The Routledge Dictionary of Modern Am. Unconventional English

Praise for *The New Partridge Dictionary of Slang and Unconventional English*

"This dictionary informs, but it also entertains" – *Booklist*

"This dictionary is huge fun." – *The Times Literary Supplement*

" ... no term is excluded because it might be considered offensive as a racia. sexual, or any kind of slur ..." – *Against the Grain*

" ... the editors have succeeded in ... observing high standards of lexicography w an accessible work." – *Choice*

" ... you can dip in just about anywhere and enjoy the exuberant, endless display of i inventiveness with language." – *BOOKFORUM*

The Routledge Dictionary of Modern American Slang and Unconventional English offers the u. mate record of modern, post-WW2 American slang.

The 25,000 entries are accompanied by citations that authenticate the words as well as offer lively examples of usage from popular literature, newspapers, magazines, movies, television shows, musical lyrics, and Internet user groups. Etymology, cultural context, country of origin and the date the word was first used are also provided.

This informative, entertaining and sometimes shocking dictionary is an unbeatable resource for all language aficionados out there.

Tom Dalzell is recognized as a leading expert on American slang. He is the author of *Flappers to Rappers: American Youth Slang* (1996) and *The Slang of Sin* (1998), both of which were alternate selections for the Book of the Month Club. He served as senior editor of *The New Partridge Dictionary of Slang and Unconventional English* (Routledge, 2006). He lives in Berkeley, California, with his family.

The Routledge Dictionary of Modern American Slang and Unconventional English

Edited by Tom Dalzell

Routledge
Taylor & Francis Group

NEW YORK AND LONDON

First published 2009 by Routledge
270 Madison Ave, New York, NY 10016

Simultaneously published in the UK
by Routledge
2 Park Square, Milton Park, Abingdon, Oxon OX14 4RN

Routledge is an imprint of the Taylor & Francis Group, an informa business

© 2009 new editorial matter and selection, Tom Dalzell material taken from *The Dictionary of Slang and Unconventional English*, 8th edition (first published 1984), E. Partridge and P. Beale estates

Typeset in India by Alden Prepress Services Private Limited, Chennai, TN
Printed by Sheridan Books, Inc.

British Library Cataloguing in Publication Data
A catalogue record for this book is available from the British Library

Library of Congress Cataloging-in-Publication Data
The Routledge dictionary of modern American slang and unconventional English / edited by Tom Dalzell.
p. cm.
Rev. ed. of: Dictionary of slang and unconventional English / by E. Partridge. 8th ed., 1984.
ISBN 978-0-415-37182-7 (alk. paper)
1. English language – Slang – Dictionaries. I. Dalzell, Tom, 1951- II. Partridge, Eric. 1894–1979. Dictionary of slang and unconventional English. III. Title: Dictionary of modern American slang and unconventional English.
PE3721.P323 2008
427'.09 – dc22
2008005409

ISBN10: 0-415-37182-1
ISBN13: 978-0-415-37182-7

CONTENTS

PREFACE

This dictionary is an intended consequence of a larger project, the *New Partridge Dictionary of Slang and Unconventional English*, in which Terry Victor and I updated the work of Eric Partridge. Contributors from around the globe supported us as we recorded and defined the slang of the English-speaking world since the end of World War 2. We worked hard to continue the Partridge tradition, observing his high standards of lexicography while producing an accessible work informed by, and infused with, the humor, mischief and energy that are endemic to slang. Partridge's body of work, scholarship and dignity of approach led the way and set the standard for every other English-language slang lexicographer of the twentieth century, and we tried to do as we thought he would have done.

Partridge limited his work to the language of Great Britain and her dominions. He explicitly decided to exclude American slang, and this decision created increasingly difficult problems for him as the years passed and the influence of American slang grew.

Because Partridge did not record American slang, my task for the *New Partridge* was to start from scratch, not to review and cull Partridge's previous work and then update it. To some extent I relied on reference works, but for the most part I read extensively from popular literature. I mined fiction, non-fiction, screenplays, scripts, newspapers (especially underground newspapers), magazines, and popular song lyrics for headwords and citations.

For this dictionary, I extracted the American entries from *New Partridge* and reviewed each entry, definition, and citation. I ultimately excluded many entries from *New Partridge*, and many others benefited from new citations or new first-usage dating information. I added several thousand new entries, and then trimmed the whole to fit our extent parameters.

Criteria for inclusion

I use three criteria for including a term or phrase in this dictionary. I include (1) slang and unconventional English; (2) used in the United States; and (3) after 1945.

Rather than focus too intently on a precise definition of slang or on whether a given entry is slang, jargon or colloquial English, I borrow the wide net cast by Partridge when he chose to record "slang and unconventional English" instead of just slang, which is, after all, without any settled test of purity. I have considered for inclusion all unconventional English that has been used with the purpose or effect of either lowering the formality of communication and reducing solemnity and/or identifying status or group and putting oneself in tune with one's company. A term recorded here might be slang, slangy jargon, a colloquialism, an acronym, an initialism, a vulgarism or a catchphrase.

In all instances, an entry imparts a message beyond the text and literal meaning. If there was a question as to

whether a potential entry fell within the target register, we erred on the side of inclusion. I present my evidence of usage to the reader who is free to determine if a candidate passes probation. I chose to avoid the slang of sports. Entire dictionaries are devoted to sports slang, and there was little that I could add to this work. Because golf and bowling are such social sports, I was tempted to dabble in their slang, but in the end chose not to.

Secondly, all entries were used in the United States. Regardless of the country of origin, if the word or phrase was used in the United States, it is a candidate for inclusion. A number of entries show countries of origin other than the United States, which simply reflects the fact that globalization has affected many facets of life, not the least of which is our language. I also include pidgin, Creolized English and borrowed foreign terms used by English-speakers in primarily English-language conversation.

Thirdly, I include slang and unconventional English heard and used at any time after 1945. I chose the end of the war in 1945 as my starting point primarily because it marked the beginning of a series of profound cultural changes that produced the lexicon of modern and contemporary slang. The cultural transformations since 1945 are mind-boggling. Television, computers, drugs, music, unpopular wars, youth movements, changing racial sensitivities and attitudes towards sex and sexuality are all substantial factors that have shaped culture and language.

No term is excluded on the grounds that it might be considered offensive as a racial, ethnic, religious, sexual or any kind of slur. This dictionary contains many entries and citations that will, and should, offend. To exclude a term or citation because it is offensive is to deny the fact that it is used.

Using *The Routledge Dictionary of Modern American Slang and Unconventional English*

I hope that my presentation is self-evident and that it requires little explanation. I use only a few abbreviations and none of the stylistic conceits near and dear to the hearts of lexicographers.

Headwords

I use indigenous spelling for headwords. For Yiddish words, I use Leo Rosten's spelling, which favors "sh-" over "sch-". An initialism is shown in upper case without periods (for example, BLT), except that acronyms (pronounced like individual lexical items) are lower case (for example, snafu). Including every variant spelling of a headword seemed neither practical nor helpful to the reader. For the spelling of headwords, I chose the form found in standard dictionaries or the most common forms, ignoring uncommon variants as well as common hyphenation variants of compounds and words ending in "ie" or "y". For this reason, citations may show variant spellings not found in the headword.

Placement of phrases

As a general rule, phrases are placed under their first significant word. However, some invariant phrases are listed as headwords; for example, a stock greeting, stock reply or catchphrase. Terms that involve a single concept are grouped together as phrases under the common headword; for example, burn rubber, lay rubber and peel rubber are all listed as phrases under the headword "rubber."

Definition

I use conventional English in the definitions, turning to slang only when it is both substantially more economical than the use of conventional English and is readily understood by the average reader. If a term used in a definition or gloss is itself defined in the dictionary, it appears in SMALL CAPS BOLD.

Gloss

The gloss is the brief explanations that Partridge used for "editorial comment" or "further elucidation." Partridge warned against using the gloss to show what clever and learned fellows we are – a warning that I tried to heed.

Country of origin

As is the case with dating, further research will undoubtedly produce a shift in the country of origin for a number of entries. I resolutely avoided guesswork and informed opinion.

Dating

Even Paul Beale, who as editor of the 8th edition of Partridge was the direct inheritor of Partridge's trust, noted that Partridge's dating "must be treated with caution." I recognise that the accurate dating of slang is far more difficult than dating conventional language. Virtually every word in our lexicon is spoken before it is written, and this is especially true of unconventional terms. The recent proliferation of electronic databases and powerful search engines will undoubtedly permit the antedating of many of the entries. Individualised dating research, such as Allen Walker's hunt for the origin of "OK" or Barry Popik's exhaustive work on terms such as "hot dog," produces dramatic antedatings: I could not undertake this level of detailed research for every entry.

Conclusion

In the preface to his 1755 *Dictionary of the English Language*, Samuel Johnson noted that "A large work is difficult because it is large," and that "Every writer of a long work commits errors." In addition to improvements in my dating of terms and identification of the country of origin, it is inevitable that some of my definitions are incorrect or misleading, especially where the sense is subtle and fleeting, defying paraphrasing, or where kindred senses are interwoven. It is also inevitable that some quotations are included in a mistaken sense. For these errors, I apologise in advance. I carry the flame for words that are usually judged only by the ill-regarded company they keep.

Just as Partridge did for the sixteenth-century beggars and rakes, for whores of the eighteenth century, and for the armed services of the two world wars, I try to do for the slang users of the last 60 years. I embrace the language of beats, hipsters, hippies, GI's in Vietnam, pimps, druggies, whores, punks, skinheads, ravers, surfers, Valley Girls, dudes, pill-popping truck drivers, hackers, rappers and more. I have tried to do what Partridge saw as necessary, which was simply to keep up to date.

Tom Dalzell, Berkeley, California
January 2008

ACKNOWLEDGEMENTS

Mary Ann Kernan launched the *New Partridge* project for Routledge in 1999 and will not be forgotten. Sophie Oliver led the project from 1999 until 2007, and her influence may be found in every word. Claire L'Enfant led from upstairs in a *sine qua non* fashion. John Williams was our instructor in matters of lexicography and all that is right about this book is because of him. Others from Routledge without whom this dictionary would not have existed are Anna Hines, Sonja van Leeuwen, James Folan, Louise Hake, Sandra Anderson, Howard Sargeant, Laura Wedgeworth, and Aine Duffy.

Those who contributed to the *New Partridge* all informed this work – Richard Allsop, Dianne Bardsley, James Lambert, Lewis Poteet, Jan Tent, and Lise Winer. Terry Victor, co-editor of the *New Partridge*, has left his imprint throughout this book. We were friends before this started and we are better friends these many words later.

My slang mentors, Paul Dickson and Madeline Kripke, led me to the path that made this work possible. Archie Green, who saved Peter Tamony's work for posterity, encouraged me throughout this project. Jesse Sheidlower, Jonathon Green and Susan Ford are slang lexicographers, friends and comrades in words.

Dr Jerry Zientara opened the incomparable library of the Institute for Advanced Study of Human Sexuality in San Francisco to me. Tom Miller, Bill Stolz, John Konzal and Patricia Walker, archivists at the Western Historical Manuscript Collection, University of Missouri at Columbia, gave help and insights during my work with the Peter Tamony archives. The late Jim Holliday was a generous source for the slang of pornography, as was Jennifer Goldstein with the slang of sex dancers. Mr. Baldwin, Mr. Muir, Mr. Lee, Dr. Robert Regan and Dr. Gordon Kelly were exemplary teachers of English and popular culture. Fellow language writers and lexicographers generous in their encouragement, advice and assistance: Reinhold Aman, the late Robert Chapman, Gerald Cohen, Trevor Cralle, Jim Crotty, Connie Eble, Jonathan Lighter, Edward MacNeal, Michael Monteleone, Pamela Munro, Geoffrey Nunberg, Judi Sanders, and Leslie Savan.

Last and far from least, my family gave nothing but patient support for nine years – Cathy most notably, also Jake, Julia, Rosalie and Charlotte. In their own ways, and from a distance, my parents guided. Audrey, Emily and Reggae started the project with me but did not stay for the end.

Aa

A *noun*

1 amphetamine *US, 1967*

- "A" is considered very bad news, "it rots your teeth and your mind." — **Ruth Bronsteen**, *The Hippy's Handbook*, p. 12, 1967
- — *Look*, p. 13, 8th August 1967
- [T]hat would come later, when he kicked A in terror after his toenails dropped off. — **Ed Sanders**, *Tales of Beatnik Glory*, p. 59, 1975

2 LSD *US, 1977*

An abbreviation of **ACID**.

- — **Walter Way**, *The Drug Scene*, p. 105, 1977
- Street names [:] A, acid, blotter[.] — **James Kay and Julian Cohen**, *The Parents' Complete Guide to Young People and Drugs*, p. 141, 1998

3 in a deck of playing cards, an ace *US, 1988*

- — **George Percy**, *The Language of Poker*, p. 4, 1988

A *adjective*

1 reserved for the best; the best *US, 1945*

- He went through what Hollywood calls Treatment A, i.e. the works for top visitors, without a mistake. — *Fortune*, p. 225, October 1945
- And part of the magic at Malibu was that Mickey's dinner was unseated which, as any "A" hostess knows, can be hazardous. — *San Francisco Chronicle*, 18th August 1975
- Oh my God Michele, look at the A group. — *Romy and Michele's High School Reunion*, 1997

2 anal *US, 1997*

- Now every scene I do is pretty much an "A" scene. (Quoting Nici Sterling.) — **Anthony Petkovich**, *The X Factory*, p. 33, 1997

a2m *noun*

a scene in a pornographic movie in which an object or body part is withdrawn from a rectum and taken into a mouth without either washing or editing *US, 2005*

Shorthand for "ass-to-mouth."

- She tea-bags his balls before an A2M. — **Editors of Adult Video News**, *The AVN Guide to the 500 Greatest Adult Films of All Time*, p. 27, 2005

AAA *noun*

an amphetamine tablet *US, 1993*

In the US, the AAA is the national automobile club, which, like an amphetamine tablet, helps you get from one place to another.

- — **Peter Johnson**, *Dictionary of Street Alcohol and Drug Terms*, p. 1, 1993

A and A *noun*

in the military, a leave for rest and recreation *US, 1966*

A jocular abbreviation of "ass and alcohol."

- They had put in two months' patrol in the steam-bath heat of the jungle and were due to go next morning to exotic old Hong Kong for some R & R—or A & A (Ass and Alcohol), as they put it. — **Elaine Shepard**, *The Doom Pussy*, p. 41, 1967
- Commonly known as R&R in the military, or rest and relaxation, some called it P&P (Pussy and Popcorn), A&A (Ass and Alcohol). — **Edmund Ciriello**, *The Reluctant Warrior*, p. 254, 2004

A and B *noun*

assault and battery *US, 1986*

- You wanna file A-and-B on the sonofabitch? — **Carl Hiaasen**, *Tourist Season*, p. 55, 1986

ab *noun*

an abscess, especially as a result of injecting drugs *US, 1952*

- — *American Speech*, p. 24, February 1952: "Teen-age hophead jargon"
- — **Eugene Landy**, *The Underground Dictionary*, p. 21, 1971

AB *noun*

the Aryan Brotherhood, a white prison gang in the US *US, 1972*

- According to the Los Angeles Police Department's Gang Awareness School training manual, "the Aryan Brotherhood (AB) is the most violent of the prison gangs." — **Bernard Campbell**, *Sexual Selection and the Descent of Man*, p. 77, 1972

- I had been disillusioned upon my return to prison with the AB, and this is when I just decided to drop out completely. — **Report to the Senate**, *California Senate Committee on Civil Disorder*, p. 38, 1975
- "But I'm aces with the A.B. here at Coldwater," Joe objected. — **Seth Morgan**, *Homeboy*, p. 369, 1990
- The AB began to structure as a whites-only prison gang and formed its own specific rules. — **Bill Valentine**, *Gangs and Their Tattoos*, p. 4, 2000

abba-dabba *noun*

chatter, gossip *US, 1961*

Undoubtedly originated with the song "The Aba-Daba Honeymoon," written in 1913 and rereleased with great success by Larry Clinton and His Orchestra in March 1948, in which "abba-dabba" is the chatter of monkeys.

- Abba-dabba: In and out of our town in a hurry this week was Guy Lewis. — *San Francisco Chronicle*, p. 50, 12th May 1967

abba-dabba *adjective*

dark-skinned, especially Arabic *US, 1975*

- This black ass, abba dabba motherfucker looked like he was gonna rabbit, so I drew down and zonked him across the gourd with my roscoe. — **Joseph Wambaugh**, *The Choirboys*, p. 31, 1975

abbott *noun*

a capsule of pentobarbital sodium (trade name Nembutal™), a central nervous system depressant *US, 1971*

From the name of the manufacturer.

- — **Eugene Landy**, *The Underground Dictionary*, p. 21, 1971
- — **Donald Wesson and David Smith**, *Barbiturates*, p. 121, 1977

Abby Singer *noun*

in television or movie making, the next-to-last shot of the day *US, 1990*

Singer was active in US television from the early 1950s until the late 1980s; his name became an eponym when he was an Assistant Director in the 1950s.

- — **Ralph S. Singleton**, *Filmmaker's Dictionary*, p. 1, 1990

ABC *noun*

1 an American-born Chinese *US, 1984*

- — **Judi Sanders**, *Faced and Faded, Hanging to Hurl*, p. 1, 1993
- "Yellow outside, White inside. Like ABC, American Born Chinese." "Jim's not marrying a gwailu (=foreign devil) or a banana. He's marrying a real Chinese." — **Howard Marks**, *Mr Nice*, p. 230, 1997

2 in poker, the ace, two and three *US, 1988*

- — **George Percy**, *The Language of Poker*, p. 4, 1988

ABC *adjective*

of a piece of chewing gum, already been chewed *US, 1983*

Childish usage.

- "ABC. Already Been Chewed. It was the best idea Alvin had heard in days." — **Stephen Manes**, *The Hooples' Haunted House*, p. 101, 1983
- "Exactly! It's ABC gum—Already Been Chewed! Get it?" — **Matt Christopher**, *Master of Disaster*, p. 2, 2003

ABC ad *noun*

a newspaper advertisement listing shows in alphabetical order *US, 1973*

- — **Sherman Louis Sergel**, *The Language of Show Biz*, p. 2, 1973

ABC's *noun*

underwear *US, 1949*

- I took off the a b c's and her stockings. — **Hal Ellson**, *Duke*, p. 11, 1949

ABC-ya

used as a farewell *US, 1947*

Intended as a clever variant of "I'll be seeing you."

- — *San Francisco Examiner*, p. 19, 5th January 1947
- — **Alonzo Westbrook**, *Hip Hoptionary*, p. 1, 2002

Abdul *noun*
any male Arab *US, 1991*
Gulf war usage.
- — *American Speech*, p. 382, Winter 1991: "Among the new words"

Abe Lincoln *noun*
a five-dollar bill *US, 1966*
The bill bears an engraving of President Lincoln.
- If these good people have no objection we'll call it an off the record sidebet. One Abe Lincoln it is. — Robert Edmond Alter, *Carny Kill*, p. 36, 1966

abercrombie *noun*
1 a person devoted to prep-school fashions and style *US, 2004*
- An Abercrombie is a gorgeous but terminally preppy boy (often blond) who looks like he just stepped out of the pages of A&F Quarterly. — Brittany Kent, *O.C. Undercover*, p. 137, 2004
2 someone who strives at creating the impression of knowing all *US, 1945*
- — Lou Shelly, *Hepcats Jive Talk Dictionary*, p. 7, 1945

Abigail *noun*
a staid, traditional, middle-aged homosexual man *US, 1972*
- — Bruce Rodgers, *The Queens' Vernacular*, p. 17, 1972
- — *Maledicta*, p. 222, 1979: "Kinks and queens: linguistic and cultural aspects of the terminology for gays"

able Grable *noun*
a sexually attractive girl *US, 1945*
- — *Yank*, p. 18, 24th March 1945

aboard *adverb*
present, part of an enterprise *US, 1957*
- McDougal led off the tenth. He turned around at the plate and shook hands with the kid. Gil said: "I'm from San Francisco, Commerce High. Glad to have you aboard." — *San Francisco Chronicle*, 11th July 1957
- They met for a couple of days in the plush Lake Tahoe layout of Henry Kaiser—deliberately without any party organization officials or other statewide Democratic candidates aboard. — *San Francisco Call-Bulletin*, p. 13, 15th August 1958

aboot *preposition*
used as a humorous attempt to duplicate a Canadian saying "about" *US, 1995*
- This is not aboot deals. This is aboot dignity. This is aboot freedom. This is aboot respect. — *South Park*, 1995

abort *verb*
to defecate after being the passive partner in anal sex *US, 1972*
- — Bruce Rodgers, *The Queens' Vernacular*, p. 17, 1972

abortion *noun*
a misfortune; an ugly person or thing *US, 1943*
- He scanned around his workshop, dropped the plane, reached for an old beaten-up thing with a lot of notches in it and lifted it up with one hand. "What about this abortion?" — Frederick Kohner, *Gidget*, p. 18, 1957
- — Collin Baker et al., *College Undergraduate Slang Study Conducted at Brown University*, p. 69, 1968

about-face *noun*
a 180-degree turn executed while driving fast *US, 1965*
- It was Junior Johnson specifically, however, who was famous for the "bootleg turn" or "about face." — Tom Wolfe, *The Kandy-Kolored Tangerine-Flake Streamlined Baby*, p. 128, 1965

about it; 'bout it *adjective*
in favor of something *US, 2001*
- — Don R. McCreary (Editor), *Dawg Speak*, 2001

abracadabra, please and thank you
used as a humorous embellishment of "please" *US, 1996*
A signature line from the *Captain Kangaroo* children's television show (CBS, 1944–84). Repeated with referential humor.
- Abracadabra. Please and thank you. Hilary took a deep sigh, closed her eyes. — Tyle Corland, *The Nurses*, p. 96, 1996

abs *noun*
the abdominal muscles *US, 1956*
- Danny and the man begin talking about the relative merits of "frog kicks" for the "abs" as opposed to regular situps[.] — John Rechy, *Numbers*, p. 66, 1967

- That is, if you mention a strong stomach, you must have cut abs. — John Preston, *Hustling*, p. 121, 1994
- He had the most awesome set of abs I'd ever seen. — Missy Hyatt, *Missy Hyatt*, p. 126, 2001

absofuckinglutely *adverb*
absolutely *UK, 1921*
- We would like to thank every single body who has made this years' Recorder so absofuckinglutely brilliant. — *Union Recorder*, 4th November 1991
- "So make absofuckinglutely sure that you don't spook 'em." — Richard Marcinko, *Rogue Warrior—Detachment Bravo*, p. 264, 2001

absotively; absitively *adverb*
certainly *US, 1914*
A jocular blend of "positively" and "absolutely."
- — Bill Davis, *Jawjacking*, p. 9, 1977
- "Absotively," he would say. — Marilyn Greene, *Finder*, p. 135, 1988

Abyssinian polo *noun*
a game of dice *US, 1962*
- — Frank Garcia, *Marked Cards and Loaded Dice*, p. 250, 1962
- Dice were sometimes called "African dominoes," and one game was dubbed "Abyssinian polo." — Karl Johnson, *The Magician and the Cardsharp*, p. 20, 2006

academy *noun*
a jail or prison *US, 1949*
- — Vincent J. Monteleone, *Criminal Slang*, p. 9, 1949
- — Marlene Freedman, *Alcatraz*, 1983

Academy Award *noun*
recognition of excelling in a field *US, 1958*
- Tuohy became a jailbird early in life and got his academy award, so to speak, when the FBI rated him Public Enemy No. 1 in 1934. — *San Francisco Call-Bulletin*, p. 10, 18th April 1958
- "We won't win any academy awards with our showing in Baltimore," he said disgustedly today. — *San Francisco Call-Bulletin*, p. 45, 17th September 1968

Academy Award *adjective*
excellent *US, 1958*
- But with the club averaging 7½ runs a game, Academy award pitching may not be necessary. — *San Francisco Call-Bulletin*, p. 19, 21st April 1958

Acapulco gold *noun*
golden-leafed marijuana from southwest Mexico *US, 1965*
A popular, well-known strain of cannabis. The song "Acapulco Gold" by the Rainy Daze was released in 1967 and had just begun its climb on the pop charts when program directors figured out what it was about and pulled it off play lists.
- "Gold. It's Acapulco Gold," White Rabbit corrected the doctor, who was mixing up the slang names for different kinds of marijuana. — Nicholas Von Hoffman, *We Are The People Our Parents Warned Us Against*, p. 23, 1967
- We are free to go, but have to be very sneaky and ditch Bruce somewhere inside the Pentagon maze so he won't find the Acapulco Gold in the car. — Abbie Hoffman, *Revolution for the Hell of It*, p. 44, 1968
- Is that Acapulco gold or Bangkok gold? — Hunter S. Thompson, *Fear and Loathing in America*, p. 40, 20th February 1968: Letter from Oscar Acosta
- About midnite she came to me and asked would I like some Acapulco gold, I said yes. — Babs Gonzales, *Movin' On Down De Line*, p. 115, 1975

accelerator *noun*
1 an amphetamine tablet *US, 1993*
- — Peter Johnson, *Dictionary of Street Alcohol and Drug Terms*, p. 1, 1993
2 an arsonist *US, 1992*
- — William K. Bentley and James M. Corbett, *Prison Slang*, p. 34, 1992

accessory *noun*
a boyfriend or girlfriend *US, 1992*
- — Lady Kier Kirby, *The 376 Deee-liteful Words*, 1992

accident *noun*
a murder that cannot be proved as such *US, 1964*
- — R. Frederick West, *God's Gambler*, p. 222, 1964

accommodation arrest *noun*
a prearranged, consensual raid of an illegal gambling operation, designed to give the appearance of strict enforcement
of laws *US*, *1961*

- And if you could impose reasonable jail sentences, I think you could
stop the stand-in and the accommodation arrest. — Special Committee
to Investigate Organized Crime, *Investigation of Organized Crime*, p. 1027, 1951
- If a juice joint is very conspicuous, an accommodation arrest may
occasionally be necessary. — New York Knapp Commission, *The Knapp
Commission Report on Police Corruption*, p. 145, 1973

according to Hoyle *adverb*
in keeping with established rules and norms *US*, *1904*
After Edmond Hoyle (1672–1769), who codified the rules for
many games.

- "Joshua doesn't count, because I'm his mother and it wouldn't be
according to Hoyle." — Mordecai Richler, *Joshua Then and Now*, p. 148, 1980

accordion act *noun*
collapsing under pressure *US*, *1989*

- Unlike their previous two games against the Rangers, the Devils
didn't do an accordion act after allowing an early goal, and scored
the next three goals of the first period. — *Record (Bergen County,
New Jersey)*, p. E1, 10th January 1989
- If Tech doesn't get things figured out in a hurry, a possible repeat of
the 1997 club's late-season accordion act looms. — *Roanoke (Virginia)
Times & World News*, p. C1, 9th November 2001

accordion war *noun*
US tactics during the Korean war: accordion-like movements
up and down Korea by land forces *US*, *1951*

- It was an accordion war where the Americans went three steps
ahead and two steps back. — Kurt Singer, *Spy Stories from Asia*, p. 180, 1955
- So MacArthur began sniping at Ridgway and his "accordion war."
— Joseph C. Goulden, *Korea*, p. 478, 1982

account executive *noun*
a pimp who procures and profits from high-price prostitutes
US, *1972*

- — Robert A. Wilson, *Playboy's Book of Forbidden Words*, p. 13, 1972

AC/DC; AC-DC *adjective*
bisexual *US*, *1960*
A pun on electricity's AC (alternating current) and DC (direct
current).

- — Frank Prewitt and Francis K. Schaeffer, *Vocabulary of Inmates' Usages*, 1963
- I don't trust any of those AC-DC guys. — Mickey Spillane, *Return of the
Hood*, p. 124, 1964
- But, all AC-DC folk welcome. — *Screw*, p. 7, 7th March 1969
- She started out in one of his deluxe AC-DC cathouses in the
suburbs of Havana. — Edwin Torres, *After Hours*, p. 325, 1979

ace *noun*
1 a police officer *US*, *1949*

- "The punk saw that ace 'n ducked without givin' me the word,"
Frankie decided bitterly. — Nelson Algren, *The Man with the Golden Arm*,
p. 182, 1949

2 a good and reliable friend *US*, *1932*

- One day after we became aces, we had our first fight in over a
year[.] — Claude Brown, *Manchild in the Promised Land*, pp. 79–80, 1965
- It really bugged me when the paddies call us Puerto Ricans the
same names they called our colored aces. — Piri Thomas, *Down These
Mean Streets*, p. 120, 1967
- "You're pals with Tommy Dunphy, right, Carlito?" "Yeah, we're aces."
— Edwin Torres, *Carlito's Way*, p. 47, 1975
- "But I'm aces with the A.B. here at Coldwater," Joe objected. — Seth
Morgan, *Homeboy*, p. 369, 1990

3 one dollar *US*, *1900*

- "An ace for two sticks." — Chandler Brossard, *Who Walks in Darkness*,
p. 11, 1952
- I want to play the nine ball for five dollars, but we decide on a fucking ace. — Jim Carroll, *Forced Entries*, p. 65, 1987

4 one-eighth of an ounce of a drug *US*, *1989*

- — Geoffrey Froner, *Digging for Diamonds*, p. 70, 1989

5 phencyclidine, the recreational drug known as PCP or angel
dust *US*, *1981*

- — Ronald Linder, *PCP*, p. 9, 1981

6 in dice games, a rolled one *US*, *1999*

- Three crap three, ace-deuce, no use. — Chris Fagans and David Guzman,
A Guide to Craps Lingo, p. 12, 1999

7 in the theater, a one-night engagement *US*, *1981*

- — Don Wilmeth, *The Language of American Popular Entertainment*, p. 3, 1981

8 in pool, the number one ball *US*, *1878*

- Fifteen in the corner. Ace in the side. — *The Hustler*, 1961
- — Mike Shamos, *The Illustrated Encyclopedia of Billiards*, p. 1, 1993

9 the grade "A" *US*, *1964*

- — Collin Baker et al., *College Undergraduate Slang Study Conducted at Brown
University*, p. 69, 1968

ace *verb*
1 to outsmart someone *US*, *1929*

- But there was something personal about it if the guy was driving
down Telegraph grinning, thinking he'd aced him. — Elmore Leonard,
Swag, p. 2, 1976

2 to work your way somewhere, to engineer something *US*,
1929

- The scheme is said to have originated among one or more influential
groups in San Francisco's Chinatown, one of which for several years
has been acing itself into a favored position with the Nationalist
China regime. — *San Francisco Call-Bulletin*, p. 1, 2nd September 1953

3 to do well in an examination *US*, *1957*

- — Collin Baker et al., *College Undergraduate Slang Study Conducted at Brown
University*, p. 69, 1968
- You may think that you aced the exam, but then you get back
scores only acceptable to a college that advertises in the back of
MAD magazine. — Joanne Kimes, *Dating Sucks*, p. 153, 2005

4 to kill someone *US*, *1975*

- Then Amalia told her about the woman's husband ripping off the
Casino Latino with Louis Palo and how Charley had to ace the
husband[.] — Richard Condon, *Prizzi's Honor*, p. 88, 1982
- A more likely scenario had the kid getting aced with a gun of his
own, a .38 taken off him in a struggle with an arresting officer.
— David Simon, *Homicide*, p. 27, 1991
- Of all the words American troops used to describe death in Vietnam,
aced, blown away, bought it, croaked, dinged, fucked up, greased,
massaged, porked, stitched, sanitized, smoked, snuffed, terminated,
waxed, wiped out, zapped—the one I heard most was "wasted."
— John Laurence, *The Cat from Hue*, p. 442, 2002

ace *adjective*
exceptional, expert, excellent *US*, *1930*

- I am glad that the newspaper boys, who later liked to refer to me as an
ace narcotic inspector, never heard the story of my first big pinch.
— William J. Spillard and Pence James, *Needle in a Haystack*, p. 7, 1945
- I became an ace young reporter for the Cincinnati Post and Times-
Star. — Jerry Rubin, *Do It!*, p. 12, 1970
- One of my ace informants tells me to see a guy at Charity in there
with a gunshot wound he says was from a hunting accident. — Elmore
Leonard, *Bandits*, p. 139, 1987

ace boon coon; ace boon poon *noun*
a very close friend *US*, *1958*

- I knew K.B. about a year before we became ace boon coons. — Claude
Brown, *Manchild in the Promised Land*, p. 79, 1965
- "What happened to your ace-boon-coon, that other writer fella?"
— John Williams, *The Man Who Cried I Am*, p. 172, 1967
- Now my ace-boon-poon / was a young boy named Spoon. — Lightnin'
Rod, *Hustlers Convention*, p. 10, 1973
- Margo got up to greet him. "Lobo. How's my ace boon coon?"
— Robert Deane Pharr, *Giveadamn Brown*, p. 14, 1978

ace cool *noun*
a very close and trusted friend *US*, *1988*

- Your client seemed to be indicating to me over the phone last night
that his "Ace Cool," which means best friend, told him that he was
part of the killing at Trenton Towers and that some Italian mobsters
did the work. — Stephen Cannell, *King Con*, p. 66, 1997

ace-deuce *noun*
a fellow prisoner upon whom you rely without question *US*,
1989

- — James Harris, *A Convict's Dictionary*, p. 28, 1989

ace-deuce *verb*
in craps, to sustain a heavy loss *US*, *1987*

- — Thomas L. Clark, *The Dictionary of Gambling and Gaming*, p. 2, 1987

ace-deuce *adjective*

1 cross-eyed *US, 1955*

- They had eleven bowlegged children whose glims[eyes] were ace-deuce and won bingo games on strangers' cards. — *San Francisco Examiner*, p. 6, 20th March 1955

2 riding a racehorse with the right stirrup higher than the left *US, 1948*

- Acaro uses what is called the "ace deuce" technique in which the right stirrup is about two inches higher than the left. — *Time*, p. 82, 17th May 1948

ace-deuce *adverb*

on an angle, with one side higher than the other *US, 1948*

- There's vomit all over the bed, all in my hat, and that's sittin' ace-deuce on my head! — Henry Williamson, *Hustler!*, p. 62, 1965
- He broke the stingy brim down and set the hat ace-deuce across his head. — Donald Goines, *Dopefiend*, p. 182, 1971

ace-douche *noun*

in craps, a first roll of three *US, 1999*

"Douche" is an intentional corruption of "deuce"; a come-out roll of three loses.

- — Chris Fagans and David Guzman, *A Guide to Craps Lingo*, p. 13, 1999

ace high; aces high *adjective*

the very best *US, 1896*

From poker.

- I said, "You're aces high with me, Duke." — Dan Jenkins, *Semi-Tough*, p. 177, 1972

ace in *verb*

to manipulate someone or something into a situation *US, 1971*

- — Eugene Landy, *The Underground Dictionary*, p. 21, 1971

ace in the hole *noun*

an undisclosed resource *US, 1908*

- Colonel Calls Gems His "Ace in Hole" — *San Francisco Examiner*, p. 3, 7th February 1947
- One of the first things I did was borrow $800 from Lillian, my rich ace in the hole. — Dick Gregory, *Nigger*, p. 112, 1964

aceman *noun*

a respected fighter in a youth gang *US, 1953*

- — Dale Kramer and Madeline Karr, *Teen-Age Gangs*, p. 174, 1953
- [A]cemen (secondary leaders or top fighters in the gang). — Howard Polsky, *Cottage Six*, p. 24, 1962

ace note *noun*

a one-dollar bill *US, 1929*

- — Joe McKennon, *Circus Lingo*, p. 11, 1980

ace out *verb*

1 to exclude someone *US, 1964*

- — J. R. Friss, *A Dictionary of Teenage Slang*, 1964

2 in poker, to win a hand by bluffing while holding a relatively low-value hand *US, 1983*

- — Thomas L. Clark, *The Dictionary of Gambling and Gaming*, p. 2, 1987

ace up your sleeve *noun*

a resource that is yet to be revealed *US, 1927*

From the popular belief that card cheats hide cards up their sleeves.

- I still had a few aces up my sleeve. — Max Shulman, *The Many Loves of Dobie Gillis*, p. 115, 1951

aces *adjective*

excellent *US, 1901*

- I said it in this very sincere voice. "You're aces, Ackley kid," I said. — J.D. Salinger, *Catcher in the Rye*, p. 50, 1951
- Paddy, why he's aces, a real saint, like; you know? — George Mandel, *Flee the Angry Strangers*, p. 56, 1952

aces in both places *noun*

in craps, a roll of two *US, 1999*

- — Chris Fagans and David Guzman, *A Guide to Craps Lingo*, p. 9, 1999

acey-deucey *noun*

a bisexual *US, 1980*

A probable elaboration of **AC/DC**.

- — Joe McKennon, *Circus Lingo*, p. 11, 1980

acey-deucey *verb*

(used of a jockey) to ride with the inside stirrup lower than the outside stirrup *US, 1948*

A riding style popularized by legendary jockey Eddie Acaro.

- — *Time*, 17th May 1948
- — Don Voorhees and Bob Benoit, *Railbird Handbook*, p. 44, 1968

acey-deucey *adjective*

1 bisexual *US, 1972*

A probable elaboration of **AC/DC**.

- — Bruce Rodgers, *The Queens' Vernacular*, p. 32, 1972
- — Alonzo Westbrook, *Hip Hoptionary*, p. 1, 2002

2 acceptable, satisfactory *US, 1975*

- — Report to the Senate, *California Senate Committee on Civil Disorder*, p. 226, 1975

acey-deucy *noun*

in craps, a roll of a one and a two *US, 1974*

- — John Savage, *The Winner's Guide to Dice*, p. 89, 1974

▸ **throw acey-deucy**

to die *US, 1960*

An allusion to a losing roll of the dice in the game of craps.

- "You're going to throw acey-deucy pretty soon, looks like. Okay, so how are your fixed for insurance?" — George Clayton Johnson, *Ocean's Eleven*, p. 77, 1960

achiever *noun*

a devoted fan of the movie *The Big Lebowski US, 2004*

In the movie, the rich Lebowski sponsors a program named the "Little Lebowski Urban Achievers."

- Many of the faithful—who call themselves Achievers after "The Little Lebowski Urban Achievers" in the movie—showed up dressed as their favorite characters. — *Tallahassee (Florida) Democrat*, p. D1, 11th April 2004

Achnard *noun*

a taxi driver *US, 1997*

New York police slang, corrupting "Ahmed" as an allusion to the preponderance of immigrants among New York's taxi-driving workforce.

- — Samuel M. Katz, *Anytime Anywhere*, p. 386, 1997

acid *noun*

LSD *US, 1965*

- [T]hen got up late that night, got loaded on acid & went bar-hopping to hear some great Rock & Roll. — Neal Cassady, *The First Third*, p. 218, 1965
- Last night as I left the U.C. theater on University Avenue, a guy walking behind me said to his friend: "That was better than acid, man." — *The Berkeley Barb*, p. 2, 17th December 1965
- I can't really recommend acid because acid has become an almost meaningless chemical. — *The Last Supplement to the Whole Earth Catalog*, p. 83, March 1971
- Well, Donny's in a coma. He had a very bad acid experience. — *Manhattan*, 1979

acid freak *noun*

a habitual user of LSD *US, 1966*

- freak: devotee: 1. originally of a particular drug: acid freak. — Ethel Romm, *The Open Conspiracy*, p. 243, 1970
- In a town full of bedrock crazies, nobody even notices an acid freak. — Hunter S. Thompson, *Fear and Loathing in Las Vegas*, p. 24, 1971

acid funk *noun*

a depression brought on by LSD use *US, 1971*

- Acid funk—an LSD induced depression. — Edward Bloomquist, *Marijuana: The Second Trip*, p. 332, 1971

acid head *noun*

a habitual user of LSD *US, 1966*

- For some in the group, it was a weekend party. For others, it was their first trip and several were true "acidheads." — Richard Alpert and Sidney Cohen, *LSD*, p. 100, 1966
- What they'll do is arrest the blacks, the acid heads, and the vagrants. — *Berkeley Barb*, p. 5, 30th December 1966
- Black militants, New Leftists, acid-heads, tribunes of the gay, families of the Mafia[.] — Norman Mailer, *Miami and the Siege of Chicago*, p. 33, 1968
- Steve gave a talk at Santa Monica Civic Auditorium, tickets were sold in the Free Press office and I met acid heads galore. — Eve Babitz, *Eve's Hollywood*, p. 192, 1974

acid mung *noun*

the sensation while under the influence of LSD of having an oily face *US, 1971*

- — Eugene Landy, *The Underground Dictionary*, p. 22, 1971

acid rock *noun*

a genre of rock music *US, 1966*

A style of music marketed to the mass audience when high-profile musicians were experimenting with LSD.

- I was talking recently to a member of one of America's top acid-rock bands, who had just returned from England. — Timothy Leary, *The Politics of Ecstasy*, p. 103, 1968

acid test *noun*

an event organized to maximize the hallucinatory experiences of LSD *US, 1966*

Ken Kesey and the Merry Pranksters organized acid tests in Palo Alto, Portland (Oregon), Los Angeles and Mexico in 1966.

- Several members of the "Acid Test" dance beneath a flashing stroboscope light which heightens the effects of LSD. — Richard Alpert and Sidney Cohen, *LSD*, p. 97, 1966
- Curiously, after the first rush at the Acid Test, there would be long intervals of the most exquisite boredom. — Tom Wolfe, *The Electric Kool-Aid Acid Test*, p. 218, 1968

ack *noun*

a pimple *US, 1968*

- — Collin Baker et al., *College Undergraduate Slang Study Conducted at Brown University*, p. 70, 1968

ack-ack *noun*

anti-aircraft artillery *US, 1926*

An initialism, using the phonetic alphabet that was current until 1941. Usage survived the new alphabet rather than being amended to "able able."

- To the south, ack-ack shells are bursting in the sky, and tracer bullets stream upwards. — Audie Murphy, *To Hell and Back*, p. 72, 1949
- And came in low with ack-ack taunting him on. — Nelson Algren, *The Neon Wilderness*, p. 177, 1960
- I had a cross-eyed cousin, an organizer for the farmworker's union, who had been with an ack-ack battery in the defense of Madrid[.] — Clancy Sigal, *Going Away*, p. 119, 1961
- Down the lazy valley where the ack-ack hides / The lazy lazy valley on the other side. — Joseph Tuso, *Singing the Vietnam Blues*, p. 75, 1990: Down the Lazy Valley

ack-ack *verb*

to shoot someone or something *US, 1947*

- They barge in ack-ack the wolf an' Ridinghood is in the groove forever after! — Harry Haenigsen, *Jive's Like That*, 1947

A-condition *noun*

air conditioning *US, 2002*

- "Cain't a muthafucka get some A-condition? It be hot as a crack ho's mouth up in here!" — Jimmy Lerner, *You Got Nothing Coming*, p. 39, 2002

acorn *noun*

in a casino, a generous tipper *US, 1984*

- — Thomas L. Clark, *The Dictionary of Gambling and Gaming*, p. 3, 1987

acorns *noun*

the testicles *US, 1975*

- "I loaned you part of the down payment!" reminded Harold and shrieked as the spray hit him in the acorns[.] — Joseph Wambaugh, *The Choirboys*, p. 213, 1975

act *noun*

the disguise and staged personality assumed by an expert card counter playing blackjack in a casino in the hope of avoiding detection and ejection *US, 1991*

- — Michael Dalton, *Blackjack*, p. 25, 1991

▸ **get into the act**

to take part *US, 1946*

If not coined by, popularized as part of the catchphrase "everybody wants to get into the act" by comedian Jimmy Durante on the radio in the 1940s.

- Lincoln was such a success that everybody wanted to get into the act. — *Time*, p. 66, 4th March 1946
- School Superintendent Robert F. Savitt said, "It's not possible to say how many just wanted to get into the act." — *San Francisco News*, p. 1, 17th January 1953

- I should have known that you can't escape the frantic desire now possessed by seemingly everyone to, as it were, "get into the act." — *San Francisco New Call-Bulletin*, p. 14, 5th September 1961

▸ **hard act to follow; tough act to follow**

something or someone who cannot be easily outdone *US, 1963*

- With his own yacht and his own island and his own particular brand of charm, Ari is a hard act to follow. — *San Francisco Examiner*, p. 16, 14th December 1963
- When Lombardi left, Bengtson was chosen. What an act to follow. — *San Francisco Chronicle*, p. 50, 28th August 1970

act *verb*

▸ **act as if**

in twelve-step recovery programs such as Alcoholics Anonymous, used as a slogan for new participants in the program *US, 1998*

- They're told to act as if they were sane, or not wanting to use, because all you can really change for the moment is your actions, not your feelings[.] — Christopher Cavanaugh, *AA to Z*, p. 43, 1998

acting Jack *noun*

a soldier temporarily appointed to higher rank, especially to serve as a platoon leader in basic training *US, 1942*

- — Carl Fleischhauer, *A Glossary of Army Slang*, p. 1, 1968
- I took my "acting jack" job most seriously, and was thought to be a shoo-in for the "best trainee" (an honor that included a promotion to PFC on completion of the course until a week before basic was over[.]) — David H. Hackworth, *About Face*, p. 41, 1989

action *noun*

1 sexual activity *US, 1956*

- As far as I'm concerned there ain't no difference. Action's action[.] — Malcolm Braly, *On the Yard*, p. 88, 1967
- I therefore denounced the idea of conjugal visits as inherently unfair; single prisoners needed and deserved action just as married prisoners did. — Eldridge Cleaver, *Soul on Ice*, p. 7, 1968
- Where did he go to study when he saw the tie placed on the door-knob of our room (the traditional signal for "action within")? — Erich Segal, *Love Story*, p. 36, 1970
- "If somebody comes into town and they want a little action, contact me over at the radio station." — Wolfman Jack (Bob Smith), *Have Mercy!*, p. 85, 1995

2 activity, especially of the kind to arouse interest or excitement *US, 1951*

Often in the greetings "where's the action?" and "what's the action?"

- Man, that chick is puttin' down some action! — William "Lord" Buckley, *Nero*, 1951
- — Richard McAlister, *Rapper's Handbook*, p. 1, 1990

3 betting, gambling *US, 1885*

- You looking for action? — *The Hustler*, 1961
- Every now and then I would go on the road looking for a little action. — Minnesota Fats, *The Bank Shot*, p. 31, 1966
- The sina qua non is that he is a good "money player," can play his best when heavy action is riding on the game (as many non-hustlers can't). — Ned Polsky, *Hustlers, Beats, and Others*, p. 55, 1967
- And I'll take all the action I can get. — *Diner*, 1982

4 the amount that a gambler is willing to bet *US, 1991*

- For example, one hundred bets of $5 each is $500 in action. — Michael Dalton, *Blackjack*, p. 25, 1991

5 in pool, a game played with wagers *US, 1990*

- — Steve Rushin, *Pool Cool*, p. 5, 1990

6 in pool, spin imparted on the cue ball to affect the course of the object ball or the cue ball after striking the object ball *US, 1913*

- — Mike Shamos, *The Illustrated Encyclopedia of Billiards*, p. 2, 1993

7 a political act, often confrontational or violent *US, 1971*

- On that same point, I'd like to say first of all, as Billy mentioned, letters are going to be going to the men whose [draft] files were destroyed, and this in itself is, I think, an action, because it is giving these men a chance to make their own choice. — *The Last Supplement to the Whole Earth Catalog*, p. 18, March 1971

▸ **piece of the action; share of the action**

an involvement in an activity; a share in the profits of something *US, 1957*

- Triads never helped anyone out without a promise of a piece of the action. — Lung Cheng, *I Am Jackie Chan*, p. 261, 1998

action beaver *noun*

a movie featuring full nudity and sexual activity short of intercourse *US, 1974*

- The action beaver, the next logical cinematic step, featured increasingly explicit sexual activity along with complete nudity. — Kenneth Turan and Stephen E. Zito, *Sinema*, p. 78, 1974

action faction *noun*

a subset of the political left that advocated forceful, confrontational tactics *US, 1968*

- The Labor Committee is sometimes referred to as the thought faction, as opposed to the action faction, of SDS. — James Simon Kunen, *The Strawberry Statement*, p. 102, 1968
- The Progressive Labor people, "the action faction," believed that nothing short of the active overthrow of the Establishment was warranted. — James Davis, *Assault on the Left*, p. 70, 1997

action player *noun*

a gambler who bets heavily, frequently and flamboyantly *US, 2003*

- — Victor H. Royer, *Casino Gamble Talk*, p. 5, 2003
- But should the credit risk pay back his gambling debts at that line and show the casino he's an action player so that he obtains a new higher line of credit, the person vouching for his credit is let off the hook as to any future credit. — Edwin Silberstang, *The Winner's Guide to Casino Gambling*, p. 54, 2005

action room *noun*

a poolhall where betting is common *US, 1967*

- Graney's was the action room—that's where the money was changing hands. — Robert Byrne, *McGoorty*, p. 118, 1972
- — Mike Shomos, *The Illustrated Encyclopedia of Billiards*, p. 2, 1993

actor *noun*

a troublemaker *US, 1964*

- — R. Frederick West, *God's Gambler*, p. 222, 1964

actor-proof *adjective*

denoting a part in a play or performance so well written that no amount of bad acting can ruin it *US, 1973*

- — Sherman Louis Sergel, *The Language of Show Biz*, p. 4, 1973

actuary *noun*

in an illegal betting operation, an oddsmaker *US, 1971*

- — Thomas L. Clark, *The Dictionary of Gambling and Gaming*, p. 3, 1987

Ada from Decatur; Ada Ross, the Stable Hoss *noun*

in a game of dice, a roll of eight *US, 1918*

A homophonic evolution of "eighter."

- In craps, the dice-thrower will call for "Ada from Decatur." — S.I. Hayakawa, *Language in Thought and Action*, p. 202, 1964
- "Ada from Decatur!" a little sawed-off MP pleaded. — John Oliver Killens, *And Then We Heard the Thunder*, p. 448, 1983

Ad Alley *nickname*

the advertising industry, especially that located in New York and commonly known in the US as "Madison Avenue" after the New York street where many advertising agencies had their offices *US, 1952*

- Ulcers now run second (along Ad Alley) to crackups among ad agency execs — *San Francisco Call-Bulletin*, p. 8G, 3rd October 1952
- The urgently felt need to "stimulate" people brought new power, glory, and prosperity to the professional stimulators or persuaders of American industry, particularly the skilled gray-flanneled suiters of New York's Madison Avenue, known as "ad alley." — Vance Packard, *The Hidden Persuaders*, p. 21, 1957

Adam *noun*

1 MDMA, the recreational drug best known as ecstasy *US, 1985*

A near-anagram.

- — Bruce Eisner, *Ecstasy*, p. 1, 1989
- CALL IT... Adam, brownies, burgers, disco biscuits, doves, eckies, tulips, X[.] JUST DON'T CALL IT... MDMA—too scientific — *Drugs An Adult Guide*, p. 34, December 2001

2 a partner in a criminal enterprise *UK, 1797*

- — *American Speech*, p. 97, May 1956: "Smugglers' argot in the southwest"

3 a homosexual's first sexual partner *US, 1972*

From Adam as the biblical first man.

- — Bruce Rodgers, *The Queens' Vernacular*, p. 18, 1972

Adam and Eve *noun*

a pill of MDEA and MDMA, the recreational drug best known as ecstasy *UK, 1996*

- — Gareth Thomas, *This Is Ecstasy*, p. 54, 2002

Adam and Eve on a raft *noun*

two eggs on toast *US, 1909*

Restaurant slang.

- "I'd like two scrambled eggs on toast, and a cup of tea with lemon, please." "Adam and Eve on a raft, wreck 'em, and a spot with a twist." — Alexandra Day, *Frank and Ernest*, 1988

Adam's off-ox *noun*

a complete stranger *US, 1894*

Used in the expression "he wouldn't know me from Adam's off-ox."

- The first time I stepped in, he was behind the counter and didn't know me from Adam's off ox. — *Christian Science Monitor*, p. 20, 29th April 1983
- You don't know me from Adam's off ox — *USA Today*, p. 6D, 24th February 2004

ADASTW *adjective*

arrived dead and stayed that way *US, 1991*

- "He didn't say anything in the ambulance or once he got here?" "A-D-A-S-T-W," says the nurse. — David Simon, *Homicide*, p. 287, 1991

addict *noun*

a victim of a confidence swindle who repeatedly invests in the crooked enterprise, hoping that his investment will pay off *US, 1985*

- — M. Allen Henderson, *How Con Games Work*, p. 217, 1985

addict waiting to happen *noun*

in twelve-step recovery programs such as Alcoholics Anonymous, used for describing the childhood of addicts of the future *US, 1998*

- — Christopher Cavanaugh, *AA to Z*, p. 45, 1998

addy *noun*

an address *US, 2002*

- — Alonzo Westbrook, *Hip Hoptionary*, p. 1, 2002
- [H]is e-mail addy disappeared due to the overwhelming flood of support against the global giant. — *Idaho Statesman*, p. 36, 27th January 2004

A-deck *noun*

a prison cell used for solitary confinement *US, 1984*

- — Inez Cardozo-Freeman, *The Joint*, p. 479, 1984

adger *verb*

in computing, to make an avoidable mistake *US, 1991*

- — Eric S. Raymond, *The New Hacker's Dictionary*, p. 31, 1991

adios motherfucker

used as a farewell *US, 1986*

Jocular or defiant; sometimes abbreviated to **AMF**.

- Ten days from now I am adios, motherfucker, so till then I'm playing catch-up. — James Ellroy, *Suicide Hill*, p. 585, 1986
- "Adios, motherfucker," he said, his voice distorted by the OBA mask. — Peter Deutermann, *The Edge of Horror*, p. 563, 1995

adjuster *noun*

a hammer *US, 1990*

- — Elena Garcia, *A Beginner's Guide to Zen and the Art of Snowboarding*, p. 121, 1990

adjust the stick!

used as a humorous admonition to casino employees at a craps table when the players are losing *US, 1983*

- — Thomas L. Clark, *The Dictionary of Gambling and Gaming*, p. 3, 1987

ad-lib *verb*

to date indiscriminately *US, 1960*

- — *San Francisco Examiner*, p. III-2, 22nd March 1960

ad man *noun*

a prisoner who is friendly or aligned with the prison administration *US, 1976*

- — John R. Armore and Joseph D. Wolfe, *Dictionary of Desperation*, p. 19, 1976

admiral's watch *noun*

a good night's sleep *US, 1918*

• Although the night's sleep was not his customary "Admiral's watch," he found himself refreshed. — Randall Platt, *The Cornerstone*, p. 221, 1998

adorkable *noun*
cute in an unconventional, slightly odd way *US, 2002*
• Mr. Neil Diamond besides being a very cute and fluffy adorkable man? — *alt.native*, 24th July 2002
• — Connie Eble (Editor), *UNC-CH Campus Slang*, Fall 2005

a-double-scribble *noun*
used as a euphemism for "ass" in any of its senses *US, 1996*
• — Claudio R. Salvucci, *The Philadelphia Dialect Dictionary*, p. 27, 1996

advance *verb*
▶ **advance the spark**
to prepare *US, 1945*
• — Lou Shelly, *Hepcats Jive Talk Dictionary*, p. 21, 1945

advertise *verb*
1 to signal your intentions unwittingly but plainly *US, 1931*
• Relax. Please. This is just another day. Stop advertising. — Horace McCoy, *Kiss Tomorrow Good-bye*, p. 8, 1948
2 in poker, to bluff in a manner that is intended to be caught, all in anticipation of a later bluff *US, 1949*
• — Albert H. Morehead, *The Complete Guide to Winning Poker*, p. 255, 1967
3 in gin, to discard in a manner that is designed to lure a desired card from an opponent *US, 1971*
• — Irwin Steig, *Play Gin to Win*, p. 138, 1971

adzine *noun*
a single-interest fan magazine containing only advertising *US, 1982*
• — *American Speech*, p. 23, Spring 1982: "The language of science fiction fan magazines"

aerial *adjective*
used as a modifier for any sexual position where at least one participant is off the ground *US, 1995*
• — *Adult Video News*, p. 40, August 1995

Aesop *noun*
in poker, any player who tells stories while playing *US, 1996*
• — John Vorhaus, *The Big Book of Poker Slang*, p. 3, 1996

AFAIC
used as shorthand in Internet discussion groups and text messages to mean "*as far as I'm concerned*" *US, 1991*
• Bottom line, AFAIC (as far as I'm concerned): All activism is needed at all levels. — *soc.motss*, 18th October 1991
• — Gabrielle Mander, *WAN2TLK?*, p. 42, 2002

AFF *noun*
an attraction to Asian females *US, 1997*
An abbreviation of "Asian female fetish."
• — Pamela Munro, *U.C.L.A. Slang*, p. 20, 1997

afgay *noun*
a homosexual *US, 1972*
• — Robert A. Wilson, *Playboy's Book of Forbidden Words*, p. 15, 1972

▷ **see: AGFAY (NOUN)**

AFK
used as shorthand in Internet discussion groups and text messages to mean "*away from keyboard*" *US, 2002*
• AFK away from keyboard — *alk.folklore.computers*, 28th November 1990
• — Gabrielle Mander, *WAN2TLK?*, p. 42, 2002

AFO *nickname*
the Arellano-Felix Organization, a criminal enterprise that functioned as a transportation subcontractor for the heroin trade into the US *US, 1998*
• Blancornelas' bodyguard was killed, as was David Barron-Corona, who recruited security and hitmen for the AFO[.] — *Newsday (New York)*, p. 40, 15th February 1998
• The drug trade, too, has its courier services, outfits such as "Nigeria Express" or Mexico's notorious A.F.O. — *New York Times*, p. SM29, 23 June 2002

afoot or ahossback *adjective*
unsure of the direction you are going to take *US, 1895*
• — Charles F. Haywood, *Yankee Dictionary*, p. 2, 1963

A for effort *noun*
praise for the work involved, if not for the result of the work *US, 1948*
From a trend in US schools to grade children both on the basis of achievement and on the basis of effort expended. Faint praise as often as not.
• If the rest of the movie were up to Miss Bergman, it could be rated very close to excellent. As it is, it rates A for effort. — *Time*, p. 102, 15th November 1948
• If President Johnson is handing our report cards today, he almost certainly is giving Secretary of State Dean Rusk and Gen Maxwell D. Taylor an "A" for effort. — *San Francisco Examiner*, p. 1, 18th February 1966

African *noun*
in US casinos, a black betting chip worth $100 *US, 1983*
• — Thomas L. Clark, *The Dictionary of Gambling and Gaming*, p. 4, 1987

African dominoes *noun*
dice *US, 1919*
• Then the colored gamblers set in to pleading with the African dominoes[.] — Guy Owen, *The Flim-Flam Man and the Apprentice Grifter*, p. 117, 1972
• — John Scarne, *Scarne on Dice*, p. 459, 1974

African golf *noun*
the game of craps *US, 1919*
• In Chicago, police arrested a twenty-year-old white girl and called her the world's best crapshooter, a designation that had hitherto been reserved for black experts at "African golf." — Roy Wilkins, *Standing Fast*, p. 73, 1994

African grape *noun*
a watermelon *US, 1980*
Based on the stereotypical association between rural black people and a love of watermelon.
• — Edith A. Folb, *runnin' down some lines*, p. 227, 1980

African guff-guff *noun*
a nonexistent disease suffered by soldiers *US, 1947*
• — *American Speech*, p. 305, December 1947: "Imaginary diseases in army and navy parlance"

African plum *noun*
a watermelon *US, 1973*
• — Malachi Andrews and Paul T. Owens, *Black Language*, p. 96, 1973

African toothache *noun*
any sexually transmitted infection *US, 1964*
• — Roger Blake, *The American Dictionary of Sexual Terms*, p. 2, 1964

Afro *noun*
a bushy, frizzy hairstyle embraced by black people as a gesture of resistance in the 1960s *US, 1966*
• — *Current Slang*, p. 1, Spring 1967
• But real Afros, not the ones that have been shaped and trimmed like a topiary hedge, and sprayed until they have a sheen like acrylic wall-to-wall—but like funky, natural, scraggly. — Tom Wolfe, *Radical Chic & Mau-Mauing the Flak Catchers*, p. 7, 1970
• I knew everything about O.J. from reading that 90-page book that third graders could order from the Weekly Reader. I remember knowing that he had a fine wife and an Afro. — Chris Rock, *Rock This!*, p. 206, 1997

Afro pick *noun*
a gap-toothed comb used for an Afro hairstyle *US, 1986*
• Two black guys are about to tear into each other with Afro picks[.] — Josh Alan Friedman, *Tales of Times Square*, p. 64, 1986

after *noun*
afternoon *US, 1974*
• "Look," Cogan said, "this after, I'm supposed to meet a kid, all right?" — George Higgins, *Cogan's Trade*, p. 184, 1974

afterburner *noun*
a linear amplifier for a citizens' band radio *US, 1976*
• — Lawrence Teeman, *Consumer Guide Good Buddy's CB Dictionary*, p. 23, 1976

after-hours *adjective*
open after bars and nightclubs close at 2am *US, 1947*
• [T]hose highways which in their time have known throngs of sight-seers, which in the heyday of Harlem hotspots housed cabarets and

after-hour joints known around the world[.] — Jack Lait and Lee Mortimer, *New York Confidential*, p. 96, 1948

- I had always stayed away from after-hours joints because I was afraid they would be busted by the police[.] — Dick Gregory, *Nigger*, p. 139, 1964
- One night, me and Reggie closed up my joint and then went over to this after-hours joint downtown Manhattan. — Edwin Torres, *Carlito's Way*, p. 81, 1975
- In the early morning hours, before the city has washed her face, people stream out of after-hours clubs like Jump-Offs along Seventh Avenue[.] — Terry Williams, *The Cocaine Kids*, p. 97, 1989

afterlater *adverb*
later *US*, *1997*
- I can't go witcha now, how about afterlater? — Amy and Denise McFadden, *CoalSpeak*, p. 1, 1997

afternoon delight *noun*
extra-marital sex *US*, *1982*
- adultery: afternoon delight — Sherri Foxman, *Classified Love*, p. 128, 1982

ag *adjective*
angry *US*, *2000*
An abbreviation of "aggravated."
- — *Ebony Magazine*, p. 156, August 2000: "How to talk to the new generation"

against the wall *adjective*
said of a confidence swindle which is perpetrated without a fake office, extras, props, etc. *US*, *1940*
- We're gonna do the play-off somewhere else. The play-off is against the wall. — Stephen Cannell, *Big Con*, p. 341, 1997

A-game *noun*
in a casino or cardroom, the poker game with the highest stakes *US*, *1949*
- — George Percy, *The Language of Poker*, p. 5, 1988

agate *noun*
1 a marble in the slang sense of sanity *US*, *1951*
- He didn't have all his agates and eventually went nuts. — *San Francisco News*, p. 22, 19th December 1951
2 a small penis *US*, *1967*
- — Dale Gordon, *The Dominion Sex Dictionary*, p. 17, 1967

A-gay *noun*
a prominent, sought-after homosexual man *US*, *1982*
- Chuck Lord's addiction to Negroes was a matter of common knowledge among the A-Gays in San Francisco. — Armistead Maupin, *Further Tales of the City*, p. 9, 1982

age *noun*
in poker and other card games, the person to the immediate left of the dealer *US*, *1963*
- — Irwin Steig, *Common Sense in Poker*, p. 181, 1963

-age *suffix*
used as an embellishment without meaning at the end of nouns *US*, *1981*
The suffix got a second wind with the US television series *Buffy The Vampire Slayer*.
- — Connie Eble (Editor), *UNC-CH Campus Slang*, p. 4, March 1981
- — Lady Kier Kirby, *The 376 Deee-liteful Words*, 1992

age card *noun*
proof of legal age *US*, *1968*
- New girl, Jane, she fresh up from Alabama an still funky—she ain't got no age card, can't buy herself a drink t'nurse[.] — Robert Gover, *JC Saves*, p. 17, 1968

agent *noun*
1 the operator of a rigged carnival game *US*, *1985*
- A good Agent can be listed among the elite super salesmen to be found in any field. Cars, vacuum cleaners or wheeling land dealers, I'll put a Carny Agent against them anytime. — Gene Sorrows, *All About Carnivals*, p. 6, 1985
2 in casino gambling, a confederate of a cheat *US*, *1996*
- — Frank Scoblete, *Best Blackjack*, p. 252, 1996

Agent Scully *noun*
oral sex *US*, *2001*
A reference to the name of the female lead in the *X-Files* television series, punning on her name and **SKULL** (oral sex).

- Brooks and his colleagues also provide police with glossaries of street slang—"Agent Scully" = "oral sex," "getting my cake" = "dating my girl." — *Washington Post*, p. A1, 20th August 2001

agfay *noun*
a homosexual man *US*, *1942*
Pig Latin for **FAG**.
- There were plenty of similar names that he had to live down: Nola, pix, flit, queer, fag, faggot, agfay[.] — Etienne Leroux, *The Third Eye*, p. 42, 1969

agged *adjective*
angry, aggravated *US*, *1998*
- — Ethan Hilderbrant, *Prison Slang*, p. 6, 1998

aggie *noun*
1 an aggressive, domineering male *US*, *1968*
From the conventional "aggressive."
- — Collin Baker et al., *College Undergraduate Slang Study Conducted at Brown University*, p. 70, 1968
2 a farm tool, especially a hoe *US*, *1972*
- — Bruce Jackson, *Outside the Law*, p. 55, 1972

aggie *adjective*
angry, agitated *US*, *2002*
- — Alonzo Westbrook, *Hip Hoptionary*, p. 2, 2002

aginner *noun*
a person morally opposed to carnivals and the circus *US*, *1981*
- — Don Wilmeth, *The Language of American Popular Entertainment*, p. 7, 1981

agitate *verb*
▸ **agitate the gravel**
to leave *US*, *1958*
Teen slang.
- — *San Francisco News*, p. 6, 25th March 1958
- Agitate the Gravel—beat it. — Art Unger, *The Cool Book*, p. 110, 1961

a good craftsman never blames his tools
used for dismissing an attempt by someone to blame a mistake on a piece of equipment or something within their control *US*, *1914*
- — Keith Olberman and Dan Patrick, *The Big Show*, p. 11, 1997

a-gunner *noun*
an assistant gunner *US*, *1981*
- It's up to my a-gunner to keep up with the situation. — Mark Baker, *Nam*, p. 61, 1981

A-head *noun*
1 an amphetamine abuser *US*, *1971*
- — Edward R. Bloomquist, *Marijuana*, p. 331, 1971
- There's A-heads and there's speedfreaks[.] — Lester Bangs, *Psychotic Reactions and Carburetor Dung*, p. 178, 1975
- She was a bit of an A-head and was a familiar figure at the fountain in her uniform after work. — Ed Sanders, *Tales of Beatnik Glory*, p. 121, 1975
2 a frequent user of LSD *US*, *1971*
- — Eugene Landy, *The Underground Dictionary*, p. 22, 1971

ahhh, Rooshan
used as a youth-to-youth greeting *US*, *1949*
A short-lived fad greeting associated with bebop jazz.
- — *Time*, 3rd October 1949

a-hole *noun*
1 the anus *US*, *1942*
"A" as in **ASS**.
- — Dale Gordon, *The Dominion Sex Dictionary*, p. 17, 1967
- — Bruce Rodgers, *The Queens' Vernacular*, p. 18, 1972
- "I'll stick that dang pecker-bat up his lard-ass A-hole!" — Terry Southern, *Texas Summer*, p. 110, 1991
- Cum dribbles down her crack, ultimately resting upon her a-hole. — Anthony Petkovich, *The X Factory*, p. 193, 1997
2 by extension, a despised person *US*, *1942*
- You know Jackie is an Aye Hole. — Howard Stern, *Miss America*, p. 192, 1995
- "If a-hole is on time, we'll be long gone 'fore it hits." — Carl Hiaasen, *Skinny Dip*, p. 428, 2004

-aholic; -oholic; -holic *suffix*
an addict of, or addicted to, the prefixed thing or activity *US*, *1964*

Usage may be literal or figurative. From "alco*holic*" (a person addicted to alcohol); the first widely recognized extended usage was "workaholic" (1968).

- World is full of chocoholics, as you can see at See's. — *San Francisco Examiner*, p. 3, 15th May 1976
- Therapy for Spendaholics. — *San Francisco Chronicle*, p. A1, 9th April 1980
- A self-confessed shopaholic, Rachel is also a real romantic[.] — *CD:UK*, p. 9, 2000
- [T]he epitome of shambolic, shirkaholic ineptitude[.] — Will Birch, *No Sleep Till Canvey Island*, p. 282, 2003

a-ight
used for expressing agreement or affirmation *US, 1995*
- — Lois Stavsky et al., *A2Z*, p. 1, 1995
- "He's aiight!" I used to yell back from my grandmother's window. — Earl "DMX" Simmons, *E.A.R.L.*, p. 167, 2002
- Roots was like, "Aight." — 50 Cent, *From Pieces to Weight*, p. 140, 2005

ain't no shame in my game
used for expressing a lack of shame when engaged in an activity that might shame others *US, 2002*
- — Alonzo Westbrook, *Hip Hoptionary*, p. 2, 2002

ain't no thang; ain't no big thang
used for dismissing something as not problematic *US, 1985*
- — Conne Eble, *UNC-CH Campus Slang*, Fall 1985
- — Richard McAlister, *Rapper's Handbook*, p. 1, 1990
- O-Dog: How's the shoulder, nigga? Caine: Fucked up, but it ain't no thang. — *Menace II Society*, 1993
- — Kenn "Naz" Young, *Naz's Dictionary of Teen Slang*, p. 2, 1993

ain't that a bite!
isn't that too bad! *US, 1951*
Teen slang.
- — *Newsweek*, p. 28, 8th October 1951

ain't the beer cold!
used for conveying that all is well in the world *US, 1982*
Popularized by baseball radio announcer Chuck Thompson, who used the phrase as the title of his autobiography. Repeated with referential humor.
- Thompson is the kind of announcer you listen to while wearing your slippers. He's homey and conversational. An Oriole hits a homer and he says, "Hmmm! Ain't the beer cold." — *Washington Post*, p. E12, 27th June 1982
- When your first two opponents lose their starting quarterbacks in August, well, ain't the beer cold? — *Washington Times*, p. F5, 3rd September 2003

AIO noun
a college student who does not belong to a fraternity *US, 1968*
- AIO, Ain't In One, is the way non-Greeks refer to themselves. — Fred Hester, *Slang on the 40 Acres*, p. 16, 1968

air noun
1 a jump while snowboarding *US, 1996*
- — Mike Fabbro, *Snowboarding*, p. 93, 1996

2 in the pornography industry, an ejaculation that cannot be seen leaving the penis and traveling through the air *US, 1995*
In a situation which calls for visual proof of the ejaculation, air is no good.
- — *Adult Video News*, p. 40, August 1995

3 the mood created by a person or persons *US, 1988*
There is "good air" and there is "bad air."
- — Michael V. Anderson, *The Bad, Rad, Not to Forget Way Cool Beach and Surf Discriptionary*, p. 2, 1988

▸ **in the air**
(used of the flank of an army) unprotected by natural or man-man obstacles *US, 1982*
- In Marine parlance, their flanks were "hanging in the air" with no contact save an occasional patrol. — Joseph C. Goulden, *Korea*, p. 348, 1982

▸ **on air**
(said of a bet) made on credit *US, 2005*
- "I let you bet on air," I told Antoine. — 50 Cent, *From Pieces to Weight*, p. 114, 2005

▸ **up in the air**
(used of a pair in a game of poker) formed with help from the communal face-up cards *US, 1992*
- — Edwin Silberstang, *Winning Poker for the Serious Player*, p. 221, 1992

airbag noun
a person who talks too much *US, 2004*
- To think. When I got out of the joint, I thought an airbag was Paulie Walnuts. — *The Sopranos (Episode 60)*, 2004

airbags noun
the lungs *US, 1945*
- — Lou Shelly, *Hepcats Jive Talk Dictionary*, p. 7, 1945

air ball noun
1 in pinball, a ball that is lost out of play without having been flipped *US, 1977*
- — Bobbye Claire Natkin and Steve Kirk, *All About Pinball*, 1977

2 in pool, a shot in which the cue ball does not hit any other ball *US, 1993*
- — Mike Shamos, *The Illustrated Encyclopedia of Billiards*, p. 3, 1993

air bandit noun
a gambling cheat *US, 1969*
- — Thomas L. Clark, *The Dictionary of Gambling and Gaming*, p. 4, 1987

air barrel noun
in pool, that which backs a bet made without money to back the bet *US, 1990*
A **BARREL** is a betting unit; an "air barrel" is thus an illusory betting unit.
- — Steve Rushin, *Pool Cool*, p. 5, 1990

air biscuit noun
a fart *US, 2001*
- — Pamela Munro, *U.C.L.A. Slang*, p. 31, 2001
- — *The A-Z of Rude Health*, 18th January 2002

airedale noun
1 a Wall Street gentleman *US, 1925*
An extension of the symbol of the Airedale as an aristocratic dog.
- — *New York Times Magazine*, p. 76, 13th March 1955

2 a navy pilot *US, 1942*
- The pilots are in fact a pleasant, easy-going, affable lot known affectionately to surface sailors as "Airedales" or "birdmen." — *Life*, p. 85, 26th March 1945
- Despite a Navy directive to cut it out, Navy pilots remain "Airedales" and Marines are still "Gyrenes." — *New York Times Magazine*, p. 76, 13th March 1955
- "Got it from a pilot over at the airstrip," the first sergeant said. "Those airedales sure live well." — Robert A. Anderson, *Cooks & Bakers*, p. 123, 1982
- Looks like you Airedale guys aren't gonna take no for an answer today, are you? — Gerry Carroll, *North S*A*R*, p. 88, 1991

3 a plane handler on an aircraft carrier *US, 1943*
- The battle-scarred hangar deck of the carrier Enterprise, cleared of planes and shouting airedales (airplane handlers), has been converted into this gigantic bunk room. — *Time*, p. 24, 10th December 1945
- The air officers, plane handlers who shift and push and manhandle the planes a dozen times a day around the deck. These are ordinarily known as "airedales," but the term isn't much used on our ship. — *San Francisco News*, p. 10, 19th March 1945

air guitar noun
an imagined guitar used to mimic a rock guitar player *US, 1982*
- The three Figures look at each other, do a ferocious AIR GUITAR, and run OUT OF FRAME. — *Bill and Ted's Excellent Adventure*, p. 91, 1989

airhead noun
a person who is not inclined to think, not equipped to think, or both *US, 1972*
- [T]here's a good proportion of air heads and space cadets in those courses, too. — *Wesleyan Alumnus*, p. 29, Spring 1981
- I'm sorry about your friend. I thought she was your usual airhead bitch. — *Heathers*, 1988
- Look at all these airheads! — *Airheads*, 1994
- What am I, some sort of mentally challenged airhead? — *Clueless*, 1995

air hog *noun*
in the language of hang gliding, the flier in a group who stays in the air longest *US, 1992*
- — Erik Fair, *California Thrill Sports*, p. 328, 1992

air junkie *noun*
in the language of hang gliding, a devoted, obsessed flier *US, 1992*
- — Erik Fair, *California Thrill Sports*, p. 328, 1992

airmail *noun*
1 garbage thrown from the upper windows of a building to the courtyard below *US, 1952*
- Throwing garbage out of windows is referred to as AIRMAIL. — Hubert Selby Jr., *Last Exit to Brooklyn*, p. 253, 1957

2 objects thrown by prisoners down onto guards or other prisoners below *US, 1992*
- — William K. Bentley and James M. Corbett, *Prison Slang*, p. 99, 1992

airmail *verb*
to throw garbage from the upper windows of a building to the courtyard below *US, 1968*
- [F]rom the back windows of the tenements beyond several people were busy "airmailing," throwing garbage out of the window, into the rubble, beer cans, red shreds, the No-Money-Down Eames roller stand for a TV set, all flying through the air into the scagg — Tom Wolfe, *The Pump House Gang*, p. 240, 1968

airplane *noun*
a device used for holding a marijuana cigarette that has burnt down to the stub *US, 1970*
An abbreviation of the fuller JEFFERSON AIRPLANE.
- — William D. Alsever, *Glossary for the Establishment and Other Uptight People*, p. 20, December 1970

airplane *verb*
to inhale through the nose the smoke of the stub of a marijuana cigarette *US, 1970*
- — *Current Slang*, p. 12, Spring 1970

airplane rule *noun*
in computing, the belief that simplicity is a virtue *US, 1991*
- Complexity increases the possibility of failure; a twin-engine airplane has twice as many engine problems as a single-engine airplane. — Eric S. Raymond, *The New Hacker's Dictionary*, p. 34, 1991

airs *noun*
a pair of Nike Air Jordan™ sneakers *US, 1990*
- — Richard McAlister, *Rapper's Handbook*, p. 1, 1990

air sucker *noun*
a jet airplane *US, 1963*
- — *American Speech*, p. 118, May 1963: "Air refueling words"

air-to-mud *adjective*
(used of shots fired or bombs dropped) from the air to the ground *US, 1961*
- We would like to give it modest air-to-mud capability — Senate Committee on Appropriations, *Department of Defense Appropriations*, p. 72, 1961
- The CF-5 hasn't got the range it needs for the air-to-mud role. — Tom Langeste, *Words on the Wing*, p. 8, 1995

airy *adjective*
marijuana-intoxicated *US, 1949*
- I just got a little high and airy with the sticks and they made me feel better[.] — Hal Ellson, *Duke*, p. 3, 1949

aitch *noun*
1 hell *US, 1950*
A euphemism.
- As he told his president who wanted to know why the aitch Fresno State wasn't good enough for the track coach's son, it broke his heart to lose a kid who had already thrown the javelin — *Fortnight*, p. 17, 6th January 1950
- "It was boring as aitch," says Hewitt, who does not use profanity, liquor, tobacco or coffee but has a weakness for candy bars. — *Life*, p. 144, 12th April 1954

2 heroin *US, 1945*
- The price of pure heroin ("aitch") has gone up from $60 an ounce to $500. — *Time*, p. 48, 16th April 1945

ai te guacho
I'll see you later *US, 1950*
"Guacho" prounounced "*watch-o*," a pure invention. Border Spanish used in English conversation by Mexican-Americans.
- — George Carpenter Baker, *Pachuco*, p. 40, January 1950
- "Ay te watcho, man." "Easy." — Thurston Scott, *Cure it with Honey*, p. 14, 1951
- Cruz shook his head and said, "Ahi te huacho," which is anglicized slang meaning I'll be seeing, or rather, watching for you. — Joseph Wambaugh, *The Blue Knight*, p. 61, 1973

ajax *noun*
in hold 'em poker, an ace and a jack as the first two cards dealt to a particular player *US, 1981*
Punning on the brand name of a cleaning agent.
- — Thomas L. Clark, *The Dictionary of Gambling and Gaming*, p. 5, 1987

AK *noun*
1 a sycophant *US, 1939*
An abbreviation of ASS KISSER.
- — Robert A. Wilson, *Playboy's Book of Forbidden Words*, p. 15, 1972

2 a mean and nasty old man *US, 1942*
An abbreviation of the Yiddish ALTER KOCKER.
- Two A.K.'s had sat in silence on their favorite park bench for hours, lost in thought. Finally, one gave a long and languid "Oy!" The other replied, "You're telling me?" — Leo Rosten, *The Joys of Yiddish*, p. 14, 1968

3 an AK-47 semi-automatic rifle *US, 1990*
- — Richard McAlister, *Rapper's Handbook*, p. 1, 1990
- — Bill Valentine, *Gang Intelligence Manual*, p. 74, 1995

AK *verb*
to curry favor by obsequious behavior *US, 1939*
An abbreviation of "ass-kiss."
- — *American Speech*, p. 154, May 1959: "Gator (University of Florida) slang"

AKA *noun*
an alias *US, 1955*
An acronym of "*also known as*"; from police jargon.
- It was the very lack of embellishment to his aka that established him as a man of distinction. — Marc Savage, *Paradise*, p. 206, 1993
- Reggie Jackson, Reggie Miller—I think 'cause he was given a movie star name at birth he has to pick celebrity names as his a.k.a.s, like they his peers. — Elmore Leonard, *Be Cool*, p. 247, 1999

▸ **go AKA**
to assume an alias *US, 1983*
- "The moral of the story," Chucky said, "the punto, any time you go a.k.a. you better be sure everybody with you does too." — Elmore Leonard, *Stick*, p. 121, 1983

ala-ala's *noun*
the testicles *US, 1981*
Hawaiian youth usage.
- Wow, da guy when keeck mah ala-alas! Ah t'ought da buggah goin bus'! — Douglas Simonson, *Pidgin to da Max*, 1981

Alabama Kleenex *noun*
toilet paper *US, 1967*
- Blood spurted form his face, so a pilot from Montgomery went to the bathroom to get some Alabama Kleenex. — Elaine Shepard, *The Doom Pussy*, p. 46, 1967

Alabama wool *noun*
cotton *US, 1949*
- American has Alabama wool for cotton. — Eric Partridge, *The World of Words*, p. 152, 1949

alambrista *noun*
a Mexican illegally present in the US *US, 1974*
Border Spanish used in English conversation by Mexican-Americans; from the Spanish for "wire."
- — Dagoberto Fuentes and Jose Lopez, *Barrio Language Dictionary*, 1974

Alameda *noun*
in bar dice games, a roll that produces no points for the player *US, 1971*
Alameda is an island city just west of Oakland. In Alameda, a worthless hand is called a "Milpitas," alluding to a small and relatively poor city just north of San Jose.
- — Jester Smith, *Games They Play in San Francisco*, p. 103, 1971

Alamo Hilton *nickname*
a heavily fortified bunker beneath the Khe Sanh base in South Vietnam during the Vietnam war *US, 1978*
- The grunts called it the Alamo Hilton and thought it was candy-assed, while almost every correspondent who came to Khe Sanh tried to get a bed there. — Michael Herr, *Dispatches*, p. 124, 1978

Alan Smitee
used as an alias for a film director who does not want his or her name used on the screen credits of a movie *US, 1969*
The Director's Guild created the term in 1969, and must approve its use; the term is an anagram of "The Alias Man."
- — *Atlanta Journal-Constitution*, p. 7F, 5th May 2006

Alaska hand *noun*
in hold 'em poker, a king and a three as the first two cards dealt to a particular player *US, 1981*
Built from the synonymous **KING CRAB**, which is found in Alaska.
- — Thomas L. Clark, *The Dictionary of Gambling and Gaming*, p. 5, 1987

Alaska strawberries *noun*
beans *US, 1991*
- — Russell Tabbert, *Dictionary of Alaskan English*, p. 82, 1991

Alaska tuxedo *noun*
a wool work suit *US, 1965*
- The Alaskan tuxedo is an ideal jacket in the woods and is commonly worn as a dress-up jacket. — Robert O. Bowen, *An Alaskan Dictionary*, p. 7, 1965
- — Mike Doogan, *How to Speak Alaskan*, p. 6, 1993

albino *noun*
in pool, the white cue ball *US, 1988*
- — Mike Shamos, *The Illustrated Encyclopedia of Billiards*, p. 4, 1993

alcohol rub *noun*
a cocktail party *US, 1968*
- Bryn Hemming, that delightful English import, gave an alcohol rub last night for Princess Ibrahim Fazil. — *San Francisco Examiner*, p. 21, 29th October 1968

alderman *noun*
1 in the circus and carnival, an office worker who informs on his fellow workers *US, 1981*
- — Don Wilmeth, *The Language of American Popular Entertainment*, p. 7, 1981
2 a big paunch. Referring to the supposed physique and appetite of local elected officials *US, 1933*
- — Bill Reilly, *Big Al's Official Guide to Chicagoese*, p. 13, 1982

alfalfa *noun*
money *US, 1917*
Circus and carnival usage.
- — Don Wilmeth, *The Language of American Popular Entertainment*, p. 7, 1981

alibi *noun*
in a rigged carnival game, the reason given by the game operator to disqualify a legitimate win *US, 1985*
- The most common alibi is to tell the player he went over the foul line. — Gene Sorrows, *All About Carnivals*, p. 8, 1985

Alice *noun*
1 the Aryan Brotherhood, a white prison gang *US, 1975*
- — Report to the Senate, *California Senate Committee on Civil Disorder*, p. 227, 1975
2 a military backpack *US, 1988*
- The only things the men had were their individual weapons and ALICE packs, rucksacks that held the bare bones necessities[.] — Harold Coyle, *Sword Point*, p. 177, 1988
- I hit the ground and grabbed my alice [backpack], then crawled to my humvee [military vehicle]. — *Washington Post*, p. A1, 1st February 1991

▸ **to have Alice**
to experience the bleed period of the menstrual cycle *US, 1968*
- — Collin Baker et al., *College Undergraduate Slang Study Conducted at Brown University*, p. 70, 1968

Alice B. Toklas brownies *noun*
chocolate brownies laced with marijuana or hashish *US, 1969*
Toklas' original 1954 recipe, which was for fudge, not brownies, carried the caution: "Should be eaten with care. Two pieces are quite sufficient."

- One close friend, a wife of a Congressman, who smokes marijuana on occasion and takes a few Alice B. Toklas brownies[.] — Myra MacPherson, *The Power Lovers*, p. 78, 1975
- Mrs. Madrigal had come to her table with a basket of Alice B. Toklas brownies. "I made too many," she had said. "Take two, but save one for later. They'll knock you on your ass." — Armistead Maupin, *Tales of the City*, p. 183, 1978

alien *noun*
in casino gambling, a betting chip from another casino *US, 1983*
- — Thomas L. Clark, *The Dictionary of Gambling and Gaming*, p. 5, 1987

A-list *noun*
used for denoting all that is associated with the greatest contemporary fame and celebrity *US, 1935*
- You know, if you do go out with Bianca, you'd be set. You'd outrank everyone. Strictly A-list. — *Ten Things I Hate About You*, 1999
- From comments McGann had overheard from the A-list guests, tomorrow's society columns would make the ambassador preen. — Philip Shelby, *Gatekeeper*, p. 144, 2000

alky; alkie *noun*
1 an alcoholic *US, 1952*
- I get high drunk, drop money on floor, am panhandled, play Ruth Brown wildjump records among drunken alky whores. — Jack Kerouac, *Letter to John Clellon Holmes*, p. 338, 8th February 1952
- If these boys don't play it just right they're liable to finish their training up in Portland at the alky hospital. — Ken Kesey, *One Flew Over the Cuckoo's Nest*, p. 145, 1962
- Jesus, you think we'd miss your wedding? This bunch of alky's? — *The Deer Hunter*, 1978
- You were never an alky, you were a cokehead. — *Something About Mary*, 1998
2 alcohol, especially methyl alcohol *US, 1844*
- Alky Orgy Kills One, Fells 8 — *San Francisco Examiner*, p. 5, 13th May 1946
- Maybe he put alky in the radiator and the chassis is snozzled[.] — James T. Farrell, *Saturday Night*, p. 37, 1947
- Long before midnight its habitues have already made sleeping arrangements or are snoring in the alleys, cheap overnight lodgings or hallways, paralyzed by alky or cheap domestic red wine. — Jack Lait and Lee Mortimer, *Washington Confidential*, p. 31, 1951
- I dug him up for Big Al, to protect our trucks and the alky we peddled to the coloreds. — Iceberg Slim (Robert Beck), *Death Wish*, p. 222, 1977

alky breather *noun*
a breath test for alcohol blood content *US, 1967*
- They had all the men who had visitors take an alky breather today. All neg. — Ken Kesey, *Kesey's Jail Journal*, p. 34, 1967

alkyed *adjective*
drunk *US, 1970*
- It was big, loud and rough and there must have been a dozen cops getting alkyed. — Red Rudensky, *The Gonif*, p. 88, 1970

alky tank *noun*
a holding cell in a jail reserved for drunk prisoners *US, 1962*
- I insist on a transfer—neurology bin, the alky tank, pediatrics, I just don't care! — Ken Kesey, *One Flew Over the Cuckoo's Nest*, p. 27, 1962

all *adverb*
so *US, 1997*
- Don't walk all slow—we have to go to class. — Pamela Munro, *U.C.L.A. Slang*, p. 20, 1997

all
▸ **be all**
used as a quotative device to report a conversation *US, 1992*
- — Connie Eble (Editor), *UNC-CH Campus Slang*, p. 1, Spring 1992
- So I was all, "What's your problem?" And he was all, "Nothing." — *Boogie Nights*, 1997
- Gimme the money, motherfucker, and I'm all, No, and he's yelling. — Lynn Breedlove, *Godspeed*, p. 200, 2002

all day *noun*
a life sentence to prison *US, 1974*
- "You're goin' in for all day on this one, my friend." — George Higgins, *Cogan's Trade*, p. 169, 1974
- One has all day [life], and a few are getting ready to get out in a couple of years. — Yusuf Jah, *Uprising*, p. 26, 1995

- "The majority of people under paperwork have all day. Life sentences, CUZ." — Colton Simpson, *Inside the Crips*, p. 128, 2005

all day *adjective*

1 in bar dice games involving up to three rolls, taking all three rolls to make the player's hand *US, 1976*
- — Gil Jacobs, *The World's Best Dice Games*, p. 191, 1976

2 in craps, said of a bet that is in effect until the shooter rolls his point or a seven *US, 1983*
- When you tell the dealer you're making an all day bet, that means it's a standard hardway bet rather than a one-roll proposition bet. — Thomas L. Clark, *The Dictionary of Gambling and Gaming*, p. 5, 1987

all day and night *noun*

a life prison sentence *US, 1976*
- — John R. Armore and Joseph D. Wolfe, *Dictionary of Desperation*, p. 19, 1976
- "He's in the big house for all day and night, a new fish jammed into a drum with a cribman, who acts like a gazoonie." — *San Francisco Examiner*, p. 26, 17th August 1976

all day from a quarter *noun*

a jail sentence of 25 years to life *US, 1992*
- — William K. Bentley and James M. Corbett, *Prison Slang*, p. 24, 1992

allelujah *noun*

a religious mission that serves food to the poor *US, 1947*
- "[M]aybe you hit the Salvation Army for a meal or knock on a back door or you go to the hallelujahs for coffee [.]" — Willard Motley, *Knock on Any Door*, p. 77, 1947

alley *noun*

a fictional place characterized by the preceding thing or activity *US, 1954*
- Today our readers are getting a preview of a case before it comes up in Alimony Alley, as the divorce courts sometimes are called. — *San Francisco News*, p. 2, 9th September 1954
- Ulcer Alley, the big time in Ad Row, is quivering at all the firings at one big agency. — *San Francisco Examiner*, p. 29, 26th January 1962

alley apple *noun*

a brick or cobblestone *US, 1927*
- — Bill Reilly, *Big Al's Official Guide to Chicagoese*, p. 13, 1982
- [W]hen the wine and beer bottles evaded easy reach, we threw half house bricks and roughed out cobblestones, "alley apples." — Odie Hawkins, *Men Friends*, p. 13, 1989

alley bourbon *noun*

strong, illegally manufactured whiskey *US, 1999*
- — *Star Tribune (Minneapolis)*, p. 19F, 31st January 1999

alley cat *noun*

a young person who idles on a street corner *US, 1945*
- — Lou Shelly, *Hepcats Jive Talk Dictionary*, p. 21, 1945
- [T]he elderly homeless and alley cats slowly circle the vegetable stalls for handouts from grocers' assistants at closing time. — Alix Shulman, *On the Stroll*, p. 4, 1981

alley-cat *verb*

to engage in a full range of vice, especially promiscuous sex *US, 1953*
- "Don't go back to your alley-catting until the Sergeant is over the horizon." — John D. McDonald, *The Neon Jungle*, p. 13, 1953

alley cleaner *noun*

a handgun *US, 1957*
- — *American Speech*, p. 192, October 1957: "Some colloquialisms of the handgunner"

alley craps *noun*

a spontaneous, loosely organized, private game of craps, rarely played in an alley *US, 1977*
- — Thomas L. Clark, *The Dictionary of Gambling and Gaming*, p. 5, 1987

alley-scoring *noun*

the recycling of food, furniture or anything else left in the garbage *US, 1997*
- — Vann Wesson, *Generation X Field Guide and Lexicon*, p. 4, 1997

alley-wise *adjective*

sophisticated in the ways of the world *US, 1968*
- As a pusher, you have more exposure than anyone else in the dope game. You have to be alley-wise. — Phil Hirsch, *Hooked*, p. 18, 1968
- One way or another, he has been a gambler all his life. Alley-wise. Street-smart. — Edward Lin, *Big Julie of Vegas*, p. 12, 1974

all-fired *adjective*

used as an intensifier *US, 1845*

Perhaps a euphemism for "hell-fired," as are INFERNAL, DAMNED, etc.
- Why are people so all-fired concerned about doing things the right way, anyway? — Dick Clark, *To Goof or Not to Goof*, p. 12, 1963
- "Well, how come you know so all-fired much about it?" Harold asked. — Terry Southern, *Texas Summer*, p. 45, 1991

all hands *adjective*

sexually aggressive *US, 1963*
- — *American Speech*, p. 273, December 1963: "American Indian student slang"

alligator *noun*

1 an enthusiastic fan of swing jazz *US, 1936*
- Bernie could well remember the "alligators" of the late swing period, those serious types, self-styled students of American jazz, who used to edge up to the orchestra shell and remain there all night, indefatigably listening. — Ross Russell, *The Sound*, p. 81, 1961

2 any unpleasant and difficult task *US, 1990*
- — Charles Shafer, *Folk Speech in Texas Prisons*, p. 197, 1990

3 in television and movie making, a clamp used to attach lighting *US, 1987*
- — Ira Konigsberg, *The Complete Film Dictionary*, p. 9, 1987

alligator *verb*

(of a painting) to crack *US, 1955*
- "Alligatoring" is the word for cracks that develop in paint. — *San Francisco Examiner*, p. 5, 22nd May 1955

Alligator Alley *nickname*

Interstate Highway 75, which connects Naples and Fort Lauderdale, Florida *US, 1966*

So named because it crosses the heart of what had been an impenetrable wilderness, the Florida Everglades. The name is thought to have been coined by the American Automobile Association in 1966 to express supreme disdain for what it considered to be an unsafe toll road.
- — Wayne Floyd, *Jason's Authentic Dictionary of CB Slang*, p. 8, 1976
- Authorities closed a 20-mile stretch of "Alligator Alley," south Florida's primary cross-state connector, and detonated a package early Friday after stopping three suspects who they believe may have been plotting a terror attack in Miami. — *CNN News*, 13th September 2002

alligator bait *noun*

1 a black person *US, 1901*
- Particularly disturbing was the recurring portrayel of African American children as "alligator bait" in southern tourist memorabilia. — Kevern Verney, *African Americans and US Popular Culture*, p. 11, 2003

2 bad food, especially fried liver *US, 1926*
- — Joseph E. Ragen and Charles Finston, *Inside the World's Toughest Prison*, p. 789, 1962

alligator burns *noun*

charrings on burnt wood in the form of scales that resemble an alligator's hide *US, 1981*
- If he'd gone in there he wouldn've known right off, the way those charrings, alligator burns, showed, he would've known you torched it. — George V. Higgins, *The Rat on Fire*, p. 22, 1981

alligator skins *noun*

paper money *US, 1949*
- I pulled the score by myself. I was gone about an hour and when I came back I got fistfuls of alligator skins. — Hal Ellson, *Duke*, p. 68, 1949

all in *adjective*

said of a poker player who has bet their entire remaining bankroll *US, 1979*
- — John Scarne, *Scarne's Guide to Modern Poker*, p. 272, 1979

all jokes and no tokes *adjective*

used by casino employees to describe poor tipping by gamblers *US, 1983*
- When I hear all jokes and no tokes, I know that everybody is having a good time but the dealers. — Thomas L. Clark, *The Dictionary of Gambling and Gaming*, p. 6, 1987

all like
▸ **be all like**
used as a quotative device, combining two other devices for "to say" *US, 1997*
- So then I was all like, "What are you gonna do?" Y' know? And he was all, like acting tough, y' know, with his friends around and stuff. — *Boogie Nights*, 1997

all-nighter *noun*
1 an engagement between a prostitute and customer that lasts all night; a prostitute's client who pays to stay all night *UK, 1960*
- I can't be takin no all night fer one fast fiver, so I start in playin roun wiff his lil ol pecker. — Robert Gover, *One Hundred Dollar Misunderstanding*, p. 21, 1961
- Three hundred and fifty scoots for an all-nighter. — James Ellroy, *Brown's Requiem*, p. 236, 1981
- He didn't know if they tricked during the evening and then took an all-nighter. — Robert Campbell, *Alice in La-La Land*, p. 263, 1987
2 a person who stays in jail all night after being arrested *US, 1992*
- He was issued a pallet to sleep on and locked up with twenty other all-nighters. — Richard Price, *Clockers*, p. 97, 1992

all over it *adjective*
in complete control *US, 2002*
- — Alonzo Westbrook, *Hip Hoptionary*, p. 3, 2002

all play *noun*
group sex in which all present participate *US, 2006*
- All play: A term describing a group sex situation (anything from a three-way to a motelful) where bench warming is strongly discouraged and all attendees must participate in some way. — Emma Taylor, *Em and Lo's Rec Sex*, p. 11, 2006

all reet *adjective*
good; all right *US, 1946*
- Well, all reet then, tell your story, man. — Ross Russell, *The Sound*, p. 10, 1961

all right *adjective*
in possession of drugs *US, 1971*
- "You all right?" one of the dopefiends yelled out of the back window. "I'll be back with some scag in less than an hour," Snake replied. — Donald Goines, *Dopefiend*, p. 174, 1971

all right!
used as a greeting among prisoners *US, 1992*
- — William K. Bentley and James M. Corbett, *Prison Slang*, p. 45, 1992

all rooters and no shooters
used at casino craps tables for encouraging a player to take a turn as a shooter *US, 1983*
- — Thomas L. Clark, *The Dictionary of Gambling and Gaming*, p. 6, 1987

all rootie
used as an expression of agreement or satisfaction *US, 1957*
Especially popular after Little Richard's 1955 hit song "Tutti Frutti."
- "All rootie," she said agreeably. — Max Shulman, *Rally Round the Flag, Boys!*, p. 47, 1957

all show and no go *adjective*
used for describing someone who cannot back appearances with action *US, 1978*
- "I think you're all show, no go," she said, and gave him a firm shove. — Willard Scott MacDonald, *Moose*, p. 158, 1978
- He's all show and no go. When he tried to act tough with us, no matter what happened, Hunter Thompson got scared. — Ralph "Sonny" Barger, *Hell's Angel*, p. 125, 2000

all that *adjective*
superlative, very good *US, 1991*
- — Lady Kier Kirby, *The 376 Deee-liteful Words*, 1992
- — Connie Eble (Editor), *UNC-CH Campus Slang*, p. 1, Spring 1993
- He thinks he's all that, Tai. — *Clueless*, 1995

all that and then some *noun*
everything *US, 1998*
- — Ethan Hilderbrant, *Prison Slang*, p. 142, 1998

all the way *adjective*
1 served with every possible condiment *US, 1999*
- Three hamburgers all the way, two bags of french fries and a jumbo vanilla shake. — Carl Hiaasen, *Sick Puppy*, p. 6, 1999
2 in the military, destined for leadership *US, 1982*
- At the time of the Ia Drang fight, Hal Moore was already being described as an "all the way" man, meaning four stars and probably Chief of Staff one day. — David H. Hackworth, *About Face*, p. 487, 1982

all the way live *adjective*
excellent, superlative *US, 1982*
- So like Andrea's sweet sixteen party was like all the way live! — Mary Corey and Victoria Westermark, *Fer Shurr! How to be a Valley Girl*, 1982
- He has a beautiful girl, a brand new car, and a college degree. That brother is definitely all the way live. — Fab 5 Freddy, *Fresh Fly Favor*, p. 6, 1992

all-time *adjective*
excellent *US, 1961*
- So, let's just say it was all time. Which, in case you're not up-to-date, means the utmost, the greatest. — Frederick Kohner, *Gidget Goes Hawaiian*, p. 6, 1961
- — John Severson, *Modern Surfing Around the World*, p. 162, 1964

all-timer's disease *noun*
used by surfers humorously to describe a person's proclivity to exaggerate when recounting surf conditions or their accomplishments *US, 1991*
- — Trevor Cralle, *The Surfin'ary*, p. 2, 1991

alone player *noun*
a card cheat who works alone *US, 1961*
- — Thomas L. Clark, *The Dictionary of Gambling and Gaming*, p. 6, 1987

alpha alpha *noun*
an automatic ambush *US, 2004*
From the phonetic alphabet.
- — David Hart, *First Air Cavalry Division Vietnam Dictionary*, p. 2, 2004

alphabet city *nickname*
an imprecisely defined area on the lower east side of Manhattan, near Avenues A, B, C, and D *US, 1980*
- A lot of poet friends have abandoned the squalor of Alphabet City and the Lower East Side for the bovine whines of this little coastal town outside San Francisco. — Jim Carroll, *Forced Entries*, p. 116, 1987
- We skate through Greenwich Village to Alphabet City. — Lynn Breedlove, *Godspeed*, p. 205, 2002

Alpo *noun*
sausage topping for a pizza *US, 1996*
An allusion to a branded dog food.
- — *Maledicta*, p. 7, 1996: "Domino's pizza jargon"

alrightnik *noun*
a person who has succeeded in material terms *US, 1968*
- An alrightnik, drowning, was pulled out of the water, and an excited crowd gathered, crying, "Stand back!" "Call a doctor!" "Give him artificial respiration!" "Never!" cried the alrightnik's wife "Real respiration or nothing!" — Leo Rosten, *The Joys of Yiddish*, pp. 12–13, 1968

also-ran *noun*
anyone not performing very well *US, 1896*
Originally applied in horse racing to any horse placed fourth or worse and thus not winning any money on the race.
- Veteran Milers Now "Also Rans" (Headline) — *San Francisco News*, p. 17, 15th January 1947
- "Also-Ran" Bags Net Upset Win (Headline) — *San Francisco Call-Bulletin*, p. 8G, 1st August 1953
- — Mel Heimer, *Inside Racing*, p. 209, 1962

altar *noun*
a toilet *US, 1962*
- — Joseph E. Ragen and Charles Finston, *Inside the World's Toughest Prison*, p. 789, 1962

alter kocker; alte kaker *noun*
a mean and nasty old man *US, 1968*
Yiddish for German for "old shitter."
- I'm doing it for Arnie Green, an alte kaker with hair in his ears. — Armistead Maupin, *Maybe the Moon*, p. 46, 1992
- His lawyer, Jesse Vogel, one of Mason's entourage of alter cocker flunkies, is propositioning blondes[.] — Josh Friedman, *When Sex Was Dirty*, p. 9, 2005

altogether *noun*
▸ **the altogether**
complete nudity *UK, 1894*
- It was then that Marcia leaped out of bed, forgetting in her excitement that she was in the "altogether," as the folks on Broadway say. — *San Francisco Call-Bulletin*, 2nd May 1946
- She would sooner have cake-walked out on the Radio City Music Hall stage in the altogether, with a red gardenia in her belly button, than put those crippled thumbs of hers on exhibit over a canasta table or anywhere. — Bernard Wolfe, *The Late Risers*, p. 93, 1954
- Strip teaser Lili St. Cyr made movieland history this week when she appeared in a scene for a new picture in the altogether—that is, absolutely nude. — *San Francisco News*, 16th August 1958
- Male & Female In the Altogether—Free Coffee! — *San Francisco Examiner*, 4th July 1968

alum; alumn *noun*
an alumnus or alumna *US, 1934*
- Mary Ann Berger, an Independent Freshman, says, "Stick around Alums—for the football game." — *Life*, p. 21, 20th December 1954
- The university [Princeton] is under growing pressure from the "alums." — *The Oregonian*, p. 15, 22nd April 1956
- Like most chancellors, Dr. Edgar had no doubt been promised by his well-to-do alums that he could scare up more endowment in the end zone than he could at all of the Christian fellowship dinners he attended. — Dan Jenkins, *Life Its Ownself*, p. 83, 1984

aluminum overcast *noun*
any very large military aircraft *US, 1961*
- Gansz never served in a command that had jet fighters, and he flew as a copilot on a C-124—a large propeller-driven troop and cargo carrier nicknamed "The Aluminum Overcast" because of its size and relatively low normal cruising speed of 272 miles per hour — *Chicago Tribune*, p. C6, 28th December 1987
- The B-17 was the bomber workhorse of World War II. When production ended in 1945, 12,726 had been built. The "Aluminum Overcast" carries the colors of the 398th Bomb Group and commemorates one shot down over France. — *Florida Times-Union*, p. B1, 14th November 2003

Alvin *noun*
a naive, easily cheated person *US, 1949*
Circus and carnival usage.
- I registered the unconscious contempt of the barkers for the Alvins and the Clydes who strolled the midway, fat silly sheep who thought it fun to be fleeced[.] — Malcolm Braley, *False Starts*, p. 69, 1976

A-man *noun*
a police officer assigned to a squad car *US, 1958*
- A-men are men in the automobile squad. — *New York Times*, p. 34, 20th October 1958

amateur night *noun*
New Year's Eve *US, 1977*
Just as amateur Christians attend church only twice a year, or amateur Jews attend services only twice a year, amateur drunks only drink to oblivion once a year.
- I was a third-rate amateur. Do you know what alcoholics call New Year's Eve? Amateur night. — Elmore Leonard, *Touch*, p. 168, 1977

Amazon Annie *nickname*
a cannon designed to fire atomic shells *US, 1958*
- The Army's 280-millimeter cannon, nicknamed "Amazon Annie," gave field artillerymen their biggest thrill last week since the first caisson was rolled into place in the Fourteenth Century. — *San Francisco Chronicle*, This World, p. 2, 31 May 1958

ambo *noun*
an ambulance *US, 1991*
- Separate ambulances took both men to the same trauma unit, with McLarney telling the medics that he felt as if was falling, as if he was going to fall off the litter. — David Simon, *Homicide*, p. 150, 1991
- "Mount and Fayette," says Eggy, watching the ambos roll up on a double shooting. — David Simon and Edward Burns, *The Corner*, p. 321, 1997

ambulance chaser *noun*
a disreputable lawyer, especially one who arrives or has an agent arrive at the scene of a disaster to seek clients from among the victims *US, 1896*
From the image of following an ambulance to an accident.

- You're a used car salesman, Daniel. You're an ambulance chaser with a rank. — *A Few Good Men*, 1992

ambulance chasing *noun*
the practice of a disreputable lawyer directly or indirectly soliciting representation status from accident victims *US, 1949*
- For the reception desks regarded ambulance chasing as some sort of felony. — Nelson Algren, *The Man with the Golden Arm*, p. 73, 1949

ambush academy *noun*
during the Vietnam war, training in jungle warfare, especially of the unconventional sort *US, 1966*
- The Tropic Lightning's Ambush Academy teaches all the basics necessary for a successful ambush. — United States Army, *The 25th's 25th in Combat*, p. 232, 1966

amebiate *verb*
to get drunk *US, 1966*
- — *Current Slang*, p. 1, Summer 1966

ameche *noun*
a telephone *US, 1941*
From actor Don Ameche's performance as Alexander Graham Bell in a 1939 movie.
- You're wanted on the Ameche, June! — *San Francisco News*, p. 13, 7 July 1945
- The Ameche approach—Friday night and you're waiting for that all important call. — *San Francisco Examiner*, p. 7, 16th November 1947

American Airlines *noun*
in hold 'em poker, the ace of diamonds and ace of hearts as the first two cards dealt to a player *US, 1981*
From the initials AA.
- — Thomas L. Clark, *The Dictionary of Gambling and Gaming*, p. 7, 1987

American taxpayer *noun*
any violator of routine traffic laws *US, 1962*
From the vociferous indignation voiced when stopped by a police officer.
- — *American Speech*, p. 266, December 1962: "The language of traffic policemen"

Amerika; Amerikkka *noun*
the United States *US, 1969*
A spelling favored by the political counterculture in the late 1960s and early 1970s; in the second form, "kkk" signifies the white supremacist Ku Klux Klan. Rap artist Ice Cube's 1990 album "AmeriKKKa's Most Wanted" gave the KKK spelling high-profile exposure.
- It wasn't until after the slave trade ended that Amerika, England, France, and the Netherlands invaded and settled in on Afro-Asian soil in earnest. — George Jackson, *Soledad Brother*, p. 236, April 1970
- The New York bombers identified themselves afterward as "revolutionary force 9" in a message to "Amerika" (a current fad in radical literature is to spell it with a German "k" to denote facism). — *San Francisco Examiner & Chronicle Datebook*, p. 18, 5th April 1970
- These black singers and magic music-makers were the real "freedom riders" of Amerika[.] — John Sinclair, *Guitar Army*, p. 12, 1972
- I believe that all three take a tremendous toll on the behavior of Blacks in Amerikkka. — Yusuf Jah, *Uprising*, p. 65, 1995

Amerikan *adjective*
American *US, 1969*
- Berkeley Cop Conspiracy: All-Amerikan Fascism (Headline) — *The Berkeley Tribe*, p. 11, 2nd August–4th September 1969
- They seem to be fighting a private holding-action against that day when the "Amerikan" technology turns into a joyless 1984. — Ethel Romm, *The Open Conspiracy*, p. 159, 1970

AMF
used as a farewell *US, 1963*
From **ADIOS MOTHERFUCKER**.
- An abbreviated form of the phrase adios mother fucker which simply means good-bye friend. — Sedley H. Martin, *College Lore*, 1963

a mighty roar went up from the crowd
used as a humorous comment on a lack of response to a joke or comment *US, 1997*

Coined by Keith Olberman on ESPN "to describe players or fans who do not seem to be as happy as they should be following a home run, touchdown, or victory."

- — Keith Olberman and Dan Patrick, *The Big Show*, p. 11, 1997

amigo *noun*
used as a term of address *US, 1974*
Spanish for "friend."

- "Let me lay it on you again, amigo," the short Mexican had whispered into Benson's ear. — Donald Goines, *Cry Revenge*, p. 80, 1974

ammo *noun*
1 ammunition *US, 1911*
Actual or figurative.

- They put the ammo clips in their jumper pockets and put their coats on the rack above them. — Darryl Ponicsan, *The Last Detail*, p. 26, 1970
- JOHN: Who's got the ammo? AXEL: Ammo! Get the ammo! — *The Deer Hunter*, 1978

2 cash *US, 2003*

- Candy, markers, ammo, liners, stocking stuffer, sweetener, garnish, and pledges are all terms for cash. — Henry Hill and Byron Schreckengost, *A Good Fella's Guide to New York*, p. 123, 2003

ammo humper *noun*
a soldier manning an artillery piece *US, 1961*

- It's so difficult to give a ugly a meaningful job if he's going to be an ammo humper in wartime. — Senate Committee on Appropriations, *Department of Defense Appropriations*, p. 326, 1961
- Private First Class Eugene Obregon, his ammo humper, tried to set up their weapon in an advanced position. — Joseph Alexander, *The Battle History of the U.S. Marines*, p. 280, 1999

ammunition *noun*
a gambler's bankroll *US, 1983*

- — Mike Shamos, *The Illustrated Encyclopedia of Billiards*, p. 7, 1993

amoeba *noun*
a Commodore Amiga™ personal computer *US, 1991*

- — Eric S. Raymond, *The New Hacker's Dictionary*, p. 35, 1991

amp *noun*
an *amp*lifier, especially one for electric instruments *US, 1967*

- Ray, we're here to buy stuff. We need pianos, amps, mikes, the works. — *The Blues Brothers*, 1980
- They were bringing their amps and instrument cases out through the load-in door, a giant illuminated martini glass on the wall above it. — Elmore Leonard, *Be Cool*, pp. 61–62, 1999

amped *adjective*
under the influence of a central nervous system stimulant, usually amphetamines or methamphetamine *US, 1972*

- — Walter L. Way, *The Drug Scene*, p. 105, 1977
- "Too much caffeine," Nell said. "I'm so amped I could jump-start Frankenstein's monster." — Joseph Wambaugh, *Finnegan's Week*, p. 160, 1993

amper *noun*
an ampersand (&) *US, 1991*

- — Eric S. Raymond, *The New Hacker's Dictionary*, p. 35, 1991

amphoterrible *nickname*
the antifungal drug Amphotericin B *US, 1994*
A nickname based on the drug's severe side effects.

- — Sally Williams, *"Strong" Words*, p. 133, 1994

amscray *verb*
to leave *US, 1934*
Pig Latin version of "scram."

- Tab Hunter coughing up a grand 50 grand to amscray out of his Warner Bros. Contract. — *San Francisco Progress*, p. 13, 3rd May 1961
- That's right, it's a free country, so amscray. — Eugene Boe (Editor), *The Wit & Wisdom of Archie Bunker*, p. 35, 1971
- I just grabbed a pear from the fruit selection and shouted, "Amscray time!" — Ethan Morden, *I've a Feeling We're Not in Kansas Anymore*, p. 61, 1985
- Amscray! Get out of here! — James Ellroy, *Hollywood Nocturnes*, p. 95, 1994

-amundo *suffix*
used as a humorous mechanism to form a slang equivalent *US, 1992*

Popularized by Fonz (Henry Winkler) on the US television program *Happy Days*, set in the 1950s, which aired from 1974 until 1984.

- JACK: Fake blood, fake fight, fake bullets, it was perfect. It was perfectamundo, perfect. JENNIFER: Well, it wasn't exactly perfectamundo. — *Days of Our Lives*, February 1992
- Correct-amundo! And that's what we're gonna be, we're gonna be cool. — *Pulp Fiction*, 1994

AMW *noun*
a vacuous female celebrity or hanger-on *US, 1988*
An abbreviation of "*a*ctress, *m*odel, *w*hatever."

- Tommy and Shelby Chong; biker-artists; music video hangers-on; assorted AMWs (actress, model, whatever). — *Los Angeles Times*, p. 2 (Part 5), 24th October 1988
- — Alon Shulman, *The Style Bible*, p. 11, 1999

amy; amie *noun*
amyl nitrite; an ampule of amyl nitrite *US, 1966*

- And have "amies" on hand too: poppers, banana splits, whatever you call them. — Angelo d'Arcangelo, *The Homosexual Handbook*, p. 115, 1968
- — Eugene Landy, *The Underground Dictionary*, p. 25, 1971
- "The place was full of 'amies' (amyl nitrite) and Locker Room (butyl nitrite). People were popping them all over the place," the officer said. — *San Francisco Chronicle*, p. 2, 9th September 1977

Amy-John *noun*
a lesbian *US, 1968*

- There are harsher and more widely used expressions: "Bulldyke," "Amy-John," "Cat-lapper," "Les," and so on. — L. Reinhard, *Oral Sex Techniques and Sex Practices Illustrated*, 196

amyl *noun*
amyl nitrate or butyl nitrate, when taken recreationally or to enhance sexual arousal *US, 1971*

- [N]o more grass, the coke bottle was empty, one acid blotter, a nice brown lump of opium hash and six loose amyls. — Hunter S. Thompson, *Fear and Loathing in Las Vegas*, p. 100, 1971
- The sexual odor of amyl permeates the misty air. — John Rechy, *The Sexual Outlaw*, p. 81, 1977
- Hunter Thompson probably put it best when he described Humphrey's campaign personality as akin to "a hen on amyls." — *New York Observer*, p. 1, 22nd December 2003

anal *noun*
anal sex *US, 2000*
A brief search of the Internet reveals an overwhelming and mainly heterosexual use of "anal" in this sense.

- Anal is a relatively new thing in porn films. It didn't become hugely popular among filmmakers and consumers alike until the mid-80s[.] — Ana Loria, *1 2 3 Be A Porn Star!*, p. 100, 2000
- Monet is proud of her scruples. "I never did anal or gang bangs." — Bill Brownstein, *Sex Carnival*, p. 63, 2000

analog *adjective*
in computing, pertaining to the world outside the Internet *US, 1997*
A figurative extension of a technical term.

- — Andy Ihnatko, *Cyberspeak*, p. 7, 1997

anchor *noun*
an examination that has been postponed *US, 1955*

- — *American Speech*, p. 299, December 1955: "Wayne University slang"

anchor *verb*
1 to stay put, to remain *US, 1906*

- What has a guy gotta do to anchor here in Sing Sing like you did? — A.S. Jackson, *Gentleman Pimp*, p. 130, 1973

2 to wait *US, 1990*

- — Charles Shafer, *Folk Speech in Texas Prisons*, p. 197, 1990

anchor clanker *noun*
a member of the US Navy *US, 1952*

- "Cheer up, Traxler. That probably won't be th' last time some Marine called ya an anchor clanker." — Michael Hodgson, *With Sgt. Mike in Vietnam*, p. 56, 1970

anchor man *noun*
in casino blackjack, the gambler immediately to the dealer's right *US, 1985*

- — Steve Kuriscak, *Casino Talk*, p. 56, 1985

ancient *adjective*
unfashionable, out of style *US, 2004*

- Your fit is ancient. — Rick Ayers (Editor), *Berkeley High Slang Dictionary*, p. 11, 2004

and a half
used for intensifying the preceding noun *UK, 1832*

- BLAST and a half—Good party. PANIC and a half—Very funny joke. — *San Francisco News*, p. 6, 25th March 1958

and away we go!
used as a humorous signal that something has just started *US, 1954*
A signature line of comedian Jackie Gleason.

- — Jackie Gleason, *And Awaay We Go!*, 1954
- And away you go! — *San Francisco Examiner*, p. II-7, 5th October 1956
- A tiny foreign car died like a dawg on the Hyde St. cable tracks nr. Vallejo—whereupon the cable's gripman and conductor got out, picked up the car, carried it over to the curb and awaaay they went! — *San Francisco Examiner*, p. II-1, 18th November 1957

Andes candy *noun*
cocaine *US, 1990*
A near reduplication based on the cocoa grown in the Andes Mountains.

- "What you puttin in my cooker?" "Lil Andes candy ... " "I hate coke," Rooski whimpered. — Seth Morgan, *Homeboy*, p. 77, 1990

and monkeys might fly out of my butt
used as a reflection of the high unlikelihood of something happening *US, 1992*

- What I'd really love, is to do "Wayne's World" for a living. It might happen—and monkeys might fly out of my butt! — *Wayne's World*, 1992

andro *noun*
the anabolic steroid 4-androstenedione *US, 2003*

- — *Microgram Bulletin (DEA)*, p. 210, 12 December 2003

andro *adjective*
androgynous *US, 1999*

- She chooses from a diverse bunch of African American masculinities, from a super-fly Isaac Hayes to a badass rapper to the andro king himself, The Artist (Prince). — *The Village Voice*, 5th October 1999

android *noun*
a patient with no normal laboratory values *US, 1994*

- — Sally Williams, *"Strong" Words*, p. 133, 1994

and will!
used for expressing a commitment to do something *US, 1947*

- — Marcus Hanna Boulware, *Jive and Slang of Students in Negro Colleges*, 1947

Andy Gump *noun*
the surgical removal of the mandible in the treatment of jaw cancer *US, 1980*
The postoperative patient looks like they have no chin, resembling the comic strip character.

- — *Maledicta*, p. 55, Summer 1980: "Not sticks and stones, but names: more medical pejoratives"

Andy Gump chin *noun*
a receding chin *US, 1970*

- At fourteen he had a poor self-image, which was reinforced whenever he looked in the mirror, by an "Andy Gump" chin. — Family Service Association of America, *Social Casework*, p. 286, 1989

and you know that!
used for expressing approval or praise *US, 1992*

- Yo, last night you had it going on, girls were treating you like a king. And you know that! — Fab 5 Freddy, *Fresh Fly Favor*, p. 6, 1992

angel *noun*
1 a soldier killed in combat *US, 2006*
Coined during the invasion and occupation of Iraq.

- The flag is then starched and ironed before it is fitted over a silver-coffin-shaped case that will hold their "angel," their name for dead service members. — *The Atlanta Journal-Constitution*, p. 1A, 25th March 2006

2 an outside investor, especially one who backs a theatrical production *US, 1891*
Theatrical origins.

- Farrell quickly became THE "angel" of the season when it was learned he was the sole backer of a musical called "Hold It!" — *The San Francisco News*, p. 11, 13th July 1948
- Frederick Vanderbilt Field, financial "angel" of left-wing groups, was called today to tell a Senate committee about the bail raised for four missing Communist leaders. — *The San Francisco Examiner*, p. 31, 11th July 1951

3 a male homosexual *US, 1927*
Originally referred to the passive partner, but later to any homosexual.

- — Joseph E. Ragen and Charles Finston, *Inside the World's Toughest Prison*, p. 789, 1962
- Angel, to some, mends the crumpled wings and pride of the denigrated fairy. — Bruce Rodgers, *The Queens' Vernacular*, p. 21, 1972

4 in aviation, a 1000-foot increment of altitude *UK, 1943*

- Thus, "angels two zero" is 20,000 feet. — Linda Reinberg, *In the Field*, p. 8, 1991
- A former Marine, Bellisario insists on authenticity in aircraft and protocol, and accurate use of military vocabulary, from Angels (altitude in thousands of feet) to Zulu (Greenwich Mean Time). — *The Stuart (Florida) News*, p. 4 (TV Pastime), 29th December 1996

5 in air combat, a misleading image or blind spot *US, 1998*

- Did I know any pilots victimized by "angels"; what? Hadn't I heard of an angel incident? — Clarence Major, *All-Night Visitors*, p. 174, 1998

Angel *noun*
a member of the Hells Angels motorcycle gang *US, 1965*

- These are the thoughts—anxieties—of anxious marchers / That the Angels will attack them. — *The Berkeley Barb*, p. 1, 5th November 1965
- The Angels and the Diggers organized it. — *The San Francisco Oracle*, 1967
- So the Angels just shrug and say, "our thing's violence." How can the V.D.C. guy answer that? — Joan Didion, *Slouching Toward Bethlehem*, p. 62, 1968
- Fighting broke out all over between Angels and monitors. Panic. — Jerry Rubin, *Do It!*, p. 43, 1970

angel cake *noun*
an attractive girl *US, 1962*

- — Dobie Gillis, *Teenage Slanguage Dictionary*, 1962

angel dust *noun*
1 phencyclidine, the recreational drug also it known as PCP *US, 1970*
A veterinary anesthetic originally; became a popular recreational drug.

- — Eugene Landy, *The Underground Dictionary*, p. 146, 1971
- Most of the football players and basketball players usually brought marijuana or angel dust. — United States Congress, House Select Committee on Crime, *Drugs in Our Schools*, p. 922, 1972
- "Ain't it some bad shit, baby? It's spiked with angel dust," she slurred as she dropped her head to his naked lap[.] — Iceberg Slim (Robert Beck), *Airtight Willie and Me*, p. 182, 1979
- All you guys do is drop ludes and then, then take Percodans and angel dust. — *Manhattan*, 1979
- The Technicolor plant, in an industrial area on Roseville Road not far from McClellan Air Force Base, was hit two weeks ago by robbers looking for drugs that could be used in the manufacture of an illegal drug known as angel dust. — *San Francisco Examiner*, p. A26, 22nd September 1983

2 money borrowed informally from a friend *US, 1976*

- — "Slingo", *The Official CB Slang Dictionary Handbook*, p. 3, 1976

angel food *noun*
a member of the US Air Force as an object of homosexual desire *US, 1988*

- — H. Max, *Gay (S)language*, p. 2, 1988

angelina sorority *noun*
the world of the young homosexual male *US, 1972*

- — Bruce Rodgers, *The Queens' Vernacular*, p. 21, 1972

angel kiss *noun*
a freckle *US, 1972*

- Ain't you ever seen somebody with angel kisses on his face before? — Emmett Grogan, *Ringolevio*, p. 80, 1972

Angel's bible *noun*
a Harley-Davidson motorcycle manual *US, 1992*

- — Paladin Press, *Inside Look at Outlaw Motorcycle Gangs*, p. 33, 1992

angel's kiss *noun*
a night breeze *US, 1961*
Korean war usage.

- The night breeze we called "Angel's Kiss" was in off Macquitti Bay, but it stayed high up in the palm fronds and scarcely moved the ten ropes. — Russell Davis, *Marine at War*, p. 121, 1961

angel track *noun*
an armored personnel carrier used as an aid station *US, 1971*

- — Ronald J. Glasser, *365 Days*, p. 242, 1971

angel wing *noun*
a cigarette dosed with phencyclidine, the drug commonly known as PCP or angel dust *US, 2002*

- Six months ago, I was guzzling rotgut and smoking angel wings at boarding school. — David Henry Sterry, *Chicken*, p. 5, 2002

angel with a dirty face *noun*
a male homosexual who due to caution or fear has yet to act upon his desire *US, 1941*
After the 1938 Warner Brothers movie *Angels With Dirty Faces*.

- — Dale Gordon, *The Dominion Sex Dictionary*, p. 20, 1967

angerball *noun*
a person who has lost their temper *US, 1998*
From the 1998 movie *Playing by Heart*.

- angerball—Someone who is excessively angry or frustrated ad a certain moment. — *Dictionary of New Terms (Hope College)*, 2002

angle *noun*
a scheme, especially an illegal one *US, 1920*

- Immediately I thought this Louie was working an angle. — Carmelo Soraci, *The Convict and the Stained Glass Window*, p. 84, 1961
- "It always makes me suspicious when people act kind to me. I always think they are working an angle of some kind." — William Lewis, *Helping the Youtful Offender*, p. 115, 1989
- "You were working an angle of your own, weren't you?" — Lawrence Block, *The Burglar in the Rye*, p. 243, 1999
- "Or else he's working an angle. If he doesn't steal a little, he's stealing big." — Alan Kaufman, *The Outlaw Bible*, p. 433, 2004

angle shooter *noun*
a poker player who exploits other players by bending the rules of the game *US, 1982*

- — David M. Hayano, *Poker Faces*, p. 185, 1982

Anglo *noun*
a white person *US, 1943*
The term was brought to the mainstream by Mexican-Americans in the southwestern US.

- I knew you'd call me a dirty Anglo hack if I told you that you have to at least pretend to be objective when you're trying to sell a book to a New York publisher. — Hunter S. Thompson, *Fear and Loathing in America*, p. 55, 22nd April 1968: Letter to Oscar Acosta
- "Anglos don't want to pay to see two colored guys fight." — Leonard Gardner, *Fat City*, p. 20, 1969
- Anglo: white, non-Mexican-American. Though normally used simply in a neutral, descriptive manner, the term sometimes has perjorative overtones. It has to some extent replaced gringo. — *Time*, p. 18, 4th July 1969
- An anglo with a last name for a first name is automatically a prick. — Edwin Torres, *Carlito's Way*, p. 117, 1975

angry *adjective*
(used of a penis) sexually aroused, erect *US, 1970*

- Ah'd purely love to see it angry. — *M*A*S*H*, 1970
- Poor little Heather! She's never seen one angry before. But it made quite an impression on her. — *Body Heat*, 1980
- Likewise for Rich Garvey, taking note of a rather well endowed male cadaver: "Oh,my goodness, I'd hate to see that thing angry." — David Simon, *Homicide*, p. 417, 1991

angry nine *nickname*
during the Korean war, an AN/GRC-9 radio *US, 1956*

- Below, M. E. Jeffus, ET2, T.T. Mongtomery and F. A. Wood set up "the angry nine." — Joseph Oglesby, *Deepfreeze*, p. 87, 1956

animal *noun*
1 in the Vietnam war, a gang-rigged set of claymore mines *US, 1983*

- [T]he men opened up with devastating force—first with an "animal," twenty claymores jury-rigged to go off all at once and loose a hailstorm of 14,000 flying steel balls[.] — Peter Goldman and Tony Fuller, *Charlie Company*, p. 114, 1983

2 a furpiece *US, 1959*

- — *Swinging Syllables*, 1959

▸ **go animal**
to act wildly, without inhibition *US, 1968*

- — Collin Baker et al., *College Undergraduate Slang Study Conducted at Brown University*, p. 71, 1968

Animals of the Army *nickname*
during the Vietnam war, used as a name for the Airborne Rangers *US, 1984*

- He was a LRRP (pronounced "lurp"—for "Long-Range Reconnaissance Patrol") with the Airborne Rangers, called by some the "Animals of the Army" due to their ferocity in combat. — Myra McPherson, *Long Time Passing*, p. 597, 1984

animal trainer *noun*
a person who engages in sexual activity with animals *US, 1978*

- — Anon., *King Smut's Wet Dreams Interpreted*, 1978

animal training *noun*
bestiality *US, 1971*

- Specialties include rubber, French and Greek cultures, and animal training. — Emile Nytrate, *Underground Ads*, p. 23, 1971

animal zoo *noun*
a rowdy college fraternity *US, 1967*

- — *American Speech*, p. 227, October 1967: "Some special terms used in a University of Connecticut men's dormitory"

ankle *verb*
1 to walk; to travel *US, 1917*

- In the Fall of 1927, when I ankled back to Chicago from my barnstorming and barn-burning tour of the West, we were still living in a fool's paradise. — Mezz Mezzrow, *Really the Blues*, p. 140, 1946
- Well, Tell ankles past and ganders the beret. — Harry Haenigsen, *Jive's Like That*, 1947
- I ankled over to the club early, about one A.M. — Edwin Torres, *After Hours*, p. 263, 1979
- Then she smiled and ankled towards the door. — James Crumley, *The Mexican Tree Duck*, p. 139, 1993

2 in television and movie making, to disassociate yourself from a project *US, 1950*

- — Ralph S. Singleton, *Filmmaker's Dictionary*, p. 8, 1990

▸ **ankle a show**
to walk out of a performance *US, 1973*

- — Sherman Louis Sergel, *The Language of Show Biz*, p. 8, 1973
- — Don Wilmeth, *The Language of American Popular Entertainment*, p. 9, 1981

ankle-biter *noun*
1 a petty, narrow-minded bureaucrat *US, 1990*

- Lieut. Gen Andrew J. Goodpaster, as West Point Superintendent, was described by James Faron in The New York Times in 1981 as "able to make the changes" because he had enough prestige to "keep the ankle-biters away," according to an aide on the administrative staff. — *The New York Times*, p. 6–8, 12th December 1990
- Ankle biters take the joy and creativity out of computing. They are negative people who spend their workday hours in a deathwatch over new initiatives. — *Computerworld*, p. 39, 20th March 1995

2 a child *US, 1963*
Also "knee biter." Humorous, not particularly kind to children.

- Well, it is a little bit of a problem to do a radioisotope procedure on a normal ankle-biter. — Millard Croll, *Recent Advances in Nuclear Medicine*, p. 76, 1966
- I gotta catch up with my wife. The settlement. The final decree. The property. Our four little ankle-biters! — Joseph Wambaugh, *Fugitive Nights*, p. 27, 1990

ankle bracelets *noun*
the < and > characters on a computer keyboard *US, 1991*

- — Eric S. Raymond, *The New Hacker's Dictionary*, p. 36, 1991

ankle express *noun*
walking *US, 1919*
- — *Current Slang*, p. 1, Spring 1969
- The same trip via ankle express took him and his Chinese mercenaries a full day to complete. — Robert Mason, *Chickenhawk*, p. 408, 1983
- Take the old ankle express down to the little communication closet under the stairs. — Henry Beard, *The Dick Cheney Code*, p. 62, 2004

ankle-slapper *noun*
a small wave *US, 1991*
- — Trevor Cralle, *The Surfin'ary*, p. 3, 1991

Annie from Arkansas *noun*
in craps, an eight *US, 1993*
- — Frank Scoblete, *Guerrilla Gambling*, p. 294, 1993

Annie Oakley *noun*
a free pass to a performance *US, 1916*
- I took them out myself on opening day and got Annie Oakleys for them to get in. — Robert Byrne, *McGoorty*, p. 136, 1972

Annie's alley *noun*
the vagina *US, 1949*
Attested by a police matron at the San Francisco Women's Detention Center in April 1949; a woman prisoner was thought to be concealing $13.00 "in Annie's Alley."

annihilated *adjective*
drunk *US, 1975*
- — *Rutgers Alumni Magazine*, p. 21, February 1986
- [B]attered s**tfaced f**cked messed up annihilated[.] — Stuart Walton, *Out of It, Cover*, 2001

annish *noun*
an anniversary issue of a single-interest fan magazine *US, 1982*
- — *American Speech*, p. 23, Spring 1982: "The language of science fiction fan magazines"

anoint *verb*
to whip someone *US, 1962*
- — Joseph E. Ragen and Charles Finston, *Inside the World's Toughest Prison*, p. 789, 1962

another country heard from
used for humorously acknowledging that someone who had previously been silent has spoken up *US, 1960*
- "So shut the hell up, everybody." "Another country heard from," said Phyllis. — John O'Hara, *Sermons and Soda-Water*, p. 36, 1960
- Mule finally speaks up. "We respectfully request to see the executive officer, sir." "Another country heard from," says the OOD. — Darryl Ponicsan, *The Last Detail*, p. 142, 1970
- Another day, another country heard from in the quest to serve as the summer home for the Washington Redskins. — *The Richmond Times Dispatch*, p. D1, 10th February 2001

another day, another dollar
a humorous expression of a day-by-day philosophy of life *US, 1939*
- He got up, yawned, and said "Well another day another dollar, goodnight" and disappeared upstairs. — Jack Kerouac, *On the Road (The Original Scroll)*, p. 361, 1951
- Well—another day—another dollar. — Joseph Kramm, *The Shrike*, p. 53, 1953
- KAFFEE: How's it going, Luther? LUTHER: Another day, another dollar, captain. — *A Few Good Men*, 1992

answer record *noun*
a rap song released in response to another song *US, 1995*
- "Answer records" between feuding rappers, once frequent, are today only sporadic. — Steven Daly and Nathaniel Wice, *alt.culture*, p. 229, 1995

antenna platoon *noun*
during the Vietnam war, a platoon with an unusually large number of radios assigned to it *US, 1989*
- I wasn't wearing brass, but with an "antenna platoon" of at least five PRC-25 radios with me, it was kind of obvious[.] — David H. Hackworth, *About Face*, p. 539, 1989

anti-frantic *adjective*
calm, collected *US, 1983*
- Yes, above all, anti-frantic. Stay cool. Hang loose. — *Esquire*, p. 180, June 1983
- He was the coolest cat, negative perspiration, the anti-frantic. — Bejamin Reed, *The Bow Tie Gang*, p. 2, 2002

Antsville *noun*
a crowded place *US, 1961*
- — Art Unger, *The Cool Book*, p. 105, 1961

antsy *adjective*
agitated, anxious *US, 1950*
- Golf duds and all, Bud Schwartz was antsy about being back on the premises so soon after the ratnapping[.] — Carl Hiaasen, *Native Tongue*, p. 133, 1991

anus bandit *noun*
a predatory male homosexual *US, 1962*
- — Joseph E. Ragen and Charles Finston, *Inside the World's Toughest Prison*, p. 789, 1962

anxious *adjective*
good *US, 1944*
- — Lou Shelly, *Hepcats Jive Talk Dictionary*, p. 7, 1945

anyhoo *adverb*
anyhow *US, 1946*
A deliberate mispronunciation.
- Anyhoo I don't want her ministering to me no more. — William Burroughs, *Letters to Allen Ginsberg 1953–1957*, p. 116, 23rd October 1955
- What wall were those Tulls coming off anyhoo? No comprende. — Lester Bangs, *Psychotic Reactions and Carburetor Dung*, p. 132, 1971
- Anyhoo, I took the kids back to my daughter's place. — Mordecai Richler, *Joshua Then and Now*, p. 419, 1980

any kine *noun*
anything *US, 1981*
Hawaiian youth usage.
- She tell any kine fo' get her way. — Douglas Simonson, *Pidgin to da Max*, 1981

anyone for tennis?
used for humorously suggesting an activity *US, 1951*
Seen as quintessentially British and enormously witty in its many variant forms.
- Anyone for tennis? Or lacrosse? — *Marion (Ohio) Daily Star*, p. 24, 19th December 1951
- Having slept that off, you wander recklessly onto the play deck with gay cries of "Anyone for shuffleboard?" — *San Francisco Examiner*, p. 21, 27th August 1952
- Anyone for gold? — *San Francisco Call-Bulletin*, p. 12, 9th July 1953

anywhere *adverb*
in possession of drugs *US, 1946*
- Hey, there, Poppa Mezz, is you anywhere? — Mezz Mezzrow, *Really the Blues*, p. 216, 1946

A-OK *adjective*
completely acceptable *US, 1959*
US Navy Captain Alan G. Shepard was widely credited for introducing the term to the general public during the first US space flight. Shepard later denied ever having said "A-OK," insisting that he had been spelling out awkward—"AWK."
- That's why George Romney enlisted and secured the support of all our [Rambler's] employees in the new "A-OK Quality Workmanship" program. — *San Francisco Chronicle*, p. 34, 8th August 1961
- "Mable told me you were A-okay, just drunk." — Joe Houston, *The Gay Flesh*, p. 92, 1965
- Big Ed said, "Uh, honey, these boys and your daughter have promised me that their behavior in the future will be A-OK." — Dan Jenkins, *Semi-Tough*, p. 60, 1972
- He winked obscenely as he made a lopsided circle of A-OK with pudgy fingers shiny greasy with bar-be-que he was gnawing. — Iceberg Slim (Robert Beck), *Airtight Willie and Me*, p. 32, 1979

A-one; A-1 *adjective*
excellent, first-class *US, 1846*
Originally of ships, then of persons and things.

- His embassy bespoke the American authorities to give him the A-1 treatment, the best. — Jack Lait and Lee Mortimer, *Washington Confidential*, p. 149, 1951
- Just you and me and thirty grand, maybe five or ten more if it's an A-1 job. — Jim Thompson, *Savage Night*, p. 73, 1953
- "[H]e's fuckin'-A-number-one stupid." — George Higgins, *Cogan's Trade*, p. 109, 1974
- I think while you were out on bond, according to my source, which is A-one reliable—you took out the jigs. — Elmore Leonard, *Stick*, p. 128, 1983

AOS
used for suggesting that there are no good options in a particular situation *US, 2001*
An abbreviation of "*all options suck*" or "*all options stink.*"

- "It's called AOS," they say, using a barracks abbreviation for "all options stink." Another senior military official said there was "no good option that wouldn't make us look useless." — *Deseret News (Salt Lake City)*, p. A2, 30th September 2001
- Add it all up for Martha Stewart it's what they call in the military an "AOS" situation (as in "all options suck")—and the hour is now at hand. — *New York Post*, 23rd February 2004

APB *noun*
in police work, an all points bulletin, broadcast to all who are listening *US, 1957*

- Guess you've often seen policemen working like this on TV or in the movies. They're sending out an APB. That's an All Points Bulletin. It's information they send to hundreds of their fellow law enforcement men to help break a case. — *Pacific Telephone, Talk*, p. 1, August 1957
- The police, pleased to have captured major game on a routine trapline, put out APB's on Caterpillar and Chilly. — Malcolm Braly, *On the Yard*, p. 236, 1967
- Your wife will give the police your truck plate number for an A.P.B. They will arrest you here, arrest me on charges of harboring a fugitive. — Iceberg Slim (Robert Beck), *Doom Fox*, p. 117, 1978

apcray *noun*
nonsense; garbage *US, 1937*
A Pig Latin version of CRAP.

- And please don't give me any of that apcray about first physics. — Harry Allen Smith, *Larks in the Popcorn*, p. 51, 1948
- [A] pigeon plopped his apcray on my shoulder. — Leo Rosten, *King Silky!*, p. 4, 1980

ape *noun*
in the entertainment industry, a technical member of a movie crew *US, 1970*

- You're gonna put up the actors and the apes in the same hotel?!? Are you outta your nut!?! — Terry Southern, *Blue Movie*, p. 66, 1970

ape *adjective*
crazed, frenzied, demonstrating rage or delight *US, 1955*
Based on the behavior of apes in movies—not in real life.

- I drive you ape, and you just don't trust yourself with me, that's what it is. — Max Shulman, *Rally Round the Flag, Boys!*, p. 58, 1957
- That's why they go ape in Viet Nam. — Darryl Ponicsan, *The Last Detail*, p. 34, 1970

ape drape *noun*
a hair style in which the hair is worn short at the front and long at the back *US, 1995*
Most commonly known as a "mullet."

- — Steven Daly and Nathaniel Wice, *alt.culture*, p. 158, 1995
- I snap, making a mental note of her hideous patch-denim maxi skirt and ridiculous ape-drape hairdo. — John Waters, *Crackpost*, p. 25, 2003

apeshit *adjective*
▸ go apeshit
to lose control; to go crazy *US, 1951*

- The ceremony was conducted by a lanky preacher who also was an ex-G.I., a former Marine chaplain gone apeshit. — Clancy Sigal, *Going Away*, p. 238, 1961
- The crowd went apeshit and the band went oompa-oomp. — Edwin Torres, *After Hours*, p. 198, 1979
- I turn around and all these cops are outside. You're right, it was like, bam! I blink my eyes and they're there. Everybody starts going apeshit. — *Reservoir Dogs*, 1992

- Nice to see Kiddo hasn't gone completely apeshit. [Screenplay, not in final cut] — *Kill Bill*, 2003

A-pie *noun*
apple pie *US, 1967*

- — *American Speech*, p. 61, February 1967: "Soda-fountain, restaurant and tavern calls"

A-plug *noun*
a plug inserted in the rectum as part of a sadomasochistic encounter *US, 1979*
An abbreviation for "*ass-'plug.*"

- My world of s/m is full of pleasure and is full of toys and goodies—hand-crafted leather dildoes, A-plugs[.] — *What Color is Your Handkerchief*, p. 17, 1979

apostles *noun*
▸ the apostles
in craps, a roll of twelve *US, 1999*

- — Chris Fagans and David Guzman, *A Guide to Craps Lingo*, p. 38, 1999

appie *noun*
an appendectomy patient *US, 1985*

- — *Maledicta*, p. 15, 1984–1985: "A medical christmas song"

applause *noun*
a sexually transmitted infection, especially gonorrhea *US, 1990*
An excruciating pun on CLAP.

- — Richard McAlister, *Rapper's Handbook*, p. 1, 1990

apple *noun*
1 a person *US, 1887*
Usually heard with a qualifying adjective such as "bad" or "rotten."

- I got a nephew. A brainy apple and a good kid. — Philip Wylie, *Opus 21*, p. 114, 1949
- You may be a rough apple, but I can make your face look like it's been run through a grinder[.] — Mickey Spillane, *My Gun is Quick*, p. 20, 1950
- "In removing what few 'bad apples' there may be, the union would be serving two good purposes." — *San Francisco Call-Bulletin*, p. 6G, 14th January 1953
- [T]he hearing should not be interpreted as an indictment of all auto dealers because of the activities of a few "bad apples." — *San Francisco Examiner*, 4th August 1960

2 the gullible victim of a confidence swindle *US, 1966*

- So I'm square, JD told himself resentfully. An apple. — Malcolm Braly, *It's Cold Out There*, p. 41, 1966

3 a Native American Indian who curries favor with the white establishment by embracing white cultural values *US, 1980*
A variation on a theme—red on the outside, white on the inside.

- — *Maledicta*, p. 124, Summer 1980: "Racial and ethnic slurs: regional awareness and variations"

4 a capsule of secobarbital sodium (trade name Seconal™), a central nervous system depressant *US, 1980*

- — Edith A. Folb, *runnin' down some lines*, p. 228, 1980
- — Richard A. Spears, *The Slang and Jargon of Drugs and Drink*, p. 13, 1986

5 a self-propelled barracks barge *US, 1971*
From the ship's official designation as an "APL."

- The men climbed out, walked over the metal roofing of the tango boats and up the ladders to the LST's and "apples." — Ronald J. Glasser, *365 Days*, pp. 28–29, 1971

6 the vagina *US, 1980*

- — Edith A. Folb, *runnin' down some lines*, p. 228, 1980

Apple *noun*
▸ The Apple
New York City *US, 1938*

- Max hadn't heard New York City referred to as "The Apple" in fifteen years. — John Williams, *The Man Who Cried I Am*, p. 224, 1967
- There was a giant black pimp from the "Apple." — Iceberg Slim (Robert Beck), *Pimp*, p. 168, 1969
- When I reached the Apple I got off the train at the 125th Street station[.] — A.S. Jackson, *Gentleman Pimp*, p. 133, 1973

▷ see also: BIG APPLE

apple box *noun*
in the television and movie industries, any device used to raise an actor or object to the desired height *US, 1977*

- — Tony Miller and Patricia George, *Cut! Print!*, p. 34, 1977

applehead *noun*
a dull, stupid person *US, 1951*

- She's not married; I don't believe that applehead. — George Mandel, *Flee the Angry Strangers*, p. 103, 1952
- Why, those apple heads! Who are they supposed to be kidding? — Mickey Spillane, *Kiss Me Deadly*, p. 109, 1952

apple-knocker *noun*
1 a rustic, especially a naive one *US, 1919*

- "I'm an apple-knocker," he [Casey Stengel] likes to say, "and I'm against all city slickers." — *Time*, p. 81, 25th October 1948
- He [Arthur Godfrey] always sounds like the apple-knocker who's in the big town for the very first time. — *San Francisco Examiner*, p. II-1, 6th July 1956
- I didn't get any serious action on Broadway for a while, because I was still an apple knocker[.] — Minnesota Fats, *The Bank Shot*, p. 61, 1966
- He was an open apple knocker from the West Side wearing plain Monkey Ward jeans rather than Levi's and high-top horsehide shit kickers. — Earl Thompson, *Tattoo*, p. 55, 1974

2 an outdoor toilet *US, 1975*
From the image of apples dropping onto the outhouse roof.

- — John Gould, *Maine Lingo*, p. 36, 1975

apple orchard *noun*
a location where police wait parked, certain that they will soon witness a driving infraction *US, 1970*

- "Do you know a good spot to sit? Some good spot where we could get a sure ticket?" "An apple orchard, huh?" — Joseph Wambaugh, *The New Centurions*, p. 293, 1970

apple pie order *noun*
complete and perfect order *US, 1975*

- — John Gould, *Maine Lingo*, p. 36, 1975

apple polisher *noun*
a person who shamelessly curries favor from those above him *US, 1927*

- Attention apple-polishers! A new Washington crop, bursting with flavor and health, is on the way to you. — *Time*, p. 95, 2nd November 1959
- What's Your Opinion of Office Apple Polishers? (Headline) — *San Francisco Chronicle*, p. 36, 20th July 1966

applesauce *noun*
nonsense *US, 1919*

- "Applesauce," said Mimsy. "Take the bus as far out as it will take you, and then you walk." — Frederick Kohner, *The Affairs of Gidget*, p. 25, 1963

apple up *verb*
to become frightened *US, 1966*

- "Okay, if you want to apple it up, I'm not going to try to pull you off it." — Malcolm Braly, *It's Cold Out There*, p. 40, 1966

application *noun*
▶ **take an application**
(used of a pimp) to probe the psyche of a woman who is a candidate to come to work for you *US, 1972*

- I take an application on a broad when I talk to her that is worse than if she was going to go out and get a job in the Pentagon. I get a mental makeup on her[.] — Christina and Richard Milner, *Black Players*, p. 88, 1972

appy *noun*
an appendectomy *US, 1994*

- — Sally Williams, *"Strong" Words*, p. 133, 1994

apron *noun*
the gross daily receipts from a carnival concession *US, 1990*

- — Lindsay E. Smith and Bruce A. Walstad, *Keeping Carnies Honest*, pp. 42–43, 1990

▶ **out of the apron**
(used of gambling in a casino) using money borrowed from the casino *US, 1982*

- — David M. Hayano, *Poker Faces*, p. 187, 1982

aqua boot *verb*
to vomit into the ocean *US, 1991*

- — Trevor Cralle, *The Surfin'ary*, p. 3, 1991

A-rab *noun*
an Arab *US, 1972*

Not flattering, but more oafish than derogatory. The slang sense of the word is gained strictly through pronunciation—a long first "A," two drawn out syllables, and a light twang with the second. In his 1962 rock/novelty record "Ahab the Arab," Ray Stevens gave a loud public voice to this pronunciation.

- You know yourself that a sumbitch who don't block or tackle is nothing but a nigger hebe spick with a little A-rab thrown in. By the way. We got any A-rabs around here? — Dan Jenkins, *Semi-Tough*, pp. 5–6, 1972
- One look at your guinea puss and this fuckin' A-rab of yours and he'll bolt like a rabbit. — Edwin Torres, *Carlito's Way*, p. 77, 1975
- Except I can't show you no Arabs on account of I do not know too many A-rabs. — George V. Higgins, *The Rat on Fire*, p. 27, 1981
- A boogie barkeep said she's got some ace A-rab tips. — James Ellroy, *Destination Morgue*, p. 349, 2004

arc *verb*
in computing, to archive something *US, 1997*

- I arced all of the code libraries and netted them over to you this morning. — Andy Ihnatko, *Cyberspeak*, p. 12, 1997

arc around *verb*
to engage in enthusiastic and energetic, if meaningless and aimless, activity *US, 1986*
US naval aviator usage.

- — *United States Naval Institute Proceedings*, p. 108, October 1986

architect *noun*
in poker, a player who bets heavily *US, 1988*
So called because his betting builds the pool of bets.

- — George Percy, *The Language of Poker*, p. 6, 1988

arctic *adjective*
in poker, said of a very poor hand or series of very poor hands *US, 1996*

- — John Vorhaus, *The Big Book of Poker Slang*, p. 4, 1996

arena rat *noun*
a woman who invites sexual relations with professional wrestlers *US, 1990*

- They are called "Arena Rats" by the boys, though I think this is a harsh name for most of them. There are some who deserve it. They come in all shapes, sizes, ages and social backgrounds. The one thing they have in common is the love of wrestlers. — Pat Barrett, *Everybody Down There Hates Me*, p. 225, 1990
- A new guy would come into the territory, and we would find him the most attractive "arena rat," or wrestling groupie[.] — Bobby Heenan, *Bobby the Brain*, p. 114, 2002

are you for real?
used for humorously questioning a person's sincerity *US, 1949*

- While [Dean] Martin sings, [Jerry] Lewis flaps around wild as a keyed-up freshman, breaking his sentences and throwing away the ends, asking the catch phrase, "Are you for real?" — *Vanity Fair*, p. 78, July 1949

are you ready to throw down?
used as a call soliciting a response ("yes, we are") at a party *US, 2002*

- — Alonzo Westbrook, *Hip Hoptionary*, p. 3, 2002

arg *noun*
in computing, an argument *US, 1981*

- — *CoEvolution Quarterly*, p. 27, Spring 1981

Arizona stop *noun*
a rolling stop at a traffic signal or stop sign *US, 1962*

- — *American Speech*, p. 266, December 1962: "The language of traffic policemen"
- — Jeffrey McQuain, *Never Enough Words*, p. 54, 1999

Arizona Territory *noun*
an area southwest of Da Nang, South Vietnam, with imprecise boundaries and a strong Vietcong presence *US, 1991*

- Americans who operated there named it the Arizona Territory. — William Le Gro, *Vietnam from Cease-Fire to Capitulation*, p. 113, 1981

Arkansas fire extinguisher *noun*
a chamberpot *US, 1958*

- — *Western Folklore*, p. 29, 1962

Arkansas flush *noun*
in poker, a worthless hand consisting of four cards in one suit and a fifth in another *US, 1950*
In earlier years, an Arkansas flush was three or four cards in combination and a Bowie knife.
- — *American Speech*, p. 97, May 1951: "The vocabulary of poker"
- — Albert H. Morehead, *The Complete Guide to Winning Poker*, p. 256, 1967

Arkansas toad stabber *noun*
a sharp knife *US, 1994*
- [A]rkansas toad stabbers drawn and pointed square at my middle[.] — James Ellroy, *Hollywood Nocturnes*, p. 283, 1994

Arkansas toothpick *noun*
a hunting knife *US, 1836*
- Beale Street (Memphis) Negroes could damage each other by exercising some ingenuity. Crump's cops shook them down nightly for pistols, Arkansas toothpicks, brass knucks, razors and ice picks. — *Time*, p. 20, 27th May 1946

Arky; Arkie *noun*
a resident of Arkansas; an unsophisticated rustic from the south central US *US, 1927*
Often used with contempt.
- "Did you hear that, chief?" the scurvy Arkie said. — Oscar Zeta Acosta, *The Autobiography of a Brown Buffalo*, p. 119, 1972
- — *Maledicta*, p. 151, Summer/Winter 1978: "How to hate thy neighbor: A guide to racist maledicta"
- Along about dawn, this Arkie bonhunk named Hutchinson actually got up and went back there[.] — Seth Morgan, *Homeboy*, p. 152, 1990

arm *noun*
1 a police officer *US, 1956*
- — *American Speech*, p. 99, May 1956: "Smugglers' argot in the southwest"

2 the penis *US, 1972*
- — Christina and Richard Milner, *Black Players*, p. 296, 1972

▸ **get your arms around**
to grasp the meaning of *US, 1989*
- In 1984, IBM decided it needed to get its arms around education. — *Development Journal*, p. 34, January 1989

▸ **off the arm**
in food and beverage servers' argot, served without a tray *US, 1950*
- In truth, it was once very stylish to have a sweetheart who served it "off the arm." — Jack Lait and Lee Mortimer, *Chicago Confidential*, p. 105, 1950

▸ **on the arm**
without charge *US, 1926*
- You can eat at the deli. They're good on the arm. — Peter Maas, *Serpico*, p. 60, 1973
- But that's cool, 'cause Dave is workin' mostly on the arm now, since at the present time I am in a financial state of insoluble. — Edwin Torres, *After Hours*, p. 161, 1979
- They had a pizza that tasted even better because it was on the arm, and then drove to Hamilton House. — William J. Cavnitz, *One Police Plaza*, p. 238, 1984

arm and a leg *noun*
a prison sentence of five to ten years *US, 1991*
- — Lee McNelis, *30 + And a Wake-Up*, p. 6, 1991

arm candy *noun*
someone good-looking enough for you to be seen out with *US, 1992*
- [Marilyn Monroe] already had mini-roles in eight movies when she turned up as George Sanders' arm candy in the party scenes of this film. — *Chicago Tribune*, 21st August 1992
- Our heroine Carrie walks off into the sunset not as a spinster, or as the arm candy of a suave Russian artist, but hand-in-hand with the guy who has always been in her heart. — *Chicago Daily Herald*, p. 1, 23rd February 2004

armchair *adjective*
removed from the action; said of an observer who acts as if he is a participant
- Coach Pappy Waldorf and his Golden Bears, in the opinion of local Cal's AA—Armchair Alumni in this case. — *San Francisco Call-Bulletin*, p. 29, 28th October 1955

- Tom Bolan, boxing promoter, called the National Boxing Association a "bunch of armchair schemers" today and suggested the body "drop out of existence along with its assinine ratings." — *San Francisco Examiner*, p. 53, 11th July 1961

armchair ride *noun*
in horse racing, an easy victory *US, 1976*
- — Tom Ainslie, *Ainslie's Complete Guide to Thoroughbred Racing*, p. 327, 1976

Armenian chrome *noun*
aluminum paint *US, 1961*
- — *American Speech*, p. 272, December 1961: "Northwest truck drivers' language"

Armo *noun*
an Armenian *US, 2006*
- "Not to mention Russkies and Armos." — Joseph Wambaugh, *Hollywood Station*, p. 181, 2006

armor *noun*
body restraints *US, 1995*
- The cops threw on full armor: cuffs, manacles, and drag chains. — James Ellroy, *American Tabloid*, p. 17, 1995

▸ **in the armor**
(used of beer) in a can *US, 1967*
- — *American Speech*, p. 62, February 1967: "Soda-fountain, restaurant and tavern calls"

armpit *noun*
an obnoxious, unfriendly person *US, 1968*
- — Collin Baker et al., *College Undergraduate Slang Study Conducted at Brown University*, p. 71, 1968

armpit of the world; armpit of the universe *noun*
the worst place *US, 1968*
- [L]ike the absolute armpit of the world[.] — James Patterson, *The Midnight Club*, p. 158, 1989
- I been to Asia and it's the armpit of the universe. — Bharati Mukherjee, *Jasmine*, p. 112, 1989

armpit theater *noun*
a shoddy, low-budget theater *US, 1962*
- "I did the Columbia wheel out of Sun time, al lthe armpit theaters where he was still selling Crackerjack between the striptease numbers." — Stephen Longstreet, *The Flesh Peddlers*, p. 213, 1962

arm-stretcher *noun*
a heavy suitcase *US, 1992*
- As best I could with my two heavy arm stretchers, fighting my way through a mob that kept congratulating me for ending the war, I arrived at the Ambassador Hotel. — Larry Rivers, *What Did I Do?*, p. 23, 1992

arm trophy *noun*
a stunning and sexually appealing companion, valued for the prestige attached to their presence *US, 1994*
- Another girl said, "They want an arm trophy who will be their personal slave." — Anka Radakovich, *The Wild Girls Club*, p. 168, 1994

army *noun*
a large bankroll *US, 1990*
Alluding to the green of currency and military uniforms.
- A player backed by an army can do battle all day. — Steve Rushin, *Pool Cool*, p. 7, 1990

army banjo *noun*
a shovel or other entrenching tool *US, 1969*
- Army Banjo. A shovel is given this name by soldiers because of its shape. — *Word Study*, 1969

army brat *noun*
a person who grew up the child of a career member of the army *US, 1931*
- Cindy had been an army brat and had lived at military posts all over the world. — John D. MacDonald, *The Deceivers*, p. 20, 1958
- I was an army brat, born in Chunking, China, where my parents, both Chinese-Americans, were stationed. — Kathryn Leigh Scott, *The Bunny Years*, p. 154, 1998

army craps *noun*
a game of craps in which the shooter serves as the banker *US, 1984*
- — Thomas L. Clark, *The Dictionary of Gambling and Gaming*, p. 8, 1987

army marbles *noun*
dice *US, 1963*
From the view that soldiers are fond of dice games.
- — Thomas L. Clark, *The Dictionary of Gambling and Gaming*, p. 8, 1987

army odds *noun*
in a dice game, the true odds, not approximate odds often used in street games *US, 1962*
- — Frank Garcia, *Marked Cards and Loaded Dice*, p. 250, 1962

Army Peace Corps *noun*
the US Army Special Forces *US, 1964*
Highly trained killers, so an ironic term.
- He asked the generals to name the officers who would be in charge of the proposed "Army Peace Corps" in Southeast Asia. — Davis Wise, *The Invisible Government*, p. 1964

army roll *noun*
a controlled roll of the dice by a skilled cheat in a game of craps *US, 1963*
- — Thomas L. Clark, *The Dictionary of Gambling and Gaming*, p. 8, 1987

Arnies *noun*
anabolic steroids *US, 2006*
- "If he was popping Arnies to get those shoulders, roid-rage might explain the multiple assault beefs." — Stephen J. Cannell, *White Sister*, p. 216, 2006

-aroo *suffix*
used as a festive if meaningless embellishment of a noun *US, 1941*
- Nino and his Cash Money Monkeys are dealin' with those spicaroos upon Broadway and 171st. — *New Jack City*, 1990

-arooni *suffix*
used as a meaningless embellishment of a word *US, 1946*
A highly affected style of speaking invented and marketed with limited success by jazz musician Slim Gaillard.
- To a word that's already jazz slang like "voot," he adds the sound "arooni" or something like that. — Capitol Records, *The Capitol*, p. 13, March 1946
- Slim Gaillard is a tall, thin Negro with big sad eyes who's always saying "Right-orooni" and "How 'bout a little bourbon-orooni." — Jack Kerouac, *On the Road*, pp. 175–176, 1957

around the world *noun*
the oral stimulation of all parts of a partner's body *US, 1949*
- — Anon., *The Gay Girl's Guide*, p. 15, 1949
- [T]hey say she gives a super around the world and also knows about massage[.] — Gore Vidal, *Myra Breckinridge*, p. 56, 1968
- "I learned that some things johns ask for, like 'a trip around the world,' don't mean any one thing—you have to find out what he wants." — Charles Winick, *The Lively Commerce*, p. 180, 1971
- The priest asked for around-the-world service and enjoyed every minute of it. — John Sayles, *Union Dues*, p. 188, 1977

arrow *noun*
an amphetamine tablet *US, 1993*
- — Peter Johnson, *Dictionary of Street Alcohol and Drug Terms*, p. 11, 1993

▸ **bust an arrow; blow an arrow**
in a carnival or small circus, to become lost when traveling from one town to another *US, 1973*
In the past, advance men would paste arrows along the roadside to show the way to the next stop; if you missed an arrow, you got lost.
- — Sherman Louis Sergel, *The Language of Show Biz*, p. 36, 1973

▸ **like an arrow**
in poker, said of a sequence of five cards conventionally known as a "straight" *US, 1988*
- — George Percy, *The Language of Poker*, p. 52, 1988

art *noun*
artillery *US, 2000*
- Captain Hewitt helped adjust the art from his vantage point atop Hill 902. — Keith Nolan, *Ripcord*, p. 22, 2000

Arthur Duffy *noun*
▸ **take it on the Arthur Duffy**
to leave quickly *US, 1905*

A sprinter, in 1902 Duffy was the first to run the 100-yard dash in 9.6 seconds; he later wrote a sports column for the *Boston Post*.
- The court there sort of had a hunch that Alfonso might take it on the Arthur Duffy, so it slapped a $50,000 don't-go-away bond on him. — *San Francisco Examiner*, 5th June 1947
- "If I were you," he whispers, "I would take it on the Arthur Duffy. Heel and toe it out of here." — Robert Byrne, *McGoorty*, p. 72, 1972

artillery *noun*
1 guns *US, 1822*
- "Why all the artillery?" I asked him. — Mickey Spillane, *I, The Jury*, p. 34, 1947
- Only there was no audience, just the guards and their artillery. — Red Rudensky, *The Gonif*, p. 13, 1970
- I ran downstairs and hid all the artillery again. — Edwin Torres, *Carlito's Way*, p. 109, 1975
- COP 1: What kind of artillery? SECRET 1: Perp's brandishing a shotgun. — *Mallrats*, 1995
2 in boxing, heavy blows *US, 1954*
- When he was ready to cut loose with his heavy artillery, Carter had no trouble scoring with sharp, hurting blows. — *San Francisco Examiner*, p. 28, 19th November 1954
- Rocky was tossing those artillery shells of his all night at Archie, who weathered them for nine rounds. — *San Francisco Call-Bulletin*, p. 12, 1st December 1956
3 in other sports, something accomplished from a distance *US, 1957*
- Dodgers Use Long-Ball Artillery to Clip Bucs 3-0 (Headline) — *San Francisco Chronicle*, 11th August 1957
- St. Mary's long range artillery, led by chief fire control officer LaRay Doss, shelled Santa Clara's zone defense into ruins last night. — *San Francisco Chronicle*, p. 1H, 17th January 1958
4 the equipment needed to inject a drug *US, 1915*
- A cabinet was filled with other "artillery"—the legal connotation addicts give shooting gadgets. — *San Francisco News*, p. 1, 5th December 1951
5 strict discipline; a greater power *US, 1954*
- But, before you bring in the heavy artillery, try a more gentle persuasion. — *San Francisco Examiner*, p. 6, 13th June 1954

artillery ears *noun*
partial deafness caused by exposure to the loud noise of the artillery *US, 1982*
- After nine years without any improvement, I realized that my "artillery ears" (as they were known by military tradition) were never going to get any better. — David H. Hackworth, *About Face*, p. 349, 1982

artsy-craftsy *adjective*
pretentiously artistic but not notably useful or comfortable *UK, 1902*
- For one, he has never moved his business out of the artsy-craftsy atmosphere of Greenwich Village. — Robert Sylvester, *No Cover Charge*, p. 243, 1956
- Doctrinaire and elitist. Artsy-craftsy. — Joan Didion, *The White Album*, p. 77, 1970
- Don't go back, it's all artsy-craftsy over there now. Hurley Brothers Funeral Home, they change the name of Death 'n Things. — Elmore Leonard, *Glitz*, pp. 119–120, 1985

artsy-fartsy *adjective*
excessively arty *US, 1964*
- [A]n artsy-fartsy director had shot a Western with such low-key lighting that it looked as though the wranglers were herding cattle inside a shoe[.] — Max Shulman, *Anyone Got a Match?*, p. 106, 1964
- "United Pictures, Ltd." was one of those mid-sized movie studios that pushed a bunch of now famous actors through, specialized in "small" pictures (nothing arsy fartsy) that made money … — Odie Hawkins, *Lost Angeles*, p. 61, 1994

arty *noun*
artillery *US, 1864*
- "Tell you what, how about some nice arty?" — Tim O'Brien, *Going After Cacciato*, p. 11, 1978
- Lootenant, they're kicking our ass, they know we're gonna bring heavy shit on 'em pretty soon so they're gonna get in tight under the arty. — *Platoon*, 1986
- They've got fists of iron and nerves of steel / If the "quick" don't get you, then the Arties will. — Sandee Shaffer Johnson, *Cadences*, p. 76, 1986
- "ARTY's being adjusted now…" — Cherokee Paul McDonald, *Into the Green*, p. 107, 2001

arty-farty *adjective*
pretentious, artificially cultural *US, 1967*
- Look for the Gangsters of the New Freedom at the arty-farty and
  big-business cocktail parties[.] — G. Legman, *The Fake Revolt*, p. 13, 1967

Arvin *noun*
any South Vietnamese soldier *US, 1968*
The South Vietnamese Army was known as the ARVN (*Army of
the Republic of Viet Nam*); it took one vowel and very little
imagination to get to Arvin.
- Sace and Handson, and a Vietnamese soldier, an Arvin, are already
  in the rear. — William Wilson, *The LBJ Brigade*, p. 33, 1966
- At dawn a company of Arvins moves into the hamlet and gathers all
  the civilians in one spot. — Martin Russ, *Happy Hunting Ground*, p. 119, 1968

Arvin *adjective*
pertaining or belonging to the South Vietnamese Army *US,
1967*
- That morning the VC had overrun an Arvin [Army of the Republic
  of Vietnam] outpost. — David Reed, *Up Front in Vietnam*, p. 35, 1967
- Did I tell you I've been trying to visit the Arvin prison compound
  in Danang? — Martin Russ, *Happy Hunting Ground*, p. 118, 1968
- "He's got fresh Arvin fatigues on every day," the first reporter
  insisted. — Robert Stone, *Dog Soldiers*, p. 32, 1974

Aryan B *noun*
the white-supremacist prison gang the Aryan Brotherhood
US, 2005
- "Tried right away to hook up with the Dirty White Boys—an Aryan-B
  farm club." — Jonathan Kellerman, *Rage*, p. 82, 2005

asbestos pants *noun*
in poker, used for describing what a player on a very good
streak of luck needs *US, 1988*
- — George Percy, *The Language of Poker*, p. 59, 1988

ash *noun*
▸ **get your ashes hauled**
to be brought to ejaculation *US, 1906*
- Then he said, "Kimberly, it's very plain to me what you need. You
  need to get your ashes hauled. This morning. If you went out and
  got your ashes hauled right now, it'd do wonders for you." — Frederic
  Wakeman, *The Hucksters*, p. 88, 1946
- I repeat this one bit of smut only to show what sort of fellows I've
  been forced to live with—they're going to get their ashes hauled!
  — Robert Gover, *One Hundred Dollar Misunderstanding*, p. 10, 1961
- I'm just from behind those gray prison walls / so you can see I'm
  got to get my ashes hauled. — Bruce Jackson, *Get Your Ass in the Water and
  Swim Like Me*, p. 125, 1965
- Even the company shitsack got his ashes hauled while we were
  there. — Larry Heinemann, *Paco's Story*, p. 126, 1986

ashcan *noun*
a depth charge *US, 1918*
- Deduct fifteen for an ashcan to sink to medium depth. — C.S. Forester,
  The Good Shepherd, p. 84, 1955
- We had ashcans on the stern of the vessel. — *New York Times*, p. 29, 1st
  January 1987

Ashcan City *nickname*
during the Korean war, a US Army processing center eight
miles from Inchon *US, 1957*
From ASCOM (*Army Service Command*) to "Ascom City" to
"Ashcan City."
- The convoy to this camp—Ascom City or Ashcan City—was absolutely the END. — Martin Russ, *The Last Parallel*, p. 43, 1957

Asian two-step *noun*
any highly venomous snake encountered in the jungles of
Southeast Asia *US, 1966*
From the belief that the venom will kill the victim within two
steps of the bite.
- The thought of running into an Asian two-step—any of a number of
  very poisonous snakes, usually a branded krait—in the grasslands
  wouldn't even enter my mind. — James Watson, *Point Man*, p. 270, 1995

Asiatic *adjective*
deranged *US, 1955*
- — *American Speech*, p. 302, December 1955: "Wayne University slang"

as if!
used as a humorous expression of extreme scepticism *US,
1981*
- — Connie Eble (Editor), *UNC-CH Campus Slang*, p. 1, March 1981
- BENJAMIN: Did you really think I wouldn't end up with the girl.
  GARTH: As if. — *Wayne's World*, 1992
- He said my debates were unresearched, unstructured, and
  unconvincing. As if! — *Clueless*, 1995
- "Then we'd get in our sleeping bags and hump our stuffed animals
  until we came." "As if." — Amy Sohn, *Run Catch Kiss*, p. 116, 1999

ask *noun*
▸ **ask for Nancy's hand**
to seek membership in Nuestra Family, a Mexican-American
prison gang *US, 1975*
- — Report to the Senate, *California Senate Committee on Civil Disorder*, p. 227, 1975

as my pappy would say ...
used as a humorous introduction or segue *US, 1957*
A signature line from Maverick, an early and popular television
western (ABC, 1957–62). Repeated with referential humor.
- Not a lot of men could do that. He fixed himself, as my pappy
  would say. — Jonathan Maberry, *Ghost Road Blues*, p. 181, 2006

asparagus *noun*
a boy's penis *US, 2003*
From the language of child pornography.
- In court Monday, Schopp said his computer had inadvertently
  downloaded some of the images as he searched the Internet for
  asparagus recipes. Wilken noted that asparagus is apparently a slang
  term for boys' genitalia. — *San Francisco Chronicle*, p. A17, 28th October 2003

asphalt jungle *noun*
a large city *US, 1920*
The title of a 1949 book by W. R. Burnett as well as an ABC
television series starring Jack Warden in 1961.
- Shall we take a new stance toward the City and its mass culture—a
  tougher stance, a more nervy one—so that we may learn to live
  more gracefully and meaningfully in this Asphalt Jungle we have
  constructed around us? (Letter to Editor) — *San Francisco Chronicle*, p. 2,
  28th December 1952
- "I'm not anxious. I've been waiting too long," her owner and
  skipper Bradford Simmons said. "I'm free of the asphalt jungle."
  — *San Francisco Examiner*, p. 17, 19th November 1964

A-squared *nickname*
Ann Arbor, Michigan *US, 1994*
- At press time, the hit Royal Oak fry shop was preparing to open
  an outlet on the corner of Main and Washington in downtown
  A-squared. — *Detroit Monthly*, p. 109, 7th November 1994

ass *noun*
1 the buttocks, the posterior *US, 1853*
- Her skirt is up over her ass, her thighs squirming underneath him,
  his penis in teriffic erection. — Thomas Pynchon, *Gravity's Rainbow*, p. 221,
  1973
- Is it his imagination, or is she pushing her ass out at him? — Candace
  Bushnell, *Four Blondes*, p. 128, 2001
2 the vagina *UK, 1684*
- Why, the day he was dropped from his mammy's ass / he slapped
  his pappy's face. — Bruce Jackson, *Get Your Ass in the Water and Swim Like Me*,
  p. 58, 1970
- I had saved my hankie that I wiped Ruth's ass out with after we had
  had our taste of sex, because I had a real freak of a nigger that I was
  gonna sell a smell of it to after I got back in the joint. — A.S. Jackson,
  Gentleman Pimp, p. 66, 1973
3 sex; a person as a sexual object *US, 1910*
- Most of them were dogs, and I had more ass lined up at the house
  than I could take care of. — Juan Carmel Cosmes, *Memoir of a Whoremaster*,
  p. 24, 1969
- The other numerous downtown clubs would not serve us, nor would
  the white prostitutes sell black G.I.s any ass. — Bobby Seale, *A Lonely
  Rage*, p. 106, 1978
- And here's what I want you to do: I want you to sell your ass. I'll be
  in the car waiting. — Chris Rock, *Rock This!*, p. 186, 1997
4 the self; a person *US, 1945*
- Not a living ass in that band could read a note except Elmer
  Schobel. — Mezz Mezzrow, *Really the Blues*, p. 51, 1946

- Gramma said you better get your filthy ass out of this garden.
  — Cecil Brown, *The Life & Loves of Mr. Jiveass Nigger*, p. 6, 1969
- Now that's a hard motherfuckin' fact of life, but it's a fact of life your ass is gonna hafta git realistic about. — *Pulp Fiction*, 1994
- My first thought is, "Hey, thanks a lot, man. Thanks for taking her ugly ass off our hands, because we didn't know what we were going to do about her." — Chris Rock, *Rock This!*, p. 129, 1997

5 a fool *UK, 1578*

- Ted's greatest asset is the ability to make a complete ass of himself on camera. — Bruce Campbell, *If Chins Could Kill*, p. 291, 2002

▸ **bring ass to get ass**
used for conveying that a person who wants to win a fight must be willing to fight *US, 1970*

- They has got to bring ass to get ass! Man, that Hiram Elliott Quinault is a bad mother-fucker. — Chuck Stone, *King Strut*, p. 58, 1970
- In the Black idiom of my Georgia childhood, I believe we must make it ever clear to the white boy that he has "to bring ass to git ass." — John Alfred Williams, *Amistad*, p. 106, 1971
- "But remember, muthafucka, you gotta bring ass to git ass—and I'm takin at least two of y'all with me!" — Nathan Heard, *A Cold Fire Burning*, p. 12, 1974
- You gotta bring ass to kick ass, so come on wid it. — *New Jack City*, 1990

▸ **bust your ass**
to hurry, to exert yourself; to work extremely hard *US, 1941*

- I bust my ass all day to take home a hundred and seventy bucks a week and I just can't swing the kind of money it costs. — George V. Higgins, *The Friends of Eddie Doyle*, p. 33, 1971
- He had always believed Hispanic girls would bust their ass to go out with a white man. — Elmore Leonard, *Maximum Bob*, p. 250, 1991
- One morning I heard my bell ring at dawn. I figured it was the UPS man with a package. I busted my ass down the stairs, trembling, because I couldn't wait to get my hands on that bubble wrap. — Chris Rock, *Rock This!*, p. 67, 1997

▸ **eat someone's ass out**
to berate someone *US, 1996*

- The magistrate, a lovely, intelligent woman, dismissed the charge and ate the ass out of the assistant U.S. attorney for being overzealous. — Elmore Leonard, *Out of Sight*, p. 64, 1996

▸ **on ass**
on credit *US, 1974*

- "Put up in advance. We don't play on ass around here." — Nathan Heard, *A Cold Fire Burning*, p. 104, 1974

▸ **take it up the ass**
to take the passive role in anal intercourse *US, 1966*

- "There's a lady lawyer at the end of the bar that likes to take it in the ass," he said. — Gerald Petievich, *To Die in Beverly Hills*, p. 93, 1983
- As long as you done your time nice, you didn't rat anybody out, and you never took it in the ass. — Vincent Patrick, *Family Business*, p. 55, 1985

▸ **your ass is grass**
used for conveying the state of being in great trouble *US, 1956*

- I never heard the man so pissed. They ass is grass, whoever it is. — Vernon E. Smith, *The Jones Men*, p. 40, 1974
- Else my ass would be grass by now. — Edwin Torres, *Carlito's Way*, p. 74, 1975
- If it all comes down, your ass is new-mown grass. — *48 Hours*, 1982

ass *verb*
to engage in prostitution *US, 1991*

- — William T. Vollman, *Whores for Gloria*, p. 139, 1991

ass *adjective*
terrible, bad *US, 1992*

- [T]he cha ("very cool") worlds include: "winded" for hung over; "craftsman" for a complete idiot; and "ass" for awful. — *Washington Times*, p. C3, 26th August 1992

-ass; -assed *suffix*
used as an intensifier for the preceding adjective or adverb *US, 1903*

- "Get up the stairs, you sassy-assed bitch," yelled Agent No. 3. — Tom Robbins, *Another Roadside Attraction*, p. 110, 1971
- Plus we're gonna send for a free specialist so you're not at the mercy of those sorry-ass state sawbones. — Seth Morgan, *Homeboy*, p. 288, 1990

- I've seen a lot of crazy-ass shit in my time — *Pulp Fiction*, 1994
- Do you know how depressing it is to sit in the same room you two sat in when you were both 14? There's the little-ass dresser, the little-ass bed, and the poster of Tony Doreset on the wall. — Chris Rock, *Rock This!*, p. 93, 1997

ass action *noun*
anal sex *US, 2005*

- Five sex scenes, starring such luscious pieces of mid '90s porn as Nikki Sinn and Kim Chambers, features ass action that is light years beyond most anal-themed efforts. — Editors of Adult Video News, *The AVN Guide to the 500 Greatest Adult Films of All Time*, p. 15, 2005

ass-and-trash *noun*
during the Vietnam war, people and cargo to be transported by plane *US, 1978*

- We flew three missions of local ass-and-trash, single-ship stuff. — Robert Mason, *Chickenhawk*, p. 394, 1983
- The first thing that happened to helicopter pilots when they arrived in Vietnam was assignment to a platoon that flew "slicks," the Hueys used for troop and and cargo transport, or "Ash and Trash" missions. — Dennis Marvicsin and Jerold Greenfield, *Maverick*, p. 36, 1990
- He asked the brigade for an additional allocation of the "ash and trash" support people, but made sure he had a hard-core infantry base. — J.D. Coleman, *Incursion*, p. 142, 1991
- "Ash and trash" means we'll be hauling anything from C rations to ammunition. — Richard Burns, *Pathfinder*, p. 125, 2002

ass antlers *noun*
a symmetrical tattoo on a woman's lower back, rising from her buttocks *US, 2002*

- Now, you can't swing a stick without hitting someone with a fucking barb wire armband or a "look at my ass" black low back piece. Ass antlers! — *rec.arts.bodyart*, 14th July 2002
- Ass antlers is a term for a kind of tramp stamp, in this case a tribal or other tattoo located on the lower back, and radiating upwards with the anus as a center. — *alt.buddha.short.fat.guy*, 4th March 2003

ass backwards *adverb*
in reverse order *US, 1942*

- With this joker, the more he lapped it up, the more he got his words ass backwards. — Bernard Wolfe, *The Late Risers*, p. 42, 1954
- "I think you got it ass-backwards," Majestyk said, returning the keys to his pocket. "I'm not going with you, you're going with me." — Elmore Leonard, *Mr. Majestyk*, p. 52, 1974
- All of my information on the Army indicated that they did things so ass backwards that if you were on the west coast they'd send you to the east (France or Italy or somewhere) and vice versa. — Odie Hawkins, *Scars and Memories*, p. 73, 1987

ass bandit; asshole bandit *noun*
a male homosexual, especially the active partner in anal sex *US, 1968*

- Which is, dear reader, the true story of this particular asshole bandit[.] — Angelo d'Arcangelo, *The Homosexual Handbook*, p. 78, 1968
- "In the joint I was an asshole bandit. The sheriff of the brown trail." — John Gregory Dunne, *Dutch Shea, Jr.*, p. 37, 1982
- "I ought to make you eat that hat, you fucking ass bandit!" — Stephen King, *It*, p. 20, 1987
- I wasn't scared of jail; the shape I was in I could smear any ass-bandit onto the wall. — Derek Bickerton, *King of the Sea*, p. 188, 1989

ass bite *noun*
harsh criticism *US, 1973*

- I felt like he was lots older and a damn sight wiser and took the assbite without looking at him. — Joseph Wambaugh, *The Blue Knight*, p. 77, 1973

ass-blow *verb*
to lick, suck and tongue another's anus *US, 1941*

- — Dale Gordon, *The Dominion Sex Dictionary*, p. 23, 1967

ass-breaker *noun*
a strict disciplinarian *US, 1966*

- — Rose Giallombardo, *Society of Women*, p. 204, 1966: Glossary of Prison Terms
- He's a real ass-breaker now so they don't dare touch me. — Josef Skvorecky, *The Engineer of Human Souls*, p. 211, 1985

ass bucket *noun*
a despised person *US, 1953*

• "Once a ass-bucket always a ass-bucket." The small-eyed waiter looked again at the man with his head resting on the table. — William Fisher, *The Waiters*, p. 65, 1953

ass burglar *noun*
the active partner in anal sex; more generally, a male homosexual *US, 1979*

• "You are at the end of your career ass burglar, said old Nadoway." — Gilbert Chesterton, *Four Faultless Felons*, p. 126, 1989

ass cache *noun*
a supply of drugs hidden in the rectum *US, 1992*

• — Jay Robert Nash, *Dictionary of Crime*, p. 12, 1992

ass chewing *noun*
a harsh reprimand or scold *US, 1954*

• Johnson paused to smile, perhaps in recollection of a particularly memorable ass chewing he had inflicted on some trembling bureaucrat. — Dan Rather, *The Palace Guard*, p. 29, 1974

• A vice president of manufacturing once quit the day Paul Allegretto took over as president of his division, complaining that he was not going to put up with Allegretto's "long hours, harsh demands and ass chewing." — *American Metal Market*, p. S5, 2nd January 1984

• "When accolades were coming, he'd give them to you," Martinez added. "And when an ass-chewing was coming, he'd give them, too, and I always appreciated that about him." — *Star Tribune (Minneapolis)*, p. 1B, 7th November 2003

ass cunt *noun*
the anus *US, 1974*

• Wowee, will you look at that little white kid's ass-cunt. That's a cherry if I ever saw one. — Piri Thomas, *Seven Long Times*, p. 67, 1974

assed out *adjective*
in severe trouble *US, 1993*

• Now if you ain't got none, you just assed out. — *Menace II Society*, 1993

• If you were light-skinned, maybe you had a shot with the honeys, but regular guys like me were assed out. — Earl "DMX" Simmons, *E.A.R.L.*, p. 80, 2002

ass end *noun*
the least desirable part of anything *US, 1947*

• — *American Speech*, p. 54, February 1947: "Pacific War language"

• [T]heir plight caught the ass end of a brief burst of black unity. — Jess Mowry, *Way Past Cool*, p. 29, 1992

ass English *noun*
the body movements and incantations of a dice shooter who believes that he can control the roll of the dice *US, 1950*

• — *The Annals of the American Academy of Political and Social Sciences*, p. 120, May 1950

ass fuck *noun*
1 anal sex *US, 1940*

• It seems like they were having more fun back then. Now it's like, um, you want to do an ass fuck for $250 real quick? — *LA Weekly*, p. 31, 19th November 1999

• Standard price on the street is twenty for head, thirty for a straight lay, and forty for an ass-fuck. — Edward Lee, *Seeds of Fear*, p. 161, 2005

2 a despicable person *US, 2001*

• He'd call her a "stupid ass-fuck" and throw her against the wall, she says. — *Cleveland Scene*, 8th November 2001

ass-fuck *verb*
to engage in anal sex, especially in the active role *US, 1940*

• Others will say that they're too busy being happily clit-tickled or ass-fucked to be bothered with any G-spot gyrations. — Susie Bright, *Sjusie Sexpert's Lesbian Sex World*, p. 23, 1990

• He denies saying he wanted to "ass fuck" the man, but agrees he was out of line. — *Cleveland Scene*, 2nd August 2001

ass fucker *noun*
the active partner in anal sex *US, 1979*

• "Don't you dare shoot that load until I say so, you little ass fucker," Derek demanded. — Ben Tyler, *Gay Blades*, p. 109, 2004

ass fucking *noun*
anal sex *US, 1970*

• Ass-fucking in general, never so much as crossed my mind until about two years ago[.] — *Screw*, p. 15, 15th March 1970

• "I love ass-fucking. It's the first time I've ever done it. It's really great." — Harold Robbins, *The Predators*, p. 62, 1999

ass gasket *noun*
a disposable paper toilet seat cover *US, 1994*

• — Michael Dalton Johnson, *Talking Trash with Redd Foxx*, p. 129, 1994

asshole *noun*
1 the anus *US, 1935*

• He thrusts into her asshole without using any lubrication. — Kathy Acker, *Great Expectations*, p. 39, 1989

• [He] has fucked her in the ass, sucked his own cum out of her asshole, and spit it back in her mouth. — Ron Scapp, *Eating Culture*, p. 229, 1998

• He put his hands under my ass and then he plunged his cock into my asshole. — Augusten Burroughs, *Running with Scissors*, p. 159, 2002

2 a fool; a person held in contempt *US, 1933*

• The phone rang, Benny O. Bliss answered. "Mort Robell? That asshole. Well, put him on." — Bernard Wolfe, *The Late Risers*, p. 26, 1954

• "Then let the asshole beef," said Matthews, and Gus realized that they used "asshole" as much here in the divisions as the instructors did in the academy and he guessed it was the favorite epithet of policemen[.] — Joseph Wambaugh, *The New Centurions*, p. 55, 1970

• You ain't nothing but an old stupid God damn fool, motherfucking asshole! — Bobby Seale, *A Lonely Rage*, pp. 24–25, 1978

• Why do girls like assholes? — Rosalind Wiseman, *Queen Bees & Wannabes*, p. 186, 2002

asshole buddy *noun*
a very close friend *US, 1945*

• I recall during the war at the Jockey Club in Cairo, me and my asshole buddy, Lud, both gentlemen by act of Congress. — William Burroughs, *Naked Lunch*, p. 92, 1957

• Meridian, you know that Mister Parnell ain't going to let them arrest his ass-hole buddy — James Baldwin, *Blues for Mister Charlie*, 1964

• I need an ass-hole buddy who can cook, clean and keep house. — Emile Nytrate, *Underground Ads*, p. 94, 1971

• I just hope I can keep playing good enough to make it a contest for our ass-hole buddy here. — Dan Jenkins, *Dead Solid Perfect*, p. 107, 1986

asshole eating *noun*
oral-anal sex *US, 1988*

• For asshole eating, I would charge, I would charge him thirty dollars extra. — Dolores French, *Working*, p. 98, 1988

asshole naked *adjective*
completely naked *US, 1969*

• I came in that hot summer day, took a shower and went to my bedroom asshole naked and layed down. — *Screw*, p. 5, 7th March 1969

asshole of creation *noun*
a remote, desolate place *US, 1964*

• Ain't it logical that I should appear here in Potts County, which is just about as close to the asshole of creation as you can get without havin' a finger snapped off? — Jim Thompson, *Pop. 1280*, p. 209, 1964

asshole of the world; asshole of the universe *noun*
the most despised place, area or location *US, 1949*

• But you can't vote until you get your citizenship. Not here, not in this Dutch-infested ass-hole of the nation. — John O'Hara, *A Rage to Live*, p. 118, 1949

• Way down here in the ass-hole of the world, the deep, black, funky South. — James Baldwin, *Blues for Mister Charlie*, p. 31, 1964

• "All I ever got in that state was shit on. California's the asshole of the universe." — Malcolm Braley, *False Starts*, p. 91, 1976

• We're from the Sixth Regiment / The asshole of the world. — Thomas Bowen, *The Longest Year*, p. 49, 1990: We're A Pack Of Bastards

assholes and elbows *noun*
said of a chaotic situation *US, 1987*

• Quickly, ladies! Assholes and elbows! — *Full Metal Jacket*, 1987

• I mean, you should've seen it. All asses and elbows flying all over the goddam place. — Robert Campbell, *Juice*, p. 29, 1988

asshole to appetite *noun*
from the anus to the stomach *US, 1992*

• Covers me from asshole t'appetite. — Robert Gover, *Here Goes Kitten*, p. 114, 1964

asshole to belly button *adjective*
said of people pressed close together, one behind the other
US, 1973
- I remember when the slime-balls used to be packed in there solid, asshole to belly button, waiting to look at the skin show in the viewer. — Joseph Wambaugh, *The Blue Knight*, pp. 26–27, 1973

ass hound *noun*
a man who obsessively engages in the pursuit of women for sex *US, 1952*
- My friends and professors thought I was quite an "ass-hound." How right they were! — Philip Barrows, *Whores, Queers and Others*, p. 156, 2005

ass in a sling
in deep trouble *US, 1943*
- [J]ust because I had my ass in a sling was no reason for them to suffer, too. — Anthony Herbert, *Soldier*, p. 3, 1973
- [I]f I made too many wrong moves, my ass was gon' be in another sling, so I had to proceed quietly. — Odie Hawkins, *Great Lawd Buddha*, p. 44, 1990

ass-in-the-grass *adjective*
used for describing infantry in combat in the field *US, 1973*
- It was a hell of a lot better than what the ass-in-the-grass grunts had that night. — Anthony Herbert, *Soldier*, p. 141, 1973

ass juice *noun*
rectal secretions and/or lubrication *US, 2001*
- This fat cock likes dark and damp places where it can gather up the stench of sweat and cum and ass-juice. — Mark Hemry, *Tales from the Bear Cult*, 2001

ass-keister *verb*
to hide contraband in your rectum *US, 2002*
- There will be a cavity check in the holding cell for the benefit of any ignorant motherfucker that thinks he can ass-keister a hypo or crack pipe[.] — Jimmy Lerner, *You Got Nothing Coming*, p. 28, 2002

ass-kicker *noun*
a challenging and difficult person, thing, or situation *US, 1972*
- "Ass-kicker, aint it?" I didn't answer, panting, chest quivering. — William Pelfrey, *The Big V*, p. 31, 1972

ass-kiss *verb*
to behave in an ingratiatingly sycophantic manner *US, 1961*
- Sure, I was ass-kissing the boss, but that's what employees do. — Walter Yetnikoff, *Howling at the Moon*, p. 192, 2004

ass-kisser *noun*
a sycophant *US, 1766*
- "This guy is an ass-kisser for the company," Johnny whispered. — Piri Thomas, *Stories from El Barrio*, p. 11, 1978

ass-kissing *noun*
sycophantic or ingratiating behavior *US, 1939*
- "Do you think I could stand a whole lifetime of this drinking, bordeom, small talk, and ass-kissing?" — Saul Bellow, *Humboldt's Gift*, p. 128, 1996
- My lips are permanently damaged from the amount of ass-kissing I did today. — Megan McCafferty, *Second Helpings*, p. 155, 2003

ass-kissing *adjective*
sycophantic *US, 1942*
- Nicky looked him up after doing his time and that was how he got to meet Jimmy Cap and went to work for him: picking up Chinese takeout, lighting his cigars, getting him young girls, generally serving on an ass-kissing basis at first. — Elmore Leonard, *Pronto*, p. 218, 1993
- You ass-kissing little snitch! — John Waters, *Desperate Living*, p. 166, 1999

assload *noun*
a large amount *US, 1957*
- One minor hitch—my gear is still at the hotel, so far as I know, containing an assload of barbiturates, amphetamines, T.O., PG—paraegoric—and assorted shit. — James Blake, *The Joint*, p. 161, 7th January 1957

ass man *noun*
a man who considers that the appearance of a woman's buttocks provides the supreme initial sexual attraction *US, 1972*
- — Helen Dahlskog (Editor), *A Dictionary of Contemporary and Colloquial Usage*, p. 4, 1972

- Fran Drescher has an earthy sensuality that permeates her entire being but seems to be localized in her wide, often-grinning libertine's mouth and he wide, all enveloping ass-man's dream of a rear end. — Mr. Skin, *Mr. Skin's Skincyclopedia*, p. 155, 2005

ass munch *noun*
a person who is easily despised *US, 1996*
- — Connie Eble (Editor), *UNC-CH Campus Slang*, p. 1, March 1996
- Debmeu was a major passive-aggressive ass-much with an MBA from Stanford. — Joseph Armstead, *Nocturnes and Neon*, p. 318, 2001

ass on fire *noun*
said of a person who is either angry or rushed *US, 1983*
- — Terrence M. Steele, *Streettalk Thesaurus*, p. 23, 1983

ass-out *adjective*
without money *US, 1999*
- "He's ass-out. He's not going anywhere." — John Ridley, *Everybody Smokes in Hell*, p. 131, 1999

ass-out *adverb*
extremely *US, 1995*
- — Lois Stavsky et al., *A2Z*, p. 2, 1995

ass over tea kettle; ass over tea cups *adverb*
head over heels *US, 1948*
- "Someday one of these things is going to wipe out New York, turn it ass-over-teakettle." — Stephen Longstreet, *The Flesh Peddlers*, p. 256, 1962
- In a matter of seconds, you're at horizon level and then you're down, ass over tea-kettle, scrambling up and after the chute, tearing out of the harness. — Anthony Herbert, *Soldier*, p. 31, 1973
- They drop four head of cattle and blow two papa-sans ass over teakettle with the fifties. — Larry Heinemann, *Close Quarters*, p. 106, 1977
- Ass over teakettle onto the concrete, right on my wrist. — Robert Campbell, *Juice*, p. 29, 1988

ass peddler *noun*
a male prostitute *US, 1950*
- — *Maledicta*, p. 231, 1979: "Kinks and queens: linguistic and cultural aspects of the terminology for gays"

ass pocket *noun*
a thin, flat glass bottle *US, 1996*
"Ass Pocket of Whiskey" is the name of an album released by R. L. Burnside and the Jon Spencer Blues Explosion in 1996.
- I ran to the liquor store and bought her an ass pocket of whiskey and a Coke. — Lynn Breedlove, *Godspeed*, p. 32, 2002
- He was out at St. Martha's kicking and screaming with an ass pocket of whiskey. — John Connolly, *Dark Hollow*, p. 197, 2002

ass queen *noun*
a homosexual man who is particularly attracted to other men's buttocks *US, 1978*
- — Anon., *King Smut's Wet Dreams Interpreted*, 1978

ass ripper *noun*
a difficult course or test *US, 1968*
- — Collin Baker et al., *College Undergraduate Slang Study Conducted at Brown University*, p. 71, 1968

ass time *noun*
time wasted sitting around *US, 1994*
- — Sally Williams, *"Strong" Words*, p. 133, 1994

assume *verb*
▸ **assume the angle; assume the position**
to kneel for punishment doled out as part of a hazing ritual *US, 1940*
- Next they told her to assume the angle—kneeling with her head down on her arms, which were flat on the floor. Her buttocks were up and her legs apart. — *Time*, p. 80, 13th January 1947
- "Assume the position." While the boy knelt and held his genitals, Roy went for the fraternity paddle — Geoffrey Wadiner, *The Asphalt Campus*, p. 83, 1963

asswipe *noun*
1 toilet paper *US, 1958*
- — Carl Fleischhauer, *A Glossary of Army Slang*, p. 2, 1968
- "Well, the old thief's got enough asswipe stashed to last a week," said someone in a loud voice. — Joseph Wambaugh, *The New Centurions*, p. 191, 1970

2 by extension, a despicable or offensive person *US, 1952*
- Hey! You asswipes, scumbags! — *Saturday Night Fever*, 1977

- FRANK: Is this the kind of language your employees use on duty? JOE: Well, Corey's usually very courteous. COREY: Asswipe. — *Empire Records*, 1995
- Hey, Puffy tried to warn you about that Steve guy you was seeing—he was a fucking asswipe—but you had to find out for yourself, didn't you. — *Something About Mary*, 1998
- "Ray was the real deal, asswipe" Drucker hissed. — Stephen J. Cannell, *The Tin Collectors*, p. 30, 2001

A-state *nickname*
Arkansas *US, 2002*
- — Alonzo Westbrook, *Hip Hoptionary*, p. 4, 2002

as the feller says
used for introducing a statement which the speaker does not necessarily accept *US, 1975*
- — John Gould, *Maine Lingo*, p. 37, 1975

Astor's pet horse *noun*
used in comparisons with a person, especially a woman, who is over-dressed *US, 1950*
- In the 1700s up pops John (Johannes) Jakob Astor (Asdour), who now has hotels, Astor Place, Astoria, the phrase "dressed up like Astor's pet horse" and lots of stuff named for him. — *New York Post*, p. 14, 27th June 2003

atari *noun*
crack cocaine *US, 1993*
- — Peter Johnson, *Dictionary of Street Alcohol and Drug Terms*, p. 11, 1993

ate out *adjective*
(of pants) worn, baggy, saggy *US, 2002*
- — Alonzo Westbrook, *Hip Hoptionary*, p. 4, 2002

ate up *adjective*
1 in the US Air Force, dedicated to service *US, 1998*
- — *Seattle Times*, p. A9, 12th April 1998
2 in the US Army, confused, dim *US, 1998*
- — *Seattle Times*, p. A9, 12th April 1998

Athenian *noun*
in homosexual usage, an anal sex enthusiast *US, 1986–1987*
- — *Maledicta*, p. 56, 1986–1987: "A continuation of a glossary of ethnic slurs in American English"

-athon *suffix*
used to create a word suggesting the root word activity carried on for a long period of time *US, 1934*
From "marathon."
- Another year of sitting on the platform at mass meetings in Madison Square Garden, of soirees in Greenwich Village and all-night talkathons at Sixth Avenue cafeterias[.] — Clancy Sigal, *Going Away*, p. 279, 1961
- The finale of this sepia strokeathon pairs all the participants in a single room, where they're unleashed and let loose. — *Adult Video*, p. 32, August/September 1986
- There's something about all these modern walkathons and bikeathons that recalls the early middle ages, when you could acquire indulgences by paying other people to say masses or make pilgrimages on your behalf. — Geoff Nunberg, *Fresh Air (National Public Radio)*, 2nd November 1999

ATL *nickname*
Atlanta, Georgia *US, 2002*
- — Alonzo Westbrook, *Hip Hoptionary*, p. 4, 2002

ATM *noun*
a generous person *US, 1997*
From the most common US name for a bank's *automatic teller machine.*
- — Anna Scotti and Paul Young, *Buzzwords*, p. 49, 1997

a toda madre!
excellent! *US, 1974*
Border Spanish used in English conversation by Mexican-Americans.
- — Dagoberto Fuentes and Jose Lopez, *Barrio Language Dictionary*, p. 10, 1974

atomic *noun*
a cigar-sized marijuana cigarette *US, 1953*
- Marijuana (we hear) is now peddled in the form of phony cigars. Called "atomics." A box (less conspicuous than ciggies) sells at $35. — *San Francisco Call-Bulletin*, p. 8G, 11th March 1953

atomic *adjective*
(of a drug) very-powerful *US, 1971*
- [I]t was an ace bomber of absolutely atomic North African marihooch[.] — Lester Bangs, *Psychotic Reactions and Carburetor Dung*, p. 80, 1971

A-town *nickname*
Atlanta, Georgia *US, 1995*
- — Lois Stavsky et al., *A2Z*, p. 2, 1995
- — Don R. McCreary (Editor), *Dawg Speak*, 2001

A train *noun*
any central nervous system depressant *US, 1975*
- Only thing i know is that you been fucking with them A trains, again. — Miguel Pinero, *Short Eyes*, p. 62, 1975

attaboy *noun*
praise, especially from a boss *US, 1970*
- [H]e likes a little "at-a-boy" once in a while just like the rest of us, despite his bitching. — Joseph Wambaugh, *The New Centurions*, p. 57, 1970
- They do not volunteer for medals or glory or attaboys. — Richard Marcinko and John Weisman, *Rogue Warrior*, p. 231, 1992

attack of the slows *noun*
in horse racing, an imaginary illness that plagues a horse midway through a race *US, 1951*
- — David W. Maurer, *Argot of the Racetrack*, p. 11, 1951

attagirl!
used for encouraging a female *US, 1924*
- "You denied it, though?" "Of course." "Attagirl." — Armistead Maupin, *Back to Barbary Lane*, p. 622, 1991

attitude *noun*
aggressive or antagonistic behavior *US, 1975*
- The White Party was hot, but the attitude in the room was a bit much. — Kevin Dillalo, *The Unofficial Gay Manual*, p. 237, 1994

attitude test *noun*
the extremely subjective criteria used by a traffic police officer in deciding whether to issue a traffic ticket or let the offending driver off with a warning *US, 1984*
- He found that the car's left tail-light was out and he began writing him a ticket, for failing the attitude test, as they say. — Joseph Wambaugh, *Lines and Shadows*, p. 114, 1984

atto- *prefix*
used as a diminishing intensifier *US, 1997*
Literally meaning "ten to the power of negative eighteen."
- I will devote nine attointerest units to your proposal. — Andy Ihnatko, *Cyberspeak*, p. 17, 1997

attractive young couple *noun*
a couple that has recently started to engage in spouse swapping *US, 1964*
- An "attractive young couple" are new swingers—novices to the swapping rites. — William and Jerrye Breedlove, *Swap Clubs*, p. 57, 1964

au contraire *adverb*
to the contrary *US, 1955*
French used by those who speak no French; adds a camp tone.
- I [Blanche Purka] am not "renouncing" the theatre, certainly not in any moody bitterness. Au contraire, I shall very probably be busier than ever before. — *New York Times*, p. 2, 6th November 1955
- No more do you prepare lavish meals with his tastes in mind. Au contraire. Now it is for the women you slave and work and cook. — *San Francisco Chronicle*, p. 13, 22nd June 1961
- "How do you talk to someone who keeps saying 'Au contraire?'" — *San Francisco Chronicle*, p. 59, 18th October 1972

Audi *noun*
► **to be audi**
to leave *US, 1992*
- — Lady Kier Kirby, *The 376 Deee-liteful Words*, 1992
- Let's just talk when we've mellowed, alright? I'm audi. — *Clueless*, 1995

auger in *verb*
to crash an airplane *US, 1957*
- For a fellow down to his last fuel, it's "bingo." If he "clanks," he's nervous and if he "augers in" he crashed. — *San Francisco Examiner*, p. 10 (II), 2nd June 1957

- There are no black pilots or white pilots, only pilots that make it and pilots that auger in. — Walter J. Boyne and Steven L. Thompson, *The Wild Blue*, 1986

au naturel *adjective*
naked *US, 1967*
French used by those who speak no French; informal, jocular, affected.

- No frustrating plots, mysteries or symbolism. Just simple, unrestricted, unrestrained action! Men & Women Au-Naturel! — *San Francisco Chronicle*, p. 45, 19th June 1967

Aunt Bettie *noun*
an overly cautious person *US, 1945*

- And so it is shocking to hear some of the old male Aunt Bettys lift their skirts in scat fashion against this one-time Andy Smith quarterback on the pretense that there are several indiscreet chapters in his past life. — *San Francisco News*, p. 16, 10th January 1945
- Prep's "Aunt Betties" Dawdle Over Age Limit Rule Change (Headline) — *San Francisco News*, p. 13, 23rd January 1951

Aunt Emma *noun*
used as a personification of a matronly aunt *US, 1947*

- Into this situation comes Waldorf, whose record is nothing to write your Aunt Emma about. — *San Francisco News*, p. 15, 21st February 1947
- Your Aunt Emma could win with a team like that. (Cartoon caption) — *San Francisco News*, p. 17, 24th May 1956

Aunt Flo *noun*
the bleed period of the menstrual cycle *US, 1954*

- — *American Speech*, p. 298, December 1954: "The vernacular of menstruation"
- — Pamela Munro, *U.C.L.A. Slang*, p. 16, 1989

Aunt Hazel *noun*
marijuana *US, 2001*

- "Grass ... Mary Jane, Aunt Hazel, African bush, bambalacha. You pick the cool name." — Stephen J. Cannell, *The Tin Collectors*, p. 60, 2001

auntie *noun*
an older, effeminate male homosexual *US, 1930*
A tad cruel, if not derogatory.

- They also think he has an in with the law because an old auntie fuzz man gets his boys through Tony. — William Burroughs, *Letters to Allen Ginsberg 1953–1957*, p. 82, 28th December 1954
- Later, when I went to the director's house with the auntie—several weeks later—the director would be redecorating his house. — John Rechy, *City of Night*, 1963
- Is this the way to treat another gay person with whom they disagree—calling him "auntie"? — *Screw*, January 1969
- To the younger homosexual, an auntie often translates as anything over thirty having lived too long with nothing to show for his age. Youth is the premium in the real world, but it is the criterion in the gay world. — Bruce Rodgers, *The Queens' Vernacular*, 1972

Aunt Jemima *noun*
a black woman who seeks approval from white people by obsequious behavior *US, 1966*
Ironically, singer/actor Ethel Ernestine Harper, who portrayed Aunt Jemima in pancake commercials from 1948 until 1966, was by all accounts anything but the stereotypical subservient black woman.

- What I [Adam Clayton Powell] cannot abide are the black "Aunt Jemimas" who snuggle up to the white power structure for approbation by denouncing "black power" and telling Mr. Charlie what he wants to hear. — *San Francisco Examiner*, 18th August 1966
- You have got to eat lunch anyway, you know, just like aunt Jemima said. — George V. Higgins, *Penance for Jerry Kennedy*, p. 170, 1985

Aunt Thomasina *noun*
a black woman who curries favor with white people by obsequious behavior *US, 1963*
An echo of the much more commonly heard **UNCLE TOM**.

- On the other side are New York activists led by Al Sharpton and Alton Maddox Jr. They savage their opponents, calling them "Uncle Toms" and "Aunt Thomasinas." — *Record (Bergen County, New Jersey)*, p. B7, 25th April 1990
- "I ain't nobody's Uncle Tom or Aunt Thomasina," said Ada Fisher, a Republican from Salisbury[.] — *Winston-Salem (North Carolina) Journal*, p. 1, 6th May 2003

Aunt Tillie; Aunt Tilly *noun*
used as the personification of a fussy old maid *US, 1960*

- They are determined that Aunt Tillie, a symbol of their most temperamental customer, shall love their parking. — *San Francisco News Call-Bulletin*, p. 49, 22nd June 1960

Aunt Tom *noun*
a woman who does not support the goals of feminism *US, 1968*
An attempt to link semantically the struggle of women with the struggle of black slaves by borrowing from the well-known **UNCLE TOM**.

- "Look who's calling who an Aunt Tom," Wolfgang retorted, "she's the real Aunt Tom, the Chamber of Commerce's Aunt Tom." — Dorothy Cobble, *The Other Women's Movement*, p. 193, 2004

Australian yo *noun*
in craps, a roll of three *US, 1999*
A roll of three is rarely a good thing, and is usually best face-down; if a three is face-down, an eleven is face-up. Eleven is "yo," with the three thus "down-under the yo."

- — Chris Fagans and David Guzman, *A Guide to Craps Lingo*, p. 11, 1999

automagically *adverb*
in computing, in an automatic but explanation-defying complicated fashion *US, 1981*

- — *CoEvolution Quarterly*, p. 27, Spring 1981
- Files that have a name ending in "TMF" are automagically deleted when you log out. — Guy L. Steele et al., *The Hacker's Dictionary*, p. 28, 1983

automaton *noun*
in poker, a player who bets and plays in an extremely predictable manner *US, 1996*

- — John Vorhaus, *The Big Book of Poker Slang*, p. 5, 1996

Av *nickname*
▸ **the Av**
Telegraph Avenue, Berkeley, California *US, 1966*

- "Things are really getting rougher," nearly every hippy on the Av will tell you. — *The Berkeley Barb*, p. 1, 2nd September 1966

AVANHI
used by the police as a description of a shooting involving black shooter and black victim *US, 1993*

- [P]artners were likely to turn to each other and shrug: "AVANHI"—Asshole Vs. Asshole, No Human Involved. — Bob Sipchen, *Baby Insane and the Buddha*, p. 19, 1993

Avenue *noun*
▸ **the Avenue**
Telegraph Avenue, Berkeley, California *US, 1966*

- Headline: Peace-Rock OK, But Not On "Avenue" / Will Rock "Off-Telly" — *The Berkeley Barb*, 15 August 1966

avgas *noun*
jet fuel *US, 1967*

- The decrease in aviation gasoline, or avgas, usage shows the shift away from piston-engined aircraft. — Carl Vansant, *Strategic Energy Supply and National Security*, p. 49, 1971

avocados *noun*
the female breasts *US, 1974*

- Mr. K is wearing new blinkers—not for reading but in tribute to her avocados, which are worth it. — Leo Rosten, *Dear Herm*, p. 149, 1974

away *adjective*
in bar dice games, counting for nothing *US, 1976*
A call of "aces away" would mean that rolls of one have no point value.

- — Gil Jacobs, *The World's Best Dice Games*, p. 191, 1976

awesome *adjective*
great, excellent *US, 1975*
An informal variation of the conventional sense.

- Like, OK, so I saw this totally awesome dude at the bonerama checkout, right, like I totally thought it was Rick Springfield. — Mary Corey and Victoria Westermark, *Fer Shurr! How to be a Valley Girl*, 1982
- But NO BIGGIE / It's so AWESOME / It's like TUBULAR, y'know. — Moon Unit and Frank Zappa, *Valley Girl*, 1982
- Awesome party! Good tunes! Good brew! Good buddies! — *Wayne's World 2*, 1993

AWOL bag *noun*
in the Korea and Vietnam wars, an overnight bag *US, 1956*
- — Carl Fleischhauer, *A Glossary of Army Slang*, p. 2, 1968
- They leave the MAA's office together and return separately, each carrying his AWOL bag. — Darryl Ponicsan, *The Last Detail*, p. 19, 1970
- A moment later Paco stands on the bottom of the coach steps with his AWOL bag in one hand and his black hickory cane in the other[.] — Larry Heinemann, *Paco's Story*, 1986

ax; axe *noun*
1 a musical instrument, especially an electric guitar *US, 1955*
Originally used in jazz circles for any instrument, particularly a saxophone or trumpet.
- Now these cats were blowing their horns, their axes, whatever they had. — Claude Brown, *Manchild in the Promised Land*, p. 229, 1965
- OK man, we'll take these axes. — *The Blues Brothers*, 1980

2 in a gambling operation, the house's cut of the bets *US, 1974*
- — John Scarne, *Scarne on Dice*, p. 459, 1974

3 the lip of a wave *US, 1991*
- — Trevor Cralle, *The Surfin'ary*, p. 4, 1991

▸ **get the axe**
in surfing, to be knocked off your board by a wave *US, 1957*
- I looked around. Only two other guys had made it. The others had got the axe. — Frederick Kohner, *Gidget*, p. 16, 1957

axe handle *noun*
an imprecise unit of measurement, especially when applied to the breadth of a man's shoulders or woman's buttocks *US, 1947*
- He is two axe handles across the shoulders, strong as the bulls of Bashan, and possessed of a temper like Jove's. — Colin Roderick, *Miles Franklin*, p. 70, 1982
- You have a poochy tummy but want to wear a rhinestone-studded belly tee; your ass—as my Gran used to say—is "six axe handles across" but you crave a pair of low-rise boot-leg distressed snakeskin jeans. — Leslie Carroll, *Play Dates*, p. 40, 2005

ayo
used as a greeting *US, 1995*
- — Lois Stavsky et al., *A2Z*, p. 3, 1995

Aztec hop; Aztec revenge; Aztec two-step *noun*
diarrhea suffered by tourists in Mexico *US, 1953*
- "If it isn't cat fever it's the Aztec two-step or some other stupid thing! You don't eat right!" — Evan Connell, *The Patriot*, p. 149, 1960
- With his luck he'd die of Aztec Revenge anyway, first time he had a Bibb lettuce salad. — Joseph Wambaugh, *The Black Marble*, p. 152, 1978
- Like a thief, traveler's diarrhea has many aliases. It is euphemistically known as "Turista," Montezuma's Revenge, "The Aztec Two Step," "Turkey Trots," and scores more. — *The Patriot Ledger (Quincy, Massachusetts)*, p. 16, 3rd June 1997

Bb

B *noun*

1 Benzedrine™ amphetamine sulfate, a central nervous system stimulant *US, 1986*
- — Richard A. Spears, *The Slang and Jargon of Drugs and Drink*, p. 18, 1986
- — Angela Devlin, *Prison Patter*, p. 23, 1996

2 a matchbox full of marijuana *US, 1971*
- — Eugene Landy, *The Underground Dictionary*, p. 27, 1971
- — Jay Robert Nash, *Dictionary of Crime*, p. 15, 1992

▸ **put the B on**
to ask for money for sex after giving the appearance of being seduced *US, 1954*
- You goddam tramp! Gettin' me up here, then puttin' the B on me! Twenty bucks! — Dev Collans with Stewart Sterling, *I was a House Detective*, p. 33, 1954

B *adjective*
(used of a movie) second-tier in terms of actors and budget *US, 1946*
- Being both profitable and meritorious, Lewton's productions are ideal B films. — *Life*, p. 123, 25th February 1946
- A falsehood has been circulating in Hollywood and across the country that B pictures are no longer being made. — *San Francisco Examiner*, p. 34, 30th August 1966

B-52 *noun*
a powerful amphetamine tablet *US, 1993*
- — Peter Johnson, *Dictionary of Street Alcohol and Drug Terms*, p. 12, 1993

BA *noun*
a *bare ass US, 1970*
Usually in the context of exposing the buttocks to shock or amuse.
- — *Current Slang*, p. 20, Summer 1970

▸ **hang a BA**
to expose your *bare ass US, 1970*
- Butt-Head turns around, drops his pants and hangs a "B.A." at the guy. — Mike Judge and Joe Stillman, *Beavis and Butt-Head Do America*, p. 20, 1997

babe *noun*

1 an attractive young woman *US, 1905*
- Tonight I got a date with a Sigma, a keen babe, for a hop at the Shoreland Hotel. — James T. Farrell, *Saturday Night*, p. 35, 1947
- [T]hree days in New York—three days of babes and booze while I waited to see The Man—hadn't helped it any. — Jim Thompson, *Savage Night*, p. 1, 1953
- Oh you beautiful babes from England, for whom we have traveled through time. — *Bill and Ted's Excellent Adventure*, 1989
- She does have a little gambling problem, she plays the football cards a bit too much, but she's a babe, a surgeon babe. — *Something About Mary*, 1998

2 an attractive young male *US, 1973*
- Well, he is a babe. — Francesca Lia Block, *I Was a Teenage Fairy*, p. 80, 1998

3 used as a term of address *US, 1906*
- Thanks, no, babe. I don't wanna take her time — Edwin Tarres, *Q & A*, 1977
- "How are you, babes?" — Bret Easton Ellis, *Less Than Zero*, p. 13, 1985
- Now, now, Babe. Not while I'm in uniform. — *Boys on the Side*, 1995

babelicious *adjective*
extremely sexually attractive *US, 1992*
Coined by Mike Myers on the US television program *Saturday Night Live* and popularized by the film *Wayne's World*, 1992.
- She's magically babelicious. — *Wayne's World*, 1992
- Having a babelicious best friend can cause you countless problems. — *Girlfriend*, p. 40, 1995

babies *noun*
dice *US, 1974*
- — Thomas L. Clark, *The Dictionary of Gambling and Gaming*, p. 9, 1987

babo *noun*
nalorphine, a morphine derivative that acts to reverse the effects of morphine and other narcotics *US, 1967*
- — John B. Williams, *Narcotics and Hallucinogenics*, p. 109, 1967

baboon butt *noun*
the red, sore buttocks of someone riding as a passenger on a motorcycle *US, 1988*
- For the doubters among you, there are pictures, one of which shows Brooke hanging on tight and grimacing, an expression described in the caption as "a serious sign of baboon butt"—the rawness that afflicts first-time chopper riders. — *Washington Post*, p. W5, 3rd January 1988

baby *noun*

1 used as a friendly term of address *US, 1921*
- "Look, baby," I said, "if you want to cut out of this joint so bad, I'll take you to Detroit." — Mezz Mezzrow, *Really the Blues*, p. 89, 1946
- The first time I heard the expression "baby" used by one cat to address another was up at Warwick in 1951. Gus Jackson used it. The term had a hip ring to it, a real colored ring. — Claude Brown, *Manchild in the Promised Land*, p. 171, 1965
- "What's happening, baby?" said the clerk, a small, wiry Negro with a goatee. — Nat Hentoff, *Jazz Country*, p. 74, 1965
- "Hey, baby, you're my main man," Davis said. — Jim Bouton, *Ball Four*, p. 86, 1970

2 a sweetheart, a girlfriend *US, 1839*
- Lord, I really miss my baby / She's in some far off land. — Bob Dylan, *Down the Highway*, 1963

3 a prostitute's customer *US, 1957*
- Still and all, she had a small minute of indecision when he brought the first hundred-dollar baby to his apartment to meet her. — John M. Murtagh and Sara Harris, *Cast the First Stone*, p. 32, 1957

4 a young, inexperienced male homosexual *US, 1954*
- The biggest crime against the "babies," who come in through the sewer, is there is usually no other route. — *One: The Homosexual Magazine*, p. 18, February 1954

5 a young performer new to the pornography industry who looks even younger than he or she is *US, 1995*
- — *Adult Video News*, p. 40, August 1995

6 in horse racing, a two-year-old horse *US, 1976*
- — Tom Ainslie, *Ainslie's Complete Guide to Thoroughbred Racing*, p. 327, 1976

7 in professional wrestling, a wrestler or other participant designed to be an audience favorite *US, 1999*
A shortened **BABYFACE**.
- "I really wish I could leave this place as a baby," I said, before adding, "This angle's going to change all that." — Mick Foley, *Mankind*, p. 280, 1999

8 marijuana *US, 1960*
- "He say, 'Man, don't forgit the baby now!' He mean bring a few sticks of it out to the field, you see, that's what he mean by that. He call it 'charge,' too. Sho'. Them's slang names." — Terry Southern, *Texas Summer*, p. 82, 1991

9 in the television and movie industries, a focused 500 watt light source *US, 1960*
- — Oswald Skilbeck, *ABC of Film and TV Working Terms*, p. 14, 1960

10 in poker, a 2, 3, 4, or 5 *US, 1979*
- — John Scarne, *Scarne's Guide to Modern Poker*, p. 272, 1979

baby batter *noun*
semen *US, 1997*
- — Vann Wesson, *Generation X Field Guide and Lexicon*, p. 10, 1997
- [I]t's because you ain't got the baby batter in your brain any more. — *Something About Mary*, 1998
- Was he any less a husband now that he could no longer produce even a drop of live baby batter? — Anthony McCarten, *Spinners*, p. 83, 2000

baby Benz *noun*
a Mercedes 190 *US, 1989*
- I wanted the big Benz because a lot of my friends have the baby Benz but the big one is what the big time is all about. — Terry Williams, *The Cocaine Kids*, p. 31, 1989
- At other times, it is wonderfully descriptive, such as when dealers talk about making "crazy dollars" with which to buy a "baby Benz," a Mercedes 190. — *Washington Post*, p. 9, 12th September 1989

baby blue *noun*
1 a tablet of Viagra™, an erection-inducing drug *US, 2002*
- — Amy Sohn, *Sex and the City*, p. 154, 2002
2 capsule of the synthetic opiate oxycodone used recreationally *US, 2003*
- Extracts reproduced in the tabloid show Limbaugh referring to "small blue babies" and "the little blues." — *Broward Business Review*, p. 1, 18th November 2003
- Prosecutors in Florida, where Limbaugh has a $24 million estate, are now investigating whether he used one of his housekeepers to obtain OxyContin painkillers, known on the street as "Baby Blues." — *The Record (Bergen County, New Jersey)*, p. 1, 23rd November 2003

baby blues *noun*
blue eyes *US, 1957*
- Play it big with the baby blues. — Stephen Sondheim, *West Side Story*, 1957

baby boomer *noun*
a person born roughly between 1945 and 1955 *US, 1974*
After World War 2, America and Europe saw a boom in the birthrate.
- A baby boomer of the Bill Clinton / Al Gore generation, he had three older sisters, the youngest of whom was ten years older than himself. — Joseph Wambaugh, *Finnegan's Week*, p. 72, 1993

baby breasts *noun*
small breasts on a woman, appreciated by small-breast fetishists *US, 1995*
- My "babybreasts," to use a stripper term, worked just fine. — Heidi Mattson, *Ivy League Stripper*, p. 181, 1995

baby bumper *noun*
a child molester *US, 1992*
- You know, usually there's nothing up there but snitches, baby bumpers, but then there was this other guy? — Richard Price, *Clockers*, p. 542, 1992

baby discovers!
used as a melodramatic reaction to another's surprise *US, 1972*
- A new kind of pill? Baby discovers! — Bruce Rodgers, *The Queens' Vernacular*, p. 26, 1972

baby doll *noun*
any central nervous system stimulant *US, 1955*
- — *American Speech*, p. 86, May 1955: "Narcotic argot along the Mexican border"

babydyke *noun*
a young or inexperienced lesbian *US, 1999*
- An innocent babydyke in college, I first heard of female ejaculation when Debi Sundahl came to campus to show her instructional video[.] — *The Village Voice*, 7th September 1999

babyface *noun*
1 in professional wrestling, the wrestler designed by the promoters to be the audience favorite in a match *US, 1958*
- In fact, even if people heard us talking above the clamor, they weren't able to understand what we were talking about. For example: wrestle is "wart"; fall is "going over"; "finish" is the routine just before the deciding fall; hero is "baby face." — Pappy Boyinton, *Baa Baa Black Sheep*, 1958
- Last fall Backlund signed on with Pro Wrestling USA, which has allowed him to perform on his own bland terms, as the ultimate babyface. — *Sports Illustrated*, p. 66, 29th April 1985
- I'd been a babyface for all of his fourteen months back with the company. — Mick Foley, *Mankind*, p. 2, 1999
- — *Washington Post*, p. N36, 10th March 2000
- As one of the leading babyface groups around, chances are they will win this match, unless their opponents are awarded the bout by trickery. — *Rampage*, p. 44, September 2000

2 by extension, any figure in the professional wrestling industry designed to be cheered or liked by the fans *US, 1999*
- Paul Bearer is a chubby individual who for years was a babyface manager for The Undertaker. — Jeff Archer, *Theater in the Square*, p. 28, 1999
- Finally, Vince McMahon, then a babyface announcer, asked Lawler, "What is wrong with people from Alabama?" — Jeff Archer, *Theater in the Square*, p. 137, 1999

baby femme *adjective*
(used of a fashion style) suggesting both youthful innocence and sexual abandon *US, 1995*
- Hair clips worn with middle-parted hair or with pig-tails as part of the "baby femme" style, with color-rimmed tight baby T-shorts or baby-doll dresses and Mary Jane shoes. — Steven Daly and Nathaniel Wice, *alt.culture*, p. 17, 1995

baby food *noun*
semen *US, 1972*
- — Robert A. Wilson, *Playboy's Book of Forbidden Words*, p. 23, 1972

baby fucker *noun*
a child molester *US, 1985*
- The third was a child molester who perhaps was not the best choice that the Colebrook Unified School District might have made as the driver of its bus for junior high school students. "The baby-fucker," I said. — George V. Higgins, *Penance for Jerry Kennedy*, p. 85, 1985
- "Yogee! Check out the baby-fucker!" — Jimmy Lerner, *You Got Nothing Coming*, p. 75, 2002

baby gangster *noun*
a young member of a youth gang *US, 1989*
- In Los Angeles, where Blood and Crip membership totals about 25,000, "baby-gangsters" as young as 9 are regularly recruited and some gangs include even younger "tiny gangsters," the report said. — *UPI*, 4th August 1989
- — Mark S. Fleisher, *Beggars & Thieves*, p. 287, 1995

baby grand *noun*
five hundred dollars *US, 1963*
Punning on the piano size and a "grand" as $1000.
- — Troy Harris, *A Booklet of Criminal Argot, Cant and Jargon*, p. 4, 1976
- — Thomas L. Clark, *The Dictionary of Gambling and Gaming*, p. 9, 1987

baby gun *noun*
a short, bullet-shaped surf board designed for big-wave conditions *US, 1970*
- — Jim Allen, *Locked in Surfing for Life*, p. 193, 1970

baby hole *noun*
the vagina *US, 1973*
- "Then I felt the relief as he withdrew his tremendous weapon from my sore baby hole." — Stanley Weber, *A Study of Sex in Prison*, p. 43, 1973

Baby Huey *noun*
a military helicopter *US, 1969*
An embellishment of the more common and simpler **HUEY**, alluding here to a comic strip character.
- We took some "Baby Hueys" / And we took a Weasel, too. — Joseph Tuso, *Singing the Vietnam Blues*, p. 46, 1990: The Battle of 18.50
- The U.S. government, in the midst of downsizing its military-equipment stockpile, sold the $1 million "Baby Huey" helicopter to the county for $3,000. — *Seattle Times*, p. B2, 15th June 1994

baby legs *noun*
in television and movie making, a low-legged tripod for supporting lights *US, 1987*
- — Ira Konigsberg, *The Complete Film Dictionary*, p. 23, 1987

baby life *noun*
a prison sentence of at least ten years *US, 2002*
- — Gary K. Farlow, *Prison-ese*, p. 1, 2002

Babylon *noun*
1 the white establishment; a symbol of all that is corrupt and evil *JAMAICA, 1943*
From the mystical "Babylon of the Apocalypse."
- The capitalistic, imperialistic, doggish pimping of the People must cease by this wanton, sadistic country or perish like Babylon. — *The Black Panther*, 6th April 1969

2 by extension, the United States *US, 1972*
- — David Claerbaut, *Black Jargon in White America*, p. 57, 1972

Babylonian *noun*
a white person *US, 2004*
- — Rick Ayers (Editor), *Berkeley High Slang Dictionary*, p. 11, 2004

baby needs a pair of shoes!
used for summoning good luck while rolling the dice in craps *US, 2003*
- — Victor H. Royer, *Casino Gamble Talk*, p. 8, 2003

baby pro *noun*
a very, very young prostitute *US, 1961*
- — Burgess Laughlin, *Job Opportunities in the Black Market*, p. 1, 1978
- Young pussy ought to draw the best; that was why he risked the dangers of baby pro. — Alix Shulman, *On the Stroll*, p. 112, 1981

baby race *noun*
in horse racing, a relatively short race for two-year-old horses *US, 1976*
- — Tom Ainslie, *Ainslie's Complete Guide to Thoroughbred Racing*, p. 327, 1976

baby raper; baby rapist *noun*
a child molester *US, 1961*
- Even the Baby Raper appeared to believe he could be forgiven. Baby raping didn't necessarily make him a bad fellow. He just forgot to ask for ID. — Malcolm Braly, *On the Yard*, p. 13, 1967
- [Y]eah, he's a child rapist . . . baby rapist, how old was she? — Miguel Pinero, *Short Eyes*, p. 30, 1975
- He was told there were guys in the regular cell blocks who were just dying to get him for being a "baby-raper." — Thomas Kiernan, *The Roman Polanski Story*, p. 228, 1980
- "Baby rapers" [child molesters], snitches, whites associating with blacks and other undesirables could no longer live in the general population. — Bill Valentine, *Gangs and Their Tattoos*, p. 10, 2000

baby rip *noun*
a small current traveling seaward from shore *US, 1990*
An abbreviation of "rip tide" or "rip current."
- He bitched about missing some rad tubes and said that old dorks shouldn't be anywhere near a rip, even a baby rip. — Joseph Wambaugh, *The Golden Orange*, p. 33, 1990

baby-san *noun*
an East Asian child; a young woman *US, 1954*
Coined during the US occupation of Japan, used frequently in Vietnam.
- Hey, baby-san, you boum-boum G.I.? — *Screw*, p. 5, 15th February 1971

baby shotgun *noun*
a sawed-off shotgun *US, 2002*
- But the coat served its purpose because Swizz had a fully loaded Glock and a baby shotgun hidden underneath it. — Earl "DMX" Simmons, *E.A.R.L.*, p. 236, 2002

babysit *verb*
1 to guide a person through an LSD or other hallucinatory drug experience *US, 1968*
- — Edward R. Bloomquist, *Marijuana*, p. 155, 1968
2 to act as a mentor or protector for newly arrived prisoners *US, 1984*
- — Ines Cardozo-Freeman, *The Joint*, p. 480, 1984

bachelor *noun*
in police work, an officer who works best alone *US, 1992*
- He was known as a bachelor, a cop who didn't work well harnessed to another cop, keeping everything to himself, going off and investigating angles on his own and sharing what he learned only when he got damned good and ready. — Robert Campbell, *Boneyards*, p. 10, 1992

bachelor pad *noun*
the apartment of a young, single, urbane, sophisticated man *US, 1976*
- For the Club's bachelor-pad look, it had been a simple matter to turn to the pages of Playboy for interior design and furnishing ideas. — Kathryn Leigh Scott, *The Bunny Years*, p. 54, 1998

back *noun*
1 an illegal gambling operation *US, 1973*
An abbreviation of "*back* office."

- We hear Red Scalotta's back offices gross from one to two million a year. And he probably has at least three backs going. — Joseph Wambaugh, *The Blue Knight*, p. 144, 1973
2 a drink taken immediately after another, a "chaser" *US, 1982*
- Next morning he went to a bar meeting, as in lawyers, and I went to my own, as in bocoo bourbon and beer backs. — Seth Morgan, *Homeboy*, p. 9, 1990
3 support, help *US, 1989*
- He told me to go to this spot with him. He said "he needed some back [backup or help] and he didn't have anybody." — Terry Williams, *The Cocaine Kids*, p. 19, 1989

▸ **get someone's back; have someone's back**
to defend or protect someone *US, 1990*
- I got your back. — *New Jack City*, 1990
- Do you get my back when she bashes me? Because I know she does. — *Chasing Amy*, 1997
- I let him roll with me, and in exchange for having his back in the street, I always had a ride. — Earl "DMX" Simmons, *E.A.R.L.*, p. 137, 2002

backasswards *adverb*
in the wrong order *US, 1951*
- "You always do everything backasswards." He looked at me. "No wonder you're flunking the hell out of here," he said. — J.D. Salinger, *Catcher in the Rye*, p. 41, 1951
- "I was born backasswards," she liked to explain, referring to her breech birth. — Seth Morgan, *Homeboy*, p. 4, 1990

backcap *noun*
an answer *US, 1945*
- — Lou Shelly, *Hepcats Jive Talk Dictionary*, p. 7, 1945

back door; backdoor *noun*
1 the anus and rectum *UK, 1694*
- The other replied, "Lawd have mercy brother, I'd go in the back door!" — Phyllis and Eberhand Kronhausen, *Sex Histories of American College Men*, 1960
- I was forced to violate everything he has been taught to regard as sacred, including the sanctity of his tiny back door. — Gore Vidal, *Myra Breckinridge*, p. 231, 1968
- She says, "Sweetie, I ain't gonna go three way with you for no saw-buck. You gotta gimme fifteen." He says, "I'll spring for that if you can guarantee a tight back door and quim." — Iceberg Slim (Robert Beck), *Doom Fox*, p. 6, 1978
- So let her explore your back door, then you can do hers — *The Village Voice*, 24th August 1999
2 in sports, the advancement of a team in a playoff situation as a result of the actions of another team *US, 1952*
- "We're lucky. That seven-point underdog stuff is steak on the platter for us," said Mr. Williamson. "They're saying we aren't up to Michigan State and only got here through the back door." — *San Francisco News*, p. 11, 30th December 1952
3 a surreptitious way of entering a protected system or web-site, made possible by a weakness in the system *US, 1990*
- — Karla Jennings, *The Devouring Fungus*, p. 218, 1990

▸ **go out the back door**
to back down from a confrontation *US, 1981*
- — *Maledicta*, p. 266, Summer/Winter 1981: "By its slang, ye shall know it: the pessimism of prison life"

back-door; backdoor *verb*
1 to commit adultery *US, 1982*
- The bawdiest story concerns a merchant who "back-doors" his partner's wife by promising to tell her his secret of turning a woman to a mare and back to a woman again. — Kent Smith et al., *Adult Movies*, p. 70, 1982
2 in surfing, to start a ride behind the peak of a wave *US, 1980*
- — John Grissim, *Pure Stoke*, p. 156, 1980

back-door; backdoor *adjective*
1 adulterous *US, 1947*
- He was your mother's back-door man, I thought. — Ralph Ellison, *Invisible Man*, p. 242, 1947
- I was getting back-door stuff from my man's rib. — A.S. Jackson, *Gentleman Pimp*, p. 45, 1973

2 in poker, describing an unexpected hand produced by drawing *US*, *1979*
- — John Scarne, *Scarne's Guide to Modern Poker*, p. 272, 1979

backdoor Betty *noun*
a woman who enjoys anal sex *US*, *2000*
- The people who've volunteered to get done are always self-proclaimed backdoor betties, but when push comes to penetration, they get shy. — *The Village Voice*, 8th August 2000
- Since anal pleasure is still taboo in American culture, anyone who admits to being a backdoor betty is on the front lines of sexual liberation. — Tristan Taormino, *Pucker Up*, p. 147, 2001

back-door bust *noun*
an arrest for one crime, usually major, after a detention or arrest for another, usually minor *US*, *1992*
- He didn't get busted against until he was thirty-two. And then it was a backdoor bust. A routine vice squad roust. They roust this bar, our buddy Lawrence is in there knocking down a few. — *Reservoir Dogs*, 1992

back door closed *adjective*
describes a convoy when the final vehicle is looking out for any police interest *US*, *1976*
Citizen band radio slang.
- — *Complete CB Slang Dictionary*, 1976

backdoor delivery *noun*
anal sex *US*, *1973*
- I find "back door deliveries" very painful—even when a man uses lots of lubricant. — Jennifer Sills, *Massage Parlor*, p. 154, 1973

backdoor parole; backgate parole *noun*
death while serving a prison sentence *US*, *1929*
A black joke.
- — Vincent J. Monteleone, *Criminal Slang*, p. 14, 1949

backdoor trots *noun*
diarrhea *US*, *1973*
- "That jail is like the inside of a toilet bowl in a place where everybody's got the backdoor trots, know what I mean?" — Joe Eszterhas, *Charlie Simpson's Apocalypse*, p. 39, 1973

backer *noun*
a high-level figure in an illegal lottery *US*, *1977*
- The highest people I know in the numbers business was the backers. — John Allen, *Assault with a Deadly Weapon*, p. 106, 1977

backfield *noun*
the supporting members of a criminal group *US*, *1970*
- What he didn't know about wires wasn't invented yet, so now we had the whole backfield. — Red Rudensky, *The Gonif*, p. 93, 1970

back flip *verb*
in pinball, to flip the ball to the same side of the playing field as the flipper *US*, *1977*
- — Bobbye Claire Natkin and Steve Kirk, *All About Pinball*, p. 110, 1977

back gate exit *noun*
death while in prison *US*, *1992*
- — William K. Bentley and James M. Corbett, *Prison Slang*, p. 104, 1992

backhouse flush *noun*
in poker, a very poor hand *US*, *1984*
From "backhouse" (an outside toilet).

back in the day *adverb*
at a time in the past that evokes a feel of nostalgia, real or conjured *US*, *1988*
- What i used to do back in the day is to record the stuff on a cheapo cassette. — *rec.music.beatles*, 30th October 1989
- — Connie Eble (Editor), *UNC-CH Campus Slang*, p. 1, March 1996
- And back in the day, they might've actually listened[.] — David Simon and Edward Burns, *The Corner*, p. 81, 1997
- Hip Hop America starts "back in the day"—the late '70s[.] — Nelson George, *Hip Hop America*, p. xi, 1998
- Back in the day, they say you had anti-freeze in them veins. — *Gone in 60 Seconds*, 2000

backlip *noun*
impertinence, talking back *US*, *1959*

- Little Jeff give you sass, Big Jeff look around like he ain't even listening, but if you gave backlip—wap!—Big Jeff laid you out. — Edwin Torres, *Carlito's Way*, p. 17, 1975

back-me-up *noun*
a friend who can be counted on for support in a confrontation *US*, *1984*
- — Inez Cardozo-Freeman, *The Joint*, p. 480, 1984

back money *noun*
money paid after delivery of the item purchased *US*, *1963*
- He demanded "front money" (an advance) and was uneasy over "back money" (arrears). — John A. Williams, *Sissie*, p. 71, 1963

back pack *noun*
a gang insignia tattooed on a gang member's back *US*, *1992*
- — Paladin Press, *Inside Look at Outlaw Motorcycle Gangs*, p. 33, 1992

back porch *noun*
a late position in a hand of poker *US*, *1996*
- — John Vorhaus, *The Big Book of Poker Slang*, p. 5, 1996

back-porch nigger *noun*
an obsequious, fawning black person *US*, *1971*
- [H]e bowed and scraped and grinned apologetically like some creaky old back-porch nigger. — Tom Robbins, *Another Roadside Attraction*, p. 61, 1971

backroom job *noun*
a tattoo on a part of the body that is usually clothed *US*, *1997*
- — *Los Angeles Times Magazine*, p. 7, 13th July 1997

back row *noun*
a prison cell used for solitary confinement *US*, *1984*
- — Inez Cardozo-Freeman, *The Joint*, p. 480, 1984

backs *noun*
money, especially counterfeit money *US*, *1945*
Probably an abbreviation of **GREENBACK**.
- — Lou Shelly, *Hepcats Jive Talk Dictionary*, p. 7, 1945

back-sass *noun*
impudent talking back to an elder *US*, *1968*
- "Don't ever give me anymore of your back sass—a girl eleven years old tellin her Pap what to do." — Jesse Stuart, *Head O' W-Hollow*, p. 36, 1979

back-sass *verb*
to talk back impudently *US*, *1950*
- "Sort of respect that, but don't back-sass me again, son, or I'll bust your spleen and you'll drown in your own blood." — Warren Ripley, *Pressing the Bet*, p. 97, 2006

back-scratching *noun*
the removal of enemy soldiers who have climbed onto a tank by shooting light-caliber weapons at the tank *US*, *1986*
- — Ralph Zumbro, *Tank Sergeant*, p. 189, 1986: Glossary

back-scuttle *verb*
to play the active role in sex, anal or vaginal, from behind *US*, *1885*
- — Dale Gordon, *The Dominion Sex Dictionary*, p. 25, 1967
- "Them square cats likes them fat-assed bitches. They likes to back scuttle 'em." — Robert Deane Pharr, *S.R.O.*, p. 274, 1971

back seat *noun*
in poker, any of the positions farther from the dealer than the third player to his left *US*, *1973*
- — Thomas L. Clark, *The Dictionary of Gambling and Gaming*, p. 11, 1987

▶ **in the back seat**
ignored, forgotten *US*, *1998*
Building on the **CAR** (clique) metaphor.
- — Ethan Hilderbrant, *Prison Slang*, p. 9, 1998

backspace and overstrike!
in computing, used for expressing alarm about a mistake that has just been made *US*, *1991*
- — Eric S. Raymond, *The New Hacker's Dictionary*, p. 45, 1991

backstop *verb*
to reinforce *US*, *1995*

- Fulo backstopped all transactions with a shotgun. — James Ellroy, *American Tabloid*, p. 351, 1995

backstrap *verb*
to wire telephone lines as part of an illegal enterprise *US, 1989*
- Buthe was also the handyman who could rewire, or backstrap, telephone lines in and out of different apartments and across rooftops to confuse investigators. — Gerard O'Neill, *The Under Boss*, p. 176, 1989

backstreet boy *noun*
a young man dressed in the trendiest of clothes with the trendiest of haircuts *US, 2001*
Not a compliment; an allusion to a band of the late 1990s that was thought to value style to the exclusion of substance.
- — Don R. McCreary (Editor), *Dawg Speak*, 2001

back time *noun*
all time spent incarcerated before sentencing *US, 1992*
- — William K. Bentley and James M. Corbett, *Prison Slang*, p. 17, 1992

back to hacking
used as a farewell, by computer enthusiast to computer enthusiast *US, 1983*
- — Guy L. Steele et al., *The Hacker's Dictionary*, p. 76, 1983

backwards *noun*
any central nervous system depressant *US, 1966*
- — J. L. Simmons and Barry Winograd, *It's Happening*, p. 167, 1966
- — Edward R. Bloomquist, *Marijuana*, p. 155, 1968

backwhack *noun*
the backslash key (\ ) on a computer keyboard *US, 1991*
- — Eric S. Raymond, *The New Hacker's Dictionary*, p. 40, 1991

backyard *noun*
1 the buttocks *US, 1972*
- — Robert A. Wilson, *Playboy's Book of Forbidden Words*, p. 23, 1972
2 the anus *US, 1967*
- — Dale Gordon, *The Dominion Sex Dictionary*, p. 25, 1967

bacon *noun*
1 the police; a police officer *US, 1974*
From PIG (a policeman). During the late 1960s and early 70s, a favored chant of the radical left youth movement in the US was "Today's pig, tomorrow's bacon."
- Publishers and stuff wouldn't even know "bacon burning" was "pigs" or "cops" coming. — Beatrice Sparks (writing as "Anonymous"), *Jay's Journal*, p. 60, 1979
- Later, bacon. — *Airheads*, 1994
- — Judi Sanders, *Da Bomb*, p. 1, 1997
2 money *US, 1957*
- The boss catered mostly to Indians who had struck oil on the reservation, beefy cattlemen who were sure to be milked, sugar-daddies with their sable-sporting chicken dinners, and butter-and-egg men with plenty of bacon. — Mezz Mezzrow, *Really the Blues*, p. 84, 1946
- We'll save your bacon for you. — Max Shulman, *Rally Round the Flag, Boys!*, p. 115, 1957

▸ **bring home the bacon**
to succeed as a wage earner, supporting one's family; to achieve success; to succeed in a given undertaking *US, 1909*
Generally thought to echo the ancient tradition in Dunmow, England, of presenting a flitch of bacon to a happily married couple but originates in the US country fair "sport" of catching a greased pig. The phrase was popularized, if not invented, by the mother of Joe Gans, a black lightweight boxer.
- Anyhow, what I'm saying, everybody depending on this new gig I got t'bring home the bacon[.] — Robert Gover, *Here Goes Kitten*, p. 53, 1964
- He is fanatical about his job. He always brings home the bacon. — Howard Stern, *Miss America*, p. 448, 1995

bacon getter *noun*
a handgun, especially a single-action revolver *US, 1957*
- — *American Speech*, p. 192, October 1957: "Some colloquialisms of the handgunner"

bad *adjective*
1 good; tough *US, 1897*

- The latest bop talk requires you to say, if you like a musician, "Man, he's real bad." Or, "he blows bad." This critical pronouncement is delivered in a monotone, with the "b-a-a-d" dragged out for emphasis. Means the exact opposite of what it says. — *Philadelphia Evening Bulletin*, 11th October 1955
- I've mentioned him before—one of Harlem's really bad Negroes. — Malcolm X and Alex Haley, *The Autobiography of Malcolm X*, p. 117, 1964
- There were cats all over East and West Oakland who had reputations for being bad, and they were known throughout the community for being bad. — Bobby Seale, *Seize the Time*, p. 15, 1970
- The Copiens, the Socialists, the Bachelors, the Comanches—all bad motherfuckers—these were the gangs that started using hardware. — Edwin Torres, *Carlito's Way*, p. 8, 1975
2 in computing, broken as designed *US, 1991*
- — Eric S. Raymond, *The New Hacker's Dictionary*, p. 46, 1991

bad ass *noun*
a tough, fearless person *US, 1956*
- Now Dolomite went on down to Kansas City kickin' asses till both shoes were shitty. / Hoboed into Chi / Who did he run into but that badass Two-Gun Pete. — Bruce Jackson, *Get Your Ass in the Water and Swim Like Me*, p. 59, 1970
- Buddusky became Bad-Ass, which in navy tolerance means a very tough customer. — Darryl Ponicsan, *The Last Detail*, p. 7, 1970
- So like I'm shooting dice on 105th Street off Madison Avenue on a Saturday afternoon when this bad-ass named Chago grabs all the money on the ground and says, "These dice are loaded." — Edwin Torres, *Carlito's Way*, p. 20, 1975
- I'm a killer and I've got a platoon of the baddest badasses in the Nam. We're bad, baaaad fuckin' killers. — Philip Caputo, *A Rumor of War*, p. 245, 1977

bad-ass *adjective*
excellent; worthy of respect, tough *US, 1955*
Originally black usage but now more widely known.
- I told him about hanging out with those bad-ass boys. — Claude Brown, *Manchild in the Promised Land*, p. 10, 1965
- My good time badass fuckaround is going out of style. — Hunter S. Thompson, *The Proud Highway*, p. 509, 18th April 1965: Letter to Paul Semonin
- Now down on the ground in a great big ring / Lived a bad-ass lion who knew he was king. — Dennis Wepman et al., *The Life*, p. 22, 1976
- You bad-ass little spick. How are you, honey? — *Boogie Nights*, 1997

bad bang *noun*
an unfortunate occurrence *US, 1960*
- Life is a bad bang for Cooney; a bum rap and no probation. — Nelson Algren, *The Neon Wilderness*, p. 12, 1960

bad beat *noun*
in poker, a disappointing loss, either with a good hand or a big bet *US, 1982*
- — David M. Hayano, *Poker Faces*, p. 185, 1982

bad boy *noun*
1 something that is impressive *US, 1974*
- I finally got this bad boy together bout six, seven months. Got the whole place furnished top to bottom. — Vernon E. Smith, *The Jones Men*, p. 139, 1974
- Well, I want two of them bad boys. Two large orders of chili fries. Two large Diet Cokes. — *True Romance*, 1993
- PIP: It's a card thing door opener. REX: I know how to handle these bad boys. — *Airheads*, 1994
- "Gimme one a them bad boys," Red Hammernut said, helping himself. — Carl Hiaasen, *Skinny Dip*, p. 119, 2004
2 a rascal, a misfit *US, 1948*
- Cincy Trades "Bad Boy" Eddie Miller to Phillies (Headline) — *San Francisco Examiner*, p. 20, 11th February 1948
- Strange Things Are Happening to Hollywood's "Bad Boy" — *San Francisco Examiner's Pictorial Review*, p. 13, 27th December 1953

bad butch *noun*
an aggressive, "mannish" lesbian *US, 1967*
- Known variously as a bull, a stomper, a bad butch, a hard dresser, a truck driver, a diesel dyke, a bull dagger and a half dozen other soubriquets, she is the one who, according to most homosexual girls, gives lesbians a bad name. — Ruth Allison, *Lesbianism*, p. 125, 1967

bad cop noun

in a pair of police, the partner who plays the aggressive and hard-nosed role during an interrogation *US, 1991*

- The one that growled is O'Shea who always looks like he's got a bad case of indigestion and plays the bad cop. — Robert Campbell, *In a Pig's Eye*, p. 23, 1991

badda bing; bada-bing; ba-da-bing

used as an embellishing intensifier *US, 1972*

The variations are nearly endless.

- You've gotta get up close like this and bada-bing! you blow their brains all over your nice Ivy League suit. — Mario Puzo and Francis Ford Coppola, *The Godfather*, 1972
- And on this farm he shot some guys. Ba-da-bip, ba-da-bing, ba-da-boom. — *The Usual Suspects*, 1995
- It was cake—8 cars. Badda-bing. — *Gone in 60 Seconds*, 2000

baddest adjective

toughest; most admired *US, 1938*

The unconventional superlative of "bad" in the "bad-as-good" sense of the word.

- "Eric [Clapton] is one of the baddest guitarists who ever lived," [Quincy] Jones concluded. — *San Francisco Chronicle*, 8th September 1971
- "I'm a killer and I've got a platoon full of the baddest badasses in the Nam. We're bad, baaaad fuckin' killers." — Philip Caputo, *A Rumor of War*, p. 245, 1977
- Then [presidential spokesman Jody] Powell turned to the statement in Tanzania, where Ali said, "There are two bad white men in the world, the Russian white man and the American white man. They are the two baddest men in the history of the world." — *San Francisco Chronicle*, p. 10, 6th February 1980

badeye verb

to glare, to stare with menace *US, 1990*

- — Charles Shafer, *Folk Speech in Texas Prisons*, p. 197, 1990

badge noun

1 a notional symbol of membership in the Mafia *US, 1987*

- "I've done more work than half the guys who were made," Guido said, meaning that he had been in on more hits, which is one of the prime considerations to getting made, "and I ain't got my badge." — Joseph Pistone, *Donnie Brasco*, p. 108, 1987

2 a police officer *US, 1925*

- — Jack Webb, *The Badge*, p. 220, 1958
- About that time along come two badges patrolling their beat/arrested this whore for prostituting on the street. — Bruce Jackson, *Get Your Ass in the Water and Swim Like Me*, p. 80, 1966
- "[B]efore I even unpacked my suitcase I'd head for the nearest police station and check in with the big badge." — Martin Gosch, *The Last Testament of Lucky Luciano*, pp. 141–142, 1975

3 a prison guard *US, 1992*

- — William K. Bentley and James M. Corbett, *Prison Slang*, p. 95, 1992

badge verb

to show a police badge, especially as part of a psychological ploy to elicit information *US, 1970*

- She thought he was a PO-lice impersonator when he finally badged her. — Joseph Wambaugh, *The New Centurions*, p. 214, 1970

badge bunny noun

a woman attracted to and sexually available for police *US, 1997*

- Being single, I started to see all the badge bunnies that were ready for the taking, but that's another story. — *alt.law-enforcement*, 29th January 1997
- [A]nd held tight to the conviction that a woman in uniform meant a badge bunny who'd found a way to stalk cops—and get a paycheck. — Gina Gallo, *Armed and Dangerous*, p. 243, 2001
- He and his partner Cash had swapped any number of the badge bunnies who liked to hang out at cop bars. — Jory Strong, *Calista's Men*, p. 37, 2005
- Sometimes badge bunnies would show up. — Joseph Wambaugh, *Hollywood Station*, p. 36, 2006

badger noun

in horse racing, an inexpensive horse that qualifies its owner for race track privileges *US, 1976*

- — Tom Ainslie, *Ainslie's Complete Guide to Thoroughbred Racing*, p. 327, 1976

badger game noun

a swindle in which a prostitute lures a customer or victim to a room where he is robbed by a confederate of the prostitute, often posing to be her husband *US, 1909*

- But cases of "badger" workers are everyday occurrences[.] — Jack Lait and Lee Mortimer, *New York Confidential*, p. 98, 1948
- [T]he street-level warrens decayed into strip tease clip joints and worthless sucker traps with carnival barkers, broads hustling tables, finger men on the prowl, lookouts for blackmail mobs on steady duty, badger game veterans[.] — Robert Sylvester, *No Cover Charge*, p. 89, 1956
- Blackmail Trap Laid to Clerk, Wife; Contractor Charges Badger Game (Headline) — *San Francisco Examiner*, p. 12, 8th February 1956
- There he met Phillipa, an orphaned teenage whiz at the badger game played with a Baton Rouge based pimp and con man on johns during Mardi Gras. — Iceberg Slim (Robert Beck), *Doom Fox*, p. 46, 1978

bad guy noun

a criminal *US, 1932*

Originally children's vocabulary from watching western movies.

- "Maybe he didn't," Raylan said. "Maybe he was abducted." They hadn't thought of that, both of them turning to look at each other. "By who," Jerry said, "the bad guys?" — Elmore Leonard, *Pronto*, p. 71, 1977

bad hair day noun

a day on which your hair is especially unruly; hence, a day on which nothing goes to plan *US, 1991*

- They said I told them I was having a bad hair day. They didn't even talk to me. (Quoting Gary Shandling) — *Seattle Times*, p. 10, 25th January 1991

bad hat noun

someone who can be counted on to misbehave *US, 1914*

- He was a thoroughly bad hat, then, but that was the kind, of course, that nice women broke their hearts over. — Mary McCarthy, *The Group*, p. 175, 1963

bad idea jeans noun

the notional clothing worn by someone who has displayed an utter lack of common sense *US, 1994*

From a skit on *Saturday Night Live*.

- And whoever thought mild-mannered milquetoast Jimmy Buffet was up for a no-holds-barred tag-team match on "Mack the Knife" should be given a pair of "Bad Idea" jeans and maybe a dose or two of electro-shock therapy. — *Philadelphia Daily News*, p. 25, 16th November 1994
- — Ben Applebaum and Derrick Pittman, *Turd Ferguson & The Sausage Party*, p. 4, 2004

bad motherfucker noun

a fearless, tough person *US, 1971*

- "Jesus Christ was a bad motherfucker." — Ronald Steel, *Imperialists and Other Heroes*, p. 270, 1971
- [H]e was a very mean and impatient man who had no respect for free enterprise, especially when some cocksucker was freely enterprising in his territory. He was a bad motherfucker[.] — Emmett Grogan, *Ringolevio*, p. 112, 1972
- "I said you were a bad motherfucker, man, like you could handle yourself." — Robert Stone, *Dog Soldiers*, p. 86, 1974

bad mouth noun

a curse, a put-down *US, 1960*

- Rudy wondered how the bad mouth about him had started, although he'd arrived at the point where he didn't much care. — Clarence Cooper Jr., *The Scene*, p. 12, 1960
- I said, "Mama, look, don't be puttin' the bad mouth on him." — Claude Brown, *Manchild in the Promised Land*, p. 287, 1965
- Just that they ken pu the bad-mouth on you, that's all. — Steve Cannon, *Groove, Bang, and Jive Around*, p. 128, 1969
- "Funny, I heard somebody put a bad mouth on me." — Gail Sheehy, *Hustling*, p. 65, 1973

badmouth verb

to insult someone, to disparage someone *US, 1941*

- "I had to beat the bitch's ass for bad mouthing you, Mollie," he said. — Dick Gregory, *Nigger*, p. 22, 1964
- Bobby Bodega Pogats, the society stock market operator, has retained Atty. Jim MacInnis to file a slander suit against the Stock

Exchange hotshot who has been badmouthing him. — *San Francisco Chronicle*, p. 29, 2nd July 1969

- "[W]hen you threatened him and bad-mouthed him and everything, you were no better than he was." — Darryl Ponicsan, *The Last Detail*, pp. 43–44, 1970
- Taylor said, "They were bad mouthing our ball players when we were on the way into the locker room. It's bush." — *San Francisco Examiner*, p. 50, 26th January 1972

bad news *noun*
something, abstract or actual, that is unpleasant or contemptible *US, 1917*
- — *American Speech*, p. 55, Spring–Summer 1975: "Razorback slang"

bad-o *adjective*
excellent *US, 1991*
- — Trevor Cralle, *The Surfin'ary*, p. 5, 1991

bad paper *noun*
1 a discharge from the military other than an honorable discharge, such as the UD (undesirable discharge) or resignations for the good of the service *US, 1971*
- I've met the bitter veterans with "bad-paper" discharges who hate themselves and everybody else, too. — *The Los Angeles Times*, 20th April 1980
- "Bad paper," that childish-sounding phrase, is loaded with all the negative connotations of leaving the military with anything less than an honorable discharge. — Myra MacPherson, *Long Time Passing*, p. 679, 1984

2 counterfeit money or securities *US, 1981*
- If told my partner, if the dude was into bad paper, you'd know who he was. — Gerald Petievich, *Money Men*, p. 13, 1981

bad-rap *verb*
to disparage *US, 2002*
- This is the first time (not the last) I have heard one C.O. "bad-rap" another to an inmate. — Jimmy Lerner, *You Got Nothing Coming*, p. 133, 2002

bads *noun*
the depression following the use of hallucinogens or amphetamines *US, 1970*
- — William D. Alsever, *Glossary for the Establishment and Other Uptight People*, p. 2, December 1970

bad scene *noun*
an unpleasant situation; a depressing experience *US, 1966*
- J. L. Simmons and Barry Winograd, *It's Happening*, p. 167, 1966
- Eugene Landy, *The Underground Dictionary*, p. 27, 1971

bad thing *noun*
an inherently bad idea *UK, 1930*
From *1066 and All That*, the history parody in which Sellar and Yeatman created the "bad thing" device: "Indeed, he had begun badly as a Bad Prince, having attempted to answer the Irish Question by pulling the beards of the aged Irish chiefs, which was a Bad Thing and the wrong answer."
- "Replacing all of the 9600-band modems with bicycle couriers would be a Bad Thing." — Eric S. Raymond, *The New Hacker's Dictionary*, p. 46, 1991

bad time *noun*
1 time served in prison that does not count toward the overall sentence; time served in a military stockade that does not count towards the overall period of service *US, 1968*
- — Carl Fleischhauer, *A Glossary of Army Slang*, p. 2, 1968
- Quinn, your young ass is gonna do some bad time for this. — Larry Heinemann, *Close Quarters*, p. 164, 1977
- The penalty of being derelict on duty was slyly unexplained but understood, the stockade, bad time, serve six months, come out and start over where you left off. — Odie Hawkins, *Scars and Memories*, p. 90, 1987

2 a jail or prison sentence for a petty, avoidable offense *US, 1977*
- He had enough to think about, the last thing he needed was the clammy friendship of a dumb sap doing bad time on an alimony beef. — Odie Hawkins, *Chicago Hustle*, p. 102, 1977

bad trip *noun*
1 an unpleasant, frightening or unnerving experience with LSD *US, 1966*
- Such precautions are thought to be insurance against bad trips. — Hunter S. Thompson, *Hell's Angels*, p. 236, 1966

- It's like the guy in Los Angeles who had a bad trip on LSD and turned himself into the police, and wrote, "Please help me. Signed, Jehovah." — *The San Francisco Oracle*, 1967
- After midnight a college kid from Wisconsin phoned requesting help on a bad trip. — Timothy Leary, *The Politics of Ecstasy*, p. 163, 1968
- There isn't much sense in trying to explain what a "bad trip" is. You simply lose your marbles. You go crazy. There is no bottom, no top. — Oscar Zeta Acosta, *The Autobiography of a Brown Buffalo*, p. 183, 1972

2 a very unpleasant experience *US, 1969*
- From running up bills to drugs, to laying bad trips on other people. — Hunter S. Thompson, *Fear and Loathing in America*, p. 214, 15th November 1969: Letter to Oscar Acosta
- The history of the Sunset Strip has been a bad trip, man, a bummer. — Arthur Blessitt, *Turned On to Jesus*, p. 103, 1971

baff *verb*
to vomit *US, 1968*
- — Collin Baker et al., *College Undergraduate Slang Study Conducted at Brown University*, p. 74, 1968

bafflegab *noun*
verbose language that is difficult to penetrate and impossible to understand *US, 1952*
The term, by all accounts, was coined by Milton A. Smith of the United States Chamber of Commerce. Smith defined the term as "Multiloquence characterized by consummate interfusion of circumlocution or periphrasis, inscrutability, incognizability, and other familiar manifestations of abstruse expatiation commonly utilized for promulgations implementing procrustean determinations by governmental bodies."
- — *Word Study*, p. 5, May 1952
- Mutual funds are diversifying to the point where you can completely lose your way in this financial industry without a bafflegab guide. — *San Francisco Chronicle*, p. 52, 7th January 1970
- Connoisseurs of bureaucratic bafflegab may salivate over this May 12 memo from Robertio Alioto. — *San Francisco Chronicle*, 15th May 1980

bag *noun*
1 an interest *US, 1964*
- Anyway you can also be a part-time new American head. That's going to be my bag. — Nat Hentoff, *I'm really dragged but nothing gets me down*, p. 19, 1968
- I mean, what the hell's the matter with you guys? You into some kind of fag bag aweady? — Terry Southern, *Blue Movie*, p. 166, 1970
- He was a painter and singer but his main bag was hustlin' in de Paris streets. — Babs Gonzales, *Movin' On Down De Line*, p. 17, 1975
- I don't even know what this [a penis-enlarger] is. This sort of this ain't my bag, baby. — *Austin Powers*, 1997

2 a way of doing things *US, 1962*
- It was clear to me that we were in two different bags; I had it "made" because I had occupied my niche from the age of five, definitely by the time I was eight. — Odie Hawkins, *Lost Angeles*, p. 89, 1994

3 a police uniform *US, 1944*
- — *New York Times Magazine*, p. 87, 16th March 1958
- I'd hate to be back in the bag, believe me. — Charles Whited, *Chiodo*, p. 54, 1973
- I tell you, it's a whole different thing when you wear a nice suit to work instead of that damn bag. — Leonard Shecter and William Phillips, *On the Pad*, pp. 166–167, 1973

4 duty as a uniformed police officer *US, 1973*
- [H]e suddenly declared that maybe he would get out of the pad someday, that if necessary he would go back to the "bag"—police slang for uniformed duty. — Peter Maas, *Serpico*, p. 187, 1973

5 the scrotum *US, 1938*
- — Anon., *King Smut's Wet Dreams Interpreted*, 1978

6 a condom *US, 1922*
- — Dale Gordon, *The Dominion Sex Dictionary*, p. 25, 1967
- She was on the pill, but I used to use a bag with her anyway. — *Screw*, p. 9, 12th April 1971
- Like Brittney Skey as super-heroine Anal Woman advising Kurt Kockwoodon safe sex and telling him to use a bag, a rubber, a condom, if the pair hasn't been tested for disease, and animated talking buttholes aplenty. — Editors of Adult Video News, *The AVN Guide to the 500 Greatest Adult Films of All Time*, p. 73, 2005

7 a diaphragm *US, 1964*
- — Roger Blake, *The American Dictionary of Sexual Terms*, p. 11, 1964

8 a package of drugs *US, 1952*
- A bag is his supply of drugs. — Clarence Cooper Jr., *The Scene*, p. 54, 1960

- Now you know it's a drag; I copped a bad bag. — Dennis Wepman et al., *The Life*, p. 78, 1976
- Jimmy went and leaned up against a building with them and watched the whores go by and a pusher said you want a bag? — William T. Vollman, *Whores for Gloria*, p. 115, 1991

9 a fuel tank on an airplane *US, 1991*
- We're loading you up with Rockeyes and giving you a full bag of gas. — Gerry Carroll, *North S*A*R*, p. 61, 1991

10 bed *US, 1969*
- — John D. Bell et al., *Loosely Speaking*, p. 2, 1969

▸ **bags are dragging**
the supply of heroin is low *US, 1971*
- Although his bags were dragging, Bud was bragging. — Michael H. Agar, *The Journal of American Folklore*, p. 177, 1971

▸ **in the bag**
1 drunk *US, 1940*
- You know. Drunk stewed, clobbered, gone, liquored up, oiled, stoned, in the bag. — Max Shulman, *Guided Tour of Campus Humor*, p. 106, 1955
- [T]he next night when he came in she was half in the bag[.] — George V. Higgins, *The Rat on Fire*, pp. 94–95, 1981
- It took him three hours and forty minutes to hike it half in the bag, from Thebes to the bridge, not seeing one goddman car on the road. — Elmore Leonard, *Killshot*, p. 287, 1989

2 as good as done *US, 1921*
- Israel-Egyptian Peace Pact Believed Virtually "in the Bag" (Headline) — *San Francisco News*, p. 2, 21st February 1949
- The butler said it was in the bag. — Charles Raven, *Underworld Nights*, p. 16, 1956

3 corrupted, bribed, beholden to someone else *US, 1926*
- I'm not asking was the fight put in the bag. — Rocky Garciano (with Rowland Barber), *Somebody Up There Likes Me*, p. 307, 1955
- As far as he's concerned, I'm in the bag. He gave me until the weekend to contact him. — Edwin Torres, *Q & A*, p. 175, 1977

▸ **on someone's bag**
in golf, working as a caddie *US, 2000*
- Angelo was on Jack's bag for years, but he eventually retired and opened a restaurant in Miami. — Hubert Pedroli and Mary Tiegreen, *Let the Big Dog Eat! A Dictionary of the Secret Language of Golf*, p. 13, 2000

▸ **to have a bag on**
to be drunk *US, 1945*
- Mrs. Doherty, according to eyewitnesses, not to mention authoritative sources, had a bag on. She was drinking champagne. — Earl Wilson, *I Am Gazing Into My 8-Ball*, p. 151, 1945

bag *verb*
1 to seduce *US, 2002*
- At seventeen, you were a real nigga if you could bag a chick that wasn't from the neighborhood on the walk-by. — Earl "DMX" Simmons, *E.A.R.L.*, p. 134, 2002

2 to disparage *US, 1991*
- "I get hyper, and I start baggin'—talkin' about somebody, everybody." — Leon Bing, *Do or Die*, p. 57, 1991

3 to arrest someone *UK, 1824*
- He wasn't taking no chances on getting bagged. — Hal Ellson, *Duke*, p. 127, 1949
- Tito and Turk said they would get bagged and sent to Warwick by the time I got there. — Claude Brown, *Manchild in the Promised Land*, p. 16, 1965
- I says pal, put that in your pocket before I bag you for bribery. — Leonard Shecter and William Phillips, *On the Pad*, p. 190, 1973
- "I might get bagged and have to go to jail." — George Higgins, *Cogan's Trade*, p. 151, 1974
- Our only chance to bag him is if he tries it again. — Gerald Petievich, *Money Men*, p. 17, 1981

4 to catch, capture or obtain something for yourself *US, 1861*
- [B]y midsummer he managed to bag 135 teachers, every one of them with impeccable credentials. — Max Shulman, *Anyone Got a Match?*, p. 66, 1964
- So, Ted, any ideas on who should we bag? Ted? — *Bill and Ted's Excellent Adventure*, 1989
- Yeah, I hear you bagged Martin Weir for Mr. Lovejoy. — *Get Shorty*, 1995

5 to disregard, dismiss or stop something *US, 1988*
Figurative use of throwing garbage in a garbage bag.

- MRS CHANDLER: We are leaving for your grandmother's. If you'd care to join us... HEATHER CHANDLER: Bag that. MRS CHANDLER: Is that a "No" in your lingo? — *Heathers*, 1988

6 to abandon or leave a place or thing *US, 1962*
- Let's bag the mall. It's boring. — *American Beauty*, 1999

7 to bribe someone; to arrange an outcome *US, 1948*
- Bagging of a baseball game down in the Carolina League came as a shock to fans and officials throughout the country. — *San Francisco Examiner*, p. 27, 3rd June 1948
- We wink and laugh at wrestling. We go for the bagged fight. — *San Francisco News*, p. 17, 28th February 1951
- He became a pigeon for the FBI and fed them information on how football games were supposed to be bagged by the mob in different parts of the country. — Vincent Teresa, *My Life in the Mafia*, p. 144, 1973

8 to leave *US, 1981*
Hawaiian youth usage.
- — Douglas Simonson, *Pidgin to da Max*, 1981

▸ **bag and tag**
(used of a prison guard) to count and account for prisoners during scheduled count times *US, 2002*
- — Gary K. Farlow, *Prison-ese*, p. 2, 2002

▸ **bag ass**
to leave, especially in a hurry *US, 1972*
- — Helen Dahlskog (Editor), *A Dictionary of Contemporary and Colloquial Usage*, p. 5, 1972

▸ **bag beaver**
to have sex with a woman *US, 1994*
Combining hunting and sexual metaphors.
- — Michael Dalton Johnson, *Talking Trash with Redd Foxx*, p. 72, 1994

▸ **bag your head**
to stop talking *US, 1962*
- — Joseph E. Ragen and Charles Finston, *Inside the World's Toughest Prison*, p. 789, 1962

bag and baggage
used for conveying to a prisoner that he is to be released from jail *US, 1977*
- He had been told, "Bag and baggage." A little later, Larry found himself outside the jail, still not believing it was all true. — Donald Goines, *Black Gangster*, p. 189, 1977

bag biter *noun*
in computing, something or someone that does not work well *US, 1981*
- — *CoEvolution Quarterly*, p. 26, Spring 1981
- This text editor won't let me make a file with a line longer than eighty characters! What a bagbiter! — Guy L. Steele et al., *The Hacker's Dictionary*, p. 28, 1983

bag case *noun*
a fatally injured motorist, especially one with gruesome injuries *US, 1962*
- — *American Speech*, p. 266, December 1962: "The language of traffic policemen"

bag-chaser *noun*
a drug user who is obsessed with getting drugs *US, 1989*
- — Geoffrey Froner, *Digging for Diamonds*, p. 7, 1989

bagel face *noun*
a Jewish person *US, 1979*
Derogatory.
- He punches some Hebe—Murray something or other. The biggest bagel face in the precinct, and Lawlor belts him. — Vincent Patrick, *The Pope of Greenwich Village*, p. 112, 1979

bag-follower *noun*
an attractive woman who carries packets of heroin for a heroin dealer while bestowing status upon him with her good looks *US, 1978*
- — Burgess Laughlin, *Job Opportunities in the Black Market*, p. 1, 1978

baggage *noun*
1 a boyfriend, agent or other male who accompanies a female pornography performer to the set *US, 1995*
Not flattering.
- — *Adult Video News*, p. 50, October 1995

2 a nonplaying observer of a card or dice game *US, 1950*
- — *The Annals of the American Academy of Political and Social Sciences*, p. 120, May 1950

bagged *adjective*
drunk *US, 1953*
- Sure, Gleason is consistently "bagged" throughout, by which is he such an angry drunk? — *Times Union (Albany, New York)*, p. S2, 13th October 2002

bagger *noun*
a poker player who does not bet aggressively when holding a good hand until late in the hand *US, 1966*
- — John D. Bell et al., *Loosely Speaking*, p. 2, 1966

baggie *noun*
1 a plastic bag filled with a variable amount of loose marijuana *US, 1980*
From the trademarked name of a brand of plastic sandwich bags.
- There wasn't any grass in the apartment anyway. Down to seeds and stems. She'd have to stop at the store on the way and pick up a baggie. — Elmore Leonard, *City Primeval*, p. 54, 1980
2 a condom *US, 1971*
- [I]f you ever run into sluts like The Rump Humpers be sure and wear a baggie. Anal sex has been linked to several serious diseases[.] — *Adult Video*, p. 66, August/September 1986

baggies *noun*
loose pants or shorts, especially loose-fitting shorts or swimming trunks popularized by surfers *US, 1963*
- You'd see 'em wearing their baggies / Huarachi sandals too. — Chuck Berry (Brian Wilson, uncredited lyricist), *Surfin' U.S.A.*, 1963
- — *Paradise of the Pacific*, p. 27, October 1963
- — J. R. Friss, *A Dictionary of Teenage Slang (Mt. Diablo High)*, 1964
- — Collin Baker et al., *College Undergraduate Slang Study Conducted at Brown University*, p. 76, 1968

Baghdad Betty *nickname*
during the US war against Iraq in 1991, a female Iraqi disk jockey who broadcast propaganda to US troops *US, 1991*
- — *Army*, p. 47, November 1991

Baghdad Boys *noun*
during the Gulf war, reporters from the Cable News Network *US, 1991*
- — *American Speech*, p. 385, Winter 1991: "Among the new words"

bag job *noun*
1 a murder in which the victim is left inside a burlap bag *US, 1951*
- It was decided that a bag job was in order, so that the motive would not be mistaken as any but the one intended. — Burton Turkus and Sid Feder, *Murder, Inc.*, p. 175, 1951
2 a cheating scheme involving a casino employee as a confederate *US, 1950*
- — *The Annals of the American Academy of Political and Social Sciences*, p. 120, May 1950
3 a burglary, especially when committed by law enforcement or intelligence agents looking for information *US, 1971*
- The bag job on his car was a waste of time — Gerald Petievich, *Shakedown*, p. 119, 1988

bag lady *noun*
a destitute woman who wanders the streets with her possessions in shopping bags *US, 1972*
- He's like the bag ladies on the Common, or some other shit like that. — George V. Higgins, *Penance for Jerry Kennedy*, p. 234, 1985
- An old bag lady with an anti-abortion poster has it grabbed and ripped up by man-hating dykes. — Josh Alan Friedman, *Tales of Times Square*, p. 166, 1986
- "We may as well start targeting bag ladies." — Glenn Savan, *White Palace*, p. 207, 1987
- I guess we've been passing a lot of bag ladies and bums, and I'm like, I don't know, they're everywhere[.] — Jay McInerney, *Story of My Life*, p. 112, 1988

bagman *noun*
1 a person who collects, makes or holds illegal payments *US, 1935*

- Tom ("Sailor") Burke had been the sheriff's "bag man," had delivered $36,000 in payoff money to the sheriff's wife and had gotten signed receipts for the boodle. — *Time*, p. 18, 24th July 1950
- The "pad" refers to regular weekly, biweekly, or monthly payments, usually picked up by a police bagman and divided among fellow officers. — *The Knapp Commission Report on Police Corruption*, p. 66, 1972
- Turns out the cop was the biggest bagman ever. — Vincent Patrick, *The Pope of Greenwich Village*, p. 247, 1979
- It's tougher to buy the cheapest bagman than it is to buy a cop. — *The Usual Suspects*, 1995

2 in the circus or carnival, a person who makes change for customers, often cheating them *US, 1980*
- — Joe McKennon, *Circus Lingo*, p. 13, 1980
3 a drug dealer; a person in possession of drugs *US, 1970*
- — Richard E. Haorman and Allan M. Fox, *Drug Awareness*, p. 463, 1970
- — William D. Alsever, *Glossary for the Establishment and Other Uptight People*, p. 26, December 1970

bag money *noun*
money for buying drugs *US, 1968*
- Girls, trying to put together bag money, approached cars that had stopped for red lights. — Phil Hirsch, *Hooked*, p. 154, 1968

bag of snakes *noun*
a business acquisition full of bad surprises *US, 1991*
- — David Olive, *Business Babble*, p. 12, 1991

bag on; bag *verb*
to insult someone in a competitive, quasi-friendly spirit *US, 1993*
- Hanging out, shooting craps, playing dominos, bagging on each other, and just plain kickin' it. — *Menace II Society*, 1993
- There are many different terms for playing the dozens, including "bagging, capping, cracking, dissing, hiking, joning, ranking, ribbing, serving, signifying, slipping, sounding and snapping." — James Haskins, *The Story of Hip-Hop*, p. 54, 2000

bag up *verb*
1 to divide a powdered drug into bags preparatory to selling it *US, 1989*
- — Geoffrey Froner, *Digging for Diamonds*, p. 7, 1989
2 to laugh *US, 1989*
- — Ellen C. Bellone (Editor), *Dictionary of Slang*, p. 2, 1989

bail *verb*
1 to leave a relationship or situation *US, 1977*
- "Maybe I just bail myself on home an watch TV or something." — Jess Mowry, *Way Past Cool*, p. 10, 1992
- I don't know how I can bail now, he's going to be here any minute. — *Something About Mary*, 1998
- [T]he funniest shit happens when I'm about to bail. — Eminem (Marshall Mathers) , *Angry Blonde*, p. 67, 2001
2 to fall while skateboarding *US, 1984*
- — *San Francisco Sunday Examiner & Chronicle*, p. 20, 2nd September 1984
3 in mountain biking, to jump off a bicycle in order to avoid an accident *US, 1996*
- A few who were born rad go too fast for their skill level—when they need to bail they won't be able to. — *Mountain Bike Magazine's Complete Guide To Mountain Biking Skills*, p. 79, 1996

bail out *verb*
to jump off a surfboard when you are about to be knocked off the board by a wave *US, 1964*
- — John Severson, *Modern Surfing Around the World*, p. 162, 1964

bait *noun*
1 in poker, a small bet that is hoped will lure another player into a larger bet *US, 1967*
- — Albert H. Morehead, *The Complete Guide to Winning Poker*, p. 256, 1967
2 in shuffleboard, a shot made to entice the opponent to try to go after the disk *US, 1967*
- — Omero C. Catan, *Secrets of Shuffleboard Strategy*, p. 64, 1967
3 a small meal *US, 1958*
- — *American Speech*, p. 268, December 1958: "Ranching terms from eastern Washington"

bait *verb*
in gin, to discard a card in a manner that is designed to lure a desired card from an opponent *US, 1971*
- — Irwin Steig, *Play Gin to Win*, p. 138, 1971

bait money *noun*
cash with prerecorded serial numbers set aside by a bank
to be included in money given to a robber *US, 1992*
- — Jay Robert Nash, *Dictionary of Crime*, p. 16, 1992
- Nothing with bank straps or rubber bands, I don't want any dyke
  packs, I don't want any bait money. — Elmore Leonard, *Out of Sight*,
  p. 87, 1996

Baja bug *noun*
a Volkswagen Beetle modified for surfer use *US, 1991*
"Baja" is a reference to Baja California, the Mexican state immediately south of California.
- — Trevor Cralle, *The Surfin'ary*, p. 6, 1991

bake *noun*
a complete and hopeless outcast *US, 1991*
An abbreviation of Bakersfield, a city at the south end of
California's San Joaquin Valley, "the other side of nowhere"
to the surfers who use this term.
- — Trevor Cralle, *The Surfin'ary*, p. 6, 1991

bake *verb*
▶ **bake biscuits**
to record and produce a phonograph record *US, 1959*
- — *Look*, p. 49, 24th November 1959

baked *adjective*
drug-intoxicated, especially by marijuana *US, 1978*
- I'm still baked. — *Clueless*, 1995
- Now Vita was lighting a joint, needing to get baked before she could
  turn herself into an International Chick. — Elmore Leonard, *Be Cool*, p. 48,
  1999

baker *noun*
1 a marijuana smoker *US, 1997*
- — Jim Emerson-Cobb, *Scratching the Dragon*, 1997
2 a grade of "B" in academic work *US, 1968*
- — Collin Baker et al., *College Undergraduate Slang Study Conducted at Brown University*, p. 76, 1968

balance *verb*
▶ **balance the books**
in an illegal betting operation, to place bets with other operations when betting is too heavy on one proposition *US,
1979*
- You have to balance the books so you don't get caught too heavy
  on one side. — Thomas L. Clark, *The Dictionary of Gambling and Gaming*, p. 11,
  1987

balcony *noun*
the female breasts *US, 1963*
- "This one's a carbon copy ... especially in the balcony, doctor."
  — Wade Hunter, *The Sex Peddler*, p. 9, 1963
- Polly's balcony might not be something to inflame the pimple-faced
  readers of Playboy, but it had exactly what a grown man wanted[.]
  — Max Shulman, *Anyone Got a Match?*, p. 248, 1964
- — Collin Baker et al., *College Undergraduate Slang Study Conducted at Brown
  University*, p. 76, 1968

baldheaded row *noun*
the front row of a burlesque or strip show *US, 1887*
- Forth Worth had a number of burlesque houses at that time, and
  we were able to obtain choice seats on the front or "baldhead" row.
  — Jim Thompson, *Bad Boy*, p. 329, 1953

Baldwin *noun*
a handsome man *US, 1995*
From the family of handsome actor brothers.
- OK, OK, so he's kind of a Baldwin, but what would he want with Tai.
  — *Clueless*, 1995
- — Judi Sanders, *Da Bomb!*, p. 2, 1997

bale *noun*
any quantity of marijuana *US, 2001*
- He exploded away from the wall and made a grab for the Baggie.
  "Hey, what you be doing with my bale, man?" — Stephen J. Cannell,
  The Tin Collectors, p. 35, 2001

bale *verb*
▶ **bale the kale**
to win a lot of money gambling *US, 1962*

From **KALE** (money).
- — Frank Garcia, *Marked Cards and Loaded Dice*, p. 250, 1962

bale of straw *noun*
a blonde white woman *US, 1928*
- — Clarence Major, *Dictionary of Afro-American Slang*, p. 23, 1970
- — Don Wilmeth, *The Language of American Popular Entertainment*, p. 14, 1981

balk *verb*
in poker, to hesitate when it is your turn to bet in the hope
of seeing whether players who follow you are prepared to
call the bet *US, 1996*
- — John Vorhaus, *The Big Book of Poker Slang*, p. 5, 1996

ball *noun*
1 a thoroughly good time *US, 1932*
- I had no time now for thoughts like that and promised myself a ball
  in Denver. — Jack Kerouac, *On the Road*, pp. 17–18, 1957
- [T]he other who had eyes for Phil and had been wooing him by
  stealing morphine styrettes from the life boats, presenting them to
  him and beseeching him to have a ball[.] — Herbert Huncke, *The Evening
  Sun Turned Crimson*, p. 101, 1980
2 an act of sexual intercourse *US, 1956*
- Well after the ball was over, he wants to stay all night and stay a
  little longer. — William Burroughs, *Letters to Allen Ginsberg 1953–1957*, p. 147,
  13th September 1956
- Ball: The accepted word for the sex act. — *Screw*, p. 7, 12th October 1970
- Yeah, she's a good ball, get with it already yet. — Babs Gonzales, *Movin'
  On Down De Line*, p. 37, 1975
3 one dollar *US, 1895*
Mainly prison slang.
- — Gary K. Farlow, *Prison-ese*, p. 2, 2002

▶ **that's the way the ball bounces**
that's how things turn out *US, 1952*
- The soldiers coined "That's the way the ball bounces," meaning
  what was forordained to be. — *East Liverpool (Ohio) Review*, 28th December
  1952
- "This week's "Spectator" will raise much hell, I'm sure—but that's
  just the way the ball bounces." — Hunter S. Thompson, *Letter to Jack
  Thompson*, 24th October 1956
- "General Hanrahan doesn't like to be kept waiting." "Few people
  do," Oliver said. "But sometimes that's the way the ball bounces."
  — W.E.B. Griffin, *The Aviators*, p. 379, 1988
- With 10 weeks until the election, it's an instructive reminder that in
  news and punditry, as in sports, that's now often just the way the
  ball bounces. — *Variety*, p. 4, 25th August 2004

ball *verb*
1 to sell drugs *US, 1995*
- For the brothers who are ballin' out of control and brothers on the
  street who generate sixty, seventy, eighty, ninety thousand dollars in
  just a short period of time, it only takes about $15,000 to open a
  little mini-market. — Yusuf Jah, *Uprising*, p. 332, 1995
2 to sell drugs *US, 1991*
- "The homie was ballin', and he was rich." — Leon Bing, *Do or Die*, p. 230,
  1991
3 to have sex *US, 1952*
- "We'll have time, baby, we'll have all the balling we can hold."
  — George Mandel, *Flee the Angry Strangers*, p. 304, 1952
- In that time, Dean is balling Marylou at the hotel and gives me time
  to change and dress. — Jack Kerouac, *On the Road*, p. 43, 1957
- Work little, eat well, ball like crazy, and use all their energy to perfect
  their own beings, and to help the perfection of others. — *The Digger
  Papers*, p. 8, August 1968
- He was there on the acid trip scene, but he wasn't there when we
  actually balled. — Jefferson Poland and Valerie Alison, *The Records of the San
  Francisco Sexual Freedom League*, p. 30, 1971
4 to fondle a man's penis *US, 1968*
- — Burton H. Wolfe, *The Hippies*, p. 203, 1968
5 to thoroughly enjoy yourself *US, 1942*
- He's the kind of a cat that balled every big swingin' main day breeze,
  all the time every day. — William "Lord" Buckley, *Nero*, 1951
6 to go or take something somewhere very quickly *US, 1939*
- But come on, let's ball up there and take a look in that little box of
  yourn! — John Clellon Holmes, *Go*, p. 105, 1952
- And he balled that thing clear to Iowa City and yelled me the funniest
  stories[.] — Jack Kerouac, *On the Road*, p. 16, 1957

7 to insert amphetamine or methamphetamine in the vagina before sexual intercourse *US, 1971*

- — Eugene Landy, *The Underground Dictionary*, p. 28, 1971
- — Jay Robert Nash, *Dictionary of Crime*, p. 17, 1992

ballad *noun*
a love letter *US, 1960*

- — *San Francisco Examiner*, p. III-2, 22nd March 1960

ball and chain *noun*
a man's wife *US, 1921*
A rare bit of rhyming slang used in the US, rhyming with "pain."

- — Lou Shelly, *Hepcats Jive Talk Dictionary*, p. 21, 1945
- What Ball and Chain could take that treatment for long? — *Whisper Magazine*, p. 37, May 1950: Anything for a Divorce
- — *Complete CB Slang Dictionary*, 1976
- — *Dictionary of Cautionary Words and Phrases*, 1989: "Multicultural Management Program Fellows"

ballbag *noun*
an athletic supporter *US, 1968*

- Whenever he saw a black person in a ballbag, he swooned. — Miriam Cooke, *Blood Into Ink*, p. 137, 1994

ballbreaker *noun*
1 a difficult task, a boring situation; any circumstance that saps your spirit *US, 1942*
The prosaic etymology leads to any task that strains the testicles; more likely that "balls" represent power or spirit in this context.

- So it was the usual day—ballbreaker? — Richard Price, *Clockers*, p. 284, 1992

2 a powerful, assertive woman; someone who demands or actively exacts a difficult requirement *US, 1944*

- See, at that time the Anglican Church were really ballbreakers. That was one of the words they used then, ballbreakers. Ballbreakers means backbreakers. — Lenny Bruce, *The Essential Lenny Bruce*, p. 210, 1967
- At least she's not a ballbreaker. Christ, if she were a ballbreaker there'd be no way. — *Diner*, 1982
- He prided himself on being as tough, as cruel, as unforgiving as any pimp, macgimper, child stealer, cutthroat, or ball breaker on the street. — Robert Campbell, *Sweet La-La Land*, p. 183, 1990

ball-busting *adjective*
harassing, dominating, controlling *US, 1954*

- — Joseph Weingarten, *American Dictionary of Slang*, p. 54, 1954
- Fuckin' nigger gets Doris Day as a parole office. But a good fella like you gets stuck with a ball-bustin' prick. — *Reservoir Dogs*, 1992
- You're just jealous, because unlike a certain ball-busting, dried-up career woman I might mention, we're all happily married. — *Romy and Michele's High School Reunion*, 1997

ball-cutter *noun*
a person who belittles and demeans others *US, 1962*

- [W]hat she is a ball-cutter. I've seen a thousand of 'em, old and young, men and women. Seen 'em all over the country and in the homes—people who try to make you weak so they can get you to toe the line, to follow their rules, to live like they want you to. — Ken Kesey, *One Flew Over the Cuckoo's Nest*, p. 58, 1962

baller *noun*
1 a drug dealer, usually of crack cocaine *US, 1991*

- "Them people can't nail down no decent jobs, and you tell me about any baller who's gonna tell 'em 'no' when they come lookin' for work." — Leon Bing, *Do or Die*, p. 223, 1991
- She tells me that when she was actively gangbanging, her father's brother, Uncle Darryl (whom she describes as a "baller," a successful drug dealer), supplied her with drugs to sell for him. — *Rolling Stone*, p. 86, 12th April 2001

2 a member of a youth gang who is prospering financially *US, 1995*

- — Bill Valentine, *Gang Intelligence Manual*, p. 74, 1995

ballhuggers *noun*
very tight pants *US, 1982*
Hawaiian youth usage.

- Whaty, Aaron, you t'ink you macho when you wear dose ball huggahs? — Douglas Simonson, *Pidgin to da Max Hana Hou*, 1982

balling *noun*
sex *US, 1960*

- I tell you there's just too much balling going on in the city itself altho I love it of course. — Jack Kerouac, *Jack Kerouac Selected Letters 1957–1969*, p. 307, September 1960: Letter to Neal Cassady

ballistic *adjective*
extremely angry; out of control *US, 1985*
Originally applied to an out-of-control missile.

- Officer Nelson Hareem went ballistic and put the hot flogger in a neck brace for three weeks. — Seth Morgan, *Fugitive Nights*, p. 32, 1990
- "Your dad was pissed, huh?" "Totally ballistic." — C.D. Payne, *Youth in Revolt*, p. 302, 1993
- I totally choked. My father is going to go ballistic on me. — *Clueless*, 1995
- Mommy goes ballistic and ends their relationship. — *Cruel Intentions*, 1999

ball of fire *noun*
a dynamic and energetic person *US, 1900*

- He is a ball of fire with the women—the sultry, slow-urning kind, of course. — Max Shulman, *Guided Tour of Campus Humor*, p. 2, 1955
- To listen to you guys tell it, my old man is one ball of fire. — Donald Goines, *El Dorado Red*, p. 32, 1974

ball of wax *noun*
a complete set of facts or situation *US, 1953*

- After 13 years of dinner plates that sports Jackie's face in colors, after writing as many as 100 letters a night in search of a rare Kennedy piece, after "lots and lots" of dollars, Steinberg is trying to sell the whole ball of wax. — *Washington Post, Potomoc Journal*, p. 1, 29th September 1979

balloon *noun*
1 a lieutenant *US, 1951*
Coined in Korea.

- Gasping, I told him that "Combat" was now a first lieutenant, and though I made it a rule not to speak to second balloons, since he'd been instrumental in my development I would make an exception. — David H. Hackworth, *About Face*, p. 211, 1989

2 used as a humorous synonym of "platoon" *US, 1967*

- — Carl Fleischhauer, *A Glossary of Army Slang*, p. 3, 1968

3 a small amount of heroin, whether or not it is actually in a balloon *US, 1967*

- — Richard Horman and Alan Fox, *Drug Awareness*, p. 463, 1970

balloon head *noun*
an empty-headed, dim-witted dolt *US, 1931*
Sometimes contracted to "balloon."

- What a fuckin' balloon head. — *Casino*, 1995

balloon juice *noun*
empty talk *US, 1900*
A play on the "hot air" typically found inside balloons.

- Tonight would have been balloon juice without a big backlog of thinking. — Bernard Wolfe, *The Late Risers*, p. 183, 1954
- — Joseph E. Ragen and Charles Finston, *Inside the World's Toughest Prison*, p. 790, 1962

ballpark *noun*
an approximate range *US, 1957*

- Yes, someone older. Yeah, I mean, you know, you know, old, not as old as I am, but in the same general ball park as me. — *Manhattan*, 1979
- Can you give me a ballpark on the time? — Robert Crais, *L.A. Requiem*, p. 42, 1999

ball player *noun*
in prison, anyone who is open to being bribed or corrupted *US, 1966*

- — Rose Giallombardo, *Society of Women*, p. 204, 1966: Glossary of Prison Terms

ballroom *noun*
a singles bar with a reputation for easy sexual conquests *US, 1985*

- — *American Speech*, p. 18, Spring 1985: "The language of singles bars"

balls *noun*
1 the testicles *UK, 1325*

- "I said I lost my balls! Can't you hear me? I'm wounded in the groin!" — Joseph Heller, *Catch-22*, p. 289, 1961
- I worked my way up to his balls, which I sucked one at a time. — Xaviera Hollander, *The Happy Hooker*, p. 181, 1972

- She held it up and kissed under it, running her tongue over my testicles and sucking my balls. — Harold Robbins, *Sin City*, p. 64, 2002

2 courage, daring *UK, 1893*

- He's a smart pitcher too, knows what he's doing out there, and as Jim Owens says, "He has the balls of a burglar." — Jim Bouton, *Ball Four*, p. 324, 1970
- You didn't hit it, but it was a big balls bet. — *Hard Eight*, 1996
- If you think something's going on, have the balls to ask someone instead of just sneaking around. — Robert Crais, *L.A. Requiem*, p. 124, 1999
- [Y]ou need one other vital ingredient for your criminal idea—balls, big balls. And that makes all the difference. — Danny King, *The Burglar Diaries*, p. 33, 2001

▶ **bust your balls; break your balls**
to harrass, to nag someone *US, 1944*

- C'mon, man, don't break my balls, I'm just trying to get along. — Darryl Ponicsan, *The Last Detail*, p. 3, 1970
- "You fucking snuck up here and did this just to break my fucking balls!" — Joseph Pistone, *Donnie Brasco*, pp. 361–362, 1987

▶ **to have someone by the balls**
to exert complete control over someone; to have complete power over someone *US, 1918*

- [E]ven though he's got me by the balls out here, Dan knows that in a courtroom, he loses this case. — *A Few Good Men*, 1992

▶ **to have someone's balls in a vice**
at an extreme disadvantage, overpowered *US, 1987*

- I'm up front with ya, Tilley. I've got my balls in a vice. — *Tin Men*, 1987

balls-ass naked *adjective*
completely naked *US, 1958*

- The two of us were balls-ass naked when they carried us to Bellevue. — Herbert Huncke, *Guilty of Everything*, p. 197, 1990

balls-to-the-walls *adjective*
unrestrained, full-out *US, 1967*
From military aviation; thrusting the throttle with its ball-shaped grip towards the firewall at the front of the cockpit achieves maximum power.

- J.L. says that motorcycle of his only has two speeds: dead still and balls to the walls. — Ken Weaver, *Texas Crude*, p. 102, 1984

ballsy *adjective*
gutsy, courageous *US, 1935*

- The minesweep guys are a real ballsy bunch. — Darryl Ponicsan, *The Last Detail*, p. 123, 1970
- That Scal, he's a ballsy guy, you know. — George V. Higgins, *The Friends of Eddie Doyle*, p. 203, 1971
- I've got to tell you, my friend: this is one of the ballsiest moves I've ever been privy to. I never would have thought you capable of such blatant disregard of store policy. — *Clerks*, 1994

ball team; baseball team *noun*
a group of gambling cheats who work in casinos *US, 1987*

- — Thomas L. Clark, *The Dictionary of Gambling and Gaming*, p. 12, 1987

ball up *verb*
to botch, to ruin *US, 1915*

- You say that the present generation has balled things up to the extent that we now face a war so terrible that the very thought of it makes hardened veterans shudder. — Hunter S. Thompson, *The Proud Highway*, p. 3, 1955: Open Letter to the Youth of our Nation

bally; bally act; ballyhoo *noun*
any method used to draw a crowd; a small, free performance given outside a place of entertainment in the hope of drawing customers inside *US, 1901*
Circus and carnival usage.

- I refused to go out in the rain and do the bally. — Ethel Waters, *His Eye is on the Sparrow*, p. 84, 1951
- Bally is used by sideshows, girlie shows, and the like to give the tip an idea of the show to be seen inside (the bally is located immediately outside the structure or tent). — Don Wilmeth, *The Language of American Popular Entertainment*, p. 15, 1981
- — Gene Sorrows, *All About Carnivals*, p. 8, 1985

ballyhoo *verb*
to draw a crowd *US, 1965*

- Said, "I've ballyhooed in a smalltown circus / throughout the middle west." — Bruce Jackson, *Get Your Ass in the Water and Swim Like Me*, p. 75, 1965

baloney *noun*
1 utter nonsense *US, 1922*

- I met Bob's brother Hank, who says he fell in love with me, which is a bunch of baloney 'cause he fell in love with anything in skirts that would pay any attention to him. — James Mills, *The Panic in Needle Park*, p. 93, 1966
- It might be a load of baloney, but I have always really liked that image. — *Varsity*, p. 6, 14th June 2002

2 the penis *US, 1928*

- Man, wouldn't I love to play hide the baloney with that. — Charles Whited, *Chiodo*, p. 224, 1973

3 a die that has been flattened on several edges to favor one surface *US, 1974*

- You watch these dice for so many years and years and years, square dice, that when you throw a pair of baloneys in, it looks like a flat tire. — Edward Lin, *Big Julie of Vegas*, p. 217, 1974

baloney pony *noun*
the penis *US, 2005*

- Bouncing butt and boobs during her Ride-'em-Cowboy impression on a lucky feller's baloney pony. — Mr. Skin, *Mr. Skin's Skincyclopedia*, p. 110, 2005

balsa boy *noun*
a male pornography performer who has trouble maintaining an erection *US, 1995*
One of many **wood** images.

- — *Adult Video News*, p. 42, August 1995

Balto *nickname*
Baltimore, Maryland *US, 1981*

- — Don Wilmeth, *The Language of American Popular Entertainment*, p. 16, 1981

bam *noun*
1 a pill or capsule of amphetamines *US, 1970*
An abbreviation of "bambita."

- — Clarence Major, *Dictionary of Afro-American Slang*, p. 23, 1970
- [A]rrested 71 persons trying to buy Preludin—known as "bam" in street slang—and Dilaudid. Both are diet pills used as heroin boosters or heroin substitutes. — *Washington Post*, p. A1, 22nd July 1981
- I am steeped in thoughts about "angel dust" and "wacky weed" and "bam" and "speed," not to mention plain old marijuana, cocaine, and heroin because I have spent weeks doing a television special on drug abuse. — *San Francisco Examiner*, p. C10, 28th March 1981

2 a female member of the US Marine Corps *US, 1948*
A "broad-assed marine."

- That was something that a general could turn to his aide and say: "Who's that BAM?" Up until, like yesterday. — Jean Zimmerman, *Tailspin*, p. 211, 1995

▷ **see:** BAMPOT; BAMSTICK

bama *noun*
a conventional person, profoundly out of touch with current trends *US, 1970*

- — *Current Slang*, p. 1, Fall 1970

bamalam *noun*
marijuana *US, 1973*

- [D]iggin' sounds after hours and smokin' your bamalam and walking down the street stark noble savage naked to the world! — Lester Bangs, *Psychotic Reactions and Carburetor Dung*, p. 117, 1973

bambalacha; bamba; bammy *noun*
marijuana *US, 1938*

- Marijuana is also known as loco weed, love weed, giggle weed, bambalacha and Indian hay. — *San Francisco Examiner*, p. 15, 19th October 1948
- Grass ... Mary Jane, Aunt Hazel, African bush, bambalacha. You pick the cool name. — Stephen J. Cannell, *The Tin Collectors*, p. 60, 2001

bambi-sexual *noun*
a homosexual whose sexual activity is characterized by kisses, caresses, and emotion *US, 1985*
Punning on the gentle deer Bambi, hero of the novel by Felix Salten and the movie by Disney.

- — Wayne Dynes, *Homolexis*, p. 147, 1985

bamboo manicure *noun*
torture using bamboo splinters forced under the fingernails
US, *1982*
Korean and then Vietnam war usage.
- — Frank Hailey, *Soldier Talk*, p. 3, 1982

bamboo telegraph *noun*
the spreading of gossip or rumours in a jungle *US*, *1929*
Vietnam war usage.
- In my country, good deeds are publicized all over by the bamboo telegraph. — William Lederer, *The Ugly American*, p. 73, 1958

bamf!
1 in computing, a notional sound during a magical transformation in a multi-user dungeon *US*, *1991*
Also an acronym produced from "*bad-ass motherfucker.*"
- — Eric S. Raymond, *The New Hacker's Dictionary*, p. 47, 1991.
2 used as Internet shorthand to mean "I am leaving this discussion" *US*, *1997*
A sound effect from the *X-Men* comic books.
- — Andy Ihnatko, *Cyberspeak*, p. 21, 1997

bammer *noun*
weak, low grade marijuana *US*, *1997*
- — Pamela Munro, *U.C.L.A. Slang*, p. 30, 1997

banana *noun*
1 in street luge, a racer who frequently crashes *US*, *1998*
- BANANA A luger who wipes out often. — Shelley Youngblut, *Way Inside ESPN's X Games*, p. 130, 1998
2 an Asian-American who rejects his Asian heritage and seeks to blend into the dominant white culture *US*, *1970*
Like a banana, the person described is yellow on the outside, white on the inside.
- — Douglas Simonson, *Pidgin to da Max*, 1981
- — Multicultural Management Program Fellows, *Dictionary of Cautionary Words and Phrases*, 1989
3 a person of mixed race, with both black and white ancestors *US*, *1945*
- — Lou Shelly, *Hepcats Jive Talk Dictionary*, p. 7, 1945
4 a hospital patient suffering from jaundice *US*, *1983*
- — *Maledicta*, p. 38, 1983: "More common patient-directed pejoratives used by medical personnel"
- — Sally Williams, *"Strong" Words*, p. 133, 1994
5 in US casinos, a $20 chip *US*, *1985*
From the yellow color.
- — Steve Kuriscak, *Casino Talk*, p. 2, 1985
6 the penis *US*, *1916*
- — Anon., *King Smut's Wet Dreams Interpreted*, 1978
7 a parenthesis sign (or) on a computer keyboard *US*, *1991*
- — Eric S. Raymond, *The New Hacker's Dictionary*, p. 39, 1991
8 the convex curvature of the bottom of a surfboard *US*, *1965*
- — D.S. Halacy, *Surfer!*, p. 216, 1965
9 a comic in a burlesque show *US*, *1953*
- Why do you think she went out and bought this army cot? Leave it to me: I'm always top banana in the shock department. — Truman Capote, *Breakfast at Tiffany's*, p. 61, 1958
- For years one of the most formidable second bananas in the comedy spectrum, Louis Nye comes into his own and attains premium solo status in his current nitery act. — *Variety*, p. 10, 23rd May 1962
- Lenny had his mother, Sally Marr—a top banana when they all worked in burlesque—fitted out with a recorder[.] — Albert Goldman, *Freak Show*, pp. 211–212, 1968
10 a crazy or foolish person *US*, *1919*
- The kid was a banana! Bonzo. Loonier than his old man. — Joseph Wambaugh, *Lines and Shadows*, p. 108, 1984
11 a dollar *US*, *1970*
- I can't help thinking about Billy the Bad-Ass, what a goodnigger, and that kid Meadows and his eight years for a lousy forty fucking bananas. — Darryl Ponicsan, *The Last Detail*, p. 182, 1970

banana *verb*
in television and movie making, to walk in a slight curve in front of the camera to preserve focus *US*, *1990*
- — Ralph S. Singleton, *Filmmaker's Dictionary*, p. 15, 1990

banana belt *nickname*
southeastern Alaska *US*, *1937*
- — Russell Tabbert, *Dictionary of Alaskan English*, p. 47, 1991

banana clip *noun*
the curved magazine or clip for a US Army carbine *US*, *1968*
- — Carl Fleischhauer, *A Glossary of Army Slang*, p. 3, 1968
- [C]licking banana clips into automatic weapons that I'd never even seen before. — Michael Herr, *Dispatches*, p. 11, 1977

banana hammock *noun*
a brief male bikini *US*, *1997*
- A member of the band roused himself from his lounge chair, gut jiggling out over his banana hammock, and strutted lazily to the edge of the water. — Rick Marin, *Cad*, p. 152, 2004

banana horse *noun*
a racehorse that is part of a cheating scheme in a fixed race *US*, *1973*
- "We'd list the banana horse on the sheet that went out to all our bookmakers and he'd then refuse to take any action on that horse from anyone in the city." — Vincent Teresa, *My Life in the Mafia*, p. 156, 1973

banana oil *noun*
nonsense; persuasive talk *US*, *1924*
- — Jerry Robertson, *Oil Slanguage*, p. 24, 1954
- — Helen Dahlskog (Editor), *A Dictionary of Contemporary and Colloquial Usage*, p. 5, 1972

banana race *noun*
a fixed horse race *US*, *1967*
- New England tracks are famous throughout the United States for their so-called "banana-races," in which the winner is known in advance to a select few. — *Saturday Evening Post*, p. 29, 18th November 1967
- "New England had—it still does—more banana races each year than any section of the world." — Vincent Teresa, *My Life in the Mafia*, p. 152, 1973

bananas *adjective*
madly excited; mad; behaving oddly *US*, *1957*
Derives from **BANANA OIL** (nonsense), which abbreviates as "bananas"; "to become mad" is "to go bananas."
- We heard the police broadcast! They say you're bananas! — L'il Abner in *San Francisco News*, p. 11, 20 March 1957
- If this dude in a pinstripe suit thinks he's going to keep her off The All-Weather Panther Committee, he's bananas. — Tom Wolfe, *Radical Chic & Mau-Mauing the Flak Catchers*, p. 63, 1970
- Was Richard Nixon mentally unstable at any time of his Presidency? Did he flip his lid, go bananas? — *San Francisco Chronicle*, p. 7, 14 May 1975
- He went totally bananas, cussin' me out instead of thankin' me for savin' his raggedy ass. — Edwin Torres, *After Hours*, p. 264, 1979

banana shot *noun*
in pool, a shot at an object ball near a cushion, with spin imparted such that the cue ball follows through after striking the object ball and comes to rest after bouncing off the cushion *US*, *1993*
- — Mike Shamos, *The Illustrated Encyclopedia of Billiards*, p. 20, 1993

bananas on bananas *noun*
too much of something, even a good something *US*, *1977*
- — Tony Miller and Patricia George, *Cut! Print! The Language and Structure of Filmmaking*, p. 39, 1977

banana split *noun*
amyl nitrite; an ampule of amyl nitrite *US*, *1968*
A reference to the banana-like smell of the drug vapors.
- And have "amies" on hand too: poppers, banana splits, whatever you call them. — Angelo d'Arcangelo, *The Homosexual Handbook*, p. 115, 1968

banana with cheese *noun*
marijuana and freebase cocaine combined for smoking *US*, *1979*
- A marijuana-and-base combo is referred to as "banana with cheese" banana is the rolling paper, usually wheat straw or yellow paper, and cheese is the base, white and crumbly like feta. — *Hi Life*, p. 78, 1979

band *noun*
in prison, a riot squad *US*, *1976*
- — John R. Armore and Joseph D. Wolfe, *Dictionary of Desperation*, p. 19, 1976

band box *noun*

a county jail *US, 1992*

- — William K. Bentley and James M. Corbett, *Prison Slang*, p. 3, 1992

band chick *noun*

a woman who is attracted to, and makes herself available to, musicians *US, 1961*

An early term for what would come to be known as a "groupie."

- Although Miriam had known enough musicians and enough Negroes to judge each one on his own, there were "band chicks" at the Savoy, as at nearly every club where jazz is played. — Nat Hentoff, *The Jazz Life*, p. 20, 1961

B and D; B/D *noun*

*b*ondage and *d*omination (or *d*iscipline) as sexual activities *US, 1973*

- The term b & d as an abbreviation for bondage and discipline is gaining currency, certainly in the underground press, for s-m. — Gerald and Caroline Green, *S-M*, p. 205, 1973
- Real-life S/M activity, unlike the cliches of S/M fiction, rarely is bizarre or extreme; most of it involves biting, hitting, slapping and the like, rather than heavy B and D (bondage and discipline). — *Playboy*, p. 183, March 1974
- Look out for terms like dominant, submissive, B/D, and S and M. — Lawrence Paros, *The Erotic Tongue*, p. 148, 1984
- The sadomasochism books, or S&M, featured whips, unlike the bondage-and-discipline (B&D) magazines[.] — Jack Weatherford, *Porn Row*, p. 8, 1986

B and E *noun*

burglary *US, 1965*

From the initials for "*b*reaking *a*nd *e*ntering."

- He said, "Mom, there's no way anybody could bust in here, even jigs I met who spent their lives doing B and Ees, pros." — Elmore Leonard, *Glitz*, p. 98, 1985
- The one where you do all your B-and-E's? — Carl Hiaasen, *Tourist Season*, p. 15, 1986

B and E; B & E *verb*

to commit a burglary *US, 2004*

- A one-armed bum B&Es the doc's pad and snuffs her. — James Ellroy, *Destination Morgue*, p. 35, 2004

Band House *nickname*

the Chicago House of Corrections *US, 1946*

- Off I went to Chicago's city prison at 26th and California, the Bridewell, known as "The Band House" in the underworld. — Mezz Mezzrow, *Really the Blues*, p. 33, 1946

bandit *noun*

1 an enemy combatant *US, 1967*

- "Four bandits on the path moving east." — Donald Duncan, *The New Legions*, p. 54, 1967

2 a hostile aircraft *US, 1942*

- Two friendly aircraft closing on the bandit to intercept, Sir! — Milton Caniff, *Steve Canyon in San Francisco Examiner*, p. 40, 15th December 1954
- I had a SAM come so close I could almost read the tail markings. You get bandit calls all the time. — *San Francisco Chronicle*, p. 10, 30th December 1971
- Bandits! Bandits! Over Thud Ridge. — Joseph Tuso, *Singing the Vietnam Blues*, p. 36, 1990: The Ballad of Robin Olds

bandit odds *noun*

betting odds that strongly, if secretly, favor one betting position *US, 1977*

- He was fleecing rich sportsmen out of a fortune by betting ringer Upshaw could beat their favorite boxers, usually at bandit odds. — Iceberg Slim (Robert Beck), *Long White Con*, p. 189, 1977

B and Q *noun*

diluted or adulterated crack cocaine *US, 1997*

- Baking soda or bonita and quinine—B-and-Q—as dope. oregano as weed, battery acid as ready rocks. — David Simon and Edward Burns, *The Corner*, p. 69, 1997

bandwidth *noun*

attention span *US, 1991*

A borrowing of a technical term with a technical meaning (the volume of information that can be handled within a time unit) for a humorous, broader usage.

- — Eric S. Raymond, *The New Hacker's Dictionary*, p. 47, 1991

bang *noun*

1 pleasure, enjoyment *US, 1929*

- Many of the younger social and diplomatic sets get a bang out of hot licks. — Jack Lait and Lee Mortimer, *Washington Confidential*, p. 17, 1951
- Boy, did I get a bang out of watching him. — Frederick Kohner, *Gidget*, p. 29, 1957
- The surfers also get a hell of a bang out of slot racing for some reason[.] — Tom Wolfe, *The Kandy-Kolored Tangerine-Flake Streamline Baby*, p. 81, 1965
- Also, I could tell these dudes got a real bang out of playing and winning at cards[.] — Bobby Seale, *A Lonely Rage*, p. 267, 1978

2 an injection of a narcotic *US, 1922*

- I found him in such a state of collapse that I had to give him a bang before he could pull himself together and locate the junk in the place where he'd hidden it. — Ethel Water, *His Eye is on the Sparrow*, p. 148, 1952
- The physician would take care of her with a "bang" in the arm, employing a strong narcotic drug. — Harry J. Anslinger, *The Murderers*, p. 185, 1961

3 the sudden effect of a drug *US, 1948*

- [T]he top grade, the gungeon, which produces a voluptuous "bang," bringing as high as a dollar. — Jack Lait and Lee Mortimer, *New York Confidential*, pp. 102–103, 1948

4 marijuana *US, 1993*

- — Kenn "Naz" Young, *Naz's Dictionary of Teen Slang*, p. 6, 1993
- "We could light up, toke some bang?" the teenager said hopefully. — Stephen J. Cannell, *The Tin Collectors*, p. 136, 2001

5 an exclamation point (!) *US, 1931*

From the slang of printers to the slang of computer enthusiasts.

- — Guy L. Steele et al., *The Hacker's Dictionary*, p. 28, 1983

bang *verb*

1 to have sex *UK, 1720*

- Because I haven't banged anybody, not anybody, since we picked up Dinah, except her, of course, and this Margo is real cute. — John Clellon Holmes, *Go*, p. 137, 1952
- At one sharp he rushes from Marylou to Camille—of course neither one of them knows that's going on—and bangs her once, giving me time to arrive at one thirty. — Jack Kerouac, *On the Road*, pp. 42–43, 1957
- I suppose she's a real gunner; bangs away, huh? — John Nichols, *The Sterile Cuckoo*, p. 88, 1965
- Even Dave Dummings, a fiftysomething ex-Army colonel, has marketed himself as the sexy older man who doesn't need Viagra and gets to bang beautiful young chicks half his age. — Ana Loria, *1 2 3 Be A Porn Star!*, p. 110, 2000

2 to stimulate a woman's vagina by introducing and withdrawing a finger in rapid order *US, 1971*

- — Eugene Landy, *The Underground Dictionary*, p. 28, 1971

3 to inhale or to inject a drug intravenously *US, 1926*

- If he'd taken an overdose of cocaine, I'd have to bang him with heroin to counteract it. — Ethel Water, *His Eye is on the Sparrow*, p. 148, 1952
- Angel nodded off immediately, hitting himself and banging it all in at once[.] — Hal Ellson, *The Golden Spike*, p. 95, 1952
- He groaned as he banged himself in the arm while the mixture was still warm. — Chester Himes, *A Rage in Harlem*, p. 38, 1957
- My habit screwed my mind up. All I wanted to do was bang "H" and "coast." — Iceberg Slim (Robert Beck), *Pimp*, p. 99, 1969

4 to engage in youth gang criminal activity *US, 1986*

- In most of Los Angeles, gang members contend that for all the publicity about the killings, the gangs themselves are pretty quiet. "Ain't nobody banging no more," they insist. — *Los Angeles Times*, p. 1, 26th June 1986
- "People who never banged in their life." — Leon Bing, *Do or Die*, p. 221, 1991
- OLDER SHERIFF: Are you a Crip or a Blood? CAINE: I don't bang. — *Menace II Society*, 1993
- I started banging when I was ten years old. — Yusuf Jah, *Uprising*, p. 25, 1995
- Curiously, the 18th Street gangsters, who have definite roots in the l.A. area, nevertheless claim norte while bangin' in EPA. — Bill Valentine, *Gangs and Their Tattoos*, p. 112, 2000

5 to make a turn *US, 1969*

- — *Current Slang*, p. 1, Summer 1969

▶ **bang ears**

to talk idly *US, 1946*

- "[T]he other day he was banging ears with the Old Man again. He tells us he hates him and every chance he gets he sneaks up there and bangs ears." — Thomas Heggen, *Mister Roberts*, p. 65, 1946

▶ **bang heads**
to fight *US, 1968*
- — Hy Lit, *Hy Lit's Unbelievable Dictionary of Hip Words for Groovy People*, p. 3, 1968

bangalore torpedo *noun*
an improvised bomb *UK, 1889*
Originally designed in India by the Royal Engineers.
- Jimmy sat in the kitchen of Tom Dragna's house and watched him make what he called a bangalore torpedo, an army term for a bomb designed to destroy barbed wire barricades. — Ovid Demaris, *The Last Mafioso*, p. 40, 1981

bang and slang *verb*
to take part in youth gang activity and sell drugs *US, 1995*
- What was that like coming from the streets of Watts, bangin' and slangin', and then going to meet Minister Farrakahn? — Yusuf Jah, *Uprising*, p. 180, 1995

bang-bang *noun*
a gun *US, 1992*
- "Well, leastways we score ourselfs a new bang-bang, huh?" — Jess Mowry, *Way Past Cool*, p. 55, 1992
- "But as long as the law says I can own bang-bangs, I will." — Jonathan Kellerman, *Rage*, p. 240, 2005

banged *adjective*
intoxicated on a drug, especially marijuana *US, 1980*
- He had me take a long, strong take, and then squat down and blow on my thumb. After a few of those, he had me floating and really banged. — Stephen Gaskin, *Amazing Dope Tales*, p. 7, 1980
- He said he should've held the meeting in here, get everybody zonked and decadent on a strong stone, get them good and banged—using all the words he knew—then present the movie deal. — Elmore Leonard, *Stick*, p. 241, 1983
- [S]o banged on ups and cocaine she fell out on the floor[.] — Clarence Major, *All-Night Visitors*, p. 201, 1998

banged up *adjective*
drug-intoxicated *US, 1981*
- Half of them was banged up high as kites. — Mark Barker, *Nam*, p. 7, 1981

banger *noun*
1 a knife *US, 2002*
- — Jeffrey Ian Ross, *Behind Bars*, p. 182, 2002: Slammer Slang

2 a boxer who relies on brute strength and aggressive tactics *US, 1968*
- The Big Banger From Parks (Headline) — *San Francisco Chronicle*, p. 42, 21st September 1968
- Robertson is a "banger," a converted southpaw whose left hook has produce 18 KO's. — *San Francisco Chronicle*, p. 46, 28th July 1973

3 a gang member *US, 1985*
Shortened form of **GANGBANGER**.
- Two of the bangers had shaved heads, two others wore knit caps; all wore black high-top sneakers, half unlaced. — Joseph Wambaugh, *Floaters*, p. 26, 1996
- "Dunas isn't a banger. He's a bookie, pure and simple." — John Ridley, *Love is a Racket*, p. 33, 1998
- [T]he Border Brothers, who outnumber both the MRU and the Sur Califas in Nevada's prisons, are aligning with the Sur Califas bangers. — Bill Valentine, *Gangs and Their Tattoos*, p. 32, 2000

4 a heavy metal music enthusiast who dances with zeal *US, 2001*
- — Don R. McCreary (Editor), *Dawg Speak*, 2001

5 a hypodermic needle and syringe *US, 1986*
- — Richard A. Spears, *The Slang and Jargon of Drugs and Drink*, p. 24, 1986

6 in pool, an unskilled if forceful player *US, 1990*
- — Steve Rushin, *Pool Cool*, p. 7, 1990

7 in the casino game Keno, the punch tool used to make holes in tickets showing the numbers bet on *US, 1978*
- — Thomas L. Clark, *The Dictionary of Gambling and Gaming*, p. 12, 1987

banging *adjective*
excellent *UK, 1788*

- Baby sister had a banging body, and she mighta been looking just a little too fly and hooched out for Vonnie's tastes. — Noire, *Candy Licker*, p. 114, 2005
- — Connie Eble (Editor), *UNC-CH Campus Slang*, Fall 2005

bang-needle gun *noun*
a contraption for injecting drugs *US, 1951*
- Later Rocky told me he made his own bang-needle gun out of those things. — Ethel Waters, *His Eye is on the Sparrow*, p. 115, 1951

bang on *verb*
in computing, to subject a piece of equipment or a new program to a stress test *US, 1991*
- I banged on the new version of the simulator all day yesterday and it didn't crash once. — Eric S. Raymond, *The New Hacker's Dictionary*, p. 48, 1991

bangtail *noun*
1 a racehorse; one of several inferior kinds of horse *US, 1921*
From the practice of bobbing the horse's tail.
- — David W. Maurer, *Argot of the Racetrack*, p. 12, 1951
- "Wherever the bangtails are running, this Banjho's there." — Ovid Demaris, *The Last Mafioso*, p. 423, 1981

2 a return-address envelope sent with a bill, containing a product offer on a detachable portion of the envelope flap *US, 1986*
- — Rachel S. Epstein and Nina Liebman, *Biz Speak*, p. 16, 1986

bang up *verb*
to end a poker game *US, 1979*
- — John Scarne, *Scarne's Guide to Modern Poker*, p. 272, 1979

bank *noun*
1 money; wealth *US, 1991*
- — Connie Eble (Editor), *UNC-CH Campus Slang*, p. 1, Spring 1991
- Hoodsters gathered in the evening to swap stories, get high, make a little bank on drug sales, and plot crimes. — Bob Sipchen, *Baby Insane and the Buddha*, p. 15, 1993
- Doing this, we make mad bank. — *Gone in 60 Seconds*, 2000
- Because if the buzz is any indication, the movie's gonna make some huge bank. — Kevin Smith, *Jay and Silent Bob Strike Back*, p. 18, 2001

2 a person who finances a gambling enterprise *US, 1964*
- — R. Frederick West, *God's Gambler*, p. 222, 1964

3 a prison cell for solitary confinement *US, 1962*
- — Joseph E. Ragen and Charles Finston, *Inside the World's Toughest Prison*, p. 790, 1962

4 a toilet *US, 1945*
- — Lou Shelly, *Hepcats Jive Talk Dictionary*, p. 7, 1945

▶ **take it to the bank; put it in the bank**
to be very sure of a fact *US, 1977*
- "One thing you can take to the bank is a white Christmas," a National Weather Service spokesman said of western Illinois and eastern Iowa. — *Washington Post*, p. A2, 22nd December 1983
- "I will never forget where I come from, and you can take that to the bank." (Quoting Senator John Edwards). — *Chicago Tribune*, p. C1, 20th February 2004

bank *verb*
to prove someone guilty of a crime *US, 1992*
- — William K. Bentley and James M. Corbett, *Prison Slang*, p. 18, 1992

banker *noun*
1 a usurer, an illegal lender of money *US, 1988*
- How can I figure Bill Ray—he knows the streets like I know the streets—gets a case of the stupids and brags to Pachoulo that he's got a new banker? — Robert Campbell, *Juice*, p. 73, 1988

2 the operator of an illegal numbers racket or lottery *US, 1959*
- A numbers banker? — Chester Himes, *The Real Cool Killers*, p. 102, 1959
- They couldn't be trusted by numbers bankers any more. — Claude Brown, *Manchild in the Promised Land*, p. 191, 1965
- There was no problem getting the free-lance Negro bankers out of business. — Mario Puzo, *The Godfather*, p. 252, 1969
- The bankers pay them [the police] off. — Louise Meriwether, *Daddy Was a Number Runner*, p. 116, 1970

3 in a functionally compartmentalized illegal drug operation, the person who receives payment for drugs bought *US, 1987*
- — Carsten Stroud, *Close Pursuit*, p. 269, 1987

banker's bit *noun*

a prison sentence of five to ten years *US, 1950*

A common sentence for bankers caught commiting fraud.

- — Hyman E. Goldin et al., *Dictionary of American Underworld Lingo*, p. 23, 1950

banker's set *noun*

in dominoes, the 3 – 2 piece *US, 1959*

So named because opponents cannot score on it.

- — Dominic Armanino, *Dominoes*, p. 15, 1959

bank job *noun*

a bank robbery *US, 1920*

- "A bank job. I pulled a bank job and I got away with it." — John Ridley, *Love is a Racket*, p. 20, 1998

bank off *verb*

to place a prisoner in a punishment cell *US, 1981*

- — *Maledicta*, p. 266, Summer/Winter 1981: "By its slang, ye shall know it: the pessimism of prison life"

bap *verb*

to shoot someone or something *US, 1966*

- Then I bapped at the first little rabbit and turned him aboutface on his pivot. — Robert Edmond Alter, *Carny Kill*, p. 2, 1966

baptism *noun*

the drenching of a prison guard with urine and/or feces *US, 1992*

- Word of the guard's "baptism" had spread through the cellhouse, sparking laughter and jeers from other Cubans. — Pete Earley, *The Hot House*, p. 116, 1992

Baptist bag *noun*

a brown paper bag in which a bottle of beer can be concealed *US, 1992*

- You want a Baptist bag with that beer, buddy? — Lewis Poteet, *Car & Motorcycle Slang*, p. 23, 1992

bar *noun*

1 a package of heroin *US, 1978*

- All I want is the stuff. Hey, wait a minute, momma, I ain't no petty nigger. Naw, baby, if I was goin' rip off something, it would be a hell of a lot bigger than a twenty-five dollar bar. — Donald Goines, *Crime Partners*, p. 43, 1978

2 used as a name for any variable object *US, 1983*

- The second metasyntactic variable, after FOO. If a hacker needs to invent exactly two names for things, he almost always picks the names "foo" and "bar." — Guy L. Steele et al., *The Hacker's Dictionary*, p. 29, 1983

BAR *noun*

a Browning automatic rifle *US, 1967*

- But today all the Oakland Angels got BARs. — Frank Reynolds, *Freewheelin' Frank*, p. 7, 1967

bar *adjective*

a "minus" attached to a grade *US, 1968*

- — Collin Baker et al., *College Undergraduate Slang Study Conducted at Brown University*, p. 76, 1968

bar; barr *noun*

a mixture of codeine-infused cough syrup and soda *US, 1998*

- I'm also trying to find out the Pharmaceutical name for a drug in Texas called syrup, lean or bar. It is a codeine based syrup, which tastes like some sweet cough syrup, but it is very strong. — *alt.drugs.chemistry*, 22nd November 1998
- In Houston, Elwood said, it has a variety of nicknames—Lean, AC/DC, barr, down, Karo and nods. "Lean because after you take it you will be definitely leaning and losing your coordination," Elwood said. — *The Commercial Appeal* (Memphis), p. F1, 9th July 2000

barb *noun*

a *barb*iturate *US, 1966*

- — John B. Williams, *Narcotics and Hallucinogenics*, p. 109, 1967
- [H]e only lets me come over when he restocks my acid supply and gives me enough grass and barbs to lasts me until I see him again. — Anonymous, *Go Ask Alice*, p. 59, 1971
- Barbiturates are also known as BARBS, BLUES, REDS, and SEKKIES. — Macfarlane, Macfarlane and Robson, *The User*, p. 97, 1996

Barbara Hutton *noun*

in hold 'em poker, a five and ten as the first two cards dealt to a player *US, 1981*

Hutton (1913 – 1979) was heiress to the Woolworth fortune; Woolworth was the foremost five and ten cent store in America.

- — Thomas L. Clark, *The Dictionary of Gambling and Gaming*, p. 13, 1987

barbecue *noun*

1 a self-immolation *US, 1963*

The term enjoyed a brief and gruesome popularity in the early 1960s.

- I am not saying that we should accept Mme. Nhu's statements at face value. Nor that we should forgive her for using that unfortunate language. If she had not referred to the Buddhist suicides as "monk barbecues," Americans would surely have greeted her. — *San Francisco News Call-Bulletin*, p. 6, 12th October 1963

2 the burning of a prisoner locked in a cell *US, 1992*

- — William K. Bentley and James M. Corbett, *Prison Slang*, p. 89, 1992

3 radiation treatment *US, 1994*

- — Sally Williams, "*Strong*" *Words*, p. 134, 1994

4 Medical slang *US, 1994*

- — Sally Williams, "*Strong*" *Words*, p. 134, 1994

5 an attractive girl or woman *US, 1938*

- — Lou Shelly, *Hepcats Jive Talk Dictionary*, p. 7, 1945
- — Jack Lait and Lee Mortimer, *New York Confidential*, p. 235, 1948: "A glossary of Harlemisms"

barbecue *verb*

to put someone to death by electrocution *US, 1990*

- — Charles Shafer, *Folk Speech in Texas Prisons*, p. 197, 1990

barbed wire city *noun*

a military stockade *US, 1964*

- — Carl Fleischhauer, *A Glossary of Army Slang*, p. 3, 1968

barber *noun*

in pool, a close miss, usually made intentionally to avoid a scratch *US, 1993*

- — Mike Shamos, *The Illustrated Encyclopedia of Billiards*, p. 21, 1993

barber pole *noun*

in casino gambling, a bet comprised of various colored chips *US, 1980*

- Barber poles are to be broken down and paid color for color. — Lee Solkey, *Dummy Up and Deal*, p. 107, 1980

Barbie; Barbie Doll *noun*

a barbiturate capsule *US, 1979*

- — Joel Homer, *Jargon*, p. 193, 1979
- — Sally Williams, "*Strong*" *Words*, p. 134, 1994

bare-ass; bare-assed *adjective*

naked *UK, 1562*

- That's what I thought, no gloves. I heard about you. The Digger goes in bare-ass. — George V. Higgins, *The Digger's Game*, p. 4, 1973
- [T]he Zorros marched off, leaving Dougie and Scottie bare-assed and shivering on the bridge. — Richard Price, *The Wanderers*, p. 23, 1974

bareback *verb*

1 to engage in sex without a condom *US, 1970*

- — *Current Slang*, p. 12, Spring 1970
- — Judi Sanders, *Faced and Faded, Hanging to Hurl*, p. 2, 1993
- The study by researchers at the CDC and San Francisco's Department of Public Health is the first serious analysis of the practice of "barebacking," in which gay or bisexual men intentionally engage in sex without a condom with someone other than their primary partner[.] — *San Francisco Chronicle*, p. A2, 4th April 2002

2 to surf without a wetsuit *US, 1991*

- — Trevor Cralle, *The Surfin'ary*, p. 6, 1991

bareback *adjective + adverb*

(used of sex) without a condom *US, 1960*

- I always ride bareback myself. Take a chance my way, though. — Joseph Wambaugh, *The Glitter Dome*, p. 165, 1981
- I never got the clap and I always went in bareback. — Mark Baker, *Nam*, p. 167, 1981
- What can I tell you, she let this jockey ride bareback. — James Ellroy, *White Jazz*, p. 113, 1992
- "Tell them not to ride bareback. Tell them to stay away from the whores." — Cherokee Paul McDonald, *Into the Green*, p. 96, 2001

barefoot *adjective*
in craps, said of a bet on the pass line without odds taken *US, 1983*
- — Thomas L. Clark, *The Dictionary of Gambling and Gaming*, p. 13, 1987

barefoot pilgrim *noun*
in the used car business, a naive, trusting, unsophisticated customer *US, 1968*
- — *Esquire*, p. 118, March 1968

bare metal *noun*
a new computer which is not equipped with even an operating system *US, 1991*
- — Eric S. Raymond, *The New Hacker's Dictionary*, p. 49, 1991

bares *noun*
the bare fists *US, 1972*
- — Helen Dahlskog (Editor), *A Dictionary of Contemporary and Colloquial Usage*, p. 5, 1972

barf *verb*
1 to vomit *US, 1958*
- — *American Speech*, p. 228, October 1967: "Some special terms used in a University of Connecticut men's dormitory"
- LaDonna said, "You want me to barf all over the car?" — Elmore Leonard, *Glitz*, p. 235, 1985
- If you think you're going to barf, walk out and get some air. — Robert Crais, *L.A. Requiem*, p. 97, 1999

2 in computing, to fail to operate *US, 1983*
- The division operation barfs if you try to divide by zero. — Guy L. Steele et al., *The Hacker's Dictionary*, p. 29, 1983

barfbag *noun*
by extension, a despicable person *US, 1973*
- I'd always tried to teach him and other young cops that you can't be a varsity letterman when you deal with these barfbags. — Joseph Wambaugh, *The Blue Knight*, p. 56, 1973

barf, beer and a cigar *noun*
a fighter pilot's breakfast *US, 1986*
- — *United States Naval Institute Proceedings*, p. 108, October 1986

barf buddy *noun*
a drinking companion *US, 1977*
- [S]ometimes longed for the uncomplicated life of lacrosse and rugby and hou-bro beevo parties, of happily hugging the toilet all night long with your barf buddies after draining a half-keg for no special occasion? — John Sayles, *Union Dues*, p. 279, 1977

barfic *noun*
an unartistic computer graphic created with keyboard characters *US, 1995*
- — Christian Crumlish, *The Internet Dictionary*, p. 19, 1995

barfly *noun*
a too-frequent frequenter of bars and saloons *US, 1906*
- In the dingy half-light, in the thick, stale miasma of tobacco smoke and alcoholic fumes which are the atmosphere of the innumerable cocktail bars of our cities, a new character has entered the American scene. It is the female bar fly. — *San Francisco Examiner*, p. 14, 10th December 1947
- Me, now, the first impression I'd had of her was that she wasn't much to look at—just a female barfly with money. — Jim Thompson, *After Dark, My Sweet*, p. 7, 1955
- The kid had still another beer, pulled the cheek of a middle-aged woman bar fly and bought her a drink. — Willard Motley, *Let No Man Write My Epitaph*, p. 73, 1958
- She couldn't bear the thought of sitting in a gin mill like a daytime barfly, avoiding the moves of local lotharios so old they were moldering. — Joseph Wambaugh, *Fugitive Nights*, p. 107, 1992

barf me out!
used for expressing disgust *US, 1982*
- Sheryl's mom, like she's a total space cadet, like barf me out, she like made Sheryl throw her dead beta fish down the garbage disposal, right? — Mary Corey and Victoria Westermark, *Fer Shurr! How to be a Valley Girl*, 1982
- He like sits there and like plays with all his rings / And he like flirts with all the guys in the class / It's like totally disgusting / I'm like so sure / It's like BARF ME OUT / Gag me with a spoon! — Moon Unit and Frank Zappa, *Valley Girl*, 1982

barf ride *noun*
a tumultuous carnival ride *US, 2005*
- Party Time Shows specialized in violent, lurching "barf"rides. — Peter Fenton, *Eyeing the Flash*, p. 132, 2005

barfy *adjective*
unpleasant, disgusting *US, 1957*
- That's what my English-comp teacher says—Mr. Glicksberg that barfy-looking character who's practically invented halitosis. — Frederick Kohner, *Gidget*, p. 3, 1957

barge *noun*
1 a large, unwieldy surfboard *US, 1963*
- — Grant W. Kuhns, *On Surfing*, p. 113, 1963
2 a large vagina *US, 1972*
- — Robert A. Wilson, *Playboy's Book of Forbidden Words*, p. 28, 1972

barge *verb*
to come; to go; to leave; to arrive; to move *US, 1929*
- "Let's barge out of here," Dopey said suddenly. — James T. Farrell, *Saturday Night*, p. 23, 1947

barge pole *noun*
a large penis *US, 1967*
- — Dale Gordon, *The Dominion Sex Dictionary*, p. 26, 1967

barhop *verb*
to move in a group from one bar to another, stopping at each for a drink or two *US, 1948*
- For the still missing mother, 18 year old Joyce Swinhart, her barhopping appeared to have been a giddy one-way, dead-end road. — *San Francisco Examiner*, p. 15, 8th January 1948
- The few who stayed, and the tourists, kept to the Gay White Way as they used to name it, clubbing, bar hopping or taking in a show. — Mickey Spillane, *Return of the Hood*, p. 60, 1964
- [T]hen they went out to bar-hop the beach bars, avoiding only the gay bars on the crossroads where the main road from the freeway joins the Coast Highway. — Roger Gordon, *Hollywood's Sexual Underground*, p. 145, 1966
- I was barhopping ... I must have hit every place on the West Side of town. — Gerald Petievich, *To Die in Beverly Hills*, p. 205, 1983

bari *noun*
a baritone saxophone *US, 1955*
- — Robert S. Gould, *A Jazz Lexicon*, p. 12, 1964

bark *noun*
the skin *UK, 1758*
- — Lou Shelly, *Hepcats Jive Talk Dictionary*, p. 7, 1945

bark *verb*
to brag *US, 1968*
- — Hy Lit, *Hy Lit's Unbelievable Dictionary of Hip Words for Groovy People*, p. 3, 1968

barker *noun*
1 a failure, a waste of time *US, 2002*
An elaboration of the common dog.
- "I just went and saw that movie. Avoid it all costs. It was a total barker." — *Dictionary of New Terms (Hope College)*, 2002
2 a person who stands at the door of a business calling out to people passing by, trying to lure them into the business *UK, 1699*
- The spiel of the leather lunged barker, a Barbary Coast fixture who continued on when Pacific St. became the International Settlement, is to be silenced. — *San Francisco Examiner*, p. 3, 9th January 1957
- Behind him, blazing lights promote a "Male and Female Love Act," topless singers, topless stewardesses, topless wrestlers. To top it off, The Colonel, a Broadway barker, wears a derby. — *San Francisco Examiner*, p. 21, 9th March 1976
- — Joe McKennon, *Circus Lingo*, p. 16, 1980
3 an unsophisticated master of ceremonies *US, 1986*
- The barker comes out and says that Hester Prime will now take off her clothes, which is what she does best. — Robert Campbell, *Junkyard Dog*, p. 132, 1986
4 in craps played in a casino, the stickman *US, 1983*
The stickman controls the pace of the game and engages in steady banter with the players.
- — Thomas L. Clark, *The Dictionary of Gambling and Gaming*, p. 14, 1987

5 a handgun *US, 1814*

- Then, holding his roscoe or barker on Mr. Mach, the policeman moseyed back to the truck and peered inside. — *San Francisco News*, p. 1, 25th August 1950
- "Then he yanks out the barker and bangs him. Smack in the biscuit." — Richard Prather, *The Peddler*, p. 67, 1952

barkers *noun*
shoes *US, 1929*
An extension of the much more commonly used **DOGS** (shoes).

- — Lou Shelly, *Hepcats Jive Talk Dictionary*, p. 7, 1945

barley *noun*
beer *US, 1972*

- — David Claerbaut, *Black Jargon in White America*, p. 57, 1972

barley water *noun*
beer *US, 1966*

- — *Current Slang*, p. 1, Summer 1966

barn *noun*
in poker, a hand consisting of three cards of the same suit and a pair *US, 1988*
Conventionally known as a "full house."

- — George Percy, *The Language of Poker*, p. 7, 1988

barnburner *noun*
an exciting idea, event or thing *US, 1934*

- All the Dub Hotchkisses looked at him with admiration bordering on awe. "A barn-burner!" said one. — Max Shulman, *Rally Round the Flag, Boys!*, p. 185, 1957

barndance card *noun*
a debriefing after combat *US, 1992*

- Sure, I'd handled Barrett's paperwork during my time at UDT-21 and UDT-22, and written "barn-dance cards" (after-action reports), fitreps, and commendation citations for my squads and platoon in Vietnam. — Richard Marcinko and John Weisman, *Rogue Warrior*, p. 147, 1992

barn door *noun*
1 the fly on a pair of pants *US, 1950*
Used in the euphemistic warning: "Your barn door is open."

- — Don R. McCreary (Editor), *Dawg Speak*, 2001
- "Your barn door is open," I said, remembering Uncle Peter's sense of humor. — V.C. Andrews, *Falling Stars*, p. 145, 2001

2 in stage lighting, and the television and movie industries, blinders used to focus a studio lamp *US, 1960*
Conventionally known as a "variable mask."

- — Oswald Skilbeck, *ABC of Film and TV Working Terms*, p. 16, 1960

barney *noun*
1 an unattractive, unpopular young man *US, 1987*

- — Mitch McKissick, *Surf Lingo*, 1987
- — Pamela Munro, *U.C.L.A. Slang*, p. 17, 1989
- I don't know where she meets these Barnies. — *Clueless*, 1995

2 a new Internet user whose interest will soon lapse *US, 1997*

- Different from a newbie in that newbies become plain decent folk through time and effort; a barney is for good once their ten free hours of AOL time are up[.] — Andy Ihnatko, *Cyberspeak*, p. 23, 1997

3 in the television and movie industries, a noise-reducing pad placed over a camera *US, 1977*

- — Tony Miller and Patricia George, *Cut! Print!*, p. 40, 1977

Barney's brig *noun*
the essence of disorder *US, 1975*
The full expression includes "both main tacks over the foreyard," showing the nautical origins if not explaining who Barney was.

- — John Gould, *Maine Lingo*, p. 6, 1975

barn money *noun*
in horse racing, money bet by purportedly informed track insiders *US, 1994*

- — Igor Kushyshyn et al., *The Gambling Times Guide to Harness Racing*, p. 211, 1994

barnstorm *verb*
to travel from town to town, performing, competing or campaigning *US, 1888*

- Murph had joined a circus band after his release and was barnstorming around the country some place. — Mezz Mezzrow, *Really the Blues*, p. 20, 1946

- After observing "Archie" I decided my troubles were small so I joined up with them barnstorming for a month. — Babs Gonzales, *I Paid My Dues*, p. 64, 1967

barnyard expression; barnyard language *noun*
profanity *US, 1968*

- What's amazing is that viewers are making it one of the highest rated shows on TV this season, so people obviously don't find the barnyard language the debutantes use distasteful. — *Daily News Leader* (Staunton, Virginia), p. 11A, 18th December 2003
- Although Hatch draws chuckles in Washington for uttering Utah-approved epithets like "Bullcorn!" his book gives readers uncensored expletives by the second page and sprinkles what the Denver Post called "barnyard expressions" throughout the narrative. — *Salt Lake Tribune*, p. A1, 16th February 2003

barnyard golf *noun*
the game of horseshoe pitching *US, 1925*

- Eighty-one contestants, who don't like to be called "barnyard golfers," gathered under the poplar trees at the county fairgrounds in Murray for the National Horshoe Pitchers Association of America's Ninth World's Championship tourney. — *Time*, p. 15, 21st August 1950
- Barnyard Golf This Week End [Headline] — *San Francisco Chronicle*, p. 1H, 30th August 1957

barnyard hen *noun*
a prostitute not favored by her pimp *US, 1957*

- [T]hey are their "head chicks" instead of just one or another of their "barnyard hens." — John M. Murtagh and Sara Harris, *Cast the First Stone*, p. 10, 1957

bar of soap *noun*
in dominoes, the double blank *US, 1959*

- — Dominic Armanino, *Dominoes*, p. 15, 1959

barracuda *noun*
an aggressive, unprincipled person *US, 1957*

- "My God," he whispered, "get a load of the barracuda with Tompkins." — Jimmy Snyder, *Jimmy the Greek*, p. 211, 1975
- — Multicultural Management Program Fellows, *Dictionary of Cautionary Words and Phrases*, 1989

barrel *noun*
1 a drum containing 50,000 central nervous system depressants for illegal sale *US, 1978*

- In this form they were called barrels, or kegs, and sold for $1,200 at the time. — Joan W. Moore, *Homeboys*, p. 79, 1978

2 a tablet of LSD *US, 1971*
Usually in the plural.

- — Richard A. Spears, *The Slang and Jargon of Drugs and Drink*, p. 28, 1986
- Acid pills roughly the shape and size of asprin tablets are called "barrels" because of their cylindrical shape. — Cam Cloud, *The Little Book of Acid*, p. 37, 1999

3 a perfect wave breaking *US, 1991*

- — Trevor Cralle, *The Surfin'ary*, p. 7, 1991

4 in pool, a betting unit *US, 1990*

- If you have $1000 and you're playing for $100 a game, you're packing ten barrels. — Steve Rushin, *Pool Cool*, p. 6, 1990

barrel-ass; barrel *verb*
to move rapidly, generally oblivious to any obstacles *US, 1930*

- Barrel-assing toward Buddhahood. — Tom Robbins, *Another Roadside Attraction*, p. 245, 1971
- "Dagos, eh, drivin' a big Cadillac from the big city—where yo all barrel-assing to?" — Edwin Torres, *Carlito's Way*, p. 33, 1975
- He was more at home on the Howard, the A or B trains that ignored risk, gathered speed, six cars, and barreled ass straight north or straight south. — William Brashler, *City Dogs*, p. 65, 1976
- I barreled through the living room, back to the kitchen[.] — Janet Evanovich, *Seven Up*, p. 82, 2001

barreled out *adjective*
in pool, depleted of money to bet *US, 1990*

- — Steve Rushin, *Pool Cool*, p. 6, 1990

barrelhouse *noun*
some combination of brothel, bar, and rooming house *US, 1883*

- I've played the music in a lot of places these last thirty years, from Al Capone's roadhouses to swing joints along 52nd Street in New York, Paris nightclubs, Harvard University, dicty Washington embassies and Park Avenue salons, not to mention all the barrel house dives — Mezz Mezzrow, *Really the Blues*, p. 4, 1946

barse-ackwards *adjective*
end-first *US, 1975*
- — John Gould, *Maine Lingo*, p. 7, 1975

bart *noun*
a criminally inclined youth, especially a youth gang member *US, 1963*
- — *San Francisco Examiner*, p. 8, 27th October 1963: "What a 'Z'! The astonishing private language of Bay Area teenagers"

bar up *verb*
to become excited *US, 1996*
- — John Vorhaus, *The Big Book of Poker Slang*, p. 6, 1996

base *noun*
freebase cocaine; basic cocaine from which the hydrochloride has been removed *US, 1982*
- After some of the fellas would step away form the blackjack table, and the bar, and get ready to buy a fiddy or a hundred dollars' worth of sniff, I would set them up with a hit of base in the back room. — *New Jack City*, 1990
- "They look around, find ten keys of base in the garage, actually in a Mercedes that happens to have my prints on the steering wheel and partials on the door handle." — Elmore Leonard, *Out of Sight*, p. 63, 1996

▸ **on base**
engaged in some degree of sexual activity *US, 1972*
- I admired her for that—it made me feel pretty sure that not too many other people had been on base. — Robert Byrne, *McGoorty*, p. 82, 1972

base *verb*
1 to smoke freebase cocaine *US, 1987*
- — Ellen C. Bellone (Editor), *Dictionary of Slang*, p. 2, 1989
- "At about five a.m. they wanted to base and shit and I knew Max didn't base either." — Terry Williams, *The Cocaine Kids*, p. 33, 1989
- — Terry Williams, *Crackhouse*, p. 146, 1992
- I tried basing a few times but thought it a waste. — Cleo Odzer, *Goa Freaks*, p. 261, 1995

2 to argue *US, 1990*
- For home boys and zimmers; This dictionary is def! — *Frederick (Maryland) Post*, p. B2, 24th May 1990

3 to verbally attack someone using sarcasm to convey an accurate if cruel appraisal of them *US, 1993*
An abbreviation of "de*base*."
- It reminded him of the way he and Keller and Cedric Pratt would base on each other back at the polliwog pool. — Bob Sipchen, *Baby Insane and the Buddha*, p. 349, 1993
- — Vann Wesson, *Generation X Field Guide and Lexicon*, p. 14, 1997

baseball *noun*
1 homosexual activity *US, 1989*
Back formation from the use of **PITCH** and **CATCH** as terms meaning "to have the active and passive roles in homosexual sex."
- — James Harris, *A Convict's Dictionary*, p. 28, 1989

2 in horse racing, a bet on one horse in one race and all horses in another *US, 1976*
- — Tom Ainslie, *Ainslie's Complete Guide to Thoroughbred Racing*, p. 328, 1976

Baseball Annie *noun*
a woman who makes herself available sexually to professional baseball players *US, 1949*
- It is permissible, in the scheme of things, to promise a Baseball Annie dinner and a show in return for certain quick services for a pair of roommates. — Jim Bouton, *Ball Four*, p. 204, 1970
- I don't like the word "groupie" or "Baseball Annie" applied to me. — Herb Michelson, *Sportin' Ladies*, p. 92, 1975
- — Richard Scholl, *Running Press Glossary of Baseball Language*, p. 13, 1977
- Roberts' agent, Seth Levinson, was at the ballpark and came out swinging against the woman, described as a "Baseball Annie" living near the Mets' minor-league affiliate in Binghamton. — *New York Post*, p. 51, 21st September 2002

baseball bum *noun*
in craps, the number nine *US, 1949*
- — Thomas L. Clark, *The Dictionary of Gambling and Gaming*, p. 14, 1987

baseball whiskers *noun*
a sparsely bearded face *US, 1952*
- "He said I had baseball whiskers," I said, blushing. "Nine on each side." It was a stale joke. — Chester Himes, *Cast the First Stone*, p. 37, 1952

base camp commando; base camp desk jockey *noun*
somebody with bellicose opinions about the way the war should be conducted but no intention of leaving their post away from combat to do it *US, 1986*
Vietnam war usage.
- I was never really fond of sports, but the life of a Base Camp Commando looked pretty good. — Paul Clayton, *Cal Melcer Goes to Vietnam*, p. 11, 2004

base crazies *noun*
obsessive searching behavior experienced by crack cocaine users *US, 1989*
- [A] kind of hallucination that leads an individual to search for the smallest particle of cocaine or crack in mistaken belief that they have lost some of the residue. — Terry Williams, *The Cocaine Kids*, p. 135, 1989

base dealer *noun*
a card cheat who deals from the bottom of a deck *US, 1993*
- — Frank Scoblete, *Guerrilla Gambling*, p. 296, 1993

base gallery *noun*
a room or building where freebase cocaine users pay to enter and then buy and smoke freebase cocaine *US, 1992*
An extension of "shooting gallery."
- — Terry Williams, *Crackhouse*, p. 146, 1992

base head *noun*
a regular smoker of freebase cocaine *US, 1986*
- — Ellen C. Bellone (Editor), *Dictionary of Slang*, p. 2, 1989
- After a month or two, the place was full of just baseheads who would stay there all day or night, day after day, spending their money. — Terry Williams, *The Cocaine Kids*, p. 108, 1989
- First you wanna be a stick-up kid, but you got shot. Now youse a basehead. You all fucked up, Pookie. — *New Jack City*, 1990
- He was a little part-time basehead though. — *Menace II Society*, 1993
- There is a lot of drug dealing and baseheads around here. — S. Beth Atkin, *Voices from the Street*, p. 86, 1996

base house *noun*
a house or apartment where freebase cocaine is sold *US, 1992*
A term and concept that all but vanished with the advent of crack cocaine in the mid-1980s.
- — Terry Williams, *Crackhouse*, p. 146, 1992

basement *noun*
▸ **in the basement**
in stud poker, dealt facing down *US, 1988*
- — George Percy, *The Language of Poker*, p. 7, 1988

baser *noun*
a user of freebase cocaine *US, 1989*
- Most of this thing about rock is really just because basers want more for their money, and regular sniffers do, too. — Terry Williams, *The Cocaine Kids*, p. 41, 1989

base rock *noun*
solid freebase cocaine *US, 1998*
- Stoney was the biggest dealer on the corner, it was nothing for him to pay off some fool with base rocks to commit felonious crimes against rival dealers or people who failed to pay off their tabs. — Renay Jackson, *Oaktown Devil*, p. 29, 1998

bases loaded *noun*
in craps, bets placed on every possible combination *US, 1974*
- There's no bigger thrill than when he's got the bases loaded and they hit the numbers[.] — Edward Lin, *Big Julie of Vegas*, p. 112, 1974

bash *noun*
a party *UK, 1901*
- — Collin Baker et al., *College Undergraduate Slang Study Conducted at Brown University*, p. 77, 1968

• Last night in town, you guys gonna have a little bash before you leave? — *American Graffiti*, 1973

bash *verb*

1 while surfing, to slam into a wave *US*, *1991*
• — Trevor Cralle, *The Surfin'ary*, p. 7, 1991

2 to eat with great fervor *US*, *1945*
• — Lou Shelly, *Hepcats Jive Talk Dictionary*, p. 7, 1945

▸ **bash ears**
to talk on the telephone *US*, *1951*
Teen slang.
• — *Newsweek*, p. 28, 8 October 1951

▸ **bash wheels**
in the usage of youthful model road racers (slot car racers), to race *US*, *1997*
• — Phantom Surfers, *The Exciting Sounds of Model Road Racing (Album cover)*, 1997

basher *noun*

1 a fast, reckless skier *US*, *1963*
• — *American Speech*, p. 205, October 1963: "The language of skiers"

2 in the television and movie industries, a simple 500 watt flood light *US*, *1960*
• — Oswald Skilbeck, *ABC of Film and TV Working Terms*, p. 16, 1960

basie; basey *noun*
a person living on a military base *US*, *1993*
• Like the adults, they developed their own social hierarchy, carving up the town into a variety of cliques: greasers, soshes, basies, and those who feel somewhere inbetween. — Kim Rich, *Johnny's Girl*, p. 154, 1993

basing gallery *noun*
a room, apartment, or house where cocaine is smoked in freebase form *US*, *1995*
• — Steven Daly and Nathaniel Wice, *alt.culture*, p. 50, 1995

basket *noun*

1 the male genitals as seen through tight pants *US*, *1941*
• A young fellow in a very tight-fitting pair of faded blue jeans walks in. Eyes follow him. "Oh my God! What a basket!" a young man shrills in feminine-like voice. — Willard Motely, *Let No Man Write My Epitaph*, p. 246, 1958
• What a low-cut gown to a faggot must be is like tight Levis with a padded basket. — Lenny Bruce, *The Essential Lenny Bruce*, p. 161, 1967
• Sure, you lock eyes while you're pounding the pavement, looking for a lay or love or both, but let's face it, the focal point is the crotch. In gay parlance, the basket. — John Francis Hunter, *The Gay Insider*, p. 119, 1971
• The local men have short hair and wear wild-looking Hawaiian-style sports shirts with wide baggy pants which totally disguise their baskets. — Gore Vidal, *Myron*, p. 252, 1974

2 a woman's labia *US*, *1949*
• — Vincent J. Monteleone, *Criminal Slang*, p. 17, 1949

3 in roulette, a bet on zero, double zero and two *US*, *1983*
Sometimes expanded to "basket bet."
• — Thomas L. Clark, *The Dictionary of Gambling and Gaming*, p. 14, 1987

▸ **the baskets**
basketball *US*, *1985*
• "Very few bookmakers get into the baskets seriously." — Nicholas Pileggi, *Wise Guy*, p. 195, 1985

basket case *noun*

1 a person who is emotionally debilitated *US*, *1952*
• After forcing himself (and his "eccentricity") upon a six-year-old basket case (a victim of pregnancy tranquilizers) he is found out[.] — Terry Southern, *Now Dig This*, p. 195, 1961
• [T]he whole thing was making a young girl who wasn't too bright to being with into some kind of a daffy basket case. — George V. Higgins, *The Rat on Fire*, p. 149, 1981
• But what we found out is that each one of us is a brain and an athlete and a basket case, a princess and a criminal. — *The Breakfast Club*, 1985
• You're a basket case. — *Sleepless in Seattle*, 1993

2 any dysfunctional organization or entity *UK*, *1973*
• "Madagascar is the basket case of the Indian Ocean," said a senior Western banker[.] — *New York Times*, p. D11, 28th December 1981

• Romania, the East bloc's basket case No. 2, recently asked Western bankers to reschedule 25 percent of its outstanding debt. — *Christian Science Monitor*, p. 5, 16th November 1981

basket days *noun*
days of good weather *US*, *1965*
• Basket days—A period of mild weather that permits men to wear garments light enough to reveal the contours of their baskets. — *Fact*, p. 25, January–February 1965

baskets *noun*
the female breasts *US*, *1968*
• — Fred Hester, *Slang on the 40 Acres*, p. 3, 1968

basket shopping *noun*
the practice of observing the crotch of a clothed male to gauge the size of his penis *US*, *1964*
Also known as "basket watching."
• — Roger Blake, *The American Dictionary of Sexual Terms*, p. 13, 1964
• — Dale Gordon, *The Dominion Sex Dictionary*, p. 26, 1967

Basra belly *noun*
diarrhea experienced by travelers in the Middle East *US*, *1976*
• In the Middle East, you'll hear such euphemisms as Gippy tummy, Aden gut, and Basra belly. — Jane Brody, *The New York Times Guide to Personal Health*, p. 581, 1982

bass *noun*
one fifth of a gallon of alcohol *US*, *1975*
• — *American Speech*, p. 56, Spring–Summer 1975: "Razorback slang"

bassackwards *adjective*
in the wrong order *US*, *1865*
An intentionally jumbled **ASS BACKWARDS**. US quotation expert Fred Shapiro recently found the term used by Abraham Lincoln in 1865, a substantial antedating.
• I was pissed at him, putting the case in bass-ackwards because that way he can start with me[.] — George V. Higgins, *The Judgment of Deke Hunter*, p. 199, 1976
• My mother came downstairs the way things usually got done in my family, culo avanti—or in regular English, bass ackwards. — Rita Ciresi, *Pink Slip*, p. 4, 1999
• "It's kinda bassackwards from the way people normally do it," he laughs. — *New Times Broward-Palm Beach (Florida)*, 25th December 2003

bastard *noun*
a despised or disrespected person; a derogatory insult or challenging form of address to someone considered objectionable *UK*, *1598*
Originally, "a person born out of wedlock."
• There are consequences to breaking the heart of a murdering bastard. You experienced some of them. — *Kill Bill*, 2003

bastardy *noun*
statutory rape *US*, *1956*
• "They give a guy twenty years for bastardy in this state." — Grace Metalious, *Peyton Place*, p. 292, 1956

basted *adjective*
drunk *US*, *1928*
• — Joseph Weingarten, *American Dictionary of Slang*, p. 18, 1954
• — Connie Eble (Editor), *UNC-CH Campus Slang*, p. 1, Fall 1988

basuco; bazuko *noun*
coca paste, the basic ingredient in the manufacturing process of cocaine; hence, cocaine *US*, *1984*
• CALL IT... Busuco, gianluca, blow, percy, lady, toot, white[.] JUST DON'T CALL IT... Charlie—too Eighties — *Drugs An Adult Guide*, p. 34, December 2001

bat *noun*

1 a foolish or eccentric person *US*, *1894*
• A bat can't go it. Bat? You mean a dingbat? [fool, incompetent]. yeah. — Bruce Jackson, *In the Life*, p. 162, 1972
• The old bat on the door who rode shotgun on the money box—really a cigar box—never did act like she was going to give me the chance to take it. — A.S. Jackson, *Gentleman Pimp*, p. 12, 1973

2 an ugly woman *US*, *1972*
• — David Claerbaut, *Black Jargon in White America*, p. 57, 1972

3 a drinking binge *US, 1846*

- One sip and I'll go on a nine-week bat. — John D.McDonald, *The Neon Jungle*, p. 21, 1953

4 in horse racing, the whip used by the jockey *US, 1951*

- — David W. Maurer, *Argot of the Racetrack*, p. 12, 1951

▸ **at bat**

said of an appearance before a judge, magistrate, or parole board *US, 1967*

- You're first a bat, Henry. Take off your cap and come along. — Malcolm Braly, *On the Yard*, p. 17, 1967

bat *verb*

▸ **bat the breeze**

to talk, chat, or gossip *US, 1941*

- Jenkins, you've been around the Hall long enough to know a murder isn't something we bat the breeze about. — Thurston Scott, *Cure it with Honey*, p. 23, 1951
- A klatsch of kids was batting the breeze about five or six cars away from his own[.] — Morton Cooper, *High School Confidential*, p. 32, 1958

bat away *verb*

in a carnival, to operate swindles aggressively and without fear of arrest *US, 1985*

A term borrowed from the game of baseball.

- The only time the order to bat away is given is when the police have been paid off. — Gene Sorrows, *All About Carnivals*, p. 9, 1985

batch *noun*

an ejaculation's worth of semen *US, 1973*

- The sounds this bitch was making damn near had me ready to unload this batch right in her hand[.] — A.S. Jackson, *Gentleman Pimp*, p. 166, 1973

batch; bach *verb*

to live as a bachelor *US, 1862*

- It came from the boys' cabin—they were batching together to save money. — Jim Thompson, *The Kill-Off*, p. 29, 1957
- For nearly six months I bached it, doing damned well what I pleased. — William Tulio Divale, *I Lived Inside the Campus Revolution*, p. 9, 1970

bath *noun*

1 a heavy loss in a business or betting proposition *US, 1936*

- — *Cars*, p. 40, December 1953
- — John Scarne, *Scarne's Guide to Modern Poker*, p. 292, 1979
- — Kathleen Odean, *High Steppers, Fallen Angels, and Lollipops*, p. 94, 1988

2 in television and movie making, any of the chemical mixtures used to develop film *US, 1987*

- — Ira Konigsberg, *The Complete Film Dictionary*, p. 26, 1987

bat house *noun*

a mental hospital *US, 1962*

- — Joseph E. Ragen and Charles Finston, *Inside the World's Toughest Prison*, p. 790, 1962

baths *noun*

Turkish baths where the main attraction is sex between homosexual men *US, 1968*

- You'll never learn to stay out of the baths, will you. — Mart Crowley, *The Boys in the Band*, p. 59, 1968
- Baths can be found in any large city. — *Screw*, p. 2, 29th September 1969
- Essentially, the baths are where gay men go for sex. — *The Village Voice*, 27 September 1976
- You betcha. None o' that nasty heterosexual role-playing for us. Lots of buddy nights at the baths. — Armistead Maupin, *Further Tales of the City*, p. 33, 1982

bathtub curve *noun*

in computing, used as a description of a notional graph of the predicted failure rate of a piece of electronic equipment *US, 1991*

Evoking a cross-section of a bathtub as the graph—briefly high, long low, high again at the end.

- — Eric S. Raymond, *The New Hacker's Dictionary*, p. 51, 1991

bathtub gin *noun*

homemade alcohol, perhaps approximating gin *US, 1930*

- [H]e had been a cab driver in Chicago during the Roaring Twenties but had left town fast due to some trouble with the police over transporting bath tub gin in his cab. — Piri Thomas, *Seven Long Times*, p. 216, 1974

Bats *nickname*

the pilots of the Iowa Air National Guard *US, 1990*

- Oh, they came form old Sioux City, widely known as bats / And they're going home tomorrow; we gotta raise our hats! — Joseph Tuso, *Singing the Vietnam Blues*, p. 212, 1990: The VC Truck Driver's Blues

bats *adjective*

crazy; very eccentric; mad, to any degree *UK, 1911*

From the phrase **HAVE BATS IN THE BELFRY**.

- You're bats. Somebody'll bust in. You can't leave it here. — Harry J. Anslinger, *The Murderers*, p. 72, 1961
- You think I'm nuts because I sew. It's to keep me from going bats. — Antony James, *America's Homosexual Underground*, p. 137, 1965
- I'm not bats, but I got to try this track. — Iceberg Slim (Robert Beck), *Pimp*, p. 102, 1969

batshit *adjective*

crazy, out of control, angry *US, 1970*

- [H]e just wanted to know whether the private standing in front of him was trying to punk out of that war, or was truly bat-shit. — Emmett Grogan, *Ringolevio*, p. 227, 1972
- "Some guys couldn't take it, they went batshit." — Robert Stone, *Dog Soldiers*, p. 237, 1974
- Nothing's working anymore, everything's changing and it's driving me fucking batshit. — James Ellroy, *Brown's Requiem*, p. 105, 1981
- These things are more likely to fuck up a shoot than trying to stick a needle [S-M piercing] through someone on camera who goes bat-shit. — Robert Stoller and I.S. Levine, *Coming Attractions*, p. 93, 1991

battery *noun*

▸ **get your battery charged**

to have sex *US, 1935*

- — *American Speech*, p. 56, February 1947: "Pacific War language"

batting average *noun*

a police officer's arrests-to-prosecution percentage *US, 1958*

- A policeman calls his arrest and summons record his batting average. — *New York Times*, p. 34, 20th October 1958

battle *noun*

an unattractive woman *US, 1948*

- — Jack Lait and Lee Mortimer, *New York Confidential*, p. 235, 1948

battle *verb*

1 to breakdance or rap competitively with the object of demonstrating the most individual style *US, 1999*

- So when you're practicing for that whole week, your goal is to hit the jam and battle. — Alex Ogg, *The Hip Hop Years* [quoting "Crazy Legs" Richie Colon], p. 32, 1999
- But how did battling come about? Well, DJs had always battled with their sound systems in New York. — J. Hoggarth, *How To Be a DJ*, p. 82, 2002
- See, I wasn't scared about battling someone on their own turf because I quickly realized that MC's thought they had an advantage on their block when they really didn't. — Earl "DMX" Simmons, *E.A.R.L.*, p. 127, 2002

2 to attack someone verbally *US, 1998*

- — Ethan Hilderbrant, *Prison Slang*, p. 10, 1998

▸ **battle the iron men**

in horse racing, to bet using pari-mutuel machines *US, 1951*

- — David W. Maurer, *Argot of the Racetrack*, p. 12, 1951

battleaxe; battleax *noun*

an old or elderly woman who is variously characterized as resentful, vociferous, thoroughly unpleasant, usually arrogant and no beauty *US, 1896*

- Hey, Estelle, ain't that that old battle ax that owns the place next door? — Helen P. Branson, *Gay Bar*, p. 57, 1957

battle happy *adjective*

emotionally imbalanced due to combat stress *US, 1949*

- "What's wrong with that joe? Battle-happy?" asks Candler. "Looks like he's taken about all he can." — Audie Murphy, *To Hell and Back*, p. 269, 1949

battle of the bulge *noun*

an effort to lose weight *US, 1956*

- They won their battle of the bulge, according to a male post commander and three foreign correspondents, also eminently male. — *San Francisco Examiner*, p. 17, 13th October 1956
- The inside story of Elvis Presley's battle of the bulge is that Presley tipped the scales at 253 pounds only a few weeks ago. — *San Francisco Chronicle*, p. 43, 27th May 1975

battle scar *noun*
a bruise on the skin caused by sucking *US, 1982*
Hawaiian youth usage.
- — Douglas Simonson, *Pidgin to da Max Hana Hou*, 1982

battle whacky *adjective*
emotionally distraught from combat stress *US, 1949*
- "You're dreaming things, Mike. You're battle whacky." — Audie Murphy, *To Hell and Back*, p. 39, 1949

batty *adjective*
eccentric, odd, insane *US, 1903*
- "Look," Coyle said, "they're all batty." — George V. Higgins, *The Friends of Eddie Doyle*, p. 132, 1971
- She's been driving me batty lately. — *Body Heat*, 1980

batwings *noun*
in the language of parachuting, surfaces applied to the arms and body to slow the rate of descent *US, 1978*
- — Dan Poynter, *Parachuting*, p. 165, 1978

bay *noun*
▸ **over the bay**
drunk *US, 1787*
- — John Gould, *Maine Lingo*, p. 8, 1975

bay and a gray *noun*
in poker, a bet involving a red chip (the bay) and a white chip (the gray) *US, 1951*
- — *American Speech*, p. 97, May 1951: "The vocabulary of poker"
- — Albert H. Morehead, *The Complete Guide to Winning Poker*, p. 256, 1967

Bay City *nickname*
the San Quentin California State Prison in San Rafael, California *US, 1975*
- — Report to the Senate, *California Senate Committee on Civil Disorder*, p. 228, 1975

bayonet *noun*
a hypodermic needle *US, 1986*
- — Sacramento Municipal Utility District, *A Glossary of Drugs and Drug Language*, 1986

▸ **take the bayonet course**
to participate in bismuth subcarbonate and neoarsphenamine therapy for syphilis *US, 1981*
- — *Maledicta*, p. 227, Summer/Winter 1981: "Sex and the single soldier"

bayonet drill *noun*
sexual intercourse *US, 1964*
- — Roger Blake, *The American Dictionary of Sexual Terms*, p. 14, 1964

Bay State *noun*
any standard medical syringe *US, 1973*
Drug addict usage.
- — David Maurer and Victor Vogel, *Narcotics and Narcotic Addiction*, p. 387, 1973

bazillion *noun*
a mythical very large number *US, 2001*
- — Pamela Munro, *U.C.L.A. Slang*, p. 35, 2001

bazooka *noun*
1 crack cocaine *US, 2003*
- "Welfare pukes hustling bazooka and blacks and South American spics and bikers muleing brown skag out of Florida." — James Lee Burke, *Last Car to Elysian Fields*, p. 31, 2003
2 in television and movie making, a light support used on a catwalk *US, 1990*
- — Ralph S. Singleton, *Filmmaker's Dictionary*, p. 16, 1990

bazookas *noun*
the female breasts *UK, 1963*
- Thonged buttage backed up by booming bazookas when Bobbie boogies on the stage at a club. — Mr. Skin, *Mr. Skin's Skincyclopedia*, p. 85, 2005

bazooms *noun*
the female breasts *US, 1936*

Originally a corruption of "bosom" with the same sense, then evolved to mean "breasts."
- How many out-of-town buyers' hands had paraded over those bazooms? How much in fees had each of these bazooms raked in per annum? — Bernard Wolfe, *The Late Risers*, p. 73, 1954
- "They're solid gold, these boozooms of mine," she said. — Gypsy Rose Lee, *Gypsy*, p. 185, 1957
- Their secondary sex characteristics are simply too conspicuous to pass without insult, and we were unmerciful towards them: tits, boobs, knockers, jugs, bubbies, bazooms, lungs, flaps and hooters we called them, and there was no way to be polite about it. — *Screw*, p. 6, 3rd January 1972
- Yeah, but howdja like them bazooms on that P.R. chick? — Richard Price, *The Wanderers*, p. 27, 1974
- "Nice bazooms. She was a good kid to talk to." — George Higgins, *Cogan's Trade*, p. 71, 1974

bazuca *noun*
the residue of smoked freebase cocaine, itself mixed with tobacco and smoked *US, 1984*
- [O]thers prefer a bazuca, in which the drug is sprinkled on cigarettes or joints and smoked. — Terry Williams, *The Cocaine Kids*, p. 110, 1989

BB *noun*
any smart person, especially a professor *US, 1947*
An abbreviation of "*big brains*."
- — Marcus Hanna Boulware, *Jive and Slang of Students in Negro Colleges*, 1947

BBA *noun*
a woman with large buttocks *US, 1968*
An abbreviation of "*broads with big asses*."
- — Fred Hester, *Slang on the 40 Acres*, p. 3, 1968

BBFN
used as shorthand in Internet discussion groups and text messages to mean "*bye-bye for now*" *US, 2002*
- — Gabrielle Mander, *WAN2TLK? ltl bk of txt msgs*, p. 43, 2002

BBL
used in computer message shorthand to mean "*be back later*" *US, 1991*
- — Eric S. Raymond, *The New Hacker's Dictionary*, p. 342, 1991

B board *noun*
an electronic newsgroup *US, 1991*
A contraction of "bulletin board."
- — Eric S. Raymond, *The New Hacker's Dictionary*, p. 52, 1991

B bomb *noun*
an amphetamine inhaler *US, 1969*
Withdrawn from the market by Smith Kline & French in 1949 after widespread abuse. A wad of Benzedrine™-soaked cotton found in an asthma inhaler would be removed, immersed in a drink until drug and drink form a single intoxicating solution, reputedly 100 times stronger than a single Benzedrine™ tablet.
- — Richard Lingeman, *Drugs from A to Z*, p. 21, 1969
- — William D. Alsever, *Glossary for the Establishment and Other Uptight People*, p. 2, December 1970
- — Eugene Landy, *The Underground Dictionary*, p. 30, 1971

B-boy *noun*
1 a breakdancer; later, anyone involved in hip-hop culture *US, 1981*
- The heroes of these legends are the B Boys, the Puerto Rican and black teenagers who invent and endlessly elaborate this exquisite, heady blend of dancing, acrobatics, and martial spectacle. — *Village Voice*, p. 31, 22nd–28th April 1981
- The "breakers," or "B boys," for rival crews at the playgrounds, discos and skating rinks where they gather. — *New York Times*, p. C1, 14th August 1981
- B-boys were inner city kids who were trying to get theirs. — William Upski Wimsatt, *Bomb the Suburbs*, p. 18, 1994
- The B-Boy, a phrase originally applied to break dancers, was, by the time I used it [1992], a catchall phrase among hip hop fans for anyone deeply involved with or influenced by hip hop culture. — Nelson George, *Buppies, B-Boys, Baps & Bohos*, p. xv, 2001
2 a streetwise young black man *US, 1995*
By extension from the previous sense.

- Most athletes are all B-boys and homeboys from the block. — Lois Stavsky et al., *A2Z [quoting Run-DMC, 1992]*, p. 4, 1995

BBW *noun*
a fat woman *US, 1988*
An abbreviation of "*big, beautiful woman*"; a fetish with a large male following.
- "Ninety-five percent of the men are average-sized but attracted to BBW" (Big Beautiful Women). — *Newsday (New York)*, p. 2 (Part II), 13th February 1988

BC *noun*
contraception; birth control *US, 1985*
- — *American Speech*, p. 19, Spring 1985: "The language of singles bars"

B cat *noun*
an ostentatiously homosexual male prisoner *US, 1989*
From the official categorization by California prison authorities.
- — James Harris, *A Convict's Dictionary*, p. 28, 1989

BCD *noun*
military eyeglasses *US, 1991*
Because they are so unattractive, they are deemed "*birth control devices.*" Also variant BCG (*birth control goggles*).
- — E.M. Flangan Jr., *Army*, November 1991
- — *American Speech*, p. 383, Winter 1991: "Among the new words"

BC Lounge *noun*
a Burger Chef fast food franchise restaurant *US, 1979*
- — *Detroit Free Press*, 4th November 1979

BCNU
used in computer message shorthand to mean "be seeing you" *US, 1991*
- — Eric S. Raymond, *The New Hacker's Dictionary*, p. 342, 1991

BD *noun*
a syringe *US, 1982*
An allusion to Becton-Dickison, a medical supplies manufacturer.
- — Ralph de Sola, *Crime Dictionary*, p. 14, 1982

BDF *noun*
a big, strong, dumb brute *US, 1997*
New York police slang; an abbreviation of "*big dumb fuck.*"
- — Samuel M. Katz, *Anytime Anywhere*, p. 386, 1997

B dog *noun*
used as a term of address between members of the Bloods gang *US, 1998*
- — Ethan Hilderbrant, *Prison Slang*, p. 11, 1998

BDSM; BD/SM *noun*
bondage, domination, sadism and masochism or sado-masochism, unified as a sexual subculture *US, 1969*
- B&D = dominant (sadist) — Stephen Lewis, *The Whole Bedroom Catalog*, p. 144, 1975

beach *noun*
▶ **the beach**
Saudi Arabia *US, 1991*
Gulf war usage.
- "Desert cherries" in "Kevlars" fly the "Sand Box Express" to the "beach" and soon are complaining about "Meals Rejected by Ethiopians" if they can't find a "roach coach" run by "Bedouin Bob." — *Houston Chronicle*, p. 15, 24th January 1991

Beach *noun*
▶ **the Beach**
Miami Beach, Florida *US, 1993*
- "You from somewhere on the East coast. New York?" "Miami. The Beach most of my life." — Elmore Leonard, *Pronto*, p. 120, 1993

beach bomber *noun*
a bicycle modified for riding on the sand *US, 1991*
- — Trevor Cralle, *The Surfin'ary*, p. 7, 1991

beach boy *noun*
a young male who spends a great deal of time at the beach *US, 1965*
- — John M. Kelly, *Surf and Sea*, p. 279, 1965

beach bum *noun*
someone whose devotion to spending a lifetime at the beach has left them destitute and an outcast *US, 1965*
- — John M. Kelly, *Surf and Sea*, p. 279, 1965

beach bunny *noun*
a young female who spends a great deal of time at the beach, surfing or associating with surfers *US, 1963*
- — *Paradise of the Pacific*, p. 27, October 1963
- — John M. Kelly, *Surf and Sea*, p. 279, 1965
- What to other people is a "pad" is called a "hutch" in surfing circles—most properly if it is the beach bunny's own apartment[.] — Roger Gordon, *Hollywood's Sexual Underground*, p. 144, 1966

beach chick *noun*
a young woman living a Bohemian lifestyle near the beach in the 1950s *US, 1958*
Peter Tamony described the term as follows: "Originally applied to girls who lived at Stinson Beach [north of San Francisco] who were bisexual. By those unfamiliar with its background, and both ways implication, it has been extended to any girl who associated with the so-called Beat Generation inhabitants of North Beach in San Francisco."
- It's [being Beat] shacking up for weeks at a time with a Beach chick, or picking up homosexuals in gay bars. — *San Francisco Chronicle, This World*, p. 4, 15th June 1958
- Nude "Beach Chick" Strangled Here [Headline] — *San Francisco Call-Bulletin*, p. 10, 18th June 1958

beached whale *noun*
an obese hospital patient *US, 1994*
- — Sally Williams, *"Strong" Words*, p. 134, 1994

beach head *noun*
a person who spends a great deal of time at the beach *US, 1991*
- — Trevor Cralle, *The Surfin'ary*, p. 9, 1991

beach rat *noun*
a person who spends a great deal of time at the beach *US, 1990*
- "I'll certainly point out that a pensioned fifteen-year veteran of the Newport Beach police Department is not just some ordinary unemployed beach rat," Chip added. — Joseph Wambaugh, *The Golden Orange*, p. 10, 1990

bead jiggler *noun*
a Roman Catholic *US, 1966*
After rosary beads.
- He has also requested that Losing Preacher Mulcahy come prepared to administer the last rites of the bead-jiggler Church. — Richard Hooker, *MASH*, p. 49, 1968

beagle *noun*
1 a sausage *US, 1927*
- — Joseph E. Ragen and Charles Finston, *Inside the World's Toughest Prison*, p. 790, 1962
2 a racehorse *US, 1923*
- — David W. Maurer, *Argot of the Racetrack*, p. 12, 1951

beak *noun*
1 the nose *UK, 1715*
- We called this kid O'Brien because his beak was so big and hooked it kept the sun out of his face and got caught on clothes lines. — Mezz Mezzrow, *Really the Blues*, p. 7, 1946
- You've been snorting coke. You been snuffling that crap up your beak again after you promised—after you swore on your mother's grave[.] — Robert Campbell, *Juice*, p. 130, 1988
2 in horse racing, a bet that a horse will win *US, 1951*
Extended from the sense as a "nose," suggesting that the horse will win by "a nose."
- Give me two tickets right on the beak. — David W. Maurer, *Argot of the Racetrack*, p. 12, 1951

beam *noun*
a good person *US, 1945*
- — Lou Shelly, *Hepcats Jive Talk Dictionary*, p. 7, 1945
▶ **off the beam**
incorrect *US, 1945*
- — Lou Shelly, *Hepcats Jive Talk Dictionary*, p. 47, 1945

▸ **on the beam**
good; to the point; balanced *US, 1941*
- — Lou Shelly, *Hepcats Jive Talk Dictionary*, p. 31, 1945
- And you can get Ann for Benny? That's on the beam. — Irving Shulman, *The Amboy Dukes*, p. 87, 1947
- I lost the argument—the part of me that was on-the-beam lost it—and I went back. — Jim Thompson, *After Dark, My Sweet*, p. 3, 1955
- The signal beam, high over the tracks, could be seen for miles from the engine cab. Three colored lights kept the engineer informed of track conditions ahead. Being on the beam really meant being well-informed. — J. Herbert Lund, *Herb's Hot Box of Railroad Slang*, p. 20, 1975

beam *verb*
in computing, to transfer a file electronically *US, 1991*
From the terminology of the original *Star Trek* television series.
- — Eric S. Raymond, *The New Hacker's Dictionary*, p. 53, 1991

▸ **beam up to Scotty; beam up; beam**
to smoke crack cocaine and become cocaine-intoxicated *US, 1986*
From the pop phrase "Beam me up, Scotty" used repeatedly on the first generation of *Star Trek* television programs from 1966 to 1969.
- On the street, they say when you're smoking crack, that you're beamin' up to Scotty, you're goin' to another world. — *New Jack City*, 1990
- "To buy crack and beam up," Kathy said. — Elmore Leonard, *Maximum Bob*, p. 232, 1991
- — Terry Williams, *Crackhouse*, p. 146, 1992

beamer *noun*
a crack cocaine user *US, 1992*
From **BEAM UP** (**TO SCOTTY**) (to smoke crack cocaine).
- — Terry Williams, *Crackhouse*, p. 146, 1992

beamers; beemers *noun*
crack cocaine *US, 1988*
After **BEAMER** (a crack cocaine user).
- They say "Beam Me Up, Scotty." They say, "I Need a Beam-Me-Up Scotty. You got some? You got some?" And the rock star say, "Looky here. Lookyhere. I got a dollar beamer. Dollar Beamer. Three dollar Beamer." — *St. Petersburg (Florida) Times*, p. 1F, 28th February 1988

beamy *adjective*
wide *US, 1961*
Originally "broad in the beam," then shortened and applied to a ship's width, and then by extension to other objects and to people, especially those wide in the seat.
- You couldn't possibly be a tadpole—your tail's too beamy. — Willie Fennell, *Dexter Gets The Point*, p. 86, 1961
- — John Gould, *Maine Lingo*, p. 9, 1975

bean *noun*
1 anything at all; very little *US, 1833*
- And another thing—the race made me feel inferior, started me thinking that maybe I wasn't worth beans as a musician or any kind of artist, in spite of all my big ideas. — Mezz Mezzrow, *Really the Blues*, p. 239, 1946
- He's makin' beans compared to what he should be makin'. — *Raging Bull*, 1980
2 a dollar *US, 1902*
- And I want four hundred beans for the Dinch and I want it soon. — George Mandel, *Flee the Angry Strangers*, p. 269, 1952
- In three weeks after they showed I got my vines out of hock and was doing about fifteen beans a day. — Babs Gonzales, *Movin' On Down De Line*, p. 6, 1975
- Pals of mine at the Ventura courthouse said he logged twenty-one hundred sixty-six beans of the ransom money into the evidence locker. — James Ellroy, *Hollywood Nocturnes*, p. 187, 1994
3 a coin *UK, 1799*
- — Lou Shelly, *Hepcats Jive Talk Dictionary*, p. 7, 1945
4 in US casinos, a $1 betting chip *US, 1967*
- — Albert H. Morehead, *The Complete Guide to Winning Poker*, p. 256, 1967
- — Steve Kuriscak, *Casino Talk*, p. 3, 1985
5 a capsule or tablet of Benzedrine™ (amphetamine sulfate), a central nervous system stimulant *US, 1967*
- After a particularly lackluster effort, I asked a friend of the Cal team what happened. "Oh, it was simple. We just ran out of beans (amphetamines)." — *San Francisco Chronicle*, p. 57, 23rd September 1971
- I ran down the pill man and bought out his supply of beans. — Donald Goines, *Whoreson*, p. 200, 1972
- "One of my first nights at Obie's, Delise asked me if I had any beans[.]" — Anne Steinhardt, *Thunder La Boom*, p. 126, 1974
- One game owner I knew goes through a daily ritual of passing out a BEAN to each of his agents before they start work[.] — Gene Sorrows, *All About Carnivals*, p. 10, 1985
6 a capsule of MDMA, the recreational drug best known as ecstasy *US, 2000*
- — Connie Eble (Editor), *UNC-CH Campus Slang*, p. 1, Spring 2000
- — Don R. McCreary (Editor), *Dawg Speak*, 2001
7 the head *US, 1905*
- [T]heir well-educated little beans[.] — Lester Bangs, *Psychotic Reactions and Carburetor Dung*, p. 42, 1970
8 the hymen *US, 1950*
- — Hyman E. Goldin et al., *Dictionary of American Underworld Lingo*, p. 24, 1950
9 the penis *US, 1967*
- — Dale Gordon, *The Dominion Sex Dictionary*, p. 27, 1967

bean-choker *noun*
a Mexican or Mexican-American *US, 1980*
- — Edith A. Folb, *runnin' down some lines*, p. 229, 1980

bean chute; bean slot *noun*
the opening in a solid prison cell door through which food is passed to the prisoner within *US, 1998*
- — Ethan Hilderbrant, *Prison Slang*, p. 11, 1998

beaned up *adjective*
under the influence of Benzedrine™ (amphetamine sulfate), a central nervous system stimulant *US, 1971*
- — Montie Tak, *Truck Talk*, p. 8, 1971

beaner *noun*
a Mexican or Mexican-American *US, 1965*
Derogatory, from the association of beans with the Mexican diet.
- I mean, here you go around apologizing to everybody cause you got a name like a beaner, and cause you're dark enough to pass for one. — Joseph Wambaugh, *The Delta Star*, p. 25, 1983
- When he made the canteen cart, the beaners ripped off his zuuzuus and whamwhams. — Seth Morgan, *Homeboy*, p. 152, 1990
- "Joey, accidents happen," Tommy pleaded. "People get hit by falling safes ... a car fulla beaners runs a light and whammo, you got avocado salad." — Stephen Cannell, *King Con*, p. 94, 1997

beanery *noun*
a low-cost, low-quality restaurant *US, 1887*
- Worked as a waitress in a beanery to keep body and soul together. — Mezz Mezzrow, *Really the Blues*, p. 88, 1946
- When he got his discharge papers he made tracks for Laguna Beach, where he landed a job as a carhop in a drive-in beanery. — Bernard Wolfe, *The Late Risers*, p. 159, 1954

beanie light *noun*
a flashing, rotating light on an emergency vehicle *US, 1969*
- — *American Speech*, p. 202, Fall 1969: "Truck driver's jargon"

beanies and weenies *noun*
c-rations of hot dogs with beans *US, 1982*
Vietnam war usage.
- By the time we finished Kobi Tan Tan, after thirty days of eating C rations, the only C rations I could even look at was beanies and weenies. — Al Santoli, *Everything We Had*, p. 27, 1982

beanmobile *noun*
a car embellished with bright colors, chrome and other accessories associated with Mexican-American car enthusiasts *US, 1981*
- I ditched the bean-mobile at the Ford lot and dropped the keys and repo order with the sales manager. — James Ellroy, *Brown's Requiem*, p. 16, 1981

bean patch *nickname*
during the Korean war, an assembly area on the northern outskirts of Masan, a seaport about 40 miles west of Pusan *US, 1982*

- The 1st Marine Brigade moved its headquarters to a new bivouac area near Masan that came to be known in marine lore as the Bean Patch. The area in calmer times had been exactly that. — Joseph C. Goulden, *Korea*, p. 182, 1982

beanpole *noun*
a tall, thin person *US*, *1837*

- Which is more beautiful, this expert asks—a bean pole or a woman? — *San Francisco Chronicle, This Week*, p. 12, 4th January 1953
- Pat Marichal—dark-skinned Paraguayan beanpole with a stark resemblance to the morgue pic of Chief Joe Running Car. — James Ellroy, *Hollywood Nocturnes*, p. 100, 1994

bean queen *noun*
a homosexual who prefers Latin Americans as sexual partners but is not Latin American himself *US*, *1988*

- — H. Max, *Gay (S)language*, p. 4, 1988

bean rag *noun*
a red flag raised on a ship during mealtime *US*, *1955*

- [T]he meal pennant is called the bean rag. — United States Naval Institute, *Proceedings of the United States Naval Institute*, p. 1020, 1955

beans and baby dicks *noun*
in the Vietnam war, beans and hot dogs *US*, *1983*

- "The crazy fucker just finishing eat six cans of beans and dicks before we got hit." — Lynda Van Devanter, *Home Before Morning*, p. 11, 1983

beans and motherfuckers *noun*
in the Vietnam war, lima beans and ham, one of the least popular c-rations *US*, *1981*

- "I'm not going to say he had some cold beans and motherfuckers for breakfast, took some shots from the other guys about being a cherry and then went out and got blown into fifty million pieces—which is what happened." — Mark Barker, *Nam*, p. xi, 1981

Beantown; Bean Town *nickname*
Boston, Massachusetts *US*, *1901*
Because Boston is known for its baked beans.

- Beantown's No. 1 bachelor, youthful, handsome Nathaniel Saltonstall, has all of Boston society buzzing over the attention he's showering on Bobo Rockefeller. — *San Francisco Examiner*, p. 14, 24 November 1954
- — Montie Tak, *Truck Talk*, p. 9, 1971
- You think this is Bean Town? You think this is New York? You make a mess in Chicago, you clean it up with your tongue. — Robert Campbell, *Junkyard Dog*, p. 49, 1986
- Beantowns premier black-owned 24 hour hip-hop station, WBOT[.] — *The Source*, p. 243, March 2002

bean up *verb*
to take amphetamines *US*, *1976*

- — *Verbatim*, p. 280, May 1976

bean wagon *noun*
a no-frills lunch counter *US*, *1960*

- We did it all in Stamford and White Plains—in the streets, the park, a bean wagon, a saloon[.] — Richard Schickel, *Elia Kazan*, p. 143, 2005

bear *noun*
1 the co-pilot or navigator in an F-4 or F-105 military aircraft *US*, *1990*

- He's a man who flies, but don't fly / Bear of the sky. — Joseph Tuso, *Singing the Vietnam Blues*, p. 52, 1990: Bear of the Sky

2 a hairy and stocky man, of a type beloved by some homosexuals *US*, *1994*

- — Kevin Dilallo, *The Unofficial Gay Manual*, p. 237, 1994
- In some cities, particularly San Francisco, "bears" are very popular. — John Preston, *Hustling*, p. 48, 1994

3 an unattractive woman *US*, *1982*

- — Arnold Shaw, *Dictionary of American Pop/Rock*, p. 30, 1982

4 a cautious and conservative poker player *US*, *1988*

- — George Percy, *The Language of Poker*, p. 8, 1988

5 a difficult task or situation *US*, *1966*

- — Andy Anonymous, *A Basic Guide to Campusology*, p. 2, 1966

beard *noun*
1 a woman's pubic hair *US*, *2005*

- [S]he strips down to bumpers and beard, then climbs aboard his Oscar Meyer-mobile. — Mr. Skin, *Mr. Skin's Skincyclopedia*, p. 188, 2005

2 in gambling, a person who bets for someone else, especially for a cheat *US*, *1962*

- — Frank Garcia, *Marked Cards and Loaded Dice*, p. 250, 1962
- — Thomas L. Clark, *The Dictionary of Gambling and Gaming*, p. 15, 1987
- — Frank Scoblete, *Guerrilla Gambling*, p. 296, 1993

3 a person used to mask the identity of the actual controlling agent; a person who escorts another to a social function in order to mask the identity of one or the other's lover or sexual orientation *US*, *1956*

- In underworld terminology, Manny Skar was a beard (front). — Ovid Demaris, *Captive City*, p. 76, 1969
- "It's supposed to look like the girls are for the clients' entertainment, not his." "Who believes that?" "Not many. He also has a respectable friend he uses as a beard." — Robert Campell, *Junkyard Dog*, p. 147, 1986
- Maya, did you hear the latest medical report on Clinton's laryngitis? They say it's just an excuse to let Hillary make all the speeches, since all he is, is her beard anyway. — Joseph Wambaugh, *Finnegan's Week*, p. 110, 1993

4 a broker who buys up stock quietly and secretly for bidders in a corporate takeover who hope to disguise their intentions *US*, *1988*

- As one colleague explained about Ivan Boesky, the most closely watched of the arbitrageurs, "He likes a beard when he trades." — Kathleen Odean, *High Steppers, Fallen Angels, and Lollipops*, p. 107, 1988

5 an intellectual or academic *US*, *1927*
Unkind if not derisive.

- — *Washington Post*, 23rd April 1961: "Man, Dig This Jazz"
- — Clarence Major, *Dictionary of Afro-American Slang*, p. 24, 1970

6 a male member of an Orthodox Jewish group *US*, *1967*

- The beards are picketing the Russian Mission. — Charles Whited, *Chiodo*, p. 154, 1973

7 an "older" surfer *US*, *1991*
In the youth culture of surfing, "old" is a relative term.

- — Trevor Cralle, *The Surfin'ary*, p. 9, 1991

beard *verb*
to serve as a beard for someone *US*, *1971*

- Bloomquist writes like somebody who once bearded Tim Leary in a campus cocktail lounge and paid for all the drinks. — Hunter S. Thompson, *Fear and Loathing in Las Vegas*, p. 139, 1971

bearded clam *noun*
the vulva *US*, *1965*
Combines **FISH** with visual imagery.

- — Dale Gordon, *The Dominion Sex Dictionary*, p. 27, 1967
- He gobbles one beaver and gets promoted. I've ate close to three hundred bearded clams in my time and never even got a commendation. — Joseph Wambaugh, *The Choirboys*, p. 22, 1975

bearded lady *noun*
the vulva *US*, *1967*

- — Dale Gordon, *The Dominion Sex Dictionary*, p. 27, 1967

beard jammer *noun*
the manager of a brothel *US*, *1962*

- — Joseph E. Ragen and Charles Finston, *Inside the World's Toughest Prison*, p. 790, 1962

bear insurance *noun*
a gun, the bigger the better the insurance *US*, *1965*

- — Robert O. Bowen, *An Alaskan Dictionary*, p. 8, 1965

bear joint *noun*
in a carnival, a game in which stuffed teddy bears are the prize *US*, *1960*

- — *American Speech*, pp. 308–309, December 1960: "Carnival talk"

bear paw *noun*
round-footed snowshoes worn while doing chores *US*, *1993*

- — Mike Doogan, *How to Speak Alaskan*, p. 7, 1993

bear trap *noun*
in television and movie making, a strong clamp used for attaching lights to rigging *US*, *1987*

- — Ira Konigsberg, *The Complete Film Dictionary*, p. 26, 1987

Bear Whiz Beer *noun*
an inferior beer *US*, *1978*

A popular beverage in Firesign Theater skits; its motto is the stunning "It's in the water! That's why it's yellow!"

- Turns it off before going to the kitchen for another can of Bear Whiz Beer. — Richard Malott, *Behavior Analysis*, p. 149, 1978

beast *noun*
1 used as an affectionate reference to an aircraft *US, 1990*
- — Joseph Tuso, *Singing the Vietnam Blues*, p. 245, 1990: Glossary

2 a sexually available female *US, 1955*
- — *American Speech*, p. 302, December 1955: "Wayne University slang"

3 anything excellent *UK, 1996*
- [I]'m say that that was the fuckin' best beast of a monster party[.] — Mike Benson, *Room full of Angels (Disco Biscuits)*, p. 25, 1996
- — Vann Wesson, *Generation X Field Guide and Lexicon*, p. 16, 1997

4 heroin; heroin addiction *US, 1958*
- — Edward R. Bloomquist, *Marijuana*, p. 332, 1971
- As long as Mable his whore was able / To satisfy his beast. — Dennis Wepman et al., *The Life*, p. 98, 1976

beast *verb*
to crave *US, 2007*
- Angry, cold, beasting for crack[.] — Treasure E. Blue, *A Street Girl Named Desire*, p. 6, 2007

beastly *adjective*
excellent *US, 1953*
- — Lavada Durst, *The Jives of Dr. Hepcat*, p. 11, 1953

beasty *noun*
a repulsive, disgusting person *US, 1985*
- "Oh, Clay, you're such a beasty," she giggles. — Bret Easton Ellis, *Less Than Zero*, p. 16, 1985

beasty *adjective*
repulsive, disgusting *US, 1982*
- Like we went to Dupars and there were all these beasty seventh grade nerds with nine million zits apiece. — Mary Corey and Victoria Westermark, *Fer Shurr! How to be a Valley Girl*, 1982

beat *noun*
1 a member of the 1950s youth counterculture *US, 1958*
- But insofar as they speak of themselves generically and are forced to choose among evils, they prefer the word "beat." — *Dissent*, p. 339, Summer 1961
- Beats avoid work. — Ned Polsky, *Hustlers, Beats, and Others*, p. 159, 1967

2 in horse racing, an unfortunate defeat *US, 1976*
- As when a horse is caught in the last stride and a losing bettor moans, "What a tough beat!" — Tom Ainslie, *Ainslie's Complete Guide to Thoroughbred Racing*, p. 328, 1976

3 a crime which has not been solved *US, 1992*
- What the fuck do I care if this goes in as a solve or a beat? — Richard Price, *Clockers*, p. 449, 1992

4 in television and movie making, the main storyline *US, 1990*
- — Ralph S. Singleton, *Filmmaker's Dictionary*, p. 16, 1990

5 a car *US, 1947*
- — Marcus Hanna Boulware, *Jive and Slang of Students in Negro Colleges*, 1947

beat *verb*
to cheat, to swindle, to steal *US, 1849*
- It was early one morning / the temperature read about twenty below / I was on my way to the Union Station to beat some sucker for his dough. — Bruce Jackson, *Get Your Ass in the Water and Swim Like Me*, p. 66, 1964
- I knew the cab driver had beat me for my bread but there was no use crying, it was gone. — Babs Gonzales, *I Paid My Dues*, p. 24, 1967
- They also beat me for a ten dollar bill. — Herbert Huncke, *The Evening Sun Turned Crimson*, p. 177, 1980
- We was over in New York and we got beat on some dope. — Richard Price, *Clockers*, p. 461, 1992

▸ **beat feet**
to leave *US, 1944*
- So he snags his blunderbuss, calls his bonecruncher, blows the barracks and beats feet for the timber. — Harry Haenigsen, *Jive's Like That*, 1947
- — Collin Baker et al., *College Undergraduate Slang Study Conducted at Brown University*, p. 78, 1968
- — Gregory Newbold, *The Big Huey*, p. 244, 1982
- Well, shit, fella, you might as well keep fuckin' beatin' feet, as they say. — Larry Heinemann, *Paco's Story*, p. 64, 1986

- "I'll be glad when all these sailboat tourists beat feet," Fortney said. — Joseph Wambaugh, *Floaters*, p. 178, 1996

▸ **beat it**
1 to leave quickly *US, 1878*
- I sneaked into the house and stole my sister's Hudson-seal fur coat out of the closet, then I beat it down to a whorehouse and sold it to a madam for $150. — Mezz Mezzrow, *Really the Blues*, p. 54, 1946
- He forgot all about the money, and beat it. — Jim Thompson, *The Kill-Off*, p. 132, 1957

2 (of a male) to masturbate *US, 1995*
- The plane started spinning around, going out of control. So my cousin decides it's all over, and he whips it out and starts beating it right there. — *Mallrats*, 1995

▸ **beat the board**
in poker, to hold the best hand showing *US, 1963*
- — Irwin Steig, *Common Sense in Poker*, p. 181, 1963

▸ **beat the bushes**
in horse racing, to race a horse in minor circuits, where the horse can be a big fish in a little pond *US, 1951*
- — David W. Maurer, *Argot of the Racetrack*, p. 13, 1951

▸ **beat the cotton**
to soak and then pound used cottons, used to strain drug doses, in an attempt to leach out enough heroin for another dose *US, 1989*
- — Geoffrey Froner, *Digging for Diamonds*, p. 8, 1989

▸ **beat the eightball**
to use heroin *US, 1971*
- — Eugene Landy, *The Underground Dictionary*, p. 31, 1971

▸ **beat the favorite**
in horse racing, to place a small bet on a horse with long odds to win rather than betting on the horse favored to win *US, 1951*
- — David W. Maurer, *Argot of the Racetrack*, p. 13, 1951

▸ **beat the man**
to sleep *US, 1990*
Prison usage suggesting that in sleep one escapes domination by prison authorities.
- — Charles Shafer, *Folk Speech in Texas Prisons*, p. 197, 1990

▸ **beat the tab; beat the check**
to leave a restaurant or hotel without paying your check *US, 1973*
- He'd check into the best New York hotels under a phoney name so he could beat the tab. — Vincent Teresa, *My Life in the Mafia*, p. 119, 1973
- I was proudest of the chuckles we got from beating checks in restaurants. — Gary Mayer, *Bookie*, p. 81, 1974

▸ **beat the till**
to grab money from a cash register when the store clerk is not watching *US, 1972*
- I walked into a supermarket and watched a girl beatin' the till. She had turned the cashier around. — Harry King, *Box Man*, p. 71, 1972

▸ **beat your baloney**
(of a male) to masturbate *US, 1969*
- One maverick among those polled got his kicks beating his baloney during TV commercials. — *Screw*, 10th November 1969

▸ **beat your bishop**
(of a male) to masturbate *US, 1916*
- In fact you can sit here and rest or beat your bishop while I go ramblin around there, I like to ramble by myself. — Jack Kerouac, *The Dharma Bums*, p. 53, 1958

▸ **beat your chops; beat up your chops**
to talk *US, 1945*
- Herbie was beating up his chops about Lend-Lease to Russian when I walked up. — Chester Himes, *If He Hollers Let Him Go*, p. 112, 1945
- When I stood around outside the Pekin, beating up my chops with Big Buster, and he put his arm around my shoulder in a friendly way[.] — Mezz Mezzrow, *Really the Blues*, p. 48, 1946
- — Sherman Louis Sergel, *The Language of Show Biz*, p. 19, 1973

▶ **beat your face**
to perform push-ups *US, 1998*
- — *Seattle Times*, p. A9, 12th April 1998

▶ **beat your gums; beat up your gums**
to talk without purpose or without effect *US, 1945*
- "Never mind, I am who I am. Just don't beat up your gums at me," I said, throwing him a newly acquired phrase. — Ralph Ellison, *Invisible Man*, p. 269, 1947
- On the way to Biff's, Betsy, dressed in a knocked-out strapless, bloobers more out than in, kept beating her gums. — Bernard Wolfe, *The Late Risers*, p. 157, 1954

▶ **beat your meat; beat the meat**
(of a male) to masturbate; to masturbate a male *US, 1936*
- Suppose you just sit down and beat your meat if you're getting anxious. — Norman Mailer, *The Naked and the Dead*, p. 124, 1948
- The young man held his fist up and agitated it meaningfully, yet with such a disinterested air that his gesture—ordinarily such a smutty one—seemed quite abstract and inoffensive. "You know— onanism—'beating your meat,'" he explained. — Terry Southern, *Candy*, p. 74, 1958
- I have affairs, Arn, and I beat my meat. — Philip Roth, *Portnoy's Complaint*, p. 197, 1969
- Beating your meat is not a substitute for fucking. — *Screw*, p. 11, 1st September 1969

beat *adjective*
world-weary, spiritual, jaded, intellectual *US, 1947*
- But he's still alive, and strange, and wise, and beat, and human, and all blood-and-flesh and starving as in benny depression forever. — Jack Kerouac, *Windblown World*, pp. 100–101, 3rd July 1948
- You know, everyone I know is kind of furtive, kind of beat. — John Clellon Holmes, *Go*, p. 38, 1952
- The beatest characters in the country swarmed on the sidewalk[.] — Jack Kerouac, *On the Road*, p. 85, 1957
- If all the unemployed had followed the lead of the beatniks, Moloch would gladly have legalized the use of euphoric drugs and marijuana, passed out free jazz albums and sleeping bags, to all those willing to sign affidavits promising to remain "beat." — Eldridge Cleaver, *Soul on Ice*, p. 72, 1968

beat artist *noun*
a swindler *US, 1973*
- "That beat artist? He's got himself a home in Westchester[.]" — Gail Sheehy, *Hustling*, p. 70, 1973
- One response to freebase buyers' increasing demand for purer and purer cocaine was a proliferation of dealers and con men ("beat artists") purporting to sell the real thing. — Terry Williams, *The Cocaine Kids*, p. 40, 1989

beat bag *noun*
a bag of drugs that is heavily adulterated or is completely counterfeit *US, 1993*
- — *Washington Post*, p. C5, 7th November 1993

beatbox *verb*
to make mouth noises that serve as the background rhythm for a rap *US, 2002*
- Seeing all of this go down, I knew that I had to find my niche, so one day I started beatboxing. — Earl "DMX" Simmons, *E.A.R.L.*, p. 76, 2002

beatdown *noun*
a brutal physical beating *US, 1993*
- The Grape Streets moved on Bingo first. The sight was inexplicable; within seconds he was unidentifiable. This was a standard beat-down. — Sanyika Shakur, *Monster*, p. 148, 1993
- Such punishment would most probably be a beat-down. — Eric Davis, *The Slick Boys*, p. 41, 1998
- George had allegedly arranged for someone to greet Jessica with a beat-down. — Adrian Nicole LeBlanc, *Random Family*, p. 121, 2003

beat generation *noun*
the alienated class of young Americans who came of age in the mid-1940s and then embraced an alternative lifestyle and values in the 1950s *US, 1950*
- It's time we thought about our material. Call them hipsters, the "beat generation," "postwar kids," or our own displaced person whatever you will. — John Clellon Holmes, *Letter to Jack Kerouac*, 28th April 1950

- They were like the man with the dungeon stone and the gloom, rising from the underground, the sordid hipsters of America, a new beat generation that I was joining. — Jack Kerouac, *On the Road (The Original Scroll)*, p. 156, 1951
- The whole beat generation is a pain in the ass after 35. — Jack Kerouac, *Jack Kerouac Selected Letters 1957–1969*, pp. 138–139, 13th April 1958: Letter to John Clellon Holmes

beat in *verb*
to initiate a new member of a youth gang by group beating *US, 1996*
- You can either get beat in or sexed in. — S. Beth Atkin, *Voices from the Street*, p. 8, 1996

beatnik *noun*
a follower of the beat generation (avant-garde "visionaries, rebels and hipsters") derided and defined by stereotypical appearance and lifestyle choices *US, 1958*
Coined in 1958 (the first popular, non-Russian use of the suffix **NIK**) by San Francisco newspaper columnist Herb Caen.
- For some reason my name has become associated with bearded beatniks with whom I never had anything to do at all. — Jack Kerouac, *Jack Kerouac Selected Letters 1957–1969*, p. 210, 13th February 1959: Letter to Stella Sampas

beat off *verb*
(of a male) to masturbate *US, 1962*
- Guys all primed by the live show could duck next door to beat off in peace and dark. — Anne Steinhardt, *Thunder La Boom*, p. 144, 1974
- [T]hen there was only emptiness and the same sort of something-wasted feeling he'd had when he was his little brother's age and beat off in the bathroom. — Jess Mowry, *Way Past Cool*, p. 33, 1992
- Just as he'd begun to beat off, there was a knock on the bedroom door, which had no lock. — John Irving, *A Widow for a Year*, p. 50, 1998
- Gypsy Rose Lee related a story about how she told a dozen guys in the front row who were beating off, "Are ya ready yet, fellas, or can you use another 12 bars?" — Josh Friedman, *When Sex Was Dirty*, p. 108, 2005

beat out *verb*
to strip someone of their membership in a youth gang, accomplished by a ritualistic beating *US, 1995*
- — Mark S. Fleisher, *Beggars & Thieves*, p. 287, 1995

beat sheet *noun*
in television and movie making, a short summary of a story *US, 1990*
- — Ralph S. Singleton, *Filmmaker's Dictionary*, p. 16, 1990

beat-up *adjective*
shoddy, shabby, worn out *US, 1946*
- He'd light up and get real high and when he was groovy as a ten-cent movie he'd begin to play the blues on a beat-up guitar. — Mezz Mezzrow, *Really the Blues*, pp. 51–52, 1946

beau *noun*
used as a term of address between young males *US, 1954*
- — *This Week Magazine, New York Herald Tribune*, p. 47, 28th February 1954

beaut *noun*
a beauty, an impressive person or thing *US, 1895*
- Interior Secretary Harold L. Ickes, who previously had been denying applications for federal tidelands oil leases on the ground that the submerged territory clearly was the property of the States, wise-cracked, "When I make a mistake, it's a beaut." — *San Francisco Examiner*, 15th April 1946
- Jimmy Kelly's, a beaut of a room specializing in fan wielders and dancing gals, is patronized chiefly by merchants and Wall Streeters. — Jack Lait and Lee Mortimer, *New York Confidential*, p. 67, 1948
- A few minutes later he was back in an entirely different car, a brand-new convertible. "This one is a beaut!" he whispered in my ear. — Jack Kerouac, *On the Road*, p. 211, 1957
- BB: You know, I hear the new Cadillac's gonna be out in a couple of months. TILLEY: You're kidding? BB: Yeah, they're changing the body. I hear it's a beaut. — *Tin Men*, 1987

beauteous maximus *noun*
something that is excellent *US, 1989*
Mock Latin.
- — *Merriam-Webster's Hot Words on Campus Marketing Survey '93*, p. 2, 13th October 1993

beautiful *adjective*

in the counterculture of the 1960s and 70s, used as an all-purpose adjective of approval *US, 1961*

A vague but central word of the hippie eta, suggesting passivity, appreciation for nature, kindness, etc.

- — Francis J. Rigney and L. Douglas Smith, *The Real Bohemia*, p. xiii, 1961
- I hear it's a very good scene there. Not much heat, beautiful people, no speed freaks, and righteous dope. — Nicholas Von Hoffman, *We Are The People Our Parents Warned Us Against*, p. 47, 1967
- For a few days, we were all in a beautiful place. Can we do it again? — *East Village Other*, 20th August 1969
- beautiful: great, marvelous, a term of approval and admiration similar to groovy and outasight. — Ethel Romm, *The Open Conspiracy*, p. 242, 1970

beautiful!

used for expressing enthusiastic agreement *US, 1975*

- "Yes, Elliot, I'll be waiting." "Beautiful, beautiful." — Donald Goines, *Inner City Hoodlum*, p. 88, 1975

beautiful people *noun*

the cream of society's crop; the wealthy, fashionable people of high society and the arts, especially those celebrated as trendsetters *US, 1964*

- Two of the Beautiful (and famous) People, actress-model Suzy Parker and her husband Brad Dillman of film, TV and stage game, flew into San Francisco airport last evening. — *San Francisco Chronicle*, p. 9, 27th February 1965
- We rent beautiful people to squares. — Emile Nytrate, *Underground Ads*, p. 112, 1971

beauty *noun*

an amphetamine *US, 1993*

A shortened **BLACK BEAUTY**.

- He popped three more beauties, and stepped on the pedal. — Carl Hiaasen, *Strip Tease*, pp. 177–178, 1993

beauty farm *noun*

a resort with a focus on improving appearances *US, 1972*

- Her old lady's at the beauty farm[.] — John Rechy, *The Fourth Angel*, p. 76, 1972

beaver *noun*

1 a beard *US, 1871*

- — Lou Shelly, *Hepcats Jive Talk Dictionary*, p. 7, 1945
- She plunged her hands into the beaver, and I decided I'd better go home and think, because I was in very big trouble. — Max Shulman, *I was a Teen-Age Dwarf*, p. 104, 1959
- "When did this all happen?" says Parker. "The beaver. When did you grow the beaver?" — Tom Wolfe, *The Kandy-Kolored Tangerine-Flake Streamline Baby*, p. 279, 1965

2 a woman's pubic region; a woman as a sex object; sex with a woman *US, 1961*

Although recorded at least as early as 1927, "beaver" did not come into its own until the mid-1960s, with an explosion of films featuring full frontal female nudity but no sexual activity and titles punning on "beaver"—*Bald Beaver, Beaver Works in the Bush Country, Hair Raising Beaver, Fine Feathered Beavers, Leave it to Beavers*, and so on. As published sexual material got more graphic, so did the association of the term. Despite the highly sexual origin of the term, it was used by truck drivers with a slightly naughty innocence to refer to women.

- Hey, you know what the cryptic term "Beaver" refers to in those nudie movie ads? Then you're sharper than a Gillette. — *San Francisco Chronicle*, p. 31, 27th September 1967
- [S]he was a professional, but the trained buttocks behind and the sheared beaver up front didn't seem like real cunt and ass. — Anne Steinhardt, *Thunder La Boom*, p. 45, 1974
- Truckers expanded the existing slang term of "beaver" into their own vocabulary and "sweet thing" and "mini skirt," two previous names used for females were discarded. Beaver became the national word for a female[.] — Gwyneth A. "Dandalion" Seese, *Tijuana Bear in a Smoke 'Um Up Taxi*, p. 45, 1977
- Beaver? You mean vagina? — *The Big Lebowski*, 1998
- Perhaps you're daring enough to make your beaver completely bare. — *The Village Voice*, 8th–14th November 2000

3 a pornographic film *US, 1969*

- The first two beavers were disappointing for a unique reason. The girls were splendidly proportioned creatures with saliva-inducing propensities for any males' libido, but they didn't do anything. — *Screw*, p. 5, 24th January 1969

4 a police officer *US, 1961*

- When the information came over the station ticker type that the Missouri state police had captured the right man, these local beavers knocked me around all the way to the edge of town[.] — Clancy Sigal, *Going Away*, p. 138, 1961

beaver bait *noun*

money *US, 1976*

- — "Slingo", *The Official CB Slang Dictionary Handbook*, p. 7, 1976

beaver film *noun*

a mildly pornographic film, featuring full frontal nudity *US, 1969*

- If the beaver film is not something like that, then what? — *Adam Film Quarterly*, p. 75, February 1969
- The original Avon was the first in New York to screen "beaver" films, i.e., those showing pubic hair, five or six years ago. — Joseph Slade, *The Sexual Scene*, p. 269, December 1971
- For a time, this genre of "beaver" film was the most explicit pornographic entertainment available. — George Paul Csicsery (Editor), *The Sex Industry*, p. 166, 1973
- The simple beaver film soon developed two significant variations. — Kenneth Turan and Stephen E. Zito, *Sinema*, p. 77, 1974

beaver flick *noun*

a pornographic film *US, 1970*

- Shortly after this, the first genuine beaver flick was shown in another dingy house on 50th Street near 8th Avenue. — *Screw*, p. 14, 27th April 1970
- "We know we've got a long way to go but we're trying not to make just beaver flicks." (Quoting Jim Mitchell). — *The Berkeley Tribe*, p. 9, 22nd–28th August 1970

beaver loop *noun*

a repeating video featuring female frontal nudity *US, 1971*

- During my career, I've probably seen close to 500 beaver loops and maybe 200 hard-core shorts[.] — *Screw*, p. 18, 2nd August 1971
- "Those early prints of the beaver loops cost thirty-five dollars a print, right?" — Carolyn See, *Blue Money*, p. 132, 1974

beaver magazine *noun*

a magazine featuring photographs of nude women, focused on their genitals, usually not engaged in sex *US, 1967*

- Guys from around the league wrote to him regularly and sent him CARE packages—cakes, cookies, video cassettes, beaver magazines—because he refused to name any of his customers. — Dan Jenkins, *Life Its Ownself*, p. 28, 1982

beaver movie *noun*

a film featuring female frontal nudity *US, 1971*

- Do you think that for many of the girls the decision to work in a beaver movie—besides just being an economic decision—is a way of saying—"Why should I be afraid of this?" — Jefferson Poland and Valerie Alison, *The Records of the San Francisco Sexual Freedom League*, p. 75, 1971
- [S]he was back down on Main Street competing with beaver movies between reels, and taxi dancing part-time down the street at the ballroom. — Joseph Wambaugh, *The Blue Knight*, p. 21, 1973
- The first beaver movies—whose main attraction was the visible pubic region of the women (and later men) who posed for them—were nothing more than short loops, several loops making up a show[.] — Kenneth Turan and Stephen E. Zito, *Sinema*, p. 77, 1974

beaver patrol *noun*

girl-watching *US, 1967*

- — *Current Slang*, p. 1, Summer 1967

beaver picture *noun*

a movie, the main attraction of which is a number of shots of women's genitals; a photograph of a woman's genitals *US, 1769*

- For those interested in semantics, the pictures with the legs in normal position showing only the pubic bush are called "beaver pictures" but if the legs are spread apart and the camera angle shows the vaginal aperture or clitoris, then it is called "spread." — *Screw*, p. 16, 18th August 1969
- Sells, I figure he sells beaver pictures. — George V. Higgins, *The Friends of Eddie Doyle*, p. 171, 1971
- Her "co-star" in the beaver picture? — *The Big Lebowski*, 1998

beaver red *noun*

a photograph or film depiction of a woman's vulva, showing a hint of pink but not the vaginal lips *US, 1970*

- No, that's what we call "beaver red." It's not prosecutable as long as you don't have the lips showing or hanging out all through the picture. — Roger Blake, *The Porno Movies*, p. 195, 1970

beaver-shooting *noun*

a concerted voyeuristic effort to find women whose genitals or pubic hair can be seen *US, 1970*

- I better explain about beaver-shooting. A beaver-shooter is, at bottom, a Peeping Tom. It can be anything from peering over the top of the dugout to look up dresses to hanging from the fire escape on the twentieth floor of some hotel to look into a window. — Jim Bouton, *Ball Four*, p. 36, 1970
- — Helen Dahlskog (Editor), *A Dictionary of Contemporary and Colloquial Usage*, p. 6, 1972

beaver shot *noun*

a photograph or filming of a woman's genitals *US, 1970*

In the early 1960s LA-based band The Periscopes recorded a rock'n'roll tune called "Beaver Shot" which was banned from the radio after two plays.

- In commercial film prior to this, other than documentaries on nudism, a view of the pubic region—the "beaver shot" it was called—occurred only as a brief glimpse[.] — Terry Southern, *Blue Movie*, p. 24, 1970
- This was about all that softcore consisted of at that point, except for the famed "beaver shot." — Tina Russell, *Porno Star*, p. 22, 1973
- A beaver shot taken with a 60-second camera takes very little artistic ability. — Stephen Ziplow, *The Film Maker's Guide to Pornography*, p. 142, 1977
- What's there to steal? Two bucks and a beaver shot. — *The Breakfast Club*, 1985

beaver-with-stick *noun*

full frontal male nudity *US, 1977*

- Back in the good old days, like the middle '60s, when female "beaver" films were all the rage, the industry catered primarily to the heterosexual trade. Oh, sure, there was the occasional male "beaver-with-stick" flick, but these were the exception. — *San Francisco Chronicle*, 24th January 1977

bebe *noun*

crack cocaine *US, 1994*

Possibly an initialism of **BEAUTIFUL BOULDERS**.

- — US Department of Justice, *Street Terms*, October 1994

bebop *verb*

to take part in gang fights *US, 1965*

- This was one way of putting down bebopping. When you were on horse, you didn't have time for it. — Claude Brown, *Manchild in the Promised Land*, p. 153, 1965

be careful, Matt!

used as a humorous caution *US, 1979*

A signature line of Miss Kitty Russell (portrayed by Amanda Blake) to Marshall Matt Dillon on the television Western *Gunsmoke* (CBS, 1955–75). Repeated with referential humor.

- "Be careful, Matt." Hendrick watched Link fixing him a drink. — Jeremy Burnham, *Children of the Stones*, p. 140, 1979

bed *noun*

▸ **put to bed**

to watch someone go home before burglarizing their business *US, 1972*

- We saw him go into his house and that's what we call putting them to bed. So we knew it was perfectly safe. — Harry King, *Box Man*, p. 49, 1972

bedbug *noun*

a person who is somewhere between amusingly eccentric and alarmingly disturbed *US, 1832*

- "Agh, Clancy is a bedbug," Solly said. — Evan Hunter, *The Blackboard Jungle*, p. 149, 1954

bedbug row; bedbug alley *noun*

a poor, crime-ridden area in a city *US, 1969*

- [T]he central business area and the red-light districts, variously known as the Levee, Hair-Trigger Block, Little Cheyenne, Gamblers' Alley, Bad Lands, Bedbug Row and Hell's Half Acre. — *Chicago Tribune*, p. 7C, 25th January 1987

bed-check Charlie *noun*

a pilot flying night air raids against US troops *US, 1964*

Korean war usage.

- Although these night raids did no major damage, they did affect the morale of the ground troops, who called the raiders "Bed Check Charlies." — Don Lawson, *The United States in the Korean War*, p. 66, 1964

beddy *noun*

1 in circus and carnival usage, the place where a person spends the winter or off-season *US, 1981*

- — Don Wilmeth, *The Language of American Popular Entertainment*, p. 19, 1981

2 a promiscuous girl *US, 1989*

- — Pamela Munro, *U.C.L.A. Slang*, p. 20, 1989

beddy-bye; beddy byes; beddie-byes *noun*

sleep or bed *UK, 1906*

A nursery term, used for effect elsewhere.

- [I]t's two o'clock in the afternoon by golly, and he, for one, is going to take his little chicks home to beddy-by. — John M. Murtagh and Sara Harris, *Cast the First Stone*, p. 13, 1957
- Mr. Cherry said he had a hard day's driving to Spokane tomorrow to purchase some varnish wholesale and he would have to go beddy-bye now. He said beddy-bye. We said goodnight to him[.] — Clancy Sigal, *Going Away*, p. 95, 1961
- Well, I better get my ass beddy-by. I'll see you in the morning. — Elmore Leonard, *Gold Coast*, p. 71, 1980
- And she's wearing her Frederick's of Hollywood silkies for beddy-bye. — Joseph Wambaugh, *Fugitive Nights*, p. 82, 1992

bed-hop *verb*

to habitually have casual sex *US, 1974*

- HI! GREAT WEEK! Mine was really great—back bed-hopping again. — *Screw*, p. 2, 4th March 1974

bed house *noun*

a brothel *US, 1973*

- — Ruth Todasco et al., *The Intelligent Woman's Guide to Dirty Words*, p. 2, 1973

Bedouin Bob *noun*

any Saudi; any desert nomad *US, 1991*

Gulf war usage.

- — *American Speech*, p. 384, Winter 1991: "Among the new words"

bedpan commando *noun*

a medic in the Medical Corps *US, 1948*

- Bedpan Commando: Slang for medical corps man. — Anna Marjorie Taylor, *The Language of World War II*, p. 33, 1948
- I was transferred to Fort Sam Houston to be turned into a Surgical Technician or, as we called it, a Bedpan Commando. — Orris Keiser, *How Can I Help You?*, p. 14, 2006

Bedrock *noun*

a common name for US armed forces camps during the Persian Gulf war *US, 1990*

An allusion to the prehistoric town on the cartoon television series *The Flinstones* (ABC, 1960–66), home to quarry worker Fred Flintstone and his wife Wilma.

- They live in a tent city nicknamed "Bedrock," for Fred Flintstone's home town, and eat two hot meals a day and packaged rations for the third in a mess tent dubbed "Dino's Diner." — *Washington Post*, p. A20, 1st October 1990

bedroom eyes *noun*

a sensual face and eyes that convey desire *US, 1947*

- "Those dreamy eyes—" she said. "Bedroom eyes, that's what they are." — Willard Motley, *Knock on Any Door*, p. 123, 1947
- Pretty, blonde Mrs. Acaro sees beyond the end of his nose, thinks the most striking thing about his face are his "big, brown bedroom eyes." — *Time*, p. 78, 17th May 1948
- They all have to have bedroom eyes. — Raymond Chandler, *The Little Sister*, p. 42, 1949
- "Why not stay here?" Nancy said and added, looking up at him with the bedroom brown eyes, "No one's home." — Elmore Leonard, *The Big Bounce*, p. 41, 1969

Bed-Stuy *nickname*

the Bedford-Stuyvesant neighborhood of New York City *US, 1989*

The area is the epitome of urban American poverty.

- G.B. ran back up to his neighborhood (Bed-Sty New Yawk) for a bag of bad smoke[.] — Odie Hawkins, *Men Friends*, p. 51, 1989
- It's one of the original ghettos. I grew up there. Bed-Stuy is such a ghetto that in Billy Joel's song, "You May Be Right," he brags about walking through Bedford-Stuyvesant by himself: "I walked through a combat zone." — Chris Rock, *Rock This*, p. 40, 1997

bee *noun*

1 a drug addiction *US, 1960*
Also known as "a bee that stings."
- A bee is what he calls his habit; it's always stinging him to get a fix. — Clarence Cooper Jr., *The Scene*, p. 54, 1960
- — David Maurer and Victor Vogel, *The Slang and Jargon of Drugs and Drinks*, p. 387, 1973

2 a barbiturate or other central nervous system depressant, especially Nembutal™ *US, 1963*
A Nembutal™ capsule is commonly known as a **YELLOW JACKET**, hence the "bee."
- I have a fine connection here, baby, and we'll get tanked on bees and pods and then I'll really show you a sex-scene. — John Rechy, *City of Night*, p. 184, 1963

3 in a deck of playing cards, a joker, especially when the deck is made by the playing card manufacturer Bee *US, 1988*
- — George Percy, *The Language of Poker*, p. 8, 1988

bee *verb*

to beg *US, 1962*
- — Joseph E. Ragen and Charles Finston, *Inside the World's Toughest Prison*, p. 790, 1962

bee-bee *noun*

crack cocaine *US, 1993*
- — Peter Johnson, *Dictionary of Street Alcohol and Drug Terms*, p. 17, 1993

beef *noun*

1 a complaint, an argument, a fight *US, 1899*
- These fellers have a beef, boss. — Chester Gould, *Dick Tracy Meets the Night Crawler*, pp. 61–62, 1945
- Man, I tell you we had some real beefs. — Hunter S. Thompson, *Hell's Angels*, p. 40, 1966
- If while living in the Honor Unit you get into a "beef" which results in action against you by the disciplinary committee, one of the certain penalties is that you are immediately kicked out of No. 5 Building. — Eldridge Cleaver, *Soul on Ice*, p. 52, 1968
- Mr. Wilson apparently has a beef against society. A serious beef. — Carl Hiaasen, *Tourist Season*, p. 195, 1986

2 conflict, feuding *US, 2002*
A wider use of the previous sense.
- Their deaths [Tupac Shakur and Notorious B.I.G] forever alter the way we look at beef, death—and life—in hip-hop. — *The Source*, p. 133, March 2002

3 an arrest or criminal charge *US, 1928*
- Satin picked up three beefs in six months, and since the High One was still an undercover bondsman he raised her each time. — A.S. Jackson, *Gentleman Pimp*, p. 121, 1973
- [P]risoners with felony beefs outranked the other prisoners. — Bobby Seale, *A Lonely Rage*, p. 268, 1978
- He's got all these drunk-driving beefs. — James Ellroy, *White Jazz*, p. 33, 1992

4 in prison, a written reprimand *US, 1967*
- They should have given you a medal instead of a beef. — Malcolm Braly, *On the Yard*, p. 183, 1967
- — Paul Glover, *Words from the House of the Dead*, 1974

5 the penis *US, 1980*
- — Edith A. Folb, *runnin' down some lines*, p. 229, 1980
- I laid her down on the sofa and placed my beef directly over her soaking split. — Renay Jackson, *Oaktown Devil*, p. 32, 1998
- The boy is masturbating [...] Beef Strokin' off[.] — Erica Orloff and JoAnn Baker, *Dirty Little Secrets*, p. 89, 2001

6 in homosexual society, a masculine man or a member of the armed forces whatever his gender preference *US, 1972*
- So he married a real girl, huh? Well, I guess he preferred fish to beef. — Bruce Rodgers, *The Queens' Vernacular*, p. 30, 1972

7 a dramatic and unintended ending of a surf ride *US, 1991*
- Dude, check out these hot beefs. — Trevor Cralle, *The Surfin'ary*, p. 9, 1991

8 a backwards fall off a skateboard *US, 1997*
- — Vann Wesson, *Generation X Field Guide and Lexicon*, p. 18, 1997

▸ **ride the beef**
to refuse to implicate others when arrested or interrogated *US, 1954*
- "I heard you rode the beef for a lot of other people when you partner squealed." — Caryl Chessman, *Cell 2456 Death Row*, p. 88, 1954
- "Yeah, ride the beef, man. Ride that motherfucker down." — James Lee Burke, *Dixie City Jam*, p. 214, 1994

beef *verb*

1 to argue, to fight *US, 1997*
- But Boys Village is way worse than Hickey, filled with D.C. niggers who like to beef with the Baltimore boys. — David Simon and Edward Burns, *The Corner*, p. 119, 1997

2 to complain *US, 1866*
From an earlier sense: to shout.
- Everything is going wrong here. My boy's family has beefed to the fuzz. — William Burroughs, *Letters to Allen Ginsberg 1953–1957*, p. 28, 13th April 1954: Letter to Jack Kerouac
- Some bitch in Newton Division beefed a policeman last week. Says he took her in a park and tried to lay her. — Joseph Wambaugh, *The New Centurions*, p. 54, 1970
- "Have you been beefed before?" "When I was on the police department a prisoner spit in my face. I was accused of punching him in the stomach so hard it knocked him out." — Gerald Petievich, *To Live and Die in L.A.*, p. 64, 1983

3 to have sex *US, 1975*
- — *American Speech*, p. 56, Spring–Summer 1975: "Razorback slang"

4 in prison, to issue a disciplinary reprimand *US, 1967*
- [O]n such nights he would literally beef you because he didn't like your looks. — Malcolm Braly, *On the Yard*, p. 70, 1967

beef and shrapnel *noun*

in the Vietnam war, a meal of beef and potatoes *US, 1972*
- I was eating sliced beef and potatoes—beef and shrapnel in the vernacular. — William Pelfrey, *The Big V*, p. 40, 1972
- I had beef and shrapnel for supper; Fi Bait had spaghetti. — Melvin Small, *International War*, p. 83, 1989

beefcake *noun*

1 artistic or photographic depictions of nude or partially nude muscular men *US, 1949*
The gender equivalent of **CHEESECAKE**.
- — Roger Blake, *The American Dictionary of Sexual Terms*, p. 14, 1964
- Doubleday Book Shops have run smirking ads for The Gay Cookbook and newsstands make room for "beefcake" magazines of male nudes. — Joe David Brown, *Sex in the '60s*, p. 66, 1968
- Lesbian periodicals, male "beefcake," pamphlets, cards, buttons, and a host of fine fiction on the homosexual theme adorn the shelves of Craig's bookstore. — *Screw*, 21st February 1969
- True, the beefcake cowboy murals struck a somewhat citified note in the overall scheme of things, but Michael didn't mind. — Armistead Maupin, *Further Tales of the City*, p. 31, 1982

2 a muscular man *US, 1949*
- — Roger Blake, *The American Dictionary of Sexual Terms*, p. 14, 1964
- Male, 26, trim, smooth-skinned, is hung-up on beefcake guys who are well-hung and wear lace briefs. — Emile Nytrate, *Underground Ads*, p. 15, 1971

beef curtains *noun*

the labia *US, 1991*
- It tastes really weird though, all those cheesy deposits in her beef curtains. — alt.tasteless, 3rd October 1991
- I parted her beef curtains with my tongue. — Stewart Home, *69 Things to Do with a Dead Princess*, p. 10, 2003
- After he universally maligned "performance" at the VMA's on Sunday, the former pop star went out partying at the Bellagio in Vegas and showed the world her hairless beef curtains, cuz she knows we just can't get enough of that. — perezhilton.com, 10th September 2007

beefer *noun*

a constant and tiresome complainer *US, 1950*
- — *The Annals of the American Academy of Political and Social Sciences*, p. 120, May 1950
- Most of the guests were pretty good about the blizzard, like they lent each other newspapers and so on, but the other people, the beefers, just hung around the lobby and stared out at the snow going up higher and higher, and made trouble. — Richard Condon, *Prizzi's Honor*, p. 24, 1982
- — George Percy, *The Language of Poker*, p. 8, 1988

beef injection; hot beef injection *noun*
sexual intercourse *US, 1968*

- [W]hat Rollo really needs is love, affection, understanding, etc. In other words, a beef injection. — Angelo d'Arcangelo, *The Homosexual Handbook*, p. 229, 1968
- Robert A. Wilson, *Playboy's Book of Forbidden Words*, p. 33, 1972
- Pamela Munro, *U.C.L.A. Slang*, p. 77, 1989
- Michael Dalton Johnson, *Talking Trash with Redd Foxx*, p. 70, 1994

beef trust *noun*
1 in sports, a group of large athletes *US, 1928*

- Defensively the 49ers came up with a beef trust on the line that really held the vaunted Browns in check. — *San Francisco News*, p. 11, 29th August 1958
- Lincoln Line More Like Beef Trust [Headline] — *San Francisco Examiner*, p. 61, 17th September 1970

2 a chorus of large women who entertain men *US, 1931*

- The beef trust was out in full force—these ladies were all shaped like barrels, wherever there wasn't a crease in their meat there was a dimple. — Mezz Mezzrow, *Really the Blues*, p. 91, 1946
- Now touring the burlesque houses is a troupe known as "The Beef Trust." The women in this aggregation weigh 250 pounds or over. — *San Francisco Examiner*, 21st June 1948

beef up *verb*
to enhance someone or something, to strengthen someone or something *US, 1944*

- I got all beefed up—and then got sick in Poland—and the beef evaporated. — Philip Wylie, *Opus 21*, p. 280, 1949
- Say I got an idea for the recording, I want to lay in some more tracks, beef it up. — Elmore Leonard, *Be Cool*, p. 8, 1999

beefy *adjective*
(used of a shot in croquet) long and hard *US, 1977*

- James Charlton and William Thompson, *Croquet*, p. 155, 1977

beehive *verb*
▶ **beehive it**
to leave hurriedly *US, 1991*
Vietnam war use.

- Linda Reinberg, *In the Field*, p. 19, 1991

beehive round *noun*
an artillery shell that scatters small nails with fins instead of shrapnel, first used in Vietnam in 1964 *US, 1991*

- The cannister, or beehive, rounds, were especially effective for final, close-in defensive fire. — J.D. Coleman, *Incursion*, p. 77, 1991

beeitch *noun*
used as a synonym of "bitch," especially as a term for a woman *US, 1963*

- "Of course. From the moment that little bee-itch moved in on us." — Frederick Kohner, *Gidget Goes to Rome*, p. 59, 1963
- Beeitch, if you ain't got no kinda chronic, yo punk ass gots to go! — Snoop Doggy Dogg, *A Day in the Life of Snoop Doggy Dogg [Cover art]*, 1993

Bee More *nickname*
Baltimore, Maryland *US, 1989*

- Ellen C. Bellone (Editor), *Dictionary of Slang*, p. 2, 1989

been around
sexually experienced *US, 1979*

- Brad and Dell both told me "for my own good" that Deb "has been around." — Beatrice Sparks (writing as "Anonymous"), *Jay's Journal*, p. 19, 1979

beep *noun*
a homing or tracking device *US, 1989*

- "There's a fucking bug or beep on it." — Gerard O'Neill, *The Under Boss*, p. 213, 1989

beep beep!
pay attention! *US, 1961*

- [U]sed in the expression "beep beep to X." — *San Francisco Examiner*, p. 21, 12th December 1961

beeper *noun*
1 the telephone *US, 1968*

- "Here's why I'm on the beeper, Ron," said the telephone voice on the all-night radio show. — Joan Didion, *Slouching Toward Bethlehem*, p. 220, 1968

2 an electronic paging device *US, 1970*

- He had an answering service and an electronic beeper that fit onto his belt. The beeper didn't make Keyes feel particularly important; every shyster lawyer, dope dealer, and undercover agent in Dade County wore one. — Carl Hiassen, *Tourist Season*, p. 33, 1986
- Max prefers to be called on the tiny beeper attached to his belt. — Terry Williams, *The Cocaine Kids*, p. 31, 1989
- Besides, everybody had a beeper these days. — Richard Price, *Clockers*, p. 6, 1992
- They [call girls] drive Porsches, live in condos, have stockbrokers, carry beepers, you know, like Nancy Allen in Dressed to Kill. — *True Romance*, 1993

beer *noun*
in the illegal production of alcohol, fermented grain, or sugar mash *US, 1887*

- David W. Maurer, *Kentucky Moonshine*, p. 114, 1974

beer belly *noun*
the protruding stomach of an excessive beer drinker *US, 1960*

- [A] large, brawny man about the shade of a chestnut with a crop of snow-white hair, a white billygoat goatee and a beer belly that hung out over his belt. — Robert Gover, *Poorboy at the Party*, p. 37, 1966

beer blast *noun*
a party organized around the consumption of beer *US, 1967*

- Not like the Socs, who jump greasers and wreck houses and throw beer blasts for kicks[.] — S.E. Hinton, *The Outsiders*, p. 5, 1967
- Collin Baker et al., *College Undergraduate Slang Study Conducted at Brown University*, p. 78, 1968

beer bottle glasses *noun*
thick eye glasses *US, 1979*

- "That ski-jumper fellow with the beer-bottle glasses and scary hair." — James Hawkins, *No Cherubs for Melanie*, p. 166, 2002

beer bust *noun*
a party organized around the consumption of beer *US, 1913*

- Police said they were called to the picnic grounds of Enrico Rosotti, favorite "beer bust" locale of Stanford students, and there found the sextette hilariously dancing about the flaming tables. — *San Francisco Examiner*, p. 32, 2nd March 1948
- Have a real beer bust, like we used to in the old days, and make a tour of the burly houses. — Jim Thompson, *Roughneck*, p. 119, 1954
- Two weeks ago the kids had a beer-bust on the beach. — Ann Landers, *Ann Landers Talks to Teen-Agers About Sex*, p. 120, 1963
- He was the only one of them who didn't like to join the beer busts after work. — Joseph Wambaugh, *Lines and Shadows*, p. 41, 1984

beer can grenade *noun*
a crude hand grenade fashioned by the Viet Cong, packed inside a beer can *US, 1990*

- Gregory Clark, *Words of the Vietnam War*, p. 53, 1990
- On the walk along deserted Grave Street toward the company, Moytz attacked Baker Company's dumpster with a beer can grenade. — William Singley, *Bragg*, p. 178, 2006

beered; beered out *adjective*
drunk on beer *US, 1930*

- She was starting into her glass and did not notice him at first. "Get beered out?" — Harold Robbins, *Never Enough*, p. 148, 2002

beer flat *noun*
an apartment where beer is sold privately and illegally *US, 1980*

- It was shortly prior to the repeal of prohibition and beer flats were popular. — Herbert Huncke, *The Evening Sun Turned Crimson*, p. 27, 1980

beer goggles *noun*
a drink-induced clouding of visual perception that enhances the sexual allure of previously unappealing companions *US, 1987*

- Connie Eble (Editor), *UNC-CH Campus Slang*, p. 1, Fall 1987
- Aside from inappropriate vomiting and public urination, one of the most puzzling effects are the "beer goggles" that accompany the latter stages of a bender. — *Drugs: An Adult Guide*, p. 32, December 2001

beer gut *noun*
the protruding stomach of an excessive beer drinker *AUSTRALIA, 1967*

- Reaney stood back with Pemberton as the director, a large, bearded man with a down-to-earth beer gut, spared Jake a few words. — Gordon Williams, *The Man Who Had Power Over Women*, p. 228, 1967
- "What's he look like? Regular old beer-gut dick?" "No, he's skinny almost." — Elmore Leonard, *City Primeval*, p. 54, 1980
- His pants hang perfectly flat, while out front his angry red beer gut balloons out like the front end of a '51 Studebaker. — C.D. Payne, *Youth in Revolt*, p. 10, 1993

beer run *noun*
a trip to a store to buy beer for a party *US, 1970*
- At supper I sat with the new girl, and that night she chose a study; I helped her move her stuff in[.] later, as somebody made a beer run, we chipped in[.] — Fielding Dawson, *The Black Mountain Book*, p. 27, 1970
- — *Current Slang*, p. 8, Spring 1971

beer-thirty *noun*
a fictional time of day, suggesting that a beer is overdue *US, 1980*
- — Don Alexander, *The Racer's Dictionary*, p. 10, 1980
- Their minds were on beer-thirty and lounge chairs, worried less about suspicious activity than asteroid collisions. — Tom Corcoran, *Octopus Alibi*, p. 242, 2003

beer up *verb*
to drink a great deal of beer *US, 1952*
- [T]he mechanics beering up with the guys and driving off to Detroit on a whim. — *New York Times Magazine*, 16th November 1952: This is the Beat Generation

bee shit *noun*
honey *US, 1984*
From the mistaken belief that bees defecate honey.
- She calls me "beeshit," 'cause I'm so sweet. — Ken Weaver, *Texas Crude*, p. 103, 1984

bee stings *noun*
small female breasts *US, 1964*
- — Roger Blake, *The American Dictionary of Sexual Terms*, p. 15, 1964
- — Michael Dalton Johnson, *Talking Trash with Redd Foxx*, p. 62, 1994

bee-stung *adjective*
(said of a woman) endowed with small breasts *US, 2005*
- For a look at Suzy's Qs, check out her striptease down to her bee-stung boobage[.] — Mr. Skin, *Mr. Skin's Skincyclopedia*, p. 14, 2005

beeswax *noun*
business *US, 1934*
- When I extricated myself from Brandon's arms and came home to take care of beeswax, I realized the full extent of my rebound. — Pamela Des Barres, *I'm With the Band*, p. 122, 1988

beetle *noun*
1 in horse racing, a poorly performing horse *US, 1915*
- — David W. Maurer, *Argot of the Racetrack*, p. 13, 1951
2 a female *US, 1931*
Circus and carnival usage.
- — Don Wilmeth, *The Language of American Popular Entertainment*, p. 20, 1981

beetle juice *noun*
soy sauce *US, 1972*
- He shook the little glass bottle and that beetle-juice came out real good for him[.] — Robert Byrne, *McGoorty*, p. 83, 1972

beevo *noun*
an alcoholic beverage *US, 1977*
- [S]ometimes longed for the uncomplicated life of lacrosse and rugby and hou-bro beevo parties, of happily hugging the toilet all night long with your barf buddies after draining a half-keg for no special occasion? — John Sayles, *Union Dues*, p. 279, 1977

beeyatch *noun*
used as an emphatic variation of "bitch," especially when used to a woman or as exclamation *US, 2001*
- One time for your mind, beeyatch[.] — Too $hort, *Tell the Feds*, 2001
- Cuz you ask the questions I got answers, beeyatch[.] — Ja Rule, *Survival of the Illest 2*, 2004

beezer *noun*
1 the nose *US, 1908*

- How many ways can you wrinkle your beezer? Do you show your teeth when you say the letter S? — Bruce Brooks, *The Moves Make the Man*, p. 62, 1984
2 in horse racing, a horse's nose *US, 1951*
- — David W. Maurer, *Argot of the Racetrack*, p. 13, 1951

before time *adverb*
long ago *US, 1982*
- "Befo' time I had real popolo kine hair, you know!" — Douglas Simonson, *Pidgin to da Max Hana Hou*, 1982

beg *noun*
in a telephone solicitation, the actual plea to purchase that which is being sold *US, 1959*
- — *American Speech*, pp. 150–151, May 1959: "Notes on the cant of the telephone confidence man"

behind *adjective*
1 imprisoned *US, 1961*
- Before I left Chicago he had been "behind" twice, once for car stealing and once, of all things, for bond forgery or something complicated like that. — Clancy Sigal, *Going Away*, p. 355, 1961
2 committed, dedicated *US, 1968*
- — Lewis Yablonsky, *The Hippie Trip*, p. 367, 1968

behind *preposition*
1 (of a drug) under the influence of *US, 1967*
- I could write behind STP, but not behind acid. — Joan Didion, *Slouching Toward Bethlehem*, p. 109, 1967
- — Edward I. Bloomquist, *Marijuana*, p. 333, 1971
- — Peter Johnson, *Dictionary of Street Alcohol and Drug Terms*, p. 17, 1993
- Simone de Beauvoir, whom I knew during her Nelson Algren period, worked very well behind absinthe, or its substitute, Pernod[.] — Terry Southern, *Now Dig This*, p. 206, 2001
2 as a result of *US, 1957*
- — Anthony Romeo, *The Language of Gangs*, p. 16, 4th December 1962
- "Well, I might have to go to jail for a while behind that roust." — Malcolm Braly, *Shake Him Till He Rattles*, p. 171, 1963
- Went to Q behind armed robbery. — Joseph Wambaugh, *The Blue Knight*, p. 27, 1973
- "That's outta line, dawg, falling behind some bitch snitch." — Jimmy Lerner, *You Got Nothing Coming*, p. 28, 2002

behind-the-behind *noun*
anal sex *US, 1967*
- — Dale Gordon, *The Dominion Sex Dictionary*, p. 27, 1967

beige *noun*
a light-skinned black person *US, 1945*
- — Lou Shelly, *Hepcats Jive Talk Dictionary*, p. 7, 1945
- Sweetheart, yo's as baij as they come. — Robert Gover, *JC Saves*, p. 68, 1968

beige *verb*
to chemically darken cocaine to give it the appearance of a purity that it does not possess *US, 1989*
- — Terry Williams, *The Cocaine Kids*, p. 135, 1989

beige frame *noun*
a light-skinned black woman *US, 1953*
- — Lavada Durst, *The Jives of Dr. Hepcat*, p. 11, 1953

be-in *noun*
an organized gathering for the celebration of counterculture lifestyles and values *US, 1967*
Originally applied to an event in San Francisco in January 1967, and then to similar events elsewhere. Organizers ("inspirers") of that event wrote: "When the Berkeley political activists and the love generation of the Haight Ashbury and thousands of young men and women from every state in the nation embrace at the gathering of the tribes for a Human Be-In at polo field in Golden Gate Park the spiritual revolution will be manifest and proven."
- And again, the beautiful thing about the Be-In was it had no leader-ship, it had no big financing, it will just grow automatically. — *The San Francisco Oracle*, 1967
- THE BEGINNING IS THE HUMAN BE-IN [Headline] — *Berkeley Barb*, p. 1, 6th January 1967
- Be-In. A kind of instant hippie evangelism. Park grass, open skies and trees is the usual church architecture. — Sidney Bernard, *This Way to the Apocalypse*, p. 58, 1968

- Like a super be-in, a live-in, real freedom. Wow! — *East Village Other*, 20th August 1969

bejabbers; bejabers *noun*
used as a jocular euphemism for "bejesus" *US, 1959*
- They arrived in time to be scared by a group of drunken townies beating the bejabbers out of three or four hippy boys they'd caught in the lot. — Nicholas Von Hoffman, *We Are The People Our Parents Warned Us Against*, p. 67, 1967
- Does he want, bejabers, to get me sacked for nothing? — Murphy Tom, *A Crucial Week in the Life of a Grocer's Assistant*, p. 155, 1989

bejesus; bejasus *noun*
used as a mild expletive *US, 1908*
An ameliorated "Jesus," originally recorded in 1908 but not widely used until the 1930s.
- I interviewed Garbo three times, and I will slap the bejesus out of anybody who says I didn't. — Earl Wilson, *I am Gazing Into My 8-Ball*, p. 63, 1945
- But stories about dykes bore the bejesus out of me. I just can't put myself in their shoes. — Truman Capote, *Breakfast at Tiffany's*, p. 21, 1958
- Did you know he got four purple hearts in Vietnam? Did he? Bejesus. — Doug Lang, *Freaks*, p. 21, 1973
- That Saturday morning, April Fool's Day, one of the lifeguards was impressing the bejesus out of a ride-along female citizen by whipping his boat into 180s on Fiesta Bay... — Joseph Wambaugh, *Floaters*, p. 22, 1996

bejiminy *noun*
used as a mild expletive *US, 1946*
- I like Rocky Graziano's way of belting the bejiminy out of his opponents without any shilly-shallying. — *San Francisco Examiner*, p. 14, 9th April 1946

Bela and Boris *noun*
in hold 'em poker, the two of clubs and the two of spades *US, 1996*
An allusion to Bela Lugosi and Boris Korloff of horror movie fame, with a nod to the horror that they visit upon a hand in hold 'em poker.
- — John Vorhaus, *The Big Book of Poker Slang*, p. 6, 1996

belch *noun*
a complaint *US, 1981*
Circus and carnival usage.
- — Don Wilmeth, *The Language of American Popular Entertainment*, p. 20, 1981

belch *verb*
to act as a police informer *US, 1901*
- — Vincent J. Monteleone, *Criminal Slang*, p. 20, 1949
- — Hyman E. Goldin et al., *Dictionary of American Underworld Lingo*, p. 25, 1950

belcher *noun*
a police informer *US, 1956*
- — *American Speech*, p. 99, May 1956: "Smugglers argot in the southwest"

bell *noun*
1 a hotel bellhop *US, 1973*
- "Three K, promo drinks and that stuff, tips for the bells," Schabb said. — George Higgins, *The Digger's Game*, p. 33, 1973
2 a telephone call *US, 1951*
Teen slang.
- — *Newsweek*, p. 28, 8th October 1951

▸ **on a bell**
in television and movie making, shooting a scene *US, 1990*
From the bell used on location to signal that shooting is about to begin.
- — Ralph S. Singleton, *Filmmaker's Dictionary*, p. 115, 1990

bell cow *noun*
in marketing, a popular, high-profit item *US, 1986*
- — Rachel S. Epstein and Nina Liebman, *Biz Speak*, p. 18, 1986

belle *noun*
a young and effeminate male homosexual *US, 1940*
- — Florida Legislative Investigation Committee (Johns Committee), *Homosexuality and Citizenship in Florida*, 1964

bell rope *noun*
the penis *US, 1969*
- — Eugene Landy, *The Underground Dictionary*, p. 31, 1971

bells!
used for expressing approval *US, 1948*
- — Robert S. Gould, *A Jazz Lexicon*, p. 17, 1964

bells and whistles *noun*
1 entertaining features that are not necessary to a computer program *US, 1983*
- "Now that we've got the basic program working, let's go back and add some bells and whistles." — Guy L. Steele et al., *The Hacker's Dictionary*, p. 29, 1983
2 extra features designed by underwriters to attract investors in a bond issue *US, 1988*
- — Kathleen Odean, *High Steppers, Fallen Angels, and Lollipops*, p. 20, 1988

Bell Telephone hour *noun*
a session of torture in which US soldiers used the electricity from field telephones to shock suspected Viet Cong *US, 1981*
The term suggests a television program, not genital-oriented electric torture.
- "Come on back, it's the Bell Telephone Hour. We're wiring somebody up." — Mark Baker, *Nam*, p. 173, 1981
- One of the favorite forms of torture was referred to as the "Bell Telephone Hour." — Lynda Van Devanter, *Home Before Morning*, p. 156, 1983

belly *noun*
1 a fat person *US, 1997*
- The labels were cruel: Gimp, Limpy–go-fetch, Crip, Lift-one-drag one, etc. Pint, Half-a-man, Peewee, Shorty, Lardass, Pork, Blubber, Belly, Blimp. Nuke-knob, Skinhead, Baldy. Four-eyes, Specs, Coke bottles. — *San Francisco Examiner*, p. A15, 28th July 1997
2 the swell in a thicker-than-normal surfboard *US, 1963*
- — Grant W. Kuhns, *On Surfing*, p. 113, 1963

bellyache *noun*
any small-town newspaper *US, 1975*
- Anything in the Bellyache this week? — John Gould, *Maine Lingo*, p. 11, 1975

bellyache *verb*
to complain *US, 1881*
- They get that idea in their heads, all they can do is stand there and bellyache Gospel at you[.] — George V. Higgins, *The Friends of Eddie Doyle*, p. 39, 1971
- Okay, hogs, I've listened to you bellyache about moving to this new town. This said bellyaching will end as of 0859 hours[.] — Lewis John Carlino, *The Great Santini*, 1979
- Now he's bellyaching in Paris and L.A. and Honolulu about the ropes and the canvas and a short count. — Bill Cardoso, *The Maltese Sangweech*, p. 304, 1984
- Quit your bellyaching, Hawkins. — *Gone in 60 Seconds*, 1992

bellyacher *noun*
a complainer *US, 1930*
- My dad wasn't a bellyacher[.] — *St. Petersburg Times*, 6th March 2004

belly board *noun*
in television and movie making, a low camera platform *US, 1990*
- — Ralph S. Singleton, *Filmmaker's Dictionary*, p. 16, 1990

belly bomber *noun*
greasy food, especially a greasy hamburger *US, 1987*
- "The next thing you know, you've got a bag full of belly-bombers on the seat of your car, and you're stuffing your face with them again." — Glenn Savan, *White Palace*, p. 13, 1987

bellybump *verb*
1 to jostle; to shove; to rough up *US, 1961*
- Most of the time, Slim said, all he did was write and mimeograph leaflets, though once or twice he was called upon to "belly bump" in the picket lines. — Clancy Sigal, *Going Away*, p. 83, 1961
2 to ride a sled face down *US, 1912*
- — Charles F. Haywood, *Yankee Dictionary*, p. 10, 1963
- — Claudio R. Salvucci, *The Philadelphia Dialect Dictionary*, p. 30, 1996

bellybuster *noun*
a greasy hamburger or other food likely to provoke indigestion *US, 1981*
- So I get myself one of Danny's bellybusters there, that a self-respecting do would not eat, and I ate it all[.] — George V. Higgins, *The Rat on Fire*, p. 102, 1981

belly fiddle *noun*
a guitar *US, 1970*
- — Clarence Major, *Dictionary of Afro-American Slang*, p. 25, 1970

belly flop *noun*
a dive into the water stomach first, intentionally or not *US, 1895*
- California's greatest exponent of the calculated belly-flop [comic diver Norman Hanley] had forgotten to eat breakfast. — *San Francisco Examiner*, p. 20, 1st September 1957
- Biggest splash in the world, according to the judges in Vancouver, B.C., where the fifth annual World Belly-Flop Championships were held, is made by Robin Gentile. — *San Francisco Examiner and Chronicle, This World*, p. 25, 12th August 1979

belly flopper *noun*
a rifleman shooting from a prone position *US, 1957*
- — *American Speech*, p. 192, October 1957: "Some colloquialisms of the handgunner"

belly gas *noun*
air injected into the abdominal cavity to raise the diaphragm *US, 1961*
- — *American Speech*, pp. 145–148, May 1961: "The spoken language of medicine; argot, slang, cant"

belly habit *noun*
severe stomach cramping suffered during withdrawal from a drug addiction; an opiate addiction *US, 1946*
- Belly habit: an opium habit that, unlike the head type, affects the addict in the stomach. — Mezz Mezzrow, *Really the Blues*, p. 371, 1946
- — Clarence Major, *Dictionary of Afro-American Slang*, p. 25, 1970

belly hit *noun*
in poker, a card drawn that completes an inside straight *US, 1951*
- — *American Speech*, p. 97, May 1951: "The vocabulary of poker"
- — Albert H. Morehead, *The Complete Guide to Winning Poker*, p. 256, 1967

bellyman *noun*
the member of a military helicopter crew who coordinates communication between the pilot and the troops being transported *US, 1992*
- The bellyman signaled me to stand in the door. — Larry Chambers, *Recondo*, p. 1, 1992

belly queen *noun*
a male homosexual who prefers face-to-face intercourse *US, 1965*
- — Robert A. Wilson, *Playboy's Book of Forbidden Words*, p. 33, 1972

belly ride *noun*
sexual intercourse *US, 1993*
- — Kenn "Naz" Young, *Naz's Dictionary of Teen Slang*, p. 7, 1993
- Roland decided he would find a way in, even if it meant forgoing the belly ride in Berkeley. — Stephen J. Cannell, *Runaway Heart*, p. 34, 2004

bellyrubber *noun*
a slow song in which partners dance close to each other *US, 1992*
- The blast of the music ended for a few counts before going on to a slower piece, a bona fide Chicago belly rubber. — Odie Hawkins, *Black Chicago*, p. 138, 1992

belly-stick; stick *noun*
in a confidence swindle involving fixed gambling, a confederate who appears to win consistently *US, 1940*
- I said, "I'll learn fast. I'll be the best stick you ever saw." — Iceberg Slim (Robert Beck), *Trick Baby*, p. 91, 1969
- "Kid, there isn't a helluva lot a belly-stick has to know. All you do is keep your belly against the joint cointer and let me make lucky on the wheel." — Iceberg Slim (Robert Beck), *Trick Baby*, p. 92, 1969

belly up *verb*
to approach and stand against something, usually a bar *US, 1907*
- [B]y the time they hit the doorway I bellied up to the bar, put a foot on the rail, one hand casually resting on the back of Susie's chair. — Larry Heinemann, *Close Quarters*, p. 175, 1977
- The road crews belly up to the bar, swilling mugs of Pabst Blue Ribbon on tap[.] — Larry Heinemann, *Paco's Story*, p. 62, 1990

belly-up *adjective*
bankrupt, out of business; dead *US, 1920*
- Air Control Union Goes Belly Up [Headline] — *San Francisco Chronicle*, p. 10, 3rd July 1982
- Your Uncle Milton lost all his money in a Puerto Rican condominium that went belly up. — *Sleepless in Seattle*, 1993
- The other Master Lee dropped the business in his lap just before he was about to go belly up. — Odie Hawkins, *Lost Angeles*, p. 25, 1994

bellywash *noun*
1 any alcoholic drink *US, 1972*
- Most of the stupid things I have done in my life I can blame on the bellywash. — Robert Byrne, *McGoorty*, p. 147, 1972
2 a soft drink, soda; colored water *US, 1926*
Originally applied to a weak drink, and then to soda.
- Many B-girls ask for "sloe gin," which is a signal to the bartender that they want some colored water ("belly wash") or tea. — Charles Winick, *The Lively Commerce*, p. 171, 1971
- So we're waiting for this kid to bring us some bellywash. — Joe Eszterhas, *Charlie Simpson's Apocalypse*, p. 36, 1973
- It's hotter than the hubs of hell today! Whatd'ya say we stop off over here and get us a bellywash? — Ken Weaver, *Texas Crude*, p. 103, 1984

belly-whop *verb*
in sledding, to dive stomach first onto the sled *US, 1955*
- There is always plenty of ice and snow for "belly-whopping." — *San Francisco Call-Bulletin*, 17th March 1955
- Belly whopping while under the influence, Sarge. — *New Yorker*, p. 53, 28th February 1968
- That was why I took the kids out to bellywhop—I was high. — John A. Williams, *The Angry Ones*, p. 153, 1969

belt *noun*
1 a gulp, especially of strong alcohol *US, 1922*
- Mrs. Larkin cried a little too and took Guido out in the garage and gave him a belt from a pint bottle of Schenley hidden behind the skid chains. — Max Shulman, *Rally Round the Flag, Boys!*, p. 14, 1957
- After a frustrating day at the office a couple of belts lift me out of the dumps. — Lenny Bruce, *How to Talk Dirty and Influence People*, p. 46, 1965
- Give me a drink, fella. Gimme a belt of Scotch. — Edwin Torres, *Q & A*, p. 51, 1977
- Hard day at the job, no lunch maybe, get so fuckin' pissed off you don't want any dinner, only thing on your mind's a good couple of belts, huh? — George V. Higgins, *The Rat on Fire*, p. 74, 1981
2 the first, strong effect of a drug *US, 1948*
- [W]hite women learned where they could get a "belt," a "jolt," or "gow." — Jack Lait and Lee Mortimer, *New York Confidential*, pp. 103–104, 1948

belt buckle polisher *noun*
a song suited for slow dancing *US, 1984*
- Now here's a belt buckle polisher, so all you lovers can dance cheek to cheek ... to cheek ... to cheek... — Ken Weaver, *Texas Crude*, p. 103, 1984

belted *adjective*
drunk or drug-intoxicated *US, 1970*
- — William D. Alsever, *Glossary for the Establishment and Other Uptight People*, p. 15, December 1970

Beltway commando *noun*
any military bureaucrat working in Washington D.C *US, 1991*
Gulf war usage.
- — *American Speech*, p. 384, Winter 1991: "Among the new words"

bench *noun*
a youth gang *US, 1951*
- — *American Speech*, p. 194, October 1951: "A study of reformatory argot"

bender *noun*
1 a prolonged session of hard drinking *US, 1845*
- Frisco Kate, who was en route to New York on a bender, came in there accompanied by a young pug she had picked up. — Jack Lait and Lee Mortimer, *Chicago Confidential*, pp. 30–31, 1950
- I was on a 5-day bender and got home long after the appointment you made to meet Nov. 25 at 3. — Jack Kerouac, *Jack Kerouac Selected Letters 1957–1969*, p. 191, 28th November 1958: Letter to Stan Issacs
- You go on a bender after all those years, it's like all that sober time never was. — Richard Price, *Clockers*, p. 274, 1992

2 a male homosexual who plays the passive role in anal sex; a homosexual *US, 1965*
- — *The Guild Dictionary of Homosexual Terms*, p. 3, 1965

bend over, brown eyes
used as a humorous instruction to a patient about to undergo a rectal examination *US, 1989*
- — *Maledicta*, p. 31, 1988–1989: "Medical maledicta from San Francisco"

bends and motherfuckers *noun*
the squat-thrust exercise drill *US, 1981*
Vietnam war usage. In gentler times, known as a "burpee."
- "You look like shit, so we're going to do a little PT now. Bends and motherfuckers. Many, many, many of them." — Mark Barker, *Nam*, p. 19, 1981

benefit *noun*
any hardship or unpleasant feature of army life *US, 1968*
Used with obvious irony.
- — Carl Fleischhauer, *A Glossary of Army Slang*, p. 3, 1968

Ben Franklin *noun*
a $100 bill *US, 1990*
From the engraving on the bill.
- Winnie looked up sharply when Buster, still staring at the pile of money, said, "That's a lot of Ben Franklins." — Joseph Wambaugh, *The Golden Orange*, p. 108, 1990

be nice!
used by US troops in Vietnam when caught by surprise or provoked by another *US, 1967*
- Sounds of Vietnam: The city: Be nice. — Ken Abood, *How to Live in Vietnam for less than $.10 a day*, p. 102, 1967
- — *Maledicta*, p. 257, Summer/Winter 1982: "Viet-speak"

benies *noun*
benefits *US, 1970*
- There sure are the benies if you don't have an education. — Darryl Ponicsan, *The Last Detail*, p. 33, 1970

Benjamin; Benjie; Benji *noun*
a $100 bill *US, 1985*
From the engraved portrait of Benjamin Franklin on the bill.
- Just go blow five benjies and stop chewing on me. — Stephen Cannell, *Big Con*, p. 208, 1997
- — Puff Daddy and the Family, *It's All About the Benjamins*, 1997
- "Fifty Grovers," I said. "Is that more than five hundred Benjamins?" — Dan Jenkins, *The Money-Whipped Steer-Job Three-Jack Give-Up Artist*, p. 235, 2001
- He dropped three stacks of Benjamins on the table. The air tightened up. — Tracy Funches, *Pimpnosis*, p. 62, 2002
- [H]avin' a Benz and a fat knot of Benji's definitely helps. — *The Source*, p. 218, March 2002

bennie *noun*
a female prostitute's customer who prefers to perform oral sex on the prostitute *US, 1964*
- — Roger Blake, *The American Dictionary of Sexual Terms*, p. 16, 1964
- — Robert A. Wilson, *Playboy's Book of Forbidden Words*, p. 34, 1972

bennie God *noun*
the sun *US, 1965*
- I learned, with the advent of the "Bennie God" to make an acceptable "bennie machine" out of aluminum foil, and use it on the flat back porch every afternoon during the spring semester to "catch a few rays" while downing some frosties. — John Nichols, *The Sterile Cuckoo*, p. 60, 1965

bennie machine *noun*
a reflector used while sunbathing *US, 1965*
- I learned, with the advent of the "Bennie God" to make an acceptable "bennie machine" out of aluminum foil, and use it on the flat back porch every afternoon during the spring semester to "catch a few rays" while downing some frosties. — John Nichols, *The Sterile Cuckoo*, p. 60, 1965

bennies *noun*
1 sun rays *US, 1965*
A shortened form of "beneficial rays."
- Nothing to do but laze around, drink beer on the back porch roof, and soak up the bennies. — John Nichols, *The Sterile Cuckoo*, p. 137, 1965

- — Collin Baker et al., *College Undergraduate Slang Study Conducted at Brown University*, p. 79, 1968
2 during the Vietnam war, basic comforts *US, 1976*
A shortened form of "benefits."
- On top of all those bennies they had ice cream and ice-cold beer! — Charles Anderson, *The Grunts*, p. 29, 1976
- The troops were always talking about service "bennies," the little perks like the BX and the commissary, as if they made much difference. — Walter Boyne and Steven Thompson, *The Wild Blue*, p. 241, 1986

benny *noun*
1 an amphetamine, especially Benzedrine™ (amphetamine sulfate), a central nervous system stimulant *US, 1945*
- I feel an incredible need to talk to you ... Not because I'm high on Benny, and lone in the cursed kitchen, but as a matter of mood. — Jack Kerouac, *Letter to Allen Ginsberg*, pp. 99–100, 13th November 1945
- Oh, I've been trying benny but its speeds everything up, it's all wrong and besides it makes you talk. — John Clellon Holmes, *John Clellon*, p. 47, 1952
- With each week of work, bombed and sapped and charged and stoned with lush, with pot, with benny[.] — Norman Mailer, *Advertisements for Myself*, p. 243, 1955
- At Bass Lake he tended the fire with the single-minded zeal of a man who's been eating bennies like popcorn. — Hunter S. Thompson, *Hell's Angels*, p. 185, 1966
2 a Benzedrine™ inhaler *US, 1970*
- — Clarence Major, *Dictionary of Afro-American Slang*, p. 25, 1970
3 an overcoat *UK, 1812*
- What size "benny" and "vine" you wear? — Iceberg Slim (Robert Beck), *Pimp*, p. 92, 1969
- 'Pon her arm she had my six-button benny / Said, "Here you are MacDaddy, here's your coat." — Roger Abrahams, *Positively Black*, p. 79, 1970
- He had a camel-hair benny with the belt in the back / Had a pair of nice shoes, and a pair of blue slacks. — Anonymous ("Arthur"), *Shine and the Titanic; The Signifying Monkey; Stackolee*, p. 1, 1971
4 a sports fan who looks back at a basketball game and analyzes what might have been *US, 1946*
Synonymous with "Monday Morning Quarterback" except basketball people like to call them "Bennys." Probably from the image of men in overcoats.
- There was nothing mysterious about the performance of Jimmy Pollard, the gangly Oakland sensation many of the tournament "Bennys" have been calling the "all-time great." — *San Francisco Examiner*, p. 18, 22nd March 1946
5 a person who looks and talks the part of a surfer but does not actually surf *US, 1991*
- — Trevor Cralle, *The Surfin'ary*, p. 9, 1991

benny blue *noun*
in craps, a roll of seven when shooting for your point *US, 1985*
From the call, "Benny blue, you're all through!"
- — Steve Kuriscak, *Casino Talk*, p. 3, 1985

benny house *noun*
a primarily heterosexual brothel that will upon request procure a male sexual partner for a male client *US, 1965*
- — *The Guild Dictionary of Homosexual Terms*, p. 4, 1965

beno *adjective*
used as a humorous description of a woman's condition while experiencing the bleed period of the menstrual cycle *US, 1954*
From the pronouncement—"There will *be no* fun tonight."
- — *American Speech*, p. 298, December 1954: "The vernacular of menstruation"

Benson Silk *noun*
counterfeit North Vietnamese currency *US, 1997*
- Benson Silk was tightly controlled, signed out on a hand receipt and usually carried only by the One-Zero. It was planted mostly to confuse the enemy. — John Plaster, *SOG*, p. 132, 1997

bent *adjective*
1 sexually deviant *UK, 1957*
- Being tall I could pass for a foreign soldier, albeit a slightly bent one. — Fiona Pitt-Kethley, *Red Light Districts of the World*, p. 53, 2000
2 homosexual *UK, 1959*
- — Eugene Landy, *The Underground Dictionary*, p. 32, 1971
- — Anon., *Ring Smut's Wet Dreams Interpreted*, 1978
- Does your family know you're bent? — Armistead Maupin, *Babycakes*, p. 214, 1984

3 drunk or drug-intoxicated *US, 1833*

- — Eugene Landy, *The Underground Dictionary*, p. 32, 1971
- CAMERON: Will Bogey get bent? MICHAEL: Are you kidding? He'll piss himself with joy. — *Ten Things I Hate About You*, 1999

4 ill-humored; grouchy *US, 1965*

- — Miss Cone, *The Slang Dictionary (Hawthorne High School)*, 1965

bent and greased *adjective*
prepared to be taken advantage of *US, 1994*
The sexual allusion is difficult to miss.

- — Michael Dalton Johnson, *Talking Trash with Redd Foxx*, p. 107, 1994

Bent Whore *nickname*
Bien Hoa, South Vietnam, site of an American air base during the Vietnam war *US, 1984*

- — John Robert Elting, *A Dictionary of Soldier Talk*, p. 23, 1984

Benz *noun*
a tablet of Benzedrine™ (amphetamine sulfate), a central nervous system stimulant *US, 1969*

- — Richard Lingeman, *Drugs from A to Z*, p. 22, 1969
- — Eugene Landy, *The Underground Dictionary*, p. 32, 1971

Benzo *noun*
a Mercedes-Benz car *US, 1986*

- That Benzo missed her ass by a red pussy hair. — Robert Campbell, *Alice in La-La Land*, p. 11, 1987
- You'd rather see, me in the pen / than me and Lorenzo rollin in a Benz-o — NWA *Fuck Tha Police*, 1988
- Who's Benzo was that I saw you rolling in yesterday? — *Boyz N The Hood*, 1990

Berb *noun*
a social outcast *US, 1993*

- — *Merriam-Webster's Hot Words on Campus Marketing Survey '93*, p. 2, 13th October 1993

Berdoo; San Berdoo; San Berdu *nickname*
San Bernadino, California, east of Los Angeles *US, 1914*

- They came from Okie flats outside Bakersfield, San Diego, Fresno and San Berdo. — Jack Kerouac, *On the Road (The Original Scroll)*, p. 206, 1951
- Anything less would forfeit the spiritual leadership back to southern California, to the San Bernadino (or Berdoo) chapter[.] — Hunter S. Thompson, *Hell's Angels*, p. 11, 1966
- I heard about you from some cops in San Berdoo. — Joseph Wambaugh, *Fugitive Nights*, p. 94, 1992
- According to Vic, the first Hell's Angels motorcycle club was formed around 1948 in Berdoo[.] — Ralph "Sonny" Barger, *Hell's Angel*, p. 30, 2000

berry *noun*
1 a dollar *US, 1916*

- Hand two hundred berries in my billfold and I couldn't afford to lose it. — Mickey Spillane, *I, The Jury*, p. 113, 1947
- "It's the berries, Phil," Dopey said. — James T. Farrell, *Saturday Night*, p. 22, 1947
- The mayor says he'll pay a thousand berries if the Pied Piper will disc his jig. — Harry Haenigsen, *Jive's Like That*, 1947
- Twenty berries an you alla roun the mothahfuggin' worl'. — Robert Gover, *One Hundred Dollar Misunderstanding*, p. 21, 1961

2 crack cocaine *US, 1993*

- — Peter Johnson, *Dictionary of Street Alcohol and Drug Terms*, p. 17, 1993

Bess *noun*
used as a term of address among male homosexuals *US, 1965*

- — *Fact*, p. 25, January – February 1965

bessie *noun*
the penis *US, 1973*

- And then I'm suddenly staring at the biggest bessie I ever seen in my life. — Richard Frank, *A Study of Sex in Prison*, p. 28, 1973

best *verb*
should *US, 1956*

- You BEST move on up. — Malachi Andrews and Paul T. Owens, *Black Language*, p. 98, 1973

▸ **give (a number) of the best**
to give (so many) betts with a cane *AUSTRALIA, 1965*

be's that way
used as a world-weary but wise acknowledgment that what is, is *US, 1968*

- — Hy Lit, *Hy Lit's Unbelievable Dictionary of Hip Words for Groovy People*, p. 4, 1968

best piece *noun*
a girlfriend or wife *US, 1937*

- — Eugene Landy, *The Underground Dictionary*, p. 32, 1971

bet *verb*
▸ **bet the dog**
in bar dice games, to bet the total amount of the pot *US, 1971*

- — Jester Smith, *Games They Play in San Francisco*, p. 103, 1971

▸ **bet the ranch; bet the farm**
to be absolutely certain about something *US, 1981*

- "I'm not a betting man, but if I was, I would bet the fuckin' ranch you don't know where the complaints are." — George V. Higgins, *The Rat on Fire*, p. 124, 1981
- But if I had a place be make a wager, I'd bet the farm on Erin's Boy in the seventh. — Robert Campbell, *Juice*, 1988

bet!
used for expressing approval *US, 1987*

- — *Washington Post Magazine*, p. 17, 28th June 1987
- — Connie Eble (Editor), *UNC-CH Campus Slang*, p. 1, Fall 1995

beta *noun*
1 a test or probationary stage *US, 1991*
Borrowed from the technical process of external testing of a product.

- "His girlfriend is in beta" means that he is still testing for compatibility and reserving judgment. — Eric S. Raymond, *The New Hacker's Dictionary*, p. 55, 1991

2 the grade "B" in academic work *US, 1968*

- — Collin Baker et al., *College Undergraduate Slang Study Conducted at Brown University*, p. 79, 1968

be there, aloha
used as a farewell *US, 1978*
Repopularized by ESPN's Keith Olberman, borrowed from the television program *Hawaii 5-0*.

- — Connie Eble (Editor), *UNC-CH Campus Slang*, April 1978
- — Keith Olberman and Dan Patrick, *The Big Show*, p. 12, 1997

better living through chemistry
used as a humorous endorsement of mind-altering recreational drug use *US, 1968*
Borrowed from an advertising slogan of DuPont Chemicals.

- While many regard psychedelic drugs as examples of "better living through chemistry," there is ample reason to be concerned[.] — American Institute of Planners, *Environment and Change*, p. 125, 1968
- Abbie Hoffman encouraged students at Columbia University to experiment further with such "better living through chemistry." — J. Anthony Lukas, *The Barnyard Epithet and Other Obscenities*, p. 10, 1970

betting tool *noun*
in horse racing, a horse that consistently wins *US, 1960*

- — Robert Saunders Dowst and Jay Craig, *Playing the Races*, p. 160, 1960

Betty *noun*
an attractive female *US, 1993*

- — Surf Punks, *Oh No! Not Them Again! (liner notes)*, 1988
- — Connie Eble (Editor), *UNC-CH Campus Slang*, p. 1, Spring 1993
- Not a total Betty, but a vast improvement. — *Clueless*, 1995

Betty Coed *noun*
the stereotypical female high school or college student *US, 1960*

- Betty Coed and her football hero—he's the coach—will be married in Richmond a week from tomorrow. — *San Francisco News Call-Bulletin*, p. 9, 6th May 1960
- "I'd never guessed—you look so—so—Betty Coed." — Frederick Kohner, *Gidget Goes Hawaiian*, p. 20, 1961
- Betty Coed passed by outside, unmindful of the drizzle and the heart that skipped a beat behind windows. — Bill Cardoso, *The Maltese Sangweech*, p. 91, 1984

between pictures *adjective*
Out of work, unemployed *US, 1954*
A euphemism, true in the entertainment industry, jocular elsewhere.

- "I'm between pictures" is a popular Hollywood phrase. But for the "Barefoot Girl with Coat of Mink"—sultry Ava Gardner—a more appropriate line is "I'm between headlines." — *San Francisco News*, p. 5, 30th August 1954

Beulah land *noun*
heaven *US, 1939*
From the book of Isaiah, 62:4.
- There ain't nothin' up there. If you would read that Bible, you would know. There is no Beulah land. — *Los Angeles Times*, p. L7, 8th January 2004

bevels *noun*
dice that have been altered by rounding off the sides slightly so as to produce a desired point *US, 1963*
- — John S. Salak, *Dictionary of Gambling*, p. 20, 1963

bewitched, bothered and bewildered *adjective*
confused *US, 1950*
The title of a song from the show *Pal Joey*, lyrics by Lorenz Hart, music by Richard Rodgers.
- [T]he bewitched, bothered and bewildered fathers and mothers of these expensively educated lads and lassies. — *San Francisco Chronicle*, p. 17, 21st May 1950
- The 49ers are bewitched, bothered, and bewildered. Plain confused too. — *San Francisco Examiner*, p. II-5, 3rd October 1955
- Bewitched, Bothered, Bewildered [Headline] — *San Francisco Examiner*, p. 23, 1st November 1967
- Bewitched, Bothered, and Bewildered [Episode Title] — Marti Noxon, *Buffy the Vampire Slayer*, 10th February 1998

beyond *adjective*
outstanding, amazing, extraordinary *US, 1999*
- Gigglepuss was so beyond. — *Ten Things I Hate About You*, 1999

BFD *noun*
a *big fucking deal US, 1966*
Sometimes euphemized from "fucking" to "fat."
- — J. W. Mays, *A Basic Guide to Campusology*, p. 2, 1966
- — *Current Slang*, p. 5, Fall 1967
- "BFD! By one stupid little minute!" — Jess Mowry, *Way Past Cool*, 1992

BFE *noun*
any remote location *US, 1989*
An abbreviation of **BUMFUCK, EGYPT**.
- — Pamela Munro, *U.C.L.A. Slang*, p. 20, 1989

BFF *noun*
best friends forever *US, 1988*
- B/F/F means Best Friends Forever — *USA Today*, 14th June 1988
- BFF: Best friends forever or a day? — Rosalind Wiseman, *Queen Bees & Wannabes*, p. 162, 2002

BFI *noun*
1 in computer technology, an approach relying on *brute force* and *ignorance* rather than elegant analysis *US, 1986*
- — Rachel S. Epstein and Nina Liebman, *Biz Speak*, p. 19, 1986
2 a massive heart attack or stroke; a *big fucking infarct US, 1994*
- — Sally Williams, *"Strong" Words*, p. 133, 1994

BG *noun*
a young member of a youth gang *US, 1995*
An abbreviate of **BABY GANGSTER**.
- — Mark S. Fleisher, *Beggars & Thieves*, p. 287, 1995
- — James Haskins, *The Story of Hip-Hop*, p. 135, 2000

B game *noun*
in a gambling establishment or cardroom, the table with the second highest betting limit *US, 1988*
- — George Percy, *The Language of Poker*, p. 9, 1988

BGF
the *Black Guerilla Family*, a black prison gang *US, 2000*
- The BGF, a radical prison security threat group, got its start in San Quentin in 1966. — Bill Valentine, *Gangs and Their Tattoos*, p. 17, 2000

B girl *noun*
1 a woman who works in a bar, encouraging customers through flirtation to buy drinks, both for themselves and for her *US, 1936*

- New York's cafes and clubs are forbidden by law to employ hostesses or "B" girls. — Jack Lait and Lee Mortimer, *New York Confidential*, p. 127, 1948
- Sunday I dropped into the Little Harlem and when the B-Girl approached me I recognized her as the fat slob who insisted she was the wife of Freddy Strong and so to avoid having her ask for a drink I casually asked if she'd heard from Freddy lately. — Neal Cassady, *Neal Cassady Collected Letters 1944–1967*, pp. 301–302, 10th August 1951: Letter to Jack Kerouac
- The B-girls (B for bar) converge on Manhattan from all over the nation, but many are native New Yorkers. — Jess Stearn, *Sisters of the Night*, p. 17, 1956
- A bunny sitting near me was more succinct. "They don't want us to look like B girls hustling drinks." — Kathryn Leigh Scott, *The Bunny Years*, p. 24, 1998
2 a young woman involved in early hip-hop *US, 2000*
From "break girl."
- — James Haskins, *The Story of Hip-Hop*, p. 135, 2000

B head *noun*
a barbiturate user or addict *US, 1979*
- — Joel Homer, *Jargon*, p. 193, 1979

bi *noun*
a *bisexual person US, 1956*
- If he were a "bi" he'd want to get into the act and maybe hump his buddy while ol' buddy is humping you. — *Screw*, p. 16, 16th May 1969
- Though the hanky code was originated by gay men, it has been adopted by cruising lesbians and bi's. — *Taste of Latex*, p. 24, Winter 1990–1991

bi *adjective*
bisexual *US, 1956*
- Met this quietly sensual "bi" friend of Martin's, wearing a clerical collar. — Jefferson Poland and Valerie Alison, *The Records of the San Francisco Sexual Freedom League*, p. 45, 1971
- This is a pretty sensual group of girls, mostly bi. — Robert Stoller and I.S. Levine, *Coming Attractions*, p. 148, 1991

Bianca blast *noun*
oral sex performed with a mouth full of Bianca™ mouthwash *US, 1993*
- — J.R. Schwartz, *The Official Guide to the Best Cat Houses in Nevada*, p. 163, 1993

Bible *noun*
1 the truth *US, 1948*
- — Jack Lait and Lee Mortimer, *New York Confidential*, p. 235, 1948
2 a fundamental source book, if not the most authoritative reference book in a given field *US, 1893*
- — Eric S. Raymond, *The New Hacker's Dictionary*, p. 56, 1991
- I'll offer up my bible for a small fee. — *Gone in 60 Seconds*, 2000
3 in circus and carnival usage, a program or souvenir magazine *US, 1981*
- — Don Wilmeth, *The Language of American Popular Entertainment*, p. 21, 1981
4 in the circus or carnival, *The Billboard*, a business newspaper *US, 1980*
- — Joe McKennon, *Circus Lingo*, p. 15, 1980

bibleback *noun*
1 a prisoner who has turned to religion, sincerely or not *US, 1953*
- Sandy's cell partner was a glib, sinister con artist, a Jew who had become a converted Baptist and posed as a Bible-toting evangelist. A type convicts called "Bible-Back." — James Blake, *The Joint*, p. 81, 1971
- There is the Bibleback, a particularly disgusting type of sycophant, who attends all the religious functions, wails the loudest, sings, prays and performs all the external functions required to become known as a Christian. — Bruce Jackson, *Outside the Law*, p. 178, 1972
2 in the circus or carnival, a folding plank used for grandstands *US, 1980*
- — Joe McKennon, *Circus Lingo*, p. 15, 1980

Bible-basher; Bible-thumper *noun*
an evangelical Christian *US, 1885*
- I could have told you for free that people think cigarettes are the road to perdition. Ain't you never heard one of them Bible-thumpers? — Max Shulman, *Anyone Got a Match?*, p. 43, 1964
- He was a real triple-threat man—boozer, Bible-thumper and box-chaser. — Joey V., *Portrait of Joey*, p. 25, 1969

- Any cheap Bible thumper on the outside has all the qualifications of a navy chaplain. — Darryl Ponicsan, *The Last Detail*, p. 46, 1970
- — Connie Eble (Editor), *UNC-CH Campus Slang*, March 1973

Bible belt *noun*
rural America, especially in the south, where fundamentalist Christians dominate the culture *US, 1924*

- Coming under the influence of the green-covered American Mercury, he looked back on home as the uncivilized "Bible belt." — James T. Farrell, *Ruth and Bertram*, p. 91, 1955
- Gonna let it rock / Let it roll / Let the Bible Belt come down / And save my soul. — John Cougar Mellencamp, *Jack and Diane*, 1982

Bible belter *noun*
a person from the rural mid-western or southern US *US, 1978*
Implies ignorance, gullibility, and backwardness.

- Harp's father is not just some eccentric Bible-belter with a little cash to give for his Jesus. — Allan Appel, *Club Revelation*, p. 122, 2001

Bible run *noun*
in television and movie making, a weekly printout of all production expenses *US, 1990*

- — Ralph S. Singleton, *Filmmaker's Dictionary*, p. 17, 1990

bicoastal *adjective*
pertaining to the west and east coasts of the US *US, 1984*
Almost always used with a sense of mocking, hyper-formality.

- To one side of us in the bleachers, as part of the audience, were the bicoastal network executives[.] — Dan Jenkins, *Life Its Ownself*, p. 174, 1984
- HBS, Stanford Forge a Bicoastal e-Alliance. — *Harvard Magazine*, p. 67, March – April 2001

bicycle *noun*
a bisexual *US, 1982*

- Only those in the know understood the reference in the 1978 Top 10 hit recording by Queen, "I want to Ride My Bicycle." — Arnold Shaw, *Dictionary of American Pop/Rock*, p. 35, 1982

▸ on your bicycle
in boxing, staying away from the opponent's punches by back pedaling *US, 1936*

- Bolden, strictly a defensive fighter, got on his bicycle in the first session and back pedaled through the entire fight. — *San Francisco Examiner*, p. 19, 13th November 1945
- So he kept me away with left hooks and got on his bicycle where I charged him. — Rocky Garciano (with Rowland Barber), *Somebody Up There Likes Me*, p. 275, 1955

bicycle *verb*
1 in television and movie making, to work on multiple projects simultaneously *US, 1977*
In the days of silent movies, to show a movie at several different theaters required transporting it from one theater to another, often by bicycle.

- — Tony Miller and Patricia George, *Cut! Print!*, p. 40, 1977
- — Ira Konigsberg, *The Complete Film Dictionary*, p. 27, 1987
- — Ralph S. Singleton, *Filmmaker's Dictionary*, p. 17, 1990

2 to ride a surfboard with a wide stance *US, 1977*
- — Gary Fairmont R. Filosa II, *The Surfer's Almanac*, p. 182, 1977

bicycle pump *noun*
a large syringe *US, 1961*
Korean war usage.

- The bicycle pump was the giant, legendary needle that Navy medics used to scare noisy Marines. When threatened with the "bicycle pump," the Marine would pretend to scorn such a story. — Russell Davis, *Marine at War*, p. 167, 1961

bid *noun*
a prison sentence *US, 2000*
A variant of the more common **BIT**.

- "Dear Sweetie," began one, which an officer had opened, "Your bid's not that long." — Ted Conover, *Newjack*, p. 167, 2000
- His stomach still had cuts from workouts during his prison bid. — Adrian Nicole LeBlanc, *Random Family*, p. 293, 2003
- He hated it. "I'd rather do my bid"—his jail sentence—he always said. — *Philadelphia Daily News*, p. Local 3, 27th December 2006

biddy *noun*
an old woman, usually one prone to complain and fuss *US, 1938*
The dominant sense of the term in the US, with the older sense of a "young woman" unknown.

- "Those old welfare biddies will find her a fine family to live with." — Chester Himes, *The Real Cool Killers*, p. 45, 1959
- The captain whispered in my ear: "Don't make any dramatic gestures to those biddies or I'll crease your head with this club." — Lenny Bruce, *How to Talk Dirty and Influence People*, p. 70, 1965
- Have you seen the way those old biddies look at you when we walk into the dining room? — Armistead Maupin, *Further Tales of the City*, p. 195, 1982
- When Bobbie questioned Fin about the age of all the fun-loving fogies, coots, geezers, codgers, duffers and biddies she'd met in the saloon, he didn't know how to tell her that the oldest fossil in the joint wasn't fifteen years his senior. — Joseph Wambaugh, *Finnegan's Week*, p. 230, 1993

bidness *noun*
business *US, 1984*
A Texas corrupted pronunciation of a Texas activity.

- He blessed Bid Ed's oil bidness, said young people were the hope of the world, acknowledged the talented tap-dance team of Jesus and Mary, forgave the Catholics and Jews, and pronounced us man and wife. — Dan Jenkins, *Life Its Ownself*, p. 65, 1984
- Doing Bidness With Roger Clinton — *Washington Post*, p. A25, 21st June 2001

biff *noun*
1 a blow, a hit, a whack *US, 1847*

- [G]et your kicks and biffs. It's your night! — Lester Bangs, *Psychotic Reactions and Carburetor Dung*, p. 38, 1970
- Then a biff from an idea that bowled him over. — Neal Cassady, *The First Third*, p. 168, 1971

2 in mountain biking, a crash *US, 1996*

- We've grimaced and chuckled simultaneously at face plants [a face-first encounter with the ground], endos [an accident in which the cyclist flies over the handlebars], biffs and crash-landings. — *Mountain Bike Magazine's Complete Guide To Mountain Biking Skills*, p. 32, 1996

3 in pinball, a forceful hit with the flipper *US, 1977*
- — Bobbye Claire Natkin and Steve Kirk, *All About Pinball*, p. 110, 1977

4 a toilet *US, 1942*
- — *The Guild Dictionary of Homosexual Terms*, p. 4, 1965
- — Collin Baker et al., *College Undergraduate Slang Study Conducted at Brown University*, p. 79, 1968

biff *verb*
in computing, to inform someone of incoming mail *US, 1991*
- — Eric S. Raymond, *The New Hacker's Dictionary*, p. 56, 1991

biffer *noun*
1 a prostitute *US, 1971*

- "Biffer," "prossie," "she-she," "pig-meat" are some other slang designations. — Charles Winick, *The Lively Commerce*, p. 41, 1971

2 an unattractive woman *US, 1932*
- — Robert George Reisner, *The Jazz Titans*, p. 150, 1957

biffy *noun*
a bathroom *US, 1942*

- [A]t a recent cocktail party Chief Justice Earl Warren, cocktail in hand, was backed up against the door leading to the biffy reserved for the children in the house[.] — *San Francisco Call-Bulletin*, p. 11, 25th March 1954
- "I'll get to inventory the rest of her when she finishes whatever she's doing in the girlies' biffy[.]" — David Gregory, *Flesh Seller*, p. 22, 1962
- There's a towel in the biffy. — Elmore Leonard, *The Big Bounce*, p. 92, 1969

big *verb*
to impregnate someone *US, 1917*

- "And tell her not to come crying around here when she gets all bigged from messing around with you!" — Herbert Simmons, *Corner Boy*, p. 99, 1957
- He tu blame fuh biggin yu. — Iceberg Slim (Robert Beck), *Mama Black Widow*, p. 184, 1969
- Damn near every man likes a girl when she's bigged and young at the same time; this makes it a double treat. — A.S. Jackson, *Gentleman Pimp*, p. 47, 1973
- — History of Medicine Society, *A Folk Medical Lexicon of South Central Appalachia*, 1990

Big A *nickname*
1 the Aqueduct Race Track in Westbury, New York *US, 1959*
- Everything about the new Aqueduct is so big that it is referred to as the Big A. — *New York Times*, p. 21, 9th September 1959

2 the US federal penitentiary in Atlanta, Georgia *US, 1982*
- — Ralph de Sola, *Crime Dictionary*, p. 15, 1982

3 in poker, an ace, especially when it is the deciding card in a hand *US, 1988*
- — George Percy, *The Language of Poker*, p. 10, 1988

4 AIDS *US, 1992*
- — Terry William, *Crackhouse*, p. 146, 1992
- — Sally Williams, *"Strong" Words*, p. 134, 1994
- [S]he wondered what diseases all these losers would bring home to their wives. Maybe the fatal one. Maybe the Big A. — Joseph Wambaugh, *Hollywood Station*, p. 155, 2006

big apple *noun*
a cap with a big visor *US, 1970*
In vogue during the "Superfly" era of the early 1970s.
- — *Current Slang*, p. 5, Fall 1970

big-ass *adjective*
very large *US, 1957*
- He left the house and didn't stop till he opened the door of his bigass Cadillac. — Hubert Selby Jr., *Last Exit to Brooklyn*, p. 304, 1957
- — Connie Eble (Editor), *UNC-CH Campus Slang*, p. 1, March 1996

big-ass bird *noun*
the Boeing B-17 military aircraft *US, 1961*
- Lt. Howard M. Park, a veteran of panzer busting in Normandy, was among the first up that morning heading for Bastogne in his famous red nosed Big Ass Bird. — Danny Parker, *To Win the Winter Sky*, p. 227, 1998

big-assed *adjective*
large *US, 1945*
- If he could think of some way not to—he's bird-brained and chicken-hearted and big-assed. — James Baldwin, *Blues for Mister Charlie*, p. 25, 1964

Big B *nickname*
Berlin *US, 1944*
- The crew couldn't make their original target in Berlin—"Big B," as they called it. — *Seattle Post-Intelligencer*, p. B2, 20th May 2003

big ball *noun*
1 in pool, an object ball that can be hit either directly or on the rebound off a cushion *US, 1913*
Because there are two ways to hit it, it is a bigger target, hence a "big ball."
- — Mike Shamos, *The Illustrated Encyclopedia of Billiards*, p. 25, 1993

2 in bowling, a roll that forcefully hooks into the standing pins *US, 1962*
- — Frank Bryan, *Tackle Tenpin Bowling This Way*, 1962

big baller *noun*
a big spender *US, 2001*
- Saturday's "Evening in Paradise" at the Hotel Inter-Continental in Miami, at $250 per person, is a big-baller special. — *Sun-Sentinel (Fort Lauderdale, Florida)*, p. 1E, 11th July 2001

big belly *noun*
a B-52 bomber *US, 1986*
- A stream of bomb trailers rolled under them, stuffing their Big Bellys with eight-four bombs. — Walter J. Boyne and Steven L. Thompson, *The Wild Blue*, p. 464, 1986

Big Ben *noun*
1 the new, large design hundred-dollar bill minted in the late 1990s *US, 1996*
The "Ben" is an allusion to Benjamin Franklin, the C18 slang lexicographer whose portrait graces the note.
- — John Vorhaus, *The Big Book of Poker Slang*, p. 6, 1996

2 Benzedrine™ (amphetamine sulfate), a central nervous system stimulant *US, 1966*
- — Mr., p. 8, April 1966: The 'Hippie's' Lexicon

3 in craps, a roll of ten *US, 1999*
Rhyming slang.
- — Chris Fagans and David Guzman, *A Guide to Craps Lingo*, p. 33, 1999

Big Ben *nickname*
the USS Franklin (heavily damaged off Japan on 19th March 1945, repaired and mothballed); the USS Bennington (commissioned in 1944, decommissioned in 1970) *US, 1954*
The Bennington was featured in the opening scene of the CBS television program Navy Log in 1956 and 1957.
- To me and many other World War II sailors, there is only one "Big Ben" and that is the U.S.S. Franklin. [Letter to Editor] — *Life*, p. 5, 28th June 1954
- The Big Blast in "Big Ben" [Headline] — *Life*, p. 36, 7th June 1954

Big Bertha *noun*
an over-sized slot machine used as a promotion for hotel guests and to lure prospective gamblers into a casino *US, 1984*
- — J. Edward Allen, *The Basics of Winning Slots*, p. 57, 1984
- Berthas, as in "Big Bertha," are giant, oversized machines sprinkled here and there around the casino. — Jim Regan, *Winning at Slot Machine*, p. 49, 1985

Big Bertha *nickname*
the Ringling Brothers, Barnum and Bailey Circus *US, 1973*
- — Sherman Louis Sergel, *The Language of Show Biz*, p. 20, 1973
- — Don Wilmeth, *The Language of American Popular Entertainment*, p. 22, 1981

big bill *noun*
a $100 bill *US, 1961*
- "Here's a big bill as a binder." Vann took a new one-hundred-dollar bill from his wallet, folded it the long way and poked it into Red's breast pocket. — Ross Russell, *The Sound*, p. 62, 1961

big bitch *noun*
the prison sentence given to habitual criminals *US, 1961*
- — Frank Prewitt and Francis Schaeffer, *Vacaville Vocabulary*, 1961–1962
- "If Chilly wasn't doing the big bitch," Nunn told Manning, "he'd own half this state." — Malcolm Braly, *On the Yard*, p. 38, 1967

Big Blue 82 *noun*
a 12,540-pound BLU-82 bomb *US, 1991*
A vicious anti-personnel weapon, developed for vegetation clearing in Vietnam, used again in the Persian Gulf war and Afghanistan.
- A unique bomb which also provides tremendous blast overpressures and was reported to have been used in the Mideast ("a favorite of the Marine Corps," according to one anonymous Pentagon spokesman) is the BLUE-82, otherwise known as "Big Blue 82." — *Boston Globe*, 16th April 1991
- The type depicted in the leaflets, and also used in Afghanistan, is the BLU-82B Commando Vault or Big Blue 82, also known as the Daisy Cutter. — *BBC News*, 6th November 2001

big-boobed *adjective*
of a female, having generously proportioned large breasts *US, 1970*
- "I gotta be bright-eyed, big-boobed and dancing at six," moaned Marion. — William Craddock, *Be Not Content*, p. 174, 1970
- He'd win at the track and some big-boobed bimbo would take it all from him. — Jackie Collins, *Rock Star*, p. 19, 1988
- Prante had told Bond, "There's a big-boobed blonde moving in next door to Dwayne." — Don Weber, *Silent Witness*, p. 182, 1993
- Tall, long-legged, and big-boobed, she was definitely built like the proverbial brick shithouse. — Beverly Barton, *The Fifth Victim*, p. 40, 2003

big book *noun*
in twelve-step recovery programs such as Alcoholics Anonymous, the book *Alcoholics Anonymous*, first published in 1939 and still the central document of the recovery movement *US, 1998*
- — Christopher Cavanaugh, *AA to Z*, p. 54, 1998

big boss *noun*
heroin *US, 1972*
- Having been an addict I know something about it, one of the narcotics especially; heroin. Some people call it "the Big Boss; Horse." — Bruce Jackson, *In the Life*, p. 210, 1972

big boy *noun*
a tank *US, 1968*

Vietnam war usage. The bigger the tank and the more weapons mounted on the tank, the more likely it was to be called a "big boy."

- — Carl Fleischhauer, *A Glossary of Army Slang*, p. 4, 1968
- I want the two big boys leading the first and third platoons. — Ronald J. Glasser, *365 Days*, pp. 113 – 114, 1971
- The Armored Cavalry battalion was also on the base so there were lots of APCs and tanks and a couple of Big Boys. — Mark Baker, *Nam*, p. 193, 1981

big brother *noun*
1 the penis, especially a large penis *US, 1965*
- — *The Guild Dictionary of Homosexual Terms*, p. 4, 1965
- — Dale Gordon, *The Dominion Sex Dictionary*, p. 28, 1967

2 the erect penis *US, 1967*
- — Dale Gordon, *The Dominion Sex Dictionary*, p. 28, 1967
- — Robert A. Wilson, *Playboy's Book of Forbidden Words*, p. 34, 1972

Big C *noun*
1 cancer *US, 1964*
- The Washington Whispers have it that Jack Ruby doesn't stand a chance of beating the Big C. — *San Francisco Examiner and Chronicle*, p. 19, 1st January 1967
- "Big C" Finally Beats John Wayne [Headline] — *San Francisco Examiner and Chronicle*, p. 14, 17th June 1979
- They don't think it's anything silly do they? Like … Big C … or any of his pals? — Dan Jenkins, *Dead Solid Perfect*, p. 26, 1986
- His wife's in the hospital, has been for a couple months. The big C. — *Fargo*, 1996
- That's when I decided I was going to beat this monster, the Big C. — Ralph "Sonny" Barger, *Hell's Angel*, p. 243, 2000

2 cocaine *US, 1959*
- — J.E. Schmidt, *Narcotics Lingo and Lore*, p. 16, 1959
- — William D. Alsever, *Glossary for the Establishment and Other Uptight People*, p. 6, December 1970
- — Donald Louria, *The Drug Scene*, p. 189, 1971

3 a female as an sexual object *US, 1963*
A hint of CUNT.
- — *American Speech*, p. 273, December 1963: "American Indian student slang"

big casino *noun*
1 the best that you can do; your greatest resource *US, 1922*
- Jimmy had written a $2,500,000 life insurance policy on Hill. Ask your insurance agent whether that would be peanuts or the big casino in the insurance. — *San Francisco Call-Bulletin*, p. 10, 17th March 1950
- The big casino in Nixon's over-all program is the next stage of the Vietnam troop withdrawals. — *San Francisco Examiner and Chronicle*, p. A-2, 14th September 1969
- Jerry Brown should go for the Big Casino [Headline] — *San Francisco Examiner*, p. 31, 16th March 1976

2 cancer *US, 1951*
- His grin was forced. He knows he's got Big Casino—cancer. — *San Francisco Examiner and Chronicle*, p. III-6, 7th May 1967
- Wee Willie Wilkin, former St. Mary's College tackle (so named because at 270 he was considered the largest item in football during the '30s) is fighting the Big Casino. — *San Francisco Chronicle*, p. 48, 14th December 1971
- "If you still want to do that book, we better get started awful sudden, because I've got cancer. Big Casino." — Robert Byrne, *McGoorty*, p. 11, 1972
- "It's true, Billy," he said, gazing bleakly at his glass. "Big casino. It's hopeless." — *San Francisco Examiner and Chronicle*, p. 5, 27th February 1983

3 any sexually transmitted infection *US, 1948*
- Nitti, like Capone, had picked up in his travels the occupational malady of the underworld, euphemistically known as the capital prize, or big casino. — *San Francisco Call-Bulletin*, p. 14, 23rd February 1948
- It was hinted that poor, departed Will had once acquired a case of what the boys call big casino, which ended in the same paresis that finished Al Capone. — *San Francisco News*, p. 11, 8th October 1951

4 capital punishment, the death penalty *US, 1960*
- Will "Call Me Bernie" for Big Casino. Yes, say the results of an informal poll of the Nation's press covering the sensational Finch murder trial here. — *San Francisco Examiner*, p. 12, 22nd January 1960

big cat *noun*
in poker, a hand comprised of five cards between eight and king and no pairs among them *US, 1963*

Also known as "big tiger."
- — Irwin Steig, *Common Sense in Poker*, p. 182, 1963

big Charlie *noun*
1 a CH-3C helicopter used during the Vietnam war for counterinsurgency airlifts *US, 1985*
- — Ian Padden, *U.S. Air Commando*, p. 104, 1985

2 an important white man *US, 1968*
- I knows they's nothin' but overseers on the big plantation, jes doin' like Big Charlie tell 'em to. — Robert Gover, *JC Saves*, p. 112, 1968

big cheese *noun*
the most important person in a given organization or enterprise *US, 1914*
- Reggie Jackson: the big cheese of the holey AL West. [Caption] — *Washington Post*, p. F8, 3rd April 1983
- Ito-san was the head honcho, the big cheese, the number-one Tomodachi … or to put it another way, the overall manager of the SPN group. — Rhiannon Paine, *Too Late for the Festival*, p. 27, 1999

big chicken dinner *noun*
a bad conduct discharge *US, 1987*
Playing with initials: armed forces usage.
- "You could have gotten a bad-conduct discharge for that." "What, the Big Chicken Dinner?" — David Poyer, *The Circle*, p. 160, 1003

big chief *noun*
the hallucinogenic drug, mescaline *US, 1971*
- — Edward R. Bloomquist, *Marijuana*, p. 332, 1971

Big D *noun*
1 dexedrine, a central nervous system stimulant *US, 1967*
- Grady will probably sleep; he has had little sleep since we've been out. Should I take a couple of "Big D's?" Better not. Want to stay awake but don't want to be jumpy or over-reactive. — Donald Duncan, *The New Legions*, p. 51, 1967

2 LSD *US, 1966*
- — Donald Louria, *Nightmare Drugs*, p. 45, 1966
- — John B. Williams, *Narcotics and Hallucinogenics*, p. 109, 1967
- — Eugene Landy, *The Underground Dictionary*, p. 33, 1971

3 the penis *US, 1998*
D as in DICK.
- — Ethan Hilderbrant, *Prison Slang*, p. 12, 1998

Big D *nickname*
1 Dallas, Texas *US, 1930*
- In Big D, do as the heteros do. — Phil Andros (Samuel M. Steward), *Stud*, p. 89, 1966
- Well, you probably have certain opinions about the security arrangements they had that bad Friday down in Big D—inadequate, I suppose. — Terry Southern, *Now Dig This*, p. 137, 2001
- Anne Frank don't make me no never mind, as they say in Big D. — David Henry Sterry, *Chicken*, p. 114, 2002

2 Detroit, Michigan *US, 1961*
- It ain't like the Big D, where so many brothers is startin' to snitch on each other. — Donald Goines, *El Dorado Red*, p. 92, 1974
- After a short run he settled in Detroit. During the early fifties, every jazz artist who played the big D, usually ran into him. — Babs Gonzales, *Movin' On Down De Line*, p. 56, 1975

3 Denver, Colorado *US, 1967*
- — *Current Slang*, p. 5, Fall 1967

big dad *noun*
a senior drill instructor *US, 1991*
Vietnam war usage.
- The senior is "Big Dad," the "Omnipotent and Omiscient One," the "Father Confessor." — Daniel Da Cruz, *Boot*, p. 72, 1987

big daddy *noun*
an immense wave *US, 1977*
- — Gary Fairmont R. Filosa II, *The Surfer's Almanac*, p. 182, 1977

big dago *noun*
a sandwich made on Italian bread *US, 1960*
- "You know the signs all over for what we call in New York 'submarines,' hero sandwich on sliced Italian bread? On the coast, they advertise 'Don's big Dagos, Red Hot Dagos!'" — *Esquire*, p. 153, 1st November 1960

big dance in Newark *noun*
in circus and carnival usage, a jocular explanation for a small
audience *US, 1981*
- — Don Wilmeth, *The Language of American Popular Entertainment*, p. 21, 1981

big day *noun*
visiting day in prison *US, 1949*
- — Vincent J. Monteleone, *Criminal Slang*, p. 21, 1949
- — *American Speech*, p. 194, October 1951: "A study of reformatory argot"
- — Troy Harris, *A Booklet of Criminal Argot, Cant and Jargon*, p. 5, 1976

big dead one *nickname*
later in the Vietnam war, the First Infantry Division *US,
1981*
A sad play on **BIG RED ONE** after heavy attrition through casualties.
- Also known as "Big Dead One" — Shelby L. Stanton, *Vietnam Order of Battle*,
p. 353, 1981

big Dick *noun*
1 in dice games, a roll of ten *US, 1949*
- "There it was—Little Joe or Phoebe, Big Dick or Eighter from Decatur,
double trey the hard way and dice be nice." — Nelson Algren, *The Man with
the Golden Arm*, p. 11, 1949
2 a 14-inch rocket *US, 1946*
- Here from 300 safe yards away we watched naval technicians fire
a free-launched 14-inch rocket known to the men developing it as
"Big Dick." That's to distinguish it from the older, smaller 11.75
inch "Tiny Tim." — *San Francisco News*, p. 1, 27th December 1946

big dog *noun*
in poker, a hand comprised of five cards between nine and
ace and no pairs among them *US, 1963*
- — Irwin Steig, *Common Sense in Poker*, p. 182, 1963

big duke *noun*
in poker, especially hold 'em poker, a strong hand *US, 1981*
- — Thomas L. Clark, *The Dictionary of Gambling and Gaming*, p. 18, 1987

Big E *nickname*
the USS Enterprise *US, 1942*
Two aircraft carriers carried the name Enterprise and the nickname "Big E," the first commissioned in 1936 and the second
in 1961.
- "Big E" Plays Cat and Mouse with Russ Sub [Headline] — *San Francisco
Examiner and Chronicle*, p. A-2, 15th September 1968
- Battleflat of "Big E" to new Enterprise [Headline] — *San Francisco Examiner*, p. 48, 18th April 1974

big ears *noun*
in the language of paragliding, an intentional collapsing of
both tips of the wing to increase speed *US, 1992*
- — Erik Fair, *California Thrill Sports*, p. 335, 1992

Big Easy *nickname*
New Orleans, Louisiana *US, 1970*
- The Big Easy, as New Orelans calls itself, regards progress with a
skeptical eye. — *New York Times*, p. 10, 4th January 1981

big eight *noun*
in poker, four twos *US, 1988*
A borrowing from the game of craps.
- — George Percy, *The Language of Poker*, p. 10, 1988

big-endian *adjective*
in computing, denoting computer architecture in which the
most significant byte is found in the lowest address *US, 1991*
- — Eric S. Raymond, *The New Hacker's Dictionary*, p. 57, 1991

big eye *noun*
1 a high-powered telescope, especially the one located on
Palomar Mountain, California *US, 1949*
- Palomar's "Big Eye'—already the apple of astronomers" eyes—is
going to be even better than expected after a final polishing. — *San
Francisco Call-Bulletin*, p. 11, 6th May 1949
- California's second "Big Eye," the 120 inch mirror for the new
telescope at Mt. Hamilton, near San Jose, is ready to probe the
heavens. — *San Francisco News*, p. 11, 26th June 1959
- Flying low over the Gulf of Mexico, pilots approaching the Florida
panhandle can see the Big Eye staring at them like some baleful
guardian of the coast. — *Los Angeles Times*, pp. 1–3, 22nd February 1968

2 a Lockheed EC-121 Warning Star aircraft *US, 1991*
Deployed in Vietnam to provide early warning and communication relay; later redesignated the **COLLEGE EYE**.
- PIRAZ was augmented by an Air Force EC-121 airborne radar aircraft,
known as "Big Eye." — John Sherwood, *Afterburner*, p. 82, 2003

big fellow *noun*
a law enforcement official of the US federal government *US,
1974*
- We best pull out. The big fellows was by here today. — David W. Maurer,
Kentucky Moonshine, p. 114, 1974

big fish *noun*
a very important person or thing *US, 1836*
- They spared most of the big fish. Congress must face up to social
security costs. — *Christian Science Monitor*, p. 1, 25th November 1981
- "I was a big fish in a little pond, but it was nice for my ego and I
learned how to win," he said. [Quoting Patrick Horgan] — *Los Angeles
Times*, p. C2, 1st February 1992
- Martha was a little fish when it comes to these crimes. We're still
waiting for the big fish at Enron, WorldCom, Tyco and Harken to pay
for their crimes. — *Post-Crescent (Appleton, Wisconsin)*, p. 7C, 11th March 2004
- Over the next few months, that same informant helped apprehend
or implicate several "big fish," such as 17 corrupt state police officers.
— *Dallas Morning News*, 14th March 2004

big foot country *noun*
the deep, rural south of the US *US, 1974*
- I heard you had went down to the big foot country and decided to
stay there for your health. — Donald Goines, *Never Die Alone*, p. 20, 1974
- You know how hard it was to get short heist up in big-foot country
before the riot. — Miguel Pinero, *Short Eyes*, p. 73, 1975
- You're a champ chump from the Big Foot Country (deep South)
and you're creaming to get laid. — Iceberg Slim (Robert Beck), *Airtight Willie
and Me*, p. 6, 1979

big friend *noun*
a bomber aircraft *US, 1946*
- — *American Speech*, p. 310, December 1946: "More air force slang"

big fucking deal *noun*
a major issue *US, 1971*
An elaboration of **BIG DEAL**. Often used to dismiss something as
not being a major issue.
- "Big deal. So they voted against the war. Big fucking deal." — Thomas
Cottle, *Time's Children*, p. 48, 1971
- Lawyer, huh? Big fuckin' deal. — Edwin Torres, *Q & A*, p. 121, 1977
- What's the big fucking deal? — *South Park*, 1999

big full *noun*
in poker, a hand consisting of three aces and two kings *US,
1978*
This hand represents the best possible variation of the hand
conventionally known as a "full house."
- — Thomas L. Clark, *The Dictionary of Gambling and Gaming*, p. 18, 1987

big general *noun*
in a bar dice game, a first roll showing five dice of the same
denomination *US, 1974*
- — Thomas L. Clark, *The Dictionary of Gambling and Gaming*, p. 18, 1987

biggie *noun*
1 a big deal; something of consequence or difficulty *US, 1945*
Often in the negative: "no biggie."
- — Connie Eble (Editor), *UNC-CH Campus Slang*, p. 5, Fall 1989
- FABIAN: You're hurt? BUTCH: I might've broke my nose, no biggie.
— *Pulp Fiction*, 1994
2 an important person *US, 1926*
- She will dance till she's dippy at the Sunset Strip cabarets, meeting
the biggies[.] — Jack Lait and Lee Mortimer, *New York Confidential*, p. 145, 1948
- He was in with all those biggies. — Edwin Torres, *After Hours*, p. 185, 1979
- So you got a biggie, Brian. — Carl Hiaasen, *Tourist Season*, p. 19, 1986

biggity *adverb*
in a haughty, arrogant or conceited way *US, 1880*
- We had a yen, every time we got away from home and school, to
strut and act biggity and shoot the works, live our whole lives out
before the sun went down. — Mezz Mezzrow, *Really the Blues*, p. 5, 1946

- Mama never acted biggety in court, but she would bow her head only so low. — Claude Brown, *Manchild in the Promised Land*, p. 95, 1965
- They were unwashed and uncombed and acted brazen-faced and biggity. — Joe Eszterhas, *Charlie Simpson's Apocalypse*, p. 28, 1973

big golden bird *noun*
an airplane transporting troops back to the United States from Vietnam *US, 1966*
- When FIGMO ("Farewell, I Got My Orders") time rolls around, some guys start marking off the days before that final one when they hop into the Big Golden Bird bound for the Land of the Big PX. — Ken Melvin, *Sorry 'Bout That*, p. 94, 1966

big green *noun*
1 large amounts of money *US, 2000*
- "If "Stunning Steve" can make more of the big green by listening to the Colonel, I can't knock him for that." — Robert Picarello, *Rules of the Ring*, p. 7, 2000

2 in sporting and music events, corporate sponsors *US, 1992*
- — Lewis Poteet, *Car & Motorcycle Slang*, p. 30, 1992

biggums *adjective*
overweight *US, 1994*
- — *Evening Sun (Baltimore)*, p. 12A, 19th January 1994

Big H *noun*
heroin *US, 1953*
- You ever hear of dope? Snow? Junk? Big H? Horse? — John D. McDonald, *The Neon Jungle*, p. 61, 1953
- Their habit of sniffing and shooting "The Big H" had reached a monumental \$500 per day. — Phil Hirsch, *Hooked*, p. 31, 1968
- "Walking with the King. Big H. If God made anything better he never let on." — Robert Stone, *Dog Soldiers*, p. 171, 1974

big hair *noun*
an extravagant, large-sized hairdo *US, 1978*
- "I think I'm more like a cartoon character, this big hair flapping all over, big hips, big bosom. It's a gimmick." [Quoting Dolly Parton] — *Washington Post*, p. B1, 8th May 1978
- — Connie Eble (Editor), *UNC-CH Campus Slang*, p. 1, Fall 1990
- I went out and bought a fall and did "big hair" for about six months—and looked horrid! — Kathryn Leigh Scott, *The Bunny Years*, pp. 265–266, 1998

big hat, no cattle
used for describing someone who appears the part but has no substance *US, 1977*
- Mr. Davis is not like a lot of Texans, big hat, no cattle. — *Lima (Ohio) News*, 15th December 1977

big-headed *adjective*
conceited, arrogant, haughty *US, 1967*
- The great thing about him is with all his talent he never became big-headed. — Babs Gonzales, *I Paid My Dues*, p. 140, 1967

big house *noun*
a prison *US, 1913*
Usually follows "the."
- "Strebhouse and Stevens spent a stretch in the big house," I said. — Mickey Spillane, *I, The Jury*, p. 111, 1947
- In fact, their fate was often worse. Suicide. Dope addiction and the d.t.'s. The big house and the nuthouse. — Jim Thompson, *The Grifters*, p. 24, 1963
- As the gates of the Atlanta big house swung open, I flippantly remarked to the guard on duty: "So long, Jim." — Red Rudensky, *The Gonif*, p. 137, 1970
- Chazz, I don't want to go to the Big House! — *Airheads*, 1994

big iron *noun*
a large, powerful, fast, expensive computer *US, 1991*
- — Eric S. Raymond, *The New Hacker's Dictionary*, p. 56, 1991

Big J *nickname*
Juarez, Mexico *US, 1970*
- — *Current Slang*, p. 13, Spring 1970

big jab *noun*
execution by lethal injection *US, 2002*
- — Jeffrey Ian Ross, *Behind Bars*, p. 182, 2002: Slammer Slang

Big Joe *noun*
a novice, especially a military recruit *US, 1947*
- — *American Speech*, p. 54, February 1947: "Pacific War language"

Big Joe from Boston *noun*
in craps, a ten *US, 1957*
- — Sidney H. Radner, *Radner on Dice*, p. 10, 1957

big John *noun*
a police officer; the police *US, 1980*
- — Edith A. Folb, *runnin' down some lines*, p. 229, 1980

big juicer *noun*
a powerful, all-night AM radio station *US, 1976*
- — Porter Bibb, *CB Bible*, p. 87, 1976

big kahuna *noun*
a top leader *US, 1990*
From a Hawaiian term for "priest" or "wise man."
- This might be the big kahuna, gentlemen. — *New Jack City*, 1990
- Because I fly a few hundred thousand miles a year, United gave me Big Kahuna status. — Sergio Zyman, *The End of Advertising as We Know It*, p. 207, 2002

Big L *noun*
love *US, 1987*
- It's love, baby. And Whatcom County residents found it at the Northwest Washington Fair in Lynden. From horse barn to the grandstand, they tell how they walked through the gates and into the big "L." — *Bellingham (Washington) Herald*, p. 1C, 13th August 2002

Big L *nickname*
the federal penitentiary in Leavenworth, Kansas *US, 1970*
- I was broke, back in stir, and the Big L was surrounding me. — Red Rudensky, *The Gonif*, p. 6, 1970

big-league *adjective*
powerful, influential, important *US, 1919*
- Being one of Yanowitz's boys made them big league. — Irving Shulman, *Cry Tough*, p. 103, 1949
- CLARENCE: Is he big league? DICK: He's nothing. — *True Romance*, 1993

big leagues *noun*
a high level in any field *US, 1941*
Also used in the singular.
- Relax. This is the big league ... — Horace McCoy, *Kiss Tomorrow Good-bye*, p. 293, 1948
- A dazzling crowd. The names escaped Reilly, but the titles and affiliations were awesome: bank trustees, Senior Wall Street lawyers, jurists, legislators. Al Reilly was in the big leagues. — Edwin Torres, *Q & A*, p. 139, 1977

Big M *noun*
1 morphine *US, 1959*
- Les, quite disheveled, still wearing his gray nut-house bathrobe, and totally strung-out in coming off the big M, had been trying to brief them as to the true nature of the movie they were producing. — Terry Southern, *Blue Movie*, p. 219, 1970

2 marriage *US, 1966*
- — *Current Slang*, p. 1, Winter 1966

big mama *noun*
the ocean *US, 1991*
- — Trevor Cralle, *The Surfin'ary*, p. 10, 1991

big man on campus *noun*
a socially prominent student *US, 1930s to 70s*
Initially used with respect, but often in later years with irony, if not scorn.
- "All the Big Men on Campus are wearing them. Where've you been?" "In the library," I said, naming a place not frequented by Big Men on Campus. — Max Shulman, *The Many Loves of Dobie Gillis*, p. 40, 1951

big meeting in the sky *noun*
heaven as characterized by those who are part of twelve-step recovery program such as Alcoholics Anonymous *US, 1998*
- — Christopher Cavanaugh, *AA to Z*, p. 54, 1998

Big Mo *nickname*
the USS Missouri *US, 1945*

- But she [Maureen Connolly] was a dynamo called Little Mo, the nickname an admiring comparison to Big Mo, the US Navy battleship Missouri famed at the time for World War II exploits. — *Boston Globe*, p. E7, 17th January 2003

big mother *noun*
a Sikorsky SH-3 helicopter used by the US Navy in Vietnam for search and rescue missions *US, 1990*
- The Sea Kings were affectionately known as "Big-Mothers" to those who flew and depended on them for rescue. — Gregory Clark, *Words of the Vietnam War*, p. 462, 1990
- The "Big Mother" SH-3 went in and picked up both survivors, although it got five bullet holes in it for its trouble. — Robert Powell, *Vigilante Units in Combat*, p. 73, 3004

Big Muddy *nickname*
1 the Mississippi River *US, 1846*
- Not only is the "Big Muddy" a long, long river, it is filled with majestic dams that create monstrous lakes. — *Mansfield (Ohio) News Journal*, p. 1B, 7th March 2004
2 the Missouri River *US, 1825*
- I told Eva-line I was going to take him over to Big Muddy, which runs into the Mississippi River around Murphysboro[.] — Minnesota Fats, *The Bank Shot*, p. 153, 1966
- Uncertain about the depth of the Missouri River over the summer, the two barge companies that move grain and fertilizer on the Big Muddy have shut down their operations, at least through 2004. — *St. Louis Post-Dispatch*, p. C1, 15th January 2004

big nickel *noun*
five hundred dollars *US, 1961*
- — John Scarne, *Scarne's Guide to Modern Poker*, p. 273, 1979

big noise *noun*
1 an important and influential person *US, 1906*
- "We want an exciting campaign, we want you to be a big noise in this campaign." [Quoting Chris Matthews] — *New York Observer*, p. 1, 2nd February 2004
2 in poker, the alpha player at a table *US, 1996*
- — John Vorhaus, *The Big Book of Poker Slang*, p. 7, 1996

bignum *noun*
any very large number, especially if greater than 2,147,483,648 *US, 1983*
- — Guy L. Steele et al., *The Hacker's Dictionary*, p. 30, 1983

big NUMBER-oh *noun*
a birthday ending with a zero, especially 30, 40, and 50 *US, 1980*
- Some women get depressed when they hit the big five-oh. Others get motivated. — *Atlanta Journal-Constitution*, p. 21JA, 27th November 2003
- Helping her ring in the big three-oh were Sean Patrick Thomas, Alanna Ubach, Tiffany Limos ... — *Hollywood Reporter*, 13th October 2003
- Brett Hawthorne hits the big "4-oh" today. — *Herald-Dispatch (Huntington, West Virginia)*, p. 9A, 28th February 2004

Big O *noun*
1 an orgasm *US, 1968*
- Then, just as I was about to reach the big O, shrieking with pleasure, he hurled me down the stairs[.] — Gore Vidal, *Myra Breckinridge*, p. 270, 1968
- One of them is the wedge-shaped "Snap-On Stimulator" which again is aimed at the Clitoral big "O." — Angelo d'Arcangelo, *The Homosexual Handbook*, p. 223, 1968
- He's got spine, but he's not the type who can't wait to leave after the big O. — Anka Radakovich, *The Wild Girls Club*, p. 21, 1994
- On the subject of the Big O, the Newsweek article gets even more infuriating. — *The Village Voice*, 13th June 2000
- For those of you who've already experienced the joys of the Big O, you know how it feels[.] — Tristan Taormino, *Pucker Up*, p. 22, 2001
2 opium; heroin *US, 1957*
- "I'm here because of opium. The big O." — United States Senate Committee on Veterans' Affairs, *Drug Addiction and Abuse Among Military Veterans.*, p. 455, 1971
- I'm not trying to hide the fact that I was smoking the Big O that night. — Ron Rosenbaum, *Murder at Elaine's*, p. 41, 1978

big one *noun*
1 one hundred dollars *US, 1961*

- "How much?" "I said, three big ones." — Ross Russell, *The Sound*, p. 135, 1961
2 one thousand dollars *US, 1863*
- He could tell a bitch he needed—not wanted—five or six big ones without her saying "Whatta you need that kinda money for?" — A.S. Jackson, *Gentleman Pimp*, p. 59, 1973
- "How the hell am I gonna deliver ten big ones in little bills right in the middle of all them cops?" — Martin Gosch, *The Last Testament of Lucky Luciano*, p. 86, 1975
- But twenty big ones each? — George V. Higgins, *Penance for Jerry Kennedy*, p. 76, 1985
- Fifteen for the vig plus the ten, that's twenty-five big ones you go for a whole year, buddy! You hear me? — *Get Shorty*, 1995
3 one million dollars *US, 1967*
- "Three big ones, baby! And final cut!" "Three million? You're kidding." — Terry Southern, *Blue Movie*, p. 47, 1970
4 World War 2 *US, 1971*
- Well, I was in Italy, fighting the Big One, one-hundred fifty-six missions over Europe, my group. — Eugene Boe (Compiler), *The Wit & Wisdom of Archie Bunker*, p. 39, 1971
5 the Ringling Brothers, Barnum and Bailey circus *US, 1973*
- — Sherman Louis Sergel, *The Language of Show Biz*, p. 20, 1973

big orange pill *noun*
during the war in Vietnam, the antimalarial pill taken once a week in addition to the daily medication *US, 1991*
Chloroquine-primaquine was taken weekly in the form of a large, orange-colored pill.
- I don't know a soul who served in Southeast Asia that didn't have some kind of problem with the big orange pill, some were just worse than others. — Stanley McGowen, *You Ain't Gonna Believe This But*, p. 93, 2004

bigot *noun*
in computing, a person who is irrationally attached to a particular operating system or computer language *US, 1991*
- True bigots can be distinguished from mere partisans or zealots by the fact that they refuse to learn alternatives even when the march of time and/or technology is threatening to obsolete the favored tool. — Eric S. Raymond, *The New Hacker's Dictionary*, p. 59, 1991
- — Christian Crumlish, *The Internet Dictionary*, p. 21, 1995

big ouch *noun*
a serious injury *US, 1962*
- — *American Speech*, p. 271, December 1962: "The language of traffic policemen"

big outpatient department in the sky *noun*
death *US, 1988–1989*
- — *Maledicta*, p. 35, 1988–1989: "More Milwukee medical maledicta"

big place *noun*
a state prison *US, 1969*
- "He's been in and out of the big place so often. And that's not including shorter stays in the county jail." — L.H. Whittemore, *Cop!*, p. 193, 1969

big pockets *noun*
wealth *US, 1971*
- "Them ole gals just comes around when I got big pockets." — Robert Deane Pharr, *S.R.O.*, p. 302, 1971

big PX in the sky *noun*
death *US, 1991*
Vietnam war usage, grim humor based on many cheerful euphemisms for death as a "big [fill in the blank] in the sky."
- No big PX in the sky for him. — Danielle Steel, *Message from Nam*, p. 223, 1991

Big Q *nickname*
the San Quentin State Prison, California *US, 1961*
Just north of San Francisco, San Quentin houses California's death chamber.
- Simpkins was convicted of five counts of robbery one with aggravated assault, for five-to-life at Big Q[.] — James Ellroy, *Hollywood Nocturnes*, p. 129, 1994

Big R *noun*
during the Korean war, rotation home *US, 1960*

Distinguished from the conventional **R AND R** (rest and recreation).
- — *American Speech*, p. 121, May 1960: "Korean bamboo English"

big red *noun*
1 secobarbitol, a sedative-hypnotic drug marketed under the brand name Seconal™ *US, 2001*
- He'd also legally scored far more interesting dope called secobarbital and sold as "Big Reds." These actually produced a slice of long-lasting silent giggles. — Howard Marks, *The Howard Marks Book of Dope Stories*, p. 113, 2001

2 adriamycin, an extremely toxic agent used in chemotherapy *US, 1994*
- — Sally Williams, *"Strong" Words*, p. 134, 1994

3 in craps, a one-roll bet on a seven *US, 1981*
If the shooter rolls a seven, he loses; "big red" thus serves as a diplomatic way to bet that the shooter will lose on the next roll.
- — N. B. Winkless, *The Gambling Times Guide to Craps*, p. 91, 1981

4 the desert sun *US, 1991*
- — *Army*, p. 47, November 1991

Big Red One *nickname*
the First Infantry Division, US Army *US, 1967*
The Division's patch is a big red number one.
- These men of the Big Red One held the record of more assault landings than any other US unit in WW II. — Elaine Shepard, *The Doom Pussy*, p. 8, 1967
- By 1969, as far as the Big Red One was concerned, tunnel rat strategy had been honed down to a sharp edge. — Tom Mangold, *The Tunnels of Cu Chi*, p. 239, 1985
- He had led a battalion, originally in the renowned 1st Infantry Division, "the Big Red One," and then a regiment flawlessly for more than two years[.] — Neil Sheehan, *A Bright Shining Lie*, p. 272, 1988
- There's the Big Red One and the First Air Cav/And all those other hordes. — Thomas Bowen, *The Longest Year*, p. 12, 1990: Ballad of Cords

Big Rock *nickname*
the US federal penitentiary on Alcatraz Island, San Francisco Bay *US, 1970*
- "Is there a blast, or are you going to the Big Rock?" He meant Alcatraz Island that we all used to joke about[.] — Red Rudensky, *The Gonif*, p. 60, 1970

bigs *noun*
in pool, the striped balls numbered 9 to 15 *US, 1990*
- — Steve Rushin, *Pool Cool*, p. 6, 1990

big shit *noun*
1 an important person, if only in their own eyes *US, 1934*
- "Ginsburg and Epstein don't pay off them welfare bigshits like they oughta." — Robert Deane Pharr, *S.R.O.*, p. 321, 1971
- "Tommy's trying to act big shit and order Italian dishes like he knows what he's doing." [Quoting James Lee Burke] — *USA Today*, p. 8D, 2nd August 1994

2 an important event or thing *US, 1960*
- We going down the road, smoking, talking cash trash, in laymen's terms, we talking big shit, right? — *Washington Post*, p. F1, 11th October 1992

big-six talk *noun*
talk unsupported by action *US, 1990*
- — Charles Shafer, *Folk Speech in Texas Prisons*, p. 198, 1990

big sleep *noun*
death; capital punishment *US, 1951*
- He told me he was going to get some one guy, even if he had to do the big sleep for it. — Thurston Scott, *Cure it with Honey*, p. 13, 1951

big slick *noun*
in hold 'em poker, an ace and a king as the first two cards dealt to a player *US, 1981*
- An ace and a king are a Santa Barbara. The older term for that is big slick, but a few years ago there was an oil spill off the coast and the California players started called it Santa Barbara. — Thomas L. Clark, *The Dictionary of Gambling and Gaming*, pp. 18–19, 1987

Big Smoke *nickname*
Pittsburgh, Pennsylvania *US, 1930*
- Today, Pittsburgh is ranked among the cleanest cities in the world and often listed as one of the five most livable cities by several national magazines. Old "Big Smoke" has finally left its cloudy legacy behind. — *Times Union (Albany, New York)*, p. J1, 2nd June 2002

big sniff *noun*
execution in the gas chamber *US, 1969*
- The D.A. made it out as a triangle slaying, and he made it stick. So Jerry was going to take the Big Sniff. — Juan Carmel Cosmes, *Memoir of a Whoremaster*, p. 66, 1969

big spark *noun*
an electric shock administered in a hospital to a patient whose heart has failed in an attempt to revive the heart *US, 1994*
- — Sally Williams, *"Strong" Words*, p. 143, 1994

big tender *noun*
a scene in a pornographic film when the participants hug each other *US, 1991*
- Now, this [on screen] is what we call "the big tender," only the dialogue is a little different[.] — Robert Stoller and I.S. Levine, *Coming Attractions*, p. 88, 1991
- — *Adult Video News*, p. 42, August 1995

big-ticket *adjective*
expensive; representing a major purchase *US, 1945*
- Dick Nichols said, "Now you're talking about a big-ticket item." — Elmore Leonard, *Bandits*, p. 192, 1987

big time *noun*
1 the highest level of achievement in a field *US, 1910*
Originally theatrical.
- "I been away." She said, "Uh-oh. You mean you were in jail?" "Jail, shit, the big time." — Elmore Leonard, *Maximum Bob*, p. 149, 1991
- They started off robbing 7/11 type stores and gas stations and later graduated to banks and the big time. — *Natural Born Killers*, 1994

2 a long sentence to state prison *US, 1939*
- "What else could you be? As much big time as you pulled?" — Malcolm Braly, *It's Cold Out There*, p. 40, 1966

3 heroin *US, 1971*
- — Eugene Landy, *The Underground Dictionary*, p. 33, 1971
- — Richard A Spears, *The Slang and Jargon of Drugs and Drink.*, p. 44, 1986

big-time *verb*
to show off *US, 1957*
- That was the way jokers in Harlem carried their money when they wanted to big-time. — Chester Himes, *A Rage in Harlem*, p. 76, 1957

Big Tom *noun*
in a carnival ball-throwing game, a big stuffed cat target that has been weighted and is thus hard to knock down *US, 1981*
- — Don Wilmeth, *The Language of American Popular Entertainment*, p. 22, 1981

big top *noun*
a prison, especially a maximum-security state prison *US, 1955*
- He went straight to the big top, Rikers Island. — Rocky Garciano (with Rowland Barber), *Somebody Up There Likes Me*, p. 76, 1955
- Fixer, I'm going to send those dirty bastards to the big-top for murder-one. — Iceberg Slim (Robert Beck), *Trick Baby*, p. 306, 1969
- This killing was witnessed by twelve hundred cons during the noon meal at the Big Top's mess hall[.] — Red Rudensky, *The Gonif*, p. 21, 1970
- — John R. Armore and Joseph D. Wolfe, *Dictionary of Desperation*, p. 20, 1976

big train *noun*
in horse racing, a great racehorse *US, 1951*
- — David W. Maurer, *Argot of the Racetrack*, p. 14, 1951

big Turk *noun*
an ostrich *US, 1981*
Circus and carnival usage.
- — Don Wilmeth, *The Language of American Popular Entertainment*, p. 22, 1981

Big Two *nickname*
World War 2 *US, 1961*
- He'd been in the Big Two and had come out a war hero, having been among those who'd fought their way up the boot of Italy and past the slaughterhouse known as Monte Cassino. — Robert Campbell, *Boneyard*, p. 10, 1992

big wheel *noun*
a prominent, powerful and important person *US, 1942*

- Heretofore I thought Kalecki was the big wheel behind the syndicate, but now I could see that he was only a small part of it. — Mickey Spillane, *I, The Jury*, p. 157, 1947
- Every one of us is a big wheel, and I don't mind telling you I'm one of the biggest. — Hal Ellson, *Tomboy*, p. 90, 1950
- The athletes and the rich boys and the brains were the big wheels at Summer High School. — Dick Gregory, *Nigger*, p. 47, 1964
- Big hara put the cuffs on me in the car, just in case a big wheel was present when they brought me in. — Piri Thomas, *Down These Mean Streets*, p. 314, 1967

big whoop!
used to mock the importance of what has just been said *US, 1981*
- I'll never drive your precious Mercedes again. Big whoop. — *American Beauty*, 1999
- I now, you're thinking, Fifty dollars! Big whoop! — Missy Hyatt, *Missy Hyatt*, p. 35, 2001

big win *noun*
complete luck *US, 1991*
- "Yes, those two physicists discovered high-temperature superconductivity in a batch of ceramic that had been prepared incorrectly according to their experimental schedule. Small mistake; big win!" — Eric S. Raymond, *The New Hacker's Dictionary*, p. 56, 1991

big yard *noun*
the main yard in a prison where the general population mingles for recreation *US, 1958*
- I, at last encountered, when first stumbling across the "Big Yard"— as the "cons" call it[.] — Neal Cassady, *Grace Beats Karma*, p. 59, 16th October 1958: Letter to Carolyn Cassady
- Jack gave him the Big Yard stare, cold and hard, set his tone low, and asked, "What did you say?" — Elmore Leonard, *Bandits*, p. 104, 1987

big yellow mama *nickname*
the electric chair *US, 2001*
- Ohio and other states call it "Old Sparky." In Alabama, it's the "Big Yellow Mama." In Mississippi, it's "Black Death." — *Cincinnati Enquirer*, p. 1F, 2nd September 2001

bike *noun*
a motorcycle police officer *US, 1958*
- — *New York Times Magazine*, p. 87, 16th March 1958

bike doc *noun*
in mountain biking, a bicycle mechanic *US, 1992*
- — William Nealy, *Mountain Bike!*, p. 162, 1992

bikini bar *noun*
a sex club where the dancer strips down to her bikini *US, 1988*
- Those exercises and her three-our shifts as an exotic dancer in bikini bars would one day give her the physical strength to hoist people twice her weight over her head. — *Los Angeles Times*, p. 1 (Part 5), 18th January 1988
- "I just want a bikini bar. Girls are going to wear beach bikinis, not tiny little strings," she said. — *Riveride (California) Press Enterprise*, p. B1, 2nd September 1994
- A Scottsdale cabaret owner is currently working on turning the property around the corner from Majerle's into a "bikini bar" (translation: topless, but with panties). — *Phoenix New Times*, 11th December 2003

bikini wax *noun*
an application of hot wax to remove a woman's pubic hair *US, 1982*
- — Mary Corey and Victoria Westermark, *Fer Shurr! How to be a Valley Girl*, 1982
- Cosmo may mention where to get a good bikini wax for that trip to the Bahamas, but what about the girl who wants to go beyond the bathing-suit line? — *The Village Voice*, 8th-14th November 2000

bilged *adjective*
worn out, tired *US, 1968*
- — Fred Hester, *Slang on the 40 Acres*, p. 15, 1968

bilingual *adjective*
bisexual *US, 1964*
- — Roger Blake, *The American Dictionary of Sexual Terms*, p. 17, 1964
- — Dale Gordon, *The Dominion Sex Dictionary*, p. 29, 1967
- — Anon., *King Smut's Wet Dreams Interpreted*, 1978

bill *noun*
1 a dollar *US, 1915*
- He'd raised one hundred sixty-five bills to buy an anti-war ad in the school paper, and then the principal, who is widely held to be a bad person, refused to let the ad run. — James Simon Kunen, *The Strawberry Statement*, p. 80, 1968
- Like I was saying about the hundred bills: the suit and shoes would run about eight bill, right? — Nathan Heard, *Howard Street*, p. 160, 1968
- They must have won eighty dollars between them last night at poker (and spent considerable time letting us be reminded of the fact on the way over here), and they walk after being shot down for a measly five bills. — Jim Carroll, *Forced Entries*, p. 65, 1987

2 one hundred dollars *US, 1929*
- I'll sound Jimmy on a stronger advance, say a bill and a half, but I can't guarantee anything. — Ross Russell, *The Sound*, p. 189, 1961
- "I only got two bills because I made it with a donkey." — Elliott Parker, *What You Always Wanted to Know About Sodomy and Perversion*, p. 256, 1972
- He's pulling down six bills a week. — *The Blues Brothers*, 1980
- If this stuff is worth twenty-five bills then I probably won't have to sell all of it. — Kenneth Lonergan, *This is Our Youth*, p. 94, 2000

▶ **do a bill**
to spend one hundred dollars *US, 1974*
- — Stewart L. Tubbs and Sylvia Moss, *Human Communication*, p. 120, 1974

Bill!
used as a warning that police are near *US, 1998*
- "Now, when they see me, they yell '5-0' or 'Bill! Bill!,' street slang for police." — *Record (Bergen County, New Jersey)*, p. L1, 24th February 1998

Bill Daley *noun*
▶ **on the Bill Daley**
in horse racing, having taken the lead at the start of the race and held it for the entire race *US, 1932*
- Tod [Sloan] got his horses away from the post fast and put them out in front. He was "off on a Bill Daly." — *San Francisco Examiner*, p. 17, 28th June 1949
- — David W. Maurer, *Argot of the Racetrack*, p. 46, 1951
- He would, as the saying goes, "be off on a Bill Daly" and get so far out in front that the foreign jockeys employed the "come from behind" technique couldn't catch him. — *San Francisco Examiner*, p. 21, 15th January 1952
- Claude was a wire-to-wire winner and as a result the phrase "on the Bill Daley" was coined and today it is uttered hundreds of times daily by racetrackers. — *San Francisco News Call-Bulletin*, p. 51, 14th April 1965

billfold biopsy *noun*
a hospital's analysis of the ability of a patient seeking admission to pay their bill *US, 1986*
- — Rachel S. Epstein and Nina Liebman, *Biz Speak*, p. 20, 1986

Billie Hoke *noun*
cocaine *US, 1959*
A personification based on **COKE**.
- — J.E. Schmidt, *Narcotics Lingo and Lore*, p. 16, 1959

billies; billys *noun*
money *US, 1982*
- I saw the kill mini, but like I totally don't have the billys to buy it[.] — Mary Corey and Victoria Westermark, *Fer Shurr! How to be a Valley Girl*, 1982

bills *noun*
1 money *US, 1997*
- Those without bills have spare change. — Vann Wesson, *Generation X Field Guide and Lexicon*, p. 18, 1997
2 the game of pool *US, 1993*
- — Mike Shamos, *The Illustrated Encyclopedia of Billiards*, p. 29, 1993

billy *noun*
1 an unsophisticated rustic *US, 1991*
An abbreviation of "hillbilly."
- To the chagrin of established white ethnic groups, the billies swarmed into the red brick and Formstone rowhouses in the southern reaches of the city. — David Simon, *Homicide*, p. 420, 1991
- Never mind that it's three black men and a white girl held hostage in the street by a red-faced billy. — David Simon and Edward Burns, *The Corner*, p. 317, 1997

2 a police officer's blackjack or club, a truncheon *US, 1850*
- I clung desperately to the back of the seat until one of the cops hit me on the arm with a billy. — Hunter S. Thompson, *Songs of the Doomed*, p. 86, 1962

- The cop came down. He had his billy out. — Nat Hentoff, *Jazz Country*, p. 129, 1965
- Back at school I eat in a restaurant full of police. As audibly as possible I compose a poem entitled "Ode to the TPF." It extols the beauty of rich wood billies, the sheen of handcuffs, the feel of a boot on your face. — James Simon Kunen, *The Strawberry Statement*, p. 45, 1968

bim *noun*

a shortened form of "bimbo" *US, 1925*

- — Lou Shelly, *Hepcats Jive Talk Dictionary*, p. 7, 1945
- I date the best-looking bims in Sigma at school, and I'm a Kapp, the best frat there. — James T. Farrell, *Saturday Night*, p. 34, 1947
- The table is so situated that the town's aging and more prosperous squab-hunters who congregate at it nightly can case the door and ogle the bims brought in by younger and more energetic men. — Jack Lait and Lee Mortimer, *New York Confidential*, p. 166, 1948
- But a bim that won't bolt while you doin' a little jolt / is just one out of a thousand my friend. — Bruce Jackson, *Get Your Ass in the Water and Swim Like Me*, p. 116, 1964

bimbette *noun*

a young, mindless, attractive woman *US, 1982*

A diminutive of the more widely known **BIMBO**.

- Shannon and the other blonde bimbettes gasp in delight as they bring this ballbusting orgy to its only possible conclusion. — *Adult Video*, p. 32, August/September 1986
- I don't need these bimbettes you got me chasing. — *Something About Mary*, 1998

bimbo *noun*

a well-built, attractive, somewhat dim woman *US, 1920*

An offensive term.

- New York has the most beautiful bimbos on earth and it will amuse you to learn that few of them come from New York. — Jack Lait and Lee Mortimer, *New York Confidential*, p. 130, 1948
- When Biff gets there with the bimbo he finds 94 of my baby turtles crawling in the bed[.] — Bernard Wolfe, *The Late Risers*, p. 13, 1954
- Then the bimbo gets kidnapped by some Zombies[.] — Joe Bob Briggs, *Joe Bob Goes to the Drive-In*, p. 156, 1987
- He had a typical Frenchman's attitude toward women—i.e., that they were all bimbos. — Terry Southern, *Now Dig This*, p. 174, 1991

bindle stiff *noun*

a migratory worker; a tramp *US, 1897*

- Every bindle stiff on the street lifted his lids, and eyed this group of black kids coming along the Bowery. — Emmett Grogan, *Ringolevio*, p. 9, 1972

bing *noun*

1 jail, especially solitary confinement in jail *US, 1932*

- Mrs. McDonnell one day passes the bing (cramped little cell where guys are stuck in solitary confinement, as punishment), finds somebody locked up there and runs to Big John screaming[.] — Mezz Mezzrow, *Really the Blues*, p. 315, 1946
- Later on, Collier made the bing again on a battery charge. — *San Francisco Examiner*, p. 16, 13th November 1947
- Boys sent to the bing (the solitary confinement cell, the punishment chamber—without mattress, light, or reading matter, an inmate must stand silently for five days and sleep on the cement floor), sent there for fighting, talking, dressing improperly, or getting seconds on food. — *Evergreen*, p. 46, April 1970
- The only game I'm going to play with you is to break your little Puerto Rican ass and slam you in the bing until you leave this place. — Miguel Pinero, *Short Eyes*, p. 104, 1975

2 an injection with a hypodermic needle and syringe *US, 1918*

- — J.E. Schmidt, *Narcotics Lingo and Lore*, p. 16, 1959

3 crack cocaine; a piece of crack cocaine *US, 1994*

- — US Department of Justice, *Street Terms*, October 1994

bingo *noun*

a prison riot *US, 1992*

- — William K. Bentley and James M. Corbett, *Prison Slang*, p. 100, 1992

bingo!

used for emphasis or for registering pleasurable surprise, success, excitement *UK, 1927*

- They take a bit here and a bit there until the picture is complete and bingo, they have something we're trying to keep under the hat. — Mickey Spillane, *One Lonely Night*, p. 94, 1951

- No way, Jose, the cop said. Bingo: nine months in the laundry at Wayside. — James Ellroy, *Suicide Hill*, p. 597, 1986
- HITCHHIKER: You see Eight-Minute Abs and right next to it you see Seven-Minute Abs—which you gonna spring for? TED: I'd go with the seven. HITCHHIKER: Bingo. — *Something About Mary*, 1998
- ELLE: Bill? BUDD: Wrong brother, you hateful bitch. ELLE: Budd? BUDD: Bingo. — *Kill Bill*, 2003

bingo field *noun*

a field in Vietnam where an American bomber could land safely if unable to return to its home aircraft carrier *US, 1984*

- It started becoming real when we started getting fewer and fewer "bingo" fields. — Wallace Terry, *Bloods*, p. 193, 1984

binky *noun*

a baby's pacifier that a heroin user has converted into a squeeze bulb for injecting a dose of heroin through an eye dropper and needle into the vein *US, 1989*

From the common childrens' nickname for a pacifier.

- — Geoffrey Froner, *Digging for Diamonds*, p. 9, 1989

binocs *noun*

binoculars *US, 1943*

- Those Germans might be some crazy, genocidal Hitler-loving bastards, but they knew how to make a great pair of binocs. — John Ridley, *Everybody Smokes in Hell*, p. 174, 1999

binos *noun*

binoculars *US, 1976*

- The platoon commanders went up on top for one last look through the binos and to hear the Captain's plan. — Charles Anderson, *The Grunts*, p. 58, 1976
- Late one afternoon, on top of the pass, my RTO squatted beside me as I swept the highway far below with my binos. — Cherokee Paul McDonald, *Into the Green*, p. 24, 2001

bip *noun*

the head; the brain *US, 1947*

- At first the good citizens say he's off his bip. — Harry Haenigsen, *Jive's Like That*, 1947

bip *verb*

to break into a house while the housewife is outside hanging laundry on the line to dry *US, 1972*

An abbreviation of **SCALLYBIP**.

- Around Christmas of that year me and a friend was going to go up through Oklahoma bipping—scallybipping [burglarizing a home when they saw the wife out back hanging clothes], you know. — Bruce Jackson, *In the Life*, p. 82, 1972

bipe *verb*

to break and enter the dwelling of another while they sleep, with the intent of stealing *US, 1990*

- — Charles Shafer, *Folk Speech in Texas Prisons*, p. 198, 1990

bippy *noun*

used as a jocular euphemism for "ass" *US, 1967*

Coined and popularized by Rowan and Martin on the television program *Laugh-In* (NBC,1968–73); a wildly popular word for several years, the key word in the title of the 1969 Rowan and Martin film *The Maltese Bippy*, and then abandoned on the junk heap of slang.

- You bet your sweet bippy I did. [Quoting Apollo 10 crew member Tom Satfford] — *San Francisco Examiner*, p. 1, 26th May 1969
- — Helen Dahlskog (Editor), *A Dictionary of Contemporary and Colloquial Usage*, p. 7, 1972

bird *noun*

1 an ordinary fellow *US, 1839*

- This is an inside job, pulled by one of the company or some bird working for them. — Chester Gould, *Dick Tracy Meets the Night Crawler*, p. 28, 1945
- You birds say that knowledge is power—yet all your knowledge turns into impotence when you want it used for human harmony and peace. — Philip Wylie, *Opus 21*, p. 58, 1949

2 the penis *US, 1969*

- — John D. Bell et al., *Loosely Speaking*, p. Addenda, 1969
- "Bird"—the male organ. Used in jovial greeting, as in "How's your bird?" — *Washington Post*, p. B1, 17th January 1985

3 a homosexual man *US, 1956*

- The muggers and the sluggers who in recent years have made it unsafe for almost anyone to walk the public streets late at night, learned about the Birds long ago. — Robert Sylvester, *No Cover Charge*, p. 268, 1956

4 a surfer who uses any bird or wings as his surfboard logo *US, 1988*

- — Michael V. Anderson, *The Bad, Rad, Not to Forget Way Cool Beach and Surf Discriptionary*, p. 3, 1988

5 a twenty-five cent betting token *US, 1974*

- — Thomas L. Clark, *The Dictionary of Gambling and Gaming*, p. 19, 1987

6 a gesture of the middle finger, meaning "fuck you" *US, 1961*

- It was Red's way of giving him the bird. — Ross Russell, *The Sound*, p. 177, 1961
- — Frank Prewitt and Francis Schaeffer, *Vacaville Vocabulary*, 1961–1962
- — Collin Baker, *College Undergraduate Slang Study Conducted at Brown University*, p. 79, 1968
- He got up the juice to give me a feeble middle-finger farewell, and when the bird was in midair I stepped on his heart and pushed down[.] — James Ellroy, *Hollywood Nocturnes*, p. 141, 1994

7 an amphetamine tablet *US, 1992*

- — Jay Robert Nash, *Dictionary of Crime*, p. 29, 1992
- — Peter Johnson, *Dictionary of Street Alcohol and Drug Terms*, p. 19, 1993

8 a kilogram of cocaine *US, 2002*

- "In the past two or three years around here, a brick, kilo of coke— 1,000 grams of the drug, they'd call a 'bird,'" Hagedorn said. — *Milwaukee Journal Sentinel*, p. 1B, 9th February 2002

9 Wild Turkey™ whisky *US, 1984*

- "I've never seen anybody that loved that ol' Bird as much as Jim Ed. When he buys a bottle, he just throws the cap away." — Ken Weaver, *Texas Crude*, p. 64, 1984
- We just chillin' out, drinking a little Bird, that's all. You want a taste? — Odie Hawkins, *Great Lawd Buddha*, p. 11, 1990

10 a helicopter *US, 1967*

- "Unless the friendlies have their ass in a crack, no raget is worth a man or a bird." — Elaine Shepard, *The Doom Pussy*, p. 51, 1967
- A total of eight birds (helicopters) could make a pick-up simultaneously. — Kenneth Mertel, *Year of the Horse*, p. 66, 1968
- Seven birds appeared from behind the resupply tent. — William Pelfrey, *The Big V*, p. 23, 1972
- But we got special permission tonight for this big shot, 'cause we had to land the bird in the middle of the street[.] — Stephen J. Cannell, *The Tin Collectors*, p. 239, 2001

▸ **for the birds**
no good, shoddy *US, 1944*

- — Arnold Shaw, *Lingo of Tin-Pan Alley*, p. 7, 1950

birdbath *noun*
a cursory washing of the body using little water *US, 1953*

- [A]fter I've finished my calisthenics and the hot water has arrived, I take me a bird (jailbird) bath in the little sink. — Eldridge Cleaver, *Soul on Ice*, p. 43, 1968

birdbrain *noun*
a human who gives the impression of possessing a bird-size brain; a fool *US, 1933*

- Leo wasn't there—probably out chasing missing persons, the birdbrain[.] — Bernard Wolfe, *The Late Risers*, p. 4, 1954
- In spite of his father's reputation as the family intellectual, Billy, at about age twelve, considered him something of a birdbrain[.] — Darryl Ponicsan, *The Last Detail*, p. 11, 1970

birdcage *noun*
1 the anus *US, 1972*

- — Bruce Rodgers, *The Queens' Vernacular*, p. 18, 1972

2 a box used for storing dice *US, 1962*

- — Frank Garcia, *Marked Cards and Loaded Dice*, p. 250, 1962

bird circuit *noun*
a prolonged group tour of gay bars; the bars themselves *US, 1956*

- The Bird Circuit—a network of saloons and small night clubs catering exclusively to the homosexuals—and what are generally known as Broad Joints. — Robert Sylvester, *No Cover Charge*, p. 265, 1956
- — *The Guild Dictionary of Homosexual Terms*, p. 4, 1965
- [R]ight after the war the bars of New York were filled with beauty, particularly along "the bird circuit" as it was then known[.] — Gore Vidal, *Myron*, p. 335, 1974

bird colonel; full-bird colonel *noun*
in the US Army, a full colonel *US, 1946*
From the eagle insignia.

- A bird colonel, commanding a brigade of the 4th Infantry Division. — Michael Kerr, *Dispatches*, p. 178, 1977
- Had NCO's all around his desk / And a full Bird Colonel in the leanin' rest. — Sandee Shaffer Johnson, *Cadences*, p. 66, 1986
- He [Oliver North] is a lieutenant colonel in the United States Marine Corps, although his chances of making bird colonel seem dim this week. — Hunter S. Thompson, *Generation of Swine*, p. 184, 1988

bird dog *noun*
1 a Cessna observation aircraft *US, 1992*

- Now Charlie didn't like the sound of that birddog / And the bullets began to fly. — Joseph Tuso, *Singing the Vietnam Blues*, p. 142, 1990: Old 97, the O-IE
- Their sister squadron, VMO-2, had light, fixed-wing Cessna observation aircraft, "Bird Dogs," for forward air control (FAC) and for controlling attack bombers[.] — Bob Stoffey, *Cleared Hot!*, p. 8, 1992
- The Navy jet jockeys loved to poke fun of Air Force forward air controllers in single engine bird dogs, which flew low and very slow. — Paul Morgan, *The Parrot's Beak*, p. 19, 2000

2 a scout *US, 1929*

- The boys had instructed their courtroom bird dogs to call that number as soon as the verdict was in. — Robert Sylvester, *No Cover Charge*, p. 205, 1956
- I had a bird dog in almost every "action" room who would tip me off for small change. — Robert Byrne, *McGoorty*, pp. 25–26, 1972
- Art says Mansell used him as a bird dog. Mr. Sweety would go in a dope house—very friendly type of guy—sit around and chat a while, pass out some angel dusty, tell a few jokes—that's the way they worked. Get 'em laid back on the dusty, then Clement comes in and takes 'em off easy... — Elmore Leonard, *City Primeval*, p. 100, 1980

3 in professional sports, a talent scout or a scout's associates who let him know about players who may be prospects for professional play *US, 1950*

- — Richard Scholl, *Running Press Glossary of Baseball Language*, p. 16, 1977
- — Bill Shefski, *Running Press Glossary of Football Language*, p. 15, 1978
- Paul's scouts also found Vada Pinson, Jim Maloney, Tony Perez and—after much cajoling from Buddy Bloebaum, a bird-dog scout who was the kid's uncle—Pete Rose. — *Cincinnati Enquirer*, p. 4D, 28th October 2003

4 a person who provides information about potential victims to a thief or group of thieves *US, 1977*

- — Robert C. Prus and C.R.D. Sharper, *Road Hustler*, p. 169, 1977

5 a navigational device in planes that points in the direction of a radio signal *US, 1956*

- — *American Speech*, p. 227, October 1956: "More United States Air Force slang"
- — *American Speech*, p. 118, May 1963: "Air refueling words"

6 a person who solicits players for gambling, whether in a casino or a private poker game *US, 1949*

- — Thomas L. Clark, *The Dictionary of Gambling and Gaming*, p. 19, 1987
- — George Percy, *The Language of Poker*, p. 10, 1988

bird-dog *verb*
1 to eavesdrop *US, 2002*

- [S]ome wood suggests I stop bird—dogging his conversation (eavesdropping—one of my many character flaws). — Jimmy Lerner, *You Got Nothing Coming*, p. 185, 2002

2 to flirt with another's date *US, 1941*

- You oughta be out running around in a convertible, bird-dogging girls. — Ken Kesey, *One Flew Over the Cuckoo's Nest*, p. 184, 1962
- — *American Speech*, p. 193, October 1965: "Notes on campus vocabulary, 1964"

3 to look for, find and return with someone or something *US, 1948*

- Old Preston was back out there bird-dogging suckers. — Iceberg Slim (Robert Beck), *Pimp*, p. 98, 1969
- [T]he pilot-mogul had me out bird-dogging quiff: prowling bus depots and train stations for buxom young girls who'd fall prey to RKO contracts in exchange for frequent nighttime visits. — James Ellroy, *Hollywood Nocturnes*, p. 199, 1994

bird egg *noun*
an amphetamine tablet *US, 1993*

- — Peter Johnson, *Dictionary of Street Alcohol and Drug Terms*, p. 18, 1993

bird food *noun*
inferior quality marijuana *US, 2001*

- "Bet he didn't sell you this crummy bag a' bird food," Shane said, holding up the bag of thin, seed-ridden grass. — Stephen J. Cannell, *The Tin Collectors*, p. 98, 2001

birdie *noun*

a passive, effeminate male homosexual *US, 1921*

- — Vincent J. Monteleone, *Criminal Slang*, p. 23, 1949
- He didn't turn around even when he heard the crunch of boots on the gravel, or felt the heavy body of the bulldog creature filling the space at his back, or even when the sodomite spoke. "You're a birdie and I'm going to have your ass." — Robert Campbell, *Alice in La-La Land*, pp. 6–7, 1987

bird in a cage *noun*

the rank of Specialist 5, in the US Army *US, 1968*
From the eagle under a curved stripe on the chevron.

- — Carl Fleischhauer, *A Glossary of Army Slang*, p. 4, 1968

bird nest *noun*

a person's room, apartment, or house *US, 1973*

- Dickie held the sting, and I split back to the bird next to get what I left. — A.S. Jackson, *Gentleman Pimp*, p. 23, 1973

bird of paradise *noun*

the US armed forces insignia designating honorable discharge *US, 1946*

- — *American Speech*, p. 153, April 1946: "GI words from the separation center and proctology ward"

bird sanctuary *noun*

any institution where traffic violators who are under pursuit are free from further pursuit once they pass the gates *US, 1962*

- — *American Speech*, p. 267, December 1962: "The language of traffic policemen"

bird's eye *noun*

a small dose of heroin *US, 1973*

- A bird's eye is generally what a junker takes in his first bang after being on vacation for a while. — David Maurer and Victor Vogel, *The Slang and Jargon of Drugs and Drinks*, p. 388, 1973

bird's nest *noun*

pubic hair that can be seen to extend from the crotch to the navel *US, 1972*

- — Bruce Rodgers, *The Queens' Vernacular*, 1972

birdwood *noun*

a cigarette *US, 1944*

- — Lou Shelly, *Hepcats Jive Talk Dictionary*, p. 7, 1945

birthday card *noun*

in poker, the one card needed and drawn to complete an unlikely good hand *US, 1996*

- — John Vorhaus, *The Big Book of Poker Slang*, p. 7, 1996

birthday present *noun*

in tiddlywinks, a stroke of good luck *US, 1977*

- — *Verbatim*, p. 525, December 1977

birthday suit *noun*

a state of nudity *UK, 1771*

- "Why don't you go back to your place and change into something comfortable?" "My birthday suit?" — Robert Gover, *This Maniac Responsible*, p. 115, 1963

biscuit *noun*

1 a good-looking member of whatever sex attracts you *US, 1990*

- My brother was seeing this biscuit out here and she almost got him shot. — *Boyz N The Hood*, 1990
- But even the grunge-wear could not dull the brilliant polished-mineral black of his eyes or lessen the effect of his lavish eyelashes, pouting lips, or leanly muscled babe-of-life body. A biscuit, as Mab would say. — Francesca Lia Block, *I Was a Teenage Fairy*, p. 73, 1998
- — Connie Eble (Editor), *UNC-CH Campus Slang*, p. 1, Spring 1998

2 the head *US, 1934*

- — Lou Shelly, *Hepcats Jive Talk Dictionary*, p. 7, 1945
- "Then he yanks out the barker and bangs him. Smack in the biscuit." — Richard Prather, *The Peddler*, p. 67, 1952

3 a watch *US, 1905*

- Think our nut will show to take his biscuit out of hock? — Iceberg Slim (Robert Beck), *Doom Fox*, p. 175, 1978

4 a phonograph record *US, 1950*

- — Arnold Shaw, *Lingo of Tin-Pan Alley*, p. 7, 1950

5 a white tablet of methadone, a synthetic narcotic used to treat heroin addicts *US, 1972*

- — Richard A. Spears, *The Slang and Jargon of Drugs and Drink*, p. 46, 1986

6 a handgun *US, 1962*

- — Joseph E. Ragen and Charles Finston, *Inside the World's Toughest Prison*, p. 791, 1962
- "You have the biscuit?" Godineaux asked, using street slang for a gun. — *New York Post*, p. 4, 28th May 2000
- I roll with groups of ghetto bastards with biscuits. — RZA, *The Wu-Tang Manual*, p. 146, 2005

7 a black prisoner *US, 1976*

- — John R. Armore and Joseph D. Wolfe, *Dictionary of Desperation*, p. 20, 1976

8 used as a euphemism for "bitch" *US, 1999*

- Drop the biscuit. (I will!) — Eminem (Marshall Mathers), *Guilty Conscience*, 1999

biscuit *adjective*

easy *US, 1997*

- — Vann Wesson, *Generation X Field Guide and Lexicon*, p. 20, 1997

biscuit bitch *noun*

a female Red Cross volunteer *US, 1983*
Vietnam war usage; less common than the more popular **DOUGHNUT DOLLY**.

- Biscuit bitch refers to a female volunteer in the American Red Cross. — Philip Herbst, *Wimmin, Wimps & Wallflowers*, p. 24, 2001

biscuit gun *noun*

a signal light given from a landing strip to aircraft *US, 1952*

- Without radio contact you have to rely on "biscuit guns" beamed from the tower. — Elaine Shepard, *The Doom Pussy*, p. 191, 1967

biscuits *noun*

1 shoes *US, 1993*

- Wearing my fresh Pendleton shirt, beige khakis, and biscuits (old-men comfort shoes, the first shoe officially dubbed a "Crip shoe"), I threw on my black bomber jacket and stepped out into the warm summer night. — Sanyika Shakur, *Monster*, p. 45, 1993

2 money *US, 1977*

- — Bill Davis, *Jawjacking*, p. 18, 1977

biscuit snatcher *noun*

the hand; a finger *US, 1953*

- — Lavada Durst, *The Jives of Dr. Hepcat*, p. 11, 1953

bishop *noun*

the penis *US, 1916*
Used in a variety of expressions that refer to male masturbation.

- — Collin Baker et al., *College Undergraduate Slang Study Conducted at Brown University*, p. 80, 1968
- I banged the bishop over this one more times than I care to count. — Armistead Maupin, *Babycakes*, p. 75, 1984

bit *noun*

1 a prison sentence *US, 1866*

- Now that I was in the money and had done two bits in the pen, I got more respect from the gang. — Mezz Mezzrow, *Really the Blues*, p. 44, 1946
- He was sent up for his first real bit when he was 16. — Hubert Selby Jr., *Last Exit to Brooklyn*, p. 42, 1957
- By the time he was twenty-three he had done four bits in the joint. — Iceberg Slim (Robert Beck), *Pimp*, p. 33, 1969
- Jack Hardy, he worked for a safe company after he did a six-year bit. — *Casino*, 1995

2 an interest; an affected mannerism; a role *US, 1955*

- "What a drag!" said Red. "What's the bit?" "Hangoversville, for all I know," said her mother. — Steve Allen, *Bop Fables*, p. 37, 1955
- She had done the champagne-and-stout bit, the Westhampton bit, the French poodle bit. — Max Shulman, *Rally Round the Flag, Boys!*, p. 71, 1957
- Kim Novak is doing the intellectual bit. Reading scads of books. — *San Francisco Call-Bulletin*, p. 24, 21st November 1957

3 an activity *US, 1968*

- — Burton H. Wolfe, *The Hippies*, p. 203, 1968

4 used as a meaningless embellishment of the preceding noun, as in "Let's do the lunch bit" *US, 1955*

- In the white-collar canyons of Manhattan, the smart-talk boys are almost constantly "doing" some kind of "bit." If they want to propose going to lunch, they say: "Let's do the lunch bit." If they see a motion picture, they "do the movie bit." — *Philadelphia Evening Bulletin*, 11th October 1955

5 twelve and a half cents *US, 1821*

- "Two bits!" he yelled to the boy who took the hat. — Irving Shulman, *The Amboy Dukes*, p. 228, 1947
- It is customary to give her four bits for the pro in the powder-room. — Jack Lait and Lee Mortimer, *New York Confidential*, p. 221, 1948
- I had to panhandle two bits for the bus. I finally hit a Greek minister who was standing around the corner. He gave me the quarter with a nervous lookaway. — Jack Kerouac, *On the Road*, p. 107, 1957

6 twelve dollars and fifty cents *US, 1929*

- "One and four bits." — Lois O'Conner, *The Bare Facts*, p. 45, 1964
- Sweet meat, you wouldn't be happy, respect me, couldn't love me if say I became a funky tire changer for six bits a week to support us and whatsit's name? — Iceberg Slim (Robert Beck), *Doom Fox*, p. 75, 1978

▸ **pull a bit**
to serve a prison sentence *US, 1969*

- I thought about Oscar and wondered if he could pull his bit or if he would go back to his parents in a pine box, or worse to the crazy farm. — Iceberg Slim (Robert Beck), *Pimp*, p. 51, 1969

bit bashing *noun*
low level, tedious computer programing *US, 1991*

- — Eric S. Raymond, *The New Hacker's Dictionary*, p. 60, 1991

bit bucket *noun*
in computing, the mythical place where lost information goes *US, 1983*

- — Guy L. Steele et al., *The Hacker's Dictionary*, p. 33, 1983

bitca *noun*
used as a euphemism for **BITCH** *US, 2001*
Coined by the writers of the television series "Buffy the Vampire Slayer" in 2001 and used outside the confines of the show with some degree of referencing.

- Trips to Ireland, house in the Hamptons, sailboat, a modest amount of fame, a loving family. I'd say ol' Spalding's a whiny little bitca. — *alt.true-crime*, 15th January 2004
- He was hilarious and she wasn't such a selfish shallow bitca when they were together. — *televisionwithoutpity.com*, 6th June 2004

bitch *noun*
1 a woman *UK, 1713*

- Johnny was always telling us about bitches. To Johnny, every chick was a bitch. Even mothers were bitches. Of course, there were some nice bitches, but they were still bitches. — Claude Brown, *Manchild in the Promised Land*, p. 113, 1965
- I know you been traveling a lot of Europe and used to "dem harems" and things so I brought you four bitches. They're going to do anything you ask them to[.] — Babs Gonzales, *I Paid My Dues*, p. 84, 1967
- Bitch involves many connotations. It is, of course, allied to White middle-class usage, but is far from synonymous with it. Sometimes it is used insultingly or as a curse, but often it is used casually and without malice[.] — Christina and Richard Milner, *Black Players*, p. 32, 1972
- And if you bitches talk shit I'll have to put the smack down[.] — Dr. Dre, *Nuthin' But a "G" Thang*, 1992

2 a despicable woman *UK, 1400*

- On the other hand, Charles Laughton kills his wife in The Suspect (1944) because she is a total bitch. — Jeanine Basinger, *A Woman's View*, p. 383, 1995

3 the person taking the passive role in a male homosexual relationship; a feminine or weak man *UK, 1726*

- He was neither a wolf nor a wolverine but just a pleasant bitch who had a crush on me. — Chester Himes, *Cast the First Stone*, p. 72, 1952
- "You think you's a man, bitch. Running off with my ho like this." — Frederique Delacoste, *Sex Work*, p. 31, 1987
- I ain't nobody's bitch, you a bitch, Bitch. You a bitch, your daddy's a bitch and your momma's a bitch! — *Boyz N The Hood*, 1990
- Archie was the bitch and Jughead was the butch. — *Chasing Amy*, 1997
- And he said you're the bitch and you're the butch. — Kevin Smith, *Jay and Silent Bob Strike Back*, p. 11, 2001

4 a remarkable person or thing *US, 1943*

- Jack, I finally made it, I was a musician. If you'll pardon my beat-up English, ain't that a bitch. — Mezz Mezzrow, *Really the Blues*, p. 56, 1946

- I hear you've decided to bite the bullet, as it were, in re: The '74 Senate race. It should be a real bitch, eh? — Hunter S. Thompson, *Fear and Loathing in America*, p. 478, 22nd February 1973: Letter to Gary Hart

5 something that is difficult or unpleasant *UK, 1814*

- "That's a bitch," Robell said sympathetically. — Bernard Wolfe, *The Late Risers*, p. 263, 1954
- And a kid like this they give eight years to for nothing. Ain't that a bitch. — Darryl Ponicsan, *The Last Detail*, p. 34, 1970
- I heard Prohibition was a bitch, but the dope rumbles sure has buried a lot of people in my time. — Edwin Torres, *Carlito's Way*, p. 93, 1975
- You can bet that Texas boy, Charles Whitman, the fella who shot all them guys from that tower, I'll bet you green money that the first little black dot that he took a bead on, was the bitch of the bunch. — *True Romance*, 1993

6 in a deck of playing cards, any queen; in hearts, the queen of spades *US, 1900*

- — Joseph Weingarten, *American Dictionary of Slang*, p. 29, 1954

7 in chess, the queen *US, 1971*

- Checkschmuck! The Slang of the Chess Player — *American Speech*, p. 232, Autumn – Winter 1971
- The guy called the queen, the most powerful and versatile piece on the board, the "bitch." — Nathan McCall, *Makes Me Wanna Holler*, p. 147, 1994

8 a complaint; an extended period of complaining *US, 1945*

- "What's your bitch? You're having an affair, one of the better ones I've seen." — Sara Vogan, *Loss of Flight*, p. 37, 1989

9 the middle position of the back seat of a car *US, 1989*

- — Pamela Munro, *U.C.L.A. Slang*, p. 62, 1989

▸ **put the bitch on you; hit you with the bitch**
to file criminal charges accusing someone of being a habitual criminal *US, 1957*

- They tell me it's possible the judge may hit me with the bitch (habitual criminal) because my record will have a possible four strikes when I go up for trial. — James Blake, *The Joint*, p. 161, 7th January 1957
- — Bruce Jackson, *Outside the Law*, p. 59, 1972

bitch *verb*
1 to complain *US, 1918*

- In early January I realize it's been weeks since anyone has bitched about the desert. — Anthony Swofford, *Jarhead*, p. 151, 2003

2 to identify and punish someone as a habitual criminal *US, 1976*

- "While you wuz on Sick Bay I got bitched," Smoothbore cried over the crashing water. — Seth Morgan, *Homeboy*, p. 122, 1990

bitch-ass *adjective*
weak, effeminate *US, 1979*

- Bitch-ass motherfucker. — Elin Schoen, *Tales of an All-Night Town*, p. 89, 1979
- "Hey, dickhead," she screamed. "Tell your bitch-ass gorilla to get off him." — John Ridley, *Love is a Racket*, p. 225, 1998

bitch bath *noun*
a cleaning of the body using little water, powder, or other odor-masking agents *US, 1999*

- I took a bitch bath while two Kraqui artillery pieces burned about four hundred meters away. — Alex Vernon, *The Eyes of Orion*, p. 247, 1999

bitch box *noun*
a public address loudspeaker system *US, 1945*

- — *American Speech*, p. 54, February 1947: "Pacific war language"
- The Karp punched the general alarm and got on the bitch box to all the towers on the perimeter. — Malcolm Braly, *On the Yard*, p. 198, 1967
- I was awakened by a loud banging on the locked door coupled with the noise coming from the loudspeaker—the bitch box, we called it, from dispatch. — Bobby Seale, *A Lonely Rage*, p. 126, 1978
- Welch called down to the ship's bridge, using the "bitch box," the intercom system that connected important parts of the ship with each other. — Gerry Carroll, *North S*A*R*, p. 56, 1991

bitchen; bitching *adjective*
excellent *US, 1957*

- It was a bitchen day, too. — Frederick Kohner, *Gidget*, p. 4, 1957
- "Wouldn't that be bitchen?' says Tom Coman. Bitchen is a surfer's term that means "great," usually. — Tom Wolfe, *The Pump House Gang*, p. 19, 1968

- It was so bitchin' mon. Everybody is talking about it. — *Fast Times at Ridgemont High*, 1982
- Encino is like SO BITCHEN! — Moon Unit and Frank Zappa, *Valley Girl*, 1982

bitchen twitchen *adjective*
excellent *US*, *1982*
- — Mimi Pond, *The Valley Girl's Guide to Life*, p. 52, 1982

bitcher *noun*
a habitual criminal *US*, *1963*
- — Marlena Kay Nelson, *Rookies to Roaches*, p. 7, 1963

bitches' Christmas *noun*
Halloween *US*, *1964*
A glorious homosexual holiday, erotic and exotic.
- — Guy Strait, *The Lavender Lexicon*, 1 June 1964
- They were singing "Don us now our gay apparel" on Bitches' Christmas. — Bruce Rodgers, *Queens' Vernacular*, p. 32, 1972
- In some homosexual newspapers it's called Bitches' Christmas. — *San Francisco Examiner*, p. 3, 1st November 1976

bitch fight *noun*
a quarrel between ostentatiously effeminate male homosexuals *US*, *1964*
- — Guy Strait, *The Lavender Lexicon*, 1964

bitch fit *noun*
a temper tantrum *US*, *1969*
- Carey-Lee, secure in his knowledge that he is loved, does not throw a "bitch fit" when his nellie neighbor, Tommy (Edward Dunn) intimates that something more than a simple "visit" may have taken place while he was away. — *Screw*, p. 20, 27th October 1969

bitching *adjective*
used as a negative intensifier *US*, *1928*
An abbreviation of "son-of-a-bitching."
- But he'd manage it somehow. He bitchin' well had to. — Tom Ronan, *Moleskin Midas*, 1956

bitch kitty *noun*
an excellent instance of, or example of, something *US*, *1944*
- I was having one bitch kitty of a time tunning out the interracial sewer mouth shucking and jiving[.] — Iceberg Slim (Robert Beck), *Airtight Willie and Me*, p. 3, 1979

bitch lamp *noun*
an improvised lamp *US*, *1956*
- Long after he had gone to bed that night the light from the bitch lamp kept him awake. — Nelson Algren, *A Walk on the Wild Side*, p. 9, 1956

bitch off *verb*
to irritate someone *US*, *1975*
- — *American Speech*, p. 56, Spring–Summer 1975: "Razorback slang"

bitch on wheels *noun*
a person, especially a woman, with a truly nasty disposition *US*, *1946*
- The girl said she was a bitch on wheels. — Jerome Weidman, *Too Early to Tell*, p. 258, 1946
- — John D. Bell et al., *Loosely Speaking*, p. 2, 1966

bitch out *verb*
to criticize someone harshly *US*, *1955*
- No, the queens would have smelled him out, bitched him out years ago. — William Burroughs, *Letters to Allen Ginsberg 1953–1957*, p. 124, 2nd November 1955
- — Connie Eble (Editor), *UNC-CH Campus Slang*, p. 1, Fall 1986

bitch pad *noun*
a small seat mounted behind the regular seat on a motorcycle or bicycle *US*, *1992*
- — Lewis Poteet, *Car & Motorcycle Slang*, p. 30, 1992
- In revenge, Stephens claims for herself the envied machismo of the outlaw Harley biker who never rides the "bitch pad." — Deborah Bright, *The Passionate Camera*, p. 15, 1998
- She sidesaddles the bitch pad, and we weave off into the night[.] — Lynn Breedlove, *Godspeed*, p. 75, 2002

bitch pie *noun*
a pizza with pepperoni, mushroom, and sausage *US*, *1996*

The initials of the toppings—PMS—suggest a cranky woman.
- — *Maledicta*, p. 8, 1996: "Domino's pizza jargon"

bitch session *noun*
a group airing of complaints *US*, *1960*
- As one dispatcher disclosed, after disconnecting from a frustrating call, dispatchers like to "have a little bitch session back and forth." — Gregory Shepherd, *Communication and Community*, p. 70, 2001

bitch sip *verb*
to sip slowly and with manners *US*, *2000*
- "But you can't just drink it down. You have to bitch-sip it. Savor it." — Paul Beatty, *Tuff*, p. 156, 2000

bitch slap *verb*
to slap someone full across the face *US*, *1995*
- Kint's lawyer comes in and five minutes later the D.A. comes out looking like he'd been bitch-slapped by the boogey man. — *The Usual Suspects*, 1995
- — Pamela Munro, *U.C.L.A. Slang*, p. 30, 1997
- Openhanded, he bitch-slapped me. — John Ridley, *Love is a Racket*, p. 206, 1998
- Dr. Evil charges at Klansman and starts to bitch slap him. — *Austin Powers*, 1999
- His old lady was screaming, so one of the Misfits bitch-slapped her, making her lay down on the floor. — Ralph "Sonny" Barger, *Hell's Angel*, p. 85, 2000
- But we bitch-slapped that little fuck and sent him packing, so it's smooth sailing. — Kevin Smith, *Jay and Silent Bob Strike Back*, p. 44, 2001
- [W]hen Knut does that kind of thing, somebody ought to "bitch-slap the motherfucker upside the head." — Dan Jenkins, *The Money-Whipped Steer-Job Three-Jack Give-Up Artist*, p. 60, 2001
- "Ah hope to God you don't try that mess in public, cuz that's a good way to git yourself bitchslapped, son." — David Henry Sterry, *Chicken*, p. 25, 2002

bitch-smack *verb*
to strike without warning and emphatically *US*, *2004*
- I wanted to walk up and bitch smack the shit out of each one of them, but that wouldn't get me any Christmas money. — Jamie Lowe, *Da Flip Side*, p. 284, 2004
- Hurricane lunged across the table and bitch-smacked the phone clear out of my hand. — Noire, *Candy Licker*, p. 75, 2005

bitch up *verb*
to ruin *US*, *1980*
- "She really bitched her life up," French said. — George Higgins, *Kennedy for the Defense*, p. 21, 1980

bitch with a capital C *noun*
a truly hideous person *US*, *2003*
A suggestion of **CUNT**.
- I was a total bitch with a capital C. — *Stuck on You*, 2003

bitchy *adjective*
malicious, spiteful *US*, *1925*
- The bitchy quality that only a female can get into a review makes Miss Wilella Waldorf, who occupies the next cage to me on the New York Post, a cruel and unusually readable critic. — Earl Wilson, *I Am Gazing Into My 8-Ball*, p. 79, 1945

bite *noun*
1 a small meal or a snack *US*, *1899*
- Think I'll go get a bite to eat, then. — Jim Thompson, *A Swell-Looking Babe*, p. 44, 1954
- "You're going to have some lunch before you go, aren't you?" "I'll get a bite downtown." — J.D. Salinger, *Franny and Zooey*, p. 117, 1961
- While I grabbed a bite, I called the Naples Cafe, got a number for me to call Art and dialed it. — Mickey Spillane, *Me, Hood!*, p. 44, 1963
- You wanna grab a bite or something like that? — *Manhattan*, 1979
- You guys go on inside, get yourselves a bite. — *The Blues Brothers*, 1980

2 the portion of the money bet by gamblers taken as the share for the establishment sponsoring the gambling *US*, *1988*
- — George Percy, *The Language of Poker*, p. 10, 1988

3 a price *US*, *1958*
- You want the blue too? The bite is two for fifty slats. — Iceberg Slim (Robert Beck), *Pimp*, p. 92, 1969
- — Kenn "Naz" Young, *Naz's Underground Dictionary*, p. 15, 1973

4 something that is very disagreeable *US, 1951*

- If they can't get the car, that's the way the ball bounces (tough luck) or ain't that a bite? (too bad). — *Newsweek*, 8th October 1951

bite *verb*

1 to copy or steal another person's style, especially a break-dancing move or a rap lyric or sound *US, 1979*

- Biting moves is really wack, but everyone does it. — Bradley Elfman, *Breakdancing*, p. 40, 1984
- You wacker than the motherfucker you bit your style from — Eminem (Marshall Mathers) *Just Don't Give a Fuck*, 1999
- At first I thought it was to discourage me from sweating him, but he thought graffiti is best learned by intuition and biting. — Stephen Power, *The Art of Getting Over*, p. 38, 1999
- Then he passed a poplock over ot Warren, who also bit my style and tried to make it look juvenile. — Linden Dalecki, *Kid B*, p. 17, 2006

2 to be unfair or extremely distasteful *US, 1966*

- — John D. Bell et al., *Loosely Speaking*, p. 2, 1966
- You know what really bites; when people watch that cafeteria stuff on TV and see all those Geeks and Metalheads jumping around, they're going to think UnCool is the Rule at Westerburg. — *Heathers*, 1988

3 to flex, and thus contract, the sphincter during anal sex *US, 1972*

- — Bruce Rodgers, *The Queens' Vernacular*, p. 32, 1972

▸ **bite feathers**

to lie on your stomach, especially in anticipation of anal sex *US, 1964*

- — Guy Strait, *The Lavender Lexicon*, 1964

▸ **bite it**

to die *US, 1977*

- She bit it. — *Drugstore Cowboy*, 1988

▸ **bite the bag**

in computing, to fail, especially in a dramatic fashion *US, 1983*

- — Guy L. Steele et al., *The Hacker's Dictionary*, p. 28, 1983

▸ **bite the big one**

to die *US, 1979*

- Most people think of the Chateau as the place where Belushi bit the big one, but it's got a lot more going for it than that. — Armistead Maupin, *Maybe the Moon*, p. 142, 1992

▸ **bite the brown**

to perform mouth-to-anus sex *US, 1972*

- — Robert A. Wilson, *Playboy's Book of Forbidden Words*, p. 38, 1972

biter *noun*

1 a copier of breakdance moves; a plagiarist of rap lyrics *US, 1999*

- Back in the days you could get booed out of the circle [...] if you looked too much like the next man. They'll tell right off you're a biter and you're wack [inferior]. — Alex Ogg, *The Hip Hop Years [quoting Jorge "Fabel" Pabon]*, pp. 32 – 33, 1999

2 the vagina *US, 1998*

- [O]ut on the floor, after a long sexy masturbatory dance, her mini-skirt around her hips; her rosy biter winking its hairy eye at me where I sat[.] — Clarence Major, *All-Night Visitors*, p. 201, 1998

3 a tooth *US, 1946*

- During this period I sat in on a recording date with the Pollack band, just a couple hours after I'd had a gang of teeth yanked, because my biters were going bad along with all my other parts. — Mezz Mezzrow, *Really the Blues*, p. 188, 1946

biting *noun*

copying another person's style *US, 1994*

- Like when did biting become cool? Onyx came out biting Busta Rhymes. It's cool. — William Upski Wimsatt, *Bomb the Suburbs*, p. 14, 1994

bit spit *noun*

any electronic communication *US, 1997*

- — Vann Wesson, *Generation X Field Guide and Lexicon*, p. 20, 1997

bitter-mouth *verb*

to speak harshly *US, 1947*

- — Marcus Hanna Boulware, *Jive and Slang of Students ,in Negro Colleges*, 1947

bitty *noun*

a girl *US, 1962*

- — Anthony Romeo, *The Language of Gangs*, p. 16, 4th December 1962

bitty *adjective*

tiny *US, 1905*

A corruption and shortening of **ITSY-BITSY**.

- [H]e was sorta convinced already that there was something odd about this little-bitty nigger who tink he can beat somebody five times his size. — Cecil Brown, *The Life & Loves of Mr. Jiveass Nigger*, p. 64, 1969
- There never was a man who could stand up to Kokomo, and he started to wonder where this little-bitty nigger could get such confidence. — Christina and Richard Milner, *Black Players*, p. 175, 1972
- Little itty-bitty things accumulate. — Susan Hall, *Gentleman of Leisure*, p. 6, 1972
- Darrol Woods was saying "Two larceny from a person reduced from larceny not armed and a little bitty assault thing ... " And Hunter was saying, "Little bitty ... little bitty fucking tire iron you used on the guy." — Elmore Leonard, *City Primeval*, p. 58, 1980

bitty box *noun*

a small computer, especially a single-tasking-only machine *US, 1991*

- — Eric S. Raymond, *The New Hacker's Dictionary*, p. 64, 1991

biz; bizz *noun*

1 business *US, 1861*

- Rumor had it that there were quite a few pinks in the publishing biz. — Mary McCarthy, *The Group*, p. 185, 1963
- Lead you to draw bad conclusions (or "bad vibes" as they say in the rock biz) about what happened. — Abbie Hoffman, *Woodstock Nation*, p. 4, 1969
- [H]e had to stay in L.A. for the music biz, and if he stayed in L.A., Bobby would find him[.] — James Ellroy, *Suicide Hill*, p. 673, 1986

2 the syringe and other equipment used by intravenous drug users *US, 1949*

- — Vincent J. Monteleone, *Criminal Slang*, p. 24, 1949
- — William D. Alsever, *Glossary for the Establishment and Other Uptight People*, p. 19, December 1970

3 a small amount of a drug *US, 1971*

- — Eugene Landy, *The Underground Dictionary*, p. 34, 1971

▸ **in the biz bag**

in trouble with police management *US, 1994*

- — *Los Angeles Times*, p. B8, 19th December 1994

bizarro *noun*

a bizarre person *US, 1980*

Influenced by, if not directly descended from, "Bizarro" a comic-book villain who first challenged Superman in the late 1950s.

- [T]he reclusive bizarro I've been goofing on for the past year wants to come on my radio show. — Howard Stern, *Miss America*, p. 60, 1995

bizarro *adjective*

bizarre *US, 1971*

- Out here in the bizarro city by the bay, things are different. — Jim Carroll, *Forced Entries*, p. 130, 1987
- Hey, this question wouldn't be that bizarro thing you were blabbing about over the phone[.] — *Heathers*, 1988

bizotic *adjective*

unexpected, out of the ordinary *US, 1984*

- — *San Francisco Sunday Examiner & Chronicle*, p. 20, 2nd September 1984
- — Vann Wesson, *Generation X Field Guide and Lexicon*, p. 20, 1997

bizzing *noun*

sliding on an icy road while hanging onto the rear bumper of a car *US, 1969*

A verbal noun with no recorded use of "bizz" as a verb.

- Not to mention bizzing in the Northwest and bum-riding in Utah; all these denote the action of daring, often foolish, children who grab a ride on the back end of a moving vehicle. — *New York Times Magazine*, p. 18, 13th March 1994

bizzo *noun*

an ill-tempered woman *US, 2001*

A corruption or evolution of "bitch."

- — Don R. McCreary (Editor), *Dawg Speak*, 2001

BJ *noun*
an act of oral sex, a blow job *US, 1949*
- — Anon., *The Gay Girl's Guide*, p. 3, 1949
- "B.J."—"Blowjob." — Richard Price, *The Wanderers*, p. 101, 1974
- And what should be this film's finest sex scene, the finale between Ashlyn and Jamie, turns out to be mainly a simple b.j. ending in a facia. — *Adult Video News*, p. 48, February 1993
- Of course, staying in town probably wasn't the best decision, but it affords *** a jailed Ava a chance to seduce sheriff Dillion Day with a through-the-bars b.j. — Editors of Adult Video News, *The AVN Guide to the 500 Greatest Adult Films of All Time*, p. 8, 2005

B joint *noun*
a bar where women coax customers to buy drinks *US, 1993*
- Ginger was my mother's nightclub name, to match her new career working as a part-time stripteaser and "B-girl" in Tenderloin "B-joints." — Kim Rich, *Johnny's Girl*, p. 48, 1993

BK's *noun*
British Knight™ shoes *US, 2000*
Favored by members of the Crips youth gang, for whom the initials also stand for "Blood Killer."
- — Bill Valentine, *Gangs and Their Tattoos*, p. 77, 2000

blabber *noun*
a very talkative hospital patient *US, 1994*
- — Sally Williams, *"Strong" Words*, p. 134, 1994

black *noun*
1 potent, unrefined black opium *US, 1978*
- Injecting "black" was risky; if the addict missed a vein, impurities lodged in the tissues. — Joan W. Moore, *Homeboys*, p. 83, 1978

2 night *US, 1947*
- — *Time Magazine*, p. 92, 20 January 1947
- About a deuce of long black and whites ago, a stud from the low lands came to the Apple. — Babs Gonzales, *"A Manhattan Fable" in Movin' On Down De Line*, p. 89, 1975

3 in American casinos, a $100 chip *US, 1980*
- I've never dealt to blacks before. — Lee Solkey, *Dummy Up and Deal*, p. 107, 1980

black *adjective*
secret *US, 1965*
- He dubbed the group his little "black box" ("black" for secret) and promised them carte blanche. — Frank Snepp, *Decent Interval*, p. 218, 1977
- When completed it filled a large spiral notebook nicknamed "the Black Book," and it covered all of Delta's skills. — Charlie A. Beckwith and Donald Knox, *Delta Force*, p. 168, 1983

black action *noun*
casino betting in $100 increments *US, 1991*
- — Michael Dalton, *Blackjack*, p. 31, 1991

black and tan *adjective*
catering to both black and white customers *US, 1887*
- Many of these small clubs have become, for all practical purposes, "black and tan" spots where whites and Negroes (of opposite sexes) mix, not furtively. — Jack Lait and Lee Mortimer, *New York confidential*, p. 45, 1948
- In some places—like Georgia—the Populists "fused" with the lily-white wing of the Republican Party, not with the so-called black-and-tan wing. — Stokely Carmichael and Charles V. Hamilton, *Black Power*, p. 68, 1967
- As one old queen—who had the apartment next to Spencer's—told me—"My dear—it was really too much. It was a regular black and tan fantasy." — Herbert Huncke, *The Evening Sun Turned Crimson*, p. 43, 1980
- My father was a regular at the Oasis as well as at the other all-black nightclubs, including bars that catered to all races, called "black and tan" bars. — Kim Rich, *Johnny's Girl*, p. 81, 1993

black and white *noun*
1 a police car *US, 1958*
From the traditional colors of police cars in the US.
- Officer Breslin and I took cover behind our, uh, black and white, and ordered the suspects to, uh, halt. — Darryl Ponicsan, *The Last Detail*, p. 153, 1970
- The policia drive black and whites, 'ey? Most towns in the States I think our policia drive black and whites too. — Elmore Leonard, *Glitz*, p. 7, 1985

- Jimmy said shit because he saw the black-and-white rolling up. — William T. Vollman, *Whores for Gloria*, p. 130, 1991
- A shitload of Hollywood division black-and-whites showed up[.] — James Ellroy, *Hollywood Nocturnes*, p. 191, 1994

2 a capsule containing both a central nervous system stimulant and a barbiturate *US, 1971*
- — Eugene Landy, *The Underground Dictionary*, p. 34, 1971

3 a soda fountain drink made with chocolate syrup, seltzer, and vanilla ice cream *US, 1947*
- "You want black and whites?" Benny asked the boys at the table. — Irving Shulman, *The Amboy Dukes*, p. 192, 1947

black and white fever *noun*
an aversion to police *US, 1970*
- Funny, how many people get black and white fever and start moving fast in the opposite direction. — Joseph Wambaugh, *The New Centurions*, p. 127, 1970

black and whites *noun*
the black pants or skirt and white shirt worn by American casino dealers *US, 1961*
- — Thomas L. Clark, *The Dictionary of Gambling and Gaming*, p. 19, 1987

black and white taxi *noun*
a police car *US, 1962*
- — *American Speech*, p. 267, December 1962: "The language of traffic policemen"

black art *noun*
in computing, an array of techniques developed and discovered for a particular system or application *US, 1991*
- The huge proliferation of formal and informal channels for spreading around new computer-related technologies during the last twenty years has made both the term black art and what it describes less common than formerly. — Eric S. Raymond, *The New Hacker's Dictionary*, p. 65, 1991

black ass *noun*
a car without working rear lights *US, 1962*
- — *American Speech*, p. 267, December 1962: "The language of traffic policemen"

black bag *noun*
a brown-haired prostitute *US, 1960*
- The telegraphic code is "black bag" for brunettes and "tan valise" for blondes. — Lee Mortimer, *Women Confidential*, p. 141, 1960

black bag job *noun*
a burglary, especially one committed by law enforcement or intelligence agents *US, 1966*
- Two months later, Gary asked me if I would like to do a black bag job. — Wesley Swearingen, *FBI Secrets*, p. 23, 1995

black beauty *noun*
1 a black amphetamine capsule *US, 1969*
- They are known as "black mollies" or "black widows" or "black beauties," because they were put in black capsules. — *San Francisco Chronicle*, p. 24, 19th January 1972
- [H]e was always in danger of being seized and booked with a pocket full of "bennies" or "black beauties" at the property desk. — Hunter S. Thompson, *The Great Shark Hunt*, p. 582, 1979
- "Processed any speed lately?" "Black beauties?" "Music to my ears." — James Ellroy, *Suicide Hill*, p. 836, 1986

2 a capsule containing both barbiturate and amphetamine *US, 1973*
- — David Maurer and Victor Vogel, *Narcotics and Narcotic Addiction*, p. 389, 1973

black belt *noun*
a neighborhood of black families that circles a city or area *US, 1951*
- But Washington's Black Belt is no belt at all. It is sprawled all over[.] — Jack Lait and Lee Mortimer, *Washington Confidential*, p. 37, 1951
- Unlike other areas in the black belt, Macon County remained relatively free of overt acts of violence and intimidation during the forties and fifties. — Stokely Carmichael and Charles V. Hamilton, *Black Power*, p. 129, 1967
- [T]he Black belt had the Blackstone Rangers, the largest gang of juvenile delinquents on earth[.] — Norman Mailer, *Miami and the Siege of Chicago*, p. 87, 1968
- There are more people starving in the U.S., in the Black Belt of southeastern U.S. in all the large cities, in the Appalachian Mountains and grape fields of California than in any other country on

earth with the possible exception of India. — George Jackson, *Soledad Brother*, p. 261, April 1970

black Betty *noun*
a van for transporting prisoners *US, 1965*
- 'Cause one day on Main she caught a convict chain / and rode Black Betty to her new pad. — Bruce Jackson, *Get Your Ass in the Water and Swim Like Me*, p. 155, 1965

blackbird *noun*
1 an unmarked military aircraft, such as a C-123 or C-130 *US, 1983*
Used by the Studies and Observations Group (SOG) in Vietnam, the highly secret, elite, unconventional warfare component of the US military presence in Southeast Asia.
- Flown in a SOG blackbird to Okinawa, the ammunition was dismantled by CIA technicians. — Peter MacInerney, *A Contagion of War*, 1983

2 an amphetamine capsule *US, 1972*
- — Carl Chambers and Richard Heckman, *Employee Drug Abuse*, p. 201, 1972

black book *noun*
1 a corporation's plan for battling a hostile takeover *US, 1988*
- — Kathleen Odean, *High Steppers, Fallen Angels, and Lollipops*, p. 111, 1988

2 in a casino, a list of persons to be excluded from the casino *US, 1991*
- — Michael Dalton, *Blackjack*, p. 32, 1991

3 a graffiti artist's notebook containing ideas, outlines, sketches and plans for future graffiti pieces *US, 1982*
- "Autographing" each other's black books (hardbound sketch pads that almost all writers carry with them.) — Craig Castleman, *Getting Up*, p. 21, 1982
- I couldn't even bring my blackbook out of my jacket. — Stephen Power, *The Art of Getting Over*, p. 38, 1999
- If you live, breathe, piss, and shit hip-hop culture, you'll feel at home hanging out at Oaklandish, checking out its weeking series and live music happenings—or maybe just collecting wildstyle hieroglyphs from local graf-heads in your black book. — *East Bay Express (Oakland, California)*, 5th May 2004

black bottom *noun*
a neighborhood where most of the population are poor black people *US, 1915*
- Eatonville has been described as a place neither ghetto, nor slum, nor black bottom[.] — *Pittsburgh Post-Gazette*, p. F1, 14th October 2001

black box *noun*
1 the notional container in which proprietary technical information is secured in dealings over industrial property rights *US, 1974*
- In dealing with the sale or purchase of industrial property rights, classified technical information can be often dealt with as proprietary knowledge without revealing the confidential know-how of what is in the black box. — Robert Kirk Mueller, *Buzzwords*, p. 47, 1974

2 any highly technical piece of electronics equipment *US, 1945*
- I think now of our first celestial computer, known commonly as the Black Box. It was a gadget with counters on it, and cranks which you turned. — Curtis E. LeMay with MacKinlay Knator, *Mission with LeMay*, p. 98, 1965

3 a linear amplifier for a citizens' band radio *US, 1976*
Sometimes embellished as "little black box."
- — Porter Bibb, *CB Bible*, p. 98, 1976

black Cadillac *noun*
an amphetamine capsule *US, 1980*
- — National Institute on Drug Abuse, *What do they call it again?*, 1980

black death *nickname*
the electric chair *US, 2001*
- Ohio and other states call it "Old Sparky." In Alabama, it's the "Big Yellow Mama." In Mississippi, it's "Black Death." — *Cincinnati Enquirer*, p. 1F, 2nd September 2001

black fever *noun*
sexual attraction felt by a white person for black people *US, 1977*
- Black Fever is when a girl, a white girl she gets this thing in her head she's got to have a black guy. — John Sayles, *Union Dues*, p. 147, 1977

black Friday *noun*
the day after Thanksgiving *US, 1975*

- Philadelphia police and bus drivers call it "Black Friday"—that day each year between Thanksgiving and the Army-Navy game. It is the busiest shopping and traffic day of the year in the Bicentennial City[.] — *New York Times*, p. 21, 29th November 1975

black gold *noun*
distilled, concentrated heroin *US, 1987*
- — Carsten Stroud, *Close Pursuit*, p. 269, 1987

Black Hand *noun*
a secret criminal organization composed of first-generation Italian immigrants to the US *US, 1898*
- The Mafia and the dread Black Hand are the same thing. The black hand was the sign over which the Mafia's threats were delivered. — Jack Lait and Lee Mortimer, *Washington Confidential*, p. 180, 1951
- The Black Hand? You think you can laugh it off? — Mickey Spillane, *Kiss Me Deadly*, p. 38, 1952

black hat *noun*
1 in a drama, or in life viewed as a drama, the villain *US, 1964*
- Why are we talking about Alfred North Whitehead when we ought to be out looking for a black hat? — Max Shulman, *Anyone Got a Match?*, p. 41, 1964
- Well, from where this peace monger sits, I'd say the black hats are succeeding. — William C. Anderson, *Bat 21*, p. 161, 1980

2 a member of Pathfinder platoon, dropped behind enemy lines to make deep reconnaissance patrols and to establish landing zones for the initial helicopter waves *US, 1982*
- "You know how to operate that thang?" asked the Black Hat, a staff sergeant member of SERTS' cadre. — John Del Vecchio, *The 13th Valley*, p. 9, 1982

3 a US Army drill instructor *US, 1986*
- Look to your left and what did you see? / A mean old black hat lookin' at me. — Sandee Shaffer Johnson, *Cadences*, p. 24, 1986
- The Black Hats are looking for any lack of motivation, and they jump, quickly and hard, on anybody they think is suspect. — Hans Halberstadt, *Airborne*, p. 34, 1988

black hole *noun*
in computing, the notional place where e-mail that is sent but not received disappears *US, 1991*
- "I think there's a black hole at foovax!" conveys suspicion that site foovax has been dropping a lot of stuff on the floor lately[.] — Eric S. Raymond, *The New Hacker's Dictionary*, p. 65, 1991

black ice *noun*
in in-line skating, a recently paved street *US, 1998*
- BLACK ICE A very smooth, recently paved street. — Shelley Youngblut, *Way Inside ESPN's X Games*, p. 84, 1998

black jack *noun*
1 a central nervous system stimulant *US, 1968*
- Some of the names describe the drugs' effects, such as "helpers," "copilots," "Los Angeles turn arounds," or their shape, color and markings—"hearts," "footballs," "blackjacks," "crossroads." — Phil Hirsch, *Hooked*, pp. 51–52, 1968

2 the penis of a black man *US, 1965*
Homosexual usage.
- — *The Guild Dictionary of Homosexual Terms*, p. 4, 1965

blackjack mission *noun*
during the war in Vietnam, an operation carried out by a mobile strike force *US, 1991*
The mobile strike forces were light infantry battalions equipped and trained to operate in remote areas without any significant logistical requirements or support.
- Jenkins, Morris, and Head went on at least one more blackjack mission. — Henry Gole, *Soldiering*, p. 161, 2005

black light *noun*
an ultraviolet light, under which fluorescent paint glows *UK, 1927*
- — Eugene Landy, *The Underground Dictionary*, p. 34, 1971

Black Lions *nickname*
a navy fighter squadron formally identified as VF-213, commissioned in 1955 *US, 1990*
- Nash was one of those rare Phantom pilots who, against the trend, had been dogfighting in the F-4 since his squadron, the V-213, nicknamed "The Black Lions," had transitioned to it in 1964. — Robert K. Wilcox, *The Scream of Eagles*, p. 45, 1990

black magic *noun*
in computing, a technique that works without any apparent reason for its success *US, 1991*
- — Eric S. Raymond, *The New Hacker's Dictionary*, p. 65, 1991

Black Maria *noun*
1 a police wagon or van for transporting those who have been arrested *US, 1843*
The etymology is uncertain beyond the color black.
- Po-lice thought it was really funny . . . two niggers fightin' over some bags of coffee on their way to the Black Maria. — Odie Hawkins, *Ghetto Sketches*, p. 123, 1972
2 in a deck of cards, the queen of spades *US, 1988*
- — George Percy, *The Language of Poker*, p. 10, 1988

black molly *noun*
1 a black amphetamine capsule *US, 1970*
- There are known as "black mollies" or "black widows" or "black beauties," because they were put in black capsules. — *San Francisco Chronicle*, p. 24, 19th January 1972
2 a barbiturate capsule *US, 1973*
- — David W. Maurer and Victor Vogel, *Narcotics and Narcotic Addiction*, p. 389, 1973

Black Monday *noun*
1 28th May 1962 *US, 1962*
The date of a dramatic stock market crash.
- Was it the "little woman" who panicked on Black Monday, May 28, in Wall Street, then in unreasoning terror dumped off her stocks in skyrocketing volume and thereby set off one of the worst stock market slumps of this century? — *San Francisco Chronicle*, p. 54, 18th June 1962
- Will 1968 see another "Black Monday" in the stock market? — *San Francisco Chronicle*, p. 58, 1 April 1968
2 19th October 1987 *US, 1987*
The date of the greatest single-day stock market crash in the US since the Depression.
- By 4 p.m., after the market bell clanged, economics reporter Mike Jensen would appear with Brokaw to intone that "today will be known as Black Monday" and NBC News consultant Donald Regan would bid "goodbye to the bull market." — *Washington Post*, p. D6, 20th October 1987
- — Kathleen Odean, *High Steppers, Fallen Angels, and Lollipops*, p. 165, 1988
- — *American Speech*, Fall 1988

black money *noun*
cash that is not accounted for in the financial records of a business *US, 1963*
- Attorney General Robert F. Kennedy is concerned about "black money"—also known as "hot money." — Ed Reid and Ovid Demaris, *The Green Felt Jungle*, p. 212, 1963

black on black *noun*
a car with a black exterior and black upholstery *US, 1980*
- — Edith A. Folb, *runnin' down some lines*, p. 229, 1980

black-out *noun*
a very dark-skinned black person *US, 1947*
- — Marcus Hanna Boulware, *Jive and Slang of Students in Negro Colleges*, 1947

black rain *noun*
rain that has been contaminated by smoke from oil field fires *US, 1991*
Gulf war usage.
- — *American Speech*, p. 384, Winter 1991: "among the new words"

blackstick *noun*
a clarinet *US, 1937*
- — Robert S. Gould, *A Jazz Lexicon*, p. 21, 1964

black syph *noun*
a virulent, fatal strain of syphillis, probably apocryphal *US, 1976*
- The GIs insisted the VC injected the whores with something called "black syph." ("You get it, man, and they just send you to this black syph camp to die"). — Jack Karmer, *Travels with the Celestial Dog*, p. 53, 1976

black tar *noun*
crude, impure, potent heroin from Mexico *US, 1986*
- — Peter Johnson, *Dictionary of Street Alcohol and Drug Terms*, p. 20, 1993
- [I]t brushes up against the competition, including Mexican-produced Black Tar, known derisively as Mexican Mud because of its poor

quality; the more superior Mexican Brown in powder form; and especially high-grade Colombian White, its biggest rival. — *New York Times*, p. SM29, 23rd June 2002
- "And this is not the black tar crap you all do either." — J.T. LeRoy, *Harold's End*, p. 31, 2004

black velvet *noun*
a black woman's vagina *US, 1967*
- — Dale Gordon, *The Dominion Sex Dictionary*, p. 30, 1967
- — Robert A. Wilson, *Playboy's Book of Forbidden Words*, p. 40, 1972

black water *noun*
sewage *US, 1993*
Euphemism used in recreational vehicle camping.
- — John Edwards, *Auto Dictionary*, p. 15, 1993

black whack *noun*
phencyclidine, the recreational drug known as PCP or angel dust *US, 1994*
- — US Department of Justice *Street Terms*, October 1994

black widow *noun*
1 a black amphetamine capsule; Benzedrine™ (amphetamine sulfate), a central nervous system stimulant *US, 1972*
- They are known as "black mollies" or "black widows" or "black beauties," because they were put in black capsules. — *San Francisco Chronicle*, p. 24, 19th January 1972
- — *American Speech*, p. 56, Spring–Summer 1975: "Razorback slang"
2 a capsule containing both barbiturate and amphetamine *US, 1973*
- — David Maurer and Victor Vogel, *Narcotics and Narcotic Addiction*, p. 389, 1973

black wings *noun*
oral sex with a black woman *US, 2000*
- You got your Red Wings by eating a girl on her period and your Black Wings by eating a black girl. — Ralph "Sonny" Barger, *Hell's Angel*, p. 99, 2000

bladder *noun*
a balloon *US, 1981*
Circus and carnival usage.
- — Don Wilmeth, *The Language of American Popular Entertainment*, p. 26, 1981

bladder bird *noun*
a tanker aircraft used for aerial bulk fuel delivery *US, 1976*
Vietnam war usage.
- A bladder-bird received major damage on the 26th. — A.J.C. Lavalle, *Airpower and the 1972 Spring Invasion*, p. 68, 1976

blade *noun*
1 a knife *US, 1896*
- He came back, pulling a blade[.] — Malcolm X and Alex Haley, *The Autobiography of Malcolm X*, p. 131, 1964
- Hip little kiddies never carry a BLADE; it's a bad scene if you meet up with your equalizer or John Law. — Hy Lit, *Hy Lit's Unbelievable Dictionary of Hip Words for Groovy People*, p. 5, 1968
- I thought only PRs went to the blades over a broad. — Edwin Torres, *Q & A*, p. 45, 1977
- Wonder why O.J. used a blade? Why not a gun with a silencer? A guy like him could get any weapon he wanted. Why a blade? — Joseph Wambaugh, *Floaters*, p. 128, 1996
2 a man *US, 1948*
- Vice does not thrive here, because the young blades seek it elsewhere. — Jack Lait and Lee Mortimer, *New York Confidential*, p. 83, 1948
3 a dollar *US, 2002*
- — Gary K. Farlow, *Prison-ese*, p. 4, 2002

blade *verb*
1 in professional wrestling, to cut yourself intentionally to produce bleeding *US, 1990*
- Real blood produced by means other than blading. — *rec.sports.pro-wrestling*, 17th July 1990
- Jericho wasn't wearing a bandaid any more (this is week four of TV, after all) and there was no scar. "This makes us think he must have bladed above the hair line." — *Herb's Smoky Mountain Fanweek 1994 Review*, 1994
- He lay there motionless. Then I noticed his hand moving slowly under his forehead. He was "blading" himself, cutting his own forehead with a razor blade. — Larry Nelson, *Stranglehold*, p. 119, 1999

- Some guys were terrified of blading. I remember William Snyder would whimper when it was time for him to blade. — Bobby Heenan, *Bobby the Brain*, p. 127, 2002

2 to skate on rollerblades *US, 1997*
- — Pamela Munro, *U.C.L.A. Slang*, p. 31, 1997

blader *noun*
a rollerblader *US, 1989*
- The most common injury to a blader is a sprained or broken wrist. — *New York Times*, p. C12, 17th April 1989
- [D]aylight shots taken down along the West Village piers among the weekend cruising population: bladers and bikers and dog walkers. — Ethan Morden, *Some Men Are Lookers*, p. 132, 1997
- — Pamela Munro, *U.C.L.A. Slang*, p. 44, 2001

blading *noun*
using rollerblades *US, 1995*
- Blading exploded in the late '80s and early '90s, appealing both to ex-joggers looking for low-impact workouts and death-defying speed freaks[.] — Steven Daly and Nathaniel Wice, *alt.culture*, p. 211, 1995

blah *adjective*
without energy, without spark, unmotivated *US, 1922*
- Part of the problem is a blah role: Steve is not a protagonist of many words, or even many revealing looks. — *Washington Post*, p. E7, 6th May 1981

blah; blah blah; blah blah blah *noun*
empty and meaningless talk; so on and so forth; used for implying that what is being said is not worth the saying or has been said too often already *UK, 1918*
Echoic of nonsense speech, possibly German *blech* (nonsense); synonymous with **RHUBARB** (nonsense) which may also be repeated two or three times for emphasis.
- "You can give me a whole ration of shit and this and that, and blah, blah, blah." — George V. Higgins, *The Friends of Eddie Doyle*, p. 75, 1971
- We all decided to chuck the idea because I'd have trouble making friends, blah-blah-blah. — *Heathers*, 1988
- This country is just one big global village with everyone out there going blah blah blah. — *Sleepless in Seattle*, 1993

blahs *noun*
a minor illness; a feeling of ennui *US, 1968*
- — Collin Baker et al., *College Undergraduate Slang Study Conducted at Brown University*, p. 81, 1968

blanca *noun*
an amphetamine or other central nervous system stimulant *US, 1967*
Border Spanish used in English conversation by Mexican-Americans; from the Spanish for "white."
- It's something like bennies—blancas—only not as good. — Malcolm Braly, *On the Yard*, p. 281, 1967
- — Dagoberto Fuentes and Jose Lopez, *Barrio Language Dictionary*, p. 17, 1974

blanco *noun*
heroin; cocaine *US, 1973*
Spanish for "white."
- — US Department of Justice, *Street Terms*, October 1994

blank *noun*
1 a package of non-narcotic white powder sold as narcotics *US, 1966*
- Heroin itself has a bitter taste and if a junkie tastes some stuff before he uses it and it's real sweet he figures he's bought a blank and gets upset. — James Mills, *The Panic in Needle Park*, p. 72, 1966
- — Richard Lingeman, *Drugs from A to Z*, p. 25, 1969

2 in a carnival, a bad day, a bad engagement or a bad customer *US, 1985*
- What a BLANK that bum was. He looked like he had money, but all he had was three lousy bucks. — Gene Sorrows, *All About Carnivals*, p. 10, 1985

3 in poker, a useless card in the dealt hand *US, 1992*
- Edwin Silberstang, *Winning Poker for the Serious Player*, p. 217, 1992

4 the top of a skateboard *US, 1976*
- — Laura Torbet, *The Complete Book of Skateboarding*, p. 105, 1976

5 a tablet of Aspirin *US, 1990*
- — Charles Shafer, *Folk Speech in Texas Prisons*, p. 198, 1990

blank; blankety; blankety-blank
used as a self-censored deletion of an expletive, regardless of part of speech *UK, 1854*
Written more often than spoken, but not without uses in speech.
- Two Judges Wish Two Thieves A Blankety-Blank Christmas [Headline] — *San Francisco News*, p. 8, 20th December 1945
- "Throw that blank blank out!" ordered Dressen angrily. "Throw him out!" — *San Francisco Examiner*, p. 33, 7th August 1953
- Oh, go ahead and inject your blankety-blank personal note, you old geezer. — *Washington Post*, p. B1, 4th July 1977

blank canvas *noun*
the body of a person who is about to get their first tattoo *US, 1997*
- — *Los Angeles Times Magazine*, p. 7, 13th July 1997

blanket *noun*
1 any sandwich *US, 1960*
- — *San Francisco Examiner*, p. III-2, 22nd March 1960

2 an overcoat; a top coat *US, 1925*
- — H. Craig Collins, *Street Gangs*, p. 221, 1979

3 in the US military, a beret *US, 1992*
- He'd always refused to wear the blanket, the green beret. — Richard Marcinko and John Weisman, *The Rogue Warrior*, p. 238, 1992

blanket-ass *noun*
a native American Indian *US, 1973*
Derogatory.
- The Native American Student Council says it will not sit by idly while slurs such as "mucket," "blanket ass," "dirty skin" and "lazy" are hurled at the school's 138 American Indians[.] — *Salt Lake Tribune*, p. D1, 10th October 1994
- "I've been called "blanket ass" and "prairie nigger" more times than I can count," he said. — *Philadelphia Inquirer*, 7th November 1999

blanket craps *noun*
an informal game of craps with the shooter acting as banker *US, 1977*
- — Thomas L. Clark, *The Dictionary of Gambling and Gaming*, p. 20, 1987

blanket drill *noun*
sex in bed *US, 1964*
- — Roger Blake, *The American Dictionary of Sexual Terms*, p. 19, 1964

blanket finish *noun*
in horse racing, a close finish between several horses *US, 1951*
So called because the horses contending for the lead could all be covered by a single figurative blanket.
- — David W. Maurer, *Argot of the Racetrack*, p. 14, 1951

blanket game *noun*
in the circus or carnival, a private gambling game for employees only, played on a blanket *UK, 1980*
- — Joe McKennon, *Circus Lingo*, p. 17, 1980

blanket party *noun*
a ritual in which the offending person is covered with a blanket, which prevents identification of the wrong-doers, and then beaten *US, 1969*
- In Washington's jail, for example, any young white man weighing less than 150 pounds is likely to be the unwilling host of a "blanket party." — Thomas Hoult, *Social Justice and its Enemies*, p. 435, 1975
- [S]ome of the others were pissed at him for thinking us so foolish as to swallow his story. They gave him a blanket party. — Malcolm Braley, *False Starts*, p. 142, 1976
- "Some of the guys just had a blanket party with the ops officer," he said. — Randy Zahn, *Snake Pilot: Flying the Cobra Attack Helicopter in Vietnam*, p. 186, 2003

blanket roll *noun*
a controlled roll of the dice by a skilled cheat, best made on a blanket spread on the ground *US, 1950*
- — *The Annals of the American Academy of Political and Social Sciences*, p. 128, May 1950

blasé blasé
and so on and so on *US, 2002*
An embellishment of the more expected **BLAH BLAH BLAH**.
- — Gary K. Farlow, *Prison-ese*, p. 4, 2002

blast *noun*

1 a telephone call *US, 1970*
- "Give us a blast on the horn sometime." — Burt Hirschfield, *Fire Island*, p. 27, 1970

2 an extremely enjoyable time *US, 1950*
- [B]efore you know it she's going tandem with you and that's the end of the whole blast. — Frederick Kohner, *Gidget*, p. 39, 1957
- It was going to be the blast to end all blasts[.] — Glendon Swarthout, *Where the Boys Are*, p. 220, 1960
- It would be such a blast for you guys to reach a half-million houses. — *Wayne's World*, 1992

3 a party, especially a loud and raucous one *UK, 1959*
- I said yes, she could have a party here—now she's inviting all her friends to come to a blast. [The Neighbors comic strip] — *San Francisco News Call-Bulletin*, p. 13, 20th June 1960
- Patrolman Charles Roberts called it "a real blast" in the usually quiet Westerview residential section on the San Mateo coast. — *San Francisco News Call-Bulletin*, p. 3, 25th September 1964

4 an injection of a drug *US, 1952*
- I want it main line for one blast. — George Mandel, *Flee the Angry Strangers*, pp. 378–379, 1952

5 an escape *US, 1970*
- Red, we need some hooks and need them quick. We've got a blast going in two weeks[.] — Red Rudensky, *The Gonif*, p. 47, 1970

blast *verb*

to use a drug, especially to smoke marijuana *US, 1943*
- At York Avenue we goofed all day ... as we've been doing for 2 weeks now, laugh ... laugh ... laugh; imitated "B" movies; blasting hay; talking. — Jack Kerouac, *Windblown World*, p. 395, 10th January 1949
- Sure, we'll be seeing you over the weekend, and we'll blast some of this tea, okay? — John Clellon Holmes, *John Clellon*, p. 106, 1952
- We were at a crazy pad before going and were blasting like crazy and were up so high that I just didn't give a shit for anyone[.] — Hubert Selby Jr., *Last Exit to Brooklyn*, pp. 39–40, 1957
- Here you'd be with a joint in your hand, and you'd be blasting before you knew what had happened. — Herbert Huncke, *Guilty of Everything*, pp. 1–2, 1990

blasted *adjective*

highly intoxicated on any drug or alcohol *US, 1928*
- Everyone would leave the Strip at 2 when the clubs closed and go to Cantor's en masse so blasted out of their heads that if you asked someone what time it was they backed away, wide-eyed, as though you'd presented them with a philosophical impossibility. — Eve Babitz, *Eve's Hollywood*, p. 234, 1974
- Cause like this one time with Eric, when we got blasted at his house. — *Kids*, 1995

blaster *noun*

1 a gun, especially a pistol *US, 1964*
- [N]either of them had the guts to go for a rod because they knew I had a blaster in my belt and would chop them down the second they moved. — Mickey Spillane, *Return of the Hood*, p. 106, 1964

2 a powerful, hard-breaking wave *US, 1964*
- — John Severson, *Modern Surfing Around the World*, p. 165, 1964

blast from the past *noun*

a song that was popular in the past and is still popular with those who were young when the song was popular *US, 1962*
- He'll be autographing copies of his great new album, "Blasts from The Past." — *Chicago Tribune*, p. 10, 19th January 1962
- Speedy went with a blast from the past: cold-storaged Kate Smith, a known quantity once, of uncertain mornings of late[.] — Bill Cardoso, *The Maltese Sangweech*, pp. 127–128, 1984

blasting oil *noun*

nitroglycerin, used by criminals to blast open safes *US, 1949*
- — Vincent J. Monteleone, *Criminal Slang*, p. 25, 1949

blast party *noun*

a gathering of marijuana smokers *US, 1958*
- — *New York Times Magazine*, p. 87, 16th March 1958

blaze *noun*

1 in a card game with five cards per hand, a hand with five face cards *US, 1962*
- — Frank Garcia, *Marked Cards and Loaded Dice*, p. 250, 1962
- — Irwin Steig, *Common Sense in Poker*, p. 182, 1963

2 in a deck of playing cards, a face card *US, 1987*
- — Thomas L. Clark, *The Dictionary of Gambling and Gaming*, p. 20, 1987

blaze *verb*

1 to leave *US, 1983*
- — *Washington Post*, 14th October 1993

2 to light a marijuana cigarette or other drug-smoking conveyance *US, 1985*
Also expressed as to "blaze up."
- Yo wastoid—you're not gonna blaze up in here! — *The Breakfast Club*, 1985
- Go behind tha curtains while my fanz they point / You know what Loc's doin', I'm blazin a joint — Tone Loc, *Cheeba Cheeba*, 1989
- So I'm blazing with my friends man. — *Dazed and Confused*, 1993

blaze full *noun*

in poker, a hand consisting of three cards of one face card rank and a pair of another *US, 1968*
The "full" is drawn from the conventional name for the hand, a "full house."
- — Thomas L. Clark, *The Dictionary of Gambling and Gaming*, p. 20, 1987

bleach *verb*

to soak and flush a hypodermic needle and syringe with bleach to prevent transmission of HIV *US, 1989*
- — Geoffrey Froner, *Digging for Diamonds*, p. 10, 1989

bleacher bum *noun*

a loud, rowdy sports fan who favors the inexpensive bleacher seats *US, 1981*
- Giant's centerfielder Bill North received an afternoon of heckling from the Wrigley Field bleacher bums. [Caption] — *San Francisco Chronicle*, p. 53, 25th June 1981
- In a booming bleacher bum voice C.C. ordered coffee from a trusty passing his open office door. — Seth Morgan, *Homeboy*, p. 106, 1990

bleat *verb*

to complain *US, 1985*
- — M. Allen Henderson, *How Con Games Work*, p. 217, 1985

bleed *noun*

in pinball, a ball that leaves play having scored few points *US, 1979*
- — Edward Trapunski, *Special When Lit*, p. 152, 1979

bleed *verb*

1 to dilute a drug *US, 1992*
- Buy four, bleed in a ounce of cut, make it five. — Richard Price, *Clockers*, p. 185, 1992

2 to be showing lipstick on your face or clothes *US, 1968*
- Sandy sat up and grinned, and said, "You're bleeding, Peter," meaning I had lipstick on my face[.] — Evan Hunter, *Last Summer*, p. 187, 1968

▶ **bleed the weasel**
(of a male) to urinate *US, 2006*
- "Come in here and play my hand, will ya? I gotta bleed the weasel." — Chris Miller, *The Real Animal House*, p. 70, 2006

bleeder *noun*

1 a casino employee or executive who worries extensively about money being lost to gamblers *US, 1974*
- He will try to avoid picking "bleeders" or "sweaters." That is executives who so hate to see the player win they may cheat the customer without the permission of the hotel, just out of sheer competitiveness. — Mario Puzo, *Inside Las Vegas*, p. 182, 1977

2 in poker, a player who methodically if undramatically drains money from the game by conservative, steady play *US, 1988*
- — George Percy, *The Language of Poker*, p. 10, 1988

3 a boxer who is prone to bleeding *US, 1975*
- [H]e was not a good defensive fighter and to cap it all, a bleeder. — Edwin Torres, *Carlito's Way*, p. 135, 1975

bleeding deacon *noun*

a person with an over-inflated sense of self-importance to an organization *US, 1988*
Usually used in the context of self-help recovery groups such as Alcoholics Anonymous.
- It will be what I call the "tradition lawyers." They find it easier to live with black and white than they do with gray. These "bleeding

deacons"—these fundamentalists—are afraid of and fight any change. — *New York Times*, p. 40 (Section 6), 21st February 1988

- People who behave in this manner in the A.A. program—those who abandon self in the effort to help others—are called "bleeding deacons." — Terence T. Gorski, *Understanding the Twelve Steps*, p. 123, 1989
- He was just one very dry and very angry alcoholic—often called a "bleeding deacon" (as contrasted to an "elder statesman") in earlier A.A. parlance. — Dick B., *That Amazing Grace*, p. 109, 1996
- Most will do the right thing and accept discussion of drugs. Those that don't will be populated mostly by "bleeding deacons" masquerading as elder statesmen, as members vote with their feet. (Letter to the editor). — *Village Voice*, p. 42, 5th June 2001

bleeding spot *noun*
an oil leak on an asphalt road *US, 1962*
- — *American Speech*, p. 267, December 1962: "The language of traffic policemen"

bleep *verb*
to superimpose an electronic noise over expletives in a television or radio broadcast *US, 1966*
- Just bleep out the fucks and shit shits. — *Natural Born Killers*, 1994
- Stern has made the same kind of threat dozens of times in the past, often in response to the way his flagship station, WXRK-FM in New York, bleeps out extreme sexual content. — *Los Angeles Times*, p. E1, 22nd March 2004

bleep
used as a euphemistic replacement for an expletive, regardless of part of speech *US, 1968*
- You could hardly hear Columnist Sheilah Graham for the "bleeps" on KPIX's "Hot Line" Wednesday morning. Once she started discussing "Portnoy's Complaint," it was bleepers' creepers all the way. — *San Francisco Chronicle*, p. 29, 7th March 1969
- When you're having trouble stopping them and you're not moving the ball, it's going to be a bleeping long day. [Quoting John Madden] — *San Francisco Chronicle*, p. 44, 4th September 1972
- I'm a bleep, "Howard said," because if you say what I think you're going to say, that's the way it'll come out. — Elmore Leonard, *Touch*, p. 220, 1977

blem *noun*
a pimple *US, 1968*
A shortened form of the conventional English "blemish."
- — Collin Baker et al., *College Undergraduate Slang Study Conducted at Brown University*, p. 82, 1968

bless *verb*
to approve the forwarding of a proposed action *US, 1986*
Military usage.
- — Department of the Army, *Staff Officer's Guidebook*, p. 56, 1986

blessed sacrament *noun*
marijuana *US, 2001*
- — Rick Ayers (Editor), *Slang Dictionary*, p. 5, 2001

bless in *verb*
to join a youth gang by consent of the membership without any physical or sexual initiation rite *US, 1996*
- You only get blessed in if you've been in the gang before or something. — S. Beth Atkin, *Voices from the Street*, p. 8, 1996

bless your pea-pickin' hearts
used for expressing thanks *US, 1956*
A catchphrase television sign-off on *The Ernie Ford Show* (NBC, 1956–61), a music variety program. Repeated with referential humor.
- Beginning in 1956 he took a prime-time TV gig on The Ford Show, where he instigated the time-worn phrase "Bless your pea-pickin' hearts." — Kurt Wolff, *Country Music*, p. 177, 2000

bletch!
used as an all-purpose, potent expression of disgust *US, 1981*
From the German *brechen* (to vomit).
- — *CoEvolution Quarterly*, p. 26, Spring 1981
- — Guy L. Steele et al., *The Hacker's Dictionary*, p. 33, 1983

bletcherous *adjective*
in computing, poorly designed, dysfunctional *US, 1981*
- — *CoEvolution Quarterly*, p. 26, Spring 1981
- — Guy L. Steele et al., *The Hacker's Dictionary*, p. 33, 1983

blimp *noun*
1 in necrophile usage, a corpse with a distended abdomen *US, 1987*
- — *Maledicta*, p. 180, Summer/Winter 1986–1987: "Sexual slang: prostitutes, pedophiles, flagellators, transvestites, and necrophiles"

2 an obese person *US, 1934*
- — *Maledicta*, p. 38, 1983: "More common patient-directed pejoratives used by medical personnel"

3 in the television and movie industries, a camera's sound-proofing housing *US, 1977*
- — Tony Miller and Patricia George, *Cut! Print!*, p. 41, 1977

4 a bus *US, 1990*
- — Charles Shafer, *Folk Speech in Texas Prisons*, p. 198, 1990

blind *noun*
1 a legitimate business used to conceal an illegal one *US, 1929*
- Why didn't you tell us Carlito was using the office as a blind? We could have all been embarrassed. — Edwin Torres, *After Hours*, p. 369, 1979
- A sports news wire, set up in a back room that displayed the latest results from thee region's horse tracks, was the shop's reason for existing. My grandfather called the shop a "blind": a front for an off track betting operation. — Kim Rich, *Johnny's Girl*, p. 33, 1993

2 an area in prison where guards cannot easily see what is going on *US, 1989*
- Allright, you lame bastard, let's go to the blind. — James Harris, *A Convict's Dictionary*, p. 34, 1989

3 a baggage carriage, usually immediately behind the engine of a passenger train *US, 1893*
- I started to buzz fast in Louis' ear, telling him that A-Number-One was the greatest hobo who ever lived, hoboes ride the rods, blinds, and tops of trains[.] — Mezz Mezzrow, *Really the Blues*, p. 256, 1946

▸ **make the blind see**
to perform oral sex on an uncircumcised man *US, 1981*
- — *Male Swinger Number 3*, p. 48, 1981: "The complete gay dictionary"

blind *adjective*
1 very drunk *UK, 1630*
- Many a night we put on the whole floor show, chorus and all, for a party of six or eight, and they were usually too blind to see it. — Mezz Mezzrow, *Really the Blues*, p. 84, 1946
- But you—being a man—don't care if the boys get blind. — Philip Wylie, *Opus 21*, p. 101, 1949
- [W]e were more than pretty well loopoed—we were blind. — John Nichols, *The Sterile Cuckoo*, p. 190, 1965

2 highly drug-intoxicated *US, 1952*
From an earlier alcohol sense.
- Later, they entered the movie house blind and sat down upstairs. — Hal Ellson, *The Golden Spike*, p. 234, 1952

3 (used of a bet) placed before seeing the cards being bet on *US, 1963*
- — Irwin Steig, *Common Sense in Poker*, p. 181, 1963

blind bat *noun*
an AC-130 aircraft used for night flare missions in Vietnam between 1964 and 1970 *US, 1971*
Bats are not, of course, blind; they see at night.
- The role of the C-123s included the Candlestick flare-drop mission that had been performed by C-47s in South Vietnam and C-130 Blind Bat aircraft out of country. — Philip Chinney, *Air Commando*, p. 167, 1997

blind link *noun*
on the Internet, a link that is misleading or false, taking you somewhere other than where you expect to go *US, 2000*
Common on pornography websites.
- Detracting from the site are a few "blind links," notably under "Contact us," which lead to annoying error messages. — *Legal Times*, p. 20, 19th June 2000

blind pig *noun*
1 a speakeasy, where alcohol is served illegally *US, 1886*
- Of the 50-odd blind pigs in 52nd Street, between Fifth and sixth, only two remained. — Jack Lait and Lee Mortimer, *New York Confidential*, p. 43, 1948
- They hadn't been able to locate him in any of the blind pigs or whorehouses where he usually holed up, but he could have found a new place. — Jim Thompson, *The Nothing Man*, p. 142, 1954

- There is no way of estimating how many night clubs, speakeasies and blind pigs existed in the Broadway sector then. — Robert Sylvester, *No Cover Charge*, p. 138, 1956
- I found out from arguments between Mama and Pap that cousin Bunny had been a fast twenty five year old hustler who was operating a blind pig and poker trap in Vicksburg's sin district that night that Mama saw Papa for the first time. — Iceberg Slim (Robert Beck), *Mama Black Widow*, p. 56, 1969

2 in poker, an unskilled but lucky player *US*, *1996*

From the adage that even a blind pig will find an acorn over time.

- — John Vorhaus, *The Big Book of Poker Slang*, 1996

blindside *verb*

to hit or attack someone without warning *US*, *1968*

Originally a term from American football, and then extended as a metaphor.

- "He got past me Rog. He blindsided me," Walter Pulaski said. — Robert Campbell, *Alice in La-La Land*, p. 45, 1987

blind tiger *noun*

an illegal drinking establishment *US*, *1909*

- Washington is loaded with bootleggers and blind tigers. — Jack Lait and Lee Mortimer, *Washington Confidential*, p. 130, 1951

bling *noun*

a vulgar or ludicrously ostentatious display of wealth *US*, *2003*

- Leave the bling and attitude at home. Abstract Rude's on the microphone. — *Anchorage (Alaska) Daily News*, p. H5, 25th April 2003
- [Jennifer] Lopez' erstwhile boyfriend [Puff Daddy/P Diddy] was "bling" personified. — *The Guardian*, p. 23, 21st May 2003

bling-bling *noun*

wealth, especially as manifested in expensive, if tasteless, jewelry *US*, *1999*

Coined by hip-hop rapper B.G. and appearing in his 1999 "Chopper City in the Ghetto."

- Like B.G.'s hit song says, it's about "Bling! Bling!" Li'l Wayne calls it "braggin' rights." A teenager whose gold teeth say "CASH MONEY," Wayne says he lives with Baby in English Turn just so he can say he does. — *Atlanta Journal and Constitution*, p. 1C, 28th November 1999
- She [Aaliyah] didn't traffic in Glocks, didn't indulge in big pimpin', didn't court the bling-bling life. — *Washington Post*, p. C1, 28th August 2001
- [T]he modern-day "bling-bling" era of hip-hop has emerged. Gold has taken a back seat to the new metal of choice—platinum. — *The Source*, p. 64, March 2002

bling-bling *verb*

to be successful, especially in hip-hop; hence, to be ostentatious; to make money *US*, *2003*

- Lyrix, Reggie, Akino and even Hank are bling-blinging it all the way to the bank. — Patrick Neate, *Where You're At*, p. 14, 2003

blinged; blinged out *adjective*

ostentatious; expensively bejeweled, especially if a tasteless display *US*, *2000*

- The Honda's driver cuts the gas, his jaw working a wad of gum as he checks out what Aviland his friends bring to the table: two Integras, a '93 and a '98, and a moderately blinged-up Benz sedan. — *Los Angeles Times*, p. B1, 9th December 2000

blink *noun*

▸ **on the blink**

1 broken, not functioning *US*, *1899*

- "Our car's on the blink," she said. "I took a bus." — Robert Campbell, *Juice*, p. 104, 1988
- My car was on the blink, so Mr. De Wilde politely asked if he could take me home from the train station. — Pamela Des Barres, *I'm With the Band*, p. 120, 1988
- Although Keb' Mo', in his Monday night performance at the Birchmore, showed hints of ownership, it appeared as if his mojo was on the blink. — *Washington Post*, p. C2, 24th March 2004

2 posing as a blind person while begging *US*, *1956*

- "Tell you what, Tex," Ford persisted, "you go on the blink with me and I give you my word of honor here and now, the day we get a stake we throw away the glasses." — Nelson Algren, *A Walk on the Wild Side*, p. 136, 1956

blink *verb*

to miss seeing a fight, attack or other cause of excitement *US*, *1976*

- — John R. Armore and Joseph D. Wolfe, *Dictionary of Desperation*, p. 20, 1976

blinkenlights *noun*

diagnostic lights on the front panel of a computer *US*, *1991*

- — Eric S. Raymond, *The New Hacker's Dictionary*, p. 66, 1991

blinker *noun*

1 a quadriplegic *US*, *1980*

Vietnam war gallows humor, suggesting that a quadriplegic is capable only of blinking his eyes.

- "You got fucked, but there's a guy who's a blinker—the quadriplegic—and he got it worse than you." — Mark Baker, *Nam*, p. 257, 1981

2 a police helicopter *US*, *1980*

- — Edith A. Folb, *runnin' down some lines*, p. 229, 1980

blinkers *noun*

eye-glasses *US*, *1974*

- Mr. K is wearing new blinkers—not for reading but in tribute to her avocados, which are worth it. — Leo Rosten, *Dear Herm*, p. 149, 1974

blinkus of the thinkus *noun*

a momentary loss of concentration *US*, *1971*

- — Dick Squires, *The Other Racquet Sports*, p. 219, 1971

blinky *noun*

a person with poor or no eyesight *US*, *1922*

- — Joseph E. Ragen and Charles Finston, *Inside the World's Toughest Prison*, p. 791, 1962

blinky *adjective*

agitated, upset *US*, *1992*

- And she gets all blinky on me. "What you say!" — Richard Price, *Clockers*, p. 366, 1992

blip *noun*

1 a minor fluctuation, usually upward, in the stock market or other measures of corporate fortunes *US*, *1988*

- — Kathleen Odean, *High Steppers, Fallen Angels, and Lollipops*, p. 97, 1988
- The rise of Reese [Witherspoon] is explicable both as a blip (she's a perky, funny, charming freak of nature) and as a trend: chick flicks are performing better than ever before. — *The Times*, 2nd August 2003

2 a source of surprise *US*, *1947*

- You young New York Negroes is a blip! I swear you is! — Ralph Ellison, *Invisible Man*, p. 330, 1947
- I lit the stick of pot. Damn, that whole scene was a blip. — Piri Thomas, *Down These Mean Streets*, p. 62, 1967

3 a nickel (five-cent piece) *US*, *1935*

- — Lou Shelly, *Hepcats Jive Talk Dictionary*, p. 7, 1945
- Even before I was in the money I togged like a fashion plate, so I could run with the hip cats who hung around the poolroom. I was always as ready as they were, although sometimes I never had a blip in my poke. — Mezz Mezzrow, *Really the Blues*, p. 22, 1946

blip *adjective*

classy *US*, *1948*

- — Jack Lait and Lee Mortimer, *New York Confidential*, p. 235, 1948

blippy *adjective*

used as a euphemism roughly meaning "damned" *US*, *1974*

- How many times have I stood on my street corner, looking out at your blippy world full of pros? — Piri Thomas, *Seven Long Times*, p. 4, 1974

bliss cup *noun*

in the usage of counterculturalists associated with the Rainbow Nation gatherings, a homemade cup or bowl for eating and drinking *US*, *1997*

- — Jim Crotty, *How to Talk American*, p. 288, 1997

bliss out *verb*

to become ecstatic *US*, *1973*

Used in a derogatory fashion, usually when applied to religious or cult zealots.

- — Connie Eble (Editor), *UNC-CH Campus Slang*, November 1973
- The trumpet fanfares in ["It's All Too Much" by The Beatles]... completely blissed-out, over the top. — *Uncut*, p. 34, July 2001

blister *noun*

1 a bump placed on a playing card by pressing it against a small sharp object, used by card cheats to identify the value of the card *US, 1991*
- — Michael Dalton, *Blackjack*, p. 33, 1991

2 a prostitute *US, 1905*
- — Dale Gordon, *The Dominion Sex Dictionary*, p. 30, 1967

blisterfoot *noun*

an infantry soldier *US, 1945*
- — Lou Shelly, *Hepcats Jive Talk Dictionary*, p. 43, 1945

blister work *noun*

extortion *US, 1950*
- When we pipe, it's a hard lay we do a little blister work. — *The New American Mercury*, p. 708, 1950

blisty *adjective*

windy, cold, not suitable for surfing *US, 1991*
- — Trevor Cralle, *The Surfin'ary*, p. 11, 1991

blitz *noun*

an intensive campaign; a concentrated effort *US, 1940*
After German *blitz* (understood in English as "all-out offensive warfare").
- The Utah Highway Patrol's recent speeding-enforcement blitz between Lehi and Provo showed there are a significant number of drivers who exceed the posted 65 mph limit along tha stretch of I-15. — *Desert Utah Morning News*, 1st April 2004

blitz *verb*

1 to defeat someone soundly *US, 1940*
- The Mountaineers led 14–9 before being blitzed 74–53. — *Charleston (West Virginia) Daily Mail*, p. B1, 22nd March 2004

2 in gin, to win and leave an opponent scoreless *US, 1971*
- — Irwin Steig, *Play Gin to Win*, p. 138, 1971

3 in bar dice games, to bet the total amount of the pot *US, 1971*
- — Jester Smith, *Games They Play in San Francisco*, p. 103, 1971

blitzed *adjective*

drunk or drug-intoxicated *US, 1966*
- If they were too drunk to get out, too blitzed to feel the heat, their skeletons were found in the debris, skulls smiling. — William Brashler, *City Dogs*, p. 56, 1976
- I get blitzed and pass out in his bedroom. Caitlan comes in and dives all over me. — *Clerks*, 1994
- I had my shirt off, I was sweaty, blitzed, everyone was. — Michelle Tea, *Valencia*, p. 49, 2000

blivet *noun*

1 an obnoxious person, especially with bad hygiene *US, 1949*
- — Sally Williams, *"Strong" Words*, p. 134, 1994

2 in computing, a problem which cannot be solved or any impossibility *US, 1991*
- — Eric S. Raymond, *The New Hacker's Dictionary*, p. 67, 1991

blizzard *noun*

1 a large amount of cocaine *US, 1999*
- So of course there was a blizzard, a never-ending, complimentary blizzard for your nasal enjoyment. — James St. James, *Party Monster*, p. 127, 1999

2 poor television reception characterized by flickering white dots *US, 1952*
- Life in this great pretzel center is distinguished by the worst television reception enjoyed by any metropolitan American city—not even barring blast-furnacy Pittsburgh, runner-up for ghosts, blizzards, fade-outs and other visual blah. — *San Francisco News*, p. 21, 22nd May 1952

3 the cloud of thick, white smoke produced when smoking freebase cocaine *US, 1992*
- — Terry Williams, *Crackhouse*, p. 147, 1992

blizzard head *noun*

in the early days of black and white television, a blonde *US, 1948*
So called because a blonde's hair takes up all the light in the picture.
- — *Time*, p. 76, 24th May 1948

blo *noun*

cocaine *US, 1993*
- — Peter Johnson, *Dictionary of Street Alcohol and Drug Terms*, p. 22, 1993

block *noun*

1 prison *US, 1983*
- He paused. Stick was looking at him now. Cornell said, "You from the block, aren't you?" — Elmore Leonard, *Stick*, p. 98, 1983

2 a watch *US, 1972*
Circus and carnival usage.
- He had an old dollar block [watch] and a few picks and he'd lay around the yard and every fish [new convict] that come in, if the fish had anything he'd con him out of it if he could. — Bruce Jackson, *In the Life*, p. 285, 1972

▸ **on the block**

engaged in prostitution on the street *US, 1941*
- Have all the players and working girls smiling on her, lapping up the news that Inez been put out on the block again, handed over her little black book and gone back in harness. — John Sayles, *Union Dues*, p. 182, 1977
- A whore had to be tough, because if she start off at sixteen out there on the block, by the time she's twenty-four or twenty-five, she's done for. — John Allen, *Assault with a Deadly Weapon*, p. 102, 1977

block and tackle *noun*

illegally manufactured whiskey *US, 1974*
- — Burgess Laughlin, *Job Opportunities in the Black Market*, p. 4, 1978
- — *Star Tribune (Minneapolis)*, p. 19F, 31st January 1999

block boy *noun*

a youth who spends his abundant free time idling on a street corner, looking or hoping for trouble *US, 1970*
- — *Current Slang*, p. 5, Fall 1970

blockbuster *noun*

1 a capsule of pentobarbital sodium (trade name Nembutal™), a central nervous system depressant *US, 1970*
Sometimes shortened to "buster."
- — Clarence Major, *Dictionary of Afro-American Slang*, p. 27, 1970

2 a .357 Magnum bullet *US, 1962*
- — *American Speech*, p. 267, December 1962: "The language of traffic policemen"

blocked *adjective*

drunk or drug-intoxicated *US, 1956*
- I knew he was getting blocked in a very methodical fashion. — James Blake, *The Joint*, p. 126, 30th June 1956
- — Eugene Landy, *The Underground Dictionary*, p. 35, 1971

blocker *noun*

a confederate who shields a casino cheat from being seen as he robs a slot machine *US, 1984*
- — Thomas L. Clark, *The Dictionary of Gambling and Gaming*, p. 22, 1987

blockhead *noun*

a stupid fool, an idiot *UK, 1549*
Originally "a wooden base for hats or wigs," hence "wooden-headed."
- Peterson's defense would have been more palatable if it had admitted to his arrogance, lecherousness, and stupidity, and argued that he was too much of a self-centred blockhead to pull off a murder. — Loretta Dillon, *Stone Cold Guilty*, p. 154, 2005

block hustle *noun*

a small-scale swindle *US, 1997*
- I prosecuted a few bunco cases, but they were just block hustles, street scams. — Stephen Cannell, *Big Con*, p. 152, 1997

blocks *noun*

dice *US, 1962*
- — Frank Garcia, *Marked Cards and Loaded Dice*, p. 262, 1962

▸ **put the blocks to someone**

to have sex with someone *US, 1888*
- — Joseph E. Ragen and Charles Finston, *Inside the World's Toughest Prison*, p. 814, 1962
- He supposed every stud on the beach was trying to put the blocks to her. — Burt Hirschfield, *Fire Island*, p. 71, 1970
- Guys who spoke of "putting the blocks to" a chick were bound to be assholes too[.] — *Screw*, p. 7, 3rd January 1972

blonde *noun*
coffee with cream *US, 1952*
- — *American Speech*, p. 232, October 1952: "The argot of soda jerks"

blonde and sweet *adjective*
(used of coffee) with cream and sugar *US, 1945*
- — *American Speech*, p. 37, February 1948: "Talking under water: speech in submarines"
- — Helen Dahlskog (Editor), *A Dictionary of Contemporary and Colloquial Usage*, p. 8, 1972
- — "Slingo", *The Official CB Slang Dictionary Handbook*, p. 9, 1976

bloober *noun*
a female breast *US, 1954*
- On the way to Biff's, Betsy, dressed in a knocked-out strapless, bloobers more out than in, kept beating her gums. — Bernard Wolfe, *The Late Risers*, p. 157, 1954

bloochie *noun*
any cumbersome object *US, 1982*
From Polish immigrants' speech.
- Bloochie—Any awkward, unwieldy object. Something without handles, making it difficult to pick up or steal. — Bill Reilly, *Big Al's Official Guide to Chicagoese*, p. 16, 1982

blood *noun*
1 a black person *US, 1965*
- — J. L. Simmons and Barry Winograd, *It's Happening*, p. 167, 1966
- Annette downtown going for broke, while Chicanos and bloods outside the bars beat the nightlight out of po' trash from across the way, driving them out their territory. — Steve Cannon, *Groove, Bang, and Jive Around*, p. 24, 1969
- They never inquired if the bloods they were giving the jobs to were the same ones who were causing the trouble. — Tom Wolfe, *Radical Chic & Mau-Mauing the Flak Catchers*, pp. 98–99, 1970
- A young blood stops him, gives him his address. — Ken Kesey, *Last Whole Earth Catalog*, p. 234, 1971
- "Okay. So he wasn't a blood." — Robert Deane Pharr, *S.R.O.*, p. 464, 1971

2 wine *US, 1959*
- — Robert George Reisner, *The Jazz Titans*, p. 151, 1960
- "Ever try blood?" Joe Richards snickered across the room. "The kind distilled from grapes, I mean." — Clarence Cooper Jr., *Black*, p. 12, 1963
- I told him like I did every stud / that it wasn't shit for me to drink two or three fifths a some real good blood. — Bruce Jackson, *Get Your Ass in the Water and Swim Like Me*, p. 89, 1964

3 pizza sauce *US, 1996*
- — *Maledicta*, p. 12, 1996: "Domino's pizza jargon"

4 tomato juice *US, 1936*
- — Lou Shelly, *Hepcats Jive Talk Dictionary*, p. 7, 1945

blood alley *noun*
an unsafe stretch of a road *US, 1978*
- "Blood Alley" Claims Victim — *San Francisco Examiner*, p. 54, 9th March 1978
- The site of the crash was a desolate desert stretch of Highway 86, a two-lane highway known as "Blood Alley" and "killer Highway" because of the hundreds of collisions there each year. — *New York Times*, p. A12, 11th August 1983
- How many injuries or deaths are required on the 74 to increase CHP and local police enforcement to improve conditions on this highway which is fast becoming Blood Alley? [Letter to Editor] — *Press Enterprise (Riverside, California)*, p. B2, 26th January 2004

blood chit *noun*
a written notice in several languages, carried by members of the American armed forces, identifying the person as American and promising a reward for help in evading the enemy *US, 1941*
The US Department of Defense Policy on Blood Chits states that the chits "are a tool used by an evader or escapee after all other measures of independent evasion and escape have failed and the evader(s) considers assistance vital to survival. Upon receiving assistance, the evader or escapee provides the assistor with the blood chit number. The blood chit represents an obligation of the U.S. Government to compensate the claimant, or his immediate family if the claimant is deceased, for services rendered to DoD personnel." The version used in the Vietnam war had the plea for "assistance in obtaining food, shelter and protection" in English, Burmese, Chinese, Thai, Laotian, Cambodian, Vietnamese, Malayan, Indonesian, Tagalog, Visayan, French and Dutch.
- None of them had dared take anything—not even the cheap barter watch from the blood-chit can. — Wallace Brown, *The Endless Hours*, p. 27, 1961
- Finally, Morton gave each man a small, plastic escape and evasion map and his personal "blood chit." — Benjamin Schemmer, *The Raid*, p. 191, 1976

bloodhound *verb*
to track someone down *US, 1963*
- That hundred and a quarter was in my fist almost, and I went bloodhoundin after you. — Clarence Cooper Jr., *Black*, p. 190, 1963

blood in *verb*
in prison, to establish your credentials for toughness by slashing another prisoner *US, 2000*
- Rikers inmates had to "blood in," or slash someone across the face. — *Village Voice*, p. 54, 19th December 2000

blood in, blood out *noun*
used for expressing the rules for entering (to kill) and leaving (to be killed) a prison gang *US, 1990*
- Entrance into the group is by election and a "blood in, blood out" oath is taken by new members. — Alfredo Mirande, *Gringo Justice*, p. 205, 1990
- — William K. Bentley and James M. Corbett, *Prison Slang*, p. 41, 1992
- "'Blood in, blood out' simply means that to join the AB, an inmate had to 'earn his bones'—in other words, had to kill someone to get in." — Pete Earley, *The Hot House*, p. 79, 1992
- A "blood-in, blood-out" entry requirement is absolute. — Bill Valentine, *Gangs and Their Tattoos*, p. 8, 2000

bloodman *noun*
a person who is at any moment capable of physical violence *US, 2002*
- — Gary K. Farlow, *Prison-ese*, p. 5, 2002

blood money *noun*
in gambling, money that is won after long, hard work *US, 1979*
- — John Scarne, *Scarne's Guide to Modern Poker*, p. 273, 1979

blood poker *noun*
poker played as business with no social trappings *US, 1988*
- — George Percy, *The Language of Poker*, p. 11, 1988

blood simple *adjective*
crazed by violence *US, 1984*
- But the caper went blood simple: guard snuffed, stray bullets flying. — James Ellroy, *Hollywood Nocturnes*, p. 286, 1984

blood stripe *noun*
a military promotion that is made possible only by the demotion of another unit member *US, 1968*
- — Carl Fleischhauer, *A Glossary of Army Slang*, p. 4, 1968
- I don't know if the blood-stripe promotion qualified Kell as a full-fledged lifer or not. — William Pelfrey, *The Big V*, p. 80, 1972

blood wings *noun*
the first set of parachute insignia that a paratrooper receives upon qualification at different levels of expertise *US, 1989*
- His master-blaster "blood wings" were on his hat and he desperately wanted them back. — David H. Hackworth, *About Face*, p. 449, 1989

blooey *adjective*
▸ **go blooey**
to go out of business; to break down completely *US, 1910*
- One More American Tradition Goes Blooey [Headline] — *San Francisco News*, p. 15, 12th June 1950
- Because fish fall in love with other fish, a wartime dream of a Sunnyvale industrial plant's employee went blooey today. — *San Francisco news*, p. 1, 18th July 1952
- Oblivious shitbird—he didn't know the whole scheme had gone blooey. — James Ellroy, *Hollywood Nocturnes*, p. 115, 1994

blooker *noun*
an M79 grenade launcher *US, 1973*
Vietnam war usage. It is a single-shot, break-open, breech-loading, shoulder-fired weapon.
- — *Maledicta*, p. 259, Summer/Winter 1982: "Viet-speak"

- "A guy who'd started lobbing blooker rounds in on us." — James Lee Burke, *Last Car to Elysian Fields*, p. 406, 2003

bloomer *noun*

in horse racing, a horse that performs well early in the morning during the workout but not in a race later in the day *US, 1951*

- — David W. Maurer, *Argot of the Racetrack*, p. 14, 1951

bloomer boy *noun*

a paratrooper *US, 1948*

- — *American Speech*, p. 319, October/December 1948: "Slang of the American paratrooper"

Bloomie's *nickname*

the Bloomingdale's department store, especially the original store located on Third Avenue between 59th and 60th Streets, New York *US, 1977*

- Pitstopping on her way to Paris, where she will shoot pix of Raquel, our heroine hit Bloomie's New York where with credit card in hand racked up a $240 bill in 15 minutes. — *New York Times*, p. B1, 22nd April 1977
- Even with the Bloomie's job, I carefully rationed myself to one 23-cent can of tuna fish a day. — Kathryn Leigh Scott, *The Bunny Years*, p. 13, 1998
- The limited-edition tees are available at all Bloomie's locations. — *Atlanta Journal-Constitution*, p. 18NE, 18th March 2004

blooper *noun*

1 an error, especially a humiliating and/or humorous one *US, 1925*

- "He would never make such a tactical mistake in a naval problem but he made bloopers with the press." — William Brinkley, *Don't Go Near the Water*, p. 45, 1956

2 in television, radio or film making, an unintentionally funny misspoken line *US, 1924*

- — Ira Konigsberg, *The Complete Film Dictionary*, p. 32, 1987

3 an M79 grenade launcher *US, 1978*

Vietnam war usage. It is a single-shot, break-open, breech-loading, shoulder-fired weapon.

- — *Maledicta*, p. 259, Summer/Winter 1982: "Viet-speak"
- — Peter Kokalis, *Solider of Fortune*, p. 57, July 1992

blooper ball *noun*

a grenade used in an M-79 grenade launcher *US, 1982*

- — *Maledicta*, p. 259, Summer/Winter 1982: "Viet-speak"

bloop tube; bloop gun *noun*

an M79 grenade launcher *US, 1971*

Vietnam war usage. It is a single-shot, break-open, breech-loading, shoulder-fired weapon.

- — Peter Kokalis, *Solider of Fortune*, p. 57, July 1992
- [M]achine guns, automatic rifles, bloop guns, occasionally the mortar tubes, maybe the recoilles if there was one—would open fire into their sector of the wire and cleared approaches. — Cherokee Paul McDonald, *Into the Green*, p. 204, 2001

blotch *verb*

to stain your underwear when what had seemed like flatulence was something more *US, 1989*

- — Pamela Munro, *U.C.L.A. Slang*, p. 21, 1989

blotter *noun*

a tiny piece of absorbent paper impregnated with LSD and ingested as such *US, 1971*

- He was rummaging around in the kit bag. "I think it's about time to chew up a blotter," he said. — Hunter S. Thompson, *Fear and Loathing in Las Vegas*, pp. 20–21, 1971
- "What kind is it?" "Blotter. Has a little numeral one on it." — Elmore Leonard, *Freaky Deaky*, p. 20, 1988
- This plan ended up with us walking up and down Haight Street in S.F. trying to sell blotter to amused and disinterested ex-hippies. — Jennifer Blowdryer, *White Trash Debutante*, p. 37, 1997
- She did some blotter when she started with the Chicks and made the mistake of telling him one time, on the phone. — Elmore Leonard, *Be Cool*, p. 79, 1999

blotto *adjective*

very drunk; in a drunken stupor *UK, 1917*

- "You can sit up and drink with me until I go blotto," I said. — Chester Himes, *If He Hollers Let Him Go*, p. 95, 1945

- "The pleasure of being blotto and not knowing for a little while what a mess everything is." — John Conway, *Love in Surbiria*, p. 56, 1960
- And the Barfers got blotto and fell in love with everything about these movie guys[.] — Joseph Wambaugh, *Lines and Shadows*, p. 336, 1984
- [H]is M.O. for the evening, I soon began to discern, was to get Donleavy so totally blotto that he could have his way with him, in terms of contracts[.] — Terry Southern, *Now Dig This*, p. 174, 1991

blow *noun*

1 cocaine *US, 1971*

- "I think I'll have a little blow before we begin," he said as he produced the folded hundred-dollar bill in which he carries his cocaine. — Christina and Richard Milner, *Black Players*, p. 177, 1972
- He says he owes you for blow and he just got some product himself. — *Heathers*, 1988
- You got some good blow, right? — *The Bad Lieutenant*, 1992
- The two of us liked to get high a lot around the house, and we used more than our share of blow during the early 1970s. — Ralph "Sonny" Barger, *Hell's Angel*, p. 113, 2000

2 heroin *US, 2003*

- "We've been sitting out here for the last couple hours and haven't heard anyone shouting about 'rocks' and 'blows,'" said Talley, 65, referring to the street slang for crack and heroin. — *Chicago Tribune*, p. C1, 3rd August 2003

3 a dose of a drug, especially a dose of cocaine to be snorted *US, 1953*

- "You goin' give me a blow, ain't you Terry?" she asked in a pleading voice. — Donald Goines, *Dopefiend*, p. 197, 1971
- I felt it getting a bit heated so I ordered another blow of cocaine and a round of drinks and I split. — A.S. Jackson, *Gentleman Pimp*, p. 58, 1973
- I'm dying, baby. If I don't get a blow I'm goin' to die. — Charles W. Moore, *A Brick for Mister Jones*, pp. 26–27, 1975
- After a while Lalin said, "Carlito where can we go for a blow?" I wasn't too much into candy anymore since I came out. — Edwin Torres, *After Hours*, p. 241, 1979

4 a confidence swindle involving the claimed ability to change the denomination on currency *US, 1957*

- It didn't surprise Goldy that Jackson had been trimmed on The Blow. — Chester Himes, *A Rage in Harlem*, p. 40, 1957

blow *verb*

1 to smoke, especially to smoke marijuana *US, 1772*

Originally "to smoke a pipe or cigar," now drugs use only. Usage often specifies marijuana thus "blow **SHIT**," "blow a **STICK**," etc.

- At times, after we had fixed and blown some pot, with a sleek thrust of my own soul, a thrust of empathy, I used to find myself identifying with him. — Alexander Trocchi, *Cain's Book*, p. 75, 1960
- Shorty would take me to groovy, frantic scenes in different chicks' and cats' pads, where with the lights and juke down mellow, everybody blew gage and juiced back and jumped. — Malcolm X and Alex Haley, *The Autobiography of Malcolm X*, p. 56, 1964
- I could not see how they were more justified in drinking than I was in blowing the gage. — Eldridge Cleaver, *Soul on Ice*, p. 4, 1968
- — Home Office, *Glossary of Terms and Slang Common in Penal Establishments*, 1978
- Did I ask if they're tooting cocaine, maybe blowing a little weed? No, I didn't ask him that either. — Elmore Leonard, *Split Images*, p. 16, 1981

2 to register on a blood alcohol breath testing device *US, 1978*

- Someone at the club that evening had said that anybody coming from Deep Run after a Saturday night party, anybody at all, would blow at least a twenty on the breathalizer. — Elmore Leonard, *Switch*, p. 1, 1978

3 to perform oral sex *US, 1930*

- I, anticipating even more pleasure, wouldn't allow her to blow me on the bus[.] — Neal Cassady, *The First Third*, p. 190, 1947
- Here, man. Blow me here! — John Rechy, *Numbers*, p. 106, 1967
- Girls will blow girls, girl will blow boys, boys will blow girls, and boys will blow boys. — *Screw*, p. 11, 5th January 1970
- Oh, if you think I'm gonna blow this guy for your sick purposes, you are sadly mistaken. — *The Sopranos* (Episode 57), 2004

4 to open something with explosives *UK, 1602*

- The guys in the mob thought I had turned snowbird when I said we would blow the Kroger safe. — Charles Hamilton, *Men of the Underworld*, p. 136, 1952
- I prefer blowing one. I blowed quite a few. — Bruce Jackson, *In the Life*, p. 96, 1972

- Convicts, they'd sit around talking about jobs, banks they'd held up, argue about how to blow a safe. — Elmore Leonard, *Maximum Bob*, pp. 107–108, 1991

5 to waste an opportunity, to bungle *US, 1907*

- I had the market on the good pot uptown sewed up; I didn't want to blow that. — Claude Brown, *Manchild in the Promised Land*, p. 161, 1965
- Anyway, she blew her whole weekend looking for someone for me to debate. — James Simon Kunen, *The Strawberry Statement*, p. 63, 1968
- You know, Billy, we blew it. — *Easy Rider*, 1969
- You blew it, asshole. — *Fast Times at Ridgemont High*, 1982

6 to be useless, unpopular, distasteful *US, 1997*
Often in the context of an exclamation such as "That blows!"

- — Anna Scotti and Paul Young, *Buzzwords*, p. 53, 1997
- — Connie Eble (Editor), *UNC-CH Campus Slang*, p. 2, Fall 1999

7 to leave *US, 1898*

- I picked up my battered hat from the desk and stretched. "Got to blow, pal." — Mickey Spillane, *I, The Jury*, p. 24, 1947
- "Go ahead," he said to her. "You can blow." — Irving Shulman, *The Amboy Dukes*, p. 43, 1947
- As far as Roamer is concerned, they blew with the dough. — Horace McCoy, *Kiss Tomorrow Good-bye*, p. 264, 1948
- "Want to blow this place now?" he said to the girl. — Chandler Brossard, *Who Walks in Darkness*, p. 12, 1952

8 to play a musical instrument *US, 1949*
Used with all instruments, not just those requiring wind.

- And the gate that rocked at the eighty-eight was blowin' "How High the Moon." — William "Lord" Buckley, *The Ballad of Dan McGroo*, 1960
- You blew piano with Jimmy Vann, huh? — Ross Russell, *The Sound*, p. 108, 1961
- This gave me a stronger urge to blow piano, or blow a box, as they used to say. — Claude Brown, *Manchild in the Promised Land*, p. 229, 1965
- [O]ne whom he intended looking up at the Capitol Theater where he was blowing with a name band (Glenn Miller's old band). — Herbert Huncke, *The Evening Sun Turned Crimson*, p. 75, 1980

▶ **blow a gasket**
to lose your temper completely *US, 1949*

- Watching it one day I saw the normally mild mannered Stuart almost blow a gasket on the air. — Sue Rhodes, *Now you'll think I'm awful*, p. 100, 1967
- — Helen Dahlskog (Editor), *A Dictionary of Contemporary and Colloquial Usage*, p. 8, 1972

▶ **blow a hype**
to become overexcited *US, 1986*

- — Gary Goshgarian (Editor), *Exploring Language*, p. 302, 1986

▶ **blow a load**
to ejaculate *US, 1995*

- Lois could never have Superman's baby. Do you think her fallopian tubes could handle his sperm? I guarantee he blows a load like a shotgun. — *Mallrats*, 1995

▶ **blow a nut**
to ejaculate *US, 1994*

- So I blow a nut on her belly, and I get out of there, just as my uncle walks in. — *Clerks*, 1994

▶ **blow a shot**
while trying to inject a drug, to miss the vein or otherwise waste the drug *US, 1966*

- You keep blowing shots like that and all you'll have for an arm is abcesses. — James Mills, *The Panic in Needle Park*, p. 80, 1966
- I blew the shot, please come back and give me another bag. — Robert Daley, *Prince of the City*, p. 21, 1978

▶ **blow a vein**
while injecting a drug, to cause a vein to collapse *US, 1974*

- — Stewart L. Tubbs and Sylvia Moss, *Human Communication*, p. 119, 1974
- — Geoffrey Froner, *Digging for Diamonds*, p. 11, 1989
- — Sally Williams, *"Strong" Words*, p. 134, 1994

▶ **blow beets**
to vomit *US, 1968*

- — Collin Baker et al., *College Undergraduate Slang Study Conducted at Brown University*, p. 82, 1968
- — Lewis Poteet, *Car and Motorcycle Slang*, p. 32, 1992

▶ **blow chow**
to vomit *US, 1988*

- — Michael V. Anderson, *The Bad, Rad, Not to Forget Way Cool Beach and Surf Discriptionary*, p. 3, 1988
- I gagged a couple of times, but I didn't blow chow so I was pretty pleased. — Janet Evanovich, *Seven Up*, p. 201, 2001

▶ **blow chunks**
to vomit *US, 1992*

- I think he's gonna blow chunks. — *Wayne's World*, 1992
- If some disco freak popped out of a trunk and blew chunks all over the hood of my car, I'd be hopping mad. — Elissa Stein and Kevin Leslie, *Chunks*, p. 3, 1997

▶ **blow dinner**
to vomit *US, 1968*

- — Collin Baker et al., *College Undergraduate Slang Study Conducted at Brown University*, p. 82, 1968

▶ **blow dust**
to shoot a gun *US, 2001*

- At one point, a woman overheard one of Mendrell's friends tell Miguel's security guard they would "blow dust also, if they have to," which is street slang for shooting a gun, police said. — *Intelligencer Journal (Lancaster, Pennsylvania)*, p. B1, 10th March 2001

▶ **blow lunch**
to vomit *US, 1965*

- I ate the porridge with onions and salt in it that had a raw egg tinted with blue vegetable coloring on top, blew my lunch, and ate some more. — John Nichols, *The Sterile Cuckoo*, p. 55, 1965
- — Collin Baker et al., *College Undergraduate Slang Study Conducted at Brown University*, p. 82, 1968

▶ **blow smoke**
to brag *US, 1946*

- — Norman Carlisle, *The Modern Wonder Book of Trains and Railroading*, p. 259, 1946

▶ **blow someone's mind**
to amaze someone; to surprise someone; to shock someone *US, 1965*
A figurative sense, extended from the sense as a "hallucinogenic experience."

- "People are already down on us because we're Hell's Angels," Zorro explained. "This is why we like to blow their minds." — Hunter S. Thompson, *Hell's Angels*, p. 117, 1966
- Who was the passenger? You guess it—Peter Fonda. It blew my mind. I couldn't believe it. — Darryl Ponicsan, *The Last Detail*, p. 83, 1970
- That she knew my name blew my mind. Some of my best friends didn't know my name. — *Something About Mary*, 1998

▶ **blow this cookie stand**
to leave *US, 1977*

- Let's blow this cookie stand and get ourselves some breakfast. — John Sayles, *Union Dues*, p. 373, 1977

▶ **blow this trap**
to leave *US, 1958*

- Why don't we all blow this trap and have us some laughs? — Morton Cooper, *High School Confidential*, p. 19, 1958

▶ **blow your cool**
to lose your mental composure *US, 1961*

- "We agreed when this shit started, that we'd just have to move it from day to day and not blow our cool and not try to think too far ahead." — James Baldwin, *If Beale Street Could Talk*, p. 197, 1974

▶ **blow your jets**
to become angry *US, 1960*

- — *San Francisco Examiner*, p. III-2, 22nd March 1960

▶ **blow your lid**
to lose your control emotionally; to become angry *US, 1935*

- We were in my room, Mrs. Winroy had come in a couple of minutes behind him, and she'd blown her lid so high we'd had to come upstairs. — Jim Thompson, *Savage Night*, p. 24, 1953

▶ **blow your lump**
to completely lose your emotional composure *US, 1951*

- — *American Speech*, p. 194, October 1951: "A study of reformatory argot"

▶ **blow your mind**
1 to have a hallucinogenic experience; to experience a psychotic break as a result of drug use *US, 1965*

- What's it like to blow you mind? [Advertisement for Look Magazine's "Hippie issue"] — *San Francisco Examiner*, p. 26, 12th September 1967

- Since that time I've had a few friends that have blown their minds on acid[.] — Leonard Wolfe (Editor), *Voices from the Love Generation*, p. 70, 1968
- One pound of LSD could therefore blow the minds of the entire population of New York City. — Timothy Leary, *The Politics of Ecstasy*, p. 74, 1968

2 to lose your mind, to go crazy *US, 1965*

- There's a man in the line / And she's blowing his mind / Thinking that he's already made her — Arlo Guthrie, *Coming into Los Angeles*, 1969

▸ **blow your stack**
to lose your temper *US, 1947*

- He waited to see what would happen and when nothing did, said, "you go blowing off your stack like you been doing and you'll be wearing a D.O.A. tag on your toe." — Mickey Spillane, *Kiss Me Deadly*, p. 65, 1952
- I want to say something to you without you blowing your stack. — *Raging Bull*, 1980

▸ **blow your top**
1 to lose emotional control *US, 1946*

- It left me so shaky I almost blew my top and got sicker than a hog with the colic. — Mezz Mezzrow, *Really the Blues*, p. 4, 1946
- The weed available in the U.S. is evidently not strong enough to blow your top and weed psychosis is rare in the States. — William Burroughs, *Junkie*, p. 32, 1953

2 to engage in inconsequential conversation *US, 1947*

- — Marcus Hanna Boulware, *Jive and Slang of Students in Negro Colleges*, 1947

▸ **blow your wheels**
to act without restraint *US, 1955*

- You feel like you want to blow your wheels right now? — *Rebel Without a Cause*, 1955

▸ **blow your wig**
to lose emotional control; to become angry *US, 1851*

- "I still think the punk's blowed his wig!" — Donald Wilson, *My Six Convicts*, p. 47, 1951
- The Chick, you may dig, may blow her wig if a lad is sad and when he visits her pad and can't talk trash and has no cash. — Dan Burley, *Diggeth Thou?*, p. 5, 1959

blow away *verb*
1 to kill someone, usually with a gun *US, 1913*

- — H. Craig Collins, *Street Gangs*, p. 222, 1979
- He should have just taken a dollar out of the wallet, given it to Joe the Grinder, and walked out, instead of blowing her away like he did. — Gerald Petievich, *Money Men*, p. 120, 1981
- That's what he has workers for, to blow people away for nothing. — Richard Condon, *Prizzi's Honor*, p. 223, 1982
- I said, "Okay, I'll give you three seconds." By the time he started to reach in his pocket I was at three and it was too late. So I blew him away. — Elmore Leonard, *Killshot*, p. 22, 1989

2 to impress or astonish someone; hence, to be impressed or astonished *US, 1975*

- "I don't know why you're so blown away, though, after the stuff Kate laid on us in group." — Cyra McFadden, *The Serial*, p. 155, 1977

blow back *verb*
in gambling, to lose all or most of your winnings *US, 1990*

- — Anthony Holden, *Big Deal*, p. 298, 1990

blow bath *noun*
during the war in Vietnam, a bath, massage, and sex *US, 1969*

- They went to whorehouses and massage parlors—steam and cream, they were called, the Old Cocksucker Shop, going to a blow bath to get a steam job. — Philip Beidler, *Late Thoughts on an Old War*, p. 32, 2004

blowboy *noun*
a male homosexual *US, 1935*

- "Else you be tellin' everybody round school tomorrow how a blowboy kick your butt." — Jess Mowry, *Way Past Cool*, p. 124, 1992
- — Michael Dalton Johnson, *Talking Trash with Redd Foxx*, p. 66, 1994

blow dart *noun*
a hypodermic needle used to inject drugs *US, 1971*

- — Edward R. Bloomquist, *Marijuana*, p. 334, 1971

blow date *noun*
a session with a prostitute enhanced by cocaine use *US, 1973*

- When you have a blow date, a couple of men come to your house for three days. — Susan Hall, *Ladies of the Night*, p. 71, 1973

blower *noun*
1 a telephone *UK, 1922*
Carried over from the "speaking tube" which was blown through to alert the receiver; has also been applied to the telegraph system when used for the transmission of racing results. During World War 2, and for some time after, applied to a public address system.

- [T]he bent bogey [corrupt policeman] was on the blower to Charley. — Charles Raven, *Underworld Nights*, p. 62, 1956

2 a respirator *US, 1994*

- — Sally Williams, *"Strong" Words*, p. 135, 1994

3 in a jazz band, a soloist *US, 1960*

- — Robert S. Gould, *A Jazz Lexicon*, p. 26, 1964

4 a handkerchief *US, 1960*

- Stout looked humiliated and ineffably sad as he pulled out his blower and began to wipe off the goo. — Timothy Crouse, *The Boys on the Bus*, p. 53, 1973

5 a party *US, 2001*

- — Don R. McCreary (Editor), *Dawg Speak*, 2001

6 a pistol *US, 1976*

- — Porter Bibb, *CB Bible*, p. 94, 1976

blowhard *noun*
a boaster, a braggart *US, 1857*

- "[A] braggart and a blowhard of the type who may climb up on a soapbox and shout for a following, the way we've all seen Mr. Ceswick do, then back down the moment there is any real danger to him personally." — Ken Kesey, *One Flew Over the Cuckoo's Nest*, p. 149, 1962

blowhole *noun*
the mouth *US, 1950*

- "You shut your blowhole," Tomboy said, turning to Liz. — Hal Ellson, *Tomboy*, p. 85, 1950

blow in *verb*
to arrive *US, 1882*

- About that time Sid Barry blew in from New York[.] — Mezz Mezzrow, *Really the Blues*, p. 21, 1946
- Well, children, the big bad wolf blew into town as advertised[.] — Steve Allen, *Bop Fables*, p. 21, 1955
- Sapphire waited until 2.30. Then she blew in by the kitchen window round at the back[.] — Charles Raven, *Underworld Nights*, p. 11, 1956
- He had blown into town with no 'ho. — Iceberg Slim (Robert Beck), *Airtight Willie and Me*, p. 21, 1979

blow job *noun*
1 an act of oral sex performed on a man, or, occasionally, a woman *US, 1972*

- That white chick—Jane—of yours—she ever give you a blow job? — James Baldwin, *Another Country*, p. 69, 1962
- Well, the least you could do is give me a blow job. — *Repo Man*, 1984
- "You've written the definite blow-job!" he kept shouting. "The definite blow-job!" — Terry Southern, *Now Dig This*, p. 13, 1986
- After all, if you're the kind of guy who'll pay for blowjobs from a black chick on the Sunset Strip, it's humiliating to have to keep saying "Oh, bugger" as if it were the most adorable thing in the world. — *LA Weekly*, p. 15, 31st May 2002

2 a safe robbery in which explosives are used to gain access to the safe *US, 1973*

- There's also the old-fashioned blow job, which nobody uses anymore. You blow the whole goddamn safe. — Leonard Shecter and William Phillips, *On the Pad*, p. 179, 1973

blowman *noun*
a member of a youth gang designated as a shooter *US, 1979*

- — H. Craig Collins, *Street Gangs*, p. 222, 1979

blown *adjective*
of a blood vein, collapsed *US, 1989*

- A vein is said to be "blown" when it can no longer be used because it has collapsed. — Geoffrey Froner, *Digging for Diamonds*, p. 11, 1989

blown away *adjective*
drunk or drug-intoxicated *US, 1981*

- I checked out an unmarked car, drove to the apartment of an informant and got blown away on hash[.] — James Ellroy, *Brown's Requiem*, p. 220, 1981

blown out *adjective*

1 said of choppy ocean conditions unfavorable for surfing *US, 1963*

- — Grant W. Kuhns, *On Surfing*, p. 114, 1963

- [H]e took first place in the U.S. Surfing Championship on a "blown-out" (rotten) day when he got one of the few decent waves. — Eve Babitz, *Eve's Hollywood*, p. 204, 1974

2 drug-intoxicated *US, 1972*

- — Helen Dahlskog (Editor), *A Dictionary of Contemporary and Colloquial Usage*, p. 8, 1972

blow-off *noun*

1 the end of a performance; the final performance in a engagement *US, 1913*

Originally circus usage.

- Feuds and angles, if successful, can last for a year or more, progressing slowly before dramatically culminating in what is known as a blow-off match, signifying the end of the wrestler's current storyline[.] — Dave Flood, *Kayfabe*, p. 30, 2000

- Actually, I was the one who came up with an angle for the blow off. — Missy Hyatt, *Missy Hyatt*, p. 87, 2001

2 in the circus or carnival, the crowd leaving a performance *US, 1980*

- — Joe McKennon, *Circus Lingo*, p. 18, 1980

3 oral sex performed on a man *US, 1972*

- Through Oregon and Washington we were cut down quite a bit; we couldn't give the blow-off and we couldn't strip all the way and things like that. — Bruce Jackson, *In the Life*, p. 390, 1972

4 the moment in a confidence swindle when the victim is left to discover his loss *US, 1969*

- White grifters call it the blowoff. — Iceberg Slim (Robert Beck), *Trick Baby*, p. 124, 1969

blow off *verb*

1 to ignore, to dismiss someone *US, 1965*

- Well then blow him off when he gets here. — *Something About Mary*, 1998

2 to fail to attend *US, 1986*

- — *Rutgers Alumni Magazine*, p. 21, February 1986

blow out *noun*

1 a party or meal unlimited by normal rules of conduct *US, 1815*

- Two summers ago he decided to throw a blowout reunion party at the China Club[.] — Elissa Stein and Kevin Leslie, *Chunks*, p. 8, 1997

2 in horse racing, a short but intense workout several days before a race *US, 1968*

- — Don Voorhees and Bob Benoit, *Railbird Handbook*, p. 44, 1968

3 an utter failure *US, 1938*

- Blowouts, both times, wiped me clean. — Elmore Leonard, *Bandits*, p. 66, 1987

blow-up *noun*

a corpse that has exploded from a build-up of internal gas *US, 1962*

- — *American Speech*, p. 267, December 1962: "The language of traffic policemen"

blow up *verb*

1 to become muscular *US, 1995*

- So when I started buffin with Jimel, I blew up to some twenties [20-inch arms], then I got sick with cancer. — Yusuf Jah, *Uprising*, p. 27, 1995

2 in an endurance sport, to reach a point of utter exhaustion *US, 1990*

- The Ultimate Warrior is said to be one of the few wrestlers who blows up on the entry ramp. — *rec.sports.pro-wrestling*, 17th July 1990

- The athlete may "bonk," "hit the wall" or "blow up," as the terminology goes. — *Washington Post*, p. A1, 11th June 2001

3 to receive repeated electronic pages *US, 2001*

- — Rick Ayers (Editor), *Slang Dictionary*, p. 5, 2001

blow-your-mind roulette *noun*

a drug activity in which a variety of pills are mixed together and individuals take a random selection of pills from the mix *US, 1970*

- — Clarence Major, *Dictionary of Afro-American Slang*, p. 29, 1970

blubber *noun*

a fat person *US, 1997*

- The labels were cruel: Gimp, Limpy–go-fetch, Crip, Lift-one-drag one, etc. Pint, Half-a-man, Peewee, Shorty, Lardass, Pork, Blubber, Belly, Blimp. Nuke-knob, Skinhead, Baldy. Four-eyes, Specs, Coke bottles. — *San Francisco Examiner*, p. A15, 28th July 1997

blubberbutt *noun*

an obese person *US, 1952*

- And watch: if Gore wins, America's blubberbutts will file a class action suit against the beer companies. — *New York Post*, p. 20, 30th July 2000

blubberhead *noun*

a fool *US, 1916*

- [E]ven jail was not a safe sanctuary for that big scar-faced blubberhead. — Harry Grey, *The Hoods*, p. 79, 1952

blue *noun*

1 a barbiturate capsule *US, 1969*

- — Norman W. Houser, *Drugs*, p. 13, 1969

- I laughed to myself as I pictured blues or dilaudid in such great amounts that the spoon would literally be overflowing. — *Drugstore Cowboy*, 1988

2 cocaine *US, 1945*

- They ordered cocaine or morphine by the pieces (ounces) and used the dope peddler's slang or code terms, red or blue identifying morphine or cocaine. — William J. Spillard and Pence James, *Needle in a Haystack*, p. 147, 1945

3 a police officer *UK, 1844*

- Couple of years ago, I just missed getting locked up myself, or maybe getting shot by a "blue." It happened on a Mardi Gras. I was walking along and looked at a "fay bitch," just a little too long. — Robert deCoy, *The Nigger Bible*, p. 234, 1967

- "If you want to be a copy, if you want to do for law and order," Schoonover said sarcastically, "why don't you put in your application? Be a blue?" — Robert Campbell, *In La-La Land We Trust*, pp. 26–27, 1986

- I'll have one of the blues park it for you in the underground garage[.] — Stephen J. Cannell, *The Tin Collectors*, p. 16, 2001

4 a black man *US, 1964*

A shortened **BLUE BOY**.

- — *New York Times Magazine*, p. 62, 23rd August 1964

- If Mathis wasn't a blue, he'd be a big movie star. — *Diner*, 1982

▸ **under the blue**

said of a rigged carnival game being operated with police protection *US, 1985*

- — Gene Sorrows, *All About Carnivals*, p. 27, 1985

blue *adjective*

sexually explicit, pornographic *UK, 1864*

- Angela Hoffa hung up her pink telephone and muttered a blue word. — Max Shulman, *Rally Round the Flag, Boys!*, p. 70, 1957

- [B]ut then one night he took us to a blue movie, and what do you suppose? There he was on the screen — Truman Capote, *Breakfast at Tiffany's*, p. 61, 1958

- [H]is material was blue and old, but after a while I was laughing too[.] — Dick Gregory, *Nigger*, p. 101, 1964

- I've always enjoyed the various "blue" French 16mm I've come across. — *Screw*, p. 2, 4th July 1969

▸ **all blue**

in poker, a flush consisting of clubs or spades *US, 1967*

- — Albert H. Morehead, *The Complete Guide to Winning Poker*, p. 255, 1967

blue and clear *noun*

an amphetamine tablet *US, 1993*

- — Peter Johnson, *Dictionary of Street Alcohol and Drug Terms*, p. 191, 1993

blue and white *noun*

a police car *US, 1974*

A variation on **BLACK AND WHITE**.

- There were three blue and whites in front of it, blocking the north side of the boulevard. — Robert Campbell, *Boneyards*, p. 36, 1992

blue angel *noun*

a tablet of Amytal™, a central nervous system depressant *US, 1967*

- Barbies, downers; for nembutal, nebbies, abbots; for amytal, amies, blue angel[.] — *Providence (Rhode Island) Journal-Bulletin*, p. 6B, 4th August 1997

blue baby *noun*
a capsule of the synthetic opiate oxycodone used recreationally *US, 2003*
- Extracts reproduced in the tabloid show Limbaugh referring to "small blue babies" and "the little blues." — *Broward Business Review*, p. 1, 18th November 2003

blue bag *noun*
a police uniform *US, 1973*
- You miss the blue bag. — Charles Whited, *Chiodo*, p. 143, 1973

blue balls *noun*
1 a pain in the testicles caused by long periods of sexual arousal without release *US, 1916*
- Know what the cure for blueballs is? Scratch them until they're red! — Bruce Rodgers, *The Queens' Vernacular*, p. 34, 1972
- [A]s though to pay me back for the case of "blue balls" I must have given him on our honeymoon excursion across Manhattan Island. — Xaviera Hollander, *Xaviera*, p. 64, 1973
- She's taken their blood pressures on a wild-goose chase, and abandoned them with blueballs. — Josh Alan Friedman, *Tales of Times Square*, p. 9, 1986
- Ho Chi Minh is a son of a bitch / Got the blueballs, crabs and the seven-year itch. — *Full Metal Jacket*, 1987
2 any sexually transmitted infection *US, 1912*
- — Roger Blake, *The American Dictionary of Sexual Terms*, p. 19, 1964

blue band *noun*
a capsule of Carbitral™, a central nervous system depressant *US, 1971*
On 27th August 1967, Brian Epstein, manager of the Beatles, was found dead from an overdose of Carbitral.
- — Edward R. Bloomquist, *Marijuana*, p. 334, 1971

bluebird *noun*
a capsule of amobarbital sodium (trade name Amytal™), a central nervous system depressant *US, 1953*
- Her equipment is a small bottle of knockout drops (chloral hydrate) or "blue-birds," (sodium amytal). — Lee Mortimer, *Women Confidential*, p. 301, 1960
- — John B. Williams, *Narcotics and Hallucinogenics*, p. 109, 1967

bluebirds *noun*
waves on the horizon, seen from near the shore *US, 1964*
- — John Severson, *Modern Surfing Around the World*, p. 165, 1964

blue bloater *noun*
1 a hospital patient suffering from chronic bronchitis *US, 1994*
The blue coloring is from lack of oxygen; the bloating is from the lungs as they retain water.
- — Sally Williams, *"Strong" Words*, p. 135, 1994
2 an overweight patient suffering from emphysema *US, 1973*
- — *American Speech*, p. 202, Fall–Winter 1973: "The language of nursing"

blue boar *nickname*
the F-4D Phantom aircraft *US, 1990*
- — Joseph Tuso, *Singing the Vietnam Blues*, p. 245, 1990: Glossary

blue book *noun*
in horse racing, a sheet showing the contenders in a day's races, the odds on the horses and the handicapping *US, 1951*
- — David W. Maurer, *Argot of the Racetrack*, p. 15, 1951

bluebottle *noun*
a Portuguese man-of-war *US, 1991*
- — Trevor Cralle, *The Surfin'ary*, p. 12, 1991

blue boy *noun*
1 an amphetamine tablet *US, 1952*
- [T]aken two or three at one time with coffee, they gave a wonderful jag. The capsules were blue so we called them blue boys. After we got jagged we found no one would know what we were talking about when we said blue boys. — Chester Himes, *Cast the First Stone*, p. 247, 1952
2 a black man *US, 1967*
- BLUE BOY—Synonym for a Nigger male. — Robert deCoy, *The Nigger Bible*, p. 29, 1967

blue bullet *noun*
a capsule of amobarbital sodium (trade name Amytal™), a central nervous system depressant *US, 1977*
- — Walter L. Way, *The Drug Scene*, p. 106, 1977

Blue Chip *nickname*
the US air base at Tan Son Nhut, Saigon *US, 1989*
- At "Blue Chip," Seventh Air Force's operational headquarters at Tan Son Nhut near Saigon, plans for the renewed attack on North Vietnam were also well advanced. — Jeffrey Ethel, *One Day in a Long War*, p. 14, 1989

blue-chip *adjective*
of the highest quality *US, 1904*
A term that spread from poker (the blue chip is the highest value) to stocks to general usage.
- T.J. soon discovered that the blue-chip athletes coming out of Texas high schools rarely chose to become Horned Frogs. — Dan Jenkins, *Life Its Ownself*, p. 21, 1984

blue-chipper *noun*
an excellent student athlete with potential for playing professionally *US, 1984*
- — Arthur Pincus, *How to Talk Football*, p. 16, 1984
- — Don R. McCreary (Editor), *Dawg Speak*, 2001

blue-clue caper *noun*
a scheme by one police officer to cause harm to another police officer *US, 1983*
- "You're talking about a blue-clue caper," Higgins said. "You're talking about going against another cop." — Gerald Petievich, *To Die in Beverly Hills*, p. 66, 1983

bluecoat *noun*
a uniformed police officer *US, 1976*
- About the weather being bad and the business being slow / And the bluecoat on the beat taking all her dough. — Dennis Wepman et al., *The Life*, p. 165, 1976
- To get locked up by a bluecoat—a uniformed cop—was an embarrassment. — Eric Davis, *The Slick Boys*, p. 37, 1998

blue devil *noun*
a capsule of amobarbital sodium (trade name Amytal™), a central nervous system depressant *US, 1967*
- — John B. Williams, *Narcotics and Hallucinogenics*, p. 109, 1967
- — Helen Dahlskog (Editor), *A Dictionary of Contemporary and Colloquial Usage*, p. 8, 1972

blue doll *noun*
a capsule of amobarbital sodium (trade name Amytal™), a central nervous system depressant *US, 1977*
- — Walter L. Way, *The Drug Scene*, p. 106, 1977

blue-eyed devil *noun*
a white person *US, 1972*
- I'm tellin' you I know what that blue-eyed devil was hooked you up on. — Odie Hawkins, *Ghetto Sketches*, p. 210, 1972
- Don't thank me, Home ... thank that blue-eyed devil. He's the one who made it mean somethin' to you. — Odie Hawkins, *Chicago Hustle*, p. 80, 1977

blue flamer *noun*
a zealot *US, 1991*
- Added to which indignity, I got three months left to retirement and they saddle me with some blue-flamer fresh out of Quantico for a partner. — *Point Break*, 1991

bluegill *noun*
the penis *US, 1990*
- — Charles Shafer, *Folk Speech in Texas Prisons*, p. 198, 1990

bluegrass *verb*
to commit someone to the Lexington (Kentucky) Federal Narcotics Hospital *US, 1953*
Kentucky's nickname is "the Bluegrass State."
- — *American Speech*, p. 86, May 1955: "Narcotic argot along the Mexican border"
- "They blue-grassed me to Lex, and all that shit," Red said sullenly. — Ross Russell, *The Sound*, p. 155, 1961

blue hair *noun*
an older person, especially an older woman *US, 1981*
- This joint is where you find busloads a blue-hairs when they get off the freaking cruise ships. — Joseph Wambaugh, *The Glitter Dome*, p. 85, 1981
- — *Multicultural Management Program Fellows, Dictionary of Cautionary Words and Phrases*, 1989
- — Connie Eble (Editor), *UNC-CH Campus Slang*, p. 7, Fall 1991

blue happiness *noun*
liquid morphine *US, 1988–1989*
- — *Maledicta*, p. 31, 1988–1989: "Medical maledicta from San Francisco"

blue haze *noun*
the sense of euphoria and distance produced by a large dose of alprazolam (trade name Xanax™), a benzodiazepine used for short term relief of symptoms of anxiety *US, 1993*
- — Peter Johnson, *Dictionary of Street Alcohol and Drug Terms*, p. 227, 1993

blue heaven *noun*
sodium amytal, a barbiturate *US, 1954*
- They also take Amytal ("blue heaven"), Nembutal ("yellow jackets") and Tuinal. — Hunter S. Thompson, *Hell's Angels*, p. 216, 1966
- — Donald Louria, *Nightmare Drugs*, p. 25, 1966
- — *Current Slang*, p. 10, Fall 1968

blue ice *noun*
frozen toilet waste from an aircraft which melts off and falls *US, 1982*
- A 30-pound chunk of ice that fell from the sky over Tecumseh, Okla., was not the world's largest hailstone but probably "blue ice" from an airliner's leaky lavatory, officials say. — *United Press International*, 15th March 1982
- 48. Blue ice falling on houses. [List of 100 things that wouldn't have occurred without development of the airplane]. — *Newsday (New York)*, p. B10, 8th December 2003

blue in the armor *noun*
a can of Pabst Blue Ribbon beer *US, 1967*
- — *American Speech*, p. 61, February 1967: "Soda-fountain, restaurant and tavern calls"

blue jay *noun*
a capsule of amobarbital sodium (trade name Amytal™), a compound used as a sedative and hypnotic *US, 1953*
- [W]e have a pretty complete exhibit of the little pills downtown. Bluejays, redbirds, yellow jackets, goofballs, and all the rest of the list. — Raymond Chandler, *The Long Goodbye*, p. 230, 1953

blue John *noun*
strong, homemade whiskey *US, 1986*
- Masters of moonshine prided themselves in their ancient, father-to-son recipes and the white lightning, blue John, red eye, happy Sally, and stumphole whiskey they made, Smith said. — *Chicago Tribune*, p. C-1, 15th January 1986
- — *Star Tribune (Minneapolis)*, p. 19F, 31st January 1999

blue juice *noun*
a powerful wave *US, 1991*
- — Trevor Cralle, *The Surfin'ary*, p. 12, 1991

blue line *noun*
a river *US, 1976*
From the designation of a river on a map.
- This is Six! Tell your people they can stop at this here blue line, but to fill only two canteens. — Charles Anderson, *The Grunts*, p. 41, 1976

Blue Max *nickname*
the Congressional Medal of Honor *US, 1988*
- Let's go flying now with the twisted hero of Hunters Tale, Bruno Stachel, who is about to sell his soul for a chance at a Blue Max. — Stephen Coonts, *On Glorious Wings*, p. 179, 2003

blue meanies *noun*
the police or other enforcement authorities; a section of society with an antifreedom point of view *US, 1969*
From so-named predatory characters in the 1968 Beatles' cartoon film *The Yellow Submarine*.
- Alas, the Blue Meanies and politicians in the area did not see Our People as separate and distinct human beings at all[.] — Raymond Mungo, *Famous Long Ago*, p. 52, 1970
- BLUE MEANIES: the deputies of the Alameda County Sheriff's Department — Robert Buckhout, *Toward Social Change*, p. 464, 1971

blue movie *noun*
a sexually themed or pornographic film *US, 1957*
- Cunts, pricks, fence straddlers, tonight I give you—that international-known impressario of blue movies[.] — William Burroughs, *Naked Lunch*, p. 88, 1957

blue mystic *noun*
the central nervous system stimulant 2,5-dimethoxy-4-(n)-propylthiophenethlyamine *US, 2000*
- Each pill of Blue Mystic contains 10mg of 2C-T-7 if I'm not mistaken but make sure you verify this with your source before you take them. — *alt.drugs.psychedelics*, 26th October 2000
- "Blue Mystic" is a common drug in the Ecstasy and club drug scene. — *Microgram Bulletin (DEA)*, p. 16, January 2004

blue nitro *noun*
the recreational drug GHB *US, 1998*
- Three young people were treated at Southwest Washington Medical Center on Thanksgiving and released apparently after taking a drug called GHB or "Blue Nitro." — *The Columbian (Vancouver, Washington)*, p. B4, 27th November 1998

blue-nosed; blue-nose *adjective*
excessively moral, puritanical, repressed *US, 1890*
- The Mann Act was invented by a Chicago blue-nosed representative named Mann, after a hophead parlor-whore in melodramatic mood threw a note out of the window of the late Harry Guzik's cathouse on which she had written "I am a white slave." — Jack Lait and Lee Mortimer, *Washington Confidential*, p. 86, 1951
- Mr. Poole was Philadelphia's blue-nose censor, and whenever he came to catch the show, all the strippers would wear big panties and opaque brassieres and would drop the bumps and grinds from their acts. — Georgia Sothern, *My Life in Burlesque*, p. 73, 1972

blue-on-blue *noun*
1 in battle, fire unintentionally directed at friendly forces *US, 1991*
- On the night of 17 February, we had the first blue-on-blue (what some call fratricide, or so -called friendly fire) in the lst Infantry Division[.] — Tom Clancy, *Into the Storm*, p. 248, 1991
- — *American Speech*, p. 384, Winter 1991: "Among the new words"

2 clear blue sky and a calm blue sea *US, 1986*
- — *American Speech*, p. 122, Summer 1986: "The language of naval fighter pilots"

blue one *noun*
in carnival usage, poor location or slow business for a concession stand *US, 1981*
- — Don Wilmeth, *The Language of American Popular Entertainment*, p. 28, 1981

blue pages *noun*
in television and movie making, additions to a script after production has started *US, 1990*
- — Ralph S. Singleton, *Filmmaker's Dictionary*, p. 19, 1990

blue pill *noun*
a very powerful handgun *US, 1957*
- — *American Speech*, p. 192, October 1957: "Some colloquialisms of the handgunner"

blue room *noun*
1 a toilet *US, 1965*
Usually applied to a portable toilet on a construction site.
- Federal Aviation Agency official had locked himself in the "blue room." He emerged on his own when the stewardess informed him the captain was coming back with an ax. — *San Francisco Examiner*, p. 13, 10th September 1965

2 a cell used for solitary confinement *US, 1976*
- — John R. Armore and Joseph D. Wolfe, *Dictionary of Desperation*, p. 21, 1976

blues *noun*
1 a deeply felt sense of sadness, rejection or depression *UK, 1741*
- They taught me the blues in Pontiac—I mean the blues, blues that I felt from my head to my shoes, really the blues. — Mezz Mezzrow, *Really the Blues*, p. 4, 1946

2 unreserved bleacher seats in a circus *US, 1980*
- — Joe McKennon, *Circus Lingo*, p. 18, 1980

3 money *US, 1976*
From blue gambling chips.
- Playing blackjack, short on blues / A game all bad motherfuckers were booked to lose. — Dennis Wepman et al., *The Life*, p. 125, 1976

blue sky *noun*
1 worthless securities; a pleasant appearance with difficulties ignored *US, 1906*
- Although fakers, known as blue sky promoters, promise to fulfill all the aspirations of the average man for a comfortable nest egg,

prudent analysts know that Ponzi and his ilk were not public bene-factors. — *San Francisco Examiner*, p. 16, 26th November 1945

- Henry A. Wallace: Apostle of Political Blue Sky [Headline] — *San Francisco Examiner*, p. 10, 14th January 1948

- It violates the blue-sky laws. — Jim Thompson, *Bad Boy*, p. 294, 1953

- I'm not selling blue sky, Gypsy! I can place you tonight! [Gordon comic strip] — *San Francisco Chronicle*, p. 14, 26th March 1958

2 heroin *US*, *1987*
- — Carsten Stroud, *Close Pursuit*, p. 269, 1987

Blue Spader *nickname*
a soldier of the 1st Battalion, 26th Infantry, 2nd Brigade, 1st Infantry Division *US*, *1990*
From the blue spade on the insignia. Served in World War 2, Berlin, Vietnam from 1965 until 1970, Bosnia, Macedonia, and Kosovo.
- The number one Blue Spader used varied methods to watch the progress of junior officers in the regiment. — Harold Meyer, *Hanging Sam*, p. 151, 1990

blue spot *noun*
a spotlight with a blue filter, sometimes required by law dur-ing striptease shows *US*, *1986*
- When Hester shows every inch she can show and struts off the floor in a blue spot, Choo-Choo gets up and hurries over towards the men's room — Robert Campbell, *Junkyard Dog*, p. 133, 1986

blue steeler *noun*
a particularly erect erection *US*, *1978*
- "Give me a blue-steeler to look at her." — Thomas Williams, *The Night of Trees*, p. 67, 1978
- Racing from droopy dick to Blue Steeler in two seconds flat was no record for a guy to be proud of, and Remy certainly wasn't. — Sandra Hill, *Tall, Dark, and Cajun*, p. 66, 2003

blue streak *noun*
an emphatic and vigorous degree *US*, *1830*
Used to modify "talk" or variations on talking.
- I'll curse up a blue streak if my heat so desires. Motherfucker—Shit—Bastard—Cocksucker—Bastard. — *Mo' Better Blues*, 1990

bluesuit *noun*
a uniformed police officer *US*, *1965*
- Bimbo and Hecto ran into a bluesuit who stiffed Bimbo in the wind with his night stick and Bimbo doubled down on his hands and knees and began to vomit. — Sol Yurrick, *The Warriors*, p. 178, 1965
- Sheee-it, man, when the bluesuits stops me, I always gets nervous. — Joseph Wambaugh, *The New Centurions*, p. 73, 1970

bluesuiter *noun*
a member of the US Air Force *US*, *1963*
- [I]t was wrong for the Air Force to fire civil service workers and replace them with former blue-suiters. — *San Antonio (Texas) Express-News*, p. 3B, 11th September 2003

blue ticket *noun*
a one-way train or bus ticket given by the police to crimi-nals whose presence in town is no longer deemed accept-able *US*, *1993*
- If your past did catch up with you, the police were more than happy to buy you a "blue ticket," the term used to describe the one way passages they'd purchase to send shady characters back to wherever they'd come from. — Kim Rich, *Johnny's Girl*, p. 53, 1993

blue tip *noun*
a capsule of amobarbital sodium (trade name Amytal™), a central nervous system depressant *US*, *1977*
- — Donald Wesson and David Smith, *Barbiturates*, p. 121, 1977

blue veiner *noun*
a rigid erection *US*, *1975*
- During his one month convalescence Rosco was unable to raise what Harold Bloomguard called a "diamond cutter" or even a "blue veiner" due to the shooting pains in his groin. — Joseph Wambaugh, *The Choirboys*, p. 45, 1975
- Otto's got a throbbing blue-veiner for Romaine Lewis's little sister, Rayette. — Terry Davis, *Vision Quest*, p. 161, 1979

blue velvet *noun*
a combination of cough syrups, especially codeine-based syrups, used as a weak heroin substitute *US*, *1994*
- — US Department of Justice, *Street Terms*, October 1994

blue water Navy *noun*
an ocean-going military vessel *US*, *1948*
Coined well before the American invasion of Vietnam, when the term became widely used.
- The desire to assert a global role through a "blue water" navy. — Rand Corporation, *Rand Report*, p. 45, 1948
- The U.S. Navy's riverine forces were commonly referred to as the "Brown Water" Navy in contrast to the Blue Water forces[.] — T.L. Bosiljevac, *SEALs*, p. 51, 1990

bluff *noun*
a lesbian who enjoys both the active and passive role in sex *US*, *1970*
- — *American Speech*, p. 56, Spring–Summer 1970: "Homosexual slang"

blunt *noun*
1 marijuana rolled and smoked in a hollowed out cigar *US*, *1988*
Generic usage but originally made with a Phillies Blunt™.
- Purchase a Philly, not the city of Philly / Silly punk, I'm talking 'bout the shit called the Philly blunt / Lick the blunt and then the Philly blunt middle you split[.] — Redman, *How To Roll A Blunt*, 1992
- We don't smoke blunts, strictly Zigzags — *The Source*, p. 64, September 1993
- Drinking beers, beers, beers, rolling fatties, smoking blunts! — Kevin Smith, *Jay and Silent Bob Strike Back*, p. 9, 2001
- There were no lingering effects of getting drunk one night off a bot-tle of malt liquor or passing a blunt with my niggas from School Street. — Earl "DMX" Simmons, *E.A.R.L.*, p. 93, 2002

2 a capsule of Seconal™ or other barbiturate in a black cap-sule *US*, *1980*
- — Edith A. Folb, *runnin' down some lines*, p. 230, 1980

3 a hypodermic syringe *US*, *1980*
- — Edith A. Folb, *runnin' down some lines*, p. 230, 1980

blunted *adjective*
marijuana-intoxicated *US*, *1997*
- Being a little blunted at the time, the first thing that came to mind was women[.] — *The Source*, p. 54, May 1993
- He can remember getting blunted up with Tae and Sean. — David Simon and Edward Burns, *The Corner*, p. 20, 1997
- — Connie Eble (Editor), *UNC-CH Campus Slang*, p. 2, Spring 1998
- I get too blunted off funny homegrown[.] — Eminem (Marshall Mathers), *Role Model*, 1999

bluntie *noun*
marijuana rolled and smoked in a hollowed out cigar *US*, *1997*
- Rucker proudly holds up a bluntie and bag of pot. — James Mangold, *Copland*, p. 91, 1997

BM *noun*
a bookmaker *US*, *1974*
- By 11:30, which is the time most BMs are settled in their joints or phone booths around the city, my ninny action is behind me[.] — Gary Mayer, *Bookie*, p. 4, 1974

BMO *noun*
used by US troops in the war against Iraq to describe Saudi women *US*, *1991*
Initialism of "*b*lack *m*oving *o*bjects."
- — *Newsweek*, 21st January 1991
- — *Army*, p. 47, November 1991

BMOC *noun*
a popular and visible college boy *US*, *1934*
A "*b*ig *m*an *o*n *c*ampus."
- — Marcus Hanna Boulware, *Jive and Slang of Students in Negro Colleges*, 1947
- "This is the most important event of the year, and if you should come up with a winning idea for us, you'd be a B.M.O.C." "A what?" "A Big Man on Campus." — Max Shulman, *I was a Teen-Age Dwarf*, p. 131, 1959
- "You know darn well that Ollie is B.M.O.C. at Cascadia." — Frederick Kohner, *The Affairs of Gidget*, p. 52, 1963
- — Collin Baker et al., *College Undergraduate Slang Study Conducted at Brown University*, p. 73, 1968

B-more *nickname*
Baltimore *US*, *1989*

- You can bet if there were baseball in the District, these very same folks would still think of "B-more" as a rest stop on their way north. — *Washington Post*, p. A26, 17th August 1989
- But like Yonkers, B-more was a small world[.] — *E.A.R.L.*, p. 219, 2002

BNF *noun*

a science fiction fan well known by other fans *US*, *1982*
A "big-name fan."
- — *American Speech*, p. 24, Spring 1982: "The language of science fiction fan magazines"

bo *noun*

a hobo *US*, *1899*
A reality and term that only barely lingered into the 1950s.
- I reclined on a flatcar reading the Sunday funnies with the other [ho]bos, and the brakemen smiled at us and waved cheerfully. — Jack Kerouac, *Letter to Allen Ginsberg*, p. 151, 18th May 1948
- Mr. Davis informs me there are no more hoboes riding the rails any more—"only a few bums and tramps passing themselves off as boes. The real boes all quit to go work during the war." — *San Francisco News*, p. 21, 16th June 1949
- There was nobody around but a bo who pointed out the freight for us[.] — James Blake, *The Joint*, p. 28, 21st June 1951

BO *noun*

body odor *US*, *1931*
An initialism coined for soap advertisements; made even more infamous by the comic strip villain B.O. Plenty in *Dick Tracy*.
- — Lou Shelly, *Hepcats Jive Talk Dictionary*, p. 21, 1945
- with bright almond-shaped eyes and a mishapen, pear-shaped head, with tremendous b.o., and endowed, through his stupidity, with a certain curious thrusting intelligence — Clancy Sigal, *Going Away*, p. 476, 1961
- The Angels' old ladies are generally opposed to B.O. — Hunter S. Thompson, *Hell's Angels*, p. 47 (note), 1966
- That don't mean I gotta die of B.O. — Darryl Ponicsan, *The Last Detail*, p. 91, 1970
- Give the big pig with the B.O. to Healy, right? — *Something About Mary*, 1998

bo *adjective*

excellent, fashionable, trendy *US*, *1963*
- — *San Francisco Examiner: People*, p. 8, 27th October 1963

board *noun*

1 a surfboard *US*, *1963*
- — Grant W. Kuhns, *On Surfing*, p. 114, 1963
- — Ross Olney, *The Young Sportsman's Guide to Surfing*, p. 88, 1965

2 in a game of poker in which some cards are dealt face-up, all face-up cards collectively *US*, *1992*
- — Edwin Silberstang, *Winning Poker for the Serious Player*, p. 217, 1992

▸ **off the board**

in horse racing, said of odds greater than 99–1 *US*, *1976*
- — Tom Ainslie, *Ainslie's Complete Guide to Thoroughbred Racing*, p. 335, 1976

▸ **take off the board**

in sports betting, to fail to establish a pointspread on a game or event *US*, *1975*
- I didn't establish a line—a point spread—on the Kansas City Chiefs. In betting parlance, they were "taken off the board." — Jimmy Snyder, *Jimmy the Greek*, p. 145, 1975

board cord *noun*

a line attached at one end to a surfer and at the other to the surfboard *US*, *1977*
- — Gary Fairmont R. Filosa II, *The Surfer's Almanac*, p. 183, 1977

boarding house reach *noun*

an effort by a diner to reach for a serving plate rather than ask for it to be passed *US*, *1908*
- Well, my old ma always said you had to have a boarding house reach if you were ever going to get your share off the table. — Robert Campbell, *Alice in La-La Land*, p. 104, 1987
- Yes, we are responsible for our own actions, our own boarding-house reach at the table, our own failure to get any exercise more strenuous than fumbling for the remote. — *Salt Lake Tribune*, p. A12, 13th November 2003

board jock; board sock *noun*

a protective surfboard cover *US*, *1977*
- — Gary Fairmont R. Filosa II, *The Surfer's Almanac*, p. 183, 1977

boards *noun*

▸ **on the boards**

in solitary confinement *US*, *1976*
- — John R. Armore and Joseph D. Wolfe, *Dictionary of Desperation*, p. 42, 1976

boast *verb*

to brag as a part of a rap performance *US*, *2000*
- Big Daddy is "boasting," a tradition in rap music derived from reggae. — James Haskins, *The Story of Hip-Hop*, p. 3–4, 2000

boat *noun*

1 a large shipment of MDMA, the drug commonly known as ecstasy *US*, *2004*
- The Royal Canadian Mounted Police (RCMP) in Vancouver, British Columbia, has noted an increase in the supply of seized MDMA, with 1,000 tablet shipments, known as "boat" shipments, the most common. — *Microgram Bulletin (DEA)*, p. 11, January 2004

2 a prison transfer; a group of prisoners being transferred; the bus used to transfer them *US*, *1956*
- — Frank Prewitt and Francis Schaeffer, *Vacaville Vocabulary*, 1961–1962
- When I heard I was on a boat to Comstock, I knew you'd be here. — Piri Thomas, *Down These Mean Streets*, p. 265, 1967
- Have you anything to say before we send you away / On the next Sing Sing boat? — Dennis Wepman et al., *The Life*, p. 59, 1976

3 phencyclidine, the recreational drug known as PCP or angel dust *US*, *1984*
A shortened form of **LOVE BOAT**.
- With a police officer on every corner directing traffic, dealers simply lined the curbs along 11th Street and silently formed the word "boat," street slang for PCP, with lips pursed like a fish. — *Washington Post*, p. B1, 29th July 1984
- — Peter Johnson, *Dictionary of Street Alcohol and Drug Terms*, p. 24, 1993

4 heroin *US*, *1993*
- — Peter Johnson, *Dictionary of Street Alcohol and Drug Terms*, p. 24, 1993

5 in poker, a hand consisting of three of a kind and a pair *US*, *1981*
Conventionally known as a "full house."
- — Jim Glenn, *Programed Poker*, p. 155, 1981

boat anchor *noun*

a crippled or useless piece of computer equipment; by extension, a useless person *US*, *1991*
- That was a working motherboard once. One lightning strike later, instant boat anchor! — Eric S. Raymond, *The New Hacker's Dictionary*, p. 71, 1991

boat in a moat *noun*

a casino that must, as a result of gambling laws, float *US*, *2003*
- — Victor H. Royer, *Casino Gamble Talk*, p. 16, 2003

boat people *noun*

people who arrive at casinos on bus excursion trips *US*, *1994*
- We are the boat people. That is casino workers' slang for the millions of Americans now arriving at their portals in smelly diesel waves. We come by bus – "motorcoach," if you want to get la-di-da about it. — *New York Times*, p. 36, 17th July 1994

boat race *noun*

a fixed horse race or other competition *US*, *1917*
- — Walter Steigleman, *Horseracing*, p. 271, 1947
- I bet crooked horse races—"boat races" we called them. My two detectives at the track would hear of a fix. They'd telephone me. I'd say get down a hundred for me. I made about $50,000 on "boat races" when I was chief of detectives. — *San Francisco News*, p. 40, 16 November 1950
- It was claimed then, reported United Press, that Berry engineered two "boat races" on Feb. 7–8. — *San Francisco News*, 26th November 1952
- — *Current Slang*, p. 4, Summer 1969

boats *noun*

shoes or feet, especially large ones *US*, *1956*
- Too small for your fat fuckin' boats. — Richard Price, *Clockers*, p. 97, 1992

bob *noun*

1 marijuana *US*, *1997*
Very likely derived from Bob Marley, a highly visible marijuana lover. A long list of derivatives play with the term—"see bob,"

"talk with bob," "bob's on the phone" – serve as a code for discussing marijuana and its use.
- — Jim Emerson-Cobb, *Scratching the Dragon*, April 1997

2 a shoplifter *US, 1962*
- — Joseph E. Ragen and Charles Finston, *Inside the World's Toughest Prison*, p. 791, 1962

bob *verb*
to perform oral sex on a man *US, 1995*
- How much more can I bob here? — *Kids*, 1995

▸ **bob for apples**
to remove impacted feces by hand *US, 1988–1989*
- — *Maledicta*, p. 31, 1988–1989: "Medical maledicta from San Francisco"

Bob *adjective*
used by US troops in the war against Iraq as an adjective for all things Saudi *US, 1991*
- Bob car, Bob clothes, and the like. — *Army*, p. 47, November 1991

bobble bumper *noun*
in pinball, a bumper that scores and kicks the ball on contact *US, 1977*
- — Bobbye Claire Natkin and Steve Kirk, *All About Pinball*, p. 111, 1977

Bobbsey Twins *noun*
1 used as a representation of either innocence or a strong resemblance *US, 1969*
From a popular series of 72 children's books created by Edward Stratemeyer in 1904 and written under the name of Laura Lee Hope by writers under contract to Stratemeyer.
- The backlot scuttle is that Mike Frankovich's "Doctors' Wives" will make the Kinsey Report look like Bobbsey Twins research. — *San Francisco Examiner*, p. 37, 3rd November 1969
- One of the questions show folks often discuss is, "Which of the British Bobbsey Twins, Tom Jones or Engelbert Humperdinck, will be around longer?" — *San Francisco Examiner*, p. 33, 2nd August 1971

2 two girls who regularly double-date *US, 1968*
- — Mary Swift, *Campus Slang (University of Texas)*, 1968

bobbysoxer *noun*
a teenage girl *US, 1944*
"Bobby socks" (ankle-high white socks, first recorded in 1927) as a generational trademark for American teenagers arrived on the national scene in June 1937, with a cover photograph in *Life* magazine. After "the socks" came "the soxer." The "bobby" is most likely constructed on "to bob" (to cut or shorten).
- Champion of the Bobby Soxers [Headline] — *San Francisco Chronicle*, p. 10, 18 February 1946
- "Occasional" prostitutes work some of the bars, and bobby soxers flirt at Washington Square. — Jack Lait and Lee Mortimer, *New York Confidential*, p. 69, 1948
- Gregory Peck, or some of the new boy friends of the bobby-soxers I'm too old to remember the names of? — Philip Wylie, *Opus 21*, p. 83, 1949
- She's been around, she knows what the score is, she ain't some punk bobby-soxer with the mood in her eyes. — Jim Thompson, *A Swell-Looking Babe*, p. 80, 1954

bobo *noun*
prison-issued canvas shoes *US, 2002*
- — Gary K. Farlow, *Prison-ese*, p. 5, 2002

bobtail *noun*
in poker, four fifths of a straight that can be completed at either end *US, 1865*
- — Oswald Jacoby, *Oswald Jacoby on Poker*, p. 141, 1947
- — Thomas L. Clark, *The Dictionary of Gambling and Gaming*, p. 23, 1987

bodacious *adjective*
amazing, impressive *US, 1843*
A C19 word from the American frontier, rediscovered by the late C20 young. The term "bodacious tatas" as descriptive of "magnificent breasts" was made widely popular by the 1982 film *Officer and a Gentleman*.
- — Helen Dahlskog (Editor), *A Dictionary of Contemporary and Colloquial Usage*, p. 8, 1972
- — Connie Eble (Editor), *UNC-CH Campus Slang*, p. 1, November 1983
- Ted, you and I have witnessed many things, but nothing as bodacious as what just happened. — *Bill and Ted's Excellent Adventure*, 1989

bo-deen *noun*
a police officer *US, 2001*
- While kids in Northwest refer to police as "one-time," Northeast teenagers call them "bo-deen" or "hot dog," and in Southeast they're "po-pos" or good old "feds." — *Washington Post*, p. A1, 20th August 2001

bodice-ripper *noun*
a sexually themed romantic/historical novel aimed at an adult female audience *US, 1980*
- Miss Faust reminds us that women, too, are a little bit beastly, that they too have their pornography: Harlequin romances, novels of "sweet savagery," bodice-rippers. — *New York Times*, p. 7–4, 28th December 1980
- A steamy bodice-ripper to help while away the hours in an airport lounge? — *Opera News*, p. 48, October 1998
- Diana Lindsay admits that Marshal's journalism is as romantic as a Harlequin bodice-ripper. — *San Diego Union-Tribune*, p. E1, 14th March 2004

bodied *adjective*
(used of a female) well built *US, 1947*
- — Marcus Hanna Boulware, *Jive and Slang of Students in Negro Colleges*, 1947

body *noun*
a person you have killed *US, 2001*
- Vega allegedly bragged to the undercover cops that he had "bodies" on his criminal resume[.] — *Daily News (New York)*, p. 1, 9th May 2001

▸ **to have a body on**
to have committed a murder in the name of a youth gang *US, 1996*
- — S. Beth Atkin, *Voices from the Street*, p. 125, 1996: Glossary

body *verb*
to kill someone *US, 1999*
- Investigators went on to learn from several other people that Parker bragged that "I bodied him for his drugs." — *Hartford (Connecticut) Courant*, p. B1, 15th October 1999

body contact squad *noun*
Korean soldiers who acted as suicide bombers *US, 1982*
- Without our knowledge, they prepared charges designed to strap around the waist of a soldier and formed some "body contact squads." Members of these squads were to move into the side of a tank, pull a fuze lighter on a two-second fuze, perhaps disable the tank and certainly join their honored ancestors. — Joseph C. Goulden, *Korea*, p. 128, 1982

body queen *noun*
a homosexual man attracted to men with muscular bodies *US, 1970*
- — *American Speech*, p. 56, Spring–Summer 1970: "Homosexual slang"

body rain *noun*
corporate executives in search of employment after a takeover, merger or business failure *US, 1988*
A macabre image recalling the suicides by jumping associated with the market crash of 1929.
- — Kathleen Odean, *High Steppers, Fallen Angels, and Lollipops*, p. 119, 1988

body shop *noun*
a bar catering to an unmarried clientele with sexual agendas *US, 1970*
- Pete Rozelle was in town this weekend. He popped into one of those body shops on Union Street Friday night, squeezing past the sweet young things and the hot-to-trot hustlers. — *San Francisco Examiner*, p. 63, 24th September 1970
- But its [Union Street's] detractors are confusing its present nature with its image of half a decade ago—when it surely was home of Dark-Glass-in-the-Rain, every girl a stewardess, and fast bucks to be picked up by operating body shops. — *San Francisco Examiner and Chronicle*, p. 10, 4th March 1973

body shot *noun*
a ritual in which a person licks salt off someone else, drinks a shot of tequila and then sucks on a lemon in the other's mouth *US, 2001*
- — Don R. McCreary (Editor), *Dawg Speak*, 2001

body snatcher *noun*
1 a morgue employee who retrieves and transports corpses to the morgue *US, 1993*
- After talking to the body snatcher, Nell wasn't sure whether she'd be better off trying to upchuck or work. — Joseph Wambaugh, *Finnegan's Week*, p. 161, 1993
2 someone who steals another's date *US, 1955*
- — *American Speech*, p. 302, December 1955: "Wayne University slang"

body snatching outfit *noun*
a military unit assigned to recover and process bodies *US, 1949*
- "Then why didn't you get hooked up with a body-snatching outfit? You look like a natural for the buzzard detail." — Audie Murphy, *To Hell and Back*, p. 3, 1949

body time *noun*
in casinos, the amount of time a player, whose playing time is being tracked, spends gambling *US, 1996*
- — Frank Scoblete, *Best Blackjack*, p. 254, 1996

body womping *noun*
body surfing *US, 1987*
- — Mitch McKissick, *Surf Lingo*, 1987

bof *noun*
a record album consisting of the "best of" the artist's previous recordings *US, 1982*
- — Arnold Shaw, *Dictionary of American Pop/Rock*, p. 47, 1982

boff *noun*
1 a hearty laugh *US, 1945*
- More to be desired, though, is the boff, which is the Homeric response to an elementary comic situation. — *Atlantic Monthly*, p. 136, April 1946
- Boff: a full, hearty burst of laughter that comes from the bottom of the stomach. — *Everybody's Digest*, p. 21, September 1951
- The producer orders a gross of assorted yaks and boffs, and sprinkles the whole sound track with a lacing of simpering snorts. — Vance Packard, *The Hidden Persuaders*, p. 204, 1957
2 sex; an act of sexual intercourse *US, 1956*
- "Well, there goes your opportunity to give the guy a boff and find out if everything I told you was correct," he said. — Georgia Sothern, *My Life in Burlesque*, p. 269, 1972
- Ladies flock to kiss him, pay respects, and, in some cases, hope for a little boff. — Josh Alan Friedman, *Tales of Times Square*, p. 108, 1986

boff *verb*
1 to have sex *US, 1937*
- Don't give me that innocent bit. I know you were boffing Virgil Tatum this afternoon. — Max Shulman, *Anyone Got a Match?*, p. 253, 1964
- Why, just the thought of boffing some hairy boy makes me sick all over. — Gore Vidal, *Myra Breckinridge*, p. 158, 1968
- And yet, go understand people—it is her pleasure while being boffed to have one or the other of my forefingers lodged snugly up her anus. — Philip Roth, *Portnoy's Complaint*, p. 116, 1969
- Then I asked him if it was true he was boffing Kate Cruikshank. — C.D. Payne, *Youth in Revolt*, p. 71, 1993
2 to kiss and caress *US, 1968*
- — Collin Baker et al., *College Undergraduate Slang Study Conducted at Brown University*, p. 84, 1968

boffo *noun*
1 a dollar *US, 1979*
- It made me feel noble and generous to donate 100 boffos to such a worthy cause. — Leo Rosten, *Silky!*, p. 91, 1979
2 a great joke *US, 1968*
- Billy Wilder's One, Two, Three was a boffo (cf. Variety) spoof of international relations. — Joan Didion, *Slouching Toward Bethlehem*, p. 157, 1968
3 a one-year prison sentence *US, 1930*
- — Frank Prewitt, *Vacaville Vocabulary*, 1961–1962

boffo *adjective*
very impressive, popular, successful *US, 1949*
Originally theatrical when it was often used of a comedic success, and in which sense it probably derives from "buffo" (a comic actor; comic).
- [S]he was going to be competing with garage sales, which got more boffo all the time. — Cyra McFadden, *The Serial*, p. 188, 1977

- They had tried in vain to convince one another and the brass that they had been boffo in the canyon. — Joseph Wambaugh, *Lines and Shadows*, p. 100, 1984

boffola *noun*
1 a hearty laugh; a joke that produces a hearty laugh *US, 1946*
- It'll sound all right. Good jokes, laughs, I'll pack the script with boffolas. — Frederick Wakeman, *The Hucksters*, p. 47, 1946
2 a smash hit, a success *US, 1947*
- Working with Dirty Eddie, Cassard thought he could make a big boffola* of Will You Marry Me? *Variant of the Hollywood term, "Boffo Terrific," big box-office smash. — *Time*, p. 86, 1st September 1947
- The new boffola of the Soviet Screen is Meeting on the Elbe, and it has everything. — *Time*, p. 30, 23rd May 1949

bogart *verb*
1 to bully *US, 1966*
As "tough guy" movies and the forceful characters portrayed by actors like Humphrey Bogart went out fashion, so the usage moved from admiring to critical. Also variant "bogard."
- — *Current Slang*, p. 1, Fall 1966
- Cool Breeze jus' bogarts his way in. — Malcolm Braly, *On the Yard*, p. 195, 1967
- "Then I'm going to Bogart some pussy," Green spouted. — Bobby Seale, *A Lonely Rage*, p. 118, 1978
- DREXL: Next time you Bogart your way into a nigger's crib, an' get all in his face, make sure you do it on white boy day. — *True Romance*, 1993
2 to selfishly keep possession of something that you are expected to return or forward, especially drugs *US, 1957*
- You've been holding on to it and I sure would like a hit/Don't bogart that joint my friend, pass it over to me — Fraternity Of Man, *Don't bogart me*, 1969
- — Connie Eble (Editor), *UNC-CH Campus Slang*, October 1972
- The one where you bogarted nine grand and flew to Vegas. — *Empire Records*, 1995
- Motherfuckers try to come up and bogard your weed at the club, and they don't wanna share theirs[.] — Cypress Hill, *Can I get a hit?*, 1999

bogey *noun*
an unidentified aircraft, presumed to be hostile until identified as friendly *US, 1943*
Coined in World War 2 and used since.
- A few minutes later came "scramble," an unidentified "bogey" had been picked up on RAF control radar. — Gregory "Pappy" Boyington, *Baa Baa Black Sheep*, p. 57, 1958

bogey *adjective*
fraudulent, bogus *US, 1977*
- "I got a great-uncle lives over to Kentucky, he's in one of them bogey locals. Bunch of old miners drawin' from the retirement fund but somehow they still got a vote." — John Sayles, *Union Dues*, p. 41, 1977

boggie bear *noun*
an ugly person *US, 1947*
- — Marcus Hanna Boulware, *Jive and Slang of Students in Negro Colleges*, 1947

Bogners *noun*
blue jeans worn when skiing *US, 1963*
Alluding to the stylish stretch pants manufactured by the German Bogner firm.
- — *American Speech*, p. 205, October 1963: "The language of skiers"

bogosity *noun*
the degree to which anything can be described as wrong or in error *US, 1973*
Computer hacker slang from BOGUS (wrong).
- Bilgewater words like "bro" for brother, "gritting down" for eating, "crib" for home, "P-ing down" for sexual intercourse, "skunk" for girl, and "bogosity" for anything he disagreed with. — Joe Eszterhas, *Charlie Simpson's Apocalypse*, p. 22, 1973
- — *CoEvolution Quarterly*, p. 27, Spring 1981

bog out *verb*
to become intoxicated on drugs *US, 1998*
- — Ethan Hilderbrant, *Prison Slang*, p. 14, 1998

bogue *verb*
to smoke a cigarette *US, 1983*

- — *Concord (New Hampshire) Monitor*, 23rd August 1983
- — Vann Wesson, *Generation X Field Guide and Lexicon*, p. 24, 1997

bogue *adjective*
wrong; sick *US, 1960*
From **BOGUS**; sometimes seen spelt as "boag."

- I'm bogue, but I ain't gonna indulge. I'm tryin' to kick. — Clarence Cooper Jr., *The Scene*, p. 13, 1960
- Whenever a kid did something that was boag, you were never told to get under the desk[.] — A.S. Jackson, *Gentleman Pimp*, p. 17, 1973
- Man, I'm as boguie as a Hong Kong coolie with his piles hangin' out! — Charles W. Moore, *A Brick for Mister Jones*, p. 32, 1975
- — Connie Eble (Editor), *UNC-CH Campus Slang*, p. 1, October 1986

bogue out *verb*
in computing, to become nonfunctional suddenly and without warning *US, 1983*

- — Guy L. Steele et al., *The Hacker's Dictionary*, p. 35, 1983

bogus *noun*
counterfeit money *US, 1798*

- There's a hell of a lot of bogus flying around in tens and twenties. — George V. Higgins, *The Friends of Eddie Doyle*, p. 87, 1971
- He was sitting in a motel room on Hollywood Boulevard waiting for the money man, and two hippies kicked in the door, tied him up, and took the bogus. — Gerald Petievich, *One-Shot Deal*, p. 218, 1981

bogus *adjective*
1 disagreeable, offensive; wrong *US, 1876*

- So, like when Jefferson went before the people what he was saying was "Hey, we left this place in England because it was bogus, and if we don't come up with some cool rules ourself, we'll be bogus, too!" — *Fast Times at Ridgemont High*, 1982
- "Heard you dropped out of U.S.C." "Oh yeah. Couldn't deal with it. It's so totally bogus." — Bret Easton Ellis, *Less Than Zero*, p. 48, 1985
- Bogus. My dad's home. — *Bill and Ted's Excellent Adventure*, 1989
- I still live with my parents, which I admit is both bogus and sad. — *Wayne's World*, 1992

2 in computing, nonfunctional, useless, false or incorrect *US, 1981*

- — *CoEvolution Quarterly*, p. 27, Spring 1981
- — Guy L. Steele et al., *The Hacker's Dictionary*, p. 34, 1983

bogus beef *noun*
idle, insincere conversation *US, 1947*

- — Marcus Hanna Boulware, *Jive and Slang of Students in Negro Colleges*, 1947

bohawk *noun*
a member of the Bohemian counterculture *US, 1952*

- "She's only a bohawk anyway," Dincher complained. "Like—one of them screwy artists." — George Mandel, *Flee the Angry Strangers*, p. 249, 1952

boho *noun*
a Bohemian, in the sense of an unconventional person *US, 1958*

- A few local bohos saw it and came out, but mainly it was the Pranksters and their friends who showed up at the Spread that night, including a lot of the Berkeley crowd that had been coming to La Honda. — Tom Wolfe, *The Electric Kool-Aid Acid Test*, p. 209
- — *Current Slang*, p. 2, Winter 1971

boho *adjective*
unconventional, bohemian *US, 1958*

- I can't say I gave her costume an honor grade, however; it was a bit too Boho for my taste. I especially loathed the Indian thing she carried for a handbag. — Erich Segal, *Love Story*, p. 3, 1970
- "Oh, he's just trying to be boho." — Chris Miller, *The Real Animal House*, p. 4, 2006

bohunk *noun*
1 a Czechoslovakian immigrant *US, 1903*

- Generally Czechs, or "Bohunks," as they once were called, are law-abiding people[.] — Jack Lait and Lee Mortimer, *Chicago Confidential*, p. 72, 1950
- Hell, when I was a kid I knew guys who were real Bohemians, I mean in the blood—Bohunks. — Darryl Ponicsan, *The Last Detail*, p. 75, 1970
- There was a bohunk girl used to hang around at the dances at the Midway Gardens. — Robert Byrne, *McGoorty*, p. 57, 1972

2 a ill-mannered, loutish person *US, 1919*

- Hey, who the hell's this bohunk, anyhow? — Robert Gover, *The Maniac Responsible*, p. 22, 1963

- "What do you mean by calling Randy Pinkerton a bohunk, you ghetto slime?" — Ethan Morden, *Buddies*, p. 140, 1986
- Along about dawn, this Arkie bohunk named Hutchinson actually got up and went back there[.] — Seth Morgan, *Homeboy*, p. 152, 1990

boil *noun*
in surfing, a turbulence or disturbance on a developing wave *US, 1980*

- — John Grissim, *Pure Stoke*, p. 156, 1980

boiled *adjective*
very drunk *US, 1884*

- — Collin Baker et al., *College Undergraduate Slang Study Conducted at Brown University*, p. 84, 1968
- Ken Kelly got boiled on vodka for courage[.] — Joseph Wambaugh, *Lines and Shadows*, p. 254, 1984

boiled owl *noun*
1 used as a representation of the ultimate drunkard *US, 1864*

- — Lou Shelly, *Hepcats Jive Talk Dictionary*, p. 21, 1945

2 the last thing in the world that you would want to eat *US, 1975*

- — John Gould, *Maine Lingo*, p. 17, 1975

boiler *noun*
the stomach *US, 1886*

- Boiler, as in "he's got the bad boiler," or upset stomach. — Jim Bouton, *Ball Four*, p. 252, 1970

boilermaker *noun*
a shot of whiskey followed by a glass of beer; a beer and whiskey combined *US, 1942*

- They are hard workers and good citizens who seldom get into trouble except on Saturday nights after too many boilermakers—whiskey and beer. — Jack Lait and Lee Mortimer, *Chicago Confidential*, p. 78, 1950
- They go to a bar and order boilermakers. — Darryl Ponicsan, *The Last Detail*, p. 149, 1970
- At four in the afternoon, two old men were huddled over boilermakers at the far end of the bar[.] — Walter Tevis, *The Color of Money*, p. 69, 1984
- While he's having his first boilermaker, he asks me what's new in my precinct. — Robert Campbell, *Junkyard Dog*, p. 17, 1986

boiler room *noun*
an office used in an elaborate swindle *US, 1931*

- "An office, a secretary, a car, juice money for the real estate people, the boiler room, bleepety, bleepety bleep." — Gerald Petievich, *Money Men*, p. 78, 1981
- Those boiler-room scams can get a guy chucked into a single room with three roommates. For about five years. — Joseph Wambaugh, *The Golden Orange*, p. 251, 1990
- He ran boiler rooms and bucket shops. — Stephen Cannell, *King Con*, p. 35, 1997
- Boca Raton supposedly had more telephone boiler rooms than Calcutta. — Carl Hiaasen, *Nature Girl*, p. 295, 2006

boiler water *noun*
whiskey *US, 1977*

- — Ramon Adams, *The Language of the Railroader*, p. 17, 1977

boing *verb*
while snowboarding, to bounce off something *US, 1990*

- — Elena Garcia, *A Beginner's Guide to Zen and the Art of Snowboarding*, p. 121, 1990: Glossary

bo-ing!
used for humorously expressing approval or delight *US, 1955*
Teen slang.

- — *American Weekly*, p. 2, 14 August 1955

boink *noun*
an in-person meeting of participants in an Internet discussion group *US, 1995*

- — Christian Crumlish, *The Internet Dictionary*, p. 24, 1995

boink *verb*
to have sex with someone *US, 1987*

- — Connie Eble (Editor), *UNC-CH Campus Slang*, p. 1, Spring 1987
- Thing was, Marty never got down to doing it. You know, it. Boinking. — Seth Morgan, *Homeboy*, p. 84, 1990

- Real pedophiles try and convince everyone it's OK to boink prepub kids. — Nancy Tamosaitis, *net.sex*, p. 113, 1995
- Was there any greater sin than this? Fantasizing about embracing—or boinking—a priest? — Rita Ciresi, *Pink Slip*, p. 64, 1999

boinking *noun*
sexual intercourse *US*, *2005*
- Julia joins a horned-up farmhand for some boinking in the barn. — Mr. Skin, *Mr. Skin's Skincyclopedia*, p. 81, 2005

boker *noun*
an unsophisticated rustic *US*, *1968*
- — Mary Swift, *Campus Slang (University of Texas)*, 1968

bold *adjective*
successful, excellent *US*, *1965*
- — Carol Covington, *A Glossary of Teenage Terms*, 1965

Bolivian marching powder *noun*
cocaine *US*, *1984*
- All might come clear if you could just slip into the bathroom and do a little more Bolivian Marching Powder. — Jay McInerney, *Bright Lights, Big City*, p. 1, 1984
- "Because," he screams over the music, grabbing me by the collar, "we need some Bolivian Marching Powder … " — Bret Easton Ellis, *American Psycho*, p. 54, 1991

bollix *verb*
to bungle something, to ruin something *US*, *1937*
- One of the three commissioners is noted for his ability to bollix everything up after a big, bad night—which is almost every night. — Jack Lait and Lee Mortimer, *Washington Confidential*, p. 235, 1951
- Write to me. The mail gets bollixed up at Xmastime. — James Ellroy, *White Jazz*, p. 167, 1992

bollixing *adjective*
used as a negative intensifier *US*, *1954*
- On top of everything else I got those bollixing poems. — Jim Thompson, *The Nothing Man*, p. 242, 1954

bolloxed *adjective*
drunk *US*, *1986*
- — *Rutgers Alumni Magazine*, p. 21, February 1986

bolo *noun*
1 a directive to be on the look-out for something *US*, *1986*
- I'm sorry, old man, but the cops put a BOLO out on the Caddy so I had Tommy get rid of the darn thing. — Carl Hiaasen, *Tourist Season*, p. 231, 1986
- Struggling frantically through traffic to get back behind the fleeing car, they radioed the dispatcher for what Fort Lauderdale police call a Bolo—"be on the lookout." — James Mills, *The Underground Empire*, p. 157, 1986

2 crack cocaine *US*, *1994*
Spanish.
- — US Department of Justice, *Street Terms*, October 1994

bolo badge *noun*
a Purple Heart military decoration for battle wounds, especially those suffered in a foolish action *US*, *1968*
- — *New York Newsday*, 14th February 1991
- — *American Speech*, p. 384, Winter 1991: "Among the new world"

bolohead *noun*
a bald person *US*, *1981*
- — Douglas Simonson, *Pidgin to da Max*, 1981

bolshie; bolshy *noun*
a Bolshevik *US*, *1919*
- Her coverage of Iraqi weapons of mass destruction (WMDs) has been quite properly thumped by both CounterPunch Bolshie Alexander Cockburn and Slate's Jack Shafer[.] — *LA Weekly*, p. 14, 6th June 2003

bolt *noun*
a blemish; a pimple *US*, *1969*
- — Richard Scholl, *Running Press Glossary of Baseball Language*, p. 17, 1977

bolt *verb*
1 to leave *US*, *1845*
- — *USA Today*, 29th September 1983

2 in poker, to withdraw from a hand *US*, *1988*
- — George Percy, *The Language of Poker*, p. 11, 1988

bolter *noun*
a landing on an aircraft carrier in which the plane misses the arresting mechanisms *US*, *1958*
- After the day's operations, pilots who have made sloppy approaches or too many bolters (missing the arresting gear) are sharply criticized by their squadron commanders. — *San Francisco Chronicle*, p. 7, 28th September 1958

bolts *noun*
a tattooed depiction of lightning bolts, symbolising a prisoner's association with a white pride prison gang *US*, *1989*
- — James Harris, *A Convict's Dictionary*, 1989

bolts and jolts *noun*
a combination of central nervous system stimulants and depressants *US*, *1946*
- Dr. Freireich's discovery was anticipated by bored Broadwayites, who had made a pastime of "bolts and jolts" – mixtures of barbiturates and Benzedrine which knock them for a loop, then slap them to. — *Time*, p. 67, 1st July 1946

bolts and nuts *adjective*
mentally unstable; crazy *US*, *1984*
- — Inez Cardozo-Freeman, *The Joint*, p. 483, 1984

bomb *noun*
1 a marijuana cigarette, especially a large one *US*, *1951*
- By the way, boy, I am of course indulging in a perfect orgy of Miss Green & can hardly see straight right at this minute, whoo! 3 bombs a day. — Jack Kerouac, *Letter to Neal and Carolyn Cassady*, p. 358, 10th May 1952
- I paid 75 cents a stick, or a dollar for a bomb. A bomb is about as big as a Pall Mall and as fat as a Pall Mall. Like a regular cigarette. — Jeremy Larner and Ralph Tettelteller, *The Addict in the Street*, p. 33, 1964
- When my buddy told me, we smoked around five bombs[.] — Bruce Jackson, *Get Your Ass in the Water and Swim Like Me*, p. 133, 1964
- [T]ake a head of this Skunk / Twist up a big bomb of this serious dope / Smoke it down to the dub or roach tip[.] — Tone Loc, *Cheeba Cheeba*, 1989

2 high potency, relatively pure heroin *US*, *1960*
- "You know," Curtis began, "if you say the stuff will take a five, then I put a four on it. That way, I always have the bomb." — Donald Goines, *Cry Revenge*, p. 107, 1974

3 crack cocaine *US*, *1994*
- — US Department of Justice, *Street Terms*, October 1994

4 potent heroin *US*, *1969*
- Lee here says he knows where to cop the bomb at. — Donald Goines, *Dopefiend*, p. 104, 1971

5 a forceful blow with the fist *US*, *1949*
- From Challenge Jake La Motta's corner, he heard the entreaties of La Motta's handlers above the buzz of 22,183 spectators: "'At's it, Jackson. 'Atta go, Jackson … put the bomb in." — *Time*, p. 53, 27th June 1949
- Johnny Summerlin planned today to "stay out of the way of the bombs" and let youth carry him to victory tonight. — *San Francisco News*, p. 27, 20th June 1956
- Moore moved quickly and threw another overhand bomb flush to the chin. — *San Francisco Chronicle*, p. 39, 9th April 1961
- Rush Bomb Decks Johnson [Headline] — *San Francisco Examiner*, p. 47, 22nd February 1967

6 in tiddlywinks, a long-distance shot *US*, *1977*
- — *Verbatim*, p. 525, December 1977

7 a skateboarding maneuver in which the rider crouches and holds the sides of the board as the board leaves the ground *US*, *1976*
- — Laura Torbet, *The Complete Book of Skateboarding*, p. 105, 1976

8 a dismal failure, especially in show business *US*, *1952*
- The 10 biggest bombs [Headline] — *San Francisco Examiner and Chronicle, Sunday Scene*, p. 12, 13th January 1974
- The title of the book was How to Talk Dirty and Influence People, and, oddly enough, it was a bomb. — Mort Sahl, *Heartland*, p. 25, 1976

9 an unexpected bass drum accent *US*, *1955*
- He taught me how to turn on what the kids now call "dropping bombs." — Nat Shapiro and Nat Hentoff, *Hear Me Talkin' to Ya*, p. 289, 1955
- He [Kenny Clarke] uses his bass drum, but only to "drop an occasional bomb," that is, he "boots" the soloist forward with an infrequent and unerringly timed explosion. — Hugh Panassie and Madeline Gautier, *Guide to Jazz*, p. 41, 1956

- Hassan dropped bombs, flailed tom-toms, rapped the snare, stirred his cymbals. — Ross Russell, *The Sound*, p. 32, 1961

▸ **the bomb; da bomb**
the very best, something that is very good *US, 1973*
- The crescent was the bomb. — A.S. Jackson, *Gentleman Pimp*, p. 13, 1973
- Smoking a spliff of high-octane chronic (street talk for pot) in the back room, he explains his bond to Dre. "He's the bomb," says Snoop. — *People*, p. 77, 23rd May 1994
- I just did a movie about teen modeling with Todd and Griffin Tyler. It's the bomb. — Francesca Lia Block, *I Was a Teenage Fairy*, p. 72, 1998
- Yeah, I'm not too big a fan either. Though Affleck was the bomb in Phantoms. — Kevin Smith, *Jay and Silent Bob Strike Back*, p. 19, 2001

bomb *verb*
1 to place graffiti with an emphasis on quantity, not quality *US, 1982*
- I did my first car in less than an hour. I was bombing. — Craig Castleman, *Getting Up*, p. 5, 1982
- What is a young man from the Hague doing bombing the one line in the 145th Street tunnel with Bode nudes? — Henry Chalfant, *Spraycan Art*, p. 7, 1987
- [A]erosol artists find a place to bomb in peace[.] — *The Source*, April 2000
- "Bombing," trying to put your name up in as many challenging and highly visible places as possible, was how a graffiti writer maintained his reputation among peers. — *Plain Dealer (Cleveland, Ohio)*, p. L1, 29th July 2001

2 in mountain biking, to travel fast downhill *US, 1992*
- — William Nealy, *Mountain Bike!*, p. 160, 1992

3 to train intensely, alternating heavy weights with light weights *US, 1984*
- — *American Speech*, p. 198, Fall 1984: "The language of bodybuilding"

4 to fail dramatically; to flop *US, 1958*
Originally theatrical.
- "They bomb and I serve their time," was Lenny's view of the situation. — Albert Goldman, *Freak Show*, p. 211, 1968

5 in computing, to cease to function completely and suddenly *US, 1991*
- Don't run Empire with less than 32K stack, it'll bomb. — Eric S. Raymond, *The New Hacker's Dictionary*, p. 73, 1991

▸ **get bombed**
to be overcome by a wave while surfing *US, 1965*
- — Duke Kahanamoku with Joe Brennan, *Duke Kahanamoku's World of Surfing*, p. 172, 1965

bombed *adjective*
extremely drunk or drug-intoxicated *US, 1955*
- With each week of work, bombed and sapped and charged and stoned with lush, with pot, with benny[.] — Norman Mailer, *Advertisements for Myself*, p. 243, 1955
- Last weekend the men got so bombed they couldn't make the stairs. [Letter to Ann Landers] — *San Francisco Examiner*, p. 24, 27th May 1966
- She gets totally bombed anyway, but having him around makes it worse. — Bret Easton Ellis, *Less Than Zero*, p. 16, 1985

bombed out *adjective*
extremely marijuana-intoxicated *US, 1967*
- Bombed-out hippies, drag queens, and the great male unwashed. — James Ellroy, *Destination Morgue*, p. 128, 2004

bomber *noun*
1 an extra large, thick or potent marijuana cigarette *US, 1949*
- I was only carrying the bombers. The bombers are big. They're just like regular cigarettes, the same size[.] — Hal Ellson, *Duke*, p. 3, 1949
- Gregor proceeded to roll the biggest bomber anybody ever saw. — Jack Kerouac, *On the Road (The Original Scroll)*, p. 383, 1951
- Satchmo making a roach of a bomber joint in two mighty drags. — Neal Cassady, *Neal Cassady Collected Letters 1944–1967*, p. 299, 20th June 1951: Letter to Jack Kerouac
- I felt its size. It was king-sized, a bomber. — Piri Thomas, *Down These Mean Streets*, p. 58, 1967
- — *Current Slang*, p. 11, Fall 1968

2 a graffiti artist *US, 1994*
- An enterprising bomber could take King of Cleveland by walking the tracks one night. — William Upski Wimsatt, *Bomb the Suburbs*, p. 43, 1994

- These guys were bombers that would do the fancy stuff only when time permitted. — Stephen Power, *The Art of Getting Over*, p. 38, 1999

3 a nicely restored older car *US, 1991*
- This used to be Bianca's brother's greatest source of pride—a fully restored Chevy Impala, what the homies call a bomber. — Leon Bing, *Do or Die*, p. 72, 1991

4 a hard-hitting, aggressive boxer *US, 1937*
- — J. E. Lighter, *Historical Dictionary of American Slang, Volume 1*, p. 226, 1994

5 a powerful, hard-breaking wave *US, 1964*
- — John Severson, *Modern Surfing Around the World*, p. 165, 1964

bomb farm *noun*
an area on a military base where bombs are stored *US, 1991*
- He made his way through the "Bomb Farm," the area where the weapons readied for loading were kept handy. — Gerry Carroll, *North S*A*R*, p. 172, 1991

bombida *noun*
a mixture of heroin and cocaine *US, 1975*
From the Spanish, literal translation "little bomb."
- "I need you to fire a bombida, Rooski," Joe said softly. — Seth Morgan, *Homeboy*, p. 77, 1990

bombilla *noun*
an ampule filled with a drug *US, 1998*
- "Absolutely!" he said emphatically and opened the second refrigerator, which was filled to overflowing with row upon row of small bombillas (glass ampules) filled with methedrine[.] — Peter Coyote, *Sleeping Where I Fall*, p. 162, 1998

bombita; bombito *noun*
a tablet of amphetamine sulfate (Dexedrine™), a central nervous system stimulant *US, 1966*
- — Donald Louria, *Nightmare Drugs*, p. 28, 1966
- He was on amphetamines, stimulants, and had been shooting bombitas, small glass ampules of a drug called Desoxyn. — James Mills, *The Panic in Needle Park*, p. 34, 1966
- One outstanding defensive back was officially known as the Gulper. He would stand there swallowing a gaudy assortment of bombitos. — *San Francisco Examiner*, p. 46, 30th March 1970

bomb line *noun*
during the Korean war, the line beyond which bombing was deemed safe *US, 1986*
- Jim called back, past "the bomb line," the arbitrary division beyond which it was safe to bomb with assurance of not hitting any United Nations patrol. — Steven L. Thompson, *The Wild Blue*, p. 137, 1986

bomb-out *noun*
in competitive surfing, early elimination *US, 1988*
- — Brian and Margaret Lowdon, *Competitive Surfing*, 1988

bomb out *verb*
to knock a surfer off a surfboard *US, 1964*
- — John Severson, *Modern Surfing Around the World*, p. 165, 1964

bombs *noun*
the female breasts *US, 1968*
- — Collin Baker et al., *College Undergraduate Slang Study Conducted at Brown University*, p. 85, 1968

bombshell *noun*
a woman who is astonishingly attractive *US, 1933*
- Kaye Stratford, "The Blond Bombshell," an international favorite, in person 3 shows nitely at Spanish Village, 54 Mason, near Market. — *San Francisco Call-Bulletin*, p. 21, 10th April 1951
- Italian Bombshell Silvana Mangano Jolts America [Headline] — *Quick Magazine*, p. 55, 13th November 1951
- I never know what she is trying to be, except noisy. Miss Tanguay is billed as a "bombshell." — *San Francisco Call-Bulletin*, p. 11, 9th January 1956

Bom-de-Bom *noun*
Ba Muoi Ba beer, a staple in Saigon during the Vietnam war *US, 1990*
- Nobody in Maverick's platoon could pronounce the name, so they just called it Bom-de-Bom. — Dennis J. Marvicsin and Jerold A. Greenfield, *Maverick*, p. 45, 1990

bomfog *noun*
dense and verbose language *US, 1965*

When Governor Nelson Rockefeller campaigned for the Republican nomination for president in 1964, he tended to end speeches with a reference to the "brotherhood of man under the fatherhood of God," a phrase which compacts into the acronym BOMFOG. Reporters covering the campaign began to refer to the end of his speeches as BOMFOG. The term survived and eventually took on a more general, less flattering meaning.

- "Do you remember Nelson Rockefeller's 'bomfog?'" asked the American. — *New York Times*, p. 1–1, 9th June 1984
- BOMFOG has now acquired a meaning along the lines of highfalutin verbiage. — *Time*, 26th April 1999

bondage *noun*
indebtedness *US, 1945*
- — Lou Shelly, *Hepcats JiveTalk Dictionary*, p. 7, 1945

bondage pie *noun*
a pizza with sausage and mushroom topping *US, 1996*
The initials of the toppings—S and M—suggest bondage.
- — *Maledicta*, p. 8, 1996: "Domino's pizza jargon"

bone *noun*
1 the penis, especially when erect *US, 1916*
- "Why, if you mean do I think I could get a bone up over that old buzzard, no, I don't believe I could … " — Ken Kesey, *One Flew Over the Cuckoo's Nest*, p. 69, 1962
- And when you fall down on your good gal and lower your bone / you got to make that pussy call your dick "Bad Mr. Al Capone." — Bruce Jackson, *Get Your Ass in the Water and Swim Like Me*, p. 135, 1964
- Torn or nicked cocks are common casualties as one endeavors to stuff a full bone into his pants and zip up. — John Francis Hunter, *The Gay Insider*, p. 191, 1971
- Let her suck me up good, till I've got a fresh bone / And then I'll come in like the sword in the stone. — *Screw*, p. 7, 15th May 1972
- Every time she'd move her big ass, my bone would ache and throb. — A.S. Jackson, *Gentleman Pimp*, p. 15, 1973

2 the active participant in homosexual sex *US, 2001*
- — AFSCME Local 3963, *The Correctional Officer's Guide to Prison Slang*, 2001

3 the middle finger raised in a gesture meaning, roughly, "fuck you!" *US, 1957*
- [A]ll Jeff did was flip the bone at his old man which is a very dirty way of telling somebody where to get off. — Frederick Kohner, *Gidget*, p. 48, 1957
- — Collin Baker et al., *College Undergraduate Slang Study Conducted at Brown University*, p. 85, 1968
- — Eugene Landy, *The Underground Dictionary*, p. 38, 1971

4 a marijuana cigarette; hence, marijuana *US, 1978*
A visual pun.
- — Richard A. Spears, *The Slang and Jargon of Drugs and Drink*, p. 62, 1986
- Take a big bone hit/Cause after tha bud, My rhymes start flowin' — Tone Loc, *Cheeba cheeba*, 1989

5 a measurement of crack cocaine sold for $50 *US, 2003*
- We got Rocks, we got Bones, we got Brown, we got Stones. — Julian Johnson, *Urban Survival*, p. 170, 2003

6 heroin *US, 1993*
- — Peter Johnson, *Dictionary of Street Alcohol and Drug Terms*, p. 25, 1993

7 a dollar *US, 1889*
- I never heard of anybody offering a twenty-bone bounty for bagging a ball-cutter. — Ken Kesey, *One Flew Over the Cuckoo's Nest*, p. 69, 1962
- I sent you two dollars of it, but don't spend it fast / 'cause those two bones will be your first and last. — Dennis Wepman et al., *The Life*, p. 141, 1976
- Thousand, yes, bones or clams or whatever you call them. — *The Big Lebowski*, 1998
- Me and Trick figured it would be at least ten bones each for gas roundtrip. — Linden Dalecki, *Kid B*, p. 137, 2006

8 one thousand dollars *US, 1988*
- They lend you a thousand and call it a bone. — Robert Campbell, *Juice*, p. 20, 1988

9 a trombone *US, 1918*
- Ross frequently lays aside his "bone" to take over the mike as Benny's vocalist. — *The Capitol*, p. 6, July 1946
- Furg's 'bone was a brass bowel hooked in his nervous system, completing some rare equation of heart and body. — Malcolm Braly, *Shake Him Till He Rattles*, p. 85, 1963

- Many of the performers belonged to a San Francisco trombone choir called the Bay Bones. — *Time*, p. 73, 5th March 1979

10 a domino *US, 1959*
Usually in the plural.
- Joe played dominoes with Smoothbore and Clovis. The thwacking of the bones punctuated desultory conversation. — Seth Morgan, *Homeboy*, p. 90, 1990

11 in private poker games or other private gambling, a white betting chip *US, 1866*
- — George Percy, *The Language of Poker*, p. 12, 1988

12 a black person *US, 1992*
- — William K. Bentley and James M. Corbett, *Prison Slang*, p. 54, 1992

bone *verb*
1 to have sex from the male point of view *US, 1971*
- You kin change the engine on your bike, you kin paint the kitchen, you kin bone your old lady twice. — Joseph Wambaugh, *The Secrets of Harry Bright*, p. 191, 1985
- It's a lot more interesting than just flinging off your clothes and boning away on the neighbor's swing set. — *Heathers*, 1988
- "Make sure you wear a raincoat when you bone them broads." — Nathan McCall, *Makes Me Wanna Holler*, p. 40, 1994
- Alone with most of the female cast, he proceeds to bone one after another after another. — Editors of Adult Video News, *The AVN Guide to the 500 Greatest Adult Films of All Time*, p. 62, 2005

2 to walk fast *US, 1999*
- We boned out of the police station and headed to the parking lot. — Eric Jerome Dickey, *Cheaters*, p. 369, 1999

3 in mountain biking, to strike the nose of your seat with your buttocks *US, 1992*
- — William Nealy, *Mountain Bike!*, p. 160, 1992: Bikespeak

4 to study intensely *US, 1859*
- I was back at State again, boning for my finals[.] — Chester Himes, *Cast the First Stone*, p. 55, 1952

bone banger; bone crusher *noun*
an orthopedist *US, 1994*
- — Sally Williams, *"Strong" Words*, p. 135, 1994

bonecrushers *noun*
the very painful symptoms of withdrawal from drug addiction *US, 1990*
- I've held off the bonecrushers two days, rationing that stuff up my nose—horned the last just an hour ago. — Seth Morgan, *Homeboy*, p. 49, 1990

bonehead *noun*
an idiot *US, 1908*
- "Anything a bonehead like me can do to study up on 'em, Doc?" — Donald Wilson, *My Six Convicts*, p. 54, 1951
- "That was a bonehead play." — Charles Perry, *Portrait of a Young Man Drowning*, p. 141, 1962
- I don't know which bonehead dreamed up this business of splitting up teams that have been working together for years. — Robert Campbell, *Juice*, p. 216, 1988

bone-on *noun*
an erection *US, 1927*
- I swear to Christ, B., I never got such a terrific bone-on in my life! Like a fucking rock[.] — Terry Southern, *Blue Movie*, p. 206, 1970

bone out *verb*
1 to relax, to idle *US, 1991*
- "I go to my mama's house like Friday through Sunday, and I bone out." — Leon Bing, *Do or Die*, p. 32, 1991

2 to back down from a confrontation; to run away from danger *US, 1993*
- — *People Magazine*, p. 72, 19th July 1993
- — Bill Valentine, *Gang Intelligence Manual*, p. 75, 1995

3 to leave quickly *US, 1993*
- I know if I had some money I'd bone the fuck out. — *Menace II Society*, 1993

4 while snowboarding, to hold your leg straight during a maneuver in the air *US, 1990*
- — Elena Garcia, *A Beginner's Guide to Zen and the Art of Snowboarding*, p. 121, 1990

bone queen *noun*
a male homosexual who favors performing oral sex *US, 1964*
- — Roger Blake, *The American Dictionary of Sexual Terms*, p. 21, 1964

boner *noun*

1 a blunder *US, 1912*

- Right here is where we pulled a boner. I didn't know at the time I was being followed, but my leaving the bandstand out of a clear sky and taking Frank's car called for a tail. — Mezz Mezzrow, *Really the Blues*, p. 66, 1946
- He had a pretty good idea that he'd pulled a boner. — Jim Thompson, *Savage Night*, p. 61, 1953
- As for Japhy he was quite pleased with anything I did provided I didn't pull any boners like making the kerosene lamp smoke from turning the wick too far up[.] — Jack Kerouac, *The Dharma Bums*, p. 147, 1958
- "Now remember you get a roust out here, crack my name. Don't repeat your boner." — Iceberg Slim (Robert Beck), *Pimp*, p. 192, 1969

2 an erection *US, 1961*

The supposed bone-like quality of an erect penis, with which you **BONE** (have sex).

- The little dog used to raise a boner every time it walked into a room where Rickie was present[.] — Clancy Sigal, *Going Away*, p. 68, 1961
- In the classroom I sometimes set myself consciously to thinking about DEATH and HOSPITALS and HORRIBLE AUTOMOBILE ACCIDENTS in the hope that such grave thoughts will cause my "boner" to recede before the bell rings and I have to stand. — Philip Roth, *Portnoy's Complaint*, p. 200, 1969
- I graduated into the "talking mood"–a group of neighborhood kids who met behind the garage to tell the same worn-out dirty jokes and recount when they (the boys) had last had a "boner." — Jefferson Poland and Valerie Alison, *The Records of the San Francisco Sexual Freedom League*, p. 111, 1971
- Don't like to look like I'm hustling, and there I am, sitting next to you with a boner. — *Diner*, 1982

bones *noun*

1 dice *UK, 1400*

The term has journeyed from colloquial to standard English and now to slang.

- And I'd take some loaded craps down there, some bones, and I would beat the paddy boys out of all their money. They were the only ones who were dumb enough to shoot craps with bones. — Claude Brown, *Manchild in the Promised Land*, p. 151, 1965
- We now had five yards to spend / so I made the same bet again / as I watched the bones fly from Spoon's hand. — Lightnin' Rod, *Hustlers Convention*, p. 52, 1973
- How bout it new kid, you wanna handle my bones, or do you just like to watch. [Screenplay, not in final cut.] — *Kill Bill*, 2003

2 heroin *US, 1984*

- Heroin is called either "bones," referring to a high level of purity, or "scramble," meaning a much less pure version, which is much cheaper. — *Washington Post*, p. B1, 29th July 1984

3 an orthopedist *US, 1892*

- — Sally Williams, *"Strong" Words*, p. 135, 1994

4 spare ribs *US, 1990*

- — Charles Shafer, *Folk Speech in Texas Prisons*, p. 198, 1990

▸ **make your bones**

by extension, to establish yourself as an equal in a group setting *US, 1996*

- She'd made her bones back in the days when there were still a lot of dinosaurs left on the job, guys who wanted women to fail. — Joseph Wambaugh, *Floaters*, p. 139, 1996

▸ **make your bones; earn your bones**

to establish yourself as a fully fledged member of a crime organization, usually by carrying out an execution-style murder *US, 1972*

- Only a few weeks before he had made his bones, a double kill of Herm and Sal Perigino[.] — Mickey Spillane, *Last Cop Out*, p. 8, 1972
- Mr. Bellini wants you to join the Family. He told me to see that you make your bones. I have the guy you need in mind already. — Iceberg Slim (Robert Beck), *Death Wish*, p. 65, 1977
- When he was thirteen he had made his bones on the Gun Hill Road in the Bronx, where he had never been before that afternoon. — Richard Condon, *Prizzi's Honor*, p. 4, 1982
- Angiulo had no scalps, never having "earned his bones," or killed a man to become a "made" Mafia member. — Gerard O'Neill, *The Under Boss*, p. 41, 1989

bone shack *noun*

any place where a couple have sex *US, 1997*

- — Pamela Munro, *U.C.L.A. Slang*, p. 42, 1997

boneshaker *noun*

a rigid-frame motorcycle, especially a rigid-frame Harley-Davidson *US, 1962*

- — *American Speech*, p. 267, December 1962: "The language of traffic policemen"

bone up *verb*

to study, especially at the last minute *US, 1918*

An American outgrowth of the C18 "bone" with the same meaning.

- Then we started boning up on the dog-ass Jets, who had dusted off Oakland thirty-five to ten for the American Conference title. — Dan Jenkins, *Semi-Tough*, p. 91, 1972

bone works *noun*

rough treatment *US, 1970*

- I wasn't leaned on too much, but I got the bone works when it came to security. They stayed on me like hawks for six months. — Red Rudensky, *The Gonif*, p. 50, 1970

boneyard *noun*

1 a cemetery *US, 1866*

- "Among other places, at the boneyard," I clued her in. — Frederick Kohner, *The Affairs of Gidget*, p. 119, 1963
- A minister funeralized over his coffin and all the tiny town's eyes were flued on the windy old boneyard. — Joe Eszterhas, *Charlie Simpson's Apocalypse*, p. 75, 1973
- So if he did the work on the plumber he would be sending the only woman he had ever really loved to a boneyard. — Richard Condon, *Prizzi's Money*, p. 90, 1994

2 in various industrial settings, the site for dumping broken vehicles and equipment which can be cannibalized for parts *US, 1913*

- — Ramon Adams, *The Language of the Railroader*, p. 18, 1977

3 in dominoes, the pile of unused tiles *US, 1897*

- — Dominic Armanino, *Dominoes*, p. 16, 1959
- Never mind the sun, Homer—help yourself to the boneyard—you're 5 pegs from a skunking. [Homer comic strip] — *San Francisco Examiner*, p. 48, 2nd April 1963

4 the area off a beach where waves break *US, 1957*

- [O]n Malibu Mac's how to get out of a "boneyard" when you're caught in the middle of a set of breakers—and on Scooterboy Miller's hot rod I learned how to avoid a pearl dive. — Frederick Kohner, *Gidget*, p. a, 1957
- — John M. Kelly, *Surf and Sea*, p. 280, 1965

5 a conjugal visit in prison *US, 1989*

- — James Harris, *A Convict's Dictionary*, p. 28, 1989

boney maroney *noun*

a very thin person *US, 1957*

In various spellings, but surely originating in the rock 'n' roll lyric from the 1957 song by Larry Williams.

- I've got a girl named Bony Maroney / She's as twiggy as a stick of macaroni. — Larry Williams, *Bony Maronie*, 1957
- — Kenn "Naz" Young, *Naz's Underground Dictionary*, p. 16, 1973

bone you! bone ya!

used as an all-purpose, defiant insult *US, 1963*

- — *American Speech*, p. 276, December 1963: "American Indian student slang"

bonfire *noun*

a burning cigarette stub *US, 1945*

- — Lou Shelly, *Hepcats Jive Talk Dictionary*, p. 8, 1945

bong *noun*

a pipe with a water-filled bowl through which marijuana or crack cocaine smoke is drawn for inhalation *US, 1971*

- I like a blunt or a big fat coal / But my double-barrel bong is gettin' me stoned / I'm skill it, There's water inside don't spill it — Cypress Hill, *Hits from the Bong*, 1993
- "Come smoke a few bhongs with the sheriff." A bhong was a vertical bamboo pipe containing water. — Cleo Odzer, *Goa Freaks*, p. 75, 1995
- If we didn't have a bong, we used to get my brother's motorcycle helmet[.] — Macfarlane, Macfarlane and Robson, *The User*, p. 79, 1996

• She wondered what misshapen bong or other embarrassment was drawn on him. — Francesca Lia Block, *I Was a Teenage Fairy*, p. 90, 1998

▸ **hit the bong**

to smoke using a water pipe *US, 1986*

• But then would any of you lame fucks give up your CD player now that you've been trained to crawl up in front of it and hit the bong every night? — *mod.music.gaffa*, 7th November 1986

• She was upstairs hitting the bong. — Michelle Tea, *Rent Girl*, p. 98, 2004

bong *verb*

to drink beer directly from a keg, using a hose and funnel *US, 1982*

• — Mary Corey and Victoria Westermark, *Fer Shurr! How to be a Valley Girl*, 1982

bongo *noun*

in skateboarding, a fall or the wounds resulting from a fall *US, 1976*

• — Laura Torbet, *The Complete Book of Skateboarding*, p. 105, 1976

bongo *adjective*

crazy *US, 1979*

• I wonder if I'm bongo to let this yo-yo try to do what I want. — Leo Rosten, *Silky!*, p. 25, 1979

bonhunkus *noun*

the buttocks *US, 1941*

• If surfing isn't vigorous enough, you can go zipping down the Sun Streaker water slide, a 220-foot nearly straight shot that you take from four stories high, sitting only on your bohunkus. — *Washington Post*, p. 5 (Weekend), 1st April 1983

bonita *noun*

milk sugar (lactose) used to dilute heroin *US, 1973* Mexican Spanish.

• — David Maurer and Victor Vogel, *Narcotics and Narcotic Addiction*, p. 390, 1973

bonk *verb*

in an endurance sport, especially cycling, to reach a point of utter exhaustion *US, 1979*

• The challenge is to fuel our bodies to meet enormous energy needs, spare glycogen stores so we don't "bonk"[.] — *Baltimore Sun*, p. 7D, 2nd August 1994

• The athlete may "bonk," "hit the wall" or "blow up," as the terminology goes. — *Washington Post*, p. A1, 11th June 2001

bonkers *adjective*

crazy *US, 1957*

• That's incredible! Richard Marks will go bonkers. — Dan Jenkins, *Life Its Ownself*, p. 198, 1984

• North rim? Man, are you bonkers! They'll shoot you. — Bill Cardoso, *The Maltese Sangweech*, p. 247, 1984

• That's when Letch devised the scheme to pee on the tree and drive the little bowwow bonkers. — Joseph Wambaugh, *Floaters*, p. 11, 1996

• This she could deal with: a woman going bonkers over a man. — Rita Ciresi, *Pink Slip*, p. 340, 1999

bonneroo; bonaroo *adjective*

good, smart, sharp *US, 1926* Largely, if not exclusively, prison slang.

• The uniform of the 10-piece ensemble was "boneroo" – that's lingo on the inside for "cool" on the outside. — *San Francisco Examiner*, p. 19, 13th June 1960

• — Board of Corrections, State of California, *A Dictionary of Criminal Language For Official Law Enforcement Use Only*, 1962

• These are boneroo free-world shoes. — Malcolm Braly, *On the Yard*, p. 140, 1967

• He had bonneroo rolls and cookies[.] — James Carr, *Bad*, p. 70, 1975

• If you weren't a Mexican, I'd call it a bonaroo taco wagon. — James Ellroy, *Suicide Hill*, p. 611, 1986

bonnet *noun*

a blasting cap *US, 1972*

• Bad-Eye's got what we call the bonnets, that's the caps which are used to set the grease off. — Harry King, *Box Man*, p. 48, 1972

Bonnie Dick *nickname*

the USS Bonhomme Richard *US, 1955* An aircraft carrier named after Capt. John Paul Jones' famous ship in the American Revolution.

• Bonnie Dick Rejoins Fleet [Headline] — *San Francisco News*, p. 12, 7th September 1955

bonzo *adjective*

crazy *US, 1979*

• The kid was a banana! Bonzo. Loonier than his old man. — Joseph Wambaugh, *Lines and Shadows*, p. 108, 1984

boo *noun*

1 marijuana *US, 1959*

• "Boo is a crutch for you," Lee snorted. — Clarence Cooper Jr., *Black*, p. 104, 1963

• Hey, really, you know my manic thing with boo. If I start seeing spiders, you can always slip me a little niacin. — Richard Farina, *Been Down So Long*, p. 66, 1966

• Well then somebody dumped an ounce of boo on the table and cats and kitties got their kicks that way and the beering halted. — Richard Meltzer, *A Whore Just Like the Rest*, p. 163, 1972

• His father had been unable to figure out any other way to ice Little Phil Terrone, the heaviest shit and boo dealer in the North Bronx. — Richard Condon, *Prizzi's Honor*, p. 4, 1982

2 a sexual partner or lover *US, 1997*

• — Connie Eble (Editor), *UNC-CH Campus Slang*, p. 2, 1997

• — *Milwaukee Journal-Sentinel*, 5th March 2001

• — Gary K. Farlow, *Prison-ese*, p. 5, 2002

3 an attractive young person *US, 1968*

• — Collin Baker et al., *College Undergraduate Slang Study Conducted at Brown University*, p. 84, 1968

4 used as a term of endearment *US, 2004*

• — Rick Ayers (Editor), *Berkeley High Slang Dictionary*, p. 13, 2004

5 anything at all *US, 1883* Usually heard in the warning—"don't say boo."

• "I've hardly had time to say boo to her today." — Glenn Savan, *White Palace*, p. 271, 1987

boo *nickname*

a C-7 Caribou aircraft *US, 2004*

• — David Hart, *First Air Cavalry Division Vietnam Dictionary*, p. 9, 2004

boob *noun*

1 a fool *US, 1907* Almost certainly from C16 "booby," meaning a "stupid fellow."

• There's another buddyship of boobs who think the earth is hollow and we live inside. — Philip Wylie, *Opus 21*, p. 85, 1949

• But wouldn't it be funny if he suddenly turned to him and said, "Phil Latham, you're a boob." — John Knowles, *A Separate Peace*, p. 175, 1959

• Your rotarian boob of a publisher has one of the most original minds I've run across in quite a while. — Hunter S. Thompson, *The Proud Highway*, p. 191, 29th October 1959: Letter to William J. Kennedy

• New York Billie dug that Willie was from Lame Junction so he figured he'd take this boob for the New York pig. — Babs Gonzales, "A Manhattan Fable" in *Movin' On Down De Line*, p. 89, 1975

2 the female breast *US, 1931* From synonymous "bub." Generally used in the plural.

• She had a nice pair of boobs and he'd like to catch her sometime — Hubert Selby Jr., *Last Exit to Brooklyn*, p. 268, 1957

• Someone would sit up and point at some sex display, "Look at those boobs!" — Frederick Kohner, *Gidget*, p. 49, 1957

• Her breasts weren't especially big, or little, or round, or pointy or any of those magazine-writer tit fetish cliches. They were just nice boobs on a nice woman. — Gurney Norman, *Divine Right's Trip (Last Whole Earth Catalog)*, p. 41, 1971

• "Oh, I wish you wouldn't use that expression [flat]," retorted Miss Andrews in her precise British voice. "Everyone including Carol Burnett knows I have bigger boobs than she does." — *San Francisco Chronicle*, p. 58, 15th December 1971

boob *verb*

to perform poorly, to botch something *US, 1919*

• The growing consensus, says the pro-American Economist, is "that American intelligence boobed." — *Tampa (Florida) Tribune*, p. 6, 9th September 1998

• "I just completely boobed three 5-irons and plunked two or three woods," Wessels said of her morning qualifying round in the Illinois Women's State Amateur. — *Rockford (Illinois) Star*, p. 1D, 8th June 1999

boob box *noun*

a television; television *US, 1968*

- [G]lomming the presidential conventions from the boob box[.] — Sidney Bernard, *This Way to the Apocalypse*, p. 72, 1968

boo-bird *noun*

a sports fan who constantly and loudly boos during a game *US*, 1948

- Cleveland Boo-Birds Backed by Veeck [Headline] — *Sporting News*, p. 1, 14th July 1948
- Philadelphia is reputed to be the biggest sports boobird city in the U.S. — *San Francisco Examiner*, p. 50, 17th November 1966
- Enraged boo birds, many fueled by beer, took over the game for about 20 minutes Sunday, making so much noise play had to be held up because the Eagles couldn't hear Garbril's signals. — *San Francisco Chronicle*, p. 46, 29th October 1974

boobitas; boobititas *noun*

small female breasts *US*, 1963

A borrowed use of the Spanish diminutive.

- — Carol Ann Preusse, *Jargon Used by University of Texas Co-Eds*, 1963

boob job *noun*

surgery to alter a woman's breast size *US*, 1986

- Half the girls get boob jobs and butt tucks. — Carl Hiaasen, *Tourist Season*, p. 259, 1986
- Cop Don Fernando, who's been trying to find Spankenstein for five years, discovers pint-sized Nasty Natasha (Courtney plus a boob job). — *Adult Video News*, p. 56, February 1993
- I've got almost three thousand dollars. I was saving it for a boob job. — *American Beauty*, 1999
- [A] week after Jake dumped me, I slept with Hawk just to get back at him. Then I got a boob job. — Missy Hyatt, *Missy Hyatt*, p. 19, 2001

boob man *noun*

a male with a primary interest in a woman's breasts as a point of attraction *US*, 1973

- "I've seen you looking at women, the big boobs … you are a big boob man and I think I can satisfy that." — Robert O'Neil Bristow, *A Faraway Drummer*, p. 232, 1973
- "Like, most of 'em got small little titties and are skinny, so if you're a boob man your hands feel kinda empty." — Cherokee Paul McDonald, *Into the Green*, p. 98, 2001

boo-boo *noun*

1 a woman *US*, 1997

- See? With the boo-boo in red? — David Chase, *The Sopranos: Selected Scripts from Three Seasons*, p. 10, 25th August 1997

2 an error *US*, 1953

Children's vocabulary.

- The other day, Mr. B. made a lamentable boo-boo. — *San Francisco Examiner*, p. 29, 24th January 1953
- How could she have made such a thundering booboo as to cut Oscar loose before she had Harry properly hooked? — Max Shulman, *Rally Round the Flag, Boys!*, p. 233, 1957
- "Now, since I made a booboo—I'll let you make one." — Frederick Kohner, *Gidget Goes Hawaiian*, p. 46, 1961
- This is a male institution. Someone's made a … booboo. — Seth Morgan, *Homeboy*, p. 251, 1990

3 a bruise or scrape *US*, 1954

- But in Springfield, Mass., you say "I fell down and got a boo-boo on my elbow" (a bruise). This boo-boo may come from a French slang word, bo-bo, any small bruise or hurt. — *Junior Parade Magazine*, p. 22, 20th June 1954
- Has the poor little girl got a Booboo? — Hubert Selby Jr., *Last Exit to Brooklyn*, p. 47, 1957
- He says, "Well, whaddaya know—Champ Pimp's got himself a boo-boo." — *Raging Bull*, 1980
- [D]on't worry about that little boo-boo on her throat / It's just a little scratch[.] — Eminem (Marshall Mathers), *'97 Bonnie and Clyde*, 1999

boo-boos *noun*

the testicles *US*, 1951

- — Dale Gordon, *The Dominion Sex Dictionary*, p. 31, 1967

boobs *noun*

in poker, a pair of queens *US*, 1988

- — George Percy, *The Language of Poker*, p. 12, 1988

boob sling *noun*

a brassiere *US*, 1968

- — Collin Baker et al., *College Undergraduate Slang Study Conducted at Brown University*, p. 85, 1968
- They raised thousands of dollars for breast cancer research by staging a strip-a-thon-cum-burlesque show and an autographed celebrity bra auction (including a multicolored boob-sling from Madonna). — Mark Ebner, *Hollywood, Interrupted*, p. 235, 2004

boob tube *noun*

television *US*, 1963

First came **THE TUBE**, and then the obvious reduplication.

- Maybe you do a few things which irritate her and she retaliates via the boob tube. — *San Francisco News Call Bulletin*, p. 11, 21st January 1963
- Hi-fi comes to the boob tube [Headline] — *Life*, p. 22, 15th May 1970
- Parked in front of the boob tube, Carol and I used to gawk and hoot at those hunks[.] — Rita Ciresi, *Pink Slip*, p. 163, 1999

booby *adjective*

foolish *US*, 1958

- [W]e'll poetize the lot and make a fat book of icy bombs for the booby public. — Jack Kerouac, *The Dharma Bums*, p. 158, 1958

booby; boobie *noun*

a female breast *US*, 1916

- Sitting in the back seat with the pudgy girl was his date – big boobies, he remembered, they jiggled. — Bernard Wolfe, *The Late Risers*, p. 46, 1954
- You can be up to your boobies in white satin, with gardenias in your hair and no sugar cane for miles, but you can still be working on a plantation. — Billie Holiday with William Dufty, *Lady Sings the Blues*, p. 95, 1956
- And pointy, stretched-out boobies from past hormone dabbling. — James St. James, *Party Monster*, p. 68, 1990
- Her eyes are still big, and her boobies are still mobile and high as she straddles her man in a girl-on-top tussle. — Mr. Skin, *Mr. Skin's Skincyclopedia*, p. 10, 2005

booby hatch *noun*

a mental hospital *US*, 1896

- If I was, they'd drive me into the booby hatch. — James T. Farrell, *Saturday Night*, p. 20, 1947
- How in the name of carnation some people go through life without their getting locked up in what we used to call the Bobby Hatch *** well, pal, it sure beats me. — Leo Rosten, *Dear Herm*, p. 17, 1974
- Frank had to content himself with getting her committed to the booby hatch for life, innocent by reason of insanity. — George V. Higgins, *Penance for Jerry Kennedy*, p. 37, 1985

booby house *noun*

a mental institution *US*, 1949

- "In the booby house you eat every day." — Nelson Algren, *The Man with the Golden Arm*, p. 274, 1949

booby trap *noun*

a dishonest carnival game *US*, 1950

- — *American Speech*, p. 235, October 1950: "The argot of outdoor booby traps"

boochie *noun*

a Japanese person *US*, 1950

- Chicago Japs refer to those from the old country and Hawaii as "Buddha heads" or "Boochies." — Jack Lait and Lee Mortimer, *Chicago Confidential*, p. 88, 1950

boo-coo; boo koo *noun*

a large number; a lot *US*, 1918

- Bama said, "Yeah, he'll be there. So what has that to do with boo koos of fine foxes?" — Iceberg Slim (Robert Beck), *Death Wish*, p. 130, 1977
- I can't remember boo koos of kilometers before we began to really hear the mortar shells singing in the curves they take, the perfection of U.S. electric magic! — Clarence Major, *All-Night Visitors*, p. 36, 1998

boo-coo; boo koo *adjective*

a large number of; a lot of *US*, 1972

- "LZ on the Cambodian border. Beaucoup dinks." You pronounce it boo-coo in the Big V. — William Pelfrey, *The Big V*, p. 12, 1972
- We got boo-coo movement. 3rd Battalion just got hit 15 kliks north of here. — *Platoon*, 1986
- He's boo-koo koo-koo. — *Gone in 60 Seconds*, 2000
- I fry boocoo buckets of chicken, and eat them by the stomachful. — David Henry Sterry, *Chicken*, p. 27, 2002

boodle *noun*

1 profits appropriated quietly, and usually illegally *US, 1858*

- Tom ("Sailor") Burke had been the sheriff's "bag man," had delivered $36,000 in payoff money to the sheriff's wife, and had gotten signed receipts for the boodle. — *Time*, p. 18, 24th July 1950
- Of the boodle with which she had skipped St. Louis, she still had several thousand dollars, plus, of course, such readily negotiable items as her car, jewelry, and furs. — Jim Thompson, *The Grifters*, p. 87, 1963
- Sister Heavenly reckoned that Gus was carrying the boodle on him. — Chester Himes, *Come Back Charleston Blue*, p. 48, 1966
- We gotta go and score for decent bennys and bread to make up a playing boodle. — Iceberg Slim (Robert Beck), *Airtight Willie and Me*, p. 5, 1979

2 a fake bankroll used in confidence swindles *US, 1985*

- — M. Allen Henderson, *How Con Games Work*, p. 218, 1985

3 a package of snacks *US, 1900*

- Those with friends or family in the military are sure to find the online Gift Shop an easy way to send "boodle," as soldiers often refer to much-anticipated packages from home. — *PR Newswire*, 17th June 2003

4 a capsule of poison disguised as a capsule of heroin *US, 1968*

- And the best way to "waste" a stoolie was to make him a conspirator in his own murder, by dropping a "boodle." — Phil Hirsch, *Hooked*, p. 15, 1968

boof *noun*

contraband hidden in the rectum *US, 2002*

- — Jeffrey Ian Ross, *Behind Bars*, p. 182, 2002: Slammer Slang

boof *verb*

to hide prison contraband in your rectum *US, 2000*

- Like prisoners everywhere, Rikers inmates use their rectums as a sort of suitcase for weapons, concealing one or two razor blades—or sometimes even 20 or 30—by "slamming" or "boofing" them. — *Village Voice*, p. 45, 19th December 2000

boog *noun*

a black person *US, 1937*

Offensive.

- "She's workin' in some boog honky-tonk," Antek told Frankie. — Nelson Algren, *The Man with the Golden Arm*, p. 231, 1949
- Christ, let's take all of them—the fucking boogs may turn cannibal any minute! — Terry Southern, *Blue Movie*, p. 182, 1970
- Everybody is doing okay, Irish, Poles, the ghinnies even, paddling along, all except the boogs. Right to the bottom. — John Sayles, *Union Dues*, pp. 22–23, 1977

boogaloo *noun*

a black person *US, 1970*

- — Clarence Major, *Dictionary of Afro-American Slang*, p. 29, 1970

booger *noun*

1 a glob of nasal mucus *US, 1891*

- Eeeeuwww! You got a booger on your shirt! — Richard Price, *The Wanderers*, p. 76, 1974
- She peered at me with fierce suspicion, so I crossed my eyes and probed for a booger. — C.D. Payne, *Youth in Revolt*, p. 36, 1993

2 the vagina; and so, woman as sexual object *US, 1959*

- I bet LaNelle got some sweet booger up top of them nice long legs. — Ken Weaver, *Texas Crude*, p. 105, 1984

booger drag *noun*

a man dressed as a woman, but revealing his masculinity by not shaving his face, arms and/or legs *US, 1997*

- — Jim Crotty, *How to Talk American*, p. 138, 1997
- What I had seen before her was what Joe called "booger drag." — Jay Quinn, *The Mentor*, p. 91, 2000

boogie *noun*

a black person *US, 1923*

Offensive.

- Strike a match, the boogy's nuts. — Ralph Ellison, *Invisible Man*, p. 566, 1947
- "Stopped both fights in the first. One was against that boogie from the Savoy." — Nelson Algren, *The Neon Wilderness*, p. 62, 1960
- She was with some boogey and then some other boogey came in and shot them both in the head. How do you like that? Fucking for boogies. — Philip Roth, *Portnoy's Complaint*, p. 197, 1969
- Make our job a lot easier, keep the boogies inside. — John Sayles, *Union Dues*, p. 22, 1977

boogie *verb*

1 to dance, especially with abandon *US, 1947*

- He could hear the hi-fi going next door, Lesley boogying around the apartment to the Bee-Gees, ignoring her aunt, who was a little deaf. — Elmore Leonard, *Gold Coast*, p. 58, 1980

2 to go, especially in a hurry *US, 1970*

- If you were lonely you could always boogie on down to the Vietnam Day Committee house and find somebody to talk to. — Jerry Rubin, *Do It!*, p. 37, 1970
- Let's boogie. — *The Blues Brothers*, 1980
- Gazing into the mirror he used an actor's trick and conjured images of middle-aged sociopaths: Fat Tony Salerno, Saddam Hussein, Ted Kennedy. Nothing worked. The killer had boogied. — Joseph Wambaugh, *Finnegan's Week*, p. 2, 1993

boogie-joogie *verb*

to fool around *US, 1968*

- Hadn't he messed up his own chances at life by boogy-joogying with them? — Nathan Heard, *Howard Street*, p. 53, 1968

boogie man; boogy man *noun*

a mythical demon, used to frighten children *US, 1905*

- Television, the early boogie-man of all forms of show business, has had a definite effect on night clubbing, Walters thinks. — Robert Sylvester, *No Cover Charge*, p. 36, 1956
- Betty, John, and I believed there was a boogie man in the church at night[.] — Bobby Seale, *A Lonely Rage*, p. 5, 1978
- Damn, you daddy mean. He worse than the boogy man himself. — *Boyz N The Hood*, 1990
- I couldn't tie my shoes until I was 9, I wet the bed until I was 13, and I still can't go to sleep without Mommy making sure the Boogie Man isn't under the bed. — Chris Rock, *Rock This!*, p. 57, 1997

boogie party *noun*

a party held to raise money to pay the rent *US, 1982*

- — Arnold Shaw, *Dictionary of American Pop/Rock*, p. 159, 1982

boojie *noun*

a middle-class person *US, 1970*

A refinement of "bourgeois" and not used with kindness.

- "We know those Boojies (bourgeois Negroes) don't want to hear about us," was their reaction, "but that's too bad: we exist!" — Christina and Richard Milner, *Black Players*, p. 11, 1972

book *noun*

1 a life sentence to prison *US, 1976*

- "What do you think we'll get?" Bob asked. "The book," Mick said. — Malcolm Braley, *False Starts*, p. 98, 1976

2 a betting operation *US, 1917*

- There are about thirty books or wheels going in Chicago alone. — Alson Smith, *Syndicate City*, p. 196, 1954
- One of my rules, forty years in the business—going back to the syndicate days—twenty years running my own book, you have to always know who you're doing business with. — Elmore Leonard, *Riding the Rap*, p. 16, 1995

3 in sports, the collective, conventional wisdom in a given situation *US, 1985*

- Williams went against the book, and sent pitching coach Galen Cisco to the mound with instructions. — *Los Angeles Times*, p. 1 (Part 3), 10th April 1985
- In sports, it is always referred to as "the Book." It doesn't exist, not in any tangible form at least, but it is referenced by coaches on every level, from little league to the NFL. — *Atlanta Journal-Constitution*, p. 7F, 2nd January 2004

4 ten thousand doses of LSD soaked into paper *US, 1999*

- Ten pages—ten thousand hits—constitute a "book," which is a common wholesale unit. — Cam Cloud, *The Little Book of Acid*, p. 34, 1999

5 one pound of drugs *US, 1976*

- — Robert Sabbag, *Snowblind*, p. 271, 1976

6 half a kilogram of drugs *US, 1976*

- — Robert Sabbag, *Snowblind*, p. 271, 1976

7 a hard-working, focused, serious student *US, 1968*

- — Collin Baker et al., *College Undergraduate Slang Study Conducted at Brown University*, p. 85, 1968

▶ **make book**

to bet *US, 1962*

- [H]e was shrugging it off like water, makin' book with the technicians on how long he could keep his eyes open after the poles touched. — Ken Kesey, *One Flew Over the Cuckoo's Nest*, p. 277, 1962

▸ **the book**
the unwritten code of style and conduct observed by pimps *US, 1972*
- During the study we only met three White pimps, and all of them mimicked the Black style in their speech, dress, and in their adherence to "The Book," the unwritten pimp's code. — Christina and Richard Milner, *Black Players*, p. 12, 1972

▸ **throw the book at; give the book**
to sentence someone to a maximum penalty allowed by law *US, 1908*
- That's what they do, give you the book. That's supposed to scare the other guys. — Chester Himes, *Cast the First Stone*, p. 12, 1952
- The assistant U.S. attorney argued that the defendant had been involved in criminal endeavors for over four decades and wanted an upward departure. Which Raylan understood to mean throw the book at him. — Elmore Leonard, *Riding the Rap*, p. 280, 1995

book *verb*
1 to study *US, 1968*
- — Collin Baker et al., *College Undergraduate Slang Study Conducted at Brown University*, p. 86, 1968
2 to depart, usually hurriedly *US, 1974*
- Belly sprang to her feet. "We gotta book—fast." — Seth Morgan, *Homeboy*, p. 66, 1990
- MARSELLUS: Whatch got? ENGLISH DAVE: He booked. — *Pulp Fiction*, 1994
- We gotta book it if we're going to make it to P.E. — *Clueless*, 1995
- We gotta book. We're catching a bus to Chi-town. — *Chasing Amy*, 1997

▸ **book a party of two**
to arrange for oral sex to be performed on two male prisoners *US, 1989*
- — James Harris, *A Convict's Dictionary*, 1989

▸ **book the action**
to accept a bet *US, 1980*
- If a player puts down a roll of dimes, you book the action. — Lee Solkey, *Dummy Up and Deal*, p. 108, 1980

book-beater *noun*
a serious, hard-working student *US, 1945*
- — *Yank*, p. 18, 24th March 1945

book 'em, Danno
used for humorous suggestion that somebody has been caught in an improper act *US, 1968*
From the US television series *Hawaii Five-O* (1968–1980), in which Detective Steve McGarrett would order Detective "Danno" Williams to arrest a suspect.
- McGarrett may have said, "Book 'em, Danno," but the audience wanted to bed 'em when it came to Anne's brunette beauty and her big kahunas. — Mr. Skin, *Mr. Skin's Skincyclopedia*, p. 24, 2005

bookend *verb*
in twelve-step recovery programs such as Alcoholics Anonymous, to speak with a fellow recovering addict both before and after confronting a difficult situation *US, 1998*
- — Christopher Cavanaugh, *AA to Z*, p. 58, 1998

book gook *noun*
a diligent, socially inept student *US, 1951*
Teen Slang.
- — *Newsweek*, p. 28, 8th October 1951

bookie *noun*
a bookmaker *UK, 1885*
Sometimes spelt "booky."
- He spotted the young Duke of Salamanca drawing stacks of white from the bookies[.] — Charles Raven, *Underworld Nights*, p. 174, 1956
- The Pope is the world's biggest bookie. Makes people bet on their own salvation. — *The Bad Lieutenant*, 1992

books *noun*
used as a figurative description of membership in a criminal organization *US, 1964*
- — *American Speech*, p. 305, December 1964: "Lingua cosa nostra"

- The bosses are sitting on millions and they say, you no do-a this, you no do-a that—meanwhile they close the books and the soldiers have to drive trucks on the side to live. — Edwin Torres, *Carlito's Way*, p. 41, 1975
- "When they open the books, they won't put you up. Don't you want to be a wiseguy?" — Joseph Pistone, *Donnie Brasco*, p. 298, 1987

book up *verb*
to study *US, 1975*
- — *American Speech*, p. 56, Spring–Summer 1975: "Razorback slang"

boola-boola *adjective*
characterized by extreme boosterism and spirited support of an institution *US, 1900*
The song "Boola Boola" has been one of Yale University's football fight songs since 1901 when it was written by Allan M. Hirsh, who explained the meaning of the word as follows: "It is interesting to note that many people have asked us what the word 'Boola' meant, and we said it was Hawaiian and meant a joy cry. We stuck to this for several years until someone came along and pointed out to us that there was no B in the Hawaiian language and therefore Boola could not possibly be Hawaiian. So the fact remains that we do not know what it means, except that it was euphonious and easy to sing and to our young ears sounded good." The song was an "adaptation" of an 1898 "La Hoola Boola" performed by Bob Cole and Billy Johnson.
- It was a real boola-boola reunion. — Edwin Torres, *After Hours*, p. 294, 1979
- — *Yale Alumni Magazine*, October 2000

boolhipper *noun*
a black leather jacket with a belt in the back *US, 1970*
- — Roger D. Abrahams, *Deep Down in the Jungle*, p. 258, 1970

boom *noun*
1 potent marijuana *US, 1946*
- Stoned Raider, in the Temple of Boom — Cypress Hill, *Stoned Raider*, 1995
- Yo, Cass, you got any boom? — *Kids*, 1995
2 fake crack cocaine *US, 2001*
- One of the officers patted him down and felt a "rock-like substance," said Sgt. Clifford Gatlin. Smith told the officer it was "boom," street slang for fake crack cocaine. — *Daily Town Talk (Alexandria, Louisiana)*, p. 3A, 25th April 2001

boom and zoom; b and z *verb*
in air combat, to use a relative altitude advantage to attack an opponent (to boom) and then return to a superior position out of danger (to zoom) *US, 1986*
- But that bunch of good old boys, big-shot lawyers, ex-Marine Corps heroes, ring-knocking fighter jocks who can't get enough of that boomin' and zoomin'[.] — Larry Heinemann, *Paco's Story*, p. 157, 1986

boom-boom *noun*
1 sex *US, 1964*
From Asian pidgin. Major use in Vietnam during the war.
- — Carl Fleischhauer, *A Glossary of Army Slang*, p. 5, 1968
- [F]rom then on the recreation area at the lake was referred to jokingly by the Jumping Mustangs as the "Boom-boom" area. — Kenneth Mertel, *Year of the Horse*, p. 213, 1968
- "Come on, we make boom boom, Joe." — William Pelfrey, *The Big V*, p. 19, 1972
- "No more boom-boom for that mamma-san," the Marine said, that same, tired remark you heard every time the dead turned out to be women. — Michael Herr, *Dispatches*, p. 199, 1977
- She love you good. Boom-boom long time. Ten dollar. — *Full Metal Jacket*, 1987
2 live music *US, 2003*
- Quirky alt-rockers The Anarchy Orchestra will provide the boom boom[.] — *The Record (Bergen County, New Jersey)*, p. 37, 24th October 2003
3 a pistol *US, 1945*
- — Lou Shelly, *Hepcats Jive Talk Dictionary*, p. 22, 1945
4 a cowboy or Western movie *US, 1947*
- — Marcus Hanna Boulware, *Jive and Slang of Students in Negro Colleges*, 1947

boom-boom *verb*
to copulate *US, 1971*
- Hey, baby-san, you boum-boum G.I.? — *Screw*, p. 5, 15th February 1971

- At least they were honest about who they were boom-booming. — Larry Chambers, *Recondo*, p. 124, 1992

boom-boom girl *noun*
a prostitute *US, 1966*
Vietnam usage.
- The rest of the day was spent in finding a boom-boom girl. — Charles Anderson, *The Grunts*, p. 159, 1976

boom-boom house; boom-boom parlor *noun*
a brothel *US, 1966*
- — *American-Statesman* (Austin, Texas), p. A7, 9th January 1966
- — Carl Fleischhauer, *A Glossary of Army Slang*, p. 5, 1968
- He had what he called "Boom-boom Parlors," a common name referring to prostitution in Vietnam. — Kenneth Mertel, *Year of the Horse*, p. 213, 1968
- A trip to the local boom-boom house not only enabled the three LRP's to relieve a lot of tension, but also provided them with the information that the air force had an enormous amount of beer stored over in their supply center. — Gary Linderer, *The Eyes of the Eagle*, p. 136, 1991

boom-booms *noun*
the female breasts *US, 2005*
- [H]er bare boom-booms are reflected mesmerizingly in the mirror. — Mr. Skin, *Mr. Skin's Skincyclopedia*, p. 207, 2005

boom-booms-a-gogo *noun*
a unit of quad-fifty machine guns *US, 1982*
Korean war usage.
- — Frank Hailey, *Soldier Talk*, p. 7, 1982

boom box *noun*
a large, portable radio and tape player *US, 1981*
- They measured their warrior cakewalk to a boombox beat as deadly and mechanical as automatic fire. — Seth Morgan, *Homeboy*, p. 18, 1990
- I could hear sirens and boom boxes and Valley kids howling at the moon as if they owned the night. — Armistead Maupin, *Maybe the Moon*, p. 138, 1992
- And there were a lot of young people on the streets, leaning into cars, chatting, listening to boom boxes. — Joseph Wambaugh, *Finnegan's Week*, p. 59, 1993
- The normal noises of the Cabrinin-Taylor projects continued to accompany their weekly sexual get together: doors slamming, boom boxes blaring raps, screams, yells, car horns blasting[.] — Odie Hawkins, *Amazing Grace*, p. 9, 1993

boom-dee-boom *noun*
sex *US, 1984*
An embellishment of the more common **BOOM-BOOM**.
- Some of the boom-dee-boom girls. Some of the owners of the boom-dee-boom clubs. — Wallace Terry, *Bloods*, p. 123, 1984

boomer *noun*
1 a portable radio, tape player, or CD player *US, 1992*
- "Hell, man, here we just tryin' to save by for scorin' usselfs a CD boomer." — Jess Mowry, *Way Past Cool*, p. 225, 1992

2 a nuclear submarine armed with missiles *US, 1976*
- On the other question, no, they've never recalled all their boomers at once, but they do occasionally reshuffle all their positions at once. — Tom Clancy, *The Hunt for Red October*, p. 88, 1984

3 a member of the baby boom generation, born between roughly 1945 and 1955 *US, 1982*
- The boomers have failed to provide or protect or prepare us for any kind of hopeful life. — *Empire Records*, 1995
- It was all so depressing. Boomers weren't supposed to get old. It sucked. — Joseph Wambaugh, *Floaters*, p. 138, 1996

4 during aerial refueling, the boom operator on the fueling plane *US, 1986*
- The bomber pilot's task was then simply to formate within a prescribed envelope while the boomer, the refueling operator, actually flew the patented Boeing boom into the receptacle. — Walter J. Boyne and Steven L. Thompson, *The Wild Blue*, p. 442, 1986

boomerang *noun*
1 a young person who moves back in with their parents after moving out *US, 1997*
- — Vann Wesson, *Generation X Field Guide and Lexicon*, p. 26, 1997

2 a repeated offender, a recidivist *US, 2002*
- — Gary K. Farlow, *Prison-ese*, p. 5, 2002

3 in television and movie making, a device that holds a filter in front of a light *US, 1987*
- — Ira Konigsberg, *The Complete Film Dictionary*, p. 33, 1987

boomerang *verb*
to return to prison shortly after being released *US, 1992*
- — William K. Bentley and James M. Corbett, *Prison Slang*, 1992

boomers *noun*
large female breasts *US, 2005*
- Kinked-up Lisa dons a leather outfit that showcases her boomers and buncakes while she drips hot wax on her man-friend. — Mr. Skin, *Mr. Skin's Skincyclopedia*, p. 79, 2005

booming *adjective*
excellent *US, 1990*
- Baby was fine, body was boomin', like right outta Jet centerfold o somethin'. — *Boyz N The Hood*, 1990
- — Kenn "Naz" Young, *Naz's Dictionary of Teen Slang*, p. 13, 1993

boom squad *noun*
the group of prison guards who are used to quell disturbances *US, 2000*
- Depending on whom you ask, the ESU, or "boom squad," is a group of dedicated officers with the toughest job on the island or a bunch of testosterone-fueled thugs who get a rush from brawling with the inmates. — *Village Voice*, p. 62, 19th December 2000

boon *noun*
1 a dollar *US, 1957*
- "Fifty dollars, sweet Jesus, fifty boons you'll never see again, lord have mercy!" — Herbert Simmons, *Corner Boy*, p. 21, 1957

2 a black person *US, 1967*
Possibly reduced from **BOON COON** (a good friend) or as outlined in the following citation.
- ["A]ll these boons just sat there laughing at me." "Boons?" I said. "What's boons?" "You know," she said. "Black guys." "Why do you call them that?" "I dunno. From 'baboons,' I guess." I didn't say anything. — Lester Bangs, *Psychotic Reactions and Carburetor Dung*, p. 272, 1978

boon *adjective*
close, intimate *US, 1969*
- They pounded each other on the back. They looked like boon buddies. — Iceberg Slim (Robert Beck), *Pimp*, p. 123, 1969

boon coon *noun*
a very close friend *US, 1958*
- He said, "About a month ago, your 'boon coon Party' caught sixty in the county." — Iceberg Slim (Robert Beck), *Pimp*, p. 79, 1977
- That's cool for you. You his boon-coon. — Edwin Torres, *Q & A*, p. 187, 1977

boondagger *noun*
a lesbian with overtly masculine mannerisms and affectations *US, 1972*
- I was mad at Loren for being loyal to a crazy old boondagger like her instead of someone who really cared about him. — John McMans, *Bitter Milk*, p. 7, 2005

boondock *verb*
in tiddlywinks, to shoot from a position far from the action *US, 1977*
- — *Verbatim*, p. 525, December 1977

boondocker *noun*
a party held in the country *US, 1966*
- — *Current Slang*, p. 1, Winter 1966

boondockers *noun*
marine-issued combat boots *US, 1942*
- In preparation for disembarking I'm wearing the following articles: scivvie shirt and drawers, long johns, flannel shirt, utility pants, cold-weather pants, pile-lined vest, park w/hood, gloves and inserts, flannel cap, socks, boondockers[.] — Martin Russ, *The Last Parallel*, p. 58, 1957

I could sure use those size-twelve boondockers of yours. — Joseph Wambaugh, *The Blue Knight*, p. 137, 1973

Kavanaugh lay next to MacCauley, his face dead white, his boondockers smelling of vomit. — Alfred Coppel, *The Burning Mountain*, p. 211, 1983

The first thing he saw was the man's shoes, black boondockers, then bell-bottom jeans, then the gym bag and the Uzi. — Stephen Coonts, *Final Flight*, p. 338, 1988

boondocks *noun*
the remote end of nowhere *US, 1909*

Schauer told me he saw the accident but it is so far out in the boondocks people were afraid to stop. — *San Francisco Examiner*, p. 125, 21st June 1964

[H]e had this thing for a P.R. chick, which in those days was unheard of, so like his uncle kept him in the boondocks. — Edwin Torres, *Carlito's Way*, p. 22, 1975

boondoggle *noun*
a business trip or venture designed for the enjoyment of those involved, not for its stated purpose *US, 1935*

It's just a big boondoggle for the Army; they're trying to get the guided missile program away from the Air Force. — Max Shulman, *Rally Round the Flag, Boys!*, p. 95, 1957

boonie hat; boonie cap *noun*
a fatigue hat, made of cotton canvas with a brim around, that kept the sun and rain off the heads of American soldiers in Vietnam *US, 1972*

There were four, with AK-47s and cloth boony hats. — William Pelfrey, *The Big V*, p. 144, 1972

[C]amouflage T-shirts for the kids, stiff-brim drill instructor hats, Ranger boonie hats and combat caps, holsters, binoculars, canteens, knives, and bayonets with sawtooth blades[.] — Elmore Leonard, *Bandits*, p. 266, 1987

He was dressed in OD fatigues and a boonie cap. — Gary Linderer, *The Eyes of the Eagle*, p. 179, 1991

As the rotor blades picked up speed, I pulled my boonie hat off my head and stuck it in my shirt. — Larry Chambers, *Recondo*, p. 51, 1992

boonie rat *noun*
a soldier serving in the jungle or other remote area *US, 1967*

In Vietnam, he goes by an assortment of names—the Grunt, Boonie Rat, Line Dog, Ground Pounder, Hill Humper, or Jarhead. — David Reed, *Up Front in Vietnam*, p. 3, 1967

Everyone has always portrayed infantryman, boonierat, as dumb. Everyone, except anyone who has ever been a boonierat. — John M. Del Vecchio, *The 13th Valley*, p. 121, 1982

The fort afforded showers, bunkers, private rooms, movies, girls, and enough equipment and supplies to make us boonie rats drool. — David Donovan, *Once a Warrior King*, p. 217, 1985

From this point on, with the possible exception of a seven-day rest-and-recuperation (R&R) leave (probably spent somewhere else in Asia), he would live each day of the next year in the surreal, virtually indescribable existence of the "boonie rat." — James L. Estep, *Company Commander, Vietnam*, p. 22, 1996

boonies *noun*
a remote rural area *US, 1956*
An abbreviation of **BOONDOCKS**.

Special Forces in remote outposts, boondocks, or "boonies," military slang for just about as far from civilization as you can get. — Elaine Shepard, *The Doom Pussy*, p. 53, 1967

In the boonies the whole time? — Ronald J. Glasser, *365 Days*, p. 130, 1971

"Anything more than six blocks from Hollywood and Vine is to you the boonies," Pachoulo said. — Robert Campbell, *Juice*, p. 168, 1988

The place was deep in the boonies, but after a few wrong turns on backcountry roads, we came to a tiny, run-down shack perched on stilts over a steep hillside. — C.D. Payne, *Youth in Revolt*, p. 37, 1993

booorrring *adjective*
very boring *US, 1981*
Slang by drawn out pronunciation. From popular entertainment.

Would you want to drive a truck all day? Boorrring! — C.D. Payne, *Youth in Revolt*, p. 217, 1993

Back in the early part of my career, I think Cleveland was the most boring city to go in and play. But now it's one of the hottest cities to go in and play. But when I came into the league, it was booorring. — *Denver Post*, p. C4, 27th July 2003

boo out *verb*
to leave *US, 1959*

— *American Speech*, p. 154, May 1959: "Gator (University of Florida) slang"

boo-reefer *noun*
marijuana *US, 1972*

— David Claerbaut, *Black Jargon in White America*, p. 58, 1972

boost *noun*
1 a theft, especially a car theft *US, 1995*

You down with the boost? — *Kids*, 1995

MEMPHIS: What kind of job? ATLEY JACKSON: A boost. A big boost. — *Gone in 60 Seconds*, 2000

2 in poker, an increased or raised bet *US, 1988*

— George Percy, *The Language of Poker*, p. 12, 1988

3 a background player in a large confidence swindle *US, 1985*

— M. Allen Henderson, *How Con Games Work*, p. 218, 1985

▸ **on the boost**
engaged in shoplifting *US, 1962*

— Joseph E. Ragen and Charles Finston, *Inside the World's Toughest Prison*, p. 810, 1962

boost *verb*
1 to steal, especially to steal a car or to shoplift *US, 1928*

Only thing I can think of is to go in the Business with Ritchie or start boosting. — William Burroughs, *Letters to Allen Ginsberg 1953–1957*, p. 67, 13th October 1954

"Pinched. Jobbed. Swiped. Stole," he says, happily. "You know, man, like somebody boosted my threads." — Ken Kesey, *One Flew Over the Cuckoo's Nest*, p. 94, 1962

Then there was boostin' in department stores—and there was dice, cards, writin' numbers (single action) for Jakie Cooperman[.] — Edwin Torres, *Carlito's Way*, p. 14, 1975

But you can't boost with no shopping bag. — Kate Millett, *The Prostitution Papers*, p. 116, 1976

2 in poker, to increase the amount bet on a hand *US, 1967*

— Albert H. Morehead, *The Complete Guide to Winning Poker*, p. 257, 1967

▸ **boost one**
to defecate *US, 1992*

— *Surfer Magazine*, p. 30, February 1992

booster *noun*
1 a thief, especially a shoplifter or car thief *US, 1908*

"Boosters," Inspector Smith explained, "pick on out-of-state cars because they know the people are traveling and have a lot of stuff with 'em." — *San Francisco Call-Bulletin*, 28th June 1949

He would have a booster someday. He had made up his mind to that. — Clarence Cooper Jr., *The Scene*, p. 31, 1960

Most male addicts are eventually pimps, boosters, or pushers. — Alexander Trocchi, *Cain's Book*, p. 158, 1960

That was the gang of organized boosters, who would deliver to order, in one day, C.O.D., any kind of garment you desired. — Malcolm X and Alex Haley, *The Autobiography of Malcolm X*, p. 66, 1964

2 a full-time, career thief *US, 1977*

— Robert C. Prus and C.R.D. Sharper, *Road Hustler*, p. 169, 1977

3 a criminal who specializes in selling stolen goods *US, 1985*

Some Boosters specialize in such wares as jewelry, cars, dope, etc. — Gene Sorrows, *All About Carnivals*, p. 11, 1985

4 a confederate of a cheat who lures players to a card game, carnival concession or other game of chance *US, 1906*

— Don Wilmeth, *The Language of American Popular Entertainment*, p. 30, 1981

— Thomas L. Clark, *The Dictionary of Gambling and Gaming*, p. 24, 1987

5 an additional dose of a drug taken to prolong intoxication *US, 1970*

— William D. Alsever, *Glossary for the Establishment and Other Uptight People*, p. 4, 1970

booster fold *noun*
a special inside jacket pocket used by shoplifters *US, 1972*

With both suits tucked under my armpits in a booster fold, I scanned the moving traffic until I saw an empty cab. — Donald Goines, *Whoreson*, p. 88, 1972

booster stick *noun*
a tobacco cigarette that has been enhanced with marijuana or marijuana extract *US, 1973*

— Jay Robert Nash, *Dictionary of Crime*, p. 40, 1992

boosting bloomers; booster bloomers *noun*
underwear designed for concealing merchandise that has been shoplifted *US, 1972*

- Boots was able to go back to work, so I stopped her from doing any more boosting. Her boosting bloomers were packed away for later use. — Donald Goines, *Whoreson*, p. 134, 1972
- Booster Bloomers—a large pair of underclothing worn under the outer pants or dress—can be used to "steal hundreds of dollars' worth of goods in a matter of a few seconds." — *San Francisco Examiner*, p. 6, 22nd February 1974

boot *noun*
1 vomit *US, 2006*

- "It's clean air—no beer or piss or boot." — Chris Miller, *The Real Animal House*, p. 136, 2006

2 a black person *US, 1954*

- What's wrong with a white broad helping two spades? She's a "boot." She looks like what she is. — Iceberg Slim (Robert Beck), *Pimp*, p. 207, 1969
- One boot got the tom-tom and the other grabbed a flute. — Steve Cannon, *Groove, Bang, and Jive Around*, p. 187, 1969
- Yet I hadn't seen a boot or a spic. — Robert Deane Pharr, *S.R.O.*, p. 12, 1971

3 a newly enlisted or drafted recruit in the armed services, especially the marines *US, 1911*

- For a good many years, as long as many an older salt can remember, the word "boot" has been synonymous with the younger and less experienced men of the Navy and Marine Corps. — *Leatherneck*, p. 7, September 1944
- A former Marine "boot" told the courtmartial of S/Sgt. Matthew McKeon that the drill instructor warned his platoon nonwinners would drown while sharks would devour the rest before they plunged into the waters of Ribbon Creek. — *San Francisco News*, p. 1, 21st July 1956
- I've never seen a more disgusting, disreputable bunch of boots in my life. — Earl Thompson, *Tattoo*, p. 141, 1974
- At 21, Laing, a quiet, dark, and handsome man from Waterloo, Iowa, just a few years out of undergraduate school in engineering at Dubuque's Catholic Loras University, was just a "boot ensign." — Robert K. Wilcox, *Scream of Eagles*, p. 50, 1990

4 in the US Army, a second lieutenant *US, 1966*

- — *True*, p. 4, July 1966
- — Carl Fleischhauer, *A Glossary of Army Slang*, p. 5, 1968
- I'm a boot lieutenant and that's the lowest thing in the Marine Corps. — Mark Barker, *Nam*, p. 40, 1981

5 amusement or pleasure *US, 1979*

- Down Atherton way, the peasants are getting a big boot out of the guy who's having a home built on Valparaiso Ave. — *San Francisco Examiner*, p. 25, 2nd January 1952
- He got such a boot out of being a big-dog fight manager, he never found out why I couldn't lose weight except in a steam bath. — Rocky Garciano (with Rowland Barber), *Somebody Up There Likes Me*, p. 261, 1955
- You'll Get a Real Boot out of this Beauty [Advertisement] — *San Francisco Examiner*, p. I-13, 30th March 1956
- I told her I packed the pipe by mistake and she said she wanted to give it to you anyway since you seemed to get a boot out of it[.] — Darryl Ponicsan, *The Last Detail*, p. 112, 1970

6 a bootleg product *US, 1999*

- He'd copy hits, big ones, Madonna, Elton John, the Spice Girls, and sell the boots down in South America at a discount. — Elmore Leonard, *Be Cool*, p. 205, 1999

7 while injecting a drug intravenously, the drawing of blood into the syringe to mix with the drug *US, 1987*

- I was just finishing up, the needle still in the vein for one last boot down the old line[.] — Jim Carroll, *Forced Entries*, p. 47, 1987

8 a cigarette *US, 1996*

- — John Fahs, *Cigarette Confidential*, p. 301, 1996

9 an error, especially in sports *US, 1913*

- — Lou Shelly, *Hepcats Jive Talk Dictionary*, p. 8, 1945

10 a linear amplifier for a citizens' band radio *US, 1976*

- — Lawrence Teeman, *Consumer Guide Good Buddy's CB Dictionary*, p. 32, 1976

11 a condom *US, 1966*

- — John D. Bell et al., *Loosely Speaking*, p. 3, 1966

12 in television and movie making, a tripod cover *US, 1987*

- — Ira Konigsberg, *The Complete Film Dictionary*, p. 33, 1987

▸ **in the boot**
drunk *US, 1980*

- Roger got a couple in the boot one night at my house (Roger does not do that anymore, since he made partner) and told me candidly what Grace thought of me[.] — George Higgins, *Kennedy for the Defense*, p. 62, 1980

boot *verb*
1 while injecting a drug, to draw blood into the syringe, diluting the drug dose so as to prolong the effect of the injection *US, 1952*

- Just look at me boot it and you will. — Hal Ellson, *The Golden Spike*, p. 139, 1952
- "Lou'll turn on next if Fay ever stops booting it." Fay's thick, dark, purplish-red blood rose and fell in the eye-dropper like a column of gory mercury in a barometer. — Alexander Trocchi, *Cain's Book*, p. 166, 1960
- The technique, known as "booting," is believed to prolong the drug's initial effect. — James Mills, *The Panic in Needle Park*, p. 78, 1966
- And as you feel this goodness take over, you start playing with your blood—that's a kick. You "boot" it awhile. — John Gimenez, *Up Tight!*, p. 44, 1967

2 to kick something, literally or in the slang sense of "breaking a habit" *US, 1877*

- — Francis J. Rigney and L. Douglas Smith, *The Real Bohemia*, p. xiii, 1961
- You think the white folks booted you in the butt? — Iceberg Slim (Robert Beck), *The Naked Soul of Iceberg Slim*, p. 203, 1971
- My girlfriend kicked me out of the apartment, I got booted out of Capitol Records, and somebody wrote "Fag-Mobile" on my gas tank. — *Airheads*, 1994

3 in horse racing, to spur or kick a horse during a race *US, 1951*

- — David W. Maurer, *Argot of the Racetrack*, p. 15, 1951

4 in a game, to misplay a ball *US, 1976*

- I think I booted one that should've been a double play[.] — George V. Higgins, *The Judgment of Deke Hunter*, p. 86, 1976

5 to vomit *US, 1971*

- Booted his insides all over my God damn shoes and my last pair of dry socks. — John Sayles, *Union Dues*, pp. 57–58, 1977
- — Connie Eble (Editor), *UNC-CH Campus Slang*, p. 2, Spring 1988
- Looking uncomfortable and defeated, he turned to his left, meaning to burp, and instead booted all over the back of a brunette we had just been talking to. — Elissa Stein and Kevin Leslie, *Chunks*, p. 37, 1997
- Boot on purpose? — Chris Miller, *The Real Animal House*, p. 88, 2006

boot *adjective*
inexperienced and untested *US, 1946*

- [H]e turned around and saw this boot ensign standing there, giving him the dirtiest kind of look. — Thomas Heggen, *Mister Roberts*, p. 23, 1946

boot-and-shoe *adjective*
(used of a drug addict) desperately addicted *US, 1936*

- He said she was "just a boot-and-shoe hype" with a $60-a-day heroin habit. — *San Francisco Examiner*, p. 12, 9th March 1962

boot and shoe thief *noun*
a criminal who robs parking meters using an adjustable key *US, 1972*

- Now they have on that by just changin' a little dial on it they can use one key and open any meter in any district. We call those kind of thieves "boot and shoe thieves." Where that's derived from is when they start stealing with a boot on one foot and a shoe on the other. — Harry King, *Box Man*, p. 71, 1972

booted *adjective*
intoxicated by marijuana, or another narcotic drug *US, 1995*

- We was too booted to see the cops comin'. — Lois Stavsky et al., *A2Z*, p. 11, 1995

booter *noun*
a jockey with an inclination to spur his mount incessantly *US, 1959*

- The number of riders in America who will give a horse of any age a chance to settle into stride is pitifully few, the great majority being strictly "whoop-de-do" booters who might have been developed by the late Bill Daly. — *Daily Racing Form*, p. 4, 27th November 1959

booth bimbo; booth bunny *noun*
an attractive, well-built, sometimes scantily clad woman hired to work in a company's booth during a trade show *US, 1989*

- Booth bunnies, flashy video displays and tacky giveaways ("Register Here To Win a Free Ounce of Gold") notwithstanding, this is indeed gold's darkest hour. — *Boston Globe*, p. 73, 31st May 1989

- Did it ever occur to you that the booth bimbos are just as proud of their work as you are proud of being a member of the plastics industry—whatever that is? [Letter to editor] — *Plastic News*, p. 7, 3rd January 1994
- Women are underrepresented among the professional-managerial types who frequent Comidex and overrepresented among the "booth bunnies," the working girls who hawk wares by looking pretty. — *San Francisco Bay Guardian*, 29th November 2000

booties *noun*
1 rubber surf boots *US, 1987*
- — Mitch McKissick, *Surf Lingo*, 1987

2 boots, especially knitted boots for a baby *US, 1965*
- Who cares? You can buy booties. — John Nichols, *The Sterile Cuckoo*, p. 186, 1965

boot it!; boot it baby!
used as an exhortation to continue *US, 1968*
- — Hy Lit, *Hy Lit's Unbelievable Dictionary of Hip Words for Groovy People*, p. 6, 1968

bootleg *noun*
illegally manufactured alcohol *US, 1898*
- It used to be a bootleg spot during prohibition[.] — Mickey Spillane, *I, The Jury*, p. 43, 1947
- We would buy five-gallon containers of bootleg, funnel it into the bottles, then deliver, according to Hymie's instructions, this or that many crates back to the bars. — Malcolm X and Alex Haley, *The Autobiography of Malcolm X*, p. 124, 1964

bootleg *verb*
1 to manufacture or provide something illegally *US, 1928*
- We finally found a guy bootlegging rides and he took us to the project where my sister Dolores lived with her three kids. — Dick Gregory, *Nigger*, p. 116, 1964

2 to manufacture or distribute illegal alcohol *US, 1922*
- He used to bootleg whiskey from the mountains[.] — Jack Kerouac, *On the Road*, p. 215, 1957

3 in roller derby, to deviate from the scripted game plan *US, 1999*
- A skater who bootlegs is viewed with disfavor, usually accused of showboating. — Keith Coppage, *Roller Derby to Roller Jam*, p. 126, 1999

bootleg *adjective*
1 smuggled; illegally copied; unofficial; counterfeit *US, 1889*
Derives from the practice of carrying a flat bottle of alcohol hidden in a boot leg.
- Another Negro industry is the sale of bootleg booze. — Jack Lait and Lee Mortimer, *Washington Confidential*, p. 55, 1951
- He got tagged smuggling a truckload of bootleg cigarettes up from Virginia[.] — Janet Evanovich, *Seven Up*, p. 3, 2001

2 imitation *US, 1893*
- Half of the Black "militants" ain't nothing but a bunch of potheads, bootleg preachers and coffeehouse intellectuals. — H. Rap Brown, *Die Nigger Die!*, p. 104, 1969

3 (used of an action paper) unofficial, advance *US, 1986*
- — Department of the Army, *Staff Officer's Guidebook*, p. 56, 1986

bootlegger *noun*
a manufacturer or a dealer in illegally manufactured alcohol *US, 1890*
- The bootlegger's product had to be good, and his prices reasonable. — Jim Thompson, *Bad Boy*, p. 391, 1953

bootlegger turn *noun*
a 180-degree turn executed while driving fast accomplished by a combination of spinning the wheel, shifting down the gears and accelerating *US, 1955*
- — *American Speech*, p. 98, May 1956: "Smugglers' argot in the southwest"
- It was Junior Johnson specifically, however, who was famous for the "bootleg turn" or "about face." — Tom Wolfe, *The Kandy-Kolored Tangerine-Flake Streamlined Baby*, p. 128, 1965

bootlick *verb*
to seek favor through obsequious behavior *US, 1845*
- [A]nd allows the television networks to recover some of the dignity they lose every time they bootlick Lewis until their tongues grow raw and grisly. — *Pittsburgh Post-Gazette*, p. B2, 9th January 2004

bootlicker *noun*
a person who seeks favor through obsequious behavior *US, 1848*

- We got inside, and here come the bootlickers, scared niggers, niggers who were jiving, niggers who were talking shit. — Bobby Seale, *Seize the Time*, p. 73, 1970
- Seale had come ambivalently, having okayed King's being called a "bootlicker" in Panther newspapers. — *Washington Post*, p. D1, 10th March 1978
- Of course, he doesn't say the number of listeners Limbaugh has and that they're coast to coast; he just refers to them as bootlickers. [Letter to Editor] — *Tampa (Florida) Tribune*, p. 10, 8th October 2003

boot mooch *noun*
a person who is always asking others for a cigarette *US, 1996*
- — John Fahs, *Cigarette Confidential*, p. 301, 1996

boots *noun*
▸ **put the boots to**
to have sex with someone *US, 1933*
- I'd rather put the boots to Mrs. A. than Mrs. S. — *Screw*, p. 9, 18th July 1969

boot scoot *verb*
to dance side-by-side in a line to country and western music *US, 1991*
- — *American Speech*, p. 177, Summer 1994: "Among the new words"

boot suppository *noun*
any strong measure taken to encourage an obnoxious patient to leave a hospital *US, 1994*
An image based on a "kick in the ass."
- — Sally Williams, *"Strong" Words*, p. 135, 1994

bootsy *adjective*
bad, unpleasant *US, 2003*
- — *San Francisco Chronicle*, p. E5, 10th August 2003
- — Rick Ayers (Editor), *Berkeley High Slang Dictionary*, p. 14, 2004

boot-up *noun*
a dose of heroin *US, 1953*
- "How about a boot-up? I got enough dough for a reefer, but I sure could do real good with a couple sniffs of the horse." — Dale Krame, *Teen-Age Gangs*, p. 55, 1953

boot up *verb*
to prepare for a fight *US, 1998*
- — Ethan Hilderbrant, *Prison Slang*, p. 15, 1998

booty *adjective*
unpleasant; unattractive *US, 1997*
- — *Maybeck High School Yearbook (Berkeley, California)*, 1997
- — *San Francisco Chronicle*, p. E5, 10th August 2003

booty; bootie *noun*
1 the buttocks *US, 1928*
- Wine-and-whisky-taster, downtown money-waster / back-binder, booty-grinder, sweetspot-finder. — Dennis Wepman et al., *The Life*, p. 148, 1976
- Big country bootie, big country titties. — *Boyz N The Hood*, 1990
- Breda knew he'd scope out the woman's booty before closing the door, and he did. — Joseph Wambaugh, *Fugitive Nights*, p. 45, 1992

2 the vagina *US, 1925*
- — Edith A. Folb, *runnin' down some lines*, p. 230, 1980

booty bandit *noun*
an aggressive, predatory male homosexual *US, 1962*
- Fat Rat had a reputation for being a "booty bandit" and thrived on weak men with tight asses. — Sanyika Shakur, *Monster*, p. 293, 1993
- Inmates subject to rape ("punks") face threats and violence perpetrated by stronger inmates ("daddies," "jockers," or "booty bandits") who initiate unwanted sexual acts. — *Corrections Today*, p. 100, December 1996

booty bump *noun*
the rectal ingestion of a drug *US, 2006*
- Booty bump: A hit of drug, such as crystal meth, taken rectally, usually as a prelude to high-risk casual sex. — Emma Taylor, *Em and Lo's Rec Sex*, p. 23, 2006

booty bump *verb*
to ingest drugs, usually methamphetamine, diluted in an enema *US, 2002*
Collected from a recovering methamphetamine addict in Los Angeles, 2002.

booty-bust *verb*
to play the active role in anal sex *US, 2000*
- "I can think of something worse than being booty-busted." — Paul Beatty, *Tuff*, p. 150, 2000

booty call *noun*
a date made for the sole purpose of engaging in sex *US, 1997*
- — Judi Sanders, *Da Bomb!*, p. 4, 1997
- Just another B.C.—booty call—to be made on weekends. — Eric Jerome Dickey, *Cheaters*, p. 29, 1999
- He cruises the streets of L.A. in one long booty call. — Ana Loria, *1 2 3 Be A Porn Star!*, p. 111, 2000

booty-chokers *noun*
very tight pants *US, 1994*
- I will admit he [R. Kelly] had too many girls in booty-chokers, shaking their butts on the screen. — *k12.chat.senior*, 10th December 1994

booty drought *noun*
a sustained lack of sex *US, 1989*
- — Pamela Munro, *U.C.L.A. Slang*, p. 23, 1989

booty hole *noun*
the anus *US, 1998*
- This meant pulling my ass cheeks apart while they looked in my booty hole. — Renay Jackson, *Oaktown Devil*, p. 89, 1998

booty juice *noun*
the drug MDMA, the recreational drug best known as ecstasy, dissolved in any liquid *US, 1997*
- — Jim Crotty, *How to Talk American*, p. 87, 1997

bootylicious *adjective*
sexually attractive, especially with reference to the buttocks *US, 2001*
A compound of **BOOTY** (the buttocks) and "delicious."
- I don't think you / Ready for this / 'Cause my body too / Bootylicious for ya babe — Destiny's Child, *Bootylicious*, 2001

booze *noun*
alcoholic drink of any kind *UK, 1859*
- Betty [Ford] herself was America's First Lady when booze got a grip on her[.] — *Drugs An Adult Guide*, p. 31, December 2001

booze balloon *noun*
a heavy drinker's protruding stomach *US, 1979*
- That's a booze balloon around his middle region, and his shoulders slope a bit. — Robert J. Williams, *Skin Deep*, p. 17, 1979

boozed; boozed up *adjective*
drunk *US, 1737*
First recorded by amateur slang lexicographer Benjamin Franklin in 1737.
- I know you've been cutting down, but you can't be boozed up or have a hangover on this job. — Jim Thompson, *After Dark, My Sweet*, p. 42, 1955
- It's kind of hard to tell with him—he acts boozed up sometimes even when he's sober. — S.E. Hinton, *The Outsiders*, p. 27, 1967
- At that same moment, in the bedroom of Erica's flat, boozed Baptiste has the problem of dressing for a grocery shopping trip with Erica. — Iceberg Slim (Robert Beck), *Doom Fox*, p. 102, 1978
- "You know in While the City Sleeps, he was so boozed up they had to write it into the character." — John Ridley, *Love is a Racket*, p. 60, 1998

booze freak *noun*
an alcoholic *US, 1968*
- And we all know what the world can expect from Kennedy boozefreaks. — Hunter S. Thompson, *Fear and Loathing in America*, p. 48, 26th March 1968: Letter to Oscar Acosta

boozehound *noun*
an alcoholic *US, 1911*
- Her mother was married again to some booze hound. — J.D. Salinger, *Catcher in the Rye*, p. 32, 1951
- The booze hounds just make a man a lot of trouble for no fun. — Raymond Chandler, *The Long Goodbye*, p. 3, 1953
- I can't read a list of my academic credentials to every booze-hound that comes in the place. — *48 Hours*, 1982
- "He was a booze hound," I said. "A perpetual drunk." — John Ridley, *Love is a Racket*, p. 60, 1998

boozer *noun*
a drinker of alcohol; a habitual drinker; an alcoholic *UK, 1606*
- That was the only way to bring back to life the sodden, shaky boozers. — Jack Lait and Lee Mortimer, *Chicago Confidential*, p. 53, 1950
- These are the boozers who still have entree to the better clubs but no credit whatever. — Robert Sylvester, *No Cover Charge*, p. 231, 1956
- You hit the liver and it doesn't give, you know the guy was a boozer, had cirrhosis. — Elmore Leonard, *Bandits*, p. 13, 1987

booze-rooster *noun*
a heavy drinker *US, 1962*
- The way she talks, you'd think I was a regular booze-rooster. — M.K. Joseph, *Pound of Saffron*, p. 253, 1962

booze snooze *noun*
a nap taken in anticipation of a night of drinking *US, 2004*
- — Ben Applebaum and Derrick Pittman, *Turd Ferguson & The Sausage Party*, p. 9, 2004

bop *noun*
1 a youth gang fight *US, 1962*
- Third is a "bop." That can be a small group, five, ten, twenty guys from one team, having it out with the same number from a different team. — Lewis Yablonsky, *The Violent Gang*, p. 78, 1962

2 liveliness, spirit, rhythm *US, 1997*
- My father also didn't want any of us to be cool. "I noticed when you walked in here you had a little bop in your walk. No bopping around here." — Chris Rock, *Rock This!*, p. 45, 1997

3 a member of a youth gang *US, 1958*
- Heart, as the bop defines it, is audacity, devil-may-care disregard for self and consequences. — Harrison E. Salisbury, *The Shook-up Generation*, p. 25, 1958
- But the alienation of the Negro poor is such that the "hustler" or "bop" or unwed ADC mother, the members of the "deviant subculture," often respond with an attitude of "include me out." — Kenneth Clark, *Dark Ghetto*, p. 49, 1965

4 phencyclidine, the recreational drug known as PCP or angel dust *US, 1995*
- — Maria Hinojas, *Crews*, p. 166, 1995

5 nonsense *US, 1973*
- "Yeah, you talk all that off the wall bop," Roger stammered. — Joseph Nazel, *Black Cop*, p. 104, 1974

▸ **on the bop**
involved in youth gang activity *US, 1949*
- On the bop—on the prowl for street brawling. — William Bernard, *Jailbait*, p. 81, 1949

bop *verb*
1 to move with rhythm *US, 1959*
- Hobie put the box in and slammed the trunk lid down and the two bopped away. — John Sayles, *Union Dues*, p. 11105, 1977
- Glenn would listen to the two morons and watch Maurice bopping around from table to table giving brothers the brother handshake, touch fists in their ritual ways, Maurice the hipster, a dude black felt cap set on his head, just right, and shades. — Elmore Leonard, *Out of Sight*, p. 287, 1996

2 to have sex with someone *US, 1974*
- Your dick been limp for a year, 'cept when you're bopping your buddy Tony up there. — *Platoon*, 1986
- It's all that accountant-meets-cowboy, muscle-beach-bop-in-the-surf shit that they churn out on the West Coast at the rate of four miles of celluloid a day. — Jim Carroll, *Forced Entries*, p. 39, 1987

3 to engage in gang fighting *US, 1950*
- What were you doing, bopping it up? — Hal Ellson, *Tomboy*, p. 122, 1950
- The Cobras are an active "bopping" or street-fighting club which has its base in one of the older Brooklyn housing projects. — Harrison E. Salisbury, *The Shook-up Generation*, p. 19, 1958
- She's the head guy's deb. You stick your nose in there any more, the Mau Maus'll slice it off. My information is they're all set up to go bopping. — *Man's Magazine*, p. 12, February 1960
- The gang reverted to a "bopping"—i.e., a fighting and generally hell-raising—pattern. — Isidor Chein, *The Road to H*, p. 187, 1964

4 to hit someone, to beat someone *UK, 1928*
- [I] hung around with a crew up there setting fire to mansions early in the morning and bopping skinheads. — Jamie Mandelkau, *Buttons*, p. 30, 1971

5 in team gambling, to move to a card table identified by a confederate counting cards there to be primed for better-than-average odds *US, 1985*
- — Steve Kuriscak, *Casino Talk*, p. 5, 1985

bop glasses *noun*
horn-rimmed eye glasses *US, 1958*
From the style favored by bop jazz musicians.
- "Bop glasses," or simply "bops," were affected by many, often with tinted "windowpane" lenses. — Ira Gitler, *The Masters of Bebop*, p. 80, 2001

bop 'n slop *verb*
to lose your inhibitions and enjoy yourself at a party *US, 1968*
- — Collin Baker et al., *College Undergraduate Slang Study Conducted at Brown University*, p. 87, 1968

bop off *verb*
to leave *US, 1959*
- — *American Speech*, p. 154, May 1959: "Gator (University of Florida) slang"

bopper *noun*
1 a preteen or young teenager *US, 2005*
An abbreviation of **TEENYBOPPER**.
- Mobs of boppers would subway into Times Square at school break to purchase fake I.D.'s. — Josh Friedman, *When Sex Was Dirty*, p. 13, 2005

2 a fighter, especially a gang fighter *US, 1958*
- You're not only expected to talk like a bopper, but to think like one, too. — Morton Cooper, *High School Confidential*, p. 13, 1958
- I owed them nine more years, which they'd probably make me do if I joined up with the boppers. — Piri Thomas, *Down These Mean Streets*, p. 282, 1967
- Annette smiled and turned to face the crowd: high-school and college dropouts, ex-Muslims, cons, boppers and bullshit hustlers with their dates[.] — Steve Cannon, *Groove, Bang, and Jive Around*, p. 4, 1969

3 a song in the style of bebop jazz *US, 1965*
- Fifteen years ago he got caught with very little of what Charlie Parker and Dizzy were doing, and until he began recording boppers fast, he lost some bread as modern jazz became moderately popular. — Nat Hentoff, *Jazz Country*, p. 110, 1965

boppers *noun*
shoes *US, 1975*
- — *American Speech*, p. 56, Spring–Summer 1975: "Razorback slang"

boppy *adverb*
in an affected gang manner *US, 1967*
- You dig people watching you an' walk a little more boppy. — Piri Thomas, *Down These Mean Streets*, pp. 58–59, 1967

Borax *noun*
any low quality retail merchandise that is impressive on first glance *US, 1929*
- — Rachel S. Epstein and Nina Liebman, *Biz Speak*, p. 25, 1986

border *noun*
a capsule of a noncommercial barbiturate compound *US, 1971*
- — Eugene Landy, *The Underground Dictionary*, p. 39, 1971
- — Edith A. Folb, *runnin' down some lines*, p. 230, 1980

border work *noun*
subtle markings on the printed edge of the back of a playing card for identification of the card by a cheat *US, 1988*
- — George Percy, *The Language of Poker*, p. 12, 1988

born-again *noun*
a devout, conservative Christian who professes to have been born again in a religious sense *US, 1986*
Often uttered without sympathy.
- Sergeants and lieutenants, all born-agains and all ambitious. — James Ellroy, *Suicide Hill*, p. 635, 1986

Boro *noun*
a Marlboro™ cigarette *US, 1996*
- — John Fahs, *Cigarette Confidential*, p. 301, 1996

boro-boros *noun*
old clothes worn for dirty tasks *US, 1981*
Hawaiian youth usage.
- — Douglas Simonson, *Pidgin to da Max*, 1981

borrow *verb*
to steal *US, 1821*

- — Vincent J. Monteleone, *Criminal Slang*, p. 31, 1949
- — Terry Williams, *The Cocaine Kids*, p. 135, 1989

borsch!
used for expressing disgust *US, 1968*
- — Fred Hester, *Slang on the 40 Acres*, p. 10, 1968

Borscht Belt *noun*
a group of resort hotels in the Catskill Mountains of the eastern US with a primarily Jewish clientele *US, 1941*
Alluding to the cold beet soup "borscht" because of the eastern European heritage of many of the Jewish guests.
- — *American Speech*, December 1949
- It is hard to believe that anybody is unfamiliar with New York's Borscht Belt. Books, movies, plays and TV skits have centered around this vacationland in Sullivan County, about 100 miles north of New York City. — *San Francisco News Call-Bulletin*, p. 6, 22nd December 1962
- Damon Runyon described it [Grossinger's] as Lindy's with trees. It has also been called the ancestral home of the bagel, the pride of the "Borscht Belt," the Waldorf of the Catskills. — *San Francisco Examiner and Chronicle*, p. 11 (Travel), 25th February 1973
- The Emcee was a slimy, bald exile from the Borscht Belt. — Seth Morgan, *Homeboy*, p. 313, 1990

Borscht circuit *noun*
the Borscht belt *US, 1936*
- Great for a couple of lads who, when we first knew them owned one Catskills' Borscht Circuit hotel. — *San Francisco Examiner*, p. 35, 21st June 1966

boson *noun*
in computing, an imaginary concept, the smallest possible unit measuring the bogus content of something *US, 1997*
- — Andy Ihnatko, *Cyberspeak*, p. 29, 1997

boss *noun*
1 a prison guard or official *US, 1970*
- Pace up and down, pace up and down you, you're gonna get through a lot of paces before you get out of here. Yes boss. Always yes boss. — Kevin Mackey, *The Cure*, p. 101, 1970
- — Bruce Jackson, *Outside the Law*, p. 55, 1972
- — David Powis, *The Signs of Crime*, 1977
- When they were in a good mood they called us "screws," "four-by-twos" or "boss"; but when they were pissed off it degenerated to "fuckin' cunts" and "fuckin' dogs." — William Dodson, *The Sharp End*, p. 11, 2001

2 the best *US, 1878*
- Angel laughed. "Horse is the boss," he said. — Hal Ellson, *The Golden Spike*, p. 51, 1952

3 in poker, the best hand at a given moment *US, 1990*
- — Anthony Holden, *Big Deal*, p. 298, 1990

4 pure heroin *US, 1961*
- — Francis J. Rigney and L. Douglas Smith, *The Real Bohemia*, p. xiii, 1961

boss *adjective*
very good, excellent *US, 1873*
The word was around for 70 years before taking off, it was popular beyond description in 1965 and 1966.
- Even the kids who aren't full-time car nuts themselves will be influenced by which car is considered "boss." They use that word a lot, "boss." — Tom Wolfe, *The Kandy-Kolored Tangerine-Flake Streamline Baby*, p. 80, 1964
- Of all the people I have spoken to, only one person really thought they (beach movies) were "boss" (great) and that was my 10-year-old kid sister. [Letter to the Editor] — *Life*, p. 59, 6th August 1965
- They left the joint and "Willie" knew that he'd scored, when she ushered him into a chauffeur-driven limousine and to a boss pad in the East Seventies. — Babs Gonzales, *I Paid My Dues*, p. 101, 1967
- Don't you think the Beach Boys are boss? — *American Graffiti*, 1973

boss Charley *noun*
a white person or white people collectively *US, 1967*
- It doesn't matter, the end result, as long as trick Whitey, fuck up Boss Charley. — Lenny Bruce, *The Essential Lenny Bruce*, p. 12, 1967

boss game *noun*
a highly developed, status-conscious sense of style *US, 1975*
- Rembrandt, Remington, ain't no difference, man. It all mounts to the same thing—boss game. — Charles W. Moore, *A Brick for Mister Jones*, p. 113, 1975

boss hoss *noun*

an admired, popular man *US, 1968*

- — Hy Lit, *Hy Lit's Unbelievable Dictionary of Hip Words for Groovy People*, p. 6, 1968

boss player *noun*

a pimp with flair, style, and success *US, 1981*

- He talked game with him at every chance, lectured him on the pimping code, instilled contempt for the small-time popcorns and respect for the real boss players[.] — Alix Shulman, *On the Stroll*, p. 56, 1981

Boston coffee *noun*

coffee with a lot of cream or milk *US, 1958*

- "Do you like Boston Coffee?" she asked the young man brightly. "You mean coffee with a lot of cream?" "Half cream, half coffee," she informed him. — Terry Southern, *Flash and Filigree*, p. 109, 1958

Boston Glob *nickname*

the *Boston Globe* newspaper *US, 1981*

- — *CoEvolution Quarterly*, p. 27, Spring 1981

Boston marriage *noun*

an arrangement in which two women live together in an outwardly platonic relationship *US, 2001*

- So-called "Boston marriages," intense but ostensibly nonsexual relationships between two women, were well recognized, and in fact, self-consciously survive. — Jeffrey Weeks, *Same Sex Intimacies*, p. 54, 2001
- To fulfill this longing, many of us have created a version of the "Boston marriage," making romantic friendships where we daily experience true love. — bell hooks, *Communion*, p. 212, 2002

Boston tea party *noun*

a sexual fetish in which the sadist defecates or urinates on the masochist *US, 1967*

- — Dale Gordon, *The Dominion Sex Dictionary*, p. 31, 1967
- — Robert A. Wilson, *Playboy's Book of Forbidden Words*, pp. 46–47, 1972
- — Thomas Murray and Thomas Murrell, *The Language of Sadomasochism*, p. 43, 1989

both ways *noun*

a bet in craps both that the shooter will win and that the shooter will lose *US, 1950*

In craps, gamblers can bet that the shooter will win, that he will lose, or both.

- — *The Annals of the American Academy of Political and Social Sciences*, p. 120, May 1950

▸ **go both ways**

1 to be willing to play both the active and passive role in homosexual sex *US, 1972*

- All the punks go both ways, the queens don't. — Bruce Jackson, *In the Life*, p. 400, 1972
- "Some guys go both ways, stud. No offense." He retreats. — John Rechy, *Rushes*, p. 99, 1979

2 to be bisexual *US, 1988*

- "Two of the guys went both ways, she told me." — Roger Blake, *Love Clubs, Inc.*, p. 149, 1967
- You trying to tell me if I don't like spiders it means I go both ways? — Elmore Leonard, *Freaky Deaky*, p. 30, 1988

bottle *noun*

1 a police officer *US, 1966*

- "A poor neighborhood, no one's got nothing; a class neighborhood, the bottles bust you on sight." — Malcolm Braly, *It's Cold Out There*, p. 71, 1966

2 a dose of crack cocaine, whether or not it is actually in a small bottle *US, 1992*

- In Tunnely, crack came in tinfoil because it was easier to hide and cheaper to package, but out of habit everybody still called it bottles. — Richard Price, *Clockers*, p. 190, 1992

3 a small container of amphetamine or methamphetamine in liquid form *US, 1980*

- — National Institute on Drug Abuse, *What do they call it again?*, 1980

▸ **the bottle, big house, or box**

in twelve-step recovery programs such as Alcoholics Anonymous, used as a description of the three options for an addict who does not recover from their addiction—a return to drinking, prison, and death *US, 1998*

- — Christopher Cavanaugh, *AA to Z*, p. 59, 1998

bottle baby *noun*

an alcoholic *US, 1925*

- We were on another plane in another sphere compared to the musicians who were bottle babies, always hitting the jug and then coming up brawling after they got loaded. — Mezz Mezzrow, *Really the Blues*, p. 94, 1946
- The dregs of society hang out here, and hustlers of both sexes intermingle with short-con men, narcotics pushers, junkies, and plain bottle babies who booze their way through life. — Johnny Shearer, *The Male Hustler*, p. 55, 1966
- "There's no use denying I'm a bottle baby." — Robert Deane Pharr, *S.R.O.*, p. 200, 1971

bottle blonde *noun*

a person whose blonde hair is the result of bleach, not nature *US, 1951*

- She was a real bottle-yellow blonde in a green dress that went on like a bathrobe. — Mickey Spillane, *The Long Wait*, p. 23, 1951
- He brings in this bottle-blond sissy, it was like getting a righteous college degree in fruitiness. — James Ellroy, *White Jazz*, p. 52, 1992

bottle-cap colonel *noun*

a lieutenant colonel in the US Army *US, 1986*

Vietnam war usage. From the insignia.

- I don't have time to tell you about it; I've got a bottle-cap colonel named Homer Kisling coming over to brief you. — Walter Boyne and Steven Thompson, *The Wild Blue*, p. 450, 1986

bottle club *noun*

a business disguised as a club in an attempt to circumvent alcohol laws *US, 1951*

- A bottle club is a resort which gets around the law which provides that all liquor dispensaries shall close at 2 a.m. — Jack Lait and Lee Mortimer, *Washington Confidential*, p. 11, 1951
- The Seventy-seventh Precinct, like all ghetto precincts, teems with illegal bottle clubs[.] — Robert Daley, *Prince of the City*, p. 188, 1978

bottle dealer *noun*

a drug dealer who sells pills in large quantities *US, 1971*

- — Edward R. Bloomquist, *Marijuana*, p. 334, 1971

bottle up and go *verb*

to leave *US, 1947*

- — Marcus Hanna Boulware, *Jive and Slang of Students in Negro Colleges*, 1947

bottom *noun*

1 the pimp's favorite of the prostitutes working for him *US, 2002*

An abbreviation of **BOTTOM BITCH** or **BOTTOM LADY**.

- His bottom was Rudy, a seasoned ho from Georgia. — Tracy Funches, *Pimpnosis*, p. 98, 2002

2 the submissive partner in a homosexual or sado-masochistic relationship *US, 1961*

- If he is said to be "tops," it means that he will assume only the active partnership in sodomy, while if he is called "tops or bottoms," he will assume either the so-called male or female role in sodomy. — New York *Mattachine Newsletter*, p. 6, June 1961
- No professional top pushes the limits of a bottom much beyond this point. — Frederique Delacoste, *Sex Work*, p. 51, 1987
- "You have contempt for bottoms, don't you?" — Ethan Morden, *Some Men Are Lookers*, p. 174, 1997
- According to no less an authority than the Marquis de Sade, there is only one hierarchy in the world: tops and bottoms. Those who like to administer pain and/or sexual pleasure are the tops. Those who like to receive are the bottoms. — Bill Brownstein, *Sex Carnival*, p. 75, 2000

Bottom *nickname*

Miami, Florida *US, 1991*

- Police say the Miami Boys had such a leader in Atlanta in Theophilus Lujuan "Big Wheel" Roker, 28, a Miami native who is suspected of recruiting personnel, drugs and weapons from "The Bottom"— street slang for Miami. — *Atlanta (Georgia) Journal and Constitution*, p. D1, 4th March 1991

bottom bitch *noun*

the pimp's favorite of the prostitutes working for him; the leader of the prostitutes *US, 1967*

- Oliver had assured her that she was his top bitch but demanded to know why she couldn't catch as many dates as Alice, his bottom bitch. — Joseph Wambaugh, *Floaters*, p. 67, 1996
- Now, that's bottom bitch right there. — *Hustle and Flow*, 2004

bottom feeder *noun*

in poker, a low-betting player who tries to eke out meagre winnings against unskilled players *US, 1996*

● — John Vorhaus, *The Big Book of Poker Slang*, p. 7, 1996

bottom fisher *noun*

a stock investor looking for stocks with a poor recent showing *US, 1988*

● — Kathleen Odean, *High Steppers, Fallen Angels, and Lollipops*, p. 86, 1988

bottom girl *noun*

the pimp's favorite of the prostitutes working for him; the leader of the prostitutes *US, 1973*

● It would just keep me too busy, and I wouldn't have the time to be free. That is, unless I had a top-notch bottom girl to check the traps for me. — A.S. Jackson, *Gentleman Pimp*, p. 82, 1973

bottom lady *noun*

the pimp's favorite of the prostitutes working for him *US, 1981*

● A sophisticated lady from Virginia, at twenty-eight she was the bottom lady of Sweet Rudy, and an old hand in the life. — Alix Shulman, *On the Stroll*, p. 133, 1981

bottom line *noun*

the final analysis *US, 1967*

● Bottom line? Elyse turns into Iceland and Eddie's not the type to look elsewhere. — *Diner*, 1982

bottom man *noun*

the passive partner in a homosexual relationship *US, 1972*

● — Bruce Rodgers, *The Queens' Vernacular*, p. 36, 1972

● His "bottom-men" must be equally masculine. — John Rechy, *Rushes*, p. 26, 1979

● Bottom man is the masochist in an S/M relationship (antonym: top man). The term refers exclusively to the hierarchical contrast of the two partners, one subject to the other, and need not correspond to the actual physical position — Wayne Dynes, *Homolexis*, p. 25, 1985

bottoms *noun*

1 dice that have been marked to have two identical faces *US, 1962*

● — Frank Garcia, *Marked Cards and Loaded Dice*, p. 265, 1962

2 the worst *US, 1955*

● I've had it. This is bottoms. I'm really locked. — Max Shulman, *Guided Tour of Campus Humor*, p. 105, 1955

bottom's up *noun*

a common position for anal and/or vaginal sex, in which the passive partner lies on their stomach *US, 1960*

● — Dale Gordon, *The Dominion Sex Dictionary*, p. 31, 1967

● — Bruce Rodgers, *The Queens' Vernacular*, p. 90, 1972

bottom woman *noun*

the pimp's favorite of the prostitutes working for him; the leader of the prostitutes *US, 1969*

● There ain't more than three or four good bottom women promised a pimp in his lifetime. — Iceberg Slim (Robert Beck), *Pimp*, p. 215, 1969

● A pimp with several women usually has a favorite or "number one" or "bottom woman." — Charles Winick, *The Lively Commerce*, p. 112, 1971

● My bottom woman, Sandy—she's been with me the longest—takes care of most of my business and helps me make decisions. — Susan Hall, *Gentleman of Leisure*, p. 10, 1972

● — Ruth Todasco et al., *The Intelligent Woman's Guide to Dirty Words*, p. 2, 1973

bougie; bouji; bouge *adjective*

bourgeois *US, 1975*

● Kenny Freeman was the one who came from the bourgie family. — Bobby Seale, *Seize the Time*, p. 25, 1970

● I pay you a thousand dollars a week and you can't even get one bougie nigga! — Charles W. Moore, *A Brick for Mister Jones*, p. 62, 1975

● Very "bouge" looking, which is an accomplishment[.] — Kate Millett, *The Prostitution Papers*, p. 117, 1976

● That didn't make Daymond happy, his bougie neighbors thinking he was a rapper. — John Ridley, *Everybody Smokes in Hell*, p. 37, 1999

boulder; boulders *noun*

crack cocaine; a piece of crack cocaine *US, 1998*

Built on the **ROCK** metaphor.

● — Ethan Hilderbrant, *Prison Slang*, p. 15, 1998

boulder baby *noun*

a crack cocaine addict *US, 2002*

From the **ROCK** metaphor.

● — Gary K. Farlow, *Prison-ese*, p. 6, 2002

boulevard *noun*

a long, straight hallway *US, 1965*

● They'd take us downstairs in the boulevard and strip us naked — Henry Williamson, *Hustler*, 1965

boulevard boy *noun*

a young male prostitute in an urban setting *US, 1986–1987*

● — *Maledicta*, p. 145, Summer/Winter 1986–1987: "Sexual slang: prostitutes, pedophiles, flagellators, transvestites, and necrophiles"

bounce *noun*

1 an instance of sexual intercourse *US, 1953*

● An invitation to the waltz. The signorina desires a bounce! — Edwin Gilbert, *The Hot and the Cool*, p. 11, 1953

2 a brainstorming session *US, 1984*

● Bounce, she thought with a weak smile, that's what they call it. Bounce is cop vernacular for a brainstorm session. — Michael Slade, *Headhunter*, p. 313, 1984

3 a jail or prison sentence *US, 1957*

● Hopefully I look for a 3 to 5 bounce. — James Blake, *The Joint*, p. 161, 7th January 1957

● With their priors, they're looking at a serious bounce. — *Gone in 60 Seconds*, 2000

bounce *verb*

1 to socialize, to carouse *US, 1985*

● "The rest of the week she was usually busy with the kids and I did my bouncing with the crew and took Linda along" — Nicholas Pileggi, *Wise Guy*, p. 144, 1985

● I would need an apartment, car, money to bounce around with, and so on. — Joseph Pistone, *Donnie Brasco*, p. 41, 1987

2 to maintain order in a bar or nightclub, ejecting people from the premises if necessary *US, 1874*

● [T]here's nothing much can be done about it, because the muddled situation of District law and law enforcement makes it impossible to bounce that sort of undesirables[.] — Jack Lait and Lee Mortimer, *Washington Confidential*, p. 14, 1951

● He cut her off with the wave of a hand. "A bouncer's job is to bounce. I pay that asshole good money." — Carl Hiaasen, *Strip Tease*, p. 22, 1993

3 to leave *US, 1996*

● — Connie Eble (Editor), *UNC-CH Campus Slang*, p. 1, March 1996

● — *Newsday*, p. B2, 11th October 1997

4 (used of a message sent electronically) to return to the sender, undeliverable as addressed *US, 1991*

● — Eric S. Raymond, *The New Hacker's Dictionary*, p. 75, 1991

5 to pay; to provide without charge *US, 1970*

● I think she'd bounce for a free meal if the boss isn't there. — Joseph Wambaugh, *The New Centurions*, p. 245, 1970

6 to activate a car's suspension system so as to cause the car to bounce up and down *US, 1980*

● — Edith A. Folb, *runnin' down some lines*, p. 230, 1980

bouncer *noun*

1 a check drawn on insufficient funds *US, 1966*

● — Rose Giallombardo, *Society of Women*, p. 205, 1966: Glossary of Prison Terms

2 a person, usually a strong man, employed to maintain and restore order in a bar, restaurant, club or performance *US, 1865*

● [W]hen your friends come around asking for you they don't get thrown out by the bouncer for not spending enough loot[.] — Mezz Mezzrow, *Really the Blues*, p. 198, 1946

● As the years gather on him, his personal temper seems to be cooling, but when he was younger and even more nervous he never needed a bouncer in any of his cafes. — Robert Sylvester, *No Cover Charge*, p. 104, 1956

● The bouncers took care of them in a hurry and a few were hustled out lengthwise. — Mickey Spillane, *Me, Hood!*, p. 63, 1963

● I used to be the head bouncer here back in the 70s. — *The Blues Brothers*, 1980

● The go-go whore starts yelling I owe her five bucks and this bouncer come running over. — Elmore Leonard, *Maximum Bob*, p. 1, 1991

bounce shot *noun*

in a dice game, a type of controlled shot by a skilled cheat
US, 1950

- — *The Annals of the American Academy of Political and Social Sciences*, p. 121, May 1950

bouncing Betty *noun*

a land-mine first used in World War 2, prevalent in Vietnam, that bounces waist high and then sprays shrapnel when triggered *US, 1943*

- "It's a Bouncing Betty," he said. "Is that the one that jumps into the air and then blows up?" Redding asked. — David Reed, *Up Front in Vietnam*, p. 93, 1967
- Kurt gritted his teeth, but kept on talking about a trooper who'd frozen on a pull-release bouncing betty. — Ronald J. Glasser, *365 Days*, p. 14, 1971
- He was going to take a patrol out in the morning and said he hoped they did not trip any Bouncing Betties. His last company commander had been hit by one. — Philip Caputo, *A Rumor of War*, p. 229, 1977

bouncy-bouncy *noun*

sexual intercourse *US, 1993*

- — Kenn "Naz" Young, *Naz's Dictionary of Teen Slang*, p. 13, 1993

bounty hunter *noun*

a police officer who measures success by the number of arrests made *US, 1975*

- If he was eager to make a reputation as a knight in blue or to install himself as a "bounty hunter," a cop who'd arrest his own mother, Sepe never showed these traits then[.] — John Sepe, *Cop Team*, p. 41, 1975

bouquet straight *noun*

in poker, a sequenced hand comprised of all red or all black suits, but not a flush *US, 1996*

It looks impressive, but is worth no more than any nonflush straight.

- — John Vorhaus, *The Big Book of Poker Slang*, p. 8, 1996

bow *noun*

the elbow *US, 1980*

Elbows used to establish position are a key part of the anatomy in basketball.

- — Chuck Wielgus and Alexander Wolff, *The In-Your-Face Basketball Book*, p. 30, 1980

bow-and-arrow *adjective*

not armed with a pistol *US, 1984*

- Keenan was currently assigned to the "bow-and-arrow squad," which meant that he would not be allowed to carry a gun until such time as his attitude improved. — Thomas Larry Adcock, *Precinct 19*, p. 38, 1984

bowl *noun*

a pipe for smoking marijuana, hashish, or crack cocaine *US, 1974*

- Jeff and I smoked a couple of bowls and then went to a screening of the new Friday the 13th movie. — Bret Easton Ellis, *Less Than Zero*, p. 130, 1985
- I'm at my best after some methical or a bowl of sense[.] — Tone Loc, *Cheeba Cheeba*, 1989
- And every day George would come home from work, she'd have a big fat bowl waiting for him, man, when'd come in the door, man. — *Dazed and Confused*, 1993
- — Pamela Munro, *U.C.L.A. Slang*, p. 44, 1997

bowlegged *adjective*

1 (of prison sentences) concurrent *US, 1990*

- Ring's public defender argued till he was blue in the face, and the judge relented just a little, running the deuces [two-year sentences] bowlegged instead, as in concurrent. — Seth Morgan, *Homeboy*, p. 85, 1990

2 (of prison sentences) consecutive *US, 2002*

- "Running wild?" "Yeah, daw—bowlegged sentences, y'understan' what I'm saying?" — Jimmy Lerner, *You Got Nothing Coming*, p. 60, 2002

bowl over *verb*

to kill *US, 1969*

- He recalled an old homicide buddy called Johnny Whales (phonetic), who "bowled over" people in the old days. — Ovid Demaris, *Captive City*, p. 66, 1969

bowser *noun*

a dog *US, 1965*

- Letch thought about slipping the bowser some barbiturates but was afraid it might croak. He didn't want an OD'd Scottie on his conscience. — Joseph Wambaugh, *Floaters*, p. 10, 1996

bowser bag *noun*

a container used by restaurants to package unfinished meals to be taken home by diners *US, 1965*

A variation on the more common **DOGGY BAG**.

- Whereupon the child asked, "Father, if you were in a whorehouse and you couldn't finish, would it be permissible to ask for a bowser bag to take the leftovers home?" — Tom Robbins, *Another Roadside Attraction*, p. 47, 1971

bow-wow *noun*

a "dog," literally and in its slang senses *US, 1935*

- [T]he network wants to burn off as soon as possible a series it considers to be a real bow-wow[.] — *Washington Post*, p. C14, 18th August 1983
- "A bow-wow," Purdue said. "Thirty to one on the morning line." — Robert Campbell, *Juice*, p. 2, 1988
- That's when Letch devised the scheme to pee on the tree and drive the little bowwow bonkers. — Joseph Wambaugh, *Floaters*, p. 11, 1996
- Judge Reinhold, whose career has spiraled downhill ever since *Home Alone*, stars in the direct-to-video installment of the St. Bernard series. It's a real bow-wow. — *Boston Globe*, p. N9, 23rd July 2003

box *noun*

1 an interrogation room *US, 1998*

- Back room. Interrogation room. "The Box," they called it. — John Ridley, *Love is a Racket*, p. 203, 1998

2 the vagina; a woman *UK, 1605*

- I grabbed her by the shoulders, kissed her, and right quick from some instinctive sense shoved my hand right up her dress and came up with her box shining golden in the golden sun. — Jack Kerouac, *Letter to Neal Cassady*, p. 298, 10th January 1951
- She has no cherry, but she thinks it's no sin / for she still has the box that the cherry came in. — Bruce Jackson, *Get Your Ass in the Water and Swim Like Me*, p. 229, 1964
- The broad was there in a short skirt with no drawers; when the guard wasn't looking—zip—she flashed her box, now you see it, now you don't—like the guy in the raincoat on the subway. — Edwin Torres, *Carlito's Way*, p. 123, 1975
- Are the billboards around town promoting Kool cigarettes' flip-top box in poor taste, pornographic—or neither? The ones that show a young woman in bathing attire floating in an inner tube under the caption: "Coolest box around." — *San Francisco Examiner*, p. 37, 15th September 1976

3 a jail or prison *US, 1995*

Usually heard as "the box."

- — Bill Valentine, *Gang Intelligence Manual*, p. 130, 1995

4 a cell used for solitary confinement *US, 1976*

- — John R. Armore and Joseph D. Wolfe, *Dictionary of Desperation*, p. 21, 1976

5 a safe *US, 1902*

- Can you bust a box, if you have to? — Robert Edmond Alter, *Carny Kill*, p. 102, 1966
- I was supposed to be the best box-man in the country and as I look back, I must have busted four hundred boxes and lifted more than a million. — Red Rudensky, *The Gonif*, p. 6, 1970
- What they weigh depends on the box you're going after. — Bruce Jackson, *Outside the Law*, p. 91, 1972
- I'm thinking about my own place, Nicky. Would you be able to put a box in? — Vincent Patrick, *The Pope of Greenwich Village*, p. 9, 1979

6 a guitar *US, 1911*

May also refer to a banjo.

- — Robert S. Gold, *A Jazz Lexicon*, p. 35, 1964
- — David Powis, *The Signs of Crime*, 1977

7 a piano *US, 1908*

- — Arnold Shaw, *Lingo of Tin-Pan Alley*, p. 8, 1950
- This gave me a stronger urge to blow piano, or blow a box, as they used to say. — Claude Brown, *Manchild in the Promised Land*, p. 229, 1965

8 a record player *UK, 1924*

- [A] record player is a "box"[.] — Harrison E. Salisbury, *The Shook-up Generation*, p. 161, 1958
- If you have a box I'll bring them in. — Jack Kerouac, *Jack Kerouac Selected Letters 1957–1969*, p. 170, 28th August 1958: Letter to Allen Ginsberg
- [W]hy did Lester [Bangs] mention that El Cajon means "The Box"? Was it because "box" is old hipster slang for record player[?] — Greil Marcus, *Psychotic Reactions and Carburetor Dung*, 1986

9 a large, portable radio and tape player *US, 1985*
A shortened **GHETTO BOX**.

- He was no legal scholar but even he knew the kids call a ghetto blaster a box. — Andrew Vachss, *Flood*, p. 342, 1985

10 television *US, 1950*
Usually after "the."

- He came on the box early, drummed home the law and order theme, honored his cops and firemen. — Sidney Bernard, *This Way to the Apocalypse*, p. 72, 1968

11 a polygraph machine *US, 1991*

- On the night that Yolanda passes the box, there is a homecoming of sorts when McLarney returns to Kavanaugh's[.] — David Simon, *Homicide*, p. 157, 1991
- She was taken to the next room and connected to "the Box." — Stephen Cannell, *Big Con*, p. 325, 1997

12 in bar dice games, a leather or vinyl cup used to shake dice before spilling them out *US, 1976*

- — Gil Jacobs, *The World's Best Dice Games*, p. 194, 1976

13 a pool table, especially a large one *US, 1990*

- — Steve Rushin, *Pool Cool*, p. 6, 1990

14 in the Vietnam war, an aerial target zone approximately ⅝ of a mile wide by 2 miles long *US, 1988*

- Every three hours around the clock, six B-52s from the Strategic Air Command bases in Guam and Thailand obliterated a "box" with 162 tons of bombs. — Neil Sheehan, *A Bright Shining Lie*, p. 706, 1988

▸ **in the box**
engaged in vaginal sex *US, 1972*

- — Helen Dahlskog (Editor), *A Dictionary of Contemporary and Colloquial Usage*, p. 9, 1972

▸ **put someone in the box**
to kill someone *US, 2000*

- There are three reasons a familiano can be put in the box [killed]: cowardice, treason, or desertion. — Bill Valentine, *Gangs and Their Tattoos*, p. 36, 2000

▸ **take someone out of the box**
to kill someone *US, 1995*

- — Bill Valentine, *Gang Intelligence Manual*, p. 78, 1995: 'Black street gang terminology'

box *verb*

1 to subject to a polygraph examination *US, 1997*

- Within months every American had been "boxed," but the ARVN was still planning its program. — John Plaster, *SOG*, p. 322, 1997

2 to confirm the death of a hospital patient *US, 1977*

- — *Philadelphia Magazine*, pp. 145–151, November 1977

3 to die *US, 1994*

- — Sally Williams, *"Strong" Words*, p. 135, 1994

4 in an illegal lottery, to bet on a group of related numbers rather than a single number *US, 1974*

- I guess you just gotta do like the Reverend I Doo Little tell the people: If you must play 'em, brothers and sisters, box 'em. — Vernon E. Smith, *The Jones Men*, p. 92, 1974

Box 100 *noun*
the notional repository for information given to police by informants *US, 1979*

- It's the rattingest fucking neighborhood in the city. Half the mail into box 100 must come from the Village. — Vincent Patrick, *The Pope of Greenwich Village*, p. 183, 1979

box bag *noun*
the amount of marijuana (the bag) which can be bought for a carton of cigarettes (the box) *US, 1992*

- — William K. Bentley and James M. Corbett, *Prison Slang*, p. 74, 1992

boxcar *noun*
any four-engine bomber *US, 1946*

- — *American Speech*, p. 310, December 1946: "More Air Force slang"
- Yeah. He was my buddy on the boxcar. — Kurt Vonnegut, *Slaughterhouse-Five*, p. 141, 1969

boxcar numbers *noun*
a lot of money *US, 1950*

- He's OK for a short tab but make sure you don't let him go into box-car numbers. — *The Annals of the American Academy of Political and Social Sciences*, p. 121, May 1950

boxcar prices *noun*
in horse racing, high odds *US, 1974*

- "I just know boxcar prices like that made somebody out there happy." — Gary Mayer, *Bookie*, p. 63, 1974

boxcars *noun*

1 in horse racing, high odds *US, 1934*
From the high numbers used to identify railroad cars.

- — *San Francisco Examiner*, p. 25, 3rd April 1953
- — Robert Saunders Dowst and Jay Craig, *Playing the Races*, p. 160, 1960

2 in a game of dice, a roll of two sixes *US, 1949*

- Abie the Jew bet the dice to win or lose, barring box cars and snake-eyes. — Chester Himes, *A Rage in Harlem*, p. 26, 1957
- — Frank Garcia, *Marked Cards and Loaded Dice*, p. 250, 1962
- I learned about percentage dice that are shaved to favor an ace-six—and a plentitude of snake eyes and boxcars. — Jimmy Snyder, *Jimmy the Greek*, p. 15, 1975

3 in poker, a pair of sixes or three sixes *US, 1988*
A borrowing from the game of craps.

- — George Percy, *The Language of Poker*, p. 12, 1988

box-chaser *noun*
a man who relentlessly pursues women *US, 1969*

- He was a real triple-threat man—boozer, Bible-thumper and box-chaser. — Joey V., *Portrait of Joey*, p. 25, 1969

boxed *adjective*

1 marijuana-intoxicated, drunk *US, 1958*

- — Robert George Reisner, *The Jazz Titans*, p. 151, 1960
- — William D. Alsever, *Glossary for the Establishment and Other Uptight People*, p. 15, December 1970
- Her pretty face was slightly flushed, the look of a woman who'd already gotten half-boxed. — Dan Jenkins, *The Money-Whipped Steer-Job Three-Jack Give-Up Artist*, p. 133, 2001

2 incarcerated *US, 1970*

- — William D. Alsever, *Glossary for the Establishment and Other Uptight People*, p. 16, December 1970

boxes *noun*
in craps, a roll of two fours *US, 1983*

- — Thomas L. Clark, *The Dictionary of Gambling and Gaming*, p. 25, 1987

boxie *noun*
a person with bleached blond hair *US, 1987*

- — *Washington Post*, p. 18, 8th November 1987

Boxie *noun*
in the Vietnam war, used as a nickname for company medics *US, 1967*
An Americanization of bac-si, Vietnamese for "doctor."

- [H]e knows his weakness and allows Boxie, medic-turned-team sergeant, to do the leading. — Donald Duncan, *The New Legions*, p. 11, 1967

box-kicker *noun*
a supply clerk in the US Marines *US, 1998*

- — *Seattle Times*, p. A9, 12th April 1998

box lunch; box lunch at the Y *noun*
oral sex on a woman *US, 1964*

- — Roger Blake, *The American Dictionary of Sexual Terms*, p. 21, 1964
- [C]omments such as "likes to make," "frigid," "the picture does her too much justice," "box lunch," "a real roller," "get laid," ad infinitum. — John Nichols, *The Sterile Cuckoo*, p. 7, 1965
- — *American Speech*, p. 228, October 1967: "Some special terms used in a University of Connecticut men's Dormitory"

box man *noun*
a criminal who specializes in breaking into safes *US, 1902*

- "I don't know, for godsake," I said. "I'm no box man." — Robert Edmond Alter, *Carny Kill*, p. 103, 1966
- I was supposed to be the best box-man in the country and as I look back, I must have busted four hundred boxes and lifted more than a million. — Red Rudensky, *The Gonif*, p. 6, 1970
- The old boxmen [safecrackers] they was not dope fiends. — Bruce Jackson, *In the Life*, p. 68, 1972
- When I was learning to be a box-man, I didn't do nothing but box work. — Harry King, *Box Man*, p. 85, 1972

box of L *noun*
a box of 100 ampules containing methamphetamine hydrochloride (trade name Methedrine™), a central nervous system stimulant *US, 1973*

- — David Maurer and Victor Vogel, *Narcotics and Narcotic Addiction*, p. 391, 1973

box shot *noun*
in a dice game in which the dice are rolled from a cup, a controlled shot *US, 1950*
- — Thomas L. Clark, *The Dictionary of Gambling and Gaming*, p. 26, 1987

box slugger *noun*
a criminal specializing in breaking into safes *US, 1970*
- Later, I heard that they had picked up a tip that two major outfits outside were in dire need of a box slugger and would collaborate to break me out. — Red Rudensky, *The Gonif*, p. 49, 1970

box tool *noun*
any tool used for breaking into a safe *US, 1972*
- [T]hey'd go in there with nothing but regular old box tools. — Bruce Jackson, *Outside the Law*, p. 96, 1972

box work *noun*
breaking into safes *US, 1972*
- When I was learning to be a box-man, I didn't do nothing but box work. — Harry King, *Box Man*, p. 85, 1972

boy *noun*
1 heroin *US, 1953*
- "I'm warning you though, you start fooling with Boy and Girl and I'm through with you." — Herbert Simmons, *Corner Boy*, p. 28, 1957
- But now he had the boy; he could lie around up in his crib, twisted, drugged to the verge of insensibility. — Clarence Cooper Jr., *The Scene*, p. 12, 1960
- Dig my man, how about dropping off two spoons of boy, and a hundred dollar bag of girl. — Donald Goines, *El Dorado Red*, p. 69, 1974
- They called it "girl" or "Jane" or "Missy" in feminine contrast to "boy" or "John" or "Mister" for king heroin. — David Simon and Edward Burns, *The Corner*, p. 62, 1997

2 a male friend *US, 1997*
Connotes affection and loyalty.
- A man gets off work, he's got to go somewhere. He's got to drink something. He's got to smoke something. He's got to watch a game. He's got to hang out with his boys. — Chris Rock, *Rock This!*, p. 169, 1997

3 a homosexual male prostitute *US, 1971*
- The boys—who are called boys and not hookers or hustlers—generally go to the john's apartment, usually staying until the john has his mind-blowing climax and not lingering for the night. — John Francis Hunter, *The Gay Insider*, p. 213, 1971
- Not being under the same financial pressures as most of the other boys, I could be a little choosy about my customers. — John Preston, *Hustling*, p. 67, 1994

4 a lesbian *US, 1997*
- Gay or straight—ugly's still ugly. And most of those boys are scary. — *Chasing Amy*, 1997

5 a boxer or wrestler *US, 1977*
- A specialist, in Berlin, told me last year to retire Upshaw after he was knocked out in the last of three boys in three days. — Iceberg Slim (Robert Beck), *Long White Con*, p. 189, 1977

6 in a deck of playing cards, a jack or knave *US, 1967*
- — Albert H. Morehead, *The Complete Guide to Winning Poker*, p. 258, 1967

7 in horse racing, a jockey *US, 1951*
- — David W. Maurer, *Argot of the Racetrack*, p. 15, 1951

boy beaver *noun*
the male sex organs and pubic hair *US, 1987*
- The job: co-manager (with Gerry Malanga) of a boy-beaver movie house operating under Andy's name. — Jim Carroll, *Forced Entries*, p. 39, 1987

boychik *noun*
a boy or young man *US, 1951*
- You see, boychick, I can spike any script with yaks, but the thing I can't do is heartbreak. — Norman Mailer, *Advertisements for Myself*, p. 159, 1951
- "Pleased to meet up with you boychiks." — Harry Grey, *The Hoods*, p. 16, 1952
- "Where you been, boychik?" chirped Joel. — Clancy Sigal, *Going Away*, p. 10, 1961
- "She's still got the sleeping mask on. Goodbye, boychik." — Stephen Longstreet, *The Flesh Peddlers*, p. 94, 1962
- Mama would say that she only hoped I would only turn into a good boychik — Red Rudensky, *The Gonif*, p. 39, 1970
- "Oh, boychik." I rub my high, fine brow. — Leo Rosten, *Silky!*, p. 2, 1979

boy-gal *noun*
a male homosexual *US, 1990*
- — Charles Shafer, *Folk Speech in Texas Prisons*, p. 199, 1990

boy-girl *noun*
a young, effeminate, male homosexual *US, 1952*
- [I]t was in that bar that I first saw flagrantly painted men congregate and where a queen boy-girl camped openly with a cop. — John Rechy, *City of Night*, p. 62, 1963

boy in the boat; little man in the boat *noun*
the clitoris *US, 1916*
- [T]hose who felt that the ladies should have big bursts but could have them only in that highly localized surface nodule known in the trade as the vestigial phallus, or button, or boy in the boat. — Bernard Wolfe, *The Magic of Their Singing*, p. 93, 1961
- I suppose I should describe the moans she moaned, the way her hot body moved into me and trembled when I touched the little man in the rowboat[.] — Leo Rosten, *Silky!*, p. 180, 1979
- Don't be afraid to spread her open with your fingers. Pull back on her mons to expose the little man in the boat. — Diana Cage, *Box Lunch*, p. 79, 2004

boyo *adjective*
mildly pornographic, featuring naked men *US, 1970*
- [A] tawdry grocery store where every known Girlie and Boyo magazine is sold; and a colorful assortment of pimps, hustlers, prostitutes, petty thieves, and alcoholics. — Raymond Mungo, *Famous Long Ago*, p. 25, 1970

boys *noun*
1 a group of homosexual male friends; collectively, the male homosexual community *US, 1972*
- You've been seeing a real woman—what will the boys think? — Bruce Rodgers, *The Queens' Vernacular*, p. 36, 1972
- They have everything for young men to enjoy/You can hang out with all the boys. — Village People, *Y.M.C.A.*, 1978

2 racketeers *US, 1979*
- The boys financed this Poker game. — John Scarne, *Scarne's Guide to Modern Poker*, p. 273, 1979

3 used by professional wrestlers to refer to other professional wrestlers *US, 1990*
- They were nasty affairs and could go on for long periods of time with the wrestlers, or "boys" as is the common term used in the business, capitalizing on the situation. A "boy" could be any age, from sixteen to sixty, as long as she wore wrestling trunks. — Pat Barrett, *Everybody Down There Hates Me*, p. 72, 1990
- A lot of AWA people live there when they move to town. Many of the boys live there now. — Larry Nelson and James Jones, *Stranglehold*, p. 55, 1999
- The last was the one that angered the boys the most. Nikita Koloff questioned this commandment at a meeting a short time later. Bill addressed the boys and asked if there were any questions. — Mick Foley, *Mankind*, p. 221, 1999
- While I enjoyed the freedom of traveling alone, the most memorable trips were those that I made with the boys[.] — Gary Cappetta, *Bodyslams!*, p. 178, 2000

▸ **do the boys**
to engage in homosexual activity *US, 2002*
- — Gary K. Farlow, *Prison-ese*, p. 17, 2002

boys and girls *noun*
heroin and cocaine, mixed and injected together *US, 1993*
- — Peter Johnson, *Dictionary of Street Alcohol and Drug Terms*, p. 27, 1993

boy scout *noun*
a person who is extremely, and usually distressingly, sincere *US, 1997*
- He's got a whole troop of Boy Scout lawyers ready to swear for him. — Stephen Cannell, *King Con*, p. 47, 1997

boys in blue *noun*
the police; sailors; US Federal troops *UK, 1851*
Rarely, if ever, occurs in the singular.
- One or two of the boys in blue will dull this lull with well-whipped heads needing white-togged meds. — Dan Burley, *Diggeth Thou?*, p. 18, 1959
- Sometime around ten or ten thirty we'll get a visit from the boys in blue. — Donald Goines, *White Man's Justice, Black Man's Grief*, p. 81, 1973

boys of Baghdad *noun*
during the Gulf war, reporters for the Cable News Network
US, 1991
- — *American Speech*, p. 385, Winter 1991: "Among the new words"

Boy's Town *noun*
a city neighborhood dominated by homosexual men, especially West Hollywood, California *US, 1984*
A play on Father Flanagan's Boys Home, a home for delinquent and homeless boys in Omaha, Nebraska.
- Officer Pig was, of course, corruption incarnate—an up-for-grabs cop who took bribes from the male prostitutes of Boy's Town, allowing them to ply their wicked craft while he and his sleazy cop buddies looked the other way. — James Ellroy, *Blood on the Moon*, p. 58, 1984
- And they were beautiful, too, all the boys in Boy's Town. — John Ridley, *Love is a Racket*, p. 228, 1998
- Through Boyz' Town, slow down at the Castro Theater, wistful, covet James Dean marathons. — Lynn Breedlove, *Godspeed*, p. 286, 2002

boy toy *noun*
a young, attractive woman or man who is the object of sexual desire of their elders, homosexual or heterosexual *US, 1989*
- They're soon joined by a wealthy local widow (Tanya Berezin) and her new "boy toy" of a lover (Brian Tarantina), an aspiring tennis star. — *New York Times*, p. C15, 18th October 1982
- Boy toy—young (18–22 years old) club kid, often seen wearing go-go outfits. — Kevin Dilallo, *The Unofficial Gay Manual*, pp. 237–238, 1994
- Our glitzy diva French-kissing a boy toy in a tongue-wrestling match that would make Madonna salivate — *Miami New Times*, 8th April 2004
- Bryant gives much joy when she flashes her bare boobies during a shower shtup with her tattooed boytoy. — Mr. Skin, *Mr. Skin's Skincyclopedia*, p. 86, 2005

bozack *noun*
1 sex *US, 1989*
Usually heard as "do the bozack."
- — Terry Williams, *The Cocaine Kids*, p. 138, 1989
2 the penis; the entire male genitalia *US, 1990*
Sometimes shortened to "zack."
- And the bitches? They'll do anything for it. I got my bozack done every day last week. Several times a time. — *New Jack City*, 1990
- I put the starter cap on the bozack, can't get with no kid rap[.] — Kwest Tha Madd Lad *Lubrication*, 1996
- a knack for grabbin' the bozack — *The Source*, p. 181, March 2002

bozo *noun*
a buffoon *US, 1916*
In the US, the older sense of "bozo" as "a fellow" was supplanted by the figure Bozo the Clown, who first appeared on record in 1946 and then became a fixture on local television programs throughout the US beginning in 1949.
- "Read it and weep, bozo—I'm the law." — Willard Motley, *Knock on Any Door*, p. 173, 1947
- It's the horn-goggled bozos who sit in swivel chairs that make wars. [Quoting Dr. Leo Eloesser] — *San Francisco Chronicle*, p. 21, 3rd December 1950
- C'mon now, Blondie, what you want to mess with these bozos for? — Ken Kesey, *One Flew Over the Cuckoo's Nest*, p. 231, 1962
- What these bozos and their friends are up to now is simply the last act in their original adoption and betrayal of any truly "beat" credo. — Jack Kerouac, *Jack Kerouac Selected Letters 1957–1969*, p. 429, 1964: Letter to Fernanda Pivano
- Hey, Murtaugh, tell these bozos to lay off. — *Lethal Weapon*, 1987

bozotic *adjective*
in computing, ridiculous *US, 1991*
- — Eric S. Raymond, *The New Hacker's Dictionary*, p. 77, 1991

BP *noun*
1 in blackjack counting teams, the player who places the large bets based on cues from other members of the team who have been counting cards at a particular table *US, 1991*
An intialism for "big player."
- — Michael Dalton, *Blackjack*, p. 31, 1991
2 in American casinos, a serious gambler *US, 1985*
The initials stand for "big player."
- — Steve Kuriscak, *Casino Talk*, p. 6, 1985

3 a young prostitute *US, 1971*
An abbreviation of "baby pro."
- So the next day she registered in school as the woman's niece and began living as a high class BP. — Anonymous, *Go Ask Alice*, p. 161, 1971

BPS *noun*
a wooden stick used by police for probing a corpse *US, 1997*
New York police slang; an abbreviation of "brain-picking stick."
- — Samuel M. Katz, *Anytime Anywhere*, p. 386, 1997

BQ *noun*
a male homosexual who favors anal sex *US, 1964*
An abbreviation of **BROWNIE QUEEN**.
- — Roger Blake, *The American Dictionary of Sexual Terms*, p. 22, 1964

BR *noun*
1 a bankroll *US, 1915*
- After finding the fat BR, I removed a few pound-notes from the center and placed it back in the same way it was when I found it. — A.S. Jackson, *Gentleman Pimp*, p. 12, 973
2 money *US, 1915*
From the term "bankroll."
- I'm broke as Lazarus, with no B.R. for the free world when I hit it. — Iceberg Slim (Robert Beck), *Doom Fox*, p. 214, 1978
3 in carnival usage, any hyperbolic story *US, 1985*
An extension of the "bankroll" sense, the roll of money used by the operator of a rigged game to distract and divert the attention of a player from how the game is rigged.
- — Gene Sorrows, *All About Carnivals*, p. 11, 1985
4 Banana Republic™, a chain of shops selling casual clothing *US, 1997*
- — Pamela Munro, *U.C.L.A. Slang*, p. 44, 1997

bra-busters *noun*
large female breasts *US, 2005*
- Raven's bra-busters are each bigger than a hog's head. — Mr. Skin, *Mr. Skin's Skincyclopedia*, p. 139, 2005

brace *verb*
to apprehend someone; to arrest someone; to accost someone *US, 1889*
- "[W]hen I braced the guy that proved that Decker had paid him back." — Mickey Spillane, *The Big Kill*, p. 45, 1951
- Then I thought: brace him at his pad? — James Ellroy, *Brown's Requiem*, p. 209, 1981
- They haven't braced Girod's killer. — Seth Morgan, *Homeboy*, p. 239, 1990

brace face *noun*
any person wearing an orthodontic brace *US, 1991*
- "Fewer people make fun of me; they want to see them," Shawn said. "And they don't call me as many names as they used to, like 'brace face' and 'metal mouth.'" — *St. Petersburg (Florida) Times*, p. 2D, 9th September 1991
- For boomers, taunts like "brace-face," tin grin' and "metal mouth" have made way for more sophisticated teasing. — *Washington Post*, p. F1, 13th January 2004

bracelet play *noun*
in poker, an exceptionally crafty play *US, 1996*
An allusion to the "bracelet prize" in the World Series of Poker.
- — John Vorhaus, *The Big Book of Poker Slang*, p. 8, 1996

bracelets *noun*
handcuffs *UK, 1661*
- I was cold, stiff, sore all over, and if I had any hands left behind me they could have been stone for all they felt the bite of the bracelets. — Thurston Scott, *Cure it with Honey*, p. 175, 1951
- I can also see us in bracelets pictured on page three of the Daily News the next day too. — Emmett Grogan, *Final Score*, p. 70, 1976
- Take off the bracelets or no deal. — *48 Hours*, 1982

bracer *noun*
any strong alcoholic drink *US, 1830*
- These first are merely "bracers," to protect them from the morning chill. — Robert deCoy, *The Nigger Bible*, p. 248, 1967

brace work *noun*
poorly executed markings on the back of cards by card cheats *US, 1961*
- — Thomas L. Clark, *The Dictionary of Gambling and Gaming*, p. 26, 1987

bra chute *noun*
a type of parachute malfunction *US, 1982*

- The bra chute or semi-inverted chute resulted when the rigging lines were routed incorrectly causing the lines to split the chute canopy into two sections. — Gregory Clark, *Words of the Vietnam War*, p. 498, 1990

braggadocious; bragadocious *adjective*
boastful *US, 1956*

- The black who caused more nightmares for white America than any other was bullet-headed, braggadocious heavyweight boxing champion Jack Johnson. — Mary Frances Berry and John W. Blassingame, *Long Memory*, p. 131, 1982
- I don't mean to sound braggadocious, but it does not strap me or hurt me to do it. — *Washington Post*, p. A1, 26th April 1983
- "It seems to me that people with these characteristics would naturally be drawn to music that is made especially braggadocious for them." — William Upski Wimsatt, *Bomb the Suburbs*, p. 24, 1994
- We're full of it. We're vain, we're braggadocious. At Passover, we try to come down to a normal level[.] — *Ledger (Lakeland, Florida)*, p. D1, 3rd April 2004

brag-rag *noun*
a military decoration in the form of a ribbon *US, 1960*

- Bill opened his jacket and flashed his brag rag. — Fran Baker, *Once a Warrior*, p. 49, 1998

brah *noun*
used as a term of address, young surfing male to young surfing male *US, 1981*
A surfer's "brother."

- — Douglas Simonson, *Pidgin to da Max*, 1981
- Chill, brah. — *Point Break*, 1991

brain *noun*
1 a police detective *US, 1958*

- Detectives are brains. — *New York Times*, p. 34, 20th October 1958

2 oral sex performed on a male *US, 1998*
An extension of **HEAD**.

- Kids say "get brain" does not mean smarts. It's slang for oral sex. — *Daily News (New York)*, 5th November 2004

3 a smart person *UK, 1914*

- The athletes and the rich boys and the brains were the big wheels at Summer High School. — Dick Gregory, *Nigger*, p. 47, 1964

brain *verb*
to hit someone on the head *US, 1938*

- Do you know when they're fulfilled? When you tell them not to go any further or you'll brain them. — Mort Sahl, *Heartland*, p. 60, 1976
- He wanted to brain Lefty and drag Millie Filbert into the bushes. — C.D. Payne, *Youth in Revolt*, p. 131, 1993
- Schmalowitz picked a kid up in a gay bar, took him home, and the kid brained him. — Richard Condon, *Prizzi's Money*, p. 146, 1994

brain bender *noun*
a strenuous, rowdy party *US, 1966*

- At least twice a year outlaws from all parts of the state gather somewhere in California for a king-size brain-bender. — Hunter S. Thompson, *Hell's Angels*, p. 116, 1966

brain box *noun*
the head; the mind *UK, 1823*

- [T]he A's portable brain-box of manager Ken Macha and general manager Bill Meane decided it would behoove them to push Ted Lilly back three days to help align the rotation for the postseason. — *San Francisco Chronicle*, p. B1, 21st September 2003

brain candy *noun*
an insignificant entertainment or diversion as opposed to something that requires thought *US, 1981*

- I was writing in a medium—the Sunday supplement—that tended to be ignored, treated like brain candy. [Quoting Tom Wolfe] — *New York Times*, pp. 6–46, 20th December 1981
- Brain candy is not something you'll find on The O.C.—if you want a show with no gray cells, that's what The King of Queens is for! — Brittany Kent, *O.C. Undercover*, p. viii, 2004

brain cramp *noun*
a mental error *US, 1982*

- Utah coach Jerry Pimm said his team seemed victimized by "brain cramps." — *United Press International*, 7th February 1982
- — Paul Dickson, *The New Dickson Baseball Dictionary*, p. 82, 1999

brain-damaged *adjective*
in computing, clearly wrong *US, 1983*

- — *CoEvolution Quarterly*, p. 27, Spring 1981
- Calling something brain-damaged is really bad; it also implies it is unusable, and that its failure to work is due to poor design rather than some accident. — Eric S. Raymond, *The New Hacker's Dictionary*, p. 77, 1991

brain derby *noun*
1 an exam or test *US, 1961*

- Brain Derby—school exams. — Art Unger, *The Cool Book*, p. 107, 1961

2 a test or examination *US, 1961*

- — *San Francisco Examiner*, p. 21, 12th December 1961

brain fade *noun*
a momentary mental lapse *US, 1980*

- — Don Alexander, *The Racer's Dictionary*, p. 11, 1980

brain fart; mind fart *noun*
a temporary mental lapse *US, 1983*

- — Connie Eble (Editor), *UNC-CH Campus Slang*, p. 2, Spring 1992
- [T]hey painted the den "grape" the first time, an embarrassing goof. "It was some kind of brain fart," said the always-blunt Peterson. — *Atlanta Journal and Constitution*, p. G5, 26th August 1994
- Did retired General Anthony Zinni really call George W. Bush's war in Iraq a "brain fart"? That seems to be the case. — *The Nation*, 26th September 2003

brain fixer *noun*
a psychotherapist *US, 1953*

- "It upsets Brownie so much that he complained to his brain fixer, who called up the probation board and asked what the hell." — Dale Krame, *Teen-Age Gangs*, p. 123, 1953

brain freeze *noun*
a searing headache experienced when eating frozen food or drinks *US, 1993*

- Though ominous-sounding, brain freeze is nothing more than the fleeting headache that befalls most of us after consuming too much ice cream too quickly. — *Columbus (Ohio) Dispatch*, p. 1C, 3rd May 1993
- Drank Slurpee too fast, got a brain freeze. (Quoting the David Letterman Show) — *Post Standard (Syracuse)*, p. D1, 25th September 1993
- Why do you get brainfreeze if you eat ice cream too fast? — *Chicago Daily Herald*, 9th July 1998
- The culprit, in most cases, isn't an ice pick, but rather an icy drink or ice cream that spawns the cold frontal lobotomy known as "brain-freeze." — *The Orlando Sentinel*, p. E1, 26th June 2001

brainiac *noun*
a very intelligent person *US, 1986*
Brainiac was introduced as an arch-enemy of Superman in 1958.

- — Ellen C. Bellone (Editor), *Dictionary of Slang*, p. 4, 1989
- Hey, brainiac. — *Clueless*, 1995
- Angela Bassett honed her considerable acting chops in productions at Yale University, where the brainiac beauty earned a scholarship. — Mr. Skin, *Mr. Skin's Skincyclopedia*, p. 45, 2005

brain-over-butt *adverb*
head-over-heels *US, 1960*

- I don't know how to tell a girl I'm crucially and brain-over-butt in love with her[.] — Glendon Swarthout, *Where the Boys Are*, p. 138, 1960

brain screw *noun*
a prison psychological counselor *US, 1951*

- Cheer up, brain screw. — Thurston Scott, *Cure it with Honey*, p. 20, 1951

brain session *noun*
a group study session *US, 1963*

- "I've been foolin' around with a lot of dames on campus, and been cuttin' out on brain sessions." — Frederick Kohner, *The Affairs of Gidget*, p. 64, 1963

brainstorm *noun*
a sudden, good idea *US, 1925*

- — Lou Shelly, *Hepcats Jive Talk Dictionary*, p. 8, 1945

brain surgeon *noun*

1 a poker player who over-analyzes every situation *US, 1982*
- — David M. Hayano, *Poker Faces*, p. 185, 1982

2 used in comparisons as the epitome of intelligence *US, 1978*
- Frank's got a decent body but he's no brain surgeon. — Jay McInerney, *Story of My Life*, p. 55, 1988

brain surgery *noun*
any difficult, demanding work *US, 1978*
Used in contrast to the job at hand.
- "I think this so-called intelligence factor is being a bit overrated," said Healy. "Let's face it, this isn't brain surgery." — *Washington Post*, p. E1, 27th July 1980
- As a coach, you have one basic tool and that is playing time. This isn't brain surgery. — *Milwaukee Journal Sentinel*, p. 7C, 21st March 2004

brain trust *noun*
a group of expert advisers *US, 1910*
Although found at least as early as 1910, not popularized until 1933 in association with US President Franklin Roosevelt's advisers.
- Oakland's new "brain trust" includes Manager Chuck Dressen, left, and Long George Kelly, former major league baseball luminaries. — *San Francisco News*, 19th January 1949
- But the strategy of the Democratic brain-trust miscarried. — Jack Lait and Lee Mortimer, *Washington Confidential*, p. 200, 1951
- It is not altogether strange that President Kennedy's brain trust should find itself under heavy fire from the Republican side of the fence. — *San Francisco Chronicle*, p. 1, 1st July 1962
- Well, he ain't popl'lar neither. He ain't no brain trust. He ain't even good-lookin'. — C.D. Payne, *Youth in Revolt*, p. 409, 1993

brake fluid *noun*
any medication used to sedate an unruly prisoner *US, 1991*
- — Lee McNelis, *30 + And a Wake-Up*, p. 6, 1991

brand X *noun*
marijuana *US, 1980*
- — Edith A. Folb, *runnin' down some lines*, p. 230, 1980

brannigan *noun*
a brawl, literal or figurative *US, 1940*
- But no matter how great the whoop-de-do, nothing in Chicago is likely to approach the heroic brannigan of 1920, when an earlier and perhaps more stalwart Democratic generation convened for the first and only time in San Francisco. — *San Francisco Chronicle*, p. 19, 20th July 1952
- Another brannigan is expected to break out for control of the Democratic party on the San Francisco county level. — *San Francisco News*, p. 3, 9th June 1956
- Next came the brannigan. — *San Francisco Examiner*, p. 7, 11th August 1960

brass *noun*

1 in the military, high-ranking officers as a collective entity *US, 1864*
- As perspiring VIPs, government guides, Navy brass and reporters stood by, the President came out, shook hands with Guzick, his wife and three children, then patted his pockets for the check. — *Washington Post*, p. B2, 19th May 1979
- [I]t is by considerations largely beyond the control of the air crews or even the Air Force Brass. — *Washington Post*, p. E7, 9th August 1981
- Secretary of Defense Donald Rumsfeld won the first argument, about the size of the invasion force; it was far smaller than Army brass wanted. — *Chicago Tribune*, p. C24, 8th April 2004

2 in carnival usage, fake jewelry *US, 1981*
- — Don Wilmeth, *The Language of American Popular Entertainment*, p. 33, 1981

3 brass knuckles *US, 1980*
- — Edith A. Folb, *runnin' down some lines*, p. 231, 1980

brass buttons *noun*
a police officer; the police in general *US, 1974*
- — John Scarne, *Scarne on Dice*, p. 462, 1974

brass-happy *adjective*
extremely anxious to be promoted within the officer corps *US, 1946*
- — *American Speech*, p. 238, October 1946: "World War II slang of maladjustment"

brass monkey *noun*
used in a number of figures of speech, especially as a basis for comparison *US, 1857*
- It would take what Kipling called the nerve of a brass monkey to talk about democracy versus totalitarianism or about fighting the anti-Christ. — George N. Crocker, *Roosevelt's Road to Russia*, p. 85, 1959
- "It's cold enough to breeze the balls off a brass monkey" (which has nothing to do with a monkey or its private parts, but rather the brass rings that held cannonballs on ships.) — *St. Petersburg (Florida) Times*, p. 1, 19th January 2003
- Clem Dubose can talk the ears off a brass monkey. — *Orlando (Florida) Sentinel Tribune*, p. K1, 29th February 2004

brass ring *noun*
an elusive but valuable prize *US, 1950*
- There are plenty of women who see me as the brass ring. — *Sleepless in Seattle*, 1993

brass tacks *noun*
the basic facts; the basic reality *US, 1895*
Rhyming slang for "facts," but not accepted as such by authorities who combine "brass tacks" with its variation "brass nails."
- Let's get down to brass tacks here. We've got a sweetheart of a deal to do. — Vincent Patrick, *Family Business*, p. 53, 1985

brat *noun*
a young and/or weak man used as a passive homosexual partner, especially in prison *US, 1961*
- Punks and brats are those prisoners who take the passive role in sodomy; there is no chronological age limit. — *New York Mattachine Newsletter*, p. 6, June 1961
- — Joseph E. Ragen and Charles Finston, *Inside the World's Toughest Prison*, p. 792, 1962

brat pack *nickname*
a group of young movie actors who played roles in John Hughes films of the 1980s *US, 1985*
Frequently mentioned as members of the group included Anthony Michael Hall, Emilio Estevez, Charlie Sheen, Judd Nelson, Molly Ringwald, Rob Lowe, and Ally Sheedy. A play on the Sinatra-centric Rat Pack of the 1950s and 60s.
- No, he insists, the Brat Pack (the name given to Estevez and some of his young actor pals) is not a tightly knit group of friends[.] — *Chicago Tribune*, p. 7C, 31st March 1989
- "Went to the movies?" "Any good?" "Tedious. Brat-pack stuff." — Joseph Wambaugh, *The Golden Orange*, p. 54, 1990

braveheart *noun*
a group activity at a heavy metal or punk concert in which dancers divided into two groups rush at each other *US, 2003*
From the scenes in Mel Gibson's movie in which the Scottish and English armies rush at each other.
- "We did the Braveheart thing. We split the crowd, and when you give the signal, you have both fronts collide, and they didn't know how to do it." — *Phoenix New Times*, 4th December 2003

bravo delta *noun*
a nonfunctioning piece of hardware *US, 1988*
A phonetic-alphabet euphemism for "broke dick."
- — Hans Halberstadt, *Airborne*, p. 130, 1988

brawl *noun*
a rowdy party *US, 1927*
- — Collin Baker et al., *College Undergraduate Slang Study Conducted at Brown University*, p. 8, 1968
- — Kenn "Naz" Young, *Naz's Underground Dictionary*, p. 17, 1973

Brazilian landing strip; Brazilian *noun*
the trimming of a woman's pubic hair such that only a narrow strip remains; the result thereof *US, 2001*
- Maybe one percent of my clients have stuck to the old conservative bikini line wax—the rest have converted to Brazilians. — *Nerve*, p. 20, December 2000–January 2001
- "I got mugged. She took everything I've got." Carrie Bradshaw in Sex and the City after a Brazilian bikini wax. — *Real Simple*, p. 65, May 2001
- The Brazilian[:] Leaves a vertical stripe in front, two or three fingers in width. — *Loaded*, p. 5, June 2002

BRB
used in computer message shorthand to mean "be right back" *US, 1991*
- — Eric S. Raymond, *The New Hacker's Dictionary*, p. 342, 1991

breach *noun*

▸ **in the breach**

in poker, first to act in a given situation *US, 1988*

- — George Percy, *The Language of Poker*, p. 47, 1988

bread *noun*

money *US, 1935*

The term was used at least as early as the 1930s, but it did not gain wide acceptance until the 1960s.

- Without bread a stud can't even rule an anthill. — William "Lord" Buckley, *Marc Anthony's Funeral Oration*, 1955
- We spent two hours in Testament waiting for Hyman Solomon to show up; he was hustling for his bread somewhere in town, but we couldn't see him. — Jack Kerouac, *On the Road*, p. 137, 1957
- "There's a lot of bread to be made gigging right around here in Roxbury," Shorty explained to me. — Malcolm X and Alex Haley, *The Autobiography of Malcolm X*, p. 45, 1964
- Black Panther Platform and Program No. 10: We want land, bread, housing, education, clothing, justice and peace. — *The Black Panther*, p. 18, 25 January 1969

breadbasket *noun*

the stomach *UK, 1785*

- I had to stand on top of the pile trying to catch four or five bricks at a time when the man below heaved them at me. The first batch caught me right in the breadbasket and bounced square on my toe. — Mezz Mezzrow, *Really the Blues*, p. 36, 1946
- I pivoted like a soldier doing an aboutface and planted my right in Pansy-face's bread basket[.] — Robert Edmond Alter, *Carny Kill*, p. 110, 1966

bread box *noun*

1 the stomach *US, 1919*

A lesser-known cousin of **BREADBASKET**.

- Also, he needed more cash—ought to see a doctor about this bum breadbox. — Bernard Wolfe, *The Late Risers*, p. 170, 1954

2 a safe that is easily broken into *US, 1949*

- — Vincent J. Monteleone, *Criminal Slang*, p. 33, 1949

breadwinner *noun*

the person responsible for supporting a family *UK, 1821*

- "I don't blame you, dear Kay," he said gravely, "for comparing your-self to me as a breadwinner." — Mary McCarthy, *The Group*, p. 87, 1963
- MICKEY: Because it's expected. He's—KAY: The breadwinner. — Elmore Leonard, *Switch*, p. 34, 1978

break *noun*

in hip-hop culture, an instrumental section from any recor-ded source that is mixed with other similar selections to make a new piece of music *US, 1993*

- [H]e plays the instrumental breakdown section—or the breaks—of his favorite funk, soul and reggae songs, sending partygoers to the dancefloor in droves. — *The Source*, p. 137, March 2002

break *verb*

1 in blackjack, to exceed 21 points, losing the hand *US, 1991*

- — Avery Cardoza, *Winning Casino Blackjack for the Non-Counter*, p. 73, 1991

2 to run away *US, 1994*

- We gon' have to get out and break. — *Menace II Society*, 1993
- — Ann Lawson, *Kids & Gangs*, p. 56, 1994

3 to steal something *US, 2003*

- — *San Francisco Chronicle*, p. E5, 10th August 2003

4 to do something to excess *US, 1989*

- — Terry Williams, *The Cocaine Kids*, p. 135, 1989

▸ **break a cap**

to shoot a gun *US, 1954*

- The bodyguard got hold of his gun and we broke a couple of caps at each other. — Caryl Chessman, *Cell 2456 Death Row*, p. 194, 1954

▸ **break bad**

to act in a threatening, menacing manner *US, 1997*

- — Anna Scotti and Paul Young, *Buzzwords*, p. 54, 1997

▸ **break his (or her) cherry**

(used of a racehorse) to win the first race in a racing career *US, 1951*

- — David W. Maurer, *Argot of the Racetrack*, p. 17, 1951

▸ **break luck**

(of a prostitute) to have sex with the first customer of the day or night *US, 1969*

- The runt was gone. She was breaking her luck with Chuck. — Iceberg Slim (Robert Beck), *Pimp*, p. 154, 1969
- A ho breaks her luck when she turns the first trick of her work day. — Christina and Richard Milner, *Black Players*, p. 297, 1972
- "I broke luck. Made fifty dollars." — Susan Hall, *Ladies of the Night*, p. 21, 1973
- Several of her stable prosses were chatting over too hot cups of coffee, eager to break luck, anxious for Leila to tell them where to turn the first trick of their workday. — Emmett Grogan, *Final Score*, p. 68, 1976

▸ **break out into assholes**

to become deeply frightened *US, 1982*

- — Arnold Shaw, *Dictionary of American Pop/Rock*, p. 54, 1982

▸ **break out the rag**

to lose your temper after losing a game *US, 1971*

- — *American Speech*, p. 232, Autumn – Winter 1971: "Checkschmuck! the slang of the chess player"

▸ **break someone's chops**

to give someone a hard time, to harass someone *US, 1953*

- We don't get those bullshit complaints and they won't break our chops on the paper work. — Peter Maas, *Serpico*, p. 175, 1973
- Kids used to call me a "hallelujah"—break my chops. — Edwin Torres, *Carlito's Way*, p. 7, 1975

▸ **break squelch**

to communicate on a radio during a period when radio use is inadvisable, given enemy locations, by tapping a key on the radio handset *US, 1981*

- I broke squelch, because I thought they would move these people out, relocate them to a POW camp. — Mark Baker, *Nam*, p. 138, 1981
- "If you're receiving me, break quelch [key your radio handset] twice, over." — James Donahue, *Mobile Guerilla Force*, p. 217, 1997

▸ **break starch**

to put on a fresh uniform. *US, 1968*

- — Carl Fleischhauer, *A Glossary of Army Slang*, p. 5, 1968
- Every day in the Airborne began in a freshly washed and starched pair of cut-down fatigues, and both officer and NCO "broke starch" —put on a fresh pair—once or twice throughout the day. — David H. Hackworth, *About Face*, p. 442, 1989

▸ **break the bank**

to divide the winnings up among members of a blackjack counting team *US, 1991*

- — Michael Dalton, *Blackjack*, p. 34, 1991

▸ **break the house**

in gambling, especially an illegal gambling enterprise, to win a great deal of money from the house *US, 1989*

- I will never forget watching him stroll across Washburne Avenue after breaking the house. — Odie Hawkins, *Men Friends*, p. 130, 1989

▸ **break the night**

to stay up all night *US, 1989*

- Then Thursday he tried to "break the night," street slang for staying up until sunrise—in search of a good time. — *Newsday (New York)*, p. 20, 14th May 1989
- "We broke night," Coco said. From their bed, they watched the morn-ing brighten. — Adrian Nicole LeBlanc, *Random Family*, p. 69, 2003

▸ **break watches**

(of a racehorse) to run very fast during a morning workout *US, 1951*

- — David W. Maurer, *Argot of the Racetrack*, p. 16, 1951

▸ **break weak**

to back down from a confrontation *US, 1992*

- — William K. Bentley and James M. Crobett, *Prison Slang*, p. 31, 1992

▸ **break wide**

to leave *US, 1992*

- — William K. Bentley and James M. Corbett *Prison Slang*, p. 48, 1992

breakage *noun*

in horse racing pari-mutuel betting, the change left over after paying off bets to the nearest nickel, dime, or dollar *US, 1947*

- — Dan Parker, *The ABC of Horse Racing*, p. 144, 1947

breakaway *noun*

1 any piece of equipment or clothing that will tear free from a police officer's body during a fight *US, 1962*

- — *American Speech*, p. 267, December 1962: "The language of traffic policemen"

2 in television and movie making, a prop designed to break easily upon impact *US, 1990*

- — Ralph S. Singleton, *Filmmaker's Dictionary*, p. 22, 1990

breakbeat *noun*

in contemporary dance culture, a sampled beat that is looped to create a rhythmic pattern; hence, a musical style *US, 1988*

- The best-stocked is the Music Factory (1476 Broadway, between 42nd and 43rd), which is jammed with the latest New York-based label rap hits, breakbeat collections (which feature hit songs with extended breaks for rap deejays or record producers)[.] — *Los Angeles Times*, p. 92, 13th March 1988
- intense breakbeat sessions — Alon Shulman, *The Style Bible*, p. 42, 1999
- — Gareth Thomas, *This Is Ecstasy*, p. 43, 2002

breakdancing *noun*

an energetic dance improvised to the rhythms of hip-hop; often danced competitively *US, 1983*

The origin of hip-hop is credited to New York DJ Kool Herc who mixed in rhythmic "*break*down parts" which dancers then interpreted.

- Breakdancing, also performed during a Nike fashion show and at the Hyde booth, is a stylized movement form, straight from New York City sidewalks, characterized by fast, robotic movements and synchronized acrobatics. — *Footwear News*, p. 1, 10th October 1983
- Breakdancing went with rap, the way graffiti went up on the subway trains and schoolyard walls. — Bonnie Nadell and John Small, *Breakdance*, p. 8, 1984
- The discipline of breakdancing/B-boying was one of four separate styles that converged through the late 70s. Up-rocking [...] pop-locking [...] and body-popping[.] — Alex Ogg, *The Hip Hop Years*, p. 14, 1999

breakdown *noun*

a shotgun *US, 1994*

- — Ann Lawson, *Kids & Gangs*, p. 56, 1994: "Common African-American gang slang/phrases"
- — Bill Valentine, *Gang Intelligence Manual*, 1995

break down *verb*

to explain something *US, 1965*

- So I clean out Margo's refrigerator of all its food and drive back over to the Communication Company where is lovely Sam and Cassandra and Claude and Helene who I break it down to. — *The Digger Papers*, p. 10, August 1968

breaker *noun*

in horse racing, a horse that starts a race with a great burst of speed *US, 1982*

- — Bob and Barbara Freeman, *Wanta Bet?*, p. 288, 1982

breakers *noun*

in certain games of poker, cards that qualify a player to open betting *US, 1988*

- — George Percy, *The Language of Poker*, p. 13, 1988

breakers ahead!

used as a general purpose warning of impending problems *US, 1963*

Of obvious nautical origin, from the cry of the masthead lookout.

- — Charles F. Haywood, *Yankee Dictionary*, p. 15, 1963

breakfast club *noun*

a nightclub operating after other clubs close at 2 a.m., staying open until the early morning when breakfast is served *US, 1954*

- Wilbur Stump, the noted pianist, opened a "breakfast club" (one of those bring-your-own bottle joints, opening at 2 a.m.) on the second floor at 207 Powell. — *San Francisco Examiner*, p. 19, 4th September 1954
- But since she began operating Guys and Dolls as a breakfast club last October, the alliances arranged there have been somewhat less permanent, Sgt. Robert Davis of the vice squad charged. — *San Francisco News Call-Bulletin*, p. 2, 20th February 1965
- Joint police-health department action has dealt almost a knockout blow to San Francisco's after-hours "breakfast" clubs, reducing their number from 14 to only two. — *San Francisco Examiner*, p. 3, 24th April 1970

breakfast of champions *noun*

beer *US, 1976*

- She handed one to Steve, then took a long drink from her own. "Breakfast of Champions" she proclaimed, holding up the can in a mock toast until Steve had taken a drink. — Jack W. Thomas, *Heavy Number*, p. 53, 1976

breakfast of losers *noun*

methaqualone, the recreational drug best known as Quaaludes™ *US, 1987*

- — Carsten Stroud, *Close Pursuit*, 1987

breaking *noun*

break dancing, especially its gymnastic and acrobatic aspect *US, 1984*

- — Bradley Elfman, *Breakdancing*, p. 11, 1984
- After breakin' died in 1986, b-boys here took revenge against house by breakin' in house clubs, which were the only clubs back then. — William Upski Wimsatt, *Bomb the Suburbs*, p. 125, 1994

break it off!

give me your money! *US, 1997*

- Just about a year ago, when Deon Jones was 17, he pulled a green Halloween mask over his face and put a gun to the head of a Fairywood neighbor. "Break it off," Jones said—street slang for "Hand over your money." — *Pittsburgh Post-Gazette*, p. A1, 7th August 1997

break-luck *noun*

a prostitute's first customer of the day *US, 1993*

- — *Washington Post*, p. C5, 7th November 1993

break man *noun*

a prison guard who orchestrates the opening of cells in the morning *US, 1977*

- Voices were raised in harsh humor, as over four hundred men joked and argued back and forth. "Break three!" the break man screamed as he reached the third gallery. — Donald Goines, *Black Gangster*, p. 7, 1977

break off *verb*

to treat someone harshly *US, 2004*

- break you off: to deal with harshly, extremely — J.G. Narum, *The Convict Cookbook*, p. 158, 2004

break out *verb*

to leave *US, 1997*

- — Vann Wesson, *Generation X Field Guide and Lexicon*, p. 28, 1997

breast check *noun*

a walk through a crowd in search of attractive female breasts *US, 1995*

- — *Maledicta*, p. 47, 1995: "Door whore and other New Mexico restaurant slang"

breath *noun*

in poker, to pass without betting *US, 1988*

- — George Percy, *The Language of Poker*, p. 13, 1988

breather *noun*

1 in sports, a game against a weak opponent *US, 1945*

From the conventional sense (a rest).

- The coaches used to talk about breathers. That's a sad excuse. There are no breathers today anyway. — *San Francisco News*, p. 18, 15th November 1945
- Da Grosa also assailed the scheduling of "breathers" as unfair to the paying public. — *San Francisco Cann-Bulletin*, p. 16, 26th December 1950
- The UCLA Bruins, toppled from No. 1 last week amid the mud and might of Maryland, drew their "breather" tomorrow and are figured to beat Washington State by three or four touchdowns. — *San Francisco Chronicle*, p. 3H, 1st October 1955
- Women Look to Get on Track With Nonconference Breather [Headline] — *Daily Tar Hee (Chapel Hill, North Carolina))*, 10th February 1995

2 the nose *US, 1973*

- — Kenn "Naz" Young, *Naz's Underground Dictionary*, p. 17, 1973
- — Charles Shafer, *Folk Speech in Texas Prisons*, p. 199, 1990

3 a person who derives sexual pleasure from telephoning someone and breathing heavily when they answer the phone *US, 1986*

- When I lift up the receiver, at first I think I got a breather. Then a voice says, "Check it out. There was a bullet in Helen Caplet." — Robert Campbell, *Junkyard Dog*, p. 75, 1986

breck *noun*
breakfast *US, 1983*
- — *Concord (New Hampshire) Monitor*, p. 17, 23rd August 1983

bree *noun*
a young woman *US, 1992*
- — Jack Lait and Lee Mortimer, *New York Confidential*, p. 235, 1992: "A glossary of Harlemisms"

breed *noun*
a person who is not white *US, 1992*
- — William K. Bentley and James M. Corbett, *Prison Slang*, p. 54, 1992

breeder *noun*
from the homosexual point of view, a heterosexual *US, 1979*
Usually used as an insult.
- "Hey, what does a breeder know?" Michael grinned. "Where did you learn that word?" The light changed. They proceeded with graceless caution across the pebbly asphalt. "One of the guys at Perry's," replied Brian. "He said that's what the faggots call us." — Armistead Maupin, *Further Tales of the City*, p. 167, 1982
- "So we defy them, see?" "Them?" I asked. "Breeders." — Ethan Morden, *Everybody Loves You*, p. 209, 1988
- We whispered "breeder" behind your breeder-backs, made fun of your bi-level haircuts, Jordache jeans, and "spare tires." — Dan Savage, *Savage Love*, p. 305, 1998
- Butt-banging breeders may even throw their own pride parade. — *The Village Voice*, 7th March 2000

breeder *adjective*
heterosexual *US, 1997*
- "Breeder bitch," I said happily; but by then she was Ignoring Me. — Ethan Morden, *Some Men Are Lookers*, p. 99, 1997
- As a breeder boy put it to me, "It's easier approaching straight women in gay bars." — Dan Savage, *Savage Love*, p. 25, 1998

breeze *noun*
1 something that is achieved easily and quickly *US, 1928*
- [T]he boosts are a breeze. — *Gone in 60 Seconds*, 2000

2 in horse racing, an easy pace during a workout or race *US, 1951*
- — David W. Naurer, *Argot of the Racetrack*, p. 16, 1951

3 a prison sentence that is nearly completed *US, 1962*
- — Joseph E. Ragen and Charles Finston, *Inside the World's Toughest Prison*, p. 806, 1962

4 a calm, collected person *US, 1992*
- — K. Bentley and James M. Corbett, *Prison Slang*, p. 48, 1992

5 used as a term of address *US, 1966*
- — *Current Slang*, p. 2, Fall 1966

breeze *verb*
1 to escape; to go *US, 1913*
- Any time I breezed down the street, cats would flash me friendly grins and hands would wave at me from all sides, and I felt like I was king of the tribe. — Mezz Mezzrow, *Really the Blues*, p. 48, 1946
- Soon as I got the angle on that I breezed. — Hal Ellson, *Duke*, p. 124, 1949
- Take the dough and breeze. — Raymond Chandler, *The Little Sister*, p. 62, 1949
- He kept breezing and getting caught and brought back into the detail building. — Claude Brown, *Manchild in the Promised Land*, p. 142, 1965

2 in pool, to only barely glance the object ball with the cue ball *US, 1990*
- — Steve Rushin, *Pool Cool*, p. 6, 1990

breezeway *noun*
the area in a prison where the most derelict of the convicts gather *US, 1984*
- — Inez Cardozo-Freeman, *The Joint*, p. 484, 1984

breezy *noun*
a young woman *US, 2004*
- What's up with you and that breezy. — Rick Ayers (Editor), *Berkeley High Slang Dictionary*, p. 14, 2004

brew *noun*
1 beer; a glass, bottle or can of beer *US, 1907*
- I shook hands with the guy and ordered a brew. — Mickey Spillane, *I, The Jury*, p. 43, 1947
- [W]ith a few brews my fingers flail and fly less than as usual. — Jack Kerouac, *Letter to Neal Cassady*, p. 318, 10th June 1951
- Awesome party! Good tunes! Good brew! Good buddies! — *Wayne's World 2*, 1993

- MAFADA: Would you like a glass of tea or something? HEALY: You got a brew? — *Something About Mary*, 1998

2 a Jewish person *US, 1997*
An abbreviation of "Hebrew."
- — Pamela Munro, *U.C.L.A. Slang*, p. 45, 1997

brewha *noun*
a glass, bottle or can of beer *US, 2001*
- — Pamela Munro, *U.C.L.A. Slang*, p. 47, 2001

brewski; brewsky *noun*
beer; a serving of beer *US, 1978*
Mock Polish.
- — *Wesleyan Alumnus*, p. 29, Spring 1981
- — Connie Eble (Editor), *UNC-CH Campus Slang*, p. 2, Spring 1982
- JD: This is Ohio. If you don't have a brewsky in your hand you might as well be wearing a dress. — *Heathers*, 1988
- "Brewskie," he said. "I got some Bud under my bed, man." — Larry Brown, *Dirty Work*, p. 49, 1989
- Dig this. They're charging for brewskies. — *Clueless*, 1995

briar patch *noun*
a female's pubic hair *US, 1967*
- — Dale Gordon, *The Dominion Sex Dictionary*, p. 32, 1967

bribe *noun*
in marketing, the initial, attractive offer to join a book or music club *US, 1986*
- — Rachel S. Epstein and Nina Liebman, *Biz Speak*, p. 27, 1986

brick *noun*
1 someone with exceptionally good credit *US, 2001*
Collected in San Rafael, California, at a car dealership, in March 2001.
2 a person lacking social skills *US, 1968*
- — Collin Baker et al., *College Undergraduate Slang Study Conducted at Brown University*, p. 88, 1968
3 a die that has been shaved on one face *US, 1950*
- — Thomas L. Clark, *The Dictionary of Gambling and Gaming*, p. 27, 1987
4 in poker, a drawn card that fails to improve the hand *US, 1996*
- — John Vorhaus, *The Big Book of Poker Slang*, p. 8, 1996
5 ten cartons of stolen cigarettes *US, 1982*
- — Bill Reilly, *Big Al's Official Guide to Chicagoese*, p. 17, 1982
6 a carton of cigarettes *US, 1981*
- — *Maledicta*, pp. 266–267, Summer/Winter 1981: "By its slang, ye shall know it: the pessimism of prison life"
- — Reinhold Aman, *Hillary Clinton's Pen Pal*, p. 22, 1996
7 a kilogram of, usually compressed, marijuana, or, less commonly, another drug *US, 1992*
- She had a brick of weed she was sellin', and she didn't want to go to the buy alone. — *Reservoir Dogs*, 1992
- Oh yeah? How much blow you do tonight? I heard they had a fuckin' brick. — *Copland*, 1997
- Here was some dude, not even a chemistry major, coming on to you with mikes [microdots], grams, bricks, kilos and hundredweights. — Robert Sabbag, *A Way with the Spoon [The Howard Marks Book of Dope Stories]*, p. 351, 2001

brick *verb*
1 to fail to deliver as promised *US, 1993*
- The delivery guy bricked. — *Dazed and Confused*, 1993
2 to hurl bricks, rocks or other hard objects *US, 1972*
A word commonly used in the 1960s in American cities during events called "riots" by the dominant power and "uprisings" by leftists.
- — David Claerbaut, *Black Jargon in White America*, p. 59, 1972
3 to miss a shot; to fail *US, 2001*
- She threw th' fuckin' case, went in the tank, intentionally bricked it. — Stephen J. Cannell, *The Tin Collectors*, p. 156, 2001

brickhouse *noun*
in poker, a full house that is not the best hand *US, 1996*
An allusion built on "brick" as a "useless card."
- — John Vorhaus, *The Big Book of Poker Slang*, p. 8, 1996

bricks *noun*
in prison, the world outside the prison walls *US, 1976*
- — John R. Armore and Joseph D. Wolfe, *Dictionary of Desperation*, p. 21, 1976

▸ **hit the bricks**
to leave, especially to leave prison *US, 1931*
- Maybe I could fly one of my magnetized copping kites (high voltage letters) when I hit the bricks, and steal a 'ho! — Iceberg Slim (Robert Beck), *Airtight Willie and Me*, p. 3, 1979
- Just say goodbye once, and then hit the bricks, you big-bottomed freaks, you. — Stuart Jeffries, *Mrs Slocombe's Pussy*, p. 10, 2000

▸ **on the bricks**
working as a street prostitute *US, 1981*
- "Oh, they might treat you real nice at first, talk to you pretty, show you a good time, buy you pretty things, but before you know what's happening they got you out on the bricks." — Alix Shulman, *On the Stroll*, p. 22, 1981

▸ **to the bricks**
extremely, utterly, completely *US, 1928*
- You sure are getting togged to the bricks, pal. [Freckles and His Friends comic strip] — *San Francisco News*, 23rd May 1946
- — Clarence Major, *Dictionary of Afro-American Slang*, p. 115, 1970

brick shithouse *noun*
a woman, or rarely a homosexual man, with a curvaceous figure; a powerfully built man *US, 1928*
Sometimes euphemized to a simple "house."
- Janet is something to write home about. Blonde with a shape like a brick shit house. — Donald Goines, *Never Die Alone*, p. 107, 1974
- She's a brick house / The lady's stacked and that's a fact. — The Commodores, *Brick House*, 1977
- This guy was built like a brick shithouse, with an elephantine mustache and smoldering brown eyes. — Armistead Maupin, *Further Tales of the City*, p. 150, 1982
- You with some fine bitch, I mean a brick shithouse bitch—you're with Jayne Kennedy. — *True Romance*, 1993

bricktop *noun*
a red-haired person *US, 1856*
- Greer, in common with all bricktops, especially those of Irish origin can be a little difficult to handle at times. — *San Francisco Examiner*, p. II-3, 21st June 1957

brick-topped *adjective*
red-headed *US, 1912*
- Whit wondered, as he ate his meal in the huge B.D.R.—boy's dining room—how this brick-topped cadet officer would go about learning him to like it. — Caryl Chessman, *Cell 2456 Death Row*, p. 88, 1954

bridal suite *noun*
a room where police assigned the late night shift can sleep *US, 1994*
- — *Los Angeles Times*, p. B8, 19th December 1994

bride's slide *noun*
in backgammon, the customary play with a first roll of 6 – 5: moving a back man 11 points *US, 1976*
- — Dave Thompson, *Play Backgammon Tonight*, p. 58, 1976

bridge *noun*
1 a holder for a marijuana cigarette *US, 1955*
A common term in the 1950s, largely supplanted by **ROACH CLIP** in the 1960s.
- — *American Speech*, p. 86, May 1955: "Narcotic argot along the Mexican border"
2 a slightly curved playing card, altered by a cheat to manipulate the cutting of a deck *US, 1991*
- — Michael Dalton, *Blackjack*, p. 34, 1991
3 a group of four in a restaurant or soda fountain *US, 1967*
An allusion to a bridge party.
- — *American Speech*, p. 61, February 1967: "Soda-fountain, restaurant and tavern calls"

▸ **under the bridge**
in a smuggling operation, across a border *US, 1956*
- — *American Speech*, p. 98, May 1956: "Smugglers' argot in the southwest"

bridge and tunnel *adjective*
said of a resident of New Jersey who commutes to New York *US, 1984*
Disparaging.
- I said to the team, "We can't go to New Jersey. What would they call us, the Bridge and Tunnels?" — Dan Jenkins, *Life Its Ownself*, p. 18, 1984

- The worst drug calamity, the worst-case scenario, was that you accidentally took too much ecstasy and were actually nice to a Bridge-and-Tunnel person. — James St. James, *Party Monster*, p. 67, 1990
- Eww! Not a bridge-and-tunnel Jersey dyke! — *Chasing Amy*, 1997
- I jam it open with my shoe and slide in between a bridge-and-tunnel babe and a lawyer. — Lynn Breedlove, *Godspeed*, p. 243, 2002

bridge jumper *noun*
in horse racing, a person who regularly bets on favorites and is distraught if the favorite does not win *US, 1951*
- — David W. Naurer, *Argot of the Racetrack*, p. 16, 1951

bridge man *noun*
a liaison *US, 1986*
- When Charley was twenty-one he was transferred to be the bridge man between the mob-owned racetracks around the country and the racehorses they had to keep buying[.] — Richard Condon, *Prizzi's Family*, p. 40, 1986

Bridge of Sighs *nickname*
an overpass connecting the New York City jail with the criminal court building *US, 1955*
A borrowing from Venice's Ponte de Sospiri, romanticized by Lord Byron.
- He walked me down this long dark corridor and then into a narrower corridor. Now I knew were I was. This was the Bridge of Sighs that led from the court building high up over the street into the old Tombs. — Rocky Garciano (with Rowland Barber), *Somebody Up There Likes Me*, p. 105, 1955
- Few lawyers alive today remember the old court house or the grey granite, twin-peaked Tombs and the famous "Bridge of Sighs" that rose over Franklin Street to connect the two buildings. — *New York Law Journal*, p. S-14, 6th May 1991

brief *noun*
a playing card that has been trimmed slightly so that a cheat can locate it within a deck by feel *US, 1988*
- — George Percy, *The Language of Poker*, p. 13, 1988

briefcase *noun*
a faceless, anonymous businessman *US, 2001*
- The briefcases stood at attention and took shit, then left. — Dan Jenkins, *The Money-Whipped Steer-Job Three-Jack Give-Up Artist*, p. 69, 2001

briggity *adjective*
arrogant, vain, stubborn *US, 1884*
- Come to think of it, you never hear briggity anymore either. Briggity-britches was one of the insults we used to hurl at one another when we were kids. — *Charleston (West Virginia) Gazette*, p. 4C, 15th August 2003

bright *noun*
1 morning *US, 1941*
- Many was the night we sniffed and philosophized, philosophized and sniffed, until the early bright was upon us. — Mezz Mezzrow, *Really the Blues*, p. 170, 1946
- — *Time Magazine*, p. 92, 20th January 1947
- With a pocketful of green I was digging the scene the other bright[.] — Dan Burley, *Diggeth Thou?*, p. 36, 1959
- Bitch, one of these "brights" you're going to shoot your "jib" [mouth] off, I'll curtsy and call you Runt the corpse. — Iceberg Slim (Robert Beck), *Pimp*, p. 136, 1969
2 a light-complexioned black person *US, 1976*
- "Break it down, you even got one set for brights and—" "Brights?" "—another for bloods." She looked at her hands before she answered the question. "Light-skinned niggers." — Robert Campbell, *Boneyards*, p. 268, 1992

bright disease *noun*
the condition of knowing too much for your own good *US, 1953*
- — Lavada Durst, *The Jives of Dr. Hepcat*, p. 11, 1953

bright-eyed and bushy-tailed *adjective*
alert and enthusiastic, lively *US, 1942*
- I'm telling you, he's bright-eyed and bushy-tailed, none of that sulking, suspicious nature. — *Washington Post*, p. D1, 28th January 1979
- Alex Rodriguez was the first Yankee at the stadium. He showed up for work ahead of every other ballplayer Thursday morning, although not exactly bright-eyed and bushy-tailed, as his droopy lids betrayed. — *Chicago Tribune*, p. C2, 9th April 2004

bright eyes *noun*

a lookout during a criminal venture *US, 1962*

- Smugglers' Argot in the Southwest — *American Speech*, p. 96, May 1956
- — Joseph E. Ragen and Charles Finston, *Inside the World's Toughest Prison*, p. 792, 1962: "Penitentiary and underworld glossary"

brightlight team *noun*

in Vietnam, a small group from the special forces sent to rescue American prisoners of war *US, 1981*

- — Shelby L. Stanton, *Vietnam Order of Battle*, p. 29, 1981
- There was enough evidence that Mike might be held in the general area where we were hit that a "bright light" team was interested to attempt to find and rescue him. — Government Printing Office, *Report of Select Committee on POW/MIA's*, p. 57, 1995

brights *noun*

white socks *US, 1969*

- — *Current Slang*, p. 5, Summer 1969

brighty *adjective*

very smart *US, 1945*

- — Lou Shelly, *Hepcats Jive talk Dictionary*, p. 8, 1945

brig rat *noun*

a prisoner *US, 1942*

- [H]e could imagine Red in the Navy, a brig rat of course, an old white hat, shipping over until the sailors' home claimed him. — Malcolm Braly, *On the Yard*, p. 211, 1967

brim *noun*

1 a police officer *US, 1957*

- This was the risky part, the exchange, if the bims should happen along right now. — Herbert Simmons, *Corner Boy*, p. 54, 1957

2 any hat *US, 1965*

- — David Claerbaut, *Black Jargon in White America*, p. 59, 1972

bring *verb*

to compel someone to do something. *US, 1972*

- — Bruce Jackson, *Outside the Law*, p. 55, 1972

▶ **bring it in**

in poker, to make the first bet of a hand *US, 1990*

- — Anthony Holden, *Big Deal*, p. 298, 1990

▶ **bring it on**

used for challenging an opponent to begin a competition *US, 1998*

- VICTOR: Game point, cousin, game point. JUNIOR POLATKIN: Bring it on, Victor, bring it on. — *Smoke Signals*, 1998
- Bring it on, Mum, bring it on! — Dave Haslam, *Adventures of the Wheels of Steel*, p. 117, 2001

▶ **bring pee**

to frighten someone severely *US, 1966*

Vietnam war usage.

- — *Post (New York)*, p. 42, 16th July 1966
- — Carl Fleischhauer, *A Glossary of Military Slang*, p. 5, 1968

▶ **bring smoke**

by extension, to reprimand someone in harsh, profane tones *US, 1968*

- — Carl Fleischhauer, *A Glossary of Army Slang*, p. 6, 1968

bringdown *noun*

an event or person that discourages or depresses you *US, 1939*

- "You'll have to go home, son," the doc said. "You've got a slight murmur in your heart." That was a bringdown. — Mezz Mezzrow, *Really the Blues*, p. 19, 1946
- And that coming right after a big bug-sized bringdown from the Naxi's put on him. — William Lord Buckley, *Hip Einie*, 1955
- We sophisticate our tastes in order to tap dance by hassles and shove the poignancy of "bring downs" into impersonal shadows. — *Berkeley Barb*, p. 6, 18th November 1966
- Now you say, "Well the world of reality is a bringdown, man. There's police brutality and there is all this stuff." — *The San Francisco Oracle*, 1967

bring down *verb*

1 to depress someone, to deflate someone *US, 1935*

- "Don't let us down." "Or bring us down." — Chandler Brossard, *Who Walks in Darkness*, p. 74, 1952

- What really brought him down was the way Danny Atlas, owner of the Broadway novelty shop called Fun, Inc., gave him the big slough-off. — Bernard Wolfe, *The Late Risers*, p. 5, 1954
- The Hare Krishna boys got up and chanted, bringing most everyone down from the super-high place we had been. — *East Village Other*, 20th August 1969
- Don't let it bring you down, it's only castles burning. — Neil Young, *Don't Let It Bring You Down*, 1970

2 to help ease someone's return from a difficult drug experience *US, 1970*

- bring down: help someone come out of a bad drug experience. — Ethel Romm, *The Open Conspiracy*, p. 242, 1970

bring it, don't sing it!

used to invite action instead of words *US, 1998*

- — Ethan Hilderbant, *Prison Slang*, p. 144, 1998

bring out *verb*

to introduce someone to homosexuality, to awaken in someone their homosexuality *US, 1941*

- — Anon., *The Gay Girl's Guide*, p. 4, 1949
- Another exception is the young man who is "brought out" by older, more sophisticated homosexuals. — Stanley Weber, *A Study of Sex in Prison*, p. 12, 1973

bring up *verb*

to try someone on a criminal charge *US, 1823*

- He's dirty, for one thing. Twice brought up on assault, the people he beat up failed to show. — Elmore Leonard, *Be Cool*, p. 179, 1999

brittle *adjective*

(used of a computer program) functional, but easily rendered dysfunctional by changes or external stimuli which should not have the effect they have *US, 1991*

- — Eric S. Raymond, *The New Hacker's Dictionary*, p. 78, 1991

bro *noun*

a *bro*ther, in the sense of a fellow in a given situation or condition; especially of a fellow black *US, 1957*

- Crazy, bro. I gotcha. — Nathan Heard, *Howard Street*, p. 88, 1968
- "What's the tab, bro?" — Piri Thomas, *Stories from El Barrio*, p. 57, 1978
- Goodnight, bro—good dreams. — Herbert Huncke, *The Evening Sun Turned Crimson*, p. 205, 1980
- Bro? You in the "Mod Squad?" — *Copland*, 1997
- If they don't feel good about me, bro, where I'm coming from, they're not gonna listen. — Elmore Leonard, *Be Cool*, p. 8, 1999
- What are you doin' to her, dude? Oh my God, bro, dude. — *American Pie*, 1999

broad *noun*

1 a woman *US, 1911*

Somewhere between derogatory and so old-fashioned as to be charming in a hopeless way.

- "I smell Arpege," said the mama bear to her mate. "Gus, you've had a broad here." — Steve Allen, *Bop Fables*, p. 8, 1955
- The only time I went out for TV was to dig the broads on Shindig and Hollywood-A-Go-Go[.] — Eldridge Cleaver, *Soul on Ice*, p. 44, 1968
- Local Women's Libbers may have been right to equate the tacky term "broad" with "nigger," and I was wrong to act snappish about it earlier this week. Let's be friends again, people—and people again, friends. — *San Francisco Chronicle*, p. 35, 21st April 1972
- This is the end result of all the bright lights and the comped trips, of all the champagne and free hotel suites, and all the broads and all the booze. — *Casino*, 1995

2 a queen piece in a chess set *US, 2005*

- "You're the first youngster that realized how to beat me without my broad." — Colton Simpson, *Inside the Crips*, p. 143, 2005

3 a male homosexual who plays the passive sexual role *US, 1984*

- — Inez Cardozo-Freeman, *The Joint*, p. 484, 1984

4 in a deck of playing cards, a queen *UK, 1781*

- — Thomas L. Clark, *The Dictionary of Gambling and Gaming*, p. 29, 1987

broadcast *verb*

to engage in conversation *US, 1959*

- — *Swinging Syllables*, 1959

broadie *noun*

a woman *US, 1932*

A slightly embellished **BROAD**.

- She don't bother no one at all. Not even little broadies going by. — George Mandel, *Flee the Angry Strangers*, p. 386, 1952
- One of the broadies (as the driver referred to the madams and girls) had a couple of sixteen-year-olds in her place. — Monroe Fry, *Sex, Vice and Business*, p. 10, 1959

broad joint *noun*

a bar where prostitutes are available along with the drinks *US, 1956*

- A Broad Joint can furnish you a cooperative-type girl if you'll make proper financial arrangements. — Robert Sylvester, *No Cover Charge*, p. 265, 1956

broadski *noun*

a woman *US, 1967*

- I hear you latched on to a broadski. — Malcolm Braly, *On the Yard*, p. 250, 1967

broad squad *noun*

in prison, a group of homosexual men *US, 1990*

- — Charles Shafer, *Folk Speech in Texas Prisons*, p. 199, 1990

broad tosser *noun*

the operator of a three-card monte game swindle *US, 1980*

- — Joe McKennon, *Circus Lingo*, p. 21, 1980

Broadway *noun*

in poker, a five-card sequence ending with an ace as the highest card of the sequence *US, 1988*

- — George Percy, *The Language of Poker*, p. 13, 1988

Broadway Arab *noun*

a Jewish person *US, 1946*

- The Pavilion catered mostly to Gentiles, and when the manager found out that three of us musicians were Broadway Arabs from the tribe of Israel he wouldn't let us blow note one. — Mezz Mezzrow, *Really the Blues*, p. 86, 1946

Brodie; Brody *noun*

1 a fall or leap from a great height *US, 1899*

An allusion to Steve Brodie, a New York bookmaker who in 1886 claimed to have survived a leap from the Brooklyn Bridge and then opened a tavern which succeeded as a result of the publicity surrounding his claimed leap.

- I wondered if the undertaker had been born yet who was slick enough to paste a sucker's ass together after a "Brodie" fifteen-stories down. — Iceberg Slim (Robert Beck), *Pimp*, p. 165, 1969

2 a feigned drug withdrawal spasm *US, 1936*

- A drug addict's life is dedicated to cheating, lying, conniving, and "conning" to obtain illegal drugs. It's an obsession. And they'll go to any length to achieve their purpose. They'll pull a "Brody" or "Cartwheel" (feigned spasms) to elicit sympathy. — San Francisco News, p. 1, 5th December 1951
- — David Maurer and Victor Vogel, *Narcotics and Narcotic Addiction*, p. 392, 1973

3 a play that is a complete failure *US, 1973*

- — Sherman Louis Sergel, *The Language of Show Biz*, p. 29, 1973

Brodie; Brody *verb*

to intentionally skid a car *US, 1995*

- Fulo brodied in close. His headlights strafed Kirpaski. — James Ellroy, *American Tabloid*, p. 59, 1995
- I was going so fast, I overshot the house and hit the brakes half a block past, squealing rubber as I brodied to a stop. — Stephen J. Cannell, *White Sister*, p. 89, 2006

brogans *noun*

heavy work shoes *US, 1835*

From the Gaelic. During the US Civil War, the sturdy and durable leather shoes issued to infantrymen were nicknamed Brogans or Jefferson Booties.

- They took one of the opened bottles with them from which Agatson drank continually, brazenly, as he stumbled along in his oversize G.I. brogans. — John Clellon Holmes, *Go*, p. 219, 1952
- [M]any of us bought him a beer and a Polish sausage when he came in with his paint-splattered cords and brown brogans, broke as ever. — Oscar Zeta Acosta, *The Autobiography of a Brown Buffalo*, p. 47, 1972

- The very next evening, Daddy came home with shoes for Betty, John and me—three pairs of black, sturdy, strong, steel-toed brogans. — Bobby Seale, *A Lonely Rage*, p. 37, 1978

broges *noun*

work shoes *US, 1990*

An abbreviation of **BROGANS**.

- — Charles Shafer, *Folk Speech in Texas Prisons*, p. 199, 1990

broke dick *adjective*

nonfunctioning *US, 1975*

- I was walking past an old jalopy when this dude gets out looking sharper than a broke-dick dog. — James Carr, *Bad*, p. 77, 1975
- — Hans Halberstadt, *Airborne*, p. 130, 1988

broke money *noun*

a small amount of money given to a gambler who has lost his entire bankroll *US, 1950*

- — *The Annals of the American Academy of Political and Social Science*, p. 122, May 1950

broken *adjective*

depressed, acting oddly *US, 1981*

- — *CoEvolution Quarterly*, p. 27, Spring 1981

broken arrow *noun*

1 an accident involving nuclear weapons *US, 1980*

- Mr. Affeldt said that he learned of the incident when he received a telephone call from a regional office saying that personnel monitoring radio traffic had overheard a message containing the code word "broken arrow," which he said indicated "a major accident with a nuclear weapon aboard." — New York Times, p. A13, 17th September 1980
- It might not have been a "broken arrow" nuclear missile accident, but a mishap that damaged a Bangor Trident submarine ballistic missile and was kept under wraps by the Navy until this week threatens broken trust on an international scale. — Seattle Post-Intelligencer, p. B1, 13th March 2004

2 in computing, an error code on line 25 of a 3270 terminal *US, 1991*

- — Eric S. Raymond, *The New Hacker's Dictionary*, p. 79, 1991

broken wrist *noun*

an effeminate male homosexual *US, 1968*

- — Mary Swift, *Campus Slang (University of Texas)*, 1968

broker *noun*

a drug dealer *US, 1962*

- — Joseph E. Ragen and Charles Finston, *Inside the World's Toughest Prison*, p. 792, 1962
- — William D. Alsever, *Glossary for the Establishment and Other Uptight People*, p. 26, December 1970

broket *noun*

on a computer keyboard, the characters < and > *US, 1983*

A contraction of "broken bracket."

- — Guy L. Steele et al., *The Hacker's Dictionary*, p. 36, 1983

broly *adjective*

conforming to surfer etiquette *US, 1991*

- — Trevor Cralle, *The Surfin'ary*, p. 15, 1991

bronco *noun*

a young male recently initiated into homosexual sex *US, 1967*

- — Dale Gordon, *The Dominion Sex Dictionary*, p. 33, 1967

Bronx cheer *noun*

a combination of booing and a derisory farting noise, expressing disgust *US, 1922*

- I mentioned that maybe he ought to save it—meaning the Bronx cheer—till he started using his title regularly. — J.D. Salinger, *Nine Stories*, p. 98, 1953
- I kept giving "p-r-rt" Bronx cheers thru the blanket[.] — Jack Kerouac, *Letter to John Clellon Holmes*, p. 407, 19th February 1953
- [A] nation of peep freaks who prefer the bikini to the naked body, the white lie to the black truth, Hollywood smiles and canned laughter to a soulful Bronx cheer. — Eldridge Cleaver, *Soul on Ice*, p. 84, 1968

Bronzeville *noun*

a city neighborhood with a largely black population *US, 1950*

- This one concerns chiefly the South Side major settlement, which its residents euphemistically call "Bronzeville." — Jack Lait and Lee Mortimer, *Chicago Confidential*, p. 32, 1950

Brooklyn clothesline *noun*
any looped lanyard and pulley system *US, 1972*
The term evokes pulleyed clotheslines strung outside apartments or houses.
- You may hear the astronauts talking to Mission Control at Houston about a "Brooklyn clothesline." They will be discussing a backup system of ropes and pulleys used to transport film to and from Skylab's huge telescope. — *Vidette (Indiana) Messenger*, p. 25, 20th June 1972

Brookulino *nickname*
Brooklyn, New York *US, 1985*
- Friends, if after this meal I die in Brookulino/ I ask to be buried with my mandolino. — Joseph Bonnano, *A Man of Honor*, p. 149, 1983

broom *noun*
1 the person who is assigned to or takes it upon himself to keep a workplace neat *US, 1984*
Sometimes embellished to "broom man."
- The only person he ever saw making up the bunks, however, was the "broom man," an elderly cop who served as the station-house janitor and sometimes cooked hot meals for the clerical staff on a stove in the basement. — Peter Maas, *Serpico*, p. 68, 1973
- Sweeping the steps was the precinct "broom," an old-timer no longer eager for street duty and working out retirement doing station-house chores. — Charles Whited, *Chiodo*, p. 129, 1973
- The stationhouse broom—a thirty-year airbag who in addition to keeping the stationhouse clean was the precinct's gofer—saw his plight and shouted to him. — William J. Cavnitz, *One Police Plaza*, p. 359, 1984
2 a hat *US, 1960*
- — Robert George Reisner, *The Jazz Titans*, p. 151, 1960

bro's *noun*
heavy work shoes *US, 1994*
An abbreviation of **BROGANS**.
- The "bros," as we called them, were good fighting shoes, used for landing a hard kick to the nuts or delivering a severe stomping to a fallen foe. — Nathan McCall, *Makes Me Wanna Holler*, p. 65, 1994

bros before hoes
used as a rallying cry for the precedence of male friendship over relationships with females *US, 1998*
Sometimes seen as the abbreviation BBH.
- When someone makes sexist comments (e.g., "Bros before hos"), uses derogatory terms for women (e.g., bimbo, bitch, slut), or tells demeaning sexist jokes around you, speak up. — Sharon Gmelech, *Gender on Campus*, p. 56, 1998
- "No," he said, "bros before hos, you're staying." — *alt.bitterness*, 12th March 1998
- — Ben Applebaum and Derrick Pittman, *Turd Ferguson & The Sausage Party*, p. 6, 2004

brothel creeper *noun*
a patron of brothels *US, 1977*
- — *Maledicta*, p. 9, Summer 1977: "A word for it!"

brothel spout *noun*
a prostitute who is physically and emotionally worn out by her work *US, 1993*
- — J.R. Schwartz, *The Official Guide to the Best Cat Houses in Nevada*, p. 164, 1993

brother *noun*
1 a black man *US, 1910*
- Young bloods wanted to be like these brothers. — H. Rap Brown, *Die Nigger Die!*, p. 15, 1969
- Both of these brothers were shot in the head. Both Brothers were members of the Central Staff of the revolutionary party. — *The Black Panther*, p. 14, 19th May 1969
- I wouldn't go so far as to call the brother fat. He's got a weight problem. What's the nigger gonna do, he's Samoan. — *Pulp Fiction*, 1994
- Because I know all you white folks are pissed off that the studio'd entrust a multi-million-dollar movie to a brother. — Kevin Smith, *Jay and Silent Bob Strike Back*, p. 112, 2001
2 a fellow member of a counter cultural or underground political movement *US, 1968*
- Each service should be performed by a tight gang of brothers and sisters whose commitment should enable them to handle an overload of work with ability and enthusiasm. — *The Digger Papers*, p. 15, August 1968

3 in carnival usage, a woman's husband or lover *US, 1981*
- — Don Wilmeth, *The Language of American Popular Entertainment*, p. 35, 1981
4 heroin *US, 1990*
A rare variant on the common **BOY**.
- — Gilda and Melvin Berger, *Drug Abuse A-Z*, p. 38, 1990

brother man *noun*
used as a term of address to establish solidarity, among black men *US, 1974*
- I understand your problem, brother man, but don't come in here comin' down on me. — Vernon E. Smith, *The Jones Men*, p. 127, 1974
- Uhhh, say, look, brother man, I know the pussy is exquisite 'n all that but I got a family down in L.A. and they're missing me. Know what I mean? — Odie Hawkins, *Lost Angeles*, p. 44, 1994

brown *noun*
1 the anus and/or rectum *US, 1916*
- — Joseph E. Ragen and Charles Finston, *Inside the World's Toughest Prison*, p. 792, 1962
- Up your brown with a Roto-Rooter— and spin it! — *Maledicta*, p. 15, Summer 1977
- Then, I'll wanna pinky you and put it in your friend's brown. — Kevin Smith, *Jay and Silent Bob Strike Back*, p. 90, 2001
2 heroin, especially if only partially refined *US, 1962*
- He explained that what addicts refer to as "The Brown" is opium which has been incompletely refined into heroin. Usually, he said, it comes from Mexico. — *San Francisco Examiner*, p. 4, 6th March 1962
3 an amphetamine tablet *US, 1972*
- — Carl Chambers and Richard Heckman, *Employee Drug Abuse*, p. 202, 1972

brown *verb*
to perform anal sex upon someone *US, 1933*
- — Donald Webster Cory and John P. LeRoy, *The Homosexual and His Society*, p. 262, 1963: A lexicon of homosexual slang
- Let's just say a little friendly browning, OK? — Angelo d'Arcangelo, *The Homosexual Handbook*, p. 173, 1968

brown Abe *noun*
a US penny *US, 1945*
From the engraving of President Abraham Lincoln on the coin.
- — Lou Shelly, *Hepcats Jive Talk Dictionary*, p. 22, 1945

brown-bag *verb*
to carry lunch to work, especially in a brown paper lunch bag *US, 1968*
- He used to brown-bag down from the Bronx in the subway. — Edwin Torres, *After Hours*, p. 187, 1979

brown bagger *noun*
a married person *US, 1947*
From the image of bringing lunch packed in a brown bag to work; originally military usage.
- — *American Speech*, p. 227, October 1956: "More United States Air Force slang"

brown bar *noun*
in the US Army, a second lieutenant *US, 1977*
The single brass bar worn by the second lieutenant was camouflaged in the field and became a single brown bar.
- I was alliteratively known as the "boot brown-bar," slang for a raw second lieutenant. — Philip Caputo, *A Rumor of War*, p. 31, 1977
- They were all with colonels and didn't want to know no brown bar out of the bush. — Mark Baker, *Nam*, p. 92, 1981
- Except that the lieutenant, that fucking brown-bar ROTC idiot no more than three days in-country, had to tag along for the ride. — John Skipp and Craig Spector, *The Scream*, p. 98, 1988

brown bomb *noun*
a laxative *US, 1990*
- — Charles Shafer, *Folk Speech in Texas Prisons*, p. 199, 1990

brown boot Army *noun*
the army as it once was *US, 1968*
- — Carl Fleischhauer, *A Glossary of Army Slang*, p. 6, 1968

brown boy *noun*
a male who derives sexual pleasure from eating the feces of others *US, 1971*
- — Eugene Landy, *The Underground Dictionary*, p. 40, 1971

brown cowboys *noun*
the Mexican Mafia, a Mexican-American prison gang *US, 1975*
- — Report to the Senate, *California Senate Committee on Civil Disorder*, p. 227, 1975

brown crown *noun*
a notional sign of one who has failed miserably *US, 1966*
- — John D. Bell et al., *Loosely Speaking*, p. 3, 1966

browned off *adjective*
depressed, angry *US, 1950*
- They tell us good ol' Hap Chandler is plenty browned off at the Hollywood Stars for coming out in those above-the-knee baseball panties. — *San Francisco Call-Bulletin*, p. 15, 3rd April 1950
- Do you wonder, Charlie, that I get a bit browned off? — Charles Raven, *Underworld Nights*, p. 56, 1956
- She'd been browned off at him ever since he dug up her tulip bulbs for kicks last spring. — Max Shulman, *I was a Teen-Age Dwarf*, p. 61, 1959
- — *American Speech*, p. 235, October 1964: "Student slang in Hays, Kansas"
- — Robert J. Glessing, *The Underground Press in America*, p. 175, 1970

brown eye *noun*
the anus *US, 1954*
- The video continues as Stag fucks Trinity's brown eye while she finishes reaming North. — *Adult Video*, August/September 1986
- "Hey baby, when you gonna gimme that brown eye?" — Nathan McCall, *Makes Me Wanna Holler*, p. 188, 1994
- I stick these little pieces of paper over my brown-eye, and bam—no shit stains in my undies. — Kevin Smith, *Jay and Silent Bob Strike Back*, p. 13, 2001
- He pushes his naked knob right in her old brown eye. — Lynn Breedlove, *Godspeed*, p. 39, 2002

brown eyes *noun*
the female breasts, especially the nipples *US, 1932*
- — Collin Baker et al., *College Undergraduate Slang Study Conducted at Brown University*, p. 89, 1968

Brown family *noun*
collectively, all passive participants in anal sex *US, 1950*
- — Hyman E. Goldin et al., *Dictionary of American Underworld Lingo*, p. 149, 1950

brown helmet *noun*
a notional sign of one who has been rejected in romance *US, 1968*
- — Fred Hester, *Slang on the 40 Acres*, p. 17, 1968

brownie *noun*
1 the anus *US, 1927*
- She bends over to pick up the suit. Look at that. Taking my picture with her brownie. — Elmore Leonard, *Split Images*, p. 193, 1981
2 a traffic police officer *US, 1987*
- — Carsten Stroud, *Close Pursuit*, p. 269, 1987
3 marijuana *US, 1966*
- The man at the door was the old dope peddler with his bag of brownie, also known as pot, shit, cannabis, or to the staid, marijuana. — Roger Gordon, *Hollywood's Sexual Underground*, p. 150, 1966

Brownie *noun*
a student, past or present, at Brown University *US, 1995*
- Tonight I was just another Brownie, partying with student friends. — Heidi Mattson, *Ivy League Stripper*, p. 218, 1995

Brownie Girls *noun*
lesbian mutual oral-anal sex *US, 1968*
- Analingus, in which one of the partners will be tongued, or playing "Brownie Girls" in which the two take turns upon each other. — L. Reinhard, *Oral Sex Techniques and Sex Practices Illustrated*, 1968

brownie point *noun*
an imaginary award or credit for a good deed *US, 1953*
- He was tryin' to make brownie points with some of the boys. — *Raising Arizona*, 1987

brownie queen *noun*
a male homosexual who enjoys the passive role in anal sex *US, 1968*
- A "brownie queen" is a homosexual male interested primarily in being the passive partner in anal intercourse. — James Harper, *Homo Laws in all 50 States*, p. 147, 1968
- We call that a brownie queen. In prison they call it under-yonder and round-brown. — Bruce Jackson, *In the Life*, p. 397, 1972

brownies *noun*
1 brown gloves *US, 1993*
- Brownies—brown garden gloves worn by gang members for fighting a shooting, hung out of my right back pocket, and a blue flag hung out my left. — Sanyika Shakur, *Monster*, p. 40, 1993
2 dice that have had their spots altered for cheating *US, 1950*
More commonly known as "busters," which leads to the cartoon character "Buster Brown," which leads to "Brown."
- — *The Annals of the American Academy of Political and Social Sciences*, p. 122, May 1950

brown job *noun*
oral-anal sex *US, 1971*
- — Eugene Landy, *The Underground Dictionary*, p. 40, 1971

brown-nose *verb*
to curry favor in a sycophantic fashion *US, 1938*
- Don't try and brownnose me Mike. — Hubert Selby Jr., *Last Exit to Brooklyn*, p. 143, 1957
- No wonder the world was going to hell when a grown man pranced around in a monkey suit, brown-nosing dames who made a big deal out of ordering a belt of booze! — Jim Thompson, *The Grifters*, p. 78, 1963
- "Nick," she said when I had finished, "six months ago you were just another brownnosing honor student. What happened?" — C.D. Payne, *Youth in Revolt*, p. 334, 1993
- Now you're gonna brown nose me? Don't be doing me any more favors, Pancho. — *Airheads*, 1994

brown nose; brown noser *noun*
a toady; a sycophant *US, 1938*
Originally military.
- "I know Stanley is the biggest goddam brown-nose in the platoon[.]" — Norman Mailer, *The Naked and the Dead*, p. 61, 1948
- I encountered far too often there a type that is familiar to anyone who has built time—the organization man of the penitentiary, the yea-sayer, the brown-nose. — James Blake, *The Joint*, p. 318, 6th November 1962
- You are such a brown-noser. — *Clueless*, 1995
- I'm sorry you've got to eat shit from a hack brownnoser like Krantz[.] — Robert Crais, *L.A. Requiem*, p. 97, 1999

brownout *noun*
a near but not complete loss of consciousness *US, 1992*
Not quite a "blackout."
- An occasional brownout on a couch where I accidentally sat on a hypodermic needle full of heroin took time too. — Larry Rivers, *What Did I Do?*, p. 47, 1992

brown shirt *noun*
a police officer *US, 1993*
- Glass had his arms loaded with three VCRs when Sneak whispered, "Hey, there's some brown shirts outside." — Bob Sipchen, *Baby Insane and the Buddha*, p. 118, 1993

brown shoes *noun*
a person who does not use drugs *US, 1970*
- — William D. Alsever, *Glossary for the Establishment and Other Uptight People*, p. 23, December 1970

brown sugar *noun*
1 grainy, poor quality heroin *US, 1971*
- But now something new and more deadly has been added to the bazaar's wares—"brown sugar," an opium derivative close to heroin. — *Washington Post*, p. A22, 26th March 1981
- Chinese-made ammonium chloride, which transforms the morphine into the lower-grade No. 3 heroin, or "brown sugar," as it is popularly known — *New York Times*, p. SM27, 23rd June 2002
2 a black woman, especially a beautiful one; a black woman's vagina *US, 1971*
- "Black ones be called brown sugar." — Jess Mowry, *Six Out Seven*, p. 93, 1993
3 by extension, a sexually desirable black man *US, 1996*
Adopted by black women.
- And what about D'Angelo? / I want some of that brown sugar / And watch this rap bitch bust all over ya nuts[.] — Lil' Kim, *Dreams*, 1996

brown trout *noun*
feces, when thrown by prisoners from their cells onto guards *US, 1992*
- — William K. Bentley and James M. Corbett, *Prison Slang*, p. 89, 1992

brown water navy *noun*

during the Vietnam war, the US Navy presence on rivers and deltas *US, 1961*

- The U.S. Navy's riverine forces were commonly referred to as the "Brown Water" Navy in contrast to the Blue Water forces[.] — T.L. Bosiljevac, *SEALs*, p. 51, 1990

brown water sailor *noun*

a Navy sailor assigned to river or delta duty *US, 1985*

- He stood out in comic contrast to the brown water sailors, who padded about their boat in cut-off fatigue shorts and a variety of faded shirts, with no helmets or flack vests. — David Donovan, *Once a Warrior King*, p. 264, 1985

brown wings *noun*

experience of anal intercourse, or anal-oral sexual contact, considered as an achievement *US, 1971*

Originally Hell's Angel usage.

- Most of the Frisco chapter earned their brown wings on this occasion. It was some shindig! The queen never had it so good! — Jamie Mandelkau, *Buttons*, p. 101, 1971
- But if you're the proud owner of an enormous penis and you still want to get your brown wings, the way is not to ask, it's to do. — *GQ*, p. 117, July 2001

Bruce *noun*

used as a stereotype of an effeminate male homosexual *US, 1973*

- Too Many "Bruce" Jokes [Headline] — *San Francisco Examiner*, p. 27, 28th May 1973

bruiser *noun*

a rugged physical specimen; a thug *UK, 1742*

- "Well, it was then this big bruiser decides to wise him up, so he eases up to Scott and kicks him—where it hurts most." — Donald Wilson, *My Six Convicts*, p. 53, 1951
- If you fell behind with your rent the prince sent a couple of bruisers round to punch seven bells out of you. — John Peter Jones, *Feather Pluckers*, p. 17, 1964
- — Collin Baker et al., *College Undergraduate Slang Study Conducted at Brown University*, p. 89, 1968
- "Christ, he'll be an incredible bruiser," I continued. — Erich Segal, *Love Story*, p. 102, 1970

brush *noun*

a technique for introducing altered dice into a game as the dice are passed from player to shooter *US, 1950*

Also known as a "brush-off."

- — *The Annals of the American Academy of Political and Social Sciences*, p. 122, May 1950

brush *verb*

to introduce marked cards or loaded dice into a game *US, 1993*

- — Frank Scoblete, *Guerrilla Gambling*, p. 299, 1993

brusher; brushman *noun*

a casino employee who tries to lure casino visitors into playing poker *US, 1988*

- — George Percy, *The Language of Poker*, p. 13, 1988

brush-off *noun*

a rejection *US, 1938*

- [S]he reminded him of Lindy whom he'd given the brush-off. — Wilda Moxham, *The Apprentice*, p. 174, 1969
- [H]e got negative responses, distinguished only by hostile looks and shakes of the head from low-rider types who made him for fuzz and annoyed brush-offs from young women who didn't like his style. — James Ellroy, *Because the Night*, p. 312, 1984

brutal *adjective*

extremely good, intense *US, 1964*

- — *Time*, p. 56, 1st January 1965
- Connie Eble (Editor), *UNC-CH Campus Slang*, p. 2, Fall 1987

brutally *adverb*

very *US, 1995*

- Christian is brutally hot, and I am going to remember tonight forever. — *Clueless*, 1995

brute *noun*

in the television and movie industries, a large spotlight used to simulate sunlight *US, 1960*

- — Oswald Skilbeck, *ABC of Film and TV Working Terms*, p. 21, 1960
- — Tony Miller and Patricia George, *Cut! Print!*, p. 44, 1977

brute force *noun*

in computing, a simplistic and unsophisticated programing style *US, 1991*

- — Eric S. Raymond, *The New Hacker's Dictionary*, p. 80, 1991

bruz *noun*

used as a term of address, man to man *US, 1958*

- — Robert S. Gold, *A Jazz Lexicon*, p. 42, 1964

BS *noun*

bullshit, in all its senses *US, 1900*

A euphemism accepted in polite society.

- The absolute B.S. I've been going through is finally over. — Neal Cassady, *Neal Cassady Collected Letters 1944–1967*, p. 141, 12th August 1950: Letter to Diana Hansen Cassady
- Elijah shared the indulgent smiles of the men who had graciously granted Monkeydude some b.s. time. — Odie Hawkins, *Chicago Hustle*, p. 7, 1979
- We have more lesbians working there, or they are bisexual. That's because they have to put up with men all night long and listen to all that BS. — Marilyn Suriani Futterman, *Dancing Naked in the Material World*, p. 57, 1992

BT *noun*

an inhalation of marijuana smoke filtered through a water-pipe *US, 1997*

An abbreviation of "*bong toke*."

- — Pamela Munro, *U.C.L.A. Slang*, p. 113, 1997

BTO *noun*

an influential and admired person *US, 1944*

A "*big-time operator*"—not without overtones of smarminess.

- — *Cosmopolitan*, p. 76, October 1949
- We'd raced tanks down hills, chased big-time operators (BTOs) who tried to screw us in our small-time forays into the black market, fought in the TRUST 15th Tank Company smokers[.] — David H. Hackworth, *About Face*, p. 219, 1989

BTW

used in computer message shorthand to mean "*by the way*" *US, 1991*

- — Eric S. Raymond, *The New Hacker's Dictionary*, p. 342, 1991
- Orient Road looks like a fucking resort, btw[.] — Eleusis, *Lightning on the Sun [The Howard Marks Book of Dope Stories]*, p. 325, 2001

Bu; the Bu; Mother Bu *nickname*

Malibu, California *US, 1961*

- I grabbed my board and tooled down to old mother Bu—meaning Malibu. — Frederick Kohner, *Gidget Goes Hawaiian*, p. 6, 1961
- — Trevor Cralle, *The Surfin'ary*, p. 16, 1991

BUAG *noun*

a simple drawing made with computer characters *US, 1995*

A "*big ugly ASCII graphic*."

- — Christian Crumlish, *The Internet Dictionary*, p. 27, 1995

bub *noun*

1 used as a term of address, usually to a stranger and usually in a condescending tone *US, 1839*

- "Having trouble, bub?" I grinned at him. — Mickey Spillane, *I, The Jury*, p. 90, 1947
- "Call it a dollar for the shirt and pants," he said. "What size you wear, bub?" — Jim Thompson, *Bad Boy*, p. 382, 1953
- "Looks like you've got a ticket, bub!" said a voice somewhere behind him. — Terry Southern, *The Magic Christian*, p. 14, 1959

2 the female breast *UK, 1826*

- A flask that fits over her bubs. — Irving Shulman, *The Amboy Dukes*, p. 99, 1947
- — Dale Gordon, *The Dominion Sex Dictionary*, p. 33, 1967

3 a blue flashing police car light *US, 1987*

- The blue flashers, called bubbles or bubs by the troopers, on top of the cruiser were dead and dark. — Stephen King, *The Tommyknockers*, p. 675, 1987

bubba *noun*

1 a stereotypical white, southern male *US, 1982*

- — *American Speech*, p. 100, Spring 1993: "Among the new words"

2 marijuana *US, 1997*
- — Jim Emerson-Cobb, *Scratching the Dragon*, April 1997

bubbie circus *noun*
a chorus line or other display of multiple women with large breasts *US, 1967*
- — Dale Gordon, *The Dominion Sex Dictionary*, p. 33, 1967

bubbies and cunt *noun*
a poor woman's dowry *US, 1967*
- — Dale Gordon, *The Dominion Sex Dictionary*, p. 33, 1967

bubblate *verb*
to idle, to pass time with friends *US, 2004*
- We weren't causing any problem. We were just bubblatin'. — Rick Ayers (Editor), *Berkeley High Slang Dictionary*, p. 14, 2004

bubble *noun*
1 an airplane cockpit *US, 1986*
- — *American Speech*, p. 122, Summer 1986: "The language of naval fighter pilots"

2 in the television and movie industries, an incandescent electric light bulb *US, 1960*
- — Oswald Skilbeck, *ABC of Film and TV Working Terms*, p. 21, 1960

3 a specialization *US, 1997*
- Don't laugh it off, buddy. Sweetheart scams are my bubble. — Stephen Cannell, *Big Con*, p. 298, 1997

▸ **on the bubble**
engaged in swindling as a career *US, 1997*
- Stuart Bates, like Carol Sesnick, was one of the few Bates family members who wasn't on the bubble. — Stephen Cannell, *Big Con*, p. 357, 1997

bubble brain *noun*
a distracted, unfocused person *US, 1981*
- — *Wesleyan Alumnus*, p. 29, Spring 1981
- [O]r maybe a blond bubble-brain to show the poor niggers that drug bucks could buy what you couldn't score with a high school diploma or a hard-muscled bod. — Jess Mowry, *Way Past Cool*, p. 25, 1992

bubble butt *noun*
large, firm buttocks *US, 1990*
A pornography fetish.
- Catalina follows her boss, swinging her bubble butt from side to side. — Jane Hill, *Street Songs 1*, p. 147, 1990
- Tony's bubble butt was next and soon he had to sit on every hard cock in the room. — *alt.sex.motss*, 19th April 1991
- Lexi, who possesses an amazing bubble butt, gets that ass fucked. — Editors of Adult Video News, *The AVN Guide to the 500 Greatest Adult Films of All Time*, p. 129, 2005

bubble chaser *noun*
a bombardier on a bomber aircraft *US, 1945*
A reference to the bubbles in the leveling device used.
- — *American Speech*, p. 310, December 1946: "More Air Force slang"

bubbledance *verb*
to wash dishes *US, 1947*
- — Marcus Hanna Boulware, *Jive and Slang of Students in Negro Colleges*, 1947

bubble dancer; bubbles dancer *noun*
a woman who performs a striptease using a bubble or bubbles to mask her nudity *US, 1954*
- A former bubble dancer, Miss Troy had made the front pages five years before[.] — Earl Wilson, *I am Gazing Into My 8-Ball*, p. 27, 1945

bubblegum *adjective*
unimaginative, highly commercial, insincere *US, 1963*
Usually used to describe music.
- We had an hysterical call from Buddah Records complaining about the way I insulted their bubblegum music. — *Screw*, p. 17, 4th July 1969
- A coke-jerking rhythm, a Woody Woodpecker voice, a scoopful of cliches from a bin labeled "sweet talk" and you've got—bubble-gum music. — *Life*, p. 13, 30th January 1970
- — Connie Eble (Editor), *UNC-CH Campus Slang*, October 1972
- If Harvey thought getting it on with some bubble-gum rocker was realizing his full human potential, well, that was his prerogative. — Cyra McFadden, *The Serial*, p. 37, 1977

bubble gum machine *noun*
the H-13 army helicopter *US, 1968*

Vietnam war usage.
- — Carl Fleischhauer, *A Glossary of Army Slang*, p. 7, 1968

bubblegummer *noun*
a preteenager or young teenager *US, 1947*
- Not one fan magazine flashbulb popped, not one autograph hound stuck his grimy book under Pete's schnozz and not one bubblegummer cooed. — *Washington Post*, p. VI-2, 21st December 1947
- Bubble-Gummer—a square, especially one who's younger than you — Art Unger, *The Cool Book*, p. 106, 1961
- — William D. Alsever, *Glossary for the Establishment and Other Uptight People*, p. 32, December 1970
- She was the force behind subversive club chapters starting on her high school campus when she was still a bubblegummer. — Joseph Wambaugh, *The Blue Knight*, p. 78, 1973
- One of the younger Joe Cool types passed by, holding hands with a bubble-gummer. — P.J. Petersen, *Good-Bye to Good Ol' Charlie*, p. 120, 1987

bubblehead *noun*
1 a person whose thinking is not grounded in reality *US, 1945*
- By now it is obvious even to the bubbleheads that we exorcised one set of devils from the earth in 1945 only to make room for another equally evil horde. — Daniel V. Gallery, *Clear the Decks*, p. 221, 1945

2 a submariner *US, 1986*
- I live in a submarine. I'm a bubblehead, and that gives me a certain point of view. — Mark Joseph, *To Kill the Potemkin*, p. 81, 1986
- — *Seattle Times*, p. A9, 12th April 1998

bubbler *noun*
a water tank or cooler *US, 1961*
Korean war usage.
- Buck must have carried a filled canteen all the way from Pavuvu. It was brackish. "Why didn't you fill it from the bubblers on the transport?" I asked him. — Russell Davis, *Marine at War*, p. 50, 1961
- Dryness gripped my throat; I went to a stone drinking fountain and drank from the bubbler. — Frank Hardy, *But The Dead Are Many*, p. 312, 1975

bubble-top *noun*
an OH-13 Sioux helicopter, used for observation, reconnaissance, and medical evacuation in the Korean war and the early years of the war in Vietnam *US, 1984*
So named because of the distinctive plexiglas canopy.
- When the sheriff's helicopter, which looked like the old military bubble-tops, finally got landed on suitable ground, Manny Lopez was ministering to the bandit[.] — Joseph Wambaugh, *Lines and Shadows*, p. 183, 1984
- — Linda Reinberg, *In the Field*, p. 29, 1991

bubbling bundle of barometric brilliance *noun*
used as the introduction for Bobbie the weather girl on AFVN television, Saigon, during the Vietnam war *US, 1990*
Officially she served as a secretary for the US Agency for International Aid in Saigon from 1967 to 1969. Her unpaid weather broadcasts, which always ended with the benediction of wishing "everyone a pleasant evening weather-wise and good wishes for other-wise," were greatly appreciated by the men in the field.
- As "Bobbie the Weather Girl" for Armed Forces Television Vietnam in Saigon, she was a "bubbling bundle of barometric brilliance" with her lighthearted nightly broadcasts to tens of thousands of Americans in Vietnam. — *USA Today*, p. 11A, 11th November 1993
- When a friend teased Bobbie unmercifully, she decided to go for the audition, and she became the weather girl, the "bubbling bundle of barometric brilliance." — Olga Gruhzit-Hoty, *A Time Remembered*, p. 238, 1999

bubbly *noun*
champagne *UK, 1920*
- The lush was a complete stranger, having been delivered by a cabdriver who steered for various joints, and Tappy had just gotten around to selling him the first bottle of bubbly. — Robert Sylvester, *No Cover Charge*, p. 213, 1956
- In the red-lit murk, there was the counterpoint bedlam of profane ribaldry as they loaded their skulls with cocaine and bubbly. — Iceberg Slim (Robert Beck), *Airtight Willie and Me*, p. 26, 1979
- Nabokov only got two-fifty. You're getting top dollar! Break out the bubbly! — Terry Southern, *Now Dig This*, p. 155, 1991

- Instead, Lefty handed her a cup and poured her some bubbly. — C.D. Payne, *Youth in Revolt*, p. 132, 1993
- Get Rex some bubbly, whatever. — *Empire Records*, 1995

bubbly *adjective*
cheerful, full of spirit *US, 1939*
- For weeks he lay in his hospital bed and cursed steadily, cheered only slightly by the bubbly letter which arrived every three days from Maggie. — Max Shulman, *Rally Round the Flag, Boys!*, p. 17, 1957

bubby *noun*
the female breast *UK, 1655*
Usually in the plural.
- — Dale Gordon, *The Dominion Sex Dictionary*, p. 33, 1967
- Their secondary sex characteristics are simply too conspicuous to pass without insult, and we were unmerciful towards them: tits, boobs, knockers, jugs, bubbies, bazooms, lungs, flaps and hooters we called them, and there was no way to be polite about it. — *Screw*, p. 6, 3rd January 1972

bubonic *noun*
potent marijuana *US, 2001*
- — Pamela Munro, *U.C.L.A. Slang*, p. 48, 2001

bubonic *adjective*
potent, extreme, intense *US, 1993*
- [A] fat ass J, of some bubonic chronic that made me choke[.] — Snoop Doggy Dogg, *Gin and Juice*, 1993

buck *noun*
1 100 pounds *US, 2006*
- "So tell me—how much does she weigh?" "A buck forty," Dealey said. — Carl Hiaasen, *Nature Girl*, p. 26, 2006

2 a dollar *US, 1856*
Originally US but applied in Hong Kong and other countries where dollars are the unit of currency.
- There was no mention of a full or partial refund of my two-hundred-buck fee for said license to said state. — Mickey Spillane, *Kiss Me Deadly*, p. 33, 1952
- She was here last night. All night. For two lousey bucks. — Harry J. Anslinger, *The Murderers*, p. 54, 1961

3 one hundred dollars; a bet of one hundred dollars *US, 1973*
- He'd go a buck and a half apiece for as many as I could get. — George V. Higgins, *Friends of Eddie Coyle*, p. 10, 1973
- — Don R. McCreary (Editor), *Dawg Speak*, 2001

4 a young black man *US, 1835*
Overtly racist; an unfortunate favorite term of US President Ronald Reagan when speaking unscripted.
- We saw one buck pull a razor on his sugar in front of Gamby's. — Jack Lait and Lee Mortimer, *Washington Confidential*, p. 272, 1951
- — *Maledicta*, p. 152, Summer/Winter 1978: "How to hate thy neighbor: a guide to racist maledicta"

5 a male homosexual *US, 1984*
- — Inez Cardozo-Freeman, *The Joint*, p. 485, 1984

6 a type of homemade alcoholic drink *US, 1951*
- To brighten the nights a little, I had started a little bootlegging operation, making "buck" (prison liquor) out of cornbread, cane syrup and water. — James Blake, *The Joint*, p. 36, 23rd December 1951
- Some pretty good shine we call buck, made of rice or orange juice with some yeast and sugar. We'd have some poor asshole keep it in his cell while it set up. — Elmore Leonard, *Maximum Bob*, p. 108, 1991
- — Gary K. Farlow, *Prison-ese*, p. 7, 2002

7 in prison, a sit-down strike by the prisoners *US, 1972*
- — Bruce Jackson, *Outside the Law*, p. 55, 1972

buck *verb*
1 to act aggressively *US, 1977*
- So now some dudes will buck on you. They'll say, "What ten cents? What you talking about?" — John Allen, *Assault with a Deadly Weapon*, p. 56, 1977

2 to shoot a gun *US, 1996*
- So once we went in a car by Mozart, a rival, Mozart Park Boys, and started bucking at them. — S. Beth Atkin, *Voices from the Street*, p. 86, 1996

3 to fight your way through a difficult surfing situation *US, 1965*
- — John M. Kelly, *Surf and Sea*, p. 281, 1965

▶ **buck it**
in craps, to roll a number that has previously been rolled *US, 1974*
- — John Scarne, *Scarne on Dice*, p. 462, 1974

▶ **buck the tiger**
to play faro, a game of chance that was extremely popular in the C19 and only rarely seen in modern times *US, 1849*
- She's right here in Atlantic City. She's been bucking the tiger in clubs off the Boardwalk. — Stephen Cannell, *King Con*, p. 120, 1997

buckeroo *noun*
one dollar *US, 1942*
An embellishment of **BUCK**.
- Thirty-five thousand buckaroos, lady. — Gerald Petievich, *Shakedown*, p. 79, 1988

bucket *noun*
1 a jail *US, 1894*
- If anybody is found carrying a gun or blackjack, he will be tossed in the bucket. — *San Francisco Examiner*, p. 1, 30th August 1946
- Those goddam girls were gigglin, righteously laughin ... you know, "Ha, ha, that's one of 'em." So off I went to the bucket, for rape. — Hunter S. Thompson, *Hell's Angels*, p. 17, 1966
- "Is Earl out of the bucket?" — Leonard Gardner, *Fat City*, p. 128, 1969
- But I really should be in the bucket with a lot of other guys. — Robert Byrne, *McGoorty*, p. 76, 1972

2 a cell used for solitary confinement *US, 1989*
- — James Harris, *A Convict's Dictionary*, p. 28, 1989

3 the buttocks; the anus *US, 1938*
- — Ellen C. Bellone (Editor), *Dictionary of Slang*, p. 5, 1989

4 a car, especially one with bucket seats *US, 1939*
- — Marcus Hanna Boulware, *Jive and Slang of Students in Negro Colleges*, 1947
- — Connie Eble (Editor), *UNC-CH Campus Slang*, p. 2, Spring 1992
- [T]hey lurched onto Market Street in a brown Bonneville bucket. — Bob Sipchen, *Baby Insane and the Buddha*, p. 150, 1993

5 a small car *US, 2000*
- There's even street slang for stealing cars such as "new buckets are being splacked." Buckets refer to small cars, such as Dodge Neons, and to splack is to steal a car using a screwdriver to break into the steering column and start it. — *Tampa (Florida) Tribune*, p. 1, 6th May 2000

6 in pool, a pocket that appears receptive to balls dropping *US, 1988*
- — Mike Shamos, *The Illustrated Encyclopedia of Billiards*, p. 36, 1993

bucketfull *noun*
▶ **have a bucket full**
said of a racehorse that has been fed heavily before a race to decrease its chances of winning *US, 1951*
- — David W. Maurer, *Argot of the Racetrack*, p. 34, 1951

bucket gunner *noun*
in carnival usage, a person who from a hidden location operates the mechanisms that determine a game's outcome *US, 1981*
- — Don Wilmeth, *The Language of American Popular Entertainment*, p. 35, 1981

bucket head *noun*
a socially inept person *US, 1906*
- — *Detroit Free Press*, 4th November 1979

bucket job *noun*
an intentional loss in an athletic contest *US, 1955*
- The Olson-Maxim bout was one of the top bucket jobs since the Carnera trail of hoaxes. — *San Francisco News*, p. 14, 24th February 1955

bucket of blood
a bar or dance hall where hard drinking and hard fighting go hand in hand *US, 1915*
- My place, before I bought it, was referred to as a bucket of blood. — Helen P. Branson, *Gay Bar*, p. 52, 1957
- You walk into a nigger bucket-of-blood bar on the wooliest corner in the state and spout stupid insults. — Iceberg Slim (Robert Beck), *Trick Baby*, p. 276, 1969
- This dislike gave the store a bucket-of-blood reputation which warned anyone who wasn't already known by, or friendly with, someone in the establishment, to stay away unless his head was made of concrete. — Emmett Grogan, *Ringolevio*, p. 99, 1972
- Peeking into the "430" club, a bucket of blood type establishment with sawdust and ground up bones on the floor[.] — Odie Hawkins, *Black Casanova*, p. 184, 1984

bucket of bolts *noun*
a dilapidated car, truck, boat or plane *US, 1942*

- — Montie Tak, *Truck Talk*, p. 20, 1971
- If the French had felt so threatened by the Rainbow Warrior (a "bucket of bolts," according to a New Zealand national security official), disabling the ship at sea with a low-charge explosive on the propeller shaft—or even tangled wire—would have been enough covert action to deter its further passage. — *American Journal of International Law*, p. 15, 1992
- The Marines got me airborne in this piece of *** that looked ragged and was shaking like a bucket of bolts. — Stephen K. Scroggs, *Army Relations with Congress*, p. 92, 2000
- Many charities can arrange to have that bucket of bolts towed right out of your driveway. — *Alameda (California) Times-Star*, 12th March 2004

bucket shop noun
an investment office that swindles its clients *US, 1879*
- "And look at all those so-called business men—these bucket-shop guys and stock swindlers and embezzlers." — Charles Hamilton, *Men of the Underworld*, p. 312, 1952
- He ran boiler rooms and bucket shops. — Stephen Cannell, *King Con*, p. 35, 1997

bucket worker noun
a swindler *US, 1949*
- [M]ush workers and lush workers, catamites and sodomites, bucket workers and bail jumpers, till tappers and assistant pickpockets[.] — Nelson Algren, *The Man with the Golden Arm*, p. 197, 1949

buck fever noun
in shuffleboard, the anxiety often experienced on the last shot *US, 1967*
- — Omero C. Catan, *Secrets of Shuffleboard Strategy*, p. 64, 1967

buckle bunny noun
a woman who seeks short-term sexual liaisons with rodeo cowboys *US, 1978*
- Baseball players call them "Annies." To riders on the rodeo circuit, they are "buckle bunnies." To most other athletes, they are just "the wannabes" or "the girls." — *Time Magazine*, p. 77, 25th November 1991
- Poem, poem on the range / Where the dudes and buckle bunnies all play. — *Denver Westword*, 26th August 2004

bucklebuster noun
a line in a performance that is guaranteed to produce loud laughter *US, 1973*
- — Sherman Louis Sergel, *The Language of Show Biz*, p. 30, 1973

buckled adjective
ugly *US, 1993*
- — *People Magazine*, p. 73, 19th July 1993

bucko noun
1 a dollar *US, 1973*
- "[S]till in pretty good shape and all, six hundred buckos left and he likes golf, he's out all day, he feels pretty good." — George Higgins, *The Digger's Game*, p. 97, 1973

2 a man, especially an unrefined or crude man *US, 1883*
- But when it came to the belligerent buckos, there'd be a house officer call. — Dev Collans with Stewart Sterling, *I was a House Detective*, p. 66, 1954

buckra noun
a white person *US, 1787*
- Whites called them "white trash" and Negros "po' buckra." — Nelson Algren, *A Walk on the Wild Side*, p. 8, 1956
- "Buckra? What's that?" "The kind of white folks ain't got time for nuthen but kicken niggers and ass-kissen rich folks," the driver said. — Robert Penn Warren, *Wilderness*, p. 84, 1961

Buck Rogers gun noun
an M-3 Tommy gun *US, 1947*
- — *American Speech*, p. 54, February 1947: "Pacific War language"

buckshot special noun
in sports betting, a game with heavy betting on one team *US, 1974*
- I raised the line to 8½ before one-thirty, but this game was what I'd heard called "a buckshot special." — Gary Mayer, *Bookie*, p. 155, 1974

buckwheat noun
a black male *US, 1978*

- — *Maledicta*, p. 153, Summer/Winter 1978: "How to hate thy neighbor: a guide to racist maledicta"

buckwheats noun
1 abuse, persecution *US, 1942*
- — Hyman E. Goldin et al., *Dictionary of American Underworld Lingo*, p. 98, 1950
- He gave me the buckwheats, this sergeant. — Rocky Garciano (with Rowland Barber), *Somebody Up There Likes Me*, p. 202, 1955

2 diminution of power or standing in an organized crime enterprise *US, 1964*
- — *American Speech*, p. 306, December 1964: "Lingua cosa nostra"

bucky noun
a shotgun *US, 1995*
- — Bill Valentine, *Gang Intelligence Manual*, p. 110, 1995

bud noun
1 the flower of the marijuana plant; hence marijuana *US, 1978*
- — Mary Corey and Victoria Westermark, *Fer Shurr!*, 1982
- Take a big bone hit/Cause after tha bud, My rhymes start flowin' — Tone Loc, *Cheeba Cheeba*, 1989
- I used to buy some bud from these Jamaicans on the west side all the time. — Yusuf Jah, *Uprising*, p. 179, 1995

2 a girl *US, 1965*
- Elsewhere, Las Vegas' beautiful little high-school buds in their buttocks-decolletage stretch pants are back on the foam-rubber upholstery of luxury broughams peeling off the entire chick ensemble[.] — Tom Wolfe, *The Kandy-Kolored Tangerine-Flake Streamline Baby*, p. 12, 1965

3 the female nipple *US, 1990*
- Your buds is as hard as two frozen huckleberries. — Robert Campbell, *Sweet La-La Land*, p. 175, 1990

4 a friend, a buddy *US, 1935*
- I'm sorry about the show. Buds? — *Wayne's World*, 1992
- Aw, be a bud, let me in. I was having a blast. — *Airheads*, 1994

budded; budded out adjective
intoxicated on marijuana *US, 1997*
- — Judi Sanders, *Da Bomb*, p. 3, 1997
- — Vann Wesson, *Generation X Field Guide and Lexicon*, p. 30, 1997

buddha noun
1 a marijuana cigarette embellished with crack cocaine *US, 1989*
- — Terry Williams, *The Cocaine Kids*, p. 135, 1989

2 potent marijuana, usually of Asian origin *US, 1988*
Also spelt "buddah" or "buda."
- I hit they' ass like the buddah thats stinkey[.] — Cypress Hill, *Stoned is the Way of the Walk*, 1991
- — Connie Eble (Editor), *UNC-CH Campus Slang*, p. 2, Spring 2000

Buddha grass noun
marijuana *US, 1975*
Vietnam war usage.
- In 1968, when heroin found its way into those Buddha grass "Marlboro" joints (eventually turning some 20 to 30 percent of the U.S. military in Vietnam into junkies before you could say "Far out, man"), it would be too late to turn the tide. — David H. Hackworth, *About Face*, p. 574, 1982

Buddhahead noun
a Japanese person *US, 1945*
Offensive.
- Chicago Japs refer to those from the old country and Hawaii as "Buddha heads" or "Boochies." — Jack Lait and Lee Mortimer, *Chicago Confidential*, p. 88, 1950
- — Eugene Landy, *The Underground Dictionary*, p. 41, 1971
- "So now if I wanna get somewhere in the department I gotta be a Buddhahead," Francis moaned to his partner. — Joseph Wambaugh, *The Choirboys*, p. 91, 1975
- — Edith A. Folb, *runnin' down some lines*, p. 231, 1980
- — Douglas Simonson, *Pidgin to da Max*, 1981

buddy noun
1 in homosexual culture, a good friend who may or may not be a lover *US, 1972*
- "Lots of buddy nights at the baths. I can't even count the number of times I rolled over in bed and told some hot stranger: 'You'd like my lover.'" — Armistead Maupin, *Further Tales of the City*, p. 22, 1982

2 a volunteer companion to a person with AIDS *US*, *1984*

- There also exist buddy programs that team a recently diagnosed person with an HIV-positive person who is more experienced in dealing with the issues. — Darrell Ward, *The Amfar AIDS Handbook*, p. 15, 1999

buddy-buddy *adjective*

friendly *US*, *1944*

- A friendly, laconic man—but definitely not the back-slapping, buddy-buddy type—Mr. Cadell politely declined to discuss these episodes. — *San Francisco News*, p. 2, 26th February 1946
- Joan and my woman probation officer real buddy buddy shaking hands[.] — Jack Kerouac, *Letter to Allen Ginsberg*, p. 459, 1st January 1955
- I have no respect for a duck who runs up to me on the yard all buddy-buddy, and then feels obliged not to sit down with me. — Eldridge Cleaver, *Soul on Ice*, p. 47, 1968
- So he tried to be buddy-buddy with me, but I wasn't buying that either. — H. Rap Brown, *Die Nigger Die!*, p. 44, 1969

buddy buddy plan *noun*

an arrangement by which friends who enlist in the armed services together serve together *US*, *1994*

- "We can go in the Marines on the buddy-buddy plan and get stationed together." — Nathan McCall, *Makes Me Wanna Holler*, p. 92, 1994

buddy check *noun*

a last-minute inspection of a parachutist's gear by his jump partner *US*, *2000*

- — Murry A. Taylor, *Jumping Fire*, p. 455, 2000

buddy-fuck *verb*

(of a male) to steal a friend's date *US*, *1966*

- — Collin Baker et al., *College Undergraduate Slang Study Conducted at Brown University*, p. 89, 1968

buddy poker *noun*

a game of poker in which two friends are playing as partners, but not in collusion *US*, *1987*

- — Thomas L. Clark, *The Dictionary of Gambling and Gaming*, p. 30, 1987

buddyro; buddyroo *noun*

a pal; used as a term of address for a friend *US*, *1951*

- Be a buddy. Be a buddyroo. Okay? — J.D. Salinger, *Catcher in the Rye*, p. 28, 1951

buddy system *noun*

during the Korean war, a plan teaming American and Korean soldiers in the hope of providing one-on-one mentoring and training *US*, *1968*

- This was the much-vaunted "buddy system" under which the Koreans were paired off with Americans who were supposed to give them on-the-job training in the soldier's craft. — Robert Leckie, *The Wars of America*, Volume II, p. 353, 1968

buddy window *noun*

a hole between private video booths in a pornography arcade designed for sexual contact where none is officially permitted *US*, *1996*

- The peep show has lost its popularity. The buddy window, glory hole. — James Ridgeway, *Red Light*, p. 212, 1996

bud head *noun*

1 a beer drinker *US*, *1972*

Not confined to drinkers of Budweiser™ beer.

- — David Claerbaut, *Black Jargon in White America*, p. 59, 1972

2 a frequent marijuana user *US*, *1997*

- — Pamela Munro, *U.C.L.A. Slang*, p. 45, 1997

buds *noun*

1 small female breasts *US*, *1967*

- — Dale Gordon, *The Dominion Sex Dictionary*, p. 34, 1967

2 marijuana, especially the most psychoactive part of the plant *US*, *1997*

Also spelled "budz."

- — Jim Emerson-Cobb, *Scratching the Dragon*, April 1997

budsky *noun*

used as a term of address *US*, *1984*

A meaninglessly decorative "buddy."

- Maybe he's looking for a job? Huh budsky? — *Repo Man*, 1984

Budweiser crest; Budweiser label *noun*

the emblem of the Navy SEALS (the sea, air and land team) *US*, *1992*

- Even when I was full commander, wet-behind-the-ears ensigns straight out of the Academy would look at the Budweiser cresty—the eagle, anchor, and trident emblem all SEALS wear—on my uniform blouse and sneer. — Richard Marcinko and John Weisman, *Rogue Warrior*, p. 147, 1992

buf; buff *noun*

any large military aircraft like a Grumman A-6, a Boeing B-52, and a Sikorsky CH-33, especially the B-52 Stratofortress *US*, *1968*

An abbreviation of "bigugly fat fucker" or, in polite company, "fellow."

- And the B-52s, or "Buffs," for Big Ugly Fuckers. If a grant humping in the boonies heard a plane, he could take comfort: it was his. — Harry Maurer, *Strange Ground*, p. 365, 1989
- Here's the story of speckled Buf, Lockheed's Super R. — Joseph Tuso, *Singing the Vietnam Blues*, p. 188, 1990: Super Constellation
- When a B-52 takes off, Flinn cocks her head to listen. "There goes a Buf," she announces. She knows not only the nickname of this plane, but its classified secrets[.] — *Washington Post*, p. D1, 29th April 1997
- Boeing and the Air Force have elicited almost half a century of widely varied service form the Buf by masterful planning. — Walter J. Boyne, *The B-52 Story*, 2001

buff *noun*

1 a graffiti-cleaning machine used on subway cars *US*, *1987*

- They were a good place on which to practice and in periods when the "buff" was operating they presented a convenient alternative to the trains. — Henry Chalfant, *Spraycan Art*, p. 8, 1987

2 a workout with weights *US*, *1989*

- — James Harris, *A Convict's Dictionary*, p. 28, 1989

3 a water buffalo *US*, *1977*

- He called Quinn and told him to put the buff out of its misery and take the farmer's name so the Army could pay him back. — Larry Heinemann, *Close Quarters*, p. 97, 1977
- The Vietnamese used the buffs for pulling plows and carts. — Gregory Clark, *Words of the Vietnam War*, p. 555, 1990

buff *verb*

1 to exercise with the aim of developing an athletic body *US*, *1995*

- So when I started buffin with Jimel, I blew up to some twenties [20-inch arms], then I got sick with cancer. — Yusuf Jah, *Uprising*, p. 27, 1995

2 in hospital usage, to make notations in a patient's chart that makes the patient look better than they are and ready for the next stage of their care *US*, *1994*

- — Sally Williams, "*Strong*" *Words*, p. 135, 1994

buff *adjective*

1 handsome, excellent *US*, *1982*

- — Lillian Glass with Richard Liebmann-Smith, *How to Deprogram Your Valley Girl*, p. 29, 1982

2 (used of a body) well-toned, well-exercised *US*, *1982*

- — *National Education Association Today*, April 1985: "A glossary for rents and other squids"
- Gorgeous, buff, volleyball player's legs? — Joseph Wambaugh, *Floaters*, p. 149, 1996
- "You're as titanic as ever. So fucking buff!" — Ethan Morden, *Some Men Are Lookers*, p. 49, 1997
- "Yeah, you're big enough. Buff enough, I mean. Real buff." — Missy Hyatt, *Missy Hyatt*, p. 112, 2001

buffalo *noun*

1 an American Indian male with especially long hair *US*, *1963*

- — *American Speech*, p. 272, December 1963: "American Indian student slang"

2 a five-cent piece *US*, *1945*

From the engraving on the coin.

- — Lou Shelly, *Hepcats Jive Talk Dictionary*, p. 8, 1945

buffalo *verb*

to confuse someone, to intimidate someone *US*, *2003*

- I never saw nobody buffalo Bill the way she buffaloed Bill. — *Kill Bill*, 2003

buffalo bagels!

used for expressing disapproval *US*, *2003*

A signature line of Colonel Sherman Potter on *M*A*S*H* (CBS, 1972–83). Repeated with referential humor.

- As far as I am concerned this is a bunch of—as Colonel Potter from MASH would say "Horse Hockey" or "Buffalo Bagels." — Steven Wunderink, *Minding Your Spiritual Business*, p. 98, 2003

buffalo grass *noun*
any grass tall enough to hide a solider *US, 2004*
- — David Hart, *First Air Cavalry Division Vietnam Dictionary*, p. 10, 2004

buffalo gun *noun*
a large caliber gun *US, 1989*
Korean war usage.
- Then two more enemy soldiers appeared out of the smoke and confusion dragging a .57 caliber antitank "buffalo gun." — David H. Hackworth, *About Face*, p. 27, 1989

buffarilla *noun*
an ugly girl *US, 1968*
A blend of "buffalo" and "gorilla."
- — Collin Baker et al., *College Undergraduate Slang Study Conducted at Brown University*, p. 89, 1968

buffed *adjective*
said of a surface chemically treated to thwart graffiti *US, 1994*
- Almost none of the walls look buffed. — William Upski Wimsatt, *Bomb the Suburbs*, p. 43, 1994

buffed; buffed up *adjective*
muscular; in very good physical condition *US, 1995*
- They can tell, just from looking at you all buffed up, that you just got outta jail. — Odie Hawkins, *Midnight*, p. 20, 1995
- — Connie Eble (Editor), *UNC-CH Campus Slang*, p. 1, Fall 1996

buffer *noun*
in the world of crack cocaine users, a woman who will perform oral sex in exchange for crack cocaine or the money to buy it *US, 1992*
- — Terry Williams, *Crackhouse*, p. 147, 1992

buffers *noun*
the female breasts *US, 1964*
- — Roger Blake, *The American Dictionary of Sexual Terms*, p. 23, 1964

buffet flat *noun*
a party held to raise rent money *US, 1982*
- — Arnold Shaw, *Dictionary of American Pop/Rock*, p. 179, 1982

buff up *verb*
to engage in strenuous exercise with a goal of body conditioning *US, 2000*
- They had to buff up and get mean. — Bill Valentine, *Gangs and Their Tattoos*, p. 10, 2000

bufu *noun*
a male homosexual *US, 1982*
An abbreviation of **BUTTFUCKER**.
- — Mary Corey and Victoria Westermark, *Fer Shurr!*, 1982
- He's like Mr. BU-FU (Valley Girl) / We're talking Lord God King BU-FU (Valley Girl). — Moon Unit and Frank Zappa, *Valley Girl*, 1982

bug *noun*
1 a hidden microphone or listening device *US, 1946*
- The Texas officers had put a "bug" (hidden microphone) in the room where Manno was to discuss terms with them[.] — Alson Smith, *Syndicate City*, p. 252, 1954

2 in the television and movie industries, a small earphone used by a sound mixer *US, 1977*
- — Tony Miller and Patricia George, *Cut! Print!*, p. 184, 1977

3 a malfunction in design, especially of a computer or computer software *US, 1978*
- — *CoEvolution Quarterly*, p. 27, Spring 1981
- — Eric S. Raymond, *The New Hacker's Dictionary*, p. 82, 1991

4 a sociopathic criminal; a crazy person *US, 1951*
- "You think a jury would convict even a cat on what a bug like Harry Rudolph says?" he taunted. — Burton Turkus and Sid Feder, *Murder, Inc.*, p. 50, 1951
- "He ties her up and beats on her. She loves it. They're both bugs." — Robert Stone, *Dog Soldiers*, p. 80, 1974
- Telano reached the "Bug" on the street side, his off-duty revolver at the ready now[.] — John Sepe, *Cop Team*, p. 60, 1975

- "Nobody takes Wick seriously. He's a fuckin' bug." — Ted Conover, *Newjack*, p. 116, 2000

5 a burglar alarm *US, 1926*
- This joint was bugged up, it was a poison joint, a drugstore. I figured out how to cut through the roof and into the ceiling and beat the bug. — Harry King, *Box Man*, p. 56, 1972
- There weren't any bugs or burglar alarms. — Vincent Teresa, *My Life in the Mafia*, p. 102, 1973

6 an illegal numbers lottery *US, 1963*
- The numbers game, or, to use the regional term, "the bug," remains the most lucrative racket. — *Saturday Evening Post*, p. 72, 9th March 1963

7 in poker, a joker played as an ace or a wild card to complete a flush or straight *US, 1967*
- — Albert H. Morehead, *The Complete Guide to Winning Poker*, p. 258, 1967

8 an enthusiastic interest; a popular craze *UK, 1902*
- [Y]ou've already been bitten by the collecting bug. — Ron Guth, *Coin Collecting for Dummies*, p. 3, 2001

9 a chameleon *US, 1973*
Circus and carnival slang.
- — Sherman Louis Sergel, *The Language of Show Biz*, p. 33, 1973

10 in horse racing, a weight handicap *US, 1941*
- They've got Imarazzo on her. He gets the five-pound bug and she's running against stiffs, except for Green Grip. — Vincent Patrick, *The Pope of Greenwich Village*, p. 82, 1979

11 a torch *US, 1980*
Circus and carnival usage.
- — Joe McKennon, *Circus Lingo*, p. 21, 1980

▸ **have a bug up your ass**
to be annoyed or angry *US, 1949*
- "Beeker's got a bug in his ass," he said. — Clarence Cooper Jr., *The Scene*, p. 25, 1960
- Sometimes Moran the cop would get a bug up his ass and grab me or Colorado on the street and put us back in the Home. — Edwin Torres, *Carlito's Way*, p. 16, 1975
- Castlebeck's got a bug up his ass over this guy. — *Gone in 60 Seconds*, 2000

▸ **put a bug in someone's ear**
to hint at something *US, 1905*
- I'm just saying maybe you should put a bug in her ear all the same. You never know. — Robert Campbell, *In a Pig's Eye*, p. 56, 1991

▸ **the bug**
HIV *US, 1997*
- Linda Taylor caught the bug and died in January. — David Simon and Edward Burns, *The Corner*, p. 148, 1997

▸ **the bug**
malaria *US, 1947*
- — *American Speech*, p. 54, February 1947: "Pacific War language"

bug *verb*
1 to bother someone, to annoy someone *US, 1947*
- You must start reading Balzac, incidentally, but don't let me rush you and bug you. — Jack Kerouac, *Letter to Neal Cassady*, p. 126, 13th September 1947
- Don't bug me with them Christian cats, let them goof off anyway they want to. — William "Lord" Buckley, *Nero*, 1951
- Goldilocks rolled over and mumbled sleepily, "Jack, don't bug me." — Steve Allen, *Bop Fables*, p. 12, 1955
- You want to bug us till we have to lock you up. — *Rebel Without a Cause*, 1955

2 to panic, to be anxious *US, 1988*
- But people came that like, did not R.S.V.P., so I was like, totally buggin'. — *Clueless*, 1995

3 to watch something *US, 1952*
- He sat forward to bug the picture—and again lost himself in fantasy. — Hal Ellson, *The Golden Spike*, p. 196, 1952

4 to talk and act in a disassociated, irrational way while under the influence of crack cocaine *US, 1992*
- — Terry Williams, *Crackhouse*, p. 147, 1992

5 to arm something with an alarm *US, 1919*
- The question is whether they got this door bugged or not. — Vincent Patrick, *Family Business*, p. 209, 1985

6 to attach or install a listening device *US, 1919*
- [T]hey are even bugging her telephone and just now sent over this tape[.] — Gore Vidal, *Myra Breckinridge*, p. 133, 1968

7 to dance *US, 1968*
- — Joan Fontaine et al., *Dictionary of Black Slang*, 1968

bugaboo *noun*
an imagined object of terror *UK, 1740*
- Selling apples on the streets became the great national bugaboo, a coast-to-coast phobia. — Max Shulman, *The Zebra Derby*, p. 109, 1946
- [W]e are having fish for supper this Friday nite because I mentioned I was Catholic—their bugaboo. — Neal Cassady, *The First Third*, p. 219, 1965

bug boy *noun*
in horse racing, a jockey who has not yet won a race and who is given a five-pound weight allowance *US, 1968*
Because of the "bug" or asterisk denoting the jockey's status in the racing program.
- — Don Voorhees and Bob Benoit, *Railbird Handbook*, p. 44, 1968

bug buster *noun*
a physician specializing in infectious diseases *US, 1984–1985*
- — *Maledicta*, p. 117, 1984–1985: "Milwaukee medical maledicta"

bug cell *noun*
a prison cell reserved for the mentally ill *US, 1949*
- The cons up there were either in bug cells or deadlock. — Nelson Algren, *The Man with the Golden Arm*, p. 205, 1949

bug chaser *noun*
a person whose unsafe sex practices suggest a suicidal wish *US, 2002*
- "You're what they call a bug chaser, aren'tcha. If you wanna die so bad, whyn'tcha just blow yer fuckin' brains out?" — Lynn Breedlove, *Godspeed*, p. 181, 2002

bug doctor *noun*
a psychiatrist *US, 1951*
- — *American Speech*, p. 194, October 1951: "A study of reformatory argot"
- — Gary K. Farlow, *Prison-ese*, p. 7, 2002

bug dope *noun*
insect repellant *US, 1993*
- — Mike Doogan, *How to Speak Alaskan*, p. 16, 1993

bug eye *noun*
in television and movie-making, a fisheye lens *US, 1987*
- — Ira Konigsberg, *The Complete Film Dictionary*, p. 36, 1987

bug flea *noun*
an epidemiologist specializing in infectious diseases *US, 1994*
- — Sally Williams, *"Strong" Words*, p. 135, 1994

bugfuck *adjective*
deranged, out of control *US, 1994*
- When he saw the cat, that old bulldog went bugfuck. — Michael Dalton Johnson, *Talking Trash with Redd Foxx*, p. 110, 1994

bugged *adjective*
angry *US, 1956*
- I guess he was bugged also, and when two bugged convicts meet head on, pressure gotta come out. — Piri Thomas, *Down These Mean Streets*, p. 259, 1967
- What's the point of being bugged if you don't have any power to change anything? — Nat Hentoff, *I'm really dragged but nothing gets me down*, p. 9, 1968

bugged up *adjective*
1 equipped with a burglar alarm *US, 1972*
- This joint was bugged up, it was a poison joint, a drugstore. — Harry King, *Box Man*, p. 56, 1972

2 anxious, nervous *US, 1949*
- I wasn't more than two blocks away from Juan's place when I started getting bugged up again. — Hal Ellson, *Duke*, p. 164, 1949

bugger *verb*
to bungle something, to ruin something *US, 1847*
- The way to handle it is to pass the word to some crabby dumb mick of a DA, and he'll bugger it up fast enough. — George V. Higgins, *The Friends of Eddie Doyle*, p. 65, 1971

bugging *adjective*
crazy *US, 1995*
- That cess [marijuana] got me buggin'. — Lois Stavsky et al., *A2Z*, p. 18, 1995

buggy *adjective*
silly, insane, or inbetween *US, 1902*
- Now, beat it, you baggy old bitch! Take your buggy boy friend and clear out of here before I forget I'm a lady. — Jim Thompson, *Pop. 1280*, p. 201, 1964
- Back in New York the place had gone Beatle buggy. — Murray Kaufman, *Murray the K Tells It Like It Is, Baby*, p. 91, 1966
- "I can tell you right now the sonofabitch weren't never right after that. Got buggy, I guess." — William Brashler, *City Dogs*, p. 60, 1976
- He had no desire to go back up to his cutting room again, get all buggy with his thoughts. — Richard Price, *Clockers*, p. 435, 1992

buggy whip *noun*
a long radio antenna on a car or truck *US, 1962*
- — *American Speech*, p. 267, December 1962: "The language of traffic policemen"

bughouse *noun*
a mental hospital *US, 1899*
- "I told you he was bug-house, didn't I?" Jinx said. — Horace McCoy, *Kiss Tomorrow Good-bye*, p. 108, 1948
- So they took him to the hospital and when he failed to improve they shipped him to the "bug house." — Caryl Chessman, *Cell 2456 Death Row*, p. 117, 1954
- I could snap up and get sent to the federal bughouse in Springfield, Missouri, or I could refuse to come out of my cell. — Edwin Torres, *Carlito's Way*, p. 124, 1975
- "Twelve years in St. Liz's bughouse," Harry said. — Elmore Leonard, *Pronto*, p. 258, 1993

bughouse *adjective*
insane, mad *US, 1894*
- Joe Castillo was, in his words, totally bughouse. — Joseph Wambaugh, *Lines and Shadows*, p. 135, 1984

bug juice *noun*
1 an insect repellant *US, 1944*
The term was coined in World War 2 and has been used since. In Vietnam, there was no shortage of bugs or "bug juice," which was also used to light fires, clean weapons, and heat cans of c-rations.
- Neither fire nor water nor bug juice nor anything except burning the bunks could get rid of them. — Chester Himes, *Cast the First Stone*, p. 77, 1952
- We never use deodorant, but we do use bug juice. Lots and lots of bug juice. — Ernest Spencer, *Welcome to Vietnam, Macho Man*, p. 90, 1987

2 Kool-Aid™ or a sugary, powdered, artificially flavored Kool-Aid-like drink *US, 1946*
Coined in World War 2, popular in Vietnam, and the title and subject of a rousing Girl Scout song sung to the tune of "On Top of Old Smokey."
- He went up to the wardroom and got a glass of "bug juice" before he returned to his room. — Gerry Carroll, *North S*A*R*, p. 255, 1991
- Amazingly, it still tasted vaguely like grape bug juice. — Elissa Stein and Kevin Leslie, *Chunks*, p. 78, 1997

3 medication given those with mental disorders *US, 2002*
- — Gary K. Farlow, *Prison-ese*; p. 8, 2002

4 any antibiotic *US, 1984*
- — *Maledicta*, p. 117, 1984–1985: "Milwaukee medical maledicta"
- — Sally Williams, *"Strong" Words*, p. 135, 1994

5 tear gas *US, 1950*
- — Hyman E. Goldin et al., *Dictionary of American Underworld Lingo*, p. 35, 1950

bugle *noun*
the nose *US, 1865*
- George Piccolo, "a guy with a tremendous bugle on him," stumbled on some gang kids in Queens who were armed with chains and switchblades. — Leonard Shecter and William Phillips, *On the Pad*, p. 84, 1973

bug-out *noun*
1 any hasty retreat; a dramatic evasive maneuver used by fighter pilots *US, 1957*
- If the feces really hit the fan, there are three points through which a man can run for the hills—rear exits in the trench called "bug-outs." — Martin Russ, *The Last Parallel*, p. 116, 1957
- In these "bug-outs" the men sometimes threw away their weapons without firing a shot. It was this "bug-out" atmosphere that caused General Walker to make his "stand-or-die" order. — Don Lawson, *The United States in the Korean War*, p. 33, 1964

- For those situations in which barrel rolling didn't work, McKeown devised a maneuver called the "bug out." — Robert K. Wilcox, *Scream of Eagles*, p. 140, 1990

2 a lively, wild time *US*, *1995*

- His parents are away. It's gonna be a bug-out. — *Kids*, 1995

bug out *verb*
1 to flee *US*, *1950*

- "Bugging out," a phrase describing unseemly and precipitate flight, was already a battlefield cliche, and one regiment had already adopted "the Bug-Out Blues" as its "theme song." — Robert Leckie, *The Wars of America, Volume II*, p. 349, 1968
- Not long before I bugged out, there was violence in St. Peter's Square. — Tom Robbins, *Another Roadside Attraction*, p. 254, 1971
- The all-black 24th Infantry Regiment had bugged out scandalously in Korea, even adopting the pop song "Bug-Out Blues" as its unofficial regimental theme[.] — Earl Thompson, *Tattoo*, p. 658, 1974
- The troops came up with a better catchword than Vietnamization, pithier, to the point. They were "bugging out." — Walter J. Boyne and Steven L. Thompson, *The Wild Blue*, p. 533, 1986

2 to go insane *US*, *1961*

- — Francis J. Rigney and L. Douglas Smith, *The Real Bohemia*, p. xiii, 1961
- Dr. Dre admitted that it "tripped me out, bugged me the fuck out" when he discovered white kids were buying his records[.] — Barney Hoskyns, *Waiting For The Sun*, p. 337, 1996

bugout unit *noun*
a military unit with a reputation for running under fire *US*, *1982*
Korean war usage.

- The 24th Regiment never overcame its reputation as a "bugout" unit—a derisive name GIs gave to troops who broke under fire. — Joseph C. Goulden, *Korea*, p. 169, 1982

bugs *adjective*
crazy *US*, *1903*

- "He's nutty." "He's bugs," said another. — Robert Gover, *The Maniac Responsible*, p. 191, 1963

bugsmasher *noun*
a Beech C-47 Expeditor, a military transport plane used from World War 2 until early in the Vietnam war *US*, *1991*

- Still, he had never actually flown in a Navy plane other than the COD, the Carrier Onboard Delivery Plane, the ugly bugsmasher that carried parts and people. — James Huston, *Balance of Power*, p. 122, 1999

build *verb*
to serve time in prison *US*, *1967*

- You mean you've built two big ones in this jailhouse and you still don't know when to leave your cell partner alone for a few minutes? — Malcolm Braly, *On the Yard*, p. 209, 1967

build-up *noun*
in horse racing, betting at the track designed to increase the odds on a bet made away from the track *US*, *1960*

- — Robert Saunders Dowst and Jay Craig, *Playing the Races*, p. 161, 1960

bukkake *noun*
a photograph or video depicting multiple men ejaculating onto a single woman *US*, *1997*
Japanese slang meaning "splash" used by English-speakers with no further knowledge of Japanese; a popular fetish.

- Bukkake Festival. Does anybody know about these Asian films? — *alt.asian-movies*, 15th March 1995
- Bizarre rituals such as bukkake videos, which feature as many as 80 men ejaculating one after another into a woman's face while she holds a bowl underneath her chin, pushed the limits even further. — *LA Weekly*, p. 18, 14th January 2000
- The porn phenomenon known as bukkake shoots homophobia and misogyny right in the face. — *Village Voice*, p. 144, 20th March 2001

bulbed *adjective*
drunk *US*, *1960*

- We were both really bulbed[.] — Glendon Swarthout, *Where the Boys Are*, p. 29, 1960
- But when it happened I was so pleasantly bulbed that the implications didn't sink in. — Frederick Kohner, *The Affairs of Gidget*, p. 113, 1963

bull *noun*
1 nonsense *US*, *1902*

An abbreviation of **BULLSHIT**.

- Not the bull they teach you in Sunday school. — John Rechy, *City of Night*, p. 327, 1963
- "So don't give me a lot of bull. Give me the truth." — Frederick Kohner, *The Affairs of Gidget*, p. 3, 1963

2 a police officer, especially a detective; a prison guard *US*, *1893*

- It's better you tell me than have the bulls drag you to the station. — Mickey Spillane, *I, The Jury*, p. 43, 1947
- There were two narcotic bulls on my back. — Jack Gerber, *The Connection*, p. 69, 1957
- Big Jeff, as usual, was the first bull through the door. Imagine, Augie Robles, cornered, with four, count 'em, four pistols, waiting on you. Shee-it. The bulls killed Augie that night[.] — Edwin Torres, *Carlito's Way*, p. 17, 1972
- The bulls are across the street. They're watching everything we do. — *Goodfellas*, 1990

3 an aggressive, mannish lesbian *US*, *1964*

- Some bull pawing over her. — Joe Houston, *The Gay Flesh*, p. 108, 1965
- Known variously as a bull, a stomper, a bad butch, a hard dresser, a truck driver, a diesel dyke, a bull dagger and a half dozen other soubriquets, she is the one who, according to most homosexual girls, gives lesbians a bad name. — Ruth Allison, *Lesbianism*, p. 125, 1967

4 in prison, a person who can withstand physical hardship *US*, *1990*

- — Charles Shafer, *Folk Speech in Texas Prisons*, p. 199, 1990

5 an aggressive poker bettor *US*, *1988*

- — George Percy, *The Language of Poker*, p. 14, 1988

6 in the circus, an elephant, male or female *US*, *1921*

- [E]lephants are called "bulls" or "pigs." — Butch Reynolds, *Broken Hearted Clown*, p. 32, 1953
- — Joe McKennon, *Circus Lingo*, p. 21, 1980

7 a battle tank *US*, *1976*

- Get that bull off us, over! — Charles Anderson, *The Grunts*, p. 119, 1976

8 in a deck of playing cards, an ace *US*, *1963*

- — Irwin Steig, *Common Sense in Poker*, p. 182, 1963

bull *verb*
in poker, to bluff repeatedly, betting in amounts designed to drive other players out of hands simply by virtue of the size of the bet *US*, *1963*

- — Irwin Steig, *Common Sense in Poker*, p. 182, 1963

bull *adjective*
when describing a military rank, full *US*, *1973*
Korean war usage.

- He finally made bull colonel: he's deserved it a long time. — Walter J. Sheldon, *Gold Bait*, p. 47, 1973
- The orders came, brawled by a bull sergeant. — Michael Shaara, *The Killer Angels*, p. 326, 1974

bull artist *noun*
a person who habitually lies or exaggerates *US*, *1918*

- "Oh, brother!" she said. "What a bull artist!!" — Jim Thompson, *Pop. 1280*, p. 209, 1964

bull boss *noun*
a superintendent *US*, *1962*

- [T]wo roustabouts and the bull boss were killed. — Stephen Longstreet, *The Flesh Peddlers*, p. 193, 1962

bullcrap *noun*
nonsense *US*, *1935*
A slightly euphemized **BULLSHIT**.

- "She's too good for me," Chico admitted. Bull-crap, Angel thought[.] — Hal Ellson, *The Golden Spike*, p. 57, 1952
- "A chance to make a lot of money and with no risk." "Bullcrap. There's always risk." — Burt Hirschfield, *Fire Island*, p. 99, 1970

bulldag *verb*
to perform oral sex on a woman *US*, *1954*

- Cause, whore, I'm gonna sleigh-ride you and bulldag you too. — Bruce Jackson, *Get Your Ass in the Water and Swim Like Me*, p. 125, 1965

bulldagger *noun*
a lesbian with masculine affectations and mannerisms *US*, *1929*
A variant of **BULLDYKE**.

- She dresses like a goddamn bull dagger. — James Baldwin, *Another Country*, p. 31, 1962
- Now the hostess of the evenin' was Free-Turn Flor / she brought fifteen bulldaggers to put on the show. — Bruce Jackson, *Get Your Ass in the Water and Swim Like Me*, p. 148, 1964
- Bev is sometimes a raging bulldagger, sometimes rabidly homophobic. — Michelle Tea, *Rent Girl*, p. 84, 2004

bull derm *noun*
any low grade of tobacco issued by the state to prisoners *US, 2001*
A corruption of Bull Durham™, an RJ Reynolds tobacco brand.
- — AFSCME Local 3963, *The Correctional Officer's Guide to Prison Slang*, 2001

bulldog *noun*
the earliest edition of a morning newspaper *US, 1986*
- — Rachel S. Epstein and Nina Liebman, *Biz Speak*, p. 28, 1986

bulldog *verb*
1 (used of a professional insider in horse racing) to falsely claim to have given good information in a completed race *US, 1968*
- — *San Francisco News*, 14th February 1968

2 in the illegal production of alcohol, to sweat whiskey out of used barrel staves *US, 1974*
- — David W. Maurer, *Kentucky Moonshine*, p. 114, 1974

3 to intimidate someone verbally and/or physically *US, 1992*
- — William K. Bentley and James M. Corbett, *Prison Slang*, p. 91, 1992

bulldog nose *noun*
a severe case of gonorrhea *US, 1967*
A truly hideous image.
- — Dale Gordon, *The Dominion Sex Dictionary*, p. 34, 1967

bulldozer *noun*
a poker player whose aggressive betting is not contingent upon holding a good hand *US, 1988*
- — George Percy, *The Language of Poker*, p. 14, 1988

bulldrunk *noun*
a drinking spree *US, 1964*
- I went to the Republican convention and put on a bulldrunk that scared the shit out of the Observer honchos sent out to put me to work. — Hunter S. Thompson, *The Proud Highway*, p. 463, 19th August 1964: Letter to Don Cooke

bulldyke; bulldike; bull *noun*
a lesbian with masculine affectations and mannerisms *US, 1931*
- You lousy bulldike! — George Mandel, *Flee the Angry Strangers*, p. 386, 1952
- He was torn in two by a bull dike. Most terrific vaginal grip I ever experienced. — William Burroughs, *Naked Lunch*, p. 91, 1957
- "Well, really, darling," she said, because I was clearly puzzled, "if it's not about a couple of old bull-dykes, what the hell is it about?" — Truman Capote, *Breakfast at Tiffany's*, p. 21, 1958
- The occasional cigar-smoking leather-jacket bull dyke may bend the regulation. — Roger Gordon, *Hollywood's Sexual Underground*, p. 25, 1966
- I looked like a bull dyke or the trick of one, with handcuffs, a leather jacket, metal belts, and levi 501's, so I would try to method act. — Jennifer Blowdryer, *White Trash Debutante*, p. 56, 1997

bulldyker; bulldiker *noun*
a lesbian with masculine affectations and mannerisms *US, 1906*
A variant of **BULLDYKE**.
- The compound bulldiker seems to stem from adjectival use of bull and ram as intensifiers among West Indians. — Peter Tamony, *Dike*, p. 6, 1972
- Last night some bulldiker tried to stab Apeman when he tried to collect. — Donald Goines, *Black Gangster*, p. 213, 1977

bullet *noun*
1 a bag of heroin packaged for retail sale *US, 2006*
- On the day that we was killed, Mr. Brown was with a friend when he received a phone call about "five bullets," street slang for a bag of heroin. — *The Capital* (Annapolis, Maryland), p. A1, 18th August 2006

2 one year of a prison sentence *US, 1967*
- He had served a bullet 'n' a deuce. — Lightnin' Rod, *Hustlers Convention*, p. 10, 1973

- Richard, you're looking at a dime minimum this time. Ten bullets. You think you can handle that? — James Ellroy, *Blood on the Moon*, p. 90, 1984
- What's another bullet, wild or bowlegged... Anyways they have to convict first. — Seth Morgan, *Homeboy*, p. 141, 1990

3 in cards, an ace *US, 1807*
- "But watch out, punk—that hand beside you is flushin' 'n' that bird with nothin' but an ace showin' is gonna cop with three concealed bullets." — Nelson Algren, *The Man with the Golden Arm*, p. 10, 1949
- Get rid of that damn ace, that black bullet. — Richard Prather, *The Peddler*, p. 65, 1952
- The banker spread his hand. A flush. "Four bullets," Rick said joyously, slapping them down. — John D. McDonald, *The Neon Jungle*, p. 57, 1953

4 a quart bottle of beer, especially of Budweiser™ beer *US, 1967*
- — *American Speech*, p. 61, February 1967: "Soda-fountain, restaurant and tavern calls"

5 a capsule of secobarbital sodium (trade name Seconal™), a central nervous system depressant *US, 1972*
- — Richard A. Spears, *The Slang and Jargon of Drugs and Drink*, p. 83, 1986

6 a narcotic suppository *US, 1984*
- — Inez Cardozo-Freeman, *The Joint*, p. 485, 1984

7 a short surfboard with a rounded nose *US, 1991*
- — Trevor Cralle, *The Surfin'ary*, p. 16, 1991

8 in skateboarding, a riding position: crouching low on the board with arms outstretched *US, 1976*
- — Laura Torbet, *The Complete Book of Skateboarding*, p. 105, 1976

▶ **put a bullet in Rover**
to stop talking and start listening *US, 1992*
- The expression "put a bullet in Rover" is common street slang for "shut up and listen," Mike explained. "It's an everyday expression, but they don't know it because they don't know the streets." — *Orlando (Florida) Sentinel Tribune*, p. E1, 23rd July 1992

bulletproof *adjective*
in computing, able to withstand any change or external stimulus *US, 1991*
- — Eric S. Raymond, *The New Hacker's Dictionary*, p. 84, 1991

bullet stabber *noun*
a loader of a combat tank crew *US, 1986*
- If you weren't a trained "tread head" when you came to us, llpha would turn you into a top-grade "bullet stabber" in no time. — Ralph Zumbro, *Tank Sergeant*, p. viii, 1986

bullet-stopper *noun*
a soldier in the infantry *US, 1998*
- — *Seattle Times*, p. A9, 12th April 1998

bull feathers *noun*
nonsense *US, 1971*
- The statement left no room for doubt. "Bullfeathers," said Charles O. Finley, owner of the Oakland A's. — *San Francisco Examiner*, p. 45, 15th June 1971
- Bull feathers. That amounts to bureaucratic blackmail. — *San Diego Union-Tribune*, p. NC2, 18th October 2003

bullfrog *verb*
in craps, to make a bet on a single roll of the dice *US, 1983*
- — Thomas L. Clark, *The Dictionary of Gambling and Gaming*, p. 30, 1987

bull goose *noun*
by extension, the person in charge of any situation *US, 1932*
- "Old Foster is the bull goose out at the Army Hospital," meaning that Colonel Foster was the commandant." — Vance Randolph, *Down in the Holler*, p. 231, 1953
- "You the bull goose here?" Dove asked. "I'm lookin' for boat-work." — Nelson Algren, *A Walk on the Wild Side*, p. 81, 1956
- Tara Reid, 26, who plays a student writing about Van at the behest of campus newspaper editor Tom Everett Scott, 31, when she's not suffering the company of her bull-goose jerk of a boyfriend, Daniel Cosgrove, also 31. — *Cincinnati Enquirer*, p. 9W, 5th April 2002
- Warren was pretty much bull goose of Magno Clique. — Linden Dalecki, *Kid B*, p. 23, 2006

bull goose looney *noun*
the leader of a group of crazy people *US, 1962*

- Ask him if he's bull goose loony. — Ken Kesey, *One Flew Over the Cuckoo's Nest*, p. 19, 1962
- The air's filled with sex, and I'm the bullgooseloony chicken. — David Henry Sterry, *Chicken*, p. 48, 2002

bullhead *noun*
an extremely large penis *US, 1973*
- I told her to make a guy think he has a bullhead for a dick even if it's not as large as her clitoris. — A.S. Jackson, *Gentleman Pimp*, p. 167, 1973

bull horrors *noun*
the terror of the police felt by a drug addict *US, 1927*
- — Vincent J. Monteleone, *Criminal Slang*, p. 36, 1949
- — Eugene Landy, *The Underground Dictionary*, p. 41, 1971

bulling *adjective*
very good *US, 1953*
- — Lavada Durst, *The Jives of Dr. Hepcat*, p. 11, 1953

bull jive *noun*
1 insincere talk *US, 1971*
- — Hermese E. Roberts, *The Third Ear*, 1971
2 marijuana that has been adulterated with catnip or another leaf-like substance *US, 1973*
- — David W. Maurer and Victor Vogel, *Narcotics and Narcotics Addiction*, p. 393, 1973

bull of the woods *noun*
a college official such as a dean *US, 1947*
- — Marcus Hanna Boulware, *Jive and Slang of Students in Negro Colleges*, 1947

bullpen *noun*
1 a holding cell in a courtroom or a jail *US, 1880*
- I stepped into the bull pen, followed him dumbly. — Chester Himes, *If He Hollers Let Him Go*, p. 200, 1945
- From there they were sent to the bullpen to await the wagon[.] — Hal Ellson, *The Golden Spike*, p. 240, 1952
- They come from the bullpen to the Tombs up to their floor. — James Mills, *The Panic in Needle Park*, p. 44, 1966
- The bailiff thrust him into the bullpen. — Seth Morgan, *Homeboy*, p. 145, 1990
2 an open area in an office with desks *US, 1983*
- The bullpen was a large room in the Field Office which was crammed with rows of gray metal desks facing one another. — Gerald Petievich, *To Live and Die in L.A.*, p. 53, 1983
- — Kathleen Odean, *High Steppers, Fallen Angels, and Lollipops*, p. 157, 1988
3 in a nightclub, chairs without tables for patrons who want only to listen to the music *US, 1956*
- These bull pens still exist in bop palaces around the country. — Robert Sylvester, *No Cover Charge*, p. 275, 1956

bull pup *noun*
the 250-pound air-to-ground missile (AGM) carried on fighter jets *US, 1990*
- — Joseph Tuso, *Singing the Vietnam Blues*, p. 246, 1990: Glossary

bullpup *noun*
a target pistol, especially one with an elaborate stock *US, 1957*
- — *American Speech*, p. 192, October 1957: "Some colloquialisms of the handgunner"

bull ring *noun*
in horse racing, a small track *US, 1976*
- — Tom Ainslie, *Ainslie's Complete Guide to Thoroughbred Racing*, p. 329, 1976

bull roar *noun*
nonsense *US, 1967*
- [H]e preached it with a brand of psychology, the sunshine-spreading, and a generous sprinkling of bull roar. — Elaine Shepard, *The Doom Pussy*, p. 49, 1967

bull-scare *verb*
(used of the police) to frighten or intimidate someone without arresting them *US, 1971*
- At four a.m. my man the grifter called to report that the gorilla had been bull scared into taking a train back to New York. — Iceberg Slim (Robert Beck), *The Naked Soul of Iceberg Slim*, p. 86, 1971

bull session *noun*
an informal group discussion *US, 1919*
- — Lou Shelly, *Hepcats Jive Talk Dictionary*, p. 22, 1945

- For instance, if you were having a bull session in somebody's room, and somebody wanted to come in, nobody'd let them in if they were some dopey, pimply guy. — J.D. Salinger, *Catcher in the Rye*, p. 167, 1951
- He said that when Kossmeyer came down the three of us ought to get together some night and have us a bull session. — Jim Thompson, *The Kill-Off*, p. 28, 1957
- Once a week, he said, a very few of the other people employed by the university dropped in at one another's houses for a bull session. — Clancy Sigal, *Going Away*, p. 244, 1961
- For instance, the bullsessions: I found that half the things they talked about were over my head[.] — Robert Gover, *Poorboy at the Party*, p. 5, 1966
- As for the college audiences, they listened to me in the early '50's because they were surprised that a comedian could have written term papers and wondered about the meaning of life in bull sessions. — Mort Sahl, *Heartland*, p. 103, 1976

bullshit *noun*
nonsense *US, 1914*
- Let's jus leave all this bullshit and beat it. — George Mandel, *Flee the Angry Strangers*, p. 205, 1952
- Efan was a man who always backed up his bullshit with action, which explains why he was always getting himself in these impossible situations. — Cecil Brown, *The Life & Loves of Mr. Jiveass Nigger*, p. 62, 1969
- Nearly everything I have ever read or been told about why people gamble is just plain bullshit. — Mario Puzo, *Inside Las Vegas*, p. 133, 1977
- Carter, Reagan and Anderson. It's all bullshit. (Radio commercial for Barry Commoner). — *San Francisco Chronicle*, p. 12, 15th October 1980

bullshit *verb*
to deceive someone, to fool someone *US, 1937*
- Through the port ... I climbed out on the bodkin ... I'm not bullshitting Chris. — Robert S. Close, *Love Me Sailor*, p. 141, 1945
- I was just bull shittin' her all the way down the line anyway to try to make peace before I get out of the house. — Babs Gonzales, *Movin' On Down De Line*, p. 126, 1975
- I took the liberty of bullshitting you, okay? — *The Blues Brothers*, 1980
- I knew he was bullshitting. — *Ferris Bueller's Day Off*, 1986

bullshit artist *noun*
a person who habitually lies or exaggerates *US, 1942*
- He seems likeable enough, but he's a typical Marine bullshit artist—an authority on everything, incapable of saying I don't know. — Martin Russ, *Happy Hutning Ground*, p. 20, 1968
- In the eyes of many of his colleagues, Apple was a compulsive bullshit artist, the kind of man who could not resist adding $5000-a-year when he told you his salary. — Timothy Crouse, *The Boys on the Bus*, p. 75, 1974
- He was a wonderful intimidator and bluffer and bullshit artist. — Nicholas Von Hoffman, *Citizen Cohn*, p. 386, 1988
- Andy would have accepted "con man" or even "bullshit artist" over "comedian." — Bob Zmuda, *Andy Kaufman Revealed!*, p. 22, 1999

bullshit-ass *adjective*
rubbishy, awful *US, 2002*
Combines **BULLSHIT** (nonsense) with **-ASS** (an intensifier for the preceding adjective).
- After reading that Mobb Deep [hip-hop artists] article and hearing that bullshit-ass album, I don't know what's going on[.] — *The Source*, p. 44, March 2002

bullshit black *noun*
the flat black paint often found on a used car's chassis *US, 1962*
- — *American Speech*, p. 267, December 1962: "The language of traffic policemen"

bullshit bomber *noun*
a plane used in a propaganda-dropping operation *US, 1980*
- Throughout Southeast Asia everybody referred to them as "bullshit bombers." — Tom Yarborough, *Da Nang Diary*, p. 22, 1990

bullshit rich *adjective*
very rich *US, 1994*
A gem from the slang of miners.
- — Michael Dalton Johnson, *Talking Trash with Redd Foxx*, p. 120, 1994

bullshitter *noun*
a liar, a braggart, a bluffer *US, 1933*

- I'm a bigger bullshitter than any of them. — Jack Kerouac, *Letter to John Clellon Holmes*, p. 200, 24th June 1949
- What a bullshitter, geez, I never—is he a bullshitter! — Jack Kerouac, *Doctor Sax*, p. 40, 1959
- He was a real bullshitter, but he was an exciting guy and as long as he wasn't bullshitting me, I didn't mind. — Marilyn G. Haft, *Time without Work*, p. 172, 1983
- A lot of Greek bullshitters read the coffee cups but I reckon my Aunt Tasia is the real thing. — Christos Tsiolkas, *Loaded*, p. 16, 1995

bullskate *verb*
to pretend, to deceive someone, to brag *US, 1947*
A euphemism for **BULLSHIT**.
- — Marcus Hanna Boulware, *Jive and Slang of Students in Negro Colleges*, 1947

bull sugar *noun*
nonsense *US, 1963*
A cleaned up **BULLSHIT**.
- "The genuine article. No bullsugar, eh." — Frederick Kohner, *The Affairs of Gidget*, p. 111, 1963

bull's wool *noun*
any stolen goods *US, 1945*
- — Lou Shelly, *Hepcats Jive Talk Dictionary*, p. 22, 1945

bullsworth *noun*
in circus usage, a lie *US, 1981*
- — Don Wilmeth, *The Language of American Popular Entertainment*, p. 37, 1981

bull thrower *noun*
an eloquent bluffer *US, 1987*
- I picked him because he was a good bull-thrower, sharp on his feet, and could really handle himself. — Joseph Pistone, *Donnie Brasco*, p. 39, 1987

bully club *noun*
a police baton *US, 1963*
- The beatman held a bully-club in his right hand and used it for short, rapid blows to Dena's head and back[.] — Robert Gover, *The Maniac Responsible*, p. 160, 1963

bully stick *noun*
a police baton *US, 1990*
- Police used bully sticks against the protesters, who rained rocks and bottles on the officers. — *USA Today*, 29th October 1990

bum *noun*
1 the buttocks; occasionally and specifically, the anus, the rectum *UK, 1387*
A good Middle English word that survived in conventional usage until the late C18. The etymology is very uncertain; possibly from Italian *bum* (the sound of an explosion), and it is suggested (elsewhere) that "bum" is echoic of buttocks slapping a flat surface. What is certain is that it is now in semi-conventional currency. It is not an abbreviation of **BOTTOM** which is a much later coinage.
- [S]he infuriated a number of men who thought that they should be able to rub her small breasts and round bum simply because she was an Indian. — Leonard Cohen, *Beautiful Losers*, p. 33, 1966
2 a bag in which classified documents which are to be destroyed are placed *US, 1986*
- — Department of the Army, *Staff Officer's Guidebook*, p. 57, 1986

bum *verb*
1 to beg; to borrow something without the expectation of returning it *US, 1857*
- Sure, I always got cigarettes. Reason is, I'm a bum. I bum them whenever I get the chance is why my pack lasts longer than Harding's here. — Ken Kesey, *One Flew Over the Cuckoo's Nest*, p. 173, 1962
- Right away he thought, "There's me three suckers over there." So he walked over to them and he bummed them. — John Gimenez, *Up Tight!*, p. 79, 1967
- I bum a cigarette from one. We're all brothers. — Abbie Hoffman, *Revolution for the Hell of It*, p. 19, 1968
- His name was Bummer Bob because he was the first person in San Francisco to call panhandling "bumming." — Pamela Des Barres, *I'm With the Band*, p. 48, 1988
2 to feel poorly or depressed *US, 1989*
- There I was, bumming about Cassandra, and out of the blue, I meet Bjergen, Bjergen Kjergen from Knuergen near the Jbergen Fjords. — *Wayne's World 2*, 1993

- Something about having to hear the woman you really like going to the toilet always bummed me. — *Airheads*, 1994
3 to have a bad experience with a hallucinogenic drug *US, 1972*
- "He's bumming," comes Manny's voice. "We have to get him out," Shell says. For them, the drug's spell has ended. And they realize that for Jerry the insane world has spilled into reality. — John Rechy, *The Fourth Angel*, p. 130, 1972
4 in computing, to improve something by removing or rearranging it *US, 1983*
- "I bummed the program not to write the file if it would be empty." — Guy L. Steele et al., *The Hacker's Dictionary*, p. 39, 1983

bum *adjective*
injured, damaged, faulty *US, 1902*
- "That trap door turned out to be a bum lead," Pat said. — Chester Gould, *Dick Tracy Meets the Night Crawler*, p. 138, 1945
- Edgar, her husband, succumbed to "bum kidneys" (his term) on Christmas Eve, 1976. — Armistead Maupin, *Further Tales of the City*, p. 16, 1982
- I got a bum prostate [...] I had to stop to take a leak. — Janet Evanovich, *Seven Up*, p. 9, 2001

bum about; bum around *verb*
to wander or live idly *US, 1926*
- I started bumming around the country, playing poker and shooting dice. — Bruce Jackson, *A Thief's Primer*, p. 75, 1972

bum beef *noun*
a complaint or accusation lacking merit *US, 1976*
- In the old prison flicks, the nice old con or the innocent kid, railroaded on a bum beef, always works in the library[.] — Malcolm Braly, *False Starts*, p. 106, 1976
- "This is a bum beef," he told the guards there. "Total bullshit." — Pete Earley, *The Hot House*, p. 15, 1992

bum-beef *verb*
to frame an innocent person *US, 1968*
- — *Current Slang*, p. 12, Fall 1968

bum bend *noun*
an unpleasant experience under the influence of a hallucinogen *US, 1971*
- — Eugene Landy, *The Underground Dictionary*, p. 42, 1971

bumbershoot *noun*
an umbrella *US, 1896*
- While the umbrella—or brolly or bumbershoot or parasol—has protected people from sun or rain for some 4,000 years, there apparently are a few rude umbrella handlers left on the planet. — *Chicago Tribune*, 6th April 2003

bumbled up *adjective*
drunk to the point of passing out *US, 1968*
- — Collin Baker et al., *College Undergraduate Slang Study Conducted at Brown University*, p. 91, 1968

bumblee *noun*
in Passaic, New Jersey, a police officer *US, 2000*
- "I know the bumblees are out tonight." "Bumblees" is street slang for the community police officers, whose uniform includes yellow shirts. — *Record (Bergen County, New Jersey)*, p. L3, 15th September 2000

bumblefuck *noun*
an inept person *US, 1990*
- Jettison the bumblefuck into the vacuum of space where no one can hear him scream. — *rec.humor*, 10th October 1990
- You didn't think about patting them down and checking them for gear, did you? Bumblefucks! — William Upski Wimsatt, *Bomb the Suburbs*, p. 51, 1994
- "I don't have time for this bumblefuck." — Carl Hiaasen, *Nature Girl*, p. 261, 2006

Bumblefuck *noun*
any remote, small town *US, 1989*
- — Pamela Munro, *U.C.L.A. Slang*, p. 26, 1989
- "So like two goofs from East Bumblefuck, Mort and I put all the pieces together." — Scott Thurow, *Personal Injuries*, p. 23, 1999
- She was certain she would end up in Bumblefuck, Illinois, where she would have to endure the self-righteous monologues of Myra Tuchbaum[.] — Adam Langer, *Crossing California*, p. 391, 2004

bum-bust *verb*
to arrest someone on false or nonexistent charges *US, 1977*

- "He doesn't look like a bad kid, be a shame the city put him up for a week, he gets bum-busted by some hood case." — John Sayles, *Union Dues*, p. 29, 1977

bumbye; bumbai *adverb*

sometime soon *US, 1981*

Hawaiian youth usage.

- Bumbye we goin' ovah Harold's, get radical. — Douglas Simonson, *Pidgin to da Max*, 1981

bumfuck *verb*

to have anal intercourse, to sodomize someone *US, 1866*

- "You wanna be bum-fucked while Don watches?" — Sonia Florens, *The Mammoth Book of Women's Fantasies*, p. 82, 2004

Bumfuck, Egypt *noun*

a mythical town that is the epitome of remoteness *US, 1972*

With variants.

- "This ... ain't ... Bumfuck, Egypt." — Jack Hawkins, *Chopper One #2*, p. 89, 1987
- After that, I went to Aberdeen Proving Grounds, and you went to ... bumfuck Saudi Arabia? — Edward Lee, *Ghouls*, p. 202, 1988
- Well, yes, in a way, but it's better than being stuck somewhere outside of Bhum Fuk Vietnam in the middle of a bomb crater the size of the Superdome under fire by determinedly hostile forces. — Dannie J. Marvicsin and Jerold A. Greenfield, *Maverick*, p. 205, 1990
- — Connie Eble (Editor), *UNC-CH Campus Slang*, p. 1, Fall 1993

bum-kicked *adjective*

depressed *US, 1974*

- Tramp's drug thing spun out of control and he was found dead from an overdose of Seconal. It happened right after the Hell's Angels '69 movie was released. Nobody knows whether he was bum-kicked or was just being his usual reckless self. — Ralph "Sonny" Barger, *Hell's Angel*, p. 74, 2000

bummed; bummed out *adjective*

depressed, irritated *US, 1973*

- "I'm sorry to dump on you like this," she said, "but it couldn't even wait for group. That's how bummed out I am." — Cyra McFadden, *The Serial*, p. 97, 1977
- That fucking mousse-haired, white-skinned, needlenose scumbag better show up, 'cause I'm getting bummed. — Howard Stern, *Miss America*, p. 74, 1995
- So we follow him to a clearing about a mile away, where they've got 2 tents set up and a bunch of bummed 'heads are standing around. — Scott Meyer, *Deadhead Forever*, 2001

bummer *noun*

1 a disappointing or depressing event *US, 1965*

- — Miss Cone, *The Slang Dictionary (Hawthorne High School)*, 1965
- But then we came outside and saw all those clippings about us, pasted up like advertisements. Man, it was a bummer, it wasn't right. — Hunter S. Thompson, *Hell's Angels*, p. 89, 1966
- If you consider that the sheer number of beautiful people struggling against the inclement weather, and basic needs of survival, turned the festival into a Nation dedicated to victory, then the bummers get put in quite a different perspective. — Abbie Hoffman, *Woodstock Nation*, p. 4, 1969
- It's a bummer about your party, man. — *Dazed and Confused*, 1993
- CHER: I failed. TAI: Oh, bummer. — *Clueless*, 1995

2 a bad experience with LSD or another hallucinogen *US, 1966*

- Is he going to put acid in everything consumable? Does he want to create a big freak out, a big bummer? — *The San Francisco Oracle*, 1966
- Some of them had a terrible bummer—bummer was the Angels' term for a bad trip on a motorcycle and very quickly it became the hip world's term for a bad trip on LSD. — Tom Wolfe, *The Electric Kool-Aid Acid Test*, p. 159, 1968
- Whatever it was, I had a bummer. One of those rare acid trips when everything caves in. I learned enough shit from it, through, that maybe it wasn't such a bummer after all. — Abbie Hoffman, *Woodstock Nation*, p. 5, 1969
- Bummers were when the acid had something in it that didn't agree with you. — Eve Babitz, *Eve's Hollywood*, p. 234, 1974

3 a beggar, a tramp, a bum *US, 1855*

- Where do you come off knowing a bummer like Billings? — Mickey Spillane, *Me, Hood!*, p. 29, 1963

bummy *noun*

a transient, penniless, dirty person *US, 1923*

- "I'm just one more poor blind bummy peddlin' pencils," he mourned[.] — Nelson Algren, *The Man with the Golden Arm*, p. 176, 1949
- I was carrying the banner down yonder in Atlanta, but watch out, keep out, stay awake—they throw bummies in for thirty days. — John Clellon Holmes, *The Horn*, p. 160, 1958

bummy *adjective*

dirty, wretched *US, 1896*

- Young and emaciated girl, dressed in a raggedy trenchcoat, bummy blue prom dress, and bummy Air Jordans—who is also in another world. — *New Jack City*, p. 28, 1990
- Strike liked her because she was clean, not bummy, a working woman with a kid, holding down the world. — Richard Price, *Clockers*, p. 75, 1992
- "I'm tired of being one of those bummy Raisin in the Sun niggers." — Paul Beatty, *Tuff*, p. 44, 2000

bummy-ass *adjective*

low, disreputable, shoddy *US, 1990*

- Gone are the days of sellin' on street corners, in dark alleys, or in the bathroom of some bummy-ass bar. — *New Jack City*, 1990

bum of the month *noun*

a person identified as a poor performer *US, 1970*

A term coined in connection with heavyweight boxer Joe Louis, who fought against a series of unworthy contenders.

- Production picks out the engineer who'll be the "bum of the month." — Gene W. Dalton et al., *Organizational Structure and Design*, p. 78, 1970
- One concern, according to some of those involved, is that an unfriendly prosecutor could make charges of political corruption a priority. "She might start a "bum of the month" club—you can indict anybody," said Mr. Diamond. — *New York Times*, p. 46, 6th September 1981

bum out *verb*

to depress someone; to disappoint someone *US, 1970*

- Having bummed out almost the entire population of one room, I took my show into another[.] — Lester Bangs, *Psychotic Reactions and Carburetor Dung*, p. 232, 1977
- "Don't look so bummed out," Wiley said. — Carl Hiaasen, *Tourist Season*, p. 101, 1986
- It would truly bum me out if this turned into a commodification of "girl zines." — Marion Leonard, *Cool Places*, p. 108, 1998
- He gets really bummed out a lot though. — Francesca Lia Block, *I Was a Teenage Fairy*, p. 95, 1998

bump *noun*

1 in a striptease or other sexual dance, a forceful pelvic thrust *US, 1931*

- A lot of white vocalists, even some with the big name bands today, are either as stiff as a stuffed owl or else they go through more wringing and twisting than a shake dancer, doing grinds and bumps all over the place[.] — Mezz Mezzrow, *Really the Blues*, p. 27, 1946
- Here she stopped, laughed out loud, and flung her hips into a series of "bumps" and "grinds." — Mark Tryon, *Of G-Strings and Strippers*, p. 7, 1953
- "You do about four bars a bumps and grinds while I chew a hunk outta the grass hut." — Gypsy Rose Lee, *Gypsy*, p. 182, 1957
- Traditional stripping involves several dance movements, including the bump, the grind, and the "hootchy-kootchy." — Marilyn Suriani Futterman, *Dancing Naked in the Material World*, p. 126, 1992

2 in professional wrestling, a fall to the mat or floor, embellished with grunts, shakes, and body spasms that create the impression that the opponent has truly hurt the victim *US, 1990*

- bump n. a fall or hit done as a spot (see spot) usually, but not necessarily, by a referee, manager or other non-wrestler. — *rec.sports.pro -wrestling*, 17th July 1990
- As a pro, Morrus took major bumps when he faced off against another super-heavyweight. — *Rampage*, p. 33, September 2000
- Even the girls in ECW took crazy bumps. — Missy Hyatt, *Missy Hyatt*, p. 150, 2001
- I started wrestling right away in addition to managing, because the promoters saw that I could take bumps. — Bobby Heenan, *Bobby the Brain*, p. 15, 2002

3 a single dose of a powdered drug *US, 1985*

- I cried out, pitifully, "PLEASE! Just one bump! One little bump, I beg of you." — James St. James, *Party Monster*, p. 75, 1990

- It's a tongue-in-cheek reference to a "bump," which is a dose of ketamine, or Special K, a surgical anesthetic snorted by clubgoers to magnify dance floor sensations lights, bass, chaos. — *Daily News (New York)*, p. 42, 8th October 1995
- You don't need to do that much. You only have to do bumps with crystal. — *Boogie Nights*, 1997
- Got a cigarette? Can I have a bump? — Michelle Tea, *Rent Girl*, p. 171, 2004

4 in poker, an increase in the bet on a hand *US, 1988*
- — George Percy, *The Language of Poker*, p. 14, 1988

5 in betting, a doubling of the bet in effect *US, 1986*
- — Sam Snead and Jerry Tarde, *Pigeons, Marks, Hustlers and Other Golf Bettors You Can Beat*, p. 110, 1986

6 in computing, an increment *US, 1991*
- — Eric S. Raymond, *The New Hacker's Dictionary*, p. 85, 1991

bump *verb*
1 to kill someone *US, 1914*
- — Lou Shelly, *Hepcats Jive Talk Dictionary*, p. 8, 1945
- But somebody was afraid of what he knew and bumped him. — Mickey Spillane, *I, The Jury*, p. 24, 1947
- Only six days after they had bumped Bannon they had almost been trapped. — Irving Shulman, *The Amboy Dukes*, p. 169, 1947
- That don't make me know who bumped him. Lots of cats didn't go for him because he was snitchin. — Clarence Cooper Jr., *The Scene*, p. 182, 1960

2 to slide a large stack of gambling chips up next to a player's bet to size the amount of chips for a payoff *US, 1991*
- — Michael Dalton, *Blackjack*, p. 34, 1991

3 in poker, to increase another player's bet *US, 1961*
- — Irv Roddy, *Friday Night Poker*, p. 216, 1961

4 in professional wrestling, to fall to the mat in feigned pain *US, 1999*
- Bumping is, without a doubt, the most valuable thing a wrestler can learn. — Mick Foley, *Mankind*, p. 65, 1999

5 in a striptease or other sexual dance, to thrust the hips forward as if copulating *US, 1936*
- "Bump, damn it! Bump! Or I'll throw you out in the street the minute you come off that stage!" — Mark Tryon, *Of G-Strings and Strippers*, p. 58, 1953
- "It just don't bump when I do—and it scratches the hell outta me." — Gypsy Rose Lee, *Gypsy*, p. 176, 1957
- You can sacrifice your sacro, workin' in the backrow / Bump in a dump till you're dead. — Stephen Sondheim, *You Gotta Get a Gimmick*, 1960
- I continued to bump and grind across the stage, forcing a smile as I unfastened my brassiere[.] — Blaze Starr, *Blaze Starr*, p. 84, 1974

6 to play music loudly *US, 1998*
- — *Columbia Missourian*, p. 1A, 19th October 1998

▶ **bump fuzz**
(used of a female) to have sex with another woman *US, 1997*
- — Pamela Munro, *U.C.L.A. Slang*, p. 46, 1997

▶ **bump heads**
to fight *US, 1971*
- — Eugene Landy, *The Underground Dictionary*, p. 42, 1971

▶ **bump pussies; bump donuts; bump fur**
(used of lesbians) to have sex, especially by engaging in vulva-to-vulva friction *US, 1967*
- What would we do—bump pussies? — Malcolm Braly, *On the Yard*, p. 296, 1967
- Two girls can, by interlacing themselves like forks, "bump pussies" as we used to say when I was a lad, and enjoy all of the thrills and chills of intercourse without even fingering themselves. — Angelo d'Arcangelo, *The Homosexual Handbook*, p. 208, 1968

▶ **bump titties**
to fight *US, 1985*
- — Jennifer Blowdryer, *Modern English*, p. 57, 1985
- — Ann Lawson, *Kids & Gangs*, p. 56, 1994

▶ **bump uglies**
to have sex *US, 1989*
- And Tango adds a phrase to the popular lexicon when Sly's Tango asks Russell's Cash, "Did you bump uglies with my sister?" — *USA Today*, p. 7D, 22nd December 1989
- — Connie Eble (Editor), *UNC-CH Campus Slang*, p. 2, Spring 1992

bump and run *noun*
a crude street robbery *US, 1976*
- But this time was different, he told himself, no cheap-ass drugstore hit, no bump and run. — William Brashler, *City Dogs*, p. 124, 1976

bumper *noun*
1 the buttocks *US, 1963*
- While I was taking a turn around the floor with Jim Bacon of the Associated Press, the Prince and I felt our bumpers collide, and he promptly marched off the floor. — *San Francisco Chronicle*, p. 24, 18th April 1963
- I'll moor it on the Chicago River and put on a big sign, "Babes with Big Bumpers Wanted." — Red Rudensky, *The Gonif*, p. 102, 1970
- He called titties "headlights" and bottoms "bumpers," and we called him "What's Happening Bob[.]" — Pamela Des Barres, *I'm With the Band*, p. 39, 1988
- In the old days, people had metaphors for what they wanted to say. Even the nasty songs aspired to a certain level of craftmanship. Remember "Pull Up to the Bumper?" For a song about anal sex, it was pretty tongue-in-cheek. — Chris Rock, *Rock This!*, p. 213, 1997

2 in pool, the cushion on the side of the table *US, 1990*
- — Steve Rushin, *Pool Cool*, p. 6, 1990

bumper kit *noun*
the female buttocks *US, 1995*
- — Bill Valentine, *Gang Intelligence Manual*, p. 75, 1995

bumpers *noun*
the female breasts *US, 1947*
- What bumpers on her. — Norman Mailer, *The Naked and the Dead*, p. 485, 1948
- [S]he strips down to bumpers and beard, then climbs aboard his Oscar Meyer-mobile. — Mr. Skin, *Mr. Skin's Skincyclopedia*, p. 188, 2005

bumper tag *noun*
1 a slight collision between cars, especially a rear end collision *US, 1980*
- And because the judge was involved in a little bumper tag with a black car that was either a Buick or an Olds. — Elmore Leonard, *City Primeval*, p. 63, 1980
- Once, while biking on a lonely road near Desert Hot Springs, two dirtbag rednecks in a raggedly pickup truck had played bumper tag, forcing her off the road. — Joseph Wambaugh, *Fugitive Nights*, p. 54, 1992

2 in pool, a shot that is made off two cushions on the side of the table *US, 1990*
Punning on a term commonly used to describe a traffic jam.
- — Steve Rushin, *Pool Cool*, p. 6, 1990

bumper-to-bumper *adjective*
(used of car traffic) moving slowly and close together *US, 1938*
- They started south on Collins and pretty soon turned west toward Washington, not much traffic yet. By December it would be bumper to bumper down here. — Elmore Leonard, *Pronto*, pp. 7–8, 1993

bumping *adjective*
excellent *US, 1985*
- — *National Education Association Today*, April 1985: "A glossary for rents and other squids"
- — *The Washington Post*, 15th March 1987
- — Connie Eble (Editor), *UNC-CH Campus Slang*, p. 2, Fall 1988
- — Vann Wesson, *Generation X Field Guide and Lexicon*, p. 30, 1997

bump list *noun*
a list of murder targets *US, 1963*
- Who's bump list you on now? — Mickey Spillane, *Me, Hood!*, p. 16, 1963

bumpman *noun*
in a pickpocket team, a confederate who bumps and distracts the targeted victim *US, 1940*
- It is understood by the police that a "bump man" or a "hook" does not operate at the Garden under the code long agreed upon between the stadium and the artistes. — Robert Sylvester, *No Cover Charge*, p. 286, 1956

bump-off *noun*
a murder *US, 1952*
- "Why the bump-off?" — Richard Prather, *The Peddler*, p. 132, 1952

bump off *verb*
to kill *US, 1907*

- [T]hey'll get out of here now, all join up in the Air Corps and become heroes and bump off fifty, a hundred, a thousand Japs[.] — Mezz Mezzrow, *Really the Blues*, p. 314, 1946
- Can I help it if somebody bumps off the teacher? — Irving Shulman, *The Amboy Dukes*, p. 91, 1947
- In it they had written the names of their enemies and the guys they were going to bump off. — Willard Motley, *Knock on Any Door*, p. 122, 1947
- You can see the processes working in the results: two of the eye witnesses recanted; the third was bumped off. — Jack Lait and Lee Mortimer, *Chicago Confidential*, p. 234, 1950

bumps *noun*
loud bass notes as amplified on a stereo *US, 1997*
- Did you hear the bumps coming from that car? — Pamela Munro, *U.C.L.A. Slang*, p. 46, 1997

bump shop *noun*
a car body repair shop *US, 1978*
- "She's out in Pontiac someplace at a bump shop, getting an estimate," Ordell said. — Elmore Leonard, *Switch*, p. 68, 1978
- Its owner sold it to the owner of the bump shop who sold it to us. — *Detroit News*, p. 2F, 7th April 2004

bum rap *noun*
1 an unfair or false accusation or reputation *US, 1952*
- I'm positive neither bartender's so much as pocketing a wrong tip. Your client may be giving these bartenders a bum rap. — Joseph Wambaugh, *Fugitive Nights*, p. 118, 1992
- I think to blame that all on Reagan is unfair. It's a bum rap. [Quoting Richard Rosenbaum] — Natalie Datlof et al., *Ronald Reagan's America, Vol. 2*, p. 634, 1997
- Let me tell you something, doctor. Chicks love a guy with a bum rap. — *Cruel Intentions*, 1999

2 a false criminal accusation; an unfair conviction *US, 1926*
- "And also, if I'm workin' for a guy, not to take his bum raps." — Irving Shulman, *Cry Tough*, p. 30, 1949
- During the trial, LaMotta denied having any part in steering the girl into prostitution, insisting that he had never seen her before and that he was being given a "bump rap" because he had a "big name." — *Confidential*, p. 29, July 1957
- They demand due process for colleagues beyond all legal necessity because they're so concerned about anyone's getting a bum rap. — Billie Wright Dziech and Linda Weiner, *The Lecherous Professor*, p. 51, 1984

bum-rap *verb*
to arrest someone without proof of guilt *US, 1947*
- I can't ever scream about being bum-rapped. — Bruce Jackson, *In the Life*, p. 160, 1972
- I was in a schoolyard, fer chrissake, maybe five, ten minutes, when these two cops from the 86th precinct bum-rap me! — Terry Southern, *Now Dig This*, p. 146, 2001

bum-rush *verb*
to swarm someone; to attack someone *US, 1987*
- Homeboys I don't know but they're part of the pack / In the plan against the man, bum rush attack / For the suckers at the door — Public Enemy *Yo! Bum Rush The Show*, 1987
- It was on a Sunday. Rick and I were kicking it upon Crenshaw. All these females rolled up in a Rabbit. Everybody started to bum rush them, trying to get their numbers and all. — *Boyz N The Hood*, 1990
- When we bum-rushed white boys, it made me feel like we were beating all white people on behalf of all blacks. — Nathan McCall, *Makes Me Wanna Holler*, p. 4, 1994

bumsicle *noun*
a hypothermic alcoholic *US, 1994*
- — Sally Williams, *"Strong" Words*, p. 135, 1994

bum steer *noun*
a piece of bad advice *US, 1924*
- [T]hey all knew me pretty well and I had never given them a bum steer. — Wade Hunter, *The Sex Peddler*, p. 146, 1963

bum trip *noun*
1 a bad experience with LSD or another hallucinogen *US, 1966*
- — Richard Alpert and Sidney Cohen, *LSD*, 1966
- — Joe David Brown (Editor), *The Hippies*, p. 217, 1967
- See, if you consider the event [Woodstock] as a festival in the traditional sense of the word ... then three people getting killed, a few

thousand injuries, lack of food and water and hundreds of bum trips lead you to draw bad conclusions — Abbie Hoffman, *Woodstock Nation*, p. 4, 1969
- Sure, there was some bad shit around and some bum trips were had, but mostly it was ok. — *East Village Other*, 20th August 1969

2 any bad experience *US, 1965*
- — Miss Cone, *The Slang Dictionary (Hawthorne High School)*, 1965
- They had been shunted off to a parched meadow nine or ten thousand feet up in the Sierras and it was obviously a bum trip. — Hunter S. Thompson, *Hell's Angels*, p. 135, 1966
- And I don't want to take my brothers on a bum trip when I go into Lovely Larry and the theory of reincarnation. — Frank Reynolds, *Freewheelin' Frank*, p. 66, 1967
- Education is another bum trip. — *Berkeley Barb*, 20th December 1968

bum tripper *noun*
a person experiencing a psychotic break while using a hallucinogenic drug *US, 1967*
- In the mornings there would be a sign on the clinic's door: BUM TRIPPERS AND EMERGENCIES ONLY. NO DOCTORS TILL 4 P.M. — Nicholas Von Hoffman, *We Are The People Our Parents Warned Us Against*, p. 12, 1967

bumwad *noun*
toilet paper, or any material used in place of toilet paper *US, 1896*
- I would climb onto a truck with seven much older boys (nine months older at least!), towing five canoes, hundreds of pounds of supplies and shovels and bumwad[.] — Marlo Thomas, *The Right Words at the Right Time*, p. 96, 2002

bum warmer *noun*
a car coat *US, 1961*
- Used to be a time when these jackets, affectionately known as "bum warmers," were for just that! Now they're just status symbols. — *San Francisco Progress*, p. 2, 18th August 1961

bun bandit *noun*
the active male in male-on-male anal sex *US, 1964*
- — Guy Strait, *The Lavender Lexicon*, 1964

bun-biter *noun*
a sycophant or toady *US, 1961*
School usage.
- — *Washington Post*, 23rd April 1961

bun boy *noun*
1 a male homosexual prostitute whose prominent feature is his buttocks *US, 1983*
- Though it was early in the day, the usual assortment of street hustlers, whores (they all seemed to be wearing straight skirts slit up the side), bun boys (tight jeans, tennis shoes and tropical shirts) and black pimps[.] — Gerald Petievich, *To Die in Beverly Hills*, p. 82, 1983

2 a sycophantic assistant *US, 1988*
- I don't want any of your bun-boys around when you and I talk business. — Gerald Petievich, *Shakedown*, p. 149, 1988

bun buddy *noun*
a homosexual *US, 2004*
- A few bun buddies said they'd "seen them around" and no more. — James Ellroy, *Destination Morgue*, p. 242, 2004

bunch punch *noun*
sex involving multiple males and a single female *US, 1975*
- — *American Speech*, p. 56, Spring–Summer 1975: "Razorback slang"

bunco *noun*
1 fraud; an act of fraud, especially a swindle by means of card-trickery; a confidence trick *US, 1914*
- The ingenuity of crooks and swindlers is being constantly exercised in the invention of new forms of bunco games or confidence games. — David Louisell, *Cases and Materials on Evidence*, p. 759, 1981

2 a squad of police assigned to confidence swindles *US, 1947*
- The graying captain of bunco was sitting behind his ornate desk in the well-appointed office, sipping coffee. — Iceberg Slim (Robert Beck), *Long White Con*, p. 68, 1977

bunco *verb*
to swindle someone, to cheat someone *US, 1875*

- "Don't give me that, man—I've been buncoed by experts!" means "Don't try to deceive me!" — David Powis, *The Signs of Crime*, 1977

bunco artist *noun*
a professional swindler *US, 1945*

- The journal kept up a steady barrage against Cox, making him well known among its readers as a bunco artist. — Dianna Davids Olien et al., *Easy Money*, p. 125, 199
- In simple terms, maskirovka combines concealment and misdirection in a way that would be familiar to bunco artists or stage magicians. — *Providence (Rhode Island) Journal-Bulletin*, p. 8F, 1st March 1998

bunco booter *noun*
an infrequent smoker *US, 1996*

- — John Fahs, *Cigarette Confidential*, p. 302, 1996

bundle *noun*
a large amount of money *US, 1903*
From an earlier sense (a roll of money).

- "One guy that owed Kattar a bundle, seventy-five grand, was a character named Willie." — Vincent Teresa, *My Life in the Mafia*, p. 131, 1973

bundle *verb*
to make someone incapable of action *US, 1976*

- — John R. Armore and Joseph D. Wolfe, *Dictionary of Desperation*, 1976

bun floss *noun*
a thong-backed bikini bottom *US, 1991*

- — Trevor Cralle, *The Surfin'ary*, p. 39, 1991

bung *noun*
the anus *UK, 1788*

- Or, maybe, having me lick her bung? — Joey V., *Portrait of Joey*, p. 118, 1969
- First, I'll want to tongue your bung while you juggle my balls in one hand and play with my asshole with the other. — Kevin Smith, *Jay and Silent Bob Strike Back*, p. 90, 2001

bunghole *noun*
1 the anus *UK, 1611*

- The way you were banging the bunghole, you damned near fell in — Jim Thompson, *Pop. 1280*, p. 192, 1964
- Just a lot of screwballs jumping bare-assed over swords and fire, kissing the master's bunghole. — Robert Campbell, *Sweet La-La Land*, p. 247, 1990
- Larry urged brutally, slapping Nora's butt-cheeks while he continued to ream her bunghole. — *Penthouse Uncensored II*, p. 646, 2001
- Butt Freak is a festival of ass and a video show that certainly knows its way around a woman's bunghole. — Editors of Adult Video News, *The AVN Guide to the 500 Greatest Adult Films of All Time*, p. 50, 2005

2 by extension, a despicable, unlikeable person *US, 1968*

- — Collin Baker et al., *College Undergraduate Slang Study Conducted at Brown University*, p. 91, 1968
- "And all of this bullshit is gonna go flying through the air, my friend, because this bunghole-hard-ass Hudson decided to grab a guy he doesn't like on a phony charge[.]" — George Higgins, *Kennedy for the Defense*, p. 197, 1980

bunghole *verb*
to sodomize someone *US, 1939*
From the noun **BUNGHOLE** (the anus).

- "Unless he was looking to get bungholed, or unless he had an appointment." — William Caunitz, *Black Sand*, p. 221, 1989

bunghole buddy *noun*
a close and trusted friend *US, 1960*

- Of course he hung out with the lieutenant all the time and he was supposed to be bunghole buddies with the piano man[.] — George Clayton Johnson, *Ocean's Eleven*, p. 46, 1960

bunhead *noun*
a dolt; an outcast *US, 1988*

- — Michael V. Anderson, *The Bad, Rad, Not to Forget Way Cool Beach and Surf Discriptionary*, p. 4, 1988

bun-huggers *noun*
tight-fitting pants *US, 1964*

- — J. R. Friss, *A Dictionary of Teenage Slang (Mt. Diablo High)*, 1964
- These goddamn Hollywood lawyers with the fag boots and bun-huggers, he thought to himself. — Michael Eberhardt, *Body of a Crime*, p. 104, 1994

bunk *noun*
1 nonsense *US, 1900*

- All that crap they have in cartoons in the Saturday Evening Post and all, showing guys on street corners looking sore as hell because their dates are late—that's bunk. — J.D. Salinger, *Catcher in the Rye*, pp. 124–125, 1951
- When Mr. Money arrived at the airport, the grifter had him paged, then introduced himself with a bunk story, such as being a friend of hotel manager, who had asked him to pick up the boob. — Jack Lait and Lee Mortimer, *Washington Confidential*, p. 277, 1951
- To Johnny, that was bunk from a punk. — Ed Sanders, *Tales of Beatnik Glory*, p. 77, 1975

2 a weak drug, especially heroin *US, 1992*

- — Jay Robert Nash, *Dictionary of Crime*, p. 50, 1992
- — Mark S. Fleisher, *Beggars & Thieves*, p. 287, 1995

3 a hiding place *US, 1950*

- I don't see how anybody could know they were there. That's a good bunk we have. — Hal Ellson, *Tomboy*, p. 24, 1950

4 a prisoner's cell or the area immediately around his bed in a dormitory setting *US, 1998*

- — Ethan Hilderbrant, *Prison Slang*, 1998

bunk *verb*
1 to sleep, to stay the night *US, 1840*
Introduces a military or Western feel.

- Or you can bunk out in the Rumpus Room. It doesn't matter to me. — Odie Hawkins, *Lost Angeles*, p. 203, 1994

2 to hide something *US, 1950*

- "I hope the cigarettes we bunked last night don't get wet," she said, avoiding his eyes. — Hal Ellson, *Tomboy*, p. 12, 1950

bunk *adjective*
worthless *US, 1990*

- Noontimes Rooski often hustled bunk hash there and Joe planned to do the same[.] — Seth Morgan, *Homeboy*, p. 59, 1990

bunk fatigue *noun*
sleep *US, 1915*

- Swimming at the beaches and bunk fatigue rounded out the day before evening chow and the usual night at the movie. — Orlando Davidson, *The Deadeyes*, p. 236, 1947

bunk flying *noun*
dramatic, on-the-ground discussions of flying exploits *US, 1933*

- That night in barracks during bunk-flying the five men of Leseur's squad talked over their instructor. — Frederic Litten, *Sinister Island Squadron*, p. 117, 2005

bunky; bunkie *noun*
in jail or prison, a cellmate *US, 1858*

- Worden rode the roommate hard, seizing on the fact that he was out working while his bunky was lazing around the house with some new man. — David Simon, *Homicide*, p. 342, 1991
- "My bunkie in County? Some cretin couldn't figure out how to open and close his Velcro jumpsuit." — Richard Price, *Samaritan*, p. 289, 2003

bunny *noun*
1 the vulva and vagina *US, 1969*

- Especially when I reached around and started playing with her big, beautiful tits and fingering her slick-furry bunny. — Joey V., *Portrait of Joey*, p. 92, 1969

2 a woman blessed with few if any sexual inhibitions *US, 1971*

- — Eugene Landy, *The Underground Dictionary*, p. 42, 1971

3 a female surfer or a male surfer's girlfriend *US, 1936*

- — Rob Burt, *Surf City, Drag City*, 1986

4 a homosexual male prostitute *US, 1967*

- — Dale Gordon, *The Dominion Sex Dictionary*, p. 35, 1967

5 the rectum *US, 1977*

- — *Maledicta*, p. 15, Summer 1977: "A word for it!"

6 in shuffleboard, the disk on a number representing the winning score *US, 1967*

- — Omero C. Catan, *Secrets of Shuffleboard Strategy*, p. 64, 1967

bunny book *noun*
a sexually explicit magazine *US, 1967*
From the *Playboy* bunny.

- — *Current Slang*, p. 7, Fall 1967

bunny boot *noun*

a large white felt boot, now usually made of rubber with an inflatable air layer for insulation *US, 1954*

- Bunny boots are the warmest footgear worn in the Northland except-ing the Eskimo mukluk. — Robert O. Bowen, *An Alaskan Dictionary*, p. 10, 1965

bunny dip *noun*

a method of serving bar customers drinks calculated to keep a woman's breasts from spilling out from a low-cut, tight bodice *US, 1985*

A technique perfected by and taught to Playboy Bunnies.

- "In a frosted glass with an umbrella," Vincent said, as the girl did the bunny dip to place the drink on the table without losing her breasts. — Elmore Leonard, *Glitz*, p. 112, 1985

bunny fuck *verb*

to have sex quickly, if not frantically *US, 1971*

- — Eugene Landy, *The Underground Dictionary*, p. 42, 1971

bunny hole *noun*

an excavation in a fox hole to provide protection from a mortar attack *US, 1957*

Korean war usage.

- These caves correspond roughly to our "bunny holes," which are only large enough for one man to huddle in during a mortar bar-rage. Bunny holes are usually dug so that a man can jump from his fighting-hold into the bunny hole[.] — Martin Russ, *The Last Parallel*, p. 115, 1957

bunny hop *noun*

the act of bouncing both wheels of a bicycle off the ground into the air *US, 1953*

- — William Nealy, *Mountain Bike!*, p. 160, 1992

bunny-hugger *noun*

an environmental activist *US, 1994*

- And in the next few years, grass-roots activists will need to pay seri-ous attention to what look like bunny-hugger issues but aren't. — Andrews Szasz, *Ecopopulism*, p. 77, 1994
- Stoat's buddies once called her a bunny hugger because she wasn't a fan of blood sports. — Carl Hiaasen, *Sick Puppy*, p. 5, 1999

buns *noun*

the buttocks *US, 1877*

- Her skirt was a short one, almost reaching the bottom of her buns which tended to hang down into her net stockings. — *Evergreen*, p. 19, 1968
- It was a drag with all the whiteys looking at a brother getting his buns kicked. — Babs Gonzales, *Movin' On Down De Line*, p. 74, 1975
- Cher, I don't wanna do this any more, and my buns, they don't feel nothin' like steel. — *Clueless*, 1995

bunt *noun*

the buttocks *US, 1967*

A blend of "buttocks" and "cunt."

- — Dale Gordon, *The Dominion Sex Dictionary*, p. 35, 1967

bunter *noun*

a prostitute *US, 1973*

- — Ruth Todasco et al., *The Intelligent Woman's Guide to Dirty Words*, p. 2, 1973

buoy *noun*

a surfer who lingers in the water, rarely catching a wave *US, 1991*

- — Trevor Cralle, *The Surfin'ary*, p. 16, 1991

bupkes; bupkis *noun*

nothing—used for expressing scorn at something deemed foolish or trivial *US, 1942*

From the Russian for "beans."

- I worked on it three hours—and what did he give me? Bubkes! — Leo Rosten, *The Joys of Yiddish*, p. 55, 1968
- Three go-rounds—zero, zilch, buppkis. — James Ellroy, *White Jazz*, p. 53, 1992
- While two volunteers said it "does make your lips appear fuller," the other two noticed "nothing, bupkis, zilch." — *Daily News (New York)*, p. 62, 15th April 2004

burble *noun*

in skysurfing, the rough air about the skysurfer *US, 1998*

- BURBLE The rough air just above a freefalling body. — Shelley Youngblut, *Way Inside ESPN's X Games*, p. 65, 1998

burble *verb*

in computing, to post an inflammatory message that displays the person's complete ignorance on the subject in question *US, 1991*

From Lewis Carroll's 1871 *Through the Looking Glass*, in which the Jabberwock "burbled" (spoke in a murmuring or rambling manner).

- — Eric S. Raymond, *The New Hacker's Dictionary*, p. 85, 1991
- — Christian Crumlish, *The Internet Dictionary*, p. 28, 1995

'burbs *noun*

the sub*urbs US, 1989*

- Everybody said we were moving to the 'burbs, and none of my friends wanted us to go where only white people stayed. — Terry Williams, *The Cocaine Kids*, p. 76, 1989

bureau-drawer special *noun*

a small, inexpensive handgun *US, 1962*

- — *American Speech*, p. 267, December 1962: "The language of traffic policemen"

burg *noun*

1 a city or town *US, 1835*

- I've got to get out of this burg. — Jim Thompson, *The Nothing Man*, p. 266, 1954
- "They're coming in from the burgs, man. Bit shooters and they're gathering around waiting for orders." — Mickey Spillane, *The Snake*, p. 37, 1964
- I want you hogs to let this burg know you're here. — Lewis John Carlino, *The Great Santini*, 1979
- That freak who tried to kill me had to have been sent by the Pimp Blimp—who, if he can get at me in the jailhouse, can reach me in this burg. — Seth Morgan, *Homeboy*, p. 115, 1990

2 a burglary *US, 1983*

- Sometimes he just sets up burg's. He doesn't do them himself, but farms out the address and steers the stolen property to his own fencing channels. — Gerald Petievich, *To Die in Beverly Hills*, p. 113, 1983
- "I'm here at camp 'cause they think I did a burg'—a robbery." — Leon Bing, *Do or Die*, p. 63, 1991

burger *noun*

1 a hamburger *US, 1924*

- President Bush got pretty cheeky with little Olivia Eoff during a visit to Cotham's Restaurant in Scott, Ark, yesterday. Cotham's is known for its 1-pound "Hubcap" burger. — *Daily News (New York)*, p. 24, 31st August 2006

2 a shapeless, uneven wave *US, 1991*

An abbreviation of **MUSHBURGER**.

- — Trevor Cralle, *The Surfin'ary*, p. 16, 1991

3 a scrape or raw bruise suffered while skateboarding *US, 1976*

- — Laura Torbet, *The Complete Book of Skateboarding*, p. 105, 1976

burger jockey *noun*

an employee in a hamburger restaurant *US, 1992*

- So you're a burger jockey. I hope your Mickey D's down in Edmonton is better than ours up here. — *k12.chat.senior*, 12th January 1992
- I must confess I felt a little nervous gazing at the minimum-wage burger jockeys as I munched my fries. — C.D. Payne, *Cut to the Twisp*, p. 13, 2001

burgher *noun*

a townsperson *US, 1957*

- This town hasn't been occupied since the Revolutionary War, and I'd just as soon not make the burghers any shakier than I have to. — Max Shulman, *Rally Round the Flag, Boys!*, p. 197, 1957

burglar *noun*

the operator of a dishonest carnival game *US, 1950*

- — *American Speech*, p. 235, October 1950: "The argot of outdoor boob traps"

buried treasure *noun*

in computing, an unexpected and usually poorly written piece of code found in a program *US, 1991*

- — Eric S. Raymond, *The New Hacker's Dictionary*, p. 85, 1991

burley; burly *noun*

burlesque *US, 1934*

- "Simon, he was always a top banana in burly, but he couldn't hold anybody alone." — Stephen Longstreet, *The Flesh Peddlers*, p. 213, 1962

burleycue; burly-Q noun
burlesque *US, 1923*

- There was also burly burleycue queen Carrie Finnell, who could make the tassels on her breasts swing in multiple directions. — Samuel L. Letter, *The Encyclopedia of the New York Stage, 1940–1950*, p. 589, 1992
- On Ruby's last day as a free citizen that November morning in '63, he was a paunchy, balding, 52-year-old burly-Q operator. — Josh Friedman, *When Sex Was Dirty*, p. 112, 2005

burly adjective
1 intimidating *US, 1993*
A surfer term used to describe a wave, brought into broader youth usage.
- — Judi Sanders, *Faced and Faded, Hanging to Hurl*, p. 6, 1993
- — Connie Eble (Editor), *UNC-CH Campus Slang*, p. 2, Spring 2003

2 very cold *US, 1991*
- — Trevor Cralle, *The Surfin'ary*, p. 16, 1991

burly show noun
in carnival usage, a burlesque show *US, 1981*
- — Don Wilmeth, *The Language of American Popular Entertainment*, p. 38, 1981

burn noun
1 a chemically straightened hairdo *US, 1957*
- "Where did you get a burn like that?" — Herbert Simmons, *Corner Boy*, p. 166, 1957

2 a swindle *US, 1960*
- Outside he got in a cab with the Puerto Rican's money and told the driver to take off. The perfect burn, he thought, humming to himself. — Clarence Cooper Jr., *The Scene*, p. 105, 1960
- There are many stories about marijuana being cut with bay leaves, oregano, etc. and about an increase in the number of "burns" (in which someone who claims he can obtain drugs takes money in advance and never returns.) — Ned Polsky, *Hustlers, Beats, and Others*, p. 171, 1967
- MR. ORANGE: Look, Eddie, he was pullin' a burn. He was gonna kill the cop and me. And when you guys walked through the door, he was gonna blow you to hell and make off with the diamonds. — *Reservoir Dogs*, 1992
- If I was really pullin' a burn, I'd have take two out, wouldn't I? — *Jackie Brown*, 1997

3 the initial flooding of sensations after injecting heroin *US, 1973*
- — David Maurer and Victor Vogel, *Narcotics and Narcotic Addiction*, p. 393, 1973

burn verb
1 to masturbate *US, 1975*
- BURN. *** To masturbate while looking at a provocative picture of a woman. — Miguel Pinero, *Short Eyes*, p. 123, 1975

2 to put someone to death by electrocution *US, 1927*
- "Listen, rat"—Benny's face paled—"one more word like that and I'll plug you too. They can only burn me once, and I'd just as soon knock you off to stay alive as not." — Irving Shulman, *The Amboy Dukes*, p. 85, 1947
- And if I burn for it, here or anywhere, at least I won't burn like a slave. — Thurston Scott, *Cure it with Honey*, p. 37, 1951
- We ain't going to let her die, get me? Not this way. I'm going to see that she burns. — Jim Thompson, *The Killer Inside*, p. 54, 1952
- He said, "Forgive this man, he knows not what he did." / I said, "Can that kill, Father, don't let them burn the kid." — Dennis Wepman et al., *The Life*, p. 120, 1976

3 to kill someone *US, 1933*
- Do you really want to burn this cat, man? — Claude Brown, *Manchild in the Promised Land*, p. 176, 1965
- The guy who burned the gook gunner was saved by a misfire. — Ernest Spencer, *Welcome to Vietnam, Macho Man*, p. 141, 1987

4 to shoot a gun at someone *US, 1953*
- — Dale Kramer and Madeline Karr, *Teen-Age Gangs*, p. 174, 1953
- Then the Wolves start burnin'. One of them got a piece. He fire 2 times[.] — Warren Miller, *The Cool World*, p. 231, 1959

5 to cheat, swindle someone *UK, 1698*
- I drank all day in a wild poolhall-bar-restaurant-saloon two-part joint, also got burned for a fin (Mexican, 5 pesos, 60 cents) by a connection. — Jack Kerouac, *Letter to Neal and Carolyn Cassady*, p. 359, 10th May 1952

- He even cut me into the good drygoods thieves, so that I would never get burned by fences. — Claude Brown, *Manchild in the Promised Land*, p. 167, 1965
- Hawaiian Chuck was handing out hepatitis-infected points to friends who'd burned him. — Nicholas Von Hoffman, *We Are The People Our Parents Warned Us Against*, p. 83, 1967
- He probably got burned trying to make a drug buy and did have to run for his life. — Joseph Wambaugh, *Finnegan's Week*, p. 301, 1993

6 to expose the identity of a person or place *US, 1959*
- He didn't want any dopefiends burning up his house, even though he paid off the vice squad monthly to allow him to operate. — Donald Goines, *Dopefiend*, p. 37, 1971
- PARK SWEEP "BURNS" L.A. GAYS — *The Advocate*, 24th October 1973
- "They'd burn me the minute I came inna door." — George Higgins, *Cogan's Trade*, p. 38, 1974
- He said I burned one of his sources. — Carl Hiaasen, *Tourist Season*, p. 201, 1986

7 in private dice games, to stop the dice while rolling, either as a superstition or to check for cheating *US, 1950*
- — *The Annals of the American Academy of Political and Social Sciences*, p. 122, May 1950

8 while playing blackjack, to place an unplayed card into the discard card holder *US, 1982*
- — Thomas F. Hughes, *Dealing Casino Blackjack*, p. 71, 1982

9 to smoke marijuana *US, 1964*
- Hey, man, Pickford's got a dube we're about to burn. — *Dazed and Confused*, 1993
- I hate standing around when everyone's burning and I ain't got none[.] — Two Fingers, *Puff (Disco Biscuits)*, p. 220, 1996

10 to infect someone with a sexually transmitted disease *US, 1967*
- — Dale Gordon, *The Dominion Sex Dictionary*, p. 35, 1967
- — Don R. McCreary (Editor), *Dawg Speak*, 2001

▸ **burn paint**
(used of a car or truck) to be engulfed in flames *US, 1977*
- — Bill Davis, *Jawjacking*, p. 24, 1977

▸ **burn the lot**
(used of a carnival) to cheat a town so badly that no carnival will be able to come to that town for some time *US, 1989*
- — Lindsay E. Smith and Bruce A. Walstad, *Sting Shift*, p. 115, 1989

▸ **burn the road up**
to leave *US, 2002*
- — Gary K. Farlow, *Prison-ese*, p. 9, 2002

▸ **burn up the wires**
to spend a great deal of time on the telephone *US, 1954*
Originally a term applying to the telegraph. As telephones become increasingly independent of wires, it will be interesting to see if the phrase survives.
- Meanwhile, the White House was burning up the wires to Wall Street. — Eliot Janeway, *The Economics of Crisis*, p. 268, 1968

▸ **enough money to burn a wet mule**
a great deal of money *US, 1895*
Slang synonyms for "money" are found in variants of the phrase.
- I also got enough bread to burn a wet mule. — Babs Gonzales, *Movin' On Down De Line*, p. 27, 1975
- As Mr. Barbour is fond of saying in such circumstances, the GOP had "enough cash to burn a wet mule." — *Washington Times*, 16th January 1997
- "We got enough money to burn a wet mule," Big Bill said. — Bill Fitzhugh, *Fender Benders*, p. 267, 2003

burn artist noun
a cheat, a conman, especially in dealings with drugs *US, 1968*
- Speed freaks have as bad a reputation as junkies for being thieves, burn artists, liars and generally unreliable and untrustworthy. — *Washington Free Press*, 29th February 1968
- "That guy's a burn artist." — Brian Boyer, *Prince of Thieves*, p. 65, 1975
- One of the burn artist's tricks is to take your money, tell you to wait and split with your dough. There are various side show gimmicks each burn artist works. — Abbie Hoffman, *Steal This Books*, p. 96, 1995

• The Barksdale gang murders people for a variety of reasons: to instill fear and respect among prospective rivals, to send a message to residents of the projects to mind their own business and keep their mouths shut, to punish thieves and burn artists. — *Tri-Valley Herald (Pleasanton, California)*, 17th August 2002

burn bag noun

a bag of adulterated or diluted drugs *US, 1991*

• "He was selling burn bags, you know. He was selling people shit." — David Simon, *Homicide*, p. 283, 1991

• He's out there on an alien corner, a dark-skinned lampost amid the Pennsie whores and the johns and the other dealers, holding a handful of B-and-Q burn bags[.]. — David Simon and Edward Burns, *The Corner*, p. 500, 1997

burn cards noun

in blackjack played in casinos, a few cards taken from the top of a newly shuffled pack and discarded *US, 1980*

• — Lee Solkey, *Dummy Up and Deal*, p. 108, 1980

burn down verb

to overuse and thus ruin something *US, 1953*

• I've about burned down all the pawnshops in New York. — William Burroughs, *Junkie*, p. 60, 1953

• Three junkies say that there have been a sharply increased number of sick junkies unable to support their habits at former levels, trying to taper off on such things as Cocinil, and hitting so often that some stores have been totally "burned down," i.e., refuse to supply even non-prescription items to known junkies. — Ned Polsky, *Hustlers, Beats, and Others*, p. 168, 1967

burned out; burnt out adjective

exhausted beyond mental or physical capacity *US, 1980*

• I had no emotions on court. I felt burned out and didn't want to play. — *UPI*, 15th December 1980

• "I was kind of burned out playing," Colbert said. — *The Columbian (Vancouver, Washington)*, p. B1, 16th April 2004

burned up adjective

1 infected with a sexually transmitted infection *US, 1971*

• "She is burned up" (has venereal disease). — Charles Winick, *The Lively Commerce*, p. 43, 1971

2 angry *US, 1934*

• At first she was shocked, the kid said, then she was burned up. — Joey V., *Portrait of Joey*, p. 127, 1969

burner noun

1 a knife *US, 2002*

• — Jeffrey Ian Ross, *Behind Bars*, p. 182, 2002: Slammer Slang

2 a criminal who specializes in breaking into safes using an acetylene torch *US, 1950*

• — Hyman E. Goldin et al., *Dictionary of American Underworld Lingo*, p. 37, 1950

• We were going to need burners for the big stuff, but there wasn't a torch man in the mob. — Charles Hamilton, *Men of the Underworld*, p. 140, 1952

3 a handgun *US, 1926*

• "What, your ass don't need a burner?" — Paul Beatty, *Tuff*, p. 4, 2000

• I made sure that I had a burner tucked in my sweatpants and Boomer was ready by my side. — Earl "DMX" Simmons, *E.A.R.L.*, p. 181, 2002

• Gray got caught up in a beef with a group of about 10 Hispanic men, one of whom was boasting about having a burner—street slang for a handgun—and trying to bait him with taunts of "You want it? You want it?" — *Boston Herald*, p. 14, 23rd June 2002

4 a very fast runner *US*

• — Bill Shefski, *Running Press Glossary of Football Language*, p. 21, 1978

• Can you imagine what it's gonna be like to have them two burners in my backfield? — Dan Jenkins, *Life Its Ownself*, p. 164, 1984

5 an extraordinary person *US, 1952*

• "He's a burner, ain't he?" he said. — Chester Himes, *Cast the First Stone*, p. 76, 1952

6 a marijuana smoker *US, 1985*

• Only burners like you get high. — *The Breakfast Club*, 1985

• Jay and Silent Bob watch as Dante passes. A small group of burners are poised around the store door. — Kevin Smith, *Clerks*, p. 125, 1994

• — Pamela Munro, *U.C.L.A. Slang*, p. 47, 1997

7 a complete piece of graffiti art *US, 1982*

• A "burner" in an autograph book reflects well on both the artist and the owner of the book. — Craig Castleman, *Getting Up*, p. 21, 1982

burnie noun

a partially smoked marijuana cigarette *US, 1952*

• — *American Speech*, p. 24, February 1952: "Teen-age hophead jargon"

• BURNIE, drug connotation, partially smoked marijuana cigarette. — *Chicago Tribune*, p. C3, 27th December 1998

burnout noun

1 a person whose mental capacity has been diminished by extended drug or alcohol use *US, 1973*

• Sure he's treated thousands of burn-outs. — Ken Kesey, *The Further Inquiry*, p. 119, 1990

2 an uninhabitable, ruined tenement, whether it has been burnt or not *US, 1987*

• — Carsten Stroud, *Close Pursuit*, p. 270, 1987

burn out verb

to make a fire in a prisoner's cell as retaliation for real or perceived cooperation with prison authorities *US, 1974*

• — Paul Glover, *Words from the House of the Dead*, 1974

burn rubber!

leave me alone! *US, 1996*

• — Reinhold Aman, *Hillary Clinton's Pen Pal*, p. 23, 1996

burnt adjective

exhausted *US, 1995*

• "I'm feeling kind of burnt," Dirk said. "You can just drop me off." — Francesca Lia Block, *Baby Be-Bop*, p. 403, 1995

burnt money noun

a bet in a dice game lost because of a rule violation *US, 1997*

• — *American Speech*, p. 398, Winter 1997: "Among the new words"

burp gun noun

a submachine gun *US, 1946*

• In general character, this one developed like the second: the same whistles and roll calling to start with, then heavy and inaccurate fire, involving several machine guns and burp guns which sprayed the hedgerow and the fields beyond. — United States War Department, *Small Unit Actions*, p. 57, 1946

• Next—and it was in this order—we heard the BRRRP! sound of one Chinese pp-S or "burp gun" as it is called. — Martin Russ, *The Last Parallel*, p. 107, 1957

burr noun

the recurring operating expenses in a circus or carnival *US, 1980*

• — Joe McKennon, *Circus Lingo*, p. 22, 1980

burrhead noun

a black person *US, 1902*

• — Helen Dahlskog (Editor), *A Dictionary of Contemporary and Colloquial Usage*, p. 11, 1972

• — *Maledicta*, p. 153, Summer/Winter 1978: "How to hate thy neighbor: a guide to racist maledicta"

• [J. Edgar] Hoover was apparently convinced that the content of these tapes would "destroy the burrhead [King]." — Ward Churchill and Jim Vander Wall, *Agents of Repression*, p. 55, 1988

• "You shut your mouth, burrhead!" — Jess Mowry, *Six Out Seven*, p. 30, 1993

burrito adjective

cold *US, 1997*

From "brrrr" as a vocalization of feeling cold.

• — Pamela Munro, *U.C.L.A. Slang*, p. 47, 1997

burrito bag noun

a mesh restraint used by police to contain a violent person *US, 1997*

• — Samuel M. Katz, *Anytime Anywhere*, p. 389, 1997

burro noun

a racehorse that does not perform well *US, 1947*

• — *San Francisco Call-Bulletin*, p. 16, 2nd April 1947

burr up your ass noun

a person with a displeased focus on something *US, 1960*

• I showed up at the rink with a burr up my ass. [Quoting Billy Smith] — *Boston Globe*, p. D1, 3rd November 2003

burst noun

a period of reenlistment in the military *US, 1968*

A "burst of six" would thus be reenlistment for six years.
- — Carl Fleischhauer, *A Glossary of Army Slang*, p. 7, 1968

bury *verb*

1 to sentence a criminal to a long or life term in prison *US, 1904*
- — William K. Bentley and James M. Corbett, *Prison Slang*, p. 18, 1992

2 in casino gambling, to place a card in the middle of a deck or in the discard pile *US, 1991*
- — Michael Dalton, *Blackjack*, p. 34, 1991

▸ **bury the stiffy**
from a male perspective, to have sex *US, 1994*
- — Michael Dalton Johnson, *Talking Trash with Redd Foxx*, p. 53, 1994

bury-the-brisket *noun*

sex (from a male perspective) *US, 1995*
- Mr. Hoover knew full well that President Kennedy was not playing bury-the-brisket with Marilyn Monroe[.] — James Ellroy, *American Tabloid*, p. 327, 1995

bus *noun*

▸ **on the bus**
part of a countercultural movement *US, 1994*
From the language of Ken Kesey, Neal Cassady, and the Merry Pranksters.
- — David Shenk and Steve Silberman, *Skeleton Key*, p. 210, 1994

bus *verb*

to shoot a gun at someone *US, 1995*
- — Bill Valentine, *Gang Intelligence Manual*, p. 75, 1995

▸ **bus one**
to leave *US, 1993*
- — *Washington Post*, 14th October 1993

bus and truck *adjective*

said of a traveling show, with the cast and crew traveling by bus, with the props and wardrobe in a truck *US, 1973*
- — Sherman Louis Sergel, *The Language of Show Biz*, p. 34, 1973
- "[T]hey forced them to tour in a bus-and-truck Porty and Bess." — Ethan Morden, *How's Your Romance?*, p. 73, 2005

bus driver *noun*

1 in poker, the player in a given hand who controls the betting *US, 1996*
- — John Vorhaus, *The Big Book of Poker Slang*, p. 9, 1996

2 a pilot, especially the pilot of a military transport aircraft *US, 1944*
- Finding pilots wasn't difficult, as all the USAF "bus drivers"—transport pilots—had to qualify regularly in CARP. — Richard Marcinko and John Weisman, *Rogue Warrior*, p. 47, 1992

bush *noun*

1 pubic hair, especially a woman's pubic hair *UK, 1650*
A source for endless punning during the US presidential election of 2000; President Bush Jr.'s lack of *gravitas* opened him up to "bush" puns to an extent that his father did not have to endure.
- The liberated chick up front appears not to be wearing any underwear and the print reveals what might be construed by some as a hairy bush. — *Screw*, p. 8, 4th April 1969
- And then Jayne Kennedy says, "First things first, nigger, I ain't suckin' shit till you bring your ass over here an' lick my bush!" — *True Romance*, 1993
- Dude—she had seventies bush. — Kevin Smith, *Jay and Silent Bob Strike Back*, p. 30, 2001
- Know what the biggest change is for me? Broads shavin' their bushes. I went over to Silvio's, it's like the Girl Scouts in there. — *The Sopranos (Episode 53)*, 2004

2 a sexually active female *US, 1966*
- — Andy Anonymous, *A Basic Guide to Campusology*, p. 5, 1966

3 a bushy hairstyle, especially on a black person *US, 1972*
- — David Claerbaut, *Black Jargon in White America*, p. 59, 1972

4 marijuana *US, 1946*
- As soon as we got some of that Mexican bush we almost blew our tops. — Mezz Mezzrow, *Really the Blues*, p. 215, 1946
- Byron smoked too much potiguaya bush for a lunger. "I was born to smoke bush," he boasted. — Nelson Algren, *A Walk on the Wild Side*, p. 14, 1956

5 the woods *US, 1997*
- "What are yez doin' tonight?" "We're gettin' some kortz and goin' upda bush." — Amy and Denise McFadden, *CoalSpeak*, pp. 2–3, 1997

▸ **make bush**
to escape from prison *US, 1966*
- — Rose Giallombardo, *Society of Women*, p. 210, 1966: Glossary of Prison Terms

bush *verb*

1 to ambush someone *US, 1947*
- You 'bush in this area near that ol' Buddhist temple we passed on the hump in. — *Platoon*, 1986

2 to deceive someone *US, 1971*
- "Don't bush me," the man said. "Don't hand me that crap[.]" — George V. Higgins, *The Friends of Eddie Doyle*, p. 198, 1971

bush *adjective*

second-rate, amateurish *US, 1959*
- Taylor said, "They were bad mouthing our ball players when we were on the way into the locker room. It's bush." — *San Francisco Examiner*, p. 50, 26th January 1972
- I'll tell you something, wise-ass, you think you're so fucking clever. You're bush. Homicide lieutenant, all that goes with it, you're still bush. — Elmore Leonard, *Split Images*, p. 65, 1981
- You're showing up my pitcher, bush—get your ass in gear. — *Bull Durham*, 1988

bush Baptist *noun*

a religious zealot lacking formal theological training *US, 1967*
- "I'm only a bush Baptist." — Dean Acheson, *Present at the Creation*, p. 338, 1969

bushboy *noun*

in the context of youth gangs, a coward *US, 1962*
- Bushboys (or punks). — Howard Polsky, *Cottage Six*, p. 74, 1962

bush dinner *noun*

oral sex on a woman *US, 1967*
- — Dale Gordon, *The Dominion Sex Dictionary*, p. 35, 1967

bus head *noun*

hair that is in complete disarray after a long bus ride *US, 1988*
- — *Washington Post Sunday Magazine*, p. 7, 3rd January 1988

bushed *adjective*

very tired *US, 1879*
- He said, "Cecil, I'm bushed. Goodnight." — Iceberg Slim (Robert Beck), *Long White Con*, p. 53, 1977
- You look bushed. What time did you get to bed? — *Clerks*, 1994

bushel-cunted *adjective*

possessing a slack and distended vagina *US, 1980*
- — *Maledicta*, p. 184, Winter 1980: "A new erotic vocabulary"

bushes *noun*

any place where sexual activity takes place, whether or not an actual bush is involved *US, 1975*
- To take a girl into the bushes means what it means, but the sense has been generalized. It may be the bushes but it doesn't have to be. — John Gould, *Maine Lingo*, p. 29, 1975

bush-league *adjective*

petty, mediocre, trivial, inconsequential, second-rate *US, 1908*
- But I now sense that it might be attained without long years of bush-league apprenticeship. — Horace McCoy, *Kiss Tomorrow Good-bye*, p. 90, 1948
- "Ton D'Andrea was a bush league bum!" — Donald Wilson, *My Six Convicts*, p. 221, 1951
- I had lost my taste even for bush league vindictiveness. — Clancy Sigal, *Going Away*, p. 5, 1961
- They were bush-league hoods known only to California cops and a few thousand cycle buffs. — Hunter S. Thompson, *Hell's Angels*, p. 37, 1966

bush light *noun*

in the pornography industry, a light used to illuminate the genitals of the performers *US, 1995*
- — *Adult Video News*, p. 50, October 1995

bush mag *noun*

a magazine featuring photographs of naked women, focusing on their pubic hair and vulvas *US, 1972*

- The "tit magazines" of the Fifties and Sixties, which were fit only for the garbage pail, have transformed themselves of late into "bush mags." — *Screw*, p. 4, 3rd July 1972

bush parole *noun*
escape from prison *US, 1957*
- [T]he Wisconsin authorities allowed him to return here to serve out a Florida bit that was interrupted when he took bush parole from a road camp at Pompano. — James Blake, *The Joint*, pp. 175–176, 1st October 1957
- — Inez Cardozo-Freeman, *The Joint*, p. 486, 1984

bush patrol *noun*
sex with a woman *US, 1964*
The **BUSH** in question here is the woman's pubic hair.
- — Roger Blake, *The American Dictionary of Sexual Terms*, p. 26, 1964
- — Kenn "Naz" Young, *Naz's Dictionary of Teen Slang*, p. 17, 1993

bush time *noun*
during the Vietnam war, the amount of time spent in combat *US, 1987*
- We didn't go to Nui Dat after our bush time because the Pioneer Platoon had to go bush and we were called to defend Brigid. — Peter Winter, *The Year I Said Goodbye*, p. 242, 2003

bushwhacker *noun*
1 a rapist *US, 1976*
Playing on the sexual meaning of **BUSH**.
- — John R. Armore and Joseph D. Wolfe, *Dictionary of Desperation*, p. 22, 1976

2 a man who enjoys sex in park bushes *US, 1966*
- We don't tolerate any of those toilet quickies or a job with a bushwhacker. — Johnny Shearer, *The Male Hustler*, p. 20, 1966

bush whiskey *noun*
strong, homemade whiskey *US, 1999*
- — *Star Tribune (Minneapolis)*, p. 19F, 31st January 1999

business *noun*
1 a syringe employed by intravenous drug users *US, 1949*
- Vincent J. Monteleone, *Criminal Slang*, p. 39, 1949
- — *American Speech*, p. 24, February 1952: "Teen-age hophead jargon"

2 the actual cheating move of a card cheat *US, 1973*
- — Thomas L. Clark, *The Dictionary of Gambling and Gaming*, p. 32, 1987

▸ **do business**
1 to engage in an illegal activity such as bribery *US, 1984*
- Coach, you don't think there's even a remote chance an official would do some business. — Dan Jenkins, *Life Its Ownself*, p. 194, 1984

2 in pool, to intentionally lose a game or other competition *US, 1989*
- Mike Shamos, *The Illustrated Encyclopedia of Billiards*, p. 38, 1993

3 in horse racing, to cooperate in the fixing of a race *US, 1951*
- David W. Maurer, *Argot of the Racetrack*, p. 24, 1951

▸ **give someone the business; do the business**
to have sex *US, 1942*
- Shimmy's buddy is in the back room giving my date the business. — Irving Shulman, *The Amboy Dukes*, p. 204, 1947

▸ **take care of business**
to have sex *US, 1966*
- Rose Giallombardo, *Society of Women*, p. 205, 1966: Glossary of Prison Terms

▸ **the business**
an argument, a confrontation, a hard time *US, 1957*
- Don't start up with me, don't give me the business. — Nat Hiken, *Sergeant Bilko*, p. 92, 1957

businessman *noun*
1 any official or witness who will accept a bribe *US, 1950*
- Hyman E. Goldin et al., *Dictionary of American Underworld Lingo*, p. 37, 1950

2 in horse racing, a jockey who may be persuaded to lose a race intentionally *US, 1951*
- David W. Maurer, *Argot of the Racetrack*, p. 17, 1951

businessman's special; businessman's lunch *noun*
DMT (dimethyltryptamine), a powerful but short-lasting hallucinogen *US, 1967*
An allusion to the fact that it can be taken, experienced, and recovered from in short order.
- — John Williams, *The Drug Scene*, p. 111, 1967

- They call this the Businessman's lunch. This is a twenty minute, half-hour psychedelic trip. — Stephen Gaskin, *Amazing Dope Tales*, p. 174, 1980

bussie *noun*
a bus driver *US, 1967*
Common among professional baseball players in the days when bus travel dominated travel between cities.
- Someone asked the bus driver, "How many miles on this baby?" "Don't know," the bussie said. "Thing's broken." — *Washington Post*, p. D1, 26th February 1983
- — Paul Dickson, *The New Dickson Baseball Dictionary*, p. 94, 1999

bust *noun*
1 an arrest *US, 1953*
- I didn't burn you, Joe, honest … I told you it was a bust, honest. — Alexander Trocchi, *Cain's Book*, p. 150, 1960
- Since a bust does not seem imminent, I climb out the window and go to crew at four. — James Simon Kunen, *The Strawberry Statement*, p. 35, 1968

2 to reduce someone in rank or standing *US, 1878*
- Word's going around that in addition to losing Ganz for the second time, and in addition to Haden busting you back to Patrolman, some jig beat the crap out of you. — *48 Hours*, 1982

3 a complete failure *US, 1842*
- Don't spend much time here himself. He's a bust. — Marvin Wald and Albert Maltz, *The Naked City*, 1947
- Them PRs are the reason my old man's gone bust. — Stephen Sondheim, *West Side Story*, 1957

4 in poker, a worthless hand *US, 1963*
- — Irwin Steig, *Common Sense in Poker*, p. 182, 1963
- — George Percy, *The Language of Poker*, p. 15, 1988

bust *verb*
1 to arrest someone *US, 1940*
- "That's because the local pushers probably got busted," Hassan cautioned. — Ross Russell, *The Sound*, p. 86, 1961
- She told the group how she had been busted. — James Mills, *The Panic in Needle Park*, p. 33, 1966
- How I came to be busted at Heathrow I don't know. — Doug Lang, *Freaks*, p. 15, 1973
- A midnight call from a friend: "I've been busted!—the guy propositioned me! Please get me out!" — John Rechy, *The Sexual Outlaw*, pp. 98–99, 1977

2 to catch someone with evidence of guilt; to report on someone *US, 1960*
- Oh, that's just great. Are you busted? — *Ferris Bueller's Day Off*, 1986
- I was sorry for busting you on that. — *As Good As It Gets*, 1997

3 to insult someone *US, 1985*
- — *National Education Association Today*, April 1985: "A glossary for rents and other squids"

4 to give someone something, to lend someone something *US, 1990*
- Tre, bust me a ride to the store. — *Boyz N The Hood*, 1990

5 in pontoon (blackjack, vingt-et-un), to exceed 21 points *UK, 1939*
- — Jerry L. Patterson, *Blackjack*, p. 20, 1978

6 in pool, to break to start a game *US, 1990*
- — Steve Rushin, *Pool Cool*, p. 6, 1990

▸ **bust a box**
to break into a safe *US, 1966*
- Can you bust a box, if you have to? — Robert Edmond Alter, *Carny Kill*, p. 102, 1966
- I was supposed to be the best box-man in the country and as I look back, I must have busted four hundred boxes and lifted more than a million. — Red Rudensky, *The Gonif*, p. 6, 1970

▸ **bust a cap**
1 to shoot a gun *US, 1965*
- The sister ran out and said, "Call the law!" / And I bust two caps right dead in her jaw. — Bruce Jackson, *Get Your Ass in the Water and Swim Like Me*, p. 49, 1965
- You better shut up fool! 'N haul ass 'less you want t'get a cap busted in it! — Odie Hawkins, *Ghetto Sketches*, p. 12, 1972
- Awww shit! Niggas is bustin' caps fuck that[.] — DAS-EFX *Hard Like a Criminal*, 1992

- Can't go to a movie the first week it opens. Why? Because niggers are shooting at the screen. "This movie is so good I gotta bust a cap in here." — Chris Rock, *Rock This!*, p. 20, 1997

2 to use drugs *US*, *1971*
- — Eugene Landy, *The Underground Dictionary*, p. 43, 1971

▶ **bust a few**
to surf *US*, *1997*
- — Vann Wesson, *Generation X Field Guide and Lexicon*, p. 32, 1997

▶ **bust a grape**
in prison, to commit a foolish act as a result of a sense of intense desperation *US*, *1990*
- — Charles Shafer, *Folk Speech in Texas Prisons*, p. 199, 1990

▶ **bust a move**
to make a move; to take action; to dance *US*, *1984*
- — Don R. McCreary (Editor), *Dawg Speak*, 2001

▶ **bust a stop sign**
to ignore a stop sign *US*, *1973*
- Let's see, did I ever tell you about the big dude I stopped for busting a stop sign out front of your place? — Joseph Wambaugh, *The Blue Knight*, p. 156, 1973

▶ **bust balls**
to tease someone relentlessly, provoking their anger *US*, *1955*
- Busting his balls? If I was busting your balls, I'd send you home for your shine box. — *Goodfellas*, 1990
- The Sheriff's lookin' to bust your balls. — *Casino*, 1995

▶ **bust jungle**
to break through a jungle with a tank or armored carrier *US*, *1977*
Vietnam war usage.
- We mounted up and moved off, and while we busted jungle I kept looking back at Stepik[.] — Larry Heinemann, *Close Quarters*, p. 68, 1977
- They called it "busting jungle" where armored vehicles literally made a road through the forest by knocking trees down. — Tom Clancy with Fred Franks Jr., *Into the Storm*, 1991

▶ **bust laugh**
to laugh out loud *US*, *1982*
Hawaiian youth usage.
- — Douglas Simonson, *Pidgin to da Max Hana Hou*, 1982

▶ **bust someone's drawers**
to have sex, seen as a conquest *US*, *1990*
- Yeah, I've bust them draws once. But I just met her. I need time to get to know her. — *New Jack City*, 1990

▶ **bust your buns**
to exert yourself; to try hard *US*, *1964*
- Don't be afraid to try the newest sport around / (Bust your buns, bust your buns now). — Jan Berry and Dean Torrance, *Sidewalk Surfin'*, 1964

▶ **bust your nut**
to experience an orgasm *US*, *1964*
- They say, "Make me hot when a sucker get up on top a me and don't make me bust my nut." — Bruce Jackson, *Get Your Ass in the Water and Swim Like Me*, p. 103, 1964
- After she had bust her nuts three or four times she wanted me to pop it to her in the ass. — A.S. Jackson, *Gentleman Pimp*, p. 109, 1973
- I became somewhat self-conscious and proceeded to move my butt around, with the head of my penis doubling her hairy lips back into her vagina. I wanted to bust my nuts now. — Bobby Seale, *A Lonely Rage*, p. 136, 1978
- Which is more important to you: a fortune in diamonds or busting a nut? — Kevin Smith, *Jay and Silent Bob Strike Back*, p. 94, 2001

bust *adjective*
without funds *US*, *1990*
- Can't play boys, I'm bust. — Steve Rushin, *Pool Cool*, p. 6, 1990

busta *noun*
a person who informs on another *US*, *2000*
- — James Haskins, *The Story of Hip-Hop*, p. 136, 2000

bust and run *noun*
a crude burglary *US*, *1976*

- It was just dumb to break ass on weekend jobs, bust-and-run jobs, when real planning, real scheming could lead to something big[.] — William Brashler, *City Dogs*, p. 73, 1976

bust developer *noun*
a singer who performs during a striptease act *US*, *1981*
- — Don Wilmeth, *The Language of American Popular Entertainment*, p. 40, 1981

busted, disgusted, and can't be trusted *adjective*
despondent *US*, *1994*
- He'd shake his head sadly and say, "Bro' Nate, I'm busted, disgusted, and can't be trusted." Cincinatti was so far away from home that he never got visits. — Nathan McCall, *Makes Me Wanna Holler*, p. 176, 1994

buster *noun*
1 pleasure, especially sexual pleasure *US*, *1973*
- It's not a thing you rush through, and it's important not to leave a girl hanging. She must reach her busters too. — A.S. Jackson, *Gentleman Pimp*, p. 164, 1973

2 used as a term of address *US*, *1866*
Lends a self-conscious, old-fashioned tone.
- "You're grounded, buster!" she screamed. — C.D. Payne, *Youth in Revolt*, p. 130, 1993

3 a social outcast, a coward *US*, *1991*
- [H]e needs to know about every other kid who's in here with him: who's a straight killer, who's a buster (a coward), who can't open his mouth to speak without lying. — Leon Bing, *Do or Die*, p. 4, 1991
- The kids across the street, despite their Raiders caps and blue sweat suits, were just busters, just wannabes. — Bob Sipchen, *Baby Insane and the Buddha*, p. 15, 1993
- In other words, "Man, you're a real buster," is not a compliment. — *Orlando (Florida) Sentinel Tribune*, p. E1, 11th May 1995
- "Either you with it, or you get got. And whatever you do, don't be a buster." "Buster?" I ask. "Coward." — Colton Simpson, *Inside the Crips*, p. 19, 2005

4 a firecracker *US*, *1952*
- When the months-old buster blew up, it scattered a profusion of filth everywhere. — John Clellon Holmes, *Go*, p. 36, 1952

5 in poker, a card that does not improve a hand *US*, *1961*
- — Irv Roddy, *Friday Night Poker*, p. 216, 1961

busters *noun*
dice that have had their spots altered to aid cheating *US*, *1962*
- — Frank Garcia, *Marked Cards and Loaded Dice*, p. 261, 1962

bust hand *noun*
in bar dice games, a roll that produces no points for the player *US*, *1971*
- — Jester Smith, *Games They Play in San Francisco*, p. 103, 1971

bust-head *noun*
potent whiskey or beer, especially if manufactured illegally *US*, *1857*
- I got so drunk I couldn't see. They were using this homemade beer, they used to call it "busthead" in Keokuk [Iowa]. — *Evergreen Review*, p. 137, 1957
- — Ramon Adams, *The Language of the Railroader*, p. 25, 1977

bus therapy *noun*
keeping a problem prisoner in transit in prison transport between prisons *US*, *1975*
- This "bus therapy" is famous in the California pens; anyone who's hard to handle without committing violent acts gets to see a lot of the state. — James Carr, *Bad*, p. 186, 1975
- When there were problems—race hassles, drugs, violence, whatever —in San Quentin, they'd grab everybody and ship 'em out, keeping their actual location in bureaucratic limbo. "Bus therapy" was another name for moving the problem rather than solving it. — Ralph "Sonny" Barger, *Hell's Angel*, p. 194, 2000

busticate *verb*
to break *US*, *1916*
- We make fun of learned or formal vocabulary by inventing and using such words as discombobulate, busticate, ruction, rambunctious (and the verb formed on the last-mentioned, rambunct). — Robert A. Hall, *Leave Your Language Alone!*, p. 126, 1950

bus ticket *noun*
a transfer from one prison to another *US*, *1989*
- — James Harris, *A Convict's Dictionary*, p. 29, 1989

bust in *verb*

in a dice cheating scheme, to introduce altered dice into a game *US, 1963*
- — John S. Salak, *Dictionary of Gambling*, p. 35, 1963

bustle rack *noun*

on a tank, welded pipe framework on the turret used as a sort of roof rack, storing food, drinks, and supplies *US, 1986*
- — Ralph Zumbro, *Tank Sergeant*, p. 189, 1986: Glossary
- I reached down into the bustle rack, grabbed a bottle, and scrambled back onto the ground. — Matthew Burden, *The Blog of War*, p. 177, 2006

bust off *verb*

to experience orgasm *US, 1996*
Derives from **BUST YOUR NUTS**.
- And watch this rap bitch bust all over ya nuts[.] — Lil' Kim *Dreams*, 1996
- [W]ant to bust off[.] — Kool Keith *Sex Style*, 1997

bust on *verb*

to shoot someone *US, 2001*
- "And then we pull heat and bust on 'em." I interrupt to ask if that means to shoot. "Shoot, yeah. Bust a cap." — *Rolling Stone*, p. 82, 12th April 2001

bust-out *noun*

1 a bankruptcy forced upon a business by organized crime, usually a lending enterprise owed money by the head of the business *US, 1969*
- In recent years, bankruptcy has become a major source of income for the underworld. New York hoodlums call it "bust-out;" in Chicago it is known as a "scam." — Ovid Demaris, *Captive City*, p. 84, 1969
- He said he had a Jewish guy, we called him Billy, who was a genius at setting up a bust-out. — Vincent Teresa, *My Life in the Mafia*, p. 99, 1973
- Forced bankruptcy is the newest golden pot. In some cities it's called scam and in some bust-out. — Robert Campbell, *Juice*, p. 238, 1988

2 in a dice cheating scheme, the substitution of altered dice for the legitimate dice; the altered dice *US, 1954*
- Max smiled and whispered to me as he rattled them together, "Bust-outs," meaning that nine out of ten times a seven would show up. — Harry Grey, *The Hoods*, p. 174, 1952
- It's an honest game, no "bust-out or flats." — Alson Smith, *Syndicate City*, p. 208, 1954

bust-out *verb*

an escape from confinement *US, 1951*
- "A bust-out! They take the deputy an' one of the doctors." — Donald Wilson, *My Six Convicts*, p. 296, 1951

bust out *verb*

1 to take over a legitimate business, exploit its credit to the maximum, and then liquidate all assets *US, 1962*
- "The whole idea behind buying and fixing this place up was to burn it down and bust it out." — Vincent Teresa, *My Life in the Mafia*, p. 101, 1973
- And, finally, when there's nothing left, when you can't borrow another buck from the bank or buy another case of booze, you bust the joint out. — *Goodfellas*, 1990

2 in a dice cheating scheme, to remove altered dice from a game and reintroduce the legitimate dice *US, 1963*
- — John S. Salak, *Dictionary of Gambling*, p. 35, 1963

bust-out *adjective*

1 in gambling, dishonest or part of a cheating scheme *US, 1937*
- That way I'll know up front if he's switched in bust-out cards of his own. — Iceberg Slim (Robert Beck), *Doom Fox*, p. 48, 1978

2 without money, broke *US, 1965*
- If this syllogism holds true, the bust-out junkie will say to his cellmate: "I am a heroin addict. I started smoking marijuana and then naturally I graduated to heroin." — Lenny Bruce, *How to Talk Dirty and Influence People*, p. 129, 1965

bust-out joint *noun*

a casino or gambling establishment that cheats gamblers *US, 1959*
- Bust-out joints, of which there are some two dozen in Newport, got their name from the recognized practice of not letting a customer out until he's "bust," one way or another. — Monroe Fry, *Sex, Vice, and Business*, p. 8, 1959

- I started in this business behind the bar in bust-out joints on Third Street. Strippers hustling drinks between their numbers. — Vincent Patrick, *The Pope of Greenwich Village*, p. 151, 1979
- — Frank Scoblete, *Guerrilla Gambling*, p. 299, 1993

bust-out man *noun*

in a dice cheating scheme, the confederate whose special skill is the switching of tampered dice with the legitimate dice *US, 1950*
- — *The Annals of the American Academy of Political and Social Sciences*, p. 122, May 1950

bust-out mob *noun*

a group of confederates gambling with altered dice *US, 1972*
- I do—and this is a divergence with what I just said—work with what they call a "bust-out" mob. Craps in conventions, picnics, things like that. There you work eight- or ten-handed. — Bruce Jackson, *In the Life*, p. 176, 1972

bus' up *verb*

to wreak havoc *US, 1981*
Hawaiian youth usage.
- Junior's face all bus' up form da fight! — Douglas Simonson, *Pidgin to da Max*, 1981

busy *adjective*

1 actively searching for, or engaged in, a sexual liaison *US, 1965*
Homosexual usage.
- "I'm busy, dear; talk to you later …" If this latter is said over the phone, it always means, "I'm in the middle of sex …" (nothing more). — *The Guild Dictionary of Homosexual Terms*, p. 6, 1965

2 (used of a card in poker) producing a pair or otherwise improving a hand *US, 1988*
- — George Percy, *The Language of Poker*, p. 15, 1988

▸ **get busy**

1 to have sex *US, 1989*
- — Terry Williams, *The Cocaine Kids*, p. 138, 1989

2 to rob someone *US, 1987*
- — Carsten Stroud, *Close Pursuit*, p. 272, 1987

busy bee *noun*

phencyclidine, the recreational drug known as PCP or angel dust *US, 1994*
- — US Department of Justice, *Street Terms*, October 1994

butch *noun*

the person fulfilling the masculine role in a homosexual relationship *US, 1954*
- Billy, the butch, squares off, putting up her fists. — Willard Motely, *Let No Man Write My Epitaph*, p. 248, 1958
- As in most homosexual encounters, the roles of the "butches" and "queens" were not strictly adhered to. — Roger Blake, *Love Clubs, Inc.*, p. 56, 1967
- A stone butch, she had a cute li'l chick, Sarita, she used to abuse for days. — Edwin Torres, *After Hours*, p. 323, 1979
- After I saw teenagers Tatum O'Neal and Kristy McNichol in Little Darlings (the perfect butch-femme dyke couple), I couldn't wait to—not to lose my virginity to Matt Dillon, but to have a sex slumber party with those two cuties. — *The Village Voice*, 17th June 2002

butch *adjective*

1 overtly masculine *US, 1936*
- "And when we got into bed, that tough butch number—he turned over on his stomach and I—…" a score had told me about a very masculine young man I had seen on the streets. — John Rechy, *City of Night*, p. 59, 1963
- I can remember when, years back, they shunted you through the side door, admitting only those who appeared "butch enough." — John Francis Hunter, *The Gay Insider*, p. 74, 1971
- Eleanor didn't wear thongs, she wore men's underwear like a normal butch girl. — Michelle Tea, *Rent Girl*, p. 217, 2004

2 fulfilling the masculine role in a male or female homosexual relationship *US, 1941*
Originally applied to male and female homosexuals, but later predominantly to lesbians.
- — Donald Webster Cory and John P. LeRoy, *The Homosexual and His Society*, p. 262, 1963: "A lexicon of homosexual slang"
- — Florida Legislative Investigation Committee (Johns Committee), *Homosexuality and Citizenship in Florida*, 1964: "Glossary of homosexual terms and deviate acts"

- I had to run out to catch the end of the Sunday-afternoon-Saturday-night recover bout at Julius'—where the oldest college sophomores in the world gather and everyone still pretends to be so butch that she just dropped in famished for one of those greasy hamburgers — *Screw*, p. 15, 22nd December 1969
- In spite of the fact that butch was not a friendly designation, it was, for the most part, adopted by the lesbian peoples. — Monique Wittig and Sande Zeig, *Lesbian People*, p. 23, 1979

3 heterosexual *US*, *1949*
- — Anon., *The Gay Girl's Guide*, p. 4, 1949

butch broad *noun*
an aggressive lesbian with masculine affectations *US*, *1966*
- Ordinarily, he wouldn't have gotten away with this behavior among the butch-broads[.] — Nathan Heard, *Howard Street*, p. 229, 1968

butch dike *noun*
an aggressive, mannish lesbian *US*, *1969*
- Rumors have it that a truly "butch dike" can whip any muscleman with her little finger. — *Screw*, p. 18, 27th June 1969

butcher *noun*
1 a surgeon *US*, *1849*
- — *Maledicta*, p. 57, Summer 1980: "Not sticks and stones, but names: more medical perioratives"

2 a prison guard captain *US*, *1983*
- — Marlene Freedman, *Alcatraz*, 1983

Butcher Brigade *nickname*
the 11th Infantry Brigade of the Americal Division, US Army *US*, *1991*
So named after the Brigade's role in the massacre at My Lai became known.
- Was this another incident like the one Calley and his Butcher Brigade perpetrated at My Lai? — Eric Van Lustbader, *The Kaisho*, p. 180, 1993

butcher charts *noun*
large pieces of paper used during a briefing or brainstorming session *US*, *1986*
Named because the paper used is similar to the paper used by butchers to wrap meat.
- — Department of the Army, *Staff Officer's Guidebook*, p. 57, 1986

butcher shop *noun*
a hospital casualty department or operating room *US*, *1918*
- — *American Speech*, p. 267, December 1962: "The language of traffic policemen"

butch it up *verb*
to act in an aggressive, manly manner *US*, *1963*
Homosexual usage, male and female.
- — Donald Webster Cory and John P. LeRoy, *The Homosexual and His Society*, p. 262, 1963: "A lexicon of homosexual slang"

butch number *noun*
a manly homosexual man desired by others as a partner in sex *US*, *1967*
- He is very masculine, and he has been described recurrently in homosexual jargon as "a very butch number"[.] — John Rechy, *Numbers*, p. 16, 1967

butch out *verb*
(used of a woman) to affect a mannish appearance *US*, *1999*
- I went over to the window and gazed down on a group of girls butched out in buzz cuts and work boots. — Rita Ciresi, *Pink Slip*, p. 11, 1999

butch pad *noun*
an apartment or house where lesbians congregate *US*, *1973*
- Then you can lay up in those butch pads with a bunch of bull daggers and a pack of smelly houses cats and drop pills and shoot junk[.] — Joseph Wambaugh, *The Blue Knight*, p. 148, 1973

butch queen *noun*
a decidedly masculine male homosexual *US*, *1966*
- — Kenneth Marlowe, *The Gay World of Kenneth Marlowe*, p. 3, 1966

butch trade *noun*
a seemingly heterosexual man who consents to homosexual sex in the male role, receiving orally or giving anally *US*, *1970*
- They want their men to be "butch trade." — *Screw*, p. 18, 22nd June 1970

butchy *adjective*
overtly masculine in affectation and mannerisms *US*, *1956*
- Then she started buying and sending me presents—slacks and jackets, suits cut and tailored like a man's with butchy accessories. — Billie Holiday with William Dufty, *Lady Sings the Blues*, p. 86, 1956
- "The public conception of a lesbian is that she's a butchy kind of person—an aggressive dyke," said Dr. Fort. — *San Francisco Chronicle*, p. 22, 30th June 1969
- No Birkenstocks or butchy buzz cuts here. — *Record (Bergen County, New Jersey)*, p. E1, 18th January 2004

but, I digress
used as a humorous end to a wandering thought *US*, *1961*
A catchphrase attributed to author Max Shulman in cigarette advertisements of the 1950s.
- But—like Max Shulman in those clever cigarette advertisements—I digress. — Robert Gover, *One Hundred Dollar Misunderstanding*, p. 12, 1961

butt *noun*
1 the buttocks *UK*, *1720*
- "you can't tell it none now but her butt was twice as big last summer." — Sylvia Wilkinson, *A Killing Frost*, p. 29, 1967
- It's the perils of coaching. You work your butt off, and then get kicked in it. — *Honolulu Advertiser*, 27th April 2003

2 by extension, the tail end of anything *US*, *1970*
- — *Current Slang*, p. 15, Winter 1970

3 the tail end of a prison sentence; the final morning in prison *US*, *1949*
- — Vincent J. Monteleone, *Criminal Slang*, p. 40, 1949
- When we were getting short and someone asked how long we had left, we said "Six days and a butt." "Four days and a butt." The butt is your last morning. — Malcolm Braley, *False Starts*, p. 199, 1976

4 a cigarette *US*, *1902*
- "Now ya can buy butts, kid," Chirechillo said. — Nathan Heard, *Howard Street*, p. 107, 1968
- I took packs of butts to the coal pile the next day. — Iceberg Slim (Robert Beck), *Pimp*, p. 260, 1969
- "I quit smoking, right? You remember that? I got off the butts." — George Higgins, *The Digger's Game*, p. 50, 1973
- It drove Rocco nuts; guys would buy ten loose cigarettes on ten trips for a dollar fifty when they could have bought a pack—twice as many butts for the same price. — Richard Price, *Clockers*, p. 264, 1992

butt *verb*
in tiddlywinks, to knock a wink off a pile *US*, *1977*
- — *Verbatim*, p. 525, December 1977

butt boy *noun*
a sycophant; a toady *US*, *1950*
- [H]e's the only one I can point to and say I'm sure I hate. Him and his butt boys. — Mickey Spillane, *My Gun is Quick*, p. 90, 1950
- Let little Eddie, the butt boy, shake him out of it. — Georgia Sothern, *My Life in Burlesque*, p. 284, 1972
- He's nothing but a pipe-smoking, draft-dodging, headquarters-carted butt-boy. — Gerald Petievich, *To Die in Beverly Hills*, p. 26, 1983
- The subcommittee's chairman, Minnesota Republican Norman Coleman, is one of the administration's leading butt boys. — Al Franken, *The Truth With Jokes*, p. 262, 2005

butt can *noun*
any improvised ashtray *US*, *1968*
- — Carl Fleischhauer, *A Glossary of Army Slang*, p. 7, 1968

butt drop *noun*
a backwards fall while snowboarding *US*, *1990*
- Are you perfecting your butt drop? — Elena Garcia, *A Beginner's Guide to Zen and the Art of Snowboarding*, p. 120, 1990

butter *noun*
crack cocaine *US*, *1998*
- Frank Sarubbi, 20, of 106 Prospect St., allegedly walked up to an undercover officer and asked if he was "looking to buy butter," street slang for crack. — *Hartford (Connecticut) Courant*, p. B5, 23rd December 1998

butter-and-egg man *noun*
an unsophisticated free spender *US*, *1924*
Coined by 1920s nightclub performer Texas Guinan for a shy, middle-aged man so flattered by her friendliness that he paid

the steep cover charge for every guest in the house and pressed $50 notes on all the entertainers. When he said he was in the dairy business, she introduced him as "the big butter-and-egg man."

- He puffed on the big cigar like he always had stuck in his face and posed back like a big butter-and-egg man. — Mezz Mezzrow, *Really the Blues*, p. 69, 1946

butter and eggs *noun*
an illegal lottery *US, 1973*
Most commonly known as a **NUMBERS** game.

- — Thomas L. Clark, *The Dictionary of Gambling and Gaming*, p. 32, 1987

butterball *noun*
a fat person or animal *US, 1941*

- Anna, sister of Huldah Purdick, was a rolypoly and a butterball, with pink-and-white plump cheeks. — Sinclair Lewis, *The God-Seeker*, p. 137, 1949
- Start your little butterball on her new diet by mixing small amounts of the canned kitten food with her dry. — *Albuquerque (New Mexico) Journal*, p. C3, 29th March 2004

butterbar *noun*
a second lieutenant in the US Army *US, 1973*
Vietnam coinage, from the gold-bar insignia.

- On April 25, 117 marched out as "butterbars"—Second Lieutenants of Marines. — *Washington Post Magazine*, p. 24, 25th May 1980
- Barbara's father pinned the gold bars—"butter bars" of a second lieutenant on the collars[.] — Lynda Van Devanter, *Home Before Morning*, p. 65, 1983
- A crusty old Sergeant major is not going to accept the indignity of becoming a "butterbar" second lieutenant. — Christopher Bassford, *The Spint-Shine Syndrome*, p. 141, 1988

butter-brain *noun*
a person of limited intelligence *US, 1968*

- So it constantly amazed him, and left him feeling much abused, to hear such nonsense—twerp, creepo, butter-brain. — Tim O'Brien, *Going After Cacciato*, p. 36, 1978

buttered up *adjective*
dressed up *US, 2002*

- "I have to go get buttered-up for the party tonight." — *Dictionary of New Terms (Hope College)*, 2002

butterfingers *noun*
a clumsy person, prone to dropping things *UK, 1837*
After the adjective.

- Those soggy chunks kept slipping out of my hands before I got them two inches off the ground. Slap my wrist and call me Butterfingers. — Mezz Mezzrow, *Really the Blues*, p. 36, 1946

butterfly *noun*
1 a person who is romantically fickle *US, 1947*
- — *American Speech*, p. 54, February 1947: "Pacific War language"

2 in television and movie-making, a large screen used to direct or diffuse light *US, 1987*
- — Ira Konigsberg, *The Complete Film Dictionary*, p. 36, 1987

butterfly *verb*
to engage in promiscuous sex *US, 1946*
- — *American Speech*, p. 120, May 1960: "Korean bamboo English"
- — Linda Reinberg, *In the Field*, p. 31, 1991

butterfly girl *noun*
a prostitute *US, 2004*
- — David Hart, *First Air Cavalry Division Vietnam Dictionary*, p. 10, 2004

butterhead *noun*
a stupid person, especially a stupid black person *US, 1963*

- Other black terms for blacks are implicitly or overtly derogating, such as butterhead for an embarrassingly stupid person. — Irving Lewis Allen, *The Language of Ethnic Conflict*, p. 111, 1983

buttermilk *noun*
beer *US, 1977*
- — Bill Davis, *Jawjacking*, p. 25, 1977

butt floss *noun*
a thong or string bikini with only a slender piece of fabric passing between the cheeks of the buttocks *US, 1991*

- — Trevor Cralle, *The Surfin'ary*, p. 17, 1991
- — Judi Sanders, *Kickin' like Chicken with the Couch Commander*, p. 4, 1992
- Young girls who sported thong swimsuits—known to Southern Californians as "butt floss" were "victims of a denigrating narcissistic society[.]" — Mark Sullivan, *Hard News*, p. 47, 1995

butt fuck *noun*
an act of anal sex *US, 1981*

- Well-hung males looking for a fix or a butt fuck—those are becoming my readers. — Robert Olen Butler, *The Alleys of Eden*, p. 151, 1981
- Tom Byron gives Francesa Le a resounding butt-fuck in a swimming pool sequence. — Editors of Adult Video News, *The AVN Guide to the 500 Greatest Adult Films of All Time*, p. 159, 2005

buttfuck *noun*
a despicable person *US, 2005*

- "So you're fired, buttfuck. Turn in your paintbrush and split." — Peter Fenton, *Eyeing the Flash*, p. 60, 2005

butt-fuck *verb*
1 to copulate anally *US, 1968*

- I hear when Caroline was living with that Greek bartender he used to butt-fuck her all the time. — Joseph Wambaugh, *The Choirboys*, p. 325, 1975
- He'll be at the Betty Ford Clinic while you and me do twenty-five at Raiford, getting butt-fucked in the showers. — Carl Hiaasen, *Tourist Season*, p. 130, 1986
- Me and Marcus Allen was butt fuckin' Nicole / When we heard a knock at the door[.] — Eminem (Marshall Mathers), *Role Model*, 1999

2 to light one cigarette with the burning butt of another *US, 2001*
- — Pamela Munro, *U.C.L.A. Slang*, p. 50, 2001

buttfucker *noun*
a homosexual male *US, 1989*

- "I was called boof, buttfucker, faggot, and queer." — Gilbert Herdt, *Gay and Lesbian Youth*, p. 168, 1989

butt fucking *noun*
anal sex *US, 1999*

- The Back Door Boys go for all the fag subtext of these homoerotic groups, exploring their interpretation of the hit song "I Want It That Way"—it's all about butt fucking. — *The Village Voice*, 5th October 1999
- I could not decide whether to give her the vigorous butt-fucking she so obviously craved[.] — Neal Stephenson, *The Confusion*, p. 35, 2004

buttfuck motel *noun*
jail or prison *US, 1995*

- "One phone call," said Whitmark, "and you're on your way to the buttfuck motel." — Carl Hiaasen, *Stormy Weather*, p. 178, 1995

butthead *noun*
a generally unlikeable, disagreeable, dimwitted person *US, 1973*

- MURTAUGH: Tell Martin what you think of crooks. CARRIE: Buttheads. They're buttheads. — *Lethal Weapon*, 1987
- "Why they don't stick around." "Because they're buttheads." — Armistead Maupin, *Maybe the Moon*, p. 44, 1992

butthole *noun*
1 the anus *US, 1951*

- [T]he man ain't never licked a female butthole! — Richard Meltzer, *A Whore Just Like the Rest*, p. 259, 1970
- He led the fellow away, got a canteen of water, washed the streak of shit off his cheek and then proceeded to wash the youth's butthole[.] — H.L. Stryker, *Obsessed!*, p. 118, 1984
- My pink butthole widened with each probing. — Dennis Cooper, *Closer*, p. 74, 1990
- Doggie style gives you a clear view of the butthole[.] — Tristan Taormino, *Pucker Up*, p. 151, 2001

2 by extension, a despicable or offensive person *US, 1962*
- — Collin Baker et al., *College Undergraduate Slang Study Conducted at Brown University*, p. 93, 1968
- Dad says you're late again, you butthole! — *Fast Times at Ridgemont High*, 1982
- This sucks more than anything has ever sucked before. We must find this butt-hole that took the TV. — Mike Judge and Joe Stillman, *Beavis and Butt-Head Do America*, p. 2, 1997

butt hut *noun*

1 a building set aside for smoking in an otherwise no-smoking atmosphere *US, 1996*

- We just go to the "Butt-hut" (a weird little hutch that leaks when it rains) to smoke and get all the best gossip from around the hospital. — *alt.showbiz.gossip*, 20th May 1996
- Your butt hut is an embarrassment. Building a fancy tent for your cigar addiction glamorizes smoking and violates California's clean indoor air law. — *smokefree.net/arnold*, 2007

2 a building or room where colonscopies are performed *US, 1999*

- We had a variety of names for it, but the "Butt Hut" was the most prevalent. — *alt.fan.mark-brian*, 4th January 1999

3 a brothel *US, 2003*

- I think it ought to be regulated and monitored. The problem is that people don't want a "butt hut" in their neighborhood. — *talk.politics.misc.*, 25th November 2003
- Thanks for the laugh, Eddy. I haven't heard the term Butt hut for 21 years or so. They don't seem to be a problem in Nevada. — *talk.politics.misc.*, 25th November 2003

buttinski; buttinsky

a meddler; a person who interferes in the affairs of others *US, 1902*

- It is said that one night a buttinsky in the audience said to her, "Say, aren't you Dorothy Parker?" — Earl Wilson, *I Am Gazing Into My 8-Ball*, p. 82, 1945
- Look who's talking about stickin' noses. You're the God-damndest buttinski I ever run into! — Garson Kanin, *Born Yesterday*, p. 131, 1946
- Are you going to let your coach have a free hand or are you going to be a buttinsky and keep trying to make him use your ideas? — *San Francisco Examiner*, p. 19, 20th December 1948
- You're a buttinsky, a guy who sticks his nose in places he shouldn't stick his nose. — Robert Campbell, *Junkyard Dog*, p. 120, 1986
- To some, Diane Vollmer is a buttinski. To others, she's the Lady Bird Johnson of her north Denver neighborhood. — *The Denver Post*, p. B1, 9th March 1997

buttlegger *noun*

a person who smuggles cigarettes from states with low or no cigarette taxes to states with high cigarette taxes *US, 1976*

- — *New York Times*, p. 2–13, 31st December 1976

buttlegging *noun*

the smuggling of cigarettes from states with low or no cigarette taxes to states with high taxes *US, 1977*

- — *Miami Herald*, p. 1, 4th July 1977

buttload *noun*

a large amount *US, 1991*

- — Connie Eble (Editor), *UNC-CH Campus Slang*, p. 2, Spring 1991
- I don't have time to fight. We have to find out what kind of algorithm we need here. I have to write a buttload of code. — Gary Dorsey, *Silicon Sky*, p. 144, 1999

buttly *adjective*

very ugly *US, 1989*

A blend of "butt" and "ugly."

- — Pamela Munro, *U.C.L.A. Slang*, p. 27, 1989

buttmunch *noun*

a contemptible person *US, 1996*

- He looks irritated and says, "Cut it out butt-munch!" — Mike Judge and Joe Stillman, *Beavis and Butt-Head Do America*, 1996
- I figure it don't take Colombo to find me guilty as charged of being a paranoid buttmunch. — Bob Janis, *Displicit*, p. 98, 2002

button *noun*

1 a police badge *US, 1929*

- He said, "Folks, you got that button? Those Mau Mau are going to maim our damn-fool host." I reached under the seat and got the fake detective badge. — Iceberg Slim (Robert Beck), *Trick Baby*, pp. 44–45, 1969

2 by extension, a police officer *US, 1953*

- It was pretty obvious that the buttons in the prowl car were about ready to drop the hook on him, so I went over there fast and took hold of his arm. — Raymond Chandler, *The Long Goodbye*, p. 6, 1953

3 a person who acts as lookout *US, 1992*

- — William K. Bentley and James M. Corbett, *Prison Slang*, p. 40, 1992

4 in organized crime, a person who kills on the orders from above *US, 1966*

Sometimes expanded as "button man" or "button guy."

- Two apartments were set up in the city and furnished with mattresses for the button men to sleep on. — Mario Puzo, *The Godfather*, p. 253, 1969
- Pete says to this button-guy with him — Edwin Torres, *Carlito's Way*, p. 23, 1975
- Vincent was arrested twice; and his three capi and about two hundred of his button men, as if they were moving through a revolving turnstile. — Richard Condon, *Prizzi's Honor*, p. 233, 1982
- The buttons had driven over from Las Vegas where they worked as freelance muscle. — Stephen Cannell, *Big Con*, p. 251, 1997

5 a small quantity of an item to be smuggled *US, 1956*

- — *American Speech*, p. 97, May 1956: "Smugglers' argot in the southwest"

6 the edible, psychoactive portion of a peyote cactus *US, 1953*

- Peyote is a small cactus and only the top part that appears above the ground is eaten. This is called a button. — William Burroughs, *Junkie*, p. 122, 1953

7 the clitoris *UK, 1900*

- [T]hose who felt that the ladies should have big bursts but could have them only in that highly localized surface nodule known in the trade as the vestigal phallus, or button, or boy in the boat. — Bernard Wolfe, *The Magic of Their Singing*, p. 93, 1961
- — Robert A. Wilson, *Playboy's Book of Forbidden Words*, p. 58, 1972

8 the chin *US, 1920*

Boxing jargon, usually in the phrase "on the button," describing a blow right on the chin.

- "I hit him right on the button. They used to stay down when I hit 'em like that." — William Kennedy, *Billy Phelan's Greatest Game*, p. 194, 1983

9 in the television industry, a dramatic or funny climax to a scene *US, 1990*

- — Ralph S. Singleton, *Filmmaker's Dictionary*, p. 24, 1990

button *verb*

▸ **button your lips**

to stop talking *US, 1947*

- — Marcus Hanna Boulware, *Jive and Slang of Students in Negro Colleges*, 1947
- When the teacher closes the door, the signal that class has begun, button your lips and open your ears. — Judith Scott, *The Art of Being a Girl*, p. 225, 1963

button-dicked *adjective*

possessing a small penis *US, 1994*

- — Michael Dalton Johnson, *Talking Trash with Redd Foxx*, p. 63, 1994

buttons *noun*

a messenger *US, 1962*

- — Joseph E. Ragen and Charles Finston, *Inside the World's Toughest Prison*, p. 793, 1962

button up *verb*

to close completely *US, 1941*

- Instead, his comrades killed the North Korean who shot him, and with that the rest of the tanks shot the pass, roaring down the road fully buttoned up and firing wildly as they went. — Robert Leckie, *The Wars of America, Volume II*, p. 340, 1968
- Also, he never learned to button up when he gets him, so if you two can get a good shot at him once, you can hurt him. — *M*A*S*H*, 1970
- The crew then "buttons up"—closes the blast doors and switches to emergency air and power. — Peter Pringle and William Arkin, *S.I.O.P.*, p. 166, 1983
- But for now, why not put everyone on full security alert and have NIS button up your house. — Richard Marcinko and John Weisman, *Rogue Warrior*, p. 306, 1992

butt out *verb*

to stop interfering *US, 1906*

Generally as an imperative.

- "Oscar, butt out!" her voice was a shriek and her eyes were swimming with tears. — Max Shulman, *Rally Round the Flag, Boys!*, p. 191, 1957
- "Will you listen if I tell you to butt out?" — Sue Grafton, *O is for Outlaw*, p. 149, 1999

butt pirate *noun*

an anal sex enthusiast *US, 1997*

- "I'm no butt pirate! I want women! Gazongas! Ass!" — Kelly Winters, *Walking Home*, p. 56, 2001

Francesca lived for butt-pirate porn and the old slap and tickle.
— Mr. Skin, *Mr. Skin's Skincyclopedia*, p. 402, 2005

butt plant *noun*
a backwards fall while snowboarding *US, 1993*
- — Doug Werner, *Snowboarders Start-Up*, p. 111, 1993

butt plug *noun*
1 a container such as a cigar tube, containing contraband, hidden in the rectum *US, 1992*
- The most common spot for prisoners to hide keys, drugs, and even hacksaw blades was inside metal cigar tubes—called "butt plugs"— inserted in the rectum. — Pete Earley, *The Hot House*, p. 56, 1992
2 a device that is inserted into the anus during sex, sometimes to retain an enema and sometimes simply for the sensation *US, 1989*
- Even today I still get a major hard-on watching Harry Reems (as "the Teacher") stick a butt plug slowly into Splevin's hot, willing anus. — Anthony Petkovich, *The X Factory*, p. 8, 1997
3 an offensive, unlikeable person *US, 1993*
- TED: But you said she was a sparkplug? HEALY: I said buttplug. She's heinous. — *Something About Mary*, 1998

butt slut *noun*
a male homosexual who takes a passive sexual role *US, 1992*
- — William K. Bentley and James M. Corbett, *Prison Slang*, p. 58, 1992
- Sometimes she likes to violate me and make her her "Butt slut." — Maxim Jakubowski, *The Mammoth Book of Sex Diaries*, p. 395, 2005

butt tuck *noun*
cosmetic surgery reducing and lifting the buttocks *US, 1984*
- Big Barb was a regal brunette with the Rolls-Royce of face lifts and butt-tucks. — Dan Jenkins, *Life Its Ownself*, p. 92, 1984
- "Half the girls get boob jobs and butt tucks," Kara Lynn said. — Carl Hiaasen, *Tourist Season*, p. 259, 1986

butt-twitcher *adjective*
revealing the shape of the wearer's buttocks *US, 1951*
- So we went and after they gave us our skates, they gave Sally this little butt-twitcher of a dress to wear. — J.D. Salinger, *Catcher in the Rye*, p. 129, 1951

butt ugly *adjective*
very ugly *US, 1986*
- If I want to know the latest slang, if I want to talk about "caps" and "marks" and "icy clothes" and "butt-ugly boys," I'll have to do it with the Other Emma. — *Los Angeles Times*, p. 5–1, 25th May 1988
- Let me tell you something. Diana Ross is butt ugly to me. — Karen A. Callaghan, *Ideals of Feminine Beauty*, p. 150, 1994
- [T]he street was lined with butt-ugly attached brick houses with tall stoops and no front lawns. — Jason Starr, *Lights Out*, p. 22, 2006

buttwipe *noun*
1 toilet paper *US, 1971*
- — Helen Dahlskog (Editor), *A Dictionary of Contemporary and Colloquial Usage*, p. 12, 1972
2 a despicable or offensive person *US, 1979*
- The buttwipe was sore, that's what. He couldn't beat Jimmy Carter. — Tom Tiede, *Welcome to Washington, Mr. Witherspoon*, p. 120, 1979
- Freeze, butt-wipe! — Mike Judge and Joe Stillman, *Beavis and Butt-Head Do America*, p. 3, 1997
- That was a New Guinea Peaberry, you Folger's-crystals-slurping buttwipe. — *Ten Things I Hate About You*, 1999
- We all got around to agreeing that Knut Thorssun was a universal buttwipe, perhaps the all-time. — Dan Jenkins, *The Money-Whipped Steer-Job Three-Jack Give-Up Artist*, p. 205, 2001

but why?
used humorously with varying meanings *US, 1963*
For example, a teacher might ask the class to pass in their homework, whereupon at least one member of the class will mutter, "But why?"
- — *American Speech*, p. 275, December 1963: "American Indian student slang"

buy *noun*
a purchase of illicit merchandise, especially drugs *US, 1906*
- [O]ur agents made a number of "buys" of opium at Chinese establishments. — Harry J. Anslinger, *The Murderers*, p. 30, 1961

buy *verb*
in poker, to draw a card or cards after the initial deal *US, 1967*
- — Albert H. Morehead, *The Complete Guide to Winning Poker*, p. 258, 1967

▶ **buy a pot**
in poker, to win a hand by betting so excessively as to drive all other players from the hand *US, 1963*
- — Richard Jessup, *The Cincinnati Kid*, p. 21, 1963

▶ **buy a suit**
to kill someone *US, 1997*
Referring to funeral attire.
- Y'see what I'm saying? Now I gotta either watch my back constantly or buy you a fuckin' suit right now. — Stephen Cannell, *King Con*, p. 25, 1997

▶ **buy it**
to die; to become a casualty *UK, 1825*
World War 1 and 2.
- Perry Chops was a long-dead narcotics pusher who bought it in a five-floor fall from a rooftop[.] — Mickey Spillane, *Last Cop Out*, p. 73, 1972
- By the time I gave it to the meat wagon, the ants had bought it! — Joseph Wambaugh, *Finnegan's Week*, p. 133, 1993

▶ **buy someone a suit**
to bribe someone *US, 1984*
- When someone "wants to buy you a suit" or "give you a hat" that means there is a payoff waiting for you if you overlook a violation of law, fail to do your job. — William J. Cavnitz, *One Police Plaza*, p. 81, 1984

▶ **buy the rack**
in horse racing, to bet on every possible combination of winners in a Daily Double bet *US, 1947*
- — Dan Parker, *The ABC of Horse Racing*, p. 144, 1947

▶ **buy the ranch**
to die *US, 1976*
A primary euphemism used by US soldiers in Vietnam.
- How can I hide my girl's pictures so no NVA ever puts his dirty commie gook hands on them if I buy the ranch? — Charles Anderson, *The Grunts*, p. 136, 1976

buy-and-bust *noun*
a police operation in which an undercover officer buys an illegal drug and then immediately arrests the seller *US, 1987*
- Typically, what an undercover cop will do, in a buy-bust situation, is try to buy something from you. — Joseph Pistone, *Donnie Brasco*, p. 52, 1987
- Officers of the San Diego Police Department were also there working an undercover "buy-bust" operation. — Bob Sipchen, *Baby Insane and the Buddha*, p. 346, 1993
- An undercover narcotics detective who minutes before had bought $30 worth of heroin in a buy-and-bust operation in Brooklyn yesterday shot and killed a man who tried to rob him, the police said. — *New York Times*, p. B3, 21st October 2000
- Before Reg went in, there was no TNT, no buy-and-bust program. — 50 Cent, *From Pieces to Weight*, p. 87, 2005

buy-down *noun*
a bribe paid to a police officer to release a criminal or to reduce the severity of the charges against him *US, 2001*
- You think it's some kinda buy-down? Some bullshit collars-for-dollars scheme? — Stephen J. Cannell, *The Tin Collectors*, p. 174, 2001

buy money *noun*
the money used to buy contraband *US, 1981*
- I will show you my ten grand buy money before you show me the funny money. — Gerald Petievich, *Money Men*, p. 5, 1981

buzz *noun*
1 a rumor; gossip; news *UK, 1821*
- It's out two days here and there, L.A., the Bay Area, San Diego today, and the buzz is better than expected. — Elmore Leonard, *Be Cool*, p. 335, 1999
- Because if the buzz is any indication, the movie's gonna make some huge bank. — Kevin Smith, *Jay and Silent Bob Strike Back*, p. 18, 2001
2 an immediate sensation of a drug or alcohol *US, 1849*
- Everybody looked like they'd got in a good buzz. There was liquor all over the place and women. — Hal Ellson, *Duke*, p. 111, 1949

- I don't get strung out on any speed; there's no chemical I need. I like the buzz. I like the rush. — Nicholas Von Hoffman, *We are the People Our Parents Warned Us Against*, p. 151, 1967
- Cold is nice going down, but I've swilled enough warm, now, so that it don't mean much. A buzz is a buzz. — Larry Heinemann, *Close Quarters*, p. 141, 1977
- See, that almost destroyed my buzz. — *Clueless*, 1995

3 a telephone call *US*, *1930*

- I'll give you a buzz in the morning, Yvonne. — Philip Wylie, *Opus 21*, p. 106, 1949
- I started toying with the idea, while I kept standing there, of giving old Jane a buzz—I mean calling her long distance at B.M., where she went, instead of calling up her mother to find out when she was coming home. — J.D. Salinger, *Catcher in the Rye*, p. 63, 1951

4 x-ray therapy *US*, *1994*

- — Sally Williams, *"Strong" Words*, p. 135, 1994

buzz *verb*

1 to feel the effects of drug intoxication *UK*, *1992*

- She was also buzzing, having taken three Eskatrol pills—amphetamines—before she left Miami. — *Vanity Fair*, p. 106, November 1993

2 to telephone someone; to summon someone by buzzer *US*, *1929*

- That's why you buzzed me so fast. — Mickey Spillane, *I, The Jury*, p. 10, 1947
- I buzz the attendant and he tells me that he notes the license number of every car he parks[.] — Gerald Petievich, *To Die in Beverly Hills*, p. 229, 1983
- When I got there, I buzzed her for at least five minutes. — Sandra Bernhard, *Confessions of a Pretty Lady*, p. 100, 1988
- A few days later the guy comes back and this time Tommy's there. She buzzes him, says the guy's here who left the photo. — Elmore Leonard, *Be Cool*, p. 183, 1999

3 to call for someone *US*, *1946*

- For three or four days I lived on fluids, and I got so raving hungry I was ready to chew on the bedclothes. Finally I buzzed Big Buster, a colored boy who worked in the hospital kitchen, and he took pity on me. — Mezz Mezzrow, *Really the Blues*, p. 38, 1946

4 to kiss someone *US*, *1945*

- — Lou Shelly, *Hepcats Jive Talk Dictionary*, p. 8, 1945

5 to fly very close to an object *US*, *1944*

- I am told that Soviet fighter planes are buzzing our air lift. — Philip Wylie, *Opus 21*, p. 146, 1949
- When he flew his plane behind a waterfall, then buzzed the diamond and broke up a baseball game. — Elaine Shepard, *The Doom Pussy*, p. 57, 1967

6 (used of a computer program or operation) to run without any sign of progress *US*, *1981*

- — *CoEvolution Quarterly*, p. 27, Spring 1981

7 to activate a remote device unlocking a door *US*, *1997*
From the buzzing sound the device often makes.

- I'm always afraid of those stores where they have to buzz you in. I'm concerned they won't buzz me in. Then I'll just have to stand there feeling like shit. — Chris Rock, *Rock This!*, p. 11, 1997

8 to anger someone; to alienate someone; to annoy *US*, *1952*

- It's your brother. I don't want to buzz him, you understand. — Hal Ellson, *The Golden Spike*, p. 30, 1952

buzzard *noun*

the eagle insignia of a full colonel or the Women's Army Corps *US*, *1931*

- An eagle for the cap was also designed, less intricate than the Army eagle and later to be familiarly known to Waacs, for reasons connected with its appearance, as "the buzzard." — Mattie E. Treadwell, *The Women's Army Corps*, p. 39, 1954

buzzard detail *noun*

a military unit assigned to recover and process bodies *US*, *1949*

- "Then why didn't you get hooked up with a body-snatching outfit? You look like a natural for the buzzard detail." — Audie Murphy, *To Hell and Back*, p. 3, 1949

buzzard's roost *noun*

the highest seats in a movie theater balcony *US*, *1920*

- We sat upstairs in the buzzard's roost 'cause it only costs a dime[.] — Louise Meriwether, *Daddy Was a Number Runner*, p. 94, 1970

buzz bomb *noun*

a person rendered emotionally unstable due to long incarceration *US*, *1976*

- — John R. Armore and Joseph D. Wolfe, *Dictionary of Desperation*, p. 23, 1976

buzz boy *noun*

a fighter pilot *US*, *1944*

- — *American Speech*, p. 310, December 1946: "More Air Force slang"

buzz-cut *noun*

a very short haircut; a person with a very short haircut *US*, *1977*
Perhaps from the sound of the electric clippers.

- She looked around, sure there would be a government sedan with two buzz-cuts somewhere nearby watching, but she saw nothing. — Stephen Cannell, *Big Con*, p. 339, 1997

buzzed *adjective*

drug-intoxicated *US*, *1972*

- STACY is getting more buzzed by the minute. He takes a drag from a big, fat joint[.] — *Menace II Society*, 1993
- She be buzzed on somethin' most the time. — Lois Stavsky et al., *A2Z*, p. 16, 1995

buzzer *noun*

1 a badge *US*, *1914*

- Next time ask to see the buzzer. — Raymond Chandler, *The Little Sister*, p. 19, 1949
- I flashed my buzzer. So did Velda. — Mickey Spillane, *One Lonely Night*, p. 91, 1951
- Grave Digger fished a felt-lined leather folder from his side coat pocket and showed his buzzer. — Chester Himes, *Come Back Charleston Blue*, p. 19, 1966
- I flashed my buzzer, is all. — Joseph Wambaugh, *Fugitive Nights*, p. 206, 1992

2 in a hospital casualty department, a defibrillator paddle *US*, *1994*

- — Sally Williams, *"Strong" Words*, p. 135, 1994

3 in horse racing, a battery-powered device used illegally by a jockey to shock a horse during a race *US*, *1942*

- Jockey Gets "Life" for Using Buzzer [Headline] — *San Francisco News*, p. 19, 26th May 1950
- — David W. Maurer, *Argot of the Racetrack*, p. 17, 1951

buzzing *adjective*

1 drunk *US*, *2003*

- — Recorded by Connie Eble (Editor), *UNC-CH Campus Slang*, p. 2, November 2003

2 manic, hyperactive *US*, *1994*

- — Sally Williams, *"Strong" Words*, p. 135, 1994

buzz job *noun*

the flying of an aircraft low to the ground to impress or scare those on the ground *US*, *1943*

- Class was interrupted when a Mosquito night fighter gave us a good buzz job. That is a beautiful aircraft. We got quite a thrill out of it. — Calvin L. Christman et al., *Lost in the Victory*, p. 62, 1998

buzz-kill *noun*

anything that suddenly deflates enjoyment *US*, *1990*

- So the free 60 minutes may not be as much as your hoping. Just a little buzz-kill. — comp.dcom.telecom, 24th March 1990
- And the National Guard! How much more of a creative buzz-kill could you get? — Isabel Rose, *The J.A.P. Chronicles*, p. 176, 2005
- Brooklyn was such a wasteland, such a downer, such a total buzz kill. — Jason Starr, *Lights Out*, p. 189, 2006
- Hinrich aims his camera at the woman covered in shaving cream. That's when he spots a serious buzz kill coming his way. — *Pitch Weekly (Kansas City)*, 31st August 2006

buzz off *verb*

to go away *UK*, *1914*

- He was drunk. Andy told him to buzz off. — Vincent Teresa, *My Life in the Mafia*, p. 165, 1973

buzztrack *noun*

in the television and movie industries, a sound track without modulations *US*, *1960*

- — Oswald Skilbeck, *ABC of Film and TV Working Terms*, p. 22, 1960

BW *noun*

an obese hospital patient *US*, *1994*

An abbreviation of BEACHED WHALE.
- — Sally Williams, *"Strong" Words*, p. 134, 1994

BW *nickname*
the Black Warriors prison gang *US, 2000*
- Borrowing from the AWs, the blacks were now organizing under the name the Black Warriors (BWs). — Bill Valentine, *Gangs and Their Tattoos*, p. 11, 2000

BWOC *noun*
a popular and visible college girl; a *big woman on campus*
US, 1947
- — Marcus Hanna Boulware, *Jive and Slang of Students in Negro Colleges*, 1947

BY *adjective*
(of a telephone line) busy *US, 1968*
- EMORY: B.Y. MICHAEL: It's busy? EMORY: Lorraine is probably talking to her mother. — Mart Crowley, *The Boys in the Band*, p. 149, 1968

by any means necessary; by whatever means necessary
used as a slogan by the radical political left of the 1960s to reflect a belief that the end justifies the means, up to and including violent action *US, 1970*
- We relate to a phrase coined by Malcom X: "By any means necessary." — Tom Wolfe, *Radical Chic & Mau-Mauing the Flak Catchers*, p. 23, 1970
- Those who make a life of seeking power, whether they are members of SDS or the Defense Department, must first establish enemies from whom they will wrest control—and then do it, By Any Means Necessary. — Raymond Mungo, *Famous Long Ago*, p. 51, 1970
- "How do you plan to go about doin' all this?" "By whatever means necessary!" Kwendi answers, jaws clenched. — Odie Hawkins, *Ghetto Sketches*, p. 213, 1972

bye Felicia!
used for inviting someone to leave *US, 2004*
From the film *Friday*.
- — Ben Applebaum and Derrick Pittman, *Turd Ferguson & The Sausage Party*, p. 10, 2004

by golly!
used as a euphemism for by God! *US, 1833*
- Betcha by golly, wow / You're the one that I've been waiting for forever — The Stylistics, *Betcha By Golly Wow*, 1971
- By golly, it's clean clear to Flagtown. — C.W. McCall, *Convoy*, 1976

by guess and by gosh *adjective*
without planning, relying on serendipity *US, 1914*
- Success in tactical field communications, Tully believed, was apt to be a "by guess and by gosh" proposition, amid the general lack of advanced information. — George Raynor Thompson, *The Signal Corps*, p. 384, 1957

by jumbo!
used as a substitute for an oath *US, 1959*
- "You've got to look ahead in this man's game," he emphasized at the first conference, "or by jumbo you're up crap creek without a paddle!" — Terry Southern, *The Magic Christian*, p. 50, 1959

by me
in poker, used for expressing a player's decision not to bet
US, 1988
- — George Percy, *The Language of Poker*, p. 16, 1988

BYO
a request that guests "*bring your own*" *US, 1968*
- — *Current Slang*, p. 13, Fall 1968
- It will commence with a BYO lunch, with gas barbecues available and plenty of off-street parking. — *Messenger*, p. 2, 1st May 1991

BYOB
used in invitations as an instruction to *bring your own booze or bottle US, 1968*
- — Collin Baker et al., *College Undergraduate Slang Study Conducted at Brown University*, p. 73, 1968

byplay *noun*
a device on a dishonest carnival game that can be activated to let players win *US, 1950*
- — *American Speech*, p. 235, October 1950: "The argot of outdoor boob traps"

Cc

C *noun*

1 the Viet Cong; a member of the Viet Cong *US, 1966*
- Vietnamese Communists, we call then Vietcong, we call them VC and C and Charlie and all the usual names[.] — William Wilson, *The LBJ Brigade*, p. 31, 1966

2 cocaine *US, 1921*
- The guy and the girl are both plenty loaded with C and feeling high. — William J. Spillard and Pence James, *Needle in a Haystack*, p. 74, 1945
- When you shoot C in main line—no other way of taking it gives the real C kick—there is a rush of pure pleasure to the head. — William Burroughs, *Letters to Allen Ginsberg 1953–1957*, p. 27, 7th April 1954
- He was a junkie for sure. He would know where to cop "C," and probably gangster for the runt. — Iceberg Slim (Robert Beck), *Pimp*, p. 126, 1969
- When the "C" hit us we started to rapping. — A.S. Jackson, *Gentleman Pimp*, p. 162, 1973

3 contraception *US, 1997*
Interview with Jim Holliday, 12th June 1997.

4 one hundred dollars *US, 1839*
- The two C's got him. — Mickey Spillane, *Kiss Me Deadly*, p. 78, 1952
- I rolled her for a C, man — John Rechy, *City of Night*, p. 140, 1963
- A fin for a number-five cap. A sixteenth for a "C." A piece for a grand. — Iceberg Slim (Robert Beck), *Pimp*, p. 128, 1969

C-47 *noun*
a clothespin *US, 2003*
Used by television and movie crews, mocking the formality of the official jargon of their craft. Collected from Discovery Channel television crew in Los Angeles, January 2003.

cab *noun*

▶ **take a cab**
to die *US, 2000*
- [H]is character suffers such a vicious beating that, as they say in New York, he took a cab. That is Big Apple street slang for saying that a person has breathed his last. — *San Diego Union-Tribune*, p. E10, 8th September 2000

caballo *noun*
heroin *US, 1970*
Spanish for "horse."
- — Richard Horman and Allan Fox, *Drug Awareness*, p. 464, 1970

cabaret *verb*

1 to lie in bed masturbating *US, 1950*
- You better knock off reading that hot stuff and going carbareting or you'll wind up bugged — Hyman E. Goldin et al., *Dictionary of American Underworld Lingo*, p. 39, 1950

2 to use an addictive drug in a semicontrolled pattern *US, 1958*
- Only he and Extra Black Johnson could cabaret—have their morning and evening fix and then take some whenever they felt like taking off and really getting charged up. — Willard Motley, *Let No Man Write My Epitaph*, p. 119, 1958

cabbage *noun*

1 money *US, 1903*
- Claims he's a human juke box and can lead the rats away if he jives the right tune which he'll do if the top squatters will put up the cabbage. — Harry Haenigsen, *Jive's Like That*, 1947
- [H]e spent the winters in Miami and dropped a wad of cabbage at the tables there. — Mickey Spillane, *Kiss Me Deadly*, p. 114, 1952
- On seeing me, he had said, Look, kid, ya gotta make the cabbage before you can carry the torch. — Clancy Sigal, *Going Away*, p. 433, 1961
- Made a little cabbage on the Tommy Bell fight too. — *Raging Bull*, 1980

2 the vagina *US, 1967*
Perhaps from the image of leaves peeling back.
- — Dale Gordon, *The Dominion Sex Dictionary*, p. 39, 1967

3 a coronary artery bypass graft *US, 1994*
A loose pronunciation of the acronym CABG.
- — Sally Williams, *"Strong" Words*, p. 136, 1994

cabbaged *adjective*
under the influence of MDMA, the recreational drug best known as ecstasy *UK, 1991*
- Ecstasy (a combination of mescaline and amphetamine) and LSD were a big help in reaching the ultimate state of "getting cabbaged." — *The Commercial Appeal (Memphis)*, p. 1C, 10th June 1994

cabbage-eater *noun*
a German or Russian immigrant *US, 1942*
Offensive.
- He did not live there, for the apartment was kept by Israel Amter, the cabbage-eater, and his wife. — Benjamin Gitlow, *The Whole of Their Lives*, p. 111, 1948
- — Irving Lewis Allen, *The Language of Ethnic Conflict*, p. 66, 1983

cabinet *noun*
a safe that is easily opened by thieves *US, 1972*
- Some of these safes you can actually open with a can opener. We call them cabinets. — Harry King, *Box Man*, pp. 30–31, 1972

cable *noun*
a chain necklace *US, 2005*
- Suddenly he's coming back with cables, a car, Gucci gear. — RZA, *The Wu-Tang Manual*, p. 32, 2005

caboodle *noun*
all of something *US, 1848*
- It wasn't the money, mind you—he was dead set against the whole caboodle. — Frederick Kohner, *Gidget*, p. 23, 1957
- I left the whole caboodle under a bench in Washington Square. — Mary McCarthy, *The Group*, p. 174, 1963

caboose *noun*

1 the buttocks; the anus *US, 1919*
- "As a matter of fact, you got what railroading folk call a mighty trim caboose." — Nelson Algren, *A Walk on the Wild Side*, p. 87, 1956
- He cussed her as he drove his needle-toed shoe into her wide caboose several times. — Iceberg Slim (Robert Beck), *Pimp*, p. 168, 1969
- Kitty bemoaned, "She's got a sexy caboose." — Seth Morgan, *Homeboy*, p. 135, 1990
- Nice knockers, plus some dark crotch and caboose. — Mr. Skin, *Mr. Skin's Skincyclopedia*, p. 13, 2005

2 the final participant in serial sex *US, 1970*
From the phrase **PULL A TRAIN** used to describe the practice.
- — *Current Slang*, p. 14, Spring 1970
- More common was the spontaneous act of gang sex: "pulling a train" on a drunken girl at the party—the boy's rank in the gang determined if he was the engine, the caboose, or somewhere in between[.] — Gini Sikes, *8 Ball Chicks*, p. 103, 1997

cabron *noun*
a guy, especially a brutish or dim-witted one *US, 1974*
Border Spanish used in English conversation by Mexican-Americans.
- — Dagoberto Fuentes and Jose Lopez, *Barrio Language Dictionary*, p. 23, 1974

ca-ca *noun*

1 excrement *US, 1952*
Probably from Spanish children's speech; used by non-Spanish speakers. Sometimes seen spelt as "kaka" or other such variations.
- All right, he made a kahkah, call a policeman. — Lenny Bruce, *How to Talk Dirty and Influence People*, p. 123, 1965
- Midget, you're doing a doo-doo job. You're fucking up. It's shit. Ca-ca. — *Mo' Better Blues*, 1990

2 nonsense *US, 1980*
- It was nothing but pure caca far as I could tell—boring isn't a good enough word. — Arturo Islas, *La Mollie and the King of Tears*, p. 20, 1986

3 heroin, especially low quality heroin *US, 1986*
- — Richard A. Spears, *The Slang and Jargon of Drugs and Drink*, p. 90, 1986
- — Gilda and Melvin Berger, *Drug Abuse A-Z*, p. 40, 1990

4 drugs, not necessarily heroin *US, 1995*
- — *Gang Intelligence Manual*, p. 40, 1995

cack; cak; kack *verb*
to fall asleep *US, 1959*
- — Robert George Reisner, *The Jazz Titans*, p. 153, 1960
- — Robert S. Gold, *A Jazz Lexicon*, p. 46, 1964

cackies *noun*
pants, especially khakis *US, 1990*
- So I then go into my Mack Daddy mode cause I'm getting a woodie in my cackies y'know. — *Boyz N The Hood*, 1990

cackle *verb*
1 to confess and/or to inform on others *US, 1949*
- — Vincent J. Monteleone, *Criminal Slang*, p. 41, 1949

2 as part of a controlled roll of dice, to give them the appearance and sound of being shaken while actually preventing their turning *US, 1963*
- — John S. Salak, *Dictionary of Gambling*, p. 37, 1963

cackle factory *noun*
a mental hospital *US, 1950*
- I didn't want to end up in the cackle factory with my meds and all. — Gerard Kuc, *Red Sex, White Drugs, Blue Rock 'N Roll*, p. 60, 2005

cacky *adjective*
in the language of striptease, overtly if not excessively sexual *US, 1981*
- — Don Wilmeth, *The Language of American Popular Entertainment*, p. 41, 1981

cactus *noun*
in hospital usage, a severely burnt patient *US, 1994*
- — Sally Williams, *"Strong" Words*, p. 136, 1994

cactus juice *noun*
tequila; mescal *US, 1971*
- If tequila spin-doctors can transform cactus juice into snob central, why not gin? — *Riverfront Times (St. Louis)*, 21st January 2004

cadaver cadet *noun*
a necrophile *US, 1986–1987*
- — *Maledicta*, p. 178, Summer/Winter 1986–1987: "Sexual slang: prostitutes, pedophiles, flagellators, transvestites, and necrophiles"

caddie shack *noun*
any small building where gold caddies congregate and wait for work *US, 1953*
- Later in the day, when the jobs were being passed out, you would engage in profane and bloody struggle behind the caddie shack. — Jim Thompson, *Bad Boy*, p. 341, 1953

caddy blackjack *noun*
a private game of blackjack *US, 1981*
- — Michael Dalton, *Blackjack*, p. 35, 1991

cadet *noun*
1 a pimp *US, 1904*
- — Hyman E. Goldin et al., *Dictionary of American Underworld Lingo*, p. 39, 1950

2 a new drug user *US, 1949*
- — Vincent J. Monteleone, *Criminal Slang*, p. 41, 1949

cadge *verb*
to beg; to wheedle something from someone *US, 1812*
- Joe told him he only needed to find Rooski this morning, who often cadged Demerols from Hymie's migraine script. — Seth Morgan, *Homeboy*, p. 59, 1990

cadillac *noun*
1 cocaine *US, 1953*
- "Are the Marmon and Cadillac working tonight?" "Yeah." "That Marmon's an eight, isn't it? And Cadillac's a twelve?" — William J. Spillard and Pence James, *Needle in a Haystack*, p. 145, 1945

2 phencyclidine, the recreational drug known as PCP or angel dust *US, 1994*
- — US Department of Justice, *Street Terms*, October 1994

3 a cup of coffee with cream and sugar *US, 1989*
- — James Harris, *A Convict's Dictionary*, p. 29, 1989

4 a note-and-string based method of communication in prison *US, 2000*
- [O]r using a cadillac [a line with the attached message and a weight that is whipped down the tier along the floor from one cell to another]. — Bill Valentine, *Gangs and Their Tattoos*, p. 38, 2000
- "I'm gonna make us a righteous Cadillac so we can score a couple of rollies from my dawg Big Bear." — Jimmy Lerner, *You Got Nothing Coming*, p. 90, 2002

5 the maximum amount which may be spent at a prison canteen *US, 1989*
- — James Harris, *A Convict's Dictionary*, p. 29, 1989

6 in the language of the homeless, a shopping cart *US, 1997*
- — Jim Crotty, *How to Talk American*, p. 262, 1997

7 the US Army M-1 tank *US, 1991*
- The generic nickname for the Army's M-1 Abrams tank is Cadillac. But most tankers give their own tank a name, too. — *Houston Chronicle*, p. 7A, 20th January 1991

8 a large surfboard used for big-wave conditions *US, 1965*
- — D.S. Halacy, *Surfer!*, p. 215, 1965

Cadillac bunk *noun*
a single prison bed in a setting where most beds are two-tiered bunk beds *US, 1989*
- — James Harris, *A Convict's Dictionary*, p. 29, 1989

cage *noun*
an abandoned house *US, 2000*
- Jackson considers herself lucky that she never had to resort to sleeping in "cages," the street slang for abandoned houses. — *Clarion-Ledger (Jackson, Mississippi)*, p. 1, 24th January 2000

cahoots *noun*
▶ **in cahoots with**
conspiring or planning with someone *US, 1829*
- O'Connor, however, is the Democratic leader of the Maryland organization, which is in cahoots with one of the tightest and biggest Mafia concentrations in the country. — Jack Lait and Lee Mortimer, *Washington Confidential*, p. 201, 1951
- Was she in cahoots with some Puerto Rican pusher who was about to make his entrance in my life? — Philip Roth, *Portnoy's Complaint*, p. 180, 1969
- [B]ecause when your father finds out your spent that money on drugs, he's gonna think I'm in cahoots with you, and then he's gonna forgive you and kill me. — Kenneth Lonergan, *This is Our Youth*, p. 88, 2000

caine; cane *noun*
cocaine, crack cocaine *US, 1983*
- I said, "Listen homeboy, what you talkin' about? / You're mistakin' my pad for a rockhouse / Well, I know to you we all look the same / But I'm not the one slingin' caine." — Toddy Tee, *Batterram*, 1985
- He's got a scale on the table, with some cut foil, some 'caine, and a bag full of money. — Terry Williams, *The Cocaine Kids*, p. 106, 1989
- I don't wanna be like my brother and shit, hanging out not doing shit, end up dealing cane just like him. — *Boyz N The Hood*, 1990
- What d'ya know. A kilo of 'caine. — *The Bad Lieutenant*, 1992

Cajun microwave *noun*
a large outdoor charcoal cooker *US, 1986*
- One kitchen, on the lower level, will be close to the outdoor barbecue and to an outdoor oven with indirect heat that he calls a Cajun microwave. — *Chicago Tribune*, p. C7, 19th March 1987

cake *noun*
1 a beautiful girl or young woman *US, 1941*
- What's on your mind, Jim-Jam? Thinkin' about that new cake you pulled from Baxter Terrace, huh? — Nathan Heard, *Howard Street*, p. 63, 1968
- — Vann Wesson, *Generation X Field Guide and Lexicon*, p. 34, 1997

2 the vagina *US, 1967*
- — Dale Gordon, *The Dominion Sex Dictionary*, p. 39, 1967

3 a meal provided as compensation in addition to wages *US, 1973*
- — Sherman Louis Sergel, *The Language of Show Biz*, p. 39, 1973

4 money; a good deal of money *US, 1965*
Extends, perhaps, from **BREAD** (money) but "cake" has traditionally been associated with wealth. *"Qu'il mangent de la brioche"*—"Let them eat cake," attributed to Queen Marie-Antoinette (1755–93) on being told that her people had no bread.
- — Hermese E. Roberts, *The Third Ear*, 1971

- She hated the job but she loved the cake. — Alix Shulman, *On the Stroll*, p. 137, 1981
- But you'd go out with her if you had the cake? — *Ten Things I Hate About You*, 1999

5 a round disc of crack cocaine *US, 1994*
- — US Department of Justice, *Street Terms*, October 1994

▸ **get your cake**
to date your girlfriend *US, 2001*
- Brooks and his colleagues also provide police with glossaries of street slang—"Agent Scully" = "oral sex," "getting my cake" = "dating my girl." — *Washington Post*, p. A1, 20th August 2001

cake *adjective*
easy *US, 1968*
- — Collin Baker et al., *College Undergraduate Slang Study Conducted at Brown University*, p. 93, 1968
- — AFSCME Local 3963, *The Correctional Officer's Guide to Prison Slang*, 2001
- "His schedule this semester is cake." — *Dictionary of New Terms (Hope College)*, 2002

cake boy *noun*
an attractive, usually younger homosexual male *US, 1995*
- Are you bitches blind or something? Your man, Christian, is a cake-boy. — *Clueless*, 1995
- — Ethan Hilderbrant, *Prison Slang*, p. 21, 1998

cake-cutting *noun*
short-changing *US, 1993*
- On the midway, he learned the art of "cake cutting," or shortchanging customers, using "sticks"—carnies posing as customers pretending to win a big prize—and "gaffs"—concealed devices such as magnets used to ensure that the house always won. — Kim Rich, *Johnny's Girl*, p. 37, 1993

cake-eater *noun*
1 an effeminate young man, who may or may not be homosexual *US, 1916*
An important word of the flapper era, but seldom heard thereafter.
- And Three-Star Hennessey, the lousy little cake-eater who used to rob girls' pocketbooks while he danced with them. — James T. Farrell, *Saturday Night*, p. 31, 1947

2 a person who enjoys performing oral sex on women *US, 1967*
- — Dale Gordon, *The Dominion Sex Dictionary*, p. 39, 1967
- — Robert A. Wilson, *Playboy's Book of Forbidden Words*, p. 58, 1972
- — Helen Dahlskog (Editor), *A Dictionary of Contemporary and Colloquial Usage*, p. 12, 1972

cake hole *noun*
the mouth *UK, 1943*
- Jeremy asks no one in particular, as he jams a slab of lox into his cake hole. — Anthony Petkovich, *The X Factory*, p. 183, 1997
- — Pamela Munro, *U.C.L.A. Slang*, p. 106, 1997

cakes *noun*
the female breasts *US, 1967*
- What they want is shows where one guy kicks another guy in the belly while a dame leans over 'em with her cakes falling out of her negligee. — Max Shulman, *Rally Round the Flag, Boys!*, p. 67, 1957

cakewalk *noun*
an easy or overwhelming success *US, 1897*
Originally a boxing term for an easy victory, then expanded to general use.
- They came out of the chute with fire in their eyes and a tiger in their tank and turned this old-fashioned, gut-bustin' sidewinder into a cakewalk! — Dan Jenkins, *Life Its Ownself*, p. 219, 1984
- Solving Iraq will not be easy, and it won't be quick. This is not a cakewalk. — *Baltimore Sun*, p. 16A, 21st April 2004

calaboose *noun*
a jail, especially a local one *US, 1792*
From the Spanish *calabozo* (dungeon).
- [T]hey'll find you and kick you out and you'll wind up in a Mexican calaboose boy. — Jack Kerouac, *The Dharma Bums*, p. 101, 1958
- Jail, man! The fuckin' calaboose. — Joseph Wambaugh, *Finnegan's Week*, p. 51, 1993

calamity howler *noun*
a person who predicts disaster *US, 1892*

- All those calamity-howlers who have been taking it for granted that downtown San Francisco is ready to fold up have been given the kind of jolt they deserved. — *San Francisco Examiner*, p. 32, 22nd March 1954

Calamity Jane *noun*
in a deck of playing cards, the queen of spades *US, 1988*
Martha Jane "Calamity Jane" Canary (1852–1903) was a legendary figure in the settling of the western US.
- — George Percy, *The Language of Poker*, p. 16, 1988

calculator *noun*
1 in horse racing, a pari-mutuel clerk who calculates odds *US, 1976*
- — Tom Ainslie, *Ainslie's Complete Guide to Thoroughbred Racing*, p. 329, 1976

2 in poker, a player skilled at assessing the hands of other players *US, 1988*
- — George Percy, *The Language of Poker*, p. 16, 1988

calendar *noun*
a prison sentence of one year *US, 1926*
- "Rough as a cob. 'Specially for you—many calendars as you pulled." — Malcolm Braly, *It's Cold Out There*, p. 39, 1966

calf *noun*
a young teenage girl *US, 1959*
- — *Look*, p. 49, 24th November 1959

Cali *noun*
California *US, 1930*
- With a flash of the Krylong emergency symbol, writers from Philly, New York, Atlanta, and Cali will be here in minutes[.] — William Upski Wimsatt, *Bomb the Suburbs*, p. 50, 1994
- — Pamela Munro, *U.C.L.A. Slang*, p. 49, 1997

Califas *nickname*
California *US, 1974*
Border Spanish used in English conversation by Mexican-Americans.
- — Dagoberto Fuentes and Jose Lopez, *Barrio Language Dictionary*, p. 27, 1974
- Some had ended up in Texas and others in Califas[.] — Jim Sagel, *El Santo Queso*, pp. 187–188, 1988
- Even Texans are surprised at California's vehemence and, being more experienced, are wooing Mexican business away from Califas. — *Los Angeles Times*, p. B7, 5th May 1995

California bankroll *noun*
a single large-denomination bill wrapped around a small-denomination bill, giving the impression of a great deal of money *US, 1980*
- — Edith A. Folb, *runnin' down some lines*, p. 231, 1980

California coffee *noun*
inexpensive wine *US, 1976*
- — *Elementary Electronics*, *Dictionary of CB Lingo*, p. 55, 1976

California cornflakes *noun*
cocaine *US, 1976*
- — *Elementary Electronics*, *Dictionary of CB Lingo*, p. 55, 1976

California Crybaby Division *nickname*
in the Korean war, the 40th California National Guard Division *US, 1989*
- [A]ll of these had only reinforced the unit's reputation as a sorry, undisciplined, ineffective fighting force. Its nickname—the California "Crybaby" Division—spoke for itself. — David H. Hackworth, *About Face*, p. 225, 1989

California pimping *noun*
working as a pimp in a relaxed, low-pressure style *US, 1972*
- California pimpin' is the relaxed style of pimping peculiar to the Golden State, also known as the slow track. — Christina and Richard Milner, *Black Players*, p. 48, 1972

California quail *noun*
a tablet of the recreational drug methaqualone, the recreational drug best known as Quaaludes™ *US, 1997*
- — *Providence (Rhode Island) Journal-Bulletin*, p. 6B, 4th August 1997

Californicator *noun*
a Californian, especially one who has moved to Oregon or Washington state *US, 1978*

- — *Maledicta*, p. 153, Summer/Winter 1978: "How to hate thy neighbor: a guide to racist maledicta"
- Watching some Californicator build a log mansion on the creek where your Dad used to take you fishing. — Arthur Kroker, *Digital Delirium*, p. 13, 1997

calipers *noun*
dice that are true to an extremely minute tolerance, approximately 1/1000th of a inch *US, 1950*
- — *The Annals of the American Academy of Political and Social Sciences*, p. 122, May 1950

call *noun*
the initial flooding of sensations after injecting heroin *US, 1973*
- — David Maurer and Victor Vogel, *Narcotics and Narcotic Addiction*, p. 394, 1973

call *verb*
▸ **call Earl**
to vomit *US, 1968*
- — Collin Baker et al., *College Undergraduate Slang Study Conducted at Brown University*, p. 93, 1968

▸ **call for the butter**
to have completed a task or arrived at your destination *US, 1975*
Fishing skippers who claimed the ability to locate fish by the taste of the bottom mud would smear butter on a lead weight, lower it to the bottom, and then taste the mud brought to the surface on the buttered lead.
- — John Gould, *Maine Lingo*, p. 30, 1975

▸ **call it on**
to challenge another gang to a gang fight *US, 1955*
- — *New York Times*, p. 2, 15th May 1955

call book *noun*
a list, formal or highly informal, kept by a pool hustler, of locations where money can be made playing pool *US, 1990*
- — Steve Rushin, *Pool Cool*, p. 7, 1990

call boy *noun*
a male prostitute whose clients book his services by telephone *US, 1942*
- There are clandestine call boy rings, operated by discreet male madams (often called "misters" in Miami) who supply male prostitutes to guests at beach hotels. — Johnny Shearer, *The Male Hustler*, pp. 123–124, 1966
- The frequent performance of fellatio on customers raises the question for the call boy of what to do with the fluid at ejaculation. — George Paul Csicsery (Editor), *The Sex Industry*, p. 32, 1973
- Students and middle-class youngmen […] become callboys (the callboy faction being safer, more "conservative")[.] — John Rechy, *The Sexual Outlaw*, p. 152, 1977
- I've witnessed various liaisons with hustlers over the years, the street kind as well as the call-boy elite[.] — Ethan Morden, *I've a Feeling We're Not in Kansas Anymore*, p. 34, 1985

call girl *noun*
a prostitute who makes bookings with customers by telephone *US, 1922*
- The girl actually was—a professional tart. A call girl. — Philip Wylie, *Opus 21*, p. 62, 1949
- The aristocrats among prostitutes are expensive call-girls who work for fancy fees and keep their pimps in luxury. — John M. Murtagh and Sara Harris, *Cast the First Stone*, p. 1, 1957
- I worked as an independent and could not imagine why a $100-a-night call girl like myself or Blossom would want or need a pimp. — Sara Harris, *The Lords of Hell*, p. 31, 1967
- Coz says he's been beefing up his East Coast staff, in part by hiring Richard Gooding, who broke the 1996 story about Dick Morris's call girl for the rival *Star*. — *Washington Post*, p. C1, 26th February 2001

call house *noun*
a brothel from which prostitutes are procured by telephone *US, 1913*
- It's the telephone number of a call house. — Mickey Spillane, *I, The Jury*, p. 61, 1947
- The call houses that specialize in sixteen-year-old virgins are doing a land-office business. — Raymond Chandler, *The Little Sister*, p. 1, 1949

- Then somebody will suggest the call houses. Address books with lists of cryptic phone numbers will be consulted. — Dev Collans with Stewart Sterling, *I was a House Detective*, p. 152, 1954
- Then Fullenwider asked, "Did you ever conduct a call house there?" Again MacInnis objected: "What is a call house? What does that phrase mean?" — *San Francisco News*, p. 8, 21st October 1955

calling card *noun*
1 a fingerprint *US, 1949*
- — Vincent J. Monteleone, *Criminal Slang*, p. 42, 1949
- Calling cards, in the form of fingerprints left at the scene of East bay holdups, led today to the arrest of two suspected big-shot partners in crime. — *San Francisco News*, p. 1, 21st March 1953
2 needle marks on a drug user's arm *US, 1971*
- — Eugene Landy, *The Underground Dictionary*, p. 45, 1971
3 during the Vietnam war, a printed card identifying the unit, left on the bodies of dead enemy soldiers *US, 1990*
- Their "calling card" featured an eagle holding the crest of the 101st ABN, and a thunderbolt. — Gregory Clark, *Words of the Vietnam War*, p. 137, 1990

calling station *noun*
in poker, an unskilled player who calls bets prematurely *US, 1979*
- — John Scarne, *Scarne's Guide to Modern Poker*, p. 274, 1979

call money *noun*
a demand for payment of a debt *US, 1989*
- Max's friends began to call him to tell him his brother was creating heavy debt, and asking Max for "call money." — Terry Williams, *The Cocaine Kids*, p. 122, 1989

call out *verb*
to challenge someone to a fight *US, 1980*
- — Edith A. Folb, *runnin' down some lines*, p. 231, 1980

Calvin Klein special *noun*
a mixture of cocaine and the recreational drug ketamine *US, 1995*
A back formation from the initials.
- Users pay from $20 to $40 per dose, or "bump," usually to be mixed with heroin or cocaine and snorted (the coke/ketamine combo is called CK or the "Calvin Klein Special")[.] — *The Record [Bergen County, New Jersey]*, p. A1, 5th December 1995

Calvins *noun*
blue jeans or underwear designed by Calvin Klein *US, 1982*
- — Connie Eble (Editor), *UNC-CH Campus Slang*, p. 2, Spring 1982
- Rock and Rap Stars Show Their Calvins — *Rolling Stone*, 4th June 1999

Cambo *adjective*
Cambodian *US, 1976*
- In May 1970, for example, when US troops in Vietnam pushed into Cambo. — EBSCO Publishing, *Discover*, p. 57, 1980

Cambode *noun*
Cambodia *US, 1986*
- Snipings had increased radically, and raids near the Cambode border had expanded to the point where A Company's particular brand of expertise was needed. — Ralph Zumbro, *Tank Sergeant*, p. 99, 1986

Cambodie *adjective*
Cambodian *US, 1964*
Vietnam war usage.
- [W]e kept smoking our Cambodie smokes and took turns trying to nap and swatted flies. — Larry Heinemann, *Close Quarters*, p. 240, 1977

camel *noun*
1 in twelve-step recovery programs such as Alcoholics Anonymous, a person who maintains sobriety *US, 1998*
From the sense of "dry as a camel."
- — Christopher Cavanaugh, *AA to Z*, p. 65, 1998
2 a marijuana cigarette *US, 1976*
- — John R. Armore and Joseph D. Wolfe, *Dictionary of Desperation*, p. 23, 1976

camel driver *noun*
an Arab *US, 1984–1985*
- — *Maledicta*, p. 117, 1984–1985: "Milwaukee medical maledicta"

camelfucker *noun*
an Arab *US, 1994*
Offensive.

- "Just make sure the girl and the camel-fucker are well done."
  — Bill Branon, *Let Us Prey*, p. 195, 1994
- Look at our current situation with that camelfucker in Iraq—pacificism is not something to hide behind. — *The Big Lebowski*, 1998
- The feds culled camel fuckers in custody. — James Ellroy, *Destination Morgue*, p. 372, 2004

camel head *noun*
an Arab *US, 2004*
- The feds culled camel fuckers in custody. Said camelheads confirmed the contretemps. — James Ellroy, *Destination Morgue*, p. 372, 2004

camel jockey; camel jock *noun*
a Arab; anyone mistaken for an Arab *US, 1961*
Used with contempt.
- The Vice President's lengthy preoccupation with that Pakistani camel-jockey, Bashir Ahmed[.] — *Reno (Nevada) Evening Gazette*, p. 4, 11th June 1961
- — Andy Anonymous, *A Basic Guide to Campusology*, p. 5, 1966
- — *Current Slang*, p. 14, Spring 1970
- Clement couldn't picture this skinny camel-jockey-looking guy shooting anybody anyway. — Elmore Leonard, *City Primeval*, p. 145, 1980
- So it must be disconcerting, and scary, for Arab-Americans and Muslims to hear Savage and his kind refer to them as "towel heads" and "camel jockeys." — *Corpus Christi (Texas) Caller-Times*, p. A7, 28th January 2004

camel toe *noun*
the condition that exists when a tight-fitting pair of pants, shorts, bathing suit, or other garment forms a wedge or cleft between a woman's labia, accentuating their shape *US, 1993*
- Beef curtains, vertical smile, flesh taco, whiskerbiscuit, cooter, cum dump, mound, camel toe. — *alt.sex.bestiality*, 15th April 1993
- Camel lips, an offensive name from the '50s when women wear their pants too tight. Also known as camel toes. The pants were designed to capitalize on that. — *USA Today*, p. 1D, 12th April 1994
- When you put them back on you knew they were tight enough if you could see the outline of your pussy, which, with the seam going up the crotch, made it sort bulge on each side, vaguely reminding one of a camel's toe. — Editors of Ben is Dead, *Retrohell*, p. 31, 1997
- "They're too tight, too revealing, and the source of both visible panty lines and camel toe"—an unsightly affliction[.] — *New York Post*, p. 12, 9th October 2003

camera-eye dick *noun*
a police officer with a good memory for faces from photographs of wanted criminals *US, 1972*
- But the minute you sit down they'll get you because it's the bull's job to know all the thieves in that town. That's what make them smart dicks. They call these guys "camera-eye dicks." — Harry King, *Box Man*, p. 106, 1972

Camille *noun*
1 a homosexual man who moves from one unfortunate, failed love affair to another *US, 1972*
- — Bruce Rodgers, *The Queens' Vernacular*, p. 40, 1972

2 a melodramatic hospital patient who always feels on the verge of dying *US, 1994*
From the novel by Alexandre Dumas.
- — Sally Williams, *"Strong" Words*, p. 136, 1994

cammies; camies *noun*
a camouflage uniform *US, 1971*
- Hey you ... you in the camies. — Ronald J. Glasser, *365 Days*, p. 201, 1971
- The uniforms may well be necessary. Even though women are barred from combat jobs, many open specialties require "cammies." — *Insight*, 28th November 1988
- A strack-looking E-6 in jungle cammies stepped up to the platform at the head of the formation[.] — Gary Linderer, *The Eyes of the Eagle*, p. 24, 1991
- Some "ground pounders" wearing "chocolate chip cookie cammies" even talk of an "Adopt-a-Pilot" campaign and cheer when the jets roar overhead. — *Shreveport (Louisiana) Journal*, p. 4B, 1st February 1991

cammo stick *noun*
an applicator for camouflage makeup *US, 2001*
- — James Kirschke, *Not Going Home Alone*, p. 239, 2001: Glossary

camo *noun*
camouflage *US, 1984*
- A pair of bearded soldiers armed with matt black machine pistols, and wearing berets and desert camo uniforms, appeared from out of a tent along the side of the road. — T.E. Cruise, *Wings of Gold III*, p. 300, 1989
- Okay. Was the shooter wearing camo gear? — Andrew Vachss, *Blossom*, p. 200, 1990
- Today he wore camo fatigues. — Carl Hiaasen, *Strip Tease*, p. 208, 1993

camouflage *noun*
the disguise and staged personality assumed by an expert card counter playing blackjack in a casino in the hope of avoiding detection and ejection *US, 1991*
- — Michael Dalton, *Blackjack*, p. 25, 1991

camp *noun*
1 ostentation, flamboyant behavior; extravagance of gesture, style etc.; also, deliberately overt effeminacy used to signal homosexuality *US, 1932*
May be further refined (or otherwise) as **HIGH CAMP** or **LOW CAMP**.
- Detractors dismiss Barlett/Brommfield collaborations as outdated high camp. — John Clum, *Still Acting Gay*, p. 348, 2000

2 a dramatically effeminate homosexual man *US, 1923*
- Still, when this assistant prop man, crew-cut kid, flit, floppy wrists and pursy lips, what they called rough trade, a real camp, when he'd begun stroking Biff's elbows and saying how gone he was on him, Biff hadn't come down with the immediate kyawkyaws. — Bernard Wolfe, *The Late Risers*, p. 202, 1954

3 jail *US, 1968*
- — Hy Lit, *Hy Lit's Unbelievable Dictionary of Hip Words for Groovy People*, p. 7, 1968

camp *verb*
to exhibit humorously exaggerated, dramatic, effeminate mannerisms (usually but not exclusively of a homosexual male) *US, 1925*
Variants are "camp around," "camp about" and "camp it up."
- She can neither act, nor even camp the role. — Sidney Bernard, *This Way to the Apocalypse*, p. 147, 1964
- So then years later they meet a fresh bloke like me who's not afraid to camp a bit. — Antony James, *America's Homosexual Underground*, p. 80, 1965
- They screamed and camped when they got on it. — Phil Andros, *Stud*, p. 39, 1966
- That's exactly what I'm talking about, Emory. No camping! — Mart Crowley, *Boys in the Band*, p. 51, 1968

camp bitch *noun*
an overtly, extravagantly effeminate male homosexual *US, 1964*
- — Roger Blake, *The American Dictionary of Sexual Terms*, p. 28, 1964

Camp Cupcake *noun*
any minimum security prison *US, 1996*
This term was widely heard during the months of Martha Stewart's incarceration.
- In coming home for the holiday from a prison known among regulars as Camp Cupcake, Sarault sent a message to criminals everywhere that it is better in the long run to steal in Brooks Brothers than in Levi Strauss. — *Providence Journal Bulletin*, p. 1B, 12th January 1996

campy *adjective*
melodramatically and blatantly homosexual *US, 1965*
- The rest were largely "campy" homosexuals who enjoyed dressing up in women's clothes and performing dirty sketches and singing off-color songs. — Antony James, *America's Homosexual Underground*, pp. 83–84, 1965

can *noun*
1 a Navy destroyer *US, 1946*
- "I just took for granted that I'd get on a can or a wagon or a carrier right in the middle of it." — Thomas Heggen, *Mister Roberts*, p. 65, 1946

2 a combat tank *US, 1986*
- "Well, then, round up three savages and put them back in their cans." — Ralph Zumbro, *Tank Sergeant*, p. 108, 1986

3 a jail or prison *US, 1912*
- The day he got out of the can he was in business in Union Station again and still was at this writing, though arrested again and out on bail. — Jack Lait and Lee Mortimer, *Washington Confidential*, p. 130, 1951

- Once you lose the hatred, then the can's got you. — Piri Thomas, *Down These Mean Streets*, p. 263, 1967
- You're gonna spend eight years in the can—minimum—and for what? — *King of Comedy*, 1976
- So there I am in the can, and not the one that says "gentlemen" on the door. I'm talking about jail. — *Raging Bull*, 1980

4 a toilet; a bathroom or water closet *US, 1914*

- In the corner I spied a bucket coated with two inches of lime inside and out, with no cover; from the tip-off my nose gave me, I figured this was the can. — Mezz Mezzrow, *Really the Blues*, pp. 33–34, 1946
- I didn't have anything special to do, so I went down to the can and chewed the rag with him while he was shaving. — J.D. Salinger, *Catcher in the Rye*, p. 26, 1951
- "He sits when he goes to the can, doesn't he?" he asked philosophically. — Evan Hunter, *The Blackboard Jungle*, p. 28, 1954
- You mean if I go into latrine to relieve myself I should take along at least seven buddies to keep me from brooding on the can? — Ken Kesey, *One Flew Over the Cuckoo's Nest*, p. 158, 1962
- Only man in history who ever found fulfillment in the ladies' can of a Boston and Maine Railroad car! — *M*A*S*H*, 1970

5 the buttocks *US, 1914*

- Yeah, sitting on your can. Ever think of working? — Hal Ellson, *The Golden Spike*, p. 22, 1952
- Sat around on our cans all evening, Brownie. — Jim Thompson, *The Nothing Man*, p. 209, 1954
- Hey motherfucker! / All you do is sit on your can / Get out in the streets and prove you're a man[.] — Lester Bangs, *Psychotic Reactions and Carburetor Dung*, p. 103, 1972
- Mr. Preston overheard him ask Miss Pliny how long she'd been "parking her pretty can at Regressive Plywood." — C.D. Payne, *Youth in Revolt*, p. 184, 1993

6 an imprecise amount of marijuana, usually one or two ounces *US, 1967*

Derived from the practice in the 1940s of selling marijuana in Prince Albert tobacco cans.

- We bought three cans of reefer for fifty dollars, and split the rest of the money. — Donald Goines, *Whoreson*, p. 36, 1972
- So frequently when you'd be going to cop a few joints or a can—a Prince Albert can of the best pot you ever smoked in your life[.] — Herbert Huncke, *Guilty of Everything*, p. 27, 1990

7 a car *US, 1970*

- — William D. Alsever, *Glossary for the Establishment and Other Uptight People*, p. 5, December 1970

8 a safe *US, 1949*

- — Vincent J. Monteleone, *Criminal Slang*, p. 42, 1949
- "He and two others planned a safe robbery with Decker opening the can while the others were lookouts or drove." — Mickey Spillane, *The Big Kill*, p. 22, 1951

▶ **in the can**

not trying to win *US, 1951*

- — David W. Maurer, *Argot of the Racetrack*, p. 37, 1951
- Somebody on the golf tour used to be a hustler who went in the can and intentionally lost a lot of amateur tournaments one time. — Dan Jenkins, *Dead Solid Perfect*, p. 47, 1986

can *verb*

to stop something, to cease something *US, 1906*

- "Let's just can the comedy and come on, huh?" said Grady. — Max Shulman, *Rally Round the Flag, Boys!*, p. 217, 1957
- Can that Uncle Tom crap. — Chester Himes, *The Real Cool Killers*, p. 99, 1959
- "Can the brochure, daddy," I said, surprising myself by the Fifties jargon that so amused Myron but rather repelled me. — Gore Vidal, *Myra Breckinridge*, p. 52, 1968
- RIGGS: Oh, brother. This is good. I like this. MURTAUGH: Can it, Martin. — *Lethal Weapon*, 1987

Canadian *noun*

a Jewish person *US, 1950*

- — Jack Lait and Lee Mortimer, *Chicago Confidential*, p. 301, 1950

Canadian bouncer *noun*

the central nervous system depressant Seconal™, manufactured in Canada *US, 1971*

- — Eugene Landy, *The Underground Dictionary*, p. 46, 1971
- — Jay Robert Nash, *Dictionary of Crime*, p. 55, 1992

Canadian passport *noun*

a hairstyle in which the hair is worn short at the front and long at the back *US, 2000*

Most commonly known as a **MULLET**.

- — Ben Sharpe, *Scooter Crazy*, p. 41, 2000
- — Don R. McCreary (Editor), *Dawg Speak*, 2001
- It's called the ape drape. The Tennessee top hat. The hockey head. The Kentucky waterfall. The Canadian passport. — *New York Times*, p. G11, 8th March 2001
- Connie Eble (Editor), *UNC-CH Campus Slang*, p. 4, Spring 2001

canary *noun*

1 a female singer *UK, 1886*

- — Arnold Shaw, *Lingo of Tin-Pan Alley*, p. 9, 1950
- But Jan Du Mond, a five-foot-three night club canary, pianist and composer, drives a cab by day. — Jack Lait and Lee Mortimer, *Washington Confidential*, p. 83, 1951
- [A] socially connected, prominently married carpet muncher with a yen for nightclub canaries was prime meat for the four-star Herald. — James Ellroy, *Hollywood Nocturnes*, p. 270, 1994
- At a time when it was hip to be cool and well-tailored, and female singers were still referred to as "songbirds" and "canaries," the Playboy Club became the most popular nightclub in town. — Kathryn Leigh Scott, *The Bunny Years*, p. 58, 1998

2 a police informer *US, 1929*

Canaries sing, as do informers.

- Jails are no sanctuaries for canaries. — Burton Turkus and Sid Feder, *Murder, Inc.*, p. 163, 1951
- "You know," Varga says very slowly, "a show-off is only a few steps away from being a canary." — Charles Perry, *Portrait of a Young Man Drowning*, p. 167, 1962
- Scott was carrying on like the MC in a lounge act, like here he is, the one and only made-guy canary in captivity. — Edwin Torres, *Carlito's Way*, p. 130, 1975

3 a person who is perceived to bring bad luck *US, 1974*

- [A]nybody who is a carrier of such disasters is known in Las Vegas as a "canary." The word canary is derived from the Yiddish word, kinnahora, which means evil eye. — Edward Lin, *Big Julie of Vegas*, p. 255, 1974

4 a capsule of pentobarbital sodium (trade name Nembutal™), a central nervous system depressant *US, 1973*

- — David W. Maurer and Victor Vogel, *Narcotics and Narcotic Addiction*, p. 394, 1973

canary *verb*

to inform to the police *US, 1958*

- He was going to canary and the pusher went around to jail and told him, "Don't talk." — Willard Motley, *Let No Man Write My Epitaph*, p. 381, 1958

cancel *verb*

to end a relationship *US, 2007*

- "I cancelled that nigga a long time ago." — Treasure E. Blue, *A Street Girl Named Desire*, p. 153, 2007

▶ **cancel someone's ticket**

to kill someone *US, 1970*

- If he uses a knife you use a gun and cancel his ticket then and there. — Joseph Wambaugh, *The New Centurions*, p. 11, 1970

cancelled stick *noun*

a tobacco cigarette that has been emptied of tobacco and refilled with marijuana *US, 1970*

- — *Mr.*, p. 8, April 1966: "The hippie's lexicon"
- — William D. Alsever, *Glossary for the Establishment and Other Uptight People*, p. 5, December 1970
- — Richard A. Spears, *The Slang and Jargon of Drugs and Drink*, p. 92, 1986

Cancer Alley *noun*

any area with high levels of environmental carcinogens *US, 1981*

- Similar threats exist in East St. Louis, in Louisiana's "Cancer Alley," on Navaho lands where uranium is mined, and in farmworker communities where laborers and their families are routinely poisoned by pesticides. — Robert D. Bullard and Benjamin Chavis, *Confronting Environmental Racism*, p. 4, 1993

cancer center *noun*

a cigar store *US, 1955*

- — *American Speech*, p. 302, December 1955: "Wayne University slang"

cancer stick *noun*

a cigarette *US, 1958*

- Dally searched his pocket for a cigarette, and finding none, said, "You gotta cancer stick, Johnny-cake?" — S.E. Hinton, *The Outsiders*, p. 71, 1967

- Later on she was lighting another cancer stick and I leaned over to get a light. — Babs Gonzales, *Movin' On Down De Line*, p. 67, 1975

- [Y]our pussy's been tampered with / Did you show him that new trick of how you can make it smoke a cancer stick? — Dr Dr, *Fuck You*, 2001

C and E *noun*

in craps, a bet on any craps and eleven *US, 1985*

- — Steve Kuriscak, *Casino Talk*, p. 9, 1985

C and H *noun*

cocaine and heroin *US, 1980*

A borrowing of a branded name for sugar; sometimes used with the sugar company's advertising slogan: "pure cane sugar from Hawaii."

- — Edith A. Folb, *runnin' down some lines*, p. 231, 1980

candlestick bird *nickname*

the Fairchild C-123 Assault Transport aircraft *US, 1990*

- These guys were pilots on C-123s, known as "Candle Stick" birds. — Tom Yarborough, *Da Nang Diary*, p. 175, 1990

can-do *adjective*

confident, optimistic *US, 1921*

- The Belgian battalion, for example, was attached to the U.S. 15th Infantry Regiment which proudly called itself the "Can Do" outfit. — Don Lawson, *The United States in the Korean War*, p. 24, 1964

candy *noun*

1 the female genitals *US, 2005*

- All the freaky things I fantasized about doing with a brother who was interested in licking my candy all night long. — Noire, *Candy Licker*, p. 136, 2005

2 any barbiturate capsule *US, 1969*

- — William D. Alsever, *Glossary for the Establishment and Other Uptight People*, p. 2, December 1970

- — Donald Wesson and David Smith, *Barbiturates*, p. 121, 1977

3 cocaine *US, 1931*

- Me he caught with some bad candy at a party years back[.] — Edwin Torres, *Carlito's Way*, p. 53, 1975

4 a sugar cube treated with LSD *US, 1972*

- — Helen Dahlskog (Editor), *A Dictionary of Contemporary and Colloquial Usage*, p. 12, 1972

5 inexpensive plastic or acrylic jewelry *US, 1949*

- — Vincent J. Monteleone, *Criminal Slang*, p. 42, 1949

- — *American Speech*, p. 96, May 1956: "Smugglers' argot in the Southwest"

6 cash *US, 2003*

- Candy, markers, ammo, liners, stocking stuffer, sweetener, garnish, and pledges are all terms for cash. — Henry Hill and Byron Schreckengost, *A Good Fella's Guide to New York*, p. 123, 2003

7 anything good or enjoyable *US, 1984*

- — Inez Cardozo-Freeman, *The Joint*, p. 487, 1984

8 a girl with extremely conservative sexual mores *US, 1961*

- — *Washington Post*, 23rd April 1961

candy *verb*

to enhance a marijuana cigarette with another drug *US, 1982*

- — Ernest L. Abel, *A Marijuana Dictionary*, p. 21, 1982

- — Jay Robert Nash, *Dictionary of Crime*, p. 56, 1992

candy-ass *noun*

a weak person *US, 1967*

- "A candy-ass is a—is a—a candy-ass," he explained. — Elaine Shepard, *The Doom Pussy*, p. 124, 1967

- Get yourselves squared away, candy-asses. — Darryl Ponicsan, *The Last Detail*, p. 102, 1970

- He (Nixon) said something to the effect, well, if Schultz thinks he's been put over there to be some sort of candy ass, he is mistaken. — *San Francisco Examiner*, p. 10, 25th July 1974

- There are places you can coach and get by, by being a candy ass (wimp). Buffalo is not one of those places. — *Buffalo (New York) News*, p. B1, 15th January 2004

candy-ass; candy-assed *adjective*

weak, ineffective, timid *US, 1952*

- I just couldn't see myself growing old and telling my children that during the war I'd been a member of such a candy-assed organization. — David H. Hackworth, *About Face*, p. 225, 1989

- — Michael Dalton Johnson, *Talking Trash with Redd Foxx*, p. 98, 1994

candy-bar punk; candy-bar fag *noun*

a male prisoner whose sexual favors are bought with purchases from the prison store *US, 1972*

- There are two classes of homos in here. You have what they call the "original" or "square" and you have what they call the "candy-bar punk["]. — Bruce Jackson, *In the Life*, p. 359, 1972

candycaine; candycane *noun*

cocaine *US, 1989*

Punning on the Christmas hard peppermint "candy cane" and "cocaine."

- — Ellen C. Bellone (Editor), *Dictionary of Slang*, p. 6, 1989

candy maker *noun*

a male homosexual who masturbates a partner to ejaculation and then licks and swallows the semen *US, 1964*

- — Roger Blake, *The American Dictionary of Sexual Terms*, p. 29, 1964

- — Dale Gordon, *The Dominion Sex Dictionary*, p. 40, 1967

candyman *noun*

a drug dealer, especially a cocaine dealer; a heavy cocaine user *US, 1969*

- Hear they had to bring the coke in a wheelbarrow. He's a real candy man, our boy Bobby Tex. — Edwin Torres, *Q & A*, p. 21, 1977

- Also there was Taffy Boyd, Helena's candy man, who'd come early in the day to ask why Pachoulo wouldn't extend Helena any more credit and was still hanging around. — Robert Campbell, *Juice*, p. 203, 1988

candy stick *noun*

a cigarette with a menthol filter *US, 1984*

- Look at that sissy, smokin' a candy stick, just like a woman. — Ken Weaver, *Texas Crude*, p. 106, 1984

candy store *noun*

a casino with rules that favor gamblers *US, 1991*

- — Michael Dalton, *Blackjack*, p. 35, 1991

candystore dice *noun*

mass-produced dice that are imperfect even when unaltered by a cheat *US, 1974*

- — Thomas L. Clark, *The Dictionary of Gambling and Gaming*, p. 219, 1987

candy wrapper *noun*

a hundred-dollar bill *US, 1983*

Probably because of its association with the snorting of cocaine, or "nose candy."

- — Thomas L. Clark, *The Dictionary of Gambling and Gaming*, p. 3435, 1987

cane *noun*

sugar *US, 1990*

- — Charles Shafer, *Folk Speech in Texas Prisons*, p. 200, 1990

can house *noun*

a brothel *US, 1906*

- The Roamer Inn was like a model of all the canhouses I ever saw around Chicago[.] — Mezz Mezzrow, *Really the Blues*, p. 22, 1946

- "Down by the railroad tracks and the flop houses and the can houses." — Willard Motley, *Knock on Any Door*, p. 77, 1947

canister *noun*

1 a jail or prison *US, 1952*

- More successful was Jack Black, whose thirty years as a burglar and robber netted him about $50,000 and a total of fifteen years in the canister. — Charles Hamilton, *Men of the Underworld*, p. 81, 1952

2 a safe *US, 1950*

- — Hyman E. Goldin et al., *Dictionary of American Underworld Lingo*, p. 40, 1950

canned *adjective*

recorded, repetitive *US, 1903*

- Mom gave him one of her canned high-volume diatribes. — C.D. Payne, *Youth in Revolt*, p. 5, 1993

canned goods *noun*

1 a virgin *US, 1967*

- — Dale Gordon, *The Dominion Sex Dictionary*, p. 40, 1967

- — Anon., *King Smut's Wet Dreams Interpreted*, 1978

2 a male who has never experienced passive anal sex *US, 1972*

- — Bruce Rodgers, *The Queens' Vernacular*, p. 21, 1972

canned heat *noun*

a gel formed with liquid ethanol and saturated calcium acet-ate solution; when ignited, the alcohol in the gel burns *US, 1950*

Used as a source of fuel in portable cooking stoves and as a source of alcohol by truly desperate derelicts.

- Dope is sold everywhere, as are denatured alcohol, bay rum, canned heat, fermented cider and anything else that will produce a jag. — Jack Lait and Lee Mortimer, *Chicago Confidential*, p. 60, 1950
- I was one of them, a guy who could talk knowingly of Four-Trey Whitey and the Half-a-Half Pint Kid, who knew how to filter canned heat through a handkerchief and rubbing alcohol through dry bread[.] — Jim Thompson, *Roughneck*, p. 65, 1954
- He drank quarts of it a day. Any kind. Gallo, sneaky pete, the distillation of canned heat. — Clancy Sigal, *Going Away*, p. 238, 1961
- And the wino cringes from the canned-heat binges / And finds his grave in the snow. — Dennis Wepman et al., *The Life*, p. 80, 1976

cannibal *noun*

a person who performs oral sex *US, 1916*

- Head-hunters, cannibals and kid-fruits are fellators[.] — *New York Mattachine Newsletter*, p. 6, June 1961
- Two to one, he is a "Cannibal" who ate her before she ate him. — Robert deCoy, *The Nigger Bible*, p. 128, 1967
- — Clarence Major, *Dictionary of Afro-American Slang*, p. 34, 1970

cannon *noun*

1 a large handgun *US, 1846*

- When Diamond came back he had a pitchfork. But Legs had a cannon. — Jack Lait and Lee Mortimer, *New York Confidential*, p. 161, 1948
- If you do that, we can stow these damn cannons and arm bands in a locker. — Darryl Ponicsan, *The Last Detail*, p. 37, 1970
- About this time, four detectives come out of an unmarked car with their cannons out. — Edwin Torres, *Carlito's Way*, p. 73, 1975
- Listen, you motherfucker, you tried to kill me with a fucking cannon. — *Traffic*, 2000

2 a large surfboard designed for big-wave conditions *US, 1965*

- — John M. Kelly, *Surf and Sea*, p. 297, 1965

3 a muscular arm *US, 1989*

- — Ellen C. Bellone (Editor), *Dictionary of Slang*, p. 6, 1989

4 a pickpocket *US, 1909*

- Jake, a con man, a cannon or a fake of any kind / make a C or so, the day after tomorrow you serving time. — Bruce Jackson, *Get Your Ass in the Water and Swim Like Me*, p. 141, 1965
- A "cannon" with a tired horse face took the vacant stool on my right. — Iceberg Slim (Robert Beck), *Pimp*, p. 91, 1969
- The cannon is the guy who actually goes in the guy's pocket. — Leonard Shecter and William Phillips, *On the Pad*, p. 159, 1973

cannon *verb*

to pick pockets *US, 1960*

- "You're too small to cannon the street cars." — Nelson Algren, *The Neon Wilderness*, p. 101, 1960

cannonball *noun*

a dive in which the diver grips and tucks their knees against their chest to maximize the splash *US, 1949*

- But a cannonball is neither aesthetic nor much fun to watch. — Barnaby Conrad, *Fun While It Lasted*, p. 46, 1969

cannon-cocker *noun*

a member of an artillery unit *US, 1952*

- The brave cannon-cockers in LZ Falcon went without sleep for three days and nights to help keep us surrounded by a wall of steel. — Harold Moore, *We Were Soldiers Once ... And Young*, p. 105, 1992
- The efforts of the cannon cockers were rewarded. — Harold Coyle, *Team Yankee*, p. 94, 1997

canoe *verb*

(used of a marijuana cigarette) to burn only on the top *US, 1989*

- Masterrap, puffing on a cocaine-laced cigarette, complains to Charlie, "Hey, it's canoeing"—burning only on top so the unburnt paper looks like a canoe. — Terry Williams, *The Cocaine Kids*, p. 86, 1989

canoe inspection *noun*

a medical inspection of a woman's genitals for signs of a sexually transmitted disease *US, 1964*

- — Roger Blake, *The American Dictionary of Sexual Terms*, p. 30, 1964
- — Robert A. Wilson, *Playboy's Book of Forbidden Words*, p. 60, 1972

canoe-maker *noun*

a forensic pathologist *US, 1970*

From the image of the body on the autopsy table, opened up to resemble a canoe.

- [T]he old canoe maker at the autopsy today claimed she punctured the aorta with a three and a half inch blade. — Joseph Wambaugh, *The New Centurions*, p. 58, 1970

Canoe U *nickname*

the US Naval Academy at Annapolis *US, 1963*

The 1998 Naval Academy yearbook included a CD-ROM sup-plement entitled *Canoe U*, providing a virtual tour of the Naval Academy.

- "Yeah, well, Canoe U has always been a little bizarre in its nomenclature." — P.T. Deutermann, *Sweepers*, p. 102, 1998

can of gas *noun*

a small butane torch used in the preparation of crack cocaine *US, 1992*

- — Terry Williams, *Crackhouse*, p. 147, 1992

can of whip-ass; can of whup-ass *noun*

a notional repository for a physical beating *US, 1984*

- She started it back in the days when I, me, Billy Clyde Puckett, your basic all-pro immortal, was expected to go out there every Sunday and crack open a 220-pound can of whipass. — Dan Jenkins, *Life Its Ownself*, p. 15, 1984
- "I remember when we were losing at halftime (Cougar All-America guard Mike) Utley said to get out a can of whip ass," he said. — *Lewiston (Idaho) Morning Tribune*, p. 1C, 7th July 1991
- — Connie Eble (Editor), *UNC-CH Campus Slang*, p. 6, Spring 1994
- So go open a can of whup-ass on that little fuck, and get me his game! — Kevin Smith, *Jay and Silent Bob Strike Back*, p. 25, 2001

canonical *adjective*

in computing, in the usual and accepted form *US, 1981*

Literally, "according to religious law."

- — *CoEvolution Quarterly*, p. 27, Spring 1981
- — Eric S. Raymond, *The New Hacker's Dictionary*, p. 88, 1991

can opener *noun*

1 a bulldozer tank *US, 1986*

- — Ralph Zumbro, *Tank Sergeant*, p. 190, 1986: Glossary

2 a curved bar used by criminals to prize open a safe *US, 1949*

- — Vincent J. Monteleone, *Criminal Slang*, p. 42, 1949
- — Hyman E. Goldin et al., *Dictionary of American Underworld Lingo*, p. 40, 1950

can or no can

used for expressing the decision-making process used by a big-wave surfers *US, 1991*

- — Trevor Cralle, *The Surfin'ary*, p. 18, 1991

cans *noun*

the female breasts *US, 1959*

- — Collin Baker et al., *College Undergraduate Slang Study Conducted at Brown University*, p. 93, 1968
- Cans up to her chin and an ass like a brick shithouse. — Oscar Zeta Acosta, *The Autobiography of a Brown Buffalo*, p. 112, 1972
- What's your breast size? I know it sounds crazy but my grandmother told me as she breathed her last breath: "Only talk to ladies with huge cans." — Howard Stem, *Miss America*, 1995
- — Judi Sanders, *Da Bomb*, p. 3, 1997
- Campbell and her cans were invited to perform full time for a two-year stint as a favorite Baywatch balloon smuggler. — Mr. Skin, *Mr. Skin's Skincyclopedia*, p. 93, 2005

can shooter *noun*

a criminal who specializes in breaking into safes *US, 1949*

- — Vincent J. Monteleone, *Criminal Slang*, p. 42, 1949

cantaloupe *noun*

a misfit; an outcast *US, 1985*

- "Clyde"—a loser, a shmendrick. Also, "a cantaloupe." — *Washington Post*, p. B1, 17th January 1985

cantaloupes *noun*

large female breasts *US, 1964*

- One of the cantaloupes bounces higher than the other. — Jerome Charyn, *Once Upon a Droshky*, p. 71, 1964
- [H]e took 1 gander at those bouncing cantalopes and gave "Bebe" the Bye-Bye. — Leo Rosten, *Dear Herm*, p. 104, 1974

- I stopped right before I gathered both of her cantaloupes together to taste. — Franklin White, *Money for Good*, p. 181, 2007

canteen punk noun
a prisoner who engages in sexual acts for payment in goods bought at the prison canteen or shop *US, 1974*
- — Paul Glover, *Words from the House of the Dead*, 1974

can't-miss noun
in horse racing, a racehorse that is a sure thing to win a race to the extent that a sure thing is a sure thing *US, 1951*
- — David W. Maurer, *Argot of the Racetrack*, p. 18, 1951

can to can't
all day, from early morning (when you can just see) to late evening (when you can't see) *US, 1919*
- His aunt worked from can to can't, and by the time she got home at night she was too tired to bend over the scrub board to wash out some clothes for J.S. to wear every day. — H. Rap Brown, *Die Nigger Die!*, p. 20, 1969
- "He's trying to learn day trading now, sits as his laptop from can to can't." — Richard Price, *Samaritan*, p. 211, 2003

Canuck noun
a Canadian, especially a French-Canadian *US, 1835*
Insulting. Most likely to be heard in portions of the US bordering Canada. During the 1972 campaign for US President, a newspaper in New Hampshire printed an anonymous letter accusing candidate Senator Muskie of having used the term "Canuck" to describe the state's French-Canadian population. The sound and fury created by the accusation stunned Muskie, and by the time it was learned that the letter had been a concoction of President Nixon's election campaign the damage had been done.
- "For God's sake, isn't it enough that we've got a whole colony of Polacks and Canucks working in the mills without letting the Greeks in?" — Grace Metalious, *Peyton Place*, p. 136, 1956
- I am a Canuck. I could not speak English till I was 5 or 6[.] — Jack Kerouac, *The Subterraneans*, p. 3, 1958
- At a heated juncture, I made the unfortunate error of referring to their center as a "fucking Canuck." — Erich Segal, *Love Story*, p. 17, 1970
- Fucking Canucks. Worse than guineas. — Robert Campbell, *Juice*, p. 149, 1988

Canuck adjective
Canadian *US, 1955*
Insulting.
- Reassure Canuck painter too. — Jack Kerouac, *Letter to Allen Ginsberg*, 1st January 1955
- [A]nd then, hunch over, holding the money close to the glove-compartment light, to look at it. "What's this, all Cannuck?" "Most of it." "It's pretty but, shit, what's it worth?" — Elmore Leonard, *Killshot*, p. 31, 1989

can-up noun
a particularly bad fall while skiing *US, 1963*
- — *American Speech*, p. 205, October 1963: "The language of skiers"

canvasback noun
a boxer or fighter whose lack of skills leads him to find himself on his back *US, 1955*
- It's a train hijack, canvasback. — James Ellroy, *Hollywood Nocturnes*, p. 138, 1994

canyon noun
the vagina *US, 1980*
- — Edith A. Folb, *runnin' down some lines*, p. 231, 1980

canyon-dive noun
oral sex performed on a woman *US, 1980*
- — Edith A. Folb, *runnin' down some lines*, p. 231, 1980

cap noun
1 a capsule of drugs *US, 1929*
- Local street sales of narcotics are concentrated on Pennsylvania Avenue in the Negro district, where individual caps of heroin, morphine and reefers are available cheap. — Jack Lait and Lee Mortimer, *Washington Confidential*, p. 271, 1951
- Lots of jive and goofballs, maybe a couple caps of Horse. — George Mandel, *Flee the Angry Strangers*, p. 56, 1952

- M-a-a-n, I'm drug by that son of a bitch MacDoud with all his routines about how he ain't got enough money for one cap[.] — Jack Kerouac, *The Subterraneans*, p. 29, 1958
- We bought one cap and we split it, y'know. It was a giant cap, it was supposed to be five hundred grams, micrograms or something. — Leonard Wolfe (Editor), *Voices from the Love Generation*, p. 172, 1968

2 a bullet; a shot *US, 1925*
- But before he got within ten feet of the door / I dropped him with a cap from my Colt .44. — Dennis Wepman et al., *The Life*, p. 42, 1976

3 a decorative tooth cap *US, 2006*
- The teeth caps are alternately called grills, fronts, shines, plates, or caps, and these glittering decorative pieces are the latest hip-hop culture trend making its way into the mainstream. — *Boston Globe*, p. C1, 31st January 2006

4 a psychoactive mushroom *US, 1999*
Conventionally, the domed upper part of a mushroom; possibly an abbreviation of "liberty cap," the name given to psilocybin mushrooms.
- I took three, she ate the other twenty-two caps[.] — Eminem (Marshall Mathers), *My Fault*, 1999

5 the amount of marijuana that will fit into the plastic cap of a tube of lip gloss *US, 1989*
- — James Harris, *A Convict's Dictionary*, p. 29, 1989

6 used as a term of address for someone whose actions are provoking physical violence *US, 1982*
Hawaiian youth usage; an abbreviated form of "capillary."
- — Douglas Simonson, *Pidgin to da Max Hana Hou*, 1982

7 captain *US, 1759*
- The cap got all pissed off and had another shit fit, and we didn't get going again until after daybreak. — Larry Heinemann, *Paco's Story*, p. 22, 1990

8 in casino gambling, a chip of one denomination on top of a stack of chips of another denomination *US, 1991*
- — Michael Dalton, *Blackjack*, p. 35, 1991

cap verb
1 to package a drug in capsules *US, 1952*
- "We got a little cappin to do," Buster told the Dinch. — George Mandel, *Flee the Angry Strangers*, p. 248, 1952
- They cut it, cap it, and retail it at about a hundred percent profit. — John D. McDonald, *The Neon Jungle*, p. 61, 1953
- If you're a good capper and cap it yourself and sell part of it and use the rest yourself you can double your money. — Willard Motley, *Let No Man Write My Epitaph*, p. 122, 1958
- Clayton also taught me how to cap. — John Allen, *Assault with a Deadly Weapon*, p. 160, 1977

2 to shoot someone *US, 1970*
- They said he got capped by a junkie; shit, but didn't die. — Elmore Leonard, *Glitz*, p. 57, 1985

3 to insult someone in a competitive, quasi-friendly spirit; to outdo someone *US, 1944*
- "Sing it you sweet cow!" some fellow shouted from the table next to ours. The chick that was with him capped this with "Yeah baby, he can't help it, it's the way you do it." — Mezz Mezzrow, *Really the Blues*, p. 26, 1946
- I would remark to Jessie that I was ready to pimp, but she would only laugh and cap: "You think you know to talk slick, boy, but that ain't the key." — Donald Goines, *Whoreson*, p. 37, 1972
- There are many different terms for playing the dozens, including "bagging, capping, cracking, dissing, hiking, joning, ranking, ribbing, serving, signifying, slipping, sounding and snapping." — James Haskins, *The Story of Hip-Hop*, p. 54, 2000

4 to steer business to someone *US, 1973*
- Herb was fired for capping for a bail bondsman and had a nice thing going until they caught him. — Joseph Wambaugh, *The Blue Knight*, p. 123, 1973

5 in casino gambling, to add to an existing bet, usually illegally *US, 1980*
- — Lee Solkey, *Dummy Up and Deal*, p. 109, 1980

Cape Cod turkey noun
salt cod *US, 1865*
- Along Cape Cod Bay in Massachusetts cod fish is sometimes called Cape Cod Turkey — George Earlie Shankle, *American Nicknames*, p. 74, 1955
- — Charles F. Haywood, *Yankee Dictionary*, p. 24, 1963

caper *noun*

a criminal undertaking, especially a swindle or theft *US, 1925*

- It always seems that way when a guy's going on a caper. — Jim Thompson, *A Swell-Looking Babe*, p. 79, 1954
- He was always and forever cooking up deals, figuring the angles, plotting a caper, with a mournful, long-faced and unhappy expression as though he knew someone would catch him. — Clancy Sigal, *Going Away*, p. 355, 1961
- No more chickenshit two- and three-grand capers that cost two or three years. — Gerald Petievich, *Money Men*, p. 85, 1981
- Finally, someone comes up with the idea, wait a minute, while we were planning this caper, all we did was sit around and tell fucking jokes. — *Reservoir Dogs*, 1992

caper *verb*

to commit a criminal undertaking, especially a swindle or theft *US, 1976*

- During the years of his cruising around the country, Leo would caper and regularly send money through Joanie to his attorney[.] — Emmett Grogan, *Final Score*, p. 22, 1976
- Harold and Joe had capered together on the streets, though petty boosting only[.] — Seth Morgan, *Homeboy*, p. 89, 1990

caper car *noun*

a car used for a crime and then abandoned *US, 1981*

- It's a caper car, for sure. — Gerald Petievich, *Money Men*, p. 99, 1981

capisce?; capeesh?

do you understand? *US, 1977*

Thanks to gangster films and television programs, almost always a blatant affectation with an organized, Sicilian ring to it.

- Mr. Collucci has got my ass dragging with all our troubles with Tat Taylor's Warriors and other serious trouble I can't talk about. Capisce? — Iceberg Slim (Robert Beck), *Death Wish*, p. 12, 1977
- In this enterprise you do as I say. Obey me, and you'll escape unscathed. Capeesh? — Jonathan Gash, *The Ten Word Game*, p. 74, 2003
- As anyone who's seen the mob melodrama knows, loose lips are likely to result in a major loss of blood, capisce? — *The News-Press (Fort Myers, Florida)*, p. 8E, 6th February 2004

capital *adjective*

attractive, good-looking *US, 2001*

- — Don R. McCreary (Editor), *Dawg Speak*, 2001

capital prize *noun*

a sexually transmitted infection *US, 1948*

- Nitti, like Capone, had picked up in his travels the occupational malady of the underworld euphemistically known as the capital prize, or big casino. — *San Francisco Call-Bulletin*, p. 14, 24th February 1948

cap man *noun*

a confederate in a swindle *US, 1971*

- Jackson's cap man (confederate) heckled the mark to blow close to a C note to Jackson with such violent enthusiasm that the mark woke up. — Iceberg Slim (Robert Beck), *The Naked Soul of Iceberg Slim*, p. 123, 1971

capo *noun*

a leader of a Mafia organization *US, 1952*

- That was an operation for any local capo, not the boss. — Mickey Spillane, *Last Cop Out*, p. 114, 1972

capon *noun*

an effeminate or homosexual male *US, 1945*

- — Lou Shelly, *Hepcats Jive Talk Dictionary*, p. 8, 1945

cap on *verb*

to look at someone or something *US, 1971*

- — Eugene Landy, *The Underground Dictionary*, p. 46, 1971

capper *noun*

1 a clincher; something that beats all others *UK, 1960*

- — Robert S. Gold, *A Jazz Lexicon*, p. 48, 1964
- You know, like the capper on a bad fuckin' day. — Richard Price, *Clockers*, p. 381, 1992

2 in a drug-selling enterprise, a person who fills capsules with a drug *US, 1958*

- If you're a good capper and cap it yourself and sell part of it and use the rest yourself you can double your money. — Willard Motley, *Let No Man Write My Epitaph*, p. 122, 1958

3 in a confidence swindle, a person who lures the victim into the swindle *US, 1753*

From the verb CAP.

- "I understand you guys are looking for a capper to rope a mark," she said as she hugged John, but only looked over at Beano. — Stephen Cannell, *King Con*, p. 138, 1997

capsule con *noun*

a prisoner convicted on drug charges *US, 1970*

- To me, he didn't look like a capsule con. — Red Rudensky, *The Gonif*, p. 17, 1970

Captain Hicks *noun*

in craps, the number six *US, 1941*

- — Vincent J. Monteleone, *Criminal Slang*, p. 44, 1949
- — Thomas L. Clark, *The Dictionary of Gambling and Gaming*, p. 36, 1987

captain of the head *noun*

an orderly assigned to latrine duty *US, 1947*

- — *American Speech*, p. 54, February 1947: "Pacific War language"

captain's man *noun*

a police officer designated to pick up bribes from criminals for his superior officers *US, 1972*

- Precinct commanders who received graft almost always designated a patrolman, "the captain's man," to make their pickups[.] — *The Knapp Commission Report on Police Corruption*, p. 76, 1972

capun *noun*

capital punishment *US, 1992*

- — William K. Bentley and James M. Corbett, *Prison Slang*, p. 104, 1992

cap work *noun*

the alteration of dice for cheating by making them resilient on certain surfaces, which makes them more likely to bounce off the altered sides *US, 1950*

- — *The Annals of the American Academy of Political and Social Sciences*, p. 122, May 1950

car *noun*

1 a clique of prisoners *US, 1989*

- — James Harris, *A Convict's Dictionary*, p. 29, 1989
- "We the L.A. Crip car, cuz. You wanta get in the car?" — Bob Sipchen, *Baby Insane and the Buddha*, p. 183, 1993
- He takes care of the Car's laundry and runs contraband from one cellblock to another. — Jimmy Lerner, *You Got Nothing Coming*, p. 216, 2002

2 a radio *US, 2002*

- — Gary K. Farlow, *Prison-ese*, p. 10, 2002

caramel *adjective*

mixed race *US, 1994*

- I noticed a lot of Jungle Fever action, with people describing themselves as "vanilla" or "chocolate" or "caramel." — Anka Radakovich, *The Wild Girls Club*, p. 43, 1994

carbolic dip *noun*

the bath or shower with carbolic dip given to prisoners when they arrive at a prison *US, 1950*

- — Hyman E. Goldin et al., *Dictionary of American Underworld Lingo*, p. 40, 1950

carbos *noun*

carbohydrates *US, 1977*

- She knew she shouldn't be munching out on carbos like this; substitute gratification wasn't the answer. — Cyra McFadden, *The Serial*, p. 87, 1977
- Three days before the Ironman "I ate carbos. Bread. Spaghetti. Anything." — *Washington Post*, p. E1, 3rd November 1982

carburetor *noun*

a tube with holes used for smoking marijuana; a hole that is designed to let air into a pipe used for smoking marijuana *US, 1976*

As its automotive namesake forces a mixture of fuel and oxygen into an engine, the marijuana-related carburetor forces a mixture of marijuana smoke and air into the smoker's lungs.

- — *High Times*, May 1976

car clout *noun*

a thief who breaks into and steals the contents of cars *US, 1962*

- — *American Speech*, p. 267, December 1962: "The language of traffic policemen"

card *verb*
to ask someone for proof of age before selling or serving them alcohol *US, 1975*
- — Sue Black, *The Totally Awesome Val Guide*, p. 21, 1982
- Whoa, he didn't even card us. — *Bill and Ted's Excellent Adventure*, 1989
- I never get carded either, have to show any proof. — Elmore Leonard, *Maximum Bob*, p. 3, 1991

card-carrying *adjective*
devout, dedicated *US, 1927*
First used in the late 1940s to describe fervent leftists in the US as "card-carrying Communists," the term was given new life in 1988 when Democratic presidential candidate Michael Dukakis described himself as a "card-carrying member of the American Civil Liberties Union."
- Donald, you are a real card-carrying cunt. — Mart Crowley, *The Boys in the Band*, p. 42, 1968
- But people in politics remembered the Communist history of the word and were careful not to apply it to a left-leaning noun. A card-carrying hawk offended nobody, but a card-carrying dove was an insult. — *The New York Times Magazine*, p. 20, 18th September 1988
- They pursued liberals, pinkos and others they suspected of being card-carrying commies[.] — *The Chicago Tribune*, p. C3, 30th September 1988
- Only a card-carrying shithead would show his face at a nudie joint in an election year. — Carl Hiaasen, *Strip Tease*, p. 11, 1993

cardenales *noun*
barbiturates *US, 1997*
From the Spanish for "cardinal" (a red bird).
- — *Providence (Rhode Island) Journal-Bulletin*, p. 6B, 4th August 1997

card mob *noun*
two or more card cheats working together *US, 1979*
- — John Scarne, *Scarne's Guide to Modern Poker*, p. 274, 1979

cards speak *noun*
in high-low poker, the rule that players need not declare whether they are playing for a low or high hand *US, 1996*
- — Peter O. Steiner, *Thursday Night Poker*, p. 409, 1996

card surfing *noun*
a criminal act in which a criminal closely observes a person using an automatic cash machine (by looking over his or her shoulder) and notes the personal identity number that is entered on the keypad *US, 1992*
Also known as "shoulder surfing."
- Mostly it starts with what is called "shoulder surfing." While you're holding your credit card at a pay phone, especially in a large public area, people can stand at your shoulder and get your card number. — *Atlanta Journal and Constitution*, p. H10, 10th May 1992
- In fact, "shoulder surfing" is an outdated, low-tech approach. Thieves no longer need to steal a debit card to gain access to a bank account through an ATM. They simply make the cards themselves. — *Baltimore Sun*, 15th April 2003

CARE package *noun*
a box of treats and/or necessities, sent to someone away from home with the hope of cheering them up *US, 1962*
Suggested by CARE packages sent by the United Nations.
- [H]e paid the priest for the funeral, arranged a CARE package for Jack in the Sierra (Hersheys and khaki socks)[.] — Richard Farina, *Been Down So Long*, p. 256, 1966
- — *Current Slang*, p. 8, Fall 1967
- "Motherfuck," he said, coming back. "No care package." — William Pelfrey, *The Big V*, p. 58, 1972
- He loves to eat, so we feed him from our care packages. — Ernest Spencer, *Welcome to Vietnam, Macho Man*, p. 42, 1987

careware *noun*
computer software offered free by its developer, with the request that the user make a contribution to a charity in place of paying a fee for the software *US, 1991*
- — Eric S. Raymond, *The New Hacker's Dictionary*, p. 89, 1991

carga *noun*
heroin *US, 1968*
Border Spanish used in English conversation by Mexican-Americans.

- Depending on who is listening, heroin can be referred to as carga (heroin), la chiva (the thing), or la madre (the mother). — George R. Alvarez, *Semiotic Dynamics of an Ethnic-American Sub-Cultural Group*, p. 4, 1965
- — *Current Slang*, p. 14, Fall 1968
- [Y]ou take your first hit of carga before you get laid. — Oscar Zeta Acosta, *The Revolt of the Cockroach People*, p. 90, 1973
- — Dagoberto Fuentes and Jose Lopez, *Barrio Language Dictionary*, p. 29, 1974

carhop *noun*
1 an employee in a drive-in restaurant who serves customers in their cars *US, 1923*
- I drove on past the gaudy neons and the false fronts behind them, the sleazy hamburger joints that look like palaces under the colors, the circular drive-ins as gay as circuses with the chipper hard-eyed car-hops[.] — Raymond Chandler, *The Little Sister*, p. 79, 1949
- [A] fancy dog palace sprawled along the highway with tables inside and out, car-hop service and a small bar if you wanted one for the road. — Mickey Spillane, *The Long Wait*, p. 120, 1951
- When he got his discharge papers he made tracks for Laguna Beach, where he landed a job as a carhop in a drive-in beanery. — Bernard Wolfe, *The Late Risers*, p. 159, 1954
- "And it's easier than being a carhop." — Madam Sherry, *Pleasure Was My Business*, p. 15, 1963
- It was a big year for a drive-in restaurant carhop. — Merle Haggard, *The Way It Was in '51*, 1975
- They don't have carhops there, they have a radio speaker into which you call your order. — Mort Sahl, *Heartland*, p. 61, 1976
- Son of a carhop in an all-night dive. — Rodney Crowell, *Ain't Livin' Long Like This*, 1978

2 a girl who chooses partners on the basis of their car *US, 1995*
- — Bill Valentine, *Gang Intelligence Manual*, p. 75, 1995

carnal *noun*
among Mexican-Americans, a very close male friend *US, 1950*
Border Spanish used in English conversation by Mexican-Americans.
- — George Carpenter Baker, *Pachuco*, p. 41, January 1950
- — Dagoberto Fuentes, *Barrio Language Dictionary*, p. 29, 1974
- [T]hey automatically became members of La Eme, the so-called Mexican Mafia, and were now sworn carnales, the Hispanic term for homeboys. — Seth Morgan, *Homeboy*, p. 176, 1990
- A carnal had to be prepared to fight at all times. — Bill Valentine, *Gangs and Their Tattoos*, p. 33, 2000

carnation *noun*
used as a humorous substitute for "damnation" *US, 1974*
- "Why in carnation is Hermie Klitcher writing me?" — Leo Rosten, *Dear Herm*, p. 2, 1974

carnival croquet *noun*
the shell game *US, 1966*
- Here we are, ladies and gentlemen! Carnival croquet, the preacher's pastime. — Robert Edmond Alter, *Carny Kill*, p. 34, 1966

carnival louse *noun*
a person who follows a carnival from town to town and associates with carnival employees, but is not one himself *US, 1981*
- — Don Wilmeth, *The Language of American Popular Entertainment*, p. 44, 1981

carny *noun*
any person employed by or associated with a traveling carnival *US, 1939*
- Itinerant short con and carny hype men have burned down the croakers of Texas. — William Burroughs, *Naked Lunch*, p. 13, 1957
- — *American Speech*, p. 279, December 1966: "More carnie talk from the West Coast"
- This girl, I think the most important thing in her background was that her family were carnies. — Bruce Jackson, *In the Life*, p. 196, 1972
- Trailers were a carny status symbol. — Peter Fenton, *Eyeing the Flash*, p. 111, 2005

carny Bible *noun*
the *Amusement Business* magazine *US, 1985*
- The *Amusement Business* magazine is such an integral tool to a carny that it is referred to as the "Carny Bible." — Gene Sorrows, *All About Carnivals*, p. 5, 1985

carny divorce *noun*

an arrangement in which a man and woman who are living together without benefit of a wedding end their relationship, often consisting of one ride backward around on a ferris wheel *US, 1985*

- — Gene Sorrows, *All About Carnivals*, p. 12, 1985

carny's Christmas *noun*

Labor Day *US, 1981*

- — Don Wilmeth, *The Language of American Popular Entertainment*, p. 45, 1981

carny wedding *noun*

an arrangement in which a man and woman live together without benefit of a wedding, often consisting of one ride around on a ferris wheel *US, 1980*

- — Joe McKennon, *Circus Lingo*, p. 23, 1980
- — Gene Sorrows, *All About Carnivals*, p. 12, 1985

Carolina *noun*

in craps, a nine *US, 1950*

- — Thomas L. Clark, *The Dictionary of Gambling and Gaming*, p. 37, 1987

Carolina pancake *noun*

a mixture of lye and bacon fat or Crisco™, heated and thrown at someone with the intent of burning them badly *US, 1985*

- What happened was that this guy was involved in a family fight and some cops showed up. He had made a Carolina pancake. — Mark Baker, *Cops*, p. 287, 1985

carp *noun*

1 anchovies as a pizza topping *US, 1996*

- — *Maledicta*, p. 99, 1996: "Domino's pizza jargon"

2 a black prisoner *US, 1989*

- — James Harris, *A Convict's Dictionary*, p. 29, 1989

carpenter *noun*

an orthopedist *US, 1994*

- — Sally Williams, *"Strong" Words*, p. 136, 1994

carpenter's dream *noun*

a flat-chested woman *US, 1974*

- Natalie Wood, a carpenter's dream. "Flat as a board an' easy to screw." — Richard Price, *The Wanderers*, p. 27, 1974
- — Michael Dalton Johnson, *Talking Trash with Redd Foxx*, p. 79, 1994

carpet and drapes that match

applied to a person, usually a woman, whose hair is neither bleached nor dyed *US, 1999*

A jocular suggestion that the hair on the head is of the same natural shade as the pubic hair.

- Gwen Stefani's wild pink hair. "Does the carpet match the drapes? Heh, heh, heh." — *OC (Orange County, California) Weekly*, p. 6, 22nd October 1999
- She then described how she and a friend discuss whether another woman's hair color is truly natural. "What do you think: Does the carpet match the drapes?" she said with a cocked eyebrow. — *Marion (Ohio) Star*, p. 1A, 17th November 2003
- Annette indulged in more bed-top squirming, was carried like a sack of stripped potatoes, posed totally reviewed from the standing rear, and dared to reveal that the carpet did not match the drapes. — Mr. Skin, *Mr. Skin's Skincyclopedia*, p. 57, 2005

carpetbagger *noun*

a person who interferes in local politics without being a true part of the local community *US, 1868*

- A fantastic notion to turn back time, to drive out the carpetbaggers, to reclaim the land by painting it as treacherous and uninhabitable. — Carl Hiaasen, *Tourist Season*, p. 159, 1986

carpet burger *noun*

oral sex performed on a woman *US, 2001*

- — Pamela Munro, *U.C.L.A. Slang*, p. 52, 2001

carpet burn *noun*

a rawness of the skin due to frictional contact with a carpet *US, 1986*

On the model of "rope-burn." Tends to be used mainly of knees and elbows and generally in the context of wounds received in the course of unconventionally located love-making.

- No fight. No shoving. Not so much as a carpet burn. — *Los Angeles Times*, p. 1 (Part 6), 15th August 1986

carpet game *noun*

a swindle in which the swindler holds and then steals the wallet of a customer going to see a nonexistent prostitute *US, 1967*

- He settled back and found himself listening to Henry Jackson describing his arrest for something he called "carpet game." — Malcolm Braly, *On the Yard*, p. 24, 1967

carpet joint *noun*

a fancy, high-class casino *US, 1961*

- [S]etting up shop in the various "carpet" joints on the Strip and "sawdust" joints downtown. — Ovid Demaris, *The Last Mafioso*, p. 57, 1981
- And he saw the "carpet joint" for what it was—an institution designed with neither windows, doors, chairs, nor wall clocks in order to mesmerize the tourists therein trapped into losing track of time and place as they squandered money. — Gerald Petievich, *Shakedown*, p. 64, 1988
- I used ta only work carpet joints 'cause the ritzy casinos didn't float the dice. — Stephen Cannell, *Big Con*, p. 215, 1997

carpet muncher *noun*

a cunnilinguist; hence, and especially, a lesbian *US, 1994*

- [A] socially connected, prominently married carpet muncher with a yen for nightclub canaries was prime meat for the four-star Herald. — James Ellroy, *Hollywood Nocturnes*, p. 270, 1994
- Lesbians and straight women are insulted as "carpet-munchers." — *New York Post*, p. 18, 13th February 1999

carpet slashing *noun*

a dance party *US, 1947*

From the more common CUT A RUG.

- One night at a carpet slashing Romeo got a gander at Julie. — Harry Haenigsen, *Jive's Like That*, 1947

Carrie; Carrie Nation; Carry; Carry Nation *noun*

cocaine *US, 1993*

- — *American Speech*, p. 86, May 1955: "Narcotic argot along the Mexican border"
- — Peter Johnson, *Dictionary of Street Alcohol and Drug Terms*, 1993

carrier pigeon *noun*

a messenger or courier *US, 1933*

- We relied on "carrier pigeons"—other Korean agents who would take messages back and forth. Damnably dangerous work but necessary. — Joseph C. Goulden, *Korea*, p. 470, 1982

carrot eater; carrot snapper *noun*

a Mormon *US, 1968*

Offensive.

- In and around the state of Utah, Mormons have been called carrot-eaters or carrot-snappers. — Irving Lewis Allen, *Unkind Words*, p. 50, 1990

carrot-top *noun*

a red-headed person *US, 1889*

- Arthur Godfrey is going to have the whole Buckeye State after his carrot top for what he did to Miss Ohio last night. — *San Francisco News*, p. 12, 6th November 1956
- Another carrot-top had been dead for over a year. — Gerald Petievich, *Money Men*, p. 97, 1981
- If only the carrottop kook were hunkered beside him on the grass. — Seth Morgan, *Homeboy*, p. 190, 1990

carrot-topped *adjective*

redheaded *US, 1899*

- [S]he's particularly tasty in Please Don't Eat My Mother (1972), in which just before her carrot-topped deliciousness gets fed to a giant flesh-eating plant, she provides an up-close organic study of her pink-tipped booby bulbs[.] — Mr. Skin, *Mr. Skin's Skincyclopedia*, p. 191, 2005

carry *noun*

any victim of a crime who must be taken from the scene by stretcher *US, 1958*

- — *New York Times Magazine*, p. 87, 16th March 1958

carry *verb*

1 to carry a firearm *US, 1971*

- I'd get three Hail Marys and the priest'd ask me confidentially if I could get him something light he could carry under his coat. — George V. Higgins, *The Friends of Eddie Doyle*, p. 7, 1971

- Turn around a lift your tail. All right, you ain' carryin'. — Robert Campbell, *In La-La Land We Trust*, p. 173, 1986

2 to lead or be in charge of something *US, 1972*
- — Bruce Jackson, *Outside the Law*, p. 56, 1972

▶ **carry it to the door**
to serve all of a prison sentence *US, 2002*
- — Gary K. Farlow, *Prison-ese*, p. 11, 2002

▶ **carry someone's bags**
to be romantically involved with someone *US, 1973*
- — Sherman Louis Sergel, *The Language of Show Biz*, p. 107, 1973

▶ **carry the banner**
to stay up all night *US, 1947*
- "Are you carrying the banner too, kid?" When Nick looked puzzled, he said, explaining, "Sitting up all night." — Willard Motley, *Knock on Any Door*, p. 144, 1947
- — Joe McKennon, *Circus Lingo*, p. 23, 1980

▶ **carry the bug**
in circus usage, to work as a night watchman *US, 1981*
From BUG (a flashlight).
- — Don Wilmeth, *The Language of American Popular Entertainment*, p. 46, 1981

▶ **carry the mail**
to commit a murder for hire *US, 1971*
- I hear they used to call up from Providence whenever they had a particularly bad piece of work and get ahold of Artie Van to carry the mail. — George V. Higgins, *The Friends of Eddie Doyle*, p. 101, 1971

▶ **carry the silks**
in horse racing, to race for a particular owner *US, 1951*
- — David W. Maurer, *Argot of the Racetrack*, p. 18, 1951

▶ **carry the stick**
to live without a fixed abode; to live in someone else's room *US, 1971*
- "Anybody that don't have a room of their own and bunks in with somebody else for free is carrying a stick, just like a tramp." — Robert Deane Pharr, *S.R.O.*, p. 181, 1971
- Carrying the stick means not having a fixed address. — Burgess Laughlin, *Job Opportunities in the Black Market*, pp. 13–2, 1978

▶ **carry the target**
in horse racing, to run in the last position for an entire race *US, 1976*
- — Tom Ainslie, *Ainslie's Complete Guide to Thoroughbred Racing*, p. 329, 1976

carry; carry along *verb*
in professional wrestling, to try to make your opponent look like they are putting up a good fight *US, 1957*
- When one man has the ability to knock the other off in a hurry, he is asked to "carry along" the other fellow for a certain length of time to give the fans their money's worth. — Helen Giblo, *Footlights, Fistfights and Femmes*, p. 241, 1957

carry-away *noun*
a robbery in which a safe is taken and opened at leisure away from the crime scene *US, 1958*
- — Jack Webb, *The Badge*, p. 220, 1958

carry day *noun*
in television and movie making, a day in which the cast and crew are paid but do not have to work *US, 1990*
- — Ralph S. Singleton, *Filmmaker's Dictionary*, p. 28, 1990

carry on *verb*
to act in an ostentatiously effeminate manner in public *US, 1963*
- — Donald Webster Cory and John P. LeRoy, *The Homosexual and His Society*, p. 262, 1963: "A lexicon of homosexual slang"

Carter's Little Liver Pills *noun*
any central nervous system stimulant *US, 1976*
- — Elementary Electronics, *Dictionary of CB Lingo*, p. 56, 1976

carton-pusher *noun*
a person who sells cigarettes that have been stolen or smuggled from a state with lower taxes *US, 1978*
- The "carton pusher" is the other kind of retailer. He attracts customers by selling below the price for legal cigarettes. — Burgess Laughlin, *Job Opportunities in the Black Market*, pp. 10–9, 1978

car trick *noun*
an act of sex between a prostitute and customer in a car *US, 1968*
- Sue never let Sadie have another room—to pay her money out finished their relationship. Now most of Sadie's tricks were car tricks. — Nathan Heard, *Howard Street*, 1968

cartwheel *noun*
1 a feigned drug withdrawal spasm *US, 1936*
- A drug addict's life is dedicated to cheating, lying, conniving, and "conning" to obtain illicit drugs. It's an obsession. And they'll go to any length to achieve their purpose. They'll pull a "Brody" or "Cartwheel" (feigned spasms) to elicit sympathy. — *San Francisco News*, p. 1, 5th December 1951

2 an amphetamine tablet *US, 1966*
- I asked what they were and somebody beside me said, "Cartwheels, man. Bennies. Eat some, they'll keep you going." — Hunter S. Thompson, *Hell's Angels*, p. 216, 1966
- — Donald Louria, *The Drug Scene*, p. 189, 1971
- Army officers pass out "cartwheels"—20-milligram dextroamphetamine pills—to keep their men alert and moving on patrol duty. — *The San Francisco Chronicle*, p. 12, 24th June 1971

3 a silver dollar piece *US, 1949*
- — Vincent J. Monteleone, *Criminal Slang*, p. 44, 1949
- — Steve Kuriscak, *Casino Talk*, p. 10, 1985

carve *verb*
1 in skateboarding, to take a turn sharply *US, 1976*
- — Albert Cassorla, *The Skateboarder's Bible*, p. 199, 1976
- Carve: To make a long, curving turn while skating. For old dudes. — Shelley Youngblut, *Way Inside ESPN's X Games*, p. 39, 1998

2 in surfing, to change the course of the surfboard by digging it into the water *US, 1980*
- — John Grissim, *Pure Stoke*, p. 156, 1980

3 in mountain biking, to travel at great speed around corners *US, 1996*
- I put a lot of weight on it and carve the turn. — *Mountain Bike Magazine's Complete Guide To Mountain Biking Skills*, p. 148, 1996

4 to outplay another musician in a competition of solos *US, 1970*
- — Clarence Major, *Dictionary of Afro-American Slang*, p. 35, 1970

▶ **carve some beef**
to grant sexual favors; to consent to sex *US, 2001*
- "So what's the deal, then? She carving you some beef?" Another gangbang sexual reference. — Stephen J. Cannell, *The Tin Collectors*, p. 34, 2001

▶ **carve someone's knob**
to make someone understand *US, 1953*
- — Lavada Durst, *The Jives of Dr. Hepcat*, p. 12, 1953

carved up *adjective*
(used of a bodybuilder) without fat *US, 1984*
- — *American Speech*, p. 198, Fall 1984: "The language of bodybuilding"

car wash *noun*
during the Vietnam war, an establishment in Vietnam where a man went for a haircut, bath, massage and sex *US, 1969*
- And finally the convoy would crank and crash past the strip of car-wash and hand-laundry whorehouses outside the Tay Ninh Base Camp gate, where the housecats got laid. — Larry Heinemann, *Close Quarters*, p. 95, 1977
- Some of us would sneak off to Tu Duc Phuc's #1 Souvenirs and Car Wash in town and get laid. — Larry Heinemann, *Paco's Story*, p. 116, 1990

casabas *noun*
the female breasts *US, 1970*
- What ever happened to comparing breasts to fruit—casabas, melons, peaches? [Letter to Editor] — *New York Times*, p. 20 (Section 6), 19th September 1993
- Kelly Bundy toplessly tongue-kisses a dude whose damn hands cup her naked casabas and thereby conceal them from the rest of us — Mr. Skin, *Mr. Skin's Skincyclopedia*, p. 23, 2005

case *noun*
1 in card games, the fourth and remaining card when the three other cards of that value have been played *US, 1949*

- [T]hey took the 52–1 chance without hesitation and went for the case king as if it were a hope of heaven. — Nelson Algren, *The Man with the Golden Arm*, p. 249, 1949

2 a patient with a sexually transmitted infection *US, 1994*
  - — Sally Williams, *"Strong" Words*, p. 136, 1994

▸ **get off my case**
  leave me alone! *US, 1970*
  - "Get off my case, will you?" he said. — Frank Bonham, *Viva Chicano*, p. 126, 1970
  - — Eugene Landy, *Underground Dictionary*, p. 88, 1971
  - "It's Michael's," she said. "Anita's new old man. And get off my case." — Cyra McFadden, *The Serial*, p. 32, 1977

case *verb*
  1 to look over a place or person, especially in anticipation of criminal activity *US, 1914*
  - [A]nd probably was frightened either for the idea I'd bust right in and pull a holdup on the spot, or was merely casing for later. — Jack Kerouac, *Letter to Neal Cassady*, p. 277, 3rd January 1951
  - Bud, after critically if surreptitiously "casing" the boy, decided to have a try at examining Sam. — Arthur V. Huffman, *New York Mattachine Newsletter*, p. 6, July 1961
  - Another principal need is someone able to "case" these places' physical layouts—to determine means of entry, the best getaway routes, and so forth. — Malcolm X and Alex Haley, *The Autobiography of Malcolm X*, p. 140, 1964
  - I went out and cruised around to case the city. — Iceberg Slim (Robert Beck), *Pimp*, p. 91, 1969

2 to tease someone, to scold someone *US, 1971*
  - — Hermese E. Roberts, *The Third Ear*, 1971

case game *noun*
  in pool, a situation in which each player can win with their next shot *US, 1985*
  - — Mike Shamos, *The Illustrated Encyclopedia of Billiards*, p. 42, 1993

case note *noun*
  1 a one-dollar bill *US, 1962*
  - — Joseph E. Ragen and Charles Finston, *Inside the World's Toughest Prison*, p. 794, 1962
  2 a gambler's last money *US, 1962*
  - — Frank Garcia, *Marked Cards and Loaded Dice*, p. 261, 1962

case of the ass *noun*
  anger; frustration *US, 1968*
  Vietnam war usage.
  - — Carl Fleischhauer, *A Glossary of Army Slang*, p. 8, 1968
  - "That kind of stuff really gave us a case of the ass about Colonel Lucas." — Keith Nolan, *Ripcord*, p. 126, 2000

case of the jaws *noun*
  a harsh reprimand *US, 1968*
  - — Carl Fleischhauer, *A Glossary of Army Slang*, p. 27, 1968

case out *verb*
  to engage in sexual foreplay *US, 1963*
  - — *American Speech*, p. 273, December 1963: "American Indian student slang"

caser *noun*
  1 a skilled card-counter in blackjack *US, 1983*
  - A good caser can track every card played in a six-deck shoe. — Thomas L. Clark, *The Dictionary of Gambling and Gaming*, p. 38, 1987
  2 in poker, the last card in a particular rank or suit in a deal *US, 1963*
  A term borrowed from the card game of faro.
  - — Irwin Steig, *Common Sense in Poker*, p. 183, 1963

Casey Jones *noun*
  1 in poker, a player who draws the last card of a rank, the case card *US, 1988*
  John Luther "Casey" Jones (1864–1900) was an American locomotive engineer whose death in a train accident made him a legend celebrated in ballad and song.
  - — George Percy, *The Language of Poker*, p. 17, 1988
  2 in pool, a case game (one that either player can win with their next shot) *US, 1993*
  - — Mike Shamos, *The Illustrated Encyclopedia of Billiards*, p. 42, 1993

cash *verb*
  1 to finish consuming something *US, 2001*
  Usage is in the context of drug or alcohol consumption.
  - — Don R. McCreary (Editor), *Dawg Speak*, 2001
  2 to pass counterfeit money *US, 1985*
  - "Before big-money holidays like Easter and Mother's Day, instead of going to school I'd go 'cashing' with Johnny Mazzolla." — Nicholas Pileggi, *Wise Guy*, p. 18, 1985

cash cow *noun*
  any business or business sector that provides a steady cash flow *US, 1972*
  - The scrap-heaps of business are littered with concepts which went—to use the Boston Group matrix—from being question marks to dogs, without the intervening periods of star and cash cow status. — Fiona Czerniawska, *Corporate-Speak*, p. 224, 1997

cashed *adjective*
  completely consumed, empty *US, 1997*
  - — Vann Wesson, *Generation X Field Guide and Lexicon*, p. 34, 1997
  - The keg was cashed at 10 o'clock so we decided to go uptown earlier than usual. — Connie Eble (Editor), *UNC-CH Campus Slang*, p. 1, Spring 2001

cashew *noun*
  a psychiatric patient *US, 1994*
  - — Sally Williams, *"Strong" Words*, p. 136, 1994

cash in *verb*
  to die *US, 1891*
  A shortened form of "cash in your chips."
  - She must have died. She must have cashed in. — Harry J. Anslinger, *The Murderers*, p. 175, 1961
  - "You got boo-koo [many] years before you cash in," Young Joe whispers. — Iceberg Slim (Robert Beck), *Doom Fox*, p. 135, 1978

cashola *noun*
  money *US, 1977*
  - This is just from ticket sales, not concessions, and still you're talking three hundred and forty thousand. Cash-ola. — Carl Hiaasen, *Native Tongue*, p. 394, 1991
  - Mickey Cohen is Skidsville, U.S.A., and he needs moolah, gelt, the old cashola. — James Ellroy, *White Jazz*, p. 7, 1992
  - I had living quarters, cashola, a job[.] — Paolo Hewitt, *Heaven's Promise*, p. 120, 1999

cash register *noun*
  the vagina *US, 1966*
  - — Rose Giallombardo, *Society of Women*, p. 206, 1966: Glossary of Prison Terms

cash sale *noun*
  a US Marine newly arrived in Vietnam and inexperienced in combat *US, 1990*
  Cash Sales was the name of an outlet found on marine bases in the US; a marine newly arrived in Vietnam looked like and smelled like a Cash Sales outlet.
  - — Gregory Clark, *Words of the Vietnam War*, p. 88, 1990

casino-hop *verb*
  to move from one casino to another *US, 1993*
  - I tried a white blouse under the blue gown, but concluded I looked like a nun out for an evening of casino-hopping in Las Vegas. — C.D. Payne, *Youth in Revolt*, p. 442, 1993

casino perfects *noun*
  high quality dice used in casinos *US, 1997*
  The dice are almost certain to roll true because they are milled to a very precise tolerance.
  - Besides letter "imperfections," the Sabre Bay casino perfects probably also have black-light marks or some other identifying device. — Stephen Cannell, *Big Con*, pp. 192–193, 1997

casper *noun*
  a very pale white person, especially a tourist at the beach *US, 1991*
  - — Trevor Cralle, *The Surfin'ary*, p. 19, 1991

Casper; Casper the ghost *noun*
  crack cocaine *US, 1994*

Based on the cartoon-strip character Casper the Friendly Ghost; from the cloud of smoke produced when smoking the product.
- — US Department of Justice, *Street Terms*, October 1994

cast *verb*

▸ **cast an eyeball**
to look *US, 1958*
Teen slang.
- — *San Francisco News*, p. 6, 25th March 1958

▸ **cast the runes**
in computing, to operate a program that will not work for anyone else *US, 1991*
- — Eric S. Raymond, *The New Hacker's Dictionary*, p. 90, 1991

casters-up mode *adjective*
in computing, broken *US, 1991*
- — Eric S. Raymond, *The New Hacker's Dictionary*, p. 90, 1991

casting couch *noun*
the notional or real sofa in a director's office, used for sex with an actor hoping for a part *US, 1931*
Based on the commonly held belief that a sexual performance is all the audition required.
- "I don't care if you go over Niagra Falls in a barrel with it," Betsy said. "You and your casting couch." — Bernard Wolfe, *The Late Risers*, p. 7, 1954
- [O]nce he starts making a living he'll be off with the cute young chicks, leaving poor old Letitia to her Scotch and casting couch. — Gore Vidal, *Myra Breckinridge*, p. 219, 1968
- Both agents profess to being proud family men who never ran casting couches. — Josh Alan Friedman, *Tales of Times Square*, p. 38, 1986
- And he, this purveyor of porn, gets her on a casting couch at first callback in an office in Midtown, the oldest gambit in the business of show. — Jim Carroll, *Forced Entries*, p. 104, 1987

cast iron college *noun*
a local jail *US, 1968*
Carnival usage.
- — E.E. Steck, *A Brief Examination of an Esoteric Folk*, p. 11, 1968

castle *noun*
a house or apartment *US, 1953*
- — Lavada Durst, *The Jives of Dr. Hepcat*, p. 12, 1953

Castro clone *noun*
a homosexual who conforms to a clean-cut, fashionable image *US, 1986*
The Castro is a predominantly gay neighborhood in San Francisco.
- If the Castro Clone* look of self-conscious masculinity, for example, seems to be the image of choice among San Francisco gay men, there is still a greater awareness that those gender symbols are assumed not inherent. (*The short hair, trimmed moustache and athletic build currently popular among many gay men in the Castro district of San Francisco.) — Wendy Chapkis, *Beauty Secrets*, p. 136, 1986
- Most of the gay men in S.F., except for my friends, were going through this generic lumberback period, and were called "Castro Clones" because they all lived or hung out in the Castro. — Jennifer Blowdryer, *White Trash Debutante*, p. 58, 1997

casual *noun*
a private party for a group of men, featuring sexual entertainment *US, 1964*
- The reason the casual does not receive much advertisement is obvious. The entertainment almost always is several steps beyond what the law allows. — Lois O'Conner, *The Bare Facts*, p. 45, 1964

casual *adjective*
excellent, fashionable, trendy *US, 1963*
Youth usage.
- — *San Francisco Examiner: People*, p. 8, 27th October 1963

cat *noun*
1 a man *US, 1920*
- I don't want to sound square or anything, but you don't look like my grandmother at all. You look like some other cat. — Steve Allen, *Bop Fables*, p. 46, 1955
- Man, he'd be blasting with every mad cat he could find. — Jack Kerouac, *On the Road*, p. 158, 1957

- The sharp-dressed young "cats" who hung on the corners and in the poolrooms, bars and restaurants, and who obviously didn't work anywhere, completely entranced me. — Malcolm X and Alex Haley, *The Autobiography of Malcolm X*, p. 43, 1964
- A strong trio of serious business-oriented cats should develop this liberation of space within the cities[.] — *The Digger Papers*, p. 15, August 1968

2 a black person *US, 1972*
- Where we grew up, you never came in contact very often with many cats. — Dan Jenkins, *Semi-Tough*, p. 11, 1972

3 the vagina *UK, 1720*
- That puckered gash looked like she had grown an extra "cat." — Iceberg Slim (Robert Beck), *Pimp*, p. 116, 1969

4 in circus and carnival usage, a trouble-making southern rustic *US, 1981*
- — Don Wilmeth, *The Language of American Popular Entertainment*, p. 47, 1981

5 heroin *US, 1993*
- — Peter Johnson, *Dictionary of Street Alcohol and Drug Terms*, p. 34, 1993

6 meth*cat*hinone *US, 1995*
- The recipe for cat, based on (widely available) ephedrine, has been widely disseminated on the Internet. — Steven Daly and Nathaniel Wice, *alt.culture*, p. 148, 1995

7 a hydraulic catapult on an aircraft carrier *US, 1962*
- — John Winton, *HMS Leviathan*, 1967

▸ **on the cat**
staying away from home at night *US, 1965*
- When I was on the cat, I knew that I was going to get caught sooner or later, but I just didn't want to get caught before I had stolen a new suit. — Claude Brown, *Manchild in the Promised Land*, p. 69, 1965

cat *verb*
1 to stay away from home overnight, prowling for sin *US, 1949*
From the alleycat as a role model for behavior.
- "But you was away?" "Catting out. I holed up with a rich lady for a while." — Hal Ellson, *Duke*, p. 154, 1949
- The older guys had been doing something called "catting" for years. That catting was staying away from home all night was all I knew about the term. — Claude Brown, *Manchild in the Promised Land*, p. 18, 1965
- He staggered into the Picket Arms to cat on Gloria and never again drew a sober breath. — Robert Deane Pharr, *S.R.O.*, p. 396, 1971

2 to pursue someone in the hopes of sexual relations *US, 1946*
- She was catting, getting me all bothered. — Hal Ellson, *Duke*, p. 112, 1949
- — Robert S. Gold, *A Jazz Lexicon*, p. 48, 1964

catalog man *noun*
a gambling cheat whose superficial knowledge of cheating is acquired from studying catalogues of cheating devices *US, 1945*
A derisive term when used by cheats who carefully hone their craft.
- — Thomas L. Clark, *The Dictionary of Gambling and Gaming*, p. 40, 1987

catapult *noun*
in the language of wind surfing, a high-speed exit from the board assisted by high winds *US, 1985*
- — Frank Fox, *A Beginner's Guide to Zen and the Art of Windsurfing*, p. 149, 1985

catatonia *noun*
in computing, the condition that exists when a computer is in suspended operation, unable to proceed *US, 1981*
- — *CoEvolution Quarterly*, p. 27, Spring 1981

catatonic *adjective*
(of a computer) caught in an inextricable operation and thus suspended beyond reach or response *US, 1991*
- — Eric S. Raymond, *The New Hacker's Dictionary*, p. 91, 1991

catawampus *adjective*
crooked, bent *US, 1851*
- Poor Buster and Sybil's trials and tribulations in building their comically catawampus house and then seeing it tossed about in a twister and finally leveled by a train build to a small masterpiece of slapstick[.] — *Tulsa (Oklahoma) World*, p. H3, 13th July 2003

catbird seat *noun*
an advantageous position *US, 1942*

Coined or at the very least popularized by humorist James Thurber in 1942.

- — *American Speech*, December 1954

- Hell, they were all finished and he was in the catbird seat now. — Mickey Spillane, *Last Cop Out*, p. 154, 1972

- "Gee, that's a shame," Harvey said, "sitting where you are, right there in the catbird seat." — Elmore Leonard, *Stick*, p. 115, 1983

- He is in the catbird seat, with time on his hands and plenty of money and handsome Danny Quayle to take his place, if anything goes wrong. — Hunter S. Thompson, *Songs of the Doomed*, p. 249, October 1988

cat box *noun*
a small interrogation room in a police station *US, 2004*

- Cool Cal Eggers—couched in a cat box—an 8 by 12 interview room. — James Ellroy, *Destination Morgue*, p. 291, 2004

catbox *noun*
the Middle East *US, 1998*

- — *Seattle Times*, p. A9, 12th April 1998

catcall *noun*
a derisive jeer *US, 1839*

- "There's no comparison to this rivalry," A-Rod had said before the game, while steeling himself for the inevitable booing and catcalls he was to get from the Fenway rabble[.] — *Daily News (New York)*, 17th April 2004

catch *noun*
1 a prostitute who has been recruited to work for a pimp *US, 1973*

- It was time for me to get another good catch and I found this edge full of fine whores. — A.S. Jackson, *Gentleman Pimp*, p. 74, 1973

2 in Keno, the number of winning numbers that a player has marked *US, 1972*

- — John Mechigian, *Encyclopedia of Keno*, p. 111, 1972

3 a hidden condition or consequence *US, 1855*

- What's the catch? — *New Jack City*, 1990

catch *verb*
1 (used of a pimp) to recruit a prostitute to work for him; to recruit a woman to work as a prostitute *US, 1972*

- I said, "What are you doing down here?" and he said, "I'm trying to catch." I said, "There's lots of women out here." — Christina and Richard Milner, *Black Players*, p. 238, 1972

- Today he had a pocketful of bills from last week's three-card monte game: enough to catch a bitch if his luck held out. — Alix Shulman, *On the Stroll*, p. 7, 1981

2 (used of a prostitute) to engage a customer *US, 1968*

- Never know it t'find her at the bar in her catchin' clothes[.] — Robert Gover, *JC Saves*, p. 112, 1968

3 to play the passive sexual role in a homosexual relationship *US, 1966*

- They say, if you pitch, you'll catch. Any truth in that? — Malcolm Braly, *On the Yard*, p. 250, 1967

- — Eugene Landy, *The Underground Dictionary*, p. 46, 1971

- The young man walked over and leaned in through the window. "It's thirty; head only, pitch or catch." — James Ellroy, *Blood on the Moon*, p. 133, 1984

- Elaine caught his slight grin and was sure Chili did too. He said, "You pitch or catch, Elliot?" "Mostly pitch." — Elmore Leonard, *Be Cool*, p. 269, 1999

4 to take calls or complaints called in to a police station; to be assigned a case *US, 1958*

- — *New York Times Magazine*, p. 87, 16th March 1958

- Gee, Blackjack's catching that case, and he's off for a couple of days. — Peter Maas, *Serpico*, p. 76, 1973

- You start our the tour with him saying, "Are you catching?" — Mark Baker, *Cops*, p. 288, 1985

5 in an illegal number gambling lottery, to win *US, 1949*

- — *American Speech*, p. 191, October 1949

6 in gin, to draw a card *US, 1971*

- — Irwin Steig, *Play Gin to Win*, p. 138, 1971

▸ catch (some) lead
to be shot *US, 1970*

- Smitty apparently caught some lead and headed out of town to recover. — Red Rudensky, *The Gonif*, p. 113, 1970

▸ catch a bullet
to be shot *US, 1992*

- But even if that was true, the woman had to be crazy, since anybody could catch a bullet. — Richard Price, *Clockers*, p. 209, 1992

▸ catch a buzz
to smoke marijuana and become intoxicated *US, 1997*

- — Jim Emerson-Cobb, *Scratching the Dragon*, 1997

▸ catch a crab
in rowing, to err in a stroke, disrupting the timing and momentum of the rowing *US, 1949*

- The famous "crab" which University of Washington oarsmen caught when they lost to California in a driving finish in Seattle is subject of a communication from Don McNary, Cal '46. — *San Francisco Chronicle*, p. 1H, 24th June 1949

- "Well ... you haven't been catching any crabs, but you haven't had your back in the stroke all the time." — John D. MacDonald, *The Deceivers*, p. 182, 1958

▸ catch a dummy
in prison, to refuse to speak *US, 1990*

- — Charles Shafer, *Folk Speech in Texas Prisons*, p. 200, 1990

▸ catch a fish
in poker, after making a small bet with a good hand (the bait), to lure another player into increasing the bet *US, 1988*

- — George Percy, *The Language of Poker*, p. 18, 1988

▸ catch a run
to wet one side of a marijuana cigarette to promote even burning *US, 1997*

- — Jim Emerson-Cobb, *Scratching the Dragon*, 1997

▸ catch a stack
to rob someone with a lot of cash *US, 1987*

- — Carsten Stroud, *Close Pursuit*, p. 270, 1987

▸ catch air
to become airborne while skateboarding or surfing *US, 1987*

- — Mitch McKissick, *Surf Lingo*, 1987

- — *Macon Telegraph and News*, p. 9A, 18th June 1989

▸ catch it
to be killed *US, 1982*

- Ask your people if they ever saw this woman on the night Louis Palo caught it. — Richard Condon, *Prizzi's Honor*, p. 169, 1982

▸ catch one
to drink or use drugs to the point of mild intoxication *US, 1997*

- — Vann Wesson, *Generation X Field Guide and Lexicon*, p. 34, 1997

▸ catch some
to engage in heavy sexual caressing *US, 1968*

- — Collin Baker et al., *College Undergraduate Slang Study Conducted at Brown University*, p. 94, 1968

▸ catch squeals
to take calls or complaints called into a police station *US, 1969*

- The detective who picks up the phone (this activity is called "catching squeals") is the man on the case, and will hold this distinction forever. — Martin Meyer, *All You Know is Facts*, p. 107, 1969

▸ catch the bumps
in a striptease act, to synchronize the dancer's pelvic thrusts with the drum and cymbal beat *US, 1981*

- — Don Wilmeth, *The Language of American Popular Entertainment*, p. 47, 1981

▸ catch thrills
to engage in an activity that excites or stimulates *US, 1982* Hawaiian youth usage.

- — Douglas Simonson, *Pidgin to da Max Hana Hou*, 1982

▸ catch time
to be sentenced to jail *US, 1947*

- "They're in the can. He caught time for jackrolling." — Willard Motley, *Knock on Any Door*, p. 173, 1947

▸ catch tricks
(used of a drummer in a performance) to create sound effects on sight *US, 1973*

- — Sherman Louis Sergel, *The Language of Show Biz*, pp. 44–45, 1973

▶ **catch wreck**
to achieve respect for your actions *US, 1995*

- My sun moon sets and catches wreck, when we be cruisin. — Digable Planets, *The May 4th Movement*, 1995
- "If I get on the stage before the other man, I'm taking all that energy, just to make sure he don't catch wreck." [Quoting Busta Rhymes] — *Daily News (New York)*, p. 35, 7th April 1996
- skilled rhyme animals who stalk the stage ready to "catch wreck" at a moments notice — Nelson George, *Hip Hop America*, p. 113, 1998

catch 22 *noun*
a self-cancelling dilemma *US, 1955*
Coined by Joseph Heller for his 1955 novel *Catch-22*, which was originally to be titled "Catch 18"—until *Mila 18* by Leon Uris was published.

- The law was one of those Catch-22 things that put you in jail. If you complied with the federal law to buy stamps, then the state law got you for being a bookmaker. If you didn't buy the stamps, the feds jugged you. — Mario Puzo, *Inside Las Vegas*, p. 291, 1977
- In other words, it was established that the [Smothers] Brothers could do what they wanted, but so could the network. In other words, grok Catch-22. — Bill Cardoso, *The Maltese Sangweech*, p. 237, 1984
- It's such a Catch-22 that I'm not sure it ain't gonna kill me. — Marilyn Suriani Futterman, *Dancing Naked in the Material World*, p. 67, 1992
- It's not gonna happen. This is a Catch-22. — *Boogie Nights*, 1997

catch driver *noun*
in harness racing, a driver hired on the day of the race *US, 1994*

- — Igor Kushyshyn et al., *The Gambling Times Guide to Harness Racing*, p. 112, 1994

catcher *noun*
1 the passive partner in homosexual sex *US, 1966*

- I've been known to pitch, but I'm no catcher. — Malcolm Braly, *On the Yard*, p. 149, 1967
- "Who would be the top man in that combination? Aren't they both natural catchers?" — Ethan Morden, *Everybody Loves You*, p. 163, 1988
- Hey, hey! I'll play your victim, but not your catcher. — *Chasing Amy*, 1997
- Frank found one the day he arrived at Folsom—a big black-beared "pitcher" (in prison jargon, the active sexual partner) whose last "catcher" (passive partner) had been paroled several weeks before. — Lora Shaner, *Madam*, p. 74, 1999

2 a peripheral member of an illegal drug enterprise hired to retrieve drugs hurriedly thrown out of a window to avoid confiscation and arrest *US, 1989*

- Chillie has hired the fourteen-year-old son of the building super-intendent as a "catcher"—he is on call to retrieve any cocaine thrown out the window during a bust. — Terry Williams, *The Cocaine Kids*, p. 28, 1989

catch you later
used as a farewell *US, 1947*

- — Connie Eble (Editor), *UNC-CH Campus Slang*, p. 2, March 1979
- Catch you men later. Enjoy yourselves. — *Platoon*, 1986

Cat City *nickname*
Cathedral City, California *US, 1981*
A resort town just south of Palm Springs in the Coachella Valley.

- I don't know, but he's got a cousin up there, in Cat city. — James Ellroy, *Brown's Requiem*, p. 184, 1981
- Our seniors have never beaten Cat City and we haven't beaten Brawley in six years. — *Desert Sun (Palm Springs, California)*, p. 1C, 25th October 2003

caterpillar *verb*
in mountain biking, to pedal with a fluctuating, inefficient cadence *US, 1992*

- — William Nealy, *Mountain Bike!*, p. 160, 1992

cat fever *noun*
1 catarrhal gastroenteritis, suffered by troops in the field in Vietnam *US, 1945*

- Cat fever caused diarrhea and cramping. — Gregory Clark, *Words of the Vietnam War*, p. 89, 1990
- They tell us it's for "cat fever" (whatever the hell that is). — Michael Helms, *Proud Bastards*, p. 27, 2004

2 any set of achy symptoms that a Navy doctor cannot readily diagnose *US, 1943*

- [T]here were only three: constipation, fungus infection, and what the Navy calls cat fever. — Thomas Heggen, *Mister Roberts*, p. 38, 1946

catfish *noun*
a person who speaks too much and thinks too little *US, 1954*

- — Jerry Robertson, *Oil Slanguage*, p. 35, 1954

catfish row *noun*
a black neighborhood in a southern city *US, 1944*
For the setting of his 1935 folk opera *Porgy and Bess*, George Gershwin used Catfish Row, a fictionalization of an alleyway named Cabbage Row off Church Street in Charleston, South Carolina.

- I think perhaps the spades are better off here, the weather is kinder, and certainly here is something softer about the Catfish Row type of thing as contrasted with the grim phalanxes of tenements one sees in Chicago. — James Blake, *The Joint*, p. 136, 22nd August 1956
- It's a night for temptation, the kind of temptation one might see on Catfish Row at the end of the cotton season on the weekend. — Claude Brown, *Manchild in the Promised Land*, p. 315, 1965
- No lights, not even porch lights in this catfish row-alley section of Augusta. — Odie Hawkins, *Men Friends*, p. 60, 1989

cat head *noun*
a biscuit *US, 1961–1962*

- — Frank Prewitt and Francis Schaeffer, *Vacaville Vocabulary*, 1961–1962

cat hole *noun*
a one-time, one-man field latrine dug by the user in Vietnam *US, 1978*

- Back to the regular cat hole, slit trench, or whatever you want to call it. — House Committee on Appropriations, *Military Construction Appropriations for 1979*, p. 265, 1978
- If troops were moving through an area the cat hole was dispensed with. — Gregory Clark, *Words of the Vietnam War*, p. 89, 1990
- A fitful night had been punctuated by several trips to his cat-hole latrine and a terrifying visit by a sand viper. — Robin Moore, *The Wars of the Green Berets*, p. 187, 2007

Catholic aspirin *noun*
a tablet of Benzedrine™ (amphetamine sulfate), a central nervous system stimulant *US, 1973*
From the cross scores on the white tablet.

- — David Maurer and Victor Vogel, *Narcotics and Narcotic Addiction*, p. 395, 1973

cathouse *noun*
a brothel *US, 1850*

- She looked as if she might have worked half those years in a cat house. — Chester Himes, *If He Hollers Let Him Go*, p. 19, 1945
- Just a while ago you were as hard as a little boy's peter in a fifty-cent cat house. — Clarence Cooper Jr., *The Scene*, p. 199, 1960
- [S]he changed back and bided her time between cat houses in Saratoga and in other towns where Eddie was riding. — Madam Sherry, *Pleasure Was My Business*, p. 118, 1963
- We're in transit, the three of us, and we could sure use the services of a decent cathouse that don't hate G.I.'s. — Darryl Ponicsan, *The Last Detail*, p. 121, 1970

cat lapper *noun*
a lesbian; someone who enjoys performing oral sex on women *US, 1967*

- There are harsher and more widely used expressions: "Bulldyke," "Amy-John," "Cat-lapper," "Les," and so on. — L. Reinhard, *Oral Sex Techniques and Sex Practices Illustrated*, 196
- — Dale Gordon, *The Dominion Sex Dictionary*, p. 41, 1967

cat-lick; cat-licker *noun*
a Roman Catholic *US, 1942*

- I remember in the third grade the kids calling me "cat licker" because I was Catholic and "four eyes" because I wore glasses. — *San Francisco Examiner*, p. 29, 14th January 1974
- He viewed such casual insults as signs of good fellowship, the easy, rude, irrevent ways of family, fellow soldiers, brothers-in-combat, laughing when they called him a harp or a cat-lick. — Robert Campbell, *Boneyards*, p. 10, 1992
- A rich kid whose big house we passed by every day in walking to and from school started calling us "cat lickers, cat lickers" and "sissies" from, he thought the safety of his front lawn. — *Chicago Sun-Times*, p. 5, 19th June 1994

catnap *noun*
a short jail or prison sentence *US, 2002*
- — Jeffrey Ian Ross, *Behind Bars*, p. 183, 2002: Slammer Slang

catnip *noun*
poor quality, adulterated or entirely fake marijuana *US, 1962*
Catmint, the botanical genus *nepeta*, known in the US as "catnip," may be passed off as marijuana to the unsuspecting, or mixed with genuine marijuana.
- — Anthony Romeo, *The Language of Gangs*, 1962

cat pack *noun*
a loosely defined group of wealthy, famous, and fashionable people *US, 1971*
- This kind of kinship between fashion and society that not too many years ago produced the Beautiful People also characterizes the newest social species on the New York scene—the Cat Pack. — *San Francisco Chronicle*, p. 23, 1st December 1971

cat rack *noun*
a game concession in a carnival in which a player throws balls at stuffed cats on a platform or fence *US, 1952*
- This is the cat rack, with three stuffed cats just waiting to be knocked over. Even Bobby Feller couldn't win this one when it's rigged. — Charles Hamilton, *Men of the Underworld*, p. 178, 1952
- — Don Wilmeth, *The Language of American Popular Entertainment*, p. 47, 1981

cat's ass *noun*
an extraordinarily good or extraordinarily bad example of something *US, 1967*
- After working on the tactical unit of the high-crime Fillmore District, protecting languorous women in bikinis was a nice change of pace. "Believe me, it was the cat's ass," Delaney digresses. — *Chicago Tribune*, p. C12, 6th March 1994
- Chiefs vs. Raiders. In football, this one is the cat's ass. — *Sporting News*, p. 6, 22nd September 2003

cat's eyes *noun*
in craps, a roll of three *US, 1945*
- — Lou Shelly, *Hepcats Jive Talk Dictionary*, p. 22, 1945

cat shit *noun*
used as a basis for comparison when describing someone who is mean *US, 1970*
- Almost anyone who has known me for a week or so will reiterate that I'm as mean as cat shit on a pump handle. — Laurie Harper, *Don Sherwood*, p. 295, 2003

cat shot *noun*
a take-off from an aircraft carrier assisted by a catapult *US, 1959*
Vietnam war usage.
- What had it been? A "cold-cat" shot, whatever that was, from a carrier. — Hank Searls, *The Big X*, p. 221, 1959
- Its squadrons of Phantoms and A-6 Intruders practiced "cat shots" (catapulted takeoffs) and landings all day long. — James W. Canan, *The Superwarriors*, p. 36, 1975

cat's nut *noun*
an extraordinary thing or person *US, 1928*
- If I ever saw a babe who's the cat's nuts, it's you. — James T. Farrell, *Ruth and Bertram*, p. 100, 1955

cat's pajamas *noun*
anything very good, superlative or exceptional; someone who is considered the best by themselves or others *US, 1922*
Coined by, or inspired by, an illustration by *New York Journal* sports cartoonist Thomas Aloysius "TAD" Dorgan (1877–1929).
- Leroy Middleton groaned. "Oh boy, this is the living end, this is really the cat's pajamas, this is sweet, oh this is really dynamite, oh we did it." — John Nichols, *The Milagro Beanfield War*, p. 301, 1974

cat's paw *noun*
the member of a group of burglars who enters a building and lets the rest of the group in *US, 1976*
- The police, finding nothing on me, toyed with the notion I was a cat's paw for a gang of larger boys who had sent me to make the entry and open the door for them[.] — Malcolm Braley, *False Starts*, p. 13, 1976

cattle call *noun*
a mass audition *US, 1952*

- Well, let's say I go to one of those cattle calls, a try out[.] — *Klute*, 1971
- One method used in casting is called the cattle call. Everybody who wants to be in your picture shows up at the specified time, and you see each person on a first-come, first-served basis. — Stephen Ziplow, *The Film Maker's Guide to Pornography*, p. 46, 1977
- I went to one of the early huge cattle calls, although I had never thought of myself as glamorous or particularly pretty. — Kathryn Leigh Scott, *The Bunny Years*, p. 137, 1998
- But the Generals are not cattle calls. Actors are cut off—"Time!" only if they surpass their three-minute limit. — *San Francisco Chronicle*, 27th February 2001

cattle truck *noun*
any large truck used to transport troops *US, 1968*
Vietnam war usage.
- — Carl Fleischhauer, *A Glossary of Army Slang*, p. 8, 1968

catty *adjective*
sly, spiteful, mean-spirited *UK, 1886*
- He and another prissy lad were in our cocktail lounge one evening, drinking, making catty and audible cracks about other patrons[.] — Dev Collans with Stewart Sterling, *I was a House Detective*, p. 105, 1954

catty-cat *noun*
the vagina *US, 1980*
- — Edith A. Folb, *runnin' down some lines*, p. 232, 1980

cauliflower ear; cauliflower *noun*
an ear that has been damaged and deformed by blows *US, 1896*
Originally and still used as a boxing term.
- All he had now were his job as a houseman, his cauliflower ears and broken nose, his precious scrapbook, the bitter memories of his former glory, and an insane temper. — Irving Shulman, *The Amboy Dukes*, p. 53, 1947
- Down the stairs a cauliflower-eared gent played doorman with a nod, a grunt and an open palm. — Mickey Spillane, *My Gun is Quick*, p. 65, 1950
- But it was a while before the hard guys turned their cauliflower ears toward the jazz bandstands[.] — Robert Sylvester, *No Cover Charge*, p. 84, 1956
- Big Tom was quizzical and oblique and had a cauliflower ear from the Peekskill riot. — Clancy Sigal, *Going Away*, p. 66, 1961

cause *verb*
▸ **cause a vacancy**
in poker, to win a hand that drives a player from the game *US, 1988*
- — George Percy, *The Language of Poker*, p. 18, 1988

cav *adjective*
cavalier *US, 1995*
In the pornography industry, an attitude towards sexually transmitted disease.
- — *Adult Video News*, p. 42, August 1995

cave *noun*
a deep sore at the site of repeated drug injections *US, 1973*
- — David Maurer and Victor Vogel, *Narcotics and Narcotic Addiction*, p. 395, 1973

cave *verb*
to have sex with someone *US, 1973*
- And Carri with your class and swiftness you can cave the bellboys and save the four outta ten[.] — A.S. Jackson, *Gentleman Pimp*, p. 84, 1973

cave bro *noun*
a white person adapting black style and mannerisms *US, 2006*
- "Cool, cave bro." Cave bro being another way to say wigger. — Linden Dalecki, *Kid B*, p. 73, 2006

caveman *adjective*
obsolete *US, 1974*
- Their computer is caveman. — Robert Kirk Mueller, *Buzzwords*, p. 51, 1974

caviar *noun*
1 residue in whatever utensils are used for manufacturing crack cocaine *US, 1993*
- — Peter Johnson, *Dictionary of Street Alcohol and Drug Terms*, p. 36, 1993

2 a mixture of marijuana and crack cocaine prepared for smoking in a cigarette *US*, *1989*

- — Geoffrey Froner, *Digging for Diamonds*, p. 33, 1989

cavvy *noun*

high-quality crack cocaine *US*, *1991*

- "I sell Yay-o, Cavvy—caviar crack—fo' my money, and on a good day I can make like six, seven hundred dollars." — Leon Bing, *Do or Die*, p. 63, 1991

Cax *noun*

the Coxsackie Correctional Facility, a prison in upstate New York *US*, *1975*

- When I was in Cax—it was terrible up there. — Miguel Pinero, *Short Eyes*, p. 74, 1975

cazooled *adjective*

drunk *US*, *1968*

- — Collin Baker et al., *College Undergraduate Slang Study Conducted at Brown University*, p. 94, 1968

CB *noun*

used as an abbreviation for "COCKBLOCK" *US*, *1980*

- — Edith A. Folb, *runnin' down some lines*, p. 231, 1980

CB *adjective*

could be *US*, *1994*

Used in tentative diagnoses, such as "could be lupus."

- — Sally Williams, *"Strong" Words*, p. 136, 1994

CC *noun*

1 Canadian Club™ whisky *US*, *1971*

- You had about two hundred cases of C.C. on that truck[.] — George V. Higgins, *The Friends of Eddie Doyle*, p. 14, 1971
- Canadian Club is a brand of rye. Not to be confused with "hockey stick," another kind of Canadian club. — Will Ferguson, *How to be a Canadian*, p. 63, 2001

2 cocaine offered as a gift by a dealer *US*, *1989*

- Generally, cocaine dealers come to after-hours clubs with "C-C," or calling card cocaine, to give out. — Terry Williams, *The Cocaine Kids*, p. 97, 1989

CCW *noun*

the criminal charge of carrying a concealed weapon *US*, *1973*

As the US moved to the right, gun enthusiasts have been successful in enacting legislation in many states that permit—not forbid—carrying concealed weapons, changing the meaning of the acronym to "concealed-carry weapon."

- He saw dozens of c-c-w cases come through the courtroom, and he knew that had Chester been white, he'd have been given a small bond or released on his own personal word. — Donald Goines, *White Man's Justice, Black Man's Grief*, p. 30, 1973
- "We have a ton of CCW (carrying concealed weapon) cases with these exact facts," McCarty said. — *Plain Dealer (Cleveland, Ohio)*, p. 4B, 8th May 1994

Cecil B. DeMille *noun*

any large job that evolves into a chaotic mess *US*, *1997*

New York police slang.

- — Samuel M. Katz, *Anytime Anywhere*, p. 387, 1997

ceiling bet *noun*

the highest bet permitted in a given game or situation *US*, *1988*

- — George Percy, *The Language of Poker*, p. 18, 1988

celeb *noun*

a celebrity *US*, *1916*

- [S]ome juvenile half-wits plant themselves outside the hotels when such celebs are in town. — Jack Lait and Lee Mortimer, *Washington Confidential*, p. 132, 1951
- I don't mean the celebs and the legit high rollers, he's got to take care of them, and he loves it. — Elmore Leonard, *Glitz*, p. 119, 1985
- Messy-haired rock stars are the celeb squeeze of choice[.] — *Sky Magazine*, p. 8, May 2001

celebrity-fucker *noun*

a person who seeks out sexual relationships with famous people *US*, *1969*

- She was always such a celebrity fucker. It must be said of Lillian that when the chips were down she'd always go for the guy who had the most clout. — George Plimpton, *Truman Capote*, p. 269, 1997

- Should I tell them that he deserves the grant because every gifted young artist does, or throw the information request back in their faces, screaming that they're just youth-hungry celebrity-fuckers like the rest of this disgusting country? — *Village Voice*, p. 119, 4th August 1998

celestial discharge *noun*

death in a hospital *US*, *1994*

- — Sally Williams, *"Strong" Words*, p. 136, 1994

cell *noun*

a wireless telephone that is part of a system in which a geographical area is divided into sections served by a limited-range transmitter *US*, *1997*

An abbreviation of "cell phone" a term first heard in the late 1980s as an abbreviation of "cellular."

- So—on the way home from the strip bar—at 0200—you get this call on your cell saying something happened to Superboy on the bridge. — *Copland*, 1997
- — Pamela Munro, *U.C.L.A. Slang*, p. 49, 1997
- — Connie Eble (Editor), *UNC-CH Campus Slang*, p. 1, Fall 2001

cell *verb*

to occupy a prison cell *US*, *1901*

- [T]he good news is that I'm now celing alone & shall do so for the balance of my sentence. — Neal Cassady, *Grace Beats Karma*, p. 162, 10th January 1960: Letter to Carolyn Cassady
- It was bad enough trying to cell with someone halfway regular, let alone some knickknacking nut. — Malcolm Braly, *On the Yard*, p. 205, 1967
- But, nine times out of ten, after they cell with the guy a while, after this relationship goes on for a while, they quit it. — Bruce Jackson, *In the Life*, p. 379, 1972
- George didn't approve of any convict preying on a weaker convict, but if Little wanted to cell with George, it was okay by him. — Pete Earley, *The Hot House*, p. 62, 1992

cellar dealer *noun*

a card cheat who deals from the bottom of a deck *US*, *1988*

- — George Percy, *The Language of Poker*, p. 18, 1988

cell block *noun*

a school classroom *US*, *1958*

Teen slang.

- — *San Francisco News*, p. 6, 25th March 1958

cell buddy *noun*

a cellmate *US*, *1949*

- That evening as I sat on the floor of my cell I got acquainted with Halfpint, my cell buddy. — John Dollard, *Criteria for Life History*, p. 193, 1949
- Absolute knowledge, I have none. But my rap-buddy's cell buddy told me one. — Stanley Mayer, *Fantasy*, 1969
- I watched one cell buddy learn to paint. — Malcolm Braley, *False Starts*, p. 240, 1976

cellie; celly *noun*

1 in jail or prison, a cellmate *US*, *1966*

- What do yeh got, a bear for a celly? — Paul Glover, *Words from the House of the Dead*, 1974
- He had hurt lots of people, but the Trasbag Man had been his cellie at Attica and the headaches had started about then[.] — James Ellroy, *Because the Night*, p. 329, 1984
- Robert "Robot" Salas, a Sureno from a street gang called Big Hazard, and Hector Padilla, a Norteno, were cellies[.] — Bill Valentine, *Gangs and Their Tattoos*, p. 24, 2000
- Charlie's old greaser cellie from Terminal Island recalls Manson as a no-good young punk motherfucker. — Bill Landis, *Sleazoid Express*, p. 257, 2002

2 a cellular telephone *US*, *1999*

- [T]he play-by-play via cellie from 7-year-old Patrick's first ball season did it. — *Sporting News*, p. 7, 20th September 1999
- — Connie Eble (Editor), *UNC-CH Campus Slang*, p. 3, October 2002
- Forty-nine percent use a "cellie" to make plans with friends. — *Chicago Daily Herald*, p. 1, 9th September 2003

cell-shocked *adjective*

deranged from life in prison *US*, *1990*

An obvious, although sharp, play on "shell-shocked."

- He's cellshocked. Done so much time he can only concentrate long enough to tie his shoe. — Seth Morgan, *Homeboy*, p. 211, 1990

cell warrior *noun*
a prisoner whose actions outside his cell do not match his aggressive words uttered in the safety of his cell *US, 2001*
- — Jim Goad, *Jim Goad's Glossary of Northwestern Prison Slang*, 2001
- cell warrior: talks boldly in cell, actions don't match up — J.G. Narum, *The Convict Cookbook*, p. 158, 2004

cement arm *noun*
an intravenous drug user's arm that is toughened with scar tissue over the veins *US, 1973*
- — David Maurer and Victor Vogel, *Narcotics and Narcotic Addiction*, p. 395, 1973

cement funeral *noun*
disposal of a murder victim's body by pouring cement around the feet and dumping the body in water *US, 1975*
- "So a little while later, Bugsy gave Sam Bloom a cement funeral." — Martin Gosch, *The Last Testament of Lucky Luciano*, p. 103, 1975

cementhead *noun*
a stupid person *US, 1949*
- For example, throwing office supplies and constantly calling women "assholes," "morons," and "cementheads" probably would not have been considered part of the hostile environment[.] — *Wisconsin Women's Law Journal*, p. 397, Summer 1997

cement mixer *noun*
1 a dancer who rotates her pelvis in a simulation of sexual intercourse *US, 1951*
- Belly down she's a cement mixer. — Thurston Scott, *Cure it with Honey*, p. 152, 1951

2 a loud car or truck *US, 1914*
- — Mary Elting, *Trucks at Work*, 1946
- — Judi Sanders, *Da Bomb!*, p. 6, 1997

cement overshoes *noun*
concrete poured around a person's feet, used to weigh them down when their body is disposed of in a body of water *US, 1962*
- For example, a defense lawyer who double-crosses a drug lord during the defense of an underling may end up in cement overshoes. — *Harvard Law Review*, p. 693, January 1992
- Onlookers whisper jokes about bumping into Jimmy Hoffa's cement overshoes. — *USA Today*, p. 6D, 30th June 2003

cent *noun*
a dollar *US, 1957*
- "Four cents for the plunge, and it's lemonade." — Herbert Simmons, *Corner Boy*, p. 55, 1957
- One cent is a dollar. — Willard Motley, *Let No Man Write My Epitaph*, p. 148, 1958
- Red came toward Bernie, menacing. "You don't understand, I gotta have twenty cent, like I tell you." Twenty cent meant twenty dollars; Red always spoke of dollars in amounts under one hundred as cents; perhaps it expressed his contempt for money. — Ross Russell, *The Sound*, p. 157, 1961
- Man, like how many times some cat's come up to me with his old man's watch or sister's coat and swap for a three-cent bag. — Piri Thomas, *Down These Mean Streets*, p. 206, 1967

centerfield *noun*
1 in craps, a field bet on the nine *US, 1985*
- — Steve Kuriscak, *Casino Talk*, p. 11, 1985

2 in blackjack played in casinos, the seat directly across from the dealer *US, 1985*
- — Steve Kuriscak, *Casino Talk*, p. 11, 1985

century *noun*
1 a $100 bill *US, 1859*
- I took them out and riffled them. Ten centuries. All new. All nice. An even thousand dollars. — Raymond Chandler, *The Little Sister*, p. 239, 1949
- The next bag had bigger bills, and the last bag had nothing but centuries—sparkling $100 greens. — Red Rudensky, *The Gonif*, p. 118, 1970

2 one hundred yards *US, 1989*
- I always ran when I was with Leonard, maybe it had something to do with the fact that he was a natural 440 man and I had the dashes covered up to the century. — Odie Hawkins, *Men Friends*, p. 117, 1989

3 one hundred miles *US, 1956*
- Years ago, there used to be bicycle clubs, meeting Sundays, who had what was termed "century" runs. — *San Francisco Progress*, p. 4, 1st August 1956

century *verb*
to save $100 *US, 1970*
- — Clarence Major, *Dictionary of Afro-American Slang*, p. 35, 1970

century note *noun*
a one-hundred dollar bill *US, 1908*
- He ended up borrowing a century-note from them. — Jack Lait and Lee Mortimer, *Washington Confidential*, p. 278, 1951
- "Oh, hell, then, let's make it for a lousy century note." — Sam Snead, *The Education of a Golfer*, p. 172, 1962

cess *noun*
marijuana, possibly of inferior quality *US, 1995*
- That cess got me buggin'. — Lois Stavsky et al., *A2Z*, p. 18, 1995
- [S]moke a pound of cess a day[.] — Eminem (Marshall Mathers), *Rock Bottom*, 1999

CFB *adjective*
very clear indeed *US, 1980*
An abbreviation of "clear as a fucking bell." Vietnam war usage.
- It wouldn't be long now until the visibility was CFB (clear as a frapping bell) and the Jolly Greens would be chattering in. — William C. Anderson, *Bat 21*, p. 77, 1980

CFM *adjective*
sexually suggestive *US, 1989*
An abbreviation of **COME-FUCK-ME**.
- — Pamela Munro, *U.C.L.A. Slang*, p. 28, 1989

CFNM *noun*
a pornographic and sexual fetish—clothed female, naked male *US, 2005*
- CFNM clothed female naked male fans will like this movie. — groups.google.com/group/cfnmhandjobs, 19th June 2005

C-H *noun*
a cheating scheme in poker involving two players; if one player signals that he is holding a good hand, his confederate raises the bet *US, 1988*
An abbreviation of "crooked-honest."
- — George Percy, *The Language of Poker*, p. 18, 1988

cha *adjective*
fashionable, trendy, stylish *US, 1992*
- [T]he cha ("very cool") words include: "winded" for hung over; "craftsman" for a complete idiot; and "ass" for awful. — *Washington Times*, p. C3, 26th August 1992

chabobs *noun*
the female breasts *US, 1962*
- McMurphy starts. "She's got one hell of a set of chabobs," is all he can think of. — Ken Kesey, *One Flew Over the Cuckoo's Nest*, p. 174, 1962

cha-cha *verb*
to have sex *US, 1980*
- — Edith A. Folb, *runnin' down some lines*, p. 232, 1980

chain *noun*
1 a bus or van used to transport prisoners *US, 1984*
- — Inez Cardozo-Freeman, *The Joint*, p. 487, 1984

2 a necklace *US, 1985*
- The girl wasn't going along with it, so he said, "To hell with it, I'll take your chains." So he ripped off her jewelry. — Mark Baker, *Cops*, p. 117, 1985

3 a group of prisoners being transferred *US, 1954*
- These transfers, incidentally, are referred to as "loads" or "chains." — Caryl Chessman, *Cell 2456 Death Row*, p. 299, 1954
- chain: a group of new inmates arriving on a bus — J.G. Narum, *The Convict Cookbook*, p. 158, 2004

▸ **off the chain**
excellent *US, 2001*
- — Don R. McCreary (Editor), *Dawg Speak*, 2001
- — Connie Eble (Editor), *UNC-CH Campus Slang*, p. 7, November 2003
- "You and the Krew were off the chain." — Linden Dalecki, *Kid B*, p. 202, 2006

▸ **pull your chain**
to tease you; to mislead you *US, 1962*
- He realized after a few weeks that the guy had been pulling his chain about the women, but that was all right. — Elmore Leonard, *The Big Bounce*, p. 111, 1969

- He's pulling your chain. And the fact that you even bought it for a second makes you look like an idiot. — *Chasing Amy*, 1997

Chain *noun*
▸ **The Chain**
the Aleutian Islands *US, 1886*

- Many a ship has been lost in The Chain, and many a man lies there with no gravestone. — Robert O. Bowen, *An Alaskan Dictionary*, p. 11, 1965
- Traveling to the Aleutians is commonly called "going out on The Chain." — Mike Doogan, *How to Speak Alaskan*, p. 20, 1993

chain-drink *verb*
to drink one beverage after another, barely pausing between drinks *US, 1976*

- Fueled by the coffee he chain-drinks, he likes to get going before dawn and often goes with little sleep. — *Washington Post*, p. D1, 22nd December 1982

chainsuck *noun*
in mountain biking, a condition that occurs when the bicycle chain doubles back on itself and gets jammed between the frame and the chain rings *US, 1996*

- Muddy water washes the lube from the chain, which leads to chainsuck, so lube your chain before and after every ride[.] — *Mountain Bike Magazine's Complete Guide To Mountain Biking Skills*, p. 126, 1996

chair *noun*
the electric chair; the death penalty *US, 1895*

- I'm going to get that louse that killed you. He won't sit in the chair. He won't hang. He will die exactly as you died[.] — Mickey Spillane, *I, The Jury*, p. 7, 1947
- A little later, just about half dead already, they put Irvin in the chair and turned on the juice. — Haywood Patterson, *Scottsboro Boy*, p. 43, 1950
- The whole town knows that if he'd been a little older he'd have gone to the chair instead of reform school. — Jim Thompson, *The Killer Inside*, p. 19, 1952
- Tell us the truth, Black, and you might beat the chair. — Clarence Cooper Jr., *The Scene*, p. 226, 1960

chairbacker *noun*
an unordained, self-taught preacher *US, 1955*

- "Chairbacker" (a preacher whose pulpit was a common chair in a slave cabin) and "floor preacher" became common appellations[.] — Mechal Sobel, *Trabelin' On*, p. 160, 1988

chairborne *adjective*
in the military, assigned to a rear-echelon support job *US, 1943*
A pun on "airborne," applied to "chairborne commandos," "chairborne generals," the "chairborne infantry," "chairborne rangers," etc.

- Mission demands led Brig. Gen. John Iffland, 146th Airlift Wing commander, to fly the 36-year-old plane, stepping away from dealing with personnel and paperwork—what GIs call the chairborne division. — *Ventura County (California) Star*, p. A1, 22nd November 1998
- Is it possible that a "chairborne" general was unhappy because he was not qualified to wear the headgear awarded to certain combat troops of the U.S. Army? — *Columbus (Ohio) Dispatch*, p. 6A, 16th January 2001

chair cheeks *noun*
the buttocks *US, 2005*

- [H]er exquisitely formed chair cheeks and her perfecting thrusting, ever-so-slightly swaying top tier are impossible to look away from? — Mr. Skin, *Mr. Skin's Skincyclopedia*, p. 64, 2005

chairwarmer *noun*
an idler, a loafer *US, 1960*

- He added "do-nothing" and "chairwarmer" to rhetorical blasts at a news conference, even as he urged Sundquist to devote half the campaign to daily debates at towns across the state. — *Knoxville (Tennessee) News-Sentinel*, p. A4, 9th August 1994

chale!
no! never! *US, 1950*
Border Spanish used in English conversation by Mexican-Americans.

- — George Carpenter Baker, *Pachuco*, p. 41, January 1950
- "Chale, chalee. Quit being a sergeant," I said. — Joseph Wambaugh, *The Blue Knight*, p. 58, 1973

chalk *noun*
1 a white person *US, 1945*

Not flattering.

- If it wasn't for Uncle Tom ass dudes like me, niggers like you wouldn't be havin' a chance to eat all the chalk pussy you want, or nothin' else, for that matter! — Odie Hawkins, *Chicago Hustle*, p. 138, 1977

2 methamphetamine or amphetamine *US, 1966*

- — J. L. Simmons and Barry Winograd, *It's Happening*, p. 173, 1966
- The most common drugs in use in industry, according to the police sergeant, are amphetamine sulfate compounds and barbiturates, known among workers in the plants as "chalk," "whites," "bennies," "reds," "jackets," "blue heavens" and "rainbows." — *The San Francisco Chronicle*, p. 5, 11th October 1966
- He was really in a bad way and begged me for some chalk or anything. — Anonymous, *Go Ask Alice*, p. 85, 1971

3 a potent homemade "wine" made from yeast, sugar, water, and rice or fruit *US, 2001*

- — AFSCME Local 3963, *The Correctional Officer's Guide to Prison Slang*, 2001

4 in sports betting, the contestant or team favored to win *US, 1991*

- — *Bay Sports Review*, p. 8, November 1991
- "You would bet against the chalk? Eighteen to one, your long shot." — John Ridley, *Love is a Racket*, p. 41, 1998

5 chocolate syrup *US, 1946*

- — *American Speech*, p. 88, April 1946: "The language of West Coast culinary workers"

chalk *verb*
1 to chemically lighten the color of cocaine for buyers who believe that the white color reflects purity *US, 1989*

- — Terry Williams, *The Cocaine Kids*, p. 136, 1989

2 to observe something or someone *US, 1959*

- "Shhhh," Choo-Choo cautioned. "Chalk the walking Jeffs." — Chester Himes, *The Real Cool Killers*, p. 120, 1959

3 to ban a gambler from a table, game or casino *US, 1950*

- — *The Annals of the American Academy of Political and Social Sciences*, p. 122, May 1950

4 to steal something *US, 2001*

- — Rick Ayers (Editor), *Slang Dictionary*, p. 6, 2001

chalk-eater *noun*
in horse racing, a bettor who consistently bets on favorites *US, 1951*
From the old custom of a bookmaker chalking odds on a blackboard.

- — David W. Maurer, *Argot of the Racetrack*, p. 18, 1951

chalked up *adjective*
under the influence of cocaine *US, 1955*

- — *American Speech*, p. 86, May 1955: "Narcotic argot along the Mexican border"

chalk hand *noun*
in poker, a hand that is almost certain to win *US, 1988*

- — George Percy, *The Language of Poker*, p. 18, 1988

chalk horse *noun*
in horse racing, the favorite in a race *US, 1951*

- — David W. Maurer, *Argot of the Racetrack*, p. 18, 1951

chalk man *noun*
the police employee who chalks the outline of a corpse where it has fallen before the body is removed *US, 1992*

- — Lewis Poteet, *Car & Motorcycle Slang*, p. 46, 1992

chalk people *noun*
people who live far from the ocean *US, 1991*

- — Trevor Cralle, *The Surfin'ary*, p. 20, 1991

chalk stick *noun*
a cigarette *US*

- — Art Unger, *The Cool Book*, p. 107, 1961

chamber of commerce *noun*
1 a toilet *US, 1960*
A pun on "chamber pot."

- — Lou Shelly, *Hepcats Jive Talk Dictionary*, p. 22, 1945
- — Clarence Major, *Dictionary of Afro-American Slang*, p. 35, 1970

2 a brothel *US, 1949*

- — Vincent J. Monteleone, *Criminal Slang*, p. 47, 1949

champ *noun*
a drug addict who does not inform on others when questioned by the police *US, 1960*
- A champ is a junkie who won't snitch or inform, although no such animal exists. — Clarence Cooper Jr., *The Scene*, p. 55, 1960
- — Eugene Landy, *The Underground Dictionary*, p. 47, 1971

champagne *noun*
human urine in the context of a sexual fetish *US, 1987*
- — Thomas E. Murray and Thomas R. Murrell, *The Language of Sadomasochism*, p. 50, 1989

champagne blonde *noun*
a woman with pale blonde hair *UK, 1904*
- As these words were being typed, a nineteen-year-old champagne blonde snatched $1500 from a Las Vegas bank and was caught only because she was so beautiful no one could forget her police description. — Lee Mortimer, *Women Confidential*, p. 25, 1960

champagne drug *noun*
cocaine *US, 1998*
- Cocaine prices dropped dramatically from 1980 onwards as the drug cartels successfully expanded their client base, bringing in many people who previously could not afford to use the "champagne drug." — Richard Rudgley, *The Encyclopedia of Psychoactive Substances*, p. 67, 1998
- After years of decline, prompted by rocketing prices and the fashion for LSD and speed, coke resurfaces and gains a reputation as the "champagne drug." — *Drugs: An Adult Guide*, p. 16, December 2001

champagne trick *noun*
a wealthy, big-spending customer of a prostitute *US, 1973*
- The call girl who earns $100 for a "champagne trick" views the streetwalker with contempt. — Ruth Rosen, *The Lost Sisterhood*, p. 171, 1982

chance 'em *verb*
while surfing, to decide to ride a big wave *US, 1991*
- — Trevor Cralle, *The Surfin'ary*, p. 20, 1991

chancre mechanic *noun*
a military medic, especially one assigned to diagnose and treat sexually transmitted infections *US, 1944*
- [H]e had been doc of Baker Company, survivor of the Makin Raid, as opposed to your typical natty, run-of-the-mill chancre mechanic. — W.E.B. Griffin, *The Corps Book II*, p. 339, 1987
- "After that first day," says the 1st Battalion surgeon Ben Sullivan, "we were no longer pill rollers or chancre mechanics. We were all beloved." — Gerald Astor, *Battling Buzzards*, p. 130, 1993

chandelier sign *noun*
a dramatic reaction to being touched in a painful area *US, 1994*
It is said that the patient "hits the ceiling" or "hits the chandelier."
- — Sally Williams, *"Strong" Words*, p. 136, 1994

chanel *noun*
cocaine *US, 1976*
A slightly forced formation, playing on the name of designer Coco Chanel.
- — Robert Sabbag, *Snowblind*, p. 271, 1976

change *noun*
an approximation or a fraction — Edwin Torres, *Carlito's Way*, p. 52, 1975

change *verb*
▸ **change water**
to engage in an unproductive activity *US, 1975*
From lobstermen, who refer to the hauling and baiting of an empty trap as "changing water."
- — John Gould, *Maine Lingo*, p. 47, 1975

▸ **change your luck**
(used of a white person) to have sex with a black person; to have sex with a person of the sex with whom one would not ordinarily have sex *US, 1916*
- The Harlem community accepts—though it despises—these Caucasians who cross the color line, or as it is known above 110th Street, "change their luck" or "deal in coal." — Jack Lait and Lee Mortimer, *New York Confidential*, p. 161, 1948

- Go to bed with a nigger and change your luck. — Willard Motley, *Let No Man Write My Epitaph*, p. 327, 1958
- "Sometimes we go over to Little Harlem," he said, and smacked his lips. "You know, when the luck's running bad there's nothing as good as changing it." — Irving Shulman, *The Short End of the Stick*, p. 26, 1959
- Hey, Flo, gonna take the little monkey home with you, change your luck? — Dick Gregory, *Nigger*, p. 10, 1964

change artist *noun*
a swindler who gives customers too little change *US, 1960*
- We will assume that the change artist is behind the cash register, and you are the customer; you hand him a bill and he takes the change from the drawer. — W.M. Tucker, *The Change Raisers*, p. 17, 1960

change machine *noun*
a prostitute who charges very little for sex *US, 1963*
- DARLING DOLLY DANE: "Two miserable bucks!" LOLA: "You've gone for less, dear." "DARLING DOLLY DANE, wiggling: "'This aint no change-machine, Mae.'" — John Rechy, *City of Night*, p. 114, 1963

change of luck *noun*
(used of a white person) sex with a black person *US, 1916*
- I know you, you after a change of luck. — Bernard Wolfe, *The Magic of Their Singing*, p. 103, 1961

change raiser *noun*
a swindler who tricks cashiers into giving him too much change *US, 1960*
- Change raisers deliberately confuse the victim by repeatedly handling the change back and forth, then they throw the change out of balance. Then they balance it again, but in the process a good portion of the change sticks to their own fingers. — W.M. Tucker, *The Change Raisers*, p. 7, 1960

changes *noun*
difficulties *US, 1973*
- She really worked me over good, she was a credit to her gender / She put me through some changes Lord, sort of like a Waring blender. — Warren Zevon, *Poor Poor Pitiful Me*, 1973
- "He's going through changes." — Cyra McFadden, *The Serial*, p. 84, 1977

channel *noun*
a vein, especially a prominent vein suitable for drug injection *US, 1994*
- — US Department of Justice, *Street Terms*, October 1994

channel fever *noun*
a strong desire by someone at sea to be back on land *UK, 1929*
- Most were infected with "channel fever," the giddiness that overcomes crew members in the days before warships return to San Diego Bay. — *Orange County (California) Register*, 3rd June 2003

channel-surf *verb*
to browse distractedly through a variety of television programs, switching from channel to channel *US, 1994*
- — Connie Eble (Editor), *UNC-CH Campus Slang*, p. 2, Spring 1994
- The TV was on for 11 hours. She channel-surfed, flicking backwards and forwards never watching anything properly. — Sally Cline, *Couples*, p. 203, 1998

chapped *adjective*
1 depressed *US, 1990*
- — *Surfing*, p. 43, 14th March 1990

2 irritated, angry *US, 1966*
- — *Current Slang*, p. 2, Fall 1966

chapped off *adjective*
very angry *US, 1963*
- — Carol Ann Preusse, *Jargon Used by University of Texas Co-Eds*, 1963

chapter and verse *noun*
complete detail; detailed knowledge *US, 1956*
- If the terrorists do not surface, the United States Government will soon be forced to lay out its evidence in chapter and verse. — *New York Times*, p. A31, 10th December 1981

character *noun*
a person with an underworld lifestyle *US, 1958*
- The only pistol you can count on is a revolver. Every real character [criminal] knows that. — Ned Polsky, *Hustlers, Beats, and Others*, p. 136, 1967

- I mean somebody who makes a living without a legitimate job. Their income is not legitimate. He might be a pimp—he's a character. — Bruce Jackson, *Outside the Law*, p. 144, 1972

charge *noun*
1 intense excitement *US, 1960*
- Ooh man! This is a great charge — William "Lord" Buckley, *Martin's Horse*, 1960

2 marijuana *US, 1941*
From an earlier sense meaning "drugs in general"; it contains a charge—produces a **KICK**.
- "Do you have any charge? Do you Diane? Dincher?" as he sat at her sister's elbow. "Do you have any hemp you could leave me?" — George Mandel, *Flee the Angry Strangers*, p. 259, 1952
- "This is really great charge. The best I know." — Chandler Brossard, *Who Walks in Darkness*, p. 11, 1952
- Some were quietly trying to borrow money from other guests while some became intoxicated as others smoked "charge" or ate pigs feet in the kitchen at $1.10 apiece. — Dan Burley, *Diggeth Thou?*, pp. 45–46, 1959

3 an injection of a drug *US, 1925*
- She applied the needle herself, jabbed quickly and gasped, then pumped the charge and drew it back with her blood[.] — George Mandel, *Flee the Angry Strangers*, p. 379, 1952
- "Why don't you let me get my charge from you?" — Herbert Simmons, *Corner Boy*, p. 56, 1957
- If he tried mainlining with the sugar in the capsule he'd find out in a hurry he had nothing going for him and would do a crazy dance to get a charge. — Mickey Spillane, *Return of the Hood*, p. 104, 1964

charge *verb*
to go surfing *US, 1991*
- Let's charge it bro, the waves are sweet. — Trevor Cralle, *The Surfin'ary*, p. 20, 1991

▶ **charge it to the rain and let the dust settle it**
to pay for something on credit without fully expecting to pay the charge *US, 1946*
- Look. Charge it to the dust and let the rain settle it. — Brian Pera, *Troublemaker*, p. 54, 2000

charged; charged up *adjective*
drug-intoxicated *US, 1942*
- Mae was charged to the gills and Marcia looked as if she'd been at the bottle the entire time. — Polly Adler, *A House is Not a Home*, p. 117, 1953
- Half marijuana, half tobacco. And he was always charged up. — Willard Motley, *Let No Man Write My Epitaph*, p. 108, 1958
- He had them confused, but they were so charged up, they could as easily knife him or accept him. — Phil Hirsch, *Hooked*, pp. 117–118, 1968

charge 'em!
used as an exortation to action *US, 1982*
Hawaiian youth usage.
- — Douglas Simonson, *Pidgin to da Max Hana Hou*, 1982

charity fuck *noun*
sexual intercourse engaged in by one partner as an act of generosity *US, 1978*
- He described the awkward union which he terms "the charity fuck." — John D. Macdonald, *The Empty Copper Sea*, p. 47, 1978
- I sort of stumbled into her. I reckon it must have been a charity fuck, to be honest. From Sally's point of view, that is. — Alan Wall, *The School of Night*, p. 268, 2001

charity girl *noun*
an amateur prostitute or promiscuous woman *US, 1916*
- — Dale Gordon, *The Dominion Sex Dictionary*, p. 42, 1967

charity goods *noun*
a promiscuous woman who does not expect payment for sex *US, 1966*
- — Rose Giallombardo, *Society of Women*, p. 206, 1966: Glossary of Prison Terms

charity stuff *noun*
a woman who, while promiscuous, does not prostitute herself *US, 1950*
- — Hyman E. Goldin et al., *Dictionary of American Underworld Lingo*, p. 42, 1950

Charles *noun*
1 a Viet Cong; the Viet Cong *US, 1966*

- Charles was tearing our ass up in front. — Harry Maurer, *Strange Ground*, p. 215, 1989
- Charles may or may not have had time to scream as he died in a hail of shot. — Cherokee Paul McDonald, *Into the Green*, p. 78, 2001

2 a female's underwear *US, 1968*
- — Collin Baker et al., *College Undergraduate Slang Study Conducted at Brown University*, p. 95, 1968

charley horse *noun*
a muscle cramp *US, 1888*
- Sure, I'm fine now, Sugar Tit. Just a bitch-kitty charley horse in the foot. — Iceberg Slim (Robert Beck), *Death Wish*, p. 196, 1977
- He jerked LaVerne up again, his muscles screaming protest, trying to knot into charley horses. — Stephen King, *Skeleton Crew*, p. 300, 1985

charleys *noun*
the testicles *US, 1964*
- — Roger Blake, *The American Dictionary of Sexual Terms*, p. 33, 1964

Charlie *verb*
in the circus or carnival, to dump posters or advertising leaflets that have not been distributed or posted *US, 1980*
- — Joe McKennon, *Circus Lingo*, p. 25, 1980

Charlie; charlie *noun*
1 cocaine *US, 1935*
The phonetic alphabet uses "Charlie" for "C" in use from around the same time that "charlie" for "cocaine" first appears. Also spelt "charley."
- More specifically, it was classified as M, C, and H—Mary, Charlie, and Harry—which stood for morphine, cocaine, and heroin. — William J. Spillard and Pence James, *Needle in a Haystack*, pp. 147–148, 1945
- "When you shoot Henry [heroin] and Charley, you can smell it going in. — William Burroughs, *Junkie*, p. 84, 1953
- We all know what a lummox Frankie Lymon was to mess with hard drugs like henry and charlie, after all, they took his life. — Richard Meltzer, *A Whore Just Like the Rest*, p. 65, 1970

2 a member of the Viet Cong *US, 1965*
- So you have to look for it, you have to check every damn hootch, even if its been burned to the ground. Cause maybe Charlie is down in a hole — John Sayles, *Union Dues*, p. 255, 1977
- "Charlie was always a gook? But a gook wasn't always Charlie?" Farley smiled for the first time. "You never knew when a gook was Charlie." — Nelson DeMille, *Word of Honor*, p. 414, 1985
- He wore a string of ears right across his chest / Just to show Charlie he was always the best. — Sandee Shaffer Johnson, *Cadences*, p. 139, 1986
- Wanna kill those Chinese Charlies! — William T. Vollman, *Whores for Gloria*, p. 124, 1991

3 the Viet Cong *US, 1966*
- We love to dine by candlelight / Since Charlie blew the power plant. — Ken Melvin, *Sorry 'Bout That*, p. 50, 1966
- There was a hell of a lot of Charlies (Communists) in here yesterday. — *San Francisco Chronicle*, p. 19, 3rd February 1966
- "How do you spot the elusive Charlie from the air?" — Elaine Shepard, *The Doom Pussy*, p. 24, 1967
- Charlie don't surf. — *Apocalypse Now*, 1979

4 a white man, or white men in general *US, 1928*
- I am perplexed and hard pressed in finding a solution or reason that will adequately explain why we are so eager to follow Charlie. — George Jackson, *Soledad Brother*, p. 67, July 1965
- "You know Charlie and Miss Ann ain't going to sit still for that—their kids in the same classroom with black kids." — John Williams, *The Man Who Cried I Am*, p. 235, 1967
- So you going back to Charlie country. — Cecil Brown, *The Life & Loves of Mr. Jiveass Nigger*, p. 206, 1969
- Sapphire is the world's foremost authority on Charlie. She has borne his children, been his servant, his mistress, his confidante, and the recipient of perversion for hundreds of years. — Carolyn Greene, *70 Soul Secrets of Sapphire*, p. 32, 1973

5 the penis *US, 1969*
- Also, if you get caught eating at the table after a game with Charley uncovered, that costs a dollar. — Jim Bouton, *Ball Four*, p. 152, 1970

6 a dollar *US, 1924*
- Hey, man, you got a couple charlies you can lend me? — Piri Thomas, *Down These Mean Streets*, p. 106, 1967
- — Eugene Landy, *The Underground Dictionary*, p. 48, 1971

7 in poker, the third player to the left of the dealer *US, 1988*
- — George Percy, *The Language of Poker*, p. 16, 1988

Charlie bird noun

during the Vietnam war, a helicopter used by a tactical commander US, 1974

- Charlie Bird—Command and control helicopter. — William Peers, *Report of the Department of Army Review*, 1974

- "Punchbowl Three, this is Firefly Four-Four. We got a Charlie bird down on Lima-Zulu Firefely. — Gil Parker, *Quest for Glory*, p. 84, 2003

Charlie Chan noun

a Chinese-American who curries favor with the dominant white culture US, 1969

- We want her replaced with a Third World person who is absolutely responsible to Third World and poor students, not to House Nigger, Uncle Tom, Tio Taco, or a Charlie Chan. — House Committee on Education and Labor, *Campus Unrest*, p. 15, 1969

charlie-charlie bird noun

a command and control aircraft US, 1982

- "You tell that muthafucka in that Charlie-Charlie bird fuck hisself." — John Del Vecchio, *The 13th Valley*, p. 287, 1982

- "They hated the commanders flying around in their charlie-charlie birds giving orders without a clue as to what it was like on the ground." — Keith Nolan, *Ripcord*, p. 205, 2000

- "Is your LZ secure enough for a touch down by a Charlie-Charlie bird now?" — Paul Morgan, *The Parrot's Beak*, p. 194, 2000

Charlie Cong noun

the Viet Cong; a Viet Cong US, 1970

- In the iconology of the Vietnam war, drugs occupy as significant a role as B-52s, napalm, free fire zones, and Charlie Cong. — *Washington Post*, p. 3 (Book World), 30th October 1983

Charlie Noble noun

an exhaust stack or chimney US, 1940

Originally nautical, referring to a ship's smokestack.

- [I]n addition to which they are often to leeward of exhaust pipes and charlie nobles and are slammed mercilessly from side to side when lying ahull to a windless seaway. — Emiliano Marino, *Sailmaker's Apprentice*, p. 99, 2001

Charlie rats noun

US Army c-rations US, 1982

A combination of the phonetic alphabet and an abbreviation of "rations."

- Ham and lima beans. Taste like shit. Worst Charlie Rat there is. — John M. Del Vecchio, *The 13th Valley*, p. 47, 1982

- PFC Eric R. Shimer, a grenadier in third squad, 3rd Platoon, dumped the paraphenalia from it and reshouldered it with only his last can of warm beer, a can of charlie rats, and thirty rounds of ammunition. — Keith Nolan, *Death Valley*, p. 140, 1987

- We ate C rations or "charlie Rats," as they were often called. The olive-drab cans contained approximately eleven ounces of solid food such as frankfurters and beans, ham and lima beans, spaghetti and meat balls, sausage patties, and corned-beef hash. — Robert W. Black, *Rangers in Korea*, p. 131, 1989

Charlie Ridge noun

a ridge in the mountainous region west of Da Nang at the base of Ba Na Mountain; during the Vietnam war, also used as a jocular, generic term for any piece of landscape in Vietnam US, 1980

- He pulled back onto "Firebase Polar Bear," located on "Charlie Ridge." — Senate Committee on Veterans' Affairs, *Vietnam Veterans' Readjustment*, p. 237, 1980

- I could see almost the entire area of my unit, the 1st Marine Division—from Elephant Valley out Route 37 in the north, stretching south past Ba Na Mountain, Charlie Ridge, and the Arizona Territory. — William Capps, *The Vietnam Reader*, p. 290, 1991

Charlie rockets noun

a marine contraption in Korea, a small cart with 144 tubes that fire 42-pound projectiles over a range of approximately 5,200 yards US, 1957

- The marines have a unit called "Charlie rockets." — Martin Russ, *The Last Parallel*, p. 280, 1957

Charlie the Gooner noun

the collective forces of the North Vietnamese Army and the Vietcong US, 1992

- The message was brought home quickly: Charlie the Gooner will fight us and fight us nose to nose, when he has to. — Bob Stoffey, *Cleared Hot!*, p. 34, 1992

charm verb

to talk to someone US, 1989

- All the Kids would rap, charm (talk to), or game to impress girlfriends; hang it up (insult) or fresh (compliment) male friends by using special words. — Terry Williams, *The Cocaine Kids*, p. 90, 1989

Charmin' noun

a timid prisoner US, 1976

From the advertising slogan for Charmin™ toilet paper—"Please don't squeeze the Charmin."

- — John R. Armore and Joseph D. Wolfe, *Dictionary of Desperation*, p. 24, 1976

charm school noun

any leadership training course US, 1971

Originally applied to officer training in the military.

- Until 1978, women attended a separate OCS, nicknamed the "charm school," at Quantico. — *Washington Post Magazine*, p. 24, 25th May 1980

- The airline picked him to head what we pilots called a charm school—a program of a couple of days that taught how to conduct oneself as an airline captain. — *Atlanta Journal-Constitution*, p. 6B, 23rd March 2004

chase verb

in poker, to play against an opponent's superior hand US, 1963

- — Irwin Steig, *Common Sense in Poker*, p. 183, 1963

▸ **chase the bag**

to engage yourself in a near constant search for drugs to buy US, 1970

- — William D. Alsever, *Glossary for the Establishment and Other Uptight People*, p. 5, December 1970

- — Geoffrey Froner, *Digging for Diamonds*, p. 16, 1989

▸ **chase the dragon**

to inhale heroin smoke, especially from heroin burnt on a piece of aluminum foil US, 1961

- — David Maurer and Victor Vogel, *Narcotics and Narcotic Addiction*, p. 396, 1973

- — Geoffrey Froner, *Digging for Diamonds*, p. 16, 1989

- It was well known that Binion liked to "chase the dragon" or smoke heroin. — Jeff German, *Murder in Sin City*, p. 120, 2001

▸ **chase the nurse; chase the white nurse**

to become addicted to morphine US, 1992

- — Jay Robert Nash, *Dictionary of Crime*, p. 62, 1992

▸ **chase your losses**

when losing at gambling, to bet more and more and with less discretion in an increasingly frustrating attempt to win back what has been lost US, 1998

- — Christopher Cavanaugh, *AA to Z*, p. 67, 1998

chaser noun

1 a drink taken immediately after another US, 1897

- Boilermaker. This is a shooter followed by a chaser. — Mardee Regan, *The Bartender's Best Friend*, p. 93, 2003

2 a military police officer assigned to escort prisoners in transport US, 1927

Short for "brig chaser."

- In August of 1969, shortly before coming home, I was made a "brig chaser" and told to escort another 19-year-old to the brig in Da Nang. — *Providence (Rhode Island) Journal-Bulletin*, p. 1E, 20th April 2000

3 a crack cocaine user with obsessive compulsive behaviors US, 1992

- — Terry Williams, *Crackhouse*, p. 147, 1992

chassis noun

1 a human body US, 1930

- She had the kind of chassis that gallant men died for, but, despite her terrific good looks and her knockout shape, she was starting to become a hell of a drag. — Morton Cooper, *High School Confidential*, p. 37, 1958

- He dropped his own drink in the act of catching her lax chassis[.] — David Gregory, *Flesh Seller*, p. 73, 1962

- "She got a real sweet chassis filling up a tight sheath dress[.]" — Roger Blake, *Love Clubs, Inc.*, p. 143–144, 1967

2 the female breasts US, 1957

- They really had no idea what was coming off—even though Barbara had a couple of fangled chassis that would put Jayne Mansfield to shame. — Frederick Kohner, *Gidget*, p. 39, 1957

3 the skull *US*, *1994*
- — Sally Williams, *"Strong" Words*, p. 136, 1994

chastity belt *noun*
in gambling, the loss limit that players some impose on themselves *US*, *1996*
- — John Vorhaus, *The Big Book of Poker Slang*, p. 9, 1996

chastity rig *noun*
a skin-colored patch worn over a woman's vulva to give the appearance of nudity *US*, *1970*
- Feral's hands, gripping her bottom, covered the adhesive strips which secured her chastity rig[.] — Terry Southern, *Blue Movie*, p. 208, 1970

chat room *noun*
a network on the Internet that hosts real-time typed conversations *US*, *1993*
- Rush Limbaugh makes regular appearances on CompuServe, although acerbic "Rush Rooms"—a Limbaugh-oriented chat room where users can discuss issues in real time—pop up on several online services. — *Boston Globe*, p. 51, 8th July 1993
- Subscribers can talk directly to one another in "chat rooms"—subnetworks in which up to two-dozen people can type comments to one another. — *New York Times*, p. 1, 20th June 1993
- When the Internet first happened, chat rooms were the place to be. — Suroosh Alvi et al., *The Vice Guide*, p. 16, 2002

Chattanooga choo-choo *noun*
a marijuana cigarette made with two or three rolling papers laid longways *US*, *1997*
- — Jim Emerson-Cobb, *Scratching the Dragon*, 1997

chatter *noun*
the flexing of a surfboard riding over choppy water or the slapping sound created *US*, *1963*
- — Grant W. Kuhns, *On Surfing*, p. 114, 1963

chatterbox *noun*
a typewriter *US*, *1950*
- — Hyman E. Goldin et al., *Dictionary of American Underworld Lingo*, p. 42, 1950

chawbacon *noun*
an unsophisticated country dweller *US*, *1834*
- It's a rule in these parts, so black chawbacons don't git took unawares! — George MacDonald Fraser, *Black Ajax*, p. 68, 1997

cheap Charlie *noun*
1 a small, neighborhood candy store *US*, *1979*
- Every street had a "Cheap Charlie." — Samuel Chotznoff, *A Lost Paradise*, p. 75, 1979
- One of the most popular among the younger generations was the candy store, or "Cheap Charlie." Every street had a "Cheap Charlie." — Mario Maffi, *Gateway to the Promised Land*, p. 85, 1991

2 a cheapskate *US*, *1972*
- "Hoa, numah fucking ten!" the kid yelled. "Cheap Charlie." — William Pelfrey, *The Big V*, p. 17, 1972
- You number fucking ten cheap charlie GI cocksucker! — *Maledicta*, p. 257, Summer/Winter 1982

cheap heart *noun*
a Purple Heart award resulting from a minor combat wound *US*, *1990*
- A "cheap heart" was a very minor wound, not requiring medical evacuation, hospitalization or any major treatment; any combat wound was grounds for a Purple Heart. — Gregory Clark, *Words of the Vietnam War*, p. 417, 1990

Cheap John *adjective*
shoddy, inferior *US*, *1855*
- "Cheap John" jewelry salesmen gulled naive countrymen with their suavity and faked generosity. — Thomas D. Clark, *The Southern Country Editor*, p. 38, 1948

cheapo *noun*
in chess, a trick move or a game won because of an opponent's error *US*, *1971*
- — *American Speech*, p. 233, Autumn–Winter 1971: "Checkschmuck! The slang of the chess player"

cheapo *adjective*
inexpensive *US*, *1972*

- It's a cheapo takeoff on porn flicks and movie musicals that might have been expected to die unheralded of its own terminal ineptitude. — *Washington Post*, p. B4, 5th September 1977
- [W]ith cheapo bullets like these it don't all the time go clear around. — Jess Mowry, *Way Past Cool*, 1992

cheap physical stuff *noun*
sexual activity short of intercourse *US*, *1958*
- Ninety-five percent of the guys here—at least for the weekend dates—are just looking for that "cheap physical stuff." — Otto Butz, *The Unsilent Generation*, p. 88, 1958
- — Collin Baker et al., *College Undergraduate Slang Study Conducted at Brown University*, p. 95, 1968
- No kissy-face-huggy-bod, there's plenty of time for the cheap physical stuff later. — J.C. Pollock, *Crossfire*, p. 271, 1985

cheap play *noun*
in dominoes, a move that scores one point *US*, *1959*
- — Dominic Armanino, *Dominoes*, p. 16, 1959

cheapshit *adjective*
inexpensive, shoddy *US*, *1978*
- "He handed her a pair of panties. Cheapshit dimestore panties." — Tony Ardizzone, *In the Name of the Father*, p. 208, 1978
- He was continuously and unceremoniously evicted form cheapshit apartments[.] — Bill Landis, *Sleazoid Express*, p. 81, 2002

cheap shot *noun*
1 a petty, unfair insult *US*, *1971*
- I resent his cheap shot at Dan Quayle. Dan Quayle has been viciously smeared by the media and comedians for spelling potato with an "e" at the end. — *Telegraph Herald (Dubuque, Iowa)*, p. A4, 12th March 1999
- She also called the flap on Bush's inability to answer questions on foreign leaders a cheap shot. Bush could not name the leaders of Chechnya, India and Pakistan. — *Lansing (Michigan) State Journal*, p. 1B, 19th November 1999
- Why aren't there more black quarterbacks? The old racist slander was that they weren't smart enough. Having had that lie thrown in their faces, the cheap-shot artists like Limbaugh would now say, Well, maybe they're good, but they're not as good as that — *Baltimore Sun*, p. 1B, 10th October 2003
- Arianna said, "Let me finish. Let me finish. Let me finish. You know this is completely impolite and"—here's the kicker—"we know how you treat women." "Okay, Arnie, so it was a cheap shot." — *Washington Post*, p. A25, 27th September 2003

2 in sports, an unnecessary, unprovoked act of violence *US*, *1970*
- [I]f anything goes wrong, if there's any cheap shots, I'll be right there for them. — *Sun-Sentinel (Fort Lauderdale, Florida)*, p. 3C, 29th October 2003

cheapskate *noun*
a miserly person *US*, *1896*
- "We'd love to take you up on that, we really would, but the bank's already got us on more payment plans than we can handle." "Fucking cheapskates." — David Sedaris, *Naked*, p. 186, 1997

cheat *verb*
in the entertainment industry, to move slightly to create a better camera angle *US*, *1991*
- The word is cheat: "Cheat your left leg out a little," or "Open to the camera." — Robert Stoller and I.S. Levine, *Coming Attractions*, p. 121, 1991

cheater five *noun*
while surfing, the toes of one foot extended over the nose of the board only because the surfer has stretched his leg far forward *US*, *1965*
- — Ross Olney, *The Young Sportsman's Guide to Surfing*, p. 88, 1965

cheaters *noun*
1 eye glasses *US*, *1908*
- Tesch mumbled in his signifying way, cocking his sorrowful eyes over those hornrimmed cheaters. — Mezz Mezzrow, *Really the Blues*, p. 177, 1946
- The eyes behind the rimless cheaters flashed. — Raymond Chandler, *The Little Sister*, p. 5, 1949
- "Take those cheaters off," Sheik said. — Chester Himes, *The Real Cool Killers*, p. 46, 1959

2 dark glasses *US*, *1938*
- — Robert S. Gold, *A Jazz Lexicon*, p. 54, 1964

3 padding that enhances the apparent size of a female's breasts *US, 1945*

- Millions and millions of men were being deceived, hoodwinked, and betrayed by scientific gadgets known as "falsies," "gay deceivers," "pads," and "cheaters." — Earl Wilson, *I Am Gazing Into My 8-Ball*, p. 70, 1945
- — Helen Dahlskog (Editor), *A Dictionary of Contemporary and Colloquial Usage*, p. 12, 1972

4 metal skis *US, 1963*

- When metal skis were first introduced by racers, they were called cheaters because of their easier maneuverability. — *American Speech*, p. 205, October 1963: "The language of skiers"

cheat sheet *noun*

1 a written memory aid, usually but not always clandestine *US, 1957*

- — *Time Magazine*, p. 46, 24th August 1959
- — Collin Baker et al., *College Undergraduate Slang Study Conducted at Brown University*, p. 95, 1968
- He [Socrates] reads from a cheat sheet under his toga. — *Bill and Ted's Excellent Adventure*, p. 93, 1989

2 in casino gambling, a listing of the payoffs for a particular ticket *US, 1982*

- — Jim Claussen, *Keno Handbook*, p. 17, 1982

cheat spot *noun*

an establishment that sells alcohol after closing hours *US, 1963*

- Few racketeers could afford to operate a cheat spot if every time a liquor-law violation was proven the court imposed the maximum penalties. — *Saturday Evening Post*, p. 72, 9th March 1963

cheat throat *noun*

oral sex performed on a man in which the person doing the performing simulates taking the penis completely into their mouth without actually doing so *US, 1995*
A play on **DEEP THROAT**, the real thing.

- — *Adult Video News*, p. 48, August 1995

check *noun*

a gambling token *US, 1974*

- And then a rush for the cage to cash in the chips (which, for whatever this information may be worth, are always called "checks" by the people who work in the casinos and "chips" by everybody else). — Edward Lin, *Big Julie of Vegas*, p. 23, 1974
- Griffin, the quiet Irishman, was fascinated by the way I handled chips—"checks" in dealers' slang. — Jimmy Snyder, *Jimmy the Greek*, p. 16, 1975

check *verb*

as a prank, to pull down a friend's bathing suit from behind *US, 1997*

- — Vann Wesson, *Generation X Field Guide and Lexicon*, p. 36, 1997

▸ **check hat**
to prepare to leave *US, 1966*

- — *Current Slang*, p. 2, Fall 1966

▸ **check the cheese**
to watch girls as they walk by *US, 1959*

- — *American Speech*, p. 154, May 1959: "Gator (University of Florida) slang"

▸ **check the war**
to stop arguing *US, 1947*

- — Marcus Hanna Boulware, *Jive and Slang of Students in Negro Colleges*, 1947

▸ **check your nerves**
to stay calm *US, 1947*

- — Marcus Hanna Boulware, *Jive and Slang of Students in Negro Colleges*, 1947

▸ **check your six**
used as a warning to a pilot to check behind his aircraft for enemy planes *US, 1963*
Based on the clock configuration, with twelve o'clock being straight ahead and six o'clock straight behind.

- "Leopard One, check your six, check your six!" — Eric Harry, *Arc Light*, p. 315, 1996

check artist *noun*

a criminal adept at forging checks *US, 1959*

- [M]y cell partner is a check artist from Maryland who has been ostensibly rehabilitated to the extent that he is leaving on parole next week. — James Blake, *The Joint*, p. 227, 25th June 1959

checkbook *adjective*

characterized by a seemingly unlimited ability and will to pay for something *US, 1975*
Applied most commonly to journalism (paying for news), but also to enterprises such as baseball.

- While this was unfolding, Police Chief Charles Gain was hit with accusations of checkbook detective work. — Bill Cardoso, *The Maltese Sangweech*, p. 13, 1984

check cop *verb*

to use an adhesive placed on a cheater's palm to steal chips while sliding a pile of chips in a poker game to the winner *US, 1988*

- — George Percy, *The Language of Poker*, p. 19, 1988

check day *noun*

the day each month when welfare checks are delivered *US, 1971*

- I did all the buying; everybody else was broke because this was the day before Checkday and everyone's last check was long since spent. — Robert Deane Pharr, *S.R.O.*, p. 120, 1971
- Today was check day; he would take it in person from the carrier and hustle down to the currency exchange. — William Brashler, *City Dogs*, p. 94, 1976
- On the first day of April, she's out on the stoop, same as she ever was, watching the check-day traffic at Mount and Fayette. — David Simon and Edward Burns, *The Corner*, p. 179, 1997

check-hiker

a forger *US, 1979*

- "Hobart Slocum was one of the most artistic check hikers in the greater Manhattan area." I unbutton my jacket and put my elbows out to the side and raise them. "Am I heeled?" — Leo Rosten, *Silky!*, p. 55, 1979

check in *verb*

1 to place yourself in protective police custody *US, 2001*

- — Don R. McCreary (Editor), *Dawg Speak*, 2001

2 to be initiated into a youth gang *US, 1994*

- — Ann Lawson, *Kids & Gangs*, p. 55, 1994

check out *verb*

1 to leave prison *US, 1950*

- — Hyman E. Goldin et al., *Dictionary of American Underworld Lingo*, p. 42, 1950

2 to die *US, 1927*

- — Sally Williams, "Strong" Words, p. 137, 1994

3 to commit suicide while in prison *US, 1992*

- — William K. Bentley and James M. Corbett, *Prison Slang*, p. 104, 1992

check, please!

used as a humorous suggestion that a conversation is at an end *US, 1971*
Popularized by Keith Olberman on ESPN, used by Woody Allen in *Annie Hall* and Catherine Keener in *Being John Malkovich*.

- — Hermese E. Roberts, *The Third Ear*, 1971
- — Keith Olberman and Dan Patrick, *The Big Show*, p. 13, 1997

check writer *noun*

a criminal who passes bad checks *US, 1972*

- And they just do not worry about check writers because they are too numerous. — Bruce Jackson, *Outside the Law*, p. 78, 1972

check you later; check ya later

used as a farewell *US, 1982*

- — Connie Eble (Editor), *UNC-CH Campus Slang*, p. 1, Fall 1982
- — *Washington Post Magazine*, p. 17, 2nd August 1988

cheddar *noun*

money *US, 1998*

- — Connie Eble (Editor), *UNC-CH Campus Slang*, p. 2, Spring 1998
- "And then I'd like to know, who in their right fucking mind walks out on that kind of cheddar, comes to Dempsy fucking New Jersey with their hands in their pockets whistling Dixie." — Richard Price, *Samaritan*, p. 49, 2003

cheeba; cheeb *noun*

a potent marijuana, now a generic term *US, 1994*

- — Judi Sanders, *Mashing and Munching in Ames*, p. 4, 1994
- Pot, grass, weed, herb, cheeba, chronic, trees, indo, doja—whatever they called it then, whatever they call it now, and whatever they'll

call it in the future, it was marijuana. — 50 Cent, *From Pieces to Weight*, p. 5, 2005

- A lot of hip-hoppers puff cheeb, man — *The Source*, p. 56, November 91

cheech noun

a leader of an Italian-American criminal organization *US*, 1977

- And the guy belonged to some downtown cheech. There was a hell of a row with the mob and with the department. — Edwin Torres, *Q & A*, p. 157, 1977

cheek noun

a sexually loose female *US*, 1955

- — *American Speech*, p. 302, December 1955: "Wayne University slang"

cheese noun

1 a powdery concoction containing heroin, designed for beginning users *US*, 2006

- A new heroin-laced powder known as "cheese" is popping up in middle and high schools in Texas. — *USA Today*, p. 1, 27th April 2006

2 smegma, matter secreted by the sebaceous gland that collects between the glans penis and the foreskin or around the clitoris and labia minora *US*, 1927

From the dull whitish color of this substance.

- — Donald Webster Cory and John P. LeRoy, *The Homosexual and His Society*, p. 262, 1963: "A lexicon of homosexual slang"
- We pushed heavily on the new moral outlook: get a VD test often or face the fact that you're just as dirty as a person who never washes the cheese off his uncircumcised cock[.] — *Screw*, p. 13, 6th November 1972
- "Some places I've worked, some guys will come in real cruddy, you know, their penis hasn't been clean for weeks. They call it 'cheese,'" she says graphically, wriggling up her nose. — George Paul Csicsery (Editor), *The Sex Industry*, p. 8, 1973

3 an attractive young woman *US*, 1959

- I got into the habit of studying at the Radcliffe library. Not just to eye the cheese, although I admit that I liked to look. — Erich Segal, *Love Story*, p. 2, 1970

4 in pool, a situation where a player needs to make only one shot to win *US*, 1993

- — Mike Shamos, *The Illustrated Encyclopedia of Billiards*, p. 49, 1993

5 money; a gambler's bankroll *US*, 1985

A locution popularized by Minnesota Fats, as in, "I never lost when we played for the cheese."

- — Mike Shamos, *The Illustrated Encyclopedia of Billiards*, p. 49, 1993
- All these niggas want cheese, is we mice or men, word up. — RZA, *The Wu-Tang Manual*, p. 164, 2005

6 freebase cocaine *US*, 1992

- — Jay Robert Nash, *Dictionary of Crime*, p. 63, 1992

7 an amphetamine user *US*, 1993

- — Peter Johnson, *Dictionary of Street Alcohol and Drug Terms*, p. 38, 1993

8 nonsense *US*, 1989

- Joe Flaherty nailed the essence of TV monster movie cheese without even using a real word from the English language[.] — Frank Zappa, *The Real Frank Zappa Book*, p. 168, 1989

9 luck *US*, 1990

- — Steve Rushin, *Pool Cool*, p. 10, 1990

cheese verb

to leave *US*, 1955

- He's going to cheese, I tell you. Nobody arrested him! — *Rebel Without a Cause*, 1955
- Cheese it! Here comes the socialite man. — Mart Crowley, *The Boys in the Band*, p. 85, 1968

cheese and crackers!

used as a nonprofane oath *US*, 1924

A euphemistic "Jesus Christ!"

- Cheese and crackers, pal! — Leo Rosten, *Dear Herm*, p. 117, 1974

cheeseball noun

a corny, socially inept person *US*, 1990

- — Connie Eble (Editor), *UNC-CH Campus Slang*, p. 2, Spring 1992
- You don't need to come to a place like Lookout Point and spout off all those cheeseball lines to be romantic. — *American Pie*, 1999

cheesebox noun

a telephone device used to transfer calls received by an illegal operation *US*, 1952

So named, according to Maas, because the first one was found by police hidden in a cheese box.

- — *Life*, p. 39, 19th May 1952
- Next he would install the cheesebox, an electrical device that connected the lines of the two phones. — Peter Maas, *Serpico*, p. 112, 1973

Cheesebox nickname

the Stateville Prison in Joilet, Illinois *US*, 1992

- — Jay Robert Nash, *Dictionary of Crime*, p. 63, 1992

cheesecake noun

a scantily clad woman as the subject of a photograph or artwork *US*, 1934

- "Hey, how about some leg shots, Georgia—some cheesecake?" — Georgia Sothern, *My Life in Burlesque*, p. 142, 1972
- Afterwards, he talked to me about posing for what he called "cheesecake photographs." — Tempest Storm, *Tempest Storm*, p. 129, 1987
- I had done only cheesecake photos before—never anything nude—but I did the centerfold for December 1959 because I knew it would please him. — Kathryn Leigh Scott, *The Bunny Years*, p. 73, 1998

cheesedog noun

a socially inept person who perceives himself in somewhat grandiose terms *US*, 1997

- — Vann Wesson, *Generation X Field Guide and Lexicon*, p. 36, 1997

cheese eater noun

an informer *US*, 1886

Playing on RAT.

- The legendary "silence" of prisons ("death to the squealer," and all) does not apply here. The joint is full of cheese-eaters and the Man usually knows what you're doing before you do. — James Blake, *The Joint*, p. 36, 23rd December 1951
- — Kenn "Naz" Young, *Naz's Underground Dictionary*, p. 20, 1973
- John Scarne, *Scarne on Dice*, p. 463, 1974
- "Slade was a cheese-eater." — Stephen J. Cannell, *White Sister*, p. 51, 2006

cheese-eating noun

an act of informing on others or betrayal *US*, 1951

- To report these unsavory and totally lost creatures is of course a violation of the rigid convict code, and is called "ratting" or "cheese-eating." — James Blake, *The Joint*, p. 21, 15th April 1951

cheese-eating surrender monkeys noun

the French; anyone who does not support American imperialism *US*, 2000

Coined on *The Simpsons* television show as a parody of American arrogance; often used by arrogant Americans unaware of the irony of their use.

- If these old gasbags really prefer to live in a nation of cheese-eating surrender monkeys (Groundskeeper Willie's delicious phrase from "The Simpsons") because they cannot lower themselves to accept the democratic judgment of their fellow Americans, then bon voyage, jerks. — *New York Post*, p. 4, 7th November 2000

cheesehead noun

a resident of the state of Wisconsin, especially a fan of the Green Bay Packers *US*, 2001

- The term "Cheesehead" to denote a Packer fan had not yet been labeled. — Gary Vasquez, *Packer Passion*, p. 22, 2001

cheese off!

go away! *US*, 1996

- — *Maledicta*, p. 99, 1996: "Domino's Pizza jargon"

cheeser noun

a police informer *US*, 1979

- — H. Craig Collins, *Street Gangs*, p. 222, 1979

cheesy adjective

of poor quality, inexpensive, shoddy *US*, 1863

- The driver asked us whether we had had fun. We said not too much, and pretty cheesy. — Jack Lait and Lee Mortimer, *Chicago Confidential*, p. 63, 1950
- Jammed between a grimy-windowed bookstore and a cheesy luncheonette was the marquee of a tiny art theater[.] — Philip Roth, *Goodbye, Columbus*, p. 22, 1959
- I started up the car and cruised along Ogden Boulevard until I found an open bar, a cheesy, small place called John's On. — Clancy Sigal, *Going Away*, p. 358, 1961

• "Faith Domergue was an Oscar hopeful when making *This Island Earth*, one of the most opulently cheesy sci-films ever." — Ethan Morden, *Some Men Are Lookers*, p. 111, 1997

chemical *noun*
crack cocaine *US, 1994*
• — US Department of Justice, *Street Terms*, October 1994

chemist *noun*
a person who uses a mainframe computer for the academic purposes for which it was designed, depriving the speaker of the chance to use it for more interesting, less academic purposes *US, 1991*
• — Eric S. Raymond, *The New Hacker's Dictionary*, p. 93, 1991

chemo *noun*
chemotherapy, a cancer treatment *US, 1978*
• Personal memos were returned to him with "chemo" written in, he said. — *Washington Post*, p. B1, 2nd December 1978
• At night the kids play video games in the den and gossip about their doctors and their current regimen of what they call "chemo." — *New York Times*, p. 27 (Section 2), 9th May 1981

cheroot *noun*
a large marijuana cigarette *US, 1993*
• — N. Peter Johnson, *Dictionary of Street Alcohol and Drug Terms*, p. 38, 1993

cherry *noun*
1 the hymen; virginity (male or female); the state of sustained sexual abstinence *US, 1918*
Combines with a variety of verbs (bust, crack, pop) to indicate the ending of a virgin condition.
• But I felt that bragging to other fellas about how many cherries I'd cracked or how many panties came down on rooftops or backyards was nobody's business but my own[.] — Piri Thomas, *Down These Mean Streets*, p. 15, 1967
• Some "cherries" completely close the cunny hole and have to be opened by surgery. — *Screw*, p. 9, 29th December 1969
• The good girls held on to their cherry. And it was a big deal. — Edwin Torres, *Carlito's Way*, p. 11, 1975
• I drove around the desolate southern perimeter of the city while Willie muledicked her and blew off his jail cherry[.] — Iceberg Slim (Robert Beck), *Airtight Willie and Me*, p. 8, 1979

2 a virgin; someone who because of extenuating circumstances has abstained from sex for a long period *US, 1942*
• A no-poot green cherry. — Bernard Wolfe, *The Late Risers*, p. 30, 1954
• "I don't think any of my damned sisters were cherries since they were thirteen anyway." — Robert Newton, *Bondage Clubs U.S.A.*, p. 69, 1967
• "Yeah man, they ain't never had no cherry before, and they think this is a cherry they'll be getting," Prince replied, and laughed. — Donald Goines, *Black Gangster*, p. 23, 1977
• BRIAN: I'm not a cherry. BENDER: When have you ever gotten laid? BRIAN: I've gotten laid lotsa times. — *The Breakfast Club*, 1985

3 by extension, any innocence that can be lost *US, 1956*
• He had no idea he was talking to a young man who cracked his cherry in the thievery business with forty times that at Ludwig's. — Red Rudensky, *The Gonif*, p. 76, 1970
• I've talked about it to other guys who've lost their cherry, and we all agree: You appreciate different things. — James Ellroy, *Blood on the Moon*, p. 33, 1984
• [As Henry leaves court after his first arrest] You broke your cherry! You broke your cherry! — *Goodfellas*, 1990
• Folks do not want to hear about Alpha Company—us grunts—busting jungle and busting cherries from Land Zone Skator-Gator to Scat Man Do (wherever that is). — Larry Heinemann, *Paco's Story*, p. 5, 1990

4 by extension, someone who is completely inexperienced *US, 1946*
• "They should a never done it, throwing a cherry in with hardened sailors like us," says Mule. — Darryl Ponicsan, *The Last Detail*, p. 74, 1970
• "Any ever been here before?" "No, all cherries." — Ronald J. Glasser, *365 Days*, p. 29, 1971
• "I'm not going to say he had some cold beans and motherfuckers for breakfast, took some shots from the other guys about being a cherry and then went out and got blown into fifty million pieces—which is what happened." — Mark Barker, *Nam*, p. xi, 1981
• We were cherries. It was my third day in-country. — Harry Maurer, *Strange Ground*, p. 148, 1989

5 of a male, the "virginity" of the anus *US, 1997*
• MISTRESS: […] Now let's dress you—let's get you ready for your defloration. DAMEN [a male "slave"]: I'm going to lose my cherry. MISTRESS: You're just a little girl, an innocent thing[.] — Terence Sellers, *Dungeon Evidence*, p. 55, 1997

6 an entry-level youth gang member *US, 1981*
• When he was old enough he hoped to be a cherry, then a cutdown, then finally, after he'd been shot and stabbed ten times and was too old to fight, a veterano. — Joseph Wambaugh, *The Glitter Dome*, p. 109, 1981

7 in pool, an extremely easy shot *US, 1993*
• — Mike Shamos, *The Illustrated Encyclopedia of Billiards*, p. 49, 1993

8 in horse racing, a horse that has yet to win a race *US, 1951*
• — David W. Maurer, *Argot of the Racetrack*, p. 19, 1951

9 a female nipple *US, 1964*
• — Roger Blake, *The American Dictionary of Sexual Terms*, p. 34, 1964

10 the flashing red light on top of a police car *US, 1973*
• [T]he squad car came tooling down the alley, its outraged cherry blazing. — Joe Eszterhas, *Charlie Simpson's Apocalypse*, p. 109, 1973
• — Warren Smith, *Warren's Smith's Authentic Dictionary of CB*, p. 59, 1976

▸ **cop a cherry**
to take someone's virginity *US, 1971*
• A young man's sexual initiation by a prostitute ("copping a cherry") was once more frequent than it is today. — Charles Winick, *The Lively Commerce*, p. 189, 1971

▸ **pop a cherry**
to have sex with a virgin *US, 1973*
• "If I were to have a son, I would definitely pop his cherry." — Xaviera Hollander, *Xaviera*, p. 21, 1973

cherry *adjective*
1 virginal *US, 1933*
• Don't forget she's cherry. — Norman Mailer, *The Naked and the Dead*, p. 551, 1948
• I know a waitress. She ain't cherry. — Willard Motley, *Let No Man Write My Epitaph*, p. 179, 1958
• I know you thought I was cherry, your number-one size / But I was balling Tony, and you weren't wise. — Dennis Wepman et al., *The Life*, p. 142, 1976

2 without a criminal record *US, 1980*
• "You lied to me, Darrold," sounding a little hurt—"try to tell me you're cherry and they got a sheet on you, man." — Elmore Leonard, *City Primeval*, p. 58, 1980

cherry bomb *noun*
a virgin *US, 2001*
• "A lot of 'em like little girls. And if I tell 'em I'm a cherry bomb ... a virgin." — J.T. LeRoy, *The Heart is Deceitful Above All Things*, p. 92, 2001

cherry boy *noun*
1 a male virgin *US, 1974*
• Some are revealed as male models and others as adolescent, self-confessed virgins who have never kissed before. "Cherry boys," the host-comics leer to the squeals of young women in the audience. — BPI Entertainment News Wire, 2nd May 2000

2 a recent arrival to combat *US, 1984*
• "You're like old Jacobs, goddamned cherry boy." — William Pelfrey, *The Big V*, p. 133, 1972
• I was still a cherry boy—and that's what you stay until you get 90 days in country. — Wallace Terry, *Bloods*, p. 239, 1984

cherry farm *noun*
a prison, or the section of a prison reserved for first-time offenders *US, 1966*
• — *Current Slang*, p. 2, Winter 1966
• — Helen Dahlskog (Editor), *A Dictionary of Contemporary and Colloquial Usage*, p. 13, 1972

cherry fine *adjective*
excellent *US, 1966*
• — Andy Anonymous, *A Basic Guide to Campusology*, p. 5, 1966

cherry girl *noun*
a virgin *US, 1982*
US military usage during the Vietnam war.
• — *Maledicta*, p. 256, Summer/Winter 1982: "Viet-speak"
• I'm still a "cherry girl" when I go live with Mac. He be the first man I go home with, first man I sleep with. — Steven DeBonis, *Children of the Enemy*, p. 163, 1995

cherry kicks *noun*

the first drug injection enjoyed by someone just released from prison *US, 1971*

- — Eugene Landy, *The Underground Dictionary*, p. 48, 1971

cherry menth; cherry meth *noun*

the recreational drug GHB *US, 1995*

- Police have identified a substance that left three people unconscious and close to death on a Fillmore sidewalk last month as a legal yet potentially dangerous drug know as "Cherry Meth." — *Los Angeles Times*, p. B2, 4th November 1995
- GHB has been marketed as a liquid or powder and has been sold on the street under names such as Grevious Bodily Harm, Georgia Home Boy, Liquid Ecstasy, Liqiud X, Liquid E, GHB, GBH, Soap, Scoop, Easy Lay, Salty Water, G-Riffick, [and] Cherry Menth. — *Morbidity and Morality Weekly Report*, p. 281, 4th April 1997

cherry orchard *noun*

a woman's college *US, 1966*

- — *Current Slang*, p. 2, Winter 1966
- — Helen Dahlskog (Editor), *A Dictionary of Contemporary and Colloquial Usage*, p. 13, 1972

cherry patch *noun*

a poker game being played by a group of poor players, ripe for the taking by a good professional *US, 1982*

- — David M. Hayano, *Poker Faces*, p. 186, 1982

cherry picker *noun*

1 a person who targets virgins for seduction *US, 1960*

- They call me Rap the dicker the ass kicker / The cherry picker the city slicker the titty licker. — H. Rap Brown, *Die Nigger Die!*, p. 28, 1969

2 a crane *US, 1987*

- — Ira Konigsberg, *The Complete Film Dictionary*, p. 47, 1987

cherry pie *noun*

in the entertainment industry, extra money earned for something other than ordinary work *US, 1955*

- — *American Speech*, pp. 310–311, December 1955: "Cherry pie"
- — Don Wilmeth, *The Language of American Popular Entertainment*, p. 51, 1981

cherry-popping *noun*

the act of taking someone's virginity *US, 1972*

- I believe there was such a thing as "cherry-popping"—an occasion when a father would send his adolescent son along to an understanding prostitute for an introduction to sex. — Xaviera Hollander, *The Happy Hooker*, p. 201, 1972

chest *noun*

a woman's breasts *US, 1986*

- Another great chest on parade in Big Bust #5 is that of Barbara Alton, a diminuitive little vixen who obviously loves fondling, squeezing, licking and just generally fiddling with her two tremendous tits[.] — *Adult Video*, p. 54, August/September 1986
- "Yeah, nice, healthy chest," Letch said, leering. — Joseph Wambaugh, *Floaters*, p. 155, 1996

chest cutter *noun*

a thoracic surgeon *US, 1983*

- — Lynda Van Devanter, *Home Before Morning*, p. 378, 1983: Glossary

Chester and Esther *noun*

in craps, a bet on any craps and eleven *US, 1985*

A back formation from the initials "c" and "e."

- — Steve Kuriscak, *Casino Talk*, p. 67, 1985

Chester the Molester; Chester *noun*

a lecherous man *US, 1977*

From a cartoon character regularly featured in *Hustler* magazine.

- They also have an ad for "Chester the Molester" T-shirts. — United States Congress, *Sexual Exploitation of Children*, p. 7, 1977
- Hustler used to run a regular kiddie corner called "Chester the Molester." — Jeanne Ballantine, *Sociological Footprints*, p. 248, 1982
- — Pamela Munro, *U.C.L.A. Slang*, p. 29, 1989
- The girl remained clothed the entire time, but Jenkins had manipulated her into various poses that revealed his Chester the Molester ways. — Alafair Burke, *Missing Justice*, p. 164, 2004

chestnuts *noun*

the testicles *US, 1971*

- — Eugene Landy, *The Underground Dictionary*, p. 48, 1971

chesty *adjective*

arrogant, conceited *US, 1899*

- Mr. Harrison stood there chesty as a peacock[.] — Mezz Mezzrow, *Really the Blues*, p. 310, 1946
- — Kenn "Naz" Young, *Naz's Underground Dictionary*, p. 20, 1973

chew *noun*

chewing tobacco *US, 1990*

- The uncles toil good-naturedly in the kitchen ("It beats the shit out of the old country," they'd tell you if they could), singing Caruso and arias and spitting chew on the floor. — Larry Heinemann, *Paco's Story*, p. 105, 1990

chew *verb*

▶ **chew face**

to kiss *US, 1980*

- "Who can tell me what petting means?" asked substitute teacher Sharon Simon, who has a master's degree in psychology. "You mean chewing face?" queried one student. — *Los Angeles Times*, pp. 2–6, 3rd February 1986

▶ **chew it**

in skateboarding, to fall from the board *US, 1976*

- — Albert Cassorla, *The Skateboarder's Bible*, p. 199, 1976

▶ **chew the fat**

to gossip, to chatter idly *US, 1907*

- The farmers were chewing the fat in feed and hardware stores, the women were chopping their gums in Five-and-tens and department stores[.] — Jack Kerouac, *Letter to Caroline and Paul Blake*, p. 143, 16th March 1948
- [I]n the course of chewing the fat we told each other all about our form. — Charles Raven, *Underworld Nights*, p. 148, 1956
- We stood around the De Soto and chewed the fat a while. — Clancy Sigal, *Going Away*, p. 258, 1961
- Now I want to create the illusion that this is just Mickey and I chewin' the fat all by ourselves. — *Natural Born Killers*, 1994

▶ **chew the scenery**

to over-act in a dramatic performance *US, 1973*

- — Sherman Louis Sergel, *The Language of Show Biz*, p. 48, 1973
- I see scenery and / chew it, chew it / that's how I do it[.] — Gerard Alessandrini, *Chew It [Forbidden Broadway Volume 3]*, 1993
- Johnny Depp and rival pirate Geoffrey Rush, both chewing the scenery with such abandon it's a wonder their vessels don't spring a leak[.] — *Bang*, p. 64, August 2003
- A surprisingly entertaining high-seas actioner with Perkins chewing the scenery as the leader of a group of terrorists who have taken over a supply ship. — David Beller, *TLA Video & DVD Guide 2004*, p. 206, 2004

▶ **chew the sugar cane**

to gossip *US, 1978*

- The family was in the living room chewing the sugar cane on what was happening in Puerto Rico. — Piri Thomas, *Stories from El Barrio*, p. 118, 1978

▶ **chew your tobacco more than once**

to repeat yourself *US, 1893*

- — Shirley Brice Heath, *Ways with Words, back matter*, 1983

chewers *noun*

the teeth *US, 1970*

- — Clarence Major, *Dictionary of Afro-American Slang*, p. 36, 1970

chewies *noun*

crack cocaine *US, 1994*

- — US Department of Justice, *Street Terms*, October 1994

chew out *verb*

to rebuke someone harshly *US, 1929*

- John Wayne chewed me out for that one. "Never play a rapist and never die in a picture," he said. — Burt Reynolds, *My Life*, p. 203, 1994

chew out; chewing out *noun*

a rebuke *US, 1964*

- Yet instead of forty lashes, or even a thorough chewing out, she had given them her car. — Max Shulman, *Anyone Got a Match?*, p. 55, 1964

chewsday *noun*

Tuesday *US, 1877*

- "I don't know how come I didn't git dere Chewsday like I promise." — Kate Chopin, *At Fault*, p. 19, 2002

Chi *nickname*
Chicago, Illinois *US, 1895*
- The news spread across an amused United States. WRITING IN SKY PANICS CHI — Philip Wylie, *Opus 21*, p. 204, 1949
- It's in a bus envelope so he must have taken a bus as far as Chi then switched to rail. — Mickey Spillane, *One Lonely Night*, p. 52, 1951
- I arrived in Chi quite early in the morning[.] — Jack Kerouac, *On the Road*, p. 14, 1957
- hours before that, we'd watched the third night of the days of Rage in Chi. — Paul and Meredith, *Chamisa Road*, 1971

chiba *noun*
marijuana *US, 1981*
Spanish slang embraced by English-speakers.
- 11 of 12 tracks are dedicated to the joys of boo, tea, dope, grass, ganga, chiba, the doob—whatever street you're on. — *Riverfront Times (Missouri)*, 21st November 2001

chiba-chiba *noun*
marijuana, especially potent marijuana from Colombia or Brazil *US, 1979*
- Over the past few years in New York, the magic moniker has been successively, Chiba-Chiba, wacky, red, red wacky, gold and Santa Marta. — *Hi Life*, p. 15, 1979
- Chiba-Chiba—a Brazilian form of pot, usually compressed into bricks. — Nick Brownlee, *This Is Cannabis*, p. 151, 2002

chibs; chips *noun*
the buttocks *US, 1957*
- I had a couple a sweet kids but they didn't have chips like this, patting her again on the ass and looking at the others, smiling, and waiting for them to smile in appreciation of his witticisms. — Hubert Selby Jr., *Last Exit to Brooklyn*, p. 44, 1957
- I ain't a profane cat, but I had to say, "Thank you God, for them fine chibs." — Edwin Torres, *Carlito's Way*, p. 94, 1975

Chicago bankroll *noun*
a single large denomination bill wrapped around small denomination bills, giving the impression of a great deal of money *US, 1966*
- — Edith A. Folb, *runnin' down some lines*, p. 232, 1980
- In the right pocket was something known in the trade as a "Chicago bankroll." This consisted of one twenty wrapped around the outside of a roll of sixty ones and secured with a rubber band. — David McCumber, *Playing Off the Rail*, p. 27, 1996

Chicago contract *noun*
a binding oral agreement, secured by honor *US, 1992*
- So we make a Chicago contract. Nothing on tape. Nothing on paper. No outside witnesses. We don't ever have to spit on our palms and shake. — Robert Campbell, *Boneyards*, p. 53, 1992

Chicago G-string *noun*
a g-string designed to break open, revealing the dancer's completely naked state *US, 1981*
- — Don Wilmeth, *The Language of American Popular Entertainment*, p. 51, 1981
- Margia Hart, for instance, is said to have worked with a Chicago G-string that could be stripped off in a trice during her show. — David Scotti, *Behind the G-String*, p. 210, 2003

Chicago leprosy *noun*
infections, scars, and abcesses caused by prolonged intravenous drug use *US, 1992*
- — Jay Robert Nash, *Dictionary of Crime*, p. 63, 1992

Chicago piano *noun*
an antiaircraft gun or other automatic weapon *US, 1941*
- A submachine gun is a Chicago piano. — *Austin (Texas) American-Statesman*, p. A15, 4th December 1999
- Floyd Farragut recalled the South Pacific and the war there, the anti-aircraft guns they called "Chicago pianos." — *Florida Times-Union*, p. B1, 31st May 1999

Chicago pill *noun*
a bullet *US, 1949*
- — Vincent J. Monteleone, *Criminal Slang*, p. 48, 1949

Chicago typewriter *noun*
a fully automatic weapon *US, 1963*

- His weapon of choice was the "Chicago typewriter," the submachine gun prized by warring Chicago mobs. — *Boston Globe*, p. A29, 24th September 1989

Chicano *noun*
a Mexican-American *US, 1947*
Originally a slur; by the later 1960s a term of self-identification and pride.
- "What business has a Chicano got to love a man like you?" — Thurston Scott, *Cure it with Honey*, p. 209, 1951
- His name is Oscar Acosta; he's a Chicano lawyer who's heavily involved in that action. — Hunter S. Thompson, *Fear and Loathing in America*, p. 83, 24th May 1968: Letter to Jim Bellows
- A few frames of Chicano heroes highlighted the corners: Cesar Chavez, the father of the United Farm Workers. — Denise Chavez, *Loving Pedro Infante*, p. 136, 2001

Chicano time *noun*
used for denoting a lack of punctuality *US, 1972*
- "He's keeping C.P. time—colored people and Chicano time" one of the postal academy sign carriers cried[.] — *San Francisco Examiner*, p. 6, 24th May 1972
- Sonny knew they were going to be late for the opening pitch. What the hell, it was summer and they were operating on Chicano time. — Rudolfo Anaya, *Zia Summer*, p. 260, 1995
- I got there "Chicano time," late. — Gary Soto, *The Afterlife*, p. 130, 2003

chi-chi *noun*
1 a person of mixed British and Indian parentage *US, 1958*
- She was an Anglo-Indian girl, or, as the American officers termed that racial mixture, a chi-chi. — John D. MacDonald, *The Deceivers*, p. 73, 1958
2 first aid *US, 1992*
- — William Nealy, *Mountain Bike!*, p. 160, 1992

▷ see: CHEE-CHEE

chi-chi *adjective*
fashionable; fussy *UK, 1932*
Also spelt "she-she."
- In some New Deal left-wing circles it is considered chi-chi to meet socially and even sexually with Negroes[.] — Jack Lait and Lee Mortimer, *Washington Confidential*, p. 39, 1951
- We drove up the mountain and found the narrow streets chockfull of chichi tourists. — Jack Kerouac, *On the Road (The Original Scroll)*, p. 153, 1951

chichi man *noun*
a lookout *US, 1977*
- The chichi man, he's outside watching. — John Allen, *Assault with a Deadly Weapon*, p. 38, 1977

chi-chis *noun*
a woman's breasts *US, 1961*
- "Oh yeah," I said, seeing only a blur and feeling one of those heavy chi-chis resting on my shoulder. — Joseph Wambaugh, *The Blue Knight*, p. 24, 1973
- Still astride him after sex in their sixdollar room at the Jupiter Hotel overlooking the Strip, she laughed: "Big ass and chichis is all you love." — Seth Morgan, *Homeboy*, p. 20, 1990
- I, on the other hand, seize the synchronous opportunity to stare at those Monster Chi-Chis for ninety splendid minutes. — Marty Beckerman, *Death to All Cheerleaders*, p. 125, 2000
- Maria's first English-language role consisted of her plump and perky chi-chis doing the talking[.] — Mr. Skin, *Mr. Skin's Skincyclopedia*, p. 475, 2005

chick *noun*
1 a young woman *US, 1899*
- To give you an idea of what a sweet thing she was, children, I'll just say she was not only a lovely little girl; she was a fine chick. — Steve Allen, *Bop Fables*, p. 36, 1955
- I met chicks who were fine as May wine, and cats who were hip to all happenings. — Malcolm X and Alex Haley, *The Autobiography of Malcolm X*, p. 56, 1964
- Says that he lived in North Beach and all that, and that he has this chick who writes him who is a member of the DuBois Club in Frisco. — Eldridge Cleaver, *Soul on Ice*, p. 46, 1968
- [S]pace should be available for chicks to sew dresses, make pants to order, recut garments to fit, etc. — *The Digger Papers*, p. 15, August 1968
2 a friendly fighter aircraft *US, 1951*
- — *Washington Post Magazine*, p. W8, 3rd February 1991

3 cocaine *US, 1990*
One of many variations on the cocaine-as-female theme.
- — Gilda and Melvin Berger, *Drug Abuse A-Z*, p. 43, 1990

chicken *noun*

1 a young prostitute *US, 2002*
- Sunny put me in charge of making a chicken out of her, and I was taking my responsibility seriously. — David Henry Sterry, *Chicken*, p. 153, 2002

2 a woman *US, 1981*
- Three of the groping, licking, grinding pairs of cops and chickens had managed everything but penetration. — Joseph Wambaugh, *The Glitter Dome*, p. 2, 1981

3 a boy, usually under the age of consent, who is the target of homosexual advances *UK, 1910*
- The drug-pitch skells would rather tear off with a wallet than transact an actual exchange, and they make the teenage chicken fags seem like the most discreet commodity on the street. — Josh Alan Friedman, *Tales of Times Square*, p. 51, 1986
- Like seeing a big new car with Ohio plates come driving up in front of that skinny little ten-year-old chicken selling his tender ass for a night's bed and board — Robert Campbell, *Alice in La-La Land*, p. 9, 1987
- And feature—him and that bottle-blond fruitcake are porking in trailers every chance they get, and chasing chicken down at the Fern Dell toilets. — James Ellroy, *White Jazz*, p. 59, 1992

4 a test of wills in which two cars drive directly at each other until one driver—the loser—veers off course *US, 1950*
- Below in "chicken" drivers race at each other; first to turn aside is "chicken." — *Whisper Magazine*, p. 23, May 1950: Flaming Youth Rides Again
- I used to play "chicken" on Miceltorena when I was a kid. Rebel Without A Cause had just come out and chicken was in. — James Ellroy, *Blood on the Moon*, p. 160, 1984

5 marijuana *US, 1997*
- — Jim Emerson-Cobb, *Scratching the Dragon*, April 1997

6 a small halibut *US, 1997*
Alaskan usage.
- — Jim Crotty, *How to Talk American*, p. 5, 1997

▷ **see: CHICKEN PERCH**

chicken *adjective*
scared, cowardly, afraid *US, 1933*
- "You're chicken," Sheik said contemptuously, sucking another puff. — Chester Himes, *The Real Cool Killers*, p. 49, 1959
- What are ya, chicken, Charlie? — *The Hustler*, 1961
- It was true that he was becoming afraid, but he was even more afraid of being called "chicken" if he refused to go with them. — Nathan Heard, *Howard Street*, p. 62, 1968
- If you passed it [a joint] on, no-one would call you chicken or anything[.] — Macfarlane, Macfarlane and Robson, *The User*, p. 32, 1996

chickenbone special *noun*
any small, local railroad *US, 1970*
- After all, the Chickenbone Special ran both ways. The Dixie Highway goes south from Ohio as well as north to it. — John Shelton Reed, *My Tears Spoiled my Aim*, p. 108, 1993

chicken colonel *noun*
in the US Army, a full colonel *US, 1918*
From the eagle insignia of the rank.
- That was the first time anybody ever told me they're proud of me, and it's a full chicken colonel in the U.S. Army! — Rocky Garciano (with Rowland Barber), *Somebody Up There Likes Me*, p. 235, 1955
- But I've seen the Air Force turn out generals and chicken colonels in brigade strength to welcome junketing congressmen. — *San Francisco Examiner*, p. 27, 9th April 1966

chicken coop *noun*
a women's jail or prison *US, 1949*
- — Vincent J. Monteleone, *Criminal Slang*, p. 49, 1949

chicken crank *noun*
an amphetamine fed to chickens to accelerate their egg-laying *US, 1989*
- — Geoffrey Froner, *Digging for Diamonds*, p. 68, 1989

chicken dinner *noun*
a pretty woman *US, 1946*

- When we saw one of buddies blowing his top over some chicken dinner we pitied him for going tangent[.] — Mezz Mezzrow, *Really the Blues*, p. 78, 1946
- — Kenn "Naz" Young, *Naz's Underground Dictionary*, p. 20, 1973

chickenfeed *noun*

1 a less than generous amount of money *US, 1836*
- — Marcus Hanna Boulware, *Jive and Slang of Students in Negro Colleges*, 1947
- He comes from one of the few states where there is no gangsterism except in picayune city and county affairs, and in those the Republicans share the chicken-feed rewards. — Jack Lait and Lee Mortimer, *Washington Confidential*, p. 195, 1951
- Harry would turn up his nose and say: "Chickenfeed. Not interested." — Charles Raven, *Underworld Nights*, p. 101, 1956

2 methamphetamine *US, 1964*
- She believes crystals are a form of Methedrine and that "they're called chicken feed because they're actually given to chickens." — *San Francisco News Call Bulletin*, p. 3, 17th February 1964

chicken fink *noun*
an unlikeable, disloyal person *US, 1973*
- You chicken fink! — *American Graffiti*, 1973

chickenguts *noun*
braided military decorations *US, 1943*
- Resplendent in feathers and loops of gold braid known locally as "chicken guts," his personal staff included Hungarians and Italians. — *Albuquerque (New Mexico) Journal*, p. 5, 1st September 2000

chickenhawk *noun*

1 during a war, someone who supports the war but avoids military service themselves *US, 1988*
Most high-profile members of the US government (President Bush and Vice President Cheney being the most prominent) and right-wing radio entertainers (Rush Limbaugh being the most prominent) who supported the 2003 invasion of Iraq avoided active military service during their youth, a fact which gave the term a second life.
- Vann had warned Komer that if he arrived with less authority and access, he would be eaten by the chicken hawks. — Neil Sheehan, *A Bright Shining Lie*, p. 656, 1988
- Calling Quayle "chicken hawk" or "yellow bird" is cruel and unfair, but I guess that's politics. — *Newsday (New York)*, p. 85, 2nd September 1988
- Limbaugh is a prime example of what is known as a Chicken Hawk—a noisy, preening master of the martial art of talking who, back when it was a question of getting anywhere near harm's way for the sake of his country, discovered that he had (as Vice President Cheney once put it, explaining his own absence from the fray) "other priorities." — *New York*, p. 39, 27th October 2003

2 a mature homosexual man who seeks much younger men as sexual partners *US, 1965*
- Basically the Flamingo Isles was a dive for pimps, chicken hawks, and hookers. — Carl Hiaasen, *Tourist Season*, p. 33, 1986
- [A]nd instead of a chicken hawk flagging him inside with a twenty-dollar bill, his old mother, wrapped in furs and flashing newly capped teeth, comes rushing out. — Robert Campbell, *Alice in La-La Land*, p. 9, 1987
- [W]e three go up there frequently, proud to still elicit, in our post-teen years, the lurid howls of chickenhawks as we pass on by. — Jim Carroll, *Forced Entries*, p. 7, 1987
- The next day Jules was in several adult magazine and book shops in downtown San Diego looking for chickenhawk and pedophile publications. — Joseph Wambaugh, *Finnegan's Week*, p. 18, 1993

3 by extension, a woman who seeks out young male lovers *US, 1978*
- "She's a chickenhawk!" Natalie sneered. "These kids come and go hourly through her zoo." — Joseph Wambaugh, *The Black Marble*, p. 306, 1978

chickenhead *noun*

1 a person performing oral sex on a man *US, 1996*
Also "chickhead." From the bobbing motion.
- Thinkin' of this chickenhead I stuck my dick in. — Originoo Gunn Clapazz, *Elite Fleet*, 1996
- Rap made slang aimed at women like "skeezer," "hootchie," "chickenhead," and the ubiquitous "bitch"[.] — Nelson George, *Hip Hop America*, p. 186, 1998

2 an aggressive or violent woman *US, 1980*
- — Edith A. Folb, *runnin' down some lines*, p. 232, 1980

3 a foolish, frivolous person *US, 1906*

- Your reviewer, who never put any chips on [bet on] the old chickenhead anyway[.] — Lester Bangs, *Psychotic Reactions and Carburetor Dung*, p. 162, 1976
- — Don R. McCreary (Editor), *Dawg Speak*, 2001

chickenkiller *noun*

a Cuban or Haitian *US, 1970s*

From the stereotype of Cubans and Haitians as voodoo practioners sacrificing chickens in religious rites; insulting.

- Somebody who thought American but worked for the chickenkillers. — Elmore Leonard, *Stick*, p. 86, 1983

chicken out *verb*

to lose courage and retreat from an endeavor *US, 1934*

- I hope he points out that Chicago Yippies also signed the permit request and all the local Yippies, even those who chickened out, are working on the Festival harder than ever. — Abbie Hoffman, *Revolution for the Hell of It*, p. 110, 1968
- I was wondering if he had chickened out again, when he came down the sidewalk and got in the Buick beside me. — Iceberg Slim (Robert Beck), *Trick Baby*, p. 223, 1969

chicken pimp *noun*

a pimp who works with young male prostitutes *US, 2002*

- "He certainly doesn't look like a chicken pimp." — David Henry Sterry, *Chicken*, p. 43, 2002

chickenplate *noun*

a steel vest that helicopter and other aircrew wore in the Vietnam war, designed as bulletproof *US, 1971*

- We don't even have the armour plate for our chests—"chicken plate"—that the helicopter pilots did in Vietnam. — Orson Scott Card, *Ender's Game*, p. xxiii, 1985
- Before we climbed in, Terzala grabbed him. "Major," he said, "today you need to wear your chicken plate. You are not getting on this helo until you put it on." Franks didn't usually wear the chicken plate, but he took Terzala's advice and put it on. — Tom Clancy with Fred Franks Jr., *Into the Storm*, p. 58, 1991
- [H]e fingered the scar on the side of his face where the AK-47 round had settled in his teeth after rifling through the small observation helicopter, up across his "chicken plate." — Kregg Jorgensen, *Very Crazy G.I.*, p. 77, 2001

chicken powder *noun*

amphetamine in powdered form *US, 1971*

- — Edward R. Bloomquist, *Marijuana*, p. 336, 1971

chicken queen *noun*

a mature male homosexual who is especially attracted to boys or young men *US, 1963*

- — Donald Webster Cory and John P. LeRoy, *The Homosexual and His Society*, p. 262, 1963: "A lexicon of homosexual slang"
- I hope you're not a chicken queen. I'm twenty-six. — Armistead Maupin, *Tales of the City*, p. 134, 1978
- Natch, he eventually leaves her for girls his own age and poor Lola becomes an anxiety ridden chicken queen. — John Waters, *Crackpot*, p. 113, 1986
- Boy prostitutes are typically referred to on the streets as chickens, while homosexual men that solicit young male prostitutes are known as chicken hawks or chicken queens. — R. Barri Flowers, *Runaway Kids and Teenage Prostitution*, p. 139, 2001

chicken ranch *noun*

a rural brothel *US, 1973*

Originally the name of a brothel in LaGrange, Texas, and then spread to more generic use.

- Hey, you don't make a thousand bucks tax-free by staying in bed unless you're working at one of those chicken ranches in Nevada. — Joseph Wambaugh, *Fugitive Nights*, p. 43, 1992

chickenshit *noun*

a coward *US, 1929*

- [A]ll the Richard Hells are chickenshits who trash the precious gift too blithely[.] — Lester Bangs, *Psychotic Reactions and Carburetor Dung*, p. 267, 1977
- When did they start hiring chickenshits like you on Robbery-Homicide, Krantz? — Robert Crais, *L.A. Requiem*, p. 44, 1999

chickenshit *adjective*

cowardly *US, 1934*

- They after my job, the chickenshit bastards! — Ralph Ellison, *Invisible Man*, p. 228, 1947
- "They want to destroy religion. They're chickenshit," Marty said. — James T. Farrell, *Saturday Night*, p. 35, 1947
- He got mad at the guys from acting too cagey—too chicken-shit, he called it. — Ken Kesey, *One Flew Over the Cuckoo's Nest*, p. 113, 1962
- Then cut to me talking about the two chickenshit pyschiatrists and straight in Dr. Reinghold laughing. — *Natural Born Killers*, 1994

chicken skin *noun*

the sensation and physical manifestation of the chills *US, 1981*

Hawaiian youth usage, instead of the more common "goose bumps."

- When we wen keess, ah got chicken skin! — Douglas Simonson, *Pidgin to da Max*, 1981

chicken switch *noun*

a switch that will abort a mission; a notional switch that will end a project *US, 1960*

- A quick-thinking sailor hit the "chicken switch" in the control room, which blew the main ballast tanks and brought the Edison to the surface. — *Chicago Tribune*, p. C1, 9th January 1991
- And a switch, the chicken switch. The purpose was that if anything at all went wrong, we could disconnect. — *Providence (Rhode Island) Journal-Bulletin*, p. 1A, 16th July 1995

chick flick *noun*

a movie that is designed to appeal to a female audience *US, 1993*

- — Connie Eble (Editor), *UNC-CH Campus Slang*, p. 2, Spring 1998
- Boys and young men will simply refuse to see the "chick flicks" their girlfriends and wives want to attend, while females will accommodate their boyfriends and husbands. — *National Review*, 16th June 2001

chickie!

used as warning *US, 1934*

- Then, almost before it began, it was over, for a lookout on the corner heard sirens, and yelled, "Chickie, the nabs!" — Hal Ellson, *Tomboy*, p. 110, 1950
- [A]s he was jumping off the fender Angus shouted chicky! — Gilbert Sorrentino, *Steelwork*, p. 53, 1970

chickie; chicky *noun*

1 a lookout or decoy *US, 1934*

- Not having anyone to lay chickie for me, I had to do it quicker than most of the time. — Claude Brown, *Manchild in the Promised Land*, p. 31, 1965
- They searched for a money belt and ripped his shoes from his feet while Butch and Brother played chickie. — Nathan Heard, *Howard Street*, p. 67, 1968
- You don't have to take part, play chickie. — Miguel Pinero, *Short Eyes*, p. 92, 1975
- I went in but now I had nobody to lie chicky for me[.] — Herbert Huncke, *Guilty of Everything*, p. 102, 1990

2 a young girl *US, 1919*

Teen slang.

- "Don't scream, chickies, or try leaving this place." — Georgia Sothern, *My Life in Burlesque*, p. 161, 1972
- Shit never been his pleasure, but as you say, maybe it's for some chickie friend. — Elmore Leonard, *52 Pick-up*, p. 146, 1974

chickie poo *noun*

a young and beautiful girl *US, 1981*

Recorded in the usage of counterculturalists associated with the Rainbow Nation.

- You didn't come home last night. What were you up to, out messing around with all the chickie-poos? — John Nichols, *The Nirvana Blues*, p. 90, 1981
- If I was a cute young chickie-poo with big boobs, I would be seen as flirtatious, looking for action. — *St. Petersburg (Florida) Times*, p. 1F, 13th April 2003

chick with a dick *noun*

a transexual or, rarely, a hermaphrodite *US, 1989*

Almost always plural.

- They got a "Chicks with Dicks" sex show I'd like to check out before I order my corn-beef sandwich with a side of potato salad. — Scott Sommer, *Still Lives*, p. 199, 1989
- Asserting that neither the "glamorized" movie stars nor the queens are desirable (they are "asexual," despite the evidence of star fan clubs and Chicks-with-Dicks phone sex numbers) Bersani condemns them to/for masturbation. — Diana Fuss, *Inside/Out*, p. 39, 1991

- All right, but your're missing out. Chicks with dicks. — *Clerks*, 1994
- Chicks with dicks are a heavy date. — Ethan Morden, *Some Men Are Lookers*, p. 37, 1997

chicle *noun*
heroin *US*, 1994
Spanish for "gum," alluding to the gummy nature of heroin that has not been processed to powder form.
- — US Department of Justice, *Street Terms*, October 1994

chiclet keyboard *noun*
a computer keyboard with small plastic keys *US*, 1991
A visual allusion to a branded chewing gum.
- Customers rejected the idea with almost equal unanimity, and chiclets are not often seen on anything larger than a digital watch any more. — Eric S. Raymond, *The New Hacker's Dictionary*, p. 94, 1991

Chicom *noun*
a soldier from the People's Republic of China; a Chinese communist *US*, 1967
- On a three-hundred-mile front, countless thousands of Chinese Communists—"Chicoms," as MacArthur's headquarters had begun to call them, had howled down from what the General had previously described as "a rugged spinal mountain range" too precipitous to shelter troops. — William Manchester, *American Caesar*, p. 726, 1978

Chicom *adjective*
Chinese communist *US*, 1964
- He had apparently never seen a "Chicom" grenade before[.] — Martin Russ, *Happy Hunting Ground*, p. 204, 1968
- The American side wanted the British to support United States political policy on China, while noting that this would "make it easier to meet the British views on some of the trade matters and the alignment of the Cocom and Chicom lists." — Michael A. Guhin, *John Foster Dulles*, p. 296, 1972
- [A] young man or a boy who wore a cap with a short visor and held a Chicom machine gun across his skinny knees[.] — Elmore Leonard, *Mr. Majesty*, p. 146, 1974
- We grabbed the weapons. I gave them a quick once-over. They were Chicom AK-47s. — Richard Marcinko, *Rogue Warrior*, p. 116, 1992

chief *noun*
1 LSD *US*, 1966
- — Donald Louria, *Nightmare Drugs*, p. 45, 1966
- — Steve Salaets, *Ye Olde Hiptionary*, 1970
2 used as a term of address *US*, 1935
Jocular, sometimes suggesting deference.
- Roll up your sleeve, chief. — *Clerks*, 1994

chief *verb*
in a group smoking marijuana, to hog the cigarette or pipe *US*, 1997
- — Jim Emerson-Cobb, *Scratching the Dragon*, April 1997

chief cook and bottle washer *noun*
used as a humorous title for someone with important duties and responsibilities *US*, 1840
Often, not always, used with irony.
- Mother as "chief cook and bottle washer," responsible for all tasks that she cannot effectively delegate. — Howard Becker, *Family, Marriage and Parenthood*, p. 545, 1948
- Suppose you had a father like me—chief cook and bottle-washer at sea, and jack-of-all-trades on land. — S.N. Behrman et al., *Fanny*, p. 127, 1955
- G.M. Allen, cocalorum firechief, the town's chief cook and bottle washer, got up and spoke with hawkshaw eloquence. — Joe Eszterhas, *Charlie Simpson's Apocalypse*, p. 23, 1973
- The dads wore aprons that said "Chief Cook and Bottle Washer," and they grilled burgers and hot dogs at backyard barbecues. — Caroline Kettlewell, *Skin Game*, p. 36, 1999

chief itch and rub *noun*
an organization's key leader *US*, 2001
- Do all successful athletic teams need an on-the-field leader, or leaders? If so, who are UTEP's chief itch and rubs this football season? — *El Paso (Texas) Times*, p. 1C, 22nd August 2001

chief of dicks *noun*
a police chief *US*, 1972

- There was a guy named Dick Shopus, he's dead, he was a chief of dicks [Chief of Police Detectives] in Portland and he was a dirty rotten bugger. — Harry King, *Box Man*, p. 44, 1972

chief of heat *noun*
a noncommissioned officer commanding an artillery battery *US*, 1988
- — Hans Halberstadt, *Airborne*, p. 130, 1988

chief of staff *noun*
a soldier's girlfriend back home *US*, 1965
Vietnam war usage.
- Yeah, I believe you numbah one soldier 'cuz you write chief of staff in states alla time. — Tony Zidek, *Choi Oi*, p. 123, 1965

chile pimp *noun*
a pimp, especially a Mexican-American pimp, who has no professional pride and only mediocre success in the field *US*, 1972
- Black pimps never solicit for their women if they are "true pimps," and call a man who does a cigarette pimp, popcorn pimp, or chile pimp. — Christina and Richard Milner, *Black Players*, p. 33, 1972
- After Vietnam they had taken up where they'd left off. Bessie working, Free Lee chili pimpin' and trying to be nickel slick[.] — Odie Hawkins, *The Busting Out of an Ordinary Man*, pp. 137–138, 1985

chili *adjective*
Mexican *US*, 1936
- "No es un problema, chiquita," he said confidently, flashing a little chili chatter he'd picked up in the tomato fields of the Youth Authority. — Seth Morgan, *Homeboy*, p. 64, 1990

chili bean *noun*
a Mexican or Mexican-American; any Spanish-speaking person *US*, 1980
Derogatory.
- — Edith A. Folb, *runnin' down some lines*, p. 232, 1980

chili belly *noun*
a Mexican or Mexican-American *US*, 1967
- Junior snarls, "Lissen to the chili bellies cheer that lucky fart." — Iceberg Slim (Robert Beck), *Doom Fox*, p. 179, 1978

chili bowl; chili-bowl haircut *noun*
an untapered haircut that looks as if the barber simply placed a bowl on the person's head and trimmed around the edge of the bowl *US*, 1960
- A group of boys with mohawks sporting leather and chains would be more likely to be asked to "leave the premises" before a bunch of boys with chili-bowl haircuts and blue jeans. — *Tulsa (Oklahoma) World*, 15th January 1999

chili chaser *noun*
an agent of the US Immigration and Naturalization Service Border Patrol *US*, 1956
- — *Maledicta*, p. 166, 1979: "A glossary of ethnic slurs in American English"

chili choker *noun*
a Mexican or Mexican-American *US*, 1990
Derogatory.
- That same night the niggers and chilichokers dragged that boy back to the showers[.] — Seth Morgan, *Homeboy*, p. 152, 1990

chili chomper *noun*
a Mexican or Mexican-American *US*, 1970
Derogatory.
- — *Current Slang*, p. 15, Spring 1970

chili eater *noun*
a Mexican or Mexican-American *US*, 1911
Derogatory.
- Mexican officials accused the Canadian catcher, Alex Andreopoulos, of provoking their players by calling them "chili-eaters." — *Los Angeles Times*, p. C8, 11th August 1991

chill *noun*
death *US*, 1975
- But they got him into the hospital and they saved Jack Fox from the chill. — James Carr, *Bad*, p. 139, 1975

chill *verb*
1 to kill someone *US*, 1947
- — Marcus Hanna Boulware, *Jive and Slang of Students in Negro Colleges*, 1947

- Remember the night Stein got chilled out front? — Raymond Chandler, *The Little Sister*, p. 247, 1949

2 to calm down; to be calm *US, 1979*

- Chill, brah. You know who this is? — *Point Break*, 1991
- "Griff," Todd said, "just chill, man." — Francesca Lia Block, *I Was a Teenage Fairy*, p. 109, 1998

3 to idle *US, 1972*

- [E]ver since I first sat chilling and rocking to things like John Coltrane's Africa / Brass[.] — Lester Bangs, *Psychotic Reactions and Carburetor Dung*, p. 104, 1972
- All are talking, drinking and chilling. — *Boyz N The Hood*, p. 67, 1990

▸ **chill like a megavillain**
to relax *US, 1992*
Especially effective in the participle form—"chillin."

- — *Surfer Magazine*, p. 30, February 1992

▸ **chill the beef; chill the rap**
to escape prosecution by bribery or intimidation of witnesses *US, 1950*

- — Hyman E. Goldin et al., *Dictionary of American Underworld Lingo*, p. 43, 1950

chill *adjective*

1 calm, unexcited *US, 1987*

- — *Washington Post Magazine*, p. 17, 13th September 1987

2 excellent *US, 1989*

- We were sniffing all night long. It was chill. — Terry Williams, *The Cocaine Kids*, p. 33, 1989

chilled *adjective*
calm, relaxed *US, 1992*

- He had a big .45 Army pistol and generally just flashing it kept the kids chilled and shit to a minimum. — Jess Mowry, *Way Past Cool*, p. 31, 1992

chill factor *noun*
a notional measure of fashionability and popularity *US, 1993*

- "Sides, man, chill factor in this hood be directly proportional to the long of your green." — Jess Mowry, *Six Out Seven*, p. 17, 1993

chill out *verb*

1 to calm down, to relax *US, 1983*

- We just chillin' out, drinkin' a little Bird, that's all. — Odie Hawkins, *Great Lawd Buddha*, p. 11, 1990
- JULES: Tell that bitch to be cool! Say, bitch be cool! Say, bitch be cool! PUMPKIN: Chill out, honey! — *Pulp Fiction*, 1994
- Chill out, Phil. Four deputies and you, I can live with that. — *Natural Born Killers*, 1994

2 to calm (someone) down *US, 1988*

- But it chills me out. I sit down in the folding chair and relax, empty my mind of all the crap. — Jay McInerney, *Story of My Life*, p. 8, 1988

chill pill *noun*
a mythical pill that will induce calm *US, 1982*

- — Connie Eble (Editor), *UNC-CH Campus Slang*, p. 8, Spring 1982
- "I ain't gonna be messin around, cuz. I'm on a chill pill." — Bob Sipchen, *Baby Insane and the Buddha*, p. 188, 1993
- Okay, you got it. Just take a chill pill, for Christ's sake. — *Jackie Brown*, 1997

chill time *noun*
time to relax *US, 2004*

- I gotta have some chill time too. — *Hustle and Flow*, 2004

chill with you later
used as a farewell *US, 1987*

- — *Washington Post Magazine*, p. 17, 13th September 1987

chilly *adjective*

1 excellent, fashionable, desirable *US, 1971*

- I was a chilly homeboy, yes / I was down because I came to school just to mess around. — *All for Love, School*, 1985

2 cold-hearted *US, 1971*

- That's awful chilly, I tol' her. — Joseph Nazel, *Black Cop*, p. 144, 1974

chilly most *adjective*
calm and collected *US, 1992*

- — William K. Bentley and James M. Corbett, *Prison Slang*, p. 48, 1992

chime *noun*
an hour *US, 1946*

- At the Mexican's we could at least get loaded on good hay and forget our misery for a couple of chimes. — Mezz Mezzrow, *Really the Blues*, p. 164, 1946
- — Jack Lait and Lee Mortimer, *New York Confidential*, p. 235, 1948: "A glossary of Harlemisms"

chimer *noun*
a clock or watch *US, 1973*

- I asked him what time was it just to see if my chimer was right[.] — A.S. Jackson, *Gentleman Pimp*, p. 128, 1973

chin *noun*
gossip, idle conversation *UK, 1862*

- Call me sometime and we'll have a good chin. I'm in the book. — Max Shulman, *Rally Round the Flag, Boys!*, p. 209, 1957

chin *verb*
to talk idly *US, 1872*

- They used to spend more time chinning than cheating, around here. — Philip Wylie, *Opus 21*, p. 112, 1949
- One night in Hutton's, Kiefer had started chinning about Leo's interest in missing heirs. — Bernard Wolfe, *The Late Risers*, p. 208, 1954
- I've got nothing to do except sit around chinning with little girls like you. — John M. Murtagh and Sara Harris, *Cast the First Stone*, p. 45, 1957

china *noun*
teeth; false teeth *US, 1942*

- — John R. Armore and Joseph D. Wolfe, *Dictionary of Desperation*, p. 24, 1976

China cat *noun*
strong heroin *US, 1994*

- — US Department of Justice, *Street Terms*, October 1994

china chin *noun*
(of a boxer or fighter) a vulnerability to blows on the chin *US, 1940*

- "Lennox has a china chin," Dundee said. — *Los Angeles Times*, p. 4 (Sports Section), 21st June 2003

China circuit *noun*
in the language of traveling performances, a circuit of small, unsophisticated towns *US, 1973*
Named after the Pennsylvania towns of Pottstown, Pottsville and Chambersburg, all of which were home to chamber pot manufacturing concerns.

- — Sherman Louis Sergel, *The Language of Show Biz*, p. 49, 1973

China clipper *noun*
a dishwasher, human or mechanical *US, 1966*
Vietnam war usage.

- — *Columbus (Ohio) Citizen-Journal*, p. 14, 21st July 1966
- — Carl Fleischhauer, *A Glossary of Army Slang*, p. 9, 1968

Chinaman *noun*

1 an addiction to heroin or another opiate *US, 1948*

- Is getting that Chinaman off his back, too. — Jack Kerouac, *Letter to Neal Cassady*, p. 175, 8 December 1948
- You know, man, Win's just about got the Chinaman off her back! — John Clellon Holmes, *Go*, p. 81, 1952
- The Chinaman's riding you, huh? — Willard Motley, *Let No Man Write My Epitaph*, p. 91, 1958
- She just kicked, she ain't got to worry about the Chinaman no more. — Donald Goines, *Dopefiend*, p. 130, 1971

2 in politics, a mentor or protector *US, 1973*
A term from Chicago, a major cradle of machine politics in the US.

- Chinaman (Polit.)—Political sponsor. Your personal clout, your man upstairs. — Bill Reilly, *Big Al's Official Guide to Chicagoese*, p. 21, 1982
- Then comes my Chinaman—who is called a rabbi in New York, a mentor in the colleges and a political sponsor elsewhere—Delvin, who has plenty of jobs to give out since the shit has to be kept moving. — Robert Campbell, *Junkyard Dog*, pp. 7–8, 1986

Chinaman's chance; Chinaman's *noun*
an absence of luck, no real chance at all *US, 1911*
Reflecting the status of the Chinese population of early C20 US.

- But I remember when I started running, my opponent's campaign headquarters had a sign with a quote: TOM DOESN'T HAVE A CHINAMAN'S CHANCE. — Culture Clash, *Culture Clash in America*, p. 21, 2003

Chinamat *noun*

an inexpensive Chinese restaurant *US, 1979*

- — *Maledicta*, p. 155, 1979: "A glossary of ethnic slurs in American English"

China white *noun*

heroin; less frequently, cocaine *US, 1974*

The presumed location of the drug's origin (although it's just as likely to come from Pakistan, Afghanistan or Thailand) plus the color.

- China White they called it when they had first seen the stuff from New York City. — Donald Goines, *Never Die Alone*, p. 53, 1974
- DEALER: Hey, man. You wanna cop some blow? / JUNKIE: Sure, watcha got? Dust, flakes or rocks? / DEALER: I got China White, Mother of Pearl...I reflect what you need. — Grandmaster Flash & The Furious Five featuring Melle Mel, *White Lines*, 1983
- They're dealing China white out of the place like they had a license. — Gerald Petievich, *The Quality of the Informant*, p. 57, 1985
- Though China White is often packaged by refiners in 700-gram bricks, known as units, the universal measure in the global narcotics business is the 1,000-gram kilo. — *New York Times*, p. SM27, 23rd June 2002

chinch; chintz *noun*

a bedbug *UK, 1625*

- I found out then that chinches never die. When they get tired of scuffling for their chow and want to retire, they just go and live happily forever after in the Band House. — Mezz Mezzrow, *Really the Blues*, p. 34, 1946
- We called them chinches, and they were all over the place, hard-biting armies in constant battle formation[.] — Ethel Waters, *His Eye is on the Sparrow*, p. 9, 1951
- One night as I awoke a little wee chintz spoke to me as I raised my head / He said, "Don't you get rough and don't you get tough, for you and I both must share this bed." — Bruce Jackson, *Get Your Ass in the Water and Swim Like Me*, p. 211, 1966
- Her dead didn't feel too good and her mouth tasted like she had been eating Harlem chinches. — Robert Deane Pharr, *S.R.O.*, p. 187, 1971

chin-chin man *noun*

a male homosexual *US, 1990*

- — Charles Shafer, *Folk Speech in Texas Prisons*, p. 200, 1990

chinch pad *noun*

an inexpensive, shoddy boarding house or hotel *US, 1958*

- — Clarence Major, *Dictionary of Afro-American Slang*, p. 36, 1970
- Vermin-infested flops were also called flea houses, flea boxes, flea traps, bug houses, louse traps, louse cages, scratch houses, and chinch pads. — Irving Lewis Allen, *The City in Slang*, p. 156, 1993

chinchy *adjective*

1 cheap; parsimonious, stingy *UK, 1400*

- I guess when you get into the atom-bomb class of brains, you get pretty chinchy everywhere else. — Philip Wylie, *Opus 21*, p. 351, 1949
- "You all are so chinchy," Lowry lectured company officials. — Daniel J. Clark, *Like Night & Day*, p. 60, 1997
- Spending by a few board members does seem high, and billing the state $151.21 for attending the funeral of a legislator's wife seems especially chinchy. [Editorial] — *Charleston (West Virginia) Daily Mail*, p. 4A, 2nd March 2000

2 infested with bedbugs *US, 1961*

- What in the world would these important big-time musicians want to hang around a chinchy old uptown joint like this for? — Ross Russell, *The Sound*, p. 216, 1961

chinee *noun*

1 a free ticket to a sporting event *US, 1981*

- — Don Wilmeth, *The Language of American Popular Entertainment*, p. 52, 1981

2 a Chinese person *US, 1871*

- [A] little Chinee impression of Judge Ito. — Howard Stern, *Miss America*, p. 138, 1995

Chinese *noun*

in circus and carnival usage, hard work, especially hard work without payment *US, 1981*

- — Don Wilmeth, *The Language of American Popular Entertainment*, p. 52, 1981

Chinese *verb*

in the circus or carnival, to perform heavy labor *US, 1980*

- — Joe McKennon, *Circus Lingo*, p. 25, 1980

Chinese *adjective*

in horse racing, said of blurred numbers on the tote board *US, 1947*

- — Dan Parker, *The ABC of Horse Racing*, p. 144, 1947

Chinese ace *noun*

a pilot who makes a landing with one wing lowered; a pilot who has a reputation for crashing planes on landing *US, 1928*

After **CHINESE LANDING**.

- — *Maledicta*, p. 156, 1979: "A glossary of ethnic slurs in American English"
- He called me a "damned Chinese ace"—a term developed from the reputation Chinese pilots had in those days for crashing more of their own planes than they shot down of the enemy's. — Carroll V. Glines, *I Could Never Be So Lucky Again*, p. 51, 1991
- A "Chinese ace" was someone who accidentally managed to destroy five planes belonging to his own air force. — *Winged Victory*, p. 384, 1993

Chinese auction *noun*

a charity auction, in which a buyer is selected at random for each item *US, 1997*

- — Amy and Denise McFadden, *CoalSpeak*, p. 4, 1997

Chinese copy *noun*

a reproduction that captures the original's defects as well as its strengths *US, 1979*

- — *Maledicta*, p. 156, 1979: "A glossary of ethnic slurs in American English"

Chinese cure *noun*

an all-natural treatment for the symptoms associated with withdrawal from heroin addiction *US, 1953*

- A variation of it is known as the Chinese cure, which is carried out with hop and Wampole's Tonic. — William Burroughs, *Junkie*, p. 63, 1953

Chinese dolly *noun*

in the television and movie industries, a dolly on slanted tracks *US, 1987*

- — Ira Konigsberg, *The Complete Film Dictionary*, p. 47, 1987

Chinese fashion *adverb*

sex with both participants lying on their sides, the active male lying behind his partner *US, 1980*

- — *Maledicta*, p. 198, Winter 1980: "A new erotic vocabulary"

Chinese fire drill *noun*

1 any situation in which confusion reigns *US, 1946*

Frequent use in the Vietnam war.

- As far as Burton was concerned, everything was fouled up like a Chinese fire drill as Hogan finished with his plus 51 to lead Lloyd Mangrum. — *Coshocton (Ohio) Tribune*, p. 8, 5 June 1946
- — *American Speech*, p. 267, December 1962: "The language of traffic policemen"
- "It must have looked like a Chinese fire drill back on the river when the shooting started," said Bill. — Donald Duncan, *The New Legions*, p. 72, 1967
- "[I]t turned into an absolute goddamned Chinese fuckin' fire drill." — George Higgins, *Kennedy for the Defense*, p. 215, 1980

2 a prank loved by generations of American youth in which a car full of people stops at a red light and the passengers suddenly leap from the car, run around it, and get back in as the light turns green *US, 1972*

- — Hugh Rawson, *Wicked Words*, p. 81, 1989
- — Lewis Poteet, *Car & Motorcycle Slang*, p. 49, 1992
- We had stopped to do Chinese fire drill, trading spots during the long ride. I was trading with Dad, taking his spot in the backseat, while he went up front to drive. — Barbara Camens, *Girls' Night Out*, p. 204, 2002

Chinese landing *noun*

the typical angling of an airplane when it lands in Antarctica, with one wing low *US, 1918*

Humor based on the premise that "one wing low" has a certain Chinese ring to it.

- — *Cool Antarctica*, 2003: "Antarctic slang"

Chinese needlework *noun*

intravenous use of narcotics *US, 1942*

- — Vincent J. Monteleone, *Criminal Slang*, p. 49, 1949
- Do you go for Chinese needlework, reindeer dust [powdered drugs], Texas tea [marijuana]—that kind of stuff? — Douglas Rutherford, *The Creeping Flesh*, p. 49, 1963
- — *Maledicta*, p. 156, 1979: "A glossary of ethnic slurs in American English"

Chinese rocks noun
relatively pure heroin US, 1975
- Wanna go cop / Wanna go get some Chinese Rock / I'm livin' on Chinese Rocks — Dee Dee Ramone and Richard Hell, *Chinese Rocks*, 1975

Chinese rong noun
a nonexistent disease suffered by soldiers US, 1947
- — *American Speech*, p. 305, December 1947: "Imaginary diseases in army and navy parlance"

Chinese rot noun
any unidentified skin disease or sexually transmitted infection US, 1940
- Imagine the worst of the fungoid-type skin diseases you have ever encountered—ringworm, Dhobie itch, athlete's foot, Chinese rot, saltwater itch, seven year itch. — *Logic of Empire, (reprinted in The Green Hills of Earth)*, p. 225, 1951

Chinese tobacco noun
opium US, 1951
- — Eugene Landy, *The Underground Dictionary*, p. 49, 1971
- — *Maledicta*, p. 156, 1979: "A glossary of ethnic slurs in American English"

chingazos noun
fisticuffs; blows US, 1965
Border Spanish used in English conversation by Mexican-Americans.
- Calo has terms for activities, such as eating (refinar), drinking (pistiar), fighting (chingazos), and dancing (borlotear). — George R. Alvarez, *Semiotic Dynamics of an Ethnic-American Sub-Cultural Group*, p. 10, 1965
- — Dagoberto Fuentes and Jose Lopez, *Barrio Language Dictionary*, p. 47, 1974

chingon noun
an important person; a leader US, 1974
Border Spanish used in English conversation by Mexican-Americans.
- — Dagoberto Fuentes and Jose Lopez, *Barrio Language Dictionary*, p. 48, 1974

Chink noun
1 a Chinese person US, 1878
Derives from "ching-ching," the phonetic interpretation of a Chinese courtesy, adopted as a racist term, now obsolete; this abbreviated, still derogatory, variation is much used in Britain and the US. Variants are "Chinkie" and "Chinky."
- "Sometimes a chink or wetback gets into the city with some; it doesn't last long." — Clarence Cooper Jr., *The Scene*, p. 83, 1960
- Only junk comin' in is with the chinks and niggers, behind them spook Air Force sergeants from Nam. — Edwin Torres, *After Hours*, p. 169, 1979
- That's no NVA man. That's a chink—look at him, the cocksucker's six and half feet tall. — *Platoon*, 1986
- Close up he looked like a light-skinned brother with a little Chinese or something in him. Strange-looking dude, Chink with nappy hair. — Elmore Leonard, *Bandits*, p. 199, 1987

2 a Vietnamese person US, 1970
- — *Current Slang*, p. 15, Summer 1970

Chink adjective
1 Chinese US, 1957
- Old Pete men suck the black smoke in the Chink laundry back room[.] — William Burroughs, *Naked Lunch*, p. 6, 1957
- "I don't have time to waste bringing in guys whose idea of a big score is hitting a Chink laundry for change of a dollar." — John Ridley, *Love is a Racket*, p. 204, 1998

2 Vietnamese US, 1970
- — *Current Slang*, Summer 1970

chinkie; chinky; chink noun
a Chinese meal US, 1948
- Hey, I got an idea. Feel like eating Chink? — Max Shulman, *Anyone Got a Match?*, p. 109, 1964

chink ink noun
an indelible ink used by card cheats to mark cards US, 1988
- — George Percy, *The Language of Poker*, p. 20, 1988

Chinks noun
Chinese food US, 1949
- "Where we gonna eat?" "Wherever you want. Spaghetti. Chinks. Steaks." — Irving Shulman, *Cry Tough*, p. 30, 1949

Chinktown noun
an Asian neighborhood US, 1996
- I churned through Chinktown. — James Ellroy, *Destination Morgue*, p. 189, 2004

chinky noun
a small firecracker US, 1997
- — Amy and Denise McFadden, *CoalSpeak*, p. 4, 1997

chin music noun
gossip, idle conversation UK, 1826
- "Cut out all that chin music!" he would holler. — Bobby Seale, *A Lonely Rage*, p. 5, 1978

chin pubes noun
sparse facial hair US, 1995
- You don't want to be the last one at the coffee house without chin pubes. — *Clueless*, 1995

chintz noun
a cheapskate US, 1949
- — *American Weekly*, p. 2, 14th August 1955

chintzy adjective
cheap, miserly, stingy UK, 1902
- There are the 1919 Chicago White Sox, infamously known as the Black Sox, who threw the World Series to make some money and to spite their chintzy owner, Charles Comiskey. — Chad Millman, *The Odds*, p. 38, 2001

chip noun
a small surfboard made from lightweight balsa wood US, 1964
Also known as a "potato chip."
- — John Severson, *Modern Surfing Around the World*, p. 166, 1964

chip verb
1 to use drugs occasionally or irregularly US, 1964
Applied to all narcotics but especially heroin.
- Well, all the studs I knew was on stuff now, and their habits was a good mile long / but I thought I could chip and never get hooked, for my will was strong. — Bruce Jackson, *Get Your Ass in the Water and Swim Like Me*, p. 91, 1964
- He was only "chipping," using drugs occasionally when they were handy, and had not yet acquired a habit. — James Mills, *The Panic in Needle Park*, p. 29, 1966
- Prince whistled. "He sure ain't chippin' then. That's a goddamn oil-burner." — Donald Goines, *Black Gangster*, p. 128, 1977
- I don't mind chipping when I know I'm chipping—that was what we called just biting off a corner of a tab just for the buzz. — Stephen Gaskin, *Amazing Dope Tales*, p. 20, 1980

2 in shuffleboard, to barely touch another disk US, 1967
- — Omero C. Catan, *Secrets of Shuffleboard Strategy*, p. 65, 1967

▸ **chip your teeth**
1 to become very angry US, 1962
- — *American Speech*, p. 268, December 1962: "The language of traffic policemen"

2 to talk incessantly US, 1973
- Okay, okay, quit chipping your teeth. You complain more than any kid I ever saw. — Joseph Wambaugh, *The Blue Knight*, p. 252, 1973

Chip; Chippie; Chippy noun
a member of the California Highway Patrol US, 1977
Thanks to the 1977–1983 television series *CHiPs*.
- "CHIPS" stands for California Highway Patrol. The "i" was added because "CHPs" is hard to pronounce and the guys don't like being called "Chippies." — *The Washington Post*, p. D13, 15th September 1977
- He couldn't understand what the Chippy wanted. Maybe he'd better pull over. Then an extraordinary thing happened. The Chip yelled at him so loudly it hurt. — Joseph Wambaugh, *The Glitter Dome*, p. 11, 1981
- The Chippie, frequently interrupted by Nelson's "Whadhesay?" learned that the husky bald man had stashed the stolen car[.] — Joseph Wambaugh, *Fugitive Nights*, pp. 69–70, 1992

chip along; chip in verb
in poker, to make the minimum bet required US, 1988
- — George Percy, *The Language of Poker*, p. 20, 1988

chip dip noun
an adhesive placed on a cheater's palm, enabling him to steal chips as he helpfully slides a pile of chips in a poker game to the winner US, 1988
- — George Percy, *The Language of Poker*, p. 19, 1988

chip head *noun*

a computer enthusiast *US, 1993*

- — *Merriam-Webster's Hot Words on Campus Marketing Survey '93*, p. 2, 13th October 1993

chippy *verb*

to use drugs occasionally and not habitually *US, 1924*

Applied particularly to heroin.

- "Hoss was his Boss." He had chippied around and gotten hooked. — Iceberg Slim (Robert Beck), *Pimp*, p. 63, 1969

chippy; chippie *noun*

1 a person who uses addictive drugs occasionally without developing a habit *US, 1924*

- She's no chippie, man. — Alexander Trocchi, *Cain's Book*, p. 29, 1960

2 a modest drug addiction *US, 1964*

- At the moment, like Sammy, he had only a chippy, and got most of the heroin he needed by hanging around other addicts who occasionally turned him on with a taste[.] — James Mills, *The Panic in Needle Park*, p. 35, 1966

3 a young woman, usually of loose morals, at times a semi-professional prostitute *US, 1886*

- That was some other quick-trick chippy. — Thurston Scott, *Cure it with Honey*, p. 143, 1951
- I deserve it for acting like a two dollar chippie! — John Clellon Holmes, *Go*, p. 134, 1952
- [W]hy would I fool around with some chippy when I had you? — Jim Thompson, *The Killer Inside*, p. 61, 1952
- A guilty furtiveness in the gray eyes. The cast of weakness across the mouth, with its sullen swollen lips. The look of the chippy. — John D. McDonald, *The Neon Jungle*, p. 26, 1953
- Also, he had gotten into the habit of falling in love with teen-age girls, like this Chippy on the Strip, for whom he had just bought a new cloth coat. — Clancy Sigal, *Going Away*, p. 3, 1961

4 a person in a gambling casino who tries to hustle or steal chips *US, 2003*

- — Victor H. Royer, *Casino Gamble Talk*, p. 32, 2003

5 an inexperienced gambler *US, 1985*

- — Steve Kuriscak, *Casino Talk*, p. 12, 1985

chippy; chippie *verb*

to be unfaithful sexually *US, 1930*

- "You ever chippied on your wife?" "Never." "Never chippied on your wife one time in eighteen years?" "Never." — Lenny Bruce, *How to Talk Dirty and Influence People*, p. 104, 1965
- But Momma's an alcoholic, chippying on Dad. — Christina and Richard Milner, *Black Players*, p. 264, 1972
- They will avoid bars and restaurants that are patronized by girls who, they feel, have inferior status as professionals or whom they consider amateurs just "chipping around"[.] — Harold Greenwald, *The Call Girl*, p. 18, 1978
- Prince Rainier and Princess Grace couldn't have afforded to get caught chippying around, but it's different here. — Joseph Wambaugh, *Fugitive Nights*, pp. 8–9, 1992

chips *noun*

money *US, 1840*

- So when the big day rolled around I spent my last chips on a taxi. — Mezz Mezzrow, *Really the Blues*, p. 152, 1946
- Nay, old dude, I don't need chips. — A.S. Jackson, *Gentleman Pimp*, p. 41, 1973

▶ **in the chips**

well funded *US, 1842*

- If you're in the chips and Burroughs feels good, all three of you could come out here for kicks sometime. — Jack Kerouac, *Letter to Neal Cassady*, p. 115, 26th August 1947

chips and whetstones *noun*

odds and ends *US, 1927*

- You're like as not famished, Mr. Birdwell, delivering trees all day and feeding and chips and whetstones. — Jessamym West, *The Friendly Persuasion*, p. 154, 1945

chirp *noun*

a female singer *US, 1944*

- — Jack Lait and Lee Mortimer, *New York Confidential*, p. 235, 1948: "A glossary of Harlemisms."
- — Robert S. Gold, *A Jazz Lexicon*, p. 56, 1964

chisel *noun*

▶ **on the chisel**

involved in a swindle *US, 1958*

- My old man owns the company. He'd be pretty sore if I was on the chisel. — Raymond Chandler, *Playback*, p. 44, 1958

chisel *verb*

1 to cheat *UK, 1808*

- And he was proud of his chiseling. He felt the crisp five-dollar bill in his pocket. — James T. Farrell, *Saturday Night*, p. 18, 1947
- Can you imagine people that can afford to drive thirty- and forty-thousand-dollar cars chiseling an insurance company for five hundred bucks? — Gerald Petievich, *To Die in Beverly Hills*, p. 209, 1983
- Serenity never tried to chisel her girls and wouldn't stand for it in return. — Joseph Wambaugh, *Floaters*, p. 13, 1996

2 to place small, conservative bets *US, 1950*

- — *The Annals of the American Academy of Political and Social Sciences*, p. 122, May 1950

chiseled *adjective*

without fat, well sculpted *US, 1984*

- — *American Speech*, p. 198, Fall 1984: "The language of body building"

chiseler *noun*

1 a cheat, a petty swindler *US, 1918*

- "I don't like competition from amateur chiselers," Dopey said. — James T. Farrell, *Saturday Night*, p. 27, 1947
- "Amboy Dukes are supposed to be regular guys"—she wept and clutched her purse with both hands—"not a bunch of chiselers." — Irving Shulman, *The Amboy Dukes*, p. 43, 1947
- [M]any a fearful and repentant chiseler has been fleeced by smart operators who told him they were wonder-workers. — Jack Lait and Lee Mortimer, *Washington Confidential*, p. 161, 1951
- Two of the worst chiselers I ever seen. Why, I'd never seen the characters before, and they tried to put the bite on me! — Jim Thompson, *Roughneck*, p. 144, 1954

2 a gambler who places small, conservative bets *US, 1950*

- — *The Annals of the American Academy of Political and Social Sciences*, p. 122, May 1950

chisme *noun*

gossip; rumors *US, 1974*

Border Spanish used in English conversation by Mexican-Americans.

- — Dagoberto Fuentes and Jose Lopez, *Barrio Language Dictionary*, p. 48, 1974

chit-chat *noun*

small talk *UK, 1605*

- Maybe later, if things cooled out a little, they could manage a little chit-chat[.] — Gurney Norman, *Divine Right's Trip (Last Whole Earth Catalog)*, p. 87, 1971
- Well, enough chitchat. Let's go to work. — Armistead Maupin, *Tales of the City*, p. 52, 1978

chit-chat *verb*

to engage in small talk *UK, 1821*

- [W]e stand in the checkout line, chit-chattin'. — Odie Hawkins, *Ghetto Sketches*, p. 126, 1972

Chitlin Circuit *noun*

the notional collection of ghetto bars and nightclubs where black musicians perform in the hope of having a hit that will launch them into better venues *US, 1967*

A term attributed to black singer Lou Rawls.

- He [Rawls] used to sing on what he calls "the chitlin' circuit"—"Places so small you had to dress in the men's room." — *Times Recorder (Zanesville, Ohio)*, p. 2-B, 28th May 1967
- Got me tourin' the chittlin' circuit all through the summer. — *Hustle and Flow*, 2004

Chitlins 101 *noun*

any black studies course *US, 1998*

A derogatory term, drawing from "chitterlings," a dish made with pork innards.

- "Normally, when people think of a black institution, they think of 'Chitlins 101'—something not very sophisticated," he added. — *Chicago Tribune*, p. CN1, 22nd July 1998

Chi-town *nickname*

Chicago, Illinois *US, 1922*

- By the time we hit that "Chi-town" / Them bears were a-gettin' smart[.] — C.W. McCall, *Convoy*, 1976
- We gotta book. We're catching a bus to Chi-town. — *Chasing Amy*, 1997

chiva *noun*
heroin *US, 1967*
From the Spanish of Mexican-Americans.
- Depending on who is listening, heroin can be referred to as carga (heroin), la chiva (the thing), or la madre (the mother). — George R. Alvarez, *Semiotic Dynamics of an Ethnic-American Sub-Cultural Group*, p. 4, 1965
- — Dagoberto Fuentes, *Barrio Language Dictionary*, p. 48, 1974
- — Geoffrey Froner, *Digging for Diamonds*, p. 18, 1989
- Next to the highgrade chiva he dealt, La Barba was proudest of his lowrider. — Seth Morgan, *Homeboy*, p. 57, 1990

chiz *noun*
in circus and carnival usage, a swindler *US, 1981*
An abbreviation of **CHISELER**.
- — Don Wilmeth, *The Language of American Popular Entertainment*, p. 52, 1981

choad *noun*
1 the penis *US, 1968*
- [N]obody to my knowledge spoke of "choad," "rod," "stem" or any other more strictly pornographic term. — *Screw*, p. 5, 3rd January 1972
- — Christian Crumlish, *The Internet Dictionary*, p. 34, 1995
2 a person who is easily despised *US, 1998*
Sometimes spelled "chode."
- — Connie Eble (Editor), *UNC-CH Campus Slang*, p. 2, Spring 1998
- "Break up with that choad," he said. — Megan McCafferty, *Second Helpings*, p. 207, 2003

choc beer *noun*
an unfiltered ale, sweeter and fruitier than traditional beer, brewed in Oklahoma *US, 1954*
From the Choctaw Indians, who are said to have taught immigrant Italians the recipe for the beer.
- A sign behind the latter fixture announced that choc beer was fifteen cents, whiskey two shots for a quarter. — Jim Thompson, *Roughneck*, p. 90, 1954

chock *noun*
home-fermented, vegetable-based alcohol *US, 1972*
- I'll tell you about chock. They used to make it here all the time. — Bruce Jackson, *In the Life*, p. 301, 1972

chockablock; chocka *adjective*
jammed close together, crammed full *UK, 1840*
From C19 nautical slang.
- I know, for example, that he was the creepiest guy in our office (which, believe you me, was choc-a-bloc full). — Terry Southern, *Now Dig This*, p. 31, 1975
- It took me forever to wend my way back south. Traffic was chocka. — Diran Abedayo, *My Once Upon A Time*, p. 93, 2000
- Portland is chockablock with beautiful, historic houses, and on the right day, you can walk right in the front door. — Chuck Palahniuk, *Fugitive and Refugees*, p. 39, 2003

chocolate *noun*
a black person *US, 1906*
- — Anon., *The Gay Girl's Guide*, 1949

chocolate *adjective*
of African heritage *US, 1906*
- I noticed a lot of Jungle Fever action, with people describing themselves as "vanilla" or "chocolate" or "caramel." — Anka Radakovich, *The Wild Girls Club*, p. 43, 1994

chocolate chips *noun*
desert camouflage uniforms *US, 1991*
- Some "ground pounders" wearing "chocolate chip cookie cammies" even talk of an "Adopt-a-Pilot" campaign and cheer when the jets roar overhead. — *Houston Chronicle*, p. 15, 24th January 1991
- — *Army*, p. 48, November 1991

chocolate highway *noun*
the anus and rectum *US, 1977*
- "You ever been fucked up the chocolate highway, Irish?" — John Gregory Dunne, *Dutch Shea, Jr.*, p. 37, 1982
- I rode her chocolate highway in eighth gear. — Zane, *Caramel Flava*, p. 237, 2006

chogie!
move out of here! *US, 1982*
Korean war usage.
- — Frank Hailey, *Soldier Talk*, p. 13, 1982

choice *adjective*
excellent *US, 1958*
- — *Washington Post*, 23rd April 1961
- — J. R. Friss, *A Dictionary of Teenage Slang (Mt. Diablo High)*, 1964
- — Miss Cone, *The Slang Dictionary (Hawthorne High School)*, 1965
- — Trevor Cralle, *The Surfin'ary*, p. 21, 1991

choiceamundo *adjective*
excellent *US, 1991*
- — Trevor Cralle, *The Surfin'ary*, p. 21, 1991
- — Vann Wesson, *Generation X Field Guide and Lexicon*, p. 38, 1997

choirboy *noun*
a newly initiated member of a youth gang *US, 1956*
- — *American Speech*, p. 99, May 1956: "Smugglers' argot in the southwest"

choir practice *noun*
an after-hours gathering of policemen, involving liberal amounts of alcohol and sex, usually in a remote public place *US, 1975*
- The first choir practice in MacArthur Park took place in the early spring when the nights became warm enough. — Joseph Wambaugh, *The Choirboys*, p. 25, 1975
- According to Hart, many officers participate in a rite of passage in many police departments—the so-called "choir practice" or heavy after-hours drinking. — *Boston Globe*, p. 16, 30th October 1991
- I can tell you this much: these cops are having choir practice with first-string girls and two guys from the mayor's staff. — Stephen J. Cannell, *The Tin Collectors*, p. 231, 2001
- They used to call it choir practice when a squad would go out together after their shift. They would hang out, blow off steam, try to pick up women, whatever. — *The Journal News (Westchester County, New York)*, p. 1A, 2nd September 2001

choke *noun*
1 a swallow or drink of alcohol *US, 1958*
- Have a choke, man. Like it might loosen up your right hand so you can really blow. — John Clellon Holmes, *The Horn*, p. 192, 1958
2 a Mexican-American *US, 1990*
Derogatory. A shortened form of **CHILI CHOKER**.
- That's Flaco de la Oilslick, a Nester General. One evil choke, yeah. — Seth Morgan, *Homeboy*, p. 185, 1990

▶ **pull your choke**
to masturbate *US, 1992*
- [M]asturbation—"pulling your choke"—becomes something to brag about. — Pete Earley, *The Hot House*, p. 42, 1992

choke *verb*
1 to forget *US, 1968*
Especially in the imperative.
- — Joan Fontaine et al., *Dictionary of Black Slang*, 1968
2 to fail to perform under pressure *US, 1986*
- A lot of pros in my position would already be thinking about the $130,000 check for winning, and they'd choke quicker on that than they would on their name in a history book. — Dan Jenkins, *Dead Solid Perfect*, p. 75, 1986
3 in computing, to reject data input *US, 1991*
- I tried building an EMACS binary to use X, but cpp(1) choked on all those #defines. — Eric S. Raymond, *The New Hacker's Dictionary*, p. 94, 1991

▶ **choke the chicken**
(of a male) to masturbate *US, 1976*
- He likes killin ... the way you like chokin your chicken. — Seth Morgan, *Homeboy*, p. 124, 1990
- "Guest home" meant "fuck pad" meant Howard Hughes left to choke his own chicken. — James Ellroy, *White Jazz*, p. 57, 1992
- Spanking the monkey. Flogging the bishop. Choking the chicken. Jerking the gherkin. — *American Beauty*, 1999

▶ **choke your chauncy**
(of a male) to masturbate *US, 1989*
- Who's sitting by himself in a room choking his chauncey to a bunch of videotapes, Graham? — *Sex, Lies and Videotape*, 1989

▶ **choke your mule**
(of a male) to masturbate *US, 1992*
- I get to choke my mule on the Mighty Man Agency's time. — James Ellroy, *White Jazz*, p. 111, 1992

choke *adjective*
many *US, 1982*
Hawaiian youth usage.
- Wow, get choke pakalolo until Green Hahvest! — Douglas Simonson, *Pidgin to da Max Hana Hou*, 1982

choke and chew *noun*
a roadside restaurant *US, 1976*
- — Elementary Electronics, *Dictionary of CB Lingo*, p. 57, 1976

choked down *adjective*
1 (of a racehorse) experiencing difficulty breathing during a race *US, 1994*
- — Igor Kushyshyn et al., *The Gambling Times Guide to Harness Racing*, p. 114, 1994
2 well-dressed *US, 1980*
- — Edith A. Folb, *runnin' down some lines*, p. 232, 1980

choked up tight *adjective*
dressed up, especially with button-down collars *US, 1976*
- He was choked up tight in a white-on-white / And a cocoa front that was down. — Dennis Wepman et al., *The Life*, p. 54, 1976

choke lover *noun*
a white person who maintains decent relationships with Mexican-Americans *US, 1976*
"Choke" is an abbreviation for **PACHUCO**.
- "You fucking Choke lover, you better learn who your own people are." — Malcolm Braley, *False Starts*, p. 53, 1976

choke out *verb*
to render someone unconscious through a choke hold that cuts off cerebral blood flow at the carotid artery in the neck, usually applied with a police officer's baton across the throat *US, 1985*
- Don't ... don't never try to choke out a ... hard-core street cop! — Joseph Wambaugh, *The Secrets of Harry Bright*, p. 199, 1985
- Once, when he'd choked out a San Bernadino County deputy D.A. who'd stopped at a minimarket to buy some nonprescription sleeping pills. — Joseph Wambaugh, *Fugitive Nights*, p. 31, 1990

choker *noun*
a necktie *US, 1945*
- — Lou Shelly, *Hepcats Jive Talk Dictionary*, p. 8, 1945
- — Clarence Major, *Dictionary of Afro-American Slang*, p. 37, 1970
- [H]er warm hands are unloosening my choker and unbuttoning my collar. — Leo Rosten, *Silky!*, p. 38, 1979

choke rag *noun*
a necktie *US, 1944*
- "Well, that's the first time I ever saw you with a choke rag on." — Francis Harper, *Okefinokee Album*, p. 171, 1981

choke up *verb*
to lose your composure; to totter on the verge of tears *US, 1941*
- And the whole damned United States gets choked up and goes into mourning. — Philip Wylie, *Opus 21*, pp. 7–8, 1949

cholly *noun*
cocaine *US, 1970*
- — William D. Alsever, *Glossary for the Establishment and Other Uptight People*, p. 6, December 1970

cholo *noun*
a young, tough Mexican-American *US, 1971*
Border Spanish used in English conversation by Mexican-Americans.
- The language of East L.A. is a speedy sort of cholo mixture of Mexican Spanish and California English. — Hunter S. Thompson, *Fear and Loathing in Las Vegas*, p. 230, 1971
- — Dagoberto Fuentes and Jose Lopez, *Barrio Language Dictionary*, p. 49, 1974
- The cholo shaded his eyes squinting into the Mission forenoon. — Seth Morgan, *Homeboy*, p. 57, 1990
- He saw a group of cholos in their oversized white T-shirts and baggy pants making their way through the yard. — Michael Connelly, *The Black Ice (in The Harry Bosch Novels)*, p. 379, 1993

chomo *noun*
a child molester *US, 1992*
- — William K. Bentley and James M. Corbett, *Prison Slang*, p. 35, 1992
- Like the "chomos" (child molesters) and rapists, he [Charles Manson] needed protection. — Edward George, *Taming the Beast*, p. 6, 1998
- "Back in the pen in Kansas we threw the fucking Chomos off the top tier, y'unnerstan?" — Jimmy Lerner, *You Got Nothing Coming*, p. 59, 2002

chomp *verb*
to eat *US, 1968*
- — Collin Baker et al., *College Undergraduate Slang Study Conducted at Brown University*, p. 96, 1968

chompers *noun*
the teeth; false teeth *US, 1950*
- "Jesus, he had fake teeth," Julia said, staring at the pink and super-white upper and lower chompers smiling up from the carpet. — Richard Condon, *Prizzi's Money*, p. 111, 1994
- I've heard those horror stories about folks with false teeth who tossed their net and watched their expensive store-bought chompers go sailing into the water with it. — *Tampa Tribune*, p. 11, 6th July 2003

chooch *noun*
a person *US, 2002*
- Count this crazy chooch out another dime. — David Chase, *The Sopranos: Selected Scripts from Three Seasons*, p. 152, 20th September 1999

choo-choo *noun*
a train *US, 1898*
Formed from the child's imitation of a steam whistle.
- "No, the choo-choo comes in, we get mostly appliances," Ordell said. — Elmore Leonard, *Switch*, p. 18, 1978

choose *verb*
(of a prostitute) to agree to work for a pimp *US, 1972*
- This bitch come over talkin' about she gon' choose me. — Christina and Richard Milner, *Black Players*, p. 87, 1972
- I was behind him with my hand in my pocket gripping the gun when Rose looked at him and said, "Ace, I've chosen Stonewall for my man." — A.S. Jackson, *Gentleman Pimp*, p. 145, 1973

choosing money *noun*
the money a prostitute pays a pimp to join his fold *US, 1972*
- Then get your choosin' money ready 'cause I don't chippy around. — Christina and Richard Milner, *Black Players*, p. 42, 1972

chop *noun*
1 approval *US, 1992*
- He taught me the intricacies of getting a superior's "chop," or approval on a draft memo that the superior might in fact not like at all. — Richard Marcinko and John Weisman, *Rogue Warrior*, p. 150, 1992
2 a scathing, cutting remark or joke *US, 1957*
- Very funny. What a chop. Ha, ha, ha. — *American Graffiti*, 1973
3 food *US, 1982*
US military usage during the Vietnam war.
- — *Maledicta*, p. 253, Summer/Winter 1982: "Viet-speak"

chop *verb*
1 to shoot someone to death *US, 1933*
- They were taking the two downtown to the D.A.'s and somebody chopped them. — Mickey Spillane, *Kiss Me Deadly*, p. 108, 1952
2 to approve something *US, 1992*
- We would scramble to do the research and draft an answer. Our superiors would "chop," or approve, our work and pass it up the ladder. — Richard Marcinko and John Weisman, *Rogue Warrior*, p. 190, 1992
3 to adulterate a powdered drug *US, 1970*
- You buy, you chop, you mix, you measure, then bag and sell. — Lanre Fehintola, *Charlie Says...*, p. 14, 2000
4 (of dice in a crap game) to pass once and then not pass *US, 1981*
- Don't count on it, they have been chopping. — N. B. Winkless, *The Gambling Times Guide to Craps*, p. 92, 1981

▶ **chop it up**
to talk with enthusiasm and energy *US, 2004*
- — Rick Ayers (Editor), *Berkeley High Slang Dictionary*, p. 15, 2004

▶ **chop your gums**
to engage in idle talk *US, 1948*

- The farmers were chewing the fat in feed and hardware stores, the women were chopping their gums in Five-and-tens and department stores[.] — Jack Kerouac, *Letter to Caroline and Paul Blake*, p. 143, 16th March 1948

chop-chop *verb*
during the Korean war, to eat *US, 1951*

- Chop-chop in World War II meant hurry up, snap into it, get on the ball, etc. In Korea, chop chop is most natives' term for eat, and many GI's are picking it up. — *The Baltimore Sun*, 24th June 1951

chop-chop *adverb*
immediately; in an instant *UK, 1836*
Pidgin or mock pidgin, sometimes used as an imperative.

- Boy, bring us three Reverend Davidsons. And boy: chop-chop! — Max Shulman, *Anyone Got a Match?*, p. 110, 1964
- At the sound of which word Little Cousin Norman would take off chop-chop at a chubby little scamper for the house. — Robert Gover, *Poorboy at the Party*, p. 102, 1966
- Wilson, take him and brief him. Chop-chop. — *Airheads*, 1994

chop house *noun*
a restaurant *US, 1956*

- [H]e conferred with three captains of waiters who were yearning to desert the fabled chophouse of James "Dinty" Moore. — Robert Sylvester, *No Cover Charge*, p. 99, 1956

chop it up *verb*
to engage in enthusiastic group conversation *US, 2001*

- — Rick Ayers (Editor), *Slang Dictionary*, p. 7, 2001

chopped *adjective*
1 marijuana-intoxicated *US, 1995*

- — Maria Hinojas, *Crews*, p. 167, 1995

2 ugly *US, 1993*

- — *Washington Post*, 14th October 1993

chopped liver *noun*
something of no consequence *US, 1954*

- MURTAUGH: Jesus. Maybe I should call for backup. RIGGS: What am I, chopped liver? — *Lethal Weapon*, 1987

chopped off *adjective*
annoyed, angry *US, 1963*

- — *American Speech*, p. 276, December 1963: "American Indian student slang"

chopped top *noun*
a hot rod that has had its roof removed *US, 1960*

- Aguilar stared at the street as a three-window '35 Ford Coupe with a chopped top rolled past. — *Los Angeles Times*, p. 3 (Calendar), 22nd June 1986

chopper *noun*
1 a machine gun; an assault rifle *US, 1929*

- Time was when you stood behind a chopper yourself, now you let a college kid do your blasting. — Mickey Spillane, *I, The Jury*, p. 18, 1947
- [Y]ou did not have to be twenty-one to press the trigger on a chopper. — Paul Gallico, *Trial By Terror*, p. 88, 1951
- Witnesses told police Neight pointed at Abernathy and said: "My boy's coming with a chopper." — *Miami Herald*, p. B3, 7th November 2006

2 a pistol *US, 1957*

- — *American Speech*, p. 193, October 1957: "Some colloquialisms of the handgunner"

3 a hacksaw; a hacksaw blade *US, 1950*

- — Hyman E. Goldin et al., *Dictionary of American Underworld Lingo*, p. 44, 1950

chopper *verb*
to fly by helicopter *US, 1977*

- "We can chopper you back to base-camp hospital in like twenty minutes." — Michael Herr, *Dispatches*, p. 15, 1977

chopper coppers *noun*
the police in helicopters *US, 1958*

- Chopper coppers are helicopter fliers. — *New York Times*, p. 34, 20th October 1958
- That game's halftime show will include an exhibition by LAPD's Special Weapons and Tactics (SWAT) unit, as well as helicopter-borne officers flying into the stadium and rappelling from the "copper choppers" to a simulated crime scene on the Coliseum floor. — *San Francisco Chronicle*, p. D6, 24th January 1990
- There's a new breed of police officer on the hunt for the menacing motorists who make highway travel an unwelcome hell ride: the chopper copper. — *Boston Herald*, p. 5, 9th June 2001

chopper jockey *noun*
a motorcycle enthusiast *US, 1971*

- Only in Hollywood's know-nothing biker movies do you see chopper jockeys in starched blue jeans and freshly ironed shirts. — Arthur Blessitt, *Turned On to Jesus*, p. 121, 1971

choppers *noun*
1 the teeth *US, 1944*

- He was smiling, grim through his cheap false choppers and blurred alcoholic face[.] — Gilbert Sorrentino, *Steelwork*, p. 153, 1970
- [A]n avenging old witch whose gorgeous smile and girlish face were courtesies of a five grand set of upper and lower choppers and a New York face lift[.] — Iceberg Slim (Robert Beck), *Doom Fox*, p. 100, 1978

2 the female legs *US, 1963*

- — *American Speech*, p. 273, December 1963: "American Indian student slang"

chops *noun*
1 the teeth or mouth *UK, 1589*

- He spit blood on the floor. "Boss, suh, please be careful with my chops—they're tender." — Chester Himes, *The Real Cool Killers*, p. 71, 1959
- A clout in the chops is what they deserved after dropping their Austin-Healey in the drink last night[.] — Max Shulman, *Anyone Got a Match?*, p. 54, 1964
- If I'd been on the outside, not being able to play until my chops healed, I'd probably have brooded the time away. — Nat Hentoff, *Jazz Country*, p. 141, 1965
- Maybe Mailer punches Vidal in the chops, maybe Vidal kicks Mailer in the cozies. — Robert Campbell, *Alice in La-La Land*, p. 52, 1987

2 musical ability *US, 1968*

- Man, your chops must've been really tight — Elmore Leonard, *Be Cool*, p. 108, 1999

► **bust your chops; break your chops**
to harass or provoke someone *US, 1953*

- Okay, Reggie, start bustin' my chops. Tell me how great you were with that chick. — *48 Hours*, 1982
- They would like to laugh and break other other's chops. — Joseph Pistone, *Donnie Brasco*, p. 90, 1987
- Jimmy's busting my chops. — *Goodfellas*, 1990
- Dad, have you been busting Ted's chops? — *Something About Mary*, 1998

chop shop *noun*
1 an autopsy room *US, 1991*

- Walking into the autopsy room on one occasion, Donald Waltemeyer made the mistake of wishing all the ghouls in the chop shop a fine good morning. — David Simon, *Homicide*, p. 410, 1991

2 a car body repair shop where stolen cars are altered or parts are stripped for sale separately *US, 1977*

- Jimmie (The Bomber) Catuara, 72, was assassinated yesterday in what police called a continuing chop-shop stolen auto parts vendetta. — *Washington Post*, 29th July 1978
- Pachoulo owned a piece of a chop shop on Alameda, near Olive Avenue Park over in Burbank, where stolen cars were dismembered with acetylene torches and the parts parceled out for sale. — Robert Campbell, *Juice*, p. 116, 1988
- The chop shop. Where are the stripped cars? The rolled-back odometers? The part bins? — *Gone in 60 Seconds*, 2000
- The only BMW's you see around here are from the chop shop. — Alisa Valdes-Rodriguez, *The Dirty Girls Social Club*, p. 204, 2003

chopsocky *noun*
martial arts; low-budget martial arts films *US, 1978*

- [Stan Shaw] got to play bone-crushers on TV cop shows, a martial arts maestro in a chopsocky melodrama called "TNT Jackson." — *The Washington Post*, 10th February 1978
- Bright spot here is Kriel, a South African star who dressed up the James Ryan chopsocky hit "Kill and Kill Again" a decade ago. — *Daily Variety*, 27th June 1990

chopstick *noun*
a South Asian person *US, 1980*
Offensive.

- — Edith A. Folb, *runnin' down some lines*, p. 232, 1980

chopsticks *noun*
mutual, simultaneous masturbation *US, 1941*
From the crossing of hands in the piano piece "Chopsticks."

- — Robert A. Wilson, *Playboy's Book of Forbidden Words*, p. 197, 1972

chop suey *adjective*
mixed up *US, 1981*
Hawaiian youth usage.

- "I get Japanese, Chinese, Filipino, Irish, German, Hawaiian, French—" "Real chop suey, yeah?" — *Douglas Simonson, Pidgin to da Max, 1981*

choptop *noun*
a crewcut haircut *US, 1959*

- — *Edd Byrnes, Way Out with Kookie, 1959*

chord-ially
used as a humorous closing in letters between singers *US, 1975*

- — *American Speech, p. 296, Autumn–Winter 1975: "The jargon of barbershop"*

chorine *noun*
a member of a theatrical chorus *US, 1922*

- Makes a change from those cottage queen chorines[.] — *The cast of Aspects of Love, Prince of Wales Theatre, Palace for Beginners, 1989–92*
- It was what looked like twelve Las Vegas chorines crowded in with one old boy who was wearing the biggest cowboy hat and the darkest Foster Grants I'd ever seen. — *Stephen King, Nightmares & Dreamscapes, p. 41, 1993*
- composing his daily letter to Maura Zell, his mistress, who was a chorine in the road company of Pearls of Broadway — *Michael Chabon, The Amazing Adventures of Kavalier & Clay, p. 81, 2000*
- With Steven Tyler, John Entwistle and Joan Jett in attendance, Jimmy Stoma marries a chorine turned professional wrestler in Las Vegas. — *Carl Hiaasen, Basket Case, p. 3, 2002*

chorizo *noun*
the penis *US, 1995*

- One girl said Castro had a 12" chorizo. — *James Ellroy, American Tabloid, p. 352, 1995*
- "A big Latino with his chorizo grande in your mouth and a hot Latina licking your pretty little hairless conyo." — *Ken Albertsen, Lali's Passage, p. 158, 2001*

chota *noun*
the police; a police officer *US, 1974*
Border Spanish used in English conversation by Mexican-Americans.

- — *Dagoberto Fuentes and Jose Lopez, Barrio Language Dictionary, p. 49, 1974*

chovies *noun*
anchovies *US, 1996*

- — *Maledicta, p. 9, 1996: "Domino's Pizza jargon"*

chow *noun*
food *US, 1856*

- "What the hell, roomy," he said. "Let's go to chow." — *Ralph Ellison, Invisible Man, p. 106, 1947*
- You tried to hurry good chow and you'd screw it up sure as hell. — *Jim Thompson, The Nothing Man, p. 245, 1954*
- Privacy exists because you pretend nothing else is there and in a chow joint you're expected to obey the rules of the game. — *Mickey Spillane, Return of the Hood, p. 82, 1964*

chow *verb*
to eat *US, 1900*

- You want something to chow? — *Airheads, 1994*

chowderhead *noun*
a fool *UK, 1819*

- — *Helen Dahlskog (Editor), A Dictionary of Contemporary and Colloquial Usage, p. 13, 1972*
- Does this chowderhead really believe Time magazine wants to hire him? — *Carl Hiaasen, Tourist Season, p. 200, 1986*

chow down *verb*
to set to eating *US, 1945*
Originally military, then spread into widespread, if affected, use.

- Most people would chow down on cheese and cold cuts before heading upstairs. — *Armistead Maupin, Tales of the City, p. 128, 1978*

chowhound *noun*
an enthusiastic eater *US, 1917*

- Not to mention such obvious rhymings as the charge-of-quarters' morning wakey-wakey call, "Okay, men. Drop your cocks and grab your socks!," or chowhound or shit list or walkie-talkie or the favorite term for those unhappy in the army, nervous in the service. — *Paul Fussell, Wartime, p. 256, 1989*
- Now you know why Marco Polo—a real chowhound—traveled clear up Rainier Avenue South to discover Aurora Avenue North. — *Seattle Post-Intelligencer, p. E2, 31st March 2004*

chowmeinery *noun*
in circus and carnival usage, a Chinese restaurant *US, 1981*

- — *Don Wilmeth, The Language of American Popular Entertainment, p. 52, 1981*

christer *noun*
a Christian who proclaims his beliefs to all, whether they wish to hear or not *US, 1921*

- "Why don't you get the hell out of here and go clean up or something?" "What are you—a christer?" — *John Nichols, The Sterile Cuckoo, p. 219, 1965*
- Bush is a Christer. He takes every opportunity to inform the American people that he is in touch with the Lord and therefore that, by deduction, what he does is the Lord's work. — *Chattanooga (Tennessee) Free Press, p. B9, 10th September 2003*

Christians in Action *nickname*
the US Central Intelligence Agency *US, 1992*
Reverse engineered from the agency's initials.

- They worked for my brothers-in-arms from the organization we fondly called Christians In Action—the CIA. — *Richard Marcinko and John Weisman, Rogue Warrior, p. 126, 1992*

Christine *noun*
cocaine *US, 1968*
Another in a long series of personifications of drugs based on the drug's first letter.

- "What is this?" I asked. "It's 'her,' man. 'Christine.' Cocaine." — *Phil Hirsch, Hooked, p. 9, 1968*
- He got up, dressed, we took a few more toots of Christine and Henry (pineapple) and split. — *A.S. Jackson, Gentleman Pimp, p. 71, 1973*

Christ-killer *noun*
a Jewish person *UK, 1861*
Offensive.

- Through the centuries, the Church has, wittingly and unwittingly, helped to nurture hate for the Jew, the "Wandering Jew," the "Christ Killer." [Letter to the editor] — *Life, p. 13, 14th January 1946*
- "No, I'm different. (Pause) I'm Jewish." "(Shocked) Christ-killer!" — *Raymond Mungo, Famous Long Ago, p. 58, 1970*

Christless *adjective*
cursed, damned *US, 1912*

- Talk about a Christless mess. And for what? — *Indianapolis (Indiana) Star, p. 1B, 28th November 1999*

Christmas present *noun*
in tiddlywinks, a stroke of good luck *US, 1977*

- — *Verbatim, p. 525, December 1977*

Christmas roll *noun*
a multi-coloured assortment of barbiturate capsules *US, 1973*

- — *David W. Maurer and Victor Vogel, Narcotics and Narcotic Addiction, p. 397, 1973*

Christmas tree *noun*
1 a busy telephone switchboard *US, 1958*

- A busy switchboard at Police Headquarters is, by poetic touch, a Christmas tree. — *New York Times, p. 34, 20th October 1958*

2 a bank of red and green-coloured lights that are part of an instrument panel *US, 1945*

- Captain Rogers? I have a green Christmas tree on board. — *Edwin Corley, The Jesus Factor, p. 167, 1970*
- First, we waited for the "Christmas tree," the bank of indicator lights showing the status of all hull openings, to change from red to green to all green, signaling that they were closed. — *Richard O'Kane, Clear the Bridge, p. 14, 1977*

3 in the car sales business, a car loaded with accessories and gadgets *US, 1953*

- — *Cars, p. 40, December 1953*

4 in the television and movie industries, a cart used for storing and carrying lighting equipment *US, 1977*

- — *Tony Miller and Patricia George, Cut! Print!, p. 51, 1977*

5 in the television and movie industries, a stand with more than one light mounted on it *US, 1987*

- — *Ira Konigsberg, The Complete Film Dictionary, p. 47, 1987*

Christmas tree lights; Christmas trees *noun*

a capsule of amobarbital sodium and secobarbital sodium (trade name Tuinal™), a combination of central nervous system depressants *US, 1968*

- — Donald Louria, *The Drug Scene*, p. 189, 1968

- A brother and sister from Michigan, eighteen and sixteen years old, whispered to me that they were turned on with CTL—Christmas Tree Lights. — Arthur Blessitt, *Turned On to Jesus*, p. 233, 1971
- Tuinal is what I like. Some people call them Christmas Trees. That's the underworld slang for them because they're a kind of a green and kind of a red[.] — Bruce Jackson, *Outside the Law*, p. 110, 1972
- Whites to wake up, yellow jackets to sleep, and a special present she called a Christmas Tree, a cap filled with red and green spansules. — Malcolm Braley, *False Starts*, p. 267, 1976

Christ on a bike!; Jesus Christ on a bike!

used as a register of shock or amazement *US, 1986*

- Brian Keyes removed the rum and dumped the ice cubes over Wiley's naked chest. "Christ on a bike!" Wiley sat up like a bolt. — Carl Hiaasen, *Tourist Season*, p. 163, 1986

Christ on a crutch!

used for expressing exasperation *US, 1928*

- Christ on a crutch, man: if you people are as hard up for writers as you appear to be, then you need help in the worst way. — Hunter S. Thompson, *The Proud Highway*, p. 113, 31st March 1958: Letter to Down Beat Magazine
- But Christ on a crutch, the news that Britney Spears and Fred Durst are hitting it has blown nearly every other coherent thought right out of our little peanut brains. — *Seattle Weekly*, p. 46, 22nd January 2003

chrome *noun*

1 handguns *US, 2006*

- "I been dealin' chrome to kids. You know, junior high, that kinda shit." — Jason Starr, *Lights Out*, p. 130, 2006
- "I don't allow no chrome in here." — Stephen J. Cannell, *White Sister*, p. 46, 2006

2 in computing, software features that attract buyers but add little functionally *US, 1991*

- The 3D icons in Motif are just chrome but they certainly are pretty chrome. — Eric S. Raymond, *The New Hacker's Dictionary*, p. 95, 1991

chrome dome *noun*

a bald man; a bald head *US, 1962*

- Hose Nose / Chrome Dome / Mr. Absent Offenhauser. — Ron Padgett, *New and Selected Poems*, p. 78, 1995
- Last month in Dallas, an Associated Press photographer at a political fund-raiser captured Bush grabbing the chrome dome of an unidentified supporter so forcefully you can see indentation marks. — *Austin (Texas) American-Statesman*, p. E1, 7th August 2003

chrome-plated *adjective*

1 nicely dressed *US, 1961*

High school student usage, borrowing from car vocabulary.

- — *San Francisco Examiner*, p. 21, 12th December 1961

2 dressed up *US, 1961*

- — Art Unger, *The Cool Book*, p. 106, 1961

chrome to the dome *noun*

a pistol held to the head *US, 1998*

- — Ethan Hilderbrant, *Prison Slang*, p. 146, 1998

chrondo *noun*

potent marijuana *US, 1997*

A blend of **CHRONIC** and **INDO**.

- — Pamela Munro, *U.C.L.A. Slang*, p. 51, 1997

chroned out *adjective*

suffering from a hangover *US, 2001*

- — Don R. McCreary (Editor), *Dawg Speak*, 2001

chronic *noun*

1 potent marijuana *US, 1993*

A word popularized in hip-hop usage. "The Chronic" by Dr Dre (1992) is one of the biggest-selling rap albums of all time.

- Beeitch, if you ain't got no kinda chronic, yo punk ass gots to go! — Snoop Doggy Dogg, *A Day in the Life of Snoop Doogy Dog [Cover art]*, 1993
- Smoking a spliff of high-octane chronic (street talk for pot) in the back room, he explains his bond to Dre. "He's the bomb," says Snoop. — *People*, p. 77, 23rd May 1994
- Gimme a taste of the mothafuckin' chronic. — *Kids*, 1995

2 marijuana mixed with crack cocaine *US, 1998*

- [A] fat ass J, of some bubonic chronic that made me choke[.] — Snoop Doggy Dogg, *Gin and Juice*, 1993

chronic bubonic *noun*

marijuana that is more potent than simple "chronic" or simple "bubonic" *US, 2001*

- — Pamela Munro, *U.C.L.A. Slang*, p. 54, 2001

chub *noun*

a moderately overweight person *UK, 1838*

- [Y]ou can be sure that plump women such as myself and many of my "chub" friends all over the country, who perhaps are contemplating weight loss, will never enter a Jenny Craig office. [Letter to the editor] — *Virginian-Pilot (Norfolk, Virginia)*, p. J4, 9th January 2000

chubbies *noun*

large female breasts *US, 1964*

- — Roger Blake, *The American Dictionary of Sexual Terms*, p. 35, 1964
- — *Current Slang*, p. 3, Winter 1971

chubby *noun*

1 an overweight man as a homosexual object of desire *US, 1971*

- If you dig chubbies and are good-looking, white male, 23—40, and groove on affection, I'm your boy. — Emile Nytrate, *Underground Ads*, p. 99, 1971
- Are there any straight bars for chubbies and chubby-chasers? — *Screw*, p. 11, 2 August 1971

2 an erection *US, 1997*

- — Pamela Munro, *U.C.L.A. Slang*, p. 51, 1997
- I woke up with a chart-busting chubby. — James Ellroy, *Destination Morgue*, p. 235, 2004
- You'll be sporting chubbies from the first glimpse of every rubber-warped aerola. — Editors of Adult Video News, *The AVN Guide to the 500 Greatest Adult Films of All Time*, p. 309, 2005

chubby-chaser *noun*

a person who is sexually attracted to overweight people *US, 1971*

- Are there any straight bars for chubbies and chubby-chasers? — *Screw*, p. 11, 2 August 1971
- — *Maledicta*, p. 227, Winter 1980: "'Lovely, blooming, fresh and gay': the onomastics of camp"
- — *American Speech*, p. 19, Spring 1985: "The language of singles bars"
- Watching Buffy Davis and Tammy White going at it with a dildo in between them is a chubby-chaser's delight. — *Adult Video*, p. 50, August/September 1986
- While there are some people out there who revel in obesity (they're called chubby-chasers), they are few and far between. — John Preston, *Hustling*, p. 48, 1994
- Chuckie's a chubby chaster that likes fat chicks. — James Ellroy, *Destination Morgue*, p. 231, 2004

chub rub *noun*

a rash from anywhere that fat body part meets fat body part *US, 1998*

- Has anyone experiences (sic) cysts or boils on inner thighs and underarms? I always thought they were just a symptom of "chub rub" though they weren't always just where I chafe. — *alt.support.pco*, 13th September 1998
- — Connie Eble (Editor), *UNC-CH Campus Slang*, p. 3, Fall 2005

chuc; chuke *noun*

a Pachuco, or young Mexican-American with a highly stylized sense of fashion and a specialized idiom *US, 1963*

The Pachuco was the Mexican zoot-suiter of the 1940s, and his legacy is seen today in Mexican-American culture. The term can be used either as a term of pride or as a term of derision.

- — *San Francisco Examiner: People*, p. 8, 27th October 1963
- They came in Packards, two of them, they dig big white cards; twelve, maybe thirteen chucs in all. — Richard Farina, *Been Down So Long*, p. 63, 1966
- — *Current Slang*, p. 15, Spring 1970

Chuck *noun*

1 a white man *US, 1965*

A diminuitive of Charles or Charlie.

- — Clarence Major, *Dictionary of Afro-American Slang*, p. 37, 1970
- A few years ago, Civil Rights workers took to calling White "Chuck." — Roger Abrahams, *Positively Black*, p. 32, 1970

2 the Viet Cong *US, 1981*

- Chuck, Charlie, Mr. Charles, VC, Viet Cong, Victor Charlie. Whom are we talking about? — Nelson DeMille, *Word of Honor*, p. 131, 1985

chuck *verb*

1 to over-eat during withdrawal from a drug addiction *US, 1966*

- — Rose Giallombardo, *Society of Women*, p. 206, 1966: Glossary of Prison Terms

2 to throw something *UK, 1593*

- Robert Jr. and I got to be tight friends—by chucking rocks at a tin can, the next day in the courtyard. — Bobby Seale, *A Lonely Rage*, p. 25, 1978

3 to throw something away, to discard something *US, 1911*

- We all decided to chuck the idea because I'd have trouble making friends. — *Heathers*, 1988
- Well maybe I should just chuck it all and go sell derby hats to women in Boliva. — Joseph Wambaugh, *Finnegan's Week*, p. 11, 1993

4 to forget *US, 1947*

Also "chuck it."

- — Marcus Hanna Boulware, *Jive and Slang of Students in Negro Colleges*, 1947

chuck habit *noun*

the strong appetite of an addict withdrawing from drug use *US, 1953*

- He had developed the familiar "chuck habit." — Phil Hirsch, *Hooked*, p. 95, 1968
- But Gloria's stomach protruded slightly and I knew that this was only temporary, coming from her recently acquired "chuck habit." — Robert Deane Pharr, *S.R.O.*, p. 53, 1971

chuck horrors *noun*

the painful symptoms and craving for sweets experienced during withdrawal from drug addiction *US, 1926*

- Back on the street at last, he'd gotten the chuck horrors; for two full days he'd eaten candy bars, sweet rolls and strawberry malteds. — Nelson Algren, *The Man with the Golden Arm*, p. 59, 1949
- So you might as well get yourself set for the steel-and-concrete and the chuck horrors. I had 'em. — *The New American Mercury*, p. 711, 1950
- "You look like you've got the chuck horrors," he commented[.] — Morton Cooper, *High School Confidential*, p. 58, 1958

chucklehead *noun*

a fool *UK, 1731*

- I enjoy a good har-dee-har-har as much as the next chucklehead[.] — *San Francisco Bay Guardian*, 4th December 2002

chuckleheaded *adjective*

simple, dim-witted *UK, 1768*

- A chuckleheaded, no-talent cook shovels food around a burned-out griddle with a warped spatula in one hand and a beat-up barbecue fork in the other, pouring sweat into the food for all to see. — Larry Heinemann, *Paco's Story*, p. 104, 1990

chuckle sticks *noun*

nunchaku sticks *US, 1988*

- "We went over and this guy pulls out these chuckle sticks [nunchaku, two wooden batons joined with a chain] like he was going to do us in." — James Vigil, *Barrio Gangs*, p. 132, 1988

chucks *noun*

1 a powerful craving for food associated with withdrawal from heroin addiction *US, 1953*

Also "chuckers."

- After eight days I got the "chucks" and developed a tremendous appetite for cream puffs and macaroons. — William Burroughs, *Junkie*, p. 40, 1953
- When you're kicking, you get what we call the chucks, and after that you're hungry all the time. — Billie Holiday with William Dufty, *Lady Sings the Blues*, p. 134, 1956
- This excessive desire for sweets is the beginning of what is known as the chucks, an enormous hunger which addicts experience in the last stages of withdrawal[.] — Emmett Grogan, *Ringolevio*, p. 63, 1972

2 the craving for food that follows the smoking of marijuana *US, 1970*

- — William D. Alsever, *Glossary for the Establishment and Other Uptight People*, p. 6, December 1970

chuck you, Farley!

used as an expression of derision *US, 1976*

An intentional Spoonerism "Fuck you, charley."

- "Chuck you, Farley," she said. "Don't you wish," Donald Ray said. — William Brashler, *City Dogs*, p. 145, 1976

chuco *noun*

a tough, urban Mexican-American youth *US, 1978*

An abbreviation of **PACHUCO**.

- The "chucos" spoke their own argot, a Spanish with words and phrases unintelligible to the outsider. — Joan W. Moore, *Homeboys*, p. 57, 1978

chud *noun*

a disgusting person *US, 1986*

From the film *Cannabalistic Humanoid Underground Dwellers*.

- Besides being the perfect film for study, it can drive home the message that these "CHUDS" ain't nothing compared to some of the people you'll have to meet in the movie business. — John Waters, *Crackpot*, pp. 131–132, 1986
- — Pamela Munro, *U.C.L.A. Slang*, p. 30, 1989

chuff *noun*

1 the anus *AUSTRALIA, 1945*

- [M]y mouth was munching and sucking her whole fur-pie, and my nose was probing her chuff like a mole trying to get into an ant hill. — Joey V., *Portrait of Joey*, p. 94, 1969

2 pubic hair *US, 1967*

- — Dale Gordon, *The Dominion Sex Dictionary*, p. 43, 1967

chug *verb*

1 to swallow a drink in a single draught *US, 1989*

An abbreviation of **CHUGALUG**.

- — Connie Eble (Editor), *UNC-CH Campus Slang*, p. 2, Fall 1989
- DeChooch chugged three fingers and got some color back into his face. — Janet Evanovich, *Seven Up*, p. 277, 2001

2 in computing, to operate slowly *US, 1991*

- The disk is chugging like crazy. — Eric S. Raymond, *The New Hacker's Dictionary*, p. 95, 1991

chugalug; chuglug *verb*

to drink without pausing to breathe *US, 1936*

- Chug-a-lug, chug-a-lug / Make you want to holler hi-de-ho / Burns your tummy, don'tcha know / Chug-a-lug, chug-a-lug — Roger Miller, *Chugalug*, 1964
- Pooks, I couldn't care less how fast Schoons can chug-a-lug a beer. — John Nichols, *The Sterile Cuckoo*, p. 163, 1965
- A little drunk, very happy, she chugalugged a beer someone handed her up, yelled "G7!" and proceeded to divest herself of veil, dress, slip, and bra. — Anne Steinhardt, *Thunder La Boom*, p. 189, 1974
- Paco fetching another bursting-full bus pan of dishes in the meantime, chugalugging his coffee, going to take a whiz[.] — Larry Heinemann, *Paco's Story*, p. 112, 1986

chumbolone *noun*

a fool *US, 2007*

- "I don't wanna look like a "chumbolone," an idiot," said Doyle, using street slang. — Jeff Coen, *Chicago Tribune*, p. Metro 1, 24th August 2007

chum buddy *noun*

a close friend *US, 1952*

- Don't forget when you gather your chum-buddies for your Friends watch party that tonight's episode has been "supersized." — *Arkansas Democrat-Gazette*, 12th February 2004

chummified *adjective*

drunk *US, 1968*

- — Collin Baker et al., *College Undergraduate Slang Study Conducted at Brown University*, p. 96, 1968

chummy *adjective*

very friendly, intimate, sociable *US, 1884*

- And, if you ask me, Trent's being awfully chummy too. — C.D. Payne, *Youth in Revolt*, p. 390, 1993

chump *noun*

a fool; a naive person who is easily duped *US, 1875*

- I'd acted like a chump. — Jim Thompson, *The Killer Inside*, p. 9, 1952
- Don't be a chump. Don't bet any more money on that damn fool shot. — *The Hustler*, 1961
- He said, "Gonzi, Miles and Vernon were trying to use me so I burned both them chumps." — Babs Gonzales, *Movin' On Down De Line*, p. 63, 1975
- I don't want to do any coke. It's a terrible drug. It's for chumps. — Kenneth Lonergan, *This is Our Youth*, p. 47, 2000

chump *verb*

1 to act foolishly *US, 1946*

- Most pimps chump off their money. They blow it on drugs, clothes, jewelry, cars and in chrome and leather cesspools. — Iceberg Slim (Robert Beck), *The Naked Soul of Iceberg Slim*, p. 68, 1971

2 to swindle someone, to cheat someone *US, 1930*

- He wouldn't be rimmed no sir, not him, because he wasn't the kind of a chump who allowed himself to be chumped by a cheap kike auctioneer. — James T. Farrell, *Willie Collins*, p. 107, 1946

chump change *noun*

a small amount of money *US, 1968*

- — *Current Slang*, p. 15, Fall 1968
- They said that Western whores were lazy and were satisfied with making "chump change." — Iceberg Slim (Robert Beck), *Pimp*, p. 285, 1969
- Why should they keep their job as a delivery boy for "chump change" when they could be making big money? — Christina and Richard Milner, *Black Players*, p. 141, 1972
- He pays you chump change. Know what a real driver gets for haulin' poison waste? — Joseph Wambaugh, *Finnegan's Week*, p. 39, 1993

chump down *verb*

to intimidate someone into backing down *US, 1994*

- I calmed down and pulled the gun away, satisfied that I'd publicly chumped him down. — Nathan McCall, *Makes Me Wanna Holler*, p. 64, 1994

chump educator *noun*

1 a trade newspaper or magazine used to educate outsiders on the industry's secrets *US, 1981*

- — Don Wilmeth, *The Language of American Popular Entertainment*, p. 53, 1981

2 in the circus or carnival, *Billboard* magazine *US, 1980*

- — Joe McKennon, *Circus Lingo*, p. 26, 1980

chump expenses *noun*

minor expenses *US, 1969*

- At least she'd make enough scratch for chump expenses. — Iceberg Slim (Robert Beck), *Pimp*, p. 252, 1969

chump heister *noun*

a carnival ferris wheel *US, 1980*

- — Joe McKennon, *Circus Lingo*, p. 26, 1980

chump job *noun*

a legal, legitimate job, especially a low-paying and menial one *US, 1972*

- Why should I work a chump job for chump change when I can make real money and be independent of the Man? — Christina and Richard Milner, *Black Players*, p. 257, 1972

chump life *noun*

a conventional, law-abiding life *US, 1993*

- Sometimes he could almost envision himself living the chump life. — Bob Sipchen, *Baby Insane and the Buddha*, p. 223, 1993

chump off *verb*

to better or out-insult someone in a verbal duel *US, 1972*

- — David Claerbaut, *Black Jargon in White America*, p. 60, 1972
- "Sergeant Stranger tells me you chumped him off in front of the assistant warden." — Jimmy Lerner, *You Got Nothing Coming*, p. 201, 2002

chump twister *noun*

a carousel *US, 1961*

- — Don Wilmeth, *The Language of American Popular Entertainment*, p. 53, 1981

chunck *verb*

in pinball, to hit the ball into a scoring bumper with such force that the bumper fails to respond *US, 1977*

- — Bobbye Claire Natkin and Steve Kirk, *All About Pinball*, p. 111, 1977

chunder *noun*

in poker, a weak hand that wins *US, 1996*

- — John Vorhaus, *The Big Book of Poker Slang*, p. 10, 1996

chunk *noun*

a large amount *US, 1889*

- WADE: Well, seven hundred and fifty thousand dollars is a lot. JERRY: Yah, well, it's a chunk. — *Fargo*, 1996

chunk *verb*

1 to throw something *US, 1835*

- "You know how to make pigeons fly?" Sonny hesitated. "Chunk rocks at 'em?" — Chester Himes, *The Real Cool Killers*, p. 51, 1959

- "Hey, quit chunkin' them balls, you little dumb-asses," Coach Popper yelled. — Larry McMurtry, *The Last Picture Show*, p. 36, 1966
- Everybody's mother knew a little boy "got his eye put out like that," whether we were chunkin' rocks at each other or fighting with homemade bullwhips. — Ken Weaver, *Texas Crude*, p. 107, 1984

2 in Americans casinos, to bet a great deal, especially to do so unwisely *US, 1985*

- — Steve Kuriscak, *Casino Talk*, p. 12, 1985

3 to engage in a fist fight *US, 1990*

- — Charles Shafer, *Folk Speech in Texas Prisons*, p. 201, 1990
- — Rick Ayers (Editor), *Berkeley High Slang Dictionary*, p. 16, 2004

chunk down *verb*

to eat *US, 1968*

- — Collin Baker et al., *College Undergraduate Slang Study Conducted at Brown University*, p. 96, 1968

chunker *noun*

an M79 grenade launcher *US, 1975*

Vietnam war usage.

- — *Maledicta*, p. 259, Summer/Winter 1982: "Viet-speak"
- "Use your chunker!" the team leader yelled to Bruce Judkins who nodded and brought the short, compact weapon up to fire. The chunker was actually an M-79 grenade launcher, a six-pound, single-shot break-open weapon like a fat sawed-off shotgun that could fire a 40mm high-explosive round up to four hundred yards. — Kregg P. Jorgenson, *LRRP Company Command*, p. 121, 2000

chunk of change *noun*

a lot of money *US, 2002*

- But believe me when I say the whole thing isn't just about a chunk of change. — Christopher Brookmyre, *The Sacred Art of Stealing*, p. 238, 2002
- — Victor H. Royer, *Casino Gamble Talk*, p. 33, 2003

chunt *noun*

a Mexican national *US, 1988*

- Mexican nationals are referred to as chuntaros or "chunts." — James Vigil, *Barrio Gangs*, p. 119, 1988

church is out

an opportunity has passed *US, 1966*

- — *Current Slang*, p. 2, Summer 1966

church key *noun*

a can and bottle opener *US, 1951*

With the advent of pull-ring (1962), the pop-top (1963), and the stay-on tab can (1974), the device and term all but disappeared.

- She hooked the church key over the top of each bottle and with a sharp rap of her hand that made a sharp, sucking pok, opened the bottles and handed them up. — Larry Heinemann, *Close Quarters*, p. 70, 1977
- The real hoods, the serious ones who'd been up the night before fighting with churchkeys and tireirons or knocking up "cheap" girls, spent the days dozing fully clothed[.] — Eve Babitz, *Eve's Hollywood*, p. 59, 1984

church mouse *noun*

in prison, a convict assigned to work in the chapel *US, 1957*

- Working in the Chapel is rather peaceful (us Chapel employees are referred to as "church mice"). — James Blake, *The Joint*, p. 177, 10th November 1957

Church of England *noun*

in craps, a bet that the next roll will be 1, 2, 11 or 12 *US, 1983*

A back-formation from C AND E, itself the initials of "crap-eleven," the conventional name of the bet.

- — Thomas L. Clark, *The Dictionary of Gambling and Gaming*, p. 44, 1987

church tramp *noun*

a student who changes his church affiliation as necessary to attend various church social functions *US, 1963*

- — *American Speech*, p. 272, December 1963: "American Indian student slang"

chute *noun*

1 the rectum *US, 1976*

- [S]lim blonde anal lover Chrissy Ann, who lets Cal Jammer slide up her chute. — *Adult Video News*, p. 56, February 1993
- He deliberately drove back onto my hand, my thumb up his chute. — Jack Hart, *My First Time*, p. 168, 1995
- Moving harder than ever against the tank barrel, with my finger jammed up her chute, she started to growl passionately. — *Penthouse International, Letters to Penthouse XV*, p. 148, 2002

2 the coin slot on a pinball machine *US, 1977*
- — Bobbye Claire Natkin and Steve Kirk, *All About Pinball*, p. 111, 1977

3 in sailing, a spinnaker *US, 1990*
- "Okay!" Winnie shouted. "Let's pop the chute!" — Joseph Wambaugh, *The Golden Orange*, p. 286, 1990

4 in the usage of youthful model road racers (slot car racers), a straight portion of track *US, 1997*
- — Phantom Surfers, *The Exciting Sounds of Model Road Racing (Album cover)*, 1997

chutzpah; chuzpah *noun*
gall, intestinal fortitude, extreme self-confidence *US, 1892*
One of the known Yiddish words in the US.
- Next to his adroitness in fleecing the philanthropic sheep was his chutzpah, his unmitigated impudence. — Nathan Ausubel, *A Treasury of Jewish Folklore*, p. 267, 1948
- The gall, the chutzpah, her bringing a girl friend along[.] — Sol Yurrick, *The Bag*, p. 214, 1968
- It takes chutzpah as well as millions to win the America's Cup. — Joseph Wambaugh, *Floaters*, p. 267, 1996
- I'm talking about Vice President Dick Cheney. For him to be questioning Sen. John Kerry's ability and/or willingness to protect this nation takes, well, chutzpah. — *Oakland Tribune*, 2nd May 2004

'cid; cid; sid *noun*
LSD *US, 1986*
An abbreviation of **ACID**.
- — Connie Eble (Editor), *UNC-CH Campus Slang*, p. 2, October 1986
- — US Department of Justice, *Street Terms*, October 1994

cig *noun*
a cigarette or cigar *US, 1894*
- [T]hey heard him say to Polly, "Have a cig?" while offering a silver cigarette-case with a flourish. — Norman Lindsay, *Halfway to Anywhere*, p. 44, 1947
- I see her standing, with her black velvet slacks, handsapockets, thin, slouched, cig hanging from lips[.] — Jack Kerouac, *The Subterraneans*, p. 50, 1958
- We carried the tax stampless cigs down into the cellar in the nick of time. — Ed Sanders, *Tales of Beatnik Glory*, p. 29, 1975
- When we finished Susie went for the john, I went for my cigs. — Larry Heinemann, *Close Quarters*, p. 187, 1977

cigar *noun*
in circus and carnival usage, any compliment *US, 1981*
- — Don Wilmeth, *The Language of American Popular Entertainment*, p. 53, 1981

cigar!
correct! *US, 1991*
An extrapolation from "Close, but no cigar."
- — Trevor Cralle, *The Surfin'ary*, p. 21, 1991

cigarette *noun*
an untalented or personality-free roller derby skater *US, 1999*
The cigarette lagged back in the pack, hence the punning term.
- Skaters who were washed up, problem children looking for a way back in, and rookies who would probably never amount to anything were cigarettes. Virtually every team had at least one. — Keith Pollage, *Roller Derby to Rollerjam*, p. 126, 1999

cigarette pimp *noun*
a pimp whose lack of professional pride leads him to solicit customers for his prostitutes *US, 1972*
- Black pimps never solicit for their women if they are "true pimps," and call a man who does a cigarette pimp, popcorn pimp, or chile pimp. — Christina and Richard Milner, *Black Players*, p. 33, 1972
- — Burgess Laughlin, *Job Opportunities in the Black Market*, p. 2, 1978

cigarette roll *noun*
a type of parachute malfunction *US, 1962*
- The cigarette roll was a rigging error which caused the parachute to unfold, but not fill with air, not opening to full deployment. — Gregory Clark, *Words of the Vietnam War*, p. 498, 1990
- The main parachute of an experienced jumper failed to open; it streamed upward in what was known as a cigarette roll. — Robert W. Black, *A Ranger Born*, p. 44, 2002

cigarette with no name *noun*
a marijuana cigarette *US, 1980*
- — Edith A. Folb, *runnin' down some lines*, p. 232, 1980

ciggy; ciggie *noun*
a cigarette *US, 1915*
- The youngsters eat at Walgreen's drugstore, 44th Street and Broadway, and the drugstore, in the Astor; instead of cocktails they sip cokes and smoke ciggies. — Jack Lait and Lee Mortimer, *New York Confidential*, p. 39, 1948
- Marijuana (we hear) is now peddled in the form of phony cigars. Called "atomics." A box (less conspicious than ciggies) sells at $35[.] — *San Francisco Call-Bulletin*, p. 8G, 11th March 1953
- "You got a ciggy?" The messenger gives him a cigarette and Billy puts one hand beneath his head and smokes. — Darryl Ponicsan, *The Last Detail*, p. 3, 1970
- "Do you know what's in those boxes?" "First-quality ciggies. You want some?" — Janet Evanovich, *Seven Up*, p. 57, 2001

ciggyboo; ciggieboo *noun*
a cigarette *UK, 1958*
- The ciggyboos are kept in counter under the trash locked behind a wooden board. — Allen Ginsberg, *Journals*, p. 204, 5th May 1961
- — Andy Anonymous, *A Basic Guide to Campusology*, p. 6, 1966
- — Collin Baker et al., *College Undergraduate Slang Study Conducted at Brown University*, p. 96, 1968

cinch *noun*
in horse racing, a horse that is virtually certain to win *US, 1960*
- — Robert Saunders Dowst and Jay Craig, *Playing the Races*, p. 161, 1960

Cincy; Cinci *nickname*
Cincinatti, Ohio *US, 1899*
- We were in Cincy in April and had a free day on our hands because this exhibition game was called off. — Bernard Malamud, *The Natural*, p. 47, 1952
- Keep out of Cincy in the fall—mean cops. — John Clellon Holmes, *The Horn*, p. 160, 1958
- Cinci, just another forlong border-south Queen City, the Gateway to something or other — Bill Cardoso, *The Maltese Sangweech*, p. 175, 1984

Cinderella liberty *noun*
a short release from military duty and from base restrictions *US, 1961*
Cinderella had to be home by midnight, as do navy and marine troops.
- Wagoner said yes, ten percent of the battalion would be allowed Cinderella liberty (ending at midnight) in Danang. — Philip Caputo, *A Rumor of War*, p. 129, 1977
- Large signs were strategically placed along the way that stated the penalty for being caught out in town after midnight, when curfew began for all enlisted men holding the pay grade of E-5 or below, and remained in effect until 5:00 a.m. This was commonly known as "Cinderella Liberty." — Bruce H. Norton, *Force Recon Diary*, p. 5, 1992
- "NoFuck Virginia." Recruits learn to say "NoFuck"on their first Cinderella liberty when they have to be back on base by midnight without getting "any." — Maria Flook, *My Sister Life*, p. 62, 1998

ciphering *noun*
arithmetic *US, 1905*
- I liked ciphering all right, but I didn't care much for spelling and studying the Bible and memorizing psalms. — James Lincoln Collier, *My Brother Sam is Dead*, p. 66, 1974

circle *noun*
1 a group of close and trusted friends *US, 2006*
- On the street, the circle was your group of tights—your buddies. — Stephen J. Cannell, *White Sister*, p. 139, 2006

2 any group of people playing footbag *US, 1997*
- — Jim Crotty, *How to Talk American*, p. 122, 1997

circle *verb*
▸ **circle a game**
(of a bookmaker) to limit the amount that may be bet on a given game or race when the bookmaker suspects that the game or race is fixed *US, 1978*
- — Burgess Laughlin, *Job Opportunities in the Black Market*, p. 5, 1978

▸ **circle the drain**
1 to be near death *US, 1994*
- — *Los Angeles Times*, p. B1, 19th December 1994

2 by extension, said of a project or enterprise that is nearing collapse *US, 1997*
- — Vann Wesson, *Generation X Field Guide and Lexicon*, p. 38, 1997

circled *adjective*

married *US, 1960*

- — *San Francisco Examiner*, p. III-2, 22nd March 1960

circle jerk *noun*

1 group male masturbation, sometimes mutual and sometimes simply a shared solitary experience *US, 1958*

- The "circle jerk," or mass masturbation, is a common sex activity. — Harrison E. Salisbury, *The Shook-up Generation*, p. 32, 1958
- He is also a participant in the circle-jerks held with the shades pulled down in Smolka's living room after school[.] — Philip Roth, *Portnoy's Complaint*, p. 194, 1969
- If there are several persons present, and somehow it has been determined that all are "O.K.," a circle jerk will result. — John Francis Hunter, *The Gay Insider*, p. 191, 1971
- Sometimes the event [a college fraternity hazing] is a circle-jerk, with each guy fisting the cock of the guy next to him. — *Drummer*, p. 73, 1977

2 any non-productive, time-wasting exercise *US, 1973*

- It all sounded unreal to me, a vicious faggot circle-jerk. — Xaviera Hollander, *Xaviera*, p. 35, 1973
- The grand jury is off on a giant circle jerk. They've got nothing. — Steven Paul Martini, *The Judge*, p. 42, 1995
- Reality was troubling and deeply relevant, a refreshing departure from the usual circle jerk of undergraduate publishing. — Tom Perrotta, *Joe College*, p. 36, 2000

3 a series of exit consoles on websites that link back on themselves, creating an infinite loop *US, 2004*

- — www.adultquarter.com/blossary.html, January 2004

circle-jerk *verb*

to participate in group male masturbation *US, 1971*

- [S]ucking, fucking, circle-jerking, all anonymously performed[.] — John Francis Hunter, *The Gay Insider*, p. 26, 1971

Circle K *noun*

the recreational drug ketamine *US, 1998*

A punning allusion to a US national chain of convenience stores.

- The stolen drugs include pentobarbital, Valium, and ketamine—known on the streets as "Circle K." — *Press Journal (Vereo Beach, Florida)*, p. A3, 14th March 1998

circuit *noun*

a series of homosexual parties held each year around the US, with participants flying from city to city for the festivities *US, 1990s*

- — Kevin Dilallo, *The Unofficial Gay Manual*, p. 238, 1994
- The gay urban scene today encompasses what has come to be known as the "circuit," a series of large gay dance parties that occur throughout the year in cities around the country and around the world, attended by tens of thousands of gay men. — Michelangelo Signorile, *Life Outside*, p. xxiv, 1997

circuit girl *noun*

a traveling prostitute *US, 2002*

- Laticia says the pimps use "tudge boys," street slang for hired enforcers, not only to rough up circuit girls who get out of line, but also to patrol Colfax, looking for crack whores out of bounds. — *Denver Westword*, 2nd May 2002

circuit queen *noun*

a male homosexual who follows the circuit from party to party *US, 1994*

- — Kevin Dilallo, *The Unofficial Gay Manual*, p. 238, 1994
- Whether you're a circuit queen or a suburban dad, just coming out or stoically postgay, Drama Queen takes you kindly by the hand and leads you on an exploration of the unique and oft-misunderstood dynamics of our daily lives. — Patrick Price, *Drama Queen*, p. xviii, 2001

circular file *noun*

a wastebasket *US, 1947*

- Cladny is one of many who has loaded the circular file with fund-raising literature from organizations to which he has already contributed. — *Washington Post*, p. C14, 24th December 1981
- It's going right into the old circular file as soon as I make a couple routine calls to the feds. — Carl Hiaasen, *Tourist Season*, p. 21, 1986

circus *noun*

1 sexual behavior that is public, fetishistic or both *US, 1878*

- [B]aby spotlights were focused on the three naked women who were participating in the circus. — Irving Shulman, *Cry Tough*, p. 176, 1949
- If they desire the kind of entertainment most ordinarily referred to as a sex circus, they do their booking through a pimp or out of a brothel. — Lois O'Conner, *The Bare Facts*, p. 45, 1964
- When I came in here, our deal included no circuses, no shows, no peeping. — Robert Leslie, *Confessions of a Lesbian Prostitute*, p. 66, 1965
- I mean, we all decided with Gwenie we could now handle "trio tricks" and put on more "shows" and "circuses" and stuff like that. — Joey V., *Portrait of Joey*, p. 131, 1969

2 feigned spasms by a drug addict to convince a doctor to prescribe a narcotic *US, 1949*

- [T]he junkie was throwing a regular circus for the boys, tossing himself about on the floor. — Nelson Algren, *The Man with the Golden Arm*, p. 206, 1949
- — J.E. Schmidt, *Narcotics Lingo and Lore*, p. 30, 1959

circus bees; circus squirrels *noun*

body lice *US, 1981*

- — Don Wilmeth, *The Language of American Popular Entertainment*, p. 54, 1981

circus simple *adjective*

obsessed with the circus *US, 1975*

- — Joe McKennon, *Circus Lingo*, p. 26, 1980

circus tent *noun*

an apartment or house where customers pay to view sexual exhibitions *US, 1959*

- And behind the respectable-looking facades of the apartment buildings were the plush flesh cribs and poppy pads and circus tents of Harlem. — Chester Himes, *The Real Cool Killers*, p. 61, 1959

citizen *noun*

1 an ordinary person outside a gang or club *US, 1987*

- Mob guys or fences I recognized were mixed in with ordinary customers, what wiseguys call "citizens," people not connected with the mob. — Joseph Pistone, *Donnie Brasco*, p. 46, 1987
- As Hell's Angels, we lived in our own underground world, barely part of the citizens' world and having as little to do with them as possible. — Ralph "Sonny" Barger, *Hell's Angel*, p. 109, 2000

2 a fellow member of a youth gang *US, 1953*

- — Dale Kramer and Madeline Karr, *Teen-Age Gangs*, p. 174, 1953
- [C]hicken, smart money man, citizen, and many more. — Howard Polsky, *Cottage Six*, p. 24, 1962

3 a prisoner who has earned the respect of other prisoners *US, 1989*

- — James Harris, *A Convict's Dictionary*, p. 30, 1989

cits *noun*

▶ **the cits**

Minneapolis and St. Paul, Minnesota *US, 1966*

- — John D. Bell et al., *Loosely Speaking*, p. 4, 1966

City *noun*

▶ **The City**

San Francisco, California *US, 1955*

Uniformly used by northern Californians, who shun **"FRISCO**.

- [F]rom LA I ride the freight on up to the City and en route I want to visit the Buddhist Monastery at Santa Barbara[.] — Jack Kerouac, *Letter to Malcolm Crowley*, pp. 502–503, 19 July 1955

-city *suffix*

a good example of the precedent noun *US, 1930*

- Fat City: an extremely favorable situation — Collin Baker et al., *College Undergraduate Slang Study Conducted at Brown University*, p. 115, 1968
- "One of my prize suckers is taking a cue stick from the rack to make the trip to trim city." — Iceberg Slim (Robert Beck), *Trick Baby*, p. 183, 1969
- This has never failed. Poon City! You are there! — Terry Southern, *Now Dig This: The Unspeakable Writings of Terry Southern 1950–1995*, p. 5, 1986
- The reporters ignored him—snore city. — James Ellroy, *White Jazz*, p. 64, 1992

city block *noun*

in horse racing, a large margin of victory or a large lead *US, 1951*

- — David W. Maurer, *Argot of the Racetrack*, p. 19, 1951

city college *noun*

a jail, especially the New York City jail *UK, 1796*

- He was sent first to the Tombs, a jail his old gangster friends called City College. — Rich Cohen, *Tough Jews*, p. 79, 1999

civilian *noun*

1 anyone who is not a member of the group with which the speaker identifies, especially a motorcycle gang *US, 1946*

- Ricky finished his glass of red while they argued who was meaner, dirtier, who'd stomped more civilians, hit more cops, got brought up on more charges. — Elmore Leonard, *Glitz*, p. 240, 1985
- "Keep the suit pressed, the shoes shined, and let them think you are a civilian." — Richard Condon, *Prizzi's Family*, pp. 32–33, 1986
- Generally, they held themselves to a higher standard of honesty and commitment than most civilians I knew. — Peter Coyote, *Sleeping Where I Fall*, p. 112, 1998

2 a non-regular officer *US, 1947*

- Patton recommended only seven full colonelcies—four Regulars, three "civilians." — Robert S. Allen, *Patton's Third U.S. Army*, p. 45, 1947

3 in twelve-step recovery programs such as Alcoholics Anonymous, a person who is not involved in and does not need to be involved in a recovery program *US, 1998*

- — Christopher Cavanaugh, *AA to Z*, p. 68, 1998

civil serpent *noun*

used as a humorous synonym for "civil servant" *US, 1980*

- If not corrupted or manipulated by development interests, pandering politicians or civil serpents, the boards hold the promise of a planning process more sensitive to the needs and desires of the city's diverse neighborhoods. — *Los Angeles Times*, p. 2 (Part 8), 23rd November 1986

civvies *noun*

civilian clothes *UK, 1889*
Military usage.

- Probably an admiral in civies, spying out the next war. — Philip Wylie, *Opus 21*, p. 142, 1949
- When she saw Harry walk in wearing his pre-war civvies, his wrists and ankles sticking out like Huck Finn's, she promptly burst into laughter. — Max Shulman, *Rally Round the Flag, Boys!*, p. 24, 1957
- He slammed a plastic bag down on the counter. "These are the civies you came in with. Put 'em on." — Gerald Petievich, *One-Shot Deal*, p. 157, 1981

c-jame *noun*

cocaine *US, 1968*

- — *Current Slang*, p. 15, Fall 1968

CK *noun*

1 a member of a youth gang that is a rival of the Crips *US, 1991*
An abbreviation of "Crip Killer."

- "He say somethin' like 'C.K.' to me and I'm like, 'What, nigger? Fuck slobs!'" — Leon Bing, *Do or Die*, p. 23, 1991

2 Calvin Klein™ clothing *US, 2000*
Favored by members of the Bloods youth gang, to whom the initials also stand for "Crip Killer."

- — Bill Valentine, *Gangs and Their Tattoos*, p. 77, 2000

3 a mixture of cocaine and the recreational drug ketamine *US, 1995*

- Users pay from $20 to $40 per dose, or "bump," usually to be mixed with heroin or cocaine and snorted (the coke/ketamine combo is called CK or the "Calvin Klein Special")[.] — *The Record [Bergen County, New Jersey]*, p. A1, 5th December 1995

4 a man who feels that he has to disparage other men in front of women *US, 2002*
An abbreviation of **COCK-KNOCKER**. Recorded in Los Angeles, August 2002.

clack *verb*

to rattle the dice when switching altered dice in or out of a game; always inadvertent and usually disastrous to the cheat *US, 1950*

- — *The Annals of the American Academy of Political and Social Sciences*, p. 123, May 1950

clacker *noun*

1 a dollar *US, 1918*

- Commencing shortly after the first of the year, he'll get some 25,000 clackers per annum[.] — *San Francisco Examiner*, p. 19, 20th December 1945
- In Alameda County, where the officials have a thrifty eye toward the public clacker, the Supervisors and their lawyers have been

recovering assessment losses. — *San Francisco Examiner*, p. 35, 3rd February 1966

2 a triggering device for claymore mines *US, 1990*

- I took out a couple of frags and placed them on the ground next to the clacker, the firing device for the claymore mine. — Larry Chambers, *Recondo*, p. 58, 1992

clackers *noun*

the teeth; false teeth *US, 1950*

- [R]emembering my father's ugly pink clackers soaking in their bedside glass of water. — Leonard Garment, *Crazy Rhythm*, p. 265, 2000

claim *verb*

to self-identify as a youth gang member *US, 1993*

- "He claim?" Jaus asked. "He's West Coast. He's OK." — Bob Sipchen, *Baby Insane and the Buddha*, p. 234, 1993
- "It was good to see some old friends, kids I knew in elementary school before I claimed Crip." — Gini Sikes, *8 Ball Chicks*, p. 83, 1997
- "Me and Smiley want him to claim the set," T.J. says. — Colton Simpson, *Inside the Crips*, p. 19, 2005

claimer *noun*

a crime victim *US, 1993*

- "You look like a claimer. A mark." — Bob Sipchen, *Baby Insane and the Buddha*, p. 94, 1993

claiming *noun*

a method of casino cheating, in which a cheat claims that a slot machine malfunctioned and they received no payment or inadequate payment from a win *US, 1985*

- It is informally called claiming and can occur in a variety of situations in which the players falsely claim that the slot machine has malfunctioned. — Jim Regan, *Winning at Slot Machine*, p. 67, 1985

clam *noun*

1 the vagina *US, 1916*

- I was gobblin' her clam like it was the last supper. — Richard Price, *The Wanderers*, p. 37, 1974
- Imagine bein' the lucky guy lucky enuff to remove her straps before nuzzlin' her knockers and then proceeding south to dig for clam! — Richard Meltzer, *A Whore Just Like the Rest*, p. 377, 1977
- I will not shake my clam in front of a tragically hip East Village audience for $35 a night when I can be doing the same in Jersey for $300 a night. — James Ridgeway, *Red Light: Inside the Sex Industry*, p. 153, 1996
- [A] hot and humid shower scene that steams Genevieve straight down to her clam. — Mr. Skin, *Mr. Skin's Skincyclopedia*, p. 88, 2005

2 the anus *US, 1983*

- — *Maledicta*, p. 197, 1983: "Ritual and personal insults in stigmatized subcultures"

3 the mouth; the lip *US, 1825*

- "You better open your clams and talk." — Herbert Simmons, *Corner Boy*, p. 225, 1957

4 a dollar *US, 1886*

- I take him for fifty clams a day. — Horace McCoy, *Kiss Tomorrow Good-bye*, p. 354, 1948
- Oh, it ain't going to cost nothing, like something like little old two million clams. — William "Lord" Buckley, *Hip Einie*, 1955
- "So I beat him for about ten thousand clams," he told Bea finally. — George Clayton Johnson, *Ocean's Eleven*, p. 102, 1960
- Thousand, yes, bones or clams or whaever you call them. — *The Big Lebowski*, 1998

5 a betting chip in a poker game *US, 1988*

- — George Percy, *The Language of Poker*, p. 21, 1988

6 in a musical performance, a missed cue or an off-key note *US, 1955*

- — Robert S. Gold, *A Jazz Lexicon*, p. 58, 1964
- — David Shenk and Steve Silberman, *Skeleton Key*, p. 39, 1994

clam; clam up *verb*

to stop talking *US, 1916*

- I haven't got enough to lean on you and make you open up, but you can believe it that I'm going to get something that'll make you give this clamming up another thought. — Robert Campbell, *The Cat's Meow*, p. 113, 1988
- Phil, I'm just scared he's gonna clam up on me with all these sheriffs all over the place. — *Natural Born Killers*, 1994

clambake *noun*

a session in which jazz musicians collectively improvise *US, 1937*

From **CLAM** (a missed note).
- — Arnold Shaw, *Lingo of Tin-Pan Alley*, p. 9, 1950
- — Robert S. Gold, *A Jazz Lexicon*, p. 58, 1964

clambaking *noun*
smoking marijuana with a group in an enclosed space *US, 2002*
- clam baking—Burning and inhaling of marijuana openly in an enclosed area with multiple people. — *Dictionary of New Terms (Hope College)*, 2002

clam-diggers *noun*
calf-length pants *US, 1947*
The suggestion is that the pants are an appropriate length for digging for clams in mud flats.
- They go over any skirt and top off all the shorts, clam-diggers and slacks combinations you have for the summer. — *San Francisco Examiner*, p. 11, 15th June 1947
- Mario Villalobos watchd the bearded young vice cop, who wore a tank top and clam diggers[.] — Joseph Wambaugh, *The Delta Star*, p. 17, 1983

clam gun *noun*
a shovel or other digging implement *US, 1927*
- — Russell Tabbert, *Dictionary of Alaskan English*, p. 165, 1991

clamp *verb*
► **clamp it to**
to have sex *US, 1963*
- "Generally, I talk about clamping it to some old girl, because you start talking about sex around here and half these guys lose their minds." [Interview with Walt Grove] — *Playboy*, p. 130, May 1963

clam-shell *verb*
► **to get clam-shelled**
to be engulfed by a wave while surfing *US, 1991*
- — Trevor Cralle, *The Surfin'ary*, p. 21, 1991

clam squirt *noun*
vaginal secretions *US, 1974*
- Anyways, I get this knife an' some bread and I stuck the knife up her ol' patoot, got a nice gob of clam squirt, an' I spread it on the bread. — Richard Price, *The Wanderers*, p. 37, 1974

Clan *noun*
► **the Clan**
a group of performers and friends surrounding Frank Sinatra in the 1950s and 60s *US, 1960*
Better known as the Rat Pack.
- "The Clan," as they've been dubbed by others, possess talent, charm, romance, and a devil-may care nonconformity that gives them immense popular appeal. — *Playboy*, p. 34, June 1960

clanger *noun*
in poker, a drawn card that does nothing to improve your hand *US, 1996*
Also known as a "clang."
- — John Vorhaus, *The Big Book of Poker Slang*, p. 10, 1996

clangers *noun*
the testicles *UK, 1961*
- You like real clangers? I'll show you a pair that gong like Big Ben! — Joseph Wambaugh, *The Secrets of Harry Bright*, p. 47, 1985

clank *verb*
1 to be nervous *US, 1955*
- For a fellow down to his last fuel, it's "bingo." If he "clanks," he's nervous and if he "augers in" he crashed. — *San Francisco Examiner*, p. 10 (II), 2nd June 1957
2 to reject a romantic overture or partner *US, 1959*
- — *Time Magazine*, p. 46, 24th August 1959

clap *noun*
gonorrhoea *UK, 1587*
From old French *clapoir* (a sore caused by venereal disease); the term was normal register for centuries, slipping into colloquial or slang in mid-C19.
- But all the way out west, to Washington, he kept worrying about whether he was going to get a clap. — Clancy Sigal, *Going Away*, p. 135, 1961
- But how do you get the clap? By doing it, and anybody who does that dirty thing obviously deserves to get the clap. — Lenny Bruce, *How to Talk Dirty and Influence People*, p. 54, 1965

- There is an awful lot of clap loose in the U.S.—and while rubbers are a drag, the clap is something else again. — *Berkeley Barb*, p. 10, 2nd June 1967
- Joy, there's no way you can get the clap unless you go to the Heart O' Texas Motel with Roy Kennerdine or Billy Bob Simpson or any of those other off-brand, drop-case guys you hang around with in the afternoons. — Dan Jenkins, *Dead Solid Perfect*, p. 77, 1986

clap *verb*
to kill someone *US, 2002*
- Check reportedly screamed obscenities at the woman and threatened to "clap" her and her sister. "Clap" is street slang for murder, police said. — *Connecticut Post*, p. 1, 8th April 2002

clap checker *noun*
a member of the Medical Corps *US, 1984*
Vietnam war usage, identifying medics by the least glorious of their duties.
- Terms for enlisted men of the Medical Corps include bedpan commando, chancre mechanic, clap checker. — John Elting et al., *A Dictionary of Soldier Talk*, p. 196, 1984

clap clinic *noun*
a medical practice that treats all sexually transmitted disease *US, 1976*
- — Susan Quist, *On the Way to the Clap Clinic*, 1976
- You were down the clap clinic so many times last season you were on first-name terms with all the doctors. — Colin Butts, *Is Harry on the Boat?*, 1997

clappy *adjective*
infected with a sexually transmitted infection, especially gonorrhea *US, 1937*
- Before I'd touch your slimy thighs / which a thousand crabs has bit / I'd drink a gallon a drunkard's puke / and suck a clappy dick. — Bruce Jackson, *Get Your Ass in the Water and Swim Like Me*, p. 124, 1964

claps *noun*
gonorrhea *US, 1965*
Largely black usage.
- "She had the claps," he said, "and those Texas claps got bigger monster bugs." — Christina and Richard Milner, *Black Players*, p. 72, 1972
- [T]hese beast ain't got NO IDEA how to help a man get rid of the claps. — A.S. Jackson, *Gentleman Pimp*, p. 62, 1973
- — John A. Holm, *Dictionary of Bahamian English*, p. 43, 1982

clap shack *noun*
a clinic or hospital ward where sexually transmitted infections are treated *US, 1952*
- The place their unfortunate owners are sent for treatment is the clap shack. — Paul Fussell, *Wartime*, p. 257, 1989

clap sticks *noun*
in the television and movie industries, the clapboard used for synchronizing sound and picture *US, 1987*
- — Ira Konigsberg, *The Complete Film Dictionary*, p. 52, 1987

claptrap *noun*
a brothel with a high incidence of sexually transmitted infections *US, 1986–1987*
- — *Maledicta*, p. 150, Summer/Winter 1986–1987: "Sexual slang: prostitutes, pedophiles, flagellators, transvestites, and necrophiles"

claret *noun*
blood *US, 1962*
- Floyd Janney balefully bubbled, spitting out a mouthful of broken teeth and claret[.] — David Gregory, *Flesh Seller*, p. 119, 1962

Clarisse *noun*
used as a term of address among male homosexuals *US, 1965*
- — *Fact*, p. 26, January-February 1965

clarity *noun*
MDMA, the recreational drug best known as ecstasy *US, 1989*
- — Bruce Eisner, *Ecstasy*, p. 1, 1989
- — *Miramonte High School Parents Club Newsletter (Orinda, California)*, p. 1, 26th November 2001

clary *noun*
a clarinet *US, 1942*
- — Robert S. Gold, *A Jazz Lexicon*, p. 59, 1964

classic *adjective*

1 excellent *US, 1964*
- — John Severson, *Modern Surfing Around the World*, p. 166, 1964
- — Connie Eble (Editor), *UNC-CH Campus Slang*, p. 2, Spring 1990

2 handsome, well-dressed *US, 1998*
- — Ethan Hilderbrant, *Prison Slang*, p. 25, 1998

classy chassis *noun*

an attractive female body *US, 1955*
- — *American Weekly*, p. 2, 14th August 1955
- — Clarence Major, *Dictionary of Afro-American Slang*, p. 37, 1970
- Joe Fabrini tells a waitress, played by Ann Sheridan, that she has a "classy chassis" and that he likes the way she "fills out" her clothes. — Thaddeus Russell, *Out of the Jungle*, p. 119, 2003
- Raven De La Croix is one of the most stacked classy chassis in history. — Mr. Skin, *Mr. Skin's Skincyclopedia*, p. 139, 2005

claw *noun*

a pickpocket *US, 1914*
- — Hyman E. Goldin et al., *Dictionary of American Underworld Lingo*, p. 44, 1950
- — Don Wilmeth, *The Language of American Popular Entertainment*, p. 55, 1981

clay eater *noun*

a poor rural dweller *US, 1841*
- "Clay-eaters" was a term often applied to far-flung denizens of the unsettled South. — Jim Goad, *The Redneck Manifesto*, p. 85, 1997

claymore clacker *noun*

the triggering device for a claymore antipersonnel mine *US, 1994*
- He squeezed the claymore clacker briskly, heard an explosion, and saw the side of the house shake as though struck by a flaming tornado. — T. Michael Booth, *Retribution*, p. 270, 1994
- "I checked my rifle and laid in on my lap, made sure the claymore clacker was close at hand, and then settled in to watching the jungle in front of me." — Kregg Jorgenson, *Very Crazy G.I.*, p. 43, 2001

clay pigeon *noun*

a person who is easily victimized *US, 1972*
- — Helen Dahlskog (Editor), *A Dictionary of Contemporary and Colloquial Usage*, p. 13, 1972

clean *verb*

1 to rid yourself of altered dice, altered cards, or any evidence of cheating *US, 1950*
- — *The Annals of the American Academy of Political and Social Sciences*, p. 123, May 1950

2 in mountain biking, to succeed in negotiating an obstacle or set of obstacles without accident *US, 1996*
- [A] series of five to seven small obstacles that I know I can clean without much thought. — *Mountain Bike Magazine's Complete Guide To Mountain Biking Skills*, p. 41, 1996

▸ **clean it up**

to clarify or explain something *US, 1942*
- — William K. Bentley and James M. Corbett, *Prison Slang*, p. 14, 1942

▸ **clean out the kitchen; clean up the kitchen**

to perform oral sex on a woman *US, 1941*
- — Roger Blake, *The American Dictionary of Sexual Terms*, p. 51, 1964

▸ **clean someone's bones**

to thrash or defeat someone soundly in a fight *US, 1963*
- — *American Speech*, p. 276, December 1963: "American Indian student slang"

▸ **clean someone's clock**

to severely defeat someone, physically or in a competition *US, 1908*
- [S]ince Turnipseed had got his clock cleaned in his own cell it wasn't difficult to determine who deserved the credit. — Malcolm Braly, *On the Yard*, p. 202, 1967
- "We played poker," added Jeremiah-Dumpling. "Cleaned his fucking clock." — Carl Hiaasen, *Native Tongue*, p. 356, 1991

▸ **clean the books**

to induce a criminal to confess to a series of unsolved crimes *US, 1984*
- — Inez Cardozo-Freeman, *The Joint*, p. 488, 1984

▸ **clean the pipes**

to ejaculate; to masturbate *US, 1998*

- DOM: You know, clean the pipes. TED: Pipes? What are you talking about? DOM: You jerk off before all big dates, right? — *Something About Mary*, 1998

▸ **clean the slate**

to confess to unsolved crimes in hopes of winning better treatment from the police *US, 1972*
- So to make it easier for everybody we'd just what we called "clean the slate" for them. — Harry King, *Box Man*, p. 97, 1972

▸ **clean the table**

in pool, to shoot all of the remaining balls in one turn *US, 1989*
- — Mike Shamos, *The Illustrated Encyclopedia of Billiards*, p. 51, 1993

▸ **clean up your hands**

in prison, to stay out of trouble *US, 1970*
- First they do this by staying out of trouble, "cleaning up their hands." — John Irwin, *The Felon*, p. 70, 1970

▸ **clean yourself**

to make sure that you are not being followed while driving *US, 1987*
- Obviously Guido had just been cleaning himself, making sure nobody was following him, with the run to Staten Island. — Joseph Pistone, *Donnie Brasco*, p. 98, 1987

clean *adjective*

1 drug free *US, 1949*
- "Look, I kicked. I'm clean, I tell yah!" Fay repeated. — Alexander Trocchi, *Cain's Book*, p. 156, 1960
- I was thinkin' about askin' you to see what you can do for me. I mean, like, when I get clean. — Nathan Heard, *Howard Street*, p. 79, 1968
- "If I don't get anything else out of all this," he said, "I'm going to get clean." — Seth Morgan, *Homeboy*, p. 102, 1990
- I have to take a drug test every six months to make sure I'm clean. — *American Beauty*, 1999

2 innocent; free of suspicion; without a trace of guilt; without a criminal record *US, 1925*
- This is clean shit. No serial numbers and never been used. — *48 Hours*, 1982
- I've been picked up a couple times. Loan sharking. Racketeering. But I was never convicted. I'm clean. — *Get Shorty*, 1995

3 not subject to police surveillance *US, 2003*
- If some punk asks you if your ride is "clean," he wants to know if it was tailed or not. — Henry Hill and Byron Schreckengost, *A Good Fella's Guide to New York*, p. 13, 2003

4 (used of an illegal betting operation) unafraid of police intervention because of bribes paid to the police *US, 1951*
- — David W. Maurer, *Argot of the Racetrack*, p. 20, 1951

5 excellent, fashionable, stylish *US, 1963*
- — *San Francisco Examiner*, p. 8, 27th October 1963
- It was the one who had a Thunderbird, and some clean vines. — H. Rap Brown, *Die Nigger Die!*, p. 9, 1969
- It was lowered to da ground, had twice-pipes, candy-apple red and button top. Ooo, clean! — Cheech Marin and Tommy Chong, *Santa Claus and his Old Lady*, 1971
- Now we were big-time pimps from the New York scene / And believe me, Jim, we were both real clean. — Dennis Wepman et al., *The Life*, p. 36, 1976

6 (used of a theatrical performance) completely sold out *US, 1973*
- — Sherman Louis Sergel, *The Language of Show Biz*, p. 49, 1973

7 in circus and carnival usage, without value *US, 1981*
- — Don Wilmeth, *The Language of American Popular Entertainment*, p. 55, 1981

8 (of an object ball in pool) directly into the pocket without touching a cushion or another ball *US, 1993*
- — Mike Shamos, *The Illustrated Encyclopedia of Billiards*, p. 51, 1993

clean and ready *adjective*

prepared; dressed nicely *US, 1980*
- — Edith A. Folb, *runnin' down some lines*, p. 232, 1980

cleaner *noun*

1 a hired killer *US, 2000*
- Tiny stars placed on the arm in any fashion indicate that the wearer is a hitter (also known as a "cleaner" or "torpedo"). — Bill Valentine, *Gangs and Their Tattoos*, p. 36, 2000

2 in circus and carnival usage, the person who retrieves money from paid players who have been allowed to win a concession game to drum up business *US, 1981*
- — Don Wilmeth, *The Language of American Popular Entertainment*, p. 55, 1981

clean freak *noun*
a person who is obsessed with cleanliness *US, 1967*
- He blamed his affliction on dirt, and he was a tireless clean freak who liked the cell spotless. — Malcolm Braly, *On the Yard*, p. 7, 1967

cleaning crew *noun*
the members of a criminal enterprise who rid the crime scene of possible evidence and at times any bodies resulting from the crime *US, 1997*
- Tommy had decided not to use a contracted cleaning crew. On some hits a crew of "sanitation specialists" would follow in right behind to wash the crime scene down with detergents and vacuum the carpets, eliminating trace evidence. — Stephen Cannell, *King Con*, p. 20, 1997

cleaning kit *noun*
the equipment needed to rid a crime scene of possible evidence *US, 1997*
- "Okay," Texaco said, "looking at the cleaning kit in a Gucci leather suitcase beside him." — Stephen Cannell, *King Con*, p. 20, 1997

clean peeler *noun*
to a surfer, a perfect wave *US, 1997*
- — Vann Wesson, *Generation X Field Guide and Lexicon*, p. 38, 1997

cleansleeve *noun*
a low-ranking military recruit *US, 1909*
- Yet only five years after graduating—"clean sleeve," with no rank chevrons—Davison had commanded a battalion in France. — Rick Atkinson, *The Long Gray Line*, p. 65, 1989

clean-the-kitchen *noun*
corned beef hash *US, 1946*
- — *American Speech*, p. 89, April 1946: "The language of west coast culinary workers"

clean time *noun*
the amount of time that has passed since a prisoner was last in trouble *US, 1975*
- I spent six months in the Paso Robles Hole because I couldn't get enough clean time together. — James Carr, *Bad*, p. 42, 1975
- — James Harris, *A Convict's Dictionary*, p. 30, 1989

clean-up *noun*
1 a good alibi *US, 1990*
- — Charles Shafer, *Folk Speech in Texas Prisons*, p. 201, 1990

2 a wave that breaks seaward of most surfers, causing them to lose their boards and thus cleaning up the area *US, 1964*
- — John Severson, *Modern Surfing Around the World*, p. 166, 1964

cleanup team *noun*
the members of a criminal enterprise who rid a crime scene of any possible evidence and at times bodies resulting from the crime *US, 1997*
- Problem was, you had to know the cleanup team was solid. — Stephen Cannell, *King Con*, p. 20, 1997

clean works *noun*
a new needle and syringe *US, 1993*
A concept and term new in the age of AIDS.
- — Peter Johnson, *Dictionary of Street Alcohol and Drug Terms*, p. 41, 1993

clear *verb*
▸ **clear the channel**
to stop talking *US, 1962*
- — *Dobie Gillis Teenage Slanguage Dictionary*, 1962

clear gravy *noun*
an unexpected bonus or profit *US, 1975*
An embellishment of the more common **GRAVY**.
- — John Gould, *Maine Lingo*, p. 52, 1975

clearinghouse *noun*
an illegal lottery *US, 1951*
More commonly known as a **NUMBERS** game.
- — Thomas L. Clark, *The Dictionary of Gambling and Gaming*, p. 44, 1987

clear light *noun*
a stage in some LSD experiences in which the user feels receptive to enlightenment *US, 1971*
- — Edward R. Bloomquist, *Marijuana*, p. 336, 1971

Clem *noun*
in the circus or carnival, a fight with customers *US, 1891*
- — Joe McKennon, *Circus Lingo*, p. 26, 1980

clerk *noun*
in American casinos, an exceptionally skilled dealer *US, 1980*
- — Lee Solkey, *Dummy Up and Deal*, p. 109, 1980
- — Steve Kuriscak, *Casino Talk*, p. 12, 1985

clerks and jerks *noun*
clerical support personnel and officers *US, 1975*
Vietnam war usage. The high degree of cynicism about officers found in enlisted men was even more intense in Vietnam.
- Running a god-damned club when there's nobody on the rear except clerks and jerks. — John M. Del Vecchio, *The 13th Valley*, p. 461, 1982
- [T]he second plane was filled with the clerks and jerks—the Ranger support company, whose weapons probably weren't even loaded. — Richard Marcinko, *Rogue Warrior*, p. 329, 1992
- "When operations gets really strapped for door gunners, they even let some of the clerks and jerks tag along!" — Richard Burns, *Pathfinder*, pp. 123–124, 2002

Cleveland portrait *noun*
a one-thousand-dollar bill *US, 1952*
- "A couple of those Cleveland portraits will do it." — Harry Grey, *The Hoods*, p. 141, 1952

cleverly *adverb*
(used of a racehorse winning a race) easily *US, 1960*
- — Robert Saunders Dowst and Jay Craig, *Playing the Races*, p. 161, 1960

click *noun*
a gang *US, 1879*
A corrupted spelling of "clique."
- You know there's a lot of streets where a whole "click" is made out of punks who can't fight[.] — Piri Thomas, *Down These Mean Streets*, p. 49, 1967
- I'd been hearing about him on the street in Harlem, he was the war counselor of some click uptown on Lenox Avenue. — Edwin Torres, *Carlito's Way*, p. 20, 1975
- Just remember, if you join a prison tip or click, you'll never fit in out there again. — Seth Morgan, *Homeboy*, p. 153, 1990
- Everyone in here is associated in "clicks" or gangs. Since I am an outsider to these "clicks" I live a fearful existence. — Miles Harvey, *The Island of Lost Maps*, p. 213, 2000

click *verb*
1 to associate with in a group *US, 1995*
- I just started clicking again with the Harlem 30's. — Yusuf Jah, *Uprising*, p. 27, 1995

2 to perform at the right moment as needed by a friend *US, 1989*
- — Terry Williams, *The Cocaine Kids*, p. 136, 1989

3 in horse racing, to win a race *US, 1951*
- — David W. Maurer, *Argot of the Racetrack*, p. 20, 1951

4 to be well accepted *US, 1982*
- — Arnold Shaw, *Dictionary of American Pop/Rock*, p. 78, 1982

click; klick; klik *noun*
a kilometer *US, 1962*
Vietnam war usage.
- So the helicopter takes off and after going out maybe four clicks it crashes, and the wounded and everybody on board dies. — John Kerry, *The New Soldier*, p. 98, 1971
- The target must have been two clicks from us anyway. — William Pelfrey, *The Big V*, p. 3, 1972
- A LOH fired up a sampan on the river at 131324, that's about a klick an a half downriver from that big tree that sticks up. — John M. Del Vecchio, *The 13th Valley*, p. 281, 1982
- [E]verything was transformed into Crispy Critters for half a dozen clicks in any direction you would have cared to point. — Larry Heinemann, *Paco's Story*, p. 15, 1986

clicker *noun*

1 crack cocaine mixed with phencyclidine, the recreational drug known as PCP or angel dust *US, 1994*
- — US Department of Justice, *Street Terms*, October 1994

2 a brick *US, 1989*
- — Ellen C. Bellone (Editor), *Dictionary of Slang*, p. 7, 1989

3 in circus and carnival usage, a free pass *US, 1981*
- — Don Wilmeth, *The Language of American Popular Entertainment*, p. 55, 1981

clicks and mortar; C&M *noun*

a business that combines trading from traditional business premises with Internet-based commerce *US, 1999*
A play on "bricks and mortar," a traditional business.
- He struck a chord with his audience by saying companies that learn how to seamlessly blend virtual and physical assets will emerge as big winners in what he called the new "clicks and mortar" economy. — *Washington Post*, p. E1, 22nd July 1999
- Such "clicks and mortar" retailers give customers the option to purchase or order on-line and then pick up the product at a bricks-and-mortar branch. — *Harvard Business Review*, *Harvard Business Review on Marketing*, p. 61, 2001

Cliffie *noun*

a student or alumna of Radcliffe College, Harvard University *US, 1961*
- Obviously the Cliffie who greeted me read the Crimson and knew who I was. — Erich Segal, *Love Story*, p. 25, 1970

C light *noun*

in the pornography industry, a light used to illuminate the genitals of the performers *US, 1991*
- This is Randy's dick here. We lit it so it wouldn't look so white and unreal: a little light called the C light. — Robert Stoller and I.S. Levine, *Coming Attractions*, p. 131, 1991
- The c-light is a light shined directly on the action (whether you want to call it crotch or cookie or cunt). It helps us see the "c" better. Makes the "c" brighter. — *The Village Voice*, 3rd April 2001

cling *verb*

▸ **cling to the belt**

(used of South Vietnamese troops) to stay close to US troops *US, 1988*
- [T]he Vietnamese did all they could to keep the killing on an infantry-against-infantry basis by staying as close to the Americans as possible, a tactic they called "clinging to the belt." — Neil Sheehan, *A Bright Shining Lie*, p. 574, 1988

clinic *noun*

1 a poker game characterized by over-analysis of each hand *US, 1988*
- — George Percy, *The Language of Poker*, p. 21, 1988

2 a poker game played by doctors *US, 1988*
- — George Percy, *The Language of Poker*, p. 21, 1988

clink *noun*

a jail; a police station *UK, 1785*
Originally an infamous prison in Southwark, London, and then by the mid-C19 applied to any jail, prison, or cell.
- Mom left a big hole in his life, which he filled by marrying Betty Bugbee when she got out of the clink. — Bernard Wolfe, *The Late Risers*, p. 301, 1954
- I heard that after the fracas in Harlem she landed in the clink[.] — Ross Russell, *The Sound*, p. 287, 1961
- [T]he western lead will be Rusty Godowsky who is aimed for stardom if he stays out of the clink[.] — Gore Vidal, *Myra Breckinridge*, p. 102, 1968
- He just laughed and said he'd probably see me in the clink before he got out. — Oscar Zeta Acosta, *The Revolt of the Cockroach People*, p. 253, 1973
- There were interviews with black neighborhood residents who said the police had to start hooking the kids up and throwing them in the clink. — Elmore Leonard, *Switch*, p. 100, 1978
- Rings was like, Wow, I never thought to find love in the clink! — Seth Morgan, *Homeboy*, p. 83, 1990
- In those days, simply being a suspicious character could land you in the clink for three days without charges being pressed, a handy method for dealing with undesirables. — Kim Rich, *Johnny's Girl*, p. 47, 1993

clinker *noun*

1 in the entertainment industry, a failure *US, 1961*

- This is, mind you, the definitive list of clinkers released in 1973. — *San Francisco Examiner and Chronicle, Sunday Scene*, p. 12, 13th January 1974

2 a wrong note in a musical performance *US, 1937*
- — Kenn "Naz" Young, *Naz's Underground Dictionary*, p. 20, 1973
- — Arnold Shaw, *Dictionary of American Pop/Rock*, p. 79, 1982

3 a mistake *US, 1937*
- — Robert S. Gold, *A Jazz Lexicon*, p. 59, 1964

clinkeroo *noun*

a jail or prison *US, 1949*
- "You are going downtown to the clinkeroo." — Gene Fowler, *Skyline*, p. 35, 1961

clip *noun*

1 an occurrence or instance *US, 1979*
- Since then, I been on half a dozen scores—three, four thousand a clip—when I'm pressed to the wall. — Vincent Patrick, *The Pope of Greenwich Village*, p. 30, 1979

2 a swindle or other act of dishonest trickery *US, 1941*
- He felt it expedient to do so each day after he had put a hard clip on some sucker who might be inclined to wake up sober and call for the bluecoats. — Robert Sylvester, *No Cover Charge*, p. 208, 1956
- [G]uys sitting around talking about the clip they'd made. — Herbert Huncke, *Guilty of Everything*, pp. 43–44, 1990

3 a string of bottles containing doses of crack cocaine *US, 1992*
- She could carry two clips down in her panties, another two up top, and the Fury couldn't do anything unless they pulled her into the precinct for a strip search. — Richard Price, *Clockers*, p. 5, 1992

4 in the circus or carnival, a patron *US, 1980*
- — Joe McKennon, *Circus Lingo*, p. 26, 1980

clip *verb*

1 to steal something; to swindle someone; to win something, especially through cheating *US, 1922*
- Generally a runner made plenty for himself, taking a chance that the dough he clipped wasn't on the number that pulled in the shekels. — Spillane, I, *The Jury*, p. 46, 1947
- I just clip a buck here and a buck there. It mounts up, but nobody gets hurt. — Jim Thompson, *The Grifters*, p. 72, 1963
- I clipped a dance moll for a swab, it paid a trey or a fin. — Bruce Jackson, *Get Your Ass in the Water and Swim Like Me*, p. 85, 1965
- Boy, you clipped me for ten grand and the others for at least another five. — Iceberg Slim (Robert Beck), *Airtight Willie and Me*, p. 112, 1979

2 to kill someone, especially by gunshot *US, 1928*
- "We've got to clip this guy." — Robert Daley, *Prince of the City*, p. 103, 1978
- "You are the only one who can get close enough to her to do it," his father said. "Zotz her? Clip Irene?" — Richard Condon, *Prizzi's Honor*, p. 304, 1982
- [S]lick or no fuckin' sick, you knew people were gonna get clipped. — *Casino*, 1995
- Hey, guys like Joe Loop get clipped all the time. It's what they do, man, they get pissed off about something or bored and shoot each other; it's their fate. — Elmore Leonard, *Be Cool*, p. 284, 1999

3 to hit someone *US, 1855*
- And I haven't had to really clip a young Negro in years. — Ralph Ellison, *Invisible Man*, p. 144, 1947

clip and clean *adverb*

completely *US, 1975*
- The jolt took out his front tooth clip and clean. — John Gould, *Maine Lingo*, p. 53, 1975

clip-a-nines *noun*

a 9 mm ammunition clip *US, 2001*
- I've seen fifteen-year-olds roll pipe bombs under taxis and peel a clip-a'-nines at a passing squad car. — Stephen J. Cannell, *The Tin Collectors*, p. 34, 2001

clip joint; clip dive *noun*

a bar, gambling house, or other business where customers are routinely cheated *US, 1932*
- Baltimore clip-dives operate more closely to the orthodox custom. — Jack Lait and Lee Mortimer, *Washington Confidential*, p. 283, 1951
- About the only real aggravation in those days, Watkins remembers, was a parking lot which separated the "legitimate" Stables from a clip joint a few yards East. — Robert Sylvester, *No Cover Charge*, p. 82, 1956
- "[M]ost of these night-clubs are just clip joints." — Monroe Fry, *Sex, Vice, and Business*, p. 65, 1959

● Ralph got a job in a clip joint on West 49th Street and soon acquired a good reputation among the whores he protected from tricks complaining about being robbed. — Babs Gonzales, *I Paid My Dues*, p. 104, 1967

clipped dick *noun*
a Jewish person *US, 1960*
Derogatory.

● He thought about his wife sitting on that clipped-dick's lap and his face twisted at the memory. — Loraine Despres, *The Scandalous Summer of Sissy LeBlanc*, p. 331, 2001

clipper *noun*
1 a thief *US, 1965*

● No security staff could hope to beat this army of clippers without a lot of help. — *I was a House Detective*, p. 120, 1954
● — *Woman*, 11th December 1965

2 a person who collects movie clips, usually of a single subject *US, 1978*

● — *American Speech*, p. 53, Spring 1978: "Star trek lives: trekker slang"

clique up *verb*
to form small groups *US, 1972*

● There's other characters, as soon as they walk in the wing, they'll just clique right up with a group. — Bruce Jackson, *Outside the Law*, p. 155, 1972

clit *noun*
the clitoris *US, 1958*

● Why, I've only to give my clit a tiny flick right now and I'd be sopping. — Terry Southern, *Candy*, p. 49, 1958
● I'll blip her clit up and I'll blip it down, and I'll blip it east and west[.] — Robert Gover, *Poorboy at the Party*, p. 82, 1966
● She told me her clit was so sensitive when I got through that she didn't think she could touch it for a week. — Roger Blake, *What you always wanted to know about porno-movies*, p. 244, 1972
● Kitt shows tit and mitts her clit, masturbating full-frontally nude while she knows someone is watching. — Mr. Skin, *Mr. Skin's Skincyclopedia*, p. 445, 2005

clit-licking *noun*
oral sex on a woman, focused on her clitoris *US, 2004*

● Normally, I can't come from clit licking alone. — Diana Cage, *Box Lunch*, p. 88, 2004

clit ring *noun*
a piece of jewelery for a clitoral piercing *US, 1995*

● Even Madonna can be shocked as one of the lesbians shows her clit ring and laughs as the star grimaces with surprise and disgust. — Linda Grant, *Sexing the Millennium*, p. 246, 1995

clit tease *noun*
a heterosexual woman who socializes with lesbians without revealing that she is heterosexual *US, 1993*

● As the boy-toy turned clit tease, she played out the notion of the gaze. — Arlene Stein, *Sisters, Sexperts, Queers*, p. 124, 1993
● — Amy Sohn, *Sex and the City*, p. 154, 2002
● "Are you just a clit-tease, Kinkade?" — Kathy Lette, *Deadly Sexy*, p. 84, 2005

clitty *noun*
the clitoris *UK, 1866*

● We got chocolate clitty onstage for ya now. — Josh Alan Friedman, *Tales of Times Square*, p. 65, 1986
● She may want you to use your best soft, sloppy tongue for caressing her clit, or if she has a tough li'l clitty, a firm tongue might be just fine. — Jamie Goddard, *Lesbian Sex Secrets for Men*, p. 142, 2000

cloak *verb*
to send an electronic message in a manner that disguises the true origin of the message *US, 1997*

● — Andy Ihnatko, *Cyberspeak*, p. 40, 1997

cloak-and-dagger *adjective*
very secret; pertaining to espionage *US, 1944*

● The capital is overrun by snoops and spies, not only using every cloak-and-dagger device for foreign transmission, but assigned and trained to catch and report inter-bureau information, rumors included. — Jack Lait and Lee Mortimer, *Washington Confidential*, p. 245, 1951

clobber *verb*
1 to strike someone forcefully *US, 1944*

● For no reason they were going to clobber us. — Nat Hentoff, *Jazz Country*, p. 54, 1965

2 in computing, to overwrite a program *US, 1991*

● — Eric S. Raymond, *The New Hacker's Dictionary*, p. 96, 1991

clobbered *adjective*
drunk *US, 1951*

● You know. Drunk, stewed, clobbered, gone, liquored up, oiled, stoned, in the bag. — Max Shulman, *Guided Tour of Campus Humor*, p. 106, 1955
● — *American Speech*, p. 156, May 1959: 'Gator (University of Florida) slang

clock *noun*
a prisoner who is at the beginning of their sentence *US, 1961–1962*

● — Frank Prewitt and Francis Schaeffer, *Vacaville Vocabulary*, 1961–1962

clock *verb*
1 to catch sight of or notice someone or something; to watch someone or something *US, 1929*

● Big, gap-toothed smile of surprise, like we wasn't clocked before we came in the door, comes up from the pool table. — Edwin Torres, *After Hours*, p. 170, 1979
● When you walked in, Eddie, did you clock the two chinks? — Vincent Patrick, *The Pope of Greenwich Village*, p. 36, 1979

2 to keep track of a slot machine in an effort to make an educated guess as to when it will pay off *US, 1984*

● There's a machine I'm clocking. Jackpot's getting up where it's getting interesting. — J. Edward Allen, *The Basics of Winning Slots*, p. 56, 1984

3 to keep track of the money involved in a game or an enterprise *US, 1977*

● — Robert C. Prus and C.R.D. Sharper, *Road Hustler*, p. 169, 1977

4 to figure something out, to evaluate something *US, 1961*

● I mean, he was already in Vegas a couple of years and he had the fuckin' place clocked. — *Casino*, 1995

5 to earn something *US, 1989*

● — Ellen C. Bellone (Editor), *Dictionary of Slang*, p. 7, 1989

6 to sell drugs on the street *US, 1992*

● This kid Strike is now out there on the streets clocking for Rodney, like his lieutenant or something, OK? — Richard Price, *Clockers*, p. 447, 1992

▸ **clock in**
to visit your boyfriend or girlfriend only out of a sense of duty *US, 2004*

● I'd love to drink and throw stuff off the roof with you guys, but I have to clock in with the boss or she''ll cut me off. — Ben Applebaum and Derrick Pittman, *Turd Ferguson & The Sausage Party*, p. 13, 2004

▸ **clock in the green room**
while surfing, to take a long ride inside the hollow of a breaking wave *US, 1991*

● — Trevor Cralle, *The Surfin'ary*, p. 21, 1991

▸ **clock the action**
to understand what is happening and what is being said *US, 1962*

● — *Dobie Gillis Teenage Slanguage Dictionary*, 1962

clocker *noun*
1 a street drug dealer, especially of crack cocaine *US, 1992*

● Strike's clockers got jumpy if they thought they were being watched. — Richard Price, *Clockers*, p. 5, 1992
● Daymond, Omar gave up, had done very well for himself, moving from clocker to pusher. — John Ridley, *Everybody Smokes in Hell*, p. 38, 1999

2 a watchman or guard, especially one who punches a time clock while making his rounds *US, 1949*

● — Vincent J. Monteleone, *Criminal Slang*, p. 52, 1949
● — Jay Robert Nash, *Dictionary of Crime*, p. 69, 1992

3 an onlooker *US, 1976*

● He bounced over and they giggled and kissed and performed a young lovers' routine for the benefit of the clockers and watchers in all the other cars. — Emmett Grogan, *Final Score*, p. 220, 1976

clock out *verb*
to act in a psychotic manner *US, 1989*

● — Terry Williams, *The Cocaine Kids*, p. 136, 1989

clockworks *noun*
the brain *US, 1947*

● — Marcus Hanna Boulware, *Jive and Slang of Students in Negro Colleges*, 1947

clocky *noun*

sudden waving arm movements of a surfer trying to get his balance *US, 1991*

- The judges took off half a point for each of those clockies you did on take-off. — Trevor Cralle, *The Surfin'ary*, pp. 21–22, 1991

clod *noun*

a stupid person *UK, 1605*

- You also need to convince yourself that there is nothing worse than stupid clods who ask pointless unnecessary questions. — Mad Magazine, *Mad About the Sixties*, p. 129, 1995

clodhopper *noun*

a person with big feet; big feet or big shoes *UK, 1836*

Evoking the image of a plowman with large, coarse boots.

- [S]o the Negro's supposed to lie down and let the paddy climb upon his chest with his clodhoppers. — Piri Thomas, *Down These Mean Streets*, p. 126, 1967
- He shifts his clodhopper feet as he exhales tension relief to discover her apparently innocent. — Iceberg Slim (Robert Beck), *Doom Fox*, p. 150, 1978

clone *noun*

1 a highly stylized, fashion-conscious homosexual male *US, 1979*

- [T]he Castro Street lot (often called clones) has a typical admixture of leather queens mostly "South of Market types." — *Maledicta*, p. 247, 1979
- First attracting attention as a definite type, it seems, in San Francisco and New York's Greenwich Village, the gay clone wears short hair and a clipped mustache, and (if possible) sports a sculpted chest with prominent pectorals. — Wayne Dynes, *Homolexis*, pp. 31–32, 1985
- It's always queens, by the way: clones don't start these scenes[.] — Ethan Morden, *Buddies*, p. 90, 1986

2 a personal computer that closely duplicates the functions and operations of a leading brand *US, 1991*

- — Eric S. Raymond, *The New Hacker's Dictionary*, p. 96, 1991
- I am writing this in the tenuous privacy of my bedroom on my annoyingly obsolete AT clone. — C.D. Payne, *Youth in Revolt*, p. 3, 1993

clone *verb*

to reconfigure a stolen cell phone so that an existing subscriber is charged for all calls *US, 1994*

- To clone a regular cellular telephone, thieves steal the over-the-air electronic signal that identifies each cellular caller for billing purposes. — *Newsday (New York)*, p. 3, 9th January 1994

close *adjective*

skilled *US, 1959*

- "Like he's close, man" (he is quite capable) and "touches home" (really makes sense). — *Look*, p. 49, 24th November 1959

close but no cigar; no cigar

incorrect *US, 1935*

From carnival games giving cigars as prizes.

- I show him the picture of Helen in the summer dress. "Still no cigar," he says. — Robert Campbell, *Junkyard Dog*, p. 163, 1986
- The red-tail youngster went after the mouse, but it scurred away—close, but no cigar. — Marie Winn, *Red-Tails in Love*, p. 229, 1999

closed *adjective*

subject to strict law enforcement; unfriendly to criminal enterprises *US, 1969*

- Here I was with four idle whores in a closed town where I had fallen [been arrested] three times. — Iceberg Slim (Robert Beck), *Pimp*, p. 279, 1969

closed door *noun*

a surf condition where waves are breaking simultaneously all along a beach, creating no shoulder to ride *US, 1963*

- — Grant W. Kuhns, *On Surfing*, p. 115, 1963

close out *verb*

(of waves) to become unsuitable for surfing, either because of their size or their breaking pattern *US, 1991*

- It's closing out completely. Let's call it. — *Point Break*, 1991

closer *noun*

in a sales team, the individual responsible for the final stages of negotiations *US, 1906*

- MASTER: Told them the job was free. Then you sent in your closer with some cover story about how you had suffered a nervous breakdown, and a sale was ultimately made for $2375.00. — *Tin Men*, 1987

closet *noun*

▸ **in the closet**

hidden, not avowed *US, 1967*

Almost always applied to homosexuality.

- Do you know what it means to be "in the closet?" — Mart Crowley, *The Boys in the Band*, p. 169, 1968
- While gays who are prominent in businesses or professions in Manhattan many live in the closet in the city, they tend to be most relaxed and casual and open while in residence in The Hamptons[.] — John Francis Hunter, *The Gay Insider*, p. 253, 1971
- It sure puts you guys in the closet for a while. — George V. Higgins, *The Friends of Eddie Doyle*, p. 46, 1971
- Okay. So he's in the closet. — Edwin Torres, *Q & A*, p. 111, 1977

▸ **out of the closet**

avowed, open *US, 1971*

- So come on outa the closet, James[.] — Lester Bangs, *Psychotic Reactions and Carburetor Dung*, p. 115, 1973
- Yeah, well the only woman of the Indians we ran into was shacked up with her dyke girlfriend. I guess she went with him before she came outta the closet. — *48 Hours*, 1982
- Especially with priests coming out of the closet and saying they're queer[.] — Robert Campbell, *The Cat's Meow*, p. 51, 1988

closet *adjective*

hidden, not admitted *US, 1952*

- — Dale Gordon, *The Dominion Sex Dictionary*, p. 45, 1967
- "Well," she said, "a closet intellectual." — Walter Tevis, *The Color of Money*, p. 52, 1984
- He was a middle-aged closet pervert from over in the Valley. He thought we didn't know. — Robert Campbell, *Alice in La-La Land*, p. 77, 1987
- Debbie thought I was just a frustrated closet bull dyke, and hung around all night, spitefully, I felt. — Jennifer Blowdryer, *White Trash Debutante*, p. 78, 1997

close-talker *noun*

a person who speaks to others without respecting the usual cultural protocols on not standing too close to someone you are talking to *US, 1994*

A term popularized on Jerry Seinfeld's television program in an episode called "The Raincoat Party" first aired on 28th April 1994.

- Jake had to back away a couple of feet because Alan was a close-talker, and his breath smelled like sardines. — Jason Starr, *Lights Out*, p. 38, 2006

closet case *noun*

1 a person who is secretly homosexual *US, 1969*

- [S]omeone from Dallas—I think he's a closet case—wrote a horrible letter, from a Christian point of view. — Dan Woog, *Jocks*, p. 211, 1998
- Oh he's the biggest closet case walking. — Michelle Tea, *The Passionate Mistakes and Intricate Corruption of One Girl in America*, p. 38, 1998

2 someone to be ashamed of *US, 1954*

Teen slang, without any suggestion of the homosexuality later associated with the term.

- — *Look*, p. 88, 10th August 1954

3 a potential romantic interest whom you are keeping away from your friends *US, 1955*

- [F]raternity and sorority has its share of closet cases. — Max Shulman, *Guided Tour of Campus Humor*, p. 75, 1955
- — *McCall's*, April 1967

closeted *adjective*

living with an unrevealed fact, especially homosexuality *US, 1992*

- It's not like he can't change. I was closeted once myself. — Armistead Maupin, *Maybe the Moon*, p. 220, 1992

close to the door *adjective*

about to be released from prison *US, 1989*

- — James Harris, *A Convict's Dictionary*, p. 30, 1989

closet queen *noun*

a male homosexual who conceals his sexual orientation *US, 1957*

- All the fairies in her town were closet queens or pinkteas[.] — Hubert Selby Jr., *Last Exit to Brooklyn*, p. 60, 1957

• They call them "closet queens." The implication is queen. It derives from the English word for lavatory, water closet. — Antony James, *America's Homosexual Underground*, p. 66, 1965
• Have you heard the term "closet queen"? — Mart Crowley, *The Boys in the Band*, p. 169, 1968
• These are the "closet queens," the "aunties" and the furtive, secretive types. — *Screw*, p. 14, 25th April 1969

close work *noun*
sexual activity *US, 1957*
• That boy up on the stage singing to them from his heart is clearly country, even as they are, and they find it not at all unthinkable that he might be available for some close work after the show. — Max Shulman, *Rally Round the Flag, Boys!*, p. 164, 1957

cloth *noun*
▸ **down to the cloth**
(used of a player in a game of poker) almost out of money *US, 1982*
• — David M. Hayano, *Poker Faces*, p. 186, 1982

clothes *noun*
in horse racing, a horse blanket *US, 1951*
• — David W. Maurer, *Argot of the Racetrack*, p. 21, 1951

clotheshorse *noun*
a person who pays a great deal of attention to fashions and the clothing they wear *US, 1850*
• Everybody in a Technicolor movie seems to feel obliged to wear a lurid costume in each new scene and to stand around like a clotheshorse with a lot of very green trees[.] — Sylvia Plath, *The Bell Jar*, p. 42, 1971
• "Don't see no reason to be a clotheshorse." Hawk was wearing white Puma track shoes with a black slash on them. White linen slacks, and a matching white linen vest with no shirt. — Robert Parker, *Promised Land*, p. 82, 1976

clothes queen *noun*
a homosexual man who is drawn to ostentatious, flamboyant clothing *US, 1963*
• — Donald Webster Cory and John P. LeRoy, *The Homosexual and His Society*, p. 263, 1963: "A lexicon of homosexual slang"

cloud *noun*
1 crack cocaine *US, 1994*
From the thick white smoke produced when smoked.
• — US Department of Justice, *Street Terms*, October 1994
2 the intoxication from smoking freebase or crack cocaine *US, 1992*
• — Terry Williams, *Crackhouse*, p. 147, 1992

cloud nine *noun*
1 a condition of perfect happiness, euphoria *US, 1935*
Probably derives as a variation of **CLOUD SEVEN**; possibly from US weather forecasting terminology which divides clouds into nine types, the highest being number nine; or, less likely, a spiritual possibility: of the ten names for Buddha, the ninth is "enlightened one." It is probable that the US radio adventure series *Johnny Dollar*, 1949–62, popularized the term's usage.
• Depressed and down-hearted, I took to Cloud 9. / I'm doing...(fine) / Up here. (On cloud nine) / Listen one more time. / I'm doing...(fine) / Up here. (On cloud nine) — The Temptations, *Cloud Nine*, 1969
• Frank is, of course, delirious way past Cloud Nine. — Stephen King, *On Writing*, p. 245, 2000
2 crack cocaine *US, 1994*
• — US Department of Justice, *Street Terms*, October 1994

clout *verb*
1 to steal; to rob *US, 1972*
• We would have left if he had just went out but we knew when he clouted this stuff that we had no rank. — Harry King, *Box Man*, p. 43, 1972
• "[T]he only thing they're gonna find out's that it got clouted in Plymouth about three days or so before." — George Higgins, *Cogan's Trade*, p. 109, 1974
• "Some shitbird clouted the Hollywood Federal at Santa Monica and Cole four days ago[.]" — James Ellroy, *Destination Morgue*, p. 228, 2004
2 to rob or steal something *UK, 1708*
• In the reformatory. They tried to clout a color TV among other things, and got busted for it. They'd been playing that caper for quite a while. — Hugh Garner, *The Intruders*, p. 83, 1976

• The Prizzis had been clouted for a gang of money! — Richard Condon, *Prizzi's Honor*, p. 59, 1982
• A black-white stick-up gang had been clouting markets and juke joints on West Adams[.] — James Ellroy, *Hollywood Nocturnes*, p. 127, 1994

clouter *noun*
a thief who steals from parked cars *US, 1993*
• — Kenn "Naz" Young, *Naz's Dictionary of Teen Slang*, p. 23, 1993
• A recent Associated Press story described a car clouter who dressed like a hiker and used his walking stick to break windows at a trailhead in a national park, snatching $9,400 worth of valuables the day he got caught with the goods. — *Statesman Journal (Salem, Oregon)*, p. 1D, 18th July 2003

clover *noun*
money *US, 1951*
• — David W. Maurer, *Argot of the Racetrack*, p. 21, 1951

clown *noun*
a fool, an incompetent person *US, 1898*
• Lieutenant Colonel Henry Braymore Blake. One of them regular army clowns. — *M*A*S*H*, 1970
• My voice shook, talking with this clown was doing me a lot of good. — Jim Thompson, *Savage Night*, p. 3, 1985
• Least of all the pushy broad, the smart Jew, and the Harvard clown. — *A Few Good Men*, 1992

clown alley *noun*
on a circus lot, the area of tents where performers, especially clowns, dress and live *US, 1956*
• "The old-fashioned clown alley ended after the 1997 season," said Renee Storey, the circus's vice president for administration. — *New York Times*, p. G11, 12th August 1999
• In clown alley, Felix Adler was preparing for the walkaround. — Stewart O'Nan, *The Circus Fire*, p. 70, 2000

club *noun*
in pool, a heavier-than-usual cue stick *US, 1990*
• — Steve Rushin, *Pool Cool*, p. 10, 1990

club *verb*
to spend an evening in a nightclub or several nightclubs *US, 1964*
• The few who stayed, and the tourists, kept to the Gay White Way as they used to name it, clubbing, bar hopping or taking in a show. — Mickey Spillane, *Return of the Hood*, p. 80, 1964
• The status-conscious dress codes of '80s clubbing dissolved in all-night raves[.] — Steven Daly and Nathaniel Wice, *alt.culture*, p. 2, 1995
• At nights we'd go clubbing and spend time in the bathroom snorting and giggling. — Cleo Odzer, *Goa Freaks*, p. 69, 1995

Club 14 *noun*
Nuestra Familia, a Mexican-Amerian prison gang *US, 1975*
"N" is the 14th letter of the alphabet.
• — Report to the Senate, *California Senate Committee on Civil Disorder*, p. 228, 1975

club crawl *verb*
to move as a group of friends from one nightclub to another *US, 1994*
• But instead of club crawling, she's been spending her nights working as a second assistant director[.] — *Vogue*, p. 86, June 1994

Club Fed *noun*
a minimum-security, well-equipped federal prison housing white-collar criminals, especially the federal prison camp in Lompoc, California *US, 1985*
A punning reference to Club Med, a group of vacation resorts.
• Big Springs has no walls and is called Club Fed by critics because of its elaborate recreational facilities and college dormitory atmosphere. — *Washington Post*, p. A1, 8th September 1985
• That was Lompoc FPC, federal prison camp, the one they used to call Club Fed. No fence, no guys with shanks or razor blades stuck in toothbrush handles. The worst that could happen to you, some guy hits you over the head with a tennis racquet. — Elmore Leonard, *Out of Sight*, p. 45, 1996
• Hopefully, you'll never experience the pleasures of a "Club Fed vacation." — Suroosh Alvi et al., *The Vice Guide*, p. 223, 2002

club-fight *verb*
to engage in youth gang warfare *US, 1949*
• I ain't club-fighting no more. I ain't sham-battling or nothing else. I'm out. — Hal Ellson, *Duke*, p. 144, 1949

club-hop *verb*

to move from one nightclub to another, especially with a group of friends *US, 1972*

- We club-hopped until dawn. — Georgia Sothern, *My Life in Burlesque*, p. 260, 1972
- Sophomore year. I'm going down on Cynthia Slater in her dorm room after we went club-hopping. — *Chasing Amy*, 1997

club kid *noun*

a young clubgoer in the late 1980s and early 1990s, known for flamboyant costumes and heavy drug use *US, 1990*

- The epithet "club kids" gained currency in 1988, when a New York magazine cover story featured a posse of young nightcrawlers who managed to parlay their exhibitionist antics and fondness for glitzy, flamboyant get ups into budding careers. — Steven Daly and Nathaniel Wice, *alt.culture*, p. 42, 1995

club sandwich *noun*

sex involving three people at once *US, 1970*

Surviving in the shortened form of a simple "sandwich."

- — *Current Slang*, p. 5, Winter 1970

clubzine *noun*

a single-interest fan magazine published by a fan club *US, 1982*

- — *American Speech*, p. 24, Spring 1982: "The language of science fiction fan magazines"

cluck *noun*

1 a gullible fool *US, 1906*

- Some other time, baby. I got to go find that cluck. — Philip Wylie, *Opus 21*, p. 288, 1949
- I find myself eating at some greasy spoon next to a liquor store and talking to the most embittered cluck this side of the Continental Divide. — Clancy Sigal, *Going Away*, p. 134, 1961
- Don't a one of you clucks know what I'm talking about enough to give us a hand? — Ken Kesey, *One Flew Over the Cuckoo's Nest*, p. 136, 1962
- Guy that's worth, easy, forty fifty million, he cheats on a hundred-dollar round of golf and all the clucks, the guys that play with him, know it. — Elmore Leonard, *Cat Chaser*, p. 27, 1982

2 a crack cocaine user *US, 1994*

- — US Department of Justice, *Street Terms*, October 1994
- — Mark S. Fleisher, *Beggars & Thieves*, p. 288, 1995

3 counterfeit money *US, 1949*

- — Vincent J. Monteleone, *Criminal Slang*, p. 53, 1949

cluck and grunt *noun*

ham and eggs *US, 1972*

- — Helen Dahlskog (Editor), *A Dictionary of Contemporary and Colloquial Usage*, p. 13, 1972

clucker *noun*

1 a crack cocaine addict *US, 1993*

- He knew that chumps who got mired in cocaine's quicksand of euphoria and depression were called "cluckers" by Seattle's gangsters. — Bob Sipchen, *Baby Insane and the Buddha*, p. 391, 1993

2 in the urban drug culture, someone who brings buyers to sellers *US, 2002*

- — *Detroit News*, p. 5D, 20th September 2002

3 a fool *US, 1945*

- — Lou Shelly, *Hepcats Jive Talk Dictionary*, p. 8, 1945

cluckhead *noun*

a crack cocaine addict *US, 1991*

- "Cluckheads just be wanderin' around, looking for more dope to smoke, anyway." — Leon Bing, *Do or Die*, p. 54, 1991
- — Bill Valentine, *Gang Intelligence Manual*, p. 75, 1995

clue; clue in *verb*

to inform someone, to update someone *UK, 1948*

- — *Newsweek*, p. 28, 8th October 1951
- "I'll clue you," said Grady. "There's gotta be a rumble." — Max Shulman, *Rally Round the Flag, Boys!*, p. 231, 1957
- Well's she's out of your price range, man. My brother's been out with her. He clued me in. — *American Graffiti*, 1973

clueless *adjective*

unaware, especially of fashion, music and other social trends *UK, 1943*

- — *USA Today*, 29th September 1983
- Would you look at that girl? She is so adorably clueless. — *Clueless*, 1995

clunker *noun*

1 an old, beat-up car *US, 1942*

The original military usage in the 1940s applied to any old vehicle or machine. By the 1960s, applied almost exclusively to a car.

- The parking lot at Devil's Slide was jammed with vehicles: flowered hippie vans, city clunkers, organic pickups with shingled gypsy houses, and a dusty pack of Harley-Davidsons. — Armistead Maupin, *Tales of the City*, p. 99, 1978
- Banged up, pounded out, dented-in old clunkers with "21" or "99" or "45" painted haphazardly on their doors and tops. — *San Francisco Examiner and Chronicle*, p. 6, 1st July 1979
- He had made friends with the few attractive women who had wandered in, deciding he was more interesting than the rusting clunkers he was selling. — Stephen Cannell, *Big Con*, p. 28, 1997

2 an inferior item *US, 1971*

- [O]ne of the all-time clunkers of history[.] — Lester Bangs, *Psychotic Reactions and Carburetor Dung*, p. 14, 1971

clunkers *noun*

the testicles *US, 1976*

- If you don't print this letter or pic, I'll cut your clunkers off! — *Punk*, July 1976

clunkhead *noun*

a dolt *US, 1952*

- The minute I ever decided to become a clunkhead enough to take a shot, the real big boys would goose me out of business[.] — Morton Cooper, *High School Confidential*, pp. 115–116, 1958
- The people in the Department of State are equally convinced that if they don't watch those clunkheads in the field who are so immersed in the problem, they will disregard policy and get everyone in trouble. — *Washington Post*, 8th February 1983
- There is a clique of right-wing cranks, yahoos and assorted clunkheads who make a career and a living off direct-mail propaganda in complaining about public broadcasting. — *Boston Globe*, p. 17, 20th January 1991
- Some wonder aloud why UTEP doesn't look for coaches like Don Haskins, who win and still stick around all 38 years of their career. Clunkheads, all. — *El Paso Times*, p. 1C, 26th December 2003

clusterfuck *noun*

1 group sex, heterosexual or homosexual *US, 1966*

- Oh, those big cluster fucks! I can't stand them. I think it's revolting, you know, more or less getting punked by anybody who happens to be standing near you, man, woman, child, or dog. — Nicholas Von Hoffman, *We Are The People Our Parents Warned Us Against*, p. 182, 1967
- You may see many of the people at your "do" only at other "cluster fucks," having nothing in common with them but a taste for orgies. — Angelo d'Arcangelo, *The Homosexual Handbook*, p. 115, 1968
- If Chris likes an occasional clusterfuck, and feels he has to do this "masculine" sex thing for himself (with the girls), remember he is doing it partly for you too. — *Screw*, p. 8, 18th August 1969
- The last scene shot was the Clusterfuck, beginning around 11 p.m. — *Cult Movies No. 17*, p. 47, 1996

2 a disorganized, chaotic situation *US, 1969*

- Now what's happenin'? We gonna get this clusterfuck in the air? — John M. Del Vecchio, *The 13th Valley*, p. 137, 1982
- "This fire's been the shits," he said, pushing back his hard hat. "Welcome to the first clusterfuck of the year." — Murry A. Taylor, *Jumping Fire*, p. 80, 2000
- "Another clusterfuck," said Patrick O'Meara under his breath as the lieutenant walked away. — Cherokee Paul McDonald, *Into the Green*, p. 125, 2001

clusterscrew *noun*

chaos; monumental lack of organization *US, 1976*

- You saw what a clusterscrew that outfit was. It only took ten gooks to fuck that Company up bad. — Charles Anderson, *The Grunts*, p. 65, 1976

clutch *noun*

in poker, a hand that is certain to win *US, 1967*

- — Albert H. Morehead, *The Complete Guide to Winning Poker*, p. 259, 1967

clutch *adjective*

1 Serving as a replacement *US, 1957*

- We have been standing "clutch duty" lately, which means that we are on call as reinforcements or replacements for the front-line troops. — Martin Russ, *The Last Parallel*, p. 143, 1957

2 unkind *US, 1991*
- "I bet the witch child ran away!" he said. Cherokke began to cry. "I've been so clutch to her." — Francesca Lia Block, *Witch Baby*, p. 136, 1991

clutch-butt *noun*
sex *US, 1967*
- "That big old gal is ready for some rib-rattling clutch butt," said Nails. — Elaine Shepard, *The Doom Pussy*, p. 113, 1967

clutched *adjective*
scared, anxious, emotional *US, 1952*
- First, the ocean. If you come form the Midwest and you've never seen it you are really clutched, that is, seized by emotion. — Glendon Swarthout, *Where the Boys Are*, p. 5, 1960

Clyde *noun*
1 a misfit; an outcast; a naive, easily cheated person *US, 1950*
- To the swinger there are two types of people: swingers and "clydes." He looks down his nose at the clydes[.] — William and Jerrye Breedlove, *Swap Clubs*, p. 58, 1964
- I registered the unconscious contempt of the barkers for the Alvins and the Clydes who strolled the midway, fat silly sheep who thought it fun to be fleeced[.] — Malcolm Braley, *False Starts*, p. 69, 1976
- You hear that, Clyde? That's got to be the most spooky-ass question I've ever heard. — *Heathers*, 1988

2 during the Vietnam war, a Viet Cong or North Vietnamese regular *US, 1966*
- VICTOR CHARLIE. Viet Cong. VC. Also shortened to "Charlie," "Clyde," etc. — Ken Melvin, *Sorry 'Bout That*, p. 96, 1966: Glossary

3 used to refer to any object the name of which you cannot remember or do not know *US, 1992*
- — Lewis Poteet, *Car & Motorcycle Slang*, p. 53, 1992

C-man *noun*
a sexually successful male student *US, 1968*
An abbreviation of "cunt-man" or **COCKSMAN**.
- — Collin Baker et al., *College Undergraduate Slang Study Conducted at Brown University*, p. 93, 1968

C-note *noun*
1 a one hundred dollar bill *US, 1930*
- Van shrugged. "I expect I'm out one C-note." — Ross Russell, *The Sound*, p. 65, 1961
- You could find a dozen punks in Harlem who'd kill him for a C-note. — Chester Himes, *Cotton Comes to Harlem*, p. 15, 1965
- She seemed to wake up, staring at that C-note. — Elmore Leonard, *Glitz*, p. 30, 1985
- [P]ast the jag-off guard who gets an extra c-note a week just to watch the door[.] — *Casino*, 1995

2 a prison sentence of 100 years *US, 1990*
- — Charles Shafer, *Folk Speech in Texas Prisons*, p. 201, 1990

C-note Charlie *noun*
in a casino, a gambler who insists on betting with hundred-dollar bills, not betting chips *US, 1949*
- — Thomas L. Clark, *The Dictionary of Gambling and Gaming*, p. 45, 1987

coal *noun*
a marijuana cigarette *US, 1993*
- I like a blunt or a big fat coal/But my double-barrel bong is gettin' me stoned. — Cypress Hill, *Hits from the Bong*, 1993

▸ **burn coal; deal in coal**
(of a white person) to have sex with a black person *US, 1922*
- The Harlem community accepts—though it despises—these Caucasians who cross the color line, or as it is known above 110th Street, "change their luck" or "deal in coal." — Jack Lait and Lee Mortimer, *New York Confidential*, p. 101, 1948
- Antoine, my contract says no niggers. I dont . . . burn . . . coal. — Seth Morgan, *Homeboy*, p. 155, 1990

coal candy *noun*
hard black licorice *US, 1997*
- — Amy and Denise McFadden, *CoalSpeak*, p. 4, 1997

coal chute *nickname*
the Harbor Freeway South in Los Angeles *US, 2004*
- Cops call it the "Coal Chute." It's a jungle-bunny juggernaut and a sleaze sluice. It connects Darktown with White Man's L.A. — James Ellroy, *Destination Morgue*, p. 327, 2004

coal cracker *noun*
a resident of the anthracite coal region of northeastern Pennsylvania *US, 1997*
- — Amy and Denise McFadden, *CoalSpeak*, p. 4, 1997

coalminer's breakfast *noun*
a shot of whiskey served in a glass of beer *US, 1990*
- [A] "Coalminer's Breakfast," or "Depth Charge" (when a shot of whiskey is dropped into a glass of beer). — Roger E. Axtell, *The Do's and Taboos of Hosting International Visitors*, p. 76, 1990

coal oil *noun*
kerosene *US, 1980*
- — Joe McKennon, *Circus Lingo*, p. 26, 1980

Coaly *noun*
the devil *US, 1950*
- "Okay, the first thing I want to do is decide on a model juror." "Black," said Lucien. "Black as old Coaly's ass," said Harry Rex. — John Grisham, *A Time to Kill*, p. 329, 1989

Coast *noun*
▸ **the Coast**
the west coast of the US *US, 1930*
- He came from the Coast. He saw a way to get back East without arousing suspicion. — Mickey Spillane, *My Gun is Quick*, p. 150, 1950
- But I'll never forget one night when we were coming in by plane from the Coast. — Billie Holiday with William Dufty, *Lady Sings the Blues*, p. 169, 1956
- Sophia's husband was away on one of his trips to the coast when I told her and her sister. — Malcolm X and Alex Haley, *The Autobiography of Malcolm X*, p. 141, 1964
- You can tell they're not from the coast. — Nicholas Von Hoffman, *We Are The People Our Parents Warned Us Against*, p. 13, 1967

coast *verb*
1 to idle; to relax *US, 1981*
- — Douglas Simonson, *Pidgin to da Max*, 1981
- — *San Jose Mercury News*, 11th May 1999

2 to relax and experience the effects of a drug *US, 1969*
- All I wanted to do was bang "H" and "coast." — Iceberg Slim (Robert Beck), *Pimp*, p. 99, 1969
- — Eugene Landy, *The Underground Dictionary*, p. 52, 1971

coaster *noun*
someone who lives near the beach; a surfer *US, 1982*
- Like you know, this beasty coaster goes, "You wanna bag some rays?" and like I totally go, "Bag your face, surf punk." — Mary Corey and Victoria Westermark, *Fer Shurr!*, 1982

Coastie; Coasty *noun*
a member of the US Coast Guard; a Coast Guard ship *US, 1970*
- And when the Strike Team Coasties have done their duty and cleaned up a mess that somebody else made, they get homage from a grateful news media[.] — Hans Halberstadt, *USCG*, p. 89, 1986
- Get the XO to set up a track to rendezvous with the Coastie. — P.T. Deutermann, *Scorpion in the Sea*, p. 122, 1992

coast-to-coast *noun*
a powerful amphetamine or other central nervous system stimulant *US, 1969*
Purportedly strong enough to keep a truck driver awake long enough to drive the 3,000 miles from coast to coast.
- — *American Speech*, p. 203, Fall 1969: "Truck driver's jargon"

coat *verb*
in tournament pool, to obscure the view of the tournament judge when making a shot, thus jeopardizing the point *US, 1972*
- — Mike Shamos, *The Illustrated Encyclopedia of Billiards*, p. 1972, 1993

coaxer *noun*
in horse racing, a battery-powered device used illegally by a jockey to shock a horse during a race *US, 1951*
- Frank Wolverton of Santa Rosa, Cal., "a track follower," today was suspended by the Lone Oak Racing Track Board of Stewards for manufacturing electrical "coaxers" allegedly used to stimulate horses in two races. — *San Francisco News*, p. 21, 7th September 1951

cob *noun*
the penis, literally and in the figurative sense of a disagreeable man *US, 1954*

- The president, a fairly rough old cob, said just a little angrily, "Look, don't be so surprised." — Clancy Sigal, *Going Away*, p. 141, 1961

▸ **off the cob**
overly sentimental *US, 1935*
A play on words to achieve "corny."
- — Jack Lait and Lee Mortimer, *New York Confidential*, p. 236, 1948

COBOL Charlie *noun*
in computing, a COBOL programer who can use the language but does not fully understand how it works *US, 1990*
- — Karla Jennings, *The Devouring Fungus*, p. 218, 1990

cocaine bugs *noun*
psychosomatic itching experienced by some heavy users of cocaine *US, 1902*
- The most common cocaine-induced hallucination is the so-called "cocaine bugs," which gives the user the sensation that there are sharp little insects crawling beneath the skin. — *Ethnic NewsWatch*, p. 1, 26th April 1996

cock *noun*
1 the penis *UK, 1450*
Probably from "cock" (a male bird).
- The success of Allen is due to the fact that no one since Henry Miller has had the guts to say cock and cunt in public. — Jack Kerouac, *Letter to Lucien Carr*, p. 563, 24th February 1956
- Jesus she was hot! I thought she'd tear the cock off me. — Henry Miller, *Tropic of Cancer*, p. 102, 1961
- What he's doing is staring at Johnny's cock[.] — John Rechy, *Numbers*, p. 41, 1967
- A hand on your cock is more moral—and more fun—than a finger on the trigger. — Richard Neville [quoting Lawrence Lipton], *Play Power*, p. 71, 1970
2 the vagina *US, 1867*
- Say, "Yes, your mama got a cock big as a whale is true / And your sister got a big cock, too!" — Roger Abrahams, *Positively Black*, p. 90, 1970
- Cock mean pussy down here, boy. so don't you go takin' no offense, y'hear. — Emmett Grogan, *Ringolevio*, p. 159, 1972
- To them, Coco said, cock meant "pussy." — Gini Sikes, *8 Ball Chicks*, p. 63, 1997
3 used as a male-to-male term of address *UK, 1837*
Decidedly casual.
- "Is that Father Christmas?" "There was a night-light burning beside the bed." "Yes, cock—I mean Sonny," hissed Sapphire[.] — Charles Raven, *Underworld Nights*, p. 207, 1956
4 a man who fights without restraint *US, 1964*
- — R. Frederick West, *God's Gambler*, p. 223, 1964

▸ **get cock**
to have sex *US, 1972*
- — Bruce Jackson, *Outside the Law*, p. 57, 1972

cock *verb*
1 to have sex *US, 1973*
- — Malachi Andrews and Paul T. Owens, *Black Language*, p. 111, 1973
- "You listening? You don't cock me without a glove." — John Ridley, *Love is a Racket*, p. 297, 1998
2 to prepare an aircraft for take-off *US, 1986*
- When the crews were not preflighting the airplanes, "cocking" them for instant takeoff, they were flying the simulator[.] — Walter J. Boyne and Steven L. Thompson, *The Wild Blue*, p. 265, 1986

cockadau *verb*
to kill someone *US, 1987*
On loan from Vietnamese.
- "Cockadau!" Harris suddenly yelled in Vietnamese. He sounded a little nuts. "Cockadau means kill," Sampson told me. — James Patterson, *Four Blind Mice*, p. 313, 2002

cockalize; kokalize *verb*
to thrash someone *US, 1947*
- I kokalized him in Scranton. — Marvin Wald and Albert Maltz, *The Naked City*, p. 107, 1947

cockamamie; cockamamy *adjective*
implausible, not credible *US, 1941*
Neither Yiddish nor Hebrew, but born of Jewish immigrants in the US.
- "How could Helen Lawrence like our cockemamie act?" — Jacqueline Susann, *Valley of the Dolls*, p. 23, 1966

- Did you ever hear such a cockamamy story? — Leo Rosten, *The Joys of Yiddish*, p. 94, 1968
- Through some cockamamie appeal you're back on the street. — Edwin Torres, *After Hours*, p. 387, 1979
- I couldn't for the life of me figure out where he had gotten that cokamamy idea[.] — Rita Ciresi, *Pink Slip*, p. 75, 1999

cock and bull story *noun*
a fanciful, exaggerated or outright untrue story *US, 1795*
- I debated about going back with some cock-and-bull story, anything to forestall her tipping him off to my deception. — Sue Grafton, *J is for Judgment*, p. 170, 1993
- Taylor shot me a look that asked, Are you going to back up this cock-and-bull story? I gave him a sheepish smile and nodded my head. — Douglas C. Waller, *The Commandos*, p. 184, 1994

Cockbang *noun*
Bangkok, Thailand *US, 1991*
Offensive to Thai people. A near-Spoonerism that aptly describes Bangkok's reputation and role as a sex destination.
- — Linda Reinberg, *In the Field*, p. 46, 1991

cock bite *noun*
an unpleasant person *US, 1971*
- — Eugene Landy, *The Underground Dictionary*, p. 53, 1971

cockblock *verb*
to interfere with someone's intentions to have sex *US, 1971*
- So you both jus' gonna set dere and cock block and neither one o' you gonna get nothin'. — Geneva Smitherman, *Talkin that Talk*, p. 85, 1999
- I wanted to tell her how pissed I was that she had cock-blocked me, but I didn't feel like we knew each other well enough for me to have a right to be mad. — Amy Sohn, *Run Catch Kiss*, p. 82, 1999
- — Connie Eble (Editor), *UNC-CH Campus Slang*, p. 2, Spring 1999
- Every night when I try to think of someone else, Javon cockblocks me. — Carol Taylor (Editor), *Brown Sugar*, p. 26, 2001

cock book *noun*
a sexually explicit book *US, 1968*
- — Carl Fleischhauer, *A Glossary of Army Slang*, p. 10, 1968

cock cheese *noun*
smegma *UK, 1961*
- — Roger Blake, *The American Dictionary of Sexual Terms*, p. 38, 1964

cock Corpsman *noun*
a military doctor or medic who inspects male recruits for signs of sexually transmitted disease *US, 1964*
- — Roger Blake, *The American Dictionary of Sexual Terms*, p. 39, 1964
- — Dale Gordon, *The Dominion Sex Dictionary*, p. 119, 1967

cock crazy *noun*
obsessed with sex with men *US, 1979*
- He had a dong like a horse, and that Betsy Ann was cock crazy. — Bruno Skoggard, *China Hand*, p. 12, 1979
- "So, out flopped the Great American Flagpole, and suddenly the neat and controlled man in the suit goes cock-crazy and blows his self-esteem and marches out of here with my career in a shambles." — Ethan Morden, *Some Men Are Lookers*, p. 118, 1997

cock-diesel *adjective*
muscular *US, 1988*
- Or "Stupid cock diesel"—slang for a boy who was muscular from lifting weights. — Tom Wolfe, *Hooking Up*, p. 1, 2000

cockeater *noun*
a person who enjoys performing oral sex on men *US, 1967*
- — Dale Gordon, *The Dominion Sex Dictionary*, p. 45, 1967

cocked *adjective*
drunk *US, 1737*
- — J.E. Lighter, *Historical Dictionary of American Slang, Volume 1*, p. 446, 1994

cocker *noun*
1 the penis *US, 1967*
- Those black cockers are the longest, the fattest, the hardest in the world. — John Folger, *Black on White*, p. 27, 1967
2 a man *US, 1946*
From the Yiddish *kakker*; used with a lack of kindness.
- Yeah, I know the old Cocker. Lives across the Avenue in those apartments. — George Pelecanos, *A Firing Offense*, p. 23, 1992

cock-eyed *adjective*
drunk *US, 1737*
First recorded by Benjamin Franklin.

- There, one night, cockeyed, he shot two inoffensive customers. — Jack Lait and Lee Mortimer, *New York Confidential*, p. 160, 1948
- Thursday night I took a bottle up to my room with me, and I got half cockeyed. — Jim Thompson, *Savage Night*, p. 124, 1953
- "Sit here and drink myself cockeyed." — John Conway, *Love in Suburbia*, p. 56, 1960

cock eyes *noun*
in craps, a three *US, 1968*

- — Thomas L. Clark, *The Dictionary of Gambling and Gaming*, p. 45, 1987

cockfest *noun*
a party with many more males than females in attendance *US, 2001*

- — Don R. McCreary (Editor), *Dawg Speak*, 2001

cock hound *noun*
a man obsessed with sex *US, 1947*

- "An' you're jus', jus' an old cock hound, Wilson. You're the goddamnedest ole lecher..." — Norman Mailer, *The Naked and the Dead*, p. 202, 1948
- He was a cockhound, and all his bitches were white. — John Williams, *The Man Who Cried I Am*, p. 136, 1967
- "Those who do go to town don't go to find a woman, even the cockhounds." — Donald Duncan, *The New Legions*, p. 67, 1967
- Everyone in Hollywood knows my father as a real cockhound. Once when I came home from boarding school he had these two Puerto Rican women in his bedroom. — Gerald Petievich, *To Die in Beverly Hills*, p. 48, 1983

cock jacket *noun*
a reputation for sexual prowess *US, 1984*

- Me, I had a cock jacket. They thought every broad that rode my bike, with the exception of my mother, got laid. — Joseph Wambaugh, *Lines and Shadows*, p. 51, 1984

cock-knocker *noun*
a despised person *US, 1959*

- Goggles so big you can't see his motherfuckin' face. Spooky old cock-knocker, ain't he? — Stephen King, *The Stand*, p. 504, 1978
- The little shit. The little brass-balled cock-knocker. Screw him. — Pat Cadigan, *Synners*, p. 281, 1991
- He started it! Fucking cock-knocker! — *Chasing Amy*, 1997

cocklicker *noun*
a despicable person *US, 1967*

- "Bunch of wet-nose cock lickers," obviously pleased with the way this younger generation is shaping up. — Ken Kesey, *Kesey's Jail Journal*, p. 34, 1967
- "Cock licker! Shit eater!" Joris bellowed. — Roberta Gellis, *The Rope Dancer*, p. 121, 1986

cockmaster *noun*
a male proud of his sexual prowess *US, 1951*

- In a jiff I was in; but for some strange reason I couldn't come; all 19-year-old cockmasters can't come, you know this as well as I do. — Jack Kerouac, *Letter to Neal Cassady*, p. 299, 10th January 1951

cockmeat *noun*
the penis, specifically or as a generality *US, 1995*

- Hey girls, who needs some cockmeat from a real man? — Howard Stern, *Miss America*, p. 15, 1995

cock movie *noun*
a pornographic film *US, 1967*

- — *American Speech*, p. 228, October 1967: "Some special terms used in a University of Connecticut men's dormitory"

cockpit *noun*
1 the vagina *UK, 1891*

- — Dale Gordon, *The Dominion Sex Dictionary*, p. 45, 1967

2 the clitoris *US, 1982*

- — *Maledicta*, p. 131, Summer/Winter 1982: "Dyke diction: The language of lesbians"

cock ring *noun*
a device worn on the penis to enhance sexual performance *US, 1977*

- The other man wears a cock ring—a current fad, a ring of metal, like his, or of studded leather, around the base of the cock and balls,

supposedly insuring harder hard-ons, better orgasms. — John Rechy, *The Sexual Outlaw*, p. 202, 1977

cockroach *verb*
to steal something *US, 1981*
Hawaiian youth usage.

- Who wen cockaroach da cookies? — Douglas Simonson, *Pidgin to da Max*, 1981

cockroach castle *noun*
a dirty, messy place *US, 1990*

- After seven years in that Texas cockroach castle, I was, I think, madam, qualified to make some judgments, even some harsh ones. — Ken Kesey, *The Further Inquiry*, p. 116, 1990

cockroach killers *noun*
pointed shoes or boots *US, 1970*

- Cockroach killers: a street term that arose to describe the narrow, pointed, and sometimes hand-tiled needle-nose boots worn in the 1960s and early 1970s. — Tyler Beard, *Art of the Boot*, p. 154, 2006

cock rock *noun*
aggressively macho heavy rock music performed with pelvic-thrusting posturing *US, 1971*
Combines **cock** (the penis) and "rock."

- As much as I hate heavy music, cock rock, macho rock, or whatever the current name for it is—I have to admit to having every Blue Cheer album ever made[.] — *Creem*, May 1971
- You get straight-up funk, vintage Seventies cock-rock, anarchic hard-core and enough psychedelia to make this the pot-smoking album of the year. — *Phoenix (Arizona) New Times*, p. 97, 23rd December 1992
- The typical guitar oriented thrashy pop would at times evolve into a sound described perfectly by the band as "cock rock." — *Beat*, p. 46, 9th July 1996

cock rot *noun*
an unspecified sexually transmitted disease *US, 1990*

- She then proceeded to curse me into hell, accusing me of not knowing my father, and hoping I succumbed to galloping cock rot. — Kevin Noble, *Baghdad Trucker*, p. 143, 2006

cocksman
1 a man who prides himself on his sexual prowess *US, 1896*

- The adolescent cocksman having made his conquest barely broods at home the loss of the love of the conquered lass[.] — Jack Kerouac, *The Subterraneans*, p. 18, 1958
- "I come to visit the girl I love and find her laying on the sand with this dumb-ass cocksman." — Burt Hirschfield, *Fire Island*, p. 505, 1970
- You know that guy, that guy is the cocksman of Bay Ridge. — *Saturday Night Fever*, 1977
- Allen was still so unsure of himself and here was Neal the confident cocksman if there ever was one. — Herbert Huncke, *Guilty of Everything*, p. 92, 1990

2 a male prostitute *US, 1970*

- — Clarence Major, *Dictionary of Afro-American Slang*, p. 38, 1970

cocksmith *noun*
a sexually expert man *US, 1959*

- He standin' in the door comin' back from Lu Ann. Cowboy a cocksmith. — Warren Miller, *The Cool World*, p. 105, 1959
- Nevertheless, the latter scene is one of the most scorching four-ways ever committed to film with Siffredi proving to be arguably the best living cocksmith in the business. — *Adult Video News*, p. 48, February 1993
- Seeing Persia getting boned up the dark side of the moon (by cocksmith supreme Sean Michaels) is mighty fine incentive to stick with the program. — Editors of Adult Video News, *The AVN Guide to the 500 Greatest Adult Films of All Time*, p. 208, 2005

cockstrong *adjective*
overtly masculine and strong *US, 2000*

- "Cockstrong nigger, nice with the hands like Tuffy, catch you right, forget about it." — Paul Beatty, *Tuff*, p. 79, 2000

cocksuck *noun*
an act of oral sex on a man *US, 1940*

- He'd grin grotesquely, rolling his eyes and darting his tongue in and out of his cadaverous mouth—more in an approximation, or so it seemed to me, of clit-lick than of cock-suck. — Terry Southern, *Now Dig This*, p. 33, 2001

cocksuck *verb*
to perform oral sex on a man *US, 1977*

- She cock-sucked him like crazy, and then he lost all control. — Roy Hawkins, *Bimbos by the Bay*, p. 105, 1977

cocksucker noun

1 used as a generalized term of abuse for a despicable person US, 1918

- I don't see how these cocksuckers could have done a better job trying to fuck me up as a first & second novelist if they had laid out a blueprint in an attic. — Jack Kerouac, *Letter to Neal Cassady*, pp. 239–240, 3rd December 1950
- I said, what if the three months comes at a time when the writing is going well? Marty said, "Cocksucker." — Clancy Sigal, *Going Away*, p. 46, 1961
- He died on account of this silly cocksucker here. So I promised him I'd have this silly cocksucker shot after the war. — Kurt Vonnegut, *SlaughterhouseFive*, p. 141, 1969
- All the way to the station house I was called 110 cocksuckers, etc. — Babs Gonzales, *Movin' On Down De Line*, p. 55, 1975

2 a person who performs oral sex on a man, especially a male homosexual UK, 1891

The most well-known use of the term in the US is in a statement attributed to former President Richard Nixon, who upon learning of the death of FBI Director J. Edgar Hoover on 2nd May 1972, is reported to have said "Jesus Christ! That old cocksucker!" Nixon was reflecting the widespread belief that Hoover was homosexual.

- I know I have always been a beat cocksucker in your imagination. — Allen Ginsberg, *Letter to Carolyn Cassady*, p. 128, 30th May 1952
- Later, in his apartment, he said, "Why are you so nervous, aint you been with a cocksucker before?" — John Rechy, *City of Night*, p. 28, 1963
- "Homosexual" is a kind of neutral, scientific term which might in a given context itself have a freight of significance or beauty or artistic merit. But it's less likely to than the word "cocksucker," which is closer to colloquial, idiomatic expression. — Lenny Bruce, *How to Talk Dirty and Influence People*, p. 117, 1965
- With an expert cocksucker, a rubber is no barrier to pleasure. — *Letters to Penthouse V*, p. 155, 1995

3 a person who performs oral sex on a woman US, 1942

- The man said, "I'm a cocksucker [a performer of cunnilingus]." — Roger Abrahams, *Positively Black*, p. 104, 1970

4 during the Vietnam war, a leech US, 1991

Especially the huge, reddish-black, slimy leeches of the Mekong Delta.

- — Linda Reinberg, *In the Field*, p. 46, 1991

cocksucker red adjective

a bright red shade of lipstick US, 1982

Not a brand name. Garish and conveying a low-life, whorish image.

- [S]o I said just let me handle this because my grandma is getting nothing less than Cocksucker Red when they put her in the ground... — Armistead Maupin, *Further Tales of the City*, p. 74, 1982
- — *Adult Video News*, p. 42, August 1995

cocksucker's teeth noun

used as the epitome of uselessness US, 1972

- — Robert A. Wilson, *Playboy's Book of Forbidden Words*, p. 73, 1972

cocksucking noun

oral sex performed on a man UK, 1895

- I don't know what it is, but the Trailways and the Greyhound people have done more to popularize impersonal cocksucking than Army chaplains. — Angelo d'Arcangelo, *The Homosexual Handbook*, p. 47, 1968
- Frank's dick was almost fully hard from the cock-sucking, it stuck halfway up from his naked lap. — Roy Hawkins, *Bimbos by the Bay*, p. 9, 1977
- Though I enjoyed sucking David's dick, it's true that I considered cocksucking to be strictly foreplay and not the main course. — *Letters to Penthouse V*, p. 58, 1995

cocksucking adjective

despicable, loathsome US, 1902

- But these next five years are not to be wasted "waiting" for these cocksucking bastards with their sheep's brains who will some day come bleating all over my premises. — Jack Kerouac, *Letter to Neal Cassady*, p. 173, 8th December 1948
- "Look out for those cocksucking cops!" — Heather Robertson, *Grass Roots*, p. 149, 1973

cocktail noun

a marijuana cigarette, partially smoked and inserted into a regular cigarette US, 1971

- — *Mr.*, p. 9, April 1966: "The hippie's lexicon"

- — Eugene Landy, *The Underground Dictionary*, p. 53, 1971
- As the cigarette began to burn his finger, Prince put the reefer out and made a cocktail out of the roach. — Donald Goines, *Black Gangster*, p. 224, 1977

cocktail verb

to insert a partially smoked marijuana cigarette into a tobacco cigarette US, 1960

- The bomber in her hand was now a "roach." I cocktailed it for her. — Iceberg Slim (Robert Beck), *Pimp*, p. 182, 1969
- Marlene sighed impatiently and cocktailed the roach, waited for a light and took a deep hit before passing it on. — Odie Hawkins, *Amazing Grace*, p. 142–143, 1993
- I cocktailed the last of a roach I had now three days in my wallet, smoked it, a mellow high, boss shit from North Africa, I think the dude said. — Clarence Major, *All-Night Visitors*, p. 54, 1998

cocktailery noun

a cocktail lounge US, 1981

- — Don Wilmeth, *The Language of American Popular Entertainment*, p. 56, 1981

cocktail hour noun

the time when all patients in a hospital ward are given medication US, 1946

- — *American Speech*, p. 154, April 1946: "GI words from the separation center and proctology ward"

cocktail party noun

the use of Molotov cocktails US, 1979

- — H. Craig Collins, *Street Gangs*, p. 222, 1979

cocktease noun

a cockteaser US, 1981

- He wanted to hit the supercilious little cocktease. — John Nichols, *The Nirvana Blues*, p. 426, 1981

cocktease verb

to tempt a man with the suggestion of sex UK, 1957

- — Angus Wilson, *A Bit off the Map*, 1957
- I knew I couldn't cocktease him any lower without walking off the lot[.] — Rita Ciresi, *Pink Slip*, p. 310, 1999

cockteaser noun

a sexually attractive woman who flaunts her sexuality UK, 1891

- Nobody likes a cockteaser. Either you put out or you don't. — Hubert Selby Jr., *Last Exit to Brooklyn*, p. 107, 1957
- The bad thing about a cockteaser like Angela is she turns her man loose on the world and lets a lot of other women in for trouble. — John Updike, *Couples*, p. 125, 1968
- JOAN: My little boy is sick, and I really should be getting home. BERNIE: Cockteaser. JOAN: I beg your pardon? BERNIE: You heard me. JOAN: I have never been called that in my life. BERNIE: Well, you just lost your cherry. — David Mamet, *Sexual Perversity in Chicago*, p. 21, 1974
- He was still with Cindy of the blond hair and cute ass. Cockteaser was a name invented specially for Cindy. — Jackie Collins, *Chances*, p. 130, 1980

co-co noun

cocaine US, 1997

- My girl at Chase says Figsy was missing payments—what with the his and her co-co problems and whatnot. — *Copland*, 1997

coconut noun

1 a Mexican-American who rejects his heritage and seeks to blend in with the white majority US, 1974

Like a coconut, brown on the outside but white on the inside.

- — Dagoberto Fuentes and Jose Lopez, *Barrio Language Dictionary*, p. 32, 1974
- Shot full of holes, he apparently only had one worry: that these coconut assholes might accidentally drop him over a cliff and kill him. — Joseph Wambaugh, *Lines and Shadows*, p. 138, 1984
- — Multicultural Management Program Fellows, *Dictionary of Cautionary Words and Phrases*, 1989

2 a clod, a dolt US, 1965

- — Miss Cone, *The Slang Dictionary (Hawthorne High School)*, 1965

coconuts noun

1 cocaine US, 1952

- — *American Speech*, p. 25, February 1952: "Teen-age hophead jargon"

2 money US, 1981

- — Don Wilmeth, *The Language of American Popular Entertainment*, p. 58, 1981

coconut telegraph *noun*

the informal way in which news travels in the tropics *US, 1961*

- Anyway you slice it, the coconut telegraph had transmitted this coup-de-something in no time around the islands and it had become history ever since. — Frederick Kohner, *Gidget Goes Hawaiian*, p. 49, 1961
- Kirk can get in touch with me on the Coconut Telegraph and I will meet you there. — Jimmy Buffett, *Tales from Margaritaville*, p. 61, 1989

code brown *noun*

used as a vaguely humorous notification that a hospital patient has defecated *US, 1988–1989*

An allusion to the color code jargon heard in hospitals.

- — *Maledicta*, p. 31, 1988–1989: "Medical maledicta from San Francisco"

code red *noun*

in the military, punishment meted out by a group of soldiers to a nonconforming peer *US, 1992*

- Sir, a Code Red is a disciplinary engagement. — *A Few Good Men*, 1992

codger *noun*

a pleasantly eccentric old man *UK, 1756*

Often found as "old codger."

- My grandfather was a tough old codger, but that's one thing you can say for him, he was always a believer in giving folks a second chance. — Gurney Norman, *Divine Right's Trip (Last Whole Earth Catalog)*, p. 49, 1971
- When Bobbie questioned Fin about the age of all the fun-loving fogies, coots, geezers, codgers, duffers and biddies she'd met in the saloon, he didn't know how to tell her that the oldest fossil in the joint wasn't fifteen years his senior. — Joseph Wambaugh, *Finnegan's Week*, p. 230, 1993

cods *noun*

1 the testicles *UK, 1632*

- He don't have cods enough to steal and all he wants to do is stand around and whip some gal, you know. — Bruce Jackson, *Outside the Law*, p. 157, 1972
- She stepped aside, reaching out and cupping his cock and cods in her lump, liver-spotted hand. — Earl Thompson, *Tattoo*, p. 195, 1974

2 courage, daring *US, 1972*

Synonymous with **BALLS**.

- He don't have cods enough to steal and all he wants to do is stand around and whip some gal, you know. — Bruce Jackson *Outside the Law*, p. 157, 1972

coffee *noun*

LSD *US, 1967*

A euphemism created in Boston, alluding to the fact that LSD was often sold in Cambridge coffee houses.

- — Richard Lingeman, *Drugs from A to Z*, p. 47, 1967

coffee-and *noun*

a light meal *US, 1901*

- — Hyman E. Goldin et al., *Dictionary of American Underworld Lingo*, p. 46, 1950
- They sprawled at the counter and at the tables and ordered coffeeand. — Hubert Selby Jr., *Last Exit to Brooklyn*, p. 239, 1957
- I drank coffee in Skid Row coffee houses, South Main Street, coffee-and, seventeen cents. — Jack Kerouac, *The Dharma Bums*, p. 93, 1958

coffee-and *adjective*

small-time, insignificant *US, 1937*

- "That coffee-an' mac you got," a French girl would crack to a straight one, and then it was on—hair came out by the handful. — Mezz Mezzrow, *Really the Blues*, p. 23, 1946
- "I'm not makin' more than coffee-an' money." — Irving Shulman, *Cry Tough*, p. 31, 1949
- [C]offee-and habit: a small drug habit[.] — Richard A. Spears, *The Slang and Jargon of Drugs and Drink*, p. 113, 1986

coffeehouse *verb*

in poker, to try to deceive your opponents by idle speech and deliberate mannerisms *US, 1949*

- — Albert H. Morehead, *The Complete Guide to Winning Poker*, p. 259, 1967
- — Thomas L. Clark, *The Dictionary of Gambling and Gaming*, p. 46, 1987

coffee pot *noun*

a lively party guest *US, 1961*

- Coffee Pot—the life of the party — Art Unger, *The Cool Book*, p. 109, 1961

coffin *noun*

1 in skateboarding, a maneuver in which the rider lies completely horizontally on the board, feet first *US, 1964*

- You can do the tricks the surfers do / Just try a Quasimodo or The Coffin too. — Jan Berry and Dean Torrance, *Sidewalk Surfin'*, 1964
- — Albert Cassorla, *The Skateboarder's Bible*, p. 199, 1976

2 a case housing weapons *US, 1978*

- In the trunk of the squad car was a wooden box known as the coffin. It contained two Remington 12-gauge automatic shotguns, with ammunition[.] — Jon A. Jackson, *The Blind Pig*, p. 7, 1978

3 in poker, the smallest possible raise in a game with a limited number of raises permitted *US, 1967*

- — Albert H. Morehead, *The Complete Guide to Winning Poker*, p. 256, 1967

coffin corner *noun*

in battle, a vulnerable position *US, 1995*

- I ain't surprised. We're flying in coffin corner to start with. And we were so goddamn low by the time we jumped that the squadron had already left us behind. — Greg Iles, *Black Cross*, p. 138, 1995

coffin nail *noun*

a cigarette *US, 1900*

From the link between smoking cigarettes and death. In the C19, it referred to "a cigar."

- "Say, got a fag?" asked Buddy. "Here's a coffin nail," Phil said, talking out of the side of his mouth and extending a pack to Buddy. — James T. Farrell, *Saturday Night*, p. 28, 1947
- And that's what the so-called Surgeon General has going for him—a black hat: cigarettes. Coffin nails, gaspers—a black hat if ever there was one. — Max Shulman, *Anyone Got a Match?*, p. 42, 1964
- It's why I didn't take a drink or smoke a coffin nail or lay a broad until I was nineteen. — Iceberg Slim (Robert Beck), *Doom Fox*, p. 199, 1978
- If I had just turned twenty-two, I wouldn't be suckin' on these ol' coffin nails myself, but I ain't got a thing to lose, not at my age. — Odie Hawkins, *The Busting Out of an Ordinary Man*, p. 143, 1985

cogs *noun*

sunglasses *US, 1945*

- — Lou Shelly, *Hepcats Jive Talk Dictionary*, p. 8, 1945

coin *noun*

money *UK, 1820*

- If you intend to seek coin or a career here (or just a job) do not come at all[.] — Jack Lait and Lee Mortimer, *New York Confidential*, p. 122, 1948
- Man it just spendin' money when whut I need is big coin so I can put some away for buyin' the Colt. — Warren Miller, *The Cool World*, p. 86, 1959
- "You're going to blow the coin?" he asked, incredulously. "You don't have to if you don't want to." — James Simon Kunen, *The Strawberry Statement*, p. 76, 1968
- Because it's not just the money I deserve. It's not just the coin. — *Jerry Maguire*, 1996

coin *verb*

to earn an amount of money *US, 1946*

- [W]ith the chuck-luck and Indian-dice games at the cigar counter I was coining at least two C-notes a week. — Mezz Mezzrow, *Really the Blues*, p. 44, 1946

coinkidink *noun*

a coincidence *US, 1979*

Multiple creative spellings are to be found.

- Is it just more of what Kendall calls "coincidence-a-dinkies?" — Beatrice Sparks (writing as "Anonymous"), *Jay's Journal*, p. 54, 1979
- NOT AN item but a heckuva coinkidink: Winifred Giannini, whose car bears plates reading "2 VJH 135," parked and 19th and Ocean behind a car with plates "2 VJH 124." — *San Francisco Chronicle*, p. E1, 6th March 1992
- What struck me as a little "coinkydinky," Colonel, is that three times in the space of ten days, you were witness to some sort of cover-up there. — *Real Time with Bill Maher*, 13th February 2004

coin-op *noun*

a coin-operated pool table *US, 1990*

- — Steve Rushin, *Pool Cool*, p. 10, 1990

cojones *noun*

the testicles; courage *US, 1932*

From Spanish.

- It had been raining like a bastard, and the baseball field was mud up to your cojones. — Truman Capote, *In Cold Blood*, p. 331, 1965

- [A]nd would be if the anthropologists had a shred of imagination or the dimmest sense of wonder, or the cojones, the bollocks to look at the big picture, to help focus and enlarge the big picture. — Tom Robbins, *Fierce Invalids Home from Hot Climates*, p. 74, 2000

coke *noun*
cocaine *US, 1903*

- H and coke. You can smell it going in. — William Burroughs, *Junkie*, p. 66, 1953
- I've got some Coke. What's you think we're celebrating for? Coke and champagne, Kitty, get champagne for everyone. — Susan Hall, *Gentleman of Leisure*, p. 130, 1972
- Wow, I don't believe it. You mean to tell me you guys have never snorted coke? — *Annie Hall*, 1977
- Here were two coke fiends who came into court because their marriage didn't seem to be working and the children were getting nervous. — Hunter S. Thompson, *Songs of the Doomed*, p. 197, 1983

cokebottle *noun*
in computing, any character that is not found on a normal computer keyboard *US, 1983*

- A program written at Stanford, for example, is likely to have a lot of "control-meta-cokebottle" commands, that is, commands that you can only type on a Stanford keyboard[.] — Guy L. Steele et al., *The Hacker's Dictionary*, p. 44, 1983

Coke bottle glasses *noun*
eyeglasses with very thick lenses *US, 1986*

- [S]ome skinny jerk-off with Coke-bottle glasses[.] — Carl Hiaasen, *Strip Tease*, p. 4, 1993
- A few weeks earlier, Senator Pothole [D'Amato] had been on the Imus radio show and done an over-the-top Japanese stereotype impression of Judge Ito. It was real Jerry-Lewis-bucktooth-Coke-bottle-glasses stuff[.] — Al Franken, *Rush Limbaugh is a Big Fat Idiot*, p. 189, 1996

Coke bottles *noun*
a person with poor eyesight and thick glasses *US, 1997*

- The labels were cruel: Gimp, Limpy-go-fetch, Crip, Lift-one-drag one, etc. Pint, Half-a-man, Peewee, Shorty, Lardass, Pork, Blubber, Belly, Blimp. Nuke-knob, Skinhead, Baldy. Four-eyes, Specs, Coke bottles. — *San Francisco Examiner*, p. A15, 28th July 1997

Coke club *noun*
a club with live sexual performances, including soda pop douches *US, 1966*

- Afterward, the girl partner would douche by using the bottle and contents of a well known commercial drink for which the club was named. Since then, the so-called "Coke clubs" have received no small amount of publicity. — Victor J. Banis, *Small Town Sex Today*, p. 28, 1966

coked; coked out; coked up *adjective*
cocaine-intoxicated *US, 1924*

- I was real hungup on it two years ago, you understand—coked most of the time. — John Clellon Holmes, *Go*, p. 121, 1952
- They're coked to the gills. — Edwin Torres, *Q & A*, p. 98, 1977
- "You look just like David Bowie," Alana, who is obviously coked up out of her mind, tells Daniel. — Bret Easton Ellis, *Less Than Zero*, p. 16, 1985
- "There was a BC party, everyone coked up, and he was sitting on the floor with this BC Chick, Patty." — Gini Sikes, *8 Ball Chicks*, p. 130, 1997

cokehead *noun*
a cocaine addict *US, 1922*

- On one occasion when I was playing the role of a very dumb cokehead, a flash little racketeer called me. — Maurice Helbrant, *Narcotic Agent*, p. 10, 1981
- [H]ard-core, career dope fiends, and even the cokeheads like the number runners from way back—Cisco Kid and Billy Bucks—be comin' into the clubs to get a taste of the base. — *New Jack City*, 1990
- You were never an alky, you were a cokehead. — *Something About Mary*, 1998
- Ye's a pyscho-cokehead-hitman. — *Traffic*, 2000

coke house *noun*
a building or dwelling where cocaine is sold *US, 1989*

- I told two of my old roomies about the coke house, but I didn't say I worked here or nothing. — Terry Williams, *The Cocaine Kids*, p. 40, 1989

coke out *verb*
to use cocaine to an excess *US, 1995*

- The ritual was to coke out every night, for the whole night, and not to stay too long with any particular group. — Cleo Odzer, *Goa Freaks*, p. 39, 1995

coke, smoke, and a puke *noun*
a fighter pilot's breakfast *US, 1986*

- — *United States Naval Institute Proceedings*, p. 108, October 1986

coke whore *noun*
a person who trades sex for cocaine *US, 1984*

- "I don't do needles and I don't fuck coke whores." — John Updike, *Rabbit at Rest*, p. 160, 1990
- After all, who many coke whore-snitches are there in Spokane who set up dates for other coke whore-snitches if the client asks them to suggest other girls? — Burt Barer, *Body Count*, p. 114, 2002

cokie *noun*
1 a frequent user of cocaine *US, 1916*

- A competitor in the same block was Wilbur Kenny, known to the cokies merely as "Y." — Jack Lait and Lee Mortimer, *Washington Confidential*, p. 51, 1951
- "Why, I wouldn't dream of teaming up with a 'cokey'!" — Charles Hamilton, *Men of the Underworld*, p. 213, 1952
- The girls never bother the alkies and cokies of the street with their joke[.] — John M. Murtagh and Sara Harris, *Cast the First Stone*, p. 4, 1957
- "Now I was a cokey pure and simple when Joey got loosed last time, but I haven't had a snort since she came home." — Robert Deane Pharr, *S.R.O.*, pp. 50–51, 1971

2 a junior member of a youth gang *US, 1949*

- I see one of their cokies standing in a doorway with his hands in his pockets. — Hal Ellson, *Duke*, p. 39, 1949

Cokomo Joe; Kokomo Joe; kokomo *noun*
a cocaine user *US, 1938*

- — J.E. Schmidt, *Narcotics Lingo and Lore*, p. 98, 1959

cold *adjective*
1 heartless, cruel *US, 1962*

- That's pretty cold, ain't it, lady? — *Basic Instinct*, 1992
- "If you do something to offend someone, then that's cold," said Ryan Hoskin, 17, a senior at Stuart. — *The Washington Post*, 19th March 2002

2 bad *US, 1934*

- And the bitch had cuffs on at the time, but I being the warm and he being the cold, I was able to get her to give up the source of her supplier which was all we wanted from the jump. — A.S. Jackson, *Gentleman Pimp*, p. 131, 1973

3 absolute *US, 1973*

- "They don't want their wives to know they're cold freaks," she explains. "They bring their sex hang-ups to us." — George Paul Csicsery (Editor), *The Sex Industry*, p. 9, 1973

4 not capable of being traced to an owner *US, 1992*
Back-formed from **HOT** (stolen).

- "He could feel the bump of Dan's service revolver, unwrapped and loaded now against his leg. A cold piece, its registry lost in a mountain of old records somewhere if they existed at all. — Robert Campbell, *Boneyards*, p. 276, 1992

5 in gambling, unlucky *US, 1892*

- Duffy ended up being the only player shooting at table three because he was so cold he had become a plague on everybody's luck. — Stephen Cannell, *Big Con*, p. 202, 1997

6 used as a substitute for "cool" in any of its senses *US, 1968*

- The dress Mary's wearing today is too cold. — Joan Fontaine et al., *Dictionary of Black Slang*, 1968
- — *Columbia Missourian*, p. 8A, 19th October 1998
- — Julian Johnson, *Urban Survival*, p. 258, 2003

7 (used of a take-off from an aircraft carrier) failed, resulting in a crash *US, 1959*

- What had it been? A "cold-cat" shot, whatever that was, from a carrier. A crash at take-off, anyway, into the waters off Iwo-Jima[.] — Hank Searls, *The Big X*, p. 221, 1959

cold *adverb*
suddenly, completely *US, 1889*

- Talking about a stretch in Atlanta, where he kicked a habit cold: "Fourteen days I was beating my head against the wall." — William Burroughs, *Junkie*, p. 68, 1953
- They had me cold. — Clarence Cooper Jr., *The Farm*, p. 63, 1967

cold and hot *noun*
cocaine and heroin combined for injection *US*, *1986*
Based on the initials.
- — Richard A. Spears, *The Slang and Jargon of Drugs and Drink*, p. 115, 1986

cold biscuit *noun*
1 a female who does not respond to sexual overtures *US*, *1972*
- — Helen Dahlskog (Editor), *A Dictionary of Contemporary and Colloquial Usage*, p. 14, 1972
2 a person lacking any apparent sex appeal *US*, *1961*
High school usage.
- — *Washington Post*, 23rd April 1961

cold-blooded *adjective*
1 competent; admirable *US*, *1992*
Also shortened to "cold."
- — William K. Bentley and James M. Corbett, *Prison Slang*, p. 31, 1992
2 in horse racing, said of any horse that is not a thoroughbred *US*, *1960*
- — Robert Saunders Dowst and Jay Craig, *Playing the Races*, p. 161, 1960

cold bluff *noun*
in poker, a large bet on a poor hand designed to mislead other players *US*, *1980*
- — Thomas L. Clark, *The Dictionary of Gambling and Gaming*, p. 46, 1987

cold-bust *verb*
to catch someone in the act; to reveal your own guilt inadvertently *US*, *1986*
- — Connie Eble (Editor), *UNC-CH Campus Slang*, p. 2, Fall 1986
- It was too late to make a run for it. We were cold busted. — L.L. Cool J, *I Make My Own Rules*, p. 56, 1997
- "I figured I was cold busted so I pulled over and was ready to give myself up," Andreas said. — Mike Seate, *Streetbike Extreme*, p. 81, 2002

cold caper *noun*
a crime with relatively little risk of being observed *US*, *1972*
- One night I took this girl out and it was what we called a cold caper. The safe was in a back room. — Harry King, *Box Man*, p. 13, 1972

coldcock *verb*
to hit someone without warning, especially with a blow to the head that knocks the person to the ground *US*, *1918*
- You killed her. You coldcocked her and set fire to her. — Jim Thompson, *The Nothing Man*, p. 172, 1954
- I wish he was a wise-ass messcook who coldcocked a commander and went over the hill. — Darryl Poncisan, *The Last Detail*, p. 148, 1970
- Jackie got up and cold cocked him with two punches and then announced, "Let 'em roll." — Babs Gonzales, *Movin' On Down De Line*, p. 47, 1975

cold comfort *noun*
in necrophile usage, sexual activity with a corpse *US*, *1986–1987*
- — *Maledicta*, p. 180, Summer/Winter 1986–1987: "Sexual slang: prostitutes, pedophiles, flagellators, transvestites, and necrophiles"

cold crotch *noun*
the application of an ice pack on the scrotum of a man who has overdosed on heroin *US*, *1993*
- — Peter Johnson, *Dictionary of Street Alcohol and Drug Terms*, p. 45, 1993

cold-cunt *verb*
(used of a woman) to treat someone with hostility *US*, *1982*
- [E]ven my female helpers if detected as not sympatica have been cold-cunted and brushed off. — *Maledicta*, p. 134, Summer/Winter 1982

cold deck *noun*
in card games, a stacked deck of cards *US*, *1857*
- — Lou Shelly, *Hepcats Jive Talk Dictionary*, p. 23, 1945
- Was back in thirty-two when times were hard/I had a sawed-off shotgun and a cold deck a cards. — Bruce Jackson, *Get Your Ass in the Water and Swim Like Me*, p. 50, 1964
- — Jim Glenn, *Programed Poker*, p. 155, 1981

cold-deck *verb*
to introduce a stacked deck into a game of cards *US*, *1962*
- "They caught his blackjack dealers cold-decking, didn't they?" — Stephen Longstreet, *The Flesh Peddlers*, p. 273, 1962

cold dope *noun*
in horse racing, information based on empirical evidence *US*, *1951*
- — David W. Maurer, *Argot of the Racetrack*, p. 21, 1951

cold feet *noun*
fear or a reluctance to proceed *US*, *1896*
- Maybe he just got cold feet. — Michael Chabon, *The Amazing Adventures of Kavalier & Clay*, p. 495, 2000

cold finger work *noun*
picking the pocket of a man preoccupied with sex *US*, *1948*
- The woman goes through the man's clothes while he is in no frame of mind to keep his hands on his pockets. This is subtly known in Harlem as "cold finger work." — Jack Lait and Lee Mortimer, *New York Confidential*, p. 99, 1948

cold fish *noun*
an unfriendly person *US*, *1924*
- He's a cold fish all right. — Jack Kerouac, *Letter to Carolina Kerouac Blake*, p. 89, 14th March 1945
- But I know I have to talk to Chichi if I want any kind of emotional angle, a point of view, because Robbie's such a cold fish. He thinks he's Mr. Personality, but he's basically a very dull person. — Elmore Leonard, *Split Images*, p. 213, 1981

cold in the dong *noun*
gonorrhea *US*, *1981*
- — *Maledicta*, p. 228, Summer/Winter 1981: "Sex and the single soldier"

cold meat party *noun*
a funeral or wake *US*, *1908*
- My favorite euphemism for a funeral wake is cold meat party, partly because the attempt at euphemistic disguise (deliberately) fails. — Andrew Goatly, *Critical Reading and Writing*, p. 109, 2000

cold one *noun*
1 a cold beer *US*, *1927*
- Hurry up Jack. Give us a carton and a cold one. I'm in a hurry. — Sam Weller, *Old Bastards I Have Met*, p. 22, 1979
- "You want a cold one?" The guy stared at him. "That means a beer. You want one? You like beer?" — Elmore Leonard, *Bandits*, pp. 106–107, 1987
2 an empty wallet, purse or safe *US*, *1962*
- — Joseph E. Ragen and Charles Finston, *Inside the World's Toughest Prison*, p. 795, 1962

cold-plate *verb*
to attach a legitimate license plate to a stolen vehicle that matches the description of the vehicle to which the license plate belongs *US*, *1993*
- The shop in Old Town might be in cahoots with Tijuana thieves who steal trucks and cold-plate them. — Joseph Wambaugh, *Finnegan's Week*, p. 132, 1993

cold-read *verb*
(used of a fortune teller) to tell a fortune without background information on the customer, relying on observations and the customer's answers for the predictions *US*, *1989*
A term borrowed from acting, where it means "to read a script out loud without having studied it."
- — Lindsay E. Smith and Bruce A. Walstad, *Sting Shift*, p. 115, 1989

cold shake *noun*
a method of preparing pills for injection by crushing and then dissolving them in cold water instead of heating with a flame *US*, *1989*
- — Geoffrey Froner, *Digging for Diamonds*, p. 20, 1989

cold spot *noun*
a glass of iced tea *US*, *1967*
- — *American Speech*, p. 61, February 1967: "Soda-fountain, restaurant and tavern calls"

cold storage *noun*
1 a morgue *US*, *1949*
- — Vincent J. Monteleone, *Criminal Slang*, p. 55, 1949
2 solitary confinement *US*, *1949*
- — Marlene Freedman, *Alcatraz*, 1983

cold turkey *noun*
1 an act of withdrawing from addictive drugs suddenly; the time period of that withdrawal *US*, *1925*
- If you didn't bring a trained nurse with you, you're just sneezed down, and it's piddle and cold turkey for you. — *The New American Mercury*, p. 711, 1950
- "Cold Turkey?" I nodded. "That's taking kind of a chance, isn't it?" — Polly Adler, *A House is Not a Home*, p. 121, 1953

- "I've tried, Tom. Honestly I have. But no-one knows what a spell of cold turkey is like—" "Cold turkey?" "Trying to kick the habit."
— Douglas Rutherford, *The Creeping Flesh*, pp. 83–84, 1963
- I'm clean now. On my children. Believe me! Two weeks cold turkey waiting for bail got my head together. — *Goodfellas*, 1990

2 in blackjack, a hand comprised of two face cards *US, 1980*
- — Lee Solkey, *Dummy Up and Deal*, p. 110, 1980

3 in poker, two kings dealt consecutively *US, 1988*
- — George Percy, *The Language of Poker*, p. 22, 1988

cold turkey *verb*
to withdraw from a habit or addiction suddenly and without any tapering off *US, 1949*
- Two days later, Chico told himself, "I'm going to cold turkey it. That's the hard way but the only way to bust my habit." — Hal Ellson, *The Golden Spike*, p. 47, 1952
- "You gonna cold-turkey it!" Dincher yelled on his feet. — George Mandel, *Flee the Angry Strangers*, p. 250, 1952

cold turkey *adjective*
(used of an attempt to break a drug addiction) sudden and complete without narcotics or medication to ease the withdrawal symptoms *US, 1953*
- Mae said she'd prefer to get the agony over with as quickly as possible so I might as well give her the Cold Turkey cure. — Polly Adler, *A House is Not a Home*, p. 155, 1953

cold turkey *adverb*
(used of an attempt to break a drug addiction) suddenly and completely without narcotics or medication to ease the withdrawal symptoms *US, 1922*
- Included as a medical record from the hospital when he had made her go cold turkey, which is dope-addict talk for an all-out cure. — Mickey Spillane, *I, The Jury*, p. 12, 1947
- They just throw you in the hospital by yourself, take you off cold turkey, and watch you suffer. — Billie Holiday with William Dufty, *Lady Sings the Blues*, p. 131, 1956
- Like the worst habit I ever had was $135 a day. And I kicked that one cold-turkey 'cause I didn't know what I was in for. — James Mills, *The Panic in Needle Park*, p. 99, 1966
- I kicked the habit "cold turkey" in city jail. — Iceberg Slim (Robert Beck), *Pimp*, p. 101, 1969

cold weather indicators *noun*
a woman's nipples *US, 2001*
- — Don R. McCreary (Editor), *Dawg Speak*, 2001

collar *noun*
1 an arrest *US, 1871*
- One of the cops, the handsomest, made the pick-up, and his confederates were supposed to crash in five minutes after he entered the room, which would give both time to disrobe, and that is enough evidence to make a collar. — Jack Lait and Lee Mortimer, *Washington Confidential*, p. 23, 1951
- In those days one big collar and you were in the Detective Bureau. — Edwin Torres, *Q & A*, p. 17, 1977
- Cocaine. Dirty cops. Hollywood. This is Crocket and Tubbs all the way. And we found it, so we want the fucking collar. — *True Romance*, 1993

2 an improvised seal between a dropper and needle used to inject drugs *US, 1960*
- Siphoning up the liquid again, applying the needle with its collar (a strip from the end of a dollar bill) to the neck of the dropper, twisting it on, resting the shot momentarily while he ties up[.] — Alexander Trocchi, *Cain's Book*, p. 81, 1960
- The hypodermic needle is secured to a common eyedropper by means of a narrow cardboard "collar." — Leonard Cohen, *Beautiful Losers*, pp. 238–239, 1966

collar *verb*
1 to grab someone by the collar, literally or figuratively; to arrest someone *UK, 1613*
- We collared everybody on campus; we applied all possible pressures. — Max Shulman, *The Many Loves of Dobie Gillis*, p. 34, 1951
- And being a girl, I supposed they figured they'd collar me. — James Mills, *The Panic in Needle Park*, p. 101, 1966
- Didn't I tell you, when I collared you, your next step was going to be the place where they're so concerned about whether you get

nightmares, that they keep guards around all night? — George V. Higgins, *The Rat on Fire*, p. 178, 1981
- He didn't look like a guy who shot alligators or collared offenders. — Elmore Leonard, *Maximum Bob*, p. 94, 1991

2 to understand something, to grasp something *US, 1938*
- I began to collar that all the evil I ever found came from ounce-brain white men who hated Negroes and me both, while all the good things in life came to me from the race. — Mezz Mezzrow, *Really the Blues*, p. 44, 1946

3 in horse racing, to run neck and neck *US, 1951*
- — David W. Maurer, *Argot of the Racetrack*, p. 21, 1951

▸ **collar a hot**
to eat a meal *US, 1947*
- — Marcus Hanna Boulware, *Jive and Slang of Students in Negro Colleges*, 1947

▸ **collar the jive**
to understand what is being said *US, 1947*
- — Marcus Hanna Boulware, *Jive and Slang of Students in Negro Colleges*, 1947

collars and cuffs *noun*
▸ **matching collars and cuffs; collars and cuffs that match**
applied to a person, usually a woman, whose hair is neither bleached nor dyed *US, 1984*
A jocular suggestion that the hair on the head is of the same natural shade as the pubic hair.
- — Ken Weaver, *Texas Crude*, p. 81, 1984
- "Do the collars match the cuffs?" "What?" "Do the curtains match the carpets?" "I don't understand." "Your pubic hair. Does it match the color of the hair on your head?" — Andrew Lewis Conn, *P: A Novel*, p. 16, 2003

collars-for-dollars *noun*
a situation in which an arresting officer trades the criminal's release for a share of the proceeds of the crime *US, 2001*
- You think it's some kinda buy-down? Some bullshit collars-for-dollars scheme? — Stephen J. Cannell, *The Tin Collectors*, p. 174, 2001

collect call *noun*
a citizens' band radio message for a specific named person *US, 1976*
- — Elementary Electronics, *Dictionary of CB Lingo*, p. 58, 1976

college *noun*
jail *UK, 1699*
- — Lou Shelly, *Hepcats Jive Talk Dictionary*, p. 9, 1945
- — Hy Lit, *Hy Lit's Unbelievable Dictionary of Hip Words for Groovy People*, p. 9, 1968

College Joe *noun*
a quintessential college student *US, 1961*
- In come this trick by hisseff. College Joe. — Robert Gover, *One Hundred Dollar Misunderstanding*, p. 19, 1961
- Being and acting like the typical college Joe seemed downright childish. — Friends' Historical Association, *Quaker History*, p. 70, 1962

college try *noun*
a sincere effort, despite the likelihood of failure *US, 1918*
Especially common as "the old college try."
- He thought of everything in terms of the old college try, and he had told students to attack their studies, their sports, religious waverings, sexual maladjustments, physical handicaps and a constellation of other problems with the old college try. — John Knowles, *A Separate Peace*, p. 174, 1954
- WAYNE: You can't escape like this. MICKEY: Probably not, but we're gonna give it the old college try. — *Natural Born Killers*, 1994
- You gave it the old college try. No hard feelings. — Stephen Cannell, *Big Con*, p. 44, 1997

college widow *noun*
a woman who lives in or near a college town and dates men from the college year after year *US, 1900*
- She made me think of a college widow. Actually, she was a serious girl, in her own inscrutable way. — Mary McCarthy, *Memories of a Catholic Girlhood*, p. 174, 1957

Colombian *noun*
extremely potent marijuana from Colombia *US, 1971*
- I think you better hit on a couple pounds of good Colombian. — Elmore Leonard, *City Primeval*, p. 107, 1980

Colombian necklace *noun*
a form of execution intended to set an example in which the victim's throat is slit *US, 2001*
Probably formed after the more elaborate **COLOMBIAN NECKTIE**.
- If I'd given them what they wanted I'd have been found in my cell wearing a very drippy Colombian Necklace years ago. — Carrie Lieber, *Buzz*, p. 144, 2001

Colombian necktie *noun*
a form of execution intended to set an example in which the victim's throat is slit and the tongue pulled down through the gaping wound *US, 1997*
From a well-dressed image in which the tongue replaces a tie.
- [T]he "Colombian necktie" in which the victim's throat is cut and his tongue is brought out through the wound. Something like that. — John E. Douglas and Mark Olshaker, *Journey into Darkness*, p. 342, 1997
- [J]ust before she kneed him in the balls and tried to give him a Colombian necktie[.] — Cherry Adair, *Kiss and Tell*, p. 59, 2000

Colonel Klink *noun*
any high-ranking prison officer *US, 2002*
A reference to *Hogan's Heroes*, a popular television comedy of the late 1960s.
- — Gary K. Farlow, *Prison-ese*, p. 14, 2002

Colonel Sanders *noun*
a mature male homosexual who is especially attracted to boys or young men *US, 1979*
An allusion to the founder of the Kentucky Fried Chicken™ franchise.
- — *Maledicta*, p. 220, 1979: "Kinks and queens: Linguistic and cultural aspects of the terminology for gays"

color *noun*
1 in roller derby, any type of theatrics that would make the skater stand out to fans *US, 1999*
- — Keith Coppage, *Roller Derby to Rollerjam*, 1999

2 in a casino, any betting token worth more than one dollar *US, 1977*
- — Thomas L. Clark, *The Dictionary of Gambling and Gaming*, p. 47, 1987

colorado *noun*
a red barbiturate capsule, especially if branded Seconal™ *US, 1971*
From Spanish *colorado* (the color red). Often abbreviated to "colie."
- — Eugene Landy, *The Underground Dictionary*, p. 54, 1971
- Got any colorados, chico? — Lous Stavsky et al, *A2Z*, p. 22, 1995

Colorado Kool Aid *noun*
Coors™ beer *US, 1972*
Brewed in Colorado, and for several decades not marketed nationally.
- "Oh, he'll drink that Colorado Kool-Aid," said Jim Tom "He don't like it any more than he likes gettin' fed and fucked before sundown." — Dan Jenkins, *Semi-Tough*, p. 24, 1972
- Well, I was sittin' in this beer joint down in Houston, Texas / Was drinking Colorado Kool-Aid and talkin' to some Mexicans. — Johnny Paycheck, *Colorado Kool Aid*, October 1977
- — Ellen C. Bellone (Editor), *Dictionary of Slang*, p. 7, 1989

colored people's time *noun*
used for denoting a lack of punctuality *US, 1967*
One of the very few instances in which the former ameliorative "colored people" is still used in the US.
- Their lives run by a clock that keeps C.P.T., Colored People's Time, which assumes that appointments won't be kept, work promised won't be delivered, jobs found won't be gone to, since those are all part of the outside world. — Paul Jacobs, *Prelude to a Riot*, p. 12, 1967
- CPT—Colored People's Time (i.e., on time when they WANT to be, otherwise NOT). — *San Francisco Examiner*, p. 33, 9th May 1967
- I be trying to hook you up, mama. So cut all the hoorah, we wain't on colored people's time here. — Stephen Cannell, *Big Con*, p. 49, 1997
- "Well, now, I don' rightly know de answer to dat. Counselor Tubbs, he operates on C.P.T." Colored People's Time. — Tom Wolfe, *A Man in Full*, p. 21, 1998

colored showers *noun*
a sexual fetish involving urination on your partner *US, 1993*
- — J.R. Schwartz, *The Official Guide to the Best Cat Houses in Nevada*, p. 164, 1993

colored town *noun*
a neighborhood with a large population of black people *US, 1964*
- Colored town. It's on fire. — Jim Thompson, *Pop. 1280*, p. 150, 1964

color for color *adverb*
in American casinos, the method of paying bets—one denomination at a time *US, 1980*
- — Lee Solkey, *Dummy Up and Deal*, p. 110, 1980

color me *verb*
used ironically in conjunction with an adjective for describing a personal condition *US, 1962*
- Color me Naive. — Erma Brombeck, *At Wit's End*, p. 121, 1967
- Color me gone. — Michael Herr, *Dispatches*, p. 250, 1977
- — Connie Eble (Editor), *UNC-CH Campus Slang*, p. 2, Spring 1980
- HEATHER CHANDLER: Grow up, Heather. Bulimia's so '86. HEATHER MCNAMARA: Color me nauseous. — *Heathers*, 1988

color of money *noun*
a green smoke grenade *US, 2000*
- Green was the color of money. — Paul Morgan, *The Parrot's Beak*, p. 205, 2000

colors *noun*
1 insignia that identify group membership, especially in motorcycle gangs *US, 1966*
- All that remained was the gathering of any loose money or marijuana that might be lying around, lashing the sleeping bags to the bikes and donning the infamous "colors." The all-important colors ... the uniform as it were, the crucial identity[.] — Hunter S. Thompson, *Hell's Angels*, p. 8, 1966
- Though I was in jail, I had my colors on, for permission had been given. — Frank Reynolds, *Freewheelin Frank*, p. 14, 1967
- "Can't fly my colors. I don't want trouble with The Man." — Arthur Blessitt, *Turned On to Jesus*, p. 121, 1971
- We got to play out of town twice, once in an ex-biker club in Sacramento that thrilled me by making me take off my Harley Wings because they were "colors"[.] — Jennifer Blowdryer, *White Trash Debutante*, p. 78, 1997

2 the colored clothing worn as a signal of gang affiliation *US, 1989*
- So we pulled off our jackets and showed them our colors[.] — Terry Williams, *The Cocaine Kids*, p. 60, 1989

color-struck *adjective*
overly conscious of skin color *US, 1965*
- I ain't got nothin' against dark-skin girls. I ain't never been color struck, and I never try to let none-a my chillun be color struck. — Claude Brown, *Manchild in the Promised Land*, p. 133, 1965
- You just color-struck, that's why you givin' your money to a white man[.] — Nathan Heard, *Howard Street*, p. 143, 1968
- Either you want a black man, or it's really true that you done got color-struck and you won't be satisfied unless you get your own white owl. — Donald Goines, *Whoreson*, p. 260, 1972

color up *verb*
in casino gambling, to trade chips of one denomination for chips of a higher denomination *US, 1991*
- — Michael Dalton, *Blackjack*, p. 39, 1991

combat fishing *noun*
sport fishing at a crowded fishing spot *US, 1993*
- — Mike Doogan, *How to Speak Alaskan*, p. 22, 1993

combat-happy *adjective*
deranged by the horrors of combat *US, 1962*
- And Leo's Duvall-like portrayal, though sometimes over the top, is an interesting study of a combat-happy maniac whose unstable emotional state is exacerbated when he's given virtual carte blanche to kill in the name of his country. — *Denver (Colorado) Westword*, 26th November 1998

combat jack *noun*
an act of masturbation by a combat soldier to relieve the tension or boredom of combat *US, 2003*
- After surviving their first ambush at Al Gharraf, a couple of Marines even admitted to an almost frenzied need to get off combat jacks. — *Rolling Stone*, 24th July 2003

Combat Zone *nickname*
an unsavory area in downtown Boston, dominated by sex shops, bars, and drug dealers *US, 1971*
- Get-down time in the Combat Zone and Inez was waiting to draw first blood. — John Sayles, *Union Dues*, p. 180, 1977
- By 1979, I had worked in Boston's Combat Zone for three years. — Lauri Lewin, *Naked is the Best Disguise*, p. 13, 1984
- The wheelchair-bound friends and the then teenaged boys ended up at a girlie show in the Combat Zone. — *Boston Herald*, p. 23, 13th January 2004

comber *noun*
a large wave that breaks on a reef or a beach *US, 1961*
- Canoe Surf is where the kookes hang out and where you get the first feel of Hawaiian combers before you set out for the real thing— Makaha or Sunset. — Frederick Kohner, *Gidget Goes Hawaiian*, p. 48, 1961
- Gary Fairmont R. Filosa II, *The Surfer's Almanac*, p. 183, 1977

combo *noun*
1 a combination of anything physical or abstract *US, 1921*
- I just told you, she's half Asian, half American. They're all good looking. You could mate Don Rickles and Yoko Ono and they're going to have a gorgeous kid. It's a foolproof combo. — *Something About Mary*, 1998
2 a small jazz band *US, 1924*
- Some skinny joker with scald burns on his face was fronting a combo. — Iceberg Slim (Robert Beck), *Pimp*, p. 95, 1969
3 in pool, a combination shot, or one in which the cue ball is shot into a numbered ball that then hits the object ball *US, 1990*
- Balls shot in combination are preceded by the call of "combo," much the same as a basketball player cries "glass" to acknowledge that he intends to make his shot off the backboard. — Steve Rushin, *Pool Cool*, p. 10, 1990

come; cum *noun*
1 semen *US, 1923*
- — Donald Webster Cory and John P. LeRoy, *The Homosexual and His Society*, p. 263, 1963: "A lexicon of homosexual slang"
- "Well, dammit, it was full of his come!" she retorted with an indignant toss of her head. — Nathan Heard, *Howard Street*, p. 20, 1968
- Jim feels the other's warm cum on his stomach, and his own cock stretches[.] — John Rechy, *The Sexual Outlaw*, p. 32, 1977
- He saw the Jimi poster in my room and goes, "That nigger looks like he's got a mouth full of cum." — Francesca Lia Block, *Baby Be-Bop*, p. 391, 1995
- I touch her pussy now, the dry hair. My sperm dry on it. Little streaks of dry cum. — Clarence Major, *All-Night Visitors*, p. 4, 1998
2 an orgasm *US, 1967*
- [W]hat these broads—the good-looking ones, that is—were after was a damned good come. — Joey V., *Portrait of Joey*, p. 117, 1969
- [In Cairo, 1992] the price was about 50 piastres (8p) for one come whether you took a minute or hours. — Fiona Pitt-Kethley, *Red Light Districts of the World*, p. 42, 2000

come; cum *verb*
to experience an orgasm *UK, 1600*
- In a jiff I was in; but for some strange reason I couldn't come; all 19-year-old cockmasters can't come, you know this as well as I do. — Jack Kerouac, *Letter to Neal Cassady*, p. 299, 10th January 1951
- "Who's talking about go?" demanded Liv. "The girls want to come! Am I right, Can?" — Terry Southern, *Candy*, p. 49, 1958
- "You came, Boston," he remarked with the air of a satisfied instructor. — Mary McCarthy, *The Group*, p. 37, 1963
- He was afraid she would come too soon; he was afraid he might come too soon. — Cecil Brown, *The Life & Loves of Mr. Jiveass Nigger*, p. 75, 1969

▶ **come down like trained pigs**
in horse racing, to finish a race exactly as predicted *US, 1951*
- — David W. Maurer, *Argot of the Racetrack*, p. 21, 1951

▶ **come from**
to emanate from; to expose the philosophical basis for a statement or action *US, 1978*
Another vague term of the 1960s.
- If you can check where I'm coming from, I'm talking about the class struggle. — Bobby Seale, *A Lonely Rage*, p. 295, 1978

▶ **come home early**
in horse racing, to establish and hold an early lead to win a race *US, 1951*
- — David W. Maurer, *Argot of the Racetrack*, p. 21, 1951

▶ **come hot**
in a confidence swindle, to complete the swindle which the victim immediately understands to have been a swindle *US, 1985*
- — M. Allen Henderson, *How Con Games Work*, p. 218, 1985

▶ **come out the side of your neck**
to speak foolishly *US, 1975*
- You know I don't stand for no lame coming out the side of his neck with me. — Miguel Pinero, *Short Eyes*, p. 13, 1975

come across *verb*
1 to have sex as the result of persuasive insistence *US, 1921*
- He had gone dancing there a week ago, picked up a dame, shot her a line, and she had come across. — James T. Farrell, *The Life Adventure*, p. 182, 1947
- "Yeah," another one agreed, "a babe would have to come across to ride in that car with us." — Irving Shulman, *The Amboy Dukes*, p. 52, 1947
- Jazz groupies in those days came across as weird but did not necessarily come across. — Larry Rivers, *What Did I Do?*, p. 50, 1992
2 to agree to become an informer *US, 1973*
- You'd better realize that if you come across, you've got to come across all the way; we don't want to hear anything from you that isn't true just because you think we'd like to hear it. — Leonard Shecter and William Phillips, *On the Pad*, p. 50, 1973

come again?
please repeat or restate what you just said *US, 1970*
- — Clarence Major, *Dictionary of Afro-American Slang*, p. 39, 1970

come-along *noun*
handcuffs with a chain lead *US, 1974*
- His pockets contained a billfold with a dozen credit cards in different names, a key ring with a great many keys on it, a Mexican switchblade, and chain manacle known to the police as a "come along." — Robert Stone, *Dog Soldiers*, p. 101, 1974

comeback *noun*
1 revenge *US, 1964*
- — *American Speech*, p. 306, December 1964: "Lingua cosa nostra"
2 an adulterant used to dilute crack cocaine *US, 1989*
- Max's recipe calls for an "eighth" of cocaine ($\frac{1}{8}$ kilo, or 125 grams), 60 grams of bicarbonate of soda (ordinary baking soda) and 40 grams of "comeback," an adulterant that has allowed Max to double his profits from crack. — Terry Williams, *The Cocaine Kids*, p. 17, 1989
- And like you Gee Money I have also been doing some experimenting and discovered by cutting the caine with comeback we make more product not less. — *New Jack City*, 1990

come back *verb*
to reply to a citizens' band radio broadcast *US, 1976*
- From the opening whistle, he'd be as mad as a redneck truckdriver who'd heard a fag come back on his CB. — Dan Jenkins, *Life Its Ownself*, p. 18, 1984

comeback kid *noun*
a thief who breaks into a hotel room where he has previously stayed, using a key he failed to return *US, 1954*
- A comeback kid was a room-rifler who operated by the simple procedure of checking in and checking right out again the next day but "forgetting" to turn in the room key when he left. — Dev Collans with Stewart Sterling, *I was a House Detective*, p. 11, 1954

come-back money *noun*
in horse racing, money from off-track betting operations that is wired to a race track just before a race *US, 1951*
- — David W. Maurer, *Argot of the Racetrack*, p. 21, 1951

come chugger *noun*
a person who performs oral sex on men *US, 1999*
- He's not a fudgepacker. Cum chugger yes, but not a fudgepacker. — *Cruel Intentions*, 1999

come day, go day; come day, go day, God send Sunday *adjective*
laid back, unruffled *US, 1918*
- "Come day, go day, God send Sunday" is more the motto of the free and go-easy life of the Boyds. — Edward L. Ayers, *Southern Crossing*, p. 19, 1995

comedown *noun*
a person, thing or event that dampens your spirits or depresses you *US*, *1952*
- Well, this is really a comedown. — John Clellon Holmes, *Go*, p. 143, 1952

come down *verb*
1 to experience the easing of drug intoxication *US*, *1959*
- — Burton H. Wolfe, *The Hippies*, p. 203, 1968
- You're high and you need to come down. Sleep it off, Dirk. — *Boogie Nights*, 1997

2 to arrive in prison *US*, *1972*
- You take a lot of guys that when they come down the first or second time to the penitentiary, they come down with a good reputation from the streets[.] — Bruce Jackson, *Outside the Law*, p. 170, 1972

come freak; cum freak *noun*
a person who is obsessed with sex *US*, *1966*
- Maybe I'm turning into a come freak. — Malcolm Braly, *On the Yard*, p. 326, 1967
- — *Current Slang*, p. 19, Fall 1968
- A pimp does not want a promiscuous woman, a "come-freak," who "lives only on the physical plane." — Christina and Richard Milner, *Black Players*, p. 89, 1972
- Body have to be stuck with a mean case of horniness to even think about it in this weather, much less do anything about it. Have to be a stone come-freak. — John Sayles, *Union Dues*, p. 180, 1977

come-fuck-me *adjective*
sexually alluring *US*, *1986*
An embellished **FUCK-ME**.
- Then Paco hears Cathy and Marty-boy leave her apartment (the two of them dressed for a hot day's traveling; Cathy in one of her famous low-cut, summery "come-fuck-me" dresses). — Larry Heinemann, *Paco's Story*, p. 187, 1986
- I buy a pair of shoes like Tiffany's—come-fuck-me shoes—with heels high as candy canes. — Cathi Hanauer, *My Sister's Bones*, p. 24, 1996
- Does Madonna walk around the house in cone bras and come-fuck-me bustiers? — Steven Pressfield, *The War of Art*, p. 86, 2002
- [T]he woman had looked away from her sketch long enough to favor him with a come-fuck-me stare so blatant it allowed for no other interpretation. — David Cray, *Partners*, p. 148, 2004

come gum; cum gum *noun*
chewing gum with a liquid center *US*, *1985*
- — *Maledicta*, p. 284, 1984–1985: "Food names"
- Around the same time, there was a gum designed with a liquid center, so it would squirt fluid in your mouth when you bit into it. It was popularly known among teenagers as ... you guessed it. "Come gum." — museumofhoaxes.com, 14th September 2005

come-in *noun*
in a circus, the hour period before the performance, during which patrons are allowed to enter the big top *US*, *1980*
- — Joe McKennon, *Circus Lingo*, p. 27, 1980

come-off *noun*
an event or result *US*, *1887*
- By this time, the Hotsy Totsy Club "come off," as the hoodlum expression describes such unfortunate occurrences, was making both press and police forget the irritating lack of an arrested culprit[.] — Robert Sylvester, *No Cover Charge*, p. 16, 1956

come-on *noun*
1 a woman who uses her sexuality to induce customers to buy drinks at a bar *US*, *1971*
- A B-girl (also called a "come-on" or "percentage girl" or "drink rustler") often spends six to seven hours in a bar every evening. — Charles Winick, *The Lively Commerce*, p. 171, 1971

2 an invitation, especially unspoken and especially sexual *US*, *1942*
- Can't a man say a woman is attractive without it being a come-on? — *When Harry Met Sally*, 1989
- She had the talent, she had the cool expression on her face, like a good stripper who doesn't overdo it, just gives you enough of a come-on. — Elmore Leonard, *Be Cool*, p. 53, 1999

come on *verb*
1 to demonstrate sexual interest *US*, *1959*
- Now Johnny Rio is not coming on with this queen—although he spoke to her and winked. — John Rechy, *Numbers*, p. 69, 1967
- This fucking pervert just came on to Nance! — *Something About Mary*, 1998
- Some of our customers—wealthy, older men—felt free to come on to us. — Kathryn Leigh Scott, *The Bunny Years*, p. 74, 1998
- But I saw her last week and she was coming on to me all over the place. — Kenneth Lonergan, *This is Our Youth*, p. 34, 2000

2 (of drugs) to start having an effect *US*, *1946*
- I make Koolaid that makes purple Owlsey come on like piss. — *Apocalypse Now*, 1979
- She hung out with me while I was coming on when I had been dosed by what I think was something approaching 3500 mikes[.] — Stephen Gaskin, *Amazing Dope Tales*, p. 115, 1980

come on snake, let's rattle!
let's dance! *US*, *1958*
Teen slang.
- — *San Francisco News*, p. 6, 25th March 1958

come on worm, let's wiggle
let's dance *US*, *1954*
- — *This Week Magazine*, New York Herald Tribune, p. 47, 28th February 1954

come out *verb*
to declare your homosexuality openly or publicly *US*, *1941*
- Not all homosexuals are "gay." That term is applied especially to those who are just "coming out" or acknowledging their membership in a minority group. — Helen P. Branson, *Gay Bar*, p. 9, 1957
- — Donald Webster Cory and John P. LeRoy, *The Homosexual and His Society*, p. 263, 1963: "A lexicon of homosexual slang"
- I was 16 when I really "came out." — Antony James, *America's Homosexual Underground*, p. 110, 1965
- I didn't come out until I left college. — Mart Crowley, *The Boys in the Band*, p. 37, 1968
- When we first "came out" we spent many happy and exciting times in gay bars from one coast to the other. — *Screw*, p. 8, 24th November 1969
- When any male anywhere "comes out" he is faced with the problem of where to find sex partners and/or lovers. — John Francis Hunter, *The Gay Insider*, pp. 5–6, 1971
- "Dig on this: Carol's come out." "Come out of what?" Kate asked, after a pause. "Her tube top?" "Not to joke," Sylvia said. "She's gay." — Cyra McFadden, *The Serial*, p. 88, 1977

comer *noun*
a promising prospect *US*, *1879*
- Bana was twenty-seven and a comer. His foot was on the ladder. — Robert Campbell, *Alice in La-La Land*, p. 195, 1987

come shot; cum shot *noun*
a scene in a pornographic film or a photograph of a man ejaculating *US*, *1972*
- The film [Deep Throat] features a couple of ass-fucking sequences and three come shots, two in that wonderful mouth. — *Screw*, p. 21, 19th June 1972
- What you see now is the "cum shot," and it has become a big item in sexflicks. You can watch his jism jettison, and this removes all doubt that there is anything simulated about this sex scene. — *Adam Film World*, p. 58, 1977
- "You know what a cum shot is?" Sabrina said she did not. Erin explained. "Yukky." — Carl Hiaasen, *Strip Tease*, p. 335, 1993
- What do you want to do about the come shot? We could go to the stock footage, get a close-up. — *Boogie Nights*, 1997

come the revolution
at some unknown point in the future everything will change for the better *US*, *1970*
Not without irony, even at the time.
- "Come the revolution," he went on, "and you report me to the Committee, try to remember that the pressures to conform are tremendous in a small town." — Ethan Morden, *Buddies*, p. 81, 1986
- When disputes erupted, "Come the revolution!" could mean "Later for that—much later." — Todd Gitlin, *The Sixties*, p. 346, 1987

come-through *noun*
in a big store confidence swindle, the stage when the victim learns that he has been swindled and goes after the swindlers *US*, *1997*
- Dakota has to remain behind after we run so she can tell the tale to Tommy and control the come-through. — Stephen Cannell, *Big Con*, p. 193, 1997

come-up *noun*

a robbery *US, 2003*

- In two expletive-laced calls to friends Jan. 5, two days after his arrest, Rawls admitted he knew Ramirez was planning a "come up," which is street slang for a robbery. — *The Oregonian*, p. B2, 10th November 2003

comfy *adjective*

comfortable *UK, 1829*

- His voice in the dark, breathing on her, said, "You comfy?" — Elmore Leonard, *Out of Sight*, p. 40, 1996

comical *adjective*

used as a humorous synonym for "chemical" *US, 1968*

- — Carl Fleischhauer, *A Glossary of Army Slang*, p. 10, 1968

comic strip *noun*

a person with many tattoos *US, 1997*

- — *Los Angeles Times Magazine*, p. 7, 13th July 1997

coming down!; coming through!

used as a warning by a surfer to other surfers that he is starting a ride on a wave *US, 1991*

- — Trevor Cralle, *The Surfin'ary*, p. 23, 1991

coming out party *noun*

discharge from prison *US, 1983*

- — Marlene Freedman, *Alcatraz*, 1983

commando *noun*

a person with rough sexual tastes *US, 1964*

- — Roger Blake, *The American Dictionary of Sexual Terms*, p. 43, 1964

commando *adjective*

▶ **go commando**

to wear no underwear *US, 2001*

Commandos are always ready for action.

- I took my shirt, shoes, and socks off, and clad only in jeans (I'd been going commando all day). — Jack Hart, *Twink*, p. 93, 2001
- "I bet you go commando." Lula and Connie fanned themselves in the backseat. — Janet Evanovich, *To the Nines*, p. 153, 2004

commando style *adverb*

without contraception *US, 2002*

- "You need a condom? Or do you like to fuck your bitches commando style?" — Marty Beckerman, *Generation S.L.U.T.*, p. 158, 2004

commercial *noun*

1 a male homosexual prostitute *US, 1949*

- Commercial—One who is a male prostitute, whether brazenly or discreetly, homosexual or not. — Anon., *The Gay Girl's Guide*, p. 5, 1949
- — Guy Strait, *The Lavender Lexicon*, 1964

2 a sex scene in a pornographic film *US, 1995*

An intentionally misleading term which makes a public discussion about the production of pornography possible without offending those nearby.

- — *Adult Video News*, p. 42, August 1995

commie *noun*

a Communist, literally or approximately *US, 1939*

- I had one, good, efficient, enjoyable way of getting rid of cancerous Commies. I killed them. — Mickey Spillane, *One Lonely Night*, p. 175, 1951
- Now there are no more dirty Japs; there are dirty Commies! — Lenny Bruce, *How to Talk Dirty and Influence People*, p. 17, 1965
- Aunt Sadie, long hair is a commie plot! Long hair gets people uptight—more uptight than ideology, cause long hair is communication. — Jerry Rubin, *Do It!*, p. 93, 1970
- Grenada Island here I come / To save you from the Commie scum. — Sandee Johnson, *Cadences: The Jody Call Book, No. 2*, p. 146, 1986

commish *noun*

a *Commiss*ioner *US, 1910*

- "Commish," he pleaded, "don't get us wrong.["] — Harry J. Anslinger, *The Murderers*, p. 101, 1961

commissary punk *noun*

a male prisoner who engages in homosexual activity in return for goods bought at the prison commissary *US, 1972*

- Bob had become a commissary punk, a boy literally bought by a wealthy convict for the extra food and few luxuries he's able to provide. — Malcolm Braley, *False Starts*, p. 105, 1976

committee joint *noun*

a honest carnival concession or game *US, 2005*

- A half-dozen "Committee Joints"—honest, straightforward games like the Milk Bottle Throw or Ring Toss, operated by local civic groups—completed the midway. — Peter Fenton, *Eyeing the Flash*, p. 133, 2005

commo *noun*

a military radio; communications *US, 1964*

- "While we were on the attack my commo (radio) went out," said one soldier to a center observer. "Then by a miracle, I got my commo back." — *Houston Chronicle*, p. 4A, 20th March 1989

commo wire *noun*

electrical wire used for a wide variety of tasks *US, 1986*

- Jones (Jonesy for short, James) had thirty-nine pairs of blackened, leathery, wrinkly ears strung on a bit of black commo wire and wrapped like a garland around that bit of turned-out brim of his steel hat. — Larry Heinemann, *Paco's Story*, p. 7, 1986

community chest *noun*

a sexually available girl *US, 1968*

- Boys look down on a "community chest," meaning a promiscuous girl. — Joe David Brown, *Sex in the '60s*, p. 19, 1968

commute *verb*

to take DMT, a short-lasting hallucinogen *US, 1970*

- — William D. Alsever, *Glossary for the Establishment and Other Uptight People*, p. 9, December 1970

comp *noun*

a *comp*limentary benefit given to valued customers *US, 1977*

- Comps, the giving away of food, rooms, drink, girls, free airplane tickets, and show entertainment, started in Vegas in the 1940s. — Mario Puzo, *Inside Las Vegas*, p. 285, 1977
- "You're gonna be a comp." "Yeah? What's that, Vincent, a comp?" "Like the champagne, a gift. You're gonna get handed out, passed around." — Elmore Leonard, *Glitz*, p. 77, 1985

comp *verb*

1 to issue something on a *comp*limentary basis *US, 1961*

- This is the end result of all the bright lights and the comped trips[.] — *Casino*, 1995
- I play long enough and hard enough to get a comped room and put food in my stomach. — *Hard Eight*, 1996

2 to accompany someone musically *US, 1949*

- — Robert S. Gold, *A Jazz Lexicon*, p. 63, 1964

compa *noun*

a very close friend *US, 1974*

Border Spanish used in English conversation by Mexican-Americans; from the more formal *compadre* (godfather to one's child).

- — Dagoberto Fuentes and Jose Lopez, *Barrio Language Dictionary*, p. 33, 1974

compadre *noun*

a close and trusted male friend *US, 1833*

From the Spanish word (the godfather of your child).

- [T]he slim blond boy continued to run like a streak toward his friends, his long lost compadres, his School pals. — James Patterson, *When the Wind Blows*, p. 340, 1998

company *noun*

sex *US, 1991*

Used as a euphemism by prostitutes soliciting customers.

- — William T. Vollman, *Whores for Gloria*, p. 139, 1991

company girl *noun*

a prostitute hired to enliven a corporate event or outing *US, 1960*

- Whores are now "call girls," "party girls" or "company girls." Instead of visiting them, they come to see you. — Lee Mortimer, *Women Confidential*, p. 140, 1960

company patsy *noun*

the person within an organization who is blamed for everything that goes wrong *US, 1973*

- — Sherman Louis Sergel, *The Language of Show Biz*, p. 56, 1973

comp list *noun*

a list kept at the door of a club or concert, identifying those who are to be admitted free of charge *US, 1999*

- Chili was on his way in, waiting for the doorman to find his name on the comp list, as Hy Gordon was coming out and they stopped to say hello. — Elmore Leonard, *Be Cool*, p. 51, 1999

comprende?
do you understand? *US, 1994*
Spanish used by English speakers without regard to their fluency in Spanish, and with multiple variations reflecting their lack of fluency.
- Fuck with me, bitch, even a little bit, even a little bit, you're gonna get accidentally shot! Comprende? — *Natural Born Killers*, 1994

comps *noun*
comprehensive college examinations *US, 1961*
- I spent most of my time boning up for my final examination, the "comps." — Clancy Sigal, *Going Away*, p. 407, 1961

compute *verb*
to make sense *US, 1964*
Almost always heard in the negative—"does not compute." Popularized in the 1960s television situation comedy *My Living Doll*, in which the robotic character played by Julie Newmar would respond to anything that she did not understand by saying "That does not compute."
- Because good news does not compute for me right now. — Anna Quindlen, *One True Thing*, p. 151, 1994
- On the very next page, we find out that in the 71 days since combat operations ended in Iraq, 77 American soldiers have died. This does not compute! [Letter to Editor] — *Times Herald (Port Huron, Michigan)*, p. 9AQ, 18th July 2003

computer geek *noun*
a person whose life is centered around computers to the exclusion of all other outlets *US, 1991*
- — Eric S. Raymond, *The New Hacker's Dictionary*, p. 102, 1991

computer nerd *noun*
a student whose enthusiasm for computers has interfered with the development of a well-rounded personality *US, 1985*
- I'm not at all impressed by those movies about computer nerds in high school who triumph in some improbable way over the jocks[.] — *Washington Post (reprinted from The Nation)*, p. C5, 22nd December 1985

compy?
do you understand? *US, 1947*
A complete corruption of the French or Spanish.
- — Marcus Hanna Boulware, *Jive and Slang of Students in Negro Colleges*, 1947

comrat *noun*
a political liberal *US, 1951*
A derogatory play on the communist use of the term "comrade."
- The Nat'l Lawyers Guild (listed as a commy front by the Cong-probers) is trying to find some way to intervene in the proceedings against the comrats by the McCarran Act. — *San Francisco Call-Bulletin*, p. 11, 12th June 1951

comred *noun*
a political liberal *US, 1953*
A play on the term "comrade."
- What this cultural group did not select is an ex-Commy such as Chambers, Budenz, Bentley, Rushmore and other one-time Reds, who proved their loyalty to the U.S. by publicly named comreds. — *San Francisco Call-Bulletin*, p. 60, 3rd February 1953

comsymp *noun*
a liberal; a communist sympathizer *US, 1964*
- Therefore, the defeat of that proposal put forward by those wild-eyed comsymps in Welfare, due to come before the board at Monday's meeting, was the big skyhook[.] — Robert Gover, *Here Goes Kitten*, p. 91, 1964

con *noun*
1 a convict or ex-convict *US, 1888*
- Shortie was a con and he was more than anxious to stay away from murder. — Mickey Spillane, *My Gun is Quick*, p. 57, 1950
- I listen to the other cons making with the patter—kidding each other about the great things they're going to do to celebrate release. — Colin Johnson, *Wild Cat Falling*, p. 4, 1965
- I was astonished to see the old grizzled cons playing marbles. — Eldridge Cleaver, *Soul on Ice*, p. 43, 1968

- In the recreation room there were some fifty gas ranges that cons used to cook on. — A.S. Jackson, *Gentleman Pimp*, p. 128, 1973

2 a convention *US, 1978*
Especially popular among fans of science fiction and comic books.
- — *American Speech*, p. 53, Spring 1978: "Star Trek lives: trekker slang"
- I swear—the next con I attend and they ask me to be on the minority panel, if I see your name anywhere near the list, I'm passing. — *Chasing Amy*, 1997

con *verb*
to subject someone to a *con*fidence trick; to dupe the victim of a criminal enterprise *US, 1892*
- He's been associated with race tracks and track people and had a great deal of school difficulties. He was quite proficient in "conning" people. — *San Francisco News*, p. 4, 5th June 1959
- But you better try and try hard. And don't try to con the parole board. — *San Francisco Chronicle*, p. 36, 16th April 1966
- She was going to con a con man. Ha! — Edwin Torres, *Carlito's Way*, p. 36, 1975

Con-Air *noun*
any airplane flown by the federal Bureau of Prisons to transport prisoners *US, 1996*
- — Reinhold Aman, *Hillary Clinton's Pen Pal*, p. 25, 1996

con artist *noun*
a skilled confidence swindler *US, 1937*
- Every con artist that has ever lived had to gain the mark's confidence during the scam. — Dennis M. Marlock, *How to Become a Professional Con Artist*, p. 34, 2001

con-con *noun*
the residue that remains after smoking freebase cocaine *US, 1992*
- — Terry Williams, *Crackhouse*, p. 147, 1992

concrete overcoat *noun*
the covering of a corpse with concrete to facilitate its disposal in a body of water *US, 1971*
- I see a few wrinkles in this scheme now (the words "concrete overcoat" come to mind), but I did not then. — Joan Didion, *The White Album*, p. 182, 1979

concrete overshoes *noun*
concrete poured around a person or body's feet to facilitate disposal in a body of water *US, 1976*
- We guessed that most of them were where you couldn't see them, at the bottom of Lake Michigan, wearing concrete overshoes. — Richard Peck, *A Long Way from Chicago*, p. 1, 1998

condom *noun*
1 in computing, the plastic bag that protects a 3.5 inch disk *US, 1991*
- — Eric S. Raymond, *The New Hacker's Dictionary*, p. 103, 1991
2 in pool, a removable rubber sleeve for a cue stick *US, 1993*
- — Mike Shamos, *The Illustrated Encyclopedia of Billiards*, p. 56, 1993

condominiums *noun*
in bar dice games, a roll from the cup in which some dice are stacked on top of others, invalidating the roll *US, 1976*
- — Gil Jacobs, *The World's Best Dice Games*, p. 201, 1976

conductor *noun*
the second active participant in serial sex with a single passive partner *US, 1975*
From PULL A TRAIN (serial sex).
- Carolina Moon announced that she was going to take her blanket into the bushes and pull the train. "I'm first! I'm the engineer!" cried Harold Bloomguard. "I'm second! I'm conductor!" cried Spencer Van Moot. — Joseph Wambaugh, *The Choirboys*, p. 333, 1975

cone *noun*
a socially inept person *US, 1990*
An abbreviation of CONEHEAD.
- — Elena Garcia, *A Beginner's Guide to Zen and the Art of Snowboarding*, p. 121, 1990

▸ **give cone**
to perform oral sex *US, 1982*
- — Mimi Pond, *The Valley Girl's Guide to Life*, p. 57, 1982

conehead *noun*
a socially inept person *US, 1990*
From a recurring skit on *Saturday Night Live*, first appearing in 1983; Dan Ackroyd played alien Beldar Conehead and Jane Curtin his wife Prymaat.
- — Elena Garcia, *A Beginner's Guide to Zen and the Art of Snowboarding*, p. 121, 1990

Coney Island *noun*
any room in a police station where suspected criminals are forcefully interrogated *US, 1949*
- — Vincent J. Monteleone, *Criminal Slang*, p. 57, 1949
- — Hyman E. Goldin et al., *Dictionary of American Underworld Lingo*, p. 47, 1950

Coney Island whitefish *noun*
a used condom *US, 1984*
The most prominent use of the term is probably in the title of the 1979 Aerosmith song "Bone to Bone (Coney Island White Fish Boy)."
- Abrams spotted a flaccid rubber sheath that in his youth had been called a Coney Island whitefish. — Nelson DeMille, *The Talbot Odyssey*, p. 346, 1984
- Coney Island also gave its name, probably in the 1930s, to the Coney-Island whitefish, a used condom floating in the water at the bathing beach—a common sight then and now. — Irving Lewis Allen, *The City in Slang*, p. 102, 1993
- I recall how surfers objected to sharing their waves with the schools of "Coney Island whitefish," the name we gave used condoms that drifted east, along Long Island's South Shore, from the city sewer system. — Russell Drumm, *In the Slick of the Cricket*, p. 212, 1997
- In Brooklyn, in what many people have been taught by crack journalists to call "a more innocent time," floating condoms were often called "Coney Island whitefish." — Gilbert Sorrentino, *Little Casino*, p. 35, 2002

conference *noun*
a poker game *US, 1988*
An intentionally misleading euphemism.
- — George Percy, *The Language of Poker*, p. 24, 1988

confidencer *verb*
an electronic device that screens out background noise from a telephone mouthpiece *US, 1985*
- — M. Allen Henderson, *How Con Games Work*, p. 219, 1985

congrats *noun*
congratulations *UK, 1894*
- This one's received with no fanfare or congrats. — Josh Alan Friedman, *Tales of Times Square*, p. 122, 1986

conk *verb*
1 to straighten hair using any number of chemical processes *US, 1935*
- The face of a colored youth with slick conked hair and beardless cheeks stared up. — Chester Himes, *The Real Cool Killers*, p. 25, 1959
- Everybody understood that my head had to stay kinky a while longer, to grow long enough for Shorty to conk it for me. — Malcolm X and Alex Haley, *The Autobiography of Malcolm X*, p. 51, 1964
- He had his hair conked, but around his ears and at the nape of his neck were the hard, tight burrs he wanted so much to hide. — Nathan Heard, *Howard Street*, p. 86, 1968
- Then you had a pimp name of Red Conk on account of he conked his hair red (hair was straight in them days one way or other—Dixie Peach or Sulfur 8). — Edwin Torres, *Carlito's Way*, p. 13, 1975

2 to kill someone *US, 1918*
- He was yellow. That's what caused him to get conked. — Horace McCoy, *Kiss Tomorrow Good-bye*, p. 41, 1948

conk; konk *noun*
1 the head *US, 1870*
- The halo that started to shape up around my conk was so big and bright, I felt like an overgrown glow-worm. — Mezz Mezzrow, *Really the Blues*, p. 89, 1946

2 a hairstyle in which naturally curly hair is chemically straightened; hence, the hair straightening process; the chemical preparation required *US, 1942*
- Even the solid cats in their pancho conks didn't ruffle me. — Chester Himes, *If He Hollers Let Him Go*, p. 43, 1945
- I couldn't get over marveling at how their hair was straight and shiny like white men's hair; Ella told me this was called a "conk." — Malcolm X and Alex Haley, *The Autobiography of Malcolm X*, p. 43, 1964

- He'd drop by the school and be vined down. He was clean, Jim. Had him a conk then and he knew he was ready. — H. Rap Brown, *Die Nigger Die!*, p. 24, 1969
- I went to a barber shop way up in the wilds of the South Bronx, recommended by some walking exponents of one hair-straightening process known as the "konk." — Piri Thomas, *Stories from El Barrio*, p. 50, 1978

conkbuster *verb*
inexpensive, potent whiskey *US, 1947*
- — Marcus Hanna Boulware, *Jive and Slang of Students in Negro Colleges*, 1947

conk out; konk out; clonk out *verb*
to fall asleep; to pass out; to stop operating *UK, 1917*
- I don't conk out on grape! — Dan Burley, *Diggeth Thou?*, p. 34, 1959
- The Plymouth conked out on La Brea avenue, and we had to take three buses out to Boyle Heights. — Clancy Sigal, *Going Away*, p. 65, 1961
- He just crawled into the back seat, said "West 45th Street," and conked out. — *Taxi Driver*, 1976
- At this point Iris lay back in her chair and konked out on him. He could slap her face all he wanted, throw water in it, hold her under the shower—he could see she wasn't about to come around for the rest of the night. — Elmore Leonard, *Glitz*, p. 190, 1985

con merchant *noun*
a confidence swindler *US, 1959*
- In short, since a con merchant must swindle his clients under those circumstances where clients appreciate that a confidence game could be employed, the con man must forestall the immediate impression that he might be what in fact he is. — Erving Goffman, *The Presentation of Self in Everyday Life*, p. 225, 1959

connect *noun*
a connection from which an illicit substance may be obtained; a drug dealer *US, 1960*
- The connect ain't come through the last week, and the Man's downtown. — Clarence Cooper Jr., *The Scene*, p. 23, 1960
- "If my connect gets the wire I gave his name to somebody," he said, "splittin' aint going to help me none." — Charles W. Moore, *A Brick for Mister Jones*, p. 34, 1975
- The price is going up, because the connect wants thirty [$30,000] for each [kilo] package, and I got to make at least ten on each package for myself. — Terry Williams, *The Cocaine Kids*, p. 34, 1989
- Because it's my connect. I'm providing the connect. — Kenneth Lonergan, *This is Our Youth*, p. 37, 2000

connect *verb*
to make a sexual conquest *US, 1985*
- — *American Speech*, p. 19, Spring 1985: "The language of singles bars"

connected *adjective*
associated with, if not a formal part of, organized crime *US, 1968*
- [O]ne day he comes up to me and says there are these guys out on Long Island who asked him if he was connected, meaning mobbed up. — Peter Maas, *The Valachi Papers*, p. 140, 1968
- You can't print me. I'm, a connected guy. — Edwin Torres, *Q & A*, p. 157, 1977
- No, I never heard that name. He could be connected, but I can tell you he's not family. — Elmore Leonard, *Killshot*, p. 230, 1989

connection *noun*
1 a drug dealer; a drug deal *US, 1928*
- "I need a jolt," one addict might remark. "I gotta see my connection." — William J. Spillard and Pence James, *Needle in a Haystack*, p. 148, 1945
- I drank all day in a wild poolhall-bar-restaurant-saloon two-part joint, also got burned for a fin (Mexican, 5 pesos, 60 cents) by a connection. — Jack Kerouac, *Letter to Neal and Carolyn Cassady*, p. 359, 27th May 1952
- I'd better go see my connection. — Piri Thomas, *Down These Mean Streets*, p. 203, 1967
- Is there a connection around, man? I have to cop. I'm alright, but my old lady is getting sick. — Herbert Huncke, *The Evening Sun Turned Crimson*, p. 72, 1980

2 a sexual partner *US, 1985*
- — *American Speech*, p. 19, Spring 1985: "The language of singles bars"

connections *noun*
in horse racing, a horse's owner, trainer and the trainer's assistants *US, 1960*
- — Robert Saunders Dowst and Jay Craig, *Playing the Races*, p. 161, 1960

connectors *noun*
in poker, several sequenced cards that might be improved to a five-card sequenced straight *US, 1990*
- — Anthony Holden, *Big Deal*, p. 299, 1990

conneroo *noun*
a confidence swindler *US, 1949*
- Glenn made Jack feel as he had around his stepfather—a master barroom conneroo who would afterwards deride those who always stood him a drink[.] — Earl Thompson, *Tattoo*, p. 227, 1974

Connie's army *noun*
the flotilla of supporters of the racing yacht *Constellation* in the 1962 America Cup races *US, 1964*
An obvious allusion to "Arnie's army."
- "Connie's Army," the spectator fleet which stayed close to the leading Constellation, affected both boats with their wakes and the British were informed that the Coast Guard would study how to remedy the situation today. — *San Francisco News Call-Bulletin*, p. 56, 19th September 1964

cons *verb*
in computing, to add an item to a list *US, 1983*
- — Guy L. Steele et al., *The Hacker's Dictionary*, p. 48, 1983

con safos
used as a warning not to deface the writer's grafitti *US, 1970*
In Spanish, literally means "with safety."
- Of course at the bottom of the wall was the inevitable "CON SAFOS," the crucial gang incantation not to be found in any Spanish dictionary[.] — Joseph Wambaugh, *The New Centurions*, p. 105, 1970

consig *noun*
in an organized crime enterprise, a trusted adviser *US, 1985*
Shortened from the Italian *consigliore*.
- Now they say he's like an honorary consig, a counsellor, reactivated while Sale's doing his two years. — Elmore Leonard, *Glitz*, p. 170, 1985

constipated *adjective*
in tiddlywinks, said of a position in which your winks are tied down and useless *US, 1977*
- — *Verbatim*, p. 525, December 1977

constitutional *noun*
a drug addict's first injection of the day *US, 1959*
- — J.E. Schmidt, *Narcotics Lingo and Lore*, p. 33, 1959

contact *noun*
a reliable source for something, especially drugs *US, 1966*
- — J. L. Simmons and Barry Winograd, *It's Happening*, p. 168, 1966

contact high *noun*
a vicarious, sympathetic experience caused by witnessing another person's drug-induced experience *US, 1955*
- — J. L. Simmons and Barry Winograd, *It's Happening*, p. 168, 1966
- — Edward R. Bloomquist, *Marijuana*, p. 157, 1968

content-free *adjective*
said of a computer message that adds nothing to the substance of a discussion or to the reader's knowledge *US, 1991*
- Though this adjective is sometimes applied to flamage, it more usually connotes derision for communication styles that exalt from over substance or are centered on concerns irrelevant to the subject ostensibly at hand. — Eric S. Raymond, *The New Hacker's Dictionary*, p. 104, 1991

contour *adverb*
(used of an aircraft) at treetop level *US, 1988*
- There would be no warning beyond a minute or two if the pilots flew "contour"—that is, at treetop level—for the last few miles, which they did whenever they could. — Neil Sheehan, *A Bright Shining Lie*, p. 74, 1988

contract *noun*
1 an order to kill someone or a reward offered to anyone who kills the target *US, 1941*
- — *American Speech*, p. 306, December 1964: "Lingua cosa nostra"
- "We'll let a contract out on him," Teddybear says. (The Haight thinks gangsters talk this way.) — Nicholas Von Hoffman, *We Are The People Our Parents Warned Us Against*, p. 45, 1967

- "I told him the whole story. 'Look, kid,' he told me, 'your name's in the hat for what you did. New Jersey wants to whack you out and Jerry's got the contract.'" — Vincent Teresa, *My Life in the Mafia*, p. 107, 1973

2 a promise made by one police officer to do a favor for another *US, 1958*
- — *New York Times Magazine*, p. 87, 16th March 1958

control C *verb*
to stop what it is that you are doing *US, 1991*
A borrowing from the command used on many computer operating systems to interrupt a program.
- — Eric S. Raymond, *The New Hacker's Dictionary*, p. 105, 1991

control freak *noun*
a person with an obsessive need to control people and events *US, 1977*
- You know that, Mike? You're a maniac control freak. — *The Deer Hunter*, 1978
- Oh, so that was it. Control freak. — Francesca Lia Block, *I Was a Teenage Fairy*, p. 77, 1998
- And why worry about the ending anyway? Why be such a control freak? — Stephen King, *On Writing*, p. 161, 2000
- John McGraw, obsessive control freak that he was, reviewed the hotel dinner checks to see what his players were eating. — Bill James, *The New Bill James Historical Baseball Abstract*, p. 426, 2001

controller *noun*
a mid-level operative in an illegal gambling enterprise who is in charge of a number of runners *US, 1964*
- A controller might have as many as fifty runners working for him, and the controller got five percent of what he turned over to the banker. — Malcolm X and Alex Haley, *The Autobiography of Malcolm X*, p. 85, 1964
- A lot of the junkies started sticking up the numbers writers and sticking up the controllers. — Claude Brown, *Manchild in the Promised Land*, p. 191, 1965
- A banker usually has working for him several "controllers," each of whom in turn controls a number of runners. — *The Knapp Commission Report on Police Corruption*, p. 79, 1972
- Then you got to be an administrator; then you got labor problems—what controller is humpin' what runner's wife. — Edwin Torres, *Carlito's Way*, p. 30, 1975

control O *verb*
to stop talking *US, 1991*
From the character used on some computer operating systems to abort output but allow the program to keep on running. Generally means that you are not interested in hearing anything more from that person, at least on that topic.
- — Eric S. Raymond, *The New Hacker's Dictionary*, p. 105, 1991

convict *noun*
in circus usage, a zebra *US, 1926*
An allusion to the zebra's striped coat, evocative of a prison uniform.
- — Don Wilmeth, *The Language of American Popular Entertainment*, p. 63, 1981

convincer *noun*
1 the stage in a confidence swindle when the victim is fully committed to the scheme *US, 1940*
- White grifters call it the convincer. When con is played for money alone, it's that point at which the sucker is hooked or convinced by actual or paper profits that he can reap a bonanza. — Iceberg Slim (Robert Beck), *Trick Baby*, p. 55, 1969

2 a weapon *US, 1979*
- "That's a holster," I explain. "With a little convincer tucked in." — Leo Rosten, *Silky!*, p. 54, 1979

con wise *adjective*
extremely sophisticated in the ways of the world based on lessons learned in prison *US, 1912*
- Why didn't he tell his jailers about this? He was an ex-con. No con-wise con squeals. — *San Francisco Examiner*, p. 4 (II), 4th August 1957
- Hence, expressions among the "con-wise" as, "Do your own time," meaning stay clear of another's tension. — Neal Cassady, *Grace Beats Karma*, p. 42, 20th August 1958: Letter to Carolyn Cassady
- He's con wise, told me what I already know. — Gerald Petievich, *Money Men*, p. 56, 1981

cooch *noun*
the vagina; sex with a woman *US, 2001*

- There are plenty of queer women who work as porn stars, strippers, and sex workers, but there are a lot fewer of us willing to fork over cash for cooch. — *The Village Voice*, 7th August 2001
- [T]he classic scene were Jen pets Gina's cooch and diddles her dingle really hits the nail on the head. — Mr. Skin, *Mr. Skin's Skincyclopedia*, p. 202, 2005
- Janine presses her breasts against her reflection in the mirror, working a vibe in and out of her cooch. — Editors of Adult Video News, *The AVN Guide to the 500 Greatest Adult Films of All Time*, p. 111, 2005

coocher *noun*
a sexually suggestive dancer *US*, 1927

- [I]mmediately after each coarse coocher has given her exhibition, your waitress solicits you for her. — Jack Lait and Lee Mortimer, *Chicago Confidential*, p. 60, 1950
- Coochers is the term applied to the solo dancers. It derives from hootchee cootchee, a descriptive label traced to Little Egypt's belly dancing at the 1893 Chicago World's Fair. — William Green, *Strippers and Coochers*, p. 161, 1977

coochie *noun*
the vagina; sex with a woman; a woman as a sex object *US*, 1999

- She ain't giving up no coochie. — *A2Z*, p. 22, 1995
- So what you had your little coochie in your dad's mouth? — Eminem (Marshall Mathers), *My Fault*, 1999
- There are '80s goths and foppish glam boys and women dressed like schoolgirls and schoolgirls dressed like hookers and endless Lil' Kim coochies in blond wigs and crop-tops that bear obtuse English phrases like "Sexy Kitty" or "Culture Style" and their eyes are manga wide and their make-up is as thick and as solid as cement. — Patrick Neate, *Where You're At*, p. 50, 2003

coochie block *verb*
to thwart a person's attempt to seduce someone *US*, 1999

- "What did I do?" "Always coochie blocking." "I do not coochie block." — Eric Jerome Dickey, *Cheaters*, p. 292, 1999

cook *noun*
a musician who plays with great passion and energy *US*, 1962

- — Robert S. Gold, *A Jazz Lexicon*, p. 65, 1964

cook *verb*
1 to melt a powdered narcotic, especially heroin, in water, prior to injecting or inhaling *US*, 1952
The drug is "cooked up" and "cooked down."

- Angel watched him begin preparations again and didn't move until all six caps were in the spoon, ready to be cooked. — Hal Ellson, *The Golden Spike*, p. 7, 1952
- I finally got enough to get me a ten-dollar bag. I came home and cooked my stuff. — Claude Brown, *Manchild in the Promised Land*, p. 259, 1965
- So cook me up when you're good and ready / And you won't remember if you're Johnnie or Eddie. — Dennis Wepman et al., *The Life*, p. 171, 1976
- Hey, man, gimme something cooked! — *The Bad Lieutenant*, 1992

2 to boil dynamite to extract nitroglycerine *US*, 1992

- — Jay Robert Nash, *Dictionary of Crime*, p. 79, 1992

3 to prepare crack cocaine, heating a mixture of cocaine, lidocaine, baking soda, and other chemicals to remove the hydrochloride *US*, 1992

- — Terry Williams, *Crackhouse*, p. 147, 1992

4 to excel; to excite people *US*, 1942

- You're cooking when you can play everything that jumps into your mind. — Nat Hentoff, *Jazz Country*, p. 25, 1965
- I got there at 1 P.M. and he took me down in the basement and staked me in the game. Between shows all that day, I really "cooked." — Babs Gonzales, *I Paid My Dues*, p. 28, 1967
- The boys proved once again this week that they can cook in the South and especially North Carolina. (From "Summer Tour News," 7/14/91). — Scott Meyer, *Deadhead Forever*, 2001

5 to execute someone by electrocution *US*, 1932

- [H]e was still going to cook in the hot squat up the river. — Mickey Spillane, *Kiss Me Deadly*, p. 139, 1952
- I think most of the guys my age looked upon them as heroes when they were getting cooked at Sing Sing. — Claude Brown, *Manchild in the Promised Land*, p. 220, 1965

▸ cook on the front burner
to excel; to go fast *US*, 1956

- — *American Speech*, p. 227, October 1956: "More United States Air Force slang"

▸ cook with gas
to perform successfully, especially after a period of trying and failing; to do very well *US*, 1941

- — Lou Shelly, *Hepcats Jive Talk Dictionary*, 1945
- He goes to the jukery to watch and wait and cut a rug with a solid gate he snatches a quail with hep and class and they go to town cooking with gas! — Harry Haenigsen, *Jive's Like That*, 1947

▸ cook your goose
to drink to the point of being drunk *US*, 1964

- — R. Frederick West, *God's Gambler*, p. 223, 1964

cookbook *noun*
in computing, a book of code segments that can be used to enhance programs *US*, 1991

- Cookbooks, slavishly followed, can lead one into voodoo programing, but are useful for hackers trying to monkey up small programs in unknown languages. — Eric S. Raymond, *The New Hacker's Dictionary*, p. 105, 1991

cooked *adjective*
1 in trouble *US*, 1956

- When I saw who was on the bench I knew I was cooked. — Billie Holiday, *Lady Sings the Blues*, p. 26, 1956
- I knew she would soon make her choice and I would be cooked for good and all. — Max Shulman, *I was a Teen-Age Dwarf*, p. 28, 1959

2 embalmed *US*, 1986–1987

- — *Maledicta*, p. 180, Summer/Winter 1986–1987: "Sexual slang: prostitutes, pedophiles, flagellators, transvestites, and necrophiles"

cooker *noun*
1 in an illegal drug enterprise, a person who tests the purity of a drug *US*, 1967

- His father was a "cooker"—a tester who finds out how pure the imported heroin is before it gets distributed to dealers. — John Gimenez, *Up Tight!*, p. 50, 1967

2 any object used to heat heroin preparatory to injecting it *US*, 1958

- The cookers are metal caps off wine bottles with the cork lining taken out. — Willard Motley, *Let No Man Write My Epitaph*, p. 157, 1958
- A gland in his neck was making the ducts in his mouth water at the thought of drugs: cooker, matches, needle, eye-dropper, and pacifier. — Clarence Cooper Jr., *The Scene*, p. 15, 1960
- When he awakes in the morning, he reaches instantly for his "works"—eyedropper, needle ("spike," he calls it), and bottle top ("cooker"). — James Mills, *The Panic in Needle Park*, p. 14, 1966
- Joe Green, better known to his friends and acquaintances as Jo-Jo, poured the rest of the heroin out of a small piece of tin foil into the Wild Irish Rose wine bottle top that had been converted into what drug users call a cooker. — Donald Goines, *Crime Partners*, p. 7, 1978

3 a person who prepares crack cocaine *US*, 1992

- — Terry Williams, *Crackhouse*, p. 147, 1992

4 a person or thing that excels or excites *US*, 1943

- Baby, this is Bernie, Bernie is a real heavy cooker on piano. — Ross Russell, *The Sound*, p. 190, 1961

cookie *noun*
1 a person *US*, 1917

- There's your answer. He's a smart cookie. — Horace McCoy, *Kiss Tomorrow Good-bye*, p. 207, 1948
- When that girl comes back she be one mad cookie, you bet! — Mickey Spillane, *One Lonely Night*, p. 146, 1951
- He was a sharp cookie, West, and Miller was just as sharp[.] — Evan Hunter, *The Blackboard Jungle*, p. 64, 1954
- Now the smart cookies line up their weekend dates on Thursdays, at the latest. — Frederick Kohner, *The Affairs of Gidget*, p. 55, 1963

2 the vagina *US*, 1970

- — Clarence Major, *Dictionary of Afro-American Slang*, p. 40, 1970
- I promise you, kiddo, if you can't get a boner, I'll let you cop a feel of my cookie. — Thomas Sanchez, *The Zoot Suit Murders*, p. 58, 1978

3 a material reward or inducement; money *US*, 1973

- Cookies are the prizes to be won in a game, and the term usually refers to money. — Christina and Richard Milner, *Black Players*, p. 48, 1972
- Now that you're on the streets, you'll need cookies in your kick [wallet], and always try to keep some there. — A.S. Jackson, *Gentleman Pimp*, p. 30, 1973

4 a large chunk of processed crack cocaine *US, 1993*
- Cocaine had to be turned into what we called a cookie. Then you could break it off and sell it as rocks. — *Menace II Society*, 1993
- I didn't even let the crack cookies dry. — 50 Cent, *From Pieces to Weight*, p. 52, 2005

5 a file that an Internet webpage leaves on the hard drive of a user's computer, that is retrieved whenever the user returns to that webpage *US, 1993*
- — Eric S. Raymond, *The New Hacker's Dictionary*, p. 117, 1993
- — Andy Ihnatko, *Cyberspeak*, p. 40, 1997

6 a blood clot traveling through the arteries *US, 1994*
- — Sally Williams, *"Strong" Words*, p. 137, 1994

7 in television and movie-making, a light screen designed to cast shadows *US, 1990*
- — Ralph S. Singleton, *Filmmaker's Dictionary*, p. 91, 1990

▸ **get your cookies**
to experience pleasure, especially in a perverted way *US, 1956*
- A fart smeller, way over in the corner, grabbed them, started sniffing, getting his cookies. — Steve Cannon, *Groove, Bang, and Jive Around*, p. 71, 1969

▸ **that's the way the cookie crumbles**
that's how things turn out *US, 1955*
- — *Independent Record* (Helena, Montana), 27th November 1955
- "How do the kids say it?" Sam continued to pat his daughter's hand; how beautiful she was in sadness! "That's the way the cookie crumbles?" — Irving Shulman, *College Confidential*, p. 168, 1960
- Well, you know what they say, that's the way the cookie crumbles sometimes. — Odie Hawkins, *Ghetto Sketches*, p. 179, 1972
- [I]f the conversation happens to turn to gossip about sex in the office, well, that's the way the cookie crumbles. — Michael Crichton, *Disclosure*, p. 223, 1993

cookie cop *noun*
a private security officer *US, 2004*
- Then up popped two swoll cookie cops. I mean, they were just fat old security guys and not real police with guns and stuff. — Linden Dalecki, *Kid B*, p. 108, 2006

cookie cutter *noun*
in circus and carnival usage, a police badge *US, 1926*
- — Don Wilmeth, *The Language of American Popular Entertainment*, p. 63, 1981

cookie duster *noun*
a mustache *US, 1930*
- One's ten, the other's four and half, living up there with their mom and a real estate man she married name of Gary, has a little cookie-duster mustache. — Elmore Leonard, *Riding the Rap*, p. 9, 1995

cookies *noun*
the contents of a person's stomach *US, 1927*
- "You can lose your cookies later." — Christopher Lane, *Tonopah*, p. 370, 1999
- The body's response to fear is simple: fight or flight. Either lose your cookies while scampering off to safety, or hope to find an incontinence pad before being embarrassed to death[.] — Karen Moline, *No Parachutes [Tart Noir]*, p. 49, 2002

▸ **blow your cookies**
to vomit *US, 1976*
- My lunch—a tahini-and-bean-sprout pita—came back into my throat, and I practically blew my cookies all over my calendar. — Rita Ciresi, *Pink Slip*, p. 54, 1999

▸ **pop your cookies**
to vomit *US, 1960*
- "Popped my cookies!" he congratulated himself, awe-struck by ihs deed. "Flashed the old hash all over Twenny-second." — Nelson Algren, *The Neon Wilderness*, p. 164, 1960

▸ **toss your cookies**
to vomit *US, 1941*
Children's vocabulary.
- The cab I had was a real old one that smelled like someone'd just tossed his cookies in it. — J.D. Salinger, *Catcher in the Rye*, p. 81, 1951
- — Collin Baker et al., *College Undergraduate Slang Study Conducted at Brown University*, p. 99, 1968

cooking *adjective*
1 in shuffleboard, used for communicating the fact that a disk is in the kitchen *US, 1967*
- — Omero C. Catan, *Secrets of Shuffleboard Strategy*, p. 65, 1967
2 (used of surf conditions) excellent *US, 1977*
- — Gary Fairmont R. Filosa II, *The Surfer's Almanac*, p. 183, 1977

cook off *verb*
(used of ammunition) to explode because of heat from a surrounding fire *US, 1985*
- The mortar bomb was just an illumination round, though, a flare that had finally cooked off in the heat. — David Donovan, *Once a Warrior King*, p. 75, 1985

cooks and bakers *noun*
any and all military support personnel *US, 1921*
- "Cooks and bakers," the battalion XO in the operations clerk called them, a mixture of clerk-typists, supply workers, mail clerks,and stranded combat marines[.] — Robert A. Anderson, *Cooks & Bakers*, p. 168, 1982

cook up *verb*
1 to concoct something; to fabricate something; to falsify something *UK, 1817*
Often in the form "cook up a story."
- "What you got cooked up?" he asked. — Chester Gould, *Dick Tracy Meets the Night Crawler*, p. 168, 1945
- The Man be cooking up the conspiracies again, but the sentences are gonna be a motherfucker—I ain't jiving you. — Edwin Torres, *Carlito's Way*, p. 66, 1975
2 to manufacture amphetamine *US, 1985*
- They cook up speed in those shacks, but it's almost impossible to get probable cause to bust them. — Joseph Wambaugh, *The Secrets of Harry Bright*, p. 108, 1985

cool *noun*
1 self-control, composure, style *US, 1953*
- An Open Letter to Tom Jones—YOU BLEW YOUR COOL, TOM JONES [Full-page advertisement] — *Record Beat*, p. 9, 12th April 1966
- Then Our Mayor hotly blew his cool and launched the now-historic raids on the North Beach nudie nooks. — *San Francisco Chronicle*, p. 29, 8th July 1966
- There was a big numbers man named James, and for a long time I dug his cool. — John Allen, *Assault with a Deadly Weapon*, p. 4, 1977
2 a truce between street gangs *US, 1958*
- A "cool" was negotiated by street club workers. But it was an uneasy truce, often broken. — Harrison E. Salisbury, *The Shook-up Generation*, p. 38, 1958

cool *verb*
1 to please *US, 1953*
- "Do you like bop?" "It cools me," he said. — Irving Shulman, *The Short End of the Stick*, p. 203, 1953
2 to calm down; to become less dangerous *US, 1972*
- Jim will last out the cops. He'll go to the hustling bar a few streets away, until the street cools. — John Rechy, *The Sexual Outlaw*, p. 48, 1977
3 to idle; to pass time doing nothing *US, 1990*
- I was coolin' with Rick. — *Boyz N The Hood*, 1990
4 to kill, or at least immobilize someone *US, 1962*
- — *American Speech*, p. 268, December 1962: "The language of traffic policemen"
5 to die *US, 1994*
- — Sally Williams, *"Strong" Words*, p. 137, 1994

▸ **cool it**
to unwind, to calm down; to slow down, to ease off; to stop whatever activity you are engaged in *US, 1953*
Often used in the imperative.
- Let's cool it — Lavada Durst, *The Jives of Dr. Hepcat*, 1953
- "Man, we'd be sitting over there in the bar," said one, "just coolin' around the pool table with a few beers[.]" — Hunter S. Thompson, *Hell's Angels*, p. 40, 1966
- [T]he black friends of the white power structure issued a pamphlet with the headline COOL IT, BABY! — Eldridge Cleaver, *Soul on Ice*, p. 90, 1968
- [S]he insisted on carrying [drugs] even after I warned her to cool it while I was heavy into my dealing changes. — Robert Bingham, *Planted, Burnt, and Busted [The Howard Marks Book of Dope Stories]*, p. 339, 1970

- "Cool it. The guard's coming," I whispered. — Bobby Seale, *A Lonely Rage*, p. 263, 1978
- Meaning we'll have to cool it for a while, right? — *Sex, Lies and Videotape*, 1989

▶ **cool it back**
to become calm and composed under pressure *US, 1984*
- — Inez Cardozo-Freeman, *The Joint*, p. 489, 1984

▶ **cool your heels**
to rest *UK, 1633*
- A half hour later Rocco walked into the amber glow of the old Juvie annex behind the Western District station house and found four kids cooling their heels[.] — Richard Price, *Clockers*, p. 591, 1992

▶ **cool your jets**
to calm down; to back off *US, 1973*
- I'm just going to cool my jets, no matter what! — Beatrice Sparks (writing as "Anonymous"), *Jay's Journal*, p. 62, 1979
- WURLITZER: How 'bout Mallory? SCAGNETTI: Coolin' her jets in a holding cell. — *Natural Born Killers*, 1994

cool *adjective*

1 fashionable, attractive, admired *US, 1947*
The word "cool" has shown remarkable staying power, never waning in the affection of young people since its entry on the scene in the 1950s. In 2005, the term faced its biggest challenge, when copies of affectionate notes from Harriet Miers, briefly nominated as Justice on the Supreme Court, to then-Governor George Bush surfaced. In one card, Mier wrote to Governor Bush, "Hopefully Jenna and Barbara recognize that their parents are 'cool'—as do the rest of us." After this near-miss, cool survived.
- — Marcus Hanna Boulware, *Jive and Slang of Students in Negro Colleges*, 1947
- He had been half-heartedly trying to explain to her what was suggested by the term "cool," as hipsters used it. — John Clellon Holmes, *Go*, p. 173, 1952
- I learned the new hipster vocabulary; "pot" for weed, "twisted" for busted, "cool," an all-purpose word indicating anything you like or any situation that is not hot with the law. — William Burroughs, *Junkie*, p. 120, 1953
- [N]ow it is no longer 1948 but 1953 with cool generations and I five years older, or younger[.] — Jack Kerouac, *The Subterraneans*, p. 9, 1958

2 acceptable, agreeable *US, 1994*
- BUTCH: So we're cool. MARSELLUS: Yeah man, we're cool — *Pulp Fiction*, 1994
- I guess he's pretty, huh, racially pretty cool. — *The Big Lebowski*, 1998
- "I'm sure you've got a million things you want to do to me, and I'm very cool with that, and I'll probably love it, okay? — Dennis Cooper, *The Sluts*, p. 180, 2006

3 used for emphasizing an amount of money *UK, 1728*
- Depending on the size of the casino and the day of the week, that sum can fluctuate between a half-million and a cool million dollars, sheer cash. — Edward Lin, *Big Julie of Vegas*, p. 80, 1974

cool beans!
used as an expression of intense approval *US, 1987*
- — Connie Eble (Editor), *UNC-CH Campus Slang*, p. 2, Spring 1987
- — Merriam-Webster's Hot Words on Campus Marketing Survey '93, p. 3, 13th October 1993
- — Vann Wesson, *Generation X Field Guide and Lexicon*, p. 40, 1997
- Cool beans, Scotty—now where's my cameo? — Bruce Campbell, *If Chins Could Kill*, p. 337, 2002

cool breeze *adjective*
calm, collected *US, 1967*
- Good when I'm cool breeze and bad when I'm down. — Piri Thomas, *Down These Mean Streets*, p. 48, 1967

cool breezer *noun*
a carefree, casual surfer *US, 1988*
- — Michael V. Anderson, *The Bad, Rad, Not to Forget Way Cool Beach and Surf Discriptionary*, p. 4, 1988

cool car *noun*
a car used by robbers for escape after leaving the scene of the crime in another car *US, 1993*
- [T]hey transferred the guns and bags of cash into a stolen Mazda RX-7 that they'd planted as their cool car. — Bob Sipchen, *Baby Insane and the Buddha*, p. 5, 1993

coolcrack *verb*
to kill someone *US, 1947*
- Give it to him, Maceo, coolcrack the motherfouler! — Ralph Ellison, *Invisible Man*, p. 488, 1947

cool dad *noun*
a well-dressed, popular male *US, 1959*
College student usage.
- — *Time Magazine*, p. 46, 24th August 1959

cooler *noun*

1 a jail or prison *US, 1872*
- [I]mmediately he sounded as if he weren't so hot about sitting in the cooler overnight after all. — Nelson Algren, *The Man with the Golden Arm*, p. 6, 1949
- I was in cooler with poor Spick husbands for 30 mins. — Jack Kerouac, *Letter to Neal Cassady*, p. 326, 1 October 1951
- "Any analysis, any time spent in any other institutions?" "Well, counting state and county coolers—" — Ken Kesey, *One Flew Over the Cuckoo's Nest*, p. 44, 1962
- While Gigi cooled his heels in the cooler, a private detective named Whelan, a retired homicide cop, was out working on his behalf. — Leonard Shecter and William Phillips, *On the Pad*, p. 214, 1973

2 a cell used for solitary confinement; a segregation unit *US, 1899*
- This little scuffle cost me my fifteen days off for good behavior and caused me to get tossed in the cooler. — Billie Holiday, *Lady Sings the Blues*, p. 28, 1956
- — John M. Murtagh and Sara Harris, *Cast the First Stone*, p. 259, 1957

3 an infirmary *US, 1983*
Where one's social activities are "put on ice."
- — *Concord (New Hampshire) Monitor*, p. 17, 23rd August 1983

4 a morgue *US, 1994*
- — Sally Williams, "Strong" Words, p. 137, 1994

5 a silencer attached to a hand gun *US, 1962*
- — Joseph E. Ragen and Charles Finston, *Inside the World's Toughest Prison*, p. 795, 1962

6 a cigarette laced with cocaine *US, 1994*
- — US Department of Justice, *Street Terms*, October 1994

7 a stacked deck of cards used by a cheat *US, 1935*
- I don't care how smart you were, Joe could set up a cooler [stacked deck] in front of you and you'd never spot it. — Vincent Teresa, *My Life in the Mafia*, p. 215, 1973

8 in horse racing, a horse that is not expected to win the race *US, 1935*
- — Dan Parker, *The ABC of Horse Racing*, p. 145, 1947

cool head main thing!
used for urging others to calm down *US, 1972*
Hawaiian youth usage.
- — Elizabeth Ball Carr, *Da Kine Talk*, p. 128, 1972
- — Douglas Simonson, *Pidgin to da Max*, 1981

coolie *noun*

1 a loner; a person who refuses to join a gang *US, 1958*
- The concept of the coolie is common to all the street gangs. The coolie is a boy who does not belong to a street club. — Harrison E. Salisbury, *The Shook-up Generation*, p. 29, 1958
- Coolies don't swing with the gang. They are out and by themselves alone. — Warren Miller, *The Cool World*, p. 9, 1959
- Coolies is something like whores, you know. Can't stop nothing because they all alone in the world. — Sara Harris, *The Lords of Hell*, p. 128, 1967

2 a hip, street-smart person *US, 1967*
- "I hear you 104th Street coolies are supposed to have heart," I said. — Piri Thomas, *Down These Mean Streets*, p. 49, 1967

3 a cigarette to which crack cocaine has been added *US, 1967*
- — Terry Williams, *Crackhouse*, p. 147, 1992

coolie-do *noun*
the vagina *US, 1972*
- — Helen Dahlskog (Editor), *A Dictionary of Contemporary and Colloquial Usage*, p. 15, 1972

cooling tank *noun*
a cold holding cell *US, 1993*
- Later, after what seemed like hours in the cooling tank—a deliberately chilled holding cell designed to keep its occupants freezing and uncomfortable—I was transported to Los Padrinos Juvenile Hall. — Sanyika Shakur, *Monster*, p. 68, 1993

cool Muther John *noun*

a boy who is fashionable, knowledgeable and trendy *US, 1955*
- — *American Weekly*, p. 2, 14th August 1955

cool off *verb*

to kill *US, 1972*
- They got a joint and the thieves there are afraid to do it because they'll cool 'em off [kill them] if they catch them. — Harry King, *Box Man*, p. 28, 1972

cool-off man *noun*

in a confidence swindling or cheating scheme, the member of the swindling group who stays with the victim calming him down after he learns that he has been swindled *US, 1953*
- "To do this you had to have mechanics who could control the games, broads who would entertain the suckers, and a cool-off man who, after a sucker had been stripped of his money, could calm the sucker down and make him feel like he'd had a good run for this money." — Vincent Teresa, *My Life in the Mafia*, p. 214, 1973

cool-out *noun*

in police interrogations, the practice of leaving the accused alone in the interrogation room before the interrogation begins *US, 1997*
- I know this routine, guys. I pulled this cool-out a hundred times myself. — Stephen Cannell, *Big Con*, p. 320, 1997

cool out *verb*

1 in police interrogations, to perform a cool-out on someone *US, 1997*
- She'd been a prosecutor for five years, so she knew that there were basically two reasons why cops cool out a suspect like this. — Stephen Cannell, *Big Con*, p. 320, 1997

2 (used of a confidence swindler or a tout who has given bad tips) to calm a bettor who has lost *US, 1951*
- — David W. Maurer, *Argot of the Racetrack*, p. 22, 1951
- — Robert C. Prus and C.R.D. Sharper, *Road Hustler*, p. 169, 1977

cool water *noun*

strong, illegally manufactured whiskey *US, 1999*
- — *Star Tribune (Minneapolis)*, p. 19F, 31st January 1999

coon *noun*

a black person *US, 1834*
Offensive.
- "Ring the bell before Jackson kills him a coon!" someone boomed in the sudden silence. — Ralph Ellison, *Invisible Man*, p. 22, 1947
- Heard these little coons are hung like horses[.] — Dick Gregory, *Nigger*, p. 10, 1964
- White people always associated watermelons with Negroes, and they sometimes called Negroes "coons" among all the other names[.] — Malcolm X and Alex Haley, *The Autobiography of Malcolm X*, p. 15, 1964
- "That coon knows his place, Zeke," Jamie answered weakly. — Donald Goines, *Swamp Man*, p. 16, 1974

coon *verb*

1 to steal something; someone to cheat *US, 1964*
- [S]ome of us boys would slip out down the road, or across the pastures, and go "cooning" watermelons. — Malcolm X and Alex Haley, *The Autobiography of Malcolm X*, p. 15, 1964
- — Clarence Major, *Dictionary of Afro-American Slang*, p. 40, 1970
- Charlie broke a window in the principle's office one night, cooned in, stumbled through the darkness, grabbed the telephone, gave it a smiling vicious tug, and ripped it from the wall. — Joe Eszterhas, *Charlie Simpson's Apocalypse*, p. 65, 1973
- Monkey said, "Find a stump to fit your rump / And I'll coon you till your asshhole jump." — Dennis Wepman et al., *The Life*, p. 33, 1976

2 to bet *US, 1947*
- — Marcus Hanna Boulware, *Jive and Slang of Students in Negro Colleges*, 1947
- Say, "Why don't you get you a deck of cards where I can coon you some?" — Bruce Jackson, *Get Your Ass in the Water and Swim Like Me*, p. 175, 1962

coon-ass *noun*

a resident of Louisiana; a Cajun *US, 1943*
Often, not always, considered a slur.
- How a coon ass like me merits the time and patience of two such eminent editors is hard to figure. — James Carville, *We're Right, They're Wrong*, p. x, 1996
- He talks like a coon-ass. — James Lee Burke, *Sunset Limited*, p. 174, 1998

- When he called the name Terry Hubert, I whispered, "A-Bear, Sir, not Hubert. That's a coon-ass name, Sir!" — Franklin D. Rast, *Don's Nam*, p. 42, 1999

coon bottom *noun*

a poor part of town, especially one where poor black people live *US, 1968*
- Others suggest that these sections are not urban at all but intolerably countrified: Frogtown and Goosetown (3 responses each), Gooseville, Coontown, and Coon Bottom (1 each). — Erin McKean (Editor), *Verbatim*, p. 37, 2001

cooney *noun*

a white resident of Louisiana *US, 1975*
A diminuitive of **COON-ASS**.
- — *American Speech*, p. 57, Spring–Summer 1975: "Razorback slang"

coon killer *noun*

a club *US, 1982*
- — Ralph de Sola, *Crime Dictionary*, p. 31, 1982

coon's age *noun*

a long time *US, 1843*
- Hell, I haven't been in a brawl in a coon's age. — Darryl Ponicsan, *The Last Detail*, p. 77, 1970
- "If it ain't Bertha Grimmitt—you ain't been in here in a coon's age," Cleve Goins shouted. — Pat Conroy, *The Great Santini*, p. 173, 1976
- I found this old address book in a jacket I ain't worn in a coon's age. Toby what? What the fuck was her last name? — *Reservoir Dogs*, 1994
- "I have a sneaking suspicion you haven't sat in a coon's age." "However the hell long that is," said Switters. — Tom Robbins, *Fierce Invalids from Hot Climates*, p. 130, 2000

coon stopper *noun*

a powerful gun *US, 1977*
- "And this, Wiftoe," he said pointing to Condo's revolver, "is a Colt Trooper .357. The kind you stop coons with. A coon-stopper." — John Sayles, *Union Dues*, p. 313, 1977

Coon Town *noun*

a neighborhood populated largely by black families *US, 1987*
Offensive.
- — *Maledicta*, p. 52, 1986–1987: "A continuation of a glossary of ethnic slurs in American English"
- [W]e cross the railroad tracks into Coon Town, as my schoolmates at George Wallace Elementary School call it. — David Henry Sterry, *Chicken*, p. 97, 2002

coop *noun*

1 a house or apartment *US, 1947*
- [S]crams on ahead to grandma's coop[.] — Harry Haenigsen, *Jive's Like That*, 1947

2 a police stationhouse *US, 1962*
- — Joseph E. Ragen and Charles Finston, *Inside the World's Toughest Prison*, p. 795, 1962

3 a place where police sleep or idle during their shift *US, 1958*
- Any spot that takes a policeman out of the rain is a coop, or a heave. — *New York Times*, p. 34, 20th October 1958
- First, though, he went down to his little coop, a room in the basement of an apartment house where police could, while on duty, rest, sleep, play cards, use a toilet, hide from the sergeant. — Leonard Shecter and William Phillips, *On the Pad*, p. 91, 1973

Coop *noun*

in craps, a roll of 12 *US, 1983*
An abbreviated nickname of Gary Cooper, star of the Western film *High Noon*.
- — Thomas L. Clark, *The Dictionary of Gambling and Gaming*, p. 90, 1987

coop *verb*

to sleep or relax while on duty *US, 1962*
- When policemen sleep on duty in New York, they "coop"; when they sleep in Washington, they "huddle." — *New York Times*, 15th February 1970
- As a rookie cop, Serpico was also introduced to the fine art of "cooping," or sleeping on duty, a time-honored police practice that in other cities goes under such names as "huddling" and "going down." — Peter Maas, *Serpico*, p. 63, 1973
- A big four cops—and two of them moonlight days driving cabs, so they spend half their shift cooping. — Vincent Patrick, *The Pope of Greenwich Village*, p. 37, 1977

- He's in there with the guy who takes your quarter, drinking. Cooping, they call it in the city, in New York. — *John Sayles, Union Dues,* p. 367, 1977

coop delight *noun*
the body of a murder victim *US, 1976*
From the Latin *corpus delicti*.
- — *John R. Armore and Joseph D. Wolfe, Dictionary of Desperation,* p. 25, 1976

coosie *noun*
a Chinese person or other South Asian *US, 1949*
- — *American Speech,* p. 30, February 1949: "A.V.G. lingo"

coot *noun*
1 a harmless simpleton, especially an old one; a fellow *US, 1766*
Probably from the behavioral characteristics of the bird.
- I hunched behind the wheel when I began thinking of the old coot who took the easy way out. — *Mickey Spillane, One Lonely Night,* p. 144, 1951
- After Howard Blakely wandered away, the old coot sat there, scattering crumbs and listening to the pings from the shooting gallery across the way. — *Bernard Wolfe, The Late Risers,* p. 33, 1954
- This coot was maybe sixty; tall and stooped, with a beaklike nose dripping in a straight line from his high liverspotted pate. — *Seth Morgan, Homeboy,* p. 168, 1990
- When Bobbie questioned Fin about the age of all the fun-loving fogies, coots, geezers, codgers, duffers and biddies she'd met in the saloon, he didn't know how to tell her that the oldest fossil in the joint wasn't fifteen years his senior. — *Joseph Wambaugh, Finnegan's Week,* p. 230, 1993
2 the vagina; a woman as a sex object; sex with a woman *US, 1975*
- — *American Speech,* p. 57, Spring–Summer 1975: "Razorback slang"

cootch dancer; cooch dancer *noun*
a woman who performs a sexually suggestive dance *US, 1910*
- A good colored singer doesn't have to wrap her sex in a package and peddle it to the customer like a cootch dancer in a sideshow. — *Mezz Mezzrow, Really the Blues,* p. 27, 1946
- In sentencing the Cootch-Dancer Schmidt to 15 years for manslaughter (Time, Beb. 2), the judges had chided her for "appearing nude on the deck of [Mee's] yacht like a nymph," and for "swimming naked in [Havana] Bay." — *Time,* 11th October 1948
- [W]e furnished hot competition for the cootch dancers[.] — *Ethel Waters, His Eye is on the Sparrow,* p. 83, 1951
- "And I thought it was a kootch dancer from a carnival." — *Helen Giblo, Footlights, Fistfights and Femmes,* p. 104, 1957

cootchy-coo; kootchy-koo; kitchy-koo *noun*
used as a lexicalization of talk used with babies *UK, 1984*
From Irish dialect *kitchy, kitchy, kaw*.
- The clerk gave the baby a hunched-up kootchy-koo, impervious to Rodney's rage. — *Richard Price, Clockers,* p. 571, 1992

cooter *noun*
the vagina *US, 1986*
- — *Connie Eble (Editor), UNC-CH Campus Slang,* p. 2, Fall 1986
- And then they shoved frozen polar bear sperm pencils up their cooters. — *Tony Kushne, Angels in America,* p. 34, 1994

cootie catcher *noun*
a somewhat intricately folded piece of paper, manipulated by the fingers, used by children to tell fortunes or to catch imaginary cooties *US, 1996*
- To American children, the salt cellar construction is traditionally known as a "cootie catcher." — *Eric Kenneway, Complete Origami,* p. 154, 1987
- Folk toys can be made by children themselves, in which case they are often temporary ("cootie catchers" and paper folded into a specific form and used to tell fortunes). — *Jan Harold Brunvand, American Folklore,* p. 712, 1996
- [A] playmate's folding paper toy (we used to call them "cootie catchers") unfolded to show him the words "dream is destiny." — *Roger Ebert, Roger Ebert's Movie Yearbook,* p. 652, 2002

cooties *noun*
an imaginary disease or infestation that could be transmitted by close contact, thus creating a stigma for the person who is said to have it *US, 1971*
A children's corruption of the older sense of the term (a body louse).

- Get your cooties off me. — *American Graffiti,* 1973
- Pretend you're a missionary saving a colony of cootie victims. — *Heathers,* 1988
- More than mouthwash would be required to slay those cooties. — *C.D. Payne, Youth in Revolt,* p. 39, 1993
- You can use my straw, I don't have kooties. — *Pulp Fiction,* 1994

cooze; coozie *noun*
1 the vulva; the female genitals *US, 1927*
- — *The Guild Dictionary of Homosexual Terms,* p. 9, 1965
- Maybe it's just something to hold on to ... an extension of her thing, you know, her cooze. — *Terry Southern, Blue Movie,* p. 37, 1970
- "Snatch," "hole," "kooze," "slash," "pussy" and "crack" were other terms referring variously to women's genitals, to women as individuals, or to women as a species. — *Screw,* p. 5, 3rd January 1972
- "Let me see a little more cooze, sweetie." — *Tina Russell, Porno Star,* p. 23, 1973
- She also possesses a truly attractive cunt: cooze lips which aren't flappy, crinkly, or rundown[.] — *Anthony Petkovich, The X Factory,* p. 16, 1997
2 a woman, especially a promiscuous woman *US, 1921*
- "Who's that fine-looking coozie?" hollered another one. — *Frederick Kohner, Gidget,* p. 15, 1957
- See, in the lounge, they got these coozie that carry lights, take you to a table. — *Robert Gover, Here Goes Kitten,* p. 25, 1964
- Brad says you're being a real coozie. — *Heathers,* 1988
- Let me tell ya what "Like a Virgin's" about. It's about some cooze who's a regular fuck machine. — *Reservoir Dogs,* 1992

cooze light *noun*
in the pornography industry, a light used to illuminate the genitals of the performers *US, 1995*
- — *Adult Video News,* p. 50, October 1995

coozie stash *noun*
contraband, especially drugs, hidden in the vagina *US, 1992*
- — *Jay Robert Nash, Dictionary of Crime,* p. 79, 1992

cop *noun*
1 a police officer *US, 1859*
False etymologies abound, with formation suggestions of "copper badges," "copper buttons," or an initialism of "Constable On Patrol" at the head of the unruly pack. The verb sense "to grab" leads to the verb sense "to arrest" which leads to **COPPER** which was shortened to "cop." No buttons, no badges, no initialisms.
- J. Edgar Hoover, director of the F.B.I., recently tried to enlist the help of a television program in what seems to be a campaign on the part of certain high-ranking cops to eliminate a word from the language. The word is "cop," as a noun, in its most popular usage. — *New Yorker,* p. 51, 18th July 1959
- The first thing he said to me, "We are police officers." I said, "You're cops to me." — *Herbert Huncke, Guilty of Everything,* p. 22, 1990
- You were doing good here. You did that nice short thing on the gay cop. — *Anna Quindlen, One True Thing,* p. 36, 1994
- Setups with regional police became routine, sparked by America's historic phobia about "niggers with guns," and in the aftermath, some thirty-eight Panthers were shot down by racist cops. — *Mumia Abu-Jamal, Live from Death Row,* p. 147, 1996
2 a plea in a criminal case *US, 1977*
- The D.A. offered me a cop to a robbery charge, but I wasn't accepting nothing. — *John Allen, Assault with a Deadly Weapon,* p. 120, 1977
3 in carnival usage, a small prize won at a game concession *US, 1980*
- — *Joe McKennon, Circus Lingo,* p. 27, 1980
- — *Don Wilmeth, The Language of American Popular Entertainment,* p. 64, 1981
4 winnings from gambling *US, 1930*
- Put that heavy cop in your mitt flat against your thigh furthest from the mark. — *Iceberg Slim (Robert Beck), Trick Baby,* p. 93, 1969

cop *verb*
1 to obtain, to take or to purchase something, especially drugs *US, 1867*
- Slicker Morrie made more dames and copped more cherries than any lad in the history of Louisa Nolan's dance hall. — *James T. Farrell, Saturday Night,* p. 30, 1947
- "Get ready to cop," I said, and dropped the caps into his hands. — *William Burroughs, Junkie,* p. 56, 1953

- Cowboy went to cop and got copped. — Jack Gerber, *The Connection*, p. 28, 1957
- [T]his is the way they have been living for months, for years, some of them, across America and back, on the bus, down to the Rat lands of Mexico and back, sailing like gypsies along the Servicenter fringes, copping urinations[.] — Tom Wolfe, *The Electric Kool-Aid Acid Test*, p. 16, 1968

2 to seduce someone, to have sex with someone US, 1965
- I played stickball, marbles, and Johnny-on-the-Pony, copped girls' drawers and blew pot. — Piri Thomas, *Down These Mean Streets*, p. 13, 1967
- A pimp brought a girl to me and said he'd copped her—which means he's gotten her to join his group. — Susan Hall, *Ladies of the Night*, p. 165, 1973
- Copped regular after that. Her desk, Kleinfeld's desk, broom closet, even on the washbasin. — Edwin Torres, *After Hours*, p. 220, 1979
- Billy Woods, like most of the dudes in and around the neighborhood wanted to cop Phyllisine. — Donald Goines, *The Busting Out of an Ordinary Man*, p. 19, 1985

3 to inform; to betray someone US, 1895
- Louis went up without copping—naming any names to have his time cut—and was respected among the population, all the homeboys up at Starke, where he met Bobby Deo. — Elmore Leonard, *Riding the Rap*, p. 55, 1995

4 (used of a rigged carnival game) to malfunction, allowing a player to win US, 1985
- — Gene Sorrows, *All About Carnivals*, p. 14, 1985

▸ **cop a breeze**
to leave, especially without calling attention to yourself US, 1950
- — Hyman E. Goldin et al., *Dictionary of American Underworld Lingo*, p. 49, 1950

▸ **cop a feel**
to touch someone sexually without their consent US, 1935
- Despite her anger she had to laugh, for the boys were gentle with her, no one took advantage and copped a feel. — Irving Shulman, *College Confidential*, p. 104, 1960
- DENOUNCE the poor Nigger male who cherishes his whiteness, and allows the Caucasian male's "copping-a-feel" his own black wife's ass, at a social. — Robert deCoy, *The Nigger Bible*, pp. 132–133, 1967
- Is this what they call copping a feel? — *American Graffiti*, 1973
- But would a company yes-man (who I suspected would never dare cop a feel unless it was written into the annual strategic plan) really risk so much to show his interest in me? — Rita Ciresi, *Pink Slip*, p. 85, 1999

▸ **cop a heel**
to leave; to run away; to escape US, 1977
- Kid said, "Then cop a heel and pee." She muttered an inaudible expletive as she gave him a filthy look and stomped away. — Iceberg Slim (Robert Beck), *Long White Con*, p. 20, 1977
- — M. Allen Henderson, *How Con Games Work*, p. 219, 1985

▸ **cop a mope**
to escape US, 1951
- — *American Speech*, p. 194, October 1951: "A study of reformatory argot"

▸ **cop a nod**
to sleep US, 1947
- — Marcus Hanna Boulware, *Jive and Slang of Students in Negro Colleges*, 1947
- — Robert S. Gold, *A Jazz Lexicon*, p. 69, 1964

▸ **cop a plea**
to enter a guilty plea to a criminal charge US, late 1920s
- Only plea I ever copped cost me three years in the slams. — Edwin Torres, *Carlito's Way*, p. 10, 1975

▸ **cop deuces**
to assume a submissive or defensive position US, 1976
- — John R. Armore and Joseph D. Wolfe, *Dictionary of Desperation*, p. 25, 1976

▸ **cop someone's joint**
to perform oral sex on a man US, 1962
- — Guy Strait, *The Lavender Lexicon*, 1 June 1964
- [S]he smiles and says, "How about if I cop your joint instead?" — Terry Southern, *Blue Movie*, p. 149, 1970
- Turned out she climbed in beside me and copped my joint for forty-five cents. — Robert Byrne, *McGoorty*, p. 124, 1972
- I kept my hands on my private parts, broke a boy's arm tried to cop my joint and came out [of prison] a two hundred and five pound virgin. — Elmore Leonard, *Gold Coast*, p. 17, 1981

copacetic; copasetic *adjective*
good, excellent; safe; attractive US, 1919
Etymology unknown; Chinook jargon, French, Italian and Yiddish sources have been suggested.
- — Bernard Wolfe, *The Late Risers*, p. 189, 1954
- It was not copacetic / It was not right. — The Rulers, *Copasetic*, 1966
- Good bread coming in. Everything was copasetic. Too good to last. — Edwin Torres, *Carlito's Way*, p. 29, 1975

cop and blow *noun*
the rule of thumb governing a pimp's *modus operandi*, acquiring and losing prostitutes US, 1967
- He reconciled himself to the name of the game, "Cop and Blow" (win and lose) and made his way uptown[.] — Babs Gonzales, *I Paid My Dues*, p. 101, 1967
- I bombarded him with street logic and begged him to recognize the hard pimp law of "cop and blow": somebody has to lose when somebody wins. — Iceberg Slim (Robert Beck), *The Naked Soul of Iceberg Slim*, p. 123, 1971
- Cop and blow is the name of the game. — A.S. Jackson, *Gentleman Pimp*, p. 100, 1973
- "Bitch, you ain't no lame, you know the Game / They call it cop and blow." — Dennis Wepman et al., *The Life*, p. 86, 1976
- With most chicks it was cop and blow, cop one week and blow the next. — Alix Shulman, *On the Stroll*, p. 109, 1981

cop and blow *verb*
to acquire something and then leave US, 1972
- But he had no hangups or any peculiarly excessive style of stealing like his two partners—his way was simply to cop and blow. — Emmett Grogan, *Ringolevio*, p. 46, 1972

cop and hold; cop and lock *verb*
(of a pimp) to acquire and retain a prostitute US, 1972
- My regulars—whom I've copped and locked—that's Sandy and Kitty and Linda—they each made around seventy-five thousand last year. — Susan Hall, *Gentleman of Leisure*, p. 13, 1972

cope *verb*
to function in normal situations while under the influence of a hallucinogenic drug US, 1966
- — J. L. Simmons and Barry Winograd, *It's Happening*, p. 169, 1966

Copenhagen capon *noun*
a transsexual US, 1972
Homosexual usage; an allusion to the sex-altering operation performed on Christine Jorgensen in Denmark.
- — Bruce Rodgers, *The Queens' Vernacular*, p. 201, 1972

cop house; cop factory *noun*
a police station US, 1928
- I have to go to the cop house just about now. — Raymond Chandler, *Playback*, p. 152, 1958

copilot *noun*
a tablet of dextroamphetamine sulfate (trade name Dexedrine™), or any other central nervous system stimulant US, 1965
- — Donald Louria, *Nightmare Drugs*, p. 28, 1966
- Some of the names describe the drugs' effects, such as "helpers," "copilots," "Los Angeles turn arounds," or their shape, color and markings—"hearts," "footballs," "blackjacks," "crossroads." — Phil Hirsch, *Hooked*, pp. 51–52, 1968
- — *American Speech*, p. 203, Fall 1969: "Truck driver's jargon"
- Jackie slipped me a couple of co-pilots in English when she passed out the test papers. — Anonymous, *Go Ask Alice*, p. 94, 1971

cop man *noun*
a low-level drug dealer who must pay cash to the supplier for the drugs to be sold US, 1989
- Many are taken on in a variety of tangential roles and work as steerers, touts, guards, runners, and "cop men"—dealers whom suppliers will only sell to on a cash basis. — Terry Williams, *The Cocaine Kids*, p. 33, 1989

cop-out *noun*
a drastic compromise of principle US, 1956
- I considered crossing over to the other side of the highway and trying to get back to New Haven for a bus. But that would be an incredible cop out. — James Simon Kunen, *The Strawberry Statement*, p. 81, 1968

- Kesey has sold out to keep from getting a five-year sentence or worse. Next he'll nail it down by calling all the kids to Winterland and telling them to stop taking LSD ... Freaking cop-out ... — Tom Wolfe, *The Electric Kool-Aid Acid Test*, p. 336, 1968

cop out *verb*

1 to avoid an issue by making excuses; to go back on your word *US, 1952*

- [O]ff we go, 2 girls and me and Neal, bleary, driving into woods of California for orgy, but one girl cops out[.] — Jack Kerouac, *Letter to John Clellon Holmes*, p. 339, 8th February 1952
- I'm not trying to cop out, but I was playing it too safe that afternoon at your house. — Nat Hentoff, *Jazz Country*, p. 32, 1965
- Even Flo Kennedy, our chief lawyer, copped out—though some of the younger legal-beagels (women, bless 'em) were ready to carry the fight to the floor of the Pageant[.] — *Screw*, p. 14, 13th October 1969
- The line between madness and masochism was already hazy; the time had come to pull back ... to retire, hunker down, back off and "cop out," as it were. — Hunter S. Thompson, *Fear and Loathing in Las Vegas*, p. 81, 1971
- All the way over here I was telling you how he would cooperate. Now, he's just copping out. — Donald Goines, *Inner City Hoodlum*, p. 60, 1975

2 to confess; to enter a guilty plea *US, 1938*

- I copped out on the larceny charges, figuring to get six months at the most[.] — James Blake, *The Joint*, p. 13, 25th February 1951
- "She's gonna cop out," Davis told him. — Clarence Cooper Jr., *The Scene*, p. 115, 1960
- I was supposed to take a jury trial, but the lawyer told me he'd get me eighteen months if I'd cop out. — Henry Williamson, *Hustler!*, p. 141, 1965
- I copped out to attempted larceny and was given one to two years in the state prison at Jackson, Michigan. — A.S. Jackson, *Gentleman Pimp*, p. 59, 1973

copper *noun*

a police officer *UK, 1846*

- [T]here was a chance that either the police might walk in on me or the little guy get suspicious enough of my being away so long he'd call a copper. — Mickey Spillane, *I, The Jury*, p. 58, 1947
- Now how did I know you were a copper? — Marvin Wald and Albert Maltz, *The Naked City*, 1947
- Sheik looked dazed. "Can't no copper hurt me," he muttered thickly[.] — Chester Himes, *The Real Cool Killers*, p. 92, 1959
- And every copper is on the take, you know, up and down the line. — Sara Harris, *The Lords of Hell*, p. 117, 1967

copper *verb*

in craps, to bet that the shooter will lose *US, 1950*

- — *The Annals of the American Academy of Political and Social Sciences*, p. 123, May 1950

copper chopper *noun*

a police helicopter *US, 1979*

- Most of it was growing outside on a porch, clearly visible to anybody at a higher elevation, such as, say, a snooping copper chopper. — Larry "Ratso" Sloman, *Reefer Madness*, p. 420, 1979
- That game's halftime show will include an exhibition by LAPD's Special Weapons and Tactics (SWAT) unit, as well as helicopter-borne officers flying into the stadium and rappelling from the "copper choppers" to a simulated crime scene on the Coliseum floor. — *San Francisco Chronicle*, p. D6, 24th January 1990

copper jitters *noun*

an excessive fear of contact with the police *US, 1953*

- Pushing junk is a constant strain on the nerves. Sooner or later you get the "copper jitters," and everybody looks like a cop. — William Burroughs, *Junkie*, p. 58, 1953

copper time *noun*

the reduction of a prison sentence for good behavior *US, 1992*

- — William K. Bentley and James M. Corbett, *Prison Slang*, p. 25, 1992

copping clothes *noun*

unusually "stylish" clothes worn by a pimp who is trying to entice a prostitute to work for him *US, 1981*

- So instead of partying, he'd got his copping clothes cleaned and pressed, had a manicure, a shave, and a shine, and prepared the rest for flashing. — Alix Shulman, *On the Stroll*, p. 8, 1981

copping neighborhood *noun*

a neighborhood where buyers and sellers know that drugs are sold *US, 1990*

- The street corners were literally teeming with sick addicts in the copping neighborhoods. — Herbert Huncke, *Guilty of Everything*, p. 130, 1990

copping zone *noun*

an area in a city where buyers and sellers of drugs know to congregate and do business *US, 1989*

- It was a place to "cop" (buy), a "copping zone." — Terry Williams, *The Cocaine Kids*, p. 14, 1989
- — Terry Williams, *Crackhouse*, p. 147, 1992

cop shop *noun*

a police station *UK, 1941*

- Outside, down the street, round a couple of corners, and I was in the local cop-shop. — John Wain, *Contenders*, p. 263, 1958
- The underworld and the cop shop (as some are wont to call police headquarters) buzzed with whispers of suicide and even murder. — Phil Hirsch, *Hooked*, p. 79, 1968
- They filed out of the local cop shop. — Chris Miller, *The Real Animal House*, p. 167, 2006

cop's rub *noun*

a frisking or pat-down for weapons or contraband *US, 1973*

- They ordered the white guys out of the car, put the cop's rub on 'em, then asked them to open the trailer. — A.S. Jackson, *Gentleman Pimp*, p. 8, 1973

cops' tank *noun*

a jail cell reserved for policemen/criminals *US, 1985*

- O.A. Jones mumbled, hoping that he would get put in the cops" tank at the county jail[.] — Joseph Wambaugh, *The Secrets of Harry Bright*, p. 33, 1985

cop-stop *verb*

(said of police) to stop someone for questioning *US, 1965*

- Because as soon as they were cop-stopped, it was a matter of the club touching on their kidneys and asses and the backs of their legs[.] — Sol Yurrick, *The Warriors*, p. 28, 1965

copy *verb*

to understand what has been said *US, 1984*

Shortwave radio slang that spread well outside the world of radio.

- I want no firing, period, unless your hear shots. Copy that, Mace? — *Airheads*, 1994

cord *noun*

corduroy *US, 1960*

- [H]is light cord suit probably cost more than Ryder's and with his bones mercifully covered he looked tall and sharp. — Glendon Swarthout, *Where the Boys Are*, p. 92, 1960

cords *noun*

corduroy pants *US, 1926*

- [M]any of us bought him a beer and a Polish sausage when he came in with his paint-splattered cords and brown brogans, broke as ever. — Oscar Zeta Acosta, *The Autobiography of a Brown Buffalo*, p. 47, 1972

corduroy *noun*

in surfing, a swell lined up like ribbing *US, 1991*

- — Trevor Cralle, *The Surfin'ary*, p. 24, 1991

core *adjective*

said of pornography that shows penetration *US, 1995*

A shortened **HARDCORE**.

- — *Adult Video News*, p. 42, August 1995

corflu *noun*

correction fluid, especially the fluid used for correcting mimeograph stencils *US, 1982*

- — *American Speech*, p. 25, Spring 1982: "The language of science fiction fan magazines"

Corine *noun*

cocaine *US, 1967*

- — John B. Williams, *Narcotics and Hallucinogenics*, p. 111, 1967

cork *noun*

▸ **pull the cork**

to inform, to betray *US, 1964*

"Like a lot of big ones that went bust," he said, "somebody pulled the cork. The department got a call." — Mickey Spillane, *The Snake*, pp. 115–116, 1964

cork *verb*
to have sex *US, 1983*
- — *Maledicta*, p. 250, 1983: "A connotative analysis of synonyms for sexual intercourse"

corker *noun*
an inconsistent, unpredictable poker player *US, 1988*
- — George Percy, *The Language of Poker*, p. 24, 1988

cork off *verb*
to sleep *US, 1959*
- Pa blew up the mattress and corked off for a couple of hours while I read the book[.] — Max Shulman, *I was a Teen-Age Dwarf*, p. 4, 1959

cork top *noun*
a surfer *US, 1963*
- — *Paradise of the Pacific*, p. 27, October 1963

corn *noun*
1 something that is excessively sentimental *US, 1936*
Originally applied to all music that was not jazz in the 1930s, and then eased into general usage.
- [A]nd, to top off the ridiculous and embarrassing performance, she threw on the corn. — Jim Thompson, *The Grifters*, p. 12, 1963

2 sentimental, maudlin, mawkish music *US, 1936*
- I thought George was going to knock out some of the usual corn. — Mezz Mezzrow, *Really the Blues*, p. 25, 1946

3 whiskey *US, 1967*
- If "Harry Belfonte" could make it after being a restaurateur, I can sure do alright "pouring the corn." — Babs Gonzales, *I Paid My Dues*, p. 157, 1967

4 a hard scar produced by repeated drug injections *US, 1971*
- — Eugene Landy, *The Underground Dictionary*, p. 58, 1971

cornball *noun*
an old-fashioned, unsophisticated person *US, 1952*
- "Don't be a cornball. You're a girl. They wouldn't take you." — Mary Chase, *Mrs. McThing*, p. 34, 1954
- "That's because you're a cornball, Dad," he said. — Malcolm Braly, *The Protector*, p. 11, 1979

cornball *adjective*
clichéd; overly sentimental *US, 1948*
- Will you stop this cornball stuff. — Jack Gerber, *The Connection*, p. 24, 1957
- I was half tempted but decided that would have been too cornball. — Clancy Sigal, *Going Away*, p. 353, 1961

corn belt *noun*
the midwestern United States *US, 1955*
- [Z]igzagged through corn belts and cotton belts (this is not too clear, I am afraid, Clarence, but I did not keep any notes)[.] — Vladimir Nabokov, *Lolita*, p. 154, 1955
- Setting out on a tour of the Corn Belt in a tubercular jalopy, Oscar informed the suckers that research had disclosed that they were descendants of the illegitimate Drake boy. — *San Francisco Examiner, American Weekly*, p. 17, 24th May 1959
- In addition, those photographs could earn those corn-belt clods a fortune in some photographic contest. — John Kennedy Toole, *A Confederacy of Dunces*, pp. 231–232, 1980
- Dean could have come out of the Corn Belt with a dismal third-placing showing. But finish third and appear un-presidential in the process? — *Arizona Republic*, p. 10B, 28th January 2004

cornbread *noun*
old fashioned music *US, 1957*
- Kenny liked boogie-woogie and Scar was not in the mood for digging corn bread. — Herbert Simmons, *Corner Boy*, p. 162, 1957

corner *noun*
1 a prisoner's group of friends *US, 2002*
- — Jeffrey Ian Ross, *Behind Bars*, p. 184, 2002: Slammer Slang

2 a youth gang *US, 1974*
- They did not like to be called "gangs," but referred to themselves as "cliques" in New York and "corners" in Philadelphia. — James Haskins, *Street Gangs*, p. 124, 1974

3 the block in a prison where the cells for solitary confinement are found *US, 1962*

- — Joseph E. Ragen and Charles Finston, *Inside the World's Toughest Prison*, p. 795, 1962

▶ **around the corner**
in poker, said of a sequence of cards that uses the ace as both a high and low card *US, 1988*
- — George Percy, *The Language of Poker*, p. 6, 1988

corner boy *noun*
1 an urban youth who idles in the street *US, 1971*
- — Hermese E. Roberts, *The Third Ear*, 1971
- Another dealer, "Donnie," 16, and his corner crew laughed when asked about murder. Donnie is proud of being a "corner boy." — *Philadelphia Daily News*, p. Local 3, 27th December 2006

2 a fellow prisoner from a prisoner's neighborhood *US, 1991*
- — Lee McNelis, *30 + And a Wake-Up*, p. 1, 1991

corner man *noun*
a person who is not part of the criminal underworld but whose sympathies lie with the underworld in its constant strife with law enforcement *US, 1964*
- — R. Frederick West, *God's Gambler*, p. 223, 1964

cornet player *noun*
a cocaine user *US, 1977*
- I can see you are a heavy cornet player, Roger. — Edwin Torres, *Q & A*, p. 114, 1977

corn-fed *adjective*
unsophisticated, simple, rustic *US, 1924*
- Certainly it generated televised images of a feminized home front—small Midwestern towns waving with yellow ribbons and corn-fed women trying to keep back the tears. — *Feminist Studies*, p. 72, 1994

cornfield clemency *noun*
escape from a rural prison *US, 1950*
- — Hyman E. Goldin et al., *Dictionary of American Underworld Lingo*, p. 50, 1950

corn game *noun*
in a carnival, a Bingo game *US, 1980*
- — *American Speech*, pp. 308–309, December 1960: "Carnival talk"
- — Joe McKennon, *Circus Lingo*, p. 27, 1980
- — Don Wilmeth, *The Language of American Popular Entertainment*, p. 64, 1981

cornhead *noun*
a long-haired adherent to the racist, fascist philosophy espoused by shaved-head skinheads *US, 2000*
- Today, most skinheads continue to wear close-cropped hair; however, there are long-haired skinheads, who are referred to as "cornheads." — Bill Valentine, *Gangs and Their Tattoos*, p. 59, 2000

cornhole *noun*
the anus *US, 1922*
- They may want you to show your corn hole. A lot of them are very anal. — James Ridgeway, *Red Light*, p. 153, 1996

cornhole *verb*
1 to take the active role in anal sex *US, 1938*
- "Now look are you going to cooperate"—three vicious diddles—"or does the ... does the Man cornhole you???" — William Burroughs, *Naked Lunch*, p. 196, 1957
- "I bet you were cornholed in kindergarten before you ever knew what it was about." — Reginald Harvey, *Park Beat*, p. 31, 1959
- Jus' take your pants down an' we jus' do a li'l corn-holin' with you-all. — Piri Thomas, *Down These Mean Streets*, p. 161, 1967
- Al had never "cornholed" before. — James Harper, *Homo Laws in all 50 States*, p. 177, 1968

2 to victimize someone; to force someone into submission *US, 1974*
A figurative use of the previous sense.
- I guess he felt safe, ninety miles away, but he was about to be cornholed by yours truly[.] — Howard Stern, *Miss America*, p. 272, 1995

cornpone *noun*
an unsophisticated, crude rural southerner *US, 1919*
Poet Lawrence Ferlinghetti regularly referred to US President Lyndon B. Johnson as "Colonel Cornpone" in his poems; cartoonist Al Capp created General Jubilation T. Cornpone, master of grabbing defeat from the jaws of victory.
- Consequently, I head Dan Rather, CBS's king of cornpone, begin the evening with his now infamous promise. — *Commonweal*, p. 1, 12th January 2001

corn row *noun*
hair tied in tight braids separated by rows of bare scalp *US,*
1946
- — *American Speech*, Fall – Winter 1971
- After several trips to Africa he decided to give up his "natural" and wear what the black brothers call "corn rows." — *San Francisco Chronicle*, p. 54, 5th June 1972
- — Edith A. Folb, *runnin' down some lines*, p. 233, 1980
- As we speak, they're braiding each other's hair into corn rows. — John Berendt, *Midnight in the Garden of Good and Evil*, p. 293, 1994

corn-row *verb*
to fix hair in tight braids *US, 1971*
- — *American Speech*, Fall – Winter 1971
- Sapphire knows how to corn-row hair. — Carolyn Greene, *70 Soul Secrets of Sapphire*, p. 25, 1973

corny *adjective*
mawkish, sentimental, hackneyed *US, 1932*
- The piano player in the band was an old maid about forty-five who knew every song that had been published in the last hundred years and could play in any key you named, each one cornier than the other. — Mezz Mezzrow, *Really the Blues*, p. 60, 1946
- Christ, I'm getting corny. — Jack Neal Cassady, *Letter to Jack Kerouac*, p. 135, 5th October 1947
- They were full of corny quips and Eastern college talk[.] — Jack Kerouac, *On the Road*, p. 227, 1957
- ["]New York meant beautiful women and street-smart guys who seemed to know all the angles." Nah, no... corny, top corny... for... my taste. — *Manhattan*, 1979

corpse cop *noun*
a homicide detective *US, 1985*
- Sidney, I realize an old corpse cop like you has instincts about dead bodies. — Joseph Wambaugh, *The Secrets of Harry Bright*, p. 168, 1985

corpuscle *noun*
used as a humorous synonym for "corporal" *US, 1968*
- — Carl Fleischhauer, *A Glossary of Army Slang*, p. 11, 1968

corral *noun*
a group of prostitutes working for a single pimp *US, 1971*
- — Eugene Landy, *The Underground Dictionary*, p. 58, 1971

corroded *adjective*
ugly *US, 1980*
- — Edith A. Folb, *runnin' down some lines*, p. 233, 1980

co-signer *noun*
a fellow prisoner who is willing to vouch for you or to defend you with action *US, 1989*
- — James Harris, *A Convict's Dictionary*, p. 30, 1989

cosmic rays *noun*
the source of an unexplained computing problem *US, 1991*
- "Hey, Eric—I just got a burst of garbage on my tube, where did that come from?" "Cosmic rays, I guess." — Eric S. Raymond, *The New Hacker's Dictionary*, p. 107, 1991

cosmos *noun*
phencyclidine, the recreational drug known as PCP or angel dust *US, 1977*
- — *Drummer*, p. 77, 1977
- — Jay Robert Nash, *Dictionary of Crime*, p. 82, 1992

cotics *noun*
narcotics, especially heroin *US, 1942*
- — US Department of Justice, *Street Terms*, October 1994

cottage cheese *noun*
cellulite *US, 1997*
A purely visual coining.
- — Pamela Munro, *U.C.L.A. Slang*, p. 53, 1997

cotton *noun*
1 cotton used for straining a dissolved narcotic (heroin, cocaine, or morphine) before injection *US, 1933*
- I was all out of junk at this point and had double-boiled my last cottons. — William Burroughs, *Junkie*, p. 37, 1953
- But when I make that big sting, I'll straighten you / If you'll save me a little on the cotton. — Dennis Wepman et al., *The Life*, p. 78, 1976

- Of course that's where Rooski would go to ground, there to run errands for the Troll and beg cottons from the other dopefiends. — Seth Morgan, *Homeboy*, p. 60, 1990
2 female pubic hair *US, 1970*
- — Roger D. Abrahams, *Deep Down in the Jungle*, p. 259, 1970

cotton-chopper *noun*
used as a term of address, especially to someone with a southern accent *US, 1977*
- Terms such as Bud, cottonpicker, cottonchopper, guy, and good buddy are affectionate-type terms used among truckers. — Gwyneth A. "Dandalion" Seese, *Tijuana Bear in a Smoke "Um Up Taxi"*, p. 18, 1977

cotton fever *noun*
an intense illness sometimes suffered after injecting heroin leached from used cottons *US, 1989*
- — Geoffrey Froner, *Digging for Diamonds*, p. 22, 1989

cottonhead *noun*
a heroin addict who habitually uses cotton used by other addicts to leach out heroin for his use *US, 1970*
- — Richard Horman and Allan Fox, *Drug Awareness*, p. 465, 1970

cotton-picking *adjective*
used as a folksy intensifier *US, 1949*
- "Okay, gourd-head. Get that cotton-picking butt off the ground and give us a hand." — Audie Murphy, *To Hell and Back*, p. 47, 1949
- That's the sum cottinpickin total[.] — Robert Gover, *Here Goes Kitten*, p. 54, 1964
- "And tell those cotton-pickin' cowboys to give me a shout when they pass the ol' Funny Farm." — E.M. Corder, *Citizens Band*, p. 33, 1977

cotton shooter *noun*
a drug addict who injects residue aggregated from cotton swatches used to strain drugs *US, 1951*
- Down-and-out addicts are "cotton shooters." They collect discarded cottons, soak out the narcotic residue and come up with an anemic shot. — *San Francisco News*, p. 1, 5th December 1951

cotton slut *noun*
a person who will attend an event for the sole purpose of obtaining a tee-shirt being given to those in attendance *US, 2001*
- — Don R. McCreary (Editor), *Dawg Speak*, 2001

couch *noun*
► **on the couch**
1 undergoing psychotherapy *US, 1961*
- — *American Speech*, pp. 145 – 148, May 1961: "The spoken language of medicine; argot, slang, cant"
2 in gambling, without further funds *US, 1996*
- — John Vorhaus, *The Big Book of Poker Slang*, p. 27, 1996

couch casting *noun*
the practice of casting roles in performances based on the actor's willingness to have sex with the casting director *US, 1973*
- — Sherman Louis Sergel, *The Language of Show Biz*, p. 60, 1973

couch checkers *noun*
sexual foreplay *US, 1967*
- What sports to you like? Couch checkers? — Elaine Shepard, *The Doom Pussy*, p. 48, 1967

couch dance *noun*
a sexual dance performed in a sex club, with the dancer grinding on the lap of a man seated on a couch *US, 2002*
- Additionally, some officers are pulling the tough duty of sitting around in topless clubs and paying for table or couch dances, waiting to be "wrongly touched." — *Seattle Times*, p. D1, 20th June 1990
- "What's a couch dance?" "You take the guy into a private room filled with couches. No door, and a bouncer standing outside, keepin' an eye on things. You dance on his lap and he gropes you for three, or four minutes." — Richard N. Cote, *The Redneck Riviera*, p. 126, 2002
- Some of the girls sashay over to chat with the generous tippers or give private "couch dances" in circular booths along back walls. — *Cincinnati Enquirer*, p. 1B, 19th May 2003

couch potato *noun*
a person who habitually idles, watching television *US, 1976*

One of the very few slang words or phrases where it is seemingly possible to trace the coining; in July 1976 a group of friends in California coined the term, which was first used in commerce in 1977 and then hit the big time with the *Official Couch Potato Handbook* (1983).

- — Connie Eble (Editor), *UNC-CH Campus Slang*, p. 2, Spring 1984
- I'd be ready to give odds he's a couch potato, sitting in watching television while the other kids are out batting the baseball around or playing soccer. — Robert Campbell, *The Cat's Meow*, p. 75, 1988

cough and die *verb*
(used of a computer program) to cease operating by virtue of a design feature *US*, *1991*

- The parser saw a control-A in its input where it was looking for a printable, so it coughed and died. — Eric S. Raymond, *The New Hacker's Dictionary*, p. 109, 1991

cough syrup *noun*
money paid to police informers *US*, *1951*

- — *American Speech*, p. 155, May 1951: "Hermann Collitz and the language of the underworld"

count *noun*
1 the ratio by which a drug is diluted *US*, *1964*

- They say it's supposed to be six and one, but if the dealer is wise, he wants everybody to keep coming to him, and he wants to give them a nice count so they can fall out, he will go and cut it two and one, or three and one, and make it nice and strong. — Jeremy Larner and Ralph Tefferteller, *The Addict in the Street*, p. 38, 1964

2 the weight or amount of a drug *US*, *1967*

- COUNT: The amount or purity of a drug. — Elizabeth Finn, *Drugs in the Tenderloin*, 1967: Glossary of Drug Slang Used in the Tenderloin

count *verb*
in pool, to make a shot *US*, *1967*

- I started in there when I was 13 and when I was 14 I got my stroke. I got my stroke and learned to count [pocket the balls]. — Ned Polsky, *Hustlers, Beats, and Others*, p. 89, 1967

▸ **count days**
in twelve-step recovery programs such as Alcoholics Anonymous, to track your recovery from addiction *US*, *1998*

- We count our days since we last incurred unsecured debt. — Christopher Cavanaugh, *AA to Z*, p. 74, 1998

▸ **count your money**
to use the toilet *US*, *1954*

- — Jerry Robertson, *Oil Slanguage*, p. 41, 1954

counter *noun*
1 in poker, a player who to the annoyance of other players repeatedly counts his chips or money *US*, *1963*

- — Irwin Steig, *Common Sense in Poker*, p. 183, 1963

2 a prostitute's customer *US*, *1964*

- — Roger Blake, *The American Dictionary of Sexual Terms*, p. 48, 1964

country *noun*
▸ **in country**
during the Vietnam war, in Vietnam *US*, *1977*

- How much longer do you have in country? — Ronald J. Glasser, *365 Days*, p. 177, 1971
- After a few months "in country," the advisers and experts usually came to the conclusion that the United States was not sending enough commodities for them to do their job properly. — Frances Fitzgerald, *Fire in the Lake*, p. 347, 1972
- And I was new, brand new, three days in-country[.] — Michael Kerr, *Dispatches*, p. 167, 1977

country *adjective*
unsophisticated, rural, not world-wise *US*, *1964*

- You know what Otis? What. You're country. It's alright. — Otis Redding, *Tramp*, 1964
- Cuz you're so country. So Bama. I didn't know niggers like you still existed. — *Mo' Better Blues*, 1990

country bama *noun*
a naive, gullible rustic *US*, *1990*

- I can't imagine no country bama muthafucka talking bout. — *Boyz N The Hood*, 1990
- But he wasn't what Tracy used to call a "country bama," either. — Felicia Mason, *Truly, Honestly*, p. 304, 2000

- Because he's a big old country bama, ain't got no good sense. — Sandra Jackso Opoku, *Hot Johnny (and the Women Who Loved Him)*, p. 172, 2001
- In fact, I was gonna ask your country Bama ass why do you put those Jheri Curl drip-drip chemicals in your Black nappy hair? — Ayana Byrd, *Hair Story*, p. 112, 2001

country club *noun*
1 a minimum security, comfortable prison generally reserved for corporate and banking criminals *US*, *1960*

- Once, when jailed briefly in the early 50's, Costello was sent to a Federal country club near Flint, Michigan[.] — Lee Mortimer, *Women Confidential*, p. 34, 1960
- Chino, California's "country club" prison, yesterday had its first murder. — *San Francisco Examiner*, p. 18, 18th July 1972
- I should be going to one of those country-club joints like where they sent those Watergate assholes[.] — Elmore Leonard, *Freaky Deaky*, p. 13, 1988

2 anything that appears to be relatively comfortable and undemanding *US*, *1973*

- His instructors had spoken of some precincts that were "country clubs"—in the quieter residential sections of the city[.] — Peter Maas, *Serpico*, p. 58, 1973

country jake *noun*
a naive rustic *US*, *1973*

- "They're all tied into together, they're all country jakes." — Joe Eszterhas, *Charlie Simpson's Apocalypse*, p. 30, 1973

country mile *noun*
a long distance or margin *US*, *1951*

- — David W. Maurer, *Argot of the Racetrack*, p. 22, 1951
- I sliced one a country mile into a chocolate factory off the right fairway. — Sam Snead, *The Education of a Golfer*, p. 36, 1962
- I love my job, it's the best I've ever had by a country mile and turning up for work is an absolute delight. — Paul Vautin, *Turn It Up!*, p. 103, 1995

country send *noun*
in a big con, sending the victim away to retrieve money *US*, *1997*

- In the old days once a mark was hooked on the con, the sharpers would always send him home to get more money. It was called "The Country Send." — Stephen Cannell, *Big Con*, p. 292, 1997

country store *noun*
in the Vietnam war, a military self-service supply center *US*, *1968*

- — Carl Fleischhauer, *A Glossary of Army Slang*, p. 11, 1968

country straight *noun*
in poker, a hand consisting of four sequenced cards which can be converted into a five-card sequence with the correct draw at either end of the sequence *US*, *1978*

- — Thomas L. Clark, *The Dictionary of Gambling and Gaming*, p. 53, 1987

count store *noun*
a rigged carnival game *US*, *1985*

- — Gene Sorrows, *All About Carnivals*, p. 15, 1985

county *noun*
any county jail, where the accused are held before trial and prisoners convicted of misdemeanors are incarcerated for short sentences *US*, *1949*

- Leaving him a reasonless desire to go hurrying out through the snow to the nearest station, whatever the cost, in the hope of getting some sort of charge at County. — Nelson Algren, *The Man with the Golden Arm*, p. 304, 1949
- So there we were in County. — William Burroughs, *Junkie*, p. 66, 1953
- Okay gentlemen, you've both been to County before, I'm sure. Here it comes. — *Pulp Fiction*, 1994
- Judge said if we go within a hundred feet of the stores, we get thrown into County. — Kevin Smith, *Jay and Silent Bob Strike Back*, p. 14, 2001

county blues *noun*
a blue uniform issued to prisoners in a county jail *US*, *1993*

- Caine is dressed in the "County Blues"; that's the jumpsuit that they give all inmates. — *Menace II Society*, 1993

county shoes *noun*
inexpensive shoes issued to prisoners by a county jail *US*, *1973*

- One of them is still wearing his "county shoes." That tells me he just got out of county jail[.] — Joseph Wambaugh, *The Blue Knight*, p. 9, 1973

county time *noun*
time served in a local county jail, as opposed to a state or federal prison *US, 1996*
Less than "state time" or "hard time."
- Add county time awaiting hearings, and that hole we just left, that's more'n a decade of correctional living. — Elmore Leonard, *Out of Sight*, p. 45, 1996

Coupe *noun*
a Cadillac Coupe de Ville car *US, 1980*
- — Edith A. Folb, *runnin' down some lines*, p. 233, 1980

coupon *noun*
an "I owe you" which has not and will not be paid off *US, 1996*
- I haven't seen Big Larry in three months; I think I'm holding a coupon. — John Vorhaus, *The Big Book of Poker Slang*, p. 11, 1996

courage pill *noun*
a capsule of heroin *US, 1933*
- — Vincent J. Monteleone, *Criminal Slang*, p. 59, 1949
- I was discovering why heroin caps are so often called "courage pills." — Douglas Rutherford, *The Creeping Flesh*, p. 149, 1963

court *noun*
▸ **hold court in the street**
to mete out what a police officer deems justice through physical beatings *US, 2001*
- He was busting heads and holding court in the street, then getting you dummies to take the heat for him if complaints came down. — Stephen J. Cannell, *The Tin Collectors*, p. 179, 2001

court *verb*
to physically assault as part of a gang initiation *US, 2005*
- Now I know. Courting means to be physically "jumped in." — Colton Simpson, *Inside the Crips*, p. 19, 2005

court card *noun*
in a deck of playing cards, any jack, queen, or king *US, 1961*
- — Irv Roddy, *Friday Night Poker*, p. 217, 1961

courtesy flush *noun*
a mid-defecation flush of the toilet as a courtesy to others in a bathroom or other prisoners in the cell *US, 1972*
- The smell is terrible, and I open the only window. I can see someone's feet beneath the commode stall door. "Give us a courtesy flush, will ya?" — Dennis Smith, *Report From Engine Co. 82*, p. 179, 1972
- — Reinhold Aman, *Hillary Clinton's Pen Pal*, p. 33, 1996
- When performing the Courtesy Flush, always lift up from your seat to avoid speckling your ass with toilet water. — Fred Pollack, *The College Senior's Survival Guide to Corporate America*, p. 125, 2002

court-in *noun*
a ceremonial beating to initiate a new member into a gang *US, 1990*
- Giggles, Shygirl and Rascal performed the initiation they call a court-in, a 13-second beating that ended with tangled hair, smudged lipstick and a bloody nose. — *Houston Chronicle*, p. 3A, 4th February 1990
- — Mark S. Fleisher, *Beggars & Thieves*, p. 288, 1995

court in *verb*
to initiate into a youth gang *US, 1993*
- I had heard about being "courted in" ("courted in" means to be accepted through a barrage of tests, usually physical, though this can include shooting people) or "jumped in[.]" — Sanyika Shakur, *Monster*, p. 9, 1993

court-out *noun*
a ceremonial beating of a person leaving a gang *US, 1990*
- If she fails to do her part as a loyal gang member—if she is not, as the girls say, down for her neighborhood—she can face a "court-out," in which there is no time limit to the beating. — *Houston Chronicle*, p. 3A, 4th February 1990

cover *noun*
1 an admission fee paid to enter a bar or club *US, 1986*
A shortened "cover charge."
- Bellamy was so snockered he didn't even blink at the ten-dollar cover. — Carl Hiaasen, *Tourist Season*, p. 2, 1986

2 a single large-denomination bill wrapped around small-denomination bills, giving the impression of a great deal of money *US, 1964*
- He loved to flash his "Kansas City roll," probably fifty one-dollar bills folded with a twenty on the inside and a one-hundred dollar bill on the outside. We always wondered what Dollarbill would do if someone ever stole his hundred-dollar "cover." — Malcolm X and Alex Haley, *The Autobiography of Malcolm X*, p. 89, 1964

3 a recording which has been popularized by someone else *US, 1970*
A shortened form of the more formal "cover version."
- Listen, it isn't bad enough, we have to do covers, we're doing the Spice Girls, and those chicks can't even fucking sing. — Elmore Leonard, *Be Cool*, p. 35, 1999

4 the disguise and staged personality assumed by an expert card counter playing blackjack in a casino in the hope of avoiding detection and ejection *US, 1991*
- — Michael Dalton, *Blackjack*, p. 25, 1991

cover *verb*
(used of a favorite by sports gamblers) to win by at least the margin established as the pointspread by the bookmakers *US, 1991*
- — *Bay Sports Review*, p. 8, November 1991

covered wagon *noun*
1 an improvised tent in a prison cell used to conceal sexual activity *US, 1950*
- They built "covered wagons" or "hunks" around the beds. That screened out what went on inside the bunks. — Haywood Patterson, *Scottsboro Boy*, p. 65, 1950
- "Prisoners, they got this thing they do called 'the covered wagon.' What they do is string up a blanket from a bunk so the guards can't see into the cell. Then they take fresh ass, a guy like you, behind the blanket and gang-fuck him." — John Ridley, *Love is a Racket*, p. 271, 1998

2 an aircraft carrier, especially the USS Langley *US, 1933*
- The nickname "covered wagon" describes the way the Langley looked with its rooflike landing strip over the deck. — *Sunday Telegram* (Worcester, Massachusetts), p. B1, 4th May 1997
- They called it a covered wagon because the flight deck was above the well deck making the ship sort of look like a covered wagon. — *Virginian-Pilot* (Norfolk, Virginia), p. 5, 5th September 1997

covered with horseshoes *adjective*
extremely lucky *US, 1988*
- — George Percy, *The Language of Poker*, p. 24, 1988

covers *noun*
▸ **pull the covers off**
to reveal someone's homosexuality *US, 1981*
- — *Maledicta*, p. 265, Summer/Winter 1981: "By its slang, ye shall know it: the pessimism of prison life"

▸ **pull your covers**
to harass *US, 2002*
- "It's all good, O.G. I ain't fittin' to pull yo covers." — Jimmy Lerner, *You Got Nothing Coming*, p. 96, 2002

▸ **to pull someone's covers**
to catch someone in a lie *US, 1967*
- "If they try to pull your covers," Fassenaux feels compelled to advise me, "retaliate. Pull their motherfucking covers." — Ken Kesey, *Kesey's Jail Journal*, p. 4, 1967

covey *noun*
a group of gullible people, likely victims for a swindle or crime *US, 1964*
- — R. Frederick West, *God's Gambler*, p. 223, 1964

cow *noun*
1 a prostitute attached to a pimp *US, 1859*
- Her tricks, when she functioned as an independent instead of a cow, had been hundred-dollar babies who came highly recommended. — John M. Murtagh and Sara Harris, *Cast the First Stone*, p. 128, 1957
- Pimps also refer to the women as "cows" and "shitkickers." — Sara Harris, *The Lords of Hell*, p. 48, 1967

2 a can of evaporated milk *US, 1975*
- When the cow is called for, the standard reply is, "Send down the milk, the calf's blattin'!" — John Gould, *Maine Lingo*, p. 62, 1975

▶ **have a cow**

to become emotionally overwrought; to lose control *US*, *1966*
- — Collin Baker et al., *College Undergraduate Slang Study Conducted at Brown University*, p. 100, 1968
- — Connie Eble (Editor), *UNC-CH Campus Slang*, April 1978
- My mom had a cow. — Francesca Lia Block, *I Was a Teenage Fairy*, p. 134, 1998
- Martha Stewart would have a cow over my apartment. — Janet Evanovich, *Seven Up*, p. 99, 2001

cowabunga; cuyabunga!

used as an expression of triumph *US*, *1955*
Originally a signature line uttered by Chief Thunderthud on *The Howdy Doody Show* (NBC, 1947–60). Embraced by surfers, American soldiers in Vietnam, and the writers of *Teenage Mutant Ninja Turtles* and *The Simpsons*.
- Those hopscotch poledads and pedestrians too, will bug ya / Shout "Cuyabunga!" now and skate right on through. — Jan Berry and Dean Torrance, *Sidewalk Surfin'*, 1964
- — Hy Lit, *Hy Lit's Unbelievable Dictionary of Hip Words for Groovy People*, p. 10, 1968
- Gene Brabender sometimes walks around bellowing "cowabunga!" So I threw some trivia at him. "Bender, who first said 'cowabunga?'" — Jim Bouton, *Ball Four*, p. 314, 1970

cowboy *noun*

1 a reckless, impulsive, undisciplined person *US*, *1926*
- A Cuban has trouble getting in and out; and besides, this is not a cowboy job. — Edwin Torres, *Carlito's Way*, p. 72, 1975
- Am I crazy? I got a business. What do I need cowboy stuff for? — Richard Condon, *Prizzi's Honor*, p. 234, 1982
- He's a good kid, but he's crazy. He's a cowboy. He's got too much to prove. — *Goodfellas*, 1990
- Myhand had a reputation as an energetic, likeable "cowboy" who, like Shoats, preferred action to talk. — Pete Earley, *The Hot House*, p. 116, 1992

2 a driver prone to breaking the rules of the road *US*, *1928*
- — *New York Times Magazine*, p. 88, 16th March 1958

3 in computing, a person with intelligence, knowledge, and dedication to programing *US*, *1991*
- Eric S. Raymond, *The New Hacker's Dictionary*, p. 109, 1991

4 in a deck of playing cards, a king *US*, *1967*
- — Albert H. Morehead, *The Complete Guide to Winning Poker*, p. 260, 1967

cowboy *verb*

1 to act in a reckless, fearless fashion *US*, *1954*
- So you cowboy it; you rob everything and anything in the way of business establishments that you happen to find open for business. — Caryl Chessman, *Cell 2456 Death Row*, p. 175, 1954

2 to murder someone in a reckless manner *US*, *1946*
- And the wops are gonna cowboy me on sight. Open contract. — Edwin Torres, *Q & A*, p. 180, 1977

3 to gang-rape someone *US*, *1957*
- They cowboyed him in the steam room. — William Burroughs, *Naked Lunch*, p. 188, 1957

cowboy *adjective*

reckless, impulsive, flamboyant *US*, *1951*
- To shoot a man off his front doorstep, without the mapped-out getaway, the "hot" car, the other fine details carefully worked out, was truly a "cowboy job." — Burton Turkus and Sid Feder, *Murder, Inc.*, p. 9, 1951

cowboy Cadillac *noun*

any pickup truck *US*, *1976*
- — Wayne Floyd, *Jason's Authentic Dictionary of CB Slang*, p. 13, 1976
- Came back to town once in a cowboy Cadillac, big old bull horns on the hood and six-shooters for door handles. — Craig Lesley, *The Sky Fisherman*, p. 78, 1995

cowboy coffee *noun*

coffee boiled in an open pot, served without milk or sugar *US*, *1943*
- I taught him how to make cowboy coffee by merely throwing the grinds into the pot, and I drank plenty of it, loving the smell of it. — Anne Rice, *Servant of the Bones*, p. 15, 1996

cowboy cool *adjective*

(used of beer) at room temperature *US*, *1984*
- I don't have any cold beers, but you're welcome to one of these if you don't mind it being cowboy cool. — Ken Weaver, *Texas Crude*, p. 63, 1984

cowboy coupe *noun*

a pickup truck decked out with accessories *US*, *1962*
- — *American Speech*, p. 268, December 1962: "The language of traffic policemen"

cowboy gun *noun*

a revolver *US*, *2006*
- He traded $50 worth of marijuana for a stolen "cowboy gun," a .22 caliber revolver. — *Philadelphia Daily News*, p. Local 3, 27th December 2006

cowboys and Indians *noun*

a prison sentence of 99 years *US*, *1990*
- — Charles Shafer, *Folk Speech in Texas Prisons*, p. 201, 1990

cow college *noun*

a small rural college, especially one offering degrees in agriculture *US*, *1906*
- Your career would have been different—you might have been stuck in some cow college. — Wallace Stegner, *Crossing to Safety*, p. 8, 1987

cow cunt *noun*

a despicable person *US*, *1988*
- Creepy cow cunt like Krystal! — Mary Mcgary Morris, *Vanished*, p. 61, 1988
- A retard. A cow cunt. — Joyce Carol Oates, *Foxfire*, p. 149, 1994

cow-cunted *adjective*

possessing a slack and distended vagina *US*, *1994*
- — *Maledicta*, p. 184, Winter 1980: "A new erotic vocabulary"
- — Michael Dalton Johnson, *Talking Trash with Redd Foxx*, p. 64, 1994

cow fence *noun*

a defensive barbed-wire fence around a military camp *US*, *1968*
- Cow fence—Applies to the Barrier—a five- to six-foot-high barbed-wire fence. — Kenneth Mertel, *Year of the Horse*, p. 320, 1968

cowgirl *noun*

a sexual position in which the woman is on top, astride and facing her partner *US*, *1995*
- — *Adult Video News*, p. 42, August 1995
- [I]n describing one of these positions (called the "cowgirl," in which the woman is facing the man and sitting up, or the "reverse cowgirl," in which she faces away from him) a pornographic director has said: "Very unnatural position. The girls hate it.["] — Gail Dines, *Pornography*, p. 76, 1998
- These include fellatio, cunnilingus, missionary-style, doggie-style, cowgirl, reverse cowgirl, double penetration, double-pussy penetration and double-anal penetration. — Carolina Vegas Starr, *Jobs Your Mother Never Wanted You to Have*, p. 77, 2002
- [S]he refuses to stand still when there is a stud to mount and romp in cowgirl superior. — Mr. Skin, *Mr. Skin's Skincyclopedia*, p. 388, 2005

cow kicker *noun*

an electric prod *US*, *1973*
- "And just to make sure he felt like a real spring chicken once he got out of the truck, I hit him with a cow kicker in the ass." — Vincent Teresa, *My Life in the Mafia*, p. 158, 1973

cow lick *noun*

in publishing, inexpensive varnish used on a book cover *US*, *1986*
- — Rachel S. Epstein and Nina Liebman, *Biz Speak*, p. 50, 1986

cowyard *noun*

an inexpensive brothel *US*, *1964*
- The worst conditions for prostitutes were found in 6-foot by 6-foot cribs and multi-story "cowyards" off Pacific Street, which was known to sailors everywhere as Terrific Street. — *San Francisco Examiner*, p. A17, 26th December 1994

cox box *noun*

an electronic device that includes an amplifier/microphone system as well as various measurement functions, used by a coxswain in competitive rowing *US*, *1999*
- Cox box: The in-boat intercom used by the coxswain to be sure all eight rowers can hear the commands. — Sue Muller Hacking, *Boatless in Seattle*, p. 76, 1999

coxey; cocksy *noun*

an inexperienced swindler working on a scam by telephone who makes the initial call to potential victims *US*, *1988*
- — Kathleen Odean, *High Steppers, Fallen Angels, and Lollipops*, p. 132, 1988

coxy *noun*

a *cox*swain *US, 1966*

- He's coxy on the Olympic crew. — Richard Farina, *Been Down So Long*, p. 39, 1966
- — Judy's Enterprises, *Coxswain Postcard*, 2001

coyote date *noun*

a date with an ugly woman *US, 1985*

- When you wake up in the morning and she's laying on your arm, you chew your arm off so she won't wake up as you leave. That's a coyote date. — Mark Baker, *Cops*, p. 231, 1985
- "Has anyone out there ever had a coyote date?" — Richard Meltzer, *A Whore Just Like the Rest*, p. 377, 2000

coyote ugly *adjective*

very ugly *US, 1985*

The conceit of the term is that a man who wakes up with a "coyote ugly" woman sleeping on his arm will, like a coyote caught in a trap, gnaw off his arm to escape.

- In an interview, [Judge Bernard] Avellino said the victim "was the ugliest girl have ever seen in my entire life ... in the top 10." Avellino was also quoted as calling the victim "coyote ugly." — *Los Angeles Times*, p. 2, 5th February 1986
- *Philadelphia Inquirer*, p. A1, 27th January 1986
- [A] judge chastised a defendant accused in an attempted rape case for having picked an "unattractive girl" and later, in a subsequent interview, described the victim as "coyote ugly," society is again sent a clear message. — Laura A. Otten, *Women's Rights and the Law*, p. 9, 1993

cozmo *noun*

phencyclidine, the recreational drug known as PCP or angel dust *US, 1994*

- — US Department of Justice, *Street Terms*, October 1994

c phone *noun*

a cell phone *US, 1997*

"C" is for "cellular."

- — Pamela Munro, *U.C.L.A. Slang*, p. 49, 1997

CPT; CP time *noun*

a notional system of time in which punctuality is not important *US, 1925*

An abbreviation of **COLORED PEOPLE'S TIME**.

- And come on time, not C.P.T. — Letter from Langston Hughes to Carl Van Vechten, 23rd September 1949
- Their lives run by a clock that keeps C.P.T., Colored People's Time, which assumes that appointments won't be kept, work promised won't be delivered, jobs found won't be gone to, since those are all part of the outside world. — Paul Jacobs, *Prelude to a Riot*, p. 12, 1967
- In recognition of the fact that a stereotype has developed regarding C.P. Time, the first 15 minutes of any meeting shall henceforth be known as J.T. (Jive Time). — Carolyn Greene, *70 Soul Secrets of Sapphire*, 1973
- Although there are cultural jokes about "CP time" (being chronically or consistently late), I was once told by a brother from Kenya that "things begin when the people gather." — Teresa L. Fry Brown, *God Don't Live Ugly*, 2000

crab *noun*

1 in the language of members of the Bloods youth gang, a member of the Crips youth gang *US, 1987*

- "We keep Crabs out of our 'hood," he said, referring to area Crip gang members. — *Los Angeles Times*, p. 6 (Metro), 8th November 1987
- "Fuck you, Crabs!" someone in the car yelled—an increasingly familiar war cry. — Bob Sipchen, *Baby Insane and the Buddha*, p. 110, 1993
- "Yeah, you, you little crab-ass punk!" (Crab is a disrespectful term used by Bloods against Crips—defacing the enemy.) — Sanyika Shakur, *Monster*, p. 22, 1993
- "There's crabs in the 'hood," she said, using the derogatory slang for "Crips," a rival gang. — *Omaha World-Herald*, p. 1A, 18th September 2002

2 a first-year college student *US, 1947*

- — Marcus Hanna Boulware, *Jive and Slang of Students in Negro Colleges*, 1947

crab *verb*

1 in the language of parachuting, to direct the parachute across the wind direction *US, 1978*

- — Dan Poynter, *Parachuting*, p. 166, 1978: "The language of parachuting"

2 in the television and movie industries, to move the camera sideways *US, 1987*

- — Ira Konigsberg, *The Complete Film Dictionary*, p. 67, 1987

crab bait *noun*

a newly arrived prisoner *US, 1976*

- — John R. Armore and Joseph D. Wolfe, *Dictionary of Desperation*, p. 25, 1976

crabby *adjective*

ill humored, perpetually mean, cross *US, 1908*

The villain of the extremely popular 1957 *Tom Terrific* cartoon series from Terry-Toon Cartoon Studios was the aptly named Crabby Appleton, who was, we remember, "rotten to the core."

- It was something else bothering her, or her life in general that made her crabby. Sitting there pissed off in her black bra and panties. — Elmore Leonard, *Glitz*, p. 188, 1985

crabs *noun*

1 pubic lice *UK, 1707*

- The Inspector opens his fly and begins looking for crabs, applying ointment from a little clay pot. — William Burroughs, *Naked Lunch*, p. 73, 1957
- I'll stay a week / And get the crabs / And take a bus back home. — Frank Zappa, *Who Needs The Peace Corps?*, 1968
- The French call them papillons d'amour, i.e., the "butterflies of love." I call them crabs, the tiny parasites of crotch. — Jim Carroll, *Forced Entries*, p. 4, 1987
- When we were kids in the Navy, he had such a bad case of crabs, we used to call him the Governor of Maryland. — *The Sopranos (Episode 60)*, 2004

2 in craps, a three *US, 1938*

- — Thomas L. Clark, *The Dictionary of Gambling and Gaming*, p. 53, 1987

3 by extension, in a deck of playing cards, any three *US, 1981*

- — Thomas L. Clark, *The Dictionary of Gambling and Gaming*, p. 53, 1987

crack *noun*

1 crystalline lumps of concentrated cocaine *US, 1985*

- When cocaine got too expensive for the 'hood, crack was invented. Now brothers with fourth-grade educations go down into their basements and become mad scientists. — Chris Rock, *Rock This!*, p. 68, 1997
- The simple technique used in the preparation of crack consists of heating cocaine hydrochloride in a baking soda and water solution[.] — Richard Rudgley, *The Encyclopaedia of Psychoactive Substances*, p. 69, 1998
- Hip hop 'bin around since 1970. It got exposed in 1979. So once it's exposed, this is it. Just like crack. Crack 'bin around, till Richard Pryor got burnt up, then it went: whoosh! — Alex Ogg, *The Hip Hop Years* [quoting Kool Herc], p. 45, 1999

2 a witticism; a quick and funny remark *US, 1884*

- I sat there in the tree-shaded yard, listening to Axel talk and Marie make cracks[.] — Clancy Sigal, *Going Away*, p. 240, 1961

3 the vagina *UK, 1775*

The imagery from which this derives should be apparent; it remains in widespread use.

- "Snatch," "hole," "kooze," "slash," "pussy" and "crack" were other terms referring variously to women's genitals, to women as individuals, or to women as a species. — *Screw*, p. 5, 3rd January 1972
- I could feel the soft hairs over her crack and they aroused me like always. — Donald Goines, *Never Die Alone*, p. 163, 1974
- He used his forefingers to gently pry her crack apart. — Jon Sharpe, *Springfield Shooters*, p. 73, 1994
- She splays wide her hairless crack before Max Hardcore (real name Max Steiner), who initiates her into the Mile-High Club. — Editors of Adult Video News, *The AVN Guide to the 500 Greatest Adult Films of All Time*, p. 199, 2005

4 an instance; one item *US, 1937*

- He and I and Alvah drove to Oakland in Morley's car and went first to some Goodwill stores and Salvation Army stores to buy various flannel shirts (at fifty cents a crack) and undershirts. — Jack Kerouac, *The Dharma Bums*, p. 84, 1958

5 an opportunity or chance *US, 1893*

- Okay, who wants to take a crack at wiring Mr. Zimm's jaw? — *Get Shorty*, 1995

crack *verb*

1 to shoot *US, 1984*

- We both had a look of surprise. And I cracked him. — Wallace Terry, *Bloods*, p. 21, 1984

2 to burglarize *US, 1972*

- We would go crack some poison joints and he would get enough stuff [drugs] to last him two or three months. — Harry King, *Box Man*, p. 48, 1972

s to speak *US, 1897*

- I said, "Have you cracked anything about me to him?" — Iceberg Slim (Robert Beck), *Pimp*, p. 155, 1969
- As I was about ready to end my spiel, my man Walter cracked "Go on and pimp, Stoney, to hell with what any black-ass pimping sonuvabitch gotta say!" — A.S. Jackson, *Gentleman Pimp*, p. 45, 1973
- When I crack on a female "how you livin'?" she got to respond to me in the positive, or I don't waste my time. — Terry Williams, *The Cocaine Kids*, p. 87, 1989

4 to ask for something *US, 1928*

- Oh yeah, you can cop a "spike" [needle] at any drug store. You gotta crack for insulin with it. — Iceberg R. Slim (Robert Beck), *Pimp*, p. 135, 1969
- When I cracked for seconds, the hack stood there looking / I said, "Serve it raw, punk. The chair'll do the cooking." — Dennis Wepman et al., *The Life*, p. 118, 1976

5 to reveal a secret; to inform on someone *US, 1922*

- [I]t was easy going through the usual jailhouse bullshit, answering a lotta things, like who's doing what, how long Joe Blow been dealing, how'd I get cracked, who cracked me. — A.S. Jackson, *Gentleman Pimp*, p. 127, 1973

6 to tease someone; to taunt someone; to insult someone *US, 1942*

- The girls used to fight over their macs. "That coffee-an' mac you got," a French girl would crack to a straight one, and then it was on—hair came out by the handful. — Mezz Mezzrow, *Really the Blues*, p. 23, 1946
- When he was new to the life he'd liked to crack on them just for the sport. — Alix Shulman, *On the Stroll*, p. 229, 1981
- Rodney, man, I was just crackin'. — Richard Price, *Clockers*, p. 181, 1992
- — Vann Wesson, *Generation X Field Guide and Lexicon*, p. 42, 1997

7 to arrrest someone *US, 1952*

- Did you know that was the time I got cracked? That the Man swooped down on me? — Clarence Cooper Jr., *The Farm*, p. 46, 1967
- I had spent the two months in County Jail where I had been taken after Captain Churchill, a "House" bloodhound, backed by city police, crashed my pad and cracked me on an ancient fugitive warrant for the escape from the "House." — Iceberg Slim (Robert Beck), *The Naked Soul of Iceberg Slim*, p. 21, 1971
- How did you get cracked on that there rape beef, anyway, Green Grass? — Charles W. Moore, *A Brick for Mister Jones*, p. 103, 1975

▸ **crack a bennie**
to break a Benzedrine™ (amphetamine sulfate) inhaler open *US, 1970*

- — William D. Alsever, *Glossary for the Establishment and Other Uptight People*, p. 7, December 1970

▸ **crack a rat**
to fart *US, 1998*

- — Peter Furze, *Tailwinds*, p. 39, 1998

▸ **crack a short**
to break into a car *US, 1970*

- — William D. Alsever, *Glossary for the Establishment and Other Uptight People*, p. 7, 1970

▸ **crack the nut**
to meet an operation's daily operating expenses *US, 1980*

- — Joe McKennon, *Circus Lingo*, p. 29, 1980

▸ **crack wise**
to insult someone with a degree of sarcasm and humor *US, 1921*
Imparts a slight air of the old gangster life.

- If he was all hopped up, cracking wise, acting big buying drinks for the house, he was on his way. — Mezz Mezzrow, *Really the Blues*, p. 59, 1946
- He came up to me cracking wise all the way and we shook hands. — Clancy Sigal, *Going Away*, p. 350, 1961
- Such a wiseass. But go ahead. Crack wise. That's why you're jockeying a register in some fucking local convenience store instead of doing an honest day's work. — *Clerks*, 1994

▸ **crack your cherry**
to lose your innocence or virginity *US, 1970*

- He had no idea he was talking to a young man who cracked his cherry in the thievery business with forty times that at Ludwig's. — Red Rudensky, *The Gonif*, p. 76, 1970

▸ **get cracking**
to start, to begin work *UK, 1937*

- In, out—let's get crackin'! — Stephen Sondheim, *West Side Story*, 1957

crack *adjective*
excellent *UK, 1793*

- I rode all the way back on The Chief, the crack train on the Santa Fe[.] — Mezz Mezzrow, *Really the Blues*, p. 137, 1946

crack attack *noun*
the intense craving for crack cocaine felt by an addict *US, 1992*

- — Terry Williams, *Crackhouse*, p. 148, 1992

crack baby *noun*
a child born with an addiction to crack cocaine *US, 1988*

- A "crack baby" addicted to cocaine because the mother was an addict. — Paul Boller, *A More Perfect Union*, p. 289, 1988
- "But they are not that much smaller that you can walk in and say that's a crack baby." — *St. Petersburg Times*, p. 3B, 23rd May 1988
- These are cocaine and crack babies. Born carrying a psychic ball and chain they didn't ask for. — *New Jack City*, 1990
- "Um … cause I a motherfuckin' crack baby, man." — Jess Mowry, *Six Out Seven*, p. 16, 1993

crack cooler *noun*
pieces of crack cocaine soaked in a wine cooler drink *US, 1994*

- — US Department of Justice, *Street Terms*, 1994

crack down *verb*
in horse racing, to be determined to win a race *US, 1994*

- — Igor Kushyshyn et al., *The Gambling Times Guide to Harness Racing*, p. 114, 1994

cracked ice *noun*
diamonds that have been removed from their settings *US, 1962*

- — Joseph E. Ragen and Charles Finston, *Inside the World's Toughest Prison*, p. 795, 1962

cracked out *adjective*
suffering symptoms of heavy crack cocaine usage *US, 1988*

- The way it is now, Ronnie could do it, play himself, some cracked out asshole. — *Get Shorty*, 1995

cracked squash *noun*
a fractured skull *US, 1984–1985*

- — *Maledicta*, p. 117, 1984–1985: "Milwaukee medical maledicta"

cracker *noun*

1 a poor, uneducated, racist white from the southern US *US, 1766*

- Tommy was another cracker bastard. — Chester Himes, *If He Hollers Let Him Go*, p. 26, 1945
- "I'm Ethel Waters," I told him, "and I'm standing on my grounds. And you or no other cracker sonofabitch can tell me what to do." — Ethel Waters, *His Eye is on the Sparrow*, p. 203, 1951
- I think we ought to just challenge for the heck of it every two hours or so, just to let those crackers know that we are on our toes and they'd better not try anything. — Stokely Carmichael and Charles V. Hamilton, *Black Power*, p. 110, 1967
- [A] number-one-all-Amerikan cracker[.] — Abbie Hoffman, *Woodstock Nation*, p. 41, 1969

2 the buttocks *US, 1948*

- And the loudest cusser is generally the first one knocked on his cracker and sent to the bench for repairs. — *Fortnight*, p. 11, 31st December 1948
- Now their fear of missing something has carried them almost, but not quite, to the point of hoping that Clay wins so that the beautiful sight they want most to see—that of Clay on his cracker—might be "saved" for their eyes at some later date. — *San Francisco Examiner*, p. 61, 23rd March 1966

3 a person who breaches a computer system's security scheme *US, 1991*
Coined by hackers in defense against journalistic misuse of their word.

- — Eric S. Raymond, *The New Hacker's Dictionary*, p. 110, 1991
- These crackers exploited a flaw in the VMS infrastructure which DEC Corporation had announced was remedied three months earlier. — The Knightmare, *Secrets of a Super Hacker*, p. 8, 1994

4 a phonograph record *US, 1947*

- — *Time Magazine*, p. 92, 20th January 1947

cracker-ass *noun*
a thin person *US, 1966*

- "He's a cracker-ass cracker." — Kevin Dole, *Tangerinephant*, p. 111, 2005

crackerbox *noun*

a plain, box-like house *US, 1945*

- The people sweltering through the early dog days of late spring ... not warm enough to stay outside all the time, but too warm to stay inside the crackerbox walls[.] — Odie Hawkins, *Ghetto Sketches*, p. 9, 1972

- The house was a frame crackerbox with a pair of dormer windows sticking out of the roof and no style at all until Richard fixed up the front with imitation ledgerock, a grillwork porch and striped aluminum awnings over the porch and windows. — Elmore Leonard, *Switch*, p. 37, 1978

- Why on earth didn't I sell this run-down little cracker box and return to my hometown[?] — Armistead Maupin, *Maybe the Moon*, p. 19, 1992

cracker-box *adjective*

plain, simple, unsophisticated *US, 1911*

- [H]earing for month after month after month of the achievements of bums like Floyd and Karpis and Nelson and Dillinger, who were getting rich off cracker-box banks. — Horace McCoy, *Kiss Tomorrow Goodbye*, p. 7, 1948

Crackerdom *noun*

an area inhabited predominantly by racist white people *US, 1987*

- My Lady saved me from Georgia, the Georgia that I had thought of, the world that represented Crackerdom, was undermined by people from another place. — Odie Hawkins, *Scars and Memories*, pp. 82–83, 1987

cracker factory *noun*

a mental hospital *US, 1970*

- You'd have me sent to a cracker factory if I told you. — Sidney Sheldon, *The Naked Face*, p. 160, 1970

- Six months in a five-star cracker factory, and that woman is home free. — Judith Kelman, *One Last Kiss*, p. 70, 1994

crackerjack *noun*

an excellent example of something *US, 1895*

- We've got a crackerjack here, Miss Chambers, who's been with us twenty years. — Mary McCarthy, *The Group*, p. 199, 1963

crackerjack *adjective*

highly skilled, excellent *US, 1899*

- Everything is shipshape, jim-dandy, and crackerjack[.] — Jim Thompson, *The Nothing Man*, p. 189, 1954

- "Yes, sir," interrupted Jefferson, "we have gone and made us a real crackerjack of a college." — Max Shulman, *Anyone Got a Match?*, p. 125, 1964

- I've been getting crackerjack reports from them, particularly in Empathy[.] — Gore Vidal, *Myra Breckinridge*, p. 48, 1968

- I know some cracker jack pool hustlers solo sharking that are starving to death. — Iceberg Slim (Robert Beck), *Mama Black Widow*, p. 158, 1969

crackers *noun*

LSD *US, 1967*

From the practice, at least in Boston, of saturating animal cracker cookies with LSD and selling it in that form.

- — John Williams, *The Drug Scene*, p. 111, 1967

crackers *adjective*

crazy, mad *UK, 1925*

- I guess he and Kurt told me all that crap just to see exactly how crackers I was! — Beatrice Sparks (writing as 'Anonymous'), *Jay's Journal*, p. 40, 1979

crack gallery *noun*

a building or room where crack cocaine is sold and smoked *US, 1989*

- — Terry Williams, *The Cocaine Kids*, p. 136, 1989

- Ques pulled the cab into the trash-strewn parking lot, and he spoke his first impression: "Place is a crack gallery, folks." — Robert McCammon, *Blue World*, p. 193, 1990

crack girl *noun*

a girl or woman addicted to crack cocaine *US, 1980s*

- If you catch the crack girl early on she can still look fine. Three weeks into the addiction, no one can tell the difference—except that a girl who would normally never talk to you ... will fuck you for five or ten dollars. — Chris Rock, *Rock This!*, p. 79, 1997

crackhead *noun*

a person addicted to crack cocaine *US, 1986*

- "I want quality young people in this organization, not crackheads, is that understood?" he said again. — *New York Times*, p. 8 (Section 11), 10th August 1986

- — Terry Williams, *Crackhouse*, p. 148, 1992

- The guy could be a crackhead. — *Sleepless in Seattle*, 1993

- Marion Barry at the Million Man March. Do you know what that means? Even in our finest hour we had a crackhead on stage. — Chris Rock, *Rock This!*, p. 187, 1997

crack house *noun*

a building or room where crack cocaine may be bought and consumed *US, 1985*

- Meanwhile, narcotics officers of the New York City Police Department have shut down a few of the so-called crack houses, the rough equivalent of heroin-shooting galleries, where sales are made and users gather for smoking binges that can last for several days. — *New York Times*, p. A1, 29th November 1985

- You know, they turned that spot into a crack house, it's just crack and more crack. — Terry Williams, *The Cocaine Kids*, p. 70, 1989

- She took me to crack houses. They stink. — S. Beth Atkin, *Voices from the Street*, p. 7, 1996

crackie *noun*

a crack cocaine user *US, 1997*

- Back in 1989–1990, I spent many nights in the East Village of New York hanging out with "crackies" of all stripes around makeshift bonfires of the insanities. — Jim Crotty, *How to Talk American*, p. 90, 1997

crack in the shack *noun*

a homosexual in a jail cell *US, 1984*

- "What's happening in there?" "We got us a crack in the shack, man. Want to get down? — Inez Cardozo-Freeman, *The Joint*, p. 490, 1984

cracko *noun*

a crazy person *US, 1981*

- Crackos pulled knives on the street[.] — Alix Shulman, *On the Stroll*, p. 8, 1981

crack out *verb*

1 to escape from prison *US, 1950*

- — Hyman E. Goldin et al., *Dictionary of American Underworld Lingo*, p. 51, 1950

2 in a swindle, to relieve the victim of his money quickly *US, 1977*

- — Robert C. Prus and C.R.D. Sharper, *Road Hustler*, p. 169, 1977

crackpot *noun*

a person who is somewhere in the continuum between odd and crazy *UK, 1883*

- When Washington was suddenly flooded with a horde of crackpots from the campuses, Communists, ballet-dancers and economic planners, there was no place for them to live. — Jack Lait and Lee Mortimer, *Washington Confidential*, p. 9, 1951

- What the hell, we were supposed to be here as observers, not as participants in any of Allen's crackpot schemes. — Terry Southern, *Now Dig This*, p. 122, November 1968

- "The Beach police think it's a crackpot," Garcia added in a noncommittal way. — Carl Hiaasen, *Tourist Season*, p. 54, 1986

- "Just remember," Rebus warned, "the person we're looking for might be a crackpot too." — Ian Rankin, *The Falls*, p. 99, 2001

crack rack *noun*

a small seat mounted behind the regular seat on a bicycle *US, 2002*

- I pat my jacket, bundled and bungeed onto the crack rack over my rear wheel for her comfort, all inviting. — Lynn Breedlove, *Godspeed*, p. 73, 2002

cracksmoker *noun*

a person whose sanity is open to question, whether or not they actually smoke crack *US, 1997*

- — *Maybeck High School Yearbook (Berkeley, California)*, p. 28, 1997

crack-up *noun*

1 a nervous breakdown *US, 1936*

- So return with us now to Los Angeles where Brenda (Griffiths) is headed for a crack-up even before she hits her mother, the crazy psychiatrist Joanna Cassidy[.] — *New York Metro*, 4th March 2002

2 a cause for laughter *US, 1961*

- Yes sir, I was definitely the life of the party. A real crack-up. — Bill Myers, *The Incredible Worlds of Wally Mcdoogle #7*, p. 33, 1994

crack up *verb*

1 to undergo a nervous breakdown *US, 1917*

- Lank lizards, as Weetzie would say. Maybe I am cracking up.
  — Francesca Lia Block, *Missing Angel Juan*, p. 293, 1993

2 to amuse someone greatly; to cause laughter *US, 1942*

- And that cracked me up, because I grew up with him. — Ben Fong-Torres, *Hickory Wind*, p. 72, 1991

crack whore *noun*

a prostitute motivated by a desire to buy crack cocaine *US, 1980s*

- A crack whore named Princess from the Forties House in South Jamaica had turned up dead in the grass near an exit ramp to Greenwich, Connecticut. — *San Francisco Chronicle*, p. 5 (Sunday Review), 19th August 1990
- See, he likes to smoke crack; she's a crackhead. There's a difference. She leaves because she's a drifting crack whore and she literally sleeps where she ends up. — Chris Rock, *Rock This!*, p. 75, 1997

cracoid *noun*

a crack cocaine addict *US, 1990*

- A turf challenge was slanting across the Strip, a precision patrol of cracoids swivelhipping between stalled bumpers straight for the Blue Note. — Seth Morgan, *Homeboy*, p. 17, 1990

cradle rape *noun*

sex with a girl under the age of consent *US, 1969*

- What's your story, morning glory? It costs three grand to fix cradle rape. — Iceberg Slim (Robert Beck), *Trick Baby*, p. 161, 1969

cradle robber *noun*

a person who is in a sexual relationship with someone who is far younger than they are *US, 1920*

- And besides that, I'm no cradle robber. — Patricia McLaine, *Love is Contagious*, p. 30, 1961
- "That woman's a cradle-robber from way back." — Glenn Savan, *White Palace*, p. 249, 1987

cradle-snatcher *noun*

a person who is in a sexual relationship with someone who is far younger than they are *US, 1907*

- She would be discreet in front of people, not wanting to cross the middle-class sensibilities of the hotel clientele by appearing to be a cradle-snatcher. — Robert Klein, *The Amorous Busboy of Decatur Avenue*, p. 152, 2005

craftsman *noun*

a socially inept dolt *US, 1992*

- [T]he cha ("very cool") worlds include: "winded" for hung over; "craftsman" for a complete idiot; and "ass" for awful. — *Washington Times*, p. C3, 26th August 1992

cram it!

used for registering an imperative rejection *US, 1957*

- "Hey, did the mirror fog up, Susan? Did you touch yourself?" "Would you just cram it?" Susan said. — Howard Stern, *Miss America*, p. 277, 1995

cramp *noun*

an unpleasant person *US, 1992*

- Stupid cramp, man! — Jess Mowry, *Way Past Cool*, p. 32, 1992

cramp *verb*

▸ **cramp someone's style**

to hamper or prevent someone from doing, or being at, their best *US, 1917*

From sporting use.

- "If you don't think it would cramp you style, Franzie, to have me around—I will." — Frederick Kohner, *Gidget Goes to Rome*, p. 109, 1963

cramper *noun*

a small cage in which a prisoner of war is confined *US, 1986*

- The cage, with a locked drop gate facing the open end of the horseshoe of buildings, was not large enough for him to stand or fully extend himself on the ground, and Veil had to shuffle on all fours in order to turn around. It was what, in Vietnam, had been called a tiger cage, or "cramper." — George C. Chesbro, *Veil*, p. 123, 1986

cranberry *noun*

a B-57 Canberra bomber *US, 1967*

- "Old Charlie harbors a special hatred for the Cranberries." — Elaine Shepard, *The Doom Pussy*, p. 38, 1967

crane *noun*

1 in skateboarding, a maneuver in which the rider crouches on one foot, extending the other leg outward *US, 1976*

- — Laura Torbet, *The Complete Book of Skateboarding*, p. 105, 1976

2 a superior with a great deal of influence *US, 1997*

New York police slang.

- The Extremely Unofficial and Completely Off-the-Record NYPD/ESU Truck-Two Glossary — Samuel M. Katz, *Anytime Anywhere*, p. 387, 1997

crank *noun*

1 methamphetamine hydrochloride in powdered form; any amphetamine; methcathinone *US, 1966*

On 15th September 1966, jazz critic Ralph J. Gleason wrote to slang lexicographer Peter Tamony, reporting that on 6th September he had heard the word "crank" used by a "young Negro pusher" in San Francisco's Fillmore district. On 9th October 1967, Gleason wrote Tamony a second note, clarifying that "crank" was the same as "meth," not "heroin." Peter Tamony heard the term again on 12th April 1968, in a speech at a meeting of the California Folklore Society in Berkeley.

- — William D. Alsever, *Glossary for the Establishment and Other Uptight People*, p. 7, December 1970
- I ain't trading no uptown crank for no downtown trash. — *Drugstore Cowboy*, 1988
- Are you saying you never made crystal meth, crank, methamphetamine, what ever you want to call it, with these chemicals? — Eleusis Lightning on the Sun [The Howard Marks Book of Dope Stories], p. 322, 2001

2 a mentally unstable person; an unreliable, unpredictable person; a person who is obsessed by a single topic or hobby *US, 1833*

- Since you seem to be unwilling to accept the note as the work of some crank who has observed Mr. Bigelow's movements and who profited by an unfortunate but by no means extraordinary coincidence. — Jim Thompson, *Savage Night*, p. 135, 1953

3 a prison guard who takes pleasure in making life difficult for prisoners *US, 1981*

- — *Maledicta*, p. 264, Summer/Winter 1981: "By its slang, ye shall know it: the pessimism of prison life"

4 the penis *US, 1968*

- Right soon after that, his crank was hard. It rose up like it wanted to have a look around. — Tom Abrams, *A Piece of Luck*, p. 47, 1994
- He pulled his zipper down, extracted his crank, and started to relieve himself. — Wolfman Jack (Bob Smith), *Have Mercy!*, p. 54, 1995
- So, to save time, he simply pulls out his crank and pisses into his now-empty Diet Coke cup. — Rick Reilly, *Who's Your Caddy?*, p. 51, 2003
- I wanted to just snatch up my crank and wrap her little hand around it and squeeze it[.] — Chris Miller, *The Real Animal House*, p. 31, 2006

crank *verb*

1 to use amphetamines or methamphetamine, central nervous system stimulants *US, 1970*

- — William D. Alsever, *Glossary for the Establishment and Other Uptight People*, p. 7, December 1970

2 to turn up the volume of music to very loud *US, 1994*

- Hey! Turn your radios up! Crank it up so's we can hear it! — *Airheads*, 1994
- I had the tunes cranked, I had nine grand sitting in front of me. — *Empire Records*, 1995
- I've got it modified with the TK 421, which is a bass unit that basically kicks in another two, maybe three quads when you really crank. — *Boogie Nights*, 1997

3 to excel *US, 1988*

- UNREAL, it's cranking out there. — Michael V. Anderson, *The Bad, Rad, Not to Forget Way Cool Beach and Surf Discriptionary*, p. 5, 1988

4 in computing, to perform well *US, 1991*

- This box cranks (or, cranks at) about 5 megaflops, with a burst mode of twice that on vectorized operations. — Eric S. Raymond, *The New Hacker's Dictionary*, p. 110, 1991

5 in a card game, to deal the cards *US, 1988*

- — George Percy, *The Language of Poker*, p. 25, 1988

▸ **crank your yanker**

(of a male) to masturbate *US, 2005*

- If you are a slave to the boob tube, you've probably cranked your yanker to thoughts of Kristian Bauer. — Mr. Skin, *Mr. Skin's Skincyclopedia*, p. 48, 2005

crank bug *noun*
an insect that is seen by someone under the influence of methamphetamine but not by others *US, 1977*
- — Walter L. Way, *The Drug Scene*, p. 107, 1977

crankcase *verb*
the head *US, 1960*
- You're not responsible to desk sergeants any more, sweets, can't you get that through your crankcase? — Clarence Cooper Jr., *The Scene*, p. 50, 1960

cranked; cranked out; cranked up *noun*
1 excited; intensified *US, 1957*
Mechanical imagery.
- Only a fool would try to explain why four thousand Japanese ran at top speed past the U.S.S. Arizona, sunken memorial in the middle of Pearl Harbor, along with another four or five thousand certified American liberals cranked up on beer and spaghetti[.] — Hunter S. Thompson, *Songs of the Doomed*, p. 189, 1980
2 stimulated by methanphetamine or amphetamines *US, 1981*
- "There's another worrier," said my attorney. "He's probably all cranked up on speed." — Hunter S. Thompson, *Fear and Loathing in Las Vegas*, p. 14, 1971
- I was half-drunk, fully cranked, and pissed off at everything that moved. — Hunter S. Thompson, *The Greak Shark Hunt*, p. 663, 1979
- They're all crazy cranked-out animals! — Joseph Wambaugh, *The Secrets of Harry Bright*, p. 243, 1985
- Akerlund rounds up a troupe of Hollywood B-listers—Mena Suvari, Brittany Murphy, Jason Schwartzman, and Patrick Fugit—for an hour and a half of cranked-out obnoxiousness. — *Boston Globe*, p. D8, 28th March 2003

cranker *noun*
a methamphetamine user *US, 2001*
- "Tweaker," "cranker," "meth monkey" – A user. — *Lewiston (Idaho) Morning Tribune*, p. 6A, 20th May 2001

crank freak *noun*
a methamphetamine addict *US, 1996*
- I should mention that I was something of a "speed" and "crank" freak in the middle 70s. — *alt.recovery.aa*, 29th June 1996
- "Cindy. She's a crank freak." — Carl Hiaasen, *Nature Girl*, p. 122, 2006

cranking *adjective*
amusing; pleasing; exciting; good *US, 1982*
- — Mary Corey and Victoria Westermark, *Fer Shurr! How to be a Valley Girl*, 1982

crank off *verb*
to consume something *US, 2001*
- I'm busy crankin' off an eight-ball, dude. — Stephen J. Cannell, *The Tin Collectors*, p. 116, 2001

crap *noun*
1 excrement *UK, 1846*
- Why is dog crap always bigger when they shit in the house than when they do their business outside? — Rick Huffman, *Graffiti Mirror*, p. 81, 2002
2 nonsense *UK, 1898*
- And I think that stuff about women wanting it just as bad is crap. — *Sex, Lies and Videotape*, 1989
3 marijuana *US, 1961*
- — Francis J. Rigney and L. Douglas Smith, *The Real Bohemia*, p. xiii, 1961
4 weak or highly diluted heroin *US, 1942*
- — Richard Lingeman, *Drugs from A to Z*, p. 51, 1969

▸ **take a crap**
to defecate *US, 1952*
- I took a crap in a 1000-year old Indian stone crapper in the outdoors. — Jack Kerouac, *Letter to Allen Ginsberg*, p. 350, 10th May 1952

crap *verb*
to defecate *UK, 1673*
- Gandhi was at the bottom of the bed and he had crapped in it. — Marion Davies, *The Times We Had*, p. 227, 1975

crap around *verb*
to idle; to pass time doing nothing; to waste time *US, 1935*
- Tell him I'm not going to crap around bargaining. — James Clavell, *King Rat*, p. 221, 1962

crap artist *noun*
a convincing liar *US, 1934*

- Oh, hell, I hate them, those crap artists. — Saul Bellow, *Humboldt's Gift*, p. 142, 1975
- Wassamatter, all the big girls found out you're a crap artist? — Jackie Collins, *Chances*, p. 577, 1980

crap-ass *noun*
a despicable person *US, 1975*
- [E]ven though architects are always trying to take credit for it—crap-asses. — Todd McEwen, *Who Sleeps with Katz?*, p. 40, 2003

crap-ass *adjective*
shoddy, inferior *US, 2000*
- I'm a dull, boring hack writing copy for crap-ass products and sucking up to a bunch of corporate dildos. — Linda Watanabe McFerrin, *Hand of Buddha*, p. 51, 2000

crap course *noun*
an easy college course *US, 1956*
- But you were having an affair with your college professor. That jerk that teaches that incredible crap course "Contemporary Crisis in Western Man!" — *Annie Hall*, 1977

crape-hanger *noun*
a doomsayer *US, 1949*
- The crapehangers love to bury me. They think I'm making more money than I should. — *Time*, p. 54, 27th June 1949
- The crape hangers were out in full force. — Vincent Curcio, *Chrysler*, p. 269, 2000

craphole *noun*
a bad place, a disgusting place *US, 1939*
- That shit was my ticket outta this craphole and every one like it. — Randy Everhard, *Tattoo of a Naked Lady*, p. 197, 284

craphouse *noun*
1 a toilet *US, 1934*
- I'm got the ol' experience, I'm smart as a craphouse rat. — Nelson Algren, *Never Come Morning*, p. 10, 1963
2 a dirty, unpleasant place *US, 1934*
- You don't need to snake their dirty whores in some enlisted man's off-limits craphouse, then cover your ass with that Jesus talk of yours. — David Poyer, *The Med*, p. 54, 1988

crapola *noun*
used as an embellished "crap" in any and all of its senses *UK, 1959*
- "The Prime Minister expressed his hope that the Greek and Turkish Governments would reconsider the British proposals in the light of..." "Crapola," Mellors said. — Derek Bickerton, *Payroll*, p. 77, 1959
- Let us cope with the preliminary part of that farrago of crapola by citing the handiest record of the net assessment of the Shah's reign[.] — *San Francisco Examiner*, p. 34, 10th December 1979
- And you got to know that statue will be some dipped-in-shit, John Wayne crapola[.] — Larry Heinemann, *Paco's Story*, p. 157, 1986
- Tell me you've finished your crapola Foreign Legion movie. — Gerald Petievich, *Shakedown*, p. 133, 1988

crap out *verb*
1 to fail to produce, to stop functioning *US, 1929*
- If so, they crap out, I can picture myself getting stoned by MacClaine, McClure etc., but actually what I'd do in such a case is get it published by Grove or New D[irections]. — Jack Kerouac, *Jack Kerouac Selected Letters 1957 – 1969*, p. 236, 10th June 1959: Letter to Philip Whalen
- "I'm sorry to crap out like this, Danny," he said, "but I don't have the vigorish for this job." — George Clayton Johnson, *Ocean's Eleven*, p. 187, 1960
2 to be completely exhausted; to go to sleep *US, 1976*
- — *American Speech*, p. 227, October 1956: "More United States Air Force slang"
- Four in the morning / crapped out, yawning — Paul Simon, *Still Crazy After All These Years*, 1976
3 to die *US, 1929*
- Suppose I crap out? — Mickey Spillane, *Me, Hood!*, p. 14, 1963

crap paper *noun*
toilet paper *US, 1952*
- I noticed that there were no orange tissue wrappers hanging on the wall. "No crap paper," I muttered. — Harry Grey, *The Hoods*, p. 19, 1952

crapper *noun*
1 a toilet *US, 1927*

- "Him, we wouldn't let a guy like him even touch the crapper," said Willie. — James T. Farrell, *Willie Collins*, p. 115, 1946
- I took a crap in a 1000-year old Indian stone crapper in the outdoors. — Jack Kerouac, *Letter to Allen Ginsberg*, p. 350, 10th May 1952
- I try and try, ma'am, but I'm afraid I'll never make my mark as head man of the crappers. — Ken Kesey, *One Flew Over the Cuckoo's Nest*, p. 151, 1962
- Inside the crapper, I ripped a wad of paper from its holder. — Iceberg Slim (Robert Beck), *Pimp*, p. 81, 1969

2 the anus and rectum *US*, *2000*
- "And the fleshier one's had it up her crapper as well," gurgled Maggie with a grin. — *alt.sex.stories*, 11th December 2000
- Both shove their bratwursts simultaneously up her cunt and crapper in a reverse, bouncing cowgirl d.p. — Editors of Adult Video News, *The AVN Guide to the 500 Greatest Adult Films of All Time*, p. 65, 2005

▸ **in the crapper**
in horse racing, finishing in fourth place or worse *US*, *1976*
- — Tom Ainslie, *Ainslie's Complete Guide to Thoroughbred Racing*, p. 333, 1976

crapper dick *noun*
a police officer who patrols public toilets in search of illegal homosexual activity *US*, *1950*
- — Hyman E. Goldin et al., *Dictionary of American Underworld Lingo*, p. 52, 1950
- A crapper dick has got to have good eyes to be able to see everything. — Bruce Rodgers, *The Queens' Vernacular*, p. 207, 1972

crappy *adjective*
of poor quality *US*, *1942*
- He'd clip out cartoons and weather reports and crappy poems and health columns. — Jim Thompson, *The Killer Inside*, p. 96, 1952
- I'm a crappy little agency with crappy little clients nobody else will touch[.] — Max Shulman, *Anyone Got a Match?*, p. 24, 1964
- Duncan and I went fishing in a crappy little catfish creek below the dirt road. — Jeffrey Golden, *Watermelon Summer*, p. 111, 1971
- Yeah, but the animation's all crappy—it probably can't sustain itself over ninety minutes. — *South Park*, 1999

craps *noun*
dice, especially used in craps *US*, *1965*
- And I'd take some loaded craps down there, some bones, and I would beat the paddy boys out of all their money. — Claude Brown, *Manchild in the Promised Land*, p. 151, 1965

crapshoot *noun*
an unpredictable, risky situation *US*, *1971*
- All oil field exploration is a crap shoot at best, with only one in ten or fifteen fields panning out. — Stephen Cannell, *Big Con*, p. 137, 1997

crap up *verb*
1 to fill something with clutter *US*, *1946*
- It was still all crapped up. Boxes of car parts were stacked all the way to the ceiling. Tires were rolled over in the corners. Oil cans and carburetors and anything else that didn't have a box were all crammed together on a bunch of shelves. — Sam Giancana, *Double Deal*, p. 65, 2003

2 to spoil something; to ruin something *US*, *1953*
- I'm sick and tired of Him and His whole choir of Guardian Angels—all they do is crap up my life! — Laura Esquivel, *The Law of Love*, p. 134, 1996

3 to address someone with a complete lack of sincerity *US*, *1950*
- "[Y]ou don't have to give me any crap." "Well, for Christ's sake, who's crapping you up?" — Hal Ellson, *Tomboy*, p. 121, 1950

crash *verb*
1 to enter a party or social event without an invitation *US*, *1921*
- The newcomers intended to crash, as everyone in the room knew. — Hal Ellson, *The Golden Spike*, p. 69, 1952
- On this particular night, the Wolf "crashed" a rather high-class party. — Max Shulman, *Guided Tour of Campus Humor*, p. 70, 1955
- Needless to say, nobody with an ounce of good manners or a thimbleful of concern for the feelings of others ever crashes a party. — Dick Clark, *To Goof or Not to Goof*, p. 130, 1963
- Frank crashed the party? — Terry Southern, *Now Dig This*, p. 220, 1978

2 to enter a place with force with the intention of committing a crime *US*, *1924*
- I told her somebody had crashed the place before I got there and liked to knock it apart. — Mickey Spillane, *My Gun is Quick*, p. 24, 1950

- We had a pretty good bunch of O'Sullivans, a torch man, a mechanic, a jigger and a hard-shell biscuit who'd been with a gopher mob. We crashed with a get-in betty. — *The New American Mercury*, p. 709, 1950
- It wasn't really fear even though he had never crashed a joint before. — Donald Goines, *Dopefiend*, p. 162, 1971

3 to stay somewhere temporarily; to sleep somewhere *US*, *1945*
- As we walked up the steps a neighbor said "Here come two more kids looking for a place to crash." — James Simon Kunen, *The Strawberry Statement*, p. 96, 1968
- Well, she lets me crash at her place. — *Airheads*, 1994
- Then I realized that I owned my own apartment and had an American Express card while he was still crashing on his friend's couch and thrilled to have a new library card. — Anka Radakovich, *The Wild Girls Club*, p. 158, 1994
- I was just planning to crash on the floor for a few days till I figure out what I'm doing. — Kenneth Lonergan, *This is Our Youth*, p. 54, 2000

4 to return to normal perceptions after a drug intoxication; to experience an associated feeling of post-intoxication depression or dismay *US*, *1967*
- WYATT: Wow! I think I'm gonna crash. BILLY: Ah, man. I think you have crashed, man. — Peter Fonda, *Easy Rider*, p. 71, 1969
- "I'm crashing, man," Manny says. He lies on the floor. — John Rechy, *The Fourth Angel*, p. 114, 1972

5 (used of a computer program) to fail completely without warning *US*, *1983*
- — Guy L. Steele et al., *The Hacker's Dictionary*, p. 49, 1983

6 to hit something, to strike something *US*, *1989*
- — Terry Williams, *The Cocaine Kids*, p. 136, 1989

7 to escape from jail or prison *US*, *1970*
- — Red Rudensky, *The Gonif*, p. a, 1970

8 in circus and carnival usage, to change money *US*, *1981*
- — Don Wilmeth, *The Language of American Popular Entertainment*, p. 66, 1981

9 to intubate a hospital patient quickly and urgently *US*, *1994*
- — Sally Williams, *"Strong" Words*, p. 137, 1994

10 to perform a high-priority job as soon as possible *US*, *1986*
- — Department of the Army, *Staff Officer's Guidebook*, p. 58, 1986

▸ **crash and burn**
in computing, to fail in a dramatic and spectacular fashion *US*, *1991*
- — Eric S. Raymond, *The New Hacker's Dictionary*, p. 110, 1991

crash car *noun*
1 an old, inexpensive car used in the distribution of illegal alcohol *US*, *1974*
- — David W. Maurer, *Kentucky Moonshine*, p. 115, 1974

2 in a robbery, a car used to crash into other cars to thwart pursuit of the robbers *US*, *1981*
- The theory of a crash car is to obstruct whatever pursuit there may be of the getaway car, regardless of the risk involved. — Ovid Demaris, *The Last Mafioso*, p. 12, 1981

crash cart *noun*
a mobile cart used to carry equipment *US*, *1982*
Originally hospital use, since expanded.
- Next to me was the "crash cart" they had used for Marcus. Rubber tourniquets hung like streamers from the black handles of the cart. — James Patterson, *Kiss the Girls*, p. 29, 1995
- Usually, the crew chief sits on top of a big box, called a crash cart, which is filled with equipment used for quick repairs[.] — Mark Martin, *NASCAR for dummies*, p. 152, 2000

crasher *noun*
a powerful, hard-breaking wave *US*, *1964*
- — John Severson, *Modern Surfing Around the World*, p. 165, 1964

crash-out *noun*
an escape from prison or jail *US*, *1940*
- He was the last guy I would have picked as a partner in a crash-out; he was very young, this would be his first break, and Christ alone knew how his reflexes would work if something went wrong. — Horace McCoy, *Kiss Tomorrow Good-bye*, p. 7, 1948

crash out *verb*
to escape from prison *US*, *1954*
- He's on the lam from a pen back east, crashed out with twenty years to serve of a thirty-year bank-robber rap. — Jim Thompson, *A Swell-Looking Babe*, p. 77, 1954

crash pad *noun*

1 a room, apartment, or house where people stay for the night or temporarily, with or without knowing the owner, with or without formal invitation *US, 1967*

- In one week, four Digger-sponsored crash pads were busted by the cops. — Abbie Hoffman, *Revolution for the Hell of It*, p. 54, 1968
- [R]ent or work deals with the urban gov't to take over spaces that have been abandoned for use as carpentry shops, garages, theaters, etc., rent whole houses, but don't let them turn into crash pads. — *The Digger Papers*, p. 15, August 1968
- Landis was taken into custody at his home at 243 Bradford street, which police said was being used as a "crash pad" for assorted homeless hippies. — *San Francisco Chronicle*, p. 3, 19th June 1968
- The White House will become a crash pad for anybody without a place to stay in Washington. — Jerry Rubin, *Do It!*, p. 256, 1970

2 a pit of soft dirt or sand used for low-level stunt falls *US, 2003*

- — John Cann, *The Stunt Guid*, p. 57, 2003

crate *noun*

a carton of cigarettes *US, 2002*

- — Jeffrey Ian Ross, *Behind Bars*, p. 184, 2002: Slammer Slang

crater *noun*

1 a deep sore caused by repeated injections *US, 1967*

- I had cultivated a crater and always shot through the same hole. It sure looked awful, though. — Piri Thomas, *Down These Mean Streets*, p. 202, 1967
- — Edward R. Bloomquist, *Marijuana*, p. 337, 1971

2 a facial blemish *US, 1968*

- — Collin Baker et al., *College Undergraduate Slang Study Conducted at Brown University*, p. 101, 1968

crater *verb*

in rock climbing, to fall and hit the ground *US, 1998*

- CRATER Hit the ground. — Shelley Youngblut, *Way Inside ESPN's X Games*, p. 209, 1998

c-rats *noun*

US Army combat rations *US, 1965*

Vietnam war coinage, used since.

- "Rain fallin' into my C-rats—A perfect example of nature pollutin' garbage. — Michael Hodgson, *With Sgt. Mike in Vietnam*, p. 31, 1970
- It brought the usual water, C-rats and mail. — Charles Anderson, *The Grunts*, p. 106, 1976
- Negative, m' man, fuck a bunch a C rats. I mean meat. — Larry Heinemann, *Close Quarters*, p. 142, 1977
- When off duty, Prince was a furry mooch, always on the lookout for C rats, fish, or whatever. — Ralph Zumbro, *Tank Sergeant*, p. 65, 1986

crawfish *verb*

to evade someone or something *US, 1842*

In nature, the only defence available to the crawfish is to bury itself in mud or silt, moving backward.

- "Aw shut up," Green said impatiently. "You're crawfishing and you know it." — Raymond Chandler, *The Long Goodbye*, p. 33, 1953

crawl *noun*

1 in television and movie-making, titles that roll from the bottom of the screen to the top *US, 1990*

- — Ralph S. Singleton, *Filmmaker's Dictionary*, p. 39, 1990

2 in pool, backspin applied to the cue ball *US, 1954*

- — Mike Shamos, *The Illustrated Encyclopedia of Billiards*, p. 63, 1993

crawl *verb*

to search somewhere *US, 1986*

- But the dresser had been pulled out, and the three scrapbooks stacked across it had been replaced unevenly, one upside down. The pad had been crawled. — James Ellroy, *Suicide Hill*, p. 740, 1986

crawling horror *noun*

in computing, obsolete hardware or software *US, 1991*

- — Eric S. Raymond, *The New Hacker's Dictionary*, p. 110, 1991

crayon *noun*

a programmer who works on a supercomputer designed by Cray Research *US, 1991*

- — Eric S. Raymond, *The New Hacker's Dictionary*, p. 111, 1991

crazies *noun*

phencyclidine, the recreational drug known as PCP or angel dust *US, 1993*

- — Peter Johnson, *Dictionary of Street Alcohol and Drug Terms*, p. 50, 1993

crazy *noun*

a person who engages in erratic or unpredictable behavior *US, 1867*

- In one room crazies planned to rent planes and fly over the Rose Bowl dropping antiwar leaflets on the crowd. — Jerry Rubin, *Do It!*, p. 38, 1970
- The "crazies" might still be winning headlines, but largely they had lost the campuses. They had taken to playing revolution mostly with themselves. — William Tulio Divale, *I Lived Inside the Campus Revolution*, p. 195, 1970
- In a town full of bedrock crazies, nobody even notices an acid freak. — Hunter S. Thompson, *Fear and Loathing in Las Vegas*, p. 24, 1971
- This town has always had its share of crazies. — *Slacker*, 1992

crazy *adjective*

1 excellent, exciting, superlative *US, 1948*

- It's "crazy," it's the "world's best." — *San Francisco Call-Bulletin*, 31st October 1947
- Isn't this the craziest! — *Rebel Without a Cause*, 1955
- Things were "cool" and cool things "gassed" the initiates and anything that was particularly cool was "crazy." — Robert Sylvester, *No Cover Charge*, p. 287, 1956
- [H]e blew his now-settled-down-into-regulated-design "crazy" notes[.] — Jack Kerouac, *The Subterraneans*, p. 13, 1958

2 (used of a particular card in poker and other card games) capable of being played as a card of any value *US, 1967*

The same as the more common "wild."

- — Albert H. Morehead, *The Complete Guide to Winning Poker*, p. 260, 1967

3 many *US, 1989*

- Everybody thinks they can make crazy dollars, but they confused. — Terry Williams, *The Cocaine Kids*, p. 86, 1989

crazy alley *noun*

the area in a prison in which mentally ill patients are confined *US, 1992*

- — William K. Bentley and James M. Corbett, *Prison Slang*, p. 3, 1992

crazy-ass *adjective*

very crazy *US, 1994*

- They're like that crazy mother in the first Dirty Harry movie. 'Member that crazy-ass mother? — *Natural Born Killers*, 1994

crazy doctor *noun*

a psychiatrist or other psychotherapist *US, 1989*

- — Leo Rosten, *The Joy of Yinglish*, p. 119, 1989

crazy Eddy *noun*

high quality phencyclidine, the recreational drug known as PCP or angel dust *US, 1993*

- — Peter Johnson, *Dictionary of Street Alcohol and Drug Terms*, p. 50, 1993

crazy eight; crazy 8 *noun*

a discharge from the US Army for mental unfitness *US, 1968*

From US Army Regulation 600–208.

- — Carl Fleischhauer, *A Glossary of Army Slang*, p. 12, 1968

crazy freak *noun*

a pretty girl *US, 1955*

- — *American Speech*, p. 302, December 1955: "Wayne University slang"

crazy house *noun*

a mental hospital *US, 1887*

- I just hope no one sees me down in those bottoms talking to a monkey. Why, they would put me in the crazy house sure as shootin'. — Wilson Rawls, *Summer of the Monkeys*, p. 120, 1976
- It was nothing to walk in her home and find Mexicans or someone from the crazy house eating dinner. — Renay Jackson, *Oaktown Devil*, p. 59, 1998

creaker *noun*

an old person *US, 1958*

- This family is full of creakers. We creak along to about the age of 96. — Flannery O'Connor, *Letter to Richard Stern*, p. 574, 14th April 1964

cream *noun*

a bribe *US, 1982*

- — Bill Reilly, *Big Al's Official Guide to Chicagoese*, p. 23, 1982

cream *verb*

1 to ejaculate; to secrete vaginal lubricants during sexual arousal *US, 1915*

- Sometimes, though, I'd go home afterwards, after having had a hard-on for four hours of making out on the floor and in the bleachers, but without creaming, and it really gave you a sore dick. — *The Berkeley Tribe*, p. 13, 5th-12th September 1969
- "I bet you're creaming all over yourself this minute, you blind freak." — Robert Deane Pharr, *S.R.O.*, p. 334, 1971
- "Jesus, nobody creams that much, especially not some guy who hasn't moved a muscle in his face for the last half hour." — Anne Steinhardt, *Thunder La Boom*, p. 148, 1974
- Leslie gives the gorgeous geisha a raunchy workout, which ends with him creaming all over her grateful face, after which he goes to work on Mai's still-smouldering snatch[.] — *Adult Video*, p. 23, August/September 1986

2 by extension, to gush with excitement *US, 1948*
- It is only "history" that today critics cream all over Moby Dick, the dear perceptive things. — Jack Kerouac, *Letter to Neal Cassady*, p. 173, 8th December 1948
- Movement, it creams me to be talking to you. — Bernard Wolfe, *The Late Risers*, p. 228, 1954
- The PD's office would cream over something like this. — Carl Hiaasen, *Tourist Season*, p. 21, 1986

3 to defeat someone convincingly *US, 1940*
- [H]e had benched his regulars and sent in his scrubs, and as a result, the Rockets had been creamed the next three times in a row. — Max Shulman, *Rally Round the Flag, Boys!*, p. 224, 1957
- We creamed them 7-0. — Erich Segal, *Love Story*, p. 11, 1970
- We're gonna get creamed. — *A Few Good Men*, 1992
- "Bruno left it on the bus after Friday's game," sniffed Fuzzy indignantly. "I guess he was bummed we got creamed again." — C.D. Payne, *Youth in Revolt*, p. 198, 1993

4 to kill someone *US, 1940*
- [W]hen she had the chance to get Evello creamed before that congressional committee she put in her bid[.] — Mickey Spillane, *Kiss Me Deadly*, p. 143, 1952
- "I dunno," Ms. Murphy said, "but he's sure got a thing about the cat he creamed." — Cyra McFadden, *The Serial*, p. 164, 1977

5 to hit someone or something *US, 1942*
- When Ali creamed him in the eighth, Foreman pirouetted, spiraled downward using the whole ring for his fall[.] — Bill Cardoso, *The Maltese Sangweech*, p. 304, 1984
- You can't strap into your seat belt, without almost getting creamed by a bus. — *Gone in 60 Seconds*, 2000

▸ **cream the rag**
to boast in an offensive manner *US, 1971*
The masturbatory image is powerful.
- — *American Speech*, p. 233, Autumn–Winter 1971: "Checkschmuck! The slang of the chess player"

▸ **get creamed**
to be knocked from your surfboard and pounded into the ocean, ocean bottom or pilings of a pier *US, 1978*
- — Dennis Aaberg and John Milius, *Big Wednesday*, p. 208, 1978

CREAM; cream *noun*
money *US, 1994*
- — Wu-Tang Clan, *C.R.E.A.M. (Cash Rules Everything Around Me)*, 1994
- "This 'cream' that they keep chanting about getting," he pointed to Sinbad and co., "what do they mean?" "C.R.E.A.M. Cash Rules Everything Around Me. It's just an old word for money." — Diran Adebayo, *My Once Upon A Time*, p. 59, 2000
- — Connie Eble (Editor), *UNC-CH Campus Slang*, p. 3, October 2002

creamdown *noun*
sex focused on the pleasure of the active male participant *US, 1997*
- "He basically liked them leaning over, braced against the wall, legs wide, a good fast pump. Back in San they call that a creamdown." — Ethan Morden, *Some Men Are Lookers*, pp. 54–55, 1997

creampie *noun*
semen seeping from a vagina, anus or mouth *US, 2002*
A fetish that oozed from US Internet pornography in the early 2000s.
- Creampie vids mean to correct this by showing sex as it actually happens, plus bodily fluids getting licked off the floor. — *Village Voice*, p. 179, 23rd April 2002
- Howard Schiffer is not the first parent to be alarmed that his teenager was learning about sex from either sniggering peers or a

deeply confused culture that veers between sexual repression and Internet "creampie" raunch. — *Salon.com*, 12th May 2004
- Diamond Foxx and Dallas Sexton go for the cream pie after rimming, doggie, and mish. — Editors of Adult Video News, *The AVN Guide to the 500 Greatest Adult Films of All Time*, p. 11, 2005

cream puff *noun*
1 an effeminate male *US, 1945*
- — Lou Shelly, *Hepcats Jive Talk Dictionary*, p. 9, 1945

2 an easy target, easy prey *US, 1915*
- Blue had been right about Frascati. He was a real cream puff. He didn't give us an anxious moment all during the play. — Iceberg Slim (Robert Beck), *Trick Baby*, p. 299, 1969

creamy *adjective*
sexually attractive *US, 1947*
- "Mike Horner—he plays the guitar. He's absolutely creamy and guess what?" — Frederick Kohner, *Gidget Goes Hawaiian*, p. 55, 1961

crease *noun*
in sports betting, a distortion created when strong fan support for one team or contestant creates an imbalance in the odds which can be exploited by a clever better *US, 1991*
- — Avery Cardoza, *The Basics of Sports Betting*, p. 43, 1991

cred *noun*
credibility *UK, 1998*
- [G]unpoint abduction didn't have enough cred to be anything more than an implausible but as-yet-uneliminated possibility. — Christopher Brookmyre, *Not the End of the World*, p. 192, 1998
- When the Hollister incident cut deep into their cred, they labeled rowdy, outlaw motorcyclists the "one-percenters." — Ralph "Sonny" Barger, *Hell's Angel*, p. 41, 2000

credit *noun*
an achievement or accomplishment *US, 1992*
From the acknowledgement of service rendered in the entertainment industry.
- He asked me if I ever done armed robbery before. I read him my credits. — *Reservoir Dogs*, 1992

credit card *noun*
a favor owed *US, 1985*
- If he wants to screw Amad he'll call in some credit cards at Vacaville. — Vincent Patrick, *Family Business*, p. 244, 1985

creek *noun*
▸ **up the creek**
in trouble *US, 1918*
Variant phrases include "up the creek without a paddle" and "up the creek with a paddle in a barbed-wire canoe."
- The local bogies [police] made inquiries and he was up the creek. — Charles Raven, *Underworld Nights*, p. 31, 1956
- If not you're up the creek without a paddle, and no mistake. — Troy Kennedy Martin, *Z Cars*, p. 135, 1962

creep *noun*
1 a prisoner who steals from other prisoners at night *US, 1951*
- We also have a group of prisoners called "creeps" or "night-crawlers," who prowl the dormitory at night and steal from the other sleeping prisoners. — James Blake, *The Joint*, p. 21, 15th April 1951

2 a sex offender *US, 1975*
- Creeps never "get a hang-out card" (command enough respect to mingle and converse freely with other prisoners). — Miguel Pinero, *Short Eyes*, p. 123, 1975

3 an objectionable or unpleasant person; a dull or insignificant person *US, 1926*
- I got this here album by this bunch of Limey creeps called Jethro Tull[.] — Lester Bangs, *Psychotic Reactions and Carburetor Dung*, p. 133, 1973

4 a prisoner who is neither respected nor liked *US, 1951*
- Very often, a "creep" to escape general harassment will pay tribute to one particular "gee" and will be taken under his protection. — *American Speech*, p. 194, October 1951: "A study of reformatory argot"

5 a thief who operates in hotels, entering unlocked rooms as the guests sleep *UK, 1877*
- Often creeps would check into the hotel, in order to have a plausible explanation if challenged by a corridor patrol. — Dev Collans with Stewart Sterling, *I was a House Detective*, p. 32, 1954
- Some Creeps wear thick woollen socks over their shoes. — Charles Raven, *Underworld Nights*, p. 11, 1956

6 a drug addict who relies on the kindness of other addicts for small amounts of drugs *US, 1971*
- — Eugene Landy, *The Underground Dictionary*, p. 60, 1971

7 a furtive arrival or departure *US, 1946*
- The Chicagoans, including some of the Austin High Gang, were pulling a creep in a dozen different directions. — Mezz Mezzrow, *Really the Blues*, p. 129, 1946

creep *verb*
1 to work as a sneak-thief *US, 1928*
- Sapphire Harris, the King of Creeps, had crept a gaff on a tip-off passed on to him by Larry[.] — Charles Raven, *Underworld Nights*, p. 191, 1956

2 to ambush someone with the intent of seriously injuring or killing them *US, 1974*
Prison usage.
- — Paul Glover, *Words from the House of the Dead*, 1974
- Y'all niggas ain't gonna creep me! — Earl "DMX" Simmons, *E.A.R.L.*, p. 236, 2002

3 to attempt to have a secret sexual relationship with someone's boyfriend or girlfriend *US, 2001*
- — Don R. McCreary (Editor), *Dawg Speak*, 2001

4 to be sexually unfaithful *US, 1972*
- — David Claerbaut, *Black Jargon in White America*, p. 61, 1972

5 to escape *US, 1967*
- Still even those who managed to creep were reapprehended with stifling regularity. — Malcolm Braly, *On the Yard*, p. 205, 1967

creep-and-cuss *adjective*
(used of car traffic) extremely congested *US, 1964*
- It was creep-and-cuss traffic for two hours, beginning at 11:30 a.m. On Bayshore Freeway, autos were bumper-to-bumper from Candlestick south to San Bruno, about eight miles. — *San Francisco Examiner*, p. 1, 17th August 1964

creep catalogue *noun*
a high school yearbook *US, 1961*
- — Art Unger, *The Cool Book*, p. 110, 1961

creeped out *adjective*
worried, disturbed *US, 2001*
Extends from THE CREEPS (a feeling of dread).
- It was midafternoon, and I was more than a little creeped out[.] — Janet Evanovich, *Seven Up*, p. 15, 2001

creeper *noun*
1 a burglar *US, 1906*
- Bill had been a creeper at one time, who had made his living by breaking into homes and apartments. — Nathan Heard, *Howard Street*, p. 36, 1968
- He was a daytime hotel creeper and hitting maybe four to six hotel rooms in the best downtown hotels every time he went to work. — Joseph Wambaugh, *The Blue Knight*, p. 20, 1973

2 a marijuana cigarette *US, 1997*
- — Jim Emerson-Cobb, *Scratching the Dragon*, April 1997

creepers *noun*
soft-soled, quiet shoes favored by burglars *US, 1949*
- — Vincent J. Monteleone, *Criminal Slang*, p. 61, 1949
- — Joseph E. Ragen and Charles Finston, *Inside the World's Toughest Prison*, p. 796, 1962
- — Inez Cardozo-Freeman, *The Joint*, p. 491, 1984

creepers!
used for expressing surprise *US, 1944*
An abbreviated version of JEEPERS, CREEPERS!
- Creepers! If any of my buddies in the lower income group could see me here, I wonder what they'd say. [Freckles and his Friends comic strip] — *San Francisco News*, p. 29, 17th October 1946

creep game *noun*
a scheme in which a prostitute and her confederate rob the prostitute's customer *US, late 1960s*
- Lying in bed, he explained to her the new hap-nings and also started to teach her in the art of using knock-out drops plus, "The Creep game" where one girl does the physical work while another would rob the victims pockets. — Babs Gonzales, *I Paid My Dues*, p. 97, 1967

creep house *noun*
a brothel where customers are routinely robbed *US, 1913*

- Warnings of immorality were probably less effective than warnings that some brothels were creep houses or panel houses wherein visitors were robbed of money and gold watches. — Irving Lewis Allen, *The City in Slang*, p. 180, 1993

creeping crud *noun*
any skin rash suffered in tropical and jungle environments *US, 1946*
- "Jungle rot," "New Guinea crud" or "the creeping crud" are U.S. servicemen's names for any & every kind of tropical skin disease. — *Time*, p. 76, 13th August 1946

creeping mocus *noun*
a nonexistent disease *US, 1947*
- — *American Speech*, p. 304, December 1947: "Imaginary diseases in army and navy parlance"

creep joint *noun*
a brothel where customers' clothes are searched and robbed *US, 1921*
- Took my public-school training in three jails and a plenty of poolrooms, went to college in a gang of tea-pads, earned my Ph.D. in more creep joints and speakeasies and dancehalls than the law allows. — Mezz Mezzrow, *Really the Blues*, p. 3, 1946
- "Whaddya going to that kind of a creep joint for?" — Irving Shulman, *Cry Tough*, p. 167, 1949
- What kinda creep joint you run here? — William Burroughs, *Naked Lunch*, p. 200, 1957
- [W]e went through plush lavender and redwood catacombs to the inner sanctum of a florid-faced wheeler dealer in a four-hundred dollar suit who was oozing distractive charm like a pickpocket whore in a creep joint. — Iceberg Slim (Robert Beck), *The Naked Soul of Iceberg Slim*, p. 142, 1971

creepo *noun*
a contemptible person *US, 1960*
- So it constantly amazed him, and left him feeling much abused, to hear such nonsense—twerp, creepo, butter-brain. — Tim O'Brien, *Going After Cacciato*, p. 36, 1978
- "Some creepo was tailing me," he was saying, "for like a hundred miles." — Carl Hiaasen, *Sick Puppy*, p. 16, 1999

creep out *verb*
to create a very uncomfortable feeling in someone *US, 1983*
- Actually, Dad, that room creeps me out. — Francine Pascal, *Tearing Me Apart (Sweet Valley High Senior Year No. 36)*, p. 87, 2001
- Ric Flair was another person who creeped me out on a regular basis. — Missy Hyatt, *Missy Hyatt*, p. 107, 2001

creep pad *noun*
a creep joint *US, 1946*
- I swear I'm no sky-pilot, but a creep pad turns into a confession booth as soon as I squat in it. — Mezz Mezzrow, *Really the Blues*, p. 88, 1946

creeps!
used as an all-purpose, nonprofane expression of surprise *US, 1971*
- Creeps! What the heck is that? [Tiffany Jones comic strip] — *San Francisco Chronicle*, p. 24, 24th May 1971

creepster *noun*
a revolting person *US, 1993*
An embellished CREEP.
- Look at this crazy girl following some stranger into his diner trying to save her boyfriend who isn't even her boyfriend anymore because of some weird creepster dream. — Francesca Lia Block, *Missing Angel Juan*, p. 349, 1993

creepy *adjective*
annoying; producing anxiety or nervousness in others *US, 1919*
- Do you have any control over how creepy you allow yourself to get? — *As Good As It Gets*, 1997

creepy-peepy *noun*
1 battlefield radar *US, 1965*
Vietnam war usage.
- — *Time*, p. 32, 10th December 1965
- — Carl Fleischhauer, *A Glossary of Army Slang*, p. 12, 1968

2 a television mini-camera *US, 1986*
- — Rachel S. Epstein and Nina Liebman, *Biz Speak*, p. 52, 1986

Creme de Menthe French *noun*

oral sex performed with a mouth full of creme de menthe alcohol *US, 1993*

- — J.R. Schwartz, *The Official Guide to the Best Cat Houses in Nevada*, p. 164, 1993

crescent fresh *adjective*

attractive, stylish *US, 2000*

A term coined by the sock puppets on Mtelevision's *Sifl and Ollie* show.

- And then Michael suddenly appeared out of nowhere, looking crescent fresh—isn't that a funny expression? I learned it from Michael—in the tux his mom made him get[.] — Meg Cabot, *The Princess Diaries*, p. 274, 2000

crest *verb*

to smile *US, 1997*

From the branded toothpaste.

- — Vann Wesson, *Generation X Field Guide and Lexicon*, p. 42, 1997

cretin *noun*

an incompetent and despicable person *US, 1991*

- — *Coevolution Quarterly*, p. 29, Spring 1981: 'Computer slang'
- — Eric S. Raymond, *The New Hacker's Dictionary*, p. 112, 1991

cretinous *adjective*

in computing, incompetent, dysfunctional *US, 1991*

- — *Coevolution Quarterly*, p. 29, Spring 1981: 'Computer slang'
- — Eric S. Raymond, *The New Hacker's Dictionary*, p. 112, 1991

crew *noun*

1 a criminal gang *US, 1946*

- Lepke and Gurrah stepped up into an exclusive crew headed by Li'l Augie Organ[.] — Burton Turkus and Sid Feder, *Murder, Inc.*, p. 291, 1951
- Most of my crew got washed on the way. — Edwin Torres, *Carlito's Way*, p. 6, 1975
- To become a member of a crew, you've got to be one hundred percent Italian so that they can trace all your relatives back to the old country. — *Goodfellas*, 1990
- They could have a lovers' quarrel, give the dope to a new boyfriend not in the crew, sell it themselves, smoke it themselves. — Richard Price, *Clockers*, p. 5, 1992

2 a tightly-knit group of close friends *US, 1957*

- [T]hose guys made me a member of the crew. — Frederick Kohner, *Gidget*, p. 37, 1957
- Quite a few of the old crew are in institutions across the country, quite a few still out on the street. — John Allen, *Assault with a Deadly Weapon*, p. 222, 1977
- So, anyway, the whole crew is going to this party in the Valley. — *Clueless*, 1995

3 a group of graffiti artists who work together *US, 1997*

- Crews are one of three things: a group of people down for each other; a group of people working for the common goal of getting up, or a group of people unified through a certain style. — Stephen Power, *The Art of Getting Over*, p. 118, 1999

crew chief *noun*

the leader of a unit of a criminal gang *US, 1992*

- It was exactly the one Andre had given to him, complete with hug, when Strike's mother had gone to Andre four years ago, after some long-gone local crew chief had taken Strike out for his haircut. — Richard Price, *Clockers*, p. 281, 1992

crew dog *noun*

a crew chief in the US Air Force *US, 1998*

- — *Seattle Times*, p. A9, 12th April 1998

crew hog *noun*

a miscellaneous member of a movie crew *US, 2000*

- The typical porn crew—camera operators, assistant directors, box-cover photographers, and other "crew hogs"—does not have as good a time as you might think. — Ana Loria, *1 2 3 Be A Porn Star!*, p. 30, 2000

crew pie *noun*

a pizza made by a pizza parlor's employees *US, 1996*

- — *Maledicta*, p. 10, 1996: "Domino's pizza jargon"

crew runner *noun*

the leader of a criminal gang *US, 2000*

- Kip's become quite the little crew runner since you left. — *Gone in 60 Seconds*, 2000

crew up *verb*

1 to join a gang; to form a group of friends *US, 2005*

- On one side of Kyle's you could still see the Krush Krew tag put up by Ruina like two years back when we first crewed up. — Linden Dalecki, *Kid B*, p. 2, 2006

2 to form a group to commit a crime *US, 2000*

- If we put out the word that we're crewing up for a one-time-only job, what do you think that'll yield. — *Gone in 60 Seconds*, 2000

crib *noun*

1 a person's dwelling; an apartment or house *US, 1809*

- He had chicks sleeping with cats in nice cribs downtown. — Claude Brown, *Manchild in the Promised Land*, p. 109, 1965
- Nat wasn't making but twenty dollars ($20) a night but he told me when I got out I could shack up at his crib for a few weeks while getting my strength back. — Babs Gonzales, *I Paid My Dues*, p. 25, 1967
- But I'll tell you what, you meet me over to my crib in about an hour. — Donald Goines, *El Dorado Red*, p. 78, 1974
- Next time you bogart your way into a nigger's crib, an' get all in his face, make sure you do it on white boy day. — *True Romance*, 1993

2 a room or shack where a prostitute plies her trade *US, 1846*

- All of nigger Chicago is lousy with police stations, gambling joints, and whore cribs. — Iceberg Slim (Robert Beck), *Mama Black Widow*, p. 74, 1969

3 a prison cell *US, 1990*

- — Charles Shafer, *Folk Speech in Texas Prisons*, p. 202, 1990

4 a safe *US, 1962*

- — Joseph E. Ragen and Charles Finston, *Inside the World's Toughest Prison*, p. 796, 1962

crib *verb*

1 to reside somewhere *US, 1969*

- I coasted the "Hog" into the curb outside the hotel where Kim, my newest, prettiest girl, was cribbing. — Iceberg Slim (Robert Beck), *Pimp*, p. 272, 1969
- All the chorus chicks from the Lido was cribbing there (20) so I knew I was gonna have a ball. — Babs Gonzales, *Movin' On Down De Line*, p. 15, 1975
- If nothing else, just knowing where Deek cribbed could be a major advantage. — Jess Mowry, *Way Past Cool*, p. 124, 1992
- [I]nstead of moving west where the rest of the LA money cribbed, they kept themselves close to their roots. — John Ridley, *Everybody Smokes in Hell*, p. 36, 1999

2 to plagiarize something; to copy something *UK, 1941*

- It's an easy act for a doctor to crib. — Philip Wylie, *Opus 21*, p. 159, 1949

crib course *noun*

a basic, easy course of study *US, 1970*

- Crib course in wireless basics. — Clint Smith, *Wireless Telecommunications FAQs*, p. Back Cover, 2001

cribhouse *noun*

a brothel *US, 1916*

- He wasn't anything, for he got cut by a coke-frisky piano player in a cribhouse where he had gone to take out a little in trade on his protection account. — Robert Penn Warren, *All the King's Men*, p. 13, 1946

cribman *noun*

a professional safecracker *US, 1976*

- — John R. Armore and Joseph D. Wolfe, *Dictionary of Desperation*, 1976
- He's in the big house for all day and night, a new fish jammed into a drum with a cribman, who acts like a gazoonie. — *San Francisco Examiner*, p. 26, 17th August 1976

crib prowl *noun*

an illicit search of a house *US, 1995*

- Black bag work—a classic FBI Commie crib prowl. — James Ellroy, *American Tabloid*, p. 28, 1995

crib sheet *noun*

a piece of paper with information used for studying or cheating in an examination or test *US, 1960*

- Finally, do not carry notes or crib sheets on your person—this can only result in the gravest of problems. — O. Ray, *Audition*, p. 33, 2003

cricket *adjective*

fair, following customs and rules *UK, 1900*

- "Why don't we just get hold of them and—It's not cricket maybe but—" — Herman Wouk, *The Caine Mutiny*, p. 85, 1951

crills *noun*
crack cocaine *US, 1995*
- — Maria Hinojas, *Crews*, p. 167, 1995

crimey *noun*
a criminal *US, 1969*
- CRIMEY A fellow prisoner who was a member of one's gang or a partner in crime. — Miguel Pinero, *Short Eyes*, p. 124, 1975
- "My crimey here thinks the way to go is more drugs," he says[.] — Terry Williams, *The Cocaine Kids*, p. 86, 1989
- They know I'm the type that never had a crime partner. I was always by myself, and the times that I did have some crimeys, we all basically got up out of it by keeping our mouths shut. — Yusuf Jah, *Uprising*, p. 29, 1995

crimp *noun*
1 a military recruiter *US, 1987*
- Uncle Sam sent the crimps (the recruiters) out when I was in college. — Ernest Spencer, *Welcome to Vietnam, Macho Man*, p. 13, 1987
2 an obstacle or impediment *US, 1896*
- I can understand that must have been a bitch of a crimp. — Iceberg Slim (Robert Beck), *Airtight Willie and Me*, p. 59, 1979

crimp *verb*
to intrude; to impede something *US, 1979*
- That hump of a husband of hers was crimpin' on my time. — Edwin Torres, *After Hours*, p. 218, 1979

crimp cut *noun*
in a card game, a cheating move in which the cheater cuts the deck of cards to an intended spot *US, 1996*
- — Peter O. Steiner, *Thursday Night Poker*, p. 409, 1996

crimper *noun*
in gambling, a person who crimps cards so as to be able to identify them in future hands *US, 1992*
- Besides dice tats and 7UPS, there were volumes for nail nickers and crimpers (card markers), hand muckers and mit men (card switchers), as well as card counters and shiner players. — Stephen Cannell, *Big Con*, p. 143, 1992

cringe *noun*
methamphetamine *US, 1993*
- Teener means one sixteenth of an ounce. One eighth is called a eightball. You ever do cringe? That's what we call meth, cringe. — Joseph Wambaugh, *Finnegan's Week*, p. 40, 1993

crink *noun*
1 a sharp, searing pain *US, 1970*
- [T]hat was the direction in which she turned in order to ease a crink in her neck. — Roger Zelazny, *Bring Me the Head of Prince Charming*, p. 187, 1991
2 methamphetamine sulfate in powdered form *US, 1967*
- Sometimes I get some crink (methedrine) or smack (heroin) and then the dough really comes in. — Elizabeth Finn, *Drugs in the Tenderloin*, p. 12, 1967
- — Walter L. Way, *The Drug Scene*, 1977

crinkle-top *noun*
a black person with natural or afro hair *US, 1980*
- — Edith A. Folb, *runnin' down some lines*, p. 233, 1980

crip *noun*
1 an easy course in school or college *US, 1923*
- — *Time Magazine*, p. 46, 24th August 1959
- — Andy Anonymous, *A Basic Guide to Campusology*, p. 7, 1966
2 a cripple *US, 1893*
- In the middle of the second month we attended a wedding of an old whore and a crip on the abandoned stage of a Main Street theater closed for repairs. — Clancy Sigal, *Going Away*, p. 238, 1961
- The stump [of a rat's foot] was ragged like a trap had hacked off the foot, or perhaps the old crip had chewed it off in a valorous escape from the trap. — Iceberg Slim (Robert Beck), *Mama Black Widow*, p. 71, 1969
- — Multicultural Management Program Fellows, *Dictionary of Cautionary Words and Phrases*, 1989
- How'd dem crips get the jack inside? — Seth Morgan, *Homeboy*, p. 331, 1990

crip *verb*
to dress and behave in a manner associated with the Crips youth gang *US, 1993*
- D-Don's mother ordered that there be no Crippin' at her son's memorial or funeral. — Bob Sipchen, *Baby Insane and the Buddha*, p. 219, 1993

- When I was in there, I was Crippin' hard. — Yusuf Jah, *Uprising*, p. 28, 1995
- "Crippin' aint' easy," Smiley says. "You gotta stay down and represent to the fullest." — Colton Simpson, *Inside the Crips*, p. 19, 2005

crippie *noun*
high quality marijuana *US, 2002*
- The top grade marijuana, known in street slang as "crippie," sold for about $5,000 a pound. — *Sun Sentinel (Fort Lauderdale, Florida)*, p. 1B, 4th June 2002

cripple *noun*
1 a Class 4, low-power radio station *US, 1995*
- It was what people in the radio business call a "cripple," a station with either a weak signal or crummy facilities. — Wolfman Jack (Bob Smith), *Have Mercy!*, p. 75, 1995
2 a knee-boarder; a surfer who rides kneeling rather than standing *US, 1988*
Derogatory, spoken with disdain by experienced surfers.
- — *Surf Punks, Oh No! Not Them Again!*, 1988
3 in pool, a shot that cannot be missed or a game that cannot be lost *US, 1964*
- — Steve Rushin, *Pool Cool*, p. 11, 1990
- — Mike Shamos, *The Illustrated Encyclopedia of Billiards*, p. 63, 1993

crippleware *noun*
computer software that operates up to a point but then is disabled until payment for a full working version is made *US, 1991*
- — Eric S. Raymond, *The New Hacker's Dictionary*, p. 112, 1991

crisp *noun*
any alcohol *US, 2001*
- — Don R. McCreary (Editor), *Dawg Speak*, 2001

crisp *adjective*
said of a table in pool where there is no need to adjust a shot to compensate for the table surface *US, 1993*
- — Mike Shamos, *The Illustrated Encyclopedia of Billiards*, p. 63, 1993

crispy *noun*
a badly burnt person or corpse *US, 1981*
An abbreviation of **CRISPY CRITTER**.
- — J.E. Lighter, *Historical Dictionary of American Slang, Volume One*, p. 523, 1994

crispy *adjective*
good, stylish, fashionable, pleasing *US, 1997*
- You're crispy, you're the shit, you really are, Joey. You're the man. — Joel Rose, *Kill Kill Faster Faster*, p. 141, 1997
- Even a Fubu sweat suit; I like it to be fresh, crispy, brand-new, looking right. — *Style*, p. 96, July 2001

crispy critter *noun*
1 a burnt corpse, especially one burnt by napalm *US, 1967*
The term was borrowed from the branded name of a sugar-frosted oat cereal cut out in animal shapes, popular in the US in the 1960s.
- [E]verything was transformed into Crispy Critters for half a dozen clicks in any direction you would have cared to point; everything smelling of ash and marrow and spontaneous combustion[.] — Larry Heinemann, *Paco's Story*, p. 15, 1986
- It's a two-story dump on North Bond Street and, of course, there are no witnesses—just a bunch of burned furniture and one crispy critter in the middle room. — David Simon, *Homicide*, p. 447, 1991
2 a badly burnt hospital patient *US, 1988–1989*
- — *Maledicta*, p. 35, 1988–1989: "More Milwaukee medical maledicta"
3 a burnt pizza *US, 1996*
- — *Maledicta*, p. 10, 1996: "Domino's pizza jargon"

criss-cross *noun*
an amphetamine tablet, especially Benzedrine™ (amphetamine sulfate) *US, 1993*
From the cross scoring on the tablet; possibly a play on **CRIS**, a central nervous system stimulant (amphetamine).
- — US Department of Justice, *Street Terms*, August 1993

cristina; cris; crist; christina *noun*
methamphetamine *US, 1971*
A personification of **CRYSTAL** (powdered methamphetamine).
- — Walter L. Way, *The Drug Scene*, 1977

- And amidst all this Crist' poppin' and wristwatches / I just sit back and just watch[.] — Eminem (Marshall Mathers), *Marshall Mathers*, 2000

critical *adjective*

1 impressive, amazing *US, 1990*
- — Connie Eble (Editor), *UNC-CH Campus Slang*, p. 3, November 1990
- — Vann Wesson, *Generation X Field Guide and Lexicon*, p. 42, 1997

2 (used of a wave) very steep, threatening to break at any moment *US, 1963*
- — Grant W. Kuhns, *On Surfing*, p. 115, 1963

croack *noun*

a mixture of crack and an amphetamine *US, 1993*
- — Peter Johnson, *Dictionary of Street Alcohol and Drug Terms*, p. 51, 1993

croagies *noun*

the testicles *US, 1985*
- She didn't do anything like that, try to kick me in the croagies or anything. — George V. Higgins, *Penance for Jerry Kennedy*, p. 191, 1985

croak *verb*

1 to die *UK, 1812*
From the death rattle.
- Old Mr. Keller croaked, but he was almost eighty years old, he shoulda croaked[.] — Darryl Ponicsan, *The Last Detail*, p. 59, 1970

2 to kill someone *UK, 1823*
- Let her go ahead and croak him. — Chester Himes, *The Real Cool Killers*, p. 45, 1959
- I recall pointing to the loaded double-barreled shotgun on my wall and replying, with a smile, that I would croak at least two of them before they go away. — Hunter S. Thompson, *Hell's Angels*, p. 143, 1966
- "Party" tried his fists and muscle until the pimp game croaked him. — Iceberg Slim (Robert Beck), *Pimp*, p. 41, 1969
- When I heard they croaked Charlie I freak out, almost went back to shootin scag. — Charles W. Moore, *A Brick for Mister Jones*, p. 105, 1975

3 to inform on someone, to betray someone *US, 1964*
- — R. Frederick West, *God's Gambler*, p. 223, 1964

croaker *noun*

a doctor, especially a company doctor *UK, 1879*
Sometimes abbreviated to "croak."
- We'll knock off this croaker. — William J. Spillard and Pence James, *Needle in a Haystack*, p. 18, 1945
- The old croaker on 102nd finally lost his mind altogether and no drugstore would fill his scripts[.] — William Burroughs, *Junkie*, pp. 25–26, 1953
- From this croaker up on 76th Street. He used to write for me, you know, scripts, prescriptions. I turned a trick with him. — James Mills, *The Panic in Needle Park*, p. 91, 1966
- He told me he knew of a couple of people who were keeping up habits making croakers. — Herbert Huncke, *The Evening Sun Turned Crimson*, p. 84, 1980

crock *noun*

1 an unpleasant or worthless person, object or experience; a waste of time *US, 1944*
Contemptuously abbreviated from the familiar **CROCK OF SHIT**.
- Your ideas are a crock, I added to myself. — Jack Kerouac, *The Dharma Bums*, p. 72, 1958

2 a person with medical problems which are the result of abusive living *US, 1978*
- — *Maledicta*, p. 68, Summer/Winter 1978: "Common patient-directed pejoratives used by medical personnel"

3 a computer program that normally functions but fails if modified at all *US, 1983*
- — Guy L. Steele et al., *The Hacker's Dictionary*, p. 50, 1983

4 nonsense *US, 1962*
An abbreviation of **CROCK OF SHIT**.
- "Now what kind of crock are you giving us?" No crock. It's every word gospel. — Ken Kesey, *One Flew Over the Cuckoo's Nest*, p. 297, 1962
- "Now, that's a crock," the kid said, cocking his head insolently. — Malcolm Braly, *It's Cold Out There*, p. 37, 1966

crocked *adjective*

drunk *US, 1917*
- In the first place, they were both slightly crocked. — J.D. Salinger, *Catcher in the Rye*, p. 86, 1951
- I had traveling money and got crocked in the bar downstairs. — Jack Kerouac, *On the Road*, pp. 76–77, 1957

- The producer arrived slightly crocked and drank a half-bottle of Scotch before he lay naked on the waterproofed bed and the bizarre scene began. — Xaviera Hollander, *The Happy Hooker*, p. 247, 1972
- Both of them were half-crocked, drunken leers on their faces. — Herbert Huncke, *The Evening Sun Turned Crimson*, p. 119, 1980

crock of shit *noun*

1 an unpleasant or worthless person, object or experience; a waste of time *US, 1951*
- Now, stop stallin', man, or else admit all this professional stuff you're talkin', about is a crock of shit. — *48 Hours*, 1982

2 nonsense, lies *US, 1945*
- They said God took her away. That's a crock of shit. God don't do evil things like that[.] — Rita Mae Brown, *Rubyfruit Jungle*, p. 27, 1973
- Now, stop stallin', man, or else admit all this professional stuff you're talking about is a crock of shit. — *48 Hours*, 1982

crop *noun*

a fifth of a gallon of wine *US, 1975*
- — *American Speech*, p. 57, Spring–Summer 1975: "Razorback slang"

crop dust *verb*

to break wind *US, 2000*
- The average person crop dusts a room about 14 times a day. — Joy Masoff, *Oh, Yuck*, p. 54, 2000

cross *noun*

▶ **in a cross**
in trouble *US, 1976*
- I go for you, Sam, I think you're boss / but don't think you can ever put me in a cross. — Dennis Wepman et al., *The Life*, p. 40, 1976

cross *verb*

1 to betray someone *UK, 1821*
- Seven years later she would tally up and happily cross me into prison. — Iceberg Slim (Robert Beck), *Pimp*, p. 110, 1969

2 to cheat a cheat *US, 1950*
- — Thomas L. Clark, *The Dictionary of Gambling and Gaming*, p. 55, 1987

cross bar hotel *noun*

a jail or prison *US, 1865*
- — *Swinging Syllables*, 1959
- the poor jerk from Camden you take up the river to the Crossbars Hotel. — Darryl Ponicsan, *The Last Detail*, p. 181, 1970
- So Butch said he could keep me out of the Crossbar Hotel for a while if I would send him another hundred[.] — Joe Bob Briggs, *Joe Bob Goes to the Drive-In*, p. 32, 1987
- "If they ignore [the laws] they're going to end up staying in the Virginia Beach crosssbar hotel," says Virginia Beach police Officer Lou Thruston. — *Washington Times*, 24th May 1996

crossfire *noun*

in confidence games, conversation between confederates in the swindle that draws the victim into the swindle *US, 1940*
Originally used to describe the quick banter of vaudeville, then adapted to criminal purposes.
- Now, when Blue came back he'd need me to set up the crossfire to make it logical to Dot that the flue and the mail-away were necessary and fair arrangements for us all. — Iceberg Slim (Robert Beck), *Trick Baby*, p. 27, 1969

crossfire *verb*

(used of a racehorse) to clip the rear hooves together while running *US, 1951*
- — David W. Maurer, *Argot of the Racetrack*, p. 22, 1951

cross my heart and hope to die

used as an oath, often with humor *US, 1926*
- No jive, cross my heart and hope to die, Darling. — Iceberg Slim (Robert Beck), *Airtight Willie and Me*, p. 75, 1979

cross my heart and hope to spit

used as an oath and pledge *US, 1957*
Popularized by Theodore "Beaver" Cleaver on the US television comedy *Leave it to Beaver* (CBS and ABC, 1957–63), in place of the more common "cross my heart and hope to die." Used with referential humor by those who had watched the show as children.
- "Cross my heart and hope to spit." He spat into the bushes. — Bess Kaplan, *The Empty Chair*, p. 189, 1978

crossover *verb*
to leave one youth gang and join a rival gang *US, 1995*
- — Bill Valentine, *Gang Intelligence Manual*, p. 75, 1995

crossroad *noun*
an amphetamine tablet identified by its cross-scoring *US, 1968*
Less commonly heard than **CROSS-TOP**.
- Some of the names describe the drugs' effects, such as "helpers," "copilots," "Los Angeles turn arounds," or their shape, color and markings—"hearts," "footballs," "blackjacks," "crossroads." — Phil Hirsch, *Hooked*, pp. 51–52, 1968
- — National Institute on Drug Abuse, *What do they call it again*, 1980

crossroader *noun*
an itinerant card cheat or thief *US, 1889*
- Most thieves are crossroaders—they travel around, so they can't have a family. — Harry King, *Box Man*, p. 76, 1972
- [I]n a court of law, if a blackjack Dealer gets terribly unlucky and his table keeps losing fifteen nights in a row, there is no legal proof that he is cheating for the benefit of an "outside" man or "crossroader," that he is "dumping out." — Mario Puzo, *Inside Las Vegas*, p. 180, 1977

cross top *noun*
a tablet of Benzedrine™ (amphetamine sulfate), a central nervous system stimulant *US, 1971*
From the appearance: white tablets with a cross cut into the surface.
- — Walter L. Way, *The Drug Scene*, 1977
- Actually, the cross tops from the early '70s were sometimes decent-grade methamphetamines, not the early '80s-style caffeine crap. — Don Bolles, *Retrohell*, p. 50, 1997
- I suspected they were speed, known on the street as "cross-tops." — Lora Shaner, *Madam*, p. 213, 1999

crosstown *noun*
the air space above Hanoi *US, 1990*
- — Joseph Tuso, *Singing the Vietnam Blues*, p. 249, 1990: Glossary

crotch *noun*
a woman *US, 1973*
- I come in here, I open the door, and there's this crotch at the desk there. — George V. Higgins, *The Digger's Game*, p. 180, 1973

Crotch *nickname*
the US Marines Corps *US, 1953*
- "There are a lot of mean sons-of-bitches in the Crotch." — Martin Russ, *Happy Hunting Ground*, pp. 33–34, 1968
- I been busted so many times I couldn't make lance corporal if I stayed in the Crotch for thirty years. — Philip Caputo, *A Rumor of War*, p. 133, 1977
- They talked about how much they hated the Marine Corps—"the Crotch," "the Green Motherfucker." — Robert A. Anderson, *Cooks & Bakers*, p. 118, 1982
- Anyway, I go, "Were you in the Crotch?" He says, "The Crotch?" I say, "Yeah, the Marine Corps. Were you around Da Nang?" — James Lee Burke, *Sunset Limited*, p. 134, 1998

crotch crickets *noun*
pubic lice *US, 1971*
- Oh shit, I've never had saber-toothed crotch crickets before. — Beatrice Sparks (writing as "Anonymous"), *Jay's Journal*, p. 130, 1979
- On top of being skinny, our crotch crickets were very prevalent, and the bedbugs were everywhere. — Donald Knox, *Death March*, p. 401, 1981
- — Michael Dalton Johnson, *Talking Trash with Redd Foxx*, p. 51, 1994

crotch light *noun*
in the pornography industry, a light used to illuminate the genitals of the performers *US, 1977*
- They said, "What am I doing here" and see all these strange faces and people holding crotch lights. — Stephen Ziplow, *The Film Maker's Guide to Pornography*, p. 14, 1977

crotch magazine *noun*
a pornographic magazine *US, 1986*
- "My name's Whistler," he said when the attendant looked up from his crotch magazine, open to the centerfold in which a girl of stunning beauty spread her legs for anyone who cared to ogle her. — Robert Campbell, *In La-La Land We Trust*, p. 95, 1986

crotch rot *noun*
any fungal infection in the crotch *US, 1967*

- Sometimes your chops for action and your terror would reach a different balance and you'd go looking for it everywhere, and nothing would happen, except a fire ant would fly up your nose or you'd grow a crotch rot[.] — Michael Herr, *Dispatches*, p. 1962, 1977
- Maybe we would be able to clear up the cases of trench foot and crotch rot that seemed to be plaguing everyone. — Gary Linderer, *The Eyes of the Eagle*, p. 118, 1991
- — Sally Williams, "Strong" Words, p. 137, 1994
- Aside from some improvement in my jungle sores, crotch rot, and immersion foot, I rejoined my unit in much worse shape than when I'd left. — Nelson DeMille, *Up Country*, pp. 280–281, 2002

crotch row *noun*
in a striptease performance, seats very near the performers *US, 1973*
- — Sherman Louis Sergel, *The Language of Show Biz*, p. 63, 1973
- — Don Wilmeth, *The Language of American Popular Entertainment*, 1981

crotch shot *noun*
a photograph focused on a person's genitals *US, 1973*
- Customer always want smiling crotch shots. — George Paul Csicsery (Editor), *The Sex Industry*, p. 163, 1973
- The explicitness of the crotch shots was made for pigs like you who need the anatomy lesson. — *The Village Voice*, 25th July 2000

crow *noun*
1 a black person *US, 1823*
Offensive.
- It was a dangerous practice to call a Negro anything that could be loosely construed as insulting because of the centuries of their having been called niggers, jigs, dinges, blackbirds, crows, boots and spooks. — Maya Angelou, *I Know Why the Caged Bird sings*, p. 106, 1969
2 a mawkish, old-fashioned person *US, 1945*
- A corny person is a "cornball" or a "crow." — *Women's Digest*, p. 40, September 1945
3 an electronic warfare specialist *US, 1980*
Vietnam war usage.
- He knew the "crows" in the back of the plane—four electronic warfare officers—were doing the same. — William C. Anderson, *Bat 21*, p. 3, 1980
4 an eagle insignia in the US Navy *US, 1905*
- She hadn't felt so powerful since those days when she'd first earned the "crow" of a petty officer, taking on the responsibility of command over subordinates. — Joseph Wambaugh, *Finnegan's Week*, p. 29, 1993

crowbait *noun*
a horse, especially an older horse *US, 1851*
- — *American Speech*, p. 270, December 1958: "Ranching terms from eastern Washington"

crowd *noun*
a fat person *US, 1970*
- — William D. Alsever, *Glossary for the Establishment and Other Uptight People*, p. 8, 1970

crowded cabin *noun*
in poker, a hand consisting of three cards of one rank and a pair *US, 1988*
Conventionally known as a "full house."
- — George Percy, *The Language of Poker*, p. 25, 1988

crowd-surf *verb*
to pass over the heads of a crowd, propelled and supported by the hands of that crowd *US, 1992*
- Men, now you can stagedive and crowdsurf, and maybe get a look at the band before the security nazis throw you off the stage. — *talk.bizarre*, 18th January 1992
- With the club's tables and chairs tucked away, the flannel-clad crowd had plenty of room to dance and crowd-surf, which the band encouraged. — *Buffalo (New York) News*, p. 5, 25th October 1993
- They had a bunch of people, and they would make guys crowd surf. — Suroosh Alvi et al., *The Vice Guide*, p. 313, 2002

crowd-surfer *noun*
a person who allows himself to be passed over the heads of a crowd, propelled and supported by the hands of that crowd *US, 1992*
- Nearly lost my earring when a crowd-surfer kicked me in the head (earring back knocked off, post bent sideways). — *talk.bizarre*, 31st January 1993

crowd-surfing *noun*

passing over the heads of a crowd, propelled and supported by the hands of that crowd *CANADA, 1989*

- [C]rowd surfing, where the stage-diver is passed over the heads of moshers in apparent gratitude for not having squashed anyone. — *The Oregonian, p. C4, 7th December 1992*

Crow Jim *noun*

anti-white racial discrimination by black people *US, 1956*

A reversal of the common term JIM CROW for anti-black discrimination.

- Even in their chosen field of "traditional" jazz the authors are unreliable due to the constant intrusion of a form of racial bias known in the trade as "Crow-Jim." — *San Francisco Examiner, p. 3 (II), 7th January 1957*
- Archie Shepp had not yet passed form Fire Music into increasingly virulent Crow-Jim nihilism. — Lester Bangs, *Psychotic Reactions and Carburetor Dung, p. 41, 1987*

crown *noun*

a hat *US, 1976*

- Sported a hand-painted tie that hung down to his fly / And he had on a gold-dust crown. — Michael H. Agar, *The Journal of American Folklore, p. 177, April 1971*
- A candy-striped tie hung down to his fly / And he sported a gold-dust crown. — Dennis Wepman et al., *The Life, p. 54, 1976*
- — Bill Valentine, *Gang Intelligence Manual, p. 110, 1995*

crown jewels *noun*

jewels, usually ostentatious if not tacky, worn by a drag queen *US, 1965*

The royalty punning thanks to "queen."

- — *Fact, p. 26, January–February 1965*

crow's feet *noun*

wrinkles at the corner of the eyes *UK, 1374*

- I told you, he's got that outdoor good-guy look. Even has crow's-feet when he squints. — Elmore Leonard, *Riding the Rap, p. 103, 1995*

crow's foot *noun*

in electric line work, a device formally known as Exaxirod tri-unit *US, 1980*

- — A.B. Chance Co, *Lineman's Slang Dictionary, 1980*

CRS disease *noun*

a sudden loss of memory *US, 1997*

The person in question "can't remember shit."

- The other guys caught the CRS disease. — Dee Holmes, *The Caleb Tree, p. 148, 2000*

crud *noun*

1 a contemptible person *US, 1930*

Originally Scottish dialect for "excrement."

- The crud pulled out his money to try to bribe me. [Steve Canyon comic strip] — *San Francisco Examiner, p. 14, 24th March 1947*
- No bums like these cruds. — Hubert Selby Jr., *Last Exit to Brooklyn, p. 123, 1957*
- The furious District Attorney of Fort Lauderdale, Fla., who describes his town's Easter vacation visitors as "College cruds," put it too mildly. — *Los Angeles Herald-Examiner, p. B3, 5th April 1967*

2 dried or sticky semen *US, 1967*

- — Dale Gordon, *The Dominion Sex Dictionary, p. 52, 1967*

3 any sexually transmitted infection *US, 1951*

- — Dale Gordon, *The Dominion Sex Dictionary, p. 52, 1967*

4 a notional disease, covering many ailments, real and imaginary *US, 1932*

- — *American Speech, p. 304, December 1947: "Imaginary diseases in army and navy parlance"*

5 snow that does not produce good snowboarding *US, 1990*

- — Elena Garcia, *A Beginner's Guide to Zen and the Art of Snowboarding, p. 121, 1990*

crudball *noun*

an odious person *US, 1987*

- A yahoo is a crudball, a stupid person. — William McQuade, *SAT Success, p. 90, 1987*
- Yes, this crudball clearly aspires to join the net.cosmic.asshole Hall of Fame. — *alt.flame, 3rd November 1987*
- I shared it with crudballs who won't give me the time of day now. — David Simon and Edward Burns, *The Corner, p. 103, 1997*

- "You were just saying, hey, you no-major, somewhere-down-the-money-list crudball, pick up my bag and be happy you know me." — Dan Jenkins, *The Money-Whipped Steer-Job Three-Jack Give-Up Artist, p. 11, 2001*

crudded up *adjective*

infected with a sexually transmitted disease *US, 1997*

- It's not possible that she's all crudded up? — *Chasing Amy, 1997*

cruddy *adjective*

1 useless, worthless, unpleasant, disgusting *US, 1947*

Created from CRUD (filth).

- "Go back to your nice little apartment and get the hell out of this cruddy dive. Just go." — Curt Cannon, *Die Hard, p. 11, 1953*
- Oh, my aching, breaking, cruddy, bloody back! — Max Shulman, *Rally Round the Flag, Boys!, p. 20, 1957*
- Is this the Mothers of Invention recording under a different name in a last ditch attempt to get their cruddy music on the radio? — Frank Zappa, *Cruising With Ruben & The Jets, 1968*

2 encrusted with dirt or filth *US, 1949*

- This is where you're heading. A cruddy lung, smoking through a hole in your throat. Do you really want that? — *Clerks, 1994*
- Can I sit on the chair? I don't want to get all cruddy. — *Airheads, 1994*

crudie *noun*

an unsophisticated rustic *US, 1968*

- — Mary Swift, *Campus Slang (University of Texas), 1968*

crud up *verb*

to foul something; to spoil something *US, 1963*

- There never was much around Houston or Dallas to crud up, but the limestone hills and fast rivers of Central Texas—that's a shame. — Molly Ivins, *Molly Ivins Can't Say That, Can She?, p. 26, 1991*

crudzine *noun*

a poorly written and/or poorly produced fan magazine *US, 1976*

- — *American Speech, p. 53, Spring 1978: "Star trek lives: trekker slang"*
- — *American Speech, p. 25, Spring 1982: "The language of science fiction fan magazines"*

cruft *noun*

any unpleasant, unidentified substance *US, 1983*

- — Guy L. Steele et al., *The Hacker's Dictionary, p. 50, 1983*

crufty *adjective*

in computing, poorly designed or poorly built *US, 1991*

- — Guy Steele, *Coevolution Quarterly, p. 29, Spring 1981: "Computer slang"*
- — Eric S. Raymond, *The New Hacker's Dictionary, p. 114, 1991*

cruise *noun*

a male homosexual who picks up multiple short-term sexual partners *US, 1950*

- That cruise we robbed looked like a bum but he went for four C's on the shake. — Hyman E. Goldin et al., *Dictionary of American Underworld Lingo, p. 53, 1950*

cruise *verb*

1 to search for a casual sex partner, usually homosexual; to pursue a person as a casual sex partner, especially by eye contact *US, 1923*

- "Oh that charming young scamp, or is it 'camp,' who passed me on the stairs on his way out cruising." — Reginald Harvey, *Park Beat, p. 76, 1959*
- [T]wo anxious fairies cruise me. — John Rechy, *City of Night, p. 194, 1963*
- I don't get it—you cruise Atlantic City or something? — Mart Crowley, *The Boys in the Band, p. 121, 1968*
- At first it simply didn't occur to me that this number was cruising me. — John Francis Hunter, *The Gay Insider, p. 35, 1971*

2 to drive *US, 1957*

With a suggestion of carefree elan.

- "Whaddya say, hey?" he said to Comfort. "Let's do some cruisin'." — Max Shulman, *Rally Round the Flag, Boys!, p. 58, 1957*
- Wait, wait, I gotta cruise by this afternoon and run a little business if you know what I'm talking about. — *Dazed and Confused, 1993*

3 to take someone, to lead someone *US, 1946*

- Rue Auberg; fly little chick gets stranglehold on my lapel, tries to cruise me up to her apartment[.] — Mezz Mezzrow, *Really the Blues, p. 197, 1946*

▶ **cruisin' for a bruisin'**
heading for trouble, especially a physical beating *US, 1947*
- — *Newsweek*, p. 28, 8th October 1951
- — *Dobie Gillis Teenage Slanguage Dictionary*, 1962
- Your dad is really cruising for a bruising, Carlotta. — C.D. Payne, *Youth in Revolt*, p. 376, 1993

cruise joint *noun*
a bar or other establishment where people gather in search of sexual partners *US, 1966*
- "We'd hit the cruise joints around Chicago looking for a well-heeled out of town faggot in the city for kicks," explained Gene. — Johnny Shearer, *The Male Hustler*, p. 36, 1966

cruisemobile *noun*
any desirable car *US, 1978*
- — Lillian Glass with Richard Liebmann-Smith, *How to Deprogram Your Valley Girl*, p. 27, 1982
- The hot exhausts of Chevy Biscaynes, Pontiac Catalinas, Mercury Montereys, and the rest of the road's superwide, electraglide, V8 cruisemobiles muddy the atmosphere[.] — William Clark, *Temples of Sound*, p. 193, 2003

cruiser *noun*
1 a prostitute *US, 1868*
- — Ruth Todasco et al., *The Intelligent Woman's Guide to Dirty Words*, p. 3, 1973
2 a surfer who approaches surfing with a casualness that borders on laziness *US, 1988*
- — Michael V. Anderson, *The Bad, Rad, Not to Forget Way Cool Beach and Surf Discriptionary*, p. 5, 1988

cruising *noun*
the recreational activity of searching for a casual sex partner, usually homosexual *UK, 1927*
- There was quite a bit of forthright cruising (that's the gay word for giving a guy "the eye") going on [.] — *Screw*, 24th November 1969
- Cruising, he had long ago decided, was a lot like hitchhiking. It was best to dress like the people you wanted to pick you up. — Armistead Maupin, *Tales of the City*, 1978

cruisy *adjective*
(of a place) characterized by a high degree of activity by homosexual men looking for sexual partners *US, 1949*
Also spelt "cruisey."
- Third Avenue is also cruisy in the later afternoon. — John Francis Hunter, *The Gay Insider*, p. 120, 1971
- A place where one can expect to find many persons on the make is termed cruisy. — Wayne Dynes, *Homolexis*, p. 39, 1985
- You can go out and make good friends without it being a cruisey scenario. — *Attitude*, p. 34, October 2003

cruit; croot *noun*
a new military recruit *US, 1897*
- — Carl Fleischhauer, *A Glossary of Army Slang*, p. 12, 1968

cruller *noun*
the head *US, 1942*
- "Toady to the turban, droop, or snipe a Stayman off your son's cruller with a bow and arrow at a hundred paces," says Mr. Big. — Harry Haenigsen, *Jive's Like That*, 1947

crumb *noun*
1 a despicable person *US, 1919*
- "One move outa you or your other crumbs and I'll have this in your guts," Crazy rasped. — Irving Shulman, *The Amboy Dukes*, p. 213, 1947
- I think I remember Larry sayin'—"Mayor Lindsay is a crumb!" — Eugene Boe, *The Wit & Wisdom of Archie Bunker*, p. 102, 1971
- "I began to realize that what I'd promised Goodman would make me nothing but a crumb, workin' and slavin' for a few bucks." — Martin Gosch, *The Last Testament of Lucky Luciano*, p. 26, 1975
- [L]andlady to a dozen or so crumbs who flopped into her furnished rooms for a week or a year[.] — William Brashler, *City Dogs*, p. 77, 1976
2 a body louse *US, 1863*
- — Joseph E. Ragen and Charles Finston, *Inside the World's Toughest Prison*, p. 796, 1962
- — Joe McKennon, *Circus Lingo*, p. 29, 1980
3 a small piece of crack cocaine *US, 1994*
- — US Department of Justice, *Street Terms*, October 1994

crumb box *noun*
in circus and carnival usage, a small suitcase or box containing personal belongings *US, 1981*
- — Don Wilmeth, *The Language of American Popular Entertainment*, p. 67, 1981

crumb bum *noun*
1 a lowly, inept person *US, 1934*
- All the guys have gone into the army; only the crumb-bums are left. — Hal Ellison, *Summer Street*, p. 15, 1953
- Spell: untoiling me from my friends at Malibu beach, referred to by my father as the beachniks or the crumbums or just plain bums[.] — Frederick Kohner, *Gidget Goes Hawaiian*, p. 2, 1961
2 a gambler who places very small and very conservative bets *US, 1950*
- — *The Annals of the American Academy of Political and Social Sciences*, p. 123, May 1950

crumb castle *noun*
in circus and carnival usage, a dining tent *US, 1981*
- — Don Wilmeth, *The Language of American Popular Entertainment*, p. 67, 1981

crumb-catcher *noun*
a young child *US, 1962*
- I said, "Well, I can dig it, buddy, 'cause I'm hooked up myself. I got a dough-roll [wife] and two crumb-catchers [children], you know." — Bruce Jackson, *In the Life*, p. 152, 1972
- What about this little crumb-catcher you got in the oven here? — Edwin Torres, *After Hours*, p. 378, 1979

crumb crunchers *noun*
the teeth *US, 1945*
- — Lou Shelly, *Hepcats Jive Talk Dictionary*, p. 23, 1945

crumb-crusher; crumb-cruncher *noun*
a child, especially a very young one *US, 1959*
- — Robert George Reisner, *The Jazz Titans*, p. 153, 1960
- — Frank Prewitt and Francis Schaeffer, *Vacaville Vocabulary*, 1961–1962
- I hadn't heard about a "crumb crusher." — Iceberg Slim (Robert Beck), *Pimp*, p. 114, 1969
- The little bitch—outta the clear blue—told me one night that she was going to have a crumb crusher! — A.S. Jackson, *Gentleman Pimp*, p. 45, 1973
- She ain't into nothin', with two crumbcrushers and no ambition. — Donald Goines, *The Busting Out of an Ordinary Man*, p. 21, 1985

crumb crushers *noun*
the lips *US, 1957*
- Just keep your crumb crushers shut, Monk said. — Herbert Simmons, *Corner Boy*, p. 219, 1957

crumbo *noun*
▶ **el crumbo**
a socially inept person *US, 1959*
Pseudo Spanish.
- — *American Speech*, p. 155, May 1959: "Gator (University of Florida) slang"

crumbs *noun*
a small amount of money *US, 1970*
An offshoot of **BREAD**.
- — Clarence Major, *Dictionary of Afro-American Slang*, p. 42, 1970
- — Kenn "Naz" W. Young, *Naz's Underground Dictionary*, p. 23, 1973

crumb-snatcher *noun*
a child; a baby *US, 1958*
- — Robert George Reisner, *The Jazz Titans*, p. 153, 1960
- — Frank Prewitt and Francis Schaeffer, *Vacaville Vocabulary*, 1961–1962
- I was about twelve strokes from a nuclear orgasm when I realized the crumb snatchers were on my front porch. — Eric Jerome Dickey, *Cheaters*, p. 13, 1999

crummy *adjective*
1 inferior *US, 1915*
- "Of all the lousy, crummy, garish, flamboyant, undisciplined, stupid, corny writing," continued Mr. Oliver, "that I have ever had the misfortune to read, this is absolutely the—Will you stop blubbering?" — Max Shulman, *The Many Loves of Dobie Gillies*, pp. 149–150, 1951
- "That's the crumby part of it." — Chandler Brossard, *Who Walks in Darkness*, p. 80, 1952
- When it came to a choice of being nice and dead or crummy and alive, the guy would work overtime at being a heel. — Jim Thompson, *Savage Night*, p. 40, 1953

- Once at Ames with Minnesota Fats and then again at Arthur's in that cheap, crummy poolroom. — *The Hustler*, 1961

2 lice-infested *UK, 1859*
- — Joe McKennon, *Circus Lingo*, p. 29, 1980

crump *verb*

1 to die *US, 1958*
- — Sally Williams, *"Strong" Words*, p. 137, 1994

2 (used of a hospital patient) to become suddenly sicker, especially without hope of recovering *US, 1980*
- — *Maledicta*, p. 31, 1988–1989: "Medical maledicta from San Francisco"

crump out *verb*

to succumb to exhaustion; to die *US, 1953*
- Just the implication that, if she keeps her equipment in regular use, she'll be all set for sex until she crumps out altogether. — Susan Rako, *The Hormone of Desire*, p. 33, 1996

crunch *noun*

1 a most severe test of strength, courage, nerve, skill, etc *UK, 1939*
- A kid points out that we've come to the big crunch. If you don't go to the dean you're suspended and you have the draft and prison. — James Simon Kunen, *The Strawberry Statement*, p. 62, 1968
- "Crunch" is a word currently favored by the keener journalists. It means the showdown, the moment of truth. — Gore Vidal, *Myra Breckinridge*, p. 202, 1968

2 a number sign (#) on a computer keyboard *US, 1991*
- — Eric S. Raymond, *The New Hacker's Dictionary*, p. 39, 1991

3 a hospital patient with multiple fractures *US, 1989*
- — *Maledicta*, p. 32, 1988–1989: "Medical maledicta from San Francisco"

crunch *verb*

1 to flirt *US, 2002*
From the 1999 movie *Never Been Kissed*.
- "Josie, Guy is totally crunching on you." — *Dictionary of New Terms (Hope College)*, 2002

2 to analyze something, especially a large amount of data *US, 1983*
- — Guy L. Steele, *Coevolution Quarterly*, p. 29, 1981: "Computer Slang"
- — Guy L. Steele et al., *The Hacker's Dictionary*, p. 51, 1983
- We did it by crunching data. — *Point Break*, 1991

crunch and munch *noun*

crack cocaine *US, 1993*
From the drug's arguable resemblance to breakfast cereal or a snack food.
- — Peter Johnson, *Dictionary of Street Alcohol and Drug Terms*, p. 51, 1993

crunch case *noun*

a hospital patient with a severe head injury *US, 1994*
- — Sally Williams, *"Strong" Words*, p. 137, 1994

cruncher *noun*

1 a dent in a surfboard that can be repaired without a resin filler *US, 1986*
- — George Colendich, *The Ding Repair Scriptures*, p. 88, 1986

2 a foot *US, 1946*
- Gee, you feel it way down to your crunchers. — Mezz Mezzrow, *Really the Blues*, p. 100, 1946

crunchy *noun*

1 the sidewalk *US, 1945*
- — Lou Shelly, *Hepcats Jive Talk Dictionary*, p. 9, 1945

2 a foot soldier, or member of the infantry *US, 1951*
Korean and then Vietnam war usage.
- Armed helicopters were especially reassuring to the "crunchies," the ground infantrymen who depended on them to deliver accurate supporting fire. — Shelby L. Stanton, *The Rise and Fall of an American Army*, p. 86, 1985

crunchy *adjective*

embodying the values or at least the trappings of the 1960s counterculture; a person who embodies these values *US, 1990*
An adjective often associated with **GRANOLA**, used to describe the throwback person.
- — Connie Eble (Editor), *UNC-CH Campus Slang*, p. 2, Spring 1990
- "A crunchy is a '90s hippie," says Scott Blasik, a young poet from Durham, New Hampshire. "A hiking-boot-wearing, granola-eating,

Grateful Dead/Blues Traveler-listening type of person." — David Shenk and Steve Silberman, *Skeleton Key*, p. 48, 1994
- — Andy Ihnatko, *Cyberspeak*, p. 48, 1997
- True, they [the Indigo Girls] are crunchy lesbian-coffeehouse-alterna-rock, and I know you hide the CD when people come over, but it's time we make these girls cool again. — Suroosh Alvi et al., *The Vice Guide*, p. 17, 2002

crunk *noun*

1 an excited state *US, 2001*
- Iconz take a geeky, white American family clubbing and they all get their crunk on. — *Mixmag*, p. 38, December 2001

2 used as a substitute for any profanity *US, 1994*
A device created by Conan O'Brien in 1994.
- "What the crunk are you talking about?" — *Dictionary of New Terms (Hope College)*, 2002

crunk *adjective*

excellent; intense *US, 1995*
Rap coinage; a variation of **CRANKED** (intensified).
- Take him out and take his money / Then I spit on the punk / Now I'm crunk[.] — Three 6 Mafia, *Tear Da Club Up*, 1996
- But around here we get it crunk when ya / Bounce with me — Lil Bow Wow, *Bounce With Me*, 2000
- I go out to clubs. I love to dance and get "crunk." — Alison Pollet, *MTV's Real World Chicago*, p. 104, 2001

crunked *adjective*

excited *US, 2001*
Rap usage; a variation of **CRUNK** (excellent).
- Best bit: When overcrunked dad grabs a podium dancer and gets a smack. — *Mixmag*, p. 38, December 2001
- — Connie Eble (Editor), *UNC-CH Campus Slang*, p. 3, October 2002

crush *noun*

1 an infatuation *US, 1884*
- RUTH: Do you remember your first crush? LIANNA: My first crush... I used to go to camp up north in the summer. There was this one counselor, she was fifteen maybe sixteen [...] I had sort of a crush on her. — John Sayles, *Lianna*, 1983

2 a hat *US, 1916*
- — Marcus Hanna Boulware, *Jive and Slang of Students in Negro Colleges*, 1947

3 in pool, the opening or break shot *US, 1993*
- — Mike Shamos, *The Illustrated Encyclopedia of Billiards*, p. 66, 1993

crushed *adjective*

ugly *US, 1993*
- — *People Magazine*, p. 73, 19th July 1993

crusher *noun*

1 a police officer *UK, 1835*
- "Look, Mr. Hyatt, I just spent three hours talking to the crushers, and I'm about talked out." — Malcolm Braly, *The Protector*, p. 131, 1979

2 a powerful, hard-breaking wave *US, 1964*
- — John Severson, *Modern Surfing Around the World*, p. 165, 1964

crush out *verb*

to escape *US, 1960*
- "Betcha he crushes outta there," he heard under the thunderous music. — George Clayton Johnson, *Ocean's Eleven*, p. 40, 1960

crust *noun*

nerve, courage, gall *US, 1900*
- You got a crust asking Allbright to use ammunition on that slob. — Raymond Chandler, *The Long Goodbye*, p. 75, 1953

crust *verb*

to insult someone *US, 1945*
- — Lou Shelly, *Hepcats Jive Talk Dictionary*, p. 9, 1945

crusty *adjective*

1 dirty, shabby *US, 1972*
- — Helen Dahlskog (Editor), *A Dictionary of Contemporary and Colloquial Usage*, p. 16, 1972
- A crustie boy examined his bourbon-and-scotch soaked pants and scratched his head, raising a small cloud of dust — Linda Jaivin, *Rock n Roll Babes from Outer Space*, p. 138, 1996
- "I couldn't stand sitting next to that crusty man in the theater." — Rick Ayers (Editor), *Berkeley High Slang Dictionary*, p. 17, 2004

2 crude, vulgar *US, 1964*
- — J. R. Friss, *A Dictionary of Teenage Slang (Mt. Diablo High)*, 1964
- — *Current Slang*, p. 2, Fall 1966

crut *noun*
a disease *US, 1947*
- Benny clutched his stomach and rolled his eyes. "Me too. I got the crut." — Irving Shulman, *The Amboy Dukes*, p. 73, 1947

crutch *noun*
1 an improvised holder for the short butt of a marijuana cigarette *US, 1938*
The term of choice before **ROACH CLIP** came on the scene.
- She doubled the empty match cover over backward and put the butt of the cigarette up in the fold to make a crutch, and she brought the cardboard up to her lips and took three deep final drags off the short roach. — Thurston Scott, *Cure it with Honey*, p. 69, 1951

2 in pool, a device used to support the cue stick for a hard-to-reach shot *US, 1990*
As the terminology suggests, the device is scorned by skilled players.
- — Steve Rushin, *Pool Cool*, p. 11, 1990

Crutches *nickname*
Las Cruces, New Mexico *US, 1970*
- — *Current Slang*, p. 16, Spring 1970

cry *noun*
▶ **the cry**
the best *US, 1955*
- Q: Charlie, how would you describe the house parties? A: It's the cry! The latest! — Max Shulman, *Guided Tour of Campus Humor*, p. 106, 1955

cry *verb*
▶ **cry a river**
to regret something deeply *US, 1994*
- And I want you to know, we'll all cry a river when you're gone. — *Natural Born Killers*, 1994

cry baby *noun*
a child swindler who appeals for money from strangers with pitiful tales of woe, accompanied if need be by tears *US, 1982*
- — Bill Reilly, *Big Al's Official Guide to Chicagoese*, p. 23, 1982

crying *adjective*
used as a negative intensifier *US, 1942*
- Yet no one came up with a crying dime. — Nelson Algren, *The Man With the Golden Arm*, p. 136, 1949

crying towel *noun*
a notional linen given to someone who is a chronic complainer *US, 1928*
- Give Challee a crying towel, with the compliments of the Caine! — Herman Wouk, *The Caine Mutiny*, p. 479, 1951
- — Zander Hollander and Paul Zimmerman, *Football Lingo*, p. 28, 1967

cry me a river!
used for expressing a lack of sympathy in the face of an implicit solicitation of same *US, 1995*
- — Connie Eble (Editor), *UNC-CH Campus Slang*, p. 3, April 1995
- Huh, cry me a river. Three kings. — David Chase, *Sopranos*, 25th August 1997

cryppie; crippie *noun*
in computing, a cryptographer *US, 1991*
- — Eric S. Raymond, *The New Hacker's Dictionary*, p. 115, 1991

crystal *noun*
1 a powdered narcotic, especially methamphetamine *US, 1964*
- She believes crystals are a form of Methedrine and that "they're called chicken feed because they're actually given to chickens." — *San Francisco News Call Bulletin*, p. 3, 17th February 1964
- Methamphetamine hydrochloride, known colloquially as methedrine or crystal, and going under such trade names as Desoxyn, is of the same chemical family as Benzedrine[.] — *The San Francisco Oracle*, 1966
- Crystal got to be real popular. — John Sinclair, *Guitar Army*, p. 291, 1972
- ROLLERGIRL: This stuff burns. DINK: It's crystal. — *Boogie Nights*, 1997

2 phencyclidine *US, 1977*
- — *Drummer*, p. 77, 1977

crystal chin *noun*
a fighter who is easily injured with blows to the chin *US, 1981*
- Redbeard Mahoney in his time had been a merchant seaman, a renowned arm wrestler, and a pretty good professional boxer, except for his crystal chin. — Joseph Wambaugh, *The Glitter Dome*, p. 83, 1981

crystal palace *noun*
an apartment or house occupied by amphetamine and/or methamphetamine abusers *US, 1997*
- — Walter L. Way, *The Drug Scene*, p. 107, 1997

c's *noun*
1 combat rations, the standard meals eaten by US troops in the field, consisting of an individual ration of packaged precooked foods which can be eaten hot or cold *US, 1968*
- We carried two kinds of hot rations: C's and long-range rations. — Martin Russ, *Happy Hunting Ground*, p. 210, 1968
- First thing that morning the Anachronism drew a case of C's for each of us — William Pelfrey, *The Big V*, p. 29, 1972
- Have your people shaved by noon tomorrow and tell them to eat up all their Cs—we gotta pallet coming in the morning. — Charles Anderson, *The Grunts*, p. 90, 1976
- "You hungry any?" "Inna sorta gen'ral way, yeah. You mean C's?" — Larry Heinemann, *Close Quarters*, p. 142, 1977

2 food *US, 1968*
An abbreviation of "calories"; "to get your c's" is "to eat."
- Collin Baker et al., *College Undergraduate Slang Study Conducted at Brown University*, p. 93, 1968

CS
used as a warning not to deface a piece of graffiti *US, 2000*
An abbreviation of **CON SAFOS**, which literally means "with safety." Used in English conversation by Spanish-speaking youth.
- Often, gang writings will be concluded with the initials c/s. — Robert Jackson and Wesley McBride, *Understanding Street Gangs*, p. 64, 2000

C sponge *noun*
a contraceptive sponge *US, 1997*
- They'd blame it on the fact that I was wearing a c-sponge, saying it would make them numb. — Anthony Petkovich, *The X Factory*, p. 99, 1997

CT *noun*
1 a woman who signals an interest in sex with a man but does not have sex with him *US, 1971*
An abbreviation of **COCK TEASE**.
- I responded by emptying my Bud on her lap, those Texas CT's sure are somethin' else. — Richard Meltzer, *A Whore Just Like the Rest*, p. 214, 1971

2 a woman who signals an interest in sex with another woman but does not have sex with her *US, 1923*
An abbreviation for **CUNT TEASE**.
- — Eugene Landy, *The Underground Dictionary*, p. 61, 1971

CTL *noun*
a capsule of amobarbital sodium and secobarbital sodium (trade name Tuinal™), a combination of central nervous system depressants *US, 1971*
An abbreviation of **CHRISTMAS TREE LIGHTS**.
- A brother and sister from Michigan, eighteen and sixteen years old, whispered to me that they were turned on with CTL—Christmas Tree Lights. — Arthur Blessitt, *Turned On to Jesus*, p. 233, 1971

CTN
used as shorthand in Internet discussion groups and text message to mean "can't talk now" *US, 2002*
- — Gabrielle Mander, *WAN2TLK? ltl bk of txt msgs*, p. 44, 2002

Cuban pumps *noun*
in homosexual usage, heavy work boots *US, 1986–1987*
- — *Maledicta*, p. 53, 1986–1987: "A continuation of a glossary of ethnic slurs in American English"

cubby *noun*
a room, apartment or house *US, 1948*
- — Jack Lait and Lee Mortimer, *New York Confidential*, p. 235, 1948: "A glossary of Harlemisms"

cube *noun*
1 a complete conformist *US, 1955*

An intensification of **SQUARE** (a conventional person).

- Youngsters of both sexes used to call a person who wasn't hip a "square," but now the phrase is "cube" (that's a square in 3-D). — *American Weekly*, p. 2, 14th August 1955
- "A cube is a new fangled square, isn't it?" she teased. — Morton Cooper, *High School Confidential*, p. 138, 1958
- "Compared to you, Big Ten boys are cubes." — Glendon Swarthout, *Where the Boys Are*, p. 69, 1960

2 LSD *US, 1966*

From the fact that LSD was often administered in sugar cubes.
- — Donald Louria, *Nightmare Drugs*, p. 45, 1966

3 a tablet of morphine *US, 1950*
- — Hyman E. Goldin et al., *Dictionary of American Underworld Lingo*, p. 54, 1950
- — Rose Giallombardo, *Society of Women*, p. 207, 1966: Glossary of Prison Terms

cubeb *noun*

a herbal cigarette, pungent and spicy, made from the cubeb berry *US, 1959*
- "Granny will smell it if you smoke in here," Sissie said. "She thinks they're cubebs." — Chester Himes, *The Real Cool Killers*, p. 93, 1959

cube head *noun*

a regular LSD user *US, 1966*
- — Eugene Landy, *The Underground Dictionary*, p. 61, 1971

cubes *noun*

1 the testicles *US, 1968*
- — Collin Baker et al., *College Undergraduate Slang Study Conducted at Brown University*, p. 103, 1968

2 dice *US, 1918*
- "You know, I'm pretty hot with the cubes, mister." — Mickey Spillane, *The Long Wait*, p. 114, 1951
- He lit a cigarette, exhaled, and said with hazel eyes ashine, "Say, Speedy, how's your cube game?" — Iceberg Slim (Robert Beck), *Long White Con*, p. 168, 1977

3 morphine *US, 1980*
- — Edith A. Folb, *runnin' down some lines*, p. 233, 1980

cub reporter *noun*

a young, naive and untrained reporter *US, 1908*

The term is a popular culture allusion to the Superman legend. When Clark Kent went to work at the *Daily Star*, Jimmy Olsen was an office boy with aspirations to be a great reporter. With help from Superman, Olsen, who was forever tagged with the label "cub reporter," became a member of the reporting staff. From the much earlier (1845) sense of a "cub" as an "apprentice."
- For two weeks out of every year, students were required to go to work as cub reporters on the downtown Minneapolis newspapers, where they covered real news stories and helped to put out a real metropolitan daily. — Max Shulman, *The Many Loves of Dobies Gillis*, p. 142, 1951
- Leon Daniel, a fine and dedicated newsman, gave me my start by hiring me as a cub reporter for UPI in London. — Thomas L. Friedman, *From Beirut to Jerusalem*, p. 573, 1995

cuckle bucks *noun*

curly or kinky hair that has not been chemically straightened *US, 1973*
- — Malachi Andrews and Paul T. Owens, *Black Language*, p. 88, 1973

cuckoo *noun*

a fool; a crazy person *UK, 1889*
- Listen, I got another one of those phone calls this morning. Some cuckoo, he'll get picked up and thrown in jail. — Elmore Leonard, *Maximum Bob*, p. 245, 1991

cuckoo *adjective*

crazy, mad, distraught *US, 1906*
- "You can't leave the kids with that girl. She's cuckoo!" "Now, Harry—" "Don't give me the 'Now Harry' bit. I tell you this girl is a certifable maniac!" — Max Shulman, *Rally Round the Flag, Boys!*, p. 82, 1957
- Look, honey, if that man is cuckoo for kids, that's his problem, not yours. — Armistead Maupin, *Further Tales of the City*, p. 223, 1982
- He's boo-koo koo-koo. — *Gone in 60 Seconds*, 2000

cuckoo house *noun*

a mental hospital *US, 1930*
- I ended up in the cuckoo house, and after that they finally realized I needed rehab. — S. Beth Atkin, *Voices from the Street*, p. 50, 1996

cuckoo's nest *noun*

a mental hospital *US, 1962*
- Her antics gave our neurology section a heady "cuckoo's nest" atmosphere. — Jean-Dominique Bauby, *The Diving Bell and the Butterfly*, p. 96, 1997

cucumber *noun*

in gambling, an ignorant victim of a cheat *US, 1962*

A play on "green," the color of the cucumber and a slang term for "inexperienced." Often shortened to "cuke."
- — Frank Garcia, *Marked Cards and Loaded Dice*, p. 261, 1962

cuda *noun*

a barracuda *US, 1949*
- "Remember what happened last time with the 'cuda." — Carl Hiaasen, *Skin Tight*, p. 283, 1989
- "Wait, don't cast yet, those are just cudas," he cautioned as he threw more live bait over the rising cloud of snook. — *Inshore Salt Water Fishing*, p. 45, 2001

cuddle bunny *noun*

an attractive girl *US, 1946*
- Hey, Cuddle-bunny, come on over. I'm tired of being a chair-warmer for this drip-bait. [Freckles and his Friends comic strip] — *San Francisco Examiner*, p. 15, 9th February 1946

cue *noun*

1 barbecued meat *US, 1992*
- Probably, Earl got to have him some 'que on Memorial Day. — Odie Hawkins, *Black Chicago*, p. 149, 1992

2 barbecue *US, 1908*
- The term barbecue (a.k.a. Bar-B-Q, BBQ, 'cue, or, to the real aficionados, simply Q) is often used synonymously with grilling. — Omaha Steaks, *Omaha Steaks*, 2001

3 a tip or gratuity *US, 1970*
- — Roger D. Abrahams, *Deep Down in the Jungle*, p. 259, 1970

cueball *noun*

1 a bald person *US, 1941*
- — Don R. McCreary (Editor), *Dawg Speak*, 2001

2 a crew-cut haircut *US, 1955*
- — *American Speech*, p. 303, December 1955: "Wayne University slang"

cue biter *noun*

an actor who proceeds with his lines without letting the audience react appropriately to the cue line *US, 1973*
- — Sherman Louis Sergel, *The Language of Show Biz*, p. 63, 1973

cue-bow *noun*

a charge of "conduct unbecoming an officer" filed against a police officer *US, 1975*
- The charge was conduct unbecoming an officer, or CUBO, called "cue-bow" by the policemen. — Joseph Wambaugh, *The Choirboys*, p. 20, 1975

cues *noun*

headphones worn by musicians overdubbing a tape *US, 1979*
- — Arnold Shaw, *Dictionary of American Pop/Rock*, p. 100, 1982

cuff *noun*

a prostitute viewed as the possession of a pimp *US, 2002*
- In the early morning dark, Twilight found himself anointing his latest cuff in the dim lights of his back room — Tracy Funches, *Pimpnosis*, p. 106, 2002

▸ **on the cuff**

1 on credit *US, 1927*
- [A]rrangers worked for us on the cuff[.] — Mezz Mezzrow, *Really the Blues*, p. 288, 1946
- Look, boys, I'm a little short. You don't mind putting this one on the cuff, do you? You know I'm good for it. — William Burroughs, *Junkie*, p. 76, 1953
- When asked for a shot on the cuff he would answer reflectively, "I wouldn't want such a good-lookin' girl like you to be goin' down State Street thirsty." — Nelson Algren, *The Neon Wilderness*, pp. 97–98, 1960
- He's got the capital, he can let you ride on the cuff a little while. — John Sayles, *Union Dues*, p. 244, 1977

2 admitted to a theater without paying for a ticket *US, 1973*
- — Sherman Louis Sergel, *The Language of Show Biz*, p. 64, 1973

cuff *verb*

1 to handcuff someone *UK, 1851*

- I just got cuffed again / Now I'm going to dizz knee land. — Dada, *Dizz Knee Land*, 1992
- You are under arrest! Cuff 'em! — *South Park*, 1999

2 to shine something, to polish something *US, 1973*

- While the cat was cuffing my boots, my brother came in. — A.S. Jackson, *Gentleman Pimp*, p. 27, 1973

3 to admit someone to an entertainment without charge *US, 1981*

- But the two assigned to keep the visitors happy had worked the bright-light belt, so they knew where they could cuff a few small night clubs. — Jack Lait and Lee Mortimer, *Washington Confidential*, p. 223, 1951
- — Don Wilmeth, *The Language of American Popular Entertainment*, p. 67, 1981

4 in an illegal betting operation, to accept bets at odds and in a proportion guaranteed to produce a loss for the bookmaker *US, 1951*

- — David W. Mauver, *Argot of the Racetrack*, p. 23, 1951

cuff link faggot; cuff link queen *noun*
a wealthy, ostentatious homosexual male *US, 1965*

- In this rarified area, johns are not johns but cuff link faggots or queens, an expression derived from their tendency to wear extravagant looking jewelry. They are also called "finger bowl faggots." — Antony James, *America's Homosexual Underground*, p. 29, 1965

cuff-up *verb*
to submit to being handcuffed *US, 1998*

- Sometimes, when an inmate refuses to cuff up, or be handcuffed, and come out of the cell, the guards—dressed in riot-type clothing, carrying large shields to protect themselves—rush in on that inmate. — Tookie Williams, *Life in Prison*, p. 72, 1998

cuke *noun*
a cucumber *US, 1903*
A domestic colloquialism.

- I got tomatoes, cukes, and a jar of mayonnaise. She wanted bacon, but all the bacon was gone. — Stephen King, *Skeleton Crew*, p. 52, 1985

CUL
used in computer message shorthand to mean "see you later" *US, 1991*

- — Eric S. Raymond, *The New Hacker's Dictionary*, p. 342, 1991

cull *noun*

1 a prisoner reassigned to an undemanding job after failing at a more challenging one *US, 1990*

- — Charles Shafer, *Folk Speech in Texas Prisons*, p. 202, 1990

2 in horse racing, a horse that is cast off by a stable because it has failed to perform well *US, 1947*

- — Dan Parker, *The ABC of Horse Racing*, p. 145, 1947

culture fruit *noun*
watermelon *US, 1973*

- Black people did not want to reject the fruit because of the white man's mechanism of perpetuating racism in relation to it, so we made it a positive thing by calling it CULTURE FRUIT cause it was too good to let go. — Malachi Andrews and Paul T. Owens, *Black Language*, p. 96, 1973

cumbucket *noun*
a despised person *US, 1975*

- "Scumbags?" "Naw." "Cumbuckets?" "Too long." — Joseph Wambaugh, *The Choir Boys*, p. 33, 1975
- She heard him call me disgusting names, like the time we were sitting in the kitchen and he yelled to me from the living room, "Hey, cumbucket, get out here with a beer." — Robert Davidson, *Fighting Back*, p. 167, 2000

cummy face *noun*
in a pornographic film or photograph, a close-up shot of a man's face as he ejaculates *US, 1995*

- — *Adult Video News*, p. 42, August 1995

cung *noun*
marijuana *US, 1995*

- — Bill Valentine, *Gang Intelligence Manual*, p. 130, 1995

cunny *noun*
the vagina *UK, 1615*
A play on **CUNT** (the vagina) and "con(e)y" (a rabbit).

- Some "cherries" completely close the cunny hole and have to be opened by surgery. — *Screw*, p. 9, 29th December 1969

- LESSEE YA LAP THAT CUNNY UP[.] — Lester Bangs, *Psychotic Reactions and Carburetor Dung*, p. 364, 1981
- I must have been wearing loose-fitting shorts because, as I was waiting to see my friend, her puppy came to me and licked me several times on my little cunny. — Nancy Friday, *Women on Top*, p. 221, 1991
- Does he ever get down there and tongue my cunny? No sir, no how, no way. — *Letters to Penthouse XV*, p. 303, 2002

cunny fingers; cunny thumbs *noun*
an awkward, clumsy person *US, 1892*
A term originally applied to a weak shooter.

- Oh, give it here, cunny-thumbs. I know my way 'round a cork. — Dewey Lambdin, *King's Captain*, p. 345, 2000

cunt *noun*

1 the vagina *UK, 1230*
The most carefully avoided, heavily tabooed word in the English language.

- I bet her cunt is juicy & ripe, hunh? — Neal Cassady, *The First Third*, p. 197, 1950
- You know: well-scrubbed, blonde bangs, china blue eyes, apple cheeks, little cunt that smells like a gouda cheese. — Tom Robbins, *Another Roadside Attraction*, p. 78, 1971
- The Melody girls orchestrate their stripteases over five-song cassette sound tracks; the generous ones reach cunt by the fourth number, while the ones who fancy themselves jazz ballerinas wait till the fifth. — Josh Alan Friedman, *Tales of Times Square*, p. 9, 1986
- Then he said, "Allright bitch, I want to taste a little bit of your cunt." — *Final Report of the Attorney General's Commission on Pornography*, p. 437, 1986

2 a woman, especially as an object of sexual desire *UK, 1674*

- And do you know that the same thing happened to that dumb little cunt. — Jack Kerouac, *On the Road (The Original Scroll)*, p. 284, 1951
- After that, Mexico, and this time a cunt will live with me. — Jack Kerouac, *Letter to Neal Cassady*, p. 400, April 1953
- Ha, you bet your sweet ass they could be improved! Get some halfway decent cunt in there for openers! — Terry Southern, *Blue Movie*, p. 25, 1970
- And all because of a stupid blond cunt in a cold water flat who knew how to assuage his sex problems[.] — Mickey Spillane, *Last Cop Out*, p. 7, 1972
- I shouted from the audience, "You're nothing but eight assholes and a token cunt!!" — Larry Flynt, *An Unseemly Man*, p. 192, 1996

3 sex with a woman *UK, 1670*

- [A]t the same time depriving him of cunt and subjecting him to homosex stimulation[.] — William Burroughs, *Naked Lunch*, p. 27, 1957
- They would run down a story to them about selling them some cunt from some of the finest bitches they ever saw. — Claude Brown, *Manchild in the Promised Land*, p. 160, 1965
- All the cats laughed at me all the way to Frisco, "Ole Babs spent Fifty Dollars and still didn't get no cunt, so that makes Babs a trick." — Babs Gonzales, *Movin' On Down De Line*, p. 22, 1975
- [P]rostitutes are our political prisoners—in jail for cunt. — Kate Millett, *The Prostitution Papers*, p. 111, 1976

4 a despicable person, female or male *UK, 1860*
When used as a reductive term of abuse, "cunt" is usually more offensive than the male equivalents.

- Do you know what that cunt said? — Eve Babitz, *Eve's Hollywood*, p. 117, 1974
- Her new husband makes potato chips. And she's a cunt. — Armistead Maupin, *Babycakes*, p. 206, 1984
- "You fucking Communist cunt, get out of here," he [Richard Mellon Scaife] said to Karen Rothmyer of the Columbia Journalism Review. — Al Franken, *Lies*, p. 132, 2003
- You're a terrific person. You're my favorite person. But every once in a while, you can be a real cunt. — *Kill Bill*, 2003

5 among homosexuals, the buttocks, anus, and rectum *US, 1972*

- Move your cunt—Mama wants to sit down. — Bruce Rodgers, *The Queens' Vernacular*, p. 57, 1972

6 among homosexuals, the mouth *US, 1972*

- Close your filthy cunt; I don't want to hear any more about it. — Bruce Rodgers, *The Queens' Vernacular*, p. 57, 1972

7 to a drug addict, a vein used for injecting a drug, especially the vein found on the inside of the elbow *US, 1960*

- [I]t looks like a small purple cyst . . . into which she drives the needle each time she fixes. "That's your cunt, Jody," I said once[.] — Alexander Trocchi, *Cain's Book*, p. 31, 1960

- CUNT: An area of vein that is favored for injections — Elizabeth Finn, *Drugs in the Tenderloin*, 1967: Glossary of Drug Slang Used in the Tenderloin
- — Stewart L. Tubbs and Sylvia Moss, *Human Communication*, p. 119, 1974

cunt book *noun*
a pornographic book, especially one with photographs or illustrations *US, 1969*
- Goldstein showed that it wasn't just perverts that bought cunt books. — *Screw*, p. 2, 4th July 1969
- You sanitize everything? Take out the rubbers and cunt books? — David Poyer, *The Passage*, p. 192, 1995

cunt breath *noun*
a despicable person *US, 1992*
- And leave those cocksucking, cunt-breath, pusnuts, shit-for-brains, pencil-pushing Pentagon assholes to me. — Richard Marcinko, *Rogue Warrior I*, p. 266, 1992
- Little five-foot-six-inch Roten stands up and says, "He said suck my shorts, cunt breath!" — Daniel E. Kelly, *U.S. Navy Seawolves*, p. 31, 2002

cunt cap *noun*
a narrow green garrison cap worn by enlisted men *UK, 1923*
Probably of World War 1 vintage. The same article as a "cow's-cunt-cap." Soldiers learn the term in the first few days of training. They now learn not to use the term in the presence of women.
- — *Argosy*, p. 81, July 1966
- — Carl Fleischhauer, *A Glossary of Army Slang*, p. 13, 1968
- Shaerbach's kid brother in his uniform, his cunt cap pushed back on his shaved, Neanderthal skull[.] — Gilbert Sorrentino, *Steelwork*, p. 59, 1970
- A white soldier, his shirttail out behind, his cunt cap crosswise on his dome, staggered along happily[.] — Earl Thompson, *Tattoo*, p. 121, 1974
- Since at least as long ago as 1940, the soldier's name for the Army's garrison cap has been cunt cap. — *Maledicta*, p. 222, Winter 1980

cunt collar *noun*
a desire for sex *US, 1965*
- But then they got so bad that even cats with long cunt collars would get tired of screwing these cold junkie bitches. — Claude Brown, *Manchild in the Promised Land*, p. 193, 1965
- He had a cunt collar around his neck bigger than this galaxy[.] — Steve Cannon, *Groove, Bang, and Jive Around*, p. 29, 1969
- Spoon's cunt collar was tight / which was understandably right / after serving three years and day. — Lightnin' Rod, *Hustlers Convention*, p. 16, 1973
- She began to wonder what made this dude uptight ... have what Ranger called a "cunt collar." — Robert Deane Pharr, *Giveadamn Brown*, p. 60, 1978

cunt eater *noun*
any person who performs oral sex on a woman *US, 1967*
- "The shiteaters, cornholers, hermaphrodites, pricks, assholes, cunts and cunteaters" — John Williams, *The Man Who Cried I Am*, p. 130, 1967
- I want so much to really get down there and examine her cunt. But I am ashamed to do it. I might be called a "Cunt Eater," for even getting that close. — Clarence Major, *All-Night Visitors*, p. 20, 1998

cunt face *noun*
a despicable person *US, 1948*
- That's the one. The little cunt face. — Mark Barker, *Nam*, p. 29, 1981
- [G]enerations of academy maintenance men had sanded away the more flagrant obscenities, although an occasional "dork-brain" or "cunt-face" was freshly etched in the wooden slats[.] — John Irving, *A Prayer for Owen Meany*, p. 111, 1989
- And I want it all, whether it's from an ugly Indian-curry-quaffing cunt-face—the Bureau butt-wiping baloney-beaters—or Michael Ei. — Robert Eringer, *Lo Mein*, p. 157, 2000

cunt-faced *adjective*
despicable *US, 1974*
- We can't let these cunt-faced white-assed motherfuckers get away with this shit no longer. — James Baldwin, *If Beale Street Could Talk*, p. 159, 1974
- He said she was a heartless lying evil cunt-faced bitch just like her goddamn fucking mother was. — Buddy Giovinazzo, *Life is Hot in Cracktown*, p. 6, 1993
- She kept her eyes off the mess he was making of her crime scene, reading the words on the wall, cocksucker, disgusting cunt-faced pig. — Michele Jaffe, *Bad Girl*, p. 295, 2003

cunt fart *noun*
a despicable person *US, 1996*
- This is your wake-up call, you cunt fart. — Bruce Wagner, *I'm Losing You*, p. 151, 1996

cunt hair *noun*
a very small distance *US, 1951*
- "I had a touch of gangrene in it and they had to amputate a cunthair tip off the end." — Jack Kerouac, *On the Road (The Original Scroll)*, p. 285, 1951
- Well, we the side of the angels in the censorship fight, won one recently by the margin of a cunt's hair[.] — *Screw*, p. 12, 8th March 1970
- [A] quick, but competent one arm chin with both hands, satisfactory enough with the right hand and a cunt hair short with the smaller left. — Neal Cassady, *The First Third*, p. 165, 1971
- Clipping a famous rat would put me a cunt hair away from being made. — David Chase, *The Sopranos: Selected Scripts from Three Seasons*, p. 114, 3rd November 1998

cunthead *noun*
a despised fool *US, 1971*
- Wilson was looking for some diversion, and he clearly didn't like Kent's looks. "Shove off, cunt-head," he snapped. — John Irving, *The Water-Method Man*, p. 239, 1972

cunt hook *noun*
the hand *US, 1994*
Usually in the plural.
- — Michael Dalton Johnson, *Talking Trash with Redd Foxx*, p. 114, 1994

cunt hound *noun*
a man obsessed with the seduction of women *US, 1960*
- It was shocking, but I knew Joe was 1 helluva cunthound, or so he said[.] — Clarence Cooper Jr., *The Farm*, p. 187, 1967
- — *Maledicta*, p. 10, Summer 1977: "A word for it!"
- Ralston is a notorious well-endowed cunthound and he's had years to work on you. — James Ellroy, *Brown's Requiem*, p. 175, 1981
- An old cunt-hound professor pal of Shark's at the prestigious feminist institution somehow secured the main auditorium at Marymount. — Josh Friedman, *When Sex Was Dirty*, p. 34, 2005

cuntish *adjective*
1 unpleasant; stupid *US, 1999*
- "Hey, man! You going cuntish on me?" — James Ellroy, *Killer on the Road*, p. 232, 1999
2 weak, cowardly *US, 1988*
- "Don't go cuntish on me!" Roscoe snarled when he drove away from the station. — Joseph Wambaugh, *The Choir Boys*, p. 53, 1975
- Danny stood up, feeling warm and loose, wondering if he should muscle Lembeck for going cuntish on him. — James Ellroy, *The Big Nowhere*, p. 83, 1988

cunt juice *noun*
vaginal secretions *US, 1990*
- Cunt juice is a perfume. — Kathy Acker, *In Memoriam to Identity*, p. 128, 1990
- My cock slides in almost too easily—her cunt is too wet, drenched with her own cunt juice and Christie's saliva, and there's no friction. — Brett Easton Ellis, *American Psycho*, p. 175, 1991
- I eased myself into her ass, very slowly, greasing myself well with her cunt juice. — Pedro Juan Gutierrez, *Dirty Havana Trilogy*, p. 5, 1998
- I could see steam rising up from the tank barrel where her warm cunt juices had bathed it. — *Letters to Penthouse XV*, p. 147, 2002

cunt-lapper *noun*
a person who performs oral sex on a woman *US, 1916*
- "Wait a minute," he yelled, "don't you cunt-lappers know that's Agnes, she's got the biggest dose in Hartford, everybody knows that." — Jack Kerouac, *Letter to Neal Cassady*, p. 298, 10th January 1951
- And don't give me (you better, you bastard) any more wonderful bullshit, you giggling cuntlapper, about my letter attempts. — Neal Cassady, *Neal Cassady Collected Letters 1944–1967*, p. 264, 8th January 1951: Letter to Jack and Joan Kerouac
- Well, cock-suckers and reluctant cunt-lappers, the revolution is here! — *Screw*, p. 5, 12th June 1972
- "You cuntlapper," the Greek said. — George Higgins, *The Digger's Game*, p. 183, 1973

cunt-lapping *noun*
oral sex on a woman *US, 1970*

- Is Cunt-Lapping Better Than the Pill? (Headline) — *Screw*, p. 13, 22nd March 1970
- His own young porno collection had swung more and more toward pictures, stories, drawings, any material having to do with cunt-lapping. — James Jones, *The Merry Month of May*, p. 53, 1971

cunt-lapping *adjective*
despised *US, 1923*

- The public-relations value of appearing to send all the pot-smoking, cunt-lapping, ad-men for the revolution to Brixton, or even Parkhurst, is enormous. — Germaine Greer, *The Madwoman's Underclothes*, p. 45, 1986
- I know you and Boyd wanted that cunt-lapping faggot to win. — James Ellroy, *American Tabloid*, p. 1, 2001

cunt-licking *noun*
oral sex on a woman *US, 2003*

- It took a good ten minutes of wrestling and another five were given over to cunt-licking before Samson got to sink his sausage in Walker's tunnel of love. — Stewart Home, *Slow Death*, p. 107, 1996
- Elsewhere there's all the stuffed cunts, finger jobs, and cunt-licking you can handle—and then some. — *The Penthouse Erotic Video Guide*, p. 196, 2003

cunt-licking *adjective*
despised *US, 1985*

- "I'm not gonna be any cunt-licking nurse," Natalie snapped. — Augusten Burroughs, *Running with Scissors*, p. 44, 2002

cunt light *noun*
in the pornography industry, a light used to illuminate the genitals of the performers *US, 1995*

- — *Adult Video News*, p. 50, October 1995

cunt pie *noun*
the vagina, especially as an object of oral sex *US, 1980*

- There, in public, making herself hotter and hotter, finger in cunt pie going round and round, as finger slips black panties lower, she breathes harder and harder. — Kathy Acker, *Portrait of an Eye*, p. 147, 1980

cunt racket *noun*
prostitution *US, 1977*

- Must be some hod times in the cunt racket. — John Sayles, *Union Dues*, p. 152, 1977

cunt rag *noun*
1 a sanitary napkin *US, 1968*

- A bitch was nothing but a bitch no matter who she was; they spread their legs the same wore cunt-rags the same when they had their periods, and sat on the toilet to do the same things[.] — Nathan Heard, *Howard Street*, p. 177, 1968
- You'd have to go to the bottom of the Hudson River and bring me back Lena Horn's cunt rag. — Dennis Wepman et al., *The Life*, p. 151, 1976
- She's putting that cunt rag back in. — James Ellroy, *My Dark Places*, p. 350, 1996

2 a despicable person or thing *US, 1997*

- You ever seen a nun call a small child a "fucking cunt rag?" Wasn't pretty. — *Chasing Amy*, 1997

cunt-simple *adjective*
obsessed with sex; easily distracted by women *US, 1982*

- With her mind, and with her body, she had to organize Louis Palo, that cunt-simple schmuck, and her own husband, to steal the money then to take the fall for her. — Richard Condon, *Prizzi's Honor*, p. 70, 1982

cunt splice *noun*
any improvised splice *US, 1956*

- — Peter Kemp, *The Oxford Companion to Ships and the Sea*, p. 218, 1976

cunt stretcher *noun*
the penis *US, 2001*

- What price now, "cunt plugger," "cunt prober," "cut prodder," "cunt rammer," "cunt stopper," "cunt stretcher," "cunt whacker?" — Ian Gibson, *The Erotomaniac*, p. 184, 2001

cunt-struck *adjective*
obsessed with sex with a woman or women *UK, 1866*

- I do not agree, for instance, that he is a philosopher, or a thinker. He is cunt-struck, that's all. — Henry Miller, *Tropic of Cancer*, p. 4, 1961
- — John D. Bell et al., *Loosely Speaking*, p. 6, 1966
- — Michael Dalton Johnson, *Talking Trash with Redd Foxx*, p. 62, 1994

cunt-sucker *noun*
1 a person who performs oral sex on women *UK, 1868*

- He can become a world-class cunt sucker who will have women standing in line waiting to be next. — Betty Dodson, *Orgasms for Two*, p. 172, 2002

2 a despised person *US, 1964*

- Meal mouthed cunt suckers flow through you. — William S. Burroughs, *The Soft Machine*, p. 47, 1966
- You ain't been here twenty minutes you finished already, you cheap quickie cuntsucker ... in and out ... that's what she likes, the cold bitch. — Grace Paley, *Enormous Changes at the Last Minute*, p. 112, 1974

cunt-sucking *noun*
oral sex on a woman *US, 1998*

- I sat right down on Joe's mouth and he gave me the most comprehensive cunt-sucking that I've ever had in my life. — Graham, Masterson, *Secrets of the Sexually Irresistible Woman*, p. 244, 1998

cunt-sucking *adjective*
despised *US, 1964*

- And you just let me tell you how much all the kids in the office and the laboratory hate you thinking heavy metal assed cunt sucking board bastards. — William S. Burroughs, *Nova Express*, p. 48, 1964
- I didn't foresee that my editors at Columbia University Press would be called "cunt-sucking maggots to let this one slighter through." — Elaine Showalter, *Hystories*, p. x, 1997

cunt tease *noun*
a woman who signals an interest in sex with another woman but does not have sex with her *US, 1971*

- — Eugene Landy, *The Underground Dictionary*, p. 61, 1971
- I pulled myself away from Shoshi, feeling like a cunt-tease. "I'm sorry. I can't. I think we need to go." — Angela Brown, *Best Lesbian Love Stories 2005*, p. 106, 2005

cunt-tickler *noun*
a mustache *US, 1967*

- I wish you was an Italianate Jew, all earthy and Levantine and suave and had a cunt-tickler of a mustache[.] — Norman Mailer, *Why Are We in Vietnam?*, p. 15, 1967

Cunt Town *nickname*
Norfolk, Virginia *US, 1982*
A major naval base, and hence a hotbed of prostitution.

- — Ralph de Sola, *Crime Dictionary*, p. 198, 1982

cunty *adjective*
unpleasant *US, 1972*

- [S]he was also smart, tough, feisty and knew her way around without being foul-mouthed and cunty. — Emmett Grogan, *Ringolevio*, p. 198, 1972

cunt zombie *noun*
a man obsessed with the female sex organs *US, 1974*

- Sometimes she made fun of the whole trip, exaggerating bumps and grinds, stopping and staring right back at the cunt zombies[. — Anne Steinhardt, *Thunder La Boom*, p. 177, 1974

cup *noun*
the vagina *US, 1973*

- Satin was a bitch that had one of those real rare fuzzy cups, the kind a man runs into once in a lifetime. — A.S. Jackson, *Gentleman Pimp*, p. 108, 1973

cupcake *noun*
1 a cute girl *US, 1939*

- It's Art Linkletter, assisted by a cupcake named Jean Lewis, setting up one of his harebrained stunts for "People Are Funny." [Caption] — *San Francisco News*, p. 4T, 25th September 1954
- He gets a look at the cupcakes and he's staggering all over the place, and he grabs her right by the left tit and gives her a nice little milkshake, on the house. — George V. Higgins, *The Rat on Fire*, p. 126, 1981
- Give me that cupcake shot first. — Robert Stoller and I.S. Levine, *Coming Attractions*, p. 195, 1991
- "Hi Nick," said Jerry, toweling his hair. "You get a piece off your cupcake yet?" — C.D. Payne, *Youth in Revolt*, p. 48, 1993

2 a haircut shaped like a box *US, 1989*

- — Ellen C. Bellone (Editor), *Dictionary of Slang*, p. 8, 1989

cupcakes *noun*
1 the female breasts *US, 2001*

- "Yeah, well, nice cupcakes!" he said, eyes locked onto the woman's breasts. — Kregg Jorgenson, *Very Crazy G.I.*, p. 159, 2001

2 well-defined, well-rounded buttocks *US, 1972*
- — H. Max, *Gay (S)language*, p. 9, 1988

cupid's itch *noun*
any sexually transmitted infection *US, 1930*
- — Joseph E. Ragen and Charles Finston, *Inside the World's Toughest Prison*, p. 796, 1962
- "So your client goes in on Monday complaining that he is," she reads from a page, "as he describes it, 'pissing battery acid,' and wondering if he has to tell his wife about a little bout of Cupid's itch." — Richard Dooling, *Brain Storm*, p. 261, 1998
- [T]he gals all had Cupid's Itch and the whiskey was two dollars a glass. — Jake Logan, *Hot on the Trail*, p. 101, 2002

cupid's measles *noun*
syphilis; any sexually transmitted infection *US, 1970*
- You say only three people know that this Prince has Cupid's measles? — George MacDonald Fraser, *Royal Flash*, p. 98, 1970

cuppie *noun*
a female hanger-on at a World Cup sailing competition *US, 1996*
- The cuppies, many of whom were dressed in upscale sailing togs, outnumbered sailors and sailing wannabes by a wide margin. — Joseph Wambaugh, *Floaters*, p. 55, 1996

cups *noun*
sleep *US, 1948*
- — Jack Lait and Lee Mortimer, *New York Confidential*, p. 235, 1948: "A glossary of Harlemisms"

▸ **in your cups**
drinking; drunk *UK, 1406*
- Well, Collie, is this part of your college training? Not to take advantage of a lady in her cups? — Jim Thompson, *After Dark, My Sweet*, p. 35, 1955
- In his cups, of course. Meant no harm. — Max Shulman, *Anyone Got a Match?*, p. 68, 1964

curb *noun*
▸ **against the curb**
without money *US, 1995*
- — Bill Valentine, *Gang Intelligence Manual*, p. 74, 1995

▸ **to the curb**
1 destitute; suffering from hard times *US, 1989*
- — James Harris, *A Convict's Dictionary*, p. 40, 1989

2 rejected in romance *US, 1993*
- — *Washington Post*, 14th October 1993

3 vomiting *US, 1989*
- — Pamela Munro, *U.C.L.A. Slang*, p. 19, 1989

curb *verb*
1 to stop or slow down *US, 1953*
- — Lavada Durst, *The Jives of Dr. Hepcat*, p. 12, 1953

2 to reject in romance *US, 1999*
- "He curbed your butterball booty and left you blowing snot bubbles and slinging boogers on your birthday." — Eric Jerome Dickey, *Cheaters*, p. 401, 1999

curb serve *verb*
to sell crack cocaine on a street corner *US, 1995*
- — Bill Valentine, *Gang Intelligence Manual*, p. 75, 1995

cure *verb*
▸ **get cured**
to get rich *US, 1957*
- Salvador, known as Sally to his friends—he always keeps a few "friends" around and pays them by the hour—got cured in the slunk business in World War 2. — William Burroughs, *Naked Lunch*, p. 156, 1957

curl *noun*
the concave face of a wave as it breaks *US, 1963*
- — Grant W. Kuhns, *On Surfing*, p. 115, 1963

curlies *noun*
pubic hair *US, 1973*
Used both literally and figuratively to suggest complete control over someone.
- You're in no position to make deals. We got you by the curlies. — Joseph Wambaugh, *The Blue Knight*, p. 146, 1973

curly do *noun*
a curly hair style popular with black men and women in the mid-1970s *US, 1975*
- It's goodbye Afro, hello curls for scads of local hip black men who are part of the international, unisex trend to curly hair. They call the style "a Superfly," "a Lord Jesus" or just "a Curly Do" and they're spending lots of time and money to get the look. — *San Francisco Examiner*, p. 34, 13th April 1975

curly lip *adjective*
▸ **to give someone the curly lip**
to say something displeasing *US, 1989*
- Most people call me Jimmy. One or two call me Jimbo when they want to give me the curly lip. — Robert Campbell, *Nibbled to Death by Ducks*, p. 2, 1989

curly wolf *noun*
an aggressive, belligerent man *US, 1910*
A term from the American west.
- I think I'll pick a flower and maybe call on the old curly wolf himself. — Kerry Newcomb, *Texas Anthem*, p. 121, 1986

curse *noun*
the bleed period of the menstrual cycle *US, 1930*
Used with "the."
- I've got the curse. But call me again. —James T. Farrell, *Rendezvous*, p. 139, 1955
- She hadn't had the curse in months—all she needed was a change-of-life kid. — Jacqueline Susann, *Valley of the Dolls*, p. 232, 1966
- — Collin Baker et al., *College Undergraduate Slang Study Conducted at Brown University*, p. 102, 1968
- I was praying all these past four days I wouldn't get the curse. I'm overdue. — Elmore Leonard, *Switch*, p. 158, 1978

curse of Mexico *noun*
in a deck of playing cards, the two of spades *US, 1949*
- — Thomas L. Clark, *The Dictionary of Gambling and Gaming*, p. 57, 1987
- — George Percy, *The Language of Poker*, p. 25, 1988

curse of Scotland *noun*
in a deck of playing cards, the nine of diamonds *UK, 1715*
- — Albert H. Morehead, *The Complete Guide to Winning Poker*, p. 260, 1967

curtain-raiser *noun*
the first game of a season *US, 1950*
- — Parke Cummings, *Dictionary of Baseball*, p. 15, 1950
- I spent last Saturday night TV surfing, going from "The Godfather" on ABC, the Corleones vs. those other families, to the XFL curtain-raiser on NVC[.] — *Times-Picayune (New Orleans)*, p. 1 (Sports), 9th February 2001

curtains *noun*
the end, implying death or dismissal *US, 1901*
Theatrical origin (the final curtain of a play).
- Now, when we get out there, you do what we say or its curtains. — *Natural Born Killers*, 1994

▸ **curtains and carpet that match; matching curtains and carpet**
said when a person's hair color matches the color of their pubic hair *US, 2003*
- "Do the curtains match the carpets?" "I don't understand." "Your pubic hair? Does it match the color of the hair on your head?" — Andrew Lewis Conn, *P: A Novel*, p. 16, 2003

curve-breaker *noun*
a diligent, smart student *US, 1955*
A student whose performance upsets the grading curve.
- A. I've had two guts all lined up, but they backfired. Q. Why? A. Too many curve breakers. — Max Shulman, *Guided Tour of Campus Humor*, p. 105, 1955

curve-killer *noun*
a student who excels *US, 1959*
A reference to the grading curve.
- — *Time Magazine*, p. 46, 24th August 1959
- — Helen Dahlskog (Editor), *A Dictionary of Contemporary and Colloquial Usage*, p. 17, 1972

cush *noun*
1 the vagina; sex; a woman as a sexual object *US, 1960*

- No, it was a walking, living round balloon with a fat "poke" [wallet] and a flaming itch for black "Cush." — Iceberg Slim (Robert Beck), *Pimp*, p. 40, 1969

2 money *US, 1900*
- — Inez Cardozo-Freeman, *The Joint*, p. 492, 1984

cush *adjective*

comfortable, unstrained *US, 1931*
A shortened form of **CUSHY**.
- I called Homeboy at Folsom, got through 'cause he got this cush orderly job. — James Ellroy, *Suicide Hill*, p. 796, 1986

cushy *adjective*

easy, comfortable, unstrained *UK, 1915*
From Hindu *khush* (pleasant) or Romany *kushto* (good).
- There was a cushy career spot in State arranged by his father Sam'l and waiting for him when he got his very own Ph.D. — Bernard Wolfe, *The Magic of Their Singing*, p. 8, 1961

cuspy *adjective*

(used of a computer program) well designed, highly functional *US, 1981*
- — Guy L. Steele, *Coevolution Quarterly*, p. 29, Spring 1981: "Computer Slang"
- — Guy L. Steele et al., *The Hacker's Dictionary*, p. 52, 1983

cuss fight *noun*

a loud, angry argument *US, 1923*
- He rushed to the White House and they had a huge cuss fight[.] — John Grisham, *The Pelican Brief*, p. 100, 1992

cuss out *verb*

to reprimand someone with a heavy reliance on profanity *US, 1863*
- She hates to drive anywhere with me because I am inclined to cuss out drivers who don't please me. — Wallace Earle Stegner, *The Spectator Bird*, p. 10, 1976

cuss word *noun*

a profanity *US, 1872*
After **cuss** (a curse).
- If I was a fat bitches thong I'd be like "Hell naw!" / If I was a hotties thong I'd be like "Awwww..." / If I was a cuss word I'd just be like "fuck" — Insane Clown Posse, *If*, 2000

custer *noun*

a person who poses as a member of a youth gang but is not accepted as a gang member *US, 1995*
- — Bill Valentine, *Gang Intelligence Manual*, p. 75, 1995

customer *noun*

a driver being stopped by a police officer for a traffic violation *US, 1962*
- — *American Speech*, p. 268, December 1962: "The language of traffic policemen"

cut *noun*

1 an adulterant used to dilute a drug; a dilution of a drug *US, 1966*
- Now today, if you buy your piece, you'd be very lucky if you could get a three-to-one cut[.] — James Mills, *The Panic in Needle Park*, p. 44, 1966
- New York Pure, no more than a one cut, if that. — Vernon E. Smith, *The Jones Men*, p. 88, 1974
- Probably all the lactose in the cut: you were shooting ten times more sugar than junk. — Seth Morgan, *Homeboy*, p. 139, 1990
- Buy four, bleed in a ounce of cut, make it five. — Richard Price, *Clockers*, p. 185, 1992

2 a reduction of a prison sentence *US, 2002*
- Gary went back to court to try to get a time cut. — Gary K. Farlow, *Prison-ese*, p. 15, 2002

3 any place where young people congregate to socialize *US, 1953*
- — Lavada Durst, *The Jives of Dr. Hepcat*, p. 12, 1953

4 in hip-hop music, a sample or part of a tune that is played repeatedly *US, 2000*
- — James Haskins, *The Story of Hip-Hop*, p. 137, 2000

5 the vagina *US, 1967*
- — Dale Gordon, *The Dominion Sex Dictionary*, p. 54, 1967

cut *verb*

1 to leave *US, 1965*
- "Like we have to cut. Hot. Movies." — Sol Yurrick, *The Warriors*, p. 18, 1965

2 in the drug trade, to dilute drugs *US, 1937*
- Ray just sat there and watched while Chico went to work cutting the horse with milk sugar. — Hal Ellson, *The Golden Spike*, p. 166, 1952
- They cut it, cap it, and retail it at about a hundred percent profit. — John D. McDonald, *The Neon Jungle*, p. 61, 1953
- I invest half a grand in cocaine and H. It's good enough so I can cut it twice with milk, sugar, and still have the best stuff on Thirty-fifth Street. — Iceberg Slim (Robert Beck), *Trick Baby*, p. 184, 1969
- It's good shit. From when they busted those Columbians uptown. You can cut it in half. — *The Bad Lieutenant*, 1992

3 to dilute anything by the addition of a secondary ingredient *US, 1985*
Extended from the previous sense (to dilute drugs).
- They're cutting the butter with Vaseline. — William Burroughs, *Queer*, p. 36, 1985

4 to fart *US, 1967*
- [S]ome American speakers use "cut" as a variant of "lay" or "let" and refer to "cutting" or "cutting a fart." — Peter Furze, *Tailwinds*, p. 55, 1998

5 to engage in an informal musical competition in which musicians attempt to better each other in extended jazz solos *US, 1937*
- When one jazz musician cuts another, he merely outplays him, does it better, shows him how, establishes who's boss of the instrument. — Robert Sylvester, *No Cover Charge*, p. 48, 1956
- Maybe he couldn't cut the cats at the Savoy in Harlem, but he sure could dance. — Billie Holiday with William Dufty, *Lady Sings the Blues*, p. 98, 1956
- "But I can still cut all these cats two choruses to one," he spat out[.] — John Clellon Holmes, *The Horn*, p. 51, 1958

6 to record a song *US, 1937*
- — Arnold Shaw, *Lingo of Tin-Pan Alley*, p. 10, 1950
- He finally came half an hour late, borne up (as it were) by a jostling, haggard bunch of hangers-on, among whom was the white boy for whose phantom company the records were to be cut. — John Clellon Holmes, *The Horn*, p. 67, 1958
- They can cut disks which are played on our Muzak-type system. — Gore Vidal, *Myra Breckinridge*, p. 52, 1968
- When you get my backups straight, then we'll talk about cutting this tune here. — *Nashville*, 1992

7 to skip something, to fail to attend something *UK, 1794*
- You're not going to cut again. Get up. — Irving Shulman, *The Amboy Dukes*, p. 19, 1947
- He cuts a lot of classes. He got thrown out of schools. — John D. McDonald, *The Neon Jungle*, p. 94, 1953
- The fact that you're cutting gym so you can T.A. Sophomore English just to hear his name, is a little without in itself if you ask me. — *Ten Things I Hate About You*, 1999

8 to leave quickly *UK, 1790*
- "Let's cut," I said. We started down the platform. — William Burroughs, *Junkie*, p. 48, 1953
- [S]uddenly he gets up and says to Miss Van Allen, "I got to cut. This isn't my scene." — Gore Vidal, *Myra Breckinridge*, p. 207, 1968

9 to tease or disparage someone *US, 1975*
- — *American Speech*, p. 57, Spring–Summer 1975: "Razorback slang"

10 to perform surgery *US, 1970*
- You just sit up front and sign the mail, and leave the cutting to us. — *M*A*S*H*, 1970

▸ **be cut out to be a gentleman**
to be circumcised *UK, 1961*
- — Roger Blake, *The American Dictionary of Sexual Terms*, p. 53, 1964

▸ **cut a chogie**
to leave quickly *US, 1988*
Korea and Vietnam war usage.
- It was time for us to "cut-a-chogie," to haul our asses out of the area. — C.S. Crawford, *The Four Deuces*, p. 251, 1989
- — Linda Reinberg, *In the Field*, p. 55, 1991
- Our pay was burning a hole in our fatigue pockets, so we "cut a chogie" down to the Dragon's Lair and exchanged a good share of it for cold cans of beer. — Robert Peterson, *Rites of Passage*, p. 473, 1997

▸ **cut a hus**
to do someone a favor *US, 1991*
Marine slang in Vietnam.
- Take what shots we wanted at the Lifers, they cut us a hus and left us alone. — George Mariscal, *Aztlan and Viet Nam*, p. 162, 1999

▶ **cut a rug**
to dance expertly *US, 1942*
- He goes to the jukery to watch and wait and cut a rug with a solid gate: he snatches a quail with hep and class and they go to town cooking with gas! — Harry Haenigsen, *Jive's Like That*, 1947
- When somebody asks you if you'd like the cut a rug, say, "Fine, you get the scissors." — Art Unger, *The Cool Book*, p. 5, 1961
- "I'm … ah, curious to know if you can still cut a bad rug." — Iceberg Slim (Robert Beck), *Doom Fox*, p. 253, 1978
- Come on. Let's cut a rug. — *Empire Records*, 1995

▶ **cut a rusty**
to show off *US, 1838*
- "You're still spunky," the voice responded. "Ain't no one able to cut a rusty like you." — Gwyn Hyman Rubio, *Icy Sparks*, p. 204, 1998

▶ **cut ass**
to leave, especially in a hurry *US, 1969*
- "Sarge, we could cut ass out." — William Eastlake, *The Bamboo Bed*, p. 60, 1969
- — Helen Dahlskog (Editor), *A Dictionary of Contemporary and Colloquial Usage*, p. 5, 1972

▶ **cut loose**
1 to leave someone alone *US, 1974*
- — Stewart L. Tubbs and Sylvia Moss, *Human Communication*, p. 120, 1974
2 to enjoy yourself unrestrained by any sense of moderation *US, 1808*
- After that, maybe I'd cut loose a little bit. — Mickey Spillane, *My Gun is Quick*, p. 6, 1950
- I guess I cut pretty loose in my day too. — *Rebel Without a Cause*, 1955

▶ **cut someone dead**
to ignore someone completely *UK, 1826*
An emphasized use of **CUT** (to ignore).
- "I seen the dweeb around," Baborak replied, cutting me dead and walking away. — C.D. Payne, *Youth in Revolt*, p. 243, 1993

▶ **cut the crap**
to stop talking nonsense *US, 1931*
- "I don't owe you a cent. I already gave her the five —" "Cut the crap, now. Let's have it." — J.D. Salinger, *The Catcher in the Rye*, p. 101, 1951
- "Cut the crap, Sid." — John O'Hara, *Instrument*, p. 103, 1967

▶ **cut the gas**
to stop talking *US, 1951*
- — *Newsweek*, p. 28, 8th October 1951

▶ **cut to the chase**
to get on with it *US, 1983*
Cinematic imagery; "to jump to the next exciting sequence."
- "Cut to the chase," he muttered irritably. "What the hell is it you want us to do?" — Carl Hiaasen, *Native Tongue*, p. 83, 1991

▶ **cut up jackies**
in the circus or carnival, to tell stories about the past *US, 1980*
- — Joe McKennon, *Circus Lingo*, p. 29, 1980

▶ **cut up jackpots**
(used of carnival workers) to engage in carnival insider conversation *US, 1985*
- — Gene Sorrows, *All About Carnivals*, p. 19, 1985

▶ **cut up old touches**
to tell stories about past triumphs *US, 1950*
- [W]e'd sit up there and cut up what we call "old touches"—that's a phrase for discussing old capers. — Harry King, *Box Man*, p. 145, 1972

▶ **cut up pipes**
in circus and carnival usage, to gossip, brag or disparage someone *US, 1981*
- — Don Wilmeth, *The Language of American Popular Entertainment*, p. 69, 1981

▶ **cut your water off**
in shuffleboard, to hold an opponent to a scoreless half round *US, 1967*
- — Omero C. Catan, *Secrets of Shuffleboard Strategy*, p. 65, 1967

cut *adjective*
1 circumcized *US, 1988*
- — H. Max, *Gay (S)language*, p. 10, 1988

- I've got six-pack abs. I'm eight inches cut. — *The Village Voice*, 4th April 2000

2 physically fit, conditioned, well toned *US, 1985*
- He had lost his nondescript straight's fleshiness; he was cut and basted. — Ethan Morden, *I've a Feeling We're Not in Kansas Anymore*, p. 17, 1985
- That is, if you mention a strong stomach, you must have cut abs. — John Preston, *Hustling*, p. 121, 1994
- "My body was shredded down, cut as they call it and I was totally ripped." — Robert Picarello, *Rules of the Ring*, p. 139, 2000

cut and paste *verb*
to open a patient's body in surgery only to discover an inoperable condition, and then to close the patient back up *US, 1994*
- — Sally Williams, *"Strong" Words*, p. 137, 1994

cutback *noun*
in surfing, a turn back into the wave *US, 1979*
- I've admired your nose-riding for years. I like your cutback too. — *Apocalypse Now*, 1979

cut buddy *noun*
a close friend *US, 1954*
- — Robert George Reisner, *The Jazz Titans*, p. 153, 1960
- We greeted each other like we were ol' cut-buddies, but after all the greeting and slapping hands, we found it hard to talk to each other. — H. Rap Brown, *Die Nigger Die!*, p. 24, 1969
- "You're my cut-buddy, buddy," Solly said drunkenly. "My real bosom boon buddy-buddy." — John Oliver Killens, *And Then We Heard the Thunder*, p. 197, 1983
- Most Black males have at least one close male friend—often called "Cuz," "Running Buddy," "Ace Boon Coon," "Cut Buddy," "Road Dog," Homeboy," or "Main Man." — Joseph L. White, *Black Man Emerging*, p. 134, 1999

cutemup *noun*
a prison doctor *US, 1961–1962*
- — Frank Prewitt and Francis Schaeffer, *Vacaville Vocabulary*, 1961–1962

cuter *verb*
a twenty-five cent piece *US, 1927*
A corruption of "quarter."
- — Lou Shelly, *Hepcats Jive Talk Dictionary*, p. 9, 1945

cuteration *noun*
the zenith of cuteness *US, 1963*
- — *American Speech*, p. 275, December 1963: "American Indian student slang"

cutesy *adjective*
cloying, annoyingly cute *US, 1914*
- Don't take all that cutesy-kitschy fuckin' retro-Sixties bullshit out in my apartment. — Kenneth Lonergan, *This is Our Youth*, p. 32, 2000

cutie *noun*
an attractive or clever young woman *US, 1911*
- "The Snake Pit" is that—the mad gathering place at cocktail time for the local celebs—the Senators, lobbyists, army brass and blondest cuties. — Jack Lait and Lee Mortimer, *Washington Confidential*, p. 132, 1951
- "If you and Gil Sullivan went and got yourselves fixed up with a pair of semi-pro cuties down in the city, I wouldn't applaud, but I think I could understand[.]" — John D. MacDonald, *The Deceivers*, p. 147, 1958

cutie-pie *noun*
an attractive woman *US, 1970*
- Les Harrison attempted to intercept her and introduce her to the cutie-pie starlet. — Terry Southern, *Blue Movie*, p. 17, 1970
- And there were leggy cutie-pie vultures and cold-blooded toothy hustlers staked out in the plush murk to ambush celebrity bankrolls. — Iceberg Slim (Robert Beck), *The Naked Soul of Iceberg Slim*, p. 80, 1971
- I only like cutie pies massaging me. When you're massaged, you like to open up your eyes and see a cutie pie there. — Susan Hall, *Gentleman of Leisure*, p. 93, 1972

cut-in *noun*
the initial contact with the intended victim in a confidence swindle *US, 1977*
- Folks left the office and went to the elevator athrob with satisfaction that the Bates cut-in had come off so sweetly. — Iceberg Slim (Robert Beck), *Long White Con*, p. 94, 1977

cut in verb

1 to attempt a romantic relationship with someone already romantically involved US, 1950

- That makes her his chick. You've both been playing around when you're not supposed to. Happy don't fancy that crap and neither do we 'cause there's not supposed to be any cutting in. — Hal Ellson, *Tomboy*, p. 76, 1950

2 to seize a share of a business or enterprise US, 1980

- I wanted to be in the swim so I cut in on a chick. She was not much to look at, but she made good money[.] — Louis Armstrong, *Satchmo*, p. 86, 1954

cut into verb

to approach someone and draw them into a swindle; to introduce someone to something US, 1940

- He doesn't know a diamond from a seashell. I've already cut into him and told him the tale. — Iceberg Slim (Robert Beck), *Trick Baby*, p. 298, 1969
- Prince cut me into a choice little crib for fifteen cents a week. — Babs Gonzales, *Movin' On Down De Line*, p. 15, 1975

cut man noun

the member of a boxer's entourage responsible for treating cuts between rounds US, 1975

- Of course he had a great cut man, Whitey Bimstein, and Charley Goldman, a great trainer, taught him to shorten up his shots and develop a left hook. — Edwin Torres, *Carlito's Way*, p. 135, 1975
- The cutman should have told him not to clear his nose after taking the shot in the eye from Palomino. — Elmore Leonard, *Out of Sight*, p. 113, 1996

cutor noun

a prosecuting attorney US, 1962

- — Joseph E. Ragen and Charles Finston, *Inside the World's Toughest Prison*, p. 796, 1962

cut out verb

1 to leave US, 1827

- Now, look, man, we ought to be cutting out. — John Clellon Holmes, *Go*, p. 98, 1952
- "This joint must have just been raided," she said. "Looks like everybody cut out." — Steve Allen, *Bop Fables*, p. 6, 1955
- With her pretty nose in the air she cut out of there[.] — Jack Kerouac, *On the Road*, p. 89, 1957
- Then E.J. and I had cut out, bumming around and fruit-picking[.] — Clancy Sigal, *Going Away*, p. 84, 1961
- Looks like you decided to cut out early. — *Empire Records*, 1995

2 to die US, 1955

- The bad jazz that a cat blows wails long after they've cut out. — William "Lord" Buckley, *Marc Anthony's Funeral Oration*, 1955

cuts noun

1 the definition of body muscle from spaces between the muscle that have no fat US, 1984

- — *American Speech*, p. 199, Fall 1984: "The language of bodybuilding"
- His stomach still had cuts from workouts during his prison bid. — Adrian Nicole LeBlanc, *Random Family*, p. 293, 2003

2 any remote location BERMUDA, 2004

- — Rick Ayers (Editor), *Berkeley High Slang Dictionary*, p. 17, 2004

3 permission from a friend to step into a line at their place US, 1989

- — Pamela Munro, *U.C.L.A. Slang*, p. 43, 1989

4 clothing US, 1978

- Whooh! This preacher got some cuts, I thought, admiring the sharp clothes he was wearing. — Bobby Seale, *A Lonely Rage*, p. 133, 1978

cutta noun

the buttocks US, 1957

- "Man, dig that crazy cutta on the big beast in the plaid skirt." — Herbert Simmons, *Corner Boy*, p. 58, 1957

cutter noun

1 a forensic pathologist US, 1991

- Julie Goodin looks nothing like a cutter, and considering the prevailing stereotype, that's probably something of a compliment. — David Simon, *Homicide*, p. 428, 1991

2 a surgeon US, 1970

- Y'all were short a couple cutters and we're what the Army sent. — *M*A*S*H*, 1970

3 a person who is proficient with the use of a knife or of a weapon US, 1947

- Crazy's reputation as a cutter and potential killer was well known in Brownsville. — Irving Shulman, *The Amboy Dukes*, p. 214, 1947

4 a pistol US, 1908

- — *American Speech*, p. 193, October 1957: "Some colloquialisms of the handgunner"

5 a musician who betters another in a competition of solos US, 1956

- Mexico's "cutters" must have played variations on it for three straight, solid hours. — Robert Sylvester, *No Cover Charge*, p. 49, 1956

6 any substance used to dilute a drug, thereby expanding volume while reducing potency US, 1995

- — Mark S. Fleisher, *Beggars & Thieves*, p. 288, 1995

7 in American casinos, twenty-five cents US, 1985

Playing on the sound of "quarter."

- — Steve Kuriscak, *Casino Talk*, p. 17, 1985

cutting house noun

a place where drugs are diluted for resale US, 1974

- Well, that was Willis McDaniel's main cuttin' house they hit. — Vernon E. Smith, *The Jones Men*, p. 54, 1974

cutting man noun

a best friend US, 1970

- — Roger D. Abrahams, *Deep Down in the Jungle*, p. 259, 1970

cutting match noun

a competition between improvizing jazz musicians US, 1963

- Cabiness knew it would turn into a cutting match, and Kovin would blow him through the door. — Malcolm Braly, *Shake Him Till He Rattles*, pp. 72–73, 1963

cutting plant noun

a shop where stolen cars are dismantled or altered US, 1978

- But wait—and both of them had been in there for grand theft auto, supplying new Sevilles and Continentals to body shops and cutting plants down near Columbus. — Elmore Leonard, *Switch*, p. 16, 1978

cutty noun

a cousin US, 2002

- On the west side, Mexicans and blacks started calling him "Cutty," street slang for cousin. — *Los Angeles Times*, p. 1, 26th August 2002

cut up verb

to behave without restraint US, 1846

- The lowlier links lam the 36 miles to Baltimore to cut up. — Jack Lait and Lee Mortimer, *Washington Confidential*, 1951

cuz noun

a friend US, 1979

- — *The Bell (Paducah Tilghman High School)*, pp. 8–9, 17th December 1993

cuz; cuzz noun

a term of address used by one member of the Crips youth gang to another US, 1990

- Thanks cuzz. — *Boyz N The Hood*, 1990
- "What's up, cuz?" Tray Ball extends his very dark, muscular, veined hand. — Sanyika Shakur, *Monster*, p. 5, 1993
- One of the Crips named Cunningham had been tagged with the moniker "Young Cousin." This was subsequently shortened to "Young Cuzz," and then to, "Cuzz." Many of the other Crips started calling each other Cuzz[.] — Bill Valentine, *Gangs and Their Tattoos*, p. 75, 2000

cwazy adjective

used as a jocular substitute for "crazy" US, 1952

- After all these years, the hamburgers at Vanessi's—when Mario makes 'em—are still the endest, the gonest, the cwaziest. — *San Francisco*, p. 29, 23rd March 1952
- Monkey Flees Its Cage and Cwazy People [Headline] — *San Francisco Examiner*, p. 5, 15th March 1956

CYA verb

to protect yourself from future criticism for actions being taken now US, 1959

An abbreviation of "cover your ass."

- In World War II, the Army coined its special code word—SNAFU, or politely translated, Situation Normal All Fouled Up. Today's Army has its code word too – CYA, or Cover Your Ass. — *New York Times*, p. SM10, 5th September 1971

- "I can't cover for you there, even if I wanted to," he said, laying out the usual C.Y.A. office ground rules. That's the way it was in the District Attorney's office. You had to "Cover Your Ass," because Gil always covered his. — Stephen Cannell, *King Con*, p. 46, 1997
- Pumping up a coalition that existed mostly in name, putting out CYA statements, refusing to concede a war plan had obvious problems, hyping one of the more dramatic (and cinematic) moments of the war—none of this was surprising behavior for the Pentagon[.] — David Corn, *The Lies of George W. Bush*, p. 267, 2003

c-ya
used in computer messages as shorthand to mean "see you" *US*, *1995*
- — Christian Crumlish, *The Internet Dictionary*, p. 44, 1995

cyclo *noun*
a rickshaw pulled by a bicycle *US*, *1988*

- [F]rom the poor cyclo drivers of Hue to the most sophisticated intellectuals[.] — Frances Fitzgerald, *Fire in the Lake*, p. 244, 1972
- He drove out of the old French cavalry camp and then maneuvered in his impatient way through Saigon's vehicular extravangza of trucks and gaudily painted buses coming and going from the countryside, Vespa scooters and Lambretta motorbikes, cyclos[.] — Neil Sheehan, *A Bright Shining Lie*, p. 41, 1988

cyclone *noun*
phencyclidine, the recreational drug known as PCP or angel dust *US*, *1994*
- — US Department of Justice, *Street Terms*, October 1994

cyring call *noun*
in poker, a bet equal to the last bet made in a hesitating fashion *US*, *1982*
- — David M. Hayano, *Poker Faces*, p. 186, 1982

Dd

D *noun*

1 a police detective *US, 2005*

- Milo briefed one of the D's very quickly, then came over to where I sat, just outside the tape. — Jonathan Kellerman, *Rage*, p. 487, 2005

2 Dilaudid™, a synthetic opiate *US, 1954*

- All right, we was just gonna shoot this little bitty bottle of D. — Bruce Jackson, *In the Life*, p. 220, 1972

3 narcotics *US, 1976*

- — John R. Armore and Joseph D. Wolfe, *Dictionary of Desperation*, p. 26, 1976

4 a member of the Disciples youth gang *US, 1969*

- "Nah, ain't no D shot me. My old-lady cousin did it." — L.H. Whittemore, *Cop!*, p. 180, 1969

D/s *noun*

in sado-masochistic sex, domination and submission *US, 1995*

- Since the D/s (Dominance/submission) and B&D (bondage and discipline) crowds often incorporate dressing for pleasure as a related part of their lifestyle, it is not surprising to find that many of the posts relate to this lifestyle. — Nancy Tamosaitis, *net.sex*, p. 99, 1995

DA *noun*

1 a hair-style popular in the early 1950s; the hair was tapered and curled on the nape of the neck like the feathers of a duck's tail *US, 1951*
Abbreviated from **DUCK'S ASS**.

- The D.A. haircut requires nothing more than finding a barber who is not a sqaure (i.e., one who would think it was named for the district attorney). — *Life*, p. 137, 25th January 1954
- [S]moothing their hair lightly with the palms of their hands, pushing their DA's gently and patting them in place. — Hubert Selby Jr., *Last Exit to Brooklyn*, p. 28, 1957
- I noticed they were dressed in peg pants with pistol pockets, wearing DA's, like everybody except me. — Bobby Seale, *A Lonely Rage*, p. 86, 1978
- Her hair was done in a salt-and-pepper DA. — Armistead Maupin, *Tales of the City*, p. 25, 1978

2 a drug addict *US, 1946*

- I sure didn't want to be classed as a junkie, no matter how many "D.A.'s" they stamped on my card. — Mezz Mezzrow, *Really the Blues*, p. 311, 1946

da

so; very *US, 1981*
Hawaiian youth usage.

- "Oh, da hot!" — Douglas Simonson, *Pidgin to da Max*, 1981

dab *verb*

in mountain biking, to touch the ground unintentionally with any part of the body *US, 1992*

- — William Nealy, *Mountain Bike!*, p. 160, 1992: 'Bikespeak'

dabble *verb*

to use addictive drugs without succumbing to the addiction *US, 1949*

- — Captain Vincent J. Monteleone, *Criminal Slang*, p. 64, 1949
- How long have you been dabblin' in stuff? — Claude Brown, *Manchild in the Promised Land*, p. 322, 1965
- Eugene Landy, *The Underground Dictionary*, p. 64, 1971

dab-dab *noun*

to participate in homosexual sex *US, 1990*
Prison usage.

- — Charles Shafer, *Folk Speech in Texas Prisons*, p. 202, 1990

dad *noun*

1 used as a term of address for a man, especially an older man. Often patronizing *US, 1928*

- — Robert S. Gold, *A Jazz Lexicon*, p. 76, 1964

2 a homosexual prisoner's "owner" (protector and lover) *US, 1992*

- — William K. Bentley and James M. Corbett, *Prison Slang*, p. 59, 1992

'Dad *nickname*

the state penitentiary in Soledad, California *US, 1993*

- "They's as cold-blooded killas as anyone you ever met in Quentin or the 'Dad." — Bob Sipchen, *Baby Insane and the Buddha*, p. 92, 1993

dad-blamed *adjective*

used as a euphemism for "damned" *US, 1844*
"Dad" is a euphemism for God.

- "What you always writing in that dad-blamed book for?" she asked with a sour little face. — Louise Fitzhugh, *Harriet the Spy*, p. 36, 1964
- When they're located, the whole dad-blamed family is going to be whisked off to a mansion in Beverly Hills[.] — *Portland Mercury*, 18th September 2002

daddy *noun*

1 the dominant partner in a homosexual relationship *US, 1932*

- They are usually long-terms and are familiarly known to inmates by such local cognomens as "wolves," "top men," "jockers" or "daddies." — *Ebony*, p. 82, July 1951
- [T]he queens will go on looking for their own legendary permanent "Daddies" among the older men who dig the queens' special brand of gone sexplay[.] — John Rechy, *City of Night*, p. 108, 1963
- The complementary role to the femme is the "stud broad" or "daddy" who assumes the male role. — Rose Giallombardo, *Society of Women*, p. 124, 1966
- It must have been your night to play daddy. — Malcolm Braly, *On the Yard*, p. 333, 1967

2 an aggressive, predatory male homosexual *US, 1972*

- "Look, if you're a kid in here it means ya gotta have a 'daddy.'" — Nathan Heard, *To Reach a Dream*, p. 30, 1972
- Inmates subject to rape ("punks") face threats and violence perpetrated by stronger inmates ("daddies," "jockers," or "booty bandits") who initiate unwanted sexual acts. — *Corrections Today*, p. 100, December 1996

3 in the US Army, your supervising officer *US, 1968*

- — Carl Fleischhauer, *A Glossary of Army Slang*, p. 13, 1968

daddy-come-to-church *noun*

an unusual event *US, 1953*

- All that hard work and deep breathing had put breasts on her like daddy-come-to-church. — Jim Thompson, *Savage Night*, p. 22, 1953

daddy mac *noun*

an attractive young man *US, 1997*

- — Vann Wesson, *Generation X Field Guide and Lexicon*, p. 48, 1997

daddy-o *noun*

1 used as a term of address for a man *US, 1947*

- You just burned down the town last Wednesday, daddy-o. — William "Lord" Buckley, *Nero*, 1951
- "Sorry, Daddy-o," said Red. "Some other time." — Steve Allen, *Bop Fables*, p. 38, 1955
- RIFF: Spread the word, Diesel. DIESEL: Right, daddy-0. — Stephen Sondheim, *West Side Story*, 1957
- Evan Hunter, author of MGM's movie "Blackboard Jungle," was sued for using the expression "daddy-o" in the script. A Midwest disc jockey claimed he coined the term. — *San Francisco Chronicle, This Week*, p. 10 (II), 26th August 1962

2 an aggressive, predatory male homosexual *US, 1951*

- He is simply the brass-brained, muscle-bound Golden Boy who appointed himself my jailhouse Daddy-o. — James Blake, *The Joint*, p. 24, 13th May 1951

3 the US Federal Communications Commission *US, 1977*

- — Bill Davis, *Jawjacking: The Complete CB Dictionary*, p. 33, 1977

daddypoo *noun*

used as an embellishment of "daddy," usually from a woman to a man *US, 1966*

- All the other girls are ahead of me this month, daddypoo! [Steve Roper comic strip] — *San Francisco Chronicle*, p. 54, 1st March 1966

daddy tank *noun*
a jail cell reserved for lesbian prisoners *US, 1971*
- — Eugene Landy, *The Underground Dictionary*, p. 64, 1971
- — Ralph de Sola, *Crime Dictionary*, p. 37, 1982
- — William K. Bentley and James M. Crobett, *Prison Slang*, p. 10, 1992

daffy *adjective*
odd, eccentric, silly *UK, 1884*
The original meaning of "slightly mad" has softened over the years.
- [T]he whole thing was making a young girl who wasn't too bright to begin with into some kind of a daffy basket case. — George V. Higgins, *The Rat on Fire*, p. 149, 1981
- Before Lynn could get into his Rambler, Nelson showed him that daffy grin and said, "If we get him, I hope you'll put in a good word for me with your ex-captain." — Joseph Wambaugh, *Fugitive Nights*, p. 103, 1992

dag *verb*
1 to engage in anal sex *US, 2001*
- — *The Correctional Officer's Guide to Prison Slang*, 2001
2 to participate in serial, reciprocal, homosexual oral sex *US, 1990*
- — Charles Shafer, *Folk Speech in Texas Prisons*, p. 202, 1990

dag!
used for expressing surprise *US, 1987*
- "I made four goals in the game yesterday." "Dag! You were hot!" — Connie Eble (Editor), *UNC-CH Campus Slang*, p. 3, Spring 1987
- Can't go nowheres without the hat. Dag. — David Simon and Edward Burns, *The Corner*, p. 102, 1997
- "Oh hell, I might as well try 'em [psychoactive mushrooms], this party is so drab." "Oh dag!" "What?" "I ain't mean for you to eat the whole bag!" — Eminem (Marshall Mathers), *My Fault*, 1999
- "Dag, I'll take it." — Richard Price, *Samaritan*, p. 33, 2003

dagga *noun*
a marijuana cigarette *US, 1955*
- — *American Speech*, p. 87, May 1955

dagger *noun*
a lesbian *US, 1980*
An abbreviation of the full **BULLDAGGER**.
- — Edith A. Folb, *runnin' down some lines*, p. 234, 1980

dago *noun*
an Italian or Italian-American *US, 1857*
A slur, originally applied to Spaniards, then to Spaniards, Portuguese and Italians, and now only to Italians.
- Angelo meant "angel" in dago. But he wasn't no angel. — Willard Motley, *Knock on Any Door*, p. 91, 1947
- "He called me a dago son of a b——," explained Sinatra as he told how he had clouted Mortimer at the entrance of Ciro's. — *Fortnight*, p. 20, 21st April 1947
- Who gets the jobs over there in the NMU Hall? American white men like you and me? No. Dagos and Spiks and Niggers. — William Burroughs, *Junkie*, p. 72, 1953
- I had so much of that hot greaser dago cock that I stopped menstruating and started minestroning! — Terry Southern, *Candy*, pp. 211–212, 1958
- In '77 he smoked a bag of dust he bought from a dago. — *New Jack City*, 1990

Dago *nickname*
San Diego, California *US, 1931*
- We don't do it in Dago. — Raymond Chandler, *Playback*, p. 13, 1958
- I made a connection with some Mexican pushers in 'Dago, and they kept me supplied. — John O'Day, *Confessions of a Male Prostitute*, p. 105, 1964
- Berdoo and Dago Chapters of the South don't think so, they really can't see it this way. — Frank Reynolds, *Freewheelin Frank*, p. 21, 1967
- I caught the six o'clock bus to Dago and walked across the border. — James Ellroy, *Brown's Requiem*, pp. 128–129, 1981

dago bomb *noun*
a type of firework *US, 1960*
- Now loo, when the Dago bomb goes off I want all of you to be ready. — Jean Shepherd, *The Ferrari in the Bedroom*, p. 187, 1972

dago red *noun*
cheap Italian red wine *US, 1945*

- They entered the back door of the Gambino's frame house on East 93rd Street, interrupting a heated conversation in the kitchen between Frank's father and a half dozen other rather threatening Italians drinking dago red out of jelly glasses. — Brian Boyer, *Prince of Thieves*, p. 18, 1975
- I mean, around here a cultured person is one that don't drink dago red from a jar. — Joseph Wambaugh, *Finnegan's Week*, p. 9, 1993

dagotown *noun*
a neighborhood dominated by Italian-Americans *US, 1960*
- Even the dago-town pusher was wary of him now, just because of Sonny. — Clarence Cooper Jr., *The Scene*, p. 12, 1960

Dagwood *noun*
a large and elaborate sandwich *US, 1948*
Named after the sandwiches made by the Dagwood Bumstead character in the *Blondie* comic strip.
- Sol had a saltine Dagwood going: peanut butter, lox spread, sardines. — James Ellroy, *Hollywood Nocturnes*, p. 96, 1994

daikon legs *noun*
short, pale, and fat legs *US, 1981*
Hawaiian youth usage. The "daikon" is also known as an Asian, Oriental, or Chinese radish; it is stubby and white.
- — Douglas Simonson, *Pidgin to da Max*, 1981

daily-daily *noun*
during the Vietnam war, antimalaria pills taken daily, in addition to a second medication taken once a week *US, 1982*
- Doc McCarthy came by with the daily-daily (anti-malaria) pills. — John M. Del Vecchio, *The 13th Valley*, p. 243, 1982

daily double *noun*
in poker, two consecutive winning hands *US, 1996*
A borrowing from horse racing.
- — John Vorhaus, *The Big Book of Poker Slang*, p. 12, 1996

dainties *noun*
underwear, especially women's underwear worn by transvestites *US, 1972*
- — Bruce Rodgers, *The Queens' Vernacular*, p. 59, 1972

daisy *noun*
an attractive young woman *US, 1876*
- Who was she? Just some blonde daisy, getting into the Jag. — John Milne, *Alive and Kicking*, p. 33, 1998

daisy chain *noun*
1 a group of people, arranged roughly in a circle, in which each person is both actively and passively engaged in oral, anal, or vaginal sex with the person in front of and behind them in the circle *US, 1927*
A term that is much more common than the practice.
- Past the Horseshoe Club, with its modified burlesque, and where for five bucks extra you can watch three naked women form a daisy chain on the floor of a basement room anytime after one a.m. — *Rogue for Men*, p. 46, June 1956
- We had sort of a daisy chain, with Ned in the middle. Ned's boyfriend performed fellatio on him while Ned used his hand on me and I masturbated his friend. — Ruth Allison, *Lesbianism*, p. 117, 1967
- The orgy scene is to involve, primarily, three different sexual activities in the following chronological order: oral sex in a "daisy-chain" configuration with all five performers involved. — Vincent Barth, *Porno Films and the People who Make Them*, p. 121, 1973
- His appearance signals a nine-person orgy that features a delicious daisy-chain of joined cocks and cunts and mouths. — *Adult Video*, p. 29, August/September 1986
2 figuratively and by extension, a series of events that return to the beginning *US, 1954*
- Randolph is suing. Stanley is suing Stuyvesant North. it's a daisy chain. — *San Francisco Call-Bulletin*, p. 15, 6th May 1954
- "But the cool nurse who's no longer cool goes immediately to the feds, who've been talking to her anyway, and now the fucking daisy chain comes around again." — Elmore Leonard, *Bandits*, p. 140, 1987
3 in computing, a network architecture in which a single cable connects all nodes *US, 1995*
- — Christian Crumlish, *The Internet Dictionary*, p. 47, 1995

4 a confidence swindle where funds from successive victims are used to keep the swindle alive with the earlier victims *US*, *1985*
- He has a girlfriend named Monica Brown, a con artist who's working a gold-mine scam, a daisy chain. — Gerald Petievich, *Shakedown*, p. 154, 1988

5 a series of (Claymore) mines attached to each other and rigged for sequential detonation *UK*, *1950*
From the general appearance.
- He carried ten extra claymore mines, and we spent the better part of the evening running a daisy chain that went forever. — Larry Chambers, *Recondo*, p. 74, 1992

daisy-chain *verb*
1 to take part in DAISY CHAIN sex *US*, *1962*
- "You didn't go in for any of that daisy-chaining with Ira?" — Stephen Longstreet, *The Flesh Peddlers*, p. 171, 1962

2 to arrange Claymore mines in a sequence *US*, *1991*
- It was too dark to daisy-chain together so we tried to at least overlap the kill zones. — Gary Linderer, *The Eyes of the Eagle*, p. 177, 1991

daisy cutter *noun*
a 10,000 to 15,000 pound bomb used to clear jungle and create an instant landing zone in Vietnam *US*, *1917*
- It can drop napalm (jellied gasoline), phosphorous bombs, 500-pound demolition and 260-pound fragmentation bombs, and a 500-pound Daisy Cutter with an attachment to detonate the bomb before it buries itself in the soft soil of the Delta. — Elaine Shepard, *The Doom Pussy*, p. 30, 1967
- The bunker complex was not secured until the air force hit it with Daisy Cutters. — Keith Nolan, *Ripcord*, p. 89, 2000
- A "Daisy Cutter" is a huge bomb that can cause massive destruction [...] The type depicted in the leaflets, and also used in Afghanistan, is the BLU-82B Commando Vault or Big Blue 82, also known as the Daisy Cutter. — *BBC News*, 6th November 2001

Daisy Dukes *noun*
very short and very tight shorts *US*, *1993*
Named after a character on the unforgettable television program *Dukes of Hazzard*.
- — Connie Eble (Editor), *UNC-CH Campus Slang*, p. 2, Spring 1993
- I trip off of these "Daisy Dukes"; they be wearing these short, biker shorts, and these little crazy outfits. — Yusuf Jah, *Uprising*, p. 103, 1995
- Randi Storm is in the classic blond bimbo mold, getting d.p'd out of her tit-sling and Daisy Dukes. — Editors of Adult Video News, *The AVN Guide to the 500 Greatest Adult Films of All Time*, p. 326, 2005

dak *noun*
a C-47A Skytrain plane, also known as a DC-3, most commonly used to transport people and cargo, but also used as a bomber and fighter *US*, *1975*
- She was known affectionately as the "Gooney Bird," "Dak," and "Dizzy Three" to the men who flew her during World War II. — *San Francisco Chronicle*, p. 60, 18th January 1975

da kine
used at any time to mean anything *US*, *1951*
Hawaiian youth usage. Can be used as a noun, pronoun, adjective, and suffix.
- — Douglas Simonson, *Pidgin to da Max*, 1981
- — Mitch McKissick, *Surf Lingo*, 1987

dama blanca *noun*
cocaine *US*, *1976*
Spanish for "white lady."
- — R.C. Garrett, *The Coke Book*, p. 200, 1984
- — US Department of Justice *Street Terms*, August 1994

damage *noun*
1 expense; cost *UK*, *1755*
Probably from damages awarded in law. Especially familiar in the (jocular) phrase, "what's the damage?" (how much?).
- What's the damage? It is one dollar and fifty all together, senor. — William Edmund Barrett, *The Lilies of the Field*, p. 26, 1967

2 a problem *US*, *1988*
- What's your damage, Heather? — *Heathers*, 1988

damaged goods *noun*
an ex-virgin *US*, *1916*
- — Vincent J. Monteleone, *Criminal Slang*, p. 65, 1949

dame *noun*
1 a woman *UK*, *1720*
While the term originally reflected on the woman involved (an implication of common status), it now reflects more on the speaker, suggesting a tough or old-fashioned viewpoint.
- Prosperous now, he drifted into Broadway life—and immediately tangled with a new breed of dames. — Bernard Wolfe, *The Late Risers*, p. 48, 1954

2 in a deck of playing cards, a queen *US*, *1996*
- — Peter O. Steiner, *Thursday Night Poker*, p. 409, 1996

damfino
used as a jocular abbreviation of "damned if I know" *US*, *1882*
- "Then why are we doing this?" "Damfino." — Jerry Pournelle and Jerry Pournelle, *Football*, p. 514, 1985

damn *noun*
something of little or no worth *UK*, *1760*
Usually in phrases like "not worth a damn," "not care a damn," and "not give a damn." There is a strongly fought historical argument that this derives from "dam" (an Indian coin of little value); the *Oxford English Dictionary* prefers "damn" (a "profane utterance") as the object of this etymology.
- Life's not worth a damn / Till you can say / I am what I am. — Jerry Herman, *I Am What I Am*, 1983
- David O. Selznick was fined $5,000 for allowing Clark Gable to say "Frankly, my dear, I don't give a damn" in Gone With The Wind (1939). — Aubrey Dillon-Malone, *I Was A Fugitive From A Hollywood Trivia Factory*, p. 99, 1999
- I mean it. I don't give a damn who you are. — James N. Frey, *How to Write a Damn Good Mystery*, p. 46, 2004

-damn- *infix*
used as an intensifier *US*, *1867*
- "And I'll guaran-damn-tee you they won't be back," and he put his hat on and left. — Fannie Flagg, *Fried Green Tomatoes at the Whistlestop Cafe*, p. 206, 1987

damnation alley *noun*
in roulette, the twelve-number column on the left of the layout *US*, *1979*
So named because a dealer may not see a cheat place a late bet in the column, which is sometimes out of the dealer's line of sight.
- — Thomas L. Clark, *The Dictionary of Gambling and Gaming*, p. 58, 1987

damned tooting
used for expressing emphatic agreement *US*, *1963*
Folksy.
- Simms said he was damned tootin' he was right. — Jim Thompson, *The Grifters*, p. 17, 1963
- You're damned tootin' ol' LB ain't gonna take no money from the members of the Bar. — Oscar Zeta Acosta, *The Autobiography of a Brown Buffalo*, p. 21, 1972

damn skippy
absolutely! without a doubt! *US*, *1994*
An intensive affirmative.
- We got them on our side and damn skippy we'll use them. — William Upski Winsatt, *Bomb the Suburbs*, p. 51, 1994
- "I'm telling you, you can't trust nobody anymore." "He snookered us." "Damn skippy." — Janet Evanovich, *Seven Up*, p. 12, 2001

damp *adjective*
allowing the importation of alcohol for personal consumption but not for public sale *US*, *1991*
A play on the extremes of "wet" and "dry."
- — Russell Tabbert, *Dictionary of Alaskan English*, p. 89, 1991

damp blanket *noun*
in the theater, a bad review *US*, *1981*
- — Don Wilmeth, *The Language of American Popular Entertainment*, p. 70, 1981

damper *noun*
1 a solitary confinement cell; a cell *US*, *1992*
- — William K. Bentley and James M. Corbett, *Prison Slang*, p. 10, 1992

2 a safe deposit box in a bank *US, 1872*
- — Clarence Major, *Dictionary of Afro-American Slang*, p. 44, 1970

3 a bank *US, 1932*
- He was a pretty good fake in his day, but he couldn't show his mug around any of the dampers in the Apple. — A.S. Jackson, *Gentleman Pimp*, p. 134, 1973

damper *verb*
to mute, to quiet *US, 1979*
- Pallies, damper the rapping! — Iceberg Slim (Robert Beck), *Airtight Willie and Me*, p. 29, 1979

dance *verb*
1 to fight *US, 1975*
- — Report to the Senate, *California Senate Committee on Civil Disorder*, p. 227, 1975

2 (used of a wink in tiddlywinks) to wobble around *US, 1977*
- — *Verbatim*, December 1977

3 to cause a car to bounce up and down by use of hydraulic lifts *US, 1980*
- — Edith A. Folb, *runnin' down some lines*, p. 234, 1980

▶ **dance in the rain room**
to take a shower in prison *US, 1989*
- — James Harris, *A Convict's Dictionary*, p. 30, 1989

dancehall *noun*
the execution chamber in a prison *US, 1928*
- — Troy Harris, *A Booklet of Criminal Argot, Cant and Jargon*, p. 8, 1976
- [T]he condemned man was moved from the regular Death Row cells to a cell near the Dance Hall, through which he would walk on in his way to the chair. — Ted Conover, *Newjack*, p. 195, 2000

dance of death *noun*
a relationship or marriage between two addicts *US, 1998*
Used in twelve-step recovery programs such as Alcoholics Anonymous.
- — Christopher Cavanaugh, *AA to Z*, p. 75, 1998

dancing academy *noun*
used as a euphemism and legal dodge for an after-hours homosexual club *US, 1974*
- Although it appears an unlikely hour for serious study, private dancing academies offering instructions between 2 a.m. and 6 a.m. have opened in San Francisco, the police reported to the Board of Supervisors yesterday. — *San Francisco Chronicle*, p. 4, 12th April 1974

dancing girls *noun*
in dominoes, the seven tiles with a five *US, 1959*
- — Dominic Armanino, *Dominoes*, p. 16, 1959

D and D *noun*
the criminal charge of being drunk and disorderly *US, 1966*
- "We better get out of this neighborhood," Doc warned. "Or we'll find ourselves with thirty days D and D." — Malcolm Braly, *It's Cold Out There*, p. 73, 1966

D and D *adjective*
deaf and dumb *US, 1937*
- "He went D and D," Loretta Fischetti said. "Yes, Deaf and Dumb, I said." — Daniel Pinkwater, *Looking for Bobowicz*, p. 59, 2004

dandy *noun*
a grade of "D" *US, 1965*
- — *Time*, p. 57, 1st January 1965: "Students: the slang bag"

dang
used as a mild oath or intensifier *US, 1821*
A euphemized "damn."
- Dang me, dang me / They oughta take a rope and hang me. — Roger Miller, *Dang Me*, 1964
- It's those dang judgment calls! — Dan Jenkins, *Life Its Ownself*, p. 193, 1984
- LUCY: Get me a beer. VELMA: Hey, we quit drinking. LUCY: Dang, that's right, enit? I forgot. — *Smoke Signals*, 1998
- Dang, can't a bro take a five-minute break? — Eric Jerome Dickey, *Cheaters*, p. 410, 1999

danged *adjective*
used as a euphemism for "damned" *US, 1962*
- When did they sneak that danged glass in there? — Ken Kesey, *One Flew Over the Cuckoo's Nest*, p. 195, 1962

- Because the danged place was being painted, and the painters had left their ladders and cans scattered all over everywhere. — Jim Thompson, *Pop. 1280*, p. 10, 1964

danger is my business
used as a humorous response to a suggestion that a proposed activity is dangerous *US, 2006*
The motto of cartoon secret agent *Cool McCool* (NBC, 1966–69), used with referential humor.
- "And who do I look like, Philip Marlowe?" "Not in the least. But it was Cool McCool who said 'Danger is my business,' not Philip Marlowe." — Michael Blair, *Overexposed*, p. 256, 2006

dangle *noun*
the penis *US, 1936*
- On the wall was a nude drawing of Dean, enormous dangle and all, done by Camille. — Jack Kerouac, *On the Road*, p. 44, 1957
- — Collin Baker et al., *College Undergraduate Slang Study Conducted at Brown University*, p. 103, 1968
- She must have featured the angle of his dangle. — J.F. Freedman, *Against the Wind*, p. 88, 1991
- When I asked Mr. Dent, the gym teacher, if the angle of his dangle was equal to the heat of her meat, he rammed my head into a locker. — Breece Pancake, *The Stories of Breece D'J Pancake*, p. 135, 2002

dangler *noun*
the penis *US, 1970*
- "I'd be scared stiff," he mutters. "Or, rather, I'd be scared limp, if you follow me. My dangler." — Paul West, *I'm Expecting to Live Quite Soon*, p. 57, 1970
- At which point he unzipped his fly and yanked out his dangler and waved it at me. — John Francis Hunter, *The Gay Insider*, p. 204, 1971
- He let down his pants and was seated, and within two minutes was bitten on his dangler by a violin spider. — Samuel Steward, *Understanding the Male Hustler*, p. 130, 1991

daniel *noun*
the buttocks *US, 1946*
- Man, we oughta git up off our daniels and dig what's goin' on. — Mezz Mezzrow, *Really the Blues*, p. 250, 1946
- — Kenn "Naz" Young, *Naz's Underground Dictionary*, p. 24, 1973

Daniel Boone mission *noun*
a small military incursion into Cambodia from Vietnam *US, 1973*
- Daniel Boone was the code name for the operations being run across the border into Cambodia[.] — Senate Committee on Armed Services, *Bombing in Cambodia*, p. 244, 1973
- A good buddy of mine on a Daniel Boone mission had been captured by the NVA crossing the Vam Co Dong River[.] — Paul Morgan, *The Parrot's Beak*, p. 49, 2000

Daniel Boone squad; Daniel Boone team *noun*
US soldiers who engaged in cross-border reconnaissance in Cambodia during the Vietnam war *US, 1991*
- [A] Special Forces "Daniel Boone" team helicoptered into the target area. — Tom Wells, *The War Within*, p. 290, 2005

Danish *noun*
sexual intercourse with full penetration *US, 1981*
- "[S]tick to Swedish massage (by hand), or French (by mouth), and only go Spanish (between the breasts), Russian (between the thighs), American (a body roll) or Danish (inside) if it's worth the money." — Alix Shulman, *On the Stroll*, p. 133, 1981

Danish pastry *noun*
a transsexual *US, 1997*
An allusion to Denmark's standing as an early pioneer in sex-change operations.
- — Jim Crotty, *How to Talk American*, p. 138, 1997

dank *noun*
a very potent marijuana *US, 1998*
- I am a mobile buffet though, plenty of meth, always 'shrooms and doses, windowpane or blotter with Disney characters on it, and Cali-diggity dank to take off the edge. — Lynn Breedlove, *Godspeed*, p. 86, 2002

dank *adjective*
excellent; brilliant *US, 1989*
BAD is "good," **WICKED** is "excellent."
- — Pamela Munro, *U.C.L.A. Slang*, p. 33, 1989
- — Connie Eble (Editor), *UNC-CH Campus Slang*, p. 2, Fall 1996

Dan O'Leary *noun*
a tour of police duty in which the police officer works every possible minute *US, 1958*
- — *New York Times Magazine*, p. 88, 16th March 1958

dap *noun*
a handshake hooking thumbs, used by black US soldiers in Vietnam *US, 1972*
- [R]ace consciousness took the form of symbolic cultural behavior, for example, involved handshakes or the "dap." — Charles R. Figley, *g*, p. 79, 1980
- This was a dap, among "in-country" vets a sign that they had been in Vietnam. — Wukkuan Diehl, *Thai Horse*, p. 249, 1987
- Dap was the Vietnamese word for beautiful, and it was this way of shaking hands. — Harry Maurer, *Strange Ground*, p. 515, 1989

dap *verb*
to greet another with a ritualistic handshake; to show respect in greeting *US, 1973*
- Even if you just hate my fuckin' guts go 'head and dap me / Cause I'm gon' dap you anyway and then go home and pray for yo' ass later. — Outkast, *Wailin'*, 1996

dap *adjective*
well-dressed, fashionable *US, 1956*
A shortened "dapper."
- — Robert George Reisner, *The Jazz Titans*, p. 153, 1960
- — *Current Slang*, p. 19, Fall 1968
- — Hermese E. Roberts, *The Third Ear*, 1971

dap down *verb*
to dress nicely *US, 1980*
- — Edith A. Folb, *runnin' down some lines*, p. 234, 1980

dapper *noun*
a person dressed in style *US, 1974*
- When she hesitated and put her hands on her hips, two young dappers yelled from the middle of the bar. — Donald Goines, *Never Die Alone*, p. 46, 1974

dapper Dan *noun*
any well-dressed man *US, 1955*
- I asked famed fashion designer Bill Blass the difference between a slob and a Dapper Dan last night at an I. Magnin party. — *San Francisco Examiner*, p. 37, 21st October 1970

daps *noun*
proper respect *US, 1997*
- — Pamela Munro, *U.C.L.A. Slang*, p. 56, 1997

darb *adjective*
in circus usage, excellent *US, 1981*
- — Don Wilmeth, *The Language of American Popular Entertainment*, p. 70, 1981

dark *noun*
▶ **in the dark**
(used of a bet in poker) made without having seen your cards *US, 1990*
- — Anthony Holden, *Big Deal*, p. 302, 1990

dark *adjective*
1 unreachable by telephone *US, 2004*
A condition usually resulting from a failure to pay your bill.
- — Ben Applebaum and Derrick Pittman, *Turd Ferguson & The Sausage Party*, p. 24, 2004
2 untelevized *US, 2000*
- Dark matches serve numerous purposes. Wrestlers who've shined on the independent circuit—cards staged by small promoters in high school gyms, Grange halls and fraternal lodges—are invited to World Wrestling Federation TV tapings to audition for Federation officials. — *Raw Magazine*, p. 48, September 2000
- Just as non televised under-card bouts are called "dark matches" non televised arena events are called "dark shows." Yeah, sure, the results show up in the rankings, but not on the boob tube. — *Rampage Magazine*, p. 18, September 2000

dark cheaters *noun*
sunglasses *US, 1949*
- Don't think for a minute those dark cheaters fool little Flackie. — Raymond Chandler, *Little Sister*, p. 65, 1949

Dark Gable *noun*
a handsome black man *US, 1959*
Punning on the name Clark Gable. The nickname has been taken by more than one, but perhaps nobody more prominent than Mohammed Ali who briefly called himself Dark Gable in 1981.
- You make like a Dark Gable but you can't dig my fable. — Dan Burley, *Diggeth Thou?*, p. 45, 1959

dark-green *adjective*
excellent *US, 1954*
- "Dark Green," he explained, "is what the hipsters are saying now instead of 'real crazy.'" — *San Francisco Examiner*, p. 31, 7th May 1954

dark horse *noun*
in horse racing, a horse that is deemed a poor performer but one that might surprise all and win *US, 1951*
- — David W. Maurer, *Argot of the Racetrack*, p. 23, 1951

dark meat *noun*
a black person as a sexual object *US, 1888*
- All white men hanker after dark meat. The reader has the preacher's word for that. — *Pacific Spectator*, p. 108, Winter 1947
- I tell them dark meat's all the same as white in the dark, but I think they can't believe it. — John M. Murtagh and Sara Harris, *Cast the First Stone*, p. 11, 1957
- Vess's remarks really started me to wondering, however, why I really did like dark meat so much. — Phil Andros (Samuel M. Steward), *Stud*, p. 89, 1966
- This torrid tribute to the joys of dark meat features a chorus line of ebony beauties bouncing and boffing through a series of raunchy, relentlessly racist, and often unbearably funny skits that mine just about every sick cliche[.] — *Adult Video*, p. 16, August/September 1986

dark thirty *noun*
late at night *US, 1984*
- To work from dawn till dark thirty. — Ken Weaver, *Texas Crude*, p. 91, 1984

dark time *noun*
night *US, 1976*
- — Elementary Electronics, *Dictionary of CB Lingo*, p. 60, 1976

darktown *noun*
a neighborhood populated largely by black people *US, 1916*
- The black ghettos of the "Darktown" slums in every Southern city were the consequence mainly of the Negro's economic status, his relegation to the lowest rung of the ladder. — C. Vann Woodward, *The Strange Career of Jim Crow*, p. 1, 1974
- "It might be a window peeper who's been working Darktown lately." — James Ellroy, *White Jazz*, p. 54, 1992
- Lorenzo had guessed as much, Gannon being the mostly white blue-collar town bordering the so-called Darktown section of Dempsy. — Richard Price, *Freedomland*, p. 37, 1998

darky; darkie *noun*
a black person *US, 1775*
Originally used in a paternalistic, condescending manner, but now mainly to disparage.
- In fact, there's a saying in Georgetown now that you're not "smart" unless darkies live next door to you. — Jack Lait and Lee Mortimer, *Washington Confidential*, p. 10, 1951
- Darkies are always singing. You people know that. — James Baldwin, *Blues for Mister Charlie*, p. 73, 1964
- Well, what the hell is your problem that you and that other darky would come here to my house with the city lousy with government agents? — Iceberg Slim (Robert Beck), *Long White Con*, p. 148, 1977
- But who was using em? Chinese immigrants. Slave labor. And the darkies up in the inner cities[.] — *Traffic*, 2000

darkytown *noun*
a neighborhood with a large population of black people *US, 1971*
- Roy felt it when he ventured out of darky town onto the broad reaches of Court Square the center of white power and prestige in Holly Springs. — J. Anthony Lukas, *Don't Shoot—We Are Your Children*, p. 79, 1971

darling *noun*
used as a term of address between male homosexuals *US, 1949*
- Darling—Meaningless vocative loosely used in "bitchy" conversation. — Anon., *The Gay Girl's Guide*, p. 6, 1949

darn!; darn it!

used for registering annoyance, frustration, etc. US, 1781
A euphemistic variation of **DAMN!**

- Well, it's my own fault, darn it, she sighed, then smiled a little smile. — Terry Southern, *Candy*, p. 149, 1958

darned *adjective*

used as an intensifier US, 1807
Euphemistic for **DAMNED**.

- "You're darned straight I'm impressed." — Donna Clayton, *Taking Love in Stride*, p. 83, 1991

darned tooting!

used as a mock oath affirming that which has just been said US, 1963
Usually used in a self-mocking way, conjuring the image of an older, confused, country bumpkin.

- Simms said he was damned tootin' he was right. — Jim Thompson, *The Grifters*, p. 17, 1963
- You're darned tootin'! — *Fargo*, 1996

dash *noun*

an escape from custody US, 1952

- *American Speech*, p. 25, February 1952: 'Teen-age hophead jargon'

date *noun*

1 a prostitute's customer US, 1961

- This John is a real honest-to-goodness hundred-dollar date, the way it used to be during the war. — Ross Russell, *The Sound*, p. 181, 1961
- I put her to work on the same edge on Hastings Street and fixed it where she could take her dates to a pal's pad to turn em. — A.S. Jackson, *Gentleman Pimp*, p. 88, 1973
- Since each girl usually had between five and twenty dates a day, the average would be about twelve. — Jan Hutson, *The Chicken Ranch*, p. 83, 1980
- They told him that he was her first date of the night, but her cunt seemed to be full of something viscous like come or corn syrup. — William T. Vollman, *Whores for Gloria*, p. 15, 1991

2 a sexual liaison between a prostitute and a customer US, 1957
An ironic euphemism.

- The men involved on these "dates" were always Chinese. — Harry J. Anslinger, *The Murderers*, p. 38, 1961
- But there were no $5 dates in my house. — Bruce Jackson, *In the Life*, p. 78, 1972
- You want a date, honey? — Vernon E. Smith, *The Jones Men*, p. 111, 1974
- Since each girl usually had between five and twenty dates a day, the average would be about twelve. — Jan Hutson, *The Chicken Ranch*, p. 83, 1980
- Oliver had assured her that she was his top bitch but demanded to know why she couldn't catch as many dates as Alice, his bottom bitch. — Joseph Wambaugh, *Floaters*, p. 67, 1996

3 a prisoner's expected date of release from prison US, 1989

- James Harris, *A Convict's Dictionary*, p. 30, 1989

date *verb*

(used of a prostitute) to have sex with a customer for pay US, 1951

- A white prostitute tried to date us at the Mai Fong restaurant, in Chinatown[.] — Jack Lait and Lee Mortimer, *Washington Confidential*, p. 26, 1951
- His name is Milt. I've dated him before, he only gets to the Apple once or twice a year. — Ross Russell, *The Sound*, p. 182, 1961
- "If a john walks up and offers seven dollars she tells him to shove it, she only dates for ten." — Robert Deane Pharr, *S.R.O.*, p. 372, 1971
- The polite form is to have a date, to turn a date, or dating. — Christina and Richard Milner, *Black Players*, p. 38, 1972

date bait *noun*

1 an attractive person of either sex who is sought after as a date US, 1944

- She was not somebody who was considered date bait, because of her weight and her presentation. — David Brock, *The Seduction of Hilary Rodham*, p. 40, 1996

2 anything that might serve as an incentive for a date US, 1986

- What a fun, sweet, terrific movie. Great date bait. — Roger Ebert, *Questions for the Movie Answer Man*, p. 163, 1997

daughter *noun*

a male homosexual in relation to the man who has introduced him to homosexuality US, 1949

- Anon., *The Gay Girl's Guide*, p. 6, 1949
- *American Speech*, p. 56, Spring–Summer 1970: 'Homosexual slang'

dauncey *adjective*

pregnant US, 1952
The "Lucy is Enceinte" episode of the television comedy "*I Love Lucy*" (CBS, 1950–57), which aired on 8th December 1952, was the first US television treatment of pregnancy. Lucy avoided the word "pregnant," instead saying that she was "feeling real dauncey," explaining that it was a word that her grandmother "made up for when you're not really sick but you just feel lousy." The word enjoyed brief popular usage.

davvy *noun*

a sofa or couch US, 1997
A corruption of "Davenport."

- Amy and Denise McFadden, *CoalSpeak*, p. 5, 1997

dawg *noun*

1 a dog US, 1979
A rural, southern "dog."

- Kleinfeld put his hand out and Carlito slapped it. "You dawg," Brigante said. — Edwin Torres, *After Hours*, p. 208, 1979

2 a fellow youth gang member US, 2003

- [Y]our Kru, or your Massive, your Thugs, or Bredrins; Dawgs, Homies, your Clique, or your Posse. — Julian Johnson, *Urban Survival*, p. 264, 2003

dawner *noun*

an engagement between a prostitute and customer that lasts all night, until dawn US, 1987

- Rialto was supposed to be waitin' on Felita to say was it going to be a quick trick or a dawner. But Rialto wasn't there. — Robert Campbell, *Alice in La-La Land*, p. 328, 1987

dawn patrol *noun*

any activity that requires staying up all night or getting up very early US, 1945
Originally a military term, later applied figuratively.

- Lou Shelly, *Hepcats Jive Talk Dictionary*, p. 44, 1945
- "I suffered through those dawn patrol meetings myself," says Masters. — *San Francisco News*, p. 23, 19th September 1951
- Therefore, I insisted that one girl work the dawn patrol. — Madam Sherry, *Pleasure Was My Business*, p. 107, 1963
- Dawn patrol—major dawn patrol. My son had a full blown attack. — *As Good As It Gets*, 1997

day com *noun*

a practice of leaving a safe locked during business hours but only requiring a slight adjustment to open US, 1976

- Day com is when the manager of a store, fearing robbery, wants to give the impression his safe is locked, and still not have to rework the entire combination every time something is needed. — Malcolm Braley, *False Starts*, p. 125, 1976

day-for-day; day-to-day *adverb*

serving a prison sentence without any reduction in the sentence for good behavior US, 1983

- "Let me explain something so you understand," Stick said. "See, I did seven years straight up day to day in a room six and half feet wide by ten feet deep." — Elmore Leonard, *Stick*, p. 84, 1983
- Charles Shafer, *Folk Speech in Texas Prisons*, p. 202, 1990

day job *noun*

a conventional job, usually used to finance a person's true interest or passion US, 1994

- HONEY BUNNY: Well, what else is there, day jobs? PUMPKIN: Not this life. — *Pulp Fiction*, 1994

daylight in the swamp!

used for rousing people from bed US, 1936
A logger term.

- My father woke us early, hours before it's light out, pounding on our doors, bellowing "Reveille, reveille, it's daylight in the swamp!" — Susan Fox Rogers, *Solo*, p. 17, 1996

day number *noun*

in an illegal number gambling lottery, a wager on a number for a single day's drawing US, 1949

- *American Speech*, p. 191, October 1949

day player *noun*
an actor who is called for a single day's work on a television program or movie set *US, 1988*
- I mean was it a pretty big part or were you just—were you a day player? — Robert Campbell, *Juice*, p. 28, 1988

days of rage *noun*
a series of violent confrontations between radical members of the Students for Democratic Society and the police in downtown Chicago in the autumn of 1969 *US, 1969*
- J. Anthony Lukas, *The Barnyard Epithet and ther Obscenities*, p. 10, 1970

daytime name *noun*
a person's legal name, as distinguished from an alias or nickname *US, 1949*
- "That's me, too, Sparrow Saltskin, it's my daytime name." — Nelson Algren, *The Man with the Golden Arm*, p. 5, 1949

DB *noun*
a *dead* body *US, 1973*
- "I think a guy might be dead upstairs." "What the hell made you think so?" I said sarcastically, as we started up the stairs and I smelled the d.b. from here. — Joseph Wambaugh, *The Blue Knight*, p. 131, 1973

DC *noun*
a hamburger with every possible trimming and condiment *US, 1966*
- American Speech, p. 280, December 1966: 'More carnie talk from the west coast'

DD *noun*
a person who is *deaf* and *dumb* *US, 1926*
- Vincent J. Monteleone, *Criminal Slang*, p. 68, 1949

DD *adjective*
by extension, said of a criminal who gives up no information at all if arrested *US, 1950*
- Hyman E. Goldin et al., *Dictionary of American Underworld Lingo*, p. 56, 1950

DDT!
used for disparaging, urging the listener to *drop dead twice US, 1947*
Youth usage; punning on the insecticide now banned but used with great effectiveness to kill mosquitos in the years after World War 2. Recorded in *Time*, 3rd October 1949.
- Last year's "drop dead" is now "D.D.T." (drop dead twice) or, more formally, "Please do me the personal favor of dropping dead." — *Life*, p. 119, 17th November 1947
- But when Batsy feels like snoozing nice ... "DDT," you all ... "Drop Dead Twice." [They'll Do It Every Time comic strip] — *San Francisco Call-Bulletin*, 10th November 1950
- American Weekly, p. 2, 14th August 1955
- He remembers Winchell's famous handwritten notes on top of wrongo items returned to the sender: "DDT" which meant "Drop Dead Twice." — *Daily Variety*, p. 2, 19th November 1998

deacon *verb*
to present a job or product in the best possible light, placing more importance on the first impression than on the actual quality *US, 1855*
- He deaconed his barn by painting the side toward the ro'd. — John Gould, *Maine Lingo*, p. 70, 1975

deacon seat *noun*
the seats nearest a fire *US, 1975*
- Because the deacons usually sat down front in church, the deacon-seat became the bench nearest the fire in a lumber camp. — John Gould, *Maine Lingo*, p. 70, 1975

dead *noun*
in any card game, cards that have been discarded *US, 1973*
- I buried their dead/ then did what they said/ dealing each man their hand. — Lightnin' Rod, *Hustlers Convention*, p. 90, 1973

dead *adjective*
1 (used of dice) weighted to have one face land up more often than the law of averages would predict *US, 1993*
- Frank Scoblete, *Guerrilla Gambling*, p. 304, 1993

2 in bar dice games, no longer wild *US, 1976*
If a game is played with "aces wild" (assuming the point value of any other die), a call of "aces dead" after the first call of a hand nullifies the "wild" status.
- Gil Jacobs, *The World's Best Dice Games*, p. 191, 1976

3 in pinball, said of a bumper that scores when hit but does not propel the ball back into play *US, 1977*
- Bobbye Claire Natkin and Steve Kirk, *All About Pinball*, p. 111, 1977

4 in pool, said of a shot made such that the cue ball stops completely after striking the object ball *US, 1990*
- Steve Rushin, *Pool Cool*, p. 11, 1990

dead as disco *adjective*
completely dead *US, 1995*
From the meteoric rise and fall of the disco fad in the 1970s.
- By Friday, man, or you're fuckin' dead as disco. — *Get Shorty*, 1995

dead ass *noun*
the buttocks in seated repose *US, 1950*
- Look, we have this date scheduled. I can't perform unless you get off your dead ass. — Rosabeth Moss Kanter, *Change Masters*, p. 81, 1983

dead-ass *adjective*
lacking energy *US, 1958*
- I gave a dead-ass performance. — Andrea Siegel, *Women in Aikido*, p. 80, 1993

dead-ass *adverb*
absolutely *US, 1971*
- "We've got three infantry brigades," he said. "Yours is dead-ass last." — Joseph Persico, *My American Journey*, p. 204, 1995

dead babies *noun*
semen *US, 1998*
- Ethan Hilderbrant, *Prison Slang*, p. 36, 1998

dead-bang *adjective*
beyond debate *US, 1934*
- We were both hungry for jurywork, and therefore we agreed to try a dead-bang loser of a rape case on reassignment from somebody smarter. — Scott Turow, *Presumed Innocent*, p. 174, 1987

dead-bang *adverb*
absolutely *US, 1919*
- I don't need to turn you, Vicky. I got you dead bang. — Stephen Cannell, *Big Con*, p. 323, 1997

deadbeat *noun*
a person who won't pay his debts, especially one who does not pay child support after divorce *US, 1871*
In modern use, often construed with "dad" or "parent."
- You sonofabitch fuck. Are you calling me a deadbeat? The money I spent here? — *Goodfellas*, 1990
- So you want a financial, is he a deadbeat? — *Sleepless in Seattle*, 1993
- There's a lot more money in getting deadbeats to pay up, isn't there? — Elmore Leonard, *Riding the Rap*, p. 158, 1995
- [T]hey knew if you let one go, then every other deadbeat on the Strip would think they could pull something, too. — John Ridley, *Stray Dogs*, p. 53, 1997

Dead board *noun*
an Internet bulletin board system designed by, and for, fans of the Grateful Dead *US, 1994*
- David Shenk and Steve Silberman, *Skeleton Key*, p. 53, 1994

dead cat *noun*
in circus usage, a lion, tiger, or leopard that is on display but does not perform *US, 1981*
- Don Wilmeth, *The Language of American Popular Entertainment*, p. 71, 1981

dead cat on the line *noun*
used as a representation of something that is wrong or immoral *US, 1970*
- There's a dead cat on the line, Eleanor. And you'd better wake up and smell it. — Candy Dawson Boyd, *Charlie Pippin*, p. 32, 1987
- If one comes in there like a scalded dog, the others in that hole know there's a dead cat on the line somewhere. — Foxfire Fund, *Foxfire 11*, p. 266, 1999

dead drop *noun*
in espionage or a sophisticated criminal venture, a location where a message can be left by one party and retrieved by another *US, 1986*
- Henry Becket, *The Dictionary of Espionage*, pp. 52–53, 1986
- That bank could be the dead-drop. — Stephen Cannell, *King Con*, p. 119, 1997

dead duck *noun*

an absolute failure, a person or thing with no possibility of success *US, 1829*

- Senator Hugh Burns (F. Fresno) said his bill to make the present closing hours permanent apparently is a "dead duck." — *San Francisco News*, p. 1, 10th June 1947

deadfall *noun*

a dishonest, disreputable, vice-ridden drinking establishment *US, 1837*

- They worked the come-on joints and dead-falls on West Fifty-second Street, between Sixth and Seventh Avenues[.] — Lee Mortimer, *Women Confidential*, p. 138, 1960

dead fish *noun*

a gambler who places small bets to prolong the inevitable *US, 1963*

- — Thomas L. Clark, *The Dictionary of Gambling and Gaming*, p. 58, 1987

dead hand *noun*

in poker, any hand held by a player who has bet all of his chips or money on the hand *US, 1947*

- — Oswald Jacoby, *Oswald Jacoby on Poker*, p. 141, 1947

deadhead *noun*

1 a person who rides free on a railroad, bus, or airplane, usually because of their employment with the carrier *US, 1841*

- — Norman Carlisle, *The Modern Wonder Book of Trains and Railroading*, p. 261, 1946
- The only other people on the plane were a half dozen or so off-duty pilots: "deadheads" as they say in the business. — Hunter S. Thompson, *Generation of Swine*, p. 137, 7th July 1986

2 a boring person; a person of limited intelligence *US, 1907*

- "But can you see me doing my top yak routines on the boat for deadheads?" — Stephen Longstreet, *The Flesh Peddlers*, p. 214, 1962
- "I'm booking and shylocking and working all kinds of scams, but I'm cutting the money with a bunch of fucking deadheads." — Ovid Demaris, *The Last Mafioso*, p. 124, 1981

3 a non-playing observer of gambling *US, 1974*

- — John Scarne, *Scarne on Dice*, p. 465, 1974

4 a person given a ticket or tickets for having performed minor services in a theatrical production *US, 1973*

- — Sherman Louis Sergel, *The Language of Show Biz*, p. 69, 1973

Deadhead *noun*

a follower of Grateful Dead, a band strongly associated with psychedelic drugs, seen by many to epitomize the hippie ideal *US, 1972*

Grateful Dead's choice of name was the result of browsing a dictionary; usually abbreviated to "The Dead"; their 30-year career as a live band came to an end in 1995 with the death of guitarist Jerry Garcia.

- — Connie Eble (Editor), *UNC-CH Campus Slang*, p. 2, Fall 1982
- Someone who loves—and draws meaning from—the music of the Grateful Dead and the experience of Dead shows, and builds community with others who feel the same way. — David Shenk and Steve Silberman, *Skeleton Key*, p. 60, 1994
- [J]ust hanging out, doing drugs with their dead-head clothes on[.] — Tim Lucas, *Cool Places*, p. 154, 1998
- Ten music-related university courses that really exist [...] 2 DEADHEAD 101, University Of North Carolina, Greensboro — *Q*, p. 38, December 2001

deadhead *verb*

(used of an airline or railroad employee) to ride as a passenger in available seating *US, 1854*

- Deadheaded up there like a bat out of fuckin' hell. — George V. Higgins, *The Rat on Fire*, p. 105, 1981

dead lice

▸ **dead lice are falling off; dead lice are dropping off**

used for describing someone who is very slow-moving or lazy *US, 1960*

- Look at those good-for-nothing loafers, so lazy that dead lice wouldn't drop off them. — Robert Ruark, *The Old Man and the Boy*, p. 119, 1957

dead line *noun*

in prison, a line the crossing of which will bring gun fire from guards *US, 1961–1962*

- — Frank Prewitt and Francis Schaeffer, *Vacaville Vocabulary*, 1961–1962

deadlock *noun*

a prison cell housing a prisoner who is temporarily not allowed to leave the cell *US, 1949*

- The cons up there were either in bug cells or deadlock. — Nelson Algren, *The Man with the Golden Arm*, p. 205, 1949

deadly *adjective*

1 excellent *US, 1970*

- — Clarence Major, *Dictionary of Afro-American Slang*, p. 45, 1970
- Right now I'm enjoying a Jolt cola with a dash of Henson's Orange soda. It's deadly. — *Wayne's World 2*, 1993

2 very boring *US, 1955*

- — *American Speech*, p. 303, December 1955: "Wayne university slang"

deadly embrace *noun*

in computing, the condition resulting when two processes cannot proceed because each is waiting for another to do something *US, 1981*

- — 'Computer slang', p. 29, Spring 1981

dead man's hand *noun*

in poker, a hand with a pair of aces and a pair of eights *US, 1886*

Although it is the modern belief that this was the hand held by Wild Bill Hickok when shot to death in 1876 in Deadwood, Dakota Territory, early uses of the term (which also sometimes referred to hands other than aces and eights) make no mention of Hickok. In 1942, Damon Runyon wrote that the hand was sometimes called the "Montana dead man's hand."

- — John Scarne, *Scarne's Guide to Modern Poker*, p. 277, 1979

dead man's pull-ups *noun*

an exercise in which a person hangs with their arms extended from a bar, lifts their chin over the bar, and then lowers themselves to the full arm-extended position *US, 1996*

- Her hands had looked like chopped sirloin from all the training, until at last she could pump out twenty. All the way down. All the way up. Dead man's pull-ups. — Joseph Wambaugh, *Floaters*, p. 140, 1996

dead man's zone; dead Marine zone *noun*

a demilitarized zone *US, 1984*

Back-formation from the initials DMZ.

- Roy tells the group that the DMZ also was known as the "Dead Marine zone." — Raymond Scurfield, *A Vietnam Trilogy*, p. 153, 2006

dead meat *noun*

used for expressing a very high degree of trouble *US, 1974*

Originally applied only in situations where death was certain, but then softened to include lesser consequences.

- "You're dead meat," I said. — Armistead Maupin, *Maybe the Moon*, p. 179, 1992
- It's a good thing you had that plane ticket to get out of the country. You'd be dead meat for sure here. — C.D. Payne, *Youth in Revolt*, p. 347, 1993
- "He's dead meat, man." "He put away people that would have died for him." — Bob Sipchen, *Baby Insane and the Buddha*, p. 378, 1993
- I'm fucking dead meat in this town. — Theresa Rebeck, *View of the Dome*, p. 54, 1998

dead money *noun*

1 obviously counterfeit paper money *US, 1956*

- — *American Speech*, p. 100, May 1956: "Smugglers' argot in the southwest"

2 in poker, money bet by a player who has withdrawn from a hand *US, 1992*

- — Edwin Silberstang, *Winning Poker for the Serious Player*, p. 218, 1992

dead-nuts *adverb*

completely *US, 1887*

- I catch you dead nuts in the middle of the act, you don't even act nervous or anything. — Elmore Leonard, *Swag*, p. 9, 1976
- Ordinarily Marine Corps noncoms were dead-nuts certain about everything. Even when they were wrong. — Stephen Coonts, *Victory*, p. 436, 2003

dead on arrival *noun*

phencyclidine, the recreational drug known as PCP or angel dust *US, 1993*

In honor of the drug's fatal overdose potential.

- — Peter Johnson, *Dictionary of Street Alcohol and Drug Terms*, p. s, 1993

dead pan *noun*

a complete lack of facial emotion *US, 1927*

- The more effective technique is dead pan. — Madeleine L'Engle, *Walking on Water*, p. 184, 1980

deadpan *adjective*

without expression; displaying no emotion *US, 1928*

- With his sunken cheeks, deadpan kisser and wig that looked like a Fuller brush, he used to give us hysterics up on the bandstand[.] — Mezz Mezzrow, *Really the Blues*, p. 85, 1946

dead pigeon *noun*

1 in a criminal enterprise, a double-crosser *US, 1964*

- — R. Frederick West, *God's Gambler*, p. 225, 1964: "Appendix A"

2 a person who is destined to lose *US, 1919*

- Well, sir, Mary is a dead pigeon, the way I see it, and Barney goes for that kind of case. — Herman Wouk, *The Caine Mutiny*, p. 377, 1951

dead presidents *noun*

money *US, 1944*

From the portraits of Washington, Lincoln, Hamilton etc., printed on the different value notes.

- — Lou Shelly, *Hepcats Jive Talk Dictionary*, p. 23, 1945
- Say, if you overhear some conversation about "a lot of dead Presidents," don't phone J. Edgar. It's accepted American slang for money—especially bills. Broadway's Gentleman Georgie Solotaire coined it. It's catching on all over. — *San Francisco Examiner*, p. 24, 17th December 1952
- I say, "Bitch, what about those dead Presidents?" — Christina and Richard Milner, *Black Players*, p. 87, 1972
- Maurice, the Blue Note's manager, no matter how often or eloquently he promised a bonus percentage of gross receipts over a certain figure, always kicked the same lousy fifty dead presidents across the bar at closing. — Seth Morgan, *Homeboy*, p. 13, 1990

dead rabbit *noun*

the penis in a flaccid state *US, 1964*

- — Roger Blake, *The American Dictionary of Sexual Terms*, p. 54, 1964

dead soldier *noun*

an empty alcohol bottle or beer can *US, 1899*

- I found a half-dead soldier in the drawer of the night stand and I poured myself a stiff one. — Curt Cannon, *Die Hard*, p. 16, 1953
- First toast: "May the war be over before this bottle becomes a dead soldier." — *San Francisco Chronicle*, p. 24, 29th June 1966
- Dead soldiers of all cheap and barely legal brands were kicked into the corners[.] — Earl Thompson, *Tattoo*, p. 23, 1974
- Nother dead soldier and the brandy's near touching bottom. — Elmore Leonard, *Cat Chaser*, p. 13, 1982

dead-stick *verb*

to land an aircraft without engine function *US, 1962*

- My only alternative was to dead-stick the plane into the chilly waters. — Bob Hoove, *Forever Flying*, p. 29, 1996

dead-stick *adjective*

(used of landing an aircraft) without engine function *US, 1999*

- The dead-stick ditching of a plane into the ocean wasn't something you could practice; you had to get it right the first time. — Elgen M. Long, *Amelia Earhart*, p. 30, 1999

Dead threads *noun*

in the language surrounding the Grateful Dead, the layers of clothes worn by a concert-goer *US, 1994*

- — David Shenk and Steve Silberman, *Skeleton Key*, p. 59, 1994

dead time *noun*

time served in jail which does not count towards fulfillment of the prisoner's sentence *US, 1973*

- It ain't dead time no more like it used to be. Now they give a man all the time he spends in the county jail. — Donald Goines, *White Man's Justice, Black Man's Grief*, p. 32, 1973
- Under California law, such time is dead time. — Malcolm Braley, *False Starts*, p. 237, 1976

dead tumble *noun*

capture during the commission of a crime *US, 1952*

- — Charles Hamilton, *Men of the Underworld*, p. 321, 1952: Glossary

deadwood *noun*

1 an incompetent or otherwise useless person *US, 1887*

- He'd have a lot of deadwood to clear out, or put some sap back into 'em. — Jim Thompson, *The Grifters*, p. 122, 1963
- Luke Zigman was surprised to see the old deadwood player being rolled by into the casino by his nephew at three in the morning. — Stephen Cannell, *Big Con*, p. 224, 1997

2 a flaccid penis *US, 1995*

Extended from **WOOD** (the erect penis).

- — *Adult Video News*, p. 51, October 1995

3 unsold tickets for a performance *US, 1934*

- — Joe McKennon, *Circus Lingo*, p. 30, 1980

4 nonplaying observers of gambling *US, 1974*

- — John Scarne, *Scarne on Dice*, p. 482, 1974

5 a person caught outright committing a crime *US, 1992*

- — William K. Bentley and James M. Corbett, *Prison Slang*, p. 92, 1992

deal *verb*

1 to sell drugs *US, 1958*

- Frankie has been dealing for six years without a bust. — Abbie Hoffman, *Woodstock Nation*, p. 66, 1969
- We are all outlaws in the eyes of America / In order to survive we steal cheat lie forge fuck hide and deal — Jefferson Airplane, *We Can Be Together*, 1970
- Seems like dealing is all I'm good at, so be it. — Edwin Torres, *Carlito's Way*, p. 66, 1975
- DANTE: How many times I gotta tell you not to deal outside the store. JAY: I'm not dealing. KID: You got anything, man? JAY: Yeah, what do you want? — *Clerks*, 1994

2 to supervise the blackjack game in a casino *US, 1980*

- How many games do you deal? — Lee Solkey, *Dummy Up and Deal*, p. 111, 1980

▶ **deal off the top**

to treat fairly *US, 1969*

From the gambling scheme of cheating by dealing off the bottom of a deck.

- After I had been in town six months, fate dealt me one off the top for a change. — Iceberg Slim (Robert Beck), *Pimp*, p. 288, 1969

dealer's band *noun*

an elastic band used by a drug dealer to secure or to facilitate the jettisoning of drugs for sale *US, 1966*

- Many addicts—especially pushers—wear a rubber band on their wrists (a dealer's band, some call it) which, if hooked properly around a deck of heroin, will send it flying if an approaching detective is spotted. — James Mills, *The Panic in Needle Park*, p. 15, 1966

dealie; dealy *noun*

a thing the correct name of which escapes or is not important to the speaker *US, 1997*

- "Oh yeah, Mr. Singh, he said I couldn't park with the handcaps even though I got the blue wheelchair dealie on the mirror." — Carl Hiaasen, *Lucky You*, p. 150, 1997
- "The book our mothers had was the Bible, not some fifty-cent dealie." — Barbara Kingsolver, *The Bean Trees*, p. 111, 1998
- — Pamela Munro, *U.C.L.A. Slang*, p. 59, 2001

dean *noun*

a skilled and experienced poker player *US, 1979*

- — John Scarne, *Scarne's Guide to Modern Poker*, p. 277, 1979

dean of men *noun*

a prison warden *US, 1949*

- — Captain Vincent J. Monteleone, *Criminal Slang*, p. 66, 1949

Dear Jane *noun*

a letter to a girlfriend or wife breaking off the relationship *US, 1963*

- Oh, you mean the "Dear Jane" routine? — Clarence Cooper Jr., *Black*, p. 64, 1963

Dear John; Dear John letter; Johnny letter *noun*

a letter from a woman to her husband or boyfriend ending their relationship *US, 1945*

- "Leave a girl behind, get a Dear John?" — Norman Mailer, *The Naked and the Dead*, p. 181, 1948
- — *American Speech*, p. 303, December 1955: "Wayne university slang"
- 389 pieces of mail (which included one birth announcement and three Dear Johns) received. — Charles Anderson, *The Grunts*, p. 121, 1976
- Aboard the nuclear-powered carrier USS Theodore Roosevelt, with a crew of 5,000, the chaplains spent hours last Sunday night

counseling men who'd received one version or another of the dreaded "Dear John" lettter. — *Washington Times*, 1st February 1991

- In Baghdad, the worst of the fighting over and the soldiers bunking in a former train station, the mail watch began again. A letter arrived for Tielbar and he recognized it wasn't what he'd hoped. It was a "Dear John" letter. She couldn't wait any longer. — *Hartford (Connecticut) Courant*, p. 6, 9th November 2003

death *noun*
someone or something that is exquisitely perfect *US, 1965*
- David Frazer said she was death. — *Diner*, 1982
- — Levi Strauss & Company, *Campus Slang*, p. 2, January 1986
- — Trevor Cralle, *The Surfin'ary*, p. 28, 1991

▸ **to death**
to the extreme; superlative *UK, 1998*
- — Gary K. Farlow, *Prison-ese*, p. 74, 2002

death benefit *noun*
in poker, money given to a player to complete a bet *US, 1996*
- — John Vorhaus, *The Big Book of Poker Slang*, p. 12, 1996

death breath *noun*
a social outcast *US, 2004*
- "Keep moving, death breath." — Brittany Kent, *O.C. Undercover*, p. 137, 2004

death cookie *noun*
in snowboarding, a rock hidden in snow *US, 1995*
- — Jim Humes & Sean Wagstaff, *Boarderlands*, p. 221, 1995

death mitten *noun*
bags slipped over the hands of murder victims to preserve evidence *US, 1992*
- Death mittens, in case something's under the nails. You know, like hair, skin, from a struggle. — Richard Price, *Clockers*, p. 137, 1992

death pen *noun*
a designated pen with black indelible ink used in hospitals for filling out death certificates *US, 1994*
- — Sally Williams, *"Strong" Words*, p. 138, 1994

death rim *noun*
any expensive car wheel rim *US, 1995*
The rim is an invitation to crime and violence, hence the name.
- — *American Speech*, p. 303, Fall 1996: "Among the new words"

death seat *noun*
the front passenger seat of a car or truck *US, 1975*
From the probability, actual or notional, that the passenger is the least likely to survive an accident.
- [Y]es, he was sitting in the death seat I think you call it in the insur, the phrase they used in the paper that is to say beside the driver. — William Gaddis, *JR*, p. 239, 1975
- I could tell Franny had taken the wheel when the car began to careen between the trees, great slithers of the spring mud flying—and the wild, half-seen gestures of Frank's arms waving in what is popularly called the death seat. — John Irving, *The Hotel New Hampshire*, p. 199, 1981

death spiral *noun*
a downward spiral of an airplane from which recovery is nearly impossible and as a result of which impact with the ground is inevitable *US, 1990*
- The two, in the course of the fight, found themselves in what some call "the death spiral." — Robert K. Wilcox, *Scream of Eagles*, p. 157, 1990

death trip *noun*
1 LSD enhanced with botanical drugs from plants such as Deadly Nightshade or Jimsonweed *US, 1970*
- — William D. Alsever, *Glossary for the Establishment and Other Uptight People*, p. 3, December 1970
2 a fascination with death *US, 1969*
- The herding tribes gradually overran the feminist states, replacing the Great Mother with God the Father, substituting the Christian death trip for the pagan glorification of life. — Tom Robbins, *Even Cowgirls Get the Blues*, p. 331, 1976

death wish *noun*
phencyclidine, the recreational drug known as PCP or angel dust *US, 1986*
- — Richard A. Spears, *The Slang and Jargon of Drugs and Drink*, p. 138, 1986

deazingus *noun*
a dingus, or eye dropper used in drug injecting *US, 1973*
- Deazingus taken from a carnival grifter's usage and an example of cezarney, an argot based on phonetic distortion. — David Maurer and Victor Vogel, *Narcotics and Narcotic Addiction*, p. 402, 1973

deb *noun*
1 a debutante *US, 1920*
- [A]ll the debs and dowagers let their hair down and danced[.] — Charles Raven, *Underworld Nights*, p. 102, 1956
- You'll meet her. She's one of the debs I invited over. — Dan Jenkins, *Life Its Ownself*, p. 127, 1984
2 a girl associated with a youth gang, either directly as a member or through a boyfriend *US, 1946*
A lovely if ironic borrowing from "debutante."
- The Debs and Sub-Debs are usually from 50 to 500 feet behind the warriors. — Jack Lait and Lee Mortimer, *New York Confidential*, p. 106, 1948
- Why isn't she like the rest of the debs in the gang, or any other girl? — Hal Ellson, *Tomboy*, p. 2, 1950
- She's the head guy's deb. You stick your nose in there any more, the Mau Maus'll slice it off. — *Man's Magazine*, p. 12, February 1960
- Our debs sat on the stoops watching for the fuzz or for any wrong shit from the Jolly Rogers. — Piri Thomas, *Down These Mean Streets*, p. 52, 1967

deball *verb*
to castrate *US, 1961*
- I'll gut and deball the old bastard if he's touched you. — Keri Hulme, *The Bone People*, p. 137, 1983

debone *verb*
to bend a playing card so that it can be identified later in another player's hand *US, 1968*
- — Thomas L. Clark, *The Dictionary of Gambling and Gaming*, p. 60, 1987

debris *noun*
marijuana seeds and stems remaining after cleaning *US, 1971*
- — Eugene Landy, *The Underground Dictionary*, p. 64, 1971

debug *verb*
to clear an area of listening devices *US, 1964*
- "We were first on the scene and concluded that Rove had hired a company to debug his office and the same company had planted the bug[.]" — Lou Dubose, *Boy Genius*, p. 34, 2003

debut *verb*
1 to subject a boy to his first homosexual experience *UK, 1978*
- — Anon., *King Smut's Wet Dreams Interpreted*, 1978
2 to acknowledge your homosexuality *US, 1964*
- — Roger Blake, *The American Dictionary of Sexual Terms*, p. 55, 1964

decaf *adjective*
decaffeinated *US, 1981*
- She stopped all her caffeine sodas and only had one decaf soda a week. — Juliana van Olphen-Fehr, *Diary of a Midwife*, p. 150, 1998

decayed *adjective*
drunk *US, 1966*
- — *Current Slang*, p. 2, Fall 1966
- — Helen Dahlskog (Editor), *A Dictionary of Contemporary and Colloquial Usage*, p. 18, 1972

decent *adjective*
good, pleasing, excellent *US, 1979*
- — *Detroit Free Press*, 4th November 1979
- — Connie Eble (Editor), *UNC-CH Campus Slang*, p. 3, November 1990
- — Lee McNelis, *30 + And a Wake-Up*, p. 7, 1991

decision *verb*
to win a boxing match by a decision of the judges as opposed to with a knock-out *US, 1979*
- One of the boys from the old neighborhood was parkin' the cars on 60th Street (used to be a good pug, had decisioned Bethea in the Garden). — Edwin Torres, *After Hours*, p. 329, 1979

deck *noun*
1 a packet of a powdered drug *US, 1916*
- The stuff is usually paid for in advance, with the peddlers hoping they come through with enough decks to make money on it. — Mickey Spillane, *I, The Jury*, p. 23, 1947
- Once he was too feeble to leave the house and sent me out for a deck of junk. — Ethel Water, *His Eye is on the Sparrow*, p. 148, 1952

- Many addicts—especially pushers—wear a rubber band on their wrists (a dealer's band, some call it) which, if hooked properly around a deck of heroin, will send it flying if an approaching detective is spotted. — James Mills, *The Panic in Needle Park*, p. 15, 1966
- The man, identified as Reynaldo Colon, 33, of Ridgewood, Queens, approached the detective with a folding Leatherman, a metal-colored multipurpose tool, and said, "Give me the decks," using street slang to refer to the small glassine packages of heroin. — *New York Times*, p. B3, 21st October 2000

2 a skateboard *US, 1993*
- Lactameon wasn't even sure Steadhams like that were made anymore, and a seriously ridden deck was lucky to last half a year no matter how good[.] — Jess Mowry, *Six Out Seven*, p. 84, 1993

3 a pack of cigarettes *US, 1923*
- I sat there until a quarter to nine trying to smoke my way through a deck of Luckies. — Mickey Spillane, *One Lonely Night*, p. 103, 1951
- — *Newsweek*, p. 98, 8th October 1951

deck *verb*
to knock to the ground *US, 1945*
- Irrigated his face with the shot of J and B I'd just poured him. Then I tried to deck the sucker. — *48 Hours*, 1982
- [I]f people weren't performing they'd get decked. — Andy McNab, *Immediate Action*, p. 48, 1995
- Doesn't say a word, walks up and decks the guy and throws him out on the street. — Elmore Leonard, *Be Cool*, p. 183, 1999

deck ape *noun*
an enlisted sailor in the US Navy *US, 1944*
- Deck apes worked in whites, not dungarees. — Earl Thompson, *Tattoo*, p. 309, 1974
- Shelby said, "Look at all them lazy deck apes, smokin n' jokin'. Can't tell me anybody works in the navy. I shoulda been a swab." — Joseph Wambaugh, *Finnegan's Week*, p. 39, 1993

decked *adjective*
dressed stylishly *US, 1972*
- — David Claerbaut, *Black Jargon in White America*, p. 62, 1972

deck monkey *noun*
a deckhand *US, 1941*
- [T]wo other "deck monkeys" besides himself, who would grind the winches and provide ballast. — Mark L. Friedman, *Everyday Crisis Management*, p. 101, 2002

deck up *verb*
to package a powdered drug for sale *US, 1964*
- We could deck up two-three hundred in an evening's time. It all depends on how much you got and how fast you deck up. — Jeremy Larner and Ralph Tefferteller, *The Addict in the Street*, p. 207, 1964
- — Eugene Landy, *The Underground Dictionary*, p. 64, 1971

declare *verb*
▶ **declare a gang**
(used of warring youth gangs) to agree to discuss a truce *US, 1953*
- — Dale Kramer and Madeline Karr, *Teen-Age Gangs*, p. 174, 1953

decomp room *noun*
the room in a morgue housing decomposed bodies *US, 1983*
- There were bunches of bodies in the "decomp" room, decomposed bodies, lying putrid under ceiling fans[.] — Joseph Wambaugh, *The Delta Star*, p. 42, 1983
- She gagged as she passed the decomp room, where decomposing bodies lay under plastic sheets, waiting for autopsies. — Stephen Cannell, *King Con*, p. 62, 1992

decorate *verb*
to pay for something at a restaurant or bar *US, 1908*
Most commonly in the phrase "decorate the mahogany" for buying drinks at a bar.
- Decorating the booths in the ice-cream parlor. — Dick Clark, *To Goof or Not to Goof*, p. 103, 1963

decoy *noun*
an undercover police officer whose appearance leads criminals to assume the officer is a promising victim *US, 1981*
- We go in teams in a hot street-crime area, inner city. Dress like you live around there. One guy's the decoy, the target. — Elmore Leonard, *Split Images*, p. 23, 1981

dedo *noun*
an informant *US, 1995*
From the Spanish for "finger," used by English speakers in the American southwest.
- — Bill Valentine, *Gang Intelligence Manual*, p. 41, 1995: "Hispanic gang terminology"

dedud *verb*
to clear unexploded artillery shells from a practice range *US, 1968*
- — Carl Fleischhauer, *A Glossary of Army Slang*, p. 14, 1968

deeda *noun*
LSD *US, 1967*
Possibly New York slang.
- John Williams, *The Drug Scene*, p. 111, 1967

deemer *noun*
a ten-cent piece *US, 1926*
From the colloquial "dime."
- "If I stepped out on that street and played chump Santa Claus to my last deemer, that would be Blue's happiness, not yours." — Iceberg Slim (Robert Beck), *Trick Baby*, p. 12, 1969

deep *adjective*
1 numerous *US, 1991*
- "Crips, man—deep!" — Leon Bing, *Do or Die*, p. 36, 1991

2 filled with the specified number of referential objects *US, 1973*
For example, "four deep" would mean "four people in a car."
- — Malachi Andrews and Paul T. Owens, *Black Language*, p. 86, 1973

3 serious, intense *US, 1990*
- Damn, Furious is deep, he used to be a preacher or something? — *Boyz N The Hood*, 1990

deep-dick *verb*
(from the male perspective) to have sex *US, 2005*
- He and Boz methodically deep-dick the willing starlets. — Editors of Adult Video News, *The AVN Guide to the 500 Greatest Adult Films of All Time*, p. 47, 2005
- The African-American porn star does his part to end simmering Mexican-black tensions by deep-dicking Mexican gals in all three inputs as they moan in English and espanol. — Gustavo Arellano, *Ask a Mexican*, p. 80, 2007

deep-dicking *noun*
(from the male point of view) sex *US, 1997*
- Can I at least tell people that all you needed was some serious deep-dicking? — *Chasing Amy*, 1997
- After I turned him down, Edd was his next target for a bit of deep dicking. — Benjamin Evans, *Tales From The Kerb*, p. 135, 2006

deep freeze *noun*
solitary confinement *US, 1958*
- And in a couple of hours form now he wouldn't have a job, even if the cops didn't grab him and toss him into the deep freeze. — Raymond Chandler, *Playback*, p. 72, 1958
- — Inez Cardozo-Freeman, *The Joint*, p. 492, 1984

deep kimchi *noun*
serious trouble *US, 1998*
Based on the unflattering comparison of the Korean pickled delicacy with excrement.
- — *Seattle Times*, p. A9, 12th April 1998: "Grunts, squids not grunting from the same dictionary"

deep magic *noun*
in computing, an understanding of a technique in a program or system not known by the average programer *US, 1991*
- Compiler optimization techniques and many aspects of OS design used to be deep magic; many techniques in cryptography, signal processing, graphics, and AI still are. — Eric S. Raymond, *The New Hacker's Dictionary*, p. 122, 1991

deep-pocket *adjective*
(used of a defendant in civil litigation) wealthy, possessing considerable financial reserves *US, 1976*
- If the latter is ever spotted, do not attempt to feed ordinary lawyer bait: i.e., greenbacks, cocaine, hookers, deep-pocket defendants, adolescent boys. — Joseph Wambaugh, *Fugitive Nights*, p. 93, 1992

deep sea fishing *noun*
exploratory surgery *US, 1994*
- — Sally Williams, *"Strong" Words*, p. 138, 1994

deep serious *adjective*
extremely critical, as bad as it gets *US, 1985*
Vietnam war coinage and usage.
- Armed helicopters were especially reassuring to the "crunchies," the ground infantrymen who depended on them to deliver accurate supporting fire whether conducting raids or in "deep serious" trouble trying to disengage. — Shelby L. Stanton, *The Rise and Fall of an American Army*, p. 86, 1985

deep shaft *noun*
strong, illegally manufactured whiskey *US, 1999*
- It is called corn liquor, white lightning, sugar whisky, skully cracker, popskull, bush whiskey, stump, stumphole, 'splo, ruckus juice, radiator whiskey, rotgut, sugarhead, block and tackle, wildcat, panther's breath, tiger's sweat, sweet spirits of cats a-fighting, alley bourbon, city gin, cool water, happy Sally, deep shaft, jump steady, old horsey, stingo, blue John, red eye, pine top, buckeye bark whisky and see seven stars. — *Star Tribune (Minneapolis)*, p. 19F, 31st January 1999

deep six *verb*
to discard; to reject *US, 1952*
- We pulled over to the side of the road, and like a couple of Mafiosi getting rid of the guy who betrayed the family honor, we deep-sixed him into the ditch. — Rita Ciresi, *Pink Slip*, p. 32, 1999

deep throat *noun*
oral sex performed on a man in which the person doing the performing takes the penis completely into their mouth and throat *US, 1972*
A term from the so-named 1972 classic pornography film.
- "Would you like to try deep throat?" — D.M. Perkins, *Deep Throat*, p. 46, 1973
- She was beaten on an almost daily basis, humiliated, threatened, including with guns, kept captive and sleep-deprived, and forced to do sex acts ranging from "deep throat" oral sex to intercourse and sodomy. — Andrea Dworkin, *Mercy*, p. 344, 1991
- On Saturday night a game of deep throat was being played. The Marines had drawn a line on the rhino's dildo and chanted, "Beat the line, beat the line," as a woman would simulate performing oral sex. — Gregory L. Vistica, *Fall from Glory*, p. 328, 1997
- Once you've mastered the basic techniques of fellatio and cunnilingus, you might want to experiment with "69," deep throat and other oral tricks for adventurous lovers! — Siobhan Kelly, *The Wild Guide to Sex and Loving*, p. 64, 2002

deep throat *verb*
to take a man's penis completely into the mouth and throat *US, 1991*
- [S]tudents expecting to see "Kermit's Wild West Adventure" were instead exposed to a mattress-level montage of Latin porn star Pina Kolada deepthroating a semi-pro soccer team. — Carl Hiaasen, *Native Tongue*, p. 47, 1991
- I know he is ready to shoot his thick creamy come down my throat, as I deep-throat him. — Nancy Friday, *Women on Top*, p. 81, 1991
- You may have to deep-throat wing a "69" position in order for his and your angles to match up. — Craig Nelson, *Finding True Love in a Man-Eat-Man World*, p. 82, 1996
- So if you're giving him head, you've got to deep throat it so you can touch that part. — Anthony Petkovich, *The X Factory*, p. 86, 1997

deep-water Baptist; deep-dip Baptsit *noun*
a member of a Baptist sect that practises full-immersion baptism *US, 1949*
- "Lives like a deep-dip Baptist. Can't be touched." — Stephen Longstreet, *The Flesh Peddlers*, p. 85, 1962
- I came to, under a steaming pile of trash / In the narrow alley-way / Behind that old Deep Water Baptist mission. — Paul Muldoon, *Immram*, p. 98, 1977

dee wee *noun*
driving while intoxicated *US, 1995*
- Dee Wee: Phonetic for DWI (Driving While Intoxicated). — Samuel Katz, *NYPD*, 1995

deez-nuts *pronoun*
me *BERMUDA, 1985*

The reference to "these nuts" is an intimate, if crude, reference to yourself.
- — Rick Ayers (Editor), *Berkeley High Slang Dictionary*, p. 18, 2004

def *adjective*
excellent, superlative *US, 1979*
- — Connie Eble (Editor), *UNC-CH Campus Slang*, p. 2, Fall 1987
- — Ellen C. Bellone (Editor), *Dictionary of Slang*, p. 9, 1989
- — Terry Williams, *The Cocaine Kids*, p. 136, 1989
- [E]ven "stoopid fresh," which could also be "def" when it wasn't "dope." — Nelson George, *Hip Hop America*, p. 209, 1998

def *adverb*
definitely *US, 1942*
- [Jim] Morrison, def, does not get a pie in the face! He 'fessed up! — Lester Bangs, *Psychotic Reactions and Carburetor Dung*, p. 36, 1970
- — Connie Eble (Editor), *UNC-CH Campus Slang*, p. 2, Fall 1996

definite *adjective*
used as a meaningless embellishment *US, 1985*
- "Definite"—all-purpose Rat Pack prefix, as in "I'll hail a definite cab." — *Washington Post*, p. B1, 17th January 1985

degennie *noun*
a degenerate gambler *US, 1974*
- Of course, you can get degennies who would like to stay in action right up until midnight by betting Sunday night hockey games[.] — Gary Mayer, *Bookie*, p. 6, 1974

dehorn *noun*
1 denatured alcohol (ethyl alcohol to which a poisonous substance has been added to make it unfit for consumption) *US, 1926*
- [H]e lived on dehorn alcohol, mulligan, dayolds, misery[.] — John Clellon Holmes, *The Horn*, p. 159, 1958
2 a person who is addicted to denatured alcohol (ethyl alcohol to which a poisonous substance has been added to make it unfit for consumption) *US, 1926*
- The Jolity Theater is a crummy burlesque house on Minneapolis's skid row. It is patronized largely by vagrants, winos, dehorns, grifters, and other such unsanitary persons. — Max Shulman, *The Many Loves of Dobie Gillis*, p. 203, 1951

dehorn *verb*
to have sex after a long period of celibacy *US, 1972*
- — Helen Dahlskog (Editor), *A Dictionary of Contemporary and Colloquial Usage*, p. 18, 1972

dehose *verb*
to return a computer that is suspended in an operation to functioning *US, 1991*
- — Eric S. Raymond, *The New Hacker's Dictionary*, p. 122, 1991

deja fuck *noun*
the unsettling sensation that the person with whom you are now having sex is a former sexual partner *US, 2002*
- — Amy Sohn, *Sex and the City*, p. 154, 2002

deja vu all over again *noun*
the same thing, once again, repeated *US, 1995*
An assault on the language attributed to baseball great Yogi Berra.
- "It's deja vu all over again," as Yogi Berra probably didn't say. We are out to get a new baseball stadium, according to the gazettes. — *The Seattle Times*, p. B1, 30th May 1995
- When his teammates Mickey Mantle and Roger Maris slugged back-to-back home runs for what he described as "the umpteenth time," he [Berra] grunted, "It's deja vu all over again." — *New York Times*, pp. 13–1, 8th August 1999
- Bush Plan: Deja Vu All Over Again — *Washington Post*, 17th May 2001

deke *noun*
a decoy *US, 1950*
- We found an unoccupied blind, put out our "dekes" and sat down to await developments. — *San Francisco News*, p. 12, 16th December 1950

Delhi belly *noun*
diarrhea suffered by tourists *US, 1944*
- Anyone suffering from art-gallery gout, Delhi belly, jaded eyeballs or other ills of the traveler on the high road, is hereby advised to relax while suffering. — *Washington Post, Times Herald*, p. F17, 24th July 1955

- When it comes to where you can get Delhi Belly, Tut's Trot, or Montezuma's revenge, there are no surprises here. — Robert Young Pelton, *The World's Most Dangerous Places*, p. 15, 2003

delicatessen book noun
a betting operation where the odds are constantly cut *US, 1947*
- — Dan Parker, *The ABC of Horse Racing*, p. 145, 1947

delish; deelish adjective
delicious *UK, 1920*
- I took her first to dinner. "Gee, that was a delish dinner," she said as we left the restaurant. — Max Shulman, *The Many Loves of Dobie Gillis*, p. 43, 1951
- "No, tell me how you like it with my hair over one eye!" "De-lish!" she exclaimed. — Eve Babitz, *L.A. Woman*, p. 119, 1982
- — Judi Sanders, *Da Bomb*, p. 5, 1997

delivery boy noun
in poker, any young, inexperienced, unskilled player *US, 1996*
- — John Vorhaus, *The Big Book of Poker Slang*, p. 13, 1996

delivery order noun
a request that a certain type of car be stolen and sold to the requesting party *US, 1983*
- [A] brand-new Corvette he could get five grand for easy, even without a delivery order. — Elmore Leonard, *Stick*, p. 67, 1983

delosis noun
a pretty girl *US, 1953*
- — Lavada Durst, *The Jives of Dr. Hepcat*, p. 12, 1953

delta noun
a helicopter used for troop transport *US, 1967*
- The true transport model, which hauls seven to nine men into battle, is called "The Slick," technically "The Delta" or UF-1D. — Elaine Shepard, *The Doom Pussy*, p. 4, 1967

delts noun
the deltoid muscles *US, 1981*
- — *American Speech*, p. 199, Fall 1984: "The language of bodybuilding"
- "Lats and delts poking around inside a dress shirt in the Park with those binoculars." — Ethan Morden, *Some Men Are Lookers*, p. 318, 1997

delurk verb
to post a message on an Internet discussion group after previously observing without posting *US, 1995*
- — Christian Crumlish, *The Internet Dictionary*, p. 51, 1995

deluxe noun
in circus usage, a box seat *US, 1981*
- — Don Wilmeth, *The Language of American Popular Entertainment*, p. 72, 1981

Dem noun
a *Democrat* *US, 1875*
- When the Dems found out he knew Republicans, and vice versa, they began to use him as a channel to square things they didn't want to talk about directly to each other[.] — Jack Lait and Lee Mortimer, *Washington Confidential*, p. 161, 1951

demented adjective
in computing, not functional and not useful *US, 1983*
In computing, the condition resulting when two processes cannot proceed because each is waiting for another to do something.
- — Guy L. Steele et al., *The Hacker's Dictionary*, p. 55, 1983

demento noun
a deranged person *US, 1977*
- "I don't have a clue about you, old sport," he says. "You're just another New York demento, as far as I can tell." — Pete Hamill, *Forever*, p. 573, 2003

demi-god noun
a person recognized by the computing community as a major genius *US, 1991*
- To qualify as a genuine demigod, the person must recognizably identify with the hacker community and have helped shape it. — Eric S. Raymond, *The New Hacker's Dictionary*, p. 123, 1991

demmie; demmy noun
meperidine, an analgesic best known by its trademarked brand name Demerol™ *US, 1956*

- "We call them demmies. If you can't buy H or M, why, demmies will do the trick." — Jess Stearn, *Sisters of the Night*, p. 59, 1956

demo noun
1 a *demonstration model or recording* *US, 1963*
- You don't happen to have a tape or a demo that we might listen to? — *King of Comedy*, 1976
- I wanted the money to make a demo [demonstration record] and go into the record business. — Terry Williams, *The Cocaine Kids*, p. 89, 1989
- You guys are an unsigned band, and you broke into the radio station to get your demo tape played on the air? — *Airheads*, 1994
- Bobby Beck, the owner, used to let me come in and play drums on the demo kit. — *Empire Records*, 1995

2 a laboratory pipette used to smoke crack cocaine *US, 1992*
- — Terry Williams, *Crackhouse*, p. 152, 1992

demon adjective
excellent *US, 1983*
- — Tom Hibbert, *Rockspeak!*, p. 47, 1983
- — Connie Eble (Editor), *UNC-CH Campus Slang*, p. 4, Spring 1988

demoto noun
a person lacking motivation; a self-non-starter *US, 1993*
- — *Washington Post*, 14th October 1993

Denmark noun
▶ **go to Denmark**
to undergo a sex change operation *US, 1957*
Homosexual usage; an allusion to the sex-altering operation performed on Christine Jorgensen in Denmark.
- I'll makeya a real woman without goin' to Denmark. — Hubert Selby Jr., *Last Exit to Brooklyn*, p. 46, 1957
- — *The Guild Dictionary of Homosexual Terms*, p. 19, 1965
- — *Maledicta*, p. 53, 1986–1987: "A continuation of a glossary of ethnic slurs in American English"

den mother noun
an older, unofficial leader of a group of homosexual men *US, 1997*
- — Jim Crotty, *How to Talk American*, p. 138, 1997

dense adjective
exciting, fashionable, popular *US, 1961*
- That's Dense—that's cool. — Art Unger, *The Cool Book*, p. 106, 1961

dentist's friend noun
in circus and carnival usage, any sweet *US, 1981*
- — Don Wilmeth, *The Language of American Popular Entertainment*, p. 72, 1981

Denver mud noun
a patent medicine applied as a poultice *US, 1970*
- Strange things surfaced, like the taste of the Denver mud Mama applied to my chest when I had a cold. She heated the mud in the lid on the burner, then spread it on my chest. — Kay Allenbaugh, *Chocolate for a Woman's Soul*, p. 215, 1997

depart verb
in the language of fighter pilots, to accelerate through the plane's limits *US, 1990*
- If that failed, McKeown would deliberately "depart" the plane (take it outside its flight envelope) as a last resort maneuver. — Robert K. Wilcox, *Scream of Eagles*, p. 140, 1990

depeditate verb
in computing, to place text in a fashion that cuts off the feet of the letters *US, 1991*
- — Eric S. Raymond, *The New Hacker's Dictionary*, p. 124, 1991

depth charge noun
a shot of whiskey served in a glass of beer *US, 1956*
- [A] "Coalminer's Breakfast," or "Depth Charge" (when a shot of whiskey is dropped into a glass of beer.) — Roger E. Axtell, *The Do's and Taboos of Hosting International Visitors*, p. 76, 1990

depth charging noun
a system of playing blackjack based not on a count of the value of cards played but on the depth of the deck dealt *US, 1991*
- — Michael Dalton, *Blackjack*, p. 42, 1991

deputy do-right *noun*
a police officer *US, 1980*
- — Edith A. Folb, *runnin' down some lines*, p. 234, 1980

derby *noun*
oral sex *US, 1969*
- Today the single most requested service is fellatio ("French" or "derby"). — Charles Winick, *The Lively Commerce*, p. 207, 1971
- — Kenn "Naz" Young, *Naz's Underground Dictionary*, p. 24, 1973

derel *noun*
a person lacking in basic intelligence *US, 1991*
An abbreviation of the conventional "derelict."
- — Trevor Cralle, *The Surfin'ary*, p. 29, 1991

DEROS; deros *verb*
to return to the US from combat duty in Vietnam *US, 1968*
From the abbreviation for the "*d*ate of *e*stimated *r*eturn from *o*verseas."
- Few of us had had the opportunity to say good-bye to each other when we DEROS'd or ETS'd. — Gary Linderer, *The Eyes of the Eagle*, p. 5, 1991
- The reduction hadn't worked, but he would DEROS Vietnam and ETS the army at the same time. — Ches Schneider, *From Classrooms to Claymores*, p. 149, 1999

'ders *noun*
oral sex *US, 1982*
An abbreviation of "headers," itself an embellishment of HEAD.
- It was a way cranking party, but I was sooo embarrassed, like I walk into the bedroom and Tricia's totally giving Sean ders! — Mary Corey and Victoria Westermark, *Fer Shurr! How to be a Valley Girl*, 1982

desert cherry *noun*
a soldier newly arrived to Kuwait or Saudi Arabia during the first Gulf war *US, 1991*
- "Desert cherries" in "Kevlars" fly the "Sand Box Express" to the "beach" and soon are complaining about "Meals Rejected by Ethiopians" if they can't find a "roach coach" run by "Bedouin Bob." — *Houston Chronicle*, p. 15, 24th January 1991

desert rat *noun*
any longtime resident of any desert area, especially, in modern usage, Las Vegas, Nevada *US, 1907*
- These confirmed desert dwellers are called "desert rats" and they wouldn't give up their carefree life in the sun for anything. — *San Francisco Examiner*, p. 1, 22nd March 1964
- In the early days of Vegas an old desert rat collapsed outside a small-town casino. — Mario Puzo, *Inside Las Vegas*, p. 327, 1977
- — *Maledicta*, p. 156, Summer/Winter 1978: "How to hate thy neighbor: a guide to racist maledicta"

designer *adjective*
(used of pornography) relatively high-brow, designed for couples and first-time viewers *US, 2000*
- — Ana Loria, *1 2 3 Be A Porn Star!*, p. 165, 2000: "Glossary of adult sex industry terms"

designer drug *noun*
a recreational drug synthesized to mimic the effects of an illegal drug *US, 1985*
- Sales of the "designer drug" called Ecstasy are booming at nightclubs in Dallas[.] — *Washington Post*, p. A10, 29th June 1985
- Designer drugs are drugs made underground, often in home based labs. The chemists making these drugs modify the molecular structure of certain types of illegal drugs to produce analogs. These analogs are what are termed "designer drugs." — Gary L. Somdahl, *Drugs and Kids*, p. 94, 1996

desk commando *noun*
a military support worker who does not face combat *UK, 1958*
- That's putting a desk commando in his place. — Paul Good, *Once to Every Man*, p. 164, 1970

desk cowboy *noun*
a military or police support worker who does not face combat or street duty *US, 1942*
- If you were an experienced investigator who'd handled a few of these before, that would be one thing. But you're a desk cowboy, okay? — Boston Teran, *God Is a Bullet*, p. 47, 1999

desk jockey *noun*
an office worker *US, 1953*
- — *American Speech*, p. 228, October 1956: "More United States Air Force slang"

- As a congressional candidate in the late 1970s, he had emphasized his desk jockey job at the Pentagon as a whiz-kid planner in the nation's conversion to a peacetime economy. — Chris Matthews, *Hardball*, p. 126, 1988

desk pilot *noun*
a military or police support worker who does not face combat or street duty *US, 1955*
- A pair of polyester desk pilots who smelled like hair oil and made grade by jamming up other cops. — James Lee Burke, *Purple Cane Road*, p. 354, 2000

desk rider *noun*
a military support worker who does not face combat; an officious bureaucrat *US, 1966*
- He'd had enough of this fat, strutting little desk rider! What did he know about the job? — Barbara Nadel, *Belshazzar's Daughter*, p. 106, 1999

desmadre *noun*
a disaster *US, 1974*
Border Spanish used in English conversation by Mexican-Americans.
- — Dagoberto Fuentes and Jose Lopez, *Barrio Language Dictionary*, p. 54, 1974

desperado *noun*
a desperate gambler *US, 1961*
- — Ned Wallish, *The Truth Dictionary of Racing Slang*, p. 22, 1989

desperate *adjective*
very good *US, 1951*
Largely dependent on a melodramatic delivery to impart the slang sense.
- Oh what a desperately wonderful affair it's going to be—Harry James and a grand march and everybody goes formal. Isn't that desperate? — Max Shulman, *The Many Loves of Dobie Gillis*, p. 55, 1951

despizable *adjective*
worse than despicable *US, 1975*
- — John Gould, *Maine Lingo*, p. 72, 1975

dessert crack *noun*
nitrous oxide *US, 2002*
Small containers of nitrous oxide used in canned dessert topping are a prime source of the gas for young users.
- Whippits: Otherwise known as "hippie crack" or "dessert crack." Either way, it's the best high a thirteen-year-old can get. — Suroosh Alvi et al., *The Vice Guide*, p. 20, 2002

destructo *noun*
in surfing, a large and powerful wave *US, 1978*
- — Dennis Aaberg and John Milius, *Big Wednesday*, p. 209, 1978

detox *noun*
a facility where an alcoholic or drug addict can begin treatment with the detoxification process *US, 1973*
- They're not patients till they're admitted somewhere for treatment, or we sent them to detox. — Elmore Leonard, *Maximum Bob*, p. 20, 1991

Detroit iron *noun*
a large, American car *US, 1950*
- — Edd Byrnes, *Way Out with Kookie*, 1959
- — Chrysler Corporation, *Of Anchors, Bezels, Pots and Scorchers*, September 1959
- "Meanwhile, you prefer a bike to a Detroit iron?" — Irving Shulman, *College Confidential*, p. 84, 1960
- It's underpowered. Two seats. Detroit iron. Nice, but compare it with a Jaguar XJS, which is quieter, smoother, handles better, is faster, and costs twenty thousand dollars less. — John McPhee, *Irons in the Fire*, p. 182, 1997

deuce *noun*
1 two of anything, such as two marijuana cigarettes, two women, etc. *US, 1943*
- I drove straight home to stash my frame between a deuce of lily-whites. — Mezz Mezzrow, *Really the Blues*, p. 101, 1946
- It hopped off with a deuce of studs jiving some buds about how strong they were — Dan Burley, *Diggeth Thou?*, p. 15, 1959
2 a two-year prison sentence *US, 1925*
- Well, the faggot draws a deuce; and in the box he meets this cat who is some species of cheap hustler. — William Burroughs, *Naked Lunch*, p. 129, 1957

- He had served a bullet 'n a deuce. — Lightnin' Rod, *Hustlers Convention*, p. 10, 1973
- My man Colorado was doing a deuce, and he had a little click waiting for me when I got up there. — Edwin Torres, *Carlito's Way*, p. 46, 1975
- He pleaded guilty anyway, expecting a deuce maximum, back on the street in eighteen months tops. — James Ellroy, *Suicide Hill*, p. 579, 1986

3 two dollars *US, 1900*
- Zaida dug in her bag. "Here's a deuce for the cab." — Ross Russell, *The Sound*, p. 240, 1961
- You'll learn; sometimes you'll stand around all day and wait for a 15-buck score, a 10-buck score, even a deuce—all day[.] — John Rechy, *City of Night*, p. 43, 1963
- The turnstile attendant thinks it might help me if I went for a little walk (the cops watch him while other cops watch the cops) and then returned to him with a deuce in my hand. — James Simon Kunen, *The Strawberry Statement*, pp. 91–92, 1968

4 an act of defecation *US, 2003*
From the children's toilet vocabulary: **NUMBER TWO** (defecation).
- "I think she's in the back dropping a deuce." — *Howard Stern Radio Show*, 24 January 2003
- Topless Deb squats on the pot and drops a deuce while making goo-goo eyes at her boyfriend as he brushes his teeth. — Mr. Skin, *Mr. Skin's Skincyclopedia*, p. 172, 2005

5 in dice games, the point two *US, 1950*
- — *The Annals of the American Academy of Political and Social Sciences*, p. 123, May 1950

6 in pool, the two-ball *US, 1878*
- — Mike Shamos, *The Illustrated Encyclopedia of Billiards*, p. 76, 1993

7 two dollars' worth of drugs *US, 1992*
Originally a $2 package of heroin; with inflation other drugs became more likely to fit the bill.
- — Robert Nash, *Dictionary of Crime*, p. 101, 1992

8 two hundred *US, 1998*
- TED: Mary's a little chubby, huh? HEALY: I'd say about a deuce, deuce and half. Not bad. — *Something About Mary*, 1998

9 two hundred dollars *US, 1973*
- This thing's worth about a deuce. — Charles Whited, *Chiodo*, p. 48, 1973

10 twenty dollars *US, 1960*
- I stood repeating, "'Tis some strange midnight stud that's sounding a money beat on my pad's door. A deuce the morrow." — William "Lord" Buckley, *The Raven*, 1960

11 in television and movie-making, a 2000 watt spotlight *US, 1990*
- — Ralph S. Singleton, *Filmmaker's Dictionary*, p. 46, 1990

12 an arrest or conviction for driving under the influence of alcohol *US, 1971*
California Penal Code Section 502 prohibits driving under the influence of alcohol, hence the "two" reference.
- I don't wanna book a deuce right now. I wanna go get a hot pastrami. — Joseph Wambaugh, *The Secrets of Harry Bright*, p. 56, 1985
- — Judi Sanders, *Don't Dog by Do, Dude!*, p. 10, 1991

13 used as a substitute for "the devil" or "hell" *UK, 1694*
- I had the deuce of a time trying to find you. — Horace McCoy, *Kiss Tomorrow Good-bye*, p. 324, 1948
- I walked on down the street and turned into the subway kiosk wondering what the deuce had happened to Washington. — Mickey Spillane, *Kiss Me Deadly*, p. 45, 1952

14 the Delta Dagger fighter aircraft *US, 1970*
- The first USAF aircraft armed only with guided missiles and unguided rockets—the Convair YF-102 Delta Dagger, always called "the Deuce"—made its first flight on 24th October 1953. — James P. McCarthy, *The Air Froce*, p. 81, 2002

▶ **chunk the deuce**
to flash a two-finger peace sign *US, 2006*
- The rest of the Clique chunked the deuce and jumped in the El C. — Linden Dalecki, *Kid B*, p. 133, 2006

Deuce *nickname*
42nd Street, New York *US, 2002*
An abbreviation of **FORTY-DEUCE**.
- [C]oming out of its doors, you'd bump into the other Deuce grindhouses whether you went left, right, or crossed the street. — Bill Landis, *Sleazoid Express*, p. 47, 2002

deuce *verb*
to back down from a confrontation *US, 1950*
- You deuced. Admit it. You deuced. — Hal Ellson, *Tomboy*, p. 3, 1950

deuce-and-a-half *noun*
a two-and-a-half ton cargo truck *US, 1944*
Military usage since World War 2.
- "Fill up that deuce and a half," hollered the loadmaster[.] — Elaine Shepard, *The Doom Pussy*, p. 61, 1967
- A deuce-and-a-half was waiting beside the orderly room. — William Pelfrey, *The Big V*, p. 16, 1972
- The gas truck, a deuce-and-a-half with two fuel tanks on the back, marked "Mo-gas," had begun moving up the line, refueling. — Larry Heinemann, *Close Quarters*, p. 17, 1977
- Going in, there were sixty of us packed into a deuce-and-a-half[.] — Michael Herr, *Dispatches*, p. 72, 1977

deuce bag; deuce *noun*
a two dollar bag of heroin *US, 1971*
- — Richard A. Spears, *The Slang of Drugs and Drink*, 1986

deuceburger *noun*
a prison sentence of two years *US, 1990*
- — Charles Shafer, *Folk Speech in Texas Prisons*, p. 202, 1990

deuce-deal *verb*
to deal the second card in a deck *US, 1965*
- — Thomas L. Clark, *The Dictionary of Gambling and Gaming*, p. 61, 1987

deuce-deuce *noun*
1 a .22 caliber weapon *US, 1990*
- I got a Deuce Deuce. My brother gave it to me before he went inna county jail. — *Boyz N The Hood*, 1990
- He say how dem guinea gray cats go got him a deuce-deuce t'carry. — Stephen Cannell, *King Con*, p. 50, 1997
- Bolden broke into the Pony Express Sports Shop in North Hills and took about 25 guns—"nines," "deuce-deuces," and "deuce-fives," Dixon, also of North Hills testified[.] — *Daily News of Los Angeles*, p. N1, 27th April 2003

2 a 22-ounce beverage, especially beer *US, 2002*
- "When driving down 17th Street in Holland, it is not uncommon to see people on their porches drinking a deuce-deuce." — *Dictionary of New Terms (Hope College)*, 2002

deuce-five *noun*
a .25 caliber gun *US, 1991*
- Sidewinder's weapons in the crime were "a 'gauge and a deuce-five automatic." — Leon Bing, *Do or Die*, p. 47, 1991
- Bolden broke into the Pony Express Sports Shop in North Hills and took about 25 guns—"nines," "deuce-deuces," and "deuce-fives," Dixon, also of North Hills testified[.] — *Daily News of Los Angeles*, p. N1, 27th April 2003

deuce gear *noun*
a soldier's rucksack and other items carried in the field *US, 1987*
- "We ain't got enough deuce gear to go around yet, but be patient." — Craig Roberts, *Crosshairs on the Kill Zone*, p. 103, 2004

deuce of benders *noun*
the knees *US, 1947*
- — Marcus Hanna Boulware, *Jive and Slang of Students in Negro Colleges*, 1947

deuce out *verb*
to withdraw from a situation out of fear *US, 1949*
- Hell, I felt like I was getting to be chicken. Deucing out. — Hal Ellson, *Duke*, p. 17, 1949

deuces *noun*
1 dice that have been altered to have two twos, the second two being where one would expect to find a five *US, 1974*
Used in combination with **fives**, likely to produce a seven, an important number in craps.
- — John Scarne, *Scarne on Dice*, p. 466, 1974

2 a double line *US, 1990*
- — Charles Shafer, *Folk Speech in Texas Prisons*, p. 205, 1990

deuce up *verb*
to line up in pairs *US, 1990*
- — Charles Shafer, *Folk Speech in Texas Prisons*, p. 202, 1990

deuceway *noun*

an amount of marijuana costing two dollars *US, 1979*

- Yeah, they got stoned on giggle-weed, zonked on grifa, zapped on yerba, bombed on boo, they were blitzed with snop, warped on twist, gay on hay, free on V—deuceways, nicels, dimes, lids, pounds and kilos of it. — *Hi Life*, p. 14, 1979

devil *noun*

1 a barbiturate or other central nervous system depressant, especially Seconal™ *US, 1969*

A truncated form of **RED DEVIL**.

- I said, "If your sick father can part with at least two dozen devils, I'll part with half a C-note." — Iceberg Slim (Robert Beck), *Trick Baby*, p. 268, 1969

2 the hallucinogen STP *US, 1971*

- — Eugene Landy, *The Underground Dictionary*, p. 65, 1971

3 a white person *US, 1980*

- — Edith A. Folb, *runnin' down some lines*, p. 234, 1980

4 in craps, a seven *US, 1993*

- — Frank Scoblete, *Guerrilla Gamblin*, p. 305, 1993

devil-dog *noun*

a member of the US Marine Corps *US, 1918*

- He spotted the joker which would have wiped out the Marine Corps in the administration Defense reorganization measure and tied the bill up until the Devil Dogs were assured of being more than a mere "police force." — Jack Lait and Lee Mortimer, *Washington Confidential*, p. 162, 1951
- "Nothing," crowed The New York Times, "could stop our gallant Devil Dogs." That was not entirely true. — William Manchester, *Goodbye, Darkness*, p. 25, 1979

devilfish *noun*

in poker, a skilled player who plays poorly to mask his skill early in a game *US, 1996*

- — John Vorhaus, *The Big Book of Poker Slang*, p. 13, 1996

devil's bedpost *noun*

in a deck of playing cards, the four of clubs *UK, 1837*

- — Albert H. Morehead, *The Complete Guide to Winning Poker*, p. 261, 1967

devil's candy *noun*

cocaine *US, 1999*

- I hate cocaine. It's the Devil's candy. I just despise it. — James St. James, *Party Monster*, p. 271, 1999

devil's dancing rock *noun*

a large, smooth, flat stone found in a pasture or meadow *US, 1963*

- — Charles F. Haywood, *Yankee Dictionary*, p. 44, 1963

devil's dandruff *noun*

cocaine; crack cocaine *US, 1981*

A simile for an "evil white powder."

- Beware the devil's dandruff, he'd heard an actress warn. — Joseph Wambaugh, *The Glitter Dome*, p. 249, 1981
- — Mike Haskins, *Drugs*, p. 280, 2003
- [H]e "made love all night" after being introduced to the Devil's dandruff by a lap dancer. — *Q*, p. 32, October 2004

devil's dick *noun*

a crack cocaine pipe *US, 1992*

- — Terry Williams, *Crackhouse*, p. 148, 1992

devil's dust *noun*

phencyclidine, the recreational drug known as PCP or angel dust *US, 1992*

- — Jay Robert Nash, *Dictionary of Crime*, p. 101, 1992

devil's half acre *noun*

a neighborhood catering to vice *US, 1959*

- In a riverside neighborhood called the Devil's Half Acre, dozen of bars, bordellos, and gambling dens competed to empty the men's pockets. — Jamie Jensen, *Road Trip USA: New England*, p. 115, 2001

dew *noun*

marijuana; hashish *US, 1971*

- — Richard A. Spears, *The Slang and Jargon of Drugs and Drink*, p. 141, 1986
- It was the first and only time I ever smoked any dew with Linderer. He was so funny. — Larry Chambers, *Recondo*, p. 182, 1992

▸ **knock the dew off the lily; shake the dew off the lily**

(of a male) to urinate *US, 1974*

- "Think I'll shake a little dew off the lily then." He turned toward the door beyond the dance floor marked HIS. — Earl Thompson, *Tattoo*, p. 75, 1974
- — Pamela Munro, *U.C.L.A. Slang*, p. 54, 1989
- "While you're doing that," Elvin said, "I'm gonna go shake the dew off my lily." He got up and walked to the men's room, all the way in back. — Elmore Leonard, *Maximum Bob*, p. 201, 1991

dewbaby *noun*

a dark-skinned black male *US, 1972*

- — David Claerbaut, *Black Jargon in White America*, p. 62, 1972

Dewey *noun*

a socially inept social outcast *US, 1988*

- — Michael V. Anderson, *The Bad, Rad, Not to Forget Way Cool Beach and Surf Discriptionary*, p. 5, 1988

dex *noun*

1 Dexedrine™, a central nervous system stimulant *US, 1961*

- "Benny" and "dex" are fairly common in large groups because they combat fatigue[.] — William and Jerrye Breedlove, *Swap Clubs*, p. 151, 1964
- In my case, I was just on dex, and occasionally on Benzedrine. — John Warren Wells, *Tricks of the Trade*, p. 16, 1970
- He said there would be two or three doctors on hand with B1 shots and Dex and penicillin to handle various things like hang-overs, fatigue and the clap. — Dan Jenkins, *Semi-Tough*, p. 125, 1972
- I had a couple of tall-ones, a change of clothes, doubled-Dexed it, and hit the street. — Terry Southern, *Now Dig This*, p. 131, 2001

2 dextromethorphan (DXM), an active ingredient in non-prescription cold and cough medication, often abused for non-medicinal purposes *US, 2003*

- Youths' nicknames for DXM: Robo, Skittles, Triple C's, Rojo, Dex, Tussin, Vitamin D. DXM abuse is called "Robotripping" or "Tussing." Users might be called "syrup heads" or "robotards." — *USA Today*, p. 1A, 29th December 2003

dexie; dexi; dexo *noun*

Dexedrine™, a central nervous system stimulant *US, 1951*

- Two or three people can get high on one joint (marijuana cigarette). Of course, you can take bennies (Benzedrine) or dexies (Dexedrine), but they make me nervous. I'm a hog. I don't just take one. I take three or four. You can get hooked on them. — *Time*, p. 19, 7th July 1952
- "I feel miserable today. I'm really dragging." SECOND WOMAN: "Here, take one of these Dexies." — Lenny Bruce, *How to Talk Dirty and Influence People*, p. 46, 1965
- She had needed two Dexies to wake up. — Jacqueline Susann, *Valley of the Dolls*, p. 285, 1966
- Meditation, shit! Cocaine or maybe a dexi was more like it. — Odie Hawkins, *The Busting Out of an Ordinary Man*, p. 156, 1985

dexing *noun*

the recreational abuse of dextromethorphan *US, 1999*

- Anyhow, hopefully this answers your questions. happy DEXing! — *rec.drugs.psychedlic*, 16th November 1999
- Kids don't have to drink entire bottles of goopy cough syrup to go "Robotripping" or "Dexing." — *USA Today*, p. 1A, 29th December 2003
- DMX can produce a euphoric feeling that some teens call "robo-tripping," "skittling" or "dexing." — Carla Di Fonzo, *Intelligencer Journal (Lancaster, Pennsylvania)*, p. A1, 19th May 2007

dexter *noun*

a diligent, socially inept student *US, 1985*

- The strongest competition to squid and grimbo as successor term of nerd is dexter, a shortening of poindexter, probably based on a cartoon character. — *New York Times Magazine*, 22nd September 1985

DFFL

dope forever, forever loaded—a slogan of the Hell's Angels motorcycle gang that enjoyed somewhat wider popularity *US, 1966*

- Others, like the patch saying "DFFL" (Dope Forever, Forever Loaded) and the Playboy Rabbit (mocking birth control) were exposed by True magazine. — Hunter S. Thompson, *Hell's Angels*, p. 117, 1966
- I wear my DFFL patch below my right front pocket. — Frank Reynolds, *Freewheelin Frank*, p. 74, 1967

DFP *noun*

in pornography, a scene in a movie or a photography showing two men ejaculating on a woman's face; a *double facial pop US, 1995*

- — *Adult Video News*, p. 44, August 1995

DG *noun*
a degenerate *US, 2005*
- "D.G.?" "Degenerate. A loser who craves more of the same thing even when it's already wrecking his life." — Peter Fenton, *Eyeing the Flash*, p. 52, 2005

D girl *noun*
a low-level female employee in a movie or television studio *US, 1999*
The "D" stands for "development." Episode 20 (27th February 2000) in the second season of the HBO series "The Sopranos" was titled "D-Girl" and brought the term some brief fame.
- But every D-girl in Hollywood drove one of those roadsters[.] — John Ridley, *Everybody Smokes in Hell*, p. 33, 1999

dial *noun*
the face *US, 1842*
- I gave the rest of the watch the once over, but there were no signs of scrapping on any other dial[.] — Robert S. Close, *Love Me Sailor*, p. 108, 1945
- [His] days as the shining light of the Ghost Squad were now over, his dial having become as familiar to the entire underworld of London as Big Ben's. — Charles Raven, *Underworld Nights*, p. 99, 1956

DIAL *adjective*
dumb *in any* language *US, 1994*
Said of truly incommunicative hospital patients.
- — Sally Williams, *"Strong" Words (Dissertation)*, p. 139, 1994

dialer *noun*
a telephone that when called automatically calls another telephone number *US, 1976*
- The line was used as an inexpensive alarm system, known as a "dialer." — Emmett Grogan, *Final Score*, p. 86, 1976

dial in on *verb*
to understand what motivates someone else; to grasp their personality *US, 1997*
- — Vann Wesson, *Generation X Field Guide and Lexicon*, p. 52, 1997

dial out *verb*
to ignore *US, 1967*
- Then I dialed him out because he seemed to advocate everything that had been said by his cohorts, and I could look in his face and tell he was afraid. — Clarence Cooper Jr., *The Farm*, p. 166, 1967

dialtone *noun*
a personality-free person *US, 1990*
- She knew Sunny Deelight, a real dialtone. — Seth Morgan, *Homeboy*, p. 296, 1990

diamond *noun*
a custom diamond-shaped car window *US, 1980*
- — Edith A. Folb, *runnin' down some lines*, p. 234, 1980
- Diamonds in the back, sunroof top/ diggin the scene with the gangster lean. — Massive Attack, *Be Thankful for What You've Got*, 1991

diamond cutter *noun*
the erect penis *US, 1975*
- During his one month convalescence Rosco was unable to raise what Harold Bloomguard called a "diamond cutter" or even a "blue veiner" due to the shooting pains in his groin. — Joseph Wambaugh, *The Choirboys*, p. 45, 1975
- Plus, in his glue-dazed condition, Chub found himself wielding something less than a world-class, diamond-cutter erection. — Carl Hiaasen, *Lucky You*, p. 368, 1997

diamonds *noun*
the testicles *US, 1964*
An evolution from the common **FAMILY JEWELS**.
- — Roger Blake, *The American Dictionary of Sexual Terms*, p. 57, 1964

diamond season *noun*
warm weather *US, 1987*
- — Carsten Stroud, *Close Pursuit*, p. 271, 1987

diamond white *noun*
a white Cadillac *US, 1998*
- — Ethan Hilderbrant, *Prison Slang*, p. 36, 1998

diaper *noun*
a sanitary napkin *US, 1980*
- — Edith A. Folb, *runnin' down some lines*, p. 234, 1980

diaper dandy *noun*
an athlete in his first year of college *US, 1993*
Coined or popularized by sports announcer Dick Vitale.
- "Dale Brown, you got a Diaper Dandy, baby! Welcome to LUS, Shaquille O'Neal." — Shaquille O'Neal, *Shaq Talks Back*, p. 33, 2002
- "You're a diaper dandy. You haven't earned the right. The front row is for veterans." — Dick Vitale, *Dick Vitale's Living a Dream*, p. 18, 2006

diaper sniper *noun*
a child molester *US, 2000*
- Cain is a diaper sniper. Boycott the WWF! — *rec.sport.pro-wrestling*, 17th March 2000
- chester: Child molestor. Also known as short eyes, diaper sniper. — Jeffrey Ian Ross, *Behind Bars*, 2002

dibbler *noun*
the penis *US, 1998*
- The attraction of my hand, my fingers at her clitoris, only distracts from her skill on my dibbler. — Clarence Major, *All-Night Visitors*, p. 6, 1998

dibs *noun*
1 first right to, first claim on *US, 1932*
Among the earliest slang a child in the US learns; derives from "dib" (a portion or a share) which was first recorded in the UK in 1889.
- The black market, meaning the dope fiends who slept in our kitchen in the winter, offered us dibs on what they stole. — Odie Hawkins, *Scars and Memories*, p. 147, 1987
- But now, you understand, Homicide will have a priority, first dibs. — Elmore Leonard, *Freaky Deaky*, p. 175, 1988
- "Vijay has his dibs in on them." "But, Frank, that's not fair!" I complained. "I know, Nick. But those are the rules. Dibs is dibs. You know that." — C.D. Payne, *Youth in Revolt*, p. 284, 1993
- RANDAL: That's the movie I came for. V.A. CUSTOMER: I have first dibs. RANDAL: Says who? V.A. CUSTOMER: Says me. I've been here for half an hour. I'd call that first dibs. — *Clerks*, p. 35, 1994
- "Dibs on that bitch," I avow. "Good luck," Dylan says. — Marty Beckerman, *Death to All Cheerleaders*, p. 13, 2000
2 a living *US, 1949*
- What do you shake them for? How do you make your dibs? — Raymond Chandler, *The Little Sister*, p. 28, 1949

dibs and dabs *noun*
small amounts *US, 1960*
- To have small dibs and dabs of time at his disposal will not be sufficient even if the total is an impressive number of hours. — Peter F. Drucker, *The Effective Executive*, p. 28, 2007

dice *noun*
Desoxyn™, a branded methamphetamine hydrochloride *US, 1977*
- — Walter L. Way, *The Drug Scene*, p. 108, 1977

dice bite *noun*
a wound on the hand of a gambler in casino craps when struck by tossed dice *US, 1983*
- The stickman shouts, "there's no cure for dice bite," as a signal for the players to keep their hands up when the dice are coming out. — Thomas L. Clark, *The Dictionary of Gambling and Gaming*, p. 62, 1987

dice mob *noun*
a group of two or more cheats in a dice game *US, 1961*
- The dice not only appeared to be constructed in two pieces, they actually were constructed in two pieces. Apparently, a dice mob had switched a batch of dice. — Jacques Noire, *Casino Holiday*, p. 166, 1968

dicer *noun*
a hat *US, 1887*
- — Lou Shelly, *Hepcats Jive Dictionary*, p. 9, 1945
- — Joseph E. Ragen and Charles Finston, *Inside the World's Toughest Prison*, p. 796, 1962: "Penitentiary and underworld glossary"

dick *noun*
1 the penis *US, 1888*
- Sometimes, though, I'd go home afterwards, after having had a hard-on for four hours of making out on the floor and in the bleachers, but without creaming, and it really gave you a sore dick. — *The Berkeley Tribe*, p. 13, 5th-12th September 1969
- The kid had a dick like a horse and could screw all night. — Dennis Havens, *Autopsy on a Living Corpse*, p. 90, 2000

- The guy with the huge dick hardly spoke any English. — Rich Merritt, *Secrets of a Gay Marine Porn Star*, p. 227, 2005
- Het let up momentarily then tried to force his dick into her ass once again. This time she felt pain and screamed out loud, "Jeremy, that's the wrong hole." — Renay Jackson, *Crack City*, p. 176, 2005

2 the clitoris *US, 1964*

- She had a dick so long she had to be circumcised. — Bruce Jackson, *Get Your Ass in the Water and Swim Like Me*, p. 148, 1964

3 a man *US, 1914*

- Hunter would remind Maureen she was a girl. Or Hunter would tell her she was just one of the dicks. — Elmore Leonard, *City Primeval*, p. 33, 1980

4 sex with a man *US, 1956*

- [H]ow could you beat two hundred dollars a night just to be there listening and now and then give up a little dick? — Alix Shulman, *On the Stroll*, p. 55, 1981
- I bet she hasn't had any dick in years and years. Judging from the type of woman she was and her age. Old women don't get a lot of dick. — Elmore Leonard, *Glitz*, p. 320, 1983
- Women are tricky. You ask a woman how many men she's fucked, and she'll tell you how many boy friends she's had instead. A woman doesn't count all the miscellaneous dick. — Chris Rock, *Rock This!*, p. 130, 1997
- Cause even if he did decide to play his self and slip on of these bitches a little dick, they ain't me. — K'Wan Foye, *Sweet Dreams*, p. 154, 2004

5 a police officer, especially a detective; a private detective *US, 1886*

- "I know you don't believe that"—he laughed shortly—"and I guess you don't like dicks. But we aren't bad guys." — Irving Shulman, *The Amboy Dukes*, p. 105, 1947
- The dicks gave her the bum's rush too. — Jack Lait and Lee Mortimer, *New York Confidential*, p. 163, 1948
- I was cooking up some stuff, bending over and this dick kicked me dead up the can. — Hal Ellson, *The Golden Spike*, p. 152, 1952
- The thought that hit my mind was that this guy was trying to get him some bread other than his dick's pay[.] — A.S. Jackson, *Gentleman Pimp*, p. 103, 1973

6 a despicable person *US, 1966*

- Don't be a dick. That stuff'll kill her. — *Heathers*, 1988
- Now, they got him dressed like a dick. He's wearing these stupid-lookin' pants, this horrible sweater. — *True Romance*, 1993
- I thought the executive producer was a total dick, and I got fired from it in the middle of the LA riots. — Drew Carey, *Dirty Jokes and Beer*, p. 31, 2000
- Republican politicians are shameless dicks. — Al Franken, *The Truth With Jokes*, p. 58, 2005

7 a fool *UK, 1553*

- "Stop being such a dick." "Well, young man, you just bought yourself a suspension." — Mark Sullivan, *Jonah Sees Ghosts*, p. 162, 2003

8 nothing, zero *UK, 1925*

- "I didn't do dick and I don't know dick. And you did way less than dick." — Jonathan Kellerman, *The Murder Book*, p. 43, 1991
- He steals from you, you don't do dick. — *Empire Records*, 1995

▸ **get your dick tender**
to have an emotional need to be with a woman at all times *US, 1972*

- I knew that as soon as she became conscious of the fact that I had weakened in that respect, as soon as I had what they call "got my dick tender"—that means you've got to be with a woman all the time—they figure they're out working and you're out chipping someplace. — Bruce Jackson, *In the Life*, p. 179, 1972

▸ **put dick**
(from the male point of view) to have sex *US, 1973*

- Damn but you know how to put dick to a bitch. — A.S. Jackson, *Gentleman Pimp*, p. 72, 1973

dick *verb*

1 to exploit; to take advantage of; to harm *US, 1964*
In the 1968 US presidential election, the bumper sticker "Dick Nixon Before Nixon Dicks You" raised eyebrows.

- I got them on one side, I got La Cosa Nostra on the other, I got more people trying to dick me than if I turned tricks for a living. — Elmore Leonard, *Glitz*, p. 289, 1985
- Compared to other law firms, Kipper Garth's had the overhead problem dicked. — Carl Hiaasen, *Skin Tight*, p. 89, 1989

- Time to play let's dick the old guys, huh, Harp? — *Point Break*, 1991
- The club owner is trying to dick me out of some money. — *Wayne's World*, 1992
- I know not to dick with him when it comes to matters PC. — Armistead Maupin, *Maybe the Moon*, p. 163, 1992

2 (from the male point of view) to have sex with *US, 1942*

- I dicked her here in Pussycat where the coffin sets. — Pietro Di Donato, *Naked Author*, p. 294, 1970
- He said, "Did I ask him, you want to know, if he's dicking her? No, I didn't." — Elmore Leonard, *Split Images*, p. 16, 1981
- Shark, a newcomer to dicking onstage, comes from Cuba, perhaps a gift from Castro's boat-people exchange. — Josh Alan Friedman, *Tales of Times Square*, p. 189, 1986
- Beat her in the day and dicked her little hole at night. — David Shorey, *Flares and Other Motor Episodes*, p. 240, 2001

dick around *verb*

1 to behave in a sexually promiscuous fashion *US, 1969*

- Wives were fools who let their husbands dick around. — Danya Rubbenberg, *Yentl's Revenge*, p. 3, 2001

2 to pass time idly *US, 1947*

- "Aw, I'm just dicking around until I head down to South America." — Nicholas Kolya, *You Never Ate Lunch in This Town to Begin With*, p. 153, 2002

dickbrain *noun*

a fool *US, 1971*

- "Think real hard, dick brain," the Punk responded derisively. — Scott Sommer, *Hazzard's Head*, p. 52, 1985
- Good place, dickbrain. Who would ever think to look there? — Stephen J. Cannell, *The Tin Collectors*, p. 6, 2001

dick-breath *noun*

used as a term of abuse *US, 1972*

- "Make her bark, dick-breath." "Who are you calling dick-breath?" "You, you dog-stealing fuck." — Daniel Lyons, *Dog Days*, p. 177, 1998
- "We're on the job." Job me, dickbreath—Donna Donahue is mine! — James Ellroy, *Destination Morgue*, p. 223, 2004

dick-dip *noun*

sex *US, 1967*

- — Dale Gordon, *The Dominion Sex Dictionary*, p. 57, 1967

dick doc *noun*

1 a urologist *US, 1994*

- — Sally Williams, *"Strong" Words: (Dissertation)*, p. 161, 1994

2 a military doctor or medic who inspects male recruits for signs of sexually transmitted disease *US, 1964*

- — Roger Blake, *The American Dictionary of Sexual Terms*, p. 58, 1964
- — Dale Gordon, *The Dominion Sex Dictionary*, p. 119, 1967

dickeroo *noun*

a police officer *US, 1945*

- — Lou Shelly, *Hepcats Jive Dictionary*, p. 9, 1945

dickey *noun*

the penis *US, 1962*

- The hair around my dickey has been there since I was fourteen, and I have hair under my arms. — Charles Perry, *Portrait of a Young Man Drowning*, p. 48, 1962
- And his albino humpback saw the traveling salesman with his dickey hanging out. — Christopher Durgan, *The Marriage of Bette and Boo*, p. 42, 1985

dickface *noun*

a contemptible fool *US, 1975*

- The shithead has all the latest shampoos and conditioners. — Jay McInerney, *Story of My Life*, p. 112, 1988
- "Queer. You dickface." — Larry Brown, *Dirty Work*, p. 46, 1989
- "Why'd you kill Patrick?" "Why not. He's a dickface." — Sue Grafton, *G is for Gumshoe*, p. 251, 1990
- I know you've been listening to some scumhead, some bald dickface up there. — Howard Stern, *Miss America*, p. 276, 1995
- Chub said, "Then where's our ticket, dickface?" — Carl Hiaasen, *Lucky You*, p. 157, 1997

dick-fingered *adjective*

clumsy *US, 1984*

- He's so dick-fingered he can't pick his nose without puttin' his eye out. — Ken Weaver, *Texas Crude*, p. 108, 1984
- — Michael Dalton Johnson, *Talking Trash with Redd Foxx*, p. 130, 1994

dick flick *noun*
an action-oriented movie that appeals to a male audience
US, *2001*
An opposite and equal reaction to **CHICK FLICK**.
- — Don R. McCreary (Editor), *Dawg Speak*, 2001

dickhead *noun*
an inept, unlikeable person; an idiot *US*, *1964*
- "Ruin our A&A will you?" he snorted. "Gahdam dickhead." — Elaine Shepard, *The Doom Pussy*, p. 142, 1967
- If it wasn't for dickheads like you, there wouldn't be any thievery in this world, would there? — *Full Metal Jacket*, 1987
- Dickheads with a family crest and a prep-school code of honor. — Jay McInerney, *Story of My Life*, p. 11, 1988
- Now we know something's rotten in Denmark, 'cause this dickhead had a big bag, and it's uncut too, so we're sweatin' him, tryin' to find out where he got it. — *True Romance*, 1993

dickie *noun*
the penis *US*, *1962*
Children's vocabulary.
- On the other hand, some corresponding euphemistic expressions (e.g., dickie, peepee, weewee, number one, number two, to move the bowels, to pass water, to make love, and so on), obviously evasive in their very structure, do have considerable usage. — *Eros*, p. 69, Autumn 1962
- "And stick his dickie up a butthole instead." — Rick Russ, *Everything You Know About Sex is Wrong*, p. 298, 2005

dickjoke *noun*
any coarse joke *US*, *1991*
- — *American Speech*, p. 167, Summer 1991: "A brief annotated glossary of standup comedy jargon"

dickless *noun*
a female police officer or detective *US*, *1984*
A shortened form of **DICKLESS TRACY** that plays on two meanings of dick—"penis" and "detective."
- "You think I'd be a good Robbery/Homicide dick?" Lloyd laughed. "No, but you'd be a great Robbery/Homicide dickless." — James Ellroy, *Blood on the Moon*, p. 100, 1984

dickless *adjective*
gutless, cowardly *US*, *1971*
- I'm fifty. That's not old, dickless. — *Lethal Weapon*, 1987
- "Listen, you dickless sack of shit," I said[.] — Janet Evanovich, *Seven Up*, p. 118, 2001

dickless Tracy *noun*
a female police officer *US*, *1963*
A neat pun on **DICK** (the penis) and the popular comic book hero-detective Dick Tracy created by Chester Gould in 1931; a contemptuous suggestion that a female cannot be as effective as a male.
- No-Balls Hadley, who was sometimes called Dickless Tracy, was also right when she declared fearlessly at a policewomen's meeting attended by chauvinist spies for Commander Moss that he, as well as most high ranking officers of the department, had little or no street experience[.] — Joseph Wambaugh, *The Choirboys*, pp. 78–79, 1975
- "They call us Dickless Tracys," said said[.] — Joan Didion, *The White Album*, p. 21, 1979
- "I expect you to make sure she doesn't fall flat on her ass," he said, glancing pointedly at Bailey. "I don't need any Dickless Tracy problems." — Gerald Petievich, *To Die in Beverly Hills*, p. 11, 1983

dickless wonder *noun*
a person of either sex who lacks courage or conviction
US, *1997*
- He dreamed he was back in boot camp, trying to do push-ups while a brawny black sergeant stood over him, calling him a faggot, a pussy, a dickless wonder. — Carl Hiaasen, *Lucky You*, p. 170, 1997

dick-lick *noun*
used as a term of abuse *US*, *1984*
- Or do you get off on pigs rubbin' their shoes on your ugly dick-lick face, you lowlife beefcake faggot! — John Patrick Shanley, *Danny and the Deep Blue Sea*, p. 24, 1984
- What are you smiling at, you dick-lick? — Don Ericson, *Charlie Rangers*, p. 3, 1989

dicklicker *noun*
a "cocksucker" in all its senses *US*, *1968*
- Ahm sho 'nuff glad they got that dicklicker, man! — Nathan Heard, *Howard Street*, p. 236, 1968
- DCT made me what I am, in a way. Fucking dicklicker. — Ethan Coen, *Gates of Eden*, p. 104, 1998
- "We got really honest and called each other 'gofers,' 'ass-kissers,' 'butt-wipes,' and 'dick-lickers.'" — Jimmy Lerner, *You Got Nothing Coming*, p. 55, 2002

dicklicking *adjective*
despicable *US*, *1978*
- He'd driven straight to the plant to get away from that dick-licking deputy[.] — Joseph Flynn, *Digger*, p. 266, 1997
- Dick-licking bastards! How could they steal our mules? — Thomas Harlan, *The Dark Lord*, p. 299, 2002

dick mittens *noun*
hands that were not washed after urination *US*, *2001*
- — Jim Goad, *Jim Goad's Glossary of Northwestern Prison Slang*, December 2001

dicknose *noun*
used as a term of abuse *US*, *1974*
- At least Lou is upfront about it, which makes him more human than the rest of those MOR dicknoses. — Lester Bangs, *Psychotic Recations and Carburetor Drugs*, p. 196, 1976

dick off *verb*
to waste time, to idle, to shun work *US*, *1948*
- "But when it comes down to a little goddam work, you're always dicking off." — Norman Mailer, *The Naked and the Dead*, p. 138, 1948

dick-skinner *noun*
the hand *US*, *1971*
- You ain't going to have no skin on those dick-skinners. Remember them hands is your best girl. Rosie Palms. — Daniel Buckman, *The Names of Rivers*, p. 58, 2003

dick-smacker *noun*
a prison guard *US*, *1984*
Not kind.
- Hey, you stupid dick-smacker, get down here and open this door. — Inez Cardozo-Freeman, *The Joint*, 1984

dicksmith *noun*
a US Navy hospital corpsman *US*, *1974*
- I never thought them nice, clean "Dicksmiths" knew that kind of language. — Edward Raymer, *Descent into Darkness*, p. 84, 1996

Dick Smith *noun*
a drug user or addict who does not socialize with other users
US, *1876*
- — *American Speech*, p. 87, May 1955: "Narcotic argot along the Mexican border"

dick-stepper *noun*
a clumsy, awkward person *US*, *1992*
- "I just don't want any dick-steppers. Don't send anyone you wouldn't want to break in on your team." — Larry Chambers, *Recondo*, p. 228, 1992

dick-string *noun*
a male's ability to achieve an erection *US*, *1953*
- If yall was battlin some rookies we know and let um git up on ya that close, they'd slit ya dick-string loose. — Mark Kennedy, *The Pecking Order*, p. 122, 1953
- Ah hopes yuh busted his dick string. — Piri Thomas, *Down These Mean Streets*, p. 157, 1967
- "If you ever get her set, she'll knock your dick-string loose." — Robert Dean Pharr, *The Book of Numbers*, p. 181, 1969
- The hill had definitely busted his dick string, so she lounged back and smoked a Salem. — Chuck Logan, *Absolute Zero*, p. 225, 2003
- Seeing her jerked hard on my dick string. — *Penthouse International, Letters to Penthouse XXI*, p. 357, 2004

dick sucker *noun*
a homosexual male *US*, *1983*
- "Every man is a homo, a dick-sucker, every woman is a dyke." — Charles Bukowski, *The Most Beautiful Woman in Town*, p. 80, 1983
- Maybe they have a problem with each other, because, you know, they look like a couple of dick suckers. — Pete Dexter, *The Paperboy*, p. 179, 1995

dicksucking *noun*

oral sex performed on man *US, 1977*

- Her beautiful face was puckered with the size of his dick, as he plunged forward and back to give him a wild dick-sucking. — Roy Hawkins, *Bimbos by the Bay*, p. 53, 1977
- "Me and my girlfriend are having a dick-sucking contest and we thought you'd be a good judge." — Chris Rock, *Rock This!*, p. 135, 1997
- I wanted to make this dick-sucking an event he would remember for the rest of his damn life. — Noire, *Thong on Fire*, p. 154, 2007

dick-sucking *adjective*

despicable *US, 1972*

- [T]he Causey I know is the C.O. of the most limp-wristed, lily-livered, dick-sucking squadron in the history of flight. — Pat Conroy, *The Great Santini*, p. 326, 1976

dicktease *noun*

a woman who creates the impression of being more sexually available than she is *US, 1989*

A variant of the more common **PRICK-TEASER**.

- — Pamela Munro, *U.C.L.A. Slang*, p. 33, 1989

dickteaser *noun*

a person who suggests that they will engage in sex with a man but will not *US, 1962*

Originally applied to women, but later to both women and men.

- — *American Speech*, p. 273, December 1963: "American Indian Student Slang"
- I wanted to, but my muscles had atrophied. I didn't want him to think of me as a dick teaser. — Maya Angelou, *Gather Together in My Name*, p. 22, 1974
- And we don't go to meat markets to buy drinks for dick teasers. — Dan Savage, *Savage Love*, p. 26, 1998
- You know Saphronia, decent women aren't dick-teasers. — Michele Andrea Bowen, *Church Folk*, p. 82, 2001

dickwad *noun*

an unlikeable or despicable person *US, 1989*

- I get dickwad in there wantin' to play wheel of fortune so I can find out their supplier! — *Break Point*, 1991
- [A] TV personality, a fucking dickwad who could screw any hot stripper he wants[.] — Howard Stern, *Miss America*, p. 11, 1995
- Who's gonna stop me, dickwad? — Stephen J. Cannell, *The Tin Collectors*, p. 8, 2001

dick-waver; dicky-waver *noun*

a male exhibitionist *US, 1973*

- Indeed, at times the station house was so peaceful that the arrest of a "dicky waver," a man who exposed himself, was the major law-enforcement event of the day. — Peter Maas, *Serpico*, p. 107, 1973

dickweed *noun*

a despicable, dim-witted person *US, 1980*

- Not even in your dreams, Dickweed. — Sandra Bernard, *Confessions of a Pretty Lady*, p. 108, 1977
- What did you say dickweed? — *Heathers*, 1988
- You killed Ted, you Medieval dick-weed! — *Bill and Ted's Excellent Adventure*, 1989
- — Connie Eble (Editor), *UNC-CH Campus Slang*, p. 2, Fall 1993

dick-whipped *adjective*

dominated by a man *US, 2005*

- I thought she was either smoking crack or totally dick whipped. — Noire, *Candy Licker*, p. 172, 2005

dickwipe *noun*

a despicable person *US, 1992*

- I would have to say a dickwipe says what? — *Wayne's World*, 1992

dicky *noun*

the penis *UK, 1891*

An extension of **DICK**.

- Your pa sticks his dicky boy in your ma, see, and shoots this stuff into the hole that your mother pees from. — Herman Wouk, *Inside, Outside*, p. 69, 1985
- "Pull his dicky and get milk," Jadie replied. "You don't get milk out of a cow's pisser." — Torey Hayden, *Ghost Girl*, p. 135, 1991

dicky-dunking *noun*

sex from the male perspective *US, 1994*

- When the frost is on the pumpkin, it's time for dicky dunkin. — Michael Dalton Johnson, *Talking Trash with Redd Foxx*, p. 39, 1994

dicty *noun*

a snob *US, 1928*

- Dictys and the others among my own people who despise Negroes who are poor and ignorant and condemned to live like animals arouse my fury as no white people ever can. — Ethel Waters, *His Eye is on the Sparrow*, p. 18, 1951

dicty *adjective*

1 arrogant, haughty *US, 1923*

Also spelt "dichty."

- She had been doing everything possible to conceal her condition from her "dicty" parents. — Ethel Waters, *His Eye is on the Sparrow*, p. 53, 1951
- It's only good for one thing—that's to be dicty. — Billie Holiday, *Lady Sings the Blues*, p. 79, 1956
- You gonna be one dicty nigger, now ain't you? — John Clellon Holmes, *The Horn*, p. 180, 1958
- I don't want no dichty gray that thinks music is a lot of hen tracks put down on a piece of paper. — Ross Russell, *The Sound*, p. 217, 1961

2 excellent *US, 1947*

- "Dicty dictionary" — *Time Magazine*, p. 92, 20th January 1947

diddle *noun*

an act of masturbation *US, 2001*

From conventional "diddle" (to jerk from side to side).

- "You can keep the twenty [dollars]." "Do you want a diddle for it?" "No!" — Janet Evanovich, *Seven Up*, p. 94, 2001

diddle *verb*

1 (from the male perspective) to have sex *US, 1870*

- You want to conk me out and diddle with me while I'm helpless. — George Mandel, *Flee the Angry Strangers*, p. 269, 1952
- How about you and Boo? Did you or did you not diddle her during the war? Are you or are you not still diddling her? — Max Shulman, *Anyone Got a Match?*, p. 253, 1964
- I mean, he's got a wonderful wife and he prefers to, diddle this little yo-yo that—that, you know. — *Manhattan*, 1979
- Any movie that starts off with a woman being diddled by a giant katydid can't be all bad. — Joe Bob Briggs, *Joe Bob Goes to the Drive-In*, p. 19, 1987

2 to masturbate *US, 1934*

- [I]f I was you I would just go right back out that door and let her diddle herself in the powder room. — George V. Higgins, *The Rat on Fire*, p. 78, 1981
- She played with herself in chapel, at Holy Communion; she diddled in the confessional even as she was asking forgiveness for diddling. — Tom Robbins, *Fierce Invalids Home From Hot Climates*, p. 261, 2000
- Let's say you are diligently diddling her clit with a well-lubed fingertip[.] — Jamie Goddard, *Lesbian Sex Secrets for Men*, p. 61, 2000

3 to cheat *US, 1972*

- "Of course, once he spied those cut glass diamonds, he'd take in how we'd diddle him goodfashion." — Guy Owen, *The Flim-Flam Man and the Apprentice Grifter*, p. 163, 1972

4 in computing, to make a minor change *US, 1983*

- Let's diddle this piece of code and see if the problem goes away. — Guy L. Steele et al., *The Hacker's Dictionary*, p. 56, 1983

5 in computing, to work half-heartedly *US, 1991*

- I diddled a copy of ADVENT so it didn't double-space all the time. — Eric S. Raymond, *The New Hacker's Dictionary*, p. 125, 1991

▸ **diddled by the dirty digit of destiny**

adversely affected by fate *US, 1977*

- — *Maledicta*, p. 15, Summer 1977: "A word for it!"

diddler *noun*

1 the penis *US, 1969*

- If I see a queer, I wave my diddler at him and show him how big it is. — *Screw*, p. 11, 4th July 1969

2 a child molester *US, 1976*

- — John R. Armore and Joseph D. Wolfe, *Dictionary of Desperation*, p. 27, 1976
- "Little girl diddler," he says. — Guy Vanderhaeghe, *The Last Crossing*, p. 96, 2002
- You diddler! Rat! Child molester! — Edward Mackenzie, *Street Soldier*, p. 287, 2003

diddly *noun*

anything at all *US, 1964*

An abbreviation of **DIDDLY-SHIT**.

- — *American Speech*, p. 117, May 1964: "Problems in the study of campus slang"
- Since Manny Lopez admitted he didn't know diddly about guns and ammo, Ernie Salgado volunteered to help with the weapons training. — Joseph Wambaugh, *Lines and Shadows*, p. 32, 1984

diddlybopper; diddybopper; dittybopper; diddley bop; diddy bop *noun*
a street thug *US, 1958*

- The Cobras dress like "real diddley bops"—first-class street fighters. — Harrison E. Salisbury, *The Shook-up Generation*, p. 27, 1958
- Just because of that diddleybop walk, there were always fights, too. — Jeremy Larner and Ralph Tefferteller, *The Addict in the Street*, p. 143, 1964
- Now the lion jumped up full of rage/ Like a ditty bopper ready to rampage. — Dennis Wepman et al., *The Life*, p. 23, 1976
- [I]dentifying in less time than it took to name the hookers, hustlers, thieves and thugs; pennyweight ponces and flyweight flimflammers; diddyboppers, deadbeats and dopefiends. — Seth Morgan, *Homeboy*, p. 13, 1990

diddly-dick *noun*
nothing at all *US, 1972*

- Balfry already told the fucker that the hooker's identification wasn't worth diddly-dick. — Robert Campbell, *Sweet La-La Land*, p. 252, 1990

diddly-shit; diddly-squat *noun*
anything at all or nothing *US, 1955*

- In the first place, he doesn't know diddly-shit, nothing about Watergate, had nothing to do with it. — Stanley Kutler, *Abuse of Power*, p. 201, 2000

diddy bag; ditty bag *noun*
a small bag issued to soldiers for carrying their personal effects *US, 1947*

- — *American Speech*, p. 54, February 1947: "Pacific War language"
- "What the hell you got in there?" Emilio asked nodding toward the ditty bags. — Richard Price, *The Wanderers*, p. 219, 1974
- Stepik said he found a bulldog hash pipe in his ditty bag. — Larry Heinemann, *Close Quarters*, p. 102, 1977

diddy bop *verb*
to walk without paying attention to or taking safety precautions *US, 1992*

diddybop *verb*
to take part in gang fights *US, 1955*

- He was going to do that life term in the penitentiary at Dannemora and Kenny made a mental note to write him a short letter and mail him some money. "The diddy-boppin' fool!" he thought[.] — Emmett Grogan, *Ringolevio*, p. 104, 1972

diddybopper *noun*
a racially ambitious black person who rejects black culture and embraces the dominant white culture *US, 1980*

- — Edith A. Folb, *runnin' down some lines*, p. 234, 1980

diddy-dum slinger *noun*
a radar operator *US, 1947*

- — *American Speech*, p. 153, April 1947: "Radar slang terms"

didge *noun*
price or cost *US, 1984*
A corruption of "digits."

- — Jonathan Roberts, *How to California*, p. 166, 1984

didi; dee-dee *verb*
to leave *US, 1964*
From the Vietnamese word *di* (for goodbye) adapted by US soldiers during the war and made into a verb.

- DI DI! Get lost! Bug out! — Ken Melvin, *Sorry 'Bout That*, p. 96, 1966
- Man, the dinks have dee-deed. They've split, Man. You ain't got nothin' to worry about. — John M. Del Vecchio, *The 13th Valley*, p. 74, 1982
- Besides, the VC are going to di di mau out of that village[.] — Stan Lee, *The 'Nam*, p. 83, 1987
- The safest thing to do was di di south down the wood line and just lay low. — Larry Chambers, *Recondo*, p. 76, 1992

dido *noun*
1 mischief, a prank *US, 1807*

- Our youngest uncle, Billy, was not old enough to join in their didoes. — Maya Angelou, *I Know Why the Caged Bird Sings*, p. 66, 1969

2 a petty complaint filed against a police officer by a superior *US, 1958*

- — *New York Times Magazine*, p. 88, 16th March 1958

die *verb*
in roller derby, to fall after an extended and dramatic fight *US, 1999*

- — Keith Coppage, *Roller Derby to Rollerjam*, 1999

▸ **die for a tie**
used as a humorous sobriquet for General MacArthur's prediction that the war in Korea would end in a stalemate unless he were given approval to attack China *US, 1976*

- Eighth Army troops called this "die for a tie" speech, and in the words of Colonel Voorhees, "its effect on their attitude toward the future was not inspirational." — Joseph C. Goulden, *Korea: The Untold Story of the War*, p. 453, 1982
- The phrase "Why die for a tie?" was frequently used by opponents of limited war. — Carter Malkasian, *The Korean War 1950–1953*, p. 71, 2001

▸ **die with your boots on**
to die while in action *US, 1874*

- You have to say that cowboy died with his boots on[.] — Joseph Wambaugh, *The Glitter Dome*, p. 165, 1981

▸ **to die for**
spectacular, wonderful *US, 1983*

- The suspense is killing me. This is to die for. — *Empire Records*, 1995

die on the floor, seven at the door; on the floor, hit the door
in casino craps, used as a prediction that the next roll after a die has bounced onto the floor will be a seven *US, 1983*

- "Dice on the floor, seven at the door." And they'll always remember when it comes back a seven. — Edward Lin, *Big Julie of Vegas*, p. 245, 1974
- — Thomas L. Clark, *The Dictionary of Gambling and Gaming*, p. 64, 1987

dies *noun*
tablets of diazepam, an anti-anxiety agent with central nervous system depressant properties *US, 1997*

- — *Providence (Rhode Island) Journal-Bulletin*, p. 6B, 4th August 1997: "Doctors must know the narcolexicon"

diesel *noun*
1 heroin *US, 1996*

- They use whatever drugs they can get, like crack, cocaine, diesel. — S. Beth Atkin, *Voices from the Street*, p. 86, 1996

2 an aggressive, "manly" lesbian *US, 1959*
An abbreviation of **DIESEL DYKE**.

- It means that if we get busted the nice, bright-eyed prosecutors are going to describe prison to you, tell you about the two-hundred-pound diesel with a smelly snatch who's going to share your cell and how you'll have to go down on half the guards[.] — Vincent Patrick, *Family Business*, p. 69, 1985

3 a man with a great physique *US, 1993*

- — *Washington Post*, 14th October 1993

diesel *adjective*
projecting an aggressive and tough image *US, 1995*
Originally applied to a lesbian type, the **DIESEL DYKE**, then to a broader field.

- I'm gonna get mad diesel. — *Kids*, 1995
- — Connie Eble (Editor), *UNC-CH Campus Slang*, p. 2, Fall 1996

diesel dork *noun*
a large penis *US, 1994*

- — Michael Dalton Johnson, *Talking Trash with Redd Foxx*, p. 77, 1994

diesel dyke; diesel dike *noun*
a strong, forceful, aggressive lesbian *US, 1959*

- Well, honey, that butch numbuh turns out to be a les-bay-an—the butchest dam diesel dike y'evuh laid yuh gay eyes on! — John Rechy, *City of Night*, p. 354, 1963
- Two cases in point are Maria and Dickie, the former a fem, the later a stompin' diesel dyke. — Ruth Allison, *Lesbianism*, p. 73, 1967
- The perfect homo companion for a junkie diesel dyke who relaxed listening to CD's of the Ontario 500 while selfirrigating with homemade herbal colonics. — Seth Morgan, *Homeboy*, p. 16, 1990
- Have you ever gotten a lipstick smeared Christmas card from a two hundred pound diesel dyke? — James Ellroy, *Hollywood Nocturnes*, p. 25, 1994

diesel therapy *noun*

the repeated transfer of a troublesome prisoner from prison to prison *US, 1996*

- — Reinhold Aman, *Hillary Clinton's Pen Pal*, p. 33, 1996

diff; dif *noun*

difference *US, 1896*

- What's the diff? You wanna get on? — George Mandel, *Flee the Angry Strangers*, p. 26, 1952
- "Pres, President. What's the dif?" Booker said. — Herbert Simmons, *Corner Boy*, p. 90, 1957
- The clerk glanced at Folks and muttered, "What the diff?" — Iceberg Slim (Robert Beck), *Long White Con*, p. 65, 1977
- Maybe when you hit maturity you'll understand the diff between a Remington University man like David and a Westerburg boy like Ram[.] — *Heathers*, 1988

different strokes for different folks

different things please different people *US, 1966*

Singer Syleena "Syl" Johnson released the song "Different Strokes" (J. Cameron & J. Zachary) with this line in it in 1967; Sly and the Family Stone's 1968 mega-hit "Everyday People" put the phrase on the map.

- "I got different strokes for different folks." [Quoting Cassius Clay] — *Great Bend (Kansas) Daily Tribune*, p. 6, 11th November 1966

dig *verb*

1 to like, to appreciate *US, 1939*

- [I]n five seconds a billiard tournament was going full blast, with spectators lined up around the table digging all the fine points of each player. — Mezz Mezzrow, *Really the Blues*, p. 20, 1946
- They rushed down the street together, digging everything in the early way they had[.] — Jack Kerouac, *On the Road*, p. 8, 1957
- I'm going to see the folks I dig/ I'll even kiss a Sunset pig/ California, I'm coming home. — Joni Mitchell, *California*, 1971
- You'll dig it [Amsterdam] the most. — *Pulp Fiction*, 1994
- He's had enough. He no longer digs her. — *The Big Lebowski*, 1998

2 to understand *US, 1934*

- [T]hat will be a different kind of thing, of course. You dig? — Jack Kerouac, *Letter to Neal Cassady*, p. 155, 27th June 1948
- He's really diggin' this scene, man. — William "Lord" Buckley, *Nero*, 1951
- Now you all better dig this and dig it the most. — Stephen Sondheim, *West Side Story*, 1957
- But you don't need to have nothing except rubbers—until you can dig who's a cop. — Malcolm X and Alex Haley, *The Autobiography of Malcolm X*, p. 48, 1964
- We didn't dig why we needed to work towards owning bigger houses? bigger cars? Bigger manicured lawns? — Jerry Rubin, *Do It!*, p. 18, 1970

3 in surfing, to paddle energetically *US, 1963*

- — Grant W. Kuhns, *On Surfing*, p. 115, 1963

digger *noun*

1 a person who buys a large number of tickets to a popular entertainment and resells the tickets to a broker *US, 1927*

- — Sherman Louis Sergel, *The Language of Show Biz*, p. 71, 1973
- — Don Wilmeth, *The Language of American Popular Entertainment*, p. 73, 1981

2 a member of the Digger hippie counterculture support-network *US, 1966*

Named for a mid-C17 English sect that practised agrarian communism.

- As they say, it's free because it's yours. In the Hashberry they're known as the Diggers. — *The San Francisco Oracle*, 1966
- They are THE DIGGERS. And everyday at four o'clock they provide anybody with anything to eat. — *Berkeley Barb*, p. 3, 21 October 1966
- The Diggers are hip to poetry. Everything is free, do your own thing. — *Trip Without a Ticket*, Winter 1966–67
- Why did the hippie take a job in the cemetery? He was a Digger! — Paul Laikin, *101 Hippie Jokes*, 1968

3 a pickpocket, especially a clumsy one *US, 1931*

- — Vincent J. Monteleone, *Criminal Slang*, p. 68, 1949
- — *The New American Mercury*, p. 707, 1950

4 a solitary confinement cell *US, 1992*

- — William K. Bentley and James M. Corbett, *Prison Slang*, p. 10, 1992

5 the grade "D" *US, 1968*

- — Collin Baker et al., *College Undergraduate Slang Study Conducted at Brown University*, p. 104, 1968

diggety

used in various combinations for expressing surprise or pleasure *US, 1928*

- John claps his hands together. "Hot diggedy dog! I'll be a god-damned monkey's psychotherapist!" — Linda Keen, *Across the Universe with John Lennon*, p. 117, 1999

diggings *noun*

lodgings *US, 1837*

- Opal and Sesame Mae live together in nice diggings in West Harlem. — Sara Harris, *The Lords of Hell*, p. 48, 1967

digi *noun*

phencyclidine, the drug best known as PCP or angel dust *US, 2005*

- AKA: angel dust, illy, super weed, stained, horror, digi. — RZA, *The Wu-Tang Manual*, p. 121, 2005

digit *noun*

a number chosen as a bet in an illegal policy bank lottery *US, 1973*

- I stopped my man that I did my dope juggling with, and who also had the number bag going for him, and placed my diggets for that day. — A.S. Jackson, *Gentleman Pimp*, p. 154, 1973

digithead *noun*

a person whose enthusiasm for mathematics or computers is never hidden *US, 1994*

- Megabyte me, Digithead! — Jim Davis, *Garfield's Insults, Put-Downs, and Slams*, p. 59, 1994

digits *noun*

1 a telephone number *US, 1995*

- Oh, Cher, he's getting her digits. — *Clueless*, 1995
- — *San Jose Mercury News*, 11th May 1999

2 a personal identification number *US, 2006*

- "Givin' me bullshit digits and shit." — Jason Starr, *Lights Out*, p. 175, 2006

digits dealer *noun*

an operator of an illegal numbers policy lottery *US, 1982*

- — Ralph de Sola, *Crime Dictionary*, p. 41, 1982

digs *noun*

lodgings, be it a room, flat, or house *UK, 1893*

An abbreviation of the earlier (1830s) "diggings."

- This is an important courtesy, and one that you will appreciate, too, if you can establish it as Standard Operating Procedure around your digs. — Dick Clark, *To Goof or Not to Goof*, p. 69, 1963
- "Having this messengered to your digs after numerous calls to reputed place of employ." — Jay McInerney, *Bright Lights, Big City*, p. 89, 1984
- The other tenants included a children's photographer, a C.P.A., an optometrist and an office for the landlord, who used the digs as a place to clip coupons and get away from his wife[.] — Joseph Wambaugh, *Fugitive Nights*, p. 44, 1992
- I am staying with a nice family in their digs across the river in the Deccan Gymkhana district. — C.D. Payne, *Youth in Revolt*, p. 404, 1993

dig you later

used as a farewell *US, 1947*

- — Marcus Hanna Boulware, *Jive and Slang of Students in Negro Colleges*, 1947

dike *noun*

stolen brass or copper sold as scrap *US, 1980*

- — Joe McKennon, *Circus Lingo*, p. 30, 1980

dike *verb*

in computing, to remove or disable something *US, 1991*

Derived from the sense of "dikes" as "diagonal cutters used in electrical work."

- A standard slogan is "When in doubt, dike it out." (The implication is that it is usually more effective to attack software problems by reducing complexity than by increasing it.) — Eric S. Raymond, *The New Hacker's Dictionary*, p. 126, 1991

Dilbert *noun*

in poker, a player with a strong grasp of the mathematics and probabilities associated with the game but a poor set of playing skills *US, 1996*

- John Vorhaus, *The Big Book of Poker Slang*, p. 13, 1996

dildo *noun*

a despicable, offensive or dim-witted person *US, 1960*

- — Collin Baker et al., *College Undergraduate Slang Study Conducted at Brown University*, p. 105, 1968
- — Helen Dahlskog (Editor), *A Dictionary of Contemporary and Colloquial Usage*, p. 18, 1972
- I take back cars from dildos who don't pay their bills. — *Repo Man*, 1984
- See, I don't think I need to sit here with you fuckin' dildos anymore! — *The Breakfast Club*, 1985

dill-dock *noun*
a dildo *US, 1949*

- Dill-dock—Artificial penis strapped on by active Lesbian partner. — Anon., *The Gay Girl's Guide*, p. 7, 1949

dill piece *noun*
the penis *US, 2001*

- — Rick Ayers (Editor), *Slang Dictionary*, p. 8, 2001

dilly *noun*
1 an excellent or remarkable thing or person *US, 1908*
Usually used in a sarcastic sense.

- Five minutes later another car drove up and a pair of dillies climbed out. — Mickey Spillane, *I, The Jury*, p. 70, 1947
- Every time I was up for a new cellmate they spin the bottle and give me a real dilly. — Rocky Garciano (with Rowland Barber), *Somebody Up There Likes Me*, p. 116, 1955
- You're the most impossible man i ever met. And I've met some dillies. — Raymond Chandler, *Playback*, p. 150, 1958
- Of course your idea is a dilly, just great. — Jack Kerouac, *Jack Kerouac Selected Letters 1957–1969*, p. 459, 21st July 1965: Letter to John Clellon Holmes

2 a capsule of Dilaudid™, a synthetic morphine used by heroin addicts trying to break their habit *US, 1971*

- — Geoffrey Froner, *Digging for Diamonds*, p. 26, 1989

dilly-dally *verb*
to dawdle; hence to waste time *UK, 1741*
A reduplication of conventional "dally" (to loiter).

- Kenny sensed something. so he dilly-dallied on the other side of the street[.] — Emmett Grogan, *Ringolevio*, p. 6, 1972

dim *noun*
the night; twilight *US, 1944*

- — Lou Shelly, *Hepcats Jive Dictionary*, p. 9, 1945
- — *Time Magazine*, p. 92, 20th January 1947: 'Dicty Dictionary'
- 'Twas the dim before Nicktide and all through the pad/ You could dig them cats waiting and praying like mad[.] — Dan Burley, *Diggeth Thou?*, p. 42, 1959

dime *noun*
1 ten dollars *US, 1958*

- "I only got a dime. But I sure would like to put it out for even a little of the horse." — Dale Krame, *Teen-Age Gangs*, p. 55, 1953
- A dime is ten dollars. — Willard Motley, *Let No Man Write My Epitaph*, p. 148, 1958
- Couldn't you borrow a dime from Moira, Joe? — Alexander Trocchi, *Cain's Book*, p. 35, 1960
- Gimme thirty-five of it, put fifteen in your stocking for mad money, and put the dime in your purse. Let it be that way all the time. A dime is the most you carry in your purse. — A.S. Jackson, *Gentleman Pimp*, p. 168, 1973

2 one hundred dollars *US, 1974*

- Since I had more than five dimes bet on the White Sox-Tiger second game, I didn't comment on the charge. — Gary Mayer, *Bookie*, p. 185, 1974
- Two hundred bucks, two small, two dimes, two C-notes, all blown away. — Robert Campbell, *Juice*, p. 9, 1988
- Twenty dimes on Columbia. — *Casino*, 1995

3 one thousand dollars *US, 1974*

- You owe almost eight dimes. You never shoulda got in so deep, but you did. — Joseph Wambaugh, *The Black Marble*, p. 39, 1978
- — Michael Knapp, *Bay Sports Review*, p. 8, November 1991
- Twenty dimes on Columbia. — *Casino*, 1995

4 ten years; a ten-year prison sentence *US, 1967*

- [B]oth doing 10 years for SALE—but Tam's dime was new and Joe's was old, and he only had a year left. — Clarence Cooper Jr., *The Farm*, p. 25, 1967
- The repeater said, "The son-of-a-bitch is stir crazy. His voice-box screwed up on him a 'dime' ago." — Iceberg Slim (Robert Beck), *Pimp*, p. 51, 1969

- He had to do a dime (ten years) for the Government. — A.S. Jackson, *Gentleman Pimp*, p. 88, 1973
- Guy did a dime—in the labor camps, froze his ass. — Edwin Torres, *After Hours*, p. 173, 1979

5 a pretty girl *US, 2002*
A product of a one-to-ten scale for rating beauty, with ten being the best; thus an updated way of saying "a ten."

- He was the man and she was a dime. — Earl "DMX" Simmons, *E.A.R.L.*, p. 13, 2002
- — Connie Eble (Editor), *UNC-CH Campus Slang*, p. 4, October 2002

▸ **on a dime**
precisely, suddenly *US, 1996*

- The order was, you see anybody run, give them a warning, and if they don't stop on a dime, shoot. — Elmore Leonard, *Out of Sight*, p. 109, 1996

dime *verb*
to betray, to inform on *US, 1970*

- Cut the crap. I know you dimed me out on this. I know you went right to Sennett when I said I'd had a thing with a judge. — Scott Turow, *Personal Injuries*, p. 199, 1999
- "The same goes if you dime me." — James Lee Burke, *Last Car to Elysian Fields*, p. 320, 2003

dime-a-dance-girl *noun*
a woman who will dance with a stranger for a payment, originally a dime *US, 1938*

- So, for instance, the sailor in "Deadline at Dawn" soon discovers that the dime-a-dance girl whom he has picked up yearns only to return to her home town while she fends off unattractive men for a living. — Wilbur Schramm, *Mass Communications*, p. 348, 1949
- She got her start as a dime-a-dance girl. The rest just came naturally. — Phil Stanford, *Portland Confidential*, p. 36, 2004

dime-a-dip dinner *noun*
a fundraising meal *US, 1967*

- He'd met Oribelle, en route, at a dime-a-dip dinner at a Baptist church in Fayetteville, Arkansas. — Sue Grafton, *F is for Fugitive*, p. 53, 1989

dime bag; dime *noun*
a packet of drugs sold for ten dollars *US, 1968*

- "I can get you a quarter-ounce of P (pure heroin) and two dime bags." — Phil Hirsch, *Hooked*, p. 153, 1968
- The apartment is shadowy, sparsely furnished ... a portable record player, two beat-up sofas, a couple of sprung loose easy chairs, a small coffee table, holding on its top a dime bag[.] — Odie Hawkins, *Ghetto Sketches*, p. 115, 1972
- [Y]ou're gonna spend an entire summer going blind on paperwork because a Signalman Second Class bought and smoked a dime bag of oregano. — *A Few Good Men*, 1992
- But we should run by the park and get a dime. — *Kids*, 1995

dime-dropper *noun*
a police informant *US, 1966*

dime note *noun*
a ten-dollar bill *US, 1938*

- — Lou Shelly, *Hepcats Jive Talk Dictionary*, p. 23, 1945

dime paper *noun*
ten dollars worth of a powdered drug, especially heroin *US, 1972*

- Sell me and Clearhead a dime paper and we can geeze in one of the pads in the abandoned building down the block. — Emmett Grogan, *Ringolevio*, p. 43, 1972

dime-stacking *noun*
a system of keeping track of drinks not rung up on a bar's cash register, enabling the bartender to calculate the amount that can be safely embezzled at the end of the shift *US, 1992*

- Both were working furiously to serve customers, as well as the waitresses at the serve bar, and neither was making any funny moves such as dime-stacking, one for every drink they didn't ring up on the register. — Joseph Wambaugh, *Fugitive Nights*, p. 116, 1992

dime store *noun*
1 a store selling a variety of small items *US, 1938*

- The looting of a train, the robbery of a dime store, those were the kind of things that Spence and Baker always seemed to find themselves hooked up with. — Donald Goines, *Inner City Hoodlum*, p. 23, 1975

2 a small casino or gambling establishment with low-stakes games *US, 1953*
- — Thomas L. Clark, *The Dictionary of Gambling and Gaming*, p. 64, 1987

Dinah *noun*
dynamite or nitroglycerin *US, 1949*
- — Vincent J. Monteleone, *Criminal Slang*, p. 68, 1949

din-din *noun*
dinner; a meal *UK, 1905*
Children's vocabulary.
- Really interesting din-din. — Odie Hawkins, *Scars and Memories*, p. 47, 1987
- I'm thinking, why don't you and I go out and have some din-din this evening. — Elmore Leonard, *Maximum Bob*, p. 245, 1991

dine *verb*
▶ dine at the Y; eat at the Y
to perform oral sex on a woman *US, 2002*
- [W]hat's known in some circles as dining at the Y. Her Y. — *The Times Magazine*, p. 43, 16th February 2002

dine and dash *verb*
to leave a restaurant without paying your bill *US, 1997*
- — Anna Scotti and Paul Young, *Buzzwords*, p. 59, 1997

ding *noun*
1 the penis *US, 1965*
- I say to you, Legion of Decency—you with your dings scrubbed with holy water and Rokeach soap—you're dirty. — Lenny Bruce, *How to Talk Dirty and Influence People*, p. 71, 1965

2 a dent, scratch, scrape or rip *US, 1945*
- — Grant W. Kuhns, *On Surfing*, p. 115, 1963
- — John Lawlor, *How to Talk Car*, p. 38, 1965
- They checked their boards for dings and stood over us as we waxed them. — Kathy Lette and Gabriel Carey, *Puberty Blues*, p. 32, 1979

3 the expenses incurred in operating a carnival concession *US, 1985*
- These are legitimate DINGS, but more and more, the poor concessionaire finds himself with paying, paying paying. — Gene Sorrows, *All About Carnivals*, p. 15, 1985

4 a mentally unstable person *US, 1929*
A shortened form of **DINGBAT**.
- You mean, dings drew these? — Thurston Scott, *Cure it with Honey*, p. 56, 1951
- "What Centennial's saying," Leo said, 'is these dings start shooting up the place, they ain't gonna pay the claim." — Emmett Grogan, *Final Score*, p. 244, 1976
- And any ding who smeared shit on his cell walls got five whacks in the ass with the lead-filled "ding-donger" Meyers carried. — James Ellroy, *Suicide Hill*, p. 585, 1986

5 a quasi-coercive request for money *US, 1982*
- — Bill Reilly, *Big Al's Official Guide to Chicagoese*, p. 24, 1982

ding *verb*
1 to dent, scratch, scrape or rip *US, 1968*
- "He's got a dinged front left fender," Raymond said. — Elmore Leonard, *City Primeval*, p. 64, 1980
- You dinged my board, kook! — *Point Break*, 1991

2 in circus and carnival usage, to borrow *US, 1981*
- — Don Wilmeth, *The Language of American Popular Entertainment*, p. 74, 1981

3 to reject *US, 1965*
- Headline: Malvina Dings Co-Op Hoot — *The Berkeley Barb*, p. 1, 24th September 1965
- — Connie Eble (Editor), *UNC-CH Campus Slang*, p. 3, April 1995

4 to wound *US, 1967*
- — Carl Fleischhauer, *A Glossary of Army Slang*, p. 15, 1968
- "I saw him just before he got to it, and dinged him." — Martin Russ, *Happy Hunting Ground*, p. 25, 1968

dingage *noun*
damage to a surfboard or a surf-related injury *US, 1991*
- — Trevor Cralle, *The Surfin'ary*, p. 30, 1991

ding-a-ling *noun*
1 the penis *US, 1972*

- I want you to play with my ding-a-ling — Chuck Berry, *My Ding-a-ling*, 1972
- I think with my ding-a-ling — Ice Cube, NWA, *I Aint Tha 1*, 1988
- She may be your wife but I stick my dingaling in her every night so that make her mine. — *Boyz N The Hood*, 1990
- Swingin' and swingin' my ding-a-ling in — Ultramagnetic MCs, *Porno Star*, 1992

2 a fool *US, 1935*
- You may think I'm a ding-a-ling, but I had fun. — Mickey Spillane, *Last Cop Out*, p. 64, 1972
- This burglar was doing ding-a-ling stuff on some of the jobs, cutting up clothing, usually women's or kids'[.] — Joseph Wambaugh, *The Blue Knight*, p. 21, 1973
- Katie, I wouldn't play a ding-a-ling like Stilwell without it. — Iceberg Slim (Robert Beck), *Long White Con*, p. 33, 1977

ding-a-ling *adjective*
foolish, crazy *US, 1959*
- What I can't understand is why professional baseball players are highly praised as bench jockeys, but professional football players are considered ding-a-ling for doing the same thing. — *San Francisco Chronicle*, p. 1H, 19th April 1959

dingbat *noun*
an odd, foolish or eccentric person *US, 1879*
- What they should do with that whole bunch of dingbats up there is toss a couple of grenades in the dorm. — Ken Kesey, *One Flew Over the Cuckoo's Nest*, p. 116, 1962
- A dingbat across the aisle and Kitty Wells on the headphones. — Hunter S. Thompson, *Songs of the Doomed*, p. 127, 18th/19th February 1969
- Oh, don't be a dingbat. — Eugene Boe (Compiler), *The Wit & Wisdom of Archie Bunker*, p. 22, 1971
- "Dingbat, what you doing at my door with your shotgun?" Joe says as he seizes the lapels of Baptiste's robe[.] — Iceberg Slim (Robert Beck), *Doom Fox*, p. 169, 1978

ding-ding *noun*
a crazy person *US, 1970*
- Red, about all you have to fear is getting castrated by the ding-ding's knife. — Red Rudensky, *The Gonif*, p. 15, 1970

dingdong *noun*
the penis *US, 1944*
- He kept sitting around and trying to figure out what all this excitement was about over his erect ding-dong. — Johnny Shearer, *The Male Hustler*, p. 27, 1966
- [T]he man had used his handkerchief to wipe up the "funny white juice that came out of his dingdong"[.] — James Harper, *Homo Laws in all 50 States*, pp. 41–42, 1968
- I quoted in repetitious sing-song the overheard limerick "King Kong plays ping pong with his ding dong." — Neal Cassady, *The First Third*, p. 67, 1971
- "Then she brought it out and began to nurse on it, mistakenly thinking it was a real ding-dong." — Stanley Weber, *A Study of Sex in Prison*, p. 80, 1973
- Gino had a slight, twenty three year old paunch, nappy hair curling fiercely on his black ass and a small ding dong. — Odie Hawkins, *Black Casanova*, p. 42, 1984
- I notice the eyes of some cats here, openly and secretly spying, measuring the length and width of the next guy's dingdong! — Clarence Major, *All-Night Visitors*, p. 31, 1998
- Truth is, I think naked men are kind of strange-looking, what with their doodles [testicles] and ding-dong hanging loose like they do. — Janet Evanovich, *Seven Up*, p. 134, 2001

ding-dong *verb*
to telephone *US, 1973*
- I got up early that morning and ding-donged Carri, and this time I caught her home. — A.S. Jackson, *Gentleman Pimp*, p. 135, 1973

dinge *noun*
a black person *US, 1848*
Derogatory, from conventional "dingy" (dark).
- That old dinge nut! — John Clellon Holmes, *The Horn*, p. 210, 1958
- "And that dinge Ira, I suppose, off in the kip someplace!" — Stephen Longstreet, *The Flesh Peddlers*, p. 197, 1962
- The dinge. The colored kid. He goofin off on you? — John Sayles, *Union Dues*, p. 56, 1977

- If there wasn't a reward for shooting the little dinge he ought to get a medal, something. — Elmore Leonard, *City Primeval*, 1980

dinge queen *noun*
a white homosexual man who finds black men attractive; a black homosexual man *US, 1964*
- — Florida Legislative Investigation Committee (Johns Committee), *Homosexuality and Citizenship in Florida*, 1964: "Glossary of homosexual terms and deviate acts"
- A white man homosexually interested in a Negro is known in homosexual parlance as a "dinge queen." — James Harper, *Homo Laws in all 50 States*, p. 147, 1968
- — *American Speech*, p. 56, Spring–Summer 1970: "Homosexual slang"

dinger *noun*
a burglar alarm, especially an intentionally visible one *US, 1931*
- — Vincent J. Monteleone, *Criminal Slang*, p. 69, 1949

dinghead *noun*
a fool, an idiot *US, 1999*
- I'll be if his face cleared up, she'd go out with him, and then he'd see for himself what a dinghead she is. — Norma Howe, *The Adventures of Blue Avenger*, p. 84, 1999

dingleberry *noun*
1 a glob of dried feces accumulated on anal hairs *US, 1938*
Although this sense is not the earliest recorded sense of the word, it is probably the original sense.
- — Bruce Rodgers, *The Queens' Vernacular*, p. 99, 1972
- At Ralph's side was his enormous, dingle-berry-decorated and constantly farting shaggy dog named Rimpoche. — John Nichols, *The Nirvana Blues*, p. 36, 1981
- What if you have extra stuff hanging around like dingleberries? — Howard Stern, *Miss America*, p. 114, 1995
- Some of your cruds are going to wipe just half-assed, so I do not want to see any—and I mean any—dingleberries in your skivvies. — Zell Miller, *Corps Values*, p. 14, 1996

2 a despicable person *US, 1924*
- — Collin Baker et al., *College Undergraduate Slang Study Conducted at Brown University*, p. 105, 1968
- You fucking little dingleberry. That's what you're like, you fucking ball of shit! — John Waters, *Pink Flamingos*, p. 19, 1972
- But Surtees' move-out drills always started with some dingleberry housecat from the Orderly Room standing in the tent doorway and blowing his brains out on a silver MP whistle. — Larry Heinemann, *Close Quarters*, p. 150, 1977
- He said he'd snap us up if the lawyers weren't such dingle-berries. — *Airheads*, 1994

3 a military decoration *US, 1953*
- You kicked some ass out there today, boy! I'll see you get a dingle-berry [personal decoration] for it! — Michael Hodgins, *Reluctant Warrior*, p. 184, 1996

dinglebody *noun*
a foolish, simple person *US, 1957*
- But then they danced down the streets like dinglebodies, and I shambled after[.] — Jack Kerouac, *On the Road*, p. 8, 1957

dingle-dangle *noun*
the penis *US, 1986*
- I won't let my dingle-dangle dangle in the dirt / Gonna pick up my dingle-dangle, tie it to my shirt. — Sandee Johnson, *Cadences: The Jody Call Book, No. 2*, p. 50, 1986

dinglefuzzy *noun*
used in place of a person's name which has been forgotten *US, 1975*
- — John Gould, *Maine Lingo*, p. 73, 1975

ding list *noun*
in female college students' slang, a notional list of boys whom the keeper of the list does not like *US, 1963*
- — Carol Ann Preusse, *Jargon Used by University of Texas Co-Eds*, 1963

ding string *noun*
a cord attached to a surfer and his surfboard *US, 1991*
The cord has the effect of reducing damage to the board after the surfer falls off.
- — Trevor Cralle, *The Surfin'ary*, p. 30, 1991

dingus *noun*
1 the penis *US, 1888*

- Gets to him pretty quick too, cause nex thing I know he's got his dingus out. — Robert Gover, *Here Goes Kitten*, p. 79, 1964
- [D]ingus pressed up against the back, hips bumping and grinding. — Joe Eszterhas, *Charlie Simpson's Apocalypse*, p. 105, 1973
- I got a real ugly dingus. — Joseph Wambaugh, *The Secrets of Harry Bright*, p. 186, 1985
- What do you got there? A bigger dingus than God gave you? — *The Sopranos (Episode 63)*, 2004

2 an artificial penis *US, 1957*
- She greases the dingus, shoves the boy's legs over his head and works it up his ass with a series of corkscrew movements of her fluid hips. — William Burroughs, *Naked Lunch*, p. 92, 1957

3 used for identifying a thing, the correct name of which escapes the speaker or is not important in context; a gadget, a contraption *US, 1876*
- I filled the lower half of the dingus and set it on the flame. — Raymond Chandler, *The Long Goodbye*, p. 22, 1953
- Flathead flips a dingus that makes the door click[.] — Leo Rosten, *Silky!*, pp. 161–162, 1979

4 an eye-dropper used in makeshift drug-injection equipment *US, 1973*
- — David Maurer and Victor Vogel, *Narcotics and Narcotic Addiction*, p. 402, 1973

ding ward *noun*
a hospital ward for the mentally ill *US, 1981*
- Why don't those unknown suspects have a little more imagination next time and come up with a surefire scheme to get Woofer in the ding ward at the Veterans' Hospital[?] — Joseph Wambaugh, *The Glitter Dome*, p. 77, 1981

ding wing *noun*
the section of a prison where mentally ill patients are housed *US, 2002*
- — Jeffrey Ian Ross, *Behind Bars*, p. 184, 2002
- The mental ward was the "ding wing" where people "bugged out." — Justin Cartwright, *The Promise of Happiness*, p. 171, 2006

dingy *noun*
a police van *US, 1970*
- — Claudio R. Salvucci, *The Philadelphia Dialect Dictionary*, p. 37, 1996

dingy *adjective*
eccentric, odd *US, 1907*
- Hey, do you think it's dingy, what I did to the girl? — Thurston Scott, *Cure it with Honey*, p. 162, 1951
- He was out in a little over six. But he was dingy after that ... real dingy. — Robert Byrne, *McGoorty*, p. 72, 1972
- — Judi Sanders, *Kickin' Like Chicken with the Couch Commander*, p. 7, 1992

dink *noun*
1 a person from South Asia; especially, in later use, a Vietnamese person *AUSTRALIA, 1938*
Possibly Australian rhyming slang, formed on CHINK (a Chinese person). It was adopted by the US military in Vietnam in 1967.
- "Hey," he said, lowering his weapon. "The dink's got cokes." — Ronald J. Glasser, *365 Days*, p. 80, 1971
- Another time we were running convoy and the road was crowded with dink kids, begging C rations just like always. — Larry Heinemann, *Close Quarters*, pp. 98–99, 1977
- Gooks could be both. Slants and slopes were civilians. Dinks could be both. — Nelson DeMille, *Word of Honor*, p. 414, 1985
- Police up your extra ammo and frags, don't leave nothing for the dinks. — *Platoon*, 1986

2 a clueless, unaware person *US, 1962*
- — Collin Baker et al., *College Undergraduate Slang Study Conducted at Brown University*, p. 105, 1968
- — *Current Slang*, p. 10, Spring 1971
- Safeway, dink. As in the supermarket. — Armistead Maupin, *Tales of the City*, p. 14, 1978
- It's an anonymous call, you dink. — Elmore Leonard, *Cat Chaser*, p. 233, 1982
- Next thing I know I'm standing over her, trying to look like a loverstudguy and not some scared-to-death dink. — David Henry Sterry, *Chicken*, p. 48, 2002

3 the penis *US, 1888*
- "I bet he still pees the bed," Rodney Harrington had been heard to say. "That is, if he's got a dink to pee with." — Grace Metalious, *Peyton Place*, p. 92, 1956

- — Collin Baker et al., *College Undergraduate Slang Study Conducted at Brown University*, p. 105, 1968
- — H. Max, *Gay (S)language*, p. 12, 1988
- Lube the shit out of her ass and your dink, and place your dink's face right at the anus. — Suroosh Alvi et al., *The Vice Guide*, p. 40, 2002

dink around *verb*
to idle or waste time *US, 1978*
- Bo said he'd like to meet the kid again when the kid learned some tennis and knew how to play instead of dinking around. — Elmore Leonard, *Switch*, p. 53, 1978

dinky *noun*
the penis *US, 1962*
- "They start to pressing him, grabbing at his dinky." — Charles Perry, *Portrait of a Young Man Drowning*, p. 203, 1962

dinky *adjective*
1 small, unassuming *US, 1895*
- I gave her the bag, mumbling awkwardly about "Merry Early Christmas," then played some dinky tune while she dug into the bag and pulled out the first one. — John Nichols, *The Sterile Cuckoo*, p. 90, 1965
- The whore was in a dinky little North Main hotel. — Larry McMurtry, *The Last Picture Show*, p. 55, 1966
- "Here you are standing in deep shit and you're worried about a little dinky melon crop." — Elmore Leonard, *Mr. Majestyk*, p. 86, 1974
- She was telling me about how she hitchhiked from some dinky little town in Illinois[.] — Clarence Major, *All-Night Visitors*, p. 3, 1998

2 wildly enthusiastic, crazy *US, 1969*
- Last week the 49ers won a (one) game and the two sports fans went dinky. — *San Francisco Examiner and Chronicle, Sunday Punch*, p. 8, 2nd November 1969

dinky dau *adjective*
crazy *US, 1965*
From the Vietnamese for "off the wall." Vietnam war usage.
- Yeah, put it on my bill! Monsieur Dinky Dau from Bung Tau! — Tony Zidek, *Choi Oi: The Lighter Side of Vietnam*, p. 24, 1965
- — Carl Fleischhauer, *A Glossary of Army Slang*, p. 15, 1968
- At various times in the play, a character named Dinky Dau pointed an M-16 straight at Michael's head. — Peter Straub, *Koko*, p. 227, 1988

dinky dau cigarette *noun*
a marijuana cigarette *US, 1977*
- Her competition were street boys, "Changee money," "Boom-boom picture, "Dinkydao cigarette[.]" — Michael Herr, *Dispatches*, p. 36, 1977

dinky inky *noun*
in television and movie-making, a low watt spotlight *US, 1990*
- — Ralph S. Singleton, *Filmmaker's Dictionary*, p. 47, 1990

dinner-pail pimp *noun*
a man living off money earned by his girlfriend prostituting herself *US, 1972*
- A dinner-pail pimp keeps her body for himself and makes her work for the groceries to boot. — Robert Byrne, *McGoorty*, p. 35, 1972

dinners *noun*
the female breasts *US, 1953*
- A schoolmarm in southwest Missouri has truly enormous breasts, and is known as "Big Dinners" by almost everybody in town. — Vance Randolph, *Down in the Holler*, p. 120, 1953

dinosaur *noun*
1 any person who is old or considered to be out of date, or both *US, 1970*
- I mean the mob is falling apart. These guys like Chick, my uncle, they're dinosaurs. — Edwin Torres, *Carlito's Way*, p. 105, 1975
- Though their popularity had peaked a long time ago, they still toured on the "dinosaur" circuit, playing their vintage hits for diehard fans like me. — Jimmy Buffett, *Tales from Margaritaville*, p. 171, 1989

2 an older heroin user *US, 2002*
- — *Detroit News*, p. 5D, 20th September 2002

3 any computer that requires raised flooring and a dedicated power source *US, 1991*
- — Eric S. Raymond, *The New Hacker's Dictionary*, p. 126, 1991

dip *noun*
1 a pickpocket *US, 1859*
- I always went with good thieves, for I had become a first-class dip[.] — Charles Hamilton, *Men of the Underworld*, p. 115, 1952

- Allie had visited Houston and Galveston, convincing a coterie of dips that the fix was in Forth Worth[.] — Jim Thompson, *Bad Boy*, p. 353, 1953
- Thus a pickpocket squad cop never molests a recognized dip at the Garden. The dip is merely there for entertainment and relaxation. — Robert Sylvester, *No Cover Charge*, p. 286, 1956
- They ran tarot scams and were excellent dips. — Stephen Cannell, *King Con*, p. 55, 1997

2 a foolish person *US, 1932*
- — Miss Cone, *The Slang Dictionary (Hawthorne High School)*, 1965
- I sat there pulling my pud like a total dip and told her to take her whatchamacallit and go home[.] — Lawrence Block, *No Score [The Affairs of Chip Harrison Omnibus]*, p. 150, 1970
- You little dip! Did you come all the way back here to fix me breakfast? — Armistead Maupin, *Tales of the City*, p. 199, 1978

3 crack cocaine *US, 1994*
- — US Department of Justice *Street Terms*, October 1994

4 an injection of a narcotic *US, 1959*
- — J.E. Schmidt, *Narcotics Lingo and Lore*, p. 39, 1959

5 a pinch of chewing tobacco; the chewing tobacco itself *US, 1997*
- — Pamela Munro, *U.C.L.A. Slang*, p. 57, 1997

▸ **on the dip**
engaged in pickpocketing *US, 1949*
- — Captain Vincent J. Monteleone, *Criminal Slang*, p. 166, 1949

dip *verb*
1 to pick pockets *UK, 1857*
- He watched the other woman's purse and wondered idly if he could dip on her before she noticed him. — Donald Goines, *Dopefiend*, p. 65, 1971
- I guess he thought he found a live one and tried to dip on me. — A.S. Jackson, *Gentleman Pimp*, p. 134, 1973

2 to display an inappropriate interest in another prisoner's business *US, 1976*
- — John R. Armore and Joseph D. Wolfe, *Dictionary of Desperation*, 1976

3 to eavesdrop *US, 1987*
- I was dippin' on my brother when he was talking to his girlfriend. — *The Washington Post*, p. W-11, 24th May 1987

4 to hurry *US, 1997*
- — Vann Wesson, *Generation X Field Guide and Lexicon*, p. 52, 1997

5 to use chewing tobacco *US, 2001*
- — Don R. McCreary (Editor), *Dawg Speak*, 2001

6 to leave *US, 1993*
- — *Washington Post*, 14th October 1993

▸ **dip your wick**
to have sex *UK, 1958*
- — Joseph E. Ragen and Charles Finston, *Inside the World's Toughest Prison*, p. 796, 1962: "Penitentiary and underworld glossary"
- — Collin Baker et al., *College Undergraduate Slang Study Conducted at Brown University*, p. 105, 1968
- — Anon., *King Smut's Wet Dreams Interpreted*, 1978
- You're gonna find out if you mastrebate (sic) instead of dippin' your wick, you'll conserve energy. — Dan Jenkins, *Life Its Ownself*, p. 111, 1984
- He tries it on this one and that one, dipping his wick along the way, and finally finds the perfect fit[.] — *Adult Video*, p. xx, August/September 1986

dip-dunk *noun*
an unpleasant person, especially one who is not in the know *US, 1992*
- SEAL Team Six trained harder than any unit had ever trained before, waiting for the opportunity to show the skeptical bureaucrat-sailors and dip-dunk bean-counters prevalent in Washington that it was possible for the U.S. Navy to fight back effectively against terrorists. — Richard Marcinko with John Weisman, *Rogue Warrior*, p. 5, 1992

diphead *noun*
a social outcast *US, 1975*
- My name's Jason, you diphead. — Jeane Okimoto, *To Jaykae*, p. 68, 2000
- All because his dizzy diphead of a sister couldn't behave herself. — Katherine Sutcliffe, *Darkling I Listen*, p. 278, 2001

diply *noun*
a socially inept outcast *US, 1965*
- — *Time*, p. 56, 1st January 1965: "Students: the slang bag"

dipped *adjective*
well-dressed *US, 2002*

- He always liked to stay dipped in the nice outfits[.] — Earl "DMX" Simmons, *E.A.R.L.*, p. 141, 2002
- When I saw him, he was clean-cut and freshly dipped. — 50 Cent, *From Pieces to Weight*, p. 25, 2005
- — Connie Eble (Editor), *UNC-CH Campus Slang*, p. 3, Fall 2005

dipper *noun*
a pickpocket *UK, 1889*
- Another less flamboyant group of habitues are those who make money through wit, skill, and guile: boosters (professional shoplifters), dippers (pickpockets) and con artists. — Terry Williams, *The Cocaine Kids*, p. 102, 1989

dipping *noun*
the act of picking pockets *UK, 1882*
- — David Powis, *The Signs of Crime*, p. 181, 1977

dippy *adjective*
foolish, unstable, silly *US, 1899*
- — Joseph E. Ragen and Charles Finston, *Inside the World's Toughest Prison*, p. 796, 1962: "Penitentiary and underworld glossary"
- Is it my fault the dippy network wants to spend a billion dollars to get a pilot they can fondle? — Dan Jenkins, *Life Its Ownself*, p. 71, 1984
- I was always too dippy, too bubbly, never serious. — Marilyn Suriani Futterman, *Dancing Naked in the Material World*, p. 104, 1992

dipshit *noun*
a person of no consequence and no intelligence *US, 1962*
- "We had this lieutenant, honest to Christ he was about the biggest dipshit fool of all time, all time." — Michael Herr, *Dispatches*, p. 26, 1977
- "This better be fucking important, dipshit!" the cop growled. — C.D. Payne, *Youth in Revolt*, p. 301, 1993
- The dipshit who's never been out of Miami. — *Get Shorty*, 1995
- [Y]ou're going to leave them alone in a jail cell with one inept guard? They'll escape, dipshit. — *Austin Powers*, 1999

dipshit *adjective*
offensive, inconsequential, lacking in intelligence *US, 1968*
- Turns out, not only am I ugly, but I have a dipshit personality. I suck. — Howard Stern, *Miss America*, p. 18, 1995

dipso *noun*
a person who suffers from an uncontrollable urge to drink *UK, 1880*
An abbreviated "*dipso*maniac."
- Consider this—my father canned me and my brother and my Mom for a twenty five year old dipso with fake tits. — *Ferris Bueller's Day Off*, 1986

dipstick *noun*
1 the penis *US, 1973*
- My dipstick wouldn't feel safe here without a wrapper, so I wrap it. — Richard Meltzer, *A Whore Just Like the Rest*, p. 431, 1991
- He knew if he kept having weeks like this one, his dipstick would be checking her oil level on a regular maintenance schedule. — Renay Jackson, *Oaktown Devil*, p. 166, 1998
- Fellatio: blowing, deep throating, frenching, getting a facial, giving head, giving lip service, hoovering, putting lipstick on one's dipstick[.] — Ruth K. Westheimer, *Sex for Dummies*, p. 166, 2001
2 an inept fool, an idiot *US, 1963*
A euphemistic **DIPSHIT**; possibly punning on the synonymous sense of **PRICK**.
- — *Current Slang*, p. 4, Spring 1968
- "What are you thinking about, dipstick?" — Robert Stone, *Dog Soldiers*, p. 279, 1974
- Sergeant Anson Trobridge, the platoon dipstick, also called Four-Eyes and Highpockets[.] — Larry Heinemann, *Close Quarters*, p. 125, 1977

dipsy *noun*
a gambling cheat *US, 1950*
- — *The Annals of the American Academy of Political and Social Sciences*, p. 124, May 1950

dipwad *noun*
an inept outcast *US, 1976*
- He don't believe no cop would give a fuck about a dipwad like me. — LaVyrle Spencer, *Family Blessings*, p. 100, 1993

dipwipe *noun*
an inept social outcast *US, 2006*
- "Come on, you dipwipes!" — Chris Miller, *The Real Animal House*, p. 162, 2006

direct action *noun*
a political act, especially a violent one, that may lead to arrest *US, 1968*
- There we sat in a corner of Central Park going through all the changes that you go through before direct action. — Abbie Hoffman, *Revolution for the Hell of It*, p. 24, 1968

dirk *noun*
1 a knife or improvised cutting weapon *US, 1950*
- Funny how ghees that ain't afraid of a roscoe chill when they see a dirk. — Hyman E. Goldin et al., *Dictionary of American Underworld Lingo*, p. 59, 1950
2 a socially unacceptable person *US, 1964*
- — *American Speech*, p. 118, May 1964: "Problems in the study of campus slang"

dirt *noun*
1 a man or group of men who will prey upon homosexuals *US, 1927*
- Dirt—Properly, a highly specialized type of criminally psychopathic youth, self-appointed nemesis of any and all homosexuals, usually not homosexual himself (but this varies greatly since some kind of sexual abnormality or inferiority is almost always at the root of it), who guilefully leads on a homosexual interested in him until in a position to do him dirt, rolling and/or beating him up (rarely fatally), alone or with others, before or after being "blown." — Anon, *The Gay Girl's Guide*, 1949
- — Florida Legislative Investigation Committee (Johns Committee), *Homosexuality and Citizenship in Florida*, 1964: "Glossary of homosexual terms and deviate acts"
- — Guy Strait, *The Lavender Lexicon*, 1964
2 gossip, criticism, rumor *US, 1844*
- Being a psychologist has a certain appeal. You get paid extravagently well to sit around and listen to the most intimate dirt. — C.D. Payne, *Youth in Revolt*, p. 426, 1993
3 heroin *US, 1973*
Slightly less judgmental than "shit."
- — David Maurer and Victor Vogel, *Narcotics and Narcotic Addiction*, p. 402, 1973
4 a tobacco cigarette *US, 1971*
- — Eugene Landy, *The Underground Dictionary*, p. 67, 1971

▸ **down in the dirt**
(used of flying) close to the ground *US, 1987*
- High-flying fighter jocks aren't terribly comfortable down in the dirt, but another bunch of tactical pilots, the close-air support specialists, are in their element. — George Hall, *Top Gun*, p. 71, 1987

dirtbag *noun*
1 a despicable or offensive person *US, 1941*
- Rachel's a dirtbag. Who else? — *Ferris Bueller's Day Off*, 1986
- "Tell me about Ernesto Cabal." "Dirtbag burglar." — Carl Hiaasen, *Tourist Season*, p. 20, 1986
- I'm some kinda dirtbag. — Howard Stern, *Miss America*, p. 456, 1995
2 a prisoner with poor personal hygiene *US, 1989*
- — James Harris, *A Convict's Dictionary*, 1989

dirtball *noun*
a dirty, despicable person *US, 1974*
- Tell them to compare to every known in the county. Anybody. Any dirtball who's ever been printed. — Scott Turow, *Presumed Innocent*, p. 26, 1987
- This look like an act of international terrorism? Or does it look like some dirtball in a junker went nuts? — Carl Hiaasen, *Skin Tight*, p. 121, 1989

dirtbox *noun*
the anus *UK, 1984*
- Jokes at the expense of gay men invariably revolve around fucking, and the gamut of derogatory terms usually play on that act (dirt box snatcher, sausage jockey, uphill gardener, shit stabber, chocolate box poker, brown hatter). — Peter Davies, *Sex, Gay Men and AIDS*, p. 129, 1993
- And how embarrassing for those poor girls, having your private parts about half an inch away from your dirt box. Planning! I mean, who thought of that? — Melvin Burgess, *Doing It*, p. 218, 2003

dirtbud *noun*
a despicable person *US, 1998*
- Hey, dirtbud, who you going to the prom with? — *Something About Mary*, 1998

dirt chute *noun*
the rectum *US, 1971*

- Proctor thought helplessly of how he could have been a big, clean career aviator instead of staring up some wise guy's dirt chute. — Thomas McGuane, *The Bushwacked Piano*, p. 198, 1971
- They'll get ya so you won't be able to tell the dirt chute from the manhole. — Martyn Burke, *Laughing War*, p. 87, 1980
- It would have been so sweet to know she'd felt that last big bang, and to feel her guts spasm as I greased her dirt chute! — Brian Lumley, *Necroscope: Invaders*, pp. 431–432, 1999

dirt-dobber *noun*
a farmer; an unsophisticated rustic *US, 1947*
- I replied that as far as I knew, we came from a line of scrawny old dirt-dobbers, Scotch-Irish with more than one or two Indians thrown in. — Susan Wittig Albert, *Writing from Life*, p. 93, 1996

dirt-eater *noun*
a soldier in the infantry *US, 2005*
- The army sought to improve the image of the infantrymen, whom Americans saw as the dirt-eaters and mud-sloggers, the guys at the bottom of the military's pecking order. — Stephen Borelli, *How About That!*, p. 53, 2005

dirt farm *noun*
the mythical source of gossip *US, 1980*
- — Edith A. Folb, *runnin' down some lines*, p. 234, 1980

dirt nap *noun*
death *US, 1981*
- Despite yourself, you glance through the folder, a compendium of bad news with references to the big sleep, the deep six, the dirt nap. — *New York Times*, p. 32, 18th January 1987
- "I'm bringing some pain, baby," Tyson said. "If he [opponent Orlin Norris] makes even one mistake, he'll be taking a dirt nap." — *Las Vegas Sun*, p. D1, 22nd October 1990
- "Then the firin pin hit an empty spot an you end up with jack." "Or a dirt nap," growled Gordon. — Jess Mowry, *Way Past Cool*, p. 7, 1992
- Foremost on their "to do" list, I imagine, is finding a way to delay for as long as possible their date with the state-sponsored dirt nap. — *News and Observer (Raleigh, NC)*, p. B1, 18th May 1998

dirt-nap *verb*
to be dead *US, 1993*
- "I been with Sabby when your dudes jump his ass, they all be dirt-nappin right now." — Jess Mowry, *Six Out Seven*, p. 111, 1993

dirt Navy *noun*
a naval unit assigned to land duty *US, 1998*
- These are the sights, sounds and smells of the "Dirty Navy," the buzz words for a new initiative that, if put into play, could thrust sailors into a domain long reserved for foot soldiers. — *The Virginian-Pilot*, p. A1, 18th October 2005

dirt road *noun*
the anus and rectum *US, 1922*
- "She lets her customers take the dirt road." — Madam Sherry, *Pleasure Was My Business*, p. 86, 1963
- "No dirt roads for me," he said with a smile. — Gerald Petievich, *To Die in Beverly Hills*, p. 93, 1983
- "Pussy business, I'll bet, or some barmaid who wants you to lay some pipe up her dirt road!" — Eric Van Hoffman, *A Venom in the Blood*, p. 125, 1990
- "That nigga just tore me a new asshole," said Rosalyn clutching her own butt cheeks. "Girl, you let him go down the dirt road?" "Oooh." She covered her mouth. "Shut up. My ass is killing me." — Antoine Thomas, *Flower's Bed*, p. 70, 2003

dirt sailor *noun*
a member of the US Navy assigned to land duty *US, 2003*
- The Navy's "dirt sailor" Seabees built bridges to nowhere in the desert yesterday that they will break up, pick up and slam together again in Iraq if war comes. — *Daily News (New York)*, p. 4, 9th March 2003

dirt surfer *noun*
a member of the counterculture who have abandoned any pretence of personal hygiene or grooming *US, 1994*
- — David Shenk and Steve Silberman, *Skeleton Key*, p. 70, 1994

dirt weed *noun*
low quality marijuana *US, 1997*

- Every time I come to Memphis, my boys hook me up with some dirt weed taste like they grown it out the ass a' some redneck. — *Hustle and Flow*, 2004

dirty *noun*
► **do the dirty**
to have sex *US, 1968*
- — *Current Slang*, p. 16, Spring 1970
- He could understand that Twelvetree's daughter had walked in on her old man doing the dirty with the make-believe schoolgirl hooker but what was the half-naked whore doing with the daughter's boyfriend, scrambling into her skirt with her tits hanging out? — Robert Campbell, *Alice in La-La Land*, p. 289, 1987
- True, she'd made no pretense of trying to keep Deandre from doing the dirty[.] — David Simon and Edward Burns, *The Corner*, p. 229, 1997
- Michelle's erect nipples indicate she's fully into doing the dirty with a man. — Mr. Skin, *Mr. Skin's Skincyclopedia*, p. 114, 2005

dirty *adjective*
1 indicative of an excrement fetish *US, 1975*
- Dirty Sex or Scat = scatology. — Stephen Lewis, *The Whole Bedroom Catalog*, p. 144, 1975
- Warning: if he tells you on the phone he wants it "dirty," he's letting you know he wants a scat scene. — John Preston, *Hustling*, p. 171, 1994

2 guilty *US, 1927*
- He said, "I try to keep an open mind. Everyone's dirty till they prove they aren't." — Elmore Leonard, *Maximum Bob*, p. 95, 1991

3 in possession of drugs or other contraband *US, 1927*
- But there was the chance that he was dirty too. — A.S. Jackson, *Gentleman Pimp*, p. 181, 1973

4 in urine testing, containing drug metabolites *US, 1990*
- One more dirty test, Miss Batista, and you're off the methadone program. — Seth Morgan, *Homeboy*, p. 187, 1990
- He had a dirty urine twice in a row so I violated him. — Elmore Leonard, *Maximum Bob*, p. 164, 1991
- "You tested dirty, and now you've got a spot waiting at Folsom." — Bob Sipchen, *Baby Insane and the Buddha*, p. 23, 1993

5 infected with a sexually transmitted infection *US, 2003*
- Dirty means diseased—a diseased girl. — *Oprah Winfrey Show*, 2nd October 2003

6 descriptive of electricity with unstable voltage that causes problems with computers *US, 1991*
- — Eric S. Raymond, *The New Hacker's Dictionary*, p. 127, 1991

dirty anal *noun*
a scene in a pornographic film or a photograph depicting anal sex where traces of feces are visible on that which is being inserted anally *US, 1995*
A pornography fetish, with movies titles such as Dirty Anal Kelly in Rome (2000) and Dirty Anal Whores (2005).
- — *Adult Video News*, p. 44, August 1995

dirty barrel *noun*
the genitals of a person infected with a sexually transmitted disease *US, 1967*
- — Dale Gordon, *The Dominion Sex Dictionary*, p. 58, 1967

dirty bird *noun*
Old Crow™ whiskey *US, 1970*
- — Clarence Major, *Dictionary of Afro-American Slang*, p. 46, 1970

dirty boogie *noun*
a sexually suggestive dance *US, 1969*
- You just didn't do the Dirty Boogie to Theresa Brewer, no sir, and not at the Totem Pole in Newton, Mass., no man, definitely not. — Abbie Hoffman, *Woodstock Nation*, p. 25, 1969
- And if anyone tried to give the Bop some joie de vivre it was immediately intercepted and was secretly known as the "dirty boogie." — Eve Babitz, *Eve's Hollywood*, p. 44, 1984

dirty case *noun*
in hospital usage, an operation in which the surgeons discover an infection *US, 1980*
- — *Maledicta*, p. 56, Summer 1980: "Not sticks and stones, but names: more medical pejoratives"

dirty-dance *verb*
to dance in an explicitly and intentionally sexual manner *US, 1994*

- Breaking from our gabfest, we dirty-danced to Tom Jones songs.
  — Anka Radakovich, *The Wild Girls Club*, 1994

dirty-dirty *nickname*
the southern United States *US, 1999*

- I love how they [OutKast] represent the dirty-dirty with more juice than Zeus[.] (Letter to the editor). — *Village Voice*, p. 82, 2nd March 1999
- Over the last decade hip-hop has inevitably branched out into its many "coastal" facets, including the dirty-dirty (South). — *University Wire*, 15th September 2004

Dirty Dora *noun*
the queen of spades *US, 1953*
Of special significance in the game of Hearts.

- Their favorite game as Hearts, and there was always an outburst of squeals when Dirty Dora (the Queen of Spades) was passed to somebody. — Polly Adler, *A House is Not a Home*, p. 85, 1953
- He was going to get Dirty Dora and every heart but one. — Catherine Reid (Editor), *His Hands, His Tools, His Sex, His Dress*, p. 78, 2001

dirty dupe *noun*
in television and movie-making, a crude, black and white, working print *US, 1990*

- — Ralph S. Singleton, *Filmmaker's Dictionary*, p. 48, 1990

dirty hustling *noun*
behavior by a prostitute during a group inspection by a potential customer that crosses the line of what is allowed by the brothel *US, 1997*

- All private parts must be covered at all times (nipples and pubic hair). It was absolutely taboo and called "Dirty Hustling" if a girl broke any of these rules during line-ups. — *Sisters of the Heart, The Brothel Bible*, p. 15, 1997
- "Any kind of moving in the line-up is considered dirty hustling, a way one girl could invite attention to herself and gain an unfair advantage over the others." — Lora Shaner, *Madam*, p. 193, 1999

dirty laundry *noun*
embarrassing information *US, 1982*

- What expectations do people learn form talk shows like those starring Jerry Springer or Jenny Jones, where people air their dirty laundry? — Keith E. Whitfield, *Fighting for Your African American Marriage*, p. 146, 2001

dirty leg *noun*
a woman with loose sexual mores; a common prostitute *US, 1966*

- — Andy Anonymous, *A Basic Guide to Campusology*, p. 7, 1966
- A dirty leg is the $5 or $10 trick. — Bruce Jackson, *In the Life*, p. 181, 1972
- — Charles Shafer, *Folk Speech in Texas Prisons*, p. 202, 1990
- "Women are dirty-legs, cunts, weaklings." — Pete Earley, *The Hot House*, p. 191, 1992

dirty mixing *noun*
sex for pay in a bar or dance club *US, 1987*

- Then there's "dirty mixing." In the past, that included being able to hide away in a dark corner with a customer and turning a regular trick[.] — Frederique Delacoste, *Sex Work*, p. 22, 1987

dirty movie *noun*
a sexual or pornographic film *US, 1969*

- As little as two years ago dirty movies, at least the kind that ran city-wide, were pitiful things indeed. — *Adam Film Quarterly*, p. 74, February 1969

dirty old man *noun*
any homosexual man older than the homosexual male speaker *US, 1964*

- — Guy Strait, *The Lavender Lexicon*, 1 June 1964

dirty side *nickname*
the eastern seaboard *US, 1976*

- — Book Craft Guild *Official CB Lingo*, p. 25, 1976
- "Hey," he broadcast, "you say how-do to all my boys at K&L when you hit the Dirty Side, all right?" — E.M. Corder, *Citizens Band*, p. 33, 1977

dirty stack *noun*
in a casino, a stack of betting tokens of different denominations *US, 1983*

- — Thomas L. Clark, *The Dictionary of Gambling and Gaming*, p. 64, 1987

dirty thirty *noun*
1 in the Vietnam war, a US soldier who had killed 30 enemy soldiers *US, 1991*

- Everyone talked about the Dirty Thirty. Every soldier worth his salt bragged he was getting closer and closer: "Killed another Charlie last night while Lurpin' thru sector seven. That brings my count to over two dozen. Only a matter of time before I'm a Dirty Thirty myself." — Jack Hawkins, *Chopper One #2: Tunnel Warriors*, p. 27, 1991

2 the US Air Force pilots who served as co-pilots with Vietnamese Airforce crews in 1963 and 1964 *US, 1990*

- Most of the Dirty Thirty were over thirty years of age, and many had flown in World War II. — Caj Ky Nguyen, *Buddha's Child*, p. 64, 2002

dirty tricks *noun*
secret tactics that are generally considered to be unfair *US, 1963*

- "Malice, Mormonism, McCarthy-Nixon dirty tricks are written all over it by extreme rightist elements in the Republican Party," Ritter wrote. — Norman Mailer, *The Executioner's Song*, p. 864, 1979
- Reverend Pat Robertson said, "Lee Atwater has used every dirty trick known to mankind." — Larry Beinhart, *American Hero*, p. 3, 1993
- A Bush family insider since 1973, when he [Karl Rove] was chairman of the College Republicans National Committee (and taught party youth "dirty tricks" according to the Washington Post), Rove worked for the elder Bush[.] — J.H. Hatfield, *Fortunate Son*, p. 264, 2001
- Instead of a dirty-tricks squad composed of over-the-hill intelligence agents, it featured a concerted effort by top Reagan officials to circumvent congressional control in order to funnel aid to rightwing Nicaraguan terrorists. — Daniel Lazare, *The Velvet Coup*, pp. 86–87, 2001

dirty work *noun*
in a strip or sex show, movements made to expose the vagina *US, 1971*

- If strippers choose a face that is shy, it is because they want their "floor work" (crouching or lying on the floor and simulating intercourse) and "dirty work" ("flashing" and spreading their legs) to remind the audience of demure girls. — Marilyn Salutin, *The Sexual Scene*, p. 173, June 1971

dirty work at the crossroads *noun*
illegal activity, especially if concealed *US, 1938*

- It sounds to me as if there's going to be dirty work at the crossroads. — Rex Stout, *Some Buried Caesar*, p. 41, 1967

DIS *noun*
death while in the saddle, or engaged in sexual intercourse *US, 1979*

- Coroners have been known to label it "D.I.S.," death in the saddle. — *Maledicta*, p. 58, 1979

dis; diss *verb*
1 to insult in a competitive, quasi-friendly spirit, especially in a competitive rap battle *US, 2000*

- There are many different terms for playing the dozens, including "bagging, capping, cracking, dissing, hiking, joning, ranking, ribbing, serving, signifying, slipping, sounding and snapping." — James Haskins, *The Story of Hip-Hop*, p. 54, 2000
- The guy from Scotland was virtually unknown, so I decided not to diss him, because I knew that would be a diss in itself! — J. Hoggarth (quoting Prime Cuts), *How To Be a DJ*, p. 101, 2002

2 to show disrespect, to disparage *US, 1982*

- — Connie Eble (Editor), *UNC-CH Campus Slang*, p. 2, Fall 1990
- You know, I'll tell you what the whole shouting match came down to. Dis. It was all about dis. The kid disrespected me by raising up in my face. I dissed him by throwing him up against the fence[.] — Richard Price, *Clockers*, pp. 368–369, 1992
- Italian people came over here. They got dissed. They said, "Yo man, fuck you! Little Italy. All right? We got our own thing." You ever heard of Little Africa? Didn't think so. — Chris Rock, *Rock This!*, p. 13, 1997
- I would never half dis somebody. — Earl "DMX" Simmons, *E.A.R.L.*, p. 128, 2002

3 to release (from prison) *US, 1990*
An abbreviation of "discharge."

- — Charles Shafer, *Folk Speech in Texas Prisons*, p. 202, 1990

disappear *verb*
to kill someone and dispose of the corpse in a manner that assures it will never be discovered *US, 1964*
As a transitive verb, a favorite term—and practice—of right wing death squads and organized criminal enterprises.

- — *American Speech*, p. 306, December 1964: "Lingua cosa nostra"
- Our two Nicaraguan doctors were disappeared one right after the other. — Elmore Leonard, *Bandits*, p. 38, 1987

discipline *noun*
fetishistic, sado-mashochistic dominating behavior *US, 1971*
- Love French and Greek, discipline, home movie-making, and anything you can name. — Emile Nytrate, *Underground Ads*, p. 18, 1971

disco biscuit *noun*
the recreational drug methaqualone, best known as Quaaludes™, a tablet of methaqualone *US, 1993*
From the popularity of the drug in the 1970s disco scene.
- — Peter Johnson, *Dictionary of Street Alcohol and Drug Terms*, p. 59, 1993
- Most of the local trade in these babies was controlled by speed-freak bikers, and these were dismissively known as Disco Biscuits. — Editors of Ben is Dead, *Retrohell*, p. 169, 1997
- Who wouldn't rather have a couple of plump, flaky lines on a mirror and half a disco biscuit than lead the lives these people are leading? — Patrick J. O'Rourke, *Parliament of Whores*, p. 118, 2003

Disco Danny *noun*
a stereotyped fashionable male of the late 1970s *US, 1986*
- In contrast to the disco Dannies, the mates wore T-shirts and sandals and deep Gulf Stream tans, and they drank mostly beer. — Carl Hiaasen, *Skin Tight*, pp. 74–75, 1989

disco dose *noun*
a mild dose of LSD *US, 1995*
- While the typical late-'60s tripper probably took about 250 mg of "acid," the average strength of the hits sold in recent years, known to old-timers as "disco doses," is less than half that. — Steven Daly and Nathaniel Wice, *alt.culture*, p. 138, 1995

disco move *noun*
any maneuver executed by a novice surfer *US, 1991*
- — Trevor Cralle, *The Surfin'ary*, p. 30, 1991

discon *noun*
the criminal charge of "disorderly conduct" *US, 1963*
- All defendants were charged with discon, disorderly conduct. — Ed Sanders, *Tales of Beatnik Glory*, p. 217, 1975
- [I]f Ray Garvey presses those pricks like he's supposed to I'll wind up with a dis-con conviction. — Vincent Patrick, *Family Business*, p. 53, 1985

disco queen *noun*
a male homosexual who frequents discos *US, 1979*
The title of a 1978 song by Paul Jabara glorifying the energy of the song's hero.
- What, asked McCormack, were the drawbacks to being a Disco Queen? "One of the problems is that you have to master the art of looking bored." — Tim Lawrence, *Love Says the Day*, p. 230, 2003

disgustitude *noun*
the state of being disgusted *US, 1990*
- — Karla Jennings, *The Devouring Fungus*, p. 219, 1990

dish *noun*
1 an attractive female *UK, 1909*
- I couldn't forget the way she looked through me the last time we met. What a dish. — Mickey Spillane, *I, The Jury*, p. 49, 1947
- Did you catch that photo on Page 1 yesterday of Liberace and his "current flame," a dish named Jan Valerie? — *San Francisco News*, p. 14, 14th January 1955
- I dreamed I was a real dish in my Maidenform bra. [Headline of advertisement]. — *Life*, p. 48, 16th May 1960
- Myra Breckinridge is a dish, and never forget it, you motherfuckers, as the children say nowadays. — Gore Vidal, *Myra Breckinridge*, p. 3, 1968
- — Collin Baker et al., *College Undergraduate Slang Study Conducted at Brown University*, p. 106, 1968
- DUKE: Just one for a start. HAWKEYE: The blonde dish. — *M*A*S*H*, 1970

2 gossip, especially when disparaging, salacious, or scandalous *US, 1976*
From the verb sense.
- This guy was awfully nice, but his dish seemed suspect. — Armistead Maupin, *Babycakes*, p. 20, 1984
- "Don't give me secret dish." — Ethan Morden, *Buddies*, p. 50, 1986
- [T]abloids are known to pay cash for good "dish." — Erica Orloff & JoAnn Baker *Dirty Little Secrets*, p. 115, 2001

dish *verb*
to gossip, to disparage *US, 1941*
Originally "dish the dirt" or "dish out the dirt."
- "Are you trying to dish me, Mary?" she says angrily. — John Rechy, *City of Night*, p. 53, 1963

- I could have dished her an earful, believe you me. — Antony James, *America's Homosexual Underground*, p. 133, 1965
- O.K., if you don't want to dish, we won't dish. — Armistead Maupin, *Tales of the City*, p. 143, 1978
- Which leads me to the most important rule of all: Never, ever dish anyone in print. — James St. James, *Party Monster*, p. 47, 1990

▸ **dish it out**
to have sex *US, 1949*
- "I got it when I was a freshman, now I'm dishing it out." — William Bernard, *Jailbait*, p. 24, 1949

▸ **dish soup**
to sell cocaine *US, 1995*
- — Mark S. Fleisher, *Beggars & Thieves*, p. 289, 1995: "Glossary"

▸ **dish the dirt; dish it**
to gossip indiscreetly or with slanderous intent *US, 1926*
- Cocktail time hang-outs for models are the bars of the St. Clair and the Croydon, and the Cloverbar, where they dish the dirt. — Jack Lait and Lee Mortimer, *Chicago Confidential*, p. 113, 1950
- They drank more bouillon, popped more bennie and dished the dirt. — Hubert Selby Jr., *Last Exit to Brooklyn*, p. 59, 1957

DI shack *noun*
the quarters where drill instructors live and the on-duty instructor works *US, 1987*
- quarterdeck: sacrosanct area outside DI shack. — Daniel Da Cruz, *Boot*, p. 298, 1987

dishonorable discharge *noun*
ejaculation achieved through masturbation *US, 1964*
- — Roger Blake, *The American Dictionary of Sexual Terms*, p. 60, 1964
- — Dale Gordon, *The Dominion Sex Dictionary*, p. 59, 1967
- When I was in the army, a sergeant caught me in the shower in the process of giving my dick a dishonorable discharge. I looked him straight in the eye and told him it was my dick and I could wash it as fast as I wanted to. — Ken Weaver, *Texas Crude*, p. 83, 1984

dish out *verb*
to dispense (abuse) *US, 1908*
- I began to feel plenty sore, doing a twenty-month stretch (that's the bit the parole board finally dished out to me). — Mezz Mezzrow, *Really the Blues*, p. 318, 1946

dish queen *noun*
a male homosexual who takes special pleasure in gossip *US, 1970*
- — *American Speech*, p. 56, Spring–Summer 1970: "Homosexual slang"
- "Let me point out that there is an incredibly vicious dish-queen in this room and it isn't me." — Ethan Morden, *I've a Feeling We're Not in Kansas Anymore*, p. 15, 1985

dish rags *noun*
in poker, poor cards *US, 1996*
- — John Vorhaus, *The Big Book of Poker Slang*, p. 14, 1996

dismo *noun*
a fanatic surfing enthusiast who never actually surfs *US, 1997*
- — Vann Wesson, *Generation X Field Guide and Lexicon*, p. 54, 1997

Disneyland *nickname*
1 the Pentagon; military headquarters in Vietnam *US, 1963*
A critical assessment of reality and fantasy in the military leadership.
- Referring to the Pentagon in such derisive terms as "Disneyland East" and "Malfunction Junction," politicans, pundits, and professional military officers have launched a barrage of complaints about every aspect of JCS activity. — Amy Zegart, *Flawed by Design*, p. 131, 1999
- MACV Headquarters: "Disneyland East" — Robert Asprey, *War in the Shadows*, p. xxx, 2002

2 the brothel district near An Khe, Vietnam, near the 1st Cavalry Division base *US, 1966*
- — *Time*, p. 29, 6th May 1966
- — Carl Fleischhauer, *A Glossary of Army Slang*, p. 15, 1968
- Although the prostitution corner ("Sin City" or "Disneyland") is run by the Vietnamese, American military police patrol the area to check the pass of every soldier entering it. — Charles Winick, *The Lively Commerce*, p. 265, 1971

3 a prison with relaxed rules that ease the difficulty of serving a sentence *US, 1992*
- — William K. Bentley and James M. Corbett, *Prison Slang*, p. 3, 1992

Disneyland North *nickname*
the Los Angeles County Juvenile Detention Center *US, 1970*
- They headed north on a freeway towards the marvelous new Juvenile Hall out in the Valley, that the kids called Disneyland North. — Hunter S. Thompson, *The Great Shark Hunt*, p. 152, 1979

dispatchers *noun*
in a dice game cheating scheme, improperly marked dice *UK, 1811*
- — John S. Salak, *Dictionary of Gambling*, p. 77, 1963

ditch *noun*
the antecubial vein inside the bend of the elbow, often used for injecting drugs *US, 1967*
- DITCH: The inside of the elbow which has two large veins. — Elizabeth Finn, *Drugs in the Tenderloin*, 1967: Glossary of Drug Slang Used in the Tenderloin
- — *Current Slang*, p. 20, Fall 1968
- — Stewart L. Tubbs and Sylvia Moss, *Human Communication*, p. 119, 1974

ditch *verb*
1 to reject, discard, abandon; to elude *US, 1899*
- You ought to ditch the Dukes while you can. — Irving Shulman, *The Amboy Dukes*, p. 62, 1947
- We are free to go, but have to be very sneaky and ditch Bruce somewhere inside the Pentagon maze so he won't find the Acapulco Gold in the car. — Abbie Hoffman, *Revolution for the Hell of It*, p. 44, 1968
- Honey, ditching class to go shopping doesn't make you a defective. — *The Breakfast Club*, 1985
- I myself have ditched and gotten so bored I did homework. Figure that shit out. — *Ferris Bueller's Day Off*, 1986

2 to release (from prison) *US, 1990*
An abbreviation and corruption of "discharge."
- — Charles Shafer, *Folk Speech in Texas Prisons*, p. 202, 1990

ditchweed *noun*
marijuana of inferior quality that grows wild in roadside ditches, especially in Mexico *US, 1982*
- Ditchweed is uncultivated marijuana that grows wild. — United States General Accounting Office, *Drug Control*, p. 47, July 1999

ditso *noun*
an absent-minded, somewhat dim person *US, 1976*
- Meantime, Zahna noticed, the ditso had left her bag, her books, and that bizarre cross on her blanket. — Kelly Lange, *The Reporter*, p. 246, 2002

ditso *adjective*
absent-minded, somewhat dim *US, 1987*
- Eddie really looked like the typical dumb blond of that era and he behaved off-camera exactly the way he did on-camera, really goofy and ditso. — Patty Duke, *Call Me Anna*, p. 118, 1987
- Gold chain wearin' fried chicken and biscuit eatin' monkey, ape, baboon, fast runnin', high jumpin', spear chuckin' basketball dunkin' ditso spade, take you fuckin' pizza and go back to Africa. — *Do the Right Thing*, 1989

ditsy *adjective*
upset, nervous *US, 1978*
- For a minute I wonder is he going to get ditsy about us living together without benefit of wedlock. — Robert Campbell, *Junkyard Dog*, pp. 61–62, 1986

ditto-head *noun*
a fan of radio entertainer Rush Limbaugh *US, 1992*
Limbaugh conditioned his callers to begin conversations on the radio with a simple "Dittos from [hometown]" instead of gushing admiration for him.
- "Ditto-heads" fall for Rush Limbaugh's specious arguments that pointy-headed, intellectual, godless, semi-Nazi, secular humanist, evolutionist, sexually permissive, environmentalist wackos are out to capture the world by stultifying the minds of our youth and destroying traditional family values. — *St. Petersburg Times*, p. 2, 8th January 1992

ditz *noun*
an absent-minded, empty-headed person *US, 1976*

- She's no longer the erratic "ditz" she used to be, and her career is blossoming, too. — *Chicago Tribune*, p. A2, 17th November 1976
- — Multicultural Management Program Fellows, *Dictionary of Cautionary Words and Phrases*, 1989

ditzy; ditsy *adjective*
(usually of a woman) scatterbrained, silly *US, 1973*
- But what about the ditzy little secretary who lives with her ditzy mother in a ditzy state? — *Los Angeles Times*, p. IV-4, 3rd August 1973
- This one was set up by Lorrie, her ditzy pal from The Fabric Barn, who knew a guy who had a friend who'd been "out of circulation for a while" (whatever that means—prison if you ask me) and wanted his ashes hauled in the worst kind of way. — Armistead Maupin, *Maybe the Moon*, p. 222, 1992
- So ditzy—but sweet. — Rosalind Wiseman, *Queen Bees & Wannabes*, p. 43, 2002

dive *noun*
1 a disreputable establishment *US, 1867*
- I've played the music in a lot of places these last thirty years, from Al Capone's roadhouses to swing joints along 52nd Street in New York, Paris nightclubs, Harvard University, dicty Washington embassies and Park Avenue salons, not to mention all the barrelhouse dives. — Mezz Mezzrow, *Really the Blues*, p. 4, 1946
- After Chicago we thought nothing could make us blink. But some of the dives on 8th Street made it. — Jack Lait and Lee Mortimer, *Washington Confidential*, p. 33, 1951
- Now you not going back on the road no more, and you ain't playing no more two bit sleazy dives. — *The Blues Brothers*, 1980
- Do you call having pizza in the same dive pizzeria every night "eating out?" — *Mallrats*, 1995

2 an intentional loss in a sporting event *US, 1916*
- Q. You think anybody is crazy who takes a dive? A. Yah. Sure. — Rocky Garciano (with Rowland Barber), *Somebody Up There Likes Me*, p. 305, 1955
- What the fuck they want? I took the dive. — *Raging Bull*, 1980

dive *verb*
to lose a contest or competition intentionally, especially in boxing *US, 1921*
From the image of a boxer diving towards the mat, feigning a knock-out blow.
- Folks said, "It's interesting about his secret control of a stable of fighters. I'd guess a hog like that would set-up to bet the ones that dived." — Iceberg Slim (Robert Beck), *Long White Con*, p. 170, 1977

diver *noun*
a hang glider *US, 1992*
- — Erik Fair, *California Thrill Sports*, p. 328, 1992

divoon *adjective*
lovely, delightful *US, 1944*
A humorous elaboration of "divine."
- Stooky! It's divoon! — S.J. Perlman, *Fly by Noon*, p. 540, 1958
- Ezzie Fenwick, who knew beauty when he saw beauty, had tears in his eyes. "Divoon," he said. — Dominick Dunne, *People Like Us*, p. 331, 1988

divvies *noun*
sharing something that is being divided *US, 1958*
- Ah get divvies though. — John Clellon Holmes, *The Horn*, p. 111, 1958
- "And you talk they got to worry about divvies?" — Robert Deane Pharr, *S.R.O.*, p. 269, 1971

divvy *noun*
a share or portion; a *divi*dend *US, 1872*
- Well, well, well, Whistler thought, not a bad night's divvy for the cops. — Robert Campbell, *In La-La Land We Trust*, p. 141, 1986

divvy up *verb*
to divide into shares *US, 1876*
A phonetic abbreviation of "divide."
- OK, we'll divvy it up . . . four ways! — *Tin Men*, 1987

Dixie *nickname*
the southeastern United States *US, 1859*
- Seniority rules in the Congress, which permit one-party Southern Senators and Representatives to control more than their share of committees, account for continuance of its Dixie slant. — Jack Lait and Lee Mortimer, *Washington Confidential*, p. 6, 1951

Dixie cup *noun*

1 the traditional navy white hat, symbol of the American sailor since the C19 *US, 1973*

- When freshmen, or "plebes" at the U.S. Naval Academy in Annapolis, Maryland, finish their summer basic training, they trade in their "dixie cups" (sailor hats) for "covers" (officer hats)[.] — Jan Harold Brunvard, *American Folklore*, p. 484, 1996
- All three wore white navy "Dixie cup" hats, while one also sported a piratical black eye patch and a foul-looking stogie cigar. — James H. Cobb, *Sea Fighter*, p. 178, 2000

2 a woman who speaks with a southern accent *US, 1977*

- — Bill Davis, *Jawjacking*, p. 34, 1977

3 a person who is considered to be utterly dispensable, who is used and then discarded *US, 1997*

- "'Cause he's a Dixie cup." Tommy grinned and refused further comment. Texaco didn't know what the hell that meant[.] — Stephen Cannell, *King Con*, p. 18, 1997

Dixie Trail *noun*

anal sex facilitated by Dixie Peach hair dressing as a lubricant *US, 1968*

- And the few times subseqeunt to my christening when circumstances brought me in contact with someone via the "Dixie Trail," I relived the keenest pleasures. — Angelo d'Arcangelo, *The Homosexual Handbook*, p. 99, 1968

dizzy three *noun*

a C-47A Skytrain plane, also known as a DC-3, most commonly used to transport people and cargo, but also used as a bomber and fighter *US, 1975*

- She was known affectionately as the "Gooney Bird," "Dak," and "Dizzy Three" to the men who flew her during World War II. — *San Francisco Chronicle*, p. 60, 18th January 1975

dj; deejay *noun*

a disc jockey *US, 1950*

- Top 40 Negro dee-jay desires position. Reliable and ambitious. — *Broadcasting*, p. 98, May – June 1964

dj; deejay *verb*

to work as a disc jockey *US, 1985*

- [T]he various hip hop expressions (graffiti, breaking, Djing, rapping)[.] — Nelson George, *Hip Hop America*, p. 18, 1992

DL *noun*

▸ **on the DL**

down low, discreetly *US, 1996*

- — Connie Eble (Editor), *UNC-CH Campus Slang*, p. 3, March 1996
- On the DL, I know where the mojo is. — Gary K. Farlow, *Prison-ese: A Survivor's Guide to Speaking Prison Slang*, p. 17, 2002

DMT *noun*

dimethyltryptamine, a hallucinogenic drug *US, 1971*

- To a client whom he feels is sound enough to handle it, he also will sell LSD, mescaline, STP, DMT or pysilocybin. — Tom Robbins, *Another Roadside Attraction*, pp. 57 – 58, 1971
- Acid is like being sucked up a tube, but DMT is like being shot out of a cannon. — Hunter S. Thompson, *Songs of the Doomed*, p. 113, 1990

DMV *verb*

(said of a male) to urinate *US, 2000*

An abbreviation of **DRAIN THE MAIN VEIN**.

- Go DMV (Drain the Main Vein). — Joy Masoff, *Oh, Yuck*, p. 120, 2000

DMZ *noun*

any place between two opposing factions or social forces, controlled by neither yet ceded by neither *US, 1976*

Originally a military term—"demilitarized zone"—for an area dividing North and South Korea.

- TRAVIS: He wanted to go to the DMZ. BETSY: The DMZ? TRAVIS: South Bronx. The worst. — *Taxi Driver*, 1976
- The back room vibrated with rock music blasting from an enormous set of speakers attached to a stereo system Miguel had stolen, piece by piece, from shops down in the Nineteenth Precinct just below Ninety-sixth Street, the "DMZ" of the East Side. — Thomas Larry Adcock, *Precinct 19*, p. 71, 1984
- The Camelot was on the DMZ between the Heights and the last vestiges of old-time German-Irish Dempsy, and cops were always welcome. — Richard Price, *Clockers*, p. 99, 1992

do *noun*

1 a party or social function *UK, 1824*

- Yoko Ono is throwing a little do in her suite at the Clift. — Armistead Maupin, *Babycakes*, p. 221, 1984
- A valet-parking girl, in a white shirt with a black bow tie and black pants, took his car, saying, "You won't need a ticket, sir." Which meant that the do wouldn't be as big as some he'd had to attend lately. — Joseph Wambaugh, *Floaters*, p. 87, 1996

2 a dose of drugs *US, 1971*

- Damn, I'm getting boogy. I hope you saved me a do, Snake, 'cause I'm sure gettin' sick. — Donald Goines, *Dopefiend*, p. 216, 1971
- Foxy left the spike sticking in the girl's arm and started to prepare his own Do. — Vernon E. Smith, *The Jones Men*, p. 20, 1974

3 in craps, a bet on the shooter *US, 1974*

- At the dice table, the professor would bet either on or against the shooter—otherwise known as do or don't, right or wrong—at $1,000 a shot on what may or may not have been a system. — Edward Lin, *Big Julie of Vegas*, p. 47, 1974

4 a hairdo *US, 1966*

- "I'm out there this morning," Darryl said, "talking to Tiffany, girl with the Indian 'do." — Elmore Leonard, *Be Cool*, p. 182, 1999

do *verb*

1 to rob *UK, 1774*

- How many banks was it you've done in your life, about fifty? — Elmore Leonard, *Bandits*, p. 97, 1987

2 to have sex with *UK, 1650*

- I tried some sex banter with him but Axel was looking fierce. "I'd like to do some of them," he whispered, "I'd like to do some of them." — Clancy Sigal, *Going Away*, p. 258, 1961
- DALLAS: I'll pay ya twenty if you go back there and do mah husband. BUTT-HEAD: Uh, you want us to do a guy? Huh huh. No way. BEAVIS: Umm, I don't know Butt-head. That is a lot of money. Maybe if we close our eyes and pretend he's a chick. — Mike Judge and Joe Stillman, *Beavis and Butt-Head Do America*, p. 29, 1997
- "I don't do divorced men." Karen gave me a tense smile and lowered her voice to a confidential whisper. "You know, Lisa, I probably shouldn't say this, but the word do sometimes has sexual connotations." — Rita Ciresi, *Pink Slip*, p. 29, 1999

3 to perform oral sex upon someone *US, 1963*

- — Donald Webster Cory and John P. LeRoy, *The Homosexual and His Society*, p. 263, 1963: "A lexicon of homosexual slang"

▸ **do me**

to live independently, to take care of yourself *US, 2006*

- "I had to do me," said Donnie, explaining in street slang that he had to survive. — *Philadelphia Daily News*, p. Local 3, 27th December 2006

▸ **do the thing**

to have sex *US, 1968*

- — *Current Slang*, p. 5, Summer 1968

▸ **do your do**

to prepare your hairdo *US, 1995*

- — *Adult Video News*, p. 44, August 1995

DOA *noun*

phencyclidine, the recreational drug known as PCP or angel dust *US, 1993*

The abbreviation is for **DEAD ON ARRIVAL**—the results of a PCP overdose.

- — Peter Johnson, *Dictionary of Street Alcohol and Drug Terms*, p. 60, 1993

doable *adjective*

sexually attractive enough as to warrant the speaker's gift of having sex *US, 1997*

- — Pamela Munro, *U.C.L.A. Slang*, p. 58, 1997
- — Don R. McCreary (Editor), *Dawg Speak*, 2001

do bears shit in the woods?

yes; a nonsense retort used as an affirmative answer to a silly question, often sarcastic *US, 1971*

Often mixed with the synonymous "Is the Pope Catholic?" to achieve **DOES THE POPE SHIT IN THE WOODS?**

- "Is it gonna be hot?" the kid said. "Does a bear shit in the woods?" Dillon said. — George V. Higgins, *The Friends of Eddie Doyle*, p. 210, 1971

dobie *noun*

a Doberman Pinscher dog *US, 1981*

- To cut the tension, he said: "Ten bucks it's a Dobie." "No way," said Danny Pogue. "I say Rottweiler." — Carl Hiaasen, *Native Tongue*, p. 170, 1991
- I was at a bachelor party for Zane where they had these two Doberman Pinschers. The Dobies were on these stairs watching everything. — Anthony Petkovich, *The X Factory*, p. 83, 1997

do-boy *noun*
a male who does whatever his girlfriend tells him to do *US, 2001*
- — Don R. McCreary (Editor), *Dawg Speak*, 2001

doc *noun*
1 a *doctor US, 1840*
- All medicine, docs cheap, very modern. — Jack Kerouac, *Letter to Carolyn Cassady*, p. 363, 3rd June 1952

2 in computing, *doc*umentation *US, 1991*
- — Eric S. Raymond, *The New Hacker's Dictionary*, p. 129, 1991

doc in the box *noun*
a walk-in medical clinic *US, 1994*
- — Sally Williams, *"Strong" Words*, p. 139, 1994

dock rat *noun*
a person who spends a great deal of time working on boats or passing time at docks *US, 2002*
- It's an eclectic, funky flow of mourners—sunburned dock rats and dive captains[.] — Carl Hiaasen, *Basket Case*, p. 72, 2002

dock walloper *noun*
a thief who steals cargo before it has been unloaded or passed through customs *US, 1986*
- — Rachel S. Epstein and Nina Liebman, *Biz Speak*, p. 65, 1986

Docs *noun*
Dr. Martens™ footwear *US, 1993*
- — Judi Sanders, *Faced and Faded, Hanging to Hurl*, p. 12, 1993
- — Steven Daly and Nathaniel Wice, *alt.culture*, p. 65, 1995
- If ever there were status symbols in the punk community, Docs rated up there with mohawks, safety pins, and black leather and flight jackets. — Editors of Ben is Dead, *Retrohell*, p. 60, 1997
- The most sought-after article of clothing, though, was the steelies, 12- to 14-hole, calf-high, steel-toed Doc Marten boots also called DMs or Docs[.] — Bill Valentine, *Gangs and Their Tattoos*, p. 58, 2000

doctor *noun*
1 (used of children) the exploration of each other's genitals *US, 1959*
- We played doctor in the woods. — Leonard Cohen, *Beautiful Losers*, p. 23, 1966
- During all those school years we children had been playing "doctor" by sticking popsicles in our underpants. — Jefferson Poland and Valerie Alison, *The Records of the San Francisco Sexual Freedom League*, p. 111, 1971
- We never played doctor—and yet, I had played this rather terrifying game with other boys and Fonny had certainly played with other girls, and boys. — James Baldwin, *If Beale Street Could Talk*, p. 55, 1974
- We didn't play "house" or "Doctor" or any of that. We had sexual intercourse. — Odie Hawkins, *Scars and Memories*, p. 136, 1987

2 a male with a large penis *US, 1964*
Homosexual usage.
- — Roger Blake, *The American Dictionary of Sexual Terms*, p. 60, 1964
- — Dale Gordon, *The Dominion Sex Dictionary*, p. 59, 1967

Doctor Blue; Dr. Blue *noun*
used in hospitals as a code announcement that a patient is in cardiac arrest *US, 1973*
- — *American Speech*, p. 203, Fall–Winter 1973: "The language of nursing"

Doctor Feelgood; Dr. Feelgood *noun*
any doctor who specializes in energy-giving injections *US, 1973*
- Dr. Feelgood is, actually, a generic term. There are four of them in New York City, all frequented by the social elite, show business folk, and artists with money. — Jim Carroll, *Forced Entries*, p. 75, 1987
- He found some Dr. Feelgoods and copped amphetamine scripts. — James Ellroy, *Destination Morgue*, p. 116, 2004

Doctor Jekyll and Mister Hyde; Dr. Jekyll and Mr. Hyde *noun*
the recreational drug methaqualone, best known as Quaaludes™ *US, 1985*

- By 1972 it was one of the most popular drugs of abuse in the United States and was known as love drug, heroin for lovers, Dr. Jekyll and Mr. Hyde, sopors, sopes, ludes, mandrakes and quacks. — Marilyn Carroll and Gary Gallo, *Methaqualone*, p. 18, 1985

doctor shopping *noun*
the practice of visiting multiple physicians to obtain multiple prescriptions for otherwise illegal drugs *US, 2003*
A common practice of drug addicts and suppliers of drug addicts.
- Doctor shopping refers to the practice of obtaining medications from more than one physician at the same time, as demonstrated in the recent case of Rush Limbaugh. — United States Senate, *Prescription Drug Abuse and Diversion*, p. 53, 2005

Doctor Thomas; Dr. Thomas *noun*
a black person who rejects black culture and takes on the culture of the dominant white society *US, 1980*
An elaboration of the common **UNCLE TOM**, coined long before Clarence Thomas became the personification of the concept.
- — Edith A. Folb, *runnin' down some lines*, p. 235, 1980

Doctor White; Dr. White *noun*
a drug addiction *US, 1959*
- — J.E. Schmidt, *Narcotics Lingo and Lore*, p. 45, 1959

Doc Yak *noun*
a doctor whose reputation is less than sterling *US, 1956*
From a syndicated comic strip that last appeared in 1935.
- I did come up to Your Honor's courtroom five weeks ago, but then Old Doc Yak—what is his name? The man from Washington—Oh, Dr. McNarry. — Meyer Levin, *Compulsion*, p. 378, 1956

dodge *noun*
a scam, a swindle *UK, 1638*
- Why, once in Cuba he even cleaned out Babe Ruth with the fixed-race dodge. — Guy Owen, *The Flim-Flam Man and the Apprentice Grifter*, p. 17, 1972
- "As a matter of fact, I have a friend who needs an operation." "Watch yourself," Torino advised. "I myself have been taken by the old 'I need an operation' dodge." — Robert Campbell, *Alice in La-La Land*, p. 88, 1987

▶ **on the dodge**
in hiding from the police *US, 1976*
- Leo had been living on the dodge for over three years with wanted sheets out in a dozen states, his photograph decorating every post office wall in America. — Emmett Grogan, *Final Score*, p. 22, 1976

Dodge *noun*
▶ **get out of Dodge; get the hell out of Dodge**
to leave, usually with some haste *US, 1965*
A loose allusion to the Wild West as epitomized by Dodge City, Kansas, and the seriousness of an order by the authorities to leave town.
- Coming off the target Jack made a gut decision. "Head straight for home plate, Thunder; let's get the hell out of Dodge." — Richard Herman, *The Warbirds*, p. 295, 1989
- The pilot had some problem, so he aimed it over the sea, trimmed up the controls to keep it that way till it ran out of fuel and splashed in, and then got the hell out of Dodge. — Dennis Marvicsin and Jerold Greenfield, *Maverick*, p. 92, 1990
- That gives us forty minutes to get the fuck outta Dodge, which, if you do what I say when I say it, should be plenty. — *Pulp Fiction*, 1994

Dodge City *nickname*
an enemy-controlled area south of Da Nang, the scene of heavy fighting in November 1968; anywhere in Vietnam with a strong Viet Cong presence *US, 1969*
- "I got a letter from him and he said he was going on an operation into 'Dodge City,' which is close to An Hoa." — Joseph T. Ward, *Dear Mom*, p. 92, 1991

dodger *noun*
a small advertising leaflet *US, 1879*
- — Joe McKennon, *Circus Lingo*, p. 30, 1980

dodo *noun*
1 a fool *US, 1898*
- Thad is acting like a complete dodo. For a man his age his daddyhood antics border on the absurd. — Sandra Brown, *Adam's Fall*, p. 31, 1988

2 an aviation cadet who has not completed basic training US, *1933*

- In normal times a cadet who had completed primary training became an upperclassmen and was encouraged to haze the young "dodos." — Charles A. Martin, *The Last Great Ace*, p. 116, 1998

doer *noun*

the person responsible for a specific crime, especially a murder US, *1992*

- Yeah, well, he says he can serve up one of the do-ers on the Henderson job. — Richard Price, *Clockers*, p. 40, 1992

dog *noun*

1 an unattractive woman or man US, *1937*

- What's the difference between a dog and a fox? About six beers. — *Maledicta*, p. 291, 1988–1989

2 a sexually transmitted infection US, *1962*

- — Joseph E. Ragen and Charles Finston, *Inside the World's Toughest Prison*, p. 797, 1962: "Penitentiary and underworld glossary"
- — *Maledicta*, p. 228, Summer/Winter 1981: "Sex and the single soldier"

3 used as a general form of friendly address (without any negative connotations) US, *1995*

A rare positive use of "dog," synonymous with "man," possibly influenced by rap artist Snoop Doggy Dogg (Calvin Broadus, b.1972). Also spelled "dogg" and "dawg."

- — Linda Meyer, *Teenspeak!*, p. 28, 1994
- — Connie Eble (Editor), *UNC-CH Campus Slang*, p. 3, April 1995
- The rap page biz [publishing] is murder, dog. — *The Source*, p. 36, March 2002

4 a freshman, or first-year college student US, *1947*

- — Marcus Hanna Boulware, *Jive and Slang of Students in Negro Colleges*, 1947

5 the grade "D" US, *1964*

- — Collin Baker et al., *College Undergraduate Slang Study Conducted at Brown University*, p. 106, 1968

6 a marijuana cigarette US, *1997*

- — Jim Emerson-Cobb, *Scratching the Dragon*, April 1997
- — Pamela Munro, *U.C.L.A. Slang*, p. 61, 2001

7 in sports betting, the underdog US, *1975*

- — *Bay Sports Review*, p. 8, November 1991

8 in poker, a worthless hand US, *1988*

- — George Percy, *The Language of Poker*, p. 29, 1988

9 in horse racing, a racehorse with little value US, *1840*

- — David W. Maurer, *Argot of the Racetrack*, p. 24, 1951
- But, anyway, a real dog had come in at a hundred-and-forty for two. — Jim Thompson, *The Grifters*, p. 63, 1963

10 in pool, a difficult shot US, *1993*

- — Mike Shamos, *The Illustrated Encyclopedia of Billiards*, p. 79, 1993

11 in horse racing, a sawhorse used to keep horses away from the rail during a workout on a muddy track US, *1976*

- — Dean Alfange, *The Horse Racing Industry*, p. 212, 1976

12 in poker, the fourth player to the left of the dealer US, *1988*

- — George Percy, *The Language of Poker*, p. 26, 1988

13 a failure of a song or movie US, *1929*

- — Arnold Shaw, *Lingo of Tin-Pan Alley*, p. 10, 1950
- The movie is a dog, but Larry likes it because Natalie Wood is in it and he says during the intermission that Carlotte looks a lot like Natalie Wood. — Darryl Ponicsan, *The Last Detail*, p. 104, 1970

▸ **like a big dog**

to an extreme US, *1987*

- — *Washington Post Magazine*, p. 9, 6th September 1987

▸ **on the dog**

on credit US, *1978*

- Some bookies let reliable customers put it on the dog ... have credit. — Burgess Laughlin, *Job Opportunities in the Black Market*, p. 10–2, 1978

▸ **put on the dog**

to assume a superior, upper-class attitude US, *1865*

- But it's really funny to watch these Californians trying to put on the dog. — Jack Kerouac, *Letter to Caroline Kerouac Blake*, p. 131, 25th September 1947
- She's always putting on the dog—saying bahth and cahn't and dahnce and like that. — Max Shulman, *I was a Teen-Age Dwarf*, p. 60, 1959

Dog *noun*

the Greyhound bus line US, *1974*

A fixture in American travel until a crippling strike in the 1990s; variants include "Grey Dog" and ol' "Grey Dog."

- — Gwyneth A. "Dandalion" Seese, *Tijuana Bear in a Smoke, Um Up Taix*, p. 14, 1977

- Well, the wife left me again. Took the ol' Grey Dog to Falfurrias last night ... thank God. — Ken Weaver, *Texas Crude*, p. 110, 1984
- — Bill Casselman, *Canadian Sayings*, p. 134, 2002

dog *verb*

1 to avoid work; to work slowly US, *1955*

- I hoped they would understand that I wasn't going what they called it—"over the hill"—because I was yellow or wanted to dog a fight. — Rocky Garciano (with Rowland Barber), *Somebody Up There Likes Me*, p. 188, 1955
- That bastard on the next line is dogging—I've made three trips to his two. — Donald Duncan, *The New Legions*, p. 131, 1967
- "He's not dogging it," Carbone said. "He's got a temperature and he's got a fever and he's got the trots." — George V. Higgins, *The Rat on Fire*, p. 90, 1981

2 to studiously ignore US, *1987*

- — *Washington Post Magazine*, p. 17, 12th April 1987: "Say wha?"

3 to abuse or harass US, *1992*

- — William K. Bentley and James M. Corbett, *Prison Slang*, p. 92, 1992
- "Why you dog 'im like that in public?" — Eric Jerome Dickey, *Cheaters*, p. 131, 1999
- "I can't dog my boys like that." — Linden Dalecki, *Kid B*, p. 141, 2006

4 to perform sexually for money US, *1989*

- — Terry Williams, *The Cocaine Kids*, p. 136, 1989

5 in pool, to miss a shot that should be made US, *1984*

- The other man won it, broke the balls wide and ran half the solids before dogging a thin cut into the corner. — Walter Tevis, *The Color of Money*, p. 114, 1984
- — Steve Rushin, *Pool Cool*, p. 11, 1990

dog; doggo *adverb*

motionless UK, *1893*

- I seem to have emotional upheavals, like Kansas has tornadoes, and when they hit I have a tendency to lie doggo, in the manner of a beast turning its posterior to a blizzard and dumbly, numbly waiting it out. — James Blake, *The Joint*, p. 187, 28th March 1958
- I must play by the rules, but I'll lie doggo and pretend I am hypnotized. — John Fowles, *The Magus*, p. 242, 1965
- I wanted to play it doggo for a month or two. — Juan Carmel Cosmes, *Memoir of a Whoremaster*, p. 74, 1969
- Two days later we were still laying dog, and it was still raining. — Larry Chambers, *Recondo*, p. 64, 1992

dog and pony show *noun*

an elaborate presentation US, *1957*

- Speaking of which, I have a dog-and-pony show for Fartface Siegel this morning. — Armistead Maupin, *Tales of the City*, p. 106, 1978
- — Department of the Army, *Staff Officer's Guidebook*, p. 58, 1986
- [He] meant the lunch to be a serious discussion, not one of those "dog and pony shows," as they were called in service parlance, which Vann put on with Cao for guided tours through My Tho. — Neil Sheehan, *A Bright Shining Lie*, p. 117, 1988

dog-ass *noun*

a despised person US, *1959*

- In a strangely kind tone of voice he said: "Okay, dog ass, come get some food." — John Howard Griffin, *Black Like Me*, p. 32, 1962

dog-ass *adjective*

1 shoddy, inferior US, *1953*

- Say, now boys, I got something to tell you, just to get it off my mind / Now your dogass pimps ought to get off the line. — Bruce Jackson, *Get Your Ass in the Water and Swim Like Me*, p. 134, 1964
- "White Plains." "That's a dog-ass town." — David Parks, *GI Diary*, p. 5, 1968
- That was a dog-ass amateur job. — George V. Higgins, *The Rat on Fire*, p. 22, 1981

2 despicable US, *1953*

- NOW WHAT DO YOU HAVE TO SAY, YOU DOG-ASS SON OF A BITCH? — David McCumber, *Playing Off the Rail*, p. 87, 1996
- I knew that despite all of Trent's good qualities, he was still a dog ass nigga, like all the other men I knew. — Brenda L. Thomas, *Threesome*, p. 94, 2002

dog bait *noun*

during a mass prison escape, a prisoner left by others to attract the attention of the tracking dogs US, *1972*

- Everybody in escaping down here, they're looking for what we call dog bait. Unless you're with a guy personally, you're going to try to feed them to the dogs so you can get away. — Bruce Jackson, *In the Life*, p. 317, 1972

dogball *noun*

in a deck of playing cards, an eight *US, 1996*

- — John Vorhaus, *The Big Book of Poker Slang*, p. 16, 1996

dog breath *noun*

1 bad-smelling breath *US, 1944*

- I had horrible dog's breath and was constantly on edge. — Suzanne Somers, *Suzanne Somer's Eat Great, Lose Weight*, p. Front Matter, 1996

2 cigarette smoke *US, 1996*

- — John Vorhaus, *The Big Book of Poker Slang*, p. 14, 1996

dog clutch *noun*

an involuntary locking of the vaginal muscles, imprisoning the penis (*penis captivus*) *US, 1967*

Common in dogs, not so common in humans, but common enough for a term to describe it.

- — Dale Gordon, *The Dominion Sex Dictionary*, p. 121, 1967

dog days *noun*

a woman's menstrual period *US, 1960*

- — Helen Dahlskog (Editor), *A Dictionary of Contemporary and Colloquial Usage*, p. 19, 1972

dog do *noun*

dog feces *US, 1979*

- Brad had somehow stuffed the right toe with dog-do. — Beatrice Sparks (writing as 'Anonymous'), *Jay's Journal*, p. 72, 1979

dog-eater *noun*

a member of the Sioux Indian tribe *US, 1963*

- — *American Speech*, p. 271, December 1963: "American Indian student slang"

dog-eye *verb*

to scrutinize carefully *US, 1912*

- — Joseph E. Ragen and Charles Finston, *Inside the World's Toughest Prison*, p. 797, 1962: "Penitentiary and underworld glossary"
- Here I am in these stripes—I stuck out like a sore thumb. He had been dog-eyeing me over, but he didn't know me. — Bruce Jackson, *In the Life*, p. 320, 1972

dogface *noun*

1 an ugly person; used as a general term of abuse *US, 1849*

- "Where you headed, Dogface?" "A face like yours could stop time." — Barbara Robinette Moss, *Change Me into Zeus's Daughter*, p. 211, 2000

2 a low ranking soldier *US, 1930*

- If there is one thing a dogface loves, it is artillery—his own. — Audie Murphy, *To Hell and Back*, p. 58, 1949
- Having served in Korea as a dogface grunt, he knew a lifer when he saw one. — Joseph Wambaugh, *Finnegan's Week*, p. 27, 1993

dog-faced *adjective*

despicable *US, 1962*

- The dog-faced security men had tracked him somehow. — F. Paul Wilson, *All the Rage*, p. 197, 2004

dog fashion; doggie fashion *adverb*

sexual intercourse from behind, vaginal or anal, heterosexual or homosexual *UK, 1900*

- I'd always drop it down and fuck her dog fashion. — A.S. Jackson, *Gentleman Pimp*, p. 110, 1973
- One time I was with Jim and we were balling doggie fashion and his roommate came home and got turned on watching us ball. — *Adam Film Quarterly*, p. 68, October 1973
- I had terrible thoughts of being caught, doggie fashion. — Odie Hawkins, *Black Casanova*, p. 37, 1984
- "I got a three-hundred-and-fifty-pounder likes to lay on top of me as it is. Can you picture that?" "How do you do it?" "Like the bow-wows, doggie fashion. Man, it's a full-time job." — Elmore Leonard, *Pronto*, p. 336, 1993

dog finger *noun*

the index finger *US, 1926*

- And it wasn't just any finger either—it was the pointer finger, the one next to the thumb, and we called it "the dog finger"—the finger you used to curse somebody. — Cornelia Walker Bailey, *God, Dr. Buzzard, and the Bolito Man*, p. 170, 2000

dog food *noun*

Italian sausage *US, 1996*

- — *Maledicta*, p. 11, 1996: "Domino's pizza jargon"

dogfuck *noun*

a despicable person *US, 1993*

- You either hand it over, or I'll have my people sign their names in your flesh. And believe me, dogfuck, they got long names. — James W. Hall, *Hard Aground*, p. 56, 1993

dogfuck *verb*

to have sex from the rear, homosexual or heterosexual, vaginal or anal *US, 1980*

- — Edith A. Folb, *runnin' down some lines*, p. 235, 1980

dogfucker *noun*

a despicable person *US, 1981*

- "I have an accident an' you curse me, gringo dog-fucker." — Jake Logan, *Hellfire*, p. 195, 1981
- "Not some white-cocksuckin Oreo dogfucka like you!" — Jess Mowry, *Six Out Seven*, p. 344, 1993

doggie *noun*

1 a sexual position in which the woman or passive male kneels and the man enters her from behind *US, 2005*

- Next up is "nurse" Chai Sun bathing Mr. Marcus, then mounting him in both cowgirl positions, divided by a bit of doggie. — Editors of Adult Video News, *The AVN Guide to the 500 Greatest Adult Films of All Time*, p. 19, 2005

2 an infantry soldier *US, 1937*

A shortened **DOGFACE**.

- It hits the doggies to see a man staring glassily at the shambles of the home he spent his life building. — Bill Mauldin, *Up Front*, p. 69, 1945
- Once in a while a doggie or seaman came in for a hamburger and played the jukebox. — Hubert Selby Jr., *Last Exit to Brooklyn*, p. 27, 1957
- I watch those brave doggies die trying to attack. — Ernest Spencer, *Welcome to Vietnam, Macho Man*, p. 135, 1987
- Some doggies—both draftees and enlisted men—frequently jumped the fence and went AWOL, wondering on why on earth they ever joined up in the first place. — Ralph "Sonny" Barger, *Hell's Angel*, p. 22, 2000

doggie cop *noun*

a police officer working with a trained dog *US, 1983*

- You wanna give up being a doggie cop, you can jist transfer over here to Ramparts. — Joseph Wambaugh, *The Delta Star*, p. 181, 1983

doggie pack *noun*

a US Army combat field pack *US, 1982*

Used derisively by US Marines during the conflict in Vietnam.

- — *Maledicta*, p. 253, Summer/Winter 1982: "Viet-speak"

doggie pouch *noun*

a small ammunition pouch used by the infantry *US, 1971*

- When my clip expended I started reaching in my little doggie pouch thing for more ammo. — John Kerry, *The New Soldier*, p. 68, 1971

doggie straps *noun*

rucksack straps *US, 1982*

Vietnam war usage.

- Doggie straps—that was the thing we used to dream about, shoulder straps. — Al Santoli, *Everything We Had*, p. 92, 1982

doggins *noun*

in the illegal production of alcohol, liquor sweated out of used barrel staves *US, 1974*

- — David W. Maurer, *Kentucky Moonshine*, p. 115, 1974

doggone *adjective*

used as a mild, folksy euphemism for "damn" *UK, 1826*

Multiple variants. Usually used with a conscious folksy effect in mind.

- Don't you talk to me that way! You owe every doggone cent of it and you know it, and by golly you're going to pay it. — Jim Thompson, *The Grifters*, p. 90, 1963
- I didn't have a doggone dime[.] — C.W. McCall, *Convoy*, 1976
- There really ain't too doggoned much difference between the Democrats 'n the Republicans. — Donald Goines, *The Busting Out of an Ordinary Man*, p. 57, 1985

doggy bag; doggie bag *noun*

a bag in which uneaten food from a restaurant is packed and taken home *US, 1947*

- They paid $3.50 each, left with enough uneaten steak in a "doggie bag" to feed themselves, not the dog, all next day. — *Life*, p. 47, 6th April 1947

- "Who gets the doggie bag?" The girl from the News waited. "Just put it there," Raymond said. "She doesn't take it, I will." — Elmore Leonard, *City Primeval*, p. 23, 1980
- You don't need to be Alan Greenspan to know that one of the nation's leading economic indicators—doggie-bag requests at upscale restaurants—suggests that we're headed for recessionary times. — *San Francisco Chronicle*, p. 1, 25th August 2001

doghouse cut *noun*
a manner of cutting a deck of cards in which a section of cards is moved from the center of the deck to the top, leaving the bottom cards undisturbed *US, 1967*
- — Albert H. Morehead, *The Complete Guide to Winning Poker*, p. 261, 1967

dog it; dog *verb*
1 to refuse to pay a lost bet or a debt *US, 1950*
- — *The Annals of the American Academy of Political and Social Sciences*, p. 124, May 1950
2 to back down from a confrontation or situation for lack of courage *US, 1979*
- — H. Craig Collins, *Street Gangs*, p. 222, 1979

dog juice *noun*
inexpensive alcohol, especially wine *US, 1980*
- — Edith A. Folb, *runnin' down some lines*, p. 235, 1980

dogleg *noun*
a nap *US, 2002*
- "Gene, all decked out for the eternal dogleg." — Carl Hiaasen, *Basket Case*, p. 54, 2002

dog meat *noun*
1 a person who is certain of defeat or death *US, 1977*
- If one of those gates accidentally popped open, I'd have been dog meat[.] — John C. Burnham, *A Soldier's Best Friend*, p. 97, 2000
2 an inept, worthless person *US, 1908*
- Miss Titania had her court, and everyone else was dogmeat when Miss Titania got through. — Ethan Morden, *I've a Feeling We're Not in Kansas Anymore*, p. 2, 1985
- An eight-year-old makes me look like dog meat. — Elizabeth Spurr, *Surfer Dog*, p. 71, 2002

dog mouth *noun*
bad breath experienced upon waking up *US, 1982*
Hawaiian youth usage.
- — Douglas Simonson, *Pidgin to da Max Hana Hou*, 1982

do-gooder *noun*
a well-intentioned person who believes in and supports charity *US, 1927*
The term suggests both a naivete and a slightly cloying sense of self-righteousness.
- He doesn't appeal to the modern worker. They smell the do-gooder in him. — Mary McCarthy, *The Group*, p. 138, 1963
- The polio boxes are the old man's old lady's personal do-gooder project. — Darryl Ponicsan, *The Last Detail*, p. 17, 1970
- But I had to visit with a number of social workers and do-gooders[.] — Herbert Huncke, *Guilty of Everything*, p. 198, 1990
- Candy Pringle and some other do-gooder seniors from my high school just dropped by with a frozen turkey and a big bag of canned goods. — C.D. Payne, *Youth in Revolt*, p. 319, 1993

dog out *verb*
to criticize harshly *US, 1986*
- You dog her out because she's White. — *Mo' Better Blues*, 1990
- — *Army*, p. 48, November 1991

Dogpatch *nickname*
a neighborhood of bars and shops near the Da Nang US Air Base during the Vietnam war *US, 1975*
Dogpatch was the stereotypical Appalachian town in Al Capp's *Li'il Abner* comic strip, which was very popular in the US during the Vietnam war.
- It's just sticks, hovels with tin roofs. It's Dogpatch. — Mark Barker, *Nam*, p. 38, 1981
- Late in 1966, Steve was in a place just below Hill 327 near Da Nang that the GIs called Dogpatch, a sprawl of native huts, some made of C-ration boxes and Coke cans stamped flat and nailed together. — Peter Collier, *Destructive Generation*, p. 126, 1996
- Them girls are the cleanest in Dogpatch. Use protection and don't leave alone. — John J. Culbertson, *A Sniper in the Arizona 2nd Battalion*, p. 145, 1999

dog pile *noun*
the pile of skiers or snowboarders produced when one falls while dismounting from a lift *US, 1990*
- — Elena Garcia, *A Beginner's Guide to Zen and the Art of Snowboarding*, p. 121, 1990: "Glossary"

dogpile *verb*
1 to jump onto someone or onto a group of people *US, 1945*
- [H]e swiveled in his chair, dropped his arms and got ready to let his son dogpile him. — James Ellroy, *The Big Nowhere*, p. 110, 1988
2 to post many critical comments in response to a posting on an Internet discussion group *US, 1995*
- — Christian Crumlish, *The Internet Dictionary*, p. 54, 1995

dog-piss *adjective*
inferior, shabby *US, 1971*
- It was a scruffy dog-piss postcard off the postcard rack of broken dreams. — Tom Robbins, *Another Roadside Attraction*, p. 75, 1971

dog race *noun*
in horse racing, a race featuring cheap racehorses *US, 1951*
- — David W. Maurer, *Argot of the Racetrack*, p. 24, 1951

dog-rob *verb*
to acquire through scrounging or pilfering *US, 1919*
- I give you Arch—that's Livingston—and Papa and anybody you can dog-rob outa some other department. — William Diehl, *Starky's Machine*, p. 92, 1978

dog-robber *noun*
1 an officer's assistant *US, 1863*
- I thought it might be stretching a point to bring the wife of the Secretary's chief horse holder, dog robber, and gofer, but Weinberger insisted. — Colin L. Powell, *My American Journey*, p. 278, 1995
- "You know he's no longer a dog-robber?" "No, I didn't." "Well, he's not. He was good at it, but he hated it." — W.E.B. Griffin, *Special Ops*, p. 94, 2001
2 a person assigned the most menial of tasks, especially the acquisition of difficult-to-acquire goods and services *US, 1974*
- Each marine hut or tent had its dog robber. Okinawans only a few months from Japanese occupation could work up a spit shine as if they had been born to it. — Earl Thompson, *Tattoo*, p. 293, 1974
- So Americans went to war with a will. They went as riflemen and machine-gunners, as cooks and dog-robbers, they went as motor-pool sergeants and as heavy equipment specialists who could reopen a bombed harbor for the Allied invasion. — *Press Enterprise (Riverside, California)*, p. A12, 11th November 1999
- Here it comes, he thought, proof I was a rear echelon dog robber. — Joseph Cody, *Imitate the Tiger*, p. 343, 2004
3 in the movie and television industries, a person whose job it is to find difficult-to-find goods for props *US, 2002*
- He is neither the biggest nor the best in his business, he tells you. There are dozens of other dog-robbers in town. Many have specialties. He's partial to military garb and gear. — *Los Angeles Times*, p. 1 (Part 6), 18th February 2002

dogs *noun*
1 the feet; shoes *US, 1914*
- "What's a-matter?" he snarls. "Pick up your dogs." — Audie Murphy, *To Hell and Back*, p. 6, 1949
- "Show 'em how you used to murder par in your bare dogs down home in the hills." — Sam Snead, *The Education of a Golfer*, p. 58, 1962
- — Joseph E. Ragen and Charles Finston, *Inside the World's Toughest Prison*, p. 796, 1962
- Preston had his bad dogs propped on a chair when I got back. I stumbled over his make-shift sandals beside the sofa. — Iceberg Slim (Robert Beck), *Pimp*, p. 98, 1969
- He thought of getting up at 5 A.M., at the bare ass of dawn, and getting his dogs down to daily pay for a dishwashing gig or a kitchen job or anything at all. — William Brashler, *City Dogs*, p. 14, 1976
- — Connie Eble (Editor), *UNC-CH Campus Slang*, p. 2, Fall 1997
2 in circus and carnival usage, the legs *US, 1981*
- — Don Wilmeth, *The Language of American Popular Entertainment*, p. 75, 1981

dog's bait *noun*
a huge amount *US, 1933*
- It's the conservatives who get up in time to milk a dairy herd and stuff their bullets with a dog's bait of eggs and sausages. — Larry King, *The One-Eyed Man*, p. 33, 2001

dogshit *noun*

1 anything or anyone considered to be worthless or disgusting *US, 1968*

- You dirty little faggot! Call the manager! I'm tired of listening to this dogshit! — Hunter S. Thompson, *Fear and Loathing in Las Vegas*, p. 107, 1971
- [E]verything that came from [San Francisco] was really important Art, and anything from anyplace else (especially L.A.) was dogshit. — Frank Zappa, *The Real Frank Zappa Book*, p. 68, 1989
- You look like dogshit. — *Basic Instinct*, 1992

2 Italian sausage *US, 1996*

- — *Maledicta*, p. 11, 1996: "Domino's pizza jargon"

dogshit *adjective*

worthless or disgusting *US, 1967*

- "I don't write any fucking dog shit poetry. Even after I've stuffed myself and have nothing else to do, I still won't crank out any of that dog shit garbage." — Alai, *Red Poppies*, p. 169, 2003

dog's lunch *noun*

a physically repulsive person *US, 1964*

- — Florida Legislative Investigation Committee (Johns Committee), *Homosexuality and Citizenship in Florida*, 1964: "Glossary of homosexual terms and deviate acts"

dog soldier *noun*

a common soldier *US, 1950*

- [T]he department was top-heavy with managers while the ranks below were so thin that the dog soldiers on the street rarely had the time or inclination to step out of their protective machines, their cars, to meet the people they served. — Michael Connelly, *The Concrete Blond*, p. 209, 1994

dog style; doggy style *noun*

a sexual position in which the woman or passive male kneels and the man enters her from behind *US, 1957*

- Greek lads white as marble fuck dog style on the portico of a great golden temple. — William Burroughs, *Naked Lunch*, p. 117, 1957
- They crawl down aisle/ While screwing dog-style. — *Eros*, p. 64, Winter 1962
- Why don't we do it doggie. — Stephen Ziplow, *The Film Maker's Guide to Pornography*, p. 90, 1977
- "I still think I might go for that anterior stuff—I may want you to fuck me doggy-style," she added. — Larry McMurtry, *When the Light Goes*, p. 190, 2007

dogtag *noun*

1 an identity disc *US, 1918*

- When Billy Pilgrim's name was inscribed in the ledger of the prison camp, he was given a number, too, and an iron dogtag on which that number was stamped. — Kurt Vonnegut, *Slaughterhouse Five*, p. 91, 1969

2 a prescription for a narcotic, possibly legal or possibly forged or illegally obtained *US, 1959*

- — J.E. Schmidt, *Narcotics Lingo and Lore*, p. 40, 1959

dog turd *noun*

a cigar *US, 1969*

- When it came around to the man sitting on Annie's right—a heavy-set man with a red face, smoking a cigar that one of the other men had called a dog turd—the man added ten more chips. — Gary Paulsen, *The Car*, p. 144, 1994

dog wagon *noun*

a bus or van used to transport prisoners from jail to prison *US, 1952*

- Somebody screaming his head off in that empty dog wagon two blocks south. — Mickey Spillane, *Kiss Me Deadly*, p. 138, 1952
- — Frank Prewitt and Francis Schaeffer, *Vacaville Vocabulary*, 1961–1962

dogwash *noun*

a task that is not particularly important but is pursued in instead of a more demanding, more important task *US, 1991*

- — Eric S. Raymond, *The New Hacker's Dictionary*, p. 129, 1991

dog water *noun*

colorless seminal fluid *US, 1861*

- Knowing that scum was white, most of the guys said that Horse was right and that it was just dog water. I said that dog water was more than he ever made. — Claude Brown, *Manchild in the Promised Land*, pp. 80–81, 1965
- Slowly the initial pain subsided, ever so slowly, then it started slowly feeling good as the dog water in her nest. — Steve Cannon, *Groove, Bang, and Jive Around*, p. 38, 1969

- "No dry spasms, piss or clear drops of 'dog water,'" according to the glib rule sheet[.] — Josh Alan Friedman, *Tales of Times Square*, p. 103, 1986

do in *verb*

to kill *UK, 1905*

- Before you do me in, Mr. McManus, you will let me finish my business with Ms. Finneran first, won' you? — *The Usual Suspects*, 1995

doink *noun*

a socially inept, out-of-touch person *US, 1968*

- — Collin Baker et al., *College Undergraduate Slang Study Conducted at Brown University*, p. 106, 1968

do it!

used as an exhortation to experience life rather than analyze it *US, 1968*

- [A]s he holds the flag staunchly in his hands and marches up the aisle and then down the aisle, signifying—what? Ne'mind! But exactly! Don't explain it. Do it! — Tom Wolfe, *The Electric Kool-Aid Acid Test*, p. 167, 1968

do-it fluid *noun*

alcoholic drink *US, 1980*

Based on the observed effect of alcohol on sexual inhibition.

- — Edith A. Folb, *runnin' down some lines*, p. 235, 1980
- Pinto went into the library, where the band was enjoying some pre-performance do-it-fluid[.] — Ralph Gessner, *Deep in My Heart*, p. 297, 2000

dojah *noun*

marijuana *US, 2004*

- — Rick Ayers (Editor), *Berkeley High Slang Dictionary*, p. 16, 2004
- Pot, grass, weed, herb, cheeba, chronic, trees, indo, doja—whatever they called it then, whatever they call it now, and whatever they'll call it in the future, it was marijuana. — 50 Cent, *From Pieces to Weight*, p. 5, 2005

doll *noun*

1 a young woman *US, 1840*

- If somebody else's dish (and we mean dish, not doll), looks particularly attractive, don't sample it unless you're asked to. — Jack Lait and Lee Mortimer, *New York Confidential*, p. 223, 1948
- Tappy then sent a couple of exquisite dolls to the drunk's table, everybody had drinks, and Tappy presented a $50 tab. — Robert Sylvester, *No Cover Charge*, pp. 213–214, 1956
- All the wise guys 'n dolls was jammed in—place was hysteria. — Edwin Torres, *Carlito's Way*, p. 23, 1975

2 a very attractive person of any sex that you find attractive *US, 1963*

- — Donald Webster Cory and John P. LeRoy, *The Homosexual and His Society*, p. 263, 1963: "A lexicon of homosexual slang"

3 used as a term of address *US, 1949*

- — Anon., *The Gay Girl's Guide*, p. 8, 1949

4 a barbiturate capsule; an amphetamine capsule or tablet *US, 1966*

- She claimed the little red "dolls" had saved her life. — Jacqueline Susann, *Valley of the Dolls*, p. 215, 1966
- — Richard Lingeman, *Drugs from A to Z*, p. 65, 1969

dollar ride *noun*

an orientation flight on a military aircraft *US, 1975*

- The next day, they'd get their dollar ride, an orientation flight around the area. — Walter Boyne and Steven Thompson, *The Wild Blue*, p. 69, 1986
- Boyd first went on what was called the "dollar ride," an orientation flight over northeastern Mississippi, where he would be flying for the next several months. — Robert Coram, *Boyd*, p. 40, 2002

dollars to doughnut

at very high odds, indicating a high degree of certainty *US, 1889*

- Why, I'll bet you a dollar to a doughnut my dog'll point five birds to your dog's one. — Ken Weaver, *Texas Crude*, p. 110, 1984
- I'm laying dollars to doughnuts we can pass the proposal in the '47 Special. — James Ellroy, *The Black Dahlia*, p. 20, 1987
- "Dollars to doughnuts he's at his social club," Vinnie said. — Janet Evanovich, *Seven Up*, p. 14, 2001

doll's eyes *noun*

eyes rolling upward, suggesting neurological depression *US, 1988–1989*

- — *Maledicta*, p. 32, 1988–1989: "Medical maledicta from San Francisco"

doll shop *noun*

a brothel *US, 1990*

- After all, Ah Toy once worked at one of Johnny Formosa's doll shops. — Seth Morgan, *Homeboy*, p. 127, 1990

doll up *verb*

to dress up, to refine *US, 1906*

- I got myself all dolled up and went down—big night at the Copa. — Edwin Torres, *Carlito's Way*, p. 26, 1975
- The head of CBS Sports called from the Bel Air Hotel to say he was on the Coast for a few days to "doll up an affiliate." — Dan Jenkins, *Life Its Ownself*, p. 159, 1984

dolly *noun*

a capsule of Dolophine™, known generically as methadone *US, 1954*

- Start dolly cure in a few days now. — William Burroughs, *Letters to Allen Ginsberg 1953–1957*, p. 25, 1st March 1954
- "Even without dollies," Tom Tear said, "I could kick it in three days." — Alexander Trocchi, *Cain's Book*, p. 31, 1960
- "Some kid smashed into a drugstore, and he sold Kove a handful of dollies." — Malcolm Braly, *Shake Him Till He Rattles*, p. 141, 1963
- I had one little bitty piece of dolly [Dolophine] in my aspirin box. — Bruce Jackson, *In the Life*, p. 84, 1972

Dolly Parton *noun*

in craps, a roll of two ones *US, 1983*

Dolly Parton is a talented and popular American country singer and songwriter with big hair and big breasts; the single dots on the two dice suggested to someone her breasts.

- — Thomas L. Clark, *The Dictionary of Gambling and Gaming*, p. 65, 1987

dolly sweetness *noun*

a pretty girl *US, 1947*

- — Marcus Hanna Boulware, *Jive and Slang of Students in Negro Colleges*, 1947

dolo *noun*

methadone *US, 1986*

A shortened form of Dolophine™, a protected trade name for methadone.

- — Richard A. Spears, *The Slang and Jargon of Drugs and Drink*, p. 148, 1986

dolphin *noun*

a flaccid penis *US, 1995*

- — *Adult Video News*, p. 51, October 1995

dolphin ball *noun*

in pinball, a ball that stays in play for a relatively long period without scoring many points *US, 1977*

- — Bobbye Claire Natkin and Steve Kirk, *All About Pinball*, p. 112, 1977

DOM *noun*

an older homosexual who is attracted to younger men and boys; a *dirty old man US, 1966*

- Yet another stereotype that Rubin examines is that of the DOM (Dirty Old Man). — Julia Braun Kessler, *Getting Even with Getting Old*, p. 145, 1980

dom; domme *noun*

1 the dominant performer in a pornographic sex scene *US, 2000*

- — Ana Loria, *1 2 3 Be A Porn Star!*, p. 164, 2000: "Glossary of adult sex industry terms"

2 a sexual dominant in sadomasochistic sexual relationships *US, 1989*

- — Thomas Murray and Thomas Murrell, *The Language of Sadomasochism*, p. 61, 1989

3 a person's room, apartment, or house *US, 1959*

A shortened variant of the more common **DOMMY**.

- The Beatnik knocked his stroll right then, went straight down to his dom[.] — Dan Burley, *Diggeth Thou?*, p. 34, 1959

dome doily *noun*

a hat *US, 1947*

- One day this top-kick hangs his dome doily on a pole in the market place and says everybody will bow to the bonnet. — Harry Haenigsen, *Jive's Like That*, 1947

do-me queen *noun*

a passive sexual partner with specific, self-oriented, sexual demands *US, 1994*

- Now, it does help that I am a do-me-queen, and have no need to have a deep, meaningful relationship with everyone I play with.

If they're willing to do me the way I want them to do me, they can do me. — *soc.subculture.bondage-bdsm*, 11th April 2001

domes *noun*

LSD *US, 1980*

- As we came walking along, on White Lightning and Purple Haze double domes, Owsley's first purple double domes, somebody walked up and said, "You guys have such pretty smiles." — Stephen Gaskin, *Amazing Dope Tails*, p. 81, 1980

domino *noun*

1 a black and white capsule containing a mixture of central nervous system stimulants and depressants *US, 1971*

- — Eugene Landy, *The Underground Dictionary*, p. 69, 1971

2 a 12.5 mg tablet of Durophet™, an amphetamine *US, 1971*

- — Carl Chambers and Richard Heckman, *Employee Drug Abuse*, p. 204, 1972

domino *verb*

to stop or finish *US, 1953*

- — Lavada Durst, *The Jives of Dr. Hepcat*, p. 12, 1953

dommo *noun*

one who performs well *US, 1997*

Applied to skateboarding, surfing and snowboarding.

- — Vann Wesson, *Generation X Field Guide and Lexicon*, p. 56, 1997

dommo *verb*

to perform well; to dominate *US, 1990*

- — *Surfing*, p. 43, 14th March 1990

dommy; dommie *noun*

a home *US, 1943*

From "*domicile.*"

- Harry Shapiro was crazy about musicians so we headed straight for his dommy. — Mezz Mezzrow, *Really the Blues*, p. 50, 1946
- Tis the gonest little dommy that a chick like you could pick. — Dan Burley, *Diggeth Thou?*, p. 33, 1959
- One more fine dommie that narco built. — Robert Deane Pharr, *Giveadamn Brown*, p. 123, 1978

Donald Duck Navy *noun*

the anti-submarine fleet of the US Navy *US, 1947*

- Most of the men and officers, Reservists and regulars, on PCs served with pride in what they called the "Donald Duck Navy." — Wm. J. Veigle, *PC Patrol Craft of World War II*, p. 79, 1998

Donald Duck suit *noun*

the blue uniform of sailors in the US Navy *US, 1972*

- He picked the Navy "because of the uniform." His friend had told him: "If you want to get into the Donald Duck suit, go down and sign up." — Robert S. La Forte, *Remembering Pearl Harbor*, p. 288, 1991

done deal *noun*

an agreement that has been reached *US, 1990*

Folksy, a hint of the American South.

- The late-night Saturday anonymous caller said it was a "done deal." The reporter winced, having been through "done deals" before. — *Arkansas Democrat-Gazette*, 22nd January 1990
- The proposed extended-stay Saybride Suites hotel and B. Smith restaurant on the 1.24-acre site between the Waterside festival marketplace and the Spirit of Norfolk berth are called "a done deal." — *The Virginian-Pilot*, p. B8, 26th April 2001

dong *noun*

the penis *US, 1900*

- Ginger's hands quickly pulled open his pants and she moaned as his long dong popped out rigid as a hammer. — James Harper, *Homo Laws in all 50 States*, pp. 117–118, 1968
- Nevertheless, I was wholly incapable of keeping my paws from my dong once it started the climb up my belly. — Philip Roth, *Portnoy's Complaint*, p. 18, 1969
- There I am with my dong in my hand when a guy come up and asks if I need any help. — *Taxi Driver*, 1976
- The entire flick leads to the moment when Constance is deemed worthy to accept the dong of her sexual mentor, Jaime Gillis. — Mr. Skin, *Mr. Skin's Skincyclopedia*, p. 384, 2005

don gee *noun*

a respected criminal *US, 1975*

- DON GEE A big shot. — Miguel Pinero, *Short Eyes*, p. 124, 1975
- I'm the Don Gee here. You know what that mean, right? Good. — Harold Augenbraum, *The Latino Reader*, p. 346, 1997

dongle *noun*

1 a security scheme for a commercial microcomputer program
US, 1991
- — Eric S. Raymond, *The New Hacker's Dictionary*, p. 129, 1991

2 any small device designed to add functionality to a computer, often plugged into a USB port *US, 1997*
- — Andy Ihnatko, *Cyberspeak*, p. 58, 1997

donkey *noun*

a black person *US, 1857*
- Tell me, Dadier, what do you think of kikes and mockies and micks and donkeys and frogs and niggers, Dadier. — Evan Hunter, *The Blackboard Jungle*, p. 209, 1954

▸ **pull your donkey**
(used of a male) to masturbate *US, 1990*
- They'd be pulling their donkeys all night, beating their meat, whispering back and forth. — Robert Campbell, *Sweet La-La Land*, p. 136, 1990

donkey dick *noun*

1 a man with a large penis; a large penis *US, 1980*
- — *Maledicta*, p. 189, Winter 1980: "A new erotic vocabulary"
- Mickey's got a big donkey dick. — *Natural Born Killers*, 1994
- Little fuckin' fag! Donkey dick! — *Boogie Nights*, 1997
- Launius called Holmes "donkey dick," which would be a compliment to most guys, but the way Launius said it, it was an insult. — Legs McNeil, *The Other Hollywood*, p. 286, 2005

2 sausage; unidentified pressed meat *US, 1968*
- — Carl Fleischhauer, *A Glossary of Army Slang*, p. 26, 1968

3 the flexible spout attached to the opening of a container *US, 2001*
- We would manhandle it up onto the tank, and we would put a donkey-dick (a flexible, screw-in spout) into the bung of the drum, open it up, and refuel the thing right there. — Oscar E. Gilbert, *Marine Tank Battles in the Pacific*, p. 247, 2001

4 a large electrical cable connector *US, 1990*
- — Gregory Clark, *Words of the Vietnam War*, pp. 150–151, 1990

5 a prolonged, insatiable erection due to extended heroin use *US, 1997*
- — Jim Crotty, *How to Talk American*, p. 94, 1997

donkey sight *noun*

an imprecise but easily maneuvered manual sight on a tank's main gun *US, 1986*
- Hazelip's method used the cupola-mounted .50 as a "donkey sight," adjusting it to be parallel with the 90mm. — Ralph Zumbro, *Tank Sergeant*, p. 43, 1986

donniker *noun*

1 a toilet *US, 1937*
- — Joe McKennon, *Circus Lingo*, p. 31, 1980
- — Gene Sorrows, *All About Carnivals*, p. 15, 1985: "Terminology"
- "And look, there are even donnickers for the patrons." He pointed to two privy-sized boxes off to one side[.] — Gary Jennings, *The Center Ring*, p. 99, 1987

2 the penis *US, 1951*
- Otherwise he would have to have a terrifically long donniker to have her fall in love with him overnight. — Todd McCarthy, *Howard Hawks*, p. 159, 1997

donniker location *noun*

a poor location on a carnival midway *US, 1985*
- — Gene Sorrows, *All About Carnivals*, p. 15, 1985: "Terminology"

Donniker Sam *noun*

a man who begs for money in a public toilet *US, 1981*
- — Don Wilmeth, *The Language of American Popular Entertainment*, p. 76, 1981

donnybrook *noun*

a riot, a tumult *UK, 1852*
- And on one such occasion we got involved in a donnybrook. I can't say how it started, and I doubt that any of the other participants could. — Jim Thompson, *Bad Boy*, p. 386, 1953

don't *noun*

in craps, a bet against the shooter *US, 1950*
- — *The Annals of the American Academy of Political and Social Sciences*, p. 124, May 1950

- At the dice table, the professor would bet either on or against the shooter—otherwise known as do or don't, right or wrong—at $1,000 a shot on what may or may not have been a system. — Edward Lin, *Big Julie of Vegas*, p. 47, 1974

don't ask, don't tell

used as a humorous, if jaded, reminder that some things are best left unknown *US, 1993*
An adage coined to describe the official approach to homosexuals in the US military under the Clinton administration; a soldier would not be asked about his or her sexual preference, but would be expected not to reveal their homosexuality.
- — Steven Daly and Nathaniel Wice, *alt.culture*, p. 64, 1995

don't call us, we'll call you

used as a catchphrase that is generally understood to be a polite, or not-so-polite, rejection of an application for employment *US, 1968*
Adopted from the world of entertainment where it is traditionally supposed to signal the end of an unsuccessful audition.
- Guards frequently complain that they are never consulted by the administrators. As one guard commented, "their attitude is don't call us, we'll call you." — Robert Melvin Carter and Daniel Glaser, *Correctional Institutions*, p. 211, 1977

don't-care-ish *adjective*

apathetic, indifferent *US, 1927*
- Well, Eleanora just went out and done what she felt like doing 'cause she was just don't-care-ish. — Donald Clarke, *Billie Holiday*, p. 27, 2000

don't do that, then

in computing, used as a stock response to a complaint that a certain action causes a problem *US, 1991*
- "When I type control-S, the whole system comes to a halt for thirty seconds." "Don't do that, then!" — Eric S. Raymond, *The New Hacker's Dictionary*, p. 129, 1991

don't go there!; don't even go there!

used for expressing a lack of interest in pursuing a topic *US, 1993*
- — Connie Eble (Editor), *UNC-CH Campus Slang*, p. 2, Spring 1993
- Harry held his palms up in a don't-go-there gesture[.] — Christopher Brookmyre, *The Sacred Art of Stealing*, p. 191, 2002

don't mean nothin'

used as an all-purpose reaction to any bad news among American soldiers in Vietnam *US, 1975*
- — Gregory Clark, *Words of the Vietnam War*, p. 149, 1990
- "It don't mean nothin'." He laughed. — John Del Vecchio, *The 13th Valley*, p. 51, 1999

don't shit a shitter

don't try to fool someone who knows how to fool others *US, 1989*
- "In California, we say, 'Don't shit a shitter,'" Carly said. — Donald McCaig, *The Bamboo Corner*, p. 219, 1989
- "Somewhere in the vicinity of seventeen thousand." Santo Junior said, "Don't shit a shitter. I'd say eight thousand tops." — James Ellroy, *American Tabloid*, p. 267, 1995

don't tense!

relax! *US, 1951*
- — *Newsweek*, p. 28, 8th October 1951
- — *American Speech*, p. 303, December 1955: "Wayne University slang"

donut bumping *noun*

lesbian sex *US, 2005*
- But wouldn't we all try to make her trade her donut-bumping for cruller-humping? — Mr. Skin, *Mr. Skin's Skincyclopedia*, p. 3, 2005

doobage *noun*

marijuana *US, 1985*
- So, Ahab, can I have my doobage. — *The Breakfast Club*, 1985
- — Connie Eble (Editor), *UNC-CH Campus Slang*, p. 4, Spring 1988
- — Ellen C. Bellone (Editor), *Dictionary of Slang*, p. 10, 1989

doober *noun*

a marijuana cigarette *US, 2000*

- "At least we can fire up a doober," he said by way of consolation, producing a fat joint from behind his ear[.] — Tom Perrotta, *Joe College*, p. 173, 2000
- But he was no head. Just a doober now and then to take the edge off. — B.A. Brittingham, *Journeys*, p. 244, 2002

doobie; dooby; doob; dube *noun*
a marijuana cigarette *US, 1967*
The earliest identification is as "Negro slang for a marijuana roach." A belief persists that the term was spawned from the 1950s American children's television show, *Romper Room*, in which children were urged to be "good do-be's." Alternative spelling with a "u" for "dubee" and "dubbe."

- Whitey had laid a few doobies on me for the occasion[.] — Anne Steinhardt, *Thunder La Boom*, p. 194, 1974
- I smoke a doobie at lunch, come back, put these babies [earphones] on and go with the flow. — Armistead Maupin, *Further Tales of the City*, p. 151, 1982
- Hey man, Pickford's got a dube we're about to burn. — *Dazed and Confused*, 1993
- It is one thing to spark up a dubie and get laced at parties, but it is quite another to be fried all day. — *Clueless*, 1995

doodad; dodad *noun*
a trivial or useless object *US, 1877*

- Sam finally, as always falling over drunk, but not really, drunk-desiring, over a little lowtable covered a foot high with ashtrays piled three inches high and drinks and doodads[.] — Jack Kerouac, *The Subterraneans*, p. 55, 1958
- I was sitting on a concrete do-dad in front of the depot restaurant during a supper break in Friarsburg, Oklahoma. — John Nichols, *The Sterile Cuckoo*, p. 7, 1965
- Chicks love to see you wearing doo-dads like that. — Darryl Ponicsan, *The Last Detail*, p. 103, 1970
- Got all the computer electronic dodads[.] — Lester Bangs, *Psychotic Reactions and Carburetor Dung*, p. 339, 1981

doodle *noun*
the penis *US, 1980*
Children's vocabulary.

- — *Maledicta*, p. 190, Winter 1980: "A new erotic vocabulary"
- Uric acid, they say is my trouble, and I don't mind telling you this, / I've to whistle "The Last Rose of Summer," to coax the old doodle to piss. — Martin Cameron, *A Look at the Bright Side*, 1988

doodle *verb*
1 to have sex *US, 1957*

- Well, Mr. Anker, you know yourself all a Jew wants to do is doodle a Christian girl. — William Burroughs, *Naked Lunch*, p. 177, 1957

2 to play music in a whimsical, relaxed manner *US, 1955*

- — Robert S. Gold, *A Jazz Lexicon*, p. 85, 1964

doodle-a-squat *noun*
in circus and carnival usage, money *US, 1981*

- — Don Wilmeth, *The Language of American Popular Entertainment*, p. 76, 1981

doodle-gaze *verb*
to stare at a woman in a lingering, lustful fashion *US, 1990*

- — Charles Shafer, *Folk Speech in Texas Prisons*, p. 202, 1990

doodly *noun*
anything at all *US, 1939*

- "Because the amount doesn't mean doodly," said the heavyset aide with the puffed face. — Robert Ludlum, *The Scorpio Illusion*, p. 27, 1993

doodly-squat *noun*
low grade marijuana *US, 1979*

- Also known as doodly-squat, salt and pepper, and "amle twigs," this female-impersonator a/d/a Headache Mary is sometimes advertised as "good commercial"[.] — *Hi Life*, p. 15, 1979

doodly-squat; diddly squat *noun*
nothing at all *US, 1934*

- She'll stay with me and the kids 'cause he ain't gonna be worth doodly squat to her after I catch 'em. — Iceberg Slim (Robert Beck), *Doom Fox*, p. 182, 1978
- She-it, she swim better than you do, Carlito. You can't do doodley-squat. — Edwin Torres, *After Hours*, p. 379, 1979
- Other than Eaton's occasional generous handouts, YOU paid diddly-squat. — Wolfman Jack (Bob Smith), *Have Mercy!*, p. 83, 1995

doo-doo *noun*
1 excrement *US, 1948*
Also as "do-do." A child's euphemism; by reduplication of "do" or "doo" (excrement).

- I came up thrashing and spitting out a mouthful of that damn duck-doodoo water[.] — Robert Edmond Alter, *Carny Kill*, p. 130, 1966
- I'm fed up with stumblin' 'round in my own doo doo every time I flush the toilet! — Odie Hawkins, *Ghetto Sketches*, p. 196, 1972
- Make sure you land on a spot where there's no dog doo-doo. — *San Francisco Chronicle*, p. 25, 22nd February 1977
- After lying in front of a freight train you can lie in bed in your underwear while two cops are visiting, asking about a certain black Buick—and while a mean-looking Walther P.38 automatic is hidden nearby at that very moment—and not worry about making doo-doo in the bed. — Elmore Leonard, *City Primeval*, p. 53, 1980

2 trouble *US, 1989*

- The Republicans have put up a man whose most memorable contribution to political rhetoric is "deep doo-doo." — Molly Ivins, *Molly Ivins Can't Say That, Can She?*, p. 187, 1991
- "Man," he says. "It was doo-doo." — David Simon and Edward Burns, *The Corner*, p. 47, 1997
- He'd be okay. I was the one who was in deep doodoo. — Joseph Finder, *Paranoia*, p. 387, 2004

doody; dooty *noun*
excrement *US, 1969*
Childish.

- On any given day I'll start with a few finely crafted doody jokes. — Howard Stern, *Miss America*, p. 137, 1995

doof *noun*
a slow-witted person, a fool *US, 1971*
Originally a Scottish dialect word.

- "How'd you get an ID so fast?" "Doofs who found her? She had her driver's license in her shorts." — Robert Crais, *L.A. Requiem*, p. 42, 1999

doofball *noun*
an inept social outcast *US, 1977*

- She looks up at the gangly doofball, spreading her arms to let him see the whole of her clingy dress, her bare legs and feet. — Brian Hall, *The Saskiad*, p. 280, 1997

doofus; dufus *noun*
a dolt, a fool *US, 1955*

- [S]miling a great big, stupid doofus grin comparable to the crease in her crackers. — Clarence Cooper Jr., *The Farm*, p. 26, 1967
- — *Current Slang*, p. 3, Spring 1967
- Whatcha do'en dufus? — Paul Glover, *Words from the House of the Dead*, 1974

doofy *adjective*
awkward, slow *US, 2002*

- There was Michael Wiznewski, Patrick Chaney, and this big, doofy white kid we used to tease about having a big nose, named Charles. — Earl "DMX" Simmons, *E.A.R.L.*, p. 74, 2002

doohickey *noun*
an object the exact name of which escapes the speaker *US, 1914*

- For no reason a pencil rolled off the desk and broke its point on the glass doohickey under one of the desk legs. — Raymond Chandler, *The Little Sister*, p. 42, 1949
- Well, it's a helluva lot better than sending away for one of those plastic doohickies. — Armistead Maupin, *Tales of the City*, p. 141, 1978
- I tried the little doohickey that worked the window and got nothing. — John Ridley, *Love is a Racket*, p. 30, 1998

doojigger *noun*
an object the name of which escapes the speaker *US, 1927*

- This chapter defines a few common things associated with your computer. It describes them by using a variety of terms, including geegaw, doojigger, and madoodle. — Dan Gookin, *DOS for Dummies*, p. 73, 1999

dooker *noun*
a member of a criminal enterprise whose job is to distract the authorities by creating a diversion *US, 1956*

- — *American Speech*, p. 98, May 1956: "Smugglers' argot in the Southwest"

dookie; dookey; dooky; dukey *noun*
excrement *US*, *1969*
Children's vocabulary.

- My fighter's got nothing on his mind but punching the dooky outta the other dude. — Iceberg Slim (Robert Beck), *Death Wish*, p. 94, 1977
- Sandra, I got the squirty dukes. — Sandra Bernhard, *Confessions of a Pretty Lady*, p. 123, 1988
- It starts out just as Kansas is announcing he needs "to drop a dookie." — Jimmy Lerner, *You Got Nothing Coming*, p. 105, 2002

doo-mommie
go fuck your mother *US*, *1983*
A phonetic approximation of the Vietnamese *du ma* (fuck your mother).

- They'd take off through the village yelling, "Wa-ky Jake No. 10. Motherfucker, motherfucker. You doo-mommie. All kinds of weird shit." — Mark Baker, *Nam*, p. 175, 1983

doom tube *noun*
the hollow of a wave that does not offer a surfer the ability to leave the hollow *US*, *1991*

- — Trevor Cralle, *The Surfin'ary*, p. 30, 1991

door *noun*
▸ **from the door**
from the outset *US*, *1967*

- But it was the fuzz's action from the door. They wanted me gone. — Malcolm Braly, *On the Yard*, p. 27, 1967

doorbell *noun*
the nipple of a woman's breast *US*, *1973*

- "She's peeved in this one," said Glenda, leaning closer, and it was pressed against my cheek, and finally one tender doorbell went right into my ear. — Joseph Wambaugh, *The Blue Knight*, p. 24, 1973

door buster *noun*
a heavily discounted item intended to draw customers into a store *US*, *1935*

- "It's part of the bedroom suite, but a lot of stores use it for a door buster, or leader." — *Memphis Business Journal*, p. 12, 21st October 1985
- With our largest selection of door busters ever. — *World News Tonight*, 2nd December 2004
- In recent years, retailers have upped the Black Friday ante, first opening earlier and earlier, and then adding door-buster promotions[.] — *Advertising Age*, p. 8, 6th December 2004

door-hugger *noun*
a girl who sits as far away from her date when he is driving as possible *US*, *1966*

- — Andy Anonymous, *A Basic Guide to Campusology*, p. 8, 1966
- — *American Speech*, p. 59, Spring–Summer 1975: "Razorback slang"

doorknob *noun*
a socially inept person *US*, *1994*

- The words they are constantly coining to describe other teens—geek, nerd, doorknob, shithead, and so on—are generally intended to be derogatory. — Marcel Danesi, *Cool*, p. 43, 1994

door pops *noun*
dice that have been altered so that they will score a 7 or 11 more frequently than normal *US*, *1950*

- — *The Annals of the American Academy of Political and Social Sciences*, p. 124, May 1950

door-pusher *noun*
a girl who stays as close as possible to the passenger door while riding in a car on a date *US*, *1959*

- — *Time Magazine*, p. 46, 24th August 1959

doorshaker *noun*
a night watchman *US*, *1942*

- It was my job to watch the joint for three or four nights and see when the door-shaker [night watchman] or the policeman would come by. — Harry King, *Box Man*, p. 10, 1972
- I know it's him because a the noises the doorshaker said he made. — Joseph Wambaugh, *The Choirboys*, p. 149, 1975

doorstop *noun*
in computing, broken or obsolete equipment *US*, *1991*

- — Eric S. Raymond, *The New Hacker's Dictionary*, p. 30, 1991

doo-wop *noun*
a musical style popular in the 1950s, featuring nonsense syllables sung in close harmony *US*, *1969*

- We stood on the corners rappin' and signifyin' ("you know what, man, yo' momma is so ugly she can't even catch a cold") 'n do'wappin' (Wop doo-dooo/doo doo doo doo wop doo ddoo). — Odie Hawkins, *Men Friends*, p. 9, 1989

doozer *noun*
an exceptional example or specimen *US*, *1930*

- Players are what's important. Personalities. You must know some doozers roundabouts? — Ken Kesey, *Sailor Song*, p. 116, 1992

doozy *adjective*
an extraordinary example of something *US*, *1916*

- Listen, there's a publicity angle rigged to Contino's participation that I can't reveal the details of, but believe me, it's a doozie. — James Ellroy, *Hollywood Nocturnes*, p. 103, 1994

dope *noun*
1 a drug, drugs, especially if illegal *US*, *1888*

- [A] great dope man, anything in the form of kicks he would want at any time and very intense[.] — Jack Kerouac, *The Subterraneans*, p. 4, 1958
- [Janis Joplin] said to a reporter not long before she died: "I wanted to smoke dope, take dope, lick dope, suck dope and fuck dope." But her mental frailty could not match her physical appetites. — Harry Shapiro, *Waiting For The Man*, 1999

2 marijuana *SOUTH AFRICA*, *1946*

- They refer to it as "weed" or "dope," shunning such hipster terminology as "grass" and "pot." — Hunter S. Thompson, *Hell's Angels*, p. 215, 1966
- We had already smoked a lot of dope[.] — Doug Lang, *Freaks*, p. 8, 1973
- You guys want something to drink, or a pill, or some coke, or some dope? — *Boogie Nights*, 1997
- Yeah, then some dope to take the edge off of a long day. — *Traffic*, 2000

3 heroin *US*, *1891*

- You ever hear of dope? Snow? Junk? Big H? Horse? — John D. McDonald, *The Neon Jungle*, p. 61, 1953

4 information, especially confidential information *US*, *1902*

- For Christ's sake, Garrity, spill the dope. — James T. Farrell, *Saturday Night*, p. 21, 1947
- "Whatsa dope, Bob?" — A.J. Liebling, *The Wayward Pressman*, p. 37, 1947
- Sometime look up my history. Any paper will supply the dope. — Mickey Spillane, *Kiss Me Deadly*, p. 82, 1952
- Plus Fuel Facts: Inside Dope on Feeding Vitamins to your Engine — *Hot Rod Comics*, June 1952
- Had The Man given me the straight dope? — Jim Thompson, *Savage Night*, p. 62, 1953

5 in oil drilling, a lubricant *US*, *1954*

- — Jerry Robertson, *Oil Slanguage*, p. 47, 1954

dope *verb*
to use recreational drugs *US*, *1889*

- As usual the party was a whirl of boozing and doping. — Jamie Mandelkau, *Buttons*, p. 73, 1971
- Doping and drinking, wisecracking and insulting[.] — Greil Marcus, *Psychotic Reactions and Carburetor Dung*, 1986

dope *adjective*
stylish, excellent, best *US*, *1981*
A word that defines and sneers at society's failures; this common hip-hop usage, credited to rap-pioneer Chief Rocker Busy Bee, rejects the negative and promotes the positive in the "bad-as-good" way.

- Hey, you know what would be so dope? If we got some really delicious take-out. — *Clueless*, 1995
- I knew I had something special because it sounded dope, real dope. — Earl "DMX" Simmons, *E.A.R.L.*, p. 126, 2002
- My determination to turn out an album full of dope singles, my discriminating ear for what's hot, and my experience with the mixtape circuit paid off big-time. — 50 Cent, *From Pieces to Weight*, p. 217, 2005

dope corner *noun*
a street corner where drugs are usually sold *US*, *1992*

- Strike preferred talking on the phone, mouth to ear—one thing about dope corners, nobody ever vandalized the phones. — Richard Price, *Clockers*, p. 6, 1992

dope daddy *noun*
a drug dealer *US, 1936*
- — *American Speech*, p. 87, May 1955: "Narcotic argot along the Mexican border"

doped up *adjective*
rigged as part of a cheating scheme *US, 1952*
- We completed the rounds by throwing a few quarters into the slot machines. They were hidden way off in a corner. Even they were doped up. — Harry Grey, *The Hoods*, p. 175, 1952

dope fiend *noun*
a drug addict *US, 1895*
- I hate it when they started using "addict" and put "fiend" aside. A funky chump who is into serious drugs is a fuckin' Dope Fiend. Fiend, as in Fiend! — Odie Hawkins, *Midnight*, p. 147, 1995

dopehead *noun*
a regular drug user *US, 1903*
- I don't be fucking no dopeheads. I might let them suck my dick but I don't be fucking 'em. Shit, they got Aids and shit. — *Boyz N The Hood*, 1990

dope house *noun*
a house or building where drugs are bought and used *US, 1968*
- Police say the shootings appear to be another one of the city's rising dope house robberies. — Vernon E. Smith, *The Jones Men*, p. 37, 1974

dopeman *noun*
a drug dealer *US, 1974*
- The dopeman they had stuck up would be getting various wires from fifty different informers, and it wouldn't take long for him to find out who was spending large sums of money. — Donald Goines, *Daddy Cool*, p. 127, 1974
- See, you shoot the dope man, you letting his henchmen know you come in there for sho nuff business. — Vernon E. Smith, *The Jones Men*, p. 9, 1974

dope off *verb*
to fail to pay attention; to fall asleep *US, 1918*
- But I can't do anything about some silly ape who dopes off on the Betelgeuse. — Herman Wouk, *Caine Mutiny*, p. 145, 1951

dope on a rope *noun*
in the language of hang gliding, a paraglider pilot *US, 1992*
- — Erik Fair, *California Thrill Sports*, p. 336, 1992

dope out *verb*
1 to deduce *US, 1970*
- And the Rock sitting two blocks away tapping his desk with a pencil and trying to dope out where Duran was hiding. — Frank Bonham, *Viva Chicano*, p. 65, 1970
2 to become, or spend time, intoxicated on recreational drugs *US, 1970*
- [G]o back the next day and dope out with the gang, grass, speed, reds, Romilar, who cares[.] — Lester Bangs, *Psychotic Reactions and Carburetor Dung*, p. 33, 1970
3 to discover, to ascertain, to comprehend; to work out *US, 1906*
- "Try and dope out their style of play and signals and let him have the jump," Cal told Schultz before they lined up for the next jump. — James T. Farrell, *Tournament Star*, p. 71, 1946
- I tried to dope it out, a screwy thing like that. — Jim Thompson, *Savage Night*, p. 70, 1953

doper *noun*
a drug user *US, 1922*
- All the animals come out at night. Whores, skunk pussies, buggers, queens, fairies, dopers, junkies, sick, venal. — *Taxi Driver*, 1976
- And hey, good work rousting those dopers! — Carl Hiaasen, *Tourist Season*, p. 151, 1986
- He acts like he's this big international arms dealer, when, come on, the only people he ever sold to were dopers. — *Jackie Brown*, 1997

dope rope *noun*
a cord attached to a surfer and his surfboard *US, 1991*
- — Trevor Cralle, *The Surfin'ary*, p. 30, 1991

dope sheet *noun*
a leaflet or pamphlet offering "inside" tips on horse betting *US, 1900*
- — Helen Dahlskog (Editor), *A Dictionary of Contemporary and Colloquial Usage*, p. 19, 1972

dope slap *noun*
a quick and unexpected slap doled out as punishment for a stupid act *US, 1992*
- Well, the first thing I'd do is give that kid a dope slap for driving home after the oil light came on. — Tom Magliozzi, *Click & Clack*, 29th March 1992

dope slope *noun*
a beginner's ski slope *US, 1963*
- — *American Speech*, p. 205, October 1963: "The language of skiers"

dopester *noun*
a person who analyzes the past performance of racehorses and athletic teams in order to predict future performance *US, 1907*
- That is, these excellent dopesters can, presumably, assess the "real probability" (as opposed to the subjective, pari-mutuel probability) that horse H will finish first[.] — Richard A. Epstein, *The Theory of Gambling and Statistical Logic*, p. 291, 1977

dope stick *noun*
a cigarette *US, 1904*
- Have you been puffing on one of those San Francisco dope sticks? — Tom Robbins, *Half Asleep in Frog Pajamas*, p. 121, 1994
- The legislative activity suggests that public attitudes were hardening, as does the proliferation of denigrating slang for cigarettes: coffin nails, dope sticks, devil's toothpicks, Satan sticks, coffin pills, joy pills, little white devils, and so forth[.] — Cassandra Tate, *Cigarette Wars*, p. 13, 1999

dope up *verb*
to use drugs *US, 1942*
- Interestingly, doping up for me has always been with older people[.] — Macfarlane, Macfarlane and Robson, *The User*, p. 2, 1996

dopey; dopie *noun*
a drug user or addict *US, 1929*
- The one thing about the Row was that it was filled with okies, weary old Wobblies, drunkies and dopies far gone, whores on their last legs—they never judged you. — Clancy Sigal, *Going Away*, p. 238, 1961
- [T]hey, none of them, giveashit for me, but they are weak dopies[.] — Clarence Cooper Jr., *The Farm*, p. 19, 1967

dor; door; dorie *noun*
a capsule of glutethimide (trade name Doriden™), a hypnotic sedative and central nervous system depressant *US, 1986*
- — Richard A. Spears, *The Slang and Jargon of Drugs and Drink*, p. 159, 1986

do-rag *noun*
a scarf worn on the head after a hair treatment process *US, 1966*
- Young called himself the "do-rag" man, referring to a bandana, or do-rag, worn around the head after applying a hair preparation. — *Newark (Ohio) Advocate*, p. 39, 17th August 1966
- — *Current Slang*, p. 7, Fall 1970
- [S]ince I had my hat conked in them days, I had my 'do rag 'round my skull. — Odie Hawkins, *Ghetto Sketches*, p. 119, 1972
- Nobody wears do-rags no more, you dumb nigger! — Joseph Wambaugh, *The Glitter Dome*, p. 60, 1981
- The guy in the do-rag. — Elmore Leonard, *Out of Sight*, p. 209, 1996

do-re-mi; dough-rey-me *noun*
money *US, 1926*
Extends from DOUGH (money), punning on "do-re-mi/doh-ray-mi" in the "tonic sol-fa" system of music. Most strongly associated with Woody Guthrie's 1937 song "(If You Ain't Got the) Do Re Mi."
- "Do I get my do-re-mi, or do I take it out of your hide?" — Audie Murphy, *To Hell and Back*, p. 31, 1949
- In the rear was the parking space crowded to capacity with expensive, chauffeured automobiles singing out "dough-re-mi." — Harry Grey, *The Hoods*, p. 172, 1952
- Jews know what to do with that old do-re-mi. — Red Rudensky, *The Gonif*, p. 107, 1970
- Joan's got lots of dough-rey-mi and bad QVC jewelry. — Howard Stern, *Miss America*, p. 146, 1995

do-right *adjective*
righteous, diligent *US, 1936*

- If I want a do-right woman/ Then I've got to be a do-right man. — B.B. King, *Lay Another Log on the Fire*, 1989

do-righter *noun*
a person who does not use drugs *US, 1970*
- — William D. Alsever, *Glossary for the Establishment and Other Uptight People*, p. 23, December 1970

dork *noun*
1 the penis *US, 1961*
- And Roscue Rules sitting there pulling on his dork wasn't doing anything to settle his queasiness. — Joseph Wambaugh, *The Choirboys*, p. 55, 1975
- Neal wore a short kimono with his dork showing underneath it—just the tip. — William Plummer, *Holy Goof*, p. 76, 1981
- He sort of matter-of-factly removed his dork, pressed the length of it against her, and jizzed on her ass[.] — Josh Alan Friedman, *Tales of Times Square*, p. 107, 1986
- I'm this innocent Jewish kid, never seen shit, and she reaches down and pulls out his dork. I mean, it's the size of a small sailboat. — Robert Stoller and I.S. Levine, *Coming Attractions*, p. 182, 1991

2 a socially inept, unfashionable, harmless person *US, 1964*
- — J. R. Friss, *A Dictionary of Teenage Slang (Mt. Diablo High)*, 1964
- I ain't nobody, dork. — *American Graffiti*, 1973
- CLAIRE: So, academic clubs aren't the same as other kinds of clubs. BENDER: Oh, but to dorks like him, they are. — *The Breakfast Club*, 1985
- I have a boyfriend, you dork. — Marty Beckerman, *Death to All Cheerleaders*, 2000
- Available for flirting, but there's a few jerks among them ... a few dorks too. — Rosalind Wiseman, *Queen Bees & Wannabes*, p. 42, 2002

dork *verb*
to act in a socially inept fashion *US, 1990*
- — Elena Garcia, *A Beginner's Guide to Zen and the Art of Snowboarding*, p. 121, 1990: "Glossary"

dorkbrain *noun*
an inept outcast *US, 1974*
- [S]he was not in the habit of discussing her private affairs with dorkbrains. — James Morrison, *Broken Fever*, p. 88, 2001

dorkbreath *noun*
used as a term of abuse *US, 1974*
- What I said, dorkbreath, is, "Are you just good at fucking?" — R.M. Ryan, *The Golden Rules*, p. 126, 1999

dorking *noun*
sexual intercourse *US, 2005*
- Marika massages her man, mounts his meat, then drops to all fours for some doggie-style dorking. — Mr. Skin, *Mr. Skin's Skincyclopedia*, p. 152, 2005

dorkus *noun*
a fool *US, Late 1970*
An embellished **DORK**.
- You wouldn't believe the dorkus she was with when I met her. — *Body Heat*, 1980

dorky *adjective*
odd; out of step with the rest; without social skills *US, 1970*
- A dorky kid with Dumbo ears and a bad habit of mangling the petunias with his Schwinn. — Armistead Maupin, *Babycakes*, p. 87, 1984
- But I was kind of dorky in high school. — Anthony Petkovich, *The X Factory*, 1997
- [W]e were marching around this really hostile neighborhood in Cambridge in our dorky pink baseball hats and t-shirts[.] — Michelle Tea, *The Passionate Mistakes and Intricate Corruption of One Girl in America*, p. 105, 1998
- In high school Dougie was the kid who wore the dorky button-down shirt when all the other kids wore T-shirts. — Janet Evanovich, *Seven Up*, p. 25, 2001

dormie *noun*
a student living in a dormitory; a person with whom you share a dormitory room *US, 1963*
- "I wish you'd promise me not to spread the word among your dormies." — Frederick Kohner, *The Affairs of Gidget*, p. 32, 1963
- Your visiting ex-dormie is going to have different needs than, say, your estranged billionaire father. — Paul Gilovich, *The Stranger Guide to Seattle*, p. 243, 2001

dorm rat *noun*
a person living in a dormitory *US, 1963*
- Just a dorm rat making grades, that's all. — Stephen King, *Night Shift*, p. 249, 1978

dorm rot *noun*
a bruise on the skin caused by a partner's mouth during foreplay; a suction kiss *US, 1970*
- — *Current Slang*, p. 6, Winter 1970

do-room *noun*
a room where drugs are used, especially injected *US, 1974*
- Man I swear, tryin' to keep this damn Do-room clean is a bitch. — Vernon E. Smith, *The Jones Men*, p. 15, 1974

dose *noun*
1 a case of a sexually transmitted infection *US, 1914*
- God might punish him with an automobile accident, death, a dose. — James T. Farrell, *Saturday Night*, p. 26, 1947
- "Wait a minute," he yelled, "don't you cunt-lappers know that's Agnes, she's got the biggest dose in Hartford, everybody knows that." — Jack Kerouac, *Letter to Neal Cassady*, p. 298, 10th January 1951
- I think she's got a dose. — Willard Motley, *Let No Man Write My Epitaph*, p. 178, 1958
- "All you got is a little dose. You'll be back on the hustle in two weeks." — Nelson Algren, *The Neon Wilderness*, p. 36, 1960

2 a single experience with LSD *US, 1967*
- I've never had a bad one and I've taken at least two hundred doses. — Nicholas Von Hoffman, *We Are The People Our Parents Warned Us Against*, p. 95, 1967

3 a dolt *US, 1969*
- — *Current Slang*, p. 6, Summer 1969

dose *verb*
1 to introduce a drug, especially LSD, into a host substance; to give a drug to someone without their knowledge *US, 1957*
- [A]nd dosed the punch with a mixture of Yage, Hashish and Yohimbine during a Fourth of July reception at the U.S. Embassy[.] — William Burroughs, *Naked Lunch*, p. 146, 1957
- His eerily profound pictures of rocks and flowers and trees convey a concentration so intense that my first time through the book I remember feeling nauseous when I found myself tripping on the pictures to such a degree that I thought I had been dosed. — *The Last Supplement to the Whole Earth Catalog*, p. 2, March 1971
- She hung out with me while I was coming on when I had been dosed by what I think was something approaching 3500 mikes[.] — Stephen Gaskin, *Amazing Dope Tails*, p. 115, 1980

2 to ingest; to take a dose of *US, 1971*
- D.R. didn't learn until later that Estelle had dosed herself heavily on downers[.] — Gurney Norman, *Divine Right's Trip (Last Whole Earth Catalog)*, p. 97, 1971

3 to infect another with a sexually transmitted disease *US, 1918*
- I'm dosed, baby. Clap, if you dig. Look, one hand. — Richard Farina, *Been Down So Long*, p. 239, 1966

dosed up *adjective*
infected with a sexually transmitted disease *US, 1969*
- — *Kiss*, 1969: "Groupie glossary"

dose up *verb*
to pass a sexually transmitted infection to someone else *US, 1950*
- — Hyman E. Goldin et al., *Dictionary of American Underworld Lingo*, p. 60, 1950

dosey-doe *verb*
to dance, literally or figuratively *US, 1961*
From a basic call in American square dancing.
- Christopher gave me a big daddy-o wink behind the client's back and doz-doed out. — Clancy Sigal, *Going Away*, p. 28, 1961

doss *noun*
1 sleep *US, 1894*
- — Jack Lait and Lee Mortimer, *New York Confidential*, p. 235, 1948: 'A glossary of Harlemisms'
- I said, "Sugar, let's cop some 'doss.'" — Iceberg Slim (Robert Beck), *Pimp*, p. 116, 1969
- After I had the fix of boy it caused me to wantta get my nuts outta pawn and since I knew Chuck was beat for doss, I told him I was gonna lay and free my nuts from the pressure they were under. — A.S. Jackson, *Gentleman Pimp*, p. 71, 1973

2 an attractive female *US, 1968*
- — *Current Slang*, p. 21, Fall 1968

dot *noun*

1 LSD; a dose of LSD *US, 1967*
- Look, I've got blue dots I'm selling for $1.75 — Nicholas Von Hoffman, *We Are The People Our Parents Warned Us Against*, p. 43, 1967
- — US Department of Justice, *Street Terms*, October 1994
- Street names [...] blotter, cheer, dots, drop[.] — James Kay and Julian Cohen, *The Parents' Complete Guide to Young People and Drugs*, p. 141, 1998
- Very tiny, often brightly-colored pills called "microdots" or "dots" still appear with some regularity in the underground acid market. — Cam Cloud, *The Little Book of Acid*, p. 38, 1999

2 the anus *US, 1964*
- — Roger Blake, *The American Dictionary of Sexual Terms*, p. 62, 1964

3 the clitoris *US, 1964*
- — Roger Blake, *The American Dictionary of Sexual Terms*, p. 62, 1964

dot *verb*

to drop a small amount of LSD on a piece of paper *US, 1970*
- — William D. Alsever, *Glossary for the Establishment and Other Uptight People*, p. 9, December 1970

dot commer *noun*

a person employed in an internet business, especially during the boom of the 1990s *US, 1999*
- And of course, if you want to live like a "dot.commer" you can always become a "dot.commer." — *ca.general*, 10th December 1999
- The hot dot-commer who still has a job and has moved in next door hasn't noticed you? — Jayne Young, *Savvy in the City San Francisco*, p. 53, 2001
- He's lanky, a bit nerdy—half yuppie, half computer geek. He's a dot-commer. — Michelle Tea, *Rent Girl*, p. 229, 2004

dot head *noun*

an Indian or Pakistani *US, 1982*
Offensive. From the caste mark which Hindu women wear on their foreheads.
- — Bill Reilly, *Big Al's Official Guide to Chicagoese*, p. 24, 1982
- Somebody oughta crack his dot-head with a baseball bat. — Eric Bogosian, *Suburbia*, p. 10, 1995
- South Asians' unique attributes are warped for use as racist artillery: attire (we are towel heads and wear loin cloths and sheets); costume (we are dot-heads). — Paula S. Rothenberg, *Race, Class and Gender in the United States*, p. 113, 1998

dotty *adjective*

eccentric, senile *UK, 1885*
- — Lou Shelly, *Hepcats Jive Dictionary*, p. 9, 1945
- You would have thought I'd left them that morning, the way their minds kept running down that same old alley. You can't teach a dotty cat new tricks. — Mezz Mezzrow, *Really the Blues*, p. 88, 1946
- St. John of the Cross was not as dotty as certain Anglicans would have had you believe. — Joan Didion, *The White Album*, p. 119, 1971

double *noun*

1 a pimp with more than one prostitute working for him *US, 1986–1987*
- — *Maledicta*, p. 148, Summer/Winter 1986–1987: "Sexual slang: prostitutes, pedophiles, flagellators, transvestites, and necrophiles"

2 a twenty-dollar bill *US, 1966*
An abbreviation of **DOUBLE SAWBUCK**.
- — *American Speech*, p. 280, December 1966: "More carnie talk from the West Coast"
- — Joe McKennon, *Circus Lingo*, p. 31, 1980

double A *noun*

simultaneous penetration of one rectum by two penises *US, 1997*
- From their little dinner meeting comes the idea of the double A club. — *alt.sex.movies*, 15th November 1997
- You simply ain't gonna see gagging, drool, felching, gape, double A's and other wondrously squalid sights in those other positively tame-by-comparison tapes. — Editors of Adult Video News, *The AVN Guide to the 500 Greatest Adult Films of All Time*, p. 175, 2005

double ace *noun*

in dominoes, the 1 – 1 piece *US, 1959*
- — Dominic Armanino, *Dominoes*, p. 17, 1959

double anal *noun*

sex in which two penises penetrate a single rectum *US, 1994*
- Chessy Moore did a couple of double anal scenes but these were a couple of years ago. — *alt.sex.movies*, 4th April 1994
- So in what movies have you done double anal? — Anthony Petkovich, *The X Factory*, p. 83, 2002
- Many d.p.s, squirting, and double anals her specialty. — Editors of Adult Video News, *The AVN Guide to the 500 Greatest Adult Films of All Time*, p. 72, 2005

double-aught buck *noun*

double-O (.32 calibre) buckshot used in police shotguns *US, 1982*
- "He filled my squad car door with double-aught buck." "What for?" "Cause he was drunk, I guess." — Kim Wozencraft, *Wanted*, p. 256, 2004

double bag *verb*

to use two condoms at once *US, 1989*
- — Geoffrey Froner, *Digging for Diamonds*, p. 27, 1989

double-bagger *noun*

an ugly woman *US, 1982*
- What's a double-bagger? A woman so ugly that before you'll screw her you put a bag over her head, and one over yours—just in case hers falls off. — Blanche Knott, *Blanche Knott's Book of Truly Tasteless Anatomy Jokes, Vol. 2*, p. 107, 1991

double-bank *verb*

to join with someone attacking a third person *US, 1994*
- One day, we double-banked a guy standing at his locker in the area where the wood-shop classes were held. — Nathan McCall, *Makes Me Wanna Holler*, p. 58, 1994

double-barreled *adjective*

extreme *US, 1867*
- I probably might just fit in one of those double-barreled accelerated courses in elementary German they've rigged up. — Sylvia Plath, *The Bell Jar*, p. 34, 1971

double belly buster *noun*

in poker, a hand that requires two cards to make a five-card sequence *US, 1987*
- — Thomas L. Clark, *The Dictionary of Gambling and Gaming*, p. 66, 1987

double bubble *noun*

1 cocaine in a smokable form *US, 1993*
Marketed as being twice as potent when inhaled.
- — Peter Johnson, *Dictionary of Street Alcohol and Drug Terms*, p. 63, 1993

2 a very attractive girl *US, 1951*
Teen slang.
- — *Newsweek*, p. 28, 8th October 1951

double call *noun*

an arrangement with two prostitutes *US, 2004*
- After a brief attempt to turn out Bev the phone girl, he asked for a double call with Allison and Tiffany. — Michelle Tea, *Rent Girl*, p. 83, 2004

double cheese *noun*

in pool, the situation when either player can win with one shot *US, 1993*
- — Mike Shamos, *The Illustrated Encyclopedia of Billiards*, p. 80, 1993

double-clutch *verb*

1 to partake of more than your share of a marijuana cigarette being passed around a group *US, 1980*
- — Edith A. Folb, *runnin' down some lines*, p. 235, 1980

2 to move quickly; to do anything quickly *US, 1968*
- — Hy Lit, *Hy Lit's Unbelievable Dictionary of Hip Words for Groovy People*, p. 12, 1968

double-clutcher *noun*

used as a humorous euphemism for "motherfucker" *US, 1967*
- Doubt if you remember this crazy ol' double-clutcher. — Jim Dodge, *Stone Junction*, p. 9, 1990

double-clutching *adjective*

used as a jocular euphemism for "motherfucking" *US, 1964*
- Guys referred to the aide as a double-dealing, double-clutching, clipboard-carrying apple polisher. — Dennis Smith, *Firefighters*, pp. 123–124, 1988

double-column *verb*

to pass another vehicle and stay in the passing lane *US, 1982*
- His driver swung over and to the left to "double-column it," in army parlance. — Joseph C. Goulden, *Korea*, p. 424, 1982

double cross noun
a double-scored tablet of amphetamine or other central nervous system stimulant *US*, *1971*
- — Edward R. Bloomquist, *Marijuana*, p. 338, 1971

double-cunted adjective
possessing a slack and distended vagina *US*, *1980*
- — *Maledicta*, p. 184, Winter 1980: "A new erotic vocabulary"

double dare; double dog dare verb
to challenge someone to do something *US*, *1849*
- And I double dare anyone to say a word against any of the adopted ones to any of the natural born members of this family. — *San Francisco Chronicle*, 23rd December 1969

double deuce noun
a .22 caliber gun *US*, *1994*
- — Ann Lawson, *Kids & Gangs*, p. 56, 1994: "Common African-American gang slang/phrases"

double dibs!
used as a strong assertion of a claim of rights to something *US*, *1947*
- Double dibs! I saw him first! [Freckels and his Friends comic strip] — *San Francisco News*, 3rd November 1947

double-digit midget noun
a soldier with fewer than 100 days left in their tour of duty *US*, *1969*
- He's a double-digit midget, he's got ninety-nine days or less to go. — Harry Maurer, *Strange Ground*, p. 209, 1989
- Specialist Four Francis Anthony Cortez was a shorttimer, a double-digit midget, which meant that the six-one, 175-pound infantryman had less than a hundred days left to go on his tour of duty in country. — Kregg P.J. Jorgenson, *MIA Rescue*, p. 78, 1995

double dime noun
twenty *US*, *1969*
- He's been the brass nuts here for a double dime, and guess how the bastard lost his "rapper?" — Iceberg Slim (Robert Beck), *Pimp*, p. 51, 1969

double dime note noun
a twenty-dollar bill *US*, *1961*
- It cost mother a double dime-note only this morning. — Ross Russell, *The Sound*, p. 45, 1961

double dimes noun
wheels that are 20 inches in diameter *US*, *2006*
- They're called "dubs"—street slang for "double dime," wheels 20 inches in diameter. — *Los Angeles Times*, p. S7, 3rd December 2006

double-dip verb
to date both sexes *US*, *2002*
- — Amy Sohn, *Sex and the City*, p. 155, 2002

double-dipping noun
payment by two different sources for the same work or reason *US*, *1975*
Slang from the ice-cream parlor, where the "double dip" cone had two scoops of ice-cream.
- Of course Ida's Otter Creek neighbors disapproved of her extravagance and thought it tacky that she boasted of her double-dipping from Social Security. — Carl Hiaasen, *Tourist Season*, p. 109, 1986

doubledome noun
an intellectual *US*, *1943*
- When those doubledomes go nuts—they still keep talking in their double-dome lingo. — Philip Wylie, *Opus 21*, p. 341, 1949
- Double-domes claim there is less juvenile delinquency in the suburbs than in the cities. — Lee Mortimer, *Women Confidential*, p. 70, 1960

double-domed adjective
intellectual *US*, *1962*
- "Skipping the scientific doubletalk—I leave that to Dr. Kurcipski, my doubled-domed headshrinker, Monte has been hit over the ego too often." — Stephen Longstreet, *The Flesh Peddlers*, p. 343, 1962

double-door verb
in pool, to beat someone quickly *US*, *1990*
The image is that the defeated player has no sooner walked in the front door than he is walking out the back door.
- — Steve Rushin, *Pool Cool*, p. 11, 1990

double duke verb
to arrange a deck of cards so that two players will be dealt good hands *US*, *1977*
- — Robert C. Prus and C.R.D. Sharper, *Road Hustler*, p. 169, 1977: "Glossary of terms"

double dump noun
the doublecrossing of a better who believes that a player will intentionally lose a game *US*, *1972*
- The next level is the double dump, where the mark thinks he is in on a fix and then is double-crossed. — Robert Byrne, *McGoorty*, p. 31, 1972

double fin noun
ten dollars or ten years *US*, *1949*
- — Vincent J. Monteleone, *Criminal Slang*, p. 73, 1949

double-fisted adjective
large, imposing *US*, *1853*
- The double-fisted burger was indeed thick and juicy. — Sandra Brown, *Charade*, p. 125, 1994

double fives noun
a hand slap of both hands used for a greeting or for expressing appreciation of that which has just been said *US*, *1977*
- "But we needs the milk," Precious finished off the sentence and gave Elijah double fives. — Odie Hawkins, *Chicago Hustle*, p. 150, 1977

double-gaited adjective
bisexual *US*, *1927*
- Probably cruising, the double-gaited sonofabitch. — Jacqueline Susann, *Valley of the Dolls*, p. 286, 1966
- Double gaited? No. [...] I never did meet any cat who was double gaited. — Lenny Bruce, *The Essential Lenny Bruce*, p. 164, 1967
- Women who go with double-gaited Romeos invariably wind up with more pain than pleasure. — *San Francisco Examiner*, p. E9, 18th December 1981
- [I]t was already an open secret in theatrical circles that Coward was gay; and after Edna Ferber described the Lunts as "double-gaited," theater historians took the Ferber report for granted. — *Los Angeles Times*, p. 11 (Part R), 21st December 2001

double-hatted adjective
serving in two positions simultaneously *US*, *1990*
- I remember we were double-hatted, because we were working very hard to put crews through the tactics phase of the RAG and still trying to build [the Fighter Weapons School] syllabus. — Robert K. Wilcox, *Scream of Eagles*, p. 164, 1990

double-header; doubleheader noun
an activity engaged in twice in a row on the same day, especially sex *US*, *1977*
- Elijah smiled and thought to himself ... doubleheaders can wear you out. Oh well ... my dick'll rot away one day, may as well use it as much as I can now. — Odie Hawkins, *Chicago Hustle*, p. 34, 1977
- Which meant that she wasn't interested in the hundred-dollar bag of bones who Juicy Lucy said was coming back at eight o'clock for a doubleheader. — Joseph Wambaugh, *The Glitter Dome*, p. 208, 1981

double infinity noun
in poker, a pair of eights *US*, *1996*
Turned on its side, a figure eight is an infinity symbol.
- — John Vorhaus, *The Big Book of Poker Slang*, p. 14, 1996

double-jointed adjective
exceptional *US*, *1974*
- "Changed my birth certificate and they accepted me." "That's double-jointed! Too much!" — Earl Thompson, *Tattoo*, p. 108, 1974

double L noun
a telephone *US*, *1976*
An extrapolation from "landline."
- — *Complete CB Slang Dictionary*, p. 5, 1976

double nickel noun
1 fifty-five; five-fifty *US*, *1976*
- Way it was, I got on the double-nickel with the load. — George V. Higgins, *The Rat on Fire*, p. 106, 1981
- Five fifty? It's only double nickels. Five fifty? — Ivan Doig, *Ride With Me, Mariah Montana*, p. 259, 1990
- What golfer and future PGA Tour winner once went microscopic with a double nickel, shooting an unheard-of 55 in the 1962 Premier

Invitational in Longview, Texas? — Mike Towle, *The Ultimate Golf Trivia Book*, p. 52, 1999

- I want to electrify the crowd like Michael Jordan droppin' a double nickel on the New York Knicks. — Todd Boyd, *Young Black Rich and Famous*, p. xii, 2003

2 a ten-year prison sentence *US*, *1998*

- You on parole for check writing now. That liquor will get you a double nickel. — James Lee Burke, *Sunset Limited*, p. 45, 1998
- "I was doing a double nickel in that fucking joint back in '71 when the Shit Jumped Off—and I'm talkin' about some serious shit."
— Jimmy Lerner, *You Got Nothing Coming*, p. 186, 2002

3 in craps, a roll of ten made with a pair of fives *US*, *1999*

- — Chris Fagans and David Guzman, *A Guide to Craps Lingo*, p. 33, 1999

double nuts *noun*
double zero *US*, *1981*

- Originator of the Commander Air Group's "00" (or "double nuts" as the marking is often irreverently referred to by junior officers), recently-promoted Cdr "Jimmy" Flatley, Jr., is seen climbing down from his personal F6F-3[.] — Barrett Tillman, *Hellcat Aces of World War 2*, p. 7, 1996

double-o *noun*
a close examination *US*, *1913*

- I gave him the double-o after I lamped the engraved card he handed me. — Mezz Mezzrow, *Really the Blues*, p. 261, 1946

double O's *noun*
Kool™ cigarettes *US*, *1981*

- — *Maledicta*, pp. 266–267, Summer/Winter 1981: "By its slang, ye shall know it: the pessimism of prison life"

double packer *noun*
a member of the Hell's Angels who is prone to take a girlfriend with him on excursions *US*, *1966*

- When I found such perennial double packers as Sonny, Terry, Tiny, Tommy and Zorro without their women, I realized the outlaws were expecting real trouble — Hunter S. Thompson, *Hell's Angels*, p. 119, 1966

double rough *noun*
a prison sentence of 50 years *US*, *1990*

- — Charles Shafer, *Folk Speech in Texas Prisons*, p. 203, 1990

double saw *noun*
a twenty-year jail sentence *US*, *1976*

- John R. Armore and Joseph D. Wolfe, *Dictionary of Desperation*, p. 27, 1976

double sawbuck; double saw *noun*
a twenty-dollar bill *US*, *1931*

- I had a check for a double sawbuck coming from a booking office in Chi[.] — Mezz Mezzrow, *Really the Blues*, p. 131, 1946
- I got five doublesawbucks out of my wallet and dropped them in front of him. — Raymond Chandler, *The Long Goodbye*, p. 11, 1953
- On the other hand, for a double-saw, I'll tell you where you get your job done if that's your bag. — *Screw*, p. 7, 7th March 1969
- A double-sawbuck is a night out for my wife and me, or new shoes for the kids, or a hundred other things we need that twenty dollars can buy. — Dennis Smith, *Report from Engine Company 82*, p. 224, 1972

double sawski *noun*
a twenty-dollar bill *US*, *1953*

- He's into us for a double sawski. — William Burroughs, *Junkie*, p. 63, 1953

double stacks *noun*
MDMA, the recreational drug best known as ecstasy *US*, *2002*

- The drug Ecstasy was called fishies or double stacks, according to the affidavit. — *Orlando Sentinel*, p. B2, 17th August 2002

double tre *noun*
six *US*, *1998*

- — Ethan Hilderbrant, *Prison Slang*, p. 40, 1998

double trouble *noun*

1 a capsule of sodium amobarbital and sodium secobarbital (trade name Tuinal™), a combination of central nervous system depressants *US*, *1967*

- — John B. Williams, *Narcotics and Hallucinogenics*, p. 111, 1967
- — Eugene Landy, *The Underground Dictionary*, p. 70, 1971

2 any combination of drugs *US*, *1990*

- — Gilda and Melvin Berger, *Drug Abuse A-Z*, p. 59, 1990

3 a member of Alcoholics Anonymous who is seeking treatment for a second psychological disorder *US*, *1990*
Those who succeed are known as "double winners."

- — Gilda and Melvin Berger, *Drug Abuse A-Z*, p. 59, 1990

double ups *noun*
vials of crack cocaine *US*, *1992*

- Several minutes later, a man walked up to them and asked, "Do you have any double-ups"—street slang for crack cocaine. — *Plain Dealer (Cleveland, Ohio)*, p. C16, 25th December 1992

double vag *noun*
simultaneous penetration of a single vagina by two penises *US*, *1994*

- Sounds like a dp or double vag to me. — *rec.arts.movies.erotica*, 2nd February 1997
- Sure, X-Traordinary left out Adkins's mind-bending double-vag extravaganza form Young and Anal 20. — Eric Danville, *The Penthouse Erotic Video Guide*, p. 55, 2003
- A couple of girls go anal, one does a d.p., and one does a double-vag. — Editors of Adult Video News, *The AVN Guide to the 500 Greatest Adult Films of All Time*, p. 111, 2005

double veteran *noun*
a soldier who has had sex with a woman and then killed her *US*, *1981*

- They'd come back a double veteran. These were not men who would normally commit rape. — Mark Baker, *Nam*, p. 166, 1981

douche *verb*

1 to take an enema before or after anal sex *US*, *1972*

- — Bruce Rodgers, *The Queens' Vernacular*, pp. 66–67, 1972

2 to reject someone's application for membership in a fraternity, sorority or club *US*, *1968*

- — Collin Baker et al., *College Undergraduate Slang Study Conducted at Brown University*, p. 107, 1968

douche bag *noun*

1 a despicable person; a socially inept person *US*, *1945*

- That douchebag? You should be able to do betteran that. — Hubert Selby Jr., *Last Exit to Brooklyn*, p. 119, 1957
- Patty ties Becky to a tree, calls her names ("pubescent scumbag," "douchebag"). — *Final Report of the Attorney General's Report on Pornography*, p. 435, 1986
- How the fuck did you get hooked up with a douche-bag like this in the first place. — *True Romance*, 1993
- Hi, my name is JT, I'm an alcoholic and an addict. I'm also a TV writer, which by default makes me a douchebag. — *The Sopranos (Episode 59)*, 2004

2 a promiscuous woman prisoner *US*, *1992*

- — William K. Bentley and James M. Corbett, *Prison Slang*, p. 59, 1992

douched *adjective*
exhausted *US*, *1968*

- — Collin Baker et al., *College Undergraduate Slang Study Conducted at Brown University*, p. 108, 1968

douche kit *noun*
a shaving kit *US*, *1970*

- Billy rinses out his razor and drops it into his douche kit. — Darryl Ponicsan, *The Last Detail*, p. 130, 1970

douche out *verb*
as a prank, to flood the floor of a room by pouring buckets of water under the crack of the door *US*, *1967*

- — *American Speech*, p. 228, October 1967: "Some special terms used in a university of Connecticut men's dormitory"

dough *noun*

1 money *US*, *1851*

- Live off the fatta the land with dough their father left them. — Mickey Spillane, *I, The Jury*, p. 12, 1947
- Too bad in a way cause most of us used to rip off the Lion Supermarket there when we had to eat and had no dough. — Abbie Hoffman, *Woodstock Nation*, p. 21, 1969
- When you figure it up, we don't have to lay out for half of it before we got more dough back than we can use. — Richard Farina, *Long Time Coming and a Long Time Gone*, p. 211, 1969
- Young man, there's a place you can go/I said, young man, when you're short on your dough. — Village People, *Y.M.C.A.*, 1978

2 an American infantryman *US, 1951*
Korean war usage; shortened from the earlier **DOUGHBOY**.
- — *The Baltimore Sun*, 24th June 1951

doughboy *noun*
a soldier in the infantry *US, 1847*
Many inventive, but unproved, explanations for the term's coining can be found.
- The wounded veteran of Vietnam gazed upon the World War I poster of the doughboy with the rifle. — Steve Thayer, *Silent Snow*, p. 81, 1999

doughfoot *noun*
an infantry soldier *US, 1943*
World War 2's answer to the **DOUGHBOY** of World War 1.
- These—and lots of ammo—were the real essentials in a dough-foot's kit, a fact that was one of those things you just had to learn. — David H. Hackworth, *About Face*, p. 79, 1989

doughnut *noun*
1 any material produced to be played on the radio which leaves a silent space in the middle for information provided by the announcer *US, 1980*
- — Walter Hurst and Donn Delson, *Delson's Dictionary of Radio & Record Industry Terms*, p. 38, 1980
2 the inside of a round, hollow wave *US, 1988*
- — Michael V. Anderson, *The Bad, Rad, Not to Forget Way Cool Beach and Surf Discriptionary*, p. 5, 1988

doughnut *verb*
to win a game without your opponent scoring *US, 1971*
- — Dick Squires, *The Other Racquet Sports*, p. 220, 1971: "Glossary"

doughnut bumper *noun*
an aggressive, dominant lesbian *US, 1992*
- — William K. Bentley and James M. Corbett, *Prison Slang*, p. 59, 1992

doughnut dolly; donut dolly *noun*
a female Red Cross volunteer in Vietnam *US, 1968*
Vietnam war usage. From the practice of Red Cross volunteers serving doughnuts and coffee to the troops.
- — Carl Fleischhauer, *A Glossary of Army Slang*, p. 16, 1968
- You know, one of the things I remember about Vietnam, besides all the war stories, are the "Doughnut Dollies" [USO girls]. They'd come out to the field to play Bingo or something. — John Kerry, *The New Soldier*, p. 78, 1971
- The Doughnut Dollies of the Red Cross had been asking for a jeep for several weeks. — Anthony Herbert, *Soldier*, p. 147, 1973
- We don't have no officer's club out here. Ain't no band. No donut dollies to fuck. — John M. Del Vecchio, *The 13th Valley*, p. 218, 1982

doughnut head *noun*
used as a term of abuse suggesting an empty head *US, 1977*
- My brain hears her talking and goes, Do it, doughnut head. — W.R. Philbrick, *Max the Mighty*, p. 37, 1998

doughnut six; donut six *noun*
the leader of a group of female Red Cross workers in Vietnam *US, 1981*
"Six" was radio code for a unit's commander.
- Doughtnut six: chief of Red Cross girls. — Shelby L. Stanton, *Vietnam Order of Battle*, p. 355, 1981

dough-pop *verb*
to hit hard *US, 1972*
- "Put in there that I'll probably catch two or three balls behind Dreamer Tatum and at least once I'll dough-pop him on his black ass," he said. — Dan Jenkins, *Semi-Tough*, p. 17, 1972

dough-roll *noun*
a wife *US, 1972*
- I said, "Well, I can dig it, buddy, 'cause I'm hooked up myself. I got a dough-roll [wife] and two crumb-catchers [children], you know." — Bruce Jackson, *In the Life*, p. 152, 1972

dough-roller *noun*
a wife or female lover *US, 1929*
- "My little dough roller be gone," sings Robert Johnson. — Donald G. Dutton, *The Batterer*, p. 139, 1995

do up *verb*
1 to inject a drug *US, 1952*

- They did up two each, then went down to the stoop. — Hal Ellson, *The Golden Spike*, p. 57, 1952
- If Porky don't act funny and stop us from taking our stuff out, we can go over there and do up. — Donald Goines, *Dopefiend*, p. 47u, 1971
- But every time you start to come down it's so terrible that you do up again. — J. Anthony Lukas, *Don't Shoot—We Are Your Children*, p. 256, 1971
2 to apply a tourniquet before injecting a drug intravenously *US, 1970*
- — William D. Alsever, *Glossary for the Establishment and Other Uptight People*, p. 19, December 1970

douse *verb*
▸ **douse the glim**
to turn off the lights *US, 1945*
- — Lou Shelly, *Hepcats Jive Talk Dictionary*, p. 24, 1945

dove *noun*
a five-dollar bill *US, 2002*
- He owes me a dove. — Gary K. Farlow, *Prison-ese: A Survivor's Guide to Speaking Prison Slang*, p. 19, 2002

do vibes *noun*
surging energy *US, 1971*
- DO-VIBES: a burst of energy, a desire to do something — Robert Buckhout, *Toward Social Change*, p. 465, 1971

dowager *noun*
an elderly, usually affluent, homosexual man *US, 1941*
- — Bruce Rodgers, *The Queens' Vernacular*, p. 67, 1972

down *noun*
1 any barbiturate or central nervous system depressant *US, 1971*
- [T]he kids take a lot of downs and dig down bands[.] — Lester Bangs, *Psychotic Reactions and Carburetor Dung*, p. 69, 1971
- "Ups" all day and "downs" at night. — Beatrice Sparks (writing as 'Anonymous'), *Jay's Journal*, p. 26, 1979
- I'd make that trip in from the cabin at least every two or three weeks for a fresh supply of inhalers. Sometimes I'd pick up a few downs to go along with it. — Herbert Huncke, *Guilty of Everything*, p. 88, 1990
- But what usually happened was that I'd be speeding like mad when the downs finally took effect. — Cleo Odzer, *Goa Freaks*, p. 148, 1995
2 a diluted alcoholic drink *US, 1971*
- "Downs" enable her to give the customer the impression that she is drinking with him. — Charles Winick, *The Lively Commerce*, p. 171, 1971
3 a mixture of codeine-infused cough syrup and soda *US, 2000*
- In Houston, Elwood said, it has a variety of nicknames—Lean, AC/DC, barr, down, Karo and nods. "Lean because after you take it you will be definitely leaning and losing your coordination," Elwood said. — *The Commercial Appeal (Memphis)*, p. F1, 9th July 2000

down *verb*
1 to conquer sexually *US, 1967*
- "I'm going to down at least four women in the next twenty-four hours." — Elliot Liebow, *Tally's Corner*, p. 144, 1967
2 to kill *US, 1977*
- Snap saved me from a murder charge because I'm sure I was going to down Rock. — John Allen, *Assault with a Deadly Weapon*, p. 65, 1977
3 to sell stolen goods *US, 1967*
- Ten minutes later he walked up to me and said, "Babs, baby, I know I downed your vines, so here's the tickets." — Babs Gonzales, *I Paid My Dues*, p. 52, 1967
- "And you won't have no trouble downing your stuff in the Logan." — Robert Deane Pharr, *S.R.O.*, p. 468, 1971
- Sooner or later they have to try downing it and I want that ice hotter than a meteor, harder to move than the Rock of Gibraltar. — Seth Morgan, *Homeboy*, p. 99, 1990

down *adjective*
1 excellent; loyal; fashionable *US, 1946*
- She didn't look like much, but she was a down chick. — Malcolm Braly, *Shake Him Till He Rattles*, p. 18, 1963
- He explained that I didn't know him but a friend of both of ours had told him I was "down people" and to turn me on when I arrived. — Babs Gonzales, *I Paid My Dues*, p. 84, 1967
- The tigers would go to the Cabo and the BC, the down P.R.'s would go to the Palladium. — Edwin Torres, *Carlito's Way*, p. 24, 1975
- Jake the Fake held up his glass for a toast. "Here's to Taco and Slick, two of the downes' sistahs that ever did it, two of the hippes' ladies

that it has ever been my purpose to meet and greet." — Donald Goines, *The Busting Out of an Ordinary Man*, p. 74, 1985

- You ain't down if you ain't heard of Method Man. — *A2Z*, p. 30, 1995
- You are a down girl. — *Clueless*, 1995

2 willing, prepared, eager *US, 1944*

- "Are you still down for it?" "I'm down for it." — Hal Ellson, *The Golden Spike*, p. 15, 1952
- He's a hype but he is very down with the current scene. — Eldridge Cleaver, *Soul on Ice* (letter dated 19th September, 1965), p. 46, 1968
- Myself, I'm down for the action anytime, and I don't want to hear this ol' bullshit about the little kids in the schoolyard. — Edwin Torres, *Carlito's Way*, p. 71, 1975
- [N]ow that I wanna flap some skins Brandi ain't down for it even if I wear a jim hat. — *Boyz N The Hood*, 1990

3 (of surf conditions) flat *US, 1977*

- — Gary Fairmont R. Filosa II, *The Surfer's Almanac*, p. 184, 1977

4 in police custody; imprisoned *US, 1927*

- The first time I was down I come down with assault with attempt to murder. — Bruce Jackson, *In the Life*, p. 61, 1972
- "You got to treat someone who has been down as long as Carl differently from some kid fresh in from the streets." — Pete Earley, *The Hot House*, p. 150, 1992
- Buck, we have here Carl Edward Colbert, escapee from the West Tennessee Reception Center, down for armed robbery and assault with a deadly weapon, a pitchfork. — Elmore Leonard, *Riding the Rap*, p. 136, 1995
- These dawgs have all been down before ,and most of them are known quantities on the yard. — Jimmy Lerner, *You Got Nothing Coming*, p. 192, 2002

down *adverb*

▶ **get down**

to inject (a drug) into a vein *US, 1969*

- — Ralph de Sola, *Crime Dictionary*, p. 57, 1982
- — Richard A. Spears, *The Slang and Jargon of Drugs and Drink*, p. 217, 1986

down and dirty *adjective*

descriptive of the final card in a game of seven-card stud poker *US, 1988*

It is dealt face-down and it greatly affects the chances of a hand winning.

- — George Percy, *The Language of Poker*, p. 30, 1988

down beat *noun*

▶ **on the down beat**

declining in popularity *US, 1947*

- — Marcus Hanna Boulware, *Jive and Slang of Students in Negro Colleges*, 1947

downblouse *noun*

a type of voyeurism devoted specifically to seeing a woman's breasts by looking down her blouse *US, 1994*

- Hey all you peepfans! survey: do you prefer upskirtpeep, down-blousepeep, windowpeep, lockerroompeep, or bathroompeep? — *alt.sex.voyeurism*, 6th October 1996
- "Upskirt" and "downblouse" tapes often end up on the Internet, where anyone over 18 can legally view and buy them. — *Charleston (West Virginia) Daily Mail*, p. 4C, 10th August 1998
- The Internet is littered with hundreds of Web sites dedicated to voyeuristsic "upskirts" and "downblouses" in which cameras are aimed in those locales to capture revealing images of unsuspecting women in public. — *Chicago Daily Herald*, p. 11, 13th April 2002

downer *noun*

1 a barbiturate or other central nervous system depressant *US, 1965*

- [E]verybody was saying, "Smoke some grass or take downers." — Nicholas Von Hoffman, *We Are The People Our Parents Warned Us Against*, p. 223, 1967
- And I can't recommend downers because I've had too many friends go down and out. — *The Last Supplement to the Whole Earth Catalog*, p. 83, March 1971
- I mean is it an upper or a downer? — Oscar Zeta Acosta, *The Revolt of the Cockroach People*, p. 192, 1973
- "I don't need no more uppers," Joanie said, "but downers I could use." — Emmett Grogan, *Final Score*, p. 81, 1976

2 a circumstance that depresses; a depressing experience *US, 1967*

- Liquor's a downer! A bad trip! It'll kill you[.] — Nicholas Von Hoffman, *We Are The People Our Parents Warned Us Against*, p. 191, 1967

- Everyone is a junglist now, and if you go and take an E on jungle stuff, you're going to have a downer, know what I mean? — Macfarlane, Macfarlane & Robson, *The User*, p. 3, 1996

3 an animal being led to slaughter that is too sick or crippled to walk into the slaughterhouse *US, 1991*

This sense of the word began to enjoy great popularity in the US in late 2003 with the publicity surrounding Mad Cow Disease in US cattle.

- In her early thirties, she is a cocktail waitress in Minneapolis whose off-hour zeal is for ministering to stockyard animals that are too sick or crippled to walk. They are called "downers." — *Washington Post*, p. F2, 14th April 1991

down for mine *adjective*

willing to stand up for your group *US, 1989*

- — James Harris, *A Convict's Dictionary*, p. 31, 1989

down head *noun*

an abuser of central nervous system depressants *US, 1984*

- — Sohnya Sayres, *The 60s Without Apology*, p. 367, 1984: Lexicon of Folk-Etymology

down hill *adjective*

during the second half of a prison sentence *US, 1950*

- — Hyman E. Goldin et al., *Dictionary of American Underworld Lingo*, p. 47, 1950

down home *adjective*

exemplifying the essence of black culture *US, 1982*

- — Arnold Shaw, *Dictionary of American Pop/Rock*, p. 111, 1982

downie *noun*

a central nervous system depressant *US, 1966*

- [T]he beautiful thing about downies is that there's no come down [...] you just go to sleep. — Ruth Bronsteen, *The Hippies' Handbook*, 1967
- — Eugene Landy, *The Underground Dictionary*, p. 70, 1971

download *verb*

to defecate *US, 2001*

Application of computer terminology to the toilet bowl.

- — Pamela Munro, *U.C.L.A. Slang*, p. 63, 2001

down on *adjective*

opposed to; holding a low opinion of something *US, 1848*

- Judaism seems less down on sex than Christianity is. — Fiona Pitt-Kethley, *Red Light Districts of the World*, p. 59, 2000

down on your uppers *adjective*

in dire financial straits *US, 1963*

When the upper of a shoe is worn down, a person might as well be walking barefoot.

- — Charles F. Haywood, *Yankee Dictionary*, p. 49, 1963

down south *noun, adverb*

below the waist; the genitals *US, 1982*

- Now for taking care of what was down south, her fingers gripped his hardness, his bare flesh, and gently squeezed, loving the feel of the thick width and length of him. — Joy King, *Mr. Satisfaction*, p. 54, 2006

▶ **it's snowing down south**

your slip is showing *US, 1955*

- — *American Weekly*, p. 2, 14th August 1955

downstairs *adjective*

below the waist *US, 2005*

- That ain't no dye in my baby's hair neither! She's a redhead downstairs too! — Noire, *Candy Licker*, p. 172, 2005

down the hatch!

used as a drinking toast, as a descriptive precursor to taking a drink and as an encouragement to take medicine *US, 1931*

- "Down the hatch!" The words come to us as we sit here looking at the picture of Mieuli. — *San Francisco Examiner*, 2nd June 1967

down there

the genitals *US, 1995*

A precious if unmistakable euphemism.

- JANE: Okay. So what do you call it? ROBIN: Down there. — *Boys on the Side*, 1995

downtown *noun*

1 heroin *US, 1983*

- First I'll put your Uptown on the spoon, then to make it more exciting I'm gonna add some Downtown. They call this thing a speedball, honey, but then you must know that. — *The Bad Lieutenant*, 1992

2 in pool, the foot end of the table *US, 1993*
- — Mike Shamos, *The Illustrated Encyclopedia of Billiards*, p. 82, 1993

3 during the Vietnam war, the airspace above Hanoi, North Vietnam *US, 1967*
- — *Current Slang*, p. 15, Summer 1970
- "Don't forget," Cole said, "we're going right downtown. It won't be any piece of cake." — Stephen Coonts, *Flight of the Intruder*, p. 277, 1986
- When you get a belly full o' Bravo and Sky Spots/ You can always go—Downtown. — Joseph Tuso, *Singing the Vietnam Blues*, p. 76, 1990: Downtown I

down trip *noun*
any unpleasant, uninspiring experience *US, 1967*
- — Joe David Brown (Editor), *The Hippies*, p. 218, 1967: "Glossary of hippie terms"

downy *noun*
a bed *US, 1843*
A reference to the "down" found in bedding.
- They're always coming around to our pad raving about how sensational you are in the downy. — Bernard Wolfe, *The Late Risers*, p. 131, 1954

doxy; doxie *noun*
a woman; a girlfriend *UK, 1530*
Originally, in C16, "a beggar's trull" (the unmarried mistress of a beggar). Beginning in C19 it took on a softer and broader sense.
- It seemed he had bungled his way through a bouquet of doxies, male and female, without anything to show for his efforts[.] — Angelo d'Arcangelo, *The Homosexual Handbook*, p. 23, 1968
- An old church doxie cracked I was cursed for killing Mama. — Iceberg Slim (Robert Beck), *Airtight Willie and Me*, p. 91, 1979
- She was an amateur doxy thinking about turning pro. — Robert Campbell, *In La-La Land We Trust*, p. 1, 1986

Doyle Brunson *noun*
in hold 'em poker, a ten and a two as the first two cards dealt to a player *US, 1982*
Poker player Doyle "Texas Dolly" Brunson won the World Series of Poker two years in a row with this hand.
- — Thomas L. Clark, *The Dictionary of Gambling and Gaming*, p. 67, 1987

do you kiss your mother with that mouth?
used as a rejoinder to profanity *US, 1990*
- Do you eat with that mouth? Do you kiss your mother with that mouth? — *comop.sys.mac.misc*, 26th July 1990
- Do you kiss your mother with that mouth? I'm gettin' out of here. — *Wayne's World*, 1992

dozens *noun*
a game of ritualistic insult *US, 1915*
- "I don't play no dozens, boy," Smitty growled. "You young punks don't know how far to go with a man." — Chester Himes, *If He Hollers Let Him Go*, p. 102, 1945
- He would play the dozens, have rock fights, and curse us out. — Claude Brown, *Manchild in the Promised Land*, p. 84, 1965
- This was the "dozens," a game of insults. The dozens is a dangerous game even among friends[.] — Piri Thomas, *Down These Mean Streets*, p. 121, 1967
- Two cats would meet on the street and start playin' the dozens; one guy would say, "Ashes to ashes, dust to dust, your mother has a pussy like a Greyhound bus." — Edwin Torres, *Carlito's Way*, p. 10, 1975

DP *noun*
1 double penetration *US, 1997*
In the pornography industry, this usually refers to a woman who is being penetrated simultaneously in the vagina and anally; viewers of American pornography have been obsessed with this type of double penetration since the 1990s. Technically, it refers to two objects or body parts inserted into the same rectum or vagina simultaneously.
- "While we're on the subject, what do you think of DP's?" "They're too hard to shoot. There's no real spontaneity in them. You know, DP actually means a double penetration in one hole—not just the pussy and the ass." — Anthony Petkovich, *The X Factory*, p. 123, 1997

- When they do sign, they specify what they will and will not do—oral, anal, girl-girl, group sex, D.P.s, gay, bi, that sort of thing. — Ana Loria, *1 2 3 Be A Porn Star!*, p. 61, 2000
- So the unattractive girls end up being the real workhorses. They're the ones who are doing all the anals and DPs. — John Bowe, *Gig*, p. 447, 2001
- It culminates in an intense d.p. and a circle jerk on Christal's face. — Editors of Adult Video News, *The AVN Guide to the 500 Greatest Adult Films of All Time*, p. 12, 2005

2 Dr. Pepper™ soda *US, 1966*
A drink favored, and hence a term heard, mostly in the southern US.
- — Andy Anonymous, *A Basic Guide to Campusology*, p. 7, 1966
- — Charles Shafer, *Folk Speech in Texas Prisons*, p. 203, 1990

DPP *noun*
a vagina simultaneously penetrated by two penises *US, 2000*
An abbreviation of "double pussy penetration."
- — Ana Loria, *1 2 3 Be A Porn Star!*, p. 164, 2000: "Glossary of adult sex industry terms"

drab *noun*
a pretty girl, especially one who is new in town *US, 1947*
- — Marcus Hanna Boulware, *Jive and Slang of Students in Negro Colleges*, 1947

drafty *noun*
draught beer *US, 1969*
- — *Current Slang*, p. 7, Summer 1969

drag *noun*
1 anything or anyone boring or tedious *US, 1863*
- That was a solid drag[.] — Mezz Mezzrow, *Really the Blues*, p. 132, 1946
- He wants two bucks a stick! What a drag! — John Clellon Holmes, *Go*, p. 101, 1952
- It's a funny thing how life can be such a drag one minute and a solid sender the next. — Louis Armstrong, *Satchmo*, p. 126, 1954
- "Honey, your grandma is feeling the least." "What a drag!" said Red. — Steve Allen, *Bop Fables*, p. 36, 1955
- Getting up early is an incredible drag, or at least I should think it would be. — James Simon Kunen, *The Strawberry Statement*, p. 69, 1968
- I can't wait until I can drive next year. I walk every day. It's such a drag. — *Fast Times at Ridgemont High*, 1982

2 female clothing worn by men; male clothing worn by women *UK, 1870*
A term born in the theater, but the nontheatrical sense has long dominated. He or she who wears "drag" may or may not be a homosexual.
- It is a law violation for entertainers to appear in "drag" (clothes of the opposite sex). — Jack Lait and Lee Mortimer, *New York Confidential*, p. 68, 1948
- [R]ipping and tearing Georgette's drag clothes, her lovely dresses and silks, stamping on her shoes. — Hubert Selby Jr., *Last Exit to Brooklyn*, p. 56, 1957
- "I may tell you in strictest confidence that some of these girls ..." with gambler fingers he shifts the photos in Three Card Monte Passee—"are really boys. In uh drag I believe is the word???" — William Burroughs, *Naked Lunch*, pp. 194–195, 1957
- I think if everyone were honest, they'd confess that the lady looks exactly like a man in drag. — *Austin Powers*, 1997

3 an event for cross-dressers *US, 1919*
- That was the time of "drags" in Harlem. In these affairs there would be fashion parades for the male queers dressed in women's clothes. — Ethel Waters, *His Eye is on the Sparrow*, p. 149, 1951

4 a conventional, narrow-minded person *US, 1947*
- — Marcus Hanna Boulware, *Jive and Slang of Students in Negro Colleges*, 1947

5 an unattractive girl *US, 1955*
- A: But that's better than being stuck. Q: Stuck? A: With a pig, a drag, a beast. — Max Shulman, *Guided Tour of Campus Humor*, p. 106, 1955

6 clout, influence *US, 1896*
- The money came in so fast and his drag was so good that he felt immune[.] — Jack Lait and Lee Mortimer, *New York Confidential*, p. 185, 1948
- I have plenty of drag around this town. — Jim Thompson, *Bad Boy*, p. 370, 1953
- How much drag do I have with Lyndon Johnson? But none. — Glendon Swarthout, *Where the Boys Are*, p. 201, 1960
- Having drag in Vietnam was very important for specialized units that required special supplies or support. — Gregory Clark, *Words of the Vietnam War*, p. 154, 1990

7 a street or road, especially a major urban street *UK, 1851*

- Man, I could see myself in a sharp uniform, strutting down the main drag blowing my sax while the chicks lined up along the curb giving me the eye all the way. — Milton Mezzrow, *Really the Blues*, p. 19, 1946
- The houses thinned out and there were fewer roads intersecting the main drag. — Mickey Spillane, *One Lonely Night*, p. 126, 1951
- [A] nosy sheriff who thought I was pretty young to be hitchhiking accosted me on the main drag. — Jack Kerouac, *On the Road*, pp. 230–231, 1957
- Linda would see him in a pickup truck on the "drag" Saturday nights, bumper to bumper from Wendy's down to Anthony's, where kids from both schools would hang out in the shopping center parking lot. — Elmore Leonard, *Be Cool*, p. 79, 1999

8 an inhalation (of a cigarette, pipe or cigar) *US, 1904*

- [W]ith the smoking of two drags of te I felt constrained to open an extra button down and so show my tanned, hairy chest[.] — Jack Kerouac, *The Subterraneans*, p. 8, 1958
- Give me a drag. — *The Hustler*, 1961
- They all take a drag on their reefers/ And say prayers to St. Konky Mohair. (Collected in 1962). — Dennis Wepman et al., *The Life*, p. 107, 1976
- Carlucci lights his cigarette and half of it disappears on the first drag. — Robert Campbell, *The Cat's Meow*, p. 50, 1988

9 a confidence game in which a wallet is dropped as bait for the victim *US, 1958*

- — *New York Times Magazine*, p. 88, 16th March 1958

drag *verb*

1 to dance *US, 1974*

- A slow number came on and I rose to my full stature as we began to slow-drag. — Nathan Heard, *A Cold Fire Burning*, p. 16, 1974

2 to bore or annoy *US, 1944*

- It's no use to piss and moan about it; if I made a Thing of it and let it drag me, I really would flip. — James Blake, *The Joint*, p. 38, 30th December 1951
- "Jokes drag me," Porter said. — Chandler Brossard, *Who Walks in Darkness*, p. 78, 1952
- It drags me to get hit on like that. — Iceberg Slim (Robert Beck), *Pimp*, p. 126, 1969
- Of course I was never more drug in my life, but you know how it goes. — A.S. Jackson, *Gentleman Pimp*, p. 100, 1973

3 to wear clothing of the opposite sex *US, 1970*

- Dragging is just about the hardest thing to do. — *Screw*, p. 9, 15th March 1970

4 in poker, to take (chips) from the pot as change for a bet *US, 1967*

- — Albert H. Morehead, *The Complete Guide to Winning Poker*, p. 261, 1967

5 in poker, to take the house percentage out of a pot *US, 1988*

- — George Percy, *The Language of Poker*, p. 30, 1988

▸ **drag your anchor**

to lose control of yourself and drift towards trouble *US, 1963*
Clearly understood nautical origins.

- — Charles F. Haywood, *Yankee Dictionary*, pp. 49–50, 1963

drag-ass *adjective*

tired, lazy *US, 1952*

- The prospect of turning into a bureaucratic, dip-dunk, whining, drag-ass paper pusher did not excite me in the least. — Richard Marcinko, *Rogue Warrior*, p. 172, 1992
- "They were near disintegration at that point, and the drag-ass depression hung over them like a bad smell," recalls Rapeman's Steve Albini. — Michael Azerrad, *Our Band Could Be Your Life*, p. 370, 2001

drag ball *noun*

a dance dominated by men dressed as women *US, 1957*

- It might simply be that Harry would like to dress up as a woman and go to a drag ball, or parade down Broadway[.] — Hubert Selby Jr., *Last Exit to Brooklyn*, p. 215, 1957
- It was certain to be a "drag ball" (where a goodly number of fellows are dressed as southern belles) and like many male homosexuals we had always found such affairs tedious and boring. — *Screw*, p. 14, 21st March 1969

dragged *adjective*

annoyed, depressed *US, 1952*

- Seemed real dragged. Gave me the pitch about the movies and the record date and all. — Ross Russell, *The Sound*, p. 100, 1961

- I felt so dragged, I missed a couple rehearsals of our band. — Nat Hentoff, *Jazz Country*, pp. 20–21, 1965
- "Daddy, I'm dragged," she told him, looking away from him. — Sol Yurrick, *The Bag*, p. 70, 1968

dragging *adjective*

boring *US, 1960*

- They thought it was only a matter of taking a long, dragging ride in an empty train. — Sol Yurrick, *The Warriors*, p. 83, 1965

draggin' wagon *noun*

a tow truck, especially a military tow truck *US, 1945*
Also known as a "dragon wagon."

- [T]he Logistical Vehicle System, nicknamed the "Dragon Waggon," a cab-unit with a variety of trailers that can carry more than 12 tons of cargo over rough terrain. — Allan R. Millett, *Semper Fidelis*, p. 620, 1980
- A few of the Dragon Wagons, tractor trailer trucks that hauled armored vehicles, carried twisted and burned-out 10th Cavalry tracks. — David G. Fitz-Enz, *Why a Soldier?*, p. 318, 2000

drag girl *noun*

a woman who engages in a confidence swindle targeting older women *US, 1973*

- A drag girl is a con girl who tries to meet old ladies. — Susan Hall, *Ladies of the Night*, p. 76, 1973

draggy *adjective*

boring, tedious *US, 1868*

- "Very draggy, those two," Cap said. "Good people to stay away from." — Chandler Brossard, *Who Walks in Darkness*, p. 181, 1952
- "I know it sounds draggy, but this is beginning to wear a little thin." — Malcolm Braly, *Shake Him Till He Rattles*, p. 40, 1963

drag it!

let's hurry up! *US, 1951*
Teen slang.

- — *Newsweek*, p. 28, 8th October 1951

drag king *noun*

a woman who impersonates a man, especially one who performs in a male persona *US, 1995*

- It takes a while before it becomes clear, when he takes off his suit, that this dildo-packing drag-king is a lesbian. — Paul Burston, *A Queer Romance*, p. 66, 1995
- Her club was the thriving New York drag king scene, and made it possible for this new art form to grow and showcase itself to the world. — *The Village Voice*, 5th October 1999
- I found all these great stores in Beverly Hills and became a drag king. Then I bought a Cadillac. — Simon Doonan, *Wacky Chicks*, p. 91, 2003

drag mag *noun*

a magazine targeted at transvestites *US, 1972*

- — Bruce Rodgers, *The Queens' Vernacular*, p. 68, 1972

drag man *noun*

the soldier at the rear of an infantry patrol *US, 1989*

- I was tail-end Charlie, drag man. Watchin' 'em go down this trail. — Harry Maurer, *Strange Ground*, p. 155, 1989

dragon *noun*

a man dressed as a woman *US, 2006*
An evolution of **DRAG QUEEN**.

- "I've been in on some drug busts as transporting officer for trannies and dragons." — Joseph Wambaugh, *Hollywood Station*, p. 155, 2006

Dragon's Jaw *nickname*

the Thanh Hoa rail-road and road bridge, spanning the Song Ma River three miles north of Thanh Hoa, the capital of Annam Province, North Vietnam *US, 1974*

- [T]he strike force contained fourteen planes that were headed for the Thanh Hoa Railroad Bridge, later nicknamed "The Dragon's Jaw," because of its near invincibility. — Robert K. Wilcox, *Scream of Eagles*, p. 16, 1990

dragonfly *noun*

an A-37 aircraft, used in the Vietnam war largely as a close air-support fighter for ground forces *US, 1985*

- — Ian Padden, *U.S. Air Commando*, p. 103, 1985

dragon lady *noun*

an aggressive, ruthless, ambitious woman *US, 1952*

Her traits make a man a leader; from a comic strip character who along with being ruthless etc., is from the far east.

- She [Madame Ngo Dinh Nhu of Viet Nam] may be a Dragon Lady—but she's OUR Dragon Lady! — *San Francisco News Call-Bulletin*, p. 6, 12th October 1963
- A stereotypical and highly objectionable characterization of Asian women depicting them as scheming and treacherous. — Multicultural Management Program Fellows., *Dictionary of Cautionary Words and Phrases*, 1989

dragon ship *noun*
any of several US helicopter gunships equipped with Gatling guns during the Vietnam war *US, 1967*

- We could hear the Dragon Ship pilots[.] — Vernon Walters, *Silent Missions*, p. 425, 1978
- Troops discovered that the "dragon ships" were especially effective in breaking up enemy night attacks. — Roger E. Bilstein, *Flight in America*, p. 252, 2001

drag queen *noun*
a man, usually but not always homosexual, who frequently or invariably wears women's clothing *US, 1941*
From **DRAG** (women's clothes when worn by men) and **QUEEN** (an effeminate homosexual man). The social conditions that prevailed when this term was coined allowed for less obvious and glamorous cross-dressing.

- Who is to say which is more pathetic—the outlandish "drag queen" who affects thick make-up, women's skirts and high heels, or the "closet queen" who, in a much more shocking fashion, flaunts his perversion. — Antony James, *America's Homosexual Underground*, p. 67, 1965
- "That's a drag queen, man. A male impersonating a female." — Joe Houston, *The Gay Flesh*, p. 22, 1965
- It was not that we were uptight about drag queens, but just that we saw no reason to associate ourselves with that tiny fringe of the gay world who dig powder puffs. — *Screw*, 21st March 1969
- At Highland and Hollywood, the queens, awesome defiant Amazons, are assuming their stations. — John Rechy, *The Sexual Outlaw*, p. 39, 1977
- Her lips are some unlikely shade of copper or violet, courtesy of her local MAC drag queen makeup consultant. — Francesca Lia Block, *I Was a Teenage Fairy*, p. 121, 1998

drag show *noun*
a performance by men dressed as women *US, 1959*

- — J.D. Mercer, *They Walk in Shadow*, p. 564, 1959: "Slang vocabulary"

drag squad *noun*
the unit providing rear-guard security behind a larger body of soldiers *US, 1981*

- The Drag Squad behind the main maneuver element to insure rear safety. — Shelby L. Stanton, *Vietnam Order of Battle*, p. 355, 1981

dragster *noun*
a person who regularly asks for a puff on others' cigarettes *US, 1963*

- — *American Speech*, p. 276, December 1963: "American Indian student slang"

drain *verb*
(used of a ball in pinball) to leave play at the bottom of the playing field *US, 1977*

- — Bobbye Claire Natkin and Steve Kirk, *All About Pinball*, p. 112, 1977

▸ **drain the lizard**
(of a male) to urinate *US, 1981*

- Treb walked into the head to drain his lizard. — Robert Lipkin, *A Brotherhood of Outlaws*, p. 134, 1981

▸ **drain the main vein**
to urinate *US, 1989*

- — Pamela Munro, *U.C.L.A. Slang*, p. 36, 1989
- — Joy Masoff, *Oh, Yuck!*, p. 120, 2000

▸ **drain the radiator**
to urinate *US, 1977*

- — Bill Davis, *Jawjacking*, p. 36, 1977

▸ **drain the train**
(used of a male) to have sex *US, 1984*

- The bartender spoke slowly, as if to an idiot child. "You know, push the push? Slake the snake? Drain the train? Siphon the python?" — James Ellroy, *Because the Night*, p. 415, 1984

▸ **drain the vein**
to urinate *US, 1968*

- — Collin Baker et al., *College Undergraduate Slang Study Conducted at Brown University*, p. 218, 1968

▸ **drain the weasel**
(used of a male) to urinate *US, 1990*

- I gotta drain da weasel. Wanna see me write my name? — John Singleton, *Boyz N The Hood*, 1990

drain pipe *noun*
in poker, a conservative player who slowly but surely accumulates winnings, draining money from other players *US, 1996*

- — John Vorhaus, *The Big Book of Poker Slang*, p. 15, 1996

drama queen *noun*
someone who creates an unnecessary or excessive fuss *US, 1981*
Originally gay usage.

- A drama queen is a fussy person who makes a scene at the slightest provocation. — Kenneth Plummer, *The Making of the Modern Homosexual*, p. 197, 1981
- Lynda was a pill-popping speed freak and drama queen. — Bertie Marshall, *Berlin Bromley*, p. 64, 2006

drape *noun*
1 clothing; a man's suit *US, 1938*

- When we stripped naked and lined up for our numbers and prison clothes, my morale hit zero and kept sinking. Jack, the drapes they handed me a jungle bum wouldn't wear on workdays. — Mezz Mezzrow, *Really the Blues*, p. 33, 1946
- Them holler drapes Vann wears out in front of his band is just too much, man. — Ross Russell, *The Sound*, p. 109, 1961

2 the sag of a suit favored by zoot suiters and their fellow travelers *US, 1954*

- What is this suit you make over and over, with the padded shoulders and the extreme drape and the pegged pants? — Bernard Wolfe, *The Late Risers*, p. 217, 1954
- Then there was Prez, a husky, handsome blond like a freckled boxer, meticulously wrapped inside his sharkskin plaid suit with the long drape and the collar falling back[.] — Jack Kerouac, *On the Road*, p. 239, 1957

drape *verb*
to dress, to attire *US, 1942*

- Safari shirt and pants, tan colored, I'm pressed, but not like them vines Cye Martin used to drape on me. — Edwin Torres, *After Hours*, p. 272, 1979

▸ **drape the shape**
to get dressed *US, 1962*

- — *Dobie Gillis Teenage Slanguage Dictionary*, 1962

drape *adjective*
said of a stylized, baggy men's suit favored by zoot suiters *US, 1967*

- With my paper route, my gambling in school and my other hustles, I was able to acquire a radio and two new drape suits. — Babs Gonzales, *I Paid My Dues*, p. 10, 1967

draped *adjective*
adorned with a lot of gold jewelry *US, 1995*

- — Bill Valentine, *Gang Intelligence Manual*, p. 76, 1995: "Black street gang terminology"

drapes *noun*
bell-bottom pants *US, 1970*

- Any kid with drapes and a duck's ass haircut on the street got his lumps right away. — Gilbert Sorrentino, *Steelwork*, p. 63, 1970
- — Douglas Simonson, *Pidgin to da Max Hana Hou*, 1982

drape shape *noun*
a baggy, loose-fitting style of clothing popular in the 1940s *US, 1955*

- During the early postwar years, the so-called "drape shape" or loose, hanging, balloon type of suit was promoted for better or for worse. — *San Francisco News*, p. 12, 11th August 1955

draw *noun*
1 a chance, a risk *US, 1969*

- "Guys like Giancana don't take a draw [chance] by giving important messages to a warden, a guard, or a probation officer." — Ovid Demaris, *Captive City*, p. 17, 1969

2 in pool, backspin applied to the cue ball *US, 1866*
- — Mike Shamos, *The Illustrated Encyclopedia of Billiards*, p. 83, 1993

draw *verb*
while injecting a drug, to pull blood into the syringe to verify that the needle has hit a blood vein *US, 1971*
- — Eugene Landy, *The Underground Dictionary*, p. 70, 1971

▸ **draw dead**
in poker, to draw cards into a hand that cannot win *US, 1990*
- — Anthony Holden, *Big Deal*, p. 300, 1990

▸ **draw down on**
to draw out and point guns at *US, 1974*
- They, when they draw down on him and tell him to jet the fuck out of the way, he just stands there sellin' wolf tickets like a goddamn fool or something (news). — Vernon E. Smith, *The Jones Men*, p. 202, 1974
- Cat on a family dispute almost draws down on Francis when he tried to lay the iron on his wrists after the dude had went upside Momma's head. — Joseph Wambaugh, *The Choirboys*, p. 314, 1975

drawers *noun*
sex *US, 1969*
- She didn't know why, but even after all this she was still gonna give him the drawers. — Steve Cannon, *Groove, Bang, and Jive Around*, p. 30, 1969

drawings *noun*
1 information; gossip; news *US, 1968*
- Sometimes I visit the shack to shoot the bull and get the latest drawings (news). — Eldridge Cleaver, *Soul on Ice*, p. 44, 1968
2 plans for a course of action *US, 1990*
- It was Joe Sing's turn to nod. "What are your drawings?" — Seth Morgan, *Homeboy*, p. 70, 1990

dreaded *adjective*
fashionable, popular, in style *US, 1998*
- — *Columbia Missourian*, p. 1A, 19th October 1998

dreads *noun*
dreadlocks, a Rastafarian hairstyle in which the hair is not combed or brushed, forming matted clumps or "locks" *US, 1977*
- — Pamela Munro, *U.C.L.A. Slang*, p. 63, 2001

dream *noun*
1 an appealing, attractive member of whatever sex attracts you *US, 1895*
- She took to me readily because she had heard of my accomplishments, and she thought I was a dream. — Phyllis and Eberhard Kronhausen, *Sex Histories of American College Men*, p. 72, 1960
2 opium *US, 1929*
- Tell me, West, do you know what a dream session is? — Evan Hunter, *The Blackboard Jungle*, p. 159, 1954

dreamboat *noun*
a sexually attractive person *US, 1944*
- How was I to know wide girls like them would turn me into a ruddy dreamboat, all three of them? — Charles Raven, *Underworld Nights*, p. 119, 1956
- Ed Lakey at twenty-eight looked just like the dreamboat he had been when he went to Hollywood High[.] — Eve Babitz, *L.A. Woman*, p. 98, 1982
- When our eyes finally met through our viewfinders, I saw my video-dating dreamboat. — Anka Radakovich, *The Wild Girls Club*, p. 95, 1994

dream book *noun*
a book that purports to interpret dreams, suggesting numbers to be played in an illegal lottery based on symbols in the dreams *US, 1890*
- But the best numbers come from "Dream Books." They are especially made for the policy trade and have a tremendous sale on the South Side of Chicago. — Alson Smith, *Syndicate City*, p. 198, 1954
- Rev. Jones went back into the room for his dream book[.] — Clarence Cooper Jr., *Black*, p. 179, 1963
- My father used to knock me out with his dreambook. — John A. Williams, *The Angry Ones*, p. 125, 1969
- What number does Madame Zora's dream book five for fish? — Louise Meriwether, *Daddy Was a Number Runner*, p. 13, 1970
- Yet in the Pennsylvania steel town where Spencer Van Moot was born, every living soul had played numbers and consulted dream books for winners[.] — Joseph Wambaugh, *The Choirboys*, p. 64, 1975

dream dust *noun*
any powdered drug *US, 1957*
- And I keep getting off the subject of the rumor I picked up today from a traveling merchant into smuggling mostly ... Red Devil and Dream Dust. — William S. Burroughs, *The Place of Dead Roads*, p. 267, 1983

dreamers *noun*
sheets for a bed *US, 1945*
- — Lou Shelly, *Hepcats Jive Dictionary*, p. 9, 1945

dreamland *noun*
sleep or an unconscious state *US, 1908*
- And let's not forget stamina. I don't want him drifting off to dreamland when I've only just begun. — John Tomkiw, *Total Sex*, p. 15, 1999

dream number *noun*
in an illegal number gambling lottery, a bet based on the better's dream, either directly or as interpreted by a dream book *US, 1949*
- — *American Speech*, p. 191, October 1949

dream powder *noun*
heroin *US, 1951*
- Rocky was jubilant until I flushed all of this dream powder down the toilet. — Ethel Waters, *His Eye is on the Sparrow*, p. 122, 1951

dream sheet *noun*
a list created by a soldier of the places where he would like to be shipped *US, 1971*
Rarely realized.
- Owen had already filled out his Officer Assignment Preference Statement—his DREAM SHEET, he called it. — John Irving, *A Prayer for Owen Meany*, p. 416, 1989

dream stuff *noun*
marijuana *US, 1949*
- "You ever smoke dream stuff?" "Charge?" "Yeah." — Hal Ellson, *Duke*, p. 34, 1949

dream wagon *noun*
an attractive person *US, 1963*
- The fellow I'm going with is 18 and a real dream wagon. — Ann Landers, *Ann Landers Talks to Teen-Agers About Sex*, p. 114, 1963

dreamy *adjective*
very attractive, beautiful, desirable *US, 1941*
- Paul A. Wagner, 33-year-old former newsreel cameraman and salesman, has made things hum at Rollins College since taking over as prexy. And the coeds think he's dreamy. — *Colliers*, p. 21, 13th January 1951

dress down *verb*
to dress up *US, 1984*
Often intensified with "for a motherfucker."
- Big man be dressing down for a motherfucker tonight cause he's got two new hoes to sport around. — Inez Cardozo-Freeman, *The Joint*, p. 491, 1984

dressed *adjective*
armed *US, 1973*
- Ted didn't see the pistol that I had but I'm sure he felt I was dressed. — A.S. Jackson, *Gentleman Pimp*, p. 80, 1973

dress in *verb*
to exchange the clothes worn upon arrival for prison-issued clothes *US, 1976*
- — Troy Harris, *A Booklet of Criminal Argot, Cant and Jargon*, p. 8, 1976
- When I dressed into Quentin, I was an old-timer. — Malcolm Braly, *False Starts*, p. 290, 1976
- He was referring to Bro, so that he could be dressed in, but since we were both Scott and we both needed to be dressed in, he let us go together. — Sanyika Shakur, *Monster*, p. 132, 1993

dressing out *noun*
throwing feces on someone *US, 2006*
- For prisoners, "gassing" had another meaning: it meant throwing shit on another person, sometimes while holding her down. A few prisoners called this "dressing out." — Justin Cartwright, *The Promise of Happiness*, p. 171, 2006

dress out *verb*
to exchange prison clothing for street clothes upon release
from prison *US, 1976*
- — Troy Harris, *A Booklet of Criminal Argot, Cant and Jargon*, p. 8, 1976

drib *noun*
an unskilled poker player *US, 1967*
- — Albert H. Morehead, *The Complete Guide to Winning Poker*, p. 262, 1967

dribble *noun*
small, weak waves *US, 1991*
- — Trevor Cralle, *The Surfin'ary*, p. 31, 1991

dribble *verb*
to meander, to walk *US, 1960*
- — Robert George Reisner, *The Jazz Titans*, p. 154, 1960

drift *verb*
to leave *US, 1853*
- "Okay for us to drift now, Chief?" — Evan Hunter, *The Blackboard Jungle*,
p. 48, 1954

drill *verb*
1 to inject (a drug) *US, 1970*
- — William D. Alsever, *Glossary for the Establishment and Other Uptight People*, p. 19,
December 1970
2 to shoot (with a bullet); to kill by shooting *UK, 1720*
- Drill the fucker. I got my attorney's .357 Magnum out of the trunk
and spun the cylinder. — Hunter S. Thompson, *Fear and Loathing in Las Vegas*,
p. 99, 1971
- They both had guns, but guess they didn't drill me because they
knew the police was keepin' watch on me and a lotta noise was the
last thing they wanted. — Martin Gosch, *The Last Testament of Lucky Luciano*,
p. 390, 1975
3 to interrogate *US, 1995*
- They drilled us all night. Somebody was pissed about that truck getting knocked off and the cops had nothing. — *The Usual Suspects*, 1995
4 in pool, to make a shot in an emphatic and convincing
manner *US, 1993*
- — Mike Shamos, *The Illustrated Encyclopedia of Billiards*, p. 83, 1993
5 to walk, to move *US, 1953*
- — Lavada Durst, *The Jives of Dr. Hepcat*, p. 12, 1953

driller *noun*
a poker player who bets very aggressively *US, 1988*
- — George Percy, *The Language of Poker*, p. 31, 1988

drink *noun*
a large body of water, especially an ocean *US, 1832*
- The guys I wanted to play with and listen to were all on the other
side of the drink. — Mezz Mezzrow, *Really the Blues*, p. 198, 1946
- A clout in the chops is what they deserved after dropping their
Austin-Healey in the drink last night[.] — Max Shulman, *Anyone Got a
Match?*, p. 54, 1964

▸ **in the drink**
in pool, said of a cue ball that falls into a pocket *US, 1990*
- — Steve Rushin, *Pool Cool*, p. 16, 1990

drinkee; drinkie *noun*
any alcoholic drink *US, 1960*
A jocular mock pidgin.
- "Not until I get me a drinkie," Delores announced. — George Clayton
Johnson, *Ocean's Eleven*, p. 48, 1960
- "Fresheners," Nancy said. "Tighteners and fresheners. Sometimes
drinkees or martin-eyes." — Elmore Leonard, *The Big Bounce*, p. 88, 1969

drinkerama *noun*
a party organized around the consumption of alcohol *US,
1968*
- — Collin Baker et al., *College Undergraduate Slang Study Conducted at Brown
University*, p. 109, 1968

drinker's hour *noun*
3 a.m. *US, 1984*
- Several were waking each night at the drinker's hour with night
sweats and irregular heartbeats. — Joseph Wambaugh, *Lines and Shadows*,
pp. 305–306, 1984
- He looked at his watch. Three A.M. The Drinker's Hour. All the grief
and agony of mankind happened at three A.M., after booze made
the blood sugar drop. — Joseph Wambaugh, *Fugitive Nights*, p. 234, 1992

drink rustler *noun*
a woman who uses her sexuality to induce customers to
buy drinks at a bar *US, 1971*
- A B-girl (also called a "come-on" or "percentage girl" or "drink
rustler") often spends six to seven hours in a bar every evening.
— Charles Winick, *The Lively Commerce*, p. 171, 1971

drinkypoo; drinki-poo *noun*
any alcoholic drink *US, 1983*
Baby talk, thought to give alcohol an innocent demeanor.
- It's time for you to have another drinky poo! — Joseph Wambaugh, *The
Secrets of Harry Bright*, p. 224, 1985

drip *noun*
1 a person lacking in social skills, fashion sense, or both; a
simpleton, a fool *US, 1932*
- "Damn 'em, this guy was supposed to be a drip. Easy, the son of a
bitch said. He'd shake in his shoes if you yelled at 'im." — Mickey
Spillane, *The Long Wait*, p. 74, 1951
- Ginnie openly considered Selena the biggest drip at Miss Basehoar's[.]
— J.D. Salinger, *Nine Stories*, p. 39, 1953
- She had called him a drip, a creep, and a primate and had said that
the best thing he could do for her was to join the French Foreign
Legion. — Max Shulman, *Rally Round the Flag, Boys!*, p. 202, 1957
- George W. Bush is, as one friend called him, a "drip" who couldn't
get a date. — *Nerve*, p. 15, October-November 2000
2 coffee *US, 1976*
- Harry headed for the Ron-Ric Cafe for a cup of coffee, the worst drip
in Uptown, or all of town, black and filmy, bitter because the pots
were never cleaned. — William Brashler, *City Dogs*, p. 32, 1976

drip and suck *verb*
to intubate a hospital patient with intravenous and naso-
gastric tubes *US, 1994*
- — Sally Williams, *"Strong" Words*, p. 140, 1994

dripper *noun*
an eye dropper, used in an improvised method of drug
injection *US, 1953*
- — *San Francisco Call-Bulletin*, p. 6, 17th August 1953

drippy *adjective*
mawkish, overly sentimental, insipid *US, 1947*
- [H]e was pretty as a picture in a drippy sort of way and wrote these
far out pieces about the movies[.] — Gore Vidal, *Myra Breckinridge*, p. 23,
1968

drippy dick *noun*
an unspecified sexually transmitted disease *US, 1990*
- "I, uh," he was sweating hard, beads of perspiration falling to the
ground. "I got the drippy-dick, okay?" — Steve Armstrong, *Officer Down*,
p. 28, 2004
- Because he caught drippy dick, he was restricted to the ship for
the mandatory 30 days. — Richard Merrell, *Gangway Regular Navy*, p. 86,
2005

drippy faucet *noun*
the penis of a man with a sexually transmitted infection
that produces a pus discharge *US, 1981*
- Do you know he has a drippy faucet? — Joseph Wambaugh, *The Glitter Dome*,
p. 6, 1981

dripsy *noun*
gonorrhea *US, 1981*
- — *Maledicta*, p. 228, Summer/Winter 1981: "Sex and the single soldier"

drive *verb*
1 to walk *US, 1956*
- — *American Speech*, p. 228, October 1956: "More United States Air Force slang"
2 to lift weights *US, 2000*
- On November 5, 1980, while driving (lifting weights) on the lower
yard, several of the Aryans spotted a white inmate who was carrying
a snitch jacket[.] — Bill Valentine, *Gangs and Their Tattoos*, p. 13, 2000
3 to borrow (a radio) *US, 2002*
From **CAR** (a radio).
- — Gary K. Farlow, *Prison-ese*, p. 20, 2002

▸ **drive the bus**
to vomit *US, 2001*
- — Pamela Munro, *U.C.L.A. Slang*, p. 63, 2001

▶ **drive wooden stake**
to irrevocably and permanently end (a project, a business, an idea) *US, 1974*
- — Robert Kirk Mueller, *Buzzwords*, p. 165, 1974

drive-by *noun*
1 a drive-by shooting, where shots are fired from a moving car *US, 1997*
- Goddamn if that dint look like the selfsame ole van what done a drive-by on us a couple days ago. — Jess Mowry, *Way Past Cool*, p. 13, 1992
- The drive-by is not a new concept, you know. The cowboys had ride-bys. They'd ride-by and shoot up a whole town. — Chris Rock, *Rock This!*, p. 77, 1997

2 by extension, a sudden attack after which the attacker flees *US, 1998*
- These drive-bys don't involve cars and guns but rather swift feet and sharp knives. — Tookie Williams, *Life in Prison*, p. 73, 1998

3 a silent, smelly fart *US, 2001*
- — Jim Goad, *Jim Goad's Glossary of Northwestern Prison Slang*, December 2001

drive-by *verb*
to shoot someone, or into a crowd, from a moving car *US, 1992*
- Yo, Gordon, tell the teacher you got em all dirty gettin' drive-byed. — Jess Mowry, *Way Past Cool*, p. 7, 1992

drive call *noun*
in a telephone swindle, a high-pressure, follow-up call to the victim *US, 1985*
- — M. Allen Henderson, *How Con Games Work*, p. 219, 1985: "Glossary"

driver *noun*
1 an amphetamine or other central nervous system stimulant *US, 1990*
- — Gilda and Melvin Berger, *Drug Abuse A-Z*, p. 59, 1990

2 in poker, a player whose aggressive betting is dominating the game *US, 1996*
- — Peter O. Steiner, *Thursday Night Poker*, p. 409, 1996

3 the leader of a prison clique *US, 1989*
Back formation from **CAR** (a clique).
- — James Harris, *A Convict's Dictionary*, p. 31, 1989
- driver: a leader, in charge — J.G. Narum, *The Convict Cookbook*, p. 158, 2004

drive-up *noun*
a fresh arrival at prison *US, 1990*
- — Charles Shafer, *Folk Speech in Texas Prisons*, p. 203, 1990

drizzles *noun*
diarrhea *US, 1943*
- And the prisoner looks like a water bed, all shuddery and quivering, as he lies on the floor bloated by about five gallons of T.J.'s H2), guaranteed to give him the drizzles. — Joseph Wambaugh, *Lines and Shadows*, p. 128, 1984

drizzling shits *noun*
dysentery *US, 1980*
- I hope that son of a bitch dies of the drizzling shits. — *Maledicta*, p. 171, Winter 1980

dro *noun*
marijuana grown hydroponically *US, 2002*
- Sean Paul borrowed American slang for the opening line. "Just gimme the light and pass the 'dro," he chants, borrowing the hip-hop term for hydroponic marijuana. — *Washington Post*, p. G01, 24th November 2002

droid *noun*
a low-level employee who is blindly loyal to his employer *US, 1980*
- Typical droid positions include supermarket checkout assistant and bank clerk; the syndrome is also endemic in low-level government employees. — Eric S. Raymond, *The New Hacker's Dictionary*, p. 134, 1991

drome *noun*
in circus and carnival usage, a motordrome *US, 1981*
- Don Wilmeth, *The Language of American Popular Entertainment*, p. 80, 1981

drone *noun*
1 a sluggard, a tedious person *UK, 1529*
- Someday, Bloodworth hoped, one of these drones would call with a hot tip, maybe even a ticket to the front page. — Carl Hiaasen, *Tourist Season*, p. 232, 1986

2 in hospital usage, a medical student *US, 1994*
- — Sally Williams, *"Strong" Words*, p. 140, 1994

droned *adjective*
simultaneously intoxicated on alcohol and marijuana *US, 1997*
A blend of "drunk" and "stoned."
- — Pamela Munro, *U.C.L.A. Slang*, p. 60, 1997

drool *noun*
nonsense; drivel *US, 1900*
- [F]or God's sake don't listen to that drool how the stuff [drugs] eat you up ... that kind of jive is for squares. — Harry J. Anslinger, *The Murderers*, p. 174, 1961

drooling the drool of regret into the pillow of remorse
used as a humorous comment on a person who has not performed up to their expectation *US, 1997*
Coined and popularized by ESPN's Keith Olberman.
- — Keith Olberman and Dan Patrick, *The Big Show*, p. 13, 1997

droop *noun*
a socially inept person *US, 1932*
- He's a 6-F droop, but has extra ration points. — Harry Haenigsen, *Jive's Like That*, 1947

droopy *adjective*
dispirited, dejected, sulky *US, 1955*
- I was not really quite prepared for her fits of disorganized boredom, intense and vehement griping, her sprawling, droopy, dopey-eyed style. — Vladimir Nabokov, *Lolita*, p. 148, 1955

droopy-drawers *noun*
a person, especially a child, with pants that are too large on a comic scale *US, 1931*
- He was wearing an old black felt hat and overalls which hung down his can as though he were little Droopy-Drawers smiling up from the play pen. — Robert Penn Warren, *All the King's Men*, p. 64, 1946

drop *noun*
1 the shortening of a military tour of duty *US, 1991*
- Most soldiers' conversations centered around the Army's policy on "drops." A "drop" was a curtailment of the normal tour for any number of bureaucratic reasons. — J.D. Coleman, *Incursion*, p. 110, 1991

2 in espionage or a criminal enterprise a place where goods, documents, or money is left to be picked up later by a confederate *US, 1922*
- Sometimes the stuff is brought in direct, while at other times a "drop" is made at an outlying area. — Clarence Cooper Jr., *The Scene*, p. 27, 1960
- "The drop is where we stash the hot car until it's needed[.]" — Charles Perry, *Portrait of a Young Man Drowning*, p. 118, 1962
- There's the neighborhood cop at the numbers drop/ Shaking down the run. — Dennis Wepman et al., *The Life*, p. 162, 1976
- It was a drop. It was a pass. It was a payoff to Ray Sharkey here. this City Hall Pimp you got yourself here is a shrewd sonofabitch. He wouldn't take the payoff where somebody could see. He took the payoff where everybody could see. — Robert Campbell, *Boneyards*, p. 192, 1992

3 a place where stolen goods or other criminal material may be temporarily stored *US, 1922*
- I laid these things on him for letting me use his pad as a drop. — A.S. Jackson, *Gentleman Pimp*, p. 24, 1973
- The owner was a horse lover and gambler, and used the store as a bookie drop. — James Ellroy, *Blood on the Moon*, p. 54, 1984

4 in horse racing, a cash-handling error that favors the racetrack *US, 1982*
- — Bob and Barbara Freeman, *Wanta Bet?*, p. 289, 1982

5 the place where players who are invited to an illegal dice game are told where the game will be held *US, 1964*
- — *American Speech*, p. 306, December 1964: "Lingua Cosa Nostra"

6 an orphan *US, 1970*
- — Clarence Major, *Dictionary of Afro-American Slang*, p. 48, 1970

7 in a casino, the amount of money taken in from betting customers *US, 1935*
- He must know that Frank Sinatra will raise the "drop" of the casino more than any other entertainer. — Mario Puzo, *Inside Las Vegas*, p. 175, 1977
- As soon as he took over, he doubled the fuckin' drop. — *Casino*, 1995

drop *verb*

1 to swallow, to ingest (a drug) *US, 1961*

A favorite word of the LSD culture, but popular for other drugs of abuse before and since; if used without a direct object, almost certainly referring to LSD.

- To take orally is to "drop it." — Francis J. Rigney and L. Douglas Smith, *The Real Bohemia*, p. xx, 1961
- Everybody dropped his acid in the kitchen and for the first half hour they sat around listening to music. — Richard Alpert and Sidney Cohen, *LSD*, p. 100, 1966
- Being too young to drink, he smoked pot, dropped acid, and at last sniffed heroin[.] — Raymond Mungo, *Famous Long Ago*, p. 30, 1970
- And we ain't dropping 'til I say so. — *Saturday Night Fever*, 1977

2 to lose (especially money) *UK, 1676*

An example of C19 flash slang that has survived.

- Frank had dropped $3,200 at craps, not even shooting, betting against the shooter. — Elmore Leonard, *Switch*, p. 111, 1978

3 to perform oral sex on a woman *US, 1997*

- I stopped dropping. It got to be too frustrating. — *Chasing Amy*, 1997

4 in pool, to hit (a ball) into a pocket *US, 1993*

- — Mike Shamos, *The Illustrated Encyclopedia of Billiards*, p. 83, 1993

▶ **drop a bomb; drop one**

to defecate *US, 2001*

- — Don R. McCreary (Editor), *Dawg Speak*, 2001

▶ **drop a dime**

to make a telephone call, especially to the police to inform on someone *US, 1966*

From the days when the price of a call from a pay phone was a dime.

- I ain't never seen so many stool pigeons in one block before in all my life. Drop a dime on you 'fore Fod can git the news. — Nathan Heard, *Howard Street*, p. 35, 1968
- He dropped a dime on you to screw me out of the six hundred grand. — Gerald Petievich, *To Live and Die in L.A.*, p. 16, 1983
- Drop a dime? Call the cops? Don't even let anybody hear such bullshit. — *Goodfellas*, 1990
- They'll hear I dropped dime. They'll probably hear it from you. — *The Usual Suspects*, 1995

▶ **drop a jewel; drop jewels**

to create rap music or lyrics *US, 1991*

- Fuck droppin' a jewel[.] — Eminem (Marshall Mathers), *Just Don't Give a Fuck*, 1999

▶ **drop a lug**

to confront someone about their conduct; to insult *US, 1973*

- — Christina and Richard Milner, *Black Players*, p. 303, 1972

▶ **drop a name**

to inform on a criminal or suspect *US, 1990*

- To drop a name on you. — *New Jack City*, 1990
- What do you think he'd say if he found out you dropped his name to the D.A.? — *The Usual Suspects*, 1995

▶ **drop a nickel**

to become involved in something *US, 1953*

- So I went over and dropped my nickel. I guess it's always a mistake to interfere with a drunk. — Raymond Chandler, *The Long Goodbye*, p. 2, 1953

▶ **drop beads**

to unintentionally disclose your homosexuality *US, 1970*

- — *American Speech*, p. 56, Spring–Summer 1970: "Homosexual slang"

▶ **drop dead**

to decrease the speed of a car when being followed by the police *US, 1958*

- The foxy motorist who slows almost to a halt when he senses pursuit drops dead. — *New York Times*, p. 34, 20th October 1958

▶ **drop some iron**

to spend money *US, 1987*

- — *Washington Post Magazine*, p. 7, 20th September 1987: "Say wha?"
- — Vann Wesson, *Generation X Field Guide and Lexicon*, p. 58, 1997

▶ **drop the belt**

in a homosexual relationship, to reverse passive-dominant roles *US, 1966*

- Sometimes the stud becomes so smitten with another stud that she "drops the belt"—she shifts from the male role to the female role. — Rose Giallombardo, *Society of Women*, p. 124, 1966

▶ **drop the hook**

to arrest *US, 1953*

- It was pretty obvious that the buttons in the prowl car were about ready to drop the hook on him, so I went over there fast and took hold of his arm. — Raymond Chandler, *The Long Goodbye*, p. 6, 1953

▶ **drop trou**

as a prank, to lower your pants, bend over and expose your buttocks to the world *US, 1966*

- — Andy Anonymous, *A Basic Guide to Campusology*, p. 8, 1966
- — John D. Bell et al., *Loosely Speaking*, p. 19, 1969

▶ **drop your oyster**

(of a woman) to experience an orgasm *US, 1971*

- "I could make Gloria drop her oyster in five minutes effen I put my mind to it." — Robert Deane Pharr, *S.R.O.*, p. 101, 1971

drop-down *noun*

in horse racing, a horse that has been moved down a class or down in claiming price *US, 1990*

- — Robert V. Rowe, *How to Win at Horse-Racing*, p. 199, 1990

drop edge of yonder *noun*

a near-death condition *US, 1939*

- Took to vomitin'. All day, all night. Hangin' on the drop edge of yonder. — William Least-Heat Moon, *Blue Highways*, p. 33, 1982

drop gun *noun*

a gun that is not registered and not capable of being traced, and thus placed by the police in the vicinity of someone whom they have shot to justify the shooting *US, 1987*

- — Carsten Stroud, *Close Pursuit*, p. 271, 1987

drop-in *noun*

in computing, characters added as a result of a voltage irregularity or system malfunction *US, 1991*

- — Eric S. Raymond, *The New Hacker's Dictionary*, p. 135, 1991

drop out *verb*

to withdraw from school, college, university, or mainstream society *US, 1952*

- "Drop out" was the message both collaborators gave the audience. — *The Berkeley Barb*, p. 2, 24th June 1966
- Why did the hippie join the Parachute Corps? So he could keep dropping out! — Paul Laikin, *101 Hippie Jokes*, 1968
- Drop Out—detach yourself from the eternal social drama which is as dehydrated and ersatz as TV. — Timothy Leary, *The Politics of Ecstasy*, p. 223, 1968
- "DROP OUT!" the yippies scream at them. — Jerry Rubin, *Do It!*, p. 115, 1970

dropper *noun*

1 a gambler who can be counted on to lose a lot of money *US, 1963*

- During his stay, hieroglyphics are secretly appended to his name on the hotel register, which catalogue him as a "dropper" (businessman and heavy loser), "producer" (businessman), or "nonproducer" (professional gambler). — Ed Reid and Ovid Demaris, *The Green Jungle*, p. 2, 1963

2 a paid killer *US, 1962*

- — Joseph E. Ragen and Charles Finston, *Inside the World's Toughest Prison*, p. 797, 1962

drop piece *noun*

a gun that is not registered and not capable of being traced, and thus placed by the police in the vicinity of someone whom they have shot to justify the shooting *US, 1991*

- In Baltimore, the drop piece became standard issue in the police districts[.] — David Simon, *Homicide*, p. 112, 1991

drop pocket *noun*

a secret pocket used by shoplifters *US, 1977*

- And I learned about drop pockets. — John Allen, *Assault with a Deadly Weapon*, p. 19, 1977

drop-the-hanky *noun*

a pickpocketing scheme in which the victim is distracted when an attractive woman member of the pickpocketing team drops a handkerchief or other small object which the victim stoops to recover *US, 1954*

- One setup engineered by troupes of three was called, some years back, drop the hanky. — Dev Collans with Stewart Sterling, *I was a House Detective*, p. 47, 1954

drop-top *noun*
a car with a convertible roof *US, 1973*

- Shiiit, nigga, the driveway look like some shit off the lifestyles of the Rich and Famous; a drop top Porsche, a big body Benz, two clover green Rovers. — Nikki Turner, *A Project Chick*, p. 22, 2004

drop your cocks and grab your socks!
used for awakening a sleeping man or men *US, 1956*
A variation of **HANDS OFF COCKS—FEET IN SOCKS!** Originally used by drill instructors to military recruits.

- "Okay, you bastards, drop your cocks and grab your socks!" — James Kubeck, *The Calendar Epic*, p. 120, 1956
- Six bells and all's well. Steady as she goes. Hit the deck. Drop your cocks and grab your socks. — Ken Kesey, *One Flew Over the Cuckoo's Nest*, p. 213, 1962
- He presses his other hand against his nose and imitates the bosun's pipe. "Now, reveille, reveille, reveille!" he shouts. "Drop your cocks and grab your socks!" — Darryl Poniscan, *The Last Detail*, p. 101, 1970
- Reveille! Drop your cocks and grab your socks! — *Full Metal Jacket*, 1987
- "COUNT TIME!" boomed from the front bars. "Drop yer cocks and pull up her socks!" — Seth Morgan, *Homeboy*, p. 88, 1990

drove *adjective*
very angry *US, 1992*

- — William K. Bentley and James M. Corbett, *Prison Slang*, p. 89, 1992

drove up *adjective*
frustrated *US, 1975*

- He got real drove up. Every day he started an argument over some insignificant point. — James Carr, *Bad*, p. 129, 1975

drown *verb*
to lose heavily gambling *US, 1974*

- — John Scarne, *Scarne on Dice*, p. 466, 1974

drown-proofing *noun*
in navy training, an exercise involving extended periods of treading water, especially while restrained to some degree *US, 1987*

- Next come fifteen nonstop minutes of "drown-proofing," the modern Navy version of treading water. — George Hall, *Top Gun*, p. 42, 1987
- He turned to Curran, "You wanted to watch the drownproofing, right sir?" — James B. Adair, *Navy Seals*, p. 99, 1990

drug; drugg; drugged *adjective*
displeased, annoyed *US, 1946*

- I paced up and down, up and down, two steps each way, fidgety as a tiger in a thimble. I was one drugg cat. — Mezz Mezzrow, *Really the Blues*, p. 301, 1946
- From the day she got me sprung from the Catholic institution, Mom and I were drug with Baltimore. — Billie Holiday, *Lady Sings the Blues*, p. 19, 1956
- M-a-a-n, I'm drug by that son of a bitch MacDoud with all his routines[.] — Jack Kerouac, *The Subterraneans*, p. 29, 1958
- When a junkie's drugged, he's mad at somebody or something. — Clarence Cooper Jr., *The Scene*, p. 55, 1960

drugged *adjective*
patently stupid *US, 1991*

- — Eric S. Raymond, *The New Hacker's Dictionary*, p. 135, 1991

druggie; druggy *noun*
a drug user, abuser or addict *US, 1966*

- There wasn't that much drug stuff then, and two of these are druggies. — George V. Higgins, *Penance for Jerry Kennedy*, p. 85, 1985
- Maybe it was a druggie out there looking for targets of opportunity. — Robert Campbell, *Juice*, p. 174, 1988
- I go in there to check up on some guy, they think I'm a druggie. — Elmore Leonard, *Maximum Bob*, p. 163, 1991
- I knew you were hanging out with druggies she spat. — Michelle Tea, *The Passionate Mistakes and Intricate Corruption of One Girl in America*, p. 41, 1998

drughead *noun*
a drug addict; a serious abuser of narcotics *US, 1968*

- It is set down squarely in the midst of the greatest single concentration of drunks, drugheads, whores, pimps, queers, sodomists in the hemisphere. — Walker Percy, *Lancelot*, p. 23, 1977

drugola *noun*
a bribe in the form of drugs given to encourage play of a particular record on the radio *US, 1973*

- CBS was soon embroiled in something called "drugola." — Ben Fong-Torres, *Not Fade Away*, p. 150, 1999

drugstore cowboy *noun*
a young man who loiters in or around a drugstore for the purpose of meeting women *US, 1923*

- Girl-watching is a sport of the ages that appeals to all ages from young drugstore cowboys to graying roues. — *Life*, p. 120, 27th October 1961
- Life was combat, and victory was not to the lazy, the timid, the slugabed, the drugstore cowboy, the libertine, the mushmouth afraid to tell pepole exactly what was on his mind[.] — Russell Baker, *Growing Up*, p. 9, 1982

drugstore dice *noun*
inexpensive shop-bought dice, not milled to casino-level tolerances *US, 1962*

- — Frank Garcia, *Marked Cards and Loaded Dice*, p. 264, 1962

drugstore handicap *noun*
in horse racing, a race in which drugs have been given to enhance performance *US, 1948*

- — David W. Maurer, *Argot of the Racetrack*, p. 25, 1951

drugstore race *noun*
in horse racing, a race in which a number of the horses involved have been drugged for enhanced or diminished performance *US, 1960*

- — Robert Saunders Dowst and Jay Craig, *Playing the Races*, p. 162, 1960

drum *noun*
1 a place of business or residence, a house, a home, an apartment, etc. *UK, 1846*

- It would have been too dodgy swagging gear into Bella's drum at 3 a.m. — Charles Raven, *Underworld Nights*, p. 22, 1956

2 by extension, a cell *UK, 1909*

- He's in the big house for all day and night, a new fish jammed into a drum with a cribman, who acts like a gazoonie. — *San Francisco Examiner*, p. 26, 17th August 1976

3 a safe *US, 1912*

- — Joseph E. Ragen and Charles Finston, *Inside the World's Toughest Prison*, p. 797, 1962

drummer *noun*
a poker player who plays only with good hands or good odds favoring his hand *US, 1988*
A play on the operative adjective of **TIGHT** used to describe such a player.

- — George Percy, *The Language of Poker*, p. 31, 1988

drummer's butt *noun*
a sweat-induced rash on the buttocks and/or genitals *US, 1998*

- We used to joke about playing long hours and getting "drummers' butt," also referred to as "swamp ass." When I played rock on a vinyl covered throne I'd get, uh, sweaty. — Colin Odden, *rec.music.makers.perscussion*, 9th March 1998

drunkalog *noun*
in twelve-step recovery programs such as Alcoholics Anonymous, a long story recounted at a program meeting, dwelling on the addiction and its manifestations rather than recovery *US, 1987*

- — Christopher Cavanaugh, *AA to Z*, p. 82, 1998
- I always cringed inside when an A.A. speaker embarked on an endless "drunkalog." — Jimmy Lerner, *You Got Nothing Coming*, p. 291, 2002

drunk as Cooter Brown *adjective*
very drunk *US, 1953*

- In Washington county, Arkansas, people used to say "drunker than Cooter Brown," but nobody seems to know who Cooter Brown was. — Vance Randolph and George P. Wilson, *Down in the Holler*, p. 175, 1953
- The last time she had seen Connie, the broad had been leaning against the front fence of a house on 132nd Street, puking her guts out. Drunk as Cooter Brown. — Robert Deane Pharr, *Giveadamn Brown*, p. 20, 1978

drunken *adjective*
(used of a wink in tiddlywinks) behaving unpredictably *US,*
1977
- — *Verbatim*, p. 526, December 1977

drunkie *noun*
an alcoholic *UK, 1861*
- Actually, I think all addiction starts with soda. Every drunkie and
  junkie did soda first. But no one counts that. — Chris Rock, *Rock This!*,
  p. 62, 1997

drunkometer *noun*
any device used to measure a motorist's blood alcohol
content *US, 1962*
- — *American Speech*, p. 268, December 1962: "The language of traffic policemen"

drunk tank *noun*
a jail cell where drunk prisoners are detained *US, 1947*
- Uncle R & J Wolf and Papa spent twenty days in the drunk tank at
  The Dalles jail[.] — Ken Kesey, *One Flew Over the Cuckoo's Nest*, p. 274, 1962
- Drunk tank full to overflowing / Motherfuckers wall to wall / Coming
  twice as fast as going / Heads get big and the tank gets small.
  — Ken Kesey, *Last Whole Earth Catalog*, p. 234, 1971
- They stop off for a shot and a beer and can't see their way home.
  End up in a drunk tank. — Elmore Leonard, *Touch*, p. 62, 1977

drunk wagon *noun*
a police van used for rounding up public drunks *US, 1970*
- [T]he thought of a drunken policeman loading drunks in the drunk
  wagon struck him as particularly funny. — Joseph Wambaugh, *The New
  Centurions*, p. 298, 1970

druthers *noun*
a preference *US, 1870*
- [I]f she had her druthers, she would be there now instead of climbing toward the place that rocked her with fear[.] — Toni Morrison, *Love*,
  p. 160, 2003

dry *noun*
▸ **on the dry**
in a state of refraining from drinking any alcohol *US, 1957*
- Jackie Gleason suffered fainting spells—and has gone "on the dry"
  for three months. — *San Francisco Examiner*, p. 3 (II), 31st May 1957

dry *adjective*
without money *US, 1942*
- — *The Annals of the American Academy of Political and Social Sciences*, p. 124, May
  1950
- — Albert H. Morehead, *The Complete Guide to Winning Poker*, p. 262, 1967
- The guys inside the counting room were all slipped in there to skim
  the joint dry. — *Casino*, 1995

dry *adverb*
in a simulated manner *US, 1975*
- You chump, if you had any smarts you'd have pieced it together, but
  they dry-humped you with a couple of quarters[.] — Edwin Torres,
  Carlito's Way, p. 49, 1975
- A few people on the ground were using the desperate infantryman's
  trick of dry firing their empty rifles and simulating a recoil in order
  to keep the approaching Ashbals ducking. — Nelson DeMille, *By the Rivers
  of Babylon*, p. 377, 1978
- C'mon sir. Just dry-shoot it once. — Robert Mason, *Chickenhawk*, p. 127, 1983
- One can dry hump the local roundheels without fear of infection,
  dry fire a pistol and spend not one day in jail. But dry snitching in
  prison carries the same mortal penalty as the real thing.
  — Seth Morgan, *Homeboy*, p. 44, 1990

dry drunk *noun*
a person who behaves like an alcoholic even though they
are abstaining from drinking *US, 1957*
A term used in twelve-step recovery programs such as Alcoholics Anonymous.
- — Christopher Cavanaugh, *AA to Z: Addictionary of the 12-Step Culture*, p. 82, 1998
- Whether George W. Bush is or was an alcoholic is not the point
  here. I am taking him at his word that he stopped what he termed
  "heavy drinking" in 1986, at age 40. The point here is that, based
  on Bush's recent behavior, he could very well be a "dry drunk."
  — *American Politics Journal*, 23rd September 2002

dry Dutch courage *noun*
drugs *US, 1986–1987*

- — *Maledicta*, p. 54, 1986–1987: "A continuation of a glossary of ethnic slurs in
  American English"

dry-fire; dry-snap *verb*
to practice shooting a pistol without live ammunition *US, 1957*
- Some Colloquialisms of the Handgunner — *American Speech*, p. 193,
  October 1957

dry fuck *noun*
sex simulated while clothed *US, 1938*
- At best we could manage a dry fuck. And go home limping, our
  balls aching like sixty toothaches. — Henry Miller, *Plexus*, p. 380, 1963
- Well, Dan said, "why don't you say that you got a dry fuck and I'll
  say that I got bare tit." — Bob Greene, *Be True to Your School*, p. 117, 1987

dry-fuck *verb*
1 to stimulate or pantomime sexual intercourse while clothed
US, 1935
- You could almost dryfuck, right there standing in the sawdust. — *The
  Berkeley Tribe*, p. 13, 5th–12th September 1969
- I lost my Frisco broad for a dame I never even dry-fucked when I
  had the chance. — Oscar Zeta Acosta, *The Autobiography of a Brown Buffalo*,
  p. 63, 1972
- Jenny and I would drive out into the country and park and neck
  and dry fuck through our clothes[.] — Larry Heinemann, *Close Quarters*,
  pp. 133–134, 1977
- I had never seen an exotic dancer who opened her act with a brief
  sermon, and then dry fucked a copy of the Bible. — Dan Jenkins, *Life Its
  Ownself*, p. 128, 1984

2 to penetrate a vagina or rectum without benefit of
lubricant *US, 1979*
- — *Maledicta*, p. 231, 1979

dry fucking *noun*
sex simulated while clothed *US, 1967*
- "I'll go, but that little bit of dry-fucking isn't what's making me go."
  — Robert Deane Pharr, *S.R.O.*, p. 110, 1971

dry goods *noun*
clothing *US, 1851*
- We go up to her trap, and she remove the dry goods. — William
  Burroughs, *Naked Lunch*, p. 119, 1957

dry heaves *noun*
nonproductive vomiting or retching *US, 1991*
- Jim had woken up with the dry heaves and the thought of a beer
  almost gave him the wet heaves[.] — William T. Vollman, *Whores for Gloria*,
  p. 9, 1991

dry-hump *verb*
to simulate sexual intercourse while clothed *US, 1964*
- The girl who has let me undo her brassiere and dry-hump her at the
  dormitory door, grew up in this white house. — Philip Roth, *Portnoy's
  Complaint*, p. 248, 1969
- Sperm will not "swim" down your belly into your cunt after dry-
  humping to a climax. — *Screw*, p. 23, 3rd November 1969
- They would swing me around, with my bad haircut and plucked
  eyebrows, and dry hump me on the dance floor. — Sandra Bernhard,
  Confessions of a Pretty Lady, p. 66, 1988
- Once, when I was being dryhumped by some other man on the hood
  of a car in the alleway, Joe was mad and said, "Don't you know they're
  just after one thing?" — Jennifer Blowdryer, *White Trash Debutante*, p. 40, 1997

dry lay *noun*
sexual intercourse simulated through clothing *US, 1951*
- You get a chance, grab the down-draft blonde bumping the Marine
  by the post there. Dry lay? Man, she'll grind it off. — Thurston Scott,
  Cure it with Honey, p. 152, 1951

dry out *verb*
1 to undergo a course of treatment designed to break depen-
dence on alcohol *US, 1908*
- "How's the old lady?" "Dryin' out," Malatesta said. — George V. Higgins,
  The Rat on Fire, p. 111, 1981

2 to detoxify from heroin addiction *US, 1966*
- — Donald Louria, *Nightmare Drugs*, p. 15, 1966
- — Eugene Landy, *The Underground Dictionary*, p. 72, 1971

dry rub *noun*
body contact, implicitly sexual *US, 1950*
- — Hyman E. Goldin et al., *Dictionary of American Underworld Lingo*, p. 63, 1950

dry run *noun*
a trip to court in which nothing happens *US, 1997*
- — Jim Crotty, *How to Talk American*, p. 54, 1997

dry snitch *noun*
a person who unintentionally or indirectly but intentionally betrays or informs on another *US, 1989*
- — James Harris, *A Convict's Dictionary*, p. 31, 1989

dry-snitch *verb*
to betray or inform on someone either unintentionally or indirectly but intentionally *US, 1967*
- [W]ho would hiply drysnitch you off in the messhall if they saw you stealing an extra chop from the stainless-steel steamtables. — Clarence Cooper Jr., *The Farm*, p. 27, 1967
- — *Maledicta*, p. 264, Summer/Winter 1981: "By its slang, ye shall know it: the pessimism of prison life"

dry waltz *noun*
masturbation *US, 1949*
- "I know you don't get detective trainin' doin' a dry waltz with yourself on somebody else's fire escape," she assured him. — Nelson Algren, *The Man with the Golden Arm*, p. 84, 1949

DT *noun*
a police officer on a street crime beat *US, 1985*
- Jonah Perry returned to the neighborhood the night of the shooting and proclaimed, "We got a DT," street slang for "detective." — *Washington Post*, p. A1, 13th August 1985
- — Carsten Stroud, *Close Pursuit*, p. 271, 1987
- — Terry Williams, *The Cocaine Kids*, p. 136, 1989

DTK *adjective*
handsome, dressed sharply *US, 1967*
An abbreviation of "down to kill," "down" meaning "ready" and "kill" in the figurative sense.
- — *Current Slang*, p. 1, Spring 1967

D town *nickname*
1 Dallas, Texas *US, 1998*
- — Ethan Hilderbrant, *Prison Slang*, p. 42, 1998
2 Denver, Colorado *US, 1986*
- I can run to Denver running like this/ All the way to "D" town running like this. — Sandee Shaffer Johnson, *Cadences*, p. 66, 1986

DTs *noun*
the withdrawal symptoms of an alcohol or drug addiction *delirium tremens US, 1857*
- If I'd acted like you do, I'd have died of tuberculosis or the d.t.s long ago. — Jim Thompson, *Roughneck*, p. 37, 1954
- Someone who smokes a few cigarettes a day is no more likely to go insane than a man who takes a few cocktails before dinner is likely to come down with the DTs. — William Burroughs, *Junky*, 1977

DU *noun*
a drug user *US, 1959*
- [T]he few times I've had occasion to see one, my visiting ducket has always DU stamped all over it; not for Denver University, for Dope User. — Neal Cassady, *Grace Beats Karma*, p. 61, 26th July 1959: Letter to Carolyn Cassady

dual *noun*
a person who is willing to play either the sadist or masochist role in a sadomasochism encounter *US, 1979*
- — *What Color is Your Handkerchief*, p. 5, 1979

dual sack time *noun*
time spent sleeping with someone *US, 1946*
- — *American Speech*, p. 310, December 1946: "More Air Force slang"
- — *American Speech*, pp. 76–79, February 1963: "'Anent 'Marine Corps Slang'"

dub *noun*
1 the last part of a marijuana cigarette that it is possible to smoke *US, 1989*
- take a head of this Skunk / Twist up a big bomb of this serious dope / Smoke it down to the dub or roach tip / So much damn resin it's startin' to drip — Tone Loc, *Cheeba Cheeba*, 1989
2 a cigarette, especially when used to extend a marijuana cigarette *US, 1975*
- — *American Speech*, p. 59, Spring–Summer 1975
3 a twenty-dollar bill *US, 2001*
An abbreviation of **DOUBLE SAWBUCK**.

- — Don Wilmeth, *The Language of American Popular Entertainment*, p. 80, 1981
- — Pamela Munro, *U.C.L.A. Slang*, p. 64, 2001
- — Don R. McCreary (Editor), *Dawg Speak*, 2001
- — Rick Ayers (Editor), *Berkeley High Slang Dictionary*, p. 19, 2004

4 an incompetent and inferior person *US, 1887*
- A well known model can easily knock down a grand a week. Even dubs make $500. — Lee Mortimer, *Women Confidential*, p. 131, 1960

dub *verb*
to have sex with *US, 1997*
- A woman doesn't count all the miscellaneous dick: the guy she met at the club; that time she fucked Keith Sweat; the local she dubbed in Jamaica. — Chris Rock, *Rock This!*, p. 130, 1997

dubber *noun*
a cigarette *US, 1975*
- — *American Speech*, p. 59, Spring–Summer 1975: "Razorback slang"

dubbies *noun*
the female breasts *US, 1966*
- Christ, the dubbies on Lumper. — Richard Farina, *Been Down So Long, Looks Like Up to Me*, p. 80, 1966

dubich *noun*
a marijuana cigarette *US, 1997*
- — Jim Emerson-Cobb, *Scratching the Dragon*, April 1997

dubs *noun*
twenty dollars; something sold for twenty dollars *US, 2001*
- — Rick Ayers (Editor), *Slang Dictionary*, p. 8, 2001

ducat *noun*
in prison, a written order given to a prisoner for an appointment *US, 1926*
- That night after dinner, when the ducat officer passed the cell, he called "Cain," laid a ducat on the bars and passed on. The boy climbed down from the upper bunk to take the slip of paper. — Malcolm Braly, *On the Yard*, p. 246, 1967
- Three days later I got a ducat to report to Dr. Schultz's office for an interview. — James Carr, *Bad*, p. 145, 1975

ducats *noun*
money *US, 1866*
- You've fucked off all your ducats gambling. — Seth Morgan, *Homeboy*, p. 238, 1990
- He's single, he's 47, and he earns minor ducats for a thankless job. — *Clueless*, 1995

duchess *noun*
a girlfriend *US, 1945*
- — Lou Shelly, *Hepcats Jive Dictionary*, p. 11, 1945

duck *noun*
1 an unrelentingly gullible and trusting person; an odd person *US, 1848*
Prison usage.
- I have no respect for a duck who runs up to me on the yard all buddy-buddy, and then feels obliged not to sit down with me. — Eldridge Cleaver, *Soul on Ice*, p. 47, 1968
- — Paul Glover, *Words from the House of the Dead: Prison Writings from Soledad*, 1974
- — James Harris, *A Convict's Dictionary*, p. 31, 1989

2 in pool, a shot that cannot be missed or a game that cannot be lost *US, 1990*
- — Steve Rushin, *Pool Cool*, p. 12, 1990

3 an attractive target for a robbery *US, 1965*
- It was considered by hustlers a duck 'cause it was on a dark corner, there usually wasn't no peoples in sight, and the traffic was slow. — Henry Williamson, *Hustler!*, p. 155, 1965

4 a stolen car discovered by police through serendipitous checking of number plates *US, 1970*
An abbreviation of **SITTING DUCK**.
- Ducks? Oh, I get one a week maybe. There's plenty of hot cars sitting around Hollenbeck. — Joseph Wambaugh, *The New Centurions*, p. 41, 1970

5 a portable urinal for male hospital patients *US, 1980*
- — *Maledicta*, p. 56, Summer 1980: 'Not sticks and stones, but names: more medical pejoratives'

6 a prison sentence of two years *US, 1990*
Probably from the shape of 2.
- — Charles Shafer, *Folk Speech in Texas Prisons*, p. 203, 1990

7 in a deck of playing cards, a two *US, 1988*
- — George Percy, *The Language of Poker*, p. 31, 1988

8 a surfer who lingers in the water, rarely catching a wave *US, 1991*
- — Trevor Cralle, *The Surfin'ary*, p. 32, 1991

9 an admission ticket for a paid event *US, 1945*
An abbreviation of DUCAT.
- — Lou Shelly, *Hepcats Jive Dictionary*, p. 11, 1945
- — Clarence Major, *Dictionary of Afro-American Slang*, p. 49, 1970

10 a firefighter *US, 1997*
New York police slang.
- — Samuel M. Katz, *Anytime Anywhere*, p. 387, 1997

11 inexpensive wine *US, 1972*
An abbreviation and then generic use of Cold Duck, a sparkling red wine that was extremely popular in the 1960s and 70s.
- — David Claerbaut, *Black Jargon in White America*, p. 63, 1972

duck verb
1 to avoid *US, 1864*
- You duckin' me Dwight? — *Natural Born Killers*, 1994

2 in pool, to miss a shot or lose a game intentionally to mislead an opponent as to your true ability *US, 1993*
- — Mike Shamos, *The Illustrated Encyclopedia of Billiards*, p. 84, 1993

▸ **duck a date**
in circus and carnival usage, to fail to perform as scheduled *US, 1981*
- — Don Wilmeth, *The Language of American Popular Entertainment*, p. 81, 1981

duck ass; duck's ass noun
a hair-style popular in the early 1950s, in which the hair was tapered and curled on the nape of the neck like the feathers of a duck's tail *UK, 1951*
- Morton, the bass player, wore shades and a duck's ass haircut. — Malcolm Braly, *Shake Him Till He Rattles*, p. 85, 1963
- Everyone tried to avoid the hook to the barber shop, at least long enough to grow the beginning of a duck ass[.] — Malcolm Braly, *False Starts*, p. 44, 1976
- Long enough for a pompadour in front and a duck's ass in the back. — Piri Thomas, *Stories from El Barrio*, p. 56, 1978

duck bucket noun
in poker, a poor hand that wins a pot, especially a pair of twos *US, 1996*
- — John Vorhaus, *The Big Book of Poker Slang*, p. 15, 1996

duck butt; duck's butt noun
1 a hair-style popular in the early 1950s, in which the hair was tapered and curled on the nape of the neck like the feathers of a duck's tail *US, 1955*
- Judge Buchanan took issue with Von Tagen's haircut, a long, lanky affair that the judge bluntly said was called a duck butt in his mountain realm. — *San Francisco Examiner*, p. 3, 15th March 1955
- His hair was long and combed into a glossy duck's-butt[.] — Malcolm Braly, *Shake Him Till He Rattles*, p. 25, 1963

2 a short person *US, 1939*
- I'll also beat the living shit out of every one of your duckbutts and my teammates will help me. — Pat Conroy, *The Lords of Discipline*, p. 207, 1980

duck butter noun
smegma or other secretions that collect on and around the genitals *US, 1933*
- Plus, his fucksman's got a big fist-raised dick that gotta be washed because it stays loaded with duckbutter and stinks like hell. — A.S. Jackson, *Gentleman Pimp*, p. 115, 1973

duck day noun
the day when a member of the US armed forces is honorably discharged *US, 1946*
An allusion to the US armed forces insignia designating honorable discharge known as the RUPTURED DUCK.
- — *American Speech*, p. 153, April 1946: "GI words from the separation center and proctology ward"

duck-dive verb
in surfing, to push the nose of the surfboard down under a breaking wave *US, 1988*
- — Brian and Margaret Lowdon, *Competitive Surfing*, 1988

duck-fucker noun
a lazy person *US, 1986*
- That accused stated in CIC that, having passed the tests for chief and being recommended by his officers, to whom he sucks up shamelessly, especially to the XO, a notorious duck-fucker and nose-picker. — David Poyer, *The Med*, p. 258, 1988

duck plucker noun
used as a euphemism for "motherfucker" *US, 1976*
- — Lanie Dills, *The Official CB Slanguage Language Dictionary*, p. 30, 1976

duck soup noun
an easy task; a cinch *US, 1902*
- — Lou Shelly, *Hepcats Jive Talk Dictionary*, p. 24, 1945
- I was duck soup there in that room with my back toward him and he missed. — Mickey Spillane, *One Lonely Night*, p. 130, 1951

duck tail noun
a hair-style popular in the early 1950s in which a boy's hair was tapered and curled on the nape of the neck like the feathers of a duck's tail *US, 1943*
- They were held on $1,000 bail each, were forced to undergo something worse than jail: short haircuts to eliminate their long sideburns and "ducktail" coiffures. — *Life*, p. 29, 6th August 1951
- — Dale Krame, *Teen-Age Gangs*, p. 188, 1953: Glossary
- In a courtroom jam-packed with zoot suiters, the 19-year-old Ranson, who affects Hollywood-type clothes and a duck-tail haircut, narrated events before and after he pumped five bullets from a 45 automatic[.] — *San Francisco Call Bulletin*, p. 1, 1st July 1953

ducky adjective
attractive, good *US, 1901*
- I could picture her ducky black body with the tiny waist and round, bucket-shaped hips. — Chester Himes, *If He Hollers Let Him Go*, p. 5, 1945
- Cupid had been very interested in Walter before he'd met Tony, and this struck him as a just ducky idea. — Xaviera Hollander, *Xaviera*, p. 60, 1973

dude noun
1 a regular fellow *US, 1883*
In the US, the term had this vague sense in the hippie culture, and then a much more specific sense in the 1970s and 80s.
- GEORGE: A dude? What does he mean, "dude?" Dude ranch? BILLY: A dude. WYATT: No, no. Dude means—uh—a nice guy, you know. Dude means a regular sort of person. — Peter Fonda, *Easy Rider*, p. 110, 1969
- "Hey man. You see these dudes right here? They were sitting out there hiding the wine bottle." — Bobby Seale, *Seize the Time*, p. 42, 1970
- During our stay we had all the white clientele coming from downtown and all the down black dudes and chicks too. — Babs Gonzales, *Movin' On Down De Line*, p. 9, 1975
- One night while I was visiting with Frankie there was a massive dude named Sol there who I eventually got to know and work with. — Herbert Huncke, *Guilty of Everything*, p. 113, 1990

2 used as a term of address *US, 1945*
- "Hey, dude," an older voice called out. — John Clellon Holmes, *The Horn*, p. 162, 1958
- With the nuances of pronunciation, dudes who said "dude" had no problem communicating. Pronounced "Duuhuhude" it meant "Right on, I'm into it if you are[.]" — Nina Blake, *Retrohell*, p. 120, 1997
- She's a mermaid, dude. — *American Pie*, 1999

dude up verb
to dress up *US, 1899*
- They were all duded up in tuxedos and patent leather so they must have made a score in New York. — Edwin Torres, *Carlito's Way*, p. 95, 1975

Dudley noun
a beginner gambler *US, 2003*
- — Victor H. Royer, *Casino Gamble Talk*, p. 53, 2003

Dudley Do-Right; Dudley Dogooder noun
the epitome of a sincere, moral, upstanding citizen, despised by those who live on the fringes of the law *US, 1990*
From a cartoon feature *Dudley Do-Right of the Mounties* first aired in 1961 as a segment on the *Rocky and Friends Show*.
- As soon as the last editorial is printed, the last speech made, and the last pulpit pounded, all the Dudley Dogooders will be the first back down here for a little fun. — Seth Morgan, *Homeboy*, p. 30, 1990

dudly; dudley *adjective*

(used of a boy) extremely boring *US, 1982*
- — Mimi Pond, *The Valley Girl's Guide to Life*, p. 55, 1982

duds *noun*

clothing *UK, 1307*
- "I left Bakersfield with the travel-bureau car and left my gui-tar in the trunk of another one and they never showed up—gui-tar and cowboy duds[.] — Jack Kerouac, *On the Road*, p. 167, 1957
- I'm the coolest of studs when it comes to duds. — Dan Burley, *Diggeth Thou?*, p. 44, 1959
- But the kind of duds you wear down at the garage, when you're tinkering with the scooter, or out on the field, when you're tossing around a football, just aren't right for Saturday night. — Dick Clark, *To Goof or Not to Goof*, p. 80, 1963
- I'm goin' downtown and buy me some new duds. — Nathan Heard, *Howard Street*, p. 68, 1968

due *noun*

the residue left in a pipe after smoking crack cocaine *US, 1989*
- — Terry Williams, *The Cocaine Kids*, p. 136, 1989

due-back *noun*

something that is borrowed, such as a cigarette, with an expectation of an ultimate return of the favor *US, 1951*
- — *Newsweek*, p. 28, 8th October 1951

duff *noun*

the buttocks, the rump *UK, 1840*

Although first recorded in the UK, modern usage began in the US in 1939.
- Let's get off our duffs and out on the road. — *Drugstore Cowboy*, 1988
- I guess I am, but shoving paper around and sitting on my duff listening to people yammer about ways and means, instead of getting out there and doing what's got to get done, could turn me into a stone. — Robert Campbell, *In a Pig's Eye*, p. 31, 1991

duff *verb*

to escape *US, 1963*
- Inside her bowels, the hot sausage and pepper on French played hell, pushing the beer, wine and juju seeds to the side so it could duff. — Steve Cannon, *Groove, Bang, and Jive Around*, pp. 5–6, 1969

duffel drag *noun*

the final morning of a soldier's service in Vietnam *US, 1991*
- For example, "four and a duffel drag" would indicate a soldier had four more days to serve and then was going home. — Linda Reinberg, *In the Field*, p. 69, 1991

duffer *noun*

a doltish old man *UK, 1730*

In recent times, the term has come to take on an emphasis on age.
- Right then this old duffer on the jury horns in, "How much you selling your stock for, mister?" — Guy Owen, *The Flim-Flam Man and the Apprentice Grifter*, p. 198, 1972
- When she asked one of the old duffers why they called their beauty contest winner "Ms. Emerson," the geezer said, "Knock-knock." — Joseph Wambaugh, *Finnegan's Week*, p. 229, 1993

duffy *noun*

1 a cigarette made with prison-issued tobacco *US, 1959*
- I topped it off with A "Duffy" (name of State-issued brand is "Bonanza," but honoring the man who instigated free tobacco, it's known as "Duffy") roll[.] — Neal Cassady, *Grace Beats Karma*, p. 152, 3rd December 1959: Letter to Carolyn Cassady

2 a spasm feigned by a drug addict in the hope of eliciting sympathy from a physician *US, 1973*
- — David Maurer and Victor Vogel, *Narcotics and Narcotic Addiction*, p. 404, 1973

duffy; duffie *verb*

to leave quickly *US, 1945*

A simpler version of **TAKE IT ON THE ARTHUR DUFFY**.
- I sometimes see it in the prison publications usually spelled "duffie" with a lower case "d." I recall reading in one prison paper the line "He duffied out of there." — *San Francisco Examiner*, p. 15, 20th March 1945

duggy *adjective*

dressed in style *US, 1993*
- — *Washington Post*, 14th October 1993

dugs *noun*

the female breasts *US, 2005*
- And then she went and misbehaved like any mutt from the neighborhood, pulling out her dugs, nipples and all, for a naked-chest make-out session[.] — Mr. Skin, *Mr. Skin's Skincyclopedia*, p. 177, 2005

duh!

used for expressing disgust at the stupidity of what has just been said *US, 1963*

A single syllable with a great deal of attitude.
- SEBASTIAN: You don't even know what it is. GRETCHEN: Duh. It's a book — *Cruel Intentions*, 1999

duji; doogie; doojie *noun*

heroin *US, 1960*
- I wasn't certain about how it was changing or what was happening, but I knew it had a lot to do with duji, heroin. — Claude Brown, *Manchild in the Promised Land*, p. 187, 1965
- He marveled dispassionately at the New Yorker's good, good doogie. — Nathan Heard, *Howard Street*, p. 174, 1968
- "Practically every night some cat I never even seen before comes up to me and wants to talk me into selling doogie for him on consignment." — Robert Deane Pharr, *S.R.O.*, p. 253, 1971
- Yo, dig this. One pound of pure Malaysian white douge. — Cleo Odzer, *Goa Freaks*, p. 85, 1995

duke *noun*

1 a regular fellow; a tough guy *US, 1939*
- A limo driver by day, Lou is a regular old duke at the Melody Burlesk—one of their up-and-coming resident uncles, a young pup of fifty-one. — Josh Alan Friedman, *Tales of Times Square*, p. 29, 1986

2 poor quality tobacco issued by the State of California to prisoners *US, 1989*

Named after former California Governor Deukmejian (1983–91).
- — James Harris, *A Convict's Dictionary*, p. 31, 1989

3 in card games, a hand (of cards) *US, 1967*
- — Albert H. Morehead, *The Complete Guide to Winning Poker*, p. 262, 1967

duke *verb*

1 to fight with fists *US, 1935*
- I was going down to the A.C. on Thirty-fifth Street, learning how to duke. — Chester Himes, *If He Hollers Let Him Go*, p. 105, 1945
- Here's your chance. Come on, let's see you duke. — Ralph Ellison, *Invisible Man*, p. 368, 1947
- Me and this black kid duked it out after he said, "Let me hold a quarter." — Edwin Torres, *Carlito's Way*, p. 9, 1975
- What am I talking about? I didn't even drive tonight. You wanna duke it? Let's go. — *Tin Men*, 1987

2 to give *US, 1926*
- I was building a model of the state cap'tol. I figured when I got it done, I'd duke it on the gov'nor. — Malcolm Braly, *On the Yard*, p. 204, 1967
- Well, let's try to duke our bet in again. — Joseph Wambaugh, *The Blue Knight*, p. 144, 1973
- "You duke a quarter on that po liddle black boy." — Malcolm Braly, *The Protector*, p. 181, 1979
- We duked the parking lot attendant a dollar and were soon among the Friday night North Beach throng. — Bill Cardoso, *The Maltese Sangweech*, p. 202, 1984
- [T]he guy that ran the men's room would then duke you whatever the doorman had written on a note. — Herbert Huncke, *Guilty of Everything*, p. 110, 1990

3 to allow *US, 2001*
- Maybe I could convince Scarlet to duke me in with this crowd. — Stephen J. Cannell, *The Tin Collectors*, p. 260, 2001

4 to fool; to deceive *US, 1975*
- Lieutenant Finque ain't trying to duke you into the Oriental community by using you as a part time community relations officer at Japanese luncheons. — Joseph Wambaugh, *The Choirboys*, p. 92, 1975
- — Don Wilmeth, *The Language of American Popular Entertainment*, p. 81, 1981
- — Gene Sorrows, *All About Carnivals*, p. 15, 1985: "All about sorrows"

5 to have sex *US, 1993*
- — *People Magazine*, p. 72, 19th July 1993

6 to short-change someone by palming a coin given as part of the change *US, 1981*
- — Don Wilmeth, *The Language of American Popular Entertainment*, p. 81, 1981

duke breath noun

bad breath US, 1993

- — People Magazine, p. 72, 19th July 1993

duked out adjective

dressed up US, 1938

- He was all duked out in a hard-boiled collar and a blue serge suit. — Jim Thompson, Savage Night, p. 81, 1953

duker noun

a person inclined to fight US, 1979

- A few arguments, but no fights (a miracle 'cause some of these guys were dukers for days). — Edwin Torres, After Hours, p. 295, 1979

dukes noun

the hands; fists US, 1859

The singular is "duke," or variant "dook," which is probably rhyming slang, formed on **DUKE OF YORK** for "forks." (the fingers).

- Slippers was a good man with his dukes. — Louis Armstrong, Satchmo, p. 114, 1954
- Come on Whalen, put up yr. dukes and fight! — Jack Kerouac, Letter to Philip Whalen, p. 542, 16th January 1956
- Then she doubled up her fists and put up her dukes and said she guessed she'd just have to teach Doyle a lesson. — Gurney Norman, Divine Right's Trip (Last Whole Earth Catalog), p. 203, 1971
- He had blown into town with no 'ho. And worse, no wheels and frozen fireworks (jewelry) exploding off his dukes, necessary to cop a star 'ho. — Iceberg Slim (Robert Beck), Airtight Willie and Me, p. 21, 1979

duke shot noun

any method by which a carnival game operator allows a customer to win a rigged game US, 1985

- — Gene Sorrows, All About Carnivals, p. 16, 1985: "Terminology"

duke's mixture noun

1 a person of mixed race US, 1961

- Blacks, tans, cinnamons, octoroons, reds and dukes mixture, moving Artis down the street. — Fannie Flagg, Fried Green Tomatoes at the Whistle Stop Café, p. 120, 1987

2 a random conglomeration US, 1914

- Palo verde trees, small fuzzy cholla trees, and a duke's mixture of other desert plants were scattered among the giant saguaro cacti. — Jim Conover, Greenhorns and Killer Mountains, p. 206, 1999

dukey noun

1 a brown paper lunch bag US, 1986

Chicago slang.

- — Bill Reilly, Big Al's Official Guide to Chicagoese, p. 24, 1986

2 in the circus, a lunch prepared for circus workers on long train journeys between towns US, 1980

- — Joe McKennon, Circus Lingo, p. 31, 1980

3 in circus and carnival usage, a meal ticket or book of meal tickets US, 1981

- — Don Wilmeth, The Language of American Popular Entertainment, p. 81, 1981

▷ see: DOOKIE

dukey rope noun

a gold chain necklace US, 1989

- — Ellen C. Bellone (Editor), Dictionary of Slang, p. 10, 1989

Dullsville noun

the epitome of a boring existence US, 1960

- But linguistically speaking, Disraeli is dullsville. — Kurt Vonnegut, Welcome to the Monkey House, p. 123, 1968

Dullsville, Ohio noun

anywhere other than Las Vegas US, 1985

- — Washington Post, p. B1, 17th January 1985

dumb adjective

(of an ordinance) unguided US, 1989

Back formation from "smart bomb."

- However, since the rail yard was an area target, unguided "dumb" bombs were selected as the proper ordinance. — Karl Eschmann, Linebacker, p. 31, 1989

dumb ass noun

1 a stupid person US, 1958

- "[A]ll I got was laughed at. I really felt like a dumb-ass." — Tempest Storm, Tempest Storm, p. 95, 1987
- Oh, the dumbass at the donut place put a chocolate cream filled I asked for in your box. — Natural Born Killers, 1994

2 stupidity US, 1972

- I'm what a lot of you spooks might think of as a red neck with a terminal case of the dumb-ass. — Dan Jenkins, Semi-Tough, p. 7, 1972

▸ **eat up with the dumb ass; ate up with the dumb ass**

very stupid US, 1984

- When I saw ol' Delbert tryin' to siphon gas uphill, I knew for sure he was eat up with the dumb ass. — Ken Weaver, Texas Crude, p. 112, 1984
- But picture if that was you layin' there because you was all ate up with the dumb ass an' didn't eat yer salt tablets an' passed out as a heat casualty. — Ted Arthurs, Land With No Sun, p. 174, 2006

dumb-ass; dumb-assed adjective

stupid, foolish US, 1957

From the noun sense.

- A whore; a slut; a bitch; a mother-fucker; a stupid, dumb-assed woman. Stupid idiot. — Court of Civil Appeals of Alabama, Stilwell v. Stilwell, p. 358, 1978
- [P]lay tricks on that dumb-ass cracker, the park ranger. — Howard Stern, Miss America, p. 430, 1995
- He screamed and hollered about how I was a fat, stupid, dumb-assed retard. — Joshua Key, The Deserter's Tale, p. 21, 2007

dumbbell noun

a stupid person US, 1918

- That's a life for bums and dumbbells. Don't be a fool! — James T. Farrell, Saturday Night, p. 16, 1947
- I wasn't a dumbbell. I didn't let that gob grow inside my neck, week after week, in silent fear. — Philip Wylie, Opus 21, p. 7, 1949
- "Because I love you, dumbbell!" she cried, abandoning civility. — Max Shulman, Anyone Got a Match?, p. 108, 1964
- They're used to dumbbells. — Darryl Ponicsan, The Last Detail, p. 120, 1970

dumbbutt noun

a dolt US, 1973

- Convert the Super Dome to microwave / Tell them its a pie. The dumbbutts can't count. — Barbara Smith, Wild Sweet Note, p. 90, 2000

dumb crooker noun

a social misfit US, 1963

- — Carol Ann Preusse, Jargon Used by University of Texas Co-Eds, 1963

Dumb Dora noun

an empty-headed woman US, 1922

- But I don't mind a Dumb Dora if she has looks and knows the tricks. — James T. Farrell, The Life Adventure, p. 180, 1947

dumb dust noun

cocaine or heroin US, 1986

- But the idea that Buckingham Palace is a warehouse for the dumb-dust market in Candlestick Park and McDonald's and Madison Square Garden is going to be hard one to sell to anybody except Ed Meese and Jan Wenner. — Hunter S. Thompson, Generation of Swine, p. 95, 1986

dumbfuck; dumb-fuck noun

a despicable, stupid person US, 1950

- "He said he don't, you dumb fuck," Dawg said. — James Miller, The Race for Home, p. 294, 1968
- You dumb fuck. Tom Spellacy had said you could've got me. Not a chance. — John Gregory Dunne, True Confessions, p. 81, 1977
- I already asked Toby Dumbfuck. Obviously, I've interrupted. — Romy and Michele's High School Reunion, 1997
- Listen Rees you dumb-fuck! I don't have to ask[.] — Jack Allen, When the Whistle Blows, p. 240, 2000

dumbjohn noun

a person of no importance, especially a military cadet US, 1951

- We could play like back at the Point, upperclassmen hazing the Dumbjohns. — James Jones, From Here to Eternity, p. 113, 1951

dumbo noun

a dolt, a fool US, 1932

- Somebody later told me it was an experiment to put together a group of dumbos and halfwits who wouldn't question orders. — Forrest Gump, 1992

Dumbo *noun*
during the war in Vietnam, a C-123 US Air Force provider
US, 1989
- [W]e and our jeeps boarded "Dumbo" choppers and headed south.
— David H. Hackworth, *About Face*, p. 378, 1989

dumbshit *noun*
an imbecile *US, 1961*
- I could call first, of course, I'd call, dumbshit, ask them if they have the speakerphone. — Dave Eggers, *A Heartbreaking Work of Staggering Genius*, p. 26, 2001

dumbshit *adjective*
stupid *US, 1967*
- Am I going to be a pathetic dumbshit Addict and continue to waste my life or am I going to say no and try to stay sober and be a decent Person. — James Frey, *A Million Little Pieces*, p. 258, 2003

dumb sock *noun*
a dolt *US, 1932*
- Jesus, I didn't want to lay it on him, the dumb sock. — James T. Farrell, *When Boyhood Dreams Come True*, p. 60, 1948

dumbwad *noun*
an imbecile *US, 1978*
- Clean your loathsome bodies, dumbwads. — Pat Conroy, *The Lords of Discipline*, p. 170, 1980

dum-dum *noun*
1 a simpleton *US, 1937*
- Boy, what dum-dums. Don't they know what's waiting for them in the Jersey swamps. — Piri Thomas, *Stories from El Barrio*, p. 24, 1978
2 Demerol™, a central nervous system depressant *US, 1984*
- — Inez Cardozo-Freeman, *The Joint*, p. 495, 1984

dummies *noun*
imitation drugs *US, 1995*
- — Maria Hinojas, *Crews*, p. 167, 1995

dummkopf *noun*
a dolt; a fool *US, 1809*
German for "dumb-head."
- [T]he Germans saw that apparently whatever we said about collective responsibility we were only going to hang those dumkopfs at Nuremberg[.] — Clancy Sigal, *Going Away*, p. 213, 1961

dummy *noun*
1 a mute *US, 1962*
- — Joseph E. Ragen and Charles Finston, *Inside the World's Toughest Prison*, p. 797, 1962
2 a substance other than narcotics sold as narcotics *US, 1992*
- — Jay Robert Nash, *Dictionary of Crime*, p. 113, 1992
3 the penis *US, 1950*
- — Hyman E. Goldin et al., *Dictionary of American Underworld Lingo*, p. 63, 1950

▸ **beat your dummy**
(used of a male) to masturbate *US, 1977*
- I'll bet some of those businessmen are licking the glass and beating their dummies for all they're worth. — *Adam Film World*, pp. 63–64, 1977

▸ **on the dummy**
quiet *US, 1971*
- I knew the punk was rank, but Jackson was crazy about him so I stayed on the dummy — Iceberg Slim (Robert Beck), *The Naked Soul of Iceberg Slim*, p. 122, 1971

dummy *verb*
to pack marijuana into a rolled cigarette butt *US, 1965*
- I used to be real slow at rolling reefers and at dummying reefers, but when I came back from Warwick I was a real pro at that. — Claude Brown, *Manchild in the Promised Land*, p. 146, 1965

dummy-chucker *noun*
a swindler who pretends to be the victim of accidents *US, 1963*
- The oranges was an item from the dummy-chuckers' workbag, a frammis of the professional accident fakers. Beaten with the fruit, a person sustained bruises far out of proportion to his actual injuries. — Jim Thompson, *The Grifters*, p. 70, 1963

dummy dust *noun*
phencyclidine, the recreational drug known as PCP or angel dust *US, 1977*
- — *Drummer*, p. 77, 1977

dummy flogger *noun*
a masturbator *US, 1985*
- [T]he theater manager, who was sick and tired of dummy floggers chasing off legitimate customers, grabbed Wingnut by the scruff of the neck and dragged him right out of his seat[.] — Joseph Wambaugh, *The Secrets of Harry Bright*, p. 61, 1985

dummy oil *noun*
Demerol™, a branded central nervous system depressant *US, 1988*
- Bob has one of the cabinets open only to find Demerol (otherwise known to drug addicts as "dummy oil"). — *Drugstore Cowboy*, 1988

dummy stick *noun*
a bamboo stick used to carry baskets on each end, carried across the shoulders *US, 1965*
- This much better than toting dummy stick! — Tony Zidek, *Choi Oi*, p. 68, 1965

dummy up *verb*
to stop talking; to be quiet *US, 1928*
- I began to see the handwriting on the wall. I began to dummy up.
— *San Francisco Call Bulletin*, p. A2, 10th December 1945
- I says, "You dummy up. I'll do the stealing and there ain't gonna be any pistols." — Bruce Jackson, *In the Life*, p. 99, 1972
- Dummy up you square ass punks. — Iceberg Slim (Robert Beck), *Airtight Willie and Me*, p. 3, 1979
- He was fired, but because he dummied up and denied everything, he never spent a day in jail. — Nicholas Pileggi, *Wise Guy*, p. 62, 1985

dump *noun*
1 an intentional loss of a game *US, 1972*
- Now when the best player throws the game it is called a dump.
— Robert Byrne, *McGoorty*, p. 31, 1972
2 a prison *US, 1966*
- — Rose Giallombardo, *Society of Women*, p. 207, 1966: Glossary of Prison Terms
3 a denial of a prisoner's request for parole *US, 2002*
- "Tooshay ain't fittin' ta catch nothin' but a dump" says the Bone. — Jimmy Lerner, *You Got Nothing Coming*, p. 246, 2002
4 the buttocks *US, 1973*
- [L]ooking down at her while she was on her knees with her well-rounded dump propped up in the air really made a freak outta me[.] — A.S. Jackson, *Gentleman Pimp*, p. 110, 1973
5 an act of defecation *US, 1942*
- I started documenting any large or unusually shaped bowel movements. I knew I was becoming obsessive when I filmed my third monster dump of the week. — Anka Radakovich, *The Wild Girls Club*, p. 86, 1994
6 an unpleasant place or location *US, 1899*
- Well, finally I gets back to this dump where I lives. A rotten little flat in a big old block[.] — John Peter Jones, *Feather Pluckers*, p. 9, 1964
7 in a smuggling operation, the place where the goods to be smuggled are assembled *US, 1956*
- — *American Speech*, p. 98, May 1956: "Smugglers' argot in the Southwest"
8 a ticket returned unsold to a theater by a ticket agency *US, 1981*
- — Don Wilmeth, *The Language of American Popular Entertainment*, p. 82, 1981
9 a large, unprocessed amount of information *US, 1991*
- — Eric S. Raymond, *The New Hacker's Dictionary*, p. 137, 1991
10 a hospital patient who is transferred from one hospital or nursing home to another *US, 1983*
- — *Maledicta*, p. 38, 1983: "More common patient-directed pejoratives used by medical personnel"
11 a fall from a surfboard, usually caused by a wave's impact *US, 1964*
- — John Severson, *Modern Surfing Around the World*, p. 169, 1964

▸ **take a dump**
1 to defecate *US, 1942*
- Jackie will go into the bathroom and take A HEARTY, SLOPPY, SMELLY DUMP complete with foul noises and splashing toilet water. — Howard Stern, *Miss America*, p. 196, 1995
- I mean, don't you think it's time you learned to take a dump at school? — *American Pie*, 1999
2 to lose a game intentionally, especially for the purpose of taking advantage of spectator betting *US, 1955*
- So get in there tonight and take a dump, go in the tank. — Rocky Garciano (with Rowland Barber), *Somebody Up There Likes Me*, p. 255, 1955

dump *verb*

1 to deny a prisoner's request for parole *US, 2002*

- The Parole Board can approve the applicant, can deny ("dump") parole for a year or more, and in the worst-case scenario they can dump a convict "to expiration." — Jimmy Lerner, *You Got Nothing Coming*, p. 246, 2002

2 to beat; to kill *US, 1960*

- "I'm just warning you to stay clear. I keep you punks from dumping (beating) each other, I'm satisfied." — *Man's Magazine*, p. 12, February 1960
- Marvin Lewis, attorney for Richard rock, one of five men indicted for murder and conspiring to murder the union official, said that "dumping" meant assaulting a man. Assistant District Attorney Walter Biubbbini argued in opposition that "dumping" is listed in lexicons of slang and criminal lingo as synonymous with "killing." — *San Francisco Chronicle*, p. 5, 27th May 1966

3 to assault *US, 1951*

- — *American Speech*, p. 194, October 1951: "A study of reformatory argot"

4 to derive sexual pleasure from sadistic acts *US, 1957*

- Tricks pay a hundred dollars to dump girls. Sometimes more. I'd never take a dumping myself for less than a hundred. — John M. Murtagh and Sara Harris, *Cast the First Stone*, p. 155, 1957

5 to lose a game intentionally, especially for the purpose of taking advantage of spectator betting *US, 1951*

- The possibility of trial and conviction for these basketball players who took dough to dump games is protected by a statute which makes it a felony to tamper with a sport. — *San Francisco News*, p. 17, 28th February 1951
- Sports Illustrated wrote a real cute article about how maybe I had dumped the game for better theater effect. — Minnesota Fats, *The Bank Shot*, p. 206, 1966
- "The players loved it because they were not dumping games." — Nicholas Pileggi, *Wise Guy*, p. 194, 1985
- "She threw th' fuckin' case, went in the tank, intentionally bricked it." "You never said that before. If she dumped it, you would've told me." — Stephen J. Cannell, *The Tin Collectors*, p. 156, 2001

6 in horse racing, to bet a large amount on a horse just before a race *US, 1951*

- — David W. Maurer, *Argot of the Racetrack*, p. 25, 1951

7 to lose a large sum of money gambling in a short period *US, 1980*

- I have dumping to stiffs. — Lee Solkey, *Dummy Up and Deal*, p. 112, 1980

8 to vomit after injecting heroin or a synthetic opiate *US, 1968*

- — *Current Slang*, p. 22, Fall 1968
- — William K. Bentley and James M. Corbett, *Prison Slang*, p. 77, 1992

9 to complete an illegal drug sale by delivering the drug *US, 1995*

- — Bill Valentine, *Gang Intelligence Manual*, p. 76, 1995: "Black street gang terminology"

▸ **dump it in**

to rev a motorcycle engine *US, 1958*

- A motorcycle policeman revving up in pursuit of a violator is dumping it in. — *New York Times*, p. 34, 20th October 1958

▸ **dump it out**

to defecate *US, 1990*

- — Charles Shafer, *Folk Speech in Texas Prisons*, p. 203, 1990

dumper *noun*

1 an athlete who dumps a game, intentionally losing *US, 1951*

- Reams of copy have already been written on big time basketball's latest smellero, involving enough Toledo and Bradley University cagers to make up a first string of "dumpers" and a second string of "dumpers." — *San Francisco Call Bulletin*, p. 11, 30th July 1951
- C.C.V.N.Y.'s Ed Warner (right, rear) one of the dumpers, had soft job waiting on tables. [Caption] — *Life*, p. 38, 5th March 1951
- — Steve Rushin, *Pool Cool*, p. 12, 1990

2 a person who takes sexual pleasure from sadistic acts *US, 1957*

- That's what one dumper told me. Boy, you should have heard him talking. "Honey," he says, "all I want to do is beat you up a little bit and then I'll be finished." — John M. Murtagh and Sara Harris, *Cast the First Stone*, p. 155, 1957
- I have always refused to take "dumpers," men who beat you. — Sara Harris, *The Lords of Hell*, p. 72, 1967

dumping *noun*

1 a beating in the context of sadistic sex *US, 1957*

- I don't take tricks for dumping unless I'm awful broke. Tricks pay a hundred dollars to dump girls. Sometimes more. I'd never take a dumping myself for less than a hundred. — John M. Murtagh and Sara Harris, *Cast the First Stone*, p. 155, 1957

2 a physical beating *US, 1972*

- Quite often we would have to give a dumping [a beating] to whoever was causing the trouble. — Harry King, *Box Man*, p. 61, 1972

dumping table *noun*

a blackjack table in a casino where players have been consistently winning *US, 1991*

- — Michael Dalton, *Blackjack*, p. 44, 1991

dump off *verb*

(used of a casino dealer) to overpay a bet made by a confederate *US, 1985*

- — Steve Kuriscak, *Casino Talk*, p. 20, 1985

dump out *verb*

(of a casino employee) to lose intentionally as part of a scheme with a gambler or gamblers *US, 1977*

- [I]n a court of law, if a blackjack Dealer gets terribly unlucky and his table keeps losing fifteen nights in a row, there is no legal proof that he is cheating for the benefit of an "outside" man or "crossroader," that he is "dumping out." — Mario Puzo, *Inside Las Vegas*, p. 180, 1977

dumps *noun*

the female breasts *US, 2001*

- — Don R. McCreary (Editor), *Dawg Speak*, 2001

dumpster *verb*

to salvage from a trash dumpster *US, 2002*

- I dumpster some lace and put it in the window. — Lynn Breedlove, *Godspeed*, p. 96, 2002

dump stroke *noun*

in pool, the minuscule adjustment to a shot that a player makes when intentionally missing a shot *US, 1990*

- — Steve Rushin, *Pool Cool*, p. 12, 1990

dump truck *noun*

1 a court-appointed public defender *US, 1984*

- My dump truck wants me to cop a second degree burglary. Fuck him! — Inez Cardozo-Freeman, *The Joint*, p. 495, 1984

2 a car filled with lesbians *US, 1970*

- — *American Speech*, p. 57, Spring–Summer 1970: "Homosexual slang"

3 a prisoner who does not hold up his end of a shared task or relationship *US, 1989*

- — James Harris, *A Convict's Dictionary*, p. 32, 1989
- dump truck: person who sells you out — J.G. Narum, *The Convict Cookbook*, p. 160, 2004

dumpy *adjective*

(used of waves) weak, erratic *US, 1988*

- — Michael V. Anderson, *The Bad, Rad, Not to Forget Way Cool Beach and Surf Discriptionary*, p. 6, 1988

dune coon *noun*

an Arab *US, 1984*

Very offensive.

- I was tryin' to deal with a Dune Coon the other day. — Dan Jenkins, *Life Its Ownself*, p. 92, 1984
- I convince Lavonne to see Israel before them doon coons take it back. — James Ellroy, *Hollywood Nocturnes*, p. 206, 1994
- Lord knows what vermin live in the butt of a dune coon. — *Three Kings*, 1999

dune duster *noun*

an Arab *US, 2004*

- We've detained these dune dusters on full felonies and Minnie Mouse misdemeanors. — James Ellroy, *Destination Morgue*, p. 372, 2004

duner *noun*

a person who enjoys driving dune buggies in the desert *US, 1974*

- The sand dunes about a quarter mile away make the campground a handy base for "duners." — Jackie Sheckler Finch, *The Unofficial Guide to the Best RV and Tent Campgrounds*, p. 111, 2002

dungarees noun
battle fatigues *US, 1979*
Marine Corps usage in World War 2 and Korea.
- Battle dress was dungarees. — William Manchester, *Goodbye, Darkness*, p. 146, 1979

dungeon noun
a nightclub catering to sado-masochistic fetishists *US, 1996*
- The theater of choice for many devotees of sadomasochism, or S/M, is the dungeon, a kind of specialized club catering to those with a taste for domination, bondage or submission. — James Ridgeway, *Red Light*, p. 81, 1996

dung-scuffer noun
a cowboy *US, 1974*
A euphemism for **SHITKICKER**.
- Drawing stares at Bardelli's: Red-headed Don Imus, togged like a real dung-scuffer in Western hat, faded Levis, red bandana and pointed cowboy boots. — *San Francisco Chronicle*, p. 27, 8th March 1974

dunker noun
an easily solved crime *US, 1991*
- [D]unkers are cases accompanied by ample evidence and an obvious suspect. — David Simon, *Homicide*, p. 42, 1991

dunzo adjective
finished, completed, out-of-style *US, 2005*
- Page Six reports that NYC nightclub SUEDE is dunzo! — *theurbansocialites.blogspot.com*, 12th February 2006

dupe noun
a duplicate *US, 1891*
- "Give me the dupe to the suite and 'Skeeter' and I will fine-tooth it while you lug her out to a restaurant or a show tonight." — Iceberg Slim (Robert Beck), *Airtight Willie and Me*, p. 177, 1979

dupe verb
to duplicate *US, 1912*
- So that no one will dupe this copy. — Robert Stoller and I.S. Levine, *Coming Attractions*, p. 151, 1991

durn adverb
used as a folksy variation of "darn" or "darned," a euphemism for "damned" *US, 1958*
- Just eager and anxious to go climbin around and so durn cheerful, I ain't never seen a better kid. — Jack Kerouac, *The Dharma Bums*, p. 176, 1958

dust noun
1 phencyclidine, the recreational drug known as PCP or angel dust *US, 1977*
An abbreviation of **ANGEL DUST**.
- — *Drummer*, p. 77, 1977
- The carpeted lobby was littered with fallen rainbows, dexis, bennies, ludes, speed, even some dust, though it had a bad rep these days[.] — Joseph Wambaugh, *The Glitter Dome*, p. 122, 1981
- The more KW we smoked, what is what they call dust in the east and midwest, the deeper we kipped into never-never land. — Robert Lipkin, *A Brotherhood of Outlaws*, p. 68, 1981
- In '77 he smoked a bag of dust he bought from a dago. — *New Jack City*, 1990

2 a powdered narcotic, especially cocaine or heroin *US, 1916*
- All of them, and most of the others mentioned so far in the case (plus others unmentioned but nevertheless involved), have dabbled in dust deals[.] — *San Francisco Examiner*, p. 23, 6th December 1948
- Do you ever get high? A walk on the wild side? Ever do dust? — *Nashville*, 1975
- He snorted dust from his diamond encrusted spoon strung on a gold chain around his neck. — Iceberg Slim (Robert Beck), *Airtight Willie and Me*, p. 171, 1979
- DEALER: Hey, man. You wanna cop some blow? / JUNKIE: Sure, watcha got? Dust, flakes or rocks? / DEALER: I got China White, Mother of Pearl...I reflect what you need. — Grandmaster Flash & The Furious Five featuring Melle Mel, *White Lines*, 1983

3 inexpensive cigarette tobacco given free to prisoners *US, 1967*
- There were two types available—a fine powdery rolling tobacco, called "Dust," and a pipe cut which wasn't quite inferior enough to warrant a derisive nickname. — Malcolm Braly, *On the Yard*, p. 46, 1967

4 the powdered malted milk used in soda fountain malt drinks *US, 1946*
- — *American Speech*, p. 88, April 1946: "The language of West Coast culinary workers"

5 money *UK, 1607*
- — Malachi Andrews and Paul T. Owens, *Black Language*, p. 89, 1973
- — Bill Davis, *Jawjacking*, p. 37, 1977
- "You get all that dust [money]?" — John Allen, *Assault with a Deadly Weapon*, p. 188, 1977

6 the condition of being doomed or finished *US, 1994*
- Oh, man, we're dust! We're so history! — *Airheads*, 1994
- They're just sitting on me till they can tell her I'm dust. — Stephen J. Cannell, *The Tin Collectors*, p. 87, 2001

dust verb
1 to shoot; to kill *US, 1972*
- "Face down! And nothing sexy, I'll dust ya, I swear you'll die." — Seth Morgan, *Homeboy*, p. 73, 1990

2 to leave *US, 1945*
- — Lou Shelly, *Hepcats Jive Dictionary*, p. 11, 1945

3 to use and become intoxicated with phencyclidine, the recreational drug known as PCP or angel dust *US, 1989*
- — Geoffrey Froner, *Digging for Diamonds*, p. 27, 1989

4 to combine marijuana and heroin for smoking *US, 1986*
- — Sacramento Municipal Utility District, *A Glossary of Drugs and Drug Language*, 1986

5 in horse racing, to administer a drug to a horse before a race *US, 1951*
- — David W. Maurer, *Argot of the Racetrack*, p. 25, 1951

▸ **dust your snoot**
to snort a powdered drug *US, 1968*
- "Hey, Willie, you want to dust your snoot?" one of the big jazz boys asked me. — Phil Hirsch, *Hooked*, p. 9, 1968

dust-biter noun
during the 1991 US war against Iraq, an infantry soldier assigned to front line duty *US, 1991*
- A dust-biter would ask the pogue if he ever set up a "T, R, double E"—referring to an antenna—and the pogue would almost always say "Yes." — *Army*, p. 48, November 1991

dust bunny noun
a cluster of dust that accumulates under furniture *US, 1966*
- FURRY STUFF WHICH COLLECTS UNDER BEDS AND ON CLOSET FLOORS: dust bunnies, dust kittens, lint balls, pussies. — Roger Shuy, *Discovering American Dialects*, p. 18, 1967
- Things got lined up next to the dust bunnies in the corner. — John Ridley, *Stray Dogs*, p. 85, 1997
- Jenny-talia, Mavis and me—watching the dusty bunnies, between each carefully doled out bumplet of cocaine. — James St. James, *Party Monster*, p. 138, 1999
- I shut my old notebook, glittered dust-bunnies and whorls of dyed hair clogging its spiral binding. — Michelle Tea, *Valencia*, p. 189, 2000

dust-eater noun
the last vehicle in a military convoy *US, 1986*
- The dust eaters in Vietnam were the rear security elements of the convoy. — Gregory Clark, *Words of the Vietnam War*, p. 158, 1990

dust-eater's position noun
the end position in a convoy *US, 1986*
- We tagged onto the end of the string, cursing the dumb ass who had forced us into the dust-eaters' position. — Ralph Zumbro, *Tank Sergeant*, p. 87, 1986

dusted out; dusted adjective
1 drug-intoxicated *US, 1959*
Originally of cocaine, then less and less discriminating.
- — Eugene Landy, *The Underground Dictionary*, p. 72, 1971
- Bitch, I don't sell crack, I smoke it / My brain's dusted; I'm disgusted at my habits[.] — Eminem (Marshall Mathers), *Weed Lacer (Freestyle)*, 1999

2 drunk *US, 1966*
- — *Current Slang*, p. 2, Summer 1966

3 under the influence of phencyclidine, the recreational drug known as PCP or angel dust *US, 1983*
- The trucker was dusted out on PCP and it was only Jane's choke hold that saved the life of a foot-beat cop who was nearly beaten to death with his own stick by the duster. — Joseph Wambaugh, *The Delta Star*, p. 10, 1983
- One of the popular ways to get "dusted" is to dip cigarettes, specifically the Sherman brand, into a liquid form of PCP. — James Vigil, *Barrio Gangs*, p. 127, 1988

duster noun

1 an escort helicopter US, 2001

- I requested a "duster"—an escort helicopter that would fire around the perimeter of the LZ. — James Kirschke, *Not Going Home Alone*, p. 198, 2001

2 a user of phencyclidine, the recreational drug known as PCP or angel dust US, 1967

- The trucker was dusted out on PCP and it was only Jane's choke hold that saved the life of a foot-beat cop who was nearly beaten to death with his own stick by the duster. — Joseph Wambaugh, *The Delta Star*, p. 10, 1983

3 the buttocks US, 1946

- Keep on wriggling your saucy duster and smelling sweet. — Mezz Mezzrow, *Really the Blues*, p. 199, 1946

dusters noun

the testicles US, 1967

- — Dale Gordon, *The Dominion Sex Dictionary*, p. 61, 1967

dust of angels noun

phencyclidine, the recreational drug known as PCP or angel dust US, 1994

- — US Department of Justice, *Street Terms*, October 1994

dust-off noun

medical evacuation by helicopter US, 1967

Vietnam war usage.

- Eighteen American soldiers, wounded in the battle, were taken out in "dustoff" medical evacuation choppers (so named because they stir up a lot of dust during takeoffs and landings). — David Reed, *Up Front in Vietnam*, p. 27, 1967
- Yes, sir, what we needs just this minute is one of them medevac choppers, a dust-off, don't ya know. — Larry Heinemann, *Close Quarters*, p. 92, 1977
- I picked up a stretcher from the Dust Off ship. — Robert Mason, *Chickenhawk*, p. 174, 1983
- They'd pass out from shock and die before the dust-off medevac chopper could haul-ass out to us. — Larry Heinemann, *Paco's Story*, p. 21, 1986

dust off verb

1 to kill US, 1940

- He tried to dust me off a little while ago. — Mickey Spillane, *I, The Jury*, p. 83, 1947

2 to evacuate (the wounded) US, 1971

- They dusted him off to the 27th evac. — Ronald J. Glasser, *365 Days*, p. 121, 1971

dust puppy noun

a cluster of soft dust that accumulates on the floor US, 1943

- Kristen who couldn't bake, couldn't clean house without leaving the corners full of dustpuppies and the wallpaper smeared where her broom had brushed down cobwebs. — Wallace Stegner, *The Big Rock Candy Mountain*, p. 57, 1943
- Dust puppies tended to clump where the pipes turned, and she stopped occasionally to clean them away. — Larry Niven, *Footfall*, p. 419, 1985

dust-up noun

a fight; a disturbance; an engagement with an enemy UK, 1897

Military coinage; the image of dust raised in a physical conflict.

- Immediate cause of the dustup was the fact that Oppermann had asked City Attorney Dion R. Holm for a ruling on legality of his issuing permits for twenty-five foot lots in two new subdivisions west of Twin Peaks. — *San Francisco Examiner*, p. 16, 25th November 1950
- I hoped Channel 8 had either ignored Teddy's police dust-up or prejudiced his case. — George V. Higgins, *Penance for Jerry Kennedy*, p. 125, 1985

dusty adjective

under the influence of phencyclidine, the recreational drug known as PCP or angel dust US, 1998

- Someone "dusty" is always dangerous, because you never know what the next puff can lead to. — Nelson George, *Hip Hop America*, p. 39, 1998

dutch noun

suicide US, 1915

- Four years ago, she was about to do a Dutch over the Brooklyn Bridge. — Mickey Spillane, *I, The Jury*, p. 8, 1947

▸ **in dutch**

in trouble US, 1851

- The door was still sealed pending further investigation and I didn't want to get in dutch with the D.A.'s office by breaking it[.] — Mickey Spillane, *I, The Jury*, p. 56, 1947
- I never got myself in Dutch by talking. — Ethel Waters, *His Eye is on the Sparrow*, p. 11, 1951
- "She got in Dutch." — Grace Metalious, *Peyton Place*, p. 196, 1956
- "I didn't want you getting in Dutch with Clara again. I thought I'd just make sure you were awake." In Dutch? You make a note to look up this expression in Partridge's dictionary of slang when you get to work. — Jay McInerney, *Bright Lights, Big City*, p. 55, 1984
- Better hurry it up. I'm in dutch with the wife. — *Raising Arizona*, 1987

Dutch verb

▸ **dutch a book**

in an illegal betting operation, to accept bets with odds and in a proportion that guarantees the bookmaker will lose money regardless of the outcome that is being bet on US, 1911

- — David W. Maurer, *Argot of the Racetrack*, p. 25, 1951

Dutch adverb

paying your own way US, 1914

- When they are eating alone or with a musician boy friend (with whom they usually go "Dutch") you'll find them at the soda fountains[.] — Jack Lait and Lee Mortimer, *New York Confidential*, p. 143, 1948
- I thought you were going to guess I wanted to go Dutch. — Philip Wylie, *Opus 21*, p. 33, 1949
- So we go dutch, and everybody eats and drinks what he wants and no hard feelings[.] — John Nichols, *The Sterile Cuckoo*, p. 91, 1965

Dutch act; Dutch route noun

suicide US, 1902

- The farewell note said she was just tired of it all, life was a bore and she was getting no place, thus the Dutch act. — Mickey Spillane, *My Gun is Quick*, p. 98, 1950
- "Why do you think she did it? The Dutch act, I mean." — Jacqueline Susann, *Valley of the Dolls*, p. 378, 1966
- — William K. Bentley and James M. Corbett, *Prison Slang*, p. 105, 1992

Dutch book noun

in a bookmaking operation, a horse race in which the odds are such that the astute better can bet on any horse and win US, 1912

- In such situations the bookmakers said they were "in Dutch." Hence the name "dutch book." — Toney Betts., *Across the Board*, p. 189, 1956

Dutch cap noun

a diaphram or pessary US, 1950

- — *Maledicta*, p. 200, Winter 1980: "A new erotic vocabulary"

Dutch courage noun

courage induced by drink UK, 1826

- [H]e was full of Dutch courage and had a breath like a distillery. — Charles Raven, *Underworld Nights*, p. 178, 1956

Dutch door action noun

bisexual activity US, 1997

- — Vann Wesson, *Generation X Field Guide and Lexicon*, p. 58, 1997

Dutch leave noun

an absence without permission US, 1898

- — Richard Lederer, *A Man of My Words*, p. 24, 2003

Dutchman's anchor noun

any very important object that cannot be found US, 1945

- We discovered now that the metal collars for the twin staysail booms had been left behind, like the proverbial Dutchman's anchor. — W. H. Tilman, *Eight Sailing/Mountain-Exploration Books*, p. 429, 1987

Dutch Mill nickname

the infiltration surveillance center at Nakhon Phonom, Thailand US, 1986

Sensors along routes of North Vietnamese infiltration into South Vietnam broadcast to an orbiting aircraft which relayed the signals to the US base at Nakhon Phonom, Thailand. Because of the distinctive shape of one of its antennas, the installation was called Dutch Mill.

- During the discussion, Air Force Col. William L. Walker, Director of Intelligence for Task Force alpha, as the Dutch Mill contingent was called, told the Marines the surveillance center could help them in two ways. — Bernard Nalty, *Air Power and the Fight for Khe Sanh*, p. 91, 1986

Dutch rub *noun*
a playground torture consisting of rubbing the head of a boy restrained in a headlock with the restrainer's knuckles *US, 1930*
- Dutch rub and enema by young athlete. Tops! Deluxe! — Emile Nytrate, *Underground Ads*, p. 35, 1971
- The headlock; the Dutch rub, they called it then; the arm bent behind the back[.] — Elmore Leonard, *Gold Coast*, p. 179, 1980

Dutch straight *noun*
in poker, a hand with five cards sequenced by twos, worth nothing but not without its beauty *US, 1963*
- — Irwin Steig, *Common Sense in Poker*, p. 184, 1963

Dutch treat *noun*
an arrangement in which each person pays their own way *US, 1887*
- "Do you want me to meet you for lunch?" she asked him. "Dutch treat." — Irving Shulman, *Cry Tough*, p. 113, 1949
- The luncheons were run on a Dutch treat basis, and each woman continued to pay her dollar fee per lesson. — Jack Lait and Lee Mortimer, *Washington Confidential*, p. 138, 1951
- "But we always go Dutch treat," said I, which we did. "Look," she said, "Did you or did your not ask me out on a date?" — Max Shulman, *I was a Teen-Age Dwarf*, p. 45, 1959
- "My treat?" "Dutch treat." — Joseph Wambaugh, *Finnegan's Week*, p. 215, 1993

Dutch uncle *noun*
a person given to pedantic lectures *UK, 1838*
- I talked like the proverbial dutch uncle to him about staying for a medical discharge but to no avail and that afternoon we watched him split. — Herbert Huncke, *The Evening Sun Turned Crimson*, p. 205, 1980

duty *noun*
a duty officer *US, 1957*
- The "Duty," as he is called, takes the business of waking the troops quite seriously because the sergeant of the guard is likely to appear in a minute or two later to see that everyone is out of the sack. — Martin Russ, *The Last Parallel*, p. 19, 1957

DV *noun*
a Cadillac Coupe de Ville car *US, 1980*
- — Edith A. Folb, *runnin' down some lines*, p. 234, 1980

dwaddle *verb*
to waste time, to dawdle *US, 1950*
- This is not time to dwaddle, his mentor said. — Flannery O'Connor, *The Violent Bear it Away*, p. 462, 1960

dweeb; dweebie *noun*
a socially inept person *US, 1968*
- But face it, you're a neo-maxi-zoom dweebie! — *The Breakfast Club*, 1985
- Get out of my face you little dweeb. — *Wayne's World*, 1992
- You're just like every other dweeb who worships Quentin Tarantino for the same reason you can't let go of the camera: because you don't know how to be a real person in real life. — *American Beauty*, 1999
- It is estimated that one hundred thousand people, many of them digital dweebs, are eventually able to check out new porno films[.] — Bill Brownstein, *Sex Carnival*, p. 18, 2000
- One student, White Mickey—an amateur pot dealer—turned around in his seat and faced Max with a condescending "dweeb." — Marty Beckerman, *Generation S.L.U.T.*, p. 119, 2004

dweeby *adjective*
foolish, inept, out of touch with current trends *US, 2004*
- Except he was popular and she was a big fucking dweeb with her two dweeby friends and dweeby problems. — Suzette Mayr, *Venous Hum*, p. 69, 2004

dwid *noun*
a social outcast *US, 1988*
- — Michael V. Anderson, *The Bad, Rad, Not to Forget Way Cool Beach and Surf Discriptionary*, p. 6, 1988

dwim *noun*
in computing, a command meaning *"do what I mean" US, 1983*
- — Guy L. Steele et al., *The Hacker's Dictionary*, p. 59, 1983

dwindles *noun*
the condition of an older hospital patient who is fading away *US, 1981*
- — Sally Williams, *"Strong" Words (Dissertation)*, p. 140, 1994

dye party *noun*
a gathering to tie-dye an assortment of clothes for personal use or sale *US, 1994*
- — David Shenk and Steve Silberman, *Skeleton Key*, p. 75, 1994

dyke; dike *noun*
a lesbian, especially a "mannish," aggressive one *US, 1931*
Safely used by insiders, with caution by outsiders.
- I use that as an excuse (because Alice dike-like silent unpleasant and strange and likes no one) to lay the two bills on Mardou's dishes at sink[.] — Jack Kerouac, *The Subterraneans*, p. 74, 1958
- This is not a queer bar—it is an outcast bar—Negroes and vagrant whites, heads and hypes, dikes and queens. — John Rechy, *City of Night*, p. 184, 1963
- It's hard to spot dikes, cause sometimes we're married to them. — Lenny Bruce, *The Essential Lenny Bruce*, p. 163, 1967
- I call myself a dyke so it's not too devastating when some throwback screams it at me as I'm leaving a bar at night. — *Chasing Amy*, 1997

dykey *adjective*
overtly lesbian, mannish *US, 1964*
- Now don't smile like that, nothing dikey has happened or will. — Gore Vidal, *Myra Breckinridge*, p. 242, 1968
- [P]arties have been getting dykier by the dance step and Red Raw on January 25 promises to be a winner. — *Lesbians on the Loose*, p. 44, 1997

dynamite *noun*
1 powerful alcohol or drugs *US, 1919*
- Even if it's only one stick of dynamite this boy is always a sly cat. — Hal Ellson, *Duke*, p. 27, 1949
- The good stuff, in its round cylinders of cigarettes, he stacked in one pile: dynamites. — Willard Motley, *Let No Man Write My Epitaph*, p. 107, 1958
- Not just any connection, but a connection who deals good quality stuff—"dynamite," not "garbage." — James Mills, *The Panic in Needle Park*, p. 15, 1966
- "We ain't got no bigger thang goin' on than you 'n Zelma," he replied finally, sprawling back on the bed, the first effects of the dynamite seeping in. — Odie Hawkins, *Chicago Hustle*, p. 33, 1977
2 nitroglycerine tablets prescribed to cardiac patients *US, 1975*
- — John Gould, *Maine Lingo*, p. 84, 1975
3 any amphetamine, methamphetamine, or other central nervous system stimulant *US, 1980*
- National Institute on Drug Abuse — *What do they call it again?*, 1980
4 cocaine *US, 1959*
- — J.E. Schmidt, *Narcotics Lingo and Lore*, p. 54, 1959
5 a blend of heroin and cocaine *US, 1937*
- Addicts sometimes blend heroin and cocaine in a mixture called dynamite. — Harry J. Anslinger, *The Murderers*, p. 271, 1961
6 something that is very good *US, 1902*
- Dynamite, baby, but get your paws out of my pockets. — Richard Farina, *Been Down So Long*, p. 119, 1966
7 in an illegal betting operation, money that one bookmaker bets with another bookmaker to cover bets that he does not want to hold *US, 1951*
- — David W. Maurer, *Argot of the Racetrack*, p. 25, 1951

dynamite *adjective*
excitingly excellent *US, 1922*
- The first bite was dynamite! — Max Shulman, *Guided Tour of Campus Humor*, p. 21, 1955
- There were also some nice Playboy shots that I kept (1 dynamite fleshy configuration from Europe that gave me an erection), and all the other essentials for clerking. — Clarence Cooper Jr., *The Farm*, p. 50, 1967
- The San Francisco bands, on the other hand, were hippies off the street who happened to play dynamite music as part of their lives[.] — John Sinclair, *Guitar Army*, p. 23, 1972
- Dynamite! This is dynamite! — *King of Comedy*, 1976
- She's really a sho' 'nuff dynamite sister. — Odie Hawkins, *Chicago Hustle*, p. 222, 1977

- Coulda been a dynamite score. — Edwin Torres, *After Hours*, p. 310, 1979
- The next gig is gonna be dynamite, huge, you'll see. — *The Blues Brothers*, 1980

dyn-no-mite!
used for expressing strong approval *US, 1978*
A stock laugh-line catchphrase used by the character J.J. Evans, played by Jimmie Walker, in the 1970s situation comedy *Facts of Life*.

- Michael moved in the direction of his quarry, overtaking two small black kids in Dyn-O-Mite T-shirts. — Armistead Maupin, *Tales of the City*, p. 125, 1978

dyno *noun*
1 a derelict *US, 1918*

- "Someday he'll shake down the wrong dino." — Nelson Algren, *The Man with the Golden Arm*, p. 20, 1949

2 alcohol *US, 1962*

- — Joseph E. Ragen and Charles Finston, *Inside the World's Toughest Prison*, p. 798, 1962

dyno *adjective*
excellent *US, 1962*
An abbreviation of **DYNAMITE**.

- — Jonathan Roberts, *How to California*, p. 168, 1984
- — Pamela Munro, *U.C.L.A. Slang*, p. 36, 1989

Ee

E *noun*
MDMA, the recreational drug best known as ecstasy *US, 1992*
Generally from the initial letter of **ECSTASY**, specifically in reference to any MDMA tablet stamped with the symbol.

- Most of the so-called E over here (irl) is in capsules and tends to be mixed with all sorts of crap. — *alt.rave*, 14th March 1992
- I could feel at least a decent amount off of 2 hits of good E. — *alt.drugs.ecstasy*, 31st March 2006
- "E is for ecstasy," she said and giggled again. Jasper swore beneath his breath. "Like you've never done it," Kelly snapped. — Justine Musk, *Uninvited*, p. 235, 2007

eager beaver *noun*
an annoyingly diligent and hard-working person *US, 1943*

- The all-time eager beaver. — Philip Wylie, *Opus 21*, p. 63, 1949
- George Katz, the eager beaver that he was, was directing the unloading of those books[.] — Evan Hunter, *The Blackboard Jungle*, p. 72, 1954

eagle *noun*
▸ **the eagle flies; the eagle screams; the eagle shits**
used for expressing payday *US, 1918*

- It was on a Thursday, the day before the Negro payday. The eagle always flew on Friday. — Dick Gregory, *Nigger*, p. 30, 1964
- But it had been a month of paydays / Since I'd heard that eagle scream. — Kris Kristofferson, *To Beat the Devil*, 1970
- [T]he weight of four more days (and maybe five) of clock punching and lockstepping ahead of them before the eagle flies. — Donald Goines, *The Busting Out of an Ordinary Man*, p. 12, 1985

eaglebird *noun*
1 the winner of any long-odds bet, such as the double zero in roulette *US, 1992*

- — Jay Robert Nash, *Dictionary of Crime*, p. 115, 1992

2 in horse racing, a long-shot winner that nobody has bet on *US, 1947*

- — Dan Parker, *The ABC of Horse Racing*, p. 145, 1947

eagle day *noun*
pay day *US, 1941*

- — *American Speech*, p. 55, February 1947: "Pacific War language"

E and E *noun*
evasion and escape *US, 1982*
Korean war usage.

- One of my responsibilities was to establish an evasion-and-escape [E&E] operation across Korea to rescue downed fliers. — Joseph C. Goulden, *Korea: The Untold Story of the War*, p. 468, 1982
- Brubaker lectured us on the importance of noise discipline, hand signaling, E & E (escape and evasion), and patrolling techniques. — Gary Linderer, *The Eyes of the Eagle*, p. 31, 1991

E and T; ET *noun*
in craps, a one-roll bet on eleven and twelve *US, 1983*
The bet was originally known as "E and T"; with the popularity of the film *E.T.*, the terminology quickly changed.

- — Thomas L. Clark, *The Dictionary of Gambling and Gaming*, p. 71, 1987

ear *noun*
1 a person who is not a part of the criminal underworld but who reports what he hears to those who are *US, 1964*

- — R. Frederick West, *God's Gambler*, p. 225, 1964: "Appendix A"

2 on a playing card, a bent corner used by a cheat to identify the card *US, 1950*

- — Hyman E. Goldin et al., *Dictionary of American Underworld Lingo*, p. 34, 1950
- He put the ear on it. — John Scarne, *Scarne's Guide to Modern Poker*, p. 277, 1979

ear angel *noun*
a very small, nearly invisible speaker in a television announcer's ear by which others can communicate with the announcer while on air *US, 1997*

- In his "ear angel," the director told him to go right to commercial. — Stephen Cannell, *King Con*, p. 84, 1997

ear banger *noun*
a person who enjoys the sound of his own voice *US, 1942*

- — Jerry Robertson, *Oil Slanguage*, p. 51, 1954

ear bender *noun*
an overly talkative person *US, 1934*

- — John Scarne, *Scarne's Guide to Modern Poker*, p. 277, 1979

ear candy *noun*
1 music that is pleasant, if not challenging *US, 1984*

- The album is a total pleasure and all of these little snippets are just good ear-candy. — *Fanfare*, p. 322, 1986
- — Vann Wesson, *Generation X Field Guide and Lexicon*, p. 60, 1997
- The ear candy comes in the form of the truly amazing soundtrack piping through every ep of The O.C. — Brittany Kent, *O.C. Undercover*, p. viii, 2004

2 a platitude *US, 1991*

- — David Olive, *Business Babble*, p. 51, 1991

earie *noun*
▸ **on the earie**
engaged in eavesdropping *US, 1950*

- — *The Annals of the American Academy of Political and Social Sciences*, p. 128, May 1950
- "That sonofabitch was on the Erie!" — Malcom Braly, *Felony Tank*, p. 20, 1961
- Carnival owners at the annual showmen's meetings in the Sherman Hotel sent lesser known employees into the lobby "to stay on the earie," and at regular intervals they reported all conversations heard to their boss. — Joe McKennon, *Circus Lingo*, p. 66, 1980

ear job *noun*
sexual talk on the telephone *US, 1978*

- — Steven Daly and Nathaniel Wice, *alt.culture*, p. 182, 1995

early eclectic *noun*
used as a humorous description of a mix of design or decorating styles *US, 1980*

- — *Maledicta*, p. 242, Winter 1980: "Lovely, blooming, fresh and gay: the onomastics of camp"

early foot *noun*
in horse racing, speed in the initials stages of a race *US, 1960*

- — Robert Saunders Dowst and Jay Craig, *Playing the Races*, p. 162, 1960

earner *noun*
a member of an organized crime enterprise who produces high profits, however unpleasant his character may be *US, 1995*

- "You gotta be a good earner and don't get into trouble, don't offend, don't insult." — Joseph Pistone, *Donnie Brasco*, p. 131, 1988
- He was a money machine. A tremendous earner for these guys. — *Casino*, 1995

ears *noun*
▸ **get your ears raised; get your ears lowered**
to have your hair cut *US, 1950*

- — Jerry Robertson, *Oil Slanguage*, p. 60, 1954
- "See you got your ears lowered." — Mark De Castrique, *Dangerous Undertaking*, p. 195, 2003

▸ **pull ears**
in the language of paragliding, to intentionally collapse both tips of the wing to increase speed *US, 1992*

- — Erik Fair, *California Thrill Sports*, p. 335, 1992

▸ **put the ears on**
to attempt a controlled roll of the dice *US, 1963*

- — John S. Salak, *Dictionary of Gambling*, p. 198, 1963

ear sex *noun*

a sexually-oriented telephone conversation with a person working for a telephone sex service *US, 1984*

- The idea in ear sex, not to be overly bashful about it, is that you call up and have a woman talk dirty to you while you masturbate. — Cecil Adams, *The Straight Dope*, p. 63, 1984

earth calling....

used for humorously suggesting that someone is not fully present *US, 1983*

- "Earth calling Claire! Anybody home?" — Karen Brownstein, *Memorial Day*, p. 41, 1983
- "Earth calling Marcy. Earth calling Marcy." Marcy shook her head and the scene came back in focus. — Lucy Diggs, *Everyday Friends*, p. 226, 1987
- "Earth calling Dennis Savage." "Yes, I hear," he said. — Ethan Morden, *Some Men Are Lookers*, p. 313, 1997

earth pads *noun*

shoes *US, 1947*

Teen slang.

- Marcus Hanna Boulware, *Jive and Slang of Students in Negro Colleges*, 1947
- *San Francisco News*, p. 6, 25th March 1958
- Art Unger, *The Cool Book*, p. 110, 1961

earth to [name]

used as a humorous suggestion that the person named is not in touch with reality *US, 1977*

- "Earth to Brian, earth to Brian." Mary Ann coaxed him back into the here and now with a bemused smile. — Armistead Maupin, *Babycakes*, p. 114, 1984
- Earth to Alice, come in. I switched the topic of conversation to football. Try to stay in the game, honey. — Jimmy Buffett, *Tales from Margaritaville*, p. 71, 1989
- "Earth-to-Archie! You're MILES away!" "Oh, I guess I was daydreaming." — *New Archie's Comics Digest Magazine*, October 1989
- Earth to Richie. Don't you wanna ask your new friend to join us? — Quentin Tarantino, *From Dusk Till Dawn*, p. 104, 1995

ease *verb*

to leave *US, 1947*

- She's the bang of the ball but has to ease at midnight or be turned back into a scarecrow. — Harry Haenigsen, *Jive's Like That*, 1947
- "Let's ease this punk," she told Leslie. — Clarence Cooper Jr., *The Scene*, p. 35, 1960

ease on *verb*

to leave with a parting gesture *US, 1959*

- *American Speech*, p. 154, May 1959: "Gator (University of Florida) slang"

ease up *verb*

to have sex *US, 1993*

- I know a couple 'a niggas that done eased up in her. — *Menace II Society*, 1993

East Coast girlie *noun*

a magazine that is mildly pornographic, featuring naked women but not sexual activity *US, 1970*

- The mass market magazines with the highest degree of sexual orientation (especially nudity) known as "men's sophisticates" (also as "girlie" or "East Coast girlie") devote a substantial portion to photographs of partially nude females[.] — *The Presidential Commission on Obscenity and Pornography*, p. 111, 1970

Easter egg *noun*

1 a message hidden in a computer program's object code *US, 1991*

- Eric S. Raymond, *The New Hacker's Dictionary*, p. 138, 1991
- An Easter Egg in the computing sense is some unexpected, secret thing you can do with a piece of software that the programer put in but doesn't tell anyone about. — The Knightmare, *Secrets of a Super Hacker*, p. 7, 1994
- Triggered by secret combinations of keystrokes, these "eggs" range from cartoons to surprise snapshots of the programer's family. — Vann Wesson, *Generation X Field Guide and Lexicon*, p. 60, 1997

2 an icon or hidden process on the menu of a DVD that, when selected or followed, leads to hidden features *US, 2002*

- Marc Salzman, *DVD Confidential*, 2002

Eastie *nickname*

East Boston, Massachusetts *US, 1979*

- Across one building was strung a banner that read: "Eastie Loves the Pope." — *Washington Post*, p. A1, 2nd October 1979

East Jesus *noun*

a fictitious place, difficult to find and peopled with uneducated and poor people *US, 1958*

There are many variants providing detail for exactly where East Jesus is.

- "So I told her she was a tub of lard and I wouldn't take her to East Jesus." — J.P. Donleavy, *The Ginger Man*, p. 11, 1958
- There is vice in London and there is vice in Paris, and in Reykjavik and in East Jesus, Kansas. — Brendan Behan, *Brendan Behan's New York*, p. 113, 1964
- This means that Teddy's brushes with the law are scattered all over East Jesus. — George Higgins, *Kennedy for the Defense*, p. 9, 1980
- Michael Dalton Johnson, *Talking Trash with Redd Foxx*, p. 15, 1994

East Los *nickname*

east Los Angeles, California *US, 1974*

- Dagoberto Fuentes and Jose Lopez, *Barrio Language Dictionary*, p. 57, 1974
- Judi Sanders, *Da Bomb*, p. 5, 1997
- Since all of the Mexican Mafia's founders came from East Los [East Los Angeles], and because most of the rank and file were also from that region, they referred to themselves as Surenos, which means southerners in Spanish. — Bill Valentine, *Gangs and Their Tattoos*, p. 23, 2000

East Overshoe *noun*

the mythical town in Maine which is the home to fools and idiots *US, 1975*

- John Gould, *Maine Lingo*, p. 199, 1975

easy *noun*

1 in craps, a point made by a combination other than a matched pair *US, 1996*

From the fuller "easy way."

- Sydney: Easy eight. A five and a three. Stickman: Eight. It came easy. The point. — *Hard Eight*, 1996

2 in poker, the fifth player to the left of the dealer *US, 1988*

A name based on the scheme of 1 = A, 2 = B, etc.

- George Percy, *The Language of Poker*, p. 32, 1988

▸ **on the easy**

without working *US, 1998*

- "How'd you start living on the easy?" "Met a guy. He knew the rackets." — John Ridley, *Love is a Racket*, p. 62, 1998

easy

used as a farewell *US, 1972*

Hawaiian youth usage; often accompanied by a hand gesture, wiggling the hand from the wrist emphasizing the thumb and little finger.

- Elizabeth Ball Carr, *Da Kine Talk*, p. 129, 1972

easy go *noun*

an unstrenuous prison job *US, 1983*

- Marlene Freedman, *Alcatraz*, 1983

easy, greasy!

take it easy! *US, 1955*

Teen slang.

- *American Weekly*, p. 2, 14th August 1955

easy mark *noun*

a person who is easily persuaded *US, 1915*

- You think religion is for suckers and easy marks and mollycoddles, huh? — Richard Brooks, *Elmer Gantry*, 1960

easy rider *noun*

a pimp *US, 1914*

- Robert A. Wilson, *Playboy's Book of Forbidden Words*, p. 96, 1972

easy street *noun*

a comfortable, affluent situation for little expenditure of effort *US, 1897*

- "Small time, but enough to start us on easy street." — John Ridley, *Everybody Smokes in Hell*, p. 23, 1999

easy time *noun*

time served in jail without undue stress or anxiety *US, 1966*

- Easy time refers to the process of relating one's thoughts and energies mainly to events within the prison while serving a sentence. — Rose Giallombardo, *Society of Women*, p. 134, 1966

easy walkers *noun*

sneakers; tennis shoes *US, 1954*

- The band's uniform consisted of long white pants turned up to look like knickers, black easy-walkers[.] — Louis Armstrong, *Satchmo*, p. 47, 1954

easy way *noun*

(used of an even-numbered point in craps) scored in any fashion other than a pair *US, 1974*

- — John Scarne, *Scarne on Dice*, p. 466, 1974

eat *noun*

eating *US, 1993*

- I just wanna get my eat on. — *Menace II Society*, 1993

eat *verb*

1 to perform oral sex *US, 1916*

- "Babe, I'd like to eat you," said the man in the ballet tights at Les Deux Freres. — John Rechy, *City of Night*, p. 405, 1963
- There is the type who likes to eat his woman up after you get through piling her. — Eldridge Cleaver, *Soul on Ice*, p. 170, 1968
- Gabriella shows a very pretty pussy as D.T. eats her[.] — *Adult Video*, p. 53, August/September 1986
- I once sucked a woman's pussy so hard I got a hangover. If you don't eat pussy your woman's going to be gone. She'll find someone else who will. — Chris Rock, *Rock This!*, p. 134, 1997

2 to swallow *US, 1970*

Used especially in the context of ingesting LSD.

- [Y]our average acid-eating freak will be getting arrested for attempting to sit in the park under General Thomas' horse in Thomas Circle[.] — Raymond Mungo, *Famous Long Ago*, p. 29, 1970
- Maybe he'll smoke a little weed or eat a pill or two. — Bruce Jackson, *In the Life*, p. 107, 1972
- You eat a lot of acid, Miller, back in the hippie days? — *Repo Man*, 1984

3 to bother *US, 1892*

- He looked over at the blonde, then raised his eyebrow at me. "Any idea what's eating him?" — Rita Ciresi, *Pink Slip*, p. 323, 1999

4 to accept a monetary loss *US, 1955*

- I ate twenty-four pairs of Blue Oyster Cult tickets last time around. — *Fast Times at Ridgemont High*, 1982

▸ **eat a stock**

to buy undesirable stock in order to maintain a standing order market in the stock *US, 1988*

- — Kathleen Odean, *High Steppers, Fallen Angels, and Lollipops*, p. 94, 1988

▸ **eat cards**

in blackjack, to draw more cards than you normally would in a given hand in order to learn more about what cards are remaining unplayed *US, 1991*

The card-eater takes a short-term loss in hope of a long-term big win.

- — Michael Dalton, *Blackjack*, p. 45, 1991

▸ **eat cheese**

to curry favor *US, 1968*

- — Mary Swift, *Campus Slang (University of Texas)*, 1968

▸ **eat cock**

to perform oral sex on a man *US, 1948*

- meet her 2 weeks later & drive her (Joy is name) to Sacramento to a whorehouse & she's there now—whoring & eating cock—the bitch. — Neal Cassady, *Neal Cassady Collected Letters 1944–1967*, p. 77, 16th June 1948: Letter to Jack Kerouac

▸ **eat cunt**

to perform oral sex on a woman *US, 1972*

- They claim they don't like girls, but when I get to eating their cunts, they love it. — Roger Blake, *What you always wanted to know about porno-movies*, p. 244, 1972
- People were fucking, eating cunt, sucking on cocks, to the left and right of me, on the floor of the cave. — *Penthouse International, Penthouse Uncensored II*, p. 176, 2001

▸ **eat dick**

to perform oral sex on a man *US, 1988*

- Instead of making him eat dick, the other prisoners kept out of his way right from the beginning. — Gerald Petievich, *Shakedown*, p. 85, 1988
- He pivots his body, and soon we're both eating dick, both having our dicks slobbered over. — Bob Vickery, *Cocksure*, p. 33, 2002

▸ **eat face**

to kiss in a sustained and passionate manner *US, 1966*

- — Andy Anonymous, *A Basic Guide to Campusology*, p. 8, 1966
- — Collin Baker et al., *College Undergraduate Slang Study Conducted at Brown University*, p. 112, 1968

▸ **eat it**

1 to die *US, 1987*

- Watching those Green Berets eat it leaves me with a new conviction; Charlie would never overrun us. — Ernest Spencer, *Welcome to Vietnam, Macho Man*, p. 135, 1987

2 to suffer an accident, especially a fall *US, 1982*

Hawaiian youth usage.

- — Douglas Simonson, *Pidgin to da Max: Hana Hou*, 1982

3 in surfing, to lose control and fall from your surfboard *US, 1991*

- You go in there, you're gonna eat it on the rocks. — *Point Break*, 1991

▸ **eat lead**

to be shot *US, 1927*

- I got news that old sidekick Dinty Colebeck had eaten lead in St. Louis. — Red Rudensky, *The Gonif*, p. 142, 1970

▸ **eat plastic**

(used of a hospital patient) to be intubated *US, 1994*

- — Sally Williams, *"Strong" Words*, p. 133, 1994

▸ **eat pussy**

to perform oral sex on a woman *US, 1963*

- Cunnilingus is, in fact, spoken of popularly as "eating pussy." — Robert Masters, *Sex Crimes in History*, p. 168, 1963
- She said, "Well, little daddy, I guess you and I are through / 'cause if you can't eat this pussy there's nothin' else you can do." — Bruce Jackson, *Get Your Ass in the Water and Swim Like Me*, p. 127, 1965
- He eats pussy! I don't. Man, I won't eat pussy unless I get well paid for it. — Christina and Richard Milner, *Black Players*, p. 218, 1972
- "Sweetheart, that's all very nice," she replies, "but if you're not going to eat pussy, you're not a dyke." — Kim Akass, *Reading Sex and the City*, p. 40, 2004

▸ **eat shit**

in surfing, to lose control of a ride and fall off your surfboard *US, 1991*

- This is a 5/6" tri-fin squash-tail thruster. You'd eat major shit on this, dude. — *Point Break*, 1991

▸ **eat someone's lunch**

to thrash; to exact revenge *US, 1968*

- — *Current Slang*, p. 4, Spring 1968

▸ **eat the cookie**

while surfing, to be pounded fiercely by a breaking wave *US, 1997*

- — Vann Wesson, *Generation X Field Guide and Lexicon*, p. 60, 1997

▸ **eat the floormat**

to throw yourself to the floor of a car *US, 1981*

- [B]oth narcs ate the floormat until the Mercedes turned west on Franklin. — Joseph Wambaugh, *The Glitter Dome*, p. 77, 1981

▸ **eat your gun**

to commit suicide by gun *US, 1983*

- A fellow cop who shot himself through the roof of the mouth—the surest way, though unpleasant for whoever found the body—was. "He ate his gun." — Barbara Gelb, *Varnished Brass*, p. 36, 1983

▸ **eatin' ain't cheatin'**

used as a jocular assertion that oral sex does not rise to the level of adultery or infidelity *US, 1994*

A maxim that enjoyed sudden and massive appeal in the US during the President Clinton sex scandals.

- — Michael Dalton Johnson, *Talking Trash with Redd Foxx*, p. 56, 1994

ea-tay *noun*

marijuana *US, 1938*

Pig Latin for "tea."

- — Julian Martin, *Law Enforcement Vocabulary*, p. 140, 1973

eat flaming death!

used as an overblown expression of hostility *US, 1975*

- — Fireside Theater, *In the Next World, You're on your Own*, 1975

eating tobacco noun
chewing tobacco US, 1901

- He would pause, wipe a nonexistent tear from the buttermilk—blue eyes, bite off a healthy chew of eating tobacco, and stand there.
  — George Korson, *Pennsylvania Songs and Legends*, p. 418, 1979

eat me!
used as a somewhat coarse expression of defiance US, 1962

The taboo component is fading if not faded.

- It is usually used by the heterosexual but does not mean to fellate although its unfriendly meaning is drawn from the heterosexual's low regard for the homosexual in this sex act. — *The Guild Dictionary of Homosexual Terms*, p. 14, 1965
- WAYNE: So, uh, everybody, uh, have fun. VOICE IN THE CROWD: EAT ME! — *Wayne's World 2*, 1993
- COP #2: So, fifty years old, huh? MURTAUGH: Eat me. — *Lethal Weapon*, 1995

eat my shorts!
used as a humorous declaration of defiance US, 1979

- BENDER: Eat my shorts. VERNON: What was that? BENDER: Eat my shorts! — *The Breakfast Club*, 1985

eat out verb
to perform oral sex, usually on a woman US, 1966

- We had been eating each other out all afternoon — *Screw*, p. 3, 21st February 1969
- Scarfing pussy gets great press, but most men know shit about eating out women. — *Screw*, p. 5, 12th June 1972
- It's laying hands on Marsellus Wallace's new wife in a familiar way. Is it as bad as eatin her out – no, but you're in the same fuckin' ballpark. — *Pulp Fiction*, 1994
- I lost my tolerance for the bullshit baggage that comes with eating girls out. What's the big deal? — *Chasing Amy*, 1997

eat the apple, fuck the Corps
used as a defiant yet proud curse of the marines by the marines US, 1976

- It was the common reaction among marines to all abrupt direction changes: "Eat the apple fuck the Corps." — Charles Anderson, *The Grunts*, p. 36, 1976
- "Eat the apple, fuck the Corps," they'd say and write it upon their helmets and flak jackets for their officers to see. — Michael Herr, *Dispatches*, p. 103, 1977

eat up verb
(used of a wave) to overcome and knock a surfer from the surfboard US, 1965

- — John M. Kelly, *Surf and Sea*, p. 283, 1965

eccy; ec noun
economics US, 1924

- "Mama," I said. "There ain't no boys in Home Ec. The boys are in the science class." — Nora Ephron and Alice Arlon, *Silkwood*, 1983

echo verb
to repeat what was just said US, 1967

- — *American Speech*, p. 62, February 1967: "Soda-fountain, restaurant and tavern calls"

ecofreak noun
a radical environmentalist US, 1970

- We're just a bunch of fascists, racists, terrorists, sexists, anarchists, communists, Young Americans for Freedom, Democrats and just plain folksy ecofreaks. — Edward Abbey, *Hayduke Lives!*, p. 188, 1990
- Your ecofreaks take over, Blanche, every job in the state will go[.]
  — David Powyer, *Down to a Sunless Sea*, p. 71, 1996

ecology freak noun
a devoted environmentalist US, 1984

- The 2.2 million ecology freaks who live there [Oregon] are reminded by their Highway Division to "thank Heaven we live in God's Country." — Bill Cardoso, *The Maltese Sangweech*, p. 88, 1984

econut noun
a zealous environmentalist US, 1972

- [T]he increasing number of paperbacks on "ecofiction" and man's position in the environmental crisis foretells more creations coming from the econuts. — Robert Kirk Mueller, *Buzzwords*, p. 70, 1974

ecstasy noun
methylene-dioxymethamphetamine, MDMA, a mildly hallucinogenic empathogen and/or entactogen, a drug of empathy and touch US, 1985

Easily the most recognizable slang name for this widely popular recreational drug; it derives from the senses of well-being and affection felt by users. The illegal status of the drug has encouraged a great many alternative names; some are generic (**E** is probably the most widely known), and some serve as brand names. Originally synthesized by German pharmaceutical company Merck some time before 1912. Since the 1980s the drug has been inextricably linked with **RAVE** culture.

- It is called MDMA—or "Ecstasy"—and users say it has the incredible power to make people trust one another[.] — *Newsweek*, p. 96, 15th April 1985
- It is called by some Ecstasy and, like LSD, it is psychedelic. — *ABC World News Tonight*, 17th April 1985
- On the street, its name is "ecstasy" or "Adam," which should tell how people on the street feel about it. — *Los Angeles Times*, p. 1 (Part 5), 29th March 1985
- Ecstasy is both a young drug and a drug embraced by the young.
  — Gareth Thomas, *This Is Ecstasy*, p. 9, 2002

e-deuce noun
an M-14 automatic rifle US, 1977

- Mac humped his automatic M-14, something like a BAR, which everyone called an E-deuce. — Larry Heinemann, *Close Quarters*, p. 46, 1977

edge noun

1 in gambling, a statistical advantage, usually expressed as a percentage US, 1974

- To me, it's simple. You got the edge. Use it. — Gary Mayer, *Bookie*, p. 88, 1974
- By the time the tax people take their bite off the top you have a 20 percent "Edge" working against you. — Mario Puzo, *Inside Las Vegas*, p. 46, 1977
- The house edge in "even money" bets in roulette (European rules) is 1.35% — David Bennet, *Know Your Bets*, p. 34, 2001

2 a knife, used or intended for use as a weapon US, 1972

- — David Claerbaut, *Black Jargon in White America*, p. 63, 1972

3 an urban area with bars, nightclubs, and prostitution US, 1973

- Since I was getting one vine out of every four from the three girls, my wardrobe was now twice as large as any nigger's on the edge.
  — A.S. Jackson, *Gentleman Pimp*, p. 32, 1973

▸ **on the edge**
in gambling, out of funds; broke US, 1963

- — Richard Jessup, *The Cincinnati Kid*, p. 127, 1963

Edge City noun
a notional place where people live on the edge of danger US, 1970

- — Robert J. Glessing, *The Underground Press in America*, p. 175, 1970: "Glossary of terms used in the underground press"

edged adjective
angry US, 1982

- Like I'm just lying there next to the pool, and my lame little brother throws the car keys into the Jacuzzi, right, and now I'm edged, fer shurr! — Mary Corey and Victoria Westermark, *Fer Shurr! How to be a Valley Girl*, 1982

edge work noun
the alteration of dice by rounding off the edges to affect the roll US, 1950

- — *The Annals of the American Academy of Political and Social Sciences*, p. 124, May 1950

edge-work verb
to round off the edges of dice to affect the roll US, 1959

- "You ever bevel, cap, or edge-work dice?" — Irving Shulman, *The Short End of the Stick*, p. 97, 1959

Edison noun
in horse racing, a hand battery used illegally by a jockey to impart a shock to his horse US, 1947

- — Dan Parker, *The ABC of Horse Racing*, p. 145, 1947

Edison medicine noun
electric shock therapy US, 1990

Alluding to Thomas Edison, a central figure in the early history of electricity; not a common phrase, although not for lack of cleverness.

- With the Edison medicine, shootin speedballs makes me double crazy[.] — Seth Morgan, *Homeboy*, p. 77, 1990

Edsel; Flying Edsel *nickname*
the US Air Force F-111 aircraft *US, 1972*
An allusion to the single greatest failure in American car manufacture.

- The result was an Edsel aircraft of monumental proportions. — John Singlaub, *Hazardous Duty*, p. 265, 1991
- Not bad for what was once called the Flying Edsel. — *Texas Monthly*, p. 14, July 1996

educated currency *noun*
in horse racing, bets placed on the basis of what is believed to be authentic, empirical tips *US, 1951*

- — David W. Maurer, *Argot of the Racetrack*, p. 26, 1951

educator *noun*
in the circus or carnival, the *Billboard* weekly newspaper *US, 1980*

- — Joe McKennon, *Circus Lingo*, p. 32, 1980

edumacation *noun*
education *US, 1833*

- Y'll know you got some radio directors with two years of edu-ma-cat-ion. — Geneva Smitherman, *Talkin and Testifyin*, p. 88, 1977
- George W.—he's the Edumacation president! — Kate Clinton, *What the L*, p. 81, 2005

eel *noun*
a spy or informer *US, 1956*

- — *American Speech*, p. 98, May 1956: "Smugglers' argot in the Southwest"

eensy-weensy *adjective*
very small *US, 1978*
A rarely heard variant of "teensy-weensy."

- C'mon. One eensy-weensy guess. — Armistead Maupin, *Tales of the City*, p. 58, 1978

eeoo-leven *noun*
in craps, an eleven *US, 1985*

- — Steve Kuriscak, *Casino Talk*, p. 21, 1985

effed up *adjective*
used as a euphemism for "fucked up" *US, 1971*

- Earlier in his talk, Murray had said that San Francisco State was nothing more than a "nigger-producing factory," and that any black student who went along with the college program was "all effed up." — Dirkan Karagueuzian, *Blow it Up*, p. 40, 1971

efficient *adjective*
▸ **get efficient**
to smoke marijuana *US, 1997*

- — Jim Emerson-Cobb, *Scratching the Dragon*, April 1997

effing; effin'; f-ing *adjective*
used as an intensifier; a euphemism for "fucking" *UK, 1929*

- Because when you were just about my age you went through something like this. I mean one hell of a big effing overnight success. (Quoting Thomas Heggen). — *Esquire*, p. 102, November 1960
- "That's the smallest effing set on the stage," said the cameraman. "I can't get three effing machines in there." — Max Shulman, *Anyone Got a Match?*, p. 218, 1964
- He said the spyer was like a f-ing phantom, and he didn't know where he was. — James Ellroy, *White Jazz*, p. 184, 1992
- I want to stay here. I f'ing told you! — Mark Powell, *Snap*, p. 222, 2001

egg *noun*
1 a hand grenade *US, 1949*

- "Eggs. Looks like you've been carrying them around so long they're about hatched." — Audie Murphy, *To Hell and Back*, p. 19, 1949

2 a person *UK, 1864*
From "bad egg" (a rascal).

- He knows all the good eggs in boxing and all the bad ones. — *San Francisco Call Bulletin*, p. 14, 2nd March 1948
- Pictures of the "suspects," "the young desperadoes," "the tough young eggs." — Caryl Chessman, *Cell 2456 Death Row*, p. 205, 1954

- Besides, the Cafeteria was a popular place and the owner was a well egg who didn't deserve getting shook by a big pinch right in the middle of his rush hour. — Mickey Spillane, *Return of the Hood*, p. 79, 1964
- "Mike's a good egg. Alex is a good egg. Frankie is an awfully good egg. But who is the best egg?" "Who rattled your cage?" Alex said. "Don't ask," Mike said. — Guy Burt, *The Hole*, p. 56, 1993

3 a fool, especially an obnoxious fool *US, 1918*
Possibly derived from **YEGG** (a criminal).

- He could have a grand in his slid with most of it being one dollar bills and this egg would break a twenty just for a pack of cigarettes. — A.S. Jackson, *Gentleman Pimp*, p. 98, 1973

4 a white person who associates with, and takes on, the culture of south Asians *US, 1997*
The egg, like the person described, is white on the outside but yellow on the inside.

- — Pamela Munro, *U.C.L.A. Slang*, p. 62, 1997

5 a billiard ball *US, 1988*

- — Mike Shamos, *The Illustrated Encyclopedia of Billiards*, p. 85, 1993

6 a bomb *US, 1950*

- Disabled Bomber Dumps its "Eggs," Terrifies Canadians [Headline] — *San Francisco News*, p. 3, 11th November 1950
- [T]his man Smith did it right before the Menehunes came over form Japan and dropped their eggs on Pearl Harbor. — Frederick Kohner, *Gidget Goes Hawaiian*, p. 78, 1961

7 a pill or capsule *US, 1977*

- "I shoot three eggs tonight, then three in the morning before I leave." — John Allen, *Assault with a Deadly Weapon*, p. 198, 1977

8 a theatrical failure *US, 1952*

- I was going to lay the biggest and smelliest egg this town had ever seen. — Georgia Sothern, *My Life in Burlesque*, p. 108, 1972

eggbeater *noun*
1 a single-rotor helicopter *US, 1936*
Coined well before the war in Korea, but used extensively by US forces in Korea.

- Known by such nicknames as "choppers," "eggbeaters," "whirlybirds," and "airedales," helicopters were flown by a single pilot and had two external pods to carry wounded. — Stanley Sandler, *The Korean War*, p. 129, 1995

2 a twin-engine training plane *US, 1946*

- — *American Speech*, p. 310, December 1946: "More Air Force slang"

3 a bad head-over-skis fall while skiing *US, 1963*

- — *American Speech*, p. 205, October 1963: "The language of skiers"

egghead *noun*
1 an intellectual, often a scientist; a very smart person *US, 1918*

- Most frightening of all is the fact that American education is controlled by females and eunuchs—eggheads. — Lee Mortimer, *Women Confidential*, p. 94, 1960
- "Sure, Stew," he said, "all the eggheads are for Stevenson. But how many eggheads are there?" — *Saturday Evening Post*, p. 30, 8th September 1962
- In high school, I was an egghead who wrote poems. — Malcolm Boyd, *My Fellow Americans*, p. 144, 1970
- [Billy the Kid addressing Freud] Way to go, egghead. — *Bill and Ted's Excellent Adventure*, p. 85, 1989

2 a bald person *US, 1907*

- As for his head? It was completley bald. Clean shaven. A total egghead. — Vincent Zandri, *Godchild*, p. 249, 2000

eggheaded *adjective*
1 intellectual yet lacking common sense *US, 1956*

- I gushed, then froze because I realized—too late as usually—that I'd been too eager and too eggheaded. — Haywood Smith, *The Red Hat Club*, p. 38, 2003

2 bald *US, 1920*

- The two boys skated and stumbled to the next staircase and grabbed on, the larger one following the eggheaded one and running into him. — Richard Dry, *Leaving*, p. 370, 2002

eggplant *noun*
a black person *US, 1934*

- — Jim Goad, *Jim Goad's Glossary of Northwestern Prison Slang*, December 2001

eggs *noun*
the testicles *US, 1976*

- I mean, even if I whacked off your eggs, I don't think I'd really get to you. — Jack W. Thomas, *Heavy Number*, p. 162, 1976

eggsucker *noun*
a sycophant *US, 1838*

- My name is Vic, you little eggsucker. — Harlan Ellison, *A Boy and His Dog*, p. 971, 1969

egg-sucking *adjective*
despicable *US, 1845*

- This way you escape possible suspicion that you are an apple-polishing, bootlicking, egg-sucking, backscratching sycophant trying to win brownie points. — Leil Lowndes, *Talking the Winner's Way*, p. 192, 1999

ego surf *verb*
to search for mentions of your name on the Internet
US, 1997

- — Vann Wesson, *Generation X Field Guide and Lexicon*, p. 62, 1997

ego trip *noun*
any activity that is motivated by self-importance *US, 1967*

- All these people away on power trips and ego trips. I'm almost to the point of being sick of it, sick of being a Digger. — Nicholas Von Hoffman, *We Are The People Our Parents Warned Us Against*, p. 97, 1967
- Yet there is a way of integrating your own ego trip with a sense of community, with a concept of the "we." — Abbie Hoffman, *Woodstock Nation*, pp. 6–7, 1969
- It might be the radioworker who's on the ego trip. — John Sinclair, *Guitar Army*, p. 134, 1972
- The three most popular reasons given for appearing in porno films are money, a chance to stardom, and the old ego trip. — Stephen Ziplow, *The Film Maker's Guide to Pornography*, p. 43, 1977

egregious *adjective*
very bad *US, 1991*
Conventional English rendered slang by attitude and drawn-out pronunciation.

- — *USA Today*, p. 1D, 5th August 1991: "A sterling lexicon of the lingo"

Egypt *noun*
a neighborhood populated largely by black people *US, 1979*

- — *Maledicta*, p. 158, 1979: "A glossary of ethnic slurs in American English"

Egyptian love *noun*
bestiality or sadomasochism *US, 1964*

- "Roman," "Greek" and "Egyptian" love are, respectively, heterosexual, homosexual and bestial or sado-masochistic. — William and Jerrye Breedlove, *Swap Clubs*, p. 58, 1964

Egyptian queen *noun*
in homosexual usage, an attractive black man *US, 1986–1987*
An incorrect racial label.

- — *Maledicta*, p. 54, 1986–1987: "A continuation of a glossary of ethnic slurs in American English"

eight *noun*
1 heroin *US, 1997*
"H" is the 8th letter of the alphabet, and there is the phonetic connection to "H."

- — *Providence (Rhode Island) Journal-Bulletin*, p. 6B, 4th August 1997

2 one-eighth of an ounce of a drug *US, 1974*

- If we can find somebody Jackson's been selling the eights to, we might be able to get Wells inside to set him up for a buy[.] — Vernon E. Smith, *The Jones Men*, p. 125, 1974

eight and out *noun*
in pool, a win achieved by sinking all eight balls in a single turn *US, 1993*

- — Mike Shamos, *The Illustrated Encyclopedia of Billiards*, p. 85, 1993

eight ball *noun*
1 one eighth of an ounce *US, 1988*

- Detectives found $5,000 worth of cocaine in powdered form that had been packaged as "eightballs," or one-eighth ounces. — *The Record*, p. A40, 24th July 1988
- Had to be, Strike reasoned, because an eight ball—just three and a half grams—wouldn't be worth the risk of selling in such a public place. — Richard Price, *Clockers*, p. 110, 1992
- Tenner means one sixteenth of an ounce. One eighth is called a eightball. You ever do cringe? — Joseph Wambaugh, *Finnegan's Week*, p. 40, 1993

- We were forever finding wads and eightballs and little expensive things they had just plum forgotten about. — James St. James, *Party Monster*, p. 133, 1999

2 a discharge from the US Army for mental unfitness *US, 1968*
From the regulation AF 600–208.

- — Carl Fleischhauer, *A Glossary of Army Slang*, p. 18, 1968

3 Old English 800™ malt liquor *US, 1992*

- — Michael Small, *Break it Down*, p. 219, 1992: "Hip-hop dictionary"
- The usual group was there, listening to EAZY-E, chugging forty-ounce bottles of Old English 800—eightballs—and playing dominos. — Bob Sipchen, *Baby Insane and the Buddha*, p. 111, 1993
- — Connie Eble (Editor), *UNC-CH Campus Slang*, p. 11, Spring 1998

4 a dark-skinned black person *US, 1919*
The "eightball" in billiards is black.

- — Lou Shelly, *Hepcats Jive Dictionary*, p. 11, 1945
- An eight-ball like him sweet on a high-yaller gal will find out where Hitler is buried at. — Chester Himes, *A Rage in Harlem*, p. 148, 1957

5 a conventional, staid, unsophisticated person *US, 1970*

- — Clarence Major, *Dictionary of Afro-American Slang*, p. 50, 1970

eight-charge *noun*
eighty pounds of gunpowder in a satchel *US, 1991*

- Cpl. Tobias Rios, 27, of Elizabeth, N.J., rammed home an "eight-charge"—80 pounds of black powder trussed in a canvas satchel. — *Boston Globe*, p. 3, 29th January 1991

eighter from Decatur *noun*
in craps, a roll of eight *US, 1949*

- "There it was—Little Joe or Phoebe, Big Dick or Eighter from Decatur, double trey the hard way and dice be nice. — Nelson Algren, *The Man with the Golden Arm*, p. 11, 1949
- I listened for a moment to the snapping of their fingers, their low intent voices. "Eighter from Decatur!" — Chester Himes, *Cast the First Stone*, p. 134, 1952
- "Eighter from decatur, eighter from Decatur." He tosses the dice again and loses, a four and a three. — Darryl Ponicsan, *The Last Detail*, p. 12, 1970
- "Eighter from Decatur," Duffy shouted. "A winner." — Stephen Cannell, *Big Con*, p. 201, 1997

eight-pager *noun*
a small pornographic comic book that placed well-known world figures or comic book characters in erotic situations *US, 1961*

- It would be very difficult at Hanson Elementary living down probation for selling "eight-pagers." — Clancy Sigal, *Going Away*, p. 356, 1961
- The turning to "eight-pagers"—prison-made booklets consisting of crude, lewd pictures depicting both heterosexual and homosexual activity—appears to be, in effect, a securing of some sex satisfaction[.] — *New York Mattachine Newsletter*, p. 6, August 1961
- When I was in high school, those little comic sex books we called "Eight Pagers" were the vogue. — Angelo d'Arcangelo, *The Homosexual Handbook*, p. 186, 1968
- Buck was reading a copy of an eight-pager about TV's Hugh Downs and Barbara Walters and, instead of pictures about discussions, poverty, pollution and revolutions, they were heavy into orgies. — Steve Cannon, *Groove, Bang, and Jive Around*, p. 142, 1969

eighty *noun*
eighty dollars worth of crack cocaine *US, 2003*

- When an undercover detective asked the 50-year-old Dean what he wanted, the chamber head allegedly said he was looking to buy some "80"—street slang for $80 worth of crack cocaine. — *Los Angeles Times*, p. 1 (Part 2), 23rd July 2003

eighty-deuce *nickname*
the 82nd Airborne Division, US Army *US, 1984*

- "I just came from the 82nd," he replied, "and now we're going to be screwing around in swamps in Georgia and the eight-deuce is going to be in Cuba." — Jim Morris, *War Story*, p. 84, 2000

eighty-eight *noun*
a piano *US, 1942*
From the 88 keys on a standard piano.

- And the gate that rocked at the eighty-eight was blowin' "How High the Moon." — William "Lord" Buckley, *The Ballad of Dan McGroo*, 1960
- "Real fine eighty-eight-box, man," Red commented, brushing his sleeve over the Steinway. — Ross Russell, *The Sound*, p. 188, 1961

eighty-eighter *noun*
a piano player *US, 1949*
Drawn from the number of keys on a piano.

- It was just a debut gig for another eighty-eighter. — Arnold Shaw, *52nd Street, the Street of Jazz*, p. 291, 1977

eighty-five *noun*
a girlfriend *US, 2001*

- They're threatening you with murder because Ray's wife was your eight-five. — Stephen J. Cannell, *The Tin Collectors*, p. 174, 2001

eighty niggers and two white men *nickname*
the 82nd Airborne Division, US Army *US, 1984*
During the Vietnam war, it was perceived that the 82nd Division enjoyed an above-average black population.

- — John Robert Elting, *A Dictionary of Soldier Talk*, p. 96, 1984

eighty-one mike mike *noun*
an 81mm medium extended-range mortar, found in the mortar platoon of an infantry battalion *US, 1991*

- One of the Seal Two lieutenants, Larry Bailey, took command of a Mike boat—an armored Landing Craft, Medium, or LCM which held an 81 mike-mike. — Richard Marcinko, *Rogue Warrior*, p. 83, 1992
- Three mortars. 81 mike-mike, looks like. A couple of boxes of mortar ammo — H. Jay Riker, *Seals*, p. 203, 1997

eighty-six; eight-six *noun*
an order barring a person from entering a bar or other establishment *US, 1943*

- I take the offender aside and warn him that another complaint will result in an eighty-six. — Helen P. Branson, *Gay Bar*, pp. 88–89, 1957
- [T]wo other versions of the Eighty-Six exist. — Bill Cardoso, *The Maltese Sangweech*, p. 149, 1984

eighty-six; eight-six *verb*
to eject; to bar from entry *US, 1948*

- The Alcoholic Beverage Control Board eighty-sixed two Ninth St. grog centers yesterday—cut off their taps. — *Washington Post*, p. M1, 1st February 1948
- "Shut your nelly mouth, Mary," said the Negro queen—"or I'll have you eight-sixed out of this bar[.]" — John Rechy, *City of Night*, p. 186, 1963
- Another journalist was eighty-sixed for being too sympathetic. — Hunter S. Thompson, *Hell's Angels*, p. 201, 1966
- Hey, I been eighty-sixed out of better situations 'n that. — George V. Higgins, *The Rat on Fire*, p. 77, 1981

elbow *noun*
a pound of marijuana *US, 1995*
A phonetic rendition of the abbreviation "lb" (pound).

- Fay allegedly asked for an "elbo," or street slang for a pound of marijuana. — *Times Union (Albany, New York)*, p. B4, 26th July 1997
- Little Italian dude from Nawlin's bring me up an elbow every couple a weeks. — *Hustle and Flow*, 2004

elbow-bending *noun*
immoderate consumption of alcohol *US, 1934*

- Leave it to the 20-somethings to break in Arizona's extra hour of elbow bending. While millions of Arizonans slept, thousands of young bar warriors strapped on their beer goggles until 2 a.m. Wednesday[.] — *Arizona Republic*, p. 1B, 26th August 2004

elbow-bending *adjective*
drinking to excess *US, 2002*

- Western bands twang happily in the St. Charles Saloon as elbow-bending good old boys raise a little harmless hell. — Don W. Martin, *The Best of San Francisco*, p. 268, 2002

elbow grease *noun*
hard manual labor; effort *UK, 1672*

- "I'd start with a little 'elbow grease.'" Norine looked absently around her. "Scrub the floor, you mean?" — Mary McCarthy, *The Group*, p. 140, 1963

elbow-tit *verb*
to graze or strike an unknown female's breast with your elbow *US, 1974*

- Anyways, he bumps into this fat lady an' starts elbow tittin. — Richard Price, *The Wanderers*, p. 88, 1974

elder days *noun*
in computing, the years before 1980 *US, 1991*

A conscious borrowing from Tolkien.

- — Eric S. Raymond, *The New Hacker's Dictionary*, p. 140, 1991

El Dog *noun*
a Cadillac El Dorado car *US, 1975*

- — Carl J. Banks Jr., *Banks Dictionary of the Black Ghetto Language*, 1975

electric *adjective*
augmented with LSD *US, 1967*

- [A]s in electric banana or electric Kool-Aid (Kook-Aid spiked with LSD)[.] — Ruth Bronsteen, *The Hippy's Handbook*, p. 13, 1967
- I checked my bag—one Yippie film, ten copies of Fuck the System; Mao's little red book; recipes for Molotov cocktails, electric Koolaid and digger stew... — Abbie Hoffman, *Woodstock Nation*, p. 33, 1969
- ELECTRIC: containing psychedelics, usually LSD. — Robert Buckhout, *Toward Social Change*, p. 465, 1971

electrician *noun*
a person who provokes or accelerates a confrontation *US, 1998*

- — Ethan Hilderbrant, *Prison Slang*, p. 44, 1998

Electric Strawberry *nickname*
the 25th Infantry Division, US Army *US, 1991*
The Division's insignia is a green taro leaf in a red circle, suggesting a strawberry.

- The group is the Twenty-fifth Infantry Division, nicknamed the Electric Strawberry. — Sharyn McCrumb, *If Ever I Return*, p. 110, 1990

elegant *adjective*
1 (used of a homosexual male) polished, effete *US, 1949*

- Elegant—Adjective used for homosexual who prides himself on his higher social level, as regards behavior, haunts, friends, conversation, etc., in comparison with his more sordid brethren. — Anon., *The Gay Girl's Guide*, p. 8, 1949
- — Bruce Rodgers, *The Queens' Vernacular*, p. 75, 1972

2 in computing, simple yet extremely efficient *US, 1990*

- — Karla Jennings, *The Devouring Fungus*, p. 220, 1990

elephant *noun*
a high-ranking Naval officer *US, 1986*
US naval aviator usage.

- — *United States Naval Institute Proceedings*, p. 108, October 1986

elephant gun *noun*
1 any powerful rifle *US, 1918*

- The first time I fired it, I was tensed up for a real jaw-shaking, something much worse than a .458 Winchester Magnum elephant gun. — John Plaster, *Ultimate Snipe*, p. 160, 1993

2 an M79 grenade launcher *US, 1964*
Vietnam war usage. It is a single-shot, break-open, breech-loading, shoulder-fired weapon.

- Then turned to with M-16 automatic rifles, M-79 "elephant gun" grenade launchers, and expert fire with M-60 machine guns. — Richard Tregaskis, *Southeast Asia*, p. 380, 1975
- — *Solider of Fortune*, p. 57, July 1992
- Scharne snatched the elephant gun, which looks like a king-size single-barrel shotgun, and broke open the breech. — Robin Moore, *The Green Berets*, p. 208, 2007

3 a surfboard designed for big-wave conditions *US, 1963*

- — Grant W. Kuhns, *On Surfing*, p. 116, 1963

Elephants' Graveyard *nickname*
the Boston Naval District headquarters *US, 1971*

- The form requested a transfer "for personal reasons" to a lackluster staff job at the Boston Naval District headquarters, "the Elephants' Graveyard" in Navy slang. — Neil Sheehan, *The Arnheiter Affair*, p. 10, 1971

elephant tranquillizer; elephant *noun*
phencyclidine, the recreational drug known as PCP or angel dust *US, 2004*

- — Hillsborough County (Florida) Sheriff's Office, www.hcso.tampa.fl.us, 2005

elevator *noun*
a false cut of a deck of playing cards *US, 1991*

- — Michael Dalton, *Blackjack*, p. 45, 1991

eleven *noun*
in a deck of playing cards, a jack or knave *US, 1996*

- — John Vorhaus, *The Big Book of Poker Slang*, p. 15, 1996

eleven bang-bang *noun*
an infantry soldier *US, 1980*
11-B was the numerical MOS code assigned to an infantry soldier.

- And what can they do to him? Send him to Nam? He's eleven bang-bang. Mortars. He's going to Nam all right. — Richard Seltzer, *Spit and Polish*, 1996
- His military job specialty is 11-B, or as some here call it, "11-bang-bang." In other words, Sharp is a rifleman, assigned to Company A, 2nds Brigade, 327th Infantry. — *Lexington (Kentucky) Herald Leader*, p. A1, 12th February 2003

eleven bravo *noun*
an infantry soldier *US, 1991*

- And in contrast with that, 11 Bravo, there are 18 infantrymen being called and 21 infantry officers, 11 Alpha. — *Meeting of the House Armed Services Committee*, 7th July 2004

eleven bush *noun*
an infantry soldier *US, 1970*

- Sure, lead the armor and look for traps. What are 11 bushes for anyway? — Stan Lee, *The 'Nam*, p. 21, 1987
- I began to wonder if they weren't in the market for a radio operator, but perhaps just looking for Eleven-Bushes (11-B the standard infantry MOS). — Don Ericson, *Charlie Rangers*, pp. 43–44, 1989

eleven-foot pole *noun*
an imagined device for touching someone whom another would not touch with a ten-foot pole *US, 1975*

- — John Gould, *Maine Lingo*, p. 85, 1975

eleven from heaven *noun*
a roll of eleven in a craps game *US, 1957*

- "Natural eleven!" the stick man sang. "Eleven from heaven. The winner!" — Chester Himes, *A Rage in Harlem*, p. 27, 1957

eleventh commandment *noun*
any rule which is seen as a mandatory guideline on a par with the Ten Commandments *US, 1975*
A term probably coined by Ronald Reagan and applied to his adage that no Republican (except him) should disparage another Republican. Eventually applied, often jocularly, to many different situations. For example: the mythical commandment but very real criminal code—thou shalt not get caught.

- — Troy Harris, *A Booklet of Criminal Argot, Cant and Jargon*, p. 9, 1976

elf *noun*
a technical market analyst *US, 1986*

- — Rachel S. Epstein and Nina Liebman, *Biz Speak*, p. 72, 1986

el foldo *noun*
an utter, relentless collapse *US, 1943*

- "We'll have to put up with Pitt again—Pitt, which has consistently done the greatest el foldo of all the teams ever to play in Pasadena." — Rube Samuelson, *The Rose Bowl Game*, p. 142, 1951
- I did a bunk from picking and rode for the Baker Brothers Show till it went el foldo." — Stephen Longstreet, *The Flesh Peddlers*, p. 53, 1962
- Honorable mention to NBC Sports boss Dick Ebersol for pulling an El Foldo and televising all future NASCAR events on a five-second delay. — *Daily News (New York)*, p. 98, 10th October 2004

Eli *nickname*
Yale University; a Yale student; a Yale sports team *US, 1879*

- He starred for the Eli hockey, baseball, and football teams and was captain of the skaters in 1926–27. — Daniel K. Fleschner, *Bulldogs on Ice*, p. 16, 2003

Eli Lilly *noun*
morphine *US, 1955*
From the drug manufacturer's name.

- — *American Speech*, p. 87, May 1955: "Narcotic argot along the Mexican border"

elite *adjective*
in the world of Internet discussion groups, offering the illegal *US, 1997*

- [A]n "elite" BBS would be a BBS which features pirated software, utilities for cracking passwords, lists of stolen credit card numbers, phreak files, etc. — Andy Ihnatko, *Cyberspeak*, p. 62, 1997

El Lay *noun*
Los Angeles, California *US, 1951*

- One message read: "Hello, El Lay; Hello, El Lay – We left Some Reds For You To Slay." — *Los Angeles Times*, p. 7, 8th June 1951
- Her roots extend much farther south of the border than those of her El Lay chicano fan base. — *Playboy*, p. 17, July 2006

Elmer *noun*
in circus and carnival usage, an unsophisticated, gullible local *US, 1926*

- — Don Wilmeth, *The Language of American Popular Entertainment*, p. 84, 1981

El Producto *noun*
oil *US, 1980s*
Texan.

- — Ken Weaver, *Texas Crude*, 1984

El Ropo *noun*
any cheap cigar *US, 1960*
Mock Spanish.

- "You're supposed to flush that, not smoke it," he says, eyeing a hood's El Ropo cigar. — Richard Schickel, *Clint Eastwood*, p. 397, 1996

El Smoggo; El Stinko *nickname*
El Paso, Texas *US, 1970*
A tribute to the city's air quality.

- — *Current Slang*, p. 17, Spring 1970

Elvis *noun*
a poker player who is nearly broke but manages to stay in a game far longer than one would predict *US, 1996*
Like Elvis Presley, the poker player refuses to die.

- — John Vorhaus, *The Big Book of Poker Slang*, p. 15, 1996

elzoo *noun*
scouting, surveillance *US, 1952*

- "You got anybody giving the joint the elzoo?" — Harry Grey, *The Hoods*, p. 102, 1952

E-man *noun*
a police officer assigned to the Emergency Service Unit *US, 1997*
New York police slang.

- — Samuel M. Katz, *Anytime Anywhere*, p. 387, 1997: "The extremely unofficial and completely off-the-record NYPD/ESU truck-two glossary"

embalmed *adjective*
very drunk *US, 1934*

- Oh and your mother's pickled, Evan. I mean I've seen her drunk before, but this is different: she's embalmed. — Richard Yates, *Cold Spring Harbor*, p. 156, 1986

embalmed beef *noun*
canned beef *US, 1898*
A term most strongly associated with profiteers during the Spanish–American war; mostly historical use.

- At one rally, a heckler asked him about the "embalmed beef" scandal of the Spanish war, in which (presumably Republican) suppliers foisted tainted meat off on the soldiers. — H.W. Brands, *T.R.*, p. 403, 1997

embalming fluid *noun*
phencyclidine, the recreational drug known as PCP or angel dust *US, 1992*

- — Jay Robert Nash, *Dictionary of Crime*, p. 116, 1992
- But "embalming fluid" is an old street slang term for PCP, Lawrence said. "There is some confusion about what people are really doing," Lawrence said. — *Cincinnati Enquirer*, p. 6A, 4th December 2003

embroidery *noun*
the punctures and sores visible on an intravenous drug user's body *US, 1973*

- — David Maurer and Victor Vogel, *Narcotics and Narcotic Addiction*, p. 405, 1973

emby *noun*
in carnival usage, a gullible player *US, 1985*

- — Gene Sorrows, *All About Carnivals*, p. 16, 1985: "Terminology"

EM club *noun*
an enlisted men's club *US, 1977*

- We sat in the EM Club that night while he told us, smiling and laughing his little laugh[.] — Larry Heinemann, *Close Quarters*, p. 97, 1977

Eme *noun*
the Mexican Mafia, a Mexican-American prison gang *US, 1978*

From the Spanish pronunciation of the letter "M."

- The "M" (or "eme," originally meaning "Mafia" but soon to be glorified as "El Mejicano Encarcelado") accepted this as a challenge and stepped up their attacks. — Joan W. Moore, *Homeboys*, p. 115, 1978
- [I]n the pen, both being members of urban barrio gangs, they automatically became members of La Eme, the so-called Mexican Mafia, and were now sworn carnales, the Hispanic term for homeboys. — Seth Morgan, *Homeboy*, p. 176, 1990
- They called themselves the Mexican Mafia, or La EME. — Bob Sipchen, *Baby Insane and the Buddha*, p. 166, 1993
- These terms were being seen with greater frequency, thrown up as graffiti throughout California's prisons along with the numeral 13, which signifies the letter M, or more precisely, La eMe. — Bill Valentine, *Gangs and Their Tattoos*, p. 23, 2000

emeffing *adjective*
used as a euphemism for "motherfucking" *US, 1958*

- Them emeffing guards is bringing it in fountain pens, selling it like hot dogs at the ball game. — Willard Motley, *Let No Man Write My Epitaph*, p. 120, 1958

Emely *noun*
the Mexican Mafia, a Mexican-American prison gang *US, 1975*

- — Report to the Senate, *California Senate Committee on Civil Disorder*, p. 227, 1975

emergency gun *noun*
an improvised method to puncture the skin and inject a drug *US, 1973*

- — David Maurer and Victor Vogel, *Narcotics and Narcotic Addiction*, p. 405, 1973

empty suit *noun*
a person of no substance *US, 1990*

- The nastiest description of the Saints is "empty suits." — *Washington Post*, p. E5, 24th October 1980
- Bush wasn't the word-scrambling empty suit that he sometimes appeared to be in front of cameras. — *Orlando (Florida) Sentinel*, p. G3, 10th October 2004

encounter studio *noun*
used as a euphemism for a brothel or a business where some degree of sexual activity is for sale *US, 1987*

- Then I read on: "massage parlors, encounter studios, escort services, pornography, street prostitution, as well as other areas of sex work." — Frederique Delacoste, *Sex Work*, p. 99, 1987

end *noun*

1 a share or portion *US, 1887*

- I say I'm not waiting. I want my end. — Malcolm Braly, *On the Yard*, p. 235, 1967
- Several years ago, Beano had sent her his end of a two-month land swindle to pay for her nursing school. — Stephen Cannell, *King Con*, p. 56, 1997

2 the best; an extreme *UK, 1938*

- "Buster," said Red gratefully, "your timing was like the end, ya know?" — Steve Allen, *Bop Fables*, p. 49, 1955
- Nothin can touch the 47 Continental convertible. They're the end. — Hubert Selby Jr., *Last Exit to Brooklyn*, p. 28, 1957
- Of course, the girls think it's the end—but these are the kinds of minutes you go through when you let your hair down. — Herbert Huncke, *Guilty of Everything*, p. 145, 1990

3 the penis *US, 1957*

- You wanna get your end wet, call me. I got broads. — Max Shulman, *Rally Round the Flag, Boys!*, p. 190, 1957

4 money *US, 1960*

- — John R. Armore and Joseph D. Wolfe, *Dictionary of Desperation*, p. 28, 1976

endo *noun*

1 a backwards fall off a surfboard *US, 1988*

- — Michael V. Anderson, *The Bad, Rad, Not to Forget Way Cool Beach and Surf Discriptionary*, p. 6, 1988

2 in the television and movie industry, any stunt in which a vehicle goes through the air end-over-end *US, 2003*

- — John Cann, *The Stunt Guide*, p. 58: "Terms and definitions"

endo *verb*
while bicycling, to flip end-over-end *US, 2002*

- I jump onto the seat, just in time so that I don't endo, that is fly ass over tits across the handlebars through the intersection. — Lynn Breedlove, *Godspeed*, p. 24, 2002

end of discussion
used as a humorous, if stock, indication that there is nothing more to be said on the subject at hand *US, 1987*

- End of discussion. We're gonna wait. — *Lethal Weapon*, 1987

end of nowhere *noun*
any very remote location *US, 1970*

- He thought it was at the very end of nowhere, filled with honky tonks and little better than the cesspool of Snyder — H.G. Bissiner, *Friday Night Lights*, p. 367, 2000

end of story
used as a way to indicate that all that needs to be told has been told, all that needs to be said has been said *US, 1999*
Often jocular.

- Mrs. Mohra heard about the homicides out here and she thought I should call it in, so I called it in. End of story. — *Fargo*, 1996
- [G]row up will you—it's over, end of fucking story[.] — Patrick Jones, *Unprotected Sex*, p. 240, 1999

end of watch *noun*
death *US, 1983*

- The thought of finally going end-of-watch as the result of something as relentless as lung cancer scared the crap out of Mario Villalobos. — Joseph Wambaugh, *The Delta Star*, p. 40, 1983

ends *noun*

1 cash in hand *US, 2001*

- — Don R. McCreary (Editor), *Dawg Speak*, 2001

2 a rich customer of a prostitute *US, 1986–1987*

- — *Maledicta*, p. 150, Summer/Winter 1986–1987: "Sexual slang: prostitutes, pedophiles, flagellators, transvestites, and necrophiles"

endsville *noun*

1 the end *US, 1962*

- I hope this book will inspire other people the way I was inspired by him in my life. Endsville. — Douglas Nason and Greg Escalante, *Rat Fink*, p. 106, 2003

2 the best *US, 1957*

- [A] large buffet, always laden with endsville goodies, mostly to eat. — Terry Southern, *Riding the Lapping Tongue*, 1973

3 the worst *US, 2003*

- As a convention town, this is strictly Endsville. — Jonathan Van Meter, *The Last Good Time*, p. 200, 2003

Ene *nickname*

1 the Northern Structure prison gang *US, 1995*
Spanish for the letter "N" used by English speakers in the American southwest.

- — Bill Valentine, *Gang Intelligence Manual*, p. 41, 1995: "Hispanic gang terminology"

2 a member of the Nuestra Familia prison gang *US, 1950*

- — George Carpenter Baker, *Pachuco*, p. 41, January 1950
- — Bill Valentine, *Gangs and Their Tattoos*, p. 36, 2000

enema queen *noun*
a male homosexual with an enema fetish *US, 1969*

- I have found that a large percentage of my discipline cases are enema queens. — *Screw*, p. 7, 20th October 1969

Enema Sue; Enema Zoo *nickname*
New Mexico State University *US, 1970*
A cheerful play on the initials NMSU.

- — *Current Slang*, p. 17, Spring 1970

enforcer *noun*
a criminal who uses violence or intimidation to enforce the will of a criminal gang *US, 1929*

- — Edward J. MacKenzie, *Street Soldier*, 2003

en fuego!
used as a humorous observation that somebody is performing very well *US, 1997*
Coined and popularized by ESPN's Dan Patrick; probably the most widely used of the ESPN-spawned catchphrases.

- — Pamela Munro, *U.C.L.A. Slang*, p. 80, 1997
- — Keith Olberman and Dan Patrick, *The Big Show*, p. 14, 1997
- — Connie Eble (Editor), *UNC-CH Campus Slang*, p. 3, April 1997

engine *noun*
the first participant in serial sex *US, 1997*

More common was the spontaneous act of gang sex: "pulling a train" on a drunken girl at the party—the boy's rank in the gang determined if he was the engine, the caboose, or somewhere in between[.] — Gini Sikes, *8 Ball Chicks*, p. 103, 1997

▸ **on the engine**
(used of a racehorse) well in front in a race *US, 1994*
- — Igor Kushyshyn et al., *The Gambling Times Guide to Harness Racing*, p. 115, 1994

engineer *noun*
the first active participant in serial sex with a single passive partner *US, 1975*
- Carolina Moon announced that she was going to take her blanket into the bushes and pull the train. "I'm first! I'm the engineer!" cried Harold Bloomguard. — Joseph Wambaugh, *The Choirboys*, p. 333, 1975

engine room *noun*
the mid-boat rowers in an eight-person racing shell *US, 1949*
- She wears a microphone attached to speakers so she can communicate with the middle of the boat, "the engine room," and the bow. — *San Francisco Chronicle*, p. D1, 16th August 2004

English *noun*
in pool, spin imparted on the cue ball to affect the course of the object ball or the cue ball after striking the object ball *US, 1869*
- You had a lot of English on it. It was rolling right for the pocket. — Max Shulman, *The Zebra Derby*, p. 54, 1946
- "More high left english," he advised the kid who was sighting for his shot. — Irving Shulman, *Cry Tough*, p. 81, 1949

English massage *noun*
sex with a sadistic character *US, 1973*
- "English massages? I don't think I know much about them," I said. — Jennifer Sills, *Massage Parlor*, p. 169, 1973

English method *noun*
the rubbing of the penis between the thighs of another boy or man until reaching orgasm *US, 1986–1987*
More commonly known in the US as the "Princeton Rub."
- — *Maledicta*, p. 54, 1986–1987: "A continuation of a glossary of ethnic slurs in American English"

English muffins *noun*
in homosexual usage, a boy's buttocks *US, 1986–1987*
- — *Maledicta*, p. 54, 1986–1987: "A continuation of a glossary of ethnic slurs in American English"

English return *noun*
dead silence after what was supposed to be a funny joke *US, 1951*
- The unlaugh, or monstrous silence; also known as the English Return. — *Everybody's Digest*, p. 21, September 1951

enit?
don't you know? *US, 1998*
One of the very few Native American expressions used by English-speaking Native Americans.
- Grandma: A good name. It means he's going to win, enit? — *Smoke Signals*, 1998

enjoy!
used as a benediction by restaurant waiters, and then mimicked in other contexts *US, 1995*
- Yeah, yeah. Enjoy. — *Casino*, 1995
- The keg's back there. Enjoy! — *American Pie*, 1999

enlisted swine *noun*
an enlisted soldier *US, 1986*
- They don't let enlisted swine fly. What they had me doing was writing the written parts. — W.E.B. Griffin, *Speical Ops (Brotherhood of War)*, p. 76, 2001
- You can't imagine what that will do for a military career of even someone who came up the "enlisted swine" route. — John Pehlham, *Sex Ring in a Small Town*, p. 13, 2005

envelope *noun*
1 a cash bribe *US, 1973*
- — Vincent Teresa, *My Life in the Mafia*, p. 360, 1973: A Glossary of Mob Terminology
2 a condom *US, 1964*
- — Roger Blake, *The American Dictionary of Sexual Terms*, p. 66, 1964

3 an airplane's performance limits *US, 1990*
- If that failed, McKeown would deliberately "depart" the plane (take it outside its flight envelope) as a last resort maneuver. — Robert K. Wilcox, *Scream of Eagles*, p. 140, 1990

EOT *adjective*
dead *US, 1998*
- A D.O.A. is someone who's gone E.O.T., end of tour. — *The New Yorker*, p. 35, 10th August 1998

EPA *nickname*
East Palo Alto, San Mateo County, California *US, 2000*
A black ghetto surrounded by Silicon Valley wealth.
- Curiously, the 18th Street gangsters, who have definite roots in the L.A. area, nevertheless claim norte while bangin' in EPA. — Bill Valentine, *Gangs and Their Tattoos*, p. 112, 2000
- Needless to say, East Palo Alto (EPA) has gotten it share of the inner-city blues. — Adrienne Anderson, *Word*, p. 65, 2003

epic *adjective*
excellent, outstanding *US, 1957*
- "What he was doing was epic." — Glendon Swarthout, *Where the Boys Are*, p. 25, 1960
- — *USA Today*, 29 September 1983
- — Judi Sanders, *Faced and Faded, Hanging to Hurl*, p. 14, 1993

epidoddle *noun*
epidural anesthesia *US, 1994*
- — Sally Williams, *"Strong" Words*, p. 140, 1994

eppis *noun*
nothing *US, 1966*
- — *American Speech*, p. 280, December 1966: "More carnie talk from the West Coast"

epsilon *noun*
a very small amount *US, 1983*
- — Guy L. Steele et al., *The Hacker's Dictionary*, p. 60, 1983

EPT *nickname*
El Paso, Texas *US, 1974*
- — Dagoberto Fuentes and Jose Lopez, *Barrio Language Dictionary*, p. 60, 1974
- In EPT, the opportunities in my field were nonexistent. — Jose Antonio Burciaga, *Drink Cultura*, p. 28, 1993

equalizer *noun*
a gun or any object that can be used in a fight *US, 1899*
Not without irony.
- "He ain't go' do nothin' t'me, not long as I got my equalizer." He patted his stomach, where a small .22 automatic pistol was hidden[.] — Nathan Heard, *Howard Street*, p. 86–87, 1968
- Why do we have to split with him? I've got the equalizer stuck in my belt for those big muscles he's got. — Iceberg Slim (Robert Beck), *Trick Baby*, p. 164, 1969
- "Don't worry. I got a new equalizer." He bought a new 12 gauge from Big T[.] — Colton Simpson, *Inside the Crips*, p. 36, 2005

equator *noun*
the waist *US, 1948*
- You dames with wide circumferences should not rumba. If you must, please don't quake below the equator. — Jack Lait and Lee Mortimer, *New York Confidential*, p. 237, 1948

equipped *adjective*
stylish and fashionable *US, 1972*
- — David Claerbaut, *Black Jargon in White America*, p. 63, 1972

E-ring *adjective*
high-ranking *US, 1986*
Military usage. Refers to the "E-ring" of the Pentagon where high-ranking officers work.
- — Department of the Army, *Staff Officer's Guidebook*, p. 60, 1986

-erino *suffix*
used as a suffix to create humorous variants understood from their base *US, 1890s*
- Well, Steverino, this looks like where I get off and join another trolley. — Odie Hawkins, *Great Lawd Buddha*, p. 85, 1990

erky-dirk *noun*
a shirt *US, 1972*
A rare instance of American rhyming slang.
- I would put on a clean fiddle and an erky-dirk. — Robert Byrne, *McGoorty*, p. 147, 1972

-eroo *suffix*
used as a meaningless embellishment; also used to intensify *US, 1931*

- Thieves, embezzlers and coneroos, all might redeem themselves in time. — Nelson Algren, *The Man with the Golden Arm*, p. 298, 1949
- A smasheroo she was—a real zinger. — Max Shulman, *I was a Teen-Age Dwarf*, p. 8, 1959
- My famous one-two, learned from Myron: first, excessive flattery with a grain of truth swatched in cultured nacre; then the lethal puncheroo. — Gore Vidal, *Myra Breckinridge*, p. 51, 1968
- Glenn made Jack feel as he had around his stepfather—a master barroom conneroo who would afterwards deride those who always stood him a drink[.] — Earl Thompson, *Tattoo*, p. 227, 1974

-erooni; -eroony *suffix*
used as a decorative intensifier *US, 1966*

- The golfers are suspicious that this is another Joe Alioto zingeroony. — *San Francisco Examiner*, p. 35, 8th August 1972
- A Smasherooni!—Eliot Fremont-Smith of the Village Voice — *San Francisco Examiner*, p. 11, 21st September 1975
- "People said the same thing about 'Superstar,'" Rice says, while Webber points to "Evita's" enormous success in England, where reviewers have called it "Another smasheroonie." — *San Francisco Chronicle*, p. 38, 3rd February 1977
- Busy schedulerooni na mean [know what I mean]. — Nick Barlay, *Curvy Lovebox*, p. 71, 1997

erp *verb*
to vomit *US, 1968*

- — Collin Baker et al., *College Undergraduate Slang Study Conducted at Brown University*, p. 112, 1968

escort service *noun*
a prostitution business operating euphemistically under the guise of providing an escort, not a prostitute *US, 1982*

- Another woman runs an "escort" service on the side, sometimes using her own mansion when her husband is gone. — Kent Smith et al., *Adult Movies*, p. 180, 1982
- Then I read on: "massage parlors, encounter studios, escort services, pornography, street prostitution, as well as other areas of sex work." — Frederique Delacoste, *Sex Work*, p. 99, 1987

ese *noun*
used as a term of address to a young male; an aware, street-wise young man *US, 1950*
Border Spanish used in English conversation by Mexican-Americans.

- — George Carpenter Baker, *Pachuco*, p. 41, January 1950
- "What'd you get into this morning, ese?" — Malcom Braly, *Felony Tank*, p. 44, 1961
- Shit, ese. I mean just one joint. — Oscar Zeta Acosta, *The Revolt of the Cockroach People*, p. 120, 1973
- "Say you've got twenty brothers and esseys in your unit." — Bob Sipchen, *Baby Insane and the Buddha*, p. 92, 1993

Eskimo *noun*
a Jewish person *US, 1989.*

- I have no plausible evidence as to why the perjorative code word for "Jew" was/is/became "Eskimo." — Leo Rosten, *The Joy of Yinglish*, p. 152, 1989

Eskimo pie *noun*
the vagina of a frigid woman *US, 1977*

- — *Maledicta*, p. 17, Summer 1977: "A word for it!"

Eskimo roll *noun*
a maneuver used by surfers to pass through a wave coming at them by rolling under their surfboard *US, 1977*

- — Gary Fairmont R. Filosa II, *The Surfer's Almanac*, p. 185, 1977

Eskimo sisters *noun*
women who have at some point had sex with the same man *US, 1994*
Used as the title of a 2002 play by Laline Paull.

- Their shared experience made them "Eskimo sisters," united by the fact that they had both slept with the same guy. — Anka Radakovich, *The Wild Girls Club*, p. 6, 1994

Esky *noun*
an Eskimo *US, 1978*

- — *Maledicta*, p. 156, Summer/Winter 1978: "How to hate thy neighbor: a guide to racist maledicta"

essence *noun*
MDMA, the recreational drug best known as ecstasy *US, 1998*

- Street names [...] E, Edward, essence, fantasy[.] — James Kay and Julian Cohen, *The Parents' Complete Guide to Young People and Drugs*, p. 136, 1998
- — *Miramonte High School Parents Club Newsletter (Orinda, California)*, p. 1, 26th November 2001

establishment *noun*
the dominant power in any society *UK, 1955*

- He said, break into the Establishment, and that he was about three quarters inclined to try it. — Clancy Sigal, *Going Away*, p. 243, 1961
- Here is a list of names, those who constitute the real creme de la creme of Los Angeles power and influence. This is "the establishment." — *Los Angeles Free Press*, p. 2, 22nd October 1964
- Damn the Establishment! — Murray Kaufman, *Murray the K Tells It Like It Is, Baby*, p. 57, 1966
- And they knew that ultimately the establishment would love to lock me up and throw away the key until that fatal day of execution. — Bobby Seale, *A Lonely Rage*, p. 269, 1978

esthole *noun*
an enthusiastic supporter of the est human growth movement *US, 1997*
An appropriate play on "asshole."

- Term originated from enlightening program sessions where the leader would challenge an initiate by referring to him or her as an asshole. — Editors of Ben is Dead, *Retrohell*, p. 69, 1997
- I enjoyed it quite a bit and managed to avoid being an "esthole." — William O'Hanlon, *Evolving Possibilities*, p. 125, 1999
- It beat primal screaming or being yelled at in a crowded motel ballroom by some esthole. — Judith Van Gieson, *The Wolf Path*, p. 23, 2006

e-tard *noun*
a person whose life has been adversely effected by excessive use of MDMA *US, 2001*

- — Pamela Munro, *U.C.L.A. Slang*, p. 65, 2001

E Team *noun*
in the language of hang gliding, expert fliers from Lake Elsinore, California *US, 1992*

- — Erik Fair, *California Thrill Sports*, p. 328, 1992

ethanolic *noun*
a drunkard *US, 1978*

- — *Maledicta*, p. 68, Summer/Winter 1978: "Common patient-directed pejoratives used by medical personnel"

E to E *noun*
a piece of graffiti art stretching from one end to the other of a subway car *US, 1982*

- Often two writers share in the creation of an E-to-E, painting together and sharing materials in order that their names will appear as a single unified work. — Craig Castleman, *Getting Up*, p. 35, 1982

E-tool *noun*
an entrenching tool with an extendable telescopic handle and folding blade *US, 1976*

- Then you grab your E-tool and hit me in the foot, right here real hard, see? — Charles Anderson, *The Grunts*, p. 93, 1976
- "But we don't have any more machetes." "They can use their e-tools, damn it!" — Robert A. Anderson, *Cooks & Bakers*, p. 90, 1982

euphoria *noun*
the illegal drug 4-methylaminorex, a relatively uncommon central nervous system stimulant *US, 2005*

- Fort Lauderdale Police officers and Drug Enforcement Administration (DEA) agents responding to an anonymous tip seized an operational laboratory used to make three illegal drugs—4-methylaminorex (also known as U4Euh, euphoria, and intellex)[.] — *Microgram Bulletin (DEA)*, p. 31, February 2005

Eurotrash *noun*
rich foreigners living in the US *US, 1980*
Taki Theodoracopulos popularized the term in society columns written for *Vanity Fair* and the *Spectator*.

- Stuff like crucifixes covered in reptile skin: from his hands to Eurotrash necks. — Jim Carroll, *Forced Entries*, p. 7, 1987
- So Dan booked them a moldy suite at this crumbling relic frequented, as far as she could tell, by Eurotrash with black socks and sandals. — Seth Morgan, *Homeboy*, p. 232, 1990

evac *noun*
an evacuation *US, 1954*
- "For the medical evacs," Moser said, "a pilot had to come in perpendicular to the ridge." — Dandridge M. Malone, *Small Unit Leadership*, p. 107, 1983

evac *verb*
to evacuate *US, 1944*
- "I'll draw them off. Evac your people." — Eric Nylund, *First Strike*, p. 263, 2003

Eve *noun*
MDMA, the recreational drug best known as ecstasy *US, 1985*
- It will be supplanted—already there is a new variation, MDE, Eve. — *Washington Post*, p. D1, 1st June 1985

evening glass *noun*
calm surf conditions in the evening after the afternoon wind has diminished *US, 1978*
- — Dennis Aaberg and John Milius, *Big Wednesday*, p. 209, 1978

even steven; even stephen; even stevens; even stephens *adjective*
even, equal *US, 1866*
"Steven" adds nothing but the rhyme.
- Al, it seemed, had a great deal of pride. He liked to keep things even-Steven, and he didn't take nothing off no one. — Jim Thompson, *Roughneck*, p. 89, 1954
- "How would be split the take, Jake?" "Even steven, baby .... even steven." — Odie Haskins, *The Busting Out of an Ordinary Man*, p. 75, 1985

ever-loving *adjective*
used as an intensifier *US, 1919*
- "Chet, are you out of your ever-loving skull?" Joe demanded. — Franklin W. Dixon, *Danger on Vampire Trail*, p. 123, 1971

Every Minute Sucks *noun*
an Emergency Medical Service unit *US, 1992*
New York police slang; back-formation from the initials EMS.
- EMS: Every Minute Sucks. — *misc.emerg.services*, 3rd June 1992
- — Samuel M. Katz, *Anytime Anywhere*, p. 387, 1997: "The extremely unofficial and completely off-the-record NYPD/ESU truck-two glossary"

everything-but girl *noun*
a woman who will engage in any and all sexual activity short of intercourse *US, 2002*
- — Amy Sohn, *Sex and the City*, p. 155, 2002
- With her Clintonion parsing of the definition of sex, Melissa is an "everything-but girl" (EBG). — Ian Kener, *Be Honest—You're Not That Into Him Either*, p. 10, 2005

everything is everything
used for conveying that all is well when asked how things are going *US, 1968*
- — Hy Lit, *Hy Lit's Unbelievable Dictionary of Hip Words for Groovy People*, p. 14, 1968
- — *Washington Post Magazine*, p. 17, 28th June 1987: "Say wha?"

everything's drawing
everything's going well, thank you! *US, 1963*
Nautical origins, suggesting that all sails are set and there is a following breeze.
- — Charles F. Haywood, *Yankee Dictionary*, p. 55, 1963

evil *adjective*
1 mean-spirited, inconsiderate *US, 1939*
- — Pamela Munro, *U.C.L.A. Slang*, p. 62, 1997
2 in computing, not designed for the speaker's purpose *US, 1991*
- We thought about adding a Blue Glue interface but decided it was too evil to deal with. — Eric S. Raymond, *The New Hacker's Dictionary*, p. 146, 1991

Ev'o'lene, the Nevada Queen *noun*
in craps, the number eleven *US, 1985*
- — Steve Kuriscak, *Casino Talk*, p. 68, 1985

ex *noun*
1 a former lover or spouse *US, 1929*
The prefix "ex-," like those so-named, stands alone.
- Even if a man thought his ex was inadequate in bed, he should not say, "You know, I've never slept with such a dead fish." — Anka Radakovich, *The Wild Girls Club*, p. 39, 1994

2 in target shooting, a bullseye *US, 1957*
From the notion, perhaps, that "X marks the spot."
- — *American Speech*, p. 193, October 1957: "Some colloquialisms of the handgunner"

exacto!
exactly *US, 1991*
Mock Spanish.
- "You want the files but you don't want to pay." "Exacto!" said Kingsbury. — Carl Hiaasen, *Native Tongue*, p. 201, 1991

excellent *adjective*
impressive, amazing *US, 1982*
Conventional English turned slang by the young. Stress is on the first syllable, which follows something close to a glottal stop; the "l" is lazy.
- — Connie Eble (Editor), *UNC-CH Campus Slang*, p. 3, Spring 1982
- Ted, I totally have a most excellent moustache. — *Bill and Ted's Excellent Adventure*, 1989
- I live in Aurora which is a suburb of Chicago. Excellent. — *Wayne's World*, 1992

ex-con *noun*
an *ex-con*vict, a former prisoner *US, 1906*
- And a little spell in the can wouldn't necessarily mean the end of his career; after all, ex-cons G. Gordon Liddy, Chuck Colson and Oliver North haven't let convictions get in the way of their right-wing talk-radio gigs. — *American Prospect*, p. 9, November 2003

excuuuuuse me!
used as a humorous admission of error *US, 1975*
Made wildly popular by comedian Steve Martin during frequent appearances on NBC's *Saturday Night Live* in the 1970 and 1980s. Repeated with referential humor.
- "Well, excuse me, ladies, excuuuuse me!" — Al Young, *Who is Angelina*, p. 182, 1975
- "Well, excuuuuse me. I shoot you on the way down?" — Lawrence Block, *Even the Wicked*, p. 288, 1998

exec *noun*
an executive military officer *US, 1898*
- "The exec up there got frostbitten, and they've asked for a replacement," said the Major. — Max Shulman, *Rally Round the Flag, Boys!*, p. 2, 1957

exhorter *noun*
an unordained preacher *US, 1843*
- He raised his hand like an exhorter at a revival meeting. — Edwin Lefevre, *Reminiscences of a Stock Operator*, p. 114, 1994

expedite *verb*
▸ **expedite into eternity**
to die *US, 1994*
- — Sally Williams, *"Strong" Words*, p. 140, 1994

expensive care unit *noun*
a hospital's intensive care unit *US, 1988–1989*
- — *Maledicta*, p. 32, 1988–1989: "Medical maledicta from San Francisco"

explorers' club *noun*
a group of LSD users *US, 1967*
Another "LSD-as-travel" metaphor.
- — John Williams, *The Drug Scene*, p. 111, 1967

exsqueeze me!
excuse me! *US, 1953*
- — Lavada Durst, *The Jives of Dr. Hepcat*, p. 12, 1953
- Excuse me is playfully pronounced Screws me, Squeeze me, or Exqueeze me. — Connie Eble, *Slang and Sociability*, p. 39, 1996

extra *noun*
1 in the coded language of the massage parlor, sex *US, 1996*
- If the man would ask if there were any extras, you'd have to say no, because he might be a cop. — James Ridgeway, *Red Light*, p. 216, 1996
2 in the language surrounding the Grateful Dead, an extra ticket for that day's concert *US, 1994*
- — David Shenk and Steve Silberman, *Skeleton Key*, p. 83, 1994

eye *noun*
1 desire, an appetite *US, 1934*
- When she has "big eyes" for you—she means she "goes" for you. — Walter Winchell, *San Francisco Call-Bulletin*, p. 7, 15th January 1946

- "You're out of your skull," said the papa bear, "although it does look as if somebody had eyes for the soup over there." — Steve Allen, *Bop Fables*, p. 9, 1955
- I would prefer if he didn't have eyes for her so obviously[.] — Jack Kerouac, *The Subterraneans*, p. 84, 1958
- There are plenty of women with big eyes for me tonight. — Richard Condon, *Prizzi's Glory*, p. 187, 1988

2 a person who is not a part of the criminal underworld but who reports what he sees to those who are *US, 1964*
- — R. Frederick West, *God's Gambler*, p. 225, 1964: "Appendix A"

3 a private detective *US, 1930*
- Listen, Propser, listen to me good, the eyes in those smooth stores have the hone for uncool threads. — Bernard Wolfe, *The Magic of Their Singing*, p. 25, 1961

4 a hand-held mirror used by a prisoner to see what is happening down their cellblock *US, 1992*
- — William K. Bentley and James M. Corbett, *Prison Slang*, p. 6, 1992

5 the anus *US, 1990*
- — Charles Shafer, *Folk Speech in Texas Prisons*, p. 203, 1990

▸ **the Eye**
1 a metal detector *US, 1967*
- When men approaching the big yard saw the Eye in operation they immediately dropped their knives, and after lock-up the guards would gather the harvest. — Malcolm Braly, *On the Yard*, p. 170, 1967

2 the US Federal Bureau of Investigation *US, 1997*
From "FBI" to "eye."
- She was in her rookie year at the Eye. — Stephen Cannell, *Big Con*, p. 315, 1997

eyeball *noun*
1 a meeting between two shortwave radio operators who have only known each other over the radio *US, 1976*
- — Radio Shack, *CBer's Handy Atlas/Dictionary*, p. 23, 1976

2 a visual observation *US, 1951*
- No sign of assault or a sexual attack, but that's just my eyeball. — Robert Crais, *L.A. Requiem*, p. 41, 1999

3 the identification of a criminal by a witness to the crime *US, 1992*
- — Jay Robert Nash, *Dictionary of Crime*, p. 118, 1992

eyeball *verb*
to see, to stare, to identify in a police line-up *US, 1901*
- When a john had eyeballed the parade and made his choice he would follow her upstairs, where the landlady sat at a little desk in the hall. — Mezz Mezzrow, *Really the Blues*, p. 22, 1946
- You brought me up here to get eyeballed, didn't you? Who're those guys. You try and put me in the Plaza today—that where they're from? — Elmore Leonard, *Split Images*, p. 110, 1981

eyeball palace *noun*
a homosexuals' bar where there is a lot of looking and not much touching *US, 1964*
- — Guy Strait, *The Lavender Lexicon*, 1964

eyeball queen *noun*
a male homosexual who looks but does not touch *US, 1964*
- — Guy Strait, *The Lavender Lexicon*, 1964

eyeballs, come back here!
used by a clever boy for expressing approval of a passing girl *US, 1955*
- — *American Weekly*, p. 2, 14th August 1955

eyeball-to-eyeball *adverb*
in direct, face-to-face confrontation *US, 1953*
- "Any leadership race is as personal as you can get," Vander Jagt said. "It's eyeball to eyeball." — *Washington Post*, p. A2, 8th December 1980

eyeball van *noun*
a police van equipped for surveillance *US, 1988*
- The other vehicle, an "eyeball van" with one-way glass and surveillance equipment, was parked on Virginia Avenue[.] — Thomas Harris, *The Silence of the Lambs*, p. 102, 1988

eye candy *noun*
an extremely attractive person, regardless of their character or intellect, regardless of their sex, regardless of their sexual orientation *US, 1981*

- Both of them may try to fill the aching void within them with the eye-candy television programs that promise them glamorous and exciting and dangerous love. — Mel Krantzler, *Creative Marriage*, p. 104, 1981
- — Connie Eble (Editor), *UNC-CH Campus Slang*, p. 3, March 1996
- [T]he eye candy refers to the sun-soaked settings, the jealousy-inducing outfits, and the most beautiful collection of skilled actors since the cast of Friends. — Brittany Kent, *O.C. Undercover*, p. viii, 2004
- Amy Adams landed her first role onscreen as some of the eye candy in the appropriately titled Drop Dead Gorgeous (1999). — Mr. Skin, *Mr. Skin's Skincyclopedia*, p. 2, 2005

eye doctor *noun*
the active participant in anal sex *US, 1949*
From **EYE** (the anus).
- — Vincent J. Monteleone, *Criminal Slang*, p. 79, 1949
- — *Maledicta*, p. 231, 1979: "Kinks and queens: linguistic and cultural aspects of the terminology for gays"

eye-fuck *verb*
1 to look at with unmasked sexual intentions *US, 1916*
- She eye-fucked me all the way home, ogling me every time I looked her way. — Maxim Jakubowski, *The Mammoth Book of New Erotica*, p. 167, 1998
- I like the girl to eye-fuck the viewer. — *East Bay (Oakland, California) Express*, 18th February 2004

2 to glare *US, 1981*
- "Are you eye-fucking me, boy?" — Mark Barker, *Nam*, p. 16, 1981
- The crowd watches Pellegrini cross the street, eyefucking him in a way that only the west side corner boys can[.] — David Simon, *Homicide*, p. 4, 1991

eyeglasses *noun*
used as a warning by an orchestra conductor to the musicians that a particularly difficult passage is coming up *US, 1973*
- — Sherman Louis Sergel, *The Language of Show Biz*, p. 82, 1973

eye in the sky *noun*
1 surveillance stations or cameras in casinos concealed above two-way mirrors on the ceiling *US, 1961*
- The Casino Manager must use the "eye in the sky" and closed circuit television to make sure his personnel remain honest. — Mario Puzo, *Inside Las Vegas*, p. 181, 1977
- Except that here you could stand upright, follow a wide catwalk with handrails, and from both sides of it look down through one-way smoked glass at the casino floor: at the tables, the slot machines, the mass of players and strollers less than ten feet below. — Elmore Leonard, *Glitz*, pp. 228–229, 1985
- The eye in the sky didn't care for that either. — John Ridley, *Everybody Smokes in Hell*, p. 192, 1999

2 a police helicopter *US, 1992*
- — Jay Robert Nash, *Dictionary of Crime*, p. 121, 1992

eye job *noun*
cosmetic surgery around the eyes *US, 1996*
- Maybe if enough San Diego citizens kept shooting, stabbing, bashing, and strangling one another she could get enough time-and-a-half to afford one [face-lift]. At least an eye-job, if not the whole cut-and-snip. — Joseph Wambaugh, *Floaters*, p. 137, 1996

eye-opener *noun*
1 a strong drink, especially early in the morning *US, 1817*
- Tomorrow I've got enough for my eye opener of wine. — Willard Motley, *Let No Man Write My Epitaph*, p. 374, 1958
- Donnell brought Mr. Woody his eye-opener, vodka and pale dry ginger ale, half and half, two of them on a silver tray. — Elmore Leonard, *Freaky Deaky*, p. 183, 1988
- J.C. on the porch, holding a tray out. "Hey! We have an eye opener!" — James Ellroy, *White Jazz*, p. 39, 1992

2 a drug addict's first injection of the day *US, 1959*
- — J.E. Schmidt, *Narcotics Lingo and Lore*, p. 57, 1959
- To wake up without an eye opener has only happened to me twice in all the time I've been on junk. — David Maurer and Victor Vogel, *Narcotics and Narcotic Addiction*, p. 405, 1973

3 the active participant in anal sex *US, 1949*
- — Vincent J. Monteleone, *Criminal Slang*, p. 79, 1949

eyes *noun*
▸ **the eyes**
in craps, a roll of two *US, 1999*
An abbreviation of **SNAKE EYES**.
- — Chris Fagans and David Guzman, *A Guide to Craps Lingo*, p. 6, 1999

Eyetalian *noun*
an Italian *US, 1840*
- "Yeah, 'cause there's only two types that fight like that, a nigger or a Eye-talian." — Joseph Pistone, *Donnie Brasco*, p. 17, 1987

Eyetalian *adjective*
Italian *US, 1840*
A spelling that follows pronunciation.
- He wears those Eyetalian clothes, off duty, doesn't he? — Troy Kennedy Martin, *Z Cars*, p. 35, 1962

Eyetie *noun*
an Italian or Italian-American *US, 1919*
Originally army use in World War 1.
- "Just having a little fun when the eytie gets upset." — Audie Murphy, *To Hell and Back*, p. 188, 1949
- Yet he was generally referred to by the town as "that Eye-tye over on the Pond Road." — Grace Metalious, *Peyton Place*, p. 414, 1956
- I know, I done business with the frogs and eyeties before. — Terry Southern, *Blue Movie*, p. 94, 1970
- [D]idn't matter if he got dumped on or made to look a fool by some Eye-tie. (Jackie would call them "guinea fucks" and one time DeLeon said, "Excuse me, my granddadddy was Italian," and had to listen to Jackie explain he meant these wise-guy schmucks, not your real Eyetalians.) — Elmore Leonard, *Glitz*, p. 236, 1985

Eyetie *adjective*
Italian *UK, 1925*
- A girl, an Eyetie, he thought. She looks at me with nothing but good in her eyes. — David Camerer, *The Damned Near Wings*, p. 149, 1958

eyewash *noun*
1 outward appearances meant to disguise an inner flaw
US, 1917
- They obviously were "eyewash" in 1952 when Truman manipulated the party machinery in favor of Adlai Stevenson. — Robert E. Thompson, *Robert F. Kennedy*, p. 197, 1962
- "They're just eyewash. Besides, they're too young for you." — Mickey Spillane, *The Body Lovers*, pp. 116–117, 1967
2 intentionally deceptive words or actions *US, 1917*
- You can't trust Tommy's tells. They're all eyewash. — John Vorhaus, *The Big Book of Poker Slang*, p. 16, 1996
3 tear gas *US, 1992*
- — Jay Robert Nash, *Dictionary of Crime*, p. 122, 1992

Eye-wreck *noun*
Iraq *US, 2001*
- Could this be the WMD that the Dodo in the White(bird)house claimed was in "Eye-Wreck" so he could play with his soldiers?
— *triangle.general*, 6th November 2003

Ff

F-40; Lilly F-40; forty *noun*
an orange-colored 100 mg capsule of secobarbital sodium (trade name Seconal™), a central nervous system depressant *US, 1977*
- — Donald Wesson and David Smith, *Barbiturates*, p. 122, 1977
- — Edith A. Folb, *runnin' down some lines*, p. 236, 1980

fab *adjective*
very good, excellent *US, 1957*
An shortening of **FABULOUS** (very good, etc.); hugely popular usage in the 1960s, in part thanks to The Beatles. Subsequently in and out of vogue, surviving between times as irony.
- And the great Kahoona. He's absolutely fab. — Frederick Kohner, *Gidget*, p. 59, 1957
- — Carol Covington, *A Glossary of Teenage Terms*, 1965
- As I sat there, getting all this fab coverage from Dolan, I began to regret having laid out the fifty on the cracker-discrimination case. — Terry Southern, *Now Dig This*, p. 145, 2001

faboo *adjective*
fabulous *US, 1999*
- Janine is known for her faboo media coverage, from Howard Stern to Jay Leno, and for her policy of appearing in only "girl-girl" scenes. — *The Village Voice*, 21st September 1999

fabric *noun*
clothing in general *US, 1972*
- — David Claerbaut, *Black Jargon in White America*, p. 64, 1972

fabulicious *adjective*
good and good tasting *US, 1997*
Usually used to describe a sexually appealing man.
- — Jeff Fessler, *When Drag Is Not a Car Race*, p. 82, 1997

fabulous *adjective*
used as a clichéd term of praise *US, 1990*
- By honoring someone like Michael Musto, he was showing the old guard who had previously snubbed him, how fabulous he was doing without them. — James St. James, *Party Monster*, p. 65, 1990
- The standard among all gay guy exclamatory cliches. — Jeff Fessler, *When Drag Is Not a Car Race*, p. 82, 1997

face *noun*
1 makeup *UK, 1946*
- I'm going to shower, dress and put a face on then we can go to Mary's for a few drinks[.] — Hubert Selby Jr., *Last Exit to Brooklyn*, p. 231, 1957
- "You up?" "Yes," she answered, "putting on my face." — Joe Houston, *The Gay Flesh*, p. 101, 1964
- "I don't want you looking at me without my face on." — Georgia Sothern, *My Life in Burlesque*, p. 258, 1972
- "Had to put on a new face." She smiled. — Earl Thompson, *Tattoo*, p. 644, 1974
2 pride, self-esteem, confidence, reputation, standing *UK, 1876*
- For a hustler in our sidewalk jungle world, "face" and "honor" were important. — Malcolm X and Alex Haley, *The Autobiography of Malcolm X*, p. 127, 1964
- He couldn't risk losing face in front of the network people. — *Mallrats*, 1995
3 in professional wrestling, a wrestler who is designed by the promoters to be seen by the audience as the hero *US, 1990*
Short for **BABYFACE**.
- No word on his heel/face status. — *Herb's Wrestling Tidbits*, 18th January 1990
- Until 1982, he had always wrestled as a face, a hero. — *World of Wrestling Magazine*, p. 7, June 1999
- — *Washington Post*, p. N36, 10th March 2000: "A wrestling glossary"
4 a professional pool player who is well known and recognized, making it impossible for him to make a living betting with unsuspecting amateurs *US, 1990*
- — Steve Rushin, *Pool Cool*, p. 12, 1990

5 a stranger; any person *US, 1946*
- — Robert S. Gold, *A Jazz Lexicon*, p. 99, 1964
6 oral sex *US, 1968*
- — Kenn "Naz" W. Young, *Naz's Underground Dictionary*, p. 28, 1973
- — Inez Cardozo-Freeman, *The Joint*, p. 495, 1984
7 a clock or watch *US, 1959*
- — *Swinging Syllables*, 1959
▸ **between the face and eyes**
where a blow or shocking news hits *US, 1975*
- — John Gould, *Maine Lingo*, p. 12, 1975

face *verb*
to humiliate *US, 1983*
- — Connie Eble (Editor), *UNC-CH Campus Slang*, p. 3, Spring 1983
- One student, White Mickey—an amateur pot dealer—turned around in his seat and faced Max with a condescending "dweeb." — Marty Beckerman, *Generation S.L.U.T.*, p. 119, 2004
▸ **in your face**
adversarial, confrontational *US, 1976*
- I'm special counsel for Internal Affairs, so my jurisdiction's pretty much in your face. — *A Few Good Men*, 1992
- L7 is an L.A. chick band known for their aggressive, in-your-face lyrics. — Robert Crais, *L.A. Requiem*, p. 96, 1999

face!
used as the stinging finale to a deliberate insult *US, 1979*
Youth slang.
- "You look nice today in that acid-washed jacket and those neon jelly shoes." "Thanks." "Face!" — Morgan and Ferris, *Retrohell*, p. 71, 1997

facebook *verb*
to ask to be added to a person's list of friends on www.facebook.com; to read about a person on their page *US, 2004*
- NONE of you losers are helping because i have you all facebooked already. — *alt.fan.hanson*, 2nd October 2004
- — Connie Eble (Editor), *UNC-CH Campus Slang*, p. 4, Fall 2005

faced *adjective*
1 drunk *US, 1968*
- — Collin Baker et al., *College Undergraduate Slang Study Conducted at Brown University*, p. 113, 1968
- Being "faced" used to mean being too stoned, short for "shit-faced" — Paul Iannone, *Retrohell*, p. 71, 1997
2 embarrassed, humiliated *US, 1993*
Youth slang.
- — Kenn "Naz" Young, *Naz's Dictionary of Teen Slang*, p. 39, 1993
- It was awful to get faced. It meant you looked awful in front of your friends. Example: "You look nice today in that acid-washed jacket and those neon jelly shoes." "Thanks." "Face!" — Morgan and Ferris, *Retrohell*, p. 71, 1997

face-fucking *noun*
oral sex, from an active perspective *US, 1990*
- Face-fucking. Engaging in oral-genital sex. — Alyson Publications, *The Alyson Almanac*, p. 63, 1990
- A bruised lip, a red eye, a scratch on my forehead (all of which, right now, are real products of a furious face-fucking I took last night and this morning from a leather-clad gentleman). — Gary Fisher, *Gary in Your Pocket*, p. 83, 1996

face job *noun*
cosmetic surgery designed to alter your appearance *US, 1974*
- "I think she has had a face job" Flo offers. — Leo Rosten, *Dear Herm*, p. 150, 1974
- No running. No face jobs or new paper. — Richard Condon, *Prizzi's Honor*, p. 278, 1982

face lace *noun*
whiskers *US, 1927*
- — Lou Shelly, *Hepcats Jive Talk Dictionary*, p. 24, 1945

face-plant *noun*
a face-first fall; in snowboarding, a face-first fall into the snow *US, 1984*
- — *San Francisco Sunday Examiner & Chronicle*, p. 20, 2nd September 1984: "Say it right"
- — Elena Garcia, *A Beginner's Guide to Zen and the Art of Snowboarding*, p. 122, 1990: "Glossary"
- We've grimaced and chuckled simultaneously at face plants, endos [an accident in which the cyclist flies over the handlebars], biffs [a crash] and crash-landings. — *Mountain Bike Magazine's Complete Guide To Mountain Biking Skills*, p. 32, 1996
- — Don R. McCreary (Editor), *Dawg Speak*, 2001

faces and spaces *noun*
joint consideration of equipment and personnel for the field and non-field positions. Military usage *US, 1986*
- — Department of the Army, *Staff Officer's Guidebook*, p. 60, 1986

face-shot *noun*
an air-to-air guided missile *US, 1991*
- — *Army*, p. 48, November 1991

face time *noun*
time spent in a meeting or conversation with an important or influential person; time spent on television *US, 1991*
- — Eric S. Raymond, *The New Hacker's Dictionary*, p. 148, 1991
- But the general rule was that action officers didn't get much—if any—face time with admirals. So much for networking. — Richard Marcinko and John Weisman, *Rogue Warrior*, p. 190, 1992
- Speaking of which, as soon as he gets back from Russia and China, we'll get you in there for some face-time, let the two of you catch up. — *Traffic*, 2000

face train *noun*
serial oral sex, from the point of view of the provider *US, 2001*
- A friend of mine recently came to Throb on her birthday and wanted a face train, where women sat on her face, one after another, and she serviced them. — *The Village Voice*, 11th July 2001

facial *noun*
ejaculation onto a person's face *US, 1993*
Depictions of the act in pornographic films and photographs promise great pleasure to the recipient.
- And what should be this film's finest sex scene, the finale between Ashlyn and Jamie, turns out to be mainly a simple b.j. ending in a facial. — *Adult Video News*, p. 48, February 1993
- Facials are common in porn, as most male viewers like to see cum on a woman's face. Many women don't like facials but put up with them. — Ana Loria, *1 2 3 Be A Porn Star!*, p. 100, 2000
- Heaven Taylor (pronounced "Tyler") also gives good bounce on Mark Davis as she cums while riding him cowgirl, then leans forward for even more mish and a facial. — Editors of Adult Video News, *The AVN Guide to the 500 Greatest Adult Films of All Time*, p. 11, 2005

factory *noun*
the equipment needed to inject drugs *US, 1971*
- — Eugene Landy, *The Underground Dictionary*, p. 76, 1971
- Get out the factory, the doctor is here. — David Maurer and Victor Vogel, *Narcotics and Narcotic Addiction*, p. 405, 1973
- — Inez Cardozo-Freeman, *The Joint*, p. 495, 1984

fade *noun*
1 a departure *US, 1942*
- The studs got cool and copped their fade. They left old Boptown in a perfect panic[.] — Dan Burley, *Diggeth Thou?*, p. 19, 1959

2 a black person who tries to lose his identity as a black person and to assume an identity more pleasing to the dominant white society *US, 1970*
- — Clarence Major, *Dictionary of Afro-American Slang*, p. 52, 1970

3 a white person *US, 1972*
- — Helen Dahlskog (Editor), *A Dictionary of Contemporary and Colloquial Usage*, p. 22, 1972
- — William K. Bentley and James M. Corbett, *Prison Slang*, p. 55, 1992

4 a haircut style in which the sides of the head are closely cut and the top of the head is not *US, 1989*
Also heard as a "fadie."
- Yo could you fix my fade? — *Boyz N The Hood*, 1990
- Look, all that Kinte cloth and zig-zag fadies and fight the power? It's fashion. — *New Jack City*, 1990

- He also had his hair molded into a sloped-back six-inch-high fade, with the words "Street" and "Smart" shaved in over his temples. — Richard Price, *Clockers*, p. 97, 1992

fade *verb*
1 to leave, to disappear *US, 1899*
- Thumper emerged from the driver's side, and the clockers faded fast. — Richard Price, *Clockers*, p. 520, 1992
- Don't fade on me now, Bear. — *Get Shorty*, 1995

2 to idle; to waste time *US, 1968*
- — Collin Baker et al., *College Undergraduate Slang Study Conducted at Brown University*, p. 113, 1968

3 to match the bet of another gambler; to bet against another gambler's success *US, 1890*
- You faded what the other man wanted to shoot—and what he often chose to shoot was the exact amount of your winnings. — Jim Thompson, *Bad Boy*, p. 368, 1953
- Nobody wanted to fade the square, but the man to the right was supposed to, if he wanted to stay in the game. — Herbert Simmons, *Corner Boy*, p. 19, 1957

4 to buy part of something *US, 2004*
- "That looks like a good pie, can I fade on that?" — Rick Ayers (Editor), *Berkeley High Slang Dictionary*, p. 20, 2004

5 to deal with, to handle *US, 1972*
- — Bruce Jackson, *Outside the Law*, p. 56, 1972: "Glossary"

▸ **fade a beef**
to cause a complaint or criminal charge to be removed *US, 1976*
- He was afraid he'd be traded in to fade a beef one of them might have with the LAPD, who were notorious. — Emmett Grogan, *Final Score*, p. 23, 1976

fade away *verb*
to become quiet *US, 1947*
- — Marcus Hanna Boulware, *Jive and Slang of Students in Negro Colleges*, 1947

faded *adjective*
drunk *US, 1998*
- — Connie Eble (Editor), *UNC-CH Campus Slang*, p. 3, Fall 1998
- — Don R. McCreary (Editor), *Dawg Speak*, 2001

fade-out *noun*
a disappearance *US, 1918*
- We began to rehearse like mad, and walked away so chesty we would have made Miss Peacock pull a fade-out. — Mezz Mezzrow, *Really the Blues*, p. 61, 1946

fag *noun*
1 a male homosexual *US, 1921*
Shortened from "faggot."
- If a sucker comes up on him, he pretends to feel his leg like he was a fag. — William Burroughs, *Junkie*, p. 44, 1953
- I have $30 to my name & hope to earn some in Xmas rush baggage room work if possible in this overcrowded frosty fag town[.] — Jack Kerouac, *Letter to Carolyn Cassady*, p. 403, 3rd December 1953
- Men shouldn't feel like fags just because they want to have nice-looking bodies. [Quoting Arnold Schwarzenegger] — *Oui*, August 1977
- "Jessie, the literature fag." — Jerry Lewis, *Labor Day Telethon for Muscular Dystrophy*, 3rd September 2007

2 a cigarette, a cigarette butt *UK, 1888*
- "Say, got a fag?" asked Buddy. "Here's a coffin nail," Phil said, talking out of the side of his mouth and extending a pack to Buddy. — James T. Farrell, *Saturday Night*, p. 28, 1947
- Scott gazed forlornly at the limp fag in his lips. — Donald Wilson, *My Six Convicts*, p. 53, 1951
- His eyes lit on Choo-Choo's half-smoked package of Camels on the table. "Dump out those fags," he ordered a cop, watching Sheik's reaction. — Chester Himes, *The Real Cool Killers*, p. 69, 1959
- He says he was sittin' in a cell in a Southwest jail/ where he landed doin' three days for vag./ A drunk came in, his eyes lit up like a hungry pup/ as I handed him a tailor-made fag. — Bruce Jackson, *Get Your Ass in the Water and Swim Like Me*, p. 82, 1966
- Perry goes to the kitchen for a glass of water, wanders away to his shared bedroom, puffing on the fag-end of his cigarette. — Odie Hawkins, *Ghetto Sketches*, p. 161, 1972

3 a despicable, unlikeable person *US, 1982*
No allegation of homosexuality is inherent in this usage.

- Ohmigod, I mean my fag little brother sees Jeff and goes, "Tiffany's got her period," and I could totally die. — Mary Corey and Victoria Westermark, *Fer Shurr! How to be a Valley Girl*, 1982
- — Connie Eble (Editor), *UNC-CH Campus Slang*, p. 3, Spring 1989

fag-bag *verb*
to rob a homosexual man *US, 1977*
- You're big and bad enough so you can play them along and get them alone and pow! There's a couple dudes around making a living from fag-bagging but you don't last long. — John Sayles, *Union Dues*, p. 290, 1977

fag bait *noun*
an effeminate boy or young man *US, 1974*
- He quotes a book reviewer from the New York Times who refused to review the book once it was published as referring to the book of pictures of Arnold as "fag bait." — Michael Blitz, *Why Arnold Matters*, p. 146, 2004

fag factory *noun*
a place where homosexuals gather *US, 1949*
Formed on **FAG** (a homosexual).
- — Vincent J. Monteleone, *Criminal Slang*, p. 80, 1949
- Fag factory (or joint) refers to a place where gay men gather. — Philip Herbst, *Wimmin, Wimps & Wallflowers*, p. 88, 2001

fagged out; fagged *adjective*
exhausted *UK, 1785*
- — Collin Baker et al., *College Undergraduate Slang Study Conducted at Brown University*, p. 114, 1968
- Playing poker on a big scale demands a lot of physical stamina when a game goes twice around the clock. I noticed all the poker players I knew looked a little fagged out. — Jimmy Snyder, *Jimmy the Greek*, p. 25, 1975

faggish *adjective*
effeminate, blatantly homosexual *US, 1958*
- [L]ike maybe Gonzales the Mexican sort of bum or hanger-on sort of faggish who kept coming up to her place[.] — Jack Kerouac, *The Subterraneans*, p. 43, 1958

faggot *noun*
a male homosexual *US, 1914*
- I never could stomach the relish with which soldiers would describe how they had stomped some faggot in a bar. — Norman Mailer, *Advertisements for Myself*, p. 223, 1954
- It was the first time I'd been around guys who weren't afraid of being faggots. They were faggots because they wanted to be. — Claude Brown, *Manchild in the Promised Land*, p. 146, 1965
- I said, "Did you know that [FBI Director J. Edgar] Hoover is a faggot—your boss?" — H. Rap Brown, *Die Nigger Die!*, p. 103, 1969
- By calling himself a faggot, he steals the thunder away from the mouthy jerks of this world who'd like to beat him to it. — *Chasing Amy*, 1997

Faggot Flats *nickname*
a neighborhood in Los Angeles, south of the Sunset Strip and north of Santa Monica Boulevard *US, 1969*
- It was an area called "Faggot Flats" by insiders because of its big homosexual population. — Vance Donovan, *High Rider*, p. 25, 1969

faggotry *noun*
male homosexuality; male homosexual practices *US, 1970*
- But the life-cry of that love has long since hissed away into no more than this idle and bitchy faggotry. — Thomas Pynchon, *Gravity's Rainbow*, p. 616, 1973
- The hunters in their pickup trucks were of the opinion that to vote for this woman was to vote for faggotry—and lesbianism, and socialism, and alimony, and New York. — John Irving, *The World According to Garp*, p. 484, 1978

faggot's lunch box *noun*
a jock strap; an athletic support *US, 1964*
- — Roger Blake, *The American Dictionary of Sexual Terms*, p. 69, 1964
- — Dale Gordon, *The Dominion Sex Dictionary*, p. 67, 1967

faggot's moll *noun*
a heterosexual woman who seeks and enjoys the company of homosexual men *US, 1969*
- Fag Hags, Fruit Flies, Faggot's Molls, is what the latter are rather unkindly called. — John Francis Hunter, *The Gay Insider*, pp. 90–91, 1971

faggoty; faggotty *adjective*
obviously homosexual *US, 1927*
- It was a young man, a rather faggotty-looking character in a Volkswagen, asleep. — Robert Gover, *Here Goes Kitten*, p. 122, 1964
- It is those faggoty intellectuals who've never gotten it up themselves[.] — Oscar Zeta Acosta, *The Revolt of the Cockroach People*, p. 31, 1973

faggy *adjective*
effeminate, blatantly homosexual *US, 1949*
- That faggy guy that let me in went for the stuff. — Hal Ellson, *Duke*, p. 111, 1949
- [Y]ou could hear them all yelling, deep and terrific on the Pencey side, because practically the whole school except me was there, and scrawny and faggy on the Saxon Hall side, because the visiting team hardly ever brought many people with them. — J.D. Salinger, *Catcher in the Rye*, p. 2, 1951
- The faggy words, the determinedly masculine tone—the latter again meant to obviate the former and render it acceptable. — John Rechy, *Numbers*, p. 67, 1967
- Now if he can just ... get ... the eyebrows ... exactly right .... Not faggy, you see. But arched, like this. — James St. James, *Party Monster*, p. 113, 1990

fag hag *noun*
1 a female cigarette smoker *US, 1944*
This sense of the term is long forgotten in the US but not the UK.
- — *American Speech*, p. 303, December 1955: "Wayne University slang"
2 a woman who seeks and enjoys the company of male homosexuals *US, 1965*
Formed on **FAG** (a homosexual). At times now used with derision, at times with affection.
- — *The Guild Dictionary of Homosexual Terms*, p. 15, 1965
- Freedom of speech does not consist of the right of noisy minorities, such as the Homosexual International and their front-men or camp critics and fag hags, to seize control of propagandistic areas such as clothing fashions[.] — G. Legman, *The Fake Revolt*, p. 11, 1967
- Fag Hags, Fruit Flies, Faggot's Molls, is what the latter are rather unkindly called. — John Francis Hunter, *The Gay Insider*, pp. 90–91, 1971
- The only other women in the bar were two fag hags and a couple of drag queens. — Michelle Tea, *Valencia*, p. 84, 2000

Fagin *noun*
1 a leader of thieves *US, 1976*
After the character created by Charles Dickens in *Oliver Twist*, 1837.
- He was a small-time fagin who set up marks for others to score. — Emmett Grogan, *Final Score*, p. 69, 1976
2 in pool, a person who backs a player financially in his bets *US, 1990*
- — Steve Rushin, *Pool Cool*, p. 13, 1990

fag loop *noun*
a loop on the back of a man's shirt *US, 2001*
- My research shows that they are also known as locker loops and fag loops, and that they have pretty much disappeared because most men no longer hang dress shirts. — *Plain Dealer* (Cleveland, Ohio), p. E4, 20th December 2001

fag moll *noun*
a woman who keeps company with homosexual men *US, 1973*
- "I've become a fag moll really," she [Loulou de la Falaise] laughs. "There's nothing like fun than fags." — *Newsweek*, 27th August 1973
- Jane Lambert (Billie) grew up in Oklahoma with Cris Alexander and was, according to him, "a midwestern fag moll from the word go." — Eric Myers, *Uncle Mame*, p. 301, 2002

fagola *noun*
a homosexual *US, 1961*
- Are you a fagola, sir? My friends and me, we got to know. — Bernard Wolfe, *The Magic of Their Singing*, p. 128, 1961
- "[Y]ou are a vicious rotten oik who is completely fagola?" — Ethan Morden, *Buddies*, p. 124, 1986

fag out *verb*
to go to bed *US, 1968*
- — Collin Baker et al., *College Undergraduate Slang Study Conducted at Brown University*, p. 114, 1968

fag roller *noun*
a criminal who preys on homosexual victims *US, 1962*

- [H]e would read in great detail how Coco Salas had been beaten almost to death by some fag-rollers in Old Havana. — Reinaldo Arenas, *The Color of Summer*, p. 369, 1990
- Some specialized as "fag rollers" and would pick up men and then rob and beat them, justifying their brutality as punishment of "fairies." — Eric C. Schneider, *Vampires, Dragons, and Egyptian Kings*, p. 134, 1999

fag show *noun*
in the circus or carnival, a performance by female impersonators *US, 1980*
- — Joe McKennon, *Circus Lingo*, p. 33, 1980

fag tag *noun*
a loop on the back of a man's shirt *US, 1980*
- The little loop of fabric on the back of a dress shirt became a "fag tag." — Patricia Munhall, *The Emergence of Man Into the 21st Century*, p. 166, 2002

failure to float *noun*
drowning or near drowning *US, 1994*
- — Sally Williams, *"Strong" Words*, p. 141, 1994

fair *adjective*
(used of a gang fight) without weapons *US, 1965*
- J.J. liked it because he couldn't beat anybody in a fair fight, and whenever we stomped somebody, all of us stomped him. — Claude Brown, *Manchild in the Promised Land*, p. 98, 1965
- He got away from the stoop and asked, "Fair one, Gringo?" — Piri Thomas, *Down These Mean Streets*, p. 50, 1967

fair fight; fair one *noun*
a fight between members of rival gangs in which weapons or at least lethal weapons are forbidden *US, 1950*
- "That's okay by us then. Do you want a fair one?" "Okay, a fair one," Tomboy said. — Hal Ellson, *Tomboy*, p. 110, 1950
- Fair one—A fist fight, without weapons, between one or more representatives of two rival gangs. — *New York Times Magazine*, p. 28, 20th October 1957
- Such a battle is usually planned as "a fair one." This means that only weapons agreed upon by the leaders are to be used. — Harrison E. Salisbury, *The Shook-up Generation*, p. 41, 1958
- "A fair fight isn't rough," Two-Bit said. "Blades are rough. So are chains and heaters and pool sticks and rumbles. Skin fighting isn't rough." — S.E. Hinton, *The Outsiders*, p. 28, 1967

fairy *noun*
a male homosexual *US, 1892*
- We sat at a table in the Iron Pot and Major said, "Sam, I don't like that fairy at the bar," in a loud voice. — Jack Kerouac, *On the Road*, p. 78, 1957
- Once, years ago, El Paso had been a crossroads, between the Eastcoast and the Westcoast, for the stray fairies leaving other cities for whatever restless reasons. — John Rechy, *City of Night*, p. 91, 1963
- All the animals come out at night. Whores, skunk pussies, buggers, queens, fairies, dopers, junkies, sick, venal. — *Taxi Driver*, 1976
- I'm a fairy too! Hey, I'm a freaking fairy too. — Francesca Lia Block, *I Was a Teenage Fairy*, p. 157, 1998

fairy dust *noun*
phencyclidine, the recreational drug known as PCP or angel dust *US, 1993*
- From the drug's perceived or imagined popularity in the gay community. — Peter Johnson, *Dictionary of Street Alcohol and Drug Terms*, p. 72, 1993

fairy hawk *noun*
a criminal who preys on homosexuals *US, 1988*
- [W]hen you have that, you have fairy hawks, muggers that specialize in gays. — Elmore Leonard, *Freaky Deaky*, p. 25, 1988

fairy loop *noun*
a cloth loop on the back of a man's shirt *US, 1970*
- Fairy loop or fairy hook would, therefore, represent a leap from the original "fag loop." — *Plain Dealer (Cleveland, Ohio)*, p. E4, 20th December 2001

fairy wand *noun*
a cigarette holder *US, 1963*
- Baby—sweetheart—would you mind retrieving her fairy-wand ... please ... for a Lady? — John Rechy, *City of Night*, p. 361, 1963

fake *noun*
1 in a magic act, a piece of equipment that has been altered for use in a trick *US, 1981*
- — Don Wilmeth, *The Language of American Popular Entertainment*, p. 88, 1981

2 a swindler; a confidence man *UK, 1884*
- He was a pretty good fake in his day[.] — A.S. Jackson, *Gentleman Pimp*, p. 134, 1973

3 a medicine dropper used by an intravenous drug user to inject the drug *US, 1973*
At times embellished as "fakus."
- Just get the fake out and let's fix. — David Maurer and Victor Vogel, *Narcotics and Narcotic Addiction*, p. 405, 1973

fake *verb*
1 to deceive *UK, 1859*
- If I was them and a man fake me like I faking them, would I believe him? — Sara Harris, *The Lords of Hell*, p. 55, 1967

2 to play music by ear *US, 1926*
- — Arnold Shaw, *Dictionary of American Pop/Rock*, p. 122, 1982

▸ **fake it till you make it**
in twelve-step recovery programs such as Alcoholics Anonymous, used as a slogan to encourage recovering addicts to modify their behavior immediately, with their emotional recovery to follow *US, 1991*
- — Christopher Cavanaugh, *AA to Z*, p. 89, 1998

fake book *noun*
a book of chords used by musicians who improvise off the basic chords *US, 1958*
- — Clarence Major, *Dictionary of Afro-American Slang*, p. 52, 1970
- I borrowed a fake-book so I could follow the chord changes, since I didn't know any of the tunes. — Frank Zappa, *The Real Frank Zappa Book*, p. 41, 1989

fake out *verb*
to bluff, to dupe *US, 1949*
- Emerson's left end faked out the opposing halfback and dashed toward the corner of the field. — Carolyn Keene, *Nancy's Mysterious Letter*, p. 130, 1968
- I faked out one defenseman, slammed the other so hard he lost his breath[.] — Erich Segal, *Love Story*, pp. 114–115, 1970

fakes *noun*
breast implants *US, 1997*
- — Anna Scotti and Paul Young, *Buzzwords*, p. 108, 1997

fakie *adverb*
backwards *US, 1998*
- Fakie Backwards, as in keeping the stance the same but riding fakie. — Shelley Youngblut, *Way Inside ESPN's X Games*, p. 39, 1998

fall *noun*
an arrest and/or conviction *US, 1893*
In the US often formed as "take a fall," in the UK "get a fall."
- Jack had taken a fall on a safe job and was in the Bronx County jail, awaiting trial. — William Burroughs, *Junkie*, p. 33, 1953
- He had peddled the stuff for Treetop Coulter before he took his first fall[.] — Mickey Spillane, *Return of the Hood*, p. 105, 1964
- He says that at home he has every copy of *The Realist* published up to the time of his fall. — Eldridge Cleaver, *Soul on Ice*, p. 46, 1968
- I've taken four falls and never ratted on anyone in my life. — Gerald Petievich, *To Live and Die in L.A.*, p. 132, 1983

fall *verb*
1 to be arrested *US, 1873*
- I've got a little over 300 bucks stashed in a safe place nearby, the remains of the proceeds from a gas station we pilfered before we fell. — James Blake, *The Joint*, p. 14, 25th February 1951
- I'd heard that he was busted about 6 months after I fell, but I didn't know they'd sent him down here. — Clarence Cooper Jr., *The Farm*, p. 10, 1967
- Even if they stop us, everybody ain't got to fall. — Donald Goines, *El Dorado Red*, p. 37, 1974
- I got enough bankroll, if you fall, to raise you for murder one with a telephone call. — Iceberg Slim (Robert Beck), *Doom Fox*, p. 30, 1978

2 to come; to go *US, 1943*
- "Let's fall upstairs," said the papa bear, "and find out what the skam is." — Steve Allen, *Bop Fables*, p. 10, 1955

- "I'll probably be packing." "Might fall by." — Richard Farina, *Been Down So Long*, p. 23, 1966
- Lar introduced him to Norman (disguised for the occasion in sweatshirt and jeans, and needing a shave) as "a poet friend of mine who just happened to fall by." — Terry Southern, *Now Dig This*, p. 242, 2001

▸ **fall into the bottle**
to become a drunkard *US*, 1990
- Maybe if I'd talked about it when it happened I wouldn't have fallen into the bottle. — Robert Campbell, *Sweet La-La Land*, p. 40, 1990

fall by *verb*
to visit *US*, 1965
- Go slow, and maybe we'll fall by some surprising afternoon. — Richard Farina, *Letter to Peter Tamony*, 3rd March 1965

fall dough *noun*
money placed in reserve by a criminal for use if arrested *US*, 1952
- A fifth rule is that the fall-dough held by the mob is to be used for any member of the mob and that is the possession of the mob. — Charles Hamilton, *Men of the Underworld*, p. 81, 1952

fall guy *noun*
a person who is set up to be blamed for a crime *US*, 1904
From **FALL** (an arrest/a conviction).
- And the eventual opinion in police circles was that the pickpockets had created him, a fictitious fall guy, in the hope of excusing their own misdoings. — Jim Thompson, *Bad Boy*, p. 353, 1953
- "It seems like every time I pick a side I end up the fall guy." — Peter Maas, *The Valachi Papers*, p. 80, 1968
- They're caught right in the middle of some kind of crazy mob war they can't do a thing about and wouldn't they just love to have a fall guy handy. — Mickey Spillane, *Last Cop Out*, p. 23, 1972
- We know they used you as a patsy, a fall guy. — Edwin Torres, *Carlito's Way*, p. 122, 1975

fall-in *noun*
a practiced swagger *US*, 1953
- "Now boys, I've polished my fall-in some more. Watch me try it on for size." — Dale Krame, *Teen-Age Gangs*, p. 134, 1953

fall in *verb*
to join; to stay *US*, 1952
- "Where'll you go?" "Oh, I'll fall in somewhere." — George Mandel, *Flee the Angry Strangers*, p. 51, 1952
- She said she had other plans for the evening but she would like to fall in some other time. — Herbert Huncke, *The Evening Sun Turned Crimson*, p. 51, 1980

fall into *verb*
to acquire by chance or without effort *US*, 1946
- [W]hen prohibition came on every piss-ant and his brother suddenly fell into big money[.] — Mezz Mezzrow, *Really the Blues*, p. 20, 1946

fall money *noun*
money placed in reserve by a criminal for use if arrested *US*, 1893
- — Franklin W. Dixon, *The Hardy Boys Detective Handbook*, p. 165, 1959

fall out *verb*
1 to be overcome with emotion *US*, 1938
- I fell out and rolled all over the floor laughing. — Chester Himes, *If He Hollers Let Him Go*, p. 2, 1945
- I almost fell out when he invited me to come along with the musicians to the Royal Garden[.] — Mezz Mezzrow, *Really the Blues*, p. 29, 1946
- She fell out when she saw my white Lincoln what I was rolling around in at the time. — Edwin Torres, *Carlito's Way*, p. 67, 1975

2 to lose consciousness due to a drug overdose *US*, 1959
- — Lawrence Lipton, *The Holy Barbarians*, p. 316, 1959
- "What the hell's a matter with you? Don't fall out on me!" He looked like he was passing out. — John Gimenez, *Up Tight!*, p. 16, 1967

fall partner *noun*
a confederate with whom you have been arrested *US*, 1951
- Briefly, my fall partner was a Southerner, with a brother on the force, and I was a Yankee ripe for burning. — James Blake, *The Joint*, p. 14, 25th February 1951
- So we got into the place and I told my fall partner, "Let's go, man, everything's packed." — Bruce Jackson, *Outside the Law*, p. 69, 1972

falls *noun*
▸ **over the falls**
said of a surfer carried over the breaking edge of a wave *US*, 1964
- — John Severson, *Modern Surfing Around the World*, p. 175, 1964

fall scratch *noun*
money set aside to cover expenses incurred in the event of an arrest *US*, 1969
- You dumb chicken-hearted bitch, whatta you think I got this ass pocket full of "fall" scratch for? — Iceberg Slim (Robert Beck), *Pimp*, p. 66, 1969

fall togs *noun*
conservative, traditional clothing worn by a seasoned criminal on trial to improve his chances with the jury or judge *US*, 1962
- — Joseph E. Ragen and Charles Finston, *Inside the World's Toughest Prison*, p. 798, 1962: "Penitentiary and underworld glossary"

fall up *verb*
to go to *US*, 1952
- He and the cat had fallen up to Vickie's and she had turned them on. — Herbert Huncke, *The Evening Sun Turned Crimson*, p. 54, 1980

false!
used for expressing doubt about the truth of the matter just asserted *US*, 1989
- — Pamela Munro, *U.C.L.A. Slang*, p. 37, 1989

falsie basket *noun*
crotch padding worn by males to project the image of a large penis *US*, 1957
- They all wear enormous falsie baskets. — William Burroughs, *Naked Lunch*, p. 135, 1957
- Still, you can use the humble tuber as a make-shift cod piece or falsie basket. — Sterling Johnson, *Watch Your F*cking Language*, p. 68, 2004

falsies *noun*
pads that aggrandize the apparent size of a girl or woman's breasts *US*, 1943
- She had a big nose and her nails were all bitten down and bleedy-looking and she had on those damn falsies that point all over the place, but you felt sort of sorry for her. — J.D. Salinger, *Catcher in the Rye*, p. 3, 1951
- [M]ost of them wear those damn falsies that stick out all over the place and I'd rather be caught dead than be a phony about a thing like your bosom. — Frederick Kohner, *Gidget*, p. 10, 1957
- Down but not out, she took up smoking and drinking and wearing falsies on account of being in love until the end of Time Immemorial with Joe Grubner[.] — John Nichols, *The Sterile Cuckoo*, p. 15, 1965
- I was really getting sick of looking at all those teensy dolls with falsies propped up in this dump. — Eve Babitz, *Eve's Hollywood*, p. 71, 1974

falsitude *noun*
a lie *US*, 2001
- — Don R. McCreary (Editor), *Dawg Speak*, 2001

family *noun*
a group of prostitutes and their pimp *US*, 1969
- "Her old man got one-to-three in the joint for burglary. She wants to join our family." — Iceberg Slim (Robert Beck), *Pimp*, p. 208, 1969
- I felt deep down in my heart that I could now sit back, relax, and enjoy the silky life and get my family of four girls in order. — A.S. Jackson, *Gentleman Pimp*, pp. 81–82, 1973
- We don't have a quota in our family. — Susan Hall, *Ladies of the Night*, p. 62, 1973

family *adjective*
homosexual *US*, 1994
- — Kevin Dilallo, *The Unofficial Gay Manual*, p. 240, 1994
- I just found out my boss was family ... and to think I have talked about hockey scores for the past six months to throw him off! — Jeff Fessler, *When Drag Is Not a Car Race*, p. 36, 1997
- "Also family," says Josef. "Family" means homosexual in gay slang. — Bart Luirink (translated by Loes Nas), *Moffies*, p. 118, 2000

family jewels *noun*
the male genitals *US*, 1922
- The first time he saw Carl, Lee thought, "I could use that, if the family jewels weren't in pawn to Uncle Junk [heroin]." — William Burroughs, *Queer*, p. 21, 1985

- Both of his hands circled her left wrist, trying to get her to release his family jewels — Ben Rehder, *Bone Dry*, p. 245, 2003

family pot *noun*
in poker, a hand in which most of the players are still betting at the end of the hand *US, 1990*
- — Anthony Holden, *Big Deal*, p. 300, 1990

family-style *noun*
sex in the missionary position *US, 2002*
- — Jeffrey Ian Ross, *Behind Bars*, p. 185, 2002

famous dimes *noun*
crack cocaine *US, 1994*
- — US Department of Justice, *Street Terms*, October 1994

fan *noun*
1 the preliminary touching of a targeted victim by a pickpocket *US, 1958*
- — *New York Times Magazine*, p. 88, 16th March 1958
2 crack cocaine *US, 1993*
- — Peter Johnson, *Dictionary of Street Alcohol and Drug Terms*, p. 72, 1993

fanac *noun*
an activity for a serious fan *US, 1978*
- — *American Speech*, p. 53, Spring 1978: "Star Trek lives: trekker slang"

fan belt inspector *noun*
an agent of the Federal Bureau of Investigations *US, 1971*
A back formation from the initials FBI.
- Ever since the disaster at the Branch Davidian compound in Waco, he referred to the FBI as "fan belt inspectors" because in his opinion only a bunch of dumb-ass grease monkeys could have let so many children get killed. — Larry Simmons, *Broken Seals*, p. 113, 2001

fancom *noun*
a convention put on by fans *US, 1976*
- — *American Speech*, p. 53, Spring 1978: "Star Trek lives: trekker slang"

fancy *noun*
a man's dress shirt with a colored pattern *US, 1986*
- — Rachel S. Epstein and Nina Liebman, *Biz Speak*, p. 80, 1986

fancy boy *noun*
in poker, a draw in the hope of completing a hand that is extremely unlikely *US, 1967*
- — Albert H. Morehead, *The Complete Guide to Winning Poker*, p. 262, 1967

fancy Dan *noun*
an elegant, conceited man *US, 1943*
- Jake was a real Fancy Dan, but he was generous with all his old friends[.] — Reginald Hill, *Pictures of Perfection*, p. 71, 1994

fancy-Dan *adjective*
pretentious *US, 1938*
- I know this is one of those fancy-Dan rooms that don't serve booze while the act is on, so set up a few bottles of the grape fast, before it's too late. — Jacqueline Susann, *Valley of the Dolls*, p. 295, 1966

fancy man *noun*
a man who lives off the earnings of a prostitute or several prostitutes; a male lover *UK, 1811*
- Many of the girls who won't service blacks have black "fancy men" waiting for them in Cadillacs when they leave the houses for a week off. — Gerald Paine, *A Bachelor's Guide to the Brothels of Nevada*, p. 92, 1978
- I'm gonna kill my baby / And blast and blast her fancy man. — Dr. Feelgood, *Shotgun Blues*, 1979

fancy pants *noun*
a dandy; a pretentious, superior, self-important person *US, 1934*
- Hauser was an intellectual fancy pants who was using the labor movement merely as a springboard[.] — Clancy Sigal, *Going Away*, p. 361, 1961

fan dancer *noun*
a sexual dancer or striptease performer who employs a large fan in her dance *US, 1936*
Most famously exemplified by Sally Rand (real name Harriet Helen "Hazel" Gould Beck), who popularized the style at the 1933 Chicago Century of Progress World Fair.

- [T]he strippers have finally divided themselves into three classes: "fan-dancers," who keep up the pretense of hiding their nakedness as they enlarge it. — Jack Lait and Lee Mortimer, *Chicago Confidential*, p. 158, 1950
- Sally Rand, who is still a star, and the late Faith Bacon, are described as fan dancers, not to be confused with fan stripping, though many peelers do both and call themselves "exotic dancers." — Lee Mortimer, *Women Confidential*, p. 134, 1960

faned *noun*
the editor of a single-interest fan magazine *US, 1982*
- — *American Speech*, p. 26, Spring 1982: "The language of science fiction fan magazines"

fan fuck *noun*
a heterosexual pornographic film in which male fans of the female pornography star are selected to have sex with her *US, 1998*
- How does the fan fuck flicks work, like Christy Lake's series? Does she pay the guys (Fans) who fuck her? Or is fucking her payment enough? — *rec.arts.movies.erotica*, 14th April 1998
- First, you join the club of the star who is hosting the "fan fuck." Then you can request an application form, fill it out, and mail it back with a photo of yourself. — Ana Loria, *1 2 3 Be A Porn Star!*, p. 66, 2000

fang *verb*
to yell furiously *US, 1962*
- They only bumped fenders, but the drivers were really fanging each other. — *American Speech*, p. 268, December 1962: "The language of traffic policemen"

fangs *noun*
musical ability *US, 1958*
An outgrowth of "chops."
- — Robert S. Gold, *A Jazz Lexicon*, p. 101, 1964

fan key *noun*
the command key on a Macintosh computer *US, 1997*
From the symbol on the key, which can be seen to resemble the blades of a fan.
- — Andy Ihnatko, *Cyberspeak*, p. 69, 1997

fanner *noun*
1 a pickpocket *US, 1950*
Likely a variant of FINGER.
- — *The New American Mercury*, p. 707, 1950
2 a fan dancer *US, 1981*
- — Don Wilmeth, *The Language of American Popular Entertainment*, p. 88, 1981

Fanny Hill *nickname*
the Los Angeles County women's jail *US, 1981*
- The Los Angeles women's jail, Sybil Brand Institute, is perched high up over the San Bernadino Freeway. The cops called it Fanny Hill. — Joseph Wambaugh, *The Glitter Dome*, p. 114, 1981

fan on *verb*
to decline an offer *US, 1997*
- — Vann Wesson, *Generation X Field Guide and Lexicon*, p. 64, 1997

fanoogie; fenugie *noun*
during the Vietnam war, a soldier freshly arrived in Vietnam *US, 1991*
A back formation from FNG (FUCKING NEW GUY).
- Franks was what the troops called a "fanoogie," abbreviated as FNG and standing for "f'ing new guy." It was a way for veterans to set themselves apart from the newcomers and to tell the new guys that they had lots to learn[.] — Tom Clancy with Fred Franks Jr., *Into the Storm*, p. 26, 1991

fantabulous *adjective*
very good *US, 1953*
A blend of "fantastic" and "fabulous."
- "Fantabulous" is the word for a Delta-C&S vacation. [Advertisement] — *Chicago Tribune*, p. 15, 23rd June 1953
- Then we still have "gung ho" (all for it), "real crazy," "riot" which to teenagers means lots of fun, "fantabulous," "real nervous," "mystery meat" (meat loaf, stew or almost any meat concoction), "nervous breakdown" (rushing around too much), and "schnook" for someone you don't like. — *Washington Post*, p. F1, 29th September 1957
- I managed to catch a fantabulous Malay bitch named Daisy and a place to hang my hat. — Odie Hawkins, *Ghetto Sketches*, p. 84, 1972

- "Fantabulous!" squealed Connie. "How long you here for?"
  — Armistead Maupin, *Tales of the City*, p. 3, 1978

fantastic buy *noun*
in poker, a card drawn to make a strong hand in a heavily bet situation *US, 1988*
- — George Percy, *The Language of Poker*, p. 33, 1988

fanzine *noun*
an inexpensively self-published magazine devoted to such topics as hobbies, music, film and politics *US, 1949*
A combination of "fantasy" and "magazine"; originally a magazine produced for science fiction fans but adopted by and produced by fans of any topic imaginable.
- — *American Speech*, October 1952
- — *American Speech*, p. 53, Spring 1978: "Star Trek lives: trekker slang"
- Examples are Thunder Road (the Bruce Springsteen fanzine) and Relix (the Grateful Dead fanzine). — Jay Saporita, *Pourin' It All Out*, p. 203, 1980
- Self publication had been a method closely associated with several art movements [...] The explosion of fanzines in response to punk rock established these publications as youth culture media. — Marion Leonard, *Cool Places*, p. 103, 1998

FAR *noun*
a hard and fast rule *US, 1991*
- They are not negotiable. Franks calls such items FARs—"flat-ass rules." — Tom Clancy, *Into the Storm*, p. 189, 1991

farmer *noun*
a member of the Nuestra Familia prison gang *US, 1975*
Many Nuestra Familia members come from rural California.
- — Report to the Senate, *California Senate Committee on Civil Disorder*, p. 230, 1975

farmer's set *noun*
in dominoes, the 6–4 piece *US, 1964*
- — Dominic Armanino, *Five-up Domino Games*, p. 2, 1964

farmer tan *noun*
a suntanned face, neck, and lower arms *US, 1996*
- Has one of those farmer tans. You see Buddy in the shower, his face and arms have color but his body's pure white. — Elmore Leonard, *Out of Sight*, p. 43, 1996

far out *adjective*
1 excellent, innovative, creative, daring *US, 1954*
Originally a jazz term with an emphasis on "experimental," and then in general use with a more general meaning.
- He's a real man, twenty, and far out. — Frederick Kohner, *Gidget Goes Hawaiian*, p. 3, 1961
- I had never seen him before but yesterday morning Gloria Gordon (who is in my Empathy I class) told me he gave "far-out" parties[.] — Gore Vidal, *Myra Breckinridge*, p. 59, 1968
- I mean, friends and neighbors, I mean he [Neal Cassady] was far out, just one hell of a hero and the tales of his exploits will always be blowing around us... — *The Last Supplement to the Whole Earth Catalog*, p. 84, March 1971
- STEPHANIE: So why did you say "far out?" TONY: It sounded like "far out." It was "far out," wasn't it? — *Saturday Night Fever*, 1977
2 drug-intoxicated *US, 1961*
- I smoked three in a gas station lavatory but they did nothing. I was not at all far out, or unattached. — Clancy Sigal, *Going Away*, p. 366, 1961

farshtinkener; fushtookanah *adjective*
stinking *US, 1968*
From German to Yiddish to American slang.
- At a dinner party, a farshtinkener anti-Semite, recounting his trip to central Africa, said, "It was wonderful. I didn't run into a single pig or Jew." — Leo Rosten, *The Joys of Yiddish*, p. 114, 1968
- David Douglas Klein, the "Douglas" a dead giveaway you are not of my kindred blood, you farshtinkener Dutch fuck. — James Ellroy, *White Jazz*, p. 61, 1992

farsighted *adjective*
said of a restaurant waiter or waitress who is intentionally ignoring a customer signalling for service *US, 1995*
- — *Maledicta*, p. 47, 1995: "Door whore and other New Mexico restaurant slang"

fart *noun*
1 an anal emission of gas *UK, 1386*

From Chaucer in 1386 through to the present day.
- And the fart I'm smellin' right now is definitely not one of mine. — George Carlin, *Napalm & Silly Putty*, p. 38, 2001
2 an unlikeable, even contemptible person *UK, 1891*
- Well, Coughlin, you old fart, what you been doin'? — Jack Kerouac, *The Dharma Bums*, p. 23, 1958
- This ol' fart Blastic, he's comin' to pieces befo' my very eyes. — Ken Kesey, *One Flew Over the Cuckoo's Nest*, p. 31, 1962
- He sure was one pissed-off old fart, but he was a smart old fart too. — Mickey Spillane, *Last Cop Out*, p. 160, 1972
- Some of them old farts out three, four days a time, you don't say squat to them. — *Saturday Night Fever*, 1977
- He's got some gadgets you old farts maybe never heard of. — *Gone in 60 Seconds*, 2000

fart *verb*
to break wind *UK, 1250*
- Incidentally, actress Whoopi Goldberg admits that she got her nickname because she farted so much as a child. — Greta Garbage, *That's Disgusting*, p. 58, 1999

▸ **fart through silk**
to live a life of luxury and ease *US, 1927*
- They want to wear wing-tipped shoes, fart through silk, and drive Cadillacs and BMW's. — Andrew Garrod et al., *Souls Looking Back*, p. 198, 1999

fart around *verb*
to waste time *US, 1931*
- Just farting around like two kids sitting on a railroad track on a hot afternoon[.] — Jack Kerouac, *Letter to Neal Cassady*, p. 114, 26th August 1947
- I follow Fink into the main lobby of the station. Everybody's farting around. — Abbie Hoffman, *Revolution for the Hell of It*, p. 19, 1968
- "So I got to go down there and everything, and fart around in some motel." — George Higgins, *Cogan's Trade*, p. 156, 1974
- Who wants to be a fuck'n forty-five-year-old rock 'n' roller farting around in front of people less than half their age? — *This is Spinal Tap*, 1984

fartblossom *noun*
a despicable person *US, 1938*
- I look upon it as my sacred duty to run as many of your fart blossoms out of the Marine Corps as I can. — Pat Conroy, *The Great Santini*, p. 205, 1976

fartbreath *noun*
a despicable person *US, 1974*
- Fart Breath starts talking about a trial, about this girl got gang-raped[.] — James Lee Burke, *Cimarron Rose*, p. 277, 1997

fartface *noun*
a despicable person *US, 1938*
- Except for the fact that that old fartface flubbed up the name of Li Po by calling him by his Japanese name and all such famous twaddle, he was all right. — Jack Kerouac, *The Dharma Bums*, p. 23, 1958
- That fart face done flipflop his Whiteass lid for sure! — Robert Gover, *One Hundred Dollar Misunderstanding*, p. 170, 1961

farthead *noun*
a despicable person *US, 1962*
- "You little snipe," he said. "You arrogant little farthead!" — Eric Gabriel Lehman, *Summer's House*, p. 243, 2000

farthole *noun*
a despicable person or thing *US, 1972*
- Piece of goddamn cockpuss farthole Navy surplus bubbleshit junk. — Dan Simmons, *The Crook Factory*, p. 433, 1999

fart hook *noun*
a worthless, useless person *US, 1973*
- Monk wore the uniform of the Burdock County High School basketball team, the Bulldogs—or, as they were variously known around Needmore, with as much despair as disparagement, the Shit-heels, the Fart-hooks, and the Turd-knockers. — Ed McClanahan, *The Natural Man*, p. 10, 1983

fart in a whirlwind *noun*
anything of no consequence *US, 1952*
- He says the brothers are all fools and the Lodge don't amount to a fart in a whirlwind. — Vance Randolph, *Pissing in the Snow*, p. 120, 1976

▷ **see: FART (NOUN)**

fartknocker *noun*

1 a despicable person *US, 1952*

- Some no-good fart-knocker is out there beatin' up on a woman. — Dorothy Garlock, *After the Parade*, p. 291, 2000

2 an incompetent blunderer *US, 1952*

Used with humor and often affection.

- — *Maledicta*, p. 254, Summer/Winter 1981: "Five years and 121 dirty words later"
- — Connie Eble (Editor), *UNC-CH Campus Slang*, p. 3, March 1996

fart sack *noun*

1 a bed; a mattress cover *US, 1982*

- "Probably in the fart-sack," Jim said. He usually takes his beauty rest around this time of day. — Douglas Fairbairn, *Down and Out in Cambridge*, p. 190, 1982
- — William K. Bentley and James M. Corbett, *Prison Slang*, p. 6, 1992
- He strips loco's bed and grabs the mattress cover that we call a fart sack and tears it open. — Colton Simpson, *Inside the Crips*, p. 193, 2005

2 a sleeping bag *US, 1943*

- — Carl Fleischhauer, *A Glossary of Army Slang*, p. 18, 1968
- — Judi Sanders, *Mashing and Munching in Ames*, p. 7, 1994

fartsucker *noun*

a despicable person *UK, 1891*

- "How about fartsuckers?" "Not rotten enough." — Joseph Wambaugh, *The Choirboys*, p. 32, 1975

fascinoma *noun*

a medical case that is unusual and thus interesting *US, 1994*

- — Sally Williams, *"Strong" Words*, p. 141, 1994

fascist; fascistic *adjective*

descriptive of a computer program with security walls or usage policies that the speaker finds excessive *US, 1991*

- — Eric S. Raymond, *The New Hacker's Dictionary*, p. 149, 1991

fast *adjective*

▶ **get fast**

in a criminal enterprise, to cheat a partner out of money or goods *US, 1987*

- — Carsten Stroud, *Close Pursuit*, p. 272, 1987

fast *adverb*

in gambling, betting large amounts without fear of loss *US, 1974*

- "Actually, I had won $3,400. That's how fast I was playing." (Note: "playing fast" has very little to do with speed of the game; it has to do with the willingness of the player to let her winnings pile up.) — Edward Lin, *Big Julie of Vegas*, p. 188, 1974

fast buck *noun*

money that is easily earned, especially if done so illicitly *US, 1949*

- An entire mini-industry has flourished out of the deaths of Tupac Shakur and the Notorious B.I.G., besieging all legitimate attempts to explore possible motives or true culprits behind both murders with a barrage of conjecture and regurgitated fantasy designed to make a fast buck[.] — Jake Brown, *Ready to Die*, pp. 16–17, 2004

fast burner *noun*

a person who is advancing quickly through the ranks *US, 1986*

US Air Force usage.

- — *Seattle Times*, p. A9, 12th April 1998

fast-count *verb*

to shortchange *US, 1949*

- — Vincent J. Monteleone, *Criminal Slang*, p. 81, 1949

fast lane *noun*

a lifestyle showing no regard for the future *US, 1976*

- Elizabeth noticed changes in herself that she didn't like—low self-esteem (which showed itself in poor personal grooming, excessive weight, compulsive overeating, and excessive alcohol consumption). She lived life in the fast lane. — Michio Kushi, *The Cancer Prevention Diet*, p. 145, 1993

fast-mouthed *adjective*

prone to talk back *US, 1966*

- Funny chick—coming on hard, fast mouthed; a tough guy. — Robert Stone, *A Hall of Mirrors*, p. 94, 1966

fast mover *noun*

in Vietnam, a jet aircraft *US, 1972*

- Right about now, top's calling some fast movers to drop napalm on that village, and we're too close for comfort. — Stan Lee, *The 'Nam*, p. 83, 1987
- This lets you operate it in the pouch, to attract the attention of those friendly passing helicopters and "fast movers," while keeping both hands free to deal with the opposing team. — Hans Halberstadt, *Green Berets*, p. 71, 1988

fast one *noun*

a trick intended to deceive or defraud *US, 1923*

- Wild and scared, Jinny had pulled so many fast ones on so many different people she lived in fear that the head screw was going to walk up someday and tell her she had to go to trial some more. — Robert Deane Pharr, *S.R.O.*, p. 187, 1971

fast pill *noun*

in horse racing, a stimulant given to a horse *US, 1947*

- — Dan Parker, *The ABC of Horse Racing*, p. 145, 1947

fast sheet setup *noun*

an apartment or motel that caters to prostitutes and their customers *US, 1969*

- In addition to being a whore, she ran a fast sheet setup for a dozen whores. They tricked out of her joint. — Iceberg Slim (Robert Beck), *Pimp*, p. 271, 1969

fast shuffle *noun*

a swindle; a deceptive act *US, 1930*

- Shawn was indeed a liar (but he had to be, in his job) and an artist at the fast shuffle (again, as he had to be). — Gardner Botsford, *A Life of Privilege, Mostly*, p. 258, 2003

fast-talking Charlie *noun*

a Jewish person, or someone who is thought to be Jewish *US, 1980*

- — Edith A. Folb, *runnin' down some lines*, p. 236, 1980

fast track *noun*

a street or area where prostitutes solicit customers *US, 1981*

- The hookers who work it know it as the stroll. Pimps call it the fast track. — Alix Shulman, *On the Stroll*, p. 3, 1981

fat *adjective*

1 good *US, 1951*

- — *Newsweek*, p. 28, 8th October 1951
- — Collin Baker et al., *College Undergraduate Slang Study Conducted at Brown University*, p. 115, 1968
- — Hy Lit, *Hy Lit's Unbelievable Dictionary of Hip Words for Groovy People*, p. 14, 1968

2 (used of a part in a dramatic production) demanding, challenging, rewarding *US, 1973*

- — Sherman Louis Sergel, *The Language of Show Biz*, p. 85, 1973

3 when said of a military unit, over-staffed *US, 1977*

Vietnam war usage.

- Theirs was a "fat" battalion, meaning a unit at over its authorized strength. — Philip Caputo, *A Rumor of War*, p. 206, 1977

fat Albert; Bert *nickname*

approximately one quarter of a gram of cocaine, sold for $25 *US, 2005*

- [T]hey'd send me down the block to Brian's house for Fat Alberts. — 50 Cent, *From Pieces to Weight*, p. 25, 2005

fat ass *noun*

a fat person *US, 1931*

- ["]You call me fatso again and I'll rearrange your face." "Fatso, fat ass, lard butt, blimpo —[."] — Janet Evanovich, *Seven Up*, p. 37, 2001

fat-ass *adjective*

of impressive dimensions *US, 1993*

- [A] fat ass J, of some bubonic chronic that made me choke[.] — Snoop Doggy Dogg, *Gin and Juice*, 1993

fatback *adjective*

lacking sophistication, rustic *US, 1934*

- "A fantastic spectacle in honor of some fatback grossero named Del Webb." — Hunter S. Thompson, *Fear and Loathing in Las Vegas*, p. 9, 1971

fat boy box *noun*

a box with enough packaged food to last several days in the wilderness *US, 2000*

- — Murry A. Taylor, *Jumping Fire*, p. 456, 2000

fat cat *noun*

a wealthy, powerful, prominent individual *US, 1925*

- The fat cats coughing up $300 a ticket give off some really good vibes. Real groovy!!! — Abbie Hoffman, *Woodstock Nation*, p. 95, 1969
- Republican fat-cat businessmen see their kids become SDS leaders. — Jerry Rubin, *Do It!*, p. 88, 1970

fat chance *noun*

no chance at all *US, 1908*

- "It stands to reason that at least one of those Board of Education members has read Elmo Goodhue Pipgrass's Thoughts of My Tranquil Hours." "Fat chance," sneered Clothilde. — Max Shulman, *The Many Loves of Dobie Gillis*, p. 7, 1951
- Personally, I feel the world would be a much better place if every radio station played Frank's version of "My One and Only Love" at least once an hour. Fat chance! — C.D. Payne, *Youth in Revolt*, p. 8, 1993

fat city *noun*

success, wealth *US, 1964*

- And then came the war—fat city, big money even for Linkhorns. — Hunter S. Thompson, *Hell's Angels*, p. 155, 1966

fat devil *noun*

a good-looking woman *US, 1978*

- "Fat devils! Fine good-looking chicks, I mean." — Bobby Seale, *A Lonely Rage*, p. 138, 1978

fat farm *noun*

a facility where people go to lose weight through a regime of exercise and proper diet *US, 1969*

- The Golden Door! America's most sumptuous and blue-blooded fat farm! A jeweled oasis of sauna baths and facials, pedicures and manicures, dancing lessons, herbal wraps and gourmet cuisine! — Armistead Maupin, *Tales of the City*, p. 186, 1978

fat grrrls *noun*

a young, radical faction of the "fat acceptance movement" *US, 1995*

- — Steven Daly and Nathaniel Wice, *alt.culture*, p. 79, 1995
- This week's Dyke TV netcast: Fat Grrls Night Out. These women are making a political point about their bodies, and having a great time in the process. — soc.support.fat-acceptance, 4th June 1997

fathead *noun*

a fool *US, 1842*

- I recall publicly gloating about the defeat of some of the noxious fatheads Texas used to send to Congress. — Molly Ivins, *You Got to Dance with Them What Brung You*, p. 118, 1998

fatherfucking *adjective*

used as a variant of "motherfucking" *US, 1963*

- Fatherfucking cops! wont leave me! alone! — John Rechy, *City of Night*, p. 353, 1963

father's day *noun*

the day each month when fathers appear in court to make child support payments *US, 1973*

- — Malachi Andrews and Paul T. Owens, *Black Language*, p. 51, 1973

Father-Son-Holy Ghost house *noun*

a style of three-story terraced house consisting of three rooms stacked vertically *US, 1996*

- — Claudio R. Salvucci, *The Philadelphia Dialect Dictionary*, p. 40, 1996

fat lip *noun*

a fist blow to the mouth *US, 1944*

- I'm warning you, Fen, break another window and you're gonna get a fat lip. — *Diner*, 1982

fatmouth *verb*

to insult, to taunt, to tease, to trade barbs *US, 1962*

- For some reason, I got a bang outta fat mouthing with 'em. — A.S. Jackson, *Gentleman Pimp*, p. 30, 1973
- What was it he said when people got pissed off and started fat mouthin' 'im? — Donald Goines, *The Busting Out of an Ordinary Man*, p. 40, 1985

fat-mouthed *adjective*

loud-mouthed *US, 1952*

- You're a liar and a fat-mouthed scoundrel. — Ralph Ellison, *Invisible Man*, p. 402, 1952

fat rat *noun*

the US Army's five-quart collapsible water bladder *US, 1990*

- "It's dextro time," Short Round whispered, swallowing water in big gulps from his fat-rat water bladder. — Don Hall, *I Served*, p. 164, 2001

fat-rat *adjective*

easy, privileged *US, 1983*

- Toward the end of his tour, he negotiated a fat-rat job off the line as a jeep driver and was thinking of extending his time in 'Nam in exchange for an early discharge. — Peter Goldman and Tony Fuller, *Charlie Company*, p. 317, 1983

fatso *noun*

an obese person; used as a common nickname or rude term of address for an obese person *US, 1933*

- You were sick, weren't you, fatso? If you'd stop fressing so much[.] — Lenny Bruce, *How to Talk Dirty and Influence People*, p. 145, 1965
- "You see a fatso old broad?" he shouted. — Iceberg Slim (Robert Beck), *Airtight Willie and Me*, p. 119, 1979
- "Who you calling fatso? You call me fatso again and I'll rearrange your face." "Fatso, fat ass, lard butt, blimpo —" — Janet Evanovich, *Seven Up*, p. 37, 2001

fat stuff *noun*

a fat person *US, 1926*

- "Thought you were tough, fat stuff." The remark rattled Boots. He didn't like to be called "fat stuff," "fatso," or any other name referring to his build. — Matthew F. Christopher, *Tough to Tackle*, p. 18, 1971

fatten *verb*

in poker, to increase a bet *US, 1963*

- — Irwin Steig, *Common Sense in Poker*, p. 184, 1963

fatty *noun*

an extra-large marijuana cigarette *US, 1969*

Also variant "fattie."

- I was just—you know—smokin' a fatty. — *Jackie Brown*, 1997
- Drinking beers, beers, beers, rolling fatties, smoking blunts! — Kevin Smith, *Jay and Silent Bob Strike Back*, p. 9, 2001

faucet nose *noun*

the condition experienced by surfers who have water forced up their nose while being pummeled by a wave *US, 1991*

- — Trevor Cralle, *The Surfin'ary*, p. 36, 1991

faunch; fawnch *verb*

to complain vociferously *US, 1911*

- I want you to quit fawnching around this house and get out there and get your grass off my yard, 'cause it ain't gettin' anything but higher, and I ain't gettin' anything but madder. — Ken Weaver, *Texas Crude*, p. 112, 1984

fausty *adjective*

unpleasant, distasteful *US, 1961*

High school usage.

- — *Washington Post*, 23rd April 1961: "Man, dig this jazz"

fav *noun*

in horse racing, the horse with the shortest odds to win a race *US, 1960*

An abbreviation of "favorite."

- — Robert Saunders Dowst and Jay Craig, *Playing the Races*, p. 163, 1960

fave; fav *adjective*

favorite *US, 1921*

A term with a definite teen magazine flavor.

- "Shit, Rodney, you're out of all my faves," said Shake. — Dan Jenkins, *Life Its Ownself*, p. 145, 1984
- They've been asked to open a show for new glam fave Suede. — *Rolling Stone*, p. 16, 27th May 1993

fave rave *noun*

a current favorite person or thing *US, 1967*

- Whenever my fave rave groups came to town, Gail was also lenient with me. — Pamela Des Barres, *I'm With the Band*, p. 203, 1988

fay *noun*

a white Caucasian *US, 1927*

- OFAY has come to mean the white man. FAY is the faster form. — Malachi Andrews and Paul T. Owens, *Black Language*, 1973

fay *adjective*

1 homosexual *US, 1928*

- "Now look are you going to cooperate"—three vicious diddles—"or does the ... does the Man cornhole you???" He raises a fay eyebrow. — William Burroughs, *Naked Lunch*, p. 196, 1957

2 white, Caucasian *US, 1927*

- I really went for Ray's roll on the drums; he was the first fay boy I ever heard who mastered the vital foundation of jazz music. — Mezz Mezzrow, *Really the Blues*, p. 62, 1946
- Loboy got a fay chick sommers. — Chester Himes, *Cotton Comes to Harlem*, p. 38, 1965
- Couple of years ago, I just missed getting locked up myself, or maybe getting shot by a "blue." It happened on a Mardi Gras. I was walking along and looked at a "fay bitch," just a little too long. — Robert deCoy, *The Nigger Bible*, p. 234, 1967
- He was a good-looking cat so we'd have a good time at my discotheque—a lot of the fay chicks would go for his revolutionary bullshit[.] — Edwin Torres, *Carlito's Way*, p. 81, 1975

▷ see: FEY

Fayette-Nam *nickname*

Fayetteville, North Carolina, home of Fort Bragg and the US Special Forces *US, 1987*

- — Connie Eble (Editor), *UNC-CH Campus Slang*, p. 3, Spring 1987
- Also nearby are five hundred camouflage-clad soldiers milling around in the parachute staging area. It's a typical day in "Fayette-nam." — Alan Diehl, *Silent Knights*, p. 194, 2002

faygeleh *noun*

a male homosexual *US, 1968*

Yiddish, literally "little bird."

- Jews use faygeleh as a discreet way of describing a homosexual—especially when they might be overheard. — Leo Rosten, *The Joys of Yiddish*, p. 115, 1968
- — H. Max, *Gay (S)language*, p. 15, 1988

fazool *noun*

one dollar *US, 1979*

- Six ounces for fifteen fazools. — Vincent Patrick, *The Pope of Greenwich Village*, p. 151, 1979

FBI *noun*

1 *f*at, *b*lack and *i*gnorant *US, 1971*

Used in ritualistic insults.

- — Hermese E. Roberts, *The Third Ear*, 1971

2 a Filipino *US, 1982*

An abbreviation of "*f*ull-*b*looded *I*locano." Ilocano is a dialect spoken in the Philippines; among Hawaiian youth, the term applies to any Filipino, no matter what dialect, if any, they speak.

- — Douglas Simonson, *Pidgin to da Max Hana Hou*, 1982

F bomb *noun*

the word "fuck," especially when used in a setting where such profanity is not expected *US, 1988*

- [Gary] Carter said he has been thrown out only twice in the majors, both times by Eric Gregg. "That was when I used to use the F-bomb." — *Newsday (New York)*, p. 146, 11th August 1988
- It's Callander's playground, where he violates listeners, airs randy prank calls, and occasionally hosts f-bomb-filled interviews with acts like Insane Clown Posse. — *Cleveland Scene*, 7th April 2004
- Vice President Dick Cheney dropped the f-bomb on the Senate floor in the fast 'n' loose days of 2004. — *Seattle Post-Intelligencer*, p. B5, 15th September 2007

fear

in twelve-step recovery programs such as Alcoholics Anonymous, used as an acronym for an addict's choices—*f*uck *e*verything *a*nd *r*un, or *f*ace *e*verything *a*nd *r*ecover *US, 1998*

- — Christopher Cavanaugh, *AA to Z*, p. 91, 1998

feasty *adjective*

excellent *US, 1958*

Teen slang.

- — *San Francisco News*, p. 6, 25th March 1958

feather *verb*

1 in horse racing, a light jockey *US, 1951*

- — David W. Maurer, *Argot of the Racetrack*, p. 26, 1951

2 in pool, to only barely glance the object ball with the cue ball *US, 1990*

- — Steve Rushin, *Pool Cool*, p. 13, 1990

featherhead *noun*

a superficial, silly and/or dim-witted person *US, 1868*

- They'd barricaded themselves in Jessie's room, talking conspiratorially, trashing the in crowd as conformists, shallow featherheads with no compassion. — Anne Lamott, *Crooked Little Heart*, p. 21, 1997

feather merchant *noun*

1 a prostitute *US, 1971*

- "Damn if you don't have those feather merchants under control, buddee. I didn't think you had it in you." — Robert Deane Pharr, *S.R.O.*, p. 360, 1971

2 a civilian employee of the military; a civilian *US, 1941*

- "You do whatever you want with those cruddy feather merchants, but let's get one thing straight: they are never going to set foot on my Army post." — Max Shulman, *Rally Round the Flag, Boys!*, p. 221, 1957
- — *Current Slang*, p. 13, Fall 1967

3 a timid, conservative poker player *US, 1996*

- — Peter O. Steiner, *Thursday Night Poker*, p. 409, 1996

feathers *noun*

1 a bed *US, 1899*

- What are you like in the feathers? Are you real great in the feathers, Movement? Do you do everything? — Bernard Wolfe, *The Late Risers*, p. 229, 1954
- You been three in the feathers before, ain' you? — Ross Russell, *The Sound*, p. 191, 1961
- Oh there may be girls who get a hundred to spend a whole night with a John—dinner and the theater and eight hours in the feathers. — John Warren Wells, *Tricks of the Trade*, p. 13, 1970

2 body hair, especially fine hair or pubic hair *US, 1966*

- "Is it true all them white women shows theyself mother naked?" the old bum grinned, exposing a couple of dung-colored snaggleteeth. "Mother naked!" he croaked. "They ain't even that. They done shaved off the feathers." — Chester Himes, *Come Back Charleston Blue*, p. 92, 1966
- "My, my," the Spook murmured, "not a feather on him. Some jocker's due to score." — Malcolm Braly, *On the Yard*, p. 35, 1967
- — Inez Cardozo-Freeman, *The Joint*, p. 496, 1984

3 sleep *US, 1977*

- — Ramon Adams, *The Language of the Railroader*, p. 58, 1977

featherwood *noun*

a white woman *US, 1989*

Formed with the more common **PECKERWOOD** in mind.

- — James Harris, *A Convict's Dictionary*, p. 32, 1989

feature *noun*

in carnival usage, the rigged game that a particular operator operates best *US, 1985*

- — Gene Sorrows, *All About Carnivals*, p. 16, 1985: "Terminology"

feature *verb*

to approve of *US, 1952*

- "A couple of fags are running it, but they're okay." "I don't feature that." — Hal Ellson, *The Golden Spike*, p. 184, 1952
- I did not feature lying next to her in bed, watching the news next to her wrath on the small bedroom TV. — George V. Higgins, *Penance for Jerry Kennedy*, p. 125, 1985

feature creature *noun*

a computer programer who enjoys adding features to programs *US, 1991*

- — Eric S. Raymond, *The New Hacker's Dictionary*, p. 152, 1991

featured dancer *noun*

a sex club performer whose appearance at the club is advertised and who travels from club to club *US, 2000*

- When I was a "house" dance I would watch all the "featured" dancers, most of whom were porn stars, come in and make all the money, get lines of people and get the beautiful pictures. — Ana Loria, *1 2 3 Be A Porn Star!*, p. 107, 2000

fecal freak *noun*

a person who derives sexual pleasure from eating the feces of others *US, 1971*

- — Eugene Landy, *The Underground Dictionary*, p. 40, 1971

fed *noun*

an agent of the federal government *US, 1916*

- That woman was under surveillance by the feds. — Mickey Spillane, *Kiss Me Deadly*, p. 18, 1952
- He could feel trouble in the air: Sonny busted by the Feds[.] — Clarence Cooper Jr., *The Scene*, p. 12, 1960
- He then called back and told me that he and his brother felt that she was a federal agent. I thought that was incredible, but then I also thought it would be incredible if she weren't a fed. — James Simon Kunen, *The Strawberry Statement*, p. 70, 1968
- I like cops. I would have liked to have been a Fed myself[.] — *The Usual Suspects*, 1995

federal *adjective*

excellent *US, 2004*

- — Ben Applebaum and Derrick Pittman, *Turd Ferguson & The Sausage Party*, p. 20, 2004

federal court *noun*

a floor manager in a casino or cardroom *US, 1996*

- When the players have a dispute, they settle it in federal court. — John Vorhaus, *The Big Book of Poker Slang*, p. 16, 1996

fee *noun*

coffee *US, 1966*

- — John D. Bell et al., *Loosely Speaking*, p. 6, 1966

feeb *noun*

1 a person who is feeble, in spirit, mind or body *US, 1911*

- Trouble was, he was a victim of chronic anxiety—the willies, the jumps, which tended to trim off only when it was comfortably past sunset and the nine-to-five feebs had all lit out for the suburbs[.] — Bernard Wolfe, *The Late Risers*, p. 34, 1954
- — Connie Eble (Editor), *UNC-CH Campus Slang*, April 1977

2 an agent of the US Federal Bureau of Investigation (FBI); the FBI *US, 1985*

- "Feebs," he said. He put the binoculars in Carr's hands. "That's my guess." — Gerald Petievich, *The Quality of the Informant*, p. 175, 1985
- He found something from the FBI fingerprint section in Washington and held it to the light, without success; the clever Feebs used opaque envelopes. — Carl Hiaasen, *Tourist Season*, p. 238, 1986

fee-bee *noun*

in craps, a five *US, 1968*

Almost certainly a corruption of the more common **PHOEBE**.

- — Thomas L. Clark, *The Dictionary of Gambling and Gaming*, p. 78, 1987

feebie *noun*

an agent of the Federal Bureau of Investigation (FBI) *US, 1942*

- Sampson and I spent the next few hours with the Feebie technicians who were searching the apartment for anything that might give the Bureau a clue about Sara Rosen. — James Patterson, *Jack & Jill*, p. 424, 1996

feed *noun*

1 a meal, especially an excellent and lavish one *UK, 1808*

- We put on a terrific feed that night, then we went bouncing around the tables. — Edwin Torres, *Carlito's Way*, p. 75, 1975

2 the chords played by a jazz band during a solo *US, 1970*

- — Clarence Major, *Dictionary of Afro-American Slang*, p. 53, 1970

feed *verb*

1 in professional wrestling, to initiate a scripted move *US, 2000*

- You don't want to "feed" yourself into the arms of an opponent who at will can easily toss you head first into the ringside fans. — Gary Cappetta, *Bodyslams!*, p. 72, 2000

2 in pinball, to put a coin into the machine *US, 1977*

- — Bobbye Claire Natkin and Steve Kirk, *All About Pinball*, p. 112, 1977

3 in a jazz band, to play a chord background for a soloist *US, 1961*

- — Robert S. Gold, *A Jazz Lexicon*, p. 104, 1964

▶ **feed the monkey**

to sustain a drug addiction *US, 1970*

- — William D. Alsever, *Glossary for the Establishment and Other Uptight People*, p. 9, December 1970

▶ **feed the ponies**

to bet on horse racing *US, 1997*

- — Jim Crotty, *How to Talk American*, p. 345, 1997

▶ **feed the warden**

to defecate *US, 1996*

- — Reinhold Aman, *Hillary Clinton's Pen Pal*, p. 37, 1996

▶ **feed your face**

to eat *US, 1968*

- — Collin Baker et al., *College Undergraduate Slang Study Conducted at Brown University*, p. 116, 1968

▶ **feed your head**

to use psychoactive drugs *US, 1970*

A phrase immortalized by the Jefferson Airplane in the 1967 song "White Rabbit," with Grace Slick's commanding vocal of "Remember, what the door-mouse said/ Feed your head, feed your head."

- We took to smoking grass in Van Cortlandt Park on upper Broadway, a nice place to feed your head[.] — Raymond Mungo, *Famous Long Ago*, p. 154, 1970

fee-grabber *noun*

a policeman paid for each arrest; a lawyer *US, 1967*

- This deputy sheriff is a fee grabber. — Slim Brundage, *From Bughouse Square to the Beat Generation*, p. 4, 1992

feel *verb*

to agree with *US, 2004*

- I think the teacher is being hypocritical, do you feel me? — Rick Ayers (Editor), *Berkeley High Slang Dictionary*, p. 21, 2004

▶ **feel no pain**

to be drunk *US, 1949*

- He took a few drinks and was feeling no pain when Mr. Coolidge returned unexpectedly to his office. — Ira Smith, *Dear Mr. President*, p. 124, 1949
- — *American Speech*, p. 303, December 1955: "Wayne University slang"
- "You weren't feeling no pain either," the waitress said. "I come over to the table, I said isn't that your beeper? He didn't even hear it." — Elmore Leonard, *City Primeval*, pp. 21–22, 1980
- Joey was feeling no pain by the time the car reached the city[.] — Joel Rose, *Kill Kill Faster Faster*, p. 24, 1997

feeler *noun*

in poker, a small bet made for the purpose of assessing how other players are likely to bet on the hand *US, 1967*

- — Albert H. Morehead, *The Complete Guide to Winning Poker*, p. 262, 1967

feel up *verb*

to fondle someone sexually *US, 1930*

- They would grab girls in the dark hallways in order to "feel them up." — Phyllis and Eberhard Kronhausen, *Sex Histories of American College Men*, p. 78, 1960
- Have you ever been felt up? Over the bra, under the blouse, shoes off, hoping to God your parents don't walk in? — *The Breakfast Club*, 1985
- Shirley Votypka, the first girl I ever felt up. — *Sleepless in Seattle*, 1993

feep *noun*

the electronic alert sound made by a computer terminal *US, 1981*

- — *Coevolution Quarterly*, p. 30, Spring 1981: "Computer slang"
- — Eric S. Raymond, *The New Hacker's Dictionary*, p. 152, 1991

feh!

used as a declaration of disapproval or disgust *US, 1990*

Yiddish, although the Yiddish etymology is not at all clear.

- Feh! You and your gun. Get out of here. Who needs you? — *Goodfellas*, 1990

felch *verb*

to suck semen from another's anus and rectum *US, 1972*

- — Bruce Rodgers, *The Queens' Vernacular*, p. 80, 1972
- [P]olished everything off by protruding his tongue into Slave's rectum to felch. — Larry Kramer, *Faggots*, p. 6, 1978
- — *Adult Video News*, p. 44, August 1995
- Suck it out. Suck it. Pucker, pucker. When I get a mouthful of that stuff, after I felch her good, I move my hands to my mama's face. — Karen Finley, *A Different Kind of Intimacy*, p. 52, 2000

felching *noun*
the act of sucking semen from another's rectum *US, 1981*
- [A]cts such as "felching." — Noretta Koertge, *The Nature and Causes of Homosexuality*, p. 93, 1981
- You simply ain't gonna see gagging, drool, felching, gape, double A's and other wondrously squalid sights in those other positively tame-by-comparison tapes. — Editors of Adult Video News, *The AVN Guide to the 500 Greatest Adult Films of All Time*, p. 175, 2005

fellow traveler *noun*
a person who sympathizes with a cause without being a full-blown member of the cause *US, 1936*
Originally applied only to communist sympathizers; translated from the Russian.
- Mr. Ferguson got sprung this afternoon, no thanks to his fellow travelers. — C.D. Payne, *Youth in Revolt*, p. 299, 1993

felony *noun*
a girl under the legal age of consent *US, 2004*
- — Ben Applebaum and Derrick Pittman, *Turd Ferguson & The Sausage Party*, p. 34, 2004

felony sneakers; felony shoes *noun*
expensive sports shoes favored by urban youth *US, 1978*
Favored by urban youth, often involved in, and more often associated with, crime.
- Most of us know them by their American handles: tennis, gym shoes, sneaks, mackerels, felony shoes, hightops or lowcuts, pussyfooters or athletic shoes. — *Washington Post*, p. B1, 18th August 1978
- Fifteen ghetto guerrillas wearing Pro-Ke4ds (what transit cops call "felony sneakers") swoop down on a victim, then scatter back into subway oblivion — Josh Alan Friedman, *Tales of Times Square*, p. 51, 1986
- These younger patrons are sensitive to the older habitues' description of them as "young turks" or "kids in felony shoes[.]" — Terry Williams, *The Cocaine Kids*, pp. 102–103, 1989

feminazi *noun*
a feminist *US, 1989*
A popular term with, and probably coined by, US radio entertainer Rush Limbaugh who uses the term in order to marginalize any feminist as a hardline, uncompromising man-hater.
- [A]nti-abortion activists holding placards reading "Thank You Lord for This Victory in Life" and "Feminazis Go Home." — *New York Times*, p. 1 (Metro), 4th July 1989
- — Connie Eble (Editor), *UNC-CH Campus Slang*, p. 4, Fall 1999

femme *adjective*
blatantly effeminate *US, 1963*
- Chuck the masculine cowboy and Miss Destiny the femme queen: making it from day to park to bar to day like all the others in that ratty world of downtown L.A. — John Rechy, *City of Night*, p. 105, 1963
- Some butches, if they really want to be with their woman, they'll act like they're femme. — Susan Hall, *Ladies of the Night*, p. 48, 1973

femme; fem *noun*
1 a young woman *US, 1871*
- "That depends on the fems you got here," said Phil. — James T. Farrell, *Saturday Night*, p. 46, 1947
2 in a homosexual relationship, the person who plays the passive, "feminine" role *US, 1934*
- "In bed, the difference between femme and butch disappears," they will say. "There everybody is ki-ki." — Donald Webster Cory, *The Lesbian in America*, p. 107, 1964
- A typical example of this type of fem lesbian is Geri, whose current liaison is with a "hard-dressing stomper" who calls herself Sam. — Ruth Allison, *Lesbianism*, p. 34, 1967
- Maggie was Bad Bob's sister's squeeze—the femme half of a dyke duo. — James Ellroy, *Hollywood Nocturnes*, p. 287, 1994
- After I saw teenagers Tatum O'Neal and Kristy McNichol in Little Darlings (the perfect butch-femme dyke couple), I couldn't wait to—not to lose my virginity to Matt Dillon, but to have a sex slumber party with those two cuties. — *The Village Voice*, 17th June 2002

femme looker *noun*
in circus and carnival usage, an attractive female *US, 1981*
- — Don Wilmeth, *The Language of American Popular Entertainment*, p. 90, 1981

femmy *adjective*
effeminate *US, 1968*

- I had always figured art was for girls and "femmy" guys and had never been interested. — Peter Jenkins, *A Walk Across America*, p. 8, 1979

fence *noun*
1 a person who trades in stolen goods *UK, 1698*
- They had made contact with a "fence" from Philadelphia, to whom they were to turn over the swag for $150,000 in currency. — Jack Lait and Lee Mortimer, *Chicago Confidential*, p. 18, 1950
- They had an exceptionally good fence, the owner of a real estate office, a highly respected citizen. — Clarence Cooper Jr., *The Scene*, p. 34, 1960
- Longshoremen, or fences for them, would come into the bars selling guns, cameras, perfumes, watches, and the like, stolen from the shipping docks. — Malcolm X and Alex Haley, *The Autobiography of Malcolm X*, p. 86, 1964
- Fenster and McManus have a fence set to take the stuff. — *The Usual Suspects*, 1995
2 the Vietnam-Cambodia or Vietnam-Laos border *US, 1990*
- Over the river, across the fence / To gomer's house we go. — Joseph Tuso, *Singing the Vietnam Blues*, p. 133, 1990: Night on the Town
- Crossing the fence? It took a moment or two for my mind to comprehend. — Richard Burns, *Pathfinder*, p. 267, 2002

▸ **hit the fence**
to escape from prison *US, 1992*
- "Every convict has three choices, but only three. He can fight [kill someone], he can hit the fence [escape], or he can fuck [submit]." — Pete Earley, *The Hot House*, p. 56, 1992

▸ **take the fence**
(used of a bookmaker) to fail to pay off a winning bet *US, 1947*
- — Dan Parker, *The ABC of Horse Racing*, p. 149, 1947

fence *verb*
to cheat in a test *US, 1955*
- — *American Speech*, p. 303, December 1955: "Wayne University slang"

fenced *adjective*
irritated, angry *US, 1982*
- So Andrea scores another ten thousand points on Centipede and beats me, right, and then like I break a nail and I'm fenced, fer shurr. — Mary Corey and Victoria Westermark, *Fer Shurr! How to be a Valley Girl*, 1982

fence painting *noun*
a scene in a pornographic film or a photograph of oral sex performed on a woman in a fashion designed to maximize the camera angle, not the woman's pleasure *US, 1995*
- Fence painting. Often totally unrealistic, but necessary for viewer coverage, so it looks as if the pussy eater is painting a fence. — *Adult Video News*, p. 44, August 1995

fence parole *noun*
a prison escape *US, 1990*
- Kool Tool suddenly clutched Joe's shirt and pointed across the Yard, crying: "Mira! Dude's goin' for a fence parole!" — Seth Morgan, *Homeboy*, p. 177, 1990

fence-to-fence *adjective*
in carnival usage, in control of all the activities in an engagement *US, 1985*
- — Gene Sorrows, *All About Carnivals*, p. 16, 1985: "Terminology"

fenderhead *noun*
a dolt *US, 1975*
- Listen, you slant eyed little fenderhead, I'm tellin' you she was lopin' my mule under the table. — Joseph Wambaugh, *The Choirboys*, p. 99, 1975

fen-phen *noun*
a combination of fenfluramine and phentermine, used as a diet drug and/or central nervous system stimulant *US, 1996*
- — *American Speech*, p. 188, Summer 1997: "Among the New words"

fern *noun*
a female's pubic hair *US, 1981*
- — *Maledicta*, p. 254, Summer/Winter 1981: "Five years and 121 dirty words later"

ferschlugginer *adjective*
used as a mildly profane intensifier *US, 1955*
A Yiddish term.
- I would suggest you invest in a current issue of it as a kind of test drive before you lay out $70 for the whole ferschlugginer mess. — *Atlanta (Georgia) Journal and Constitution*, p. 4P, 10th October 1999

fer shur; fur shur *adverb*
certainly *US, 1982*
A staple of the Valley Girl lexicon, often used as an exclamation.

- • — Mary Corey and Victoria Westermark, *Fer Shurr! How to be a Valley Girl*, 1982
- • Fer sure, fer sure / She's a Valley Girl — Moon Unit and Frank Zappa, *Valley Girl*, 1982
- • Rings fur shur knew she had a career, as in like the Original Gig, though how much choice was less clear. — Seth Morgan, *Homeboy*, pp. 4–5, 1990

fertilize *verb*
▶ **fertilize the vegetables**
to feed or medicate neurologically depressed hospital patients *US, 1984–1985*

- • — *Maledicta*, p. 118, 1984–1985: "Milwaukee medical maledicta"

fess; fess up *verb*
to confess *US, 1840*

- • [Jim] Morrison, def, does not get a pie in the face! He 'fessed up! — Lester Bangs, *Psychotic Reactions and Carburetor Dung*, p. 36, 1970
- • Get 'em to fess up that it's pretty much prisons or casinos in terms of their choices for economic growth. — *Traffic*, 2000

-fest *suffix*
a gathering together of, or a concentration of, or an event celebrating the modifying noun with which it combines *US, 1865*
Abbreviated from "*festival*."

- • I was always on the lookout for new records to pep up those wax-fests of ours. — Mezz Mezzrow, *Really the Blues*, p. 118, 1946
- • Etc., then finally disintegrating into a wild talkfest and yellfest and finally songfest with people rolling on the floor in laughter[.] — Jack Kerouac, *The Dharma Bums*, p. 23, 1958
- • The Gasworks. An excellent heavy metal bar. Always a babe fest. — *Wayne's World*, 1992
- • What's with the screamfest? — *Airheads*, 1994

festivity *noun*
a drinking party *US, 1955*

- • — *American Speech*, p. 302, December 1955: "Wayne university slang"

fetch *verb*
in computing, to retrieve and import a file from an Internet site to your computer *US, 1995*

- • — Christian Crumlish, *The Internet Dictionary*, p. 68, 1995

fever *noun*
1 five *US, 1985*
An intentional corruption of **FIVER**.

- • On the four-part number six Otto actually sank his second putt for a bogey-five. "Fever!" Otto cried. "Gimme a fever!" "Five for Otto!" Archie said[.] — Joseph Wambaugh, *The Secrets of Harry Bright*, p. 150, 1985

2 in craps, a roll of five *US, 1898*
Sometimes embellished as "fever in the South."

- • — *The Annals of the American Academy of Political and Social Sciences*, p. 124, May 1950

3 in a deck of playing cards, any five *US, 1951*

- • — Albert H. Morehead, *The Complete Guide to Winning Poker*, p. 262, 1967

4 a five-dollar bill *US, 1961*

- • — George Percy, *The Language of Poker*, p. 34, 1988

fews and twos *noun*
very little money *US, 1948*

- • — Jack Lait and Lee Mortimer, *New York Confidential*, p. 235, 1948: "A Glossary of Harlemisms"
- • — Clarence Major, *Dictionary of Afro-American Slang*, p. 53, 1970

fey *adjective*
effeminate *US, 1952*

- • He arched his shoulder and made a fey grimace of imitation. — John Clellon Holmes, *Go*, p. 7, 1952
- • This is all a bit fey for my taste. — Gore Vidal, *Myra Breckinridge*, p. 61, 1968
- • If he was a true pothead—and sometimes he thought that he was—this fey sixty-year-old with the flyaway hair and the old kimonos was the fiend who had led him down the garden path. — Armistead Maupin, *Babycakes*, p. 29, 1984
- • Dodie called the entire group [the Bee Gees] fey in the worst of ways and proof that lightning could strike more than once in the same family. — Rita Ciresi, *Pink Slip*, p. 107, 1999

FI *noun*
a police field interrogation, often used to harass and deter suspected criminals *US, 1993*

- • Some of the young marines found the FI's an easy outlet for their frustrations. — Bob Sipchen, *Baby Insane and the Buddha*, p. 48, 1993

Fibber McGee's closet *noun*
any large mess *US, 1948*
From the weekly radio show *Fibber McGee and Molly*, with a running gag featuring Fibber's cluttered closet.

- • Life was chaotic as Fibber McGee's closet, into which I kept stuffing more and more awful mistakes. — Jean Stein, *Edie*, 1982

fiddle and flute; fiddle *noun*
a man's suit *US, 1972*
A rare example of American rhyming slang.

- • I would put on a clean fiddle and an erky-dirk. — Robert Byrne, *McGoorty*, p. 147, 1972

fiddlefart around *verb*
to waste time doing little or nothing *US, 1972*

- • — Pamela Munro, *U.C.L.A. Slang*, p. 63, 1997

fiddlefuck *verb*
to waste time *US, 1949*

- • Maybe these guys were here for business after all, not just to party and fiddle-fuck around. — Robert Lipkin, *A Brotherhood of Outlaws*, p. 181, 1981
- • Boys, Grandmother was slow, but she was crippled and born blind. But you've been fiddlefuckin' around here for three hours and ain't accomplished Jack Shit. — Ken Weaver, *Texas Crude*, p. 112, 1984

fiddler's bitch *noun*
used for comparisons involving a lack of moderation *US, 1899*

- • "Lucy brought me to the Veterans Hospital in Charleston drunk as a fiddler's bitch." — John Berendt, *Midnight in the Garden of Good and Evil*, p. 192, 1994

fiddler's fuck *noun*
a notional item of no value *US, 1961*

- • Didn't make a fiddler's fuck and all they could was to hang tough and hope the scene would break soon. — Hubert Selby Jr., *Requiem for a Dream*, p. 183, 1978

fiddler's green *noun*
a notional paradise *US, 1891*

- • Like Shangri-La or Fiddler's Green, the lee rail is something of a mythical place[.] — Charles Mazel, *Heave Ho*, p. 89, 1992
- • Reagan, out of water, smiled, "Here we are at Fiddler's Green." — Paul Morgan, *The Parrot's Beak*, p. 51, 2000

fiddlesticks!
used as an all-purpose cry of frustration *UK, 1600*
Considered inoffensive, although it is possibly a pun on "penis," via "sword," the Shakespearean "fiddlestick," although the bawdy pun itself is not made by Shakespeare.

- • "Careful, fiddlesticks!" she snapped. — Jim Thompson, *Savage Night*, p. 119, 1953

fido!
used for suggesting that a group overcome an obstacle *US, 1983*
An abbreviation of "*fuck it, drive on.*"

- • — Connie Eble (Editor), *UNC-CH Campus Slang*, p. 2, November 1983
- • — Linda Reinberg, *In the Field*, p. 79, 1991
- • His best friend, Brian Turner, had adopted "fido" as his favorite expression: fuck it—drive on. — Richard Herman, *The Last Phoenix*, p. 48, 2003

field buck *noun*
a simple, naive, hard-working person *US, 1993*
From the 19th century delineation of field slaves from house slaves.

- • "Shit, there be more logic an science to magic than you two field-bucks ever dream." — Jess Mowry, *Six Out Seven*, p. 31, 1993

field circus *noun*
in computing, field service *US, 1991*

- • Q. How can you recognize a DEC field circus engineer with a flat tire? A: He's changing each tire to see which one is flat. Q: How can you recognize a DEC field circus engineer who is out of gas? A: He's changing each tire to see which one is flat. — Eric S. Raymond, *The New Hacker's Dictionary*, p. 154, 1991

field goal *noun*
in pool, a shot in which the cue ball passes between the object ball and another ball, touching neither *US, 1993*
An allusion to football.
- — Mike Shamos, *The Illustrated Encyclopedia of Billiards*, p. 93, 1993

field music *noun*
a military bugler *US, 1957*
Last used in the Korean war.
- Each infantry battalion rates a bugler or "field musik." — Martin Russ, *The Last Parallel*, p. 153, 1957
- A cleanup of barracks, no matter how long it lasted, was a field day; a neck tie was a field scarf, drummers and trumpeters were field musics. — William Manchester, *Goodbye, Darkness*, p. 146, 1979

field nigger *noun*
a black person who does not curry favor from white people and thus is afforded no degree of privilege *US, 1965*
- "That where you show you're just a field nigger." — Frank Bonham, *Durango Street*, p. 61, 1965
- Professors are house niggers and students are field niggers. — Jerry Rubin, *Do It!*, p. 215, 1970
- Malcolm X extended and popularized the concept; a field nigger was more likely to become a revolutionary while the house nigger was more likely to be an Uncle Tom. — Clarence Major, *Dictionary of Afro-American Slang*, p. 53, 1970
- A term used by young Black Revolutionaries in the late 1960s as a way of identifying the slave who wasn't ready for slavery. (The term went out with the 70's, but the feeling remains.) — Malachi Andrews and Paul T. Owens, *Black Language*, p. 78, 1973

field scarf *noun*
a necktie *US, 1940*
Marine Corps usage in World War 2 and Korea.
- A cleanup of barracks, no matter how long it lasted, was a field day; a necktie was a field scarf[.] — William Manchester, *Goodbye, Darkness*, p. 146, 1979

field-strip *verb*
1 to disassemble; to take apart *US, 1947*
- They must, as well, memorize ... how to field strip its seventeen major components at speed. — Daniel Da Cruz, *Boot*, p. 62, 1987

2 to break tobacco loose from a smoked cigarette and disperse it in the wild without leaving a trace of the cigarette *US, 1963*
- If you don't want to put the butt in your pocket because of loose tobacco, you can "field strip" it. — Mark Harvey, *The National Outdoor Leadership School's Wilderness Guide*, p. 162, 1999

fiend *verb*
when arresting an unruly person, to use a choke hold *US, 1987*
- — Carsten Stroud, *Close Pursuit*, p. 271, 1987

fiendish *adjective*
excellent *US, 1900*
- — *Current Slang*, p. 23, Fall 1968
- — Carl J. Banks Jr., *Banks Dictionary of the Black Ghetto Language*, 1975

fiend on *verb*
to show off; to better *US, 1980*
- — Edith A. Folb, *runnin' down some lines*, p. 237, 1980

fierce *adjective*
very, very good *US, 1994*
- I love RuPaul. She is fierce. — Kevin Dilallo, *The Unofficial Gay Manual*, p. 240, 1994
- Gaultier's fall line is fierce! — Jeff Fessler, *When Drag Is Not a Car Race*, p. 83, 1997

fifi bag *noun*
a home-made contraption used by a masturbating male to simulate the sensation of penetration *US, 1969*
- Jail birds, cons, and other unfortunate victims of bad laws call this ingenious invention a Fifi Bag. — *Screw*, p. 23, 27th October 1969
- Males, bereft of female comfort, sometimes resort to a fi-fi bag, a plastic sack containing a warm, wet towel used as a vagina. — *Maledicta*, p. 265, Summer/Winter 1981

- They take orange juice cartons from the Commissary, yeah, cut em in half and stuff em with a baggie loaded with hand lotion. That's your basic fifi bag. — Seth Morgan, *Homeboy*, p. 211, 1990

fifteen fucker *noun*
a military disciplinary reprimand *US, 1989*
- Instead, each of them was reprimanded, fined $300, and given an Article 15—an administrative punishment known within the ranks as a Fifteen Fucker—"for conduct totally unbecoming an officer." — Rick Atkinson, *The Long Gray Line*, p. 295, 1989
- At 6:00 a.m. on May 1, Joe missed reveille formation, resulting in a Fifteen Fucker that sentenced him to forfeit $163 for one month. — Peter Maslowski, *Looking for a Hero*, p. 618, 2005

fifteen minutes of fame *noun*
the brief period of celebrity that Andy Warhol saw as an element of pop culture *US, 1968*
- AUSTIN: If you can become famous, everyone will have their fifteen minutes of fame, man. ANDY WARHOL: "Fifteen minutes of fame?" I'm going to use that quote and not give you any credit for that, either. — *Austin Powers*, 1968

fifth *noun*
▶ **take the fifth**
to listen to a fellow alcoholic recount their worst misdeeds without comment or judgment *US, 1990*
- You want to take the fifth with me? — Robert Campbell, *Sweet La-La Land*, p. 40, 1990

fifth gear *noun*
a state of intoxication *US, 1968*
- — *Current Slang*, p. 7, Spring 1968

fifty *noun*
a .50 caliber machine gun *US, 1977*
- I wrapped my blanket around my shoulders and sat behind my fifty with my knees drawn up[.] — Larry Heinemann, *Close Quarters*, p. 201, 1977
- No-one had told him, I'm quite sincere / That a fifty will put a hole / In a Centurion's rear. — Martin Cameron, *A Look at the Bright Side*, 1988

fifty-eleven *noun*
a mythical large number *US, 1970*
- — Clarence Major, *Dictionary of Afro-American Slang*, p. 53, 1970
- He was still standing there looking pitiful and getting turned down by fifty-eleven hoochies. — Zane, *The Heat Seekers*, p. 24, 2002

fifty-fifty *noun*
in the television and movie industries, a shot of two actors facing each other, each taking up half the screen *US, 1977*
- — Tony Miller and Patricia George, *Cut! Print!*, p. 73, 1977

fifty-five *noun*
in craps, a roll of two fives *US, 1974*
- — Thomas L. Clark, *The Dictionary of Gambling and Gaming*, p. 79, 1987

fifty-mission cap *noun*
a cap similar to that worn by bomber crews during World War 2 *US, 1956*
- He grinned, doffing his fifty-mission cap. — Stephen J. Cannell, *The Plan*, p. 235, 1995

fifty-one; one fifty-one *noun*
small pieces of crack cocaine sprinkled in a tobacco or marijuana cigarette *US, 1994*
- — US Department of Justice, *Street Terms*, October 1994
- Terrence Moore is standing in the men's room in the concrete catacombs of Houlihan's Stadium, doing his business and talking about how it feels to smoke a 51—street slang for a cocaine and marijuana cigarette. — *St. Petersburg (Florida) Times*, p. 1B, 18th May 1997

fifty-two *noun*
in craps, a roll of five and two—a seven *US, 1973*
- I faded his bet / and to my regret / watched him throw fifty-two. — Lightnin' Rod, *Hustlers Convention*, p. 58, 1973

fifty-two/twenty club *noun*
US military veterans who were entitled to benefits of $20 a week for a year after World War 2, making a life of bohemian leisure possible *US, 1946*

- My reason for going to the Veteran's Administration was the 52–20 Club. The Government gave all ex-GIs $20 a week for a year or until you could find a job. — Lenny Bruce, *How to Talk Dirty and Influence People*, p. 27, 1965
- He had socked away his mustering-out pay and was a member in good standing of the 52–20 club. — John Williams, *The Man Who Cried I Am*, p. 102, 1967
- Mac ran around with all the 52–20 madmen in Papa Joe's[.] — Gilbert Sorrentino, *Steelwork*, p. 73, 1970

fig *noun*
1 hardly anything at all *UK, 1400*
- "But a fig to them all!" cried Linden-Evarts, breaking into Jefferson's reverie. — Max Shulman, *Anyone Got a Match?*, p. 69, 1964

2 an effeminate male *US, 1963*
An amelioration of FAG.
- — *San Francisco Examiner: People*, p. 8, 27th October 1963: "What a 'Z'! The astonishing private language of Bay Area teenagers"

figging *adjective*
used as a euphemism for the intensifying "fucking" *US, 1999*
- Hope of Chateau-roux is worth a figging king's ransom to Philip and the Pope. — Katherine Sutcliffe, *Hope and Glory*, pp. 66–67, 1999

fighter jock *noun*
a military aviator *US, 1967*
- "A fighter jock entering the landing pattern picked it up[.]" — Elaine Shepard, *The Doom Pussy*, p. 190, 1967

Fightertown USA *nickname*
the Miramar Naval Air Station, Miramar, California *US, 1988*
- They were beginning to call the base "Fightertown," as the U.S. military increased its readiness in response to the growing war in Southeast Asia. — Robert K. Wilcox, *Scream of Eagles*, p. 15, 1990

fightinest *adjective*
toughest, scrappiest *US, 1871*
- They had one time named John L. Sullivan cause it was the fightinest little thing you ever seen. — Cormac McCarthy, *Suttree*, p. 128, 1979

Fighting Hannah *nickname*
the U.S.S. Hancock *US, 1945*
An aircraft carrier that saw service in World War 2 and Vietnam.
- Fightin' Hannah Has Proud Record [Headline] — *Treasure Island Digest*, p. 7, 27th October 1945

figmo; fuigmo *noun*
fuck it, got my orders; fuck you, I got my orders US, 1957
Korean and then Vietnam war usage. Descriptive of a somewhat defiant attitude. The sanitized version is FIGMOH: *"finally I got my orders home."*
- — *American Speech*, p. 121, 2nd May 1960: "Korean bamboo English"
- When FIGMO ("Farewell, I Got My Orders[.] — Ken Melvin, *Sorry 'Bout That*, p. 94, 1966
- It was very hard to get figmo people to do a job well. They were just plain complacent. So what are the factors that lead pilots to become figmo? — R. Randall Padfield, *Flying in Adverse Conditions*, p. 245, 1994

figmo chart *noun*
a record which a soldier kept of the number of days remaining until he was rotated home from Korea or, later, Vietnam *US, 1966*
- The FIGMO chart is an innovation of the Vietnam war. — Ken Melvin, *Sorry 'Bout That*, p. 94, 1966
- — *True*, p. 81, August 1966
- I wonder if he keeps a figmo chart to count the days till he can go home. — Abood Ken, *How to Live in Vietnam for less than $.10 a day*, p. 77, 1967

figures *noun*
an illegal lottery in which winners are those who have bet on a number chosen by some random method *US, 1967*
Best known as "the numbers" or "policy racket."
- Every year for the next five, he opened another restaurant chain to his empire, while all the time dabbling in the figures (Numbers game). — Babs Gonzales, *I Paid My Dues*, p. 83, 1967

fiji *noun*
a member of the Phi Delta Gamma college fraternity *US, 1963*
- He invited even the youngest midshipmen to the FIJI house for parties. — *The Virginian-Pilot*, p. A1, 6th November 1994

file *noun*
a pickpocket *UK, 1665*
- — Vincent J. Monteleone, *Criminal Slang*, p. 83, 1949
- — Joseph E. Ragen and Charles Finston, *Inside the World's Toughest Prison*, p. 798, 1962: "Penitentiary and underworld glossary"

filet *noun*
an attractive female *US, 1989*
- — Pamela Munro, *U.C.L.A. Slang*, p. 38, 1989

fillet *noun*
cocaine *US, 1993*
A metaphor alluding to the drug's high cost and status.
- — Peter Johnson, *Dictionary of Street Alcohol and Drug Terms*, p. 74, 1993

Fillmore *noun*
a potent mixture of alcoholic beverages *US, 1993*
- Sidney Hill, 24, says he stayed wasted on "Fillmores"—street slang for a mixture of Olde English, St. Ides, gin and orange juice—before hitting bottom and coming to Recovery House. — *San Francisco Chronicle*, p. A19, 3rd June 1993

fills *noun*
dice which have been weighted for cheating *US, 1950*
- — *The Annals of the American Academy of Political and Social Sciences*, p. 124, May 1950

fill up *verb*
in poker, to complete a desired hand by drawing cards *US, 1951*
- — *American Speech*, p. 98, May 1951

filly *noun*
1 a young woman *UK, 1614*
- [S]ome of his I.W.W. constituents would probably kick over the traces if they saw the highfalutin' fillies he runs with in Washington. — Jack Lait and Lee Mortimer, *Washington Confidential*, p. 87, 1951
- Seriously, I wish I had Super Bowl seats for every time I had some filly just come up and start talking to me without the slightest provocation. — *Sex, Lies and Videotape*, 1989

2 in poker, a hand consisting of three of the same suit and a pair *US, 1951*
Conventionally known as a "full house."
- — *American Speech*, p. 98, May 1951

filthy *adjective*
attractive, fashionable, stylish *US, 1993*
- — *People Magazine*, p. 73, 19th July 1993
- — Linda Meyer, *Teenspeak*, p. 29, 1994

Filthy McNasty *noun*
a dirty, rude person *US, 1969*
The name comes from a character also known as Repulsive Rogan in W.C. Fields' 1940 *The Bank Dick*.
- — John D. Bell et al., *Loosely Speaking*, p. 8, 1969

fimps *noun*
in craps, a roll of two fives *US, 1968*
- — Thomas L. Clark, *The Dictionary of Gambling and Gaming*, p. 79, 1987

fin *noun*
1 a five-dollar bill *UK, 1868*
- I drank all day in a wild poolhall-bar-restaurant-saloon two-part joint, also got burned for a fin (Mexican, 5 pesos, 60 cents) by a connection. — Jack Kerouac, *Letter to Neal and Carolyn Cassady*, p. 359, 27th May 1952
- He was a kid trying to get a fin or a sawbuck a day to keep his habit up. — Willard Motley, *Let No Man Write My Epitaph*, p. 369, 1958
- So he pressed a fin into her palm. — William "Lord" Buckley, *The Bad-Rapping of the Marquis de Sade*, 1960
- "How 'bout it, my mannnnn?" he called out to Elijah above the clatter of the balls being racked, "shoot one for a fin?" — Odie Hawkins, *Chicago Hustle*, p. 85, 1977

2 a five-year prison sentence *UK, 1925*
- — Joseph E. Ragen and Charles Finston, *Inside the World's Toughest Prison*, p. 798, 1962: "Penitentiary and underworld glossary"
- I said, "It isn't a little trouble. Under the 'Max' I could get a 'fin.'" — Iceberg Slim (Robert Beck), *Pimp*, p. 46, 1969

finagle *verb*
to obtain in a manipulative manner *US, 1922*
- They spent what remained of their honeymoon on deck, learning how to finagle their way through Ellis Island. — Jeffrey Eugenides, *Middlesex*, p. 73, 2002

final *noun*

the moment in a confidence swindle when the victim is left to discover his loss *US, 1969*

- Folks, black con men call this the final. — Iceberg Slim (Robert Beck), *Trick Baby*, p. 124, 1969

final curtain *noun*

in carnival usage, death *US, 1985*

The obituary section in the *Amusement Business* magazine is named "Final Curtain."

- — Gene Sorrows, *All About Carnivals*, p. 16, 1985: "Terminology"

finale-hopper *noun*

a young man who goes to a dance without a partner, cutting in on another's partner at the end of the evening in the hope of leaving the dance with her *US, 1922*

- Petted and indulged by the old man, Julio grows up into a sleek-haired finale hopper who tangos sinuously[.] — S.J. Perlman, *Most of the Most of S.J. Perlman*, p. 546, 1958

find them, fool them, fuck them, forget them

used as a formula for male relationships with females *US, 1966*

The earliest form is "find, feel, fuck and forget," also known as the "four F method." Multiple variants exist.

- "Find 'em, fool 'em, fuck 'em, and forget 'em," he was often heard to say[.] — Larry McMurtry, *The Last Picture Show*, p. 103, 1966
- Peggy Gravel: Go ahead, feel her up! Just like you did to me! Find em, feel em, fuck em, forget em ... is THAT your new motto?? Grizelda Brown: Zip that gaping hole of a mouth up, Peggy, before I plug it up with my fist. Peggy Gravel: You're just like all the rest of the common dykes in this town! — John Waters, *Desperate Living*, 1977

fine *adjective*

1 sexually attractive *US, 1944*

- He's so fine (doo-lang-doo-lang-doo-lang) / Wish he were mine (doo-lang-doo-lang-doo-lang) — The Chiffons, *He's So Fine*, 1963
- Damn, you looking good. You're fucking fine. You're a fine-looking woman. — Chris Rock, *Rock This!*, p. 185, 1997

2 in twelve-step recovery programs such as Alcoholics Anonymous, *f*ucked-up, *i*nsecure, *n*eurotic and *e*motional *US, 1998*

- — Christopher Cavanaugh, *AA to Z*, p. 93, 1998

▶ **fine as May wine**

excellent *US, 1964*

- I met chicks who were fine as May wine, and cats who were hip to all happenings. — Malcolm X and Alex Haley, *The Autobiography of Malcolm X*, p. 56, 1964

▶ **fine like wine**

very good *US, 1967*

- "How are you doing, brother?" "You tell me," Max said. "Fine, fine, fine like wine, jack." — John Williams, *The Man Who Cried I Am*, p. 43, 1967

fine and dandy *adjective*

splendid, excellent *US, 1910*

- Nice moves, very stylish; made the prosecutor look like a high-school football coach. Sent from the man? Andre nodding, pleased. Fine of fine and dandy, man. — Elmore Leonard, *Gold Coast*, p. 27, 1980
- Everything I do is fine and dandy to you, Miss Celie she say. — Alice Walker, *The Color Purple*, p. 57, 1982

fine and dandy, like sugar candy *adjective*

splendid, excellent *US, 1949*

- Although, if the sausage hadn't slipped out of the sandwich, everything would have been fine and dandy, like sugar candy. — Nelson Algren, *The Man with the Golden Arm*, p. 125, 1949

fine how-d'ya do *noun*

a dilemma, a problem *US, 1946*

- Jay was talking to a police captain and some detectives. "Ain't this a fine how-d'ya-do?" he said glumly. — Mezz Mezzrow, *Really the Blues*, p. 290, 1946

finest *noun*

the police *US, 1914*

Used with irony, alluding to the popular phrase identifying a city's policemen as "the city's finest citizens." In 1875, New York began to claim it had the "finest police force in the world," a phrase borrowed from the claim of General Joseph Hooker during the US Civil War that he commanded "the finest army on the planet." In the early C20, New York began to refer to its fire department as "the bravest" and the police simply as "the finest."

- Those two representatives of New York's finest stared at me as though I had two heads. — Mezz Mezzrow, *Really the Blues*, p. 301, 1946
- And two of Berkeley's finest marched Mario Savio off from amidst a crowd of demonstrators. — *Berkeley Barb*, p. 3, 2nd December 1966
- And then it was our turn and sure enough, in charged four of the finest, with expressions of rage such as I have never seen. — Terry Southern, *Now Dig This: The Unspeakable Writings of Terry Southern 1950–1995*, p. 126, November 1968
- New York's finest, Chiodo thought. The phrase covered a lot of ground. — Charles Whited, *Chiodo*, p. 147, 1973

fine weather *noun*

a pretty girl *US, 1947*

- — Marcus Hanna Boulware, *Jive and Slang of Students in Negro Colleges*, 1947

finger *noun*

1 the identification of a criminal by a witness *US, 1947*

- He didn't get a finger. He was free. — Willard Motley, *Knock on Any Door*, p. 176, 1947

2 a gesture of contempt, the index finger raised from a fist with the palm inwards as the hand jerks upward *US, 1961*

- To give the finger to man like Flint Granite was, of course, reprehensible[.] — Max Shulman, *Anyone Got a Match?*, p. 25, 1964
- [S]he says something rude that I can't hear and Julian gives her the finger. — Bret Easton Ellis, *Less Than Zero*, p. 178, 1985
- But he felt the other boys' eyes on him and flipped the finger anyhow. — Jess Mowry, *Way Past Cool*, p. 20, 1992

▶ **on the finger**

on credit *US, 1951*

- — Swen A. Larsen, *American Speech*, p. 97, May 1951: "The vocabulary of poker"
- — Albert H. Morehead, *The Complete Guide to Winning Poker*, p. 262, 1967
- — David M. Hayano, *Poker Faces*, p. 185, 1982

finger *verb*

1 to cast a spell, to curse *US, 1960*

- "He handles the bucket 'n sponges 'n in between he fingers the guy I'm fightin', 'n if it's close he fingers the ref 'n judges." — Nelson Algren, *The Neon Wilderness*, p. 62, 1960

2 to manipulate and penetrate a vagina or anus for sexual purposes *US, 1988*

- Instead I slid my hand between her thighs and fingered her cunt until she begged me, "Oh, Charlie, now! Do it to me!" — Charles Manson, *Manson in His Own Words*, p. 93, 1988
- Jake treated her like dirt, always bragging to guys on the baseball team about other girls he'd fingered or fucked. — Jason Starr, *Lights Out*, p. 32, 2006

3 to identify; to name; to inform upon somebody *US, 1930*

- Waiting at the airport was one of the junior officers of the Jacksonville chapter who was to "finger" the victim to be. — Burton Turkus and Sid Feder, *Murder, Inc.*, p. 7, 1951
- I had extricated her from some really bad jams with an ugly element, did some fronting and fingering for me. — Caryl Chessman, *Cell 2456 Death Row*, p. 173, 1954
- Some kid I had helped out fingered me. — Herbert Huncke, *Guilty of Everything*, pp. 82–83, 1990
- The Hungarians were going to buy the one guy that could finger Soze for them. — *The Usual Suspects*, 1995

finger artist *noun*

a lesbian *US, 1970*

- — Clarence Major, *Dictionary of Afro-American Slang*, p. 53, 1970

fingerbang *verb*

to insert a finger or fingers into a partner's vagina or rectum for their sexual pleasure *US, 1990*

- I mean I've sucked some titties and finger banged a couple of hunnies but I never stuck it in. — *Boyz N The Hood*, 1990
- I'm gonna finger-fuck her tight little asshole! Finger-bang ... and tea-bag my balls ... in her mouth! — Kevin Smith, *Jay and Silent Bob Strike Back*, p. 50, 2001
- "You wanna fingerbang me?" I cooed. "Let's mess around." — Sarah Katherine Lewis, *Indecent*, p. 69, 2006

finger bowl faggot *noun*
a wealthy, ostentatious, homosexual male *US, 1965*

- In this rarified area, johns are not johns but cuff link faggots or queens, an expression derived from their tendency to wear extravagant looking jewelry. They are also called "finger bowl faggots." — Antony James, *America's Homosexual Underground*, p. 29, 1965

fingerfuck *verb*
to insert a finger or fingers into a partner's vagina or rectum *UK, 1793*
Plain-speaking former US President Lyndon Johnson (1963–1969) was said to have said "Richard Milhouse Nixon has done for the United States of America what pantyhose did for finger-fucking."

- I was a guest at Aly Khan's for dinner, when you were still back in Newark, New Jersey, finger-fucking your little Jewish girl friend. — Philip Roth, *Portnoy's Complaint*, p. 239, 1969
- "Who taught you to kiss like that, Cousin Alldean?" "Yes, as a matter of fact, he did." "He fingerfuck you too?" — Earl Thompson, *Tattoo*, p. 475, 1974
- His finger-fucking talents were obviously driving her crazy, because her entire body began to move spasmodically. — *Adam Film World*, p. 54, August 1978
- "Then Irwin began to finger-fuck me to make my hole bigger," Millie continued. — Lora Shaner, *Madam*, p. 89, 1999

fingerfuck; finger fucking *noun*
the manual stimulation of another's vagina or anus *US, 1962*

- Finger fucking, not sucking or anything. — *Body, Mind, and the Sensory Gateways*, p. 68, 1962
- — Eugene Landy, *The Underground Dictionary*, p. 77, 1971
- After an hour or two of the above activities, we may wish to reach orgasm by either fellatio or penis-anal intercourse, or maybe finger fucking and fellatio. — *The Hite Report on Male Sexuality*, p. 823, 1987
- Putting a latex glove on your hand for finger fucking protects both you and your partner[.] — Tristan Taormino, *Pucker Up*, p. 47, 2001

finger-fucker *noun*
a person who fingerfucks *US, 1969*

- Up here in the airways, down there on the ground, you're the best finger-fucker around. — Steve Cannon, *Groove, Bang, and Jive Around*, p. 131, 1969
- As he worked his fingers inside C, like the master finger-fucker that he was, and as a big-titted blonde was being eaten by Roachmen from Mars on "Shock Theater," he grabbed the slippery vegetable with his other hand[.] — Richard Price, *The Wanderers*, p. 40, 1974

finger job *noun*
1 digital stimulation of the vagina or anus *US, 1963*

- There have been times during a new movie that turned me on, I wished somebody would give me a finger job. I've gone back to the bathroom and done it myself. — Roger Blake, *The Porno Movies*, p. 200, 1970
- — Eugene Landy, *The Underground Dictionary*, p. 77, 1971

2 an act of betrayal *US, 1974*

- "No, it wasn't exactly a finger job. What she did was sit at the bar, keeping an eye on the guy." — Elmore Leonard, *Mr. Majestyk*, p. 62, 1974

finger line *noun*
a line-up in which crime victims or witnesses attempt to identify the criminal(s) *US, 1976*

- — Troy Harris, *A Booklet of Criminal Argot, Cant and Jargon*, p. 10, 1976

finger louse *noun*
a police informer *US, 1956*

- — *American Speech*, p. 98, May 1956: "Smugglers' argot in the southwest"

finger man *noun*
1 a person who provides criminals with inside information to aid a robbery or other crime *US, 1930*

- These are finger men for the hold-up gangs, who scrape up acquaintances with the girls, then lift their house-keys from their purses. — Jack Lait and Lee Mortimer, *Chicago Confidential*, p. 70, 1950
- His activities as the "finger-man" of the terrorizing gang meant he had used his occult skills nefariously to draw the gang's victims out of hiding. — Donald Wilson, *My Six Convicts*, p. 322, 1951
- Our finger man is a junkie punk. — Iceberg Slim (Robert Beck), *Pimp*, p. 252, 1969
- [W]e even used to pay off a bunch of finger men who lined up jobs like a hijacking or a robbery. — Martin Gosch, *The Last Testament of Lucky Luciano*, p. 79, 1975

2 a professional killer *US, 1930*

- George P. Harding, a 39-year-old gunman and underworld fingerman, was shot to death by Joe Nesline[.] — Jack Lait and Lee Mortimer, *Washington Confidential*, p. 129, 1951

finger off *verb*
to bring a woman to orgasm by hand *US, 1969*

- I mean she laid right there on the floor and fingered herself off three more times. — Joey V., *Portrait of Joey*, p. 123, 1969

finger poker *noun*
a game of poker bet on credit *US, 1951*

- — *American Speech*, p. 98, May 1951
- — Albert H. Morehead, *The Complete Guide to Winning Poker*, p. 262, 1967

fingerprint *noun*
in poker, a player's signature move *US, 1996*

- Albert always raises Big Maxx in early position. It's his fingerprint. — John Vorhaus, *The Big Book of Poker Slang*, p. 16, 1996

finger sheet *noun*
in horse racing, a publication giving the entries and odds for a day's races *US, 1951*

- — David W. Maurer, *Argot of the Racetrack*, p. 26, 1951

fingers to fingers
used as an oath and pledge *US, 1950*
The original pledge was heard on the US television comedy *The Life of Riley* (NBC, 1949–58); the full pledge, used by the Brooklyn Patriots of Los Angeles fraternal group, was "Fingers to fingers, toes to toes, if I break this pact, break my nose." On the comedy *The Honeymooners* (CBS, 1955–56), the toast version used by the fraternal order of Raccoons was "Fingers to fingers, thumbs to thumbs, watch out below, here she comes."

fingertips *noun*
someone adept at masturbating others *US, 1990*

- — Charles Shafer, *Folk Speech in Texas Prisons*, p. 204, 1990

finger-walk *verb*
with one hand, to roll a coin over and through the knuckles *US, 1981*

- Red removed a half-dollar-size gambling chip from his pocket and tried to make it finger-walk on the back of his hand. — Gerald Petievich, *Money Men*, p. 26, 1981

finger wave *noun*
1 a digital examination of the rectum, either as part of an prostate examination or a drug search *US, 1962*

- Have you ever gone to the doctor for a finger wave? — Angelo d'Arcangelo, *The Homosexual Handbook*, p. 83, 1968
- When they check out cells we always have to take it [a mascara pencil] and stick it up our butt so we can hide it. They never give us a finger wave here [anal inspection], it's against the rules. — Bruce Jackson, *In the Life*, p. 400, 1972
- Jack, walking into the house with his glass, heard Cullen say, "... give it the old finger wave," but didn't hear what Harby thought about it. — Elmore Leonard, *Bandits*, p. 261, 1987
- Convicts called it a "finger wave." — Pete Earley, *The Hot House*, p. 56, 1992

2 a gesture with the middle finger, usually interpreted to mean "fuck you!" *US, 1976*

- — Porter Bibb, *CB Bible*, p. 93, 1976

finif *noun*
1 a five-dollar bill *US, 1859*
From the Yiddish finif (five).

- Widely used in colloquial English, especially by sports fans, gamblers, Broadway types, nightclub habitues, and newspaper columnists, who memorialize these gaudy provinces of diversion. — Leo Rosten, *The Joys of Yiddish*, p. 117, 1968
- Ray saw plenty of people he knew, but nobody he could tap for a finnif or a sawbuck. — Robert Campbell, *Juice*, p. 11, 1988

2 a prison sentence of five years *US, 1904*

- — Vincent J. Monteleone, *Criminal Slang*, p. 84, 1949

3 in dice games, a five on one die *US, 1950*

- — *The Annals of the American Academy of Political and Social Sciences*, p. 124, May 1950

finish verb

▶ **finish on the chinstrap**
in horse racing, to win a race easily under restraint US, 1951
- — David W. Maurer, *Argot of the Racetrack*, p. 26, 1951

finishing school noun
a reformatory for juvenile delinquents US, 1976
- — Troy Harris, *A Booklet of Criminal Argot, Cant and Jargon*, p. 10, 1976

fink noun

1 an informer US, 1902
- He looks like a dirty fink to me. A first-class enameled fink! — Ralph Ellison, *Invisible Man*, p. 219, 1947
- The conversation turned to finks. — William Tulio Divale, *I Lived Inside the Campus Revolution*, p. 111, 1970
- They never go into detail, they say here's the name of the fink, do him. — Elmore Leonard, *Glitz*, p. 179, 1985
- Don't you know you're working with one of the biggest finks in the city? — Herbert Huncke, *Guilty of Everything*, p. 195, 1990

2 a nonunion job or worker US, 1917
- "With all your education, you can't even keep a fink job driving a taxicab," Ruth screamed. — James T. Farrell, *Ruth and Bertram*, p. 95, 1955

3 in circus and carnival usage, a broken piece of merchandise US, 1981
- — Don Wilmeth, *The Language of American Popular Entertainment*, p. 91, 1981

fink verb
to inform on US, 1925
- Doolie will fink if he has to. — William Burroughs, *Junkie*, p. 56, 1953
- "And your partner finked on you." — Elmore Leonard, *Mr. Paradise*, p. 212, 2002

fink out verb
to betray; to inform US, 1962
- Took part in a payroll heist and got finked out. — Elmore Leonard, *Mr. Paradise*, p. 122, 2002

finky adjective
disloyal, cowardly US, 1948
- "It would serve the finky bastard right," said the fat, gruff colonel. — Joseph Heller, *Catch 22*, p. 441, 1955

finski noun
a five-dollar bill US, 1952
- "I want to live—at least until I drink up this Finski." — Malcolm Braly, *It's Cold Out There*, p. 102, 1966

fin-up noun
a prison sentence of five years to life US, 1961–1962
- — Frank Prewitt and Francis Schaeffer, *Vacaville Vocabulary*, 1961–1962

FIP noun
a scene in a pornographic film or a photograph of a man pretending to ejaculate inside a vagina or rectum US, 1995
An initialism for "fake internal pop-shot"; used in softcore pornography.
- — *Adult Video News*, p. 44, August 1995

fire noun

▶ **on fire**
(used of a homosexual) patently, obviously US, 1994
As in **FLAMING**.
- — Kevin Dilallo, *The Unofficial Gay Manual*, p. 243, 1994

fire verb

1 to light up a cigarette or a marijuana cigarette US, 1950
Literally "to apply a flame."
- While I fired a cig he called an extension number and was connected. — Mickey Spillane, *My Gun is Quick*, p. 13, 1950

2 to inject a drug intravenously US, 1936
- — David Maurer and Victor Vogel, *Narcotics and Narcotic Addiction*, p. 406, 1973
- Ever fire when you were in the joint? — Joseph Wambaugh, *The Blue Knight*, p. 30, 1973
- Clayton was to fire in his leg—he had a big vein in his calf. — John Allen, *Assault with a Deadly Weapon*, p. 168, 1977

3 to destroy by arson US, 1957
- So bad he'd fire his hotels if he could collect on them. — Jim Thompson, *The Kill-Off*, p. 27, 1957

4 to ejaculate UK, 1891
- The last time that Hans fired too early in the motel room, the sneering groupie said, "You better start carrying two jizz rags." — Joseph Wambaugh, *The Delta Star*, p. 105, 1983

▶ **fire the ack-ack gun**
to smoke a cigarette dipped in a heroin solution US, 1969
- — Richard Lingeman, *Drugs from A to Z*, p. 78, 1969

fire-and-forget adjective
(used of a missile) guided automatically US, 1991
- — *American Speech*, p. 389, Winter 1991: "Among the new words"

fireball noun

1 an extremely energetic person US, 1949
- Children who were once seen as "bundles of energy," "daydreamers," or "fireballs," are now considered "hyperactive," "distractible," and "impulsive." — Thomas Armstrong, *The Myth of the A.D.D. Child*, p. 4, 1995

2 in pinball, a ball that leaves play without scoring any points US, 1977
- — Bobbye Claire Natkin and Steve Kirk, *All About Pinball*, p. 112, 1977

3 a tracer bullet US, 1962
- — *American Speech*, p. 268, December 1962: "The language of traffic policemen"

fireball verb
to drive fast US, 1953
- The top was down and they were fireballing it back. — Edwin Gilbert, *The Hot and the Cool*, p. 16, 1953
- Ten days later the strip was in use and Lieutenant Ken Walsh was fireballing a Corsair down the strip. — Robert Leckie, *Strong Men Armed*, p. 153, 1962

firebug noun

1 an arsonist; a person with a pathological love of fire US, 1872
- It was wonderfully exhilarating. I guess everybody has a little of the instinct of a firebug. — Harry Grey, *The Hoods*, p. 209, 1952
- You are going to catch all the firebugs and make everybody safe in their beds. — George V. Higgins, *The Rat on Fire*, p. 7, 1981
- Jesus Bernal yearned to abandon Skip Wiley's circus and rejoin his old gang of dedicated extortionists, bombers, and firebugs. — Carl Hiaasen, *Tourist Season*, p. 135, 1986

2 in poker, a player who bets and plays in a reckless fashion US, 1996
- — John Vorhaus, *The Big Book of Poker Slang*, p. 16, 1996

fireburner noun
a zealot US, 1972
- I like to have me a little bitty young lawyer, a fire-burner. — Bruce Jackson, *Outside the Law*, p. 130, 1972

firecan noun

1 a Soviet-built radar system used against US aircraft during the Vietnam war US, 1987
- — Joseph Tuso, *Singing the Vietnam Blues*, p. 250, 1990: Glossary

2 a type of radar system in a military aircraft US, 1999
- Arranged in a circle around a "Firecan" radar, these 85-millimeter guns spat shells at Rasimus one gun at a time in a circular pattern. — John Darrell Sherwood, *Fast Movers*, p. 57, 1999
- "I got a Firecan in search mode." A Firecan was an old AAA radar. — Richard Herman, *The Last Phoenix*, p. 385, 2002

fire crotch noun
a true redhead with red pubic hair US, 1993
- Millie, a 10th-grade student with red hair, was called "fire crotch" by several sixth-grade boys, who giggled and snickered among themselves. — *New York Times*, p. C-11, 24th February 1994
- It's kinda become more of a routine for Lindsay Lohan to bare her fire crotch once in a while now ... the babe just doesn't seem to care whether it's a nip-slip or baring her pussy!!! — lindsaylohan.celebden.com, 18th November 2006

fired adjective
excited, eager, sexually aroused US, 1968
- — Collin Baker et al., *College Undergraduate Slang Study Conducted at Brown University*, p. 117, 1968

fire-eater noun
a ferociously brave person US, 1808
- I don't deal blackjack so good, hobbled like this, but I maintain I'm a fire-eater in a stud game. — Ken Kesey, *One Flew Over The Cuckoo's Nest*, p. 232, 1962

firefly noun
a helicopter equipped with a powerful search light, usually teamed with several gunships in the Vietnam war *US, 1991*
- The Firefly backed off as a couple of Huey gunships swung in from the north. — Gary Linderer, *The Eyes of the Eagle*, p. 93, 1991

fire in the hole!
1 used as a warning that an explosive is about to be detonated *US, 1986*
- Fire in the hole! — *Platoon*, 1986
- If we were moving along with another unit and an explosive device was spotted, one would usually hear, "Fire in the hole!" three times[.] — James Kirschke, *Not Going Home Alone*, p. 204, 2001
2 in the illegal production of alcohol, used as a warning of approaching law enforcement officials *US, 1974*
- Adapted from the coal mines, where it is used to indicate that the fuse has been lit and a powder charge is about to explode. — David W. Maurer, *Kentucky Moonshine*, p. 118, 1974

fireless cooker noun
a gas chamber *US, 1962*
- The gas chamber—or, as the prisoners call it, "the fireless cooker"—has only two seats. — *San Francisco Chronicle*, p. 27, 30th September 1962

fire on verb
1 to excite sexually *US, 1969*
- Girls with long legs fire me on. — *Screw*, p. 5, 7th March 1969
2 to punch someone *US, 1970*
- In a fight, if someone strikes you or you strike them with your fist, you "fire on" them. — Bobby Seale, *Seize the Time*, p. 410, 1970

firetop noun
a redhead *US, 2005*
- [T]hat didn't stop this five-foot-ten-inch hottie from becoming the first fire-top on the cover of Glamour magazine. — Mr. Skin, *Mr. Skin's Skincyclopedia*, p. 170, 2005

fire up verb
to light and smoke a cigarette *US, 1962*
- "Don't be firin' that thing up in the house." — Leon Bing, *Do or Die*, p. 216, 1991

firewater noun
1 strong alcohol *US, 1817*
A term associated with Native Americans, often pronounced with an ambiguous accent approximating an accent used by Indian actors in old cowboy movies.
- "This fire water is not his usual beverage." — Frederick Kohner, *Gidget Goes Hawaiian*, p. 59, 1961
- Will you look at the Big Chief slug down on that firewater! — Ken Kesey, *One Flew Over the Cuckoo's Nest*, p. 227, 1962
- Firewater brings out the real browness of this buffalo. — Oscar Zeta Acosta, *The Autobiography of a Brown Buffalo*, p. 36, 1972
- Firewater, Tonto? Is that what you— — *48 Hours*, 1982
2 GBL, a drug that is nearly identical in molecular structure to the recreational drug GHB *US, 1999*
- Another case involved a 14-year-old Bernalillo County boy whose heart rate slowed after drinking bright red "Firewater." — *Santa Fe New Mexican*, p. A1, 29th January 1999

fireworks noun
an exchange of gunfire *US, 1864*
- — Joseph E. Ragen and Charles Finston, *Inside the World's Toughest Prison*, p. 799, 1962: "Penitentiary and underworld glossary"

first base noun
1 in teenage categorization of sexual activity, a level of foreplay, most commonly referring to kissing *US, 1928*
The exact degree varies by region and even by school.
- Anyhow, you're just saying that 'cause you're jealous and can't get to first base with Lucky. — Hal Ellson, *Tomboy*, p. 76, 1950
- Maybe I don't like the idea of another guy making time with Fay when I've never been able to get to first base. — Jim Thompson, *After Dark, My Sweet*, p. 31, 1955
- "So did you get to first base?" — Frederick Kohner, *The Affairs of Gidget*, p. 33, 1963
- They've all tried. Nobody's got to first base. — *M*A*S*H*, 1970

2 in blackjack played in American casinos, the seat immediately to the dealer's left *US, 1985*
- — Steve Kuriscak, *Casino Talk*, p. 23, 1985

first horse nickname
the First Cavalry Division, US Army *US, 1968*
- — Carl Fleischhauer, *A Glossary of Army Slang*, p. 19, 1968
- The Viet Cong and the NVA would also come to know this "First Horse" well. — Kenneth Mertel, *Year of the Horse*, p. 250, 1968

first Louie noun
a first lieutenant *US, 1963*
- A first louie (even a Marine first louie) didn't rate much attention at an air force base. — Frank Owens, *Soldiers Such as We*, p. 203, 2003

first-of-May noun
1 an inexperienced worker *US, 1961*
A circus word, based on the start of the circus season.
- "Some of the fellows in the shop laugh about you behind your back. Know what they call you? 'First of May.' That's an old carnival term for someone who comes out in the spring but doesn't last through the winter. They don't think you have the stuff to stick[.]" — Earl Thompson, *Tattoo*, p. 573, 1974
- More common certainly than having some first-of-May, fucking-new-guy rookie triage medic sit there picking at a million slivers of shrapnel with a manicure scissors, a magnifying glass, and a bottle of hydrogen peroxide. — Larry Heinemann, *Paco's Story*, p. 51, 1986
2 a newcomer to a circus or carnival *US, 1926*
- — Joe McKennon, *Circus Lingo*, p. 34, 1980

First of the First noun
the First Battalion of the First Regiment, US Marine Corps *US, 1982*
Korean war usage.
- So the "First of the First" was rested and scrappy when they moved north through darkness and a swirling snowstorm at two o'clock on the morning of December 8. — Joseph C. Goulden, *Korea*, p. 376, 1982
- I witnessed the fighting from the vantage point of Company Commander, H&S Company, 1st Battalion, 1st Marines—which we called "the 1st of the 1st of the 1st." — William B. Hopkins, *One Bugle No Drums*, p. x, 1986

first pig noun
a first sergeant, the most senior noncommissioned officer in the US Army *US, 1975*
- "The first pig, sir. He's got himself down on the jump manifest." — William Singley, *Bragg*, p. 176, 2006

first sergeant noun
your wife *US, 1976*
- — Wayne Floyd, *Jason's Authentic Dictionary of CB Slang*, p. 16, 1976

first shirt noun
a first sergeant in the US Army *US, 1969*
- The "first shirt" spent the next fifteen minutes feasting on the young buck sergeant's behind. — Gary Linderer, *The Eyes of the Eagle*, p. 85, 1991
- I made a beeline for the tactical operations center to keep my appointment with the new first shirt. — Larry Chambers, *Recondo*, p. 226, 1992
- Secondly, gunnies have enough rank that few people screw with them, and they do not have to be an asshole like the first shirt (sergeant) to get the job done. — John Culbertson, *A Sniper in the Arizona*, p. 104, 1999

first sleeve noun
a first sergeant *US, 1956*
- — *American Speech*, p. 227, October 1956: "More United States Air Force slang"
- — Carl Fleischhauer, *A Glossary of Army Slang*, p. 19, 1968

first soldier noun
a first sergeant in the US Army *US, 1946*
- Now first sergeants are renowned in the army for being the "Top Kick," the "First Soldier," the senior NCO in the unit, and usually he's the toughest man in the company. — Larry Gwin, *Baptism (A Vietnam Memoir)*, p. 74, 1999

first today and last tomorrow
in horse racing, said of an inconsistent performer *US, 1951*
- — David W. Maurer, *Argot of the Racetrack*, p. 26, 1951

fish *noun*

1 a pimp *US, 1963*
- "Jean wouldn't waste two minutes talking to a fish." — Malcolm Braly, *Shake Him Till He Rattles*, p. 40, 1963

2 a professional wrestler who is regularly assigned to lose to advance the careers of others *US, 1990*
- Sometimes known as fish, redshirts or PLs (professional losers). — rec.sports.pro-wrestling, 17th July 1990

3 a woman, usually heterosexual *UK, 1891*
- — Anon., *The Gay Girl's Guide*, p. 9, 1949
- — Donald Webster Cory and John P. LeRoy, *The Homosexual and His Society*, p. 264, 1963: "A lexicon of homosexual slang"
- But a jealous bartender, who Knows, tells three sailors who want to make it with her that shes not a fish, shes a fruit[.] — John Rechy, *City of Night*, p. 118, 1963
- I know that women are referred to as "fish" in fag-lang. But that's defamation. — Angelo d'Arcangelo, *The Homosexual Handbook*, p. 210, 1968

4 a prisoner who has recently arrived in prison *US, 1864*
- Word buzzed through the grapevine about the new "fish[.]" — Mezz Mezzrow, *Really the Blues*, p. 10, 1946
- Much more, however, responsibility for lifting me from that blue funk of depression this place must naturally impinge on "Fish"—new convicts—can be attributed to an increasing awareness[.] — Neal Cassady, *Grace Beats Karma*, p. 61, 16th October 1958
- Bud was between romances, the Parole Board having sent his previous inamorata out several weeks prior to the time Sam showed up in his group of "fish." — *New York Mattachine Newsletter*, p. 6, July 1961
- As a "fish" (prison slang for a new inmate) at Charlestown, I was physically miserable and as evil-tempered as a snake, being suddenly without drugs. — Malcolm X and Alex Haley, *The Autobiography of Malcolm X*, p. 152, 1964

5 a drug addict who supports his habit by pimping *US, 1955*
- — *American Speech*, p. 87, May 1955: "Narcotic argot along the Mexican border"

6 in poker, an unskilled player who is a likely victim of a skilled professional *US, 1996*
- — Peter O. Steiner, *Thursday Night Poker*, p. 411, 1996

7 a poor chess player *US, 1971*
- — *American Speech*, p. 233, Autumn – Winter 1971: "Checkschmuck! The slang of the chess player"

8 a torpedo *US, 1948*
- — *American Speech*, p. 38, February 1948: "Talking under water: speech in submarines"

9 a dollar *US, 1950*
- — Hyman E. Goldin et al., *Dictionary of American Underworld Lingo*, p. 70, 1950
- The clients of the Carne Organization were charged a minimum, of one hundred fish per diem and they expected service in their homes. — Raymond Chandler, *The Long Goodbye*, p. 97, 1953

fish *verb*

1 to dance in a slow and sexual manner, moving the body but not the feet *US, 1952*
- "Something slow and sweet so we can fish." The music came on, and he took her in the close, tight embrace of the dance[.] — Hal Ellson, *The Golden Spike*, p. 28, 1952
- You ever dance fish, West? — Evan Hunter, *The Blackboard Jungle*, p. 159, 1954
- We fished real close and felt each other up. — Piri Thomas, *Down These Mean Streets*, p. 223, 1969
- — Kenn "Naz" Young, *Naz's Underground Dictionary*, p. 29, 1973

2 in gin, to discard in a manner that is designed to lure a desired card from an opponent *US, 1965*
- — Irwin Steig, *Play Gin to Win*, p. 138, 1965

3 in poker, to stay with a bad hand in the hope of drawing the only card that can possibly make the hand a good one *US, 2003*
- — Victor H. Royer, *Casino Gamble Talk*, p. 57, 2003

4 to use a prison's plumbing system to pass a note from cell to cell *US, 2000*
- [F]ishing (passing messages from one cell to another by flushing a line attached to a kite down the toilet, to be retrieved by another inmate housed in another cell[.]) — Bill Valentine, *Gangs and Their Tattoos*, p. 38, 2000

▶ **fish for food**
to gossip *US, 1947*
- — Marcus Hanna Boulware, *Jive and Slang of Students in Negro Colleges*, 1947

▶ **fish or cut bait; fish, cut bait or go ashore**
make up your mind! *US, 1860*

The shorter, two-option phrase is more popular today than the longer original.
- — Charles F. Haywood, *Yankee Dictionary*, p. 59, 1963

fish *adjective*
newly arrived *US, 1974*
- New or "fish" bulls do it a lot as part of their orientation. — Tim Findley, *The Rolling Stone Reader*, p. 87, 1974

fish and chips *noun*
in poker, a group of unskilled players with a lot of money to lose *US, 1996*
- — John Vorhaus, *The Big Book of Poker Slang*, p. 17, 1996

fishbed-D *nickname*
the Soviet MiG-21 fighter aircraft *US, 1990*
- Flak on the left, flak on the right/ Fishbeds-D and the old launch light. — Joseph Tuso, *Singing the Vietnam Blues*, p. 68, 1990: Cloudy Night, No Moonlight

fishbelly *noun*
a white person *US, 1985*
- "Heavenly days," I said, "talk about ethnic stereotyping." "You go on back to Boston, fishbelly, and stay there and don't come near my lady again." — Robert Parker, *Taming a Seahorse*, p. 39, 1986

fish-burner *noun*
a sled dog *US, 1967*
An extension of the early C20 "hay-burner" (horse).
- — Russell Tabbert, *Dictionary of Alaskan English*, p. 205, 1991

fish cake *noun*
five dollars *US, 1985*
- — Steve Kuriscak, *Casino Talk*, p. 23, 1985

fish-eater *noun*
a Roman Catholic *US, 1975*
From the largely forgotten practice of abstaining from eating meat on Fridays.
- "How do you know I'm Catholic?" Tony asked him. "You look like a fish-eater," the priest said to him. — Brian Boyer, *Prince of Thieves*, p. 56, 1975

fish eye *noun*
an expressionless stare *US, 1941*
From the appearance.
- I gets a big charge going in there with these two birds, seeing people give me the fish eye, thinking what's this herbert doing in our boozer[.] — John Peter Jones, *Feather Pluckers*, p. 43, 1964

fish eyes *noun*
tapioca *US, 1918*
- "Rubber heels 'n fisheyes again" was the word on the meatloaf and tapioca[.] — Nelson Algren, *The Man with the Golden Arm*, p. 208, 1949
- Compare what other people are eating to gross things their food looks like. Examples: tapioca pudding—fish eyes. — Matt Groening, *Bart Simpson's Guide to Life*, p. 24, 1993

fish gallery *noun*
the area in a prison where newly arrived prisoners are kept *US, 1962*
- — Joseph E. Ragen and Charles Finston, *Inside the World's Toughest Prison*, p. 799, 1962: "Penitentiary and underworld glossary"

fishhead *noun*
a person from Southeast Asia *US, 1971*
- I can hear what they are saying but all I can think of is pig, white, guinea, spic, hebe, motherfucker, nigger, donkey, mick, fishhead. — Dennis Smith, *Report from Engine Co. 82*, p. 62, 1972

fish-hook *noun*
1 in a deck of playing cards, any seven *US, 1967*
- — Albert H. Morehead, *The Complete Guide to Winning Poker*, p. 262, 1967
2 in a deck of playing cards, a jack or knave *US, 1981*
- — Jim Glenn, *Programed Poker*, p. 156, 1981

fishies *noun*
MDMA, the recreational drug best known as ecstasy *US, 2002*
- The drug Ecstasy was called fishies or double stacks, according to the affidavit. — *Orlando Sentinel*, p. B2, 17th August 2002

fishing expedition *noun*
a litigation tactic of requesting a broad range of probably irrelevant information in the hope of discovering something helpful *US, 1874*

- I was wondering why so many judges accuse—there is no other word—why they accuse lawyers of going on fishing expeditions. — *The Lawyers Weekly*, 8th July 1994

fishing pole *noun*

any contrivance fashioned to pass or retrieve items from cell to cell *US, 2001*

- — AFSCME Local 3963, *The Correctional Officer's Guide to Prison Slang*, 2001

fish line *noun*

in a prison, a string used to pull objects from one cell to another *US, 1989*

- — James Harris, *A Convict's Dictionary*, p. 32, 1989

fish queen *noun*

a homosexual male who spends a great deal of time in the company of heterosexual women *US, 1941*

- Fish-Queen—Properly a "cunt-sucker," but in general usage applied to any homosexual who makes a point of bringing women with him[.] — Anon, *The Gay Girl's Guide*, p. 9, 1949
- — Guy Strait, *The Lavender Lexicon*, 1st June 1964

fish row *noun*

a section of a jail housing newly arrived inmates *US, 1982*

- The new inmates stay on "fish row" approximately three to four weeks. — Wayne S. Wooden, *Men Behind Bars*, p. 101, 1982
- "I'ma come holler at you when you get to Fish Row." — Colton Simpson, *Inside the Crips*, p. 225, 2005

fish scale *noun*

crack cocaine *US, 1989*

From the appearance.

- The kids out here don't know a flake from a fish—if you asked them what fishscale is, they wouldn't know. [Fishscale is high-grade cocaine powder with few rock-like chunks.] — Terry Williams, *The Cocaine Kids*, p. 41, 1989

fish scales *noun*

cocaine *US, 2002*

- The wiretaps recorded a primer of street slang for powder cocaine: white lady, white fingers, soft, fish scales and sand. — *Orlando Sentinel*, p. B2, 17th August 2002

fishskin *noun*

a condom *US, 1936*

- In my memory the image of him standing by the car and holding up that transparent sack of rubber or fishskin was the finale—CURTAIN. — Mary McCarthy, *How I Grew*, pp. 80 – 81, 1987

fishtail *verb*

to cause the rear of an airplane or car to swerve from side to side *US, 1927*

- I wrenched the wheel over, felt the rear end start to slide, brought it out with a splash of power and almost ran up the side of the cliff as the car fishtailed. — Mickey Spillane, *Kiss Me Deadly*, p. 7, 1952
- [W]hen his hand came out empty he began fishtailing across three lanes of highway. — Richard Price, *Clockers*, p. 517, 1992
- The boys had almost reached the lower corner when the cop car skidded around the intersection behind them, fishtailed, recovered sloppily[.] — Jess Mowry, *Way Past Cool*, p. 15, 1992

fish tank *noun*

a holding cell for newly arrived prisoners *US, 1954*

A wonderful pun with independently formed terms.

- We had our heads shaved (a practice soon discontinued), were mugged, measured for Bertillon indexing, fingerprinted, and then assigned single cells in what was then the "Fish tank" section of the Old Prison. — Caryl Chessman, *Cell 2456 Death Row*, p. 217, 1954
- Even when I was in the fish tank (the thirty days of processing and classification in lock-down you go through before you enter the main population), I heard about the man[.] — James Lee Burke, *The Lost Get-Back Boogie*, p. 6, 1986
- "[T]hey will let you know your disposal options when you get to the Fish Tank." — Jimmy Lerner, *You Got Nothing Coming*, p. 36, 2002

fish tier *noun*

a section of a prison housing new inmates *US, 1981*

- Someone I knew from the reform school slipped me a boning knife when I arrived on fish-tier. — Jack Henry Abbott, *In the Belly of the Beast*, p. 85, 1981
- [H]e boldly led Little past the guards in the fish tier back to his own cell. — Pete Earley, *The Hot House*, p. 58, 1992

fish train *noun*

a van or bus filled with new prisoners *US, 2002*

- All of them screaming at the van. "Motherfucking fish train!" — Jimmy Lerner, *You Got Nothing Coming*, p. 41, 2002

fish wife *noun*

a married male homosexual's wife *US, 1971*

- — Eugene Landy, *The Underground Dictionary*, p. 78, 1971

fishy *adjective*

inducing suspicion *US, 1840*

- We didn't catch you with the goods tonight, but ... if we ever do catch anything fishy goin' on in here, we're gonna bust the bunch o' ya. — Odie Hawkins, *Ghetto Sketches*, p. 36, 1972

fish yard *noun*

a prison yard reserved for newly arrived prisoners *US, 2002*

- He whispers this to me in the fish yard. — Jimmy Lerner, *You Got Nothing Coming*, p. 114, 2002

fist and skull *noun*

a fight without weapons *US, 1832*

- Or they'd get in an argument, and then they'd have fist and skull there. — Eliot Wigginton, *Foxfire 5*, p. 30, 1979

fist city *noun*

a physical fight *US, 1930*

- Jump down Jackson if you want to go to fist city you can naturally take off. — Lavada Durst, *The Jives of Dr. Hepcat*, p. 1, 1953

fister *noun*

a person who inserts their hand into another's vagina or rectum for sexual gratification *US, 1999*

- An old-school fister, Bert's into getting high on pot and poppers and stuffing gobs of Crisco, whereas I am into endorphin highs and a nice, thick water-based lubricant — *The Village Voice*, 2nd November 1999

fist fuck; fist *verb*

to insert your lubricated fist into a partner's rectum or vagina, leading to sexual pleasure for both *US, 1969*

- — Bruce Rodgers, *The Queens' Vernacular*, p. 81, 1972
- Then he asked if she'd ever been fisted. — Anka Radakovich, *The Wild Girls Club*, p. 165, 1994
- I remember once I was being fisted by Sebastian Cabot—but here's where the story gets interesting. — *Austin Powers*, 1999
- If you are fisting her (have all five fingers or your entire hand inside her vagina), and you want to make her ejaculate, you need to change your hand position. — Tristan Taormino, *Pucker Up*, p. 115, 2001

fist-fucker *noun*

1 a practitioner of fist fucking *US, 1972*

- Another ugly extreme of S & M is the burgeoning of a "group" calling itself the F.F.A. (Fist Fuckers of America). — John Rechy, *The Sexual Outlaw*, p. 256, 1977
- A group known as FFA (Fist Fuckers of America) now usurped the pool tables for a demonstration of their infamous activity. — *The World of S & M*, p. 131, 1981

2 a frequent, obsessive masturbator *US, 1962*

- I feel plumb sorry for you poor Wichita fistfuckers, bein' deprived of growin' up without an ole cow, sheep er sow er somethin'. — Earl Thompson, *Tattoo*, p. 133, 1974

fist-fucking *noun*

1 masturbation *UK, 1891*

- FIST FUCKING! [Headline] — *Screw*, p. 11, 1st September 1969

2 the practice of inserting the hand (and part of the arm) into a partner's anus (or vagina) for the sexual pleasure of all involved *US, 1972*

Predominantly gay usage but also found in heterosexual practice.

- Now presumably all the rage, fist-fucking can be extremely dangerous. — Stephen Lewis, *The Whole Bedroom Catalog*, p. 60, 1975
- Vaginal fisting, also known as fist-fucking or handballing, is one of those sexual practices that still carries with it a taboo. — Deborah Addington, *A Hand in the Bush*, p. 5, 1997

fisting *noun*

the practice of inserting the hand (and part of the arm) into a partner's anus (or vagina) for the sexual pleasure of all involved *US, 1972*

- The fisting experts greased up their arms. — *The World of S & M*, p. 131, 1981
- If you don't know a lot about fisting, don't advertise it. — John Preston, *Hustling*, p. 171, 1994
- KYLE'S MOTHER: What is "fisting"? CARTMAN'S MOTHER: That's when the fist is inserted into the anus or vagina for sexual pleasure. — *South Park*, 1999

fist it!
be quiet! *US, 1994*
- — Linda Meyer, *Teenspeak!*, p. 31, 1994

fist sandwich *noun*
a punch in the mouth *US, 1982*
- Bronk offers Artie a fist sandwich. — Joe Bob Briggs, *Joe Bob Goes to the Drive-In*, p. 47, 1987

fit *noun*
1 the equipment needed to inject a drug *US, 1959*
A shortened form of **OUTFIT**.
- I'm waiting for you to finish cleaning your fit and get away from the basin, so I can use mine. — Clarence Cooper Jr., *The Scene*, p. 249, 1960
- I don't know what they had planned, but they sure was making a fit. — Joseph Wambaugh, *The Blue Knight*, p. 30, 1973
- — William K. Bentley and James M. Corbett, *Prison Slang*, p. 80, 1992

2 an outfit of clothing *US, 1972*
- — David Claerbaut, *Black Jargon in White America*, p. 64, 1972
- — Connie Eble (Editor), *UNC-CH Campus Slang*, p. 7, Spring 1994

fitted *adjective*
well-dressed *US, 2003*
- — *San Francisco Chronicle*, p. E5, 10th August 2003
- — Rick Ayers (Editor), *Berkeley High Slang Dictionary*, p. 21, 2004

five *noun*
1 a slap of the hand in greeting *US, 1959*
- They exchange fives and remain in the window, checking out the mid-afternoon scene. — Odie Hawkins, *Ghetto Sketches*, p. 111, 1972

2 an amphetamine tablet *US, 1993*
- — US Department of Justice, *Street Terms*, August 1993

3 Chanel No. 5™ perfume *US, 1994*
- I don't care if the world buys Opium until it comes to an end; I'm gonna always have me some 5. — Odie Hawkins, *Lost Angeles*, p. 188, 1994

▸ **give five**
to shake hands or to slap hands in a greeting *US, 1935*
- "Hyuh, Larry, give me five." Larry refuses the outstretched hand. — Darryl Ponicsan, *The Last Detail*, p. 60, 1970
- Murphy leaned forward to give his partner five. "Right on, brother! Right on!" — Odie Hawkins, *Chicago Hustle*, pp. 98–99, 1977
- I had it because a week later Chillie gave me five [a stylized hand slap] and the coke was in his hand. — Terry Williams, *The Cocaine Kids*, p. 78, 1989
- No jive, gimme five. — (Editors of Ben is Dead), *Retrohell*, p. 202, 1997

five and dime *noun*
in poker, a hand with a five and a ten and three other unpaired cards in between *US, 1968*
- — Thomas L. Clark, *The Dictionary of Gambling and Gaming*, p. 80, 1987

five and two *noun*
used as a formula for the services of a prostitute—her fee and the room fee *US, 1970*
- He lies back in the chaise and shuts his eyes and sees all the whorehouses, all the bar hookers he's had—the five and two's: five for the girl and two for the room. — Darryl Ponicsan, *The Last Detail*, p. 126, 1970

five-by-five; five-by *adverb*
loud and clear *US, 1954*
- "This is Gilded Cage. Read you five-by." — Donald Duncan, *The New Legions*, p. 17, 1967
- "Roger, I read you five by five. Thank you. Out." — Martin Russ, *Happy Hunting Ground*, p. 202, 1968
- "This is Rattlesnake one. Read you five by. How me? Over." "This is Rattlesnake two. Read you five by." — James N. Rowe, *Five Years to Freedom*, p. 22, 1971
- Lima Charlie and five-square mean the same thing as five by five. — *Atlanta (Georgia) Journal-Constitution*, p. 2D, 26th April 2002

five-card Charlie *noun*
in casino blackjack games, a bonus paid to a player who draws five cards and still has a total count of 21 or less *US, 1996*
- — Frank Scoblete, *Best Blackjack*, p. 261, 1996

five-cent paper *noun*
five dollars' worth of a drug *US, 1971*
- — Eugene Landy, *The Underground Dictionary*, p. 78, 1971

five-finger *verb*
to shoplift *US, 1919*
- We've five-fingered most of the action figure aisle. — *Airheads*, 1994

five-finger discount *noun*
theft by shoplifting *US, 1966*
- — *Current Slang*, p. 7, Summer 1969
- I folded the note and put it in Lefty's grungy backpack (veteran of countless shoplifting capers and itself acquired through a past five-finger discount). — C.D. Payne, *Youth in Revolt*, p. 67, 1993

five-fingered Mary *noun*
a man's hand as the means of masturbation *US, 1971*
- Poor bastards, they can't get a woman from one month to the next, and so it's five-fingered Mary and her horny-palmed sister in their hammock each night. — Christopher Peachment, *Caravaggio*, p. 171, 2002

five-knuckle shuffle *noun*
masturbation *US, 1972*
- — Helen Dahlskog (Editor), *A Dictionary of Contemporary and Colloquial Usage*, p. 23, 1972
- — Connie Eble (Editor), *UNC-CH Campus Slang*, p. 7, Fall 1987

five-o *noun*
1 fifty *US, 1983*
- That big five-o would have pretty well covered a high-stepping evening on the town with the nifty Mike Hammer secretary. — Terry Southern, *Now Dig This*, p. 145, 2001

2 the police; a police officer *US, 1983*
From *Hawaii Five-O*, a police television series that aired from September 1968 to April 1980, featuring an elite four-man police unit.
- Yo! Yo! You 5-0. This dude is a cop! A cop! — *New Jack City*, 1990
- The best he could do was to get somebody to spot them sneaking into a building from the rear, yell out "Five-oh" so nobody did anything stupid. — Richard Price, *Clockers*, p. 4, 1992
- [L]ookouts actually shout "Bob Brown," rather than the generic "Five-Oh" or "Time Out!" — David Simon and Edward Burns, *The Corner*, p. 16, 1997
- "I'll bring Five-O with me when I come." — Eric Jerome Dickey, *Cheaters*, p. 174, 1999

five o'clock follies *noun*
during the Vietnam war, the daily military press briefings *US, 1966*
- The daily sessions were soon known as "The Five O'Clock Follies." — Elaine Shepard, *The Doom Pussy*, p. 82, 1967
- He resolved to meander by MACV headquarters later in the day, perhaps in time for the famous Five O'clock Follies, the chest-thumping press briefing that so amused the collected media cynics every afternoon. — Lucian K. Truscott, *Army Blue*, p. 89, 1989
- In the view of correspondents who reported from Vietnam, it is considerably less useful than the much-satirized "Five o'Clock Follies," the daily briefing in Saigon, because far fewer facts are made available. — *New York Times*, p. A9, 4th February 1991

five o'clock shadow *noun*
fast-growing, dark facial whiskers, which give the appearance of needing a shave by late in the afternoon *US, 1937*
President Richard Nixon was known and ridiculed for his.
- I shaved then. We are all afraid of Five O'clock Shadow. — Philip Wylie, *Opus 21*, p. 76, 1949
- I told his burly man with the five-o'clock shadow next to me that I had been to a reunion of some of my old clubhouse friends. — Clancy Sigal, *Going Away*, p. 358, 1961
- Still, his perpetual five o'clock shadow remains zit-free, so he has no real reason for complaint. — C.D. Payne, *Youth in Revolt*, pp. 179–180, 1993

five of clubs *noun*
the fist *US, 1947*

Often used in constructions such as "I dealt him the five of clubs."
- — Ken Weaver, *Texas Crude*, p. 55, 1984
- — Michael Dalton Johnson, *Talking Trash with Redd Foxx*, p. 98, 1994

five on the sly; five on the soul side *noun*
a mutual slapping of palms as an "inside" greeting *US, 1980*
- — Edith A. Folb, *runnin' down some lines*, p. 240, 1980

fiver *noun*
1 a five-dollar bill *US, 1843*
- This is going to cost you about a fiver. — Willie Fennell, *Dexter Gets The Point*, p. 114, 1961
- I can't be takin' no all night fer one fast fiver, so I start in playin' roun wiff his lil ol pecker. — Robert Gover, *One Hundred Dollar Misunderstanding*, p. 21, 1961
- Reggie got out of the car and walked up the highway and gave the cop a ten-spot, and all the way to Detroit Reggie and One-Eye argued, I mean vehemently, about whether we could have gotten away with only a fiver. — Clancy Sigal, *Going Away*, p. 156, 1961
- Rialto handed him a folded fiver. "Quit while you're ahead." — Robert Campbell, *Alice in La-La Land*, p. 276, 1987

2 in craps, the number five *US, 1985*
- — Steve Kuriscak, *Casino Talk*, p. 68, 1985

fiver, fiver, racetrack driver *noun*
in craps, the number five *US, 1985*
- — Steve Kuriscak, *Casino Talk*, p. 68, 1985

fives *noun*
dice that have been altered to have two fives, the second five being where one would expect to find a two *US, 1974*
Used in combination with **DEUCES**, likely to produce a seven, an important number in the game of craps.
- — John Scarne, *Scarne on Dice*, p. 466, 1974

fives artist *noun*
an expert at a shortchanging scheme using a five-dollar bill *US, 1953*
- My fives artist would have skipped the show immediately and gone in quest of another sucker. — Jim Thompson, *Bad Boy*, p. 351, 1953

five-spot *noun*
1 a five-dollar bill *US, 1892*
- If I had a five-spot or a ten, they always knew that I was good for it. — Herbert Huncke, *Guilty of Everything*, p. 189, 1990

2 a prison sentence of five years *US, 1901*
- A felony. It rates up to a five-spot in Quentin. — Raymond Chandler, *The Long Goodbye*, p. 53, 1953
- Trial February 19, at which time with some luck I'll get hit with a five spot. — James Blake, *The Joint*, p. 163, 7th January 1957
- I'll take a five-spot and go on down. A five-spot does this for him: on his record, it shows that he really did get a conviction, and that is all that ever really matters. — Bruce Jackson, *Outside the Law*, p. 135, 1972

five-square *adverb*
loud and clear *US, 1956*
- Lima Charlie and five-square mean the same thing as five by five. — *Atlanta (Georgia) Journal-Constitution*, p. 2D, 26th April 2002

five-to-lifers *noun*
a pair of shoes issued to prisoners by the state *US, 1989*
Purported to last at least five years.
- — James Harris, *A Convict's Dictionary*, p. 32, 1989

five twenty-nine *noun*
a jail sentence of one day less than six months *US, 1953*
The maximum sentence for a misdemeanor charge in some jursidictions.
- So Mike spent at least half of his time on the Island doing "five-twenty-nine" for jostling. — William Burroughs, *Junkie*, p. 26, 1953

five will get you ten
used for an expression of confidence in the assertion that follows *US, 1990*
- GIANT: Five will get you ten he's with Jeanne. — *Mo' Better Blues*, 1990

fivezies *noun*
in poker, a pair of fives *US, 1988*
- — George Percy, *The Language of Poker*, p. 35, 1988

fix *noun*
1 an injection of a drug, especially heroin *US, 1936*
- How about a fix? How about a fix, man? — John Clellon Holmes, *Go*, p. 7, 1952
- "Angel will give me a fix," he told himself. "He'll have the stuff." — Hal Ellson, *The Golden Spike*, p. 3, 1952
- Life telescopes down to junk, one fix and looking forward to the next[.] — William Burroughs, *Junkie*, p. 35, 1953
- Do we take a fix here? — John D. McDonald, *The Neon Jungle*, p. 48, 1953
- I saw the best minds of my generation destroyed by madness, starving hysterical naked, / dragging themselves through the negro streets at dawn looking for an angry fix[.] — Allen Ginsberg, *Howl*, 1956
- Suddenly he grew tired and quiet and went in the house and disappeared in the bathroom for his prelunch fix. — Jack Kerouac, *On the Road*, pp. 151–152, 1957

2 by extension, what a person craves or needs *US, 1993*
- I guess in a way Angel Juan is my fix and I've been jonesing for him. — Francesca Lia Block, *Missing Angel Juan*, p. 332, 1993

3 an illegal arrangement *US, 1948*
- You might buy one guy and you might put the fix in for two, but not four. — Horace McCoy, *Kiss Tomorrow Good-bye*, p. 263, 1948
- I told her where to meet me, a hotel on West forty-seventh where the fix was in strong. — Jim Thompson, *Savage Night*, p. 52, 1953

4 in the slang of pool players, proper position for the next shot or shots *US, 1970*
- — Roger D. Abrahams, *Deep Down in the Jungle*, p. 261, 1970

▸ **get a fix on**
to make a plan of action *US, 1955*
- These people also are habitually "getting a fix" on things, a phrase presumably borrowed from navigation. If one of these boys is in a muddle as to how he and the girl friend are going to spend the evening, he says, "Let's get a fix on this evening." — *Philadelphia Evening Bulletin*, 11th October 1955

fix *verb*
to inject or otherwise ingest a drug, especially heroin *US, 1936*
- Trials have been held, with girls in bobbysox and sweaters testifying in childish voices to the sickening details of "blasting pot" (smoking marijuana) and fixing (use of heroin). — *San Francisco Call-Bulletin*, p. 23, 19th August 1953
- Then they fixed up. I found out later it was heroin. — Henry Williamson, *Hustler!*, p. 67, 1965
- Goddamnit, Bob, what you got to fix in the car for? — *Drugstore Cowboy*, 1988
- As for her health, Kitty hadn't fixed for twelve days. — Seth Morgan, *Homeboy*, p. 135, 1990

▸ **be fixing to do something**
preparing to do something; about to do something *US, 1855*
- — Hermese E. Roberts, *The Third Ear*, 1971

▸ **fix someone's pipe**
in the usage of counterculturalists associated with the Rainbow Nation gatherings, to give someone marijuana *US, 1997*
- — Jim Crotty, *How to Talk American*, p. 288, 1997

▸ **fix your bones**
to use drugs, especially while suffering withdrawal pains *US, 1992*
- — William K. Bentley and James M. Corbett, *Prison Slang*, p. 72, 1992

fixer *noun*
1 an embassy or other building that is provided police protection *US, 1985*
- Fixers are embassies and such that they assign a cop to stand in front of. You stand there for eight hours like a doorman. — Mark Baker, *Cops*, p. 65, 1985

2 a person who can solve problems informally *US, 1972*
- When you want a lawyer, you don't want a trial lawyer, you want a fixer. You don't care how good he is in a courtroom, you want to fix it; you don't want to go to trial. — Bruce Jackson, *Outside the Law*, p. 130, 1972

3 a person who takes care of legal problems encountered by a circus or carnival *US, 1900*
- — Joe McKennon, *Circus Lingo*, p. 34, 1980

fizz *verb*
to lose your temper *US, 1961*
- — Art Unger, *The Cool Book*, p. 105, 1961

flabby labby *noun*
sagging labia *US, 2007*

- Recently made popular because of a photograph of Britney Spears.
— Connie Eble (Compiler), *UNC-CH Campus Slang*, p. 3, April 2007
- "Flabby labby"—The term actually refers to female genitals, hence "labby" being short for "labia." There was recently some hype about Britney Spears' private parts being caught on camera. — *slebalete.livejournal.com*, 25th April 2007

flack *noun*
a publicist; a spokesperson *US, 1939*

- Obviously, Eisner wrote the letter himself—no PR flack in his right mind would've sent out such hyperbolic twaddle. — Carl Hiaasen, *Team Rodent*, p. 41, 1998

fladanked *adjective*
drug-intoxicated *US, 1997*

- — *Maybeck High School Yearbook (Berkeley, California)*, p. 28, 1997

flag *noun*
1 while injecting a drug into a vein, the flow of blood up into the syringe, indicating that the vein has been pierced *US, 1989*

- — Geoffrey Froner, *Digging for Diamonds*, p. 29, 1989

2 a variable which changes value when a certain condition is reached *US, 1991*

- — Eric S. Raymond, *The New Hacker's Dictionary*, p. 157, 1991

3 the grade "F" *US, 1968*

- — Collin Baker et al., *College Undergraduate Slang Study Conducted at Brown University*, p. 117, 1968

4 the ground floor of a tiered prison cellblock *US, 1992*

- — William K. Bentley and James M. Corbett, *Prison Slang*, p. 7, 1992

▸ **have your flag in port**
to experience the bleed period of the menstrual cycle *US, 1966*

- After the end of the month rolls around and that bitch's flag jump back in port/ then keep every inch a your natural prick right down her pricksucken throat. — Bruce Jackson, *Get Your Ass in the Water and Swim Like Me*, p. 129, 1966

flag *verb*
1 to masturbate *US, 1976*
Seemingly a misheard "flog."

- Just as I'm writing this letter O'Neil's probably in some back alley flagging it with a National Geographic opened up on the ground next to him. — *Punk*, p. 3, March 1976

2 of an older homosexual, to attempt to seduce a younger man *US, 1966*

- — Rose Giallombardo, *Society of Women*, p. 207, 1966: Glossary of Prison Terms

3 to label or categorize someone *US, 1992*

- — William K. Bentley and James M. Corbett, *Prison Slang*, p. 32, 1992

4 in the military, to make an entry on a soldier's record which will prevent further promotion *US, 1970*

- Wilson was authorized to order Colonel James D. Kiersey, chief of staff at Fort Benning, to "flag" Calley's record, an Army procedure freezing any promotion or transfer for a soldier. — Seymour M. Hersh, *My Lai 4*, p. 120, 1970

5 to give a student in college a notification of academic deficiency *US, 1968*

- — *American Speech*, pp. 76–77, February 1968: "Some notes on flunk notes"

6 to wear an article of clothing signifying sexual taste *US, 1896*

- If you wear (or "flag") a hankie on the right, you're a bottom; on the left, a top. — *The Village Voice*, 17th-23rd November 2002

7 to wear an article of clothing signifying gang membership *US, 1995*

- — *American Speech*, p. 391, Winter 1995: "Among the new words"
- "So why you flaggin' blue?" He points to the bandana hanging from my back pocket. — Colton Simpson, *Inside the Crips*, p. 133, 2005

8 to arrest *US, 1927*

- They got me up tight, and you know that ain't right / In fact, they even flagged me wrong. — Dennis Wepman et al., *The Life*, p. 62, 1976
- — John R. Armore and Joseph D. Wolfe, *Dictionary of Desperation*, p. 29, 1976

9 to fail (a test or course) *US, 1965*

- — *Time*, p. 57, 1st January 1965: "Students: the slang bag"

10 to skip, as in missing a class *US, 1997*

- — Vann Wesson, *Generation X Field Guide and Lexicon*, p. 66, 1997

flag country *noun*
in the US Navy, the area where an admiral works *US, 1991*

- Climbing the ladders up to Flag Country, as the area where the admiral and his staff worked and lived (lurked would be a better word, Boyle thought) was torture. — Gerry Carroll, *North S*A*R*, p. 32, 1991

flag day *noun*
the bleed period of the menstrual cycle *US, 1968*

- — Collin Baker et al., *College Undergraduate Slang Study Conducted at Brown University*, p. 117, 1968

flag football *noun*
a friendly, noncompetitive game of poker *US, 1996*
Flag football is played with a tame set of rules which forbid most of the physical contact associated with the game.

- — John Vorhaus, *The Big Book of Poker Slang*, p. 17, 1996

flagging *adjective*
said of a woman experiencing the bleed period of her menstrual cycle *US, 1954*

- — *American Speech*, p. 298, December 1954: "The vernacular of menstruation"

flagging, sagging and bragging
used for describing the primary activities of some urban youth—wearing gang colors, wearing low-hanging pants, and boasting *US, 1991*

- "Flaggin'. Saggin'. Braggin'. Lettin' people know you're part of something that is powerful." — Leon Bing, *Do or Die*, p. 243, 1991

flagpole *noun*
the erect penis *US, 1922*

- Not only was he a faggot, but his flagpole was not quite the standard-bearer a Bronstein boy was meant to hoist in battle. — Larry Kramer, *Faggots*, p. 46, 2000
- I could feel my flagpole coming right to attention. — Sharleen Cohen, *Innocent Gestures*, p. 280, 2003
- It was impossible for her to keep my flagpole up in her. — Thomas Larsen, *Mr. Cucumber Goes Bananas*, p. 57, 2003

flag's up!
in circus and carnival usage, used for conveying that a meal is ready *US, 1981*

- — Don Wilmeth, *The Language of American Popular Entertainment*, p. 93, 1981

flag-waver *noun*
1 a rousing, patriotic song or performance *US, 1937*

- John Oatis went out on a dark siding behind a tin baling-shed and my engine, with all the flag-wavers and brass bands, boiled on toward dawn. — Ray Bradbury, *Bradbury Stories*, p. 655, 2003

2 in horse racing, a horse that flicks its tail up and down while racing *US, 1951*

- — David W. Maurer, *Argot of the Racetrack*, p. 28, 1951

flail *verb*
to surf awkwardly *US, 1990*

- — *Surfing*, p. 43, 14th March 1990

flak *noun*
abuse, criticism *US, 1963*
From the original sense (anti-aircraft fire).

- But there was some heavy flak from the manager and we had to satisfy ourselves with the shots of Marsha on the staircase. — Fred Baker, *Events*, p. 11, 1970
- Clinton gets too much flack. Every move he makes, his enemies are right up his ass. — Chris Rock, *Rock This!*, p. 192, 1997

flake *noun*
1 cocaine *US, 1961*

- To read you your rights! When was the last time you bought a quarter of flake? Empty your purse on the desk! — Joseph Wambaugh, *Finnegan's Week*, p. 113, 1993

2 the shavings off a solid mass of crack cocaine *US, 1983*

- DEALER: Hey, man. You wanna cop some blow? / JUNKIE: Sure, watcha got? Dust, flakes or rocks? / DEALER: I got China White, Mother of Pearl ... I reflect what you need. — Grandmaster Flash & The Furious Five featuring Melle Mel, *White Lines*, 1983
- There is also disagreement on how much of a kilo should be "flake off the rock" as opposed to the more valued crystalline form. — Terry Williams, *The Cocaine Kids*, p. 35, 1989

3 an unreliable, unstable person *US, 1959*

- There is no bigger flake in organized baseball than Drabowski. — Jim Bouton, *Ball Four*, p. 148, 1970
- Wheaties now has larger flakes but there are no larger flakes than Marty Balin. — Richard Meltzer, *A Whore Just Like the Rest*, p. 79, 1970

- Harp must be fucking desperate if he's listening to you two flakes. — *Point Break*, 1991
- You're a flake, man, you don't care about this band. — *Airheads*, 1994

4 the planting of evidence on a suspected criminal *US, 1973*

- Thus we have the flake, which is planting evidence by a policeman upon a—what can he be called? Suspect? Victim? — Leonard Shecter and William Phillips, *On the Pad*, p. 115, 1973

flake *verb*

1 to plant evidence on a suspected criminal *US, 1972*

- They were rather casual about this, sometimes flaking bookmakers with numbers slips or numbers runners with bookmaking records, a practice which infuriated the gamblers more than being arrested. — *The Knapp Commission Report on Police Corruption*, p. 83, 1972
- Serpico would see a plainclothesman count the plays carried by someone he had searched, and when the number fell short of the required hundred, "flake" his prisoner—add additional plays to make up the difference. — Peter Maas, *Serpico*, p. 113, 1973
- "And with the pancake flour you threatened to flake some junkie in the street, is that right?" — Robert Daley, *Prince of the City*, p. 331, 1978

2 to fall asleep; to pass out *US, 1955*

Often used as the variant "flake out."

- Q: What will you do until then? A: I'm gonna flake out. Q: What? A: Pat the pad, sack out, lay in the sun — Max Shulman, *Guided Tour of Campus Humor*, p. 106, 1955
- — Robert George Reisner, *The Jazz Titans*, p. 155, 1960
- A. I had caught him sleeping on watch before and found him flaked out again a few minutes before the collision. Q. Please define "flaked out." A. Asleep on watch. — David Poyer, *The Circle*, p. 428, 1993

flake artist *noun*

a police officer inclined to plant evidence on a suspected criminal *US, 1973*

- But Otto Oberman, that flake artist, fucked it up for me. — Leonard Shecter and William Phillips, *On the Pad*, p. 118, 1973

flaked out *adjective*

exhausted, unconscious *US, 1958*

- — *American Speech*, p. 155, May 1959: "Gator (University of Florida) slang"
- We were flaked out from no-food and no-sleep. — Glendon Swarthout, *Where the Boys Are*, p. 205, 1960
- "He's on tubes in a nursing home, all flaked out." — Carl Hiaasen, *Skin Tight*, p. 79, 1989

flake off *verb*

to go away *US, 1957*

- "Chuckles with you?" she hooted. "Oh, flake off, little man!" — Max Shulman, *Rally Round the Flag, Boys!*, p. 58, 1957

flake off and die, dude!

used as an all-purpose insult *US, 1988*

- — Michael V. Anderson, *The Bad, Rad, Not to Forget Way Cool Beach and Surf Discretionary*, p. 7, 1988

flak shack *noun*

a military hospital or hospital ward where soldiers suffering from war-related psychological problems are treated *US, 1944*

- Before we established "flak shacks" for their rehabilitation, it was a very real problem. — Ian Hawkins, *B-17s over Berlin*, p. 260, 1990
- [F]light crews were given a week of rest and recuperation at various rest homes, sometimes known as flak shacks, that were operated by the Red Cross. — Tim Russert, *Big Russ and Me*, p. 14, 2004

flak trap *noun*

a decoying tactic used by the North Vietnamese, especially one in which antiaircraft fire is withheld from the area of a downed US aircraft until the rescue aircraft get near *US, 1955*

- "Something coming up at eleven o'clock. Might be a flak trap." — Judson Jerome, *New Campus Writing*, p. 127, 1959
- Known to pilots as the "Pyonggang flak trap," the airfield was dotted with 12 to 18 damaged Russian aircraft. — James T. Stewart, *Airpower*, p. 65, 1980
- The truck on the red cliffs sure is hell is a flak trap. — Tom Yarborough, *Da Nang Diary*, p. 43, 1990

flaky *adjective*

inattentive, distracted, unreliable *US, 1959*

Partridge suggested a connection between the adjective and cocaine, which was "flaky" in nature.

- But if I begin to sense that she won't because she's flaky or immature, then I try to get as much money as I can before she blows. — Susan Hall, *Gentleman of Leisure*, p. 8, 1972
- "She's a good kid, but flaky." "Well, nobody says you got to talk to 'em." — Elmore Leonard, *Split Images*, p. 175, 1981
- He's flaky, but you might want to question him. — Robert Crais, *L.A. Requiem*, p. 74, 1999

flam *noun*

fake heroin *US, 1971*

- He also knew that a flam wouldn't do/ And that he would have to come up with the real thing. — Michael H. Agar, *The Journal of American Folklore*, p. 178, April 1971

flamage *noun*

incendiary rhetoric used in a computer posting or internet discussion group *US, 1991*

- — Eric S. Raymond, *The New Hacker's Dictionary*, p. 158, 1991

flame *noun*

an insulting or aggressive e-mail or Internet discussion group posting *US, 1983*

The collective noun is **FLAMAGE**.

- — Guy L. Steele et al., *The Hacker's Dictionary*, p. 65, 1983

flame *verb*

to post insulting personal attacks on others posting messages on an Internet bulletin board or in an Internet discussion group, or to send an insulting personal attack by e-mail *US, 1981*

From an earlier sense of simply "insulting," in the absence of any computer technology.

- — *Coevolution Quarterly*, p. 31, Spring 1981: "Computer slang"
- — Guy L. Steele et al., *The Hacker's Dictionary*, p. 65, 1983
- A newbie with the nerve to post in alt.sex.bondage, without taking the time to lurk (read, not post) for several weeks, can expect to be flamed to blackened perfection. — Nancy Tamositis, *net.sex*, p. 75, 1995
- — Connie Eble (Editor), *UNC-CH Campus Slang*, p. 4, April 1995

flamebait *noun*

a message posted in an Internet discussion group for the express purpose of soliciting insulting messages *US, 1985*

- However, I just sent this in as flamebait. — *net.women*, 18th August 1985
- One person will post flamebait. Idiots take the bait. — Nancy Tamositis, *net.sex*, p. 113, 1995

flame bath *noun*

the dropping of 55-gallon drums of combustible liquids from a utility helicopter, followed by flares that ignite the fuel *US, 1970*

- Company A, 25th Aviation Battalion (Little Bear)—CS and Flame Bath drops, resupply and MEDEVAC. — Department of the Army, *Combat After Action Interview Report, 18th Military History Detachment, 25th Infantry Division*, 31st January 1970

flamefest *noun*

a protracted exchange of insulting and inflammatory messages on an Internet discussion group *US, 1985*

- For example, if I am engaged in a flamefest on an Arpanet discussion group, I sometimes check on my target until he appears to have logged out and gone to bed. — *fa.human-nets*, 29th June 1985
- — Christian Crumlish, *The Internet Dictionary*, p. 71, 1995

flamer *noun*

1 a blatant and conspicuous homosexual *US, 1948*

- The three young boys sitting together on one side of the booth were flamers, with big Windsor knots in their gaudy ties and shirt collars four sizes too big[.] — Horace McCoy, *Kiss Tomorrow Good-bye*, p. 278, 1948
- — Collin Baker et al., *College Undergraduate Slang Study Conducted at Brown University*, p. 118, 1968
- I thought I smelled smoke—here comes that huge flamer Dennis. — Jeff Fessler, *When Drag Is Not a Car Race*, p. 8, 1997

2 an Internet user who posts vitriolic, insulting messages in Internet discussion groups *US, 1983*

- — Guy L. Steele et al., *The Hacker's Dictionary*, p. 65, 1983
- While We like to encourage aspiring flamers, wading through a 250 line article by an untalented flamer is a little much. (If you already *had* talent, you wouldn't *need* 250 lines to flame somebody.) — *net.flame*, 10th December 1984

- A flamer is an incendiary on-liner who delights in inciting trouble by chiming in whenever possible with derisive commentary. — Nancy Tamosaitis, *net.sex*, p. 5, 1995

flame war *noun*
a virulent exchange of insulting messages in an Internet discussion group *US, 1984*
- So I would like this discussion to be viewed more as an self-exploratory experiment rather than a flame war since this has proved in the past (so I've heard) to be completely unproductive. — *net.women*, 16th February 1984
- Given the raunchiness of the subject matter, the posts are generally rather civil, and flame wars are few and far between. — Nancy Tamosaitis, *net.sex*, p. 115, 1995

flaming *adjective*
(used of a homosexual) patently, obviously *US, 1941*
- Why would anybody want to go to bed with a flaming little sissy like you? — Mart Crowley, *The Boys in the Band*, p. 159, 1968
- Flaming queens like Maude often have that effect[.] — Gore Vidal, *Myron*, p. 297, 1974
- These were the flaming swishes of his prison days; "Bernice" and "Joan." — Odie Hawkins, *Midnight*, p. 159, 1995
- For all I know, all five members could be flaming homos who are good at playing breeders. — *The Village Voice*, 25th July 2000

flaming asshole *noun*
a truly despicable person *US, 1968*
- — John D. Bell et al., *Loosely Speaking*, p. 2, 1969
- "Mr. Gitche is a flaming asshole." "Hardly a professional evaluation, Robbins." "Oh no? I thought you Freudians were really big on assholes." — Tom Robbins, *Even Cowgirls Get the Blues*, p. 240, 1976
- I was a flaming asshole. — Howard Stern, *Private Parts*, p. 100, 1994
- What a flaming asshole you are. I don't even know why we're talking. — Carl Hiaasen, *Basket Case*, p. 314, 2002

flaming coffin *nickname*
a DH-4 bomber aircraft *US, 1919*
- We were given de Havilland DH-4s to fly, known as "flaming coffins," and Curtiss JN-4 "Jennys." — James Doolittle, *I Could Never Be So Lucky Again*, p. 57, 1991
- Airmen had become "pawns," forced to fly antiquated biplanes like the De Havilland DH-4, which they nicknamed "the flaming coffin" because they claimed it easily caught fire when it crashed. — Douglas C. Waller, *A Question of Loyalty*, p. 20, 2004

flaming piss pot *nickname*
the Ordnance Corps of the US Army *US, 1980*
From the flaming grenade insignia.
- Thus the ignited old-fashioned bomb constituting the insignia of the US Ordnance Corps becomes the flaming horse turd (sometimes flaming piss-pot). — Paul Fussell, *Wartime*, p. 81, 1989

flange-head *noun*
a Chinese person *US, 1949*
- — *American Speech*, p. 30, February 1949: "A.V.G. lingo"

flangehead *noun*
an Asian person *US, 2007*
- "He [Duane Chapman] called Mexican people 'beaners' or 'wetbacks' and Asian people 'flangeheads.'" — *perezhilton.com*, 6th November 2007

flanger *noun*
in target shooting, a shot that strikes outside a close group of shots on the target *US, 1957*
- — *American Speech*, p. 193, October 1957: "Some colloquialisms of the handgunner"

flanker *noun*
a tall person *US, 1956*
- Whether flanker (tall person) or gnome (member of a runt company), he's sure to have an O.A.O. (One and Only Her). — *Chicago Daily Tribune*, p. N4, 23rd December 1956

flannelmouth *noun*
a loudmouth; an insincere, silver-tongued talker *US, 1881*
- The bartender was a flannelmouth. Everyone in the war was a flannelmouth. — Nelson Algren, *The Neon Wilderness*, p. 51, 1960
- I don't ever want to hear some Dallas flannelmouth compare the Cowboys of today—or any other day—to the "perfect" Dolphins of that era. — Bert Sugar, *I Hate the Dallas Cowboys*, p. 157, 1997

flannel-mouthed *adjective*
thick-tongued, especially as the result of drinking to excess *US, 1973*
- — Sherman Louis Sergel, *The Language of Show Biz*, p. 87, 1973

flap *noun*
a disturbance or crisis *UK, 1916*
- I suggested informally, when the Korean flap started in 1950, that we go north immediately with incendiaries and delete four or five of the largest towns[.] — Curtis E. LeMay with MacKinlay Kantor, *Mission with LeMay*, p. 382, 1965
- Over the course of a year, Nesbit had seen both Blevins and Gomez in action during a number of crises, or "flaps." — Richard Herman Jr., *The Warbirds*, p. 24, 1989

flap *verb*
while surfing, to make awkward flapping arm motions trying to gain your balance *US, 1991*
- — Trevor Cralle, *The Surfin'ary*, p. 38, 1991

▸ **flap skin**
to have sex *US, 1990*
- [N]ow that I wanna flap some skins Brandi ain't down for it even if I wear a jim hat. — *Boyz N The Hood*, 1990

flapjaw *noun*
a person who talks incessantly *US, 1950*
- "Well, flapjaw, what now?" Boo asked herself, sitting again. — Max Shulman, *Anyone Got a Match?*, p. 252, 1964

flapper *noun*
1 the penis in a flaccid state *US, 1980*
- — *Maledicta*, p. 195, Winter 1980: "A new erotic vocabulary"

2 the ear *US, 1933*
- To his thinkin', what they don't know they can't buzz in the narcops' wide flappers. — Bernard Wolfe, *The Magic of Their Singing*, p. 77, 1961

flappers *noun*
the female breasts *US, 2005*
- Janet flashed her fine, full flappers again in Aragosta a colazione (1982). — Mr. Skin, *Mr. Skin's Skincyclopedia*, p. 5, 2005

flapper steak *noun*
a pig's ear sandwich *US, 1947*
- — Marcus Hanna Boulware, *Jive and Slang of Students in Negro Colleges*, 1947

flaps *noun*
the female breasts *US, 1972*
- Their secondary sex characteristics are simply too conspicuous to pass without insult, and we were unmerciful towards them: tits, boobs, knockers, jugs, bubbies, bazooms, lungs, flaps and hooters we called them, and there was no way to be polite about it. — *Screw*, p. 6, 3rd January 1972

flare *noun*
a type of scratch (a manipulation of a record to create a musical effect) that cuts out the middle of a sample *US, 2002*
Named after DJ Flare who invented the move in the late 1980s.
- Yeah, a chirp sounds like: chig-chig, chig-chig, whereas a flare sounds like: dibbet, dibbet, dibbet—it doubles it with only one click! — J. Hoggarth (quoting DJ Olsen), *How To Be a DJ*, p. 95, 2002

flare kicker *noun*
the crew member who operates an airship's flare dispenser *US, 1997*
- When it was secure, one of the other guys climbed onto the door to take his place as the flare kicker while another stood by with a flare in his hand ready to put it in the chute when the pilot called for it. — SamC130, *First Flight Up North (1966)*, 1997

flash *noun*
1 a sudden onset of drug-induced effects *US, 1946*
- I didn't get a flash, Cowboy. — Jack Gerber, *The Connection*, p. 75, 1957
- He's gonna get a flash, let me tell you. — Richard Farina, *Been Down So Long*, p. 115, 1966
- His last flash had been all about time, it had taken him down the passageway to the very door of the rose garden, but as he was about to go in the flash had started to wear off. — Gurney Norman, *Divine Right's Trip (Last Whole Earth Catalog)*, p. 123, 1971
- No, Bob, really, this is good stuff, clears right up in the spoon, no residue, hair-raising flash. — *Drugstore Cowboy*, 1990

2 a revelation; an epiphany; a satori *US, 1924*
- You can get flashes all kinds of ways. I got a flash once when my parachute didn't open. — *Whole Earth Catalog*, p. 116, 1971

- The fact that her fears were misplaced in this case meant less to me than the flash that Marion can't get it together to walk into a restaurant in her home state. — Jeffrey Golden, *Watermelon Summer*, p. 40, 1971

3 in a striptease show, the stripper's entrance onto the stage *US, 1945*

- In succession as the Flash or entrance; the Parade or march across the stage, in full costume; the Tease or increasing removal of wearing apparel; and the climactic Strip or denuding down to the G-String[.] — *Saturday Review of Literature*, p. 28, 18th August 1945: "Take em off!"

4 inexpensive, showy jewelry *US, 1927*

- Everybody in both worlds kissed your ass black and blue if you had flash and front. — Iceberg Slim (Robert Beck), *Pimp*, p. 118, 1969

5 an inexpensive carnival prize that is so appealing that people will spend great sums trying to win it *US, 1927*

- The prizes I used as "flash"—percolators, blankets, clocks—were also numbered. — Charles Hamilton, *Men of the Underworld*, p. 178, 1952
- Blue had dismantled the wheel and taken the flash dolls and stuffed animals off the back wall when the dapper hoodlums finished their counting. — Iceberg Slim (Robert Beck), *Trick Baby*, p. 98, 1969

6 the appearance of wealth or success *US, 1975*

- The money's just for flash. You spend as little as you have to and bring the rest back. — Joseph Wambaugh, *The Choirboys*, p. 252, 1975

7 in horse racing, a last-minute change in odds *US, 1951*

- — David W. Maurer, *Argot of the Racetrack*, p. 28, 1951

flash *verb*

1 to exhibit as naked a part or parts of the body that are usually clothed *UK, 1893*

- She would also "flash"—that is, at one or two appropriate moments she would remove her G string and present herself to the audience naked as a jaybird. — *Eros*, p. 30, Spring 1962
- [W]hen you go off to do something so very simple as exchanging money for goods, it isn't necessary to flash your snatch at everyone this side of the horizon. — Philip Roth, *Portnoy's Complaint*, p. 242, 1969
- In N.Y.C. topless is O.K. but total nudity is out but on some nights the girls do flash a raw pussy. — *Screw*, p. 9, 18th April 1969
- And every year, a coed would have to flash at least one cop by lifting her T-shirt to reveal her address written across her tits. — Joseph Wambaugh, *Fugitive Nights*, p. 133, 1992

2 to show off *UK, 1754*

- Silky's off flashing with the other guys and trying to cop girls. — Susan Hall, *Gentleman of Leisure*, p. 174, 1972
- They wouldn't miss the opportunity to flash at something like this fight. — Vernon E. Smith, *The Jones Men*, p. 151, 1974
- "Oh, you see him in the neighborhood every now 'n then, flashin', ... he don't want nobody to know where he's stayin'," Taco added. — Donald Goines, *The Busting Out of an Ordinary Man*, p. 74, 1985

3 while dealing blackjack in a casino, to briefly and unintentionally expose the down card *US, 1980*

- Bill says I'm flashing my hole card, but I can't see how I could be. — Lee Solkey, *Dummy Up and Deal*, p. 113, 1980

4 to display prizes in a carnival game in order to attract customers *US, 1966*

- — *American Speech*, p. 280, December 1966: "More Carnie Talk from the West Coast"
- Fluorescent tubing lit an interior "flashed" with plush stuffed animals dangling on hooks and stacked boxes of "slum," or cheap giveaways. — Peter Fenton, *Eyeing the Flash*, p. 101, 2005

5 to vomit *US, 1968*

- — Collin Baker et al., *College Undergraduate Slang Study Conducted at Brown University*, p. 118, 1968

6 to vomit after injecting heroin or while withdrawing from heroin use *US, 1957*

- I gave her a hypodermic. She "flashed"—to use the slang expression; barely made it to the sink before she started vomiting. — Jim Thompson, *The Kill-Off*, pp. 41–42, 1957
- — David Maurer and Victor Vogel, *Narcotics and Narcotic Addiction*, p. 406, 1973

7 to inhale glue or industrial solvents for the psychoactive effect *US, 1970*

- — William D. Alsever, *Glossary for the Establishment and Other Uptight People*, p. 11, December 1970

8 to remember an event from the past in a sudden and powerful manner *US, 1984*
An abbreviation of "flashback."

- He wondered if the canyons at night would make him flash to Nam. — Joseph Wambaugh, *Lines and Shadows*, p. 41, 1984

9 to break light bulbs in their sockets, either as an act of vandalism or preparatory to a crime *US, 1953*

- — Dale Kramer and Madeline Karr, *Teen-Age Gangs*, p. 175, 1953

10 to commit a social gaffe *US, 1963*

- — Carol Ann Preusse, *Jargon Used by University of Texas Co-Eds*, 1963

▸ **flash a joint**
to display prizes in a carnival game *US, 1968*

- To "flash the joint" means to put up the prizes for display at any of the give-away (or gambling) games[.] — E.E. Steck, *A Brief Examination of an Esoteric Folk*, p. 8, 1968

▸ **flash the gallery; flash the range**
in prison, to use a small mirror to watch out for approaching guards while conducting some prohibited activity in your cell *US, 1981*

- — *Maledicta*, p. 267, Summer/Winter 1981: "By its slang, ye shall know it: the pessimism of prison life"

▸ **flash the hash**
to vomit *US, 1960*

- "Popped my cookies!" he congratulated himself, awe-struck by his deed. "Flashed the old hash all over Twenny-second." — Nelson Algren, *The Neon Wilderness*, p. 164, 1960
- — *American Speech*, p. 194, October 1965: "Notes on campus vocabulary, 1964"
- — Collin Baker et al., *College Undergraduate Slang Study Conducted at Brown University*, p. 118, 1968
- — Michael Dalton Johnson, *Talking Trash with Redd Foxx*, p. 47, 1994

▸ **flash your ass**
to commit a social gaffe *US, 1968*

- — Fred Hester, *Slang on the 40 Acres*, p. 10, 1968

flashback *noun*
a relapse into a hallucinatory drug experience long after the effect of the drug has worn off *US, 1971*

- — Edward R. Bloomquist, *Marijuana*, p. 339, 1971
- The myth of the flashback was widely promoted by the media and government as one of the severe dangers of LSD. — Cam Cloud, *The Little Book of Acid*, p. 18, 1999

flash-bang *noun*
an explosive device designed to deafen and blind without otherwise injuring *US, 1999*

- A couple more of his people are being treated for severe concussion. It was determined they got in the way of a flash-bang. — Elmore Leonard, *Be Cool*, p. 245, 1999

flash cash *noun*
a large, ostentatious bankroll *US, 1979*

- At least until I got the bread to lay down on a far-out ride (maybe a vintage Rolls, fur-trimmed) B.R. (flash cash) and threads to dazzle and lure whores[.] — Iceberg Slim (Robert Beck), *Airtight Willie and Me*, p. 4, 1979

flash cloth *noun*
colorful draping used in a carnival concession *US, 1985*

- — Gene Sorrows, *All About Carnivals*, p. 17, 1985: "Terminology"

flash dough *noun*
counterfeit money *US, 1949*

- — Captain Vincent J. Monteleone, *Criminal Slang*, p. 85, 1949

flasher *noun*

1 a person with a psychopathological need to expose his or her genitals *US, 1962*

- You know those guys in the park, the flashers? — Lenny Bruce, *The Essential Lenny Bruce*, p. 157, 1967
- The patients include an introverted neurotic with a penchant for the one-liner, a psychosomatically blind muscle man (who believes masturbation has done it to him), a jealous lesbian, a couple of transvestites, a flasher, and others. — Kent Smith et al., *Adult Movies*, p. 163, 1982
- The guy could be a crackhead, a psychopath, a flasher, a junkie[.] — *Sleepless in Seattle*, 1993

2 a casino dealer who inadvertently reveals his down card *US, 1991*

- — Michael Dalton, *Blackjack*, p. 48, 1991

flash flood *noun*
in poker, a sudden sequence of good cards *US, 1996*

- — John Vorhaus, *The Big Book of Poker Slang*, p. 17, 1996

flash house *noun*
a room, apartment or house where amphetamine addicts gather to inject the drug *US, 1970*
- — William D. Alsever, *Glossary for the Establishment and Other Uptight People*, p. 11, December 1970

flash mob *noun*
a large crowd that materializes in a public place to perform a scripted action for several minutes before dissolving *US, 2003*
- They probably don't realize it, but they've just witnessed San Francisco's second "flash mob," a phenomenon that was born in New York and is spreading across the United States and Europe with the speed of an Internet virus. — *San Francisco Chronicle*, p. D1, 11th August 2003
- Once there, participants in flash mobs, the compulsively deconstructed geek-chic game of the summer, briefly perform some collective activity, then flee. — *New York Times*, p. WK5, 17th August 2003
- Organizing a "flash mob" basically involves e-mailing a bunch of people with instructions to show up at a certain place for a few moments, then disappear. — *Ventura County (California) Star*, p. E1, 1st July 2003
- One blog proprietor gave the concept a name—"flash mobs"—after a 1973 science-fiction short story, "Flash Crowd," which deals with the unexpected downside of cheap teleportation technology. — *Harper's Magazine*, pp. 57–58, March 2006

flash mobber *noun*
a participant in a flash mob *US, 2003*
- Flash mobbers make no apologies for their lack of political mission, but stake a claim to significance nonetheless. — *New York Times*, p. WK5, 17th August 2003

flash money *noun*
money, especially in a bankroll, intended for impressing, not spending *US, 1970*
- He had retrieved it and arrested Big Dog, taking him to the detectives who, since Big Dog was a pimp, and had a five-page rap sheet, decided to book him for robbery, impound his car, and book his roll of flash money as evidence. — Joseph Wambaugh, *The New Centurions*, p. 223, 1970

flash on *verb*
to think about with great intensity and focus *US, 1968*
- — Lewis Yablonsky, *The Hippie Trip*, p. 367, 1968: "Glossary"

flash paper *noun*
paper that dissolves completely and quickly when exposed to water *US, 1973*
- You mean like flash paper? I've heard of that. — Joseph Wambaugh, *The Blue Knight*, p. 195, 1973
- You won't find the bottom line for the Super Bowl only on the scoreboard. Some of it will be scrawled hastily on flash paper by bookies across the country. — *Chicago Tribune*, p. C11, 24th January 1987
- They had been printed on flash paper, which bookies used to keep their betting records. Victoria had scooped them up on her way to the bathroom and dropped them in the toilet. — Stephen Cannell, *Big Con*, p. 384, 1997
- The most important rule; Listen to Johnson or you're gone quicker than flash paper. — *Fresno (California) Bee*, p. D1, 13th July 2003

flash roll *noun*
a large number of small-denomination bills with a large-denomination bill showing, giving the impression of a great deal of money *US, 1987*
- Neil unfolded and fanned out the rest of the bundle. It was mostly fives and tens, maybe adding up to another hundred, two hundred bucks at most. "You take the five, all I've got left is a flash roll." — Robert Campbell, *Alice in La-La Land*, p. 21, 1987

flash trash *noun*
a gaudy, cheap woman *US, 1992*
- She wears a black motorcycle jacket, a very short skirt, stiletto heels. Her hair is up. Her make-up is severe. In the darkness, in the shadows, she looks about 19. A hot 19. A hot flash-trash 19. — *Basic Instinct*, 1992

flash up *verb*
in circus and carnival usage, to add embellishments to a piece of clothing *US, 1981*
- — Don Wilmeth, *The Language of American Popular Entertainment*, p. 95, 1981

flat *noun*
1 in an illegal number gambling lottery, a bet that two digits will appear in the winning number *US, 1949*
- — *American Speech*, p. 191, October 1949
2 a smooth-sided subway train that lends itself to graffiti art *US, 1997*
- — Jim Crotty, *How to Talk American*, p. 141, 1997

flat *adjective*
1 (of a prison sentence) full, unqualified *US, 1972*
- So the minute the pop comes, one of the guys that was out in front during all this, he offered a ten-flat [ten-year sentence]. — Bruce Jackson, *In the Life*, p. 170, 1972
- So I did the five years flat. — Harry King, *Box Man*, p. 21, 1972
- Those were the good ole days of the indeterminate sentence. Mayhem's a flat four now. — Seth Morgan, *Homeboy*, p. 150, 1990
2 (used of a bet) unvarying in amount *US, 1978*
- — Jerry L. Patterson, *Blackjack*, p. 20, 1978

flat *adverb*
completely *US, 1883*
- Deek had scored them a room and gotten them flat puking drunk that night[.] — Jess Mowry, *Way Past Cool*, p. 40, 1992

flat-ass *adverb*
absolutely *US, 1964*
- Say something about my family and I will flatass stretch you out! — Ken Weaver, *Texas Crude*, p. 112, 1984

flatback *noun*
a prostitute *US, 2002*
- [U]nlike some of his peers, he didn't take just any ho—he liked his flatbacks clean and innocent-looking. — Tracy Funches, *Pimpnosis*, p. 77, 2002

flat-back *verb*
to engage in prostitution *US, 1967*
From the image of a prostitute having sex lying on her back.
- She can "flat-back" and so long as she keeps breathing you can get some scratch. — Iceberg Slim (Robert Beck), *Pimp*, p. 105, 1969
- But to me, at this stage of my life, I didn't want anything but a flat-backing whore. — Donald Goines, *Whoreson*, p. 134, 1972
- [W]hen push comes to shove, it is easier to rob than to flatback. — Gail Sheehy, *Hustling*, p. 95, 1973

flatbacker *noun*
a prostitute of an undiscerning nature *US, 1969*
- A "flat-backer" who offers only coitus ("old-fashioned" or "straight") is likely to lose customers. — Charles Winick, *The Lively Commerce*, p. 207, 1971
- The street-walker has nothing but slurs for "those lazy flatbackers." — Gail Sheehy, *Hustling*, p. 33, 1973
- I wasn't scoring a big buck from the streets with one flat-backer. — Iceberg Slim (Robert Beck), *Airtight Willie and Me*, p. 47, 1979

flat dog *noun*
bologna *US, 1990*
- — Charles Shafer, *Folk Speech in Texas Prisons*, p. 204, 1990

flatfoot *noun*
a police officer, especially one assigned on foot patrol *US, 1912*
- That dumb flatfoot, Tracy, will beat us up. — Chester Gould, *Dick Tracy Meets the Night Crawler*, p. 1945
- I'll bet you a sandwich against a marriage license he's got a flatfoot downstairs covering every exit in the place[.] — Mickey Spillane, *I, The Jury*, p. 15, 1947
- But the subway is moving. "So long flatfoot!" I yell[.] — William Burroughs, *Naked Lunch*, p. 2, 1957
- "Go chew on your banana, flatfoot." — William Brashler, *City Dogs*, p. 47, 1976

flatfoot *verb*
to walk *US, 1974*
- I say that you niggers better flat-foot it on back home. — Joseph Nazel, *Black Cop*, p. 98, 1974

flat fuck *noun*
sex without loss of semen *US, 1970*
- [S]he got to opening up the other girl's pussy and they did a flat fuck together. — Roger Blake, *The Porno Movies*, pp. 168–169, 1970

- — *Maledicta*, p. 132, Summer/Winter 1982: "Dyke diction: the language of lesbians"
- One or two only, said they'd had a flat fuck with a friend, and what harm was there? — Terry Castle, *The Literature of Lesbianism*, p. 543, 2005

flat-hat *verb*
to fly very close to the ground at a high speed *US, 1939*
- "Roger that, Boss," said Slim, as he felt his juices flowing. "Did you hear that, Sundance? We've got our flat-hatting license!" — William M. La Barge and Robert Lawrence, *Sweetwater Gunslinger 201*, p. 79, 1983

flat joint; flat store *noun*
an illegal gambling operation where players are cheated as a matter of course *US, 1914*
- — *American Speech*, pp. 308–309, December 1960: "Carnival talk"
- Folks, we play short on the flat-joint. — Iceberg Slim (Robert Beck), *Trick Baby*, p. 111, 1969
- — Gene Sorrows, *All About Carnivals*, p. 17, 1985: "Terminology"

flatline *verb*
to die *US, 1981*
An allusion to the flat line on a medical monitoring device that indicates death.
- They knew that Shelby was vibrating from having done a teener of go-fast, and that he'd chill pretty soon. Or else he'd flat-line, and they wouldn't mind that either. — Joseph Wambaugh, *Finnegan's Week*, p. 235, 1993
- [G]ot Ketamine for the nutters (oh, that'll make you flatline). — Julian Johnson, *Urban Survival*, p. 170, 2003

flatliner *noun*
in poker, an unskilled and uninspired player *US, 1996*
The moral equivalent of "brain dead."
- — John Vorhaus, *The Big Book of Poker Slang*, p. 17, 1996

flat-out *adjective*
absolute, complete *US, 1959*
- It was an absolute flat-out fabrication. — Janet Evanovich, *Seven Up*, p. 63, 2001

flat passers *noun*
shaved dice used in cheating schemes *US, 1997*
- Then I started using flat passers; they're basically shaved dice so the four, five, nine, and ten turn up more frequently. — Stephen Cannell, *Big Con*, p. 215, 1997

flats *noun*
1 the lowest tier of cells in a prison *US, 1976*
- — John R. Armore and Joseph D. Wolfe, *Dictionary of Desperation*, p. 29, 1976
2 dice, the surfaces of which have been altered for cheating *US, 1950*
- — *The Annals of the American Academy of Political and Social Sciences*, p. 124, May 1950
- It's an honest game, no "bust-out or flats." — Alson Smith, *Syndicate City*, p. 208, 1954
- He had another set of "six-ace flats," too, which were weighted so that seven would come up frequently. — James Carr, *Bad*, p. 99, 1975

flatten out *verb*
to serve a prison sentence completely *US, 1976*
- — John R. Armore and Joseph D. Wolfe, *Dictionary of Desperation*, p. 29, 1976
- Man I only got to flatten out six years in prison and I'll be out. — Inez Cardozo-Freeman, *The Joint*, p. 497, 1984

flattie *noun*
the operator of a carnival flat store (gambling operation) *US, 2005*
- I'd learned a lot about Flatties—the carnies who worked the Flat Store—by listening and watching. — Peter Fenton, *Eyeing the Flash*, p. 116, 2005

flattop *noun*
an aircraft carrier *US, 1942*
- With the U.S. flattops busy pursuing the decoy, two Japanese battleship groups would close on Leyte from the north and south[.] — James D. Hornfischer, *The Last Stand of the Tin Can Sailors*, p. 3, 2004

flatty *noun*
a person who works in a flat joint (an illegal gambling operation where players are cheated as a matter of course) *US, 1981*
- Flatties are considered, even among carnival performers, as common thieves and unlike the performers who give the marks

something for their money. — Don Wilmeth, *The Language of American Popular Entertainment*, p. 95, 1981
- — Gene Sorrows, *All About Carnivals*, p. 17, 1985: "Terminology"

flava; flavor *noun*
style, especially when unique *US, 1982*
- [C]ome hear the brand new flava in / Ya ear ... — Craig Mack, *Flava In Ya Ear*, 1994
- I got all kinda flavors; I got styles that I didn't even start doin' yet. — *A2Z (quoting KRS-One, 1992)*, p. 36, 1995

flavor *noun*
1 in computing, a type or variety *US, 1983*
- — Guy L. Steele et al., *The Hacker's Dictionary*, p. 65, 1983
2 cocaine *US, 1995*
- — Bill Valentine, *Gang Intelligence Manual*, p. 75, 1995: "Black street gang terminology"

flavorful *adjective*
in computing, pleasing *US, 1991*
- — Eric S. Raymond, *The New Hacker's Dictionary*, p. 160, 1991

flavor of the month *noun*
the latest, short-lived trend or fashion or relationship *US, 1946*
Derisive, even contemptuous; originally conceived as a marketing strategy for ice cream.
- It's like your flavor of the month, and then it suddenly changes. — *Boston Globe*, 17th March 2002

flavor of the week *noun*
the latest short-lived trend or fashion or relationship *US, 2001*
- — Don R. McCreary (Editor), *Dawg Speak*, 2001

flavur *noun*
a factory-made cigarette *US, 2002*
- — Jeffrey Ian Ross, *Behind Bars*, p. 186, 2002: Slammer Slang

flawless *adjective*
1 flawed *US, 1982*
- — Connie Eble (Editor), *UNC-CH Campus Slang*, p. 3, Spring 1982
- Flawless apartment, Sydney. Have you named the cockroaches yet? — Jeff Fessler, *When Drag Is Not a Car Race*, p. 83, 1997
2 handsome *US, 1972*
- — Bruce Rodgers, *The Queens' Vernacular*, p. 82, 1972

flea *noun*
1 in American casinos, a gambler who places very small bets *US, 1985*
- — Steve Kuriscak, *Casino Talk*, p. 24, 1985
2 in a hospital, an internist *US, 1994*
- — Sally Williams, *"Strong" Words*, p. 142, 1994

flea bag *noun*
an utterly destitute person *US, 1971*
- The older prostitute who continues working into her sixties and seventies may be reduced to seeking clients on the local Skid Row and end up as a "flea bag." — Charles Winick, *The Lively Commerce*, p. 74, 1971

fleabag *noun*
1 a low-cost, run-down motel, room, boarding house or apartment *US, 1924*
- [H]e fled after he saw, he swore, a red ribbon tied across the open commode, fled to a Fifth Street fleabag. — Clancy Sigal, *Going Away*, p. 206, 1961
- They were working in the room next to his in that fucking fleabag hotel and that hole in the wall came from a slug[.] — Mickey Spillane, *Last Cop Out*, p. 96, 1975
- Two of them dirty niggers carried her out to the back door of the flea bag across the street. — Iceberg Slim (Robert Beck), *Long White Con*, p. 164, 1977
- Some damn tribe of withered old bitches doesn't want us to terminate that fleabag hotel. All because Glenn Miller and his band once took a shit there. — *Heathers*, 1988
2 a dishonest, disreputable carnival *US, 1980*
- — Joe McKennon, *Circus Lingo*, p. 35, 1980

flea powder *noun*
weak and/or diluted heroin *US, 1956*
- — *American Speech*, p. 87, May 1955: "Narcotic argot along the Mexican border"
- — Peter Johnson, *Dictionary of Street Alcohol and Drug Terms*, p. 75, 1993

flea trap *noun*
an inexpensive, shoddy hotel or boarding house *US, 1942*

- The Spanish Trail Inn didn't offer luxury accommodations, but it was far better than some of the flea traps Angie had frequented in her time. — J.A. Jance, *Desert Heart*, p. 237, 1993

flesh *noun*

an actor who appears on stage *US, 1981*

- — Don Wilmeth, *The Language of American Popular Entertainment*, p. 96, 1981

flesh *adjective*

in the music industry, appearing and performing live *US, 1948*

- There are scores of men and women infesting every radio station and theater where "flesh" performances still remain. — Jack Lait and Lee Mortimer, *New York Confidential*, p. 32, 1948

flesh agent *noun*

a talent agent *US, 1986*

- How do the old flesh agents tell an old stripper when she's ready to be put out to pasture? "You just stop booking her," says Anthony. — Josh Alan Friedman, *Tales of Times Square*, p. 42, 1986

flesh market *noun*

an area where prostitution and other sex businesses thrive *US, 1987*

- In La-La Land the premier hole in the wall was Nifty Shiftie's, at the top end of Hollywood, just out of the flesh market. — Robert Campbell, *Alice in La-La Land*, p. 251, 1987

flesh peddler *noun*

1 a pimp *US, 1942*

- "'I'm a king-size pimp, an honest-to-God flesh peddler, and I thought I might be able to do something with you.'" — Richard Prather, *The Peddler*, p. 123, 1952

2 an entertainer's business manager or agent *US, 1935*

- All right, being flesh peddlers, it's not as neat and fancy as writing War and Peace. — Stephen Longstreet, *The Flesh Peddlers*, p. 239, 1962
- Outside of San Francisco, most rock managers were just flesh peddlers; the last thing they cared about was the music. — Alice Echols, *Scars of Sweet Paradise*, p. 172, 1999

fleshpit *noun*

a bar or nightclub where people come in search of sexual partners *US, 1991*

- [A]nd then McGarr talking later, at the Luau, a Beverly Hills flesh pit, about how he could remember when Farmer was a radical and it scared him to see how far he'd drifted from the front lines. — Hunter S. Thompson, *Songs of the Doomed*, 1991
- Certain people have characterized the farm as a kind of Bacchanalian flesh pit, which was simply not so. — Lee Underwood, *Blue Melody*, p. 127, 2002

fleshpot *noun*

a brothel *US, 1954*

- Men on leave find they save a half-hour on their way to the fleshpots by getting off at Wilson Avenue. — Jack Lait and Lee Mortimer, *Chicago Confidential*, p. 67, 1950
- "If you mean that in Korea soldiers had more time to unwind before they had a chance at the fleshpots, it's a good point." — Donald Duncan, *The New Legions*, p. 68, 1967
- Amanda's papa refused to take his pubescent daughter into the Parisian fleshpots, but he did point them out to her from the window of a taxi. — Tom Robbins, *Another Roadside Attraction*, p. 47, 1971
- Here, then, are some devious path ways to Manhattan's fleshpots. — Bernhardt J. Hurwood, *The Sensuous New York*, p. 86, 1973

flex *verb*

1 to display power by a show of strength *US, 1993*

- Saw the police and they rolled right past me / No flexin' / Didn't even look in a nigga's direction as I ran / The intersection[.] — Ice Cube, *It Was a Good Day*, 1993

2 to leave *US, 1993*

- — *Washington Post*, 14th October 1993
- — Vann Wesson, *Generation X Field Guide and Lexicon*, p. 66, 1997

flick *noun*

1 a film *UK, 1926*

- The only drag is that since they really made it, they never gave me any gigs in their flicks even when they are powerful enough to order the casting director to. — Babs Gonzales, *Movin' On Down De Line*, p. 60, 1975
- A black porno flick is the sorriest thing on earth. No actors, no actresses, just a bunch of people sitting in a hotel room waiting for somebody to yell, "Action." — Chris Rock, *Rock This!*, p. 26, 1997

- But put that bad boy in a flick, every motherfucker out there want one. — *Jackie Brown*, 1997

2 a photograph *US, 1962*

- She took dynamite flicks but didn't think of herself as a real artist with a camera. — John Sinclair, *Guitar Army*, p. 298, 1972
- It was a helluva price to pay for having a white woman's flick in my wallet. — Odie Hawkins, *Scars and Memories*, p. 54, 1987
- Flicks proved that you existed and that you were still connected to the world outside. — Adrian Nicole LeBlanc, *Random House*, p. 87, 2003

flicker *noun*

1 a movie *US, 1926*

- — Lou Shelly, *Hepcats Jive Dictionary*, p. 11, 1945
- — Marcus Hanna Boulware, *Jive and Slang of Students in Negro Colleges*, 1947
- I spoke about leaving for the last roundup in the ranch house up yonder, an idea I got from a Johnny Mack Brown cowboy flicker. — Piri Thomas, *Down These Mean Streets*, p. 15, 1967

2 the clitoris *US, 2005*

- I'd sit back in the chair with my hand in my panties as he described all the delicious ways he could lick my flicker. — Noire, *Candy Licker*, p. 136, 2005

flier *noun*

1 in target shooting, a shot that strikes outside a close group of shots on the target *US, 1957*

- — *American Speech*, p. 193, October 1957: "Some colloquialisms of the handgunner"

2 a prisoner who commits suicide by jumping or is murdered by being thrown from the top tier of a prison *US, 1942*

- — John R. Armore and Joseph D. Wolfe, *Dictionary of Desperation*, p. 29, 1976

▶ **take a flier**

1 to attempt something *US, 1914*

- Remembers his mama stopped slaving in white folk's mansions ... took a flyer in show biz ... exotic dancer[.] — Iceberg Slim (Robert Beck), *Long White Con*, p. 25, 1977

2 to have an affair *US, 1966*

- "But that didn't mean that once in a while he wouldn't take a flier with a nice-looking girl on the bill. He just needed sex." — Jacqueline Susann, *Valley of the Dolls*, p. 23, 1966

flight skins *noun*

military flight pay *US, 1945*

- I was also paid air crew flight pay, or "flight skins," for an additional $50 a month. — Don Hoover, *The Road to 311 No. York St.*, p. 146, 2003

flight time *noun*

in auto racing, the elapsed time a car unintentionally spends in the air, usually upside down *US, 1980*

Grim humor.

- — Don Alexander, *The Racer's Dictionary*, p. 27, 1980

flik *noun*

a song from which the lyrics have been changed for humorous consumption by science fiction fans *US, 1991*

- — Eric S. Raymond, *The New Hacker's Dictionary*, p. 155, 1991

flimflam *noun*

a swindle involving a supposedly lost wallet supposedly found on the ground near the victim *US, 1960*

- This is one of the oldest of the confidence games; and was called "pigeon-trapping" in years gone by, but is usually called the flimflam these days. — W.M. Tucker, *The Change Raisers*, p. 24, 1960

flimflam *verb*

to shortchange, to swindle *US, 1881*

- Then I wouldn't have to flimflam poor crazy Zelda any more, and I would tell her the whole hideous truth. — Max Shulman, *I was a Teen-Age Dwarf*, p. 121, 1959
- He said, "Blue, I'll die and go to the bottomless pits of hell before I let you flimflam me out of my two grand." — Iceberg Slim (Robert Beck), *Trick Baby*, p. 33, 1969
- He had been up in Harlem flimflamming a colored woman preacher out of $935 and thought he would take a little vacation. — *The Life & Loves of Mr. Jiveass Nigger*, p. 15, 1969
- After all these years of flimflamming, it's time to get real. — Odie Hawkins, *Great Lawd Buddha*, p. 196, 1990

flimflam man *noun*

a confidence swindler *US, 1918*

- Everyone in Hollywood is a phony, a fruit, or a flim-flam man, a partner had warned him. — Joseph Wambaugh, *The New Centurions*, p. 151, 1970
- You see, Mr. Chin thought of himself as the Orient's version of the flim-flam man. — Gary Mayer, *Bookie*, p. 211, 1974

flimflammer *noun*
a swindler who engages in the flimflam swindle (a swindle involving a supposedly lost wallet supposedly found on the ground near the victim) *US, 1960*
- The flim-flammer often goes to a bank or a bus station in order to spot a victim with a fat billfold. — W.M. Tucker, *The Change Raisers*, p. 24, 1960
- There's lesbians, masochists, hypes, whores, flim flammers, paddy hustlers, hugger muggers, ex-cons of all descriptions, and anybody else with a kink of some kind or other. — Joseph Wambaugh, *The New Centurions*, p. 174, 1970

flinger *noun*
1 an impulsive poker player who is inclined to raise bets without regard to the quality of his hand *US, 1988*
- — George Percy, *The Language of Poker*, p. 35, 1988

2 in target shooting, a shot that strikes outside a close group of shots on the target *US, 1957*
- — *American Speech*, p. 193, October 1957: "Some colloquialisms of the handgunner"

fling-wing *noun*
a helicopter *US, 1943*
- One, I know absolutely nothing about fling-wing flying. — Howard Fried, *Beyond the Checkride*, p. 184, 1997

flip *noun*
1 a condition of mental instability *US, 1953*
- [S]he'd walk down the street in her flip and actually feel the electric contact with other human beings[.] — Jack Kerouac, *The Subterraneans*, p. 29, 1958

2 a person who has lost touch with reality *US, 1952*
- Just frantic people, all of us. Just flips. — George Mandel, *Flee the Angry Strangers*, p. 373, 1952

3 a male homosexual who plays the passive role in sex *US, 1992*
- — William K. Bentley and James M. Corbett, *Prison Slang*, p. 49, 1992

4 a police informer *US, 1967*
- Then some little junker flip bitch oh-deed. — Malcolm Braly, *On the Yard*, p. 28, 1967
- The flip's name is Francis Kingsbury. — Carl Hiaasen, *Native Tongue*, p. 313, 1991

Flip *noun*
a Filipino *US, 1931*
- — Multicultural Management Program Fellows *Dictionary of Cautionary Words and Phrases*, 1989
- — Judi Sanders, *Da Bomb*, p. 6, 1997

flip *verb*
1 to convert someone to homosexuality *US, 1994*
- That a guy was even more of a man if he could "flip" another man, turn him into a homosexual. — Nathan McCall, *Makes Me Wanna Holler*, p. 188, 1994

2 to become very angry or agitated; to go temporarily crazy *US, 1950*
- Wigged? Christ, it looks like he flipped. — Thurston Scott, *Cure it with Honey*, p. 57, 1951
- "You look like some other cat." "Baby," said the wolf, "you're flippin'!" — Steve Allen, *Bop Fables*, p. 46, 1955
- Whereas if you goof (the ugliest word in Hip), if you lapse back into being a frightened stupid child, or if you flip, if you lose your control[.] — Norman Mailer, *Advertisements for Myself*, p. 351, 1957
- That he's getting married has her flipped. — Philip Roth, *Goodbye, Columbus*, p. 47, 1958

3 to become enthusiastic and excited *US, 1950*
- She was as ugly as a pan of worms, but when I saw those sandwiches with the crusts cut off, boy, I flipped! — Max Shulman, *I was a Teen-Age Dwarf*, p. 59, 1959
- They all came in to congratulate me. The whole campus flipped. — Dick Gregory, *Nigger*, p. 92, 1964
- She really flipped over you. — Hunter S. Thompson, *Fear and Loathing in Las Vegas*, p. 124, 1971

4 to induce a betrayal *US, 1980*
- If there ever was a time to flip him against his old crew it was at that moment. — Nicholas Pileggi, *Wise Guy*, p. 265, 1985

- The mission: Save LaFreniere first, and flip him as a witness against Angiulo second. — Gerard O'Neill, *The Under Boss*, p. 210, 1989
- You don't see what that motherfucker's doing? How he's trying to flip you, turn you against me? — Elmore Leonard, *Be Cool*, p. 230, 1999

5 to betray; to inform on *US, 1960*
- You don't have to larceny me—I won't flip on you. I'll never flip on nobody again. — Clarence Cooper Jr., *The Scene*, p. 14, 1960
- They wanted me to flip on the guy who had sold the stuff to me. — Henry Williamson, *Hustler!*, p. 138, 1965
- Before Barboza "flipped" in 1967, no one had laid a glove on the wily Angiulo. — Gerard O'Neill, *The Under Boss*, p. 72, 1989
- 10–4 flipped in less than a week. — Adrian Nicole LeBlanc, *Random Family*, p. 76, 2003

▸ **flip a trick**
(of a prostitute) to have sex with a customer *US, 1979*
Far less common than to "turn" a TRICK.
- She was scratching and nodding and flipping car tricks at Sunset and La Brea when I got back to L.A. two months later. — Iceberg Slim (Robert Beck), *Airtight Willie and Me*, p. 169, 1979

▸ **flip the bird**
to gesture in derision with a raised middle finger *US, 1968*
- Did he flip her the bird again? — Armistead Maupin, *Tales of the City*, p. 344, 1978
- I just flip 'em the bird / And keep goin', I don't take shit from no-one[.] — Eminem (Marshall Mathers), *Criminal*, 2000

▸ **flip the bone**
to extend the middle finger in a rude gesture of defiance *US, 1957*
- [A]ll Jeff did was flip the bone at his old man which is a very dirty way of telling somebody where to get off. — Frederick Kohner, *Gidget*, p. 48, 1957

▸ **flip the grip**
to shake hands *US, 1945*
- — Lou Shelly, *Hepcats Jive Talk Dictionary*, p. 24, 1945

▸ **flip the lip**
to talk *US, 1947*
- And she is always flippin' the lip about him bein' such a weary Willie, the citizens of the burg, even the hepcats, mark him solid. — Harry Haenigsen, *Jive's Like That*, 1947

▸ **flip your lid; flipflop your lid**
to lose emotional control *US, 1952*
- She must have flipped her lid if she likes that. — Margaret Weiss, *The TV Writer's Guide*, p. 103, 1952
- Ever since he passed his written test for the police force he flipped his lid! — Ernest Pendrell, *Seven Times Monday*, p. 20, 1961
- "People are always flipping their lids around here," Minelli observed[.] — L.H. Whittemore, *Cop!*, p. 84, 1969
- He finally flipped his lid. He walked around with a bible in his hands, would come up to you and ask, "What did you say?" — Herbert Huncke, *Guilty of Everything*, p. 178, 1990

▸ **flip your stick**
to move your penis during an all-cavity strip search *US, 2002*
- — Gary K. Farlow, *Prison-ese*, p. 21, 2002

▸ **flip your wig**
to lose your mental composure *US, 1959*
- He flipped his wig when it was finished and they took him to a sanitarium. — Chandler Brossard, *Who Walks in Darkness*, p. 52, 1952
- Nate took away her emotional security and she flipped her wig and snuck into the locker room and hacked up his athletic equipment. — Max Shulman, *I was a Teen-Age Dwarf*, p. 33, 1959
- "The trial's been postponed because the Puerto Rican chick, dig, has lost her baby and look like she flipped her wig too, lost her mind." — James Baldwin, *If Beale Street Could Talk*, p. 202, 1974

flip *adjective*
pleasant, fashionable, popular *US, 1955*
- — *American Speech*, p. 302, December 1955: "Wayne university slang"

flip act *noun*
feigned insanity *US, 1967*
- Jimmy was trying to beat the rap by pulling a flip act. He was good. He told me to go crazy and I'd beat the chair. — Piri Thomas, *Down These Mean Streets*, p. 243, 1967

flip case *noun*
a Filipino *US, 2002*
- "We got a shortage of flip cases this year," he explains. — Jimmy Lerner, *You Got Nothing Coming*, p. 180, 2002

flipflap *noun*
in circus usage, a back handspring *US, 1981*
- — Don Wilmeth, *The Language of American Popular Entertainment*, p. 96, 1981

flipflop *noun*
1 a sandal that is not bound to the foot, usually worn around a swimming pool *US, 1970*
From the sound made when walking on concrete.
- Blew out my flip flop, stepped on a pop-top/ Cut my heel, had to cruise on back home. — Jimmy Buffett, *Margaritaville*, 1977
- She will take black spikes or Capezios or even foam-rubber flip-flops. — Hunter S. Thompson, *A Generation of Swine*, p. 109, 28 April 1986
- The dozen or so trustees who had run of the place and were walking around in T-shirts, drawstring gym pants and rubber flip-flops. — Richard Price, *Clockers*, p. 96, 1992
- "If my nine wasn't drying out," Fortney said to the lifeguards, "I'd blast you moondoggies right outta your flip-flops." — Joseph Wambaugh, *Floaters*, p. 83, 1996

2 a homosexual who will reverse sexual roles *US, 1975*
- Flip-flops, also called "knickknacks," are dudes that begin by making the homos but wind up playing the female role themselves. — James Carr, *Bad*, p. 155, 1975

flip-flop *verb*
1 to change positions on a political issue or issues in response to changing public opinion *US, 1965*
- A day after a top administration official announced the National Office of AIDS Policy had become obsolete, President Bush flipflopped and said he was keeping the office open. — *San Francisco Chronicle*, p. A3, 8th February 2001
- In just the last few weeks, for example, the Bush administration flip-flopped on a campaign promise to limit carbon-dioxide emissions[.] — *Daily Sun*, 31st March 2001
- The Bush Administration has flip-flopped on North Korea. — *Time Magazine*, p. 38, 28th October 2002
- She said President Bush had flipflopped on America's global role: "For a man who said it was not our job to police the world, he seems to be pretty at ease with this." — *USA Today*, p. 12A, 21st March 2003

2 (used of two homosexuals) to reverse sexual roles after sexual satisfaction is achieved by the "active" partner *US, 1961*
- Many snide remarks would be passed to the effect that they were most probably "flipflopping," another way of saying that they were interchanging their roles in the sex act. — *New York Mattachine Newsletter*, p. 7, July 1961

3 to have sex with both men and women *US, 1992*
- — William K. Bentley and James M. Corbett, *Prison Slang*, p. 59, 1992

4 (used of two homosexuals) to reverse sexual roles *US, 1972*
- It's hard to tell who's doing what. You'd be surprised. Some of it that you would swear is strictly aggressive type is what they call flip-flop. — Bruce Jackson, *In the Life*, p. 393, 1972

flip-flopping *noun*
changing positions on an issue or issues *US, 1976*
- But his flip-flopping from con to pro on Federal aid to New York could hurt him in a September primary race[.] — *Newsweek*, p. 25, 12th January 1976

flipped *adjective*
smart, attractive *US, 1955*
- You're really flipped—aren't you. — *Rebel Without a Cause*, 1955

flipped lid *noun*
an emotionally disturbed or mentally ill person *US, 1959*
- "To lock me up with flipped lids—that's evil." — Irving Shulman, *The Short End of the Stick*, p. 95, 1959

flipped out *adjective*
drug-intoxicated *US, 1970*
- [T]wo groovy flipped out teenage fans were just sitting there digging each other, one boy, one girl. — Richard Meltzer, *A Whore Just Like the Rest*, p. 74, 1970

flipper *noun*
1 the hand *UK, 1812*

- Reach out to the clerk, shake his flipper, and say, "Hi ya, glad to see you again." — Jack Lait and Lee Mortimer, *New York Confidential*, p. 201, 1948

2 the ear *US, 1905*
- — Lou Shelly, *Hepcats Jive Dictionary*, p. 11, 1945

flippers *noun*
anchovies *US, 1996*
- — *Maledicta*, p. 12, 1996: "Domino's pizza jargon"

flipping *adjective*
used as an intensifier *UK, 1911*
- [W]hen the bogies were about to search him on some very hot sus, he swallowed a flipping great sapphire and diamond star pendant[.] — Charles Raven, *Underworld Nights*, p. 9, 1956
- I've read it through myself and then I'll suddenly scrap it and say, "Well, that's no flipping good" and start again. — *Human Studies*, p. 332, 1983

flippity *adjective*
sassy *US, 1998*
- Johnson was getting irritated with the girl's flippity mouth[.] — Renay Jackson, *Oaktown Devil*, p. 32, 1998

flippy *adjective*
eccentric, crazy *US, 1965*
- Everyone knew his mother and father were flippy. — Richard Price, *The Wanderers*, p. 33, 1974

flip-side *noun*
► **on the flip-side**
later on *US, 1977*
- "You stay close to that rig and we'll modulate with you on the flip side. We Down." — E.M. Corder, *Citizens Band*, p. 33, 1977
- — Connie Eble (Editor), *UNC-CH Campus Slang*, p. 4, October 2002

flip top *noun*
the top of a canned food or beverage that peels open without resort to an opening device *US, 1972*
- I ripped the flip top off another one. — Oscar Zeta Acosta, *The Autobiography of a Brown Buffalo*, p. 169, 1972

flit *noun*
an effeminate homosexual male *US, 1935*
- The other end of the bar was full of flits. They weren't too flitty-looking—I mean they didn't have their hair too long or anything—but you could tell they were flits anyway. — J.D. Salinger, *Catcher in the Rye*, p. 142, 1951
- Still, when this assistant prop man, crew-cut kid, flit, floppy wrists and pursy lips, what they called rough trade, a real camp, when he'd begun stroking Biff's elbows and saying how gone he was on him, Biff hadn't come down with the immediate kyawkyaws. — Bernard Wolfe, *The Late Risers*, p. 202, 1954
- The reason she married Oscar in the first place was that she had been bored silly with the flits and lushes of cafe society. — Max Shulman, *Rally Round the Flag, Boys!*, p. 72, 1957
- "Has he been married?" "I bet he has been. He's not flit." "Flit?" "Stands for faggot." — Frederick Kohner, *Gidget*, p. 115, 1957

fliv *verb*
in circus and carnival usage, to fail or to perform poorly *US, 1917*
- — Don Wilmeth, *The Language of American Popular Entertainment*, p. 96, 1981

flivver *noun*
an old, worn car, especially a Ford car *US, 1910*
The term was, by the early 1980s, chiefly associated with the early model Ford cars, and had thus become historical.
- The hustlers would be waiting in flivvers to haul people with gunny sacks home. — Iceberg Slim (Robert Beck), *The Naked Soul of Iceberg Slim*, p. 97, 1971

FLK *noun*
a strange-looking child; a funny-*looking* kid *US, 1961*
- [O]nly have come up with the residents' slang expression FLK for "funny-looking kid." — *Archives of Neurology*, p. 32, 1969
- — *Maledicta*, p. 117, 1984–1985: "Milwaukee medical maledicta"

float *verb*
1 (said of an illegal gambling operation) to move from place to place *US, 1973*
- "Now the games in town floated from location to location each week." — Vincent Teresa, *My Life in the Mafia*, p. 73, 1973

- Some of the games floated, meaning players met in an alley near Cross and Salem streets in the North End to be escorted either by foot or in a car to the secret location of that night's gathering. — Gerard O'Neill, *The Under Boss*, p. 181, 1989

2 to introduce into circulation *US, 1975*
- "They cash checks in there, and I've always thought about popping in there and floating some paper." — Brian Boyer, *Prince of Thieves*, p. 102, 1975

▸ **float dice**
to drop dice suspected of having been weighted into a glass of water to see if they roll over on one side *US, 1997*
- If you're winning too much, he'll also float the dice. — Stephen Cannell, *King Con*, p. 136, 1997

▸ **float someone's boat**
to please someone; to make someone happy *US, 1984*
- — Connie Eble (Editor), *UNC-CH Campus Slang*, p. 3, Fall 1984
- [L]et us know which new bands are floating your boat the most. — *Kerrang!*, p. 3, 1st December 2001
- [W]e have to defend the rights of homosexuals to nail each other's gonads to planks of wood if that's what floats their boat. — Christopher Brookmyre, *The Sacred Art of Stealing*, p. 244, 2002

floater noun
1 a corpse found floating in a body of water *US, 1890*
- We pulled a floater out of the Quabbin Reservoir a couple years ago, one of the Mackling gang[.] — George V. Higgins, *The Judgment of Deke Hunter*, p. 7, 1976
- Floater comes up at Waterworks Park, makes your fucking day. — Elmore Leonard, *Split Images*, pp. 65–66, 1981
- Valentine wouldn't soon forget the floater call. — Thomas Larry Adcock, *Precinct 19*, p. 17, 1984
- Another floater. The water was warm enough for the bacteria to have cooked fast, and after several days methane gas had brought it bobbing to the surface, bobbing lazily against the rocks. — Joseph Wambaugh, *Floaters*, p. 147, 1996

2 in circus and carnival usage, a slice of imitation fruit floating on the top of imitation fruit juice *US, 1981*
- — Don Wilmeth, *The Language of American Popular Entertainment*, p. 96, 1981

3 the recreational drug methaqualone, best known as Quaaludes™ *US, 1997*
- SOUTHERN: [C]hicks love Quaaludes—makes them less self-conscious, I suppose, about fucking. The druggist says it's a great favorite with hookers. With students and hookers. They must have something in common. BURROUGHS: Intense pain. SOUTHERN: They call them "floaters"—I guess they float above the pain. — Victor Bockris, *The Howard Marks Book of Dope Stories*, p. 35, 1997

4 a person who is a poor credit risk because of constantly changing employment *US, 1975*
- — *American Speech*, p. 312, Autumn–Winter 1975: "The jargon of car salesmen"

5 an early release from jail, usually with an order to leave town immediately *US, 1914*
- The copper agreed to give him a floater [out-of-state probation] for $50, but crossed him after the plea as entered[.] — Charles Hamilton, *Men of the Underworld*, p. 124, 1952
- When I got a floater out of the state, I planned to ride as far as El Paso. — Nelson Algren, *The Neon Wilderness*, p. 128, 1960
- Father was released on a "floater" and came for me with chastisement and shame flooding his florid features. — Neal Cassady, *The First Third*, p. 123, 1971

6 a river-rafting enthusiast *US, 1997*
- — Jim Crotty, *How to Talk American*, p. 213, 1997

7 in the language of wind surfing, a sailboard that can support the weight of a person in the water *US, 1985*
- — Frank Fox, *A Beginner's Guide to Zen and the Art of Windsurfing*, p. 151, 1985: "A short dictionary of wind surfing terms"

8 a big, buoyant surfboard *US, 1964*
- — John Severson, *Modern Surfing Around the World*, p. 169, 1964

9 a pinball machine which is nearly level, lacking the playfield pitch needed for a good game *US, 1977*
The fact that the playfield is nearly level makes it seem as if the ball floats on the playfield.
- — Bobbye Claire Natkin and Steve Kirk, *All About Pinball*, p. 112, 1977

floaties noun
feces floating in the sea *US, 1991*
- — Trevor Cralle, *The Surfin'ary*, p. 39, 1991

floating adjective
1 moving; not settled in a definite place *US, 1918*
- Clean-up or no, there usually are more floating crap-games, illegal bookies and after-hour spots in Prince Georges than there are in Reno, where all such things are legal. — Jack Lait and Lee Mortimer, *Washington Confidential*, p. 66, 1951
- Somewhere in Cook County, just a hoe-handle and a half from Chicago's busy Loop, the granddaddy of all floating crap games is going into its fifth successive year. — Alson Smith, *Syndicate City*, p. 202, 1954
- Up in the Bronx, a Negro held up some Italian racketeers in a floating crap game. — Malcolm X and Alex Haley, *The Autobiography of Malcolm X*, p. 124, 1964
- What do you think they was doing down there, having a floating crap game? — Robert Campbell, *Junkyard Dog*, p. 65, 1986

2 drunk or marijuana-intoxicated *US, 1938*
- "Man, when I see you floating, that'll be the day I quit. That'll be all. See old preacher Kipper floating!" — Edwin Gilbert, *The Hot and the Cool*, p. 34, 1953

floating shotgun noun
a rocket-armed landing craft *US, 1982*
Korean war usage.
- "Floating shotguns," someone in the invasion fleet called these vessels (LSMRs, for landing ships, medium rocket). — Joseph C. Goulden, *Korea*, p. 210, 1982

float-out noun
a jail sentence suspended contingent upon the criminal leaving town *US, 1968*
- This here one don't fall off that luv an ack like a lady she gonna get a floatout. — Robert Gover, *JC Saves*, p. 18, 1968

floats noun
dice that have been hollowed out to affect their balance *US, 1950*
Because most dice used in casinos are now transparent, the practice and term are almost obsolete.
- — *The Annals of the American Academy of Political and Social Sciences*, p. 125, May 1950

flock noun
a group of unskilled poker players *US, 1996*
- John Vorhaus, *The Big Book of Poker Slang*, p. 17, 1996

flog verb
to endorse, to promote, to sell *US, 1983*
- Hymie used to print and sell his own tip sheet titled Gift Horses at Bay Meadows until cataracts sealed the dapper little horse savant within a white waxen world and he was reduced to flogging forms. — Seth Morgan, *Homeboy*, p. 58, 1990

▸ **flog the bishop**
(of a male) to masturbate *US, 1999*
- Spanking the monkey. Flogging the bishop. Choking the chicken. Jerking the gherkin. — *American Beauty*, 1999

▸ **flog your dong**
(used of a male) to masturbate *US, 1994*
- Meanwhile, every Tom, Dick and Dick outside is trying to flog my dong. — *Airheads*, 1994

▸ **flog your dummy**
(used of a male) to masturbate *US, 1922*
- I'll be seeing you in March in Paris and don't flog your dummies, and save some girls for me. — Jack Kerouac, *Jack Kerouac Selected Letters 1957–1969*, p. 101, 10th December 1957: Letter to Allen Ginsberg
- [W]hen I left I told him not to flog his damn dummy too much[.] — Jack Kerouac, *The Dharma Bums*, p. 178, 1958
- What if he blabs to the Daily News? ASST HUMAN OPP'Y COMMISH FLOGS DUMMY. — Philip Roth, *Portnoy's Complaint*, p. 197, 1969
- Then he confesses that when he was little he flogged his dummy maybe a thousand times and didn't tell the priest in confession. — Joseph Wambaugh, *Lines and Shadows*, p. 129, 1984

flo is coming to town
used as a code phrase for the bleed period of the menstrual cycle *US, 2002*
- SEE (C) YOU (U) NEXT TUESDAY (slang): Charlotte's term for the place where Flo stays when she comes to town (see also "Flo is coming to town"). — Amy Sohn, *Sex and the City*, p. 155, 2002

flood *verb*

1 (used of professional wrestlers) to rush into the ring or arena in large numbers *US, 1992*

- All the faces (Pillman, Biff Wellington, Owen Hart, Bruce Hart etc.) flooded the ring and poured champagne over Benoit and Chris did a great victory interview. — *Herb's Wrestling Tidbits*, 20th August 1992

2 to wear pants that don't reach the shoes *US, 1998*

- — *Columbia Missourian*, p. 1A, 19th October 1998

floods *noun*

long pants that are too short or shorts that are too long *US, 1982*

- — Douglas Simonson, *Pidgin to da Max Hana Hou*, 1982

flooey *adverb*

awry *US, 1905*

- Why not go over and help Nelson run the lot? Something's going flooey over there. — John Updike, *Rabbit at Rest*, p. 171, 1990

floof *noun*

a fool *US, 1919*

- "Good practice for a pair of old floofs," he said. — John D. MacDonald, *The Deceivers*, p. 9, 1958

flookum *noun*

in circus and carnival usage, an artificially flavored and colored "fruit" drink; the syrup used to make the drink *US, 1966*

- — Raymond Oliver, *American Speech*, p. 280, December 1966: "More carnie talk from the west coast"

floor *noun*

▶ **take off the floor**

to remove a prostitute from service in a brothel *US, 1978*

- The price for removing a girl from service, "taking her off the floor," as they say, is one hundred fifty bucks. — Gerald Paine, *A Bachelor's Guide to the Brothels of Nevada*, p. 112, 1978

floor *verb*

to push a vehicle's accelerator to the floorboard *US, 1953*

- But the guy got the Mustang started, jammed it into reverse, and floored it. — Joseph Wambaugh, *Fire Lover*, p. 35, 2002

floorburners *noun*

shoes *US, 1972*

- — David Claerbaut, *Black Jargon in White America*, p. 64, 1972

floor lamp *noun*

a woman actor with good looks but not blessed with acting ability *US, 1973*

- — Sherman Louis Sergel, *The Language of Show Biz*, p. 88, 1973

floor name *noun*

the nickname or alias used by a prostitute in a brothel *US, 1999*

- I can't remember either her real name or her floor name. — Lora Shaner, *Madam*, p. 103, 1999

floor work *noun*

in a strip or sex show, movements made on the floor simulating sexual intercourse, offering strategic and gripping views as the dancer moves her legs *US, 1965*

- Meanwhile, back at the strip show, I knew that according to all true Christian standards nudity in itself was certainly not lewd, but burlesque—with its "subtle" charades of grabbing, "floor work," pulling and touching—was lewd. — Lenny Bruce, *How to Talk Dirty and Influence People*, p. 53, 1965
- If strippers choose a face that is shy, it is because they want their "floor work" (crouching or lying on the floor and simulating intercourse) and "dirty work" ("flashing" and spreading their legs) to remind the audience of demure girls. — Marilyn Salutin, *The Sexual Scene*, p. 173, June 1971
- Great girl. Oh, and remember, Nick likes floorwork. — George Paul Csicsery (Editor), *The Sex Industry*, p. 116, 1973
- The five-day Pure Talent School allowed Burana to polish her "floor work" skills on the dance stage—skills that Burana forthrightly

acknowledges she lacked in the early years of her career—and refine her "pole work." — *Denver Post*, p. E1, 10th October 2001

flooze *noun*

a woman or girl *US, 1952*

- The flooze down in Florida had tired of his mooching and sent him packing northward. — Ben Hamper, *Rivethead*, p. 21, 1991

floozie; floozy; floosie; floosy *noun*

a woman, especially one with few sexual inhibitions; a prostitute *US, 1902*

- [T]hey were all wobbling around the floor with their floozies, so drunk they could hardly stand. — Mezz Mezzrow, *Really the Blues*, p. 183, 1946
- And do not think that it is the abode, the stomping ground, of only the pimp, sharpie, and floozy set. — John D. McDonald, *The Neon Jungle*, p. 6, 1953
- You going with that little Mexican floozy? — Jack Kerouac, *On the Road*, p. 101, 1957
- My parents are in an uproar over Paul. He's moved some floozie in with him up in the studio over the garage. — C.D. Payne, *Youth in Revolt*, p. 254, 1993

flop *noun*

1 a place to spend the night *US, 1910*

- "I ain't got a flop. Can you let me have the price?" — Willard Motley, *Knock on Any Door*, p. 157, 1947
- [H]e himself is completely conscious not only of the old barbershop and the old B movie and bouncing his tennis ball downtown streets of Denver and the bum flops and poolhalls. — Jack Kerouac, *Letter to Carl Solomon*, p. 329, 27th December 1951
- I decided to grab a bite before I scouted up a flop for the night[.] — Robert Edmond Alter, *Carny Kill*, p. 12, 1966
- If he had a dollar he could get him a 52 cent flop and a bowl of soup. — John Gimenez, *Up Tight!*, p. 79, 1967
- [A]nd a regretful return to the monotonous rounds of one-nighter, or at most, bi-monthly, exchange of flops[.] — Neal Cassady, *The First Third*, p. 133, 1971
- I tailspinned down to Tijuana, found a flop and a bottle of drugstore hop, and went prowling for Maggie Cordova. — James Ellroy, *Hollywood Nocturnes*, p. 291, 1994

2 a drunk sleeping in public *US, 1949*

- A sleeping lush—known as a "flop" in the trade—attracts a hierarchy of scavengers. — William Burroughs, *Junkie*, p. 43, 1953

3 a complete, dismal failure *US, 1919*

- "Just another flop," he said to nobody in particular. — Robert Sylvester, *No Cover Charge*, p. 74, 1956
- He enjoyed a succession of resounding flops, and each night he came home screaming like a wounded thing. — Max Shulman, *Anyone Got a Match?*, p. 62, 1964

4 a demotion *US, 1973*

- Once the flop is in the record only the heaviest of hooks—the PC or the mayor himself—could ever restore the policeman to his previous eminence. — Leonard Shecter and William Phillips, *On the Pad*, p. 171, 1973

5 the denial of a release on parole by a prison parole board *US, 1944*

- I been to the parole board and they hit me with a year flop. — A.S. Jackson, *Gentleman Pimp*, p. 130, 1973

6 an arrest, conviction and/or imposition of a prison sentence *US, 1904*

- He act like he knows ... That man ever took a flop there people would pass him around, everybody have a piece. — Elmore Leonard, *Stick*, p. 99, 1983

7 in hold 'em poker, the first three cards dealt face-up in the centre of the table *US, 1990*

- — Anthony Holden, *Big Deal*, p. 300, 1990

8 in a dice game, a roll of the dice *US, 1962*

- — Frank Garcia, *Marked Cards and Loaded Dice*, p. 262, 1962

9 the ear *US, 1945*

- — Lou Shelly, *Hepcats Jive Dictionary*, p. 11, 1945

flop *verb*

1 to reside temporarily; to stay overnight *US, 1907*

- You ever flop into some cat's pad? — Evan Hunter, *The Blackboard Jungle*, p. 1954, 1954

- [T]he landlord flipped when he heard I was going to flop on the couch for three days. — William Burroughs, *Letters to Allen Ginsberg 1953–1957*, p. 13, 2nd January 1954
- "I got nowhere to flop and nothing to get wet with." — Malcolm Braly, *It's Cold Out There*, p. 68, 1966
- A nice old guy didn't have a dime and never hurt nobody, gets shot in the back while he's floppin' in a doorway on Seventh Avenue, and you call it a tough break! — Emmett Grogan, *Final Score*, p. 5, 1976

2 to go to sleep *UK, 1936*
- [W]aiting for householders to flop. — Charles Raven, *Underworld Nights*, p. 68, 1956

3 to fail completely *US, 1900*
- Your plan flopped, boss. — Chester Gould, *Dick Tracy Meets the Night Crawler*, p. 89, 1945
- Whenever they flopped, I sank way down in the dumps. — James T. Farrell, *They Ain't the Men They Used to Be*, p. 81, 1955

4 in police work, to demote in rank or assignment *US, 1970*
- — *New York Times*, 15th February 1970
- Serpico was resigned to the fact that he would be transferred back—"flopped," a cop would say—to the uniformed force sooner or later. — Peter Maas, *Serpico*, p. 97, 1973
- The reason it was a mistake is that Martin, who was subsequently flopped out of the bureau for seeking the help of Hugh Mulligan, bookmaker, loan shark, fixer, in getting a Police Department promotion, fell in love with the place. — Leonard Shecter and William Phillips, *On the Pad*, p. 134, 1973
- In those days, one big collar and you were in the Detective Bureau. But now they flop you for nothing. — Edwin Torres, *Q & A*, p. 17, 1977

5 in bar dice games, to shake the dice in the dice cup and then roll them onto a surface *US, 1971*
- — Jester Smith, *Games They Play in San Francisco*, p. 104, 1971

flophouse *noun*
an inexpensive, shoddy, tattered, dirty place to stay, catering to transients *US, 1909*
- He was not living in a flophouse this time—he lived in a Park Avenue hotel at $4.50 per day. — Jack Kerouac, *Letter to Allen Ginsberg*, p. 91, 23rd August 1945
- They were three noisy blocks, filled with pawn-shops, second-hand stores, pool-rooms, bail-bond brokers, beer joints, sidewalk hamburger stands, flop-houses, oil stations and narrow, messy parking lots[.] — Horace McCoy, *Kiss Tomorrow Good-bye*, p. 177, 1948
- No home, twenty-five cents a night in a flophouse. — Bobby Seale, *A Lonely Rage*, p. 295, 1978
- It's not a flop house. It's basic and simple. That doesn't make it a flop house. — Quentin Tarantino, *From Dusk Till Dawn*, p. 42, 1995
- Fuckin' flophouse. We're still short on the rent. — *Kids*, 1995

flopjoint *noun*
a flophouse *US, 1928*
- But now, thank heaven if you get in a flop joint. — Jack Lait and Lee Mortimer, *New York Confidential*, pp. 201–202, 1948
- For example, two of the ladies pick up some joker at a sleazy bar and end up having a threesome in his flop-joint apartment. — Kent Smith et al., *Adult Movies*, p. 180, 1982

flop over *verb*
to deny a prisoner's request for parole *US, 1976*
- If you're flopped over, they simply write Denied on an angle in red pencil. — Malcolm Braly, *False Starts*, p. 253, 1976

flopper *noun*
the arm *US, 1945*
- — Lou Shelly, *Hepcats Jive Dictionary*, p. 11, 1945

flopperoo *noun*
a failure *US, 1931*
- — Lou Shelly, *Hepcats Jive Dictionary*, p. 11, 1945
- "Why did Groucho Marx, Private Eye, do a flopperoo? Lousy ratings, I heard." — Ron Goulart, *Elementary, My Dear Groucho*, p. 35, 1999

flop sweat *noun*
a panic associated with the possibility of failure, whether or not actual perspiration is involved *US, 1966*

- I've got flopsweat! — Charles Ludlum, *Stage Blood*, p. 121, 1974
- "Flop sweat," they call it in the theater. Many capable, decent people are so frightened of failure that they won't even try for success. — Harvey Reese, *How to License Your Million Dollar Idea*, p. 183, 2002

Florida Hilton *nickname*
the federal prison camp at Eglin Air Force Base, Eglin, Florida *US, 1974*
- The place where the Watergate burglars spent much of their time in confinement is a white collar prison dubbed "The Florida Hilton." — *San Francisco Chronicle*, p. 6, 19th March 1974

Florida snow *noun*
cocaine *US, 1994*
- From Florida's standing as the major entry point for cocaine into the US. — US Department of Justice, *Street Terms*, August 1994

floss *noun*
1 cotton candy *US, 1960*
The spun sugar is known as "candy floss" in the UK but not known as such in the US, making what would be a simple UK abbreviated form to be a piece of slang in the US.
- — *American Speech*, pp. 308–309, December 1960: "Carnival talk"
- — Joe McKennon, *Circus Lingo*, p. 35, 1980

2 a thong-backed bikini bottom *US, 1991*
- — Trevor Cralle, *The Surfin'ary*, p. 39, 1991

floss *verb*
1 to wash *US, 1999*
- The sky was gray out this way, so not many people were getting their hoopties flossed[.] — Eric Jerome Dickey, *Cheaters*, pp. 225–226, 1999

2 to show off; to behave with ostentatious style and flair *US, 1999*
- Super John Doe needed a vehicle to floss in. — Stephen Power, *The Art of Getting Over*, p. 26, 1999
- Just because you have a new car, you don't have to floss. — Connie Eble (Editor), *UNC-CH Campus Slang*, p. 3, Spring 1999
- Wes grinned, flossin' his gold tooth with the princess-cut rock. — Linden Dalecki, *Kid B*, p. 9, 2006

flossy *adjective*
1 in circus and carnival usage, showy *US, 1895*
- — Don Wilmeth, *The Language of American Popular Entertainment*, p. 97, 1981

2 excellent *US, 2004*
- — Rick Ayers (Editor), *Berkeley High Slang Dictionary*, p. 21, 2004

flow *noun*
1 the style in which a rap artist creates lyrics and/or performs *US, 1995*
"Flow" is a term used to express a quality of conventional poetry.
- All these other females are there trying to flow and everyone can't do it. — A2Z [quoting Smooth, 1993], p. 36, 1995
- — Alex Ogg, *The Hip Hop Years*, p. 209, 1999

2 money *US, 1997*
An abbreviation of the conventional "cash flow."
- — Pamela Munro, *U.C.L.A. Slang*, p. 65, 1997
- — *Ebony Magazine*, p. 156, August 2000: "How to talk to the new generation"

flower *noun*
1 a male homosexual *US, 1949*
- — Hal Ellson, *Duke*, p. viii, 1949: "Partial glossary of gang terminology"

2 in poker, a hand made up of cards of the same suit *US, 1988*
Conventionally known as a "flush."
- — George Percy, *The Language of Poker*, p. 36, 1988

flower child *noun*
a participant in the 1960s youth movement promoting peace and love *US, 1967*
- Many of the flower children are teenage runaways from normal homes all over the United States. — James Holledge, *The Flower People*, p. 36, 1967

flower key *noun*
in computing, the comma key on a Macintosh computer *US, 1991*
- — Eric S. Raymond, *The New Hacker's Dictionary*, p. 160, 1991

flower patch *noun*

a woman's vulva and pubic hair *US, 1986*

- If they get into long skirts, they got a slit up the front almost to the flower patch, and their tits is fallin' out of the tops of their blouses. — Robert Campbell, *In La-La Land We Trust*, p. 180, 1986

flower person; flower people *noun*

a member, or members, of the 1960s counterculture *US, 1968*

- The Ancient Struggle of the Metal Men against the Flower People. — Timothy Leary, *The Politics of Ecstasy*, p. 76, 1968
- The hippies or the flower people or whatever you want to call 'em are nothing but people who've dropped these hangups. — Lewis Yablonsky, *The Hippie Trip*, p. 153, 1968
- Businessmen, fringe groups, beatniks and the flower people all use hashish. — Donald Louria, *The Drug Scene*, p. 72, 1968

flower power *noun*

the amorphous creed or philosophy of the hippie movement, based on drugs, sex, music, nonviolence and a rejection of all things material *US, 1967*

- Flower power. The power of love and peace; term and concept were originated in San Francisco. — Ruth Bronsteen, *The Hippy's Handbook*, p. 13, 1967
- Flower Power Sucks! — Frank Zappa, *Absolutely Free*, 1968

flower seeker *noun*

a member of the US armed forces in search of a Vietnamese prostitute *US, 1966*

- FLOWER SEEKER. Local newspaper phrase meaning "a man looking for a girl." — Ken Melvin, *Sorry 'Bout That*, p. 95, 1966: Glossary

flowers of spring *noun*

used condoms in a sewage system *US, 1973*

- In the old days, a Dept. of Public Works veteran tells me, they used to overflow with those rubbery objects euphemistically termed "the flowers of spring," but as he observes, "I guess nobody uses those things any longer." — *San Francisco Chronicle*, p. 23, 19th January 1973

flub *verb*

to botch *US, 1916*

- Except for the fact that that old fartface flubbed up the name of Li Po by calling him by his Japanese name and all such famous twaddle, he was all right. — Jack Kerouac, *The Dharma Bums*, p. 23, 1958
- — *Dobie Gillis Teenage Slanguage Dictionary*, 1962
- "A big ticket and the rod back and nobody puts the bull on me until I flub it royally." — Mickey Spillane, *The Snake*, p. 17, 1964

▶ **flub the dub**

to masturbate *US, 1922*

- — *American Speech*, p. 238, October 1946: "World war II slang of maladjustment"

flubadub *noun*

a fool *US, 1975*

From the name of a puppet on the *Howdy Doody Show*.

- [H]ost Gena Davis can't help but be better informed than perennial flubadub Joan Rivers. — *Houston Chronicle*, p. 8, 14th March 1999

flubdub *noun*

nonsense *US, 1888*

- And so on. All this flubdub, this flattery[.] — Henry Miller, *Nexus*, p. 285, 1960

flue *noun*

1 a room *US, 1972*

- And most of the flues [rooms] around have a open light bulb which hide nothing from view so he wants the lights turned off. — Christina and Richard Milner, *Black Players*, p. 117, 1972

2 a confidence swindle involving money in an envelope; the envelope used in the swindle *US, 1969*

- Ordinarily we used the flue as a short con game on barkeeps and small businessmen in the small towns surrounding the city. — Iceberg Slim (Robert Beck), *Trick Baby*, p. 27, 1969
- — M. Allen Henderson, *How Con Games Work*, p. 220, 1985: "Glossary"

3 the stomach *US, 1946*

- I woke up frisky and frolicsome as a two-year-old, lined my flue with some fine chocolate and brioche dished by this gay old lady[.] — Mezz Mezzrow, *Really the Blues*, p. 191, 1946

fluff *noun*

1 a woman, especially an attractive woman of no further consequence than her sexual availability *UK, 1903*

Usually used with "a bit of" or "a piece of." Combines the sense as "pubic hair," with an image of "fluff" as something of no consequence. Not kind.

- Until I sat down and looked in the mirror behind the shelves of pie segments, I didn't notice the fluff sitting off to one side at a table. — Mickey Spillane, *My Gun is Quick*, p. 6, 1950
- For another, you can't for the life of you recall this excited bit of fluff who seems so delighted to see you again. — Dev Collans with Stewart Sterling, *I was a House Detective*, p. 15, 1954
- Falling for some little ass-shaker, cute little mindless fluff who probably didn't wear a bra and said "groovy" and "cool" and smoked pot. — Elmore Leonard, *52 Pick-up*, p. 41, 1974

2 an effeminate lesbian *US, 1972*

- But now the fluff, maybe she's been in there three or four days and her habits just coming down on her and she wants to get a little something on. — Bruce Jackson, *In the Life*, p. 118, 1972

3 to a homosexual who practises sado-masochism, a homosexual of simpler tastes *US, 1985*

- — Wayne Dynes, *Homolexis*, p. 123, 1985

fluff *verb*

1 to botch, to ruin *US, 1958*

- "When and if you fluff something, I'll take the blame." — John D. MacDonald, *The Deceivers*, p. 184, 1958

2 to perform oral sex on a male pornography performer who is about to be filmed so that he will enter the scene with a full erection *US, 1977*

- Even though the term "fluffing" is used a lot on the set, I have never actually been on a shoot where someone was paid for this service. — Stephen Ziplow, *The Film Maker's Guide to Pornography*, p. 85, 1977
- They want help, they want fluffing. Hey, I'm sorry but I don't get off on getting a guy ready to go. — Anthony Petkovich, *The X Factory*, p. 99, 1997
- The Houston 500 gang bang actually produced a spinoff video entitled The Fluff Girls of the Houston 500—so maybe "fluffing" is coming back. — Ana Loria, *1 2 3 Be A Porn Star!*, p. 31, 2000

3 to ignore; to discard *US, 1959*

- — Robert S. Gold, *A Jazz Lexicon*, p. 110, 1964

4 to fail (an examination) *US, 1955*

- — *American Speech*, p. 303, December 1955: "Wayne University slang"

fluff and buff *noun*

a fluff-dried battle dress utility uniform with buff-polished boots, the standard uniform of the US Airborne *US, 1988*

- — Hans Halberstadt, *Airborne*, p. 130, 1988: "Abridged dictionary of airborne terms"

fluffer *noun*

in the making of a pornographic movie, a person employed to bring the on-camera male performers to a state of sexual readiness *US, 1977*

Extension of the conventional sense of "fluff" (to make fuller or plumper).

- A fluffer is a girl who is hired to play with the men while they're off-camera so that they can keep their erections and stay in a state of readiness. — Stephen Ziplow, *The Film Maker's Guide to Pornography*, p. 85, 1977
- [T]he theaters use a guy known as a "fluffer," whose job it is to help the boys achieve an erection for each stage appearance. — Jack Weatherford, *Porn Row*, p. 153, 1986
- Older lingo referring to the days when an extra babe was hired just to be the FLUFFER. She gave blow jobs to male actors to keep them up during transitions in sex scenes[.] — *Adult Video News*, p. 48, August 1995
- "Fluffers," or young women who offer fellatio to the male talent to prepare them for a sex scene, are mainly a thing of the past. — Ana Loria, *1 2 3 Be A Porn Star!*, p. 31, 2000

fluff girl *noun*

a fluffer *US, 1991*

- In the old days, you used to have fluff girls on the set who kept the guys worked up in between. — Robert Stoller and I.S. Levine, *Coming Attractions*, p. 55, 1991

fluff off *verb*

1 to dismiss, to reject *US, 1944*

- But the old man is dead now and his son fluffed me off. — Babs Gonzales, *Movin' On Down De Line*, p. 132, 1975

2 to evade work or duty *US, 1962*

- If you persist in thinking about fluffing off, I'll come over there and pinch a nerve that will electrify you with pain. — Odie Hawkins, *Lost Angeles*, p. 16, 1994

flug; phlug *noun*

junk *US, 1952*

- I drove us up the hill, making small talk and surreptitiously looking the rearview mirror to make sure there were no bits of flug in my nose or eyes[.] — Anne Lamott, *Hard Laughter*, p. 39, 1980

fluid *noun*

whiskey *US, 1843*

- "Say, have you boys any fluid? Another drink and I'll be just rarin' to go, and any mother's sonofabitch can just try and get tough with me," Red Murphy said. — James T. Farrell, *Saturday Night*, p. 38, 1947

fluids and electrolytes conference *noun*

used in a hospital as humorous code for a drinking party to be held on hospital grounds *US, 1988–1989*

- — *Maledicta*, p. 33, 1988–1989: "Medical maledicta from san francisco"

fluked out *adjective*

drug-intoxicated *US, 1952*

- You're real fluked out, Dinch; take it easy, be cool. — George Mandel, *Flee the Angry Strangers*, p. 131, 1952

fluke out *verb*

to become drug-intoxicated *US, 1958*

- Then she slides off the bed, her big body toppling over sideways. She has fluked out. — Willard Motley, *Let No Man Write My Epitaph*, p. 160, 1958

flummadiddle *noun*

nonsense *US, 1905*

- Gilly talks to hear his head rattle. He passes the time with flummadiddles. — Dorothy Garlock, *Larkspur*, p. 246, 1997

flunk *noun*

1 a locked and fortified compartment within a safe *US, 1928*

- — Hyman E. Goldin et al., *Dictionary of American Underworld Lingo*, p. 72, 1950

2 a soldier killed in action *US, 1987*

- I get a call from the battalion. He arrived a flunk. — Ernest Spencer, *Welcome to Vietnam, Macho Man*, p. 86, 1987

flunky *verb*

to work as a low-level assistant *US, 1968*

- All he did now was drink cheap wine and flunky for anyone who'd give a damn to help him along toward the forty-nine cents it cost to buy a pint. — Nathan Heard, *Howard Street*, p. 50, 1968
- Twenty years ago he hung out and flunkied in the joints around Thirty-Ninth and Cottage Grove. — Iceberg Slim (Robert Beck), *Trick Baby*, p. 42, 1969

flush *verb*

1 to leave work *US, 1991*

- — Eric S. Raymond, *The New Hacker's Dictionary*, p. 160, 1991

2 to fail (a test or course) *US, 1964*

- — *Time*, p. 57, 1st January 1965: "Students: the slang bag"

▸ **flush the john**

in a casino, to play slot machines *US, 1979*

- — Thomas L. Clark, *The Dictionary of Gambling and Gaming*, p. 82, 1987

flute *noun*

a soda bottle filled with liquor *US, 1971*

- Patrolman Phillips testified that it was not uncommon for policemen assigned to a radio car to pick up a "flute"—a Coke bottle filled with liquor—which they would deliver to the station house. — *The Knapp Commission Report on Police Corruption*, p. 172, 1972
- It was responsible for bringing sandwiches and beer to the station house's administrative and clerical personnel, and "flutes"—Coca-Cola bottles filled with liquor supplied by bars in the precinct—to the lieutenants and sergeants. — Peter Maas, *Serpico*, p. 60, 1973
- Cop calls the station house and the sergeant says, pickup a flute for the lieutenant. — Leonard Shecter and William Phillips, *On the Pad*, p. 94, 1973
- Hanrahan would send a patrolman out to a nearby bar for what he called a "flute"—a Coke bottle filled with gin. — Vincent Patrick, *The Pope of Greenwich Village*, p. 114, 1979

fluter *noun*

a male homosexual *US, 1962*

- — Joseph E. Ragen and Charles Finston, *Inside the World's Toughest Prison*, p. 799, 1962: "Penitentiary and underworld glossary"
- — *Maledicta*, p. 16, Summer 1977: "A word for it!"

flutter bum *noun*

a good-looking and popular boy *US, 1955*

Teen slang.

- — *American Weekly*, p. 2, 14th August 1955

flutter-finger *noun*

in the usage of youthful model road racers (slot car racers), a person who fluctuates speed constantly *US, 1997*

- — Phantom Surfers, *The Exciting Sounds of Model Road Racing (Album cover)*, 1997

flutterhead *noun*

an absent-minded person *US, 1911*

- [J]ust as she was expected to do, being an adorable flutterhead. — William Johnston, *The Brady Bunch*, p. 142, 1969

fly *verb*

1 (said of a police officer) to transfer stations *US, 1958*

- A transfer from one police command to another is flying. — *New York Times*, p. 34, 20th October 1958

2 to act cautiously *US, 1965*

- — Miss Cone, *The Slang Dictionary (Hawthorne High School)*, 1965

▸ **fly bad paper**

to pass counterfeit money or forced checks *US, 1976*

- He had flown a lot of bad paper and knew it was only a matter of time before it drifted back to sting him. — Malcolm Braley, *False Starts*, p. 327, 1976

▸ **fly right**

to behave in a manner appropriate to the situation *US, 1984*

- — Inez Cardozo-Freeman, *The Joint*, p. 467, 1984

▸ **fly someone's dome**

to shoot someone in the head *US, 2007*

- Police said Matthews' mother told them Mason had previously telephoned her son and told him he was going to "fly his dome." — *Connecticut Post Online*, 5th February 2007

▸ **fly the red flag**

to experience the bleed period of the menstrual cycle *US, 1954*

- — *American Speech*, p. 298, December 1954: "The vernacular of menstruation"
- — Collin Baker et al., *College Undergraduate Slang Study Conducted at Brown University*, p. 119, 1968

▸ **fly the rod**

to gesture with the middle finger, roughly conveying "fuck you!" *US, 1968*

- — Collin Baker et al., *College Undergraduate Slang Study Conducted at Brown University*, p. 119, 1968

fly *adjective*

good, pleasing, fashionable *US, 1879*

A term which has enjoyed three bursts of popularity—in the swing jazz era of the late 1930s, the emergence of black exploitation films in the early 1970s, and with the explosion of hip-hop culture in the 1980s.

- I had planned to get next to the colored maid there, who's pretty hip, but not hip enough to be fly, if you know what I mean. — James Blake, *The Joint*, p. 17, 18th March 1951
- I'm runnin' round with these fly broads from 111th Street and Fifth Avenue. — Edwin Torres, *Carlito's Way*, p. 11, 1975
- And his fabulous sky was broke so fly/ That the city had it banned. — Dennis Wepman et al., *The Life*, p. 48, 1976
- This is some fly shit, huh? Like some James Cagney, George Raft-type shit. — *New Jack City*, 1990

flybait *noun*

1 an unattractive girl *US, 1947*

- "She's not my type." "Me neither. To me, she's flybait." — Harry Haenigsen, *Jive's Like That*, 1947

2 a corpse *US, 1992*

- My first kills! They are now what undertakers call their clients: Flybait. — Richard Miller, *Mosca*, p. 207, 1997

flyboy *noun*

a military aviator *US, 1937*

- The flyboys're apeshit. — William Wilson, *The LBJ Brigade*, p. 77, 1966

- From an elevation of 200 feet or so, and in a gray overcast, a helicopter came buzzing back and forth. Stokely Carmichael of Snick had quipped over the microphone, "CIA's flyboys." — Sidney Bernard, *This Way to the Apocalypse*, p. 33, 1967
- But it took the fly-boys, the 415th Artillery, and our APC's to clear the decks. — David Parks, *GI Diary*, p. 108, 1968
- I made contact with some flyboys at a nearby SAC base[.] — Joey V., *Portrait of Joey*, p. 147, 1969
- Them goddamn Navy fly-boys always thought they were hot shit, but the surface Navy is the Navy. — Jimmy Buffett, *Tales from Margaritaville*, p. 132, 1989

fly-by *noun*
a missile that misses its target and does no damage *US, 1991*
- A seventh Scud was what battalion commander Lt. Col Leroy Neel called a "flyby," falling harmlessly into the Persian Gulf. — *Missourian*, p. 5A, 22nd January 1991

fly-by-night *adjective*
unreliable; likely to disappear *US, 1914*
- They was a fly-by-night bunch, I think. — Mickey Spillane, *My Gun is Quick*, p. 138, 1950

fly chick *noun*
an attractive woman *US, 1945*
- — Lou Shelly, *Hepcats Jive Talk Dictionary*, p. 24, 1945

flyer *noun*
1 a conversational line used to start conversation when seeking a sexual encounter *US, 1972*
- Flyers—opening statements; ice-breakers used when cruising. — Bruce Rodgers, *The Queens' Vernacular*, p. 83, 1972

2 a person who threatens to or has jumped to his death *US, 1986–1987*
- — *Maledicta*, p. 180, Summer/Winter 1986–1987: "Sexual slang: prostitutes, pedophiles, flagellators, transvestites, and necrophiles"

fly-fly boy *noun*
a military aviator *US, 1949*
- When my Army unit went to Vietnam in 1966, the Navy took us there in a troop ship and kept our supplies coming. When our bases came under attack, the "fly-fly boys" of the Air Force lent their support. — *Richmond (Virginia) Times Dispatch*, p. A16, 13th June 2002

fly gee *noun*
in circus and carnival usage, a clever, sarcastic, sophisticated man with a flexible approach to the truth *US, 1981*
- — Don Wilmeth, *The Language of American Popular Entertainment*, p. 97, 1981

flygirl *noun*
an attractive, sexually alluring young woman *US, 1986*
- — Connie Eble (Editor), *UNC-CH Campus Slang*, p. 4, Fall 1986
- — Ellen C. Bellone (Editor), *Dictionary of Slang*, p. 10, 1989
- I see they are mini flygirls with skin like a dark pony's velvetness. — Francesca Lia Block, *Missing Angel Juan*, p. 303, 1993
- In the ad for this line two fly girls are sitting in a hot tub talking on the phone. — Anka Radakovich, *The Wild Girls Club*, p. 56, 1994

fly-in *noun*
an extravagant party for homosexual men in which men fly in to the party from all parts of the country *US, 1982*
- The realtor nodded. "We did a fly-in together once. Gamma Mu." He tossed out the name like bait, Michael noticed, as if everyone had heard of the national gay millionaires' fraternity. — Armistead Maupin, *Further Tales of the City*, p. 7, 1982

flying *adjective*
in poker, full, as in a full house *US, 1967*
- — Albert H. Morehead, *The Complete Guide to Winning Poker*, p. 263, 1967

flying A *noun*
an extremely obnoxious person *US, 1968*
The "a" is usually understood as **ASSHOLE**.
- — Collin Baker et al., *College Undergraduate Slang Study Conducted at Brown University*, p. 120, 1968

flying banana *nickname*
a military transport helicopter, especially the Piasecki HRP *US, 1950*
- In August, HMX-1 received the Piasecki HRP-i. Nicknamed the "Flying Banana" due to its shape, the twin-rotor aircraft had a payload of 900 pounds at a speed of 100 miles per hour. — Jon T. Hoffman, *USMC*, p. 428, 2002

flying boxcar *nickname*
a transport aircraft, especially a C-119 *US, 1958*
- Santa Claus headed north driving a sleigh, in the shape of a C-119 Flying Boxcar, from 435 (Transport) Squadron at Namao, Alberta. — *Arctic Spotter*, p. 4, January 1958
- I lead out, double timing after the jumpmaster toward a C-119, a Flying Boxcar. — Donald Duncan, *The New Legions*, p. 140, 1967
- They called the C-119's flying boxcars. — Larry Chambers, *Recondo*, p. 8, 1992

flying brick *noun*
any heavy aircraft that is difficult to control *US, 1944*
- The pilots called it the "flying brick"—heavy, with no engines, gliding in on delta-wing slivers. — Tess Gerritsen, *Gravity*, p. 195, 1999

flying carpet *noun*
a taxi *US, 1997*
New York police slang; an allusion to the large number of immigrant drivers.
- — Samuel M. Katz, *Anytime Anywhere*, p. 388, 1997: "The extremely unofficial and completely off-the-record NYPD/ESU truck-two glossary'"

flying coffin *noun*
any dangerous aircraft, such as a glider used by paratroopers *US, 1918*
A reference to the gliders' vulnerability to artillery.
- — *American Speech*, p. 310, December 1946: "More air force slang"

flying douche *noun*
▸ **take a flying douche**
used as an intense expression of "go to hell" *US, 1965*
- How can a guy stand aside twiddling his planagos, and watch his bosom buddy take a flying douche? — John Nichols, *The Sterile Cuckoo*, p. 88, 1965

flying flapjack *nickname*
the XF5 U-1 experimental military hovering aircraft *US, 1973*
- [T]he United States Navy was working on its own version: a prop-driven, circular machine, the XF5U-1, otherwise known as the "flying flapjack." — Curt Sutherly, *UFO Mysteries*, p. 4, 2001

flying fuck *noun*
nothing at all, the very least amount *US, 1946*
Usually couched in the negative.
- John Simon is trying to tell us that a flying f— is less offensive than to say between you and I. (Quoting Leon Botstein). — *San Francisco Examiner*, p. 22, 12th November 1979
- Well, I don't give a flying fuck what you think! — *Reservoir Dogs*, 1992
- You're a bad person with an ugly heart, and we don't give a flying fuck what you think. — *Romy and Michele's High School Reunion*, 1997

▸ **take a flying fuck**
get lost! *US, 1926*
- So I told him to go take a flying fuck at a rolling donut[.] — Joey V., *Portrait of Joey*, p. 52, 1969
- "And you can go pack your feet in a cement block," she imagined she was saying to her father, "and take a flying fuck to the moon." — Richard Condon, *Prizzi's Money*, p. 197, 1994

flying gas station; gas station in the sky *nickname*
a KC-135 aircraft used for inflight refueling of jet aircraft *US, 1991*
- Wiggins asked, "Where the hell is our flying gas station?" — Nelson DeMille, *The Lion's Game*, p. 150, 2000

Flying Horsemen *nickname*
during the war in Vietnam, the First Air Cavalry Division *US, 1989*
An elite reconnaissance unit.
- Throckmorton made a few calls, and the next thing we knew the "Flying Horsemen" 1st Air Cav came galloping to the rescue. — David H. Hackworth, *About Face*, p. 471, 1989

flying Jenny *noun*
a US Army shortwave radar set *US, 1947*
- — *American Speech*, p. 153, April 1947: "Radar slang terms"

flying lesson *noun*
1 the reported US and South Vietnamese practice of pushing suspected Viet Cong or captured North Vietnamese soldiers from helicopters to their death *US, 1991*

- According to the folklore, there were "Bell Telephone hours," interrogation sessions in which electric jolts were administered to captured VC sympathizers, which ended in the prisoners taking their first "flying lesson" out of a helicopter. — Carol Burke, *Camp All-American, Hanoi Jane, and The High-and-Tight*, p. 110, 2004

2 the act of throwing a prisoner or guard off a high tier in a prison cellblock *US, 1992*
- — William K. Bentley and James M. Corbett, *Prison Slang*, p. 90, 1992

flying prostitute *nickname*
a B-26 bomber aircraft *US, 1943*
Like the lady of the night, the B-26 had no visible means of support.
- — *American Speech*, p. 310, December 1946: "More air force slang"

flying saucer *noun*
a morning glory seed, thought to have psychoactive properties *US, 1971*
- — Eugene Landy, *The Underground Dictionary*, p. 81, 1971

flying saucer cap *noun*
a military service cap *US, 1971*
- Standing in the light from the streetlight was The Fist in his courtroom blazer and flying saucer cap. — Jimmy Breslin, *I Don't Want to go to Jail*, p. 340, 2001

flying squad *noun*
a fast-moving, versatile group *US, 1967*
- He alerted the flying squad and phoned the warden, who authorized an emergency count. — Malcolm Braly, *On the Yard*, p. 198, 1967

flying suck *noun*
nothing at all; the very least amount *US, 1974*
- [T]hey knew managers don't give a flying suck what a girl looks like with clothes on[.] — Anne Steinhardt, *Thunder La Boom*, p. 14, 1974

flying telephone pole; telephone pole *nickname*
a surface-to-air missile, especially an SA-2 *US, 1977*
Vietnam war usage.
- He glanced down and saw two SAMS lifting, dust and dirt swirling behind the 35-foot "telephone poles." — Robert K. Wilcox, *Scream of Eagles*, p. 221, 1990
- No SAMS came at him. It seemed that absolutely everyone else had seen the front end of one of those deadly "telephone poles." — Gerry Carroll, *North S*A*R*, p. 15, 1991

flying ten *noun*
a ten-dollar advance on pay given a to soldier when newly assigned to a base *US, 1956*
- — Carl Fleischhauer, *A Glossary of Army Slang*, p. 19, 1968

Flying Tiger Air Force *noun*
a collection of American mercenaries who flew air raids in support of Chiang Kai-shek's losing effort on mainland China *US, 1971*
- Several years earlier the CIA had taken control of General Clair Chennault's old "Flying Tiger" air force from the Second World War—American mercenaries and regulars who fought for Chiang Kaishek against the Communists[.] — Joseph C. Goulden, *Korea*, p. 470, 1982

flying twenty-five *noun*
a pay advance in the military *US, 1956*
- Recruits were given a pay advance, the so-called flying twenty-five, with which they purchased toilet articles and brass and shoe polish. — James Ebert, *A Life in a Year*, p. 28, 1993

flying wedge *noun*
a group of people in a wedge-shaped formation, advancing rapidly into a crowd *US, 1953*
A practice and term used by police, security workers, and American football players.
- Thirty cops formed a flying wedge to drive us off. — Jerry Rubin, *Do It!*, p. 33, 1970

Flynn
► **in like Flynn**
1 easily, quickly, without effort *US, 1945*
Originally a reference to the legendary sexual exploits of actor Errol Flynn.
- Then I'm golden, man. I go ape. I'm in like Flynn. — Max Shulman, *Guided Tour of Campus Humor*, p. 106, 1955

- "Well, how'd you make out?" "In like Flynn, Louie." — Piri Thomas, *Down These Mean Streets*, p. 102, 1967
- "Because most men do make passes, you find, he's suddenly in like Flynn." Rags grinned widely. "And I do mean Errol Flynn." — Georgia Sothern, *My Life in Burlesque*, p. 259, 1972

2 in poker, said of a player who bets before it is his turn *US, 1951*
- — *American Speech*, p. 99, May 1951

flyspeck 3 *noun*
any miniscule, unreadable font *US, 1991*
- — Eric S. Raymond, *The New Hacker's Dictionary*, p. 162, 1991

flytrap *noun*
the mouth *UK, 1795*
- "Nigger, shut your old flytrap and get to work." — Haywood Patterson, *Scottsboro Boy*, p. 187, 1950
- Nobody calls Larry Haugen "Larry"; they call him "Fly Trap," as in "Shut your fly trap for a change." — Shawn Wong, *American Knees*, p. 130, 1995

FNG *noun*
a newly arrived soldier in Vietnam *US, 1966*
A "*fucking new guy.*"
- I was an FNG, but I never fell out. I'd keep up. — Mark Baker, *Nam*, p. 77, 1981
- Initially, the "f.n.g's" [fucking new guy] anxiety is likely to be increased by the group's asking him extremely personal questions and telling him "war stories." — Robert Fullinwider, *Conscripts and Volunteers*, p. 192, 1983
- The FNG was usually avoided and shunned by others in the unit for fear of his making a serious mistake or having an accident that could affect others. Because soldiers were often transferred individually into units, being an FNG was particularly lonely — Linda Reinberg, *In the Field*, p. 84, 1991

FOAD
used as shorthand in Internet discussion groups and text messages to mean "*fuck off and die*" *US, 1994*
- FOAD Fuck Off And Die — soc.culture.thai, 17th January 1994
- FOAD Fuck off and die (use of this is generally OTT). — Eric Raymond, *The New Hacker's Dictionary*, p. 436, 1996
- — Gabrielle Mander, *WAN2TLK? ltl bk of txt msgs*, p. 44, 2002

FOAF *noun*
a friend of a friend *US, 1991*
The most common source for an urban legend or other apocryphal story.
- — Eric S. Raymond, *The New Hacker's Dictionary*, p. 162, 1991
- FOAF friend of a friend. — rec.arts.sf-lovers, 15th March 1991

foam *noun*
beer *US, 1908*
- [S]ome raggedy kid on the Corner who hasn't got the price of admission to see the stage show at the Apollo or a deuce of blips to buy himself a glass of foam. — Mezz Mezzrow, *Really the Blues*, p. 333, 1946

foamer *noun*
1 a railroad fan whose love for railways is obsessive *US, 2004*
- The most widely used term is foamer, which may have been used first by Amtrak employees to refer to rail fans who grew so excited when looking at trains they seemed to be rabid. Another theory holds that this term was adapted from the acronym FOMITE, which stood for "fanatically obnoxious mentally incompetent train enthusiast." — Randy Kennedy, *Subwayland*, pp. 18–19, 2004

2 a glass of beer *US, 1959*
- — *Swinging Syllables*, 1959

foamie *noun*
a surfboard made from polyurethane *US, 1965*
- — John M. Kelly, *Surf and Sea*, p. 285, 1965
- After school the break in front of the village is packed with kids riding pieces of marine ply. Standing up, doing back flips and angling across the foamies. — *Tracks*, p. 63, October 1992

foamy *noun*
a glass of beer *US, 1983*
- — *Esquire*, p. 180, June 1983

FOB *adjective*
fresh off the boat *US, 1981*

An initialism usually applied to recent immigrants, but in the usage of Hawaiian youth applied to visitors to the islands.
- — Douglas Simonson, *Pidgin to da Max*, 1981

fobbit *noun*
a soldier stationed behind the lines *US, 2004*
A blend of the initials FOB (forward operating base) and the Tolkien hobbit.
- For fobbits, deployment is a lot like life in the States, only they wear uniforms and occasionally carry weapons. — *The Village Voice*, p. 36, 1st March 2005
- Some joked that whenever VIP's come to visit they just go to the main bases and meet the "fobbits," the nickname given to troops who do not go outside the barbed wire. — *CNN.com*, 27th April 2006

focus *noun*
vision, eyesight *US, 1947*
- — Marcus Hanna Boulware, *Jive and Slang of Students in Negro Colleges*, 1947

FOD *noun*
foreign object damage to an aircraft *US, 1989*
- "We police the flight deck for anything lying around that might cause an aircraft to FOD-out." "Foreign object damage," Carmen said. "I guess something that might get sucked into the jet engine." — Elmore Leonard, *Killshot*, p. 90, 1989

fofarraw *noun*
trinkets *US, 1848*
- "All that fofarraw is fine and dandy, Missy." — David Robbins, *Do or Die*, p. 117, 2003

fog *noun*
1 a person who is profoundly out of touch with current trends and his social peers *US, 1983*
- — *Concord (New Hampshire) Monitor*, p. 17, 23rd August 1983: "Slang slinging: an intense and awesome guide to prep school slanguage"
2 steam *US, 1954*
- — Jerry Robertson, *Oil Slanguage*, p. 55, 1954

fog *verb*
to shoot and kill someone *US, 1913*
- — Lou Shelly, *Hepcats Jive Dictionary*, p. 11, 1945

fogey *noun*
an increase in military pay *US, 1878*
- Typically, every two years, military members receive a years-of-service, or fogey, pay raise. — P.J. Budahn, *Military Money Guide*, p. 7, 1996

fogy; fogey *noun*
an old person with out-dated ideas and values *UK, 1720*
- What on earth had possessed Father to send him as P.G. to these old fogies? — Douglas Rutherford, *The Creeping Flesh*, p. 11, 1963
- Then all the fogies had a good snuffle and cackle, and Bobbie found herself with three Bacardis and two more brandies, compliments of the geezer gang. — Joseph Wambaugh, *Finnegan's Week*, p. 229, 1993
- He's a really cool guy. I hope I'm doing shit like this when I'm a fogey. — Francesca Lia Block, *I Was a Teenage Fairy*, p. 88, 1998

foilhead *noun*
a person with highlighted hair *US, 2001*
- — Don R. McCreary (Editor), *Dawg Speak*, 2001

fold *noun*
money *UK, 2000*
- [F]lash a few of your folds and maybe one of those flowers you're so keen on, and you'll get all the ladies you can deal with. — Diran Adebayo, *My Once Upon A Time*, p. 9, 2000
- — Don R. McCreary (Editor), *Dawg Speak*, 2001

fold *verb*
in poker, to withdraw from a hand, forfeiting your bet *US, 1963*
- — Irwin Steig, *Common Sense in Poker*, p. 184, 1963

folding; folding stuff; folding green *noun*
paper money, hence money *US, 1930*
- Just put this hunk of folding back in your saddlebag and forget you ever met me. — Raymond Chandler, *The Little Sister*, p. 38, 1949

folkie *noun*
a folk singer or musician; a folk music enthusiast *US, 1966*
- [A] decided majority of the rising bands were composed of ex-folkies[.] — Lester Bangs, *Psychotic Reactions and Carburetor Dung*, p. 41, 1970

folknik *noun*
a member of the folk music counterculture of the 1950s and 60s *US, 1958*
- "All the folkniks were running around the schmucky coffeehouses," said Young, "and the nightclub owners were giving people folk music—and booze." — David Hajdu, *Positively 4th Street*, p. 48, 2001

folks *noun*
a group of your friends *US, 1997*
- — *Maybeck High School Yearbook (Berkeley, California)*, p. 28, 1997
- — *San Jose Mercury News*, 11th May 1999

Follie *nickname*
the Folsom State Prison at Folsom, California *US, 1975*
- — Report to the Senate, *California Senate Committee on Civil Disorder*, p. 228, 1975

foo *noun*
in computing, used as an arbitrary, temporary name for something *US, 1983*
- — Guy L. Steele et al., *The Hacker's Dictionary*, p. 66, 1983

foodaholic *noun*
a compulsive eater *US, 1965*
- We couldn't possibly wear the same size. She was massive. She was probably some foodaholic who stuffed her face day and night. — Cherie Bennett, *Life in the Fat Lane*, p. 123, 1998

food chain *noun*
a pecking order or hierarchy *US, 1998*
- She joined the usual gaggle of overworked pack journalism bodies who, at the bottom of the food chain, are at the back of the plane, having to file every hour to their radio stations or TV outlets or newspaper editors, as each alleged sensation breaks out. — *Edmonton Sun*, p. 11, 7th March 1998

foodie *noun*
a person who has a passionate interest in the latest trends in gourmet food *UK, 1982*
- — Rachel S. Epstein and Nina Liebman, *Biz Speak*, p. 88, 1986
- Foodies are also overfed, which makes them cranky and jaded. — *New York Times Magazine*, p. 53, 29 July 2001

food stamps *noun*
in poker, a player's cash reserved for household expenses pressed into action after he has lost his betting money *US, 1996*
- — John Vorhaus, *The Big Book of Poker Slang*, p. 18, 1996

foo-foo *noun*
to wear cologne or perfume *US, 2002*
- — Jeffrey Ian Ross, *Behind Bars*, p. 186, 2002: Slammer Slang

foofoo *noun*
1 a prissy or girlish man *US, 1848*
- Fortney shaved closer than usual that afternoon. He even splashed on a little foo-foo cologne. — Joseph Wambaugh, *Floaters*, p. 170, 1996
2 cologne, perfume *US, 1928*
- Keep cleaners, perfumes, deodorants, and any other foofoo stuff locked up. — Sandra Hardin Gookin, *Parenting for Dummies*, p. 224, 2002
3 something that is purely decorative without adding functional value *US, 1986*
- — *United States Naval Institute Proceedings*, p. 108, October 1986

foo gas; phou gas *noun*
an explosive mixture in a buried steel drum serving as a defense around the perimeter of a military base *US, 1978*
- Fu-gas is the best. — Mark Baker, *Nam*, p. 162, 1981

fool *noun*
used as a term of address, sometimes suggesting foolishness and sometimes not *US, 1986*
- Shit, King, it ain't d-e-r-e man, it's d-e-a-r, and Sara don't have no two r's in it, fool. — *Platoon*, 1986

fool file *noun*
the mythical library of the stupidest things ever said *US, 1991*
- — Eric S. Raymond, *The New Hacker's Dictionary*, p. 164, 1991

foolio *noun*
a fool; a social outcast *US, 1994*

- And to all you youngsters out there, acting like little "foolios" that think this can't happen to you, think again! — *Los Angeles Times*, p. B1, 6th December 1994
  - — Pamela Munro, *U.C.L.A. Slang*, p. 66, 1997
  - — Rick Ayers (Editor), *Berkeley High Slang Dictionary*, p. 22, 2004

fool killer *noun*
a notional creature called upon to dispose of fools *US, 1853*
- It was the kind of crowd that would have made the Fool Killer lower his club and shake his head and walk away, frustrated by the magnitude of the opportunity. — Tom Wolfe, *The Right Stuff*, p. 246, 1979

fooper *noun*
a homosexual male *US, 1975*
Apparently back-slang of POOF.
- — *American Speech*, p. 59, Spring–Summer 1975: "Razorback slang"

foot *verb*
to run fast *US, 1965*
- "[F]oot it, Sonny! Foot it!" I said, "Like, what's wrong, man?" He said, "Run!" — Claude Brown, *Manchild in the Promised Land*, p. 131, 1965

foot army *noun*
the infantry *UK, 1702*
- "Was you in the foot army?" — Irving Shulman, *The Short End of the Stick*, p. 34, 1959

football *noun*
1 a tablet of Dilaudid™, a central nervous system depressant manufactured by the Knoll Pharmaceutical Company *US, 1972*
- So I had some footballs, some Dilaudid. I think it's a full grain. I gave this girl some. She got mad because I broke a football in two; she wanted the whole thing. — Bruce Jackson, *Outside the Law*, p. 107, 1972
- Supposed to put you to sleep tough. I think he called them footballs. — Emmett Grogan, *Final Score*, p. 81, 1976

2 a tablet of dextroamphetamine sulfate and amphetamine sulfate (trade name Diphetamine™), a central nervous system stimulant *US, 1966*
- — Donald Louria, *Nightmare Drugs*, p. 28, 1966
- Some of the names describe the drugs' effects, such as "helpers," "copilots," "Los Angeles turn arounds," or their shape, color and markings—"hearts," "footballs," "blackjacks," "crossroads." — Phil Hirsch, *Hooked*, pp. 51–52, 1968
- footballs: combination of dextroamphetamine and amphetamine. — Ethel Romm, *The Open Conspiracy*, p. 243, 1970

3 a simple musical accompaniment used when a performer is ad libbing *US, 1973*
- The orchestrator will cooperate by scoring the orchestra on one note (a whole note) in each bar. A whole note looks like a very small football. — Sherman Louis Sergel, *The Language of Show Biz*, p. 90, 1973

4 the briefcase carrying the communication equipment that enables the president of the US to launch a nuclear attack *US, 1968*
- They carry the "football," a briefcase that contains reference documents that outline U.S. strategic attack options, communications instructions, and the codewords that the President would use to authorize the release of nuclear weapons[.] — Michael K. Bohn, *Nerve Center*, p. 50, 2003

Football Annie *noun*
a woman who makes herself available sexually to professional football players *US, 1975*
- I think I'm known as a Football Annie, or an Athlete Annie. — Herb Michelson, *Sportin' Ladies*, p. 23, 1975

foot burner *noun*
a walking plow *US, 1958*
- — *American Speech*, p. 269, December 1958: "Ranching terms from eastern Washington"

foot-coffin *noun*
a shoe *US, 1993*
- "Try ridin' on your own natural God-give feet stead of smotherin' 'em in them show-time foot-coffins." — Jess Mowry, *Six Out Seven*, p. 31, 1993

foot-in-mouth disease *noun*
the tendency to say that which ought not to be said *US, 1968*
- Attentive listening is the best antidote for foot-in-mouth disease. — Jo-Ellan Dimitrius, *Put Your Best Foot Forward*, p. 226, 2000

footsie *noun*
foot-to-foot contact, usually out of sight such as under a restaurant table *US, 1944*
- His wife, who was the quiet type, sat playing footsie with Pancho under the table. — Steve Cannon, *Groove, Bang, and Jive Around*, pp. 131–132, 1969

foot-slogger *noun*
an infantry soldier *UK, 1916*
- The call went out for the closest company of foot-sloggers, and their choppers were soon on the way. — Ralph Zumbro, *Tank Sergeant*, p. 67, 1986

footwarmer *noun*
a linear amplifier for a citizens' band radio *US, 1976*
- — Warren Smith, *Warren's Smith's Authentic Dictionary of CB*, p. 38, 1976

for days *adjective*
to a great degree *US, 1981*
- "He get hair fo' days!" — Douglas Simonson, *Pidgin to da Max*, 1981
- That guy has arms for days. — Kevin Dilallo, *The Unofficial Gay Manual*, p. 240, 1994

for days!
1 that's the truth! *US, 1968*
- — *Current Slang*, p. 24, Fall 1968

2 used for expressing amazement *US, 1970*
- — *American Speech*, p. 57, Spring–Summer 1970: "Homosexual slang"

fore-and-after hat *noun*
a military garrison cap *US, 1931*
- Roy Barksdale advised that they had a lifeboat mounted on a truck bed and an admiral's uniform, complete with fore and aft hat. — James Dolittle, *I Could Never Be So Lucky Again*, p. 101, 1991

foreground *verb*
to assign a high priority to a task *US, 1991*
- If your presentation is due next week, I guess I'd better foreground writing up the design document. — Eric S. Raymond, *The New Hacker's Dictionary*, pp. 165–166, 1991

foreign *adjective*
(used of a betting chip) from another casino *US, 1982*
- — Thomas F. Hughes, *Dealing Casino Blackjack*, p. 72, 1982

forever-forever
used as a motto by the Black Guerrilla Family prison gang *US, 2000*
- The 415 motto is "Forever-Forever." This term is used to close the oath and to open and close serious business meetings. — Bill Valentine, *Gangs and Their Tattoos*, p. 19, 2000

fork *verb*
used as a euphemism for "to fuck" *US, 1999*
- How could I tell her I had already let more than a dozen boys fork me by the time I was eighteen? — Rita Ciresi, *Pink Slip*, p. 11, 1999
- "What the fork you doing down there?" — Arthur Nersesian, *Chinese Takeout*, p. 124, 2003

forked *adjective*
in computing, unacceptably slow or dysfunctional *US, 1991*
Probably a euphemism for FUCKED.
- — Eric S. Raymond, *The New Hacker's Dictionary*, p. 166, 1991

forked-tongued *adjective*
duplicitous *US, 1961*
Ascribing stereotypical snake-like qualities; best remembered (although possibly apocryphal) from cowboy films in the phrase "white man speak with forked tongue."
- "What a forked-tongued phoney you are," I told him, "coming here and trying to put the arm on me for the Mafia." — Harry J. Anslinger, *The Murderers*, p. 238, 1961

forklift *noun*
in poker, a substantial win *US, 1996*
- — John Vorhaus, *The Big Book of Poker Slang*, p. 18, 1996

fork over *verb*
to hand over *UK, 1820*
- This landlady would hand out a metal check and a towel to the girl, while the customer forked over two bucks. — Mezz Mezzrow, *Really the Blues*, pp. 22–23, 1946

forks *noun*
the fingers *UK, 1812*
Originally a pickpocket's term.
• — Lou Shelly, *Hepcats Jive Dictionary*, p. 11, 1945

formerly known as
known as *US, 1993*
A wildly popular construction after recording artist Prince announced in 1993 that he had changed his name to The Artist Formerly Known as Prince.
• "The person you are addressing," the Educated One corrected, is "the Writer Formerly Known as the Columnist." — *The Cattanooga Times*, p. B5, 11 February 1997
• The Once-Proud Franchise Formerly Known as the Bears was outscored 38-0 in the second half, giving up more points in a half than a Once-Proud Franchise Formerly Known as the Bears ever has. — *Chicago Tribune*, p. C1, 20th November 1997

for Pete's sake
used as a mild, non-profane oath used in times of exasperation or annoyance *US, 1924*
• Oh, for pete's sake, you two are psychological! — John Clellon Holmes, *Go*, p. 141, 1952
• Oh for Pete's sake. For Pete's s- He's fleein' the interview. — *Fargo*, 1996

for shame!
used as a humorous admission that you have been cleverly ridiculed *US, 1963*
• — *American Speech*, p. 275, December 1963: "American Indian student slang"

for sure!
used as an enthusiastic, stylish affirmation *US, 1978*
• BRIDESMAID 2: Look at all the holes in the lapel! AXEL: For sure! — *The Deer Hunter*, 1978

Fort Apache *nickname*
the police station in the 41st precinct, New York *US, 1976*
An allusion to the American West and the wild, lawless character of the neighborhood.
• 41st Precinct—Fort Apache. Located in the South Bronx, this precinct was in the middle of burned out, devastated wilderness where hope was a rarity. — Scott Baker, *The Funniest Cop Stories Ever*, p. 128, 2006

Fort Bushy *noun*
the vulva and female pubic hair *US, 1961*
• — Dale Gordon, *The Dominion Sex Dictionary*, p. 71, 1967

Fort Head *nickname*
Fort Hood, a US Army installation *US, 1968*
From the preponderance of drug use there during the Vietnam war.
• Soon, similar problems cropped up at home. Fort Hood, Texas, became known as Fort Head[.] — Rick Atkinson, *The Long Gray Line*, p. 367, 1989

forthwith *noun*
an order to a police officer to report immediately *US, 1958*
• — *New York Times Magazine*, p. 88, 16th March 1958

Fort Knox *noun*
in shuffleboard, a number that is well hidden or guarded *US, 1967*
• — Omero C. Catan, *Secrets of Shuffleboard Strategy*, p. 66, 1967: "Glossary of terms"

Fort Liquordale *nickname*
Fort Lauderdale, Florida *US, 1961*
A nickname earned first from the availability of liquor during Prohibition and then from the invasion of heavy-drinking college students each spring.
• So we lose ourselves in bottles and blonds at Fort Liquordale. — Jesuits of the United States and Canada, *America*, p. 547, 1961
• A nice judge in Fort Liquordale actually issued a restraining order against the Hacienda Village PD enjoining them for harrassing me! — *rec.music.gdead*, 21st April 1994

Fort Lost in the Woods *nickname*
Fort Leonard Wood, Missouri *US, 1974*
• I did my basic and my AIT at Fort Leonardwood, Missouri. "Lost in the Woods," yeah. — Wallace Terry, *Bloods*, p. 19, 1984

• Basic Training was at Fort Leonard Wood, Missouri. Sometimes referred to as Fort Lost-in-the-Woods or Little Korea, the post was isolated in the Missouri Ozarks. — George E. Dooley, *Battle for the Central Highlands*, p. 11, 2000

Fort Piss *nickname*
Fort Bliss, Texas *US, 1991*
Home to the US Army Air Defense Artillery Center.
• Destination: Fort Bliss, Texas. It was in El Paso but I soon found out that everyone knew it as "Fort Piss" in "El Pisso." — Brian Finkle, *Burny's Journeys*, p. 27, 2004

Fort Pricks *nickname*
Fort Dix, New Jersey *US, 1974*
A major training, mobilization, and deployment center. The scene of frequent demonstrations against the Vietnam war.
• Many of the forts occupied by US Army units have been given uncomplimentary nicknames: Fort Dicks or Fort Pricks (Fort Dix, New Jersey). — John Robert Elting, *A Dictionary of Soldier Talk*, p. 115, 1984

Fort Puke *nickname*
Fort Polk, Louisiana *US, 1974*
Home to the JRT Operations Group, the 2nd Armored Cavalry Regiment, the 519th Military Police Battalion, and the Warrior Brigade.
• Fort Puke (Fort Polk, Louisiana). — John Robert Elting, *A Dictionary of Soldier Talk*, p. 115, 1984

Fortrash *noun*
the FORTRAN computer language *US, 1991*
• — Eric S. Raymond, *The New Hacker's Dictionary*, p. 166, 1991

Fort Turd *nickname*
Fort Ord, Monterey, California *US, 1984*
• Fort Turd (Fort Ord, California). — John Robert Elting, *A Dictionary of Soldier Talk*, p. 115, 1984

fortune cookie *noun*
1 an aphorism or joke that appears on a computer screen when a user logs in *US, 1991*
• — Eric S. Raymond, *The New Hacker's Dictionary*, p. 166, 1991
2 in poker, a bet made without having seen all of your cards *US, 1996*
• — John Vorhaus, *The Big Book of Poker Slang*, p. 19, 1996

forty; 40 *noun*
a forty-ounce bottle of malt liquor *US, 1990*
• All I had was two forties. — *Menace II Society*, 1993
• [W]ake up with a 40 / Mixed up with Alka-Seltzer[.] — Eminem (Marshall Mathers), *Greg*, 1999
• I was gliding up 18th Street with a brand new girl and a 40, while the June sun was still high and shining. — Michelle Tea, *Valencia*, p. 41, 2000
• I drank forties with cats on corners, smoked whatever weed I came across, and experimented with bullshit drugs like mescaline when the mood arose[.] — Earl "DMX" Simmons, *E.A.R.L.*, p. 93, 2002

forty-deuce *nickname*
42nd Street, New York *US, 1981*
• Three-card monte players speak of Forty-Deuce. — Alix Shulman, *On the Stroll*, p. 3, 1981
• [E]specially in New York's Forty-Deuce area around Times Square and Eight Avenue hustler havens. — *Maledicta*, p. 156, Summer/Winter 1986–1987: "Sexual slang: prostitutes, pedophiles, flagellators, transvestites, and necrophiles"
• Tonight we find that place, right on Forty-deuce itself, between Seventh and Sixth. — Jim Carroll, *Forced Entries*, pp. 7–8, 1987
• This being New York, of course, there are plenty of curmudgeons around who bewail the death of the old sleazy Forty Deuce with its porn shops, XXX cinemas, and ragged street people. — Holly Hughes, *Frommer's New York City with Kids*, p. 187, 2003

forty-dog *noun*
a 40-ounce bottle of malt liquor *US, 1993*
• "Go an snag yourself a forty-dog, Sabby." Sebastian gave Hobbes a long look, but then went back into the main room and took a bottle from the fridge. — Jess Mowry, *Six Out Seven*, p. 435, 1993

forty-gallon Baptist *noun*
a member of a Baptist sect that practices full-immersion baptism *US, 1871*

- Among the most prominent opponents of the temperance cause were the primitive Baptists, sometimes called Hard Shells or Forty Gallon Baptists. — W.J. Rorabaugh, *The Alcoholic Republic*, p. 207, 1979

forty-going-north *adjective*
leaving or moving quickly *US, 1993*
- — *Washington Post*, p. C5, 7th November 1993

forty-miler *noun*
a new and inexperienced carnival worker or one who never travels far from home with the carnival *US, 1935*
- — Gene Sorrows, *All About Carnivals*, p. 17, 1985: "Terminology"

forty-rod *noun*
strong, cheap whiskey *US, 1861*
- It [hootchinoo] was sometimes referred to as Forty-Rod Whisky because it was supposed to kill a man at that distance. — Pierre Berton, *Klondike*, p. 23, 1958

forty-weight *noun*
1 strong coffee *US, 1976*
Inviting a comparison with motor oil.
- — Wayne Floyd, *Jason's Authentic Dictionary of CB Slang*, p. 32, 1976
2 beer, especially Iron City™ *US, 1976*
- — *Dictionary of CB Lingo*, p. 67, 1976: "Elementary electronics"

forward *noun*
any amphetamine or other central nervous system stimulant *US, 1966*
- — J. L. Simmons and Barry Winograd, *It's Happening*, p. 170, 1966: "glossary"

FOS *adjective*
full of shit, literally or figuratively *US, 1978*
- — *Maledicta*, p. 68, Summer/Winter 1978: "Common patient-directed pejoratives used by medical personnel"

fo' sheezy; fo' sheazy; fa' sheezy; fo' sho sho
Certainly *US, 1999*
- Still packing fo sho / Yeezy Weezy off of the heezy to sheezy / Cruise with the top off of the 'Ghini[.] — Lil Wayne *Fo Sheezy*, 1999
- Fa sheezy my neezy keep my arm so greasy / Can't leave rap alone the game needs me[.] — Jay Z, *to the Izzo*, 2001
- — Connie Eble (Editor), *UNC-CH Campus Slang*, p. 4, October 2002

fossil *noun*
1 an old person with outmoded ideas and values *US, 1952*
- [H]e didn't know how to tell her that the oldest fossil in the joint wasn't fifteen years his senior. — Joseph Wambaugh, *Finnegan's Week*, p. 230, 1993
2 a parent *US, 1957*
- "Cause it'll be my eighteenth birthday, and the fossils promised to buy me a Harley if I pass math." — Max Shulman, *Rally Round the Flag, Boys!*, p. 59, 1957
3 in computing, a feature that is retained after it is no longer needed in order to preserve compatibility *US, 1991*
- — Eric S. Raymond, *The New Hacker's Dictionary*, p. 166, 1991

fougasse *noun*
napalm-thickened gas, used in an improvised flame-thrower *US, 1989*
Korean and Vietnam war usage.
- Right in front of the triple concertina we had 55-gallon drums cut in half and filled with fougasse—a sort of napalm mixture. — Eric Hammel, *Khe Sanh: Siege in the Clouds*, p. 146, 1989

foul *adjective*
unpleasant, unfriendly *US, 1999*
Conventional English rendered slang with attitude.
- The people at this school are so incredibly foul. — *Ten Things I Hate About You*, 1999

foulball *noun*
a despised person *US, 1925*
- I got snaky last night on Waley's bum gin, and some big foulball of a dick came along. — James T. Farrell, *Saturday Night*, p. 28, 1947
- The Social Chairman of the boys' dorm calls the Social Chairman of a girls' dorm and says he need some flesh for Friday night, no foul balls, nothing too brainy, all queens and amenable, can she supply? — Glendon Swarthout, *Where the Boys Are*, p. 3, 1960
- [T]o be honest, there wasn't anyone much interested in a foul ball like me—except FDA. — Max Shulman, *Anyone Got a Match?*, p. 230, 1964

foul up *verb*
to botch, to ruin *US, 1942*
- Thou hadst a chance to be beautiful, yet thou hadst fouled it up. — Bel Kaufman, *Up the Down Staircase*, p. 145, 1964
- "I'd like for you not to foul it up for me." — George Higgins, *The Digger's Game*, p. 90, 1973

fountains of Rome *noun*
in homosexual usage, urinals in a public toilet *US, 1986–1987*
- — *Maledicta*, p. 60, 1986–1987: "A continuation of a glossary of ethnic slurs in American English"

four *noun*
a capsule of Empirin™ with codeine, designed for pain relief but abused by users of central nervous system depressants and opiates *US, 1977*
- — Walter L. Way, *The Drug Scene*, p. 108, 1977

four bits *noun*
a fifty-year prison sentence *US, 1990*
- — Charles Shafer, *Folk Speech in Texas Prisons*, p. 204, 1990
- — Ethan Hilderbrant, *Prison Slang*, p. 51, 1998

four by too's *noun*
in twelve-step recovery programs such as Alcoholics Anonymous, used for describing why recovering addicts don't attend program meetings—too busy, too tired, too lazy or too drunk *US, 1998*
A play on "two-by-four," the dimensions of the most common timber used in construction.
- — Christopher Cavanaugh, *AA to Z*, p. 99, 1998

four-color glossies *noun*
any literature that contains some useful information but which emphasizes style over substance *US, 1991*
- Often applied as an indication of superficiality even when the material is printed on ordinary paper in black and white. Four-color glossy manuals are never useful for finding a problem. — Eric S. Raymond, *The New Hacker's Dictionary*, p. 167, 1991

four-cornered *adjective*
caught in the commission of a crime *US, 1992*
- — William K. Bentley and James M. Corbett, *Prison Slang*, p. 92, 1992

four-deuce *noun*
an M-30 4.2 inch heavy mortar *US, 1968*
Vietnam war usage.
- — Carl Fleischhauer, *A Glossary of Army Slang*, p. 20, 1968
- "Four deuce sure beats humpin' the boonies." — William Pelfrey, *The Big V*, p. 6, 1972
- The Viet Cong were maintaining their usual invisibility—but the four-deuces would at least suppress the VC rifle fire. — Phil Caputo, *A Rumor of War*, p. 281, 1977

four-eyed *adjective*
wearing glasses *US, 1878*
- Tryin' to shop us, eh, you four-eyed git! — Charles Raven, *Underworld Nights*, p. 18, 1956
- 4F, the terminal draft classification, was wryly spelled out as Fat, Flabby, Forty, and Four-eyed[.] — Malcolm Braley, *False Starts*, p. 69, 1976
- He's got scoliosis and a clubfoot but the guy's an engineer, he pulls down seventy-five thousand a year, and that four-eyed fuck never cracked a schoolbook in his life. — Richard Price, *Clockers*, p. 523, 1992

four-eyes *noun*
a person who wears glasses *US, 1865*
- Even the so-called nice guys / Called us four-eyes. — Lenny Bruce, *The Essential Lenny Bruce*, p. 127, 1967
- One a tall tennis-anyone type, the other a bespectacled mouse type. I opted for Minnie Four-Eyes. — Erich Segal, *Love Story*, p. 2, 1970
- Four eyes. People with glasses give me a peculiar feeling. — Darryl Ponicsan, *The Last Detail*, p. 121, 1970
- — Connie Eble (Editor), *UNC-CH Campus Slang*, November 1976

four five *noun*
a 45 caliber handgun *US, 1994*
- — Ann Lawson, *Kids & Gangs*, p. 56, 1994: "Common African-American gang slang/phrases"

fourflusher *noun*
a liar, a fraud *US, 1904*

- Even Kelly laughed at the four-flusher. — Harry Grey, *The Hoods*, p. 266, 1952
- Mooches, fags, fourflushers, stool pigeons, bums—unwilling to work, unable to steal, always short of money, always whining for credit. — William Burroughs, *Junkie*, p. 54, 1954
- "Four-flushers are nil in my book." — Elaine Shepard, *The Doom Pussy*, p. 151, 1967
- "I've put you down as a fourflusher. And I've had it with you." — Burt Hirschfield, *Fire Island*, p. 267, 1970

four f's *noun*
used as a jocular if cynical approach to male relationships with women—find them, feel them, fuck them, forget them *US, 1942*
A pun on 4F draft status, which meant that a man was physically unfit to serve.
- — Roger Blake, *The American Dictionary of Sexual Terms*, p. 76, 1964
- — Dale Gordon, *The Dominion Sex Dictionary*, p. 71, 1967
- — Robert A. Wilson, *Playboy's Book of Forbidden Words*, p. 110, 1972
- — Kenn "Naz" Young, *Naz's Underground Dictionary*, p. 65, 1973

four-letter man *noun*
a male homosexual *US, 1949*
- — Vincent J. Monteleone, *Criminal Slang*, p. 90, 1949

four-oh *adjective*
excellent *US, 1919*
- "I think the whole idea is four O!" Lieutenant Commander Gladney said suddenly. — William Brinkley, *Don't Go Near the Water*, p. 10, 1956

four-one-one; 411 *noun*
gossip, information *US, 1991*
- — Connie Eble (Editor), *UNC-CH Campus Slang*, p. 7, Fall 1991
- He grinned with big teeth at Lactameon. "S' the 411, brother-mine?" — Jess Mowry, *Six Out Seven*, p. 78, 1993
- Here's the four-one-one on Mr. Hall. — *Clueless*, 1995
- "I mean, I said it real loud so he could hear and know that I didn't have the 4–1–1, right?" — Eric Jerome Dickey, *Cheaters*, p. 241, 1999

four-on-the-floor *noun*
use of the bass drum on every beat, especially in disco music *US, 1980*
Playing on the automotive term.
- — Walter Hurst and Donn Delson, *Delson's Dictionary of Radio & Record Industry Terms*, p. 54, 1980
- But then with a disco style beat of "four on the floor" the whole place starts to jump and jive. — Jack Allen, *When the Whistle Blows*, p. 134, 2000

four plus *adverb*
to the utmost degree *US, 1961*
- That accident is four plus drunk. I can't get a decent history from him. — *American Speech*, pp. 145–148, May 1961: "The spoken language of medicine; argot, slang, cant"

four-point *verb*
to handcuff a prisoner's arms and ankles to the four corners of a cot *US, 1992*
- "Better four-point him for a while. We can't have him starting fires." — Pete Earley, *The Hot House*, p. 137, 1992

fours and dors *noun*
a combination of number four codeine tablets and Doriden™ sleeping pills, which produces an opiate-like effect on the user *US, 1989*
- — Geoffrey Froner, *Digging for Diamonds*, p. 30, 1989

four-striper *noun*
a captain in the US Navy *US, 1914*
- Temporary or not, I was a four-striper. And I had clout. — Richard Marcinko, *Rogue Warrior*, p. 334, 1992

fourteen *noun*
1 an M-14 rifle *US, 1985*
- They made us switch to the M-16 during our tour. I liked the fourteens much better. — Al Santoli, *To Bear Any Burden*, p. 106, 1985
2 the Grumman F-14 Tomcat, a long-range strike-fighter aircraft *US, 1978*
Vietnam war usage.

- "You using your 14's for escort?" "Of course." The Grumman F-14 Tomcat was the best fighter craft in the world. — Nelson DeMille, *By the Rivers of Babylon*, p. 25, 1978

fourteenth street *noun*
▸ **go below fourteenth street**
to perform oral sex on a woman *US, 1971*
- Anal intercourse ("Greek") is popular, as is cunnilingus ("going below 14th Street"). — Charles Winick, *The Lively Commerce*, p. 207, 1971

four-trey, the country way *noun*
a roll of seven in a craps game *US, 1957*
- "Four-trey, the country way," the stick man san, raking in the dice. "Seven! The loser!" — Chester Himes, *A Rage in Harlem*, p. 26, 1957

four-twenty *noun*
marijuana *US, 1969*
Also written as "4:20." False etymologies abound; the term was coined by teenagers in Marin County, California, and does not refer to any police code.
- With the cocaine kangarooing me, and this booby-trapped nest of low-life suckers I stumbled into I had more than a frantic yearning for maybe four-twenty at the Haven. — Iceberg Slim (Robert Beck), *Pimp*, p. 143, 1969
- "Four-twenty"—once an obscure Bay Area term for pot—is showing up nationally in the advertisements and business names of concert promoters, travel agencies, even high-tech companies. — *Los Angeles Time*, 20th April 2002

four-way *adjective*
willing to engage in four types of sexual activity, the exact nature of which depends up on the person described and the context *US, 1971*
- I was taught early that suffering is inevitable and necessary for an aspiring pimp, pickpocket or con man and even just a nigger compelled to become a four-way whore for the Establishment. — Iceberg Slim (Robert Beck), *The Naked Soul of Iceberg Slim*, pp. 17–18, 1971
- A racehorse goes four ways. She gets tricked two ways. She eats the person up and also—actually, she does anything a man wants, that's what she does, she's all the way around. — Bruce Jackson, *In the Life*, p. 181, 1972

four-year lesbian *noun*
a woman who takes lesbian lovers in college, planning to return to the safer waters of heterosexuality after graduation from college *US, 1995*
- — Steven Daly and Nathaniel Wice, *alt.culture*, p. 138, 1995
- Pretty soon I was eating more pussy than a four-year lesbian. — Taigi Smith, *Sometimes Rhythm, Sometimes Blues*, p. 203, 2003

fox *noun*
1 an attractive male *US, 1977*
- Wasp Afro, puka shells, Che Guevara T-shirt. Joan thought Spenser was "a fox." — Cyra McFadden, *The Serial*, p. 30, 1977
- He would have blond, curly hair and deep blue eyes. He would be a fox, no doubt about it. — Robert Lipkin, *A Brotherhood of Outlaws*, p. 137, 1981
2 a beautiful woman or girl *US, 1961*
- Since there were two Negro colleges near his town, why not cut out all the old time "handkerchief head waitress" and recruit all young college "foxes." — Babs Gonzales, *I Paid My Dues*, p. 83, 1967
- Name's Dee-Dee. She a fox, too. I think Jimmy strung out behind her. — Nathan Heard, *Howard Street*, p. 63, 1968
- Your sister is really turning into a fox. — *Fast Times at Ridgemont High*, 1982
3 in poker, the sixth player to the left of the dealer *US, 1988*
- — George Percy, *The Language of Poker*, p. 33, 1988

foxie *noun*
an attractive girl *US, 1979*
- — H. Craig Collins, *Street Gangs*, p. 222, 1979

foxy *adjective*
attractive, beautiful *US, 1895*
Usually but not always applied to a woman.
- I mean all the studs in fancy duds and foxy chicks togged to the bricks is gonna be there. — Ross Russell, *The Sound*, p. 218, 1961
- George looked and saw a very foxy Danish girl sitting down. — Cecil Brown, *The Life & Loves of Mr. Jiveass Nigger*, p. 113, 1969
- He went on to say that "she was a foxy little thing" and "better than your average piece of ass." — Elmore Leonard, *City Primeval*, p. 8, 1980

- Offensive description of a woman's physical appearance.
  — Multicultural Management Program Fellows, *Dictionary of Cautionary Words and Phrases*, 1989
- You're the foxiest bitch I've ever known. — *Boogie Nights*, 1997

foxy-methoxy *noun*
the drug 5-methoxy-N, a synthetic hallucinogenic drug in the tryptamine family *US, 2005*
- 5-MeO-DIPT, also known as "Foxy-Methoxy." — *Microgram Bulletin (DEA)*, p. 46, March 2005

fracture *verb*
to have a strong, favorable effect upon someone *US, 1946*
- "You fracture me," she said. — Max Shulman, *The Many Loves of Dobie Gillis*, p. 123, 1951
- — Robert George Reisner, *The Jazz Titans*, p. 155, 1960

fractured *adjective*
drunk *US, 1953*
- They had already annihilated kegs of beer and started to get fractured on Gallo wine. — Frederick Kohner, *Gidget*, p. 123, 1957
- — Eugene Landy, *The Underground Dictionary*, p. 81, 1971

frag *noun*
1 a *fragmentation hand grenade or bomb US, 1943*
- You peep through that skinny-ass embrasure with your M-16 on full rock and roll, a double armful of fragmentation grenades—frags we called them[.] — Larry Heinemann, *Paco's Story*, p. 10, 1986
- We got two men need attention here. Police up your extra ammo and frags. — *Platoon*, 1986
- To answer, he opened his jungle shirt, revealing a shoulder-holstered Colt and a half-dozen M26 frags. — Ralph Zumbro, *Tank Sergeant*, p. 57, 1986
2 a *fragment from a bullet or artillery shell US, 1966*
- "They got frags from the woman and two good ones from Guy, the casing intact..." — Elmore Leonard, *City Primeval*, p. 60, 1980
3 a *fragmentary order US, 1962*
- Major Henri (Pete) Mallet, the 3rd Brigade operations officer, flew in with a half-page "frag" from Colonel Brown. — Harold G. Moore, *We Were Soldiers Once ... And Young*, p. 56, 1992

frag *verb*
1 to kill a fellow soldier, usually an officer and usually with a fragmentation grenade *US, 1970*
A term coined in Vietnam to describe a practice that became common if not widespread in Vietnam.
- Don't "frag" that cute little Second Lieutenant—fuck the daylights out of him! — *Screw*, p. 11, 21st June 1971
- [O]thers in prisons for fragging officers who ordered them about[.] — Emmett Grogan, *Ringolevio*, p. 231, 1972
- I say we frag the fucker. — *Platoon*, 1986
- He had been convicted of being an accessory to murder for having held open a hooch door while another Marine threw in a fragmentation grenade and killed their company commander. It was a time when "fragging" had become a new and frightening threat[.] — *Providence (Rhode Island) Journal-Bulletin*, p. 1E, 20th April 2000
2 to dispatch by a fragmentary order *US, 1967*
- The Marines arranged for a special helicopter (or "fragged a chopper," as we used to call it) to take him in and out of Khe Sanh one afternoon. — Michael Herr, *Dispatches*, p. 223, 1977
- And don't frag me for Old Package Six / I'll be in one hell of a fix. — Joseph Tuso, *Singing the Vietnam Blues*, p. 118, 1990: Just Give Me Operations

fragging *noun*
the intentional killing of an officer by his own troops *US, 1972*
- There is a word for it, "Fragging," if it would become necessary. — House Committee on Internal Security, *Investigation of Attempts to Subvert the United States Arm*, 1972
- Fragging, the deliberate attack on a noncom or ofifcer by an enlisted man or men, was not unknown in the 173d. — Anthony Herbert, *Soldier*, p. 153, 1973
- Fragging became an occupational hazard for officers and NCOs. — Harry Maurer, *Strange Ground*, p. 161, 1989

frag list *noun*
a frag order *US, 1986*
Vietnam war usage.

- I just wanted to hit them harder than the frag list allowed. — Stephen Coonts, *Flight of the Intruder*, p. 358, 1986

frag order *noun*
an order setting the day's specific military objectives *US, 1961*
Shortened "fragmentation order." Vietnam war usage.
- "However, two days later we got a frag order directing us to bomb the jungle area six miles east of the town of Bau Ngua." — Elaine Shepard, *The Doom Pussy*, p. 124, 1967
- Some frag order, Jack thought, as he tried to decipher the long message detailing the targets for the wing's next mission. — Richard Herman, *The Warbirds*, p. 266, 1989

fraho; frajo *noun*
marijuana *US, 1952*
Originally a "cigarette" or "marijuana cigarette."
- — *American Speech*, p. 25, February 1952: "Teen-age hophead jargon"

fraid hole *noun*
a cellar built for protection from cyclones *US, 1914*
- A warning was promptly issued in Woodward for everyone to go to their "fraid holes" or storm-cellars, but I had not heard about it. — Seigniora Laune, *Sand in My Eyes*, p. 142, 1956

'fraid so
I'm afraid so *US, 1895*
Often answered with "'fraid not."
- "And Michael Landon?" "'Fraid so," Al Garcia said. — Carl Hiaasen, *Tourist Season*, p. 196, 1986

fraidy cat *noun*
a coward *UK, 1910*
- He would go to Gramma and be hugged because he wasn't a crybaby fraidycat. — Stephen King, *Skeleton Crew*, p. 491, 1985
- "Timmy's a fraidy-cat," Lex called. "What a stupid jerk," Tim said. — Michael Crichton, *Jurassic Park*, p. 237, 1990

frail *noun*
a woman *US, 1899*
- [L]eaning over to brush some crumbs off the table, he'd bump up against some pretty young frail with his rear end and send her flying. — Mezz Mezzrow, *Really the Blues*, p. 85, 1946
- It is lined with walls of men waiting for the frails to come out of the bars, strip dives, and burlesque houses. — Jack Lait and Lee Mortimer, *Washington Confidential*, p. 268, 1951
- And the Frail was named Stella, a fraud Cinderella, out trying to trick any citified Hick[.] — Dan Burley, *Diggeth Thou?*, p. 47, 1959
- I'm hip to the ways you pimps try to play / And the lugs you drop on a frail. — Dennis Wepman et al., *The Life*, p. 86, 1976

frame *noun*
the body *US, 1952*
- Some poontang to cradle my lonesome frame. — George Mandel, *Flee the Angry Strangers*, p. 59, 1952
- I left the tavern, returned to the dormitory, and put my miserable frame into the sack. — Max Shulman, *Guided Tour of Campus Humor*, p. 60, 1955

frame *verb*
to incriminate a person by contriving false evidence *US, 1899*
- I never do nothin' wrong but every time I get the blame/ I been framed! — Cheech Marin and Tommy Chong, *Framed*, 1976

frame job *noun*
a conspiracy, especially one where blame for a misdeed is placed on someone *US, 1973*
- "Assuming a frame job and murder, where is Lee's body?" Sam asked neutrally. — Elizabeth Lowell, *The Color of Death*, p. 79, 2004

frames *noun*
eyeglasses *US, 1972*
- — David Claerbaut, *Black Jargon in White America*, p. 64, 1972

frammis *noun*
a commotion *US, 1954*
- Probably a dozen people saw that little frammis this morning. — Jim Thompson, *A Swell-Looking Babe*, p. 69, 1954

frank *noun*
a *frank*furter, a hot dog *US, 1925*
- We had a farewell meal of franks and beans in a Seven month Avenue Riker's[.] — Jack Kerouac, *On the Road*, p. 9, 1957

- I'm at the supermarket, I bought a pack of franks. — Chris Rock, *Rock This!*, p. 164, 1997

Franken- *prefix*

in combination with a noun denotes a freakish, genetically modified or ugly form of that thing *US, 1992*

After Mary Shelley's 1818 novel *Frankenstein* but from the images provided by C20 Hollywood.

- If they want to sell us Frankenfood, perhaps it's time to gather the villagers, light some torches and head to the castle. [Letter to the Editor] — *New York Times*, p. A24, 16th June 1992
- An Atlanta chef is leading the charge against "Frankenfood"— genetically altered foods that are expected on store shelves soon. — *Atlanta Constitution*, p. G2, 16th October 1992
- Hello Kitty or Frankenpet? — *San Francisco Chronicle*, 20th April 2004

frantic *adjective*

exciting, thrilling *US, 1934*

- Monkey Pollack was a frantic cat, small, tough, and game as they make them. — Mezz Mezzrow, *Really the Blues*, p. 69, 1946
- "But I'm seeing her again tonight and it's going to be frantic, Bill. Real frantic." — Irving Shulman, *The Short End of the Stick*, p. 110, 1959
- *Dobie Gillis Teenage Slanguage Dictionary*, 1962
- Shorty would take me to groovy, frantic scenes in different chicks' and cats' pads, where with the lights and juke down mellow, everybody blew gage and juiced back and jumped. — Malcolm X and Alex Haley, *The Autobiography of Malcolm X*, p. 56, 1964

frap *verb*

to whip *US, 1894*

- — Charles Shafer, *Folk Speech in Texas Prisons*, p. 204, 1990

frapping *adjective*

used as a euphemism for "fucking" in its different senses *US, 1968*

- So push those frappin' throttles up and head across the sky. — Joseph Tuso, *Singing the Vietnam Blues*, p. 37, 1990: The Ballad of the C-130
- I can't say that I think too much of your frapping Chemlites, John. — James H. Kyle, *The Guts to Try*, p. 343, 1995

frat *noun*

a college fraternity *US, 1895*

- Alpha Cholera is a darn swell frat and it's loads of fun. — Max Shulman, *The Zebra Derby*, p. 64, 1946
- I've completely neglected to mention—it was the weekend of the big frat formal. — Robert Gover, *One Hundred Dollar Misunderstanding*, p. 9, 1961
- The "misunderstanding" develops when James C. Holland, having been badgered into it by some of his frat brothers, goes to "this Negro ill-repute house." — Terry Southern, *Now Dig This: The Unspeakable Writings of Terry Southern 1950–1995*, p. 201, 17th November 1962
- They were blocking the sidewalk and encouraging a frat brother to do a semi-striptease for the benefit of a coed hanging out the window of a restaurant overhead. — Joseph Wambaugh, *Finnegan's Week*, p. 279, 1993

frat around *verb*

to idle, to gossip instead of studying *US, 1963*

- — Carol Ann Preusse, *Jargon Used by University of Texas Co-Eds*, 1963

frat dick *noun*

a boorish member of a college fraternity *US, 1989*

- — Pamela Munro, *U.C.L.A. Slang*, p. 40, 1989

fraternity brother *noun*

a fellow prisoner *US, 1949*

- — Vincent J. Monteleone, *Criminal Slang*, p. 90, 1949

frat rat *noun*

an obnoxious, aggressive, arrogant example of a college fraternity member *US, 1958*

- — Collin Baker et al., *College Undergraduate Slang Study Conducted at Brown University*, p. 121, 1968

frat tuck *noun*

a shirt worn tucked into the pants in the front but hanging loose in the back *US, 2001*

- — Don R. McCreary (Editor), *Dawg Speak*, 2001

frazzle-assed *adjective*

worn out *US, 1951*

- I don't give a fuck for them, see? Not a single, goddarn solitary frazzle-assed fuck. — James Jones, *From Here to Eternity*, p. 397, 1951

frazzled *adjective*

1 confused *US, 1883*

- I'm getting plumb frazzled out of my wits. — Jim Thompson, *Pop. 1280*, p. 19, 1964

2 drunk *US, 1906*

- — Ramon Adams, *The Language of the Railroader*, p. 64, 1977

freak *noun*

1 a person with strong sexual desires, often fetishistic *US, 1922*

- Say, there was asshole shellackers and shitpackers/ and freaks who drunk blood from a menstruatin' womb. — Bruce Jackson, *Get Your Ass in the Water and Swim Like Me*, p. 146, 1964
- A freak is basically anyone who needs fantasy, degradation, or punishment in order to his achieve his interpretation of erotic gratification. — Xaviera Hollander, *The Happy Hooker*, p. 208, 1972
- That girl is pretty wild now / The girl's a super freak / The kind of girl you read about / In New-wave magazines — Rick James, *Super Freak*, 1981
- This girl's a freak! You can fuck her in the ass, fuck 'er in the mouth. Rough stuff, too. She's a freak for it. — *True Romance*, 1993

2 a devotee, an enthusiast *US, 1895*

- It seems like a pose, or even a perversion—and maybe it is, but to bike freaks it is very real. — Hunter S. Thompson, *Hell's Angels*, p. 94, 1966
- [F]reak referred to styles and obsessions, as in "Stewart Brand is an Indian freak" or "the zodiac—that's her freak[.]" — Tom Wolfe, *The Electric Kool-Aid Acid Test*, p. 10, 1968
- "Beware of structure-freaks, they do not understand." — Sol Yurrick, *The Bag*, p. 341, 1968
- He was the co-editor with S.I. Hayakawa of ETC., the magazine put out by those word freaks. — Oscar Zeta Acosta, *The Autobiography of a Brown Buffalo*, p. 100, 1972
- The 2.2 million ecology freaks who live there [Oregon] are reminded by their Highway Division to "thank Heaven we live in God's Country." — Bill Cardoso, *The Maltese Sangweech*, p. 88, 1984
- They were degenerate gamblers, coke freaks. — *Casino*, 1995

3 a member of the 1960s counterculture *US, 1960*

Originally a disparaging negative, turned around and used in a positive, complimentary sense. Widely used from the mid-1960s; hurled as abuse at the original hippies, the term was adopted by them and turned back on the critics by the self-confessed "freaks" with an ability to **FREAK OUT** themselves and others.

- They are the fringe whites ... outcasts ... worse than being a Negro or Puerto Rican. Assistant Chief Inspector Joseph McLaughlin, boss of Manhattan South detectives, is tempted to send all these freaks to Hell. — *The Digger Papers*, p. 12, August 1968
- The university became a fortress surrounded by our foreign culture, longhaired, dopesmoking, barefooted freaks who were using state-owned university property as a playground. — Jerry Rubin, *Do It!*, p. 26, 1970
- [Y]our average acid-eating freak will be getting arrested for attempting to sit in the park under General Thomas' horse in Thomas Circle[.] — Raymond Mungo, *Famous Long Ago*, p. 29, 1970
- it's really impressive and hopeful to see a beautiful place built by freaks and the houses up there are out of sight. — Paul and Meredith *Chamisa Road*, 1971

4 used as a term of endearment *US, 1954*

Teenslang.

- — *Look*, p. 88, 10th August 1954

5 a dance with strong suggestions of sexual movement, first popular as a 1975 disco dance and then again in the late 1990s and early 2000s *US, 1979*

Used with "the" unless used as a verb.

- Freak: 1) Also known as free-style. The latest and possibly the greatest form of disco dancing. — Bruce Pollack, *The Disco Handbook*, p. 6, 1979
- Freak, The/La Freak/The Freaky Deaky: A 1975 disco dance often done in lines with movements like the Mashed Potato, the Shimmy, and the Twist of the 1960s and the Dirty Boogie of the 1950s. The dancer leads with the hips, but there is a lot of body touch[.] — Mari Helen Schultz, *May I Have This Dance?*, p. 38, 1986
- The latest version of dirty dancing is called "freaking" and while it's been a mainstay at high school dances and teen parties for the last five years, now the moves are getting hotter and kids as young as 12 are doing them. — *San Francisco Chronicle*, p. A23, 3rd June 2001

6 a nonsensical novelty song *US, 1948*

- All crazy songs which make no sense are "freaks." — Jack Lait and Lee Mortimer, *New York*, p. 33, 1948

7 a wrestler whose huge size is obviously the result of the use of anabolic steroids *US*, *1996*

- The WWF has just shown old clips of UW, reminding people of the steroid freak that existed in the WWF years ago. — *Herb's Wrestling Tidbits*, 28th March 1996

8 in poker, a wild card, which may be played as a card of any value *US*, *1949*

- — Albert H. Morehead, *The Complete Guide to Winning Poker*, p. 263, 1967

▸ **get your freak on**
to enjoy a sexual perversion *US*, *1998*

- It wasn't always negative or always positive. It didn't really matter —I didn't care about anything but getting my freak on — Karen Hunter, *I Make My Own Rules*, p. 106, 1998
- The price is seventy five dollars a fuck, gentlemen, you gittin your freak on or what? — *Kill Bill*, 2003
- I hadn't had sex in five days—a long-ass time when you like to get your freak on as much as I do. — Zane, *The Sisters of APF*, p. 80, 2003

freak *verb*
1 to panic *US*, *1964*

- I'm going to freak. I'm going to freak. I have to freak. I will freak. I must freak. I am freaking, and that's official. — Nicholas Von Hoffman, *We are the People Our Parents Warned Us Against*, p. 149, 1967
- The liberals try to get everyone freaked at Wallace so we won't notice that they do precisely what he advocates... — Jerry Rubin, *Do It!*, p. 145, 1970
- I said for her to be there alone and you freaked! — *Ferris Bueller's Day Off*, 1986
- Alright, I'm, freaking too. But they need you to stay calm. — *Jerry Maguire*, 1996

2 to have sex *US*, *1999*

- Later him and her would freak in the back of his tricked-out Chevy, but for now Carmen stormed off, shoving her tit back into her bra as she went[.] — John Ridley, *Everybody Smokes in Hell*, p. 5, 1999

freak *adjective*
1 in jazz, unorthodox *US*, *1955*

- — Robert S. Gold, *A Jazz Lexicon*, p. 112, 1964

2 attractive *US*, *1994*

- — Linda Meyer, *Teenspeak!*, p. 29, 1994

freaked *adjective*
very upset *US*, *1967*

- But not anybody can walk out in the market place and not get freaked. — *The San Francisco Oracle*, 1967
- A big ass rat. I keep a watch out for it, but I don't tell my brother so he won't get freaked (like I am). — Scott Meyer, *Deadhead Forever*, 2001

freak house *noun*
1 an abandoned building used as a temporary residence for drug addicts who have been evicted from their own dwelling *US*, *1995*

- — Mark S. Fleisher, *Beggars & Thieves*, p. 289, 1995: "glossary"

2 a room, apartment, or house where amphetamine addicts gather to inject the drug *US*, *1970*

- — William D. Alsever, *Glossary for the Establishment and Other Uptight People*, p. 11, December 1970

freaking *adjective*
used as an intensifier where "fucking" is to be avoided *US*, *1928*

- "You point that freakin' finger at me 'n you're one dead pointer." — Nelson Algren, *The Man with the Golden Arm*, p. 105, 1949
- "Freakin' fruit," said Fuzzy, pulling off the wide-brimmed hat and throwing back his long blond hair. — Joseph Wambaugh, *The Blue Knight*, p. 137, 1973
- On top of being a freaking pig, you gotta add insult to injury. — Piri Thomas, *Stories from El Barrio*, p. 87, 1978
- I'm a fairy too! Hey, I'm a freaking fairy too. — Francesca Lia Block, *I Was a Teenage Fairy*, p. 157, 1998

-freaking- *infix*
used as an intensifier *US*, *1983*

- "You guys coming up to the dance tonight?" he asked. "Un-freaking-likely," I said. — Christ Crutcher, *Running Loose*, p. 72, 1983
- "Un-freaking-believable. You won't even show me where the kayaks are?" — Carl Hiaasen, *Nature Girl*, p. 208, 2006

freaking A!
used as a euphemism for "fucking A!" in expressing surprise *US*, *2002*

- "Lineup time!" shouted Kevin, "Freaking A!" as they carried the kicking boy over to the wall. — Peter Meinke, *The Ponoes*, p. 163, 1986
- — Connie Eble (Editor), *UNC-CH Campus Slang*, p. 4, October 2002
- "And that time was pretty freaking-A fantastic!" — Rachel Gibson, *See Jane Score*, p. 308, 2003

freakish *adjective*
sexually perverted *US*, *1929*

- Shug say, Wellsah, and I thought it was only whitefolks do freakish things like that. — Alice Walker, *The Color Purple*, p. 112, 1989

freak jacket *noun*
a reputation for unconventional sexual interests *US*, *1967*

- Maybe you can ease from under the freak jacket you've been carrying. — Malcolm Braly, *On the Yard*, p. 32, 1967

freaknasty *noun*
a sexually active woman who shares her activity with multiple partners *US*, *2001*

- — Don R. McCreary (Editor), *Dawg Speak*, 2001

freaknik *noun*
a mass celebration of black students in the streets of Atlanta, Georgia, during college spring break *US*, *1992*

- For all of you that sleep and did not come down here to Atlanta for freaknik. It was all that. — *alt.rap*, 27th April 1993
- "Freaknik" festivities have come to the streets of Atlanta, as the 16th annual Black College Spring Break turns the town into a party. — *San Francisco Sunday Examiner and Chronicle*, p. A17, 19th April 1998

freako *noun*
a weirdo; a sexual deviant; a habitual drug-user *US*, *1963*

- [T]he quack doctor who services every freako and housewife on Woodward Ave. threw me out of his offices. — Lester Bangs, *Psychotic Reactions and Carburetor Dung*, p. 172, 1975
- That I'm not some freako sex machine who can't cut it on the big screen. — Jackie Collins, *Vendetta*, p. 241, 1997

freak-off *noun*
a sexual deviate *US*, *1973*

- Darlene happened to draw a real freak-off one night around two-thirty in the morning. — Jennifer Sills, *Massage Parlor*, p. 80, 1973

freak off *verb*
to have sex, especially with vigor and without restraint *US*, *1967*
An extremely subjective verb, perhaps referring to homosexual sex, perhaps to oral sex, perhaps to heterosexual anal sex.

- I love to freak off, but get strung out? That's something else. — Malcolm Braly, *On the Yard*, p. 326, 1967
- Hey, let's all go up my room, get high an freak off. — Robert Gover, *JC Saves*, p. 17, 1968
- Pepper is a rotten freak broad. You ain't the only stud she freaks off with. I could name a half dozen who ride her. — Iceberg Slim (Robert Beck), *Pimp*, p. 67, 1969
- "When a junky speaks of having normal sexual relations, heterosexual sexual relations, he will invariably speak of it as 'freaking off,'" Sinman said. — Robert Deane Pharr, *S.R.O.*, p. 147, 1971
- Tenderloin Tim and his lady "were like married," according to Queenie, "but sometimes he would let her freak off with another woman." — Christina and Richard Milner, *Black Players*, p. 156, 1972

freak-out *noun*
1 a celebratory event, a gathering together of counterculturists to enjoy music and drugs *US*, *1970*

- The Hog Farm Freakout at NYU, March 1969, which took place the evening of the first day of shooting on Events. — Fred Baker, *Events*, p. 11, 1970

2 an uninhibited sexual exhibition *US*, *1969*

- "Man, these motherfuckers have this restaurant, a Greek restaurant and jack if a chick wants a workout, I mean a freakout, that's where they go. These Greeks work in teams, man. They fuck the chick between the toes, in the nose, and shit like that." — Cecil Brown, *The Life & Loves of Mr. Jiveass Nigger*, p. 148, 1969

3 a temporary loss of sanity and control while under the influence of a psychoactive drug *UK, 1966*

- Besides the freak-out in the bathroom they are expecting a psychiatrist to look at Bob. — Joan Didion, *Slouching Toward Bethlehem*, p. 108, 1967

4 a complete panic and loss of control *US, 1966*

- Is he going to put acid in everything consumable? Does he want to create a big freak out, a big bummer? — *The San Francisco Oracle*, 1966
- 1967 is the Year of the Overall Freak-Out. — Hunter S. Thompson, *Fear and Loathing in America*, p. 12, 3rd January 1968: Letter to Gerald Walker
- Mothers and little kids dropped their picnic baskets and fled when they saw the signs. Near freakout. — Jerry Rubin, *Do It!*, p. 38, 1970

freak out *verb*

1 to engage in deviant sexual behavior *US, 1973*

- It turned out that Dirk was utterly impotent and got his kicks freaking out on the phone with other girls in between performing cunnilingus on me. — Xaviera Hollander, *The Happy Hooker*, p. 77, 1972

2 to lose sanity while under the influence of LSD or another hallucinogen *US, 1967*

- Freaking out is erratic behavior resulting from a bum trip. — Nicholas Von Hoffman, *We Are The People Our Parents Warned Us Against*, p. 225, 1967
- — Joe David Brown (Editor), *The Hippies*, p. 218, 1967: "glossary of hippie terms"
- Sometimes that gets tested on acid—when somebody freaks out. — Leonard Wolfe (Editor), *Voices from the Love Generation*, p. 33, 1968
- [Y]ou can go out into the country free so you can straighten your head out or freak out among true friends. — *The Digger Papers*, p. 3, August 1968
- No, I haven't freaked out. — Tom Robbins, *Another Roadside Attraction*, p. 77, 1971

3 to panic *US, 1964*

- — Joe David Brown (Editor), *The Hippies*, p. 218, 1967: "glossary of hippie terms"

4 to make someone feel unsettled, astonished, or bizarre *US, 1964*

- I mean, I like it and everything, it just doesn't freak me out. — *Sex, Lies and Videotape*, 1989
- Why don't you man? Too freaked out? — Francesca Lia Block, *Cherokee Bat*, p. 209, 1992

5 to behave in a crazed manner as a response to an emotional stimulus *US, 1966*

- I'd just tell Hugh that I wanted to sleep with this guy. He freaked out. Total freak-out! — Sally Cline, *Couples*, p. 136, 1998

freak show *noun*

a fetishistic sexual performance *US, 1973*

- "I dig what you're doing, but I think you're a little too good for a freak show." — Susan Hall, *Ladies of the Night*, p. 78, 1973
- And yet at this perverse freak show, the people I met were extraordinarily ordinary[.] — Dolores French, *Working*, p. 209, 1988
- Court documents state that 50 patrons were watching 25 strippers inside a red, one-story building where West Lanvale Street dead-ends into a fenced-in industrial complex. Sources familiar with the investigation said the event was advertised as a "Freak Show." — *Baltimore Sun*, p. 1B, 30th May 2001

freak trick *noun*

a prostitute's customer who pays for unusual sex *US, 1971*

- — Eugene Landy, *The Underground Dictionary*, p. 82, 1971
- A scrawny white hooker who had been the victim of a "freak trick" —a customer who gets his kicks from brutally beating his girls—was nursing her wounds. — Xaviera Hollander, *The Happy Hooker*, p. 4, 1972

freaky *adjective*

1 odd, bizarre *US, 1895*

- — Hy Lit, *Hy Lit's Unbelievable Dictionary of Hip Words for Groovy People*, p. 16, 1968
- The Be-in: a new medium of human relations. A magnet drawing together all the freaky, hip, unhappy, young, happy, curious, criminal, gentle, alienated, weird, frustrated, far-out, artistic, lonely, lovely people to the same place at the same time. — Jerry Rubin, *Do It!*, p. 56, 1970
- Oh, you see lots of freaky stuff in a cab. Especially when the moon's out. — *Taxi Driver*, 1976

2 characteristic of the 1960s counterculture *US, 1971*

- The freaky, zoned-out style being developed on the misty slopes of the Haight had still made few inroads into intense, political Berkeley. — J. Anthony Lukas, *Don't Shoot—We Are Your Children*, p. 386, 1971
- Maybe they didn't like my freaky clothes. — Cleo Odzer, *Goa Freaks*, p. 103, 1995

▶ **get freaky**

to have sex *US, 1996*

- — Connie Eble (Editor), *UNC-CH Campus Slang*, p. 3, March 1996
- She's a good woman. Feeds me. Loves me. Gets freaky on my birthday. — *Hustle and Flow*, 2004

freaky-deaky *adjective*

acting without restraint, especially in a sexual way *US, 1981*

- Originally a discofunk style of music and dance. That's where Spinks has been for more than a month, in the woods of Michigan conditioning himself relentlessly, stripping every ounce of fat off and renouncing those old "freaky deaky" ways of his wherein he often could be found liberally enjoying the wine and young ladies. — *United Press International*, 11th June 1981
- Quite a few freaky-deaky messages played before my trite conversation with Tammy. — Eric Jerome Dickey, *Cheaters*, p. 74, 1999
- — Rick Ayers (Editor), *Berkeley High Slang Dictionary*, p. 22, 2004
- The 1960s was a revolutionary decade led by brave, freaky-deaky hippie chicks[.] — Mr. Skin, *Mr. Skin's Skincyclopedia*, p. 66, 2005

freakyfluky *noun*

▶ **on the freakfluky**

unexpectedly, randomly *US, 1977*

- The whole rotten deal—could come in on the freakfluky as easily as in the so-called expected ways[.] — Michael Herr, *Dispatches*, p. 14, 1977

freddy *noun*

an amphetamine tablet, especially a capsule of ephedrine *US, 1992*

- — Jay Robert Nash, *Dictionary of Crime*, p. 138, 1992
- — *Providence (Rhode Island) Journal-Bulletin*, p. 6B, 4th August 1997: "Doctors must know the narcolexicon"

Freddy Fraternity *noun*

a stereotypical college fraternity member who looks, dresses, talks, and lives the part *US, 1995*

- So I became a G.D.I., which stands for God Damn Independent, and that's the way I like it and to hell with all the Betty Coeds, Sally Sororities and Freddy Frats. — Frederick Kohner, *The Affairs of Gidget*, p. 8, 1963
- "Suzi Sorority" and "Freddie Fraternity," if they ever existed, are not quite as clean or wholesome as might appear at first glance. — *Maledicta*, p. 133, 1995

free *noun*

the world outside prison *US, 1966*

- USA Today: Do you have any special advice or words to inmates when they leave the prison? HAMBRICK: Yes, I tell them that, "If I see you again, may it be in the free." — *USA Today*, p. 11A, 5th December 1988

free *adjective*

unaffected by any conventional values *US, 1967*

A critical if vague word from the 1960s counterculture.

- During the convention I wore a sign that said free on it. — Nicholas Von Hoffman, *We Are The People Our Parents Warned Us Against*, p. 131, 1967
- All the petty bullshit things that before kept us apart vanished and for the first time we were free. — *East Village Other*, 20th August 1969

freeball *verb*

(used of a male) to dress without underwear *US, 1990*

- And when you freeball in fatigues you're a walking hard-on anyway just because of the feeling of that coarse material against you all day long. — Steven Zeeland, *Sailors and Sexual Identity*, p. 261, 1995
- I might wear underwear more often than my other freeballing associates, but I will use my own judgment on this matter. — *The Arizona Republic*, p. 9, 31st August 2000
- — Pamela Munro, *U.C.L.A. Slang*, p. 70, 2001

freebase *noun*

nearly pure cocaine alkaloid which can be obtained from powdered cocaine hydrochloride and is then burnt and inhaled *US, 1976*

- 9:15: Psychological and Environmental Determinants of Relapse for Compulsive Freebase Cocaine Smokers. — *Annual Meeting of the American Public Health Association*, p. 12, 1976
- They were smoking free base, also known as the "white tornado"—the form of cocaine favored by those beyond the nasal stage of evolution. — *Hi Life*, p. 78, 1979

- CAROLINE: What is this, like freebase? SETH: Not like. It is. — *Traffic*, 2000

freebase *verb*
to remove the impurities from cocaine to advance and heighten the effect *US, 1980*
By ellipsis from "free the base."

- Besides, the idiot uses a blowtorch to freebase. — Bret Easton Ellis, *Less Than Zero*, p. 81, 1985
- John found a coke connection and started free-basing—smoking a purified form of cocaine. — Cleo Odzer, *Goa Freaks*, p. 261, 1995

freebaser *noun*
a user of freebase cocaine *US, 1979*

- [M]ost free basers in North America smoke either through a fire base pipe or off foil[.] — *Hi Life*, p. 78, 1979

freebie *adjective*
free of charge *US, 1946*

- [I]t's the brakeman who throws freebie passengers off[.] — Mezz Mezzrow, *Really the Blues*, p. 256, 1946
- The clubhouse here is kind of cramped and the Yankees would probably sneer at it, but there's a soda fountain—Coca-Cola, root beer, 7-Up, cold, on tap, freebie. — Jim Bouton, *Ball Four*, p. 14, 1970
- [H]e had received no end of crank calls from women wanting freebie obscene phonecalls. — Kitty Churchill, *Thinking of England*, p. 162, 1995

freebie; freeby *noun*
something that is given away at no cost *US, 1928*

- Maybe it was because the meal was a freebie and didn't cost me anything but a song—or I should say, a hymn. — Louis Armstrong, *Satchmo*, p. 92, 1954
- [T]his place is sold out. Freebies are rife[.] — Lester Bangs, *Psychotic Reactions and Carburetor Dung*, p. 209, 1977
- The first freebie I ever gave started with an obscene phone call. — Dolores French, *Working*, p. 39, 1988
- The son of a bitch never paid me. The first time in my life I didn't ask for it up front, that's what happens. I go, "Hey, come on, man, I don't give freebies." He says it was for fun, like I get laid on my day off. — Elmore Leonard, *Maximum Bob*, p. 238, 1991

freedom bird *noun*
an airplane bringing troops back to the US from Vietnam *US, 1971*

- It is traditional for every grunt leaving the bush for the last time—for the freedom bird, home—to get the glory ride. — William Pelfrey, *The Big V*, p. 120, 1972
- Sitting in foxholes that night watching the moon, watching shooting stars and sipping the new clean water, the Freedom Bird and the World didn't look like lies anymore[.] — Charles Anderson, *The Grunts*, p. 77, 1976
- [E]ven as the freedom birds began flying the first 25,000 boys home in June, Charlie Company and scores of line outfits like it were obliged to linger behind[.] — Peter Goldman and Tony Fuller, *Charlie Company*, p. 122, 1983
- And when that year was over, when the "Freedom Bird" took me back to "the world," I learned that my war was just beginning. — Lynda Van Devanter, *Home Before Morning*, p. 4, 1983

free green peppers *noun*
a sneeze by a food preparer *US, 1996*
Limited usage, but clever.

- — *Maledicta*, p. 12, 1996: "Domino's pizza jargon"

freek *noun*
a member of the counter-culture *US, 1972*
The intentional misspelling was seen as a political act.

- Trans-Love Energies Unlimited includes six or eight working communes of freeks of various disciplines[.] — John Sinclair, *Guitar Army*, p. 67, 1972
- None of these [ironies] is greater than the fact that a group of counterculture "freeks," who in search of radical certification, created a largely fictional White Panther Myth[.] — Peter Braunstein, *Imagine Nation: The American Counterculture of the 1960's and 1970's*, p. 151, 2002

freelancer *noun*
a prostitute unattached to either a pimp or a brothel *US, 1973*

- Freelancers operate out of their own apartments, which are usually, like those of madams, located in good buildings in the better neighborhoods. — Bernhardt J. Hurwood, *The Sensuous New York*, p. 17, 1973

- In addition to the freelancers who swiveled past him, rimming their bloody red lips with lascivious tongues, there were ladies of the windows. — Odie Hawkins, *Great Lawd Buddha*, p. 181, 1990

freeload *verb*
to cadge; to subsist at other people's expense *US, 1942*

- I couldn't freeload off her anymore. She was beginning a whole new life, I was just grateful for the time she let me stay with her. — Christy Canyon, *Lights, Camera, Sex!*, p. 205, 2003

freeloader *noun*
a person who manages to eat, drink, and socialize at the expense of others *US, 1936*

- Tell him you don't like freeloaders, either, especially that roommate you had in college who never lifted a finger to pickup a damn thing. — Michael Moore, *Dude, Where's My Country?*, p. 188, 2003

free lunch *noun*
used as a symbol of something that is provided freely *US, 1949*

- It is said that there's no such thing as a free lunch. But the universe is the ultimate free lunch. — Stephen Hawking, *A Brief History of Time*, p. 134, 1996

Freep *nickname*
the Los Angeles *Free Press*; the Detroit *Free Press* *US, 1971*

- — Eugene Landy, *The Underground Dictionary*, p. 83, 1971
- Back at the Trop, Meisner and the boys remained one step above panhandling by selling copies of "the Freep," the Los Angeles Free Press, an alternative weekly newspaper, on the streets of Sunset Boulevard. — Marc Eliot, *To the Limit*, p. 31, 1998
- Clem Grogan was standing with his arms around the ten- or eleven-year-old daughter of a Freep staffer (unbeknownst to her mother), chanting "There is no good, there is no evil." — Ed Sanders, *The Family*, p. 324, 2002

free ride *noun*
1 used as a metaphor for attaining something without effort or cost *US, 1899*

- I wanted the free ride and I wanted to be paid in my own coin[.] — John D. MacDonald, *Free Fall in Crimson*, p. 174, 1981

2 in poker, the right to stay in a hand without further betting, most commonly because the player has bet his entire bankroll on the hand *US, 1963*

- — Irwin Steig, *Common Sense in Poker*, p. 184, 1963

3 an orientation flight on a military aircraft *US, 1983*

- The IP who came to our table would take the four of us on our orientation flight, the only "free ride" in the course. — Robert Mason, *Chickenhawk*, p. 29, 1983

Free Shoes University *noun*
Florida State University *US, 2000*
A back-formation from the initials FSU, playing on the role of athletics and the sponsorship of athletics by a major shoe company at the university.

- Speaking—or in this case thinking—of football, I then wondered, "Who will win the NCAA football title next year?" The Nebraska Cornthuggers (sorry, Huskers) or the Free Shoes University (FSU) Seminoles, or, if you prefer, Free Shirts University. — *The Daily Illini*, p. 1, 5th May 2000

freeside *adjective*
outside prison *US, 1960*

- And I wished I could stop thinking about the free side. The free side—dig that! In the beginning I'd said "outside"; now I said "free side" just like a con. — Piri Thomas, *Down These Mean Streets*, p. 254, 1967

freestyle *verb*
to improvise and perform a rap lyric, often a capella *US, 1995*

- My record is mainly a freestyle album. — *A2Z [quoting Shaquille O'Neal, 1994]*, p. 37, 1995

freeware *noun*
computer software provided free of charge *US, 1983*

- A number of electronic bulletin boards offer "freeware"of various sorts for the cost of copying the program. — *Christian Science Monitor*, p. 17, 22nd March 1983
- Cybersurfers are used to getting things for free online. They regularly download shareware or freeware programs. — Greg Holden, *Starting an Online Business for Dummies*, p. 48, 2002

freeway *noun*
in a prison dormitory, the aisle through the center of the room *US, 1996*

Alluding to the constant foot traffic.

• — Reinhold Aman, *Hillary Clinton's Pen Pal*, p. 38, 1996

freeway surfer *noun*

a person who embraces the mannerisms of surfing, owns the equipment needed to surf, but who chooses to watch from the safety of the car *US, 1987*

• — Mitch McKissick, *Surf Lingo*, 1987

free, white, and 21 *adjective*

possessing free will and able to exercise self-determination *US, 1949*

• "I'm free, white and twenty-one," she said. — Raymond Chandler, *The Little Sister*, p. 75, 1949

• "You don't care what I do, do you?" she cried out. "You're free, white, and twenty-one," Bert answered. — James T. Farrell, *Ruth and Bertram*, p. 105, 1955

• From what I hear they were all free, white and twenty-one. They knew what they were getting into. They were big boys. — George V. Higgins, *The Friends of Eddie Doyle*, pp. 200–201, 1971

• She was free, white and nearly twenty-one. She thought she had nothing to fear from the police. — Charles W. Moore, *A Brick for Mister Jones*, p. 172, 1975

free world *noun*

life outside prison *US, 1960*

• — Bruce Jackson, *Outside the Law*, p. 57, 1972: "glossary"

• I was in the free world for six weeks. — Jack Henry Abbott, *In the Belly of the Beast*, p. 4, 1981

free-world *adjective*

civilian; from outside prison *US, 1966*

• "These free-world people would crawl over their dying mammies to whip you out of two bucks." — Malcolm Braly, *It's Cold Out There*, p. 160, 1966

• One day a week a free-world dentist comes in to do the major work. — Bruce Jackson, *Outside the Law*, p. 159, 1972

free-world gal *noun*

a male prisoner who practiced homosexuality before entering prison *US, 1972*

• A free-world gal, she's not going to mess with any of them rums anyway. — Bruce Jackson, *Outside the Law*, p. 173, 1972

• — Charles Shafer, *Folk Speech in Texas Prisons*, p. 204, 1990

free-world punk *noun*

a male prisoner who engaged in homosexual sex before prison *US, 1972*

• We classify them two ways: penitentiary punk and free-world punk. — Bruce Jackson, *Outside the Law*, p. 176, 1972

freeze *noun*

1 cocaine *US, 1984*

From the numbing, cooling effect.

• — R.C Garrett et al., *The Coke Book*, p. 200, 1984

2 a small amount of cocaine placed on the tongue *US, 1989*

• They snort a bit, "take a freeze" (place a pinch of cocaine on the tongue), chat another minute or two, then go in to see Chillie. — Terry Williams, *The Cocaine Kids*, p. 29, 1989

3 a rejection of affection *US, 1942*

Colder than the proverbial "cold shoulder."

• For nights that seemed like years the Dukes had given Frank the freeze. — Irving Shulman, *The Amboy Dukes*, p. 188, 1947

• She gave me the big freeze when I said hello that day, though. — J.D. Salinger, *Catcher in the Rye*, p. 77, 1951

freeze *verb*

in draw poker, to decline the opportunity to discard and draw any new cards *US, 1971*

• — Thomas L. Clark, *The Dictionary of Gambling and Gaming*, p. 85, 1987

▸ **freeze your nose**

to use cocaine *US, 1972*

From the drug's numbing effect on mucus membranes.

• But almost all I know like to sniff coke—they call it freezing their noses — Bruce Jackson, *Outside the Law*, 1972

freeze-out *noun*

a poker game in which all participants must play until they lose all their money or win all the other players' money *US, 1975*

• Nick and Ryan, it developed, had been in a poker game in Las Vegas, a 250,000-dollar freeze-out. — Jimmy Snyder, *Jimmy the Greek*, p. 197, 1975

freezer *noun*

in poker, an early call made even as other players continue to raise their bets *US, 1967*

• — Albert H. Morehead, *The Complete Guide to Winning Poker*, p. 263, 1967

freeze up *verb*

to become paralyzed with fear *US, 1989*

An occupational hazard of those who work high above the ground.

• "You can see he isn't doing nothing but standing there," the raising-gang foreman said. "He's froze-up. He wouldn't stand there like that if he wasn't froze-up. Would he?" — Elmore Leonard, *Killshot*, p. 140, 1989

freight *noun*

the cost of something, especially a bribe *US, 1950*

• — Hyman E. Goldin et al., *Dictionary of American Underworld Lingo*, p. 74, 1950

freight bomber *noun*

a graffiti artist specializing in writing on freight train cars *US, 1994*

• The Red Line runs alongside freight tracks (Conrail, for all your freight bombers). — William Upski Wimsatt, *Bomb the Suburbs*, p. 43, 1994

freight burner *noun*

graffiti on a freight train car *US, 1994*

• Futura 2000, one of Graffiti's early visionaries, who in 1986 helped paint the Detroit Art Train, a permission piece which was the first multi-car freight burner. — William Upski Wimsatt, *Bomb the Suburbs*, p. 135, 1994

freight train *noun*

a wave breaking powerfully in perfect formation *US, 1987*

• — Mitch McKissick, *Surf Lingo*, 1987

French *noun*

1 oral sex, especially on a man *US, 1916*

• I say, Yoo-hoo, pitty baby, you wanna lil french? Haff an haff? How about jes a straight? I say, Twenty berries an you alla roun the mothahfuggin worl'. — Robert Gover, *One Hundred Dollar Misunderstanding*, p. 21, 1961

• "[I]f he just wants a straight fuck or a straight French, then I say, "Why don't you spend a little extra, and we have a good time?" — John Warren Wells, *Tricks of the Trade*, p. 63, 1970

• And it was so funny, because they would describe you as Greek, active/passive; French, active/passive—French being blow jobs and Greek being fucked. — James Ridgeway, *Red Light*, p. 222, 1996

• Neither she or Marie talked of "French" (i.e., oral sex) being in demand with Dublin men. — Fiona Pitt-Kethley, *Red Light Districts of the World*, p. 36, 2000

2 an open-mouthed, French kiss *US, 1978*

• "Yes," I said grimly, "a French kiss, he tried for French." — Terry Southern, *Now Dig This*, p. 220, 1978

3 profanity *US, 1865*

• Pardon my French but you're an asshole! — *Ferris Bueller's Day Off*, 1986

• And I said yeah, walked straight into the fucking twilight zone. Pardon my French. — Carl Hiaasen, *Skin Tight*, p. 115, 1989

French *verb*

1 to perform oral sex *US, 1923*

The term derives from the widely held belief that the practice is very common in France.

• All I needed to do was to French just one. She then passed on the word to the others. — *Screw*, p. 5, 7th March 1969

• Here, again, is an advantage of Frenching. If a man's not hard, you can't have intercourse with him, but you can suck him. — John Warren Wells, *Tricks of the Trade*, p. 27, 1970

• "I thought I Frenched him to death," she said. "Oh, mercy." "You may have Frenched him into a coma," I told her. — Lawrence Block, *Chip Harrison Scores Again*, p. 222, 1971

• All other junky prostitutes I knew preferred to french their dates. In fact, getting on their back was the last thing they ever wanted to do. — Robert Deane Pharr, *S.R.O.*, p. 147, 1971

2 to French kiss; to kiss with open lips and exploratory tongues *US, 1955*

• Dr. Sommers narrated as the two Frenched, fondled, and took a bubble bath[.] — Anka Radakovich, *The Wild Girls Club*, p. 114, 1994

• I can't believe you let him French you! — *200 Cigarettes*, 1999

French artist *noun*
a person skilled at oral sex US, 1963
- And she was the first french artist to work there for less than $5 a throw. — Madam Sherry, *Pleasure Was My Business*, p. 147, 1963

French culture *noun*
oral sex US, 1975
- French Culture (Fr) = oral sex — Stephen Lewis, *The Whole Bedroom Catalog*, p. 144, 1975

French date *noun*
oral sex performed on a man by a prostitute US, 1972
- At the hotel, if it's a straight date it's usually $10, and a French date, a blow job, is $20. — Bruce Jackson, *Outside the Law*, p. 186, 1972

French deck *noun*
a deck of cards decorated with art ranging from naughty and nude to pornographic US, 1963
- At the end of 1966, he bought thirteen of the old machines, offering fifty-fifty splits to the several existing bookshops whose most extreme material were under-the-counter nudist volumes, girlie playing cards (French Decks), and Times Square standards[.] — Josh Alan Friedman, *Tales of Times Square*, pp. 74–75, 1986

French dip *noun*
precoital vaginal secretions US, 1986–1987
- — *Maledicta*, p. 55, 1986–1987: "A continuation of a glossary of ethnic slurs in American English."

French dressing *noun*
semen US, 1986–1987
An allusion to FRENCH (oral sex).
- — *Maledicta*, p. 55, 1986–1987

French Embassy *noun*
a premises of the Young Men's Christian Association US, 1963
An allusion to the association between the YMCA and homosexual men who enjoy FRENCH (oral sex).
- "They don't call this Y the French Embassy for nothing," the merchant marine laughs. — John Rechy, *City of Night*, p. 25, 1963
- — *Maledicta*, p. 218, 1979: "kinks and queens: linguistic and cultural aspects of the terminology for gays."

French fries *noun*
3 inch sticks of crack cocaine with ridged edges US, 1993
- — Peter Johnson, *Dictionary of Street Alcohol and Drug Terms*, p. 77, 1993

French harp *noun*
a harmonica US, 1983
- [T]he French harp was given to him by a "colored shoeshine boy" he met in a barbershop. — Joe Klein, *Woody Guthrie*, p. 27, 1980

French inhale *verb*
to draw cigarette smoke into the mouth and then allow it to drift out and upwards for inhalation through the nose US, 1957
The French credit is presumably to signal how sophisticated such a technique is thought to be.
- She lifts up her sunglasses and then French-inhales while she stares at Mrs. Williams' hair. — Rebecca Wells, *Little Altars Everywhere*, p. 87, 1992

French joint *noun*
an over-sized, conical marijuana cigarette US, 1997
- — Jim Emerson-Cobb, *Scratching the Dragon*, April 1997

French kiss *verb*
to kiss with the mouth open and the tongue active US, 1918
- One of the boys had a lot of experience with girls, and he told me about French or tongue kissing[.] — Phyllis and Eberhard Kronhausen, *Sex Histories of American College Men*, p. 124, 1960
- The only thing suspect about his innocence was his tendency to French-kiss given the slightest opening[.] — Glendon Swarthout, *Where the Boys Are*, p. 112, 1960
- Any American schoolboy knows what a French kiss is, and a bright one can also describe a French tickler. — Allan Sherman, *The Rape of the APE*, p. 5, 1973

French lay *noun*
oral sex US, 1972
- All the sex is extra. How about a French lay? / (But, but, my massage!) Well, here goes my pay. — *Screw*, p. 7, 15th May 1972

French lessons *noun*
oral sex US, 1970
- — Robert J. Glessing, *The Underground Press in America*, p. 176, 1970: "Glossary of terms used in the underground press"
- Instead of soliciting passing males, the hookers of London remained out of sight, if not out of mind, advertising their services on discreetly euphemistic postcards in the windows of local newsagents. "French Lessons," "Large Chest for Sale," "Stocks and Bonds," "Remedial Discipline by Stern Governess"—the oblique side of obvious, with a local phone number. — Mick Farren, *Give the Anarchist a Cigarette*, 2001

French postcard *noun*
a photographic postcard depicting anything ranging from simple female nudity to full-blown sexual activity US, 1926
- "I thought you had some French postcards," Rick said jokingly. — Evan Hunter, *The Blackboard Jungle*, p. 179, 1954
- — *Maledicta*, p. 159, 1979: "A glossary of ethnic slurs in American English"

French safe *noun*
a condom US, 1870
- "French safes" (meaning condoms), they were uncharitably called. — Robert MacNeil, *Looking for My Country*, p. 33, 2003

French tickler *noun*
a condom with external protrusions marketed as giving pleasure to the wearer's partner US, 1916
- I was heading out the door when he called after me, "And don't come back without French ticklers." — *Eros*, p. 39, Autumn 1962
- Because of the uncertain legal status of the real French tickler in this country, I have been unable to find a U.S. manufacturer or distributor who sells them openly. — Roger Blake, *The Stimulators*, p. 177, 1968
- Any American schoolboy knows what a French kiss, and a bright one can also describe a French tickler. — Allan Sherman, *The Rape of the APE*, p. 5, 1973
- The "french tickler" has a noble heritage[.] — Stephen Lewis, *The Whole Bedroom Catalog*, p. 105, 1975

French trick *noun*
oral sex performed by a prostitute US, 1972
- A quick French trick for $10 and if they wanted to stand up and perform the act, it was $20. — Bruce Jackson, *In the Life*, p. 389, 1972

Frenchy; Frenchie *noun*
1 a fundamentally honest gambler who will cheat occasionally if the right opportunity arises US, 1961
- — Thomas L. Clark, *The Dictionary of Gambling and Gaming*, p. 85, 1987

2 an act of oral-genital sex US, 1957
- — John M. Murtagh and Sara Harris, *Cast the First Stone*, p. 259, 1957: "Glossary"
- Okay, but only a quick Frenchie. Give me the hundred. — Edwin Torres, *Q & A*, p. 169, 1977

frequency *noun*
a level of understanding US, 1959
- Marv felt the warm heat of her heart through his crossed hands. "I'm on your frequency, doll." — Irving Shulman, *College Confidential*, p. 79, 1960
- He's just not on my frequency, period. — Frederick Kohner, *Gidget Goes Hawaiian*, p. 2, 1961
- We are tuning in to one another more and more, and finding, to our communal delight, that we are all on the same frequency! — Sue Ellen Cooper, *The Red Hat Society*, p. 89, 2004

frequently outwitted by inanimate objects *adjective*
extremely incompetent US, 1986
US naval aviator usage.
- — *United States Naval Institute Proceedings*, p. 108, October 1986

fresh *verb*
to flatter US, 1989
- All the kids would rap, charm (talk to), or game to impress girlfriends; hang it up (insult) or fresh (compliment) male friends by using special words. — Terry Williams, *The Cocaine Kids*, p. 90, 1989

fresh *adjective*
good, sharp, stylish US, 1984
Possibly shortened from "We're fresh out the pack / so you gotta stay back, / we got one Puerto Rican / and the rest are black," an early 1980s signature routine by Grand Wizard Theodore and the Fantastic 5 MCs.

- — Bradley Elfman, *Breakdancing*, p. 40, 1984
- — Connie Eble (Editor), *UNC-CH Campus Slang*, p. 3, Fall 1984
- It must be a secret place to keep the squares out and let the hip, fresh and chill crowds in. — Terry Williams, *The Cocaine Kids*, p. 97, 1989
- Lookin' fresh tonight, Pussy-Kat. — *Ten Things I Hate About You*, 1999

freshener *noun*
any alcoholic drink *US, 1969*
- "Fresheners," Nancy said. "Tighteners and fresheners. Sometimes drinkees or martin-eyes." — Elmore Leonard, *The Big Bounce*, p. 88, 1969

fresh-fucked *adjective*
energized and happy, whether the result of recent sex or not *US, 1994*
- — Michael Dalton Johnson, *Talking Trash with Redd Foxx*, p. 69, 1994

fresh meat *noun*
1 a newly arrived prisoner, seen as a sexual object *US, 1998*
- "Fresh meat, fresh meat," we heard the inmates shouting almost as soon as we walked into the section assigned for sixteen- and seventeen-year-olds. — Eric Davis, *The Slick Boys*, p. 95, 1998
2 a newly met candidate for sexual conquest *US, 1967*
- The man also sees himself performing better with "new meat" or "fresh meat" than with someone familiar to him sexually. — Elliot Liebow, *Tally's Corner*, p. 122, 1967
3 a newly arrived soldier *US, 1908*
Also referred to as "new meat."
- Well I'll be dipped in shit—new meat! — *Platoon*, 1986
- "Was countin' my days from the moment I stepped off the plane with all the other 'fresh meat.'" — Lynda Van DEvanter, *Home Before Morning*, p. 76, 2001

fresh money *noun*
in horse racing, the cash actually brought to the track and bet on a given day *US, 1947*
- — Dan Parker, *The ABC of Horse Racing*, p. 146, 1947
- — Bob and Barbara Freeman, *Wanta Bet? A Study of the Pari-Mutuels System in the United States*, p. 290, 1982

fresh stock *noun*
an underage prostitute *US, 1971*
- Younger girls were often called "stock," and those under fifteen were "fresh stock." — Charles Winick, *The Lively Commerce*, p. 140, 1971

fress *verb*
to eat greedily or to excess *US, 1968*
From the German for "devour."
- — Leo Rosten, *The Joys of Yiddish*, p. 120, 1968
- We're still doing OK on the fressing front. — *San Francisco Chronicle*, 21st October 1987

frick and frack *noun*
the testicles *US, 1980*
Frick and Frack (Werner Groebli and Hans Mauch) were a Swiss comedy skating duo from the 1930s.
- — Edith A. Folb, *runnin' down some lines*, p. 238, 1980

fridge *noun*
a refrigerator *US, 1926*
- Do you like the kitchen? There's an enormous fridge, and they give you all your silver. — Richard Farina, *Been Down So Long*, p. 20, 1966
- It's nice to meet you all. There's Cokes in the fridge. — *Bill and Ted's Excellent Adventure*, 1989
- They'd bug my sisters, look for porno tapes in my dad's closet, raid our fridge. — *Chasing Amy*, 1997

fried *adjective*
1 drunk or drug-intoxicated *US, 1923*
- "A customer comes out," Frank said, "Absolutely fried." — Elmore Leonard, *Swag*, p. 67, 1976
- [H]e and Aunt Helen drove down from San Francisco high on peyote all night and showed up at our front door the next morning fried out of their minds. — Eve Babitz, *L.A. Woman*, p. 66, 1982
- On Saturday night, Shelby lost most of his in a biker's bar in National City, too fried on crystal meth to be gambling on a game of pool, but doing it nonetheless. — Joseph Wambaugh, *Finnegan's Week*, p. 137, 1993
- It is one thing to spark up a dubie and get laced at parties, but it is quite another to be fried all day. — *Clueless*, 1995

2 in computing, not working because of a complete hardware failure *US, 1981*
- — Guy L. Steele, *Coevolution Quarterly*, p. 31, Spring 1981: "Computer slang"

fried, dried, and swept aside *adjective*
said of bleached hair that suggests straw *US, 1997*
- — Anna Scotti and Paul Young, *Buzzwords*, p. 104, 1997

fried, dyed, combed (swooped) to the side *adjective*
used as a description of a black person's hair that has been chemically straightened *US, 1980*
- — Edith A. Folb, *runnin' down some lines*, p. 238, 1980

fried egg *noun*
the insignia of the US Military Academy *US, 1908*
- — Lou Shelly, *Hepcats Jive Talk Dictionary*, p. 45, 1945

friend *noun*
in poker, any card that improves a hand *US, 1988*
- — George Percy, *The Language of Poker*, p. 37, 1988

friendlies *noun*
allied military forces or those serving under the same flag *US, 1967*
- "Unless the friendlies have their ass in a crack, no target is worth a man or a bird." — Elaine Shepard, *The Doom Pussy*, p. 51, 1967

friendly *adjective*
used as a coded euphemism for "passive" in sadomasochistic sex *US, 1986–1987*
- — *Maledicta*, p. 164, Summer/Winter 1986–1987: "Sexual slang: prostitutes, pedophiles, flagellators, transvestites, and necrophiles"

fries *noun*
pieces of crack cocaine *US, 1994*
Shortened from **FRENCH FRIES**.
- — US Department of Justice, *Street Terms*, October 1994

frig *verb*
1 to masturbate *UK, 1598*
- The joy-juice flies as these girls suck, frig their clits, and ready their assholes for cock. — *Adult Video*, p. 66, August/September 1986
2 to dawdle or waste time *US, 1975*
- A Maine lady of unimpeachable gentility once described her late husband as nervous and ill at ease in public, and said he would sit "frigging with his necktie." — John Gould, *Maine Lingo*, p. 102, 1975
3 used now as a euphemism for "fuck" in all its senses *UK, 1879*
- Yeah, that's a gone coat, but frig it, where's the water? — Hal Ellson, *The Golden Spike*, p. 138, 1952

frigging *adjective*
used as a euphemism for "fucking," usually as an intensifier *UK, 1893*
With variant "fricking."
- It don't make a damn frigging difference whether you're in The Place or hiking up Matterhorn, it's all the same old void, boy. — Jack Kerouac, *The Dharma Bums*, p. 45, 1958
- Especially when a bunch of friggin' Texans got together to kill the Indian agent and scare the bands off the Brazos. — Clancy Sigal, *Going Away*, p. 108, 1961
- [I]t's getting so I can't install the simplest frigging component but what I need a bracer. — Ken Kesey, *One Flew Over the Cuckoo's Nest*, p. 55, 1962
- I have one simple request—sharks with friggin' laser beams attached to their heads, and it can't be done? — *Austin Powers*, 1997

frig off *verb*
to go away, to leave *US, 1961*
Often in the imperative.
- He gave me the look. "Frig off," I said. "Bite me," he whispered. — Sheree Fitch, *One More Step*, p. 22, 2002

frig up *verb*
to botch, to ruin *US, 1933*
- Sometimes it does an even better job when the person in charge isn't there to frig it up[.] — Stephen King, *Dolores Claiborne*, p. 62, 1993

fringe *noun*
thin strips of material attached to the G-string worn by a striptease dancer *US, 1981*
- — Don Wilmeth, *The Language of American Popular Entertainment*, p. 97, 1981

fringe *verb*
to get something from somebody else by imposing on their hospitality or generosity *US*, *1947*
- — Marcus Hanna Boulware, *Jive and Slang of Students in Negro Colleges*, 1947

fringed *adjective*
excluded *US*, *1961*
- Fringed—left out of something. — Art Unger, *The Cool Book*, p. 106, 1961

fringes *noun*
the eyes *US*, *1947*
- — Marcus Hanna Boulware, *Jive and Slang of Students in Negro Colleges*, 1947

fringie *noun*
a person on the fringes of a gang, not a hardcore member *US*, *1966*
- — Jennifer Blowdryer, *Modern English*, p. 61, 1985

frip *adjective*
lousy *US*, *1949*
Youth usage.
- — *Time*, 3rd October 1949

Frisco *nickname*
San Francisco, California *US*, *1849*
Never used by San Franciscans.
- In which case, if you came to Frisco, I could still see you and Allen, but couldn't ship out. — Jack Kerouac, *Letter to Neal Cassady*, p. 114, 26th August 1947
- Frantic Frisco, yes, frenzied Frisco, yes, Fateful Frisco. Frisco of frivolous folly. — Neal Cassady, *Neal Cassady Collected Letters 1944–1967*, p. 122, 3rd July 1949: Letter to Jack Kerouac
- Hell, I could get a farm someplace, maybe out near Frisco with Hart Kennedy. — John Clellon Holmes, *Go*, p. 51, 1952
- She had me out to Frisco for two weeks over the New Year's holidays. — Babs Gonzales, *Movin' On Down De Line*, p. 148, 1975

Frisco speedball; Frisco special; San Francisco bomb *noun*
a combination of cocaine, heroin, and LSD *US*, *1969*
Up, down and out—all at once; a combination of a **SPEEDBALL** (cocaine and heroin) with the drug that made **FRISCO** (San Francisco) psychedelic.
- — Carl D. Chambers and Richard D. Heckman, *Employee Drug Abuse*, p. 205, 1972
- FRISCO SPEEDBALL: cocaine, LSD, and heroin. — Michael V. Reagen, *Readings on Drug Education*, p. 57, 1972
- His range was extensive—beginning with New Jersey pot, and ending with something called a "Frisco Speedball," a concoction of heroin and cocaine, with a touch of acid ("gives it a little color"). — Terry Southern, *Red Dirt Marijuana*, p. 240, 1990

frisky powder *noun*
cocaine *US*, *1955*
- Cocaine is referred to in the underworld as: "Snow," "Cecil," "Cob," "Frisky powder[.]" — Senate Committee on the Judiciary, *Illicit Narcotics Traffic*, 1955
- — *American Speech*, p. 87, May 1955: "Narcotic argot along the Mexican border"
- It is known by such names as snow, cecil, frisky powder, coke, chalk, Carrie Nation, and C. — John G. Nelson, *Preliminary Investigation and Police Reporting*, p. 414, 1970

Frito *noun*
a woman who is sexually expert *US*, *1967*
A pun on the Frito Lay company name—a "good lay."
- — *Current Slang*, p. 14, Fall 1967

fritterware *noun*
computer software that is seductive to users, consumes time, and adds little to functionality *US*, *1991*
- — Eric S. Raymond, *The New Hacker's Dictionary*, p. 168, 1991

fritz *noun*
► **on the fritz**
broken *US*, *1902*
- Even though the air conditioning in Dad's Beamer was on the fritz, he made us ride over with the windows up so the other motorists wouldn't think he didn't have any. — C.D. Payne, *Youth in Revolt*, p. 14, 1977
- His car's been on the fritz and he borrowed a Cadillac from someone. — Janet Evanovich, *Seven Up*, p. 43, 2001

fritz *verb*
to break *US*, *1918*
- [S]omething fritzed the gates. Goddamn things closed on the Rolls before it was through. — Robert Campbell, *In La-La Land We Trust*, p. 49, 1986

friznaughti *adjective*
drug-intoxicated *US*, *1995*
- I got me a dubie and I'ma get friznaughti tonight — *A2Z, the Book of Rap and Hip-Hip Slang*, 1995

'fro *noun*
a bushy Afro hair style *US*, *1970*
- — *Current Slang*, p. 7, Fall 1970
- I don't know how anybody could've recognized us, you especially with that 'fro. — Elmore Leonard, *Freaky Deaky*, p. 35, 1988

frob *noun*
any small object *US*, *1991*
- — Eric S. Raymond, *The New Hacker's Dictionary*, p. 168, 1991

frob *verb*
to manipulate dials or settings *US*, *1983*
- When I questioned our local computer wizard about what she meant when she said she was going to frob my workstation, she gave me this tutorial on hackerese. — Steven Pinker, *The Language Instinct*, p. 163, 1994

frobnicate *verb*
to manipulate dials or settings *US*, *1983*
- — Gilbert Held, *The Complete Cyberspace Reference*, p. 6, 1994

frobnitz *noun*
any device the name of which is unknown, escapes the speaker's mind, or is not relevant *US*, *1991*
- — Eric S. Raymond, *The New Hacker's Dictionary*, p. 169, 1991

frock *verb*
to decorate as a military officer *US*, *1986*
From the C19 sense of "investing with priestly office."
- The message announced tersely that Lieutenant Commander Robert A. Toland, III. USNR, had been "frocked" as a commander, USNR, which gave him the right to wear the three gold stripes of a commander[.] — Tom Clancy, *Red Storm Rising*, p. 124, 1986
- Regardless of the H's and I's on my fitreps, I'd finally been frocked for captain in February 1985. — Richard Marcinko and John Weisman, *Rogue Warrior*, p. 284, 1992

frog *noun*
1 a social outcast *US*, *1968*
- Frog originally meant a first semester freshman, but this use is becoming archaic. Its use today is usually derisive or derogatory. — Fred Hester, *Slang on the 40 Acres*, p. 6, 1968
2 a promiscuous girl *US*, *1995*
- — Bill Valentine, *Gang Intelligence Manual*, p. 76, 1995: "Black street gang terminology"
3 one dollar *US*, *1962*
- — Frank Garcia, *Marked Cards and Loaded Dice*, p. 262, 1962

Frog *noun*
a person from France *UK*, *1778*
Like all the "frog" terms for the French, it refers to the eating of frogs.
- You went the distance for the fab frog poet. — Terry Southern, *Now Dig This*, p. 232, 1989
- This was the same Frog who threatened to phone the consulate every time he got stopped for ripping around Mission Bay like a Paris cabbie in one of those dopey little Citroens, fit only for delivery of car bombs by neurotic Arabs. — Joseph Wambaugh, *Floaters*, p. 2, 1996

frog *verb*
to fail (a test or exam) *US*, *1968*
- — Mary Swift, *Campus Slang (University of Texas)*, 1968

Frog *adjective*
French *US*, *1910*
Said with unkind intentions.
- Back to Chicago we drove that very night to prepare for our grand tour of the Continent, Danny coaching us in the Frog lingo all the way home so we could gab with the parlay-voo's when we landed in good old Paree. — Mezz Mezzrow, *Really the Blues*, p. 129, 1946
- I suppose the Frog movie must be over by now. — C.D. Payne, *Youth in Revolt*, p. 403, 1993

frog!
used for expressing disgust *US, 1991*
- — Eric S. Raymond, *The New Hacker's Dictionary*, p. 169, 1991

Froggie; Froggy *noun*
a person from France *US, 1870s*
- The Froggie scampered across the boatyard to the fence, yelling, "No! You shall not to fo-toe le keel!" — Joseph Wambaugh, *Floaters*, p. 2, 1996

froggy *adjective*
aggressive *US, 1939*
- There were a couple of other guys in the group that might get froggy if someone leaped[.] — Joseph Wambaugh, *The Blue Knight*, p. 68, 1973
- — Edith A. Folb, *runnin' down some lines*, p. 238, 1980

frog hair *noun*
a very short distance *US, 1958*
- He'd jump all over the stage swiping wildly at the air, come within a frog hair of splatting his fist in to the chafing dish a dozen times[.] — Katherine Dunn, *Greek Love*, p. 250, 1989

frog-march; frog's march *verb*
to push someone forward holding them by their collar and the seat of their pants *UK, 1884*
- I wonder what the cop would think if I began jumping with glee and yelling: "Frog's march him! For God's sake, frog's march him!" — Terry Southern, *Now Dig This*, p. 158, 1972
- Gripping Archie under the arm, the undercover cop frogmarched him to the end of the causeway and down the steep steps to Kearny Street. — Seth Morgan, *Homeboy*, p. 205, 1990

frog salad *noun*
in carnival usage, any performance that features scantily clad women *US, 1981*
Originally recorded (1904) by Farmer and Henley as American slang for a ballet.
- It is an old joke in the United States that whenever there is a great "leg piece," sometimes called a "frog salad" (i.e., a ballet with unusual opportunities for studying anatomy), the front seats are invariably filled with veteran roués. — Sherman Louis Sergel, *The Language of Show Biz*, p. 15, 1973
- — Don Wilmeth, *The Language of American Popular Entertainment*, p. 101, 1981

frogskin *noun*
money; paper money; a one-dollar bill *US, 1902*
- Forty thousand frogskins went flying down the fairway. — Sam Snead, *The Education of a Golfer*, p. 168, 1962
- Why couldn't it be me up there in that crazy pad with my mitt out for all those frog skins? — Iceberg Slim (Robert Beck), *Pimp*, p. 135, 1969

frogskins *noun*
a wetsuit and other cold-water garments *US, 1991*
- — Trevor Cralle, *The Surfin'ary*, p. 42, 1991

frogsticker *noun*
a knife *US, 1972*
- "Lee-roy," the Kingfish says, icy, "put that damn frog-sticker away." — Guy Owen, *The Flim-Flam Man and the Apprentice Grifter*, p. 113, 1972

frog-strangler *noun*
a torrential downpour *US, 1942*
- Now I really understood what the phrases "coming down in buckets," "raining in sheets," and "frog strangler" meant. — Frank E. Walton, *Once They Were Eagles*, p. 31, 1986

frog-walk *verb*
to forcefully carry somebody face down *US, 1960*
- Bernard B. O'Hare, of course, was the young man who had captured me at the end of the war, who had frog-walked me through the death camp at Ohrdruf[.] — Kurt Vonnegut, *Mother Night*, p. 61, 1966

from here to there without a pair
in poker, used for describing a hand of sequenced cards *US, 1951*
Conventionally known as a "straight."
- — *American Speech*, p. 98, May 1951

frompy *adjective*
unattractive *US, 1948*
- — Jack Lait and Lee Mortimer, *New York Confidential*, p. 235, 1948: "A glossary of Harlemisms"

from way downtown—bang
used as a humorous comment on a witty remark, a correct answer, or other verbal victory *US, 1997*
Coined by ESPN's Keith Olberman to describe three-point shots in basketball.
- — Keith Olberman and Dan Patrick, *The Big Show*, p. 14, 1997

frone *noun*
an ugly woman *US, 1947*
- — Marcus Hanna Boulware, *Jive and Slang of Students in Negro Colleges*, 1947

front *noun*
1 a decorative tooth cap *US, 2006*
- The teeth caps are alternately called grills, fronts, shines, plates, or caps, and these glittering decorative pieces are the latest hip-hop culture trend making its way into the mainstream. — *Boston Globe*, p. C1, 31st January 2006

2 a man's suit jacket *US, 1971*
- Had on a cocoa front. — Michael H. Agar, *The Journal of American Folklore*, p. 177, April 1971

3 a person's public appearance; stylish clothing *US, 1899*
- A European charm of manner and a slight Scandinavian accent completed his front. — William Burroughs, *Junkie*, p. 43, 1953
- I layed off for another four months, but I was able to keep up a front by doing weekends in "Jersey" and "Connecticut." — Babs Gonzales, *I Paid My Dues*, p. 61, 1967
- Everybody in both worlds kissed your ass black and blue if you had flash and front. — Iceberg Slim (Robert Beck), *Pimp*, p. 118, 1969
- Despite his four years in The Life, Mojo has not yet been able to get his "front" together[.] — Christina and Richard Milner, *Black Players*, p. 146, 1972

4 the beginning *US, 1959*
Especially in the phrase "from the front."
- — Lawrence Lipton, *The Holy Barbarians*, p. 316, 1959

▸ **break your front**
to deviate from a projected image of yourself *US, 1981*
- Nothing ever tempted him to break his front. Nothing riled him[.] — Alix Shulman, *On the Stroll*, p. 159, 1981

▸ **out front**
owing someone who has extended goods to you for payment later *US, 1989*
- People be telling him nobody be staying out front for too long. — Terry Williams, *The Cocaine Kids*, p. 44, 1989

▸ **up front**
in advance *US, 1970*
- "I want the five up front," Joe Loop said, "or Nick can do the guy himself." — Elmore Leonard, *Be Cool*, p. 127, 1999

front *verb*
1 to vouch for *US, 1951*
- I was glad to have a convict with Connie's prestige "front" for me with the general population[.] — Donald Wilson, *My Six Convicts*, p. 26, 1951

2 to lie; to project a false image of yourself *US, 1967*
- And everyone is observing, but they're all fronting. They don't want to show anyone they're cowards. — John Gimenez, *Up Tight!*, p. 38, 1967
- And if you want to be there, in that club, The Society of Big-Dicked Agents, then you gotta front like you belong. — John Ridley, *Everybody Smokes in Hell*, p. 33, 1999

3 to provide something of value to someone with the expectation of being paid later *US, 1989*
- Various terms are employed to describe this: suppliers may say they give cocaine "on credit" or as a "loan" to distributors; at all levels, it is called "fronting." — Terry Williams, *The Cocaine Kids*, p. 34, 1989

4 to back down from a physical confrontation *US, 1987*
- — Carsten Stroud, *Close Pursuit*, p. 272, 1987

5 to pretend, to fake *US, 1993*
- So don't front like you don't know what my name is[.] — Akinyele *Checkmate*, 1993

front butt *noun*
an obese pelvic area *US, 2002*
- "Is that woman pregnant or does she have a front butt?" — *Dictionary of New Terms (Hope College)*, 2002
- "You wanna see some front butt, honey? When I wear my orange stretch capris, you can't tell whether I'm a-comin' or a'goin'!" — Celia Riverbank, *Stop Dressing Your Six-Year-Old Like a Skank*, p. 148, 2006

front door *noun*

the vagina *UK, 1890*

As opposed to the **BACK DOOR** (the rectum).

- Though advised Dale to get laid tonight; be his last shot at some front-door lovin'. Dale wouldn't talk about it. — Elmore Leonard, *Maximum Bob*, p. 200, 1991

front doormat *noun*

a woman's pubic hair *UK, 1980*

- — *Maledicta*, p. 183, Winter 1980: "A new erotic vocabulary"

fronter *noun*

1 an inexperienced swindler working on a scam by telephone who makes the initial call to potential victims *US, 1988*

- — Kathleen Odean, *High Steppers, Fallen Angels, and Lollipops*, p. 132, 1988

2 a person who appears to be something he is not and who does not deliver on promised action *US, 1997*

- — *Newsday*, p. B2, 11th October 1997

front-liner *noun*

a person in a youth gang who is capable of murder *US, 1995*

- — Bill Valentine, *Gang Intelligence Manual*, p. 110, 1995: "Jamaican Gang Terminology"

front man *noun*

someone who is employed to cover for a criminal operation by posing as the legitimate owner/leader or by acting as spokesperson *US, 1934*

- "Legally, a 'front man' could eliminate the actual owner, but this is seldom if ever done." — Frederic Sondern Jr., *Brotherhood of Evil*, p. 43, 1959

front money *noun*

1 money paid in advance for the purchase of drugs *US, 1963*

- He demanded "front money" (an advance) and was uneasy over "back money" (arrears). — John A. Williams, *Sissie*, p. 71, 1963
- "I need front money for the first load of snow," Mona said. — Gerald Petievich, *The Quality of the Informant*, p. 6, 1985

2 money needed to start a venture *US, 1925*

- "Here's some of the front money," he said. "Bet you thought I was gonna try and use your maxed-out Visa card." — Stephen Cannell, *King Con*, p. 110, 1997

front off *verb*

1 to place yourself in a highly visible position *US, 1960*

- "Yeah, you! You go." "Why me? Why do I have to front myself off when it's my idea?" — Clarence Cooper Jr., *The Scene*, p. 61, 1960
- All they wanted to do was front off being in the Panther Party and rap to the sisters. — Bobby Seale, *Seize the Time*, p. 367, 1970
- "Hey, aren't you the one who likes to lecture me about not fronting people off?" — Jimmy Lerner, *You Got Nothing Coming*, p. 86, 2002

2 to sell drugs on credit *US, 1995*

- — Mark S. Fleisher, *Beggars & Thieves*, p. 289, 1995: "Glossary"

front porch *noun*

1 the area immediately outside a prison cell *US, 2002*

- [T]he cell door cracked open and we put the empty trays outside (on the "front porch") for the porters to pick up. — Jimmy Lerner, *You Got Nothing Coming*, p. 72, 2002

2 in poker, the earliest position in a hand *US, 1996*

- — John Vorhaus, *The Big Book of Poker Slang*, p. 19, 1996

front-row Charlie *noun*

a regular audience member at a striptease show *US, 1972*

- The lines the strippers threw at the front-row Charlies: "Take your hot little hands outta your pockets, boys." — Georgia Sothern, *My Life in Burlesque*, p. 32, 1972

front-running *noun*

support given to a person or team only when they are doing well *US, 1970*

- Front running is not limited to coaches. — Jim Bouton, *Ball Four*, p. 157, 1970

fronts *noun*

legitimate, square, unaltered dice *US, 1950*

- — *The Annals of the American Academy of Political and Social Sciences*, p. 125, May 1950

front saddlebags *noun*

the female breasts *US, 2005*

- Allegra takes off her top, showing her front saddlebags. — Mr. Skin, *Mr. Skin's Skincyclopedia*, p. 126, 2005

front street *noun*

▶ **on front street**

in the open; in public *US, 1992*

- — William K. Bentley and James M. Corbett, *Prison Slang*, p. 32, 1992
- I'll never tell Mary anything again. She always puts my business on Front Street. — Connie Eble (Editor), *UNC-CH Campus Slang*, p. 3, November 2002

▶ **put on front street**

to inform on, to betray *US, 1995*

- — Bill Valentine *Gang Intelligence Manual*, 1995: "Black street gang terminology"

front wedgie *noun*

the condition that exists when a tight-fitting pair of pants, shorts, bathing suit, or other garment forms a wedge between a woman's labia, accentuating their shape *US, 2001*

The **WEDGIE** brought around to the front of the body.

- I think it's like a very um … visible front wedgie. — *alt.tv.sopranos*, 28th May 2001

frosh *noun*

a freshman (first-year student), either in high school or college *US, 1915*

- I'm glad I use Dial whenever I wash / I've used it to clean me since I was a frosh. — Max Shulman, *Guided Tour of Campus Humor*, p. 49, 1955
- The upperclassmen were vastly impressed that a couple of frosh could make themselves so much at home in so short a time with such apparent ease[.] — John Nichols, *The Sterile Cuckoo*, p. 49, 1965
- — Connie Eble (Editor), *UNC-CH Campus Slang*, p. 4, Spring 1982

frost *verb*

to anger *US, 1895*

Often in combination with a body part.

- What was frosting her ass was the fact that he was queering her pitch. — Robert Campbell, *Alice in La-La Land*, p. 245, 1987

▶ **frost someone's balls**

to anger someone *US, 1981*

- That really frosted Mike's balls. What the hell could those assholes in Washington possibly be thinking? — Robert Lipkin, *A Brotherhood of Outlaws*, p. 71, 1981
- The kid's only been here two months and they make him foreman. Doesn't that frost your balls? — Michael Dalton Johnson, *Talking Trash with Redd Foxx*, p. 128, 1994

frosted *adjective*

angry *US, 1956*

- First I was frosted that he went off on my birthday night. — Lynn Hall, *Uphill All the Way*, p. 106, 1984

frosted face *noun*

the photographic depiction of a woman's face covered with semen *US, 1999*

American heterosexual pornography has long shown a fascination for ejaculations on a woman's face. In the late 1990s, this fascination expanded to embrace the depiction of multiple ejaculations on a woman's face. Any Internet search engine will uncover dozens of sites boasting "frosted faces," a term that puns on the branded cereal "Frosted Flakes" while inviting a visual comparison with the cereal's sugar glaze.

- Caroline's cum frosted face is a thing of beauty. — *rec.arts.movies.erotica*, 16th April 1999
- I'd love to dump a load on your face and in your mouth you fucking cocksucking fag boy. Love to give you a hot frosted face bitch. — *alt.sex.wanted*, 21st January 2000

frost freak *noun*

a person who inhales freon, a refrigerant, for its intoxicating effect *US, 1970*

- — William D. Alsever, *Glossary for the Establishment and Other Uptight People*, p. 12, December 1970

frosty *noun*

a cold beer *US, 1961*

- I learned, with the advent of the "Bennie God" to make an acceptable "bennie machine" out of aluminum foil, and use it on the flat back porch every afternoon during the spring semester to "catch a few rays" while downing some frosties. — John Nichols, *The Sterile Cuckoo*, p. 60, 1965
- — *American Speech*, p. 59, Spring–Summer 1975: "Razorback Slang"

frosty *adjective*

cool, calm, collected *US, 1970*

- Stay frosty. Relax. That's the way to do this job. — Joseph Wambaugh, *The New Centurions*, p. 77, 1970
- Come on, let's stay frosty here, Ray. — Stephen J. Cannell, *The Tin Collectors*, p. 8, 2001

frothing *adjective*
(used of a party) populated by many girls *US, 1988*
- — Surf Punks, *Oh No! Not Them Again!*, 1988

frou-frou *adjective*
fussy, overly fancy *US, 1951*
- Tell me the truth. Is that what you want in a girl—chic-chi, frou-frou, fancy clothes, permanent waves? — Max Shulman, *The Many Loves of Dobie Gillis*, p. 64, 1951

frown *noun*
lemon syrup or fresh lemon added to a coca-cola *US, 1946*
- — *American Speech*, p. 88, April 1946: "The language of West Coast culinary workers"

frowney; frowney face *noun*
the emoticon depicting a frown—:(*US, 1991*
- — Eric S. Raymond, *The New Hacker's Dictionary*, p. 169, 1991

froyo *noun*
frozen yogurt *US, 1996*
- — Pamla Munro, *U.C.L.A. Slang*, p. 40, 1998
- — *Columbia Missourian*, p. 8A, 19th October 1998

froze *adjective*
cocaine-intoxicated *US, 1974*
Evocative of the C18 meaning of the word as "drunk."
- But I did manage to cop on her that if she liked to get froze, to get in touch. I left her with my phone number, and knowing bitches, they all like a little coke now and then. — Donald Goines, *Never Die Alone*, p. 157, 1974

frozen *adjective*
1 excellent *US, 1954*
Teen slang.
- — *Look*, p. 88, 10th August 1954
2 in pool, directly touching (a ball or the rail of the table) *US, 1984*
- The cue ball was nearly frozen to the top rail. — Walter Tevis, *The Color of Money*, p. 57, 1984
- — Steve Rushin, *Pool Cool*, p. 13, 1990

frozen Chosin *nickname*
the Chanjin Reservoir, identified on Japanese maps as the Chosin Reservoir, scene of heroic military action by the US Marine Corps in the winter of 1950–51 *US, 1952*
- The Chinese indeed ran X Corps out of "Frozen Chosin" but at a price that effectively took its Ninth Army Group out of the war for crucial weeks. — Joseph Goulden, *Korea*, p. 381, 1982
- It was good at Pusan perimeter / I was good at Frozen Chosen. — Sandee Johnson, *Cadences: The Jody Call Book, No. 2*, p. 77, 1986: That Ol' Marine Corps Spirit

frozen feline *noun*
a popular, stylish person *US, 1957*
A forced, short-lived extension of "cool cat."
- [Y]ou'd better learn the new mystery words or you'll never be a frozen feline (the superlative of cool-cat). — *Washington Post*, p. F1, 29th September 1957

frozen fireworks *noun*
jewelry *US, 1979*
- He had blown into town with no 'ho. And worse, no wheels and frozen fireworks exploding off his dukes, necessary to cop a star 'ho. — Iceberg Slim (Robert Beck), *Airtight Willie and Me*, p. 21, 1979

frugal Freddie *noun*
a conventional, frugal person *US, 1969*
- First off, even though I'd never been a real Frugal Freddie, I still had enough loot from my civilian life to finance a little gambling. — Joey V., *Portrait of Joey*, p. 146, 1969

fruit *noun*
a homosexual, especially an obviously homosexual male person *US, 1900*
- [T]old us about conditions there, how when girls go fruit they put 'em in cottages alone, all girls go fruit, black girls go fruit for Mexican girls. — Jack Kerouac, *Letter to John Clellon Holmes*, p. 338, 8th February 1952
- It was an uninviting prospect. The old fruit must be forty. — Mary McCarthy, *The Group*, p. 89, 1963
- And malehustlers ("fruithustlers"/"studhustlers"): the various names for the masculine hustlers looking for lonely fruits to score from[.] — John Rechy, *City of Night*, p. 100, 1963
- The nuns, he explained as cavalierly as possible, were "some crazy friends of Mona's." And, yes, they were men. "Fruits?" — Armistead Maupin, *Tales of the City*, p. 268, 1978

fruitbait *noun*
a man who attracts the attention of other men *US, 1973*
- Nick, always a man of few words, said "Siddown, fruitbait." — Joseph Wambaugh, *The Blue Knight*, p. 140, 1973

fruitbar *noun*
1 an eccentric, a crazy person *US, 1987*
- "A real fruitbar. I fished with him once on the St. John's." — Carl Hiaasen, *Double Whammy*, p. 71, 1987
2 a bar patronized by homosexuals *US, 2004*
- Said kid gets popped at a fruit bar later. — James Ellroy, *Destination Morgue*, p. 62, 2004

fruit basket *noun*
the male genitalia when offered to view from behind *US, 2001*
- Fruit basket for Russell Woodman! — David Duchovny, *Evolution*, 2001

fruit boot *noun*
a style of shoe popular in the 1950s and 60s, ankle-high suede shoes with crepe rubber soles conventionally known as "desert boots" *US, 1954*
English mods embraced desert boots made by Clarks, and their popularity spread to the US, where they were labeled "fruit boots" because of their perceived popularity with perceived homosexuals. The 1957 example reflects either poor adult hearing or an original "boat," not "boot."
- Also added to the teen dictionary is "fruit boats" (the new colored suede shoes)[.] — *Washington Post*, p. F1, 29th September 1957
- — Guy Strait, *The Lavendar Lexicon*, 1st June 1964
- Then he sat down and took off his fruitboots and socks, and wiggled his toes in the cool air. — John Nichols, *The Sterile Cuckoo*, p. 71, 1965

fruitcake *noun*
1 an eccentric or even mentally unstable person *US, 1942*
- Easy, feller, easy. She's a fruitcake. — Mickey Spillane, *Kiss Me Deadly*, p. 7, 1952
- Hey you, Blondie, you like fruitcake kids like that? — Ken Kesey, *One Flew Over the Cuckoo's Nest*, p. 230, 1962
- United fruitcake outlet. — *Repo Man*, 1984
- People are starting to hate you, I mean, really hate you. Not just the usual fruitcakes, either. — Carl Hiaasen, *Tourist Season*, p. 25, 1986
2 a blatantly homosexual man *US, 1960*
- I'd dress up like a fruitcake and stroll through the park, you know, asking for it. — Elmore Leonard, *Freaky Deaky*, p. 25, 1988
- The fascist fruitcake gasped when he saw the handcuffs securing the Tender Trap's door handles. — Seth Morgan, *Homeboy*, p. 67, 1990
- "We're calling that fruitcake display of yours strike one," he announced. — C.D. Payne, *Youth in Revolt*, p. 165, 1993
- — Angela Devlin, *Prison Patter*, p. 54, 1996

fruiter *noun*
a homosexual *US, 1918*
- No one yells "fruiter" faster'n an undercover fruiter. — Malcolm Braly, *On the Yard*, p. 31, 1967
- — Inez Cardozo-Freeman, *The Joint*, p. 498, 1994

fruit fly *noun*
a heterosexual woman who befriends homosexual men *US, 1965*
- — *The Guild Dictionary of Homosexual Terms*, p. 17, 1965
- The fag hag, sometimes known as a fruit fly, is a girl or woman who, although she is more than likely homosexual herself, has never admitted it. — Ruth Allison, *Lesbianism*, p. 112, 1967
- Fag Hags, Fruit Flies, Faggot's Molls, is what the latter are rather unkindly called. — John Francis Hunter, *The Gay Insider*, pp. 90–91, 1971

fruit hustler *noun*
a homosexual prostitute; a criminal who preys on homosexual victims *US, 1959*

- And malehustlers ("fruithustlers"/"studhustlers:" the various names for the masculine hustlers looking for lonely fruits to score from[.] — John Rechy, *City of Night*, p. 100, 1963
- I'd remember the contemptuous look on the cold hearted fruit hustler's face as he patted my twenty dollar bill in his pocket. — Iceberg Slim (Robert Beck), *Mama Black Widow*, p. 23, 1969
- I stopped by the arcade and saw a big muscle-bound fruit hustler standing there. — Joseph Wambaugh, *The Blue Knight*, p. 26, 1973
- He looked more like a rock musician or a high-priced fruit hustler; sensitive in an arrogant way. — James Ellroy, *Brown's Requiem*, p. 107, 1981

fruiting *noun*
promiscuous behavior *US*, *1982*
- — *Maledicta*, p. 131, Summer/Winter 1982: "dyke diction: the language of lesbians"

fruit jacket *noun*
a prison record identifying a person as a homosexual *US*, *1986*
- Not wanting a fruit jacket, he agreed. — James Ellroy, *Suicide Hill*, p. 584, 1986

fruit loop *noun*
1 an effeminate homosexual man *US*, *1989*
An elaboration of **FRUIT**, from the brand name of a popular breakfast cereal.
- Silly little fruitloop woke me up this mawnin all excited. — Seth Morgan, *Homeboy*, p. 16, 1990

2 a psychiatric patient *US*, *1994*
- — Sally Williams, *"Strong" Words (Dissertation)*, p. 136, 1994

3 the cloth loop on the back of a man's shirt *US*, *1966*
- Collecting fruit loops is in. These are the tiny tabs from the backs of ivy league shirts. — *San Francisco Examiner*, p. 17, 17th June 1966

Fruit Loop *nickname*
an area in Las Vegas where many gay bars and clubs are located *US*, *2002*
- There's a scattering of gay bars and clubs throughout the city, but the main concentrations are in what's known as the "Fruit Loop," around the intersection of Paradise Road and Naples Drive[.] — *The Rough Guide Las Vegas*, p. 267, 2002
- Britney paid a visit to 8½ one of the homo hotspots in the "fruit loop" area of Vegas. — *perezhilton.com*, 14th January 2006

fruit pinch *noun*
an arrest of a homosexual man *US*, *1970*
- "Let's go over to the park and bust a quick fruit or two," said Ranatti. We haven't made a fruit pinch for a few days. — Joseph Wambaugh, *The New Centurions*, p. 186, 1970

fruit ranch *noun*
a mental hospital or a psychiatric ward *US*, *1984*
- — *Maledicta*, p. 117, 1984–1985: "Milwaukee medical maledicta"
- — *"Strong Words"*, p. 142, 1994

fruit roll *noun*
the violent robbing of a homosexual *US*, *1973*
- I didn't think the defense counsel was succeeding too well in trying to minimize the thing as just another fruitroll[.] — Joseph Wambaugh, *The Blue Knight*, p. 164, 1973

fruit salad *noun*
1 a display of military medals *UK*, *1943*
- — Lou Shelly, *Hepcats Jive Talk Dictionary*, p. 24, 1945
- — *American Speech*, p. 55, February 1947: "pacific war language"

2 a pooled mix of different types of pills contributed by several people and then consumed randomly *US*, *1969*
- — William D. Alsever, *Glossary for the Establishment and Other Uptight People*, p. 12, December 1970
- — *Current Slang*, p. 12, Spring 1971

3 a group of stroke patients who cannot care for themselves *US*, *1978*
- — *Maledicta*, p. 68, Summer/Winter 1978: "common patient-directed pejoratives used by medical personnel"

▸ **do the fruit salad**
to expose your genitals in public *US*, *1994*
- Flashing, or as they say in California, "doing the fruit salad," is also curious because one almost has to ask why, out of all the sexual deviations, somebody would choose this. — Anka Radakovich, *The Wild Girls Club*, pp. 12–13, 1994

fruit tank *noun*
a jail cell reserved for homosexual prisoners *US*, *1981*

- Gloria la Marr says there's some queen down in the fruit tank who tricked with your boy Bozwell. — Joseph Wambaugh, *The Glitter Dome*, p. 157, 1981
- Trusties wearing slit-bottomed khakis listlessly pushing brooms down the corridor, a group of them standing outside the fruit tank, cooing at the drag queens inside. — James Ellroy, *Suicide Hill*, p. 575, 1986

fruity *adjective*
obviously homosexual *US*, *1940*
- As soon as he could decently do so he took me into his private office, which was lavishly furnished and interiorly decorated in Alfred's own inimitably fruity way. — Clancy Sigal, *Going Away*, p. 386, 1961
- "You fruity shit, lay off!" Chas focused his rage. — John Rechy, *Rushes*, p. 67, 1979
- But he had this nasal, sort of flute-y, fruity voice. — Wolfman Jack (Bob Smith), *Have Mercy!*, p. 101, 1995
- Al wouldn't be caught dead in platform shoes. He thinks they're fruity and the Bee Gees are too. — Rita Ciresi, *Pink Slip*, p. 107, 1999

frumpy *adjective*
poorly dressed, rumpled, messy *US*, *1947*
- — Marcus Hanna Boulware, *Jive and Slang of Students in Negro Colleges*, 1947
- "I don't like being cast as the interfering fusspot—how frumpy—who moralizes." — Tracy Quan, *Diary of a Mahattan Call Girl*, p. 125, 2001

fry *noun*
1 crack cocaine *US*, *1994*
- — US Department of Justice, *Street Terms*, October 1994

2 LSD *US*, *1992*
- — Jay Robert Nash, *Dictionary of Crime*, p. 141, 1992

3 a car accident in which an occupant or occupants of the car are burnt *US*, *1962*
- — *American Speech*, p. 269, December 1962: "the language of traffic policemen"

▸ **to get a fry on**
to get angry *US*, *1956*
- "Listen, Griffin," he told the lieutenant, "don't get a fry on. Don't let Nash make you feel insecure." — William Brinkley, *Don't Go Near the Water*, p. 87, 1956

fry *verb*
1 to put to death by electrocution *US*, *1928*
- You don't know what it feels like, waitin' in your cell to find out if you goin' to fry or not. — Mezz Mezzrow, *Really the Blues*, p. 267, 1946
- Well, they fried Tough Tony last night / The man who didn't know the meaning of fright. — Dennis Wepman et al., *The Life*, p. 117, 1976
- "If they [the Menendez brothers] were black, they'd be fried by now." — Gini Sikes, *8 Ball Chicks*, p. 12, 1997
- In 1966, Ronald Reagan was elected governor of California, promising to punish the mouthy students acting up in Berkeley and to fry the inmates on San Quentin's death row. — Peter Coyote, *Sleeping Where I Fall*, p. 116, 1998

2 in computing, to fail completely *US*, *1983*
- — Guy L. Steele et al., *The Hacker's Dictionary*, p. 69, 1983

3 to use and be under the influence of LSD *US*, *1993*
- — *People Magazine*, p. 72, 19th July 1993
- — Linda Meyar, *Teenspeak*, p. 31, 1994

4 to alter the mind irreparably *US*, *1972*
- [T]he [Rolling] Stones and feedback and Trout Mask Replica [by Captain Beefheart]. All these were milestones, each one fried my brain a little further[.] — Lester Bangs, *Psychotic Reactions and Carburetor Dung*, p. 12, 1971

5 to straighten your hair, chemically or with heat *US*, *1945*
- — Lou Shelly, *Hepcats Jive Dictionary*, p. 11, 1945
- You ain't had your hair fried, is you boy? Where'd you get them pretty waves? — Mezz Mezzrow, *Really the Blues*, p. 115, 1946
- — Jack Lait and Lee Mortimer, *New York Confidential*, p. 235, 1948: "A glossary of Harlemisms"
- I mean, she went to the beauty shop to have her hair fried, oiled, curled, or straightened to make it look like Lady Clairol[.] — Clarence Major, *All-Night Visitors*, p. 65, 1998

fry daddy *noun*
a marijuana and crack cocaine cigarette *US*, *1989*
- — Geoffrey Froner, *Digging for Diamonds*, p. 30, 1989
- — US Department of Justice, *Street Terms*, October 1994

frying size *noun*

said of children of elementary school age *US, 1954*

- — Jerry Robertson, *Oil Slanguage*, p. 56, 1954

FSH!

used by fighter pilots for expressing strong feelings *US, 1990*
Perhaps an abbreviation of "fight, shit, hate" or perhaps of "fuckin' shit hot!."

- Well, Colonel Meroney / Picked himself off the ceiling / Screaming loudly "FSH!!!" — Joseph Tuso, *Singing the Vietnam Blues*, p. 88, 1990

FTA

fuck the army US, 1962
A popular sentiment shared by those both in and not in the army during the Vietnam war. Country Joe McDonald of "Look's Like I'm Fixin' To Die Rag" fame, took an antiwar show named "FTA!" on the road to GI coffee houses in 1971.

- "And what does FTA stand for, Specialist?" * * * He seemed embarrassed. "The initials stand for 'Fuck the Army.'" — Thomas Doulis, *Paths for our Valor*, p. 36, 1962
- — Carl Fleischhauer, *A Glossary of Army Slang*, p. 20, 1968
- "The slogan is FTA, which means Fuck the Army. — Ward Just, *Military Men*, p. 67, 1970
- Typical of the military resistance, the meaning was reversed to "free" or "fuck the Army." FTA became one of the most common slogans expressing soldier discontent. — Richard Moser, *The New Winter Soldiers*, p. 87, 1996

FTW

used as a defiant stance against everything—*fuck the world US, 1972*

- Both of them were heavily and inexpertly tattooed with such epithets as "loser" and "FTW" which stands for "Fuck The World." — John Aitken, *Conversations*, p. 8, 1978
- "That FTW is what's on the T-shirt out there on Mits. What is it?" — John D. MacDonald, *Free Fall in Crimson*, p. 96, 1981
- "Fuck the World" (FTW) is their motto and arrogant attitude by which this sub-culture attains its goals and objectives. — Paladin Press, *Inside Look at Outlaw Motorcycle Gangs*, p. 14, 1992
- — Bill Valentine, *Gangs and Their Tattoos*, p. x, 2000
- He noted that Jessie had several tattoos, including one on his right arm that said "FTW" (it was noted that that stood for "Fuck the World"). — Mara Leveritt, *Devil's Knot*, p. 76, 2002

fubar; FUBAR *adjective*

used as an expression of disgust because a situation is *fucked up beyond all recognition US, 1944*
Of the many military acronyms with a prominent "F" coined during World War 2, one of the few to survive.

- "Not only profanity has crept into your speech," she said, "but also the peculiar jargon of the Army." "Snafu," I said, "tarfu, fubar, and weft." — Max Shulman, *The Zebra Derby*, p. 174, 1946
- The young men didn't need a recruiter to tell them that things at home were about the same as they'd been in 'Nam, which was to say, in marine parlance, FUBAR. — Bob Sipchen, *Baby Insane and the Buddha*, p. 46, 1993
- I clearly saw three blackened dwarf figures curled into fetal twists, FUBAR. — Cherokee Paul McDonald, *Into the Green*, p. 63, 2001

fubb; FUBB *adjective*

badly botched *US, 1975*

- In Vietnam, we called it a FUBB, fucked up beyond belief. — Paul Morgan, *The Parrot's Beak*, p. 143, 2000

fuck *noun*

1 the act of sex *UK, 1675*

- I ain't had a fuck in ages & no new girl (except whores) since 1945. — Neal Cassady, *The First Third*, p. 197, 1950
- "We had a great fuck. What's that supposed to mean?" — William Kinsolving, *Born with the Century*, p. 466, 1979
- The hand cream produces a kind of airless suction on my genitals which simulates the sensation of a great fuck. — Nancy Friday, *Men in Love*, p. 148, 1982
- A great fuck is one thing, but if you're falling in love, you need to know more about him. — Jackie Collins, *Thrill!*, p. 262, 1998

2 a person objectified as a sex-partner *UK, 1874*

- Even if I was the fastest fuck in the east, which I was. — Larry Rivers, *What Did I Do?*, p. 49, 1992

- "You got that right—you were the worst fuck I've ever had, and I've had some lousy ones in my life!" — Don Olson, *The Councilman*, p. 100, 2000
- "She was the best fuck I'd ever had, that's why!" — Annie Solomen, *Like a Knife*, p. 225, 2003

3 a despicable or hapless person *UK, 1927*

- "That evil little fuck is so guilty that I should probably kill him myself, on general principles." — Hunter S. Thompson, *Fear and Loathing in Las Vegas*, p. 125, 1971
- Give ya some cash, get that Scagnetti fuck off your back, and we'll be talking to ya. — *Reservoir Dogs*, 1992
- Okay you freshmen fucks, listen up. — *Dazed and Confused*, 1993
- It all started getting crazy when Charlie Magoo was having a beer in one of the Porterville bars and some fuck in the bar said something stupid to him. — Ralph Sonny Barger, *Hell's Angel*, p. 150, 2000

4 used as an intensifier *US, 1934*

Often used with "the," as in "Get the fuck out of here!."

- She may not be beautiful to look at—whatever the fuck that means, in this kingdom of the blind. — James Baldwin, *If Beale Street Could Talk*, p. 29, 1974
- Now how the fuck am I supposed to get out of debt? — Eminem (Marshall Mathers), *Still Don't Give a Fuck*, 1999
- "Where the fuck you been?" — John Del Vecchio, *The 13th Valley*, p. 333, 1999

5 an extreme *UK, 1928*

- I deal with a lot of people pick their teeth after they eat, and they eat a fuck of a lot of pasta. — John Gregory Dunne, *Dutch Sheat, Jr.*, p. 222, 1982
- "Thanks a fuck of a lot," he answered with a jolting coarseness. — John Updike, *The Witches of Eastwick*, p. 248, 1985

6 something of no value *UK, 1790*

- I don't give a fuck any more what's behind me, or what's ahead of me. — Henry Miller, *Tropic of Cancer*, p. 50, 1961
- Why should they give a fuck? — Mario Puzo, *Inside Las Vegas*, p. 145, 1977
- Just like banks, these places are insured. The managers don't give a fuck, they're just tryin' to get ya out the door before you start pluggin' diners. — *Pulp Fiction*, 1994

▸ **like fuck**

like hell; very much *UK, 1995*

- "You're being executed in the morning." "Like fuck I am." — Mark Kendrick, *Desert Sons*, p. 71, 2001

fuck *verb*

1 to have sex *UK, 1500*

- I've met a lot of girls out here, and at least two of them are anxious for me to fuck them, but I never get around to it. — Jack Kerouac, *Letter to Neal Cassady*, p. 127, 13th September 1947
- I've heard that until you've fucked on cocaine you just haven't fucked. — Herbert Huncke, *Guilty of Everything*, p. 8, 1990
- "Fucking" is not limited to penetration, Banky. For me it describes any sex when it's not totally about love. — *Chasing Amy*, 1997
- We talked and fucked and talked some more about why we were fucking[.] — Anne Heche, *Call Me Crazy*, p. 146, 2001

2 to damage beyond repair *UK, 1775*

- Before we left the cafe Ginger made a phone call to Harley Pete and said, "I'm going to fuck you." — Jamie Mandelkau, *Buttons*, p. 31, 1971
- Before he fucked the savings and loan industry, Keating tried to prevent the portrayal of fucking in magazines. — Larry Flynt, *An Unseemly Man*, p. 123, 1996

3 used as an intense verb of abuse, as in "Fuck the police" *UK, 1915*

- Fuck him seventy eight times. Fuck the literateurs too. Fuck the whole lot. — Jack Kerouac, *Letter to Neal Cassady*, p. 175, 8 December 1948
- It's called "I Put the Dick in Dixie and the Cunt in Country," but my label hates that shit. They'll never let me record it. So fuck them. Fuck them all. — Harold Evans, *The Best American Magazine Writing 2001*, p. 296, 2001

▸ **fuck a duck**

to shirk, to avoid work *US, 1933*
Vietnam war usage.

- I met a man in the Cav who'd been "fucking the duck" one afternoon, sound asleep in a huge tent with thirty cots inside[.] — Michael Herr, *Dispatches*, p. 57, 1977
- Jonesy raised his head from his rucksack, where he was taking one of his famous naps—fucking the duck, we called it—and stage-whispered right back[.] — Larry Heinemann, *Paco's Story*, p. 6, 1986

▶ **fuck the dog**
to idle instead of working *US, 1935*

- He could work out his own system, "fuck the dog," stretch the time out by taking an extra ten minutes on a banana break. — Joe Rosenblatt, *Top Soil*, p. 228, 1976
- "Naw, we're just sitting here fucking the dog." — Elmore Leonard, *Bandits*, p. 338, 1997

▶ **fuck the fucking fuckers**
used for expressing contempt and defiance of and towards just about everyone *US, 1980*

- Well, fuck the fucking fuckers. You keep every fucking scrap of paper ever crosses your desk. — Richard Marcinko, *Task Force Blue*, p. 81, 1997
- "Fuck the fucking fuckers. Strap on your chutes: we'll just jump from here." — Alexander Danzig, *Mohammed at Mono Lake*, p. 74, 2006

▶ **fuck them if they can't take a joke**
during the Vietnam war, used as a cynically humorous retort when things went wrong *US, 1980*
Multiple variants.

- — *Maledicta*, p. 170, Winter 1980: "A brief survey of some unofficial prosigns used by the United States Armed Forces"
- "We're not going on any wild-goose chase in those boonies tonight and get mortared for three hours like the last time. Fuck him if he can't take a joke." — Lucian K. Truscott, *Army Blue*, p. 11, 1989
- If not, well, screw the camel drivers if they can't take a joke. — T.E. Cruise, *Wings of Gold III*, p. 362, 1989

▶ **fuck your fist**
to masturbate *US, 1966*

- But therefor I was not Samson, so I fucked my fist once more/ but I taken good aim and shot it—through this keyhole in the door. — Bruce Jackson, *Get Your Ass in the Water and Swim Like Me*, p. 222, 1966
- Fuck Your Fist with Me [Headline] — *Partner Magazine*, p. 27, December 1980
- "I'll be fucking my fist to relax for the geometry test." — Lonnie Coleman, *Mark*, p. 166, 1981

▶ **who do you have to fuck?**
used as an impatient enquiry: who do I have to persuade? *US, 1968*

- Who do you have to fuck to get a drink around here? — Mart Crowley, *Boys in the Band*, p. 48, 1968
- Reilly proved them all wrong by becoming so omnipresent he admits to once thinking, "Who do I have to fuck to get off TV?" — *The Village Voice*, 15th October 2001

fuckaholic *noun*
a person obsessed with sex *US, 1981*

- He was a fuckaholic given his first taste. — George Rabasa, *Floating Kingdom*, p. 307, 1997
- I used to think that you did, and now you're just a regular fuckaholic! — Kevin E. Young, *Ghett Oh Luv*, p. 138, 2004

fuckaround *noun*
idling, wasting time *US, 1970*

- In a nut, my total inability to deal with the small success of the H.A. book has resulted—after three years of a useless, half-amusing rural fuckaround—in just about nothing except three wasted years. — Hunter S. Thompson, *Fear and Loathing in America*, p. 258, 13th January 1970: Letter to Jim Silberman

fuckass *noun*
a despicable person *UK, 1960*

- Don't touch me, you fuckass, I'll kill you with my bare hands. — Gregg Easterbrook, *The Here and Now*, p. 133, 2002
- "I only hope her Puerto Rican fuckass ain't got the same blood type I have." — Paul Maher, *Kerouac*, p. 424, 2004

fuckass *adjective*
despicable *US, 1961*

- Any man'd leave it layin around's a fuckass soldier anyway. — James Jones, *The Thin Red Line*, p. 21, 1962
- She was curled up on the prep table reading the fuckass book. — John Sheppard, *Small Town Punk*, p. 24, 2002

fuckathon *noun*
an extended bout of sex *US, 1968*

- How could he confess to her that he had been on a fuckathon. — John M. Del Vecchio, *The 13th Valley*, p. 336, 1982
- Tell her how much he'd loved their fuckathon this morning. — Barbara Plum, *Queen of the Universe*, p. 51, 2005

fuckbag *noun*
a despicable person *US, 1989*

- They were, undoubtedly, rancid Welsh fuckbags like himself. — Robert McLiam Wilson, *Ripley Bogle*, p. 8, 1989

fuck book *noun*
a sexually explicit book, usually heavily illustrated *US, 1944*

- Fuckbooks, in the space of about three years in this country, have become so numerous that it is not within the scope of any one reader to even thumb through them all, let alone read them — *Screw*, p. 13, 7th February 1969
- A Barney Google fuck book. Barney's cock like a whole bologna, radiating ee-lectric squiggles and flecking great airdrops of jiss as he galled at and rammed the thing into the cartoon women with equally electric cunts that looked like toothless mouths. — Earl Thompson, *Tattoo*, p. 25, 1974
- The ephemeral fuckbook, ground out by the thousands in the last ten years, come and go, never to be seen again[.] — Stephen Lewis, *The Whole Bedroom Catalog*, p. 70, 1975
- I got two letters from Jenny and the two fuck books, the ones with yellow covers, I had sent for back in December. — Larry Heinemann, *Close Quarters*, p. 259, 1977

fuck booth *noun*
a booth in a pornographic video arcade *US, 2000*

- Felicia was referring to nights when Tuffy used to escort Antoine to the cab stand after long nights of working the peep show and fuck booths. — Paul Beatty, *Tuff*, p. 145, 2000

fuck boy *noun*
a young man as the object of homosexual desire *US, 1971*

- They were known as pussyboys, galboys, fuckboys, and all had taken girls' names like Betty, Fifi, Dotty, etc. — James Blake, *The Joint*, p. 67, 1971
- In prison, the convicts who are sexually assaulted are the sissies, the effeminate, and they are called "punks" or "fuckboys." — Fox Butterfield, *All God's Children*, p. 289, 1996
- The lowest form of fuck-boy will give it up for a cup of coffee. — B. Forrest Spink, *After Midnight in Savannah*, p. 153, 2005

fuckbrain *noun*
an idiot *US, 1993*
A variation of the equally derisive **FUCKWIT**.

- "I asked you a question, fuckbrain," said Skinny. — Jonathan Kellerman, *Over the Edge*, p. 373, 1993
- That was the first time I actually considered the possibility that we might lose to that fuckbrain Nixon. — Anonymous, *Primary Colors*, p. 336, 1996

fuck buddy *noun*
a friend who is also a sex companion *US, 1972*

- While we were looking the whore spots over, we ran into an old fuck buddy of mine. We pulled up on her and after a few minutes of rapping she slid her big tasty ass in the car. — A.S. Jackson, *Gentleman Pimp*, p. 71, 1973
- "He thinks of me as as a fuck buddy. Period." How romantic." "Exactly." — Armistead Maupin, *Further Tales of the City*, p. 121, 1982
- "This is my hot little fuck buddy, bet you wished you had one, right, Chad?" — Ethan Morden, *Everybody Loves You*, p. 112, 1988
- She's insatiable and eager to please her handsomely hung fuck buddy. — Editors of Adult Video News, *The AVN Guide to the 500 Greatest Adult Films of All Time*, p. 38, 2005

fuck button *noun*
the clitoris *US, 1969*

- There were times when I could make her come just from the feel of my lips tugging on that little fuck-button of hers[.] — Joey V., *Portrait of Joey*, p. 84, 1969
- As I sucked her fuck button I brought her quickly and helplessly to the brink of orgasm. — *alt.sex.stories*, 5th March 1995
- Having completed the task at hand I was continuously stimulating her by kissing her and giving her now swollen fuck button a lick and rub. — *alt.sex.stories*, 8th October 1998

fucked *adjective*
drunk or drug-intoxicated *US, 1965*

- Enough of the hangovers that were so bad at times it felt like I was fucked on mescaline. — Al Lovejoy, *Acid Alex*, p. 287, 2005

fucked up *adjective*
1 drunk or drug-intoxicated *US, 1944*

- I wouldn't get fucked up with them [the Hell's Angels] any more than I would with the FBI or the Lyndon Johnson Fan Club. — Hunter S. Thompson, *Fear and Loathing in America*, p. 19, 15th January 1968: Letter to Kelly Varner
- I'm not even fuckin' joking with you, don't you be bringing some fucked up pooh-butt to my house. — *Pulp Fiction*, 1994
- Check this out. You get a baby's bottle, right? Fill it up with high-test gasoline and a week-old lima bean. Let it sit overnight. Suck it all down. Man, you'll get fucked up! — Chris Rock, *Rock This!*, p. 79, 1997
- I could have walked it, but I was too fucked up to walk. — John Ridley, *Love is a Racket*, p. 168, 1998

2 mentally unstable; depressed; anguished *UK, 1939*

- I hear he is like completely fucked up. — Bret Easton Ellis, *Less Than Zero*, p. 17, 1985
- Kids of shrinks are completely fucked up from the start. — Meg Wolitzer, *The Wife*, p. 157, 2003
- "I'm just completely fucked up and I don't want you to feel bad and I don't want anyone to think about me here, okay?" — Marty Beckerman, *Generation S.L.U.T.*, p. 124, 2004

3 despicable *US, 1945*

- Suddenly one of the cats near the door we had entered through spoke up, looking contemptuously at me, saying "you are fucked up man." — Herbert Huncke, *The Evening Sun Turned Crimson*, p. 134, 1980

4 ruined, spoiled, broken *US, 1951*

- We have a lot of fun together and our lives are fuckt up and so there it stands. — Jack Kerouac, *On the Road (The Original Scroll)*, p. 317, 1951
- It was back in the time of nineteen hundred and two / I had a fucked-up deck a cards and I didn't know what to do. — Bruce Jackson, *Get Your Ass in the Water and Swim Like Me*, p. 46, 1965

fucker *noun*

1 a man, a spirited person *UK, 1893*

- "Send Falwell in here. I want to see the look on the fucker's face." — Larry Flynt, *An Unseemly Man*, p. 222, 1996
- I was going to have this fucker by the balls. — Neva Gardner, *Take Your Shirt Off*, p. 78, 2003

2 a contemptible person *UK, 1890*

- "Is the fucker alone?" Scum runs in packs. — Marc 'Animal' MacYoung, *Street E&E*, p. 38, 1993
- "The fucker [Henry Kissinger] doesn't perform surgery or make house calls, does he?" [Quoting President George H. W. Bush] — Kitty Kelley, *The Family*, p. 350, 2004

3 a nuisance, an awkward thing *US, 1945*

- "So here I am," said the whale, pointing to his cheek, "with a real fucker of a problem." — Antonio Lobo Antunes, *Act of the Damned*, p. 18, 1996

fuckery *noun*

oppression; the inherent corruption of a dominant society *JAMAICA, 1979*

- That wasn't any act of God. That was an act of pure fuckery. — Stephen King, *The Stand*, p. 702, 1978

fuckface *noun*

an offensive or despicable person *US, 1945*

- Go fix the flowers fuck-face was the King's reply. — Norman Nailer, *Cannibals and Christians*, p. 155, 1966
- "Hey, Fuck Face, put out your cigar." — Malcolm Braley, *False Starts*, p. 193, 1976
- Laugh away fuckface. That picture is going to be on the cover of every major newspaper in two days time. — *Repo Man*, 1984
- Hey, fuckface. Give me that. — Cleo Odzer, *Goa Freaks*, p. 264, 1995

fuckfaced *adjective*

despicable, ugly *US, 1940*

- "You fuckfaced twerp. Go feebleminded with me and I'll roast you." — Marc Olden, *Kisaeng*, p. 265, 1992

fuck film; fuck flick *noun*

a pornographic film *US, 1970*

- Well, you were talking to me in bed about making fuck films. — Fred Baker, *Events*, p. 50, 1970
- [T]he Orientals seem to prefer to keep their hard-core "fuck films" to themselves[.] — Roger Blake, *The Porno Movies*, p. 75, 1970
- '69's Best & Worst Fuckfilm Fare (Headline) — *Screw*, p. 14, 19th January 1970

- Floods the screen with banal Pat Rocco films from Hollywood, but now and then shows a homoerotic winner like Man and Man, a full-length fun fuck film that will have you aghast and horny. — John Francis Hunter, *The Gay Insider*, p. 147, 1971

fuckhead *noun*

used as an all-purpose insulting term of address or descriptive noun for a despicable, stupid person *US, 1966*

- A week later I received a letter from some fuck head called "Lon" of Research and man, like this jasper really poured the shit out thick. — *Screw*, p. 13, 27th June 1969
- Come on, fuckhead! — *Saturday Night Fever*, 1977
- Shut up fuck head! I hate that Mongoloid voice. — *Pulp Fiction*, 1994
- A hippie fuckhead did my horoscope. — James Ellroy, *Destination Morgue*, p. 114, 2004

fuckhole *noun*

the vagina *UK, 1893*

- — Dale Gordon, *The Dominion Sex Dictionary*, p. 73, 1967
- — *Maledicta*, p. 131, Summer/Winter 1982: "Dyke diction: the language of lesbians."
- I never thought I would plug her fuckhole with such a thick, creamy load. — Christopher Szatkowski, *Mushrooms and Applesauce*, p. 26, 2002
- Four young wannabe sex stars get their nearly cherry fuckholes stretched, slammed, and jizzed on by big-dicked professional porn studs in the latest installment of this raunchy, hot series. — Penthouse Magazine, *The Penthouse Erotic Video Guide*, p. 232, 2003

fucking *noun*

sexual intercourse *UK, 1568*

- No thinking, no cogitation, no intellectual bullshit—just plain, old-fashioned fucking. — Allan Sherman, *The Rape of the APE (American Puritan Ethic)*, p. 94, 1973
- Note that the two men pictured by Chester are seemingly oblivious to the presence of the camera, that their spectacular fucking has been caught in medias res. — Henry Abelove, *The Lesbian and Gay Studies Reader*, p. 368, 1993
- After a few minutes of this slow fucking, his huge pole would disappear inside her almost completely on every stroke. — Penthouse International, *Letters to Penthouse XIII*, p. 42, 2001
- Maybe we'd been brother and sister, some sort of familial relationship that charged our frenzied fucking with taboos violated just beyond the bounds of our recognition. — Michelle Tea, *Rent Girl*, p. 162, 2004

fucking *adjective + adverb*

used as an attention-getting intensifier *US, 1857*

- I am King fucking MONTEZUMA, that's who, and this is the coin of my kingdom. — Richard Farina, *Been Down So Long*, p. 32, 1966
- Brad, I really fuckin' hate McDonald's, man. — *Fast Times at Ridgemont High*, 1982
- I fucking saw that you little sack of shit. — *Dazed and Confused*, 1993
- You're fucking twenty minutes late. What the fuck is that. — *The Big Lebowski*, 1998

-fucking- *infix*

used as an intensifier *US, 1921*

One of the very few infix intensifiers used in the US.

- Somebody better be careful, he gets himself infuckingvolved. — Richard Farina, *Been Down So Long*, p. 79, 1966
- Tony was delighted. "Fan-fucking-tastic!" — Terry Southern, *Blue Movie*, p. 95, 1970
- You gonna love the Nam, man, for-fucking-ever. — *Platoon*, 1986
- Do you realize that in 1997 some women still don't give head? Ninety-fucking-seven. — Chris Rock, *Rock This!*, p. 133, 1997

fucking A!

used as an expression of surprise, approval or dismay *US, 1947*

- Schoons thought this was the fuckin'-A twitty-bird funniest thing the Regals (Himself) had ever heard[.] — John Nichols, *The Sterile Cuckoo*, p. 66, 1965
- "Yeah, yeah, fuckin' A," Kenyon said[.] — John Wikiany, *The Man Who Cried I Am*, p. 132, 1967
- Or if somebody said, "Are you taking Louise to the dance," you had to say, "Fuckin' ay I am." — Jim Bouton, *Ball Four*, p. 361, 1970
- Fucking A it worked, that's what I'm talkin' about! — *Pulp Fiction*, 1994

fucking new guy *noun*

a recent arrival to combat *US, 1977*

A key term and key concept in Vietnam.

- Then he looked over at me. "Who's the fucken new guy?" — Larry Heinemann, *Close Quarters*, p. 34, 1977
- Me being the fucking new guy and the top banana, I had to make up my mind. — Mark Baker, *Nam*, p. 125, 1981

fuck-knuckle grip *noun*

the use of the knuckles as a bridge while playing pool *US, 1972*

- Instead of making a solid, professional-looking bridge for the cue with my left hand, I might just lay it over the back of my hand —the "fuck-knuckle grip," we used to call it. — Robert Byrne, *McGoorty*, pp. 26–26, 1972

fuck load *noun*

a considerable quantity *US, 1988*

- "Him and Marty pulled a righteous fuckin' fuckload of burglaries together." — James Ellroy, *The Big Nowhere*, p. 80, 1988
- I wanted his attention so badly and drank fuckloads to impress him, and tried so hard to be an outlaw. — Margaret Cho, *I'm the One That I Want*, p. 179, 2001
- "I don't have any money. Just a fuck load of cocaine." — Keith Blenman, *Biotechnology vs. The Teenage Schoolgirl*, p. 80, 2002

fuck machine *noun*

a very active sexual partner *US, 1981*

- He was nothing but a fuck machine. Her loins and anus felt swollen and aching[.] — Harold Robbins, *Goodbye, Janette*, p. 244, 1981
- MR BROWN: The pain is reminding the fuck machine what it was like to be a virgin. — *Reservoir Dogs*, 1992
- I don't know how much longer I can take it, being abused by this powerful little fuck machine. — Simon Sheppard, *Hotter Than Hell*, p. 160, 2001

fuck-me *adjective*

extremely sexually suggestive *US, 1974*

- There was a time when no self-respecting queen could be ignorant of Carmen Miranda's hats, Joan Crawford's ankle-strap wedgies (called fuck-me shoes). — *Maledicta*, p. 237, Winter 1980
- She wore blood-red lipstick, gold hoop earrings, a white miniskirt, fuck-me pumps and a sleeveless salmon blouse. — Carl Hiaasen, *Strip Tease*, p. 285, 1993
- I know I'm better than what I've been doing the last ten years, walking around in a tank top and fuck-me pumps waiting till it's time to scream. — *Get Shorty*, 1995
- I think Ginger pictured Lady Larue in that mental institution in her fuck me stripper shoes and a huge blonde wig[.] — Jennifer Blowdryer, *White Trash Debutante*, p. 67, 1997

fuck me blue!

used as an elaborate variant of "fuck me!" *US, 1988*

- I've told them and told them to get the hell out once we've made our goddamn move. Fuck me blue! — *Drugstore Cowboy*, 1988
- Fuck me blue. Little Kieran. Little Kieran has come home to roost. I was sure they couldn't kill you. — Jesse Hajicek, *The God Eaters*, p. 260, 2006

fuck-me's *noun*

very tight, form-fitting pants on a man *US, 1972*

- — Bruce Rodgers, *The Queens' Vernacular*, p. 53, 1972

fuck movie *noun*

a pornographic film *US, 1967*

- "I got some fuck-movies at home," the man tries to entice him[.] — John Rechy, *Numbers*, p. 105, 1967
- Maybe should get it all out front and show fuck movies in Times Square. — *Screw*, p. 16, 23rd May 1969
- "We made a few fuck movies," says brother Art [Mitchell]. — Kenneth Turan and Stephen E. Zito, *Sinema*, p. 167, 1974

fucknut *noun*

a contemptible person *US, 1988*

- First they draft all the fucknuts who flunk out of school, and then they take the douchebags who bring home report cards like this. — Peter Farrelly, *Outside Providence*, p. 68, 1988
- You think I'd go away for shooting a fucknut like you? — Tom Corcoran, *Gumbo Limbo*, p. 217, 1999
- [H]e asked me what kind of fucknut I was[.] — Jill Davis, *Girls' Poker Night*, p. 208, 2002

fucko *noun*

used as a jocular if derisive term of address *US, 1973*

- "You fucko!" the kid yelled. — Jimmy Breslin, *Table Money*, p. 115, 1986
- Hey! Fucko! You want something? — *Goodfellas*, 1990
- McMANUS: What truck? VOICE: The truck with the guns, fucko. — *The Usual Suspects*, 1995
- "Yeah, right, fucko," J.W. said under his breath after he raised his window. — Ralph "Sonny" Barger, *Dead in 5 Heartbeats*, p. 288, 2003

fuck-off *noun*

a person who shirks their responsibility and duty *US, 1947*

- Diggers are more politically oriented but at the same time bigger fuckoffs. — Abbie Hoffman, *Revolution for the Hell of It*, p. 26, 1968
- "He's a fuck-off." "You think that matters to me?" — Michael Crichton, *A Case of Need*, p. 354, 1994
- I'm just a fuck-off in a world that takes itself too serious — Angelo Jaramillo, *The Darker*, p. 50, 2006

fuck-off *adjective*

incompetent *US, 1953*

- [A] fuckoff group like Deep Purple[.] — Lester Bangs, *Psychotic Reactions and Carburetor Dung*, p. 47, 1970

fuckola

used as an embellished "fuck" in any of its senses *US, 1998*

- Fuck me! Fuckola, man. — *The Big Lebowski*, 1998

fuck over *verb*

to treat another person with contempt or cruelty in any way; to mistreat, to hurt emotionally or physically, to betray, to victimize, to cheat *US, 1961*

- Get smart and I'll fuck you over—sayeth the Lord. — Frank Zappa, *The Real Frank Zappa Book*, p. 298, 1989
- It's about a girl who is very vulnerable and she's been fucked over a few times. — *Reservoir Dogs*, 1992
- You fucked me over. I flew myself here for you. I rented a fucking car for this—for this what? For this fucking treatment? — Anne Heche, *Call Me Crazy*, p. 172, 2001

fuck pad *noun*

a room, apartment, or house maintained for the purpose of sexual liaisons *US, 1975*

- When I walk into his combination office and fuck pad I see this little jive broad from Howard or Tuskegee. — Babs Gonzales, *Movin' On Down De Line*, p. 36, 1975
- A young white peeper spotted roof-prowling fuck-pad motels, jazz clubs. — James Ellroy, *White Jazz*, p. 192, 1992
- "It's actually a fuck pad a couple of greaseballs out of Houston use." — James Lee Burke, *Last Car to Elysian Fields*, p. 173, 2003

fuck pole *noun*

the penis *US, 1966*

- She had two rusty nuts that swung from her butt / and a fuck-pole longer than mine. — Bruce Jackson, *Get Your Ass in the Water and Swim Like Me*, p. 159, 1966
- "Oh, yeah, slick it up, stud, get that big fuck-pole ready to do that fine piece a favor." — Patrick Califia-Rice, *Macho Sluts*, p. 120, 1988
- The verse, what I could recall, moved him, and he would idly play with what he called his "fuck-pole," but in no provocative way. — Gore Vidal, *Palimpsest*, p. 94, 1995
- She humped up and down on my fuckpole, loving it. — Penthouse International, *Letters to Penthouse X*, p. 308, 2000

fuck stick *noun*

1 the penis *US, 1976*

Used by Saigon prostitutes during the Vietnam war, adopted by US soldiers.

- My pistol is like my fuck-stick. Don't go nowhere without it. — Edwin Torres, *Q & A*, p. 195, 1977
- "Would you love to lick the goo off my fuck stick?" — Dan Anderson, *Sex Tips for Gay Guys*, p. 188, 2001
- "Oh, baby," she moaned, "listen to your white slut's pussy talking to your big black fuck stick!" — Penthouse Magazine, *Letters to Penthouse XVIII*, p. 220, 2003

2 a despicable person *US, 1958*

- Do you love this place, fuckstick? — Pat Conroy, *The Lords of Discipline*, p. 164, 1980
- "Get down and die, fuckstick ... get down and die." — Cherokee Paul McDonald, *Into the Green*, p. 41, 2001

- "Fuck sticks?" Kansas was indignant. "That's outta line, dawgs. That's straight-up disrespectful." — Jimmy Lerner, *You Got Nothing Coming*, p. 51, 2002

fuck-struck *noun*

infatuated or obsessed with someone because of their ability in sex *US, 1967*

- "He's fuck-struck," observed the Swede to no one in particular. — Elaine Shepard, *The Doom Pussy*, p. 139, 1967
- He's very generous. He's fuck-struck. — Thomas Sanchez, p. 120, 1989
- I was duly fuck-struck as I waved him off[.] — Julian Barnes, *Love, etc.*, p. 67, 2000

fuck-up *noun*

a chronic, bungling, dismal failure (person or thing) *US, 1944*

- [F]ixed the plug fuck-up there & roared. — Neal Cassady, *The First Third*, p. 218, 1965
- We nonstudent fuck-ups say, "Excuse me, student. Did you know the sun is shining?" — Jerry Rubin, *Do It!*, p. 209, 1970
- But if you were a fuck-up you made the cemetery gang, and were known as a "ghoul." — Herbert Huncke, *Guilty of Everything*, p. 47, 1990
- He was a serious fuck-up. I'm glad the son-of-a-bitch is dead. — *Slacker*, 1992

fuck up *verb*

1 to spoil, to destroy *UK, 1916*

- Let me tell you about this machine, a real dream; whether or not turned nitemare—the best truck I ever fucked up. — Neal Cassady, *The First Third*, p. 207, August 1965
- Scum office and factory workers, in addition to fucking up their work, will secretly destroy equipment. — Valeria Solanas, *S.C.U.M. Manifesto*, p. 73, 1968
- "Fuck it. They're dead. No big fucking deal. Move on." " – 's dead." "Fucking – fucked up. He's dead." "He shouldn't have fucked up. He wouldn't be fucking dead." — Jonathan Shay, *Achilles in Vietnam*, p. 38, 1995
- We battled long and hard for about a year, and it wasn't pretty. Oakland and Frisco Hell's Angels would fuck each other up at every chance. — Ralph "Sonny" Barger, *Hell's Angel*, p. 148, 2000

2 to make a mistake *US, 1945*

- I told Neal, "And don't fuck up with this car." — Jack Kerouac, *On the Road (The Original Scroll)*, p. 323, 1951
- Nixon beat Humphrey on what should & could have been Hubert's strongest argument—to end the war in Vietnam at once, because LBJ fucked up. — Hunter S. Thompson, *Fear and Loathing in America*, p. 404, June 1971: Letter to Jann Wenner
- He says he remembers all the little ways he fucked up when he built your place. — Richard Russo, *Straight Man*, p. 38, 1998

3 to fail dismally *US, 1970*

- So you fuck up and you know what. — Darryl Ponicsan, *The Last Detail*, p. 21, 1970
- I completely fucked up the whole thing. — Cicil Von Ziegesar, *You Know You Love Me*, p. 168, 2002

fuckwad *noun*

a contemptible fool; a despicable person; used as a general purpose pejorative *US, 1974*

The negative suffix "-wad" intensified.

- "You're dead, fuckwad," Primo yelled at the stacks of metal sheets, twisted car bodies, and rusting piping. — Ian Ludlow, *Vigilante*, p. 139, 1985
- Why don't you just go piss up a rope, fuckwad. — *Drugstore Cowboy*, 1988
- "Listen, you fuckwad, if you want to know what happened, go ask the cops." — Jimmy Buffet, *Where is Joe Merchant*, p. 184, 1992

fuckwit *noun*

a fool *AUSTRALIA, 1974*

- It is suicide to count on the next bad guy being such a fuckwit as Saddam Hussein. — David H. Hackworth, *Hazardous Duty*, p. 91, 1997

fuck with *verb*

to impress *US, 2001*

- [T]he level of perfection that he [Dr. Dre] works at is amazing. Fuckin' with the best producer in hip-hop music, I had to be more on point. — Eminem (Marshall Mathers), *Angry Blonde*, p. 4, 2001

fucky-fucky *noun*

sex *US, 1961*

Vietnam war usage.

- She used the word, absurdly baby-talk, that the whores used with the soldiers. "... fucky fucky." — Jackson Burgess, *The Atrocity*, p. 52, 1961
- "Fucky-fucky, five bucky,"he chanted in a high-pitched voice. "Who?" I asked. "You or your sister?" — Cyrus Leo Sulzberger, *Tooth Merchant*, p. 224, 1973
- I didn't want any of that "Say hey, slopehead, fuckie-fuckie?" — Larry Heinemann, *Close Quarters*, p. 176, 1977
- "You know, short time, boom-boom, fuckie fuckie." — Jim Stewart, *The Ghosts of Vietnam*, p. 69, 2005

fucky-fucky sauce *noun*

semen *US, 1972*

- Most of the guy's load hits her chin but she gets some of the fucky-fucky sauce down. — *Screw*, p. 15, 6th November 1972

fuck you and the horse you rode in on!

used as an emphatic and insulting rejection *US, 1971*

- Eddie Coyle smiled. "Fuck you, lady," he said, "and the horse you rode in on." — George V. Higgins, *The Friends of Eddie Doyle*, p. 108, 1971
- Reagan treated Baker to one of his favorite lines: "Fuck you and the horse you rode in on." — Richard Reeves, *President Reagan*, p. 239, 2005

fuck-you lizard *noun*

a Vietnamese Tokay Gecko lizard *US, 1970*

US soldiers in Vietnam thought that the gecko's call sounded as if the gecko was saying "fuck you." In polite company, the lizard was called an "insulting lizard."

- A 2nd Brigade chaplains' assistant is trying to put his outdoorsman's skills to work on a somewhat embarrassing problem at the 4th Inf. Div.'s Highlander Chapel. The nemesis in this case was the infamous Vietnamese "insulting Lizard"[.] — *Pacific Stars and Stripes*, 15th May 1970
- And there were the reptiles, especially the "fuck-you" lizard. — John Ketwig, *And a Hard Rain Fell*, p. 119, 2002

fuck-your-buddy week *noun*

a notional designation of the present week, explaining rude behavior by your superiors *US, 1960*

- "What is this, fuck-your-buddy week?" — Thomas Berger, *Crazy in Berlin*, p. 303, 1970
- "What is this," Bruce snarled, "Fuck-Your-Buddy Week?" — Paul Krassner, *Confessions of a Raving, Unconfined Nut*, p. 247, 1993

fuck you very much! *verb*

used as a humorous expression of defiance *US, 1980*

- — *Maledicta*, p. 170, Winter 1980: "A brief survey of some unofficial prosigns used by the United States Armed Forces"
- Good luck to the first team and fuck you very much. — Joseph Wambaugh, *The Glitter Dome*, p. 41, 1981
- I told him Arnie thought I sounded like Teresa Brewer. "No," he said, "more like the Bee Gees." "Well, fuck you very much." — Armistead Maupin, *Maybe the Moon*, p. 64, 1992
- "Because this is the deal of a lifetime, and I was gonna cut you in. So fuck you very much!" — Wolfman Jack (Bob Smith), *Have Mercy!*, p. 147, 1995

fucky-sucky *noun*

a combination of oral and vaginal sex *US, 1974*

- You likee me? You likee fuckee-suckee? — Earl Thompson, *Tattoo*, p. 336, 1974
- The cops in Portshead called it "the fucky-sucky beat" and competed for the opportunity to patrol it. — Walter Walker, *A Dime to Dance By*, p. 34, 1985
- "Fuckee suckee?" I pushed a bill at her. "You too much woman for me." — Harlen Campbell, *Monkey on a Chain*, p. 103, 1999
- That was a joke with them,the long-time, short-time, the number-one fucky-sucky. — Daniel Buckman, *Morning Dark*, p. 46, 2003

fucky-sucky *verb*

to engage in oral and then vaginal sex *US, 1985*

- You like fucky-sucky me, man? — Robert Abel, *The Progress of a Fire*, p. 365, 1985
- The bottom line is how many can you fucky-sucky. — James Ridgeway, *Red Light*, p. 204, 1996

fud *noun*

a fussy, old-fashioned, narrow-minded person *US, 1958*

- I'm going to take very great care to stay out of sight of that old raging fud. — Jack Kerouac, *Jack Kerouac Selected Letters 1957–1969*, p. 128, 4th February 1958: Letter to Joyce Glassman

FUD *noun*
uncertainty and doubt *US, 1997*
- The FUD factor is popularly used to explain why IBM sold so many mainframes. That middle manager couldn't understand the features of all the different systems, and ultimately decided that nobody ever got fired for buying an IBM. — Andy Ihnatko, *Cyberspeak*, pp. 77–78, 1997

fuddy *noun*
an old-fashioned person *US, 1958*
An abbreviation of FUDDY-DUDDY.
- Well, here's my point, Eleanor: the girls are cooped in here the whole day with all old sick fuddies—then a young man pops up! — Terry Southern, *Flash and Filigree*, p. 57, 1958

fuddy-dud *noun*
a fussy, old-fashioned, narrow-minded person *US, 1904*
- But my wife thinks it's the other way; call me a fuddy-dud, but I must admit I don't consider it fitting for my wife to tell me what to do in bed. — Judge John M. Murtagh and Sara Harris, *Cast the First Stone*, p. 166, 1957
- Come on, don't be a fuddy dud. We'll have a party. You and me. — Jill Smolinski, p. 220, 2002

fuddy-duddy *noun*
a fussy, old-fashioned, narrow-minded person *US, 1904*
- Father is a fuddy duddy! — Harry Haenigsen, *Jive's Like That*, 1947
- They're old fuddy-duddies who think that what was a good salary a hundred years ago — Nat Hiken, *Sergeant Bilko*, p. 74, 1957
- Aw, it's O.K., Alice. Christ, we're not a couple of old fuddy-duddies. I remember what I was like at Mike's age. — Armistead Maupin, *Tales of the City*, p. 263, 1978
- What would an old fuddy-duddy like me know about the fashions of young women? — Robert Campbell, *Sweet La-La Land*, p. 221, 1990

fuddy-duddy *adjective*
fussy, old-fashioned, narrow-minded *US, 1907*
- At least seeing Candy romantically would give him more reason to come home than seeing his fuddy-duddy parents. — Alison Kent, *Larger Than Life*, p. 68, 2005

fudge *verb*
to cheat *US, 1958*
- Perhaps he has been fudging on his tax returns. — Raymond Chandler, *Playback*, p. 83, 1958
- Bush fudged figures in his fiscal 1990 budget proposal, which said the deficit would be "only" $100 billion. — Robert Cwikik, *House Rules*, p. 82, 1991
- It is interesting that both Disney and Reagan fudged their own history, bathing fairly wretched childhood experiences in a Norman Rockwell glow. — Mike Wallace, *Mickey Mouse History*, p. 268, 1996
- Just as Powell fudged on what the question is, Rumsfeld fudged on there being no alternative to war. — James Carroll, *Crusade*, p. 163, 2005

fudge
used as a euphemism for "fuck" *UK, 1766*
Based on the opening sound (as is "sugar" for "SHIT").
- "Fudge," I said. "Land o'Goshen, heck, tarnation, crim-a-nentlies." — Max Shulman, *The Zebra Derby*, p. 174, 1946
- Twenty fudging bucks would put a gang of relief in sight for my personal smog. — Bernard Wolfe, *The Late Risers*, p. 5, 1954

fudge factor *noun*
an allowance made for possible error in estimating the time, material, or money needed for a job *US, 1956*
- Today is that fudge factor jammed into the calendar every four years to allow for time we gain on the sun during our normal calendar year. — *Ironwood (Michigan) Daily Globe*, p. 12, 29th February 1956
- — John Edwards, *Auto Dictionary*, p. 66, 1993

fudgepacker *noun*
a homosexual man *US, 1985*
A graphic description of a participant in anal intercourse.
- Horrible little fudge-packer. — Doug Lucie, *Progress*, p. 8, 1985
- Well, yeah—J. M. Barrie was a fudgepacker from way back, and clearly some of that forbiddenness sneaks into every version. — Nicholson Baker, *Vox*, p. 36, 1992
- You wanna celebrate because some fudgepacker that you date has been elected the first queer President of the United States — *As Good As It Gets*, 1997

- Can you imagine the humiliation your father's going to feel when he finds our his pride and joy is a fudgepacker! — *Cruel Intentions*, 1999

fuel *noun*
1 cocaine *US, 1984*
- But clearly you are not the only person in here to take on fuel. Lots of sniffing going on in the stalls. — Jay McInerney, *Bright Lights, Big City*, p. 5, 1984
2 marijuana *US, 1993*
- — Peter Johnson, *Dictionary of Street Alcohol and Drug Terms*, p. 78, 1993

fuel cell *noun*
the gas tank of a race car *US, 2000*
- — Mark Martin, *NASCAR for Dummies*, p. 285, 2000

fuel up *verb*
to eat quickly *US, 1991*
- — Eric S. Raymond, *The New Hacker's Dictionary*, p. 171, 1991

fug
used as a euphemism for "fuck" in all its variant uses and derivatives *US, 1948*
The source of an anecdote that has assumed urban legendary proportions, in which a witty woman (usually Dorothy Parker), when introduced to Norman Mailer, quipped "Oh, you're the young man who can't spell 'fuck'."
- "Even they can't fug me this time," he thought. — Norman Mailer, *The Naked and the Dead*, p. 7, 1948
- "I told you about fugging with that pod." — Herbert Simmons, *Corner Boy*, p. 58, 1957
- I mean have a real flower of something and not just the usually American middleclass fuggup with appearances. — Jack Kerouac, *The Dharma Bums*, p. 161, 1958
- Ah, what the fug, held others; it's only a game, it's not sacred. — Bill Cardoso, *The Maltese Sangweech*, p. 141, 1984

Fugawi *noun*
a mythical tribe or people, so named because after years of wandering they asked, "Where the fuck are we?" *US, 1989*
Military origins. Now the trademarked name of navigational software.
- In the 1/18th, the Fugawi Award went to the company or individual staff officer responsible for the biggest snafu or screwup of the week. — David H. Hackworth, *About Face*, p. 364, 1989

fugazi *adjective*
crazy *US, 1980*
Coined during the Vietnam war.
- We didn't know anything was fugazi until we got to a certain place in the South China Sea. — Mark Barker, *Nam*, p. 29, 1981

fugging *adjective + adverb*
used as a euphemism for the intensifier "fucking" *US, 1948*
- "You're only gonna get your fuggin head blown off tomorrow." — Norman Mailer, *The Naked and the Dead*, p. 7, 1948
- And if I was in the way that was just too fuggin' bad. — Gerald Petievich, *To Die in Beverly Hills*, p. 185, 1983

fugly *adjective*
very ugly *US, 1984*
A blending of FUCKING (or "funky") and "ugly."
- — Connie Eble (Editor), *UNC-CH Campus Slang*, p. 4, Fall 1988
- — Eric S. Raymond, *The New Hacker's Dictionary*, p. 171, 1991
- Her face dropped when she saw that the mingle consisted of our group plus ten fugly women and two cute guys[.] — Anka Radakovich, *The Wild Girls Club*, p. 72, 1994

full *adjective*
drunk *US, 1844*
- Another pub? Too early to get full. — Eric Lambert, *The Veterans*, p. 18, 1954
- — Joseph E. Ragen and Charles Finston, *Inside the World's Toughest Prison*, p. 800, 1962: "Penitentiary and underworld glossary"
- — Connie Eble (Editor), *UNC-CH Campus Slang*, p. 4, Spring 1990

full-auto *adjective*
(used of a firearm) fully automatic *US, 1992*
- There be them big dudes with their full-auto Uzis, an go bailin warp-seven cause Gordy gots the balls to shoot back with this! — Jess Mowry, *Way Past Cool*, 1992

full battle rattle *noun*
full battle gear *US, 2003*

- Maintain the standard for the duration—full battle rattle and alert troops[.] — Russell Glenn, *Capital Preservation*, p. 213, 2001
- Johnny-come-lately commands deem it necessary for all troops in northern Kuwait bases to wear full battle rattle—Kevlar helmet, flak vest, load-bearing vest and weapon. — *Air Force Times*, p. 60, 23rd June 2003

full bull *noun*
a colonel in the US Army *US, 1962*

- "A couple of full-bull colonels passed through Blytheville and got so caught up they wanted to know how they could get some hats." — Elaine Shepard, *The Doom Pussy*, p. 145, 1967
- A full bull earned maybe twenty-three thousand in retirement pay; she earned that every six months, and she was just getting going. — Walter Boyne Steven Thompson, *The Wild Blue*, p. 487, 1986

full Cleveland *noun*
a pastel-colored leisure suit, white belt, and white leather shoes *US, 1977*

The stereotyped wardrobe of a stereotyped 1970s American labor leader.

- The "Full Cleveland" is a celebration of bad—no, rotten, taste in clothing: a powder blue double knit leisure suit, bright blue and yellow flower-patterned shirt with cuffs turned back over the jacket sleeves, white vinyl belt and matching loafers. — *Washington Post*, p. A6, 13th June 1986
- The days of the "full Cleveland"—that classic male retiree ensemble of white shoes, white belt and after-dinner-mint-colored polyester jacket—are numbered. — *Pittsburg Post-Gazette*, p. G8, 25th July 2004

full French *noun*
oral sex performed on a man until he ejaculates *US, 1973*

- Before you walk a trick you must give half and half or full french for the minimum price. — George Paul Csicsery (Editor), *The Sex Industry*, p. 48, 1973
- Blowjob to orgasm? They call it "full French" here. — Gerald Paine, *A Bachelor's Guide to the Brothels of Nevada*, p. 15, 1978

full Greek *noun*
in pinball, a shot up and then back down a lane with a scoring device, scoring twice *US, 1977*

- — Bobbye Claire Natkin and Steve Kirk, *All About Pinball*, p. 112, 1977

full guns *adverb*
to the maximum *US, 1947*

- At any rate, I'm glad to hear everything's going full guns. — Jack Kerouac, *Letter to Caroline Kerouac Blake*, p. 132, 25th September 1947

full hand *noun*
the state of being infected with multiple sexually transmitted diseases *US, 1964*

- — Roger Blake, *The American Dictionary of Sexual Terms*, p. 81, 1964

full house *noun*
1 a combination of several nonexistent diseases *US, 1947*

- Soldiers at a port of embarkation have been told in detail about the foregoing ailments and then told: "If you get a full house, you might just as well stay over there." — *American Speech*, p. 305, December 1947: "Imaginary diseases in army and navy parlance"

2 infection with both gonorrhea and syphilis *US, 1981*

- — *Maledicta*, p. 228, Summer/Winter 1981: "Sex and the single soldier"

full house and no flush *noun*
the situation in which all available latrines are occupied *US, 1947*

- — *American Speech*, p. 55, February 1947: "Pacific war language"

full load *noun*
a long jail sentence *US, 1971*

- For I copped a full load because I strayed from the code. — Michael H. Agar, *The Journal of American Folklore*, p. 181, April 1971

full moon *noun*
1 a woman's menstrual period *US, 1954*

- — *American Speech*, p. 298, December 1954: "The vernacular of menstruation"

2 a large slice of peyote cactus *US, 1970*

- — William D. Alsever, *Glossary for the Establishment and Other Uptight People*, p. 12, December 1970

full mooner *noun*
a mentally unstable person *US, 1951*

From the belief that a full moon brings out psychotic behavior.

- A full mooner's wheels do not go around in proper synchronization. — Burton Turkus and Sid Feder, *Murder, Inc.*, p. 24, 1951

full of run *adjective*
(used of a racehorse) in good racing form *US, 1951*

- — David W. Maurer, *Argot of the Racetrack*, p. 30, 1951

full of shit *adjective*
(of a person) deliberately or congenitally stupid, misleading or misinformed *US, 1954*

- "Mothers are full of shit," Miss Lee observed and took off her leather coat. — John Kenedy Toole, *A Confederacy of Dunces*, p. 24, 1980
- I'm full of shit about what? — David Mamet, *The Woods. Lakeboat, Edmond*, p. 192, 1987
- I know people will read this and say, "Aww, he's full of shit[.]" — Howard Stern, *Miss America*, p. 129, 1995
- Parents are full of shit, teachers are full of shit, clergymen are full of shit, and law enforcement is full of shit. — George Carlin, *Napalm & Silly Putty*, p. 26, 2001

full-on *adjective*
maximum, complete, absolute, very *US, 1970*

- — Jonathan Roberts, *How to California*, p. 168, 1984
- Course, if they come, it with their screamer full on, just like now. — Jess Mowry, *Way Past Cool*, p. 15, 1992
- No, she's a full-on Monet. — *Clueless*, 1995

full out *adverb*
completely, intensely *US, 1918*

- — Leonard Wolfe (Editor), *Voices from the Love Generation*, p. 278, 1968

full tub *noun*
in poker, a hand consisting of three cards of the same rank and a pair *US, 1988*

Conventionally known as a "full house."

- — George Percy, *The Language of Poker*, p. 38, 1988

full weight *noun*
a package of drugs that weighs as much as it is claimed to weigh *US, 1992*

- [A]nd sold full weights—or at least never bitched that Ty packed full weights. — Jess Mowry, *Way Past Cool*, p. 30, 1992

fully *adverb*
very *US, 1982*

- — Mimi Pond, *The Valley Girl's Guide to Life*, p. 55, 1982
- If they threw a party, the chances are it would be "fully geeking." — *New York Times*, 12th April 1987

fumble *verb*
in college, to do poorly and receive a notification of academic deficiency *US, 1968*

- — *American Speech*, pp. 76–77, February 1968: "Some notes on flunk notes"

fumble fingers *noun*
clumsy hands; a clumsy person *US, 1905*

- I figure it's because there are people who might not agree with such a violent way of making a protest, but who do not want the perpetrator—who did not mean to hurt anyone, just a building—to go to jail for having fumble fingers. — Robert Campbell, *Junkyard Dog*, p. 120, 1986
- Do not be a fucking fumble-fingers, Marcinko. — Richard Marcinko, *Red Cell*, p. 32, 1994

fumigate *verb*
to take an enema before or after anal sex *US, 1972*

- — Bruce Rodgers, *The Queens' Vernacular*, p. 91, 1972

fummydiddle *verb*
to waste time or to bungle *US, 1975*

- — John Gould, *Maine Lingo*, p. 103, 1975

fun *noun*
a grain of opium *US, 1964*

- They'd give you a tin that was a little smaller than a tin of salve, and it weighed exactly twelve "fun." — Jeremy Larner and Ralph Tefferteller, *The Addict in the Street*, p. 159, 1964

fun *verb*
to tease, to joke *US, 1950*

- "You're funning me," I said. — Max Shulman, *Sleep Till Noon*, p. 100, 1950
- "Damn, boy," he said, "we's only funnin' with you-all." — Piri Thomas, *Down These Mean Streets*, p. 162, 1967

fun bags *noun*
the female breasts *US, 1965*

- Every time her instructor let himself be thrown, he did a number on her fun bags you wouldn't believe. — Jack W. Thomas, *Heavy Number*, p. 1, 1976
- — Judi Sanders, *Cal Poly Slang*, p. 4, 1990
- She later flashed out her fun bags in Into the Fire (1987). — Mr. Skin, *Mr. Skin's Skincyclopedia*, p. 21, 2005
- "My fun bags need to be played with," … and, indeed, fans of fun bags will be pleased with what this vid has to offer. — Mike Ramone, *The AVN Guide to the 500 Greatest Adult Films of All Time*, p. 128, 2005
- Just her fondling her fun bags. — Pat Mulligan, *The Life and Times of a Hollywood Bad Boy*, p. 278, 2006

fun book *noun*
a collection of discount coupons given to guests by casinos *US, 1991*

- — Michael Dalton, *Blackjack*, p. 49, 1991

fun button *noun*
the clitoris *US, 1973*

- "The little fun button is down at the bottom of your throat." — D.M. Perkins, *Deep Throat*, p. 44, 1973
- This is a clitoris, but she refers to her clitoris as her "fun button." — Cynthia Willett, *Theorizing Multiculturalism*, p. 228, 1998
- She plunged one finger into her tight little hole, her thumb grinding against her fun-button. — alt.sex.stories, 13th November 2004

funch *noun*
sex during lunch *US, 1976*

- Baths vary in character, from the Wall Street Sauna, where businessmen go to get their rocks off during the lunch hour (it's called "funch"), to the Beacon[.] — *The Village Voice*, 27th September 1976

Fun City *nickname*
New York *US, 1965*
Coined by Mayor John Lindsay in 1965.

- Remember Fun City? That's what New York was called when it had a glamorous mayor named Lindsay who seemed destined for even higher office, maybe the White House. — *Washington Post*, p. A2, 19th August 1979
- Meanwhile, the phrase "Fun City" became something of a sick joke[.] — Robert A. M. Stern, *New York 1960*, p. 32, 1995

fungoo!
fuck you! *US, 1942*
Often accompanied by graphic body language.

- Union placard shakers—Chick Vecchio facing them off—the stiff-arm fungoo up close. — James Ellroy, *White Jazz*, p. 58, 1992

fungous *adjective*
disgusting *US, 1960*

- I clue you, nobody can be more fungous than middle-agers on the grape. — Glendon Swarthout, *Where the Boys Are*, p. 93, 1960

fungus *noun*
▸ **there's a fungus among us**
used for disparaging a social outcast *US, 1954*

- Some of the expressions are "such rot," "real cool," "what are you, a bargain?" "he's out of it," "out to lunch," "who needs it?" and "there's a fungus among us." — *Post Standard (Syracuse)*, p. 16, 1954
- "There's a fungus among us" is taking the place of "creepy character." — *Washington Post*, p. F1, 29th September 1957

fun hog *noun*
an obsessed enthusiast of thrill sports *US, 1992*

- — William Nealy, *Mountain Bike!*, p. 161, 1992: "Bikespeak"

funk *noun*
1 a strong human smell; the smell of human sexual activity *US, 1917*

- Better to suffocate, he reasoned, than to die from an overload of funk. — Donald Goines, *White Man's Justice, Black Man's Grief*, p. 20, 1973

2 semen; smegma *US, 1976*

- They had fried shit choplets and hot funk custard/ Drank spit out of cocktail glasses and used afterbirth for mustard. — Dennis Wepman et al., *The Life*, p. 112, 1976

3 a genre of dance music that combines soul, blues, gospel and jazz with irresistible beats and rhythms *US, 1958*
From the sense as "the smell of sex."

- Ambassadors of Funk went out to conquer America and the world. — Alan Shulman, *The Style Bible*, p. 99, 1999
- "I was lucky enough to be the one who created real funk […]," says James Brown, who, as the godfather of funk, should know. — Ben Osborne, *The A-Z of Club Culture*, p. 102, 1999

4 a depressed state of mind *UK, 1820*

- He fell into a black funk, then snatched the record off the turntable and shattered it with the hammer he kept in the tool box under the kitchen sink. — Armistead Maupin, *Further Tales of the City*, p. 39, 1982
- Lefty came over in a blue funk. His sister heard on the grapevine about his penile eccentricity and told his parents. — C.D. Payne, *Youth in Revolt*, p. 12, 1993

funk!
used for expressing anger or disgust *US, 1963*

- — Carol Ann Preusse, *Jargon Used by University of Texas Co-Eds*, 1963

funked out *adjective*
drug-intoxicated *US, 1971*

- — Eugene Landy, *The Underground Dictionary*, p. 84, 1971

funky *adjective*
1 sexual in a primal sense, earthy *US, 1954*

- It was dark in here and loud, the sound cranked way up, but he liked it, the heavy beat, the girls' funky moves as they belted the lyrics, each holding a mike. — Elmore Leonard, *Be Cool*, p. 52, 1999

2 bad, distasteful, dirty, smelly *US, 1946*

- Long underwear that looked like the housing project of some gophers on a fresh air kick, about ten sizes too big and five quarts of creosote too funky. — Mezz Mezzrow, *Really the Blues*, p. 33, 1946
- The shop will be open from eight to eight and she'll be setting and washing peoples' funky hair. — Susan Hall, *Gentleman of Leisure*, p. 158, 1972

3 earthy, fundamental, emotional, and when applied to music, characterized by blues tonalities *US, 1954*

- She didn't want to dance to the blues, the gut bucket, the funky songs. — Dick Gregory, *Nigger*, p. 60, 1964
- On the other hand one does not want to arrive "poormouthing it" in some outrageous turtleneck and West Eight Street bell-jean combination, as if one is "funky" and of "the people." — Tom Wolfe, *Radical Chic & Mau-Mauing the Flak Catchers*, p. 13, 1970
- Kate showed Martha the lead-glass windows, the claw-footed tub and the blackened fireplace, large enough to smoke a salmon. "Is this funky, or is this funky?" — Cyra McFadden, *The Serial*, p. 151, 1977
- The place was musty with cigar smoke and sherry, funky in the Black jazz man's sense of the word. — Odie Hawkins, *The Life and Times of Chester Simmons*, p. 30, 1991

4 fashionable *US, 1969*

- [F]unky boots[.] — *SMTV LIVE it's wicked*, p. 19, 2000

5 in computing, descriptive of a feature that works imperfectly but not poorly enough to justify the time and expense to correct it *US, 1991*

- The Intel i860's exception handling is extraordinary funky. — Eric S. Raymond, *The New Hacker's Dictionary*, p. 171, 1991

funky-fresh *adjective*
fashionable, stylish *US, 1982*

- Scott and Kris were a funky-fresh brand of b-boy—they waved the culture's contradictions in your face like a dare. — Alan Light, *The Vibe History of Hip-Hop*, p. 148, 1999

funny *noun*
counterfeit money *US, 1974*
An abbreviation of **FUNNY MONEY**.

- "Never occurred to them, race track's a good place to pass funny." — George Higgin, *Cogan's Trade*, p. 32, 1974

funny *adjective*
1 counterfeit *US, 1980*

- "No," I said. "It's not funny, though. I inspected it closely and the serial numbers are all different. The paper looks good." — George Higgins, *Kennedy for the Defense*, p. 113, 1980

2 homosexual *US, 1962*

- — Anthony Romeo, *The Language of Gangs*, p. 18, 4th December 1962

funny bomb *noun*
a fragmenting explosive *US, 1991*
Army use.
- The funny bomb was an awesome weapon, and lethal against trucks or guns. — Phillip Chinnery, *Air Commando*, p. 172, 1997

funny book *noun*
a pornographic book or magazine *US, 1976*
- — Len Buckwalter, *CB Radio*, p. 106, 1976

funny boy *noun*
a male homosexual *US, 1977*
- Next to loneliness the biggest problem the trucker encounters on the highway is the "queer," the lollipop artist, the funny boys. They harrass a trucker unmercifully. — Gwyneth A. "Dandalion" Seese, *Tijuana Bear in a Smoke 'Um Up Taxi*, p. 75, 1977

funny bunny *noun*
an eccentric *US, 1966*
- Abominating the cops, crooks, scavengers and funny-bunnies of the twentieth century, he abandons civilization and takes the family to live in the Honduran jungle. — Paul Theroux, *The Great Railway Bazaar*, 1975

funny cigarette *noun*
a marijuana cigarette *US, 1949*
- "Funny cigarettes ain't all that one pushes, it ain't no big secret." — Nelson Algren, *The Man with the Golden Arm*, p. 23, 1949
- He looked for new faces standing around on corners and talked to them, and told them he didn't like funny cigarettes or worse sold on his beat and that he had a good memory for faces. — W.E.B. Griffin, *The Murderers*, p. 304, 1994
- Well, the Rock is standing there staring at Stone Cold Steve Austin like he's got three heads, thinking What kind of funny cigarettes have you been smoking? — Rock, *The Rock Says*, p. 231, 2000

funny farm *noun*
a hospital for the mentally ill *US, 1959*
- "He's my new headshrinker. Wants me to go to Connecticut to some fancy funny farm." — Jacqueline Susann, *Valley of the Dolls*, p. 359, 1966
- I said, "Not too well. She's on a funny farm." — Iceberg Slim (Robert Beck), *Trick Baby*, p. 173, 1969
- On a Michigan funny farm there are three inmates, each of whom believes he is Jesus Christ. — Tom Robbins, *Another Roadside Attraction*, p. 269, 1971
- The only obstacle is they're shipping me out to the funny farm in four days. — *Natural Born Killers*, 1994

funny ha-ha; ha-ha funny *adjective*
amusing, inviting of laughter, as opposed to "funny" in the sense of peculiar *UK, 1938*
From the oft-cited contrast of **FUNNY PECULIAR** and "funny ha-ha" by British novelist and dramatist Ian Hay.
- "That bird gives me the creeps. He's funny. Not ha ha funny, but koo koo funny." — Iceberg Slim (Robert Beck), *Mama Black Widow*, p. 33, 1969

funny kine *adjective*
strange, unexpected, abnormal *US, 1981*
Hawaiian youth usage.
- Oh, he ac' real funny kine. — Douglas Simonson, *Pidgin to da Max*, 1981

funny money *noun*
1 counterfeit or play currency *US, 1938*
- I tore open the bandana! It was a dummy loaded with funny-money. — Iceberg Slim (Robert Beck), *Airtight Willie and Me*, p. 16, 1979
- I will show you my ten grand buy money before you show me the funny money. — Gerald Petievich, *Money Men*, p. 5, 1981
2 during the Vietnam war, military payment certificates *US, 1965*
The certificates were handed out to the military instead of currency to prevent black market use of the US dollar. Denominations of the certificates ranged from five cents to 20 dollars.
- — *Time*, p. 34, 19th December 1965
- — Carl Fleischhauer, *A Glossary of Army Slang*, p. 20, 1968
- The boy was counting MPC, Military Payment Certificates, GI funny money, which he stuffed into the pockets of his shorts. — Larry Heinemann, *Close Quarters*, p. 40, 1977
3 promotional coupons issued by casinos to match money bets *US, 2003*
- — Victor H. Royer, *Casino Gamble Talk*, p. 57, 2003

funny papers *noun*
topographical maps *US, 1980*
Vietnam war usage; a tad cynical about the accuracy of the military's maps.
- "It must been a Montegnard ville, but it's collapsed and there's new growth over it all. Over." "Any indication of it on your funny papers? Over." "Negative that." — John M. Del Vecchio, *The 13th Valley*, p. 464, 1982
- — David Hart, *First Air Cavalry Division Vietnam Dictionary*, p. 27, 2004

funny puff *noun*
a marijuana cigarette *US, 1976*
- — Warren Smith, *Warren's Smith's Authentic Dictionary of CB*, p. 39, 1976

funny valentine *noun*
a tablet of Dexedrine™, a central nervous system stimulant *US, 1966*
A reference to the tablet's heart shape.
- Still popular among the non-psychedelics are the "funny valentines," so called because of their heart shape. — Roger Gordon, *Hollywood's Sexual Underground*, p. 58, 1966

funny ward *noun*
a hospital ward reserved for the mentally ill *US, 1963*
- Once again, Lilah's husband had been summoned to the "funny" ward at City General. — Marci Blackman, *Po Man's Child*, p. 6, 1999

funny water *noun*
any alcoholic beverage *US, 1974*
- Don Nickles admonished me to stop drinking whatever funny water I had found. — James M. Jeffords, *An Independent Man*, p. 271, 2003

funster *noun*
a joker; a person who reminds you how much fun we are having *US, 1974*
- To succeed in this society of professed funsters a man must be on the make. — Bill Cardoso, *The Maltese Sangweech*, p. 115, 1984

funsy-wunsy *adjective*
fun, cute *US, 1995*
- [M]ostly the cameras just observed "a lot of things that really go down on a tour that are not cute or funsy-wunsy." — David Downing, *A Dreamer of Pictures*, p. 195, 1995

fun tickets *noun*
money *US, 1997*
- Can't make happy hour, Bro. I'm all out of fun tickets. — Vann Wesson, *Generation X Field Guide and Lexicon*, p. 70, 1997

funzine *noun*
a purportedly humorous single-interest fan magazine *US, 1982*
- — *American Speech*, p. 26, Spring 1982: "The language of science fiction fan magazines"

fur *noun*
1 the female pubic hair; a woman as a sex object *US, 1959*
Contemporary use mainly in **FURBURGER, FUR PIE**, etc.
- Nothin to do now but smoke unless they knows some place else to buy some fur. — Warren Miller, *The Cool World*, p. 121, 1959
- — *Maledicta*, p. 131, Summer/Winter 1982: "Dyke diction: the language of lesbians"
- It's a hoot of a performance, with Leslie's hooters flopping all over the place, her perfect posterior, and even a fleeting flash of fur. — Mr. Skin, *Mr. Skin's Skincyclopedia*, p. 53, 2005
2 a woman's hairpiece *US, 1972*
- — David Claerbaut, *Black Jargon in White America*, p. 65, 1972

furball *noun*
an airial dogfight involving several planes *US, 1983*
- During furball, close-in dogfighting, the Vector-A system remained off, and the fighter's original equipment gun sight was used to aim its brace of 20-millimeter cannons. — T.E. Cruise, *Wings of Gold III*, p. 354, 1989

fur beef *noun*
a prison sentence for rape *US, 1976*
- — John R. Armore and Joseph D. Wolfe, *Dictionary of Desperation*, p. 30, 1976

furburger *noun*
the vagina, especially as an object of oral pleasure-giving; a woman as a sex object *US, 1965*
A term that is especially popular with Internet pornographers.
- I found it not at all disagreeable to mix up a few "tinis sours, or stumplifters" in a milk jug, jump into a "flip-top motivatin' unit," and "flazz off" in search of "furburgers." — John Nichols, *The Sterile Cuckoo*, p. 60, 1965

- — Eugene Landy, *The Underground Dictionary*, p. 85, 1971
- Whether it's Looking for Eileen (1988) and its full-frontal juicy furburger, or her wet goodies bouncing delightfully in Switch (1991) and Save Me (1993), Lysette is a carnal craftsman. — Mr. Skin, *Mr. Skin's Skincyclopedia*, p. 21, 2005

fur cup *noun*
the vagina *US, 1966*
- — John D. Bell et al., *Loosely Speaking*, p. 9, 1966
- Why the Fur Cup is Not Just an Inside-Out Cock (Headline) — *Screw*, p. 9, 8th December 1969

▶ **drink of the fur cup**
to perform oral sex on a woman *US, 1966*
- — John D. Bell et al., *Loosely Speaking*, p. 9, 1966

furniture *noun*
a knife *US, 1975*
- — Report to the Senate, *California Senate Committee on Civil Disorder*, p. 230, 1975

fur pie *noun*
the vulva and pubic hair *US, 1934*
- Candy lay back again with a sigh, closed-eyed, hands joined behind her head, and Grindle resumed his fondling of her sweet-dripping little fur-pie. — Terry Southern, *Candy*, p. 207, 1958
- "[M]y mouth was munching and sucking her whole fur-pie." — Joey V., *Portrait of Joey*, p. 94, 1969
- His face is maybe twelve inches from Sabrina's fur pie, and the guy is fucking snoring. — Carl Hiaasen, *Strip Tease*, p. 19, 1993
- Lee is mistaken for Dweller by Devon Shore, who is as fresh-faced a slice of fur pie you're likely to see in this kinky a video. — Penthouse Magazine, *The Penthouse Erotic Video Guide*, p. 29, 2003

further *noun*
▶ **in the further**
in the future *US, 1973*
Used when saying goodbye.
- Catch you on the FURTHA. — Malachi Andrews and Paul T. Owens, *Black Language*, p. 76, 1973

furthermucker *noun*
used as a humorous euphemism for "motherfucker" *US, 1965*
- He beats everybody in the place once on the pool table and circles around to the first boy he beat and says to him, "Rack 'em up, furthermucker." — Padgett Powell, *Aliens of Affection*, p. 187, 1998

fur-trapper *noun*
a thief who distracts hotel guests in the lobby or at the hotel desk long enough to steal their furs *US, 1954*
- The fur-trappers were older and bolder. — Dev Collans with Stewart Sterling, *I was a House Detective*, p. 97, 1954

fuselighter *noun*
an artillery soldier *US, 1988*
- — Hans Halberstadt, *Airborne*, p. 130, 1988: "Abridged dictionary of airborne terms"

fuss *verb*
used as a euphemistic replacement for "fuck" *US, 1974*
- "POK. Fuss you, sisser," Glenn said, drawing himself up. — Earl Thompson, *Tattoo*, p. 59, 1974

fussbudget *noun*
a chronic worrier *US, 1904*
- Old Janson is a fussbudget. — Mary McCarthy, *The Group*, p. 326, 1963

fusspot *noun*
a very fussy person *UK, 1921*
- "And I was the fusspot, about letting her leave school." — Herman Wouk, *The Winds of War*, p. 240, 1971

futz around *verb*
to waste time; to tinker with no results *US, 1930*
- "What's up to you sir, is not to waste time futzin' around" — Leo Rosten, *Silky!*, p. 123, 1979
- So I'm futzing around with her new kitten while she's making tea. — Robert Stoller and I.S. Levine, *Coming Attractions*, p. 78, 1991

futz up *verb*
used as a euphemism for "fuck up," meaning to bungle *US, 1947*
- The deal was futzed up enough as it was, and it didn't make sense. — Jim Thompson, *The Nothing Man*, p. 282, 1954

fuzz *noun*
a police officer; the police *US, 1924*

- By the way they knocked he knew it was the fuzz[.] — Alexander Trocchi, *Cain's Book*, p. 235, 1960
- Fuzz, man, they want to bust you, they bust you, doesn't matter what the charges, that's the whole fuzz syndrome right there. — Richard Farina, *Been Down So Long*, p. 64, 1966
- Hey, watch it, fuzz ahead. — *American Graffiti*, 1973
- Wasn't that like a cop? Didn't trust the local fuzz, had to come here and see for himself. — Elmore Leonard, *Glitz*, p. 100, 1985

fuzz *verb*
to shuffle (a deck of playing cards) by simultaneously drawing cards from the bottom and top of the deck *US, 1967*
- — Albert H. Morehead, *The Complete Guide to Winning Poker*, p. 264, 1967

fuzzburger *noun*
the vagina as an object of oral pleasure-giving *US, 1967*
- — *American Speech*, p. 228, October 1967: "Some special terms used in a University of Connecticut men's dormitory"

fuzzed *adjective*
drug-intoxicated *US, 1961*
- I was so fuzzed on White Horse, dexedrine, Miltown and the rages of brain music which beat with alternating triumph and despondency inside my head that my legs and arms felt encased in frozen concrete. — Clancy Sigal, *Going Away*, p. 400, 1961

fuzzie *noun*
a girl or young woman *US, 1974*
- Get ride of the fuzzies. We got something to talk about. — Elmore Leonard, *52 Pick-up*, p. 131, 1974

fuzz one; fuzz two; fuzz three *noun*
used as a rating system by US forces in Vietnam for the films shown on base; the system rated films on the amount of pubic hair shown *US, 1990*
The more, the better.
- — Gregory Clark, *Words of the Vietnam War*, pp. 21–22, 1990

fuzztail *noun*
a horse *US, 1958*
- — *American Speech*, p. 270, December 1958: "Ranching terms from eastern Washington"

fuzzy *noun*
1 in horse racing, a horse that is seen as certain to win a race *US, 1956*
- — Toney Betts, *Across the Board*, 1956

2 in a deck of playing cards, the joker *US, 1988*
- — George Percy, *The Language of Poker*, p. 38, 1988

fuzzy-wuzzy *noun*
a dust ball *US, 1947*
- The windows hadn't been washed in months, and the rooms were full of dust and fuzzy-wuzzies. — Irving Shulman, *The Amboy Dukes*, p. 24, 1947

f-word *noun*
the word "fuck" *US, 1970*
The intent is to specify one word, out of thousands that begin with "f," that the speaker will not use.
- Pressed by Mr. Kuntsler, all she would say was: "Every other word was that 'f' word." — J. Anthony Lukas, *The Barnyard Epithet and Other Obscenities*, p. 29, 1970
- I'd use the F word but Ice Cube got the copyright[.] — MC Serch, *Mic Techniques*, 1991
- Let me help you Bashful, did it involve the F-word? — *Pulp Fiction*, 1994
- MR. GARRISON: Eric! Did you just say the "F" word? CARTMAN: Fragile? KYLE: No, he's talking about fuck, dude. You can't say fuck in front of Mr. Garrison. — *South Park*, 1999

FYA
used as Internet shorthand to mean "for your amusement" *US, 1997*
- — Andy Ihnatko, *Cyberspeak*, p. 78, 1997

FYI
used in business and computer message shorthand to mean "for your information" *US, 1941*
Also used archly in conversation.
- [S]he will hand me a bowl of rice pudding, indicate the whipped cream with a spy's nod, and murmur, "FYI, friend." — Ethan Morden, *Everybody Loves You*, p. 136, 1988
- — Eric S. Raymond, *The New Hacker's Dictionary*, p. 342, 1991

Gg

G *noun*

1 one thousand dollars; one thousand *US, 1928*

From **GRAND**.

- She needs doctors and nurses and a place to live and something to eat for maybe years. Take six or seven gees for that... — Horace McCoy, *Kiss Tomorrow Good-bye*, p. 62, 1948
- I'll even take care of the babe's ten g's out of my end. — Jim Thompson, *A Swell-Looking Babe*, p. 80, 1954
- Gonzalo's regular tip for headwaiters and bandleaders was a "G." — Lee Mortimer, *Women Confidential*, p. 79, 1960
- Suppose you had killed him for $75,000—would that have been worth it? Ain't no bartender got 75 gees, I answered. — Piri Thomas, *Down These Mean Streets*, p. 219, 1967
- And where'd the Church get the 50 G in the first place? — *The Bad Lieutenant*, 1992

2 a cheating device *US, 2005*

An abbreviation of **GAFF**.

- The "G," or gaff, was that some nails were altered so that they bent immediately under the force of the hammer. — Peter Fenton, *Eyeing the Flash*, p. 129, 2005

3 one grain (of a narcotic) *US, 1966*

- — *Mr.*, p. 9, April 1966: "The hippie's lexicon"

4 a generic manufactured cigarette *US, 1992*

- — William K. Bentley and James M. Corbett, *Prison Slang*, 1992

5 a gang member *US, 1990*

- "This is upper level warfare; a G won't even take a youngster with him when he sets out to grab another G." — Leon Bing, *Do or Die*, p. 231, 1991
- [T]he small army of junior G's. — Karline Smith, *Moss Side Massive*, p. 8, 1994
- They know I'm the type that never had a crime partner. I was always What do you say to the other OG's about getting with the younger Gs to make things better? — Yusuf Jah, *Uprising*, p. 56, 1995

6 a close friend *US, 1989*

- — James Haskins, *The Story of Hip-Hop*, p. 137, 2000

7 a G-string *US, 1992*

- For a long time, all you can get is belly dancers willing to strip down to their G's. — Robert Campbell, *Boneyards*, p. 191, 1992

▸ **pull a G**

to engage in serial sex with many men *US, 1977*

- [T]hey would get her drunk, and then Rock and B.K. and all their boys would have sex with her. That's called a gang bang, or pulling a G. — John Allen, *Assault with a Deadly Weapon*, p. 62, 1977

gab *noun*

unimportant conversation *UK, 1790*

- "Give it to me," said Frost, "and cut that hipster gab. It's making me sick." — Terry Southern, *Flash and Filigree*, p. 145, 1958

gabacho; gavacho *noun*

a white person *US, 1950*

Derogatory border Spanish used in English conversation by Mexican-Americans.

- — George Carpenter Baker, *Pachuco*, p. 41, 1950
- — *Current Slang*, p. 18, Spring 1970
- Oscar Acosta—an old friend, who was under bad pressure at the time, from his super-militant constituents, for even talking to a gringo/gabacho journalist. — Hunter S. Thompson, *The Great Shark Hunt*, p. 119, 1979
- — Multicultural Management Program Fellows, *Dictionary of Cautionary Words and Phrases*, 1989

gabber *noun*

any central nervous system stimulant *US, 1987*

- The pills are actually nothing but rounded bits of plastic with a yellow dust of pure meth. One simply takes thirty or so of these little gabbers, leaving them in their little pill bottle. — Jim Carroll, *Forced Entries*, p. 29, 1987

Gabby Hayes hat *noun*

the field hat worn by US soldiers in Vietnam *US, 1977*

Likened to the narrow brim and low crown of the hat worn by the US western film star Gabby Hayes.

- I dress and gather up my forty-five web belt and Gabby Hayes bush hat. — Larry Heinemann, *Close Quarters*, p. 134, 1977

gabfest *noun*

a group talk, usually about gossip or trivial matters *US, 1897*

- I would have been unaware of this cigarette gesture being a signal if Bob McClurg had not told me during one of these gab-fests. — Gregory "Pappy" Boyington, *Baa Baa Black Sheep*, p. 197, 1958
- Jane DePugh to Sandra Giles—pitch-girl for Mark C. Blome Tires, semi-regular on Tom Duggan's TV gabfest. — James Ellroy, *Hollywood Nocturnes*, p. 104, 1994

gack *noun*

a despised person *US, 1997*

- — Vann Wesson, *Generation X Field Guide and Lexicon*, p. 72, 1997

gack *verb*

in poker, to fold holding a hand that have would have won had the player stayed in the game *US, 1996*

- — John Vorhaus, *The Big Book of Poker Slang*, p. 19, 1996

gadget *noun*

1 used as a general term for any cheating device used in a card game *US, 1988*

- — George Percy, *The Language of Poker*, p. 38, 1988

2 in poker, any special rule applied to a game using wild cards *US, 1967*

- — Albert H. Morehead, *The Complete Guide to Winning Poker*, p. 264, 1967

3 a G-string or similar female article of clothing *US, 1980*

- — Joe McKennon, *Circus Lingo*, p. 38, 1980

4 a US Air Force cadet *US, 1944*

- — *American Speech*, p. 310, December 1946: "More Air Force Slang"

gaff *noun*

1 a cheating device *US, 1893*

- — Frank Garcia, *Marked Cards and Loaded Dice*, p. 262, 1962
- There are fellows who laugh when they use the gaff / To take a sucker's dough. — Dennis Wepman et al., *The Life*, p. 162, 1976
- On the midway, he learned the art of "cake cutting," or shortchanging customers, using "sticks"—carnies posing as customers pretending to win a big prize—and "gaffs"—concealed devices such as magnets used to ensure that the house always won. — Kim Rich, *Johnny's Girl*, p. 37, 1993
- "On the Swinger, your pinkie is the gaff, so don't get it chopped off in a bar fight." — Peter Fenton, *Eyeing the Flash*, p. 2, 2005

2 a counterfeit watch *US, 1973*

- We call them gaffs in the mob or one-lungers. The mob's jewelers can make any kind of watch you want. — Vincent Teresa, *My Life in the Mafia*, p. 59, 1973

3 a device used to hide the shape of a male transvestite's penis *US, 1973*

- Another device is the "gaff," a cradle, usually made of canvas or denim, to which elastic hoops are attached. The gaff is pulled up tight at the crotch, the effect being to flatten the genitals[.] — George Paul Csicsery (Editor), *The Sex Industry*, p. 74, 1973

gaff *verb*

1 to fix or rig a device *US, 1934*

- Say a mark is right beside you in the joint. Blue is gonna gaff that wheel on your number and heave you a heavy cop to excite the mark. — Iceberg Slim (Robert Beck), *Trick Baby*, p. 93, 1969

2 to cheat *UK, 1811*

- — Lou Shelly, *Hepcats Jive Dictionary*, p. 11, 1945

gaffer *noun*

in circus and carnival usage, a manager *US, 1981*

- — Don Wilmeth, *The Language of American Popular Entertainment*, p. 105, 1981

gaffle *noun*

in street gambling, a protocol under which the winner shares his winnings with other players *US*, *1997*

- — *American Speech*, p. 406, Winter 1997: "Among the new words"

gaffle *verb*

1 to steal *US*, *1900*

- Go in and gaffle the money and run to one of your aunt's cribs[.] — Eminem Marshall Mathers, *Guilty Conscience*, 1999

2 to arrest; to catch *US*, *1954*

- I heard they had you gaffled. The goon squad. Someone said they marched you right across the yard. — Malcolm Braly, *On the Yard*, 1967
- Far as she was concerned, the feds who gaffled him up were angels of mercy. — Seth Morgan, *Homeboy*, p. 49, 1990
- Besides, the way we got gaffled up by the sheriff's at the muthafucka? — *Menace II Society*, 1993

3 to cheat, to swindle, to defraud *US*, *1998*

- — Ethan Hilderbrant, *Prison Slang*, 1998

gaffs *noun*

dice that have been altered for cheating *US*, *1950*

- — *The Annals of the American Academy of Political and Social Sciences*, p. 125, May 1950

gaff shot *noun*

in pool, an elaborate shot, especially an illegal one *US*, *1985*

- — Mike Shamos, *The Illustrated Encyclopedia of Billiards*, p. 106, 1993

gag *noun*

1 a manner of doing something, a practice *US*, *1890*

- John McEnroe used that gag in every successful tennis match. — Joseph Wambaugh, *Finnegan's Week*, p. 110, 1993

2 in the television and movie industries, a stunt *US*, *1988*

- — John Cann, *The Stunt Guide*, p. 59: "Terms and definitions"
- [He would] watch movies on cable TV, cars burning in flames, stunt men being shot off of high places—see if he could recognize the work, or how it was done if it was a new gag[.] — Elmore Leonard, *Freaky Deaky*, p. 179, 1988

3 any artifice employed by a beggar to elicit sympathy *US*, *1962*

- — Joseph E. Ragen and Charles Finston, *Inside the World's Toughest Prison*, p. 800, 1962: "Penitentiary and underworld glossary"

4 an indefinite prison sentence *US*, *1958*

- — *New York Times Magazine*, p. 88, 16th March 1958

5 in craps, a bet that the shooter will make his even-numbered point in pairs *US*, *1950*

- — *The Annals of the American Academy of Political and Social Sciences*, p. 125, May 1950

gag *verb*

to panic in the face of a great challenge *US*, *1988*

- — Michael V. Anderson, *The Bad, Rad, Not to Forget Way Cool Beach and Surf Discriptionary*, p. 7, 1988

gage *noun*

1 marijuana *US*, *1934*

Also variants "gayge" and "gages."

- I was really high on fine gage when I wrote pages 1 & 2—as you could guess I suppose. — Neal Cassady, *Neal Cassady Collected Letters 1944–1967*, p. 106, 22nd September 1948: Letter to Jack Kerouac
- Shorty would take me to groovy, frantic scenes in different chicks' and cats' pads, where with the lights and juke down mellow, everybody blew gage and juiced back and jumped. — Malcolm X and Alex Haley, *The Autobiography of Malcolm X*, 1964
- I could not see how they were more justified in drinking than I was in blowing the gage. — Eldridge Cleaver, *Soul on Ice*, p. 4, 1968
- The lion let out with a mighty rage / Like a young cocksucker blowing his gauge. — Anonymous ("Arthur"), *Shine and the Titanic; The Signifying Monkey; Stackolee*, p. 1, 1971

2 alcohol, especially whisky *US*, *1932*

- — Lou Shelly, *Hepcats Jive Dictionary*, p. 11, 1945

gaged *adjective*

drug-intoxicated *US*, *1932*

- Jodie was gaged on heroin and kept snapping that knife open and shut and looking at me as if he'd like to cut my throat. — Chester Himes, *A Rage in Harlem*, p. 225, 1957

gagers; gaggers *noun*

methcathinone *US*, *1998*

- — US Office of National Drug Control Policy, *Drug Facts*, February 2003

gagged *adjective*

disgusted *US*, *1968*

- — Collin Baker et al., *College Undergraduate Slang Study Conducted at Brown University*, p. 123, 1968

gaggle *noun*

a formation of several military aircraft flying the same mission *US*, *1942*

- — *American Speech*, p. 118, May 1963: "Air refueling words"

gag me!; gag me with a spoon!

used for expressing disgust *US*, *1982*

A quintessential Valley Girl expression of disgust.

- He like sits there and like plays with all his rings / And he like flirts with all the guys in the class / It's like totally disgusting / I'm like so sure / It's like BARF ME OUT / Gag me with a spoon! — Moon Unit and Frank Zappa, *Valley Girl*, 1982
- — Connie Eble (Editor), *UNC-CH Campus Slang*, p. 2, Fall 1982

gagster *noun*

a comedian *UK*, *1935*

- The gagster and his girl staggered out of the place and reported in at the nearest hospital[.] — Robert Sylvester, *No Cover Charge*, p. 205, 1956

Gainesburger *noun*

in the military, canned beef patties *US*, *1983*

Alluding to a dog food product. Vietnam war usage.

- "Gainesburgers," said Banjo. We had named the army's canned ground beef patties, served in gravy, after the dog food. — Robert Mason, *Chickenhawk*, p. 81, 1983

gal block *noun*

a section of a prison reserved for blatantly homosexual prisoners *US*, *1972*

- One night they was here and everybody in the gal block knew about it and he called me out. — Bruce Jackson, *In the Life*, p. 398, 1972

gal-boy *noun*

an effeminate young man *US*, *1950*

- He liked nature in a different way. Inside the prison we called him a punk gal-boy. — Haywood Patterson, *Scottsboro Boy*, p. 45, 1950
- They were known as pussyboys, galboys, fuckboys, and all had taken girls' names like Betty, Fifi, Dotty, etc. — James Blake, *The Joint*, p. 67, 1971
- You willing to fight anybody wants you as their gal-boy? — Elmore Leonard, *Bandits*, p. 144, 1987

Galilee stompers *noun*

in homosexual usage, sandals *US*, *1986–1987*

- — *Maledicta*, p. 56, 1986–1987: "A continuation of a glossary of ethnic slurs in American English"

gallery 13 *noun*

a prison graveyard *US*, *1982*

- — Ralph de Sola, *Crime Dictionary*, p. 56, 1982
- — William K. Bentley and James M. Corbett, *Prison Slang*, 1992

gallery girl *noun*

a woman who makes herself available sexually to professional golfers *US*, *1975*

- Now that the fairways are roped off during a tournament, it's a lot harder for the gallery girls to make contact with a golfer. — Herb Michelson, *Sportin' Ladies*, p. 138, 1975

gallery god *noun*

a theater-goer who sits in the uppermost balcony *US*, *1947*

- During the early part of my career as a theater fan I was a "gallery god." All gallery seats were unreserved. — *San Francisco Examiner*, p. 21, 12th August 1947

galloping bones *noun*

dice *US*, *1920*

- Kate and I were right at home with all those little clicking wheels and felt tables and galloping bones and slot machines. — Albert Murray, *Godd Morning Blues*, p. 364, 1985

galloping dandruff *noun*

body lice *US*, *1920*

- No point in sending squad cars screaming around the countryside if granny's demise had been by galloping dandruff and not the hand of a desperate ruffian. — Keith McCarthy, *A Feast of Carrion*, p. 22, 2003

galmeat *noun*
the vulva *US, 1991*
- Two marginally attractive white women with tan lines, only one shaved, rub their respective galmeats together. Their galmeats are wet. — Richard Meltzer, *A Whore Just Like the Rest*, p. 423, 1991

gal pal *noun*
1 a woman's female friend *US, 1969*
- [S]he'd found out about me and her old lady when she'd overheard Momma confiding in one of her koffee-klatch gal-pals. — Joey V., *Portrait of Joey*, pp. 126–127, 1969
- Angela was not only married, she was a friend of Maria's. Needless to say, it created a bit of tension between gal pals. — Erica Orloff and JoAnn Baker *Dirty Little Secrets*, p. 141, 2001
2 a female friend of a male homosexual *US, 1977*
- — Bruce Rodgers, *The Queens' Vernacular*, p. 92, 1977

gal tank *noun*
a holding cell in a jail reserved for homosexual prisoners *US, 1972*
- There's punks all over the place in the gal tank. — Bruce Jackson, *In the Life*, p. 399, 1972

gam *noun*
the leg *UK, 1785*
Originally applied to a crippled leg, later to a woman's leg.
- For the rest of her career in Hollywood, while her gams are still straight and her figure otherwise, she'll pose cheesecake for fanmags and Sunday sheets[.] — Jack Lait and Lee Mortimer, *New York Confidential*, p. 145, 1946
- Those gams. Next to her, Diedrick is a pellagra case. — Bernard Wolfe, *The Late Risers*, p. 143, 1954
- A flash of the harlequin's crotch-zinging legs reminded him of Rachel's gams. — Iceberg Slim (Robert Beck), *Death Wish*, p. 113, 1977
- Beats looking at Bonny Prince Charles's skinny gams under a kilt. — Rita Ciresi, *Pink Slip*, p. 50, 1999

gam *verb*
to boast *US, 1970*
- — Clarence Major, *Dictionary of Afro-American Slang*, p. 57, 1970

gamahuche *noun*
an act of oral sex *UK, 1865*
Possibly a combination of Scots dialect words *gam* (gum, mouth) and *roosh* (rush), hence a "rushing into the mouth"; more likely from French *gamahucher* which shares the same sense.
- [S]he always did it with her men, and said they were made for it; it's what they call gamahuching, the French pleasure. — William Gibson, *The Difference Engine*, p. 236, 1991
- Sitting there, he's watched himself on the editing machine fall out of bed and out of focus, go limp in a stockyard, sneeze in the middle of a gamahuche[.] — Robert Coover, *The Adventures of Lucky Pierre*, p. 120, 2002

gambler's bankroll; gambler's roll *noun*
a bankroll consisting of a large-denomination bill on the outside of a number of small-denomination bills *US, 1986*
- Whistler took out his gambler's roll. A fifty was on top. You'd think he was carrying big money if you didn't know the rest was ones with maybe a couple of fives. — Robert Campbell, *In La-La Land We Trust*, p. 96, 1986

game *noun*
1 a person's style, visual and oral *US, 1976*
- Now the monkey had practiced his game till it was sharp as glass / And keep in his heart he knew he could kick the baboon's ass. — Dennis Wepman et al., *The Life*, p. 31, 1976
- You look at any dude out here got a real strong game together like I do, it's cause they got theyself a strong lady like this one. — John Sayles, *Union Dues*, p. 183, 1977
- He talked game with him at every chance, lectured him on the pimping code[.] — Alix Shulman, *On the Stroll*, p. 56, 1981
- But I gotta keep my game tight like Kobe on game night. — *Hustle and Flow*, 2004
2 a criminal activity; crime as a profession *UK, 1739*
- Once these guys got hip to themselves and went into the bootlegging game, big money started to show up. — Mezz Mezzrow, *Really the Blues*, p. 20, 1946

3 an attempt to con *US, 1975*
- Bart, I know game when I hear it. You're trying to hustle me for two grand. — Charles W. Moore, *A Brick for Mister Jones*, p. 142, 1975

▸ **out of the game**
married, engaged or dating only one person *US, 2001*
- — Don R. McCreary (Editor), *Dawg Speak*, 2001

▸ **run a game**
to fool, to swindle *US, 1940*
- Jinx had a pretty long run, then he tried to run a game on a friend of mine. Shakedown. So much per week 'cause I'm bad. — Edwin Torres, *Carlito's Way*, p. 15, 1975
- Oh, so you trying run that game, huh? — *Boyz N The Hood*, 1990

▸ **the Game**
the criminal lifestyle *US, 1976*
- Well it's all the same, 'cause it's all in the Game / As I dug when I set out to play. — Dennis Wepman et al., *The Life*, p. 59, 1976

game *verb*
1 to deceive, to mislead, to trick *US, 1963*
- I have the vague hope that he's "gaming," playing the con, for the heartless white folks for some personal benefit or advantage. — Iceberg Slim (Robert Beck), *The Naked Soul of Iceberg Slim*, p. 19, 1971
- Obviously you do not know that you are in the presence of a superior jailhouse intellect that does not enjoy being gamed. — James Ellroy, *Suicide Hill*, p. 576, 1986
2 to flirt; to woo *US, 1988*
- Cause I'm gamin' on a female that's gamin' on me — NWA, *I Ain't Tha 1*, 1988
- You think you gaming on 'em and they the ones that gaming you. — *Boyz N The Hood*, 1990

game face *noun*
in sports, a serious expression and demeanor reflecting complete concentration on the competition at hand *US, 1972*
Now used outside of sports, extended to any serious situation.
- I guess I'm up early because this is Friday and it will be our last serious work-out of the week. I believe I'm getting my game-face on. — Dan Jenkins, *Semi-Tough*, p. 90, 1972

gamer *noun*
1 a video game or role-playing game enthusiast *US, 1977*
- Wars are declared at home, in library basements and in hotel rooms in weekends, where gamers stockpile cases of beer and munchies and barricade themselves against the world. — *Washington Post*, p. 3 (Weekend), 14th October 1977
- — Connie Eble (Editor), *UNC-CH Campus Slang*, p. 4, November 2003
2 an athlete who can always be counted on for a gritty, all-out effort *US, 1977*
- She [Chris Evert] doesn't say anything because she doesn't like to have any excuses. She's a gamer. — *Washington Post*, p. C1, 9th September 1977
- But he [Rob DiMaio] is, the Bruins believe, a gamer. — *The Boston Globe*, p. D3, 3rd October 1996
3 a person engaged in swindles and hustles as a way of life *US, 1975*
- All of New York's biggest gamers saw a bitch whip this cat's ass and she didn't come on the scene for weeks. — Babs Gonzales, *Movin' On Down De Line*, p. 45, 1975

game refuge *noun*
any institution where traffic violators who are under pursuit are free from further pursuit once they pass the gates *US, 1962*
- — *American Speech*, p. 267, December 1962: "The language of traffic policemen"

gamma delta iota *noun*
a college student who is not a fraternity or sorority member; a notional fraternity or sorority comprised of students who don't belong to fraternities or sororities *US, 2000*
A back-formation from **GDI** (god damn independent).
- I got around fifteen desirable pledges to quit the three major sororities and form our own, GDI—Gamma Delta Iota or God Damn Independents. — Leorge Tanenbaum, *Slut! Growing Up Female with a Bad Reputation*, p. 61, 2000
- [T]hey so dictated the terms of student life that the Gamma Delta Iota movement began. — Murray Sperber, *Beer and Circus*, p. 4, 2001

gammon *noun*

one microgram *US, 1969*

The unit of measurement for LSD doses, even in the non-metric US.

- — Richard Lingeman, *Drugs from A to Z*, p. 81, 1969

gamoosh *noun*

a fellow, usually not referring to a winner in the zero-sum game of life *US, 1988*

- "There's Bill Ray. Happy-go-lucky gamoosh, ain't he," Sam's Man said. — Robert Campbell, *Juice*, p. 16, 1988

gander *noun*

a look *US, 1914*

- Let's have a gander under that plaster. — Barry Oakley, *A Salute to the Great McCarthy*, p. 152, 1970

gandies *noun*

underwear *US, 1970*

- — *Current Slang*, p. 7, Winter 1970

gang *noun*

1 a work crew *US, 1989*

Still heard on occasion, but largely replaced with the standard English "crew."

- I'm finished at Standard Federal. They want to put me on the detail gang, plumbing up. I said no way, I'm a connector... — Elmore Leonard, *Killshot*, p. 44, 1989

2 a great many *US, 1811*

- We spent a gang of mornings after that trying to learn the number[.] — Mezz Mezzrow, *Really the Blues*, p. 13, 1946
- "He give them a coupla hundred thousand and he get us a gang of dope." — Leon Bing, *Do or Die*, p. 34, 1991
- He pushed so hard my booty landed a gang of feet from where I was standing. — Linden Dalecki, *Kid B*, p. 26, 2006

gangbang *noun*

1 successive, serial copulation between a single person and multiple partners *US, 1945*

- "Now that you're here, what do you plan to do?" "We were thinking along the lines of a gang-bang," Schoons said[.] — John Nichols, *The Sterile Cuckoo*, p. 69, 1965
- With luck, he'll get off with nothing more than a few fights, broken glasses or a loud and public sex rally involving anything from indecent exposure to a gang-bang in one of the booths. — Hunter S. Thompson, *Hell's Angels*, p. 116, 1967
- Tara Alexander, the heroine of the night, successfully balled, sucked, and jerked off eighty two strange men and her husband for a gang-bang total of eighty-three. — Josh Alan Friedman, *Tales of Times Square*, p. 89, 1986
- Gang bangs used to happen all the time. — Ralph "Sonny" Barger, *Hell's Angel*, p. 99, 2000

2 an orgy at which several couples have sex *US, 1965*

- Sometimes these small rooms, cubby holes really, entertain as many as a dozen homosexuals engaging in what is called a gang-bang. — Antony James, *America's Homosexual Underground*, pp. 62–63, 1965

3 a group of friends talking together on citizens' band radio *US, 1977*

- — Bill Davis, *Jawjacking*, p. 43, 1977

4 a television writing session involving multiple writers *US, 1997*

- — Anna Scotti and Paul Young, *Buzzwords*, p. 4, 1997

5 the utilization of a large number of computer programers to create a product in a short period of time *US, 1991*

- Though there have been memorable gang bangs (e.g., that over-the-weekend assembler port mentioned in Steven Levy's Hackers), most are perpetrated by large companies trying to meet deadlines and produce enormous buggy masses of code[.] — Eric S. Raymond, *The New Hacker's Dictionary*, pp. 172–173, 1991

6 a fight between youth gangs *US, 1967*

- — Hermese E. Roberts, *The Third Ear*, 1971
- The last man standing won a nominal prize that hardly compensated for the broken teeth and fractured bones resulting from these gang bangs. — Nelson George, *Hip Hop America*, p. vii, 1998

gangbang *verb*

1 to engage in successive, serial copulation with multiple partners *US, 1949*

Also in figurative use.

- I used to do it myself, but these preverts would want to gang-bang your broad. — Edwin Torres, *Carlito's Way*, p. 12, 1975
- She got fucked up on Chivas Regal and gang-banged the dudes who didn't bring dates, which was very polite of her. — Larry Heinemann, *Close Quarters*, p. 132, 1977

2 to be an active part of a gang; to battle another gang *US, 1968*

- Homies all standin' around, just hangin' / Some dope-dealin', some gang-bangin — NWA, *Gangsta Gangsta*, 1988
- We were a tagging crew [graffiti artists] and we would do gang banging [fight with other crews over wall turf] and other shit like that. — Terry Williams, *The Cocaine Kids*, p. 60, 1989
- It's the environment the kids live in. This kid may not be gang-banging and that's the problem with the cops. — Tim Lucas, *Cool Places*, p. 155, 1998

gangbanger *noun*

a youth gang member *US, 1969*

- — David Claerbaut, *Black Jargon in White America*, p. 65, 1972
- [H]e ripped a board away from a wooden two-story covered with graffiti trumpeting the local gangbangers. — William Brashler, *City Dogs*, p. 56, 1976
- A lot of cops think that the kids are gangbangers. We know they're not, and the cops assume they're gangbangers because of the way they dress. — Tim Lucas, *Cool Places*, p. 155, 1998

gangbuster *noun*

a zealous, energetic police official or prosecutor who targets organized crime *US, 1936*

- [I]t was only natural for those two canny gang-busters of the Chicago police department, Old Shoes and John Stege, to feel confident[.] — Alson Smith, *Syndicate City*, p. 67, 1954
- At least they didn't run around like a bunch of Gestapos like most cops, crashing in and playing gangbusters. — Robert Lipkin, *A Brotherhood of Outlaws*, p. 51, 1981
- Ever since Tom Dewey, every damn prosecutor in the country's been playing gangbusters, figuring they put enough Mafia skells in jail they could get to be president or some damn thing. — Robert K. Tannenbaum, *Immoral Certainty*, p. 57, 1991

▸ **like gangbusters**

aggressively, with force *US, 1940*

- "Boy, you sure come on like Gangbusters. I hope you're protecting yourself." — Mickey Spillane, *The Snake*, p. 26, 1964
- But I'm a player and I'm gonna conquer some young fine fox and come back like gang busters. — Iceberg Slim (Robert Beck), *The Naked Soul of Iceberg Slim*, p. 125, 1971
- He's coming after you, like gangbusters. Special task force. — Edwin Torres, *After Hours*, p. 434, 1979

gang cheats *noun*

two or more people working as confederates in a cheating scheme *US, 1988*

- — George Percy, *The Language of Poker*, p. 39, 1988

gang-fuck *verb*

to engage in serial, consecutive sex, homosexual or hetereo-sexual *US, 1916*

- These cops will go fifty bucks a head to beat her into submission and then gang-fuck her. — Hunter S. Thompson, *Fear and Loathing in Las Vegas*, p. 114, 1971

gangles *noun*

the arms *US, 2002*

- "That girl has some gangles." — *Dictionary of New Terms (Hope College)*, 2002

gangplank fever *noun*

in the military, a fear of transfer to an assignment overseas *US, 1945*

- — *American Speech*, p. 238, October 1946: "World War II slang of maladjustment"

gang-shag *noun*

successive, serial copulation between a single person and multiple partners *US, 1927*

- "Gang shag" was a term I had heard before. But I had never managed to believe in the reality of it until I became an actual witness to such an affair. — Artie Shaw, *The Trouble with Cinderella*, p. 161, 1952

- In Bryant Park, just behind the public library one night recently, a girl was reported to have been assaulted by a whole gang of boys who took turns on her in what has become known in the psychopathic fringe as a "gang shag." — *Esquire*, p. 112, September 1954
- The gangshag is a homosexual project? Interesting. — Bernard Wolfe, *The Magic of Their Singing*, p. 167, 1961
- If a good gang-shag has any advantage over any other sort of sexual performance, it seems to me to be its indifference to and rather neutralizing effect upon emotional love. — Angelo d'Arcangelo, *The Homosexual Handbook*, p. 116, 1968

gangsta *noun*
a member of a youth gang *US*, 1988
- The song "Gangsta Gangsta" seems to be glorifying gang stuff, though, and is harder to swallow. — *rec.music.misc*, 1st February 1990

gangsta-lette *noun*
a female gang member *US*, 2001
- See, I was the kinda gansta-lette would take a bullet fo' my set. — *Rolling Stone*, p. 86, 12 April 2001

gangster *noun*
1 marijuana *US*, 1960
- Just go on and smoke that gangster and be real cool. Drink that juice and smoke that gangster and keep them needles outta your arm. — Clarence Cooper Jr., *The Scene*, p. 219, 1960
- His eyes were glazed. He was sucking a stick of "gangster." — Iceberg Slim (Robert Beck), *Pimp*, pp. 96–97, 1967
2 a cigarette *US*, 1972
- — David Claerbaut, *Black Jargon in White America*, p. 65, 1972
3 HIV *US*, 2002
- — Jeffrey Ian Ross, *Behind Bars*, p. 186, 2002: Slammer Slang

gangster bitch *noun*
a female who associates with youth gang members *US*, 2001
- — Don R. McCreary (Editor), *Dawg Speak*, 2001

gangster down *adjective*
dressed in youth gang attire *US*, 1993
- G-down (short for "gangster down," or dressed in gang attire) in my gear, I had on blue khaki pants, white canvas All-Stars, and a blue sweatshirt, with my hair in braids. — Sanyika Shakur, *Monster*, p. 40, 1993

gangster lean *verb*
to drive a car leaning on an arm rest towards the right side of the car, steering with the left hand *US*, 1994
- Imitating Goldie, the pimp in the movie, guys cruised down the street gangster-leaning so hard to the right of the steering wheel that it looked like they were actually sitting in the middle of the car rather than in the driver's seat. — Nathan McCall, *Makes Me Wanna Holler*, p. 102, 1994

gangster pill *noun*
any barbiturate or other central nervous system depressant *US*, 1994
- U.S. Department of Justice, *Street Terms*, August 1994

gangster whitewalls *noun*
showy, flashy, whitewalled tires *US*, 1972
- Though you may not drive a great big Cadillac / Gangster whitewalls, TV antennas in the back. — Curtis Mayfield, *Just Be Thankful (For What You've Got)*, 1972
- Elijah had added gangster whitewalls and now he was on the scene, stylin' for the people who could really dig such things. — Odie Hawkins, *Chicago Hustle*, p. 147, 1977
- He put gangster whitewall tires on his ride and cruised through Cavalier Manor hawking drugs and supervising the guys working for him. — Nathan McCall, *Makes Me Wanna Holler*, p. 124, 1994

gang-up *noun*
serial sex between multiple active participants and a single passive one *US*, 1951
- This is the gang-up. Men like that put you to sleep with their drops. Then one man after another goes in and takes you. — Ethel Waters, *His Eye is on the Sparrow*, p. 83, 1951

gangy *noun*
a close friend; a fellow member of a clique *US*, 1982
Hawaiian youth usage.
- — Douglas Simonson, *Pidgin to da Max Hana Hou*, 1982

ganja *adjective*
white-skinned *US*, 2000
- — James Haskins, *The Story of Hip-Hop*, p. 139, 2000

gank *noun*
1 marijuana *US*, 1989
- — Ellen C. Bellone (Editor), *Dictionary of Slang*, p. 11, 1989
2 a substance sold as an illegal drug that is actually fake *US*, 1994
- Before Pitman tests it, however, he says he figures it's "gank." — *Union Leader*, p. 1, 1st August 1994
- [P]olice checked it out and found Smith in possession of the gank, which Dallavia said is a wax or soap substance that sometimes can be passed off as crack. — *Buffalo (New York) News*, p. 5B, 19th January 1999

gank *verb*
to steal *US*, 1994
- They've been ganked so bad by the time they end up here. — William Upski Wimsatt, *Bomb the Suburbs*, p. 99, 1994
- — Connie Eble (Editor), *UNC-CH Campus Slang*, p. 3, Fall 1996
- — *Columbia Missourian*, p. 1A, 19th October 1998

GAP *noun*
the Great American Public *US*, 1965
- Already traffic streamed through Thayer Gate as the GAP—the Great American Public—poured onto the reservation for the parade and the football game. — Rick Atkinson, *The Long Gray Line*, p. 57, 1989

gape *noun*
a gaping anus with a completely relaxed sphincter and distended anus *US*, 1999
A term used by anal sex fetishists, especially on the Internet.
- In the adult industry, the post-fucking state of openness of an ass which you refer to as called "the gape," as in the popular vid series "Planet of the Gapes." People write to me about seeing the gape in porn videos all the time, but usually it's in fear. — Tristan Taormino, *puckerup.com*, 1999
- Gape, of course, refers to the art of stretching one's asshole to impossible circumferences. — Editors of Adult Video News, *The AVN Guide to the 500 Greatest Adult Films of All Time*, p. 237, 2005

gape *verb*
to idle, to wander *US*, 1966
- John D. Bell et al., *Loosely Speaking*, p. 9, 1966

gaper *noun*
1 a dolt *US*, 1966
An abbreviation of **GAPING ASSHOLE**.
- John D. Bell et al., *Loosely Speaking*, p. 9, 1966
2 a mirror *US*, 1931
- — Clarence Major, *Dictionary of Afro-American Slang*, p. 57, 1970

gapers' block *noun*
a traffic jam caused by curious motorists slowing to see an accident *US*, 1961
- He also did not measure the time lost from "gapers' blocks"—delays caused when passing motorists go slowly past the wreckage. — *Chicago Daily Tribune*, p. 20, 27th November 1961
- — Don Dempsey, *American Speech*, p. 269, December 1962
- — Helen Dahlskog (Editor), *A Dictionary of Contemporary and Colloquial Usage*, p. 26, 1972
- In St. Louis, one such policeman has invented (apparently) a term for the traffic-jam caused by drivers slowing down to gawk at an accident or incident: gaper-block. — *Verbatim*, p. 627, May 1978

gaping and flaming *adjective*
(used of a party) wild, rowdy, fun *US*, 1968
- — Collin Baker et al., *College Undergraduate Slang Study Conducted at Brown University*, p. 124, 1968

gaping asshole *noun*
a dolt *US*, 1966
- John D. Bell et al., *Loosely Speaking*, p. 9, 1966

GAPO *noun*
used as an abbreviation of *gorilla armpit odor* *US*, 1967
- — *Current Slang*, p. 4, Spring 1967

gaposis *noun*
a notional disease involving a gap of any kind *US*, 1942
- Go one step further and pull the tape tighter to prevent "gaposis" of the neckline and force the lapel to roll. — Pati Palmer, *Easy, Easier, Easiest Tailoring*, p. 54, 1977

- Baste the bodice together to check for "gaposis" at this point.
  — Susan Andrinks, *Bridal Gowns*, p. 97, 2000

gapper *noun*
a mirror *US, 1934*
Prisoner usage to describe a mirror used to watch for approaching guards as the prisoners do something which they ought not to do.
- — Troy Harris, *A Booklet of Criminal Argot, Cant and Jargon*, p. 12, 1976

gappings *noun*
a salary *US, 1955*
- — Robert S. Gold, *A Jazz Lexicon*, p. 119, 1964

gap up *verb*
to fill capsules with a powdered narcotic *US, 1971*
- — Eugene Landy, *The Underground Dictionary*, p. 86, 1971

gar *noun*
a black person *US, 1962*
An abbreviation of **NIGGER**.
- — Eugene Landy, *The Underground Dictionary*, p. 86, 1971

garage *noun*
a subset of a criminal organization *US, 1975*
- Rocco was from another garage—but a boss-type. — Edwin Torres, *Carlito's Way*, p. 21, 1975

garage band *noun*
an amateur rock group with a basic, three-chord approach to music *US, 1977*
From the custom of practising in the garage at the home of the parents of a band member.
- Zehn Archar came from Baltimore. They represent the ultimate garage band. Actually, the insertion of the second letter of the alphabet smack in the middle of the garage would give a better inkling of their performance Wednesday. — *Washington Post*, p. C5, 21st July 1978
- Like the time Joe and his garage band won the "Battle of the Bands" at El Monte Legion Stadium. — James Ellroy, *Suicide Hill*, p. 597, 1986
- Girlfriends come and go faster than bass players in a garage band, but guy friends are forever. — *Wayne's World 2*, 1993
- Telling him they were kids, a garage band, not very good—if he happened to notice. — Elmore Leonard, *Be Cool*, p. 61, 1999

garans!
certainly *US, 1981*
Hawaiian youth usage; shortened from "guaranteed."
- — Douglas Simonson, *Pidgin to da Max*, 1981

garbage *noun*
1 heroin; low quality heroin *US, 1962*
- "Tony never had anything but garbage, you know that, and I'll put him right out of business." — James Mills, *The Panic in Needle Park*, p. 41, 1966
- Just stay away from the garbage. You know what I mean. — *Goodfellas*, 1990

2 any and all food, usually low in protein and high in carbo-hydrate, not in a bodybuilder's diet *US, 1984*
- — *American Speech*, p. 199, Fall 1984: "The language of bodybuilding"

3 cocktail garnishes *US, 1998*
- I was mesmerized watching them at the service bar as they called in their drink orders and dredged the fruit containers for cocktail gar-nishes. (I remember we had called in "garbage.") — Kathryn Leigh Scott, *The Bunny Years*, 1998

4 in poker, the cards that have been discarded *US, 1967*
- — Albert H. Morehead, *The Complete Guide to Winning Poker*, p. 264, 1967

garbage barge *noun*
a tuna fish sandwich *US, 1984–1985*
- — *Maledicta*, p. 284, 1984–1985: "Food names"

garbage down *verb*
to eat quickly *US, 1959*
- — *American Speech*, p. 154, May 1959: "Gator (University of Florida) slang"

garbage head *noun*
an addict who will use any substance available *US, 1970*
A term used in twelve-step recovery programs such as Alco-holics Anonymous.

- — William D. Alsever, *Glossary for the Establishment and Other Uptight People*, p. 12, December 1970
- — Christopher Cavanaugh, *AA to Z*, p. 99, 1998

garbage in – garbage out
a catchphrase employed as an admonition to computer users: if you program mistakes into a computer then an output of rubbish will surely result *US, 1959*
- The technicians have come up with an acronym to epitomize this computer limitation. The word is "GIGO." It stands for "garbage in, garbage out." — United States Senate Committee on Labor, Subcommittee on Employment, *Nation's Manpower Revolution*, p. 1464, 1963
- Well, you know the old saying about garbage in, garbage out. If wrong assumptions go in, wrong predictions come out. — *Forbes*, p. 71, 15th July 1976

garbage shot *noun*
in pool, a shot made with luck, not with skill *US, 1979*
- — Mike Shamos, *The Illustrated Encyclopedia of Billiards*, p. 108, 1993

garbage stand *noun*
in circus and carnival usage, a novelty concession *US, 1981*
- — Don Wilmeth, *The Language of American Popular Entertainment*, p. 106, 1981

garbage up *verb*
1 to eat *US, 1955*
- — *American Speech*, p. 303, December 1955: "Wayne University slang"

2 in bodybuilding, to eat food that is not in your regular diet *US, 1984*
- — *American Speech*, p. 199, Fall 1984: "The language of bodybuilding"

garbanzos *noun*
the female breasts *US, 1982*
- H&S sales, based in College Point, Queens, N.Y., is the premiere manufacturer and distributor of "big breast oriented material"—videotapes and magazines fixated on woman with gigantic knockers, huge garbzanos[.] — *Adult Video*, p. 47, August/September 1986

Gardena miracle *noun*
in a game of poker, a good hand drawn after a poor dealt hand *US, 1982*
Gardena is a city near Los Angeles where poker rooms are legal.
- — David M. Hayano, *Poker Faces*, p. 186, 1982

gardener *noun*
in pool, a betting player who wins *US, 1990*
- — Steve Rushin, *Pool Cool*, p. 14, 1990

gar-mouth *verb*
to issue threats which cannot and will not be implemented *US, 1984*
In honor of the "gar," a fish of the pike family with long jaws—a big mouth.
- "I'll knock your ass up so high you'll have to climb a stepladder to shit!" is a classic gar-mouth line. — Ken Weaver, *Texas Crude*, p. 55, 1984

garnish *noun*
cash *US, 2003*
- Candy, markers, ammo, liners, stocking stuffer, sweetener, garnish, and pledges are all terms for cash. — Henry Hill and Byron Schreckengost, *A Good Fella's Guide to New York*, p. 123, 2003

Garrison finish *noun*
in horse racing, a sprinting finish by a horse that has lagged back until the final moment *US, 1890*
- — David W. Maurer, *Argot of the Racetrack*, p. 30, 1951

Gary Cooper *noun*
in craps, a roll of 12 *US, 1983*
From Cooper's starring role in the western movie *High Noon*.
- — Thomas L. Clark, *The Dictionary of Gambling and Gaming*, p. 90, 1987

gas *noun*
1 a pleasing and/or amusing experience or situation *US, 1953*
A jazz term that slipped into mainstream youth slang.
- "Wasn't that a gas!" Zaida cried, breathless[.] — Ross Russell, *The Sound*, p. 13, 1961
- We panhandled a few cigarettes, which is really a gas. — Abbie Hoffman, *Revolution for the Hell of It*, p. 34, 1968

- It would have been a gas for me to sit on a pillow beneath the womb of Baldwin's typewriter and catch each newborn page as it entered this world of ours. — Eldridge Cleaver, *Soul on Ice*, p. 97, 1968
- This is a gas! Too bad nobody'll believe it. — *King of Comedy*, 1976

2 anabolic steroids *US, 1994*

The term drew national attention in the US on 14th July 1994, when Terry Bollea (aka Hulk Hogan) testified in criminal proceedings against wrestling promoter Vince McMahon in Uniondale, New York. Asked if he had heard any slang for steroids, Bollea/Hogan answered "Juice. Gas."

- "If you're going to get big naturally, then that's what you need to do, and not on gas, because it does have the side effects and I just choose not to deal with that." [interviewing 2 Cold Scorpio] — *Wrestling Flyer*, 1st January 1994
- You had a team of guys who were 6'4" tall and 240 pounds when they were dry; however, they went on the gas and went from 240 to 280. — Jeff Archer, *Theater in a Squared Circle*, p. 117, 1999

3 batteries *US, 2002*

From the radio as **CAR** metaphor.

- — Gary K. Farlow, *Prison-ese*, p. 23, 2002

4 in pool, momentum or force *US, 1993*

- — Mike Shamos, *The Illustrated Encyclopedia of Billiards*, p. 108, 1993

▸ **cut the gas**

to stop talking *US, 1951*

- Cut the gas has replaced shut up. — *Newsweek*, 8th October 1951

▸ **take gas**

to be knocked from a surfboard by a wave; to fall from a skateboard *US, 1963*

- — *Paradise of the Pacific*, p. 27, October 1963
- — John Severson, *Modern Surfing Around the World*, p. 183, 1964
- Takin' gas in a bush takes a lotta nerve. — Jan Berry and Dean Torrance, *Sidewalk Surfin'*, 1964
- — Hy Lit, *Hy Lit's Unbelievable Dictionary of Hip Words for Groovy People*, p. 39, 1968

▸ **take the gas**

to lose your composure *US, 1961*

- It seems Lloyd's of London has finally "taken the gas." That's a golfing term for a player who chokes up or "swallows the olive." — *San Francisco Examiner*, p. 6, 5th February 1961

gas *verb*

1 to talk idly; to chatter *US, 1847*

The "gas" is hot air.

- Twice he stopped to gas with some character and I made like I was interested in a menu pasted on the window of a joint. — Mickey Spillane, *My Gun is Quick*, p. 70, 1950
- Quit gassing and start working — John M. Murtagh and Sara Harris, *Cost the First Stone*, 1957
- We gassed a while and the husband asked me, half in joke, whether I wanted to go out to The Dalles with them. — Clancy Sigal, *Going Away*, p. 86, 1961

2 to tease, to joke, to kid *US, 1847*

- In six months, Satin? You ain't gassing me, baby? — Sara Harris, *The Lords of Hell*, p. 49, 1967

3 to please, to excite *US, 1941*

- And man, that was something would gas the folks back home in Lynton Bridge, Mass.! — Edwin Gilbert, *The Hot and the Cool*, p. 73, 1953
- Just the same the game gassed me. — Louis Armstrong, *Satchmo*, p. 123, 1954
- Things were "cool" and cool things "gassed" the initiates and anything that was particularly cool was "crazy." — Robert Sylvester, *No Cover Charge*, p. 287, 1956
- He said he gassed him, but we were too far out for the people. — Babs Gonzales, *I Paid My Dues*, p. 40, 1967

4 to inhale glue or any volatile solvent for the intoxicating effect *US, 1970*

- — William D. Alsever, *Glossary for the Establishment and Other Uptight People*, p. 13, December 1970

5 to straighten (hair) with chemicals and heat *US, 1953*

- — Lavada Durst, *The Jives of Dr. Hepcat*, p. 12, 1953
- You could tell that he was a pimping motherfucker by the way his hair was gassed. — Bruce Jackson, *Get Your Ass in the Water and Swim Like Me*, p. 162, 1965
- Those two pimps? That style is just called a process, some call it a marcel. Old-time policemen might refer to it as gassed hair[.] — Joseph Wambaugh, *The New Centurions*, p. 66, 1970

gasbag *noun*

a very talkative individual, a boaster, a person of too many words *US, 1862*

- And you implied that I was a gasbag, a do-nothing liberal. — Mort Sahl, *Heartland*, p. 138, 1976
- Rush Limbaugh, the drug-addled gasbag of right-wing talk radio, does believe in something positive: He believes in marriage. In fact, he believes in it so strongly that he does more than simply talk about it. He has actually gotten married three times. — *The Courier-Journal (Louisville)*, p. 6A, 18th June 2004

gash *noun*

1 the vagina; sex with a woman; a woman as a sex object *US, 1866*

- A fucking veritable GASH—a great slit between the legs lookin' more like murder than anything else. — Jack Kerouac, *Letter to Allen Ginsberg*, p. 499, 14th July 1955
- Son, for ya survivin' ya gotta git it solid in ya noggin all gash is the same, hairy or bald, tight or loose[.] — Iceberg Slim (Robert Beck), *Doom Fox*, p. 230, 1978
- "Couple hours away from Mr. Vesci, and you go love simple for the first gash you see." — John Ridley, *Stray Dogs*, p. 113, 1997
- Non-stop, gorgeous footage of gorgeous girlies playing with each other's gorgeous gashes. — Editors of Adult Video News, *The AVN Guide to the 500 Greatest Adult Films of All Time*, p. 156, 2005

2 a male homosexual who is sexually passive *US, 1950*

- — Hyman E. Goldin et al., *Dictionary of American Underworld Lingo*, p. 77, 1950

gash *verb*

to have sex *US, 1989*

- — Pamela Munro, *U.C.L.A. Slang*, p. 41, 1989

gas-head *noun*

a person with chemically straightened hair *US, 1968*

- — *Current Slang*, p. 25, Fall 1968
- — David Claerbaut, *Black Jargon in White America*, p. 65, 1972

gash hound *noun*

a man who is obsessed with women *US, 1955*

- "How can you stand this gash hound?" Wolf asked Mosca, his voice deliberately quiet, insulting. "He's had so many dames sitting on his head, his brain's gone soft." — Mario Puzo, *The Dark Arena*, p. 138, 1955
- They're all gash-hounds in New Hampshire, but California is a different story, eh? — Hunter S. Thompson, *Better Than Sex*, p. 111, 19th August 1992
- "I noticed," said Karras. "Sure you did," said Recevo. "Gash-hound like you." — George P. Pelecanos, *The Big Blowdown*, p. 58, 1996

gasket *noun*

1 any improvised seal between the end of a dropper and the hub of a needle *US, 1970*

- — William D. Alsever, *Glossary for the Establishment and Other Uptight People*, p. 19, December 1970

2 a doughnut *US, 1942*

- — Ramon Adams, *The Language of the Railroader*, p. 67, 1977

gasoline *noun*

a mixture of alcohol and heroin *US, 1993*

- Willie had been tempted by friends to try a new concoction sweeping the ghetto, a mix of heroin and alcohol known as "gasoline." — Bob Sipchen, *Baby Insane and the Buddha*, p. 106, 1993

gas-passer *noun*

an anesthesiologist *US, 1961*

- — *American Speech*, pp. 145–148, May 1961: "The spoken language of medicine; argot, slang, cant"
- So find the gas-passer and tell him to premedicate the patient. — *M*A*S*H*, 1970
- "When you get Mitchell into the OR, tell the gas passer to be careful putting him under." — Lynda Van Devanter, *Home Before Morning*, p. 11, 1983

gasper *noun*

something that is astonishing *US, 1970*

- "You know what that's from?"—and he looks out at everyone and hesitates before laying this gasper on them—"That's from the Declaration of Independence." — Tom Wolfe, *Radical Chic & Mau-Mauing the Flak Catchers*, p. 24, 1970

gassed *adjective*

drunk or drug-intoxicated *US, 1919*

World War 1 military use from the stupefying effects of gas; then, its origins soon forgotten, just another synonym for "drunk."

- Let's go over to Beer Can Boulevard and get gassed! — Max Shulman, *Rally Round the Flag, Boys!*, p. 173, 1957
- They play the juke box circuit and get gassed on beer, but New York has few such emporiums and even beer is expensive. — Lee Mortimer, *Women Confidential*, p. 41, 1960
- As far as they knew, all they did in port was visit around the Spanish-speaking sections and get gassed up. — Mickey Spillane, *Me, Hood!*, p. 47, 1963
- I was gassed by game time, which irritated Cochran. — Robert Byrne, *McGoorty*, p. 167, 1972

gasser *noun*
something wonderful, very exceptional; extraordinarily successful *US, 1944*
- He got this great Mexican shit, man. It's a gasser. — Bernard Wolfe, *The Late Risers*, p. 168, 1954
- "Yeah," said the wolf. "It's a gasser." — Steve Allen, *Bop Fables*, p. 44, 1955
- But the last set was a gasser. They really came on then, man! — Ross Russell, *The Sound*, p. 14, 1961
- We're killing this guy, he thought. What a gasser. — Phil Hirsch, *Hooked*, p. 45, 1968

gassing *noun*
throwing feces on someone *US, 2006*
- For prisoners, "gassing" had another meaning: it meant throwing shit on another person, sometimes while holding her down. — Justin Cartwright, *The Promise of Happiness*, p. 171, 2006

gassy *adjective*
excellent, pleasant, humorous *US, 1962*
- Always used to show up at the parties with some gassy thing, a gopher snake or a white mouse or some gassy thing like that in his pocket? — Ken Kesey, *One Flew Over the Cuckoo's Nest*, p. 218, 1962
- — Eugene Landy, *The Underground Dictionary*, p. 87, 1971

gas tank *noun*
a cell with poor ventilation where prisoners are tear-gassed as punishment for violations of prison rules *US, 1981*
- It was the "gas tank"—where you were tear-gassed and there was no ventilation. — Jack Henry Abbott, *In the Belly of the Beast*, p. 39, 1981

gat *noun*
a gun, especially a pistol *US, 1897*
- We're just curious why a couple of hard guys like you two weren't carrying your gats. — Irving Shulman, *The Amboy Dukes*, p. 164, 1947
- When he had been in town a few weeks he took Nick up there and showed him a gat. — Willard Motley, *Knock on Any Door*, p. 284, 1947
- "Five hundred plus the gat?" I asked. He looked down at it rather absently. Then he dropped it into his pocket. — Raymond Chandler, *The Long Goodbye*, p. 21, 1953
- He excused himself and left Molly standing there with the gat in her hand, the first she had ever handled. — Elaine Shepard, *The Doom Pussy*, p. 28, 1967

gat *verb*
to shoot *US, 1990*
- Oh shit somebody gonna get gatted! — *Boyz N The Hood*, 1990

gate *noun*
1 a jazz musician; hence a fashionable man *US, 1936*
- And the gate that rocked at the eighty-eight was blowin' "How High the Moon." — William "Lord" Buckley, *The Ballad of Dan McGroo*, 1960
2 used as a term of address among jazz lovers of the 1930s and 40s *US, 1936*
- Friends are addressed as gate or slot, verbal shorthand for gate-mouth and slotmouth, which are inner-circle racial jokes to begin with[.] — Mezz Mezzrow, *Really the Blues*, p. 220, 1946
3 a young person *US, 1936*
- — Lou Shelly, *Hepcats Jive Dictionary*, p. 11, 1945
4 release from prison *US, 1966*
- So to even the score, they gave the rat four / when he should have got the gate. — Bruce Jackson, *Get Your Ass in the Water and Swim Like Me*, p. 82, 1966
5 a vein into which a drug is injected *US, 1986*
- — Richard A. Spears, *The Slang and Jargon of Drugs and Drink*, p. 214, 1986
6 the mouth *US, 1936*
- She's just big-gatin', boss, tryna run up de price. — Chester Himes, *Cotton Comes to Harlem*, p. 38, 1965

gate *verb*
in private dice games, to stop the dice while rolling, either as a superstition or to check for cheating *US, 1963*
- — John S. Salak, *Dictionary of Gambling*, p. 109, 1963

gate fever *noun*
the anxiety suffered by prisoners as they approach their release date *UK, 1958*
- — John R. Armore and Joseph D. Wolfe, *Dictionary of Desperation*, p. 30, 1976

gatekeeper *noun*
a person who introduces another to a first LSD experience *US, 1967*
- — John Williams, *The Drug Scene*, p. 112, 1967

gate money *noun*
the cash given to a prisoner upon release from prison *US, 1931*
- [H]e signed his parole papers and was issued a hundred dollars in gate money. — Seth Morgan, *Homeboy*, p. 388, 1990
- Foley came out with his fifty dollars gate money and took a bus to L.A. where Buddy was waiting for him in a car he'd boosted for the occasion. — Elmore Leonard, *Out of Sight*, p. 25, 1996
- The career burglar had previously lived in the Crenshaw area and the Inland Empire, but he had only $200 in "gate" money and needed a quick place to shower and sleep. — *The Los Angeles Times*, p. 1, 30th November 2002

gatemouth *noun*
a gossip *US, 1944*
- — Clarence Major, *Dictionary of Afro-American Slang*, p. 57, 1970

gate out *verb*
to leave prison after being released *US, 2002*
- — Jeffrey Ian Ross, *Behind Bars*, p. 186, 2002: Slammer Slang

gates *noun*
1 used as a term of address, male-to-male, usually collegial *US, 1936*
- Then I said to him, "Gates leave your vibes, ain't no need to set them up every night." — Babs Gonzales, *Movin' On Down De Line*, p. 69, 1975
2 marijuana *US, 1966*
- — Ernest L. Abel, *A Marijuana Dictionary*, p. 42, 1982

gator *noun*
1 an alligator *US, 1844*
- Crocs are meaner, more aggressive. Gators get fat and lazy. — Carl Hiaasen, *Tourist Season*, p. 115, 1986
- One of the deputies said, "Well, it's a fact, gators love dog." — Elmore Leonard, *Maximum Bob*, p. 74, 1991
2 an all-purpose male form of address *US, 1944*
- The little number will pull you dead to the kerb. Gators she is a panic. — Lavada Durst, *The Jives of Dr. Hepcat*, 1953
3 a swing jazz enthusiast *US, 1944*
- — Lou Shelly, *Hepcats Jive Dictionary*, p. 11, 1945

gator boy; gator girl *noun*
a member of the Seminole Indian tribe *US, 1963*
- — *American Speech*, p. 271, December 1963: "American Indian student slang"

gator grip *noun*
in television and movie-making, a clamp used to attach lights *US, 1987*
An abbreviation of "alligator grip," from the resemblance to an alligator's jaws.
- — Ira Konigsberg, *The Complete Film Dictionary*, p. 141, 1987

gauge *noun*
a shotgun *US, 1991*
- Sidewinder's weapons in the crime were "a 'gauge and a deuce-five automatic." — Leon Bing, *Do or Die*, p. 47, 1991
- Eight Ball had been lent the gauge to bust on some Brims but had never returned it. — Sanyika Shakur, *Monster*, p. 247, 1993

gawk *noun*
in circus and carnival usage, a local who loiters as the show is assembled or taken down *US, 1981*
- — Don Wilmeth, *The Language of American Popular Entertainment*, p. 107, 1981

gay *noun*
a homosexual *US, 1953*
- An Perry—he's a gay—June found him layin' on the road one night about a week ago. — Robert Gover, *Here Goes Kitten*, p. 154, 1964

- — Collin Baker et al., *College Undergraduate Slang Study Conducted at Brown University*, p. 124, 1968
- Gay: The acceptable term for homosexuals, male or female. — *Screw*, p. 7, 12th October 1970

gay *adjective*
1 homosexual *US, 1941*

- Not all who call their flats in Greenwich Village "studios" are queer. Not all New York's queer (or, as they say it, "gay") people live in Greenwich Village. — Jack Lait and Lee Mortimer, *New York Confidential*, p. 65, 1948
- Now you see, I always thought that being gay was about the most iconoclastic, minority thing there was. — Bernard Wolfe, *The Late Risers*, p. 213, 1954
- Also met other gay cats, had many talks with them. — Jefferson Polard and Valsie Alison, *The Records of the San Francisco Sexual Freedom League*, 1971
- Yes, maybe Hoover and top aide Clyde Tolson had a gay thing going on. — *Florida Today (Brevard County, Florida)*, 24th October 1999

2 catering to or patronized by homosexuals *US, 1954*

- "I heard from a girl friend it was a gay place." "What does the word 'gay' mean to you?" asked Falvery. Her head still averted, she said, "Homosexual." "Does the word 'gay' refer to the premises?" "Yes." — *San Francisco News*, p. 1, 20th December 1954
- I own a homosexual bar. In the nomenclature of the homosexual, it is called a Gay Bar. — Helen P. Branson, *Gay Bar*, p. 23, 1957
- Advertising itself as the "the world's first gay sacramental church," the Beloved Disciple Parish of the American Orthodox Church of the United States celebrates the most ancient Western Christian Mass. — John Francis Hunter, *The Gay Insider*, p. 169, 1971
- He ain't got no girls no more. He's sinking down. He goes to gay bars and throws champagne bottles against the wall. — Susan Hall, *Gentleman of Leisure*, p. 54, 1972

3 bad, stupid, out of style *US, 1978*

General pejorative in juvenile use; a reversal of the politically correct norm much as "good" is **BAD** and **WICKED** is "good."

- — Connie Eble (Editor), *UNC-CH Campus Slang*, p. 3, Spring 1987
- — Pamela Munro, *U.C.L.A. Slang*, p. 41, 1989
- — Kenn "Naz" Young, *Naz's Dictionary of Teen Slang*, p. 48, 1993
- Man, that shit was so gay—fucking eighties style. — Kevin Smith, *Jay and Silent Bob Strike Back*, p. 10, 2001

gay bar *noun*
a bar catering to a homosexual clientele *US, 1953*

- At that time it was a gay bar—that means a bar where homosexuals go—and he could do us a lot of good or a lot of harm. — *San Francisco News*, p. 13, 14th October 1953
- I own a homosexual bar. In the nomenclature of the homosexual, it is called a Gay Bar. — Helen P. Branson, *Gay Bar*, p. 23, 1957
- In that shadowed world of dim bars characterized by nervous gestures, furtive looks, masked Loneliness—the World of the Gay Bars[.] — John Rechy, *City of Night*, p. 197, 1963
- When we first "came out" we spent many happy and exciting times in gay bars from one coast to the other. — *Screw*, p. 8, 24th November 1969

gay boy *noun*
a homosexual male, especially one who is flamboyant and young *US, 1945*

- — Elisabeth Lambert, *The Sleeping House Party*, 1951
- She shoulders some of the little gay boys out of her way, in contempt. — Willard Motely, *Let No Man Write My Epitaph*, p. 248, 1958
- "Each year—new hustlers, new queens, new—..." she hesitated, "—new gay boys just out for kicks[.]" — John Rechy, *City of Night*, p. 330, 1963

gaycat *verb*
to have a good, carefree time *US, 1924*

- I wasn't working then and didn't have much money left to gaycat with, but I couldn't refuse to light my friends up. — Mezz Mezzrow, *Really the Blues*, p. 215, 1946

gay chicken *noun*
a young homosexual male *US, 1959*

- — J.D. Mercer, *They Walk in Shadow*, p. 564, 1959: "Slang vocabulary"

gaydar; gadar *noun*
the perceived or real ability of one homosexual to sense intuitively that another person is homosexual *US, 1982*

- — Connie Eble (Editor), *UNC-CH Campus Slang*, p. 4, April 1995

- I may not have—a new expression I read several times in the Blade in the last few weeks—the best gaydar around. — William Leap, *Word's Out*, p. 52, 1996
- After he [Lou Pearlman] chose 25 semifinalists, he hugged these boys he didn't even know a little too much for my gaydar. — *The Village Voice*, 25th July 2000

gay for pay *adjective*
said of a heterosexual man who portrays a homosexual man in a movie or other theatrical performance *US, 1997*

- "Gay-for-pay" performers—proclaimed heterosexual men who slide up the Kinsey Scale when the money is right—are discussed and dissed as well. — *Variety*, p. 96, 23rd June 1997
- Dylan McDermott is going gay—for pay. McDermott, the ex-"The Practice" star, has signed on to play Will's love interest on "Will & Grace" for an episode airing Oct. 30. — *Chicago Tribune*, p. 44, 18th September 2003

gay ghetto *noun*
a section of a city largely inhabited by openly homosexual men *US, 1971*

Probably coined by Martin Levine, who wrote "Gay Ghetto," published in *Journal of Homosexuality*, Volume 4 (1979). Examples include Greenwich Village and Chelsea in New York, the North Side in Chicago and the Castro in San Francisco. Unlike all other ghettos, they are affluent.

- When one thinks of gay ghettos across the country, his mind leaps to the Pansy Patch of West Hollywood[.] — John Francis Hunter, *The Gay Insider*, p. 172, 1971

gay-marry *verb*
to commit to a lifelong relationship with someone of the same sex *US, 1999*

- Maybe you should just get gay-married to somebody. — Rita Ciresi, *Pink Slip*, p. 42, 1999

gayola; gay-ola *noun*
extortion of homosexuals by the police *US, 1960*

- The existence of these laws also affords constant opportunities for blackmail and for shakedowns by real or phony cops, a practice known as "gayola." — Joe David Brown, *Sex in the '60s*, p. 73, 1968
- Investigators from the State Franchise Tax Board have joined the hue & cry in the "gayola" quiz here. — *San Francisco Examiner*, p. 1 (II), 15th May 1970
- [I]n the late Fifties it was the "Gay-ola" affair, involving pay-offs to city authorities. — John Francis Hunter, *The Gay Insider*, p. 196, 1971

gazebbies *noun*
the female breasts *US, 1965*

Vietnam war usage.

- Gazebbies!! Ga-za-beys—most always plural—but not in dictionary! — Tony Zidek, *Choi Oi*, p. 95, 1965

gazillion *noun*
a very large, if indefinite, number *US, 1975*

- While I was out of the room, we were going through a gazillion member-adds for different types of things. — House Committee on Armed Services, *Hearings Before Committee on Armed Services*, p. 228, 1975
- Suddenly, Daddy had a case that had to be solved right away, so some clerks and Josh came to help go through a gazillion depositions. — *Clueless*, 1995
- "So you're sure you're okay?" Ken Jarvis, the Pittsburgh Pirates owner, asked Jake for what seemed like the gazillionth time. — Jason Starr, *Lights Out*, p. 228, 2006

gazongas *noun*
the female breasts *US, 1978*

- — Judi Sanders, *Faced and Faded, Hanging to Hurl*, p. 16, 1993
- Jesus of Nazareth, are those Gazongas ever plump. Christ, how can she even walk with those things? — Marty Beckerman, *Generation S.L.U.T.*, p. 21, 2004
- In between, she put together an awesome array of skin and scantily clad scenes, somehow maintaining her superhuman sexiness and those gravity-mocking gazongas along the way. — Mr. Skin, *Mr. Skin's Skincyclopedia*, p. 21, 2005

gazoo *noun*
the anus and rectum *US, 1973*

A variant of the more common **WAZOO**.

- "Now you're getting the idea: when you got airplanes up the gazoo, I'm going to be a nice fellow to know." — George Higgins, *The Digger's Game*, p. 28, 1973

gazook *noun*
1 a loud lout *US, 1901*
- The head gazook made me rent a tie. — Larry Heinemann, *Close Quarters*, p. 190, 1977
- It was that long-haired gazook in Chinatown. — Henry Miller, *Moloch*, p. 39, 1992
2 a boy *US, 1949*
- — Vincent J. Monteleone, *Criminal Slang*, p. 95, 1949

gazookus *noun*
in carnival usage, a genuine article *US, 1924*
- — Don Wilmeth, *The Language of American Popular Entertainment*, p. 107, 1981

gazoony *noun*
1 a fellow, especially a low-life *US, 1914*
- "The gazooney bother you much, Frannie?" Jinni said. — Bernard Wolfe, *The Late Risers*, p. 130, 1954
- — Joe McKennon, *Circus Lingo*, p. 38, 1980
- "That's enough for some gazoony out on the pavement to cut your throat and drink your blood," Whistler said. — Robert Campbell, *Alice in La-La Land*, p. 21, 1987
2 a manual laborer in a carnival *US, 1966*
- — *American Speech*, p. 281, December 1966: "More carnie talk from the West Coast"
3 the passive participant in anal sex *US, 1918*
- — Dale Gordon, *The Dominion Sex Dictionary*, p. 75, 1967
- He's in the big house for all day and night, a new fish jammed into a drum with a cribman, who acts like a gazoonie. — *San Francisco Examiner*, p. 26, 17th August 1976

GB *noun*
1 sex between one person and multiple, sequential partners *US, 1972*
An abbreviation of **GANG BANG**.
- There was some debate between my chief advisers and myself, regarding the need to devote an entire chapter to the G.B.— gangbang, that is. — Larry Townsend, *The Leatherman's Handbook*, p. 201, 1972
2 any barbiturate or central nervous system depressant *US, 1966*
An abbreviation of **GOOFBALL**.
- He was high on barbiturates, goofballs, GB's. — James Mills, *The Panic in Needle Park*, p. 27, 1966
- — Donald Wesson and David Smith, *Barbiturates*, 1977
3 goodbye *US, 1945*
- — Lou Shelly, *Hepcats Jive Dictionary*, p. 11, 1945

G bit *noun*
a prison sentence to a federal penitentiary *US, 1950*
- — Hyman E. Goldin et al., *Dictionary of American Underworld Lingo*, p. 77, 1950

G-car *noun*
a federal law enforcement agency car *US, 1981*
- True guided the G-car through stop-and-go airport traffic, across the Sepulveda bridge, and onto Century Boulevard. — Gerald Petievich, *One-Shot Deal*, p. 204, 1981

GDI *noun*
a college student who is not a fraternity or sorority member, a *god-damn independent US, 1960*
- Then you have the GDI, or Goddam Independent, who is anti-Greek, in school strictly for the sake of an education[.] — Glendon Swarthout, *Where the Boys Are*, p. 110, 1960
- So I became a G.D.I., which stands for God Damn Independent, and that's the way I like it and to hell with all the Betty Coeds, Sally Sororities and Freddy Frats. — Frederick Kohner, *The Affairs of Gidget*, p. 8, 1963
- GDI is what the dormies call themselves. People who aren't in frat or sorority houses. — Jeffrey Wilds Deaver, *The Lessons of her Death*, p. 23, 1993
- Even though I'm not in a sorority—I am a GDI (God Damn Independent)—I still dance at every set. — April Sinclair, *Ain't Gonna Be the Same Fool Twice*, pp. 39–40, 1996

G-dog *noun*
a good friend *US, 1998*
- — *Columbia Missourian*, p. 1A, 19th October 1998

G-down *adjective*
dressed in youth gang attire *US, 1993*
- G-down (short for "gangster down," or dressed in gang attire) in my gear, I had on blue khaki pants, white canvas All-Stars, and a blue sweatshirt, with my hair in braids. — Sanyika Shakur, *Monster*, p. 40, 1993

GE *noun*
the electric chair *US, 1990*
Homage to General Electric.
- — Charles Shafer, *Folk Speech in Texas Prisons*, p. 205, 1990

gear *noun*
1 stuff, things *UK, 1415*
- The hitch-hiker hoisted his gear in and stuffed it on the floor. — Gurney Norman, *Divine Right's Trip (Last Whole Earth Catalog)*, p. 11, 1971
2 (of a woman) the obvious physical attributes *US, 1953*
Extended from the purely genital sense.
- "Wonder gear," it developed, is an attractive girl, in Navy lingo[.] — *San Francisco News*, 14th October 1953
- So, obviously, is Joey Heatherton. Her gear is mobile, shapely and slender. — *San Francisco Examiner*, p. 19, 14th January 1965
3 a homosexual *US, 1972*
- A couple of gears own it; they dress in drag. — Bruce Jackson, *Outside the Law*, p. 113, 1972

▶ **get your ass into gear**
to stop idling, to apply yourself to an activity, to start doing something useful *US, 1914*
- I'm not gonna stand around here when I got to get my ass in gear tomorrow morning[.] — George V. Higgins, *The Judgment of Deke Hunter*, p. 50, 1976

gear *adjective*
1 obsessed with, fanatic about *US, 1972*
- — Bruce Jackson, *Outside the Law*, p. 57, 1972: "Glossary"
2 very good, outstanding *UK, 1951*
Brought to the world by the Beatles, dropped from fashionable use in the mid-1960s.
- — J. R. Friss, *A Dictionary of Teenage Slang (Mt. Diablo High)*, 1964
- "No. We never expected anything like this—it was really gear." "Gear?" "Fab," he explained, translating quickly from his native Beatle-ese, "you know—really great." — *Life*, p. 34, 21st February 1964
- "It was so gear, I cried." — Murray Kaufman, *Murray the K Tells It Like It Is, Baby*, p. 27, 1966

geared *adjective*
available for homosexual relations *US, 1935*
- — *New York Mattachine Newsletter*, p. 6, June 1961: "Sex deviation in a prison community"
- Bob and I were pretty tight in the joint, a wholly platonic intellectual friendship—he was geared and I just don't groove sackwise with another geared one, no chemistry. — James Blake, *The Joint*, p. 333, 17th February 1963

gear head *noun*
in mountain biking, a bicycle mechanic *US, 1992*
- — William Nealy, *Mountain Bike!*, p. 162, 1992: "Bikespeak"

gears *noun*
the testicles *US, 1952*
- About the only part of an old pig we don't eat is his pizlum. That's his auger. But we did eat the other part of his male self—we call them his gears. Some will stay away from those things. — Earl Conrad, *Rock Bottom*, p. 246, 1952

gear up *verb*
to get dressed *US, 1993*
- "You may tie your shoes in the morning, but the mortician may untie them at night," Alma, Crazy De's mother, was telling us as we waited for De to gear up. — Sanyika Shakur, *Monster*, p. 175, 1993

gedanken *adjective*
in computing, impractical or poorly designed *US, 1983*
From the German for "thought."
- A gedanken thesis is usually marked by an obvious lack of intuition about what is programmable and what is not, and about what does and does not constitute a clear specification of an algorithm. — Guy L. Steele et al., *The Hacker's Dictionary*, p. 71, 1983

gedunk *noun*
ice cream, candy, potato chips, and other junk food; the ship store where junk food can be bought *US, 1927*

A US Navy term.

- Maybe they have a gedonk there where he can get some candy, I don't know. — Darryl Ponicsan, *The Last Detail*, p. 167, 1970

gedunk truck *noun*

a catering truck *US*, *1992*

- It begins with a catering truck, like hundreds that ply San Diego work sites. Yes, but this is no ordinary roach coach, ptomaine wagon or gedunk truck. — *Los Angeles Times*, p. 1, 8th July 1992

gee *noun*

1 a man, a fellow *US*, *1907*

- From the first letter of "guy"; sometimes spelling "ghee." To some people you're a wrong gee. — Raymond Chandler, *The Long Goodbye*, 1953
- We was the gees on the first bench and what we said was law. — Hubert Selby Jr., *Last Exit to Brooklyn*, p. 43, 1957
- After all, I'm not a heavy gee. — Iceberg Slim (Robert Beck), *Trick Baby*, p. 14, 1969
- He was one of six Mafia ghees in my conspiracy trial in 1970. — Edwin Torres, *After Hours*, p. 159, 1979

2 a stolen car *US*, *2005*

An abbreviation of GTA (grand theft auto).

- "We're gonna roll to the store in gees." — Colton Simpson, *Inside the Crips*, p. 36, 2005

3 opium; heroin *US*, *1938*

Possibly a respelling of the initial letter of a number of synonyms, or from Hindi *ghee* (butter), or playing on the sense as **HORSE** (heroin).

- — Richard A. Spears, *The Slang and Jargon of Drugs and Drink*, p. 214, 1986

4 a strong, respected, manipulative prisoner *US*, *1951*

- A "gee" is not necessarily the most formidable physical specimen of his group. He may achieve his position by virtue of superior craftiness in "making connections" or "pulling deals." — *American Speech*, p. 194, October 1951: "A study of reformatory argot"

5 any device used to secure a needle to an eye dropper as part of an improvised mechanism to inject drugs *US*, *1960*

- You hold the needle on by tearing the edge of a dollar bill and wrapping it around the small end of the dropper. You call that the "G." — Clarence Cooper Jr., *The Scene*, p. 82, 1960
- They pulled out two spikes, laid out two hypes / And rolled some one-dollar-bill gees. — Dennis Wepman et al., *The Life*, p. 56, 1976

gee!; jee!

an exclamation used for expressing surprise, astonishment or shock *US*, *1895*

Probably a euphemism for "Jesus!" Later use is often ironic.

- Gee, Officer Krupke, / We're down on our knees, / 'Cause no one wants a fella with a social disease. / Gee, Officer Krupke, / What are we to do! / Gee, Officer Krupke, / Krup you! — Stephen Sondheim, *Gee, Officer Krupke!*, 1957

geech *noun*

money *US*, *1968*

- — Hy Lit, *Hy Lit's Unbelievable Dictionary of Hip Words for Groovy People*, p. 17, 1968

geechee *noun*

an uneducated, rural black person, especially one who is not easily understood *US*, *1905*

- One of the funniest things I ever heard was mac spieling in Yiddish, because he spoke it with a thick Southern drawl, piling on more "you-alls" than a Geechee senator. — Mezz Mezzrow, *Really the Blues*, p. 70, 1946
- Thought you might be one of those salt-water Gitchies. — Earl Conrad, *Rock Bottom*, p. 98, 1952
- Daddy was a Geechee so we had rice every day. — Louise Meriwether, *Daddy Was a Number Runner*, p. 99, 1970
- Gullah people, known as Geechee in Georgia and Florida, occupied the Lowcountry coast from the Cape Fear River in North Carolina to the St. John's River in northern Florida. — *Post and Courier (Charleston, South Carolina)*, p. 2C, 18th December 2003

gee'd up *adjective*

1 drug-intoxicated *US*, *1936*

Originally of opium (**GEE**), gradually less discriminating.

- — *American Speech*, p. 25, February 1952: "Teen-age hophead jargon"

2 dressed in clothing associated with youth gangs *US*, *1995*

- — Bill Valentine, *Gang Intelligence Manual*, p. 76, 1995: "Black street gang terminology"

geedus *noun*

in circus and carnival usage, money *US*, *1981*

- — Don Wilmeth, *The Language of American Popular Entertainment*, p. 107, 1981

gee head *noun*

a frequent Paregoric user *US*, *1970*

- — William D. Alsever, *Glossary for the Establishment and Other Uptight People*, p. 24, December 1970
- — Eugene Landy, *The Underground Dictionary*, p. 87, 1971

geek *noun*

1 a carnival freak, usually an alcoholic or drug addict, who would sit and crawl in his own excrement and occasionally bite the heads off snakes and chickens *US*, *1928*

Perhaps from German *gucken* (to peep, to look) or synonymous German slang or dialect *kieken*.

- My mother said, "So nice meeting you," but my old man just stared at him like he was a geek out of a sideshow. — Frederick Kohner, *Gidget*, p. 92, 1957
- They're used by the rummies who swamp up the lot and by the alk-paralyzed geek. — Robert Edmond Alter, *Carny Kill*, p. 8, 1966
- [H]e knew the india-rubber man—the fat woman—the bearded lady—the sword swallower—the snake charmer—geeks—midgets[.] — Herbert Huncke, *The Evening Sun Turned Crimson*, p. 37, 1980
- "They were a special breed the geeks preferred. They could bite their heads off easier." — Peter Fenton, *Eyeing the Flash*, p. 2, 2005

2 a student whose devotion to study excludes all other interests or society; someone who is considered too studious; someone obsessed with computers *US*, *1976*

Pejorative.

- Ever wondered what was on the other side of Central Square besides the MIT geeks with pocket computers and the NECCO factory? — *The Harvard Crimson*, 10th August 1976
- I'd used it on the poor geek in the bar[.] — Hunter S. Thompson, *The Great Shark Hunt*, p. 26, 1979
- Do I look like Mother Theresa? If I did, I probably wouldn't mind talking to the Geek Squad. — *Heathers*, 1988
- The library—a haven for the real geeks, the ones who don't have real friends. — Rosalind Wiseman, *Queen Bees & Wannabes*, p. 43, 2002

3 an offensive, despicable person; a clumsy person; a socially awkward person *UK*, *1876*

- The only answer he got was "I'll lay a baseball bat on you, you underage geek." — Bernard Wolfe, *The Late Risers*, p. 5, 1954
- [A]s opposed to the "frustration" of fat-assed American geeks safe at home worrying over whether to have bacon, ham, or sausage with their grade-A eggs in the morning[.] — Eldridge Cleaver, *Soul on Ice*, p. 18, 1968
- Here's this poor geek living in a world of convertibles zipping past him on the highways all the time, and he's never even ridden in one. — Hunter S. Thompson, *Fear and Loathing in Las Vegas*, p. 17, 1971
- [T]heir mothers apparently won't let 'em watch the whole movie out there in the city of geeks and weirdos. — Joe Bob Briggs, *Joe Bob Goes to the Drive-In*, p. 67, 1987

4 a prostitute's customer with fetishistic desires *US*, *1993*

- — *Washington Post*, p. C5, 7th November 1993

5 an awkward skateboarder or a pedestrian who gets in the way *US*, *1976*

- — Albert Cassorla, *The Skateboarder's Bible*, p. 200, 1976

geek *verb*

1 to display severe anxiety when coming off cocaine intoxication *US*, *1995*

- — *Washington Post*, p. C5, 7th November 1993
- — Mark S. Fleisher, *Beggars & Thieves*, p. 289, 1995: "Glossary"

2 to act foolishly *US*, *1998*

- — *Columbia Missourian*, p. 1A, 19th October 1998

geek-a-mo *noun*

a geek *US*, *1991*

- — Trevor Cralle, *The Surfin'ary*, p. 43, 1991

geeked *adjective*

1 in a psychotic state induced by continuous use of amphetamine or methamphetamine *US*, *1989*

- Last Saturday I did a sixteenth of speed and was totally geeked. — Geoffrey Froner, *Digging for Diamonds*, p. 31, 1989

2 sexually aroused while under the influence of a central nervous system stimulant *US*, *1989*

- Geeked means to be so hungry for sex that your tongue hangs down to your feet. — Geoffrey Froner, *Digging for Diamonds*, p. 31, 1989

3 marijuana-intoxicated *US, 2002*

- Tyrone says he still gets "geeked"—street slang for being high on marijuana[.] — *Milwaukee Journal Sentinel*, p. 1A, 17th March 2002

4 jittery, excited *US, 1984*

- I relished everything about it, right down to the pregame rituals: dressing, taping, listening to my music (always rap on game days to get me geeked). — The Rock, *The Rock Says...*, p. 133, 2000

geeker *noun*

a user of crack cocaine *US, 1990*

- Indeed, some students said crack smokers they see on the streets—known here as "geekers"—are mostly in their 30s and are objects of ridicule. "We all make fun of geekers." — *Washington Post*, p. A1, 2nd April 1990

geeker rental *noun*

a car stolen by a crack cocaine addict who then trades use of the car for drugs *US, 2002*

- Many car thefts are "geeker rentals," said Assistant Prosecutor Paul Scarsella. That's street slang for a crack addict who steals a vehicle and rents it out in exchange for drugs, he said. — *Columbus (Ohio) Dispatch*, p. 1A, 7th January 2002

geeking *adjective*

inept; unfashionable; awkward *US, 1987*

- If they threw a party, the chances are it would be "fully geeking." — *New York Times*, 12th April 1987

geekosaurus *noun*

a socially inept person *US, 2002*

- Why you think that anyone online must be a hairy palmed geekosaurus is beyond me. — *rec.sport.pro-wrestling.fantasy*, 26th December 2002

geek out *verb*

to enter a highly technical mode which is too difficult to explain *US, 1991*

- Pardon me while I geek out for a moment. — Eric S. Raymond, *The New Hacker's Dictionary*, p. 175, 1991

geekster *noun*

a geek *US, 1991*

- — Trevor Cralle, *The Surfin'ary*, p. 43, 1991

geek up *verb*

to intimidate *US, 1998*

- My boys were geeking me up. "Did you tell him where we come from, man?" one said. — Eric Davis, *The Slick Boys*, p. 61, 1998

geeky *adjective*

socially inept; overly involved with computers *US, 1981*

- People are just a little bit "geeky," but they mind their own business in great little Spanish houses off Moorpark. — Sandra Bernhard, *Confessions of a Pretty Lady*, p. 117, 1988
- Kia (T. Wendy McMillan) sets her up with geeky granola-type Ely (V.S. Brodie). — *Vogue*, p. 91, June 1994
- Her first role was the geeky best friend in Adventures in Babysitting. — *Mademoiselle*, p. 68, June 1994
- "Where's the little geeky guy?" Benny asked. — Janet Evanovich, *Seven Up*, p. 98, 2001

geese *noun*

a burglary *US, 1962*

- He talked primarily about his P.O., the "geese" (burglary) for which he was on probation, and I asked him if I could help him get off probation. — Lewis Yablonsky, *The Violent Gang*, p. 95, 1962

geeser *noun*

a small amount of an illegal drug *US, 1952*

- — *American Speech*, p. 25, February 1952: "Teen-age hophead jargon"

geet *noun*

a dollar *US, 1947*

- [T]he same can be said of pert Dorothy Shay, who is so hot at the b-o these days that she isn't required to do any feudin', fussin' or fightin' to land the same bundle of geets. — *Capital News from Hollywood*, p. 2, November 1947

geeter *noun*

a dollar *US, 1946*

- Belli harbors the conviction that the famous actor is going to have to decorate the mahogany with about thirty-five thousand geeters. — *San Francisco Examiner*, p. 21, 9th December 1946

geets *noun*

money *US, 1949*

- — Babs Gonzales, *Be-Bop Dictionary and History of its Famous Stars*, p. 9, 1949
- — Robert George Reisner, *The Jazz Titans*, 1960

geetus *noun*

money *US, 1926*

- The geetis taken in from that source couldn't possibly keep anything but bush baseball alive. — *San Francisco Call-Bulletin*, p. 17, 2nd May 1947
- Anselms testified that once Dahl came to him for a $100 advance, and another time walked up and said, "Where's the geitus?" — *San Francisco Call-Bulletin*, p. 4, 2nd February 1950
- "I got enough geetus that I don't have to live up here if I don't want," he said all at once. — Robert Edmond Alter, *Carny Kill*, p. 41, 1966
- Pay me back when your Chi Town lawyer unties the geeters your father left you from the I.R.S. — Iceberg Slim (Robert Beck), *Doom Fox*, p. 91, 1978

gee whiz!

used for registering shock, surprise, disappointment, or for emphasis *US, 1876*

- I'd had a deadly relationship the previous summer with another media maiden who was a self-declared faghag so gee whiz I didn't mean to be prejudiced[.] — Lester Bangs, *Psychotic Reactions and Carburetor Dung*, pp. 291–292, 1979

gee willikers!

used as a mock oath *US, 1851*

There are countless variants.

- She screwed her mouth sideways. Gee willikers was it dry. — Seth Morgan, *Homeboy*, p. 274, 1990

geeze; geaze *verb*

to inject by hypodermic needle *US, 1966*

- "I thought you said you geezed stuff?" — Ken Kesey, *Kesey's Jail Journal*, p. 68, 1967
- I have a trial going on right now for possession of paraphernalia, consisting of an outfit which is points which you use to geeze amphetamine drugs with[.] — Frank Reynolds, *Freewheelin Frank*, p. 51, 1967
- We had just finished geazin' / when the bitches started teasin' / for us to split and lay. — Lightnin' Rod, *Hustlers Convention*, p. 16, 1973
- I'll stop geezing while we're at war, man. — Oscar Zeta Acosta, *The Revolt of the Cockroach People*, p. 125, 1973

geeze; geaze; greaze *noun*

heroin; an injection of heroin; narcotics *US, 1967*

- The greaze is nice / and at a decent price — Lightnin' Rod, *Hustlers Convention*, p. 15, 1973
- "I could use a little geeze right now," Pelon says. — Oscar Zeta Acosta, *The Revolt of the Cockroach People*, p. 124, 1973
- — Inez Cardozo-Freeman, *The Joint*, 1984

geezer *noun*

1 a drink of whiskey *US, 1957*

- He walked up to the engineer and said, "You got a geezer?" — Helen Giblo, *Footlights, Fistfights and Femmes*, p. 60, 1957

2 an old person, somewhat infirm *UK, 1885*

An objectionable reference to a senior citizen.

- They look like harmless old geezers. — Chester Gould, *Dick Tracy Meets the Night Crawler*, p. 31, 1945
- That smart old geezer owned buildings, dry cleaning stores, groceries, you name it. — Edwin Torres, *Carlito's Way*, p. 28, 1975
- Why don't you geezers take your game over to the park. — *Get Shorty*, 1995
- Even a dumb geezer should know that emergency automatically pulls up your name. — *As Good As It Gets*, 1997

3 an intravenous drug user *US, 1967*

Sometimes spelled "geazer" from the variant verb spelling geeze; geaze.

- See, before I geeze, I always clean the area where I'm going to do it with alcohol. You won't see most geezers doing that, but look at my veins, clean, good, not sore, nothin'. — Nicholas Von Hoffman, *We are the People Our Parents Warned Us Against*, p. 153, 1967
- Every geezer in Soho knew what went down with Matt[.] — Emmett Grogan, *Ringolevio*, p. 203, 1972

4 a small amount of a drug *US, 1971*
- — Eugene Landy, *The Underground Dictionary*, p. 87, 1971

geezo *noun*
1 a hardened prison inmate *US, 1951*
- He wished he could be a hot geezo like the big-time con he once heard about who yelled when sentenced to 20 years: "That's a cinch, Judge; I can do that standing on my head!" — *San Francisco Chronicle*, p. 10, 27th May 1951
- — *American Speech*, p. 100, May 1956: "Smugglers' argot in the Southwest"

2 an armed robbery *US, 2001*
- And what he did along the way was become a drug dealer and a geezo artist just like the people he was supposed to lock up. — *Chicago Sun-Times*, p. 19, 12th April 2001

geezy *adjective*
drug-intoxicated *US, 1970*
- "Man, I was geezy for thirty days at Preston, and I never got hooked." — Frank Bonham, *Viva Chicano*, p. 68, 1970

gehuncle *noun*
a cripple *US, 1954*
- Ah, what was that gehuncle going for? — Bernard Wolfe, *The Late Risers*, p. 169, 1954

gel *noun*
1 dynamite used for opening a safe *US, 1972*
- — Bruce Jackson, *Outside the Law*, p. 57, 1972: "Glossary"

2 a socially inept person *US, 1991*
- — Trevor Cralle, *The Surfin'ary*, p. 43, 1991

gelt; geld *noun*
money *UK, 1529*
Originally conventional English, then out of favor, then back as slang. German, Dutch, and Yiddish claims on its origin.
- How is he to collect all this gelt? — Charles Raven, *Underworld Nights*, p. 52, 1956
- She still ignored the drunks figuring somebody with gelt would pop up. — Hubert Selby Jr., *Last Exit to Brooklyn*, p. 120, 1957
- Mickey Cohen is Skidsville, U.S.A., and he needs moolah, gelt, the old cashola. — James Ellroy, *White Jazz*, p. 7, 1992

gender mender *noun*
a computer cable with either two male or two female connectors *US, 1991*
- — Eric S. Raymond, *The New Hacker's Dictionary*, p. 175, 1991

generic *adjective*
stupid, dull, boring *US, 1988*
- — Connie Eble (Editor), *UNC-CH Campus Slang*, p. 5, Spring 1988
- — Vann Wesson, *Generation X Field Guide and Lexicon*, p. 76, 1997

geni-ass *noun*
a smart and diligent student *US, 1968*
A play on "genius."
- — Collin Baker et al., *College Undergraduate Slang Study Conducted at Brown University*, p. 124, 1968

genius *noun*
in computing, an obvious or easily guessed password *US, 1990*
- — Karla Jennings, *The Devouring Fungus*, p. 220, 1990

gentleman jockey *noun*
in horse racing, an amateur jockey, especially in a steeple-chase event *US, 1947*
- — Dan Parker, *The ABC of Horse Racing*, p. 146, 1947

gentleman's call *noun*
in pool, an understanding that a shot need not be called if it is obvious *US, 1992*
- — Mike Shamos, *The Illustrated Encyclopedia of Billiards*, p. 108, 1993

gents *noun*
a public men's restroom *US, 1960*
- Drunk now, he went to the gents', took the tooth out, and ran cold water over it. — Robert Stone, *Dog Soldiers*, p. 79, 1974

geologist *noun*
a physician who considers his patients to be as intelligent as a rock *US, 1978*
- — *Maledicta*, p. 68, Summer/Winter 1978: "Common patient-directed pejoratives used by medical personnel"

George *noun*
1 a gambler who tips the dealer or places bets in the dealer's name *US, 1974*
- Sitting there with people that are Georges, which means a good toker, you want them to win—even though you're a house person. — Edward Lin, *Big Julie of Vegas*, p. 210, 1974
- — Lee Solkey, *Dummy Up and Deal*, p. 114, 1980
- In Nevada jargon, "George" is a gambling term for a big tipper, but it means more than that at a brothel: an all-around generous straight-shooting stand-up guy. — Lora Shaner, *Madam*, p. 219, 1999

2 a skilled and lucky gambler *US, 1985*
- — Steve Kuriscak, *Casino Talk*, p. 27, 1985

George *adjective*
excellent *US, 1930*
- "She's real George all the way," one teen-ager remarked. — *Newsweek*, p. 28, 8th October 1951
- Ginny got the sticks and the horse. She says they're both real george. — John D. McDonald, *The Neon Jungle*, p. 44, 1953
- — James Harris, *A Convict's Dictionary*, p. 32, 1989

George Spelvin *noun*
used in a theater program as a fictitious name for an actor *US, 1908*
- — Sherman Louis Sergel, *The Language of Show Biz*, p. 96, 1973

Georgia; Georgie *verb*
to cheat, to swindle; (of a prostitute) to have sex with a customer without collecting the fee *US, 1969*
Especially used in the context of prostitution.
- One of the girls georged him, just for kicks, just to see if he was as good a producer as a braggart. — Clarence Cooper Jr., *The Scene*, p. 31, 1960
- She ain't got no man. She's a "come" freak. She's "Georgied" three bullshit pimps since she got here a month ago. — Iceberg Slim (Robert Beck), *Pimp*, p. 79, 1969
- What I wanted was for a white whore to hit on me to spend some money with her, that way I'd have a chance to "georgia" her out of some cock. — Donald Goines, *Whoreson*, p. 203, 1972
- Don't let no bitch georgia you. Don't fuck a bitch 'til the bread is right. In short, Little Willie, sell that dick! — A.S. Jackson, *Gentleman Pimp*, p. 27, 1973

Georgia ham *noun*
a watermelon *US, 1971*
- — Hermese E. Roberts, *The Third Ear*, 1971
- — *American Speech*, p. 153, Spring–Summer 1972: "An approach to Black slang"

Georgia homeboy *noun*
the recreational drug GHB *US, 1993*
A disguise for the initials **GHB**.
- — *American Speech*, p. 84, Spring 1995: "Among the new words"
- GHB, a drug whose street names include "liquid ecstacy," "Grievous Bodily Harm," and "Georgia Homeboy," is available in a liquid form for drinking. — Merril D. Smith, *Encyclopedia of Rape*, p. 85, 2004

Georgia ice cream *noun*
grits *US, 1972*
- "That's the worst Cream of Wheat I've ever tasted." "That's Georgia ice cream," Doc Ratteree said. — Pat Conroy, *The Great Santini*, p. 175, 1976

Georgia scuffle *noun*
in carnival usage, rough handling of an extremely naive customer in a swindle *US, 1950*
- — Hyman E. Goldin et al., *Dictionary of American Underworld Lingo*, p. 78, 1950

Georgie *noun*
a casual girlfriend *US, 1975*
- I knew he had Georgies in other cities. — Herb Michelson, *Sportin' Ladies*, p. 111, 1975

germ *noun*
a despised person *US, 1942*
- — *San Francisco Examiner*, p. III-2, 22nd March 1960

Germans *noun*
drug dealers from the Dominican Republic as perceived by African-American drug dealers competing for the same market—the enemy *US, 1992*
- — Terry Williams, *Crackhouse*, p. 148, 1992

Geronimo *noun*

1 an alcoholic drink mixed with a barbiturate *US, 1970*

A dangerous cross reaction.

- — William D. Alsever, *Glossary for the Establishment and Other Uptight People*, p. 12, December 1970
- — Donald Wesson and David Smith, *Barbiturates*, p. 122, 1977

2 a barbiturate *US, 1990*

- When we lifted her up, out of her pocket spilled about fifty geronimos. — Herbert Huncke, *Guilty of Everything*, p. 193, 1990

get *verb*

▸ **get any; get anything; get enough; get a little bit**

to have sex *US, 1947*

- I'm getting enough, and the only thing I wish is that I could stay at Park for about three more years. — James T. Farrell, *Saturday Night*, p. 36, 1947
- Outside of the football team and the basketball team, there were only a few going steady who were getting any. [Interview with Walt Grove] — *Playboy*, p. 130, May 1963
- And another time. Every time me and my old lady try to get a little bit / You come 'round here with that roaring shit. — Anonymous ("Arthur"), *Shine and the Titanic; The Signifying Monkey; Stackolee*, p. 1, 1971
- How come when you're nineteen you can't get any? [Note from Joe Bob: I just went to ask the editor if I can explain what "get any" means and he said no sireee, Joe Bob.] — Joe Bob Briggs, *Joe Bob Goes to the Drive-In*, p. 27, 1987

▸ **get it**

1 to have sex *US, 1958*

- "But at least you get it steady. And I've never got it at all." — J.P. Donleavy, *The Ginger Man*, p. 6, 1958

2 to be punished, especially physically *UK, 1851*

- I would usually hide under the porch until it came time to "get it." "You just wait till your father comes, then you're really gonna get it." — Lenny Bruce, *How to Talk Dirty and Influence People*, p. 2, 1965

3 to be killed *US, 1964*

- — R. Frederick West, *God's Gambler*, p. 226, 1964: "Appendix A"
- Several guys got it while I was on R and R. — David Parks, *GI Diary*, p. 121, 1968
- The wife of one of their people got it. — Richard Condon, *Prizzi's Honor*, p. 237, 1982

▸ **get it on**

1 to have sex *US, 1970*

- And if you feel, like I feel baby / Come on, oh come on / Let's get it on. — Marvin Gaye, *Let's Get It On*, 1973
- If Harvey thought getting it on with some bubble-gum rocker was realizing his full human potential, well, that was his prerogative. — Cyra McFadden, *The Serial*, p. 37, 1977
- Hey, don't you think a hair stylist's got any interest in gettin' it on? — *48 Hours*, 1982
- I don't have a real relationship right now, so when I'm not making a film, I ain't getting it on at all. — *Adult Video*, p. 9, August/September 1986

2 to fight *US, 1959*

- I would back out then because I was tight with both clicks and couldn't take sides when they'd get it on. — Edwin Torres, *Carlito's Way*, p. 25, 1975

▸ **get it up**

to achieve an erection *US, 1943*

- Feivel couldn't get it up with splints. — Irving Shulman, *The Amboy Dukes*, p. 53, 1947
- Well the Buyer comes to look more and more like a junky. He can't drink. He can't get it up. His teeth fall out. — William Burroughs, *Naked Lunch*, p. 15, 1957
- I'm surprised you could even get it up—look at the way you sweating now. — James Baldwin, *Blues for Mister Charlie*, p. 101, 1964
- "I didn't sleep with ladies for years because I couldn't get it up! But with you, I did." — D.M. Perkins, *Deep Throat*, p. 63, 1973

▸ **get some**

1 to have sex *US, 1970*

- So he goes to England and all his pals are getting some but he stays true to his wife, and he goes to Paris and all his pals are getting some, but he stays true to his wife. — Darryl Poncsan, *The Last Detail*, p. 15, 1970

2 to kill enemy soldiers *US, 1976*

- [T]he grunts back on the perimeter looked at each other and grinned—"Get some, Man, oh get some!" — Charles Anderson, *The Grunts*, p. 131, 1976

▸ **get well**

to make money *US, 1995*

- This way we hit the cops where it hurts and get well in the meantime. — *The Usual Suspects*, 1995

▸ **get with**

to have sex with *UK, 1987*

- Even if a bloke was hot for me, there was no way I would get with him unless he came with a medical. — Kathy Lette, *Girls' Night Out*, p. 71, 1987
- I've wanted to get with her for a while now. — *Kids*, 1995
- I tried to get with her for four years, without much success. Then I went on "The Joan Rivers Show." It was my first TV break. Right away she slept with me. — Chris Rock, *Rock This!*, p. 126, 1997

▸ **get you!; get him!; get her!**

used for expressing disbelief at what has just been said *US, 1949*

Homosexual.

- — Anon, *The Gay Girl's Guide*, p. 10, 1949

▸ **get yours**

to get the punishment you deserve *US, 1905*

- "He'll get his some day," I said. — Chester Himes, *Cast the First Stone*, p. 124, 1952
- I read that The Enforcer got his finally, with a .32 Smith & Wesson and a .38 Colt, in the barbershop of the Park Sheraton Hotel in New York City[.] — Clancy Sigal, *Going Away*, p. 472, 1961

get a life!

used to tease someone who is revealing a lack of grounding in reality or who is too obsessed with something *US, 1989*

- Jesus, Ann, get a life. I just asked what he looked like. — *Sex, Lies and Videotape*, 1989
- — Connie Eble (Editor), *UNC-CH Campus Slang*, p. 3, Fall 1989
- — Eric S. Raymond, *The New Hacker's Dictionary*, p. 176, 1991
- DONNY ASTRICKY: You ever notice how it [the show "Dukes of Hazzard"] had a different interior every week? That bugged me. MIRROR MAN: Three words. Get A Life. — *Gone in 60 Seconds*, 2000

get a roll of stamps and mail it in

used as a humorous comment on a lack of effort *US, 1997*

Coined by ESPN's Keith Olberman to describe "a lackluster effort on the part of a player or team."

- — Keith Olberman and Dan Patrick, *The Big Show*, p. 15, 1997

get a room!

used for discouraging public displays of affection *US, 1999*

- OK, Mini-Me, why don't you and the laser get a frickin' room. — *Austin Powers*, 1999

getaway *noun*

the last morning of a military tour of duty *US, 1968*

- — Carl Fleischhauer, *A Glossary of Army Slang*, p. 21, 1968

getaway day *noun*

in horse racing, the last day of a racing meet *US, 1962*

- — Mel Heimer, *Inside Racing*, p. 211, 1962

get-back *noun*

an act of revenge *US, 1984*

- Those guys got some get-backs coming for what they done to Johnny last week. — Inez Cardozo-Freeman, *The Joint*, p. 499, 1984
- You do to me and I do to you. Get-back. — Robert Campbell, *Nibbled to Death by Ducks*, p. 248, 1989
- When I got home, I telephone all the fellas to talk about getting some get-back. — Nathan McCall, *Makes Me Wanna Holler*, p. 64, 1994
- "The word is out. We need some get-back with the Bloods." — Colton Simpson, *Inside the Crips*, p. 99, 2005

get bent!

used as an exclamation of defiance, roughly along the lines of "go to hell!" *US, Early 1970s*

- We also talked about the expressions we used in high school. Things like "Get bent," which was meant to put a guy down. — Jim Bouton, *Ball Four*, p. 361, 1970
- — *Esquire*, p. 180, June 1983

get down *verb*

1 to have sex *US, 1973*

- [W]e catch a cab, zoom up to my apartment in the East eighties, get down, catch a cab, and zoom back down. — Susan Hall, *Ladies of the Night*, p. 51, 1973

2 in sports betting, to place a bet *US, 1974*

- By the way, ask him what the odds are on the Giants? I want to get down for a hundred. — Edward Lin, *Big Julie of Vegas*, p. 99, 1974
- I seen a couple of guys I know, had a couple of pops, got something down on it. — John Sayles, *Union Dues*, p. 24, 1977

get-down time; git-down time *noun*

the time of day or night when a prostitute starts working *US, 1972*

- As the "git-down" time neared, the women complained about having to go to work on public transportation rather than in a car. — Christina and Richard Milner, *Black Players*, p. 149, 1972
- Get-down time in the Combat Zone and Inez was waiting to draw first blood. — John Sayles, *Union Dues*, p. 180, 1977
- "It's way past git-down time. Why aren't you down on the street?" — Alix Shulman, *On the Stroll*, p. 151, 1981

geters *noun*

money *US, 1975*

- — Carl J. Banks Jr., *Banks Dictionary of the Black Ghetto Language*, 1975

get-go; git-go; gitty up *noun*

the very start *US, 1962*

- A clicker from the get-go, the sheet has become must reading for every deejay who sees it. — *New Pittsburgh Courier*, 19th May 1962
- I want it be understood from the git-go that this is my plan[.] — Odie Hawkins, *The Busting Out of an Ordinary Man*, p. 170, 1985
- Everything about the Irish cop was a threat, right up front, Leddy thought. Right from git-go. — Robert Campbell, *Boneyards*, p. 49, 1992
- I just find out the nigger stealing me blind since the gitty-up. — Richard Price, *Clockers*, p. 67, 1992

get-high *noun*

crack cocaine; any drug *US, 1990*

- I hooked you up for that last get-high. — *New Jack City*, 1990
- She says, "I was by Darius' house, and he said y'all just left. You got any get-high?" — Chris Rock, *Rock This!*, p. 74, 1997
- Like a lot of get-highs, some get stoned while others barely feel the effects. — Stephen Power, *The Art of Getting Over*, p. 66, 1999
- "I just want to smoke my get-high and chill, know what I'm saying?" — Paul Beatty, *Tuff*, p. 158, 2000

get-in Betty *noun*

a crowbar used by burglars *US, 1950*

- We had a pretty good bunch of O'Sullivans, a torch man, a mechanic, a jigger and a hard-shell biscuit who'd been with a gopher mob. We crashed with a get-in betty. — *The New American Mercury*, p. 709, 1950

get off *verb*

1 to achieve sexual climax *US, 1867*

- When you're turned out, pimps put that in your head. "You don't get off with tricks." — Susan Hall, *Ladies of the Night*, p. 29, 1973
- "You mean you didn't get off once?" — D.M. Perkins, *Deep Throat*, p. 32, 1973
- Harry Reems made a reputation as one of those rare people with "the ability to always get it off." — Kenneth Turan and Stephen E. Zito, *Sinema*, p. 182, 1974
- Q: "She can't get off"—"getting off" meaning in this context what? A: "Getting off" in this context indicates that she has trouble achieving an orgasm. MR. JUSTICE MOCATTA: She has what? A: She has trouble achieving an orgasm, a sexual climax. — Frank Zappa, *The Real Frank Zappa Book*, pp. 136–137, 1989

2 to use a drug; to feel the effects of a drug *US, 1952*

- We got a free bag, and he asked me if I ever got off before. — Jeremy Larner and Ralph Tefferteller, *The Addict in the Street*, p. 210, 1964
- "How many mikes?" Papa All wanted to know. "Ahh, I dunno. They'll get ya off." — Nicholas Von Hoffman, *We Are The People Our Parents Warned Us Against*, p. 26, 1967
- That woman knew he hadn't got off since six this evening, and it was close to eleven now. — Nathan Heard, *Howard Street*, p. 15, 1968
- And this would get the reindeer off, man? — Cheech Marin and Tommy Chong, *Santa Claus and his Old Lady*, 1971

3 by extension, to take pleasure from something *US, 1952*

- Well, I don't know if you knew this, but half the girls in this place are take-home whores anyway, they get off on shit like that. — *Hard Eight*, 1996

get-off house *noun*

a place where you can both purchase and inject heroin *US, 1990*

- He points out two empty units as "get-off houses"—$10 for the drug, $2 for a needle, $2 for use of the premises. — *St. Petersburg (Florida) Times*, p. 1D, 14th January 1990

get off the stove, I'm ridin' the range tonight!

used for expressing enthusiasm about an upcoming date *US, 1951*

- — *Philadelphia Evening Bulletin*, 11th November 1951

get on *verb*

1 to use drugs *US, 1952*

- You wanna get on? I got some pot stashed by the subway. — George Mandel, *Flee the Angry Strangers*, p. 26, 1952

2 to have *US, 1990*

- TRE: Say, pop, can I get on one of those stamps? FURIOUS: If you mean can you have one, yes. — *Boyz N The Hood*, 1990

get-out *noun*

an extreme degree of something *US, 1838*

- We've passed the danger mark and I'm pleased as all get-out! — Gore Vidal, *Myra Breckinridge*, p. 258, 1968

get out *verb*

(used of a bettor) to recoup earlier losses *US, 1951*

- — David W. Maurer, *Argot of the Racetrack*, p. 31, 1951

get out of here!

used for expressing disbelief at what has just been said *US, 1994*

- SMOKER: I ask the kid how come nobody called the manager, and he says it happens twice a week, sometimes more. RANDAL: Get out of here. SMOKER: I kid you not. — *Clerks*, 1994

get out of here, Mary!

used for expressing doubt *US, 1987*

- — "Say Wha?", *Washington Post Magazine*, p. 16, 26th December 1987

get-over *noun*

success through fraud *US, 1997*

- People don't look at show business as a job. They think it's the ultimate get-over. The ultimate "you got lucky." — Chris Rock, *Rock This!*, p. 83, 1997

get over *verb*

to take advantage of someone, making yourself look good at their expense *US, 1981*

- — *Maledicta*, p. 266, Summer/Winter 1981: "By its slang, ye shall know it: the pessimism of prison life"

▶ **get over on**

to seduce *US, 1987*

- I was switching gears ... forget about being a conceited asshole ... I was now trying to get over on her. — Jim Carroll, *Forced Entries*, p. 52, 1987

get over it!

used as a suggestion that the hearer move on from the issue that is dominating the moment *US, 1994*

- — Kevin Dilallo, *The Unofficial Gay Manual*, p. 240, 1994

get over you!

used in order to deflate a person's excessive sense of importance *US, 1997*

- — Jeff Fessler, *When Drag Is Not a Car Race*, p. 83, 1997

get real!

used for expressing scorn at that which has just been said *US, 1982*

- — Connie Eble (Editor), *UNC-CH Campus Slang*, p. 3, Fall 1982
- How many people in this state been executed in the last thirty years? One, maybe? Two? Get real! — Joseph Wambaugh, *Floaters*, p. 169, 1996

getting any?

used as a male-to-male greeting *US, 1958*

Instantly jocular due to the inquiry as to the other's sex life.

- It read: "Gittin' any? Hee-hee." — Terry Southern, *Candy*, p. 211, 1958
- Did you get any yet? I say, Get any what? He says, You know, man. I say, No man, I didn't get any ... get any what? He says, Did you get any ... any p-u-s-s-y? — Frank Robinson, *Sex American Style*, p. 282, 1971

- COWBOY: Been getting any? JOKER: Only your sister. — *Full Metal Jacket*, 1987

get-up noun

1 an outfit or costume *UK, 1847*

- DeDe was wearing a Hermes scarf on her head and oversized sunglasses. Mary Ann was reminded of Jackie O's old shopping get-up for Greece. — Armistead Maupin, *Further Tales of the City*, p. 147, 1982
- His get-up consisted of a black lacy teddy with no underwear and a visible penis. — Anka Radakovich, *The Wild Girls Club*, p. 225, 1994

2 the last morning of a jail sentence or term of military service *US, 1967*

- "A getup and coffee," Little Junior said. — Clarence Cooper Jr., *The Farm*, p. 88, 1967
- *Maledicta*, p. 267, Summer/Winter 1981: "By its slang, ye shall know it: the pessimism of prison life"

get up verb

1 to be released from prison *US, 1967*

- When does she get up? — Clarence Cooper Jr., *The Farm*, p. 37, 1967
- The old man shook his head and walked away. "I should have remembered you're gettin' up in the morning," he answered over his shoulder. — Donald Goines, *Black Gangster*, p. 12, 1977

2 to succeed in painting your graffiti tag in a public place *US, 1982*

- Style, form, and methodology, major concerns of most writers, are secondary in significance to the prime directive in graffiti: "getting up." — Craig Castleman, *Getting Up*, p. 19, 1982
- "If you can get up on a heaven, then the other taggers coming by, like the ones from Miami especially, they can see your tag," he says. — *New Times Broward-Palm Beach (Florida)*, 12th December 2002

get with the words!

explain yourself! *US, 1965*

- — Miss Cone, *The Slang Dictionary (Hawthorne High School)*, 1965

GFY

go fuck yourself *US, 1987*

Used when discretion suggests avoiding the word "fuck."

- — Carsten Stroud, *Close Pursuit*, p. 272, 1987

GG noun

in transsexual usage, a genuine or genetic girl *US, 1986–1987*

- — *Maledicta*, p. 173, Summer/Winter 1986–1987: "Sexual slang: prostitutes, pedophiles, flagellators, transvestites, and necrophiles"

GHB noun

Gamma hydroxybutyrate, a pharmaceutical anesthetic used as a recreational drug *US, 1990*

Gamma hydroxybutyrate is a foul-tasting liquid, invented in the 1960s by Dr. Henri Laborit, who swore by its powers as an aphrodisiac. The drug has been marketed as an anesthetic and a health supplement. A heightened sense of touch, sustained erections, and longer orgasms make it popular with "up-for-it clubbers."

- — *American Speech*, p. 84, Spring 1995: "Among the new words"
- — Angela Devlin, *Prison Patter*, p. 56, 1996
- GHB is said to increase sensuality and can lead to great sex. — Simon Napier-Bell, *Black Vinyl White Powder*, p. 329, 2001

gheid noun

a Paregoric user *US, 1971*

- — Eugene Landy, *The Underground Dictionary*, p. 87, 1971

ghetto noun

the anus *US, 1973*

- Nearly in tears, he bent over and fairly begged me to penetrate his ghetto. — Richard Frank, *A Study of Sex in Prison*, p. 36, 1973

ghetto adjective

inferior, shoddy, bad *US, 1995*

- — Connie Eble (Editor), *UNC-CH Campus Slang*, p. 5, April 1995
- — *Columbia Missourian*, p. 1A, 19th October 1998
- We were so wasted we passed out. / I got that gnarly sunburn, it was so ghetto[.] — Me First and the Gimme Gimmes, *End of the Road*, 2003

ghetto bird noun

a police helicopter, especially one flying at night with a bright spotlight *US, 1993*

- Police and media helicopters, known in south-central Los Angeles as ghetto birds, saw nothing but calm. — *CNN News*, 17th April 1993
- — *Ebony Magazine*, p. 156, August 2000: "How to talk to the new generation"

ghetto blaster; ghetto box noun

a large, portable radio and tape player; a portable music system *US, 1981*

Can be considered offensive because it is culture-specific and stereotypical.

- That sucker's the fifth thief I seen this morning with brand new ghetto blasters glued to his fuckin' ears. — Joseph Wambaugh, *The Delta Star*, p. 22, 1983
- Out in the bus lane, a kid in a Blessed Mother High School sweatshirt turns down the volume on his ghetto-blaster. — Jay McInerney, *Bright Lights, Big City*, p. 150, 1984
- [W]atching some street kids with shaved heads huddling around a ghetto blaster as if it were a fire. — Francesca Lia Block, *Witch Baby*, p. 143, 1991
- Now he went to talk to a man who prepared cafe Cubano and smoked Cohiba panatelas listening to Radio Mambi on his ghetto box[.] — Elmore Leonard, *Out of Sight*, p. 108, 1996

ghetto bootie noun

large buttocks *US, 2001*

- — Don R. McCreary (Editor), *Dawg Speak*, 2001

ghetto fabulous adjective

ostentatious, exemplifying the style of the black hip-hop community *US, 1996*

- Founded by Andre Harrell, it merged the softer approach of rhythm and blues with the hard edge of hip-hop to create what Mr. Harrell called "New Jack Swing" – or, as he describes it, "high-style urban black life a.k.a. ghetto fabulous." — *New York Times*, p. 4 (Section 13), 14th January 1996
- In the "gettin' jiggy with it," ghetto fabulous '90s, it's all about flexing the strength of hip hop's newfound pop status. — *Vibe Magazine*, *The Vibe History of Hip Hop*, p. 278, 1999
- — Don R. McCreary (Editor), *Dawg Speak*, 2001
- — Connie Eble (Editor), *UNC-CH Campus Slang*, p. 4, November 2003

ghetto lullaby noun

inner-city nighttime noises—sirens, gunfire, helicopters, etc. *US, 1993*

- I ain't raisin' no family down here. The ghetto lullaby puttin' my kids to sleep. Copters and shit flyin' by all night. — *Menace II Society*, 1993

ghetto rags noun

clothing typical of the inner-city ghetto *US, 1970*

- When you go downtown, y'all wear your ghetto rags ... see ... Don't go down there with your Italian silk jerseys on and your brown suede and green alligator shoes and your Harry Belafonte shirts. — Tom Wolfe, *Radical Chic & Mau-Mauing the Flak Catchers*, p. 99, 1970

ghetto sled noun

a large, luxury automobile *US, 1997*

- — Vann Wesson, *Generation X Field Guide and Lexicon*, p. 78, 1997

ghetto star noun

a youth gang leader *US, 1991*

- Rider goes on to explain that the people actually involved in the attack on B-Dog were "ghetto stars"—O.G.'s with very, very serious reputations. — Leon Bing, *Do or Die*, p. 226, 1991
- "Ain't nothin'," I respond, trying to hide my utter admiration for this cat who is quickly becoming a Ghetto Star. — Sanyika Shakur, *Monster*, p. 5, 1993
- His years there would galvanize his legend on the streets as a "ghetto star," but they would also eventually propel him toward a renunciation of gang life[.] — *New York Times*, p. C27, 23rd July 1993
- — Bill Valentine, *Gang Intelligence Manual*, p. 76, 1995: "Black street gang terminology"

ghetto stick noun

a sawed-off shotgun *US, 2006*

- This time I saw that she thumbed buckshot into the cut-down 12-gauge, known on the street as a ghetto stick. — Stephen J. Cannell, *White Sister*, p. 309, 2006

ghost noun

1 a faint, secondary duplicate video image in a television signal, caused by the mixing of the primary signal and a delayed version of the same signal *US, 1942*

- Life in this great pretzel center is distinguished by the worst television reception enjoyed by any metropolitan American city—not even barring blast-furnacy Pittsburgh, runner-up for ghosts, blizzards, fade-outs and other visual blah. — *San Francisco News*, p. 21, 22nd May 1952

2 a blank stop on a casino slot machine *US, 1993*
- — Frank Scoblete, *Guerrilla Gambling*, p. 310, 1993

3 in poker, a player who frequently absents himself from the table *US, 1996*
- — John Vorhaus, *The Big Book of Poker Slang*, p. 20, 1996

4 LSD *US, 1967*
Usually used with "the."
- — John Williams, *The Drug Scene*, p. 112, 1967

▸ **do a ghost**
to leave quickly *US, 1995*
- — Bill Valentine, *Gang Intelligence Manual*, p. 75, 1995: "Black street gang terminology"

ghost *verb*

1 to write an article, story, or book on behalf of and under the name of someone else *UK, 1932*
- "You were AA and slipped as all such persons do until their autobiographies are ghosted." — Irving Shulman, *College Confidential*, p. 164, 1960
- "You think he won't notice that someone was ghosting the paper for you?" — Frederick Kohner, *The Affairs of Gidget*, p. 62, 1963

2 to ambush *US, 1992*
- Ghosting the dude wouldn't be hard. — Jess Mowry, *Way Past Cool*, p. 124, 1992

3 to transfer a prisoner from one prison to another at night after the prison has been secured *US, 1982*
- — Ralph de Sola, *Crime Dictionary*, p. 57, 1982
- — William K. Bentley and James M. Corbett, *Prison Slang*, p. 10, 1992

4 to vanish *US, 1969*
- Their skulls won't let 'em believe a Nigger was clever enough to ghost outta here. — Iceberg Slim (Robert Beck), *Pimp*, p. 265, 1969

ghostbust *noun*
to search in an obsessive and compulsive way for small particles of crack cocaine *US, 1992*
- — Terry Williams, *Crackhouse*, p. 148, 1992

ghost hand *noun*
in poker, a hand or part of a hand that is dealt to the same player twice in a row *US, 1988*
- — George Percy, *The Language of Poker*, p. 39, 1988

ghoulie *noun*
a movie based on violent exploitation *US, 1970*
- Still others were known as "kinkies" (dealing with fetishes) and "ghoulies" (minimizing nudity and maximizing violence). — *The Presidential Commission on Obscenity and Pornography*, p. 109, 1970

ghoulie *adjective*
ghoulish *US, 1993*
- "Who was that ghoulie guy?" I ask the Bat Man back at the apartment. — Francesca Lia Block, *Missing Angel Juan*, p. 341, 1993

GI *noun*

1 an enlisted soldier in the US Army *US, 1939*
- The slang expression "GI" has been barred for the Army public relations officers. They'll have to refer to a soldier as a soldier. — *The Milwaukee Star*, 28th June 1951

2 an American Indian who has abandoned his indigenous culture and language in favor of mainstream American culture; a government Indian *US, 1963*
- — *American Speech*, p. 272, December 1963: "American Indian student slang"

GI *verb*

1 to clean thoroughly *US, 1944*
- At night, he would bring the dings their chow, G.I. their cells and stroll the catwalk exchanging words with them through the bars. — James Ellroy, *Suicide Hill*, p. 585, 1986

2 to strip *US, 1968*
- Jackie nervously G.I.ed his cigarette[.] — Nathan Heard, *Howard Street*, p. 208, 1968

GI *adjective*
neat, orderly *US, 1929*

- Just have your barracks clean and your men G.I. when I bring the Congressman around. — Nat Hiken, *Sergeant Bilko*, p. 154, 1957
- "I want evry thing polished an sharp an GI." — Warren Miller, *The Cool World*, p. 146, 1959

gib *noun*
a man's buttocks *US, 1986*
- Looked at Whistler's thigh and asked the white mugger if he liked "gibs," which the mugger said he liked all right when there was nothing else available. — Robert Campbell, *In La-La Land We Trust*, p. 112, 1986

GIB *noun*
the back seat member of the crew on a fighter aircraft *US, 1967*
An initialism for "guy in back."
- Now let me tell you the story / Of a GIB named Richard. — Joseph Tuso, *Singing the Vietnam Blues*, p. 87, 1990: GIB Named Richard

GIB *adjective*
skilled in sex *US, 1977*
An initialism for "good in bed."
- — Kevin DiLallo, *The Unofficial Gay Manual*, p. 218, 1988

gibbs *noun*
the lips *US, 1990*
- — Charles Shafer, *Folk Speech in Texas Prisons*, p. 205, 1990

giblet *noun*
a stupid, foolish or inept person *US, 1984*
Playing on a turkey image.
- And it is a heartbreak to be sitting waiting for the truck and the giblet comes out and drives it away. — *Repo Man*, 1984

Gibson girl *noun*
an emergency radio used when a military aircraft is shot down over a body of water *US, 1943*
- — *American Speech*, p. 310, December 1946: "More Air Force slang"

giddyap; giddyup *noun*
the beginning; the inception *US, 1974*
- He told us right from the giddyap what he was willing to put into acquisition of the siding property. — George V. Higgins, *Penance for Jerry Kennedy*, p. 25, 1985

giffer *noun*
a pickpocket *US, 1949*
- — Vincent J. Monteleone, *Criminal Slang*, p. 97, 1949

gift *noun*
in a sex club, used as a coded euphemism for payment for special services *US, 1997*
- And it's hers because this is a girl who wakes up, comes to work, and hustles. "Do you have a gift for me?" "Do you want some company?" — Anthony Petkovich, *The X Factory*, p. 40, 1997

gig *noun*

1 a musical performance or concert *US, 1926*
Originally musicians' slang for an engagement at a single venue.
- We'll put the band back together, do a few gigs, we get some bread. — *The Blues Brothers*, 1980
- We got that gig in L.A., we'll just leave a little early. — *Boys on the Side*, 1995
- You'd look for punks who'd driven up to a gig in cars or, the best, punks whose Mom had dropped them off. — Susan Ruddick, *Cool Places*, p. 354, 1998

2 a job *US, 1908*
- What's your gig in all this? — *Ten Things I Hate About You*, 1999

3 a party *US, 1954*
- Let's get that sneaky pete [wine] and have us a gig. — Harrison E. Salisbury, *The Shook-up Generation*, p. 29, 1958
- — Malachi Andrews and Paul T. Owens, *Black Language*, p. 55, 1973

4 a prison or jail sentence *US, 1977*
- I saved him a gig for a shirttail hanging out on an IG inspection. — Larry Heinemann, *Close Quarters*, p. 133, 1977
- He was at FPC doing a gig for fraud, I think credit cards. — Elmore Leonard, *Out of Sight*, p. 57, 1996

5 the vagina *US, 1967*
- — Dale Gordon, *The Dominion Sex Dictionary*, p. 76, 1967

6 a demerit or other indication of failure *US, 1968*
- — Carl Fleischhauer, *A Glossary of Army Slang*, p. 21, 1968
- "I'll take the gig and the ass-chewing." — Anthony Herbert, *Soldier*, p. 136, 1973

7 in an illegal number gambling lottery, a bet that a specific three-digit number will be drawn *US, 1846*
- — *American Speech*, p. 191, October 1949
- In order to win the player has to pick a "gig"—three numbers between 1 and 78. — Alson Smith, *Syndicate City*, p. 197, 1954
- It's the prospect of the big payoff that hooks them. A dime played on a gig that hits brings eight-six dollars. A buck on a lucky gig or bet pays eight hundred and sixty dollars. — Iceberg Slim (Robert Beck), *Mama Black Widow*, p. 97, 1969

gig *verb*

1 to work; to have a job *US, 1937*
- "They got into a jam with the locals last place they gigged, so you got to play it chilly." — Herbert Simmons, *Corner Boy*, p. 54, 1957
- "There's a lot of bread to be made gigging right around here in Roxbury," Shorty explained to me. — Malcolm X and Alex Haley, *The Autobiography of Malcolm X*, p. 45, 1964
- So like what, a cat with heart is gonna gig in some shoulder-pad factory? — Edwin Torres, *Carlito's Way*, p. 144, 1975
- He doesn't gig in the store any more. — Iceberg Slim (Robert Beck), *Doom Fox*, p. 132, 1978

2 to go out to bars, clubs and/or parties *US, 2000*
- — *Ebony Magazine*, p. 156, August 2000: "How to talk to the new generation"

3 in carnival usage, to win all of a player's money in a single transaction *US, 1985*
- The step by step process of beating a player is considered a work of art and a good agent prides himself with this skill, therefore the practice of GIGGING is frowned upon by these professionals. — Gene Sorrows, *All About Carnivals*, p. 18, 1985

giggle juice *noun*
alcohol *US, 1939*
- — Judi Sanders, *Kickin' like Chicken with the Couch Commander*, p. 10, 1992
- His sibilants were slurring; Stuart had been knocking back the giggle juice. — Eric Garcia, *Cassandra French's Finishing School for Boys*, p. 40, 2004

giggles; good giggles *noun*
marijuana *US, 1986*
- — Richard A. Spears, *The Slang and Jargon of Drugs and Drink*, p. 219, 1986

giggle smoke *noun*
marijuana; a marijuana cigarette *US, 1952*
- The "performance enhancing" capabilities of giggle smoke became the hot topic among snowboarders. — Todd Richards, *P3*, p. 208, 2004

giggle soup *noun*
any alcoholic beverage *US, 1972*
- I guess they both reasoned my pardner was still stewed from the Kingfish's gigglesoup. — Guy Owen, *The Flim-Flam Man and the Apprentice Grifter*, p. 116, 1972
- I could settle my nerves by swilling a little giggle-soup. — Robert Byrne, *McGoorty*, p. 30, 1972

giggle water *noun*
alcohol, especially champagne *US, 1926*
- With his rotten luck, perhaps a shot of giggle water now and then would have been helpful. — Helen Giblo, *Footlights, Fistfights and Femmes*, p. 15, 1957

giggle weed *noun*
marijuana *US, 1937*
- Giggle weed is a well-known term for marijuana. — Senate Committee on Energy and Natural Resources, *Nominations*, p. 164, 1977

giggling academy *noun*
a mental hospital *US, 1949*
- Wolfe winked at Bob again. Bob eyed him as if he had just escaped from the Bellevue Giggling Academy. — Bill Fitzhugh, *Pest Control*, p. 124, 1996

giggy; gigi *noun*
the anus and rectum *US, 1953*
- — *Maledicta*, p. 15, 1977: "A word for it!"
- Whereas Roland, who had the world by the giggy at the present time, had a piss-poor view of the ocean down a street and between some apartments. — Elmore Leonard, *Gold Coast*, p. 130, 1980

GI gin *noun*
cough syrup *US, 1964*
- I reached into the pocket of my loose jungle fatigues for the bottle of GI gin. A good slug of this 80 proof terpin hydrate elixir guarantees an hour free of coughing. — Robin Moore, *The Green Berets*, p. 170, 1965
- The guys had showed me how to drink GI gin—cough syrup with codeine—a nasty high but a powerful buzz[.] — Art Neville, *The Brothers*, p. 81, 2000

gig line *noun*
the vertical alignment of shirt buttons, belt buckle, and pants fly on a soldier *US, 1970*
- What is referred to as the "gig line" on the uniform? The alignment of the shirt, belt buckle, and trouser fly. — Walter Jackson, *Soldier's Study Guide*, p. 179, 2004

GIGO
in computing, used as a reminder that output is only as good as input—(garbage in, garbage out) *US, 1959*
- As a matter of fact, they have coined a word, "Gigo" (garbage in garbage out) to defend their position. — *Los Angeles Times*, p. III-5, 11th December 1961
- The technicians have come up with an acronym to epitomize this computer limitation. The word is "GIGO." It stands for "garbage in, garbage out." — United States Senate Committee on Labor, Subcommittee on Employment, *Nation's Manpower Revolution*, p. 1464, 1963
- — Robert Kirk Mueller, *Buzzwords*, p. 87, 1974
- — Karla Jennings, *The Devouring Fungus*, p. 220, 1990

gig shot *noun*
in carnival usage, the method used by an operator to win all of a player's money in a single transaction *US, 1985*
- — Gene Sorrows, *All About Carnivals*, p. 18, 1985: "Terminology"

gigunda *adjective*
very large *US, 1972*
- Here they've been talking about how gigunda these women have to be so their skin is all loose, and she's just a size 14. — Wendy Shanker, *The Fat Girl's Guide to Life*, p. 171, 2004

GI haircut *noun*
a very short haircut *US, 1941*
- "And as fast as you can, grow some hair on your head. That GI haircut looks ridiculous." — Oliver North, *Mission Compromised*, p. 20, 2002

GI Jane *noun*
a stereotypical female soldier *US, 1944*
- She sometimes compares herself to GI Jane. She's incredibly neat and diligent. — David Lipsky, *Absolutely American*, p. 33, 2003

GI Joe *noun*
a quintessential American soldier *US, 1935*
A term fueled by a cartoon in the 1940s, a Robert Mitchum movie in 1945, and a line of toys starting in 1964.
- Charlie Company was a "grunt" unit; its men were the foot soldiers, the "GI Joes," who understood they were to take orders, not question them. — Seymour Hersh, *My Lai 4*, p. 18, 1970

gill; gills *noun*
in circus and carnival usage, a customer, especially a gullible one *US, 1981*
- — Don Wilmeth, *The Language of American Popular Entertainment*, p. 111, 1981

gillie suit *noun*
camouflaged uniforms used by the US Army Special Forces *US, 1992*
Gulf war usage.
- — *American Speech*, p. 87, Spring 1992: "Gulf War words supplement"

Gilligan *noun*
a hapless, socially inept person *US, 1991*
From the *Gilligan's Island* television program, in which Gilligan was a hapless, socially inept person.
- — Trevor Cralle, *The Surfin'ary*, p. 44, 1991

gillion *noun*
ten to the ninth power; untold millions *US, 1991*
- — Eric S. Raymond, *The New Hacker's Dictionary*, p. 177, 1991
- Okay, we all know it's a gemstone and was there lurking in the ground these gillion years[.] — Jonathan Gash, *The Ten Word Game*, p. 21, 2003

gilly-galloo noun
in circus and carnival usage, an outsider US, 1981
- — Don Wilmeth, *The Language of American Popular Entertainment*, p. 112, 1981

GI marbles noun
dice US, 1950
Because of the love for dice games displayed by American soldiers, especially during World War 2.
- — *The Annals of the American Academy of Political and Social Sciences*, p. 125, May 1950

gimcrack noun
a showy person UK, 1785
- Oh, well, just another gimcrack. I let him fasten it around my wrist and I could have yawned. — Georgia Sothern, *My Life in Burlesque*, p. 273, 1972

gimme noun
1 an easy victory or accomplishment US, 1986
- He was one of the city's biggest hijackers. Clothes. Razor blades. Booze. Cigarettes. Shrimp and lobsters were the best. They went fast. And almost all of them were gimmie's. — *Goodfellas*, 1990
2 a pistol US, 1994
- A "gimme" is a pistol—because they're often seen in the hands of somebody saying "gimme your money." — *Los Angeles Times*, p. B1, 19th December 1994
3 in pool, a shot that cannot be missed or a game that cannot be lost US, 1990
- — Steve Rushin, *Pool Cool*, p. 14, 1990

gimme cap noun
a baseball cap advertising a business, given away as a promotion US, 1978
- He had long blond hair which cascaded out from under the gimme cap he was wearing and all the way down to his shoulders. — Stephen King, *The Stand*, p. 338, 1978

gimmick noun
1 characteristics such as costume, haircut, or entrance music that collectively make a professional wrestler stand out as a unique marketable commodity US, 1993
- What a gimmick they had! Lord Blearas, with his pageboy haircut and monocle, seemed to be constantly looking down his nose. Holmes, his manager, was impeccably upper class, with black bowler hat and walking stick. They never failed to rile a crowd. — Ted Lewin, *I Was a Teenage Professional Wrestler*, p. 22, 1993
- A gimmick may be owned by a wrestler or by a promoter; at Gleason's one afternoon the rumor circulated that the Undertaker gimmick was purchased by the WWF for $75,000. — Sharon Mazer, *Professional Wrestling*, p. 48, 1998
- A wrestler's gimmick is determined early in his career, and if it's a good one, the bookers will continue to have him use it. — Dave Flood, *Kayfabe*, p. 27, 2000
- The gimmick Vince had come up with was for me to become a Federette. — Missy Hyatt, *Missy Hyatt*, p. 72, 2001
2 the actual device used to rig a carnival game US, 1968
- The device used to gaff a game is the "gimmick" and is not to be confused with something one might pick up at the dime-store. — E.E. Steck, *A Brief Examination of an Esoteric Folk*, p. 9, 1968
3 in poker, a special set of rules for a game US, 1988
- — George Percy, *The Language of Poker*, p. 39, 1988

gimmick verb
to rig for a result US, 1922
- So he fix up two ropes—one gimmicked to stretch, the other the real McCoy. — William Burroughs, *Naked Lunch*, pp. 79–80, 1957
- "The only man in the U.S. Army who could gimmick a walkie-talkie so you could get the Ray Scott Quintet on the B.B.C." — George Clayton Johnson, *Ocean's Eleven*, p. 60, 1960
- "This wheel isn't gimmicked." — Stephen Longstreet, *The Flesh Peddlers*, p. 334, 1962
- Jake Roberts vs. Sting in a "Spin the Wheel, Make the Deal" match, where Sting will apparently spin a gimmicked wheel to determine which type of match takes place. — Herb Kunze, *Herb's Wrestling Tidbits*, 10th September 1992

gimmicks noun
the equipment needed to inject drugs US, 1967
- — Richard Horman and Allan Fox, *Drug Awareness*, p. 466, 1970
- — Eugene Landy, *The Underground Dictionary*, p. 89, 1971

- He had his gimmicks with him, and he began his regular procedure of turning on. — Emmett Grogan, *Ringolevio*, p. 55, 1972

gimmie noun
marijuana and crack cocaine mixed together for smoking in a cigarette US, 1994
- — US Department of Justice, *Street Terms*, October 1994

gimp noun
a limp; a cripple US, 1925
- Leo wasn't there—probably out chasing missing persons, the birdbrain—but the gimp officer manager, Gil Lazarro, was at his desk. — Bernard Wolfe, *The Late Risers*, p. 4, 1954
- Just another ugly refugee from the Love Generation, some doom-struck gimp who couldn't handle the pressure. — Hunter S. Thompson, *Fear and Loathing in Las Vegas*, p. 63, 1971
- Well, goddamn, the gimp caught me—at the same time slouching more and sliding out of the chair. — Larry Heinemann, *Paco's Story*, pp. 148–149, 1986
- What I want to know is, who's the gimp? — *The Usual Suspects*, 1995

gimped up adjective
crippled, infirm US, 1948
- [E]verybody would just be staring at poor, feckless, gimped-up Cap'm Charlie. — Tom Wolfe, *A Man in Full*, p. 78, 1998

gimper; gimpster noun
a cripple US, 1974
- "Before I go get the gimper," said the rent-a-cop, pinching harder, "how about you telling me some portion of the truth." — Carl Hiaasen, *Native Tongue*, p. 73, 1991

gimp out verb
to panic in the face of great challenge US, 1988
- — Michael V. Anderson, *The Bad, Rad, Not to Forget Way Cool Beach and Surf Discritionary*, p. 7, 1988

gimpty adjective
crippled, infirm US, 1934
- "Who touched yer hump, yuh gimpty fu-" — Henry Roth, *Call It Sleep*, p. 420, 1962

gimpy adjective
1 crippled; handicapped US, 1929
- Like for you, hey, you don't want to have a gimpy leg no more. — Michael Chabon, *The Amazing Adventures of Kavalier & Clay*, p. 145, 2000
- Buckner nearly ruined his career. The gimpy left ankle caused him to put excessive weight on his right leg, which led to a series of debilitating injuries. — Jeff Pearlman, *The Bad Guys Won!*, p. 208, 2004
2 inferior US, 1970
- [T]hey could grow up to drink and eat and fuck gimpy. — Gilbert Sorrentino, *Steelwork*, p. 147, 1970
- — Connie Eble (Editor), *UNC-CH Campus Slang*, p. 5, October 2002

gims noun
the eyes US, 1945
- — Lou Shelly, *Hepcats Jive Dictionary*, p. 12, 1945

gin noun
1 a black prostitute US, 1962
- — Joseph E. Ragen and Charles Finston, *Inside the World's Toughest Prison*, p. 800, 1962: "Penitentiary and underworld glossary"
2 cocaine US, 1971
- — Donald Louria, *The Drug Scene*, p. 190, 1971

gin verb
1 (used of a woman) to have sex US, 1976
- Now my deadliest blow came when the whore / Took sick and couldn't gin. — Dennis Wepman et al., *The Life*, p. 84, 1976
2 to fight US, 1972
- — David Claerbaut, *Black Jargon in White America*, p. 66, 1972

ginch noun
the vagina; a woman; a woman as a sex object US, 1936
- Of the thirty or so outlaws at the El Adobe on a weekend night, less than half would take the trouble to walk across the parking lot for a go at whatever ginch is available. — Hunter S. Thompson, *Hell's Angels*, p. 193, 1966
- I'd been feelin' and nuzzlin' tit and ass and stealing kisses (including tongues) all night but now it was time for some GINCH. — Richard Meltzer, *A Whore Just Like the Rest*, p. 362, 1975

- Jesus Christ, a cop can't afford that kind of ginch. — George V. Higgins, *The Rat on Fire*, p. 114, 1981
- I got a half-decent lead on a ginch Maggie used to whore with[.] — James Ellroy, *Hollywood Nocturnes*, p. 274, 1994

ginchy *adjective*
fashionable, attractive, pleasing *US, 1959*
- — Dobie Gillis, *Teenage Slanguage Dictionary*, 1962
- "Everything groovy?" Janice yelled up at me. "Ginchy," I called back, and went into my apartment. — Harlan Ellison, *The Resurgence of Miss Ankle-Strap Wedgie*, p. 624, 1968

gin flat *noun*
an apartment where alcohol is served illegally to a paying not-so public *US, 1951*
- We have already referred to the gin-flats in Black Town, where home-made gin—raw ethyl alcohol flavored with juniper and sometimes diluted with apple cider—is sold. — Jack Lait and Lee Mortimer, *Washington Confidential*, p. 130, 1951

ginger peachy *adjective*
lovely, wonderful *US, 1950*
Intentionally old-fashioned.
- That was tough, 'cause Ursula kept telling her everything was just ginger-peachy. — W.E.B. Griffin, *The Aviators*, p. 136, 1988

gink *noun*
a naive rustic; a dolt *US, 1906*
- The gink was scared stiff. — Willard Motley, *Knock on Any Door*, p. 154, 1947
- I got them running around the block night making a gink of myself for the other stables to see. — Wilda Moxham, *The Apprentice*, p. 122, 1969

ginky *adjective*
out of style *US, 1969*
- — *Current Slang*, p. 7, Winter 1969

gin mill *noun*
a bar *US, 1866*
The term has shed most of its unsavory connotations of the past and is now generally jocular.
- Look, to most whites the ginmills of Harlem mean only one thing, the underworld. — Mezz Mezzrow, *Really the Blues*, p. 228, 1946
- At three-thirty the word went out in the back of gin mill off Forty-second and Third. — Mickey Spillane, *Kiss Me Deadly*, p. 56, 1952
- [T]hese are mostly ginmills featuring bootleg and the white liquor called King Kong. — Robert Sylvester, *No Cover Charge*, pp. 67–68, 1956
- When they got to Fin's favorite gin mill they were lucky to grab a parking space only half a block away. — Joseph Wambaugh, *Finnegan's Week*, p. 226, 1993

ginned *adjective*
drunk *US, 1900*
- — Joseph E. Ragen and Charles Finston, *Inside the World's Toughest Prison*, p. 801, 1962: "Penitentiary and underworld glossary"

ginny barn *noun*
a prison for females or a section of a prison reserved for females *US, 1967*
- But the most fascinating thing about the ward: the women's section, the Ginnybarn, was situated a mere 100 feet from the UT unit[.] — Clarence Cooper Jr., *The Farm*, p. 22, 1967

ginzo *noun*
an Italian-American or Italian *US, 1931*
Offensive. Probably a derivative of GUINEA.
- "The people in this country think there is no such thing as a decent Italian. They're all wops and ginzoes." — Chandler Brossard, *Who Walks in Darkness*, p. 173, 1952
- "But then after, somebody, everybody's gonna have at least eight hot ginzos out looking for me." — George Higgins, *Cogan's Trade*, p. 34, 1974
- A crazy ginso with a horseshoe up his ass. Suspicious of his own mother. — Edwin Torres, *Carlito's Way*, p. 56, 1975
- "This isn't back when we were kids, beating up on the yids and ginzos," Pat said. — Robert Campbell, *Juice*, p. 171, 1988

GI party *noun*
cleaning a barracks or latrine *US, 1942*
- [H]e never returned later than 6:00 p.m. except on Friday, which was "GI party night," when they scrubbed the latrines and cleaned the barracks. — Peter Guralnick, *Careless Love*, p. 12, 1999

girl *noun*
1 a prostitute *US, 1987*
- The street is empty except for the fire and us "girls." — Frederique Delacoste, *Sex Work*, p. 29, 1987

2 cocaine *US, 1953*
- "I'm warning you though, you start fooling with Boy and Girl and I'm through with you." — Herbert Simmons, *Corner Boy*, p. 28, 1957
- Leslie thought of copping—four girls and four boys. A speed-ball. — Clarence Cooper Jr., *The Scene*, p. 36, 1960
- She had taught me to snort "girl," and almost always when I came to her pad, there would be big sparkling rows of crystal cocaine on the glass top of the cocktail table. — Iceberg Slim (Robert Beck), *Pimp*, p. 61, 1969
- From Timbuctoo to London Dell / They toasted the best girl in town. — Dennis Wepman et al., *The Life*, p. 105, 1976

3 a lesbian *US, 1995*
A term used by lesbians.
- But you know, she's got that "back off" thing goin' on so I just assumed that she was one of the girls. — *Boys on the Side*, 1995

4 a homosexual male, especially an effeminate one *US, 1912*
- — Bruce Rodgers, *The Queens' Vernacular*, p. 96, 1972

5 in a deck of playing cards, a queen *US, 1967*
- — Albert H. Morehead, *The Complete Guide to Winning Poker*, p. 264, 1967

girl-deb *noun*
a girl who spends time with a boy's youth gang, whether or not she is a gang member's girlfriend *US, 1967*
- And all the change we could beat out of our girl-debs. — Piri Thomas, *Down These Mean Streets*, p. 18, 1967

girlfriend *noun*
1 a male homosexual's lover or friend *US, 1965*
- I got them wholesale from a girl friend of mine, Bill S., who ran one of those head parlors off Broadway. — Antony James, *America's Homosexual Underground*, p. 133, 1965
- He hoped for early release, but got in trouble, injured a hack and shanked some cons for picking on his girlfriend—a cute guy he'd see once in a while now in West Hollywood—and had to do six years straight up, no time off. — Elmore Leonard, *Be Cool*, p. 175, 1999

2 used as an affectionate term of address for a friend or acquaintance *US, 1997*
- You're gonna knock 'em dead, girlfriend. — Stephen Cannell, *King Con*, p. 17, 1997

girl-girl *noun*
a scene in a pornographic movie, or an entire pornographic film, involving two women *US, 2000*
- "Girl-girl" has always been a thriving subgenre in porno. — Ana Loria, *1 2 3 Be A Porn Star!*, p. 101, 2000

girl-girl *adjective*
in pornography, involving two women *US, 1973*
- Say you're shooting a girl-girl hard-core and you want to shoot an extreme close-up of one girl masturbating another with her finger. — *Porno Films and the People who make them*, p. 101, 1973
- Janine is known for her faboo media coverage, from Howard Stern to Jay Leno, and for her policy of appearing in only "girl-girl" scenes. — *The Village Voice*, 21st September 1999

girlie *noun*
a magazine that is mildly pornographic, featuring naked women but not sexual activity *US, 1969*
- [T]he stories in the "girlies" got right down to the nitty-gritty, like they say now, when it came to the screwing. — Joey V., *Portrait of Joey*, p. 156, 1969
- The mass market magazines with the highest degree of sexual orientation (especially nudity) known as "men's sophisticates" (also as "girlie" or "East Coast girlie") devote a substantial portion to photographs of partially nude females[.] — *The Presidential Commission on Obscenity and Pornography*, p. 111, 1970

girlie *adjective*
mildly pornographic, featuring naked women but not sexual activity *US, 1921*
Mainly in use from the mid 1950s.
- In girlie magazines, nudity stops only at the mons Veneris—and sometimes not even there. — Joe David Brown, *Sex in the '60s*, p. 14, 1968
- Back in the neolithic days of 1969, most sex theaters were running loops of ten-minute girlie films. — George Paul Csicsery (Editor), *The Sex Industry*, p. 165, 1973

- "I was the east coast rep for one of the biggest distributors of girlie magazines in the country, and as I sold magazines to wholesalers I began to notice that big boob material was always a consistent seller[.] — *Adult Video*, p. 47, August/September 1986
- [T]he dresser was cluttered with scraps of paper, a model of the starship Enterprise, girlie magazines, food-encrusted dishes and mugs. — Janet Evanovich, *Seven Up*, p. 51, 2001

girlie bar *noun*
a drinking place at which "hostesses" are available *US, 1971*
- At first, only the girlie bars let it all hang out. — *The Advocate*, p. 13, 31st March—13th April 1971
- — *New Society*, 17th January 1980

girls *noun*
a woman's breasts *US, 2001*
From the television situation comedy *Anything but Love* (1989–92), in which the character played by Jamie Lee Curtis proudly nicknamed her breasts "the girls."
- — Pamela Munro, *U.C.L.A. Slang*, p. 121, 2001

girls' school *noun*
a reformatory for female juvenile offenders *US, 1982*
- — Ralph de Sola, *Crime Dictionary*, p. 57, 1982

girl's week *noun*
the bleed period of the menstrual cycle *US, 2001*
- — Don R. McCreary (Editor), *Dawg Speak*, 2001

girl thing *noun*
the various hygiene steps taken by a female pornography performer before a sex scene *US, 1995*
Also called "girl stuff."
- — *Adult Video News*, p. 48, August 1995
- "You do your girl thing and then you go out and they start to shoot you." (Quoting Jill Kelly) — Ana Loria, *1 2 3 Be A Porn Star!*, p. 27, 2000

girly-girl *noun*
a female friend *US, 1997*
- — *Newsday*, p. B2, 11th October 1997

GI's; GI shits *noun*
diarrhea *US, 1944*
- In the morning I had the dry heaves and GI shits. — William Pelfrey, *The Big V*, p. 127, 1972
- Cures heartburn, jungle rot, the Gee-fucken-Eyes, all them things. — Larry Heinemann, *Close Quarters*, p. 26, 1977
- Every last man on KP has a job to do, even the guy who boils the water to keep us from getting the GI shits! — Martin Blumenson, *Patton*, p. 222, 1985

GI shower *noun*
1 a military hazing or punishment in which a group of soldiers forcibly clean a dirty peer with wire brushes *US, 1956*
- DAWSON: Sir, a marine has refused to bathe on a regular basis. The men in his squad would give him a G.I. shower. KAFFEE: What's that? DAWSON: Scrub brushes, brillo pads, steel wool. — *A Few Good Men*, 1992
- These men got a GI shower. A number of us would strip them and drag their nude bodies to the shower. They were forced to lather with carbolic soap, and we then scrubbed them with the stiff bristle scrub brushes that we used on the floor. — Robert W. Black, *A Ranger Born*, p. 27, 2002

2 an improvised washing of the armpits and crotch *US, 2006*
- I took a G.I. shower, which I always do when I'm in a rush. — Linden Dalecki, *Kid B*, p. 48, 2006

gitbox *noun*
a guitar *US, 1937*
- I got a soft spot for any guy who'll go out to meet Judgment Day packed up with a battered old git-box and as much hay as he can carry. — Mezz Mezzrow, *Really the Blues*, p. 169, 1946
- Scat Man Crothers, as zany as they come, plucks his gitbox and hums like a hummingbird. — *Capitol News*, p. 15, March 1949

git-fiddle *noun*
a guitar *US, 1935*
A decidedly rural term.
- "Ah brought muh git-fiddle." He slung his gorgeously decorated guitar around his neck. — Max Shulman, *Rally Round the Flag, Boys!*, p. 229, 1957

- That Chet Atkins can make that gitfiddle stand up and talk, can't he? — Ken Weaver, *Texas Crude*, p. 113, 1984

Gitmo *nickname*
the US naval base at Guantanamo Bay, Cuba *US, 1949*
- Before coming home, Midshipman Balint went on a summer cruise for seven and one-half weeks with a week's stopover in England and several weeks in Gitmo, Cuba. — *Indiana Evening Gazette*, p. 8, 26th August 1949
- Arrive at Gitmo at 2 plus 36. On arrival Guantanamo Bay, you will be further briefed on specific missions and targets[.] — Pat Conroy, *The Great Santini*, p. 227, 1976
- We took off in April '65 with our first stop in Guantanamo Bay, Cuba. "Gitmo." — Ed Kugler, *Dead Center*, p. 16, 1999
- They would have skinned Clinton alive and thrown what was left of his carcass in Gitmo. — Michael Moore, *Dude, Where's My Country?*, p. 11, 2003

G-Ivan *noun*
a Russian enlisted soldier *US, 1946*
- — *American Speech*, p. 74, February 1946: "Some words of war and peace from 1945"

give *verb*
to consent to have sex *US, 1935*
- That's the problem with men: we always think we can buy sex. "If I take her here she'll give me some. If I buy her this she'll give me some." Nothing gets you nothing. — Chris Rock, *Rock This!*, p. 124, 1997

▶ **give it away**
to engage in sex without pay; to engage in sex promiscuously *US, 1945*
- She looked as if she might have worked half those years in a cat house, and if she hadn't she must have given a lot of it away. — Chester Himes, *If He Hollers Let Him Go*, p. 19, 1945

▶ **give it the nifty fifty**
(used of a male) to masturbate *US, 1983*
- One of the chaplains found that out the hard way, when he was caught in his cabin one afternoon with a girlie magazine in one hand and his wife's best friend in the other. In the Marines such a practice is known as "giving it the nifty fifty." — Robert McGowan and Jeremy Hands, *Don't Cry For Me Sergeant-Major*, p. 42, 1983

▶ **give it to**
to copulate with *US, 1992*
- A couple punks tore up the place and then gave it to the nuns but good. — *The Bad Lieutenant*, 1992

▶ **give it up**
to applaud *US, 1990*
Often as an imperative to an audience.
- — Connie Eble (Editor), *UNC-CH Campus Slang*, p. 4, Spring 1998
- I gotta give it up to y'all for showing love to [hip-hop artists] Mobb Deep. — *The Source*, p. 42, March 2002

▶ **give me a break; gimme a break**
used as an expression of dismay at that which has just been said *US, 1931*
Ubiquitous in the 1990s.
- "It's just navy, Mom," Bobbie had insisted. "Gimme a break!" — Joseph Wambaugh, *Finnegan's Week*, p. 26, 1993

▶ **give skin**
to slap hands in greeting *US, 1964*
- He nearly dropped the powder can. "My homeboy! Man, gimme some skin! I'm from Lansing." — Malcolm X and Alex Haley, *The Autobiography of Malcolm X*, p. 44, 1964

▶ **give someone the reds**
to anger *US, 1951*
Teen slang.
- — *Newsweek*, p. 28, 8th October 1951

▶ **give someone their hat**
to release from prison *US, 1976*
- Well, baby, I got busted, just like that / So I hope this toast helps you when they give you your hat. — Dennis Wepman et al., *The Life*, p. 53, 1976

▶ **give the office**
to signal or give information *UK, 1804*
- The boss almost shook his wig off giving me the office from behind a post[.] — Mezz Mezzrow, *Really the Blues*, p. 178, 1946

- We keep this up much longer we're a cinch to give 'em the office. — Horace McCoy, *Kiss Tomorrow Good-bye*, p. 242, 1948

▶ **give the skins**
to have sex with someone *US, 1990*
- So you gonna give me the skins or what? — *Boyz N The Hood*, 1990

▶ **give wings**
to inject someone else with heroin or to teach them to inject themselves *US, 1968*
- — Donald Louria, *The Drug Scene*, p. 190, 1968
- [H]e knew he was going to join the hyp class and become a full-out junkie now that he had given himself his wings—his first mainline fix. — Emmett Grogan, *Ringolevio*, p. 40, 1972
- He gave me my wings, that dirty rat fuck / He thought he was slick, charging a buck. — Dennis Wepman et al., *The Life*, p. 171, 1976

give-up *noun*
a robbery accomplished with the cooperation of the victim *US, 1985*
- "Lots of our jobs were called 'give-ups'—as opposed to stickups—which meant the driver was in on it with us." — Nicholas Pileggi, *Wise Guy*, p. 99, 1985

giz *noun*
the vagina *US, 1975*
- [H]is mouth was dry as Rose Bird's giz[.] — Joseph Wambaugh, *The Delta Star*, p. 127, 1983

gizmo *verb*
to outfit with a device *US, 1977*
- The limo back seat is gizmoed, and I copped Jake's hundred and twenty grand in "queer" and the valises. — Iceberg Slim (Robert Beck), *Long White Con*, p. 212, 1977

gizmo; gismo *noun*
a gadget, device or contraption, the exact name of which is forgotten by, or unimportant to, the speaker *US, 1942*
- Now we're getting down to where the rubber meets the road. Identification! That's the gizmo! — Max Shulman, *Rally Round the Flag, Boys!*, p. 182, 1957
- It had to be a compressed air gizmo. — Iceberg Slim (Robert Beck), *Pimp*, p. 143, 1969
- And, I gotta admit, the MCC is a fancy building with a lot of electronic gadgets and gismos. — Edwin Torres, *After Hours*, p. 158, 1979

gizzuts *noun*
guts, courage *US, 1993*
- — *The Bell* (Paducah Tilghman High School), pp. 8–9, 17th December 1993: "Tilghmanism: the concealed language of the hallway"

GJ *noun*
grand jury *US, 1997*
- Fuck the GJ. You're Superboy. You saved what six black babies? That shit plays. — *Copland*, 1997

G-joint *noun*
1 a federal penitentiary *US, 1992*
- — Jay Robert Nash, *Dictionary of Crime*, p. 150, 1992

2 a crooked carnival game *US, 1946*
"G" is for "gaffed" (rigged).
- — Lindsay E. Smith and Bruce A. Walstad, *Keeping Carnies Honest*, pp. 42–43, 1990: "Glossary"

GLA *noun*
a car theft; grand *l*arceny *a*utomobile *US, 1973*
- Then get the ten latest GLA's off the hot sheet. — Charles Whited, *Chiodo*, p. 27, 1973

glad bag *noun*
a body bag, used to cover corpses *US, 1983*
Coined in Vietnam; still in use in the Gulf war and after.
- Bodies were strewn all over the place, some still in litters and others in Glad bags. — Lynda Van Devanter, *Home Before Morning*, p. 189, 1983

glad eye *noun*
a come-hither look *US, 1903*
- Getting excited because a newspaper seller had given her the glad eye? — Marian Keyes, *Sushie for Beginners*, p. 103, 2003

glad hand *noun*
a welcome, rousing if not always sincere *US, 1873*

- They sure gave me the glad-hand when they laid their peepers on my new car. — Mezz Mezzrow, *Really the Blues*, p. 88, 1946

glad-hand *verb*
to greet with profuse, if insincere, enthusiasm *US, 1895*
Often found in the context of politicians.
- All they can do is go around all the time, glad-handing people and acting like jerks, and nobody remember them five minutes after they see them. — George V. Higgins, *The Judgment of Deke Hunter*, p. 17, 1976
- After a moment of glad-handing and stowing my AWOL bag and settling in, Stepik arrived. — Larry Heinemann, *Close Quarters*, p. 123, 1977
- Baby Jewels gladhanding politicos, grabassing showgirls, squeezed into nightclub booths with minor celebrities, lolling in his box at Candlestick Park. — Seth Morgan, *Homeboy*, p. 29, 1990
- Then Bob Bix, glad-handing president of the senior class, introduced the queen's court in ascending order of beauty, popularity, and personality. — C.D. Payne, *Youth in Revolt*, p. 437, 1993

gladiator school; gladiator camp *noun*
a violent prison or juvenile detention facility *US, 1975*
- — Report to the Senate, *California Senate Committee on Civil Disorder*, p. 228, 1975
- I had been trained from a youth spent in a gladiator school for this. — Jack Henry Abbott, *In the Belly of the Beast*, p. 94, 1981
- Kevin first heard stories about YA—"the gladiator school"—from older 'Hoodsters. — Bob Sipchen, *Baby Insane and the Buddha*, p. 92, 1993
- He called these prisons "gladiator schools." He said prisons were places a man could prove his toughness. — Tookie Williams, *Life in Prison*, p. 13, 1998

glad lad *noun*
an attractive male *US, 1945*
- — *Yank*, p. 18, 24th March 1945

glad plaid *noun*
a bright plaid pattern *US, 1947*
Mexican-American youth (Pachuco) usage in the American southwest.
- — *Common Ground*, p. 81, Summer 1947

glad rag *noun*
a piece of cloth saturated with glue or an industrial solvent, used for recreational inhaling *US, 1971*
- — Eugene Landy, *The Underground Dictionary*, p. 89, 1971
- — Ralph de Sola, *Crime Dictionary*, p. 5758, 1982

glad rags *noun*
your best clothes *US, 1899*
- The handbags and the gladrags / That your poor old Grandad had to sweat to buy you. — Mike D'Abo, *Handbags and Gladrags*, 1964
- — Hy Lit, *Hy Lit's Unbelievable Dictionary of Hip Words for Groovy People*, p. 18, 1968

glam *adjective*
flamboyant, especially in dress and appearance *US, 1993*
- A few glam drag queens in miniskirts and high heels are strutting in the shadows cooing and hollering. — Francesca Lia Block, *Missing Angel Juan*, p. 345, 1993
- They've been asked to open a show for new glam fave Suede. — *Rolling Stone*, p. 16, 27th May 1993
- Leitch and Skye are in the midst of cutting their first album with their glam-rock band, Nancy Boy[.] — *Vogue*, p. 86, June 1994

glamor boy *noun*
a US Air Force flier *US, 1946*
- — *American Speech*, p. 310, December 1946: "More Air Force slang"

glamor groovie *noun*
a fashion-conscious person *US, 1947*
- Once upon a time in Switzerland there was a glamour groovie named William Tell. — Harry Haenigsen, *Jive's Like That*, 1947

glamor-puss *noun*
a sexually attractive person, especially one who has enhanced a natural beauty with artificial glamor *US, 1941*
- Speaking as a newspaperman, I've found the glamor pusses of Hollywood to be a fine crowd. — Earl Wilson, *I am Gazing Into My 8-Ball*, p. 33, 1945
- Hey, hey, glamorpuss. I'm sorry. — *Rebel Without a Cause*, 1955
- [A]n endless succession of glamorpusses in figure-hugging gleaming leather and latex and PVC. — Claire Mansfield and John Mendelssohn, *Dominatrix*, p. 10, 2002

glamottle *noun*
a 13 ounce bottle of Budweiser™ beer *US, 1948*
Budweiser advertised that it was a "glass that holds more than
a bottle," which is corrupted here.
- — *American Speech*, p. 62, February 1967: "Soda-fountain, restaurant and tavern
callss"

glark *verb*
to decipher a meaning from context *US, 1991*
- The System III manuals are pretty poor, but you can generally glark
the meaning from context. — Eric S. Raymond, *The New Hacker's Dictionary*,
p. 177, 1991

glass *noun*
1 a shop window *US, 1973*
- This usually occurred about one o'clock in the morning, and did not
happen again until six, when a patrolman was required to check all
the "glass"—shop windows—in his post. — Peter Maas, *Serpico*, p. 63,
1973
2 a smooth water surface *US, 1979*
- Like to finish up operations early and fly down to Vung Tau for the
evening glass. — *Apocalypse Now*, 1979

glassbrain *noun*
a person of limited intelligence *US, 1951*
- Clearly I am a neurotic glassbrain, mired in "nostalgie de la boue."
— James Blake, *The Joint*, p. 37, 30th December 1951

glass chin *noun*
a window built in the area immediately below and slightly
behind the nose of a bomber *US, 1988*
- An Antonov AN-12 Cub, all right, with a glass chin for the navigator
to peer out of. — Stephen Coonts, *Final Flight*, p. 369, 1988

glass dick *noun*
a pipe used to smoke crack cocaine *US, 1997*
- — Mark S. Fleisher, *Beggars & Thieves*, p. 289, 1995: "Glossary"
- [B]ut he always been one boned-out nigga, spen' way too much
time suckin' da glass dick. — Stephen Cannell, *King Con*, p. 50, 1997
- One who would risk everything just for an opportunity to earn some
loot to hit that glass dick. — Treasure E. Blue, *A Street Girl Named Desire*, p. 5,
2007

glass house *noun*
in surfing, a smooth ride inside the hollow of a wave *US, 1987*
- — Mitch McKissick, *Surf Lingo*, 1987

Glass House *nickname*
the Parker Center police headquarters in Los Angeles *US, 1963*
- [T]he vice grabs her and off she goes in a very real coach to the
glasshouse[.] — John Rechy, *City of Night*, p. 104, 1963
- The police station was a brand-new structure of shining blue tile
and glass. Natives called it the Glass House. — Frank Bonham, *Viva
Chicano*, p. 33, 1970
- They call it the Glass House because the block-square building looks
like solid glass, a cute architectural trick. — Oscar Zeta Acosta, *The Revolt
of the Cockroach People*, p. 51, 1973
- I pass through drunk tanks and the "Glass House." — James Ellroy,
Destination Morgue, p. 42, 2004

glass itch *noun*
irritation of the skin by fiberglass dust *US, 1978*
Surfing usage.
- — Dennis Aaberg and John Milius, *Big Wednesday*, p. 209, 1978

glass jaw *noun*
a weak jaw in the context of boxing or fighting *US, 1955*
- I didn't think it was right I should hit a guy hard who played on the
violin like Golden Boy. But he had a glass jaw. — Rocky Garciano (with
Rowland Barber), *Somebody Up There Likes Me*, p. 271, 1955

glass work *noun*
in poker, the use of a small mirror or other reflective surface to cheat *US, 1968*
- — Thomas L. Clark, *The Dictionary of Gambling and Gaming*, p. 91, 1987

glassy *adjective*
(used of an ocean condition) smooth, not choppy *US, 1963*
- — Grant W. Kuhns, *On Surfing*, p. 117, 1963

glazed *adjective*
drunk *US, 1972*
- — Helen Dahlskog (Editor), *A Dictionary of Contemporary and Colloquial Usage*, p. 27,
1972

gleamer *noun*
any reflective surface used by the dealer for cheating in a
card game *US, 1969*
- — Thomas L. Clark, *The Dictionary of Gambling and Gaming*, p. 91, 1987

gleek *noun*
in poker, three of a kind *US, 1967*
- — Albert H. Morehead, *The Complete Guide to Winning Poker*, p. 264, 1967

gleep *noun*
a social outcast *US, 1947*
- He said it hooked into the library files and, since only gleeps and
nerds actually spent more than fifteen minutes in the library, I could
sit here at home, access the library's on-line encyclopedias. — Carol
Plum-Ucci, *The Body of Christopher Creed*, p. 33, 2001

glim *noun*
1 a light *UK, 1676*
- — Lou Shelly, *Hepcats Jive Dictionary*, p. 12, 1945
- He ganders glims up in the steeple! — Harry Haenigsen, *Jive's Like That*,
1947
2 the eye *UK, 1789*
- — Vincent J. Monteleone, *Criminal Slang*, p. 101, 1949

glim *verb*
to see *US, 1912*
- Yeh Rocky, just to "glim" him and you know he's rough, but what in
the Hell cut his box off? — Iceberg Slim (Robert Beck), *Pimp*, p. 51, 1969

glimmer *noun*
1 a light *UK, 1566*
- A paper bag was wrapped around the overhead glimmer to curb
the brightness[.] — Mezz Mezzrow, *Really the Blues*, p. 117, 1946
2 any reflective surface used by a dealer to cheat in a game
of cards *US, 1962*
- — Frank Garcia, *Marked Cards and Loaded Dice*, p. 262, 1962
- — Thomas L. Clark, *The Dictionary of Gambling and Gaming*, p. 91, 1987

gliss around *verb*
to make small talk *US, 1947*
- — *Time Magazine*, p. 92, 20th January 1947: "Dicty Dictionary"

glitch *noun*
a malfunction *US, 1962*
From the Yiddish for "slip."
- — Guy L. Steele, *Coevolution Quarterly*, p. 31, Spring 1981: "Computer Slang"

glitter *noun*
salt *US, 1981*
- — *Maledicta*, p. 267, Summer/Winter 1981: "By its slang, ye shall know it: the
pessimism of prison life"

glitterati *noun*
the fashionable class *US, 1940*
- Buffet jetted from coast to coast like one of the glitterati. — Roger
Lowenstein, *Buffet*, p. 358, 1995

glitter fairy *noun*
a style-conscious, effeminate homosexual man *US, 1978*
Usually derogatory.
- I get a lotta calls. Collegiate types. Lotta guys get sick of the glitter
fairies in this town. — Armistead Maupin, *Tales of the City*, p. 114, 1978

glittergal *noun*
in circus and carnival usage, a female performer *US, 1960*
- — Louis M. Ackerman, *American Speech*, p. 308–309, December 1960: "Carnival
Talk"
- — Don Wilmeth, *The Language of American Popular Entertainment*, p. 112, 1981

glitter gulch *noun*
downtown Las Vegas, Nevada *US, 1953*
- The commercial center of Las Vegas is Glitter Gulch, the two blocks
of Fremont Street which comprise the most concentrated gambling
complex in the world. — Ed Reid and Ovid Demaris, *The Green Jungle*, p. 3,
1963
- "Glitter Gulch," as some call it, was the brightest main drag I'd ever
seen anywhere. — *Screw*, p. 7, 7th March 1969

- Downtown. Glitter Gulch. The old Strip lit up by all the neon and dancing lights on Fremont Street. — John Ridley, *Love is a Racket*, p. 89, 1998

glo *noun*
crack cocaine *US, 1994*
- — US Department of Justice *Street Terms*, October 1994

glob *noun*
expectorated sputum *US, 1988–1989*
- — *Maledicta*, p. 32, 1988–1989: "Medical maledicta from San Francisco"

globber *noun*
an expectoration *US, 1988*
- Maybe we could cough a phlegm globber in it or something. — *Heathers*, 1988

globes *noun*
the female breasts *US, 1889*
- "I resent that," said Sheila Gomez, glancing at the little crucifix that dangled its gold-skinned heels above her globes. — Tom Robbins, *Jitterbug Perfume*, p. 57, 1984
- — Pamela Munro, *U.C.L.A. Slang*, p. 43, 1989
- A nice gander at Drew's gargantuan globes in the shower[.] — Mr. Skin, *Mr. Skin's Skincyclopedia*, p. 44, 2005

globetrotter *noun*
a heroin addict who contacts many heroin dealers in search of the best heroin *US, 1970*
- — William D. Alsever, *Glossary for the Establishment and Other Uptight People*, p. 13, December 1970

glom *noun*
a stupid person *US, 1985*
- We'd gotten taken like chumps. We were two dumb gloms. — Nicholas Pileggi, *Wise Guy*, p. 84, 1985

glom *verb*
1 to stare at, to glare at *US, 1979*
- He is glomming me with double hate, but he gets his billfold out of his inner breast pocket and drops it on the blotter[.] — Leo Rosten, *Silky!*, p. 116, 1979
2 to steal, to snatch, to grab *US, 1897*
Scots dialect *glam, glaum,* (to clutch or grasp).
- "Hell, he ain't there," the big one said. "Somebody must of glommed him off.["] — Raymond Chandler, *Farewell My Lovely*, p. 125, 1940
- They shoulda iced him as soon as he come out and glommed the money—they take this mafia shit too serious. — Edwin Torres, *Carlito's Way*, p. 52, 1975
- [C]ut the coke with some of the bennies I glom from the narco guys[.] — James Ellroy, *Blood on the Moon*, p. 172, 1984
- [M]eanwhile running around glomming anything on the island of Manhattan wasn't nailed down. — Vincent Patrick, *Family Business*, p. 37, 1985
3 to eat hastily *US, 1990*
- — Charles Shafer, *Folk Speech in Texas Prisons*, p. 205, 1990

gloom note *noun*
in college, a notification of academic deficiency *US, 1968*
- — *American Speech*, pp. 76–77, February 1968: "Some notes on flunk notes"

gloomy Gus *noun*
any chronically negative person *US, 1904*
- I am absolutely not crying anymore, ever again. Nobody likes a Gloomy Gus. — Janet Evanovich, *Seven Up*, p. 117, 2001

glop *noun*
any mucky substance *US, 1945*
- I discovered the keys sunk into some yellow-brown glop. I didn't see any Pampers nearby, so I hoped the glop was mustard. — Janet Evanovich, *One for the Money*, p. 163, 1994

glop *verb*
to pour or apply with gusto *US, 1992*
- Poor Renee, the last of the true believers, glopped the stuff on her thighs for three weeks and got nothing for her troubles but a nasty rash. — Armistead Maupin, *Maybe the Moon*, p. 14, 1992

glorioski
used for expressing surprise *US, 1972*
- "Glorioski, Sandy, there it is," Dryman yelled enthusiastically. — William Diehl, *The Hunt*, p. 408, 1990

glory hole *noun*
1 a hole between private video booths in a pornography arcade or between stalls in a public toilets, designed for anonymous sex between men *US, 1949*
- Glory-hole—Phallic size hole in partition between toilet booths. Sometimes used for a mere peep-hole. — Anon., *The Gay Girl's Guide*, p. 10, 1949
- Some reports have been received that police themselves have cut the so-called "glory holes" in booth partitions which invite the curiosity of the man who believes himself to be in privacy. — *Mattachine Review*, p. 7, November 1961
- Why are they named "glory-holes"? Possibly because of the glorious sexual release of being blown, standing with your erect prick stuck through it and being sucked off by a warm, hot mouth on the other side. — *Screw*, p. 5, 19th March 1971
- The anonymity provided by the "glory holes" allows the participants to fantasize about the gender and other characteristics of their partners. — *Final Report of the Attorney General's Report on Pornography*, p. 377, 1986
2 the officer's sleeping quarters on a navy ship *US, 1889*
- Shaking, he rose from the chair, shut the window, and hobbled into the glory-hole that had been his father's bedroom. — Emmett Grogan, *Final Score*, p. 43, 1976

glory hound *noun*
a person determined to be seen as a hero *US, 1945*
- "Cross strikes me as a pro at least. He's not just some glory hound." — James Patterson, *Kiss the Girls*, p. 225, 1995

glory ride *noun*
a tradition for troops departing Vietnam, in which the helicopter taking them from the line circles the base, explodes two smoke grenades, and then speeds away *US, 1972*
- It is traditional for every grunt leaving the bush for the last time—for the freedom bird, home—to get the glory ride. — William Pelfrey, *The Big V*, p. 120, 1972

gloss *noun*
a shine *US, 1969*
- I looked down at my "Stomps" [shoes]. They could stand a gloss all right. — Iceberg Slim (Robert Beck), *Pimp*, p. 118, 1969

glossy *noun*
a photograph *US, 1931*
- — *Swinging Syllables*, 1959

glove *noun*
a condom *US, 1958*
- Lundgren talks about condoms ("No glove, no love" is a popular class mnemonic), and abortion is presented as a fact of life. — *Time Magazine*, p. 54, 24th November 1986
- "You listening? You don't cock me without a glove." — John Ridley, *Love is a Racket*, p. 297, 1998
- — Pamela Munro, *U.C.L.A. Slang*, p. 76, 2001
- The gift shop offers "No Glove, No Love" coffee mugs and "In Rubber We Trust" key chains and T-shirts[.] — *USA Today*, p. 1D, 12th July 2004

glove *verb*
to examine a prisoner's rectum for contraband *US, 1972*
- I've got it stashed. If they don't glove [examine the rectum] me, I'm through. — Bruce Jackson, *In the Life*, p. 223, 1972

glow *noun*
a pleasant, warming sense of intoxication *US, 1942*
- I think I'll get a glow on. — Willard Motely, *Let No Man Write My Epitaph*, p. 279, 1958
- He had a right good glow on, old Boxcar[.] — Guy Owen, *The Flim-Flam Man and the Apprentice Grifter*, p. 115, 1972
- Lynn didn't fail to notice that Breda was getting a glow. — Joseph Wambaugh, *Fugitive Nights*, p. 146, 1992

glue *noun*
1 in computing, any interface protocol *US, 1991*
- — Eric S. Raymond, *The New Hacker's Dictionary*, p. 180, 1991
2 a police detective *US, 1950*
- But no one knows why a "broadman" is a crooked card-player or why "glues" are detectives. — *The New American Mercury*, p. 708, 1950

glued *adjective*
drunk *US, 1957*
- — Collin Baker et al., *College Undergraduate Slang Study Conducted at Brown University*, p. 126, 1968

gluehead *noun*
a person who inhales glue or any volatile solvent for the intoxicating effect *US, 1970*
- "[H]e's a glue head." "Any port in a storm." — Joseph Wambaugh, *The New Centurions*, p. 258, 1970
- — William D. Alsever, *Glossary for the Establishment and Other Uptight People*, p. 13, December 1970
- The city let the Pagoda rot and punks and drunks and whores and glue-heads started getting up inside of it, doing things that made the paint peel. — *Sun (Baltimore)*, p. 9 (Sunday Magazine), 10th July 1994
- Mama's Pride walked into the sound of Gregg playing with a backup band made up of, as Liston remembers, "local glue-head losers." — *Riverfront Times (St. Louis)*, 17th December 2003

gluepot *noun*
a racehorse that performs very, very poorly *US, 1924*
- — *San Francisco Call-Bulletin*, p. 16, 2nd April 1947

gluey *noun*
a person who inhales glue or any volatile solvent for the intoxicating effect *US, 1967*
- — William D. Alsever, *Glossary for the Establishment and Other Uptight People*, p. 13, December 1970

glug *noun*
a swallow, a mouthful, a swig of a drink *US, 1971*
Echoic.
- [R]ight in the middle of a glug of champagne at some jet-set hot spot. — Lester Bangs, *Psychotic Reactions and Carburetor Dung*, p. 13, 1971

GMOF *noun*
a grossly obese hospital patient *US, 1988–1989*
A "great mass of flesh."
- — *Maledicta*, p. 35, 1988–1989: "More Milwukee medical maledicta"

gnarlatious *adjective*
extremely impressive *US, 1991*
- — Trevor Cralle, *The Surfin'ary*, p. 45, 1991

gnarly *adjective*
1 treacherous, challenging *US, 1977*
Originally surfer slang applied to waves and surf conditions, and then broadened to an all-purpose adjective.
- — Gary Fairmont R. Filosa II, *The Surfer's Almanac*, p. 186, 1977
- "None of those gnarly grease-burgers and NO OKI DOGS!" Duck said. — Francesca Lia Block, *weetzie bat*, p. 62, 1989
- I remember that day—gnarly fucking ass! — *Break Point*, 1991
- Creator of a gnarly incestual sicko freak scene read by every preteen girl I hung out with[.] — Editors of Ben is Dead, *Retrohell*, p. 5, 1997
2 bad, disgusting *US, 1978*
- — Connie Eble (Editor), *UNC-CH Campus Slang*, p. 5, Fall 1985
- FEMALE STONER IN ARMY JACKET: I heard it was really gnarly. She sucked down a bowl of multi-purpose deodorizing disinfectant then she smashed[.] — *Heathers*, 1988
- Don't go soft on me now, you gnarly old fart. — Carl Hiaasen, *Basket Case*, p. 325, 2002
- We were so wasted we passed out. / I got that gnarly sunburn, it was so ghetto[.] — Me First and the Gimme Gimmes, *End of the Road*, 2003
3 excellent *US, 1979*
- And one recent visitor from Southern California reported that 14-year-olds out there ... are approving things not as boss, hot, neat, bad, or tough but—are you ready?—"gnarly." — *Washington Post*, p. B3, 29th May 1979
- That was gnarly, dude, like really bodacious. — John Nichols, *The Voice of the Butterfly*, p. 159, 2001

gnat's eyelash *noun*
a very small distance *US, 1937*
The variant bodyparts are seemingly infinite, with "eyelash" as the earliest recorded.
- They have those calculations down to a gnat's eyelash. — *Florida Today*, p. 4, 1st February 2003

gnome *noun*
a socially inept outcast *US, 1959*
- — *Time Magazine*, p. 46, 24th August 1959

G-note *noun*
a $1000 bill *US, 1930*
- "I could use a G-note." So he gave me the grand and I told him I'd pay it back within a week. — Vincent Teresa, *My Life in the Mafia*, p. 58, 1973

go *noun*
approval, agreement *US, 1878*
- But Sheldon Gurtz and Kitty Feldman were the people who would stay with Rita's Limo Stop if the network gave it a "go" and "ordered thirteen [episodes]." — Dan Jenkins, *Life Its Ownself*, p. 156, 1984

go *verb*
1 when reporting a conversation, to say *US, 1942*
A thoroughly annoying quotative device found as early as 1942, favored by teenagers in the 1970s and 80s.
- So I said, "What's your name?" And she goes, "My name's Sandra." — Leonard Wolfe (Editor), *Voices from the Love Generation*, p. 171, 1968
- He [Roman Polanski] showed me a Vogue Magazine that he had done and he said, "Would you like me to take your pictures?" And I went, "Yes." — Testimony of Samantha Jane Gailey to Los Angeles County Grand Jury, 24th March 1977
- I go hello and this guy goes, hi, I'm whatever-his-name-is, I'm a friend of Skip's. — Jay McInerney, *Story of My Life*, p. 2, 1988
- He goes "Hey, quit hassling me cause I don't speak French or whatever," and the other guy goes something in Paris talk, and I go, "Um, just back off," and he goes "Get out" and I go "Make me." — *Austin Powers*, 1997
2 to take on the mannerisms and customs of a place or group of people *US, 1917*
- Andy Warhol has "gone Hollywood." — *The Advocate*, p. 13, October 1967
- Assuring his friends back at Dartmouth that even though he'd gone to Hollywood, he had not gone Hollywood. — Eve Babitz, *Eve's Hollywood*, p. 177, 1974
3 to race *US, 1965*
- You know, a guy goes up to another guy's car and looks it up and down like it has gangrene or something, and he says: "You wanna go?" — Tom Wolfe, *The Kandy-Kolored Tangerine-Flake Streamline Baby*, p. 88, 1965
4 in a casino, to earn in tips *US, 1980*
- What did we go last night? — Lee Solkey, *Dummy Up and Deal*, p. 114, 1980
5 to weigh *US, 1999*
- Built like one of those giant Samoans you saw, this one going at least two-sixty in his tanktop, a do-rag down on his eyebrows, thick black hair to his huge shoulders. — Elmore Leonard, *Be Cool*, p. 58, 1999

▸ **go some**
to fight *US, 1968*
- — Joan Fontaine et al., *Dictionary of Black Slang*, 1968

▸ **go south**
1 to deteriorate; to break *US, 2000*
- Once we got to SoCal, my transmission went south too. — Ralph "Sonny" Barger, *Hell's Angel*, p. 30, 2000
2 in a gambling cheating scheme, to take dice or money off the gaming table *US, 1997*
- "Time to go south," Duffy said. — Stephen Cannell, *Big Con*, p. 197, 1997

▸ **go to bat**
to stand trial *US, 1965*
A baseball metaphor.
- I went up to bat on the sale first. — Henry Williamson, *Hustler!*, p. 141, 1965
- "He went to bat for wasting [killing] three of 'em, but he beat those raps." — Iceberg Slim (Robert Beck), *Airtight Willie and Me*, p. 94, 1979

▸ **go to ground**
to go into hiding *US, 1990*
- Of course that's where Rooski would go to ground[.] — Seth Morgan, *Homeboy*, p. 60, 1990

▸ **go to higher game**
to launch a legitimate business after a period in an under-world enterprise *US, 1972*
- They never have been able to get enough money together to retire or go on to higher game[.] — Christina and Richard Milner, *Black Players*, p. 157, 1972

▸ **go to the wall**
to exert yourself at all costs without regard to the consequences *US, 1976*
- — John R. Armore and Joseph D. Wolfe, *Dictionary of Desperation*, p. 31, 1976

▶ **go upside someone's head**
to hit someone on the head *US, 1959*
- If she hollers cop, all yo do is bop—her by going up side her head with your fist hard as lead! — Dan Burley, *Diggeth Thou?*, p. 5, 1959
- He was ready to go up side her head (beat her) when she threw $2,200 on the bed. — Babs Gonzales, *I Paid My Dues*, p. 97, 1967

go!
used for expressing approval and encouraging further effort *US, 1957*
- Therefore one finds words like go, and make it, and with it, and swing: "Go with its sense that after hours or days or months or years of monotony, boredom, and depression one has finally had one's chance[.]" — Norman Mailer, *Advertisements for Myself*, p. 350, 1957

GOA *adjective*
(said of a criminal) no longer at the scene of a crime *US, 1975*
An initialism of "gone on arrival."
- "Unit 2544 to Central, K ... that rate is GOA at that time, K." — John Sepe, *Cop Team*, p. 44, 1975

go ahead, make my day
used to summon defiance *US, 1983*
From the movie character Dirty Harry played by Clint Eastwood. US President Ronald Reagan used the line in a speech to the American Business Conference in March 1985: "I have only one thing to say to the tax increasers. Go ahead—make my day!" He liked the line so much that he repeated it in a speech at his 83rd birthday in 1994.
- Like that line Dirty Harry said in that picture, "Make my day." The writer who wrote that line didn't think it up. He heard it somewhere. I heard it a long time before Dirty Harry said it. But he said it and then a hundred million people said... — Robert Campbell, *Juice*, p. 213, 1988

go-ahead man *noun*
in horse racing, a person working with someone selling "inside" information on the horses and races *US, 1962*
- — Mel Heimer, *Inside Racing*, p. 211, 1962

go-aheads *noun*
thong sandals *US, 1962*
- — *American Speech*, p. 288, December 1962: "Marine corps slang"
- Two wear homemade go-aheads and two are barefooted; all wear the flyless black shorts which serve Vietnamese men as outer and under garment. — Donald Duncan, *The New Legions*, p. 178, 1967

goalie *noun*
the clitoris *US, 1972*
- — Robert A. Wilson, *Playboy's Book of Forbidden Words*, p. 124, 1972

goat *noun*
a person responsible for a failure or loss, especially a player in an athletic contest *US, 1894*
A short form of "scapegoat."
- It was in the 1963 Series that he lost a throw from third base in the shirts of the crowd and was the goat of the game. — Jim Bouton, *Ball Four*, p. 313, 1970

▶ **get someone's goat**
to succeed in making someone lose their temper *US, 1904*
- Got his goat properly, I can tell you, way I offered him out on the spot. — Norman Lindsay, *Halfway to Anywhere*, p. 200, 1947
- [H]e went with a woman once who kept acting like she couldn't remember his name right and calling him Hooligan just to get his goat. — Ken Kesey, *One Flew Over the Cuckoo's Nest*, p. 44, 1962

goat fuck *noun*
a colossal, confused mess *US, 1971*
- This op is a Larry Bailey goatfuck—we're gonna come up dry. I can't see six feet in front of me. — Richard Marcinko and John Weisman, *Rogue Warrior*, p. 96, 1992
- Bush would never say no to a friend, so then they'd have the Free world's Leader-to-be in a YR goat fuck. — Richard Ben Cramer, *What It Takes*, p. 1020, 1993
- What a goat-fuck that turned out to be. We're all lucky a nuclear war didn't break out. — Dale Brown, *Air Battle Force*, p. 154, 2003

goat hair *noun*
illegally manufactured alcoholic drink *US, 1970*
- — Roger D. Abrahams, *Deep Down in the Jungle*, p. 261, 1970

goat land *noun*
in oil drilling, non-productive land *US, 1954*
- — Jerry Robertson, *Oil Slanguage*, p. 59, 1954

goat locker *noun*
in the US Navy, the kitchen and dining hall reserved for officers *US, 1990*
- We knew why he'd done it; if he hadn't, he would have taken grief in the chief's goat locker, so to keep the peace he reamed us out. — Richard Marcinko and John Weisman, *Rogue Warrior*, p. 55, 1992

goat pasture *noun*
any worthless land sold as part of a confidence swindle *US, 1985*
- — M. Allen Henderson, *How Con Games Work*, p. 220, 1985: "Glossary"

goat-roper *noun*
a rustic *US, 1970*
- Another goat roper with an attitude, tanked up on cheap whiskey. — Catherine Anderson, *Forever After*, p. 18, 1998

goat screw *noun*
a disorganized, confusing situation *US, 1988*
- — Hans Halberstadt, *Airborne*, p. 130, 1988: "Abridged dictionary of airborne terms"
- The op was a classic goat-screw. — Gary Stubblefield, *Inside the US Navy Seals*, p. 139, 1995

go away *verb*
to be sent to jail or prison *US, 1990*
- That's what happens when you go away. We're on our own. — *Goodfellas*, 1990
- They bring him to trial he's going away. — Elmore Leonard, *Riding the Rap*, p. 107, 1995

gobble *verb*
1 to perform oral sex on a man *US, 1966*
- Hell, I'd rather let some score do a little gobbling on my joint than spend all day cleaning some guy's latrine. — Johnny Shearer, *The Male Hustler*, p. 16, 1966
- "She gobbles about twenty joints a night," said Ranatti. — Joseph Wambaugh, *The New Centurions*, p. 182, 1970
- This sort is so anxious to gobble a joint that he doesn't even take his own pants off. — *Screw*, p. 12, 13th July 1970
2 to talk *US, 1947*
- — Marcus Hanna Boulware, *Jive and Slang of Students in Negro Colleges*, 1947

▶ **gobble the goop**
to perform oral sex on a man *US, 1918*
- — Roger Blake, *The American Dictionary of Sexual Terms*, p. 88, 1964
- [S]he got right down in broad daylight standin' outside the car, me layin' back in the seat and gobbled the goop. — Earl Thompson, *Tattoo*, p. 225, 1974

gobble alley *noun*
the upper balcony in a movie theater favored by homosexuals *US, 1966*
- In Chicago, they're called "Gobble Alley." In Los Angeles, some studs refer to the balconies as the "Last Chance." — Johnny Shearer, *The Male Hustler*, p. 77, 1966

gobble down *verb*
in computing, to obtain *US, 1983*
- — Guy L. Steele et al., *The Hacker's Dictionary*, p. 73, 1983

gobbledygook *noun*
dense, pompous, and unintelligible jargon *US, 1944*
- Why do you bother going through this legal gobbledegook? — Robert Campbell, *Juice*, p. 264, 1988

gobble hole *noun*
in pinball, a hole near the center of the playing field which takes a ball from play while scoring a large number of points *US, 1979*
- — Edward Trapunski, *Special When Lit*, p. 153, 1979

gobbler *noun*
1 a person who performs oral sex *US, 1969*
- She was a gobbler. And, I guess, a pretty damned expert one, too. — Joey V., *Portrait of Joey*, p. 28, 1969
2 a hospital patient with petty complaints *US, 1980*
- — *Maledicta*, p. 56, Summer 1980: "Not sticks and stones, but names: more medical pejoratives"

gobs *noun*
a great deal of *US, 1839*
In the C16, a "gob" or "gubbe" referred specifically to a "great deal of money" or a "large mouthful of fatty meat." By World War 2, the term had acquired this broader meaning, as evidenced by the title of Johnny Viney's 1943 wartime humorous novel *Sailors are Gobs of Fun, Hattie*.

- And every time the train stopped, Cole would hop off and buy gobs of candy and cold drinks and cookies and everything else he could lay his hands on. — Jim Thompson, *The Grifters*, p. 79, 1963
- — Collin Baker et al., *College Undergraduate Slang Study Conducted at Brown University*, p. 126, 1968
- They have washed, gobs of people in front of me, alongside me, behind me, and I'm still standin'. — Edwin Torres, *After Hours*, p. 335, 1979

go-by *noun*
a passing by *US, 1949*
- I wasn't going in. I was going to give it the go-by but I don't see anybody inside so I went in and ordered a coke. — Hal Ellson, *Duke*, p. 145, 1949

God-awful *adjective*
terrible, dreadful *US, 1897*
- [T]he lead singer's twerpy attempts at Doctor John-ish mumbo-jumbo [...] were godawful. — Lester Bangs, *Psychotic Reactions and Carburetor Dung*, p. 98, 1972

God bless you *noun*
used as a mnemonic device in snooker for remembering the correct spotting of ball colors—green, brown, yellow *US, 1993*
- — Mike Shamos, *The Illustrated Encyclopedia of Billiards*, p. 109, 1993

-goddamn- *infix*
used as an intensifier *US, 1968*
- This is the most, baby. I mean abso-goddamn-lute most! — Nathan Heard, *Howard Street*, p. 68, 1968
- You fuck up in a firefight and I guaran-goddamned-tee you, a trip out of the bush—in a bodybag. — *Platoon*, 1986
- If it isn't, c'est-la-goddamn-guerre. — James Ellroy, *Hollywood Nocturnes*, pp. 60–61, 1994
- This is ri-goddamn-diculous. — *Austin Powers*, 1999

Godfrey *noun*
used in oaths in place of "God" *US, 1904*
- No by Godfrey, I won't take it to the office. — Max Shulman, *I was a Teen-Age Dwarf*, p. 108, 1959
- By Godfrey and Godfrey Mighty! are the commonest ways to use Godfrey. — John Gould, *Maine Lingo*, p. 111, 1975

God hates a coward
in poker, used for luring a reluctant bettor to bet *US, 1951*
- — *American Speech*, p. 99, May 1951

go down *verb*
1 to be arrested *US, 1968*
- If a Boston Globe reporter goes down for holding on the job, there'll be such a vicious outcry against the "drug-maddened press" that free-lancers like me—who look a bit strange anyway—will be locked up on sight. — Hunter S. Thompson, *Fear and Loathing in America*, p. 99, 20th June 1968: Letter to Bill Cardoso
2 to happen *US, 1946*
- There's not that much truth going down in the straight world. — Leonard Wolfe (Editor), *Voices from the Love Generation*, p. 33, 1968
- With all the other shit going down in Chicago during the week, it should be kept in mind that the Festival of Life is NOT a "protest" of any kind. — John Sinclair, *Guitar Army*, p. 90, 1972
- Number one contender for the middleweight crown / Had no idea what kinda shit was about to go down. — Bob Dylan, *Hurricane*, 1975
- Me and Mr. Orange jumped in the car and Mr. Brown floored it. After that, I don't know what went down. — *Reservoir Dogs*, 1992
3 while working as a police officer in a patrol car, to park and sleep *US, 1973*
- As a rookie cop, Serpico was also introduced to the fine art of "cooping," or sleeping on duty, a time-honored police practice that in other cities goes under such names as "huddling" and "going down." — Peter Maas, *Serpico*, p. 63, 1973

go-down man *noun*
in an illegal betting operation, the employee designated to identify himself as the operator in the event of a police raid, accepting risk in place of the actual operator *US, 1951*
- — David W. Maurer, *Argot of the Racetrack*, p. 32, 1951

go down on; go down; go down south *verb*
to perform oral sex *US, 1914*
- I remembered—and I felt that strange, numb, helpless, cold fear when you realize you cant change the past—the first time someone had gone down on me in a public restroom. — John Rechy, *City of Night*, p. 381, 1963
- Q Then what happened? A And then he [Roman Polanski] went down and he started performing cuddliness. Q What does that mean? A It means he went down on me or he placed his mouth on my vagina. — *Testimony of Samantha Jane Gailey to Los Angeles County Grand Jury*, 24th March 1977
- I simply had to stay in L.A. and learn how to go down on him. — Eve Babitz, *L.A. Woman*, p. 11, 1982
- If you went down on a horse, you'd tell me, right? — *South Park*, 1999

God's flesh *noun*
psilocybin, a hallucinogenic mushroom *US, 1970*
- — William D. Alsever, *Glossary for the Establishment and Other Uptight People*, p. 26, December 1970

God shop *noun*
a church *US, 1965*
- "God-Shop" for "Church" — *American Speech*, p. 234, October 1965

God-size *adjective*
very, very large *US, 1968*
- — *Current Slang*, p. 7, Summer 1968

God's medicine; God's own medicine *noun*
morphine; opium *US, 1925*
- "Melt it," he pleaded with the punk, "melt me God's medicine." — Nelson Algren, *The Man with the Golden Arm*, p. 256, 1949
- I'm several kinds of jerk for not writing sooner to thank you for the heaven-sent god's medicine. — James Blake, *The Joint*, p. 148, 28th October 1956

God squad *noun*
1 church authorities; evangelical enthusiasts *US, 1965*
- — Stephen H. Dill (Editor), *Current Slang*, p. 7, Summer 1968
2 the US military Chaplains Corps *US, 1965*
- [T]his member of the general's "God squad" was actually going to hump with them, share the merciless heat with them. — Charles Anderson, *The Grunts*, p. 53, 1976

God's waiting room *noun*
a nursing home; a rest home *US, 1988–1989*
- — *Maledicta*, p. 32, 1988–1989: "Medical maledicta from San Francisco"

godzillion *noun*
used as a notional large number *US, 1982*
- "Do you know what a fine chef makes in New York?" "A godzillion times what I make." — Kevin Wilson, *The Route*, p. 221, 2001

go-fast *noun*
any amphetamine or other central nervous system stimulant *US, 1993*
- I can let you have a quarter a go-fast for twenny bucks. This special sale can't be repeated. — Joseph Wambaugh, *Finnegan's Week*, p. 138, 1993
- "Don't trip, he's got more than smack. Go-fast, weed, crack." — Lynn Breedlove, *Godspeed*, p. 41, 2002

go-faster *noun*
any amphetamine or other central nervous system stimulant *US, 1986*
- — Richard A. Spears, *The Slang and Jargon of Drugs and Drink*, p. 223, 1986

gofer; gopher; go-for *noun*
a low-level assistant who typically runs petty errands *US, 1930*
He or she *goes for* this and *goes for* that.
- Some gopher forgot to lock the gate. — Raymond Chandler, *The Long Goodbye*, p. 105, 1953
- Of course I'm just a gopher but that's cool. — Beatrice Sparks (writing as "Anonymous"), *Jay's Journal*, p. 90, 1979
- She had just been promoted to stage manager from "broadcast associate," which used to be called "production assistant," or "PAS," or more to the point, "go-fer." — Dan Jenkins, *Life Its Ownself*, p. 186, 1984

- "Say in the paper this Chili Palmer used to be a wiseguy." "He was a gofer, a hired hand." — Elmore Leonard, *Be Cool*, p. 109, 1999

go for *verb*
to pay for *US, 1975*

- I would have gone for the funeral, but he had insurance. — Edwin Torres, *Carlito's Way*, p. 74, 1975

go for it!
used as a general exhortation *US, 1978*

- CARRIE: Make a wish, Daddy. RIANNE: Go for it, Dad. — *Lethal Weapon*, 1987

go for the gusto!
used as an exhortation to take risks and live life fully *US, 1988*
From a slogan for Schlitz beer; often used ironically.

- It was an 89–69 Seam play, when you go for the gusto. — *Milwaukee Journal*, p. 3C, 7th November 1988

go-getter *noun*
a very active, enterprising person *US, 1910*

- All women want the go-getter. The conqueror. But after he's made the conquest they get mad because he won't stick around — Chris Rock, *Rock This!*, p. 125, 1997

goggle *verb*
▸ **goggle the horizon**
used by motorcyclists to mean a number of things, most commonly to keep an eye out *US, 2006*

- — Donna Madden, *Sweet Machines & Bike Night Scenes*, p. 25, 2006

goggler *noun*
a male homosexual *US, 1970*

- — Robert J. Glessing, *The Underground Press in America*, p. 176, 1970: "Glossary of terms used in the underground press"

go-go *noun*
a discotheque; a venue for erotic-dance performance *US, 1965*

- — Smokey Robinson & The Miracles, *Going to a Go-Go*, 1965
- Soon as I had jettisoned my bags I went to a go-go bar on a steamy Bangkok street colled Soi Cowboy. — Sean Thomas, *Millions of Women Are Waiting to Meet You*, p. 249, 2007

go-go *adjective*
associated with a discotheque *UK, 1964*
A very big word for a very few years.

- He had gone to a go-go bar to meet a buddy of his, had one beer, that's all, while he was waiting, minding his own business and this go-go whore came up to his table and starting giving him a private dance he never asked for. — Elmore Leonard, *Maximum Bob*, p. 1, 1991

go-go bird *noun*
a CH-47 transport helicopter fitted with window-mounted machine guns and used as a gunship *US, 1984*
Not a successful experiment.

- — John Robert Elting, *A Dictionary of Soldier Talk*, p. 134, 1984

go-go boy *noun*
an attractive, usually homosexual, young man who is a paid dancer at a nightclub or bar *US, 1971*

- Thus the phenomenon of the orgy bars with their nude go-go boys is likely to persist. — John Francis Hunter, *The Gay Insider*, p. 11, 1971
- The entertainment consists of several go-go boys in skin-tight pants who dance harder than any topless girl I've ever seen. — Arthur Blessitt, *Turned On to Jesus*, p. 122, 1971
- The other go-go boys joined in. — James St. James, *Party Monster*, p. 51, 1990
- It's a really dreadful experience. I mean, the go-go boys in strip joints here. — James Ridgeway, *Red Light*, p. 160, 1996

go-go dance *verb*
to dance for pay at a nightclub in a cage or platform above the patrons *US, 1993*

- While my father had been seeing Tammy, my mother was under contract, go-go-dancing at a club in Kodiak. — Kim Rich, *Johnny's Girl*, p. 84, 1993

go-go dancer *noun*
a paid dancer at a nightclub *US, 1996*

- Many go-go dancers come to Come Again to buy G-strings and costumes[.] — James Ridgeway, *Red Light*, p. 122, 1996

go-go pill *noun*
a central nervous system stimulant *US, 1957*

- And he did like those go-go pills. — Jack Gerber, *The Connection*, p. 79, 1957

gohong *noun*
during the Korean war, food or chow *US, 1951*
From the Korean word for "rice" applied by American soldiers to food in general.

- — *The Baltimore Sun*, 24th June 1951

goie *noun*
a central nervous system stimulant such as Dexedrine™ or Benzedrine™ *US, 1960*

- — Robert George Reisner, *The Jazz Titans*, p. 157, 1960

going!
used for encouraging another's action *US, 1982*
Hawaiian youth usage.

- "Should I tank dis beer o' wot?" "Going, brah, going!" — Douglas Simonson, *Pidgin to da Max Hana Hou*, 1982

go-juice *noun*
alcohol *US, 1968*

- — Collin Baker et al., *College Undergraduate Slang Study Conducted at Brown University*, p. 126, 1968

gold *noun*
1 money *US, 1940*

- A lot of the guys who hung around were squares who worked for their gold, more gamblers than gangsters[.] — Mezz Mezzrow, *Really the Blues*, p. 20, 1946
- I got back all right with all the gold and gave it to Juan. He threw me the twenty[.] — Hal Ellson, *Duke*, p. 73, 1949
- "Can you lend me some gold?" he asked Porter. — Chandler Brossard, *Who Walks in Darkness*, p. 11, 1952
- Just give me the gold. — Ross Russell, *The Sound*, p. 93, 1961

2 potent marijuana *US, 1968*
Often combined with a place name for the formation of place plus color.

- Claude asks me if I want to smoke some gold and lays a joint on me—I take it and put in on Billy. — *The Digger Papers*, p. 10, August 1968

Goldberg *noun*
used as a stereotype of a Jewish merchant *US, 1965*

- This was the first time I'd ever heard "Goldberg" used this way. I said, "Who's Goldberg?" "You know, Mr. Jew. That's the cat who runs the garment center." — Claude Brown, *Manchild in the Promised Land*, p. 295, 1965
- Making money off of women just as high as making it off doing Goldberg's dirty work in some damn dress factory downtown. — Sara Harris, *The Lords of Hell*, p. 136, 1967
- — Christina and Richard Milner, *Black Players*, p. 301, 1972
- At least three different poems and articles that have some mention of "offing Goldberg" or "wasting the kikes." — John Sayles, *Union Dues*, p. 154, 1977

goldbrick *noun*
a person who shuns work or duty *US, 1918*

- — Lou Shelly, *Hepcats Jive Talk Dictionary*, p. 45, 1945
- "Jesus, you guys are a bunch of goldbricks. Why the hell don't you do your share?" — Norman Mailer, *The Naked and the Dead*, p. 186, 1948
- Jack, the plumber I was assigned to, was a prize goldbrick, a man who saw no virtue in work whatsoever. — Jim Thompson, *Bad Boy*, p. 338, 1953
- "You goldbrick." Landa's teeth were clenched. "We had word of this at oh eight hundred." — John Gobbell, *When Duty Whispers*, p. 61, 2004

goldbrick *verb*
to avoid a work detail *US, 1918*

- Just the thought of marching around all afternoon while they sweated their asses off made me feel sort of inferior, a gold-bricking weakling. — Mezz Mezzrow, *Really the Blues*, p. 321, 1946
- Goldbricking cocksuckers. Where's a man without his Nubians? — William Burroughs, *Naked Lunch*, p. 151, 1957

goldbricker *noun*
a swindler *US, 1902*

- I've seen a lot of spinals, Dude, and this guy is a fake. A fucking goldbricker. — *The Big Lebowski*, 1998

goldbug *noun*
a person who buys and hoards gold *US, 1981*
- The two old geezers were goldbugs from Spring Street in Los Angeles. — Joseph Wambaugh, *The Glitter Dome*, p. 88, 1981

Gold Coast *nickname*
1 a high-rise, high-rent district on Lakeshore Drive bordering Lake Michigan in northern Chicago, Illinois *US, 1950*
- Smooth adventurers set up swank apartments on the chi chi North Side gold Coast[.] — Jack Lait and Lee Mortimer, *Chicago Confidential*, p. z, 1950
- Behind me, the outline of the wealthy Gold Coast: luxurious apartments glistening goldenly in the sun[.] — John Rechy, *City of Night*, p. 293, 1963
- Alex lived on the Gold Coast of Chicago, and the night I drove out there the police stopped me three times along the way. — Dick Gregory, *Nigger*, p. 145, 1964
- I found the Gold Coast lifestyle incredible. — Odie Hawkins, *Scars and Memories*, p. 34, 1987

2 an area in Harlem, New York, where police bribes are common and lucrative *US, 1972*
- At the time of the investigation, certain precincts in Harlem, for instance, comprised what police officers called "the Gold Coast" because they contained so many payoff-prone activities[.] — *The Knapp Commission Report on Police Corruption*, p. 67, 1972

3 the Atlantic coast of South Florida *US, 1983*
- Money is cheap on the Gold Coast, and there is a lot of it floating around. — Hunter S. Thompson, *Songs of the Doomed*, p. 193, 1983
- He's got the entire Gold Coast terrified, your venerable newspaper included. — Carl Hiaasen, *Tourist Season*, p. 191, 1986

gold-digger *noun*
someone who pursues another romantically because of their wealth *US, 1916*
Used to characterize women as predators of men.
- I shambled out of the dormitory, cursing her for a heartless gold-digger and myself for an idiot. — Max Shulman, *The Many Loves of Dobie Gillis*, p. 56, 1951
- "Unless they were wealthy, she wasn't interested." "Gold digger?" "What an archaic term," Cleo told me. — Mickey Spillane, *The Body Lovers*, p. 31, 1967
- Who the fuck wants a gold-digger around. — Edwin Torres, *After Hours*, p. 297, 1979
- As Erin grew older, she accepted the fact that her mother was a restless gold digger who would never be happy[.] — Carl Hiaasen, *Strip Tease*, p. 26, 1993

gold dust *noun*
cocaine *US, 1998*
- — Joseph E. Ragen and Charles Finston, *Inside the World's Toughest Prison*, p. 801, 1962: "Penitentiary and underworld glossary"
- Street names [...] dust, gold dust, lady[.] — James Kay and Julian Cohen, *The Parents' Complete Guide to Young People and Drugs*, p. 134, 1998

golden *adjective*
successful, excellent, charmed *US, 1958*
- — *Current Slang*, p. 4, Spring 1967
- Once we get airplay we're golden. — *Airheads*, 1994
- If I live a hundred fucking years, he thought wistfully, I'll never top that delicatessen blow job. It was golden. A classic. — Carl Hiaasen, *Nature Girl*, p. 109, 2006

golden arm *noun*
in craps, a player with a long streak of good luck rolling the dice *US, 1993*
- — Frank Scoblete, *Guerrilla Gambling*, p. 310, 1993

golden BB *noun*
the bullet or antiaircraft round that hits you *US, 1969*
- Unfortunately it was the "Golden BB," the lucky shot, the aircrews often joked about, and it struck the LOX bottle under Johnny Nelson's seat in the pit. — Richard Herman Jr., *The Warbirds*, p. 258, 1989
- A damned golden BB met up with my plane / Hey Coach, I think I will drop out of the game! — Joseph Tuso, *Singing the Vietnam Blues*, p. 229, 1990: Wingman's Lament
- So far, it seemed that he had avoided the "Golden BB," the one lucky round that would bring him down. — Gerry Carroll, *North S*A*R*, p. 207, 1991

golden boy *noun*
in homosexual usage, a handsome young man at his sexual prime *US, 1981*
- — *Male Swinger Number 3*, p. 45, 1981: "The complete gay dictionary"

golden bullet *noun*
the bullet or antiaircraft round that hits your combat plane *US, 1991*
- Since then, the main danger has been what the pilots call the golden bullet. "That's the aimed or unaimed bullet that you run into because there are so many bullets," said a lieutenant colonel named Greg. — *Washington Times*, p. B4, 23rd January 1991

golden flow *noun*
the urine test given to US soldiers upon their return to the US from Vietnam *US, 1971*
- The Air Force took over the task of handling the "Golden Flow" flights. (This name referred to the urinalysis tests that were used to reveal drug levels.) — Elizabeth Norman, *Women at War*, p. 101, 1990

golden ghetto *verb*
a large, comfortable US Army divisional base camp *US, 1959*
A term used with derision by the marines.
- "You're the one everyone is supposed to be watching out for and talking to parties at the embassy and the Golden Ghetto." — Danielle Steel, *Message from Nam*, p. 225, 1991

golden girl *noun*
1 high quality cocaine *US, 1980*
- — Edith A. Folb, *runnin' down some lines*, p. 240, 1980
2 heroin *US, 1994*
- — US Department of Justice, *Street Terms*, October 1994

golden glow *noun*
a luminous daub used by card cheats to mark cards *US, 1988*
- — George Percy, *The Language of Poker*, p. 49, 1988

golden leaf *noun*
marijuana of excellent quality *US, 1925*
- "Man, this is some golden-leaf I brought up from New Orleans, it'll make you feel good, take a puff." — Mezz Mezzrow, *Really the Blues*, p. 51, 1946

golden oldie *noun*
a song from the past that is still popular, especially a rock and roll song from the 1950s or 60s *US, 1980*
- I'll do three golden oldies for every one I want to play[.] — Elmore Leonard, *Glitz*, p. 73, 1985

golden shower *noun*
a shared act of urine fetishism; the act of urination by one person on another for sexual gratification *US, 1943*
- One famous television producer wants to pay through the nose for what girls do through the bladder—which is otherwise known as the "golden shower." — Xaviera Hollander, *The Happy Hooker*, p. 246, 1972
- Another large percentage of the pictures have to do with urination or, as we call them, "golden showers." — Stephen Ziplow, *The Film Maker's Guide to Pornography*, p. 14, 1977
- An extreme form of humiliation involves receiving the dominant partner's urine on the masochist's body. This practice, sometimes called "golden showers," is described by Scott (1983) as "the ultimate insult." — Roy F. Baumeister, *Masochism and the Self*, pp. 159–160, 1989
- And he would like for me to give 'im golden showers. He liked for me to drink like a sixpack of beer and then after about a good hour then he'd want me to piss all in his mouth[.] — William T. Vollman, *Whores for Gloria*, p. 54, 1991

golden shower queen *noun*
a male homosexual who derives sexual pleasure from being urinated on *US, 1971*
- — Florida Legislative Investigation Committee (Johns Committee), *Homosexuality and Citizenship in Florida*, 1964: "glossary of homosexual terms and deviate acts"
- Yes, there are those who like to be peed on (Golden Shower Queens, they were once known as)[.] — John Francis Hunter, *The Gay Insider*, p. 190, 1971
- Encountered a golden shower queen but I couldn't handle it. — Daniel McVay, *The Vanilla Kid*, p. 794, 1986

golden spike *noun*
a hypodermic needle *US, 1955*
- — *American Speech*, p. 87, May 1955: "Narcotic argot along the Mexican border"

golden T *nickname*
in New York, Fifth Avenue from 47th Street north to 57th Street, and 57th Street between Madison and Sixth Avenues *US, 1989*
- — *The New York Times*, p. B1, 13th July 1989

golden time; golden hours *noun*
in the entertainment industry, time worked at a premium overtime rate *US, 1970*
- Christ, may, it's seven-ten Saturday night—that's one hour and forty minutes of golden time! — Terry Southern, *Blue Movie*, p. 187, 1970
- — Sherman Louis Sergel, *The Language of Show Biz*, p. 98, 1973
- But we were pushing golden time, where the rates triple, and that hadn't been budgeted. — Robert Stoller and I.S. Levine, *Coming Attractions*, p. 82, 1991

goldfish bowl *noun*
a jail's interrogation room *US, 1962*
- — *American Speech*, p. 269, December 1962: "The language of traffic policemen"

gold mine *noun*
an establishment that sells liquor illegally, by the drink *US, 1978*
- Shot-house operators run informal (and illegal) taverns in their own homes (shot-house operators are often women). The houses go by other names too; gold mine, good-time house, blind tiger, shine parlor, or juicejoint. — Burgess Laughlin, *Job Opportunities in the Black Market*, pp. 10–9, 1978

gold nuggets *noun*
in dominoes, the 5–5 piece *US, 1959*
- — Dominic Armanino, *Dominoes*, p. 17, 1959

gold room *noun*
a room in the Pentagon where the Joint Chiefs and Staff meet with the Operations Deputies *US, 1986*
- — Department of the Army, *Staff Officer's Guidebook*, p. 67, 1986

gold rush *noun*
1 the frantic searching for jewelry or coins that follows a shift in the slope of a beach, exposing lost articles *US, 1986*
- — Ken Suiso and Rell Sunn, *A Guide to Beach Survival*, p. 70, 1986

2 in hold 'em poker, a hand consisting of a four and a nine *US, 1996*
An allusion to the California gold rush of 1849.
- — John Vorhaus, *The Big Book of Poker Slang*, p. 20, 1996

Goldstein *noun*
a Jewish person *US, 1980*
- — Edith A. Folb, *runnin' down some lines*, p. 240, 1980

golfball *noun*
1 crack cocaine; a large piece of crack cocaine *US, 1994*
- — US Department of Justice, *Street Terms*, October 1994

2 a changeable sphere with 88 different characters used on IBM Selectric typewriters *US, 1991*
- — Eric S. Raymond, *The New Hacker's Dictionary*, p. 181, 1991

golfballs *noun*
dice *US, 1962*
- — Frank Garcia, *Marked Cards and Loaded Dice*, p. 262, 1962

Golf Course *nickname*
Camp Radcliff, base camp for the Fourth Infantry Division near An Khe, South Vietnam *US, 1968*
From its large helicopter airfield with low-cut grass.
- — *Life*, p. 33, 25th February 1966
- — Carl Fleischauer, *A Glossary of Army Slang*, p. 22, 1968
- The Golf Course, the heliport cleared of all its trees, stood out against the green. Golf Course control, Preacher eight-seven-niner, five miles east for landing instructions. — Robert Mason, *Chickenawk*, p. 72, 1983
- There were bases like An Khe with its famous Golf Course, with tons of troops and hundreds of tons of hardware, but the VC were all around them. — Dennis Marvicsin and Jerold Greenfield, *Maverick*, p. 89, 1990

golly gee, Buffalo Bob
used for expressing mock astonishment *US, 1969*
- — John D. Bell et al., *Loosely Speaking*, p. Appendix, 1969

gomer *noun*
1 an unsophisticated and uneducated person from rural America, especially the south *US, 1987*
- "So the bottom line is, these Gomers are murdering each other over fish." — Carl Hiaasen, *Double Whammy*, p. 212, 1987

2 a Vietnamese enemy *US, 1990*
- A non-Christian gomer who didn't speak English / Was shooting at us with a Communist gun. — Joseph Tuso, *Singing the Vietnam Blues*, p. 80, 1990: Escorting a Spectre

3 a US Marine, especially a clumsy trainee *US, 1984*
Terminology used with affectionate derision by the US Army during the Vietnam war. From the television show *Gomer Pyle*, which is not a completely flattering image of the marines.
- — *American Speech*, Summer 1989
- — Linda Reinberg, *In the Field*, p. 95, 1991

4 a repulsive, non-compliant hospital patient *US, 1993*
From the plea—"get out of my emergency room!"
- — Sally Williams, *"Strong" Words*, p. 143, 1994

go-minh money *noun*
compensation payment to Vietnamese civilians by the US military for accidental losses resulting from military actions *US, 1990*
From the Vietnamese for "extract yourself from a predicament."
- Thence, in the idea of applying for and receiving compensation directly from the Americans, arose the local nickname: go-minh money. — Phillip Beidler, *Late Thoughts on an Old War*, p. 43, 2004

gommed up *adjective*
dirty *US, 1982*
- — Sam McCool, *Pittsburghese*, p. 13, 1982

gonads *noun*
▸ **to have someone by the gonads**
to exert control over someone *US, 1919*
- He had me by the gonads and he knew it. — T. Brigman, *Limberger on Wry*, p. 48, 2004

gone *adjective*
1 superlative, profoundly in touch with current trends *US, 1946*
Nellie Lutcher's 1947 recording of "He's a Real Gone Guy" did as much as anything to introduce the term into the language.
- "That's Bop language!" he laughed and handed me a Bop dictionary which translates the slang used by "real gone Boppers." — *San Francisco Examiner*, Pictorial Review, 3rd December 1948
- I had a pad on tenth street living with a gone little chick from Newark. — Jack Kerouac, *Letter to Neal Cassady*, p. 234, 6 October 1950
- Isn't this wild, isn't this crazy, ain't this gone, this sure is! — William "Lord" Buckley, *Nero*, 1951
- Mary selected some gone numbers and beat on the table with the expression of a masturbating idiot. — William Burroughs, *Junkie*, p. 29, 1953
- "Your grandma," he said, "is gone." "I'm hip," said Red. "She is the swingin'est, but let's take it from the top again." — Steve Allen, *Bop Fables*, p. 47, 1955

2 drunk or drug-intoxicated *US, 1933*
- You know. Drunk stewed, clobbered, gone, liquored up, oiled, stoned, in the bag. — Max Shulman, *Guided Tour of Campus Humor*, p. 106, 1955
- — Connie Eble (Editor), *UNC-CH Campus Slang*, p. 5, April 1995

3 completely destitute and physically ruined because of crack cocaine addiction *US, 1994*
- — US Department of Justice, *Street Terms*, October 1994

4 infatuated *US, 1957*
- Dig Number one: being gone on a boy is more important than having a boy gone on you. — Frederick Kohner, *Gidget*, p. 103, 1957

goner *noun*
1 someone who is doomed to failure *US, 1970*
- That does it. The goddamn F.B.I. We're goners. — Darryl Ponicsan, *The Last Detail*, p. 159, 1970

2 a person who excels *US, 1949*
- They were all good records: Frankie Lane, Sarah Vaughn, Billy Eckstein, all gone, good singers. They were goners. — Hal Ellson, *Duke*, p. 105, 1949

gone up *adjective*
drunk or drug-intoxicated *US, 1970*
- — William D. Alsever, *Glossary for the Establishment and Other Uptight People*, p. 15, December 1970

gong *noun*
a gun *US, 1995*
- — Bill Valentine, *Gang Intelligence Manual*, p. 110, 1995: "Jamaican gang terminology."

gonies *noun*
the testicles *US, 1970*
A diminuitive of "gonads."
- "And if I'm permitted to state one more fact," says Mule, "my goddam gonies are frozen." — Darryl Ponicsan, *The Last Detail*, p. 132, 1970

gonk *verb*
to lie *US, 1991*
- — Eric S. Raymond, *The New Hacker's Dictionary*, p. 182, 1991

gonnif; gonif; ganef *noun*
a thief; a crook *UK, 1839*
Yiddish from Hebrew. Depending on the tone, can range from laudatory to disdainful.
- "Where they pickin' up these type gonifs?" — Donald Wilson, *My Six Convicts*, p. 63, 1951
- The little bulb-nosed goneff who used to play clarinet and had three fingers and his teeth shot out at Omaha Beach[.] — Clancy Sigal, *Going Away*, p. 352, 1961
- Then New York with Jimmy Walker—a heavy gonif, a master gonif, man. — Lenny Bruce, *The Essential Lenny Bruce*, p. 57, 1967
- I'm on the floor in the back of a car with somebody's shoe on my neck before I know what hits me. It's a black shoe, well-polished and with a pointy toe. A dancer's shoe. A gonif's shoe. A shoe which belongs to a man who knows how to damage a man's ribs with a kick. — Robert Campbell, *Junkyard Dog*, p. 126, 1986

go-no-go *noun*
the point on a runway where a pilot taking off must decide whether to abort a take-off or to take off *US, 1963*
- — *American Speech*, p. 118, May 1963: "Air refueling words"

gonzo *adjective*
1 crazed; having a bizarre, intensely personal style *US, 1970*
Apparently coined by US journalist and author Bill Cardoso, close friend and partner in adventure with the late Hunter S. Thompson, in a 1970 letter to Thompson: "I don't know what the fuck you're doing, but you've changed everything. It's totally gonzo." Thompson first used the term in print and the term is irrevocably linked with him in the US. Speculation about the term's etymology is speculation.
- [T]here was no avoiding the stench of twisted humor that hovered around the idea of a gonzo journalist in the grip of a potentially terminal drug episode being invited to cover the National District Attorneys' Conference on Narcotics and Dangerous Drugs. — Hunter S. Thompson, *Fear and Loathing in Las Vegas*, p. 80, 1971
- So in terms of Gonzo Journalism (pure), Part One is the only chunk that qualifies. — Hunter S. Thompson, *Fear and Loathing in America*, p. 375, 20th April 1971: Letter to Tom Wolfe
- The mother tried to save the kid, but the Reaper turned gonzo and knifed her in the stomach. — Joe Bob Briggs, *Joe Bob Goes to the Drive-In*, p. 13, 1987
- Soon enough, other porn directors caught on and his style of filming was dubbed "Gonzo." — Ana Loria, *1 2 3 Be A Porn Star!*, p. 119, 2000
2 gone *US, 1974*
- "And then, after, I'm gonzo." — George Higgins, *Cogan's Trade*, p. 49, 1974

Gonzo Station *noun*
the Indian Ocean *US, 1980*
- They'd been on Bonzo Station off Iran for three months, and he didn't seem to be making headway. — Robert Wilcox, *Wings of Fury*, p. 150, 1997

goo *noun*
any semi-liquid or viscous stuff, especially of an unknown origin *US, 1903*
- On the wall was more of his goo, with the plaster cracked from where the bullet entered. — Mickey Spillane, *I, The Jury*, p. 76, 1947
- And just how many of these chicks make enough to pay eight a month for a sleeping room and take all their meals in restaurants and buy clothes and lots of frigging goo to smear on the faces that the good Lord gave 'em... — Jim Thompson, *The Grifters*, p. 14, 1963
- Only the bombs of flaming hot goo entered the villages where the little people lived. — Oscar Zeta Acosta, *The Revolt of the Cockroach People*, p. 175, 1973

goob *noun*
1 a fool, an idiot, a dolt *US, 1919*
- The yappy goobs rendered speechless at last. — Carl Hiaasen, *Sick Puppy*, p. 267, 1999
2 a large facial blemish *US, 1976*
- — *Verbatim*, p. 280, May 1976
3 methcathinone *US, 1998*
- — US Office of National Drug Control Policy, *Drug Facts*, February 2003

goober *noun*
1 an uneducated, unsophisticated rustic *US, 1862*
- "They're talking to some dumb goober from Alabama, but I don't know." — Carl Hiaasen, *Stormy Weather*, p. 106, 1995
2 in the usage of young street racers, anyone who drives a car with an automatic transmission *US, 2003*
- The cop was a Goober, street slang for some fool who runs with an automatic transmission[.] — *Los Angeles Times*, p. A1, 6th June 2003
3 an accumulation of phlegm *US, 1970*
- [H]e was looking at my shoe and moving his mouth around like he was putting together a big goober. — Katherine Hannigan, *Ida B*, p. 138, 2004

gooberhead *noun*
a fool, an eccentric *US, 1970*
- Apparently these gooberheads actually expected wild applause from a grateful public, but instead folks were widely appalled. — Jim Hightower, *There's Nothing in the Middle of the Road*, p. 174, 1998

gooch *noun*
an inept, unaware person *US, 1976*
- — Warren Smith, *Warren's Smith's Authentic Dictionary of CB*, p. 41, 1976

gooch-eyed *adjective*
blind in one eye *US, 1972*
- I said, "I don't want to meet that gooch-eyed bitch." — Bruce Jackson, *In the Life*, p. 74, 1972

good and plenty *noun*
heroin *US, 1994*
Playing with a trademarked candy name.
- — US Department of Justice, *Street Terms*, October 1994

good buddy *noun*
used as a term of address *US, 1956*
A term that enjoyed meteor-like ascendancy in popularity with the citizens' band radio craze that swept the US in 1976. Still used with jocular irony.
- — Wayne Floyd, *Jason's Authentic Dictionary of CB Slang*, p. 17, 1976
- "Hey, good buddy," he said. (He'd been car-pooling during the Marin Transit strike with a fellow banker who had a CB radio.) — Cyra McFadden, *The Serial*, p. 85, 1977

goodbuddy lizard *noun*
a prostitute who works at truck stops *US, 2000*
- Glad's little bits don't have to stand outside the truck stop like other goodbuddy lizards usually do. — J.T. LeRoy, *Sarah*, p. 1, 2000

good-bye kiss *noun*
the repurchase at a premium of stock by a target company from the company attempting a takeover *US, 1988*
- — Kathleen Odean, *High Steppers, Fallen Angels, and Lollipops*, p. 117, 1988

good choke *noun*
intentional deprivation of oxygen as a sexual fetish *US, 1998*
- You can give "good choke"—erotic asphyxia—without actually exerting all that much pressure. — Dan Savage, *Savage Love*, p. 182, 1998

good chute *noun*
a successful ejection of pilot and crew from a downed US aircraft *US, 1990*
- I've got a good chute. I'm comfortable. I'm conscious. I've survived. — David Fisher, *Wild Blue*, p. 45, 2000

good cop *noun*
in a pair of police, the partner who plays the sympathetic, understanding role during an interrogation *US, 1975*
- Rourke, who's got a very sweet face and disposition, plays the good cop but between the two, if I had to face it out or duke it out, I'd rather go up against O'Shea than Rourke any day of the week. — Robert Campbell, *In a Pig's Eye*, p. 23, 1991

good cop, bad cop *noun*
a police interrogation method in which one interrogator plays the role of a hardliner, while the other plays the role of a sympathetic friend *US, 1975*

- Was this a bad-cop-good-cop routine? — *New York Times*, p. 4–1, 21st October 1973
- Bitsy looked at Canaan sidelong, suspicious that they were going to play the good-cop-bad-cop game on him. — Robert Campbell, *Sweet La-La Land*, p. 189, 1990

good day *noun*
a day of reduced prison sentence for good behavior *US, 1992*

- He was sentenced to 65 days in the Hole, stripped of 485 "good days" that had been previously deducted from his prison sentence because of good behavior[.] — Pete Earley, *The Hot House*, p. 209, 1992

goodfella *noun*
a member of an organized crime enterprise *US, 1990*

- Vincent "Vig" Vigliano was a "Goodfella" who ran numbers and book for one of New York's five families. — Bell Chevigny, *Doing Time*, p. 149, 1999

good fun *noun*
a great deal of fun *US, 1981*
Hawaiian youth usage.

- — Douglas Simonson, *Pidgin to da Max*, 1981

good gravy!
used as an utterly unprofane exclamation *US, 1971*

- Good gravy, I've never seen anything that came close to this. — Iceberg Slim (Robert Beck), *The Naked Soul of Iceberg Slim*, pp. 65–66, 1971
- Good gravy, why are people so boring? — Eugene Boe (Compiler), *The Wit & Wisdom of Archie Bunker*, p. 28, 1971

good grief!
used as an all-purpose expression of surprise, anger, disappointment, dismay *US, 1937*
Given great popularity in the 1960s by Charles Schultz's *Peanuts* comic strip.

- "Good Grief," cried Candy, in a very odd voice, "it's Daddy!" pushing her hands violently against the gardner's chest. "It's Daddy!" — Terry Southern, *Candy*, p. 41, 1958

good hitter *noun*
in pool, an excellent cue stick *US, 1990*

- "Hitter" is never used in reference to a poor stick, so the only time you'll hear someone speak of a "bad hitter" is in a predominantly black poolroom, where the expression is synonymous with "good hitter." — Steve Rushin, *Pool Cool*, p. 14, 1990

goodie *noun*
1 something that is special and good *US, 1975*

- I'll go for the goodies, but I can't compete with my brains or family or education, so I do it with my balls. — Edwin Torres, *Carlito's Way*, p. 42, 1975
- Well, you can either take your goodies home and get high, or, you can stay at The Enterprise. — *New Jack City*, 1990
- Chester, this is your agent, how ya' doing—great. Looks like we got a goodie for you! — Odie Hawkins, *Lost Angeles*, p. 103, 1994

2 a person on the side of right, especially in works of fiction *US, 1873*

- The question uppermost in my mind was whether Tam and her monsters were baddies or goodies. — Martin Waddell, *Otley*, p. 29, 1966

3 in poker, a card that improves a hand *US, 1961*

- — Irv Roddy, *Friday Night Poker*, p. 218, 1961

goodies *noun*
1 the vagina *US, 1959*

- — Edith A. Folb, *runnin' down some lines*, p. 240, 1980

2 the female breasts *US, 1963*

- "So you got a pretty good look at her goodies." — Wade Hunter, *The Sex Peddler*, p. 93, 1963
- God you wouldn't believe it what some of them around the house, showing you the goodies, boy, some of them just asking for it. — Elmore Leonard, *The Big Bounce*, p. 111, 1969
- "But for your crowd I've got to have all my goodies flying to the four winds." — Georgia Sothern, *My Life in Burlesque*, p. 228, 1972

good man Friday *noun*
a pimp *US, 1953*

- But I would never take a girl if I knew she had a Good Man Friday, more commonly known as a pimp. — Polly Adler, *A House is Not a Home*, p. 132, 1953

good money!
used for expressing approval *US, 2004*

- good money: that was a good move — J.G. Narum, *The Convict Cookbook*, p. 160, 2004

Good night Chet. Good night David.
used as a humorous exchange of farewells *US, 1956*
The signature sign-off of television news anchors Chet Huntley and David Brinkley (1956–1970). Repeated with referential humor.

- He left as quickly as he came, saying "good night Chet, good night David" and before long I fell back to sleep. — Elizabeth Swados, *The Myth Man*, p. 22, 1994

good-night nurse *noun*
a smoker's last cigarette of the night before going to sleep *US, 1996*

- — John Fahs, *Cigarette Confidential*, p. 301, 1996: "Glossary"

good old boy *verb*
a white male from the southern US who embraces the values of his region and race *US, 1948*

- E.J. was a good old boy. — Clancy Sigal, *Going Away*, p. 83, 1961

good people *noun*
a person who can be trusted and counted on *US, 1894*

- That's all right, kid, you're good people. — Willard Motley, *Let No Man Write My Epitaph*, p. 243, 1958
- God only knows what he's writin', but he's good people. — Hunter S. Thompson, *Hell's Angels*, p. 242, 1966
- Kenny could see that he was good people and a likable dude and he was smart and had a quick-witted way which made you laugh. — Emmett Grogan, *Ringolevio*, p. 136, 1972
- She was good people. Her trouble was she was waitin' on some guy to solve her problem. — Edwin Torres, *After Hours*, p. 280, 1979

goods *noun*
1 positive evidence of guilt *US, 1900*

- They had the goods on me, all right, and there was nothing I could do about it. — Clancy Sigal, *Going Away*, p. 214, 1961

2 any drug *US, 1971*

- — Eugene Landy, *The Underground Dictionary*, p. 91, 1971

good thing *noun*
a sucker; someone who is easily tricked *US, 1909*

- "Man," Cowboy said, "didn't I just see you with a bottle 'bout an hour ago? What you think I am—a good thing or somethin'?" — Nathan Heard, *Howard Street*, p. 53, 1968

good time *noun*
1 a reduction of a prison sentence for good behavior in jail *US, 1951*

- Each man had to have his own calendar on which his Good Time was accumulated and his parole anticipated. — Donald Wilson, *My Six Convicts*, p. 88, 1951
- Through this, the Administration took away from a girl a number of her good days; that is days that constituted her conditional release date. — Helen Bryan, *Inside*, p. 250, 1953
- I was released after twenty-one months. I got three months "good time" for good conduct. — Iceberg Slim (Robert Beck), *Pimp*, p. 75, 1969
- I got a pencil and paper down and figured my good time, and I wouldn't have but about two and a half years to do if I can get it all back. — Bruce Jackson, *In the Life*, p. 322, 1972

2 time that counts towards a soldier's military commitment *US, 1971*

- It's considered good time if you are in a medical facility even if you spend your whole tour there—the Army simply counts it as Vietnam time. — Ronald J. Glasser, *365 Days*, p. 7, 1971

3 a period of incarceration that does not destroy the prisoner's spirit *US, 1975*

- In the Joint I always get in top shape; no coke, no pot, no pussy, so you work out. I always do good time. — Edwin Torres, *Carlito's Way*, p. 41, 1975

good-time Charlie *noun*
a person who enjoys a good time at the expense of more serious pursuits *US, 1927*

- She sneaks off to a hotel room with her good-time-Charlie boyfriend, who wears a captain's cap. — Bill Landis, *Sleazoid Express*, p. 112, 2002

good-time house *noun*
an establishment that sells alcohol illegally, especially by the drink *US, 1978*

- Shot-house operators run informal (and illegal) taverns in their own homes (shot-house operators are often women). The houses go by other names too; gold mine, good-time house, blind tiger, shine parlor, or juicejoint. — Burgess Laughlin, *Job Opportunities in the Black Market*, pp. 10–9, 1978

good wood *noun*
a dependable, trustworthy white prisoner *US, 1989*
Derived from **PECKERWOOD**.

- — James Harris, *A Convict's Dictionary*, p. 33, 1989

goody drawer *noun*
any drawer in a bedroom containing contraceptives, lubricants, or sex toys *US, 2001*
Illegal in Alabama.

- "I could show him the goody drawer in my nightstand." "Goody drawer?" "It's where I keep all those nice, little, colorful packages my friend." — Cynthia Appel, *The Fixer-Uppers*, p. 109, 2001
- — Amy Sohn, *Sex and the City*, p. 155, 2002

goody-goody *noun*
an excessively good person *UK, 1871*
Usually uttered with some degree of derision.

- Because you shouldn't get mad. (Says the goody-goody.) — Elmore Leonard, *Switch*, p. 56, 1978
- While preserving a goodie goodie image I frequently did a whole bunch of stuff. — Odie Hawkins, *Scars and Memories*, p. 154, 1987

goody two-shoes *noun*
a person of excessive virtue *US, 1934*

- Oh, stop with the goodytwoshoes bit. It's a war out there. — Seth Morgan, *Homeboy*, p. 108, 1990
- Ramona Spelling in high school was the traditional version of Miss Goodie Two Shoes. — Odie Hawkins, *Black Chicago*, p. 139, 1992
- "Good," said Sheeni. "I hoped you'd say that. I was worried you might be a bit of a Goody Two-Shoes." "Hardly," I said. "I'm in a state of permanent open revolt around here." — C.D. Payne, *Youth in Revolt*, p. 87, 1993
- Are you shitting me—Mr. Goody Two Shoes? He was like a fucking eagle scout. — *Something About Mary*, 1998

gooey *noun*
in computing, a graphic user interface (GUI) such as one with windows and icons *US, 1995*

- — Steven Daly and Nathaniel Wice, *alt.culture*, p. 140, 1995

gooey *adjective*
viscous or semiviscous *US, 1903*

- It so happens I haven't been to this restaurant before. I don't know how they do their eggs. . . If they're over easy and they're gooey, I'm not happy with it. — *Tin Men*, 1987

gooey ball *noun*
any sticky confection made with marijuana or hashish *US, 2001*

- — Rick Ayers (Editor), *Slang Dictionary*, p. 10, 2001

goof *noun*
1 a barbiturate *US, 1944*
An abbreviation of **GOOFBALL**.

- Hell, no, man, none of that goof for me! — John Clellon Holmes, *Go*, p. 101, 1952
- People's first introduction to things like goofs and speed was by way of newspapers. — Herbert Huncke, *Guilty of Everything*, p. 9, 1990

2 a frequent marijuana smoker *US, 1950*

- — Hyman E. Goldin et al., *Dictionary of American Underworld Lingo*, p. 84, 1950

3 a silly, soft or stupid person *US, 1916*

- It was just bad luck. He'd simply caught a goof, and goofs couldn't be figured. — Jim Thompson, *The Grifters*, p. 7, 1963

4 a joke, a prank *US, 1958*

- Is it you & Tiny's personal goof, or really what you all want? — *The Berkeley Barb*, p. 2, 19th November 1965
- I went to my room and decided to call a Trustee, more for a goof. — James Simon Kunen, *The Strawberry Statement*, p. 164, 1968

goof *verb*
1 to botch, to ruin *US, 1952*

- But we goofed our stuff! — Hal Ellson, *The Golden Spike*, p. 32, 1952
- [T]he cool little pig goofed altogether and at the last possible minute built himself a real blue-lights shack out of clarinet reeds and scotch tape. — Steve Allen, *Bop Fables*, p. 21, 1955
- Whereas if you goof (the ugliest word in Hip), if you lapse back into being a frightened stupid child, or if you flip, if you lose your control[.] — Norman Mailer, *Advertisements for Myself*, p. 351, 1957
- She can rattle a pimp into goofing his whole game. — Iceberg Slim (Robert Beck), *Pimp*, p. 159, 1969

2 to tease, to joke *US, 1931*

- It never occurs to you that life is serious and there are people trying to make something decent out of it instead of just goofing all the time. — Jack Kerouac, *On the Road*, p. 194, 1957
- Yo Thumper, man, I was goofin', I was goofin'. — Richard Price, *Clockers*, p. 36, 1992

3 to smoke marijuana *US, 1970*

- — William D. Alsever, *Glossary for the Establishment and Other Uptight People*, p. 20, December 1970

4 to enter what appears to be a near coma as a result of drug intoxication *US, 1951*

- He was, in the junkies' word, "goofing." — James Mills, *The Panic in Needle Park*, p. 27, 1966
- I was goofing so bad, I couldn't hold my head up and just kept going into my nod. — Piri Thomas, *Down These Mean Streets*, p. 205, 1967

goof around *verb*
to pass time enjoyably but unproductively *US, 1931*

- Dean and I goofed around San Francisco in this manner until I got my next GI check and got ready to go back home. — Jack Kerouac, *On the Road*, p. 177, 1957
- [W]e had time to go over to the drugstore in the shopping center and goof around. — S.E. Hinton, *The Outsiders*, p. 20, 1967
- MEL GIBSON Said he was goofing around all his life anyway, so he thought he might as well get paid for it. — Aubrey Dillon-Malone, *I Was a Fugitive from a Hollywood Trivia Factory*, p. 4, 1999

goofball *noun*
1 a barbiturate used for nonmedicinal purposes *US, 1939*

- [O]f course I can't sleep, I want free goofballs. — Jack Kerouac, *Letter to Neal Cassady*, p. 325, 31st August 1951
- "Don't goof with no goof-balls," Juan remembered Seldom Seen telling him once. "You goof with them and pretty soon you're riding the Horse." — Willard Motley, *Let No Man Write My Epitaph*, p. 87, 1958
- I've got some goofballs and we can get a bottle of cough syrup. — Alexander Trocchi, *Cain's Book*, p. 79, 1960
- He was high on barbiturates, goofballs, GB's. — James Mills, *The Panic in Needle Park*, p. 27, 1966
- "Doc," Wanger said. "Look, Doc, how about a goofball?" — Malcolm Braly, *On the Yard*, p. 59, 1967

2 a central nervous system stimulant *US, 1966*

- "As for my not being in shape, it was The Head who first got me the green goof balls—when I was eighteen—to kill my appetite." — Jacqueline Susann, *Valley of the Dolls*, p. 316, 1966

3 a silly and/or dim-witted person *US, 1944*

- Hey, goofball, are you listening to me? — Robert Gover, *Poorboy at the Party*, p. 91, 1966
- He had pinned his grandiose hope of redemption on his last home-made bomb, only to see it claim the wrong victim, some goofball news reporter. — Carl Hiaasen, *Tourist Season*, p. 294, 1986

goofball *adjective*
quirky, eccentric *US, 1956*

- "Your goofball friends park in front of my place and broadcast their music to the entire neighborhood[.]" — Martha Davis, *The Messages Workbook*, p. 40, 2004

goof butt; goof-butt; goofy butt *noun*
a marijuana cigarette *US, 1938*

- And marijuana has legal standing, so the next time some fifteen-year-old sucks a goof butt and walks through a glass patio slider, me and the other old hippie selling nickel bags are defendants in a gigantic class-action lawsuit[.] — Mike Gray, *Busted*, p. 194, 2002

goofed; goofed up; goofed-up *adjective*
1 wrong *US, 1952*

- Any sound concept of living is goofed-up. — George Mandel, *Flee the Angry Strangers*, p. 3, 1952

2 experiencing the effects of drugs, especially barbiturates or marijuana; drunk *US, 1944*

- I guess I just wanted them for myself to get goofed a little. — Hal Ellson, *Duke*, p. 3, 1949
- [T]hese guys ain't gay, they're goofed up[.] — Lester Bangs, *Psychotic Reactions and Carburetor Dung*, p. 101, 1972

goofer *noun*

1 a central nervous system stimulant *US, 1967*

- Benzedrine (benies, Doriden, goofers). — Elizabeth Finn, *Drugs in the Tenderloin*, p. 4, 1967

2 a barbiturate capsule, especially glutethimide *US, 1969*

- — Walter L. Way, *The Drug Scene: Help or Hang-up?*, p. 109, 1977
- — Richard A. Spears, *The Slang and Jargon of Drugs and Drink*, p. 227, 1986

3 a person who regularly uses drugs in pill form *US, 1952*

- — Eugene Landy, *The Underground Dictionary*, p. 92, 1971

4 a homosexual male prostitute who assumes the active role in sex *US, 1941*

- — *Male Swinger Number 3*, p. 45, 1981: "The complete gay dictionary"

goofer dust *noun*

a barbiturate *US, 1954*

- And that blood was loaded with the goofer dust. — Jim Thompson, *The Nothing Man*, p. 282, 1954

go off *verb*

to ejaculate *UK, 1866*

- One man who wanted to go off using my rear end, when I told him I would not allow this, sneered, "You think it's a perversion, don't you?" — Sara Harris, *The Lords of Hell*, p. 72, 1967

goofies *noun*

LSD *US, 2001*

- — Don R. McCreary (Editor), *Dawg Speak*, 2001

goof-off *noun*

a lazy person *US, 1945*

- Somewhere along the line, the pack decided that Al Gore was a sanctimonious, graspy exaggerator running against a likeable if dim-witted goof-off. — Al Franken, *Lies*, p. 40, 2003

goof off *verb*

to waste time, to idle *US, 1943*

- Spent days with Vicki just "goofing off" and then I came out of it walking two miles in Manhattan. — Jack Kerouac, *Windblown World*, p. 37, 12th December 1947
- Honey, you can sit the next set out in the back yard if you promise not to goof off and get lost. — Steve Allen, *Bop Fables*, p. 4, 1955
- I stay loose. I hit the flicks, goof off a little, quaff a few brews with the boys. — Max Shulman, *Guided Tour of Campus Humor*, p. 105, 1955
- "Yes, I think so," said the dark-haired girl, then added with a frown: "Unless they're goofing off. We've had a lot of goofing off lately—especially among the boys." — Terry Southern, *Candy*, p. 179, 1958
- The doctors said I was a malingerer. I said I only liked regular sex. Then I found out they meant I was goofin' off. Okay. — Edwin Torres, *After Hours*, p. 360, 1979
- You could go down on the corner and pick up on any of those Puerto Rican kids you seen goofing off and they could give you a rundown on that scene that would put me to shame. — Herbert Huncke, *Guilty of Everything*, p. 9, 1990

goof on *verb*

to joke about, to make fun of *US, 1956*

- I first started goofing on Michael Jackson when he started showing up in the tabloids[.] — Howard Stern, *Miss America*, p. 61, 1995

goof-up *noun*

a blunder, an error of judgement *US, 1956*

- I made a goof-up. She took it the wrong way. — Richard Francis, *The Rialto*, p. 96, 1999

goofus *noun*

1 a fool *US, 1917*

- [H]er mother and goofus of a 7th grade brother[.] — Lester Bangs, *Psychotic Reactions and Carburetor Dung*, p. 59, 1971
- Michael Ventura—what a goofus—once wrote: "Our generation will never get old, because we dance." — Richard Meltzer, *A Whore Just Like the Rest*, p. 437, 1992

2 in circus and carnival usage, an extremely gullible customer who demonstrates great potential as a victim *US, 1981*

- — Don Wilmeth, *The Language of American Popular Entertainment*, p. 116, 1981

goofy *adjective*

gawky, clumsy, foolish, eccentric *US, 1919*

- In high school he had planned to be one, but most guys thought that artists were goofy, and he couldn't stand being laughed at as an artist. — James T. Farrell, *Saturday Night*, p. 25, 1947
- I'd like to check around Portland and Hood River and The Dalles to see if there's any of the guys I used to know back in the village who haven't drunk themselves goofy. — Ken Kesey, *One Flew Over the Cuckoo's Nest*, p. 311, 1962
- That's what makes you so goofy, banging her so much. — Jim Thompson, *Pop. 1280*, p. 191, 1964
- There is a seriously goofy man behind this. — *As Good As It Gets*, 1997

-goofy *suffix*

mentally imbalanced as a result of the preceding activity *US, 1969*

- I said, "Blue, what did you mean about Dirty Red going con goofy?" — Iceberg Slim (Robert Beck), *Trick Baby*, p. 125, 1969

goofy grape *noun*

a smoke grenade that emits purple smoke *US, 1989*

- "Smoke out." "Roger that, got goofy grape," replied Bird Dog. — Don Ericson, *Charlie Rangers*, p. 91, 1989
- At which DiGrezio rolled in and dropped a 1.5-pound purple-smoke grenade (a "goofy grape") over the NVA soldier's head from about 700 feet. — Gregory Bayer, *Cessna Warbirds*, p. 98, 1995

googan *noun*

in pool, someone who plays for fun *US, 1990*

- — Steve Rushin, *Pool Cool*, p. 14, 1990

google *verb*

to search for something on the Internet by means of a search engine; to check a person's credentials by investigating websites that contain that person's name *US, 1999*

A generic use of Google™ (a leading Internet search engine).

- For some reason it made me laugh that grown men are discussing frog levitation and if lycos is better than google. I googled and got the frog. — *alt.fifty-plus.friends*, 25th June 1999
- Eggers is owner of probably the most Googled name out there right now. — *Denver Post*, p. L-02, 10th September 2000
- The most popular application is to Google a potential date. — *Telegraph Herald (Dubuqe, Iowa)*, p. E1, 14th January 2001

Google bomb *noun*

an effort to create a great number of Internet pages with links to a specific website so that it achieves a position near the top of a *Google* search directory for seemingly unrelated words *US, 2002*

- Mathes' original Google Bomb remains the classic of the genre. It's pretty funny to see your friend come up in Google as the No. 1 talentless hack in the whole world. — *Slate Magazine*, 23rd March 2002

Google bombing *noun*

the deliberate creation of a great number of Internet pages with links to a specific website with an intent that the website achieves a position near the top of a *Google* search directory for seemingly unrelated words *US, 2002*

Google™ is an Internet search engine.

- BBC News reports of Google bombing (often referred to as "Google juice") by the infamous Crackmonkey subscribers. — *alt.comp.freeware. discussion*, 13th March 2002
- Mathes even invented a name for his joke: Google Bombing. — *Slate Magazine*, 23rd March 2002

googlewhack *verb*

among Internet users, to search for any webpage that, uniquely, contains a combination of two randomly chosen words and is therefore indexed by the by the search-engine *Google* as "1 of 1" *US, 2002*

- Have you Googlewhacked lately? — Janet Kornblum, *USA Today*, 30th January 2002

googobs *noun*

a great quantity *US, 1964*

- I'd been out hustling all day, shining shoes, selling newspapers, and I had googobs of money in my pocket. — Dick Gregory, *Nigger*, p. 32, 1964
- "We talking googobs of money. Scads o' cash." — Paul Beatty, *Tuff*, p. 17, 2000

goo-goo eyes *noun*

romantic glances *US, 1897*

- [T]he oldest of the 8 urchins, a good-looking blonde about 17 or so has discontinued the goo-goo eyes & has gone to the show with boy friend[.] — Neal Cassady, *The First Third*, p. 213, 1965
- Some of the women who came once a week to Connie's Beauty Salon said they gave them googoo eyes[.] — Joe Eszterhas, *Charlie Simpson's Apocalypse*, p. 10, 1973

googs *noun*

in circus and carnival usage, eyeglasses *US, 1924*

A corruption of "goggles."

- — Joe McKennon, *Circus Lingo*, p. 40, 1980
- — Don Wilmeth, *The Language of American Popular Entertainment*, p. 116, 1981

gook *noun*

1 a Vietnamese person; an Asian, especially a Filipino, Japanese, or Korean; any dark-skinned foreigner *US, 1919*

A derogatory term, too all-encompassing to be directly racist but deeply xenophobic. Coined by the US military; the Korean and Vietnam wars gave the word a worldwide familiarity (if not currency). Etymology is uncertain, but many believe "gook" is Korean for "person."

- When arrested for sodomy in Indonesia, Clem said to the examining magistrate: "Tain't as if it was being queer. After all they's only Gooks." — William Burroughs, *Naked Lunch*, p. 158, 1957
- "We've been stomping from one village to the next. Flushing out them gooks." — *The Berkeley Barb*, p. 3, 3rd December 1965
- Kill 'em, kill 'em, strafe those gook creeps! — The Fugs, *Kill for Peace*, 1966
- But he didn't think of it as hurting a person. It was just a gook and they were not people, you know. — John Kerry, *The New Soldier*, p. 60, 1971

2 the Vietnamese language; any Asian language *US, 1981*

- Bozwell was with a dink the night Violet met him and they talked a few words of gook. — Joseph Wambaugh, *The Glitter Dome*, p. 157, 1981

3 an unspecified, unidentified, unpleasant, viscous substance *US, 1942*

Sometimes spelt "guck."

- [T]his kind of gas has a great deal of O-Octane gook in it[.] — Jack Kerouac, *On the Road*, p. 209, 1957
- "How long's this gonna take?" "Until we get all this guck off the top," she said. — Phil Hirsch, *Hooked*, p. 145, 1968
- I never want to be stuck with some hag with gook falling off her face and me taking it. — *Ask*, p. 65, 21st April 1979
- You messed up the wall the last time—all that guck you slicked your hair down with. — Elmore Leonard, *City Primeval*, p. 84, 1980

4 nonsense *US, 1960*

- "I think all that gook is self-evident. I don't think he's been around much." — Glendon Swarthout, *Where the Boys Are*, pp. 150–151, 1960

5 the recreational drug GHB *US, 1996*

- Investigators say GHB is a powerful drug that also goes by the nicknames of Gook, Easy Lay, Gamma 10 and Liquid X. — *The Houston Chronicle*, p. 17, 10th September 1996

gook *adjective*

Vietnamese *US, 1979*

- What's the name of the goddamn village—Vin Drin Drop or Lopu; damn gook names all sound the same. — *Apocalypse Now*, 1979

Gookland *noun*

Asia; Southeast Asia *US, 1921*

- "You oughta write home about this. The Americanization of Gookland." — John M. Del Vecchio, *The 13th Valley*, p. 14, 1982

gook sore *noun*

any skin infection suffered by a US soldier in Vietnam *US, 1989*

- As well, most of the grunts had scars on their legs and arms called "Gook sores." — John Culbertson, *Operation Tuscaloosa*, p. 41, 1997

Gookville *noun*

a neighborhood, hamlet, or city occupied by Vietnamese people *US, 1967*

- You guys just marched right through the middle of Gookville like you was comin down the middle a Main Street. — John M. Del Vecchio, *The 13th Valley*, p. 394, 1982
- [T]hose girls—the short tails of their high-school uniform blouses loose around their hips—remind him of the Viet girls at the hand-

laundry whorehouse at Ham Lom (Gookville, we called it), across the road from fire Base Harriette. — Larry Heinemann, *Paco's Story*, p. 86, 1986

goola *noun*

a piano *US, 1944*

- — Robert S. Gold, *A Jazz Lexicon*, p. 128, 1964

goombah *noun*

a loyal male friend; an Italian-American *US, 1954*

An Italian-American usage, sometimes used in a loosely derogatory tone.

- "I will beat this Giambra," he insists, "and prove Italy still produces fine fighters. It's hard to see how he can be proved wrong. Joey is a goombah, too!" — *Coshocton (Ohio) Tribune*, p. 8, 2nd December 1954
- He was a mean, cruel, brutal heavyweight of a goomba who would just as soon have strangled you as look at you[.] — Emmett Grogan, *Ringolevio*, p. 96, 1972
- Brigante. Where'd you get that name? Goombah? — Edwin Torres, *After Hours*, p. 162, 1979
- [H]e got into a beef with some old goombah down at Benny's Lounge over his video games. — Richard Price, *Clockers*, p. 381, 1992

goon *noun*

1 a unintelligent or slow-witted person *US, 1921*

From Alice the Goon, a character in the comic strip *Thimble Theatre* (1919), via a large and stupid character known as "the goon" in Elzie Segar's comic strip *Popeye the Sailor* (1935–38), which popularized the word. Originally English dialect *gooney* (a simpleton), possibly from Middle English *gonen* (to gape) and Old English *ganian* (to gape, to yawn).

- "I'll clout you again, you goon," Frank drew back his fist, but Black Benny held him — Irving Shulman, *The Amboy Dukes*, p. 49, 1947
- Tightened them, rather, against the multimillion goons who would as soon sell all of liberty down any creek as their own two-big integrity. — Philip Wylie, *Opus 21*, p. 148, 1949
- I mean, that could have been really nice, only the goon that played the Playboy spoiled any fun it might have been. — J.D. Salinger, *Franny and Zooey*, pp. 28–29, 1961
- The goons grab the girl and take off in Sparky's car. — Carl Hiaasen, *Tourist Season*, p. 11, 1986

2 a hired thug *US, 1938*

A broadening of the original sense.

- The goon who drove the car was still running around loose and if I had to go after somebody it'd might as well be him. — Mickey Spillane, *The Big Kill*, p. 29, 1951
- He had told them they were a pair of stupid goons who had got their training in violence on the New York police force and had been "broken" for extortion or sheer witlessness. — Mary McCarthy, *The Group*, p. 137, 1963

3 a C-47A Skytrain plane, also known as a DC-3, most commonly used to transport people and cargo, but also used as a bomber and fighter *US, 1937*

An abbreviation of **GOONEY BIRD**.

- I haven't logged more than twenty hours of piston-engine time in the last four years, and only a little of that was in a Goon. — Walter Boyne and Steven Thompson, *The Wild Blue*, p. 212, 1986
- Half a day of boredom in / A silly, fuckin' goon! — Joseph Tuso, *Singing the Vietnam Blues*, p. 160, 1990: Puff

4 a North Korean soldier *US, 1960*

- — *American Speech*, p. 120, May 1960: "Korean bamboo English"

5 phencyclidine, the recreational drug known as PCP or angel dust *US, 1977*

- — *Drummer*, p. 77, 1977
- — Ronald Linder, *PCP: The Devil's Dust*, p. 9, 1981
- — US Department of Justice, *Street Terms*, October 1994

goonboards; goonieboards *noun*

short, homemade skis *US, 1963*

- — *American Speech*, p. 206, October 1963: "The language of skiers"

goon boy *noun*

a socially inept, unpopular person *US, 1955*

- — *American Speech*, p. 302, December 1955: "Wayne University slang"

goon dust *noun*

phencyclidine, the recreational drug known as PCP or angel dust *US, 2001*

- — *Q Magazine*, p. 75, February 2001

gooned out *adjective*
under the influence of a drug *US, 1968*

- I think he's gooned out most a the time. On ludes or something. — Joseph Wambaugh, *The Delta Star*, p. 17, 1983

gooner *noun*
a North Vietnamese soldier *US, 1969*

- Be advised that you have two groups of gooners approaching your pos, one from the north and one from the west. — B.H. Norton, *Force Recon Diary, 1969*, p. 108, 1991
- "That'll have us coming in from two different directions with less exposure from the gooners." — Bob Stoffey, *Cleared Hot!*, p. 41, 1992
- These men were chopper pilots who had reenlisted for their second or third tours of duty in Vietnam. Their war had been reduced to gooks, dinks, slant-eyes, and gooners. — Ted Bartimus, *Warn Torn*, p. 257, 2002

gooney; goonie *noun*
a communist Chinese soldier; a North Korean soldier *US, 1957*

- People began yelling all sorts of cheerful things: "Get down!" "Goonies!" (Chinese). — Martin Russ, *The Last Parallel*, p. 140, 1957

gooney bird *noun*

1 a C-47A Skytrain plane, also known as a DC-3, most commonly used to transport people and cargo, but also used as a bomber and fighter *US, 1942*

- "To three-point-land a gooney bird you have to pull the yoke back far enough to stall in a nose-high attitude." — Elaine Shepard, *The Doom Pussy*, p. 143, 1967
- She was known affectionately as the "Gooney Bird," "Dak," and "Dizzy Three" to the men who flew her during World War II. — *San Francisco Chronicle*, p. 60, 18th January 1975
- These craft were affectionately known as "Gooney Birds" to the American fighting men, "Dakotas" to the British soldiers, and DC-3s to most civilians. — Ian Padden, *U.S. Air Commando*, p. 6, 1985
- Weather like this makes we wish to hell I'd never told them I could fly Gooney Birds. — Walter Boyne and Steven Thompson, *The Wild Blue*, p. 212, 1986

2 a foolish or dim-witted person *US, 1956*

- That's shroud music, boy, that's goony-bird music. — John Clellon Holmes, *The Horn*, p. 67, 1958
- Strike stayed mute, glancing over at Futon doing the gooney bird. — Richard Price, *Clockers*, p. 13, 1992

goon platoon *noun*
a notional collection of fools *US, 1978*

- You end up with the city bureaucracy looking at them as "goon platoons" and actually tying their hands behind their backs. — Kevin Dockey, *Navy Seals*, p. 39, 2003

goon squad *noun*
a group of prison guards who use force to quash individual or group rebellions *US, 1967*

- [B]ut somebody called out the Goon Squad, who, all 4, look exactly what they're called. — Clarence Cooper Jr., *The Farm*, p. 139, 1967
- In less than a minute the door flew open and three guards entered on the double. "The goon squad," Nunn whispered to Manning. — Malcolm Braly, *On the Yard*, p. 34, 1967
- The Hole was run by the Paso Robles goon squad[.] — James Carr, *Bad*, p. 42, 1975
- I was once carried to the hole in Leavenworth by the security force (goon squad). — Jack Henry Abbott, *In the Belly of the Beast*, pp. 51–52, 1981

goon stand *noun*
in the television and movie industries, a large stand for supporting large equipment or devices *US, 1977*

- — Tony Miller and Patricia George, *Cut! Print!*, p. 83, 1977

goony *adjective*

1 silly, doltish *US, 1939*

- "And, man, oh, man," he clucked suddenly, "am I lushed. I'm goony." — John Clellon Holmes, *The Horn*, p. 55, 1958
- You know, one good thing about having Hovely up there, he's too goony to be scared. — Jim Bouton, *Ball Four*, p. 246, 1970

2 brutish, thuggish *US, 1939*

- "My guess is that you know exactly where i can locate this goony hit man." — Carl Hiaasen, *Skin Tight*, p. 273, 1989

goonyland *noun*
territory controlled by the North Korean Army and/or Chinese troops during the Korean war *US, 1957*

- The words "goonie" and "goonyland" are used exclusively around here. — Martin Russ, *The Last Parallel*, p. 286, 1957

goop *noun*

1 any sticky, viscid, unpleasant substance the exact chemical composition of which is unknown *US, 1918*

- Skink said, "I got some goop if want it. Great stuff." — Carl Hiaasen, *Native Tongue*, p. 155, 1991
- I bet your toxic goop got dumped in T.J. — Joseph Wambaugh, *Finnegan's Week*, p. 144, 1993

2 the chemical jelly used in incendiary bombs *US, 1944*

- — *American Speech*, p. 74, February 1946: "Some words of war and peace from 1945"

3 liquid resin used in surfacing surfboards *US, 1965*

- — John M. Kelly, *Surf and Sea*, p. 286, 1965

4 the recreational drug GHB *US, 1999*

- Gamma-hydroxybutyrate (GBH, Goop), flunitrazepam (Roofies) and ketamine (Special K) are new additions to a long list of substances that have often been encountered in these settings. — *Testimony of Terrance Woodworth to the United States Congress*, 11th March 1999

5 a fool *US, 1915*

- "You goop," said her brother. "That pamphlet was written for slum women; by a Vassar graduate, I bet." — Mary McCarthy, *The Group*, p. 229, 1963

gooper *noun*
lung phlegm *US, 1978*

- Hey, fella, go and spit your goopers in the gutter, not on my property. — Joseph Wambaugh, *The Black Marble*, p. 264, 1978

goop gobbler *noun*
a person who enjoys and/or excels at performing oral sex on men *US, 1981*

- — *Male Swinger Number 3*, p. 45, 1981: "The complete gay dictionary"

goopy *adjective*
syrupy, sentimental *US, 1957*

- There's no way to talk about that without sounding goopy. — Tom Wolfe, *The Electric Kool-Aid Acid Test*, p. 275, 1968

goose *noun*

1 a socially inept, out-of-fashion person *US, 1968*

- — Collin Baker et al., *College Undergraduate Slang Study Conducted at Brown University*, p. 126, 1968

2 in poker, an unskilled player who is a likely victim of a skilled professional *US, 1996*

- — Peter O. Steiner, *Thursday Night Poker*, p. 412, 1996

3 in television and movie-making, the truck carrying the cameras and sound equipment *US, 1990*

- — Ralph S. Singleton, *Filmmaker's Dictionary*, p. 76, 1990

goose *verb*

1 to jab or poke someone, especially between the buttock cheeks *US, 1906*

- Henri Cru and I rushed out with our clubs, gun and flashlights, laughing like hell and goosing each other on the way[.] — Jack Kerouac, *Letter to Neal Cassady*, p. 114, 26th August 1947
- He was always saying, "Try this for size," and then he'd goose the hell out of you while you were going down the corridor. — J.D. Salinger, *Catcher in the Rye*, p. 143, 1951
- And whoops and slaps his leg and gooses Billy with his thumb till I think Billy will fall in a dead faint from blushing and grinning. — Ken Kesey, *One Flew Over the Cuckoo's Nest*, p. 99, 1962

2 by extension, to urge into action; to taunt *US, 1934*

- Goosing the cops is not a practice rich in wisdom for a professional car thief. — George Higgins, *Kennedy for the Defense*, p. 7, 1980
- Keyes goosed his little MG convertible across the causeway and made it to the motel in eighteen minutes flat. — Carl Hiaasen, *Tourist Season*, p. 33, 1986

▸ **goose the ghost**
to hitchhike *US, 1953*

- No money for a train ticket. So I had to hop freights and goose the ghost—we never said "hitchhike." — Robert Byrne, *McGoorty*, p. 122, 1972
- I was traveling on freights or hitchhiking ("goosing the ghost" as Jesse calls it, a bit of slang left over from his days as a Bible salesman). — Robert Coover, *Whatever Happened to Gloomy Gus of the Chicago Bears*, p. 121, 1987

gooseberry ranch *noun*
a rural brothel *US, 1930*

- — Dr. R. Frederick West, *God's Gambler*, p. 226, 1964: "Appendix A"

- You think I'm going to let some goddamned chippie come up here and tell me how to run a gooseberry ranch? — *McCabe and Mrs. Miller*, 1971

goose-drowner; goose-drownder *noun*
a heavy rain *US, 1929*

- That rain started coming down harder than a goose-drowner.
  — Monique Peterson, *Home on the Range*, p. 96, 2004

goose egg *noun*
1 zero; nothing *US, 1866*
Originally baseball slang.

- The 4/23 F.I.s and the snitch feedback are goose-egg. — James Ellroy, *Because the Night*, p. 336, 1984

- The more homicides a prison successfully prosecutes, the sexier a warden's bonuses and prettier his commendations. My string of goose eggs makes me look soft, Mel. — Seth Morgan, *Homeboy*, p. 215, 1990

- A real heavy investigation. Zilch. Goose egg. — *Basic Instinct*, 1992

2 a swollen bump *US, 1953*

- Jesus, that's gonna be a goose egg. Hang on ... I've got some alcohol and Band-Aids in my travel kit. — Armistead Maupin, *Babycakes*, p. 170, 1984

goose-egg *verb*
to leave an opponent scoreless *US, 1892*

- Fowler goose-egged the Cubs in the last of the ninth and got credit for the win. — Bernard Malamud, *The Natural*, p. 142, 1952

goose eye *noun*
in the illegal production of alcohol, a perfect formation of bubbles on the meniscus of the product, indicating 100 proof *US, 1974*

- — David W. Maurer, *Kentucky Moonshine*, p. 119, 1974

goose grease *noun*
KY jelly, a lubricant *US, 1984–1985*

- — *Maledicta*, p. 117, 1984–1985: "Milwaukee medical maledicta"

goose juice *noun*
powerful sedative medication given to mental patients *US, 1986*

- Besides, I can sell that goose juice on the street, make a few bucks and serve law and order by keeping the Negro element sedated.
  — James Ellroy, *Suicide Hill*, p. 584, 1986

goosey *adjective*
jumpy, wary, nervous *US, 1906*

- I have to pay Dawn. She called, she's getting goosey. — Elmore Leonard, *Riding the Rap*, p. 206, 1996

go-out *noun*
a surfing session *US, 1988*

- — Surf Punks, *Oh No! Not Them Again!*, 1988

go out *verb*
to suffer a relapse while participating in a twelve-step recovery program such as Alcoholics Anonymous *US, 1998*

- — Christopher Cavanaugh, *AA to Z*, p. 101, 1998

gopher *noun*
1 a person who is easily swindled, who "goes for" the pitch *US, 1959*

- — *American Speech*, pp. 150–151, May 1959: "Notes on the cant of the telephone confidence man"

2 a poker player who plays with a high degree of optimism *US, 1996*
So named because of the player's willingness to "go for" a draw in almost any situation.

- — John Vorhaus, *The Big Book of Poker Slang*, p. 20, 1996

3 a criminal who tunnels into a business to rob it *US, 1928*

- — Vincent J. Monteleone, *Criminal Slang*, p. 105, 1949

go-pill *noun*
any amphetamine or other central nervous system stimulant *US, 1957*

- I gave her two "go" pills and took her to the street for the cut into Phyllis and Ophelia. — Iceberg Slim (Robert Beck), *Pimp*, p. 213, 1969

gorge *noun*
in circus and carnival usage, food *US, 1981*

- — Don Wilmeth, *The Language of American Popular Entertainment*, p. 116, 1981

gorilla *noun*
1 a criminal who relies on brute strength and force *US, 1861*

- People started saying that he was a gorilla, that he was going around shaking down people, shaking down numbers controllers and cats who were dealing drugs. — Claude Brown, *Manchild in the Promised Land*, p. 213, 1965

- She had been working six days a week for a month, turning more than half a dozen tricks a night, and had never once pulled a cop, a gorilla, or a freak. — Alix Shulman, *On the Stroll*, p. 144, 1981

- "Hey, dickhead," she screamed. "Tell your bitch-ass gorilla to get off him." — John Ridley, *Love is a Racket*, p. 225, 1998

2 a prisoner who obtains what he wants by force *US, 1958*

- In the argot of the inmates, an individual who takes what he wants from others by force is known as a gorilla. — Gresham M. Sykes, *The Society of Captives*, p. 91, 1958

3 a beating *US, 1971*

- Some pimps regard a "gorilla" (beating) as the best way to demonstrate love, and there are prostitutes who share such views. — Charles Winick, *The Lively Commerce*, p. 118, 1971

4 in the entertainment industry, a technical member of a movie crew *US, 1970*

- It is classic Hollywood protocol that the actors be quartered separately from the technicians ("apes" or "gorillas,") as they are affectionately called[.] — Terry Southern, *Blue Movie*, p. 66, 1970

5 in the music industry, a very popular bestselling song *US, 1982*

- — Arnold Shaw, *Dictionary of American Pop/Rock*, p. 143, 1982

gorilla *verb*
to manhandle, to beat *US, 1922*

- "Daddy, what happens now. Maybe 'Poison' will come back and gorilla me." — Iceberg Slim (Robert Beck), *Pimp*, p. 239, 1969

- "And after I turns the trick and the john's split, Kingfish comes in my room and tries to gorilla me." — Robert Deane Pharr, *S.R.O.*, p. 89, 1971

- I'd travel for blocks to duke with a cat that would try to gorilla a friend. — Edwin Torres, *Carlito's Way*, p. 14, 1975

gorilla *adjective*
thuggish, brute *US, 1972*

- "I don't like to be gorilla an' rough it off—but then, I do a lotta things I don't like, anyway." — Nathan Heard, *To Reach a Dream*, p. 32, 1972

gorilla biscuit *noun*
any strong central nervous system depressant or stimulant *US, 1972*

- [E]verybody was walking on their knuckles from marching powder, whiskey, and gorilla biscuits. — Kinky Friedman, *Blast from the Past*, p. 236, 1998

gorilla dust *noun*
intimidating bluffing *US, 1986*

- Perot called other issues brought up by GM "gorilla dust," referring to the way gorillas throw dust at their opponents to distract them during a fight. — Associated Press, 8th December 1986

- He said his competitors were creating "gorilla dust." — *The State (Columbia, South Carolina)*, p. A1, 21st May 2004

gorilla grip *noun*
a tight grip *US, 2005*

- Verbal killas, gorilla grip. — RZA, *The Wu-Tang Manual*, p. 170, 2005

gorilla-grip *verb*
in skateboarding, to jump holding the ends of the board with the toes *US, 1976*

- — Laura Torbet, *The Complete Book of Skateboarding*, p. 105, 1976

gorilla pill *noun*
a barbiturate capsule or other central nervous system depressant *US, 1969*

- — Richard Lingeman, *Drugs from A to Z*, p. 86, 1969

gorilla pimp *noun*
a brutish pimp who relies heavily on violence to control the prostitutes who work for him *US, 1972*

- One who uses brutality and threats is a gorilla pimp or hard Mack.
  — Christina and Richard Milner, *Black Players*, p. 35, 1972

- The Red Velvet Turtle was the 430 Club without sawdust on the floor, Pitts Pub, without the "Brutality Booth" where the gorilla pimps used to go and slug their women in the chops. — Odie Hawkins, *Men Friends*, p. 108, 1989

gorilla salad *noun*

thick pubic hair *US, 1981*
- — *Male Swinger Number 3*, p. 45, 1981: "The complete gay dictionary"

gork *noun*

1 a patient with severe mental deficiencies *US, 1964*
- — *Maledicta*, p. 68, Summer/Winter 1978: "Common patient-directed pejoratives used by medical personnel"
- gork: a slang expression for a patient who is brain-dead. — Lynda Van Devanter, *Home Before Morning*, p. 379, 1983: Glossary

2 a fool; a contemptible person *US, 1970*
- Of course they were staring at me. I'm a six foot-five gork. — Howard Stern, *Miss America*, p. 101, 1995
- The stupid gork was huddled there, wet and miserable, sticking out his thumb. — Chris Miller, *The Real Animal House*, p. 161, 2006

gorked *adjective*

stupefied from anesthetic *US, 1973*
- — *American Speech*, p. 205, Fall-Winter 1973: "The language of nursing"

gorm *verb*

to bungle; to act awkwardly *US, 1975*
- — John Gould, *Maine Lingo*, p. 114, 1975

gorp *noun*

1 a complete social outcast *US, 1976*
- — *Verbatim*, p. 280, May 1976

2 a snack of nuts and dried fruit favored by hikers *US, 1991*
From "*good old raisins and peanuts.*"
- — Eric S. Raymond, *The New Hacker's Dictionary*, p. 182, 1991

go-see *noun*

in modeling, an visual "interview" *US, 1969*
- The really big ones will invite you to their studios for an interview (in modeling jargon such an appointment is euphemistically known as a "go-see"). — *Screw*, p. 11, 15 December 1969

gosh darned *adjective*

used as an intentionally folksy, mock-profane intensifier *US, 1906*
- "No pillow fighting in the Green Room, you'll break the gosh-darned antiques!" — P.J. O'Rourke, *Parliament of Whores*, p. 42, 2003

gospel bird *noun*

chicken *US, 1935*
From the custom of eating chicken on Sundays.
- Too much praise of one sister's cooking tells the congregation that the preacher is availing himself of more than her gospel bird. — John T. Edge, *Fried Chicken*, p. 106, 2004

gotcha *noun*

in computing, a misfeature that generates mistakes *US, 1991*
- — Eric S. Raymond, *The New Hacker's Dictionary*, p. 183, 1991

Gotham *noun*

New York City *US, 1807*
Alluding to a mythical village inhabited by wise fools.
- Gotham chicks are different, according to Jenni Dean, the definitive New York girl of rock. — John Burks, *Groupies and Other Girls*, p. 82, 1970
- I hadn't believed we would leave Gotham, even after the New Jersey stadium was under construction. — Dan Jenkins, *Life Its Ownself*, p. 17, 1984

got it!

used for urging another surfer not to catch this wave, which you claim as yours *US, 1991*
- — Trevor Cralle, *The Surfin'ary*, p. 46, 1991

go-to-godamn *adjective*

damned *US, 1961*
- I'll be go-to-goddam if a police car didn't draw up next to me near 66th Street. — Clancy Sigal, *Going Away*, p. 435, 1961

Go to Hell *nickname*

Go Dau Ha, home to a US Naval Advanced Base from 1969 to 71, close to the Cambodian border on the Vam Co Dong River, South Vietnam *US, 1990*

- The road continued through Go Dau Ha, which everyone, of course, referred to as "Go to Hell." — Dennis Marvicsin and Jerold Greenfield, *Maverick*, p. 225, 1990

go-to-hell cap; go-to-hell hat *noun*

a jungle hat *US, 1966*
- The go-to-hell hats are centered on the head, with precisely the width of two fingers between the forward peak and the eyebrows. — Daniel Da Cruz, *Boot*, p. 154, 1987
- Combat troops sported berets and boonie hats, go-to-hell caps and Kevlar helmets. — Rick Atkinson, *In the Company of Soldiers*, p. 33, 2004

go-to-hell rag *noun*

a neckerchief worn by an infantry soldier *US, 1988*
- A field dressing covered the man's calf and someone's go-to-hell rag served as his blindfold. — Eric Helm, *Moon Cusser*, p. 108, 1988

Gotrocks *noun*

used as the name of a notional rich person *US, 1938*
- [E]ven though they were never exactly what her mother called "the Gotrocks family," they made out. — Stephen King, *Nightmares & Dreamscapes*, p. 326, 1993

got you covered!

I understand! *US, 1955*
- — *American Speech*, p. 303, December 1955: "Wayne University slang"

gouge *verb*

to surf expertly and stylishly *US, 1990*
Applied to a ride on a wave.
- — *Surfing*, p. 43, 14th March 1990

goulash *noun*

an illegal cardroom that is open 24 hours a day *US, 1974*
- To give himself something to do, he had roused himself, at last, to invest in one of the local Goulashes, Goulash being a generic term for the round-the-clock, never-closing card houses that had been springing up around New York[.] — Edward Lin, *Big Julie of Vegas*, pp. 12–13, 1974

go up *verb*

1 to be sentenced to prison; to be sent to prison *US, 1872*
- One that went up for murder—he was an Army Sergeant. — *Apocalypse Now*, 1979
- Louis was letting it become "we" to get next to Bobby and know what he was thinking, and because they were both in the life and had done state time, Bobby for shooting a man Bobby said pulled a gun on him instead of paying what he owed and went up on a manslaughter plea deal. — Elmore Leonard, *Riding the Rap*, p. 54, 1995

2 while acting, to miss your cue or forget a line *US, 1973*
- — Sherman Louis Sergel, *The Language of Show Biz*, p. 107, 1973
- — Don Wilmeth, *The Language of American Popular Entertainment*, p. 115, 1981

gourd *noun*

the head *UK, 1829*
- "Sure," said Sid, "nothing that a kick in the gourd won't fix," and he raised his foot to deliver a simulated stomp on the face of the fallen Rex. — Terry Southern, *Blue Movie*, p. 35, 1970

▸ **out of your gourd**

1 extremely drug-intoxicated *US, 1967*
- He'd come in his mohair suit and his attache case, trying to play electronics executive, but he'd be stoned outa his gourd. — Nicholas Von Hoffman, *We Are The People Our Parents Warned Us Against*, p. 157, 1967
- And he was stoned out of his fucking gourd! — James Ellroy, *White Jazz*, p. 177, 1992

2 crazy *US, 1963*
- Chester! Are you outta your fuckin' gourd! You think we're gonna bite ourselves in the ass? — Odie Hawkins, *Lost Angeles*, p. 63, 1994

gourdhead *noun*

a dolt *US, 1949*
- "Okay, gourd-head. Get that cotton-picking butt off the ground and give us a hand." — Audie Murphy, *To Hell and Back*, p. 47, 1949

gourmet ghetto *noun*

north Berkeley, California; any neighborhood featuring speciality food shops and gourmet restaurants *US, 1983*
Originally applied to a two-block stretch of Shattuck Avenue between Cedar Street and Rose Street in Berkeley.

- The geographic focus of the new sensibility is a broad, sunny section of Shattuck Avenue dubbed "the gourmet ghetto." At its center, guarded only by a modest redwood fence and a narrow, shaded courtyard, is Chez Panisse[.] — *Newsweek*, p. 42, 22nd August 1983
- And I also destroyed half of Berkeley's gourmet ghetto. — C.D. Payne, *Youth in Revolt*, p. 158, 1993
- [Y]ou'll find everything from Marczyk's burger blowouts to happy hour specials at restaurants and coffeehouses up and down what Marczyk calls Denver's "gourmet ghetto." — *Denver Westword*, 31st July 2003

govern *verb*
to play the active role in sex, sadomasochistic or not *US, 1985*
- — *American Speech*, p. 19, Spring 1985: "The language of singles bars"

government-inspected meat *noun*
a soldier as the object of a homosexual's sexual desire *US, 1970*
- — Clarence Major, *Dictionary of Afro-American Slang*, p. 61, 1970
- — *Male Swinger Number 3*, p. 45, 1981: "The complete gay dictionary"

government job *noun*
poor craftsmanship *US, 1965*
- — Robert O. Bowen, *An Alaskan Dictionary*, p. 16, 1965

Governor Green *noun*
freedom (from prison) *US, 1952*
- I give you a picture of the hospital layout so that you'll thoroughly understand what I had to contend with and what I had to do before I reached what the Southerners called "Governor Green" (liberty). — Charles Hamilton, *Men of the Underworld*, p. 267, 1952

gow *noun*
1 a drug, especially opium *US, 1922*
- [W]hite women learned where they could get a "belt," a "jolt," or a "gow." — Jack Lait and Lee Mortimer, *New York Confidential*, pp. 103–104, 1948
2 sauce *US, 1967*
- [I]t was some of that gow you smear all over our good state food. — Malcolm Braly, *On the Yard*, p. 221, 1967

gowhead *noun*
a drug addict *US, 1988*
- Juicemen are too smart to lend money to people with habits like booze and skag, though sometimes an alkie or a gow-head in a three-piece suit puts one over on them. — Robert Campbell, *Juice*, p. 21, 1988

gowster *noun*
a drug addict or heavy drug user *US, 1936*
- Reefer-smokers are called "gowsters." — Jack Lait and Lee Mortimer, *New York Confidential*, p. 104, 1948
- "This pretty 'gowster' is sure pimping his ass off," I thought. — Iceberg Slim (Robert Beck), *Pimp*, p. 129, 1969
- Listening to the developing roar of the crowd as the horses headed into the stretch, and the old gowster's tall, sad story of what the old days used to be like was exciting, disturbing, interesting. — Odie Hawkins, *Chicago Hustle*, p. 151, 1977

goy *noun*
a Gentile *UK, 1841*
Yiddish.
- He worships me because I'm a goy. — Mary McCarthy, *The Group*, p. 344, 1963
- I like to talk Yiddish in front of him, especially if there are goy cops in hearing distance. — Abbie Hoffman, *Revolution for the Hell of It*, p. 18, 1968
- He drank—of course, not whiskey like a goy, but mineral oil and milk of magnesia[.] — Philip Roth, *Portnoy's Complaint*, p. 3, 1969
- If a goy told it, you'd get all bent out of shape — Rita Ciresi, *Pink Slip*, p. 191, 1999

goyish; goyische *adjective*
Gentile *US, 1965*
- It doesn't matter even if you're Catholic; if you live in New York you're Jewish. If you live in Butte, Montana, you're going to be goyish even if you're Jewish. — Lenny Bruce, *How to Talk Dirty and Influence People*, p. 5, 1965
- [E]very spring they sent him and my mother for a hotsy-totsy free weekend in Atlantic City, to a fancy goyische hotel no less. — Philip Roth, *Portnoy's Complaint*, p. 5, 1969

- The carol playing in the background, "Rudolph the Red-Nosed Reindeer," seemed loud and ridiculous, and I listened to it—and resented the way he made me hear it—through Strauss's ears, as tacky and goyish. — Rita Ciresi, *Pink Slip*, p. 328, 1999

GP *noun*
a general principle *US, 1944*
- Sometimes they would stop you on just G-P, or give you a bullshit ticket just so they could try and tear up your car on the pretext of searching for drugs. — Donald Goines, *Whoreson*, p. 211, 1972

G-pack *noun*
one thousand dollars worth of a drug *US, 1997*
- A G-pack of a hundred coke vials, sold on consignment, can make you one thousand dollars. — David Simon and Edward Burns, *The Corner*, p. 67, 1997
- Sincere would give me half a G-pack—five hundred dollars' worth of crack, or fifty vials as opposed to a hundred[.] — 50 Cent, *From Pieces to Weight*, p. 34, 2005

grab *noun*
a person who has been arrested *US, 1992*
- Strike sat tight, just watched as Crunch stepped out and escorted his grab to the rear of the Fury. — Richard Price, *Clockers*, p. 9, 1992

grab *verb*
1 to impress *US, 1970*
- — William D. Alsever, *Glossary for the Establishment and Other Uptight People*, p. 13, December 1970
2 in horse racing, to win a race with a long shot *US, 1951*
- — David W. Maurer, *Argot of the Racetrack*, p. 33, 1951

▸ **grab a dab**
to engage in male-on-male rape *US, 1990*
- — Charles Shafer, *Folk Speech in Texas Prisons*, p. 205, 1990

graba *noun*
dried khat, a psychoactive shrub or small tree *US, 2005*
- These are the first submissions of khat seen by the laboratory in eight years, and the first ever submission of dried khat ("graba"). — *Microgram Bulletin (DEA)*, p. 46, March 2005

grab and go *noun*
attending multiple colleges in search of a degree *US, 2006*
- Officials call it swirling, mix and match, grab and go. Today's students attend two colleges, three colleges, even four. — *New York Times*, p. A1, 22nd April 2006

grab-ass *noun*
horseplay *US, 1947*
- That don't mean you should play grab-ass for five days before showing up at Portsmouth. — Darryl Ponicsan, *The Last Detail*, p. 21, 1970
- He quit all grabass in the barracks, pursued his job and studied with new purpose[.] — Earl Thompson, *Tattoo*, p. 651, 1974
- When the pace of the action was broken by periods like this, we sometimes compensated by indulging in what the army called "grab-ass." — Robert Mason, *Chickenhawk*, p. 289, 1983
- "You know what the son of a bitch did? He started playing grab-ass with me out there." — Glenn Savan, *White Palace*, p. 159, 1987

grab-ass *verb*
to engage in physical horseplay *US, 1953*
- Shoving and grab-assing with each other, and braying like a bunch of mules. — Jim Thompson, *Savage Night*, p. 75, 1953
- Jerry and the girl were dancing and making nice, sort of grabassing each other, when her husband walked up[.] — Juan Carmel Cosmes, *Memoir of a Whoremonger*, p. 64, 1969
- They'll fuck around and fart around and grab-ass around, and jack that thing up so's it'll be some horse's ass of a hero's statue. — Larry Heinemann, *Paco's Story*, p. 157, 1986

grab bag *noun*
1 a pooled mix of different types of pills contributed by several people and then consumed randomly *US, 1970*
- — William D. Alsever, *Glossary for the Establishment and Other Uptight People*, p. 12, December 1970
2 the theft of a suitcase or briefcase accomplished by placing a look-alike bag near the bag to be stolen and then picking up and leaving with the bag to be stolen; the suitcase or briefcase stolen in such a theft *US, 1977*
- He looked at the grab bag closely. Nice grained leather, expensive make. — Odie Hawkins, *Chicago Hustle*, p. 28, 1977

- Elijah sometimes felt like the only man in the world when he did the grab bag ... because it was as though everyone knew what he was doing... — Odie Hawkins, *Chicago Hustle*, p. 27, 1977

grabber *noun*

1 the hand *UK, 1859*

- She held those chopsticks in her grabbers with her arms raised in front of her. — Mezz Mezzrow, *Really the Blues*, p. 102, 1946

2 a surfer who ignores surfing etiquette and catches rides on waves "owned" by other surfers *US, 1991*

- — Trevor Cralle, *The Surfin'ary*, p. 46, 1991

3 a story that captures the imagination *US, 1966*

- Read it. It's a grabber. — *Get Shorty*, 1995

4 a shame; a pity *US, 1977*

- — William J. Bradley, *CB Fact Book and Language Dictionary*, p. 16, 1977

grab joint *noun*

an eating concession in a circus or carnival *US, 1904*

- "Grab joints," or food stands, were scattered along the breadth of the midway. — Peter Fenton, *Eyeing the Flash*, p. 131, 2005

grad *noun*

1 an ex-convict *US, 1950*

- — Hyman E. Goldin et al., *Dictionary of American Underworld Lingo*, p. 86, 1950

2 a *grad*uate *US, 1871*

- Sweet dreams, all you flophouse grads. — Mezz Mezzrow, *Really the Blues*, p. 317, 1946

grade-grubber *noun*

a student whose only goal is to get good grades *US, 1966*

- — John D. Bell et al., *Loosely Speaking*, p. 9, 1966
- He'll be the better citizen than the selfish grade grubber of a kid who just coasts through. — Theodore Sizer, *Horace's Compromise*, p. 53, 1984

graduate *noun*

an ex-convict *US, 1949*

- — Vincent J. Monteleone, *Criminal Slang*, p. 106, 1949

graduate *verb*

1 to complete a prison sentence *US, 1945*
A construction built on the jocular "college" as "jail."

- — Lou Shelly, *Hepcats Jive Dictionary*, p. 12, 1945

2 to be cured of a sexually transmitted infection *US, 1949*

- — *American Speech*, p. 31, February 1949: "A.V.G. lingo"

3 (used of a racehorse) to win a race for the first time *US, 1976*

- — Tom Ainslie, *Ainslie's Complete Guide to Thoroughbred Racing*, p. 332, 1976

grad wrecks *noun*

the Graduate Records Examinations *US, 1966*
The standardized testing given to undergraduate students seeking admission to graduate school in the US.

- — John D. Bell et al., *Loosely Speaking*, p. 10, 1966

graf *noun*

1 graffiti *US, 1991*

- My old company had a long-standing BBS called "graf" (short for "graffiti"). — *comp.risks*, 9th June 1991
- Graf is switching because of the suburbs. — William Upski Wimsatt, *Bomb the Suburbs*, p. 137, 1994
- Suroc had a lot of great ideas about the directions graff could go, but before he could go far on that train of thought, he caught an 11,000 volt bad one on the tracks. — Stephen Power, *The Art of Getting Over*, p. 39, 1999
- To distance themselves from rap's negative perceptions, those involved in the underground scene promote its four elements: MC-ing, DJ-ing (what DJ's do), graf (graffiti) art and break dancing. — *Orange County (California) Register*, p. F7, 24th March 2000

2 a paragraph *US, 1970*

- Before I tack on a final graf or so, I want to go back and read over what I've said. — Hunters S. Thompson, *Fear and Loathing in America*, p. 268, 13th January 1970: Letter to Jim Silberman
- Never mind that, just read the last three grafs. — Carl Hiaasen, *Native Tongue*, p. 41, 1991

graffer *noun*

a graffiti artist who produces complete works, not just a stylized signature *US, 1993*

- — Jim Crotty, *How to Talk American*, p. 141, 1997

graf squad *noun*

a police anti-graffiti unit *US, 1994*

- I was running desperately through an El station, pursued by Lt. Arnold Schwarzenegger, the newest member of the Chicago graf squad. — William Upski Wimsatt, *Bomb the Suburbs*, p. 48, 1994

grafter *noun*

a thief, a crook, a swindler *US, 1866*

- But petty hick grafters like Chester Miller, who extended his hand and called out his named to David, could never be dangerous[.] — Irving Shulman, *The Short End of the Stick*, p. 25, 1959

graf-write *verb*

to write or draw in the style of graffiti *US, 2000*

- "Underground Vandal" puts Freestyle up front in a song that finds him representing the best underground rappers by graf-writing their names on walls throughout New York City. — *Denver Westword*, 20th April 2000

grain *noun*

a heavy drinker *US, 1963*

- — *American Speech*, p. 276, December 1963: "American Indian student slang"

grain and drain train *noun*

solitary confinement *US, 1982*

- Twenty days on the grain and drain train for Andy down there in solitary. — Stephen King, *Different Seasons*, p. 66, 1982

grand *noun*

a unit of 1,000, usually applied to dollars *US, 1915*

- A fin [five dollars] for a number-five cap. A sixteenth [of an ounce] for a "C" [one hundred dollars]. A piece [ounce] for a grand. — Iceberg Slim (Robert Beck), *Pimp*, p. 128, 1969
- A.J.: How much? Lucas: Nine grand! — *Empire Records*, 1985

grand bag *noun*

in homosexual usage, a large scrotum *US, 1981*

- — *Male Swinger Number 3*, p. 45, 1981: "The complete gay dictionary"

grand canyon *noun*

in homosexual usage, a loose anus and rectum *US, 1981*

- — *Male Swinger Number 3*, p. 45, 1981: "The complete gay dictionary"

grand duchess *noun*

a heterosexual woman who enjoys the company of homosexual men *US, 1970*

- — *American Speech*, p. 57, Spring–Summer 1970: "Homosexual slang"

grandma *noun*

1 the lowest gear in a truck, or car *US, 1941*
The lowest gear is the slowest gear, hence the reference to grandmother.

- — Mary Elting, *Trucks at Work*, 1946
- Put it where Grandpa put it: in Grandma. — Ken Weaver, *Texas Crude*, p. 9, 1984

2 an older homosexual man *US, 1964*

- — Roger Blake, *The American Dictionary of Sexual Terms*, p. 91, 1964

grandma's peepers *noun*

in dominoes, the 1–1 piece *US, 1959*

- — Dominic Armanino, *Dominoes*, p. 17, 1959

grandpappy *noun*

grandfather *US, 1952*

- We even had a couple of grandpappys drawing pensions from the Spanish American War. — Chester Himes, *Cast the First Stone*, p. 183, 1952

grandstand *verb*

to perform in a flashy manner, with an eye towards audience perception rather than the level of performance *US, 1900*

- He had made us learn strategy all over again, made us promise to lay off the grandstanding. — Dick Gregory, *Nigger*, p. 70, 1964
- Why didn't you call in for backup instead of makin' a grandstand play. — *48 Hours*, 1982
- BLEEK: Shadow, when are you gonna stop grandstanding? SHADOW: The people eat it up. — *Mo' Better Blues*, 1990

grannies *noun*

the bleed period of the menstrual cycle *US, 1929*

- I've got the grannies. — Karen Houppert, *The Curse*, 1999

granny noun

1 the bleed period of the menstrual cycle US, 1929

- [A] funny term my grandmother (who is 73) uses. She calls menstruation "granny," and it was used by the women in her family. — a contributor, *The Museum of Menstruation and Women's Health*, August 2001

2 a bungled knot; anything that has been bungled US, 1975

- — John Gould, *Maine Lingo*, p. 115, 1975

granny-dodger noun

1 a rapist whose victims are older women US, 1976

- Daniel was a multiple rapist, and though he was in his early thirties, his victims were all over fifty. We had all heard of granny dodgers, they were large in our folklore, but there were seldom really encountered. — Malcolm Braley, *False Starts*, p. 236, 1976

2 a despicable person US, 1969

- Certainly, alternative, made-for-TV dialogue which substituted "granny-dodger" for "motherfucker" was far more conducive to bringing about a meeting of the minds than some of his earlier outbursts. — William Van Deburg, *Black Camelot*, p. 172, 1997

granny-grunt noun

a fussy, fastidious person US, 1968

- When speaking in his Granny Grunt voice, Richie would hobble around with one fist against the small of his back[.] — Stephen King, *It*, p. 304, 1998

granny's here for a visit

experiencing the bleed period of the menstrual cycle US, 1968

- — Collin Baker et al., *College Undergraduate Slang Study Conducted at Brown University*, p. 129, 1968

granola; granola-eater noun

a throw-back to the hippie counterculture of the 1960s US, 1982

- — Connie Eble (Editor), *UNC-CH Campus Slang*, p. 3, Fall 1982
- Thick with granola-eaters, Sonoma State was about as far from inner-city San Francisco as a young man could get in California[.] — Bob Sipchen, *Baby Insane and the Buddha*, p. 349, 1993
- Kia (T. Wendy McMillan) sets her up with geeky granola-type Ely (V.S. Brodie). — *Vogue*, p. 91, June 1994
- Welcome to Padua High School, your typical urban-suburban high school in Portland, Oregon. Smarties, Skids, Preppies, Granolas, Loners, Lovers, the In and the Out Crowd rub sleep out of their eyes and head for the main building. — *Ten Things I Hate About You*, 1999

Grant noun

a fifty-dollar bill US, 1961

From the engraving of Ulysses S. Grant, a distinguished general and less-than-distinguished president, on the bill.

- With shaking fingers she showed Bernie two new crisp fifty-dollar bills tucked into the lining of her glove. New bills always seemed to have such a lovely pale green color, apple-green. "Real U.S. Grants, baby," she told him[.] — Ross Russell, *The Sound*, p. 181, 1961
- "I see you again," Slick had told her, "it better be behind a pile of dead Presidents. Take a load of Jacksons and Grants get you off my shit list, girl." — John Sayles, *Union Dues*, p. 181, 1977
- There were twenty fifty-dollar bills. Nice new crisp U.S. Grants. — James Ellroy, *Brown's Requiem*, p. 42, 1981

grape noun

1 wine US, 1898

Often used in the plural.

- I don't conk out on grape! — Dan Burley, *Diggeth Thou?*, p. 34, 1959
- I ordered one of those Hawaiian punch drinks—sans grape, natch. — Frederick Kohner, *Gidget Goes Hawaiian*, p. 35, 1961
- He was just a Deep South chump driven to the grape by the confusion and disappointment of a big city. — Iceberg Slim (Robert Beck), *Trick Baby*, p. 42, 1969
- The wine bottle, the reefer, or Jesus. A taste of grape, the weed or the cross. — H. Rap Brown, *Die Nigger Die!*, p. 17, 1969

2 gossip US, 1864

A shortening of **GRAPEVINE** (the source of gossip).

- — Don R. McCreary (Editor), *Dawg Speak*, 2001

3 a member of a flight deck refueling crew US, 1986

- The "grapes," the purple-shirted members of a refueling crew, hauled out a heavy hose from the catwalk alongside the flight deck[.] — Gerry Carroll, *North S*A*R*, p. 170, 1991
- — *Seattle Times*, p. A9, 12th April 1998: "Grunts, squids not grunting from the same dictionary"

grapefruits noun

large female breasts US, 1964

- — Roger Blake, *The American Dictionary of Sexual Terms*, p. 91, 1964
- — Dale Gordon, *The Dominion Sex Dictionary*, p. 79, 1967

grapes noun

1 the testicles US, 1985

- Tried to kick him in the grapes, at least. Not sure if I connected. — George V. Higgins, *Penance for Jerry Kennedy*, p. 227, 1985

2 the female breasts US, 1980

- — Edith A. Folb, *runnin' down some lines*, p. 240, 1980

3 a percent sign (%) on a computer keyboard US, 1991

- — Eric S. Raymond, *The New Hacker's Dictionary*, p. 39, 1991

grapes of wrath noun

wine US, 1947

- — Marcus Hanna Boulware, *Jive and Slang of Students in Negro Colleges*, 1947

grapevine noun

a network of rumor or gossip; the mysterious source of rumors US, 1862

- Word buzzed through the grapevine about the new "fish"[.] — Mezz Mezzrow, *Really the Blues*, p. 10, 1946
- How should I know? The grapevine don't come from one guy. — Mickey Spillane, *My Gun is Quick*, p. 38, 1950
- She realizes it wasn't grapevine magic that tipped Baptiste to her mother's visit. — Iceberg Slim (Robert Beck), *Doom Fox*, p. 99, 1978

grappler noun

a wrestler US, 1949

More of a fan word than an insider's word, but heard.

- If he was to be considered the best grappler ever, he would have to join the WWF and beat the likes of the Ultimate Warrior and Hulk Hogan. — *Herb's Wrestling Tidbits*, 12th July 1990
- Today the wrestling faithful don't care if they get a "Hell, yeah!" or the middle finger from Stone Cold, as long as the badass grappler gives them some kind of response. — Robert Picarello, *Rules of the Ring*, p. xii, 2000

grass noun

1 marijuana US, 1943

The term of choice during the 1960s and 70s.

- Don't nobody come up thataway when he picks up on some good grass. — Mezz Mezzrow, *Really the Blues*, p. 213, 1946
- "Movement," Solly said, "how's about stashing a couple ounces for me? This new grass doublebanks me." — Bernard Wolfe, *The Late Risers*, p. 84, 1954
- WYATT: No, man—this is grass. GEORGE: You—you mean marijuana? WYATT: Yeah. — Peter Fonda, *Easy Rider*, p. 121, 1969
- Grass gets you through times of no money better than money gets you through times of no grass. — Stephen Gaskin, *Amazing Dope Tails*, p. 90, 1980

2 a woman's pubic hair US, 1964

- — Roger Blake, *The American Dictionary of Sexual Terms*, p. 91, 1964
- — *Maledicta*, p. 131, Summer/Winter 1982: "Dyke diction: the language of lesbians"

grassback noun

a promiscuous girl US, 1969

- — *Current Slang*, p. 7, Winter 1969

grasshead noun

a habitual marijuana smoker US, 1958

- Laughing like a grasshead now, she made another determined lunge and this time successfully caught her hands around the wheel, forcing Tony to swerve into the rod on their right. — Morton Cooper, *High School Confidential*, p. 89, 1958
- It seemed Proppo was one of the first big grass heads in New York[.] — Gary Mayer, *Bookie*, p. 65, 1974

grasshopper noun

a helicopter US, 1987

- No fucking around and packing. Just get your ass on the grasshoppers and go. — Ernest Spencer, *Welcome to Vietnam, Macho Man*, p. 210, 1987

grasstop noun

an influential community leader US, 1992

An allusion to grass-roots politics.

- A better way to influence legislation is what we call the "grassTOPS" approach—mobilizing influential leaders in each community[.] — *Public Relations Quarterly*, p. 24, 22nd December 1992

- CoMPASS is tasked with raising between 15 and 20 million for the grass roots and grasstops part of the reform effort. — *Washington Post*, p. A15, 28th February 2005

grave *noun*

a work shift at night, usually starting at or after midnight *US, 1980*

An abbreviation of **GRAVEYARD SHIFT**.
- — Lee Solkey, *Dummy Up and Deal*, p. 114, 1980

gravedigger *noun*

in circus usage, a hyena *US, 1981*
- — Don Wilmeth, *The Language of American Popular Entertainment*, p. 56, 1981

gravel *noun*

1 an air-delivered mine introduced by the US in Vietnam *US, 1980* Formally known as an XM42 mine dispensing system.
- Gravel was a little Marquis de Sade touch introduced in the Vietnam War. A tiny, innocent looking explosive about the size of a lemon, it was a mine released in large numbers from low-flying aircraft. — William C. Anderson, *Bat-21*, p. 20, 1980

2 crack cocaine *US, 1994*
- — US Department of Justice, *Street Terms*, October 1994
- Crack is known as base, freebase, gravel, ice, rock and wash. — James Kay and Julian Cohen, *The Parents' Complete Guide to Young People and Drugs*, p. 134, 1998

gravel agitator *noun*

an infantry soldier *US, 1898*
- — *American Speech*, p. 55, February 1947: "Pacific war language"
- We used to call non-pilots, Ground Pounders, Paddle Feet, Gravel Agitators, Grunts. — Charlie Cooper, *Tuskegee's Heroes*, p. 3, 2001

gravel cruncher *noun*

a nonflying officer in the US Air Force *US, 1929*
- — *American Speech*, p. 310, December 1946: "More air force slang"
- You're not bad for a gravel cruncher, Captain. — Pat Conroy, *The Great Santini*, p. 408, 1976
- Those damned gravelcrunchers back at the base already had their lunch, and by the time we land the chow hall will be close. — Chuck Yeager, *Yeager*, p. 66, 1985

graveyard *noun*

the area of a beach where waves break *US, 1965*
- — John M. Kelly, *Surf and Sea*, p. 280, 1965

graveyard cough *noun*

a serious, deep cough *US, 1873*
- Mama listened to the Christ Cure Radio Show and my daddy sucked on a piece of coal to help his graveyard cough. — J.T. LeRoy, *Sarah*, p. 19, 2000

graveyard spiral *noun*

a downward spiral of an airplane from which recovery is nearly impossible and as a result of which impact with the ground is inevitable *US, 1988*
- He may think he is flying level, when actually he is turning and descending steeply in what airmen call "the graveyard spiral." — Neil Sheehan, *A Bright Shining Lie*, p. 787, 1988
- Gunfighter One watched the MiG nose over, then disappear through the clouds in a classic graveyard spiral. — Joe Weber, *Defcon One*, p. 250, 1989

gravy *noun*

1 money, especially money that is easily and/or illegally obtained *US, 1930*
- We were in the gravy once more[.] — Mezz Mezzrow, *Really the Blues*, p. 131, 1946
- And what does Christ think of the easy-money boys who do none of the work and take all of the gravy? — Budd Schulberg, *On the Waterfront*, 1954
- "You getting all the gravy?" — Ross Russell, *The Sound*, p. 189, 1961
- "And all that gravy you'd be missing." "Right on! And all that unsopped up gravy." — Odie Hawkins, *The Busting Out of an Ordinary Man*, p. 156, 1985

2 an unexpected benefit *US, 1910*
- A big turnover is the gravy for these guesthouses. — Jack Lait and Lee Mortimer, *Washington Confidential*, p. 68, 1951
- After this it's all gravy. I've done it for five innings and nobody could ask for more. — Jim Bouton, *Ball Four*, p. 315, 1970

3 in poker and other games that are bet on, winnings *US, 1967*
- — Albert H. Morehead, *The Complete Guide to Winning Poker*, p. 264, 1967

4 a mixture of blood and drug solution in a syringe *US, 1971* Perhaps from "gravy" as "blood" in C19 boxing slang.
- Addicts call this "shooting gravy" "Because that's what it is—right? Cooked blood?" — James Mills, *The Panic in Needle Park*, p. 78, 1966
- — Edward R. Bloomquist, *Marijuana*, p. 341, 1971

5 pasta sauce *US, 1976* Mid-Atlantic Italian-American usage.
- — Claudio R. Salvucci, *The Philadelphia Dialect Dictionary*, p. 43, 1996

gravy train *noun*

a money-making opportunity, a generous situation *US, 1914*
- Ten percent and I furnish the car! You think this is a gravy train you're riding? — Horace McCoy, *Kiss Tomorrow Good-bye*, p. 46, 1948
- "The little beaver is derailing the gravy train, I think." — William Brinkley, *Don't Go Near the Water*, p. 87, 1956
- You're upset that you're missing the gravy train? — *Airheads*, 1994

gray *noun*

1 a white person *US, 1944*
- You know, I've spent a lot of time wondering what it is you spades have and us grays are looking for? — Ross Russell, *The Sound*, p. 101, 1961
- Thus, for a time, the most common term for whites in Negro parlance was "gray." — Roger Abrahams, *Positively Black*, p. 32, 1970

2 a white betting token usually worth one dollar *US, 1983*
- — Thomas L. Clark, *The Dictionary of Gambling and Gaming*, p. 93, 1987

3 a police officer *US, 1967*
- A gray—A Nigrite name reserved for police or law enforcement officers. — Robert deCoy, *The Nigger Bible*, p. 28, 1967

gray *adjective*

white, Caucasian *US, 1944* Derogatory.
- Say, chief, what's that gray boy doing in yo' job? — Chester Himes, *If He Hollers Let Him Go*, p. 102, 1945
- I came up to the cab, and he had two gray bitches in it. — Claude Brown, *Manchild in the Promised Land*, p. 163, 1965
- "What about that gray girl in San Jose who had your nose wide open?" — Eldridge Cleaver, *Soul on Ice*, p. 9, 1968
- Baby, it's a hip little supper club on Third Avenue and a lotta actors are the tricks and most of the girls are gray and classy and the bread is long. — A.S. Jackson, *Gentleman Pimp*, p. 161, 1973

Graybar hotel; Graybar motel *noun*

a jail or prison *US, 1970*
- "Pardon me, Officers," said the Greek, who certainly didn't want to share accommodations at the graybar hotel with a Turk. — Joseph Wambaugh, *The Glitter Dome*, p. 66, 1981
- At California's newest Graybar Hotel, the Centinela State Prison in Imperial County, a search is a search. — *Los Angeles Times*, p. A3, 1st April 1994
- So for a six-month stint in the "graybar hotel," an inmate could rack up a $12,000 tab. — *Salt Lake Tribune*, p. C2, 31st January 2003

gray boy *noun*

a white male *US, 1951*
- I had copped him a lawyer / a grayboy named Sawyer. — Lightnin' Rod, *Hustlers Convention*, p. 12, 1973
- "These gray-boys and Indians have been taking advantage of us for too long." — James Carr, *Bad*, p. 88, 1975
- A gray boy called him a "savage" once, Leroy drove a maiming fist between his eyes. — Clarence Major, *All-Night Visitors*, p. 27, 1998

gray cat *noun*

a white male *US, 1997*
- Das why I call you up, on account'a you was tryin' t'splash on dem guinea gray cats. — Stephen Cannell, *Big Con*, pp. 49–50, 1997

graymail *noun*

a tactic used by defendants in espionage cases *US, 1979*
- "Graymail" is the term used for a defendant's effort to force the termination of a prosecution by threatening exposure of secrets. — Lawrence Walsh, *Firewall*, p. 170, 1997

grayspace *noun*

the brain *US, 1982*
- — *American Speech*, p. 27, Spring 1982: "The language of science fiction fan magazines"

Graystone College *noun*

a jail or prison *US, 1933*

- — Vincent J. Monteleone, *Criminal Slang*, p. 106, 1949
- "Graystone College, they call it," the coach announced. *** "It's real name is Saint Cloud State Penitentiary," the coach added. — Will Weaver, *Hard Ball*, p. 26, 1998

Graystone Hotel *noun*

a jail *US, 1972*

- I wound up in the San Francisco Bastille between Washington and Clay streets on Kearny. The Graystone Hotel, we called it. — Robert Byrne, *McGoorty*, p. 147, 1972

graze *verb*

(used of an amphetamine user) to search obsessively in a carpet for pieces of amphetamine or methamphetamine *US, 1989*

- — Geoffrey Froner, *Digging for Diamonds*, p. 33, 1989

grease *noun*

1 nitroglycerin *US, 1949*

- — Vincent J. Monteleone, *Criminal Slang*, p. 106, 1949
- If you really want to get good as a touch man, you got to study grease and explosives for a couple of years. — Red Rudensky, *The Gonif*, p. 80, 1970

2 any lubricant used in anal sex *US, 1965*

- — Donald Webster Cory and John P. LeRoy, *The Homosexual and His Society*, p. 264, 1963: "A lexicon of homosexual slang"
- — *The Guild Dictionary of Homosexual Terms*, p. 19, 1965
- — *Male Swinger Number 3*, p. 45, 1981: "The complete gay dictionary"

3 food, especially US Army c-rations *US, 1991*

- — E.M. Flanagan Jr., *Army*, p. 48, 1991

4 a young, urban tough *US, 1967*

An abbreviation of **GREASER**.

- I'm a grease, same as Dally. — S.E. Hinton, *The Outsiders*, p. 25, 1967

5 a black person *US, 1971*

- — Hermese E. Roberts, *The Third Ear*, 1971

6 in pool, extreme spin imparted on the cue ball to affect the course of the object ball or the cue ball after striking the object ball *US, 1993*

- — Mike Shamos, *The Illustrated Encyclopedia of Billiards*, p. 110, 1993

▸ **shoot the grease**

to make the initial approach in a confidence swindle *US, 1982*

- — Bill Reilly, *Big Al's Official Guide to Chicagoese*, p. 51, 1982

grease *verb*

1 to shoot or kill *US, 1964*

Vietnam war usage.

- He was runnin' around outside yellin' "Troi Oi! Troi Oi! (Oh God)" and then Crowe greased him and he didn't do no more yellin. — Philip Caputo, *A Rumor of War*, p. 302, 1977
- You'll come out now or we grease you on the spot. — Alfred Coppel, *The Apocalypse Brigade*, p. 245, 1981
- They greased half the 4th platoon and Lieutenant Stennett's brand-new radioman, and we greased so many of them it wasn't even funny. — Larry Heinemann, *Paco's Story*, p. 7, 1986
- I'm gonna grease somebody in here I swear to God! — *Airheads*, 1994

2 to perform a favor in return for a bribe *US, 1951*

- It isn't as hard as it might seem, because one of the guards will grease for twenty-five bucks. — James Blake, *The Joint*, p. 14, 25th February 1951

3 to have sex *US, 1988*

- Keith and I went through ninety thousand trips about how I can't grease him because of Michael. — Pamela Des Barres, *I'm With the Band*, p. 259, 1988

4 to eat *US, 1984*

- — Inez Cardozo-Freeman, *The Joint*, p. 502, 1984

5 to use nitroglycerin to break into a safe *US, 1949*

- — Vincent J. Monteleone, *Criminal Slang*, p. 106, 1949

6 to barely pass a course in school or college *US, 1959*

- — *Time Magazine*, p. 46, 24th August 1959

▸ **grease the skids**

to facilitate something, especially by extra legal means *US, 1930*

- If you need me to grease the skids obtaining the various licenses and permits, all you got to do is say the word. — Robert Campbell, *Nibbled to Death by Ducks*, p. 275, 1989

▸ **grease your chops**

to eat *US, 1946*

- [T]here wasn't a gas-meter between them all, and they couldn't remember when they'd greased their chops last. — Mezz Mezzrow, *Really the Blues*, p. 177, 1946
- — Paul Glover, *Words from the House of the Dead*, 1974

greaseball *noun*

1 a person of Latin-American or Mediterranean extraction *US, 1922*

A derogatory generic derived from a swarthy complexion.

- "The hell you are, baby. With that greaseball? My aching back!" — Frederick Kohner, *Gidget Goes to Rome*, p. 84, 1963
- Three kikes, one guinea, one greaseball. — Lenny Bruce, *The Essential Lenny Bruce*, p. 11, 1967
- The second time around she was standing with some monster guinea with a leather jacket and no teeth. She pointed at Buddy. The big greaseball lumbered over to the car[.] — Richard Price, *The Wanderers*, p. 186, 1974
- It was among the Italians. It was real greaseball shit. — *Goodfellas*, 1990

2 an odious, unappealing, unattractive person *US, 1917*

Derives from racist usage.

- The greaseball on the floor was awake now, but he wasn't looking at me. — Mickey Spillane, *My Gun is Quick*, p. 10, 1950
- I'll pay you when I'm good and ready, you dirty leech. Until then, stay out of my way. God, what a greaseball. — Bernard Wolfe, *The Late Risers*, p. 10, 1954

3 in circus and carnival usage, a food concession stand *US, 1981*

- — Don Wilmeth, *The Language of American Popular Entertainment*, p. 117, 1981

greaseburger *noun*

1 a despicable person *US, 1991*

- "He is such a greaseburger!" Duck told Dirk. — Francesca Lia Block, *Witch Baby*, p. 107, 1991

2 a greasy hamburger *US, 1961*

- We sit eating oniony greaseburgers and ignoring the persistent sound of the running showers. — John Rechy, *City of Night*, p. 22, 1963

grease gun *noun*

the US Army's M-3 submachine gun *US, 1984*

Based on **GREASE** (to kill).

- They carry a shotgun, a .38 caliber pistol and .45 caliber semiautomatic rifle—known in the military as a grease gun. — Bill Cardoso, *The Maltese Sangweech*, p. 4, 1984
- Grease gun, K-bar at my side / These are tools that make men die. — Sandee Johnson, *Cadences: The Jody Call Book, No. 2*, p. 134, 1986
- My trusty M3A1 submachine gun was called a great gun because of its resemblance to a hand-held grease gun used for lubricating automobiles. — Bob Stoffey, *Cleared Hot!*, p. 80, 1992

grease joint *noun*

a low-cost, low-quality restaurant *US, 1917*

- The sidewalks were as hot as a grease-joint griddle, and just as dirty, but I didn't care. — Elaine Viets, *The Pink Flamingo Murders*, p. 108, 1999

grease man *noun*

a criminal with expertise in using explosives to open safes *US, 1970*

- Since I was considered one of the top grease men in the country, it was natural that I would be contacted. — Red Rudensky, *The Gonif*, p. 7, 1970
- So everybody quit using it. There were only a few good grease men left anyway. — Harry King, *Box Man*, p. 12, 1972

grease orchard *noun*

an oil field *US, 1954*

- — Jerry Robertson, *Oil Slanguage*, p. 62, 1954

grease out *verb*

to enjoy good luck *US, 1990*

- — Charles Shafer, *Folk Speech in Texas Prisons*, p. 205, 1990

grease pit *noun*

a low-quality, low-price restaurant *US, 1995*

- What the hell would I do with that grease pit? — Quentin Tarantino, *From Dusk Till Dawn*, p. 3, 1995

greaser *noun*

1 a Mexican or any Latin American *US, 1836*

Offensive.

- "Mexicans, greasers," his father replied. "It's one and the same." — John Conway, *Love in Suburbia*, p. 26, 1960
- Then she begins to explain about some greasers, "sort of like the Black Panthers," who are kicking up dust in East L.A. — Oscar Zeta Acosta, *The Revolt of the Cockroach People*, p. 25, 1973
- I do not look down on niggers, kikes, wops or greasers. Here you are all equally worthless. — *Full Metal Jacket*, 1987
- [H]e's going by the name Edward Mallon, but you could tell by looking at him he was a greaser. Excuse me, I mean a Latin. I have to watch that. — Elmore Leonard, *Killshot*, p. 182, 1989

2 a hamburger, especially one from a fast-food restaurant *US*, *1982*
- — Bill Reilly, *Big Al's Official Guide to Chicagoese*, p. 28, 1982

3 a young, poor tough *US*, *1997*
- — J. R. Friss, *A Dictionary of Teenage Slang (Mt. Diablo High)*, 1964
- I am a greaser and most of my neighborhood rarely bothers to get a haircut. — S.E. Hinton, *The Outsiders*, p. 5, 1967
- The greasers seemed to be attending a non-stop party to which I was not invited, and I quickly decided that even if I couldn't sniff glue and drunk-drive with them, at least I could entertain. — Jennifer Blowdryer, *White Trash Debutante*, p. 11, 1997

greasy *adverb*
▸ **do greasy**
to mistreat *US*, *2002*
- Fuck that. You are not going to do me greasy. — Earl "DMX" Simmons, *E.A.R.L.*, p. 156, 2002

greasy luck *adjective*
good luck *US*, *1963*
A whaling expression that persisted after whaling in New England.
- — Charles F. Haywood, *Yankee Dictionary*, p. 71, 1963

greasy spoon *noun*
an inexpensive and all-around low-brow restaurant *US*, *1912*
- They duck out for smokes at the same time, have their crullers and java in the same lunchrooms or greasy spoons. — Jack Lait and Lee Mortimer, *New York Confidential*, p. 142, 1948
- I find myself eating at some greasy spoon next to a liquor store and talking to the most embittered cluck this side of the Continental Divide. — Clancy Sigal, *Going Away*, p. 134, 1961
- [I]t would have gone under because the people seemed to prefer a little greasy-spoon joint down the street from their place. — Nathan Heard, *Howard Street*, p. 83, 1968
- Tonight I got a date to lay a cute hashslinger that works in the greasy spoon around the corner. — Iceberg Slim (Robert Beck), *Trick Baby*, p. 219, 1969

great balls of fire!
used as a mockingly profane expression of surprise *US*, *1951*
Found in *Gone With The Wind* (1939) but made famous by Jerry Lee Lewis in his 1957 hit song written by Jack Hammer and Otis Blackwell.
- "Great balls of fire, don't make me go now!" I cried. — Max Shulman, *The Many Loves of Dobie Gillis*, p. 120, 1951
- Too much love drives a man insane / You broke my will, but what a thrill / Goodness, gracious, great balls of fire! — Jerry Lee Lewis, *Great Balls of Fire*, 1957

great Caesar's ghost!
used as a non-profane oath *US*, *1876*
The non-profane outburst of the *Metropolis Daily Planet* editor, Perry White, in *The Adventures of Superman* (1951–1957). Repeated with referential humor.
- "Great Caesar's ghost, you're as prickly as Ada!" — Peni Griffin, *Switching Well*, p. 155, 1993

Great Runes *noun*
in computing, text displayed in UPPER CASE ONLY *US*, *1991*
A legacy of the teletype.
- — Eric S. Raymond, *The New Hacker's Dictionary*, p. 183, 1991

great white father *noun*
any unpopular authority figure *US*, *1963*
- — *American Speech*, p. 272, December 1963: "American Indian student slang"

great white light *noun*
LSD *US*, *1966*
- — Richard Alpert and Sidney Cohen, *LSD*, 1966

great white way; gay white way *noun*
Broadway and the theater district of New York *US*, *1901*
- The color line along the Great White Way wasn't broken, exactly, but it sure got dented some, during the weeks we blew our lumps down there. — Mezz Mezzrow, *Really the Blues*, p. 286, 1946
- To everyone, everywhere, the Great White Way is synonymous with Glamour, Gaiety—and Girls. — *Whisper Magazine*, p. 24, May 1950: How Hot is Broadway?
- The few who stayed, and the tourists, stayed to the Gay White Way, as they used to name it, clubbing, bar hopping, or taking in a show — Mickey Spillane, *Return of the Hood*, p. 80, 1964
- With my second [pay check] I decided to hit the Great White Way and see what all the fun was about. — Antony James, *America's Homosexual Underground*, p. 113, 1965

greaze *verb*
to eat *US*, *1968*
- — Collin Baker et al., *College Undergraduate Slang Study Conducted at Brown University*, p. 129, 1968

greed head *noun*
a person motivated largely by greed *US*, *1972*
- The greedheads might be able to buy off the musicians, but they can't buy off the people who live the music[.] — John Sinclair, *Guitar Army*, p. 29, 1972

greefa; grifa; griff; griffa; griffo *noun*
marijuana *US*, *1931*
Originally border Spanish used in English conversation by Mexican-Americans.
- Grefa was kid-stuff to me, but opium meant dope and I was really scared of it. — Mezz Mezzrow, *Really the Blues*, p. 98, 1946
- — George Carpenter Baker, *Pachuco*, p. 41, January 1950
- Tea. Grifa. Yesca. Marijuana. Whatever you want to call it. — Thurston Scott, *Cure it with Honey*, p. 4, 1951

Greek *noun*
1 unintelligible language *UK*, *1600*
- "What about stelfactiznide chloride?" "What? Now you're talking Greek to me." — James Ellroy, *White Jazz*, p. 44, 1992

2 anal sex; a practitioner of anal sex *US*, *1964*
- — Dale Gordon, *The Dominion Sex Dictionary*, 1967
- Anal intercourse ("Greek") is popular, as is cunnilingus ("going below 14th Street"). — Charles Winick, *The Lively Commerce*, p. 207, 1971
- Love French and Greek, discipline, home movie-making, and anything you can name. — Emile Nytrate, *Underground Ads*, p. 18, 1971

3 in pinball, a shot up a lane with a scoring device with sufficient force to activate the scoring device *US*, *1977*
- — Bobbye Claire Natkin and Steve Kirk, *All About Pinball*, p. 112, 1977

Greek *adjective*
(of sex) anal *US*, *1934*
- — Dale Gordon, *The Dominion Sex Dictionary*, p. 79, 1967
- They'll give a beating, they'll take a beating, they'll go Greek—and all for the same fifteen, or twenty, or whatever it is. — John Warren Wells, *Tricks of the Trade*, p. 24, 1970
- The film's raunchiest scene takes place in the kitchen, where C.J. Laing engages in "water sports" and "Greek" coupling. — Kent Smith et al., *Adult Movies*, p. 31, 1982
- And it was so funny, because they would describe you as Greek, active/passive; French, active/passive—French being blow jobs and Greek being fucked. — James Ridgeway, *Red Light*, p. 222, 1996

Greek culture; Greek love; Greek style; Greek way *noun*
anal sex *US*, *1967*
- "Roman," "Greek" and "Egyptian" love are, respectively, heterosexual, homosexual and bestial or sado-masochistic. — William and Jerrye Breedlove, *Swap Clubs*, p. 58, 1964
- — Dale Gordon, *The Dominion Sex Dictionary*, p. 79, 1967
- Of course there are requests, especially again from the older men, for the around-the-world trip—the Greek style—and those requests in general. [Quoting Xaviera] — *Screw*, p. 6, 6th March 1972
- Greek Culture (Gr) = anal sex — Stephen Lewis, *The Whole Bedroom Catalog*, p. 144, 1975

Greek lightning *noun*
arson financed by the owner of a failing business *US*, *1982*

In Chicago, Greeks enjoy the reputation of being arsonists. Chicago residents cite a rule of Three Ns—"never give matches to a Greek, whiskey to an Irishman, or power to a Polack."

- — Bill Reilly, *Big Al's Official Guide to Chicagoese*, p. 28, 1982

Greek rodeo *noun*

anal sex between men *US, 1968*

- Holding on with both hands, we bounced through the night. The Greek Rodeo! — Angelo d'Arcangelo, *The Homosexual Handbook*, p. 79, 1968

Greek Row *noun*

a neighborhood with many fraternity houses *US, 1969*

- [T]he big papier-mache floats (in collaboration with selected fraternity boys) that are a traditional display of "Greek Row" for the homecoming game. — Mark Abrahamson, *Introductory Readings on Sociological Concepts*, p. 350, 1969
- Mistaken for Greek Row's rearguard. — Jeffrey Golden, *Watermelon Summer*, p. 91, 1971

Greek shot *noun*

in dice games, a controlled roll with a controlled result *US, 1962*

- — Frank Garcia, *Marked Cards and Loaded Dice*, p. 262, 1962
- "In the old days, I used to skip- roll the dice," he said as he worked. "Perfected my Greek shot. That's a controlled roll where the dice hit the rail one on top of the other so the bottom cube doesn't roll over." — Stephen Cannell, *Big Con*, p. 215, 1997

green *noun*

1 money *US, 1898*

- With a pocketful of green I was digging the scene the other bright[.] — Dan Burley, *Diggeth Thou?*, p. 36, 1959
- How 'bout it, pal—got a taste for the easy green? — Terry Southern, *The Magic Christian*, p. 15, 1959
- These were fifteen-thousand-a-year guys—not paying with plastic, either: hard-earned green. — Vincent Patrick, *The Pope of Greenwich Village*, p. 13, 1979
- JOSH: It's about the green. MOE: It's about da money. — *Mo' Better Blues*, 1990

2 in American casinos, a $25 chip *US, 1985*

- — Steve Kuriscak, *Casino Talk*, p. 28, 1985

3 marijuana, especially with a low resin count *US, 1955*

- Threw green down the toilet, getting ready to visit you. — Jack Kerouac, *Letter to Allen Ginsberg*, p. 512, 1st, 6th September 1955
- Royo had left Los Angeles with a kilo of long Mexican green, lately smuggled across the border at Tijuana. — Ross Russell, *The Sound*, p. 86, 1961
- Billy got some light green, Whoreson, while Eddie's smoke is good, it's got a lot of sticks and stuff in it. — Donald Goines, *Whoreson*, p. 130, 1972
- They gave Donna a bulging bag of green and we left. — Michelle Tea, *Valencia*, p. 92, 2000

4 phencyclidine, the recreational drug known as PCP or angel dust *US, 1981*

From the practice of sprinkling the drug on parsley or mint.

- — Ronald Linder, *PCP*, p. 9, 1981

5 the felt surface of a pool table *US, 1990*

- — Steve Rushin, *Pool Cool*, p. 15, 1990

6 an unbroken wave *US, 1964*

- — John Severson, *Modern Surfing Around the World*, p. 169, 1964

▶ **in the green**

flying with all instruments recording safe conditions *US, 1963*

- — *American Speech*, p. 119, May 1963: "Air refueling words."

green *verb*

to smoke marijuana *US, 1957*

- Didn't even green [smoke marijuana], or looked for any, put it down now. — Jack Kerouac, *Jack Kerouac Selected Letters 1957–1969*, p. 84, October 1957: Letter to Neal Cassady

green; greenie *noun*

a green capsule containing drugs, especially a central nervous system stimulant *US, 1966*

Also variant "Greenie."

- Or he'll say, "How fabulous are greenies?" (The answer is very. Greenies are pep pills—dextroamphetamine sulfate—and a lot of baseball players couldn't function without them.) — Jim Bouton, *Ball Four*, p. 80, 1970

green-and-white *noun*

a green and white police car *US, 1991*

- Gary watched a green-and-white creeping toward them from the far end of the house, coming past sabal palms, dipping over the uneven ground in low gear. — Elmore Leonard, *Maximum Bob*, p. 78, 1991

green apple quick-step *noun*

diarrhea *US, 1994*

- — Michael Dalton Johnson, *Talking Trash with Redd Foxx*, p. 47, 1994

green around the gills *adjective*

giving an appearance of being about to vomit *US, 1985*

- Kind of green around the gills. Claimed he felt all right, felt fine. — George V. Higgins, *Penance for Jerry Kennedy*, p. 267, 1985

green-ass *adjective*

inexperienced, novice *US, 1950*

- "As far as cool, ya little green-ass nigga, we decide who gets that label." — K'wan Foye, *Street Dreams*, p. 103, 2004

greenback *noun*

1 a one-dollar bill *US, 1862*

- The only relic of their brief courtship is a postcard photograph of them taken in Las Vegas in 1956 at the Horseshoe Club and Casino in front of the club's landmark, a giant horeshoe containing a million dollars in greenbacks. — Kim Rich, *Johnny's Girl*, p. 26, 1993

2 in surfing, a swell that has not broken *US, 1963*

- — Grant W. Kuhns, *On Surfing*, p. 117, 1963

green beanie *noun*

1 a green military beret *US, 1963*

- "Oh, now you've got your green beanie," I said. — Mohn McCain, *Glory Denied*, p. 43, 2001

2 a member of the Army Special Forces *US, 1966*

- [H]e and the other ASA guys were sick of being fucked with by every other Green Beanie with a room-temperature IQ. — W.E.B. Griffin, *Special Ops*, p. 469, 2001

green boys *noun*

currency *US, 2005*

- I got into law for the same reason most people do. Cheese. Green-boys. Money. — Noire, *Candy Licker*, p. 185, 2005

green door *noun*

the door leading to an execution chamber *US, 1976*

- When we reach the green door, I happen to look in / I didn't mind the silence, but the lights were so goddamn dim. — Dennis Wepman et al., *The Life*, p. 119, 1976

green dragon *noun*

1 LSD enhanced with botanical drugs from plants such as Deadly Nightshade or Jimsonweed *US, 1970*

- — William D. Alsever, *Glossary for the Establishment and Other Uptight People*, p. 3, December 1970

2 any barbiturate or other central nervous system depressant *US, 1971*

- — US Department of Justice, *Street Terms*, August 1994

3 heroin *US, 1990*

- — Charles Shafer, *Folk Speech in Texas Prisons*, p. 205, 1990

green-eye *noun*

a reconnaisance patrol *US, 1972*

- I remember the dried muddy clothes and expressionless faces as the first green-eye filed down. — William Pelfrey, *The Big V*, p. 27, 1972

green eyes *noun*

jealousy, envy *UK, 1845*

From Shakespeare's "green-eyed jealousy."

- "You got green eyes," Liz said, taking no offense. "You wish you had what I had." — Hal Ellson, *Tomboy*, p. 28, 1950

green game *noun*

in a casino, a game with a minimum bet of $25 (the green betting token) *US, 1983*

- — Thomas L. Clark, *The Dictionary of Gambling and Gaming*, p. 94, 1987

green hornet *noun*

1 a capsule combining a central nervous stimulant and a central nervous system depressant *US, 1942*

- There were also green and brown capsules, known to pill heads as green hornets. — Roger Gordon, *Hollywood's Sexual Underground*, p. 55, 1966

2 a central nervous system stimulant *US, 1997*

- At dusk I gave each American a "Green Hornet," a powerful SOG-issue amphetamine, which, like the old OSS "B Tablet," ensured twelve hours' stamina[.] — John Plaster, *SOG*, p. 180, 1997

greenhouse *noun*

1 a small room or enclosed space where marijuana is being smoked *US, 2001*

- — Pamela Munro, *U.C.L.A. Slang*, p. 77, 2001

2 in surfing, a smooth ride inside the hollow of a wave *US, 1987*

- — Mitch McKissick, *Surf Lingo*, 1987

greenie *noun*

1 a novice *US, 1953*

- "He wants to know how he can get to Forty-seventh and Broadway from here, so I figure him for a greenie." — Curt Cannon, *The Death of Me*, p. 97, 1953

2 a soldier recently arrived at a combat zone *US, 1987*

- Guys, here's a present for you. A new greenie, with top's compliments. — Stan Lee, *The 'Nam*, p. 15, 1987

3 any paper money *UK, 1982*

- — George Percy, *The Language of Poker*, p. 41, 1988

greenie beanie; green beanie *noun*

a member of the US Army Special Forces *US, 1967*
An extension of the more common green beret.

- "Those GreenBeanie guys are overrated. Too lazy to work, too nervous to steal." — Elaine Shepard, *The Doom Pussy*, p. 46, 1967
- There went the good advisors / And some "Greenie Beanies" too / To save the little country / For the likes of Madame Nhu! — Thomas Bowen, *The Longest Year*, p. 22, 1990: Ghost Advisors By and By

green ink *noun*

time spent in arial combat *US, 1991*

- [I]t was decided that it was time for him to get some combat decorations on his chest and in his record, and some green ink, signifying combat flight time. — Gerry Carroll, *North S*A*R*, p. 139, 1991

green light *noun*

in prison, permission to kill *US, 2000*

- To reinforce their goal of becoming the most feared gang in San Quentin, the AB, which numbered around 100 members, put out the green light [open season to hit] on all blacks[.] — Bill Valentine, *Gangs and Their Tattoos*, p. 6, 2000

green-light *verb*

in prison, to give permission to kill *US, 2006*

- "If you're 'in the hat' or 'green-lighted,' it means you're targeted." — Joseph Wambaugh, *Hollywood Station*, p. 242, 2006

green machine *noun*

1 the US Army *US, 1969*
Vietnam war usage.

- [T]hey called the hierarchy "motherfuckers" and printed "Fuck the Green Machine" on their jackets and hats. — Anthony Herbert, *Soldier*, p. 127, 1973
- We're the fighting Green Machine / Better than any old Marine. — Sandee Johnson, *Cadences: The Jody Call Book, No. 2*, p. 128, 1986
- "The Green Machine," as the American soldier had come to so aptly name the Army of this war, had demanded and been given 841,264 draftees by Christmas 1967[.] — Neil Sheehan, *A Bright Shining Lie*, p. 717, 1988

2 a computer built to military specifications for field use *US, 1991*

- — Eric S. Raymond, *The New Hacker's Dictionary*, p. 185, 1991

green man *noun*

1 marijuana *US, 1997*
To "see the green man" is to smoke or buy marijuana.

- — Jim Emerson-Cobb, *Scratching the Dragon*, April 1997

2 a bottle of Ballantine™ ale *US, 1965*

- "The Regs'll take a grasshacker (lawnmower) and the fuzz (head) off a little green man (Ballantine Ale)," Schoons said. — John Nichols, *The Sterile Cuckoo*, p. 66, 1965

green motherfucker *noun*

the United State Army or Marine Corps *US, 1968*

- They talked about how much they hated the Marine Corps—"the Crotch," "the Green Motherfucker." — Robert A. Anderson, *Cooks & Bakers*, p. 118, 1982

- "This green motherfucker. Nice fuckin' rest they give us." — W.D. Ehrhart, *Vietnam-Perkasie*, p. 242, 1983

green paper *noun*

money *US, 1979*

- "I knew there was something funny about it," bellowed a delighted Willie Nebille Jr., as he thrust his hand deep into a pile of the green paper. — *Washington Post*, p. A1, 29th July 1979
- — Bill Valentine, *Gang Intelligence Manual*, p. 130, 1995: "Asian street gang terminology"
- Bill Gates is rich beyond measure because we all agree that his green paper and the numbers in his account ledgers mean something. — *Rockford (Illinois) Register*, p. 19D, 5th January 2004

green queen *noun*

a male homosexual who takes pleasure in outdoor sex in public parks *US, 1981*

- — *Male Swinger Number 3*, p. 45, 1981: "The complete gay dictionary"

green room *noun*

1 in surfing, a smooth ride inside the hollow of a wave *US, 1987*

- — Mitch McKissick, *Surf Lingo*, 1987
- — Judi Sanders, *Don't Dog by Do, Dude!*, p. 14, 1991

2 an execution chamber *US, 1981*

- A cheap ploy to avoid the green room at San Quentin that isn't going to work. — James Ellroy, *Brown's Requiem*, p. 206, 1981

greens *noun*

the green US Army dress uniform *US, 1968*

- — Carl Fleischhauer, *A Glossary of Army Slang*, p. 23, 1968

greens and beans *noun*

basic groceries *US, 1994*

- I was going to be forced to get out into the streets, back into all that dripping drama, for the sake of some greens and beans. — Odie Hawkins, *Lost Angeles*, p. 146, 1994

greenseed *noun*

a US soldier freshly arrived in Vietnam *US, 1988*

- I've had ten telexes from San Francisco this week about some Greenseed who must be someone's nephew. — Danielle Steel, *Message from Nam*, p. 193, 1990

greens fee *noun*

the amount charged by a pool room to play pool *US, 1990*
Punning on a conventional term found in golf, alluding to GREEN (the surface of a pool table).

- — Steve Rushin, *Pool Cool*, p. 15, 1990

green shirt *noun*

a member of a support crew on the flight deck of a Navy aircraft carrier *US, 1989*

- To Airman Loren Bidwell, a "green-shirt" whose task was to attach planes to the catapult, this brought welcome relief. — Jeffrey Ethel, *One Day in a Long War*, p. 104, 1989

green slime *noun*

green peppers *US, 1996*
Limited usage, but clever.

- — *Maledicta*, p. 13, 1996: "Domino's pizza jargon"

green snow; green tea *noun*

phencyclidine, the recreational drug known as PCP or angel dust *US, 1986*
The color reference is to the parsley or mint on which the drug is often sprinkled.

- — Richard A. Spears, *The Slang and Jargon of Drugs and Drink*, p. 235, 1986

greenstamp *noun*

a traffic ticket for speeding *US, 1975*

- — Wayne Floyd, *Jason's Authentic Dictionary of CB Slang*, p. 18, 1976

green stuff *noun*

currency bills *US, 1887*

- Where'd you get all that green stuff? — Hal Ellson, *Duke*, p. 74, 1949

green teen *noun*

an environmentally conscious young person *US, 1995*

- — Steven Daly and Nathaniel Wice, *alt.culture*, p. 95, 1995

green thumb *noun*

in pool, the ability to make money playing for wagers *US, 1990*

- — Steve Rushin, *Pool Cool*, p. 15, 1990

green-to-green *adjective*
running smoothly, without problem *US, 1975*
Nautical origins—ships following the rules of navigation.
- — John Gould, *Maine Lingo*, p. 116, 1975

green weenie *noun*
a United States Army commendation ribbon *US, 1975*
- Soldiers called it the "Green Weenie." As a medal, it ranked one notch above the Good Conduct Ribbon, which soldiers could earn for staying in uniform three years without catching VD. — Benjamin Schemmer, *The Raid*, p. 260, 1976

▸ **eat the green weenie; suck the green weenie**
to be terrible *US, 1944*
- Of course, the actual Thomas Jefferson recipe sucks the green weenie, so use this one instead. — Ted Taylor, *Cook Your Way Into Her Pants*, p. 53, 2003

green womb *noun*
the inside of a hollow breaking wave *US, 1991*
- — Trevor Cralle, *The Surfin'ary*, p. 47, 1991

green worms *noun*
the undulating green lines on a radar screen *US, 1947*
- — *American Speech*, p. 153, April 1947: "Radar slang terms"

gremlin *noun*
an inexperienced surfer who does not respect surfer etiquette *US, 1961*
- One who, due to objectionable actions both in and out of the water, causes public surfing bans and the closing of private beaches to all surfers. — Grant W. Kuhns, *On Surfing*, p. 117, 1963

gremmie *noun*
1 an unpopular, unfashionable person *US, 1962*
- — *Current Slang*, p. 3, Fall 1966
- For months, Pat was the outsider, the "gremmie" in the water[.] — Bob Sipchen, *Baby Insane and the Buddha*, p. 175, 1993
2 an unskilled surfing or skateboarding novice *AUSTRALIA, 1962*
- — Albert Cassorla, *The Skateboarder's Bible*, p. 200, 1976
- It was a remarkable win for a sixteen year old who as a gremmie years earlier had been considered rather too tall and gangling to ever become a first-rate surfer. — Clint Willis, *Big Wave*, p. 237, 2003
3 marijuana and crack cocaine mixed for smoking in a cigarette *US, 1989*
- — Geoffrey Froner, *Digging for Diamonds*, p. 33, 1989
- Lorraine held a fresh gremmie she had lifted from the console in her hand, twirling it around. — Renay Jackson, *Crack City*, p. 75, 2006

grette *noun*
a cigarette *US, 1966*
- — *Current Slang*, p. 3, Winter 1966

grey broad *noun*
a white woman *US, 1966*
- — Rose Giallombardo, *Society of Women*, p. 208, 1966: Glossary of Prison Terms

grey goose *noun*
a grey California Department of Corrections bus used for transporting prisoners *US, 1974*
- — Paul Glover, *Words from the House of the Dead*, 1974
- The night before the gray goose flew he came back with some more rum[.] — Malcolm Braly, *False Starts*, p. 99, 1976
- Through a grimy window of the old gray goose, the bus that shuttled prisoners from the Chino Guidance Center to Folsom, Jimmy stared at the world passing by. — Ovid Demaris, *The Last Mafioso*, p. 110, 1981

Greyhound *noun*
an M-8 armored car *US, 1980*
World War 2 vintage, used at the beginning of the Vietnam war by the Army of the Republic of Vietnam.
- Several ARVN armored car units employed the M-8 Greyhound. — Donn A. Starry, *Armored Combat in Vietnam*, p. 5, 1980

greyhound *verb*
(used of a black person) to pursue a white person in the hopes of a romantic or sexual relationship *US, 1972*
From a **GREY MAN** as a white person.
- — David Claerbaut, *Black Jargon in White America*, p. 67, 1972

grey matter *noun*
brains, thus intelligence *US, 1899*
- I'm gonna make him think his grey matter depends on it. — *Natural Born Killers*, 1994

greys on trays *noun*
adult snowboarders *US, 1997*
- Derisively called "the grays on trays" by a Gen-Xer riding a ski-lift last year, the group of eight has proudly adopted the name. — *Plain Dealer (Cleveland, Ohio)*, p. 3J, 9th February 1997
- Grays on trays: Your parents on snowboards. — *Rock River Times (Illinois)*, 21st April 2004

grick *noun*
a Greek immigrant or Greek-American *US, 1997*
- And those given a name were stuck with it forever: Svade, Svenska, Lugan, Schnapps, Moishe, Stosh, Henie, Mockie, Guinea, Canuck, Bohunk, Pork-dodger, Limey, Greaseball, Krauthead, Dutchie, Squarehead, Grick, Mick, Paddy, Goombah, Polski, Dago, Hunkie, Wop and Frog. — *San Francisco Examiner*, p. A15, 28th July 1997

G-ride *noun*
a stolen car *US, 1985*
- — Jennifer Blowdryer, *Modern English*, p. 61, 1985
- — *Los Angeles Times*, p. B8, 19th December 1994

grief *noun*
▸ **give someone grief**
to tease or criticize someone *US, 1968*
- — Collin Baker et al., *College Undergraduate Slang Study Conducted at Brown University*, p. 125, 1968

grievous bodily harm *noun*
the recreational drug GHB *US, 1993*
Extended from the punning **GBH**.
- — *American Speech*, p. 84, Spring 1995: "Among the new words"
- GHB has been marketed as a liquid or powder and has been sold on the street under names such as Grievous Bodily Harm, Georgia Home Boy, Liquid Ecstasy, Liquid X, Liquid E, GHB, GBH, Soap, Scoop, Easy Lay, Salty Water, G-Riffick, [and] Cherry Menth. — *Morbidity and Morality Weekly Report*, p. 281, 4th April 1997

g-riffick *noun*
the recreational drug GHB *US, 1997*
- GHB has been marketed as a liquid or powder and has been sold on the street under names such as Grievous Bodily Harm, Georgia Home Boy, Liquid Ecstasy, Liquid X, Liquid E, GHB, GBH, Soap, Scoop, Easy Lay, Salty Water, G-Riffick, [and] Cherry Menth. — *Morbidity and Morality Weekly Report*, p. 281, 4th April 1997

grift *verb*
to make a living by confidence swindles, especially short cons *US, 1998*
- I worked, conned, grifted. However you want to call it. — John Ridley, *Love is a Racket*, p. 55, 1998

grifter *noun*
1 a person who makes their living by confidence swindles, especially short cons *US, 1915*
Widely familiar from Jim Thompson's 1963 novel *The Grifters* and its 1990 film adaptation.
- Its 200 yards are lined almost unbrokenly by cheap hotels and rooming-houses sheltering all manner of strange characters: retired vaudevillians, down-and-out horse players, dope fiends, grifters and grafters[.] — Jack Lait and Lee Mortimer, *New York Confidential*, p. 13, 1948
- I don't want you messing with the grifters around here. — George Mandel, *Flee the Angry Strangers*, p. 52, 1952
- In town, Kid's woman, Rita, the fledgling grifter in the minor role of Lance Wellington's Baroness sister, stood impatiently on the front porch of the mob's museum-mansion set-up in a secluded area of the city. — Iceberg Slim (Robert Beck), *Long White Con*, p. 125, 1977
2 in horse racing, a bettor who makes small, conservative bets *US, 1951*
- — David W. Maurer, *Argot of the Racetrack*, p. 33, 1951

grill *noun*
1 the teeth *US, 2001*
- — Jim Goad, *Jim Goad's Glossary of Northwestern Prison Slang*, December 2001
2 a decorative tooth cap *US, 2005*
- Rob a jewelry store and tell 'em make me a grill / Had a whole top diamonds and da bottom rows gold / Yo we bout to start an epidemic wit dis one / Y'll know what dis is so, so def. — Nelly, *Grillz*, 2005

- He flashed a mouthful of bling set in a platinum grill. — Linden Dalecki, *Kid B*, p. 168, 2006
- The teeth caps are alternately called grills, fronts, shines, plates, or caps, and these glittering decorative pieces are the latest hip-hop culture trend making its way into the mainstream. — *Boston Globe*, p. C1, 31st January 2006

3 a car accident in which an occupant or occupants of the car are burnt *US, 1962*
- — *American Speech*, p. 269, December 1962: "The language of traffic policemen"

4 the bars or mesh of a prison cell *US, 1992*
- — William K. Bentley and James M. Corbett, *Prison Slang*, p. 7, 1992

grimbo *noun*
a social misfit *US, 1988*
- [T]he real reason we're not dating them is that physically they're grimbos. — John Townsend, *What Women Want*, p. 93, 1998

grin *noun*
used as Internet shorthand to mean "your message amused me" *US, 1997*
- — Andy Ihnatko, *Cyberspeak*, pp. 83–84, 1997

grinchy *adjective*
unpleasant, distasteful, bad *US, 1961*
High school usage.
- — *Washington Post*, 23rd April 1961: "Man, dig this jazz"

grind *noun*
1 in a striptease or other sexual dance, a rotating movement of the hips, pelvis, and genitals *US, 1931*
- A lot of white vocalists, even some with the big name bands today, are either as stiff as a stuffed owl or else they go through more wringing and twisting than a shake dancer, doing grinds and bumps all over the place[.] — Mezz Mezzrow, *Really the Blues*, p. 27, 1946
- "You do about four bars a bumps and grinds while I chew a hunk outta the grass hut." — Gypsy Rose Lee, *Gypsy*, p. 182, 1957
- With a few more suggestive bumps, grinds, and agitated jerks, the G-string came off and she capered around naked. — Monroe Fry, *Sex, Vice, and Business*, p. 21, 1959
- I gave one bump and one grind and ran offstage. — Tempest Storm, *Tempest Storm*, p. 113, 1987

2 sexual intercourse; an act of sexual intercourse *UK, 1870*
- That thoroughfare, once the home of a dozen proud theaters, including the New Amsterdam of red plush and wonderful memories, is now devoted to "grind" movie houses[.] — Jack Lait and Lee Mortimer, *New York Confidential*, p. 30, 1948
- Yeah, well, she got knocked up. At a grind session. — Evan Hunter, *The Blackboard Jungle*, p. 158, 1954

3 the vagina; a woman as a sex object; sex with a woman *US, 1962*
- "The trim, the grind, the scratch—in plain, everyday English—the pussy!" — Charles Perry, *Portrait of a Young Man Drowning*, p. 195, 1962

4 a serious, dedicated, diligent student *US, 1889*
- But mummy didn't want any daughter of hers turning into a grind. — John M. Murtagh and Sara Harris, *Cast the First Stone*, p. 35, 1957
- "If you are gung-ho and shoot for A's, that puts you in the grind category." — Glendon Swarthout, *Where the Boys Are*, p. 55, 1960
- Finally he settles on Donna Horowtiz, Beth Shields, and Sally Burdett, grinds who remain until after dark each day in the Chem Lab[.] — James Ellroy, *Because the Night*, p. 519, 1984

5 a style of hard rock appealing to the truly disaffected, featuring a fast, grinding tempo, bleak lyrics and relentlessly loud and distorted guitars *US, 1994*
Also known as "grindcore."
- Well, it's not exactly speed or thrash or grunge or grind. — *Airheads*, 1994

grind *verb*
1 in a striptease or other sexual dance, to rotate the hips, pelvis, and genitals in a sensual manner *US, 1928*
- Dancing boys strip-tease with intestines, women stick severed genitals in their cunts, grind, bump, and flick it at the man of their choice. — William Burroughs, *Naked Lunch*, pp. 37–38, 1957
- You can pull all the stops out / Till they call the cops out / Grind your behind till you're banned. — Stephen Sondheim, *You Gotta Get a Gimmick*, 1960
- Slowly grinding to the native beat, I flipped my skirt back and forth across my body. — Lois O'Conner, *The Bare Facts*, p. 14, 1964

- I continued to bump and grind across the stage, forcing a smile as I unfastened my brassiere[.] — Blaze Starr, *Blaze Starr*, p. 84, 1974

2 to have sex *UK, 1647*
- I'm busy grindin' so you can't come in. — Mezz Mezzrow, *Really the Blues*, p. 45, 1946
- She said, "Well, you know, daddy, you know you can find a grinder any time that can grind a while." — Bruce Jackson, *Get Your Ass in the Water and Swim Like Me*, p. 127, 1966
- I can find a grinder any time, that can grind for a while / But tonight I want my love done the Hollywood style. — Roger Abrahams, *Positively Black*, p. 95, 1970
- The overpowering rapture of just grinding gently with her, without compassion[.] — Clarence Major, *All-Night Visitors*, p. 4, 1998

3 to serve a jail sentence *US, 2002*
- There was not a mod, the hole is where you have to grind for real. — Earl "DMX" Simmons, *E.A.R.L.*, p. 121, 2002

4 to study hard *US, 1955*
- I'm completely faked out in my two departmentals, but I'll be damned if I'll grind. — Max Shulman, *Guided Tour of Campus Humor*, p. 105, 1955
- — *Wesleyan Alumnus*, p. 29, Spring 1981

5 in computing, to format code so that it looks attractive *US, 1983*
- — Guy L. Steele et al., *The Hacker's Dictionary*, p. 74, 1983

6 to eat *US, 1981*
Hawaiian youth usage.
- — Douglas Simonson, *Pidgin to da Max*, 1981
- Students there [Hawaii] do not eat, they "grind." — *New York Times*, 12th April 1987

7 to call out and invite patrons to enter a performance *US, 1968*
- For a game, however, the operator usually grinds for his own tip, but he also has help. — E.E. Steck, *A Brief Examination of an Esoteric Folk*, p. 9, 1968

grinder *noun*
1 a sexual partner *US, 1996*
- She said, "Well, you know, daddy, you know you can find a grinder any time that can grind a while." — Bruce Jackson, *Get Your Ass in the Water and Swim Like Me*, p. 127, 1966
- I can find a grinder any time, that can grind for a while / But tonight I want my love done the Hollywood style. — Roger Abrahams, *Positively Black*, p. 95, 1970
- Precious Percy, the pimp, the ladies' good time grinder and weak spot finder. — Odie Hawkins, *Chicago Hustle*, p. 35, 1977

2 a striptease *US, 1950*
- [T]he strippers have finally divided themselves into three classes: "fan-dancers," who keep up the pretense of hiding their nakedness as they enlarge it; "grinders," also known as bumpers and belly dancers, who feature undulations and various wiggles and squirms[.] — Jack Lait and Lee Mortimer, *Chicago Confidential*, p. 158, 1950
- This was Times Square's aristocratic era, before Prohibition, before honky-tonk emerged out of the Depression, a twenty-five year epoch, before the grand theaters of 42nd Street, converted to B-movie grinders. — Josh Alan Friedman, *Tales of Times Square*, p. 47, 1986

3 a person who calls out and invites patrons to enter a performance *US, 1968*
- The man standing in front of a "freak store" talking interminably is a "grind man" or "grinder." — E.E. Steck, *A Brief Examination of an Esoteric Folk*, p. 9, 1968
- — Joe McKennon, *Circus Lingo*, p. 42, 1980

4 a pornographic movie with poor production values and little plot or dialogue, just poorly filmed sex *US, 1995*
- — *Adult Video News*, p. 48, August 1995

5 the drill field in an armed forces training camp *US, 1963*
- — *American Speech*, pp. 76–79, February 1963: "Marine corps slang"

6 in competition sailing, a person who in tandem operates a winch-like device to raise a large sail very quickly *US, 1996*
- Next Thursday we can say we're grinders with Team Dennis Conner. — Joseph Wambaugh, *Floaters*, p. 56, 1996

grinders *noun*
the teeth *UK, 1676*
- Hey, there, old buddy, what's my chance of gettin' some toothpaste for brushin' my grinders? — Ken Kesey, *One Flew Over the Cuckoo's Nest*, p. 90, 1962

grind film *noun*
a pornographic movie, usually with crude production values and no plot or character development *US*, *1977*
- Just keep that crumpled sepia 1947 grind film in the basement and enjoy it next time one of your friends gets married. — Stephen Ziplow, *The Film Maker's Guide to Pornography*, p. 12, 1977

grind house *noun*
a theater exhibiting continuous shows or movies of a sexual or violent nature *US*, *1929*
- Past the souvenir shops, past the grind houses where the fags hang out[.] — *Rogue for Men*, p. 46, June 1956
- If it's raining I have to work the theaters and grind-houses, and it's dark in there so the most I can expect is five dollars for a movie job. — Johnny Shearer, *The Male Hustler*, p. 72, 1966
- Ain't another grind house in the big apple that can match that. — *Screw*, p. 7, 12th January 1970
- The Anco was the raunchiest, most dilapidated Deuce grindhouse of them all. — Bill Landis, *Sleazoid Express*, p. 79, 2002

grinding *adjective*
(used of surf conditions) powerful, breaking consistently *US*, *1987*
- — Mitch McKissick, *Surf Lingo*, 1987

grind joint *noun*
1 a casino dominated by slot machines and low-limit tables *US*, *1991*
- — Michael Dalton, *Blackjack*, p. 52, 1991
2 a brothel *US*, *1962*
- "It's the snazziest grind joint you ever heard of. And if you happen to catch clap from one of the broads over there, you don't have to worry because it's a higher class of clap." — Charles Perry, *Portrait of a Young Man Drowning*, p. 180, 1962

grind man *noun*
a person who calls out and invites patrons to enter a performance *US*, *1968*
- The man standing in front of a "freak store" talking interminably is a "grind man" or "grinder." — E.E. Steck, *A Brief Examination of an Esoteric Folk*, p. 9, 1968

grinds *noun*
▸ **get your grinds**
to have sex *US*, *1966*
- — John D. Bell et al., *Loosely Speaking*, p. 10, 1966

grinds; grines *noun*
food *US*, *1981*
- — Douglas Simonson, *Pidgin to da Max*, 1981

grind show *noun*
a carnival attraction that relies on a relentless patter to attract customers inside *US*, *1927*
- — Gene Sorrows, *All About Carnivals*, p. 18, 1985: "Terminology"
- Of course there were the cheapies and grind shows and old theater houses fallen to movie status. — Lawrence J. Quirk, *Bob Hope*, p. 17, 2000

grind store *noun*
an illegal gambling operation where players are cheated as a matter of course *US*, *1953*
- — Gene Sorrows, *All About Carnivals*, p. 18, 1985: "Terminology"
- But it was easy enough to find out that he ran a flat joint, also called a flat store or sometimes a grind store or simply a flat. — Nathaniel Knaebel, *Step Right Up*, p. 52, 2004

gringo *noun*
a white person *US*, *1849*
The source of considerable false etymology based on the marching song "Green grow the rushes, o." Often used with a lack of affection.
- I almost liked the big gringo. — Piri Thomas, *Down These Mean Streets*, p. 215, 1967
- It is unimportant that I poisoned brothers in Panama with the gringo's venomous Christ-shit. — Oscar Zeta Acosta, *The Revolt of the Cockroach People*, p. 47, 1973
- Multicultural Management Program Fellows, *Dictionary of Cautionary Words and Phrases*, 1989

- Abel knew that a real driver would be a gringo, not a former "Rodino" like himself, who felt lucky to have such a job. — Joseph Wambaugh, *Finnegan's Week*, p. 39, 1993

gringo gallop *noun*
diarrhea suffered by tourists in Mexico or Latin America *US*, *1960*
- [T]hey admit that, like most Americans, they suffered a three-day gastric upset described by a variety of names like the Gringo Gallop and Montezuma's revenge. — *Washington Post, Times Herald*, p. AW8, 24th January 1960

grip *noun*
1 a small suitcase *US*, *1879*
A shortened form of "gripsack."
- I drove my car down the alley in back of his place and he lowered his grips into the rumble seat with the aid of a clothesline[.] — Mezz Mezzrow, *Really the Blues*, p. 129, 1946
- I got clean, put my riding habit in a grip and went to Artie's beat up wheel and pulled around in front of Robin's place and parked. — A.S. Jackson, *Gentleman Pimp*, p. 110, 1973
2 money *US*, *1991*
- "He gonna go out and try to get a grip for his sisters and brothers." — Leon Bing, *Do or Die*, p. 219, 1991
- — *Washington Post*, 14th October 1993
- "Goddamn powder cost me a grip." — John Ridley, *Everybody Smokes in Hell*, p. 39, 1999
3 a large amount *US*, *1995*
- Before I went to jail I had a grip of money[.] — Yusuf Jah, *Uprising*, p. 28, 1995
- — Judi Sanders, *Da Bomb!*, p. 13, 1997
- — Jim Goad, *Jim Goad's Glossary of Northwestern Prison Slang*, December 2001

▸ **get a grip**
to get control of your emotions and actions *US*, *1971*
- BRIDGET: Eric, will you please get a grip? ERIC: Fine, I've got a grip! Now I want an explanation! — *200 Cigarettes*, 1999
- "Damn it, get a grip. This is about Doug, and that's all." — Reed Arvin, *The Last Goodbye*, p. 91, 2004

grip *verb*
1 to flatter and curry favor with those in power *US*, *1981*
- — *Maledicta*, p. 264, Summer/Winter 1981: "By its slang, ye shall know it: the pessimism of prison life"
2 to masturbate *US*, *1971*
- — Eugene Landy, *The Underground Dictionary*, p. 93, 1971

grip and grin *adjective*
used of posed photographs of smiling people shaking hands *US*, *1982*
- Too often photos of more than one person are either grip-and-grin or stand-em-in-a-line. — Mark Beach, *Editing Your Newsletter*, p. 72, 1982
- It is the job of the photographer to seek out and record such evidence rather than unleashing the flash on a "grip and grin" shot. — Kathleen Rummel, *Persuasive Public Relations for Libraries*, p. 133, 1983
- Grip-and-grin photographs of commissioners and deputy commissioners shaking hands with whichever cop managed to survive the last police shooting. — David Simon, *Homicide*, p. 46, 1991

gripester *noun*
a chronic complainer *US*, *1962*
- — Joseph E. Ragen and Charles Finston, *Inside the World's Toughest Prison*, p. 802, 1962: "Penitentiary and underworld glossary"

gripped *adjective*
in rock climbing, frozen with fear *US*, *1998*
- GRIPPED Paralyzed with fear. — Shelley Youngblut, *Way Inside ESPN's X Games*, p. 209, 1998

gripy *adjective*
miserable *US*, *1946*
- Well, we all laid around in that fleabag-with-room-service for a couple of gripy weeks[.] — Mezz Mezzrow, *Really the Blues*, pp. 177–178, 1946

grit *noun*
1 a narrow-minded if not reactionary person *US*, *1972*
- — *Washington Evening Star and Daily News (Teen Weekender)*, p. 12, 2nd December 1972: "For adults: solid slang"

2 food *US*, *1959*

- [B]esides she got some good grit waiting for me. — Piri Thomas, *Down These Mean Streets*, p. 139, 1967

3 crack cocaine *US*, *1994*

Another rock metaphor, based on the drug's appearance.

- — US Department of Justice, *Street Terms*, October 1994

grit *verb*

to eat *US*, *1968*

- — Collin Baker et al., *College Undergraduate Slang Study Conducted at Brown University*, p. 130, 1968

gritch *noun*

a complaint *US*, *1983*

- — Guy L. Steele et al., *The Hacker's Dictionary*, p. 74, 1983

gritch *verb*

to complain *US*, *1966*

- He sleeps every night, and doesn't cry or gritch very often. — Anne Lamott, *Operating Instructions*, p. 135, 1993

gritchy *adjective*

prone to complain *US*, *1966*

- Nobody wants a grumpy, gritchy, or complaining martyr mom. — Carol Kuykendall, *Real Moms*, p. 62, 2002

grit down *verb*

to eat *US*, *1973*

- Bilgewater words like "bro" for brother, "gritting down" for eating[.] — Joe Eszterhas, *Charlie Simpson's Apocalypse*, p. 22, 1973

gritter *noun*

a lower class, unsophisticated person *US*, *2002*

- gritter—Someone who is generally lower class; would attend monster truck rallies, wear jeans with holes and heavy metal rock band t-shirts. — *Dictionary of New Terms (Hope College)*, 2002

groan *noun*

a standup bass fiddle *US*, *1945*

- — Lou Shelly, *Hepcats Jive Dictionary*, p. 12, 1945

groan box *noun*

an accordion *US*, *1919*

- It was a strange red instrument, sometimes called a groan box, with many pleated folds[.] — Elizabeth Haydon, *Prophecy*, p. 603, 2000

groats *noun*

the epitome of unpleasant *US*, *1979*

- I guess they had to do it, especially after dad became suspicious and found out what I'd been doing with the caps. It's the groats! — Beatrice Sparks (writing as 'Anonymous'), *Jay's Journal*, p. 32, 1979

groceries *noun*

1 the genitals, breasts and/or buttocks, especially as money-earning features *US*, *1965*

- — Dale Gordon, *The Dominion Sex Dictionary*, p. 79, 1967
- — H. Max, *Gay (S)language*, p. 18, 1988

2 in horse racing, horse feed *US*, *1951*

- — David W. Maurer, *Argot of the Racetrack*, p. 33, 1951

grocery boy *noun*

a heroin addict who is craving food *US*, *1973*

- — David Maurer and Victor Vogel, *Narcotics and Narcotic Addiction*, p. 412, 1973
- — Richard A. Spears, *The Slang and Jargon of Drugs and Drink*, p. 235, 1986

grody *noun*

a dirty, homeless hospital patient infested with lice *US*, *1984–1985*

- — *Maledicta*, p. 15, 1984–1985: "A medical Christmas song"

grody; groady; groaty *adjective*

messy, unkempt, disgusting *US*, *1961*

- Grody—square, awful, nowhere, phew! — Art Unger, *The Cool Book*, p. 106, 1961
- — Carol Ann Preusse, *Jargon Used by University of Texas Co-Eds*, 1963
- I'm sitting there, and like this crispo waitress serves me hot tea in a Styrofoam cup, right, and it's like so grody, the Styrofoam is melting in the tea, like barf me out! — Mary Corey and Victoria Westermark, *Fer Shurr! How to be a Valley Girl*, 1982
- And the lady like goes, oh my God, your toenails are like so GRODY. — Moon Unit and Frank Zappa, *Valley Girl*, 1982

grody to the max *adjective*

extremely disgusting *US*, *1982*

- Like all the stuff like sticks to the plate / And it's like, it's like somebody elses food, y'know / And it's like GRODY / GRODY TO THE MAX. — Moon Unit and Frank Zappa, *Valley Girl*, 1982
- — Connie Eble (Editor), *UNC-CH Campus Slang*, p. 4, Fall 1984

groggery *noun*

a disreputable bar *US*, *1822*

- Eighth Street runs into Sailors' Row proper, a line of groggeries and lunch-rooms that hit bottom. — Jack Lait and Lee Mortimer, *Washington Confidential*, p. 33, 1951

groinplant *noun*

in mountain biking, an unintended and painful contact between the bicycle and your groin *US*, *1992*

- — William Nealy, *Mountain Bike!*, p. 161, 1992: "Bikespeak"

grok *verb*

to understand, to appreciate *US*, *1961*

Coined by Robert Heinlein (1907–88) for the science-fiction novel *Stranger in a Strange Land*, 1961; adopted into semi-mystical use by the counterculture.

- — Steve Salaets, *Ye Olde Hiptionary*, 1970
- — Guy L. Steele et al., *The Hacker's Dictionary*, p. 74, 1983
- In other words, it was established that the [Smothers] Brothers could do what they wanted, but so could the network. In other words, grok Catch-22. — Bill Cardoso, *The Maltese Sangweech*, p. 237, 1984
- Hard Drugs: Like I said, at first no one grokked how hard they were. — Amy Wallace, *Retrohell*, p. 61, 1997

grom *noun*

a beginner surfer *US*, *1992*

An abbreviation of **GROMMET**.

- — *Surfing*, p. 43, 14 March 1990
- The white water is barely visible but the sound of surf is enough to lure any half-stoked grom to the shore. — *Tracks*, p. 65, October 1992

grommet *noun*

a novice surfer, especially one with a cheeky attitude *AUSTRALIA*, *1981*

- — Nat Young, *Surfing Fundamentals*, p. 127, 1985
- Lockie is a grommet (a young surfer) and, according to the codes of surfing, his actions when other surfers "drop in" on him are socially inappropriate. — Dudley Jones, *A Necessary Fantasy?*, p. 353, 2000

gromp *verb*

in tiddlywinks, to move a pile of winks as a whole onto another wink or pile of winks *US*, *1977*

- — *Verbatim: The Language Quarterly*, p. 526, December 1977

gronk *verb*

1 to disable (a device) *US*, *1962*

- Gronk—To adjust a device so as to render its original function inoperable; i.e., to "gronk" a pay telephone. — *Voo Doo Magazine (MIT)*, pp. 10–11, January 1962

2 in computing, to shut down and restart a computer whose operation has been suspended *US*, *1981*

A term popularized by Johnny Hart in his *B.C.* newspaper comic strip.

- — Guy L. Steele, *Coevolution Quarterly*, p. 31, Spring 1981: "Computer slang"
- — Eric S. Raymond, *The New Hacker's Dictionary*, p. 187, 1991

groove *noun*

a profound pleasure, a true joy *US*, *1946*

- It's your special groove; you can be away from the world with your special language and special pleasures. — George Mandel, *Flee the Angry Strangers*, p. 341, 1952
- "Aren't they a groove," she was saying, "they're so funny." — Terry Southern, *Candy*, p. 139, 1958
- It's a groove if we decided to be Mr. or Mrs. Clean. — Jack W. Thomas, *Heavy Number*, p. 29, 1976
- Charlie was kind of a groove in many ways, an intelligent dude. — Stephen Gaskin, *Amazing Dope Tails*, p. 79, 1980

groove *verb*

1 to enjoy *US*, *1950*

- Word had gone out that this was going to be a head-knocking run anyway, and the idea of having a writer in two didn't groove anybody. — Hunter S. Thompson, *Hell's Angels*, p. 116, 1966

- I get up and shave with Grayson Kirk's razor, use his toothpaste, splash on his after-shave, grooving on it all. — James Simon Kunen, *The Strawberry Statement*, p. 34, 1968
- I groove on Hollywood movies—even bad ones. — Jerry Rubin, *Do It!*, p. 12, 1970
- "Most of us have too many friends outside that we groove on," she insisted. — Malcolm Boyd, *My Fellow Americans*, p. 147, 1970

2 to please, to make happy *US, 1952*

- This enabled him to get enough morphine to keep "grooved" for several weeks. — John Clellon Holmes, *Go*, p. 198, 1952

3 to have sex *US, 1960*

- [H]ere was a man who could do a lot of good, who had the bread to support her bee and give her almost face value for the goods she pulled, all for a little grooving. — Clarence Cooper Jr., *The Scene*, p. 34, 1960

groover *noun*

a drug user who enjoys psychedelic accessories to his drug experience *US, 1971*

- — Eugene Landy, *The Underground Dictionary*, p. 93, 1971

groovy *noun*

a fashionable, trendy person *US, 1974*

- The girls used to yell down to boys on the street, to all the nice free funky Village groovies they saw walking around down there. — Sheridan Baker, *The Crowell College Reader*, p. 39, 1974
- "All young people are hippies in these times. I work in a dress shop, making clothes for the groovies." — Brian Boyer, *Prince of Thieves*, p. 153, 1975

groovy *adjective*

very good, pleasing *US, 1937*

The word enjoyed two periods of great popularity, first in the early 1940s and then in the mid-to-late 1960s, where it caught on both in the mainstream and in hip circles. Since then, it has become a signature word for mocking the attitudes and fashions of the 1960s.

- "I pitched a no-hit game last summer," said Georgie. "Hey, groovy," said Sally. — Max Shulman, *The Many Loves of Dobie Gillis*, p. 83, 1951
- It's not a big motorcycle / Just a groovy little motorbike — The Beach Boys, *Little Honda*, 1964
- Shorty would take me to groovy, frantic scenes in different chicks' and cats' pads, where with the lights and juke down mellow, everybody blew gage and juiced back and jumped. — Malcolm X and Alex Haley, *The Autobiography of Malcolm X*, p. 56, 1964
- Everything groovy. Everything with style ... must be first class. — *The Digger Papers*, p. 15, August 1968

gross *adjective*

disgusting *US, 1959*

- His conversation was soon loaded with "brew" and "beevo," with talk of "hometown honeys" and things being "gross." — John Sayles, *Union Dues*, p. 278, 1977
- He's like so GROSS / He like sits there and like plays with all his rings / And he like flirts with all the guys in the class / It's like totally disgusting. — Moon Unit and Frank Zappa, *Valley Girl*, 1982
- "My mom went out with this gross trucker guy once," Pup told him. — Francesca Lia Block, *Baby Be-Bop*, p. 391, 1995
- Gross. I hate it when my mom does that. — *American Beauty*, 1999

gross out *verb*

to disgust, to shock *US, 1965*

- — Collin Baker et al., *College Undergraduate Slang Study Conducted at Brown University*, p. 130, 1968
- I had a "gross-out contest" (what the fuck is a "gross-out contest"?) with Captain Beefheart and we both ate shit on stage. — Frank Zappa, *The Real Frank Zappa Book*, p. 14, 1989

grouch *noun*

an ill-tempered person *US, 1900*

- She was a grouch. She didn't seem afraid of him or even care he was here. — Elmore Leonard, *Glitz*, p. 188, 1985

grouch bag *noun*

literally, a small bag hidden on the person with emergency funds in it; figuratively, a wallet or a person's supply of money *US, 1908*

- He could tell carnie hands and circus roustabouts because they took their money out of grouch-bags, pouches drawn by string, like tobacco pouches. — Nelson Algren, *A Walk on the Wild Side*, p. 18, 1956

- "How's the grouch bag holding?" he asked. "All right. I've got a few bucks." — Robert Edmond Alter, *Carny Kill*, p. 8, 1966
- — Joe McKennon, *Circus Lingo*, p. 42, 1980

ground *noun*

the territory controlled or claimed by a youth gang *US, 1992*

- "He in our ground now. By rules, his ass ours!" — Jess Mowry, *Way Past Cool*, p. 45, 1992

▸ **back on the ground; on the ground**

freed from prison *US, 1982*

- — Ralph de Sola, *Crime Dictionary*, p. 107, 1982
- — William K. Bentley and James M. Corbett, *Prison Slang*, p. 108, 1992

▸ **on the ground**

in horse racing, said of a jockey serving a suspension *US, 1976*

- — Tom Ainslie, *Ainslie's Complete Guide to Thoroughbred Racing*, p. 335, 1976

ground *verb*

to punish a child by refusing to let them leave the house for any social events *US, 1950*

- So I said, "What's the deal, Uncle Jeff? In wartime you want to be a pacifist and in peacetime you want to be a soldier. It took you twenty years to figure out you don't believe in anything?" Grounded. Just like that. Two weeks. — *Ferris Bueller's Day Off*, 1986
- What are you going to do, ground me? — *American Beauty*, 1999

ground apple *noun*

a brick *US, 1945*

- — Lou Shelly, *Hepcats Jive Talk Dictionary*, p. 25, 1945

ground control *noun*

a person who guides another through an LSD experience *US, 1967*

Another LSD-as-travel metaphor.

- — John Williams, *The Drug Scene*, p. 112, 1967
- If there is not one person with more experience than the others, it is probably better to have a "ground-control," that is one person who does not take the psychedelic and takes care of the mechanics of changing records, keeping off distractions, etc. — *The San Francisco Oracle*, 1967
- It was the only trip where I had somebody who acted as a guide or a ground control. — Stephen Gaskin, *Amazing Dope Tails*, p. 86, 1980

ground crew *noun*

friends who guide someone through an LSD experience *US, 1966*

- Have an experienced ground crew standing by. They may be present or easily contacted. — *The San Francisco Oracle*, 1966

grounder *noun*

a crime that does not demand much effort by the police to solve *US, 1984*

- An easy arrest is a grounder[.] — *New York Times*, p. 34, 20th October 1958
- They pulled in sixty, seventy, most of them grounders, somebody doing his wife or his best friend, the occasional fag stabbing, although the solve rate was slipping a little. — Richard Price, *Clockers*, p. 99, 1992
- [H]e and Shane had shared a few easy grounders back when Shane was still working uniform in Southwest. — Stephen J. Cannell, *The Tin Collectors*, p. 15, 2001

ground gripper *noun*

a nonaviator in the Air Force *US, 1944*

- I temporarily became a ground-gripper, a derisive Army Air Corps term applied to nonflyers. — James Brooks, *North to Wolf Country*, p. 183, 2003

groundhog *noun*

in the language of parachuting, anyone who has not parachuted *US, 1978*

- — Dan Poynter, *Parachuting*, p. 170, 1978: "The language of parachuting"

groundhog case *noun*

a desperate situation *US, 1885*

- You see it was a groundhog case. The soil was here, the climate was here, but along with them was a curse, the curse of slavery. — Broadus Mitchell, *The Rise of Cotton Mills in the South*, p. 26, 2001

ground joker *noun*

any nonflying personnel in the Air Force *US, 1946*

- — *American Speech*, p. 310, December 1946: "More air force slang"

ground-pounder noun

an infantry soldier US, 1942

Coined in World War 2, and used in every war since.

- In Vietnam, he goes by an assortment of names—the Grunt, Boonie Rat, Line Dog, Ground Pounder, Hill Humper, or Jarhead. — David Reed, *Up Front in Vietnam*, p. 3, 1967
- "Lose pilots in combat" was a groundpounder's euphemism for "We won't need pilots anymore." — Walter Boyne and Steven Thompson, *The Wild Blue*, p. 413, 1986
- Some "ground pounders" wearing "chocolate chip cookie cammies" even talk of an "Adopt-a-Pilot" campaign and cheer when the jets roar overhead. — *Houston Chronicle*, p. 15, 24th January 1991
- I'm beginning to feel like a groundpounder. Sure will feel good to feel that old prop pulling you along again. — Calvin L. Christman et al., *Lost in the Victory*, p. 62, 1998

ground rations noun

sex on the ground US, 1942

- "Or will be, once we're back on ground rations." — Robert Heinlein, *I Will Fear No Evil*, p. 211, 1970

ground stash noun

a drug dealer's supply of drugs hidden outdoors, near where sales are made US, 1997

- [T]he slingers work ground stashes hidden in used tires, behind cinder blocks, or in the tall grass by the edge of a rear wall. — David Simon and Edward Burns, *The Corner*, p. 5, 1997

ground zero noun

1 the center of action US, 1946

From the lingo of atomic weapons, literally meaning "the ground where a bomb explodes."

- "Ground zero," said Heff, shaking out his soaking jacket. — Richard Farina, *Been Down So Long*, p. 112, 1966

2 an untidy bedroom US, 2002

Teen slang.

- Their bedrooms are "ground zero." Translation? A total mess. — *The Washington Post*, 19th March 2002

grouper trooper noun

a fish and game warden US, 1987

The grouper is a fish in a family that includes the sea bass.

- "Hey, even the grouper troopers got a computer." — Carl Hiaasen, *Skin Tight*, p. 21, 1989

group grope noun

sex involving more than two people US, 1967

- I remember the first group grope I went to was with some guy and his girl friend. — Nicholas Von Hoffman, *We Are The People Our Parents Warned Us Against*, p. 183, 1967
- — *American Speech*, p. 57, Spring–Summer 1970: "Homosexual slang"
- — Eugene Landy, *The Underground Dictionary*, p. 93, 1971
- Kind of gal Alyssa is, you don't think she's been in the middle of an all-girl group grope? — *Chasing Amy*, 1997

groupie; groupy noun

1 a girl who trades her sexual availability to rock musicians in exchange for hanger-on status US, 1966

- They're called Groupies and can be found on the Sunset Strip in Los Angeles, on Macdougal Street around the Night Owl Cafe, or on Carnaby Street in London. The run of the mill Groupie has long blonde hair and heavily made-up eyes. — *The Berkeley Barb*, p. 5, 2nd September 1966
- Like a groupie who gets her hots not from being fucked by a rock star but from the image of herself getting fucked by a star[.] — *Screw*, p. 8, 24th November 1969
- The little blonde groupie with the film crew! You think he sodomized her? — Hunter S. Thompson, *Fear and Loathing in Las Vegas*, p. 54, 1971
- That night I was twenty-three and a daughter of Hollywood, alive with groupie fervor, wanting to fuck my way through rock'n'roll[.] — Eve Babitz, *L.A. Woman*, p. 15, 1982

2 a follower or hobbyist devoted to a preeminent person within a given field, or to a genre or subject type US, 1967

An extension of the previous sense, this usage is not restricted to rock groups or music, nor is there a suggestion that sex is a prerequisite; the tone may be derogatory, jocular, or ironic.

- "Any station groupies with tits that big?" pondered Lieutenant Grimsley[.] — Joseph Wambaugh, *The Choirboys*, p. 370, 1975

- A thrilled female De Lorean trial groupie jostled her way through the wedge of TV cameramen and news photographers to a better vantage point to proclaim, "Yeah, John!" — *United Press International*, 17th August 1984
- A younger generation knows her as the witch in "Rosemary's Baby," for which she won an Academy Award; the funeral groupie in "Harold and Maude"[.] — *New York Times*, p. 28, 11th November 1984
- She wondered if cop groupies out at the Polo Lounge would go for Gary Hammond or think he was impersonating a police officer. — Elmore Leonard, *Maximum Bob*, p. 88, 1991

grovel verb

1 in computing, to work with great diligence but without visible success US, 1981

- — Guy L. Steele, *Coevolution Quarterly*, p. 31, Spring 1981: "Computer slang"
- The file scavenger has been groveling through the file directories for ten minutes now. — Guy L. Steele et al., *The Hacker's Dictionary*, p. 75, 1983

2 to ride a wave even as it runs out of force US, 1990

- — *Surfing*, p. 43, 14th March 1990

Grover noun

a one-thousand dollar bill; one thousand dollars US, 1984

From the portrait of President Grover Cleveland on the bills, first issued in 1928.

- It was nothing Big Ed couldn't handle with Grovers. — Dan Jenkins, *Life Its Ownself*, p. 163, 1984

growler noun

1 in the language of barbershop quartets, a strident bass singer US, 1975

- — *American Speech*, p. 298, Autumn–Winter 1975: "The jargon of barbershop"

2 a prison cell used for solitary confinement US, 1984

- — Inez Cardozo-Freeman, *The Joint*, p. 502, 1984

3 a wrestler US, 1945

- — Lou Shelly, *Hepcats Jive Dictionary*, p. 12, 1945

4 a hotel's activity log US, 1953

- In the indictments lodged against bellboys in the hotel "growler," the rough equivalent of a ship's log, one word appeared over and over—caught. — Jim Thompson, *Bad Boy*, p. 356, 1953

5 a beer can US, 1949

- — Captain Vincent J. Monteleone, *Criminal Slang*, p. 108, 1949

grrl noun

a woman US, 1992

A radical postfeminist term.

- Part of the grrl riot and they are very active supporters of grrl issues. — *alt.music.alternatives*, 25th October 1992
- Clean, grrl-positive kids with short hair and little sweaters, pegged pants and deliberate ethics. — Michelle Tea, *Valencia*, p. 155, 2000

grrr, whirr, thank you sir

sex with a man carried out in very short order US, 1997

- "It was just Grrr, whirr, thank you sir, every time." — Ethan Morden, *Some Men Are Lookers*, p. 22, 1997

grub noun

an inferior, lowly person UK, 1845

- — Miss Cone, *The Slang Dictionary (Hawthorne High School)*, 1965

grub verb

1 to eat US, 1999

- I let Chante's chair out for her, got ready to grub and relax a bit. — Eric Jerome Dickey, *Cheaters*, p. 309, 1999

2 to kiss with passion US, 1963

- — Carol Ann Preusse, *Jargon Used by University of Texas Co-Eds*, 1963
- — Connie Eble (Editor), *UNC-CH Campus Slang*, p. 3, March 1981

3 to engage in sexual foreplay US, 1976

- — *Verbatim*, p. 280, May 1976

grubber noun

a disgusting person US, 1941

- — *American Speech*, p. 60, Spring–Summer 1975: "Razorback slang"
- I don't want to be a grubber. A hustler. A parasite. — Cleo Odzer, *Goa Freaks*, p. 39, 1995

grubbies noun

old, worn, comfortable clothes US, 1966

- — John D. Bell et al., *Loosely Speaking*, p. 10, 1966
- They wore cutoffs and jeans and grubbies of all kinds. — Joseph Wambaugh, *The Delta Star*, p. 217, 1983

grubby *adjective*
not neat, not clean *US, 1965*
- — Carol Covington, *A Glossary of Teenage Terms*, 1965

grubs *noun*
old, worn, and comfortable clothes *US, 1966*
- — *Current Slang*, p. 4, Winter 1966

grudge fuck *noun*
sex out of spite or anger *US, 1977*
- "Go somewhere else for your grudge fuck." — Anthony Mancini, *Minnie Santangelo and the Evil Eye*, p. 116, 1977
- Was it a grudge fuck? A mutual grudge fuck. — John Gregory Dunne, *Dutch Shea Jr.*, p. 320, 1982
- "But I'm afraid it was a grudge fuck," Joey said. — Carl Hiaasen, *Skinny Dip*, p. 239, 2004

grudge-fuck *verb*
to have sex out of spite or anger *US, 1990*
- To avenge the crack about Joe, she grudgefucked Dan. — Seth Morgan, *Homeboy*, p. 171, 1990

gruesome twosome *noun*
a couple who date steadily *US, 1941*
- The gruesome twosome. That's been going on since 1948 when they graduated from Bryn Mawr. — Rita Mae Brown, *Rubyfruit Jungle*, p. 165, 1973
- We became the gruesome twosome. The pair that everyone wanted at parties because we were so entertaining together. Always high on life, on each other. — Jane Green, *Straight Talking*, p. 40, 2003

Grumman Greyhound *noun*
the C-2A aircraft *US, 1979*
Manufactured by Grumann, a twin engine, prop-driven plane used by the US Navy to transport troops (hence the "Greyhound" as an allusion to the bus company) or cargo.
- Jack sat hunched in a bucket seat on the port side of a Grumman Greyhound. — Tom Clancy, *The Hunt for Red October*, p. 119, 1984

grundy *adjective*
mediocre *US, 1959*
- Some feel he is "real crazy" (fine), but others find him "just grundy" (not good, not bad). — *Look*, p. 49, 24th November 1959

grunge *noun*
an obnoxious, graceless person *US, 1968*
- — Collin Baker et al., *College Undergraduate Slang Study Conducted at Brown University*, p. 131, 1968

grungejumper *noun*
used as a euphemism for "motherfucker" *US, 1958*
- I picked him out real careful, ya grungejumper! — Jack Kerouac, *The Dharma Bums*, p. 145, 1958

grungy *adjective*
filthy, dirty, unpleasant, untidy *US, 1962*
- Grungy—Grubbiness to an extent known only to Techmen and Hoboes. — *Voo Doo Magazine (MIT)*, pp. 10–11, January 1962
- — *Current Slang*, p. 4, Winter 1966
- Fine and professional, yet intensely driving and almost grungy [...], it was truly exciting music[.] — Lester Bangs, *Psychotic Reactions and Carburetor Dung*, p. 17, 1971
- I went to the University of Miami three years, majored in psychology, and I worked as a stripper for three years in topless bars in Miami, but not the grungy joints. — Elmore Leonard, *Pronto*, pp. 332–323, 1993

grunt *noun*
1 an infantry soldier, especially but not necessarily a marine *US, 1962*
An important piece of slang in the Vietnam war.
- In Vietnam, he goes by an assortment of names—the Grunt, Boonie Rat, Line Dog, Ground Pounder, Hill Humper, or Jarhead. — David Reed, *Up Front in Vietnam*, p. 3, 1967
- Charlie Company was a "grunt" unit; its men were the foot soldiers, the "GI Joes," who understood they were to take orders, not question them. — Seymour Hersh, *My Lai 4*, p. 18, 1970
- Now according to some people, folks do not want to hear about Alpha Company—us grunts—busting jungle and busting cherries from Landing Zone Skator-Gator to Scat Man Do[.] — Larry Heinemann, *Paco's Story*, p. 5, 1986

- Grunts walk hard and they walk far / In Artillery we ride by car. — Sandee Shaffer Johnson, *Cadences*, p. 80, 1986

2 a member of the US Marine Corps *US, 1968*
- Listen, us guys are goddam saints compared to the grunts. — Darryl Ponicsan, *The Last Detail*, p. 15, 1970
- — *Current Slang*, p. 16, Summer 1970
- Having served in Korea as a dogface grunt, he knew a lifer when he saw one. — Joseph Wambaugh, *Finnegan's Week*, p. 27, 1993

3 marijuana *US, 1993*
- — Peter Johnson, *Dictionary of Street Alcohol and Drug Terms*, p. 86, 1993

grunt *verb*
to eat *US, 1968*
- — Collin Baker et al., *College Undergraduate Slang Study Conducted at Brown University*, p. 131, 1968
- — Michael Dalton Johnson, *Talking Trash with Redd Foxx*, p. 44, 1994

grunts *noun*
food *US, 1968*
- — Collin Baker et al., *College Undergraduate Slang Study Conducted at Brown University*, p. 131, 1968
- — Dennis Aaberg and John Milius, *Big Wednesday*, p. 209, 1978

GS *noun*
a shared act of urine fetishism; the act of urination by one person on another for sexual gratification *US, 1979*
Used in personal advertising; an abbreviation of **GOLDEN SHOWER**.
- — *What Color is Your Handkerchief*, p. 6, 1979

G-star *noun*
a youth gang member *US, 1995*
- — Bill Valentine, *Gang Intelligence Manual*, p. 76, 1995: "Black street gang terminology"

g-ster *noun*
a youth gang member *US, 1991*
- If you have been wearing your hair in one of the prescribed g-ster do's—rows of skinny French braids secured with red (or blue) barrettes, it is cropped close to the scalp. — Leon Bing, *Do or Die*, p. 8, 1991
- "Adios, g-sters." — Stephen J. Cannell, *White Sister*, p. 48, 2006

G-string *noun*
a small patch of cloth passed between a woman's legs and supported by a waist cord, providing a snatch of modesty for a dancer *US, 1936*
A slight variation on the word "gee-string" used in the late C19 to describe the loin cloth worn by various indigenous peoples.
- One or two Oasis girls strip completely, without G-strings, plaster or anything on. — Jack Lait and Lee Mortimer, *Washington Confidential*, p. 264, 1951
- G-strings like phosphorescent badges etched across the thighs; spread legs radiating their unfulfilled invitation[.] — John Rechy, *City of Night*, p. 297, 1963
- I felt for the snap on my strip panties ... soon I would be left with just my g-string, not much for warmth but the legal limit. — Lois O'Conner, *The Bare Facts*, p. 16, 1964
- The 6–3 votes allows local or state governments to require that dancers wear at least pasties and a G-string so long as everyone else also is forbidden to appear naked in public. — *Washington Post*, 30th March 2000

G suit *noun*
an inflatable garment that counteracts G-pressure on a pilot *US, 1990*
- And the jocks all trembled as they zipped on their G-suits / Said "I really ain't believ' that!" — Joseph Tuso, *Singing the Vietnam Blues*, p. 156, 1990: The Phu Cat Alert Pad

GTA *noun*
the criminal charge of grand theft, auto *US, 1993*
The punch-line of an oft-repeated joke: "What do you call four [ethnic minority of choice at the moment] in a brand new Cadillac?"
- "For GTA once," Shelby said. "Drove a hot Porsche for six months 'fore they nailed me." — Joseph Wambaugh, *Finnegan's Week*, p. 40, 1993

GTG
used as shorthand in Internet discussion groups and text messages to mean "*got to go*" *US, 2002*
- — Gabrielle Mander, *WAN2TLK? ltl bk of txt msgs*, p. 45, 2002

G-top *noun*

a tent or trailer in a carnival reserved exclusively for carnival employees *US, 1980*

Employees can drink and gamble out of sight of the public and police.

- — Joe McKennon, *Circus Lingo*, p. 42, 1980
- — Gene Sorrows, *All About Carnivals*, p. 18, 1985: "Terminology"

GTT

used as an abbreviation for "gone to Texas" *US, 1839*

- They didn't have a thing to lose, so they put up signs on their fences—GTT. — Michael Lee West, *American Pie*, p. 82, 1996

guardhouse lawyer *noun*

a military prisoner with a strong interest in law and legal arguments *US, 1888*

- Eisenhower described Slovik as "one of those guardhouse lawyers who refused to believe that he'd ever be executed." — Carlo D'Este, *Eisenhower*, p. 629, 2002

guard puke *noun*

a US National Air Guard pilot *US, 1990*

- Oh I'm stuck here in Sun Valley and they're bombing me / Just keep sending those old Guard pukes, I know I'll get home free. — Joseph Tuso, *Singing the Vietnam Blues*, p. 212, 1990: The VC Truck Driver's Blues

Guatemala dirt dobbers *noun*

sandals *US, 1970*

- — *Current Slang*, p. 18, Spring 1970

guava *adjective*

very good, superlative *US, 1991*

- — Trevor Cralle, *The Surfin'ary*, p. 48, 1991
- Guava tunes, kid. — *Empire Records*, 1995

gubbish *noun*

in computing, nonsense *US, 1983*

A blend of "garbage" and "rubbish."

- — Guy L. Steele et al., *The Hacker's Dictionary*, p. 75, 1983

gudentight; goot-n-tight *adjective*

tight, especially in a sexual context *US, 1969*

A mock German or Dutch construction.

- Goot-n-tight! Annette's sister. — Steve Cannon, *Groove, Bang, and Jive Around*, p. 45, 1969

guest star *noun*

a last-minute replacement to take the place of someone who has cancelled a date *US, 2002*

- — Amy Sohn, *Sex and the City*, p. 155, 2002

guff *noun*

1 foolish nonsense, usually spoken or sung *US, 1888*

From "guff" (empty talk).

- "Don't take any guff from these swine," I said as he slammed the phone down. — Hunter S. Thompson, *Fear and Loathing in Las Vegas*, p. 12, 1971

2 back-talk, verbal resistance *US, 1879*

- Just because I went to college don't make me take any guff from a nit like you. — Raymond Chandler, *The Long Goodbye*, p. 35, 1953
- You can tell the colonel your phone's been out of order if he gives you any guff. — Jim Thompson, *The Nothing Man*, p. 202, 1954

guide *noun*

a person who monitors the LSD experience of another, helping them through bad moments and caring for their physical needs *US, 1966*

- He gazes at the lights coming through the window as a guide comforted a friend. — Richard Alpert and Sidney Cohen, *LSD*, p. 116, 1966
- [W]e're asking for a court order allowing the priests, in our religion who we call "guides," to import and distribute psychedelic chemicals. — *The San Francisco Oracle*, 1966
- It was the only trip where I had somebody who acted as a guide or a ground control. — Stephen Gaskin, *Amazing Dope Tails*, p. 86, 1980

guido *noun*

an Italian or Italian-American, especially a macho one *US, 1988*

Disparaging.

- — Connie Eble (Editor), *UNC-CH Campus Slang*, p. 5, Spring 1988
- Guido's of the world unite. — *New Jack City*, 1990

- In the locker rooms of the Eighteenth District Station and around the cop bars, he called Italians guidos or wops, Poles polacks, Bohemians hunkies, Mexicans spicks or greasers, and African-Americans niggers or darkies. — Robert Campbell, *Boneyards*, p. 10, 1992
- Al Dante was the ultimate in guido. — Rita Cirtesi, *Pink Slip*, p. 2, 1999

guillotine *noun*

the lip of a wave crashing down on a surfer's head *US, 1991*

- — Trevor Cralle, *The Surfin'ary*, p. 48, 1991

guilt trip *noun*

an effort to make someone else feel guilty *US, 1970*

- Derisively, she berated her fellow Weathermen for having (obscenity, obscenity) a lot and being motivated by a white guilt trip. — *Lima (Ohio) News*, pp. 6–7, 29th January 1970
- "You poor baby, Harvey," she said. "You must have been on an incredible guilt trip." — Cyra McFadden, *The Serial*, p. 170, 1977
- And how dare you try to lay a guilt trip on me about it—in public, no less! — *Chasing Amy*, p. 99, 1997

guilt-trip *verb*

to attempt to make someone feel guilty *US, 1974*

- Black women can't be guilt-tripped any more about consciousness-raising groups. — *Off Our Backs*, p. 11, 30th September 1974
- I have a lot of trouble with gay activists who try to guilt-trip people into doing something when they don't know the consequences. — *AM Cycle*, 27th July 1977
- I mighta known. You've got a black belt in guilt-tripping. — Joseph Wambaugh, *Finnegan's Week*, p. 244, 1993

guinea *noun*

1 an Italian or Italian-American *US, 1890*

- "The agent's a goddam guinea, just like the owner," Red charged. — Ross Russell, *The Sound*, p. 144, 1961
- Know he would stand in the ghinny corner of the yard with his boss, Pete Amadeo[.] — Edwin Torres, *After Hours*, p. 159, 1979
- This little guinea fuck. Someday he's gonna be a boss. — *Goodfellas*, 1990
- He certainly didn't need to worry about tripping and spraying fizz on my highly unprofessional outfit: a pair of cutoffs and a man's white V-neck T-shirt that Dodie proclaimed was the equivalent of a neon sign that said guinea. — Rita Ciresi, *Pink Slip*, p. 39, 1999

2 in horse racing, a horse groom *US, 1962*

- — Mel Heimer, *Inside Racing*, p. 211, 1962

Guinea football *noun*

a homemade bomb *US, 1918*

- — Hyman E. Goldin et al., *Dictionary of American Underworld Lingo*, p. 87, 1950

guinea pig *noun*

a person used as the subject of an experiment *US, 1920*

- [I]nmates from both Hart's and Riker's were being shipped over to King's County Hospital, where they were being used as guinea-pigs by some city doctors to find out what the score was with marijuana. — Mezz Mezzrow, *Really the Blues*, p. 317, 1946

guinea red *noun*

cheap Italian red wine *US, 1933*

Offensive because of the national slur.

- "We still call it Guinea red." — Harry Grey, *The Hoods*, p. 125, 1952
- "What's the matter? You think I can't talk?" Felita said. "I ain't a pair of shoes or a jug of guinea red." — Robert Campbell, *Alice in La-La Land*, p. 276, 1987

guinea stinker *noun*

a strong-smelling cigar *US, 1956*

- "Here, have a guinea stinker. Special tobacco, cured in Torino." — Richard Farina, *Been Down So Long It Seems Like Up to Me*, p. 288, 1966

Guineatown *noun*

a neighborhood dominated by Italian-Americans and/or Italian immigrants *US, 1992*

- He left his own car back in Guineatown. — Richard Price, *Clockers*, p. 248, 1992

gully washer *noun*

a heavy rainstorm *US, 1903*

- Seconds later an honest-to-God Missouri gully washer would come crashing down hard and fast[.] — Fannie Flagg, *Standing in the Rainbow*, p. 8, 2002

gum *noun*

1 crude, unrefined opium *US, 1986*
- — *American Speech*, p. 100, May 1956: "Smugglers' argot in the southwest"
- — Richard A. Spears, *The Slang and Jargon of Drugs and Drink*, p. 237, 1986

2 in pool, a cushion *US, 1993*
Cushions were once fashioned with rubber gum.
- — Mike Shamos, *The Illustrated Encyclopedia of Billiards*, p. 111, 1993

gum *verb*
▸ **gum it**
to perform oral sex on a woman *US, 1971*
- — Eugene Landy, *The Underground Dictionary*, p. 94, 1971

gumball *noun*
the flashing colored lights on a police car *US, 1971*
- — Helen Dahlskog (Editor), *A Dictionary of Contemporary and Colloquial Usage*, p. 29, 1972
- [A]nd if the guy didn't sideswipe some cars and pile up he'd be on him before he hit Woodward, nail him with the gumballs flashing blue and siren turned up to high yelp. — Elmore Leonard, *Switch*, p. 150, 1978
- A lone gumball sits perched atop the passenger side of the roof. — *Menace II Society*, 1993
- [T]he amateur photographer turned on the patrol boat's gumball-blue light and hit them with a few siren yelps. — Joseph Wambaugh, *Floaters*, p. 3, 1996

gumball *verb*
to activate the flashing colored lights on a police car *US, 1983*
- Within five minutes, there were a dozen police cars blocking the street, their red and blue lights gumballing in all directions. — Joseph Wambaugh, *The Delta Star*, p. 114, 1983

gum-beat *verb*
to talk, to chat *US, 1942*
- Like practically all jazz disciplines they really came to listen, not to dance or gumbeat around the table. — Mezz Mezzrow, *Really the Blues*, p. 77, 1946

gum-beater *noun*
a talkative person *US, 1942*
- "You are four sad gum-beaters." — Nalo Hopkinson, *Mojo*, p. 19, 2003

gum-beating *noun*
idle conversation *US, 1945*
- "Mike," I said softly, "private now. What is this gum-beating?" — Robert Heinlein, *The Moon is a Harsh Mistress*, p. 318, 1966

gumbie *verb*
a transvestite or transgender person *US, 2002*
- — Jeffrey Ian Ross, *Behind Bars*, p. 187, 2002: Slammer Slang

gumbies *noun*
black tennis shoes *US, 1969*
- — *Current Slang*, p. 6, Spring 1969

gumbo *noun*

1 in horse racing, thick mud *US, 1947*
- — Dan Parker, *The ABC of Horse Racing*, p. 146, 1947

2 in oil drilling, any viscous or sticky formation encountered in drilling *US, 1954*
- — Jerry Robertson, *Oil Slanguage*, p. 62, 1954

gumby *noun*
in computing, an inconsequential but highly visible display of stupidity *US, 1991*
A borrowing from Monty Python.
- — Eric S. Raymond, *The New Hacker's Dictionary*, p. 188, 1991

gumdrop *noun*
a capsule of secobarbital, a central nervous system depressant; any drug in capsule form *US, 1980*
- — Edith A. Folb, *runnin' down some lines*, p. 241, 1980

gump *noun*

1 a simple, foolish person *US, 1994*
- You gumps have taken this power thing too far. — William Upski Wimsatt, *Bomb the Suburbs*, p. 50, 1994

2 a passive homosexual man *US, 1996*
- — *Maledicta*, p. 265, Summer/Winter 1981: "By its slang, ye shall know It: the pessimism of prison life"
- — Reinhold Aman, *Hillary Clinton's Pen Pal: A Guide to Life and Lingo in Federal Prison*, 1996

3 a chicken (of the fowl persuasion) *US, 1981*
- — Don Wilmeth, *The Language of American Popular Entertainment*, p. 121, 1981

gump stump *noun*
the rectum *US, 1967*
- "You got time up the gump stump." — Ken Kesey, *Kesey's Jail Journal*, p. 20, 1967
- We got time up the gump stump, we're on per diem, let's just check the hell into a hotel and catch the early train tomorrow morning. — Darryl Ponicsan, *The Last Detail*, p. 41, 1970
- "I know we've all been studiously reading our message traffic on the way over from EASTPAC and that we've had briefings up the gumpstump back in Pearl." — Peter Deutermann, *The Edge of Honor*, p. 17, 1994

gums *noun*
overshoes *US, 1996*
- — Claudio R. Salvucci, *The Philadelphia Dialect Dictionary*, p. 43, 1996

▸ **flap your gums; beat your gums; beat up your gums**
to talk *US, 1955*
- "I just got tired of hearing the two of you flap your gums." — Jon Sharpe, *Rogue River Feud*, p. 97, 1995
- "Are you gonna get on, or are you gonna stand there and beat your gums?" — Virgia DeBerry, *Tryin' to Sleep in the Bed You Made*, p. 207, 1997

gumshoe *noun*
a private investigator or detective *US, 1908*
- We were in the gravy once more, and we looked that gumshoe square in the eye again. — Mezz Mezzrow, *Really the Blues*, p. 131, 1946
- I thought you'd be out of that uniform by now, doing gumshoe work. — Horace McCoy, *Kiss Tomorrow Good-bye*, p. 189, 1948
- That's why I'm upset to find out that you think that I've been a detective with this club, a gumshoe. — Jim Bouton, *Ball Four*, p. 258, 1970
- This kid, looks like a girl, is a private eye. A shamus. A gumshoe. — Robert Campbell, *Alice in La-La Land*, p. 202, 1987

gun *noun*

1 a hired gunman *US, 1920*
- "He was a free-lance gun that did muscle for small bookies on bettors who didn't want to pay off." — Mickey Spillane, *The Snake*, p. 11, 1964
- She said the two guns who had guarded the truck were known as Four-Four and Freddy[.] — Chester Himes, *Cotton Comes to Harlem*, p. 85, 1965
- "McLean was with two guns at the time, Tony Blue [Anthony D'Agostino] and America Sacramone." — Vincent Teresa, *My Life in the Mafia*, p. 173, 1973

2 a pickpocket *US, 1965*
- It was on that Sixth Street to Market, between Central Avenue and Plum / that's the worst old place in ragtown for a shuckman or gun. — Bruce Jackson, *Get Your Ass in the Water and Swim Like Me*, p. 85, 1965

3 a hypodermic needle and syringe *US, 1899*
- Said, "Let's have a party, have some fun / for God's sake, fellas, don't forget the gun / 'cause man, I want some two in one." — Bruce Jackson, *Get Your Ass in the Water and Swim Like Me*, p. 149, 1964
- I emptied the dropper. I pulled out the gun. — Iceberg Slim (Robert Beck), *Pimp*, p. 183, 1969

4 the upper arm; the bicep muscle *US, 1973*
- — Malachi Andrews and Paul T. Owens, *Black Language*, p. 79, 1973
- — James Harris, *A Convict's Dictionary*, 1989
- — Connie Eble (Editor), *UNC-CH Campus Slang*, p. 3, Fall 1998

5 the penis *UK, 1675*
- This is my rifle / This is my gun / One's for fightin' / One's for fun. — *Screw!*, p. 16, 11th January 1971
- — Anon., *King Smut's Wet Dreams Interpreted*, 1978

6 any instrument used for tattooing *US, 1989*
- — James Harris, *A Convict's Dictionary*, 1989

7 a brass horn *US, 1960*
- — Robert George Reisner, *The Jazz Titans*, 1960

8 a large surfboard used for big-wave conditions *US, 1965*
- — D.S. Halacy, *Surfer!*, p. 215, 1965

9 in the language of wind surfing, a sailboard that is moderately long and tapered at the rear *US, 1985*
- — Frank Fox, *A Beginner's Guide to Zen and the Art of Windsurfing*, p. 151, 1985: "A short dictionary of wind surfing terms"

10 in horse racing, a complete effort by a jockey *US, 1976*
- — Tom Ainslie, *Ainslie's Complete Guide to Thoroughbred Racing*, p. 332, 1976

▶ **get your gun**
to experience an orgasm *US, 1967*
- When I got my gun I thought my whole insides were comin' out. — Frank Reynolds, *Freewheelin' Frank*, p. 118, 1967

▶ **on the gun**
engaged in crime as a profession *US, 1950*
- — *The New American Mercury*, p. 710, 1950

▶ **under the gun**
1 (used of a prison) under armed guard *US, 2002*
- — Gary K. Farlow, *Prison-ese*, p. 77, 2002

2 in poker, said of the player who must act first in a given situation *US, 1947*
- — Oswald Jacoby, *Oswald Jacoby on Poker*, p. 142, 1947

gun *verb*
1 to look over, to examine *UK, 1812*
- Al always showed up surrounded by a gang of trigger men—they sat in a corner, very gay and noisy but gunning the whole situation out of the corners of their eyes. — Mezz Mezzrow, *Really the Blues*, p. 63, 1946
- "Why are you gunning me?" Chllly asked. — Malcolm Braly, *On the Yard*, p. 244, 1967
- "Look at her," he said, indicating Jackie Onassis, "she's been gunning me all night." — Ovid Demaris, *The Last Mafioso*, pp. 417–418, 1981

2 to have sex with *US, 1951*
- "I was probably the only guy in the world who went to such trouble to see an old ballgame and trying to gun cunts along the way." — Jack Kerouac, *On the Road (The Original Scroll)*, p. 329, 1951

3 to be associated with or engage in criminal activity *US, 1997*
- Never mind that you were gunning with the dead man for a decade. — David Simon and Edward Burns, *The Corner*, p. 72, 1997

4 in computing, to use a computer's force-quit feature to close a malfunctioning program *US, 1983*
- Some idiot left a useless background program running, soaking up half the cycles. So I gunned it. — Guy L. Steele et al., *The Hacker's Dictionary*, p. 75, 1983

gun belt *noun*
the American defense industry *US, 1991*
- — David Olive, *Business Babble*, p. 75, 1991

gunboats *noun*
large, heavy shoes *US, 1862*
- Hobnailed, high-topped gunboats weighing about ten pounds each, with one-inch soles as flexible as a petrified tree. — Mezz Mezzrow, *Really the Blues*, p. 33, 1946

gun-bull *noun*
an armed prison guard *US, 1928*
- High on the north block wall he glimpsed a gun bull[.] — Malcolm Braly, *On the Yard*, p. 4, 1967
- — Marlene Freedman, *Alcatraz*, 1983

gun bunny *noun*
an artilleryman *US, 1980*
- — Hans Halberstadt, *Airborne*, p. 130, 1988: "Abridged dictionary of airborne terms"
- He passed it to the gun bunnies serving the six trailed guns, and they were readied. — Cherokee Paul McDonald, *Into the Green*, p. 49, 2001
- And because gun bunnies are too dumb to navigate, you're doing the navigating and scouting[.]. — Michael Takiff, *Brave Men, Gentle Heroes*, p. 59, 2003

gun down *verb*
(used of a male) to masturbate while looking directly at somebody else *US, 2002*
- They say John got caught on the third shift gunnin' down the C.O. — Gary K. Farlow, *Prison-ese*, p. 27, 2002

gunfighter seat *noun*
in a public place, a seat with the back against the wall, overlooking the room *US, 1997*
From the caution exercised by gunfighters in the West.
- Tommy had the gunfighter seat, with his back to the wall so he could scope out the hot-looking talent coming up from the pool. — Stephen Cannell, *Big Con*, p. 206, 1997
- It was the gunfighter's seat—a clear vision of the entrance and no one could sneak up behind her. — Sandra Carlotta Paige, *Beyond Heaven*, p. 89, 2005

gun for *verb*
to be on the lookout for with the intent of hurting or killing *US, 1878*
- This cat, Eddie Carter, who was gunning for Kelsey, had heard about Jim. — Claude Brown, *Manchild in the Promised Land*, p. 217, 1965

gun from the gate *noun*
in horse racing, a racehorse that starts races quickly *US, 1951*
- — David W. Maurer, *Argot of the Racetrack*, p. 33, 1951

gunge *noun*
any tropical skin disease affecting the crotch area *US, 1977*
- [Rule] 5. Do not get the gunge. When the Army wants you to have it, it will be issued to you. — Larry Heinemann, *Close Quarters*, p. 272, 1977

gungeon; gunja; gunjeh; gunga *noun*
marijuana, especially from Jamaica *US, 1944*
A corruption of GANJA. Used to describe the most potent grade of marijuana in the 1940s.
- R.S.V.P., and bring your own gunja. — Mezz Mezzrow, *Really the Blues*, p. 128, 1946
- [A]nd the top grade, the "gungeon," which produces a voluptuous "bang," bringing as high as a dollar[.] — Jack Lait, *New York Confidential*, p. 118, 1948
- [T]he best marijuana cigarettes to be had were made of the gunja and kisca that merchant sailors smuggled in from Africa and Persia. — Malcolm X and Alex Haley, *The Autobiography of Malcolm X*, p. 86, 1964
- I flew all the way to Jamaica to get you this gunja. — Snoop Doggy Dogg, *A Day in the Life of Snoop Doogy Dog [cover art]*, 1993

gung-ho *adjective*
dedicated, spirited, enthusiastic *US, 1942*
Originally coined as a slogan understood to mean "Work together!" by the US Marines during World War 2, then embraced as an adjective.
- There was the FBI in heavy numbers guarding the National Security and all that other gung-ho shit. — Abbie Hoffman, *Woodstock Nation*, p. 56, 1969
- Nat says you were a gung ho guy in uniform, Al, always up in the squad room, asking questions, y' know. — Edwin Torres, *Q & A*, p. 154, 1977
- Semper fi, do or die! / Gung ho, gung ho, gung ho! — *Full Metal Jacket*, 1987
- Now Neal was a hard guy to get to know intimately because he lived very much within himself, as gung-ho as he was. — Herbert Huncke, *Guilty of Everything*, p. 94, 1990

gungy; gungi *adjective*
enthusiastic, spirited, brave *US, 1961*
Formed from GUNG-HO.
- "If someone is 'gungi,' he's all right, it's good to have him on our side, he's afraid of nothing, he never gets tired[.]" — Charles Anderson, *The Grunts*, p. 29, 1976

gunk *noun*
1 an unidentified and unpleasant substance *US, 1938*
- She looks cheap in that sleazy red dress, and she's wearing gunk on her eyelashes. — Grace Metalious, *Peyton Place*, p. 172, 1956
- She wanted—repeat wanted—yours truly to drive this gangster's Imperial, just take it out for a spin, I suppose, and blow the gunk out of its huge engine. — Robert Gover, *One Hundred Dollar Misunderstanding*, p. 142, 1961
- [T]here's a thingamajig they can put on the projector that'll cut through that gunk like Bruce Lee's foot through Velveeta cheese. — Joe Bob Briggs, *Joe Bob Goes to the Drive-In*, p. 9, 1987
- You just get them all covered with gunk on the next load. — C.D. Payne, *Youth in Revolt*, p. 291, 1993

2 any industrial solvent inhaled for its psychoactive effect *US, 1982*
- — Ralph de Sola, *Crime Dictionary*, p. 60, 1982

gun moll *noun*
a female gangster *US, 1908*
- "You thought any about becoming a gun moll?" I asked. — Max Shulman, *The Many Loves of Dobie Gillis*, p. 9, 1951
- Don't worry, I'm not a gun moll. — Jack Kerouac, *On the Road*, p. 121, 1957

gunner *noun*
1 a person with sexual expertise and experience *US, 1965*
- I suppose she's a real gunner; bangs away, huh? — John Nichols, *The Sterile Cuckoo*, p. 88, 1965

● — Collin Baker et al., *College Undergraduate Slang Study Conducted at Brown University*, p. 132, 1968

2 in poker, the player with the best hand or who plays his hand as if it were the best hand *US, 1951*

● — *American Speech*, p. 99, May 1951

3 the person shooting the dice in craps *US, 1930*

● He never paid back loans, would stand at the edges of a crap game and bet his dime or quarter on the gunner if he was on a hot roll. — Gilbert Sorrentino, *Steelwork*, p. 156, 1970

4 a student who takes competition to an aggressive level *US, 1994*

● — Sally Williams, *"Strong" Words*, p. 145, 1994

gunny *noun*

1 a US Marine Corps gunnery sergeant *US, 1931*

● The gunny called the platoon sergeants and assigned each of the newcomers. — Charles Anderson, *The Grunts*, p. 106, 1976

● The gunny yelled, "Anyone who has R&R coming and wants it, jump on that bird." — Mark Baker, *Nam*, p. 98, 1981

2 a door gunner on an airship, or a crew member of a gunship *US, 1980*

● A door gunner's best friend was his hatch M-60, which many gunnies took to calling Hog-60's[.] — Jack Hawkins, *Chopper One #2*, p. 27, 1987

3 a gun enthusiast *US, 1957*

● — *American Speech*, p. 193, October 1957: "Some colloquialisms of the handgunner"

4 potent marijuana *US, 1970*

● I don't know where my head was, behind that jive wine and that bad gunny. — Odie Hawkins, *Ghetto Sketches*, p. 119, 1972

gun pet *noun*

a parapet fortified to protect artillery *US, 1990*

● The "gun pets" were circular and large enough to allow the gun and its tail to be rotated full circle. — Greg Clark, *Words of the Vietnam War*, p. 391, 1990

guns *noun*

the fists *US, 1981*

● — *Maledicta*, p. 266, Summer/Winter 1981: "By its slang, ye shall know it: the pessimism of prison life"

guns a go-go *nickname*

the CH-47 Chinook helicopter *US, 1987*

● He coordinated the firepower of artillery, aerial rocket helicopters, regular gunships, Navy and Air Force tactical airstrikes, naval gunfire, medium battle tanks, M42 Duster guns and even CH47 "Guns-A-Go-Go." — Shelby L. Stanton, *Anatomy of a Division*, p. 94, 1987

● — David Hart, *First Air Cavalry Division Vietnam Dictionary*, p. 29, 2004

gunsel *noun*

1 a young homosexual man *US, 1918*

● But punishment varies in almost all prisons and sometimes both "wolf" and "gunsel" are "sent to the hole." — *Ebony*, p. 82, July 1951

● The term gunsel is derived from the heyday of safe crackers when it referred to a criminal who specialized in this form of thievery and was accompanied by a youthful apprentice. — *New York Mattachine Newsletter*, p. 6, June 1961

● But no matter what, Dio must be snuffed. Him and his fucking gunsel. — Gerald Petievich, *Money Men*, p. 148, 1981

● "So why was this gunsel so runny-mouthed with you?" "I was doing him and he had the idea him talking about doing you would arouse me to greater efforts, if you know what I mean!" — Robert Campbell, *Boneyards*, p. 249, 1992

2 a thug *US, 1943*

● We shot out under the electric horshoe and the big gunsel in the front seat made a sharp right turn onto the highway back to Oakland. — Thurston Scott, *Cure it with Honey*, p. 120, 1951

● A gunsel, he thought immediately, using the term they applied to any kid on the make for trouble or a reputation as a hard rock. — Malcolm Braly, *On the Yard*, p. 243, 1967

● "A lousy little punk. A stupid gunsel." — Georgia Sothern, *My Life in Burlesque*, p. 157, 1972

● How much more of this cheapjack bullshit can we be expected to take from that stupid little gunsel? — Hunter S. Thompson, *The Great Shark Hunt*, p. 383, 1979

gunship *noun*

a van used in a drive-by shooting *US, 1988*

● The vans they go around in? They call 'em gunships. Drive by a house and spray it up with an Uzi. — Elmore Leonard, *Freaky Deaky*, p. 129, 1988

gunslinger *noun*

a chronic masturbator *US, 2002*

● — Gary K. Farlow, *Prison-ese*, p. 27, 2002

gun up *verb*

to prepare to fight, either with fists or weapons *US, 1981*

● — *Maledicta*, p. 266, Summer/Winter 1981: "By its slang, ye shall know it: the pessimism of prison life"

g up *verb*

to dress in youth gang attire *US, 1997*

● Coco complained it took them hours to get "G'd-up," or gangster dressed in Crip blue. — Gini Sikes, *8 Ball Chicks*, p. 10, 1997

guppies *noun*

anchovies *US, 1996*

Limited usage, but clever.

● — *Maledicta*, p. 13, 1996: "Domino's pizza jargon"

gush *verb*

in professional wrestling, to bleed *US, 1992*

● Steve Armstrong gushes. — *Herb's Wrestling Tidbits*, 19th October 1992

gussy up *verb*

to dress up *US, 1952*

● "Aw, gee, Annie, I wanted to get all gussied up." — Jacqueline Susann, *Valley of the Dolls*, p. 89, 1966

● They were gussied up to look like sensible townandcountry doggers. — Seth Morgan, *Homeboy*, p. 268, 1990

gusto *noun*

money *US, 1984*

● To have gangster style you have to get "getting paid"—making so much gusto (money) until it's goofy. — Nelson George (quoting Teddy Riley, 1988), *Hip Hop America*, p. 166, 1998

gut *noun*

1 a school course that requires little effort *US, 1916*

● I've had two guts all lined up, but they backfired. — Max Shulman, *Guided Tour of Campus Humor*, p. 105, 1955

● Couple of guys in the house took that one-o-one course for their science requirement, said it was a real gut. — Richard Farina, *Been Down So Long*, p. 35, 1966

2 a main street through town *US, 1968*

● — *Current Slang*, p. 4, Spring 1968

gut bomb *noun*

any greasy, tasty, heavy food, especially a greasy hamburger *US, 1968*

● — *Current Slang*, p. 6, Spring 1968

● We met Steve for lunch and celebrated with a hamburger. The old gut-bomb never tasted so good! — Mary Shields, *Sled Dog Trails*, p. 76, 1984

● After the movie last night, the two of them had stayed in the wardroom and waited for the stewards to open up the "Mid-rats" line, the midnight snack service where officers could purchase the infamous "gut bombs." These were double cheeseburgers topped with nearly everything that science was still attempting to classify. — Gerry Carroll, *North S*A*R*, p. 193, 1991

gut box *noun*

a safe *US, 1972*

● They never call them a safe, but a pete or a box. They have names like this spindle and gutbox. — Harry King, *Box Man*, p. 56, 1972

gut bucket *noun*

1 an earthy style of jazz music combining elements of ragtime and blues *US, 1929*

A "gutbucket" was a cheap saloon from the name given to a bucket placed beneath a barrel of gin to catch and recycle leakages. The musicians in these type of places played for tips, and the style of music they played there became known as "gutbucket."

● People want gut bucket orchestras ... the hip liquor toter wants sensational noise. — Frederic Ramsay Junior, *Chicago Documentary*, p. 28, 1944

● We sopped up a lot of learning at Capone's University of Gutbucket Arts. — Mezz Mezzrow, *Really the Blues*, p. 62, 1946

● She didn't want to dance to the blues, the gut bucket, the funky songs. — Dick Gregory, *Nigger*, p. 60, 1964

● [L]ots of people still care about getdown gutbucket rock 'n' roll passionately[.] — Lester Bangs, *Psychotic Reactions and Carburetor Dung*, p. 69, 1971

2 a rough and rowdy bar with rough and rowdy patrons *US, 1970*
- I mean, like sho' nuff groovy gut bucket Black. — Odie Hawkins, *Great Lawd Buddha*, p. 29, 1990

3 a fish bait boat; by extension a messy space of any kind *US, 1975*
- — John Gould, *Maine Lingo*, p. 119, 1975

gut card *noun*
in gin, a card that completes a broken sequence *US, 1965*
- — Irwin Steig, *Play Gin to Win*, p. 140, 1965

gut check *noun*
a test of courage or determination *US, 1968*
- — Fred Hester, *Slang on the 40 Acres*, p. 15, 1968
- "Say a prayer for Jack and Jill." This was gut-check time. — James Patterson, *Jack & Jill*, p. 15, 1996

gut-eater *noun*
a native American Indian *US, 1925*
- Comments of whites who lived there at the time referred to the Utes as "gut eaters." This was the result of the meager rations supplied by the Government. — V.S. Fitzpatrick, *Red Twilight*, p. 94, 1991

gut-fighter *noun*
an aggressive political candidate *US, 1962*
- Alderman Keane, an instinctive gut fighter, went on television and made snide remarks about the divorce. — Mike Royko, *Boss*, p. 94, 1971

gut hammer *noun*
a dinner bell *US, 1925*
- Everyone felt good when the gut hammer rang to announce breakfast. — Edward Langenau, *Lumberjacks and Ladies*, p. 129, 2003

gut hopper *noun*
a student who moves from one easy course to another *US, 1955*
- I'm not a gut hopper, but this term is the worst. — Max Shulman, *Guided Tour of Campus Humor*, p. 105, 1955

gut issue *noun*
the one most important issue in a discussion *US, 1986*
- — Department of the Army, *Staff Officer's Guidebook*, p. 61, 1986

gutless wonder *noun*
an outstanding coward *US, 1900*
- "Some kind of gutless wonder?" This too was the title of a book by Trout. — Kurt Vonnegut, *Slaughterhouse-Five*, p. 213, 1969

gut reamer *noun*
the active participant in anal sex *US, 1949*
- — Joseph E. Ragen and Charles Finston, *Inside the World's Toughest Prison*, p. 802, 1962: "Penitentiary and underworld glossary"

gut-ripper *noun*
1 an antipersonnel grenade that explodes at waist level *US, 1991*
- These hit the ground, jump into the air and explode at about stomach level. Gut rippers, they are called, the scourge of infantrymen. — *Boston Globe*, 29th January 1991

2 a sharp knife *US, 1960*
- His own double-edged double-jointed spring-blade cuts-all genuine Filipino twisty-handled all-American gut-ripper. — Nelson Algren, *The Neon Wilderness*, p. 56, 1960

gut-robber *noun*
a cook *US, 1919*
- No son of a bitching Texas gut robber was going to tell Milton Anthony Warden what woman he could go out with and what one he couldn't. — James Jones, *From Here to Eternity*, p. 458, 1951

guts *noun*
courage *US, 1891*
- A couple of drinks'll give us some guts. — Irving Shulman, *The Amboy Dukes*, p. 77, 1947

guts and butts doc *noun*
a gastroenterologist *US, 1994*
- — Sally Williams, *"Strong" Words*, p. 145, 1994

guts ball *noun*
any action demanding courage and aggression *US, 1966*
- He said guts ball. They're out there. Black boys in white suits peeing under the door on me. — Ken Kesey, *One Flew Over the Cuckoo's Nest*, p. 241, 1966

gut-shoot *verb*
to shoot in the stomach *US, 1935*
- "Then I gutshoot him. Then I gutshot him again." — George Higgins, *The Digger's Game*, p. 196, 1973
- "Some people aim for the heart, some people like to gut-shoot a man, but I always aim for the privates." — Janet Evanovich, *The Rocky Road to Romance*, p. 77, 1991
- "It was really pretty what you wrote. Except where that old man got gut-shot." — John Ridley, *Love is a Racket*, p. 98, 1998

gut shot *noun*
1 the use of an explosive placed in a lock to open a safe *US, 1972*
- The gut shot is when you take the combination, you knock the column off and you make a cup there and you pour the nitro-glycerin into this cup and it runs into the combination. — Harry King, *Box Man*, p. 34, 1972

2 a bullet wound in the stomach, painful and often fatal *US, 1981*
- They always aimed for a gut shot so the living would have to care for the one that was shot. — Robert Lipkin, *A Brotherhood of Outlaws*, p. 109, 1981

3 in poker, a drawn card that completes an inside straight *US, 1951*
- — *American Speech*, p. 97, May 1951: "The vocabulary of poker"
- If the player (with queens) wins the pot, they are "ladies"; but if he loses the pot, they are "whores." — Albert H. Morehead, *The Complete Guide to Winning Poker*, p. 264, 1967

gutsy *adjective*
courageous *UK, 1893*
- Look, we can be scientific from now to doomsday, but we gotta be gutsy and go for the big one. — *Tin Men*, 1987

gutter *noun*
a vein, especially a prominent one suitable for drug injection *US, 1994*
- — US Department of Justice, *Street Terms*, October 1994

gutter ball *noun*
in pool, a shot in which the cue ball falls into a pocket *US, 1993*
Homage to bowling.
- — Mike Shamos, *The Illustrated Encyclopedia of Billiards*, p. 111, 1993

gutter hype *noun*
a desperate, down-and-out drug addict *US, 1924*
- Not when Synanon has come far too expensive for the ordinary gutter-hype. — Guy Endore, *Synanon*, p. 248, 1968

gutter junkie *noun*
a drug addict who relies on others to obtain his drugs *US, 1983*
- — Michael M. D'Auria, *Legal Terms and Concepts in Criminal Justice*, p. 145, 1983
- But as a private citizen, he was something else, a prescription drug addict, not much different from a gutter junkie, except in his drugs of choice. — Alanna Nash, *The Colonel*, p. 313, 2003

gutter wear *noun*
fashionably shabby clothing *US, 1988*
- — *Washington Post Magazine*, p. 21, 21st August 1988: "Say wha?"

guy *noun*
a man or a boy; a general form of address; in the plural it can be used of and to men, women or a mixed grouping *US, 1847*
- Guys and gals, it knocks me out to be able to elucidate — Lavada Durst, *The Jives of Dr. Hepcat*, 1953
- Guys, uh, what exactly does third base feel like? — Paul Herz, *American Pie*, 1999

guyed out *adjective*
drunk *US, 1973*
An allusion to the tightness achieved through guy wires.
- — Sherman Louis Sergel, *The Language of Show Biz*, p. 100, 1973

guy thing *noun*
a problem or subject best understood by males *US, 1975*
- When I got all done, I kept thinking, maybe it is a guy-thing. — United States Congress, *Hearings Before and Special Reports Made by Committee on Armed Service*, p. 243, 1975

"And do you or do not agree that, by your definition, driving is a 'guy thing.'" — Carrie Fisher, *Surrender the Pink*, p. 218, 1990

guzzle-and-grab *noun*
eating and drinking, with an emphasis on fast, low-brow food and alcohol *US, 1951*
- A favorite after-work guzzle-and-grab spot is the Cafe of All Nations[.] — Jack Lait and Lee Mortimer, *Washington Confidential*, p. 78, 1951

gweep *noun*
an overworked computer programer *US, 1990*
- — Karla Jennings, *The Devouring Fungus*, p. 220, 1990

G-wheel *noun*
in a carnival, a game wheel that has been rigged for cheating *US, 1990*
"G" is for "gaffed" (rigged).
- — Lindsay E. Smith and Bruce A. Walstad, *Keeping Carnies Honest*, pp. 42–43, 1990: "Glossary"

gym bunny *noun*
a male homosexual devoted to physical conditioning *US, 1993*
- Why conjure up derisive terms like "gym bunny" (what is one, by the way?), or fratwink, or even *shudder* the concept of a "twink tautology"? — *soc.motss*, 1st March 1993
- "You'd rather read than fuck, is that it?" asked Blue's current boy friend, a glorious gym bunny with a single flaw, a slightly Hogarthian nose. — Ethan Morden, *How Long Has This Been Going On?*, p. 507, 1997
- Charlie straightened up, the gym bunny's cock clenched tight inside his ass. — Hank Edwards, *Flufers, Inc.*, p. 40, 2002

gymmed *adjective*
having well-defined muscles, fit, trim *US, 1988*
- "Straight dark hair. Twenty-five. Boyishly handsome. Very gymmed. Very style." — Ethan Morden, *Everybody Loves You*, p. 179, 1988

gym queen *noun*
a man who spends a great deal of time at a gym *US, 1994*
- And Genre's going after the white boy, gym queen, partyboys who don't really want to read too much. — *San Francisco Examinier*, p. C19, 4th December 1994
- [S]o too is the gym queen: a thing that needs to be exhaustively manicured and viewed publicly in a little diorama-box, with a proud groomer next to it[.] — *San Francisco Examiner*, p. C19, 22nd August 1997
- There are some deficiencies that the gym queens definitely don't have. — Suroosh Alvi et al., *The Vice Guide*, p. 272, 2002

gym rat *noun*
an exercise fanatic *US, 1978*
- In a grim twist that could fit into one of his songs, in the past year Zevon has been a gym rat ("I was working out more than Vin Diesel," he says) and assumed that his shortness of breath and the tightness in his chest were side effects of his regimen. — *Los Angeles Times*, 13th September 2002

gynormous *adjective*
very large *UK, 1992*
A blend of "giant" and "enormous."
- The Army Corps of Engineers has what must be a gynormous working model of San Francisco Bay in Sausalito. — *rec.boats*, 16th January 1994
- — Connie Eble (Editor), *UNC-CH Campus Slang*, p. 6, Fall 2005

gyno shot; gyno *noun*
a close-up scene in a pornographic movie or a photograph showing a woman's genitals *US, 1995*
- — *Adult Video News*, p. 48, August 1995
- Susan shows it all off in this infamous sequence, including a glimpse at the Gates of Venus when she swings her legs to get up out of bed. Great gyno! — Mr. Skin, *Mr. Skin's Skincyclopedia*, p. 68, 2005

gyp; gip *noun*
1 in horse racing, someone who owns only a few horses *US, 1938*
An abbreviation of "gypsy" not derogatory.
- — Mel Heimer, *Inside Racing*, p. 211, 1962
2 in oil drilling, gypsum *US, 1954*
- — Jerry Robertson, *Oil Slanguage*, p. 63, 1954

gyp; gip *verb*
to cheat (someone), to swindle *US, 1880*
- VOICE: I'm going to shoot. Don't move, eh? AGENT: No, that thing—VOICE: I've been gypped—AGENT: But, listen, that money — Harry J. Anslinger, *The Murderers*, p. 153, 1961
- They got to be going to a white fish market, that's got by gypping them. — Claude Brown, *Manchild in the Promised Land*, p. 339, 1965
- Now I'm the one gettin' gyped. — *Pulp Fiction*, 1994

gyp joint *noun*
a dishonest store or establishment *US, 1927*
- "I just hate those lousy saloonkeepers who run gyp joints as clubs and turn us into B-girls if we want to eat." — Monroe Fry, *Sex, Vice, and Business*, p. 65, 1959
- A good rule is to avoid the bargain gyp joints and go to a place that deals in electronic equipment. — Abbie Hoffman, *Steal This Books*, p. 155, 1996

gyppy tummy *noun*
diarrhea *UK, 1943*
- I shall tell all, if heat prostration and a bout of Gyppy tummy don't finish me off first. — Herman Wouk, *War and Remembrance*, p. 395, 1978

gypsy *noun*
in circus and carnival usage, an undependable employee, especially a drunk *US, 1981*
- — Don Wilmeth, *The Language of American Popular Entertainment*, p. 122, 1981

gypsy *adjective*
unlicensed, unregulated, usually owned by the operator *US, 1979*
Most often applied to a taxicab or truck, although originally to a racehorse owner/jockey.
- There are five half-mile tracks in Maryland, which run almost all year with unknown plugs and has-beens, raced by "Gypsy" horsemen. — Jack Lait and Lee Mortimer, *Washington Confidential*, p. 273, 1951
- I see this gypsy cab doubleparked in front of the club. — Edwin Torres, *After Hours*, p. 263, 1979
- "Gypsy cab" drivers who have stopped to drink beer and snort a little perico talk near the barbershop[.] — Terry Williams, *The Cocaine Kids*, p. 24, 1989

gypsy bankroll *noun*
a roll of money in which the top several bills are real large-denomination bills and the rest are counterfeit, plain paper, or small-denomination bills *US, 1981*
- It's a fucking gypsy bankroll! The hundreds are counterfeit! — Gerald Petievich, *Money Men*, p. 89, 1981

gyrene *noun*
a US Marine *US, 1894*
- Despite a Navy directive to cut it out, Navy pilots remain "Airedales" and Marines are still "Gyrenes." — *New York Times Magazine*, p. 17, 5th June 1955
- "Jist some nudie gy-rene," Gibson Hand said. — Joseph Wambaugh, *The Glitter Dome*, p. 170, 1981

gyro; gyro wanker *noun*
a surfer who constantly flaps his arms to gain balance on the surfboard *US, 1991*
- — Trevor Cralle, *The Surfin'ary*, p. 49, 1991

Hh

H *noun*
heroin *US, 1926*
- More specifically, it was classified as M, C, and H—Mary, Charlie, and Harry—which stood for morphine, cocaine, and heroin. — William J. Spillard and Pence James, *Needle in a Haystack*, pp. 147–148, 1945
- I'll see what I can do about giving you a smack of H today. — Jack Kerouac, *Beat Generation*, p. 42, 1957
- Pinky's got the habit. He's on H. — Chester Himes, *Come Back Charleston Blue*, p. 22, 1966
- I tried hard to be like him, so I got hooked on "H." — Iceberg Slim (Robert Beck), *Pimp*, p. 99, 1969

▸ **the H**
Houston, Texas *US, 1998*
- — Ethan Hilderbrant, *Prison Slang*, p. 127, 1998

HA *noun*
a member of the Hell's Angels motorcycle club *US, 1981*
- He is the one that settled the war between the H.A. and the Breed in New York. — Robert Lipkin, *A Brotherhood of Outlaws*, p. 40, 1981

hab *noun*
a habitual criminal *US, 1963*
- — Marlena Kay Nelson, *Rookies to Roaches*, p. 7, 1963

habes *noun*
a writ of habeas corpus *US, 1974*
- "We had about nine hundred habes. Every time I turn around that monkey's pulling out something else I go to sign." — George Higgin, *Cogan's Trade*, p. 5, 1974

habitch *noun*
a habitual criminal *US, 1949*
- "This one don't count toward the habitch act," Sparrow spoke up confidently. — Nelson Algren, *The Man With The Golden Arm*, p. 276, 1949

habitual *noun*
▸ **the habitual**
a criminal charge alleging habitual criminal status *US, 1972*
- They filed the habitual on me and I jumped bond. — Bruce Jackson, *In the Life*, p. 85, 1972

hache *noun*
heroin *US, 1955*
The Spanish pronunciation of the letter "h."
- — *American Speech*, p. 87, May 1955: "Narcotic argot along the Mexican border"

hachi; hodgy *noun*
the penis *US, 1954*
- But "eat a hodgy" must have been nationwide, because Norm was saying "eat a hodgy" out on the coast while I was saying it in Bloom Township High in Chicago Heights. — Jim Bouton, *Ball Four*, p. 361, 1970

hack *noun*
1 a prison guard *US, 1914*
- The boy sneered. "It's the goddamn hack." — Clarence Cooper Jr., *The Scene*, p. 224, 1960
- He killed a hack, and they had to send him to Materwann. — Claude Brown, *Manchild in the Promised Land*, p. 370, 1965
- The van went through the gates manned by rock-faced "hacks" carrying scoped, high-powered rifles. — Iceberg Slim (Robert Beck), *Pimp*, p. 49, 1969
- At that moment the hack motioned for me to leave, so I told Willie I had to split. — A.S. Jackson, *Gentleman Pimp*, pp. 62–63, 1973
- He smelled up the joint something awful and the hacks used to die. — *Goodfellas*, 1990
2 a solution to a computer problem; an impressive and demanding piece of computer work *US, 1991*
- — *Co-Evolution Quarterly*, p. 31, Spring 1981: "Computer slang"
- — Eric S. Raymond, *The New Hacker's Dictionary*, p. 189, 1991
- [A] palindromic music composition was considered a good hack (thus making Haydn, with his Palindrome Symphony, an honorary hacker). — Katie Hafner & John Markoff, quoted in *Wired Style*, p. 70, 1996

3 in computing, a quick, often temporary, fix of a problem *US, 1983*
- — Guy L. Steele et al., *The Hacker's Dictionary*, p. 75, 1983
4 a single act of unlawfully invading and exploring another's computer system by remote means *US, 1983*
- Any serious hack will involve some preparatory research long before the hacker sets foot near a computer. — The Knightmare, *Secrets of a Super Hacker*, p. 19, 1994
- The information was the trophy—the proof of the hack. — Kevin Mitnick, *The Secret History of Hacking*, 22nd July 2001

▸ **in hack**
confined to quarters *US, 1946*
- To say that ten days in hack was considered a reward of almost unbearable loveliness is not to exaggerate. — Thomas Heggen, *Mister Roberts*, p. 114, 1946

hack *verb*
1 to tolerate, endure, survive *US, 1952*
Usually used with "it."
- The reason I couldn't hack it was I really didn't want to write a thesis. — Gurney Norman, *Divine Right's Trip (Last Whole Earth Catalog)*, p. 107, 1971
- "Anyway," Elvin said, "here's this boy has to do a mandatory twenty-five on a life sentence and he's, I mean, depressed, doesn't think he can hack it." — Elmore Leonard, *Maximum Bob*, p. 50, 1991
- Much as I can hack a few nights in the cells, I really don't fancy straight porridge [prison time]. — Danny King, *The Burglar Diaries*, p. 235, 2001
2 to bother, to annoy *US, 1893*
- You know, people have been stealing his riffs for all these years. That's one of the things that hacks him up so bad[.] — Ross Russell, *The Sound*, p. 177, 1961
3 to investigate the possibilities of a computer purely for the pleasures of discovery; to create new possibilities for a computer without commercial consideration *US, 1983*
Almost certainly from the language of model railroaders at MIT in the 1950s.
- Hacking [...] exploring the boundaries of computing experiments—even if they didn't own it. — *The Secret History of Hacking*, 22nd July 2001
4 to work with a computer *US, 1981*
- — *Co-Evolution Quarterly*, p. 31, Spring 1981: "Computer slang"
- — Guy L. Steele et al., *The Hacker's Dictionary*, p. 76, 1983

hack around; hack off; hack *verb*
to waste time, usually in a context where time should not be wasted *US, 1888*
- — Collin Baker et al., *College Undergraduate Slang Study Conducted at Brown University*, p. 142, 1968
- I got to stop hacking around, is all. — George V. Higgins, *The Friends of Eddie Doyle*, p. 33, 1971

hack driver *noun*
in horse racing, a jockey *US, 1951*
- — David W. Maurer, *Argot of the Racetrack*, p. 33, 1951

hacked; hacked off *adjective*
annoyed *US, 1936*
- — Robert S. Gold, *A Jazz Lexicon*, p. 135, 1964
- Our front door is always unlocked in case one of the boys is hacked off at his parents and needs a place to lay over and cool off. — S.E. Hinton, *The Outsiders*, p. 93, 1967
- — Eugene Landy, *The Underground Dictionary*, p. 95, 1971

hacker *noun*
1 a person who uses their computer expertise in any effort to breach security walls and gain entry to secure sites *US, 1963*
- — Guy L. Steele et al., *The Hacker's Dictionary*, p. 79, 1983
2 a person with a profound appreciation and affection for computers and programing *US, 1981*
- — *Co-Evolution Quarterly*, p. 31, Spring 1981: "Computer slang"

hackie *noun*
a taxi driver *US, 1899*
- Bell-boys and hackies can steer you to anything. — Jack Lait and Lee Mortimer, *Washington Confidential*, p. 270, 1951
- The hackie left me off in front of the theater. — Georgia Sothern, *My Life in Burlesque*, p. 166, 1972

hack mode *noun*
while working on or with a computer, a state of complete focus and concentration *US, 1991*
- — Eric S. Raymond, *The New Hacker's Dictionary*, p. 190, 1991

had-it *adjective*
exhausted; completely worn out *US, 1981*
Hawaiian youth usage.
- — Douglas Simonson, *Pidgin to da Max*, 1981

hagged out *adjective*
exhausted *US, 1968*
- — Collin Baker et al., *College Undergraduate Slang Study Conducted at Brown University*, p. 133, 1968

hag-ride *verb*
to scold, to nag, to harass *US, 1909*
- But some people—people we call "depressives"—do not manage to free themselves from denominators that hag-ride them into depression[.] — Julian Simon, *Good Mood*, p. 15, 1993

Haight *nickname*
▸ **the Haight**
the Haight-Ashbury neighborhood of San Francisco *US, 1967*
- The fog came every day and destroyed the sunshine, and then the Haight was left to itself. — Nicholas Von Hoffman, *We Are The People Our Parents Warned Us Against*, p. 9, 1967
- I came to the Haight in the beginning of 1966. — Leonard Wolfe (Editor), *Voices from the Love Generation*, p. 100, 1968

hail *noun*
1 crack cocaine *US, 1994*
Based on the drug's resemblance to pieces of hail.
- — US Department of Justice, *Street Terms*, October 1994
2 in soda fountain usage, ice *US, 1935*
- — *American Speech*, p. 88, April 1946: "The language of West Coast culinary workers"

hailer *noun*
in the television and movie industries, a bullhorn *US, 1977*
- — Tony Miller and Patricia George, *Cut! Print!*, p. 85, 1977

Hail Mary *noun*
1 a last-minute, low-probability maneuver *US, 1965*
- But what the hell, why not try? I flung a Hail Mary to the shortest end I'd ever seen, the producer they had assigned to me/my project, a neurotic little bastard named Teddy. — Odie Hawkins, *Lost Angeles*, p. 61, 1994
- McVeigh's lawyers, she said, were "in a Hail Mary situation, not by their own doing but by the government's control of the timetable." — *Contra Costa Times*, p. A24, 8th June 2001
2 in poker, a poor hand that a player holds into high betting in the hope that other players are bluffing and have even worse hands *US, 1996*
- — John Vorhaus, *The Big Book of Poker Slang*, p. 21, 1996

hair *noun*
1 courage *US, 1959*
- — J. R. Friss, *A Dictionary of Teenage Slang (Mt. Diablo High)*, 1964
- — John M. Kelly, *Surf and Sea*, p. 286, 1965
- — *American Speech*, p. 194, October 1965: "Notes on campus vocabulary, 1964"
- You never would have worked up the hair to hit on her, but she came right up and started talking to you. — Jay McInerney, *Bright Lights, Big City*, p. 69, 1984
2 in computing, intricacy *US, 1981*
- — Guy L. Steele, *Coevolution Quarterly*, p. 31, Spring 1981: "Computer Slang"
- — Guy L. Steele et al., *The Hacker's Dictionary*, p. 80, 1983

hairbag *noun*
a veteran police officer *US, 1958*
- — *New York Times Magazine*, p. 88, 16th March 1958
- — *New York Times*, 15th February 1970

hairbagger *noun*
an experienced police officer *US, 1958*

- They'll probably put you on patrol with some hairbagger. — Charles Whited, *Chiodo*, p. 45, 1973

hairball *noun*
1 an obnoxious, boorish person, especially when drunk *US, 1981*
- She glanced at the two hairballs in leather jackets[.] — Joseph Wambaugh, *The Glitter Dome*, p. 144, 1981
- — Pamela Munro, *U.C.L.A. Slang*, p. 46, 1989
2 a large, powerful wave *US, 1981*
- — Trevor Cralle, *The Surfin'ary*, p. 49, 1991

hair band *noun*
a metal rock band whose male members sport long, carefully groomed hair *US, 1991*
A derisive term that arose as the alternative grunge movement found traction.
- But the better groups are breaking from the pack, looking to expand the perception of what a pop-metal "hair band" can do, plumbing new dynamics for the style. — *St. Petersburg Times*, p. 1D, 17th June 1991
- Right, the "hair band" of the 80's: (from left, rear) Andy King, Uosikkinen, Lilley, Bazilian (front left) Hyman. — *Philadelphia Inquirer*, p. D5, 5th February 2008

hairburger *noun*
the vulva, especially in the context of oral sex *US, 1971*
- — Eugene Landy, *The Underground Dictionary*, p. 96, 1971
- "Dont be surprised, though, if you catch him having a hairburger." — Kris Nelscott, *War at Home*, p. 82, 2006

hair burner; hair bender *noun*
a hair stylist *US, 1964*
- — Guy Strait, *The Lavender Lexicon*, 1 June 1964
- — *Male Swinger Number 3*, p. 45, 1981: "The complete gay dictionary"

hair-dry *adjective*
without getting your hair wet *US, 1991*
- I paddled out hair dry. — Trevor Cralle, *The Surfin'ary*, p. 49, 1991

haired up *adjective*
angry *US, 1914*
- — John Gould, *Maine Lingo*, p. 122, 1975
- "Now, let's not get all haired up," said Officer Drum. — Van Reid, *Fiddler's Green*, p. 46, 2004

hair fairy *noun*
a homosexual male with an extravagant hairdo *US, 1964*
- — Guy Strait, *The Lavender Lexicon*, 1 June 1964
- "Swish" bars for the effeminates and "hair fairies" with their careful coiffures. — Joe David Brown, *Sex in the '60s*, p. 70, 1968
- That is as unrepresentative of the spectrum of lesbians as the male "hairy fairy" or "queen" is of the male homosexual population. — *San Francisco Chronicle*, p. 22, 30th June 1969
- During this period of homosexuality all the girls relate that they were "hair fairies." That is, they would wear their hair long and tease it. — George Paul Csicsery (Editor), *The Sex Industry*, p. 67, 1973

hairhead *noun*
a person with long hair, representing counter-culture values *US, 1971*
- Although she still had her shirt on, her naked thighs and her naked head made her as naked as a hairhead wearing no clothes at all. — William Vollman, *Rainbow Stories*, p. 46, 1989

hair in the gate *noun*
in television and movie-making, any foreign object in the camera gate *US, 1990*
- — Ralph S. Singleton, *Filmmaker's Dictionary*, p. 79, 1990

hair pie *noun*
1 the vulva; oral sex performed on a woman *US, 1938*
Also spelled "hare" pie or "hairy" pie.
- "He goes in for hair pie," Goo-Goo added. — Harry Grey, *The Hoods*, p. 88, 1952
- Are you accusin' me of bein' a hair-pie man, Nathan? — Edwin Torres, *Q & A*, p. 155, 1977
- No actual dripping beaver is shown however, so all you've got is the shorthaired externals (good hair-pie but, y'know, big deal). — Richard Meltzer, *A Whore Just Like the Rest*, p. 366, 1977
- You won't believe it when I tell you I haven't seen the old hair pie in twenty-seven years. — Elmore Leonard, *Bandits*, p. 281, 1987

2 a pizza with an errant hair embedded in it *US*, *1996*

Limited usage, but clever.

- — *Maledicta*, p. 13, 1996: "Domino's pizza jargon"

hairpins *noun*

homosexual code phrases inserted casually into a conversation, trolling for a response *US*, *1950*

- — Florida Legislative Investigation Committee (Johns Committee), *Homosexuality and Citizenship in Florida*, 1964: "Glossary of homosexual terms and deviate acts"
- Keep your hairpins up, dearies. There's a "straight" inside. — Antony James, *America's Homosexual Underground*, p. 142, 1965
- — Dale Gordon, *The Dominion Sex Dictionary*, p. 61, 1967
- — Robert A. Wilson, *Playboy's Book of Forbidden Words*, p. 95, 1972

hairy *noun*

heroin *US*, *1973*

A phonetic distortion of **HARRY**.

- — David Maurer and Victor Vogel, *Narcotics and Narcotic Addiction*, p. 413, 1973

hairy *adjective*

1 dangerous; scary (especially if thrilling) *US*, *1945*

- We came out of that deal with more than sixty grand and Henry got at least as much, but it was a hairy one. — Vincent Teresa, *My Life in the Mafia*, p. 109, 1973
- I saved her from a hairy situation into which her "friend to man" attitude had cast her. — Nathan Heard, *A Cold Fire Burning*, p. 10, 1974

2 bad, difficult, undesirable *UK*, *1848*

A popular term in C19, resurrected in later C20 youth usage.

- — *Time*, 3rd October 1949
- It got a little hairy at the end when we drove him to the bus, however. — Erich Segal, *Love Story*, p. 74, 1970
- It's cool. I'll handle the hairy ones. Most of the time they're just trying to get your attention. — Armistead Maupin, *Tales of the City*, p. 155, 1978
- I mean it's hairy—they got some pretty heavy ordnance, boy. — *Apocalypse Now*, 1979

3 in computing, complicated *US*, *1983*

- — Guy L. Steele et al., *The Hacker's Dictionary*, p. 80, 1983

4 good, impressive *US*, *1959*

- In teen-age jargon, he is still "the hairiest" (the coolest, the greatest). — *Look*, p. 49, 24th November 1959
- — J. R. Friss, *A Dictionary of Teenage Slang (Mt. Diablo High)*, 1964

hairy belly *noun*

in dominoes, the 6–6 piece *US*, *1959*

- — Dominic Armanino, *Dominoes*, p. 17, 1959

hairy canary *noun*

a temper tantrum *US*, *1969*

- "Relax, don't have a hairy canary." — Ralph Fletcher, *Spider Boy*, p. 114, 1997

half a C *noun*

fifty dollars *US*, *1967*

A shortened allusion to $100 as a "C-note."

- Look my man, when you was in my town, you ate free at my joint, misused my hospitality and left town owing my "Mom" fifty dollars. You don't have to have a drink with me, but I'll take the "half a C" for Mom. — Babs Gonzales, *I Paid My Dues*, p. 88, 1967

half a case *noun*

fifty cents *US*, *1950*

- — Hyman E. Goldin et al., *Dictionary of American Underworld Lingo*, p. 90, 1950

half a dollar *noun*

a prison sentence of 50 years *US*, *1990*

- — Charles Shafer, *Folk Speech in Texas Prisons*, p. 205, 1990

half-a-man *noun*

a short person *US*, *1997*

- The labels were cruel: Gimp, Limpy–go-fetch, Crip, Lift-one-drag one, etc. Pint, Half-a-man, Peewee, Shorty, Lardass, Pork, Blubber, Belly, Blimp. Nuke-knob, Skinhead, Baldy. Four-eyes, Specs, Coke bottles. — *San Francisco Examiner*, p. A15, 28th July 1997

half and half *noun*

1 oral sex on a man followed by vaginal intercourse *US*, *1937*

- I say, Yoo-hoo, pitty baby, you wanna lil french? Haff an haff? How about jes a straight? I say, Twenty berries an you alla roun the mothahfuggin' worl'. — Robert Gover, *One Hundred Dollar Misunderstanding*, p. 21, 1961

- [A] lot of them will want half-and-half, starting with a blow job and finishing off with straight intercourse. — John Warren Wells, *Tricks of the Trade*, p. 19, 1970
- Half-and-half still costs you more than straight, so if you need the girl's mouth on your dingus to get you up it will set you back a total of thirty dollars[.] — Gerald Paine, *A Bachelor's Guide to the Brothels of Nevada*, p. 26, 1978
- The young guy who chose her wanted half and half. — Lora Shaner, *Madam*, p. 207, 1999

2 a hermaphrodite *US*, *1935*

- — Joe McKennon, *Circus Lingo*, p. 44, 1980

half and half *adjective*

bisexual *US*, *1975*

- — *American Speech*, p. 60, Spring–Summer 1975: "Razorback slang"

half-apple *noun*

in television and movie-making, a standard-sized crate used for raising objects or people, half as high as a standard "apple" *US*, *1990*

- — Ralph S. Singleton, *Filmmaker's Dictionary*, p. 79, 1990

half-assed *adjective*

incomplete, not serious, half-hearted *US*, *1933*

- They got a bang out of things, though—in a half-assed way, of course. — J.D. Salinger, *Catcher in the Rye*, p. 6, 1951
- We're talking about murder, man, not a little half-assed assault. — Elmore Leonard, *City Primeval*, p. 59, 1980
- East St. Louis, for example, was a half-assed gangster town. — Herbert Huncke, *Guilty of Everything*, p. 38, 1990

half a yard *noun*

fifty dollars *US*, *1961*

- — Gene Sorrows, *All About Carnivals*, p. 19, 1985: "Terminology"
- — Thomas L. Clark, *The Dictionary of Gambling and Gaming*, p. 95, 1987

halfback *noun*

a retiree from the northern United States living in rural Georgia *US*, *2007*

- HALFBACKS are Yankees (often retirees) who descended to live in Florida, didn't like it there (who WOULD?!), so moved "half(-way)back" northward to the hill country of Georgia. — Charles Doyle, *ads-l@listserv.uga.edu*, 29th January 2007

half-buck *noun*

fifty dollars *US*, *1992*

- His mom paid the half-buck a month for his room[.] — Jess Mowry, *Way Past Cool*, p. 120, 1992

half-cocked *adjective*

not fully capable; not completely thought out; unfinished; incomplete *US*, *1833*

- You know, we're not going into that thing half-cocked. I made a thorough survey of the consumer situation before I laid my plans. — Max Shulman, *The Zebra Derby*, p. 54, 1946
- But I wasn't rushing off half-cocked. — Malcolm X and Alex Haley, *The Autobiography of Malcolm X*, p. 140, 1964

half colonel *noun*

a lieutenant-colonel *US*, *1956*

- "What's the SAS commanded by?" "A half colonel." "Well, we'll use a full colonel." — Charlie A. Beckwith, *Delta Force*, p. 109, 1983

half-cut *adjective*

drunk *UK*, *1893*

- Scotty had turned up at the meet half cut[.] — Charles Raven, *Underworld Nights*, p. 30, 1956

half-man *noun*

a kneeboarder, or a surfer who rides without standing *US*, *1991*

- — Trevor Cralle, *The Surfin'ary*, p. 49, 1991

half-mast *adjective*

1 (used of a penis) partially but not completely erect *US*, *1972*

- — Robert A. Wilson, *Playboy's Book of Forbidden Words*, p. 134, 1972
- — Anon., *King Smut's Wet Dreams Interpreted*, 1978

2 partially lowered *US*, *1871*

- My fly is at half mast; my hands look shaky. — James Ellroy, *Hollywood Nocturnes*, p. 6, 1994

half-pint *noun*
a short person *US, 1876*
From the nonmetric measure of volume.
- "Say, Melvin, who is that half-pint con with the magazine?" Joe asks, to halt Melvin. — Iceberg Slim (Robert Beck), *Doom Fox*, p. 220, 1978

half smart *adjective*
stupid *US, 1927*
- Card-watchers, however, are half-smart. — Jacques Noir, *Casino Holiday*, p. 85, 1968

half-step *verb*
to make a half-hearted, insincere effort *US, 1990*
- — Richard McAlister, *Rapper's Handbook*, p. 1, 1990
- — William K. Bentley and James M. Corbett, *Prison Slang*, p. 15, 1992
- — Mark S. Fleisher, *Beggars & Thieves*, p. 289, 1995: "Glossary"

half-stepper *noun*
a person who does things only halfway and cannot be counted on *US, 1981*
- — *Maledicta*, p. 265, Summer/Winter 1981: "By its slang, ye shall know it: the pessimism of prison life"

halibut head *noun*
to the indigenous peoples of Alaska, a white person *US, 1965*
- — Robert O. Bowen, *An Alaskan Dictionary*, p. 17, 1965

halter *noun*
a necktie *US, 1960*
- — *San Francisco Examiner*, pp. III–2, 22nd March 1960

halvsies *noun*
1 half a share of something that is to be divided *US, 1927*
Variants include "halfsies" and "halfies."
- The blackjack Dealer goes "halfies" with a player who is also a friend of his. — Mario Puzo, *Inside Las Vegas*, p. 224, 1977
- Just figured you wanted halfies. — Piri Thomas, *Stories from El Barrio*, p. 87, 1978
- Maybe we'll go halfsies on a keg. — Carl Hiaasen, *Native Tongue*, p. 401, 1991
2 mutual oral sex performed simultaneously *US, 1985*
- — *American Speech*, p. 19, Spring 1985: "The language of singles bars"

ham *noun*
1 an amateur shortwave radio operator and enthusiast *US, 1919*
- A civilian Navy employee working on Siapan yesterday was expressing gratitude for two radio hams who put him in indirect contact with members of his family in Richmond. — *San Francisco Examiner*, p. 27, 27th March 1947
2 theatrical antics *US, 1930*
- The afternoon will be pure ham. — Oscar Zeta Acosta, *The Revolt of the Cockroach People*, p. 95, 1973
3 in circus and carnival usage, food or a meal *US, 1981*
- — Don Wilmeth, *The Language of American Popular Entertainment*, p. 123, 1981
4 any type of alcoholic drink *US, 1997*
- — Vann Wesson, *Generation X Field Guide and Lexicon*, p. 86, 1997

ham *verb*
to walk *US, 1962*
- — Joseph E. Ragen and Charles Finston, *Inside the World's Toughest Prison*, p. 802, 1962: "Penitentiary and underworld glossary"

▶ **ham it up**
to behave theatrically, to exaggerate *US, 1955*
- One day, unknown to Rae and me, he got out on the field and started hamming it up. — Jackie Robinson, *I Never Had It Made*, p. 88, 1995

ham actor; ham actress; ham *noun*
an unsubtle actor *US, 1881*
- "Let this wise-ass ham hang himself." — Donald Wilson, *My Six Convicts*, p. 45, 1951

ham-and-egger *noun*
1 an inconsequential person who has achieved little *US, 1966*
- You've got out-and-out ham-and-eggers running around today claiming they're world champions, but on a five-by-ten in the olden days, they wouldn't have beat Frank the Drunk, who cleaned toilets at Kreuter's. — Minnesota Fats, *The Bank Shot*, p. 88, 1966
- "Got himself this bunch of ham-and-eggers and he sends them down where he does his business and he goes away." — George Higgins, *Cogan's Trade*, p. 108, 1974
2 in professional wrestling, a wrestler whose regular role is to lose to help the careers of others *US, 1999*

A slight variation on the boxing original.
- Naively, I expected to be furnished with the vital statistics of every wrestler, including the unknown ham and eggers who got pounded by the stars for TV. — Larry Nelson and Jim Jones, *Strangehold*, p. 42, 1999
3 in oil drilling, an operator who has suffered loss after loss and is now burdened with poor credit *US, 1954*
- — Jerry Robertson, *Oil Slanguage*, p. 63, 1954

hambone *noun*
1 a show-off *US, 1952*
- I figured that was the last time I'd ever see that hambone. — Jerry Spinelli, *Crash*, p. 4, 1996
2 a trombone *US, 1934*
- — Lou Shelly, *Hepcats Jive Dictionary*, p. 12, 1945
3 a black prisoner *US, 1989*
- — James Harris, *A Convict's Dictionary*, p. 29, 1989

hamburger *noun*
a socially inept outcast *US, 1949*
High school usage.
- — *Washington Post*, 23rd April 1961: "Man, did this jazz"

hamburger heaven *noun*
a diner *US, 1944*
- They got summer jobs at the same hamburger heaven[.] — Nadine Gordimer, *Telling Tales*, p. 96, 2004

hamburger helper *noun*
crack cocaine *US, 1994*
The drug bears some resemblance to a brand name food product.
- — US Department of Justice, *Street Terms*, October 1994

hame; haim; haym *noun*
a job, especially a menial or unpleasant one *US, 1941*
- A haim is a job, but junkies don't bother with 'em. — Clarence Cooper Jr., *The Scene*, p. 55, 1960
- His bread (money) had dwindled by this time and he knew that he had to cop him a haym (job). — Babs Gonzales, *I Paid My Dues*, p. 95, 1967

hamfat *noun*
an amateur performer *US, 1911*
- Around the poolroom I defended the guys I felt were my real brothers, the colored musicians who made music that sent me, not a lot of beat-up old hamfats who sang and played a commercial excuse for the real thing. — Mezz Mezzrow, *Really the Blues*, p. 49, 1946

hamhock circuit *noun*
a tour of black bars and nightclubs *US, 1975*
- B.B. has been out here twenty years playing the ham-hock circuit. — Babs Gonzales, *Movin' On Down De Line*, p. 105, 1975

Hamilton *noun*
a ten-dollar bill *US, 1948*
From the engraving of Alexander Hamilton on the bill.
- Having counted ten Hamiltons out of the corner of her eye, and knowing what good times they would buy, Lacy was about to do as requested[.] — Robert Campbell, *In La-La Land We Trust*, p. 1, 1986

hammed *adjective*
drunk *US, 1997*
- — Pamela Munro, *U.C.L.A. Slang*, p. 75, 1997

hammer *noun*
1 the penis *US, 1967*
- — Dale Gordon, *The Dominion Sex Dictionary*, p. 81, 1967
- They had lost all fear of his hammer. Earlier they had teased it mercilessly, using both pairs of hands to stroke the shaft while passing the head from one mouth to the other. — Lexy Harper, *Bedtime Erotica for Men*, p. 49, 2006
- "Shut up," I whispered back as I shoved my hammer into her hole. — Shaun Mathis, *This Hurts*, p. 251, 2007
2 a handgun *US, 1994*
- Hours after the shooting death of graduate student Al-Moez Alimohamed, two of his alleged teen-age killers reportedly sat in jail laughing and singing. "Yo, I got my hammer," Ollie "Homicide" Taylor, 15, and Anthony Archer, 15, rapped through their laughter. — *Times-Picayune (New Orleans)*, p. A11, 2nd October 1994
3 an attractive girl or young woman *US, 1970*
- — David Claerbaut, *Black Jargon in White America*, p. 67, 1972
- — *American Speech*, p. 154, Spring–Summer 1972: "An approach to Black slang"

4 a pizza with ham topping *US, 1996*
- — *Maledicta*, p. 13, 1996: "Domino's pizza jargon"

5 in shuffleboard, the eighth and final shot *US, 1967*
- — Omero C. Catan, *Secrets of Shuffleboard Strategy*, p. 67, 1967: "Glossary of terms"

6 in bar dice games, the player who wins the chance to play first *US, 1971*
- — Jester Smith, *Games They Play in San Francisco*, p. 104, 1971

hammer *verb*
▸ **get hammered**
1 while surfing, to be knocked from your surfboard and violently thrashed by the surf *US, 1988*
- — Michael V. Anderson, *The Bad, Rad, Not to Forget Way Cool Beach and Surf Discriptionary*, p. 6, 1988

2 in mountain biking, to experience a violent accident *US, 1992*
- — William Nealy, *Mountain Bike!*, p. 161, 1992: "Bikespeak"

hammered *adjective*
drunk *US, 1960*
- — Collin Baker et al., *College Undergraduate Slang Study Conducted at Brown University*, p. 133, 1968
- "Fin!" she cried suddenly. "I got a flash for you. We're hammered. Smashed. Fried. Tanked." — Joseph Wambaugh, *Finnegan's Week*, p. 157, 1993
- [F]irst we hammered out a peace treaty, then we all got hammered and laughed about the end of the war. — Ralph "Sonny" Barger, *Hell's Angel*, p. 149, 2000
- "I was pretty hammered, that's true. Maybe I did get confused about the time Joey left." — Carl Hiaasen, *Skinny Dip*, p. 128, 2004

hammerheaded *adjective*
stupid *UK, 1552*
- You are still the same hammerheaded clown you always were. — John Patrick Shanley, *Danny and the Deep Blue Sea*, p. 29, 1984

hammers *noun*
the female thighs *US, 1980*
- — Edith A. Folb, *runnin' down some lines*, p. 241, 1980

hammer-slammer *noun*
an airframe technician *US, 1998*
US Army usage.
- — *Seattle Times*, p. A9, 12th April 1998: "Grunts, squids not grunting from the same dictionary"

hammer time *noun*
a decisive point; the time to launch a military attack *US, 2003*
Adapted from a catchphrase attached, in the late 1980s, to California rapper MC Hammer.
- But make no mistake, when the president says go, look out, it's hammer time, OK? It is hammer time. — Vice Admiral Timothy Keating, Commander, US 5th Fleet, *CNN*, 19th March 2003

hammock for two *noun*
a brassiere *US, 1963*
- — *American Speech*, p. 273, December 1963: "American Indian student slang"

hammy *adjective*
melodramatic, theatrical *US, 1899*
- A little at a time at first, a first hammy gestures, a few mugging expressions. — Evan Hunter, *The Blackboard Jungle*, p. 122, 1954

ham stealer *noun*
a thief who steals to eat, rather than for profit *US, 1976*
- Now he's known as Greasy Wheeler, the boss ham stealer. — Dennis Wepman et al., *The Life*, p. 78, 1976

hamster *noun*
a discrete piece of computer code that does what it is supposed to do well *US, 1991*
- The image is of a hamster happily spinning its exercise wheel. — Eric S. Raymond, *The New Hacker's Dictionary*, p. 194, 1991

Hancock *verb*
to sign *US, 1967*
A shortened version of **JOHN HANCOCK**. From his admirable signature on the Declaration of Independence.
- I'm gonna stick him up for a hundred grand before I Hancock a fucking contract. — Iceberg Slim (Robert Beck), *Long White Con*, p. 180, 1977

hand *noun*
a professional wrestler with potential for career advancement *US, 2001*

- He was a "hand"—a guy who was being groomed for bigger things. — Missy Hyatt, *Missy Hyatt*, p. 21, 2001

H and B *adjective*
sexually aroused; *hot and* bothered *US, 1968*
- — Collin Baker et al., *College Undergraduate Slang Study Conducted at Brown University*, p. 132, 1968

handball *verb*
to insert your lubricated hand into your partner's rectum or vagina, providing sexual pleasure for both *US, 1979*
- — *What Color is Your Handkerchief*, p. 5, 1979
- Wayne Dynes, *Homolexis*, p. 64, 1985

handballing *noun*
the insertion of a hand and fist into a person's rectum or vagina for sexual gratification *US, 1988*
- Fist-fucking, known affectionately as fisting, hand-balling, or punching, has emerged as a variety of sexual pleasure only in the last decade. — Seymour Kleinberg, *Alienated Affections*, p. 157, 1988
- Vaginal fisting, also known as fist-fucking or handballing, is one of those sexual practices that still carries with it a taboo. — Deborah Addington, *A Hand in the Bush*, p. 5, 1997
- Men at hand-balling parties don't usually cruise each other's dicks. — Larry Gross, *The Columbia Reader on Lesbians and Gay Men*, p. 93, 1999
- Anal fisting, also known as handballing, is the gradual process of putting your hand (and for very experienced players, sometimes your forearm) inside someone's ass. — *The Village Voice*, 2nd November 1999

handbook *noun*
a bookmaker who operates on the street, without the benefit of a fixed office *US, 1954*
- Capone had said his income was only $75 a week, his one-sixth share in the profits of one place alone, the Hawthorne Smoke Shop (a hand-book). — Alson Smith, *Syndicate City*, p. 134, 1954
- Like all handbooks though, he was scared of plain-clothes vice-cops but completely ignored uniformed policemen. — Joseph Wambaugh, *The Blue Knight*, p. 47, 1973

H and C *noun*
a mixture of *heroin and* cocaine *US, 1971*
A play on "hot and cold," shown on faucets as H and C.
- — US Department of Justice, *Street Terms*, October 1994

hand cannon *noun*
a large pistol *US, 1929*
Used for effect, quaintly old-fashioned.
- Why the fuck didn't you tell us about that guy in the bathroom? Slip your mind? Forget he was in there with a goddamn hand cannon? — *Pulp Fiction*, 1994

handcuff *noun*
an engagement or wedding ring *US, 1926*
- — Marcus Hanna Boulware, *Jive and Slang of Students in Negro Colleges*, 1947
- — Vincent J. Monteleone, *Criminal Slang*, p. 112, 1949

handcuffed *adjective*
married *US, 1945*
- — Lou Shelly, *Hepcats Jive Dictionary*, p. 12, 1945

handcuffs *noun*
a teenager's parents *US, 1961*
- — Art Unger, *The Cool Book*, p. 106, 1961

hand-doodle *noun*
to masturbate *US, 1968*
- Bab, the most beautiful Jew ever to come out of Fex, took exception to all this hand-doodling. But I maintained that masturbation is an end in itself. — Angelo d'Arcangelo, *The Homosexual Handbook*, p. 88, 1968

H and E *noun*
high explosives *US, 1971*
- Pressed into the ground, Mayfield saw the shadow pass by, heard the same deafening roar, and this time the incredible explosions of H and E. — Ronald J. Glasser, *365 Days*, p. 34, 1971

hand finish *noun*
masturbation of a man by another *US, 1987*
- So I figure I won't give him the hand finish. — Frederique Delacoste, *Sex Work*, p. 64, 1987

hand fuck *verb*
1 to stimulate another's genitals *US, 2004*

He went with a tough young man he could grab and handfuck and even kiss so long as it was some kind of boys' play, not sex but wrestling[.] — China Mieville, *Iron Council*, p. 353, 2004

2 to insert a lubricated fist into a partner's rectum or vagina, leading to sexual pleasure for both *US, 1979*

- — *What Color is Your Handkerchief*, p. 5, 1979
- Tracy took the direction and her hand fucked Den harder, unconsciously matching Cole's strokes. Den felt her cunt trying to swallow Tracy's hand. — March Sheiner, *Best of Women's Erotica*, p. 320, 2005

handful *noun*

1 a prison sentence of five years *US, 1930*

- — Hyman E. Goldin et al., *Dictionary of American Underworld Lingo*, p. 90, 1950

2 in a restaurant or soda fountain, five *US, 1967*

- — *American Speech*, p. 62, February 1967: "Soda-fountain, restaurant and tavern calls"

hand gallop *noun*

an act of male masturbation *US, 1971*

- In Lewisburg he used to tell me he was saving it up, no hand-gallops for him[.] — George V. Higgins, *The Friends of Eddie Doyle*, p. 43, 1971

hand-hump *verb*

to masturbate *US, 2004*

- More horndogs hand-humped, more tables tipped. — James Ellroy, *Destination Morgue*, p. 354, 2004

H and I *noun*

harassment and interdiction *US, 1981*

- Our artillery went two and half months one time without firing a round except for H&I. — Mark Baker, *Nam*, p. 82, 1981
- The danger of running into friendly forces, being strafed by our own gunships, or being hit by our own artillery firing H and I (harrassment and interdiction) was a real possibility. — Gary Linderer, *The Eyes of the Eagle*, p. 58, 1991

handicrapper

a handicap-accessible toilet *US, 1998*

- The Thinker is stripped off his pedestal and temporarily relocated to a spacious handicrapper. — *The Stanford Daily*, 20th April 1998

hand jig; hand gig *noun*

masturbation *US, 1972*

- — Joseph E. Ragen and Charles Finston, *Inside the World's Toughest Prison*, p. 802, 1962: "Penitentiary and underworld glossary"
- You know most of the punks, they don't take it in the ass at all. They just give hand-jigs or they'll give blowjobs. — Bruce Jackson, *In the Life*, p. 399, 1972
- — *Male Swinger Number 3*, p. 45, 1981: "The complete gay dictionary"
- — Charles Shafer, *Folk Speech in Texas Prisons*, p. 205, 1990

hand jiving *noun*

the exchange of illegal drugs for money in a secretive fashion *US, 1975*

- [T]hey observed known drug users and addicts approaching the two men and going through the motions police call "hand jiving." — John Sepe, *Cop Team*, p. 56, 1975

hand job *noun*

manual stimulation of another's genitals *US, 1937*

- The handjob is so basic it is like reading and writing. — *Screw*, 6th October 1969
- C carved it in with a nail the night she gave him his first hand job in Big Playground. — Richard Price, *The Wanderers*, p. 5, 1974
- "I only give locals." "Locals?" "Hand jobs," she explained. "Okay," he said, "I'll have a local." — Guy Talese, *Thy Neighbor's Wife*, p. 431, 1980
- I had to give all the guys in the service department hand jobs. — *Romy and Michele's High School Reunion*, 1997

hand-job *verb*

to masturbate another person *US, 1969*

- In other words, she'd be blowing, fucking, and handjobbing four guys simultaneously, an act that would make her Queen of the Gang-Bang. — Josh Alan Friedman, *Tales of Times Square*, p. 90, 1986

handkerchief head *noun*

a black person, especially one who curries favor with white people by obsequious behavior *US, 1942*

- [B]y the time it was all over, Martin Luther King was a stupid music-hall Handkerchief Head on the New Left. — Tom Wolfe, *The Electric Kool-Aid Acid Test*, p. 226, 1968

- "He made you a handkerchief-head." — Sol Yurrick, *The Bag*, p. 65, 1968
- "Swamp Guinea," shot back Ray Barrett. "Han'kerchief Head," said Ricky Leopoldi. — Richard Price, *The Wanderers*, p. 160, 1974
- Although the AJ-C had its share of handkerchief-heads, many of the blacks were cool and down to earth. — Nathan McCall, *Makes Me Wanna Holler*, p. 293, 1994

handle *noun*

1 a name, a nickname *US, 1837*

- [I]t was so irreverent, so aw-go-to-hell, that I seized it as my handle. — Earl Wilson, *I am Gazing Into My 8-Ball*, p. 12, 1945
- Two of them go as Morgan and Walker. I don't know the slim stud's handle. — Chester Himes, *A Rage in Harlem*, p. 74, 1957
- "I read you wall to wall. What did you say your handle was?" — E.M. Corder, *Citizens Band*, p. 9, 1977
- Here's what a guy who goes by the chick-magnet Net handle of "Wampa-One" thinks about Bluntman and Chronic. — Kevin Smith, *Jay and Silent Bob Strike Back*, p. 20, 2001

2 the net amount taken in a gambling operation *US, 1987*

- I would deliver the figures, how much we won over the weekend, how much we got hit for, what the total "handle" was—the total taken in. — Joseph Pistone, *Donnie Brasco*, p. 132, 1987

3 a big nose *US, 1750*

- — Lou Shelly, *Hepcats Jive Dictionary*, p. 12, 1945

4 in horse racing, the total amount bet, either on a given race or an entire season *US, 1951*

- — David W. Maurer, *Argot of the Racetrack*, p. 34, 1951

handle *verb*

to stay in control *US, 1981*

Hawaiian youth usage as an intransitive verb.

- Oh, wow, man, I too loaded! I cannot handle! — Douglas Simonson, *Pidgin to da Max*, 1981

handler *noun*

a drug dealer who deals in large quantities to retail-level sellers *US, 1953*

- — Dale Kramer and Madeline Karr, *Teen-Age Gangs*, p. 175, 1953

handle-slammer *noun*

a person who manipulates the handles of a slot machine that is in need of repair, forcing the machine to pay out regardless of the spin *US, 1984*

- — J. Edward Allen, *The Basics of Winning Slots*, p. 57, 1984

handmade *noun*

a hand-rolled cigarette *US, 1988*

- I don't know what smoking handmades has to do with horse races[.] — Robert Campbell, *The Cat's Meow*, p. 50, 1988

handmade dick *noun*

a large or curved penis *US, 1967*

An allusion to the belief that excessive masturbation will produce a larger-than-average or curved penis.

- — Dale Gordon, *The Dominion Sex Dictionary*, p. 81, 1967
- His dick was curved to the right, as if the use of his right hand had fixed the curve in it. Masturbation, or too much tender handling made it what men called a handmade dick. — Donald Goines, *Swamp Man*, p. 67, 1974

hand mucker *noun*

in gambling, a cheat who switches cards *US, 1979*

- — John Scarne, *Scarne's Guide to Modern Poker*, p. 280, 1979
- Besides dice tats and 7UPS, there were volumes for nail nickers and crimpers (card markers), hand muckers and mit men (card switchers), as well as card counters and shiner players. — Stephen Cannell, *Big Con*, p. 143, 1997

hand problem *noun*

a tendency towards physical fighting *US, 1985*

- "The guy has a little hand problem and most guys don't like to work with him." — Mark Baker, *Cops*, p. 291, 1985

hand queen *noun*

a male homosexual who favors masturbating his partner *US, 1964*

- — Roger Blake, *The American Dictionary of Sexual Terms*, p. 94, 1964

hand ride *noun*

in horse racing, a race run without using a whip *US, 1974*

- — Les Conklin, *Payday at the Races*, p. 205, 1974

hand-rolled *noun*
a marijuana cigarette *US, 1978*
Mildly euphemistic, and thus mildly humorous.
- You want a hand-rolled? — Elmore Leonard, *Switch*, p. 169, 1978

handshake *noun*
the synchronization mechanism of two computers or two programs *US, 1991*
- — Eric S. Raymond, *The New Hacker's Dictionary*, p. 195, 1991

handshaking *noun*
mutual masturbation *US, 1961*
- Mutual masturbation, or "hand-shaking," however, presents a different situation and would seem to constitute a perverted act. — *New York Mattachine Newsletter*, p. 7, June 1961

hand-sitter *noun*
an unenthusiastic member of an audience *US, 1959*
- Saturday night patrons (not the late, late show) are known as "hand sitters," for the husband dares not applaud too enthusiastically or leer too longingly. — Monroe Fry, *Sex, Vice, and Business*, p. 63, 1959

hand thing *noun*
the act of masturbating a man *US, 2001*
A variation of **HAND-JOB**.
- Twenty [dollars] for a hand thing. You go into overtime if you take all day. — Janet Evanovich, *Seven Up*, p. 94, 2001

handwave *verb*
to oversimplify or give a cursory explanation of a complicated point *US, 1983*
- — Guy L. Steele, *Coevolution Quarterly*, p. 31, Spring 1981: "Computer Slang"
- If someone starts a sentence with "Clearly..." or "Obviously..." or "It is self-evident that...," you can be sure he is about to handwave. — Guy L. Steele et al., *The Hacker's Dictionary*, p. 81, 1983

hane *adjective*
disgusting *US, 1993*
An abbreviation of **HEINOUS**.
- — *Washington Post*, 14th October 1993

hang *noun*
a little bit *UK, 1861*
Used as a euphemism for "damn"; always in the negative.
- Mike, you're too damned big and tough to give a hang what people say. — Mickey Spillane, *One Lonely Night*, p. 15, 1951
- Shoot, my old man don't give a hang whether I'm in jail or dead in a car wreck or drunk in the gutter. — S.E. Hinton, *The Outsiders*, p. 78, 1967

hang *verb*
1 to make a turn while driving a car *US, 1966*
- You said "Hang a Roscoe" or "Hang a Louie" was "Turn to the right" or "left" while you're driving. — *Coshocton (Ohio) Tribune*, p. 4, 15th March 1966
- — *Current Slang*, p. 6, Spring 1968
- Quick. Hang a right! — *American Graffiti*, 1973
- Bobby nudged him out of his reverie. "Hang a right." — James Ellroy, *Suicide Hill*, p. 600, 1986

2 to tolerate, to keep up with *US, 1993*
- He looks down at me frowning like, How can this will-o'-the-wisp white child think she can hang with this? — Francesca Lia Block, *Missing Angel Juan*, p. 330, 1993

3 to idle *US, 1941*
- — *Newsweek*, p. 28, 8th October 1951
- The other two always hang. — *Break Point*, 1991
- You know. It's boring with just my mom to hang with. — Francesca Lia Block, *I Was a Teenage Fairy*, p. 128, 1998

4 (used of a computer program) to wait in suspension for something that will not occur *US, 1983*
- — Guy L. Steele et al., *The Hacker's Dictionary*, p. 82, 1983

▸ **hang crepe**
in a hospital, to manage a patient's expectations by leading them to expect the very worst *US, 1994*
- — Sally Williams, *"Strong" Words*, p. 145, 1994

▸ **hang five**
to surf with five toes extended over the front edge of the board *US, 1963*
- — Grant W. Kuhns, *On Surfing*, p. 117, 1963

▸ **hang heels**
to surf with your heels extended backward over the tail of the surfboard *US, 1977*
- — Gary Fairmont R. Filosa II, *The Surfer's Almanac*, p. 187, 1977

▸ **hang it up**
1 to insult *US, 1989*
- All the Kids would rap, charm (talk to), or game to impress girlfriends; hang it up (insult) or fresh (compliment) male friends by using special words. — Terry Williams, *The Cocaine Kids*, p. 90, 1989

2 to stop talking; to shut up *US, 1963*
- — *San Francisco Examiner: People*, p. 8, 27 October 1963: "What a 'Z'! The astonishing private language of Bay Area teenagers"

3 to retire *US, 1936*
Or "hang them up."
- I quit. Hit my dinger and hang 'em up. — *Bull Durham*, 1988

4 to escape from jail *US, 1951*
- I have carefully considered all the ways of hanging it up, believe me, and the simplest easiest way is to be picked up by a car. — James Blake, *The Joint*, p. 15, 4th March 1951

▸ **hang loose**
to do little and to do it without angst *US, 1955*
- Reading over the Book I'm giving the impression that I'm hanging loose and bemused and don't overly care about anything. — James Simon Kunen, *The Strawberry Statement*, p. 110, 1968

▸ **hang on the leg**
(used of a prisoner) to associate and curry favor with prison authorities *US, 1992*
- — William K. Bentley and James M. Corbett, *Prison Slang*, p. 32, 1992

▸ **hang on the wall**
(used of a groupie) to loiter at a rock and roll club in the hopes of making contact with a musician *US, 1969*
- — *Kiss*, 1969: "Groupie glossary"

▸ **hang paper**
to pass counterfeit money *US, 1976*
- I've hung a little paper, not much, there's no excitement in it. — Elmore Leonard, *Swag*, p. 14, 1976
- Better call bunco-forgery. The Czech's trying to hang bad paper. — Joseph Wambaugh, *The Delta Star*, p. 91, 1983
- But when I was hanging paper, I never scored from him. — Gerald Petievich, *The Quality of the Informant*, p. 54, 1985

▸ **hang ten**
to surf with all the toes of both feet extended over the front of the board *US, 1963*
- — Grant W. Kuhns, *On Surfing*, p. 117, 1963

▸ **hang the moon**
to be talented, important, or self-important *US, 1953*
- "Lucy thinks that fool boy of hern is God's own cousin! She thinks he hung the moon." — Vance Randolph, *Down in the Holler*, p. 250, 1953
- Someone highly thought of is said to "hang the moon." — Dorothy Morrison, *Everyday Moon Magic*, p. 4, 2003

▸ **hang tight**
to stay put, to stay resolved *US, 1947*
- This is Ian with you. Hang tight, we'll be back with you after these messages. — *Airheads*, 1994

▸ **hang up your jock**
to quit or retire *US, 1983*
- "Either hang up our jocks and admit he's untouchable or be slicker than he is," Chance said. — Gerald Petievich, *To Live and Die in L.A.*, p. 123, 1983

▸ **hang your hat**
to live, to reside *US, 1997*
- — Marvin Gaye, *Wherever I Lay My Hat (That's My Home)*, 1969
- Look, I've got to get a hold of Frank and see where I'm hanging my hat. — *As Good As It Gets*, 1997

▸ **hang your own**
in circus and carnival usage, to brag *US, 1981*
A metaphor derived from the image of the braggart hanging posters advertising himself.
- — Don Wilmeth, *The Language of American Popular Entertainment*, p. 125, 1981

hang around *verb*

to idle, to pass time aimlessly, to socialize *US, 1830*

- Students started hanging around nonstudent tables, and forgetting to go to their classes. — Jerry Rubin, *Do It!*, p. 25, 1970
- He says I should just hang around my apartment and wait for a phone call. — *Reservoir Dogs*, 1992
- I been hangin' around this town on the corner / I been bummin' around this old town for way too long. — Counting Crows, *Hanging Around*, 2000

hangar queen *noun*

an aircraft that spends an inordinate amount of time being repaired *US, 1943*

- — *American Speech*, p. 228, October 1956: "More United States Air Force slang"

hangar rat *noun*

a person who associates with aviators *US, 1954*

- Paul was at the restaurant counter ranting to a row of hangar rats how the small coffee shops of America were being wiped out[.] — Boston Teran, *The Prince of Deadly Weapons*, p. 114, 2002

hanged up *adjective*

drug-intoxicated *US, 1949*

- Any time you want to get hanged up, let me know. I got connections. — Hal Ellson, *Duke*, p. 34, 1949

hanger *noun*

1 a piece of paper currency that has not fallen all the way through the slot on a casino table where cash is dropped *US, 1980*

- — Lee Solkey, *Dummy Up and Deal*, p. 114, 1980

2 in pool, a ball that is at rest right at the edge of a pocket *US, 1937*

- — Steve Rushin, *Pool Cool*, p. 15, 1990

3 a handgun cartridge that fails to detonate immediately after being struck by the firing pin *US, 1957*

- — *American Speech*, p. 193, October 1957: "Some colloquialisms of the handgunner"

4 a handbag with a strap *US, 1950*

- — Hyman E. Goldin et al., *Dictionary of American Underworld Lingo*, p. 90, 1950

hanger banger *noun*

a thief who targets women with over-the-shoulder purses *US, 1958*

- A cutpurse who goes after women's off-the-shoulder bags is a hanger banger. — *New York Times*, p. 34, 20th October 1958

hangers *noun*

the female breasts *UK, 1967*

- Chubby took in her jugs again. Nice big hangers. — Richard Price, *Blood Brothers*, p. 13, 1976

hangin' and clangin' *adjective*

said of a man's genitals when he is wearing no underwear *US, 2001*

- Just leave 'em hangin' and clangin', they air out better that way. — Cherokee Paul McDonald, *Into the Green*, p. 221, 2001

hanging, banging and slanging

used for summarizing the pastimes of some inner city youth—idling, engaging in gang fighting, and selling drugs *US, 1991*

- "He got a job and a family, he ain't out there hangin', bangin' and slangin'." — Leon Bing, *Do or Die*, p. 77, 1991

hanging buddy *noun*

a close friend *US, 1994*

- "He s'pposed to be one of your hanging buddies and he won't even give you a ride home?" — Nathan McCall, *Makes Me Wanna Holler*, p. 50, 1994

hanging Johnny *noun*

the penis in a flaccid state *US, 1980*

- — *Maledicta*, p. 195, Winter 1980: "A new erotic vocabulary"

hang-loose *adjective*

relaxed, informal *US, 1970*

- Even so, SDS was strictly hang-loose. — William Tulio Divale, *I Lived Inside the Campus Revolution*, p. 61, 1970

hang on *verb*

to make a criminal charge against *US, 1957*

- He'd been pushing for five years, and they couldn't hang one on him. — William Burroughs, *Naked Lunch*, p. 211, 1957

hangout *noun*

a place where people gather to socialize *US, 1892*

At times a negative connotation.

- That had become our hangout, when we weren't jamming at The Deuces[.] — Mezz Mezzrow, *Really the Blues*, p. 159, 1946
- One of the most colorful and successful of the Swing Street hangouts opened in 1938 in a former stable in West 51st Street[.] — Robert Sylvester, *No Cover Charge*, p. 81, 1956
- Betty's was the after-hours hangout for the Foxy Lady crew and the older night crawlers of the Providence area. — Heidi Mattson, *Ivy League Stripper*, p. 141, 1995
- You know. Rest areas are homosexual hangouts. — *Something About Mary*, 1998

hang out *verb*

to spend time with someone, usually a friend or friends *US, 1867*

- Jim Morrison used to sit outside my door when I lived in Laurel Canyon, wanting to hang out with me. — Arthur Lee, *quoted in Waiting For The Sun*, p. 124, 1969
- I was double leery when I left her because I knew "hang out" was New York white hippie argot for you know what. — Iceberg Slim (Robert Beck), *Death Wish*, p. 9, 1977

hang-out card *noun*

respect from other prisoners *US, 1975*

- Creeps never "get a hang-out card" (command enough respect to mingle and converse freely with other prisoners). — Miguel Pinero, *Short Eyes*, p. 123, 1975

hang up *verb*

▸ **hang up a shingle**

to go into business for yourself *US, 1997*

- You hang up a shingle. I know some people who will throw work your way. — Stephen Cannell, *King Con*, p. 90, 1997

hangup; hang-up *noun*

an emotional problem, neurosis, or inhibition *US, 1952*

- "And what about all these maniac hangups you've got—secretly, mind you, but got all the same—with Morality and Conduct, and like that?" "Hangups?" "This whole neurotic syndrome about love." — Richard Farina, *Been Down So Long*, p. 109, 1966
- But seriously here are some of the real "hang-ups" of being a teen-age girl that must be quite frustrating. — Murray Kaufman, *Murray the K Tells It Like It Is, Baby*, p. 33, 1966
- Max is telling me how he lives free of all the old middle-class Freudian hang-ups. — Joan Didion, *Slouching Toward Bethlehem*, p. 97, 1967
- Cassady brought in a Scandanavian-style blonde who was always talking about hangups. Everybody had hangups. — Tom Wolfe, *The Electric Kool-Aid Acid Test*, p. 118, 1968

hank *noun*

▸ **take your hank**

to masturbate *US, 1967*

- If taking your hank could destroy someone, I'd of been boiled down to a grease spot years ago. — Malcolm Braly, *On the Yard*, p. 209, 1967

hank book *noun*

a pornographic book or magazine *US, 1967*

- Page smuggled 'em past the kickout clerk in cutout compartments in his collections of hank books. — Ken Kesey, *Kesey's Jail Journal*, p. 105, 1967
- — Paul Glover, *Words from the House of the Dead*, 1974

hank freak *noun*

a person obsessed with masturbating *US, 1967*

- [N]ightly the hank freak would read of one coupling after another while he masturbated. — Malcolm Braly, *On the Yard*, p. 152, 1967

Hank Snow *noun*

▸ **to pull a Hank Snow**

to leave *US, 1962*

From Snow's recording "Movin' On."

- "You gonna pull a Hank Snow and be Movin' On." — Kevin O'Kelly, *Richland Street*, p. 259, 1992

hankty *adjective*

suspicious *US, 1966*

- He stopped into Lewis' place where all the boys was having fun / Brock got kind of hankty and he felt for his gun. — Bruce Jackson, *Get Your Ass in the Water and Swim Like Me*, p. 56, 1966

- I don't know if she was hankty [suspicious] or what, because she handed the syrup in, in a cup, and kept her hand on the grill. — Bruce Jackson, *In the Life*, p. 115, 1972

hanky; hankie *noun*
a handkerchief; a tissue (often qualified as a paper hankie) *UK*, *1895*

- Not the way Richie, bleeding all over himself, kept moaning, saying to him, "Bird, you have a hanky? Man, I'm cut bad." — Elmore Leonard, *Killshot*, p. 69, 1989
- Not even if you hear a thud from inside my home and a week later there's a smell from in there that can only come from a decaying body and you have to hold a hanky against your face because the stench is so thick[.] — *As Good As It Gets*, 1997

hanky code; hankie code *noun*
a designation of a person's sexual preferences, signaled by the color of the handkerchief and the pocket in which it is worn *US*, *1991*

- Though the hanky code was originated by gay men, it has been adopted by cruising lesbians and bi's. — *Taste of Latex*, p. 24, Winter 1990–1991
- To make matters worse, after we've spent years figuring out an entire, ever expanding hanky code of fun things to do, now we hear about "safe sex." — Cindy Patton, *Fatal Advice*, p. 92, 1996
- [T]he big article in the Boston Globe that listed their nazi bootlace code, similar to the fag hanky code but entirely different. — Michelle Tea, *The Passionate Mistakes and Intricate Corruption of One Girl in America*, p. 28, 1998
- See, the Hankie Code, that's how you said what you wanted and who you were. — Lynn Breedlove, *Godspeed*, p. 211, 2002

hanky pank *noun*
a carnival game in which the customer is allowed to win small, inexpensive prizes *US*, *1985*

- So even though a player usually wins every time, there is still some HANKY PANK as to the size of the prize. — Gene Sorrows, *All About Carnivals*, p. 19, 1985

hankypank *adjective*
(used of a carnival game) inexpensive *US*, *1950*

- — *American Speech*, p. 235, October 1950: "The argot of outdoor boob traps"

hanky-panky; hankie-pankie *noun*
trickery, mischief, especially of a sexual nature *UK*, *1841*

- As long as our guests are quiet about it, we'll put up with a little hanky-panky. — Jim Thompson, *A Swell-Looking Babe*, p. 1, 1954
- He imprisoned her in a tower in rags, and on her sixteenth birthday, the King decided to make any hankie-pankie impossible. — Iceberg Slim (Robert Beck), *Long White Con*, p. 41, 1977
- "It's the sexual hankypanky the board frowns on most," he explained. — Seth Morgan, *Homeboy*, p. 308, 1990
- There was more hanky-panky in a church pew than in my clubs. — Larry Flynt, *An Unseemly Man*, p. 68, 1996

Hanoi Hannah *noun*
a composite character on Radio Hanoi who broadcast during the Vietnam war with a target audience of US troops and a goal of lessening troop morale *US*, *1967*

- The more I thought about it, the less I could distinguish "Hanoi Hannah" from my news shows in Saigon on Armed Forces Radio and Television. — John Steinbeck, *In Touch*, p. 46, 1969
- Here she is, men—the gook you love to hate—Hannoi Hannah. — Gregory Sarno, *When Johny Comes Marching Home Again*, p. 188, 2005

Hanoi Hilton *nickname*
a North Vietnamese prisoner of war camp, formally known as the Hoa Lo Prison (1964–1973) *US*, *1970*
The title of a 1987 film starring Michael Moriarty and Jeffrey Jones as US prisoners of war trying to survive in the camp.

- The only facility North Vietnamese have taken newsmen to visit is one wryly known among American Pilots as the "Hanoi Hilton." — *New York Times*, p. 16, 24th November 1970
- The next place I end up was Hoa Lo Prison, which we called the Hanoi Hilton. — Wallace Terry, *Bloods*, pp. 273–274, 1984
- I'm a guest at Hanoi Hilton, with luxury sublime / The only thing's that not so great, I'll be here a long, long time. — Joseph Tuso, *Singing the Vietnam Blues*, p. 71, 1990: Cruising Over Hanoi

- When cruelly exploiting Cindy's brief addiction to prescription painkillers didn't work, they [President George W. Bush's operatives] said McCain was crazy—too long at the Hanoi Hilton as a POW. — John W. Dean, *Worse Than Watergate*, p. 4, 2004

happening *noun*
an unstructured event built around music, drugs, and a strong sense of bonding *US*, *1959*

- In Japan, the Gutai group started off the current wave of happenings in the early 1950s with an art show in the sky (balloons, kites, etc., from the roof of a department store). — *Los Angeles Free Press*, p. 6, 19th February 1965
- "We're gonna stage a street happening Saturday, carol singers, motorcycle gangs, the works." — *The San Francisco Oracle*, 1966
- Balls, Happenings, Theatre, Dance, and spontaneous experiments in joy. — *The Digger Papers*, p. 15, August 1968
- We simply told them we wanted to have a "happening," which they assumed would be something like the colorful street fairs the Artists' Liberation Front had been sponsoring, and agreed to let us use their building. — Peter Coyote, *Sleeping Where I Fall*, p. 77, 1998

happening *adjective*
modern, fashionable, chic *US*, *1977*
In common with many words that define the times, "happening" is now deeply unfashionable, surviving in irony and the vocabularies of those who were there when it was "happening."

- — Connie Eble (Editor), *UNC-CH Campus Slang*, p. 3, Fall 1982
- [H]e looks like he's "happening." We'll make him an A&R man[.] — Frank Zappa, *The Real Frank Zappa Book*, p. 204, 1989
- — Trevor Cralle, *The Surfin'ary*, p. 50, 1991

happily *adverb*
in computing, operating without awareness of an important fact *US*, *1991*

- The program continues to run, happily unaware that its output is going to /dev/null. — Eric S. Raymond, *The New Hacker's Dictionary*, p. 196, 1991

happy camper *noun*
used as a humorous description of a contented person *US*, *1981*
Often said with sarcasm or used in the negative.

- Time for luncheon, happy campers. — George V. Higgins, *Penance for Jerry Kennedy*, p. 168, 1985
- Vice President Dan Quayle, in an exchange of letters with American Samoa's representative in Congress, has sought to clear up his puzzling reference to Samoans as "happy campers." — *Baltimore Sun*, 16th May 1989

happy dust *noun*
cocaine, morphine, or any powdered mind-altering drug *US*, *1922*
Imparts a sense of nostalgia, not unlike **WACKY BACCY** (marijuana). The term of choice for cocaine in George Gershwin's *Porgy and Bess*.

- — *American Speech*, p. 26, February 1952: "Teen-age hophead jargon"
- "Sportin' Life," said Mona. "Happy dust. This stuff is an American institution." — Armistead Maupin, *Tales of the City*, p. 46, 1978

happy farm *noun*
a mental institution *US*, *1985*

- That stuff is happy farm. It's crazy. — Mark Baker, *Cops*, p. 268, 1985

happy hacking
used as a farewell *US*, *1981*

- — *Co-Evolution Quarterly*, p. 32, Spring 1981
- — Guy L. Steele et al., *The Hacker's Dictionary*, p. 76, 1983

happy happy joy joy
used as a humorous, often sarcastic, celebratory remark *US*, *1997*
First heard in the *Ren and Stimpy* cartoon (1991–1995), and then popularized with a broader audience by Keith Olberman on ESPN.

- — Keith Olberman and Dan Patrick, *The Big Show*, p. 17, 1997

happy herb *noun*
marijuana *UK*, *1998*

- Queen Elizabeth gladly accepts a "kind" bouquet of marijuana buds (left) from legalization advocate Colin Davies (above) whose efforts to loosen her royal highness' view on the happy herb were snuffed

by her pot-poaching chauffeur. [Caption] — *New York Post*, p. 3, 15th
October 2000

happy horseshit *noun*
nonsense *US, 1971*

- "What? Cain't talk? What's this happy horseshit?" — Stephen King,
  The Stand, p. 73, 1990

happy hour *noun*
a period of time in the late afternoon when a bar serves
free snacks and drinks at reduced prices *US, 1959*

- He knew he shouldn't mix the drug with the happy-hour booze, but
  what the hell, George Bush took them and hadn't expired yet.
  — Joseph Wambaugh, *Finnegan's Week*, p. 108, 1993

happy hunting ground *noun*
the afterlife *US, 1837*
From the native American Indian view of life after death.

- Many years after Prescott joined Geronimo in the happy hunting
  ground, this story rose up like a ghost in chains to smack the
  fortunes of Prescott's political son, George. — Kitty Kelley, *The Family*,
  p. 11, 2004

happy juice *noun*
any alcoholic drink; any mood-elevating drug *US, 1921*

- It turned out Bill didn't need anything to cheer him because Bill
  was shot up with painkillers and happy juice for the ride home.
  — Janet Evanovich, *Metro Girl*, p. 190, 2004

happy pie *noun*
the vagina *US, 1974*

- [G]roping under skirts between bare, plump young thighs, getting a
  finger or two in someone's happy pie. — Earl Thompson, *Tattoo*, p. 156,
  1974

happy Sally *noun*
strong, homemade whiskey *US, 1986*

- Masters of moonshine prided themselves in their ancient, father-to-
  son recipes and the white lightning, blue John, red eye, happy Sally,
  and stumphole whiskey they made, Smith said. — *Chicago Tribune*,
  p. C-1, 15th January 1986
- It is called corn liquor, white lightning, sugar whiskey, skully cracker,
  popskull, bush whiskey, stump, stumphole, 'splo, ruckus juice,
  radiator whiskey, rotgut, sugarhead, block and tackle, wildcat,
  panther's breath, tiger's sweat, Sweet spirits of cats a-fighting, alley
  bourbon, city gin, cool water, happy Sally, deep shaft, jump steady,
  old horsey, stingo, blue John, red eye, pine top, buckeye bark
  whiskey and see seven stars. — *Star Tribune (Minneapolis)*, p. 19F, 31st
  January 1999

happy shop *noun*
a liquor store *US, 1972*

- — *American Speech*, p. 153, Spring–Summer 1972: "An approach to Black slang"

happy talk *noun*
a "human interest" news story *UK, 1973*

- It spills over to the cheerful exchanges of the happy talk news
  shows[.] — Geoffrey Nunberg, *Going Nucular*, p. 267, 2004

happy trails *noun*
cocaine *US, 1993*
From the cowboy song known by those who came of age in the
US in the 1950s and 60s.

- — Peter Johnson, *Dictionary of Street Alcohol and Drug Terms*, p. 89, 1993

happy valley *noun*
the cleft between the buttock cheeks *US, 1970s*

- — Bruce Rodgers, *The Queens' Vernacular*, p. 103, 1972

Happy Valley *nickname*
the Vinh Thanh Valley, during the war a dangerous area
northeast of An Khe, South Vietnam *US, 1983*

- The mission we had been assigned was simple: an early-morning
  flight over the An Khe pass toward Qui Hnon; a left turn up
  between two skinny ridges into Vinh Thanh Valley, known to us as
  Happy Valley[.] — Robert Mason, *Chickenhawk*, p. 95, 1983

haps *noun*
the latest; something that is popular *US, 1961*
Often heard as "the haps."

- — Andy Anonymous, *A Basic Guide to Campusology*, p. 13, 1966
- — Connie Eble (Editor), *UNC-CH Campus Slang*, p. 5, Fall 1990

hard *noun*
1 an erection *US, 1961*

- What good are the fancy ties and the fine suits if you can't get a
  hard on any more? — Henry Miller, *Tropic of Cancer*, p. 116, 1961
- — Helen Dahlskog (Editor), *A Dictionary of Contemporary and Colloquial Usage*, p. 30,
  1972
- He lifts his blanket and he's lying there with a hard. — Herbert Huncke,
  Guilty of Everything, p. 48, 1990

2 hardcore sexual material *US, 1977*

- I put in parts of Ohio where they don't run hard, and it ran 6 weeks
  in one theater. — Stephen Ziplow, *The Film Maker's Guide to Pornography*, p. 78,
  1977

3 coins *US, 1950*

- — Hyman E. Goldin et al., *Dictionary of American Underworld Lingo*, p. 91, 1950

hard *adjective*
1 of drinks, intoxicating, spiritous, "strong" *US, 1789*

- Look, mister, we serve hard drinks in here for men who want to get
  drunk fast. — *USA Today*, 17th January 2000

2 (used of drugs) powerfully addictive *US, 1955*

- I read him the riot law—if I find out you're using hard shit I'm
  gonna pull your tongue out yo' ass, etc. — Edwin Torres, *Carlito's Way*,
  p. 73, 1975
- The hard-stuff trade is dead. — Edwin Torres, *After Hours*, p. 247, 1979
- Hard drugs were for running away from life, for altering your mind
  or searching your soul—heroin, morphine and barbiturates. Acid lay
  somewhere between soft and hard. — Simon Napier-Bell, *Black Vinyl White
  Powder*, p. 124, 2001

3 fine, excellent *US, 1948*

- — Jack Lait and Lee Mortimer, *New York Confidential*, p. 235, 1948: "A Glossary of
  Harlemisms."
- I was givin' him some balls off too, but their game was not as hard
  as mine! — Henry Williamson, *Hustler!*, p. 128, 1965
- — Judi Sanders, *Da Bomb*, p. 7, 1997

4 in craps, a point made with a matching pair *US, 1930*
A bet on a "hard" number means that the only combination
that will win is a pair. Often used in the phrase "the hard way."

- With equal ease, I could quote the Roman lyric poet, Catullus, or the
  odds against making four the hard way. — Jim Thompson, *Roughneck*,
  p. 2, 1954
- It was hot and dry, and they pay 10 to 1 on eight the hard way.
  — Max Shulman, *Rally Round the Flag, Boys!*, p. 187, 1957
- Two thousand dollar hard eight. — *Hard Eight*, 1996

5 (used of straightened hair) heavily greased *US, 1970*

- — Clarence Major, *Dictionary of Afro-American Slang*, p. 64, 1970

6 in blackjack, said of a hand without an ace or with an ace
and a value of 12 or higher *US, 1978*

- — Jerry L. Patterson, *Blackjack*, p. 19, 1978

7 (used of a theater ticket) reserved for a specific seat *US, 1973*

- — Sherman Louis Sergel, *The Language of Show Biz*, p. 104, 1973

hard *adverb*
▸ **go hard**
  to engage in gunfire *US, 2003*

- Trainum and Garrett were looking for robbers who "went
  hard"—street slang for gunplay—and started shooting when they
  lost control[.] — *Washington Post*, p. W14, 2nd May 2003

hard-ass *noun*
a strict, unforgiving, unrelenting person *US, 1966*

- I bet you played the hardass, didn't you. Show 'em no fucking
  mercy. — Elmore Leonard, *Freaky Deaky*, p. 276, 1988
- I'm always talking to them and playing with them, but Silent Bob
  won't join in. He's a fucking hard-ass. — *Mallrats*, 1995
- You were a hard ass and you took his dad out, Sydney. — *Hard Eight*,
  1996
- She had proved herself to be less of a hard-ass than I first imagined.
  — Rita Ciresi, *Pink Slip*, p. 41, 1999

hard-ass *verb*
1 to endure a difficult situation *US, 1967*

- You did it the easiest way you could and hard-assed the difference.
  — Malcolm Braly, *On the Yard*, p. 10, 1967

2 to treat harshly *US, 1961*

- But the captain didn't hard-ass worth a damn. — Malcom Braly, *Felony
  Tank*, p. 70, 1961

- Do you think we're gonna stand here and be hard-assed because some dude in Norfolk forgot to endorse our orders? — Darryl Ponicsan, *The Last Detail*, p. 143, 1970
- "The last thing Joey wants is nosy cops hard-assing him over the merchandize." — Elizabeth Lowell, *Running Scared*, p. 188, 2001

hard-ass; hard-assed *adjective*
uncompromising, unyielding, tough, stubborn *UK, 1903*

- The original Oakland Angels were hard-ass brawlers[.] — Hunter S. Thompson, *Hell's Angels*, p. 131, 1966

hardball *noun*
competition or conflict with no holds barred *US, 1972*

- This guy's looking to play tit-for-tat. That's not my game. I'm gonna play hardball. — *Tin Men*, 1987
- It's a hardball world, son. We've got to keep our heads until this peace craze blows over. — *Full Metal Jacket*, 1987

hardballer *noun*
a person who competes or pursues an interest with an intense focus and little thought as to the consequences *US, 1984*

- Chief of Police Kolender, true to his word, did come to Southern Division to reassure Manny's men of what a hell of a bunch of gutsy hardballers they really were[.] — Joseph Wambaugh, *Lines and Shadows*, p. 294, 1984

hardbelly *noun*
a teenage girl or young woman *US, 1988*
Biker (motorcycle) usage.

- "There was no confusin' her with the other hardbellies [slim biker chix] at the bar," the article says. [Quoting an article in the November 1987 issue of Outlaw Biker.] — *Washington Post*, p. W5, 3rd January 1988

hardbody *noun*
a trim, physically fit person *US, 1984*

- "Suzie, she's blond, she's twenty-four, she's a hardbody and a total babe." — Jane Green, *Jemima J.*, p. 46, 1999

hardboot *noun*
a person from Kentucky *US, 1923*

- — Dan Parker, *The ABC of Horse Racing*, p. 146, 1947

hard case *noun*
a hardened, tough person *US, 1836*

- Juvey judge Thomas A. Laskin III—a former D.A. with experience prosecuting gang members—had a rep as a hard case. — Jonathan Kellerman, *Rage*, p. 17, 2005

hard cat *noun*
a well-dressed, popular male *US, 1959*

- — *Time Magazine*, p. 46, 24th August 1959

hard charger *noun*
an aggressive, hard-working person *US, 1960*

- After all that, I guess they thought of him as a combat liability, but he was such a hard charger that they gave him the EM Club to manage. — Michael Herr, *Dispatches*, p. 171, 1972

hardcore *adjective*
of pornography, graphic, explicit *US, 1970*
The gradations between **SOFTCORE** and "hardcore" vary over time and place; in general, the erect penis, penetration and ejaculation are the hallmarks of hardcore pornography.

- "In hard-core pornography," Aileen said, "the man's core is hard." "That's an old gag," Gregor said. "Professional humor," she said. — Lawrence Block, *No Score [The Affairs of Chip Harrison Omnibus]*, p. 62, 1970
- Like the little girl who posed shyly in a nudist magazine and then graduated into hardcore porn, most are totally anonymous. — *Associated Press, PM cycle*, 14th April 1977

hard dick *noun*
a tough, uncompromising person *US, 1975*

- "The old man, he's a hard dick, he comes by every coupla years for his money[.]" — George Pelecanos, *Shoedog*, p. 13, 1996

hard dresser *noun*
an aggressive, "mannish" lesbian *US, 1967*

- Known variously as a bull, a stomper, a bad butch, a hard dresser, a truck driver, a diesel dyke, a bull dagger and a half dozen other soubriquets, she is the one who, according to most homosexual girls, gives lesbians a bad name. — Ruth Allison, *Lesbianism*, p. 125, 1967

har-de-har-har
used as a vocalization mocking laughter *US, 1957*

- "I drive you ape, and you just don't trust yourself with me, that's what it is." "Har-de-har-har!" replied Comfort. — Max Shulman, *Rally Round the Flag, Boys!*, p. 58, 1957
- "Har-de-har-har," said Wilson. — Chris Miller, *The Real Animal House*, p. 20, 2006

hard guy *noun*
a serious, violent criminal *US, 1916*

- Such veteran hard guys as are still extant differ as to what contretemps the Dutchman and The Mick's brother involved themselves. — Robert Sylvester, *No Cover Charge*, p. 60, 1956

hard hat *noun*
an elite, full-time Viet Cong soldier *US, 1965*

- Named from the metal helmets they wore, not worn by guerilla fighters. The advisors tended to group both together, calling them "hard hats" because they wore turtle-shaped sun helmets, an imitation of the colonial sun helmet that one saw in Lipingesque movies of British India on late-night television[.] — Neil Sheehan, *A Bright Shining Lie*, p. 66, 1988

hard head *noun*
a criminal who uses explosives to break into safes *US, 1949*

- — Vincent J. Monteleone, *Criminal Slang*, p. 112, 1949

Hard John *noun*
1 an agent of the Federal Bureau of Investigation (FBI) *US, 1945*

- — Lou Shelly, *Hepcats Jive Talk Dictionary*, p. 25, 1945

2 a tough, uncompromising person *US, 1961*

- [T]he "hard Johns" from the federal narcotics bureau had invaded this most neighborly of neighborhoods[.] — Ross Russell, *The Sound*, p. 219, 1961

hard leg *noun*
an experienced, cynical prostitute *US, 1967*

- "That old whore is a 'hard leg.'" — Charles Winick, *The Lively Commerce*, p. 43, 1971
- Kenn "Naz" Young, *Naz's Underground Dictionary*, p. 35, 1973

hard-look *verb*
to stare at aggressively *US, 1994*

- — Ann Lawson, *Kids & Gangs*, p. 55, 1994: "Common Mexican gang slang/phrases"

hard mack *noun*
a brutish pimp who relies on force and the threat of force to control his prostitutes *US, 1972*

- One who uses brutality and threats is a gorilla pimp or hard Mack. — Christina and Richard Milner, *Black Players*, p. 35, 1972

hard man *noun*
a professional thug; a person not afraid of violent action *US, 1970*

- [S]treet-corner society has a typology of its own denizens, pointing not only to H "hard men" or "gorillas"[.] — Roger Abrahams, *Positively Black*, p. 85, 1974

hard money *noun*
cash *US, 1972*

- A lot of times it's not too much—you'd be surprised how small an amount they can open on—but as long as they're handling hard money, you're going to get some. — Bruce Jackson, *Outside the Law*, p. 104, 1972

hard nail *noun*
a hypodermic needle *US, 1955*

- — *American Speech*, p. 87, May 1955: "Narcotic argot along the Mexican border"

hard-on *noun*
1 the erect penis; an erection *US, 1888*

- I got immediately a hardon, told Bob, ordered him in fact to drive to the woods. — Jack Kerouac, *Letter to Neal Cassady*, p. 298, 10th January 1951
- One incident which I recall rather vividly was my first understanding of the slang expression "hard-on," which I got from another boy in the sixth grade. — Phyllis and Eberhard Kronhausen, *Sex Histories of American College Men*, p. 77, 1960
- Sometimes, though, I'd go home afterwards, after having had a hard-on for four hours of making out on the floor and in the

bleachers, but without creaming, and it really gave you a sore dick. — *The Berkeley Tribe*, p. 13, 5th–12th September 1969

- It's not so cool to leave me with a hard-on. — *Boogie Nights*, 1997

2 a grudge *US, 1931*

- Just that you got a hard on for ofays. — Ross Russell, *The Sound*, p. 91, 1961
- There's a lot you don't know about, like the old man's old lady having a hard-on for him. — Darryl Ponicsan, *The Last Detail*, p. 94, 1970
- He knows I'm a cop, of course, and he knows I'm a federal cop, so he's got to figure I got a hard-on for Panthers. — George V. Higgins, *The Friends of Eddie Doyle*, p. 29, 1971
- God has a hard-on for marines because we kill everything we see! — *Full Metal Jacket*, 1987

3 a stubborn, belligerent person *US, 1968*

- "Oh come on, Day Tripper, don't be a hard-on." — Michael Herr, *Dispatches*, p. 130, 1977
- Nah, not now, all those hard-ons around. I'll wait. — *Raging Bull*, 1980
- You don't want to act like a hard-on. You're standing there in your undies. You know what I'm saying? — *Get Shorty*, 1995
- Look, I don't wanna be a hard-on about this, and I know it wasn't your fault, but I just thought it was fair to tell you that Gene and I will be submitting this to the League[.] — *The Big Lebowski*, 1998

4 a desire for *US, 1971*

- You got some hardon for Cokes, kid—I like 'em, Sprenger said. — Gilbert Sorrentino, *Steelwork*, p. 21, 1970

hard one *noun*
in necrophile usage, a corpse that has stiffened with rigor mortis *US, 1986–1987*

- — *Maledicta*, p. 180, Summer/Winter 1986–1987: "Sexual slang: prostitutes, pedophiles, flagellators, transvestites, and necrophiles"

hard pimp *noun*
a pimp who relies on violence and the threat of violence to control his prostitutes *US, 1973*

- I then went to Dian and got her gun because he was a hard pimp and just might not accept this kinda shit. — A.S. Jackson, *Gentleman Pimp*, p. 143, 1973

hard rice *noun*
during the Vietnam war, weapons and ammunition *US, 1985*

- It probably belonged to Air America and was making a hard rice drop, as munitions were called, to the Meo tribesmen in the mountains around the Plaines Des Jars. — Barry Sadler, *Casca #14: The Phoenix*, p. 37, 1985

hardshell Baptist; hard-shell Baptist *noun*
a member of the Primitive Baptist Church, or any other rigidly orthodox Baptist *US, 1838*

- Bill Hill's ex-wife, Barbararose, who was a hard-shell Baptist out of Nashville, where there were 686 different Fundamentalist churches, had called the whole Uni-Faith setup "a mockery in the eyes of God." — Elmore Leonard, *Touch*, p. 90, 1977

hard shells *noun*
powerfully addictive drugs, such as heroin, morphine and cocaine *US, 1960*

- — Robert George Reisner, *The Jazz Titans*, p. 157, 1960

hard stripe *noun*
a military chevron signifying noncommissioned officer status *US, 1970*

- There were three other guys who were hard-stripe sergeants, a respected rank for a short-termer. — Mark Baker, *Nam*, p. 124, 1981

hard stuff *noun*
1 addictive drugs such as heroin or cocaine *US, 1950*

- After they become habituated to them, they are forced to seek the more expensive reefers or go to "hard stuff"—cocaine and heroin. — Jack Lait and Lee Mortimer, *Chicago Confidential*, p. 148, 1950
- Most of the girls are into hard stuff, and Lamont is an important source—finding junk for them[.] — David Freeman, *U.S. Grant in the City*, p. 23, 1971
- They were using hard stuff so I cut out fast. — Babs Gonzales, *Movin' On Down De Line*, p. 117, 1975

2 coins *US, 1788*

- — Hyman E. Goldin et al., *Dictionary of American Underworld Lingo*, p. 91, 1950

hard time *noun*
a long prison sentence, whether in absolute terms or relative to the crime or relative to the prisoner's ability to survive *US, 1927*

- Manning did hard time and the time was hard on him. — Malcolm Braly, *On the Yard*, p. 172, 1967
- Besides, if you ain't dead, you'll be doing one hell of a lot of hard time. — Mickey Spillane, *Last Cop Out*, p. 168, 1972
- Another was doing time up state. Long hard time for murder one. — Joseph Nazel, *Black Cop*, p. 76, 1974
- JODIE: He got two years back inside for that. FREDDY: Goddamn, that's hard time. — *Reservoir Dogs*, 1992

hard-timer *noun*
a prisoner serving a long sentence *US, 1986*

- These boys were fish and Foley as a celebrity hard-timer who'd robbed more banks than they'd been in to cash a check. — Elmore Leonard, *Out of Sight*, p. 10, 1996

hardware *noun*
1 weapons, usually guns *US, 1865*

- "Do I go for the hardware?" — Dale Krame, *Teen-Age Gangs*, p. 143, 1953
- The Copiens, the Socialists, the Bachelors, the Comanches—all bad motherfuckers—these were the gangs that started using hardware. — Edwin Torres, *Carlito's Way*, p. 8, 1975
- I got to pick up my hardware from my room, then we can pull up. — Donale Goines, *Black Gangster*, p. 44, 1977
- He bolted reflexively, but stopped when he realized it was hardware digging into his backside. — James Ellroy, *Brown's Requiem*, p. 211, 1981

2 ostentatious jewelry *US, 1939*

- — Lou Shelly, *Hepcats Jive Dictionary*, p. 12, 1945

3 silverware *US, 1962*

- — Joseph E. Ragen and Charles Finston, *Inside the World's Toughest Prison*, p. 802, 1962: "Penitentiary and underworld glossary"

4 any medal or trophy awarded in a competition *US, 1921*

- — *American Speech*, p. 206, October 1963: "The language of skiers"

hardware store *noun*
a poker game in which players generally bet based on the value of their hands and do not bluff *US, 1996*
An allusion to the True Value chain of hardware stores in the US.

- — John Vorhaus, *The Big Book of Poker Slang*, p. 21, 1996

hard-way *verb*
in professional wrestling, to bleed from a cut that was not self-inflicted for dramatic effect *US, 1990*

- Real blood produced by means other than blading, i.e., the hard way. — *rec.sports.pro-wrestling*, 17th July 1990
- Eddie hard-wayed one time and bled on and off for two days. — Missy Hyatt, *Missy Hyatt*, p. 54, 2001

Harlem heater *noun*
any improvised source of heat, such as leaving an oven door open to heat the room *US, 1997*
New York police slang.

- — Samuel M. Katz, *Anytime Anywhere*, p. 387, 1997: "The extremely unofficial and completely off-the-record NYPD/ESU truck-two glossary"

Harlem sunset *noun*
the blood-red line on freshly razor-slashed skin *US, 1940*

- But don't come limping back here with an armload of bloody doctor bills if she carves a Harlem sunset in your face with a pearlhandled straight razor. — Scott Rubin, *National Lampoon's Big Book of Love*, p. 9, 2004

Harlem tennis *noun*
the game of craps *US, 1983*

- — Thomas L. Clark, *The Dictionary of Gambling and Gaming*, p. 97, 1987

Harlem toothpick *noun*
a pocket knife; a switchblade *US, 1944*

- — Lou Shelly, *Hepcats Jive Talk Dictionary*, p. 25, 1945
- — *Rhythm and Blues*, p. 28, June 1955
- — Clarence Major, *Dictionary of Afro-American Slang*, p. 64, 1970

harness *adjective*
uniformed *US, 1903*

- [H]e began fancying the aces waiting for him, harness bulls and soft-clothes dicks, on every West Side platform. — Nelson Algren, *The Man with the Golden Arm*, p. 329, 1949

- A tough-faced harness bull clomped into the arcade and handed Ferris a shoebox[.] — Robert Edmond Alter, *Carny Kill*, p. 31, 1966
- With all the harness bulls from the local precinct who're never supposed to go near the place standing round us in a circle jerk, smiling their jive asses off. — Emmett Grogan, *Final Score*, p. 70, 1976
- I was in a schoolyard, fer chrissake, maybe five, ten minutes, when these two cops from the 86th precinct bum-rap me! Can you imagine? Two dumb harness-bulls run me in for "loitering with sexual intent." — Terry Southern, *Now Dig This*, p. 146, 2001

harnessed up *adjective*
bribed and cooperating *US, 1972*
- We had a detective harnessed up, fixed, and he was our point man. — Harry King, *Box Man*, p. 54, 1972

harp *noun*
1 a harmonica *US, 1887*
- Singing Elmore James tunes and blowing the harp for us down here. — *The Blues Brothers*, 1980
2 an Irish-American or an Irish person *US, 1898*
- He viewed such casual insults as signs of good fellowship, the easy, rude, irrevent ways of family, fellow soldiers, brothers-in-combat, laughing when they called him a harp or a cat-lick. — Robert Campbell, *Boneyards*, p. 10, 1992

harpoon *noun*
a needle used to inject drugs intravenously, especially a hollow needle used in an improvised contraption *US, 1938*
- — David Maurer and Victor Vogel, *Narcotics and Narcotic Addiction*, p. 413, 1973

Harry *noun*
heroin *US, 1954*
Giving a personal identity and disguise to **H** (heroin).
- More specifically, it was classified as M, C, and H—Mary, Charlie, and Harry—which stood for morphine, cocaine, and heroin. — William J. Spillard and Pence James, *Needle in a Haystack*, pp. 147–148, 1945
- — Richard Lingeman, *Drugs from A to Z*, p. 83, 1969
- — Eugene Landy, *The Underground Dictionary*, p. 99, 1971

Harry Selby *noun*
used in a theater program as a fictitious name for an actor *US, 1973*
Less common than **GEORGE SPELVIN**, but serving the same purpose.
- — Sherman Louis Sergel, *The Language of Show Biz*, p. 96, 1973

harsh *verb*
to criticize or disparage *US, 1988*
- — Connie Eble (Editor), *UNC-CH Campus Slang*, p. 5, Spring 1988
- — *People Magazine*, p. 72, 19th July 1993

harsh *adjective*
disagreeable, forbidding, severe *US, 1984*
Conventional English rendered slang by the young.
- — Connie Eble (Editor), *UNC-CH Campus Slang*, p. 4, Fall 1987
- Mr. Hall was way harsh! He gave me a C minus. — *Clueless*, 1995
- You're really harsh, man. — Kenneth Lonergan, *This is Our Youth*, p. 44, 2000

Hart, Schaffner, and Marx *noun*
in poker, three jacks *US, 1988*
An allusion to a men's clothing manufacturer.
- — George Percy, *The Language of Poker*, p. 42, 1988

Harvard lie *noun*
a lie *US, 1941*
The lyric of "Harvard Blues," best known as a 1940's recording by Count Basie, contains the line "But I love my Vincent, and that's no Harvard lie."
- The truth of the matter is, you die, all you do is die, and yet you live, and that's no Harvard lie. — Jack Kerouac, *On the Road (The Original Scroll)*, p. 279, 1951
- I took off out of his sight, he had to turn his head to watch me pass around his left, and that's no Harvard lie. — Ashbel Green, *My Columbia*, p. 239, 2005

has-been *noun*
a person whose best days and greatest achievements are in the past *UK, 1606*
- [N]ow they say that he was just a bag of wind, a guy with a big mouth, a punch-drunk pug, a has-been. — Irving Shulman, *The Amboy Dukes*, p. 57, 1947

- James Mason wading into the sundown on account of being a has-been and all. — Frederick Kohner, *Gidget*, p. 4, 1957
- Some guy might boast about how he is going to get out next time and stay out, and some will put him down by saying he'll soon be back, playing marbles like a hasbeen[.] — Eldridge Cleaver, *Soul on Ice*, p. 43, 1968
- The first four were aging has-beens and never-weres. They were so grateful for this one more job ... that their biggest worry was not to lose control and piss all over their master's leg. — Robert Campbell, *Alice in La-La Land*, p. 195, 1987

hasbian *noun*
a former lesbian; a woman who took lesbian lovers in college, but who reverted to hetero sexuality after graduation from college *US, 1995*
- — Steven Daly and Nathaniel Wice, *alt.culture*, p. 138, 1995

hash *noun*
1 hashish (cannabis resin or pollen) *US, 1948*
Variant spellings include "hashi," "hashis" and "haschi." Derived from the Arabic word for "herb" or "grass," as though it were the herb "par excellence" (Sadie Plant, "Writing On Drugs," 1999).
- "And a little hash," added Jean-baby. "There was a little hashish in the can, too." — Terry Southern, *Flash and Filigree*, p. 121, 1958
- "I and a friend of mine spent three days dropping acid [taking LSD] and smoking hash [hashish] on top of it." — Franklin Stevens, *If This Be Treason*, p. 75, 1970
- I remember sitting on a rug in their cozy attic, quietly talking, listening to music, smoking hash. — Steve Bhaerman, *No Particular Place to Go*, p. 147, 1972
- He had been drinking aquavit and smoking hash all day and was feeling too exotic to tackle the possibility of disillusioning himself. — Odie Hawkins, *Scars and Memories*, p. 186, 1987
2 a number sign (#) on a computer keyboard *US, 1991*
- — Eric S. Raymond, *The New Hacker's Dictionary*, p. 39, 1991

hash *verb*
to serve alcoholic drink that is not the brand claimed *US, 1979*
- Some asshole wants a Chivas sour, charge him for it but pour Chivas. And whatever the label says is what's going to be in the bottle. No hashing. — Vincent Patrick, *The Pope of Greenwich Village*, p. 150, 1979

Hashbury *nickname*
the Haight-Ashbury neighborhood of San Francisco *US, 1966*
A blending of the two street names and an allusion to the drug-using propensities of the area's residents.
- As they say, it's free because it's yours. In the Hashberry they're known as the Diggers. — *The San Francisco Oracle*, 1966
- Beyond the 44-block area, though, another 4,000 hippies are living in side-street pads and gravitating to "the Hashbury" when they want to make the scene. — Joe David Brown, *The Hippies*, p. 29, 1967
- The "Hashbury" is the capital of the hippies. — Hunter S. Thompson, *The Proud Highway*, p. 599, 14th May 1967: New York Times Magazine
- On the corner, a group of long-haired residents of Hashbury had surrounded a charter bus full of tourists. — L.H. Whittemore, *Cop!*, p. 263, 1969

hash cannon *noun*
a device for smoking marijuana or hashish, used to force smoke deep into the lungs *US, 1970*
- — Ernest L. Abel, *A Marijuana Dictionary*, p. 48, 1982

hashery *noun*
a low-cost, low-quality restaurant *US, 1870*
- I was her footpad son, returning from gaol to haunt her honest labors in the hashery. — Jack Kerouac, *On the Road*, p. 174, 1957

hash head *noun*
a chronic user of hashish; a drug user *US, 1959*
- So we got laughing so hard we piss all over ourselves and the waiter says, "You bloody hash-heads, get out of here!" — William Burroughs, *Naked Lunch*, p. 84, 1959

hash house *noun*
a restaurant that serves inexpensive, simply prepared food, catering to working men *US, 1868*
- I called the Globe office from a hash house down the street. — Mickey Spillane, *One Lonely Night*, p. 23, 1951
- It was a hash house run by a Greek, Mike Manos, and he was nice. — Willard Motley, *Let No Man Write My Epitaph*, p. 43, 1958

- Just after Santa Barbara, I walked into a drive-in hash house. — Clancy Sigal, *Going Away*, p. 63, 1961

hash joint *noun*

a hash house *US, 1895*

- Right up the street under the el was an all-night hash joint, and what I needed was a couple mugs of good black java to bring me around. — Mickey Spillane, *My Gun is Quick*, p. 6, 1950

hash mark *noun*

a military service stripe *US, 1907*

- It could be worn on the lower left sleeve above hash marks and overseas bars[.] — Mark Bando, *Vanguard of the Crusade*, p. 17, 2003

hassle *noun*

a problem, trouble, harrassment *US, 1946*

- He's Mrs. Jenks' boy; what's the hassle? — George Mandel, *Flee the Angry Strangers*, p. 56, 1952
- And I knew what a hassle it was to keep your foot out of your mouth on the road on the salary that chick was making. — Billie Holiday with William Dufty, *Lady Sings the Blues*, p. 99, 1956
- And like after all these hassles out here Red will have big eyes to blow as soon as he hits the Apple. — Ross Russell, *The Sound*, p. 96, 1961
- — J. L. Simmons and Barry Winograd, *It's Happening*, p. 170, 1966: "glossary"
- What's the hassle babe? — *Airheads*, 1994

hassle *verb*

1 to harass, annoy *US, 1959*

- The nightclub acts haven't been paid in so long that they're hassling with me and with each other. — Dick Gregory, *Nigger*, p. 118, 1964
- Widows and divorcees don't get ... what's Mona's word? ... hassled. We don't get hassled as much as single girls. — Armistead Maupin, *Tales of the City*, p. 49, 1978
- Try obeyin' the law once in a while and I won't have to hassle you. — *48 Hours*, 1982
- Anywhere else in the country, I was a bookie, a gambler, always lookin' over my shoulder, hassled by cops, day and night. — *Casino*, 1995

2 to engage in mock plane-to-plane air combat *US, 1979*

- Those jets were fighting—hassling—he was sure of it. He banked his jet, and accelerated toward them. — Robert K. Wilcox, *Scream of Eagles*, p. 3, 1990

hasta la bye-bye

goodbye *US, 1990*

Intentionally butchered Spanish.

- — Connie Eble (Editor), *UNC-CH Campus Slang*, p. 1, Spring 1990
- "Hasta la bye-bye," she said sardonically. — Elizabeth Lowell, *Remember Summer*, p. 255, 1999

hasta lumbago

used as a humorous farewell *US, 1977*

An intentional corruption of the Spanish *hasta luego* (until later).

- "I'll see you in the morning." "Hasta lumbago." — Edwin Torres, *Q & A*, p. 30, 1977

hasty banana

used as a farewell *US, 1949*

An intentional butchering of the Spanish "hasta manana."

- Otherwise monolingual whites use made-up terms such as no problemo, el cheapo, and hasty banana, and phrases like hasta la vista, baby. — Joe Feagin, *Racist America*, p. 119, 2000

hat *noun*

1 a condom *US, 1992*

- — Judi Sanders, *Kickin' like Chicken with the Couch Commander*, p. 11, 1992
- Well I hope you wore a hat. — *Menace II Society*, 1993
- "I just want me some real black cunt, out no goddamn hat on my dick!" — Jess Mowry, *Six Out Seven*, p. 361, 1993
- — Connie Eble (Editor), *UNC-CH Campus Slang*, p. 3, Spring 1993

2 a woman *US, 1963*

- — Robert S. Gold, *A Jazz Lexicon*, p. 140, 1964

3 anything bought with a bribe, used as code for a bribe *US, 1971*

- A "hat" is a twenty-dollar bribe, named in honor of former New York Police Commissioner William P. O'Brien's distinguished instruction to his force[.] — David Freeman, *U.S. Grant in the City*, p. 26, 1971

- "Here," he said lazily, "get yourself a hat." A "hat" was a code word for a bonus above regularly scheduled payoffs. — Peter Maas, *Serpico*, p. 158, 1973
- For the price of a "hat," which is to say $25, one of the clerical men he knew there introduced him to a clerk in division. — Leonard Shecter and William Phillips, *On the Pad*, p. 32, 1973
- We got some rules that go along with giving you this hat. — Stephen J. Cannell, *The Tin Collectors*, p. 246, 2001

4 the up-arrow or caret key (^) on a computer keyboard *US, 1991*

- — Eric S. Raymond, *The New Hacker's Dictionary*, p. 40, 1991

5 in pinball, a piece of plastic that indicates a value when lit *US, 1977*

Conventionally known as a "playfield insert."

- — Bobbye Claire Natkin and Steve Kirk, *All About Pinball*, p. 113, 1977

▸ **get hat**

to leave *US, 1966*

- The wise thing for you to do would be to get hat. And not be found in this area again, you dig? — Joseph Nazel, *Black Cop*, p. 155, 1974

▸ **in the hat**

marked for murder *US, 1973*

- "I told him the whole story. 'Look, kid,' he told me, 'your name's in the hat for what you did. New Jersey wants to whack you out and Jerry's got the contract.'" — Vincent Teresa, *My Life in the Mafia*, p. 107, 1973
- State and federal authorities confirmed last week that the man called "the most dangerous man in California" in the wake of Diane Whipple's brutal death in January 2001 has been marked for assassination—or "placed in the hat," in the parlance of the white supremacist gang. — *San Francisco Chronicle*, p. C1, 28th October 2003

hatch *noun*

1 a mental hospital *US, 1974*

- "So my status was weird because I'm just out of the hatch." — Robert Stone, *Dog Soldiers*, p. 251, 1974
- After a week in the hatch they let me use the phone. — Jay McInerney, *Story of My Life*, p. 187, 1988

2 the vagina *US, 1967*

- — Dale Gordon, *The Dominion Sex Dictionary*, p. 82, 1967

3 the mouth *US, 1968*

- — Hy Lit, *Hy Lit's Unbelievable Dictionary of Hip Words for Groovy People*, p. 49, 1968

Hatch *nickname*

the California State Prison at Tehachapi *US, 1975*

- — Report to the Senate, *California Senate Committee on Civil Disorder*, p. 230, 1975

hatch *verb*

▸ **hatch it**

to forget about something *US, 1968*

- — Joan Fontaine et al., *Dictionary of Black Slang*, 1968

hatchery *noun*

a psychiatric ward or mental institution *US, 1994*

- — Sally Williams, *"Strong" Words (Dissertation)*, p. 137, 1994

hatchet job *noun*

a ruthless attack on a person aimed to destroy their confidence and reputation *US, 1944*

- At the same time Vanity Fair picked this moment to do one of those full-blown hatchet jobs on me, a mortifying piece[.] — James Cramer, *Confessions of a Street Addict*, p. 246, 2002
- Or how about the despicable hatchet job by Swift Boat Veterans for Truth on decorated war hero John Kerry? — *The Capital Times (Madison, WI)*, p. 9A, 1st January 2005

hatchet man *noun*

1 a person who is called upon to perform distasteful tasks *US, 1937*

- Some years earlier this man had been a "hatchet"—paid executioner—for the Hip Sing Tong. — Harry J. Anslinger (US Commissioner of Narcotics), *The Murderers*, p. 123, 1961
- Claw was the hatchet man. — Howard Polsky, *Cottage Six*, p. 33, 1962
- He's Butcher Knife Brown's ace runner and hatchet man since Brown has got elderly and half-blind. — Iceberg Slim (Robert Beck), *Trick Baby*, p. 305, 1969

2 a physically aggressive athlete, especially one who is tasked with roughing up an opponent *US, 1971*

- — Zander Hollander and Sandy Padwe, *Basketball Lingo*, p. 54, 1971
- — Bill Shefski, *Running Press Glossary of Football Language*, p. 54, 1978

hated *adjective*

(used of a girl) beautiful beyond imagination *US, 1988*

Usually as "hated **BETTY**."

- — Surf Punks, *Oh No! Not Them Again! (liner notes)*, 1988

hat out; hat up *verb*

to leave *US, 1970*

- — David Claerbaut, *Black Jargon in White America*, p. 68, 1972
- I had scrounged up 'bout $600,000 worth o' diamonds, some really good 'n some really bad, and I was gettin' ready to hat up. — Odie Hawkins, *The Busting Out of an Ordinary Man*, p. 89, 1985

hatpin Mary *noun*

a female professional wrestling fan who prodded wrestlers designated as villains *US, 1975*

- "See, there was this type of wrestling fan back then called a Hatpin Mary, ladies who would do this type of thing, and man, I tell you, it scared the crap out of me, seeing her do that." — Richard Price, *Samaritan*, p. 304, 2003

hats and bats *noun*

said of a squad of prison guards formed to extract a violent prisoner from a cell or police officers formed to squelch a riot *US, 1985*

- They came with their hats and bats—helmets and nightsticks. Within ten minutes of the initial 10:14, one hundred reinforcements and a dozen ambulances had been on the scene. — William Caunitz, *One Police Plaza*, p. 151, 1985
- I had seen video of the Hats and Bats outfit at the Academy; it was much more intimidating seen up close. — Ted Conover, *Newjack*, p. 132, 2000

hat up!

used for urging departure *US, 1971*

- — Hermese E. Roberts, *The Third Ear*, 1971

haul *verb*

▸ **haul ass**

to go swiftly *US, 1918*

- So let's haul ass, Sergeant. — *M*A*S*H*, 1970
- "Now haul ass," he says, "and pray God I never see you two brought in here." — Darryl Ponicsan, *The Last Detail*, p. 143, 1970
- Told Sweeney, forget the landlord and haul ass to Bristol. — George V. Higgins, *The Rat on Fire*, p. 182, 1981
- Mr. Hall, I was surfing the crimson wave. I had to haul ass to the ladies'. — *Clueless*, 1995

▸ **haul butt**

to move quickly *US, 1968*

- — Collin Baker et al., *College Undergraduate Slang Study Conducted at Brown University*, p. 134, 1968

▸ **haul coal**

(used of a white person) to have sex with a black person *US, 1972*

- Some of the relationships in here are interracial, about 25 percent. The whites say, "Okay, if you wanna haul coal." — Bruce Jackson, *In the Life*, p. 359, 1972
- Listen, punk, you keep hauling coal and one day you'll wake up dead. — Malcolm Braley, *False Starts*, p. 222, 1976

hauler *noun*

in the usage of youthful model road racers (slot car racers), a fast model road car *US, 1997*

- — Phantom Surfers, *The Exciting Sounds of Model Road Racing (Album cover)*, 1997

have *verb*

▸ **have a no**

I don't have *US, 1951*

Korean war usage from Japanese pidgin; a supply officer's perfect answer to a requisition for supplies not in stock.

- — *The Baltimore Sun*, 24th June 1951

have a good one

goodbye *US, 1984*

Slightly cooler than urging someone to "have a good day."

- — Jonathan Roberts, *How to California*, p. 168, 1984
- — Connie Eble (Editor), *UNC-CH Campus Slang*, p. 5, Spring 1989
- Thanks. Have a good one. — *Clerks*, 1994

have been!

I'll see you later! *US, 1949*

Youth usage.

- — *Time*, 3rd October 1949

Hawaiian disease *noun*

sexual abstinence due to an absence of women *US, 1987*

An allusion to the mythical illness "lakanuki" (lack of sex).

- "Granddaddy says she is suffering from some terrible old maid's Hawaiian disease." "Oh really? What?" "Something called lackanookie," she said perfectly straight and with no recognizable humor. — Shirley MacLaine, *It's All in the Playing*, p. 139, 1987

Hawaiian muscle fuck; muscle fuck *noun*

to rub and slide the penis in the compressed cleavage between a woman's breasts *US, 1974*

A term used widely in internet "purity tests."

- "Been involved in breast fucking? (aka 'The Hawaiian Muscle Fuck')" — *alt.sex*, 17th July 1989

Hawaiian number *noun*

any elaborate production number in a show or movie *US, 1973*

- The derivation seems to stem from those old technicolor movie musicals in which there cropped up every so often elaborate, complicated, costly, and essentially inane production numbers of a "Hawaiian" or "Polynesian" genre. — Sherman Louis Sergel, *The Language of Show Biz*, p. 105, 1973

Hawaii five-O *noun*

fifty dollars *US, 2006*

- "I'll give you an extra fifty bucks apiece." "Aw right!" Carlos shouted. "A Hawaii five-O sounds cool to me," Franky said. — Jason Starr, *Lights Out*, p. 9, 2006

hawg *noun*

a large motorcycle, especially a Harley-Davidson *US, 1981*

- I pulled my Hawg out of the pack and motioned Rom to lead them to where the police had set aside parking. — Robert Lipkin, *A Brotherhood of Outlaws*, p. 4, 1981
- Thirty or so hawgs are parked in front, many of their owners (One Percenters, as they're known) pissing into the night highway. — Bill Cardoso, *The Maltese Sangweech*, p. 243, 1984

hawk *noun*

1 a strong wind that blows off Lake Michigan across Chicago *US, 1946*

- It wasn't bad at all in the summer, that wind, but in the winter it was gruesome. The Hawk, it was called ironically. Lou Rawls sings about it, calls it a giant razor blade. — Odie Hawkins, *Black Casanova*, p. 119, 1984
- The wind Chicagoans called the Hawk flew over the empty lots, the eyeless windows, flying low, talons scraping the big painted plate-glass windows, prying into doorways where derelicts sought shelter, chattering in rage down the alleys. — Robert Campbell, *Boneyards*, p. 184, 1992
- I'm wearing no coat against the frontline urgency of the Hawk of Lake Michigan. — Clarence Major, *All-Night Visitors*, p. 142, 1998

2 any cold night wind *US, 1946*

Often with "the."

- "He so tough, man, li'l fucker, the hawk is out, an' he's in here bare-ass." — Michael Herr, *Dispatches*, p. 129, 1977
- — Connie Eble (Editor), *UNC-CH Campus Slang*, p. 4, Spring 1982
- As if on cue, the ramp behind Evans began to open, letting in the cold night air, known to the paratroopers as "the Hawk." — Harold Coyle, *Sword Point*, p. 83, 1988
- Paratroopers call it "The Hawk," a piercing chill that cuts through the flesh to the bone with a talon-like grip. — *Washington Times*, 30th January 1991

3 a racetrack scout *US, 1985*

- "We usually reached the drivers through 'hawks,' back-stretch regulars who lived and drank with the drivers and trainers." — Nicholas Pileggi, *Wise Guy*, p. 64, 1985

4 LSD *US, 1966*

May be used with "the."

- — Donald Louria, *Nightmare Drugs*, p. 45, 1966
- Street names [...] Gorbachovs, hawk, L, lightning flash[.] — James Kay and Julian Cohen, *The Parents' Complete Guide to Young People and Drugs*, p. 141, 1998

5 a lookout *US, 1956*

- — *American Speech*, p. 98, May 1956: "Smugglers' argot in the southwest"

hawk *verb*

1 to play *US, 1994*

- Those who could hawk ball were respected almost as much as those who could dress well, rap, and fight. — Nathan McCall, *Makes Me Wanna Holler*, p. 53, 1994

2 to walk fast *US, 1974*

Probably from the noun sense of the word as a cold winter wind.

- Hawk—To walk rapidly. — James Haskins, *Street Gangs*, p. 149, 1974

3 to expectorate sputum *US, 1988–1989*

- — *Maledicta*, p. 32, 1988–1989: "Medical maledicta from San Francisco"

4 to watch closely, to check out *US, 1886*

- All I have to do is pull around the corner where nobody can hawk the license plate. — Clarence Cooper Jr., *The Scene*, p. 61, 1960
- Yeah, she looked at me like I was duck under glass and I hawked her likewise. — A.S. Jackson, *Gentleman Pimp*, p. 77, 1973
- I'm hawkin' the three guys at the pool table, but all I see is cuesticks. — Elmore Leonard, *After Hours*, p. 170, 1979

5 to make an aggressive romantic approach *US, 1987*

- "If you want to ask her out for a drink or something, feel free." I said, "Thanks, but I'm not really hawking it, you know?" — Joseph Pistone, *Donnie Brasco*, p. 51, 1987
- — Kenn "Naz" Young, *Naz's Dictionary of Teen Slang*, p. 56, 1993

hawker *noun*

expectorated sputum *US, 1974*

- — *Maledicta*, p. 32, 1988–1989: "Medical maledicta from San Francisco"

hawk-eye *verb*

to watch closely *US, 1979*

- I had agreed to hawk-eye (from my modest pad down the hall) and occupy the suite during prime burglar time. — Iceberg Slim (Robert Beck), *Airtight Willie and Me*, p. 47, 1979

hawkins *noun*

cold weather *US, 1934*

An embellishment and personification of **HAWK**.

- — Marcus Hanna Boulware, *Jive and Slang of Students in Negro Colleges*, 1947

hawkshaw *noun*

a detective *US, 1888*

From the name of a detective in the 1863 play *The Ticket of Leave Man* by Tom Taylor, and later and more relevantly from the comic strip *Hawkshaw the Detective*, drawn by Gus Mager (1913–22, 1931–48).

- — Vincent J. Monteleone, *Criminal Slang*, p. 114, 1949
- — David Powis, *The Signs of Crime*, 1977
- — Ralph de Sola, *Crime Dictionary*, p. 62, 1982

hawkshaw *verb*

to snoop, to inquire *US, 1946*

- When the German censor came hawkshawing around to see what Hughes was doing on his program, he was shown a record labeled La Tristesse de St. Louis[.] — Mezz Mezzrow, *Really the Blues*, p. 195, 1946

hay *noun*

1 a bed, either in the context of sleep or of sex *US, 1903*

- The difference was that the one named Al had the reputation of being great in the hay. — Norman Mailer, *Advertisements for Myself*, p. 392, 1950
- In the good old days, the consecrated left-wingers used to go to the Soviet Embassy, where they proved their party loyalty by getting in the hay with the men from Moscow. — Jack Lait and Lee Mortimer, *Washington Confidential*, p. 152, 1951
- My wife says I'm a bastard, but she still likes me in the hay. — Mary McCarthy, *The Group*, p. 48, 1963
- We ate on the run and ran back for the hay. — Antony James, *America's Homosexual Underground*, p. 115, 1965

2 marijuana *US, 1934*

A play on **GRASS**.

- At the Mexican's we could at least get loaded on good hay[.] — Mezz Mezzrow, *Really the Blues*, p. 164, 1946
- At York Avenue we goofed all day ... as we've been doing for 2 weeks now, laugh ... laugh ... laugh; imitated "B" movies; blasting hay; talking. — Jack Kerouac, *Windblown World*, p. 395, 10th January 1949
- The boys had roughed him up pretty badly bringing him in and now, what with the hay and all, he was a regular wild man. — Jim Thompson, *The Killer Inside*, p. 37, 1952

- Be a living doll, will you, and go in the other room and see can you contact this lad to bring up some hay? — Bernard Wolfe, *The Late Risers*, p. 203, 1954

haybag *noun*

1 a lazy, despicable woman *UK, 1851*

- [H]e dunked his cruller and confessed that he still had his doubts about one Mrs. Hubbard, a feisty old haybag he was certain had secret links to the DA. — Jerry Stahl, *I, Fatty*, p. 226, 2004

2 a horse *US, 1963*

- "That last haybag at Santa Anita ran dead last." — Wade Hunter, *The Sex Peddler*, p. 6, 1963

hayburner *noun*

a horse, especially a poor-performing racehorse *US, 2005*

- "It would be nice if I had a hayburner to impress her with. Is there a hayburner you like?" — Michael Connolly, *Murder in Vegas*, p. 146, 2005

hayed up *adjective*

marijuana-intoxicated *US, 1952*

- A Mexican pipeliner had got all hayed up on marijuana and stabbed another Mexican to death. — Jim Thompson, *The Killer Inside*, p. 37, 1952

hay head *noun*

a marijuana user *US, 1942*

- — *American Speech*, p. 87, May 1955: "Narcotic argot along the Mexican border"

haymaker *noun*

a powerful fist blow to the head *US, 1902*

- BRAD casually sets himself, then delivers the most powerful right haymaker in the history of cinema. — Terry Southern, *Now Dig This*, p. 96, 1967
- Felix lashed back with a haymaker, right off the ghetto streets. — Piri Thomas, *Stories from El Barrio*, p. 138, 1978

hayo *noun*

cocaine *US, 1984*

From a Caribbean name for the coca plant.

- — R.C. Garrett et al., *The Coke Book*, p. 200, 1984

hayseed *noun*

a rustic or country yokel *US, 1851*

Strongly suggests a high degree of unsophistication.

- [A] hayseed from Jersey who went on to great heights in the glamor field as a teacher of modeling, a radio commentator and a fashion editor, before hitting the diplomatic set. — Lee Mortimer, *Women Confidential*, p. 133, 1960
- Cocaine, my dear hayseed, is the most expensive high there is. — Iceberg Slim (Robert Beck), *Trick Baby*, p. 167, 1969
- Sometimes a hayseed from Chattanooga, Tennesse, is too confused to make a suggestion, so I make it for him. — Xaviera Hollander, *The Happy Hooker*, p. 179, 1972
- Looks like a hayseed bank and, tell you the truth, it is a hayseed bank. — *Raising Arizona*, 1987

haywire *adjective*

out of control; crazy; in wild disorder; chaotic *US, 1920*

The image of wire on a bale of hay that flails wildly when cut.

- — Collin Baker et al., *College Undergraduate Slang Study Conducted at Brown University*, p. 135, 1968
- My mind was running haywire, and then I stopped thinking and just sat there. — James Mill, *The Seventh Power*, p. 189, 1976

hazed *adjective*

drug-intoxicated *US, 2001*

- — Pamela Munro, *U.C.L.A. Slang*, p. 80, 2001

Hazel *noun*

heroin *US, 1949*

Abbreviated **WITCH HAZEL** (heroin), and subsequently disguised as "Aunt Hazel."

- — J.E. Schmidt, *Narcotics Lingo and Lore*, p. 8, 1959

H cap *noun*

a capsule of heroin *US, 1990*

- — Gilda and Melvin Berger, *Drug Abuse A-Z*, p. 73, 1990

HE *noun*

high explosives *US, 1986*

- "What would you do if every time one of your buddies shot at a tank a 90mm shell and a burst of .50 blew him out of her perch, and white phosphorous and H.E. was indiscriminately tossed into the village?" — Ralph Zumbro, *Tank Sergeant*, p. 6, 1986

- At the speed of sound it goes on down / A killer missile with an H.E. round. — Sandee Johnson, *Cadences: The Jody Call Book, No. 2*, p. 140, 1986
- We had taken with us a great number of illumination and HE (high explosive) rounds with various types of fuses. — James Kirschke, *Not Going Home Alone*, p. 38, 2001

head *noun*

1 a habitual user of drugs *US, 1953*

In the Vietnam war, the term differentiated between a person who smoked marijuana and a **JUICER** who abused alcohol.

- I mean everyone's a head—you know, just everyone! — John Clellon Holmes, *The Horn*, p. 107, 1958
- This is not a queer bar—it is an outcast bar—Negroes and vagrant whites, heads and hypes, dikes and queens. — John Rechy, *City of Night*, p. 184, 1963
- Take hippies and straights, heads and narcos, put them together for 36 hours—under a church roof. — *Berkeley Barb*, p. 3, 25th February 1967
- He was a friend of the sergeant's. They were the "juicers" [alcohol drinkers] and I was the "head" [pot smoker]. — Myra MacPherson, *Long Time Passing*, p. 398, 1984

2 a member of the counterculture, usually involving drugs *US, 1966*

- And that South American ring-ding with his sequined rodeo shirt, they couldn't be heads. — Richard Fariña, *Been Down So Long*, p. 114, 1966
- What are heads interested in? They're interested in color, clothes, in dope, they're interested in lots of fresh fruit, and good natural foods[.] — Leonard Wolfe (Editor), *Voices from the Love Generation*, p. 12, 1968
- A few thousand of the absolutely most together and peaceful and loving and beautiful heads in the world are gathered in a grand tribal new beginning. — *East Village Other*, 20th August 1969
- So, if heads on the land are responsible to their environment and its inhabitants (and not all of them are), then potential opponents at the barricades may have second thoughts. — *The Last Supplement to the Whole Earth Catalog*, p. 90, March 1971

3 a devoted fan of the Grateful Dead *US, 2001*

An abbreviation of **DEADHEAD**.

- Later, JB took us to a pre-concert party at a friend's house, who didn't hide that he was pissed at JB for showing up with a crew of well-burnt 'heads. — Scott Meyer, *Deadhead Forever*, 2001

4 oral sex *US, 1941*

- [Y]ou were talking so brave and so sweet / Giving me head on the unmade bed. — Leonard Cohen, *Chelsea Hotel*, 1968
- Excuse me, mademoiselle, to give you some head. — Steve Cannon, *Groove, Bang, and Jive Around*, p. 108, 1969
- (Quoting Linda Lovelace) Just from guys saying that I was, like, the best, that I gave the best head they ever had. — *Screw*, p. 4, 9th October 1972
- I love to give head. I love to make a guy come with my mouth. — *Adult Video*, p. 10, August/September 1986
- But what happens when you get in the car, and you don't make with the head? Don't they kick your ass to the curb? — Kevin Smith, *Jay and Silent Bob Strike Back*, p. 26, 2001

5 a state of drug intoxication *US, 1952*

- Chico shot up immediately, but there was no real kick in the drug. Still, it got him a "head" and made him feel better. — Hal Ellson, *The Golden Spike*, p. 194, 1952
- "Have you been using smack?" "Yeah. I've been using smack [...] It's an unbelievable smack, man. THE best. Unbelievable." — Doug Lang, *Freaks*, pp. 119–120, 1973

6 a crime victim *US, 1987*

- — Carsten Stroud, *Close Pursuit*, p. 272, 1987

7 a toilet *US, 1942*

- It seems Edith (bah) arrived at the bus depot early & while waiting for Patricia, feeling sleepy, retired to the head to sleep on a sofa. — Neal Cassady, *The First Third*, p. 190, 7th March 1947
- [F]inally Wallenstein going to the head for a leak[.] — Jack Kerouac, *The Subterraneans*, p. 77, 1958

8 music played without a musical score *US, 1946*

- The music they were turning out, thanks to Bix's head arrangements, was ten years ahead of its time. — Mezz Mezzrow, *Really the Blues*, p. 79, 1946
- But maybe if we do a whole set of heads, old ones — John Clellon Holmes, *The Horn*, p. 193, 1958
- Our whole book is made up of heads. — Ross Russell, *The Sound*, p. 58, 1961

▶ **have your head up your ass**

to be stupid, unaware, uninformed *US, 1944*

- That desk clerk's got his head up his ass—the man never left. — Elmore Leonard, *Bandits*, p. 145, 1987

-head *suffix*

a habitual user of the indicated substance; hence an enthusiast, a fan *US, 1953*

- Now get your ass in the bathroom and wash your mouth out. I want you to kill that fuckin' odor. Where I'm gettin' ready to take you, I don't want the people to think I brought a juice head along with me. — Donald Goines, *Daddy Cool*, pp. 95–96, 1974
- Florence and I both didn't want to be invaded by amphets heads. — Herbert Huncke, *The Evening Sun Turned Crimson*, p. 174, 1980
- "I'm Department of Corrections," Kathy said. "What are you?" A rockhead for one thing, no doubt lights popping in his brain. — Elmore Leonard, *Maximum Bob*, p. 65, 1991

headache *noun*

1 your spouse *US, 1933*

- — Lou Shelly, *Hepcats Jive Dictionary*, p. 12, 1945
- Always some John Family or silk moll with bookoo toadskins playing around with a yuk who'll ante to keep the knockdown from the bundleman or headache. — *The New American Mercury*, p. 708, 1950

2 a journalist *US, 1991*

Gulf war usage.

- — *American Speech*, p. 391, Winter 1991: "Among the new words"

headache Mary *noun*

low grade marijuana *US, 1979*

- Also known as doodley-squat, salt and pepper, and "male twigs," this female-impersonator a/k/a Headache Mary is sometimes advertised as "good commercial"[.] — *Hi Life*, p. 15, 1979

headache stick *noun*

a police nightstick *US, 1919*

- Hold your piechopper, "don't vip another vop" or I'll take my headache stick and "massage your top." — Lavada Durst, *The Jives of Dr. Hepcat*, p. 9, 1953
- — Clarence Major, *Dictionary of Afro-American Slang*, p. 80, 1970
- The other guy was busy trying to kick in some kid's ribs and he didn't notice Kenny take the headache-stick away from his partner, but he heard the sound it made when Kenny crushed in the side of his friend's face with it. — Emmett Grogan, *Ringolevio*, p. 160, 1972
- Jim Garrison and John Ed Cothran admire a stick tapered like a baseball bat (called a "headache stick" by Southern police) days before a riot after James Meredith's attempt to integrate the University of Mississippi in 1962. — *San Francisco Chronicle*, p. M1, 6th April 2003

head artist *noun*

a person skilled at giving oral sex *US, 1979*

- — *Maledicta*, p. 231, 1979: "Kinks and queens: linguistic and cultural aspects of the terminology for gays"

head-bang *verb*

to jerk your head up and down to add to the enjoyment of fast music *US, 1995*

Collected from fans of heavy metal music by Seamus O'Reilly, January 1995.

headbanger *noun*

a devotee of heavy metal music *US, 1979*

- In England devoted heavy-metal fans, called "headbangers" or "punters," often crowd the stage, flailing away on imaginary guitars[.] — *Washington Post*, p. G1, 13th July 1980
- — Connie Eble (Editor), *UNC-CH Campus Slang*, p. 6, Spring 1988
- — Ellen C. Bellone (Editor), *Dictionary of Slang*, p. 13, 1989

headbreaker *noun*

a brutal policeman *US, 1959*

- "Motheren headbreakers—3 of 'em beatin' up on me hittin' me on the head all the time with their goddam fists." — Warren Miller, *The Cool World*, p. 37, 1959

headbuster *noun*

a brutish police officer *US, 1959*

- The thing to do was to sweat it out till it broke or cooled over. Let the headbusters come to them and interrogate. — Sol Yurick, *The Warriors*, p. 117, 1965

head candler *noun*

psychotherapist *US, 1955*

- [O]r in S.J. Perelman's term, "head candlers" (after poultry farmers' practice of judging eggs by holding them up to candlelight). — Allen Hess, *The Handbook of Forensic Psychology*, p. 678, 1999

head case *noun*

an emotionally troubled or mentally disturbed person *UK, 1966*

- "Eddie, he's a head case," says Parillo, waving back. — Josh Alan Friedman, *Tales of Times Square*, p. 138, 1986
- The bottom line is neither of us are going to get her if we don't do something about that headcase she's with now. — *Something About Mary*, 1998

head cheese *noun*

prepuce smegma in a male *US, 1941*

- I gasped so hard up my nose the head cheese locked into place and he let me breathe, still holding my hair. — Jack Fritscher, *Stand By Your Man*, p. 150, 1999

head chick *noun*

the dominant and favored prostitute among a group of prostitutes working for a pimp *US, 1957*

- [T]hey are their "head chicks" instead of just one or another of their "barnyard hens." — Judge John M. Murtagh and Sara Harris, *Cast the First Stone*, p. 10, 1957

headcrusher *noun*

a thug, an enforcer *US, 1973*

- — Vincent Teresa, *My Life in the Mafia*, p. 360, 1973: A Glossary of Mob Terminology

head dab *noun*

in mountain biking, a face-first fall *US, 1992*

- — William Nealy, *Mountain Bike!*, p. 160, 1992: "Bikespeak"

header *noun*

oral sex *US, 1976*

An embellishment of the more common **HEAD**.

- — Mary Corey and Victoria Westermark, *Fer Shurr! How to be a Valley Girl*, 1982

headfuck *verb*

to confuse intentionally *US, 1978*

- "You want it set to the wrong time, to headfuck that fucker in the back seat." — Matt Ruff, *Set This House in Order*, p. 303, 2003

head game *noun*

a psychological ploy *US, 1979*

- But I realized I was just playing head games, justifying an escape because of my stage fright. — Jim Carroll, *Forced Entries*, p. 62, 1987

head gee *noun*

a prison warden *US, 1976*

- — John R. Armore and Joseph D. Wolfe, *Dictionary of Desperation*, p. 32, 1976

head-hunt *verb*

in boxing, to try to hit the opponent in the head *US, 1960*

- Sometime I rubbed resin on my gloves between rounds so I could fuck—so I would waste the guy's eyes when I went head-hunting. — James Ellroy, *Suicide Hill*, p. 781, 1986

headhunter *noun*

1 a person who recruits others for specific jobs with specific firms, especially professionals and executives *US, 1960*

- "My father would never take a job I found for him. It would violate his competitive Type A standards." "You're probably right," said Sheeni. "OK. I'll pretend to be a headhunter and I'll call him up." — C.D. Payne, *Youth in Revolt*, p. 99, 1993

2 a psychiatrist *US, 1972*

- "Ah, fuck off you lousy bums. What do you know about death?" I scream at my two head-hunters. — Oscar Zeta Acosta, *The Autobiography of a Brown Buffalo*, p. 134, 1972

3 an oral sex enthusiast *US, 1961*

- Head-hunters, cannibals and kid-fruits are fellators[.] — *New York Mattachine Newsletter*, p. 6, June 1961
- Hidden safely behind anthropological images of Amazonian tribes hunting enemy skulls for religious and decorative purposes, as the initiated of the jazz world knew, were the real headhunters, hip guys constantly seeking to receive or administer blow jobs. — Larry Rivers, *What Did I Do?*, p. 57, 1992

4 a homosexual male *US, 1990*

- — Charles Shafer, *Folk Speech in Texas Prisons*, p. 206, 1990

5 a police officer assigned to investigate complaints of misconduct by other police *US, 1965*

- I wonder if Lieutenant Grimsely and all them IAD headhunters get a finder's fee when they nail a cop. — Joseph Wambaugh, *The Choirboys*, pp. 155–156, 1975

6 a female who trades sex for money or drugs *US, 1995*

- — Bill Valentine, *Gang Intelligence Manual*, p. 76, 1995: "Black Street Gang Terminology"

head job *noun*

an act of oral sex *US, 1963*

- — Donald Webster Cory and John P. LeRoy, *The Homosexual and His Society*, p. 264, 1963: "A lexicon of homosexual slang"
- Most guys would rather have head jobs and that's a lot easier for her. — Joseph Wambaugh, *The New Centurions*, p. 182, 1970
- "Are you sure you won't do a head job? I was really hoping to get one." — Frederique Delacoste, *Sex Work*, p. 67, 1987
- Tiffany Clark, in a supporting role, made us melt as she gives a smokin' head-job to Michael Bruce. — Editors of Adult Video News, *The AVN Guide to the 500 Greatest Adult Films of All Time*, p. 154, 2005

headknocker *noun*

a foreman, supervisor, director, boss *US, 1896*

- My grandfather used to say that you'd learn more about a business by sizing up the "headknocker" (his word for CEO) than you would from the company's balance sheet. — Alan Farnham, *Forbest Great Success Stories*, p. 5, 2000

headlights *noun*

1 the female breasts *US, 1919*

- He called titties "headlights" and bottoms "bumpers," and we called him "What's Happening Bob[.]" — Pamela Des Barres, *I'm With the Band*, p. 39, 1988
- During a [radio] show on breasts, Infinity was fined because I said: "Boobs, xonkers, headlights, watermelons, sweater puppies, pointers, knockers, jugs, tatas—these are some of the words to describe women's breasts." — Howard Stern, *Miss America*, p. 441, 1995

2 large jewels, especially diamonds *US, 1899*

- — Lou Shelly, *Hepcats Jive Dictionary*, p. 12, 1945

3 LSD *US, 1994*

- — US Department of Justice, *Street Terms*, October 1994

head motherfucker in charge *noun*

the leader of an enterprise *US, 1988*

- Now the head motherfucker in charge. — Steven Thompson, *Airburst*, p. 53, 1988

head nigger in charge *noun*

the leader of an enterprise *US, 1968*

- The black policemen accept the role of being the head nigger in charge. — Hearings of the Congressional Committee on Education, p. 266, 1968
- — *Maledicta*, p. 159, Summer/Winter 1978: "How to hate thy neighbor: a guide to racist maledicta"
- Finally, it dawned on one of those superduper crackers that I was actually the Head Nigger in Charge. — Odie Hawkins, *The Busting Out of an Ordinary Man*, p. 90, 1985
- The orderly hooked me up with Craig's commanding officer. That was the HNIC—Head Negro in Charge—I was trying to find. — Eric Jerome Dickey, *Cheaters*, p. 373, 1999
- — Connie Eble (Editor), *UNC-CH Campus Slang*, p. 3, Spring 2001

head on *adverb*

in gambling games such as twenty-one, playing directly against the dealer without other players *US, 1963*

- Thorp claims he could bust the state of Nevada in eighty days "if the casinos did not cheat him, if he could play head on (alone against a dealer) for eight hours a day[.]" — Ed Reid and Ovid Demaris, *The Green Felt Jungle*, p. 207, 1963

head phones *noun*

a stethoscope *US, 1982*

- — *American Speech*, pp. 152–154, Summer 1982: "More on nursing terms"

head plant *noun*

to fall face first while snowboarding *US, 1993*

- — Doug Werner, *Snowboarders Start-Up*, p. 113, 1993: "Glossary"

headquarters puke *noun*

a member of the military assigned to the rear echelon staff *US, 1992*

Gulf war usage.

- — *American Speech*, p. 87, Spring 1992: "Gulf war words supplement"

- "Headquarters puke. Eight-hour day," the Assistant Director in Charge of the Washington Field Office grumped. — Tom Clancy, *Executive Orders*, p. 454, 1997
- He had now become one of them, what he and his fellow CIA case officers in the field had called a headquarters puke. — Dick Couch, *Mercenary Option*, p. 52, 2003

head rag *noun*
a bandana or piece of cloth worn with straightened or processed hair *US, 1973*
- Sapphire usually sleeps with a head rag. — Carolyn Greene, *70 Soul Secrets of Sapphire*, p. 24, 1973

heads down *adjective*
in computing, so focused on a task as to be ignorant of all else *US, 1991*
- — Eric S. Raymond, *The New Hacker's Dictionary*, p. 197, 1991

head session *noun*
a lecture *US, 1998*
- He used to give long head sessions, where he'd just spit out knowledge that was real. — Eric Davis, *The Slick Boys*, p. 56, 1998

head shed *noun*
a military headquarters *US, 1960*
Vietnam war usage.
- The official word, "right out of the head shed in Washington," is that the Air Force will cut its 190,250 overseas dependents to about 81,600. — *Washington Post, Times Herald*, p. A14, 5th December 1960
- — Carl Fleischhauer, *A Glossary of Army Slang*, p. 24, 1968
- The head shed has decided that you're going to have to make like Charley Tuna. — William C. Anderson, *Bat 21*, p. 126, 1980
- [T]he head-shed wanted some experienced observer to get a good look[.] — Chris Ryan, *Stand By, Stand By*, p. 93, 1996

head shop *noun*
a shop that retails drug paraphernalia, incense, posters, lights, and other products and services associated with drug use *US, 1967*
- — Joe David Brown (Editor), *The Hippies*, p. 218, 1967: "Glossary of hippie terms"
- The head shop is the liquor store of the hippies. Most often it is a small airless place, with a locked-in scent not unlike that of burning tapioca. Carries a thousand items for the head-hippie fraternity, from Tarot cards to paper wrappers for tea. — Sidney Bernard, *This Way to the Apocalypse*, p. 58, 1968
- On the other side of the hill, separated by a small wood where all the head shops are located and where dope is only dealt along the paths, lies Movement City/Hog Farm. — *East Village Other*, 20th August 1969
- There were all kinds of new institutions shooting up anyway—head shops, underground papers, the Ballroom[.] — John Sinclair, *Guitar Army*, p. 153, 1972

headshrinker *noun*
a pyschiatrist or other therapist *US, 1950*
- GENE: You know if the boy ever talked to a psychiatrist? PLATO: Head-shrinker? — *Rebel Without a Cause*, 1955
- I once discussed this problem with Larry who is my sister's husband and a professional headshrinker. — Frederick Kohner, *Gidget*, p. 11, 1957
- Go first to a headshrinker. Andy and me went last year and he said we ought to leave Mama, remember, Andy? — Clancy Sigal, *Going Away*, p. 11, 1961
- I knew we were on the way to a headshrinker—the Army psychiatrist. — Malcolm X and Alex Haley, *The Autobiography of Malcolm X*, p. 106, 1964
- Mom and Dad are sending me to a headshrinker beginning next Monday. — Anonymous, *Go Ask Alice*, p. 92, 1971
- But he was working at it, breaking down my defense in a way only a headshrinker could have explained. — Georgia Sothern, *My Life in Burlesque*, p. 129, 1972
- But, frankly, pal, I think you'd better go see a headshrinker. — Charles Whited, *Chiodo*, p. 62, 1973

heads-up *adverb*
(of a game of pool) with no handicaps in effect *US, 1993*
- — Mike Shamos, *The Illustrated Encyclopedia of Billiards*, p. 114, 1993

head trip *noun*
1 a pleasant, ethereal drug experience *US, 1966*
- An example of a "head trip" on LSD would be Foss's first in 1967. — Sohnya Sayres, *The 60s Without Apology*, p. 361, 1984

2 a puzzle or challenging thought process *US, 1974*
- The more clearance you have, the more you're at risk of falling into the head trip I just described. — Thomas Barnett, *The Pentagon's New Map*, p. 343, 2004

head up *verb*
to start a fight *US, 1991*
- "So if anybody try to head up with me, I got 'em." — Leon Bing, *Do or Die*, p. 25, 1991

head up *adjective*
1 one-on-one *US, 1993*
- Everyone wanted to rat-pack him, but Monk insisted on it being head up. — Sanyika Shakur, *Monster*, p. 149, 1993
2 straightforward, direct *US, 2001*
- We don't use no weapons, no razors or nothin', it's just a head-up fight, and sometimes I come out all covered in knots and bruises. — *Rolling Stone*, p. 85, 12th April 2001

head-walk *verb*
to walk from head-top to head-top at a punk or postpunk concert *CANADA, 1991*
- Pearl Jam lead singer Eddie Vedder will watch as the daredevils in the crowd stage dive and head-walk. — *San Francisco Chronicle*, p. E7, 28th October 1993

head-walker *noun*
a person who literally walks from head-top to head-top at a punk or postpunk concert *US, 1993*
- "That's a good general rule when it comes to dealing with head-walkers and stage-divers. Stay alert." — *San Francisco Chronicle*, p. E7, 28th October 1993

head-walking *noun*
literally walking from head-top to head-top at a punk or postpunk concert *US, 1989*
- "Sometimes I do head-walking, too." Come again? "I walk on people's heads." — *Houston Chronicle*, p. 15, 22nd September 1989
- They even climb up from the crowd and dive off the lip of the stage into the undulating ocean of bodies, only to be tossed here and there like so much human flotsam—an activity known as "head walking." — *San Francisco Chronicle*, p. E7, 28th October 1993

heal *verb*
▸ **heal with steal**
to perform surgery *US, 1994*
- — Sally Williams, *"Strong" Words*, p. 146, 1994

health cure *noun*
a stay in jail or prison *US, 1966*
- Steve DeCanio came by last night and told me how much you are enjoying your health cure. — Hunter S. Thompson, *The Proud Highway*, p. 570, 2nd June 1966: Letter to Sonny Barger

healthy *adjective*
(used of a girl) well built *US, 1970*
- — *Current Slang*, p. 8, Winter 1970

heap *adjective*
very *US, 1958*
A crude borrowing of the speech of Native American Indians as portrayed by pulp fiction and movie screenwriters.
- J.L.'s the heap big kingpin around the joint, I gather. — Morton Cooper, *High School Confidential*, p. 22, 1958

heart *noun*
1 physical courage, especially as displayed in the commission of a crime *US, 1937*
- "Here come Duke. He cool. He got heart." — Warren Miller, *The Cool World*, p. 9, 1959
- He had great skill and daring—what junkies call "heart." — James Mills, *The Panic in Needle Park*, p. 21, 1966
- I gotta admit he's got a lot of heart—I mean besides being a nut. — Piri Thomas, *Stories from El Barrio*, p. 100, 1978
- — William K. Bentley and James M. Corbett, *Prison Slang*, p. 32, 1992

2 an amphetamine capsule, especially dextroamphetamine sulfate (trade name Dexedrine™) *US, 1965*
From the shape of the pill.
- Some of the names describe the drugs' effects, such as "helpers," "copilots," "Los Angeles turn arounds," or their shape, color and

markings—"hearts," "footballs," "blackjacks," "crossroads." — Phil Hirsch, *Hooked*, pp. 51–52, 1968

- I suspect she knows a little about drugs, because she's given me hearts a couple of times when I've been really low. — Anonymous, *Go Ask Alice*, p. 53, 1971

heartbeat *noun*

1 any of several signals produced by a computer or software *US*, *1991*
- — Eric S. Raymond, *The New Hacker's Dictionary*, p. 197, 1991

2 a short measure of time *US*, *1985*
- — Hans Halberstadt, *Airborne*, p. 130, 1988: "Abridged dictionary of airborne terms"

heart check *noun*

a test of courage *US*, *1995*
- — Mark S. Fleisher, *Beggars & Thieves*, p. 288, 1995: "Glossary"

- Sooner or later all new fish receive a "Heart Check" from the Yard Rats. — Jimmy Lerner, *You Got Nothing Coming*, p. 170, 2002

heart check!

I defy you!; I dare you!; I challenge you! *US*, *2001*
- — Jim Goad, *Jim Goad's Glossary of Northwestern Prison Slang*, December 2001

heartthrob *noun*

a very attractive man *US*, *1926*
- — Donald F. Reuter, *Heartthrob*, 1998

heat *noun*

1 the police *US*, *1931*
- Generally, whores are not a good deal. They attract heat, and most of them will talk. — William Burroughs, *Junkie*, p. 53, 1953
- Last night I pinned the heat, I see them. They were sitting there. — Lenny Bruce, *The Essential Lenny Bruce*, p. 202, 1967
- They split threatening an ambulance and, for all we know, the Heat, so everybody settles down again with "Come on baby" going very strong. — *The Digger Papers*, p. 10, August 1968
- This part of town, they'll make us for heat the second we walk in. — *48 Hours*, 1982

2 a firearm *US*, *1926*
- "Man, you oughta seen old Fuss-face scratching for his heat," one of them said, jubilantly. — Chester Himes, *Cast the First Stone*, p. 33, 1952
- We both reached for our heat at the same time[.] — Babs Gonzales, *I Paid My Dues*, p. 43, 1967
- "What kinda heat you got?" Benny's eyes glittered a little in the shadows as he recited the pieces in his artillery. — Odie Hawkins, *Chicago Hustle*, p. 39, 1977

3 pressure, stress *US*, *1929*
- Fruit Jar had been sitting pretty with no heat on him and a swell income, and The Man had hauled him in on something that could be very hot. — Jim Thompson, *Savage Night*, p. 61, 1953
- We even started drinking at the Sinners Club because it had a back door and a window we could get out of. I mean the heat was on, man. We were hurtin'. — Hunter S. Thompson, *Hell's Angels*, p. 28, 1966
- We take married heat, kid heat, boss heat, car heat, bank heat, credit heat, political heat, IRS heat, health heat, appliance heat, and every other kind of heat you can think of. — Dan Jenkins, *Life Its Ownself*, p. 132, 1984
- The problem was, Nicky was not only bringing heat on himself, but on me too. The FBI watched every move he made. — *Casino*, 1995

4 gunfire *US*, *1977*
- I went through that thing a number of times and only got a fast return on my fear once, a too classic hot landing with the heat coming from the trees about 300 yards away[.] — Michael Herr, *Dispatches*, p. 15, 1977

5 crowd or audience reaction *US*, *1958*
An entertainment industry term embraced by professional wrestling.
- [B]uilding a hysterical crowd up to a climax is called "heat." — Pappy Boyington, *Baa Baa Black Sheep*, p. 375, 1958
- heat n. enthusiasm, a positive response. — *rec.sports.pro-wrestling*, 17th July 1990
- You know, head down to L.A., get some gigs going, get the heat happening. — *Boys on the Side*, 1995
- On the indy scene, when you want to get heat, you pick out a small group of fans and work on them. — *Raw Magazine*, p. 49, September 2000

6 in roller derby, a fight, be it scripted or spontaneous, staged or real *US*, *1999*
- — Keith Coppage, *Roller Derby to Rollerjam*, 1999

7 in pinball, the part of the pinball machine that rises as a panel in the front of the machine *US*, *1977*
Conventionally known as the "lightbox."
- — Bobbye Claire Natkin and Steve Kirk, *All About Pinball*, p. 113, 1977

8 a dildo *US*, *1999*
- [I]f she's packin' heat (wielding a dildo), which you know they imagine she is, well, there you have it. — *The Village Voice*, 5th October 1999

▸ **take the heat**
to sunbathe *US*, *1968*
- — Collin Baker et al., *College Undergraduate Slang Study Conducted at Brown University*, p. 135, 1968

heated *adjective*

angry *US*, *2002*
- I told Kasun how heated I was about being stood up[.] — Earl "DMX" Simmons, *E.A.R.L.*, p. 156, 2002

heated hell *noun*

the worst of the worst *US*, *1945*
- — Lou Shelly, *Hepcats Jive Talk Dictionary*, p. 26, 1945

heater *noun*

1 a revolver *US*, *1926*
- I'll say what it takes to make you point that heater someplace else. — Mickey Spillane, *Kiss Me Deadly*, p. 50, 1952
- "Man, if I had my heater I bet I could shoot that sergeant down there dead between the eyes," he said. — Chester Himes, *The Real Cool Killers*, p. 49, 1959
- When he came in I cold cocked him with an iron pipe and took the heater, a grand in foreskin and the dope out of his pockets. — Iceberg Slim (Robert Beck), *Mama Black Widow*, p. 100, 1969

2 a linear amplifier for a citizens' band radio *US*, *1976*
- You might also be interested to know that while Uncle Charlie permits Class B transmissions up to 150 miles, you'd need one cotton pickin heater to do it. — *Complete CB Slang Dictionary*, p. 2, 1976

3 a large cigar *US*, *1918*
- He had this huge heater shoved in his mouth, and was puffing away with gusto. — Frederick Kohner, *The Affairs of Gidget*, p. 26, 1963
- He went back to the terrace puffing on the big heater. — Richard Condon, *Prizzi's Honor*, p. 84, 1982

4 a cigarette *US*, *1993*
- — Merriam-Webster's *Hot Words on Campus Marketing Survey '93*, p. 2, 13th October 1993

▸ **take a heater**
to defecate *US*, *2001*
- — Don R. McCreary (Editor), *Dawg Speak*, 2001

heater and cooler *noun*

a shot of whiskey and a glass of beer *US*, *1982*
- — Bill Reilly, *Big Al's Official Guide to Chicagoese*, p. 28, 1982

heat machine *noun*

recorded crowd or audience reaction *US*, *1990*
- The WWF uses a heat machine for its televised shows which make them somewhat of a work. — *rec.sports.pro-wrestling*, 17th July 1990

heat station *noun*

a police station *US*, *1963*
From HEAT (the police).
- [T]he driver says have you been clipped or raped lady?—and: I will take you to the heat station. — John Rechy, *City of Night*, p. 118, 1963

heaty *adjective*

under police surveillance or the subject of police interest *US*, *1967*
- It is enforced only in that the proprietor sometimes may ask players to keep payoffs out of sight—not to toss the money on the table after the game—if the room is currently "heaty," e.g., if an arrest as recently been made there. — Ned Polsky, *Hustlers, Beats, and Others*, p. 48, 1967

heave *noun*

any place that a police officer hides to rest or sleep while on duty *US*, *1958*
- Any spot that takes a policeman out of the rain is a coop, or a heave. — *New York Times*, p. 34, 20th October 1958

heave *verb*

to vomit *US*, *1832*

- — Collin Baker et al., *College Undergraduate Slang Study Conducted at Brown University*, p. 135, 1968
- — Helen Dahlskog (Editor), *A Dictionary of Contemporary and Colloquial Usage*, p. 31, 1972
- — Connie Eble (Editor), *UNC-CH Campus Slang*, p. 5, April 1995

heave-ho *noun*
an ejection, a dismissal *US, 1932*
- The gambling was unorganized—the syndicate boys who tried to move in got the fast heave-ho. — Jim Thompson, *Roughneck*, p. 142, 1954
- "My last job, I was fired. Canned. Given the old heave-ho." — Burt Hirschfield, *Fire Island*, p. 262, 1970
- One pitch earlier, St. Louis manager Whitey Herzog got the heave-ho from home plate umpire Don Denkinger for protesting a call in Andujar's defense. [Caption] — *Chicago Tribune*, 28th October 1985
- Clemens is one of the few players even to have been ejected from a playoff game, getting the heave-ho from a 1990 game in Oakland by plate umpire Terry Cooney for abusive language while arguing balls and strikes. — *Chicago Tribune*, p. 1C, 23rd October 2003

heaven *noun*
a billboard in the language of graffiti artists *US, 2002*
- "We're, like, riding bikes down the highway and looking for heavens," Dems says, using the graffiti slang for billboards. "If we see a nice heaven that hasn't been hit yet, we'll leave our bikes to the side, climb up, and hit it." — *New Times Broward-Palm Beach (Florida)*, 12th December 2002

heavenly blues *noun*
morning glory seeds as a psychoactive agent *US, 1982*
- — Ralph de Sola, *Crime Dictionary*, p. 63, 1982

heaves and squirts *noun*
symptoms of heroin withdrawal *US, 1973*
A rather graphic way of describing vomiting and diarrhea.
- — David Maurer and Victor Vogel, *Narcotics and Narcotic Addiction*, p. 414, 1973

heavies *noun*
large waves *US, 1961*
Always in the plural.
- — *Paradise of the Pacific*, p. 27, October 1963
- — John Severson, *Modern Surfing Around the World*, p. 171, 1964

heavy *noun*
1 an experienced criminal who relies on violence and force *US, 1930*
- Not that her word wouldn't be plenty against us, a bellboy and three heavies, but there's a lot more than that. — Jim Thompson, *A Swell-Looking Babe*, p. 69, 1954

2 in the television and movie industries, an antagonist *US, 1926*
- — Tony Miller and Patricia George, *Cut! Print!*, p. 86, 1977

3 an officer *US, 1976*
Vietnam war coinage.
- Them fucking heavies back in their air-conditioned bunkers at Quang Tri just sit there drinking beer and throwing darts at the map. — Charles Anderson, *The Grunts*, p. 43, 1976
- The "heavies"—CAG, the squadron C.O.'s, Capt. Andrews, and the staff—had been watching closely for signs of deterioration. — Gerry Carroll, *North S*A*R*, pp. 192–193, 1991

4 an important person *US, 1925*
- Some of the heavies in the mob have hit the mattress, the big names are surrounding themselves with soldiers and a few have dropped out of sight entirely. — Mickey Spillane, *Last Cop Out*, p. 84, 1972

5 heroin *US, 1971*
- — Edward R. Bloomquist, *Marijuana*, p. 342, 1971

6 a potent dose or a potent drug or both *US, 1988*
- Don't give her no heavy, Rick. We've got work to do tonight. — *Drugstore Cowboy*, 1988

7 an aircraft carrier *US, 1959*
- Under my command, during a naval maneuver in European waters, we picked up what we thought was a "heavy," or aircraft carrier, on our sonar. — William R. Anderson and Clay Blair, *Nautilus 90 North*, p. 37, 1959

heavy *adjective*
1 very serious, very intense *US, 1963*
- I learned enough shit from it, though, that maybe it wasn't such a bummer after all. All I can say is, man, I took a heavy trip! — Abbie Hoffman, *Woodstock Nation*, p. 5, 1969
- I think Workingman's Dead is the heaviest thing since Highway 61 and "Mr. Tambourine Man." — Hunter S. Thompson, *Fear and Loathing in America*, p. 343, 11th December 1970: Letter to John Lombardi

- Three years ago I used to know a lot of heavy blacks. — Oscar Zeta Acosta, *The Uncollected Works*, p. 10, 1971
- Death. It's so incredibly heavy, it's like so much heavier than like ninety-five percent of the shit you deal with in the average day that constitutes your supposed life. — Kenneth Lonergan, *This is Our Youth*, p. 118, 2000

2 (of drugs) addictive *US, 1959*
- But its subject matter, ranging as it does from heavy drugs to transvestism and sodomy, will seem bold enough to many or most people. — *New York Times*, p. 5 (Section 2), 10th June 1984
- The music they played was unmistakeably heavy and the group did heavy drugs to go with it. — Simon Napier-Bell, *Black Vinyl White Powder*, p. 78, 2001

3 violent, inclined to use violence *US, 1902*
- And I was just as determined not to become a suicidal stickup artist or other "heavy" hustler. — Iceberg Slim (Robert Beck), *The Naked Soul of Iceberg Slim*, p. 26, 1971
- And when the revolution did get heavy, they would not know our methods nor would they have the stamina to even move to fight white racists. — Bobby Seale, *A Lonely Rage*, 1978
- I know you have been cool, but then this penis stepped in and had to get all heavy. — *Airheads*, 1994

4 rough, sadistic *US, 1986*
- "Because heavy sex is fire, and some people are made of stone and some of paper." — Ethan Morden, *Buddies*, p. 145, 1986

▸ **get heavy**
to study *US, 1955*
- — *American Speech*, p. 303, December 1955: "Wayne University slang"

heavy A *noun*
an assistant drill instructor, US Marine Corps *US, 1987*
- Starting as Third Hat with a platoon on graduation, whatever his rank, the D.I. can look forward to promotion after one or two series to Heavy A, and after several more, to senior drill instructor. — Daniel Da Cruz, *Boot*, p. 71, 1987

heavy closer *noun*
in a swindle, a person who makes the final deal with the victim *US, 1986*
- They were the "heavy closers"—psychological intimidation specialists who sized up weaknesses on the follow-up calls and made the sucker sign. — James Ellroy, *Suicide Hill*, p. 596, 1986

heavy cream *noun*
a hefty, large-breasted woman *US, 1960*
- — Robert George Reisner, *The Jazz Titans*, p. 158, 1960

heavy cruising *noun*
a search of a sexual partner with a taste for sado-masochism *US, 1979*
- It is the most popular of the "heavy cruising" bars that pock the area. — John Rechy, *Rushes*, pp. 17–18, 1979

heavy-duty *adjective*
serious, intense *US, 1935*
- Heavy duty shit, Augie. Heavy duty. — James Ellroy, *Brown's Requiem*, p. 171, 1981

heavy foot *noun*
a motorist who speeds *US, 1958*
- [A] speed violator is a heavy foot. — *New York Times*, p. 34, 20th October 1958

heavy hammer *noun*
any powerful pain medication *US, 1994*
- — Sally Williams, *"Strong" Words*, p. 146, 1994

heavy hitter *noun*
1 a person with a deserved reputation for violence *US, 1970*
A baseball metaphor.
- But his uncle was a made-guy, a lieutenant with the Mulberry Street crew—a heavy hitter[.] — Edwin Torres, *Carlito's Way*, pp. 21–22, 1975
- His guy walks and the other two heavy hitters have to convey their sympathies to their clients. — George V. Higgins, *The Judgment of Deke Hunter*, p. 240, 1976
- Because we start out, all we see are heavy hitters, all your suspects. — Elmore Leonard, *Glitz*, p. 252, 1985

2 a prominent and important person *US, 1976*
- And I also got to fraternize with and observe some of the real heavy hitters of political journalism. — Maria Shriver, *Ten Things I Wish I'd Known*, p. 5, 2000

heavy lifter *noun*
a dangerous, tough person *US, 2001*
- You'll be slappin' skin with the heavy lifters from south of Hawthorn. — Stephen J. Cannell, *The Tin Collectors*, p. a, 2001

heavy metal; HM; metal *noun*
a music genre, characterized by loud amplification, the primacy of electric guitars and simple, powerful—if occasionally lumbering—rhythmic patterns *US, 1970*
The term was originally coined by Beat novelist William Burroughs in 1946, reintroduced into the pop vocabulary by Steppenwolf in their hit "Born to Be Wild," and subsequently redefined by rock critic Lester Bangs.
- This album, more of the same 27th-rate heavy metal crap, is worse than the first two put together, though I know that sounds incredible. — *Rolling Stone*, 12th November 1970

heavy paintwork passers *noun*
in a dice cheating scheme, dice that have been altered by drilling the spots and filling them with heavy metallic paint *US, 1963*
- — John S. Salak, *Dictionary of Gambling*, p. 121, 1963

heavy roller *noun*
a very important person *US, 1974*
- Word of advice to Heavy Rollers: a peacock today, a featherduster tomorrow. — Robert Kirk Mueller, *Buzzwords*, p. 91, 1974

heavy scene *noun*
sado-masochistic sex *US, 1979*
- During one of his periodic excursions to other cities in search of new "heavy scenes"—and his reputation as a top-man precedes his forays—Chas was asked to play an auctioneer at a simulated "slave auction[.]" — John Rechy, *Rushes*, p. 27, 1979

heavy thumb *noun*
in the usage of youthful model road racers (slot car racers), a fast, reckless racer *US, 1997*
- — Phantom Surfers, *The Exciting Sounds of Model Road Racing (Album cover)*, 1997

heavyweight Jones *noun*
a drug dealer who sells drugs in a manner calculated to lead his customers to addiction *US, 1971*
- — Eugene Landy, *The Underground Dictionary*, p. 101, 1971

heavy wizardry *noun*
in computing, designs or code that demand a specialized and deep practical understanding *US, 1991*
- Writing device drivers is heavy wizardry; so is interfacing to X without a toolkit. — Eric S. Raymond, *The New Hacker's Dictionary*, p. 198, 1991

Hebe; Heeb *noun*
a Jewish person *US, 1926*
Derogatory.
- "Who's that Hebe doctor?" Livia said loudly before Krankeit was well out the door. — Terry Southern, *Candy*, p. 113, 1958
- His first name is John and those Hebes don't name their kids John. — Eugene Boe (Compiler), *The Wit & Wisdom of Archie Bunker*, p. 46, 1971
- And wops 'n micks 'n slopes 'n spics 'n spooks are on my list / And there's one little Hebe from the heart of Texas—is there anyone I missed? — Kinky Friedman, *They Ain't Jews Like Jesus Anymore*, 1974
- A million times I wanted to yell in his fuckin' ear: "This is Las Vegas! We're supposed to be out here robbin', you dumb fucking Hebe!" — *Casino*, 1995

Hebrew hoppers *noun*
sandals *US, 1970*
From the images of Jesus Christ wearing sandals.
- — *Current Slang*, p. 19, Spring 1970

hecka *adverb*
very *US, 1989*
A euphemized **HELLA**.
- — Pamela Munro, *U.C.L.A. Slang*, p. 48, 1989

heck-city *adverb*
very *US, 2004*
- — Rick Ayers (Editor), *Berkeley High Slang Dictionary*, p. 24, 2004

hecksa *adverb*
very *US, 2004*
- — Rick Ayers (Editor), *Berkeley High Slang Dictionary*, p. 24, 2004

he-coon *noun*
an important person *US, 1897*
- To be able to say you'd once worked for Ol' Paul marked you as a real he-coon among loggers[.] — *Tall Tales*, p. 12, 1976

hectic *adjective*
(used of a wave) fairly treacherous *US, 1988*
- — Surf Punks, *Oh No! Not Them Again! (liner notes)*, 1988

hector!
used as a euphemism for "heck," itself a euphemism for "hell" *US, 1965*
- — Miss Cone, *The Slang Dictionary (Hawthorne High School)*, 1965

H'ed *adjective*
addicted to heroin *US, 1997*
- — Vann Wesson, *Generation X Field Guide and Lexicon*, p. 88, 1997

hedgehop *verb*
to fly at low altitudes *US, 1918*
- Kimmel chose to stay under the clouds and hedgehop over the countryside, hoping to locate himself visually and find someplace to land. — James Doolittle, *I Could Never Be So Lucky Again*, p. 356, 1991

heebie-jeebies *noun*
1 the jitters, a sense of anxiety *US, 1923*
Thought to have been coined by US cartoonist Billy DeBeck (1890–1942) for the comic strip *Barney Google*.
- The apartment was so quiet that it gave her the heebie-jeebies. — James T. Farrell, *Ruth and Bertram*, p. 113, 1955
- I was still sitting in my chair getting the cold heeby-jeebies and trying to figure out my exit line. — Martin Waddell, *Otley*, pp. 133–134, 1966
- "Them niggers shouting and talking in them spooky tongues gives me the heebie jeebies and the hives." — Iceberg Slim (Robert Beck), *Doom Fox*, p. 56, 1978

2 symptoms of withdrawal from an addictive drug *US, 1987*
- The thing is, I'm still fighting back the heebie-jeebies from this drop in my dose of mojo juice [methadone]. — Jim Carroll, *Forced Entries*, p. 144, 1987

heebies *noun*
jitters *US, 1926*
- There was a conspiracy in Manhattan, headed by him, to give all Windy City musicians the heebies until they were ready to be bugged. — Mezz Mezzrow, *Really the Blues*, p. 181, 1946

Heeeeere's Johnny......
used as a humorous introduction *US, 1980*
The drawn-out introduction of US late-night talk show host Johnny Carson by sidekick Ed McMahon from 1962 until 1992. Widely repeated, with variations and referential humor.
- "You ever watch Johnny Carson, the way they do it? You say, 'And now ... heeeeeere's Brad!'" — Elmore Leonard, *Gold Coast*, p. 51, 1980

hee-haw *noun*
loud and braying laughter *UK, 1843*
- [A]in't but four of us out here but I bet y'all see a whole bunch o' niggers hangin' 'round outside a poolroom, heehawin' 'n wastin' time. — Odie Hawkins, *Chicago Hustle*, p. 6, 1977

hee-haw *adjective*
without betting *US, 1972*
- "I don't play hee-haw. I'm looking for somebody who wants to make it interesting." — Robert Byrne, *McGoorty*, p. 98, 1972

heel *noun*
1 in professional wrestling, a wrestler designed by the promoters to be seen by the audience as a villain *US, 1958*
- For example: wrestle is "work;" fall is "going over;" "finish" is the routine just before the deciding fall; hero is "baby face;" villain is "heel." — Pappy Boyington, *Baa Baa Black Sheep*, p. 375, 1958
- "It's rough out there," panted television's Mr. T., who joined good-guy wrestling champion Hulk Hogan in stomping two heels in a tag-team grudge match. — *Associated Press*, 31st March 1985
- "Heel" is the name given to wrestlers that blatantly break the rules, thus becoming the object of the fans' hatred. — Pat Barrett, *Everybody Down There Hates Me*, p. 221, 1990
- Types of heels: the rulebreaker, the underhanded fop, the interfering manager, the nasty foreigner, the diabolic brat, the disloyal sibling, the braggart, the evolutionary throwback. — *Herb's Wrestling Tidbits*, 28th September 1995

2 by extension, any figure in the wrestling business designed by the promoters to be disliked by the fans *US, 1998*

- He was riding on this moment of fame in his local gigs, where he would appear as heel manager "Big Daddy Money Bucks"[.] — Sharon Mazer, *Professional Wrestling*, p. 161, 1998
- When Smoky began an interpromotional feud with the USWA, Brian had finally gotten a chance to wrestle, and as a vicious heel referee turned wrestler, was finally able to truly showcase his talents. — Mick Foley, *Herb's Wrestling Tidbits*, p. 301, 1999
- He is still a superb heel announcer, yet his sharp edge has been honed, and at times he almost comes across as a normal guy. — Jeff Archer, *Theater in a Squared Circle*, p. 36, 1999

heel *verb*
to leave; to leave without paying a bill *US, 1962*

- "You're still here. I told you to heel." — Charles Perry, *Portrait of a Young Man Drowning*, p. 325, 1962
- We managed to heel that motel before they could give us the bill. — *American Speech*, p. 281, December 1966: "More Carnie Talk from the West Coast"
- — Joe McKennon, *Circus Lingo*, p. 46, 1980

heeled *adjective*
1 armed *US, 1866*

- I nudged him with the gun, ran my hand over his pockets and beltline to make sure he wasn't heeled[.] — Mickey Spillane, *Return of the Hood*, p. 107, 1964
- "I'd feel a hell of a lot better if I was heeled," Grave Digger confessed. — Chester Himes, *Come Back Charleston Blue*, p. 84, 1966
- I unbutton my jacket and put my elbows out to the side and raise them. "Am I heeled?" I unbutton my jacket and put my elbows out to the side and raise them. "Am I heeled?" — Leo Rosten, *Silky!*, p. 54, 1979
- "This private-eye fucker—is he gonna be heeled?" Ronnie broke a swizzle stick in half. "Always. Waxman buys him a gun permit from a judge every year." — Gerald Petievich, *Money Men*, p. 82, 1981

2 provided with funds *US, 1873*

- — Joseph E. Ragen and Charles Finston, *Inside the World's Toughest Prison*, p. 803, 1962: "Penitentiary and underworld glossary"

3 in possession of drugs *US, 1970*

- — William D. Alsever, *Glossary for the Establishment and Other Uptight People*, p. 15, December 1970

heeler *noun*
1 an opportunistic sneak thief *US, 1931*

- I went around with a heeler one time and he just shook me to pieces when he'd go in there and reach under people's pillows while they're sleeping and steal their wallet. — Harry King, *Box Man*, p. 87, 1972

2 in poker, an unmatched card retained in a player's hand when drawing *US, 1967*

- — Albert H. Morehead, *The Complete Guide to Winning Poker*, p. 264, 1967

heeling *noun*
stealing drugs from a pharmacy while a confederate distracts the pharmacist *US, 1968*

- Heeling, as it is called in the trade, is often the quickest way to score. But that takes a girl to distract the druggist while the thief slips behind the prescription counter and pries open the narcotics cabinet. — Phil Hirsch, *Hooked*, p. 73, 1968

heelish *adjective*
in professional wrestling, villainous *US, 1996*

- Owen Hart broke his heelish character to praise his father for raising great kids. — *Herb's Wrestling Tidbits*, 24th October 1996

heel list *noun*
a list of persons unwelcome as guests at a hotel *US, 1953*

- So his name was entered on the "heel list"—a catalogue of undesirables—and he ceased to be a guest. — Jim Thompson, *Bad Boy*, p. 358, 1953

heel up *verb*
to arm yourself *US, 1966*

- — Rose Giallombardo, *Society of Women*, p. 208, 1966: Glossary of Prison Terms

heezy *noun*
▸ **off the heezy**
wonderful, cool, amazing *US, 1999*

- Still packing fo sho / Yeezy Weezy off of the heezy fo sheezy / Cruise with the top off of the 'Ghini[.] — Lil Wayne, *Fo Sheezy*, 1999

hefty *noun*
in circus and carnival usage, a performer in a strongman act *US, 1981*

- — Don Wilmeth, *The Language of American Popular Entertainment*, p. 128, 1981

hefty *adjective*
wellfunded at the moment *US, 1958*
Teen slang.

- — *San Francisco News*, p. 6, 25th March 1958

he-girl *noun*
a person with mixed sexual physiology, usually the genitals of a male and surgically augmented breasts *US, 2004*

- — www.adultquarter.com/blossary.html, January 2004: "Glossary of adult Internet terms"

he-hooker *noun*
a male prostitute *US, 1969*

- A lot of people out there in Mom's-Apple-Pie-Land aren't going to buy it— me being a he-hooker. — Joey V., *Portrait of Joey*, p. 21, 1969

HEI *noun*
a high-explosive incendiary *US, 1990*

- Willie Peter showed us where / To roll in to displease 'em / One more pass with HEI / Pop goes the Weasel! — Joseph Tuso, *Singing the Vietnam Blues*, p. 159, 1990: Pop Goes the Weasel

Heidi *noun*
a young woman with back-to-the-earth, 1960s values, and fashion sense, especially one with pigtails *US, 2001*

- — Don R. McCreary (Editor), *Dawg Speak*, 2001

heifer *noun*
a stocky girl or woman *US, 1835*
An insult, if not a fighting word.

- "I got a babe for the top role. From you, all I want is a bunch of good-looking heifers." — Wade Hunter, *The Sex Peddler*, p. 22, 1963
- No, I'm talking about that old light-skin heifer that's always comin' around here to see your daddy. — Claude Brown, *Manchild in the Promised Land*, p. 383, 1965
- I feel like such a heifer. I had two bowls of Special K, three pieces of turkey bacon, a handful of popcorn, five peanut butter M&M's, and like three pieces of licorice. — *Clueless*, 1995
- "His wife had his kids out at three in the morning?" "Yes, the heifer did." — Eric Jerome Dickey, *Cheaters*, p. 34, 1999

heifer dust *noun*
nonsense *US, 1927*
A euphemism for **BULLSHIT**.

- — William D. Alsever, *Glossary for the Establishment and Other Uptight People*, p. 14, December 1970
- "I feel fine." "Heifer dust," he said, using her word for it. — John L'Heureux, *An Honorable Profession*, p. 103, 1991

heigh-ho!
used as a signal of enthusiasm *US, 1930s to 50s*

- "Let us taste all the joys that this great city as to offer." "Heigh-ho," she replied airily and linked her pretty arm in mine. — Max Shulman, *The Many Loves of Dobie Gillis*, p. 28, 1951

Heinie; heiny *noun*
a German; German *US, 1904*

- Later—when lists of Nazis were released—we saw many of these stolid heinies on record. — Jack Lait and Lee Mortimer, *New York Confidential*, p. 81, 1948
- I remember a booby trap they set on a Heinie general's car once. — Mickey Spillane, *Kiss Me Deadly*, p. 79, 1952

Heinies *noun*
Heineken™ beer *US, 1982*

- — Dr. Lillian Glass with Richard Liebmann-Smith, *How to Deprogram Your Valley Girl*, p. 27, 1982

heinous *adjective*
offensive, unpleasant *US, 1982*
Conventional English elevated to slang by attitude.

- — Connie Eble (Editor), *UNC-CH Campus Slang*, p. 5, March 1986
- We are in danger of flunking most heinously tomorrow, Ted. — *Bill and Ted's Excellent Adventure*, 1989
- I believe "heinous bitch" is the term used most often. — *Ten Things I Hate About You*, 1999

Heinz dog *noun*
a mixed breed dog *US, 1950*
From the Heinz advertising slogan (57 varieties).

- "He is a Heinz dog," said Mrs. Peters. "Fifty-seven varieties!" — Judy Delton, *Lucky Dog Days*, p. 14, 1988

heist *noun*
a theft or robbery *US, 1976*

- Punks shooting up a delicatessen on their first heist. — Emmett Grogan, *Final Score*, p. 68, 1976

heist *verb*
1 to steal, especially to shoplift *UK, 1815*
There are enough Hollywood heist films to make a genre. Also spelt "hyste."

- I gotta hyste a fish market tonight. — George Mandel, *Flee the Angry Strangers*, p. 387, 1952
- We traced it to a group heisted from an armory in Illinois. — Mickey Spillane, *Kiss Me Deadly*, p. 109, 1952
- Until finally I heisted a gold watch off one of the girl dancers in the show[.] — Ross Russell, *The Sound*, p. 195, 1961
- If you're heisted, the worst thing is not to have any money on you[.] — Jimmy Snyder, *Jimmy the Greek*, p. 63, 1975

2 to rob *US, 1951*

- "Me and Sal heisted that joint so Sal could get some dough, for a getaway, on account of the Chippy job." — Burton Turkus and Sid Feder, *Murder, Inc.*, p. 168, 1951
- He came back and said, "Some day we're gonna heist this joint." — Harry Grey, *The Hoods*, p. 24, 1952
- "You scared they'll heist you?" — Leo Rosten, *Silky!*, p. 153, 1979

heist artist *noun*
a professional robber or burglar *US, 1949*

- "How would you like to set a trap for our heist artist?" — Ed McBain, *Let's Hear it for the Deaf Man*, p. 182, 1973

heister *noun*
a thief or robber *UK, 1865*
From the earlier "hoister."

- I described the two heisters as well as I could. — Jimmy Snyder, *Jimmy the Greek*, p. 67, 1975
- "Jungle" John Lembeck, white male, age thirty-four, two-time convicted strong-arm heister, lived in a bungalow court on Serrano just off the Boulevard. — James Ellroy, *Hollywood Nocturnes*, p. 188, 1994

heist man *noun*
a robber or burglar *US, 1931*

- "It's like in a fight," said Peter David, a heist man serving five years, once said to Socrates in the Indiana state penitentiary. — Walter Mosley, *Walkin' the Dog*, p. 77, 1999

Helen *noun*
heroin *US, 1971*
Giving an identity and disguise to **H** (heroin).

- — US Department of Justice *Street Terms*, October 1994

helium head *noun*
an aviator in a lighter-than-air airship *US, 1952*

- [W]ith the others—the other helium heads—he gradually became disillusioned , and ultimately, bitter in the feeling that the Navy had sold them out. — John McPhee, *The Deltoid Pumpkin Seed*, p. 248, 1973

hell *noun*
▸ **from hell**
used for intensifying *US, 1965*
Humorous, hyperbolic.

- We were ushers from hell. Nobody smoked in our section. — Connie Eble (Editor), *UNC-CH Campus Slang*, p. 4, Spring 1989
- "I know, Lacey," I said. "They're the all-time Parents from Hell." — C.D. Payne, *Youth in Revolt*, p. 256, 1993

hella *adverb*
extremely *US, 1992*

- — Judi Sanders, *Kickin' like Chicken with the Couch Commander*, p. 11, 1992
- For an all-purpose superlative, use "hella" as in "He's hella fine," (he's good-looking) or "that test was hella-hard." — *San Francisco Chronicle*, p. A9, 17th November 1992
- I bet he makes hella money. — *Kids*, 1995
- — Connie Eble (Editor), *UNC-CH Campus Slang*, p. 3, Fall 1998

hellacious *adjective*
especially nasty or difficult *US, 1929*

- — Collin Baker et al., *College Undergraduate Slang Study Conducted at Brown University*, p. 136, 1968
- I struck Frank Robinson out on four absolutely hellacious knuckleballs[.] — Jim Bouton, *Ball Four*, p. 169, 1970

hell and gone; hell-and-gone *noun*
a far-distant place or point in time *US, 1938*

- The ignoramus has been shooting up churches from here to hell-and-gone. Now he speaks of respect. — Audie Murphy, *Hell and Back*, p. 23, 1949
- [T]hey'd be able to stymie the cops—who could search to hell and gone and find no hard evidence[.] — Elizabeth Sims, *Holy Hell*, p. 128, 2002

hell around *verb*
to carouse *US, 1897*

- It's a goddam shame the helling around I do, cheating on her and writing lovey-dovey letters. — Norman Mailer, *The Naked and the Dead*, p. 553, 1948
- He had a laugh here, remembering an old story about a football quarterback who was out helling around and his wife caught him sneaking in around seven in the morning[.] — Stephen Hunter, *Dirty White Boys*, p. 374, 1994

hell-bender *noun*
a formidable person or thing *US, 1812*

- [C]oming home I gave him a hellbender of a ride around mountain curves. — Sam Snead, *The Education of a Golfer*, p. 16, 1962
- "He must be a hell-bender in a fight," Andy admitted. — Elmer Kelton, *Texas Vendetta*, p. 88, 2004

hell-bent *adjective*
recklessly determined *US, 1835*

- To get drunk, doped up and ride hell bent and carefree[.] — Jamie Mandelkau quoting Ken Kesey, *Buttons*, p. 154, 1971
- I've tried dragging him into the bedroom and he performs reluctantly but next time is hell bent in getting me in the water. — *Attitude*, p. 146, October 2003

hell buster *noun*
any difficult thing, task, or person *US, 1949*

- "Is it such a hell-buster of a trip, Dick?" — A.B. Guthrie, *The Way West*, p. 29, 1949

hell-cat *noun*
a woman who is quick to anger *UK, 1605*

- Miss Moore is often pictured as a bit of a hellcat as far as temperament is concerned[.] — Earl Wilson, *I am Gazing Into My 8-Ball*, p. 49, 1945
- Now it might not look like it, but lemme tell you something. She's a hellcat. — *Raising Arizona*, 1987
- "I bet she fucked like a hellcat, too." — John Ridley, *Love is a Racket*, p. 16, 1998

heller *noun*
a wild, uninhibited party *US, 1975*

- — *American Speech*, p. 61, Spring–Summer 1975: "Razorback slang"

hell-fired *adjective*
used for emphasis; damned *UK, 1756*

- Ninth, the miraculous hell-fired kitchen! — Ray Bradbury, *The October Country*, p. 185, 1955

hell-for-leather *adjective*
full speed *UK, 1889*

- It had been great fun for a kid to be part of the hell-for-leather spirit that made up the 752nd[.] — David Hackworth, *About Face*, p. 34, 1989

hell-hole *noun*
1 a horrible, infernal place *UK, 1882*

- Bay Ridge ain't the worst part of Brooklyn, you know. It ain't like a hellhole. — *Saturday Night Fever*, 1977
- I'm even talking hellholes where the warden's as hard as a bar of iron. — *Natural Born Killers*, 1994

2 in a combat helicopter, an approximately 34-inch-square opening in the floor, used for emergencies and roping down to and up from the ground *US, 1976*

- They had tried to sabotage the ship, I guess, because they had spent the time slashing the seats to ribbons, smearing shit on the instruments, piling dirt into the cockpit and cramming sticks down the hell hole. — Robert Mason, *Chickenhawk*, p. 84, 1983

hellicop *noun*
a police helicopter *US, 1971*
- HELLICOP: surveillance helicopter flown by the Berkeley police during campus and Southside uprisings. — Robert Buckhout, *Toward Social Change*, p. 465, 1971

hellifying *adjective*
used as an adjectival intensifier *US, 1973*
- Legs is what a man looks for, not faces, and you got one hellifying pair of legs. — Gail Sheehy, *Hustling*, p. 55, 1973

hell-jelly *noun*
napalm *US, 1946*
- [N]ow they were terrified of the "hell-jelly" bombs filling the air with gouts of sticky flame. — Robert Leckie, *Strong Men Armed*, p. 369, 1962

hell night *noun*
a night filled with sadistic hazing as part of a fraternity initiation ritual *US, 1956*
- The boy reported that on "hell night" he was taken to a faraway golf course "where the cops could not hear you yell." — Louis Kitzer, *Allied Activities in the Secondary School*, p. 100, 1956
- John agreed that it was wonderful to have something to warm us after the misery of hell night. — Robert Smithdas, *Life at My Fingertips*, p. 165, 1958
- They had no idea what the Fires was—just that it was the famous, scary AD hell night, and they had to go through it. — Chris Miller, *The Real Animal House*, p. 80, 2006

hello!
used for signaling disbelief when said as if speaking to someone slow-witted *US, 1984*
- Hello! That was a stop sign! — *Clueless*, 1995
- ROBIN: Jane's gay? HOLLY: Like, hello? You didn't know? — *Boys on the Side*, 1995
- — Connie Eble (Editor), *UNC-CH Campus Slang*, p. 5, April 1995
- I mean, hello. You've barely even spoken to me for months. — *American Beauty*, 1999

hell of *adverb*
extremely *US, 1995*
A reverse correction of the corrupted **HELLA**.
- "That is hell of cool," said Pup. — Francesca Lia Block, *Baby Be-Bop*, p. 391, 1995

Hell on the Hudson *noun*
the United States Military Academy *US, 1969*
- Like most cadets, he had often daydreamed about how pleasant it would be to pursue his education somewhere other than Hell on the Hudson. — Rick Atkinson, *The Long Gray Line*, p. 93, 1989

hell on wheels *noun*
an overly energetic, aggressive person *US, 1843*
- "He claims he's hell on wheels with women," explains Horse Face. — Audie Murphy, *To Hell and Back*, p. 71, 1949

hello phone *noun*
a telephone number given to supply references, which are given as part of a deception *US, 1987*
- We set up a couple of "hello phones," just numbers people could call to check my references. — Joseph Pistone, *Donnie Brasco*, p. 43, 1987

Hell Pass Hole *nickname*
El Paso, Texas *US, 1970*
- — *Current Slang*, p. 19, Spring 1970

hellride *noun*
in mountain biking, any bad trail or bad ride *US, 1992*
- — William Nealy, *Mountain Bike!*, p. 161, 1992: "Bikespeak"

hell-roaring *adverb*
extremely *US, 1878*
- There, hell-roaring drunk, his one good leg firmly planted on the bar rail, stood the redheaded chieftain of Brooklyn's Irish "White Hand." — John Kobler, *Capone*, p. 163, 1971

hell's bells
used as a mild oath *UK, 1832*
- Hell's bells, green nail polish? — Hal Ellson, *Summer Street*, p. 23, 1953
- So that's how you work this democratic bullshit—hell's bells! — Ken Kesey, *One Flew Over the Cuckoo's Nest*, p. 135, 1962
- Hells Bells! Don't stop now sugar. — *Natural Born Killers*, 1994

hell's half acre *noun*
any large, remote area *US, 1864*
- From then on, we were all kept busy running all over hell's half acre looking for new reading material for Father. — Helen Giblo, *Footlights, Fistfights and Femmes*, p. 13, 1957
- "I don't want anyone changing my mind this time or driving me all over hell's half acre." — Ann-Marie MacDonald, *Fall on your Knees*, p. 363, 1996

hell to breakfast *noun*
here to there, all over *US, 1930*
- — John Gould, *Maine Lingo*, p. 130, 1975

helluva
hell of a *US, 1910*
- Anyway, he gave me a helluva quote. — Carl Hiaasen, *Tourist Season*, p. 201, 1986

hell week *noun*
a period of extreme harassment, especially of new recruits to a college fraternity by their older fraternity brothers *US, 1930*
- Had it really been eighteen years—Christ, half his life!—since Nelson Schwab had cornered him during Hell Week at the Deke House to impart the privileged information that "Puff" was really an underground parable about—no shit—smoking marijuana? — Armistead Maupin, *Further Tales of the City*, p. 38, 1982

hell west and crooked *adverb*
to the extreme *US, 1898*
- They was out all winter and the saddles didn't fit and them horses would buck all hell west and crooked till we could get 'em rode. — Thomas McGuane, *The Cadence of Grass*, p. 29, 2002

helmet *noun*
the head of the circumcized penis *US, 1970*
From the similarity in shape to a World War 2 German Army helmet.
- You get bored you might amuse yourselves by betting quarters whether the next guy in will be a helmet or an anteater. — Joseph Wambaugh, *The New Centurions*, p. 262, 1970

helo *noun*
a helicopter *US, 1965*
- After the troops in our helo were buckled into low canvas streets, the helos took off[.] — James Kirschke, *Not Going Home Alone*, p. 52, 2001
- "Captain Harper" (who had been listening to the radio chatter on the bridge) burst into CIC and asked me "who was that person talking to the helos with that great voice." — Douglas Brinkley, *Tour of Duty: John Kerry and the Vietnam War*, p. 86, 2004

helpcat *noun*
a tutor; a student assistant *US, 1955*
A punning allusion to **HEP CAT**.
- — *American Speech*, p. 303, December 1955: "Wayne University slang"

helper *noun*
any amphetamine or other central nervous system stimulant *US, 1963*
- Some of the names describe the drugs' effects, such as "helpers," "copilots," "Los Angeles turn arounds," or their shape, color and markings—"hearts," "footballs," "blackjacks," "crossroads." — Phil Hirsch, *Hooked*, pp. 51–52, 1968
- — Montie Tak, *Truck Talk*, p. 82, 1971

hemp *noun*
marijuana *US, 1883*
- [H]e pulled out a cigarette and puffed on it, imitating a cat pulling on some hemp. — Mezz Mezzrow, *Really the Blues*, p. 298, 1946
- Now, smoking hemp, she let out the laughter she'd choked back with food. — George Mandel, *Flee the Angry Strangers*, p. 130, 1952
- And when he wasn't digging their fine silhouettes, he was busy peddling filtered hemp cigarettes. — Dan Burley, *Diggeth Thou?*, p. 22, 1959
- Your "people" are white, suburban high school boys who smoke too much hemp. — *Ten Things I Hate About You*, 1999

hemp head *noun*
a frequent user of marijuana *US, 1980*
- It goes on and on like that, until we became morally certain that it had been written by some hemp-head[.] — Stephen Gaskin, *Amazing Dope Tales*, p. 161, 1980

hen *noun*
in a deck of playing cards, a queen *US, 1988*
- — George Percy, *The Language of Poker*, p. 43, 1988

hen apple *noun*
an egg *US, 1938*
- I'll wager he never went hunting for diamonds in hen apples again anytime soon. — Guy Owen, *The Flim-Flam Man and the Apprentice Grifter*, p. 163, 1972

hen fruit *noun*
an egg *US, 1854*
- I never saw a man look so hard-down disappointed in hen fruit before. "What's wrong with them eggs, mister?" — Guy Owen, *The Flim-Flam Man and the Apprentice Grifter*, p. 157, 1972

hen mill *noun*
a women's jail or prison *US, 1960*
- We arraign you tomorrow on this evidence, we hold trial two weeks from now—next month you're doing twenty to life in the hen mill. — Clarence Cooper Jr., *The Scene*, p. 113, 1960

henny penny *noun*
a female player in a low stakes game of poker *US, 1988*
- — George Percy, *The Language of Poker*, p. 43, 1988

hen party *noun*
a social gathering restricted to women *UK, 1887*
- Jack took his mama down to N. Carolina this week; so Joan his wife threw a "hen party" last nite for Liz, marian holmes, etc. — Allen Ginsberg, *Letter to Neal Cassady*, p. 100, February 1951
- If he hates red, wear your red dress only to hen parties. — Art Unger, *The Cool Book*, p. 51, 1961

hen pen *noun*
a women's prison *US, 1992*
- — William K. Bentley and James M. Corbett, *Prison Slang*, p. 4, 1992

Henry *noun*
heroin *US, 1953*
From "heroin" to **H** to Henry.
- All that good Henry and Charley. When you shoot Henry and Charley, you can smell it going in. — William Burroughs, *Junkie*, p. 84, 1953
- We all know what a lummox Frankie Lymon was to mess with hard drugs like henry and charlie, after all, they took his life. — Richard Meltzer, *A Whore Just Like the Rest*, p. 65, 1970
- He got up, dressed, we took a few more toots of Christine and Henry (pineapple) and split. — A.S. Jackson, *Gentleman Pimp*, p. 71, 1973

Henry IV *noun*
the human immunodeficiency virus *US, 2001*
- — Don R. McCreary (Editor), *Dawg Speak*, 2001

Henry the Eighth *noun*
eight grams of cocaine *US, 1993*
- — Peter Johnson, *Dictionary of Street Alcohol and Drug Terms*, p. 91, 1993

Henry the Fourth *noun*
four grams of cocaine *US, 1993*
- — Peter Johnson, *Dictionary of Street Alcohol and Drug Terms*, p. 91, 1993

hep *noun*
hepatitis *US, 1967*
- The Communications Company printed up a thing about serum hep, that lays it out there, that lays the information out[.] — Leonard Wolfe (Editor), *Voices from the Love Generation*, p. 135, 1968
- It ain't been too busy a year, but maybe that's cause I was zonked with the hep for three months. — Abbie Hoffman, *Woodstock Nation*, p. 11, 1969
- — Walter Way, *The Drug Scene*, p. 110, 1977

hep *adjective*
1 aware *US, 1903*
- These older girls, knowing I was hep to sex, trusted me not to tell on them. — Ethel Waters, *His Eye is on the Sparrow*, p. 44, 1951
- As the days rolled on I commenced getting hep to the jive. — Louis Armstrong, *Satchmo: My Life in New Orleans*, p. 192, 1954
- [L]ike I'd never heard anywhere and which bore resemblance to Bartok modern chords but were hep wise to bop[.] — Jack Kerouac, *The Subterraneans*, p. 67, 1958
- I guess all of you already know just about what I'm going to say, but you're not really hep to what the rewards are going to be. — Donald Goines, *Black Gangster*, p. 25, 1977

2 in step with the latest fashion, latest music, and latest slang *US, 1942*
- On December 1st LuAnne arrived here; she was quite changed, affected a more sophisticated air, came on hep and moved with improved poise. — Neal Cassady, *Neal Cassady Collected Letters 1944–1967*, p. 66, 25th December 1947: Letter to Jack Kerouac
- Walters didn't want to open a typical New York cafe, appealing to the "smart" set and the heavy spenders and the "hep" crowd. — Robert Sylvester, *No Cover Charge*, p. 28, 1956
- "Don't mind Eddie. He's hep." — Wade Hunter, *The Sex Peddler*, p. 99, 1963

hepatic rounds *noun*
used in a hospital as a humorous code for a drinking party to be held on hospital grounds *US, 1988–1989*
- — *Maledicta*, p. 33, 1988–1989: "Medical maledicta from San Francisco"

hep cat; hepped cat *noun*
a fan of jazz or swing music; a stylish and fashionable man *US, 1938*
- There was probably not a single hep-cat in the auditorium, but that bass droom was strictly for hep-cats. — Mark Tryon, *Of G-Strings and Strippers*, p. 102, 1953
- The customers were the hepped-cats who lived by their wits— smooth Harlem hustlers with shiny straightened hair, dressed in lurid elegance, along with their tightly draped queens, chorus girls and models[.] — Chester Himes, *A Rage in Harlem*, p. 88, 1957
- We come in and I see this weird hepcat wearing a black robe with hood, barefoot, sitting crossleg on corner bench[.] — Jack Kerouac, *Jack Kerouac Selected Letters 1957–1969*, p. 22, 25th March 1957: Letter to Neal Cassady
- Swaggering, hepcat, ala Hollywood leading man type. — Robert Gover, *The Maniac Responsible*, p. 82, 1963

hepped up *adjective*
excited *US, 1939*
- [E]specially since the whole race was so hepped-up about appliances, he was not a hell of a lot more dependent than others[.] — Saul Bellow, *The Adventures of Augie March*, p. 69, 1953

hep square *noun*
a person who lives a conventional life but has some awareness of unconventional lifestyles *US, 1972*
- There's another thing. You have kind of a "hep square" we call them. A hep square is a person that knows a little bit of what's going on. — Bruce Jackson, *Outside the Law*, p. 145, 1972

hepster *noun*
a person at the stylish edge of fashionable; a jazz lover *US, 1938*
- Scoby and Psycho Loco would soon abandon my hepster front for the chase[.] — Paul Beatty, *The White Boy Shuffle*, p. 117, 1996

her *noun*
cocaine *US, 1968*
- "What is this?" I asked. "It's 'her,' man. 'Christine.' Cocaine." — Phil Hirsch, *Hooked*, p. 9, 1968

herb *noun*
marijuana *US, 1962*
- "You been smokin' herb at Two Day's!" Hip accused. — Nathan Heard, *Howard Street*, p. 98, 1968
- A pocket full of money and head full of herb / A Cadillac coupe parked at the curb. — Dennis Wepman et al., *The Life*, p. 31, 1976
- [H]e was stoked to the gills, having scored some primo Jamaican herb off a busboy at the hotel. — Carl Hiaasen, *Tourist Season*, p. 169, 1986
- Gets some of his herb at his mama's nursing home, from one of them Rasta fellas work there. — Elmore Leonard, *Riding the Rap*, p. 131, 1995

herb *verb*
to assault a weak person *US, 1995*
- — Maria Hinojas, *Crews*, p. 167, 1995: "Glossary"

herbal *adjective*
pertaining to marijuana *US, 1995*
- I could really use some sort of a herbal refreshment. — *Clueless*, 1995
- Leon lit a herbal cigarette and blew smoke out of the open window. — John Milne, *Alive and Kicking*, p. 12, 1998

Herc; Herk; Herky Bird *noun*
the Hercules C-130 medium cargo transport aircraft manufactured by Lockheed *US, 1980*

The primary transport aircraft used for US military forces in Vietnam.

- The first production C-130, often called the "Herky Bird," made its first flight on 7 April 1955. — Fred J. Pushies, *U.S. Air Forces Special Ops*, p. 41, 2000

herd *noun*
a packet of Camel™ cigarettes *US, 1945*
- — Lou Shelly, *Hepcats Jive Dictionary*, p. 12, 1945

herder *noun*
1 a prison guard assigned to a prison yard *US, 1992*
- — William K. Bentley and James M. Corbett, *Prison Slang*, p. 96, 1992

2 in horse racing, a jockey or horse that forces the other horses to bunch up behind it *US, 1951*
- — David W. Maurer, *Argot of the Racetrack*, p. 35, 1951

herky-jerky *adjective*
erratic, uncoordinated *US, 1943*
- [H]e knows he has Garrett Stephenson's number and has no reason to get all herky-jerky and hyperventilated. — Buzz Bissinger, *Three Nights in August*, p. 53, 2005

hermit *noun*
a poker player wearing headphones during play *US, 1996*
- — John Vorhaus, *The Big Book of Poker Slang*, p. 22, 1996

hero *noun*
1 heroin *US, 1953*
- — H.J. Ainslinger, *The Traffic in Narcotics*, p. 310, 1953
- — Eugene Landy, *The Underground Dictionary*, p. 101, 1971
- — US Department of Justice, *Street Terms*, October 1994

2 a surfer whose opinion of his own skills exceeds his actual skills *US, 1985*
- — John Blair, *The Illustrated Discography of Surf Music 1961–1965*, p. 123, 1985

hero gear *noun*
enemy paraphernalia taken from the battlefield *US, 1961*
- I swap the pastry to the troops for "hero gear" (battle souvenirs) and I swap the hero gear to the swabbies for pogey bait (candy). — Russell Davis, *Marine at War*, p. 172, 1961

herring choker *noun*
1 a person from New Brunswick or elsewhere in the Canadian Maritime Provinces *US, 1899*
- "We'll go someplace, and you'll get custard pie, and then you'll cut the damned thing up and pour vinegar on the plate and let it all soak through the crust. I know you herring-chokers." — George V. Higgins, *The Judgment of Deke Hunter*, p. 169, 1976

2 a Scandinavian *US, 1936*
- — Vincent J. Monteleone, *Criminal Slang*, p. 117, 1949
- Hear that herring chokers? You Norskis may need some supplements if you are eating the Standard American Diet. — Lendon Smith, *Happiness is a Healthy Life*, p. 89, 1992

herring snapper *noun*
a Scandinavian *US, 1930*
- — Vincent J. Monteleone, *Criminal Slang*, p. 117, 1949

Hershey Bar route *noun*
the rectum and anus *US, 1973*
- I ordered him into the shower because of the idea of sleeping with him after he'd gone the Hershey Bar route hardly turned me on. — Xaviera Hollander, *Xaviera*, p. 44, 1973

Hershey Highway *noun*
the rectum *US, 1973*
- "She thinks I killed that Hershey Highway jockey back on East Jefferson." "What?" "That fairy director you blew away—she thinks I did it." — Carl Ramm, *Detroit Combat*, p. 72, 1985
- Then she taught me how to drive the Hershey highway and she masturbated her own clitoris until we both collapsed together in a wave of orgasms. — Harold Robbins, *The Predators*, p. 196, 1998

Hershey road *noun*
the rectum *US, 1974*
- There's been so much stick pussy shoved up that Hershey road they could rent it out for a convention center. — Seth Morgan, *Homeboy*, p. 179, 1990

Hershey squirts *noun*
diarrhea *US, 1972*

A joking if unpleasant allusion to Hershey™ chocolate.
- Damn. I got Hershey squirts in my shorts. — Joseph Wambaugh, *The Secrets of Harry Bright*, p. 54, 1985
- As for her health, Kitty hadn't fixed for twelve days but still had the geewillies and was running to the bathroom every fifteen minutes with the Hershey squirts. — Seth Morgan, *Homeboy*, p. 135, 1990
- — Michael Dalton Johnson, *Talking Trash with Redd Foxx*, p. 45, 1994
- It's oddly comforting to discover that all-girl rock bands would contract "the Hershey squirts" while drinking their way through Europe and Japan. — *SF Weekly*, 3rd July 1996

he-she *noun*
a man living as a woman, either as a transvestite or transsexual; an effeminate male *US, 1871*
- England is the homo's paradise where he—she's are proud members of society. — Lee Mortimer, *Women Confidential*, p. 186, 1960
- A he-she across the way giving someone a show. — Paul Glover, *Words from the House of the Dead*, 1974
- The place was full of scum, smelly old hags, detectives, he-shes, perverts. — Alix Shulman, *On the Stroll*, p. 7, 1981
- The Bone has also advised me to never stop and talk to a "he/she" on the yard. — Jimmy Lerner, *You Got Nothing Coming*, p. 237, 2002

hesher; heshen; hesh *noun*
a fan of heavy metal music *US, 1993*
- I like those groups so I guess I'm a hesher too. I knew wish I knew what one was. — *alt.skate-board*, 28th May 1993
- [S]toner blacklight parties in his room with the scraggly hesher chicks. — *Editors of Ben is Dead, Retrohell*, p. 95, 1997
- She seemed a hesher beside their streamlined aesthetic[.] — Michelle Tea, *Valencia*, p. 155, 2000

het *adjective*
*het*erosexual *US, 1972*
- — Bruce Rodgers, *The Queens' Vernacular*, p. 190, 1972
- I'm a het male who wants a real relationship with a good woman[.] — Dan Savage, *Savage Love*, p. 29, 1998
- [A]lthough he himself was what the Americans would term "absolutely het," he found himself in the curious position of fancying the transvestite before him[.] — Fiona Pitt-Kethley, *Red Light Districts of the World*, p. 49, 2000

hetboy *noun*
a *het*erosexual male *US, 1995*
Internet shorthand.
- — Christian Crumlish, *The Internet Dictionary*, p. 88, 1995

hetero *noun*
a *het*erosexual *UK, 1933*
- Anyway, what's so special about being gay except a lot of heartaches and headaches? Heteros don't brag about the novels and paintings they've produced because they go to bed with the opposite sex. — *One: The Homosexual Magazine*, p. 19, February 1953
- In Big D, do as the heteros do. — Phil Andros (Samuel M. Steward), *Stud*, p. 89, 1966
- Did they make it with each other at all, or was it strictly hetero? — Jefferson Poland and Valerie Alison, *The Records of the San Francisco Sexual Freedom League*, p. 27, 1971
- A little more enlightened about their own captivity, cognizant of their Augustinian heritage, the heteros there have lived on a somewhat egalitarian basis with the homosexuals. — John Francis Hunter, *The Gay Insider*, p. 263, 1971

hetgirl *noun*
a *het*erosexual female *US, 1995*
Internet shorthand.
- — Christian Crumlish, *The Internet Dictionary*, p. 88, 1995

het up; all het up *adjective*
excited *US, 1909*
From a dialect variation of "heated" or "heated up."
- From the mail we got we knew people were het up about us. — Haywood Patterson, *Scottsboro Boy*, p. 19, 1950

he-whore *noun*
a male prostitute *US, 1952*
- "That's being a man—instead of a he-whore like your fine Cousin Jed." — Madison Cooper, *Sironia, Texas*, p. 819, 1952
- I'm a hooker, a prostitute. Yeah, a he-whore. — Joey V., *Portrait of Joey*, p. 20, 1969

- "Goddamn it woman, you're calling me a he-whore!" — Frank Yerby, *The Girl from Storyville*, p. 314, 1972
- "But how she does do it, and the husband nothing but a he-whore?" — Paule Marshall, *Brown Girl, Brownstone*, p. 73, 1981

hex *noun*

a number sign (#) on a computer keyboard *US, 1991*
- — Eric S. Raymond, *The New Hacker's Dictionary*, p. 39, 1991

hey

used as a discourse break that raises emphasis or focus *US, 1974*
- Up until that point, Pennzoil had been arguing that, hey, they are reasonable people, the court in Texas is reasonable and they don't need any Federal action. — *New York Times*, p. 20, 13th January 1986

hey-hey *noun*

a good time *US, 1985*
- "A little hey-hey"—a good time. — *Washington Post*, p. B1, 17th January 1985

hey now

used as a greeting *US, 1946*
- A group of zoot-suiters greted me in passing, "Hey now, daddy-o," they called. "Hey now!" "Hey now!" I said. — Ralph Ellison, *Invisible Man*, p. 485, 1947
- The "Hello!' that says you're on the bus. From the chorus of "iko Iko." — David Shenk and Steve Silberman, *Skeleton Key*, p. 143, 1994

hey rube *noun*

a fight between swindlers of any sort and their victims *US, 1900*
- Whether an event is a close call or a "hey rube" depends not so much on what is detected or suspected as on the reactions of the audience and the ability of the hustlers to cool out the other players. — Robert C. Prus and C.R.D. Sharper, *Road Hustler*, p. 114, 1977

hey, rube!

used as an insider request for help in a fight *US, 1900*
Originally and principally an expression used in the circus and carnivals.
- Early day circus troupers may have used the cry "hey rube," but during my twenty five years on the road with the larger circuses and carnivals, I have never heard it used one time. — Joe McKennon, *Circus Lingo*, p. 46, 1980
- "You better git your friend outta here right quick sonny, 'cause if I have to pull a 'Hey, Rube,' you boys will be in more trouble than you ever thought was possible." — Terry Southern, *Texas Summer*, p. 110, 1991

HFH

used as a jaded abbreviation of a jaded "ho-fucking-hum" *US, 1990*
- "What is this?" she said, finally. "An H.F.H. good-bye?" — Joseph Wambaugh, *The Golden Orange*, p. 153, 1990

HHOJ; HHOK

used in computer message shorthand to mean "*ha-ha only joking*" or "*ha-ha only kidding*" *US, 1991*
- — Eric S. Raymond, *The New Hacker's Dictionary*, p. 342, 1991

hi-ball *noun*

a central nervous system stimulant, especially dextroamphetamine (trade name Dexamyl™) *US, 1971*
- — Eugene Landy, *The Underground Dictionary*, p. 65, 1971

hiccup *verb*

in computing when transferring data, to inadvertently skip some data or send some data twice *US, 1995*
- — Christian Crumlish, *The Internet Dictionary*, p. 88, 1995

hick *noun*

an unsophisticated, simple person from the far rural reaches *UK, 1565*
A familiar form of "Richard." Now chiefly US use.
- He decided that they'd have to try and get a quick lead over these hicks. — James T. Farrell, *Tournament Star*, p. 69, 1946
- It's about a hick ... a hick like you, if you please. — Robert Rossen, *All the King's Men*, 1949
- If someone had hung a sign, "HICK," around my neck, I couldn't have looked much more obvious. — Malcolm X and Alex Haley, *The Autobiography of Malcolm X*, p. 34, 1964

- JOE: She used to be a regular on Hee-Haw. You know that country show with all those fuckin' hicks. — *Reservoir Dogs*, 1992

Hickalulu *nickname*

Hickam Field, Honolulu *US, 1967*
- Hickam Field in Honolulu is Hickalulu. — Elaine Shepard, *The Doom Pussy*, p. 110, 1967

hickey *noun*

1 a bruise caused by a suction kiss *US, 1942*
- — Donald Webster Cory and John P. LeRoy, *The Homosexual and His Society*, p. 264, 1963: "A lexicon of homosexual slang"
- My best girl friend was always showing off the hickeys on her stomach. — Jefferson Poland and Valerie Alison, *The Records of the San Francisco Sexual Freedom League*, p. 112, 1971
- Hickeys. They were fun to give but a curse to receive [...] And if my parents asked what the hell that was, the answer was always that the faithful curling iron burned me (again). — Editors of Ben is Dead, *Retrohell*, p. 95, 1997

2 in pool, a rule infraction *US, 1992*
- — Mike Shamos, *The Illustrated Encyclopedia of Billiards*, p. 115, 1993

Hicksville *noun*

any remote small town *US, 1942*
- Massachusetts, like Myron's home state of New Jersey, can quickly turn from big city to full-fledged town to hicksville. — Harlan Coben, *The Final Detail*, p. 330, 1999

hicky *adjective*

rural, unsophisticated, rustic *US, 1960*
- "May be hicky," I confessed, "coming from a small town'n stuff but I'm not really." — Glendon Swarthout, *Where the Boys Are*, p. 105, 1960
- [H]e felt genuinely sorry about taking up the valuable time of worthy people with his Southern hicky trash. — Jeffrey Golden, *Watermelon Summer*, p. 106, 1971

hiddy *adjective*

1 drunk *US, 1989*
- — Pamela Munro, *U.C.L.A. Slang*, p. 49, 1989

2 hideous *US, 1990*
- — *Surfing*, p. 43, 14th March 1990

hide *noun*

1 the human skin *UK, 1607*
- [Y]ou'll never toss and turn again in a Bowery scratchpad, digging the lice and chinches out of your hide. — Mezz Mezzrow, *Really the Blues*, p. 317, 1946

2 a wallet *US, 1932*
- So he hands over his hide, better'n a hundred in it, and I tell him some door to go knock on and splits. — Malcolm Braly, *On the Yard*, p. 25, 1967
- There's the cool old shot at the busy bus stop / Scanning on a hide. — Dennis Wepman et al., *The Life*, p. 162, 1976

3 a horse *US, 1934*
- — *American Speech*, p. 270, December 1958: "Ranching terms from Eastern Washington"

hide *verb*

▸ **hide the salami**

to have sex *US, 1983*
- Then Candy Kane goes solo as she takes on a hunky study who seems gratefully awestruck at the abundance of flesh Candy presents, and who shows his gratitude by promptly hiding the salami deep inside Candy's spectacular cleavage. — *Adult Video*, p. 54, August/September 1986
- Lets play some serious hide the salami. — Seth Morgan, *Homeboy*, p. 156, 1990
- Now that I'm dating but not yet playing hide-the-salami, I wanted to further my adult education[.] — Anka Radakovich, *The Wild Girls Club*, p. 110, 1994
- We whipped the doors open and came face-to-face with Ronald DeChooch playing hide-the-salami with the clerical help. — Janet Evanovich, *Seven Up*, p. 212, 2001

hideaway *noun*

a pocket *US, 1945*
- — Lou Shelly, *Hepcats Jive Dictionary*, p. 12, 1945
- — Clarence Major, *Dictionary of Afro-American Slang*, p. 65, 1970

hideout gun *noun*

a small gun hidden for emergency use *US, 1969*

- Not the .38s or .44s that they'd have been carrying if they were working, but little hideout guns. — Juan Carmel Cosmes, *Memoir of a Whoremaster*, p. 65, 1969
- "Keep him in your purse alongside the hideout gun." — Joseph Wambaugh, *Hollywood Station*, p. 153, 2006

hide-the-baloney *noun*
sexual intercourse *US, 1973*

- Man, wouldn't I love to play hide the baloney with that. — Charles Whited, *Chiodo*, p. 224, 1973

hide-the-weenie *noun*
sexual intercourse *US, 1968*

- He must have flipped because he has a heart-to-heart with his mother about how he's been playing hide-the-weenie with his tutor. — Angelo d'Arcangelo, *The Homosexual Handbook*, p. 230, 1968

hidey hole *noun*
a place for hiding objects *US, 1851*

- "Had the driver pull him into his hidey hole and shot him in the head." — Mickey Spillane, *The Snake*, pp. 157–158, 1964
- But the hidey-hole Bill had built was in the smaller bedroom. — Mary Janice Davidson, *Undead and Unwed*, p. 276, 2004

high *noun*
1 the sensation produced by consuming drugs or alcohol *US, 1944*

- Not a whiskey high, I could tell it was something else. — Malcolm X and Alex Haley, *The Autobiography of Malcolm X*, p. 129, 1964
- I take the stuff because I did the high, that's all. — James Mills, *The Panic in Needle Park*, p. 102, 1966
- My high was on full blast and I stretched out in the back seat and studied the passing scenes. — Piri Thomas, *Down These Mean Streets*, p. 231, 1967
- The first high is always the best high. After that, you're just trying to get back to the original feeling. — Chris Rock, *Rock This!*, p. 61, 1997

2 a sense of exhilaration, unrelated to drugs *US, 1970*

- My acceptance was an incredible high not only for me but for the whole Frisco Chapter. — Jamie Mandelkau, *Buttons*, p. 80, 1971
- The high I get at 2001, just dancing, not just being the best. I wanta get, have, that high someplace else in my life, ya know what I mean. — *Saturday Night Fever*, 1977

High *noun*
Miller High Life™ beer *US, 1967*

- *American Speech*, p. 62, February 1967: "Soda-fountain, restaurant and tavern calls"

high *adjective*
under the influence of a drug, especially marijuana *US, 1931*

- Sure, man, that cat's real high on tea! Look at those big, starin' eyes. Get that! — John Clellon Holmes, *Go*, p. 100, 1952
- We get some frantic kicks out of that wheel when we're high. — William Burroughs, *Junkie*, p. 28, 1953
- Jumpsteady always keyed himself up high on dope when he worked. — Malcolm X and Alex Haley, *The Autobiography of Malcolm X*, p. 90, 1964
- My cousin Kendall from Indiana, he got high once and you know, he started eating like really weird foods. — *The Breakfast Club*, 1985

high and light *adjective*
pleasantly drug-intoxicated *US, 1952*

- *American Speech*, p. 26, February 1952: "Teen-age hophead jargon"

high and tight *noun*
a man's haircut in which the sides of the head are shaved and a quarter-inch of hair is left on top *US, 1988*
A military term for a military haircut.

- Hans Halberstadt, *Airborne*, p. 130, 1988: "Abridged Dictionary of Airborne Terms"
- After that, they'd been checked into a recruit barracks, issued uniforms, and herded through a thirty-second haircut that left each recruit "high and tight." — Ian Douglas, *Luna Marine*, p. 127, 1990

high as a kite *adjective*
very drunk or drug-intoxicated *US, 1939*

- Percy was higher than a kite. — Charles Raven, *Underworld Nights*, p. 85, 1956
- They get high as a kite on this dangerous stuff. — Harry J. Anslinger, *The Murderers*, p. 231, 1961

high-ass *adjective*
haughty; arrogant *US, 1931*

- Hey Odessa, ain't you never comin' back an see us no more? You gone highass? — Robert Gover, *JC Saves*, p. 116, 1968

highball *noun*
1 a salute *US, 1958*

- A salute to a superior officer is a slam, or a highball. — *New York Times*, p. 34, 20th October 1958

2 a glass of milk *US, 1946*

- *American Speech*, p. 88, April 1946: "The language of West Coast culinary workers"

highball *verb*
1 to travel fast *US, 1912*

- As they highballed it southbound without lights or siren, Lloyd told the cops he was flagged for the October class at the academy[.] — James Ellroy, *Blood on the Moon*, p. 32, 1984

2 to see *US, 1965*
Probably playing on EYEBALL.

- I didn't know that old squarejohn highballed the trick and I continued on the play. — Bruce Jackson, *Get Your Ass in the Water and Swim Like Me*, p. 85, 1965

high beams *noun*
1 erect nipples on a woman's breasts seen through a garment *US, 1986*

- Connie Eble (Editor), *UNC-CH Campus Slang*, p. 5, Fall 1986
- The dramatic tension of the film derives from the constant threat of the male divers becoming so distracted by the Bisset high beams that they unwittingly take several deep breaths of saltwater and die. — Mr. Skin, *Mr. Skin's Skincyclopedia*, p. 66, 2005

2 the wide open eyes of a person under the influence of crack cocaine *US, 1994*

- US Department of Justice, *Street Terms*, October 1994

high cap *verb*
to brag, to banter, to gossip *US, 1990*

- Charles Shafer, *Folk Speech in Texas Prisons*, p. 206, 1990

high diver *noun*
a person who enjoys or excels at performing oral sex on women *US, 1981*
A construction built on the image of going down.

- *Male Swinger Number 3*, p. 46, 1981: "The complete gay dictionary"

high drag *noun*
elaborate female clothing worn by a man *US, 1963*

- I went to this straight party in High Drag (and I mean High, honey—gown, stockings, ostrich plumes in my flaming hair)[.] — John Rechy, *City of Night*, p. 103, 1963
- Guy Strait, *The Lavender Lexicon*, 1st June 1964

highfalutin; hifalutin *adjective*
absurdly pompous, snobbish *US, 1839*
Probably an elaboration of "high-flown" or similar; "highfaluting" (the "g" is optional) was originally hyphenated which lends strength to this etymology. Yiddish *hifelufelem* (ostentatious, self-glorifying) is also possible.

- [S]ome of his I.W.W. constituents would probably kick over the traces if they saw the highfalutin' fillies he runs with in Washington. — Jack Lait and Lee Mortimer, *Washington Confidential*, p. 87, 1951
- He wondered if they understood any of the high-falutin' language therein[.] — Evan Hunter, *The Blackboard Jungle*, p. 86, 1954
- Her old man was one of those highfalutin Nigger doctors. — Iceberg Slim (Robert Beck), *Trick Baby*, p. 102, 1969

high five *noun*
1 a greeting or sign of approval accomplished by slapping open palms with arms extended above head-level *US, 1980*
The greeting and term originated in sport but quickly spread.

- Aguirre gave him a high five that came straight from his toes, then shuffled to the bench, grabbed Coach Ray Meyer and bearhugged him[.] — *Washington Post*, p. D11, 28th December 1980
- The Montrealers exchanged "high fives," "low fives" and "sidearm fives." — *Washington Post*, p. D1, 15th September 1980
- How does a blonde do a high five? — *Sleepless in Seattle*, 1993

2 HIV *US, 2003*
A semantic pun based the Roman numeral five.

- *Oprah Winfrey Show*, 2nd October 2003

high five *verb*
to raise your open hand above your head and slap it against the open hand of someone else *US, 1981*

- The woof chorus went through the roof, everybody high-fiving, bopping in glee. — Richard Price, *Clockers*, p. 203, 1992
- The fielders and two-eighths of the ground high-fived and jigged merrily. — Diran Abedayo, *My Once Upon A Time*, p. 224, 2000

high fur *noun*
the refueling of a hovering helicopter *US, 1991*
- This technique is known as "Helicopter In-Flight Refueling" or, HIFR, pronounced "High-fur." — Gerry Carroll, *North S*A*R*, p. 76, 1991

high-grade *verb*
to steal in small increments *US, 1904*
- There are always people who high-grade the cashews from bowls of mixed nuts. — Stuart Pimm, *The World According to Pimm*, p. 99, 2001

high-grader *noun*
a person who steals in small increments *US, 1904*
- The high-graders who did not get them are now demanding the even more expensive Macadamia nuts. — Stuart Pimm, *The World According to Pimm*, p. 99, 2001

high hard one *noun*
forceful sex *US, 1986*
- Here she is at her quintessential best, laying virtually still for sex scene after sex scene, even as she gives blow-jobs, gets her cunt swabbed, or lifts her legs for the high hard one. — *Adult Video*, p. 72, August/September 1986
- What I want you to do is close your eyes and remember, remember the last time ol' Mickey gave you the high hard one. — *Natural Born Killers*, 1994

high-hat; high-hatted *adjective*
snobbish, superior, supercilious *US, 1924*
- [T]he local pig sheriff stormed in and got all high hatted and hotted up about us being there. — Jamie Mandelkau, *Buttons*, p. 84, 1971

high-heel boy *noun*
a paratrooper *US, 1948*
- — *American Speech*, p. 319, October/December 1948: "Slang of the American paratrooper"

high holy *noun*
in the usage of counterculturalists associated with the Rainbow Nation gatherings, an older, experienced member of the counterculture *US, 1997*
Often used with a degree of irony and lack of reverence.
- — Jim Crotty, *How to Talk American*, p. 289, 1997

high horse *noun*
a position of arrogant superiority *US, 1947*
- But the thing about California is this: everybody is on their high horse trying to imitate Eastern high society[.] — Jack Kerouac, *Letter to Caroline Kerouac Blake*, p. 131, 25th September 1947

high-jive *verb*
to tease, to taunt, to belittle *US, 1938*
- Dinch, they'll highjive you till you get hooked with them. — George Mandel, *Flee the Angry Strangers*, p. 26, 1952

highlighter *noun*
a political leader or spokesman among prisoners *US, 1976*
- — John R. Armore and Joseph D. Wolfe, *Dictionary of Desperation*, p. 33, 1976

highly *adverb*
used as an intensifier with an attitude *US, 1991*
- As in: highly nonoptional, the worst possible way to do something; highly nontrivial, either impossible or requiring a major research project; highly nonlinear, completely erratic and unpredictable[.] — Eric S. Raymond, *The New Hacker's Dictionary*, p. 200, 1991

highly illogical *adjective*
illogical *US, 1968*
A signature line of the Vulcan Mr. Spock on the first incarnation of *Star Trek* (NBC, 1966–69). Repeated with referential humor.

high maintenance *adjective*
(used of a person) requiring a great deal of attention and/or money; needy *US, 1989*
- There are two kinds of women: high maintenance and low maintenance. — *When Harry Met Sally*, 1989
- — Connie Eble (Editor), *UNC-CH Campus Slang*, p. 3, Fall 1990

- I have a high-maintenance selling painter coming through. — *As Good As It Gets*, 1997
- "And Jim's a handful. High-maintenance, they all say. It's like marriage, life with him." — Ethan Morden, *How's Your Romance?*, p. 237, 2005

high noon *noun*
in craps, a roll of twelve *US, 1982*
- — Thomas L. Clark, *The Dictionary of Gambling and Gaming*, p. 99, 1987

high-nose *verb*
to snub; to ignore *US, 1954*
- You know I wouldn't high-nose you, Allie. — Jim Thompson, *Roughneck*, p. 116, 1954

high-octane *adjective*
powerful *US, 1956*
- "Any time he mentions the Navy, there's a ballast tank full of high-octane publicity." — William Brinkley, *Don't Go Near the Water*, p. 11, 1956

high off the hog *adverb*
prosperously *US, 1970*
- I love the goddam navy. I get three squares a day, a pad to lie down on, roof over my head, tuxedo to wear. We're living high off the hog. — Darryl Ponicsan, *The Last Detail*, p. 33, 1970
- I was livin' high off the hog, so it didn't really matter. — Odie Hawkins, *Ghetto Sketches*, p. 91, 1972

high play *noun*
showy spending designed to impress *US, 1972*
- — Bruce Jackson, *Outside the Law*, p. 58, 1972: "Glossary"

high pockets *noun*
the stature of a tall, thin man *US, 1912*
- — Jerry Robertson, *Oil Slanguage*, p. 66, 1954

high puller *noun*
a devoted player of casino slot machines, especially those with higher bets and higher payouts *US, 1985*
A play on the term **HIGH ROLLER**.
- The slot players, the "high pullers" at the dollar machines; only the crap shooters animated. — Elmore Leonard, *Glitz*, p. 228, 1985

high-riders *noun*
pants worn above the waist *US, 1975*
- — Carl J. Banks Jr., *Banks Dictionary of the Black Ghetto Language*, 1975

highroll *verb*
to spend freely and to live fast *US, 1975*
- When you're highrollin' in the bread you're bound to be out there jumpin' come midnight every night. — Edwin Torres, *Carlito's Way*, p. 30, 1975

high roller *noun*
1 a drug dealer *US, 1991*
- "I ain't no high roller, but I make money for myself." — Leon Bing, *Do or Die*, p. 33, 1991
- Back in 1980, unlike today, there were no "high rollers," or "ballers," substantially anchored in any particular 'hood[.] — Sanyika Shakur, *Monster*, p. 72, 1993

2 a gambler who makes large bets and spends freely *US, 1881*
- And when Sinatra opened in Vegas, the high rollers gathered, along with the not so high rollers who enjoyed rubbing elbows with the rich. — Donald Goines, *Kenyatta's Last Hit*, p. 204, 1975
- [T]op-hatting his way around race meetings, sipping fine wines with the high rollers. — Diran Abedayo, *My Once Upon A Time*, p. 33, 2000

3 in television and movie-making, a large, tall, three-legged light stand *US, 1990*
- — Ralph S. Singleton, *Filmmaker's Dictionary*, p. 81, 1990

highs *noun*
in pool, the striped balls numbered 9 to 15 *US, 1990*
- — Steve Rushin, *Pool Cool*, p. 15, 1990

high-school Harriet *noun*
a high-school girl who is dating a college boy *US, 1966*
- — *Current Slang*, p. 3, Fall 1966
- It was like High School Harriet stuff, and here I am—twenty-six years old. — Herb Michelson, *Sportin' Ladies*, p. 153, 1975

high-school Harry *noun*
an immature college male; a typical high-school student *US, 1959*

- — *Time Magazine*, p. 46, 24th August 1959
- — Collin Baker et al., *College Undergraduate Slang Study Conducted at Brown University*, p. 137, 1968

high-school horse *noun*

in horse racing, a racehorse that seems to win only when the odds are very high *US, 1951*

Based on the humorous suggestion that the horse is so smart it can read the posted odds.

- — David W. Maurer, *Argot of the Racetrack*, p. 35, 1951

high shots *noun*

in the illegal production of alcohol, liquor that exceeds 100 proof *US, 1974*

- — David W. Maurer, *Kentucky Moonshine*, p. 119, 1974

high side *noun*

1 the outside of a curve in a road *US, 1966*

- We've all been over the high side, baby. You know what that is? It's when your bike stars sliding when you steam into a curve at seventy or eighty. — Hunter S. Thompson, *Hell's Angels*, p. 98, 1966

2 in craps, the numbers over 7 *US, 1950*

- — *The Annals of the American Academy of Political and Social Sciences*, p. 126, May 1950

high-side *verb*

to show off *US, 1965*

- So call yourself lucky and knock off the highsiding. — Malcolm Braly, *On the Yard*, p. 249, 1967
- They walking in fours and kicking in doors; dropping Reds and busting heads; drinking wine and committing crime, shooting and looting; high-siding and low-riding[.] — Eldridge Cleaver, *Soul on Ice*, p. 27, 1968
- A boss player may occasionally indulge in stylin' and high sidin' matches as a Black cultural ritual for the fun of it[.] — Christina and Richard Milner, *Black Players*, p. 105, 1972
- — Mark S. Fleisher, *Beggars & Thieves*, p. 289, 1995: "Glossary"

high speed, low drag *adjective*

competent, reliable, dependable *US, 1991*

Vietnam war usage.

- The "Three" is likely to be the "high-speed, low-drag" officer destined for great things. — Hans Halberstadt, *US Marine Corps*, p. 53, 1993

high sphincter tone *noun*

said of a person with a high degree of inhibition and a conservative nature *US, 1994*

- — Sally Williams, *"Strong" Words*, p. 146, 1994

hightail *verb*

to move very quickly *US, 1919*

Almost always used with "it."

- [S]uddenly his pet ferret rushed out and bit an elegant teacup queer on the ankle and everybody hightailed it out the door[.] — Jack Kerouac, *On the Road*, p. 144, 1957
- So I got back in the car and hightailed it out of Cheyenne[.] — Clancy Sigal, *Going Away*, p. 169, 1961
- Next he hightails to Angie's to apologize for being pigheaded last night. — Lester Bangs, *Psychotic Reactions and Carburetor Dung*, p. 125, 1973
- We'll be putting all this junk on a truck Saturday mornin', hightailin' it to the land of saddidy niggers. — Odie Hawkins, *The Busting Out of an Ordinary Man*, p. 144, 1985

high tea *noun*

a social gathering of male homosexuals *US, 1981*

- — *Male Swinger Number 3*, p. 46, 1981: "The complete gay dictionary"

high-test *adjective*

excellent, powerful *US, 1995*

- Taste #16 felt high-octane. Jack's smile was high-test. — James Ellroy, *American Tabloid*, p. 389, 1995

high tide *noun*

the bleed period of the menstrual cycle *US, 1970*

- — *Current Slang*, p. 8, Winter 1970
- Cause the moon is full and look out baby / I'm at high tide [...] I've got a hundred and five fever / and it's high tide — Laurie Anderson, *Beautiful Red Dress*, 1989

high warble *adjective*

angry, especially without justification *US, 1986*

Naval aviator usage.

- — *United States Naval Institute Proceedings*, p. 108, October 1986

high-waters; high-water pants *noun*

long pants that are too short or short pants that are too long *US, 1902*

- — *Current Slang*, p. 6, Winter 1971
- — Douglas Simonson, *Pidgin to da Max: Hana Hou*, 1982
- If a guy came to school in high-water pants, they joined him hard. — Nathan McCall, *Makes Me Wanna Holler*, p. 23, 1994

highway salute *noun*

a gesture with the middle finger meaning "fuck you" *US, 1977*

- — Bill Davis, *Jawjacking*, p. 51, 1977

highway surfer *noun*

a person who adopts the mannerisms of surfers, buys the equipment, but never seems to get out of the car into the water *US, 1963*

- — *Paradise of the Pacific*, p. 27, October 1963
- — John Severson, *Modern Surfing Around the World*, p. 171, 1964

high, wide and handsome; high, wide and fancy *adjective*

excellent; first-rate *US, 1953*

The title of a 1937 musical/romance film starring James Burke.

- "I'm stepping out, high, wide and fancy with something better than Clara Bow," Phil said. — James T. Farrell, *Saturday Night*, p. 21, 1947
- Jake married her after he left here and moved to New York—after he was riding high, wide and handsome. — Jim Thompson, *Savage Night*, p. 4, 1953
- We were going high and wide and handsome over on 6th Street. — Herbert Huncke, *Guilty of Everything*, p. 154, 1990

high yellow; high yaller; high yella *noun*

a light-skinned black person, especially female; a Creole; a mulatto *US, 1923*

"Objectionable when referring to lighter-colored black persons" according to *Dictionary of Cautionary Words and Phrases*, 1989.

- The high yellow and the tall coal black next to me were giving me nasty looks[.] — Mickey Spillane, *I, The Jury*, p. 43, 1947
- On'y hiyellas leff is Flow an Francine, so I spect this mothah gonna go up wiff Flow. — Robert Gover, *One Hundred Dollar Misunderstanding*, p. 19, 1961

high yellow; high yaller; high yella *adjective*

light-skinned *US, 1958*

- A high-yella woman, with a knife scar going along the whole length of her cheek and trying to repeat itself further down on her chin, her skirt hiked up[.] — Willard Motley, *Let No Man Write My Epitaph*, p. 90, 1958
- He couldn't stay away from the high-yellow whores with their big asses and bitch-dog sexual antics. — Iceberg Slim (Robert Beck), *Pimp*, 1969
- [H]e was twenty years older than Mrs. Edwards and should have known better than to marry a high-yaller hot-blooded Creole from New Orleans. — Louise Meriwether, *Daddy Was a Number Runner*, p. 56, 1970
- [T]heir daughter, Charlotte, is high yella, it puzzles me[.] — Clarence Major, *All-Night Visitors*, p. 18, 1998

hijo de la chingada *noun*

son of a fucked woman *US, 1974*

Border Spanish used in English conversation by Mexican-Americans; highly insulting.

- — Dagoberto Fuentes and Jose Lopez, *Barrio Language Dictionary*, p. 75, 1974

hike *verb*

to insult in a competitive, quasi-friendly spirit, especially by reference to your opponent's family *US, 2000*

- There are many different terms for playing the dozens, including "bagging, capping, cracking, dissing, hiking, joning, ranking, ribbing, serving, signifying, slipping, sounding and snapping." — James Haskins, *The Story of Hip-Hop*, p. 54, 2000

hill *noun*

▸ **go over the hill**

to desert military duty; to escape from prison *US, 1912*

- "I'm going over the hill. I've got it all figured out." — Thomas Heggen, *Mister Roberts*, p. 186, 1946
- We had hung out together for a couple of days before and he told me he was over the hill from some camp down South somewhere

and wasn't going back. — Billie Holiday with William Dufty, *Lady Sings the Blues*, p. 154, 1956

- You know, a couple of years ago, and this was in Norfolk too, a lieutenant supply officer lifted six thou and went over the hill. — Darryl Ponicsan, *The Last Detail*, p. 30, 1970

- "But if he was against the Marine Corps why didn't he do something about it? Like refuse an order. Or go over the hill." — Robert Stone, *Dog Soldiers*, p. 207, 1974

▶ **on the hill**
in pool, needing only one more score to win *US, 1993*
- — Mike Shamos, *The Illustrated Encyclopedia of Billiards*, p. 161, 1993

▶ **over the hill**
past your prime *US, 1950*
- At least it won't break my heart, Alexander Monet turning out to be an over-the-hill asshole. — Elmore Leonard, *Be Cool*, p. 311, 1999

hillbilly armor *noun*
improvised defensive armor fashioned by US troops in Iraq *US, 2004*
Underfunding and lack of body and vehicle armor led to widespread improvization by US ground forces in Iraq.
- Millican only briefly spoke of the "horrible sand," unrelenting heat, "hillbilly armor" they initially wore and camel spiders as big as a Frisbee. — *Bismarck Tribune*, p. 1A, 30th August 2004

hillbilly craps *noun*
craps played on the sidewalk or otherwise as a private game *US, 1950*
- — *The Annals of the American Academy of Political and Social Sciences*, p. 126, May 1950

hillbilly hell *noun*
used as an embellished, intensified "hell" *US, 1970*
- He'll have a hillbilly hell of a time ever making captain. — Darryl Ponicsan, *The Last Detail*, p. 146, 1970

hillbilly heroin *noun*
the synthetic opiate oxycodone used recreationally *US, 2001*
When dissolved in water and injected, or crushed and inhaled, it has a similar effect to heroin. The drug's popularity in the rural Appalachian Mountains region led to the "hillbilly" reference. It came to the forefront of the American national consciousness in late 2003 when radio entertainer Rush Limbaugh was reported to be addicted to OxyContin™.
- Many in Appalachia call OxyContin "Hillbilly heroin." Its abuse may not have started in the mountains, but it exploded in Appalachia. — *The Houston Chronicle*, 1st July 2001

- A few months ago, OxyContin abuse was considered a regional problem and confined to areas from the nation's population centers. — *The New York Times Magazine*, p. 35, 29th July 2001

- In one missive, Limbaugh pushed Cline to get more "little blues"—code for OxyContin, the powerful narcotic nicknamed hillbilly heroin, she said. — *(New York) Daily News*, 2nd October 2003

hill game *noun*
in pool, a situation where either player can win with a single pocket *US, 1993*
- — Mike Shamos, *The Illustrated Encyclopedia of Billiards*, p. 117, 1993

hill humper *noun*
an infantry soldier *US, 1967*
- In Vietnam, he goes by an assortment of names—the Grunt, Boonie Rat, Line Dog, Ground Pounder, Hill Humper, or Jarhead. — David Reed, *Up Front in Vietnam*, p. 3, 1967

him *noun*
heroin *US, 1969*
- — Richard Lingeman, *Drugs from A to Z*, p. 109, 1969

himbo *noun*
a man objectified by his good looks and presumed lack of intellectual qualities; a man who trades on this image; a gigolo *US, 1988*
Plays on contemporary use of **BIMBO** (a beautiful and available young woman—if you are a rich older man).
- Sex was commonplace, from a Melanie Griffith look-alike stuffed into her gown like salami in spandex to the macho himbo who strutted the Croisette wearing a 16-foot python like a stole around his shoulders and neck. — *Washington Post*, p. F1, 29th May 1988

- Musclebound hunks were transformed into the newest sex symbol archetype; the himbo. — Steven Daly and Nathaniel Wice, *alt.culture*, p. 104, 1995

Hinckley; Hinkley *noun*
phencyclidine, the recreational drug known as PCP or angel dust *US, 1984*
- This summer, one brand of PCP is available as "Hinckley" (referring to John W. Hinckley Jr., who shot President Reagan) or "the Keys to St. E's"—both references to the "craziness" induced by the drug. — *Washington Post*, p. B1, 29th July 1984

- — US Department of Justice *Street Terms*, October 1994

hincty *adjective*
conceited, vain, arrogant *US, 1924*
- I had to cut loose some way, to turn my back once and for all on that hincty, killjoy world of my sister's and move over to Bessie Smith's world body and soul. — Mezz Mezzrow, *Really the Blues*, p. 54, 1946

- Handsome queer boys who had come to Hollywood to be cowboys walked around, wetting their eyebrows with hincty fingertip. — Jack Kerouac, *On the Road*, p. 86, 1957

- Obviously these people come from Tucson or Albuquerque or one of those hincty adobe towns. — Tom Wolfe, *The Pump House Gang*, p. 15, 1968

- "But we all in the hands of white men and I know some very hincty black cats I wouldn't trust, neither." — James Baldwin, *If Beale Street Could Talk*, p. 70, 1974

hind tit *noun*
▶ **on the hind tit; suck the hind tit**
to be last in order of standing *US, 1940*
- Way the college business is going these days, wherever I went I'd be hind tit to a bunch of deans. — Max Shulman, *Anyone Got a Match?*, p. 65, 1964

- He's got another year before he goes to bat again, and therefore naturally he is sucking every minority and majority hind tit he can find. — George V. Higgins, *The Rat on Fire*, p. 5, 1981

- I guess Jerry Lee'd be suckin' hind tit in a Van Cliburn competition, but I like his playin' just fine. — Ken Weaver, *Texas Crude*, p. 129, 1984

- Purdue and Ray, twenty-five years younger than the other two cronies, were still around. Still sucking hind tit. — Robert Campbell, *Juice*, p. 3, 1988

hiney; heiny; heinie *noun*
the buttocks *US, 1921*
- Ma car is fast, my teeth're shiney / I tell all the girls they can kiss my heinie[.] — Frank Zappa, *Bobby Brown Goes Down*, 1979

- He turned me over so's I couldn't [resist], got my heinie up in the air and my face pressed down in the bedspread. — Elmore Leonard, *Freaky Deaky*, p. 81, 1988

- ROBIN: He does have a nice heiny. JANE: Heiny? What is he, two years old? He has a nice heiny? — *Boys on the Side*, 1995

- Heaping helpings of heinie as Samantha has her ass photographed from about 19 different angles. — Mr. Skin, *Mr. Skin's Skincyclopedia*, p. 188, 2005

hinge *noun*
the elbow *US, 1945*
- — Lou Shelly, *Hepcats Jive Dictionary*, p. 12, 1945

hinked up *adjective*
suspicious, afraid *US, 2000*
- You seem a little hinked up. — *Gone in 60 Seconds*, 2000

- The passenger, a 23-year-old citizen of Yemen, was "acting very strangely, and the flight attendants got real hinked up," said FBI Agent LaRae Quy. — *San Francisco Chronicle*, p. B4, 4th August 2004

hinky *adjective*
1 nervous, anxious *US, 1956*
- They make you hinky. What's their secret? You always wonder. — Joseph Wambaugh, *The New Centurions*, p. 127, 1970

- My aide thought he looked hinky and coup-wise, so he kept an eye on him. — James Ellroy, *Because the Night*, p. 484, 1984

- I think it's too hinky for a crackpot. — Carl Hiaasen, *Tourist Season*, p. 54, 1986

- [A]round the time Carlisle got hinky, J.C. told Dudley that Stemmons was acting crazy[.] — James Ellroy, *White Jazz*, p. 304, 1992

2 suspicious *US, 1968*
- I was always hinky about a couple of things. I never sold to sexy-looking prostitutes, for example. — Phil Hirsch, *Hooked*, p. 19, 1968

• My father later told me he first suspected something was hinky with my mom when he found a book in bag she packed for a trip with her new friend she'd moved into my vacated room. — David Henry Sterry, *Chicken*, p. 16, 2002

hinky-dee *noun*

a form of comedic song *US, 1949*

• In his dressing room, Byrnie, who was trouping with his old man, Eddie Foy, and all his six brothers, jotted down what in trouper's parlance is called a "hinky dee"—one short verse and many short choruses, each with a comedy punch-lline. — *San Francisco Call-Bulletin*, p. 15, 18th August 1949

hinky-dinky *adjective*

small-time, second class, outmoded *US, 1967*

A cousin of the more famous **RINKY-DINK**.

• What are we doing sitting here boiling our balls off for some hinky-dinky little bootleg tape operation? — Robert Campbell, *Juice*, p. 5, 1988

hip *noun*

1 a member of the 1960s counterculture *US, 1967*

• The burned hips leave and Teddybear turns back to lecture. — Nicholas Von Hoffman, *We Are The People Our Parents Warned Us Against*, p. 45, 1967

• Why is the typical middleclass person hostile to hips? — *The San Francisco Oracle*, 1967

• Some are owned by three or four hips who've pooled their money. — Arthur Blessitt, *Turned On to Jesus*, pp. 119–120, 1971

2 a heroin addict *US, 1953*

• Ike explained to me that the Mexican government issued permits to hips allowing them a definite quantity of morphine per month at wholesale prices. — William Burroughs, *Junkie*, p. 103, 1953

hip *verb*

1 to explain, to bring up to date, to inform *US, 1932*

• Al Sublette is the boy who could hip you on all the latest, especially if he has enuf money to stock his phone with records. — Jack Kerouac, *Letter to Philip Whalen*, p. 548, 7th February 1956

• He called in his flunkies and hipped 'em real good[.] — Dan Burley, *Diggeth Thou?*, p. 25, 1959

• People depend on the radio to hip them to the whole cultural scene. — John Sinclair, *Guitar Army*, p. 133, 1972

• How about if I come with you and you hip me? — Bobby Seale, *A Lonely Rage*, p. 65, 1978

2 to figure out, to become aware *US, 1975*

• Trouble is too many guys get wasted before they hip up. Shame on them. — Edwin Torres, *Carlito's Way*, p. 77, 1975

▸ **hip your ship**

to let you know *US, 1953*

• — Lavada Durst, *The Jives of Dr. Hepcat*, p. 12, 1953

hip *adjective*

1 knowing, understanding *US, 1902*

• And these children threw around swear words I'd never heard before, even, and slang expressions that were just as new to me, such as stud and cat and chick and cool and hip. — Malcolm X and Alex Haley, *The Autobiography of Malcolm X*, p. 43, 1964

• The Diggers are hip to property. — *The Digger Papers*, p. 3, August 1968

• But the PLP's squeals grow weaker and weaker as the people are now hip to their slimy snakelike TACTICS. — *The Black Panther*, p. 9, 2nd August 1969

• Parents are generally pretty hip to the fever scams. — *Ferris Bueller's Day Off*, 1986

• ALABAMA: That's a long time. CLARENCE: I'm hip. — *True Romance*, 1993

2 in style, fashionable, admired *US, 1944*

• It was a world of dingy backstairs "pads," Times Square cafeterias, bebop joints, night-long wanderings, meetings on street corners, hitchhiking, a myriad of "hip" bars all over the city, and the streets themselves. — John Clellon Holmes, *Go*, p. 37, 1952

• One is Hip or one is Square (the alternative which each new generation coming into American life is beginning to feel), one is a rebel or one conforms[.] — Norman Mailer, *Advertisements for Myself*, p. 339, 1957

• Why do you come here? Because it's hip to come on as if jazz meant something to you? — Nat Hentoff, *Jazz Country*, p. 97, 1965

• Well, everybody's saying/ that hell's the hippest way to go/ Well I don't think so[.] — Joni Mitchell, *Blue*, 1971

• "I'm not hip," he [Meatloaf] gloats, "and I'm glad. Because I hate hip. Hip doesn't last. I was never hip. It's not my style." — *Ask*, p. 53, 19th December 1981

• Now do you think she would prefer laidback Jim, or cool, hip Jim? — *American Pie*, 1999

▸ **hip to all happenings**

profoundly aware of the latest trends and happenings *US, 1964*

• I met chicks who were fine as May wine, and cats who were hip to all happenings. — Malcolm X and Alex Haley, *The Autobiography of Malcolm X*, p. 56, 1964

hip cat *noun*

a fan of jazz or swing music; a stylish and fashionable man *US, 1947*

• All the hip cats on the corner / They don't look so sharp no mo — Jimmy Witherspoon, *Skid Row Blues*,

• — Lavada Durst, *The Jives of Dr. Hepcat*, 1953

hip deep to a tall Indian *adjective*

used for describing a short person or tall pile *US, 1958*

• The area had had a terrible storm the night before and snow was hip deep to a tall Indian. — Richard Killblane, *Filthy Thirteen*, p. 200, 2003

hipe *verb*

in a cheating scheme in a game of cards, to restore a deck to its original position after a cheating move *US, 1962*

• — Frank Garcia, *Marked Cards and Loaded Dice*, p. 264, 1962

hip-flinger *noun*

a dancer in any type of overtly sexual dance *US, 1981*

• — Don Wilmeth, *The Language of American Popular Entertainment*, p. 131, 1981

hip-hop *noun*

a loose amalgamation of black urban youth culture, encompassing breakdancing, graffiti, DJing, and rap music *US, 1982*

Combining **HIP** (fashionable) and **HOP** (dance); like **ROCK 'N' ROLL** before it, "hip-hop" is an American phenomenon that has had a worldwide impact.

• I have watched him slip effortlessly from hip-hop street patter to a Brooks Brothers accent — Lawrence Block, *Even the Wicked*, p. 2, 1997

• Hip hop is nothing, however, if not resilient. While snubbed by high-brow critics, graffiti art found new followers in cutting-edge circles. — Nelson George, *Hip Hop America*, p. 12, 1998

• AFRIKA BAMBAATAA: On our flyers we used to say, "Come to the hip hop jam this, or the be bop jam that." [...] MICHAEL HOLMAN: Everyone picked it up from [Grandmaster Flash MC] Cowboy—"the hip, a hippy, a hippy hop, you don't stop." — Alex Ogg, *The Hip Hop Years*, p. 29, 1999

hip kick *noun*

the rear pocket on a pair of pants *US, 1981*

• — Don Wilmeth, *The Language of American Popular Entertainment*, p. 131, 1981

hipky-dripky *noun*

mischief *US, 1959*

• Now my mother and father gave each other a look because they knew that Mrs. Spencer was up to some hipky-dripky. — Max Shulman, *I was a Teen-Age Dwarf*, p. 62, 1959

hipped *adjective*

1 aware of, knowledgeable of *US, 1920*

• — Marcus Hanna Boulware, *Jive and Slang of Students in Negro Colleges*, 1947

2 carrying a gun *US, 1920*

• All you boys were hipped except you and Frank. What's the matter? Get scared after Mr. Bannon was knocked off? — Irving Shulman, *The Amboy Dukes*, p. 163, 1947

hipped to the tip *adjective*

aware of everything *US, 1947*

• — Marcus Hanna Boulware, *Jive and Slang of Students in Negro Colleges*, 1947

hippie; hippy *noun*

1 a follower of jazz and the jazz scene who strives to be hip *US, 1952*

• Lot of these hippies here is still in high school. — Ross Russell, *The Sound*, p. 86, 1961

• A few of the white men around Harlem, younger ones whom we called "hippies," acted more Negro than Neegroes. — Malcolm X and Alex Haley, *The Autobiography of Malcolm X*, p. 94, 1964

- The jazz musicians liked me. I was the only hippy around. — Lenny Bruce, *How to Talk Dirty and Influence People*, p. 93, 1965
- The young broad with the hippy jut in front of me turned her head back toward me. — Iceberg Slim (Robert Beck), *Trick Baby*, p. 86, 1969

2 a person with 1960s counterculture values or accessories *US, 1965*

- Five untroubled young "hippies," sprawled on floor mattresses and slouched in an armchair retrieved from a debris box, flipped cigarette ashes at a seashell in their Waller Street flat and pondered their next move. — *San Francisco Examiner*, p. 5, 5th September 1965: A New Paradise for Beatniks
- By 8:00 p.m. the crowd had swelled to about 200 children, hippies & just bystanders. — *The San Francisco Oracle*, 1966
- While the Fifth Estate and The Barb tend to focus on the hippie element, some of the new papers are looking beyond this substratum. — *New York Times*, p. 30, 1st August 1966
- But the hippies and teenieboppers on the Sunset Strip are not beatniks. — *Los Angeles Herald Examiner*, p. Second Front Page, 9th April 1967

hippie crack *noun*
nitrous oxide *US, 1992*
A substance of abuse favored by hippies and neo-hippies, seductive if not addictive.

- The gas, also referred to as "hippie crack," is sold at such parties — or "underground raves" — for \$43 to \$5 a balloonful, those familiar with the parties said. — *Los Angeles Times*, p. A1, 7th March 1992
- — Judi Sanders, *Da Bomb*, p. 8, 1997
- WHIPPITS: Otherwise known as "hippie crack" or "dessert crack." Either way, it's the best high a thirteen-year-old can get. — Suroosh Alvi et al., *The Vice Guide*, p. 20, 2002

hippie-flipping *noun*
using an inorganic drug immediately after an organic drug, especially ecstasy after psychotrobic mushrooms *US, 1997*

- Do any people out there in raver land have a preferred ratio of shrooms/X when they're hippie-flipping at a rave? — *alt.rave*, 24th March 1997
- I have no experience with the other drug combos you mention. Hippie flipping (MDMA + shrooms) is the most ecstatic thing that I have ever experienced. — *alt.drugs.mushrooms*, 4th April 2000

hippy *adjective*
1 full-hipped *US, 1963*

- He never stopped to wonder why Grace Anderson, the prettiest, the ripest, the hippiest young hussy on Lomax Street had consented henceforth to share her daily bread and nightly bed with the homeliest man in the city[.] — Clarence Cooper Jr., *Black*, p. 179, 1963

2 mentally dulled by years of imprisonment *US, 1950*

- — Hyman E. Goldin et al., *Dictionary of American Underworld Lingo*, p. 96, 1950

hippy-dippy *noun*
a hippy or hippie, in either sense *US, 1969*
Derogatory.

- A pair of hippy-dippys came into the car. — Iceberg Slim (Robert Beck), *Trick Baby*, p. 86, 1969

hippy-dippy *adjective*
used to describe the "peace and love" philosophy of the hippy movement *US, 1960*

- He couldn't stand the hippy-dippy voice any longer[.] — Clarence Cooper Jr., *The Scene*, p. 220, 1960
- In an out-of-style hippydippy strut he went into the bedroom. — Clarence Major, *All-Night Visitors*, p. 112, 1998
- Few came cooler and hung looser than hippie-dippy blonde sex kitty Jennifer Billingsley. — Mr. Skin, *Mr. Skin's Skincyclopedia*, p. 64, 2005

hippy hill *nickname*
a hill in Golden Gate Park, San Francisco, between the Stanyan Street entrance and Dinosaur Valley *US, 1967*

- There were about three hundred on Hippy Hill as the song from the Psychedelic Shop reverberated and the sitting people expelled their breath to make the slow sound of the god-centering ommmmmmm. — Nicholas Von Hoffman, *We Are The People Our Parents Warned Us Against*, p. 89, 1967

hippy witch *noun*
a girl who 30 years later still dresses in the styles popular with the late 1960s counterculture *US, 1997*

- — Vann Wesson, *Generation X Field Guide and Lexicon*, p. 90, 1997

hip-square *noun*
a conventional person who at moments adopts the drapings of the jazz lifestyle without fully embracing it *US, 1961*

- At each new knock on the door the callers would be screened to keep out such undesirables as squares, fuzz, and hip-squares. — Ross Russell, *The Sound*, p. 109, 1961
- Degrees of "squareness" are recognized by the Alderson inmates ranging from the inmate who is thought to be "so square that she's a cube" to the inmate designated as "hip square." — Rose Giallombardo, *Society of Women*, p. 115, 1966

hipster *noun*
a devotee of jazz and the jazz lifestyle *US, 1940*

- Well, she kept yelling across the room to some hipster, "How about a fix!" — John Clellon Holmes, *Go*, p. 7, 1952
- I talk to this Spade hipster who knows everyone in the Village. — William Burroughs, *Letters to Allen Ginsberg 1953–1957*, p. 169, 20th December 1956
- [F]uck Norman Mailer he's trying to get in the act. Why wasn't he a hipster when it counted? — Jack Kerouac, *Jack Kerouac Selected Letters 1957–1969*, p. 184, 28th October 1958: Letter to Allen Ginsberg
- I will be out of touch. I am 39 and already I can't relate to Fabian. There's nothing sadder than an old hipster. — Lenny Bruce, *How to Talk Dirty and Influence People*, p. 35, 1965

hir
used as a gender-neutral third-person singular pronoun *US, 1997*

- Any programer worth his salt knows that Hawaiian Punch is the best system for delivering the most sugar and caffeine within the shortest amount of time. — Andy Ihnatko, *Cyberspeak*, p. 92, 1997

hirsute *adjective*
in computing, complicated *US, 1983*
Used as a jocular synonym for "hairy."

- — Guy L. Steele et al., *The Hacker's Dictionary*, p. 82, 1983

hi-si *noun*
high society *US, 1957*

- She's real hi-si, see, and if word ever got out about this, she'd be ruined with the Four Hundred. — Max Shulman, *Rally Round the Flag, Boys!*, p. 172, 1957

history *noun*
1 the condition of being doomed or finished *US, 1978*

- Monday morning you're history. I'll tell everyone about tonight. — *Heathers*, 1988
- The boss is sellin' the business, and as soon as the new owner shows up, we're history. — Joseph Wambaugh, *Finnegan's Week*, p. 127, 1993
- Oh, man, we're dust! We're so history! — *Airheads*, 1994
- I mean, the guy is history as far as I'm concerned. History. — *Casino*, 1995
- "He's fucking history!" — Jimmy Lerner, *You Got Nothing Coming*, p. 352, 2002

2 in a swindle, the background on a victim, people likely to be encountered, a location or event *US, 1977*

- — Robert C. Prus and C.R.D. Sharper, *Road Hustler*, p. 170, 1977: "Glossary of terms"

hit *noun*
1 a stylized signature spray-painted in public places *US, 1982*

- Early Writers—Taki 183, Frank 207, and Julio 204—did not seem to care much what their "hits" (early term for tags) looked like as long as they got them up and people could read them. — Craig Castleman, *Getting Up*, p. 53, 1982

2 a single inhalation of marijuana, hashish, crack cocaine, or any drug's smoke *US, 1952*

- If somebody hands you a joint and you don't take a hit off of it, it's like sticking out your hand and not having someone shake it. — Leonard Wolfe (Editor), *Voices from the Love Generation*, p. 241, 1968
- Man, I am so fucking messed up and ripped! I got off on the first hit, man!? — John Rechy, *The Fourth Angel*, p. 32, 1972
- You're gonna have to put some gum around of the base of that if you want to get a good hit, man. — *Dazed and Confused*, 1993
- I want to have sex and do a hit right as we're coming. — *Traffic*, 2000

3 a dose of a drug *US, 1952*

- The only concern she had at the moment was whether or not she could get a hit. — Donald Goines, *Dopefiend*, p. 9, 1971
- They used to deal acid, while on acid. Big deals, gram deals, thousands of hits. — Stephen Gaskin, *Amazing Dope Tails*, p. 5, 1980

- When Masterrap missed an appointment with his girlfriend he came back to the apartment and said he wanted a "hit" because the girl was "messing him around." — Terry Williams, *The Cocaine Kids*, p. 48, 1989
- Lorna finally took two hits and told me I looked like an Orange Elephant. — Jennifer Blowdryer, *White Trash Debutante*, p. 37, 1997

4 a meeting with a drug dealer and a drug user *US, 1952*
- — *American Speech*, p. 26, February 1952: "Teen-age hophead jargon"

5 in the eastern US in the early 1990s, prescription medication with codeine *US, 1993*
- — Peter Johnson, *Dictionary of Street Alcohol and Drug Terms*, p. 93, 1993
- I got hits, hash, weed, and later on I'll have 'shrooms. We take cash or stolen MasterCard and Visa. — *Clerks*, 1994

6 a blast of euphoria, joy, excitement *US, 1971*
Figurative use of a drug term.
- Another is elation, the hit that comes when you've brought it off, an argument or whatever. — *The Last Supplement to the Whole Earth Catalog*, p. 23, March 1971

7 the electronic registration of a visit to a website *US, 1995*
- As proof, he mentioned the experience on Valentine's Day, when his firm's "build a car" application was noted as the "Cool Site of the Day" and received more than 10,000 hits on its WebSite server. — *Computerworld*, p. 53, 29th May 1995
- Hits are a common measure of the popularity of a Web site, though more sophisticated measures are evolving. — *Wired Style*, 1996

8 a planned murder *US, 1950*
- For a regular fee, The Troop would administer either a "schlammin" (Yiddish slang for a beating) or a "hit"—killing. — Alson Smith, *Syndicate City*, p. 90, 1954
- So far the cops can't find anybody who heard a damn thing and whoever pulled off the hits must be either an expert at disguise or different guys altogether. — Mickey Spillane, *Last Cop Out*, p. 11, 1972
- Hits never bothered him. It was business. — *Goodfellas*, 1990
- There were no drugs on that boat. It was a hit. — *The Usual Suspects*, 1995
- Mrs. Ayala, is it true your husband has ordered a hit on Eduardo Ruiz? — *Traffic*, 2000

9 a winning bet in an illegal lottery *UK, 1818*
- With the odds at six hundred to one, a penny hit won $6, a dollar won $600, and so on. — Malcolm X and Alex Haley, *The Autobiography of Malcolm X*, p. 84, 1964
- Once he got the club over Pepper's head, he would force her to sneak in phony "hit" slips against the policy wheel. — Iceberg Slim (Robert Beck), *Pimp*, p. 69, 1969
- Them's my last two dollars, Francie, so you bring me back a hit tonight, you hear? — Louise Meriwether, *Daddy Was a Number Runner*, p. 14, 1970
- [H]e'd stake people who needed money, helped a whole lot of people and he always paid his hits, no hedging. — Edwin Torres, *Carlito's Way*, pp. 28–29, 1975

10 in blackjack, a card that a player requests from the dealer to add to his hand *US, 1980*
- — Lee Solkey, *Dummy Up and Deal*, p. 114, 1980

▸ **on hit**
excellent *US, 1997*
- — Vann Wesson, *Generation X Field Guide and Lexicon*, p. 124, 1997

hit *verb*

1 to inject drugs into a vein *US, 1949*
- If one of them was nervous and he couldn't hit himself, if he would asks me I would hit him myself. I hit a lot of guys in my day. — Jeremy Larner and Ralph Tefferteller, *The Addict in the Street*, p. 37, 1964
- But the trouble began when I ranked my hand / And stopped blowing and started to hit. — Dennis Wepman et al., *The Life*, p. 84, 1976
- Arnie gave her stuff and asked me to hit her. — Herbert Huncke, *The Evening Sun Turned Crimson*, p. 173, 1980

2 to smoke (marijuana) *US, 1949*
- You hit a stick and you're gay. — Hal Ellson, *Duke*, p. 3, 1949

3 to guess correctly the day's number in an illegal lottery *US, 1947*
- Here I been playing for years and the first drop of the bucket you hits for that kinda money. — Ralph Ellison, *Invisible Man*, p. 325, 1947
- And when people hit, they would give you some. — Claude Brown, *Manchild in the Promised Land*, p. 191, 1965
- It's an everyday grind for that rice and grits / A constant watch for that number that never hits. — Dennis Wepman et al., *The Life*, p. 164, 1976

- Bed-Stuy is the kind of neighborhood where the only people with money are drug dealers; people who hit the daily number; and people who got hit by cars, sued, and got paid. — Chris Rock, *Rock This!*, p. 41, 1997

4 to kill in a planned, professional manner *US, 1949*
- There is no doubt, however, that The Mick's brother was "hit." In hood talk, when you are hit, you are killed dead. Completely dead. — Robert Sylvester, *No Cover Charge*, p. 60, 1956
- "Let's hit this damn Arthur Blessit," one of the Syndicate men declared. — Arthur Blessitt, *Turned On to Jesus*, p. 39, 1971
- "Who hit him?" "Outta town talent. It was a specialist kind of job." — Richard Condon, *Prizzi's Honor*, p. 20, 1982
- Even if he survives the trial without going insane or being hit like Lee Harvey Oswald by his own people, he will be better off marrying a Miskito Indian or even a fat young boy from some cannibal tribe in Ecuador than crawling out of the courtroom[.] — Hunter S. Thompson, *Generation of Swine*, p. 169, 13th October 1986

5 to rob *US, 1970*
- "What'd he hit?" asks Mule. "The commissary store." — Darryl Ponicsan, *The Last Detail*, p. 17, 1970
- The store had never been hit and naturally this permitted a laxity of surveillance. — Red Rudensky, *The Gonif*, p. 7, 1970

6 to cover with graffiti *US, 1974*
- Yes, they started three years ago and would hit four or five names a day. — Norman Mailer, *The Faith of Graffiti*, p. Section 1, 1974
- We were gonna hit on Bear Mountain. — Craig Castleman, *Getting Up*, p. 53, 1982

7 to visit, to go to a place *US, 1995*
- I've gotta hit the bathroom. — *Mallrats*, 1995

8 to serve a drink *US, 1932*
- Jack paused, touching his glass. "Why don't you hit it one more time." — Elmore Leonard, *Bandits*, p. 20, 1987

9 to have sex *US, 2004*
- — Rick Ayers (Editor), *Berkeley High Slang Dictionary*, p. 26, 2004

▸ **be hit with a bit**
to be sentenced to prison *US, 1961–1962*
From **BIT** (a prison sentence).
- — Frank Prewitt and Francis Schaeffer, *Vacaville Vocabulary*, 1961–1962

▸ **hit a lick**
to masturbate *US, 2002*
- — Jeffrey Ian Ross, *Behind Bars*, p. 188, 2002: Slammer Slang

▸ **hit a lick**
to commit a robbery *US, 2001*
- Jones and Stark approached him and asked him if he wanted to go "hit a lick at the old folks' home." — *Tampa (Florida) Tribune*, p. 1, 4th January 2001

▸ **hit daylight**
to be released from prison *US, 1988*
- He'll tell you that if there's one thing in the world I hate to do, it's lock up a man who's just hit daylight. — Gerald Petievich, *Shakedown*, p. 91, 1988

▸ **hit it**
1 to leave *US, 1930*
- No, we're gonna be hittin' it. I'll take care of the check. — *Reservoir Dogs*, 1992
- Clarence says we gotta be hittin' it. — *True Romance*, 1993

2 to have sex *US, 2006*
- "So just 'cause you been hittin' it with his ho he capped you?" — Jason Starr, *Lights Out*, p. 83, 2006

▸ **hit it a lick; hit it**
in poker, to raise a bet *US, 1988*
- — George Percy, *The Language of Poker*, p. 44, 1988

▸ **hit the books**
to study hard *US, 1968*
- — Collin Baker et al., *College Undergraduate Slang Study Conducted at Brown University*, p. 137, 1968
- Hey look, Paps, really. I've got to hit the books this semester. I'm carrying eighteen hours and I'm on pro. — Richard Farina, *Been Down So Long*, p. 26, 1996

▸ **hit the bottle**
1 to bleach your hair blonde *US, 1955*

Teen slang, punning on a term associated with drinking.
- — *American Weekly*, p. 2, 14th August 1955

2 to drink excessively *US, 1957*
- Everybody knew his reputation for hitting the bottle. — Helen Giblo, *Footlights, Fistfights and Femmes*, p. 31, 1957
- As bad as things are now, can you imagine how much worse a fix we'd be in if Bush were still hitting the bottle? — Al Franken, *The Truth With Jokes*, p. 128, 2005

▸ **hit the bricks**
to work on the street *US, 1973*
- Can't you recall telling me when I first hit the bricks to "always use a safety?" — A.S. Jackson, *Gentleman Pimp*, p. 45, 1973

▸ **hit the burner**
to draw upon all of your inner resources and stamina *US, 1986*
US naval aviator usage.
- — *United States Naval Institute Proceedings*, p. 108, October 1986

▸ **hit the deck**
to fall or throw yourself to the ground *US, 1925*
- Then I saw all black and the last thing I remember is hitting the deck. — *A Few Good Men*, 1992

▸ **hit the hay**
to go to bed *US, 1912*
- He said he guessed he was pretty shot and thought he'd hit the hay. — Ken Kesey, *One Flew Over the Cuckoo's Nest*, p. 243, 1962

▸ **hit the moon**
to reach the highest plateau of a drug experience *US, 1971*
- — Eugene Landy, *The Underground Dictionary*, p. 104, 1971

▸ **hit the pipe**
to smoke crack cocaine *US, 1992*
- They had some argument out in the parking lot. Looked like she was hitting the pipe. — Richard Price, *Clockers*, p. 197, 1992
- I [Coolio] hit the pipe again and felt a head rush. Next thing I knew I was hooked. — *The Source*, p. 74, October 1994
- People against drugs say it all starts with beer. ADDICT: "Ahh, man. I'm hitting the pipe. Can't fuck with that beer no more." — Chris Rock, *Rock This!*, p. 62, 1997

▸ **hit the pit**
to be incarcerated *US, 1992*
- — William K Bentley and James M. Corbett, *Prison Slang*, 1992

▸ **hit the prone**
to throw yourself to the ground *US, 1977*
- The three of us hit the prone and waited, then looked behind us to see two troopers from the new seven-six half pushing, half carrying a VC. — Larry Heinemann, *Close Quarters*, p. 65, 1977

▸ **hit the sack**
to go to bed, to go to sleep *US, 1912*
- "Do you want to hit the sack? I can't sleep, so I may as well take over." — Audie Murphy, *To Hell and Back*, p. 33, 1949
- He gets between the sheets and tells me I better hit the sack myself[.] — Ken Kesey, *One Flew Over the Cuckoo's Nest*, p. 81, 1962
- Every night I hit the sack / Oh my aching Airborne back! — Sandee Shaffer Johnson, *Cadences*, p. 19, 1986

▸ **hit the sauce**
to drink alcohol *US, 1997*
- As a result, I hit the sauce uncharacteristically hard that day. — Elissa Stein and Kevin Leslie, *Chunks*, p. 26, 1997

▸ **hit the sewer**
to inject heroin or another drug intravenously *US, 1973*
- — David Maurer and Victor Vogel, *Narcotics and Narcotic Addiction*, p. 415, 1973

▸ **hit the silk**
in card games, to withdraw from or end a game or hand *US, 1972*
From the military slang for bailing out of an aircraft by parachute (silk).
- I was lucky that I had Uncle Kenneth to take me to all the football games I wanted to see, and to teach me how to run the six ball in snooker and that the best thing to do in gin was hit the silk when you got ten or under. — Dan Jenkins, *Semi-Tough*, p. 50, 1972

▸ **hit the skids**
to deteriorate *US, 1958*
- She began to hit the skids harder. — Willard Motely, *Let No Man Write My Epitaph*, p. 275, 1958

▸ **hit the slab**
to be killed *US, 1950*
- — Hyman E. Goldin et al., *Dictionary of American Underworld Lingo*, p. 96, 1950

▸ **hit the spot**
to find the vein when injecting a drug *US, 1971*
- Now the cat tried real hard, but he was too scarred / He just couldn't hit the spot. — Michael H. Agar, *The Journal of American Folklore*, p. 179, April 1971

▸ **hit the wall**
to reach a point of exhaustion beyond which lesser athletes will fail to continue, especially of long-distance and marathon runners *US, 1982*
- Believe what you've read about "hitting the wall." — *Washington Post*, p. G7, 18th August 1977
- Among marathoners, hitting the wall is the term for what happens when your body runs out of glycogen. Any runner who's hit the wall during a previous race will know to take in between three and ten energy gels on a marathon. — *CNN*, 31st October 2001

hit and run *noun*
a betting technique in which a player places a single bet and withdraws from the game if he wins *US, 1950*
- — Thomas L. Clark, *The Dictionary of Gambling and Gaming*, p. 101, 1987

hit and run *verb*
1 in casino blackjack, to enter a game when the count is advantageous to the players, to play a few games, and then to move to another table *US, 1991*
- — Michael Dalton, *Blackjack*, p. 54, 1991

2 in poker, to play for a short time, win heavily, and quit the game *US, 1982*
- — David M. Hayano, *Poker Faces*, p. 186, 1982

hit and run *adjective*
(used of entertainment engagements) in one city one night, another city the next *US, 1976*
- They had a lot of "hit and run" jobs, as the musicians called them in those days, which meant that they would close one day in, say, Orlando, Florida, and have to open up the next night in Vancouver. — Mort Sahl, *Heartland*, p. 57, 1976

hit-and-split *noun*
a quick air attack followed by a quick retreat *US, 1991*
- He pressed closer now, deciding to use his gun and do a hit-and-split followed by a reattack. — Richard Herman Jr., *Firebreak*, p. 393, 1991

hitch *noun*
1 a period of duty or service *US, 1905*
- Another hitch in prison and you'll be put away for life. — Jack Kerouac, *On the Road*, p. 257, 1957
- "What's this I hear about you wanting to get out of the Army now that your hitch is almost up?" he asked. — David Reed, *Up Front in Vietnam*, p. 77, 1967
- Three hitches of four years each. — Darryl Ponicsan, *The Last Detail*, p. 2, 1970
- Yes, but how many ex-baton twirlers with only high school, two seasons with a religious revival show, and a nine-year hitch in a rodeo trailer made twenty grand a year and expenses? — Elmore Leonard, *Touch*, p. 25, 1977

2 a jail sentence *US, 1964*
- Well, I sent here a kite by my cellmate / the boy who just finished his hitch and was free. — Bruce Jackson, *Get Your Ass in the Water and Swim Like Me*, p. 116, 1964
- I did three hitches in Leavenworth and I did a ten-year bit here, and now I've got life here. — Bruce Jackson, *In the Life*, p. 97, 1972

hitch *verb*
to hitchhike *US, 1929*
A colloquial shortening.
- Okay, I asked myself—now, now, are you sorry you hitched? — James Simon Kunen, *The Strawberry Statement*, p. 82, 1968

hitchhiker *noun*
a commercial message played at the end of a radio program
US, *1980*
- — Walter Hurst and Donn Delson, *Delson's Dictionary of Radio & Record Industry Terms*, 1980

hit in the seat *verb*
an act of anal intercourse *US*, *1976*
- — John R. Armore and Joseph R. Wolfe, *Dictionary of Desperation*, p. 33, 1976

hit kiss *noun*
the exchange of crack cocaine smoke from one user to another through a kiss *US*, *1989*
- Another example is the "hit kiss" ritual: after inhaling deeply, basers literally "kiss"—put their lips together and exhale the smoke into each other's mouths. — Terry Williams, *The Cocaine Kids*, p. 108, 1989

hit list *noun*
a list of targets for retaliation, either physical or otherwise *US*, *1972*
- — *American Speech*, Spring 1980

hit man *noun*
a professional killer *US*, *1963*
- But I thought Scalisi was pretty much of a hit man, didn't do much of anything else. — George V. Higgins, *The Friends of Eddie Doyle*, p. 99, 1971
- "We have hit men like that," Shelby reminded him. — Mickey Spillane, *Last Cop Out*, p. 10, 1972
- None of us is about to deal face-to-face with a couple of guinea hit men. — Vincent Patrick, *The Pope of Greenwich Village*, p. 205, 1979
- He's a psycho-cokehead hitman. — *Traffic*, 2000

hit on *verb*
to flirt; to proposition *US*, *1954*
- [H]e took her to dinner, never mentioned it again, took her home, didn't hit on her in any way. — Terry Southern, *Now Dig This*, p. 19, 1981

hit or sit *verb*
used for describing a player's two choices in blackjack or twenty-one—draw another card or not *US*, *1962*
- Who's got five bucks they want to lose? You hit or you sit[.] — Ken Kesey, *One Flew Over the Cuckoo's Nest*, p. 120, 1962

hits *noun*
a pair of dice that have been altered so that they will not roll a total of seven *US*, *1962*
- — Frank Garcia, *Marked Cards and Loaded Dice*, p. 262, 1962

hit squad *noun*
a death squad *US*, *1969*
- There exist certain hit squads. They are sometimes dressed in khaki uniform and turban though they can be in plain clothes. — Jeffrey Sluka, *Death Squad*, p. 208, 2000

hitter *noun*
1 a big-time bettor *US*, *1974*
- Sometimes young ninnies grow into hitters later in life. — Gary Mayer, *Bookie*, p. 4, 1974

2 a hired killer *US*, *1959*
- He had put a group together in Miami, all hitters, all veterans of the Batista wars, all hungry. — Edwin Torres, *Carlito's Way*, p. 59, 1975
- And the woman was a contract hitter. — Richard Condon, *Prizzi's Honor*, p. 88, 1982
- Then the guy who sent the hitter gets hit, the macaronis are shooting each other, and it's hard to tell who's on whose side. — Elmore Leonard, *Glitz*, p. 108, 1985
- Tiny stars placed on the arm in any fashion indicate that the wearer is a hitter (also known as a "cleaner" or "torpedo"). — Bill Valentine, *Gangs and Their Tattoos*, p. 36, 2000

hittin' *adjective*
excellent *US*, *1991*
- For example, after a session Sambro is hungry, and when given a steaming hot bowl of home-cooked beans, he takes a bite and exclaims, "Dude! These beans are hittin'!" — Trevor Cralle, *The Surfin'ary*, p. 53, 1991

hitting fluid *noun*
heroin *US*, *1973*
- "Mother Coco," I says, "I gotta get some hitting fluid." — Richard Frank, *A Study of Sex in Prison*, p. 26, 1973

hivey *noun*
a person who is quick to learn *US*, *1956*
- The low ranking plebe, who has to brace (assume correct military carriage), spoon up (put in order), tour (hour's walk),might be a hivey (quick to learn), army brat (son of officer), but he must not get B.J. (bold before June). — *Chicago Daily Tribune*, p. N4, 23rd December 1956: West Point's Slang Used in Video Series

Hizzoner *nickname*
used as a jocular reference to a mayor, especially Richard J. Daley, mayor of Chicago from 1955 until his death in 1976
US, *1882*
A slurred "his honor."
- Delvin says, "It's time for new blood in this party, especially now that Hizzoner—God rest his soul—Richard J. Daly's kid, is sitting in the mayor's office." — Robert Campbell, *In a Pig's Eye*, p. 4, 1991
- A buffet of cliches, Franklin's piece invokes Ed Koch, better known as Hizzoner, subway buskers, cabbies who drive too fast, the intolerable condition of public schools, the majesty of Central Park and the New York Public Library and the tension between Manhattan's haves and have-nots. — *Jewish World Review*, 24th February 1999
- Hizzoner's Digs. "Why are you taking this tour?" I ask the young guy behind me as we await our walk-through of Getty House, Los Angeles' official mayoral residence. — *LA Weekly*, 6th-12th April 2001
- Atkins widow fumes at Hizzoner's "fat" joke. The widow of Dr. Robert Atkins went on national television Friday to demand that New York Mayor Michael Bloomberg apologize for calling the late diet guru "fat." — *Commercial Appeal (Memphis, Tennessee)*, p. A13, 24th January 2004

HMFIC *noun*
a commanding officer, or *head motherfucker in charge* *US*, *1990*
- Marinelli smirked and glanced around, as if to say, "Here's the new HMFIC" ("Head Motherfucker In Charge") and we'll eat him up, just like all the others. — William Hoffer, *Victor Six*, p. 40, 1990
- — *The Retired Officer Magazine*, p. 39, January 1993

HNIC *noun*
the leader of an enterprise, the *head nigger in charge* *US*, *1970*
- Unofficially, the special assistant was the "head nigger in charge" (HNIC) of the other Negroes. — Leslie Alexander Lacy, *The Rise and Fall of a Proper Negro*, p. 58, 1970
- — Malachi Andrews and Paul T. Owens, *Black Language*, p. 81, 1973
- The orderly hooked me up with Craig's commanding officer. That was the HNIC—Head Negro in Charge—I was trying to find. — Eric Jerome Dickey, *Cheaters*, p. 373, 1999
- I see you the HNIC, (head Negro in charge) and I know if anybody can make it happen, you can. — Nikki Turner, *A Project Chick*, p. 82, 2004

HO *verb*
to withhold more than your share of something *US*, *1950*
An initialism of "*hold out*."
- — Hyman E. Goldin et al., *Dictionary of American Underworld Lingo*, p. 98, 1950
- I suspected that Talking Tony had started to "H.O.," or hold out money from Jackie. — Peter Fenton, *Eyeing the Flash*, p. 101, 2005

ho; hoe *noun*
1 a sexually available woman; a woman who may be considered sexually available; a prostitute *US*, *1959*
Originally black usage, from the southern US pronunciation of "whore;" now widespread through the influence of rap music.
- Aw, man, white ho's are dumb. — Cecil Brown, *The Life & Loves of Mr. Jiveass Nigger*, p. 146, 1969
- "You want to get laid, go get a good ho and get laid." — George Higgins, *The Digger's Game*, pp. 103–104, 1973
- She turned on the waterworks to cop her license to do me but I was immune to ho tears. — Iceberg Slim (Robert Beck), *Long White Con*, 1977
- Let these ladies eat. Hoes gotta eat too. — *Boyz N The Hood*, 1990

2 a woman *US*, *1959*
A weakened variation of the previous sense.
- Street girls are down 'hos—they don't know nothing but how to whore. — Susan Hall, *Ladies of the Night*, p. 14, 1973
- Them ho's had bodies like goddesses, and knew it too. — *Menace II Society*, 1993

3 a weak or effeminate man *US*, *1996*
- "Fuck you, hoe." "Don't call me that." "What?" "Hoe!" — Two Fingers, *Puff (Disco Biscuits)*, p. 220, 1996

ho; hoe *verb*
to work as a prostitute *US, 1972*
- But then some again treat them nice, but my cousin even treats his wife like a dog and she's Black, but she got out there and hoed for him. — Christina and Richard Milner, *Black Players*, p. 233, 1972
- I said if you gonna be hoeing [whoring] for a rap you ain't nothing but a dog bitch anyway. — Terry Williams, *The Cocaine Kids*, p. 87, 1989

hoagons *noun*
the female breasts *US, 1968*
- — Collin Baker et al., *College Undergraduate Slang Study Conducted at Brown University*, p. 137, 1968

ho, babe
used as a student-to-student greeting *US, 1959*
- — *American Speech*, p. 154, May 1959: "Gator (University of Florida) slang"

hobnail express *noun*
travel by walking *US, 1918*
- How am I going to get to town? By hobnail express, of course. — Ian Sinclair, *Boot in the Stirrup*, p. 55, 1973

hobo *noun*
a homing bomb, one with a targeting capability *US, 1975*
- But six months earlier, in May 1973, a 2,000 "Hobo" (Homing Bomb) had obliterated a bridge just north of Hanoi which had withstood repeated onslaughts of conventional bombs. — James W. Canan, *The Superwarriors*, p. 311, 1975

hobo bet *noun*
in craps, a bet on the number twelve *US, 1985*
From the number's association with boxcars.
- — Steve Kuriscak, *Casino Talk*, p. 31, 1985

hobo cocktail *noun*
a glass of water *US, 1947*
- — Marcus Hanna Boulware, *Jive and Slang of Students in Negro Colleges*, 1947
- — Clarence Major, *Dictionary of Afro-American Slang*, p. 66, 1970

hobo coffee *noun*
coffee made by boiling coffee grounds in water *US, 1959*
- They shucked their wet gear and clothes, drank some of our gritty hobo coffee, and tried to shake the knots out of their muscles. — David Donovan, *Once a Warrior King*, p. 66, 1985
- "Only thing she drank hobo coffee, just boil the water and run it over the coffee in a strainer." — Greg Sarris, *Keeping Slug Woman Alive*, p. 137, 1993

hobo's birthday *noun*
a beating administered to a person covered with a blanket *US, 2006*
The beating is meant to extinguish your figurative candle.
- "Bunch a no-good quality of life criminals put me down with a hobo's birthday." — Stephen J. Cannell, *White Sister*, p. 134, 2006

hobosexual *noun*
a person who is sexually active with several partners in a short period of time *US, 1985*
- — *American Speech*, p. 19, Spring 1985: "The language of singles bars"

Hobo Woods *noun*
an area in South Vietnam which was a major staging area for the North Vietnamese to launch attacks on Saigon or Cu Chi City *US, 1986*
- Did myself a tour with the 173rd Airborneski! Iron fucking Triangle, Hobo Woods, the Bo Loi Woods. — Larry Heinemann, *Paco's Story*, p. 152, 1986

hobs of hell *nickname*
the epitome of heat *US, 1939*
- "Hot?" Tom whispered to her. "As the hobs of hell, I imagine," she said. — Maeve Binchy, *Scarlet Feather*, p. 543, 2002

Ho Chi Minh Motel *noun*
a rest house used by the Viet Cong along a trail or route *US, 1967*
- He outlined, with a map and a pointer, the objective: a reported Vietcong rest house on a route traversing the area. "The Ho Chi Minh motel," someone said, a used but still popular joke. — David Halberstam, *One Very Hot Day*, p. 8, 1967

Ho Chi Minh oven *noun*
a stove with an exhaust pipe that extends far from the kitchen *US, 1967*
- The kitchen was equipped with what are known as "Ho Chi Minh ovens"—ovens whose flues extend out for a hundred yards in all directions with smoke-dissipating vents at regular intervals. — David Reed, *Up Front in Vietnam*, pp. 43–44, 1967

Ho Chi Minh sandals *noun*
slip-on sandals made from the treads of discarded tires, designed and worn by the Viet Cong during the Vietnam war *US, 1968*
- We crossed a wide cart-track and saw the prints of Ho Chi Minh sandals in the mud. — Martin Russ, *Happy Hunting Ground*, p. 160, 1968
- [G]oing through the gear, snatching up the silver belt buckles with the embossed star and the little pouches of smoke and the cash, the Ho Chi Minh tire-track sandals and letters from home[.] — Larry Heinemann, *Close Quarters*, p. 239, 1977
- He wore Ho Chi Minh sandals, khaki shorts and shirt and a pith helmet. — John Del Vecchio, *The 13th Valley*, p. 266, 1982
- "For a pair of Ho Chi Minh sandals?" — Kregg Jorgenson, *Very Crazy G.I.*, p. 224, 2001

Ho Chi Minh's curse *noun*
diarrhea *US, 1984*
An existing formation of "somebody's curse" adapted in Vietnam.
- During the Vietnam War, the venerable GI's took on several modernizations: Ho Chi Minh's curse (probably influenced by Montezuma's revenge). — John Robert Elting, *A Dictionary of Soldier Talk*, p. 132, 1984

Ho Chi Minh's revenge *noun*
diarrhea *US, 1968*
- "For Christ's sake, sir, I've got Ho Chi Minh's revenge. What do you expect me to do, dump a load in my pants[?]" — Philip Caputo, *A Rumor of War*, p. 231, 1977
- "I was really sick when I first got here. We call it Ho Chi Minh's revenge." — Nelson DeMille, *Up Country*, p. 138, 2002

Ho Chi's *noun*
slip-on sandals made from the treads of discarded tires, designed and worn by the Viet Cong during the Vietnam war *US, 2001*
An abbreviation of HO CHI MINH SANDALS.
- "Yeah. Ho Chis," the veteran said. "Tire-tread sandals." — Kregg Jorgenson, *Very Crazy G.I.*, p. 225, 2001

hock *noun*
the foot *UK, 1785*
- — Lou Shelly, *Hepcats Jive Dictionary*, p. 12, 1945

▶ **in hock**
1 in debt, especially to a pawnbroker *US, 1883*
- What's the kid in hock for so far? — *The Hustler*, 1961
- [T]he suit didn't fit either one of them but they figured they might be able to get it in hock. — Herbert Huncke, *Guilty of Everything*, p. 3, 1990
2 in prison *US, 1859*
- — Lou Shelly, *Hepcats Jive Talk Dictionary*, p. 26, 1945

hock *verb*
1 to pawn *US, 1878*
- They were hungry. I dunno. They didn't want to hock the Host, they wanted to hock that golden chalice. — *The Bad Lieutenant*, 1992
2 to clear the throat of phlegm *US, 1992*
From a confusion with conventional "hawk."
- He hocked such a huge looie that I had a spiderweb of saliva running from my dark glasses onto my hair. — Howard Stern, *Miss America*, p. 340, 1995
3 to nag *US, 1961*
From the Yiddish.
- She hocks me nice. But it's still hocking. — Clancy Sigal, *Going Away*, p. 18, 1961
- Stop already hocking us to be good! Hocking us to be nice! Just leave us alone. — Philip Roth, *Portnoy's Complaint*, p. 136, 1969

hocus *noun*
a solution of heroin that has been heated and is ready to inject *US, 1967*
- — John B. Williams, *Narcotics and Hallucinogenics*, p. 113, 1967

hocus *verb*

to alter legitimate dice for cheating purposes *US, 1950*

- — *The Annals of the American Academy of Political and Social Sciences*, p. 126, May 1950

hodad *noun*

a nonsurfer who associates with surfers and poses as a surfer *US, 1961*

- — J. R. Friss, *A Dictionary of Teenage Slang (Mt. Diablo High)*, 1964
- — Mary Corey and Victoria Westermark, *Fer Shurr! How to be a Valley Girl*, 1982

hod of shit *noun*

a great deal of trouble *US, 1981*

- Looks to us like our old friend Lieutenant Billy is getting himself into a hod of shit the Lord couldn't save him from. — George V. Higgins, *The Rat on Fire*, p. 113, 1981

hoe *noun*

a fellow black man, usually in context of sexual bragging *US, 1987*

From **HOMEBOY** (close friend), punning on "hero."

- The Super Hoe is loose in your section / And he's armed with a powerful erection — Boogie Down Productions *Super Hoe*, 1987
- — Funkdoobiest, *Superhoes*, 1995
- — Sadat X Fat Joe & Diamond D, *Nasty Hoes*, 1996

hoffing *noun*

a fight, especially between youth gangs *US, 1971*

- — Hermese E. Roberts, *The Third Ear: A Black Glossary*, 1971

hog *noun*

1 used as an affectionate reference to an aircraft *US, 1990*

- — Joseph Tuso, *Singing the Vietnam Blues*, p. 253, 1990: Glossary

2 a utility helicopter equipped with rockets and machine guns *US, 1991*

- "Hogs," Kell yelled. "They ain't nothin'. Wait till you see the Cobras work out. They bring the max." — William Pelfrey, *The Big V*, p. 21, 1972

3 the penis *US, 1968*

- — Collin Baker et al., *College Undergraduate Slang Study Conducted at Brown University*, p. 137, 1968
- [S]he snuggled right up to them guys and said to them: "Come on, fellas, take me out in the woods and stick your big black hogs in my mouth and fuck me about twelve times[.]" — George V. Higgins, *The Judgment of Deke Hunter*, p. 41, 1976

4 a police officer *US, 1970*

A variation on **PIG** (a police officer).

- As I was saying, while in my quest for the honest buck, this fat hog runs into me and calls me a fireplace pimp. — *Screw*, p. 3, 7th February 1969
- The Hogs, spits Bobby. The trio scan for the fire exit and clatter through a single door. — Mark Powell, *Snap*, p. 87, 2001

5 a US Marine Corps recruit during basic training *US, 1968*

Contemptuous.

- Okay, hogs, I've listened to you bellyache about moving to this new town. This said bellyaching will end as of 0859 hours[.] — Lewis John Carlino, *The Great Santini*, 1979

6 a leader; a strong personality *US, 1989*

- — James Harris, *A Convict's Dictionary*, 1989

7 a drug addict who requires large doses to sustain his habit *US, 1952*

- — *American Speech*, p. 26, February 1952: "Teen-age hophead jargon"

8 heroin *US, 2000*

- Baker was the central figure in Metro's massive "Operation Boss Hog" (Hog is street slang for heroin) in 1983[.] — *Las Vegas Review-Journal*, p. 1B, 10th September 2000

9 phencyclidine, the recreational drug known as PCP or angel dust *US, 1971*

- — Eugene Landy, *The Underground Dictionary*, p. 104, 1971

10 a strong sedative, trade name Benaceyzine™ *US, 1977*

- — Walter L. Way, *The Drug Scene*, 1977

11 a computer program that uses a high degree of a computer's resources *US, 1991*

- — Eric S. Raymond, *The New Hacker's Dictionary*, p. 201, 1991

▸ **beat the hog**

(used of a male) to masturbate *US, 1971*

- No, I think they go home and beat the hog over them, is what I think. — George V. Higgins, *The Friends of Eddie Doyle*, p. 173, 1971

▸ **on the hog**

homosexual *US, 1976*

- — John R Armore and Joseph D. Wolfe, *Dictionary of Desperation*, 1976

hog *verb*

1 to rape *US, 1972*

- This boy that I was with, him and this other boy hogged this Mexican that wasn't a punk. They threw him in the shitter and took all his good time. — Bruce Jackson, *In the Life*, p. 397, 1972

2 in high-low poker, to declare for both high and low *US, 1996*

- — Peter O. Steiner, *Thursday Night Poker*, p. 412, 1996

Hog-60 *noun*

an M-60 machine gun *US, 1987*

Each squad in Vietnam was assigned an M-60, the army's general purpose machine gun which entered the service in the 1950s. It was designed to be lightweight (23 pounds) and easy to carry. It produced a low "grunting" sound.

- A door gunner's best friend was his hatch M-60, which many gunnies took to calling Hog-60's, though the old-timers complained a hog was a gunship and not just a small piece of the gunship's armament; but the younger hot dogs refused to listen[.] — Jack Hawkins, *Chopper One #2*, p. 27, 1987

hogback *noun*

a ridge *US, 2000*

- I moved with companies L and K, which patrolled up and down narrow, mostly dry river gorges and across "hogbacks" (narrow ridges). — James Kirschke, *Not Going Home Alone*, p. 67, 2001

hog board *noun*

a bulletin board where soldiers post pictures of their families and girlfriends *US, 1974*

Marine usage in Vietnam.

- [C]lear the "hog board" of pictures of sweethearts and parents. — Daniel De Cruz, *Boot*, p. 96, 1987

hogging *noun*

a romantic interest in heavy people *US, 2004*

- — Ben Applebaum and Derrick Pittman, *Turd Ferguson & The Sausage Party*, p. 30, 2004

hog heaven *noun*

a state of great happiness *US, 1944*

- I was in hog heaven; all I had to do was hang out, get high, and play music. — Phil Lesh, *Searching for the Sound*, p. 91, 2005

hog-leg hog leg *noun*

1 an oversized handgun *US, 1919*

- [A]nd the girl from the News would see it as his Dodge city pose: the daguerreotype peace officer, now packing a snub-nosed .38 Smith with rubberbands around the grip instead of a hogleg .44. — Elmore Leonard, *City Primeval*, p. 35, 1980
- Spencer was holding a hog leg in his hand, the long shiny barrel pointed in his companion's direction. Loop hadn't even known that the Yankee had a hand-gun. — George Bowering, *Caprice*, 1987
- Counting the cylinder and grip, the shiny revolver is about 15 inches long and weighs seven pounds. It is, as they as, a real hogleg. — *Dallas Morning News*, p. 1A, 16th April 1995
- It's already legal in our state to strap on a hogleg; in fact, the firearms industry is free to think up new and stylish ways women and men could accessorize their Pradas and Armanis with big iron and leather. — *Santa Fe New Mexican*, p. A-7, 15th March 2001

2 a large marijuana cigarette *US, 1997*

- — Jim Emerson-Cobb, *Scratching the Dragon*, April 1997
- — Connie Eble (Editor), *UNC-CH Campus Slang*, p. 5, Spring 1998

hog pen *noun*

a prison guards' control room *US, 1984*

- — Inez Cardozo-Freeman, *The Joint*, 1984

hog-tie *verb*

to bind the hands and feet *US, 1894*

- And if I ever catch ya whackin' in here again I'm gonna hog-tie ya! — Mike Judge and Joe Stillman, *Beavis and Butt-Head Do America*, p. 85, 1997

hog wallow *noun*

the slot used as a sighting plane on the topstrap of a Colt or Smith and Wesson pistol *US, 1957*

- — *American Speech*, p. 193, October 1957: "Some colloquialisms of the handgunner"

hogwash *noun*
nonsense *US, 1882*
- Sure, you can sit down at night and read about the hogwash they hand out. — Mickey Spillane, *One Lonely Night*, p. 79, 1951

hog-wild *adjective*
without restraint *US, 1904*
- If you start to go hog wild on potato chips, the effects will show up on your hips. — Elizabeth Warren, *All Your Worth*, p. 14, 2005

ho-ho *noun*
a fat teenage girl *US, 1982*
- — Mary Corey and Victoria Westermark, *Fer Shurr! How to be a Valley Girl*, 1982

ho house *noun*
a brothel *US, 1991*
- If you really want the sound of a broken-down, jangly old 'ho-house piano have you considered *getting* a broken-down, jangly old 'ho-house piano? — *alt.msic.synth*, 15th September 1991
- "They got this new ho house open on Argyle Road." — Jason Starr, *Lights Out*, p. 167, 2006

hoi polloi *noun*
the common people; the unwashed masses *UK, 1822*
- [I]n Chicago, horny-handed, wilted hoi polloi are seen in lobbies of such swell hotels as the Ambassador and Drake in shirt-sleeves. — Jack Lait and Lee Mortimer, *Washington Confidential*, p. 4, 1951
- Not to mention, they carried germs after contact with the hoi polloi[.] — Guy Owen, *The Flim-Flam Man and the Apprentice Grifter*, p. 197, 1972

hoist *verb*
to rob with guns *US, 1928*
- What are you going to do, man? Hoist it? — *Dazed and Confused*, 1993

hoister *noun*
in circus and carnival usage, a ferris wheel *US, 1981*
- — Don Wilmeth, *The Language of American Popular Entertainment*, p. 131, 1981

hoity-toity *adjective*
snobbish, haughty, assuming, uppish *UK, 1720*
Directly from the earlier form "highty-tighty."
- The prime spot for a pick-up (if you're not hoity-toity) is the Central Park Mall[.] — Jack Lait and Lee Mortimer, *New York Confidential*, p. 115, 1948
- The San Remo crowd was there, virtually hanging from the rafters; the queers and phonies and hoity-toities. — Clancy Sigal, *Going Away*, p. 405, 1961
- That good-looking thing traveling with the hoity-toity blonde? — Armistead Maupin, *Further Tales of the City*, p. 222, 1982

Ho Jo's *nickname*
a Howard Johnson restaurant *US, 1965*
A fixture along US motorways in the 1950s and 60s.
- [G]reet me at the hangar and whisk me off to a Ho-Jo's for a shake and fries. — John Nichols, *The Sterile Cuckoo*, p. 33, 1965

hoke *noun*
an overly dramatic embellishment *US, 1959*
- Another bit of "hoke" which has stood the test of time is one where the master of the house opens the door to a pretty girl who asks demurely, "Is this the house where I am to be maid?" — Monroe Fry, *Sex, Vice, and Business*, p. 62, 1959

hokey; hoky; hokie *adjective*
sentimental; mawkish; in poor taste *US, 1927*
- "What is all this?" asked Polly, indicating the hokey Polynesian motif. — Max Shulman, *Anyone Got a Match?*, p. 115, 1964

hokey-pokey *noun*
in circus and carnival usage, any shoddy, inexpensive merchandize *US, 1981*
- — Don Wilmeth, *The Language of American Popular Entertainment*, p. 132, 1981

hokum *noun*
nonsense *US, 1921*
- The outfit, the syndicate wanted us dead? It had to be hokum. — Iceberg Slim (Robert Beck), *Trick Baby*, p. 15, 1969

hold *noun*
in casino gambling, the amount of money bet that is retained by the casino *US, 1977*
- A table should win 20 percent of the drop. This 20 percent is called a "hold." — Mario Puzo, *Inside Las Vegas*, p. 187, 1977

▶ **in the hold**
hidden in a pocket or elsewhere on the body *US, 1961*
- You still got a dollar in the hold? — Bernard Wolfe, *The Magic of Their Singing*, p. 39, 1961

hold *verb*
1 to be in possession of drugs *US, 1935*
- "This is a real stroke of luck. Maybe he is holding something." — Chandler Brossard, *Who Walks in Darkness*, p. 217, 1952
- For christ's sake, do me and every other ill-dressed journalist in the world a huge favor, and don't get busted for holding. — Hunter S. Thompson, *Fear and Loathing in America*, p. 99, 20th June 1968: Letter to Bill Cardoso
- That wasn't even my stuff, I was holding it for a friend, man. — Cheech Marin and Tommy Chong, *Framed*, 1976
- HOLDING. User's term, relative to possession of the drug. — Lenny Bruce, *The Unpublished Lenny Bruce*, p. 70, 1984

2 to be in possession of money *US, 1967*
- I've got a thousand dollars on me. I'm afraid to go to my pad, 'cause I think some of these cats in here know what I'm holding. — Nicholas Von Hoffman, *We Are The People Our Parents Warned Us Against*, p. 37, 1967
- That means he came back, again and again. And since he wasn't the type to be holding, he avoided paying his tabs. — Leonard Shecter and William Phillips, *On the Pad*, p. 134, 1973
- — Don Wilmeth, *The Language of American Popular Entertainment*, 1981

▶ **hold court**
to get in a shoot-out with police *US, 1974*
- Are you out of your fuckin' mind? We ain't got no reason to hold court. — Donald Goines, *El Dorado Red*, pp. 36–37, 1974

▶ **hold heavy**
to have a lot of money *US, 1966*
- "Hey"—Doc hurried to catch up—"now that you're holding heavy, why don't you spring for another jug?" — Malcolm Braly, *It's Cold Out There*, p. 80, 1966

▶ **hold the bag**
the take the blame *US, 1985*
- Your son, unfortunately, is holding the bag. — Vincent Patrick, *Family Business*, p. 247, 1985

▶ **hold the phone!**
wait a minute! *US, 1975*
- Now, hold the phone, counselor, you ain't talkin' to no Eighty Avenue pimp here. — Edwin Torres, *Carlito's Way*, p. 127, 1975

▶ **hold your mud**
to stand up to pressure and adversity *US, 1966*
- "And the old man here—he'd never hold his mud if anyone came around leaning on him." — Malcolm Braly, *It's Cold Out There*, p. 95, 1966
- He's in his forties, he's a high roller, and for a long time he beat the hell out of us. You've got to respect the guy for that. And plus he held his mud. — James Mills, *The Underground Empire*, p. 539, 1986
- Just remember, homeboy. Do your own time, hold your own mud. — Seth Morgan, *Homeboy*, p. 151, 1990

▶ **hold your mug**
to keep a secret *US, 1970*
- — William D. Alsever, *Glossary for the Establishment and Other Uptight People*, p. 15, December 1970

hold down *verb*
to control (a block or neighborhood) *US, 1985*
Youth gang usage.
- — Jennifer Blowdryer, *Modern English*, p. 64, 1985

holder *noun*
a prisoner, usually not a gang member, entrusted with storing drugs controlled by a prison gang *US, 1992*
- — William K Bentley and James M. Corbett, *Prison Slang*, 1992

holding ground *noun*
a position, literally or figuratively, where you can weather adversity *US, 1963*
From the nautical term for an area where the sea bottom provides a firm hold for anchors.
- — Charles F. Haywood, *Yankee Dictionary*, p. 79, 1963

holding pen *noun*

a cell in a local jail where prisoners are held when they first arrive, pending a decision on whether criminal charges will be filed against them or not *US, 1981*

- "Where is Leo this fine afternoon," Roscommon said. "In the holding pen," Carbone said. — George V. Higgins, *The Rat on Fire*, p. 182, 1981

holding tank *noun*

a cell at a local jail where the recently arrested are held before being processed *US, 1994*

- You're in a large holding tank; you sign in, go stand in front of another gate. — Odie Hawkins, *Lost Angeles*, p. 159, 1994

hold-it *noun*

a gratuitous television view of a pretty girl or woman, usually a spectator at a sporting event *US, 1986*

- They do this a lot, they told me, and they call it "hooking a barracuda," or a "honey shot," or, as a matter of fact, a "hold it." — Dan Jenkins, *Dead Solid Perfect*, p. 152, 1986

hole *noun*

1 in prison, a cell designed for solitary confinement *UK, 1535*
Always with "the."

- When I asked for books to read in this particular hole, a trustee brought me a list from which to make selections. — Eldridge Cleaver, *Soul on Ice*, p. 34, 1968
- Zuzu said we was only playing, but they gave me thirty days in the hole. — Edwin Torres, *Carlito's Way*, p. 46, 1975
- "I want this punk in the hole," the black guard breathed heavily, tired by his bloody workout. — Bobby Seale, *A Lonely Rage*, p. 258, 1978
- Next thing I know I'm in the hole. Solitary confinement. — *Raging Bull*, 1980

2 the mouth *US, 1865*

- Shut your hole about my old man. — Irving Shulman, *The Amboy Dukes*, p. 26, 1947
- Aw, shut your big hole! — George Mandel, *Flee the Angry Strangers*, p. 247, 1952
- Shut your hole, Mae; youre swishing so much youre going to make a hurricane[.] — John Rechy, *City of Night*, p. 203, 1963
- [H]e's a goddam nigger-lover ... now, jest shut your hole an' git on over yonder an' check them leg-irons. — Terry Southern, *Texas Summer*, p. 75, 1991

3 in carnival and circus usage, a job *US, 2005*

- Tony had started the season with a hole (that is, a job) in one of the big money games. — Peter Fenton, *Eyeing the Flash*, p. 124, 2005

4 a pretty homosexual man *US, 1975*

- Brown was the punk man: he had about six homos working for him selling pills, and he had three top-notch holes, homos who looked like beautiful women, whom he was pimping. — James Carr, *Bad*, p. 73, 1975

5 the vagina; sex with a woman; a woman; women *UK, 1592*

- "Snatch," "hole," "kooze," "slash," "pussy" and "crack" were other terms referring variously to women's genitals, to women as individuals, or to women as a species. — *Screw*, p. 5, 3rd January 1972
- — Edith A. Folb, *runnin' down some lines*, p. 242, 1980

6 a passive, promiscuous, unattached lesbian *US, 1992*

- William K. Bentley and James M. Corbett, *Prison Slang*, 1992

7 any place where a supply of illegal drugs is hidden *US, 1993*

- "The homies talking about getting back the 'hole,' so if you see it on fire, don't trip (panic)." A "hole" is street slang for a place where drugs are stashed. — *Los Angeles Times*, p. B3, 27th May 1993

8 the subway *US, 1933*

- That's why there was so much fury when they were taken out of "the hole" and replaced by Transit Authority cops. — Leonard Shecter and William Phillips, *On the Pad*, p. 159, 1973

9 a tobacco cigarette *US, 1971*

- — Eugene Landy, *The Underground Dictionary*, p. 67, 1971

▸ **go in the hole**

to fall from a pole, tower, rig, or building under construction *US, 1989*

- If you had to fall, he told her, try to do it inside the structure, because they decked in every other floor as they bolted up. But either way, falling inside or out, it was called "going in the hole." — Elmore Leonard, *Killshot*, p. 35, 1989

▸ **in the hole**

in police usage, hiding and avoiding work *US, 1973*

- He was telling me things he probably told his young partners during lonely hours after two a.m. when you're fighting to keep awake or when you're "in the hole" trying to hide your radio car, in some alley where you can doze uncomfortably for an hour, but you never really rest. — Joseph Wambaugh, *The Blue Knight*, p. 92, 1973

hole bit *noun*

while in prison, a sentence to solitary confinement *US, 1967*

- That's enough to get you a holebit in any joint. — Clarence Cooper Jr., *The Farm*, p. 78, 1967

hole card *noun*

1 a resource in reserve *US, 1926*

- I also know that if I give up that gun it's a probation violation vis-a-fucking-vis harboring contraband items. You know what a "hole card" is? — James Ellroy, *White Jazz*, p. 73, 1992

2 the key to a person's character *US, 1968*
From the game of stud poker, in which a "hole card" is a card dealt face-down.

- People peeped your hole card then, knew where you were at. — Nathan Heard, *Howard Street*, p. 181, 1968
- I've seen him damn near every day and I wasn't hip to his hole card. — A.S. Jackson, *Gentleman Pimp*, p. 104, 1973
- I thought you were a mackman, a master at the Game; but I peeped your hole card, you're a funny-time lame. — Dennis Wepman et al., *The Life*, p. 39, 1976
- I regarded him flatly and said, "Yeah, you did. Now I know your hole card." — Peter Coyote, *Sleeping Where I Fall*, p. 313, 1998

hole-in-one *noun*

sexual intercourse on a first date *US, 1972*
A puerile golf metaphor.

- — Robert A. Wilson, *Playboy's Book of Forbidden Words*, p. 140, 1972

hole olie *noun*

in stud poker, a card dealt face-down *US, 1967*
A jocular embellishment of "hole card."

- — Albert H. Morehead, *The Complete Guide to Winning Poker*, p. 265, 1967

holetime *noun*

solitary confinement in prison *US, 1967*

- doing holetime. — Clarence Cooper Jr., *The Farm*, p. 81, 1967

hole to bowl *noun*

the path taken during defecation on a toilet *US, 1969*

- Annette belched, grunted and farted; the turds said SWOOSH and shot from hole to bowl. — Steve Cannon, *Groove, Bang, and Jive Around*, p. 6, 1969

holler *adjective*

stylish *US, 1961*

- Them holler drapes Vann wears out in front of his band is just too much, man. — Ross Russell, *The Sound*, p. 109, 1961

Hollyweird *nickname*

Hollywood, California *US, 1953*

- Playing on the at times bizarre nature of the city. John Wayne (of Hollyweird) doing the La Vie En Rose sector with a big party; Wayne, Women & Song. — *Nevada State Journal*, 8th February 1953
- We're going to Hollyweird, homeboys, he said. — James Ellroy, *Suicide Hill*, p. 722, 1986

Hollywood *noun*

used as a teasing term of address for someone whose clothes and mannerisms suggest a high level of showmanship *US, 1973*

- — Malachi Andrews and Paul T. Owens, *Black Language*, p. 86, 1973

Hollywood glider *noun*

the B-17 Flying Fortress *US, 1946*
The B-17 appeared frequently in films.

- — *American Speech*, p. 310, December 1946: "More Air Force slang"

Hollywood Marine *noun*

a member of the United States Marine Corps trained in San Diego *US, 1949*

- I was a Hollywood Marine. I went to San Diego, but it was worse in Parris Island. — Wallace Terry, *Bloods*, p. 3, 1984
- [H]e was considered to be a "pussy," or a "Hollywood Marine," as only Marines who had graduated from boot camp at Parris Island were "real Marines." — Bruce Norton, *Force Recon Diary 1969*, p. 54, 1991

Hollywood no *noun*
an answer of "no" implicit in the failure to return a phone
call *US, 1992*
- Confused because the production executive hot in pursuit of your
  screenplay last week isn't returning your calls this week? Well, meet
  the Hollywood "no." "Hollywood is the most masterful town in
  regard to saying 'no' without saying 'no'." — *Los Angeles Times*, p. 19
  (Calendar), 16th August 1992

Hollywoods *noun*
dark glasses *US, 1966*
- — Andy Anonymous, *A Basic Guide to Campusology*, p. 14, 1966

Hollywood shower *noun*
in the Navy, a shower lasting more than a few minutes *US,*
1985
- [S]ometime I can take a "Hollywood shower" and stay in there all
  I want. — Maria Flook, *My Sister Life*, p. 70, 1995

Hollywood stop *noun*
a rolling stop at a traffic signal or a stop sign *US, 1986*
- — Jeffrey McQuain, *Never Enough Words*, p. 54, 1999

Holmes *noun*
used as a term of address from male-to-male *US, 1975*
Playing on the term "homes."
- Look here, Holmes, you got to dig yo'self. — Edwin Torres, *Carlito's Way*,
  p. 21, 1975
- I think they just got out the cop car, Holmes. — *Menace II Society*, 1993

holy city *noun*
in poker, a high-value hand *US, 1988*
- — George Percy, *The Language of Poker*, p. 44, 1988

holy cow!
used as a mild oath, expressing surprise *US, 1917*
Popularized by baseball radio announcers Harry Caray and Phil
Rizzuto.
- "And then and there he assaulted the widow four times, you should
  excuse the expression." "Holy cow!" whistled Nebbice. "Four times!"
  — Max Shulman, *The Zebra Derby*, p. 79, 1946
- James McParlan II. Junior. James McParlan. Holy Cow. — Clancy Sigal,
  Going Away, p. 179, 1961
- Holy cow! — *Lethal Weapon*, 1987

holy crap!
used for registering surprise *US, 2001*
A variation of **HOLY SHIT**.
- Our mouths all dropped open. And we all made the sign of the
  cross. "Holy crap," Carolli said. "You shot Jesus. That's gonna take
  a lot of Hail Marys." — Janet Evanovich, *Seven Up*, p. 88, 2001

Holy Joe *noun*
any religious leader *US, 1864*
The term suggests a lack of sincerity.
- — Jerry Robertson, *Oil Slanguage*, p. 66, 1954
- I tried, of course to enlist Jeff as a fellow conspirator but he was
  the most violent Holy Joe of the bunch. — Frederick Kohner, *Gidget*,
  p. 80, 1957
- — R. Frederick West, *God's Gambler*, p. 226, 1964: "Appendix A"

holy jumper *noun*
any Pentacostal *US, 1933*
A derogatory term used by Christians to describe members of
Pentacostal sects, which they deem to be non-Christian.
- A cartoon ridiculed the worshippers as "holy rollers," "holy
  jumpers," and "holy kickers." — Larry Martin, *The Life and Ministry of
  William J. Seymour*, p. 248, 1999

holy moley!
used for expressing surprise *UK, 1958*
- Some communicated their astonishment with awkward
  exclamations: "Holey moley!" — Alexa Albert, *Brothel*, p. 18, 2001

holy moo cow!
used as an expression of complete surprise *US, 1968*
A jocular embellishment of the more common **HOLY COW!**
- — Collin Baker et al., *College Undergraduate Slang Study Conducted at Brown
  University*, p. 138, 1968

holy of holies *noun*
1 the vagina *US, 1994*

A crude pun on **HOLE**.
- Look, maybe your method of massage differs from mine, but
  touchin' his lady's feet, and stickin' your tongue in her holyiest of
  holyies, ain't the same ballpark, ain't the same league, ain't even
  the same fuckin' sport. — *Pulp Fiction*, 1994
2 any inner sanctum *US, 1995*
- And their cash flows from the tables to our boxes, through the cage
  and into the most sacred room in the casino, the place where they
  add up all the money, the holy of holies, the count room. — *Casino*,
  1995

holy oil *noun*
an oil applied to the skin or clothing in the belief that it
will bring the bettor luck in an illegal number gambling
lottery *US, 1949*
- — *American Speech*, p. 192, October 1949

holy olie *noun*
in stud poker, the hole card *US, 1951*
- — *American Speech*, p. 99, May 1951: "The vocabulary of poker"

holy roller *noun*
a member of a Pentacostal sect *US, 1841*
Used disparagingly by Christians.
- It's scary enough that we've got an ideological Holy Roller like John
  Ashcroft in charge of the FBI. — *Newsday (New York)*, p. A25, 4th May 2003

holy shit!
used for registering astonishment *US, 1961*
- "You said you only know how to jump out of them." "Holy shit."
  — Robert Ludlum, *The Bourne Supremacy*, p. 499, 1986
- "Who's his sister? Do I know her?" "Estelle Colucci. Benny Colucci's
  wife." Holy shit. "Small world." — Janet Evanovich, *Seven Up*, p. 81, 2001

holy smoke!
used as a exclamation of surprise and wonder *UK, 1892*
- Holy smokes, goddamn and all ye falling candles of heaven smash[!]
  — Jack Kerouac, *The Dharma Bums*, p. 94, 1958

holy Toledo!
used for registering surprise *US, 1951*
A little bit of Holy Toledo goes a long way. A trademark of Milo
Hamilton, radio broadcaster for the Houston Astros baseball
team, and often used by Skipper, the son of Jungle Jim on
Jungle Jim (1955).
- "Holy Toledo!" said Petey reverently. He plunged his hands into the
  racoon coat and then his face. "Holy Toledo!" he repeated fifteen or
  twenty times. — Max Shulman, *The Many Loves of Dobie Gillis*, p. 42, 1951

holy war *noun*
a debate among computer enthusiasts about a question
which has no objective answer *US, 1991*
- The characteristic that distinguishes holy wars from normal technical disputes is that in a holy war most of the participants spend
  their time trying to pass off personal value choices and cultural
  attachments as objective technical evaluations. — Eric S. Raymond,
  The New Hacker's Dictionary, p. 201, 1991

holy water *noun*
official approval *US, 1986*
US naval aviator usage; to give such approval is to "sprinkle
holy water."
- — *United States Naval Institute Proceedings*, p. 108, October 1986

holy week *noun*
the bleed period of a woman's menstrual cycle *US, 1964*
- — Roger Blake, *The American Dictionary of Sexual Terms*, p. 98, 1964
- — Robert A. Wilson, *Playboy's Book of Forbidden Words*, p. 140, 1972

hombre *noun*
a man *US, 1846*
Spanish *hombre* (a man), spread worldwide by Hollywood
Westerns such as *Hombre*, 1967, starring Paul Newman.
- At one point the battalion XO, Major Charles Brown, took me aside
  to tell me Colonel Locke was one mean hombre, the worst-
  tempered, toughest guy he'd ever worked for. — David H. Hackworth,
  About Face, p. 233, 1989

home *noun*
1 a very close male friend *US, 1944*
An abbreviation of **HOMEBOY**.

- You know you fuck with me you got the whole population of homes on your untainted ass. — Elmore Leonard, *Riding the Rap*, p. 55, 1995

2 the vein into which an intravenous drug user injects a drug *US, 1973*

- — David Maurer and Victor Vogel, *Narcotics and Narcotic Addiction*, p. 415, 1973

▸ **at home in the going**
in horse racing, said of a horse that is running a track that complements the horse's skills and preferences *US, 1951*

- — David W. Maurer, *Argot of the Racetrack*, p. 11, 1951

▸ **go home**
1 in professional wrestling, to finish a match *US, 2001*

- So Sunshine would pick up the cue, usually from the ring announcer, to wind up our catfight, and then she'd whisper to me, "All right, let's go home." — Missy Hyatt, *Missy Hyatt*, p. 35, 2001
- But the wrestlers wouldn't "go home." "Home" signifies the dressing room and "going home" means that you end the match. — Bobby Heenan, *Bobby the Brain*, p. 92, 2002

2 to be released from prison *US, 1967*

- [O]ne of the blocks of numbers that made up the new year was the date on which he would leave the prison—"go home" was the universal expression[.] — Malcolm Braly, *On the Yard*, p. 160, 1967

▸ **send home**
to sentence to prison *US, 1990*

- He'd be sporting shanks like a human porcupine before he was processed through Receiving and Release the next time he was sent home. — Seth Morgan, *Homeboy*, p. 44, 1990

home base; home run *noun*
in the teenage categorization of sexual activity, sexual intercourse *US, 1963*

- Why bother with first base? I'd go right to the home run. — *M*A*S*H*, 1970
- "Did you at least get to home base?" "Who knows. I couldn't tell with that lousy condom." — C.D. Payne, *Youth in Revolt*, p. 157, 1993

home box *noun*
a computer enthusiast's own computer *US, 1991*

- Yeah? Well, my home box runs a full 4.2 BSD, so there! — Eric S. Raymond, *The New Hacker's Dictionary*, p. 201, 1991

homeboy *noun*
a very close male friend, often but not always from the same neighborhood *US, 1899*

- He nearly dropped the powder can. "My homeboy! Man, gimme some skin! I'm from Lansing." — Malcolm X and Alex Haley, *The Autobiography of Malcolm X*, p. 44, 1964
- Home boy, them Brothers is taking care of Business! — Eldridge Cleaver, *Soul on Ice*, p. 26, 1968
- Like, "you my homeboy, and the dude who ain't from around here, he ain't one of us." — H. Rap Brown, *Die Nigger Die!*, p. 16, 1969
- Listen up man, me an' my homeboy are in some serious shit. — *Pulp Fiction*, 1994

home cooking *noun*
sex with your spouse *US, 1964*

- — Roger Blake, *The American Dictionary of Sexual Terms*, p. 98, 1964
- — Dale Gordon, *The Dominion Sex Dictionary*, p. 83, 1967

home ec *noun*
home economics, in which the theory and practice of homemaking are studied *US, 1899*

- Nobody but a queer would teach home ec anyway. — Larry McMurtry, *The Last Picture Show*, p. 59, 1966
- MRS. CHASEN: What are you studying? CANDY: Poli sci. With a home ec minor. — *Harold and Maude*, 1971

home-ec-y *adjective*
(used of a girl) conventional, out of touch with current fashions, styles, and trends *US, 1970*

- — *Current Slang*, p. 19, Spring 1970

homegirl *noun*
a very close female friend, usually from the same neighborhood, gang, or faction of a gang, usually applied to a black girl *US, 1934*

- You really playin' with power there, homegirl! — Jess Mowry, *Way Past Cool*, p. 28, 1992
- The white home-girl ebonics had vanished now. — Francesca Lia Block, *I Was a Teenage Fairy*, p. 78, 1998
- I just called my homegirl, Amber, just before you got here, and she was talkin' crazy about how she was gonna kill herself and how I should get her funeral clothes together. — *Rolling Stone*, p. 80, 12th April 2001

homemade *noun*
1 a cigarette rolled by hand from loose tobacco *US, 1954*

- [F]ellow who would take the news of the Apocalypse with corrugated eyes and two fingers rolling a homemade and a drawleed "Ay-uh." — Bernard Wolfe, *The Late Risers*, p. 162, 1954

2 a home-made pistol *US, 1949*

- Well, one thing, he can make as pretty a home-made as you want. — Hal Ellson, *Duke*, p. 75, 1949

home plate *noun*
an airplane's home base or carrier *US, 1991*

- While there's a break here we'd like to run out and get some gas from our home plate. — Gerry Carroll, *North S*A*R*, p. 75, 1991

homer *noun*
a sports official or reporter who favors the home team *US, 1888*

- — Zander Hollander and Sandy Padwe, *Basketball Lingo*, p. 56, 1971
- Nothing made him angrier than small-town newspapermen —"homers"—who came up to him during campaigns and told him that he was ignoring "local factors." — Timothy Crouse, *The Boys on the Bus*, pp. 40–41, 1973

Homer *noun*
any Iraqi soldier *US, 1991*
Gulf war usage; an allusion to the doltish Homer Simpson of television cartoon fame.

- — *American Speech*, p. 391, Winter 1991: "Among the new words"

home run *noun*
the journey of a circus from the final engagement of the season to the winter quarters *US, 1980*

- — Joe McKennon, *Circus Lingo*, p. 4649, 1980

homes *noun*
used as a term of address, usually establishing comrade status *US, 1971*

- I'm gonna call a coupla pipe-hittin' niggers who'll go to work on homes here with a pair of pliers and a blow torch. — *Pulp Fiction*, 1994

home skillet *noun*
a close friend *US, 1993*

- — *Merriam-Webster's Hot Words on Campus Marketing Survey '93*, p. 2, 13th October 1993

homeslice *noun*
1 a close friend *US, 1984*

- A good friend is a homeslice, dog or, simply, G. — *Chicago Tribune*, p. C7, 9th January 1994
- — Ethan Hilderbrant, *Prison Slang*, 1998
- "They're my brown brothers. My home slice." — Stephen J. Cannell, *The Tin Collectors*, p. 36, 2001

2 a prisoner from your home city *US, 1992*

- — William K Bentley and James M. Corbett, *Prison Slang*, 1992

homestead *noun*
▸ **the homestead**
San Quentin State Prison, San Rafael, California *US, 1975*

- — Report to the Senate, *California Senate Committee on Civil Disorder*, p. 230, 1975

homesteader *noun*
1 an American who had been in Vietnam for more than a few years *US, 1991*

- Some homesteaders stayed in Vietnam for up to 10 years and raised families there. — Linda Reinberg, *In the Field*, p. 107, 1991

2 a person who is dating one person steadily *US, 1961*
High school usage.

- — *Washington Post*, 23rd April 1961: "Man, dig this jazz"

home sweet home *noun*
in circus and carnival usage, the final performance of a season *US, 1981*

- — Don Wilmeth, *The Language of American Popular Entertainment*, p. 132, 1981

hometown honey *noun*
a college student's date from their hometown *US, 1968*

- — Collin Baker et al., *College Undergraduate Slang Study Conducted at Brown University*, p. 138, 1968
- His conversation was soon loaded with "brew" and "beevo," with talk of "hometown honeys" and things being "gross." — John Sayles, *Union Dues*, p. 278, 1977
- Is Britney Spears lovesick? Two weeks after the pop tart married and then dumped a hometown honey in Las Vegas, photos have emerged of her leaving a hospital. — *Daily News (New York)*, p. 3, 18th January 2004

homewrecker *noun*
a person whose affair with a married person leads to divorce, especially when there are children involved *US, 1968*

- Oh, he was nice, of course, and she did like him, but she wasn't a homewrecker. — Nathan Heard, *Howard Street*, p. 113, 1968
- "You don't think she's better-looking than your average homewrecker?" I said. — Dan Jenkins, *Life Its Ownself*, p. 230, 1984
- Shocked, Mom flew off the handle and called Joanie a "home wrecker." Joanie got livid and said, "Oh, really? I understand your last boyfriend didn't exactly qualify as bachelor of the month!" — C.D. Payne, *Youth in Revolt*, p. 77, 1993
- Contrast that with Henry "Homewrecker" Hyde's dismissing revelations of his extramarital dalliance with a married mother of three as a "youth indiscretion" committed when he was in his 40s and you get an idea of how the debate has deteriorated. — *Sunday Gazette Mail (Charleston, West Virginia)*, p. 8B, 11th October 1998

homey; homie *noun*
a person from your neighborhood; a close male friend; a fellow youth gang member *US, 1929*

- — Lou Shelly, *Hepcats Jive Dictionary*, p. 12, 1945
- I moved back to my small pad and ran into a homey of mine, James Moody. — Babs Gonzales, *Movin' On Down De Line*, p. 19, 1975
- That's my lady homey. Her name's Brandi. — *Boyz N The Hood*, 1990
- Called up the homies and I'm askin' y'all / Which park are y'all playing basketball[.] — Ice Cube *It Was a Good Day*, 1993

homey mine *noun*
a very good friend from your neighborhood *US, 1993*

- "Here, homey-mine. Wipe your face." — Jess Mowry, *Six Out Seven*, p. 20, 1993

homie *noun*
a homosexual *US, 1990*

- — Charles Shafer, *Folk Speech in Texas Prisons*, p. 206, 1990

homing pigeon *noun*
the US armed forces insignia designating honorable discharge *US, 1946*

- — *American Speech*, p. 153, April 1946: "GI words from the separation center and proctology ward"

homintern *noun*
an aggressive, loyal homosexual subculture *US, 1968*
A term coined by W.H. Auden, punning on the Marxist "comintern" or Communist International.

- The notion that the arts are dominated by a kind of homosexual Mafia—or "Homintern," as it has been called—is sometimes exaggerated, particularly by spiteful failures looking for scapegoats. — Joe David Brown, *Sex in the '60s*, p. 67, 1968

homo *noun*
1 a homosexual, especially a male homosexual *US, 1922*

- One corner of 52nd and Sixth Avenue is particularly obnoxious, a hangout for prostitutes and homos, dark and light. — Jack Lait and Lee Mortimer, *New York Confidential*, p. 45, 1948
- It is also the hustlers' bar—the boys who make a living among the sad old homos of the Eight Avenue night. — Jack Kerouac, *On the Road*, p. 131, 1957
- Makes you think homos are suckers for punishment, right? — John Francis Hunter, *The Gay Insider*, p. 78, 1971
- The local homos threw a lovely little potluck brunch for us in Antelope Park. — Armistead Maupin, *Further Tales of the City*, p. 128, 1982

2 used as an insulting term of address to someone who is not homosexual *US, 1993*

- God you are terrible. Okay, homo, I hope you are ready to take the agonizing, bitter humiliation of defeat. — *Dazed and Confused*, 1993

homo heaven *noun*
1 a public area where homosexuals congregate in hopes of quick sex *US, 1965*

- Central Park has certain sections known as homo heavens. — Antony James, *America's Homosexual Underground*, p. 60, 1965

2 the upper balcony in a theater patronized by homosexual men *US, 1966*

- — Johnny Shearer, *The Male Hustler*, p. 72, 1966

homosexual adapter *noun*
a computer cable with either two male or two female connectors *US, 1991*

- — Eric S. Raymond, *The New Hacker's Dictionary*, p. 175, 1991

hon *noun*
used as a term of endearment *US, 1906*
A shortened "honey." Fiercely claimed by Baltimore, Maryland, as a Baltimore-coinage.

- I'm sorry I brought it up, hon. — Irving Shulman, *The Amboy Dukes*, p. 175, 1947
- "What's the answer, hon?" Guide had asked, dreading the answer. — Max Shulman, *Rally Round the Flag, Boys!*, p. 223, 1957
- How you bin, hon? — Jean Brooks, *The Opal Witch*, 1967
- Take me to the party hon. — Kevin Mackey, *The Cure*, 1970
- A player brings in a lot of cash, hon, we have to look at it impartially, only as money, nothing else. — Elmore Leonard, *Glitz*, p. 153, 1985
- Thank you, hon. How's Fargo? — *Fargo*, 1996
- Teddy, hon, are you okay? — *Something About Mary*, 1998

hon bun *noun*
used as a term of endearment *US, 1940s*
A shortened "honey bunny."

- I want you clear-headed, hon bun. — Elmore Leonard, *City Primeval*, p. 54, 1980

honcho *noun*
a boss, a big-shot *US, 1945*
From the Japanese term for "a group or squad leader."

- This prisoner is the "honcho," or group headman, in the POW stockade. — *Coshocton (Ohio) Tribune*, 1st September 1945
- "Okay, Buddy," says the chief, "you're the honcho." — Darryl Ponicsan, *The Last Detail*, p. 20, 1970
- We called the few tough aggressive pilots "honchos" and the rest "students." — Walter Boyne and Steven Thompson, *The Wild Blue*, p. 172, 1986
- Ito-san was the head honcho, the big cheese, the number one Tomodachi[.] — Rhiannon Paice, *Too Late for the Festival*, p. 27, 1999

Honda rice *noun*
IR8, a high-yielding variety of rice introduced in Vietnam in the 1960s, doubling rice production yields *US, 1985*

- They used to call it "Honda rice" in the Delta because everybody earned enough money to buy a Honda motorbike by raising a second or third crop per year. — Al Santoli, *To Bear Any Burden*, p. 203, 1985

hondo *noun*
1 an attractive, popular male *US, 1986*
- — Levi Straus & Company, *Campus Slang*, January 1986
2 a zealous enthusiast *US, 1968*
- — *Current Slang*, p. 6, Summer 1968

hondo *adjective*
excellent, exciting *US, 1991*

- [T]hey've got the world's most hondo (and, real often, most gorgeous) whiskey-river twin-ax attack[.] — Chuck Eddy, *Stairway to Hell*, p. 13, 1991

honest *noun*
cherry syrup added to a soda fountain drink *US, 1946*
From the legend of George Washington's honesty when asked as a child if he cut down a cherry tree.

- — *American Speech*, p. 88, April 1946: "The language of West Coast culinary workers"

honest *adjective*
(used of a drug) relatively pure and undiluted *US, 1970*

- — William D. Alsever, *Glossary for the Establishment and Other Uptight People*, p. 16, December 1970

honest injun'

used as a pledge of complete honesty *US, 1851*

- He held up his hand like a Boy Scout. "Honest injun. You didn't miss a thing." — Armistead Maupin, *Further Tales of the City*, p. 217, 1982
- "Don't blame me. I kept my word." "Right." "Honest Injun." — Rita Ciresi, *Pink Slip*, p. 323, 1999
- "Honest Injun?" I can't believe what a pushover you are. — Kevin Smith, *Jay and Silent Bob Strike Back*, p. 38, 2001

honest John *noun*

1 a decent, upstanding, law-abiding citizen *US, 1884*

- [Y]ou long-suffering, honest Johns[.] — Charles Raven, *Underworld Nights*, p. 36, 1956
- He put on his best honest-John smile, and held out the license, being helpful. — Donald Goines, *White Man's Justice, Black Man's Grief*, p. 13, 1973

2 in a shoplifting operation, an honest-looking confederate who distracts the store personnel *US, 1974*

- It stated an "Honest John" is a person used to divert the attention of a clerk while an accomplice dips into the cash register. — *San Francisco Examiner*, p. 6, 22nd February 1974

honest kine?

is that right? *US, 1981*

Hawaiian youth usage.

- — Douglas Simonson, *Pidgin to da Max*, 1981

honest reader *noun*

a playing card with an unintentional imperfection that enables an observant player to identify it in another player's hand *US, 1988*

- — George Percy, *The Language of Poker*, p. 45, 1988

honest squeeze *noun*

a cherry squeeze soda fountain drink *US, 1952*

An allusion to the George Washington myth involving the cutting down of a cherry tree.

- — *American Speech*, p. 232, October 1952: "The argot of soda jerks"

honey *noun*

1 a sexually attractive young woman *US, 1930*

Sometimes spelled "hunny."

- Yeah, and there's two swingin' honeys for every guy. — Jan Berry and Dean Torrance, *Surf City*, 1963
- Officer Peters is not the first man who took a look at some young honey and decided he might like to try a little of that. — George V. Higgins, *The Rat on Fire*, p. 88, 1981
- I mean I've sucked some titties and finger banged a couple of hunnies but I never stuck it in. — *Boyz N The Hood*, 1990

2 a female surfer or a male surfer's girlfriend *US, 1986*

- — Rob Burt, *Surf City, Drag City*, 1986

3 an "effeminate" lesbian *US, 1978*

- — Anon., *King Smut's Wet Dreams Interpreted*, 1978

4 anything considered pleasing, attractive, effective, etc. *US, 1888*

- That's a honey of an anklet you're wearing, Mrs Dietrichson. — Fred McMurray, *Double Indemnity*, p. 49, 1944

honey barge *noun*

a garbage scow *US, 1941*

- Highly commended was Chief Boatswain's Mate L.M. Jansen, commander of YG-t7, who brought his "honey barge" (garbage lighter) alongside and helped fight the fires[.] — Samuel Eliot Morison, *History of the United States Naval Operations in World War II*, p. 103, 1948

honey box *noun*

1 the anus *US, 2005*

- He measures them all up and down, including parts you didn't expect, like their nipple size or even their honey box. — Ethan Morden, *How's Your Romance?*, p. 12, 2005

2 the vagina, *US, 1969*

- Ain't none of 'em my bitch unless I got my cock in her honey box. — Cecil Brown, *The Life & Loves of Mr. Jiveass Nigger*, p. 143, 1969

honey bucket *noun*

1 a portable toilet *US, 1976*

- — Porter Bibb, *CB Bible*, p. 96, 1976

2 a chamberpot *US, 1931*

- [E]xcept for a brief visit once a day to feed us and change our honey buckets, we were left in darkness. — Malcolm Braley, *False Starts*, p. 115, 1976

honey cart *noun*

1 a vehicle hauling human excrement; a portable toilet *US, 1929*

- — *American Speech*, p. 118, May 1960: "Korean bamboo English"

2 a portable toilet *US, 1929*

- In early dawn after finishing at Ciro's, he leaned against buildings retching as "honey carts" passed by. — Kiana Davenport, *Song of the Exile*, p. 120, 1999

honeycomb *noun*

a type of altered dice *US, 1975*

- Doc brought out some dice and explained how these were house dice—honeycombs they called them. In the center of each is a little bit of honey which gets hot as the dice are used, making the dice stick on four and seven. — James Carr, *Bad*, p. 99, 1975

honey dip *noun*

an attractive woman, especially one with a light brown skin color *US, 1993*

- — *Washington Post*, 14th October 1993

honey dipping *noun*

vaginal secretions *US, 1949*

- — Captain Vincent J. Monteleone, *Criminal Slang*, p. 121, 1949

honey-do *adjective*

(said of a list of chores) compiled by one spouse for the other *US, 1990*

- You will probably have a "honey-do" list for him most of the time. — Jerry Hardin, *Getting Ready for Marriage Workbook*, p. 1, 1992

honeyfuck *verb*

1 to have sex with a Lolita-aged nymphet *US, 1967*

- — Dale Gordon, *The Dominion Sex Dictionary*, p. 85, 1967

2 to have sex in a slow, affectionate manner *US, 1964*

- — Roger Blake, *The American Dictionary of Sexual Terms*, p. 101, 1964

honey, I'm home!

used for humorously announcing an entrance *US, 1988*

From the *Dick Van Dyke Show* (1961 – 66), a centerpiece in the golden age of the situation comedy on US television.

- Honey! I'm home! — *Drugstore Cowboy*, 1988
- Honey, I'm home! — *Natural Born Killers*, 1994

honeyman *noun*

a procurer of prostitutes; a man who makes his living off the earnings of prostitutes *US, 1982*

- — Ralph de Sola, *Crime Dictionary*, 1982
- — *Maledicta*, p. 148, Summer/Winter 1986–1987: "Sexual slang: prostitutes, pedophiles, flagellators, transvestites, and necrophiles"

honeymoon *noun*

1 sex *US, 1976*

Used by prostitutes in Southeast Asia during the Vietnam war.

- Dropped a hundred-thirty last night, on the same broad, and all he got outa the deal was a steam bath. She wouldn't go honeymoon with him. — Charles Anderson, *The Grunts*, p. 19, 1976

2 the early period in a drug addiction *US, 1952*

- — *American Speech*, p. 27, February 1952: "Teen-age hophead jargon"

3 the first few hands played by a new player in a poker game *US, 1996*

- — John Vorhaus, *The Big Book of Poker Slang*, p. 22, 1996

honey oil *noun*

the recreational drug ketamine *US, 1994*

- — US Department of Justice US, *Street Terms*, October 1994

honeypot *noun*

1 the vagina *US, 1958*

Found once in the UK in 1719, and then in general slang usage with "Candy."

- "Now I am inserting the member," he explained, as he parted the tender quavering lips of the pink honeypot and allowed his stout member to be drawn slowly into the seething thermal pudding of the darling girl. — Terry Southern, *Candy*, p. 208, 1958
- [A]ll he wanted was a fast duck of the dick in and out of Franny's Zen-immaculate honeypot in the back seat. — Lester Bangs, *Psychotic Reactions and Carburetor Dung*, 1971
- "I'll make that hot little honeypot or yours feel real good." — Jennifer Sills, *Massage Parlor*, p. 28, 1973

- Meanwhile, she sits astride me, easing her honeypot down around the throbbing upstanding round rod. — Clarence Major, *All-Night Visitors*, p. 7, 1998

2 in male homosexual usage, the anus and rectum *US, 1981*
- — *Male Swinger Number 3*, p. 46, 1981: "The complete gay dictionary"

3 a chamber pot *US, 1954*
- Sitting on "honeypots" on lawn, half-Japanese children receive toilet training. — *Ebony*, p. 20, July 1954

4 in Maine, a muddy hole in the road *US, 1975*
- — John Gould, *Maine Lingo*, p. 135, 1975

honey shot *noun*
a gratuitous television view of a pretty girl or woman, usually a spectator at a sporting event *US, 1968*
- — *American Speech*, Spring–Summer 1973
- They do this a lot, they told me, and they call it "hooking a barracuda," or a "honey shot," or, as a matter of fact, a "hold it." — Dan Jenkins, *Dead Solid Perfect*, p. 152, 1986

honey wagon *noun*
1 a vehicle hauling human excrement; a portable toilet *US, 1923*
- — John T. Algeo, *American Speech*, May 1960: "Korean bamboo English"

2 a catering truck *US, 1992*
- We just started gabbing outside the honey wagon one day. — Armistead Maupin, *Maybe the Moon*, p. 33, 1992

Hong Kong *noun*
padding used by Vietnamese bar girls to enhance their figures *US, 1966*
- HONG KONG. Something false or artificial, employed to improve a girl's figure and ease her mind by helping her put up a good front. — Ken Melvin, *Sorry 'Bout That*, p. 94, 1966: Glossary

honk *noun*
pleasure; enjoyment *US, 1964*
- My boyfriend and I do it at least once a day, generally oftener, but every now and then he gets a honk out of watching one of his friends throw it to me. — *Screw*, p. 16, 16th May 1969

honk *verb*
1 to vomit *UK, 1967*
- If you need to honk, honk into this. — *Wayne's World*, 1992

2 to inhale drugs, originally through the nose *US, 1968*
- [T]he slight scratching-sounds of bankers writing checks and cocaine honked through ivory straws on yachts. — Ed Sanders, *Tales of Beatnik Glory*, p. 92, 1975
- One day he was honking spray Pam and had a heart attack. — Eric Davis, *The Slick Boys*, p. 58, 1994

3 when flying an airplane or helicopter, to pull, to jerk, to yank *US, 1946*
- Richards "honked" back on the controls, powering the helicopter up into an arc, hoping to escape into one of the scud clouds. — Neil Sheehan, *A Bright Shining Lie*, p. 774, 1988

► **honk your horn**
to grab a man's penis *US, 1970*
- "She groped you, huh, Rosso?" "Honest to God, she honked my horn," said Ranatti, raising a rather stubby right hand heavenward. "Gave it two toots with a thumb and forefinger before I laid the iron on her wrists." — Joseph Wambaugh, *The New Centurions*, pp. 175–176, 1970

honked off *adjective*
angry *US, 1958*
- I never seen a man get so honked off over losin' a pool game. — Ken Weaver, *Texas Crude*, p. 114, 1984

honker *noun*
1 the nose *US, 1942*
- Elvin and Dale had to wait before the door was opened by a stocky little guy Elvin judged to be light-skinned colored, except he had a big honker on him and maybe was trying to pass. — Elmore Leonard, *Maximum Bob*, p. 60, 1991

2 the penis *US, 1968*
- That honker of yours was as ready for me as mine was ready for your slick butt. — James Harper, *Homo Laws in all 50 States*, p. 36, 1968
- He gasps, amazed that I can really choke his honker all the way down and keep it plugged in. — Simon Sheppard, *Roughed Up*, p. 76, 2003
- "His honker is homegrown." — Camika Spencer, *He Had It Coming*, p. 81, 2005

3 expectorated sputum *US, 1981*
- — *Maledicta*, p. 32, 1988–1989: "Medical maledicta from San Francisco"

4 a goose *US, 1841*
- "Canada honkers up there," Papa says, squinting up. — Ken Kesey, *One Flew Over the Cuckoo's Nest*, p. 91, 1962

5 a large and powerful wave *US, 1991*
- — Trevor Cralle, *The Surfin'ary*, p. 54, 1991

honking *adjective*
very large *US, 1995*
- — Connie Eble (Editor), *UNC-CH Campus Slang*, p. 5, April 1995
- And then those honkin' hooters had to grow in and ruin the whole coltish silhouette! — Mr. Skin, *Mr. Skin's Skincyclopedia*, p. 490, 2005

honk on *verb*
in the usage of youthful model road racers (slot car racers), to race fast *US, 1997*
- — Phantom Surfers, *The Exciting Sounds of Model Road Racing (Album cover)*, 1997

honky; honkie; honkey *noun*
a white person *US, 1946*
Usually not said with kindness, especially when used to describe a member of the white ruling class.
- They couldn't care less about the old, stiffassed honkies who don't like their new dances[.] — Eldridge Cleaver, *Soul on Ice*, p. 81, 1968
- no honky, liberal, bleeding heart, guilt-ridden advocates of justice, but first-class case-winners. — *The Digger Papers*, p. 15, August 1968
- The residents of this ghetto housing project clearly show us that guerilla warfare is the key: Their uprising put six honkies out of commission, only one brother was injured, and no black people were killed. — *The Black Panther*, p. 9, 4th May 1968
- You come back here and kill one racist, red-necked honkey camel-breathed peckerwood who's been misusing you and your people all your life and that's murder. — H. Rap Brown, *Die Nigger Die!*, p. 38, 1969

honky-tonk *noun*
a saloon, dance-hall, or gambling-house *US, 1894*
Also used as an adjective.
- We did meet, and we drove out to a couple of honky-tonks. — Herbert Huncke, *Guilty of Everything*, p. 88, 1990

honyocker *noun*
an unsophisticated rustic *US, 1912*
From the German slang ("chicken chaser").
- Not the captains of industry he had hoped for, but a crowd of honyockers and wahoos and lady shoppers and old galoots with an afternoon to kill. — Garrison Keillor, *Wit*, p. 28, 1991

hoo-ah!
used for expressing enthusiastic approval *US, 1991*
- The soldier had been digging foxholes for two days. "Hoo-ah!" he yelled, repeating the signature call of the American Forces. — *Houston Post*, 28th February 1991
- — *American Speech*, p. 391, Winter 1991: "Among the new words"

hoobly goobly *noun*
nonsense *US, 1956*
- — *American Speech*, p. 228, October 1956: "More United States Air Force slang"

hooch; hootch *noun*
1 alcohol *US, 1915*
- Most through trains carry clubs cars, in which excellent hooch is sold at moderate prices. — Jack Lait and Lee Mortimer, *New York Confidential*, p. 198, 1946
- He's got himself all jammed up with some floozy and a bottle of hooch. — Raymond Chandler, *Little Sister*, p. 13, 1949
- He used to drink a bottle of hootch a day and I suppose the New York people thought he was a weak link in their security chain. — Clancy Sigal, *Going Away*, p. 36, 1961
- Mama frowned and scolded, "Bunny, why yu mixin' cansur with hooch? Yu gonna' die." — Iceberg Slim (Robert Beck), *Mama Black Widow*, p. 72, 1969
- Alright—bring on the free hootch! — *Chasing Amy*, 1997

2 a peasant hut; a small, improvised shelter *US, 1952*
Korean and then Vietnam war usage.
- In a hootch, three battle-seasoned warriors, Reggie, Jake and Crunch, slept through it all. — Elaine Shepard, *The Doom Pussy*, p. 41, 1967
- A small clearing and on the far side a "hootch" tucked under the trees. — Donald Duncan, *The New Legions*, p. 42, 1967

- Folks do not want to hear about the night at Fire Base Hariette—down the way from LZ Skator-Gator, and within earshot of a ragtag bunch of mud-and-thatch hooches everyone called Gookville—when the whole company, except for one guy, got killed. — Larry Heinemann, *Paco's Story*, pp. 13–14, 1986
- The hooches were still up, and we were envious of the relative comfort the Marines on Khe Sanh base seemed to have. — Eric Hammel, *Khe Sanh: Siege in the Clouds*, p. 100, 1989

hooched out *adjective*
dressed in a sexually suggestive manner *US, 2002*
- [A] hooched-out 2 Live Crew video dancer. Couldn't get any less skin than that. — Natalie Darden, *All About Me*, p. 288, 2002
- Baby sister had a banging body, and she mighta been looking just a little too fly and hooched out for Vonnie's tastes. — Noire, *Candy Licker*, p. 114, 2005

hooch girl *noun*
a young Vietnamese woman who worked as a maid or did laundry for US troops *US, 1969*
- Dottie was no hooch girl. She was a clever little prostitute, who knew all the tricks of her trade. — Pearl Buck, *The Good Deed*, p. 199, 1969
- If the General knew about the hooch-girls, Angel explained, then the General would be responsible. — Anthony Herbert, *Soldier*, pp. 119–120, 1973
- There were mama-sans and hooch girls all over the place. Everything was clean. — Mark Barker, *Nam*, p. 31, 1981
- [T]he hooch girl, who cleaned up and took care of the laundry, stopped in her work, shook her broom at me, and started yelling, "You go kill VC! Numba fucking ten." — Paul Young, *First Recon—Second to None*, p. 195, 1992

hooch-head *noun*
a drunkard *US, 1946*
- "I done tole you," he said to Mickey, "not to rent them goddamned rooms on the top floor to them Kong-cookin' hootchhead son-of-a-bitches." — Mezz Mezzrow, *Really the Blues*, p. 250, 1946

hoochy koochy *noun*
a sexually suggestive dance *US, 1895*
- Sol Bloom, as an entrepreneur at the Chicago World's Fair, celebrating the 400th anniversary of the discovery of America, presented "Little Egypt" in a series of contortions while she stayed on her feet, known as the "hoochy koochy." — Jack Lait and Lee Mortimer, *Chicago Confidential*, p. 157, 1950
- But we forgot that and headed straight for North Clark Street, after a spin in the Loop, to see the hootchy-kootchy joints and hear the bop. — Jack Kerouac, *On the Road*, p. 138, 1957
- [S]top to watch the hoochiekoo dancer, whose name is Carmelita[.] — Lester Bangs, *Psychotic Reactions and Carburetor Dung*, p. 124, 1973

hood *noun*
1 a neighborhood, especially in an urban ghetto *US, 1967*
- The fire never goes out on the steam... in the 'hood. — Odie Hawkins, *Ghetto Sketches*, p. 75, 1972
- They either don't know, don't show, and don't care what be going on in the hood. — *Boyz N The Hood*, 1990
- Hood they got no better'n ours. — Jess Mowry, *Way Past Cool*, p. 14, 1992
- When cocaine got too expensive for the 'hood, crack was invented. — Chris Rock, *Rock This*, p. 68, 1997

2 a rough street youth; a criminal *US, 1880*
A shortened "hoodlum."
- [T]he people he'd worked with were just lowdown grafting hoods[.] — Derek Raymond (Robin Cook), *The Crust on its Uppers*, p. 57, 1962
- "When I was thirteen, I was considered a hood, even though I didn't hang out with any hoodish people." — Nicholas Von Hoffman, *We Are The People Our Parents Warned Us Against*, p. 56, 1967
- [M]y congregation, most of them under thirty—hoods, bikers, dopers, pushers, run-aways, teeny-boppers[.] — Arthur Blessitt, *Turned On to Jesus*, p. 1, 1971
- You know you walk around like you're Mr. Cool or Mr. Wisdom but you're not ... you're just an old hood. — *Hard Eight*, 1996

3 the chest *US, 1989*
- — James Harris, *A Convict's Dictionary*, p. 33, 1989

4 a 12 ounce bottle of beer *US, 1967*
- — *American Speech*, p. 62, February 1967: "Soda-fountain, restaurant and tavern calls"

▸ **under the hood**
literally, flying by instrumentation; figuratively, operating without knowing exactly what is going on *US, 1956*
- — *American Speech*, p. 229, October 1956: "More United States Air Force slang"

hoodie *noun*
a sweatshirt or jacket with a hood *US, 1993*
- — Maria Hinojas, *Crews*, p. 167, 1995: "Glossary"
- Delgadillo glared at the boys in their hoodies and baggy jeans[.] — Gini Sikes, *8 Ball Chicks*, p. 71, 1997
- She wore a cranberry-striped hoodie and matching green leggings. — Adrian Nicole LeBlanc, *Random Family*, p. 159, 2003

hoodish *adjective*
tough, criminal *US, 1967*
- "When I was thirteen, I was considered a hood, even though I didn't hang out with any hoodish people." — Nicholas Von Hoffman, *We Are The People Our Parents Warned Us Against*, p. 56, 1967

hoodrat *noun*
1 a tough youth who prowls the streets of his inner-city neighborhood, in search of trouble and fun *US, 1997*
- — Judi Sanders, *Da Bomb*, p. 15, 1997
- "You ain't a 'hood rat, are ya?" — Joseph Wambaugh, *Hollywood Station*, p. 6, 2006

2 a promiscuous girl *US, 1997*
- — Pamela Munro, *U.C.L.A. Slang*, p. 78, 1997
- — Connie Eble (Editor), *UNC-CH Campus Slang*, p. 6, Fall 1999
- Talk about how you wanna get back with that tramp and how you forgive that hoodrat broad/dickhead. — *Hip-Hop Connection*, p. 22, July 2002

hoody *adjective*
inclined to juvenile delinquency *US, 1960*
- Two hoody boys in our class put on a race one night with their cars full of kids and smashed up and the school board made a large odor. — Glendon Swarthout, *Where the Boys Are*, p. 4, 1960

hooey *noun*
nonsense *US, 1912*
- Maybe this brother-and-sister stuff was just hooey, just like everything else. — James T. Farrell, *Saturday Night*, p. 19, 1947
- If Duffy wants a seven, he pulls the ace from this side, the six from the other, and holds 'em for a minute, doing some player hooey to stall long enough for the gas to warm up and turn solid. — Stephen Cannell, *King Con*, p. 138, 1997

hoof *noun*
a foot or shoe *UK, 1598*
- — *Current Slang*, p. 10, Summer 1969

▸ **on the hoof**
1 working as a prostitute on the streets *US, 1977*
- She had no sense of it anymore, no idea of who the plainclothes might be, now fast the track was, whether she still had the heart to keep up her game out on the hoof. — John Sayles, *Union Dues*, p. 180, 1977

2 on the spot, spontaneously *US, 1992*
From the literal sense of the term, applied to cattle or swine, meaning "alive."
- I just made that up on the hoof. — Richard Price, *Clockers*, p. 270, 1992

hoof *verb*
1 to dance *US, 1916*
- The highly paid babes who pose for the photographers are prettier but dumber than their sisters who hoof in the choruses. — Jack Lait and Lee Mortimer, *New York Confidential*, p. 134, 1948
- Carrie Nugent, the sensational Negro tap dancer who'd hoofed her way around the world and been admired and acclaimed everywhere. — Ethel Waters, *His Eye is on the Sparrow*, p. 53, 1951
- [A]ll propped up by the copper wages of streetsinging, coffeehouse hoofing, bit parts in transient flicks, and the going rate for what I choose to call High Adventure. — Richard Farina, *Long Time Coming and A Long Time Gone*, p. 37, 1969

2 to walk *UK, 1641*
- Meanwhile, the goat takes off down West Street. Guess he didn't want to get locked up. We hoofed too — Edwin Torres, *After Hours*, p. 231, 1979

hoofer *noun*
a professional dancer, especially a tap dancer *US, 1916*

- A friend of ours, a newspaperman, was married to a red-headed hoofer in a Broadway night club. — Jack Lait and Lee Mortimer, *New York Confidential*, p. 127, 1948
- Clem and Jody, two oldtime vaudeville hoofers, cope out as Russian agents[.] — William Burroughs, *Naked Lunch*, p. 158, 1957
- The hoofer had originally bought it from a drag queen she worked with at the Greenwich Village Inn when they had straight acts. — Lenny Bruce, *How to Talk Dirty and Influence People*, p. 33, 1965
- Making direct eye contact, he matches them step for step, dancing along, belly abounce, a real hoofer. — Josh Alan Friedman, *Tales of Times Square*, p. 55, 1986

hoofprint *noun*

footprints that could be identified as or surmised to be made by Viet Cong or North Vietnamese soldiers *US, 1989*

- "Well, the usual stuff: strung-out commo wire, spider holes—those are gook-size foxholes—smothered cooking fires—hoofprints—what we called hoofprints: fresh VC sandal prints; they made their sandals out of old tires. And North Vietnamese Army boots—actually black sneakers. — Nelson DeMille, *Word of Honor*, p. 131, 1989

hoo-ha *noun*

a fuss or commotion; nonsense *UK, 1931*

- Let me just say right now that I'm well aware of all the current hoo-ha about the sun and all. — Jill Conner Browne, *The Sweet Potato Queens' Book of Love*, p. 27, 1999
- I think it's a lot of hoo-ha. — Jeffrey Eugenides, *Middlesex*, p. 362, 2002

hook *noun*

1 a person who serves as a liaison between someone seeking to buy drugs and someone with drugs for sale *US, 2006*

- "Dealers hang out by the trains, and the hooks hang around the boulevard." — Joseph Wambaugh, *Hollywood Station*, p. 9, 2006

2 a social outcast; a perpetual victim *US, 1993*

- I just couldn't imagine living the life of a "hook," those seemingly spineless nerds who were always victims of someone's ridicule or physical violence, who never responded to an affront of any type. — Sanyika Shakur, *Monster*, p. 100, 1993
- The other dudes that weren't hanging around us were playing ball, and we looked at them as punks, as hooks. — Yusuf Jah, *Uprising*, p. 164, 1995

3 in a pickpocket team, the confederate who actually makes the theft *UK, 1863*

- — Hyman E. Goldin et al., *Dictionary of American Underworld Lingo*, p. 100, 1950
- It is understood by the police that a "bump man" or a "hook" does not operate at the Garden under the code long agreed upon between the stadium and the artistes. — Robert Sylvester, *No Cover Charge*, p. 286, 1956
- Most often, the thieves work in teams. In police parlance, the "stall" distracts the victim while the "hook" takes the merchandize. — *The New York Times*, p. B1, 13 July 1989

4 a finger, the hand *UK, 1829*
Usually used in the plural.

- — Lou Shelly, *Hepcats Jive Dictionary*, p. 12, 1945
- The skinny was that bohemian chicks couldn't keep their hooks off soulful, lonely sailors. — Darryl Ponicsan, *The Last Detail*, p. 75, 1970
- Now get your goddamn hooks off the blanket. — Gerald Petievich, *Money Men*, p. 48, 1981

5 a key or lockpick *US, 1970*

- Red, we need some hooks and need them quick. We've got a blast going in two weeks[.] — Red Rudensky, *The Gonif*, p. 47, 1970

6 a person who strives to be that which he is not *US, 1989*

- — James Harris, *A Convict's Dictionary*, p. 39, 1989

7 a prostitute *US, 1918*
A shortened **HOOKER**.

- This was a thing where we got a few friends and a few light hooks to come in, get drunk, take naked, and have what we called an Eastern Regional Eat-Off. — Dan Jenkins, *Semi-Tough*, p. 64, 1972
- The rich are the worst tippers, hooks are lousy. — *Taxi Driver*, 1976

8 a contact in the police department with influence *US, 1973*

- There was an uneasy break in the dialogue until Inspector Sachson said, as if it were a perfectly sound explanation, that the man had a "hook"—an influential contact in the department. — Peter Maas, *Serpico*, p. 247, 1973

9 a superior with influence and the ability to protect *US, 1997*
New York police slang.

- — Samuel M. Katz, *Anytime Anywhere*, p. 388, 1997: "The extremely unofficial and completely off-the-record NYPD/ESU truck-two glossary"

10 a telephone or telephone call *US, 1975*

- — *American Speech*, p. 61, Spring–Summer 1975: "Razorback slang"

11 a CH-47 Chinook helicopter *US, 1968*
Vietnam war usage.

- — Carl Fleischhauer, *A Glossary of Army Slang*, p. 26, 1968
- "I'd have that son-of-a-bitch long before the Hook gets here." — Anthony Herbert, *Soldier*, p. 314, 1973

12 a razor *US, 1962*

- — Joseph E. Ragen and Charles Finston, *Inside the World's Toughest Prison*, p. 803, 1962: "Penitentiary and underworld glossary"

13 the concave part of a wave *US, 1963*

- — Grant W. Kuhns, *On Surfing*, p. 117, 1963

14 a chevron insignia *US, 1947*

- — *American Speech*, p. 55, February 1947: "Pacific war language"

15 the grade "C" *US, 1968*

- — Collin Baker et al., *College Undergraduate Slang Study Conducted at Brown University*, p. 138, 1968

16 a feature in a computer or computer program designed to facilitate later changes or enhancements *US, 1991*

- — Eric S. Raymond, *The New Hacker's Dictionary*, p. 201, 1991

17 in a confidence swindle, the stage in the swindle when the victim is fully committed to the scheme *US, 1969*

- He was approaching that stage in his tale that black grifters call the hook. — Iceberg Slim (Robert Beck), *Trick Baby*, p. 55, 1969

18 in pointspreads established by bookmakers in sports betting, half a point *US, 1991*

- — *Bay Sports Review*, p. 8, November 1991

19 in a deck of playing cards, a jack or knave *US, 1961*

- — Irv Roddy, *Friday Night Poker*, p. 218, 1961

▸ **on the hook**
1 in debt *US, 1957*

- A shaky guy ... but on the hook for enough money he can't say no to anyone. — Gerald Petievich, *One-Shot Deal*, pp. 193–194, 1981

2 in love *US, 1951*
Teen slang.

- — *Newsweek*, p. 28, 8th October 1951

3 skipping school *US, 1906*

- For three and a half hours they sat in the Paramount balcony with the two high school babes who were also on the hook. — Irving Shulman, *The Amboy Dukes*, p. 29, 1947

hook *verb*
1 to addict *US, 1922*

- The goal of every narcotics pusher is to "hook" a wealthy adult—the wife of a prominent businessman perhaps—who can be blackmailed as well as forced to pay exorbitant prices for dope. — Alson Smith, *Syndicate City*, p. 173, 1954
- I knew that the first shot could not hook you physically. — Jeremy Larner and Ralph Tefferteller, *The Addict in the Street*, p. 53, 1964

2 to inject by hypodermic needle *US, 1953*

- "You've been hooking that spot so much it's about to get infected," he said, pointing to a needle welt. — William Burroughs, *Junkie*, p. 81, 1953

3 to steal *UK, 1615*

- I hooked it from Callahan's bunk. — Norman Mailer, *The Naked and the Dead*, p. 613, 1948
- — *American Speech*, p. 194, October 1951: "A study of reformatory argot"
- [S]ome of the gang may have more technical knowledge than I do about hooking cars and trucks, but I knew about planning, organization, security. — Joseph Pistone, *Donnie Brasco*, p. 27, 1987

4 to engage in prostitution *US, 1959*

- She was hooking when I met her. So I didn't go for that at all. 'Cause I never made it with a hooker before. — James Mills, *The Panic in Needle Park*, p. 56, 1966
- While girls all over the room were murmuring, "What's she talking about?" one of the tougher, older Bunnies bellowed, "Hooking!" — Kathryn Leigh Scott, *The Bunny Years*, p. 138, 1998

5 to arrest *US, 1928*

- It's life if you get hooked with it and you can't really do much of anything with it except fight a war, maybe. — George V. Higgins, *The Friends of Eddie Doyle*, p. 8, 1971
- He knew what he was going to do, but it was a felony and he didn't think he should confide in her, for fear she'd hook him upon the spot. — Stephen J. Cannell, *The Tin Collectors*, p. 262, 2001

▸ **hook a barracuda**
to locate and show a gratuitous television view of a pretty girl or woman, usually a spectator at a sporting event *US, 1986*

- They do this a lot, they told me, and they call it "hooking a barracuda," or a "honey shot," or, as a matter of fact, a "hold it." — Dan Jenkins, *Dead Solid Perfect*, p. 152, 1986

▶ **hook it**
to drive fast *US, 1981*
- We didn't know where the hell we were, but we knew we had to hook it fast. — Robert Lipkin, *A Brotherhood of Outlaws*, p. 171, 1981

hook and book *verb*
to handcuff and arrest a criminal suspect *US, 1994*
- — *Los Angeles Times*, p. B8, 19th December 1994

hook and bullet crowd *noun*
hunters and recreational fishermen, collectively as a lobbying force *US, 1990*
- Since 1976, that constituency is no longer just the hook-and-bullet crowd that the department still seems to believe it is. — *St. Louis Post-Dispatch*, p. 2C, 27th September 1990
- In the next few weeks, the Bush and Kerry camps will be rolling out their over what is often called the "hook and bullet" crowd. — *Washington Post*, p. A4, 28th June 2004

hooked *adjective*
1 addicted to drugs *US, 1922*
Originally a transitive verb—the drug hooking the person—but that formation is long forgotten in the US, 1946.
- Is it junk? Are you hooked, Diane? — George Mandel, *Flee the Angry Strangers*, p. 285, 1952
- When you are hooked, the effects of a shot are not dramatic. — William Burroughs, *Junkie*, p. 55, 1953
- GEORGE: Oh, no, no, no, no. I—I—I couldn't do that. I mean, I've got enough problems with the—the booze and all. I mean I—I can't afford to get hooked. WYATT: Oh, no—you won't get hooked. — *Easy Rider*, p. 122, 1969
- Only a skag high ain't but good the first few times out, then you hooked, all they gotta do is reel you in, by the crotch now, and squeeze till you cough up another five dollars for a bag. — Edwin Torres, *Carlito's Way*, p. 10, 1975
2 (of a shot in pool) obstructed *US, 1979*
- — Mike Shamos, *The Illustrated Encyclopedia of Billiards*, p. 117, 1993

hooker *noun*
1 a prostitute *US, 1845*
Probably derives from the conventional sense of "hook" (to lure); possibly reinforced by now obsolete slang: "hook" (to rob); and with reference to Corlear's Hook, popularly The Hook, an area of New York City known for prostitution.
- Who's going to take the word of a five-buck hooker against Elmer Gantry[.] — Richard Brooks, *Elmer Gantry*, 1960
- "'Cause like every hooker I've ever met—I've never made it with a hooker before." — James Mills, *The Panic in Needle Park*, p. 51, 1966
2 in a deck of playing cards, a queen *US, 1967*
An evolved form of the more common **WHORE**.
- — Albert H. Morehead, *The Complete Guide to Winning Poker*, p. 265, 1967
3 the hand *US, 1959*
A variant of the more common **HOOK**.
- He then threw his deuce of hookers high and a big black cloud dropped from the sky. — Dan Burley, *Diggeth Thou?*, p. 28, 1959
4 a cigarette *US, 1951*
Teen slang.
- — *Newsweek*, p. 28, 8th October 1951

hook shop *noun*
a brothel *US, 1889*
From **HOOKER** (prostitute).
- He thought of the time he and Ricky were present when the big guys in the neighborhood were going to a hookshop[.] — Jose Antonio Villarreal, *Pocho*, p. 178, 1959
- And he never comes back, Mr. Dillon, he's damned well told that it ain't necessary, because this is a hotel not a hook shop. — Jim Thompson, *The Grifters*, p. 15, 1963

hook up *verb*
1 to meet someone; to meet someone and have sex *US, 1986*
- Jonathan'll take you out and show you what you wanna see, then we can all hook up for lunch. — *A Few Good Men*, 1992
- Like I care about your shit. Maybe I'll hook up myself. — *Chasing Amy*, 1997

- He's already called me to hook up. — *Cruel Intentions*, 1999
- However, hooking up also refers to a spectrum of behavior, from hanging out to make out to having sex. — Rosalind Wiseman, *Queen Bees & Wannabes*, p. 236, 2002
- "It's kind of annoying when you get too drunk to remember the guy's name the morning after you hook up or whatever." — Marty Beckerman, *Generation S.L.U.T.*, p. 17, 2004
2 to work in partnership *US, 1996*
- Many punks "hook up" in protective pairing relationships, staying with one jocker in exchange for protection. — *Corrections Today*, p. 100, December 1996
3 to arm yourself *US, 1973*
- The three men were hooked up and wore their guns police style. — A.S. Jackson, *Gentleman Pimp*, p. 123, 1973
4 to provide *US, 1993*
- Na man, c'mon, hook me up just this once. — *Menace II Society*, 1993

hooky house *noun*
a house or apartment where students who are skipping school gather to pass time *US, 2003*
- In one of the early scenes of the film, a boy who looked suspiciously like Little Star did a speedy break dance at a hooky house. — Adrian Nicole LeBlanc, *Random Family*, p. 8, 2003

hooligan navy *noun*
the United States Coast Guard *US, 1922*
- "I was in the hooligan Navy." "What's the hooligan Navy?" "Where hooligans did the dirty work." — William Least Heat-Moon, *Blue Highways*, p. 367, 1982

hoonah light *noun*
in the pornography industry, a light used to illuminate the genitals of the performers *US, 1995*
- — *Adult Video News*, p. 50, October 1995

hoop *noun*
1 a car *US, 1993*
- "Get yo' black ass out of the hoop. Park that piece of shit." — Sanyika Shakur, *Monster*, p. 258, 1993
2 in criminal circles, a finger ring *US, 1856*
Conventional English for three centuries, and then ascended to criminal slang.
- — Captain Vincent J. Monteleone, *Criminal Slang*, p. 121, 1949
- That's a twenty-five ... maybe even thirty-gee ($30,000) hoop, and you miss the point? — Iceberg Slim (Robert Beck), *Death Wish*, p. 93, 1977
3 the rectum as a place to hide prison contraband *US, 1989*
- He's gone to the hoop with it. — James Harris, *A Convict's Dictionary*, p. 34, 1989

hoop-de-doo *noun*
a loud and raucous event *US, 1973*
- It would be a redletter day, the biggest hoop-de-doo on the square since those horseshoe-pitching contests they once held. — Joe Eszterhas, *Charlie Simpson's Apocalypse*, p. 33, 1973

hoopdee *noun*
a new, late-model car *US, 1971*
- — Eugene Landy, *The Underground Dictionary*, p. 105, 1971

hoop freak *noun*
a basketball enthusiast *US, 1974*
- So while knowing that nine times out of ten an honest ninny will not slip a BM's number to a dishonest hoop freak isn't everything, at least it comes close. — Gary Mayer, *Bookie*, p. 88, 1974

hoopla *noun*
a commotion *US, 1877*
Originally, the cry associated with the fairground game of tossing hoops over blocks.
- "As Americans like to say, there was much hoopla about nothing," [George] Michael said about the lyrics in his song. — *New York Daily News*, 11th March 1988

hoople *noun*
a fool, a dolt *US, 1928*
- That's some hoople goin' to pick up his girl. — Charles Whited, *Chiodo*, p. 123, 1973
- Are you a comedian or something? He says no, I'm serious, it's a good blanket. The guy's a Hoople. — Leonard Shecter and William Phillips, *On the Pad*, p. 215, 1973

- There was so many lawyers they was stumbling all over one another, bunch of hooples. — Edwin Torres, *Carlito's Way*, p. 125, 1975

hoople head *noun*
an idiot *US, 1985*
- He still sounds like a fucking hoople head half the time. — Vincent Patrick, *Family Business*, p. 54, 1985

hoopster *noun*
a basketball player *US, 1934*
- Canadian hoopster Steve Nash supposedly dated Elizabeth Hurley, but she's about ten times more famous than he is, even in Canada. — Chuck Closterman, *Sex, Drugs, and Cocoa Puffs*, p. 79, 2004

hoopty *noun*
a run-down, shoddy car *US, 1970*
- The sky was gray out this way, so not many people were getting their hoopties flossed[.] — Eric Jerome Dickey, *Cheaters*, pp. 225–226, 1999
- I'm talking serious, hoopty shakin' shit. — *Hustle and Flow*, 2004

hoopy *adjective*
emotionally imbalanced *US, 1974*
- "That broad's hoopy. I'd, if I was you, I'd stay away form that broad, Frankie." — George Higgins, *Cogan's Trade*, p. 49, 1974

hooride *verb*
in a group, to berate and humiliate someone *US, 1997*
- — *Maybeck High School Yearbook (Berkeley, California)*, p. 29, 1997
- — Rick Ayers (Editor), *Berkely High Slang Dictionary*, p. 11, 2001

hoose *noun*
in poker, a hand consisting of three cards of the same rank and a pair *US, 1951*
Known conventionally as a "full house."
- — *American Speech*, p. 99, May 1951

hoosegow *noun*
a jail or prison *US, 1908*
A corruption of the Spanish *juzgado* (court or tribunal).
- [I]t would be the happiest day of my life if I can find out she really wasn't married to him and put her in the damned hoosegow for fraud[.] — Gore Vidal, *Myra Breckinridge*, pp. 82–83, 1968
- "If they catch you, they'll put you in the hoosegow," He'd tell us[.] — Oscar Zeta Acosta, *The Autobiography of a Brown Buffalo*, p. 79, 1972
- The hit just ordered on the hooker in the hoosegow proved that. — Seth Morgan, *Homeboy*, p. 98, 1990
- This kid got his load on, staggered out of there with his piece like he's in Tombstone Arizona and now he's in the hoosegow — Richard Price, *Clockers*, p. 382, 1992

hoosier *noun*
an unsophisticated, gullible person *US, 1848*
- Agnes offered him three cartons of cigarettes, which was a fair price, but you didn't let a hoosier off with a fair price. — Malcom Braly, *Felony Tank*, p. 24, 1961
- See, there's nothing out in this area here. This is Hoosier country. — Harry King, *Box Man*, p. 86, 1972

hoosier *verb*
to defraud, to cheat *US, 1954*
- Nobody tried to hoosier him out of his money. — Caryl Chessman, *Cell 2456 Death Row*, p. 114, 1954

hoot *noun*
1 a cause for laughter *US, 1942*
A bit old-fashioned, often used in a sarcastic or condescending tone.
- Anna suggested they lunch at the Washington Square Bar & Grill. "It's a hoot," she laughed over the phone. — Armistead Maupin, *Tales of the City*, p. 74, 1978
- You're a hoot and a half, Gino. Really a fuckin' riot. — Seth Morgan, *Homeboy*, p. 188, 1990
- I remember sitting in front of the makeup mirror in the Bunny dressing room, carefully gluing on three pairs of false eyelashes, and laughing so much. Everything about being a bunny was a hoot! — Kathryn Leigh Scott, *The Bunny Years*, p. 143, 1998

2 a little bit *US, 1878*
Generally used in phrases that have a negative intent, such as "not give a hoot," "not care two hoots," etc.
- "I don't give a hoot. They don't have the right to say those things." — Mickey Spillane, *One Lonely Night*, p. 30, 1951

hootch; hooch *noun*
a young woman, especially when easily available for sex *US, 1999*
An abbreviation of **HOOTCHIE**.
- "You left me sitting at the dinner table while you ran outside behind a hooch who has her pants stuck all up the crack of her butt." — Eric Jerome Dickey, *Cheaters*, p. 315, 1999

hootchie; hoochie; hootchy mama *noun*
a young woman, especially when easily available for sex *US, 1990*
- I wanted to get over with one of the hootchies over there. — *Boyz N The Hood*, 1990
- She was looking hootchie-mama foin. — John Ridley, *Everybody Smokes in Hell*, p. 198, 1999
- I told her about that half-breed hoochie from Palm Springs who came storming up there and claimed Stephan as her man. — Eric Jerome Dickey, *Cheaters*, p. 327, 1999
- "Actually, the one I'm interested in, Ray, is the hootchie." — Richard Price, *Samaritan*, p. 66, 2003

hootchie-coo *noun*
sex *US, 1990*
- Y'all gonna do the hootchie-coo? — *Boyz N The Hood*, 1990

hootchy-kootchy; hootchie-coochie *noun*
a sexually attractive person *US, 1969*
- He was such a hoochie-coochie she didn't know what to do. — Steve Cannon, *Groove, Bang, and Jive Around*, p. 139, 1969

hooter *noun*
1 a large marijuana cigarette *US, 1986*
- Enuff bud to keep tha whole party high on / I might get ill and roll an 8th in one hooter. — Tone, *Cheeba Cheeba*, 1989
- — Jim Emerson-Cobb, *Scratching the Dragon*, April 1997

2 a party *US, 1978*
- — Dennis Aaberg and John Milius, *Big Wednesday*, p. 208, 1978

hooters *noun*
female breasts *US, 1972*
- Their secondary sex characteristics are simply too conspicuous to pass without insult, and we were unmerciful towards them: tits, boobs, knockers, jugs, bubbies, bazooms, lungs, flaps and hooters we called them, and there was no way to be polite about it. — *Screw*, p. 6, 13th January 1972
- But below the neck is an odd set of hooters that leave some in confusion as she treats the old boys with flashes of them by her second song. — Josh Alan Friedman, *Tales of Times Square*, p. 11, 1986
- She thrust out her chest when she said it, and he had to admit she had pretty nice hooters. — Joseph Wambaugh, *Finnegan's Week*, p. 170, 1993
- Playing with Ken or Barbie made it even more confusing because neither had genitals of any kind, even though Barbie had perky hooters. — Anka Radakovich, *The Wild Girls Club*, 1994

hooting *noun*
in surfing, shouts that compliment the quality of a wave or a ride on the wave *US, 1988*
- — Brian and Margaret Lowdon, *Competitive Surfing*, 1988

hoots *noun*
the female breasts *US, 2002*
- She showed off her luscious hoots again in a topless turn[.] — Mr. Skin, *Mr. Skin's Skincyclopedia*, p. 191, 2005

hoover *verb*
1 to extract; to draw out *US, 1985*
- David Macklin had hoovered us for thousands to insure Mack would be a rich widow if I checked out back when we were young and stupid. — George V. Higgins, *Penance for Jerry Kennedy*, p. 14, 1985

2 to inhale drugs *US, 1982*
- Whenever there are dances to be danced, drugs to be hoovered, women to be allagashed. — Jay McInerney, *Bright Lights, Big City*, p. 44, 1984

3 to perform an abortion *US, 2003*
An allusion to the branded vacuum cleaner.
- — *Oprah Winfrey Show*, 2nd October 2003

Hoover blankets *noun*
newspapers *US, 1948*
- Men on benches ("Hoover bed") near a rabbit ("Hoover dog"), slept under a paper ("Hoover blanket"). — Curth Smith, *Voices of Summer*, p. 271, 2005

Hoover flag *noun*

an empty pocket turned out *US, 1977*

- The empty, out-turned pockets of the unemployed were called "Hoover flags." — Blanche Barrow, *My Life With Bonnie & Clyde*, p. 8, 2004

Hoover hog *noun*

any wild game as a potential meal *US, 1940*

- Cottontail rabbits and armadillos became "Hoover hogs." — Randolph Campbell, *Gone to Texas*, p. 380, 2003

Hooverville *noun*

a neighborhood of shacks *US, 1933*

- And now in my mind I stood upon the walk looking across the hole past a Hooverville shanty of packing cases and bent tin signs[.] — Ralph Ellison, *Invisible Man*, p. 322, 1952

hop *noun*

1 a narcotic—opium, morphine or heroin *US, 1886*

- Over and over he kept heating this small hunk of hop, rolling it on the thumb of his left hand until it was compact and looked like a tight little wad of cotton. — Mezz Mezzrow, *Really the Blues*, p. 98, 1946
- "We go up dark stairways to get a gun punk with a skinful of hop and sometimes we don't get all the way up, and our wives wait dinner that night and all the other nights. — Raymond Chandler, *The Little Sister*, p. 218, 1949
- "Not perfume, honey, hop," she said. And when I still didn't get it, "Opium, don't you know?" — Polly Adler, *A House is Not a Home*, p. 35, 1953
- They jumped from the sticks to St. Louis, and when he wasn't dead drunk he was shotting himself full of hop. — Jim Thompson, *The Grifters*, p. 82, 1963

2 a dance, a party *UK, 1731*

- Tonight I got a date with a Sigma, a keen babe, for a hop at the Shoreland Hotel. — James T. Farrell, *Saturday Night*, p. 35, 1947
- Some characters tap the female college alumnae lists for recent graduates resident in Washington, then pick names at random and phone with an invitation to a Yale or Princeton hop which never seems to come off. — Jack Lait and Lee Mortimer, *Washington Confidential*, p. 89, 1951

3 in craps, a one-roll bet on the next roll *US, 1987*

- — Thomas L. Clark, *The Dictionary of Gambling*, p. 103, 1987

hop *verb*

1 to work as a car hop at a drive-in restaurant where customers are served in their cars *US, 1972*

- She wore lots of cheap wigs, waited tables or hopped cars, was truly hung, might chew gum, posed for pictures, and got most of her fun in groups. — Dan Jenkins, *Semi-Tough*, p. 72, 1972

2 in horse racing, to administer an illegal drug to a horse, either a stimulant or a depressant *US, 1976*

- — Tom Ainslie, *Ainslie's Complete Guide to Thoroughbred Racing*, p. 333, 1976

▸ **hop 'n' pop**

in the language of parachuting, to pull the ripcord within three seconds of clearing the aircraft *US, 1978*

- — Dan Poynter, *Parachuting*, p. 167, 1978: "The language of parachuting"

▸ **hop a hole**

(used of a ball in pinball) to fall into and then keep moving out of an ejecting hole because of high velocity *US, 1977*

- — Bobbye Claire Natkin and Steve Kirk, *All About Pinball*, p. 113, 1977

▸ **hop and pop**

to wake up and spring into action *US, 1998*

- — *Seattle Times*, p. A9, 12th April 1998: "Grunts, squids not grunting from the same dictionary"

▸ **hop the train**

to ride the subway (underground) without paying the fare *US, 1995*

- — Maria Hinojas, *Crews*, p. 167, 1995: "Glossary"

hopdog *noun*

an opium addict *US, 1946*

- — Mezz Mezzrow, *Really the Blues*, p. 94, 1946

hope-to-die *noun*

your spouse or romantic partner *US, 1971*

- — Eugene Landy, *The Underground Dictionary*, p. 105, 1971

hophead *noun*

1 an opium addict, or, less precisely and more commonly, a user of marijuana or other drug *US, 1901*

- I always knew she was a hop-hop-head with no more morals than a hound-bitch in heat. — Truman Capote, *Breakfast at Tiffany's*, p. 95, 1958
- Chenault had the look of a hophead, ready to turn on. — Hunter S. Thompson, *Songs of the Doomed*, p. 96, 1962
- A junkie, a dope addict, a hop-head, a mainliner—a dope fiend! — James Baldwin, *Blues for Mister Charlie*, p. 45, 1964
- New Mexico, man, I finally found him, right where every hophead in the country figured he'd be. — Richard Farina, *Been Down So Long*, p. 60, 1966

2 in horse racing, a horse that only performs well when under the influence of a stimulant *US, 1947*

- — Dan Parker, *The ABC of Horse Racing*, p. 146, 1947
- — David W. Maurer, *Argot of the Racetrack*, p. 36, 1951

hop joint *noun*

a place where opium is smoked *US, 1957*

- There was no occasion to be concerned about the safety of the jewels in the hop-joints. — Helen Giblo, *Footlights, Fistfights and Femmes*, p. 30, 1957

hop off *verb*

to launch an attack *US, 1918*

- When that shit hops off at that A&P market, no telling who the police will end up bustin'. — Donald Goines, *Black Gangster*, p. 150, 1977

hop out *verb*

to crash (an airplane) *US, 1986*

- — *American Speech*, p. 123, Summer 1986: "The language of naval fighter pilots"

hop-pad *noun*

an opium den *US, 1946*

- That was the name we gave to a little old six-foot square coal bin down in the cellar of Mike's tenement that we cleaned out and converted into our hop-pad. — Mezz Mezzrow, *Really the Blues*, p. 245, 1946

hopped; hopped up *adjective*

1 under the influence of drugs *US, 1918*

- Some guys were so hopped on tea they were rocking on their heels. — Irving Shulman, *The Amboy Dukes*, p. 52, 1947
- He drove out north to a tea pad where everybody was already hopped up. — Willard Motley, *Let No Man Write My Epitaph*, p. 109, 1958
- Johnny turns the radio on, hoping for one of those miraculously lunatic stations that spew out the blessedly mesmerizing wailing of young groups with lovely names, the hopped-up disc jockeys making bad jokes[.] — John Rechy, *Numbers*, p. 11, 1967
- He wasn't hopped up on horse, but he was tripping just the same. — John Ridley, *Love is a Racket*, p. 129, 1998

2 agitated, excited *US, 1920*

- "Excitable" sounds cute, but in the real world it means hopped up, crabby, and absolutely unable to sleep. — Sheri Lynch, *Hello, My Name is Mommy*, p. 170, 2004

3 drunk *US, 1957*

- [O]thers were hopped up just enough to become cantankerous[.] — Helen Giblo, *Footlights, Fistfights and Femmes*, p. 25, 1957

hopper *noun*

a drug addict *US, 2007*

- Time to go before they start digging some hopper's bullet from my lonesome black ass. — David Simon and Edward Burns, *The Corner*, p. 5, 1997

hopper fill heist *noun*

an attempt to defraud a casino by sitting at a slot machine with a winning combination showing that has paid off partially but requires additional coins to be added to complete the payoff *US, 1999*

- I even know a few individuals who have been caught attempting a hopper fill heist. — Charles W. Lund, *Robbing the One-Armed Bandits*, p. 121, 1999

hopping John *noun*

a stew made of boiled pig's feet, black-eye peas, and rice *US, 1838*

- "Ain't nothin' but hoppin' john," Goldy said. "I like hoppin' john, all right," Jackson replied. — Chester Himes, *A Rage in Harlem*, p. 53, 1957

hops *noun*

beer *US, 1902*

- My own taste for the hops is very powerful, and I had no intention of spending a beerless weekend in the withering sun. — Hunter S. Thompson, *Hell's Angels*, p. 141, 1966
- — David Claerbaut, *Black Jargon in White America*, p. 68, 1972

hopscotcher *noun*
a carnival worker who moves from one carnival to another
US, 1966
- — *American Speech*, p. 281, December 1966: "More carnie talk from the west coast"

hop squad *noun*
a narcotics squad within a police department *US, 1958*
- — Jack Webb, *The Badge*, p. 221, 1958

hop stop *noun*
in pinball, a brief release of an extended flipper to prevent a ball from rolling up off the end *US, 1977*
- — Bobbye Claire Natkin and Steve Kirk, *All About Pinball*, p. 113, 1977

hoptoads *noun*
any dice altered for cheating *US, 1950*
- — *The Annals of the American Academy of Political and Social Sciences*, p. 126, May 1950

horizontal bop *noun*
sexual intercourse *US, 2001*
- Whether he [George Washington] and Sally [Fairfax] ever did the horizontal bop has remained a point of speculation for historians[.] — Erica Orloff & JoAnn Baker *Dirty Little Secrets*, p. 139, 2001

horizontal exercise *noun*
sexual intercourse *US, 1918*
- "Everybody here," she wrote to one of her friends, "is busy talking about breaking new records, getting drunk and keepin' up with their horizontal exercise." — Lauren Kessler, *The Happy Bottom Riding Club*, p. 61, 2000
- "I'm not quite so young as I used to be," Leino said at some point that morning when, after several days of horizontal exercises, he failed to rise to the occasion. — Harry Turtledove, *Rulers of the Darkness*, p. 321, 2002

horizontal frolicking *noun*
sex *US, 1982*
- sexual relationship: horizontal frolicking — Sherri Foxman, *Classified Love*, p. 128, 1982

horizontal hustle *noun*
sex *US, 2005*
- [S]he sent co-star Mark Wahlberg into a tailspin while doing the horizontal hustle completely naked except for her skates. — Mr. Skin, *Mr. Skin's Skincyclopedia*, p. 208, 2005

hormone queen *noun*
a man taking female hormones, usually in the course of a transgender transformation *US, 1972*
- Sometimes a hormone queen will decide she is TS and then have the operation. — *alt.personals.transgendered*, 24th July 1998

horn *noun*
1 the telephone *US, 1941*
- He was on the horn most of the night explaining the incident. — Elaine Shepard, *The Doom Pussy*, p. 15, 1967
- Right away Claude is on the horn talking here and there. — *The Digger Papers*, p. 10, August 1968
- "Give us a blast on the horn sometime." — Burt Hirschfield, *Fire Island*, p. 27, 1970

2 the penis; the erect penis; lust *UK, 1594*
- I could pole-vault to the bathroom on my own horn there. — George V. Higgins, *Penance for Jerry Kennedy*, p. 157, 1985

3 the nose *UK, 1823*
- — Lou Shelly, *Hepcats Jive Dictionary*, p. 12, 1945

4 any implement used for snorting powdered narcotics *US, 1977*
- They snorted sparkling rows of cocaine with a mother-of-pearl horn. — Iceberg Slim (Robert Beck), *Long White Con*, p. 97, 1977

5 a pipe used to smoke crack cocaine *US, 1994*
- — US Department of Justice, *Street Terms*, October 1994

▸ **around the horn**
1 the oral stimulation of all parts of a partner's body *US, 1976*
- She was a three-way wench, played Jasper in a pinch / And took 'em around the horn. — Dennis Wepman et al., *The Life*, p. 81, 1976

2 from one location to another, in quick succession *US, 1942*
- That's why they've been sending me around the horn. In the past eighteen months I've been stationed in Detroit, Providence, Miami, and now Los Angeles. — Gerald Petievich, *One-Shot Deal*, p. 205, 1981

3 in craps, a single-roll bet on the 2, 3, 11, and 12 *US, 1962*
- — Frank Garcia, *Marked Cards and Loaded Dice*, p. 250, 1962

▸ **put the horns on; put horns on**
(used of a superstitious gambler) to engage in a personal ritual designed to break a streak of bad luck *US, 1949*
- — George Percy, *The Language of Poker*, p. 72, 1988

horn *verb*
to inhale (a drug) through the nose *US, 1967*
- — Richard Horman and Allan Fox, *Drug Awareness*, p. 467, 1970
- I been hornin' coke all evenin', I'd hate to mess that up with anything else. — Odie Hawkins, *Chicago Hustle*, p. 201, 1977
- Before closing time I hit on her and she goes for the "horn-a-little-coke-at-my-place" act. — Gerald Petievich, *To Die in Beverly Hills*, p. 93, 1983
- I've held off the bonecrushers two days, rationing that stuff up my nose—horned the last just an hour ago. — Seth Morgan, *Homeboy*, p. 49, 1990

horn colic *noun*
an erection *UK, 1785*
- A fellow named Taylor come down with the horn colic one night, but he didn't have the two dollars. — Vance Randolph, *Pissing in the Snow*, p. 149, 1976

horndog *noun*
a person who is obsessed with sex *US, 1984*
- "I'm a horn-dog," I say. "I'm into some pretty kinky stuff to be honest." — Marty Beckerman, *Death to All Cheerleaders*, p. 24, 2000
- Horndogs browsed all night. It was cheap entertainment. — James Ellroy, *Destination Morgue*, p. 127, 2004

horndog *adjective*
sexually aggressive *US, 1984*
- "[A]nd this no matter what kind of scumbag, slutbucket, horndog chick we end up boffing." — Bret Ellis, *American Psycho*, p. 34, 1991

horned up *adjective*
excited *US, 1968*
- He'd been so horned up over Jacks that he'd hallucinated the snog, the breasts, the urgent hands. — Melvin Burgess, *Doing It*, p. 43, 1992

horn movie *noun*
a pornographic film *US, 1967*
- — *American Speed*, p. 228, October 1967: "Some special terms used in a University of Connecticut men's dormitory"

hornrim *noun*
an intellectual *US, 1974*
- Derisive implications are due to the fact that the hornrims tend to get bogged down in the technology of fact-gathering and lose sight of the realities of advertising and the real-life marketplace. — Robert Kirk Mueller, *Buzzwords*, p. 93, 1974

hornswoggle *verb*
to deceive *US, 1829*
- All Ellen G. White knew, Pete said, was how to hornswoggle religious people—who are the most hornswogglable people on earth. — David James Duncan, *The Brothers K*, p. 43, 1992

horny *adjective*
desiring sex *US, 1826*
- Those girls in juvenile were horny as they could be. — Willard Motley, *Let No Man Write My Epitaph*, p. 20, 1958
- I know this because when I was pregnant I was able to ball anyone and I was never more horny. — Jefferson Poland and Valerie Alison, *The Records of the San Francisco Sexual Freedom League*, p. 103, 1971
- That creep's not a friend of mine, he's just horny. — *American Graffiti*, 1973
- You'd get horny too if all you ever got to look at were grasshoppers and ants and toads. — Francesca Lia Block, *I Was a Teenage Fairy*, p. 60, 1998

horny man *noun*
a federal law enforcement official *US, 1974*
A euphemistic allusion to the devil by those engaged in the illegal production of alcohol.
- — David W. Maurer, *Kentucky Moonshine*, p. 119, 1974

horny porny *noun*
pornography *US, 1981*
- — *Male Swinger Number 3*, p. 46, 1981: "The Complete gay dictionary"

horrendioma *noun*
a notional disease *US, 1977*

- The suffix "-oma" may be combined with the word "horrendous," to form "horrendioma." — Jan Harold Brunvard, *American Folklore*, p. 467, 1996

horror *noun*
phencyclidine, the drug best known as PCP or angel dust *US, 2005*

- AKA: angel dust, illy, super weed, stained, horror, digi. — RZA, *The Wu-Tang Manual*, p. 121, 2005

horrors *noun*
sickness associated with withdrawal from alcohol or drug addiction *US, 1839*
Noted specifically of withdrawal from amphetamines or heroin.

- I'm not staying, Sticks. I got the horrors. — George Mandel, *Flee the Angry Strangers*, p. 377, 1952
- Knocked out on barbiturates 4 days. After that all the usual, plus a substantial case of the horrors. — William Burroughs, *Letters to Allen Ginsberg 1953–1957*, p. 99, 17th May 1955
- I've got the horrors. — Jack Gerber, *The Connection*, p. 47, 1957

hors d'oeuvre *noun*
drugs in capsule form *US, 1980*

- — Edith A. Folb, *runnin' down some lines*, p. 242, 1980

horse *noun*
1 heroin *US, 1948*

- Paddy's on Horse, that don' mean I got to. — George Mandel, *Flee the Angry Strangers*, p. 26, 1948
- He was a cheap hood from the east side who did errands for the Stipetto brothers and lived off the white Horse he peddled around the neighborhood. — Mickey Spillane, *Return of the Hood*, p. 88, 1964
- He was sitting on the small of her back as he opened the box. Inside was a glycerin suppository filled with Motherball's uncut horse. — Richard Farina, *Been Down So Long*, p. 266, 1966
- I seen the horse play with them junkies like a cat with a rubber mouse. — Edwin Torres, *Carlito's Way*, p. 11, 1975

2 a prostitute *US, 1957*
An evolution of the **STABLE** as a group of prostitutes.

- But not for that new horse. I wouldn't give her one of my tricks if she stood on her head. — John M. Murtagh and Sara Harris, *Cast the First Stone*, p. 114, 1957

3 a large man *US, 1947*
- — Marcus Hanna Boulware, *Jive and Slang of Students in Negro Colleges*, 1947

4 in circus and carnival usage, one thousand dollars *US, 1981*
- — Don Wilmeth, *The Language of American Popular Entertainment*, p. 134, 1981

5 a person who smuggles contraband into prison *US, 1981*
- — *Maledicta*, p. 264, Summer/Winter 1981: "By its slang, ye shall know it: the pessimism of prison life"

6 in bar dice games, a turn of rolling the dice *US, 1976*
- Boss is won by the player who wins two of three horses (hands). — Gil Jacobs, *The World's Best Dice Games*, p. 196, 1976

7 a poker player with a reputation for stinginess *US, 1988*
- — George Percy, *The Language of Poker*, p. 45, 1988

8 in television and movie-making, a stand that holds movie reels while the movie is fed through a viewer *US, 1990*
- — Ralph S. Singleton, *Filmmaker's Dictionary*, p. 82, 1990

horse and buggy; horse and wagon *noun*
heroin and the equipment needed to prepare and inject it *US, 1984*

- — Inez Cardozo-Freeman, *The Joint*, p. 506, 1984

horse apple *noun*
horse excrement *US, 1931*

- "Not a fresh cow turd, or a horse apple." — Peter Bowen, *Thunder Horse*, p. 11, 1998

horse around *verb*
to fool around *US, 1900*

- If we were working we wouldn't 'a been cuttin' classes and horsing around and we wouldn't be sittin' here now. — Irving Shulman, *The Amboy Dukes*, p. 106, 1947
- Gimme Foley and quit horsing around. — George V. Higgins, *The Friends of Eddie Doyle*, p. 107, 1971

horsecock *noun*
1 a sausage *US, 1942*

- The sandwiches were thick slices of bologna sausage (reviled as "horsecock" by sailors and marines) on bread plastered with artificial butter. — I.J. Galantin, *Take Her Deep!*, p. 133, 1987

2 a wooden club *US, 1970*

- You can take your hand off the horsecock you're holding under the bar. — Darryl Ponicsan, *The Last Detail*, p. 39, 1970

3 nonsense *US, 1981*

- No use dumping some sidewalk commando and listening to the government turkeys harp on unsafe riding or other such horsecock. — Robert Lipkin, *A Brotherhood of Outlaws*, p. 4, 1981

horsecollar *noun*
1 a rescue sling lowered from a hovering helicopter to the ground or sea below *US, 1969*

- The crewmen in the back dropped the rescue sling, or "horse collar," to the survivor and watched as he put it around his back. — Gerry Carroll, *North S*A*R*, p. 89, 1991

2 the vagina, especially large or distended external female genitals *US, 1994*
The shape provides a simile.

- — Michael Dalton Johnson, *Talking Trash with Redd Foxx*, p. 62, 1994

3 in an athletic contest, a failure to score *US, 1907*

- — Parke Cummings, *Dictionary of Baseball*, p. 29, 1950
- Yet horse collars were never hung on an opponent by a team trying to out-score its basketball team. — *Spokesman Review (Spokane, Washington)*, p. C4, 3rd October 2002

horse cop *noun*
a horse-mounted police officer *US, 1942*

- The horse cop was gone and the park was empty. — Christopher Hyde, *The Second Assassin*, p. 19, 2002

horse crap *noun*
nonsense *US, 1934*

- I would hate to go to all this horsecrap and lose out on any of the exposure. — Robert Lipkin, *A Brotherhood of Outlaws*, p. 3, 1981
- [S]omething that has so demoralized them that they will be their most inclined to believe a load of horse crap. — Greg Behrendt, *He's Just Not That Into You*, p. 63, 2004

horse dookie *noun*
nonsense *US, 1973*

- There were no points not addressed by my term "horse-dookie," since the sum total of the "points amount to that." — *alt.politics.bush*, 23rd December 2002

horse feathers *noun*
nonsense *US, 1927*
A transparent euphemism for **HORSESHIT**.

- Oh, horse feathers! I just can't believe that about your father. — Iceberg Slim (Robert Beck), *Doom Fox*, p. 146, 1978

horse feed *noun*
in circus and carnival usage, poor business *US, 1981*

- — Don Wilmeth, *The Language of American Popular Entertainment*, p. 134, 1981

horsefuck *verb*
to have sex from behind and with great vim *US, 1973*

- I'd like to break her open like a shotgun and horsefuck her. — Joseph Wambaugh, *The Blue Knight*, p. 96, 1973

horsehead *noun*
a heroin user *US, 1952*

- They knew he was on drugs, a real horsehead who hit the main. — Hal Ellson, *The Golden Spike*, p. 68, 1952

horse heart *noun*
a tablet of Dexedrine™, a trade name for dextroamphetamine sulfate, a central nervous system stimulant *US, 1977*

- — Walter L. Way, *The Drug Scene*, p. 110, 1977

horse hockey *noun*
nonsense *US, 1964*
As an exclamation, a signature line of Colonel Sherman Potter on *M*A*S*H* (CBS, 1972–83), repeated with referential humor.

- "There sure is a lot of horse hockey in the papers about pickets and guys that don't think we belong over here." — Elaine Shepard, *The Doom Pussy*, p. 18, 1967
- If they were after the tourist set it would be called the Tropical Inn or some other horsehockie name. — Robert Lipkin, *A Brotherhood of Outlaws*, p. 135, 1981

- Horse hockey, Counselor. You can't be that drunk. — Austin Davis, *Shoveling Smoke*, p. 146, 2003

horse-holder *noun*
an assistant to a high-ranking military officer *US, 1982*
- — Department of the Army, *Staff Officer's Guidebook*, p. 61, 1986

horse hooey *noun*
nonsense *US, 1989*
- "C'mon supper, enough of this horse-hooey." — Luanne Armstrong, *Annie*, p. 104, 1995

horse manure *noun*
nonsense *US, 1928*
- "Sounds like a load of horse manure to me." — Dee Davis, *Dark of the Night*, p. 167, 2002

horse marine *noun*
a member of the Marine Corps when the cavalry still rode horses *US, 1878*
- My gran' daddy was a Horse Marine / When he was born he was wearing green. — Sandee Johnson, *Cadences: The Jody Call Book, No. 2*, p. 62, 1986

horse opera *noun*
a cowboy movie *US, 1927*
- The movie, a horse opera named Rawhide, had its premiere in March 1938[.] — Ray Robinson, *Iron Horse*, p. 231, 1990

horse pill *noun*
the large, orange anti-malarial pill (chloroquine-primaquine) taken once a week by US troops in Vietnam *US, 1990*
- — David Hart, *First Air Cavalry Division Vietnam Dictionary*, p. 31, 2004

horse piss; horse pee *noun*
1 weak coffee *US, 1957*
- The coffee she handed me was delicious and she had long-fingered hands, thin and beautiful I suppose. "Not horse piss like the English madams drink," she said. — Jean Rhys, *Wide Sargasso Sea*, p. 85, 1966
2 cheap alcoholic drink, or a brand you don't drink *US, 1970*
- They were inveterate gamblers and accomplished scroungers, who drank hair tonic in preference to post exchange beer ("horse piss")[.] — William Manchester, *Goodbye, Darkness*, p. 132, 1980
- Here's ten dollars for a case of beer and don't come back with any of that horse piss you brought last time. When I say beer I mean beer. — Ken Weaver, *Texas Crude*, p. 59, 1984

horse pucky *noun*
nonsense *US, 1995*
- "This is horse pucky. Feds don't investigate nigger homicides." — James Ellroy, *American Tabloid*, p. 142, 1995

horse radish *noun*
heroin *US, 1997*
- — *Providence (Rhode Island) Journal-Bulletin*, p. 6B, 4th August 1997: "Doctors must know the narcolexicon"

horse room *noun*
an illegal betting operation where bets can be placed and collected on horse races *US, 1950*
- Northside shopping street, with usual quota of horse rooms, taverns, and dope peddlers at principal corners. — Jack Lait and Lee Mortimer, *Chicago Confidential*, p. 289, 1950
- — *Life*, p. 39, 19th May 1952
- A week from now half the horse rooms in Brooklyn, for example, will be out of business and the people will be held on high bail. — Richard Condon, *Prizzi's Honor*, p. 216, 1982

horses *noun*
dice that have been altered for cheating by omitting key losing combinations *US, 1964*
- — Dr. R. Frederick West, *God's Gambler*, p. 226, 1964: "Appendix A"

horse's ass *noun*
a person who is not liked or trusted; an idiot; someone deserving of a generally abusive epithet *UK, 1865*
- [I]t still couldn't be worth making a horse's ass of yourself[.] — Lawrence Block, *No Score [The Affairs of Chip Harrison Omnibus]*, p. 151, 1970

horse's cock *noun*
a despicable person *US, 1974*
- "You horse's cock," Frankie said. — George Higgins, *Cogan's Trade*, p. 134, 1974

horseshit *noun*
nonsense *US, 1923*
- "Horseshit," the man said gently. — William Brinkley, *Don't Go Near the Water*, p. 48, 1956
- For Christs sake dont give us any of that horseshit. — Hubert Selby Jr., *Last Exit to Brooklyn*, p. 113, 1957
- I don't want to abandon my solitude and reading and quietude for just a lot of horseshit showing-off in public. — Jack Kerouac, *Jack Kerouac Selected Letters 1957–1969*, p. 416, 29th June 1963: Letter to Allen Ginsberg
- Horseshit. I look like hell. — Carl Hiaasen, *Tourist Season*, p. 228, 1986

horseshit *verb*
to deceive, to tease *US, 1954*
In the nature of **BULLSHIT**.
- Don't try to horse-shit me, buster. You ain't even half-way smart enough. — Jim Thompson, *A Swell-Looking Babe*, p. 85, 1954

horseshit *adjective*
shabby, unsatisfactory *US, 1939*
- He said, "Huh. Horseshit photo." "It wasn't a goddamn portrait studio," Hubbard rasped. — John Standford, *Broken Prey*, p. 42, 2005

horseshit luck *noun*
good luck *US, 1970*
- It was plain horseshit luck that ever got us through this[.] — Jake La Motta, *Raging Bull*, p. 22, 1997

horse's patoot; horse's patootie *noun*
a fool *US, 1949*
- "You horse's patoot, pass over my dough." — Audie Murphy, *To Hell and Back*, p. 27, 1949
- "If you think that's love, then you're a horse's patootie." — Susan Douglas, *Where the Girls Are*, p. 203, 1995

horse-to-horse *adjective*
in a direct comparison or competition *US, 1950*
- Get rodded up. Horse-to-horse we can muscle that mob out of the grift. — Hyman E. Goldin et al., *Dictionary of American Underworld Lingo*, p. 102, 1950

horspital *noun*
a hospital *US, 1917*
- "Since I be out the horspital." — Scott Turow, *The Laws of Our Fathers*, p. 145, 1996

horticulturalist *noun*
in pool, a player who wins money betting *US, 1990*
- — Steve Rushin, *Pool Cool*, p. 16, 1990

hose *noun*
the penis *US, 1928*
- I'm goin' to the toilet, to let some water out of this fine hose of mine, and when I come out I don't wanna see yo' lazy, triflin' ass nowhere in sight. — Odie Hawkins, *Chicago Hustle*, p. 34, 1977
- He'd been bragging about what a hose he had. — Robert Campbell, *Sweet La-La Land*, p. 200, 1990
- Jasmin sucks hose as if she's being intubated with anesthesia (and on the verge of nodding off). — Anthony Petkovich, *The X Factory*, p. 192, 1997

hose *verb*
1 to copulate, vaginally or anally *US, 1935*
- — Collin Baker et al., *College Undergraduate Slang Study Conducted at Brown University*, p. 139, 1968
- — Connie Eble (Editor), *UNC-CH Campus Slang*, April 1977
- "Even if I was inclined to seduce the bitch into my bed again, which I'm not, and even if I hosed her, as you so romantically put it, a thousand times, it wouldn't take." — Sandra Brown, *White Hot*, p. 2004, 2004
2 to shoot with an automatic weapon *UK, 1917*
Sometimes heard as the more elaborate "hosepipe."
- There was no time for accurate, steady ranging if I was to save my pilot, so allowing plenty of lead, I "hosepiped" the 190 with a long continuous burst. — J. E. Johnson, *Wing Leader*, p. 228, 1956
- Their fire on the Rangers did not last long, as they were dealt a shattering blow when a Spectre effectively "hosed" them down with 20-mm and 40-mm fire. — Ian Padden, *U.S. Air Commando*, p. 131, 1985

hosebag *noun*
a prostitute or promiscuous woman *US, 1978*
- — Connie Eble (Editor), *UNC-CH Campus Slang*, p. 4, March 1981

- Every time he looked at his wrist he thought about that junkie hose-bag and wondered if he should get a blood test. — Joseph Wambaugh, *Finnegan's Week*, p. 41, 1993
- I just wasted an hour seducing this hosebag and she has a fucking headache? — Howard Stern, *Miss America*, p. 17, 1995

hosehead *noun*
a fool *US, 1978*

- Hosehead (n): A name that jocky collegey beer drinkers call other jocky, collegey beer drinkers. — Jennifer Blowdryer, *Modern English*, p. 22, 1985
- "Sorry, Charlie, FA's are for hoseheads." — Douglad Macdonald, *The Best of Rock and Ice*, p. 48, 1999

hose job *noun*
1 oral sex on a man *US, 1978*

- Looks like the hooker was doing a hose job on one of the truckers up at the market. — Carsten Stroud, *Close Pursuit*, p. 33, 1987
- There was an extensive trade in quick hose jobs for businessmen on the way home. — Robert K. Tannenbaum, *Reversible Error*, p. 71, 1992

2 a bad situation; a situation in which you are cheated or swindled *US, 1989*

- Everybody was having such a good time in "flower-power-land" they didn't realize what kind of hose job they were getting. — Frank Zappa, *The Real Frank Zappa Book*, p. 83, 1989

hose monster *noun*
a sexually aggressive woman *US, 1984*

- But who wants to admit being a hose monster? — Rajen Persaud, *Why Black Men Love White Women*, p. 162, 2004
- "You gotta take your mind off your ex and her lawyer and that hose monster that dumped you." — Joseph Wambaugh, *Hollywood Station*, p. 89, 2006

hose nose *noun*
a Corsair F4U-1A fighter airplane *US, 1977*

- Corsair pilots sometimes called their plane "Nose-nose" — Eric Bergerud, *Fire in the Sky*, p. 256, 2000

hose queen *noun*
a sexually active woman *US, 1984*

- You suddenly realize that he has already slipped out with some rich hose queen. — Kenneth Jackson, *Empire City*, p. 846, 2002

hoser *noun*
a male with sexual experience and expertise *US, 1968*
- — Collin Baker et al., *College Undergraduate Slang Study Conducted at Brown University*, p. 139, 1968

hosing *verb*
a defeat *US, 1947*

- You guys are really giving us a hosing. Why don't you let us alone? — Irving Shulman, *The Amboy Dukes*, p. 166, 1947

hospital *noun*
1 jail *US, 1959*
An unabashed euphemism.
- — *American Speech*, pp. 150–151, May 1959: "Notes on the cant of the telephone confidence man"

2 in a smuggling operation, the place where the smuggled goods are picked up *US, 1956*
- — *American Speech*, p. 100, May 1956: "Smugglers' argot in the southwest"

hoss *noun*
1 used as a term of address, man to man *US, 1834*

- "Howdy, hoss," said Opie genially. "Have a snort." He extended a bottle of whisky to Private Roger Litwhiler. — Max Shulman, *Rally Round the Flag, Boys!*, p. 261, 1957

2 heroin *US, 1953*
A shortened form of **HORSE** (heroin).

- "Sniff out the hoss, and you'll find Jerry standing there with his spoon." — Curt Cannon, *Die Hard*, p. 17, 1953
- She went back in her purse and wrapped her fingers about her hoss. — Clarence Cooper Jr., *The Scene*, p. 36, 1960
- "Hoss was his Boss." He had chippied around and gotten hooked. — Iceberg Slim (Robert Beck), *Pimp*, p. 63, 1969

hostess *noun*
a prostitute *US, 1954*

- She was now a "hostess" in a combination whore house-blind pig[.] — Jim Thompson, *Roughneck*, p. 89, 1954

hostess with the mostest *noun*
a good hostess *US, 1957*
An apparently irresistible reduplication, going "host with the most" one better.

- How did I know she would play hostess with the mostest to every chorine in my chorus? — Helen Giblo, *Footlights, Fistfights and Femmes*, p. 76, 1957
- It was the only time in all our marriage that Eva-line had the opportunity to come on as the hostess with the mostest[.] — Minnesota Fats, *The Bank Shot*, p. 140, 1966
- I had heard stories about "My Sister Eileen" and the "Hostess With the Mostest"[.] — Red Rudensky, *The Gonif*, p. 159, 1970
- I invited them. Me and the hostess with the mostest. — Robert Deane Pharr, *Giveadamn Brown*, p. 21, 1978
- Yes, Bobbi Flekman, the hostess with the mostest. — *This is Spinal Tap*, 1984

hostile!
used for expressing strong approval *US, 1995*
Collected from fans of heavy metal music by Seamus O'Reilly, January 1995.

hot *noun*
a hot meal *US, 1926*

- For a day's work, each youth is paid 50 cents plus earning his room and board, or "three hots and a cot," as one youth described it. — *New York Times*, p. 51, 28th September 1969
- Real beds. Sheets once a week. Three hots a day. Round-eyed pussy, reasonable. — Larry Heinemann, *Close Quarters*, p. 270, 1977
- Three hots a day, white sheets, dem pretty white nurses give you blowjobs too you pay them enough. — *Platoon*, 1986

hot *adjective*
1 stolen *US, 1924*

- One night, we were cruising about and just happened to rive by a lot where I'd parked a hot car some months before, in the summer. — Neal Cassady, *The First Third*, p. 194, 3rd July 1949
- I was also worried about a hot car connected at my mother's home. — Jack Kerouac, *Jack Kerouac Selected Letters 1957–1969*, p. 422, 16th August 1963: Letter to Carolyn Cassady
- You could walk into one or another room in the house and get a hot fur coat, a good camera, fine perfume, anything from hot women to hot cars[.] — Malcolm X and Alex Haley, *The Autobiography of Malcolm X*, pp. 90–91, 1964
- We also gotta get rid of all those cars. It looks like Sam's hot car lot outside. — *Reservoir Dogs*, 1992

2 wanted by the police *US, 1928*

- Don't laugh so loud, Buster. I'm hot—I busted out. — George Mandel, *Flee the Angry Strangers*, p. 121, 1952
- Even if I wasn't actually what was called "hot," I was now going to be under surveillance[.] — Malcolm X and Alex Haley, *The Autobiography of Malcolm X*, p. 97, 1964
- I soon got hot and the police were looking for me all over town. — A.S. Jackson, *Gentleman Pimp*, p. 96, 1973

3 dangerous for criminal activity *UK, 1618*

- "That neighborhood is too hot," he said loudly. — William Burroughs, *Junkie*, p. 79, 1953
- "Man, I told you before I don't want you all coming to turn on here," Lou said to Geo. "This pad's getting too hot." — Alexander Trocchi, *Cain's Book*, p. 166, 1960

4 dangerous to other criminals because of cooperation with the police *US, 2003*

- "He was hot," Veal said, explaining that "hot" was street slang for cooperating with police. "The word was out, he had to go, too." — *Washington Post*, p. C1, 14th December 2003

5 under enemy fire *US, 1864*
Although a critical term in the Vietnam war, it was coined not there, but in the US Civil War 100 years earlier.

- "The new landing zone was hot." — Kenneth Mertel, *Year of the Horse*, p. 180, 1968
- One of the helicopter's pilots had reported that the LZ was "hot," that is, Viet Cong were waiting below. — Seymour Hersh, *My Lai 4*, p. 45, 1970
- We're down, Eagle Thrust—we're hit. We got a hot L.Z. here. — *Apocalypse Now*, 1979
- It was what they called a hot LZ, a landing zone swarming with enemy troops and alive with sniper fire from the moment they set down[.] — Peter Goldman and Tony Fuller, *Charlie Company*, p. 69, 1983

6 (used of a weapons system) activated, armed *US, 1962*
- He watched his weapons indicators go green, signifying that his ordinance was "hot." — T.E. Cruice, *Wings of Gold III*, p. 196, 1989
- Maverick pulls up, makes a quick turn, takes all the weapons off safe, "going hot" and they throw everything that gunship carries right into the exact middle of the camp. — Dennis Marvicsin and Jerold Greenfield, *Maverick*, p. 136, 1990

7 good *US, 1970*
- Stroudsburg wasn't such a hot school anyway[.] — Darryl Ponicsan, *The Last Detail*, p. 10, 1970

8 excellent; used for describing music or musicians that create excitement *US, 1866*
- [A]in't that boy hot! — Frederic Ramsey Junior, *Chicago Documentary*, p. 31, 1944
- WAYNE: What do you think of Mickey and Mallory? CHUCK: Hot. JEFF: Hot. STEVE: Totally hot. — *Natural Born Killers*, 1994
- "I never had any intention of disappearing," he [rapper, Too Short] says now, "that's why I appeared on all the hottest shit" — *Hip-Hop Connection*, p. 35, March 2001

9 (used of jazz) traditional and spirited, as opposed to modern *US, 1924*
- When we talked about a musician who played hot, we would say he could swing or he couldn't swing, meaning what kind of effect did he have on the band. — Mezz Mezzrow, *Really the Blues*, p. 142, 1946

10 popular *US, 1961*
- I had lunch with him a couple of weeks ago. A real schnorrer, but sort of likeable, and apparently he's hot over there right now. — J.D. Salinger, *Franny and Zooey*, pp. 136–137, 1961
- We's so much hotter now. Bob Marley, Jimi Hendrix, Jim Morrison, Elvis. — Francesca Lia Block, *Cherokee Bat*, p. 232, 1992

11 sexual, sensuous *US, 1931*
- Don't try to get too hot with a girl in public, or you'll wind up with the cold shoulder. — Jack Lait and Lee Mortimer, *New York Confidential*, p. 222, 1948
- "Well, this guy ... he'll need something a little gamier. Dig?" "Hotter, you mean?" "That's about it." — Wade Hunter, *The Sex Peddler*, p. 112, 1963
- [I] even had my special favorites that always got me hotter while there were others I always avoided. — Lester Bangs, *Psychotic Reactions and Carburetor Dung*, p. 334, 1980

12 (used of a striptease dance) very sexual *US, 1977*
- A stripper who can maximize the quantity of bumps and grinds she can do during the chorus of a popular song is known in the profession as working "hot." — William Green, *Strippers and Coochers*, p. 165, 1977

13 attractive, good-looking *US, 1982*
- He was hot, wasn't he? — *Fast Times at Ridgemont High*, 1982

14 angry *UK, 1225*
- MR. WHITE: Joe, trust me on this, you've made a mistake. He's a good kid. I understand you're hot, you're super-fuckin' pissed. — *Reservoir Dogs*, 1992

15 brief, quick *US, 1946*
- He may have been hip to his hop, but the muta made him fly right for a hot minute. — Mezz Mezzrow, *Really the Blues*, p. 96, 1946

16 in sports betting, generating heavy betting; favored *UK, 1882*
- This judge bets college games through a buddy of his, a lawyer. All Southeast Conference. He lays it on the hot side, the favorite, every time. — Elmore Leonard, *Pronto*, p. 9, 1993

17 (used of a set in the television and movie industries) fully prepared for filming *US, 1977*
- — Tony Miller and Patricia George, *Cut! Print!*, p. 88, 1977
- — Ralph S. Singleton, *Filmmaker's Dictionary*, p. 82, 1990

hot and bothered *adjective*
sexually aroused *UK, 1821*
- — Collin Baker et al., *College Undergraduate Slang Study Conducted at Brown University*, p. 139, 1968

hot and cold *noun*
heroin and cocaine combined for injection *US, 1970*
Based on the initials.
- — William D. Alsever, *Glossary for the Establishment and Other Uptight People*, p. 14, December 1970
- — Richard A Spears, *The Slang and Jargon of Drugs and Drink*, p. 271, 1986

hot and heavy *adjective*
passionate *US, 1971*
- — *Current Slang*, p. 14, Spring 1971

hot and stuck *adjective*
said of a player who is losing badly in a game of poker *US, 1982*
- — David M. Hayano, *Poker Faces*, p. 186, 1982

hot bed *noun*
a motel room rented without following proper registration procedures and rented more than once a day; a room in a cheap boarding house *US, 1940*
- — Lou Shelly, *Hepcats Jive Talk Dictionary*, p. 26, 1945
- "They're hot-bed hotels," Maria Elena explains. "They make believe they're renting to you for the night, but they know they ain't." — Judge John M. Murtagh and Sara Harris, *Cast the First Stone*, p. 6, 1957
- Or you can wait till I talk to Dawn Coyote about how you rented her a hot bed tonight. Again. — Joseph Wambaugh, *Floaters*, p. 39, 1996

hot-bed *verb*
to have sex in a motel *US, 2005*
- "Okay, they discovered that hot-bedding it is more fun than going domestic." — Jonathan Kellerman, *Rage*, p. 272, 2005

hot book *noun*
a pornographic book or magazine *US, 1942*
- Hal Griffin has six hot books hidden in the back of his closet which he masturbates over at every opportunity[.] — Stephen King, *Salem's Lot*, p. 228, 1975

hot box *noun*
1 a sexually excited vagina; a sexually excited female *US, 1964*
- — Roger Blake, *The American Dictionary of Sexual Terms*, p. 103, 1964

2 a prison cell used for solitary confinement *US, 1983*
- — Marlene Freedman, *Alcatraz*, 1983

3 a small room or enclosed space where marijuana is being smoked *US, 2001*
- — Pamela Munro, *U.C.L.A. Slang*, p. 84, 2001

4 a small, enclosed space in which marijuana is smoked *US, 1998*
- I was there and it was basically a hotbox. You know, where they would close off the room and all this smoke[.] — *CNN Newsday*, 13th April 1998

hotbox *verb*
to smoke marijuana in a small, enclosed space *US, 1994*
- Haw should have just done what my roommates did freshmen year: Hotbox the bathroom. — *The Lantern*, 23rd May 2005

hotboxing *noun*
the practice of smoking marijuana or using other drugs in an enclosed space *US, 1999*
- Our younger, hip readers inform us that "hotboxing" is the practice of locking yourself in a confined space—a car or trunk will do—and smoking or sniffing hallucinogenic drugs. — *San Francisco Chronicle*, p. 1 (Contra Costa Friday Section), 12th February 1999

hot-bunk *verb*
to sleep in turns or rotation on a bunk or in a sleeping bag *US, 1945*
- Rather than Folk rolling up his sleeping bag and Bannon rolling out another, they hot bunked with Bannon using Folk's sleeping bag tonight. It was a normal practice in a tactical environment. — Harold Coyle, *Team Yankee*, p. 86, 1987

hot buns *noun*
a male homosexual *US, 1990*
- — Charles Shafer, *Folk Speech in Texas Prisons*, p. 206, 1990

hot cakes *noun*
phencyclidine, the recreational drug known as PCP or angel dust *US, 1994*
- — US Department of Justice, *Street Terms*, October 1994

hot cha cha!
used for expressing approval *US, 1931*
- "I now name you Princess Naked-as-a-Jaybird." The Princess goes wild. "Hot-cha-cha!" Teensy screams. — Rebecca Wells, *Divine Secrets of the Ya-Ya Sisterhood*, p. 72, 1996

hot chair *noun*
the electric chair; death by electrocution in an electric chair *US, 1926*
- — Joseph E. Ragen and Charles Finston, *Inside the World's Toughest Prison*, p. 804, 1962: "Penitentiary and underworld glossary"

hot check *noun*
a forged check or one intentionally drawn with insufficient
funds to cover payment *US, 1972*

- I read a few years ago that in Dallas they lost $1,740,000 in hot
  checks in the first three months of the year and it way down.
  — Bruce Jackson, *Outside the Law*, p. 80, 1972

hot chrome *noun*
a car that appeals to girls *US, 1954*

- — *American Speech*, p. 101, May 1954

hot damn, Vietnam!
used for expressing surprise, shock, or dismay *US, 1972*
"Vietnam" is lengthened to three syllables.

- Busted for stealing some fucking meat! "Hot damn, Vietnam!" as
  the man said. — Emmett Grogan, *Ringolevio*, p. 341, 1972

hot dog *noun*
1 a skilled and cocky person defined as much by their cocki-
ness as their skill *US, 1894*

- Jessie Luker is a hot dog from Alcorn A&M who's got hands on him
  like snowshoes. — Dan Jenkins, *Semi-Tough*, p. 92, 1972
- You might be more of a team player and a little less of a hot dog
  on this one, Jack. — *48 Hours*, 1982
- [T]his pilot was a hot dog, and good. — Joseph Wambaugh, *Lines and Shadows*, p. 321, 1984

2 a police officer *US, 2001*

- While kids in Northwest refer to police as "one-time," Northeast
  teenagers call them "bo-deen" or "hot dog," and in Southeast
  they're "po-pos" or good old "feds." — *Washington Post*, p. A1, 20th
  August 2001

3 a pornographic book or magazine *US, 1974*

- — Paul Glover, *Words from the House of the Dead*, 1974

hot-dog *adjective*
1 obsessed with sex *US, 1975*

- I'd known a lot of hot-dog guys before I got to Bullion, but never
  had I seen the likes of Maynard Farrell. — James Carr, *Bad*, p. 56, 1975

2 given to showing off *US, 1923*

- Kathy looked over to see one of his bodyguards from TAC in the
  doorway: a young, hot-dog cop named Wesley, blond hair down on
  his forehead. — Elmore Leonard, *Maximum Bob*, p. 217, 1991

hot dog board *noun*
a design of surf board favored by surfers who surf with flair
US, 1963

- He had been able to buy some of the visiting team's "hot dog"
  boards. — Nat Young, *History of Surfing*, p. 89, 1983

hot dog book *noun*
a book used for stimulating sexual interest while masturbating *US, 1967*

- Most of these books were L and L's, derived from Lewd and Lascivious Conduct, hotdog books heavy with sex, and they were always
  in demand. — Malcolm Braly, *On the Yard*, p. 152, 1967

hot dogger *noun*
an expert surfer *US, 1963*

- — *Paradise of the Pacific*, p. 27, October 1963

hot dog magazine *noun*
a pornographic magazine *US, 1975*

- [T]he homo convinced him to bring in Playboy and every other
  hot-dog magazine imaginable. — James Carr, *Bad*, p. 133, 1975

hot dose *noun*
a fatal injection of a narcotic that has been adulterated with
a poison *US, 1995*

- I had a private doctor do another autopsy. He said they gave her a
  hot dose. — *Casino*, 1995

hotel *noun*
a jail *US, 1845*

- — John R. Armore and Joseph D. Wolfe, *Dictionary of Desperation*, p. 34, 1976

Hotel de Gink *noun*
inexpensive rooming run by a charity *US, 1939*

- He stayed briefly at the transient quarters ("the famous Hotel De
  Gink, a real rat hole") before moving into a tent city near the Lunga
  River. — Bruce Gamble, *Black Sheep One*, p. 241, 1958

hotels *noun*
in bar dice games, a roll from the cup in which some dice
are stacked on top of others, invalidating the roll *US, 1976*

- — Gil Jacobs, *The World's Best Dice Games*, p. 201, 1976

hotfoot *noun*
a prank in which a matchbook is lit and inserted in to an
unsuspecting victim's shoe *US, 1934*

- [T]he sight of Max Baer, the former heavyweight champ, crawling
  under tables sticking lighted matches in the shoes of friends or
  acquaintances—in short, applying the infuriating "hot foot" which is
  now blessedly out of fashion—was one of the truly hilarious comedy
  bits in all history. — Robert Sylvester, *No Cover Charge*, pp. 103–104, 1956
- One of the great hot-foots (hot feets?) of all time was administered
  to Joe Pepitone by Phil Linz. — Jim Bouton, *Ball Four*, p. 118, 1970

hotfoot *verb*
to move quickly *US, 1896*

- I hotfooted it outside and back to my car[.] — James Ellroy, *Brown's
  Requiem*, p. 32, 1981
- He smiled at me and hotfooted it out to the street. — James Ellroy,
  Because the Night, p. 397, 1984
- The cops began hotfooting it down Darwin Way and they started
  feeling like pollos. — Joseph Wambaugh, *Lines and Shadows*, p. 61, 1984

hot fudgey *noun*
a savory piece of gossip *US, 1994*

- — Michael Dalton Johnson, *Talking Trash with Redd Foxx*, p. 136, 1994

hot-fuel *verb*
to fuel an aircraft while the engine is running *US, 1990*

- [T]heir roaring Phantoms "hot fueling": taking on gas as fast as they
  burned it, in order to be "topped off" when they were launched.
  — Robert K. Wilcox, *Scream of Eagles*, p. 228, 1990

hot hay *noun*
marijuana *US, 1952*

- — *American Speech*, p. 27, February 1952: "Teen-age hophead jargon"

Hot House *nickname*
the federal penitentiary at Leavenworth *US, 1992*

- The Hot House is the Harvard of them all. It is the oldest, the most
  famous. — Pete Earley, *The Hot House*, p. 27, 1992

hot item *noun*
a couple in lust *US, 1981*

- And the unlikely couple became a hot item. — Sherry Argov, *Why Men
  Love Bitches*, p. 198, 2002

hot lead *noun*
bullets *US, 1949*

- — Vincent J. Monteleone, *Criminal Slang*, p. 123, 1949

hot list *noun*
a list of stolen cars maintained by the police *US, 1972*

- During the year we would steal license plates and put them in storage until they cool off. By the time we were ready to use them they
  were off the hot list. — Harry King, *Box Man*, p. 37, 1972

hot load *noun*
a heavily charged cartridge *US, 1975*

- I changed clips in the .22 so I would have three rounds of rat shot
  above six rounds of hollow-point hot loads[.] — James Crumley, *The Last
  Good Kiss*, p. 90, 1978

hot-lot *verb*
to move quickly; to hurry *US, 1972*

- But he almost didn't get a chance to buy one because, as he was
  saying his farewells to Truman, two police patrol cars came hot-
  lotting it up to the front of the house. — Emmett Grogan, *Ringolevio*,
  p. 207, 1972

hot minute *noun*
a very short period of time *US, 1932*

- "Just a hot minute, as one of my suitors used to say" — Brendan Lemon,
  Last Night, p. 24, 2002

hot-nose *verb*
in arial combat, to approach from behind and below, rising
up in front of and ahead of the target plane *US, 1990*

- Another trick was "hot-nosing." From a hidden approach
  underneath, a plane would pull up right in front of you. — Robert K.
  Wilcox, *Scream of Eagles*, p. 156, 1990

hot number *noun*
an attractive person *US, 1896*
- "If Justine was such a hot number, why were you marrying Paula?"
  — Janice Weber, *Hot Ticket*, p. 207, 1998

hot nuts *noun*
intense male sexual desire *US, 1935*
- — Robert A. Wilson, *Playboy's Book of Forbidden Words*, p. 142, 1972

hot one *noun*
a murder in the first degree *US, 1993*
- I came back to the phone and told him I'd found it and asked how many hot ones—murders—it had on it. — Sanyika Shakur, *Monster*, p. 245, 1993

hot pants *noun*
sexual desire *US, 1929*
- I've still got hot pants for her, if you want to call that love. — Mary McCarthy, *The Group*, p. 48, 1963
- He'll think I have hot pants. — Elmore Leonard, *The Big Bounce*, p. 178, 1969
- When a woman's glands is actin' up and she can't control certain urges—they say she's got hot pants! Same as the meathead there. Hot trousers, hot pants, same thing! — Eugene Boe (Compiler), *The Wit & Wisdom of Archie Bunker*, p. 153, 1971
- I'm not going to screw it up just because you people got hot pants. — George V. Higgins, *The Friends of Eddie Doyle*, p. 74, 1971

hot paper *noun*
forged securities *US, 1952*
- Obtaining the signatures of half a dozen prospects, Benton wrote his first "hot paper," copying beneath the indorsement the signature of his involuntary benefactor. — Charles Hamilton, *Men of the Underworld*, p. 154, 1952

hot patootie *noun*
a sexually attractive woman *US, 1919*
- "He the older man with the younger wife? The hot patootie?" — Al Sarrantonio, *999*, p. 472, 1999

hot peckers *noun*
hot peppers *US, 1996*
Limited usage, but clever.
- — *Maledicta*, p. 14, 1996: "Domino's pizza jargon"

hot-pillow *adjective*
said of a hotel or motel that rents rooms for sexual liaisons for cash, without registering the guests using the room *US, 1954*
- He operated what is known as a hot pillow motel. That means a motel that is conducted on an immoral basis. — Senate Committee on the Judiciary, *Juvenile Delinquency*, p. 62, 1956
- [T]heir idea of a good time was grabbing a case of beer and heading for the nearest hot pillow joint. — Martin Boyle, *Yanks Don't Cry*, p. 10, 1963
- Until after World War II, the tourist court was considered the poor cousin of the hotel—a place which catered to the "hot pillow trade," to use J. Edgar Hoover's eloquent phrase. — *Washington Post*, p. 1 (Weekend), 12th January 1979
- Doohan could hardly keep from telling the man that the beautiful woman everyone was admiring was the woman who spent time with him in a certain hot-pillow motel at least once a week, sometimes more. — Robert Campbell, *Juice*, p. 221, 1988

hot pot *noun*
in poker, a large amount of money bet on a hand *US, 1988*
- — George Percy, *The Language of Poker*, p. 45, 1988

hot prowl *verb*
to burglarize a home with the residents present in the house *US, 1954*
- I stood guard duty while Al, silent as a cat, hot prowled a mansion. — Caryl Chessman, *Cell 2456 Death Row*, p. 248, 1954

hot prowl *adjective*
said a burglary of a house whose occupants are at home *US, 1933*
- One evening, Birse asked Willie to help him track down a couple of hot prowl burglars. — Bob Sipchen, *Baby Insane and the Buddha*, p. 105, 1993
- Grady was a hot-prowl burglar who cased his jobs when he cleaned carpets. — Stephen Cannell, *The Viking Funeral*, p. 46, 2002
- "He's been telling street creeps I gave him up to the Sheriff's on a hot-prowl job." — James Ellroy, *Destination Morgue*, p. 238, 2004

hot-prowl man *noun*
a burglar who specializes in breaking into houses whose occupants are at home *US, 2004*
- "We call burglars who break into residences with people inside them 'hot-prowl men,'" he said. — James Ellroy, *Destination Morgue*, p. 260, 2004

hot rail *noun*
a group of prisoners surrounding two prisoners having sex *US, 2002*
- — Jeffrey Ian Ross, *Behind Bars*, p. 188, 2002: Slammer Slang

hot ringer *noun*
a burglar alarm that advises police that an armed robbery is in progress *US, 2001*
- He had accepted a call on a "hot ringer" in Southwest. A Hoover Street jewelry store was being robbed. It was a "There Now" call. — Stephen J. Cannell, *The Tin Collectors*, p. 110, 2001

hot rock *noun*
a person who through dress or manner strives to be noticed *US, 1945*
- — *American Speech*, p. 228, October 1956: "More United States Air Force slang"

hot rod *verb*
to masturbate *US, 1971*
- — Eugene Landy, *The Underground Dictionary*, p. 106, 1971

hot roller *noun*
a stolen car that is being driven *US, 1970*
- "How about roller's?" asked Serge. "How many hot cars do you get rolling?" "Hot rollers? Oh, maybe one a month." — Joseph Wambaugh, *The New Centurions*, p. 42, 1970
- — *Los Angeles Times*, p. B8, 19th December 1994

hots *noun*
1 sexual desire, intense interest *US, 1947*
- You ain't in love with Angela. You just got a case of the hots, that's all. — Max Shulman, *Rally Round the Flag, Boys!*, p. 190, 1957
- They think I have a secret hot for her. — Clancy Sigal, *Going Away*, p. 409, 1961
- And besides, she doesn't even have the hots for me. — Darryl Ponicsan, *The Last Detail*, p. 113, 1970
- He's a total asshole and he's got the hots for my friend Angela and it's disgusting. — *American Beauty*, 1999
2 electric hair curlers *US, 1975*
- — *American Speech*, p. 61, Spring–Summer 1975: "Razorback slang"

hot seat *noun*
1 the electric chair; death by electrocution in the electric chair *US, 1925*
- And if either of you are tapped for the hot seat, you'd do a lot better by letting Pat pick you up. — Mickey Spillane, *I, The Jury*, p. 19, 1947
- "He said if I didn't"—Nick's eyes fastened the jurors—"he was going to see that I got the hot seat." — Willard Motley, *Knock on Any Door*, p. 432, 1947
- His buttocks, in creased midnight-blue parts, for the hot seat. — Willard Motley, *Let No Man Write My Epitaph*, p. 164, 1958
- I could've got life or the hot seat for what I did. — A.S. Jackson, *Gentleman Pimp*, p. 130, 1973
2 a high-pressure situation *US, 1935*
- First thing Monday morning McCaleb would be on the hot seat, the focus of intense scrutiny. — Michael Connelly, *Blood Work*, p. 245, 1998

hot seat game *noun*
a swindle in which all the players in a game except the victim are confederates *US, 1989*
- — Lindsay E. Smith and Bruce A. Walstad, *Sting Shift*, p. 116, 1989: "Glossary"

hot sheet *noun*
a list of cars reported as stolen *US, 1926*
- "How often you pick up a sitting dick?" asked Serge, to change the subject, checking a license plate against the numbers on the hot sheet. — Joseph Wambaugh, *The New Centurions*, p. 41, 1970
- Then get the ten latest GLA's off the hot sheet. — Charles Whited, *Chiodo*, p. 27, 1973

hot-sheet *adjective*
said of a motel or hotel that rents rooms for sexual liaisons for cash, without registering the guests using the room *US, 1977*

- Lang returned briefly to his job loading trucks, until one night when he picked up another prostitute at a bar and they slipped into a "hot-sheet" hotel. — *Newsweek*, p. 89, 7th November 1977
- I've got peeper reports nailed at my burglary location and all over the Southside—hot-sheet motels and jazz clubs. — James Ellroy, *White Jazz*, p. 51, 1992
- He's a pervy Italian who looks like he'd run a hot-sheet hotel. — Bill Landis, *Sleazoid Express*, p. 230, 2002

hot shit *noun*
an exceptionally good person or thing *US*, 1960
- — Collin Baker et al., *College Undergraduate Slang Study Conducted at Brown University*, p. 140, 1968

hot-shit *adjective*
exciting; fashionable *US*, 1962
- Go see Hot Tuna because Hot Tuna is hot shit. — Richard Meltzer, *A Whore Just Like the Rest*, p. 215, 1971
- Goddamn New York teams, think they're hot shit. — *Diner*, 1982
- Then some hot-shit doctor comes in and revives them. — Jim Carroll, *Forced Entries*, p. 52, 1987

hotshot *noun*
1 an adulterated dose of a drug that is designed to be fatal when injected *US*, 1936
- — *American Speech*, p. 27, February 1952: "Teen-age hophead jargon"
- New York detectives assigned to the Narcotics Squad are convinced that he died of what the trade calls "a hot shot"—heroin or cocaine purposely mixed with rat poison. — Robert Sylvester, *No Cover Charge*, p. 47, 1956
- "I can tell you in confidence he is due for a hot shot." (Note: This is a cap of poison junk sold to addicts for liquidation purposes. Often given to informers. Usually the hot shot is strychnine since it tastes and looks like junk.) — William Burroughs, *Naked Lunch*, p. 2, 1957
- That creepin' bastard Fink! He gets so much for what they call "makin' a case" ... someone's goin' to slip him a hotshot... — Alexander Trocchi, *Cain's Book*, p. 243, 1960
- The coroner says she O.D.'d on smack. She wasn't murdered—unless somebody gave her a hotshot on purpose. — Gerald Petievich, *Money Men*, p. 94, 1981

2 a gun shot fired after an emergency call to police *US*, 1994
- — *Los Angeles Times*, p. B8, 19th December 1994

3 an electric cattle prod *US*, 2003
- — John Cann, *The Stunt Guide*, p. 60: "Terms and definitions"

4 execution by electrocution in the electric chair *US*, 1951
- — *American Speech*, p. 155, May 1951: "Hermann Collitz and the language of the underworld"

5 a flashy, successful person whose self-esteem is perhaps excessive *US*, 1927
- If you're such a hotshot patriot, why didn't you reenlist? — Max Shulman, *Rally Round the Flag, Boys!*, p. 115, 1957

hotshot *verb*
to inject someone with a poisoned dose of a drug *US*, 1963
- "Why would he hotshot me?" — Malcolm Braly, *Shake Him Till He Rattles*, p. 146, 1963

Hot Shot Charlie *noun*
a brash, flamboyant person *US*, 1944
From the Terry and the Pirates newspaper comic strip.
- I wished I could talk as fast as the wisecracking Hot Shot Charlie, with his red hair, freckles, Boston accent, corncob pipe, and flight cap worn with a swagger[.] — Pete Hamil, *A Drinking Life*, p. 89, 1994

hot spike *noun*
a dose of a drug that has been adulterated and produces serious injury or death when injected *US*, 1974
- I'm gonna dig you out of whatever trash heap you're hidin' in and stick a hot spike in your ass! — Joseph Nazel, *Black Cop*, p. 145, 1974

hot squat *noun*
the electric chair; execution by electrocution *US*, 1928
- If you smear her all over the papers as a number-one candidate for the hot squat you and me are going to have it out. — Mickey Spillane, *I, The Jury*, p. 22, 1947

hot stop *noun*
a police stop of criminals fleeing the scene of a crime *US*, 1993
- "This is the first time I've ever been on this side of a hot stop," Kevin grinned. — Bob Sipchen, *Baby Insane and the Buddha*, p. 339, 1993

hot stuff *noun*
1 a sexually attractive and active person *US*, 1967
- He knew of a girl four years his senior, Doris, who had a reputation for being "hot stuff." — Mark Holden, *Sodom 1967 American Style*, p. 45, 1967

2 promotional literature produced as part of a telephone sales swindle *US*, 1988
- Anyone who succumbs to a sales pitch—due to the hot stuff or a phone call—becomes, in the yaks' slang, a mooch. — Kathleen Odean, *High Steppers, Fallen Angels, and Lollipops*, p. 132, 1988

3 coffee *US*, 1977
- — Bill Davis, *Jawjacking*, p. 53, 1977

hotsy-totsy *adjective*
fancy *US*, 1926
- [E]very spring, in the fullness of their benevolence, they sent him and my mother for a hotsy-totsy free weekend in Atlantic City. — Philip Roth, *Portnoy's Complaint*, p. 5, 1969

hotsy-totsy; hotsy *noun*
an attractive young woman *US*, 1928
- "This is your mother you're talking to and not one of your little hotsy-totsies." "Hotsy-totsies!" — Walker Percy, *The Movie Goer*, p. 155, 1960

hot taco *noun*
1 an attractive woman *US*, 1974
- "They do not know it is instead because I spend my nights with one hot taco." — Stephen Burns, *Call from a Distant Shore*, p. 11, 2000

2 an attractive man *US*, 2003
- "This wouldn't be you and the hot taco, now would it?" — Laura Ruby, *Lily's Ghosts*, p. 115, 2003

hot tamale *noun*
an attractive woman *US*, 1897
- My sisters were hot tamales, as well. — Jenifer Estess, *Tales from the Bed*, p. 161, 2004

hottentots *noun*
the buttocks *US*, 1974
- A white soldier, his shirttail out behind, his cunt cap crosswise on his dome, staggered along happily, held up by a chunky black whore with an enormous Hottentot can[.] — Earl Thompson, *Tattoo*, p. 121, 1974
- — *Maledicta*, p. 52, 1986–1987: "A continuation of a glossary of ethnic slurs in American English"

hotter than Dutch love *adjective*
very hot *US*, 1950
- [W]idowers teasing that the weather was hotter than Dutch love. — Mary Potter Engel, *A Woman of Salt*, p. 40, 2001

hot ticket *noun*
1 something that is extremely popular and in demand *US*, 1978
- Rings 'n' Things also has stores in hot-ticket towns like Vegas, Reno, and Atlantic City. — Stephen Cannell, *King Con*, p. 113, 1997

2 a very popular show or event *US*, 1936
- Because the tykes just can't get enough, it has been a hot ticket. — Bob Sehlinger, *The Unofficial Guide to Disneyland*, p. 212, 2005

hottie *noun*
1 an attractive, sexually appealing young person *US*, 1991
- — Connie Eble (Editor), *UNC-CH Campus Slang*, p. 5, Spring 1994
- You guys are so pathetic. I'm gonna find myself a little hottie. — *American Pie*, 1999
- We see him rolling around in the sheets with some hottie[.] — *The Village Voice*, 6th February 2001
- [H]is brothers, fraternal twins (and major hotties) Matt and Sean. — Brittany Kent, *O.C. Undercover*, p. 60, 2004

2 a great wave or surfer *US*, 1991
- — Trevor Cralle, *The Surfin'ary*, p. 55, 1991

hot to trot *adjective*
ready and eager, especially for sexual activity *US*, 1951
- Here he is hot to trot and suddenly stricken by a flash that's a sure-fire dong-wilter. — Lester Bangs, *Psychotic Reactions and Carburetor Dung*, p. 77, 1971
- So, it got to be too much for him, and he got himself this hot-to-trot bimbo, and it turns out—he was talking about it, in detail—there wasn't anything she couldn't do, wouldn't do or didn't want done. — George V. Higgins, *The Judgment of Deke Hunter*, p. 131, 1976
- Hot to trot, make any man's eyes pop[.] — Salt 'N' Pepa, *Let's Talk About Sex*, 1991

- I said to myself a while ago that Loretta was looking for trouble. She was real hot to trot. — Janet Evanovich, *Seven Up*, p. 17, 2001

hot up *verb*
to increase the power, speed and performance (of a car) *UK, 1928*

- Many people think that a rodder is a character who spends all his time hotting up his roadster. — *Hot Rod Comics*, June 1952

hot walker *noun*
in horse racing, a groom who walks a horse after a race, letting it cool down *US, 1974*

- "He knows everybody, the jocks, the hot-walkers, everybody." — George Higgins, *Cogan's Trade*, p. 107, 1974
- — Tom Ainslie, *Ainslie's Complete Guide to Thoroughbred Racing*, p. 333, 1976

hot wire *noun*
a linear amplifier for a citizens' band radio *US, 1976*

- — Porter Bibb, *CB Bible*, p. 96, 1976

hou-bro *noun*
a fellow fraternity member *US, 1977*
An abbreviation of "house brother."

- [S]ometimes longed for the uncomplicated life of lacrosse and rugby and hou-bro beevo parties, of happily hugging the toilet all night long with your barf buddies after draining a half-keg for no special occasion? — John Sayles, *Union Dues*, p. 279, 1977

hound *noun*
a person who is obsessed with the preceding combining noun *US, 1911*
Not, as the definition might suggest, a grammarian.

- Tall, slender, with regular features, dark and personable, Legs was a night club hound, even owned some himself. — Jack Lait and Lee Mortimer, *New York Confidential*, p. 160, 1948
- But he knew all about Estes Kefauver whom he described as a publicity hound. — Clancy Sigal, *Going Away*, p. 160, 1961
- I was a big pussy-hound. Ain't changed much either. — Edwin Torres, *Carlito's Way*, p. 12, 1975
- Once upstairs in the Melody lobby, Raven is instantly surrounded by admirers and tit hounds. — Josh Alan Friedman, *Tales of Times Square*, p. 23, 1986

hound-dog *verb*
to track down, to follow, to find *US, 1998*

- Bud and I were sent to hound-dog them on the way, in the direction I saw them take. — Clarence Major, *All-Night Visitors*, p. 39, 1998

house *noun*
1 a prisoner's cell or the area immediately surrounding the prisoner's bed in a prison dormitory *US, 1970*

- [V]iolations of prison rules that range from sticking a shank in somebody to having an extra sandwich in your "house" or cell. — Tim Findley, *The Rolling Stone Reader*, p. 87, 1974
- It seemed to anger him most that Cherokee had beaten me in his cell. "Black motherfucker, fucking over my house like that." — Malcolm Braley, *False Starts*, p. 227, 1976
- "I think I'll head back to my house to read," he said. — Seth Morgan, *Homeboy*, p. 257, 1990
- This is one of the most important aspects of prison life as a person's house is his home, his solitude, where he achieves his privacy. — William Bentley, *Prison Slang*, p. 7, 1992

2 a police station *US, 1909*

- "How come we're taking this guy to the house?" Chiodo asked his partner. — Charles Whited, *Chiodo*, p. 47, 1973

3 in poker, a hand consisting of three cards of the same rank and a pair *US, 1990*
An abbreviation of the conventional "full house."

- — Anthony Holden, *Big Deal*, p. 301, 1990

▸ **go under the house**
to perform oral sex on a woman *US, 1981*

- — *Male Swinger Number 3*, p. 45, 1981: "The complete gay dictionary"

▸ **in the house**
here and now, present, currently *US, 1993*

- — Judi Sanders, *Faced and Faded, Hanging to Hurl*, p. 22, 1993
- — *Merriam-Webster's Hot Words on Campus Marketing Survey '93*, p. 3, 13th October 1993

▸ **on the house**
paid for by management of the establishment *US, 1889*

- They flew him up from Miami in their private jet, comped the room, meals, everything. If you can afford to lose a hundred grand, Vincent, it's all on the house. — Elmore Leonard, *Glitz*, p. 129, 1985

▸ **the house**
the New York House of Detention for female prisoners *US, 1966*

- "She just got out of the house," Helen said, meaning the Women's House of Detention in Greenwich Village. — James Mills, *The Panic in Needle Park*, p. 33, 1966

house *verb*
to steal *US, 1989*

- — Ellen C. Bellone (Editor), *Dictionary of Slang*, p. 14, 1989

house ape *noun*
a child *US, 1968*

- A bunch a blue-eyed spad house apes inta the bargain. — Robert Gover, *JC Saves*, p. 127, 1968

house ball *noun*
in pinball, a ball that leaves play without having scored any points *US, 1977*

- — Bobbye Claire Natkin and Steve Kirk, *All About Pinball*, p. 113, 1977

housecat *noun*
a soldier not assigned to combat duty *US, 1977*
Vietnam war usage.

- I spent two and a half days at the Tan Son Nhut Air Base, explaining about my brother and the emergency leave to a running variety of housecats behind the ticket counter [.] — Larry Heinemann, *Close Quarters*, p. 118, 1977

house dancer *noun*
a sex club dancer who regularly appears at one club *US, 2000*

- When I was a "house" dancer I would watch all the "featured" dancers, most of whom were porn stars, come in and make all the money, get lines of people and get the beautiful pictures. — Ana Loria, *1 2 3 Be A Porn Star!*, p. 107, 2000

house dick *noun*
a private detective working for a hotel or other establishment *US, 1951*

- The "security officer" (refined designation for a house dick) of one of the oldest and most famous hotels in Washington, near the White House, was recently fired because he ran a shakedown racket[.] — Jack Lait and Lee Mortimer, *Washington Confidential*, pp. 285–286, 1951
- Are you going peacefully, or do I call the house dick? — Max Shulman, *Anyone Got a Match?*, p. 197, 1964
- I picked her up, and carried her into the dining room, oblivious even of the house dick. — Red Rudensky, *The Gonif*, p. 114, 1970

house doctor *noun*
a person who for a fee will help a needle-using drug addict find a vein for injecting a drug *US, 1997*

- At last, when you're equipped and ready but can't seem to find a vein, help is as near as the house doctor. — David Simon and Edward Burns, *The Corner*, pp. 69–70, 1997

house fee *noun*
the amount charged for entering a crack house *US, 1992*

- — Terry Williams, *Crackhouse*, p. 149, 1992

house girl *noun*
1 a prostitute working in a brothel *US, 1957*

- After the call-girls come the house-girls. Houses today are not the elaborate affairs that they used to be. — Judge John M. Murtagh and Sara Harris, *Cast the First Stone*, p. 2, 1957

2 in a sex club, a local dancer who regularly works at the club, as distinguished from pornography stars who make limited engagements at the club *US, 1997*

- The DJ, the manager, the owner, all such "interested" parties basically didn't want a headline dancer making them look bad in front of the house girls. — Anthony Petkovich, *The X Factory*, p. 37, 1997

housekeeper *noun*
in prison, the passive, weaker partner in a relationship who is subservient to his dominant partner's needs and wants *US, 1991*

Prison ain't that bad, you get the hang of it... find yourself some buddies, a little housekeeper to take care of your wants... — Elmore Leonard, *Maximum Bob*, p. 197, 1991

housemaid's knees *noun*
the condition caused by Osgood-Schlatter disease, calcium deposits on the lower outside quadrant of the knee *US*, 1973
- — William Desmond Nelson, *Surfing*, p. 226, 1973

houseman *noun*
the best regular player in a pool hall *US*, 1990
- — Steve Rushin, *Pool Cool*, p. 16, 1990

house mother *noun*
a madame in a brothel *US*, 1966
- — Rose Giallombardo, *Society of Women*, p. 209, 1966: Glossary of Prison Terms
- — *Maledicta*, p. 150, Summer/Winter 1986–1987: "Sexual slang: prostitutes, pedophiles, flagellators, transvestites, and necrophiles"

house mouse *noun*
1 a fastidious cleaner *US*, 1981
- It's always kind of neat to have a house mouse to cook and clean up[.] — Robert Lipkin, *A Brotherhood of Outlaws*, p. 36, 1981
2 a prisoner who takes or accepts responsibility for cleaning a prison cell, dormitory, or common room *US*, 1989
- — James Harris, *A Convict's Dictionary*, p. 33, 1989
3 an American soldier who explored Viet Cong tunnels *US*, 1989
- Every company had what they called their "house mouse," who was usually the smallest guy in the bunch. — *The Houston Chronicle*, 27th October 1989

house nigger; house nigga *noun*
a black person who curries favor from white people and in return is given some small degree of privilege *US*, 1933
An updated "house slave."
- Professors are house niggers and students are field niggers. — Jerry Rubin, *Do It!*, p. 215, 1970
- Malcolm X extended and popularized the concept; a field nigger was more likely to become a revolutionary while the house nigger was more likely to be an Uncle Tom. — Clarence Major, *Dictionary of Afro-American Slang*, p. 53, 1970
- Van was doing a Tom act that would've put any old time house nigger to utter shame. — Odie Hawkins, *Scars and Memories*, p. 158, 1987
- [W]hen she refused to talk to him, he started berating her and Sing Sing's two black captains as "house niggers." — Ted Conover, *Newjack*, p. 133, 2000

house nut *noun*
in the movie business, the weekly operating expenses of the movie theater *US*, 1990
- — Ralph S. Singleton, *Filmmaker's Dictionary*, p. 83, 1990

House of D *nickname*
the New York Women's House of Detention, Greenwich Avenue *US*, 1964
- "How'd you do it?" "House of D," Gloria said. — Robert Deane Pharr, *S.R.O.*, p. 50, 1971
- "The House of D" as it was unaffectionately nicknamed, stood on a triangular block in the heart of Greenwich Village. — Karla Jay, *Tales of the Lavender Menace*, p. 103, 1999

House of Do Right *nickname*
the New York City jail *US*, 1967
- They gave up and then I was sent to the Tombs, the House of Do-Right, on 125 White Street, to await some kinda trial. — Piri Thomas, *Down These Mean Streets*, p. 243, 1967

house of joy *noun*
a brothel *US*, 1925
- It is difficult and dangerous to fall in with streetwalkers on the avenues, and next to impossible to locate a gambling den or a house of joy. — Jack Lait and Lee Mortimer, *New York Confidential*, p. 206, 1948

house of wax *noun*
a prison *US*, 1973
- I hit the old edge and saw a lotta my old pals who all gave me the usual bullshit niggers give a guy when he's just outta the house of wax. — A.S. Jackson, *Gentleman Pimp*, p. 69, 1973

house piece *noun*
a gift of a dose of crack cocaine, given to the owner of a crack house in appreciation for the use of the premises *US*, 1992
- — Terry Williams, *Crackhouse*, p. 149, 1992

houser *noun*
a person who is part of the club music and party set *US*, 1994
- Houser: the members of this clique assigned great value to house music and to the dance club scene connected with it. — Marcel Danesi, *Cool*, pp. 56–57, 1994
- — Judi Sanders, *Da Bomb*, p. 8, 1997

house wizard; house guru *noun*
the technical expert in a business or organization *US*, 1991
- A really effective house wizard can have influence out of all proportion to his/her ostensible rank and still not have to wear a suit. — Eric S. Raymond, *The New Hacker's Dictionary*, p. 203, 1991

house-wrecker *noun*
in surfing, a large and powerful wave *US*, 1978
- — Dennis Aaberg and John Milius, *Big Wednesday*, p. 209, 1978

Howard Johnsons *noun*
an outdoor street food vendor in Vietnam during the war *US*, 1965
From the name of a roadside restaurant which at the time of the Vietnam war was immensely popular in the US.
- All over Saigon you find conveniently located portable food vendors affectionately dubbed "Howard Johnsons" by the GI. — Tony Zidek, *Choi Oi*, p. 32, 1965

how bad is that?
that's great! *US*, 1965
- — *Time*, p. 56, 1st January 1965: "Students: the slang bag"

how can I tell?
used in prison to question the truth of that which has just been said *US*, 1992
- — William K. Bentley and James M. Corbett, *Prison Slang*, p. 46, 1992

how come?
why *US*, 1848
- "How come her parents didn't show?" the woman continued, lowering her voice — Mary McCarthy, *The Group*, p. 22, 1963
- "How come?" He loved that. How come? — Joseph Wambaugh, *Finnegan's Week*, p. 205, 1993

how-do
used as a folksy greeting *US*, 1977
- "Hey," he broadcast, "you say how-do to all my boys at K&L when you hit the Dirty Side, all right?" — E.M. Corder, *Citizens Band*, p. 33, 1977

Howdy Doody *noun*
an unspecified chemical agent used in Vietnam *US*, 1991
- I've found out that those other men were drenched by a chemical spray we called Howdy Doody—because it made you stiffen up and jerk like you were hanging on strings. — Robert R. McCammon, *Blue World*, p. 81, 1991

how goes it?
used as a greeting *US*, 1966
- Easy now, stick to vernaculars: "Hello there, Gorzy, how goes it?" — Richard Farina, *Been Down So Long*, p. 34, 1966

howgozit
used as a greeting *US*, 1945
- "Howgozit at NSA?" — Stephen Coonts, *Liars & Thieves*, p. 140, 2004

howl *noun*
a source of great amusement *US*, 1930
- [W]ouldn't that have been a howl? — Mary McCarthy, *The Group*, p. 95, 1963

howling *adjective*
superlative *UK*, 1865
- "Oh, dig that howling Cadillac!" Zaida cried ecstatically. — Ross Russell, *The Sound*, p. 15, 1961

how's hacking?
used as a greeting *US*, 1981
- — *Co-Evolution Quarterly*, p. 32, Spring 1981
- — Guy L. Steele et al., *The Hacker's Dictionary*, p. 76, 1983

how's it hanging?
used as a greeting, usually male-to-male *US*, *1974*
Sometimes testically inclusive and increased to "they."

- Gennaro! How's she hangin'? — Richard Price, *The Wanderers*, p. 36, 1974
- "So how they hanging, Bilal?" — Jess Mowry, *Six Out Seven*, p. 322, 1993
- [W]ho always inexplicably greeted her with the gender-inappropriate phrase, hey, how's it hanging? — Rita Ciresi, *Pink Slip*, p. 363, 1999

how-so?
how is that so? *US*, *1980*
Found in the C14, but not a complete path to the current usage.

- "But this is different." "And I ask you how-so?" — Elmore Leonard, *Gold Coast*, p. 75, 1980

howzit?
used as a greeting *US*, *1949*
- — Hyman E. Goldin et al., *Dictionary of American Underworld Lingo*, p. 104, 1950
- — Douglas Simonson, *Pidgin to da Max*, 1981
- Eddie there to greet us with a "Hey, howzit?" — John Ridley, *Love is a Racket*, p. 49, 1998

hubba noun
crack cocaine *US*, *1988*
- — Geoffrey Froner, *Digging for Diamonds*, p. 36, 1989
- — William T. Vollman, *Whores for Gloria*, p. 139, 1991

hubba-hubba!
used for expressing enthusiastic appreciation of a good-looking woman *US*, *1941*
- — *Chicago Tribune* ("Harold the Teen" comic), 24th March 1945

hubba pigeon noun
a crack cocaine addict who searches for bits of crack cocaine on the ground *US*, *1995*
- — Bill Valentine, *Gang Intelligence Manual*, p. 77, 1995: "Black street gang terminology"
- Some long-term users are also plagued by the constant sense that they can see bits of crack on the ground, causing them to try frantically to pick them up. In New York City, such obsessed addicts are called "hubba pigeons" because their hunched-over bodies resemble pigeons pecking for food[.] — *New Times Los Angeles*, 19th September 1996

hubbly-bubbly noun
a water pipe used for smoking marijuana, hashish, or crack cocaine *US*, *1970*
- — William D. Alsever, *Glossary for the Establishment and Other Uptight People*, p. 16, December 1970
- We managed to get it [a small fire] out though, with the water from the hubbly-bubbly. — Macfarlane, Macfarlane and Robson, *The User*, p. 89, 1996

hubby; hubbie noun
a husband *UK*, *1688*
Often used in a sardonic sense.

- Hey girls, hubby's gonna strike it rich, so bye-bye now, I'm moving to the suburbs. — Max Shulman, *Guided Tour of Campus Humor*, p. 40, 1955
- What she didn't know was that I had been having an affair with her hubby for a long time[.] — Jefferson Poland and Valerie Alison, *The Records of the San Francisco Sexual Freedom League*, p. 56, 1971
- Quiet bedroom in the afternoon, hubby's off building houses — Elmore Leonard, *Switch*, p. 106, 1978
- Fortunately, Mom lives in one of the crime capitals of America, so her dim new hubby-cop is unlikely to suspect an inside job. — C.D. Payne, *Youth in Revolt*, p. 199, 1993

hubcap noun
1 an important person *US*, *1960*
Playing on WHEEL (a very important person).

- — Robert George Reisner, *The Jazz Titans*, p. 158, 1960

2 a person whose sense of importance outweights his actual importance *US*, *1951*
- — *Newsweek*, 8th October 1951

hudda noun
a police officer; the police *US*, *1993*
- While the literal translation of the shirt is the police code for homicide ("187") followed by gang slang for police ("hudda"), many Valley police, school officials and gang experts see it another way: "Murder a Cop." — *Los Angeles Times*, p. B3, 13th May 1993

huddle verb
while working as a police officer in a patrol car, to park and sleep *US*, *1973*
- As a rookie cop, Serpico was also introduced to the fine art of "cooping," or sleeping on duty, a time-honored police practice that in other cities goes under such names as "huddling" and "going down." — Peter Maas, *Serpico*, p. 63, 1973

hudge verb
in pinball, to apply physical force to a machine to affect the trajectory of the ball without activating the tilt mechanism *US*, *1977*
- — Bobbye Claire Natkin and Steve Kirk, *All About Pinball*, p. 113, 1977

huevon noun
a very lazy person *US*, *1974*
Border Spanish used in English conversation by Mexican-Americans; from the image of the man who is so lazy that his testicles (HUEVOS) grow large.

- — Dagoberto Fuentes and Jose Lopez, *Barrio Language Dictionary*, p. 76, 1974

huevos noun
1 the testicles; courage *US*, *1974*
Border Spanish used in English conversation by Mexican-Americans; literally "eggs."

- — Dagoberto Fuentes and Jose Lopez, *Barrio Language Dictionary*, p. 76, 1974
- At one of their impromptu Barf parties Manny guzzled five shots of mescal in one minute to show them how big his huevos were. — Joseph Wambaugh, *Lines and Shadows*, p. 150, 1984
- I was marveling at your huevos for standing up to our hometown police when they ran amok through your roost at Owl Farm. — Hunter S. Thompson, *Kingdom of Fear*, p. 277, 15th June 2002: Letter from Gerald Goldstein

2 waves *US*, *1991*
Spanish for "eggs," but a near-homophone for "waves," hence the play.

- — Trevor Cralle, *The Surfin'ary*, p. 55, 1991

Huey nickname
a Bell utility military helicopter *US*, *1962*
- Finally the pilot found a hole no more than fifty feet in diameter and he took the Huey—the nickname for the UH-1D helicopter—down[.] — David Reed, *Up Front in Vietnam*, p. 85, 1967
- Yeah—fishing village—helicopters over there. Hueys, lots of 'em. — *Apocalypse Now*, 1979
- We lined up with our beltkit and bergens and clambered aboard the Hueys that were going to take us in. — Andy McNab (writing of the late 1970s/early 80s), *Immediate Action*, p. 90, 1995

Huey shuffle noun
a common hesitation in the flight pattern by an inexperienced helicopter pilot *US*, *1983*
- I overcontrolled the pedals, making the tail wag back and forth. This was a common reaction to the sensitive controls, and was called the "Huey shuffle." — Robert Mason, *Chickenhawk*, p. 44, 1983

huff verb
to inhale household or industrial chemicals for recreational purposes *US*, *1969*
- — William D. Alsever, *Glossary for the Establishment and Other Uptight People*, p. 11, December 1970
- The brothers were among seven young men who repeatedly "huffed" or inhaled lacquer thinner to get a brief "high" as part of a small group of huffers in the Tampa Area. — *San Francisco Examiner*, p. 25, 19th November 1974
- [E]xplaining to young boys in confederate flag t-shirts why it was dangerous to huff gas. — Michelle Tea, *Valencia*, p. 97, 2000
- "When he was little he huffed paint and glue." — Jonathan Kellerman, *Rage*, p. 217, 2005

huff and puff verb
to breathe heavily *UK*, *1890*
From the childhood tale of *The Three Little Pigs*.

- [A]nd the guys out by the volleyball net, huffing and puffing in twelve-year-old Madras bermudas their wives have let out at least twice[.] — Armistead Maupin, *Tales of the City*, p. 245, 1978

huff duff noun
a radio direction finder *US*, *1946*

- Tonight, however, as he picked up a burst of chatter on the DAQ huff duff set that, even in its encrypted state, he could recognize[.] — Michael Chabon, *The Amazing Adventures of Kavalier & Clay*, p. 447, 2000

huffer *noun*

1 an act of oral sex on a man *US*, *1973*
Probably a mistaken understanding of **HUMMER**.

- Afterwards, she explained that little extras could be provided for a "tip"—$15 for a "huffer," the quaint idiom for oral sex. — *San Francisco Examiner*, p. 6, 15th January 1973

2 a person who inhales household or industrial chemicals for recreational purposes *US*, *1969*

- — *Current Slang*, p. 8, Winter 1969
- The brothers were among seven young men who repeatedly "huffed" or inhaled lacquer thinner to get a brief "high" as part of a small group of huffers in the Tampa Area. — *San Francisco Examiner*, p. 25, 19th November 1974

hug *verb*

▶ **hug the bowl**
to vomit *US*, *1997*

- — Pamela Munro, *U.C.L.A. Slang*, p. 79, 1997

hugger-mugger *noun*

1 chaos *US*, *1972*

- — Helen Dahlskog (Editor), *A Dictionary of Contemporary and Colloquial Usage*, p. 32, 1972

2 a prostitute who beats and robs customers or who serves as a decoy for someone who beats and robs the customer *US*, *1970*

- There's lesbians, masochists, hypes, whores, flim flammers, paddy hustlers, hugger muggers, ex-cons of all descriptions, and anybody else with a kink of some kind or other. — Joseph Wambaugh, *The New Centurions*, p. 174, 1970
- I took away the first stud's revolver easier than I could disarm a fourteen-year-old hugger-mugger in D.C. — James Patterson, *Kiss the Girls*, p. 334, 1995
- Hollywood. Home of hipsters, hugger-muggers, and hermaphrodites. — James Ellroy, *Destination Morgue*, p. 207, 2004

hugging *adjective*
bad, crazy *US*, *1997*

- — *Newsday*, p. B2, 11th October 1997

huggy-bear *noun*
prolonged hugging and kissing *US*, *1964*

- — *Time*, p. 57, 1st January 1965: "Students: the slang bag"

hulk *noun*
an unusually large bodybuilder *US*, *1980*

- — *Maledicta*, p. 234, Winter 1980: "'Lovely, blooming, fresh and gay': The onomastics of camp"
- — *American Speech*, p. 200, Fall 1984: "The language of bodybuilding"

human sea *noun*
an infantry tactic of the North Korean Army, of swarming enemy positions in overwhelming numbers *US*, *1964*

- The North Korean "Human Sea" attacks were also new to the G.I.'s—new and frightening. — Don Lawson, *The United States in the Korean War*, p. 35, 1964

humble *noun*
a false criminal accusation or charge *US*, *1940*

- It was a jive tip, but there were a whole lot of cats up there on humbles. — Claude Brown, *Manchild in the Promised Land*, p. 142, 1965

humbug *noun*

1 false or trumped-up criminal charges *US*, *1972*

- My old lady didn't say nothin' to the dude, man. He gave her a case on a humbug. — Christina and Richard Milner, *Black Players*, p. 302, 1972
- "Sheee-it, this is a humbug, we ain't done nothin'," said the procurer. — Joseph Wambaugh, *The Blue Knight*, p. 205, 1973
- The FBI arrested my wife on a humbug ... something about a fraud. It's a nothing deal. — Gerald Petievich, *Shakedown*, p. 177, 1988
- Not surprisingly, Dennis insists that the whole murder case was a humbug, anyway. — *St. Louis Post-Dispatch*, p. D1, 2nd December 2001

2 a fight, especially between youth gangs *US*, *1962*

- — Hermese E. Roberts, *The Third Ear*, 1971

humbug *verb*
to fight *US*, *1968*

- — David Claerbaut, *Black Jargon in White America*, p. 69, 1972

humdinger *noun*
a remarkable thing or person *US*, *1905*

- One was a humdinger about a gal that meets a detective in a big city. — Mickey Spillane, *I, The Jury*, p. 39, 1947
- Not too skinny, she's not too fat / She's a real humdinger and I like it like that. — Mitch Ryder, *Devil with the Blue Dress*, 1966
- ANNIE: It was really great! ALVY: Oh, humdinger. — *Annie Hall*, 1977

hum job *noun*
oral sex performed on a male *US*, *1964*

- A hum-job is the same as a blow-job however in this case the blower hums a tune, preferably a patriotic one, bringing the blowee off. — *Screw*, p. 9, 29th December 1969
- About a year ago—no, two years ago—there was this big craze for what was called a "hum job." — John Warren Wells, *Tricks of the Trade*, p. 26, 1970
- Can be by putting another testicles in one's mouth and humming, causing a pleasurable sensation. — Eugene Landy, *The Underground Dictionary*, p. 106, 1971

hummer *noun*

1 an act of oral sex performed on a man *US*, *1971*

- Did you check that poony out? I could parlay this into a hummer at least! — *Airheads*, 1994
- He was getting a hummer. — Stephen J. Cannell, *White Sister*, p. 155, 2006

2 an arrest for something the person did not do; an arrest for a minor violation that leads to more serious charges *US*, *1932*

- — Francis J. Rigney and L. Douglas Smith, *The Real Bohemia*, p. xv, 1961
- "You know the lieutenant doesn't want any hummer pinches." "Aw, it was no hummer, Jake," said Simeone. — Joseph Wambaugh, *The New Centurions*, p. 175, 1970
- I got busted on a hummer, something like that, my first day in. — Odie Hawkins, *Ghetto Sketches*, p. 123, 1972

3 a minor mistake *US*, *1959*

- — Robert S. Gold, *A Jazz Lexicon*, p. 154, 1964

4 a joke, a prank *US*, *1990*

- — Charles Shafer, *Folk Speech in Texas Prisons*, p. 207, 1990

5 the Grumman E-2, an early warning aircraft *US*, *1989*
Given the official nickname "Hawkeye," it was instantly renamed by the troops.

- The Hawkeye early warning aircraft, nicknamed "Hummer," had just informed him of unidentified "bogies" approaching the battle group. — Joe Weber, *Defcon One*, p. 3, 1989
- It is nearly impossible to flip on a TV set without seeing one—the new workhouse of the ground trooper nicknamed the Hummer. — *Washington Times*, p. G4, 22nd February 1991

6 an army weapons carrier *US*, *1983*
The official designation is a High Mobility Multipurpose Wheeled Vehicle. The slang is easier.

- He drove the camouflaged High Mobility Multipurpose Wheeled Vehicle (or "Hummer") through Washington streets as he was chased by several patrol cars. — Chuck Shepherd, *News of the Weird*, p. 124, 1989

hummingbird ass *noun*
used for suggesting that a person lacks the courage to back up his taunts *US*, *1977*

- — Richard Scholl, *Running Press Glossary of Baseball Language*, p. 44, 1977
- Sometimes he let his alligator mouth override his hummingbird ass. — *Star Tribune (Minneapolis)*, p. 1B, 16th January 2003

humongo *adjective*
very large *US*, *1981*

- I had a number in my mouth or was stuffing food into it to satiate the super humungo munchies. — Robert Lipkin, *A Brotherhood of Outlaws*, p. 192, 1981

humongous; humungous *adjective*
very large *US*, *1967*

- Maybe at the bottom there will be something worthwhile that us humble sheep, your poor, blind flock, will gather around that humongous soapbox in the sky to listen to. — *Cosmos*, p. 2, 5th May 1967
- Not humongous titties but nice pointy ones. — Carl Hiaasen, *Skin Tight*, p. 297, 1989
- "I felt all the Crips oughta have a big, humongous meeting." — Leon Bing, *Do or Die*, p. 35, 1991
- I'm allergic to bees. I get a humungous rash. — *Wayne's World 2*, 1993

hump *noun*

1 an offensive or despicable person *US, 1963*

- Didya hear what them humps in Congress did? They voted a special tax bill for themselves so that they don't have to pay any more taxes. — William Cavnitz, *One Police Plaza*, p. 337, 1984
- "What're you doing for me, you fucking hump?" — Mark Baker, *Cops*, p. 304, 1985
- Pull that shit with old ladies. Not with me, you fuckin' hump. — David Chase, *The Sopranos: Selected Scripts from Three Seasons*, p. 150, 20th September 1999

2 a dolt, a dull person *US, 1963*

- The hump pleads guilty, off he goes. — Leonard Shecter and William Phillips, *On the Pad*, p. 84, 1973
- You fuckin' hump—we went to question you, you stumbled, fell against me. — Edwin Torres, *Carlito's Way*, p. 73, 1975
- "Anyway," Garcia said, "this hump Bloodworth says he heard there's some connection between Bellamy and Sparky Harper." — Carl Hiaasen, *Tourist Season*, p. 89, 1986
- Which doesn't seem too likely with those Armenian humps holed up with Fed surveillance outside their house. — James Ellroy, *White Jazz*, p. 257, 1992

3 an act of sexual intercourse *US, 1918*

- "Say, I bet you ain't even had your first hump yet!" — Charles Perry, *Portrait of a Young Man Drowning*, p. 59, 1962
- "I'll stand for you giving your wife a hump now and then." — Jacqueline Susann, *Valley of the Dolls*, p. 496, 1966
- "Why don't you go into the business, Judd? Sell it outright. So much a hump." — Burt Hirschfeld, *Fire Island*, p. 442, 1970
- If you are the dumper, make this last hump so enjoyable that your ex will forget how much he hates your guts. — Anka Radakovich, *The Wild Girls Club*, p. 41, 1994

4 a Camel™ cigarette *US, 1989*

- — James Harris, *A Convict's Dictionary*, p. 33, 1989

5 the air route over the Himalaya Mountains during World War 2 *US, 1942*

- Civilian pilots were the first to fly the "hump" missions that kept the Chinese army linked to its U.S. supply bases in China. — *Insight*, p. 39, 17th April 1989

6 the middle section of a prison sentence *US, 1962*

- — Joseph E. Ragen and Charles Finston, *Inside the World's Toughest Prison*, p. 804, 1962: "Penitentiary and underworld glossary"

7 a large wave *US, 1963*

Surfer usage.

- When you graduate from Malibu you move down to San Onofre or Tressle where the real big humps come blasting in. — Frederick Kohner, *Gidget*, p. 4, 1957
- — Grant W. Kuhns, *On Surfing*, p. 118, 1963

8 a military combat patrol *US, 1971*

Recorded in Australia in the C19, but not again until the US war in Vietnam.

- The first day's hump was to be of moderate length, 6000 meters, or six "clicks," and there was a road most of the way so it should have been easy, a skate. — Charles Anderson, *The Grunts*, p. 35, 1976
- You 'bush in this area near that ol' Buddhist temple we passed on the hump in. — *Platoon*, 1986
- "Fuck the LT, fuck this trail, fuck this hump ... and fuck the Army." — Cherokee Paul McDonald, *Into the Green*, p. 112, 2001

9 in circus usage, a camel *US, 1926*

- — Don Wilmeth, *The Language of American Popular Entertainment*, p. 136, 1981

▶ **over the hump**

while gambling, having won enough to be gambling now with the house's money *US, 1950*

- — *The Annals of the American Academy of Political and Social Sciences*, p. 128, May 1950

hump *verb*

1 to take part in an infantry patrol *US, 1972*

- "Four deuce sure beats humpin' the boonies." — William Pelfrey, *The Big V*, p. 6, 1972

2 to earn money working as a prostitute *US, 1973*

- Satin and Nell were doing their thing together in grand style and Satin was doing her humping bit at night. — A.S. Jackson, *Gentleman Pimp*, p. 101, 1973
- Back in the days when bad girls humped good bread into my pockets, con man, Airtight Willie and pimp ... me ... lay in a double bunk cell on a tier in Chicago Cook's County Jail. — Iceberg Slim (Robert Beck), *Airtight Willie and Me*, p. 3, 1979

▶ **hump it**

in poker, to raise the maximum bet allowed *US, 1988*

- — George Percy, *The Language of Poker*, p. 46, 1988

▶ **hump the dog**

to waste time completely *US, 1980*

Similar construction to the synonymous "fuck the dog."

- "Meanwhile," Roland said, "we're sitting here humping the dog, huh?" — Elmore Leonard, *Gold Coast*, p. 50, 1980

hump and thump *noun*

cardiovascular resuscitation *US, 1994*

- — Sally Williams, *"Strong" Words*, p. 147, 1994

hump date *noun*

during the Vietnam war, the date when half of a soldier's tour of duty in Vietnam is completed *US, 1965*

- Most everyone has a short-timers calendar of some sort after he had reached the hump date signifying half his tour is completed. — Tony Zidek, *Choi Oi*, p. 124, 1965

hump day *noun*

the precise middle day of a tour of duty *US, 1983*

- It was a few days before my hump day, the exact middle of my tour when I would be "over the hump." — Lynda Van Devanter, *Home Before Morning*, p. 193, 1983

humper *noun*

1 a biscuit *US, 1950*

- "How many humpers you eat this morning?" — Haywood Patterson, *Scottsboro Boy*, p. 77, 1950

2 an infantry soldier *US, 1973*

- The humpers knew that ice cream in the jungle isn't the best present in the world. — Anthony Herbert, *Soldier*, p. 298, 1973

3 a large and unbroken wave *US, 1977*

- — Gary Fairmont R. Filosa II, *The Surfer's Almanac*, p. 187, 1977

hump-hump *verb*

to have sex *US, 1997*

Mock pidgin.

- Where'd they teach you to talk like this, some Panama City "Sailor want to hump-hump" bar? — *As Good As It Gets*, 1997

hump night *noun*

Wednesday night *US, 1955*

- — *American Speech*, p. 226, October 1955: "An aircraft production dispatcher's vocabulary"
- — *Current Slang*, p. 4, Winter 1966

humpy *adjective*

handsome, sexy *US, 1968*

Homosexual usage.

- Myself, I like looking at pictures of people doing it, and I prefer it when the people involved are men. Humpy men. — Angelo d'Arcangelo, *The Homosexual Handbook*, p. 183, 1968
- Humpy young longhairs; students with shining evening faces; Puerto Ricans fighting machismo, with wives at home[.] — John Francis Hunter, *The Gay Insider*, p. 137, 1971
- — Wayne Dynes, *Homolexis*, p. 69, 1985

humpy-bump *verb*

to have sex *US, 1974*

- I didn't know if you had to humpy-bump for a job or just know him. — Edward Lin, *Big Julie of Vegas*, p. 209, 1974

hun *noun*

one hundred dollars; a one hundred dollar bill *US, 1895*

- — Christina and Richard Milner, *Black Players*, p. 296, 1972

hunch *verb*

to bring someone up to date; to inform *US, 1973*

- I hunched him to the fact that I had left my girl with his piece on the edge and asked her to break him in to the action. — A.S. Jackson, *Gentleman Pimp*, p. 98, 1973

hundo; hundoe *noun*

one hundred dollars; a one-hundred dollar bill *US, 1998*

- Need some hundos? Come on, I got some hundos here. Take a couple. — *Dateline NBC*, 26th May 1998
- — Pamela Munro, *U.C.L.A. Slang*, p. 31, 2001

hundred-yard stare noun

a lost, unfocused look, especially as the result of brutal combat US, 1991

A variant of the more common **THOUSAND-YARD STARE**.

- The only way I was able to get him to abandon his "hundred yard stare" was by suggesting every few hundred meters that he be evacuated. — James Kirschke, *Not Going Home Alone*, p. 93, 2001

hung adjective

1 endowed with a large penis UK, 1600

Shakespeare punned with the term 400 years ago.

- Heard these little coons are hung like horses[.] — Dick Gregory, *Nigger*, p. 10, 1964
- From a certain unevenly rounded thickness at the crotch of his blue jeans, it is safe to assume that he is marvelously hung. — Gore Vidal, *Myra Breckinridge*, p. 31, 1968
- Robbie leaned forward in his chair, toward the television set. "He's not hung at all." Sounding surprised. "I thought he was supposed to be hung." — Elmore Leonard, *Split Images*, p. 211, 1981
- The men are lean and hung, and the women look like they like to do naughty and even dirty things. — *Adult Video*, p. 29, August/September 1986

2 fascinated or obsessed with US, 1950

- I remember the red air and the sadness—"the strange red afternoon light" Wolfe also was hung on—with peculiar eternity-dream vividness[.] — Jack Kerouac, *Letter to Neal Cassady*, 28th December 1950
- Mike didn't mind because, although he didn't play anything himself, he had a lot of records and he was almost as hung on jazz as I was. — Nat Hentoff, *Jazz Country*, p. 8, 1965

3 (used of a computer program) suspended, waiting for something that will not happen US, 1983

- — Guy L. Steele et al., *The Hacker's Dictionary*, p. 82, 1983

Hungarian cinch noun

a certainty US, 1966

- I had already studied the situation from every side, and I knew I had a Hungarian cinch or I never would have gone for it in the first place. — Minnesota Fats, *The Bank Shot*, p. 64, 1966

hungries noun

the craving for food that follows the smoking of marijuana US, 1970

- — William D. Alsever, *Glossary for the Establishment and Other Uptight People*, p. 6, December 1970

hung up adjective

1 obsessed, infatuated US, 1950

- Not to get hung up on the effects of this vision, let me tell you what it was. — Jack Kerouac, *Letter to Neal Cassady*, 28th December 1950
- A white man will come to the Negro club, so hung up in this race problem, so nervous and afraid of the neighborhood and the people that anything the comic says to relieve his tension will absolutely knock him out. — Dick Gregory, *Nigger*, p. 131, 1964
- I'm not hung up on you. I'm in love with you. — *Manhattan*, 1979
- It's a terrible thing to marry an Egyptologist and find out he's hung up on his mummy. — Charles Ludlum, *The Mystery of Irma Vep*, p. 44, 1984

2 addicted US, 1950

- I was just about eighteen, you know, and I got hung up on the habit myself. — John Clellon Holmes, *Go*, p. 122, 1952
- We have helped thousands hung up on drugs. — Arthur Blessitt, *Turned On to Jesus*, p. 21, 1971

3 inhibited, neurotic US, 1952

- — J. L. Simmons and Barry Winograd, *It's Happening*, p. 171, 1966: "glossary"
- Yeah, listen, uh, are you ....? ARE YOU HUNG UP? — Frank Zappa, *Are You Hung Up?*, 1968

4 while surfing, caught along the steep wall of a wave and unable to pull out US, 1963

- — Grant W. Kuhns, *On Surfing*, p. 118, 1963

hungus adjective

in computing, extremely large US, 1981

- — *Co-Evolution Quarterly*, p. 32, Spring 1981
- — Eric S. Raymond, *The New Hacker's Dictionary*, p. 204, 1991

hunk noun

1 a good-looking, muscular boy or man US, 1945

- — Lou Shelly, *Hepcats Jive Talk Dictionary*, p. 13, 1945
- — *Current Slang*, p. 3, Summer 1966
- Cherry Dilday said to mention that the Biller is a hunk. — Joe Bob Briggs, *Joe Bob Goes to the Drive-In*, p. 42, 1987

- Starlets as mermaids, Hollywood hunks covered with leaves, politicians as circus performers. — Francesca Lia Block, *I Was a Teenage Fairy*, p. 147, 1998

2 an improvised tent in a prison cell used to conceal sexual activity US, 1950

- They built "covered wagons" or "hunks" around the beds. That screened out what went on inside the bunks. — Haywood Patterson, *Scottsboro Boy*, p. 65, 1950

hunka chunka noun

sexual intercourse US, 2005

- [A]t the age of 64, Paul Theroux has decided what he's really interested in is "hunka chunka"—people getting it on. — *Esquire*, p. 25, July 2005

hunk up verb

to have sex inside an improvised tent in a prison cell US, 1950

- Usually you could hunk up with a gal-boy for two or three dollars. — Haywood Patterson, *Scottsboro Boy*, p. 67, 1950

hunky adjective

attractive, muscular US, 1972

- — Bruce Rodgers, *The Queens' Vernacular*, p. 110, 1972
- Several years ago, while I was on holiday with several girlfriends, tucked away at a seaside Florida bar, the hunky bartender poured us all vodka shots "on the house," and asked if we wanted to "party after closing." "Define 'party,'" was my retort. — Nancy Tamosaitis, *net.sex*, p. 123, 1995
- Guess what happens when a hot-and-hunky boy from the wrong side of the tracks (my new word for that is a drooligan) accepts an invite from his legal eagle to become a member of the family? — Brittany Kent, *O.C. Undercover*, p. 19, 2004

hunky; hunkie noun

1 an Eastern European; a Slav; a Hungarian US, 1909

Disparaging, but usually more illustrative of the speaker's lack of geographic knowledge.

- She'd been teaching sixth-grade Polacks and Hunkies so long that she thought she could treat everybody as if they were one of her sixth-grade pupils. — James T. Farrell, *Saturday Night*, p. 9, 1947
- He played the line with a cigarette dangling out of his Hunky mouth. — Clancy Sigal, *Going Away*, p. 52, 1961
- [W]hich brought them to the Negroes or whites, usually huge, the whites most often Polish or Hunkies[.] — Norman Mailer, *Miami and the Siege of Chicago*, p. 88, 1968
- In the locker rooms of the Eighteenth District Station and around the cop bars, he called Italians guidos or wops, Poles polacks, Bohemians hunkies, Mexicans spicks or greasers, and African-Americans niggers or darkies. — Robert Campbell, *Boneyards*, p. 10, 1992

2 a white person US, 1959

Derogatory.

- The night before I had let a hunky called Big John have a dollar's worth of chips in the poker game for a monkey which he had carved from a peach seed[.] — Chester Himes, *Cast the First Stone*, p. 66, 1952
- He said, "I'm going to buy this building and turn this into a Nigger bar. I'm going to bar all you laughing hunkies." — Iceberg Slim (Robert Beck), *Trick Baby*, p. 149, 1969
- Dem hunkies couldn't care less if a nigger was born on Mars. — J. Ashton Brathwaithe, *Niggers—This is Canada*, p. 24, 1971
- I guess every hunkie in the neighborhood must've called the po-lice soon as they saw us walkin' down the street. — Odie Hawkins, *Ghetto Sketches*, pp. 119–120, 1972

hunky dory adjective

satisfactory, fine US, 1861

- I was doing the easiest time I ever did. Everything was hunky-dory. — Chester Himes, *Cast the First Stone*, p. 112, 1952
- I saw the man once, and that's all it took for me to see he was a wrong number, but I kept my peace because you acted like everything was hunky-dory. — Robert Campbell, *Boneyards*, p. 224, 1992
- You fall in love with me and want a romantic relationship, nothing changes for you with the exception of feeling hunky-dory all the time. — *Chasing Amy*, 1997

hunt verb

▶ **hunt rabbits**

in a game of poker, to go through the cards that were not played after a hand is finished in search of what might have been US, 1951

- — *American Speech*, p. 100, May 1951: "The vocabulary of poker"

hunting license *noun*

an assignment given by a prison gang to kill someone *US, 1992*

- — William K. Bentley and James M. Corbett, *Prison Slang*, p. 94, 1992

hunyak *noun*

an immigrant from eastern Europe *US, 1910*

- It was built by old Sigmund in the free-lunch days, when he was tossing away the stockholder's dough like a hunyak on Saturday night. — Ellery Queen, *The Hollywood Murders*, p. 150, 1957

hurler *noun*

a person who suffers from bulimia nervosa *US, 1998*

- Well, from her figure and her appetite, I'm guessing she's either got a bowel disorder or we've got a hurler on our hands. — *Something About Mary*, 1998

hurrah *noun*

in a big store confidence swindle, the stage of the swindle when the victim is fully duped *US, 1997*

- "The Hurrah," Beano explained to Victoria, "is that point in the confidence game where the mark has completely committed himself. From this point forward there's no way he's going to pull out." — Stephen Cannell, *Big Con*, p. 339, 1997

hurryup wagon *noun*

a police van *US, 1893*

- — Claudio R. Salvucci, *The Philadelphia Dialect Dictionary*, p. 45, 1996

hurt *adjective*

undesirable, unattractive, inept *US, 1973*

- — Connie Eble (Editor), *UNC-CH Campus Slang*, p. 4, Fall 1980
- — Ellen C. Bellone (Editor), *Dictionary of Slang*, p. 14, 1989

husband *noun*

in a homosexual relationship (male or female), the more aggressive and domineering partner *US, 1941*

- — Donald Webster Cory and John P. LeRoy, *The Homosexual and His Society*, p. 264, 1963: "A lexicon of homosexual slang"
- — *Male Swinger Number 3*, p. 46, 1981: "The complete gay dictionary"

hush-em *noun*

a silencer attached to a handgun *US, 1949*

- — Captain Vincent J. Monteleone, *Criminal Slang*, p. 126, 1949

hush money *noun*

a bribe paid to obtain silence *UK, 1709*

- [A] former sweetheart of gambler Attilio Acalotti charged she had seen hush-money slipped to three cops. — Jack Lait and Lee Mortimer, *Washington Confidential*, p. 225, 1951
- "In hindsight, I can see why it has the appearance of 'hush money.' Perhaps I should have handled this situation differently." (Quoting Archbishop Rembver G. Weakland) — *Milwaukee Sentinel Journal*, p. 5A, 1st June 2002

hush puppy *noun*

a Smith and Wesson 9 mm pistol; the silencer attached to the pistol *US, 1982*

Carried by US Navy SEALS. So named, the legend goes, because of its use in killing guard dogs.

- Factory-modified. They call it a Hush-Puppy. — Elmore Leonard, *Cat Chaser*, p. 247, 1982
- I carried a 9mm pistol with a hush-puppy—silencer—and my M16, with lots of extra ammo. — Richard Marcinko and John Weisman, *Rogue Warrior*, p. 129, 1992

hush-puppy *adjective*

(used of jazz) old-fashioned, conventional *US, 1958*

- Yah, what's this "alabam" written up here? I ain't gonna play none of that hush-puppy jazz. — John Clellon Holmes, *The Horn*, p. 134, 1958

husk *verb*

to undress *US, 1945*

- — Lou Shelly, *Hepcats Jive Talk Dictionary*, p. 13, 1945

huss; hus; huz *noun*

a favor *US, 1971*

Vietnam war usage, especially by marines.

- — Eugene Landy, *The Underground Dictionary*, p. 63, 1971
- If they gotta put down their cold beer for five minutes to cut somebody a hus they won't do it. — Charles Anderson, *The Grunts*, p. 29, 1976
- — Connie Eble (Editor), *UNC-CH Campus Slang*, November 1976

hustle *noun*

1 an illegal enterprise, especially one involving swindling *US, 1943*

- Pickin' pockets, why that's a hustle for a lame. — Bruce Jackson, *Get Your Ass in the Water and Swim Like Me*, p. 66, 1964
- Even though he was only twenty-three years old, he'd gotten big time without a hustle. — Claude Brown, *Manchild in the Promised Land*, p. 214, 1965
- He introduced me to the sweetest "hustle" I'd ran into. — Babs Gonzales, *I Paid My Dues*, p. 73, 1967
- Get into a hustle that pays on account of he don't have a trade, only a rich mama forgot who he is. — Elmore Leonard, *Riding the Rap*, p. 54, 1995

2 effort, exertion, desire *US, 1898*

- There are times you have to show hustle, even if it's false. — Jim Bouton, *Ball Four*, p. 16, 1970

▸ **on the hustle**

1 engaged in a career of swindling *US, 1997*

- The Bates family is sort of well known. There are three thousand of them. Most of the family is on the hustle. — Stephen Cannell, *King Con*, p. 91, 1997

2 engaged in prostitution *US, 1952*

- "Well, what do you think, Tony?" "About what?" "Me being ... on the hustle." — Richard Prather, *The Peddler*, p. 7, 1952
- "All you got is a little dose. You'll be back on the hustle in two weeks." — Nelson Algren, *The Neon Wilderness*, p. 36, 1960

hustle *verb*

1 to seduce *US, 1970*

- "I think you are trying to hustle me," he said, making sure to smile, to let her know that he didn't mind at all. — Burt Hirschfield, *Fire Island*, p. 40, 1970

2 to engage in prostitution *US, 1895*

- All right, she was a hustler, but she wasn't hustling for me and I did her a favor. — Mickey Spillane, *My Gun is Quick*, pp. 13–14, 1950
- Like me, he was there almost every night; and like me, too, he was, I knew, hustling. — John Rechy, *City of Night*, p. 40, 1963
- [S]he said, "I'm going out hustling tonight." — Kate Millett, *The Prostitution Papers*, p. 48, 1976
- She told me she had been doing quite well—until but recently working as a model—doing a little hustling on the side[.] — Herbert Huncke, *The Evening Sun Turned Crimson*, p. 58, 1980
- Margo goes out and hustles a couple nights a week and that's the only money they've got coming in. — Elmore Leonard, *Split Images*, p. 90, 1981

3 to obtain after a diligent effort, especially one using unorthodox, if not illegal, means *US, 1840*

- I came to New York to start Liberty House in the West Village, which I designed, hustled the bread for, painted, and got sore fingers banging in the nails. — Abbie Hoffman, *Revolution for the Hell of It*, p. 200, 1968

hustler *noun*

1 a prostitute, especially a male homosexual *US, 1924*

- You go around telling people I'm a hustler and I'll break your skinny head. — George Mandel, *Flee the Angry Strangers*, p. 243, 1952
- [S]he would not have me hold her arm for fear people of the street here would think her a hustler[.] — Jack Kerouac, *The Subterraneans*, p. 68, 1958
- [B]oth those girls are workin' shimmy dancers and hustlers I know from Portland. — Ken Kesey, *One Flew Over the Cuckoo's Nest*, p. 210, 1962
- It was Myron who observed in 1964 that all of the male hustlers were supporting Goldwater for President. — Gore Vidal, *Myra Breckinridge*, p. 43, 1968
- Male prostitutes are currently called "hustlers." — Angelo d'Arcangelo, *The Homosexual Handbook*, p. 27, 1968
- I'm not like the average hustler you'd meet. — Mart Crowley, *The Boys in the Band*, p. 177, 1968
- It had all the types in the hustling scene: the new hustler, the aging hustler, the old queen, the fag-hag, etc. — *Screw*, pp. 8–9, 24th January 1969
- There'd usually be a couple of chicks, maybe a few good-looking hustlers from the Square, a friend of mine—a car thief—and a partner or two. — Herbert Huncke, *Guilty of Everything*, p. 84, 1990
- Any hustler who forgets that he must provide more than a hard cock and a willing ass and mouth is not going to make a go of it for long. — John Preston, *Hustling*, p. 41, 1994

2 a person who lives by his charm and wits, dishonest but usually not violent *US, 1896*

- Call Roy Bartholomew Beavers what you will, he never represented himself—unless it suited his immediate plans—as anything other than he was: a hustler. — Clarence Cooper Jr., *Black*, p. 233, 1963
- It's very interesting; they make the best hustlers too. Guys from the South, they make the best con men. — Kate Millett, *The Prostitution Papers*, p. 117, 1976

3 a person who makes his living by playing pool for wagers, feigning a skill level below his true level to secure bets *US, 1967*

- The poolroom hustler makes his living by betting against his opponents in different types of pool or billiard games, and as part of the playing and betting process he engages in various deceitful practices. — Ned Polsky, *Hustlers, Beats, and Others*, p. 41, 1967

hustling bar *noun*
a bar frequented by prostitutes *US, 1979*

- He traverses the city to the hustling bar he often frequents. Only hustlers there and those who buy them. — John Rechy, *Rushes*, p. 134, 1979

hustling gal *noun*
a prostitute *US, 1954*

- Later that same year Harry Tennisen was killed by a hustling gal of the honky-tonks called Sister Pop. — Louis Armstrong, *Satchmo*, p. 91, 1954
- You take a lot of people, a lot of thieves, they have a hustling gal working for them and she's always in and out of jail. — Bruce Jackson, *Outside the Law*, p. 137, 1972

hut *noun*
a house *US, 1989*

- Are we going to your hut tonight? — Ellen C. Bellone (Editor), *Dictionary of Slang*, p. 14, 1989

hutch *noun*
1 a domicile, be it a room, apartment or house *US, 1966*

- What to other people is a "pad" is called a "hutch" in surfing circles—most properly if it is the beach bunny's own apartment[.] — Roger Gordon, *Hollywood's Sexual Underground*, p. 144, 1966
- Shiela's hutch was on the top floor. — Robert Campbell, *In La-La Land We Trust*, p. 129, 1986

2 a prison *US, 1956*

- — *American Speech*, p. 100, May 1956: "Smugglers' argot in the Southwest"

hybolic *adjective*
pompous, wordy, bombastic *US, 1972*
Hawaiian youth usage.

- — Elizabeth Ball Carr, *Da Kine Talk*, p. 134, 1972

hydro *noun*
marijuana which is grown *hydro*ponically *US, 1996*

- Nugs is a word of marijuana. Other words include: buds, mota, chocolate tai, skunk, bunk, swag, hydro, dank, wando and crypt. — *Riverside (California) Press Enterprise*, p. D1, 8th May 1996
- That shit was hydro, man. — Stephen J. Cannell, *The Tin Collectors*, p. 35, 2001

hydroponic *noun*
marijuana that is cultivated hydroponically *US, 1989*
The soilless culture of cannabis results in plants that are up to ten times as potent as those grown outdoors.

- Two weeks ago when I was writin' this rhyme / I had some hydroponic, Boy that shit was fine — Tone Loc, *Cheeba Cheeba*, 1989

hyke *noun*
1 codeine *US, 1997*
From the brand name Hycodan™.

- — *Providence (Rhode Island) Journal-Bulletin*, p. 6B, 4th August 1997: "Doctors must know the narcolexicon"

2 hydrocodone, a synthetic codeine *US, 1967*

- HYKE: Hycodan, Dioxycodinone — Elizabeth Finn, *Drugs in the Tenderloin*, 1967: Glossary of Drug Slang Used in the Tenderloin
- — William D. Alsever, *Glossary for the Establishment and Other Uptight People*, p. 16, December 1970

Hymie *noun*
a Jewish male *US, 1973*
Like Mick (for Mickey) as a label for the Irish, Hymie is a shortened Hyman. Not used kindly.

- Had he stayed there in Ismailiya, man his size, he'd be loading ships 'stead of wearing a $400 sharkskin suit, pearl gray, and working for this little Hymie fool. — Elmore Leonard, *Glitz*, p. 137, 1985
- — Multicultural Management Program Fellows, *Dictionary of Cautionary Words and Phrases*, 1989

Hymietown *noun*
New York city *US, 1984*

- In private conversations, Jackson has referred to Jews as "Hymie" and to New York as "Hymietown." "I'm not familiar with that," Jackson said Thursday. — *The Washington Post*, p. A1, 13th February 1984

hype *noun*
1 a syringe *US, 1910*

- They pulled out two spikes, laid out two hypes / And rolled some one-dollar-bill gees. — Dennis Wepman et al., *The Life*, p. 56, 1976
- On the wall alongside Randy's head was a starburst of rust-brown dots where someone had booted the blood from their hype. — Richard Price, *Clockers*, p. 232, 1992

2 a needle-using drug addict *US, 1924*

- This is not a queer bar—it is an outcast bar—Negroes and vagrant whites, heads and hypes, dikes and queens. — John Rechy, *City of Night*, p. 184, 1963
- The one thing that broke me out of the big bind in the restaurant winds up in a hype's pocket and I'm worse off than I ever was. — Mickey Spillane, *Return of the Hood*, p. 88, 1964
- He's a hype but he is very down with the current scene. — Eldridge Cleaver, *Soul on Ice (letter dated 19th September, 1965)*, p. 46, 1968
- He was a "hype" even then. — Iceberg Slim (Robert Beck), *Pimp*, p. 99, 1969

3 exaggeration, nonsense *US, 1938*

- But that Danny laid down a super hype, and blow my nose and call me Snorty if we didn't wind up with him giving notice to the Goldkette office[.] — Mezz Mezzrow, *Really the Blues*, p. 129, 1946
- They pick up on each bopster's hype just like a simple child. — Dan Burley, *Diggeth Thou?*, p. 34, 1959

4 a swindle or cheat *US, 1980*

- — Joe McKennon, *Circus Lingo*, p. 50, 1980

▸ **put the hype on**
to raise prices because of demand without regard to fairness of the price *US, 1980*

- — Joe McKennon, *Circus Lingo*, p. 73, 1980

hype *verb*
to lie, to swindle *US, 1914*

- I'd be the last guy in the world to try and hype a Pachuco. — Thurston Scott, *Cure it with Honey*, p. 33, 1951
- No hustler could have it known that he'd been "hyped," meaning outsmarted or made a fool of. — Malcolm X and Alex Haley, *The Autobiography of Malcolm X*, p. 127, 1964

hyped up *adjective*
1 stimulated or excited, especially if by artificial means *US, 1946*

- I was so hyped up I couldn't sit still. — Mezz Mezzrow, *Really the Blues*, p. 54, 1946
- I was so hyped up that anything that moved was a threat. — Andy McNab, *Immediate Action*, p. 41, 1995

2 tense *US, 2005*

- But when things got hyped he'd keep cool under the stress. — Linden Dalecki, *Kid B*, p. 3, 2006

hype guy *noun*
in circus and carnival usage, a short-change swindler *US, 1981*

- — Don Wilmeth, *The Language of American Popular Entertainment*, p. 137, 1981

hype marks *noun*
scars and sores on a drug addict's body indicating intravenous drug use *US, 1973*

- [T]he tall one is wearing a long-sleeved shirt buttoned at the cuff. To hide his hype marks, of course. — Joseph Wambaugh, *The Blue Knight*, p. 9, 1973

hyper *noun*
in circus and carnival usage, a short-change swindler *US, 1981*

- — Don Wilmeth, *The Language of American Popular Entertainment*, p. 137, 1981

hype tank *noun*
a jail holding cell reserved for drug addicts *US, 1964*

- He remembered the hype tank. It was the coldest tank in the city prison, and it was deliberately kept that way. — Malcolm Braly, *Shake Him Till He Rattles*, p. 94, 1963
- They put me in the hype tank, I guess, because they saw the tracks (from hypodermic needles) on my arms. — *San Francisco News Call-Bulletin*, p. 3, 17th February 1964

hypo *noun*
1 a hypodermic syringe *US, 1905*

- You dissolve all the tablets—five grains—and fill the barrel of the hypo. — Philip Wylie, *Opus 21*, p. 67, 1949
- A few minutes later a nurse came in with a hypo. — William Burroughs, *Junkie*, p. 91, 1953
- I want four caps and a hypo. — John D. McDonald, *The Neon Jungle*, p. 75, 1953
- Shoot me up / Every damn day / With a hypo full of love — Alabama 3, *Hypo Full of Love*, 1997

2 a needle-using drug addict *US, 1904*

- If some hypo finds out that another hypo is a stool pigeon they give him what is called a hot shot. — Willard Motley, *Let No Man Write My Epitaph*, p. 151, 1958

3 a swindle *US, 1949*

- If you don't know who to get it from they pull a lot of hypos on you. — Hal Ellson, *Duke*, p. 3, 1949

hysteria *noun*
in street luge, out-of-control wobbling *US, 1998*

- HYSTERIA Uncontrolled speed wobbles. — Shelley Youngblut, *Way Inside ESPN's X Games*, p. 130, 1998

Hy-town *nickname*
Hyannis, Massachusetts *US, 1998*

- "Nobody messes with Hy-town," Delancey cooed, using the street slang nickname for the town. — *Boston Globe*, p. B1, 19th June 1998

Ii

I ain't even tryin' to hear you!
I am not listening *US, 1993*
- — *The Bell (Paducah Tilghman High School)*, pp. 8–9, 17th December 1993: "Tilghmanism: the concealed language of the hallway"

I ain't here to brag
used for demonstrating that the speaker understands that he is bragging *US, 2003*
A paralipsis of the first order. Many grammatical variants exist, as well as the simpler, "Not to brag."
- I ain't here to brag about my title, he yelled. I'm here to get my new pants. — John McManus, *Born on a Train*, p. 111, 2003
- I ain't here to brag, I'm just here to pop tags. — Kevin Federline, *Lose Control*, 2006

I am so sure!
used for expressing strong doubt about what has just been said *US, 1982*
- — Mimi Pond, *The Valley Girl's Guide to Life*, p. 59, 1982

I and I *noun*
used in the military as a jocular substitute for the official "R and R" (rest and recreation) *US, 1960*
An abbreviation of "*intercourse and in*toxication," the main activities during rest and recreation.
- — *American Speech*, p. 121, May 1960: "Korean bamboo English"
- [M]en going to Japan turned R&R into the great debauch that came to be known as I&I—intercourse and intoxication. — T.R. Fehrenbach, *This Kind of War*, p. 347, 1963
- Soldiers always call it I and I, which means "intercourse and intoxication." — Walter J. Sheldon, *Gold Bait*, p. 31, 1973

IBM *noun*
a smart, diligent student *US, 1960*
- — *San Francisco Examiner*, p. III-2, 22nd March 1960

IBM discount *noun*
a price increase *US, 1991*
- — Eric S. Raymond, *The New Hacker's Dictionary*, p. 206, 1991

IC *noun*
during the Vietnam war, an innocent civilian *US, 1985*
- The people appeared to be civilians, "ICs or good actors." Simcox remarked, "Yeah, I have seen a real innocent civilian since I left San Francisco." — Nelson DeMille, *Word of Honor*, p. 125, 1985

I can read his lips, and he's not praying
used as a humorous comment on a profanity *US, 1997*
Popularized by ESPN's Keith Olberman.
- — Keith Olberman and Dan Patrick, *The Big Show*, p. 19, 1997

I can't fight that!
used by a clever boy for expressing approval of a girl who has just passed by *US, 1955*
- — *American Weekly*, p. 2, 14th August 1955

I can't HEAR you!
used as a humorous solititication of more enthusiastic support *US, 1966*
A signature line of marine drill instructor Vince Carter on the television situation comedy *Gomer Pyle, USMC* (CBS, 1964–69). Repeated with referential humor.

I can't take you anywhere
used as a humorous, if stock, tease of someone who has committed a faux pas *US, 1994*
- I can't take you anywhere. — *Natural Born Killers*, 1994

ice *noun*
1 diamonds *UK, 1905*
- Mrs. M. wore lots of ice, which I'll tell you about later. — Earl Wilson, *I Am Gazing Into My 8-Ball*, p. 23, 1945

- It's nothing hot like you think. No ice. No emerald pendants. — Raymond Chandler, *The Little Sister*, p. 41, 1949
- I knew that Jerry was Chicago's top hot-ice dealer. — Iceberg Slim (Robert Beck), *Trick Baby*, p. 18, 1969
- Can you move the ice afterwards? I don't know nobody who can move ice. — *Reservoir Dogs*, 1992

2 cocaine, especially in blocks *US, 1971*
- Don't get me wrong; there is some herb you know, but no rocks, no heroin or ice that I could spot. — Odie Hawkins, *Midnight*, p. 123, 1995

3 smokeable amphetamine or methamphetamine *US, 1989*
- It is most likely that ice is simply methamphetamine that is being marketed with an exciting new image. — Geoffrey Froner, *Digging for Diamonds*, p. 37, 1989
- [A]s crack is to cocaine, so ice is to speed (methamphetamine)—the drug in a smokable, more potent crystal form. — Steven Daly and Nathaniel Wice, *alt.culture*, p. 109, 1995
- Sort of a cross between smack, E and ice. You've got to smoke it in a little pipe. — Will Self, *The Sweet Smell of Psychosis*, p. 39, 1996
- On an average night, I binge Es or ice with amyl nitrite, followed by tranx and spliffs. — Macfarlane, Macfarlane & Robson, *The User*, p. 91, 1996

4 heroin *US, 1987*
- I was dancing with Wren at Max's tonight ("Sympathy for the Devil"), waiting for my man (who happens to be a woman) to show with the ice[.] — Jim Carroll, *Forced Entries*, p. 24, 1987

5 protection money paid by a business to criminals or by criminals to the police *US, 1887*
- — *The Annals of the American Academy of Political and Social Sciences*, p. 126, May 1950
- Policemen assigned the posts the whores patrolled. Their "ice" was $1.40 a week per girl. — Lee Mortimer, *Women Confidential*, p. 178, 1960
- The ice has got to stop for you, today. — Richard Condon, *Prizzi's Honor*, p. 217, 1982
- "There was 'ice'—about seven hundred dollars a week—for the cops." — Nicholas Pileggi, *Wise Guy*, p. 118, 1985

6 a pay-off, a bribe; an added charge *US, 1963*
- That's the first rule when it comes to paying off ice. — Madam Sherry, *Pleasure Was My Business*, p. 55, 1963
- The cat gets ICE for hard to get seats for the World Series games. — Hy Lit, *Hy Lit's Unbelievable Dictionary of Hip Words for Groovy People*, p. 23, 1968

7 the difference between the listed price and the price actually paid for theater tickets for a very popular show *US, 1973*
- — Sherman Louis Sergel, *The Language of Show Biz*, p. 111, 1973

8 in poker, a stacked deck *US, 1967*
- — Albert H. Morehead, *The Complete Guide to Winning Poker*, p. 265, 1967

9 solitary confinement in prison *US, 1972*
- I was on to her and we got in a fight and I went to ice [solitary]. — Bruce Jackson, *In the Life*, p. 408, 1972
- — Charles Shafer, *Folk Speech in Texas Prisons*, p. 207, 1990

10 any computer program designed as a system security scheme *US, 1995*
- — Christian Crumlish, *The Internet Dictionary*, p. 92, 1995

▸ **on ice**
incarcerated *US, 1931*
- — Ralph de Sola, *Crime Dictionary*, p. 106, 1982
- — William K. Bentley and James M. Corbett, *Prison Slang*, p. 28, 1992
- — *Detroit News*, p. 5D, 20th September 2002

ice *verb*
1 to kill *US, 1941*
- "You're gonna end up in a bag, fool," the man said. "If that's the case," Hicks said, "I better ice you fellas." — Robert Stone, *Dog Soldiers*, p. 101, 1974
- And in making my exit, I iced a cop / 'Cause the motherfucker shot at me when I wouldn't stop. — Dennis Wepman et al., *The Life*, p. 118, 1976

- I was in the news media and I was charged with "icing," as the prisoners say, a suspected agent of the CIA or FBI. — Bobby Seale, *A Lonely Rage*, p. 269, 1978
- [H]is father had been unable to figure out any other way to ice Little Phil Terrone, the heaviest shit and boo dealer in the North Bronx. — Richard Condon, *Prizzi's Honor*, p. 4, 1982

2 to place in solitary confinement *US, 1933*
- — Clarence Major, *Dictionary of Afro-American Slang*, p. 69, 1970

3 to give up; to stop *US, 1962*
- And this time, I want you to ice the rubber and let him get a shot of pure honey. — A.S. Jackson, *Gentleman Pimp*, p. 47, 1973

4 to reject; to stand up *US, 1997*
- — Pamela Munro, *U.C.L.A. Slang*, p. 80, 1997

▸ **ice it**
1 to stop doing something *US, 1974*
- — Stewart L. Tubbs and Sylvia Moss, *Human Communication*, p. 121, 1974

2 to forget something *US, 1960*
- — *San Francisco Examiner*, p. III-2, 22nd March 1960

iceberg *noun*
a sexually frigid woman *US, 1949*
- — Vincent J. Monteleone, *Criminal Slang*, p. 127, 1949

iceberg act *noun*
unfriendly treatment *US, 1953*
- — Lavada Durst, *The Jives of Dr. Hepcat*, p. 12, 1953

icebox *noun*
1 a morgue *US, 1928*
- — Troy Harris, *A Booklet of Criminal Argot, Cant and Jargon*, p. 16, 1976

2 a jail or prison *US, 1938*
An extension of the more common **COOLER** (jail).
- He also makes good and with my fond help he has so far stayed out of the icebox. — Raymond Chandler, *The Long Goodbye*, p. 100, 1953

ice-cream habit *noun*
the irregular consumption of drugs by an occasional user *US, 1970*
"Ice-cream eater" and "ice-creamer" are obsolete slang terms for an irregular user of opium, an earlier application (late C19 to the 1930s) based on the notion that ice-cream is an occasional pleasure and not an every-day diet.
- — Richard Horman and Allan Fox, *Drug Awareness*, p. 468, 1970

ice-cream man *noun*
a drug dealer, especially one selling opiates *US, 1952*
- — *American Speech*, p. 27, February 1952: "Teen-age hophead jargon"
- — William D. Alsever, *Glossary for the Establishment and Other Uptight People*, p. 26, December 1970

ice-cream pants *noun*
light-colored or pastel pants *US, 1908*
- They were in summer uniform—tight ice-cream pants and red T-shirts. — Sol Yurick, *The Warriors*, p. 7, 1965

ice-cream suit *noun*
a lightweight, light-colored or pastel men's suit *US, 1890*
- That morning, there had been another meeting of the Southern Caucus in Richard Russell's office, Ellender and Byrd in ice cream suits[.] — Robert Caro, *Master of the Senate*, p. 960, 2002

ice cube *noun*
crack cocaine *US, 1994*
- — US Department of Justice *Street Terms*, October 1994

iced *adjective*
drunk, drug-intoxicated *US, 1953*
- "Sylvia dead drunk, paralyzed, spifflicated, iced to the eyebrows," I said harshly. — Raymond Chandler, *The Long Goodbye*, p. 25, 1953

iced down *adjective*
wearing many diamonds *US, 1998*
- — Ethan Hilderbrant, *Prison Slang*, p. 68, 1998

icehouse *noun*
a jewelry store *US, 1949*
- — Vincent J. Monteleone, *Criminal Slang*, p. 127, 1949

ice luge *noun*
a block of ice used in a drinking game in which a shot of vodka, tequila, or other alcoholic drink is poured down the ice into the drinker's mouth *US, 2001*
- — Don R. McCreary (Editor), *Dawg Speak*, 2001

iceman *noun*
a person who bribes a government official or otherwise "fixes" difficult situations *US, 1981*
From **ICE** (a bribe).
- — Don Wilmeth, *The Language of American Popular Entertainment*, p. 139, 1981

ice money *noun*
money used to bribe *US, 1993*
- The operation worked well provided that when he was raided, his case went before a judge, who, like some of the beat cops, was paid off with so-called ice money. — Kim Rich, *Johnny's Girl*, p. 142, 1993

ice pack *noun*
high quality marijuana *US, 1971*
- — Eugene Landy, *The Underground Dictionary*, p. 108, 1971

ice palace *noun*
a jewelry store *US, 1956*
- — *American Speech*, p. 99, May 1956: "Smugglers' argot in the Southwest"

ice princess *noun*
a woman who shows no emotion or passion *US, 1985*
- Then Lee'd get angry, once again call her an ice princess, and take her home. — Jude Deveraux, *Twin of Ice*, p. 8, 1985

ice queen *noun*
a woman who shows no emotion or passion *US, 1857*
- "Don't pull that ice queen routine on me." — Nora Roberts, *Born in Ice*, p. 354, 1995

ichiban *adjective*
excellent *US, 1900*
- "So you ichiban big whale kahuna, like Clay say, hey?" — Christopher Moore, *Fluke*, p. 21, 2003

icing *noun*
cocaine *US, 1984*
- — R.C. Garrett et al., *The Coke Book*, p. 200, 1984

ick *noun*
1 a social outcast *US, 1942*
- I had to accept him, as there's a special college ruling that you can't refuse a date with one of them. He's an ick anyhow. — Max Shulman, *Guided Tour of Campus Humor*, p. 72, 1955

2 in the language surrounding the Grateful Dead, a bacterial or viral infection that quickly spreads among those following the band on tour *US, 1994*
Always with "the."
- — David Shenk and Steve Silberman, *Skeleton Key*, p. 155, 1994

icky *noun*
a rich person *US, 1953*
- Jackson if you are tamping the stroll pinning the fly chicks and the ickies as they fall from their gone castles on all cuts and stems[.] — Lavada Durst, *The Jives of Dr. Hepcat*, p. 3, 1953

icky *adjective*
1 unattractive, distasteful *US, 1929*
First found in jazz to describe oversweet music other than jazz, then migrated into general use with the more general meaning.
- After class, however, she confessed to me that she thought Mr. Obispo was icky. — Max Shulman, *The Many Loves of Dobie Gillis*, pp. 97–98, 1951
- It was one of those icky desert winds we call the Santa Ana[.] — Frederick Kohner, *Gidget*, p. 124, 1957
- "It was a pretty icky scene, I can tell you." — Robert Newton, *Bondage Clubs U.S.A.*, p. 72, 1967
- Your true feelings were too gross and icky for you to face. — *Heathers*, 1988

2 overly sentimental, especially of music or of a taste in music *US, 1929*
Originally from jazz.
- There's a cheesy dance floor in the bar, so it's icky, old-fashioned music. — Leslie O'Kane, *Death of a PTA Goddess*, p. 239, 2002

ICL
used as shorthand in Internet discussion groups and text messaging to mean "*in Christian love*" *US, 2002*
- — Gabrielle Mander, *WAN2TLK? ltl bk of txt msgs*, p. 46, 2002

ID *noun*

an identity card or other means of identification *US, 1941*

- You got an I.D. for the liquor? — *American Graffiti*, 1973
- Stephie, we got money and we got fake ID's. — *200 Cigarettes*, 1999

idiot blocks *noun*

options placed at the end of a staffing paper designed to allow the reader simply to tick the option which describes his decision *US, 1986*

- — Department of the Army, *Staff Officer's Guidebook*, p. 61, 1986

idiot board *noun*

a teleprompter *US, 1952*

- He delivers the lines as if his eyes have just peeled the words from some mystical idiot board. — Steven Paul Martini, *Compelling Evidence*, p. 60, 1992

idiot box *noun*

the television *US, 1955*

- I get tired of the idiot box. — Antony James, *America's Homosexual Underground*, p. 137, 1965
- — Collin Baker et al., *College Undergraduate Slang Study Conducted at Brown University*, p. 142, 1968
- If you were to take your eyeballs and ears out of that idiot box for a hot minute and pay attention to... — Odie Hawkins, *Ghetto Sketches*, p. 152, 1972
- "Chill out. Watch the idiot box till I'm done." — Eric Jerome Dickey, *Cheaters*, p. 162, 1999

idiot card *noun*

in the television and movie industries, a poster board with the dialogue written in large letters for actors to read *US, 1957*

- Tomorrow she'd have to sue the "idiot cards." — Jacqueline Susann, *Valley of the Dolls*, p. 329, 1966

idiot juice *noun*

any alcoholic beverage brewed in prison, especially a nutmeg/water mixture *US, 1974*

- — Ralph de Sola, *Crime Dictionary*, p. 69, 1982
- — William K. Bentley and James M. Corbett, *Prison Slang*, p. 70, 1992

idiot loop *noun*

an aerial maneuver used to avoid disruption after dropping a load of bombs *US, 1961*

- It's called a Half Cuban Eight. We called it an idiot loop. — Anthony Thornborough, *Iron Hand*, p. 10, 2002

idiot pill *noun*

a barbiturate or central nervous system depressant *US, 1953*

- — Donald Wesson and David Smith, *Barbiturates*, p. 122, 1977

idiot's delight *noun*

in dominoes, the 5-0 piece *US, 1959*

- — Dominic Armanino, *Dominoes*, p. 16, 1959

idiot sheet *noun*

any published summary used for quick overview *US, 1956*

- "They put out a so-called idiot sheet every day during the [state] legislative session," former suburban Democratic committeeman Lynn Williams recalled. — Adam Cohen, *American Pharaoh*, p. 306, 2000

idiot stick *noun*

a rifle *US, 1962*

- The insignia of the infantry was crossed rifles, which people called "idiot sticks." — Larry King, *Love Stories of World War II*, p. 68, 2001

idiot tube *noun*

a television; television *US, 1968*

- Children are becoming obese and anti-social from the inactivity and lack of interaction from sitting in front of the "idiot tube" for hours each day[.] — Aya Eneli, *Live Your Abundant Life*, p. 101, 2004

I don't think so

used as a humorous rejection of the sentiment that has been expressed *US, 1969*

- Can Amerika absorb smoke-ins, fuck-ins, liberated zones, what have you, inside its borders? I don't think soooo. — Abbie Hoffman, *Woodstock Nation*, p. 97, 1969
- It looks like they just fell out of bed and put on some baggy pants, and take their greasy hair—ew!—and cover it up with a backwards cap and like, we're expected to swoon? I don't think so. — *Clueless*, 1995

iffy *adjective*

tenuous, uncertain *US, 1937*

- Though I doubt that, being a visitor with an iffy passport. — Elmore Leonard, *Bandits*, p. 197, 1987

if I'm lying, I'm dying

I am telling the truth *US, 1981*

There are multiple reduplicative variations.

- "If I'm lyin, I'm flyin." "If you're lyin, you're fryin," the Weasel corrected him. "If you're lying, your dyin," the Ferret corrected them both[.] — Joseph Wambaugh, *The Glitter Dome*, p. 71, 1981
- BB: He's bluffing. CHEESE: If I'm lying, I'm dying. CARLY: I'm out. — *Tin Men*, 1987
- Oh, yes, trust me, Grum. They will be 19 and 0. If I'm lying, I'm dying. — *The Denver Post*, p. D1, 14th November 2003

If it ain't broke, don't fix it

used as a humorous suggestion to leave well enough alone *US, 1961*

- "If it ain't broke, don't fix it"—ain't tells you that you're dealing with a nitty-gritty verity that you don't need a college education to understand. — Geoffrey Nunberg, *Going Nucular*, p. 273, 2005

if it's too loud, you're too old

used for dismissing complaints of loudness at rock concerts *US, 1995*

A saying attributed to Kiss.

ifs, ands, or buts *noun*

conditions, contingencies, exceptions *US, 1982*

- Tonight, Boogie. No ifs-ands-or-buts. — *Diner*, 1982

if ya wonders, then ya is

used in twelve-step recovery programs such as Alcoholics Anonymous as a judgment on those who stop to wonder if they might be an addict *US, 1998*

- — Christopher Cavanaugh, *AA to Z*, p. 109, 1998

ig *verb*

to ignore *US, 1946*

- — Jack Lait and Lee Mortimer, *New York Confidential*, p. 235, 1948: "A glossary of Harlemisms"
- I igged her like I usually did. I acted like I didn't even hear. — Nathan McCall, *Makes Me Wanna Holler*, p. 123, 1994

iggie *noun*

a feigned ignorance *US, 1961*

Circus and carnival usage. Often used in the phrase "give them the iggie."

- — Don Wilmeth, *The Language of American Popular Entertainment*, p. 139, 1981

igloo *noun*

a shipping container *US, 1985*

- "Charlie Flip ran most of the business and he used to buy and sell dozens of 'igloos,' or metal shipping crates, of swag." — Nicholas Pileggi, *Wise Guy*, p. 103, 1985

ignorant end *noun*

in poker, the low card in a five-card sequence *US, 1990*

- — Anthony Holden, *Big Deal*, p. 301, 1990

ignorant oil *noun*

alcohol, especially cheap and potent alcohol *US, 1954*

- The last time I'd seen him he was downing a quarter of "ignorant oil" a day in Paris. — Babs Gonzales, *I Paid My Dues*, p. 144, 1967
- — David Claerbaut, *Black Jargon in White America*, p. 69, 1972
- That's pennant fever for you. And ignorant oil. — Bill Cardoso, *The Maltese Sangweech*, p. 152, 1984

ignuts *noun*

an ignorant fool *US, 1934*

- It's always freebies with that ignatz. — Bernard Wolfe, *The Late Risers*, p. 130, 1954

I hate it when that happens

used for introducing humor, usually after someone else has described an extremely unlikely situation *US, 1987*

- — Connie Eble (Editor), *UNC-CH Campus Slang*, p. 4, Spring 1987
- — Pamela Munro, *U.C.L.A. Slang*, p. 35, 1989
- Into this delightfully revolting garbage heap steps Judd Nelson as a seriously untalented comic who, along with his buddy the accordion

player (Bill Paxton), enjoys a brief career after growing a third arm. I hate it when that happens. — *Billboard*, p. 59, 22nd February 1992

I have nothing more to say about this that is either relevant or true

used as a humorous comment when there is nothing worth-while to say *US, 1997*

Popularized by ESPN's Keith Olberman, paraphrasing Winston Churchill's claimed reaction when confronting an entrance essay at Eton.

- — Keith Olberman and Dan Patrick, *The Big Show*, pp. 10–20, 1997

I heard ya

used for expressing assent *US, 1992*

- — William K. Bentley and James M. Corbett, *Prison Slang*, p. 46, 1992

IHTFP

used as an abbreviation for "*I Hate This Fucking Place*" *US, 1969*

- During the middle years of the Vietnam War one saw the cryptic abbreviation IHTFP scrawled throughout I Corps. — James Ebert, *A Life in a Year*, p. 187, 1993

Ike jacket *noun*

a waist-length military field jacket *US, 1956*

So named because the style was favored by President Eisenhower when in the military.

- They are dressed in Levis and slacks, "Ike" jackets and sport coats, open shirts and white shirts with ties, loafers, oxfords, sneakers. — Donald Duncan, *The New Legions*, p. 3, 1967
- POW's were wearing brand-new U.S. Army officers' gear—pink and greens (the current classy officers' dress uniform) as well as Ike jackets[.] — David Hackworth, *About Face*, p. 199, 1989

I kid you not

used for humorously assuring the truth of the matter asserted *US, 1967*

The signature line of Jack Parr, host of the late-night *Jack Parr Show* (NBC, 1957–62). Repeated with referential humor.

- Next day, I kid you not, it snowed. — Sue Rhodes, *Now You'll Think I'm Awful*, p. 61, 1967
- RANDAL: Get out of here. SMOKER: I kid you not. — *Clerks*, 1994

ill *verb*

to undergo severe mental stress *US, 1989*

- — Terry Williams, *The Cocaine Kids*, p. 137, 1989

ill *adjective*

good, pleasing, desirable, admirable *US, 1990*

- Oh, it was such an ill coat! — James St. James, *Party Monster*, p. 54, 1990
- His voice is what's so ill about him. — Q-Tip, *The Source*, p. 84, April 1994
- — Ethan Hilderbrant, *Prison Slang*, p. 68, 1998

ill-ass *adjective*

excellent, superb *US, 2001*

- I finally made it. Not as a superstar rapper, not as an ill-ass white boy, but as a respected emcee. — Eminem (Marshall Mathers), *Angry Blonde*, p. 4, 2001

ill-behaved *adjective*

said of a computer program that becomes dysfunctional because of repeated error *US, 1991*

- — Eric S. Raymond, *The New Hacker's Dictionary*, p. 206, 1991

I'll bet you a fat man

used for expressing supreme confidence *US, 1963*

- — Robert S. Gold, *A Jazz Lexicon*, p. 157, 1964

illegit *noun*

a person or thing of questionable legality *US, 1954*

- It's the illegits, the ones you might call the semi-pros, who send house officers to the aspirin bottle. — Dev Collans with Stewart Sterling, *I was a House Detective*, p. 39, 1954

illegit *adjective*

illegitimate *US, 1945*

- No matter what anybody thinks of the product, there is legit stuff and illegit stuff out there. — Michael Connolly, *The Concrete Blonde*, p. 99, 1994

illegits *noun*

dice that have been altered for cheating *US, 1977*

- — Robert C. Prus and C.R.D. Sharper, *Road Hustler*, p. 170, 1977: "Glossary of terms"

illest *adjective*

best *US, 2002*

- [T]wo of the illest rappers in the world[.] — *The Source*, p. 44, March 2002

illing *adjective*

bad, troubling *US, 1980*

- — Connie Eble (Editor), *UNC-CH Campus Slang*, p. 3, October 1986
- — *Newsday*, p. B2, 11th October 1997

ill piece *noun*

a male homosexual despised by his peers *US, 1970*

- — *American Speech*, p. 57, Spring–Summer 1970: "Homosexual slang"

I'll tell you what I'm gonna do

used as a humorous, self-explanatory if nonce announcement of intent *US, 1948*

Popularized by Sid Stone, announcer on the *Texaco Star Theater*, hosted by Milton Berle (1948–1951). One of the very first television-spawned catchphrases to become part of the national vocabulary.

illy *noun*

1 phencycledine, the drug better known as PCP or angel dust *US, 2005*

- AKA: angel dust, illy, super weed, stained, horror, digi. — RZA, *The Wu-Tang Manual*, p. 121, 2005

2 marijuana, especially sensimillia (a very potent marijuana from a plant with seedless buds) *US, 1995*

- — Bill Valentine, *Gang Intelligence Manual*, p. 110, 1995: "Jamaican gang terminology"

I mean

used for emphasis on that which follows *US, 1967*

- And I went up there, I said, "Shrink, I want to kill. I mean, I wanna, I wanna kill. Kill. I wanna." — Arlo Guthrie, *Alice's Restaurant*, 1967
- Instead of using Cockney or Liverpool slang for humorous effect, narked, knickers-job and all that, he began using American hip-lower-class slang, like, I mean, you know, baby, and a little late Madison Avenue. — Tom Wolfe, *The Pump House Gang*, p. 44, 1968
- "I mean," D.R. was saying, "I mean, like, if you take this tent down, you know, take the poles down, fold the whole thing up, and move it fifteen yards." — Gurney Norman, *Divine Right's Trip (Last Whole Earth Catalog)*, p. 29, 1971
- — David Claerbaut, *Black Jargon in White America*, p. 69, 1972
- This we had to have made special. I mean, sit in it. — *Goodfellas*, 1990

I'm gone

used as a farewell *US, 1993*

- Nigga, I'm gone. — *Menace II Society*, 1993

IMHO

in my humble opinion US, 1991

A ubiquitous piece of computer shorthand.

- — Eric S. Raymond, *The New Hacker's Dictionary*, p. 206, 1991

immortal *noun*

in stud poker, any hand that is certain to win; the best possible hand *US, 1947*

- — Oswald Jacoby, *Oswald Jacoby on Poker*, p. 142, 1947
- — Irwin Steig, *Common Sense in Poker*, p. 184, 1963

IMNSHO

used as Internet shorthand to mean "*in my not so humble opinion*" *US, 1995*

- — Christian Crumlish, *The Internet Dictionary*, p. 94, 1995

IMO

used as Internet shorthand to mean "*in my opinion*" *US, 1995*

- — Christian Crumlish, *The Internet Dictionary*, p. 94, 1995

import *noun*

a date who comes from out of town *US, 1926*

- And if a player, coach or manager should bring a girl with him to another city, she's called an import. — Jim Bouton, *Ball Four*, p. 252, 1970

I'm sideways

used as a farewell *US, 1993*

- — *People Magazine*, p. 73, 19th July 1993
- — *Evening Sun (Baltimore)*, p. 12A, 19th January 1994

I'm sure!; I'm so sure!

used for expressing great doubt *US, 1982*

- I am SO SURE / He's like so GROSS. — Moon Unit and Frank Zappa, *Valley Girl*, 1982

in noun

1 an inside connection *US, 1929*

- [T]he guy buys another TV set, another fur for his wife, and a couple of watches, everything at a discount because he's a big shot and has all kinds of ins. — Elmore Leonard, *The Big Bounce*, p. 113, 1969

2 an introduction *US, 1945*

- — Lou Shelly, *Hepcats Jive Talk Dictionary*, p. 13, 1945

3 in a casino, the amount of cash collected at a table in exchange for chips *US, 1980*

An abbreviation of "buy-in."

- — Lee Solkey, *Dummy Up and Deal*, p. 115, 1980

in adjective

1 socially accepted; popular *US, 1929*

- I'm in with the in crowd / I go where the in crowd goes / I'm in with the in crowd / And I know what the in crowd knows. — Bryan Ferry, *The In Crowd*, 1964
- There was always a big band from New York staying at the "Dunbar" Hotel and since I had money to buy drinks and hang out with the "In" people, everything was cool. — Babs Gonzales, *I Paid My Dues*, p. 20, 1967

2 incarcerated *US, 1903*

- Guess what I've been in for? — S.E. Hinton, *The Outsiders*, p. 22, 1967

-in suffix

used in combination with a simple verb to create a communal activity as a means of protest, as in "love-in" or "teach-in" *US, 1937*

- The "puff-in" calls for a large group to light up marijuana cigarettes in the police station, challenging the law. — *Los Angeles Free Press*, p. 5, 24th September 1964
- I'm goin' to a love-in / To sit and play my bongos in the dirt. — Frank Zappa, *Flower Punk*, 1968
- [T]he disruption of traffic by staging a mass stall-in of vintage cars on the express ways[.] — Richard Neville, *Play Power*, p. 54, 1970
- It is curious that whites have spoken thousands of times in the Vietnam teach-ins but have done so little to take the issue of the Panthers to the same audience. — *The Black Panther*, p. 18, 20th June 1970

in preposition

owing money to *US, 1998*

- "I'm in deep to a guy this time." — John Ridley, *Love is a Racket*, p. 93, 1998

in a minute

used as a farewell *US, 1992*

- — William K. Bentley and James M. Corbett, *Prison Slang*, p. 49, 1992

in-and-out noun

sex at its most basic *US, 1974*

- "Never any tenderness. Just in-and-out." — Anne Steinhardt, *Thunder La Boom*, p. 71, 1974
- These shot-on-video features will now follow the usual formulas and should offer interesting alternatives to the usual in-and-out fare most companies are putting on tape. — *Adult Video*, p. 7, August/September 1986
- Just in town on business. Just in and out. Ha! A little of the old in-and-out. — *Fargo*, 1996
- After a minute of the ol' in-and-out, he yanks his dick out of her cunt, fumbles with his rubber (eventually snapping it off like a wet dishwashing glove), and releases tapioca onto Jasmin's belly. — Anthony Petkovich, *The X Factory*, p. 190, 1997

in a pig's valise!

used for expressing how very unlikely something is *US, 1957*

The title of a late-1990s play by Eric Overmyer.

- You think a built like that comes walking down the street every day in the week? In a pig's valise, buddy! — Max Shulman, *Rally Round the Flag, Boys!*, p. 12, 1957

in betweens noun

amphetamine tablets; depressant tablets; a mixture of amphetamines and barbiturates *US, 1975*

- — Richard A. Spears, *The Slang and Jargon of Drugs and Drink*, p. 271, 1986

incantation noun

in computing, an esoteric command *US, 1991*

- This compiler normally locates initalized data in the data segment, but if you meter the right incantation they will be forced into text space. — Eric S. Raymond, *The New Hacker's Dictionary*, p. 207, 1991

incense noun

amyl nitrite or butyl nitrite *US, 1980*

The pungent vapors are inhaled, hence the term.

- — *Maledicta*, p. 227, Winter 1980: "'Lovely, blooming, fresh and gay': the onomastics of camp"

incest noun

sex between two similar homosexual types, such as two effeminate men *US, 1972*

- — Bruce Rodgers, *The Queens' Vernacular*, p. 113, 1972

include war noun

a prolonged inflammatory debate in an Internet discussion group in which the mass of former postings and counter-postings included make it impossible to follow who is saying what and when *US, 1995*

- — Christian Crumlish, *The Internet Dictionary*, p. 94, 1995

income tax noun

fines paid by prostitutes *UK, 1947*

- — *New Statesman*, 10th May 1947
- — Roger Blake, *The American Dictionary of Sexual Terms*, p. 107, 1964

incoming noun

enemy fire, especially artillery or mortar fire that is about to land *US, 1977*

- "This way," I said. "C'mon, move. We've got incoming." — Philip Caputo, *A Rumor of War*, p. 279, 1977
- There was a barbecue. Then there was incoming. It wasn't very close, but it was close enough. — Mark Barker, *Nam*, p. 32, 1981
- This incredible fuckin' noise—I mean I've heard incoming, but that must have been the all-time prize. — Larry Heinemann, *Paco's Story*, p. 22, 1986

incoming!

used as a warning of impending enemy mortar or rocket fire *US, 1976*

- The scream went round the perimeter—"Incoming, hit it!"—and one hundred thirty-eight young filthy bodies scrambled for seventy foxholes. — Charles Anderson, *The Grunts*, p. 144, 1976
- Incoming! — *Apocalypse Now*, 1979
- And one of them soldiers squirting us shouts, "incoming," and he takes off running. — *Forrest Gump*, 1992

increase the peace!

used as a call for an end to violence *US, 1990*

- — *Boyz N The Hood*, 1990

indeedy adverb

indeed *US, 1856*

An intentionally folksy and intensifying addition of a syllable.

- Joe said, "Yes, indeedy. Just turn right on Fourteenth Place and go to Newberry, then turn left." — Iceberg Slim (Robert Beck), *Trick Baby*, p. 46, 1969

index noun

the face *US, 1945*

- — Lou Shelly, *Hepcats Jive Talk Dictionary*, p. 13, 1945

Indiana pants noun

boots *US, 1964*

- — George Sullivan, *Harness Racing*, p. 104, 1964

Indian burn noun

a chafing of the skin on the arm inflicted by twisting the victim's skin in opposing directions *US, 1987*

- [T]he rest of us gave him, or her, Indian burns; we wrung a bare arm with both hands close together till the skin chafed. — Annie Dillard, *An American Childhood*, 1987

Indian Country; Injun Country; Indian territory noun

during war, any area with a strong enemy presence *US, 1945*

- Area noted by reference A is definite Indian Country. — John Kerry, *The New Soldier*, p. 82, 1971
- In Vietnam, American officers liked to call the area outside GVN control "Indian country." — Frances Fitzgerald, *Fire in the Lake*, p. 368, 1972
- There is no front in this war, but we are aware that we have crossed an undefined line between the secure zone and what the troops call "Indian country." — Philip Caputo, *A Rumor of War*, p. 102, 1977

- They were way out in "Indian territory[.]" — David Donovan, *Once a Warrior King*, p. 139, 1985

Indian giver *noun*
a person who retracts a gift *US, 1892*
From an earlier sense of one who expects a gift in return when giving a gift. Given the treatment of Native American Indians by white Europeans and Americans, this is one of the most richly ironic terms in the lexicon.

- [O]ur only problem is that the world is an Indian giver. — Glendon Swarthout, *Where the Boys Are*, p. 183, 1960

Indian Indian *noun*
an American Indian who has retained his indigenous culture and language *US, 1963*

- — *American Speech*, p. 272, December 1963: "American Indian student slang"

Indian rub *noun*
a chafing of the skin on the arm inflicted by twisting the victim's skin in opposing directions *US, 1989*

- If he bogeys, you can give him one hard punch in the shoulder. Indian rubs, noogies, and other pain-provokers can be deployed at will according to score. — Becker & Manley Ltd., *Manly Golf*, p. 57, 2002

Indian steak *noun*
bologna *US, 1963*

- — *American Speech*, p. 272, December 1963: "American Indian student slang"

Indian time *noun*
used for denoting a lack of punctuality *US, 1963*

- This is why he is not embarrassed when he is late for an appointment by white man's standards, for he kept that appointment by Indian time, which could be defined as some unspecified time following a specified time. — *American Speech*, p. 276, December 1963: "American Indian student slang"

Indian up *verb*
to get very quiet *US, 1965*

- "They're around the corner and all we have to do is indian up and jap them quick and take those cunts." — Sol Yurrick, *The Warriors*, p. 80, 1965

indie; indy *noun*
an independent league or production *US, 1928*

- He toiled in the indies for two short years before World Championship Wrestling came knocking at his front door and offered him a tryout. — Robert Picarello, *Rules of the Ring*, p. 155, 2000

indie; indy *adjective*
independent *US, 1928*

- As soon as I find that Chevy I'm going indy. I'm going to buy myself a two truck, a couple of pitbulls, and run a yard. — *Repo Man*, 1984
- In the "let's be regular" indie milieu they inhabit, these flaming Lake Erie fashion plates are some kinda godsend. — Chuck Eddy, *Stairway to Hell*, p. 70, 1991
- Based on how I worked my ass off to become one of the highest paid indie promoters in the industry, and to where I am now, with my own lable, NTL Records, Inc. — Elmore Leonard, *Be Cool*, p. 11, 1999

indig *noun*
an indigenous person *US, 1990*

- Still, our indig would enjoy a hearty feast of pork and fowl over the next several days. — Tom Yarborough, *Da Nang Diary*, p. 181, 1990
- SOGs "indig" as they were called, were mercenaries, plain and simple, and were well paid. — John Plaster, *SOG*, p. 32, 1997

Indo *noun*
marijuana, especially that purportedly cultivated in Indonesia *US, 2005*

- Pot, grass, weed, herb, cheeba, chronic, trees, indo, doja—whatever they called it then, whatever they call it now, and whatever they'll call it in the future, it was marijuana. — 50 Cent, *From Pieces to Weight*, p. 5, 2005

inexplicable mob *noun*
a large crowd that materializes in a public place to perform a scripted action for several minutes before dissolving *US, 2003*

- "There seems to be something inherently political about an inexplicable mob," he said. — *Wired.com*, 5th July 2003

- Well, many of us were milling around waiting for it to be exactly 7:27 and sort of steeling glances at each other and wondering who was there for this inexplicable mob[.] — *All Things Considered (National Public Radio)*, 20th June 2003

infant mortality *noun*
the tendency of computer components to fail within the first few weeks of operation *US, 1991*

- — Eric S. Raymond, *The New Hacker's Dictionary*, p. 208, 1991

infinitely fine *adjective*
in computing, used as the ultimate praise *US, 1990*

- — Karla Jennings, *The Devouring Fungus*, p. 222, 1990

Ingersol Willie *noun*
in horse racing, the track's official timer of morning workouts *US, 1951*

- — David W. Maurer, *Argot of the Racetrack*, p. 38, 1951

ink *noun*
1 a tattoo *US, 2006*

- "No wallet but he's got gang ink all over him[.]" — Stephen J. Cannell, *White Sister*, p. 20, 2006

2 space or coverage in a newspaper *US, 1953*

- Got plenty of ink. Maybe we can brainwash us some famous white bitch. — Carl Hiaasen, *Tourist Season*, p. 106, 1986

3 inexpensive wine *US, 1917*

- — Clarence Major, *Dictionary of Afro-American Slang*, p. 69, 1970

ink-and-paper man *noun*
a counterfeiter who uses a printing press *US, 1985*

- You're an ink-and-paper man and you always have been. — Gerald Petievich, *The Quality of the Informant*, p. 6, 1985

ink in the pen *noun*
the ability to achieve erection and to ejaculate *US, 1967*

- — Dale Gordon, *The Dominion Sex Dictionary*, p. 90, 1967

ink stick *noun*
a fountain pen *US, 1942*

- — Don Wilmeth, *The Language of American Popular Entertainment*, p. 140, 1981

inland squid *noun*
a surfer who does not live at or near the beach *US, 1987*

- — Mitch McKissick, *Surf Lingo*, 1987

inmate *noun*
used as a term of derision, applied to a prisoner who follows prison rules and curries favor with the prison administration *US, 1984*

- — Inez Cardozo-Freeman, *The Joint*, p. 508, 1984

inner space *noun*
a person's deepest psychological being *US, 1967*

- — Joe David Brown (Editor), *The Hippies*, p. 218, 1967: "Glossary of hippie terms"

innie *noun*
an inward-turned navel *US, 1966*

- — John D. Bell et al., *Loosely Speaking*, p. 11, 1966
- Erin's mother had paid a plastic surgeon $1,500 to transform her "outie" belly button to an "innie." — Carl Hiaasen, *Strip Tease*, p. 56, 1993

insane *adjective*
1 excellent *US, 1955*

- — Robert George Reisner, *The Jazz Titans*, p. 159, 1960
- — Trevor Cralle, *The Surfin'ary*, p. 59, 1991

2 fearless; willing to try anything for fun *US, 1997*

- — Vann Wesson, *Generation X Field Guide and Lexicon*, p. 96, 1997

insanely great *adjective*
in computing, magnificent to a degree that can be fully grasped by only the most proficient practitioners *US, 1991*

- — Eric S. Raymond, *The New Hacker's Dictionary*, p. 209, 1991

insanity stripe *noun*
in the US armed forces, the insignia designating a three-year enlistment *US, 1946*

- — *American Speech*, p. 238, October 1946: "World War II slang of maladjustment"

insensitive care unit *noun*
a hospital's intensive care unit *US, 1988–1989*

- — *Maledicta*, p. 32, 1988–1989: "Medical maledicta from San Francisco"

inside man *noun*

in a big con swindle, a confederate to whom the victim is turned over once he has been lured into the enterprise *US, 1940*

- The inside man is the guts of a store. He makes one mistake and he's lost the mark and the score. — Iceberg Slim (Robert Beck), *Trick Baby*, p. 119, 1969

insider *noun*

a pocket *US, 1945*

- — Lou Shelly, *Hepcats Jive Talk Dictionary*, p. 13, 1945

inside work *noun*

any internal alteration of dice for cheating *US, 1963*

- — John S. Salak, *Dictionary of Gambling*, p. 131, 1963

Instamatic *noun*

a police radar unit used for measuring vehicle speed *US, 1976*

A brand name extrapolation from **CAMERA** (a generic term for radar).

- — *Complete CB Slang Dictionary*, p. 8, 1976

instant LZ *noun*

a 10,000- to 15,000-pound bomb used to clear jungle and create an instant landing zone in Vietnam *US, 1981*

The bomb was designed to create a wide but shallow crater in the jungle, literally creating an instant landing zone.

- The 10,000-pound "Instant LZ" opened up larger swathes of demolished jungle. — Shelby L. Stanton, *Anatomy of a Division*, p. 219, 1987

instant zen *noun*

LSD *US, 1972*

- — Carl Chambers and Richard Heckman, *Employee Drug Abuse*, p. 206, 1972

insulation *noun*

protection from police interference with a criminal scheme *US, 1978*

- It has much more to do with what the dealers call "insulation," or safety from the "heat" of law enforcement. — Joan W. Moore, *Homeboys*, p. 90, 1978

intelligence center *noun*

a field latrine *US, 1991*

Gulf war usage.

- — *American Speech*, p. 392, Winter 1991: "Among the new words"

intense *adjective*

extreme, wild *US, 1982*

A conventional adjective rendered slang by attitude and pronunciation, emphasis on the second syllable.

- — Douglas Simonson, *Pidgin to da Max Hana Hou*, 1982
- — Connie Eble (Editor), *UNC-CH Campus Slang*, p. 4, Fall 1984

interesting *adjective*

in computing, annoying or difficult *US, 1991*

- — Eric S. Raymond, *The New Hacker's Dictionary*, p. 210, 1991

interrogation by altitude *noun*

the reported practice by US troops of interrogating a group of suspected Viet Cong in a helicopter, throwing those who refused to answer to their death below and thus encouraging cooperation from those left *US, 1990*

- — Gregory Clark, *Words of the Vietnam War*, p. 249, 1990

in there; in thar *adjective*

excellent *US, 1991*

Inside the hollow of a breaking wave.

- — Trevor Cralle, *The Surfin'ary*, p. 57, 1991

into *preposition*

1 in debt to *US, 1893*

- "Dupre lost his job," Pat said. "He's already into me for twenty dollars." — William Burroughs, *Junkie*, p. 78, 1953
- "Into him is right. It's up to an even two grand now." — Wade Hunter, *The Sex Peddler*, p. 6, 1963
- "You are into me for twenty-five of the big ones." — Burt Hirschfield, *Fire Island*, p. 49, 1970
- I was into him for over a hundred and he threatened to tell my boss I was usin' stuff. — Emmett Grogan, *Ringolevio*, p. 53, 1972

2 interested in; participating in *US, 1965*

- — Joe David Brown (Editor), *The Hippies*, p. 218, 1967: "Glossary of hippie terms"
- Q: What are you into? LENORE: People and words, dreams and visions. But I'm not really into science and machines. — Leonard Wolfe (Editor), *Voices from the Love Generation*, p. 33, 1968
- Into: To be involved with. — *Screw*, p. 7, 12 October 1970
- Julie had been the only other woman on the block who was heavily into macrame, and Kate missed her and the raps they'd had on lazy summer afternoons while they sat out on Julie's patio tying knots in plant hangers. — Cyra McFadden, *The Serial*, p. 17, 1977

3 in organized crime, in control of *US, 1985*

- "The problem is, they also do business with us, indirectly. By that I mean by controlling some of our suppliers. I don't have to mention any names, I think you know what I'm talking about. Basic materials and services you need to run a hotel. Not to mention they're into a couple of unions." — Elmore Leonard, *Glitz*, p. 155, 1985

intown *noun*

the air space above Hanoi *US, 1990*

- — Joseph Tuso, *Singing the Vietnam Blues*, p. 249, 1990: Glossary

in-your-face; in-yo-face *adjective*

aggressive, provocative *US, 1998*

- Yet its fast tempos [...], in-yo-face word, and down home flavor made it [...] the South's hottest rape record. — Nelson George (writing in 1988), *Hip Hop America*, p. 132, 1998

IOW

used as Internet shorthand to mean "*in other words*" *US, 1997*

- — Andy Ihnatko, *Cyberspeak*, p. 102, 1997

I owe you money or what?

why are you looking at me that way? *US, 1981*

Hawaiian youth usage.

- — Douglas Simonson, *Pidgin to da Max*, 1981

IQ Charley *noun*

a half-wit *US, 1955*

Teen slang; unkind.

- — *American Weekly*, p. 2, 14th August 1955

Irish *noun*

fighting spirit *US, 1834*

- "Sweetheart, don't get your Irish up. We only want to help." — Elaine Flinn, *Dealing in Murder*, p. 82, 2003

Irish apple *noun*

a potato *UK, 1896*

- — *Maledicta*, p. 162, 1979: "A glossary of ethnic slurs in American English"

Irish baby buggy *noun*

a wheelbarrow *US, 1919*

- — *Maledicta*, p. 162, 1979: "A glossary of ethnic slurs in American English"

Irish clubhouse *noun*

a police stationhouse *US, 1904*

- — Vincent J. Monteleone, *Criminal Slang*, p. 129, 1949

Irish confetti *noun*

1 semen spilled on a woman's body *US, 1986–1987*

- — *Maledicta*, p. 57, 1986–1987: "A continuation of a glossary of ethnic slurs in American English"

2 stones, bricks, etc., when used as offensive missiles *US, 1913*

- The cops called these bone-breaking showers "Irish confetti." — George F. Will, *The Leveling Wind*, p. 392, 1994

Irisher *noun*

a person of Irish descent *US, 1807*

- We have seventy percent Jewish on the junkets, thirty percent Italian, and we bring along a couple of Irishers and Polacks to drink the booze. — Edward Lin, *Big Julie of Vegas*, p. 95, 1974
- An old man hands me a paper yarmulke, but I ask him is it all right I wear my crushed tweed hat. "You want you should look like an Irisher in a kosher house, so what difference is that to God?" he says sweetly. — Robert Campbell, *Junkyard Dog*, p. 34, 1986

Irish horse *noun*

1 salted beef *UK, 1748*

- — John Gould, *Maine Lingo*, p. 142, 1975

2 a flaccid or impotent penis *US, 1986–1987*

- — *Maledicta*, p. 57, 1986–1987: "A continuation of a glossary of ethnic slurs in American English"

Irish hurricane *noun*
a flat calm sea *US, 1803*
- — John Gould, *Maine Lingo*, p. 142, 1975

Irish lace; Irish lace curtains *noun*
a spider's cobweb *US, 1950*
- — Claudio R. Salvucci, *The Philadelphia Dialect Dictionary*, p. 45, 1996

Irish linen *noun*
in pool, the cloth used as a grip on the end of a cue stick *US, 1993*
- — Mike Shamos, *The Illustrated Encyclopedia of Billiards*, p. 124, 1993

Irish pennant *noun*
a dangling thread on a recruit's uniform *US, 1840*
Marine humor, Marine usage.
- Charging up and down the line through the barracks, Sergeant Carey pulls a hanging threat—what the Marines call an "Irish pennant"—from the starched camouflage uniform of Tony Wells[.] — Thomas Ricks, *Making the Corps*, p. 107, 1997

Irish picnic wagon *noun*
a police van *US, 1996*
- — Claudio R. Salvucci, *The Philadelphia Dialect Dictionary*, p. 46, 1996

Irish pop *noun*
a shot of whiskey and glass of beer *US, 1982*
- — Bill Reilly, *Big Al's Official Guide to Chicagoese*, p. 28, 1982

Irish Riviera *noun*
the South Shore of Massachusetts, spreading south and east from Boston along the south shore of Massachusetts Bay toward Cape Cod *US, 1967*
Favored by the Irish-Americans of the Boston area.
- It was a gorgeous day on the Irish Riviera. — George Higgins, *Kennedy for the Defense*, p. 222, 1980

Irish shave *noun*
an act of defecation *US, 1979*
- — *Maledicta*, p. 163, 1979: "A glossary of ethnic slurs in American English"

Irish toothache *noun*
1 a hangover *US, 1985*
- — Ernest Abel, *Dictionary of Alcohol Use and Abuse*, p. 95, 1985
2 an erection *UK, 1882*
- And in case you haven't heard, an Irish toothache is an erection. — Richard Farina, *Letter to Peter Tamony*, 24th August 1959
3 pregnancy *US, 1972*
- — Robert A. Wilson, *Playboy's Book of Forbidden Words*, p. 147, 1972

Irish turkey *noun*
corned beef *US, 1915*
- — Joseph E. Ragen and Charles Finston, *Inside the World's Toughest Prison*, p. 805, 1962: "Penitentiary and underworld glossary"

Irish wedding *noun*
masturbation *US, 1986–1987*
- — *Maledicta*, p. 57, 1986–1987: A continuation of a glossary of ethnic slurs in American "English"

iron *noun*
1 a gun, especially a handgun *US, 1838*
- The town's full of old iron. — Raymond Chandler, *The Little Sister*, p. 19, 1949
- "I ain't payin' that kind of bread for no iron like that." — Warren Miller, *The Cool World*, p. 2, 1959
- Then he stood up, flicked his iron to rock and roll and gave the little zero a long burst through the Playboy mag. — *Apocalypse Now*, 1979
- [O]ne of the Sticker and Ramsay boys—Sherman Smith by name—tilted the table and came out with his iron. — David Simon and Edward Burns, *The Corner*, p. 30, 1997
2 money *UK, 1705*
- — *Washington Post Magazine*, p. 7, 20th September 1987
3 an older mainframe computer *US, 1991*
- — Eric S. Raymond, *The New Hacker's Dictionary*, p. 211, 1991

▶ **push iron; bump iron; drive iron; pump iron; throw iron**
to lift weights *US, 1965*
Prison use.
- "You best stick to rasslin', and"—he back-handed Cat's softening belly—"pushing iron." — Malcolm Braly, *On the Yard*, p. 342, 1967
- And sometimes I go to the weight-lifting area, strip down to a pair of trunks, and push a little iron for a while and soak up the sun. — Eldridge Cleaver, *Soul on Ice*, p. 44, 1968

- He'd been to the joint, and had been throwin' iron up there. — Bobby Seale, *Seize the Time*, p. 17, 1970
- Gordon [Liddy] is gone now—he went off to prison and pumped iron for three years and gave them nothing but his name and his Social Security number. — Hunter S. Thompson, *Generation of Swine*, p. 104, 14 April 1986

Iron Age *noun*
in computing, the period approximately between 1961 (the first PDP-1) and 1971 (the first commercial microprocessor) *US, 1991*
- — Eric S. Raymond, *The New Hacker's Dictionary*, p. 211, 1991

iron ass *noun*
a stern, demanding, unrelenting person *US, 1942*
- I was always the iron ass. — Leonard Shecter and William Phillips, *On the Pad*, p. 237, 1973

iron-ass; iron-assed *adjective*
tough, unrelenting *US, 1948*
- The commanding general of the 15th Air Force was an iron ass real Air Force general—General Curtis LeMay. — Henry Yunick, *Best Damn Garage in Town*, p. 37, 2003

iron bar hotel *noun*
jail or prison *US, 1963*
- John the Bastard found himself in the iron bar hotel courtesy of the G-men on the charge of bringing girls across the state lines for reasons other than travel. — Madam Sherry, *Pleasure Was My Business*, p. 103, 1963

iron bird *noun*
an airplane *US, 1945*
- It was as though they were suspended in the sky, somehow carried aloft by an iron bird weighing many tons. — David Baldacci, *Wish You Well*, p. 35, 2000

iron bomb *noun*
a conventional bomb that is simply dropped from the sky without any targeting capability in the bomb *US, 1962*
- The bombs that Bush knew firsthand over 40 years ago are what the military calls "iron" or "dumb" bombs, those used since World War 1 to terrify the enemy from the air by opening bomb bay doors and letting them loose. — *The Houston Chronicle*, 19th January 1991

iron box *noun*
a computer program that attempts to trap illegitimate users long enough to trace their location *US, 1994*
- An iron box is a restrictive or otherwise special environment set up on a system to trap unwary hackers into staying on the line long enough to trace. — The Knightmare, *Secrets of a Super Hacker*, p. 176, 1994

iron brassiere *noun*
body armor *US, 1967*
- Next came a fifteen-pound chest protector of laminated steel and plastic, called "the iron barssiere." — Elaine Shepard, *The Doom Pussy*, p. 3, 1967

iron compass *noun*
railroad tracks as used by a flier as a navigation guide *US, 1933*
- Got lost on purpose, followed the "iron compass" home, catching up with and overtaking freight trains below. — Ann-Marie MacDonald, *The Way the Crow Flies*, p. 43, 1997

iron cure *noun*
the sudden and complete deprivation of a drug to an addict in jail who suffers intensely *US, 1973*
- — David Maurer and Victor Vogel, *Narcotics and Narcotic Addiction*, p. 418, 1973

iron curtain *noun*
a girdle *US, 1968*
- — Collin Baker et al., *College Undergraduate Slang Study Conducted at Brown University*, p. 142, 1968

iron door *noun*
▶ **behind the iron door**
in prison *US, 1992*
- — William K Bentley and James M. Corbett, *Prison Slang*, 1992

iron duke *noun*

in poker, a hand that is either certain to win or at least played as if it is certain to win *US, 1967*

- — Albert H. Morehead, *The Complete Guide to Winning Poker*, p. 266, 1967

iron freak *noun*

a weight-lifting enthusiast *US, 1966*

- He had the massive arms and chest of a dedicated iron freak. — Doug Hornig, *The Boys of October*, p. 120, 2003

iron God *noun*

the Burroughs B-550 computer *US, 1968*

- — *Current Slang*, p. 1, Spring 1968

iron horse *noun*

a tank or other armored vehicle *US, 1918*

- — Lou Shelly, *Hepcats Jive Talk Dictionary*, p. 46, 1945

iron man *noun*

one US silver dollar ($1) *US, 1908*

From the metal coin.

- — Lou Shelly, *Hepcats Jive Talk Dictionary*, p. 26, 1945
- — Don Wilmeth, *The Language of American Popular Entertainment*, p. 142, 1981

Iron Mike *noun*

a pair of brass knuckles *US, 1949*

- — Vincent J. Monteleone, *Criminal Slang*, p. 130, 1949

iron mouth *noun*

any person with orthodontia *US, 1979*

- I would be in school, and notice that if a girl had braces on her teeth the other kids would call her "tinsel-teeth" or "iron mouth." — *Washington Post*, p. D1, 24th November 1979

iron pile *noun*

the area in a prison recreation yard where the weightlifting equipment is kept *US, 1962*

- — Frank Prewitt and Francis Schaeffer, *Vacaville Vocabulary*, 1961–1962
- He went over to the iron pile. We had two complete sets of York dumbbells[.] — Malcolm Braley, *False Starts*, p. 157, 1976
- They agreed to eat together in the culinary, to work out together on the iron pile or handball court, and to have a weapon within easy reach at all times. — Bill Valentine, *Gangs and Their Tattoos*, p. 27, 2000

iron pipeline *noun*

a network for transporting guns from states where they are easily purchased to states where they are not easily purchased *US, 1993*

- They are legally purchased and sent up Interstate 95's "Iron Pipeline" to cities where gun-control laws are generally tighter. — *The Atlanta Constitution*, p. A1, 11st October 1993
- Having failed to pass off gang murders as "children killed by guns," anti-gun organizations now tell tales about "rogue gun dealers" feeding "iron pipelines" of illegal gun trafficking. — *News & Observer (Raleigh, North Carolina)*, p. A15, 30th June 2006

iron pony *noun*

a motorcycle *US, 1945*

- — Lou Shelly, *Hepcats Jive Talk Dictionary*, p. 46, 1945

Iron Queen *nickname*

the jail in the District of Columbia *US, 1977*

- See, when you first come in the D.C. Jail—the Iron Queen we call it—you don't usually raise no lot of hell. — John Allen, *Assault with a Deadly Weapon*, p. 123, 1977

irons *noun*

1 handcuffs *US, 1929*

Also used in the singular.

- "Pull the sleeves down over the irons and put on that there overcoat," he directed. — Chester Himes, *The Real Cool Killers*, p. 48, 1959
- I want this bastard in irons so we can put a call in and have a car pick them up. — Donald Goines, *Daddy Cool*, p. 151, 1974
- Cat on a family dispute almost draws down on Francis when he tried to lay the iron on his wrists after the dude had went upside Momma's head. — Joseph Wambaugh, *The Choirboys*, p. 314, 1975

2 in horse racing, stirrups *US, 1951*

- — David W. Maurer, *Argot of the Racetrack*, p. 38, 1951
- I believe that this is partly because he rides with his irons ridiculously short[.] — *Daily Racing Form*, p. 4, 27th November 1959

iron worker *noun*

a criminal who specializes in breaking into safes *US, 1949*

- — Vincent J. Monteleone, *Criminal Slang*, p. 130, 1949
- — Hyman E. Goldin et al., *Dictionary of American Underworld Lingo*, p. 108, 1950

iron yard *noun*

the area where weight lifting equipment is left and used, especially in prison *US, 1995*

- They pulled up on each other in the Chino maximum security facility iron yard. — Odie Hawkins, *Midnight*, p. 16, 1995

I see, said the blind man (and he saw)

used for expressing sudden comprehension in a teasing and humorous way *US, 1873*

- The Liberian glanced around nervously. "Oh, it is nothing, I assure you. Just a few people letting off steam." "I see, said the blind man." — Odie Hawkins, *The Life and Times of Chester Simmons*, p. 194, 1991

ish *noun*

an *i*ssue (of a magazine, especially a single-interest fan magazine) *US, 1967*

- — Patricia Byrd, *American Speech*, Spring 1978: "Star trek lives: Trekker slang"
- — *American Speech*, p. 27, Spring 1982: "The language of science fiction fan magazines"

I shit you not

I am very serious *US, 1969*

- "I shit you not, Juan, I'm afraid to go." — Juan Carmel Cosmes, *Memoir of a Whoremaster*, p. 66, 1969
- She looked like Gracie. I shit you not. — *Platoon*, 1986

ish kabibble

I don't care! *US, 1913*

- I kept my goggles down, shrugged my shoulders mentally and muttered an expression in vogue at the time, "Ish kabibble." — Preston Sturges, *Preston Sturges by Preston Sturges*, p. 164, 1990

ishy *adjective*

disgusting, unappealing *US, 1968*

- — Collin Baker et al., *College Undergraduate Slang Study Conducted at Brown University*, p. 144, 1968

island fever *noun*

the restlessness and anxiety felt by someone who is living on an island *US, 1977*

- The battalion was suffering from an epidemic of island fever when I joined it in January 1965. — Philip Caputo, *A Rumor of War*, p. 30, 1977

island happy *adjective*

restless and anxious after living on an island *US, 1946*

- It was the heebie-jeebies or the screaming meemies. It was rock-jolly, or island happy, or G.I. fever, or the purple moo-moo. — James A. Michener, *Tales of the South Pacific*, p. 144, 1947

Isro *noun*

bushy hair as worn by a Jewish person *US, 1975*

- [I]t had to be her, that was the same skinny teenager with an Isro he'd seen her with before, so who else could it be. — Adam Langer, *Crossing California*, p. 284, 2004

issue *noun*

a problem *US, 1999*

Often used in a mocking way, borrowing from the lexicon of self-improvement and popular psychotherapy. Most often heard in the plural.

- — Connie Eble (Editor), *UNC-CH Campus Slang*, p. 4, Spring 1999
- — Don R. McCreary (Editor), *Dawg Speak*, 2001

it *noun*

1 sex *UK, 1599*

- It took us some time to figure out why there were so many pretty young girls whoring in Baltimore. If they left home to sell it, why didn't they go to New York? — Jack Lait and Lee Mortimer, *Washington Confidential*, p. 274, 1951
- Was there something—uh—wrong with me, perhaps? Didn't I like "it"? — Jim Thompson, *Roughneck*, p. 89, 1954

2 the penis *US, 1846*

- MARY'S DAD: You got what stuck? TED: It. MARY'S DAD: It? Oh, it. — *Something About Mary*, 1998

3 in male homosexual usage, a heterosexual male or a homosexual male who is not part of the speaker's inner circle *US, 1981*

- — *Male Swinger Number 3*, p. 46, 1981: "The complete gay dictionary"

it ain't over 'til the fat lady sings
used as a humorous aphorism meaning that something is not over until it is over *US, 1969*
The battle cry of those who are about to lose.

- Yeah, well, it ain't over til the fat lady sings. — *A Few Good Men*, 1992

Italian airlines *noun*
walking *US, 1986–1987*

- — *Maledicta*, p. 57, 1986–1987: "A continuation of a glossary of ethnic slurs in American English"

Italian mausoleum *noun*
a car trunk *US, 1982*
From the stereotype of the corpses of Mafia murder victims being stuffed in car trunks.

- — Bill Reilly, *Big Al's Official Guide to Chicagoese*, p. 38, 1982

Italian rope trick *noun*
murder by rope garrote *US, 1981*

- Like all the other victims, Frank Borgia died with a surprised expression on his face. — Ovid Demaris, *The Last Mafioso*, p. 74, 1981

Italian salute *noun*
a type of obscene hand gesture *US, 1967*

- The kid gave him the Italian salute, slapping his biceps hard enough to bruise. — Ed Dee, *14 Peck Slip*, p. 200, 1994

item *noun*
a romantically-linked couple *US, 1981*
Expressing a commitment that the two individuals be considered as a single item.

- Said he thought we were an item! We were but we hadn't ever talked. — Sally Cline, *Couples*, p. 136, 1998

-itis *suffix*
used to create imaginary medical conditions, such as lazyitis (congenital laziness) and cobitis (an aversion to prison food) *US, 1912*

- Maybe the Premier was suffering from a bad case of electionitis. What is electionitis? I have never once suggested that the Premier suffered from a case of electionitis. I don't even know what it is. — *Hansard (British Columbia, Canada)*, 12th May 1982

it's all good
used for expressing optimism or a sense that all is well in the world *US, 1995*

- — Connie Eble (Editor), *UNC-CH Campus Slang*, p. 6, April 1995
- — Don R. McCreary (Editor), *Dawg Speak*, 2001

it's been great
used as a farewell *US, 1969*

- — John D. Bell et al., *Loosely Speaking*, p. Appendix, 1969

it's been real
used as a farewell, suggesting that the time spent together has been enjoyable *US, 1982*

- — Connie Eble (Editor), *UNC-CH Campus Slang*, p. 7, Spring 1982
- "It's been real." I held out my hand for him to shake. "It's been real," Ralph repeated. — Wally Lamb, *I Know This Much Is True*, p. 398, 1998

it's dead
the issue being discussed need not be discussed any further *US, 2002*

- — Gary K. Farlow, *Prison-ese*, p. 33, 2002

it's on!
used for announcing the start of hostilities between youth gangs *US, 1953*

- — Dale Kramer and Madeline Karr, *Teen-Age Gangs*, p. 175, 1953

itsy-bitsy *adjective*
tiny *US, 1938*

- Two, three, four, tell the people what she wore / It was an itsy-bitsy, teen-weeny yellow polka-dot bikini / That she wore for the first time today. — Brian Hyland, *Itsy-Bitsy Teeny-Weeny Yellow Polka-Dot Bikini*, 1960

- He's shorter than me, and I'm only six! He was this little, itsy-bitsy man. He was a little, little man. — *Avalon*, 1990

it's you
used as a greeting *US, 1973*

- — Malachi Andrews and Paul T. Owens, *Black Language*, p. 86, 1973

itty bitty titties *noun*
small breasts on a female *US, 1992*

- To be held in a blouse with a safety pin or breasts that qualify their owners for membership in the Itty Bitty Titty Committee. — Susan Newman, *Oh God!*, p. 52, 2002
- She wore a backpack with straps in the middle, lying between and defining where her breasts ought to have been. Itty-bitty-titty club, Benn thought. — Steven Sherrill, *Visits from the Drowned Girl*, p. 9, 2004

Ivan *noun*
a Russian, especially a soldier; the nation of Russia *US, 1944*
Originally military; the popular male forename is the Russian equivalent to John.

- Aim my M-16 downrange / If Ivan survives it'll be real strange. — Sandee Johnson, *Cadences: The Jody Call Book, No. 2*, p. 140, 1986

ivories *noun*
1 dice *US, 1962*

- — Frank Garcia, *Marked Cards and Loaded Dice*, p. 262, 1962

2 billiard or pool balls *UK, 1875*

- I threw a set of ivories out and started batting them around. — Robert Byrne, *McGoorty*, p. 132, 1972
- — Steve Rushin, *Pool Cool*, p. 17, 1990

ivory flake *noun*
cocaine *US, 1983*

- DEALER: Hey, man. You wanna cop some blow? / JUNKIE: Sure, watcha got? Dust, flakes or rocks? / DEALER: I got China White, Mother of Pearl, ivory flake. What you need? — Grandmaster Flash & The Furious Five featuring Melle Mel, *White Lines*, 1983

ivory soap *noun*
in dominoes, the double blank piece *US, 1959*

- — Dominic Armanino, *Dominoes*, p. 17, 1959

ivory tickler *noun*
a piano player *US, 1911*

- "I really thought once I'd be an ivory tickler but I am glad my money ran out before I got too far." — David McCullough, *Truman*, p. 87, 1992

ivory tower *noun*
used as a metaphor for an attitude that is elitist, intellectual, and removed from the real world *US, 1911*

- Nobody, "said Pearl," can accuse you of being an ivory-tower professor. Political science is a living, breathing subject, and the way you teach it is real and vital. — Max Shulman, *The Many Loves of Dobie Gillis*, 1951
- The piece was crutched and flawed by the usual contrived soul shit that white writers and Ivory Tower black scribes use when writing about street Niggers. — Iceberg Slim (Robert Beck), *The Naked Soul of Iceberg Slim*, p. 199, 1971

Ivy League *nickname*
the Fourth Infantry Division, US Army *US, 2001*

- He was assigned to the grunt units of the Fourth Infantry Division— the Ivy League. — Cherokee Paul McDonald, *Into the Green*, p. 187, 2001

I wouldn't fuck her with your dick
used as a jocular disparagement of a woman's sexual attractiveness *US, 1974*

- "I wouldn't fuck her with your dick!" was the consensus. — Earl Thompson, *Tattoo*, p. 291, 1974

ixnay
no *US, 1929*
Pig Latin for "nix."

- Ixnay, soldier. Or I'll have three guards on you before you can say Jesus. — Robert Edmond Alter, *Carny Kill*, p. 3, 1966
- I swear by the time he got around to askin' me for it you could hear his brain sizzlin' through his ears, and like a fool I told him ixnay[.] — Seth Morgan, *Homeboy*, p. 8, 1990

- Ixnay, dude, I tried that. She's out for the night. — *Airheads*, 1994

- Ixnay on the big appetite. — *Something About Mary*, 1998

-iz- *infix*

used as an infix to hide the meaning of a word *US, 1972*
Used in prison and other fields with a tentative relationship to
the law. "Dope" becomes "dizope."

- Language play form. ("Get me a bizzag of skizzag." "Get me a bag
  of heroin.") — Seymour Fiddle, *New York Addict Argot*, 1972
- — John R Armore and Joseph D. Wolfe, *Dictionary of Desperation*, 1976

-iz-i *infix*

an embellishment that adds no meaning to a word *US, 1999*
Popularized by Frankie Smith in the 1999 song "Double Dutch
Bus."

Jj

J *noun*

a marijuana cigarette *US, 1967*

"J" is for **JOINT**.

- Sorry old bus, he said to Urge as he felt his shirt pocket for a J. — Gurney Norman, *Divine Right's Trip (Last Whole Earth Catalog)*, p. 13, 1971
- And a fat ass J, of some bubonic chronic that made me choke — Snoop Doggy Dogg, *Gin and Juice*, 1993
- Mind if I smoke a jay? — *The Big Lebowski*, 1998
- Tammy took a hit, gagged a bit, then passed the potent J my way. — Eric Jerome Dickey, *Cheaters*, p. 37, 1999

jab *noun*

an intravenous drug injection *US, 1914*

- — David Maurer and Victor Vogel, *Narcotics and Narcotic Addiction*, p. 419, 1973

jabber *noun*

1 a drug user who injects drugs *US, 1973*

- — David Maurer and Victor Vogel, *Narcotics and Narcotic Addiction*, p. 419, 1973

2 a boxer *US, 1904*

- Big-time Mex jabber—incomprehensible. — James Ellroy, *White Jazz*, p. 258, 1992

jab-off *noun*

the flooding sensations of exhilaration and euphoria following a heroin injection *US, 1973*

- — David Maurer and Victor Vogel, *Narcotics and Narcotic Addiction*, p. 419, 1973

jack *noun*

1 money *US, 1890*

- What you need is a vacation. A decent one—with jack to spend—maybe at the seashore or up at Lake George. — Philip Wylie, *Opus 21*, p. 335, 1949
- All the jack he'd made in the rackets was gone. — Jim Thompson, *Savage Night*, p. 5, 1953
- We lived for these fantastic sums of jack. — James Carr, *Bad*, p. 136, 1975
- And then He said, "Let there be a bunch of sleazy guys hanging around Camden, New Jersey, trying to hustle up enough jack so they can move to Atlantic City." — Joe Bob Briggs, *Joe Bob Goes to the Drive-In*, p. 5, 1987

2 a homemade alcoholic beverage, usually applejack or raisinjack *US, 1894*

- Since that time they had been into a jug of Jack together a few times. — Odie Hawkins, *The Busting Out of an Ordinary Man*, p. 56, 1985

3 anything at all; nothing at all *US, 1973*

- Junior Stebbens, I recently realized, don't know jack about brakes. — Joe Bob Briggs, *Joe Bob Goes to the Drive-In*, p. 48, 1987
- Then the firin' pin hit a empty spot an you end up with jack. — Jess Mowry, *Way Past Cool*, p. 7, 1992

4 a cellular phone *US, 2005*

- Everybody get the fuck back, excuse me bitch, gimme your jack. — RZA, *The Wu-Tang Manual*, p. 170, 2005

5 an act of masturbation *US, 2003*

- After surviving their first ambush at Al Gharraf, a couple of Marines even admitted to an almost frenzied need to get off combat jacks. — *Rolling Stone*, 24th July 2003

6 tobacco *US, 1949*

- — Vincent J. Monteleone, *Criminal Slang*, p. 130, 1949

7 a small heroin pill *UK, 1967*

- Dr. Feelgood's cure had apparently intensified my problem, and the little white "jacks," tiny pills of pure heroin, made some contribution as well. — Peter Coyote, *Sleeping Where I Fall*, p. 166, 1998

8 a robbery *US, 1988*

- The Cadillac is rolling up to the intersection where the "jack" is taking place. — *Menace II Society*, 1993
- Parker told the investigators she and friends stopped to buy a bottle of soda, then decided to "do a jack," street slang for a robbery. — *Tampa (Florida) Tribune*, p. 1, 19th August 1997

jack *verb*

1 to steal, to take by force—especially of street crime *US, 1930*

Adopted from "jack" (to hijack).

- I knew that Bobo had snuck in again, and now he was trying to jack me for a dollar. — Joe Bob Briggs, *Joe Bob Goes to the Drive-In*, p. 14, 1987
- Who was it nigga? Who jacked you? — *Menace II Society*, 1993
- Li'l G.C. and I had jacked a civilian for his car one night. — Sanyika Shakur, *Monster*, p. 193, 1993
- Even Al Gore can't muster enough balls to admit the fact that he got jacked. — Suroosh Alvi et al., *The Vice Guide*, p. 196, 2002

2 (of a male) to masturbate *US, 1995*

- I wanted to take my dick out and start jacking right there. — *Kids*, 1995

3 to serve (a prison sentence) *US, 1966*

- Said, "Gee, judge, that's no time / I got a brother on Levenworth jackin' ninety-nine." — Bruce Jackson, *Get Your Ass in the Water and Swim Like Me*, p. 52, 1966

▸ **jack your jaw**

to talk incessantly *US, 1983*

- "My problem is that I'd rather put people in jail than sit around the Field Office all day jacking my jaws about how much the federal cost-of-living pay raise is going to be," Chance said. — Gerald Petievich, *To Live and Die in L.A.*, p. 27, 1983

jack *adjective*

used for describing any medium used for inspiration while masturbating *US, 1990*

Followed by the medium—"jack pictures," "jack flick," "jack book," etc.

- — Charles Shafer, *Folk Speech in Texas Prisons*, p. 208, 1990

Jack; Jack D; Jack's *nickname*

Jack Daniels™ whiskey *US, 1972*

- I listened at first, sipping my Jack's and water[.] — Lester Bangs, *Psychotic Reactions and Carburetor Dung*, p. 109, 1972
- "A whole fuckin' quart of Jack D!" — Jess Mowry, *Six Out Seven*, p. 46, 1993
- Pull me down a bottle of Jack. I'm gettin' tanked tonight. — Quentin Tarantino, *From Dusk Till Dawn*, p. 2, 1995
- "How about a shot of Jack?" I said as I dropped onto a bar stool. — John Ridley, *Love is a Racket*, p. 12, 1998

jack around *verb*

1 to idle, to fool around *US, 1962*

- For one thing, he likes to jack around in the stock market with our money. — Dan Jenkins, *Semi-Tough*, p. 63, 1972
- "There's before people starting jacking around with it." — William Least Heat-Moon, *Blue Highways*, p. 12, 1983

2 to engage in horseplay *US, 1963*

- — *American Speech*, p. 276, December 1963: "American Indian student slang"

jack benny *noun*

in hold 'em poker, a three and a nine as the first two cards dealt to a player *US, 1981*

Comedian Benny perpetually claimed that he was 39 years old.

- — Thomas L. Clark, *The Dictionary of Gambling and Gaming*, p. 109, 1987

jack boy *noun*

a street criminal who relies almost exclusively upon force and terror *US, 1989*

- He liked jackboys because they were crazy. They made their living ripping off street dealers for their blow and change and busting into crackhouses with assault weapons. — Elmore Leonard, *Rum Punch*, p. 27, 1992

jacked up; jacked *adjective*

drunk, drug-intoxicated, exhilarated *US, 1935*

- [T]his whole show and all its floodlit drug-jacked realer-than-life trappings[.] — Lester Bangs, *Psychotic Reactions and Carburetor Dung*, p. 36, 1970
- Yeah we'll show her what it's all about / We'll get her jacked up on some cheap champagne[.] — Scissor Sisters, *Take Your Mama*, 2004

jacker *noun*

1 a robber, a hijacker *US, 1965*

- You're certain this bale of cotton was carried by the meat delivery truck used by the jackers? — Chester Himes, *Cotton Comes to Harlem*, p. 108, 1965
- That was three days after those jigaboo dope jackers muscled Mack and Bone while they were delivering the eight kilos to Southside wholesalers. — Iceberg Slim (Robert Beck), *Death Wish*, p. 38, 1977
- I tried to get it in my head I really was a jacker and not just some desperate con with a finger in his pocket. — John Ridley, *Love is a Racket*, p. 123, 1998

2 a camouflage expert *US, 1956*
- — *American Speech*, p. 97, May 1956: "Smugglers' argot in the Southwest"

jacket *noun*

1 a personnel file, especially in prison or the military *US, 1944*
- The jacket said she was 38 years old, and her number was J-019 – 20 and she lived in KB-2 of the women's unit. — Clarence Cooper Jr., *The Farm*, p. 42, 1967
- If you ever get the chance, see what reason they have in my jacket for the 1962 transfer to San Quentin from Tracy. — George Jackson, *Soledad Brother*, p. 220, 24th March 1970
- The general's going to put a letter of reprimand in your jacket, but hell, all that'll do is hurt your chances for promotion to captain. — Philip Caputo, *A Rumor of War*, p. 319, 1977
- Two-time loser with a Quentin jacket. — James Ellroy, *Blood on the Moon*, p. 83, 1984

2 a jail sentence *US, 1960*
- Three days later Christy got a three-year jacket and was on his way. — Nelson Algren, *The Neon Wilderness*, p. 195, 1960

3 a capsule of Nembutal™, a central nervous system depressant *US, 1952*
- — *American Speech*, p. 27, February 1952: "Teen-age hophead jargon"

▸ **put the jacket on someone**
to frame someone, setting them up to take the blame *US, 1982*
- — Bill Reilly, *Big Al's Official Guide to Chicagoese*, p. 38, 1982

jacket *verb*
(used of a school boy) to give a girl your school jacket, signifying a steady dating relationship *US, 1954*
- — *Look*, p. 88, 10th August 1954

jack flaps *noun*
fancy clothes worn by a man in pursuit of female companionship *US, 1976*
- — *Elementary Electronics, Dictionary of CB Lingo*, p. 79, 1976

jackie *noun*
in the circus or carnival, a story of past deeds or escapades *US, 1980*
- — Joe McKennon, *Circus Lingo*, p. 51, 1980

jack in; jack it in *verb*
to log onto the Internet *US, 1995*
- — Christian Crumlish, *The Internet Dictionary*, p. 103, 1995

Jack-in-the-black *noun*
black-labeled Jack Daniels™ whiskey *US, 1983*
- "Jack in the Black." "You got it, Tennessee." — James Webbs, *A Country such as This*, p. 59, 1983
- He had some Jack in the Black in his bag, and they kept on drinking. — Brandon Stosuy, *Up is Up*, p. 260, 2006

jack-jaw *verb*
to talk incessantly *US, 1977*
- "She's been jack-jawin' for two days straight and she's still got another sixty years to tell." — E.M. Corder, *Citizens Band*, p. 36, 1977

jack-jawed *adjective*
dim-witted *US, 1985*
- They're dope dealers, a bunch of jack-jawed no-good hophead motherfuckers. — Gerald Petievich, *The Quality of the Informant*, p. 18, 1985

jack-knife *verb*
to double up at the waist *US, 1951*
- I lay between the Waldorf's excellent sheets jack-knifed with panic. — Max Shulman, *The Many Loves of Dobie Gillis*, p. 29, 1951

▸ **jack-knife your legs**
(used of a man) to straighten your legs so that the crease of the pants stands out and the turn-ups fall over the shoes *US, 1994*

- This is fight night. Shoot cuffs, boy, jack-knife yo' legs. Get down. — *Buzz*, p. 76, May 1994

jackleg *noun*
a gambler who cheats *US, 1949*
- — Vincent J. Monteleone, *Criminal Slang*, p. 130, 1949

jackleg *adjective*
unschooled, untrained *US, 1837*
- Mrs. Rogers—who was also a jackleg preacher (she did not have a church) called everybody "child," "brother," or "sister." — Claude Brown, *Manchild in the Promised Land*, p. 24, 1965
- His movements were just like a jackleg minister's; in fact, I've always thought that there is a strong personality link between a pimp and an ignorant preacher. — Robert Deane Pharr, *S.R.O.*, p. 41, 1971
- But as far as taking a jackleg lawyer, you don't use them for anything but errand boys. — Bruce Jackson, *Outside the Law*, p. 134, 1972
- His father had been a jack-leg preacher who dispensed his sermons from the mount of a storefront church on Prince street[.] — Nathan Heard, *To Reach a Dream*, p. 16, 1972

jack Mormon *noun*
a lapsed Mormon *US, 1843*
- Nails was a Jack Mormon of Welsh and Italian descent. — Elaine Shepard, *The Doom Pussy*, p. 51, 1967
- Every town had a few jack Mormons—those who smoked tobacco, drank tea or coffee or hard liquor, and perhaps even joined the Democratic Party. — Edward Abbey, *Desert Solitaire*, p. 296, 1968

jack-off *noun*

1 an act of masturbation *US, 1952*
- Whenever I can slip into my office and log on, I'm doing a quick jack-off session. — Howard Stern, *Miss America*, p. 27, 1995

2 a despised person *US, 1938*
- And never mind those jack-offs who keep saying you'll never make it as a sportswriter. — Hunter S. Thompson, *Songs of the Doomed*, p. 235, 1981

jack off *verb*

1 (used of a male) to masturbate *US, 1916*
Derives from "jack" (an erection) now obsolete, combined with **JERK OFF** (to masturbate).
- Still, having jacked off in the toilet, feeling rested & tonite's sleep (not to spoil it) being a long one, will write anyhow. — Neal Cassady, *The First Third*, 30th August 1965
- The one alternative amusement was watching the Melly brothers, George and Ed, who ordinarily spent their lunch hour jacking off in the boy's rest room. — Larry McMurtry, *The Last Picture Show*, p. 35, 1966
- "Shit, you mean you don't know how to jack off?" "You mean pull it?" I asked my guide. — Oscar Zeta Acosta, *The Autobiography of a Brown Buffalo*, p. 82, 1972
- So you're gonna go out there, drink your drink, say "Goodnight, I've had a very lovely evening," go home, and jack off. And that's all you're gonna do. — *Pulp Fiction*, 1994

2 to manipulate the injection of a drug such that the drug enters the blood stream slowly *US, 1967*
- When the blood reached the top of the dropper, she backed it up into her veins, working the blood in the dropper slowly as she jacked the works off. — Donald Goines, *Dopefiend*, p. 10, 1971
- Once it was in that was it to me. A lotta fellows liked jacking it off once they struck red. They would play with it 'til the point would plug up on 'em[.] — A.S. Jackson, *Gentleman Pimp*, p. 99, 1973

jack-off artist *noun*
a masturbator *US, 1991*
- "Any creeps call in?" Of course creeps had called—who else would bother. "The usual jack-off artists," Nina reported. — Carl Hiaasen, *Native Tongue*, p. 30, 1991

jack-off flare *noun*
a small, hand-launched aerial flare *US, 1987*
The term is based on comparing images.
- We light out LZ with jack-off flares, which are formally referred to as Flare Hand-held Illuminations. A jack-off flare looks like a silver baton about a foot and a half long. To fire it, you take the firing cap off one end, attach it to the other, and slam it against the palm of your hand. — Ernest Spencer, *Welcome to Vietnam, Macho Man*, p. 96, 1987

jack of the dust *noun*
aboard ship, a storekeeper of cleaning supplies *US, 1986*
- — Hans Halberstadt, *USCG: Always Ready*, p. 128, 1986: "Glossary"

jack-pack *noun*
a contraption used by a masturbating male to simulate the sensation of penetration *US, 1979*
- — *Maledicta*, p. 218, 1979: "Kinks and queens: linguistic and cultural aspects of the terminology for gays"

jack picture *noun*
a photograph used while masturbating *US, 1972*
- Cause all the punks, every punk that's in our tank has a jack picture, every one of them. A jack picture / Some picture of a woman. Some of them have just the head of a woman but they jack off with it anyway. — Bruce Jackson, *In the Life*, p. 403, 1972

jack pine savage *noun*
a person from the back woods *US, 1957*
- To most of the people I knew in Minneapolis, David would be considered a kind of jack-pine savage. — Gary Paulsen, *Popcorn Days and Buttermilk Nights*, p. 63, 1983

jackpot *noun*
1 serious trouble *US, 1887*
- Sooner or later Jessie's going to cook up something with you and you're going to wind up in a jackpot. — Vincent Patrick, *Family Business*, p. 40, 1985
2 in the circus or carnival, a story of past deeds *US, 1980*
- — Joe McKennon, *Circus Lingo*, p. 51, 1980
- After the countless "jackpots" (that is, wild stories) about Party Time Shows that Jackie had told me, I had been digging at him to give me a shot on the midway. — Peter Fenton, *Eyeing the Flash*, p. 96, 2005

jackrabbit parole *noun*
escape from prison *US, 1992*
- — William K. Bentley and James M. Corbett, *Prison Slang*, p. 108, 1992

jack ready *adjective*
sexually aroused *US, 1990*
- — Charles Shafer, *Folk Speech in Texas Prisons*, p. 208, 1990

jack-roll *verb*
to rob or pick a pocket, especially to rob a drunk *US, 1916*
- "Where are we going?" Nick asked. "Jack-rolling," Vito said. — Willard Motley, *Knock on Any Door*, p. 129, 1947
- "But she forgits the guys we used to jackroll." — Donald Wilson, *My Six Convicts*, p. 94, 1951
- After a few days or weeks the girls are told some big spenders wouldn't miss a few dollars if a girl picked up his change or even his wallet. This "jackrolling" works well on drunks. — Lee Mortimer, *Women Confidential*, p. 144, 1960

jackroll artist *noun*
a criminal specializing in robbing sleeping drunks *US, 1976*
- [A]t any time a jackroll artist might be confronted with a problem that would turn them into a killer. — William Brashler, *City Dogs*, p. 28, 1976

jack-roller *noun*
a person who robs drunks *US, 1922*
- [O]ther denizens of the underworld and the half-world who are also social pariahs—the prostitute, the dopey, the panhandler, the jack-roller, and the pimp. — Noel Gist, *Urban Society*, p. 439, 1953
- Jackrollers and pimps walked wise-eyed. — Willard Motley, *Let No Man Write My Epitaph*, p. 59, 1958
- According to Attorney General Lynch's own figures, California's overall crime picture makes the Angels look like a gang of petty jack-rollers. — Hunter S. Thompson, *Hell's Angels*, p. 35, 1966
- "But I ain't no jack-roller, 'cause that don't take no skill or nothing." — L.H. Whittemore, *Cop!*, p. 144, 1969

jack shit *noun*
nothing, a pittance *US, 1969*
- I'm strictly a club caddy, and proud of it. Those tour baggies ain't nothin'. Carrying single bags for a good player ain't jack shit. — James Ellroy, *Brown's Requiem*, p. 43, 1981
- MR. WHITE: Without medical attention, this man won't live through the night. That bullet in his belly is my fault. Now while that might not mean jack shit to you, it means a helluva lot to me. — *Reservoir Dogs*, 1992
- We didn't know jack shit about any riot. It just happened. — *Natural Born Killers*, 1994

Jackson *noun*
1 a twenty-dollar bill *US, 1969*
From the portrait of US President Andrew Jackson on the bill.

- He said, "A Jackson frogskin! Whr'd yu git it, Mama?" — Iceberg Slim (Robert Beck), *Mama Black Widow*, p. 114, 1969
- "I see you again," Slick had told her, "it better be behind a pile of dead Presidents. Take a load of Jacksons and Grants get you off my shit list, girl." — John Sayles, *Union Dues*, p. 181, 1977
- For a jackson Belly scored an eight milligram jug, half her normal dose[.] — Seth Morgan, *Homeboy*, p. 188, 1990
2 used as a male-to-male term of address *US, 1941*
- Cook with gas and go to town! Solid Jackson! Ride on down! — Harry Haenigsen, *Jive's Like That*, 1947
- — Lavada Durst, *The Jives of Dr. Hepcat*, p. 1, 1953

Jackson five *noun*
one hundred dollars in twenty-dollar bills *US, 1983*
A portrait of US President Andrew Jackson is found on the face of a $20 bill, enabling this pun on the 1970s Motown recording group.
- — Thomas L. Clark, *The Dictionary of Gambling and Gaming*, p. 109, 1987

jack-up *noun*
a tablet of sodium amobarbital (trade name Amytal™), a central nervous system depressant *US, 1973*
- — David Maurer and Victor Vogel, *Narcotics and Narcotic Addiction*, p. 419, 1973

jack up *verb*
1 to raise *US, 1904*
- Viceroy Wilson adjusted his Carrera sunglasses, lit up a joint, jacked up the a/c, and mellowed out behind the Caddy's blue-tinted windows. — Carl Hiaasen, *Tourist Season*, p. 58, 1986
- And this is preferable to you because Music-Town jacks up their prices, and some of this money goes in your pocket. — *Empire Records*, 1995
2 to rob with force *US, 1965*
- If you give those evil bastards a dime they'll jack you up for the whole thing. — Hunter S. Thompson, *Fear and Loathing in America*, p. 85, 31st May 1968: Letter to Carol Hoffman
- By Thursday they'll jack somebody up to get money for the weekend. — Edwin Torres, *After Hours*, p. 332, 1979
3 to arrest or detain for questioning by police *US, 1967*
- On each fall he had been "jacked up" for either strong-arm robbery or "till tapping" [stealing money from a cash register drawer]. — Iceberg Slim (Robert Beck), *Pimp*, p. 33, 1969

jack-up fence *noun*
a large wire fence with barbed wire across the top *US, 2000*
Criminals lift victims and hang them on the top of the fence as they rob them.
- — Fiona Pitt-Kethley, *Red Light Districts of the World*, p. 85, 2000

Jacob's ladder *noun*
a sturdy rope ladder dropped from a hovering helicopter for descent to and ascent from the ground *US, 1985*
- Early the next morning engineers and medical personnel reached the unit, descending through the jungle canopy on "Jacob's ladders" dropped from the rear of the hovering CH-47 Chinook helicopter. — Shelby L. Stanton, *The Rise and Fall of an American Army*, p. 94, 1985

jag *noun*
1 a state of alcohol or drug intoxication *UK, 1678*
- [T]aken two or three at one time with coffee, they gave a wonderful jag. The capsules were blue so we called them blue boys. After we got jagged we found no one would know what we were talking about when we said blue boys. — Chester Himes, *Cast the First Stone*, p. 247, 1952
- 300 jags seems kinda fantastic. — Clarence Cooper Jr., *The Farm*, p. 192, 1967
2 a drinking or drug binge *US, 1892*
- It was like waiting for the accentuated heat of your heart when you're on a reefer jag[.] — Mezz Mezzrow, *Really the Blues*, p. 181, 1946
- It was past midnight, and Frank was coming out of the marijuana jag and feeling lousy. — Irving Shulman, *The Amboy Dukes*, p. 44, 1947
- When oral administration or intramuscular injection no longer provides a "jag," he becomes a "main line shooter." — Donald Wilson, *My Six Convicts*, p. 337, 1951
- They stood at the bar like two cats having a sip of something cold to dampen their dry jag, and ordered beer. — Chester Himes, *Cotton Comes to Harlem*, p. 129, 1965
3 a loner lacking social skills *US, 1993*
- — *Washington Post*, 14th October 1993

jag *verb*

to work as a male prostitute *US, 1972*

- — Helen Dahlskog (Editor), *A Dictionary of Contemporary and Colloquial Usage*, p. 34, 1972

jagged *adjective*

drunk or drug-intoxicated *US, 1737*

First recorded by Benjamin Franklin.

- [T]aken two or three at one time with coffee, they gave a wonderful jag. The capsules were blue so we called them blue boys. After we got jagged we found no one would know what we were talking about when we said blue boys. — Chester Himes, *Cast the First Stone*, p. 247, 1952
- "Jagged to the gills," the sergeant said, looking minutely about the room. — Chester Himes, *The Real Cool Killers*, p. 69, 1959

jagger *noun*

a tattoo artist *US, 1947*

- — Don Wilmeth, *The Language of American Popular Entertainment*, p. 143, 1981

jag house *noun*

a brothel that caters to male homosexuals *US, 1972*

- — Helen Dahlskog (Editor), *A Dictionary of Contemporary and Colloquial Usage*, p. 34, 1972
- From being an inn, the jag house became a brothel and is now used of one which caters to male homosexuals. — R.W. Holder, *How Not To Say What You Mean*, p. 213, 2002

jag-off *noun*

a despicable, offensive or dim-witted person *US, 1938*

- Cops were nothing special in a landscape of winos, hustlers, hillbillies, Indians, niggers, spics, and any other assortment of jagoffs who came to Wilson Avenue[.] — William Brashler, *City Dogs*, p. 5, 1976
- Great idea jag-off! — *The Breakfast Club*, 1985
- Past the jag-off guard who gets an extra C-note a week just to watch the door. — *Casino*, 1995
- Shut up, jagoff! — *Austin Powers*, 1999

jag off *verb*

to manipulate the injection of a drug such that the drug enters the blood stream slowly *US, 1958*

- Extra Black Johnson, like so many of them, likes to jag off. — Willard Motley, *Let No Man Write My Epitaph*, p. 158, 1958

jail *noun*

in horse racing, the first month after a claimed horse is in a new stable *US, 1976*

Racing rules limit the conditions under which the horse may be raced during the first month.

- — Tom Ainslie, *Ainslie's Complete Guide to Thoroughbred Racing*, p. 333, 1976

▸ **in jail**

in pool, said of a cue ball that is touching another ball or the rail, leaving the player with no good opportunity to make a shot *US, 1990*

- — Steve Rushin, *Pool Cool*, p. 16, 1990

jail *verb*

to serve a prison sentence, especially without losing hope or sanity *US, 1967*

- But you like jailing, Red. Nunn didn't. — Malcolm Braly, *On the Yard*, p. 325, 1967
- Jailin' was an art form and lifestyle both. The style was walkin' slow, drinkin' plenty of water, and doin' your own time; the art was lightin' cigarettes from wall sockets, playin' the dozens, cuttin' up dream jackpots, and slowin' your metabolism[.] — Seth Morgan, *Homeboy*, p. 122, 1990
- Elvin, eating pizza, said he'd give him some pointers on how to jail. — Elmore Leonard, *Maximum Bob*, p. 47, 1991
- [A]fter the first few months of watching the calendar go by, banging his fists on the wall in blind rage and disbelief, he learned to "jail" the rest of his time. — Tracy Funches, *Pimpnosis*, pp. 42–43, 2002

▸ **jail it**

to wear your pants with the belt-line below the top of your underpants *US, 2002*

- The end fashion statement is calling "jailing it"—a five-to-eight-inch revelation of white boxer tops precariously embraced by the string-tightened pants below. — Jimmy Lerner, *You Got Nothing Coming*, p. 173, 2002

jail arithmetic *noun*

in prison, any method used to keep track of your time served and the time remaining on your sentence *US, 1949*

- — Vincent J. Monteleone, *Criminal Slang*, p. 131, 1949

jailbait *noun*

a sexually alluring girl under the legal age of consent *US, 1930*

- "Now they start in grammar school, and the streets are full of jail bait," Jack said. — James T. Farrell, *Saturday Night*, p. 36, 1947
- The girls are mostly jailbait chicks, radically underage and looking it in their baby fat, pedal pushers, unskillful mascara, and ponytails. — Herbert Gold, *The Age of Happy Problems*, p. 211, 1962
- Morty, that fucking chick is jail bait if I ever seen it! I mean, she's a fucking child, for Christ fucking sake! — Terry Southern, *Blue Movie*, p. 149, 1970
- Then I heard a forty-seven-year-old guy named Herman searching for jailbait. — Anka Radakovich, *The Wild Girls Club*, p. 67, 1994

jailhouse daddy *noun*

a prisoner who is a sexual predator *US, 1951*

- [L]ike most jailhouse daddies, Bowles portrays himself as a misunderstood, caring guy, improvising as best he can in an inhuman system. — Elizabeth Abbot, *A History of Celibacy*, p. 285, 2000

jailhouse flowers *noun*

the solicitation of sexual relations by nonlexical verbalization *US, 1974*

- I heard someone making squeaky sounds from between compressed lips. A sound that was a universal expression in prison, it meant getting hit on. I went on working, vaguely wondering who was getting the jailhouse flowers. — Piri Thomas, *Seven Long Times*, p. 168, 1974

jailhouse lawyer *noun*

a prisoner with some expertise, real and/or perceived, in the criminal justice system *US, 1926*

- "Jerry the Jew," as he was called, was a principal "jailhouse lawyer" at Attica, and he frequently advised the rebel committee on legal technicalities. — Russell Oswald, *Attica*, p. 26, 1972
- [A]ll the cons went ape, everybody writing papers, and the jailhouse lawyers were ridin' high talking all that jive about searching and seizing illegal evidence. — Edwin Torres, *Carlito's Way*, p. 50, 1975
- I don't know if you are listening to any of these jailhouse lawyers. — Miguel Pinero, *Short Eyes*, p. 107, 1975
- The guy I shot's got a brother was in Jackson, was in Marquette, and learned a few things there talking to the jailhouse lawyer. — Elmore Leonard, *Split Images*, p. 28, 1981

jailhouse punk *noun*

a man who becomes a passive homosexual while in prison *US, 1963*

- A common result of such experience is that when the prisoner graduates into the adult prison he arrives accompanied by the reputation of a "jailhouse punk." — Vincent Hallinan, *A Lion in Court*, p. 305, 1963
- The hacks would hear about it and they would put Tico on A1 tier where all the faggots were, and he'd be a jailhouse punk. — James Trupin, *In Prison*, p. 114, 1975
- "If you don't stand up to them now, they're gonna go ahead and fuck you and you're gonna end up a jailhouse punk." — Georgelle Hirliman, *The Hate Factory*, p. 42, 1982

jailhouse turnout; penitentiary turnout *noun*

a previously heterosexual person who becomes homosexual in prison *US, 1965*

- The "penitentiary turnout" refers to homosexuality in the prison because heterosexual relationships are not available. — Rose Giallombardo, *Society of Women*, p. 123, 1966
- Your jailhouse turnouts are treated like a machine; when someone wants sex and they haven't got a free-world queen of their own then they go to the jailhouse turnouts. — Bruce Jackson, *In the Life*, p. 365, 1972
- — *Male Swinger Number 3*, p. 47, 1981: "The complete gay dictionary"

jail-wise *adjective*

sophisticated with respect to survival in prison *US, 1922*

- I was jail-wise in picking my friends. — Piri Thomas, *Down These Mean Streets*, p. 257, 1967
- I wasn't what you would call jail-wise or nothing like that but I knew how to take care of myself. — Darrell Steffensmeier, *The Fence*, p. 39, 1986

jake *noun*

1 Jamaica ginger, a potent and dangerous illegally manufactured alcohol *US, 1923*

- — Jerry Robertson, *Oil Slanguage*, p. 72, 1954

2 a person identified as a potential crime victim *US, 1997*

- Prosecutors allege that Everybody talks about and Lopez were drinking in Pioneer Square with several other people that morning when someone said they'd spotted a "Jake." — *Seattle Times*, p. B3, 13th February 1997

3 a uniformed police officer *US, 1987*

- — Carsten Stroud, *Close Pursuit*, p. 273, 1987
- Every day I escape from jakes givin' chase, sellin' base. — RZA, *The Wu-Tang Manual*, p. 152, 2005

4 a Jamaican *US, 1991*

- A real street name for a real Jake, a homeboy in his late twenties who you know lives maybe a block or so from the Fullards. — David Simon, *Homicide*, p. 613, 1991
- [T]he Jakes are gone, melting into the city's warm darkness. — David Simon and Edward Burns, *The Corner*, p. 220, 1997

jake *verb*

to feign illness or injury *US, 1946*

- No one left his team in midyear. He accused Johnson of jaking it. He called him names. He absolutely refused him permission to go. "I never jaked in my whole life," Johnson said. — Robert Whiting, *You Gotta Have Wa*, p. 165, 1989

jake *adjective*

honest, upright, equitable, correct *US, 1914*

- He had enough money to marry one, and with her teaching too, they could get on jake, save, have a little apartment, and they ought to be happy. — James T. Farrell, *Saturday Night*, p. 26, 1947
- Everything's jake here. — Jim Thompson, *Savage Night*, p. 38, 1953
- "He's quite a nice person." "You can say that shit again," I spoke, pulling her giggling body in to me. "He's jake with me." — Jim Carroll, *Forced Entries*, p. 98, 1987
- When he was finished, he took a machine gun as evidence, promising to return it in a few days if everything was jake. — Kim Rich, *Johnny's Girl*, p. 165, 1993

jake-leg *adjective*

unschooled, untrained *US, 2004*

A variant of the more common **JACKLEG**.

- She divorced him and moved back to Fort Worth and went to work for Red Taggert, the jake-leg criminal lawyer downtown who likes to keep killers and armed robbers out of jail. — Dan Jenkins, *The Money-Whipped Steer-Job Three-Jack Give-Up Artist*, p. 11, 2001

jakey *adjective*

odd looking *US, 1964*

- — *American Speech*, p. 235, October 1964: "Student slang in Hays, Kansas"

jam *noun*

1 a recorded song *US, 1937*

- Fuck dat honky shit. Got to get me some motown jams, dig it? — *Platoon*, 1986
- I push it the way it is, the record'll get some nods, yeah, it's pretty good stuff, slightly different, but you won't get the buzz you need—hey shit, this jam reaches out and moves you. — Elmore Leonard, *Be Cool*, p. 280, 1999
- Radio won't even play my jam / 'Cause I am whatever you say I am[.] — Eminem (Marshall Mathers), *The Way I Am*, 2000

2 a party with loud music *US, 1993*

- This is an all-the-way-live ghetto jam. — *Menace II Society*, 1993
- There was park jams going on. — *A2Z [quoting KRS-One, 1994]*, p. 56, 1995
- The high point at the jam [was] where everyone starts battling each other, trying to do the dopest moves and get the most props. — Alex Ogg, *The Hip Hop Years [quoting 'Crazy Legs' Richie Colon]*, p. 16, 1999

3 cocaine *US, 1972*

- If that man goes out and does a hundred dollars jam a night, that is her fault. — Christina and Richard Milner, *Black Players*, p. 85, 1972

4 sex *US, 1949*

- Everybody plays jam in that park, gets their trim. — Hal Ellson, *Duke*, p. 61, 1949

5 the vagina *US, 1980*

- — Edith A. Folb, *runnin' down some lines*, p. 243, 1980

6 in homosexual usage, any heterosexual man *US, 1981*

An abbreviation of "*just a man*."

- — *Male Swinger Number 3*, p. 47, 1981: "The complete gay dictionary"

7 the corpse of a person who has died with massive injuries *US, 1986–1987*

- — *Maledicta*, p. 180, Summer/Winter 1986–1987: "Sexual slang: prostitutes, pedophiles, flagellators, transvestites, and necrophiles"

8 a fight, especially a gang fight *US, 1992*

- — William K. Bentley and James M. Corbett, *Prison Slang*, p. 90, 1992

9 a gathering of skateboarders *US, 1976*

- — Albert Cassorla, *The Skateboarder's Bible*, p. 201, 1976

10 petty smuggling *US, 1956*

- — *American Speech*, p. 96, May 1956: "Smugglers' argot in the Southwest"

jam *verb*

1 to rob *US, 1992*

- "I remember the first time she jammed a guy. I was hiding in the closet, and after we got the money we went to another room in the hotel[.]" — Pete Earley, *The Hot House*, p. 191, 1992

2 to play music with others, improvising *US, 1935*

- We hung out on the beach all day long, jamming our heads off, while the people gathered around us like sandflies. — Mezz Mezzrow, *Really the Blues*, p. 87, 1946
- We have a combo going at the school and I sometimes jam in Springfield and Worcester. — Nat Hentoff, *Jazz Country*, p. 139, 1965
- Jamming the next day we got totally shitfaced[.] — Lester Bangs, *Psychotic Reactions and Carburetor Dung*, p. 219, 1977

3 to have sex *US, 1972*

- — Robert A. Wilson, *Playboy's Book of Forbidden Words*, p. 149, 1972
- I knew what a train was. It was what happened when a bunch of guys got together and jammed the same girl. — Nathan McCall, *Makes Me Wanna Holler*, p. 42, 1994

4 to coerce, to threaten, to pressure *US, 1971*

- Meanwhile, the Puerto Ricans been gettin' jammed since the forties and ain't nobody said nothin'. — Edwin Torres, *Carlito's Way*, p. 5, 1975
- The big problem was the big "If" involved with trying to jam fifteen or twenty dudes who did a lot of jamming themselves. — Odie Hawkins, *Chicago Hustle*, p. 39, 1977
- Cameron, I'm sorry. I didn't mean to jam you. — *Ferris Bueller's Day Off*, 1986

5 to leave quickly; to travel at high speeds *US, 1965*

- There is nothing on the road—with the exception of a few sports or racing cars—that can catch an artfully hopped-up outlaw 74 as long as there's room to "jam it" or "screw it on." — Hunter S. Thompson, *Hell's Angels*, p. 97, 1966
- As soon as the last shot was fired, he threw himself back into the car. "C'mon man, jam it!!!" he screamed to Buddy. — Donald Goines, *Inner City Hoodlum*, p. 153, 1975
- Heather, I feel awful, like I'm going to throw up. Can we jam, please? — *Heathers*, 1988
- [H]e can keep up with me on my skates and I'm jamming through the crowds of people like a hell cat. — Francesca Lia Block, *Missing Angel Juan*, p. 299, 1993

6 in gambling, to cheat (another player) *US, 1997*

- Poor Soapy got caught jammin' some players at the Purple Tiger, which was a little card club down on the wharf, by the pier. — Stephen Cannell, *King Con*, pp. 3–4, 1997

7 in surfing, to obstruct or block another surfer's ride *US, 1967*

- — Midget Farrelly and Craig McGregor, *The Surfing Life*, p. 191, 1967

8 to surf with speed and intensity *US, 1988*

- — Michael V. Anderson, *The Bad, Rad, Not to Forget Way Cool Beach and Surf Discriptionary*, p. 9, 1988

jam *adjective*

heterosexual *US, 1935*

Eventually supplanted by **STRAIGHT**.

- — Donald Webster Cory and John P. LeRoy, *The Homosexual and His Society*, p. 265, 1963: "A lexicon of homosexual slang"
- — *Fact*, p. 26, January–February 1965

JAM

used as Internet shorthand to mean "*just a minute*" *US, 1997*

- — Andy Ihnatko, *Cyberspeak*, p. 106, 1997

Jamaican assault vehicle *noun*

any sports utility vehicle *US, 1997*

New York police slang; SUV's are favored by Jamaican criminals.

- — Samuel M. Katz, *Anytime Anywhere*, p. 388, 1997: "The extremely unofficial and completely off-the-record NYPD/ESU truck-two glossary"

Jamaican bomber *noun*

a large marijuana cigarette, made with what is claimed to be Jamaican marijuana *US, 1997*

- — Vann Wesson, *Generation X Field Guide and Lexicon*, p. 98, 1997

Jamaican switch *noun*

a type of confidence swindle *US, 1973*

There are many variations of the swindle, but the common element is the swindler pretending to be a foreigner with a lot of money in need of help.

- He used to hang around downtown and work with a Gypsy dame on pigeon drops and once in a while a Jamaican switch. — Joseph Wambaugh, *The Blue Knight*, p. 158, 1973
- Police warned residents of South Los Angeles to beware of an elaborate fraud scheme involving suspects who feign a Jamaican or other foreign accent and pretend to be worried about holding money in a big city. The so-called "Jamaican Switch" is usually aimed at elderly people[.] — *Los Angeles Times*, p. 2, 23rd May 1985
- "Jamaican switch" is a con played by a person who fakes a foreign accent and tells a trusting individual he has a sum of money saved from his country but doesn't trust U.S. banks[.] — *Daily Oklahoman*, p. 25, 15th December 1996
- Roy and Frank plan to spring the old "Jamaican switch" on a wealth mark ("you're the rope, I'm inside") even as Roy experiments with his new parental role. — *The Village Voice*, p. 79, 16th September 2003

jam band *noun*

a musical band known for long improvisations *US, 1981*

- It will include the well-known pianists Marian McPartland and Dorothy Donegan, a quintet of women led by the saxophonist Willene Barton, Melba Liston and Company, an ensemble of four women and three men, and a women's jam band. — *New York Times*, p. C14, 3rd July 1981
- First came the announcement that the mightiest jam band of them all, Phish, will end a 21-year run at the end of their summer tour[.] — *Guitar Player*, p. 30, 1st September 2004

jammed up *adjective*

1 under great pressure; in trouble *US, 1973*

- Phillip's wife didn't know how jammed up he was. — Leonard Shecter and William Phillips, *On the Pad*, p. 48, 1973
- [H]e'd told Henry he would not help if Henry got jammed up. — Nicholas Pileggi, *Wise Guy*, p. 264, 1985

2 experiencing a drug overdose *US, 1971*

- — Eugene Landy, *The Underground Dictionary*, p. 111, 1971

jammer *noun*

1 in American casinos, a skilled and adaptable dealer *US, 1985*

- — Steve Kuriscak, *Casino Talk*, p. 33, 1985

2 a popular, trend-setting, respected person *US, 1982*

Hawaiian youth usage.

- — Douglas Simonson, *Pidgin to da Max Hana Hou*, 1982

jammies *noun*

pajamas *US, 1967*

- I'll bet it takes you longer to get into your jammies at night than it does to throw on that blue suit[.] — Joseph Wambaugh, *The New Centurions*, p. 52, 1970
- A dinner jacket! Wuddya think, he was wearing his damn jammies! — *Raising Arizona*, 1987
- And I in my jammies with the holes in the toes / had just sipped my latte and started to doze. — *Seattle Times*, p. A14, 25th December 1992
- It might be a matter of waiting until you hear that familiar rumble coming down the street, then running out in your puka shirt jammies with 10 bucks in an envelope to give to the driver. — *Honolulu Advertiser*, p. 1B, 30th December 2003

jamming; jammin' *adjective*

excellent *US, 1982*

- — Douglas Simonson, *Pidgin to da Max: Hana Hou*, 1982
- — Connie Eble (Editor), *UNC-CH Campus Slang*, p. 5, Spring 1982

jammy-jams; jam-jams *noun*

pajamas *US, 1976*

- If you got her kitty outfit off, you might as well've put her jammy-jams on, she was through for the evening. — Elmore Leonard, *Swag*, p. 137, 1976
- Now you caught me in my jam-jams. — Joseph Wambaugh, *The Secrets of Harry Bright*, p. 247, 1985

jamoke *noun*

1 a despicable or ignorant person *US, 1946*

- "I don't think bringing in them jamokes was such a hot idea." — George Higgins, *The Digger's Game*, p. 41, 1973
- When he had calmed down, Mazilli nodded in the direction that Touhey had gone. "Fuckin' jamoke," he said. — Richard Price, *Clockers*, p. 104, 1992
- And the poor jamoke's T-shirt keeps threatening to soak up this nasty fluid. — Anthony Petkovich, *The X Factory*, p. 195, 1997
- This jamoke'll go where his mother tells him. — David Chase, *The Sopranos: Selected Scripts from Three Seasons*, p. 137, 20th September 1999

2 coffee *US, 1895*

- — Jerry Robertson, *Oil Slanguage*, p. 72, 1954
- [L]ike Dixon, who is able to sip the most degradedly awful pos's-end poison and yet beam like an Idiot, "Mm-m m! Best Jamoke west o' the Alleghenies!" — Thomas Pynchon, *Mason & Dixon*, p. 467, 1997

jampot *noun*

in homosexual usage, the anus and rectum *US, 1941*

- — *Male Swinger Number 3*, p. 47, 1981: "The complete gay dictionary"

jams *noun*

1 pajamas *US, 1973*

- "Oh, hi, Nick," said Dwayne, exhibiting everything except embarrassment. "Whatcha got those 'jams on for?" — C.D. Payne, *Youth in Revolt*, p. 272, 1993

2 long shorts *US, 1992*

- Most of the black inmates sitting in the bleachers were dressed in "jams," long shorts made from gray and blue sweatpants chopped off at the knee. — Pete Earley, *The Hot House*, p. 92, 1992

3 pants *US, 1968*

- — Collin Baker et al., *College Undergraduate Slang Study Conducted at Brown University*, p. 144, 1968

jam session *noun*

1 a gathering of musicians who play in a collective, improvized fashion *US, 1933*

- I think the term "jam session" originated right in that cellar. Long before that, of course, the colored boys used to get together and play for kicks, but those were mostly private sessions, strictly for professional musicians[.] — Mezz Mezzrow, *Really the Blues*, p. 148, 1946
- I'm arranging a jam session to make an album for Jerry Newman's record company, with Allen Eager on tenor[.] — Jack Kerouac, *Letter to Neal Cassady*, p. 471, April 1955
- It is probable that the elongated Mexico was the father of what today is known as the jam session. — Robert Sylvester, *No Cover Charge*, p. 48, 1956
- [M]usicians would come to some prearranged Harlem after-hours spot and have thirty- and forty-piece jam sessions that would last into the next day. — Malcolm X and Alex Haley, *The Autobiography of Malcolm X*, p. 83, 1964

2 an informal, unstructured group discussion *US, 1963*

- Would you want your mother hanging around one of your jam sessions? — Dick Clark, *To Goof or Not to Goof*, p. 113, 1963

jam shot *noun*

the use of an explosive around the edge of a safe's door *US, 1972*

- There is the jam shot which is around the edge. You soap up the crack and make a cup on the top and pour your nitroglycerin in this little cup. — Harry King, *Box Man*, p. 34, 1972

jam up *verb*

1 to cause trouble; to place in a troubling situation *US, 1836*

- He took a job. And he fumbled it. Now he's jammed up. Jammed up bad. — *Gone in 60 Seconds*, 2000

2 to confront *US, 1992*

- — William K. Bentley and James M. Corbett, *Prison Slang*, p. 93, 1992

jam-up *adjective*

1 excellent, pleasing *US, 1823*

- It made my smeller tingle, got me scared and excited me too, put me on edge – it promised a rare jam-up kick, some once-in-a-lifetime thrill. — Mezz Mezzrow, *Really the Blues*, p. 97, 1946
- It was jam-up. Jelly-tight. It was, it was a really a kick joint. — Bruce Jackson, *In the Life*, p. 122, 1972

2 in pool, playing well and luckily *US, 1990*

- — Steve Rushin, *Pool Cool*, p. 17, 1990

Jane; jane *noun*

1 a woman, a girlfriend *US, 1865*

Generic use of popular name. Also "Janie."

- In the old days when Nolan's dance hall was here on the corner, every decent-looking jane who came to the Sunday-afternoon dances was gone on him. — James T. Farrell, *Saturday Night*, p. 30, 1947
- One of the sights of Washington is the outpouring of the janes at five o'clock. — Jack Lait and Lee Mortimer, *Washington Confidential*, p. 78, 1951
- Come here little Queenie... or ah / Has the cat got your tongue? My best shot for a C note baby she said / That's why this Janie's got a gun — Aerosmith, *Black Cherry*, 1973

2 a female customer of a prostitute *US, 1969*

- Some of the "johns" and "janes" who liked to be watched, liked to be watched in a different way. — Joey V., *Portrait of Joey*, p. 115, 1969

3 cocaine *US, 1997*

- They called it "girl" or "Jane" or "Missy" in feminine contrast to "boy" or "John" or "Mister" for king heroin. — David Simon and Edward Burns, *The Corner*, p. 62, 1997

Jane Q. Public *noun*

a prototypical woman *US, 1977*

- Joan's jewelers had copied it so that Jane Q. Public could have her own version of the tiny, enameled egg charms[.] — Mary Jane Clark, *Do You Promise Not To Tell?*, p. 98, 1999

Jane Wayne Day *noun*

a day on which wives of US Marines go through a series of exercises designed to give them a sense of what their husbands go through *US, 1989*

- Shanna Reed got a major workout for tonight's Major Dad when her character, Polly, joins other Marine wives in Jane Wayne Day. — *USA Today*, 23rd October 1989

janfu *noun*

chaos caused by both the Army and Navy *US, 1944*

- "Looks to me more like a janfu," West said. "Janfu? I ain't heard that one before." "Joint Army-Navy Fuck-Up," Richardson put in blandly. — H. Jay Riker, *Silver Star*, p. 161, 1993

jang *noun*

the penis *US, 1972*

- — Helen Dahlskog (Editor), *A Dictionary of Contemporary and Colloquial Usage*, p. 34, 1972

janitor *noun*

an ordinary infantry soldier *US, 1991*

Gulf war usage.

- — *American Speech*, p. 392, Winter 1991: "Among the new words"

jank *verb*

to steal *US, 2001*

- — Rick Ayers (Editor), *Slang Dictionary*, p. 11, 2001

jankity *adjective*

old, broken down *US, 2004*

- — Rick Ayers (Editor), *Berkeley High Slang Dictionary*, p. 28, 2004

janky *adjective*

broken, dysfunctional, inoperative *US, 1999*

- Janky (adj.)—Cheap, raggedy or just improper in some sort of way. — *Corpus Christi (Texas) Caller-Times*, p. H1, 24th October 1999
- "Lou got all kind a janky shit goin' on with you." — Stephen J. Cannell, *White Sister*, p. 154, 2006

Jap *noun*

an attack from behind and/or without warning *US, 1962*

- Second kind is a "Jap." That's when a group of guys, two guys or three guys, go down in a different club's territory, get in fast, beat up one or two guys and get out. — Lewis Yablonsky, *The Violent Gang*, p. 78, 1962

JAP *noun*

a spoiled Jewish girl or woman; a Jewish-American princess *US, 1972*

- The resident chaplain is a shy rabbi, one of the sexually active girls describes herself smugly as a Jewish American Princess and remnants of excruciating ethnic humor litter the comic junkheap. The parents of the J.A.P. are exploited for kneejerk ridicule[.] — *Washington Post*, p. D4, 26th May 1980
- Trent stops by and tells me about how "a couple of hysterical J.a.p.'s" in Bel Air have seen what they called some kind of monster, talk of a werewolf. — Bret Easton Ellis, *Less Than Zero*, p. 77, 1985
- Q: What do J.A.P.'s most often make for dinner? A: Reservations. — Leo Rosten, *The Joys of Yinglish*, p. 250, 1989

- He laid romantic bullshit onto 17-year-old JAPs from Great Neck[.] — Josh Friedman, *When Sex Was Dirty*, p. 37, 2005

Jap *noun*

1 a Japanese person *US, 1854*

Derogatory.

- Jack, the guy who said he'd give his right arm for a friend and did when he stopped a bastard of a Jap from slitting me in two. — Mickey Spillane, *I, The Jury*, p. 5, 1947
- But then came the influx of Japs from the West Coast states. — Jack Lait and Lee Mortimer, *New York Confidential*, pp. 77–78, 1948
- I wished I were a Denver Mexican, or even a poor overworked Jap, anything but what I was[.] — Jack Kerouac, *On the Road*, p. 180, 1957
- And I even liked the Japs. Whenever you waved to them they'd bow a little bit. — Joseph Wambaugh, *Floaters*, p. 98, 1996

2 someone who attacks from behind and/or without warning *US, 1949*

- But if you're a Jap or a turkey or you're going to punk out it's going to be bad stuff for you. — Hal Ellson, *Duke*, p. 31, 1949

3 an unannounced test *US, 1967*

- — Collin Baker et al., *College Undergraduate Slang Study Conducted at Brown University*, p. 144, 1968

jap *verb*

to attack without warning *US, 1942*

An allusion to the Japanese attack at Pearl Harbor.

- They going to Jap us if they get the chance, only we ain't going to let them. — Hal Ellson, *Duke*, p. 76, 1949
- [O]ne side or another may at any sudden moment "jap" an unwary alien. — Harrison E. Salisbury, *The Shook-up Generation*, p. 23, 1958
- "Look out, ya gonna get japped," she shouted. — Piri Thomas, *Down These Mean Streets*, p. 53, 1967
- "Well, of course the Times japped them, but they expected that." — Malcolm Braly, *The Protector*, p. 90, 1979

Jap *adjective*

Japanese *US, 1869*

Unkind.

- It was that crazy, wild-eyed, unleashed hatred that the first Jap bomb on Pearl Harbor let loose in a flood. — Chester Himes, *If He Hollers Let Him Go*, p. 4, 1945

Jap crap *noun*

imports from Japan, especially motorcycles *US, 1986*

- His shop, Kicked Back Motor Works, is a mama-and-pop operation, where he and Sandy repair and rebuild Harleys and only Harleys. "No Jap Crap," reads his business card. — *People*, p. 82, 4th August 1986
- Epithets such as "rice burner," and "Jap crap" are frequent. — *Orlando Sentinel Tribune*, p. A1, 28th February 1993

japland *noun*

Japan *US, 1919*

- So, as everybody knows, what with the whole whirl economy o' Russia 'n them dwarf Chink bastards from Japland goin' down the tubes hourly[.] — L.D. Brodsky, *Leaky Tubs*, p. 33, 2001

Jappo *noun*

a Japanese person *US, 1942*

- Every five minutes it seems that someone white in the movie is calling the Japanese "Jappos." — Cara Lockwood, *Dixieland Sushi*, p. 37, 2005

jap scrap *noun*

a motorcycle manufactured in Japan *US, 1988*

- — Connie Eble (Editor), *UNC-CH Campus Slang*, p. 6, Spring 1988
- — Paladin Press, *Inside Look at Outlaw Motorcycle Gangs*, p. 36, 1992

Jap-slaps *noun*

a sandal that is not bound to the foot, usually worn around swimming pools or at the beach *US, 1982*

Hawaiian youth usage.

- — Douglas Simonson, *Pidgin to da Max: Hana Hou*, 1982

jar *verb*

▶ jar the deck

to wake up and get up *US, 1962*

- — *American Speech*, p. 288, December 1962: "Marine Corps slang"

jar dealer *noun*

a drug dealer who sells pills in large quantities *US, 1971*

- — Edward R. Bloomquist, *Marijuana*, p. 343, 1971

jar ears *noun*
a United States Marine *US, 1985*
- He insisted upon calling them "jar heads" and "jar ears." — Nicholas Pileggi, *Wise Guy*, p. 44, 1985

jarhead *noun*
1 a US Marine *US, 1943*
Originally an army mule, then a member of the US Army, especially a member of the football team (1931).
- "And then pickets at home scream bloody murder when the jarheads don't hold their fire because of the women." — Elaine Shepard, *The Doom Pussy*, p. 64, 1967
- The jar-heads were there for three days playing war. — Darryl Ponicsan, *The Last Detail*, p. 15, 1970
- "I hear there're so many fruit marines being busted, the jarheads at Camp Pendleton are afraid to be seen eating a banana," said Ranatti. — Joseph Wambaugh, *The New Centurions*, p. 178, 1970
2 a habitual user of crack cocaine *US, 1993*
- — Peter Johnson, *Dictionary of Street Alcohol and Drug Terms*, p. 101, 1993

jasper *noun*
1 a lesbian or a bisexual woman *US, 1954*
Robert Wilson hypothesises that the Reverend John Jasper, a pious man of God, lent his name in this good-is-bad etymology.
- 2 got seriously hurt and a jasper cut 1 on the arm with a bottle. — Clarence Cooper Jr., *The Farm*, p. 139, 1967
- Eventually, the craftier of the two jaspers wore the doll down and turned her out. They had to keep the secret of their romance from the other jasper because she was tough and built like a football player. — Iceberg Slim (Robert Beck), *Pimp*, p. 44, 1969
- She was a three-way wench, played Jasper in a pinch / And took 'em around the horn. — Dennis Wepman et al., *The Life*, p. 81, 1976
- One jasper even cut another one over me! — Clarence Major, *All-Night Visitors*, p. 212, 1998
2 a person of no consequence *UK, 1896*
From a stereotypical rural name.
- A week later I received a letter from some fuck head called "Lon" of Research and man, like this jasper really poured the shit out thick. — *Screw*, p. 13, 27th June 1969
- Dot is just as cold, or colder, than any jasper we could put on the case. — Donald Goines, *Black Gangster*, p. 124, 1977

jasper broad *noun*
a lesbian or bisexual woman *US, 1972*
- You ever hear of what they call a "jasper broad?" That is one who is bisexual, she likes both men and women. — Bruce Jackson, *In the Life*, p. 178, 1972

java *noun*
coffee *US, 1850*
- They duck out for smokes at the same time and have their crullers and java in the same lunchroom or greasy spoon. — Jack Lait and Lee Mortimer, *New York Confidential*, p. 142, 1948
- "They went into a shack to heat up some java and got a direct hit from an 88." — Audie Murphy, *To Hell and Back*, p. 106, 1949
- Right up the street under the el was an all-night hash joint, and what I needed was a couple mugs of good black java to bring me around. — Mickey Spillane, *My Gun is Quick*, p. 6, 1950
- Foxes young and old sitting on front porches and in back yards along with dogs, cats, chickens and ducks, eating boiled shrimp, chitterlings and drinking java[.] — Steve Cannon, *Groove, Bang, and Jive Around*, p. 154, 1969

jaw *verb*
1 to talk, especially in an argumentative or scolding fashion *UK, 1748*
- The boys were jawing in the office by the stove and the cash register[.] — Jack Kerouac, *Letter to Neal Cassady*, p. 296, 10th January 1951
- It was a slow morning for my friend and we jawed around. — Clancy Sigal, *Going Away*, p. 165, 1961
- Several months passed before I drove by the Conqueror's favorite bar and decided to drop in and jaw a bit with him. — Iceberg Slim (Robert Beck), *The Naked Soul of Iceberg Slim*, p. 126, 1971
- He stared at the man's back as he took his place on the fringe of a circle of dudes arguing, jawing at each other, as usual. What else was there to do in the county jail, after the watery oatmeal, crusty toast, and slimy coffee? — Odie Hawkins, *Chicago Hustle*, p. 103, 1977

2 in pool, to hit a ball that bounces off the sides of a pocket without dropping *US, 1990*
- — Steve Rushin, *Pool Cool*, p. 17, 1990

jaw artist *noun*
a person skilled at the giving of oral sex *US, 1972*
- — Robert A. Wilson, *Playboy's Book of Forbidden Words*, p. 150, 1972

jawblock *verb*
to chat, to talk *US, 1946*
- I used to see Scarface around there and jawblock with him sometimes. — Mezz Mezzrow, *Really the Blues*, p. 24, 1946
- Leo was in no mood for jawblocking but he sat down anyhow. — Bernard Wolfe, *The Late Risers*, p. 242, 1954

jawfest *noun*
1 a long, aimless conversation *US, 1915*
- — Joseph E. Ragen and Charles Finston, *Inside the World's Toughest Prison*, p. 805, 1962: "Penitentiary and underworld glossary"
2 a prolonged session of oral sex *US, 1967*
- — Dale Gordon, *The Dominion Sex Dictionary*, p. 93, 1967

jawflap *noun*
a gossip *US, 1952*
- First thing you know, that Steerman be back gettin' us busy with one of those Village jawflaps make you feel like you sat through a bad double feature eatin' sourballs. — George Mandel, *Flee the Angry Strangers*, p. 78, 1952

jaws *noun*
1 the buttocks *US, 2002*
- — Gary K. Farlow, *Prison-ese*, p. 34, 2002
2 in dominoes, the 6–6 piece *US, 1959*
- — Dominic Armanino, *Dominoes*, p. 17, 1959

jay *noun*
1 a bank *US, 1950*
An abbreviation of JUG (a bank).
- — Hyman E. Goldin et al., *Dictionary of American Underworld Lingo*, p. 110, 1950
2 coffee *US, 1962*
Probably an abbreviation of JAVA.
- — Joseph E. Ragen and Charles Finston, *Inside the World's Toughest Prison*, p. 805, 1962: "Penitentiary and underworld glossary"

jay-naked *adjective*
completely naked *US, 1975*
- I been taken for spook, wop, and one faggot (used to come to the door jay-naked when I was delivering clothes for a cleaner) said I was Armenian. — Edwin Torres, *Carlito's Way*, p. 19, 1975

jazz *noun*
1 nonsense *US, 1951*
The term jazz was first used by a San Francisco sportswriter in 1912 to describe a pitch, the "jass curve," and then applied to a new form of music in 1916.
- "Don't hand me that jazz," said the wolf impatiently. — Steve Allen, *Bop Fables*, p. 22, 1955
- The lawyers stepped forward to cop pleas for another chance, mercy and all that jazz. — Piri Thomas, *Down These Mean Streets*, p. 246, 1967
- You hear a lot of jazz about Soul Food. — Eldridge Cleaver, *Soul on Ice*, p. 29, 1968
2 stuff *US, 1951*
- They want him to make the radio and the video and all that jazz—he can't make all that jazz. — William "Lord" Buckley, *The Nazz*, 1951
- I could walk out this fuckin' store with half a shelf fulla this jazz if I wanted to. — Odie Hawkins, *Ghetto Sketches*, p. 125, 1972
3 semen *US, 1932*
Those who have seriously studied the etymology of "jazz" concur that it almost certainly derives from "jasm," a variant of "jism." Examples of "jasm," however, meaning semen, have not been found, leaving the connection as after-the-fact, not before.
- Momo wipes the jazz off Jasmin. — Anthony Petkovich, *The X Factory*, p. 190, 1997

jazz *verb*
1 to have sex with someone *US, 1918*
- I dont jazz cops. — Jim Thompson, *The Killer Inside*, p. 10, 1952
- Hey, Austin boy-ee-ee, let's jazz her. — John Clellon Holmes, *The Horn*, p. 110, 1958
- I say, Baby this daddy was not drinkin', he was on top a me, jazzin'! — Robert Gover, *Here Goes Kitten*, p. 117, 1964

- De Boya does that to a spray-painter, what's he gonna do to a guy he finds out's been jazzing his wife, room one sixty-seven the Holiday Inn. — Elmore Leonard, *Cat Chaser*, p. 206, 1982

2 to drug *US, 1973*

- "So they jazzed the hore with an overdose, and it finally just laid down and died." — Vincent Teresa, *My Life in the Mafia*, p. 162, 1973

jazz around *verb*
to cause trouble, to annoy *US, 1917*

- We don't want no jazzing around with them. — Hal Ellson, *Duke*, p. 81, 1949

jazzbo *noun*

1 a fervent jazz enthusiast *US, 1921*

- Though powerless to dispense club dates, the dopers has the power of youth, looks, exuberance, suicidal tendencies, and the PR edge of being hotshot jazzbos. — Larry Rivers, *What Did I Do?*, p. 22, 1992

2 a black person *US, 1918*

- And he slowed down the car for all of us to turn and look at the old jazzbo moaning along. — Jack Kerouac, *On the Road*, p. 115, 1957

jazzed *adjective*
excited, enthusiastic *US, 1918*

- I'm so fuckin' jazzed! — *Jerry Maguire*, 1996

jazzed up *adjective*
pregnant *US, 1973*

- Another seventeen-year-old gal, one of the hippies' hussies, was jazzed up, and Everett Wade was dutybound to send her to a home. — Joe Eszterhas, *Charlie Simpson's Apocalypse*, p. 136, 1973

jazzing *noun*
sex *US, 1965*

- They were lying, fat cheeks pressed together, smiling, and the light gave them a sweet cherubic look now, as they rested up for the next jazzing. — Sol Yurrick, *The Warriors*, p. 218, 1965

jazzy *adjective*
showy; ostentatious *US, 1923*

- We've got to go and get our hair done. Get henna'd up real jazzy for Connie boy. — Bernard Wolfe, *The Late Risers*, p. 132, 1954
- I could buy the jazziest board this side of the great divide. — Frederick Kohner, *Gidget*, p. 23, 1957

J-bird *noun*

1 a person in or recently released from jail *US, 1971*
An abbreviation of JAILBIRD.

- — Eugene Landy, *The Underground Dictionary*, p. 112, 1971

2 in a deck of playing cards, a jack or knave *US, 1951*
An elaboration of J.

- — *American Speech*, p. 99, May 1951: "The vocabulary of poker"
- — Albert H. Morehead, *The Complete Guide to Winning Poker*, p. 266, 1967

JBM *adjective*
in horse racing, said of a horse that has only won one race *US, 1976*
An abbreviation of "*just beaten maiden.*"

- — Tom Ainslie, *Ainslie's Complete Guide to Thoroughbred Racing*, p. 333, 1976

JC *noun*
overt racial segregation *US, 1967*
An abbreviation of JIM CROW.

- It had been Jim Crow for much too long, and if J.C. was virulent in the nation's capital, did it not have the excuse to run rampant throughout the country? — John Williams, *The Man Who Cried I Am*, p. 296, 1967

J-cat *noun*
a person who is more crazy than eccentric *US, 1997*

- — Jim Crotty, *How to Talk American*, p. 353, 1997
- We called these men "J-cats." It's slang for Category J, the official term used by prison staff to identify inmates in need of mental-health care. — Tookie Williams, *Life in Prison*, p. 31, 1998

JCL *noun*
used as an abbreviation of *Johnny Come Lately US, 1942*

- In the interval, Towers had to endure seeing combat commands going to "JCLs" [Johnny-come-latelys, senior officers who entered flying school late in life] and, even worse, to nonflyers like Spruance. — Walter Boyne, *Clash of Titans*, p. 284, 1995

JC maneuver *noun*
in aviation, any desperate evasive tactic *US, 1979*

- It was another of the Hun's "JC maneuvers"—one that caused the pilot involuntarily to explode over the radio with a "Jesus Christ." — Robert Coram, *Boyd*, p. 79, 2002

J C water-walkers *noun*
sandals *US, 1970*
An allusion to Jesus Christ (JC) walking on water, presumably in sandals.

- — *Current Slang*, p. 20, Spring 1970

JD *noun*

1 a juvenile delinquent *US, 1956*

- None of us wanted to be lawbreakers and we would have been shocked silly had anyone called us j.d.'s. — Dick Clark, *To Goof or Not to Goof*, p. 181, 1963
- In my book, they range next to J.D.'s. — Frederick Kohner, *The Affairs of Gidget*, p. 52, 1963
- Greasers. You know, like hoods. JD's. — S.E. Hinton, *The Outsiders*, p. 85, 1967
- Johnny Havilland has heard from the J.D.'s at school that an auto graveyard on the edge of Ossining niggertown is a chrome treasure trove. — James Ellroy, *Because the Night*, p. 514, 1984

2 Jack Daniels™, a brand name Tennessee sourmash whiskey *US, 1981*
Initialism.

- [A] JD and Coke[.] — *GQ*, p. 68, July 2001
- [P]lus J.D. on the rocks and Crown Royal straight for people serious about their liquor. — Peter Fenton, *Eyeing the Flash*, p. 151, 2005

JD card *noun*
a police citation issued to a transgressing juvenile, requiring participation in a Police Athletic League team to avoid incarceration *US, 1972*

- Cool Breeze lived somewhere in Harlem, and had gotten his JD card at about the same time as Kenny. — Emmett Grogan, *Ringolevio*, p. 13, 1972

Jean *noun*
a female customer of a prostitute *US, 1976*
An extrapolation of JOHN.

- No Jean or John this whore couldn't con / 'Cause that trick was never born. — Dennis Wepman et al., *The Life*, p. 81, 1976

jeans at half mast *noun*
engaged in the passive role in anal sex *US, 1950*

- — Hyman E. Goldin et al., *Dictionary of American Underworld Lingo*, p. 110, 1950

Jedi master *noun*
in the language of hang gliding, an experienced, expert flier *US, 1992*

- — Erik Fair, *California Thrill Sports*, p. 328, 1992

jeep *noun*
an inexperienced enlisted man *US, 1970*
Air Force usage during the Vietnam war.

- — *Current Slang*, p. 16, Summer 1970

Jeep girl *noun*
a Chinese prostitute attached to US armed forces *US, 1946*

- — *American Speech*, p. 74, February 1946: "Some words of war and peace from 1945"
- American servicemen also appear prominently on the scene and contribute significantly to the general chaos: an American jeep with a "jeep girl" and a GI holding a huge liquor bottle. — Hong Zhang, *America Perceived*, p. 232, 2002

jeeter *noun*
a lieutenant *US, 1941*

- — Lou Shelly, *Hepcats Jive Talk Dictionary*, p. 46, 1945

jeez!; jeese!; geez!
used as a mild oath *US, 1830*
A euphemized "Jesus."

- Geez, on my prom night I went around this park five, six times. — *Manhattan*, 1979
- The nuns got off easy. Jeez. Cigarette burns. — *The Bad Lieutenant*, 1992
- VELMA: Oh man, I love this song. LUCY: Jeez, you love every song. — *Smoke Signals*, 1998
- Jeez, Warren, you know you're not supposed to leave the yard by yourself. — *Something About Mary*, 1998

jeezer *noun*
a fellow *US, 1972*

- — John Gould, *Maine Lingo*, p. 146, 1975

Jeez Louise!
used as a mild oath *US*, *1957*
- [J]eeze Louise, what a crazy notion. — Frederick Kohner, *Gidget*, p. 141, 1957

Jeff *noun*
1 used as an all-purpose name for a man *US*, *1953*
- Don't be a bear and act like a square get with the jeffs that are going somewhere — Lavada Durst, *The Jives of Dr. Hepcat*, 1953
2 a white person, especially one who is hostile towards black people *US*, *1959*
- Chalk the walking Jeffs. — Chester Himes, *The Real Cool Killers*, p. 120, 1959
- "The agent's a goddam guinea, just like the owner," Red charged. "Them Jeffs is workin' together." — Ross Russell, *The Sound*, p. 144, 1961

jeff *verb*
1 to behave obsequiously in the hope of winning approval *US*, *1960*
- "Naturally," the saleslady said, doing what Masha Lee called "jeffing." — Clarence Cooper Jr., *The Scene*, p. 34, 1960
- Then he said, "Well kiss my dead mammy's ass, if it ain't Macking Youngblood. The whore's pet and the pimp's fret." The junkie bastard was jeffing on me[.] — Iceberg Slim (Robert Beck), *Pimp*, p. 63, 1969
2 to lie or at least to exaggerate *US*, *1992*
- — William K. Bentley and James M. Corbett, *Prison Slang*, p. 46, 1992

Jelke girl *noun*
a high-price, out-call prostitute *US*, *1956*
Named after a New York scandal of the early 1950s.
- [T]he Jelke girls bitterly resented everyone who had anything to do with their exposure. — Jess Stearn, *Sisters of the Night*, p. 141, 1956

jell *noun*
a person with few thoughts and no sense of fashion *US*, *1982*
- — Sue Black, *The Totally Awesome Val Guide*, p. 21, 1982

jellies *noun*
soft, plastic, apparently edible sandals *US*, *1995*
- By employing another '90s tactic of loading a single item with as many styles as possible, the jelly evolved beyond the simple flat heel into a chunky high heel that was sometimes flecked with glitter. — Steven Daly and Nathaniel Wice, *alt.culture*, p. 119, 1995

jello arms *noun*
in surfing, exhausted, rubbery arms from paddling *US*, *1987*
- — Mitch McKissick, *Surf Lingo*, 1987

jelly *noun*
1 the vagina *US*, *1926*
- The damage had already been done, and what was left just had to be pure jelly. — Donald Goines, *The Busting Out of an Ordinary Man*, p. 19, 1985
2 sexual intercourse *US*, *1926*
- "Nothin', ain't nothin' wrong" ... he answered her lamely, revving himself back up to a slow jelly, trying to come again. — Odie Hawkins, *Chicago Hustle*, p. 110, 1977

jelly baby *noun*
an amphetamine tablet *US*, *1971*
- — Eugene Landy, *The Underground Dictionary*, p. 112, 1971
- — Carl Chambers and Richard Heckman, *Employee Drug Abuse*, p. 206, 1972

jellybag *noun*
a large fuel cell made of rubber or plastic *US*, *1965*
Vietnam war usage.
- — *Army Information Digest*, January 1965
- — Carl Fleischhauer, *A Glossary of Army Slang*, p. 27, 1968

jelly roll *noun*
1 the vagina; a woman; sex with a woman *US*, *1914*
- Say now, if you don't believe my jellyroll is fine / ask Good-Cock Lulu, that's a bitch a mine. — Bruce Jackson, *Get Your Ass in the Water and Swim Like Me*, p. 139, 1964
- We just kept staring at that nice little jellyroll looking us in the face. — Robert Lipkin, *A Brotherhood of Outlaws*, p. 163, 1981
2 a used tampon or sanitary napkin *US*, *1972*
- — Helen Dahlskog (Editor), *A Dictionary of Contemporary and Colloquial Usage*, p. 34, 1972

jelly sandwich *noun*
a sanitary napkin *US*, *1980*
- — Edith A. Folb, *runnin' down some lines*, p. 243, 1980

jelly tight *adjective*
excellent *US*, *1972*
- It was jam-up. Jelly-tight. It was, it was a really a kick joint. — Bruce Jackson, *In the Life*, p. 122, 1972

jelly tot *noun*
a young boy who tries to act older than he is *US*, *1951*
Teen slang.
- — *Newsweek*, p. 28, 8th October 1951

jenny *noun*
a merry-go-round *US*, *1985*
- Terminology — Gene Sorrows, *All About Carnivals*, p. 20, 1985

Jenny barn *noun*
the ward for women in a narcotic treatment hospital *US*, *1955*
- — *American Speech*, p. 87, May 1955: "Narcotic argot along the Mexican Border"

jerk *noun*
in a gambling establishment, a hanger-on who runs errands for gamblers *US*, *1979*
- — John Scarne, *Scarne's Guide to Modern Poker*, p. 282, 1979

jerk *verb*
▸ **jerk the gherkin**
of a male, to masturbate *UK*, *1962*
- Spanking the monkey. Flogging the bishop. Choking the chicken. Jerking the gherkin. — *American Beauty*, 1999
- "The boy is masturbating" [...] Jerking the gerkin[.] — Erica Orloff and JoAnn Baker, *Dirty Little Secrets*, p. 65, 2001

▸ **jerk your chain**
to mislead someone *US*, *1976*
- "Come on, willya please, Mr. Struve . . . quit jerking my chain." — Emmett Grogan, *Final Score*, p. 166, 1976

jerk-ass *noun*
an obnoxious person *US*, *1970*
- "Who does he think he is, Mr. Big-Shot Jerk-Ass Quarterback, well he can kiss my butt is what he can do." — Joshilyn Jackson, *Gods in Alabama*, p. 35, 2005

jerked up *adjective*
worthless *US*, *1962*
- "Oh, I thought you were my jerked-up agent's office." — Stephen Longstreet, *The Flesh Peddlers*, p. 34, 1962

jerkface *noun*
used as an all-purpose term of abuse *US*, *1977*
- "I keep telling you, jerkface, I don't care about her." — Jerry Spinelli, *Fourth Grade Rats*, p. 47, 1991

jerkhead *noun*
a stupid person *US*, *1984*
- M.J. went on to graduate with honors, far away from the voices of those nasty children from Holy-fucking-Angel that she privately referred to as a bunch of aggie-dork-brained jerkheads from the sticks. — Denise Chavez, *Face of an Angel*, p. 124, 1994

jerko *noun*
an obnoxious person *US*, *1948*
- "Every one of you jerkos used that phone." — Robert Daley, *Prince of the City*, p. 80, 1978
- "No, jerko, I was talking about something altogether else." — Tom Robbins, *Fierce Invalids Home from Hot Climates*, p. 316, 2000

jerk-off *noun*
1 a single act of masturbation, especially by a male *US*, *1928*
- The Jerk-off! If you don't know how, let me explain it. — Angelo d'Arcangelo, *The Homosexual Handbook*, p. 88, 1968
2 a contemptible fool *US*, *1932*
- [I]t worked for the role he was playing, because that's what her ex-boyfriend in the movie was supposed to be, a total jerk-off. — Jackie Collins, *Hollywood Kids*, p. 261, 1995

jerk off *verb*
1 to masturbate *UK*, *1896*
A reasonably accurate description of the physical activity involved.
- The climax of this conversation was in a question he posed to me. "Do you know how to 'jerk off'?" — Phyllis and Eberhard Kronhausen, *Sex Histories of American College Men*, p. 79, 1960

- Suddenly Johnny realizes the man is jerking off looking at him. — John Rechy, *Numbers*, p. 154, 1967
- You jerk off before all big dates, right? — *Something About Mary*, 1998
- But she knew boys had her picture up over their beds to look at when they jerked off. — Francesca Lia Block, *I Was a Teenage Fairy*, p. 78, 1998

2 to tease; to mislead *US, 1968*
- I think Coyle was jerking you off. — George Higgins, *The Friends of Eddie Coyle*, p. 97, 1971

3 to cause the withdrawal (of a criminal charge, a witness scheduled to testify, etc.) *US, 1950*
- — Hyman E. Goldin et al., *Dictionary of American Underworld Lingo*, p. 110, 1950

jerk-silly *adjective*
obsessed with masturbation *US, 1962*
- — Joseph E. Ragen and Charles Finston, *Inside the World's Toughest Prison*, p. 805, 1962: "Penitentiary and underworld glossary"

jerkwater *noun*
a dull-minded person *US, 1958*
- — William K. Bentley and James M. Corbett, *Prison Slang*, p. 35, 1992

Jerkwater *noun*
used as a contemptuous name for a remote location *US, 1982*
- Killed for vagrancy in Jerkwater, USA. — *Rambo, First Blood*, 1982

jerkwater *adjective*
provincial *US, 1897*
- He'd killed half a dozen people before he picked up a jerkwater Ph.D., and edged into psychiatry. — Jim Thompson, *The Killer Inside*, p. 167, 1952
- "What," he asked, "are we going to do for broads in a jerkwater town like Putnam's Landing?" — Max Shulman, *Rally Round the Flag, Boys!*, p. 157, 1957
- Harrisonville and the fastblink jerkwater towns clustered about it—Peculiar, Lone Jack, Gunn City, attract more funnel clouds each hardluck year than anyplace else. — Joe Eszterhas, *Charlie Simpson's Apocalypse*, p. 5, 1973
- Here I come to your jerkwater little country and spend my good American dollars[.] — William Burroughs, *Queer*, p. 59, 1985

Jerry; Gerry *nickname*
a German; the Germans *US, 1915*
Derogatory, often as an abstract reference to Germans as the enemy whether at war or football. Possibly derived from "Jerry" (a chamber pot) in reference to the shape of German military helmets; more likely, as "Gerry," an elaborated abbreviation of "German."
- The two best wars this country has fought were against the Jerries. — *Harold and Maude*, 1971

Jersey *noun*
the state of New Jersey *US, 1949*
- I was even over in Jersey for a while. — Philip Wylie, *Opus 21*, p. 111, 1949
- They was supposed to go someplace in Jersey. — Mickey Spillane, *Return of the Hood*, p. 87, 1964
- What do people from Jersey drink? — *King of Comedy*, 1976

Jersey girls *nickname*
a small group of women living in New Jersey whose husbands were killed in the World Trade Center on 11th September 2001, and who pressured a reluctant Bush administration into appointing a commission to investigate the attack *US, 2002*
Evocative of an unrelated song by Bruce Springsteen.
- The commission grew largely out of pressure from families of victims, including four New Jersey widows who call themselves "the Jersey girls." — *New York Times*, p. 43, 22nd December 2002
- Kristen Breitweiser, one of the three widows known as "the Jersey girls," who helped pressure Congress into creating the commission, said the White House's actions are often at odds with its assurances it is providing the commission with "unprecedent cooperation." — *Chicago Tribune*, p. C1, 8th April 2004

Jersey highball *noun*
a glass of milk *US, 1947*
- — Marcus Hanna Boulware, *Jive and Slang of Students in Negro Colleges*, 1947

Jersey lightning *noun*
inexpensive, inferior whiskey *US, 1848*

- Here, this contains deadly poison, the effect is frightening. It's sometimes called Bourbon, oftener Jersey Lightening. — Susan Kattwinkel, *Tony Pastor Presents*, p. 103, 1998
- In the evenings, the men he was with played cards and drank "Jersey Lightning." — Francis Hartigan, *Bill W.*, p. 47, 2000

Jersey side of the snatch play *noun*
middle age *US, 1961*
Borrowed from the slang of bowlers, where the "Jersey side" is to the left of the head pin.
- They were introduced to an insignificant, graying man—"on the Jersey side of the snatch play," in hipster language, meaning that Narco was over forty and wondering if life would ever begin again. — Ross Russell, *The Sound*, p. 113, 1961
- — Clarence Major, *Dictionary of Afro-American Slang*, p. 71, 1970
- "I'm on the Jersey side of snatch." Likely it had been years since his swinging lingam had nudged itself into the sweet enclosing lips of the yoni. — Brian Preston, *Pot Planet*, p. 26, 2002

Jesse James *noun*
1 in craps, a nine rolled with a four and a five *US, 1985*
Jesse James was shot with a 45 caliber handgun.
- — Steve Kuriscak, *Casino Talk*, p. 69, 1985

2 in hold 'em poker, a four and a five as the first two cards dealt to a player *US, 1981*
- — Thomas L. Clark, *The Dictionary of Gambling and Gaming*, p. 110, 1987

jessie *noun*
a pretty red-headed girl *US, 1947*
- — Marcus Hanna Boulware, *Jive and Slang of Students in Negro Colleges*, 1947

jesum crow!
used for expressing surprise, dismay, or disgust *US, 1971*
- — *Current Slang*, p. 15, Spring 1971

Jesus *noun*
▸ **pull a Jesus**
to return from seeming oblivion to a functional state *US, 1998*
- Either the snake ate it, or the mouse pulled a "Jesus" on me and came to live (sic) and went into hiding. — *rec.pets.herp*, 7th May 1998
- — Connie Eble (Editor), *UNC-CH Campus Slang*, p. 10, Fall 2005

Jesus boots; Jesus shoes; Jesus slippers *noun*
sandals *US, 1942*
- — *American Speech*, p. 235, October 1964: "Student slang in Hays, Kansas"
- — Helen Dahlskog (Editor), *A Dictionary of Contemporary and Colloquial Usage*, p. 34, 1972
- He was wearing a bright aloha shirt, khaki shorts, Jesus boots and mirrored sky-shooters[.] — Kinky Friedman, *Steppin' on a Rainbow*, p. 103, 2001

Jesus freak *noun*
a fervent Christian, especially a recent convert *US, 1966*
The quintessential use of the term was in Elton John's 1971 song "Tiny Dancer."
- These goddman Jesus freaks! They're multiplying like rats! — Hunter S. Thompson, *Fear and Loathing in Las Vegas*, p. 134, 1971
- JESUS FREAK: a person who has found Jesus to be the "ultimate trip," e.g., a head who has gone beyond acid to Christ. — Robert Buckhout, *Toward Social Change*, p. 465, 1971
- "Jesus Freaks" harassed the third annual Christopher Street West Parade in Los Angeles — *The Advocate*, p. 5, 19th July 1972
- Stout did his twenty-five interviews, and he was on his way out of Zanesville when he came upon an encampment of Jesus freaks. — Timothy Crouse, *The Boys on the Bus*, p. 49, 1973

Jesus fucking Christ!
used as an all-purpose oath of surprise, approval, disapproval, anger, etc. *US, 1969*
The most common use of the intensifying infix in the US.
- "Jesus fucking Christ. I'm sorry I said it." — Cecil Brown, *The Life & Loves of Mr. Jiveass Nigger*, p. 132, 1969

Jesus H. Christ!
used in oaths *US, 1892*
Occasional substitutions of the middle initial, which is nothing more than a humorous, intensifying embellishment.
- Jesus Christ, Jesus H. Christ, goddamn it man. — Neal Cassady, *Neal Cassady Collected Letters 1944–1967*, p. 265, 8th January 1951: Letter to Jack and Joan Kerouac

- I wouldn't be able to go out to Malibu for at least ten days! Jesus H. Christ! — Frederick Kohner, *Gidget*, p. 58, 1957
- Jesus H. Christ! And to think he actually gets twenty-five bucks an hour—or rather, forty-five minutes—for that nonsense. — Oscar Zeta Acosta, *The Autobiography of a Brown Buffalo*, p. 15, 1972
- I mean, Jesus H. Christ. Day after day, night after night, it just doesn't stop. — George V. Higgins, *The Rat on Fire*, p. 105, 1981

Jesus juice *noun*
1 white wine *US, 2005*
Allegedly coined by singer Michael Jackson. It was also claimed, in a *Vanity Fair* article, that Jackson called red wine "Jesus blood." Within months the term was widespread.
- The boy and his siblings have said that "all the kids around Michael" knew about "Jesus juice" and that Jackson told them, "Jesus drank it, so it must be good." — *Houston Chronicle*, p. 12, 29th January 2005
2 a mixture of grape juice and gin *US, 1981*
- [H]er comrades learned they could drop in, sit on the floor, exchange ideas, and sometimes drink beer or "Jesus juice," their own concoction of grape juice and gin. — Emily Toth, *Inside Peyton Place*, p. 29, 1981

Jesus nut *noun*
the main nut and bolt holding a helicopter's rotor blade to the body of the aircraft *US, 1967*
Presumably one prayed to Jesus that the nut and bolt did not fail.
- "If it comes off we lose the main rotors. At that point a helicopter has all the aerodynamic characteristics of a footlocker. We call it the Jesus nut." — Elaine Shepard, *The Doom Pussy*, p. 2, 1967
- A lot of people thought it opened you to some kind of extra danger, like ground fire spilling in on you instead of just severing the hydraulic system or cutting off the Jesus nut that held the rotor on. — Michael Herr, *Dispatches*, pp. 255–256, 1977

Jesus punch *noun*
a wine-based alcoholic punch *US, 2000*
- Butchy and his crew threw a huge party the next day complete with black decorations and big vat of purple jesus punch. — Ralph Gessner, *Deep in My Heart*, p. 119, 2000
- Downstairs, Hardbar and Moses were concocting the Jesus punch. — Chris Miller, *The Real Animal House*, p. 250, 2006

Jesus stiff *noun*
a person who feigns religion to obtain food, lodging, or better privileges in prison *US, 1950*
- — Hyman E. Goldin et al., *Dictionary of American Underworld Lingo*, p. 110, 1950

Jesus to Jesus and eight hands around!
used as a cry of disbelief *US, 1975*
- — John Gould, *Maine Lingo*, p. 146, 1975

Jesus weejuns *noun*
sandals *US, 1969*
- — *Current Slang*, p. 7, Spring 1969

jet *noun*
the recreational drug ketamine *US, 1994*
- — US Department of Justice *Street Terms*, October 1994

jet *verb*
1 to leave in a hurry *US, 1968*
- — Collin Baker et al., *College Undergraduate Slang Study Conducted at Brown University*, p. 145, 1968
- Disgusted, the knock [narcotics officer] grabbed Rodney's arm. "C'mon, motherfucker. Let's jet, let's jet." — Richard Price, *Clockers*, p. 258, 1992
- [S]ay you're going to take a piss and jet up out that bitch through the emergency exit. — *Hip-Hop Connection*, p. 22, July 2002
2 to use crack cocaine, especially in a sustained binge *US, 2005*
- She started hanging out with crackheads and jetting for days at a time. — Noire, *Candy Licker*, p. 171, 2005

jet bumper *noun*
in pinball, a bumper that upon impact with the ball scores and then propels the ball back into play *US, 1977*
- — Bobbye Claire Natkin and Steve Kirk, *All About Pinball*, p. 113, 1977

jet fuel *noun*
phencyclidine, the recreational drug known as PCP or angel dust *US, 1994*
- — US Department of Justice, *Street Terms*, October 1994

jet jock *noun*
a jet pilot *US, 1992*
- "Dash Two, its the big antiaircraft stuff they throw up at our jet jocks." — Bob Stoffey, *Cleared Hot!*, p. 22, 1992

Jew; Jew down *verb*
to bargain aggressively about a price *US, 1818*
- "I jewed the landlord down." — John A. Williams, *Sissie*, p. 231, 1963
- Through some "Jewing down" I bought it for $10,500, studio possibilities and all, about a stone's throw from Toylsome Lane. — Larry Rivers, *What Did I Do?*, p. 329, 1992
- Don't ever try to out-Jew me, little man. I'm twice the Jew you'll ever be. — Kenneth Lonergan, *This is Our Youth*, p. 38, 2000
- I don't dodge guilt. And I don't Jew outta payin' my comeuppance. — *Kill Bill*, 2003

Jewboy *noun*
a Jewish man *UK, 1796*
Not said kindly.
- Proper little jewboy was Henry. — John Peter Jones, *Feather Pluckers*, p. 118, 1964
- [H]e could picture the guy now: little Jew-boy with a cowboy hat, string tie and high-heeled boots, and horn-rimmed glasses and a big fucking cigar. — Elmore Leonard, *Mr. Majestyk*, p. 104, 1974
- We always had a stray wop or Jew-boy and plenty of spades with our gangs. — Edwin Torres, *Carlito's Way*, p. 9, 1975

jewels *noun*
the genitals *US, 1987*
An abbreviation of **FAMILY JEWELS**.
- But most blacks, and myself, and a few other guys cover the jewels. — Ernest Spencer, *Welcome to Vietnam, Macho Man*, p. 46, 1987

Jew flag *noun*
paper money *US, 1915*
- — Joseph E. Ragen and Charles Finston, *Inside the World's Toughest Prison*, p. 805, 1962: "Penitentiary and underworld glossary"

Jewish Alps *noun*
the Catskill mountains *US, 1966*
The Catskills were a favorite vacation destination for urban Jewish people.
- Fun, before I discovered women, consisted of swimming at Hauto and summer vacations in the Catskill Mountains—the Jewish Alps[.] — Richard Marcinko, *Rogue Warrior*, p. 34, 1992

Jewish by hospitalization *noun*
in homosexual usage, circumcized but not Jewish *US, 1986–1987*
- — *Maledicta*, p. 58, 1986–1987: "A continuation of a glossary of ethnic slurs in American English"

Jewish champagne *noun*
celery-flavored soda *US, 1939*
- They will glory in the mention of dairy restaurants, half-sour pickles, and that "Jewish champagne," the celery-flavored soft drink called Dr. Brown's Cel-Ray Soda. — *Newsday (New York)*, p. B2, 8th December 2004

Jewish corned beef *noun*
in homosexual usage, a circumcized penis *US, 1986–1987*
- — *Maledicta*, p. 58, 1986–1987: "A continuation of a glossary of ethnic slurs in American English"

Jewish deal *noun*
dealing cards left-handed *US, 1949*
- "Look at the Jewish deal," Louie marveled, for the punk dealt left-handed. — Nelson Algren, *The Man with the Golden Arm*, p. 101, 1949

Jewish foreplay *noun*
pleading without results *US, 1987*
- — *Maledicta*, p. 58, 1987: "A continuation of a glossary of ethnic slurs in American English"

Jewish lightning *noun*
an act of arson as a part of a fraudulent insurance claim *US, 1983*
- When I was covering neighborhoods for the City News Bureau, the black term for insurance arson was "Jewish lightning." — Richard Stern, *A Father's Words*, p. 176, 1990
- Had 'em a little case of Jewish lightning. — Harry Hunsicker, *Still River*, p. 76, 2005

Jewish penicillin *noun*
chicken soup *US, 1968*

- I had made lunch for him ... feeling poorly as he was ... you know, a little Jewish penicillin (chicken soup). — Angelo d'Arcangelo, *The Homosexual Handbook*, p. 94, 1968

Jewish people's time *noun*
used for denoting a lack of punctuality *US, 1967*
- Like Mexican Time and the onetime JPT, Jewish People's time, C.P.T. is a phrase that draws the lines of the ghetto. — Paul Jacobs, *Prelude to a Riot*, p. 12, 1967

Jewish prince *noun*
a spoiled Jewish male *US, 1982*
An engrained cultural stereotype.
- "The standard recipe for the Jewish prince," observed Flo. — Paula Cohen, *Jane Austen in Boca*, p. 88, 2002

Jewish princess *noun*
a spoiled Jewish female *US, 1972*
A deeply engrained cultural stereotype.
- How often have we been scapegoated as Jewish mothers, Jewish princesses, source of all Jewish male neuroses? — Judith Kates, *Beginning Anew*, p. 239, 1997

Jew sheet *noun*
an accounting, literal or figurative, of money owed by friends *US, 1986–1987*
- — *Maledicta*, p. 57, 1986–1987: "A continuation of a glossary of ethnic slurs in American English"

Jewtown *noun*
a neighborhood inhabited predominantly by Jewish people *US, 1955*
- But I'm scouting some promising territory over in Jew Town when I see a janitor wheel a bike into the basement of a tenement house. — Rocky Garciano (with Rowland Barber), *Somebody Up There Likes Me*, p. 32, 1955
- Two years later Sissie and Ralph moved to Jewtown. — John A. Williams, *Sissie*, p. 215, 1963
- I'd always go in Jew town and pick pockets on Sundays. — Henry Williamson, *Hustler!*, p. 89, 1965
- Jewtown. That's exactly what it was, the place where the Jews lived and worked. — Odie Hawkins, *Scars and Memories*, p. 27, 1987

Jew York *nickname*
New York city *US, 1931*
- "You can get outta here and go right back to Jew York and sleep with all the filthy kikes you can." — Patrick Dennis, *Auntie Mame*, p. 217, 1955

jib *noun*
the mouth *UK, 1860*
- Don't let the word pimp come outta your "jib" in my presence. — Iceberg Slim (Robert Beck), *Pimp*, p. 122, 1969
- If a bitch ever made love to a nigger's dick, by hugging, kissing, and placing it in her jib, this one did. — A.S. Jackson, *Gentleman Pimp*, p. 72, 1973

jiboney; jabroni; jabroney *noun*
1 a newly immigrated foreigner; hence someone inexperienced or unsophisticated *US, 1960*
- — *San Jose Mercury News*, 11th May 1999

2 a low-level gangster, a tough *US, 1921*
- You, you fucking jaroney. One more word out of you and I'm bringing you in. — Edwin Torres, *Q & A*, p. 122, 1977
- "I doubt that," the tall jaboney says, and he looks me up and down like he's ready to squash me like a bug. — Robert Campbell, *Nibbled to Death by Ducks*, p. 97, 1989
- "Probably ratted out some Colombian or other to County in order to avoid any kind of serious time. Just like every other jibone out there." — Richard Price, *Samaritan*, p. 160, 2003

3 a professional wrestler who is usually scripted to lose *US, 1995*
- A star simply uses this medium to build his stature and display his style by manhandling a "gibroni"—an unknown or habitual loser. — Larry Nelson, *Stranglehold*, p. 45, 1999
- "Sorry 'bout barging in, but the jabroni airline that I was booked on delayed all of their flights out of Newark." — Gary Cappetta, *Bodyslams!*, p. 270, 2000
- Now it's time for The Rock to lay a little smack down on another fat-ass jabroni[.] — The Rock, *The Rock Says...*, p. 282, 2000

jibs *noun*
the teeth *US, 1970*
- — Roger D. Abrahams, *Deep Down in the Jungle*, p. 261, 1970

jiffy *noun*
in computing, a tick of the computer clock, usually one millisecond *US, 1983*
- "The swapper runs every six jiffies" means that the virtual memory management routine is executed once for every six ticks of the computer's clock, or ten times a second. — Guy L. Steele et al., *The Hacker's Dictionary*, p. 85, 1983

jiffy *adjective*
instant *US, 1949*
- The jiffy coffee lay in my stomach like a solid and the heat of it ran from my pores. — Philip Wylie, *Opus 21*, p. 226, 1949

jig *noun*
1 a black person *US, 1922*
Offensive.
- Anyway, since you beat up the two jigs nobody will talk to me. — Mickey Spillane, *I, The Jury*, p. 90, 1947
- Think of the thousand names hung on them trailing back into the darkest alleys of our racist past: coon; jig; darky; shine; Sambo; Jim Crow; buck; spearchucker etc. — Ken Kesey, *Kesey's Jail Journal*, p. 14, 1967
- Then after that if a guy was a Spic or a Jig it was his business. I mean it was his business, if he wanted to cling with his own kind. — Eugene Boe (Compiler), *The Wit & Wisdom of Archie Bunker*, p. 183, 1971
- That fuckin' jig's gonna wish he never came outa the jungle. — *Raging Bull*, 1980

2 a deception; trickery; mischief *US, 1777*
- God knows what kind of jig he was dreaming up for himself. — Clancy Sigal, *Going Away*, p. 215, 1961

jigaboo *noun*
a black person *US, 1926*
Offensive.
- You know those "dancing jigaboo" toys that you wind up? — Malcolm X and Alex Haley, *The Autobiography of Malcolm X*, p. 57, 1964
- [A]nd kissed his ithyphallic jigaboo ass! and played the parts of people their parents hated worse even than niggers. — Joe Eszterhas, *Charlie Simpson's Apocalypse*, p. 92, 1973
- No, you and that big jigaboo sat there laughing with each other—oh boy, are we having fun, taking Mr. Magic to jail. — Elmore Leonard, *Glitz*, p. 317, 1985
- "Fine," Culver said. "You sit out here in the parking lot with all these jigaboos." — Carl Hiaasen, *Double Whammy*, p. 179, 1987

jig-a-jig; jig-jig
sexual intercourse *US, 1896*
- I tell 'em how Cholly give me that jig-jig or jail jive[.] — Robert Gover, *JC Saves*, p. 55, 1968

jigger *noun*
1 a lookout during a crime *US, 1925*
- — Bruce Jackson, *Outside the Law*, p. 58, 1972: "Glossary"
- But Bucklew needed a "jigger," someone to watch for the guard. — Pete Earley, *The Hot House*, p. 254, 1992

2 a bank robber *US, 1950*
- We had a pretty good bunch of O'Sullivans, a torch man, a mechanic, a jigger and a hard-shell biscuit who'd been with a gopher mob. We crashed with a get-in betty. — *The New American Mercury*, p. 709, 1950

3 a woman who will dance with a man for a fee *US, 1951*
- The dance floor was jammed. The dime jiggers were of every age and every type and a lot of them wore cheap formals and the smiles on their faces were hard and false. — Thurston Scott, *Cure it with Honey*, p. 151, 1951

jigger *verb*
1 to adjust, especially of numbers or statistics *US, 1997*
- If the annuity also covers your spouse, payments can be jiggered to reflect your changing joint life expectancy. — Jane Bryant Quinn, *Making the Most of Your Money*, p. 927, 1997
- President Clinton had cunningly jiggered with the tax code to squeeze enormous sums of money out of comparatively tiny numbers of people. — David Frum, *The Right Man*, p. 50, 2003

2 to serve as a lookout during a crime *US, 1995*
- — Mark S. Fleisher, *Beggars & Thieves*, p. 290, 1995: "Glossary"

jigger moll *noun*
a female lookout for a criminal operation who can also serve as a diversion or distraction *US, 1956*
- — *American Speech*, p. 97, May 1956: "Smugglers' argot in the Southwest"

jiggers!

used as a warning to confederates that a prison guard is approaching *US, 1911*

- If the matron came long the hall someone yelled jiggers! and they ditched the butt. — Willard Motley, *Let No Man Write My Epitaph*, p. 21, 1958
- — Inez Cardozo-Freeman, *The Joint*, p. 509, 1984

jiggle *noun*

visual sexual content *US, 1978*

- Then again, if "sexy" in the 1970s meant a dash of the "jiggle factor" popularized by Aaron Spelling's Charlie's Angels, she wasn't doing that, either. — Maria Raha, *Cinderella's Big Score*, p. 38, 2005

jiggles and wires *noun*

excitement *US, 1984*

- "I'm all jiggles and wires!" Ken Kelly whispered to Joe Castillo. — Joseph Wambaugh, *Lines and Shadows*, p. 160, 1984

jigglies *noun*

the female breasts *US, 2002*

- "Udders," he said. "Jigglies," she countered. "Chi-chis. Kazooms[.]" — Clive Barker, *Coldheart Canyon*, p. 231, 2002
- This bubbly blonde with mammoth jigglies has made appearances on Everybody Loves Raymond[.] — Mr. Skin, *Mr. Skin's Skincyclopedia*, p. 48, 2005

jiggy *adjective*

1 rich; hence fashionable, stylish; attractive *US, 1995*

- DKNY / Oh my I'm jiggy — Junior MAFIA *Player's Anthem*, 1995
- — *Newsday*, p. B2, 11th October 1997
- A woman or a record both "got me open" but at the moment I write this they both better be "jiggy" if I'm supposed to pay attention. — Nelson George, *Hip Hop America*, p. 209, 1998

2 crazy *US, 1933*

- "Except one was kind of dead and the other was getting jiggy with a serrated blade." — Lisa Gardner, *Alone*, p. 125, 2005

▸ **get jiggy; get jiggy with it**

1 to dance, or feel the need to dance to the music *US, 1997*

- [W]ish you nig was dancin' the jig / here with this handsome kid / [...] illway to 'ami [Miami] on the interstate floorway / give it up jiggy make it feel like foreplay — Will Smith, *Gettin' Jiggy wit' it*, 1997

2 to have sex; to become sexually intimate *US, 2003*

- [W]hen we first got jiggy it was great to go in the shower but when you do it day in day out the novelty wears off. — *Attitude*, p. 146, October 2003

jig lover *noun*

a white person who, in the eyes of the racist using the term, treats black people as equals *US, 1950*

- — Hyman E. Goldin et al., *Dictionary of American Underworld Lingo*, p. 110, 1950
- "The chickenshit jig-lover," Lips said. — Bernard Brunner, *Six Days to Sunday*, p. 220, 1975

jig time *noun*

a short period of time *US, 140*

- We blew the vault in jig time and then I got out a new tool I wanted to try. — Charles Hamilton, *Men of the Underworld*, p. 140, 1952

jigtown *noun*

a neighborhood populated largely by black people *US, 1898*

- But that knowledge helped him only slightly as he tossed about and fought for sleep in a lonely Jigtown hotel room. — Bruce Jay Friedman, *The Dick*, p. 172, 1970
- — *Maledicta*, p. 52, 1986–1987: "A continuation of a glossary of ethnic slurs in American English"
- Lorna gigged the Katydid Klub, Bido Lito's, Malloy's Next, and a host of dives on the edge of jigtown. — James Ellroy, *Hollywood Nocturnes*, p. 271, 1994
- If you want to grill a jig outside his backyard you don't use a hotel room in jigtown. — Loren D. Estleman, *Jitterbug*, p. 20, 1998

jillion *noun*

a large, imagined number *US, 1939*

- We've got about ninety jillion sea gulls in our neighborhood[.] — Max Shulman, *I was a Teen-Age Dwarf*, p. 22, 1959
- [A] chance like this wouldn't come along in a jillion years. — Frederick Kohner, *Gidget Goes to Rome*, p. 2, 1963
- Goddamnit, Shapian. I'm paying you a jillion dollars for a show about food poisons. — Max Shulman, *Anyone Got a Match?*, p. 226, 1964

jill off *verb*

(of a woman) to masturbate *US, 1989*

Derivative of the male JACK OFF, and used far less frequently.

- All proceeds from this jack- and jill-off fest and the finish-line party went to From Our Streets With Dignity[.] — *The Village Voice*, 13th June 2000
- She stretches her feet out to the camera and curls her toes as she artfully jills off. — Editors of Adult Video News, *The AVN Guide to the 500 Greatest Adult Films of All Time*, p. 138, 2005

Jim *noun*

used as a name given to a friend or offered as a gesture of friendliness *US, 1899*

Black/jazz slang subverting the racism of JIM CROW.

- Jim, this jive you got is gassed. — Mezz Mezzrow, 1946, quoted in *Waiting For The Man* by Harry Shapiro, 1999

Jim *nickname*

Jim Beam whiskey *US, 1998*

- "Smirnoff, Absolut, Jim, or Jack?" — John Ridley, *Love is a Racket*, p. 163, 1998

Jimbroni *noun*

in American casinos, a dealer with neither great skills nor great reactions to situations *US, 1985*

- — Steve Kuriscak, *Casino Talk*, p. 33, 1985

jim cap; jim hat *noun*

a condom *US, 1990*

- [N]ow that I wanna flap some skins Brandi ain't down for it even if I wear a jim hat. — *Boyz N The Hood*, 1990
- — Pamela Munro, *U.C.L.A. Slang*, p. 82, 1997

Jim Crow *noun*

racial segregation; a racially segregated facility *US, 1921*

- You riding back here in the Jim Crow just like me. — Ralph Ellison, *Invisible Man*, p. 155, 1947
- Bop was so weird, and so apart from any attraction in night club history, that the breaking of the Jim Crow line went unnoticed. — Robert Sylvester, *No Cover Charge*, p. 284, 1956
- I am not like these pseudo-hip characters who immolate themselves in the Negro race which, if you ask me, really is Jim Crow in reverse. — Clancy Sigal, *Going Away*, p. 60, 1961
- [P]erhaps there are fewer breadlines in America, but is Jim Crow gone? — Students for a Democratic Society, *Port Huron Statement*, 15th June 1962

Jim-Crow *verb*

to segregate racially *US, 1918*

- He too good to come in? Tell him we don't Jimcrow nobody. — Ralph Ellison, *Invisible Man*, p. 76, 1947

Jim Crow *adjective*

racially segregated, reserved for black people *US, 1842*

- The District has a single Jim Crow law, segregating Negros and whites—in schools. — Jack Lait and Lee Mortimer, *Washington Confidential*, p. 35, 1951
- The chapel was Jim Crow; white girls pray in front, black girls in back. — Billie Holiday with William Dufty, *Lady Sings the Blues*, p. 131, 1956
- The accommodations are block blooked, with a no Jim Crow clause. — Ross Russell, *The Sound*, p. 60, 1961
- I been light enough to sit in the front of a Jim Crow bus but dark enough to be worried about it. — Edwin Torres, *Carlito's Way*, p. 19, 1975

Jim Dandy *noun*

an excellent example or instance of something *US, 1887*

- Folks, I sure hope these goddamn things work. To make sure, I'll put on both of them, one at the back and one on the end of my Jim Dandy. — Iceberg Slim (Robert Beck), *Trick Baby*, p. 219, 1969

jim-dandy *adjective*

excellent *US, 1887*

- "And even if you're jimdandy you still wait years until they've finished building." — Dale Krame, *Teen-Age Gangs*, p. 117, 1953
- He seemed surprised when he saw most of the back yard in the front yard, but he said we had done a jim-dandy job. — Harper Lee, *To Kill A Mockingbird*, p. 76, 1960
- I went on about how my cousin was a jim-dandy hunter, a heap better than Roscoe's Nelly. — Guy Owen, *The Flim-Flam Man and the Apprentice Grifter*, p. 55, 1972

jimjams *noun*

a heightened sense of anxiety *US, 1896*

- Made me so jimjam jittery, I near nutty already. — Robert Gover, *One Hundred Dollar Misunderstanding*, p. 121, 1961
- Now it seemed like someone was pressing an electric cattle prod against him. "Jimjams," he muttered. — Phil Hirsch, *Hooked*, p. 10, 1968
- Arthur Skidmore was wildly awake with the jimjams[.] — Emmett Grogan, *Final Score*, p. 36, 1976

jimmy *noun*

1 the penis *US, 1973*

- "I was always disappointed at the fact that I had no jimmy to play with." — Stanley Weber, *A Study of Sex in Prison*, p. 78, 1973
- "Gimme gimme gimme" / Jumped on my jimmy and rode me like the wild west — Ice-T, *The Girl Tried To Kill Me*, 1989
- Never sleep alone because my Jimmy is a magnet — Beastie Boys, *3 Minute Rule*, 1989

2 a condom *US, 1990*

- — Judi Sanders, *Faced and Faded, Hanging to Hurl*, p. 23, 1993
- Bitch, stop lyin'! Besides, I had the jimmy on extra tight. — *Menace II Society*, 1993
- He rolled on a jimmy and I sat on top of him. — Amy Sohn, *Run Catch Kiss*, p. 111, 1999
- "And the fool didn't even snatch the jimmy off before he ran out." — Eric Jerome Dickey, *Cheaters*, p. 35, 1999

3 an injection of an illegal drug into the skin, not a vein *US, 1952*

- — *American Speech*, p. 27, February 1952: "Teen-age hophead jargon"

jimmy *verb*

to pry open *US, 1854*

- So I jimmied open the lock and there's like rows and rows of cash just staring at me. — Kenneth Lonergan, *This is Our Youth*, p. 14, 2000

jimmy cap; jimmy hat *noun*

a condom *US, 1988*

Worn on a JIMMY (penis).

- It's "Jimmy Hats" by BDP — Boogie Down Productions, *Jimmy*, 1988
- Jimmy hat is street slang for condom and is also the title of a rap music hit. — *Boston Globe*, p. 27, 15th April 1989
- Condoms. Prophylactics. Rubbers. Jimmy caps. — John Ridley, *Love is a Racket*, p. 297, 1998

jimmyhead *noun*

a fool *US, 1976*

- Do they let jimmyheads like that walk around the streets in New York? — *Punk*, p. 3, March 1976

Jimmy Hicks; Jimmy Hix *noun*

1 in craps, a roll of six *US, 1898*

From the rhyme.

- — *The Annals of the American Academy of Political and Social Sciences*, p. 126, May 1950

2 in a deck of playing cards, a six *US, 1951*

- — *American Speech*, p. 99, May 1951: "The vocabulary of poker"

jimmy jacket *noun*

a condom *US, 1997*

Jimmy joint *noun*

the penis *US, 1976*

- — John R. Armore and Joseph D. Wolfe, *Dictionary of Desperation*, p. 36, 1976

jimmy protector *noun*

a condom *US, 1989*

- Dude, I wear the jimmy protector with all women—though in truth I'm thinking more about pregnancy than disease. — *alt.sports.basketball.nba.la-lakers*, 22nd August 2005

Jimson *noun*

used as a male-to-male term of address *US, 1953*

- Jimson, you can believe that cat's wings are not clipped because he is naturally buzzing cuzin. — Lavada Durst, *The Jives of Dr. Hepcat*, p. 1, 1953

jing *noun*

money *US, 1973*

A shortened "jingle."

- Got any jing? I told you. They fucked up my pay record in Nam. — Charles Anderson, *The Grunts*, p. 17, 1976

Jing Bao juice *noun*

rice wine or plum wine *US, 1943*

- "One night over our daily allowance of Jing Bao juice, "Bonnie" and I decided we should name the plane after his girlfriend and my wife[.]" — Carl Molesworth, *P-40 Warhawk Aces of the CBI*, 2000

jing-jang *noun*

the penis *US, 1960*

- — *Fact*, p. 26, January–February 1965

jingle *noun*

1 a telephone call *US, 1949*

- Well, I mean, I was going to give you a jingle. I was going to let you know I was back in town. — Robert Campbell, *Boneyards*, p. 129, 1992

2 money, coins *US, 1966*

- "Every time I rack up a little jingle, I race myself to the store." — Malcolm Braly, *It's Cold Out There*, p. 69, 1966

jingle *verb*

to make a telephone call *US, 1959*

- — Edd Byrnes, *Way Out with Kookie*, 1959
- I'm angling to fix Rochester for us, so jingle me at the Sherry Netherlands at least once a week. — Iceberg Slim (Robert Beck), *Long White Con*, p. 205, 1977

jingle bell crew *noun*

a team of pickpockets *US, 1982*

- Now mostly applied to the professionals from Colombia, South America, the city's most adroit. The term comes from the way they practice their craft: attaching bells to clothes dummies, which jingle when they "clumsy up" the lift. — Bill Reilly, *Big Al's Official Guide to Chicagoese*, p. 38, 1982

jingles *noun*

pocket change *US, 1989*

- — James Harris, *A Convict's Dictionary*, p. 34, 1989

jingle truck *noun*

an Afghani or Pakistani transport truck *US, 2002*

US soldiers occupying Afghanistan coined the term because of the clanging noise made by the chains and parts hanging off the bottom of the truck.

- Barreling down the road are "jingle trucks," brightly painted and exuberantly decorated lorries from Pakistan that will more often than not squeeze passengers on the top[.] — *United Press International*, 7th June 2002

jink *verb*

to make sudden, evasive movements *UK, 1785*

- Jink through the jungle / Make the ABs rumble. — Joseph Tuso, *Singing the Vietnam Blues*, p. 137, 1990
- The separation gave them the room to "jink," to move around up and down, left and right. The rule was never to stay straight and level for long and give the enemy a chance to hit you. — Gerry Carroll, *North S*A*R*, p. 202, 1991

jinky *adjective*

unlucky *US, 1969*

From "jinx."

- Don't catch any crippled or cross-eyed marks. They're jinky. — Iceberg Slim (Robert Beck), *Trick Baby*, p. 146, 1969

jinx note *noun*

a two-dollar bill *US, 1970*

- — Claudio R. Salvucci, *The Philadelphia Dialect Dictionary*, p. 46, 1996

jism trail *noun*

semen on a partner's body after ejaculation *US, 2007*

A pun on the Chisholm Trail, the major route for cattle drives from Texas to Abilene.

- Cal ambled closer and eased his throbbing rod into Lynn's heated chest canyon, began churning his hips in a dosey-do as old as the Jism Trail itself. — Cathryn Cooper, *Sex & Submission*, p. 69, 2007

jit *noun*

a nickel; five cents *US, 1913*

- — Lou Shelly, *Hepcats Jive Talk Dictionary*, p. 13, 1945
- "Got a jit? I need a couple more jits to get a bottle," he said. — James T. Farrell, *Saturday Night*, p. 27, 1947
- — John Scarne, *Scarne on Dice*, p. 471, 1974

jitney *noun*

in poker, a $5 chip *US, 1988*

- — George Percy, *The Language of Poker*, p. 49, 1988

jitterbug *noun*

a swing jazz enthusiast *US, 1938*

- Dance floors are crowded with jitterbugs. — Jack Lait and Lee Mortimer, *Washington Confidential*, p. 133, 1951

jitterbug *verb*

1 to fool around *US, 1942*

- Walk calm. No jitterbugging. Wear your cap straight. — Hal Ellson, *Duke*, p. 71, 1949
- You're just jitter-buggin' down there with them three bricks. — Henry Williamson, *Hustler!*, p. 146, 1965

2 to fight, especially between gangs *US, 1958*

- By the early 1960's, a new phenomenon had presented itself—female "bopping" or "jitterbugging" gangs. — James Haskins, *Street Gangs*, p. 96, 1974

jitters *noun*

uncontrolled shaking; extreme nervousness *US, 1929*

- "Hope you can clear this up quick, Mr. Tracy," he said. "I'm getting the jitters." — Chester Gould, *Dick Tracy Meets the Night Crawler*, p. 24, 1945
- The place was a bad spot to be in at night if you had the jitters. — Mickey Spillane, *I, The Jury*, p. 75, 1947
- Now, Folks, our play together is going to be ragged as hell for a while. But don't let it give you the jitters. — Iceberg Slim (Robert Beck), *Trick Baby*, p. 145, 1969

jive *noun*

1 insincere talk; nonsense *US, 1928*

- [I]f they got mad about it he gave them a line of his soft Southern jive. — Chester Himes, *If He Hollers Let Him Go*, p. 24, 1945
- Show me where the kitty lives and I'll believe that jive. — Hal Ellson, *The Golden Spike*, p. 40, 1952
- And also how much I would esteem myself once I got rid of them somewhere in the Loop, how I had put myself out for my fellow man and all that jive. — Clancy Sigal, *Going Away*, p. 162, 1961
- But back he came, more dead than alive / And the monkey came up with more of his jive. — Dennis Wepman et al., *The Life*, p. 24, 1976

2 a highly stylized vernacular that originated with black jazz musicians *US, 1928*

Spoken by **HEP CAT(S)**, incorporating a mix of new coinages or meanings with older adoptions; few original words remain in circulation.

- The night wound up with them accusing me of trying to pass for white, because they couldn't believe that any white man could be as hip to the jive as I was. — Mezz Mezzrow, *Really the Blues*, p. 204, 1946

3 swing jazz *US, 1937*

- Hero-worship of Americans and the flashier aspects of American life seem to be the most immediate reason for the popularity of jive[.] — William Sansom, *A Public for Jive [The Public's Progress]*, 1947
- The Blue Mirror, around the corner, specializes in hot jive. — Jack Lait and Lee Mortimer, *Washington Confidential*, p. 132, 1951

4 heroin or, less often, opium *US, 1946*

- Boy, leave me tell you one thing, if you knew like we know, you'd leave this jive alone[.] — Mezz Mezzrow, *Really the Blues*, p. 248, 1946
- You've been taking dope, horse, jive, anything you want to call it. — Hal Ellson, *The Golden Spike*, p. 22, 1952
- "What started you on the jive?" Jake asked. — Herbert Simmons, *Corner Boy*, p. 55, 1957
- He was a dope fiend, and he told me he had just beat a rap, and needed some jive. — Henry Williamson, *Hustler!*, p. 149, 1965

5 marijuana or a marijuana cigarette *US, 1963*

- It's oney gauge he's on, a little jive. Marijuana ain't no habit like heroin. — George Mandel, *Flee the Angry Strangers*, p. 20, 1948
- I mean, the main studs could have called a conference and set down and worked the whole thing out over a few sticks of this mellow jive. — Ross Russell, *The Sound*, p. 22, 1961
- We can cop some jive anyplace. — Donald Goines, *Cry Revenge*, p. 41, 1974

6 a handgun *US, 1969*

- [T]hey had fought over a woman and then over a gun, which one of the men referred to at different times as "my piece," "my thing," "my roscoe," "my jive," "my cannon," "my shit," "my pipe," and "my heater." — L.H. Whittemore, *Cop!*, p. 197, 1969

jive *verb*

1 to speak with a lack of sincerity *US, 1928*

- Monkey wasn't jiving about that bartender. He wasn't exactly a rabbi[.] — Mezz Mezzrow, *Really the Blues*, p. 74, 1946

- Let's hold class for the squares on how to properly jive a chick. — Dan Burley, *Diggeth Thou?*, p. 5, 1959
- The cops put me in the back room. I'm jiving with the spades. — Abbie Hoffman, *Revolution for the Hell of It*, p. 19, 1968
- Sapphire puts her hands on her hips to indicate that she ain't jivin' and does mean to be taken seriously. — Carolyn Greene, *70 Soul Secrets of Sapphire*, 1973

2 to dance *US, 1938*

- When a band plays one [a rumba], flabbergasted hoofers try to jive to it. — Jack Lait and Lee Mortimer, *Washington Confidential*, p. 133, 1951
- It was Danny and the Juniors singing "At the Hop," which gave Esme and me a chance to do some cool jiving all the way down the corridor to the history class[.] — Max Shulman, *I was a Teen-Age Dwarf*, p. 10, 1959

jive *adjective*

insincere, phony, pretentious *US, 1946*

- This was my first thing on my own since going up there with that jive shit with the Rev. — Babs Gonzales, *Movin' On Down De Line*, p. 32, 1975
- Rack 'em up, house man, and check my gun / I don't want to kill the jive motherfucker; I want to shoot him one. — Dennis Wepman et al., *The Life*, p. 31, 1976
- I felt, no man cared if I were alive/I felt the whole world was so jive. — Village People, *Y.M.C.A.*, 1978
- I would just be cool, I planned, carry my knife, stop running around with that jive Village Gang, and stay out of the way of other fools who would want to jump on me for nothing. — Bobby Seale, *A Lonely Rage*, p. 64, 1978

jive-ass *noun*

an insincere, unreliable person *US, 1967*

- No, he became a hustler, a jiveass, a jazz player who could never quite get the versatility to match the humming in his head[.] — Cecil Brown, *The Life & Loves of Mr. Jiveass Nigger*, p. 8, 1969

jive-ass *adjective*

worthless, unreliable *US, 1959*

- I wasn't weighted down and barred from vicarious ecstasy by no jiveass junior logarithm trash[.] — Lester Bangs, *Psychotic Reactions and Carburetor Dung*, p. 59, 1971
- We goin' take this whole fuckin' jiveass town by the fuckin' throat and make it ours! — Donald Goines, *Inner City Hoodlum*, p. 8, 1975

jive at five *noun*

the daily press briefings by the US military in Vietnam during the war *US, 1977*

- Five O'Clock Follies, Jive at Five, war stories. — Michael Herr, *Dispatches*, p. 37, 1977

jive bitch *noun*

a troublemaker *US, 1966*

- The deviance of the "jive bitch," on the other hand, is a deliberate, calculated strategy to cause conflict. — Rose Giallombardo, *Society of Women*, p. 116, 1966

jive bomber *noun*

a skilled dancer *US, 1945*

- — *Yank*, p. 18, 24th March 1945

jiver *noun*

an inveterate flatterer *US, 1947*

- — Marcus Hanna Boulware, *Jive and Slang of Students in Negro Colleges*, 1947

jive stick *noun*

a marijuana cigarette *US, 1945*

- — *American Speech*, p. 87, May 1955: "Narcotic argot along the Mexican Border"

jivetime *adjective*

worthless *US, 1962*

- "Jivetime Uncle Tom motherfucker!" said someone from the back of the room. — James Alan McPherson, *Hue and Cry*, p. 175, 1969

jiz biz *noun*

the sex industry *US, 2005*

- She has quit the jiz biz three times since then but always seems to come back for more. — Mr. Skin, *Mr. Skin's Skincyclopedia*, p. 179, 2005
- Are these girls still in the jiz biz? — board.freeones.com, 26th August 2006

jizz *verb*

to ejaculate *US, 1983*

- The Bad Czech came running into the watch commander's office, took a look and cried, "Ludwig jizzed all over the lieutenant's floor." — Joseph Wambaugh, *Delta Star*, p. 105, 1984

- He sort of matter-of-factly removed his dork, pressed the length of it against her, and jizzed on her ass[.] — Josh Alan Friedman, *Tales of Times Square*, p. 107, 1986
- Then, I want you to flick at my nuts while your friend spanks me into the same Dixie cup Silent Bob jizzed in. — Kevin Smith, *Jay and Silent Bob Strike Back*, p. 90, 2001
- "Because he jizzed on your skirt?" Gretchen asked. — Joe Meno, *Hairstyles of the Damned*, p. 113, 270

jizz; jizzum; jism; jiz; jizm; gism; gizzum *noun*
semen *US, 1941*
Links to an earlier use as "life-force, energy, spirit"; a meaning that, occasionally, may still be intended.

- The world network of junkies, tuned on a cord of rancid jissom, tying up in furnished rooms, shivering in the junk-sick morning. — William Burroughs, *Naked Lunch*, p. 6, 1957
- Swallowing gism is rather like getting used to raw clams: you have to give it a chance and before you know it, you're addicted. — *Screw*, p. 9, 1st March 1970
- I didn't much like the sounds of romance the first time I saw jizz. — Oscar Zeta Acosta, *The Autobiography of a Brown Buffalo*, p. 83, 1972
- When he finally spurts his thick jiz, she looks at you, the viewer, with a naughty smile. — *Adult Video*, p. 13, August/September 1986
- How would you like to gargle rat jiz? — *South Park*, 1999
- You have a lot of jizz being launched in Porn Valley. — Editors of Adult Video News, *The AVN Guide to the 500 Greatest Adult Films of All Time*, p. 231, 2005

jizzbag *noun*
an offensive and disgusting person *US, 1993*
Literally, "a condom."

- Who is this jizzbag judge? Bibe quotes—from what, the Book of Dick? — Carl Hiaasen, *Strip Tease*, p. 71, 1993

jizzbucket *noun*
a despicable person *US, 1987*

- For all of you who want to get rid of these jizzbucket assholes as badly as I do, I have a few words of advice. — *alt.sports.football.pro.sf-49ers*, 10th October 1995
- He remembered some jizzbucket he'd picked up in Annapolis a few years ago[.] — Edward Lee, *Portrait of the Psychopath as a Young Woman*, p. 167, 2003

jizzer *noun*
a scene in a pornographic film or single photograph showing a man ejaculating *US, 1995*

- — *Adult Video News*, p. 42, August 1995

jizz joint *noun*
a sex club *US, 2000*

- Because of the way it positions itself, this particular jizz joint is not a haven for working-class girls in a dead-end town or junkies supporting a habit. — *Village Voice*, 31st October 2000

jizz-mopper *noun*
an employee in a pornographic video arcade or sex show who cleans up after customers who have come have left *US, 1994*

- You know how much money the average jizz-mopper makes per hour? — *Clerks*, 1994

jizz rag *noun*
a rag used for wiping semen *US, 1983*

- "I think you oughta start carrying a jizz rag, Hans," Cecil Higgins said. — Joseph Wambaugh, *The Delta Star*, p. 105, 1983
- Booths seem less private, uh, more open, wider entry, but they do each have a mini-trashcan for jizz-rag disposal. — Richard Meltzer, *A Whore Just Like the Rest*, p. 427, 1991
- I got a jizz-rag, cleaned her up and got dressed. — Pat Mulligan, *The Life and Times of a Hollywood Bad Boy*, p. 69, 2006

JO *noun*
1 an act of male masturbation *US, 1972*
An abbreviation of **JERK-OFF**.

- I went two weeks with j/o so I would be really hot. [Letter] — *Drummer*, p. 73, 1979

2 a job *US, 1993*

- — *Washington Post*, 14th October 1993

JO *verb*
(used of a male) to masturbate *US, 1959*
An abbreviation of the oh-so-common **JERK OFF**.

- I tried to "read between the lines" in the famous Nancy Drew books, searching for some deep secret insinuation of erotica so powerful and pervasive as to account for the extraordinary popularity of these books, but alas, was able to garner no mileage ("J.O." wise) from this innocuous, and seemingly endless, series. — Terry Southern, *Now Dig This*, p. 2, 1986
- This venture falls in the middle range of JO tapes—good enough for aficionados of the format, but not likely to impress viewers who prefer heavier action. — *Adult Video News*, p. 95, February 1993
- — Pamela Munro, *U.C.L.A. Slang*, p. 87, 2001

joan; jone *verb*
to insult in a competitive, quasi-friendly spirit *US, 1939*

- Guys built respectable reps in the community if they could jone hard. — Nathan McCall, *Makes Me Wanna Holler*, p. 23, 1994
- There are many different terms for playing the dozens, including "bagging, capping, cracking, dissing, hiking, joning, ranking, ribbing, serving, signifying, slipping, sounding and snapping." — James Haskins, *The Story of Hip-Hop*, p. 54, 2000

Joanie *adjective*
profoundly out of touch with current fashions and trends *US, 1982*

- — Mary Corey and Victoria Westermark, *Fer Shurr! How to be a Valley Girl*, 1982

job *noun*
1 used as a substitute for a noun which is apparent from context, especially of cars *US, 1896*
Sometimes embellished to "jobby."

- The transport, a lumbering C-47, like the jobs shot down by the South Slavs, could not possibly have been mistaken for a bomber[.] — A.J. Liebling, *The Wayward Pressman*, p. 195, 1947
- He just got a Jaguar. One of those little English jobs that can do around two hundred miles an hour. — J.D. Salinger, *Catcher in the Rye*, p. 1, 1951
- "Let's take the Caddy," he said, walking toward the black four-door job[.] — Wade Hunter, *The Sex Peddler*, p. 85, 1963
- Is that the new car out there? The little red Wop job? — *The Graduate*, 1967
- Rico Carty hit two home runs off him. One of them was a two-run job in the last of the eighth[.] — Jim Bouton, *Ball Four*, p. 341, 1970

2 a criminal venture, usually a robbery *US, 1928*

- [W]hen he got home he would find them lounging about his living room, just back from one of these jobs somewhere in the city[.] — John Clellon Holmes, *Go*, p. 213, 1952
- We pulled the first job that night[.] — Malcolm X and Alex Haley, *The Autobiography of Malcolm X*, p. 143, 1964
- He pulled that job to pay for the band's room service tab from that Chiwanous gig in Pols city. — *The Blues Brothers*, 1980
- She hooked up with Fred McGar, they've done a couple jobs together. Helluva woman. Good little thief. — *Reservoir Dogs*, 1992

3 a medical procedure *US, 1943*
A variant of "job" (a variety), usually combined with a body part: "nose," "boob," etc.

- I know you and Sicora got plastic jobs. — James Ellroy, *Hollywood Nocturnes*, p. 260, 1994

4 an act of defecation *US, 1975*

- — *American Speech*, p. 62, Spring–Summer 1975: "Razorback slang"

5 in professional wrestling, a planned, voluntary loss *US, 1990*

- job n. a staged loss. A clean job is a staged loss by legal pinfall or submission without resort to illegalities. — *rec.sports.pro-wrestling*, 17th July 1990
- But even though I'm writing about a sport that some feel is not "real," this is a real story, and the real truth is I did the job that night (lost the match). — Mick Foley, *Mankind*, p. 7, 1999
- His real name was Bill Howard, and he was known for "doing jobs" (losing). — Bobby Heenan, *Bobby the Brain*, p. 35, 2002

6 the injection of a drug for nonmedicinal purposes *US, 1970*

- — William D. Alsever, *Glossary for the Establishment and Other Uptight People*, p. 17, December 1970
- — Eugene Landy, *The Underground Dictionary*, p. 113, 1971

job *verb*
1 to rob, to steal, to cheat *US, 1889*

- "Pinched. Jobbed. Swiped. Stole," he says, happily. "You know, man, like somebody boosted my threads." — Ken Kesey, *One Flew Over the Cuckoo's Nest*, p. 94, 1962
- So, the Red Sox were jobbed out of Game Three and the bubble-gum chewing Big Red Machine took the Series lead. — Bill Cardoso, *The Maltese Sangweech*, p. 178, 1984

- "He says he's sure he's being jobbed," Breda said. — Joseph Wambaugh, *Fugitive Nights*, p. 118, 1992

2 to suffer a planned, voluntary loss in a professional wrestling match *US, 1990*

- In any case, rumors have Hogan facing someone else (who's willing to job?) in place of Gordy. — *Herb's Wrestling Tidbits*, 4th April 1990
- — *Washington Post*, p. 36, 10th March 2000: "A wrestling glossary"
- When Backlund refused to hand over the belt, he was screwed out of it in a setup with the Iron Sheik, who in turn jobbed it to Hogan. — *Rampage Magazine*, p. 71, September 2000

3 to inject a drug *US, 1967*

- — John B. Williams, *Narcotics and Hallucinogenics*, p. 113, 1967

▶ **job a line**
in sports betting, to change the odds without bettors' knowledge *US, 1974*

- I mean, I'd heard about BMs jobbing lines, but Barry had the kind of customers you didn't do it with on a whim. — Gary Mayer, *Bookie*, p. 172, 1974

jobber *noun*
a professional wrestler who is regularly assigned to lose to advance the careers of others *US, 1990*

- Flair pummeled a jobber and then goaded Sting to come to the ringside. — *Herb's Wrestling Tidbits*, 5th July 1990
- Professional jobbers are unique in their trade. In no other sport is one paid to lose and make his opponent look good while doing so. — Jeff Archer, *Theater in a Squared Circle*, p. 113, 1999
- They ran him through a small army of jobbers. — *Rampage Magazine*, September 2000
- He'd squash the jobbers on television, but then he'd lose to the babyface in the house show. — Missy Hyatt, *Missy Hyatt*, p. 21, 2001

jobber to the stars *noun*
a moderately talented professional wrestler who is assigned to lose to the most popular wrestlers *US, 1996*

- These guys will be given a few wins before becoming jobbers to the stars, unless they do the unlikely and magically get over. — *Herb's Wrestling Tidbits*, 4th July 1996

jobbie *noun*
a racehorse *US, 1974*

- — David W. Maurer, *Argot of the Racetrack*, p. 38, 1951

jobo; joro *noun*
a woman, mistress or prostitute *US, 1968*
From the Japanese, used by US military in Korea.

- — Carl Fleischhauer, *A Glossary of Army Slang*, p. 28, 1968

job out *verb*
to assign a wrestler to lose intentionally to advance the career of another *US, 1990*

- Perhaps the sub will be Tom Zenk, who they seem to be jobbing out. — *Herb's Wrestling Tidbits*, 25th October 1990

jobroni; jobrone; gibroni *noun*
a professional wrestler who is regularly assigned to lose *US, 1999*
Embellishments of the standard **JOBBER**.

- A star simply uses this medium (television) to build his stature and display his style by manhandling a "gibroni"—an unknown or habitual loser. — Larry Nelson and James Jones, *Stranglehold*, p. 45, 1999
- Bounty Hunters have been beating up jobronis for weeks now and they freaked when Fuller announced Gordy. — Georgiann Makropoulos, *Chatterbox*, 8th August 2000

jock *noun*
1 an athlete, especially a student athlete *US, 1957*
Originally referred to a man's genitals, leading to "jock strap" as an athletic support, leading to a clipped "jock" for the support, leading to application to the man wearing the support. Usually, but not always, suggestive of a certain mindlessness.

- Despite its current appellation as the "Jock" House, Winthrop remains one of the most versatile yet homogeneous houses at Harvard. — *Harvard Crimson*, 22nd March 1957
- Jocks, as everyone who ever came within shouting distance of a campus knows, are the college athletes. — Frederick Kohner, *The Affairs of Gidget*, p. 52, 1963

- As with the demonstrations against Marine campus recruiting in the spring of '67, threats of violence from the right will bring hundreds of the usually moderate to the SDS ranks just to align themselves against jock violence. — James Simon Kunen, *The Strawberry Statement*, p. 27, 1968
- I guess you could call a tennis player a jock. I think they do wear them. At least the guys do. — C.D. Payne, *Youth in Revolt*, p. 210, 1993

2 a jockey *UK, 1826*

- She's hanging around the track every day. I'm interested, professionally. I find out she's some jock's regular, she's living with the shrimp. — Truman Capote, *Breakfast at Tiffany's*, p. 31, 1958
- He was a senior jock who had ridden in all parts of the globe. — Wilda Moxham, *The Apprentice*, p. 48, 1969

3 a disc jockey *US, 1947*

- After the Battle of Bermuda, I prepared a resume that painted me as a jock of all trades. — Cousin Bruce Morrow, *Cousin Brucie*, p. 57, 1987

4 a fighter pilot *US, 1959*

- As the chopper lifted off, the two figures on the ground grew smaller and smaller—the helicopter jock from Little Rock keeping vigil over a fellow soldier, a Vietnamese peasant. — Elaine Shepard, *The Doom Pussy*, p. 13, 1967
- — *American Speech*, p. 123, Summer 1986: "The language of Naval fighter pilots"
- Once three was an F-4 jock by the name of Heinz E. Coordes. — Joseph Tuso, *Singing the Vietnam Blues*, p. 28, 1990: The Ballad of Heinz E. Coordes

5 the penis; the male genitals *UK, 1790*

- The ugly big-tit broad would stand there [in the dream] buck naked with a jock three times the size of my own. — Iceberg Slim (Robert Beck), *Trick Baby*, p. 114, 1969
- [O]nce club beats and mediocre lyrics become the fashionable norm it seems everyone, your magazine included, is on the rappers' jocks. — *Hip-Hop Connection*, p. 9, July 2002

6 an athletic supporter *US, 1985*
An abbreviation of "jock strap."

- Like the baseball players that they're always catching on the on-deck circle, got their hands down in their jocks, moving their balls around. — George V. Higgins, *Penance for Jerry Kennedy*, p. 31, 1985

7 a computer programer who enumerates all possible combinations to find the one that solves the problem *US, 1983*

- — Guy L. Steele et al., *The Hacker's Dictionary*, p. 85, 1983

jock *verb*
1 to have sex *UK, 1699*

- — Pamela Munro, *U.C.L.A. Slang*, p. 53, 1989

2 to like; to find attractive *US, 1986*

- Watch, I'm 'a roll up, and y'all niggas gon' be jockin'. — *Menace II Society*, 1993
- — Rick Ayers (Editor), *Berkeley High Slang Dictionary*, p. 28, 2004

jock collar *noun*
a rubber ring fitted around the base of the penis *US, 1969*
Later and better known as a **COCK RING**.

- Pocket was at the back of the poolroom with an old Jewish peddler of French ticklers, Spanish fly, and jock collars. — Iceberg Slim (Robert Beck), *Trick Baby*, p. 218, 1969

jocker *noun*
1 an aggressive, predatory male homosexual *US, 1893*

- They are usually long-terms and are familiarly known to inmates by such local cognomens as "wolves," "top men," "jockers" or "daddies." — *Ebony*, p. 82, July 1951
- So far as possible, prison wolves or "jockers" are kept from preying on the young, frightened and physically or morally weak inmate. — Caryl Chessman, *Cell 2456 Death Row*, p. 220, 1954
- Jockers and wolves are synonymous terms to describe the active partners in sodomy. — *New York Mattachine Newsletter*, p. 6, June 1961
- "My, my," the Spook murmured, "not a feather on him. Some jocker's due to score." — Malcolm Braly, *On the Yard*, p. 35, 1967
- Others entered into a permanent relationship—a jocker-kid relationship—with a homosexual. — John Irwin, *The Felon*, p. 28, 1970

2 an older homosexual male living with and by virtue of the earnings of a younger companion *US, 1890s to 1970s*
Originally tramp slang.

- — *Fact*, p. 26, January–February 1965

jockey *verb*
to drive, to operate *US, 1948*

- That's why you're jockeying a register in some fucking local convenience store instead of doing an honest day's work. — *Clerks*, 1994

jock itch noun

a sweat-induced rash in the crotch *US*, *1950*

- He'd developed incurable jock itch, and to his astonishment, his leather gear had independent sweat rings. — Joseph Wambaugh, *Fugitive Nights*, pp. 33–34, 1992

jocko noun

an athlete, a jock *US*, *1970*

- He was just another jocko, but he was an ace because he was always out with Mickey Mantle and the boys[.] — Jim Bouton, *Ball Four*, p. 81, 1970

jock rot noun

a rash in the crotch *US*, *1982*

- "I, ah, got some cuts en some jock rot. That's all." — John Del Vecchio, *The 13th Valley*, p. 419, 1982

jock-slap verb

to knee someone in the face *US*, *1994*

- I learned how to jock-slap a man, grab him by the head and ram a knee into his face. — Nathan McCall, *Makes Me Wanna Holler*, p. 55, 1994

jock-sniffer noun

an obsequious sports fan who tries to associate with athletes *US*, *1971*

- Or you see him at Lindell's with the jock sniffers. Every couple of years he offers to buy the Tigers and in between he buys 'em drinks. — Elmore Leoanrd, *Split Images*, p. 50, 1981

jock sniffing noun

sycophantic behavior towards athletes *US*, *2001*

- For a while that evening, the all-time jock-sniffing record was in serious jeopardy. — Dan Jenkins, *The Money-Whipped Steer-Job Three-Jack Give-Up Artist*, p. 214, 2001

jockstrap noun

an athlete *US*, *1944*

- "BB a jockstrap, Neil?" "Well, no. Concentrates on the books." — Burt Hirschfield, *Fire Island*, p. 17, 1970
- He's this nine year old jockstrap in the Little League, see, really far-out kid. — Gurney Norman, *Divine Right's Trip (Last Whole Earth Catalog)*, p. 193, 1971

jock strapper noun

an athlete *US*, *1970*

- Franklin was an all-American jock strapper. a high school letterman according to the conversations they had the first few days in the academy. — Joseph Wambaugh, *The New Centurions*, p. 23, 1970

Jody noun

1 the anonymous seducer of a soldier's girlfriend back home *US*, *1944*

- The servicemen were always hostile towards a Jodie, especially a black Jodie in his fine Jodie clothes. — Chester Himes, *If He Hollers Let Him Go*, p. 79, 1945
- Then old Jody he turned over with his eyes all red / he said, "I beg your pardon, baby," says, "now what is that you said?" — Bruce Jackson, *Get Your Ass in the Water and Swim Like Me*, p. 93, 1964
- "Your best friend, Jody, is already pumping your girlfriend, Mary Jane Rottencrotch, asshole." — Lynda Van Devanter, *Home Before Morning*, p. 68, 1983
- Ain't no use in going home / Jody's got your girl and gone. — Sandee Shaffer Johnson, *Cadences*, p. 15, 1986

2 a male civilian during wartime *US*, *1944*

- I tried to go to college but I couldn't stand it. I felt I was the only Jodie there. — Chester Himes, *Cast the First Stone*, p. 256, 1952

3 a black seducer of white women *US*, *1967*

- "Jody" is a contraction of "Joe-the-Grinder" ("Sweet spot finder"), whose balls weighed forty-four pounds, whose penis was gigantic. — Robert deCoy, *The Nigger Bible*, p. 32, 1967

Jody call noun

a marching rhyme or cadence *US*, *1963*

- The troops in unison answered a sergeant's jody call. — Rick Atkinson, *In the Company of Soldiers*, p. 32, 2004

Joe noun

1 coffee *US*, *1927*

Originally tramp slang.

- Won't even trust me for a cup of joe until I get a job. — Mickey Spillane, *My Gun is Quick*, p. 7, 1950

- I do enjoy a good cuppa joe. — *Austin Powers*, 1999
- Right at that moment everyone in Editorial suddenly seemed to crave a good strong cup of joe[.] — Rita Ciresi, *Pink Slip*, p. 107, 1999
- You expect Clark Gable to swagger in for a cup of Joe[.] — Josh Friedman, *When Sex Was Dirty*, p. 119, 2005

2 a regular fellow *US*, *1911*

- I knew him well. A nice Joe that had a heart of gold. — Mickey Spillane, *I, The Jury*, p. 44, 1947
- "This Angelo guy, he's about the biggest joe in the Frisco rackets, isn't he?" — Richard Prather, *The Peddler*, p. 11, 1952
- He was a good old joe, fat, happy, middlewestern. — Jack Kerouac, *The Dharma Bums*, p. 101, 1958
- And others who seem to represent none but themselves, quirky joes, who shouted to the crowds to buy the Militant, or Sparticist, or National Liberation Front buttons. — Sidney Bernard, *This Way to the Apocalypse*, pp. 60–61, 1965

3 a new worker who cannot perform up to expected standards *US*, *1989*

- "Don't ever get hit on the head with one of these, some Joe happens to drop it." He told her a Joe was an ironworker who couldn't hack it. — Elmore Leonard, *Killshot*, p. 34, 1989

4 used to create an imaginary person, first name Joe, last name the quality or characteristic that is personified *US*, *1912*

- I meet the star of the show, Bill Leighton, whom I recognize as the typical Joe Moderator of countless afternoon programs. — James Simon Kunen, *The Strawberry Statement*, p. 56, 1968

5 a member of the Navajo Indian tribe *US*, *1963*

An abbreviation of Nava-Joe.

- — *American Speech*, p. 271, December 1963: "American Indian student slang"

6 a police officer *US*, *1987*

- Straite, who later stood outside the store, warned of Remington's approach by yelling: "Here comes the Joes!"—street slang for police officers. — *Washington Post*, p. B3, 30th May 1987

Joe Average noun

a notional, average man *US*, *1936*

- Rather than offering up an illuminating case of Mr. and Mrs. Joe Average, the Bush campaign was casting a political freak show in order to present a tiny minority as the norm. — Al Franken, *Lies and the Lying Liars Who Tell Them*, p. 291, 2003

Joe Balls noun

used as a derogatory personification of the typical US soldier *US*, *1946*

- — *American Speech*, p. 238, October 1946: "World War II slang of maladjustment"

Joe Blow noun

1 an average, typical citizen *US*, *1924*

- "If that isn't a natural my name just isn't Joe Blow and we might as well closeup shop right now and go to sea!" — William Brinkley, *Don't Go Near the Water*, p. 12, 1956
- [I]f Joe Blow has promised to come by and run him home in the chuggedy-chug, he may hang around longer than usual[.] — Dick Clark, *To Goof or Not to Goof*, p. 85, 1963
- I can find a better way of spending my life than behind Joe Blow's desk for twenty-five, thirty dollars a day, you know. — Christina and Richard Milner, *Black Players*, p. 258, 1972
- [T]he Joe Blows and their housewives who went about life as usual while the grunts had been counting off their hours and days in the paddies and hills. — Charles Anderson, *The Grunts*, p. 177, 1976

2 an excellent musician *US*, *1945*

- — Lou Shelly, *Hepcats Jive Talk Dictionary*, p. 28, 1945

Joe Blow biography noun

a glowing biographical story about a soldier in his hometown newspaper *US*, *1946*

- — *American Speech*, p. 74, February 1946: "Some words of war and peace from 1945"

Joe Chink noun

1 a heroin addiction *US*, *1973*

A further personification of the older **CHINAMAN** (a heroin addiction).

- And Stoney, believe me, I'm gonna git Joe Chink off my back. — A.S. Jackson, *Gentleman Pimp*, p. 73, 1973

2 a soldier in the armed forces of the People's Republic of China *US*, *1950*

- [M]ud and rain, big numbers and all, we were set for Joe Chink. — David Hackworth, *About Face*, p. 97, 1989

Joe Citizen noun

a notional, average male citizen US, 1985

- Detective Chris Cagney and victim Joe Citizen are the only witnesses willing to testify against bad guy Moe Mugger. — net.politics, 7th February 1985
- And while a high murder rate is deplorable, it doesn't always mean that Joe Citizen stands a greater chance of being randomly gunned down on his way to the K mart. — Carl Hiaasen, Kick Ass, p. 33, 1999

Joe College noun

a stereotypical male college student US, 1932

- They'd throw big wine parties and have girls and end up jumping out of windows and playing Joe College pranks up and down town. — Jack Kerouac, The Dharma Bums, p. 22, 1958
- Joe College has finally arrived. — Mart Crowley, The Boys in the Band, p. 41, 1968
- More important, he was the real enemy, we thought, since he was our competition for the hearts and minds of Joe and Susie College, who were naively jumping on his clean-cut haywagon. — Raymond Mungo, Famous Long Ago, p. 80, 1970
- "I was expecting an older man, but he looked like Joe College," she recalled. — Kathryn Leigh Scott, The Bunny Years, p. 52, 1998

Joe Cool noun

used for expressing the ultimate in fashion and modernity US, 1971

- I smiled my best fucking suave Joe Cool look. — Oscar Zeta Acosta, The Autobiography of a Brown Buffalo, p. 41, 1972

Joe Doakes noun

a notional, average if anonymous person US, 1926

- That's what they want, not what Joe Doakes had for breakfast in the morning. — Leigh Montville, Ted Williams, p. 6, 2004

Joe Doe; Joe Roe noun

used as a name for a male blind date US, 1951

Teen slang.

- — Newsweek, p. 28, 8th October 1951

Joe Goss noun

a boss US, 1923

- They killed a Joe Goss that time, blew the whole thing wide open. — Richard Stark, The Man with the Getaway Face, p. 10, 1963

Joe Hero noun

a typical hero US, 1977

- What the fuck was I supposed to do? Be Joe Hero? — Edwin Torres, Q & A, 1977

Joe Patriot noun

a prototypical patriot US, 1994

- I froze on Joe Patriot: booze-flushed, Legion cap, Legion armband. — James Ellroy, Hollywood Nocturnes, p. 20, 1994

Joe-pot noun

a coffee pot US, 1979

Korean war usage.

- Coffee was Joe; a coffeepot, a Joe-pot. — William Manchester, Goodbye, Darkness, p. 146, 1979

Joe Public noun

an average citizen; the regular man on the street US, 1942

Originally theatrical of an audience member; gently derogatory.

- Their jazz was only a musical version of the hard-cutting broadsides that two foxy studs named Mencken and Nathan were beginning to shoot at Joe Public in the pages of The American Mercury[.] — Mezz Mezzrow, Really the Blues, p. 103, 1946

Joe Sad noun

an unpopular person US, 1932

- Blue may be a Joe Sad but he knows what I sell. — Susan Wheeler, Record Palace, p. 199, 2005

Joe Schmo; Joe Shmo noun

an average, if dull and dim, person US, 1947

- Joe Schmo, who shares an office with six other guys in a Broadway loft, is in the business of publicizing such pillars of the American scene as second-rate movie, radio and flea circus stars and unpopular potmaine parlors. — Traverse City (Michigan) Record Eagle, p. 1, 23rd May 1947
- Like I might find old Joe Schmoe today and buy three bags from him and find that one bag straightens me out. — James Mills, The Panic in Needle Park, p. 46, 1966

- How come in former lifetimes, everybody was someone famous. How come nobody ever says that were Joe Schmo? — Bull Durham, 1988
- "Weighing in at a combined total weight of 437 pounds, Joe Schmo and John Doe!" — Heidi Mattson, Ivy League Stripper, p. 122, 1995

Joe Shit noun

a notional, stereotypical person of no consequence US, 1942

- Private Joe Shit? Number zero-zero-zero? — Donn Pearce, Nobody Came Back, p. 111, 2005

Joe Sixpack noun

a stereotypical working-class male US, 1973

- In this Dougherty is not all that different, having an idea to sell Joe Sixpack on tax reform and Sen. George McGovern[.] — Coshocton (Ohio) Tribune, p. 6, 10th September 1973
- Archie Bunker/Joe Sixpack is simply not going to answer these questions. — The Hite Report on Male Sexuality, p. 1052, 1981

Joe the grinder noun

used as a generic term for the man that a prisoner's wife or girlfriend takes up with while the man is in prison US, 1964

- Jody say, "Don't front me with that shit because it's not anywhere / and this is Joe the Grinder and damn that square." — Bruce Jackson, Get Your Ass in the Water and Swim Like Me, p. 97, 1964
- The inmates hailed him as Joe the Grinder, giving him the same wry name they gave to the man who made it into their wife's bed while they were locked, hopeless and despairing, in jail. — Malcolm Braly, On the Yard, p. 73, 1967
- He should have just taken a dollar out of the wallet, given it to Joe the Grinder, and walked out, instead of blowing her away like he did. — Gerald Petievich, Money Men, p. 120, 1981

Joe Zilch noun

a notional, average person US, 1925

- No, Joe Zilch is not stupid. He absorbs just exactly what he's being taught. — Ayn Rand, Letters of Ayn Rand, p. 298, 1995

jog verb

to push with one foot while skateboarding US, 1984

- — San Francisco Sunday Examiner & Chronicle, p. 20, 2nd September 1984: "Say it right"

john noun

1 a prostitute's customer US, 1906

From the sense as "generic man," probably via the criminal use as "dupe" or "victim."

- The johns lined up for Marcelle like it was payday. — Mezz Mezzrow, Really the Blues, p. 23, 1946
- Our hustlers sat on their steps and called to the "Johns" as they passed by — Louis Armstrong, Satchmo: My Life in New Orleans, p. 95, 1954
- Freddie had done less shoeshining and towel-hustling than selling liquor and reefers, and putting white "Johns" in touch with Negro whores. — Malcolm X and Alex Haley, The Autobiography of Malcolm X, p. 49, 1964
- So you take a call and you go to a hotel room and there's some John you've never seen before, but he wants you. — Klute, 1971

2 a toilet US, 1942

- And when I went to see Tristano I overheard some of the cats discussing him in the john. — Jack Kerouac, Letter to Allen Ginsburg, p. 141, 2nd January 1948
- Oh, I mean I want to go to the john. — Sue Rhodes, And when she was bad she was popular, p. 117, 1968
- [S]he had said, Wait a minute, and got up and went to the john to piss and came back and got in the same position again. — Cecil Brown, The Life & Loves of Mr. Jiveass Nigger, p. 79, 1969
- He pulled up his pants, flushed the john, and stretched out on a steel cot. — Carl Hiaasen, Tourist Season, p. 14, 2000

3 a lieutenant US, 1937

- — Carl Fleischhauer, A Glossary of Army Slang, p. 28, 1968
- This had disabused Mr. Ripley of the notion that, for some inexplicable reason, the Raiders had turned their armory over to a baby-faced candy-ass second john fresh from Quantico. — W.E.B. Griffin, The Corps Book II, p. 300, 1987

4 in a deck of playing cards, a jack US, 1967

- — Albert H. Morehead, The Complete Guide to Winning Poker, p. 266, 1967

John noun

1 heroin US, 1997

- They called it "girl" or "Jane" or "Missy" in feminine contrast to "boy" or "John" or "Mister" for king heroin. — David Simon and Edward Burns, The Corner, p. 62, 1997

2 a plainclothes police officer *US, 1951*

- Any of us slum children could smell out a cop even though he was a John, a plain-clothes man. — Ethel Waters, *His Eye is on the Sparrow*, p. 16, 1951

john book *noun*

a prostitute's list of customers *US, 1973*

- Also in this class are the freelance call girls with "John Books" (address books with the names and telephone numbers of well-to-do clients who come back as regular customers) or their own. — Bernhardt J. Hurwood, *The Sensuous New York*, p. 17, 1973

John D *noun*

kerosene *US, 1975*

An allusion to John D. Rockefeller and hence petroleum-based products.

- — John Gould, *Maine Lingo*, pp. 147–148, 1975

John Hancock *noun*

a person's signature *US, 1887*

From the attention-getting manner in which Hancock signed the Declaration of Independence.

- [W]hy is that doctor so nervous and unwilling to put his John Hancock to any sort of document[?] — Gore Vidal, *Myra Breckinridge*, p. 137, 1984
- It could be Westerberg's if we can get everyone's John Hancock. — *Heathers*, 1988

John Henry *noun*

1 a person's signature *US, 1972*

A variant of the more common **JOHN HANCOCK**.

- [Y]ou don't have to put up any cash and you don't have to forfeit any cash, all you have to do is write your John Henry. — Bruce Jackson, *Outside the Law*, p. 132, 1972

2 the penis *US, 1888*

- My John Henry would start to sag, but when she felt that happening, she would grab me. — Robert Byrne, *McGoorty*, p. 57, 1972

John Law *noun*

the police *US, 1906*

- I was made the lookout man and told to stick around out front with my eyes peeled for any signs of John Law. — Mezz Mezzrow, *Really the Blues*, p. 20, 1946
- Tuffy climbed over into the back seat, got his guns ready, knowing what to expect if John Law got within range. — Caryl Chessman, *Cell 2456 Death Row*, p. 186, 1954
- I don't tell them other bitzes this, but being a lone outlaw in this life, with the johnlaws up one side an the pimps down the other, everybody mouth-waterin' for a taste—well you catchin' too much mojo at once[.] — Robert Gover, *JC Saves*, p. 55, 1968

johnny *noun*

1 the penis *US, 1972*

- Or a girl would pick a guy out of the audience—it was always a pimp but she would let on that he was just an average tourist—pull his johnny out of his pants and start treating it like a lollipop. — Robert Byrne, *McGoorty*, p. 39, 1972

2 a toilet *UK, 1850*

- He was taking the only way our directors ever take—you know, from the card room to the—er—thing, the johnny. — Horace McCoy, *Kiss Tomorrow Good-bye*, p. 355, 1948
- "Oh my God," Jenny said, pleasurably titillated. "I hope I don' have to go use the johnny." — Robert Campbell, *Alice in La-La Land*, p. 271, 1987

3 a prison guard *US, 1950*

- — Hyman E. Goldin et al., *Dictionary of American Underworld Lingo*, p. 111, 1950

Johnny Black *nickname*

Johnny Walker™ Black Label whiskey *US, 1990*

- Buster was trying to look jaunty but his hands were shaking. "Gimme a Johnny Black," he said. "Neat." — Joseph Wambaugh, *The Golden Orange*, p. 49, 1990

Johnny Ham *noun*

a private investigator *US, 1986*

- We're hard on private Johnny Hams what come aroun' totin' iron. — Robert Campbell, *In La-La Land We Trust*, p. 173, 1986

Johnny Jihad *noun*

a notional militant, antiwestern Muslim *US, 2006*

The term was originally a journalistic nickname for John Walker Lindh, an American combatant captured on the battle field with Taliban forces in Afghanistan.

- He and his cousins learned to ignore the pejoratives of war, words like "haji," "camel jockey" and "Johnny Jihad." — *New York Times*, p. A1, 7th August 2006

Johnny Long Shoes *noun*

the man who steals a prisoner's girlfriend or wife after incarceration *US, 1991*

- — Lee McNelis, *30 + And a Wake-Up*, p. 15, 1991

Johnny-on-the-spot *noun*

1 a person who is available whenever needed *US, 1896*

- "There's nothing like being johnny-on-the-spot," Dr. Sherwood says. "Being right there so that when a kid is in trouble he can come and ring your bell at eleven o'clock at night and know that you will answer it." — Harrison E. Salisbury, *The Shook-up Generation*, p. 178, 1958
- No telling what might have happened if I hadn't been right here Johnny-on-the-spot when the fire broke out. — Jim Thompson, *Pop. 1280*, p. 151, 1964

2 a portable toilet *US, 1973*

- When Bengie saw the "johnny-on-the-spot," a light lit up inside his head[.] — Tina Russell, *Porno Star*, p. 157, 1973

Johnny pump *noun*

a fire hydrant *US, 1955*

- One day when the pavements are like sausage griddles, me and Romolo have our trunks on, looking to open a johnny pump or two and cool off. — Rocky Garciano (with Rowland Barber), *Somebody Up There Likes Me*, p. 77, 1955

Johnny Reb *noun*

any rural white male from the southern US *US, 1884*

- — *Maledicta*, p. 162, Summer/Winter 1978: "How to hate thy neighbor: a guide to racist maledicta"

John Q. Citizen *noun*

a notional, average member of the public *US, 1937*

- Y'know, Castro being assassinated sounds pretty wild to John Q. Citizen. — Oliver Stone, *JFK*, p. 136, 1991

John Q. Law *noun*

the personification of law enforcement *US, 1950*

- John Q. Law don't have no idea what Fifty Ferris looks like. — Walter Bullock, *Mr. Barry's Etchings*, p. 50, 1950
- Now if we cross the path of any John Q. Laws, nobody does a fuckin' thing 'til I do something. — *Pulp Fiction*, 1994

John Q. Public *noun*

a notional, average member of the public *US, 1927*

- If he stopped to track down every half-assed theory the John Q. Public volunteered, he wouldn't get anything else done. — Sue Grafton, *Q is for Quarry*, p. 117, 2002

johnson *noun*

1 the penis *UK, 1862*

Despite an 1862 citation, the word was not widely used in this sense until the 1970s.

- He pulled on his johnson, with his right hand, and closed the door with his left. — Steve Cannon, *Groove, Bang, and Jive Around*, p. 7, 1969
- One of the black guys was nearly demanding a warm-up, some contrivance to stiffen his johnson before the main event. — Josh Alan Friedman, *Tales of Times Square*, p. 94, 1986
- I wanna set Heather on my Johnson and just start spinning her like a fucking pinwheel. — *Heathers*, 1988
- Ready to spout, he yanks his berubbered johnson out of Jasmin's snatch and fumbles nervously with the condom. — Anthony Petkovich, *The X Factory*, p. 193, 1997

2 coffee *US, 1962*

- — Joseph E. Ragen and Charles Finston, *Inside the World's Toughest Prison*, p. 806, 1962: "Penitentiary and underworld glossary"

Johnson bar *noun*

any heavy bar *US, 1931*

- "You take the Johnson bar and shove it forward, that means it's going forward." — Richard Greene, *Inside the Dream*, p. 102, 2001

Johnson family *noun*

1 collectively, the underworld *US, 1926*

- — Hyman E. Goldin et al., *Dictionary of American Underworld Lingo*, p. 111, 1950

2 a mythical family, all of whose members believe that everything is legitimate and righteous *US, 1982*

- — Bill Reilly, *Big Al's Official Guide to Chicagoese*, p. 39, 1982

Johnson grass *noun*

marijuana *US, 1971*

Johnson grass is a ubiquitous weed in the US, hence the pun.

- — Eugene Landy, *The Underground Dictionary*, p. 113, 1971

Johnson Ronson *noun*

the penis *US, 1975*

- I had to put down the damn book because was Johnson Ronson was ripping through my cheap underwear. — Miguel Pinero, *Short Eyes*, pp. 75–76, 1975

John Wayne *noun*

1 in the television and movie industries, an exaggerated punch *US, 2003*

- — John Cann, *The Stunt Guide*, p. 60: "Terms and definitions"

2 a small, collapsible can opener for use in the field *US, 1973*
Officially known as a P-38.

- — *Maledicta*, p. 260, Summer/Winter 1982: "Viet-speak"
- — Gregory Clark, *Words of the Vietnam War*, pp. 387–388, 1990

John Wayne *verb*

to act with reckless disregard for life and safety *US, 1973*
One of several military slang terms based on John Wayne (1907–79), the US actor who portrayed a series of tough Western and army heroes.

- Nothing I like better than John Wayne-ing a goddamn door. — Joseph Wambaugh, *The Blue Knight*, p. 137, 1973
- Why, you can even John Wayne it and pull the son of a bitch with your fucken eyetooth. — Larry Heinemann, *Close Quarters*, p. 45, 1977
- — *Maledicta*, p. 260, Summer/Winter 1982: "Viet-speak"
- "I'm gonna John Wayne these bastards," and tried to jump to his feet[.] — John Plaster, *SOG*, p. 344, 1997

John Wayne *adjective*

reckless, confusing courage with stupidity *US, 1987*
A tribute to the lack of common sense inspired in some American troops in Vietnam who had grown up watching John Wayne's reckless heroics as a movie soldier.

- Nice job, Marks. A little John Wayne though, don't you think? — Stan Lee, *The 'Nam*, p. 91, 1987

John Wayne bar *noun*

a military-issued candy bar *US, 1986*

- Each LURP ration also included a chocolate, vanilla, or coconut candy wafer that was generally called a "John Wayne bar" by the troops. — Michael Lee Lanning, *Inside the LRRUPs*, p. 120, 1988
- Albee and I split a John Wayne bar (a chocolate bar from our C's). — Richard Burns, *Pathfinder*, p. 192, 2002

John Wayne cookie *noun*

a US Army c-ration cookie or candy bar *US, 1986*

- The GIs would slam the jam, peanut butter, and John Wayne cookie together and call them PB&Js. — Donald Gazzaniga, *The No-Salt, Lowest-Sodium Light Meals Book*, p. 62, 2006

John Wayne course *noun*

a combat training course *US, 1990*

- We suddenly have targets, many targets, boo-coo targets and god it's just like being back at Geiger on the John Wayne course with all those pop-up targets[.] — E. Michael Helms, *The Proud Bastards*, p. 190, 1990

John Wayne hat *noun*

a bush hat *US, 1987*

- Not far down the street, some wild-ass cowboy, silver studded boots, John Wayne hat, stepped out of a bar[.] — Tom Spanbauer, *In the City of Shy Hunters*, p. 283, 2001

join *verb*

▸ **join the Air Force**

to die *US, 1994*

- — Sally Williams, "Strong" *Words* (Dissertation), p. 147, 1994

joint *noun*

1 a marijuana cigarette *US, 1942*
For 50 years, the top of the slang pile, easily deposing its predecessors and fending off challengers.

- Enrique rolled enormous Indian joints, laughed at my American sticks I rolled. — Jack Kerouac, *Letter to Allen Ginsberg*, p. 351, 10th May 1952

- I don't get too high, not on a little middlin' joint like that one. — Ken Kesey, *One Flew Over the Cuckoo's Nest*, p. 286, 1962
- I was 22 years of age and shacking with a chick named Julie, I gave her one "joint" which she stashed and later turned over to the cops—a joint that netted me one of the 5-to-life sentences. — *The Berkeley Tribe*, p. 5, 5th-12th September 1969
- Yeah, it's legal, but it ain't a hundred percent legal. I mean you can't walk into a restaurant, roll a joint, and start puffin' away. — *Pulp Fiction*, 1994

2 the penis *US, 1931*

- Inez called up Camille on the phone repeatedly and even had long talks with her; they even talked about his joint, or so Dean claimed. — Jack Kerouac, *On the Road*, p. 250, 1957
- [L]eaving my joint like a rocket it makes right for the light bulb overhead, where to my wonderment and horror, it hits and it hangs. — Philip Roth, *Portnoy's Complaint*, p. 20, 1969
- I had to admit that it was one of the biggest joints I'd ever seen; it must have been nearly a foot long. — Jennifer Sills, *Massage Parlor*, p. 75, 1973
- What you want more of is boys with nice long joints. I know what you are—you're a fag. — Herbert Huncke, *The Evening Sun Turned Crimson*, p. 135, 1980

3 a prison *US, 1933*

- [Y]ou can be charged in State on one and Federal on the other so that when you walk out of the State joint the Federals meet you at the door. — William Burroughs, *Junkie*, p. 95, 1953
- I was arrested in Arizona, in that joint absolutely the worst joint I've ever been in. — Jack Kerouac, *On the Road*, p. 231, 1957
- "Why should I go to the joint?" — Clarence Cooper Jr., *The Scene*, p. 14, 1960
- In the Joint I always get in top shape; no coke, no pot, no pussy, so you work out. — Edwin Torres, *Carlito's Way*, p. 41, 1975
- Well, yeah honey, but these boys tell me they just got outta the joint. — *Raising Arizona*, 1987
- He had been death on basing before he went to the joint[.] — Terry Williams, *The Cocaine Kids*, p. 44, 1989
- You like being out of the joint, fucking a beautiful woman. — Joel Rose, *Kill Kill Faster Faster*, p. 11, 1997

4 an establishment that sells alcohol illegally; any disreputable establishment *US, 1877*

- And here comes the openin' night! And the joint is jumping! — William "Lord" Buckley, *Nero*, 1951
- Jesus wouldn't be afraid to walk into this joint or any other speakeasy to preach the gospel. — Richard Brooks, *Elmer Gantry*, 1960
- Dad knew where most of the joints in the neighborhood were and many times we had to go from one to another for what seemed like hours. — Claude Brown, *Manchild in the Promised Land*, p. 29, 1965

5 a stethoscope *US, 1966*

- But when he put the joint (the stethoscope) on my heart, he was amazed beyond compare. — Minnesota Fats, *The Bank Shot*, p. 24, 1966

6 the equipment used to smoke opium *US, 1946*

- I called up Mike and pleaded with him to bring me the joint (the layout) and put me out of my misery. — Mezz Mezzrow, *Really the Blues*, p. 253, 1946

7 a syringe *US, 1953*

- She hit the joint [hypodermic syringe] and knocked it out of the vein and by the time she got herself in, I'm already into a thing. — Bruce Jackson, *In the Life*, p. 223, 1972

8 a pistol *US, 1949*

- I'm packing no joint. — Hal Ellson, *Duke*, p. 2, 1949
- He said he got the gun, which he called "a sweet joint," because a guy named "Binky" had threatened his life. — Matt Gryta, *Buffalo (New York) News*, p. 5, 19th November 1994

9 an artistic creation *US, 1988*

- CROOKLYN, a Spike Lee Joint! — *publicity poster*, 1994
- I remember when attractive women were simply "fly" and great records were "da joint." — Nelson George, *Hip Hop America*, p. 209, 1998
- For six years they [Def Jam] were putting out joints, and every single one of those records was either going gold or platinum. — Alex Ogg, *The Hip Hop Years [quoting Bobbito 'The Barber']*, p. 91, 1999
- [T]he multi-million-pound, state-of-the-art sportswear facility, showcasing the latest in hi-tech imported "boxfresh" minty joints[.] — Julian Johnson, *Urban Survival*, p. 67, 2003

10 a hip-hop recording that features more than one leading rapper *US, 2001*
Clipped from "joint recording."

- Have they recorded any new joints? — *Hip-hop Connection*, p. 20, March 2001

- Even on that first joint, "Method Man," you hear him change it up almost every other line. — RZA, *The Wu-Tang Manual*, p. 17, 2005

11 in horse racing, a battery-powered device used illegally by a jockey to shock a horse during a race *US*, *1951*

- Frank Wolverton of Santa Rosa, Cal., "a track follower," today was suspended by the Lone Oak Racing Track Board of Stewards for manufacturing electrical "coaxers" allegedly used to stimulate horses in two races. The gimmick is a "joint," or an electric battery held in the palm of the jockey's hand. — *San Francisco News*, p. 21, 7th September 1951

joint girl *noun*

a prostitute working in one specific disreputable establishment *US*, *1972*

- And I've had what I call "joint girls," and I'm one of the kind of pimps that over the years I've felt if a girl will be a good whore she will work in a joint. — Bruce Jackson, *In the Life*, p. 185, 1972

joints *noun*

a pair of any popular brand of athletic shoes *US*, *1993*

- — *Washington Post*, 14th October 1993

joint-wise *adjective*

sophisticated and skilled at the ways and means of serving a prison sentence gracefully *US*, *1950*

- — Hyman E. Goldin et al., *Dictionary of American Underworld Lingo*, p. 111, 1950
- When I returned to my housing unit I discussed this with some of the older joint-wise cons. — Wayne Wooden, *Men Behind Bars*, p. 211, 1984

JOJ *adjective*

just off the jet *US*, *1981*

Applied to a recent immigrant or, in the usage of Hawaiian youth, to a tourist recently arrived in Hawaii.

- — Douglas Simonson, *Pidgin to da Max*, 1981
- — Judi Sanders, *Kickin' like Chicken with the Couch Commander*, p. 13, 1992

joker poker *noun*

any game of poker played with 53 cards, including the joker *US*, *1988*

- — George Percy, *The Language of Poker*, p. 50, 1988

Joliet Josie *noun*

a sexually attractive girl under the legal age of consent *US*, *1950*

Joliet is the site of the major prison in Illinois.

- — Jack Lait and Lee Mortimer, *Chicago Confidential*, p. 301, 1950: "Loop lexicon"

jollies *noun*

pleasure *US*, *1956*

- "I'd be scared," McMurphy said, "that just about the time I was getting my jollies she'd reach around behind me with a thermometer and take my temperature." — Ken Kesey, *One Flew Over the Cuckoo's Nest*, p. 289, 1962
- Let's face it, a lot of women can't make it with just one guy at a time, they can't get their jollies. — Hunter S. Thompson, *Hell's Angels*, p. 192, 1966
- He lags his response to bang the pain junkie with suspense jollies as he stares into her face — Iceberg Slim (Robert Beck), *Doom Fox*, p. 155, 1978
- Serena plays a love object in a house of pleasure, where she is used over and over for other people's jollies. — Kent Smith et al., *Adult Movies*, p. 216, 1982

jolly *noun*

the HH-53 rescue helicopter *US*, *1990*

A common abbreviated form of **JOLLY GREEN GIANT**.

- "How 'bout scrambling a Jolly and get him inbound while we continue the search." — Tom Yarborough, *Da Nang Diary*, p. 264, 1990
- And he came back with, "Jolly's got PI's, they'll soon be down." — Joseph Tuso, *Singing the Vietnam Blues*, p. 29, 1990: The Ballad of Jeb Stewart

jolly bean *noun*

an amphetamine tablet *US*, *1969*

- — Carl Chambers and Richard Heckman, *Employee Drug Abuse*, 1972

Jolly Green Giant; Jolly Green *noun*

any of several large military helicopters, especially the CH-3C helicopter, used during the Vietnam war for counterinsurgency airlifts *US*, *1965*

- 21 Hueys, holding 7–8 people each, are now available to lift us off the rooftops & out to the 3 main pickup points where the Jolly Green Giants can land. — Hunter S. Thompson, *Fear and Loathing in America*, p. 617, April 1975
- The typical rescue force was comprised of two HH-53C "Jolly Green Giant" helicopters[.] — Karl Eschmann, *Linebacker*, p. 49, 1989
- "These Jolly Green boys are breed all by their lonesome." — Joseph Tuso, *Singing the Vietnam Blues*, p. 32, 1990

jolt *noun*

1 an injection or dose of a drug *US*, *1907*

- "I need a jolt," one addict might remark. "I gotta see my connection." — William J. Spillard and Pence James, *Needle in a Haystack*, p. 148, 1945
- A fix. A cap. A jolt. A pop. What do they call it in your group, dear? — John D. McDonald, *The Neon Jungle*, p. 71, 1953
- And Doc Parker in the back room in his drugstore shooting horse heroin, three grains a jolt. — William Burroughs, *Naked Lunch*, p. 85, 1957
- What he did find was a great gym near his hotel where he could get illegal steroid shots in the ass for fifty bucks a jolt. — Stephen Cannell, *Big Con*, p. 160, 1997

2 a prison sentence *US*, *1912*

- "Funny, that I got less of a jolt in the can than you got." — Irving Shulman, *Cry Tough*, p. 28, 1949
- But a bim that won't bolt while you're doin' a little jolt / is just one out of a thousand my friend. — Bruce Jackson, *Get Your Ass in the Water and Swim Like Me*, p. 116, 1964
- That was the jolt when he blew his pickets. — Malcolm Braly, *On the Yard*, p. 7, 1967
- You tell me now, or when Amp Heywood is eventually indicted for that grand larceny, I'll see to it he gets the full jolt. — Stephen Cannell, *King Con*, p. 75, 1997

3 a shock *US*, *1966*

- There are very few angels who won't go far out of their way to lay a bad jolt on the squares[.] — Hunter S. Thompson, *Hell's Angels*, p. 118, 1966

4 a strong and bracing alcoholic drink *US*, *1904*

- The Juicehead Kid was a' takin' a jolt. — William "Lord" Buckley, *The Ballad of Dan McGroo*, 1960
- He poured a stiff jolt of bourbon and knocked it back. — Max Shulman, *Anyone Got a Match?*, p. 14, 1964

jolt *verb*

1 to shock *US*, *1961*

- "He jolted me to some unpleasant facts," Bernie said. — Ross Russell, *The Sound*, p. 237, 1961

2 to inject a drug *US*, *1953*

- The first time they jolted together, it was the beginning of the end. — Phil Hirsch, *Hooked*, p. 29, 1968

Jonah *noun*

a superstitious gambler; a gambler perceived by other gamblers to bring bad luck *US*, *1849*

- — *The Annals of the American Academy of Political and Social Sciences*, p. 126, May 1950

Jonah *verb*

in craps, to try to influence the roll of the dice with body movements, hand gestures or incantations *US*, *1974*

- — John Scarne, *Scarne on Dice*, p. 471, 1974

jones *noun*

1 an addiction *US*, *1962*

- Carmen explained she had a jones and since she spoke Spanish, could cop all the stuff Ralph needed very easily. — Babs Gonzales, *I Paid My Dues*, p. 106, 1967
- Bam and Baby June shuffle past … already a half hour away from pain … trying, with all their dopefiend cunning, to head Jones off at the pass. — Odie Hawkins, *Ghetto Sketches*, p. 39, 1972
- The only time the High One had seen me without a habit was during our school days, but ever since we were adults I had a Jones. — A.S. Jackson, *Gentleman Pimp*, p. 134, 1973
- The Barker drilled that into his head; never cop to your jones. — Seth Morgan, *Homeboy*, p. 42, 1990

2 an intense craving or yearning *US*, *1970*

- Yes, I am the victim of a basketball Jones. — Cheech Marin and Tommy Chong, *Basketball Jones*, 1973
- There was this terrible cigarette called "Bizonte" that I developed a Jones for. — Odie Hawkins, *Lost Angeles*, p. 83, 1994
- When you've got a love jones, you're like Mr. Magoo: legally blind, always bumping into something, and so deep in it that you have no time for the rest of life. — Chris Rock, *Rock This!*, p. 114, 1997

- The situation is, my man Cameron here has a major jones for Bianca Stratford. — *Ten Things I Hate About You*, 1999

3 heroin *US, 1970*

- Jones had always been an escape for people who were hopelessly oppressed — John Sinclair, *Guitar Army*, p. 286, 1972
- Then I heard a knock on the door so I placed a New York News over the Jones and got up to answer the door. — A.S. Jackson, *Gentleman Pimp*, p. 145, 1973
- No more jones, see? I just want a portion of the west side dealin' nothin' but coke. — Vernon E. Smith, *The Jones Men*, p. 8, 1974

4 the penis *US, 1966*

- The words stuck in Dip's mind like bubble gum on the brain, and slowly worked their way down to his jones. — Steve Cannon, *Groove, Bang, and Jive Around*, p. 25, 1969
- "Bitch," I yelled. "Enough is enough, turn my jones loose." — Donald Goines, *Whoreson*, p. 145, 1972
- He crossed his legs, trying to push his hardening jones down between his thighs. To keep his thang cooled out, like, after all, three months was a pretty good piece of time to remain unfucked. — Odie Hawkins, *Chicago Hustle*, p. 106, 1977
- Your jones, the quality of your erection was low, low Daddy, Dear. — Iceberg Slim (Robert Beck), *Long White Con*, p. 22, 1977

jones *verb*
to crave *US, 1974*

- I guess in a way Angel Juan is my fix and I've been jonesing for him. — Francesca Lia Block, *Missing Angel Juan*, p. 332, 1993
- I'm jonesin' for "the Dew," bigtime! — David Shenk and Steve Silberman, *Skeleton Key*, p. 167, 1994

Joneser *noun*
a heroin addict *US, 1989*

- "Aside from a wife beater, Blindman's a drug dealer, shoplifter, ex-Moonie, ex-Joneser, a contributor to the delinquency of minors, and after that bridge incident, a murder suspect." — Robert Mailer Anderson, *Boonville*, p. 75, 2001

jones man *noun*
a heroin dealer *US, 1972*

- "Everybody wanta be the jones man," he said. — Vernon E. Smith, *The Jones Men*, p. 32, 1974

joog *noun*
the jugular vein *US, 1994*
Also spelt "jug."

- — Sally Williams, *"Strong" Words*, p. 148, 1994

joog *verb*
to tease *US, 2002*

- — Gary K. Farlow, *Prison-ese*, p. 35, 2002

joot ball *noun*
stale food served in prison *US, 2005*

- "Joot balls"—yesterday's food ground up and scooped on a plate with an ice-cream scoop—are slid in the slot in my door. — Colton Simpson, *Inside the Crips*, p. 88, 2005

jostle *verb*
to engage in petty swindles *US, 1953*

- So Mike spent at least half of his time on the Island doing "five-twenty-nine" for jostling. — William Burroughs, *Junkie*, p. 26, 1953
- I had heard about jostling and the Murphy for a long time, but I didn't know what it was all about. — Claude Brown, *Manchild in the Promised Land*, p. 160, 1965

jostler *noun*
the member of a pickpocket crew whose clumsy bumping into the victim distracts him while a confederate picks the pocket *US, 1929*

- — Hyman E. Goldin et al., *Dictionary of American Underworld Lingo*, p. 111, 1950
- — John M. Murtagh and Sara Harris, *Cast the First Stone*, p. 261, 1957: "Glossary"

jounts *noun*
clothing *US, 1987*

- — *Washington Post Magazine*, p. 11, 29th March 1987: "Say wha?"

joxy *noun*
the vagina *US, 1967*

- — Dale Gordon, *The Dominion Sex Dictionary*, p. 95, 1967

joy *noun*
marijuana *US, 1980*

- — Edith A. Folb, *runnin' down some lines*, p. 244, 1980

joy bags *noun*
the female breasts *US, 2005*

- Joey bares her juicy little joy-bags in a dressing room before a guy's head comes crashing through the wall. — Mr. Skin, *Mr. Skin's Skincyclopedia*, p. 3, 2005

joy bang *noun*
an injection of a narcotic, especially heroin, without succumbing to the drug's addictive nature *US, 1953*

- Nick also scored for some respectable working people in the Village who indulged in an occasional "joy bang." — William Burroughs, *Junkie*, p. 61, 1953

joy booter *noun*
an infrequent smoker *US, 1996*

- — John Fahs, *Cigarette Confidential*, p. 302, 1996: "Glossary"

joybox *noun*
a piano *US, 1942*

- At the Pekin they had Tony Jackson, a New Orleans musician, one of the greatest blues piano players that ever pounded a joybox. — Mezz Mezzrow, *Really the Blues*, p. 45, 1946

joyboy *noun*
a young male homosexual, especially a young male homosexual prostitute *UK, 1961*

- — Dale Gordon, *The Dominion Sex Dictionary*, p. 95, 1967
- There were many other ways; masturbation was first but homosexuals or prisonmade "joy-boys" came in second. — Piri Thomas, *Seven Long Times*, p. 137, 1974
- — *Male Swinger Number 3*, p. 47, 1981: "The complete gay dictionary"

joy button *noun*
the clitoris *US, 1972*

- Although it's sometimes called "the joy button," the clitoris is actually more than a single spot. — Boston Women's Health Book Collective, *Our Bodies, Ourselves*, p. 195, 1984
- I refused to cease my administrations on her joy button, and was rewarded with another lashing howl, a frantic cry, and a plea to allow her release to end. — *alt.sex.stories*, 25th May 1993
- When I returned to her joy button, Molly soared to even greater heights, grabbing me by the hair and mashing my face into her vulva. — Penthouse International, *Penthouse Uncensored IV*, p. 291, 2004

joy girl *noun*

1 a prostitute *US, 1931*

- I knew it had changed a great deal from the days when they had the gatehouse at the entrance and the private police force, and the gambling casino on the lake, and the fifty-dollar joy girls. — Raymond Chandler, *The Long Goodbye*, p. 85, 1953
- When a community's indirect income from brothels threatens a bigger income such as gambling, the joy girls are chased, as they were chased out of Las Vegas and Reno. — Monroe Fry, *Sex, Vice, and Business*, p. 69, 1959

2 in a deck of playing cards, any queen *US, 1973*

- — Thomas L. Clark, *The Dictionary of Gambling and Gaming*, p. 111, 1987

joy hole *noun*
the vagina *US, 1939*

- At first I slowly pumped her joy hole, but it wasn't long before the momentum picked up. — *alt.sex.stories*, 4th April 1993
- "That'll be me in your joy hole, baby." — John Ridley, *The Drift*, p. 68, 2002

joy juice *noun*

1 semen *US, 1969*

- Suddenly his legs stiffened, his asshole closed, and the joy-juice shot. — Steve Cannon, *Groove, Bang, and Jive Around*, p. 24, 1969
- There, bitch, if you get hungry tonight, there's some joy juice for you to lick on. — Donald Goines, *White Man's Justice, Black Man's Grief*, p. 73, 1973
- He wanted her ass to be good and strong and filled to the brim with the joy juice of the men she'd had that day, and the more the merrier. — A.S. Jackson, *Gentleman Pimp*, p. 154, 1973
- The joy-juice flies as these girls suck, frig their clits, and ready their assholes for cock. — *Adult Video*, p. 66, August/September 1986

- Why do you have to talk dirty like that? Joy juice. I mean, for chrissake. — Robert Campbell, *Juice*, p. 214, 1988
- With the sensation of having my cock in her mouth and the stroking of my balls, I began to deliver my joy juice. — C.J. Amato, *The Royal Hotel*, p. 32, 2004

2 any alcoholic beverage, especially whiskey *US, 1907*
- — Lou Shelly, *Hepcats Jive Talk Dictionary*, p. 28, 1945
- That didn't mean nothing as his son, Rosita's husband upstairs had his own still and made his own joy juice. — Babs Gonzales, *Movin' On Down De Line*, p. 106, 1975

3 a central nervous system depressant *US, 1954*
- "Listen, she'll be so full of joy juice, she won't mind a thing." — John D. MacDonald, *The Deceivers*, p. 15, 1958

4 chloral hydrate, used to render someone unconscious *US, 1971*
- — Eugene Landy, *The Underground Dictionary*, p. 113, 1971

joy knob *noun*
1 the penis *US, 1960*
- Mike's joy knob let go and I had to swallow fast to get down his massive load of sweet boy-cream. — *alt.sex.stories.gay*, 31st May 2002

2 the prostate gland *US, 1997*
- I found his joy knob on about the second poke and started working it, his grunts of sheer animal pleasure making my balls tingle. — *alt.sex.stories.gay*, 2nd August 1997

3 the clitoris *US, 1998*
- I imagined licking her clitoral bone until her joy knob stood straight out, then I'd lick until she screamed. — *alt.sex.stories.moderated*, 23rd December 1998

joy pipe *noun*
an opium pipe *US, 1957*
- [T]hey would lie on decrepit mattresses, smoking the joy pipe. — Helen Giblo, *Footlights, Fistfights and Femmes*, p. 30, 1957

joy pop *noun*
an injection of a drug into the skin, not a vein *US, 1922*
- This time I mean to get cured and stay cured. No joy pops. — William Burroughs, *Letters to Allen Ginsberg 1953–1957*, p. 100, 17th May 1955
- The Royal Roost—swinging up to Harlem—eventually picking up a steady with a cat who was a junky—beginning to take an occasional joy-pop herself. — Herbert Huncke, *The Evening Sun Turned Crimson*, p. 53, 1980

joy-pop *verb*
to inject a drug under the skin, not into a vein *US, 1936*
- Fran joy-popped. Just hit with the stuff under her skin. — Willard Motley, *Let No Man Write My Epitaph*, p. 159, 1958
- I'm glad I don't do nothin' but joy pop. — Clarence Cooper Jr., *The Scene*, p. 77, 1960
- What really tore it was they turned the place into a regular shooting gallery—blowing pot and joy popping all over the place. — Ross Russell, *The Sound*, p. 199, 1961

joy popper *noun*
an intravenous drug user *US, 1936*
- "Just a joy-popper, eh?" "Well, I find it helps when things are rough[.]" — Douglas Rutherford, *The Creeping Flesh*, 1963
- She [an apartment] was sleazed and greasy from the legions of junkie joy poppers who had fouled her rotten with their shooting galleries. — Iceberg Slim (Robert Beck), *Airtight Willie and Me*, p. 61, 1979
- By this definition I was only a weekend joy popper who had no right to so grandiose a title as Junkie. — Larry Rivers, *What Did I Do?*, p. 194, 1992

joy ride *noun*
an impulsive excursion in a car that is, from the point of view of the riders, borrowed, but from the point of view of the law, stolen *US, 1915*
- In those days, when automobiles were still a novelty, we got a big kick out of joyriding in somebody else's car. — Mezz Mezzrow, *Really the Blues*, 1946
- Seventy-five percent of all car thefts in the United States are by teen-agers out for "joy rides." — Tom Wolfe, *The Kandy-Kolored Tangerine-Flake Streamline Baby*, p. 33, 1965
- I saw this bus and half-stoned I decided to go for a joyride—next thing I know these crazy hippies are banging into the car. — Edwin Torres, *Carlito's Way*, pp. 137–138, 1975
- Must've been a joyride situation; they abandoned the car once they hit the retaining wall. — *The Big Lebowski*, 1998

joyride *verb*
to steal a car for a joy-ride *US, 1949*

- Usually we went for girls, but this time we just went joy riding. — Hal Ellson, *Duke*, p. 113, 1949
- I had had illegally in my possession about 500 cars—whether just for the moment and to be taken back to its owner before he returned (i.e., on Parking lots) or whether taken for the purpose of so altering its appearance as to keep it for several weeks but mostly only for joyriding. — Neal Cassady, *The First Third*, p. 170, 1971
- You have pleaded guilty to "joy-riding" as a lesser charge to Grand Theft Auto. — *Menace II Society*, 1993

joy rider *noun*
an infrequent user of an addictive drug *US, 1950*
- — Hyman E. Goldin et al., *Dictionary of American Underworld Lingo*, p. 111, 1950
- — Eugene Landy, *The Underground Dictionary*, p. 113, 1971

joy smoker *noun*
an opium smoker *US, 1957*
- "James, you'll hear all over town that I'm a heavy drinker and joy smoker." — Helen Giblo, *Footlights, Fistfights and Femmes*, p. 31, 1957

joy stick *noun*
1 the penis *US, 1916*
Probably derived from mechanical imagery.
- Help me get a hard on, Patricia. Help me get my joystick up so I don't go crazy. — Sara Harris, *The Lords of Hell*, p. 93, 1967
- She may have one arm around him, or have one hand busy squeezing his gonads and the other hand busy rubbing his joystick augmenting the sucking action of her lips — *Screw*, p. 4, 1st December 1969
- Although the title would have you believe it's a flesh romp to cruise through with one hand on your joystick, the flick only offers brief looks at several actresses' breasts. — Mr. Skin, *Mr. Skin's Skincyclopedia*, p. 13, 2005

2 the pole used to carry a pair of balanced objects on your shoulders *US, 1968*
- — Carl Fleischhauer, *A Glossary of Army Slang*, p. 28, 1968

joy water *noun*
vaginal secretions produced as a result of sexual arousal *US, 1973*
- [W]hen she climaxed she hollered and screamed and her tasty ass became quite sloppy with joy water. — A.S. Jackson, *Gentleman Pimp*, p. 109, 1973

JPT *noun*
used for denoting a lack of punctuality *US, 1967*
An abbreviation of JEWISH PEOPLE'S TIME.
- Like Mexican Time and the onetime JPT, Jewish People's time, C.P.T. is a phrase that draws the lines of the ghetto. — Paul Jacobs, *Prelude to a Riot*, p. 12, 1967

J. Random *noun*
used as a humorous first initial and middle name of a mythical person *US, 1983*
- Would you let J. Random Loser marry your daughter? — Guy L. Steele et al., *The Hacker's Dictionary*, p. 86, 1983

J school *noun*
journalism school *US, 1968*
- I eventually became a tour guide for the J-school[.] — Laura Jeanne Hammond, *Your Life After High School*, p. 22, 2004

J-town *noun*
a neighborhood populated by a large number of Japanese-Americans *US, 1973*
An abbreviation of "Japan Town."
- I've been coming to the Geisha Doll and every other restaurant here in J-town for twenty years so it was no wonder. — Joseph Wambaugh, *The Blue Knight*, p. 40, 1973

Juan Doe *noun*
an unidentified Hispanic male *US, 1993*
- They knew all about trunk jobs, John Does, Juan Does, gun-shots, accidentals and naturals. — Carl Hiaasen, *Strip Tease*, p. 100, 1993

jubilee *noun*
the buttocks *US, 1967*
- — Dale Gordon, *The Dominion Sex Dictionary*, p. 95, 1967

Judas goat *noun*
an animal trained to lead other animals into slaughter *US, 1941*

- But I will not be his Judas goat because me and the Bug have been right. — Charles Perry, *Portrait of a Young Man Drowning*, p. 277, 1962
- You're Judas goats, both of you. — Darryl Ponicsan, *The Last Detail*, p. 95, 1970

Judas hole; Judas eye; Judas window; Judas *noun*
a small peep-hole in a door through which one can see who is outside the door without been seen from outside *US, 1865*

- Inside the steel door of the cell block was a basket of steel bars around the Judas window. — Raymond Chandler, *The Long Goodbye*, p. 44, 1953
- She got her copy of the New York Herald-Tribune from the mat outside her door, first peeping through the Judas window to make certain the coast was clear[.] — Chester Himes, *The Primitive*, p. 12, 1955
- "Like a jail," said Kay. "'Judases,' don't they call them?" — Mary McCarthy, *The Group*, p. 310, 1963
- Upstairs, at the end of a long corridor of doors with painted windows on both sides, there's another door all wood with a Judas hole in the middle of it. I knock and the slide clicks back. — Robert Campbell, *Junkyard Dog*, p. 68, 1986

Judas priest!
used as an expression of surprise or outrage *US, 1914*
Multiple embellishments.

- "Your friend here seems to have some pretty fancy cravings," added Harry. "Judas Priest!" — Elaine Shepard, *The Doom Pussy*, p. 113, 1967
- After an uncomfortable ten minutes passed, a voice called from the top of the stairs. "Judas Priest on a pony!" — Marilyn Manson, *The Long Hard Road Out of Hell*, p. 11, 1998
- "Well shit. Just shit." We all looked at her in amazement. She never cussed. "Judas priest!" — Haywood Smith, *The Red Hat Club*, p. 20, 2003

Judge Duffy; Judge Dean *noun*
in poker, three tens *US, 1963*
The suggestion is that the mythical Judge Duffy, Judge Dean, or whoever, commonly handed out sentences of thirty days.

- — Irwin Steig, *Common Sense in Poker*, p. 185, 1963
- — George Percy, *The Language of Poker*, p. 50, 1988

Judy *noun*
the meal fed to a prisoner in solitary confinement *US, 1992*

- Judy is a ground patty 4" × 4" × 3" that is made up of the entire meal's ingredients and is run through a grinder. They are traditionally served burned on the outside and raw on the inside. — William K. Bentley and James M. Corbett, *Prison Slang*, 1992

Judy *adjective*
locked in on a target *US, 1990*

- "We were both 'Judy,' meaning locked on," recalled J.C. They next activated their missiles. — Robert K. Wilcox, *Scream of Eagles*, p. 26, 1990

jug *noun*
1 a jail or prison *US, 1816*

- And don't forget they threw some musicians in the jug out in California for ten days[.] — Mezz Mezzrow, *Really the Blues*, 1946
- Then I'd rip off my blouse, give a scream, and run for the telephone or door, hysterically threatening to have him jugged for trying to rape an innocent young girl. — Whisper Magazine, p. 20, May 1950
- You want to go to the jug, it's your funeral, but I ain't sending any flowers. — Jim Thompson, *A Swell-Looking Babe*, p. 39, 1954
- We were rounded up and brought down to the jug. — Joe Houston, *The Gay Flesh*, p. 69, 1965

2 a Republic P-47 bomber aircraft *US, 1944*

- The Jug's short range was also criticized. — Jerry Scutts, *P-47 Thunderbolt Aces*, p. Back Cover, 1998

3 a bank *US, 1848*

- He could have a million in the jug. — Iceberg Slim (Robert Beck), *Trick Baby*, p. 111, 1969
- — Bill Reilly, *Big Al's Official Guide to Chicagoese*, 1982

4 a glass ampule holding liquid drugs *US, 1971*

- — Eugene Landy, *The Underground Dictionary*, p. 24, 1971

5 a small container of amphetamine or methamphetamine in liquid form *US, 1967*

- JUG: Ampule of liquid drugs, also a multi-dose container. — Elizabeth Finn, *Drugs in the Tenderloin*, 1967: Glossary of Drug Slang Used in the Tenderloin
- — National Institute on Drug Abuse, *What do they call it again?*, 1980

jug *verb*
1 to arrest or imprison *US, 1841*

- Thanks for the plug, but that wasn't why I got jugged. — Raymond Chandler, *The Long Goodbye*, p. 95, 1953
- "I'll have the cops send over the squad cars the night before the election and jug all the hoodlums[.]" — Alson Smith, *Syndicate City*, p. 104, 1954
- The law was one of those Catch-22 things that put you in jail. If you complied with the federal law to buy stamps, then the state law got you for being a bookmaker. If you didn't buy the stamps, the feds jugged you. — Mario Puzo, *Inside Las Vegas*, p. 291, 1977
- The judge was perplexed by his behavior because there was no chance whatsoever that he would have jugged the kid if he'd come in[.] — George V. Higgins, *Penance for Jerry Kennedy*, p. 112, 1985

2 to have sex with *US, 1965*

- There were few women around the neighborhood that Jonny wanted to jugg and didn't juff, even if they were married. — Claude Brown, *Manchild in the Promised Land*, p. 115, 1965
- You ain't been me, Panther, playing possum boo-koo [many] times she's come in way late ... don't take no bath 'cause she's done had one after he finished jugging in her. — Iceberg Slim (Robert Beck), *Doom Fox*, p. 183, 1978

3 to stab *US, 1970*

- — William D. Alsever, *Glossary for the Establishment and Other Uptight People*, p. 17, December 1970

juge *verb*
1 to have sex *US, 1967*

- Ask him did he want to juge a colored girl. — Malcolm Braly, *On the Yard*, p. 24, 1967

2 to stab *US, 2000*

- Juge said Cooper told him during questioning that was not recorded that he "juged" labi, which is street slang for stabbed. — *Times-Picayune (New Orleans)*, p. C1, 31st March 2000

juggle *verb*
to sell (drugs) *US, 1969*

- Look, Stonewall, you been juggling dope around the corner for a long time now, and you ain't gave me a hot dime. — A.S. Jackson, *Gentleman Pimp*, p. 182, 1973

juggler *noun*
a retail-level drug dealer *US, 1969*

- The street dealer sells to pushers (sometimes called jugglers). — Burgess Laughlin, *Job Opportunities in the Black Market*, p. 6–6, 1978
- — *Detroit News*, p. 5D, 20th September 2002

juggles *noun*
the female breasts *US, 2005*

- Jen's juggles make a nice appearance when she's in bed with her dude[.] — Mr. Skin, *Mr. Skin's Skincyclopedia*, p. 94, 2005

jughead *noun*
a dolt *US, 1899*

- The airline is offering regular jugheads like you and me the chance to, among other choices, "accelerate faster than the speed of sound[.]" — Celia Rivenback, *We're Just Like You, Only Prettier*, p. 223, 2004

jug heavy *noun*
a criminal who specializes in robbing bank vaults and safes *US, 1949*

- — Vincent J. Monteleone, *Criminal Slang*, p. 135, 1949

jug it!
save your prattle for someone who cares! *US, 1951*

- When the chit-chat's a bit on the dry side, tell them to "jug it"— or leave holding your ears and muttering, "my nerves." — *Philadelphia Evening Bulletin*, 11th November 1951

jugs; milk jugs *noun*
the female breasts *US, 1957*

- Some jugs! — Frederick Kohner, *Gidget*, p. 49, 1957
- "She doesn't even have a pair of decent jugs!" "Jugs," I haughtily replied, "aren't everything." — John Nichols, *The Sterile Cuckoo*, p. 88, 1965
- In other words, she was a fox with big jugs. — Edwin Torres, *After Hours*, p. 178, 1979
- You'd never know how large and in charge Meredith's mammaries are from her memorable but milk-jugless movies. — Mr. Skin, *Mr. Skin's Skincyclopedia*, p. 50, 2005

jug up *verb*
to eat *US, 1992*

- — William K Bentley and James M. Corbett, *Prison Slang*, 1992

juice noun

1 a bribe *UK, 1698*

- Thousands of dollars were spent on bribes—"juice"—blanketing the police force from top to bottom[.] — Ed Reid and Ovid Demaris, *The Green Jungle*, p. 19, 1963
- You really didn't know top wanted some juice? — Stan Lee, *The 'Nam*, p. 15, 1987

2 alcohol *US, 1932*

- At any rate, I've fixed up a real wild basket of ribs and a bottle of juice. — Steve Allen, *Bop Fables*, p. 37, 1955
- But what he was doing the whole time was mixing up this juice he calls Summer Snow. — Richard Farina, *Been Down So Long*, p. 62, 1966
- Folks, this is it for tonight. I've locked the juice cabinet. I can't let you kill yourself. Call me if you want anything except more juice. — Iceberg Slim (Robert Beck), *Trick Baby*, p. 263, 1969
- "And furthermore," I said, "you know that was my juice you drank there." — James Carr, *Bad*, p. 142, 1975

3 semen *US, 1969*

- She was afraid, because he'd shot a lot of juice into her, that she might get knocked up. — Juan Carmel Cosmes, *Memoir of a Whoremaster*, p. 32, 1969
- He'd been having trouble keeping himself from spewing his hot juice into her mouth since very shortly after she'd started in on him. — Tabor Evans, *Longarm and the Last Man*, p. 45, 1994
- Aurora coughed a little when Dante's cock shot his juice into her mouth. — Justus Roux, *Mistress Angelique*, p. 74, 2004

4 credibility, respect *US, 2007*

- They convert because Muslims in prison, even though not a gang, still have a certain amount of "juice"—street slang for "respect and credibility." — *Baltimore Sun*, p. 1B, 9th June 2007

5 methadone, used to break an opiate addiction *US, 1981*

In many US clinics, the methadone given to recovering heroin addicts is mixed in orange juice so that it cannot be injected.

- — Geoffrey Froner, *Digging for Diamonds*, p. 39, 1989
- Gino was dispensed juice at clinics in two counties and always had doses to sell. — Seth Morgan, *Homeboy*, p. 188, 1990

6 a powdered narcotic dissolved for injection; morphine *US, 1962*

- — Anthony Romeo, *The Language of Gangs*, p. 19, 4th December 1962
- "Somebody get the juice." — Tim O'Brien, *Going After Cacciato*, p. 38, 1978
- "I can only give him so much juice, and only so often." — Cherokee Paul McDonald, *Into the Green*, p. 91, 2001

7 crack cocaine mixed with marijuana *US, 1993*

- [A] fat ass J, of some bubonic chronic that made me choke[.] — Snoop Doggy Dogg, *Gin and Juice*, 1993

8 anabolic steroids *US, 1992*

- But if one guy stays on the juice, then ego makes the rest stay on, since they want The Look. — *Herb's Wrestling Tidbits*, 28th May 1992
- The Juice, a slang term for steroids, the use of which will now result in player suspensions. — *The Boston Herald*, 4th January 2004

9 blood; an intentional letting of blood *US, 1938*

Among others, professional wrestling usage.

- juice n. blood v.i. to bleed, usually as a result of blading. — *rec.sports.pro-wrestling*, 17th July 1990
- Great brawl in concession stand, quadruple juice. — *Herb's Wrestling Tidbits*, 23rd May 1992
- I climbed into the ring and the match continued. "Nice juice, huh?" I said to Vader as he set me up for a monstrous forearm to the head. — Mick Foley, *Mankind*, p. 6, 1999
- I mean, it was one of the all time juices; he was gushing like a stuck pig. — Missy Hyatt, *Missy Hyatt*, p. 53, 2001
- He'd get a lot of juice, which meant he bled a lot. — Bobby Heenan, *Bobby the Brain*, p. 114, 2002

10 nitroglycerin, used by thieves to blow open vaults or safes *US, 1924*

- — Joseph E. Ragen and Charles Finston, *Inside the World's Toughest Prison*, p. 806, 1962: "Penitentiary and underworld glossary"

11 power, influence, sway *US, 1957*

- The Hoffa juice in Las Vegas came from the Teamsters Central States, Southeast and Southwest Areas Pension Fund[.] — Ed Reid and Ovid Demaris, *The Green Felt Jungle*, p. 83, 1963
- Upstairs at Apple there is this one room where you make it if you got juice enough to get past the receptionist. — *The Last Supplement to the Whole Earth Catalog*, p. 70, March 1971
- The vic [victim's] father has juice with the City Council[.] — Robert Crais, *L.A. Requiem*, p. 44, 1999

12 interest paid to an loan shark *US, 1935*

- A hundred a week juice for as long as the loan is out. — Vincent Patrick, *The Pope of Greenwich Village*, p. 69, 1979
- You owe fifteen plus the fifteen hundred juice and another fifteen hundred for expenses, driving here from Miami. — Elmore Leonard, *Riding the Rap*, p. 19, 1995
- You owe me the dry cleaner's fifteen grand plus the juice which is what, another—ahh— — *Get Shorty*, 1995

13 in sports betting, the bookmaker's commission *US, 1975*

- All you are betting is the "juice," the one point to win twenty. — Jimmy Snyder, *Jimmy the Greek*, p. 208, 1975
- — *Bay Sports Review*, p. 8, November 1991

14 in pool, spin imparted to the cue ball to affect the course of the object ball or the course of the cue ball after it strikes the object ball *US, 1993*

- — Mike Shamos, *The Illustrated Encyclopedia of Billiards*, p. 127, 1993

15 surging surf with big waves *US, 1981*

- — Douglas Simonson, *Pidgin to da Max*, 1981
- — Trevor Cralle, *The Surfin'ary*, 1991

16 in a deck of playing cards, a two *US, 1951*

An intentional corruption of **DEUCE**.

- — *American Speech*, p. 99, May 1951: "The vocabulary of poker"

▸ **get some juice on**

to achieve a drug intoxication *US, 1980*

- Give me another tab so I can get some juice on — Stephen Gaskin, *Amazing Dope Tails*, p. 110, 1980

juice verb

1 to drink, especially to the point of intoxication *US, 1893*

- I don't think an orange ever tasted any sweeter to me; it was like some nectar the angels juice up on[.] — Mezz Mezzrow, *Really the Blues*, pp. 100–101, 1946
- I'd just like to caution you that the old days when a musician could juice on the job, try to make all the dames in the joint, and play when and how he pleased are gone. — Ross Russell, *The Sound*, p. 132, 1961
- Shorty would take me to groovy, frantic scenes in different chicks' and cats' pads, where with the lights and juke down mellow, everybody blew gage and juiced back and jumped. — Malcolm X and Alex Haley, *The Autobiography of Malcolm X*, p. 56, 1964
- I would fool with stuff a little bit and I'd see a Chinaman coming—that is, I'd see a habit coming on—and I would back away and smoke reefers for a while, then I'd juice a while. — Bruce Jackson, *In the Life*, p. 180, 1972

2 to drug *US, 1973*

- "One might have bought a jockey, another might have juiced a horse and bought the spit box." — Vincent Teresa, *My Life in the Mafia*, p. 153, 1973

3 to energize *US, 1977*

- Check out the methane level fore we get back up there and juice the machinery. — John Sayles, *Union Dues*, p. 17, 1977

4 to bleed *US, 1990*

Professional wrestling usage.

- juice n. blood v.i. to bleed, usually as a result of blading. — *rec.sports.pro-wrestling*, 17th July 1990
- The referee juiced from a nonchaku blow. — *Herb's Wrestling Tidbits*, 21st May 1992
- He drops to the canvas and juices, and now he's bleeding all over the place. — Missy Hyatt, *Missy Hyatt*, p. 53, 2001

5 to bribe; to pay for influence *US, 1953*

- I got to make lots of dough to juice the guys I got to juice in order to make lots of dough to juice the guys I got to juice. — Raymond Chandler, *The Long Goodbye*, p. 65, 1953

6 to obtain something through the influence of another *US, 1980*

- He got juiced into the Grand. — Lee Solkey, *Dummy Up and Deal*, p. 115, 1980

juice bar noun

a clinic where recovering heroin addicts are administered methadone *US, 1989*

Playful, alluding to **JUICE** (methadone).

- — Geoffrey Froner, *Digging for Diamonds*, p. 39, 1989

juice card noun

a favor performed by a guard for a prisoner *US, 2002*

- — Jeffrey Ian Ross, *Behind Bars*, p. 189, 2002: Slammer Slang

juiced; juiced up *adjective*

drunk *US, 1941*

- One stud got juiced and played the flunky, to a very surprised old Brazilian monkey. — Dan Burley, *Diggeth Thou?*, p. 17, 1959
- You've gone to the finest school all right, Miss Lonely / But you know you only used to get juiced in it. — Bob Dylan, *Like a Rolling Stone*, 1965
- This town's got four hundred people that stay juiced out of their minds—cause they're depressed because they're there. — Lenny Bruce, *The Essential Lenny Bruce*, p. 95, 1967
- He got juiced and almost ran into a trailer truck coming back. — Babs Gonzales, *Movin' On Down De Line*, p. 117, 1975

juiced in *adjective*

enjoying powerful political connections *US, 1995*

- He's juiced in. He's the County Commissioner's cousin. — *Casino*, 1995

juiced out *adjective*

dehabilitated by excessive drinking *US, 1971*

- Hector, juiced out at nineteen, according to friends, was so filled with wine that his brain started going soft. — David Freeman, *U.S. Grant in the City*, p. 33, 1971
- Hurricane drank all damn night, and by the time we got back to Long Island he was mean and juiced out. — Noire, *Candy Licker*, p. 235, 2005

juice freak *noun*

an alcoholic *US, 1969*

- Other science fiction writers, such as J.G. Ballard and Roger Zelazny, have joined the druggie panoply of literary heroes, which includes that old acid-head John Barth, that old juice-head Malcolm Lowry. — Michael Crichton, *Sci-Fi and Vonnegut*, 1969
- "He is a juice freak like you." — Harold Robbins, *Lonely Lady*, p. 347, 1983

juice head *noun*

an alcoholic *US, 1954*

- The Juicehead Kid was a' takin' a jolt. — William "Lord" Buckley, *The Ballad of Dan McGroo*, 1960
- "Thing you got to understand about her is she a juice head." — Leonard Gardner, *Fat City*, p. 155, 1969
- Now get your ass in the bathroom and wash your mouth out. I want you to kill that fuckin' odor. Where I'm gettin' ready to take you, I don't want the people to think I brought a juice head along with me. — Donald Goines, *Daddy Cool*, pp. 95–96, 1974
- A fat-ass juice head who was liable to melt with a little heat and a bad-ass spade gunslinger who blew fifty bucks a week on his highs. — Elmore Leonard, *52 Pick-up*, p. 121, 1974
- I'm a junkie. I know you can understand a little because you're a juicehead. — Herbert Huncke, *Guilty of Everything*, p. 131, 1990

juice joint *noun*

1 an establishment where alcohol is served illegally *US, 1932*

- "You know that juice joint up on the second floor?" she said. — Mezz Mezzrow, *Really the Blues*, p. 266, 1946
- Officers Phillips and Droge both testified that they, their fellow patrolmen, and in some cases, their supervisors, had accepted regular payments from bottle clubs and "juice joints." — *The Knapp Commission Report on Police Corruption*, p. 144, 1972
- Shot-house operators run informal (and illegal) taverns in their own homes (shot-house operators are often women). The houses go by other names too; gold mine, good-time house, blind tiger, shine parlor, or juice joint. — Burgess Laughlin, *Job Opportunities in the Black Market*, p. 10–9, 1989

2 a crooked gambling operation *US, 1950*

- — Frank Garcia, *Marked Cards and Loaded Dice*, p. 262, 1962

juice man *noun*

1 a usurer, loan-shark, illegal lender *US, 1961*

- The fear of the juice victim of criminal prosecution is far less than his fear of the juicemen. — Ovid Demaris, *Captive City*, p. 56, 1969
- "Tony the juice man has a long memory, doesn't he?" the lawyer asked. — Gerald Petievich, *Money Men*, p. 78, 1981
- Sometimes the average working stiff can find another juiceman who'll lend him enough dimes to pay off the first juiceman, interest and principal, with maybe a couple of C-notes left over. — Robert Campbell, *Juice*, p. 21, 1988
- Master wanted to borrow some bread to keep the dojang going, but the juice man's rates were too high. — Odie Hawkins, *Lost Angeles*, p. 26, 1994

2 an AM radio disc jockey who broadcasts on a powerful, all-night station heard by truckers *US, 1976*

- — Porter Bibb, *CB Bible*, p. 97, 1976

juice money *noun*

a bribe *US, 1981*

- An office, a secretary, a car, juice money for the real estate people, tee boiler room, bleepety, bleepety bleep. — Gerald Petievich, *Money Men*, p. 78, 1981

juicer *noun*

1 a person who abuses alcohol *US, 1960*

- And as he continued to be alone, to be apart from the reefer-smokers and juicers and Happy Others who did nothing but be square, his drive to be needed made him seek out a companion[.] — Clarence Cooper Jr., *The Scene*, p. 64, 1960
- Juicers on the wagon are all big coffee fiends. — James Ellroy, *Brown's Requiem*, p. 43, 1981
- He was a friend of the sergeant's. They were the "juicers" [alcohol drinkers] and I was the "head" [pot smoker]. — Myra MacPherson, *Long Time Passing*, p. 398, 1984

2 a persuasive and resourceful woman sent out to acquire crack cocaine for others *US, 1992*

- — Terry Williams, *Crackhouse*, p. 149, 1992

3 in hot rodding, hydraulic brakes *US, 1954*

- — *American Speech*, p. 99, May 1954

juice racket *noun*

usury, loan-sharking, illegal lending *US, 1988*

- But this other mess, the juice racket, is ours. — Robert Campbell, *Juice*, p. 213, 1988

juices *noun*

in poker, a pair of twos *US, 1951*

Probably a corruption of DEUCE(S).

- — *American Speech*, p. 99, May 1951

juice the hard way; hardway juice *noun*

in professional wrestling, blood from a cut suffered unintentionally *US, 1990*

Almost all bleeding in professional wrestling is intentionally produced in keeping with a script for the match.

- hardway juice n. real blood produced by means other than blading, i.e., the hard way — *rec.sports.pro-wrestling*, 17th July 1990
- If someone's bleeding from the mouth, it's probably real (or hardway). — Dave Flood, *Kayfabe*, p. 24, 2000
- But there's also juicing "the hard way." — Missy Hyatt, *Missy Hyatt*, p. 53, 2001

juice up; juice *verb*

1 to make exciting or powerful *US, 1964*

- I had a friend over juicing it up[.] — Lester Bangs, *Psychotic Reactions and Carburetor Dung*, 1972

2 to drink to intoxication *US, 1971*

- The kids got a little wild. Some of the boys were juicing it up. — Anonymous, *Go Ask Alice*, p. 19, 1971

juicy *noun*

the vagina *US, 2002*

- "The Holy Grail," she said. "You know. The juicy." — Dan Jenkins, *The Money-Whipped Steer-Job Three-Jack Give-Up Artist*, p. 207, 2001

juicy *adjective*

1 (used of a woman) sexually aroused *US, 1970*

- Over in the corner sat Sweet Jaw Lucy, looking all juicy. — Roger Abrahams, *Positively Black*, p. 122, 1970

2 a low-skill poker game or poker play *US, 1982*

- — David M. Hayano, *Poker Faces*, p. 186, 1982

3 (of a wave) powerful, with a large fringing crest *US, 1977*

- — Gary Fairmont R. Filosa II, *The Surfer's Almanac*, p. 188, 1977

ju-ju sign *noun*

a curse *US, 1949*

- "I'll make a ju-ju sign on you," he threatened. — Nelson Algren, *The Man with the Golden Arm*, p. 105, 1949

juke *noun*

a jukebox *US, 1941*

- "You like the groovy music on the juke?" Barrelhouse said. — Ralph Ellison, *Invisible Man*, p. 425, 1947

- He got up and went over to the juke, dropped a quarter in on "Whispering Grass," and everybody turned to look at him when the lyrics began. — Clarence Cooper Jr., *The Scene*, p. 103, 1960
- Shorty would take me to groovy, frantic scenes in different chicks' and cats' pads, where with the lights and juke down mellow, everybody blew gage and juiced back and jumped. — Malcolm X and Alex Haley, *The Autobiography of Malcolm X*, p. 56, 1964

juke; jug *verb*

1 to dance in a boisterous fashion *US, 1933*
It is theorized that the word, today only recognized in the formation **JUKE BOX**, was derived from the African Wolof, Banut, or Bambara languages. The term spread through southern blacks from the Gullah, and then into wider slang usage, although with a distinctly southern flavor.
- Now the big black guy said something, grinning, and the whores laughed and started juking around, feeling something about to happen. — Elmore Leonard, *Switch*, p. 23, 1978

2 to fool, to trick *US, 1873*
- Aw, Franchot, who you think you juggin' by tryin' to be so hard? — Nathan Heard, *Howard Street*, p. 30, 1968
- Call Wilhite and Narco more dangerous; call me a bent cop juking their meal ticket. — James Ellroy, *White Jazz*, p. 57, 1992

3 to hit *US, 1872*
- "I'll jug you," he yelled, "by God, I'll jug you." — Ralph Ellison, *Invisible Man*, p. 274, 1947

juke house *noun*

a brothel *US, 1945*
- Juke House. Slang: A house of prostitution. — Julian Martin, *Law Enforcement Vocabulary*, p. 124, 1973

juke joint *noun*

a bar or club with a jukebox; usually rowdy and teeming with sin *US, 1937*
- A black-white stick-up gang had been clouting markets and juke joints on West Adams[.] — James Ellroy, *Hollywood Nocturnes*, p. 127, 1994

jumbo *noun*

1 the penis *US, 2000*
- "Uh-huh, you stepped on my jumbo too." — Paul Beatty, *Tuff*, p. 250, 2000

2 a large vial of crack cocaine *US, 1986*
- The dealers' pitch, "Yo, man, got them jumbos!" echoed from almost every corner surrounding the park. — *Record (Bergen County, New Jersey)*, p. A21, 28th September 1986
- — Terry Williams, *The Cocaine Kids*, p. 137, 1989

jump *noun*

1 an act of sexual intercourse *US, 1931*
- Everybody cleared out, I left, it wasn't fifteen minutes after you did, Benavides went in a bedroom there with the broad, gave her a jump, that was it. — Elmore Leonard, *Glitz*, p. 139, 1985
- I was just showering your mother's stink off me after I gave her a quick jump and sent her home. — Kevin Smith, *Jay and Silent Bob Strike Back*, p. 17, 2001

2 a party, especially a party with music *US, 1954*
- You meet your boys and make it to a jump, where you can break night dancing. — Piri Thomas, *Down These Mean Streets*, p. 58, 1967

3 the start *US, 1848*
- In fact, he sincerely believed that she'd known from the jump what he'd eventually ask her to do. — Nathan Heard, *Howard Street*, p. 166, 1968
- I mounted her and asked her to fit the pipe and as always it was a bit tight from the jump. — A.S. Jackson, *Gentleman Pimp*, p. 109, 1973
- She was fascinating to watch and she and I got along splendidly from the jump, the first night I was up there. — Herbert Huncke, *Guilty of Everything*, p. 127, 1990

4 in the entertainment industry, a move in between engagements, especially by rail *US, 1916*
- With a seven-hundred-mile jump there was no time to waste on roadside repairs[.] — Gypsy Rose Lee, *Gypsy*, p. 234, 1957
- No matter how far the jumps between one-nighters, or how remote the town, she was there, ready for the night's musical adventure. — Ross Russell, *The Sound*, p. 82, 1961
- — Joe McKennon, *Circus Lingo*, p. 52, 1980

jump *verb*

1 to have sex *US, 1949*
- "I sure woulda liked to jump her." — Irving Shulman, *Cry Tough*, p. 85, 1949

- "Now it gonna cost everytime you jump her." — Warren Miller, *The Cool World*, p. 41, 1959
- On the bright Sunday afternoon we visited West Point, Strauss wore a pair of tortoiseshell prescription sunglasses that made me want to jump him. — Rita Ciresi, *Pink Slip*, p. 109, 1999

2 to be lively, wild, full of activity *US, 1938*
- We got hold of a piano somewheres, put up some tables on the porch, and inside of two weeks we had the joint jumping. — Mezz Mezzrow, *Really the Blues*, p. 86, 1946
- [H]e said she was a marvelous cook and everything would jump. — Jack Kerouac, *On the Road*, p. 11, 1957
- Havana was really jumpin' in those days—best town I was ever in. — Edwin Torres, *Carlito's Way*, p. 35, 1975

3 to travel from an engagement in one town to the next town where an engagement is scheduled *US, 1975*
- He knows what it means to jump five and six hundred miles a night. — Babs Gonzales, *Movin' On Down De Line*, p. 105, 1975

▸ **jump salty**
to become angry *US, 1961*
- "Don't jump salty with me." — Malcom Braly, *Felony Tank*, p. 125, 1961
- Broads jumped salty and called attention to their ol' man's ears. — Steve Cannon, *Groove, Bang, and Jive Around*, p. 71, 1969
- I had no intentions of ever being their muscle man if a john happened to jump salty. — Robert Deane Pharr, *S.R.O.*, p. 369, 1971

▸ **jump someone's bones**
to have sex *US, 1964*
- Failing that, he would have thoroughly enjoyed jumping on her elegant bones. — Max Shulman, *Anyone Got a Match?*, p. 38, 1964
- I wondered why I didn't just go in and jump her bones. — Jim Carroll, *Forced Entries*, p. 173, 1987
- Once in a while I'll have a dancer come on to me—with the expectation that simply because I'm a lesbian I'm dying to jump her bones. — Frederique Delacoste, *Sex Work*, p. 24, 1987
- He's just another guy who wants to jump your bones. — *American Beauty*, 1999

▸ **jump sore**
to anger *US, 1960*
- "Jack," I said, "O Jilly, if I've crossed you, don't jump sore." — William "Lord" Buckley, *The Raven*, 1960

▸ **jump stink**
to become angry *US, 1946*
- Everything seemed to be going wrong for me and Bud—the whole town jumped stink on us. — Mezz Mezzrow, *Really the Blues*, p. 130, 1946
- Macho, their president, jumped stink and said, "Time man, we got heart[.]" — Piri Thomas, *Down These Mean Streets*, p. 52, 1967

▸ **jump the shark**
of a television program, to pass a peak of popularity *US, 1998*
Coined after a 1977 episode of long-running comedy *Happy Days* in which a central character in need of fresh impetus took to water-skis and attempted to leap over a shark.
- Has "SP" [Southpark] "jumped the shark" with its April Fools' episode? — *Los Angeles Times*, p. F48, 9th April 1998

▸ **jump yellow**
to act in a cowardly manner *US, 1974*
- At least he had heart, he fought it out, but you jumped yellow and dove for the bar. — Piri Thomas, *Seven Long Times*, p. 38, 1974

jump back *verb*

1 to initiate a fight *US, 1975*
- — Carl J. Banks Jr., *Banks Dictionary of the Black Ghetto Language*, 1975

2 to relent, to ease off *US, 1986*
- Jump back, Ferris. Cameron's been a good sport. — *Ferris Bueller's Day Off*, 1986

jump ball *noun*

in pool, a ball that leaves the surface of the table *US, 1850*
- — Mike Shamos, *The Illustrated Encyclopedia of Billiards*, p. 127, 1993

jump collar *noun*

an arrest made for show, which will not produce a conviction *US, 1953*
- "Don't worry," I said to them. "This is only a jump collar." "Jump collar!" said the Inspector. "Huh! We've got you cold and you know it." — Polly Adler, *A House is Not a Home*, p. 252, 1953

jump CP *noun*
a hastily created, very temporary command post *US*, *1991*
- Take your jump CP and a company up there first thing tomorrow.
  — Edward F. Murphy, *The Hill Fights*, p. 69, 2003

jump down *verb*
to attack physically *US*, *2001*
- But we had on different colors, and they thought we was Bloods—until we jumped down on 'em. — *Rolling Stone*, p. 82, 12th April 2001

jumper *noun*
a person who threatens to or has jumped to his death, either from heights or in front of a train *US*, *1964*
- We got a call one day, a jumper. So we go to the building and the floor[.] — Mark Baker, *Cops*, p. 99, 1985
- Had a jumper last night, Sarge. Dixie here was walking by, saw the whole thing. — *Lethal Weapon*, 1987

jumpers *noun*
sports shoes *US*, *1972*
- — David Claerbaut, *Black Jargon in White America*, p. 70, 1972

jump in *verb*
to initiate (someone) into a youth gang through a timed group beating *US*, *1988*
- "When they would jump us in, they would start a fight. Some other guy jumps in, then another." — James Vigil, *Barrio Gangs*, p. 105, 1988
- I had heard about being "courted in" ("courted in" means to be accepted through a barrage of tests, usually physical, though this can include shooting people) or "jumped in[.]" — Sanyika Shakur, *Monster*, p. 9, 1993
- "We're not going to jump you in because you'll probably kick one of our asses." — S. Beth Atkin, *Voices from the Street*, p. 72, 1996
- Now I know. Courting means to be physically "jumped in." — Colton Simpson, *Inside the Crips*, p. 19, 2005

jump-in; jumping in *noun*
a timed beating used as an initiation into a youth gang *US*, *1987*
- It's called a "jump-in." That's gang vernacular for a handful of gang members jumping on a prospective member and beating him up for 45 seconds. — *Los Angeles Times*, p. Metro Section 1, 20th November 1987
- "The jumping-in process of a gang member is similar to the training process of a police cadet." — Leon Bing, *Do or Die*, p. 13, 1991

jumping *adjective*
used as an intensifier in mild oaths *US*, *1815*
- Scared the shit outa me. Jumpin' Jehosophat. — Edwin Torres, *After Hours*, p. 235, 1979

jumping judas!
used or expressing surprise *US*, *1962*
- "Jumping Judas!" yelled Bradley. "Wait'll I tell Babe Ruth about this." — Sam Snead, *The Education of a Golfer*, p. 14, 1962

jump joint *noun*
a brothel *US*, *1939*
- "Son, here's twenty dollars; I want you to go to a good whore and get a piece of ass off her." So they drive to this plush jump joint, and the father say, "All right, son. You're on your own." — William Burroughs, *Naked Lunch*, p. 119, 1957

jump juice *noun*
anabolic steroids *US*, *1997*
- He alternated between four-hundred-pound dead-lifts, shots of jump-juice, and the great Italian cuisine. — Stephen Cannell, *Big Con*, p. 160, 1997

jump off *verb*
1 to happen; to begin *US*, *1946*
- Wham! The fanfare jump off! — William "Lord" Buckley, *Nero*, 1951
- It's past ten o'clock, and ain't nothing jumped off yet. — Donald Goines, *White Man's Justice, Black Man's Grief*, p. 81, 1973

2 to assault *US*, *1975*
- "You keep fat mouthin, bitch, I'm going to jump off up in your black ass," he warned. — Charles W. Moore, *A Brick for Mister Jones*, p. 27, 1975

jump out *verb*
to mark a departure from a youth gang by a group beating *US*, *1988*

- An exit rite also exists, and gang youths typically maintain that, just as one must be "jumped in" to gain membership, he must be "jumped out" to leave. — James Vigil, *Barrio Gangs*, p. 106, 1988

jump-out squad *noun*
a unit of police-officers in a cruising, unmarked police-vehicle, detailed to jump out of their car and apprehend drug dealers *US*, *1980*
- "That was no fun," said Detective Dave Hayes, whose wrist is still sore from a fall he took dodging bullets on a chase through Condon Terrace. Hayes' unit became laughingly known among the youths as "The Jump Out Squad." — *The Washington Post*, 28th January 1980
- Police call them "corner deployment units." Local residents refer to them as "jump-out squads." — *The New York Times*, 15th December 2002

jumpsack *noun*
a parachute *US*, *1990*
- That's all, brother, hit the jumpsack. — Joseph Tuso, *Singing the Vietnam Blues*, p. 128, 1990: My Darling F-4

jump-start *verb*
to light a fresh cigarette with the ember of one being finished *US*, *1984*
- — Ken Weaver, *Texas Crude*, p. 116, 1984

jump-steady *noun*
1 strong, illegally manufactured whiskey *US*, *1923*
- It is called corn liquor, white lightning, sugar whiskey, skully cracker, popskull, bush whiskey, stump, stumphole, 'splo, ruckus juice, radiator whiskey, rotgut, sugarhead, block and tackle, wildcat, panther's breath, tiger's sweat, Sweet spirits of cats a-fighting, alley bourbon, city gin, cool water, happy Sally, deep shaft, jump steady, old horsey, stingo, blue John, red eye, pine top, buckeye bark whiskey and see seven stars. — *Star Tribune (Minneapolis)*, p. 19F, 31st January 1999

2 a drink of gin *US*, *1950*
- Nine or ten jump-steadies and a couple of muggles and up goes your gage. — Hyman E. Goldin et al., *Dictionary of American Underworld Lingo*, p. 112, 1950

jump street *noun*
the inception; the very beginning *US*, *1972*
- — William K. Bentley and James M. Corbett, *Prison Slang*, 1992

jump wire *noun*
a wire designed for starting a car engine while bypassing the key and ignition system *US*, *1970s*
- "I don't do it anymore," Stick said. "That was a long time ago." "You just happen to have the jump-wire in your bag." — Elmore Leonard, *Stick*, p. 78, 1983

Juneau sneakers *noun*
slip-on rubber boots *US*, *1982*
- — Russell Tabbert, *Dictionary of Alaskan English*, p. 97, 1991

Junebug *noun*
used as a nickname for a male named after his father *US*, *1970*
- — Clarence Major, *Dictionary of Afro-American Slang*, p. 72, 1970

jungle *noun*
1 a dangerous, rough part of town, especially one where black people live *US*, *1926*
- See, it was in the jungle there and he was looking for somebody that could sit in a car without looking like he didn't belong there, you know? — George V. Higgins, *The Friends of Eddie Doyle*, pp. 21–22, 1971
- If he thinks I'm going up into the Jungle this time of night, he can shove it. — *Taxi Driver*, 1976

2 an outdoor area favored by homosexuals for sexual encounters *US*, *1963*
- I discovered the jungle of Central Park—between the 60s and 70s on the west side. — John Rechy, *City of Night*, p. 62, 1963

3 a tramp encampment *US*, *1908*
- They had gone about fifteen miles down the railroad tracks and holed-up in a jungle. — Chester Himes, *Cast the First Stone*, p. 275, 1952

4 a prison's recreation yard *US*, *1983*
- — Marlene Freedman, *Alcatraz*, 1983

jungle bunny *noun*
a black person *US*, *1959*
Highly offensive.

- The dozen or so jungle bunnies I have trafficked with were perfectly ordinary in that department[.] — Gore Vidal, *Myra Breckinridge*, p. 88, 1968
- "Greaseball," said one of the Dukes. Angry glances. "Jungle Bunny," said Peter Udo. — Richard Price, *The Wanderers*, p. 160, 1974
- You mean by the jungle-bunnies, dontcha Smallwood? — John Sayles, *Union Dues*, p. 283, 1977
- Never ceases to amaze me. Fuckin' jungle bunny goes out there, slits some old woman's throat for twenty-five cents. — *Reservoir Dogs*, 1992

jungle busting *noun*
using tanks and other heavy combat equipment to break through a jungle *US, 1986*
- The concept of "jungle busting" was also new. — Ralph Zumbro, *Tank Sergeant*, p. 16, 1986

jungle fever *noun*
a strong attraction towards black people *US, 1990*
The prominent title of a Spike Lee film (1991).
- But they definitely didn't have a case of "jungle fever," then or now. — Odie Hawkins, *Black Chicago*, p. 159, 1992
- The week after we returned from Catalina was spent convincing him that I'd slept with him out of affection and respect, not out of Jungle Fever. I howled when we suggested this, since weeks before we'd both agreed that the movie was a crock of shit[.] — Armistead Maupin, *Maybe the Moon*, p. 206, 1992
- One girl reported that she'd slept with Robert De Niro, who made "puppy eyes" in bed, then mentioned his incurable case of Jungle Fever. — Anka Radakovich, *The Wild Girls Club*, 1994

jungle fuck *noun*
energetic, even athletic sex *US, 1994*
- — Michael Dalton Johnson, *Talking Trash with Redd Foxx*, p. 72, 1994

jungle-happy *adjective*
deranged from prolonged combat in the jungle *US, 1944*
- — *American Speech*, p. 55, February 1947: "Pacific War language"

jungle job *noun*
sex outdoors *US, 1966*
- Studs in New York, particularly those working the Public Library and Bryant Park areas, call a frantic quickie in the bushes a "jungle job" or a "Tarzan." — Johnny Shearer, *The Male Hustler*, p. 17, 1966

jungle juice *noun*
1 any improvised alcoholic beverage *US, 1946*
- At any given time there were apt to be brewing on the ship fifteen different batches of jungle juice, but it was agreed that Olson made the most distinctive brand. — Thomas Heggen, *Mister Roberts*, p. 31, 1946
- — *American Speech*, p. 55, February 1947: "Pacific War language"
- "Is it real whisky or is it jungle juice?" — Norman Mailer, *The Naked and the Dead*, p. 204, 1948

2 in prison, serious talk about serious situations *US, 1990*
- — Charles Shafer, *Folk Speech in Texas Prisons*, p. 208, 1990

jungle light *noun*
in the pornography industry, a light used to illuminate the genitals of the performers *US, 1995*
- — *Adult Video News*, p. 50, October 1995

jungle meat *noun*
in homosexual usage, a black man *US, 1981*
- — *Male Swinger Number 3*, p. 47, 1981: "The complete gay dictionary"
- — *Maledicta*, p. 52, 1986–1987: "A continuation of a glossary of ethnic slurs in American English"

jungle mouth *noun*
very bad breath *US, 1975*
- — *American Speech*, p. 62, Spring–Summer 1975: "Razorback slang"

jungle pussy *noun*
a black woman's vagina; hence black women objectified sexually *US, 1974*
- "Hey," said another sick voice, "cop a look at the fat ass on that one. Hairy as a jungle pussy." — Piri Thomas, *Seven Long Times*, p. 67, 1974
- First she said the black thing, like she understood his urge to check out some jungle pussy. — John Williams, *Cardiff Dead*, p. 61, 2000

jungle rot *noun*
any skin rash suffered in tropical and jungle environments *US, 1945*

- "Jungle rot," "New Guinea crud" or "the creeping crud" are U.S. servicemen's names for any & every kind of tropical skin disease. — *Time*, p. 76, 13th August 1946
- I also have a good case of jungle rot—a sprawling fungus Down There, or rather on either side of it. — Martin Russ, *Happy Hunting Ground*, p. 173, 1968
- Cures heartburn, jungle rot, the Gee-fucken-Eyes, all them things. — Larry Heinemann, *Close Quarters*, p. 26, 1977
- All of us had done something really brave and stupid to get this three-day R&R, and all of us had varying degrees of jungle rot, which was helped by the sun and salt water. — Nelson DeMille, *Up Country*, p. 280, 2002

jungle rules *noun*
a code of competition or combat in which all is fair *US, 1990*
- The more active ones participated in roughouse games of volleyball, playing by "jungle rules"—anything goes. — Tom Yarborough, *Da Nang Diary*, p. 198, 1990

jungles *noun*
1 a jungle camouflage uniform *US, 1981*
- "The lieutenant told me to get jungles out of there." — Mark Baker, *Nam*, p. 51, 1981

2 a neighborhood controlled by the Bloods youth gang *US, 2005*
- Then one night Huckabuck and I are at the Skate City when we find out K.B. is in the jungles. — Colton Simpson, *Inside the Crips*, p. 161, 2005

junior *noun*
1 a young hanger-on with a youth gang *US, 1949*
- A count is difficult because the larger gangs have "seniors," "juniors," and young auxiliaries known by such names as "Tiny Tims." — William Bernard, *Jailbait*, p. 80, 1949
- "All they got is juniors and midgets." — Herbert Simmons, *Corner Boy*, p. 140, 1957
- We start hangin' aroun' an become a junior an then we grow up some more an get takin' in the gang. — Warren Miller, *The Cool World*, p. 224, 1959

2 in television and movie-making, a 1000-watt or 2000-watt light *US, 1990*
- — Ralph S. Singleton, *Filmmaker's Dictionary*, p. 89, 1990

junior birdman *noun*
a member of a flight crew *US, 1944*
- As a "junior birdman" in a new unit that had precious few planes, Lyle found it difficult to get on the Group's flying schedule. — Brian O'Neill, *Half a Wing*, p. 362, 1999

junk *noun*
1 heroin; morphine; cocaine *US, 1918*
- My first experience with junk was during the War, about 1944 or 1945. — William Burroughs, *Junkie*, p. 19, 1953
- The poor fellow took so much junk into his system he could only weather the greater proportion of his day in that chair with the lamp burning at noon[.] — Jack Kerouac, *On the Road*, p. 150, 1957
- Sometimes I wondered why I bothered to go to see her, and that was the way it was with most of my friends who didn't use junk. — Alexander Trocchi, *Cain's Book*, p. 18, 1960
- That was the question on a lot of them corners, 'cause the junk was still a new scene in the forties. — Edwin Torres, *Carlito's Way*, p. 10, 1975

2 any illegal drug *US, 1967*
- Some kids call all dope "shit" or "junk," terms that were once synonyms for heroin. — Nicholas Von Hoffman, *We Are The People Our Parents Warned Us Against*, p. 65, 1967

3 the genitals *US, 1985*
- "That's when the top man lays you face down on your junk, and after he starts to punk you he turns you on your side and locks his arms around you so you can't pull away." — Ethan Morden, *I've a Feeling We're Not in Kansas Anymore*, p. 69, 1985
- She was all over my junk. — Judi Sanders, *Da Bomb!*, p. 16, 1997

4 in theater usage, a monologue *US, 1981*
- — Don Wilmeth, *The Language of American Popular Entertainment*, p. 149, 1981

junk bonds *noun*
in poker, a hand that appears attractive but is in fact a poor hand *US, 1996*
- — John Vorhaus, *The Big Book of Poker Slang*, p. 24, 1996

junked; junked up *adjective*
under the influence of heroin *US, 1930*

- When she's not junked up, she's too busy figuring ways to get the stuff she needs to think about sex or anything else. — Judge John M. Murtagh and Sara Harris, *Cast the First Stone*, p. 39, 1957
- The night man was junked to the eyes. — Raymond Chandler, *Playback*, p. 73, 1958

junker *noun*

1 a heroin addict *US, 1922*
- In one small town while we were making a check I found a junker and had him arraigned before a county judge for commitment to take a cure. — William J. Spillard and Pence James, *Needle in a Haystack*, p. 89, 1945
- I later learned that all junkers talk in terms of beauty and unreality when they've been "smoking." — Ethel Waters, *His Eye is on the Sparrow*, p. 113, 1951

2 in competitive surfing, an extremely low score *US, 1991*
- — Trevor Cralle, *The Surfin'ary*, p. 61, 1991

junk food *noun*

food with a high calorific and low nutritional content *US, 1971*
- Harry had never been a junk-food junkie. — Cyra McFadden, *The Serial*, p. 41, 1977
- I haven't had a good TV-and-junk-food pig-out in ages. — Armistead Maupin, *Further Tales of the City*, p. 156, 1982

junk hawk *noun*

a heroin addict whose life is completely controlled by the addiction *US, 1972*
- Kenny Wisdom was becoming what is known as a junk hawk, that is to say, all he ever did from then on pertained to junk, as his tolerance for the stuff grew even beyond his greed for it. — Emmett Grogan, *Ringolevio*, p. 42, 1972

junk hog *noun*

an opium addict *US, 1950*
- — Jack Lait and Lee Mortimer, *Chicago Confidential*, p. 301, 1950: "Loop lexicon"

junkie *noun*

1 a drug addict, specifically one addicted to heroin *US, 1922*
- I was cutting up to Harlem to see a junkie that Little Rock used to know in Atlanta. — John Clellon Holmes, *Go*, p. 201, 1952
- There were wild Negro queers, sullen guys with guns, shiv-packing seamen, thin, noncommittal junkies, and an occasional well-dressed middle-aged detective[.] — Jack Kerouac, *On the Road*, p. 131, 1957
- The motorized patrol was usually made twice a day, cop teams making constant saunters along the border streets to check IDs, roll up sleeve and pant legs for junkie spot checks[.] — Clancy Sigal, *Going Away*, p. 235, 1961
- All the animals come out at night. Whores, skunk pussies, buggers, queens, fairies, dopers, junkies, sick, venal. — *Taxi Driver*, 1976

2 by extension, a person fiercely devoted to an activity *US, 1962*
- A symbol junkie. People like him—that is, the majority—are strung out on symbols. They're so addicted that they prefer abstract symbols to the concrete things which symbols represent. — Tom Robbins, *Another Roadside Attraction*, p. 227, 1971
- She's a young girl out of Berkeley ... a television junkie. — Dan Jenkins, *Life Its Ownself*, p. 294, 1984
- He wondered if he qualified as a full-fledged TV junkie, a chronic escapist who needed the tube to fill a void he was no longer capable of filling himself. — Armistead Maupin, *Babycakes*, p. 13, 1984

junk in the trunk *noun*

prominent buttocks *US, 1995*
- She be wearin' some little shorts and her butt meat be hangin' out a little bit. Yellow whisper to me, "Girl got some junk in the trunk." — Percival Everett, *Erasure*, p. 90, 2001
- "I like a girl with a little junk in the trunk." — Megan McCafferty, *Second Helpings*, p. 252, 2003
- "She's a definite woman—she's got junk in the trunk." — *USA Today*, p. 10D, 6th February 2006

junk mooch *noun*

a heroin addict who trades information for heroin *US, 1972*
- He was also a junk mooch, who maintained his habit by trading information to the cops for heroin which they had confiscated from arrested addicts and pushers. — Emmett Grogan, *Ringolevio*, p. 54, 1972

junk-on-the-bunk *noun*

a military inspection of a soldier's gear displayed on his bed *US, 1957*
- Then the word was passed around the battalion that the fucking colonel also wanted "junk on the bunk." — Martin Russ, *The Last Parallel*, p. 322, 1957

junks *noun*

expensive, brand name basketball shoes *US, 1987*
- — *The Washington Post*, 15th March 1987
- — Kenn "Naz" Young, *Naz's Dictionary of Teen Slang*, p. 68, 1993

junk tank *noun*

a jail cell reserved for drug addicts *US, 1966*

A play on the earlier and more common **DRUNK TANK**.
- — Eugene Landy, *The Underground Dictionary*, p. 114, 1971
- — William K. Bentley and James M. Corbett, *Prison Slang*, p. 7, 1992

junk up *verb*

to drug *US, 1973*
- "You know, in order to junk up a horse, he's got to be a sound horse to begin with." — Vincent Teresa, *My Life in the Mafia*, p. 156, 1973

junkwagon *noun*

a motorcycle that does not meet the speaker's standards *US, 1966*
- And those silly goddamn junkwagon bikes? — Hunter S. Thompson, *Hell's Angels*, p. 87, 1967

junkyard dog *noun*

1 a ferocious, territorial person *US, 1983*
- I tell myself I got to learn not to let some vague notion get fixed in my head so there's nothing for it but to run it down like I was some crazy junkyard dog[.] — Robert Campbell, *The Cat's Meow*, p. 93, 1988

2 a junkyard operator with connections to organized crime *US, 2003*
- "Junkyard dogs" are connected guys in scrapyards. — Henry Hill and Byron Schreckengost, *A Good Fella's Guide to New York*, p. 189, 2003

junt *noun*

a large marijuana cigarette *US, 1997*
- — Jim Emerson-Cobb, *Scratching the Dragon*, April 1997

jury tax *noun*

the perceived penalty of an increased sentence for an accused criminal who refuses a plea bargain, takes his case to jury trial, and loses *US, 1997*
- — Jim Crotty, *How to Talk American*, p. 51, 1997
- Will the defendant who insists on a trial be required to pay a "trial penalty" or a "jury tax?" — Cassia C. Spohn, *How Do Judges Decide?*, p. 94, 2003

just for today *adverb*

used in twelve-step recovery programs such as Alcoholics Anonymous to describe an addict's commitment to refraining from his addiction *US, 1998*
- — Christopher Cavanaugh, *AA to Z*, p. 113, 1998

just the facts, m'am

used for expressing a wish that the speaker confine their remarks to factual matters *US, 1985*

A catchphrase from the 1960s US television series *Dragnet*.
- Just the facts, ma'am. "Remember that show? Sergeant Friday?" — Elmore Leonard, *Glitz*, p. 104, 1985

juvie; juvey *noun*

1 a juvenile delinquent *US, 1941*
- It's run by the Forest Rangers with only a few cops around to watch the juvies. — James Carr, *Bad*, p. 55, 1975

2 a juvenile detention hall where young offenders are housed or juvenile court where they are tried *US, 1965*
- — Miss Cone, *The Slang Dictionary (Hawthorne High School)*, 1965
- You're my best friend. Because you always fucking came to see me while I was in Juvie. — *Repo Man*, 1984
- A half hour later Rocco walked into the amber gloom of the old Juvie annex behind the Western District station house and found four kids cooling their heels. — Richard Price, *Clockers*, p. 591, 1992
- My father made her stay in Juvey until the dishes were stack so high—hell—someone had to come back home to clean the house. — Ralph "Sonny" Barger, *Hell's Angel*, p. 18, 2000

Kk

K *noun*

1 one thousand dollars *US, 1965*
Also spelt "kay."
- Just his luck to have them discover he was carrying twenty K and cut his throat. — Joseph Wambaugh, *The Black Marble*, p. 380, 1978
- For a K note and two grams of righteous blow you can call me anything short of Sambo. — James Ellroy, *Because the Night*, p. 355, 1984
- Come on, my brother. God is with you, right? Fourteen kay. — *New Jack City*, 1990
- "It's all there," he said. "Fifty K in fives, tens and twenties. All used bills." — Kinky Friedman, *Steppin' on a Rainbow*, p. 103, 2001

2 a kilogram, especially of an illegal drug *US, 1974*
- I know people who wanta get rid of some Ks, you dig? — Vernon E. Smith, *The Jones Men*, p. 167, 1974

3 the recreational drug ketamine *US, 1996*
Ketamine hydrochloride is an anesthetic used recreationally for its hallucinogenic properties.
- It is widely known that drugs like cocaine, the amphetamine derivative Ecstasy, and ketamine, an anesthetic often called "K," have become an integral part of the Morning Party[.] — *New York Times*, p. 22, 17th August 1996
- K is a displacer—you are outside of your head, and everything, everything is new. — James St. James, *Party Monster*, p. 10, 1999

K2 *noun*
phencyclidine, the recreational drug known as PCP or angel dust *US, 1970*
- — William D. Alsever, *Glossary for the Establishment and Other Uptight People*, p. 28, December 1970

KA *noun*
a known associate of a criminal *US, 1986*
- The K.A.s are being checked out. — James Ellroy, *Suicide Hill*, p. 713, 1986
- [T]hen Stan put on a UA flight attendant's jacket and walked down the passenger ramp and onto the plane with a clipboard to see if she was seated with any K.A.'s. — Stephen Cannell, *Big Con*, pp. 317–318, 1997

kabillion *noun*
a notional, large number *US, 1987*
- "How was your Rotary shoot?" "Same as a kabillion others." — Ivan Doig, *Ride with Me, Mariah Montana*, p. 16, 1990

ka-ching
used as a representation of the sound of a sale entered on a cash register *US, 1976*
- In the months ahead, sales for presidents' birthdays, for days exhalting romance, the Easter bunny and who knows what else will hit the marketplace like the resounding ka-ching of a cash register drawer. — *Bucks County Courier Times*, p. A5, 5th January 1976
- You win the jackpot. Ka-ching. — *Empire Records*, 1995

kahuna *noun*
1 a great or important person or thing *US, 1987*
From a Hawaiian term for "priest, wise man"; in this sense often used with "big."
- I decided the only way to really hallucinate was to take LSD. That was the big kahuna. — Howard Stern, *Miss America*, p. 95, 1995

2 in computing, an intelligent and wise practitioner *US, 1991*
- — Eric S. Raymond, *The New Hacker's Dictionary*, p. 215, 1991

kaks *noun*
khaki trousers *US, 1968*
- [A]nd in the gloaming there are about 250 boys and girls, in sex kaks, you know[.] — Tom Wolfe, *The Pump House Gang*, p. 78, 1968

kale *noun*
money *US, 1902*
- — Marcus Hanna Boulware, *Jive and Slang of Students in Negro Colleges*, 1947

- I say, Ain't you got no skins, no kale? No bread? No bones, no berries, no boys? — Robert Gover, *One Hundred Dollar Misunderstanding*, p. 22, 1961
- And some lawyer's come and shook you down for every cent of your cocksucken kale. — Bruce Jackson, *Get Your Ass in the Water and Swim Like Me*, p. 88, 1965

kangaroo *noun*
crack cocaine *US, 1994*
- From the image of the beast hopping. — US Department of Justice, *Street Terms*, October 1994

kangaroo court *noun*
a body that passes judgment without attention to due process *US, 1853*
- Talk about a kangaroo court, Rocco—that's a hell of a legal system you guys got. — Edwin Torres, *Carlito's Way*, p. 105, 1975
- The two psychologists they used for their pyschiatric kangaroo court won't talk to us, which always looks bad. — *Natural Born Killers*, 1994

kangaroo ticket *noun*
a political ticket in which the running mate is more popular than the head of the ticket *US, 1967*
- The mayor of Blanco, who made the introductions from the speaker's platform, called the Kennedy-Johnson ticket a "kangaroo ticket, one with all its strength in the hind legs." — Willie Morris, *North Toward Home*, p. 234, 1967

Kansas City roll *noun*
a single large-denomination bill wrapped around small-denomination bills, giving the impression of a great deal of money *US, 1964*
- He loved to flash his "Kansas City roll," probably fifty one-dollar bills folded with a twenty on the inside and a one-hundred dollar bill on the outside. — Malcolm X and Alex Haley, *The Autobiography of Malcolm X*, p. 89, 1964

Kansas yummy *noun*
an attractive woman who is not easily seduced *US, 1985*
A term that need not, and usually does not, apply to a woman actually from Kansas.
- — *American Speech*, p. 19, Spring 1985: "The language of singles bars"

kaput; caput *adjective*
used up, useless, destroyed *US, 1919*
From the German.
- His role in the affair might, after all, be to draw me on in conversation into revealing that I had nothing to reveal, then... kaput! — Martin Waddell, *Otley*, p. 78, 1966
- Listen, young lady, I'm almost ten years older than you are. Another bout like that, and I'll be done for, kaput. — Doug Lang, *Freaks*, p. 105, 1973
- We were through, kaput. — Odie Hawkins, *Black Casanova*, p. 125, 1984
- Into the toilet for good! Kaput! Fini! Nada! — Terry Southern, *Now Dig This*, p. 12, 1986
- The scene continued on all that summer and into fall, and then it went kaput. — Herbert Huncke, *Guilty of Everything*, p. 158, 1990

karma *noun*
fate, luck, destiny *US, 1967*
A Buddhist concept adopted by hippies, vaguely understood, simplified and debased in all-purpose usage.
- If you help us clean up you will be rewarded with karma and extra brain cells. — Nicholas Von Hoffman, *We are the People Our Parents Warned Us Against*, p. 146, 1967

karo *noun*
a mixture of codeine-infused cough syrup and soda *US, 2000*
- In Houston, Elwood said, it has a variety of nicknames—Lean, AC/DC, barr, down, Karo and nods. "Lean because after you take it you will be definitely leaning and losing your coordination," Elwood said. — *The Commercial Appeal (Memphis)*, p. F1, 9th July 2000

Kate *noun*
used as a term of address among male homosexuals *US, 1965*
- — *Fact*, p. 26, January-February 1965

kate *verb*
to act as a pimp *US, 1976*
- — John R. Armore and Joseph D. Wolfe, *Dictionary of Desperation*, p. 37, 1976

Katy bar the door!
used for warning of a dire situation *US, 1902*
- "Is that with utilities included?" "No." "Well, Katy-bar-the-door." — Glenn Savan, *White Palace*, p. 201, 1987
- Sergeant Howard feared it was "Katy-bar-the-door." — Ray Hildreth, *Hill 488*, p. 225, 2003

Kaybecker *noun*
a French-speaking Canadian *US, 1975*
An intentional "Quebec" corruption.
- — John Gould, *Maine Lingo*, p. 100, 1975

kayfabe *noun*
the protection of the inside secrets of professional wrestling *US, 1990*
- What is this "kayfabe"? * ** Nowadays it simply refers to insider info. — *rec.sport.pro-wrestling*, 6th May 1990
- Jesse Ventura then said something like "Sid doesn't have the guts to violate a restraining order," which has to be taken as a kay fabe comment about puscho Sid's confrontations with Brian Pillman and Arn Anderson. — *Herb's Wrestling Tidbits*, 11th November 1993
- McMahon was reportedly livid that "kayfabe" (the insider term for the act of keeping up the illusion of reality that is wrestling) had been so blatantly broken[.] — Scott Edelman, *Warrior Queen*, pp. 59–60, 1999
- Dutch Mantel once told me that story about how Jerry Lawler fired him for talking to the press about wrestling out of kayfabe. — *World of Wrestling Magazine*, June 1999

kayfabe *verb*
in professional wrestling, used as an all-purpose verb *US, 2001*
- "Kayfabe the headlock" means "Let's finish this up and go on to the next move." Or "Kayfabe the mark!" means "Check out that guy in the front row." — Missy Hyatt, *Missy Hyatt*, p. 29, 2001
- To "kayfabe" basically means that the wrestler keeps the inner workings of the business to himself and doesn't share them with the fans. — Bobby Heenan, *Bobby the Brain*, p. 33, 2002

kazh; kasj; cazh *adjective*
pleasant in a casual sort of way *US, 1981*
A word deeply rooted in the Valley Girl ethic.
- — Connie Eble (Editor), *UNC-CH Campus Slang*, p. 2, March 1981
- Short for "casual," but can also mean "bitchen." — Jodie Ann Posserello, *The Totally Awesome Val Guide*, p. 21, 1982
- Attractive or desirable; used (as are most terms of praise in the Valley) of possessions. — Jonathan Roberts, *How to California*, p. 166, 1984
- Nothing kasj about those brown and yellow stains. — Seth Morgan, *Homeboy*, p. 4, 1990

kazoo *noun*
the rectum *US, 1965*
- You're supposed to put sour cream on top but that just seemed like calories up the kazoo. — Barbara Kingsolver, *The Bean Trees*, p. 112, 1988

KB *noun*
high quality marijuana *US, 1997*
- Initials for kind bud or killer bud. — Jim Emerson-Cobb, *Scratching the Dragon*, April 1997

KBA *noun*
an enemy combatant killed from the air *US, 1992*
- This UH-1E flight gave me my first KBA, or killed by air, that I actually was sure that I had killed the enemy. — Bob Stoffey, *Cleared Hot!*, p. 105, 1992

k-bar *noun*
a US Marine Corps survival knife *US, 1979*
- Before you sit down you take out your K-bar, or your bayonet. — Mark Baker, *Nam*, p. 83, 1981
- Grease gun, K-bar at my side / These are tools that make men die. — Sandee Johnson, *Cadences: The Jody Call Book, No. 2*, p. 134, 1986

K-boy *noun*
in a deck of playing cards, a king *US, 1943*
- — Peter O. Steiner, *Thursday Night Poker*, p. 413, 1996

KC; Kay Cee *nickname*
Kansas City, Missouri *US, 1895*
- Somewhat younger than Lester Young, also from KC, that gloomy, saintly goof in whom the history of jazz was wrapped[.] — Jack Kerouac, *On the Road*, p. 239, 1957
- [O]nce again she saw him in some little town outside KayCee[.] — John Clellon Holmes, *The Horn*, p. 95, 1958
- His only friends in K.C., the ones he wrote about, were the pimps, clochards, whores, dope pushers, cattle stunners, pickpockets, and he saw no reasonable motive for changing his style[.] — Clancy Sigal, *Going Away*, p. 206, 1961
- I'd say, "Ah, no good, mine comes in from KC, just came up from Memphis." — Herbert Huncke, *Guilty of Everything*, p. 1, 1990

KCK *nickname*
Kansas City, Kansas *US, 1985*
As opposed to the larger, better-known Kansas City, Missouri.
- "Everybody give a cheer to KCK throughout the year!" — *Los Angeles Times*, p. 33, 6th December 1987

KC Mo *nickname*
Kansas City, Missouri *US, 1989*
As opposed to Kansas City, Kansas, smaller and less well known. The "mo" (the abbreviation of Missouri) is spoken as a word.
- Ditto here in Kansas City MO!! Let me know net (sic) what I need to do to link in a KCMO chapter. — *alt.cosuard*, 24th December 1989

keebler *noun*
a white person *US, 1992*
- — Terry Williams, *Crackhouse*, p. 149, 1992

keed *noun*
used as a term of address *US, 1920*
A humorous imitation of a Spanish speaker pronouncing "kid."
- "You're not responsible for Harold Lauder's actions, keed." — Stephen King, *The Stand*, p. 845, 1978

keel over *verb*
to fall to the ground suddenly *US, 1932*
- Darren nearly keels over with shock. — Adele Parks, *Game Over*, p. 131, 2001

keen *adjective*
good, fashionable *US, 1915*
Still heard, but by the late 1960s used almost exclusively with irony, especially when intensified with "peachy."
- Tonight I got a date with a Sigma, a keen babe, for a hop at the Shoreland Hotel. — James T. Farrell, *Saturday Night*, p. 35, 1947
- "Tell me some more of this keen stuff," she said eagerly. — Max Shulman, *The Many Loves of Dobie Gillis*, p. 45, 1951
- "Nice time?" "Keen." — Glendon Swarthout, *Where the Boys Are*, p. 73, 1960
- Next thing you know he'll find you keen and peachy, you know? — *Annie Hall*, 1977

keeno *adjective*
stylish, exciting, fashionable *US, 1918*
An elaboration of **KEEN**.
- The keeno things were that it was under the hotel and beside the swimming pool and had large windows so that you can see subsurface into the blue, floodlit water. — Glendon Swarthout, *Where the Boys Are*, p. 93, 1960
- I wouldn't be a bit surprised if such keeno sports like surfboard riding or skiing represents some dirty symbol for them. — Frederick Kohner, *Gidget Goes Hawaiian*, p. 18, 1961
- "Wow! Neato-keeno!" — Stephen King, *The Tommyknockers*, p. 575, 1987

keep *noun*
▶ for keeps
permanently *US, 1861*
- If he put her out for keeps, he'd never have the chance to see her when she became sick, and he had no doubt about her one day having to come to him for help. — Donald Goines, *Dopefiend*, p. 46, 1971

keep *verb*
to be in possession of drugs *US, 1966*
- Shooting up the Peanut Shit / Of all we need to keep. — Leonard Cohen, *Beautiful Losers*, p. 238, 1966

▶ **keep him honest**
in poker, to call a player who is suspected of bluffing *US*, *1963*
- — Irwin Steig, *Common Sense in Poker*, p. 185, 1963

▶ **keep the peek**
to serve as a lookout during a criminal act *US*, *1976*
- — John R. Armore and Joseph D. Wolfe, *Dictionary of Desperation*, p. 37, 1976

keeper *noun*
1 something or someone worth keeping *US*, *1984*
- And occasionally there would even be the unique entry—the keeper—that Barb might adopt as a friend. — Dan Jenkins, *Life Its Ownself*, p. 57, 1984
2 any weapon or instrument that can be used as a weapon *US*, *1992*
- — William K. Bentley and James M. Corbett, *Prison Slang*, p. 87, 1992
3 an arrest that results in criminal charges being filed *US*, *1987*
- — Carsten Stroud, *Close Pursuit*, p. 273, 1987

keep it real!
stay honest!, tell the difficult truth! *US*, *1987*
- Before the populist (Joan Jett) swoops off to her next campaign stop, she utters a phrase that could be her slogan, pointing her finger in emphasis: "It's important to keep it real." — *Philadelphia Inquirer*, 6th February 1987
- — Connie Eble (Editor), *UNC-CH Campus Slang*, p. 5, April 1997

keep-lock *noun*
a prisoner confined to his cell as a disciplinary measure *US*, *2000*
- Last is the list of "keep-locks." — Ted Conover, *Newjack*, p. 10, 2000

keep up your front to make your game!
don't give up! *US*, *1968*
- — Hy Lit, *Hy Lit's Unbelievable Dictionary of Hip Words for Groovy People*, p. 25, 1968

keg *noun*
1 a drum containing 50,000 central nervous system depressants for illegal sale *US*, *1978*
- In this form they were called barrels, or kegs, and sold for $1,200 at the time. — Joan W. Moore, *Homeboys*, p. 79, 1978
2 25,000 capsules of an illegal drug such as amphetamine, or more generally, a drum containing a very large amount of this or similar drugs *US*, *1970*
- — William D. Alsever, *Glossary for the Establishment and Other Uptight People*, p. 17, December 1970
3 in television and movie-making, a 750-watt spotlight that resembles a beer keg *US*, *1990*
- — Ralph S. Singleton, *Filmmaker's Dictionary*, p. 89, 1990

kegger *noun*
a party with a generous supply of beer *US*, *1966*
- — *Current Slang*, p. 4, Fall 1966
- We'll have to start going to keggers, or getting someone to make the beer-run out to the junction or maybe get our stuff off the streets. — Beatrice Sparks (writing as 'Anonymous'), *Jay's Journal*, p. 30, 1979
- Blow it tonight girls and it's keggers with kids all next year. — *Heathers*, 1988
- The Beaver Patrol—USC frat boys fresh from late keggers. — James Ellroy, *Destination Morgue*, p. 128, 2004

keg-legs *noun*
generously oversized thighs or calves *US*, *1999*
- Joel, a construction worker, had dropped eighty-five pounds, losing what he called his "keg legs" and slimming his beer-bellied waist from forty inches to thirty. — Tony Horwitz, *Confederates in the Attic*, 1999

keister *verb*
to hide (contraband) in your rectum *US*, *1993*
- "I keistered it and brought it from L.A. County Jail." — Sanyika Shakur, *Monster*, p. 324, 1993

keister; keester; keyster *noun*
1 the buttocks *US*, *1931*
From the German.
- "And for all of that a lot of those top dogs are paying through the kiester starting now." — Mickey Spillane, *Kiss Me Deadly*, p. 67, 1952
- Want a goddam branding iron up your goddamn keyster? — Bernard Wolfe, *The Late Risers*, p. 200, 1954
- He said, "I ain't paying you a 'fin' a night to sit on your keister." — Iceberg Slim (Robert Beck), *Pimp: The Story of My Life*, p. 104, 1969

- I don't want to hear about resurrection or Easter / You can shove that Bible up your kiester. — Dennis Wepman et al., *The Life*, p. 119, 1976
2 a traveling bag or satchel *US*, *1881*
- — William Bysshe Stein, *American Speech*, pp. 150–151, may 1959: "Notes on the cant of the telephone confidence man"
- — Ramon Adams, *The Language of the Railroader*, p. 89, 1977
- — Don Wilmeth, *The Language of American Popular Entertainment*, p. 150, 1981
3 a safe *US*, *1913*
- Wilson experimented in his garage, blasting and re-blasting the safe door until the keister was a twisted ruin. — Charles Hamilton, *Men of the Underworld*, p. 136, 1952
- I figured that they had a little floor keyster somewhere. — Bruce Jackson, *Outside the Law*, p. 99, 1972
- The guys apprenticed under Denver Dick were good at what they called a keister. It's a small safe inside of a big one. — Harry King, *Box Man*, p. 35, 1972
4 a jail or prison *US*, *1949*
- — Joe McKennon, *Circus Lingo*, p. 53, 1980

keister bandit *noun*
an aggressive male homosexual who takes the active role in anal sex *US*, *1950*
- — Hyman E. Goldin et al., *Dictionary of American Underworld Lingo*, p. 114, 1950

keister stash *noun*
a container of contraband hidden in the rectum *US*, *1967*
- [H]e smuggled out over two hundred dollars in the barrel of a fountain pen, converted to a keister stash. — Malcolm Braly, *On the Yard*, p. 229, 1967

keister stash *verb*
to hide (contraband) in your rectum *US*, *1967*
- You think he might have something keister stashed? We can X-ray. — Malcolm Braly, *On the Yard*, p. 35, 1967

kelly *noun*
a hat *US*, *1908*
- — Joseph E. Ragen and Charles Finston, *Inside the World's Toughest Prison*, p. 806, 1962: "Penitentiary and underworld glossary"

kelsey hair *noun*
straight hair *US*, *1976*
- She was a stomp-down mud-kicker with kelsey hair / A jive-ass bitch but her face was fair. — Dennis Wepman et al., *The Life*, p. 147, 1976

Kelsey's nuts *noun*
used in various one-off comparisons *US*, *1955*
- [I]f every other thing in Steve's career had been the same, the names would have killed him deader than poor Kelsey's nuts. — Mick Foley, *Have a Nice Day!*, p. 523, 2000

kelt; keltch *noun*
a white person *US*, *1912*
- — Clarence Major, *Dictionary of Afro-American Slang*, p. 73, 1970

kemo sabe *noun*
used as a term of address *US*, *1933*
Used with referential humor to the radio and television show "The Lone Ranger," in which the Lone Ranger's native American Indian sidekick Tonto refers to the ranger as kemo sabe.
- Close enough for government work, kemo sabe. — Stephen King, *Bag of Bones*, p. 157, 2000

kennel *noun*
a house *US*, *1947*
- Pigeon, hop this over to grandma's kennel in the woods. — Harry Haenigsen, *Jive's Like That*, 1947

Kentucky right turn *noun*
a move to the left before making a righthand turn while driving *US*, *1999*
- — Jeffrey McQuain, *Never Enough Words*, p. 55, 1999

Kentucky waterfall *noun*
a hairstyle in which the hair is worn short at the front and long at the back *US*, *2001*
Best known as a **MULLET**.
- — Don R. McCreary (Editor), *Dawg Speak*, 2001
- — Connie Eble (Editor), *UNC-CH Campus Slang*, p. 4, Spring 2001

Kentucky windage *noun*
an adjustment of the aim of a rifle based on intuition *US*, *1945*

- "Hey, what kinda windage was you using, Skipper?" "Kentucky," I answer back over my shoulder. — Ernest Spencer, *Welcome to Vietnam, Macho Man*, p. 73, 1987
- I didn't want to take a chance on Kentucky windage, so I adjusted my M-1 rifle sights down four clicks and got into a firing position. — David Hackworth, *About Face*, p. 29, 1989

keptie *noun*
a kept woman supported by a rich benefactor *US*, *1950*
- The goal of every chorine is to end up here as a keptie. — Jack Lait and Lee Mortimer, *Chicago Confidential*, p. 290, 1950

kerflooey!
used as an all-purpose exclamation, especially of frustration *US*, *1918*
- Kerflooey! Wouldn't that be great? — James Gardner, *Radiant*, p. 218, 2004

kerplop *noun*
used for imitating the sound of something being dropped *US*, *1969*
- I heard him stumble down the hall to the bedroom and soon his shoes hit the floor, kerplop. — Iceberg Slim (Robert Beck), *Mama Black Widow*, p. 114, 1969

kewl *adjective*
good, sophisticated, self-possessed *US*, *1998*
Variation of **COOL**.
- Girls are not girls, but grrrls, super kewl (cool) young women who have the tenacity and drive to surf the net[...] ("Friendly Grrrls Guide To The Internet—Introduction"). — Marion Leonard, *Cool Places*, p. 110, 1998
- [H]ip-hop style, artists and attitude were "kewl" in the land of the now defunct Beavis and Butthead[.] — *The Source*, p. 66, March 2002

key *noun*
a kilogram *US*, *1966*
From the first syllable of "kilogram"; the one unit of the metric system that at least some Americans have grasped.
- Not that it's small in the Haight, where grass is available in five-hundred-kilogram lots (2.2 pounds per kilo, or "key" as they say in the trade). — Nicholas Von Hoffman, *We Are The People Our Parents Warned Us Against*, p. 31, 1967
- It was nothing real heavy though the price of a key in one-thousand-ton lots went from fifty to seventy-five dollars and drove the street price in the U.S. from one hundred to two hundred dollars per single key. — Abbie Hoffman, *Woodstock Nation*, pp. 68–69, 1969
- Coming in to Los Angeles / Bringing in a couple of keys / Don't touch my bags if you please / Mister Customs Man — Arlo Guthrie, *Coming in to Los Angeles*, 1969
- He [the killer] is a big time dealer now with keys [kilograms] and shit, and he shot my uncle seven times. — Terry Williams, *The Cocaine Kids*, p. 33, 1989

key *adjective*
excellent, great *US*, *1980*
- — Connie Eble (Editor), *UNC-CH Campus Slang*, p. 4, Spring 1980
- — Rick Ayers (Editor), *Berkeley High Slang Dictionary*, p. 29, 2004

keyed *adjective*
1 excited *US*, *1968*
- — *Current Slang*, p. 7, Spring 1968
2 drug-intoxicated *US*, *1972*
From an earlier sense as "drunk."
- — Richard A. Spears, *The Slang and Jargon of Drugs and Drink*, p. 301, 1986
- — *San Francisco Chronicle*, p. E5, 10 August 2003: "Decoding the unique dialect of Berkeley High"

key picker *noun*
a thief who operates in hotels, stealing keys left at the front desk for safekeeping by guests before they are retrieved by a hotel clerk *US*, *1954*
- He knew all about key pickers; he'd learned the hotel business through the process as "coming up through the front of the house." — Dev Collans with Stewart Sterling, *I was a House Detective*, p. 31, 1954

keystone *noun*
in circus and carnival usage, a local prosecutor *US*, *1981*
- — Don Wilmeth, *The Language of American Popular Entertainment*, p. 150, 1981

keys to St. E's *noun*
phencyclidine, the recreational drug known as PCP or angel dust *US*, *1984*

A phencyclidine user in Washington might well find himself at St Elizabeth's hospital for treatment.
- This summer, one brand of PCP is available as "Hinckley" (referring to John W. Hinckley Jr., who shot President Reagan) or "The Keys to St. E's"—both references to the "craziness" induced by the drug. — *Washington Post*, p. B1, 29th July 1984
- — Peter Johnson, *Dictionary of Street Alcohol and Drug Terms*, p. 104, 1993

key up *verb*
1 to unlock a door *US*, *1991*
- — Lee McNelis, *30 + And a Wake-Up*, p. 9, 1991
2 to become drug-intoxicated *US*, *1964*
- Jumpsteady always keyed himself up high on dope when he worked. — Malcolm X and Alex Haley, *The Autobiography of Malcolm X*, p. 90, 1964

KG *noun*
a known gambler *US*, *1972*
- He has twelve previous KG arrests, bookmaking, policy. — Robert Daley, *To Kill a Cop*, p. 46, 1976

KGB *noun*
the security office of a prison *US*, *1991*
- — Lee McNelis, *30 + And a Wake-Up*, p. 2, 1991

K grave *noun*
a state of extreme intoxication with the recreational drug ketamine *US*, *2002*
- For about forty-five minutes he was doing really bad. He was in K-hole, a K-grave. — Suroosh Alvi et al., *The Vice Guide*, p. 66, 2002

khaki *noun*
a uniformed police officer *US*, *1986*
- There were blues and county khakis and detectives and DA's men all over. — Robert Campbell, *In La-La Land We Trust*, p. 109, 1986

khaki down *verb*
to dress like other members of a youth gang, including khaki trousers *US*, *1985*
- — Jennifer Blowdryer, *Modern English*, p. 64, 1985

khaki wacky *adjective*
attracted to men in military uniform *US*, *1944*
- — Lou Shelly, *Hepcats Jive Talk Dictionary*, p. 28, 1945
- — *Yank*, p. 18, 24th March 1945

Khe Sanh shuffle *noun*
a method of walking honed by combat, always on the lookout for enemy fire *US*, *1989*
Referring to the US air base in Vietnam during the war.
- When we got near the runway, we did what everyone called "the Khe Sanh shuffle." You looked the way you were going, and you never went more than fifty meters in one shot. It was half-slouched combined with the opposite of being cross-eyed: One eye always looked where you were going and the other always looked at an alternate route, where you would go if the rounds came in. — Eric Hammel, *Khe Sanh*, p. 245, 1989

K-hole *noun*
a state of intense confusion induced by use of the recreational drug ketamine *US*, *1993*
- The club has a 100-foot twisting slide lined with flashing lights. It's called the "K-hole," the slang term for the episodes of numbed confusion that ketamine can induce. — *Newsweek*, p. 62, 6th December 1993
- Everybody needs some time away / Just stuck in the k-hole again / An 18-hour holiday / Just stuck in the k-hole again. — NOFX, *Kids in the K Hole*, 1997
- And then: eyes—open. But they've been open. You're in the K-hole now. — James St. James, *Party Monster*, p. 10, 1999
- "That high you were feeling, that's the K-hole." — John Ridley, *The Drift*, p. 166, 2002

ki *noun*
a kilogram *US*, *1966*
- The kis cost Champ eight grand each for three, but he sold the stepped-on six for twenty-five grand each to his lieutenants, making a profit of a hundred thousand dollars a week for a few hours' work. — Richard Price, *Clockers*, p. 53, 1992
- But there's a ki under the back seat. — *The Bad Lieutenant*, 1992

KIA Travel Bureau *noun*
any organization responsible for transporting bodies of those killed in action home *US*, *1977*

- I couldn't help wondering which of them the KIA Travel Bureau would be bagging up for the return trip home. — David Hackworth, *Steel My Soldiers' Hearts*, p. 3, 2002

kibbles and bits; kibbles *noun*

small pieces of crack cocaine *US*, *1993*

A reference to a popular dog food product, suggesting that the pieces of crack cocaine bear some resemblance to the product.

- When the rock was gone, after frantically searching the carpet for nonexistent kibbles and bits of cocaine, he turned on her. — Bob Sipchen, *Baby Insane and the Buddha*, p. 405, 1993
- — *People Magazine*, p. 72, 19 July 1993
- — US Department of Justice, *Street Terms*, October 1994

kibitz *verb*

to comment while others play a game *US*, *1927*

From Yiddish (ultimately German) *kiebitzen* (to look on at cards).

- He came over to our table and kibbitzed at the Klobbiotsch [a card game] for a bit. — Charles Raven, *Underworld Nights*, p. 9, 1956
- Mary and Allerton were playing chess. "Howdy," he said. "Don't mind if I kibitz?" — William Burroughs, *Queer*, p. 69, 1985

kibitzer *noun*

a watcher rather than a participant, especially one who offers unsolicited advice *US*, *1922*

From Yiddish *kibitser*. *The Kibitzer*, a play by Jo Swerling (1929), made both the title and Edward G. Robinson, its star, famous in the US.

- We are a race of grandstand managers, Monday morning quarterbacks and chronic, incurable kibitzers. — Robert Sylvester, *No Cover Charge*, p. 192, 1956
- All through voir dire, he had his jury selection experts spread around him like card kibitzers, whispering, pointing, and pushing pieces of paper in front of him. — Stephen Cannell, *King Con*, p. 14, 1997

kibosh; kybosh *verb*

to put an end to *UK*, *1884*

- Davis kiboshed his stage chuckles; snatch jobs were meat and potatoes to him—the kind of cases he loved to work. — James Ellroy, *Hollywood Nocturnes*, p. 162, 1994

kick *noun*

1 pleasure, fun *US*, *1928*

- It's like the kick I used to get from bein' a Jet. — *West Side Story*, 1957
- Dean was having his kicks; he put on a jazz record, grabbed Marylou, held her tight, and bounced against her with the beat of the music. — Jack Kerouac, *On the Road*, p. 125, 1957
- Yeah, I'll play you a couple. Just for kicks. — *The Hustler*, 1961
- [I]t was Crane's kick to blow those sailors he encountered along the squalid waterfronts of that vivid never-to-be-recaptured prewar world[.] — Gore Vidal, *Myra Breckinridge*, p. 97, 1968

2 a fad, a temporary preference or interest *US*, *1946*

- Were you on this religious kick back home, or did you start to crack up here on the post? — *M*A*S*H*, 1970

3 the sudden onset of the effects of a drug *US*, *1912*

- They're reefers. If you're gonna smoke y'might's well get a kick out it. — Max Shulman, *The Amboy Dukes*, p. 3, 1947
- There is nothing quite like a kick on dexedrine. — Clancy Sigal, *Going Away*, p. 297, 1961

4 a pants pocket *US*, *1846*

- Some nights I'd try my luck in the crap game, and wind up with a grand or more in my kick. — Mezz Mezzrow, *Really the Blues*, p. 44, 1946
- [H]er mind couldn't lose sight of the fragile druggist lying where they'd left him, bleeding from the head, or of the bloodied nickel plated pistol Angie had in his kick. — George Mandel, *Flee the Angry Strangers*, p. 400, 1952
- He reached in my kick and came out with my prop, then sent one of the salesgirls to get some water. — A.S. Jackson, *Gentleman Pimp*, p. 54, 1973

5 money *US*, *1947*

- — Marcus Hanna Boulware, *Jive and Slang of Students in Negro Colleges*, 1947

6 a bribe *US*, *1953*

- All bellboys paid a daily "tax" or "kick" to the captains for the privilege of working. — Jim Thompson, *Bad Boy*, p. 366, 1953

7 anything that is shared with another *US*, *1995*

- — Mark S. Fleisher, *Beggars & Thieves*, p. 290, 1995: "Glossary"

kick *verb*

1 to stop using; to break an addiction *US*, *1927*

- Winnie was "kicking her morphine habit" out in some walk-up in Astoria. — John Clellon Holmes, *Go*, p. 10, 1952
- I'm not hooked. And if I was, I could kick it easy. — George Mandel, *Flee the Angry Strangers*, p. 399, 1952
- Georgia and Walter had some dollies to kick with, and the Feds came and confiscated them. They don't want anyone to kick. — William Burroughs, *Letters to Allen Ginsberg 1953–1957*, p. 68, October 1954
- Heroin had been the thing in Harlem for about five years, and I don't think anybody knew anyone who had kicked it. — Claude Brown, *Manchild in the Promised Land*, p. 187, 1965

2 to kill *US*, *1993*

- So his gang had finally kicked someone. — Jess Mowry, *Six Out Seven*, p. 85, 1993

3 to defer the gratification of a drug injection by slowly injecting the drug while drawing blood from the vein to mix with the drug in the syringe *US*, *1952*

- He was waiting anxiously but she took her time, as if dazed, then began to kick it, mixing her blood with the drug and then watching the syringe with eyes that never blinked. — Hal Ellson, *The Golden Spike*, p. 42, 1952

4 to complain *US*, *1857*

- So I kick to the paymaster. He says, "Look, you get three squares a day, don't you?" — Harry Haenigsen, *Jive's Like That*, 1947
- So what had she to kick about? — Clarence Cooper Jr., *The Scene*, p. 86, 1960

5 to release from police custody *US*, *1994*

- One officer said he planned to "kick" a suspect when he got back to the station. — *Los Angeles Times*, p. B1, 19th December 1994

6 in surfing, to force the nose of the surfboard up out of the water *US*, *1973*

- — William Desmond Nelson, *Surfing*, p. 222, 1973

7 in gambling, to raise a bet *US*, *1963*

- — Richard Jessup, *The Cincinnati Kid*, p. 4, 1963
- — Albert H. Morehead, *The Complete Guide to Winning Poker*, p. 266, 1967

▸ **kick A**

to trounce, to defeat handily *US*, *2004*

- The O.C. was now kicking major A against reality shows like Cupid and Dog Eat Dog. — Brittany Kent, *O.C. Undercover*, p. 17, 2004

▸ **kick ass**

1 to use force, to beat up *US*, *1976*

- Now the monkey had practiced his game till it was sharp as glass / And deep in his heart he knew he could kick the baboon's ass. — Dennis Wepman et al., *The Life*, p. 31, 1976
- They take him to the police station. And he starts kickin' all the cops' asses. — *True Romance*, 1993

2 to be especially energetic and exciting; to succeed by your vigorous efforts *US*, *1979*

- Every night I cried before I went on stage but I still kicked ass when I got out there. — Ted Nugent, *Ask*, p. 47, 5th May 1979

▸ **kick ass and take names**

to overwhelm someone or something in a methodical and determined fashion *US*, *1962*

- Some scumbags, all they respect is force. You just gotta kick ass and collect names. — Joseph Wambaugh, *The Blue Knight*, p. 74, 1973
- We had a great night. The cats were kickin' ass and takin' names; wish you could have been there. — *Mo' Better Blues*, 1990

▸ **kick it; kick**

to idle, to relax *US*, *1983*

- It was on a Sunday. Rick and I were kicking it up on Crenshaw. — *Boyz N The Hood*, 1990
- Kevin was kickin' with some homeboys, walking down Market Street in the 'Hood when the SED units came swarming in. — Bob Sipchen, *Baby Insane and the Buddha*, p. 291, 1993
- Fight through that shit, cause a year from now when you're kickin' it in the Caribbean you're gonna say, Marsellus Wallace was right. — *Pulp Fiction*, 1994
- "I'll kick it with you and Tammy tomorrow." — Eric Jerome Dickey, *Cheaters*, p. 196, 1999

▸ **kick mud**

to work as a prostitute *US*, *1963*

- He had a stable of whores kicking mud for him. — Iceberg Slim (Robert Beck), *Trick Baby*, p. 178, 1969

- Chuck had two girls kicking mud around the city of Detroit. — A.S. Jackson, *Gentleman Pimp*, p. 26, 1973

▸ **kick out the jams**
to remove all obstacles, to fight for freedom *US, 1968*
- [T]here is a generation of visionary maniac white motherfucker country dope fiend rock and roll freaks who are ready to get down and kick out the jams—ALL THE JAMS—break everything loose and free everybody from their very real and imaginary prisons — John Sinclair, *White Panther Statement*, 1st November 1968
- Kick out the jams, motherfuckers! — MC5 (Motor City Five), *Kick Out the Jams*, 1969
- I'm gonna rock it up and kick out the jams with Psychotic Reaction forever. — Lester Bangs, *Psychotic Reactions and Carburetor Dung*, p. 14, 1971

▸ **kick sawdust**
in circus and carnival usage, to follow or join a show *US, 1981*
- — Don Wilmeth, *The Language of American Popular Entertainment*, p. 150, 1981

▸ **kick the bucket**
to die *UK, 1785*
- The porter had picked the sickest guy in the ward, some poor guy who had it so bad he kicked the bucket a few days later. — Mezz Mezzrow, *Really the Blues*, p. 41, 1946
- If I haven't kicked the bucket by then, maybe we'll be able to get together on something. — Clarence Cooper Jr., *Black*, p. 170, 1963

▸ **kick the gong**
1 to engage in sex; to fool around *US, 1945*
- She'd come up to my room that night, that Sunday, and we'd kicked the gong around for almost an hour[.] — Jim Thompson, *Savage Night*, p. 123, 1953
- I ain't saying she's yarding but we both know she could very well be kicking the gong around. — A.S. Jackson, *Gentleman Pimp*, p. 90, 1973
2 to smoke opium *US, 1952*
- I was beginning to feel drowsy in a sort of half sleep like when we kicked the gong around at the Chinaman's. — Harry Grey, *The Hoods*, p. 114, 1952

▸ **kick to the curb**
to break off a relationship *US, 1991*
- Kick her to the curb. — *Chasing Amy*, 1997
- [A]ll it took was one femme assistant to get past her shock and over her fear of being blackballed from Hollywood forever and report one of Chad's actual dirty jokes, salacious looks, or untoward moves for Chad to get kicked to the Wilshire curb. — John Ridley, *Everybody Smokes in Hell*, p. 40, 1999
- But what happens when you get in the car, and you don't make with the head? Don't they kick your ass to the curb? — Kevin Smith, *Jay and Silent Bob Strike Back*, p. 26, 2001
- "A bitch gives me any static, O.G.—tries to dis me in any way—I just kick her to the fucking curb." — Jimmy Lerner, *You Got Nothing Coming*, p. 83, 2002

▸ **kick up; kick upstairs**
in an organized crime enterprise, to pass some of your earnings to your superior *US, 1985*
- [H]e was supposed to keep some and kick the rest upstairs. It was like tribute. — Nicholas Pileggi, *Wise Guy*, pp. 55–56, 1985

kick *adjective*
1 excellent *US, 1972*
- It was jam-up. Jelly-tight. It was, it was a really kick joint. — Bruce Jackson, *In the Life*, p. 122, 1972
2 out of style *US, 1999*
- — *San Jose Mercury News*, 11th May 1999

kickapoo juice *noun*
any potent alcoholic drink *US, 1952*
Coined by comic strip writer Al Capp.
- "Christ, this stuff is strong, it's real kickapoo juice." — Willard Manus, *The Fighting Man*, p. 16, 1981

kick around *verb*
1 to discuss something *US, 1939*
- Q. Who actually said, "How about we call this movie '8 Mile'?" A. Marshall did. We kicked it around and we were very specific that it should not be "8 Mile Road"[.] — *The Detroit News*, 26th October 2002
2 to idle; to pass time doing nothing *US, 1993*
- "I was just kickin' around," I say. — Francesca Lia Block, *Missing Angel Juan*, p. 347, 1993

kick-ass *adjective*
fantastic, excellent, thrilling *US, 1980*
- — Connie Eble (Editor), *UNC-CH Campus Slang*, p. 4, October 1986
- I got out and looked at the Porsche. It was perfect. It was a totally kick-ass car. — Janet Evanovitch, *High Five*, 1999
- It's like, "Oz, he's just the kick-ass lacrosse player." — *American Pie*, 1999
- [A] kick-ass red lipstick. — Aubrey Dillon-Malone, *I Was a Fugitive from a Hollywood Trivia Factory [quoting Gwyneth Paltrow]*, p. 20, 1999

kickback *noun*
1 a commission on a more or less shady deal *US, 1930*
- There have been rumored cases of Casino Managers actually being in cahoots with gamblers to extend them big credit for kickbacks. — Mario Puzo, *Inside Las Vegas*, p. 209, 1977
- Another reason Hy says the promo guy does so well, the label exec who hires him could be getting a kickback. — Elmore Leonard, *Be Cool*, p. 152, 1999
2 the resumption of drug use after a prolonged period of nonuse *US, 1971*
- — Eugene Landy, *The Underground Dictionary*, p. 115, 1971

kick back *verb*
to relax *US, 1972*
- You think you can put your feet up now, kick back and celebrate with an ice cold 6-pack 'o' suds? — *Sick Puppy*, p. 20, 1998

kick down *verb*
to give, to provide *US, 1992*
- When one inmate buys a "box bag" of marijuana, he may kick his friend down a "join." — William K. Bentley and James M. Corbett, *Prison Slang*, p. 15, 1992

kicker *noun*
1 an unforeseen complication *US, 1941*
- Maybe they were playing real cute and sent her in for the kicker. — Mickey Spillane, *One Lonely Night*, p. 89, 1951
- The real kicker came the following year. — Jim Bouton, *Ball Four*, p. 6, 1970
- "Here it comes," said Binky, nudging DeDe under the tablecloth. "She's always got a kicker." — Armistead Maupin, *Tales of the City*, p. 120, 1978
- If you played out your contract with the team you belonged to—because they drafted you out of college—you couldn't go to another club unless that club "compensated" the club you were with. That was the kicker. — Dan Jenkins, *Life Its Ownself*, p. 74, 1984
2 in poker, an unmatched card held in the hand while drawing *US, 1963*
- — Irwin Steig, *Common Sense in Poker*, p. 185, 1963
3 in the illegal production of alcohol, any nitrate added to the mash *US, 1974*
- — David W. Maurer, *Kentucky Moonshine*, p. 120, 1974
4 a small, yeast-rich amount of an alcoholic beverage used to start the fermentation process in a homemade alcohol-making venture *US, 1992*
- — William K. Bentley and James M. Corbett, *Prison Slang*, p. 70, 1992
5 in television and movie-making, a small light used to outline objects in the foreground *US, 1990*
- — Ralph S. Singleton, *Filmmaker's Dictionary*, p. 90, 1990
6 in dominoes, the 6–1 piece or any piece with a 5 *US, 1959*
- — Dominic Armanino, *Dominoes*, p. 17, 1959
7 a linear amplifier for a citizens' band radio *US, 1976*
- — Porter Bibb, *CB Bible*, p. 97, 1976

kick in *verb*
to contribute, to share an expense *US, 1906*
- 'Cause you're kicking in for food, don't mean you don't gotta eat. — *Saturday Night Fever*, 1977

kicking; kickin' *adjective*
excellent, wonderful *US, 1988*
- My hair was kickin'. — (Quoting Pauly Shore), *Spin Magazine*, 1999
- — Connie Eble (Editor), *UNC-CH Campus Slang*, p. 7, Fall 1999
- [T]he place [Blackpool] he various refers to as "kickin'" and "pony" [awful]. — *Hip-Hop Connection*, p. 34, July 2002

kick in the ass; kick in the pants *noun*
in horse racing, a horse heavily favored to win a race *US, 1951*
- — David W. Maurer, *Argot of the Racetrack*, p. 39, 1951

kick off *verb*

1 to sleep off the effects of an illegal drug *US, 1951*
- — *American Speech*, p. 27, February 1952: "Teen-age hophead jargon"

2 to die *US, 1908*
- The officers on the scene first aren't talking so it's my guess again that he talked before he kicked off. — Mickey Spillane, *Me, Hood!*, p. 23, 1963

kick out *verb*

while surfing, to step on the rear of the surfboard while raising the lead foot and then to pivot the board to end a ride *US, 1962*
- They're kicking out in Dohini too. — Brian Wilson and Mike Love, *Surfin' Safari (performed by the Beach Boys)*, 1962
- — Grant W. Kuhns, *On Surfing*, p. 118, 1963

kickout clerk *noun*

a jail or prison official involving in the discharge of prisoners *US, 1967*
- Page smuggled 'em past the kickout clerk in cutout compartments in his collections of hank books. — Ken Kesey, *Kesey's Jail Journal*, p. 105, 1967

kickout hole *noun*

in pinball, a hole in the playfield that registers a score and then ejects the ball back into play *US, 1977*
- — Bobbye Claire Natkin and Steve Kirk, *All About Pinball*, p. 113, 1977

kick pad *noun*

a drug rehabilitation facility *US, 1973*
- I went to a kick pad over on the east side and asked them to sign me in. — Joseph Wambaugh, *The Blue Knight*, p. 30, 1973

kick partner *noun*

a prisoner involved in a semipermanent relationship with another prisoner *US, 1966*
- To the extent that kick partners are "discreet," their behavior is not looked down upon by the inmates. — Rose Giallombardo, *Society of Women*, p. 127, 1966

kick rocks!

go away! *US, 2001*
- — Jim Goad, *Jim Goad's Glossary of Northwestern Prison Slang*, December 2001

kicks *noun*

shoes *US, 1897*
- I suddenly remembered that Railroad Cox wore nothing but tan knob-toed "kicks." — Iceberg Slim (Robert Beck), *Mama Black Widow*, p. 118, 1969
- Let's see now, them kicks you're wearing got to go for eighty dollars. — Edwin Torres, *Carlito's Way*, p. 54, 1975
- He was always pressed; nothing but the best / Vines and kicks he had. — (Collected in 1958.) Dennis Wepman et al., *The Life*, p. 97, 1976

kick stick *noun*

a marijuana cigarette *US, 1967*
- Joints are pulled out of the brims of hats and soon there's no noise except the music and the steady hiss of cats blasting away on kick-sticks. — Piri Thomas, *Down These Mean Streets*, p. 59, 1967

kicky *adjective*

amusing, entertaining *US, 1942*
- — *American Weekly*, p. 2, 14th August 1955
- I've heard it's really getting to be a kicky bar. — John Rechy, *City of Night*, p. 183, 1963
- It had been a kicky experience[.] — Jennifer Sills, *Massage Parlor*, p. 233, 1973
- — *Male Swinger Number 3*, p. 47, 1981: "The complete gay dictionary"

kid *noun*

the passive member of a male homosexual relationship, especially in prison *US, 1893*
- "This is my kid," Blocker would say. "Don't you bother this kid." — Chester Himes, *Cast the First Stone*, p. 169, 1952
- Paradoxically, after the seduction is complete and Sam takes his place as Bud's "kid," he may punch Bud in the eye every morning before breakfast. — *New York Mattachine Newsletter*, p. 5, August 1961
- It is believed in prison that the punk or kid would not necessarily be a homosexual if he had not come to prison[.] — John Irwin, *The Felon*, p. 28, 1970

- A guy'll get him a kid and he'll go to all extremes to treat this cocksucker just as though he was a wife. — Bruce Jackson, *In the Life*, p. 359, 1972

kid *verb*

▸ **kid on the square**

to mask a serious comment in humor *US, 1907*
- She smiled, but her eyes stayed the same. I recalled her phrase, "Kidding on the square." — John A. Williams, *The Angry Ones*, p. 72, 1969
- Which I thought was funny. I think he was "kidding on the square," a phrase I hope will catch on. — Al Franken, *Lies and the Lying Liars Who Tell Them*, p. 212, 2003

kiddie court *noun*

juvenile court *US, 1975*
- His destination would be Children's Court, or, as police call it, "Kiddie Court." — John Sepe, *Cop Team*, p. 9, 1975

kiddie raper; kiddy raper *noun*

a child molester *US, 2001*
- "We found a kiddie raper living one street over." — T. Jefferson Parker, *Red Light*, 2001
- "The guy with the earlocks is a rabbi with a kiddy-raper jacket." — James Ellroy, *Destination Morgue*, p. 274, 2004

kiddles *noun*

a young woman *US, 1947*
- I'm glad Paul's finishing his schoolwork for now, and I knew he'd get high marks—seeing as how he's married to a smart "kiddles." — Jack Kerouac, *Letter to Caroline and Paul Blake*, p. 105, 2nd March 1947

kiddo *noun*

1 used as a term of address, often affectionately *US, 1905*
- "Hi, kiddo," he said in a tired, cheerful voice. — Ross Russell, *The Sound*, p. 54, 1961
- Hey, what's up, kiddo? Daddy say's you're wearin' a sad face. — *Paper Moon*, 1973
- Good work, kiddo. — Carl Hiaasen, *Tourist Season*, p. 326, 1986
- Take a run at 'er, kiddo. — *Natural Born Killers*, 1994

2 a youngster, a teenager *US, 1942*
An elaboration of **KID**.
- [A] group of kiddos coming clicking, cracking prattling by. — Colin MacInnes, *Absolute Beginners*, 1959

kiddy cop *noun*

a police officer assigned to juvenile crime *US, 1975*
- I just hated being a kiddy cop. — Joseph Wambaugh, *The Choirboys*, p. 186, 1975

kiddy court *noun*

juvenile court *US, 1975*
- In what they colloquially refer to as the "kiddies' court," sentences are perceived to be lenient[.] — Phillip Alston, *Children, Rights and the Law*, p. 86, 1992

kiddy cruise *noun*

enlisting in the US Navy until age 21 *US, 1955*
- I had joined the navy, because I could get in on a kiddy cruise, which meant you just go for three years. — Bernie Glassman, *Street Zen*, p. 2, 1992

kiddy porn *noun*

child pornography *US, 1977*
- I mean real kiddy porn. The illegal kind. — Joseph Wambaugh, *The Glitter Dome*, p. 240, 1981
- But rumors still run wild: conspiracy buffs in that kiddy porn ring starring Williams as chief procurer for unnamed fat cats. — *Washington Post*, p. H1, 10th February 1985
- Hakuta, a father of three, says she wants marketers who do controversial things to just create a stir to draw the line at kiddy porn. — *St. Louis Post-Dispatch*, p. 8, 11th September 1995
- "Kiddy porn is like a drug to the perverts who prey on our kids," he says[.] — *Chicago Daily Herald*, p. 40, 17th October 2003

kid fruit *noun*

a male homosexual who achieves gratification from performing oral sex on young men or boys *US, 1961*
- Head-hunters, cannibals and kid-fruits are fellators[.] — Arthur V. Huffman, *New York Mattachine Newsletter*, p. 6, June 1961

kidlet *noun*

a child *UK, 1889*

- "Has he ever been married or engaged or does he have any out-of-wedlock kidlets?" — Laura Schlessinger, *Ten Stupid Things Couples Do*, p. 187, 2001

kidney-buster *noun*

a truck, especially a military truck, that rides roughly *US, 1938*

- "Kidney buster" was a common term. Today the picture is different. — *The Commercial Car Journal*, p. 100, 1963

kids *noun*

a group of homosexual men friends *US, 1972*

- — Bruce Rodgers, *The Queens' Vernacular*, p. 120, 1972

kid show *noun*

a circus or carnival side show *US, 1980*

- — Joe McKennon, *Circus Lingo*, p. 53, 1980

kid-simple *adjective*

obsessively attracted to young men and boys *US, 1914*

- — Joseph E. Ragen and Charles Finston, *Inside the World's Toughest Prison*, p. 806, 1962: "Penitentiary and underworld glossary"
- — *Male Swinger Number 3*, p. 47, 1981: "The complete gay dictionary"

kidvid *noun*

a television show aimed at a child market *US, 1955*

- In 1979 NBC picked up the show for its own kidvid lineup[.] — Cecil Adams, *More of the Straight Dope*, p. 15, 1988

kielbasa *noun*

the penis *US, 1978*

From *kielbasa* (a red-skinned Polish sausage).

- Believing I could do something for her career, she would be ready to please my kielbasa[.] — Howard Stern, *Miss America*, p. 153, 1995

kife *verb*

in circus and carnival usage, to swindle *US, 1931*

- — Don Wilmeth, *The Language of American Popular Entertainment*, p. 151, 1981

kike *noun*

a Jewish person *US, 1904*

Not much room for anything but hate with this word. It is believed that the term originated at the Ellis Island immigration facility in New York harbor, where Jewish immigrants who could not write were instructed to make a circle, or *kikel* in Yiddish.

- Tell me, Dadier, what do you think of kikes and mockies and micks and donkeys and frogs and niggers, Dadier. — Evan Hunter, *The Blackboard Jungle*, p. 209, 1954
- [I]ts attitude toward homosexuals bears correspondence to the pain of the liberal or radical at hearing someone utter a word like "nigger" or "kike"[.] — Norman Mailer, *Advertisements for Myself*, p. 223, 1954
- "Son of a bitch kike!" Bubbles screams. "You got gissum all over the couch!" — Philip Roth, *Portnoy's Complaint*, p. 203, 1969
- The crazy kikes had their own ideas. — Mickey Spillane, *Last Cop Out*, p. 51, 1972
- "I've got that kike by the balls," said Lou [Reed], who is Jewish himself. — Lester Bangs, *Psychotic Reactions and Carburetor Dung*, p. 192, 1976

kikey *adjective*

Jewish *US, 1936*

- [Y]ou got to pay out of your own pocket, or maybe even borrow it from one of those kikey loan agencies. — Stephen King, *Different Seasons*, p. 43, 1982

kiki *noun*

a homosexual male *US, 1935*

A derisive, short-lived insider term; sometimes spelt "kai-kai."

- Kai-Kai—As an adjective, anally-minded. — Anon., *The Gay Girl's Guide*, pp. 11–12, 1949

kiki *adjective*

1 in a homosexual relationship, comfortable with playing both roles in sex *US, 1941*

- "In bed, the difference between femme and butch disappears," they will say. "There everybody is ki-ki." — Donald Webster Cory, *The Lesbian in America*, p. 107, 1964
- She says she is "ki-ki," a frequently heard expression denoting the ability to change roles from passive to aggressive and back again. — Ruth Allison, *Lesbianism*, p. 54, 1967

2 bisexual *US, 1970*

- — *American Speech*, p. 57, Spring–Summer 1970: "Homosexual slang"

kill *noun*

1 in roller derby, an extended attack on the other team's jammer (a skater who is eligible to score) *US, 1999*

- — Keith Coppage, *Roller Derby to Rollerjam*, 1999

2 semen *US, 1998*

- — Ethan Hilderbrant, *Prison Slang*, p. 78, 1998

kill *verb*

1 to excite, to please, to thrill *US, 1844*

- Joe "King" Oliver was killing them after hours at the Pekin with the same band that played with him at the Dreamland, the New Orleans Creole Jazz Band. — Mezz Mezzrow, *Really the Blues*, p. 46, 1946

2 to excel *US, 1900*

- Work is great. I kill at work. — *Fast Times at Ridgemont High*, 1982
- It was totally Pauly, I did like 20 minutes, killed. — (Quoting Pauly Shore), *Spin Magazine*, October 1999

3 in pool, to strike the cue ball such that it stops immediately upon hitting the object ball *US, 1984*

- The cue ball rolled too far; he still had a shot on the nine, but not as easy as what simply killing the cue ball would have given him. — Walter Tevis, *The Color of Money*, p. 143, 1984
- — Steve Rushin, *Pool Cool*, p. 18, 1990

4 in bar dice games, to declare that a formerly wild point is no longer wild *US, 1976*

- — Gil Jacobs, *The World's Best Dice Games*, p. 197, 1976

5 to finish consuming something *US, 1995*

- Damn bitch, don't kill it. — *Kids*, 1995

▸ **kill big six**

to play dominoes *US, 1990*

- — Charles Shafer, *Folk Speech in Texas Prisons*, p. 208, 1990

kill *adjective*

excellent *US, 1982*

- — Heidi Steffens, "*National Education Association Today*", April 1985: "A Glossary for rents and other squids"
- This new store is so hot, like totally rad, like I got these kill Guess jeans with a split at the ankle, you know, the kind Courtney has. — Mary Corey and Victoria Westermark, *Fer Shurr! How to be a Valley Girl*, 1982

kill 'em and count 'em

used as a creed by US troops in Vietnam, referring to the importance attached to body counts of enemy dead *US, 1984*

- Added to that "kill 'em and count 'em" policy was a special hype about going in for the kill at My Lai. — Myra MacPherson, *Long Time Passing*, p. 585, 1984

killer *noun*

1 an extraordinary example of something *UK, 1835*

- Also I would like to see this Fall's Texas-Rice game, which is always a killer (among us football characters). — Jack Kerouac, *Letter to William S. Burroughs*, p. 109, 14th July 1947

2 hair pomade *US, 1945*

- — Lou Shelly, *Hepcats Jive Talk Dictionary*, p. 13, 1945

killer *adjective*

1 very good *US, 1951*

- [T]he righteous women's movement has done its killer job of raising people's consciousness about sexism and male chauvinism. — John Sinclair, *Guitar Army*, p. 295, 1972
- Eventually, I want to be headlining my own tour, have the number one record on Billboard, have a killer video directed by some hip young guy who's not afraid to take a chance[.] — *Wayne's World 2*, 1993
- Okay, with this pad, the killer wheels? Looks like you really cleaned up your act. — *Something About Mary*, 1998
- We told Pit those would be killer shows, because they were secret. — Scott Meyer, *Deadhead Forever*, 2001

2 extremely difficult *US, 1982*

- I added a couple killer questions to the test. — *Diner*, 1982

killer-diller *noun*

a remarkably attractive or successful thing; a wildly good time or thrill *US, 1938*

- — Jack Lait and Lee Mortimer, *New York Confidential*, p. 235, 1948: "A glossary of Harlemisms"

killer green bud *noun*
a potent strain of marijuana *US, 1980s*
- To score the KGB (killer green bud), you have to have a connection up here. — Brad Olsen, *World Stompers*, p. 151, 2001

killer rim *noun*
a gold-plated or chrome-plated spoked car wheel *US, 1994*
- — *American Speech*, p. 92, Spring 1996: "Among the new words"

killer weed *noun*
1 marijuana *US, 1967*
- — Ernest Abel, *A Marijuana Dictionary*, p. 60, 1982

2 phencyclidine mixed with marijuana or another substance in a cigarette *US, 1978*
- They were in Snake Alley selling homemade killer weed, parsley flakes sprinkled with PCP, telling a gay couple in jogging suits and headbands how the dust would stretch their minds, their bodies, grow actual fucking wings on them, man. — Elmore Leonard, *Glitz*, p. 238, 1985

killer whiffer!
used for acknowledging an especially bad-smelling fart
US, 1982
Hawaiian youth usage.
- — Douglas Simonson, *Pidgin to da Max Hana Hou*, 1982

kill fee *noun*
a fee paid when a creative project is canceled *US, 1982*
- In fact, at twenty-seven everything I did was rejected and I lived on kill fees—one third of their usual three hundred or five hundred dollars[.] — Eve Babitz, *L.A. Woman*, p. 149, 1982

kill-fire *noun*
an aggregation of Claymore land mines *US, 1986*
- And we set up a kill-fire, a series of Claymores along a road in what's called a phase Claymore. — James Mills, *Words of the Vietnam War*, p. 302, 1986

kill game!
used as warning to end a conversation *US, 2000*
- In a prison setting, when a group of 415s are having a meeting and a correctional officer approaches, the one who first sees him will say, "Kill game." — Bill Valentine, *Gangs and Their Tattoos*, p. 19, 2000

killing *noun*
a great financial success *US, 1888*
- "Nope, I made a killing, and it was strictly on the legit," Phil said emphasizing his words with a slicker gesture. — James T. Farrell, *Saturday Night*, p. 32, 1947
- On his visit to Hollywood, Fifie told me that Schylomo had made one big killing; he had robbed a big fur store in the company of some other thief who had promptly collapsed of a heart attack a day afterwards. — Clancy Sigal, *Going Away*, p. 355, 1961

killing box *noun*
a strategic situation in which it is relatively easy to kill a group of enemy soldiers *US, 1988*
- Anyhow, after that, Underhill surprised their point man out in the bushes, and we got the rest of 'em in a killing box. — Peter Straub, *Koko*, p. 232, 1988

kill rag *noun*
a cloth used by a male to clean up after masturbating *US, 1998*
- From kill (semen). — Ethan Hilderbrant, *Prison Slang*, p. 78, 1998

kills *noun*
in the language surrounding the Grateful Dead, the very best concert tapes *US, 1994*
- "They can have my car," he says, "but they can't have my kills." — David Shenk and Steve Silberman, *Skeleton Key*, p. 169, 1994

kill team; killer team *noun*
a small unit of highly trained scouts sent on a mission to kill enemy *US, 1984*
- Green was part of a "killer team" that searched out the enemy in a roaming, random manner. In intensely hostile areas, they were ordered to "get some." — Myra MacPherson, *Long Time Passing*, p. 593, 1984

kill-time joint *noun*
in circus and carnival usage, a cocktail lounge or bar *US, 1981*
- — Don Wilmeth, *The Language of American Popular Entertainment*, p. 151, 1981

kilo man *noun*
a drug dealer who deals at the wholesale level, buying and selling kilograms *US, 1959*
- They are known in the trade as "kilo-men" because they handle nothing less than a kilogram (approximately two pounds) of heroin at a time. — Frederic Sondern Jr., *Brotherhood of Evil*, p. 87, 1959
- All the kilo men and ounce men around town talked about real estate, about getting out, but Strike knew they were all full of shit. — Richard Price, *Clockers*, p. 57, 1992

kimchi *noun*
trouble *US, 1979*
"Kimchi" is used as a euphemism for **SHIT**, with the comparison between excrement and the Korean dish made with salted and fermented cabbage not particularly favorable to the dish.
- "We're in deep kimsche," said Slim. — William H. LaBarge and Robert Lawrence Holt, *Sweetwater Gunslinger 201*, 1983
- Think our crews can hack it? We'll be in deep kimshi with Sundown if we lose another bird. — Richard Herman, *The Warbirds*, p. 220, 1989

kind *noun*
marijuana, especially high quality marijuana *US, 1997*
As is the case with many drug slang terms, "kind" is a bit amorphous, at times referring to a marijuana cigarette, at times to the smoker, at times to the drug itself.
- — Jim Emerson-Cobb, *Scratching the Dragon*, April 1997

kinda *adjective*
approximately, sort of *US, 1963*
A ubiquitously contracted "kind of."
- He's kinda big and he's awful strong. — *My Boyfriend's Back*, 1963
- As Donald Fagan [of Steely Dan] was heard to say, "It is kinda strange, isn't it?" — Jay Saporita, *Pourin' It All Out*, p. 101, 1980
- Well, it's kinda waste for all of us to write our papers, don't you think? — *The Breakfast Club*, 1985

kinder *noun*
high quality marijuana *US, 2002*
- His plan was to peddle one last batch of kinder (street slang for excellent marijuana, pronounced to rhyme with "tinder"), get out of the drug business for good, and be living the surf life in California by Independence Day. — *Denver Westword*, 24th January 2002

kinderwhore *noun*
a young woman whose dress suggests both youthful innocence and sexual abandon *US, 1994*
- Courtney Love and her late husband, Kurt Cobain, started the craze—the kinderwhore look as she calls it—when they frolicked together in little-girl dresses in the early '90s. — *People*, p. 53, 1st August 1994
- Hole's Courtney Love, who called her own slut-infant fashion combo "kinderwhore." — Steven Daly and Nathaniel Wice, *alt.culture*, p. 15, 1995

kineahora!
God forbid! *US, 1968*
From the German (not one) and Hebrew (evil eye).
- "We should only live, kineahora, to see that day." — Leo Rosten, *The Joys of Yiddish*, p. 171, 1968

king *noun*
an aggressive, "mannish" lesbian *US, 1967*
- — Florida Legislative Investigation Committee (Johns Committee), *Homosexuality and Citizenship in Florida*, 1964: "Glossary of homosexual terms and deviate acts"
- — Anon., *King Smut's Wet Dreams Interpreted*, 1978

king bird *noun*
an HC-130 Hercules search-and-rescue control aircraft *US, 1989*
- "One of the F-4s coming out called King Bird[.]" — Jeffrey Ethel, *One Day in a Long War*, p. 157, 1989

king-bitch *noun*
the ultimate *US, 1971*
- [T]he king-bitch stud of them all was "The Duke," John Wayne, a cowboy movie actor whose only real talent was an almost preternatural genius for brainless violence. — Hunter S. Thompson, *Fear and Loathing in America*, p. 437, 12th August 1971: Letter to Margaret Harrell

king crab *noun*
in hold 'em poker, a king and a three as the first two cards dealt to a particular player *US, 1981*

In the game of craps, a three is sometimes referred to as a "crab."
- — Thomas L. Clark, *The Dictionary of Gambling and Gaming*, p. 5, 1987

kingfish *noun*
a powerful or political figure *US, 1926*
Predates but influenced by the adoption as a nickname for the governor of Louisiana, Huey P. Long (1893–1935).
- Warring is kingfish of Georgetown. He controls its local police precinct as well as its local crime — Jack Lait and Lee Mortimer, *Washington Confidential*, p. 10, 1951

king george *noun*
a gambler who tips generously *US, 1979*
- — Thomas L. Clark, *The Dictionary of Gambling and Gaming*, p. 114, 1987

king-hell *adjective*
intense *US, 1968*
- My king-hell desire, at this point, is to hear one of your lectures on the New Journalism. — Hunter S. Thompson, *Fear and Loathing in America*, p. 143, 26th October 1968: Letter to Tom Wolfe

King Kong *noun*
1 cheap and potent alcohol, usually illegally manufactured *US, 1940*
- On the second floor was a King Kong speakeasy, where you could get yourself five-cent and ten-cent shots of homebrewed corn[.] — Mezz Mezzrow, *Really the Blues*, p. 247, 1946
- There was Betty who had a double chin and blamed her homely red complexion on Monkey's King Kong. — John M. Murtagh and Sara Harris, *Cast the First Stone*, pp. 15–16, 1957
- "Not even a little taste of King Kong," he whined. — Chester Himes, *The Real Cool Killers*, p. 29, 1959
- It was true that Pap Dan did wallow in King Kong until he fell out from the stuff. — Louise Meriwether, *Daddy Was a Number Runner*, p. 28, 1970
2 a powerful drug addiction *US, 1970*
- — Gilda and Melvin Berger, *Drug Abuse A-Z*, p. 81, 1990

King Kong pill *noun*
any barbiturate or central nervous system depressant *US, 1977*
- — Donald Wesson and David Smith, *Barbiturates*, p. 122, 1977

kingpin *noun*
an indispensable leader *US, 1867*
- So if Gregor had been the Kingpin of Filth in Chicago, or if he at least tried to be the Kingpin, I would have respected him. — Lawrence Block, *No Score [The Affairs of Chip Harrison Omnibus]*, p. 88, 1970
- No one enjoyed giving the tall Black kingpin information that was bad. — Donald Goines, *Inner City Hoodlum*, p. 39, 1975
- Sonny Roberts was the biggest dope kingpin in the Bronx and also parts of Harlem in which Doll Baby was not strong. — Robert Deane Pharr, *Giveadamn Brown*, p. 27, 1978

king's elevator *noun*
monumental mistreatment *US, 1969*
A back-formation from "the royal shaft."
- — *Esquire*, p. 180, June 1983

King Shit *noun*
an important person, if only in his own mind *UK, 1944*
- Whitcraft wasn't one of their own: he lived in Belton, he used to be a kingshit lawyer in Kansas City. — Joe Eszterhas, *Charlie Simpson's Apocalypse*, p. 137, 1973
- Every one of them a ninety-day wonder, King Shit of Turd Mountain. — Stephen King, *Firestarter*, p. 254, 1980

kingshit nigger *noun*
a black person who is in charge of an enterprise or event *US, 1978*
- — *Maledicta*, p. 159, Summer/Winter 1978: "How to hate thy neighbor: a guide to racist maledicta"

kink *noun*
1 a criminal *US, 1962*
- — Hyman E. Goldin et al., *Dictionary of American Underworld Lingo*, p. 117, 1950
- — Joseph E. Ragen and Charles Finston, *Inside the World's Toughest Prison*, p. 806, 1962: "Penitentiary and underworld glossary"
- "That kink didn't put you on any of those tables up there, did he?" Shane asked. — Stephen J. Cannell, *The Tin Collectors*, p. 325, 2001
2 in a deck of playing cards, a king *US, 1951*
- — *American Speech*, p. 100, May 1951

kinker *noun*
a circus performer, especially an acrobat or contortionist *US, 1909*
Not praise.
- — Sherman Louis Sergel, *The Language of Show Biz*, p. 122, 1973
- — Joe McKennon, *Circus Lingo*, p. 53, 1980

kinkie *noun*
a movie depicting fetishistic sexual conduct *US, 1970*
- Still others were known as "kinkies" (dealing with fetishes) and "ghoulies" (minimizing nudity and maximizing violence). — *The Presidential Commission on Obscenity and Pornography*, p. 109, 1970

kink pie *noun*
a pizza with sausage and mushroom toppings *US, 1996*
From the initials for the toppings: S & M. Limited usage, but clever.
- — *Maledicta*, p. 15, 1996: "Domino's pizza jargon"

kinky *adjective*
1 (of sexual activity) deviant *US, 1942*
- In earlier days, an American stripper ordinarily did not book Juarez, Mexico, unless she was on the run from the law, or unless she had been hung out to dry by some kinky agent or slimy night club operator. — Lois O'Conner, *The Bare Facts*, p. 85, 1964
- [K]inky divertissements as velvet whips, wet towels, leather fetishism, spanking and other sadomasochistic pursuits. — Frank Robinson, *Sex American Style*, p. 35, 1971
2 illegal; dishonest *US, 1903*
In prison, used without a sense of perversion.
- — Inez Cardozo-Freeman, *The Joint*, p. 511, 1984
3 stolen *US, 1950*
- — Hyman E. Goldin et al., *Dictionary of American Underworld Lingo*, p. 117, 1950

kip *noun*
a bed *US, 1859*
- No Hinky Dink, no Pendergast caters to him, gives him free beer and rot-gut or a kip in the flop on the joint. — Jack Lait and Lee Mortimer, *Washington Confidential*, p. 30, 1951
- "And that dinge Ira, I suppose, off in the kip someplace!" — Stephen Longstreet, *The Flesh Peddlers*, p. 197, 1962
- "He may be lousy in the kip. You're going to have a trial run first, aren't you?" — Jacqueline Susann, *Valley of the Dolls*, p. 107, 1966

▸ **on the kip**
asleep *US, 1950*
- — Hyman E. Goldin et al., *Dictionary of American Underworld Lingo*, p. 117, 1950

kip *verb*
to sleep *UK, 1889*
- It would have been more restful kipping on a pile of hardtack, unbuttered. — Mezz Mezzrow, *Really the Blues*, p. 34, 1946
- [A] friend in the second-hand car business who let him kip on his sofa, and lent him some clobber. — Charles Raven, *Underworld Nights*, p. 19, 1956
- "Why didn't you kip alongside me?" "You were tossing about." — Stephen Longstreet, *The Flesh Peddlers*, p. 241, 1962

kip bag *noun*
a bedroll or sleeping bag *US, 1949*
- — Vincent J. Monteleone, *Criminal Slang*, p. 139, 1949

kip dough *noun*
money to be spent on lodging *US, 1950*
- On cold nights, 500 to 600 wrecks, who couldn't even summon a coin for a flop (called "kip dough") slept in the old station house on the floor. — Jack Lait and Lee Mortimer, *Chicago Confidential*, p. 59, 1950

kipe; kype *verb*
to steal *US, 1934*
- Charlie kypped a few loaves of bread and boxes of donuts and never got caught. — Joe Eszterhas, *Charlie Simpson's Apocalypse*, p. 115, 1973
- [S]he had so many clothes that it was then that I learned what the word "kype" meant. It meant going to the Broadway and leaving without paying. — Eve Babitz, *Eve's Hollywood*, p. 47, 1984

kishkes *noun*
the intestines *US, 1902*
Yiddish, from the Russian.
- His kishkes, nothing but water since that terrible hour, started turning solid. — Robert Campbell, *Juice*, p. 163, 1988

kismet *noun*

fate, luck, predestination *US, 1849*

From Turkish, Farsi and/or Arabic.

- Kismet, my friend. Maybe you're lucky. — Mickey Spillane, *Return of the Hood*, p. 99, 1964
- "But you probably would have wound up the same way. Kismet." — Jacqueline Susann, *Valley of the Dolls*, p. 100, 1966
- It was like kismet, but not, if you see what I mean. — *Sleepless in Seattle*, 1993
- We didn't know jack shit about any riot. It just happened. It was kismet. — *Natural Born Killers*, 1994

kiss *noun*

1 in games such as pool and marbles, a shot that barely touches another *US, 1973*

- But his hell was my heaven / when I sighted the eleven / and sank it on a rail shot kiss. — Lightnin' Rod, *Hustlers Convention*, p. 70, 1973
- On the third rack the young man made the nine-ball but scratched on an unlucky kiss[.] — Walter Tevis, *The Color of Money*, p. 202, 1984

2 a student who curries favor with the teacher *US, 1963*

An amelioration of KISS ASS.

- — What a "Z"! The astonishing private language of Bay Area teenagers, *San Francisco Examiner: People*, p. 8, 27th October 1963

kiss *verb*

1 to say that all is well and that you have no problems *US, 1966*

- — Rose Giallombardo, *Society of Women*, p. 209, 1966: Glossary of Prison Terms

2 in games such as pool and marbles, to cause one object to barely touch another *US, 1978*

- When Babe lagged, he kissed the closest toy, and Babe got first shot. — Bobby Seale, *A Lonely Rage*, p. 31, 1978

3 in pool, to try to make a shot by bouncing the object ball off another ball *US, 1990*

- — Steve Rushin, *Pool Cool*, p. 18, 1990

▸ **kiss goodbye**

to concede defeat; to accept an involuntary loss *US, 1906*

- It's my experience that once a mug's been taken by the corner game [a con trick] he's kissed his dough goodbye. — Charles Raven, *Underworld Nights*, p. 91, 1956

▸ **kiss Mary**

to smoke marijuana *US, 1968*

- — *Current Slang*, p. 32, Fall 1968

▸ **kiss the eighth pole**

in horse racing, to finish far behind the leader *US, 1976*

- — Tom Ainslie, *Ainslie's Complete Guide to Thoroughbred Racing*, p. 334, 1976

▸ **kiss the porcelain**

to vomit *US, 1984*

- Joe Castillo tried it and kissed the porcelain at once. — Joseph Wambaugh, *Lines and Shadows*, p. 150, 1984

▸ **kiss your sister**

in poker, to come out even in a game *US, 1996*

- — John Vorhaus, *The Big Book of Poker Slang*, p. 25, 1996

KISS

used as a reminder to keep it simple, stupid *US, 1960*

- Rear Adm. Paul D. Stroop, chief of the navy's weapons bureau, has instituted "Project KISS" to increase the reliability and reduce the cost of the military gadgets his organization produces. — *Chicago Daily Tribune*, p. 43, 4th December 1960
- Which brings us full circle back to the basic Claiborne philosophy: KISS—Keep It Simple, Stupid. — *Washington Post*, p. D7, 10th October 1979
- Her primary role model seems to be Gwen Stefani at her fluffiest, and the guiding musical principle here is the time-honored "KISS"—keep it simple, stupid. — *Los Angeles Times*, p. E3, 22nd August 2006

kiss-ass *noun*

a sycophant; one who curries favor in a self-demeaning fashion *US, 1973*

- Little kiss-ass with the big horn-rim glasses on to show how smart he is. — Elmore Leonard, *Swag*, p. 4, 1976
- [T]elling himself this was all for the better, that he somehow deserved this for betraying his own integrity and becoming a celebrity kiss-ass. — Richard Price, *Clockers*, p. 275, 1992
- BARBARA WALTERS IS SUCH A KISS-ASS. — Howard Stern, *Miss America*, p. 60, 1995

- I was polite, I played kiss-ass to a degree, I'd stand in the phone line for him; we're out gardening, I'd do the stoop work and let him rake. — Elmore Leonard, *Out of Sight*, p. 60, 1996

kisser *noun*

1 the mouth *UK, 1860*

Originally boxing slang.

- "That what my aunt needs, a poke in the kisser," Dopey said. — James T. Farrell, *Saturday Night*, p. 34, 1947
- There was a sketch of what he might have looked like before the bullet got him smack in the kisser. — Mickey Spillane, *One Lonely Night*, p. 27, 1951
- I could at least get the satisfaction of belting you on the kisser—too many glasses to take off. — Jack Kerouac, *Letter to Allen Ginsberg*, p. 363, 8th October 1952
- Wham! Right in the kisser. — Oscar Zeta Acosta, *The Autobiography of a Brown Buffalo*, p. 149, 1972

2 the face *US, 1904*

- They paraded around in teddies or gingham baby rompers with big bows in the back, high-heel shoes, pretty silk ribbons twice as big as their heads, and rouge an inch thick all over their kissers. — Mezz Mezzrow, *Really the Blues*, p. 22, 1946
- It wasn't that my kisser would stop clocks, understand, or anything like that. — Jim Thompson, *Savage Night*, p. 2, 1953
- He is a dark, middle-sized, middle-aged geezer with an ugly, oh but definitely ugly, kisser and a navy blue, chiv-scarred jowl. — Charles Raven, *Underworld Nights*, p. 9, 1956

3 a sycophant *US, 1951*

Shortened "ass-kisser."

- MR. HALL: Janet Huon, no tardies. CLASSMATES: Kisser! — *Clueless*, 1995

kiss-off *noun*

a complete rejection *US, 1926*

- Blue came home from Tanja's kiss-off. He looked drawn and tired. — Iceberg Slim (Robert Beck), *Trick Baby*, p. 189, 1969

kiss off *verb*

to dismiss, to reject *US, 1904*

- [H]e hasn't got enough time in to retire and take the pension and get another job, but too much time in to retire and kiss off the pension. — George V. Higgins, *The Rat on Fire*, p. 41, 1981
- He'd finally kissed off Bobbie by telling her that for the sake of the children, he had to go back home. — Joseph Wambaugh, *Finnegan's Week*, p. 121, 1993

kiss up *verb*

to curry favor *US, 1965*

- — Collin Baker et al., *College Undergraduate Slang Study Conducted at Brown University*, p. 148, 1968

kissy *noun*

an effeminate male *US, 1964*

- — J. R. Friss, *A Dictionary of Teenage Slang (Mt. Diablo High)*, 1964

kissy *adjective*

in homosexual usage, exciting, worthy of enthusiasm (usually of an inanimate object) *US, 1949*

- — Anon., *The Gay Girl's Guide*, p. 12, 1949
- The new house is heaven—it 'as the kissiest closets. — Bruce Rodgers, *The Queens' Vernacular*, p. 121, 1949

kissy-face *noun*

prolonged kissing *US, 1958*

Introduces a childish tone.

- — *Current Slang*, p. 5, Winter 1966
- Billy hugged her and gave her kissy-face. — George V. Higgins, *The Rat on Fire*, p. 95, 1981
- Playing kissy face with him the way she was doing was a game for someone considerably younger. At her age either you did it or you didn't do it. — Robert Campbell, *Alice in La-La Land*, p. 248, 1987
- Tess's playing kissy face with a guy that wears sneakers a Shanghai longshoreman wouldn't be caught dead in. — Joseph Wambaugh, *The Golden Orange*, p. 222, 1990
- The boat was a single's nightmare, made worse by an overabundance of kissy-face honeymooner couples. — Anka Radakovich, *The Wild Girls Club*, p. 73, 1994

kit *noun*

the equipment needed to prepare and inject heroin or another drug *US, 1959*

- A packet of smack and a kit! Innocent my ass! — Donald Goines, *Kenyatta's Last Hit*, p. 72, 1975

Kit *noun*

a former Viet Cong who has become a scout or translator for the US Army *US, 1973*

An abbreviation of **KIT CARSON**.

- I felt that way about Zin, the Kit along with us today. — Anthony Herbert, *Soldier*, p. 253, 1973

kit and caboodle *noun*

all of something *US, 1888*

- I think I've had it, kit and caboodle. — John Nichols, *The Sterile Cuckoo*, p. 177, 1965

Kit Carson *noun*

a former Viet Cong or North Vietnamese regular who has become a scout or translator for the US Army *US, 1970*

The allusion is to the scouting abilities of Kit Carson (1809–68), a legend of the US West.

- "Lieutenant Jackson, go over to the ARVNs and pick up that Kit Carson Scout." — William Pelfrey, *The Big V*, p. 138, 1972
- The new troops had a Kit Carson along, one of the hundreds of North Vietnamese who had surrendered and been reindoctrinated and were not working for us. — Anthony Herbert, *Soldier*, p. 253, 1973
- He would never be made into a Kit Carson, one of those former VC who had turned coats and chosen to work for the Americans in exchange for amnesty and money. — Barry Sadler, *Casca: The Phoenix*, p. 147, 1985
- American infantry platoons came increasingly to depend upon Hoi Chanh Kit Carson scouts[.] — Tom Mangold, *The Tunnels of Cu Chi*, p. 197, 1985

kitchen *noun*

1 the hairs on the back of the neck *US, 1974*

- Her hair is turning gray, but only way down on the nape of her neck, in what her generation called the "kitchen." — James Baldwin, *If Beale Street Could Talk*, p. 29, 1974
- I can close my eyes and see women (my Aunt and other ladies getting their hair done) squirming slightly as the hot combs probed the "kitchens." — Odie Hawkins, *Scars and Memories*, p. 12, 1987

2 a person's private matters *US, 1975*

From the custom of only allowing intimate friends visiting your home into your kitchen.

- "Don't go into my kitchen without permission." — Miguel Pinero, *Short Eyes*, p. 125, 1975

3 in pool, the end of the table where the cue ball is placed at the start of the game *US, 1990*

Technically, it is the area between the head string and the head rail of the table.

- — Steve Rushin, *Pool Cool*, p. 18, 1990

4 in shuffleboard, the scoring area of the court *US, 1967*

- — Omero C. Catan, *Secrets of Shuffleboard Strategy*, p. 68, 1967: "Glossary of terms"

kitchen bait *noun*

in shuffleboard, a shot made to entice the opponent to try to go after the disc *US, 1967*

- — Omero C. Catan, *Secrets of Shuffleboard Strategy*, p. 64, 1967: "Glossary of terms"

kitchen lab; kitchen *noun*

a laboratory where illegal drugs are manufactured, whether or not it is located in a kitchen *US, 1970*

- — William D. Alsever, *Glossary for the Establishment and Other Uptight People*, p. 21, December 1970
- — Geoffrey Froner, *Digging for Diamonds*, p. 40, 1989

kite *noun*

1 a letter, note or message *US, 1859*

Largely prison usage.

- I saw several kites; two were left by mistake in books returned to me in the library, and others were received by girls in our cottage. — Helen Bryan, *Inside*, p. 279, 1953
- One phenomenon not mentioned, which appears peculiar to correctional institutions, are the "kites" or love letters written by one inmate to another. — *New York Mattachine Newsletter*, p. 5, August 1961
- I decide maybe it'd have been better if I'd dropped the whole business after the first kite. — Clarence Cooper Jr., *The Farm*, p. 43, 1967
- He caught Harold at the tank gate. "Here. Fly this kite to Kitty." — Seth Morgan, *Homeboy*, p. 89, 1990

2 an ounce of drugs *US, 1958*

- "The Wolf was around today. He was holding a kite." "A ounce!" — Willard Motley, *Let No Man Write My Epitaph*, p. 117, 1958
- — Eugene Landy, *The Underground Dictionary*, p. 116, 1971

kite *verb*

1 to obtain money or credit from a check that is drawn against uncollected funds in a bank account *US, 1839*

- He kited the receipted bills and took the difference from the register. — John D. McDonald, *The Neon Jungle*, p. 40, 1953
- There's a chance I might make some when the paperback version comes out in early 1967, but until then I'm still kiting checks. — Hunter S. Thompson, *The Proud Highway*, p. 571, 2nd June 1966: Letter to Sonny Barger
- Hicky Demarra and Butcher-boy Messino bragged about how they kited their betting slips, raising the wagers by a factor of ten, and getting paid off the larger beg... — Robert Campbell, *Juice*, pp. 156–157, 1988
- I think you do it all, Roman—girls, protection, fraud, you kite checks, steal cars and you shoot people. I leave anything out? — Elmore Leonard, *Be Cool*, p. 186, 1999

2 to send a note or letter *US, 1924*

- Incoming mail is not opened at all, and it's easy to kite a letter out, as I'm doing with this. — James Blake, *The Joint*, p. 14, 25th February 1951
- I'll kite you a postcard. — Ross Russell, *The Sound*, p. 95, 1961

kitschy *adjective*

vulgarly sentimental *US, 1967*

- Don't take all that cutesy kitschy fuckin' retro-Sixties bullshit out in my apartment. — Kenneth Lonergan, *This is Our Youth*, p. 32, 2000

kitten *noun*

a young girl *US, 1923*

- — *Mr.*, p. 55, April 1966: "The hippie's lexicon"

kitty *noun*

1 a pool of money *US, 1887*

Originally a poker term.

- Barger went off to get a beer kitty going. — Hunter S. Thompson, *Hell's Angels*, p. 140, 1966
- Walberto was mad at me because he ain't had a chance to chip into my comin'-home kitty. — Edwin Torres, *After Hours*, p. 209, 1979
- At first I reckoned the lack of food in the fridge was 'cause some cheapskate scabs were not putting into the kitty. — Kathy Lette, *Girls' Night Out*, p. 41, 1987
- By sunrise a lot of the players would have blown off all of the night's street profits, some even losing their re-up kitty too. — Richard Price, *Clockers*, p. 171, 1992

2 the vagina *US, 2000*

A diminutive of **PUSSY**.

- When it comes to mowing our lickable lawns, the hairstyle you choose for your kitty can be an expression of your personal taste. — *The Village Voice*, 8th–14th November 2000
- Lit by a single police cruiser light, flickers of Kim's kettle drums, kiester, and kitty are illuminated. — Mr. Skin, *Mr. Skin's Skincyclopedia*, p. 170, 2005

3 a woman *US, 1936*

- But many a kitty has gone for me even when I didn't have big bread behind me. — Edwin Torres, *Carlito's Way*, p. 19, 1975

4 a guy, a young man *US, 1952*

An extension of **CAT**.

- "Hey, I don't know that kitty at all," Chico said. — Hal Ellson, *The Golden Spike*, p. 39, 1952

5 a jail or prison *US, 1950*

- — Hyman E. Goldin et al., *Dictionary of American Underworld Lingo*, p. 117, 1950

6 a Cadillac car *US, 1970*

- — Clarence Major, *Dictionary of Afro-American Slang*, p. 73, 1970

kiwi *noun*

a nonflying officer in the United States Air Force *US, 1918*

From the non-flying bird.

- To bend the Air Service to his will, though, he couldn't remain a kiwi, a nonflying officer. — Geoffrey Perret, *Winged Victory*, p. 6, 1993

kiyoodle *noun*

a person without value *US, 1903*

- "I'm through with the whole lot of you stinking goddam insensitive kiyoodles." — Daniel Fuchs, *Summer in Williamsburg*, p. 307, 1961

KJ *noun*

1 high quality marijuana *US, 1997*
From "kind joint."
- — Jim Emerson-Cobb, *Scratching the Dragon*, April 1997

2 a marijuana cigarette enhanced by phencyclidine *US, 2001*
- Dalaison later said the male pit bull was named "K.J.," which is street slang for "Krystal Joint," a marijuana cigarette laced with PCPC, an illegal tranquilizer. — *San Francisco Chronicle*, p. A13, 6th February 2001

3 phencyclidine, the recreational drug known as PCP or angel dust *US, 1972*
- — US Department of Justice, *Street Terms*, October 1994

K land *noun*
the catatonic intoxication experienced when taking the recreational drug ketamine *US, 1995*
- It reportedly resurfaced as "Special K" last year at Manhattan "rave parties," taking users to mental territory called "K Land" and the "K hole." — *The Record [Bergen County, New Jersey]*, p. A1, 5th December 1995
- Then I waited, and as I slipped into K-land, I think the pain subsided. — James St. James, *Party Monster*, p. 204, 1999

kleenex *noun*

1 a youthful, sexually inexperienced male who is temporarily the object of an older homosexual's desire *US, 1986–1987*
Based on a pun—blow once and then throw away.
- — *Maledicta*, p. 157, Summer/Winter 1986–1987: "Sexual slang: prostitutes, pedophiles, flagellators, transvestites, and necrophiles"

2 MDMA, the recreational drug best known as ecstasy *US, 1994*
- — US Department of Justice *Street Terms*, October 1994

klepto *noun*
a kleptomaniac *US, 1953*
- "Christ, you really are a klepto, ain't you?" says Billy. — Darryl Ponicsan, *The Last Detail*, p. 108, 1970

klika *noun*
a faction or chapter of a youth gang *US, 1978*
- The gang and the klika remain salient lifelong membership and reference groups for some, but not all, members of the gang. — Joan W. Moore, *Homeboys*, p. 35, 1978

Klondike *noun*

1 a prison cell used for solitary confinement *US, 1982*
An allusion to Klondike, Alaska, the epitome of remoteness.
- — Ralph de Sola, *Crime Dictionary*, p. 79, 1982
- — William K. Bentley and James M. Corbett, *Prison Slang*, p. 11, 1992

2 brass or copper, often stolen, sold for scrap *US, 1980*
- — Joe McKennon, *Circus Lingo*, p. 53, 1980

kluge; kludge *noun*
in computing, a makeshift solution to a hardware or software problem *US, 1962*
- — Guy L. Steele, *Coevolution Quarterly*, p. 31, Spring 1981: "Computer Slang"
- — Guy L. Steele et al., *The Hacker's Dictionary*, p. 86, 1983

kluge; kludge *verb*
to repair; to improvise a solution to a computer problem *US, 1969*
- "I've kluged this routine to get around that weird bug, but there's probably a better way." — Eric Raymond, *The New Hacker's Dictionary*, p. 217, 1991
- Of course, there are still those companies that kludge together half-hearted efforts and call it Six Sigma. — Thomas Pyzdek, *The Six Sigma Handbook*, p. 26, 2003

klutz; clutz *noun*
a clumsy, awkward person *US, 1956*
Yiddish, from German.
- — *Current Slang*, p. 2, Summer 1966
- — Collin Baker et al., *College Undergraduate Slang Study Conducted at Brown University*, p. 148, 1968
- Sergio was always charging some foreign clutz 10,000 lire ($16) for two liters of gas. — Emmett Grogan, *Ringolevio*, p. 141, 1972
- I'm lagging behind, and she says to me, get this – "Hurry up, klutz." — *Jerry Maguire*, 1996

klutzy; clutzy *adjective*
clumsy, awkward *US, 1965*
- He's a klutzy scientist, she helps him get less klutzy[.] — Nicholson Baker, *Vox*, p. 67, 1992

- [S]he can hear good enough to do that klutzy ballet routine. — Howard Stern, *Miss America*, p. xi, 1995

knee-bangers *noun*
long shorts *US, 1991*
- — Trevor Cralle, *The Surfin'ary*, p. 65, 1991

kneecap *verb*
to break someone's kneecap or shoot them in the kneecap, almost always as a planned act of retribution *US, 1974*
- All he had to worry about was that nobody should take the notion to kneecap him and leave him for dead. — Robert Campbell, *Alice in La-La Land*, p. 195, 1987
- Jeff Gillooly would have to kneecap half the field to get Tonya into medal contention. — *Washington Post*, p. D1, 24th February 1994
- He's supposed to have a filthy temper. I don't know how many people he's kneecapped — Chris Ryan, *Stand By, Stand By*, p. 103, 1996

kneehigh to a grasshopper *adjective*
very young *US, 1914*
Many variations on this theme have been recorded since "knee-high to a toad," 1814, and continue to be coined.
- It had always made me feel better to come here, back from the time I was kneehigh to a grasshopper. — Jim Thompson, *The Killer Inside*, p. 27, 1952

kneel *verb*
▶ **kneel at the altar**

1 to engage in anal sex *US, 1962*
- — Joseph E. Ragen and Charles Finston, *Inside the World's Toughest Prison*, p. 806, 1962: "Penitentiary and underworld glossary"

2 to kneel while performing oral sex on a man *US, 1965*
- — *The Guild Dictionary of Homosexual Terms*, p. 26, 1965

knee machine *noun*
a short surfboard, a kneeboard, or bellyboard *US, 1977*
- — Gary Fairmont R. Filosa II, *The Surfer's Almanac*, p. 189, 1977

kneesies *noun*
knee-to-knee contact, usually out of sight such as under a restaurant table *US, 1947*
- Mary started playing kneesy under the table. — Mickey Spillane, *I, The Jury*, p. 123, 1947
- [S]o I let him play kneesie under the table, because frankly I didn't find him at all banal; but then one night he took us to a blue movie, and what do you suppose? — Truman Capote, *Breakfast at Tiffany's*, p. 61, 1958
- A lot of the customers like to play kneesies with the hustlers. Maybe it's love foreplay for them. — Johnny Shearer, *The Male Hustler*, p. 78, 1966
- It is a good place for hand-holding, kneesies, and what have you. — Bernhardt J. Hurwood, *The Sensuous New York*, p. 36, 1973

knee-slapper *noun*

1 a small, white-water wave *US, 1991*
- — Trevor Cralle, *The Surfin'ary*, p. 65, 1991

2 something that is very funny *US, 1966*
- "A real scream." "A rib-splitting knee-slapper." "My sides hurt." — George Carlin, *Brain Droppings*, p. 258, 1997

knee-walking drunk *adjective*
very drunk *US, 1973*
- Obviously, they're far beyond knee-walking drunk; I had never seen Jerry that plastered, before or since. — Phil Lesh, *Searching for the Sound*, p. 63, 2005

knick-knack *noun*

1 a trinket; a small trivial article pleasing for ornament *UK, 1682*
- I've got all these antique knick-knacks. — *As Good As It Gets*, 1997

2 a small penis *US, 1981*
- — *Male Swinger Number 3*, p. 47, 1981: "The complete gay dictionary"

3 a homosexual who will reverse sexual roles *US, 1975*
- Flip-flops, also called "knickknacks," are dudes that begin by making the homos but wind up playing the female role themselves. — James Carr, *Bad*, p. 155, 1975

knickknacker *noun*
a petty, inconsequential person *US, 1967*
- Many of us—over half of us—have no driver's license, because of the knickknackers in white shirts in the DMV. — Frank Reynolds, *Freewheelin Frank*, p. 136, 1967

knife and fork *noun*
the money that a betting pool player leaves in reserve for living expenses *US, 1990*
- — Steve Rushin, *Pool Cool*, p. 18, 1990

knife and gun club *noun*
a hospital casualty department *US, 1994*
- — Sally Williams, *"Strong" Words*, p. 154, 1994

knife-happy *adjective*
(used of a surgeon) over-eager to treat with surgery *US, 1961*
- — *American Speech*, pp. 145–148, May 1961: "The spoken language of medicine; argot, slang, cant"

knight *noun*
in homosexual usage, a person with syphilis *US, 1981*
- — *Male Swinger Number 3*, p. 47, 1981: "The complete gay dictionary"

knit *noun*
a shirt or sweater *US, 1972*
- — David Claerbaut, *Black Jargon in White America*, p. 70, 1972

knitting circle *noun*
in homosexual usage, a group of men who are too engaged in conversation to seek sex *US, 1981*
- — *Male Swinger Number 3*, p. 47, 1981: "The complete gay dictionary"

knob *noun*
1 the penis *UK, 1961*
- He pushes his naked knob right in her old brown eye. — Lynn Breedlove, *Godspeed*, p. 39, 2002

2 the head *UK, 1673*
- If he isn't a murderer he's liable to be one if you don't use your knob and tell me where I can find the room. — Mickey Spillane, *I, The Jury*, p. 101, 1947

3 the knee *US, 1970*
- — Clarence Major, *Dictionary of Afro-American Slang*, p. 74, 1970

▸ **polish a knob**
to perform oral sex on a man *US, 1947*
- When you finish with them come on back around to me, and I'll let you polish this knob until it spits. — Donald Goines, *Dopefiend*, p. 111, 1971
- "I haven't seen you in such a good mood since that big-haired Karen chick was polishing your knob." — Carl Hiaasen, *Basket Case*, p. 272, 2002

knobber *noun*
1 a transvestite prostitute *US, 1973*
- Knobbers are men dressed as female hookers who have figured out their own ripoff on prostitution. — Gail Sheehy, *Hustling*, p. 16, 1973
- In the meantime, prostitution continued unabated there and elsewhere, transvestite or "knobbers" crowing that they needed only hallways in which to satisfy their patrons efficiently and manually. — William Taylor, *Inventing Times Square*, p. 363, 1991

2 oral sex performed on a male *US, 1989*
- — Pamela Munro, *U.C.L.A. Slang*, p. 54, 1989
- "What a knobber?" she asked. "Help you to sleep." — Joseph Wambaugh, *Hollywood Station*, p. 23, 2006

knob-gobbling *noun*
oral sex on a man *US, 1980*
- — *Maledicta*, p. 198, Winter 1980: "A new erotic vocabulary"

knob job *noun*
oral sex performed on a man *US, 1968*
- Woody took off with Carmen. "Tongolele." Knob-job. — Edwin Torres, *After Hours*, p. 214, 1979
- "They're only the best pictures anybody ever took of a knob job." — John Sandford, *Rules of Prey*, p. 33, 1989
- Joe dropping his pants in the car for a quick knob job during my "smoke break" at the restaurant. — R.J. March, *Hard*, p. 220, 2002

knobs *noun*
1 the female breasts, especially the nipples *US, 1968*
- — Collin Baker et al., *College Undergraduate Slang Study Conducted at Brown University*, p. 148, 1968
- His hands reach under her sweater and fondle her knobs to his heart's content and her nipples harden real quick[.] — Richard Meltzer, *A Whore Just Like the Rest*, p. 89, 1970
- Fawcett parlayed the appeal of her thick, stand-up knobs into one of the best-selling pinup posters in the history of infatuated maledom. — Mr. Skin, *Mr. Skin's Skincyclopedia*, p. 175, 2005

2 shoes *US, 1970*
- We all have some sharp clothes, but Bunchy was always sharp— clean, with a sharp suit, pimp socks, and shined knobs. — Bobby Seale, *Seize the Time*, p. 269, 1970
- The Farmers dressed up in overalls, white shirts, homburg hats, and knobs, which'd buy two sizes too big[.] — James Carr, *Bad*, p. 37, 1975

knobslobber *noun*
a person who performs oral sex on a man *US, 1993*
- Did you learn this back in yours of renting your mother out to the lumber camps of the northwest, duck, or was it YOUR days working as a knobslobber. — *alt.flame*, 16th September 1993
- "Call me a fag, het boy, c'mon." Call me a knobslobber. — Lynn Breedlove, *Godspeed*, p. 99, 2002

knob squad *noun*
a police prostitution task force *US, 1973*
- The inspector had created a "knob squad." — Gail Sheehy, *Hustling*, p. 95, 1973

knock *verb*
1 to criticize, to disparage *US, 1865*
- [H]e comes in, in his little button-down collar shirt and striped tie, and starts knocking Turgenev for about half an hour. — J.D. Salinger, *Franny and Zooey*, p. 15, 1961
- I mean, who are you to knock what you've never experienced. — *Cruel Intentions*, 1999

2 to arrest *US, 1987*
- — Carsten Stroud, *Close Pursuit*, p. 273, 1987
- "Yonkers incite riot..." that's what the local newspaper, the Herald Statesman, said after I got knocked in a Toyota Corolla in front of my building. — Earl "DMX" Simmons, *E.A.R.L.*, p. 111, 2002

3 to disclose that a pool player is a professional *US, 1990*
- — Steve Rushin, *Pool Cool*, p. 18, 1990

4 to mail (a letter) *US, 1947*
- For the last six months listeners had "knocked" 2,500 to 3,000 "hunks of linen" a week to the 1290 Club's M.C., young (28) vacant-faced Fred Robbins. — *Time Magazine*, p. 92, 20th January 1947

▸ **knock a chunk off**
to have sex from the male perspective *US, 1973*
- I was alone because my partner, a piss-poor excuse for a cop named Syd Bacon, was laying up in a hotel room knocking a chunk off some bubble-assed taxi dancer he was going with. — Joseph Wambaugh, *The Blue Knight*, p. 203, 1973

▸ **knock a scarf**
to eat a meal *US, 1947*
- — Marcus Hanna Boulware, *Jive and Slang of Students in Negro Colleges*, 1947

▸ **knock at the door**
in horse racing, to have nearly won several recent races *US, 1960*
- — Robert Saunders Dowst and Jay Craig, *Playing the Races*, p. 165, 1960

▸ **knock boots**
to have sex *US, 1994*
- I tell you what, though, I don't care if she is my cousin, I'm gonna knock those boots again tonight. — *Clerks*, 1994
- And Rex, he just wants to go on tour and knock the boots. — *Airheads*, 1994
- "Tell me you don't want her to wrap her long legs around your black neck and knock your boots from here to Tijuana." — Eric Jerome Dickey, *Cheaters*, p. 177, 1999
- — Gary K. Farlow, *Prison-ese*, p. 37, 2002

▸ **knock it out**
to have sex *US, 1980*
- — Edith A. Folb, *runnin' down some lines*, p. 244, 1980

▸ **knock one off**
to have sex, especially in a perfunctory manner *US, 1924*
- The moment was there. I wanted to, but I couldn't just ... knock one off. Okay? — Elmore Leonard, *Be Cool*, p. 332, 1999

▸ **knock out tongue**
to kiss with open mouths *US, 1993*
- Some brother has a girl all pinned up against the side of the house knocking out much tongue. — *Menace II Society*, 1993

▶ **knock your wig**
to comb your hair *US*, *1947*
- — Marcus Hanna Boulware, *Jive and Slang of Students in Negro Colleges*, 1947

knock around *verb*
to spend time (with someone); to idle *US*, *1846*
- Knocking around with Rapp the Rhythm Kings put the finishing touches on me and straightened me out. — Mezz Mezzrow, *Really the Blues*, p. 53, 1946
- Not long afterwards, Arnie and I were out walking and just sort of knocking around the streets and, being near 16th Street where she lived, we visited her. — Herbert Huncke, *The Evening Sun Turned Crimson*, p. 173, 1980

knockaround *adjective*
experienced in the ways of the world, especially the underworld *US*, *1949*
- "Here we have a couple of real East Side hard-boiled knock-around guys, guys that know every swindle and conniving racket that was ever pulled." — Harry Grey, *The Hoods*, p. 137, 1952
- Whores galores. But I could take a knock-around broad only so long. — Edwin Torres, *Carlito's Way*, p. 11, 1975
- I know the score, Vito, I'm a knockaround girl. — Vincent Patrick, *Family Business*, p. 241, 1985

knock back *verb*
to drink *UK*, *1931*
- Glen won't mind, and I'll just duck out with the boys, knock back a couple of uh, Co' Colas. — *Raising Arizona*, 1987

knockdown *noun*
an introduction (to someone) *US*, *1959*
- — Edd Byrnes, *Way Out with Kookie*, 1959

knock down *verb*
1 to rob *US*, *1976*
- You ever hear of somebody knocking down a post office? — Elmore Leonard, *Swag*, p. 76, 1976

2 to introduce *US*, *1953*
- — Lavada Durst, *The Jives of Dr. Hepcat*, p. 13, 1953
- Playboy could knock him down (introduce him) to those worth knowing. — Caryl Chessman, *Cell 2456 Death Row*, p. 95, 1954

knocked *adjective*
drunk *US*, *1974*
- — Stewart L. Tubbs and Sylvia Moss, *Human Communication*, p. 121, 1974

knocked out *adjective*
excellent *US*, *1952*
- "You should dig that surf. It is really something. Knocked out." — Chandler Brossard, *Who Walks in Darkness*, p. 197, 1952

knocker *noun*
1 a plainclothed police officer *US*, *2007*
- "Knockers," he whispers. "I don't know none of them." — David Simon and Edward Burns, *The Corner*, p. 16, 1997

2 in circus and carnival usage, a member of the audience who warns others that something is a fraud *US*, *1981*
- — Don Wilmeth, *The Language of American Popular Entertainment*, p. 152, 1981
- A well-patched cop would sooner run a "knocker" off the lot than cite Party Time Shows' personnel for stealing the heart medicine. — Peter Fenton, *Eyeing the Flash*, p. 127, 2005

3 someone who discloses that a pool player is in fact a professional *US*, *1990*
- — Steve Rushin, *Pool Cool*, p. 18, 1990

4 in pinball, a sound effect when an additional ball is won *US*, *1977*
- — Bobbye Claire Natkin and Steve Kirk, *All About Pinball*, p. 113, 1977

knockers *noun*
1 the testicles *UK*, *1889*
- He run right down the road and told it all over the neighborhood how the crazy woman tried to cut his knockers off. — Vance Randolph, *Pissing in the Snow*, p. 37, 1976

2 the female breasts, especially large ones *US*, *1934*
- "Did you ever see a pair of knockers like that in your life?" asked Hiff. — Max Shulman, *Sleep Till Noon*, p. 33, 1950
- Her name was Lillian Simmons. My brother D.B. used to go around with her for a while. She had very big knockers. — J.D. Salinger, *Catcher in the Rye*, p. 86, 1951

- Give me Sofia Loren. Man, oh man! Some knockers. — Frederick Kohner, *Gidget*, p. 50, 1957
- In that picture you sent, looked like she had great knockers. — *Diner*, 1982

3 dice that have been loaded with mercury that shifts when the dice are tapped *US*, *1950*
- — *The Annals of the American Academy of Political and Social Sciences*, p. 127, May 1950

knockin' *adjective*
great *US*, *2004*
- — Rick Ayers (Editor), *Berkeley High Slang Dictionary*, p. 30, 2004

knocko *noun*
a narcotics police officer *US*, *1992*
- Knockos making street buys usually came in colors, or at least Italian trying to be Puerto Rican, but not piney-woods white, and they usually acted cool or sneaky, not jumpy. — Richard Price, *Clockers*, p. 3, 1992

knock-off *noun*
1 a product that is designed to be mistaken for an expensive, brand name product *US*, *1963*
- The availability of extensive merchandising displays from manufacturers, coupled with enticing trade deals, have made knock-off fragrances an attractive category for retailers. — *Supermarket News*, p. 22, 10th August 1987
- After Fin followed Orson Ellis into his private office, the fat man removed his size 52, double-breasted Armani knockoff, and plopped his bulk into an executive chair. — Joseph Wambaugh, *Finnegan's Week*, p. 6, 1993
- [C]hances are he wasn't talking about one of the Italian designer's $150-plus originals, but one of the thousands of knock-offs that were appearing on New York streets. — Steven Daly and Nathaniel Wice, *alt.culture*, p. 27, 1995
- This latest action against "knock-off" businesses adds momentum to Cobra's successful campaign to thwart the importation, distribution and sale of "knock-off" [golf] clubs to the marketplace. — *PR Newswire*, 7th September 1995

2 a murder *US*, *1928*
- "So the outfit uses Nigger gorillas like Butcher Knife Brown for the petty knockoffs in Niggertown." — Iceberg Slim (Robert Beck), *Trick Baby*, p. 183, 1969

knock off *verb*
1 to cease; to stop *UK*, *1649*
- These girls worked hard—some of them didn't knock off for a single night. — Mezz Mezzrow, *Really the Blues*, p. 23, 1946
- So when he suggested knocking off, I didn't have any reason for staying. — Jim Thompson, *Savage Night*, p. 125, 1953

2 to kill *US*, *1879*
- "When you going to knock Tracy off?" Ripple asked nervously. — Chester Gould, *Dick Tracy Meets the Night Crawler*, p. 40, 1945
- "Listen, rat"—Benny's face paled—"one more word like that and I'll plug you too. They can only burn me once, and I'd just as soon knock you off to stay alive as not." — Irving Shulman, *The Amboy Dukes*, p. 85, 1947
- So why should I knock you off? — Marvin Wald and Albert Maltz, *The Naked City*, 1947
- One day rival gangsters caught up with Cunningham in an alley in I Street, and there he was knocked off. — Jack Lait and Lee Mortimer, *Washington Confidential*, p. 145, 1951

3 (of police) to arrest; to raid *US*, *1925*
- We'll knock off this croaker. — William J. Spillard and Pence James, *Needle in a Haystack*, p. 18, 1945

4 to rob, to steal *US*, *1917*
- Diamond watched with an air of professional concern. "This stuff could get knocked off too," he warned Bacula. — Harry J. Anslinger, *The Murderers*, p. 72, 1961
- I have a great talent for knocking off things[.] — Jamie Mandelkau, *Buttons*, p. 77, 1971
- For now we got to knock the fuckin' joint off. After that, then we'll worry 'bout spendin' the cash. — Donald Goines, *Daddy Cool*, p. 172, 1974
- Somebody was pissed about that truck getting knocked off and the cops had nothing. — *The Usual Suspects*, 1995

5 to reproduce a branded item, less expensively and usually illegally *US*, *1963*

• "Knocking off" is trade slang for copying a competitor's dress, cutting corners to sell it for a lower price. — *Saturday Evening Post*, p. 30, 21st September 1963

▸ **knock off a piece**
to have sex *US, 1921*

• Doin' the short change scene with the Geech, the grabbing, back to the pad, knocking off a li'l piece with Leelah... — Odie Hawkins, *Chicago Hustle*, p. 64, 1977

knock out *verb*
to have a very powerful effect on, to impress profoundly *US, 1890*

• I was really knocked-out by her generosity in parting with all the "good" records she'd had for years, etc. — Neal Cassady, *Neal Cassady Collected Letters 1944–1967*, p. 60, 5th November 1947: Letter to Jack Kerouac

• "But Dobie," wailed Clothilde. "It's Montgomery Clift. He knocks me out. Doesn't he knock you out?" — Max Shulman, *The Many Loves of Dobie Gillis*, p. 4, 1951

• Guys and gals, it knocks me out to be able to elucidate — Lavada Durst, *The Jives of Dr. Hepcat*, 1953

• It really knocked me out to hear him give directions. — Lenny Bruce, *How to Talk Dirty and Influence People*, p. 40, 1965

knockout man *noun*
a member of a youth gang who enforces gang rules *US, 1962*

• Guys like Bimbo and Claw were the enforcers or the knockout men. — Howard Polsky, *Cottage Six*, p. 33, 1962

knock over *verb*
1 to rob *US, 1925*

• You snatched a pimp here; you knocked over a bookie or gambling joint there. — Caryl Chessman, *Cell 2456 Death Row*, p. 184, 1954

• I'll admit under duress that he fucked my mother ... but shikses? I can no more imagine him knocking over a gas station. — Philip Roth, *Portnoy's Complaint*, p. 94, 1969

• We're going to knock over a bank so stiff it'll never get up. — Red Rudensky, *The Gonif*, p. 76, 1970

• To keep an eye on things, I brought in my kid brother Dominick and some desperados from back home and started knockin' over high rollers, casino bosses, bookmakers[.] — *Casino*, 1995

2 to raid an establishment *US, 1929*

• "Sure," Phillips said. "Give me the location and we'll knock him over." — Leonard Shecter and William Phillips, *On the Pad*, p. 150, 1973

3 to arrest *US, 1924*

• [T]his is not the first time she gets knocked over so she will be cooling it there for quite a while! — John Rechy, *City of Night*, p. 128, 1963

knock up *verb*
to impregnate *US, 1813*

• Yeah, well, she got knocked up. At a grind session. — Evan Hunter, *The Blackboard Jungle*, p. 158, 1954

• I probably knocked up your daughter is all. I wanted you to know. — Richard Farina, *Been Down So Long*, p. 226, 1966

• Pauline, this girl, I think maybe I knocked her up. — *Saturday Night Fever*, 1977

• Now I want you to level with me: did you knock this skirt up? — *Something About Mary*, 1998

• She said it was a serviceman from Fort Bliss knocked her up. — Elmore Leonard, *Be Cool*, p. 221, 1999

knockwurst *noun*
the penis *US, 1972*

• "Well, I shined my light in there and here's these two down on the seat, the old boy throwing the knockwurst to his girlfriend." — Joseph Wambaugh, *The Blue Knight*, p. 303, 1972

knot *noun*
1 the head *US, 1973*

• Since I had a not knot by nature, you can understand what this kinda exciting female did to a nigger like me. — A.S. Jackson, *Gentleman Pimp*, p. 109, 1973

• Cause if you come up weak, I'm going for your knot and gut / And throw you in the gutter like an ordinary slut. — Dennis Wepman et al., *The Life*, p. 40, 1976

2 a large sum of money *US, 1977*

• I'm well off. I'm dressing nice and keeping a knot in my pocket. — John Allen, *Assault with a Deadly Weapon*, p. 162, 1977

• — Judi Sanders, *Faced and Faded, Hanging to Hurl*, p. 24, 1993

• — Gary K. Farlow, *Prison-ese*, p. 37, 2002

• He had fat knots in his pockets and was even known to pay people's bills when they got too far behind. — Noire, *Candy Licker*, p. 6, 2005

know *noun*
▸ **in the know**
trendy, fashionable *US, 1958*

• — Vic Fredericks, *Who's Who in Rock 'n Roll*, p. 96, 1958

know *verb*
▸ **know the score**
to understand what is going on *US, 1946*
Referring to a musical score, not the score of a sports contest.

• Murph was a professional musician now, and he knew the score[.] — Mezz Mezzrow, *Really the Blues*, p. 50, 1946

knowed-up *adjective*
lucky, and believing that skill not luck produced success *US, 1954*

• — Jerry Robertson, *Oil Slanguage*, p. 21, 1954

knowledge box *noun*
1 the head; the brain *UK, 1785*

• For a busted smeller, a couple of shiners, and a few creases in the knowledge-box he made himself ten grand. — Mezz Mezzrow, *Really the Blues*, p. 21, 1946

2 a school or college *US, 1903*

• Knowledge box: school. — Franklin W. Dixon, *The Hardy Boys Detective Handbook*, p. 167, 1959

knowledge factory *noun*
a school or college *US, 1905*

• And individual teacher's interests—much less Barth's romantic serendipity—have no place in an efficient knowledge factory. — Roland Barth, *Improving Schools From Within*, 1990

knuck game *noun*
the ability to fight *US, 1994*

• So we all worked on our knuck games to earn our reps. — Nathan McCall, *Makes Me Wanna Holler*, p. 55, 1994

knuckle *verb*
to fight with bare fists *US, 2007*

• Chanel and Jasmine were already knuckling too hard to notice. — Treasure E. Blue, *A Street Girl Named Desire*, p. 97, 2007

knuckledusters *noun*
a pair of brass knuckles *US, 1858*

• Whitey crouched beside him, homemade knuckle dusters coiled in his right fist. — James Ellroy, *Blood on the Moon*, p. 20, 1984

knucklehead *noun*
a fool, an idiot *US, 1942*

• Why, you goddamn knucklehead! Who're you trying to kid? — Thomas Heggen, *Mister Roberts*, p. 61, 1946

• "You're inviting those knuckleheads to the party too?" — Nat Hiken, *Sergeant Bilko*, p. 18, 1957

• Every now and then I get a letter from some knuckle-head who tells me if I really want to befriend teen-agers, I should give them some helpful hints on how to avoid pregnancy[.] — Ann Landers, *Ann Landers Talks to Teen-Agers About Sex*, p. 47, 1963

• Knucklehead walks in a bank with a telephone, not a pistol, not a shotgun, but a fuckin' phone, cleans the place out, and they don't lift a fuckin' finger. — *Pulp Fiction*, 1994

knuckleheaded *adjective*
stupid *US, 1939*

• [E]ven an 8–1 laugher against Tampa Bay can turn—in a matter of a couple of base runners, a couple of knuckleheaded pitching changes—into pure torture. — Stewart O'Nan, *Faithful*, 2004

knuckle junction *noun*
fisticuffs *US, 1994*

• If you use any of these lines you better be joking or willing to take that quick trip to knuckle junction. — Michael Dalton Johnson (quoting Redd Foxx), *Talking Trash with Redd Foxx*, p. 87, 1994

knuckleknob *noun*
a foolish or dim person *US, 1950*

• I tried to think of Vester, a slim knuckle-knob of a fellow, my size and age[.] — James Still, *River of Earth*, p. 124, 1978

knuckle sandwich *noun*
a punch in the mouth *US, 1955*
- *— American Weekly*, p. 2, 14th August 1955
- Look, creep, you want a knuckle sandwich? *— American Graffiti*, 1973
- I'll give you a knuckle sandwich I ever see you around here again. *— Elmore Leonard, Gold Coast*, p. 179, 1980
- Nurse comes in tomorrow an she got 'er a shiner—or less some teeth, jig's up. So no knuckle sandwiches under no circumstances. *— Kill Bill*, 2003

knuckle up *verb*
to fight *US, 1968*
- *— People Magazine*, p. 72, 19th July 1993

knucks *noun*
knuckles; brass knuckles *US, 1858*
- Crump's cops shook them down nightly for pistols, Arkansas toothpicks, clubs, brass knucks, razors and ice picks. *— Time*, p. 20, 27 May 1946
- Carrying a knife and knucks is like wearing peg pants and a sharp hat. It's like a part of a uniform. *— Irving Shulman, The Amboy Dukes*, p. 165, 1947
- "There's going to be a knuck or pipe in each group." *— Herbert Simmons, Corner Boy*, p. 134, 1957
- [T]he powerful swing of this brutal bull's fist was made further effective by shiny new heavy brass "knucks" inserted over the fingers—probably being tested for the first time. *— Neal Cassady, The First Third*, p. 25, 1971

KO; kayo *noun*
in boxing, a knock-out *US, 1911*
- The Mexican shook, for a moment, like a cerebral palsy victim before he crashed backward to the canvas and lay motionless in kayo slumber. *— Iceberg Slim (Robert Beck), Long White Con*, p. 199, 1977

Kodak courage *noun*
a brief burst of fearlessness encountered when being photographed *US, 1997*
- *— Vann Wesson, Generation X Field Guide and Lexicon*, p. 104, 1997

Kodak moment *noun*
a clichéd moment or event *US, 1991*
From a series of Kodak advertisements, urging consumers to take pictures at "Kodak moments."
- *— Judi Sanders, Don't Dog by Do, Dude!*, p. 19, 1991
- Look, I really don't feel like having a Kodak moment here. *— American Beauty*, 1999

Kojak *noun*
in hold 'em poker, a king and a jack as the first two cards dealt to a player *US, 1981*
The sound of "king-jack" suggests the name of this popular police television program (1973–78) starring Telly Savalas.
- *— Thomas L. Clark, The Dictionary of Gambling and Gaming*, p. 114, 1987

Kojak light *noun*
a removable flashing police car light *US, 2006*
- I have a Kojak light in my glove box and a siren under the hood. *— Stephen J. Cannell, White Sister*, p. 19, 2006

kong *noun*
cheap and potent alcoholic drink *US, 1945*
An abbreviation of **KING KONG**.
- *— Lou Shelly, Hepcats Jive Talk Dictionary*, p. 13, 1945

kooch *noun*
a sexually suggestive dance move by a female dancer *US, 1946*
- In this country the strippers adapted the kooch as an element of the strip and sounded out all the suggestive and provocative possibilities[.] *— Jack Lait and Lee Mortimer, Chicago Confidential*, p. 157, 1950

kook *noun*
1 a mentally disturbed person; an eccentric *US, 1922*
- [S]omeone reads a request from the Monterey County Board of Supervisors that citizens fly American flags to show that "Kooks, Commies, and Cowards do not represent our County." *— Joan Didion, Slouching Toward Bethlehem*, p. 70, 1968
- The attorney for the prosecution did his best to make Dale and Ed appear as kooks and freaks who dealt only with other kooks and freaks. *— Arthur Blessitt, Turned On to Jesus*, p. 3, 1971

- So, maybe we're not the kook capital we thought we were. *— Joe Bob Briggs, Joe Bob Goes to the Drive-In*, p. 67, 1987
- Now, Bruce is no kook. *— Howard Stern, Miss America*, p. 118, 1995

2 an unskilled novice surfer or snowboarder *US, 1961*
- The word among the kooks is that lifeguards are nothing but plain mackerels. *— Frederick Kohner, Gidget Goes Hawaiian*, p. 48, 1961
- Move it, kook! *— Point Break*, 1991

3 in television and movie-making, a light screen designed to cast shadows *US, 1990*
- *— Ralph S. Singleton, Filmmaker's Dictionary*, p. 91, 1990

kook box *noun*
a paddle board, used by beginner surfers *US, 1964*
- *— John Severson, Modern Surfing Around the World*, p. 172, 1964

kook cord *noun*
a line that attaches a surfer's ankle to his surfboard *US, 1991*
- *— Trevor Cralle, The Surfin'ary*, p. 66, 1991

kooky *adjective*
eccentric, if not crazy *US, 1959*
- That's what so kookie about life that one moment you feel like Dante's Inferno and the next like Milton's Paradise. *— Frederick Kohner, Gidget Goes Hawaiian*, p. 43, 1961
- A kooky generation? No. *— Ann Landers, Ann Landers Talks to Teen-Agers About Sex*, p. 20, 1963
- Married a kooky sucker fan of the manure-and-bruises circuit. *— Iceberg Slim (Robert Beck), Long White Con*, p. 87, 1977

Kools *noun*
cigarettes made with tobacco mixed with marijuana *US, 1990*
- Kools were regular cigarettes stuffed with a mixture of regular tobacco and marijuana. *— Gregory Clark, Words of the Vietnam War*, p. 392, 1990

Korean forklift *noun*
an A-frame backpack used by Koreans to carry large and heavy objects *US, 1982*
Korean war usage.
- *— Frank Hailey, Soldier Talk*, p. 36, 1982

kosher *adjective*
1 fair, square, proper, satisfactory *UK, 1896*
Yiddish, technically meaning "fit to eat" (ritually clean in keeping with religious dietary laws). Brought into English slang originally in the East End of London.
- Pop was chopping a stud's mop and Mom was in her favorite squat behind the stove, which meant the time was kosher for me to do my famous Jimmy Valentine thing. *— A.S. Jackson, Gentleman Pimp*, p. 11, 1973
- She knew things wasn't kosher between me and this crew. *— Edwin Torres, After Hours*, p. 403, 1979
- Naw, I ain't taking no money from you. That don't look too kosher, me taking cash from you. *— Richard Price, Clockers*, p. 331, 1992
- And I'm gonna pop the ignition and wire it to make it look kosher? *— Joseph Wambaugh, Finnegan's Week*, p. 55, 1993

2 in homosexual usage, circumcized *US, 1986–1987*
- *— Maledicta*, p. 58, 1986–1987: "A continuation of a glossary of ethnic slurs in American English"

Kosher Canyon *nickname*
a neighborhood dominated by Jewish people *US, 1975*
The most famous is the Fairfax neighborhood in Los Angeles.
- I could easier put up with all the Hebes in Kosher Canyon chippin their teeth every time you give them a ticket. *— Joseph Wambaugh, The Choirboys*, p. 98, 1975
- It took Irwin forty minutes to make the run from Kosher Canyon. *— James Ellroy, Brown's Requiem*, p. 12, 1981
- In the heart of "Kosher Canyon," Canter's has long served as a meeting place for rockers. *— Art Fein, The L.A. Musical History Tour*, p. 26, 1998

K-pot *noun*
the standard US Army helmet *US, 1990*
- Jamison jumped when his K-Pot, the Army Kevlar helmet, appeared in front of his face. *— Richard Herman Jr., Force of Eagles*, p. 326, 1990

kraut *noun*
1 a German *US, 1841*
From the German dish *sauerkraut*; not necessarily disparaging.

- Isn't it niggers, Dadier? And spics? And krauts, Dadier? — Evan Hunter, *The Blackboard Jungle*, p. 209, 1954
- The lousy slob ratted on me to the M.P.'s about liberating 10 grand of some kraut's gold hoard back in '45[.] — Mickey Spillane, *Me, Hood!*, p. 15, 1963
- Now I saw, get the Krauts on the other side of the fence where they belong, and let's get back to the kind of enemy worth killing and the kind of war this whole country can support. — *Harold and Maude*, 1971
- I've read his stuff, Plimpl, he's heavy duty. I think he's a kraut. — Terry Southern, *Now Dig This*, p. 234, 1984

2 the German language *US, 1948*

- Another guy don't speak nothing but Kraut, he comes all the way from West Germany. — Elmore Leonard, *Split Images*, p. 109, 1981

krauthead noun
a German-American or German immigrant *US, 1928*

- And Mosca playing the game would say, "They wouldn't even look at your krautheads." — Mario Puzo, *The Dark Arena*, p. 90, 1955
- I doubt if the Krautheads could have handled this bunch of hoods. — Red Rudensky, *The Gonif*, p. 38, 1970
- "That phony krauthead," Francis complained[.] — Joseph Wambaugh, *The Choirboys*, p. 112, 1975
- And those given a name were stuck with it forever: Svade, Svenska, Lugan, Schnapps, Moishe, Stosh, Henie, Mockie, Guinea, Canuck, Bohunk, Pork-dodger, Limey, Greaseball, Krauthead, Dutchie, Squarehead, Grick, Mick, Paddy, Goombah, Polski, Dago, Hunkie, Wop — *San Francisco Examiner*, p. A15, 28th July 1997

krautland noun
Germany *US, 1955*

- "Every German in this part of Krautland is going to be looking for me when they find my plane." — Pat Conroy, *The Prince of Tides*, p. 68, 1986

krauty adjective
German *US, 1965*

- The Professor began a long speech in a krauty accent, crumbs yelling out of his mouth. — Sol Yurick, *The Warriors*, p. 93, 1965

kreeble verb
to ruin, partially or completely *US, 1970*

- — Steve Salaets, *Ye Olde Hiptionary*, 1970

kress adjective
cheap, inexpensive *US, 1947*
From the name of a chain of dime stores.

- — Marcus Hanna Boulware, *Jive and Slang of Students in Negro Colleges*, 1947

krills noun
crack cocaine *US, 2000*

- When [Detective Anderson] Moran went over to Dorismond, he asked whether Dorismond had any "krills"—street slang for crack cocaine. — *New York Post*, p. 4, 28th July 2000

krump; krumping noun
a volatile, expressive, stylized type of competitive dancing to a hip-hop beat *US, 2004*

- Photographer and vid helmer David LaChapelle makes his film-making debut with 24-min. short "Krumped," which documents an underground L.A. dance movement called krumping or clowning. — *Variety*, p. 1A, 14th January 2004
- Still straddling his bike, Ruina shook out a few krump-style pops. — Linden Dalecki, *Kid B*, p. 75, 2006

krumper noun
a dancer of the **KRUMP** school of dancing *US, 2005*

- What emerges is a series of rituals and competitions between groups of "clowns" and "krumpers" who perform, compete, and build community together. — *talk.politics.liberation*, 23rd August 2005
- Most Third Coast b-boys respect what krumpers and clowners did for L.A. — Linden Dalecki, *Kid B*, p. 151, 2006

ku klux klan noun
in poker, three kings *US, 1967*
From the klan's initials: KKK.

- — Albert H. Morehead, *The Complete Guide to Winning Poker*, p. 267, 1967

kumquats noun
the testicles *US, 1999*

- "Wouldn't that be a kick in the kumquats!" — Carl Hiaasen, *Sick Puppy*, p. 421, 1999

kupper noun
money *US, 1952*

- "They say he has very heavy kupper. He lends out thousands and thousands every day." — Harry Grey, *The Hoods*, p. 79, 1952

kush noun
in circus and carnival usage, money *US, 1981*

- — Don Wilmeth, *The Language of American Popular Entertainment*, p. 153, 1981

kvell verb
to overflow with joyful pride *US, 1967*
Yiddish.

- Despite having done a thousand lunch meetings at Nate 'n Al's, Orson never got the Yiddish right. He said kvel when he meant kvetch, schmutz when he mean schvitz and schlmeil for schlemazel. — Joseph Wambaugh, *Finnegan's Week*, p. 6, 1993
- CHER: My heart is totally bursting. DIONNE: I know. I'm kvelling! — *Clueless*, 1995

kvetch noun
a chronic complainer *US, 1964*

- [T]he Jew who complains about oppression is not a martyr but a kvetch[.] — Maurianne Adams, *Readings for Diversity and Social Justice*, p. 171, 2000

kvetch verb
to complain, gripe, whine *US, 1950*
Yiddish, used by those who know only five words of the language.

- — Collin Baker et al., *College Undergraduate Slang Study Conducted at Brown University*, p. 149, 1968
- I don't want to have to listen to him kvetch about how nobody ever does anything for anybody but themselves. — Mart Crowley, *The Boys in the Band*, p. 23, 1968
- Is this truth I'm delivering up, or is it just plain kvetching? Or is kvetching for people like me a form of truth? — Philip Roth, *Portnoy's Complaint*, p. 105, 1969

kvetchy adjective
prone to complaining *US, 1981*

- I felt like I could hardly be nice to Sam because I was so tired and he was such a kvetchy little bundle of shitty diapers and bad attitude. — Anne Lamott, *Operating Instructions*, p. 79, 1993

KW noun
phencyclidine, the recreational drug known as PCP or angel dust *US, 1981*
An abbreviation of **KILLER WEED**.

- The more KW we smoked, what is what they call dust in the east and midwest, the deeper we kipped into never-never land. — Robert Lipkin, *A Brotherhood of Outlaws*, p. 68, 1981

KY nickname

1 the federal narcotic treatment hospital in Lexington, Kentucky *US, 1962*

- Roy had kicked at K-Y [Lexington, Kentucky] but he started in again. — Jeremy Larner and Ralph Tefferteller, *The Addict in the Street*, p. 236, 1964
- "Tired of shooting dope. Think I'll go to "KY" tomorrow and get cleaned up. Gonna kick this habit, Johnny." — John Gimenez, *Up Tight!*, p. 16, 1967

2 any sexual lubricant *US, 1971*
From the branded name of KY Jelly™.

- — Eugene Landy, *The Underground Dictionary*, p. 117, 1971

kyaw-kyaw noun
sarcastic laughter *US, 1954*
Also used as a verb.

- The whole court kyaw-kyawed, and back to the Island I went. — Mezz Mezzrow, *Really the Blues*, p. 319, 1946
- Biff hadn't come down with the immediate kyawkyaws. — Bernard Wolfe, *The Late Risers*, p. 202, 1954

LI

L *noun*

1 a life sentence to prison *US, 2002*

- — Jeffrey Ian Ross, *Behind Bars*, p. 189, 2002: Slammer Slang

2 marijuana *US, 1993*

Rap and hip-hop slang.

- If you smoke L, you'll enjoy listening to it more[.] — *The Source*, p. 43, December 1993

3 elevation *US, 1991*

A surfer "gets L" when his surfboard soars high into the air on an aerial move.

- — Trevor Cralle, *The Surfin'ary*, p. 43, 1991

L-12 *noun*

a social outcast who is profoundly out of touch with trends *US, 1993*

The suggestion is "loser times twelve."

- — *People Magazine*, p. 73, 19th July 1993
- — *Evening Sun (Baltimore)*, p. 12A, 19th January 1994

LA *nickname*

Los Angeles, California *US, 1901*

- As you say, the novel is more important & promising now, and I'll get to see L.A. if nothing else. — Jack Kerouac, *Letter to Caroline Kerouac Blake*, p. 133, 25th September 1947
- "L.A." I loved the way she said "LA"; I love the way everybody says "LA" on the Coast[.] — Jack Kerouac, *On the Road*, p. 81, 1957
- RANCHER: Where you fellas from? WYATT: L.A. RANCHER: L.A.? WYATT: Los Angeles. — Peter Fonda, *Easy Rider*, p. 60, 1969

label *noun*

the name by which a person is known *US, 1928*

- — Hyman E. Goldin et al., *Dictionary of American Underworld Lingo*, p. 121, 1950

labial contact *noun*

a kiss; kissing *US, 1947*

- — Marcus Hanna Boulware, *Jive and Slang of Students in Negro Colleges*, 1947

labonza *noun*

the stomach *US, 1934*

- People refer to your stomach as "the labonza"[.] — Steve Friedman, *The Gentleman's Guide to Life*, p. 99, 1997

labor faker *noun*

a trade union leader *US, 1907*

- From the gallery, radicals shouted "Get out of Vietnam!" and "labor fakers!" and demanded a debate on the war. — Peter Levy, *The New Left and Labor in the 1960s*, p. 48, 1994

lace *noun*

money *US, 1971*

- — Eugene Landy, *The Underground Dictionary*, p. 118, 1971

lace *verb*

to have sexual intercourse *US, 1996*

- Think that I should lace her "Nah it's much safer orally" — Sadat X, Fat Joe & Diamond D, *Nasty Hoes*, 1996

▸ **lace up your boots**

to prepare for a fight *US, 1998*

- — Ethan Hilderbrant, *Prison Slang*, p. 156, 1998

lace card *noun*

1 a computer punch card with all the holes punched out *US, 1991*

- — Eric S. Raymond, *The New Hacker's Dictionary*, p. 219, 1991

2 the foreskin of an uncircumcized penis *US, 1941*

- — Donald Webster Cory and John P. LeRoy, *The Homosexual and His Society*, p. 265, 1963: "A lexicon of homosexual slang"
- — *American Speech*, p. 57, Spring–Summer 1970: "Homosexual slang"
- — *Maledicta*, p. 218, 1979: "Kinks and queens: linguistic and cultural aspects of the terminology for gays"

lace-curtain Irish *noun*

middle-class Irish-American or Irish immigrants *US, 1934*

- Two guineas, one hunky funky lace-curtain Irish mick. — Lenny Bruce, *The Essential Lenny Bruce*, p. 11, 1967
- Like you said, lace curtains all the way. — Edwin Torres, *Q & A*, p. 140, 1977

lace-curtain lesbian *noun*

a lesbian whose mannerisms and affectations do not suggest her sexual preference *US, 1969*

- Your fifth grade school teacher or your favorite aunt could be a lesbian. So could any pretty secretary in your office. So could your wife. "Lace curtain" lesbians pass with no difficulty. — *San Francisco Chronicle*, p. 22, 30th June 1969

laced *adjective*

drug-intoxicated, especially marijuana-intoxicated *US, 1988*

- It is one thing to spark up a dubie and get laced at parties, but it is quite another to be fried all day. — *Clueless*, 1995

lace queen *noun*

a homosexual who prefers men with uncircumcized penises *US, 1980s*

- — H. Max, *Gay (S)language*, p. 25, 1988

lack *adjective*

lacking money, style or both *US, 1982*

Hawaiian youth usage.

- Oh, Harold, so lack, you! — Douglas Simonson, *Pidgin to da Max: Hana Hou*, 1982

lack-a-nookie *noun*

a notional disease resulting from a lack of sex *US, 1952*

- Peggy said, "And you look like you're suffering from that rare Hawaiian disease." "What disease?" Cockeye was concerned. Peggy looked at Cockeye, smiling at him from head to toe. "Lack a nooky, Chump." — Harry Grey, *The Hoods*, pp. 103–104, 1952

laddie *noun*

in a deck of playing cards, a jack *US, 1988*

- — George Percy, *The Language of Poker*, p. 50, 1988

la-di-da; la-di-dah *adjective*

pertaining to the affectedly cultured speech and manners of the upper classes, especially when noted from a lower social station; hence, pretentious *US, 1890*

Jocular or pejorative usage.

- What you look for in a greasy spoon is not cookery. There is nothing la-di-da on the premises. The food is plain; that's the deal. — *The New York Times*, 22nd June 2001

ladies' *noun*

a women's public toilet *US, 1918*

- When they came out of the ladies', they saw Holy-o and Stanley Projectionist going over the vacant rows of seats for lost articles. — Robert Stone, *Dog Soldiers*, p. 62, 1974

ladies' aid *noun*

in pool, a device used to support the cue stick for a hard-to-reach shot *US, 1966*

As the terminology suggests, the device is scorned by skilled players.

- Now let's talk about the mechanical bridge. Some guys call it the Ladies Aid. — Minnesota Fats, *The Bank Shot*, p. 234, 1966

ladies' drinks *noun*

drinks bought for female hostesses by male customers at a bar *US, 1987*

- In between shows, we are required to hustle seven dollar "ladies' drinks," for which we are paid a dollar commission if we make or exceed the daily quota of twelve. — Frederique Delacoste, *Sex Work*, p. 22, 1987

lady *noun*

1 a prostitute *US, 1972*

- Ladies is the polite form, and carries the connotations of "ladies of the evening" and "sportin'" lady, that is, a kind of gallant euphemism. "This is Sheila, one of my ladies." — Christina and Richard Milner, *Black Players*, p. 37, 1972

2 in a deck of playing cards, a queen *US, 1900*
- If the player (with queens) wins the pot, they are "ladies"; but if he loses the pot, they are "whores." — Albert H. Morehead, *The Complete Guide to Winning Poker*, p. 264, 1967

3 cocaine *US, 1974*
- — Robert Sabbag, *Snowblind*, p. 271, 1976
- Street names [...] gold dust, lady, snow, white. — James Kay and Julian Cohen, *The Parents' Complete Guide to Young People and Drugs*, p. 134, 1998

ladyfinger *noun*
a 500-pound conventional bomb *US, 1990*
- Ladyfingers did their job / Did more than just tease 'em. — Joseph Tuso, *Singing the Vietnam Blues*, p. 159, 1990: Pop Goes the Weasel

lady five fingers *noun*
a boy's or man's hand in the context of masturbation; masturbation *US, 1969*
- I wondered if it were a capital crime in this joint to get caught having an affair with "lady five fingers." — Iceberg Slim (Robert Beck), *Pimp*, pp. 50–51, 1969

lady in waiting *noun*
in male homosexual usage, a man who loiters in or near public toilets in the hope of sexual encounters *US, 1981*
- — *Male Swinger Number 3*, p. 47, 1981: "The complete gay dictionary"

Lady Lex *nickname*
the USS Lexington, an aircraft carrier *US, 1948*
- This triggered a series of explosions, but so staunch was "Lady Lex" that not until shortly after 1700 did Captain Frederick C. "Ted" Sherman reluctantly order the ship abandoned. — Gordon Prange, *Miracle at Midway*, p. 42, 1982

lady-lover *noun*
a lesbian *US, 1921*
- The suave lady lovers who can pass for straight in the work day world, arriving. — Red Jordan Arobateau, *Lay Lady Lay*, p. 35, 1991

Lady Snow *noun*
cocaine *US, 1967*
- "That's my woman, Lady Snow," he told me once. "I sure wish I could cop some." — Piri Thomas, *Down These Mean Streets*, p. 258, 1967

lagger *noun*
a contact man in a smuggling enterprise *US, 1956*
- — *American Speech*, p. 97, May 1956: "Smugglers' argot in the Southwest"

LA glass *noun*
a smokeable methamphetamine that does not dissolve rapidly *US, 1989*
- — Geoffrey Froner, *Digging for Diamonds*, p. 69, 1989: "Types of speed"

laid-back *adjective*
relaxed, passive, easy-going *US, 1969*
- She sat back in the Eames chair, forced herself to ignore the roar of Harvey's compost grinder, pounding the split-level and rattling the windows, and concentrated on her mantra until she was feeling laid back again. — Cyra McFadden, *The Serial*, p. 12, 1977

laid in the aisle *adjective*
very well dressed *US, 1971*
- — Hermese E. Roberts, *The Third Ear*, 1971

laid out *adjective*
drunk to the point of passing out *US, 1928*
- — Collin Baker et al., *College Undergraduate Slang Study Conducted at Brown University*, p. 149, 1968

laid, relayed, and parlayed *adjective*
thoroughly taken advantage of *US, 1957*
There are multiple variants of the third element—"waylaid," "marmalade," etc.
- We been laid, relayed, and waylaid and nobody wants to hear about it. — Edwin Torres, *Carlito's Way*, p. 5, 1975

lakanuki *noun*
a prolonged period of sexual abstinence *US, 1944*
An imitation pidgin "lack of **NOOKIE**."

- — *American Speech*, p. 305, December 1947: "Imaginary diseases in Army and Navy parlance"
- — Robert A. Wilson, *Playboy's Book of Forbidden Words*, pp. 157–158, 1972
- — *Maledicta*, p. 56, 1986–1987: "A continuation of a glossary of ethnic slurs in American English"

Lake Acid *nickname*
Lake Placid, New York *US, 1983*
Coined during a concert stop by the Grateful Dead in 1983.
- — David Shenk and Steve Silberman, *Skeleton Key*, p. 173, 1994

Lake Atlantic *nickname*
the Atlantic Ocean on the Florida coast *US, 1991*
A tribute to the flat surf conditions found in summer.
- — Trevor Cralle, *The Surfin'ary*, p. 67, 1991

La-La Land *noun*
Los Angeles, California *US, 1972*
- (Headline) Earl the Voyeur From La La Land — *Screw*, p. 9, 28th August 1972
- "And you're in El-A?" "Yeah, La-La Land." — Odie Hawkins, *Lost Angeles*, p. 166, 1994

lalapalooze *noun*
in poker, a hand that entitles the player to special payment from all other players *US, 1988*
- — George Percy, *The Language of Poker*, p. 51, 1988

lam *noun*
1 in cheating schemes, a victim *UK, 1668*
The victims are like "lambs to slaughter" (easily duped).
- — Frank Garcia, *Marked Cards and Loaded Dice*, p. 262, 1962

2 a young, innocent-looking male prisoner recently arrived at prison, identified as an easy sexual conquest by the population of sexual predators *US, 1922*
- — *Male Swinger Number 3*, p. 47, 1981: "The complete gay dictionary"

▸ **on the lam**
running away; trying to escape *US, 1928*
- I will have to sub-lease this house to some sucker, and then take it on the lam to Frisco. — Jack Kerouac, *Letter to John Clellon Holmes*, p. 196, 24th June 1949
- Baltimore is a favorite hide-out for Mafiastas on the lam from other towns[.] — Jack Lait and Lee Mortimer, *Washington Confidential*, p. 259, 1951
- He's on the lam from a pen back east[.] — Jim Thompson, *A Swell-Looking Babe*, p. 77, 1954
- She got ten years. She's still on the lam. — Edwin Torres, *After Hours*, pp. 376–377, 1979
- [A]n Australian on the lam from a bad life and taken up with a neurotic kibbutznik with three kids. — Sandra Bernhard, *Confessions of a Pretty Lady*, p. 122, 1988

▸ **take it on the lam**
to escape, to run away *US, 1990*
- One morning I woke up and found that Joel had helped himself to a good part of the cash, and had taken it on the lam. — Herbert Huncke, *Guilty of Everything*, p. 167, 1990
- I suppose this is where you, what's the word, Lovejoy... scarper? Take it on the lam. — Jonathan Gash, *The Ten Word Game*, p. 139, 2003

lam *verb*
to escape, especially from prison *US, 1886*
- Why the hell don't you lam out of here, bud? — Raymond Chandler, *The Little Sister*, p. 107, 1949
- The lowlier links lam the 36 miles to Baltimore to cup up. — Jack Lait and Lee Mortimer, *Washington Confidential*, 1951
- She reported him to the police, some false trumped up hysterical crazy charge, and Neal had to lam from Hoboken. — Jack Kerouac, *On the Road (The Original Scroll)*, p. 110, 1951
- I'm not lamming from pitiful pittance but my last week's script pay was 18 bucks and I gotta get a bigger job. — Jack Kerouac, *Letter to Neal Cassady*, p. 326, 1st October 1951
- But—why did Connie lam so fast? — Bernard Wolfe, *The Late Risers*, p. 242, 1954

lamb fry *noun*
a necktie *US, 1972*
An example of American rhyming slang.
- Lamb-fry is the tie. — Robert Byrne, *McGoorty*, p. 147, 1972

lame *noun*
a naive, conventional, law-abiding person *US, 1960*

- The bar was filling with the lames and fools of the Saturday-workday, loud and boisterous, living it up and acting like people. — Clarence Cooper Jr., *The Scene*, p. 40, 1960
- [S]ome good Pump House souls are busted, but that is The Life, the world divided into surfer heads and surfer lames[.] — Tom Wolfe, *The Electric Kool-Aid Acid Test*, p. 321, 1968
- A whole lotta lames'll / fall victim to the game. — Lightnin' Rod, *Hustlers Convention*, p. 24, 1973
- Then some lame was puffing on a joint one night, got next to a kitty and said she had to take a poke. — Edwin Torres, *Carlito's Way*, p. 26, 1975
- "When I'm through with you, you're not only going to be able to talk to the lames, you're going to be able to talk to anyone." — Bob Sipchen, *Baby Insane and the Buddha*, p. 83, 1993

lame *adjective*

1 unfashionable, weak, unspirited *US, 1935*
- — *American Speech*, p. 302, December 1955: "Wayne University slang"
- Yeah, it's lame, but I've had this idea. — *Empire Records*, 1995
- Cat, that's the lamest idea I've ever heard. — *Get Shorty*, 1995
- Dude, this is seriously lame. I didn't know we were gonna get all dirty and stuff. — *South Park*, 1999

2 short of money *US, 1988*
- — George Percy, *The Language of Poker*, p. 51, 1988

lamebrain *noun*

a fool, an idiot *US, 1919*
- Lame-brains like to point out that only colored people are confined to "slums" in Washington[.] — Jack Lait and Lee Mortimer, *Washington Confidential*, p. 122, 1951
- "Don't forget, our audience will be made up of every lamebrain in the country." — William Johnston, *The Brady Bunch*, p. 145, 1969
- [H]e said the playoff games had made it clear to him that the players had not packaged their best product, as it would have been clear to anyone but a lamebrain owner. — Dan Jenkins, *Life Its Ownself*, p. 309, 1984

lame-o *noun*

a fool, an idiot *US, 1977*
- I wish I had a dime for every job that lame-o Florio gave out to his friends. — Howard Stern, *Miss America*, p. 461, 1995
- What a lame-o. Somebody should put him out of his misery. — *American Beauty*, 1999

lame-o *adjective*

weak, pathetic *US, 1988*
- [I]t meant get lost with this lame-o situation, or how disgusting, or forget this shit[.] — Pamela Des Barres, *I'm With the Band*, p. 64, 1988

lamer *noun*

an uninformed Internet user who passes himself off as an expert *US, 1997*
- — Andy Ihnatko, *Cyberspeak*, p. 110, 1997

lame stain *noun*

a completely inept, despised person *US, 1997*
- — Vann Wesson, *Generation X Field Guide and Lexicon*, p. 104, 1997

lamister *noun*

a fugitive from justice *US, 1955*
- I lived like a lamister. — Rocky Garciano (with Rowland Barber), *Somebody Up There Likes Me*, p. 92, 1955

lamo *noun*

a person lacking fashion sense and social skills *US, 1993*
- — *Washington Post*, 14th October 1993

lamp *noun*

a look *US, 1926*
- I knew it as soon as that Nancy walked into your office and put the lamps on you. — Edwin Torres, *Q & A*, p. 90, 1977

lamp *verb*

to look *US, 1907*
- I gave him the double-o after I lamped the engraved card he handed me. — Mezz Mezzrow, *Really the Blues*, p. 261, 1946
- "Crazy, man, crazy," spieled his pal, one eye lamping a real gone gal. — Dan Burley, *Diggeth Thou?*, p. 18, 1959
- He nipped me by my coatsleeve and lamped me with a wicked eye. — Bruce Jackson, *Get Your Ass in the Water and Swim Like Me*, p. 85, 1965

- [W]hen Joe extended his condolences for Archie, the Chinese gangster just lamped him with a freezedried smile. — Seth Morgan, *Homeboy*, p. 264, 1990

lamster *noun*

a fugitive from justice or retribution *US, 1904*
- The owner would accept no payment for keeping the jobs lamster. — Burton Turkus and Sid Feder, *Murder, Inc.*, p. 158, 1951
- Tourists, servicemen, merchant seamen, gamblers, perverts, drifters, and lamsters from every State in the Union. — William Burroughs, *Junkie*, pp. 70–71, 1953
- I later learned that they put a shadow on Gay and checked her calls, hoping she would lead them to the lamster. — Lee Mortimer, *Women Confidential*, p. 35, 1960
- He's a lamster Jap, he's a youth gang member, he did a deuce for B and E and when last seen he was passing out anti-American leaflets. — James Ellroy, *Hollywood Nocturnes*, p. 275, 1994

land *noun*

a neighborhood *US, 1989*
- — Ellen C. Bellone (Editor), *Dictionary of Slang*, p. 15, 1989

landing deck *noun*

the top of the head *US, 1947*
- Tell comes in on the down beat, draws a bead and bounces the Baldwin off Junior's landing deck! — Harry Haenigsen, *Jive's Like That*, 1947

landing gear *noun*

the legs *US, 1941*
- — Lou Shelly, *Hepcats Jive Talk Dictionary*, p. 46, 1945

landing strip *noun*

a woman's pubic hair trimmed into the shape of a narrow vertical bar *US, 1997*

A visual comparison.
- Like a nice landing strip! It's more sexy. I prefer it unshaved. — alt.tv.real-world, 3rd June 1997
- Crop your hair into a vertical so-called "landing strip" (obviously named by a jet-setting man). — *The Village Voice*, 8th–14th November 2000
- Take a chance on surviving the big, bulging expanses of chest slope, the sleek landing strip muff, and round mounds of butt meat[.] — Mr. Skin, *Mr. Skin's Skincyclopedia*, p. 110, 2005

landlady *noun*

a brothel madame *US, 1879*
- LANDLADIES' NIGHT AT THE CLUB ALABAM!—FUN AND FROLIC!—COME ONE AND ALL! — Mezz Mezzrow, *Really the Blues*, p. 91, 1946

land line *noun*

a conventional telephone line, as distinguished from a cell phone or radio *US, 1987*
- — Carsten Stroud, *Close Pursuit*, p. 273, 1987

land of the big PX *noun*

the United States *US, 1968*

The US seen in its commercial glory as one big PX (supermarket/department store). From Vietnam.
- — Carl Fleischhauer, *A Glossary of Army Slang*, p. 30, 1968
- The other half, since they had already been there, were certain of their survival; they were headed for the fantasyland of the Bix PX, the World, Man—Stateside! — Charles Anderson, *The Grunts*, p. 13, 1976
- I'm going home, back-in-the-world, the land of the big PX and the twenty-four-hour generator. — Larry Heinemann, *Close Quarters*, p. 262, 1977
- Oh, I'm just waiting to get back to the land of the big PX. — *Full Metal Jacket*, 1987

Land of the Round Doorknob *noun*

the United States *US, 1970*
- So he'd fall in love, they'd get married, and the blushing bride got her coveted passport back to the Land of the Round Doorknob. — David Hackworth, *About Face*, p. 213, 1989

lane; lain; laine *noun*

a sucker, a gullible victim *US, 1933*
- Lemme take a sawbuck, man. I got a lain hooked down here[.] — Chester Himes, *If He Hollers Let Him Go*, p. 43, 1945
- The only time the aldermen ever had a meeting was when enough of the waiters ganged up around the bar to talk about the laines they clipped, and the police chief was too busy mixing drinks to bust himself under the prohibition act. — Mezz Mezzrow, *Really the Blues*, p. 66, 1946

- He knew his fortune was surely made / If he didn't do business lanes. — Dennis Wepman et al., *The Life*, p. 105, 1976

Laotian red *noun*
a reddish marijuana, purported to have been grown in Laos *US, 1974*

- He also showed Converse the file cabinet in which he kept his pornography collection and the movie film can that was loaded with Laotian Red. — Robert Stone, *Dog Soldiers*, p. 45, 1974
- A friend of mine whose trippin' around in Southeast Asia can mail me a lil' stick or some Laotian red from time to time. — Odie Hawkins, *Great Lawd Buddha*, p. 69, 1990

lap dance *noun*
an intimate sexual performance, involving some degree of physical contact between a female performer and a sitting male *US, 1988*

- Tanya says she immediately discerned that we are extremely nice guys and is therefore prepared to offer us a bargain price (two for 30) on the regular $20 lap dances, a house specialty that need not be described in detail for the purposes of this column. — *St. Petersburg (Florida) Times*, p. 1D, 8th May 1988
- Any time you want a lap dance with that broad, say the word. — Quentin Tarantino, *From Dusk Till Dawn*, p. 94, 1995
- It was the kind of warm, personal loving you could only get a dollar at a time, or for twenty bucks a lap dance. — John Ridley, *Love is a Racket*, p. 131, 1998
- There's no constitutional right to a lap-dance. That's the gist of a divided Oregon Court of Appeals ruling[.] — *Associated Press*, 31st October 2002

lap dance *verb*
to engage in a sexual performance in which a woman dancer, scantily clad if at all, grinds her buttocks into a sitting male customer's lap *US, 1993*

- In the Starlight Room, nude girls would dance incredibly fast on a stage, then come out into the audience and do lap dancing— squirming around in a guy's lap for an extra $5. — Annie Ample, *The Bare Facts*, p. 9, 1988
- I progressed from sitting on his lap to no-charge lap dancing. — Anka Radakovich, *The Wild Girls Club*, p. 96, 1994
- My Best Friend Pays My Girlfriend to Lap Dance (Headline) — *San Francisco Examiner*, p. C2, 7th October 1994
- Lap dancing—where the dancer rubs herself against the customer for a longer time—brings in more money. — James Ridgeway, *Red Light*, p. 176, 1996

lap dancer *noun*
a woman who performs lap dances in a sex club *US, 1985*

- Sometime around midnight I stopped in Novato to pay my respects at a bachelor party for a male stripper who was marrying a lap dancer from the O'Farrell Theatre. — Hunter S. Thompson, *Generation of Swine*, p. 20, 1985

lap job *noun*
an act of oral sex on a woman *US, 1969*

- Like my second lap job a year later was on a neighborhood chick, a year older than me. — *Screw*, p. 5, 7th March 1969

larceny *verb*
to manipulate through insincere flattery *US, 1960*

- You don't have to larceny me—I won't flip on you. I'll never flip on nobody again. — Clarence Cooper Jr., *The Scene*, p. 14, 1960

lard-ass *noun*
an overweight person *US, 1918*

- At school, kids keep comin' up to him and sayin' Hey Lard Ass, how many pies ya gonna eat? — Stephen King, *Different Seasons*, p. 364, 1983

lard-assed *adjective*
fat; in the manner of a fat person *US, 1967*

- Forget the lard-assed, cynical, doughnut-gulping slobs you see waddling around like paramilitary Pillsbury doughboys. — Gina Gallo, *Armed and Dangerous*, p. 16, 2002

lard-butt *noun*
a fat person *US, 1968*

- "You call me fatso again and I'll rearrange your face." "Fatso, fat ass, lard butt, blimpo—" — Janet Evanovich, *Seven Up*, p. 37, 2001

larf *noun*
nonsense, rubbish *US, 1966*

- — John D. Bell et al., *Loosely Speaking*, p. 12, 1966

large *adjective*
1 a lot of *US, 2002*

- I have large cash money in my pocket. — David Henry Sterry, *Chicken*, p. 104, 2002

2 enthusiastic *US, 1967*

- — Hy Lit, *Hy Lit's Unbelievable Dictionary of Hip Words for Groovy People*, p. 26, 1968

3 impressively, (of a lifestyle) in an excessive, successful, comfortable, or self-indulgent manner *US, 1883*

- — Connie Eble (Editor), *UNC-CH Campus Slang*, p. 5, Spring 1989
- When you were "in effect" you were truly "large" [doing well]. — Nelson George, *Hip Hop America*, p. 209, 1998

large charge *noun*
a big thrill *US, 1951*

- — *Newsweek*, p. 28, 8th October 1951
- — Hy Lit, *Hy Lit's Unbelievable Dictionary of Hip Words for Groovy People*, p. 50, 1968

large one; large *noun*
one thousand dollars *US, 1972*

- The guy worked around the clock for free, plus he threw five large into the war chest. — Richard Price, *Clockers*, p. 269, 1992
- Guy owes me fifteen large and takes off, I go after him. — *Get Shorty*, 1995
- For that he gets 200 large. — *Gone in 60 Seconds*, 2000

larry *noun*
1 in a card game, the player who has the last chance to act in a given situation *US, 1950*

- — Thomas L. Clark, *The Dictionary of Gambling and Gaming*, p. 115, 1987

2 in carnival usage, an unprofitable day or engagement *US, 1966*

- — *American Speech*, p. 281, December 1966: "More carnie talk from the West Coast"

Larry *adjective*
in circus and carnival usage, worthless *US, 1939*

- — Don Wilmeth, *The Language of American Popular Entertainment*, p. 155, 1981

Larry Cadota *noun*
a worthless novelty sold in the circus or carnival *US, 1980*

- — Joe McKennon, *Circus Lingo*, p. 54, 1980

larval stage *noun*
the initial burst of enthusiastic and single-minded focus experienced by computer enthusiasts *US, 1991*

- A less protracted and intense version of larval stage (typically lasting about a month) may recur when one is learning a new OS or programing language. — Eric S. Raymond, *The New Hacker's Dictionary*, p. 220, 1991

lase *verb*
to print a document on a laser printer *US, 1991*

- — Eric S. Raymond, *The New Hacker's Dictionary*, p. 220, 1991

lash-up *noun*
a person who fails at all he tries *US, 1980*
From the earlier naval sense of a failure or fiasco.

- "Now he thinks he's in therapy, rehabilitation, that lash-up, he's not gonna have to go to jail." — George Higgins, *Kennedy for the Defense*, p. 205, 1980

last call *noun*
death *US, 1977*

- — Ramon Adams, *The Language of the Railroader*, p. 92, 1977
- — John Vorhaus, *The Big Book of Poker Slang*, p. 25, 1996

last-card Louie *noun*
in stud poker, a player who stays in a hand until his last card, improbably hoping for the one card that can produce a winning hand *US, 1951*

- — *American Speech*, p. 100, May 1951: "The vocabulary of poker"
- — Albert H. Morehead, *The Complete Guide to Winning Poker*, p. 267, 1967

last chance *noun*
the upper balcony in a movie theater favored by homosexuals *US, 1966*

- In Chicago, they're called "Gobble Alley." In Los Angeles, some studs refer to the balconies as the "Last Chance." — Johnny Shearer, *The Male Hustler*, p. 77, 1966

lasting mark *noun*
a welt or bruise produced in sadomasochistic sex *US, 1987*
- If a man says "no lasting marks" he is put through a gradual build-up of increasingly painful procedures. — Frederique Delacoste, *Sex Work*, p. 51, 1987

lastish *noun*
the most recently published issue of a single-interest fan magazine *US, 1982*
- — *American Speech*, p. 27, Spring 1982: "The language of science fiction fan magazines"

last mile *noun*
in prison, the walk from the death cell to the execution chamber *US, 1950*
- — Hyman E. Goldin et al., *Dictionary of American Underworld Lingo*, p. 122, 1950
- But those are memories from long before my trial / And now it's time to walk that last mile. — Dennis Wepman et al., *The Life*, p. 118, 1976

LA stop *noun*
a rolling stop at a traffic signal or stop sign *US, 1999*
- — Jeffrey McQuain, *Never Enough Words*, p. 54, 1999

last rose of summer *noun*
a hospital patient with an ever-melodramatic belief that death is near *US, 1994*
- — Sally Williams, *"Strong" Words (Dissertation)*, p. 149, 1994

last waltz *noun*
the walk taken by a prisoner condemned to death from the death cell to the execution chamber *US, 1945*
- — Lou Shelly, *Hepcats Jive Talk Dictionary*, p. 28, 1945
- — William K. Bentley and James M. Corbett, *Prison Slang*, p. 105, 1992

latch *verb*
to understand *US, 1938*
- — Lavada Durst, *The Jives of Dr. Hepcat*, p. 13, 1953

late-night *noun*
1 a bus ticket found on the street that is still valid *US, 1989*
Prized by drug addicts desperate to raise funds to buy their next dose.
- A street vendor will call out: "Hey, late-night, late night." — Geoffrey Froner, *Digging for Diamonds*, p. 41, 1989
2 a party after a party *US, 2001*
- — Don R. McCreary (Editor), *Dawg Speak*, 2001

later; laters; lates; later on; late
goodbye *US, 1954*
- — *American Speech*, p. 303, December 1955: "Wayne University slang"
- — Robert George Reisner, *The Jazz Titans*, p. 160, 1960
- I dug right away what the kick was, so I said, "later," and he split. — Eldridge Cleaver, *Soul on Ice*, p. 46, 1968
- Why? Because you are more scared to be locked up than we are—later! — Bobby Seale, *A Lonely Rage*, p. 272, 1978
- — *San Jose Mercury News*, 11th May 1999

latex *noun*
a condom *US, 1992*
- — Judi Sanders, *Kickin' like Chicken with the Couch Commander*, p. 15, 1992
- [T]hese guys would grudgingly comply, slap on the latex and wake up in the morning to find that Melissa spends the best part of her daylight hours asleep. — John Birmingham, *He Died With a Felafel in his Hand*, p. 22, 1994

Latin *noun*
a Mexican, Latin American or Spanish-speaking person *US, 1964*
- She's my pretty little baby / Litte Latin Lupe Lu — The Kingsmen, *Little Latin Lupe Lu*
- [H]e's going by the name Edward Mallon, but you could tell by looking at him he was a greaser. Excuse me, I mean a Latin. I have to watch that. — Elmore Leonard, *Killshot*, p. 182, 1989

latrine Gene *noun*
a soldier with a pathological need to be clean *US, 1946*
- — *American Speech*, p. 238, October 1946: "World War II slang of maladjustment"

latrine lawyer *noun*
an argumentative soldier who is familiar with military rules and regulations *US, 1943*

- I can split hairs with the best latrine lawyer ever born. — Rick Shelley, *Special Operations Squad*, p. 8, 2001

latrine rumor *noun*
a common rumor *US, 1918*
- The word would spread instantly through the latrine rumor network. — Harry Harrison, *A Stainless Steel Trio*, p. 301, 2002

latronic
used as a farewell *US, 1991*
A corruption of **LATER ON**.
- — Trevor Cralle, *The Surfin'ary*, p. 68, 1991

lats *noun*
the *latissimus dorsi* muscles on the lower back *US, 1939*
- He stands very straight, spreading his "lats" like batwings. — John Rechy, *Numbers*, p. 61, 1967
- "You were great in the hayfork scene." "My lats were great in the hayfork scene." — Armistead Maupin, *Further Tales of the City*, p. 104, 1982
- — *American Speech*, p. 200, Fall 1984: "The language of bodybuilding"
- "Lats and delts poking around inside a dress shirt in the Park with those binoculars." — Ethan Morden, *Some Men Are Lookers*, p. 318, 1997

LA turnabout; LA turnaround *noun*
a long-lasting amphetamine *US, 1970*
- From the image of driving from the East Coast of the US to Los Angeles and back again without resting. — Montie Tak, *Truck Talk*, p. 97, 1971
- — Peter Johnson, *Dictionary of Street Alcohol and Drug Terms*, p. 107, 1993

laugher *noun*
in sports, an easy and overwhelming victory *US, 1961*
- — Zander Hollander and Sandy Padwe, *Basketball Lingo*, p. 63, 1971

laughing academy *noun*
a mental institution *US, 1947*
- — Lawrence Lipton, *The Holy Barbarians*, p. 316, 1959
- Thoughts of straitjackets, of a Gestapo setup, of ex-Nazi male nurses, of Dr. F. smiling sinister when he got me into the laughing academy, oh no, oh no no no. — Kevin Mackey, *The Cure*, p. 43, 1970

laughing farm *noun*
a mental institution *US, 1965*
- Hey, Joe said, hey, Ziggy, you better go back to the laughin' farm. — Gilbert Sorrentino, *Steelwork*, p. 75, 1970

laughing tobacco *noun*
marijuana *US, 1981*
- There were big bonfires all over the place and numbers were being passed like they were trying to get rid of their laughing tobacco before it went out of style. — Robert Lipkin, *A Brotherhood of Outlaws*, p. 182, 1981

launching pad *noun*
a place where LSD is taken *US, 1966*
Punning both on **PAD** (a place) and LSD as "travel."
- Carefully check out your launching pad before lift-off. It is best to clean it off as much as possible. — *The San Francisco Oracle*, 1966

laundry *noun*
1 a business used by organized crime to give illegally gained money the appearance of legitimacy *US, 1997*
- I want to get the front money by hitting their laundry, 'cause they can't squeal to the law afterward for fear they'll give up the operation. — Stephen Cannell, *King Con*, p. 111, 1997
2 in homosexual usage, a bulge in a man's crotch *US, 1964*
Humorous, suggesting that the bulge is produced by something other than the man's genitals.
- — Guy Strait, *The Lavender Lexicon*, 1st June 1964
- — *Male Swinger Number 3*, p. 47, 1981: "The complete gay dictionary"

laundry queen *noun*
in circus and carnival usage, a female dancer *US, 1981*
- — Don Wilmeth, *The Language of American Popular Entertainment*, p. 155, 1981

lavaliers *noun*
the female breasts *US, 1969*
- — John D. Bell et al., *Loosely Speaking*, p. 12, 1969

lavender *adjective*
effiminate, homosexual *US, 1929*
- The lavender boys hang around the far end of the bar[.] — Roger Gordon, *Hollywood's Sexual Underground*, p. 18, 1966

- Ever anxious to parsimoniously pinch pennies, Mickey has cast lavender loverboy Touch Vecchio in a key role[.] — James Ellroy, *White Jazz*, p. 7, 1992

law *noun*
your parents *US, 1955*
Teen slang.
- — *American Weekly*, p. 2, 14th August 1955

▶ **the law**
the police, the law enforcement authorities *US, 1893*
- All I could think of was the law had nailed Mike and Mackey in The Bunk. — Mezz Mezzrow, *Really the Blues*, p. 266, 1946
- The Law's after her and we'd better find her before they do. — George Mandel, *Flee the Angry Strangers*, p. 159, 1952
- Two detectives walked in and leaned on the bar, talking to the bartender. Jack jerked his head in their direction. "The law. Let's take a walk." — William Burroughs, *Junkie*, p. 21, 1953
- The men grumble and reluctantly spread themselves along the wall, prodded by the Law. — Odie Hawkins, *Ghetto Sketches*, p. 31, 1972

law *verb*
to arrest *US, 1935*
- "Time was," said Pappy Dan, "young fella left town, he was about to be lawed or about to be a father." — John Sayles, *Union Dues*, p. 65, 1977

law dog *noun*
a law enforcement official *US, 1962*
- The big law dog in the hills where I grew up was Sheriff Charley Gumm. — Sam Snead, *The Education of a Golfer*, p. 34, 1962

lawn *noun*
a woman's pubic hair *US, 1964*
- — Roger Blake, *The American Dictionary of Sexual Terms*, p. 118, 1964
- — *Maledicta*, p. 131, Summer/Winter 1982: "Dyke diction: the language of lesbians"
- When it comes to mowing our lickable lawns, the hairstyle you choose for your kitty can be an expression of your personal taste. — *The Village Voice*, 8th–14th November 2000

lawyer up *verb*
to refuse to cooperate with a police investigation until provided with legal counsel *US, 1995*
- Lawyering up: A suspect's decision to stop answering questions and ask for legal counsel. — Samuel Katz, *NYPD*, 1995
- An eyewitness who says she saw two Italians matching the descriptions of the killers chasing a Puerto Rican earlier that day calls in, and two suspects are brought in—and quickly lawyered up[.] — *alt.tv.nypd-blue*, 16th March 1995
- "A grieving husband doesn't run out the moment his wife is murdered and get an attorney he's never hired before. That's what we call 'lawyering up,' and grieving husbands don't do that." — Gary King, *Murder in Hollywood*, p. 175, 2001
- "I really don't want to do this either, but if I have to, I can lawyer up as soon as I get off this phone." — Richard Price, *Samaritan*, p. 289, 2003

lay *noun*
an act of sexual intercourse *US, 1928*
- "I don't know why I'm not more popular with the girls. I'm such an easy lay." — Norman Mailer, *The Naked and the Dead*, p. 185, 1948
- I was about ten and she was probably less, and at the time a lay seemed like such a big deal[.] — Ken Kesey, *One Flew Over the Cuckoo's Nest*, p. 244, 1962
- "Don't push me, Jen. You're the best lay I ever had, but—" — Jacqueline Susann, *Valley of the Dolls*, p. 265, 1966
- I felt one's culo and asked, "How about a lay?" Imagine, just for that she started yelling for her boys. — Piri Thomas, *Down These Mean Streets*, p. 51, 1967

lay *verb*
to have sex *UK, 1800*
Most often heard in the passive.
- You know, all I really want is to get laid. That's what I'm really complaining about. — John Clellon Holmes, *Go*, p. 8, 1952
- I found this irksome, as I was beginning again to feel lonely and like laying half Manhattan island (the half that was female). — Clancy Sigal, *Going Away*, p. 420, 1961
- "[T]hey discussed how it would be to lay that little nurse with the birthmark who went off at midnight." — Ken Kesey, *One Flew Over the Cuckoo's Nest*, p. 289, 1962
- Thus it was that I got laid for the first time in my life in February of that new year[.] — John Nichols, *The Sterile Cuckoo*, p. 96, 1965

▶ **lay a batch**
to accelerate a car quickly and in so doing to leave rubber marks on the road *US, 1969*
- — Capitol Records, *Hot Rod Jargon*, 1963
- — Kenn "Naz" Young, *Naz's Dictionary of Teen Slang*, p. 71, 1993

▶ **lay a fart**
to pass gas *US, 1951*
- This guy sitting in the row in front of me, Edgar Marsalla, laid this terrific fart. — J.D. Salinger, *The Catcher in the Rye*, 1951

▶ **lay chilly**
to relax *US, 1981*
- Finally he decided, "We'll crawl down the streambed. Stay low, find a good spot, lay chilly." — A.D. Horne, *The Wounded Generation*, p. 67, 1981
- "Wait!" I said. "Get the ARVN up here first, and tell these guys to lay chilly." — Michael C. Hodgins, *Reluctant Warrior*, p. 152, 1996

▶ **lay dead**
1 to remain silent *US, 1976*
- — John R. Armore and Joseph D. Wolfe, *Dictionary of Desperation*, p. 38, 1976
2 to stay in one place; to stay still *US, 1949*
- — Babs Gonzales, *Be-Bop Dictionary and History of its Famous Stars*, p. 9, 1949

▶ **lay eggs**
to drop bombs *US, 1998*
- Anyway, the air force drivers were laying eggs all over the designated VC installations zone we wuz s'pose to move in on and sop up being grunts which is what you do with shit—that's the way they seed us[.] — Clarence Major, *All-Night Visitors*, p. 36, 1998

▶ **lay in the cut**
to wait in hiding *US, 1976*
- I laid in the cut on Carmen's big butt / And kept her on her knees all night. — Dennis Wepman et al., *The Life*, p. 49, 1976

▶ **lay it down**
to explain the rules of a carnival midway game to a potential customer *US, 1985*
- — Gene Sorrows, *All About Carnivals*, p. 21, 1985: "Terminology"

▶ **lay it on**
to inform, to report or explain fully *US, 1975*
- You know what to do with the stiffs, and remember to call Amos' ol' lady and lay it on her. — Donald Goines, *Inner City Hoodlum*, p. 108, 1975
- Well, I'm gonna lay it on you one time, for the record. — Edwin Torres, *Carlito's Way*, p. 5, 1975

▶ **lay paper**
to pass counterfeit money or bad checks *US, 1972*
- [H]e goes over there and starts laying this paper [writing checks]. — Bruce Jackson, *In the Life*, p. 286, 1972

▶ **lay pipe**
(used of a male) to have sex *US, 1939*
- "No more overhauls, and you're going to hafta stop laying pipe with all the guys." — Jose Antonio Villarreal, *Pocho*, p. 141, 1959
- — Collin Baker et al., *College Undergraduate Slang Study Conducted at Brown University*, p. 150, 1968
- Gonna lay some pipe, six inches at a time. — Joseph Wambaugh, *The Choirboys*, p. 313, 1975

▶ **lay the leg**
to seduce or attempt to seduce *US, 1981*
- — Don Wilmeth, *The Language of American Popular Entertainment*, p. 155, 1981

▶ **lay the note**
to shortchange someone *US, 1977*
- — Robert C. Prus and C.R.D. Sharper, *Road Hustler*, p. 170, 1977: "Glossary of terms"

▶ **lay track**
to lie *US, 1992*
- — William K. Bentley and James M. Corbett, *Prison Slang*, p. 33, 1992

lay and pay *noun*
in casino blackjack games, the practice of laying hands down, turning them over, and paying or collecting all bets at once *US, 1980*
- — Lee Solkey, *Dummy Up and Deal*, p. 115, 1980

lay bear *noun*
in the carnival, a stuffed bear given to a girl by a game operator in return for sex *US, 1985*

- More times that I care to remember, I've witnessed a thirteen or fourteen year old girl being guided to a screened area behind a game booth by one of these perverts, whispering in her ear the promise of a LAY BEAR. — Gene Sorrows, *All About Carnivals*, p. 21, 1985

lay dead!
wait just a minute! *US, 1958*
Teen slang.
- — *San Francisco News*, p. 6, 25th March 1958

lay down verb
to play in a musical performance *US, 1943*
- They laid down not only some of the heaviest music, but a message that was so then and there that it was incredible and uncanny. — *East Village Other*, 20th August 1969

layer noun
a bookmaker *UK, 1937*
- — David W. Maurer, *Argot of the Racetrack*, p. 39, 1951

layette noun
the equipment necessary to prepare and inject a narcotic drug *US, 1882*
- — Richard A. Spears, *The Slang and Jargon of Drugs and Drink*, p. 310, 1986

lay-for-pay noun
sex with a prostitute *US, 1956*
- "Who's behind all the muscle, Mamie?" I was going too fast for her. "In the past two weeks we've hauled at least three of you lay-for-pay dames into Bellevue to get patched up." — *Rogue for Men*, p. 45, June 1956

lay-in noun
permission from prison authorities to remain in bed in your cell instead of working *US, 1972*
- We had a ole doctor, one guy went up there and asked him for a lay-in [permission to stay in the building during the work day] and he told him, "I'm not gonna lay you in." — Bruce Jackson, *In the Life*, p. 307, 1972
- — Reinhold Aman, *Hillary Clinton's Pen Pal: A Guide to Life and Lingo in Federal Prison*, p. 47, 1996

layoff noun
a bookmaker who takes secondary bets from other bookmakers to protect them against large losses *US, 1973*
- "If you're a bookmaker and you get a sudden flood of bets that you figure you can't pay off if things go wrong, you phone part of your action to someone who can. That someone is a layoff." — Vincent Teresa, *My Life in the Mafia*, p. 145, 1973

lay of the land noun
in circus and carnival usage, a lead dancer in a sexually oriented dance show *US, 1981*
- — Don Wilmeth, *The Language of American Popular Entertainment*, p. 155, 1981

lay on verb
to give *US, 1936*
- I'd like you to fall by grandma's joint this afternoon and lay the stuff on her. — Steve Allen, *Bop Fables*, p. 37, 1955
- You gotta bring the cat down and lay one on him and you don't know if they're gonna pull out a French 75 or a Walther. — William "Lord" Buckley, *His Majesty the Policeman*, 1960
- Yes, but who donated it? Who's laying it on? — *Berkeley Barb*, p. 3, 21st October 1966
- "Nutmeg seeds," said Tarzan, grinning. "Here, I'll lay some on you." — Tom Robbins, *Another Roadside Attraction*, p. 272, 1971

layout noun
1 an apartment or house *US, 1883*
- I said, "Jim, you sure ain't jiving. Your layout is a sonuvabitch." He said, "I got five bedrooms here." — Iceberg Slim (Robert Beck), *Pimp*, p. 130, 1969

2 the equipment used to prepare and inject, or smoke, narcotic drugs *US, 1881*
- Mike and me grabbed our layout and out into the airshaft we climbed[.] — Mezz Mezzrow, *Really the Blues*, p. 249, 1946

3 a soldier who lies hidden in a hole observing enemy movements *US, 1957*
Korean war usage.
- These two "lay-outs," as they are called, are relieved by the next squad that night. I am interested in standing this particular watch. I can't determine what their function is, since they must hide in a hole all day. — Martin Russ, *The Last Parallel*, p. 90, 1957

lay up verb
to relax, especially after using drugs *US, 1962*
- — Anthony Romeo, *The Language of Gangs*, p. 19, 4th December 1962
- — Hermese E. Roberts, *The Third Ear*, 1971
- After the drug has been smoked, the addict goes into a state of suspended animation. Laying up is not to be confused with nodding. — Lenny Bruce, *The Unpublished Lenny Bruce*, p. 73, 1984

Lazarus ball noun
in pinball, a ball that passes between the flippers but then miraculously bounces back into play *US, 1979*
- — Edward Trapunski, *Special When Lit*, p. 153, 1979

LBFM noun
an Asian woman seen purely as a sex partner *US, 1971*
An abbreviation of *Little Brown Fucking Machine*.
- LBFM's never come. What's an LBFM? A little brown fucking machine. — Robert Reisner, *Encyclopedia of Graffiti*, p. 298, 1974
- At my quarters, when I ordered "dessert," number one houseboy Sothan would produce a LBFM, and I'd eat my "dessert" in bed. — Richard Marcinko, *Rogue Warrior*, p. 193, 1992

LBJ noun
piperidyl benzilate, a hallucinogen *US, 1970*
- — William D. Alsever, *Glossary for the Establishment and Other Uptight People*, p. 17, December 1970

LBJ nickname
during the Vietnam war, the Long Binh military stockade, South Vietnam *US, 1977*
- Yeah, you two chickenshits are gonna do about a thousand years in LBJ. — Larry Heinemann, *Close Quarters*, p. 151, 1977
- He's in the L.B.J.—didn't give him no medals or nothing. — *Apocalypse Now*, 1979
- Playing on US President Johnson's initials and nickname. — Linda Reinberg, *In the Field*, p. 125, 1991

LBJ Ranch nickname
the Long Binh military stockade, South Vietnam *US, 1973*
Playing on US President Lyndon B. Johnson's ranch in Johnson City, Texas, outside Austin.
- I drove to Long Binh, which was not only USARV headquarters, but the site of the LBJ ranch to which Franklin had threatened to send me if I didn't mend my ways. — Anthony Herbert, *Soldier*, p. 395, 1973
- Most platoon leaders, unwilling to ship half their guys to the LBJ Ranch, as the troops sardonically referred to Long Binh Jail, drew the line when it came to pot in the bush[.] — Keith Nolan, *Ripcord*, p. 106, 2000

LCN noun
organized crime *US, 1970*
An abbreviation of "La Cosa Nostra."
- Perhaps this is why many LCN members are sending their sons to universities. — United States Congress, *Federal Effort Against Organized Crime*, p. 298, 1970
- While this is standard LCN practice, there is no indication that an LCN family is based in the District. — Robert Hunter Williams, *Vice Squad*, p. 43, 1973

lead noun
▸ eat lead
to be shot *US, 1927*
- "Well, it isn't like I'm gonna eat lead tomorrow," Grandma said. — Janet Evanovich, *Hot Six*, p. 51, 2000

▸ get the lead out
to stop dawdling, to hurry up *US, 1919*
- Get the lead out, fat boy! — Stephen Sondheim, *West Side Story*, 1957
- This goddamn meal is late! Get the fucking lead out, boy! — Iceberg Slim (Robert Beck), *The Naked Soul of Iceberg Slim*, p. 47, 1971
- Come on you guys! Get the lead out. — *Repo Man*, 1984

lead cocktail noun
bullets *US, 1949*
- — Vincent J. Monteleone, *Criminal Slang*, p. 143, 1949

lead-foot verb
to drive fast *US, 1986*
- He made the trip in thirty-five, lead-footing it code Three all the way[.] — James Ellroy, *Suicide Hill*, p. 683, 1986

lead in the pencil *noun*

the ability of a man to achieve an erection and ejaculate *UK, 1925*

- — Roger Blake, *The American Dictionary of Sexual Terms*, p. 118, 1964
- I am eating oysters tonight. That will put lead in my pencil, as they say. — Gore Vidal, *Myron*, p. 251, 1974
- Drink this, Superman. It'll put some lead in your pencil. — *New Jack City*, 1990

lead joint *noun*

in circus and carnival usage, a shooting gallery concession on the midway *US, 1981*

- — Don Wilmeth, *The Language of American Popular Entertainment*, p. 156, 1981

lead pants *noun*

a slow-moving, work-averse person *US, 1947*

- This Rip is a lead pants, strictly from fatigue, allergic to work, no git up and git. — Harry Haenigsen, *Jive's Like That*, 1947

lead-pipe cinch *noun*

an absolute certainty *US, 1894*

- "Not early enough to move no tables, that's a lead-pipe cinch." — Nelson Algren, *The Man with the Golden Arm*, p. 23, 1949
- I got a lead pipe cinch … you game? — Odie Hawkins, *Chicago Hustle*, p. 38, 1977

lead poisoning *noun*

wounds inflicted by a gun *US, 1883*

From the lead in bullets.

- Three days later, when she came to, Sugarfoot was croaked from lead poisoning, like forty SWAT-issue rounds worth[.] — Seth Morgan, *Homeboy*, p. 3, 1990

lead sprayer *noun*

a machine gun *US, 1952*

- "He just walked in with the lead sprayer and almost cut the kid in half." — Harry Grey, *The Hoods*, p. 118, 1952

leaf *noun*

1 marijuana *US, 1961*

- It's a cryin' shame they outlawed the leaf. — Ross Russell, *The Sound*, p. 23, 1961
- Man, this is some golden leaf I brought up from New Orleans. — Leon Rappolo, *quoted in Waiting For The Man by Harry Shapiro*, 1999

2 cocaine *US, 1942*

- — Eugene Landy, *The Underground Dictionary*, p. 119, 1971
- The drug and this name derive from the leaves of the coca bush (Erythroxylon coca). — R.C. Garrett et al., *The Coke Book*, p. 200, 1984

leaf colonel *noun*

a lieutenant colonel *US, 1946*

- — *American Speech*, p. 55, February 1947: "Pacific War language"

leaf-peeper *noun*

a tourist drawn to autumn foliage *US, 1990*

- Veteran leaf-peepers say the colorful autumn displays of reds, yellows and oranges throughout the state are the best in recent memory. — *New Hampshire Sunday News*, p. A1, 7th October 1990

leak *noun*

1 an act of urination *US, 1918*

The verb "leak," found in Shakespeare as a vulgar synonym for "urinate," has been supplanted by the noun use of the term.

- Can't a man take a leak, Chief? — Evan Hunter, *The Blackboard Jungle*, p. 47, 1954
- [F]inally Wallenstein going to the head for a leak[.] — Jack Kerouac, *The Subterraneans*, p. 77, 1958
- Oh, God, not even to take a leak in private. — Jacqueline Susann, *Valley of the Dolls*, p. 416, 1966
- I was taking a leak! — *Something About Mary*, 1998

2 an unauthorized disclosure of confidential or secret information; the person making such a disclosure *US, 1939*

- Thought there was a leak in the Manhattan District. The only leak was in their heads. — Philip Wylie, *Opus 21*, p. 53, 1949

3 in casino gambling, any dealer error or weakness *US, 1991*

- — Michael Dalton, *Blackjack*, p. 61, 1991

leak *verb*

1 to weep *US, 1883*

- Put her in a taxi still leaking. — Jeremy Cameron, *Brown Bread in Wengen*, p. 127, 1999

2 to reveal secret or confidential information in an underhanded, secret manner *US, 1859*

- Once the cops heard Wiley's name they'd leak like the Haitian navy. — Carl Hiaasen, *Tourist Season*, p. 189, 1986

leakage *noun*

in a casino or gambling operation, the money lost to cheats and thieves *US, 1963*

- — Thomas L. Clark, *The Dictionary of Gambling and Gaming*, p. 117, 1987

leaker *noun*

in gambling, a bettor who loses large amounts of money quickly *US, 1997*

- He lived indoors and loved to see leakers like Harry Stanton Price show up. He lived for dumb bettors with systems. — Stephen Cannell, *Big Con*, p. 203, 1997

leak light *noun*

in television and movie making, unwanted light *US, 1990*

- — Ralph S. Singleton, *Filmmaker's Dictionary*, p. 93, 1990

leaky faucet *noun*

a urinary tract or reproductive system disorder causing a urinary or vaginal discharge *US, 1988*

- I go back to bed, to find I have a "leaky faucet," so I return to the kitchen, open the freezer and take out a package of vaginal suppositories. — Sandra Bernhard, *Confessions of a Pretty Lady*, p. 84, 1988

lean *noun*

a mixture of codeine-infused cough syrup and soda *US, 1998*

- — Ethan Hilderbrant, *Prison Slang*, p. 80, 1998
- I'm also trying to find out the Pharmaceutical name for a drug in Texas called syrup, lean or bar. It is a codeine based syrup, which tastes like some sweet cough syrup, but it is very strong. — *alt.drugs.chemistry*, 22nd November 1998
- In Houston, Elwood said, it has a variety of nicknames—Lean, AC/DC, barr, down, Karo and nods. "Lean because after you take it you will be definitely leaning and losing your coordination," Elwood said. — *The Commercial Appeal (Memphis)*, p. F1, 9th July 2000
- [D]rinking what's referred to there as sizzurp, or lean, a cocktail of alcohol, soda, and codeine-infused cough syrup. — *Playboy*, 1st March 2006

▶ **get your lean on**

to become intoxicated drinking a combination of codeine cough syrup and soda *US, 2005*

- "You come to me to get your lean on, huh?" — Linden Dalecki, *Kid B*, p. 10, 2006

lean on *verb*

to physically assault *US, 1911*

- — Hermese E. Roberts, *The Third Ear*, 1971

leap *verb*

▶ **leap (somone) up**

to flatter *US, 1975*

- Don't try to leap me up. — Miguel Pinero, *Short Eyes*, p. 87, 1975

leaper *noun*

1 any central nervous system stimulant, especially amphetamine *US, 1961*

- — Francis J. Rigney and L. Douglas Smith, *The Real Bohemia*, p. xv, 1961
- So no pussy, no money (Gypsy had spent it buying a shotgun in Ely, Nev.) no leapers, etc. — Neal Cassady, *The First Third*, p. 215, 30th August 1965
- [A]mphetamine sulfate, also known as SPEED, UPPERS, SULFATE, SULPH, WHIZZ, LEAPERS, and BILLY. — Macfarlane, Macfarlane and Robson, *The User*, p. 95, 1996

2 a cocaine user after sustained cocaine use *US, 1973*

From the nervousness produced by cocaine use.

- — David Maurer and Victor Vogel, *Narcotics and Narcotic Addiction*, p. 423, 1973

3 a person who threatens to or actually does jump to their death *US, 1954*

- Now, one of the surest indications of a genuine attempt at self-destruction by jumping is the collection of valuables intended to be left behind in the room after the leaper has gone out the window. — Dev Collans with Stewart Sterling, *I was a House Detective*, p. 113, 1954

leapers *noun*

wads of cotton soaked in Benzedrine™ (amphetamine sulfate, a central nervous system stimulant) extracted from an inhaler *US, 1967*

- The wads of charged cotton were known as leapers because of the energy and optimism they released in the men who choked them down[.] — Malcolm Braly, *On the Yard*, p. 85, 1967

leaping lizards!

used for expressing surprise *US, 1924*
Popularized in the Little Orphan Annie newspaper comic strip.

- Leaping lizards! I was supposed to get Melissa Sue a lock of Chad's hair! — Bill Myers, *The Incredible Worlds of Wally Mcdoogle*, p. 80, 1993

leap up *verb*

to flatter *US, 1975*

leash *noun*

a line attached at one end to a surfer and at the other to the surfboard *US, 1977*

- — Gary Fairmont R. Filosa II, *The Surfer's Almanac*, p. 189, 1977

leather *noun*

1 a wallet or purse *US, 1972*

- — Vincent J. Monteleone, *Criminal Slang*, p. 143, 1949
- What we did, every so often we'd pull off the pigeon drop for maybe twenty-five dollars, with me planting the leather, or work the twenties for a five. — Guy Owen, *The Flim-Flam Man and the Apprentice Grifter*, p. 151, 1972

2 in circus and carnival usage, a pickpocket *US, 1936*

- — Don Wilmeth, *The Language of American Popular Entertainment*, p. 157, 1981

3 in homosexual usage, the anus *US, 1941*

- — *Male Swinger Number 3*, p. 48, 1981: "The complete gay dictionary"

4 in horse racing, the small whip carried by jockeys *US, 1951*

- — David W. Maurer, *Argot of the Racetrack*, p. 40, 1951

leather *adjective*

used for denoting leather fetishistic and sadomasochistic symbolism in sexual relationships *US, 1964*

- The hostility of the minority "leather" crowd toward the rest of the "gay" world is exceeded by the bitterness of individual homosexuals toward the "straight" world. — *Life*, p. 70, 26th June 1964
- "Leather" bars for the tough-guy tops with their fondness for chains and belts. — Joe David Brown, *Sex in the '60s*, p. 70, 1968
- "Leather" articles and guidebooks—usually written, significantly, by older, perhaps not terribly attractive homosexuals[.] — John Rechy, *The Sexual Outlaw*, p. 259, 1977

leather ass *noun*

in poker, the bodily manifestation of great patience *US, 1981*

- — Thomas L. Clark, *The Dictionary of Gambling and Gaming*, p. 117, 1987

leather bar *noun*

a bar with a homosexual clientele whose fashion sense is leather-oriented and whose sexual tastes are sadomasochistic *US, 1963*

- And there are, too, the "leather bars": black-jacketed mesh inside, moving pictures of young men wrestling realistically, murals of motorcyclists at a race[.] — John Rechy, *City of Night*, p. 192, 1963
- I forgot for a moment that we were both in a leather bar. — Phil Andros, *Stud*, p. 50, 1966
- It's a typical leather bar, one of those supermasculine hangouts for people in armor and in revolt against everything in the world that might be thought of as feminine. — Angelo d'Arcangelo, *The Homosexual Handbook*, p. 137, 1968
- Afterwards, one of the members of our group wanted to be driven across town to be dropped off for the evening at a gay leather bar[.] — Jefferson Poland and Valerie Alison, *The Records of the San Francisco Sexual Freedom League*, p. 149, 1971

leather boy *noun*

a homosexual with a leather fetish *UK, 1963*

- It is also noted for its male prostitutes, leather boys and drag queens who populate the district around Forty-fifth Street. — Bruce Porter, *Blow*, p. 12, 1993

leather daddy *noun*

a male homosexual with a sadistic/masochistic fetish *US, 1991*

- Dominant Topman, a real Leather Daddy, GWM, enjoys exciting scenes. — *alt.personals*, 3rd October 1991
- "Well, I didn't get buttfucked by a buncha SM leatherdaddies doing bloodsports and shootin' up all night." — Lynn Breedlove, *Godspeed*, p. 102, 2002

leather fag *noun*

a male homosexual whose predilection for sadomasochism is manifested in leather clothing *US, 1994*

- [H]e had a pair of suspenders, leather, that made him look like a leather fag. — Michelle Tea, *The Passionate Mistakes and Intricate Corruption of One Girl in America*, p. 63, 1998

leather freak *noun*

a homosexual with a leather fetish *US, 1969*

- The militants feel the film negatively stereotypes gay male sex culture as nothing more than a bunch of crazed fist-fucking S&M leather freaks performing violent sex in the backrooms of creepy dimly-lit bars across America. — Brendan Mullen, *Lexicon Devil*, p. 292, 2002

leather hustler *noun*

a male prostitute willing to engage in sadomasochistic sex *US, 1994*

- The most important thing in being a leather hustler, he explained to me, was the costuming. — John Preston, *Hustling*, pp. 25–25, 1994

leather man *noun*

a male homosexual involved in sadomasochism *US, 1994*

- Not many men who were attracted to my self-description as a leather man would call for anything other than some version of S/M. — John Preston, *Hustling*, p. 162, 1994

leatherneck *noun*

a US Marine *US, 1890*
Possibly from an earlier usage as "Royal Marine" (a **BOOTNECK**); ultimately from a leather collar, part of the historical uniform of both services.

- They came from opposite sides of the Missouri-Pacific tracks, the hayseed asthmatic and the merchant's leatherneck son. — Joe Eszterhas, *Charlie Simpson's Apocalypse*, p. 77, 1973

Leatherneck Square *nickname*

four US Marine bases in South Vietnam that formed a quadrilateral *US, 1976*

- Patrols were keyed to debris left over from the hot summers of '67 and '68—days when Leatherneck Square was filled with battles[.] — Charles Anderson, *The Grunts*, p. 161, 1976
- They coined a phrase, "Leatherneck Square," for the area we worked in—Dong Ha, Quang Tri, Hue, Cam Lo—the DMZ—all up north. — Al Santoli, *To Bear Any Burden*, p. 134, 1985

leather queen *noun*

a homosexual with a leather fetish *US, 1972*

- Wealthy and perfectly coiffed men sauntered to their seats with leather queens and drag queens and lesbians in fashionable attire. — Randy Shilts, *And the Band Played On*, p. 282, 1988

leave *verb*

▸ **leave seeds**
to impregnate *US, 1998*

- — Ethan Hilderbrant, *Prison Slang*, p. 81, 1998

lee-gate *verb*

to peep *US, 1975*

- I didn't mind a guy lee-gating (peeping). — Edwin Torres, *Carlito's Way*, p. 12, 1975

leet *noun*

an Internet user who is categorized, often self-categorized, as "elite" *US, 1998*
A reduction of "elite"; used (especially on bulletin-boards) as an antonym for **LAMER**.

- The "leet" (the elite, or most accomplished hackers) boast about the hundreds of "boxes" (computers) they have successfully broken into. — *San Francisco Chronicle*, p. A19, 27th April 1998

leet talk; leet; l33t; leet speak; l33t 5p34k *noun*

a written slang used for Internet and text communications in which numerals and nonalphabet characters replace letters *US, 2001*
After **LEET** (an "elite" Internet user).

- Leet Talk/Leet Speak. L33t, d00d. Online vocabulary using shortened versions of words, phonetic and numbers in place of letters [...] In it's [sic] most extreme form "leet speak" would look like this: "133+ 543/-\1<." — Chris McCubbin, *Anarchy Online*, back matter, 2001
- Leet speak is a very flexible language, meaning that there are several ways to spell the same word. — *Anchorage (Alaska) Daily News*, p. F6, 19th March 2004

left field noun

▸ **out of left field**

unexpected, unforeseen, from nowhere US, 1946

- So, I had this thought and—it may seem like it's way out of left field. — *American Pie*, 1999

left-handed adjective

homosexual US, 1929

- — Helen Dahlskog (Editor), *A Dictionary of Contemporary and Colloquial Usage*, p. 37, 1972

left-handed cigarette noun

a marijuana cigarette US, 1989

- I asked what did he mean wacky tobacco. Left-handed cigarettes. Boo-shit-tea. — Larry Brown, *Dirty Work*, p. 16, 1989
- When we got in their car, Marvin pulled out one of those "left-handed cigarettes" and lit it. — Odie Hawkins, *The Life and Times of Chester Simmons*, p. 156, 1991

lefty; leftie noun

a political left-winger UK, 1939

- But this slum is permitted to remain behind the Capitol only so the lefties will have something to breast-beat over. — Jack Lait and Lee Mortimer, *Washington Confidential*, pp. 38–39, 1951

lefty; leftie adjective

politically left-wing, liberal UK, 1939

- There were plenty of red-diaper babies—children of commie parents—in lefty politics at Berkeley, but I was not among them. — Robert Cohen, *The Free Speech Movement*, p. 185, 2002

leg noun

1 sex; women as sex objects US, 1966
The functional equivalent of "ass."

- They were loaded and they wanted to get off some leg, but it just got to be too many guys. — Hunter S. Thompson, *Hell's Angels*, p. 16, 1966
- Them cats wearing themselves out on some broad that couldn't do nuthin' but give up a little leg is crazy. — Joseph Nazel, *Black Cop*, p. 96, 1974
- I mean, shit, let's face it, the naughtiest thing I've done in twenty four years is to give a dude some leg without using a condom. — Odie Hawkins, *Great Lawd Buddha*, p. 88, 1990
- A place like college—all that leg around campus—you should be sowing your wild oats. — *Mallrats*, 1995

2 a straight-leg or infantry soldier US, 1964

- "He's a 'leg' but he's trying to be honest." The last is a reference to my being a nonjumper[.] — Donald Duncan, *The New Legions*, p. 118, 1967
- We sit around practicing with the guns while the "legs" walk all day. — David Parks, *GI Diary*, p. 37, 1968
- If I was President and had my way / There wouldn't be a leg in the Army today. — Sandee Johnson, *Cadences: The Jody Call Book, No. 2*, p. 127, 1986
- Even within the services there are rivalries, such as the distinction between the airborne Army soldiers who jump out of airplanes and the "legs"—soldiers who don't. — *Houston Chronicle*, p. 15, 24th January 1991

▸ **around the leg**

currying favor with prison administration US, 1989

- — James Harris, *A Convict's Dictionary*, p. 36, 1989

▸ **give someone leg**

to tease someone US, 1971

- "Hey," Dillon said, "remember last time I saw you, you're giving me a little leg about there's nothing going on?" — George V. Higgins, *The Friends of Eddie Doyle*, p. 79, 1971

leg verb

to shoplift by hiding merchandise between your legs under a skirt US, 1972

- Stuff I legged [boosted by hiding it between her legs under her skirt]. — Bruce Jackson, *In the Life*, p. 93, 1972

▸ **leg a hand**

in poker, to reserve the right to make a bet even though the player has a good hand US, 1979

- — John Scarne, *Scarne's Guide to Modern Poker*, p. 283, 1979

leg-breaker noun

a paid thug US, 1975

- He was also wondering what attracted her to an old former mobster, a killer and leg-breaker[.] — Margaret Truman, *Murder at Union Station*, p. 211, 2004

leggins noun

the rubbing of the penis between the thighs of another man until reaching orgasm US, 1934

- [I]n leggins men reach ejaculation from the insertion of the penis between one another's legs in a face-to-face, usually horizontal, position. — *New York Mattachine Newsletter*, p. 6, June 1961

leggy noun

a cord attached to a surfer and their surfboard US, 1987

- — Mitch McKissick, *Surf Lingo*, 1987

legit noun

▸ **on the legit**

legitimate; legitimately US, 1930

- Once Side got a shipment of a hundred cases of booze on the legit, and that's when he showed up as nervous as some jello-pudding. — Mezz Mezzrow, *Really the Blues*, p. 21, 1946
- "Nope, I made a killing, and it was strictly on the legit," Phil said emphasizing his words with a slicker gesture. — James T. Farrell, *Saturday Night*, p. 32, 1947

legit adjective

legitimate UK, 1909

- Just before the war he went legit. — Mickey Spillane, *Kiss Me Deadly*, p. 60, 1952
- If she's legit, Lucky Luciano was in the paper-bag business. — Bernard Wolfe, *The Late Risers*, p. 274, 1954
- I don't mean the celebs and the legit high rollers, he's got to take care of them and he loves it. — Elmore Leonard, *Glitz*, p. 119, 1985
- You gotta go legit, at least for a minute. — Terry Williams, *The Cocaine Kids*, p. 86, 1989

legits noun

dice that have not been altered US, 1977

- — Robert C. Prus and C.R.D. Sharper, *Road Hustler*, p. 170, 1977: "Glossary of terms"

legman noun

an assistant who does the leg work US, 1923

- "Ronnie's a nice guy. No legmen ... gets all his own items." — Jacqueline Susann, *Valley of the Dolls*, p. 45, 1966

lego noun

an infantry soldier, not attached to an airborne division US, 1971

- — Ronald J. Glasser, *365 Days*, p. 243, 1971

leg piece noun

a dance performance in which the female dancers are scantily dressed or naked US, 1973

- — Sherman Louis Sergel, *The Language of Show Biz*, p. 15, 1973
- — Don Wilmeth, *The Language of American Popular Entertainment*, p. 158, 1981

legs noun

1 in the entertainment industry, staying power and continuing popularity US, 1978

- Yeah, I know we lost the bullet, spins are down slightly, but that record still has legs, man. — Elmore Leonard, *Be Cool*, p. 106, 1999

2 the duration of the intoxication from a central nervous system stimulant US, 1989

- Either the speed "has good legs" or it "doesn't have legs." — Geoffrey Froner, *Digging for Diamonds*, p. 41, 1989

3 (of a shot in pool) momentum, force US, 1835

- — Mike Shamos, *The Illustrated Encyclopedia of Billiards*, p. 135, 1993

leg show noun

1 a stage performance featuring bare-legged female dancers UK, 1882

- Not leg shows, either; Dad's favorite playwright, after Shakespeare, was Bernard Shaw. — Mary McCarthy, *The Group*, p. 58, 1963

2 a striptease show US, 2004

- Like all leg shows, as they were called, the Star had a buzzer system to warn the girls if cops were in the house. — Phil Stanford, *Portland Confidential*, p. 59, 2004

leg-spreader noun

a military aviator's wings insignia US, 1967
The suggestion is that women find fliers sexually irresistible.

- "Women are just impressed with these fliers. There's a reason those wings they wear are known as leg spreaders." — Harry Stein, *The Girl Watchers Club*, p. 83, 2004

lemac *noun*

a Camel™ cigarette *US, 1989*

- Reverse spelling. — James Harris, *A Convict's Dictionary*, p. 33, 1989

lemon *noun*

1 a heavily diluted narcotic *US, 1952*

- He handed me a lemon and I went looking for him. There wasn't nothing in the stuff but sugar[.] — Hal Ellson, *The Golden Spike*, pp. 150–151, 1952
- Then he walks off with two bags of junk and the money, and I got two empty bags—two lemons in my pocket! — John Gimenez, *Up Tight!*, p. 52, 1967
- You the fourth cat who been in here lookin' for that stud. He sellin' lemons again? — Nathan Heard, *Howard Street*, p. 117, 1968
- "Six pushers with the weakest bags in Harlem," Jackie said bitterly. "They might as well be lemons." — Robert Deane Pharr, *S.R.O.*, p. 346, 1971

2 in pool, a person who loses intentionally *US, 1990*

- — Steve Rushin, *Pool Cool*, p. 19, 1990

3 a light-skinned black person *US, 1970*

- — Clarence Major, *Dictionary of Afro-American Slang*, p. 76, 1970

lemon 714 *noun*

a tablet of the recreational drug methaqualone, best known as Quaaludes™ *US, 1993*

Quaaludes™ were originally manufactured by Rorer, and were stamped "Rorer 714." Lemon eventually bought the patent from Rorer, continuing the "714" stamp. Virtually all pills stamped with "714" today are counterfeit.

- — Peter Johnson, *Dictionary of Street Alcohol and Drug Terms*, p. 109, 1993
- A later brand: Lemon 714. It was like achieving the perfect drunken state without the sick feeling or hangover with the mere pop of a $10 pill. — Editors of Ben is Dead, *Retrohell*, p. 169, 1997

lemonade *noun*

1 poor quality heroin *US, 1957*

Often shortened to "lemon."

- "Son-of-a-bitch sold me some lemonade," Scat said. — Herbert Simmons, *Corner Boy*, p. 55, 1957
- Francis J. Rigney and L. Douglas Smith, *The Real Bohemia*, p. xx, 1961: Glossary of Beat Terms
- — Sidney Cohen, *The Drug Dilemma*, p. 129, 1969

2 manipulating play on which money is bet *US, 1972*

- But using partners and pulling dumps and double dumps and all that stuff—the lemonade it is called—is bunco, real con. — Robert Byrne, *McGoorty*, p. 32, 1972

lemonade *verb*

in poolroom betting, to miss a shot or lose a game intentionally *US, 1967*

- By "stalling" (deliberately missing some shots, leaving himself out of position, etc.) and by "lemoning" or "lemonading" an occasional game in the session (winning in a deliberately sloppy and seemingly lucky manner, or deliberately losing the game), the hustler keeps his opponent on the work. — Ned Polsky, *Hustlers, Beats, and Others*, pp. 56–57, 1967
- I was on the losing end one time when someone else was lemonading. — Robert Byrne, *McGoorty*, p. 32, 1972

lemonade *adjective*

(of drugs), impure, adulterated, low quality *US, 1972*

- A friend of mine whom I copped from all the time had scored some lemonade reefer[.] — John Sinclair, *Guitar Army*, p. 192, 1972

lemon drop *noun*

a birth control pill *US, 1970*

- — *Current Slang*, p. 9, Winter 1970

lemon player *noun*

a person who plays lemon pool *US, 1969*

- No, I doubt it, although sometimes two lemon players will pretend to be bitter rivals and play each other while a third and maybe a fourth member of the team will lay bets among the onlookers. — Iceberg Slim (Robert Beck), *Mama Black Widow*, pp. 157–158, 1969

lemon pool *noun*

a pool swindle in which a skilled player lets an opponent win until high stakes are bet and then wins, making it look like he was extremely lucky *US, 1969*

- "Soldier, what is lemon pool?" He said, "Little Brother, it's cue stick con played by a shark who never lets the sucker know his true ability." — Iceberg Slim (Robert Beck), *Mama Black Widow*, p. 157, 1969

lemon pop *noun*

a piece of plastic or thin metal used to slip between the molding and the top of the window on push-button locking cars, from which a loop of dental floss is dropped over the post on the door and yanked to open the door *US, 1996*

- He told them he'd spot the car a customer wanted and use a slim jim or lemon pop to get in, a slap hammer to yank the ignition, a side kick to extract steering column locks and usually liquid nitrogen to freeze the alarm system. — Elmore Leonard, *Out of Sight*, p. 56, 1996

lens *noun*

a dose of LSD; LSD *US, 1994*

- — US Department of Justice, *Street Terms*, October 1994

lens louse *noun*

a person who is prone to working their way into a photograph *US, 1928*

- His enjoyment of the limelight played into his marketing of his favorite woman pilot and caused reporters to dub him "the lens louse," since whenever they sought a picture of Amelia, Putnam found a way to be included[.] — Lori Van Pelt, *Amelia Earhart*, p. 116, 2005

lergy; lerg *noun*

a completely nonexistent disease *US, 1947*

- — *American Speech*, p. 304, December 1947

▷ see: DREADED LURGI

les *noun*

a lesbian *US, 1952*

- "I'm coming up," the les shouted. — Chandler Brossard, *Who Walks in Darkness*, p. 187, 1952
- There are harsher and more widely used expressions: "Bulldyke," "Amy-John," "Cat-lapper," "Les," and so on. — L. Reinhard, *Oral Sex Techniques and Sex Practices Illustrated*, 1968

lesb *adjective*

lesbian *US, 1968*

- The leader of the lesb-pack, who has been off trying to capture the third girl, walks into camp just as the two are about to consummate the feelings aroused by the dance. — *Adam Film Quarterly*, p. 9, July 1968

lesbian bed death *noun*

a marked drop in libido experienced in some long-term lesbian relationships *US, 1994*

- Obviously, urban folklore tells us, you're suffering from that legendary affliction, Lesbian Bed Death. — *San Francisco Examiner*, p. C1, 20th October 1994
- Some comics call this phenomenon "lesbian bed death." While the phrase is politically incorrect in the extreme, many lesbians report that their experiences bear out the stereotype. — *Los Angeles Times*, p. E2, 31st January 2000

lesbie *noun*

a lesbian *US, 1974*

- "You think they're Lesbies?" — Anne Steinhardt, *Thunder La Boom*, p. 74, 1974

lesbo; lezbo *noun*

a lesbian *US, 1927*

- Ex-whore, ex-addict, ex-con, ex-lesbo. — Robert Deane Pharr, *Giveadamn Brown*, p. 69, 1978
- A fat white lezbo songbird would stick out, even in a pus pocket like T.J. — James Ellroy, *Hollywood Nocturnes*, p. 291, 1994
- I'm the lesbo. I used to live here until your daughter threw me out. — *Boys on the Side*, 1995
- A steady parade of fashion models, crack dealers, whore ladies, limp-wrists holding hands, tugboat lesbos holding hands[.] — Dan Jenkins, *The Money-Whipped Steer-Job Three-Jack Give-Up Artist*, p. 91, 2001

les girls *noun*

lesbians *US, 1982*

- — *Maledicta*, p. 132, Summer/Winter 1982: "Dyke diction: the language of lesbians"

lesionaire *noun*

an AIDS patient *US, 1988–1989*

Gallows-humor to an extreme.

- — *Maledicta*, p. 33, 1988–1989: "Medical maledicta from San Francisco"

lessie *noun*

a lesbian *US, 1938*

- "[S]he whispers to me she's a lessie, hands me a five-dollar bill, and wants me to get her an instant girl friend." — Roger Blake, *Love Clubs, Inc.*, p. 143, 1967

- I dun' play that there; that's for faggots and sissies, lessies and dykes. — Steve Cannon, *Groove, Bang, and Jive Around*, p. 46, 1969

letch; lech *noun*
a sudden, powerful sexual urge *UK, 1796*

- In his ten years of marriage he had, like any red-blooded American boy, had an occasional letch for a woman other than his wife. — Max Shulman, *Rally Round the Flag, Boys!*, p. 100, 1957

let it lay!
forget about it! *US, 1947*

- — Marcus Hanna Boulware, *Jive and Slang of Students in Negro Colleges*, 1947

let's squirm, worm
used as an invitation to dance *US, 1945*

- — Lou Shelly, *Hepcats Jive Talk Dictionary*, p. 28, 1945

let's talk trash
used as a formulaic greeting *US, 1951*

- — *Philadelphia Evening Bulletin*, 11th November 1951

letterbomb *noun*
a piece of e-mail with features that will disrupt the computers of some or all recipients *US, 1991*

- — Eric S. Raymond, *The New Hacker's Dictionary*, p. 221, 1991

letter from home *noun*
a black African *US, 1972*

- — *American Speech*, p. 154, Spring–Summer 1972: "An approach to black slang"

letterhack *noun*
a fan who corresponds with many other fans *US, 1978*

- — *American Speech*, p. 53, Spring 1978: "Star trek lives: trekker slang"

letterzine *noun*
a fan magazine that only publishes letters *US, 1976*

- — *American Speech*, p. 53, Spring 1978: "Star trek lives: trekker slang"

lettuce *noun*
money, especially paper money *US, 1903*

- "Close to three bills, Curt. That's a nice chunk of lettuce." — Curt Cannon, *The Death of Me*, p. 97, 1953
- After taxes Jack had just enough lettuce to buy himself an old cow. — Steve Allen, *Bop Fables*, p. 68, 1955
- All I looked at was the lettuce while I sipped a beer. — Red Rudensky, *The Gonif*, p. 96, 1970
- "The natural look will make ya more lettuce than a face palette." — J.T. LeRoy, *Sarah*, p. 18, 2000

levels *noun*
legitimate, square, unaltered dice *US, 1950*

- — *The Annals of the American Academy of Political and Social Sciences*, p. 127, May 1950

Lex *nickname*
the Federal Narcotics Hospital in Lexington, Kentucky *US, 1960*

- I'm not a junkie. Lexi is for junkies. I ain't hooked. — Clarence Cooper Jr., *The Scene*, p. 100, 1960
- Carver would probably be shipped off to Lex ... hooked in the line of duty. — Malcolm Braly, *Shake Him Till He Rattles*, p. 166, 1963
- I think Lex [Lexington—the Federal narcotics hospital/prison] did that for me. — Bruce Jackson, *In the Life*, p. 122, 1972

lez *noun*
a lesbian *US, 1929*

- "I wonder if she's a lez," Danny is saying. — John Rechy, *Numbers*, p. 63, 1967
- It turned out she wasn't really a lez. I mean, at least not as far as making it with me was concerned. — Joey V., *Portrait of Joey*, p. 112, 1969
- "I want to use Arabell for the lez," said Boris. "Can you get her?" — Terry Southern, *Blue Movie*, p. 73, 1970

lez *adjective*
lesbian *US, 1969*

- Few, if any, are the cities of sizable population which do not have their "homo" or "lez" bars[.] — W.D. Sprague, *Sexual Rebellion in the Sixties*, p. 70, 1965
- I quit working for this outfit when the bad shit that was coming down became too much to take—a friend of the theater-owner, whose apartment we were using to film a lez flick—attacked one of the other chicks as she was leaving the pad. — *The Berkeley Tribe*, p. 9, 22th-28th August 1969

- She'll lick Levenson's perineum, but she scruples at lez cunt-sucking. — Josh Alan Friedman, *Tales of Times Square*, p. 121, 1989

lez out *verb*
to act in an overtly masculine or lesbian fashion *US, 2004*

- I just figured a two-girl call and you'd have to lez out for them. — Michelle Tea, *Rent Girl*, p. 85, 2004

lezzie; lezzy *noun*
a lesbian *US, 1938*
Usually offensive.

- Lezzy, dike, queer—the pejoratives are heard, but they are out of context, they are simple descriptive words, devoid of contempt and scorn[.] — Donald Webster Cory, *The Lesbian in America*, p. 209, 1964
- Or you get two love-bird lezzies together, and you get a few drinks in them and they want that dough[.] — Roger Blake, *The Porno Movies*, p. 176, 1970
- Butch looks up through bloodshot eyes—was the lezzie scene worth losing five grand for? — Josh Alan Friedman, *Tales of Times Square*, p. 121, 1986
- To Iris it was like playing a trick on her extended family, sneaking her lezzie girlfriend in under their noses. — Michelle Tea, *Valencia*, p. 87, 2000

lezzy *adjective*
lesbian *US, 1969*

- Maybe because she was a little on the lezzy side. — Joey V., *Portrait of Joey*, p. 83, 1969

liar's bench *noun*
a sofa in front of a country store *US, 1963*

- — Charles F. Haywood, *Yankee Dictionary*, p. 99, 1963

libber *noun*
a feminist *US, 1970*
From "Woman's Liberation" as the name for the feminist movement of the late 1960s.

- It didn't want me want to burn my bra—but it did send me back to those early women's libbers who said it all so much better: Ibsen and Shaw. — *New York Times*, 10th May 1970
- "Probably a libber," said Rose Rules. — Joseph Wambaugh, *The Choirboys*, p. 319, 1975
- "I'll get you later," he hissed menacingly, marking them as dykes or libbers from the way they screamed. — Alix Shulman, *On the Stroll*, p. 127, 1981
- They said these complaints were ridiculous. He was a fine person and we were a bunch of women's libbers. — *Seattle Times*, p. A1, 15th December 2003

libe; libes *noun*
a library *US, 1915*

- — Collin Baker et al., *College Undergraduate Slang Study Conducted at Brown University*, p. 151, 1968

liberate *verb*
1 to steal *US, 1944*
Coined in irony by US soldiers during World War 2, and then recycled by the political and cultural left of the 1960s.

- [T]he lousy slob ratted on me to the M.P.'s about liberating 10 grand of some kraut's gold hoard back in '45[.] — Mickey Spillane, *Me, Hood!*, p. 15, 1963
- Scavenger Corps and Transport Gang is responsible for garbage collection and the picking up and delivery of items to the various services, as well as liberating anything they think useful for one project or another. — *The Digger Papers*, p. 15, August 1968
- Stew and I liberated their last few copies. — Jerry Rubin, *Do It!*, p. 61, 1970
- In the rear of the Frederick Street Free Frame of Reference was the free store, brimming over with liberated goods to be shared with whoever needed them. — Emmett Grogan, *Ringolevio*, p. 266, 1972

2 to take control of *US, 1968*

- The news comes in that Avery Hall, the architecture school, has been liberated. We mark it as such on Grayson's map. — James Simon Kunen, *The Strawberry Statement*, p. 33, 1968

liberated *adjective*
free from narrow, conventional thinking *US, 1970*

- New Left women are of a different stripe. They're "liberated." What they've liberated themselves from are their mother's apron strings and also their mother's moral hypocrisy. — William Tulio Divale, *I Lived Inside the Campus Revolution*, p. 76, 1970

It's not very liberated, I know—I want a husband with a decent job, you know. — *Boys on the Side*, 1995

liberation *noun*
1 theft in the name of a cause *US*, 1970
Said either with irony or a complete lack of humor, depending on the self-righteousness of the speaker.

- Needless to say, we stole where we could, calling it "liberation of urgently-needed materials" and we left many bills unpaid. — Raymond Mungo, *Famous Long Ago*, p. 34, 1970

2 left-wing politics *US*, 1968

- We are on strike, of course. There are "liberation classes" but the scene is essentially no more pencils, no more books. — James Simon Kunen, *The Strawberry Statement*, p. 46, 1968

liberty *noun*
a twenty-five-cent piece *US*, 1947
From the inscription on the coin.

- — Marcus Hanna Boulware, *Jive and Slang of Students in Negro Colleges*, 1947

liberty act *noun*
in the circus, an act in which horses perform without riders *US*, 1973

- — Sherman Louis Sergel, *The Language of Show Biz*, p. 125, 1973

liberty hound *noun*
a sailor on shore leave *US*, 1939

- "You two liberty hounds decided that these California split-tails and the good times are more important than your duty[.]" — Charles Henderson, *Silent Warrior*, p. 25, 2000

lice bin *noun*
a dirty, unsanitary place *US*, 1971

- That's why I'm in this lice bin. — Tom Robbins, *Another Roadside Attraction*, p. 15, 1971

license *noun*
freedom to break the law in an area by virtue of having bribed the police *US*, 1967

- — Hyman E. Goldin et al., *Dictionary of American Underworld Lingo*, p. 24, 1950
- [W]e pay for them to work, your people give them their license to work. — Richard Condon, *Prizzi's Honor*, p. 217, 1982

lick *noun*
1 a liquor store *US*, 1993

- "Let's got peep a lick, Salt," Little Rock said, using street slang for casing a liquor store to rob. — Bob Sipchen, *Baby Insane and the Buddha*, p. 197, 1993

2 a musical phrase *UK*, 1932

- Many of the younger social and diplomatic sets get a bang out of hot licks. — Jack Lait and Lee Mortimer, *Washington Confidential*, p. 17, 1951
- Some big symphony trumpet player came up and asked me how I done it, said I was doing everything all wrong, but playing licks he couldn't play himself. — Ross Russell, *The Sound*, p. 196, 1961

3 a robbery *US*, 1991

- "I do jewelry licks. I go in jewelry stores, jack 'em up, go sell the jewelry." — Leon Bing, *Do or Die*, p. 33, 1991
- Smith admitted he heard Stroud and others planning "a lick" (street slang for robbery) at a white house in the country after Payne was at a house in the 1700 block of South Walnut Street. — *South Bend (Indiana) Tribune*, p. D1, 16th July 2002
- "Man," Huckabuck says, "we gotta hit a lick so we can buy better guns." — Colton Simpson, *Inside the Crips*, p. 34, 2005

lick *verb*
to shoot and kill *US*, 1994

- Two women with Brockington told police he had asked them if they had seen the TV news and told them that he and two other men had "licked" the brother of the girl killed near Tamarind Avenue last year[.] — *Palm Beach (Florida) Post*, p. 1B, 15th September 1994

lick-box *noun*
a person who performs oral sex on women *US*, 1949

- — Vincent J. Monteleone, *Criminal Slang*, p. 144, 1949

lickety-split *adverb*
speedily, headlong *US*, 1831
In recognizable variations from 1831 and uncertain spelling from 1848.

- They couldn't drive lickety-split all day and see everything they should see. — Jim Thompson, *After Dark, My Sweet*, p. 63, 1955

licorice stick *noun*
a clarinet *US*, 1935

- She called his clarinet a "licorice stick." Was she corny. — J.D. Salinger, *Catcher in the Rye*, p. 75, 1951
- Well, a-reading, writing, arithmetic / Taught to the tune of a licorice stick / No education is ever complete / Without a boogie-woogie-woogie beat[.] — Bill Haley, *ABC Boogie*, 1954

lid *noun*
1 a hat *US*, 1896

- "May I take your hat?" I snapped out of it long enough to hand over my lid. — Mickey Spillane, *I, The Jury*, p. 63, 1947
- "We don't want to be around when old Mushmouth comes after his lid." — Jim Thompson, *Bad Boy*, p. 363, 1953
- The kid with the lid and the proper dark glasses, will soon dig which chick will go for the passes. — Dan Burley, *Diggeth Thou?*, p. 7, 1959
- He was always pressed; nothing but the best / Vines and kicks he had / A thirty-dollar lid and gloves of kid / Man his threads were bad. — Dennis Wepman et al., *The Life*, p. 97, 1976

2 an approximate measure (variously twenty-two grams, or one to two ounces) of loose, uncleaned marijuana *US*, 1966
Derived from the lid of a tobacco tin, a convenient measure of sufficient marijuana to roll about forty cigarettes.

- The fact that I make more money than the cat who sells one lid of grass a week—now, that's his choice and this is my choice. — Leonard Wolfe (Editor), *Voices from the Love Generation*, 1968
- The kidnappings were nothing fancy: a young surfer at the Pompano Pier, lured to a waiting Cadillac with a lid of fresh Colombian red[.] — Carl Hiaasen, *Tourist Season*, p. 178, 1986
- The $10 lid was fading into the '60s, to be replaced by Bud and Thai stick — Editors Ben is Dead, *Retrohell*, p. 60, 1997
- He hit you with lids, caps, keys, tabs, nickel bags, blotters, buttons, spoons and everything from milligrams to boatloads. — Robert Sabbag, *A Way with the Spoon [The Howard Marks Book of Dope Stories]*, p. 351, 1998

3 the maximum prison sentence allowed by law *US*, 1993

- "Give him the lid," Peed said. "I'm not sure that's a good idea, Garland," Brise said. "His priors don't add up." — Bob Sipchen, *Baby Insane and the Buddha*, p. 377, 1993

4 in a card game, the top card of the deck *US*, 1988

- — George Percy, *The Language of Poker*, p. 52, 1988

lid-lifter *noun*
the first game of a season *US*, 1991
The image evoked is of a cook lifting the lid off a pot to see how a dish is turning out.

- The Twins' Dave Engle homered down the leftfield line in the first inning of the lid-lifter. — *Sports Illustrated*, p. 53, 19th April 1982

lid-poppers *noun*
an amphetamine or other central nervous system stimulant *US*, 1971

- — Eugene Landy, *The Underground Dictionary*, p. 119, 1971
- — Ralph de Sola, *Crime Dictionary*, p. 84, 1982

lid-propper *noun*
an amphetamine or other central nervous system stimulant *US*, 1967

- — John B. Williams, *Narcotics and Hallucinogenics*, p. 114, 1967

lie *verb*
to talk *US*, 1973

- We ain't doing nothin' 'cept sittin around an doin' some LYIN'. — Malachi Andrews and Paul T. Owens, *Black Language*, p. 95, 1973

lie box *noun*
a polygraph *US*, 1955

- According to the warden, the entire jail staff volunteered to take polygraph tests to clear themselves. The first "liebox" casualties were two jail guards[.] — Ovid Demaris, *Captive City*, p. 17, 1969
- Eventually we may end up sitting on the lie box. It's better not to have discussed such things. — Gerald Petievich, *Money Men*, p. 121, 1981

lie down *verb*
in pool, to play below your skill level to lure strangers into playing against you for money *US*, 1993

- — Mike Shamos, *The Illustrated Encyclopedia of Billiards*, p. 136, 1993

lieut; loot *noun*
a lieutenant *US*, 1759

- Ordinarily, a loot wouldn't bother with anything so trivial, but Roberts was bucking for captain[.] — Malcolm Braley, *False Starts*, p. 186, 1976

- "Talk slow, the loot is an edgy type." Lloyd took a deep breath and spoke into the mouthpiece. "Lieutenant, this is Hopkins[.]" — James Ellroy, *Because the Night*, p. 392, 1984
- Telephone for the lieut. — Robert Campbell, *Sweet La-La Land*, p. 237, 1990

lieuty *noun*
a lieutenant *US, 1998*
- It was OK that I couldn't tell him much about anything he understood, having been just a "leg," hahaha. That's what his buddy, this second lieuty, calls infantrymen. — Clarence Major, *All-Night Visitors*, p. 175, 1998

life *noun*

▶ **have a life; get a life**
to enjoy a well-rounded life including work, family, friends, and interests *US, 1995*
- How come he's not making this trek down memory lane? Or does he have a life? — *Boys on the Side*, 1995

▶ **in the life**
homosexual *US, 1981*
- — Donald Webster Cory and John P. LeRoy, *The Homosexual and His Society*, p. 265, 1963: "A lexicon of homosexual slang"
- — *Male Swinger Number 3*, p. 46, 1981: "The complete gay dictionary"

▶ **the life**
1 the criminal lifestyle; the lifestyle of prostitution *US, 1916*
- If a good gal—a sweethearted dame who had no stomach for the life—had started living with Paul, I'd have objected. — Philip Wylie, *Opus 21*, p. 297, 1949
- Willie was in the life and he couldn't return to gigging (working) everyday, so through friends he began to sell a little pot to make ends meet. — Babs Gonzales, *I Paid My Dues*, p. 96, 1967
- The hardest thing for me was leaving the life. I still love the life. We were treated like movie stars with muscle. — *Goodfellas*, 1990
- VINCENT: So you're serious, you're really gonna quit? JULES: The life, most definitely. — *Pulp Fiction*, 1994
2 the business and lifestyle of professional wrestling *US, 1999*
- It was rough at first, leaving the life, but DiBiase persevered. — *World of Wrestling Magazine*, p. 7, June 1999

lifeboat *noun*
release from prison as a result of parole board action or a commutation of sentence *US, 1908*
- — Vincent J. Monteleone, *Criminal Slang*, p. 144, 1949
- — Marlene Freedman, *Alcatraz*, 1983

life jacket *noun*
a condom *US, 1989*
Safe sex saves lives.
- — Pamela Munro, *U.C.L.A. Slang*, p. 55, 1989
- — Kevin DiIallo, *The Unofficial Gay Manual*, p. 242, 1994

life on the installment plan *noun*
a series of prison sentences with brief periods of freedom between, which have the cumulative effect of a life sentence *US, 1949*
- — Vincent J. Monteleone, *Criminal Slang*, p. 145, 1949
- Big Bird is a jailhouse lawyer who is also doing Life on the Installment Plan. — Jimmy Lerner, *You Got Nothing Coming*, p. 243, 2002

lifer *noun*
1 a career member of the armed forces *US, 1962*
- There was a lifer in San Diego who was dumped for indebtedness. — Darryl Ponicsan, *The Last Detail*, p. 13, 1970
- And they played songs like "Good Night Irene" and "I Wonder Who's Kissing Her Now" and "I Love You a Bushel and a Peck"—music nobody ever heard of but the gray-headed lifers. — Larry Heinemann, *Paco's Story*, p. 12, 1986
- A collection of "Lifers"; what the hell was I doing there, a reluctant draftee? — Odie Hawkins, *Men Friends*, p. 58, 1989
- Having served in Korea as a dogface grant, he knew a lifer when he saw one. — Joseph Wambaugh, *Finnegan's Week*, p. 27, 1993
2 a drug addict *US, 1971*
- — Eugene Landy, *The Underground Dictionary*, p. 120, 1971

lifer dog *noun*
a career member of the military *US, 1989*
- "I'm talking about some big time, lifer dog case of the butt." — Raul Correa, *I Don't Know But I've Been Told*, p. 27, 2002

lift *noun*
the act of shoplifting *US, 1971*
- I don't want to go on the lift. Not today, please. — Bernard Wolfe, *The Magic of Their Singing*, p. 25, 1961

liftbird *noun*
any troop transport plane *US, 1982*
Vietnam war usage.
- An officer from 4/3 walked over, asking for Downey, and said, "Your lift birds should be coming in about an hour." — Keith William Nolan, *Into Laos*, p. 187, 1986

lifted *adjective*
drug-intoxicated *US, 1942*
- Man I got to get high before I can have a haircut. I got to get lifted before I can face it! — John Clellon Holmes, *The Horn*, p. 35, 1958

lift-one-drag-one *noun*
a person with a pronounced limp *US, 1997*
- The labels were cruel: Gimp, Limpy–go-fetch, Crip, Lift-one-drag one, etc. Pint, Half-a-man, Peewee, Shorty, Lardass, Pork, Blubber, Belly, Blimp. Nuke-knob, Skinhead, Baldy. Four-eyes, Specs, Coke bottles. — *San Francisco Examiner*, p. A15, 28th July 1997

light *noun*
a tracer bullet *US, 1965*
- "I got light," Coffin Ed said. Grave Digger nodded in the dark and took out his long-barreled, nickelplated .38-caliber revolver and replaced the first three shells with tracer bullets. — Chester Himes, *Cotton Comes to Harlem*, p. 94, 1965

light *adjective*
1 short of funds, especially in the context of a payment owed *US, 1955*
- I had the infantile audacity to cheat. I dealt the Ace of Spades from the bottom of the deck; I stacked the cards, I went "light" in the stud poker pot. — Mario Puzo, *Inside Las Vegas*, p. 146, 1977
- He heard Ricky say, "You're still light," as the old man handed him money. — Elmore Leonard, *Glitz*, p. 172, 1985
2 in poker, owing chips to the collective bet on a hand *US, 1967*
- — Albert H. Morehead, *The Complete Guide to Winning Poker*, p. 267, 1967
3 (used of an arrest warrant) susceptible to attack by a skilled defense attorney *US, 1973*
- "A light one" meant an arrest affidavit prepared in such a way that a defense lawyer could easily pick holes in it and get the case thrown out. — Peter Maas, *Serpico*, p. 153, 1973
4 unarmed; without a weapon *US, 1974*
- He was walking light again. He was stupid, he told himself. Only a stupid cop would let a broad talk him out of his gun. — Joseph Nazel, *Black Cop*, p. 129, 1974

light artillery *noun*
1 the equipment needed to inject a drug *US, 1950*
- — Hyman E. Goldin et al., *Dictionary of American Underworld Lingo*, p. 125, 1950
2 beans *US, 1946*
- — *American Speech*, p. 89, April 1946: "The language of West Coast culinary workers"

light bird *noun*
a lieutenant colonel *US, 1974*
- "I'm looking for Major Lowell," the light bird said. — W.E.B. Griffin, *The Colonels*, p. 384, 1983

light, bright, damn near white; bright, white and dead white *adjective*
(used of a black person) very light-skinned *US, 1945*
- [S]ome stud said, "Light, bright and damn near white; how does that nigger do it?" — Chester Himes, *If He Hollers Let Him Go*, p. 43, 1945
- Hey, lots a spades runnin' with the ofay, making out they's jes bright white an dead right as old El Beejay. — Robert Gover, *JC Saves*, p. 69, 1968
- And always the one in charge was light, bright and almost white. — H. Rap Brown, *Die Nigger Die!*, p. 20, 1969
- "Tammy, you're light-bright-and-damn-near-white, so you're not going to bear witness to the truth." — Eric Jerome Dickey, *Cheaters*, p. 36, 1999

light colonel *noun*
a lieutenant colonel *US, 1954*
- While the old gent napped away the afternoons upstairs in the White House, a light colonel of Marines had run a secret government in the basement[.] — Richard Condon, *Prizzi's Glory*, p. 139, 1988

- It would mean that they have let poor Ollie, a lowly former light colonel, be a fall guy. — *Chicago Tribune*, p. C3, 26th April 1989
- Don Sheehan of Tewksbury is 71, a retired Air Force light colonel who served from 1956–1979. — *Lowell (Massachusetts) Sun*, 27th September 2003

lightem *noun*
crack cocaine *US, 1993*
Evocative of the urging "light 'em up."
- — Peter Johnson, *Dictionary of Street Alcohol and Drug Terms*, p. 116, 1993

lighter *noun*
a crewcut haircut *US, 1951*
Teen slang.
- — *Newsweek*, p. 28, 8th October 1951

light green *noun*
marijuana, especially inexpensive, low grade marijuana *US, 1973*
- After we checked in, I sent the bellboy out to cop some light green. — A.S. Jackson, *Gentleman Pimp*, p. 33, 1973

lighthouse *noun*
1 a lookout *US, 1971*
- The "wigwagger," also called a "lighthouse," was a lookout for police. — Charles Winick, *The Lively Commerce*, p. 122, 1971

2 in dominoes, a double played by a player who has no matching pieces *US, 1964*
- — Dominic Armanino, *Five-up Domino Games*, p. 3, 1964

light housekeeping *noun*
cohabitation as an unmarried couple *US, 1971*
- — Hermese E. Roberts, *The Third Ear*, 1971

light in the loafers *adjective*
homosexual *US, 1967*
A wonderful, old-fashioned euphemism.
- "Men of my group are either married or, as SP would say, 'light in the loafers.' Homosexuals, you would call them." — Helen Van Slyke, *No Love Lost*, p. 213, 1980
- "He was definitely light in the loafers." — Wally Lamb, *I Know This Much is True*, p. 365, 1998
- "Nah, unless my instincts have gone south, I pegged that guy for being light in the loafers." — Dixie Cash, *Since You're Leaving Anyway, Take Out the Trash*, p. 187, 2004

light load *noun*
a small-caliber handgun *US, 2006*
- "All we got is department-issued iron and a pocket full of light loads." — Stephen J. Cannell, *White Sister*, p. 219, 2006

lightly and politely *adverb*
with respect *US, 1933*
- We get checked over anyway, but lightly and politely, while sharing a bit of banter about the sort of contraband people might want to bring in. — Tara McCall, *This Is Not a Rave*, p. 7, 2001

lightning and thunder *noun*
whiskey and soda *US, 1945*
- — Lou Shelly, *Hepcats Jive Talk Dictionary*, p. 28, 1945

lightning bug *noun*
a helicopter equipped with a powerful search light or flares, usually teamed with several gunships *US, 1990*
- "Think the flares went up?" Myers asked. A lightning-bug mission involves loading up a Huey with a ridiculous number of aerial flares, whose job it is to be highly flammable. — Dennis Marvicsin and Jerold Greenfield, *Maverick*, p. 252, 1990

light off *verb*
1 to shoot *US, 1980*
- "Guy pulls out the Walther and lights one off at Kid Number One and misses him." — George Higgins, *Kennedy for the Defense*, p. 202, 1980

2 to experience an orgasm *US, 1971*
- The broad's great in the sack and she lights off real easy. — George V. Higgins, *The Friends of Eddie Doyle*, p. 132, 1971

light out *verb*
to leave, especially in a hurry *US, 1865*
- I stopped for a moment on the highway, put the top down and lit out. — Clancy Sigal, *Going Away*, pp. 187–188, 1961

light pipe *noun*
fiber optic cable *US, 1991*
- — Eric S. Raymond, *The New Hacker's Dictionary*, p. 222, 1991

lights *noun*
in poker, the chips owed by a player who bet without sufficient funds to back his bet *US, 1996*
- — Peter O. Steiner, *Thursday Night Poker*, p. 413, 1996

lights on but there's nobody home; lights on but nobody home
said of someone who appears to be normal but is empty-headed *US, 1980*
- I wish I could say the same for you. The lights are on, but nobody's home! — Robert Moore, *King, Warrior, Magician, Lover*, p. 148, 1990

lights out!
used to warn of the presence of police *US, 1997*
- Its progress throughout the neighborhood is marked by a steady escort of warning sounds: car alarms set off by drug lookouts, signals from teens on bikes, youthful cries of "Five-oh!" and "Lights out!"—street slang indicating cops are in the neighborhood. — *Chicago Tribune*, p. 1N, 24th May 1997

light up *verb*
1 to share drugs with others *US, 1922*
- I couldn't refuse to light my friends up. — Mezz Mezzrow, *Really the Blues*, p. 215, 1946

2 to shoot someone *US, 1967*
- Whichever way you come into it, they got you; any way you move they can light you up. — Ronald J. Glasser, *365 Days*, p. 41, 1971
- "I lit his ass up! I killed him—shot his baby in the leg—crippled his wife!" — Leon Bing, *Do or Die*, p. 43, 1991
- — Ann Lawson, *Kids & Gangs*, p. 56, 1994: "Common African-American gang slang/phrases"

light-up man *noun*
a gunman in a youth gang *US, 1959*
- There is usually a war counselor, an assistant war counselor, and occasionally a "light-up" man whose function is to carry the pistols and initiate the war by "shooting up" the rival gangs. — Earl Raab, *Major Social Problems*, p. 124, 1959
- A light-up man was responsible for the club's arsenal of weapons. — Sophia Robison, *Juvenile Delinquency*, p. 125, 1960
- Each division had its own officers including a president, vice-president, war counselor, and "light-up" man. — Lewis Yablonsky, *The Violent Gang*, p. 167, 1962
- Lightup Man—Street gang member whose job is doing the shooting. — James Haskins, *Street Gangs*, p. 149, 1974

lightweight *noun*
a person who is not taken as a serious threat *US, 1878*
- A guy's a lightweight, sooner or later it shows. He gets nervous, starts to look around; he thinks, Jesus Christ, maybe I'm over my head. — Elmore Leonard, *Gold Coast*, p. 15, 1981

like *verb*
▸ **like a price**
in horse racing, to hold a horse back from winning unless the odds on the horse are high *US, 1951*
- Sand Bag won't win in the fifth; his stable likes a price, and he is running at even money. — David W. Maurer, *Argot of the Racetrack*, p. 40, 1951

like
used for reducing the specificity, precision or certainty of what is being said, e.g., "could you like help me?" *US, 1950*
In the wake of disaster, use of "like" all but disappears. Linguist Geoffrey Nunberg first observed this after shootings at a San Diego high school in March 2001, and language columnist Jan Freeman of the *Boston Globe* made the same observation after the terrorist attacks in New York and Washington on 11th September 2001. There is no need for distance in certain situations.
- Know what Louie says about Be-bop? Like-anybody can play mistakes; it's what Louie says, so it must be like-true; right, doll? — George Mandel, *Flee the Angry Strangers*, p. 261, 1952
- "Buster," said Red gratefully, "your timing was like the end, ya know?" — Steve Allen, *Bop Fables*, p. 49, 1955

- For example, the hippies in his circle peppered all their choppy, laconic sentences with the word "like," as though they lived in a world not of events but of similitudes, as though there was no reality for them but reminiscence. — Bernard Wolfe, *The Magic of Their Singing*, p. 125, 1961

- [I]t hit me kind of hard. Like it dispelled my dominant illusion. (We youths say "like" all the time because we mistrust reality. It takes a certain commitment to say something is. Inserting "like" gives you a bit more running room.) — James Simon Kunen, *The Strawberry Statement*, pp. 101–102, 1968

▸ **be like**
used for indicating a quotation, or a paraphrase of what was said, or an interpretation of what was said, or a projection of what was thought but not said *US, 1982*

- I was like, naw man, I got a son on the way. — *Boyz N The Hood*, 1990

- — *American Speech*, pp. 215–227, Fall 1990: "I'm like, 'Say what?!': A new quotative in American oral narrative"

- This weekend he called me up and he's all, "Where were you today?" and I'm like, "I'm at my grandmother's house." — *Clueless*, 1995

- And maybe one night me and Lunchbox'll be macking some bitch, and she'll be like, "Oooo! I want to suck youse guys's dicks off. What's your names?" And I'll be like, "Jay and Silent Bob." — Kevin Smith, *Jay and Silent Bob Strike Back*, p. 21, 2001

like beef?
do you want to fight? *US, 1981*
Hawaiian youth usage.

- — Douglas Simonson, *Pidgin to da Max*, 1981

likkered up *adjective*
drunk *US, 1949*

- "I got likkered up with him once in Africa." — Audie Murphy, *To Hell and Back*, p. 2, 1949

lillies *noun*
the hands *US, 1973*

- — Joseph E. Ragen and Charles Finston, *Inside the World's Toughest Prison*, p. 807, 1962: "Penitentiary and underworld glossary"

lily *noun*
the penis *US, 1974*
Most commonly heard when describing urination as **KNOCK THE DEW OFF THE LILY**.

- "Raise up, little pud, you're bending my lily," Buck slurred. — Earl Thompson, *Tattoo*, p. 242, 1974

Lily; Lily Law; Lilly Law; Lillian; Lucy Law *noun*
used as a personification of a police officer, especially a policeman; the police. An example of **CAMP** trans-gender assignment. Sometimes accompanied by Inspector Bestly *US, 1949*

- — *Fact*, p. 26, January–February 1965

- — *American Speech*, p. 57, Spring–Summer 1970: "Homosexual slang"

- The fairies looked up suddenly and one of them screamed, "There comes Lilly Law!" — Herbert Huncke, *Guilty of Everything*, p. 184, 1990

lily-white *adjective*
populated entirely by white people; discriminating against black people *US, 1903*

- — Helen Dahlskog (Editor), *A Dictionary of Contemporary and Colloquial Usage*, p. 38, 1972

- The word had its origin with the Lily-white movement in the Republican Party in 1888. — Malachi Andrews and Paul T. Owens, *Black Language*, p. 101, 1973

lily whites *noun*
bed sheets *US, 1946*

- I sent a substitute in my place and drove straight for home, to stash my frame between a deuce of lily-whites. — Mezz Mezzrow, *Really the Blues*, p. 101, 1946

limbo log *noun*
in mountain biking, a tree limb overhanging the trail at approximately face height *US, 1992*

- — William Nealy, *Mountain Bike!*, p. 161, 1992: "Bikespeak"

limey *noun*
a Briton *US, 1917*
Derives, as an abbreviation of "lime-juicer," from the compulsory ration of lime juice that was issued in the British Navy; originally used of British immigrants in Australia, New Zealand, and South Africa; in this more general sense since 1918.

- [A] new pack of slimy Limeys was coming on over the transistors[.] — Lester Bangs, *Psychotic Reactions and Carburetor Dung*, p. 57, 1970

Limey Land *noun*
England, Great Britain, the United Kingdom *US, 1920*

- "You would be back in limey-land with all them other tub-gutted old English fishermen." — Ken Kesey, *Sailor Song*, p. 238, 1992

limit *noun*
▸ **go the limit**
to have sexual intercourse *US, 1922*

- Several times then, she had nearly gone the limit, as they used to call it, but something had always saved her—once a campus policeman but mostly the boy himself, who had scruples. — Mary McCarthy, *The Group*, p. 256, 1960

- — Kenn "Naz" Young, *Naz's Dictionary of Teen Slang*, p. 72, 1993

limp *verb*
in poker, to reserve the right to make a bet even though holding a good hand *US, 1979*

- — John Scarne, *Scarne's Guide to Modern Poker*, p. 283, 1979

limp-dick; limp-dicked *adjective*
weak, pathetic, timid *US, 1984*

- "After forty days in this limp-dick outfit, I'm convinced you could not run a good Boy Scout Troop." — David Hackworth, *About Face*, pp. 231–232, 1989

limp dick; limp prick *noun*
someone who is weak or cowardly *US, 1970*
The flaccid **DICK** (penis) as a symbol of impotency.

- Vinnie, you limp dick, I saw you sneak back into your office. — Janet Evanovich, *Seven Up*, p. 37, 2001

limp out; limp *verb*
to relax *US, 1997*

- — Vann Wesson, *Generation X Field Guide and Lexicon*, p. 106, 1997

limp wrist *noun*
an effeminate man, almost always homosexual; used as a symbol of homosexuality *US, 1950*

- Manifestations of this are seen in the number of jokes about the limp wrist set, and the occasional reports of homosexuals. — *Berkshire (Massachusetts) Evening Eagle*, 18th September 1950

- "[A]t the same time depriving him of cunt and subjecting him to homosex stimulation. Then drugs, hypnosis, and—" Benway flipped a limp wrist. — William Burroughs, *Naked Lunch*, p. 27, 1957

- I reminded her that Boke Kellum was a limp wrist. — Dan Jenkins, *Semi-Tough*, p. 172, 1979

- He looked like a peroxided limpwrist from Santa Monica Boulevard is what he looked like. — Joseph Wambaugh, *The Delta Star*, p. 130, 1983

limp-wristed *adjective*
effeminate *US, 1957*

- [T]he others kept making fun of him, obviously laughing and chattering with limp-wristed affection[.] — Roger Blake, *Love Clubs, Inc.*, p. 50, 1967

- "You evil scumsucker! You're through! You limp-wristed Nazi moron!" — Hunter S. Thompson, *Fear and Loathing on the Campaign Trail*, p. 358, 1973

- I don't care how much the limp-wrist critics panned it, calling it Pop Architecture or an Edifice Complex. — Leo Rosten, *Silky!*, p. 188, 1979

limpy-go-fetch *noun*
a disabled person *US, 1997*

- The labels were cruel: Gimp, Limpy–go-fetch, Crip, Lift-one-drag one, etc. Pint, Half-a-man, Peewee, Shorty, Lardass, Pork, Blubber, Belly, Blimp. Nuke-knob, Skinhead, Baldy. Four-eyes, Specs, Coke bottles. — *San Francisco Examiner*, p. A15, 28th July 1997

Lincoln *noun*
1 a five-dollar bill *US, 1945*

- — Lou Shelly, *Hepcats Jive Talk Dictionary*, p. 13, 1945

- Then, when we get out of this cold shack we'll make a pile of Lincolns. — Red Rudensky, *The Gonif*, p. 22, 1970

2 a five-dollar prostitute *US, 1965*

- A resident prostitute of any stature won't take his clothes off for less than $10. And frequently they get $15 and $20. Sailors are usually what are called LINCOLNS. They are eager to supplement their income with homosexual acts for as little as five dollars. — *KFRC radio, San Francisco*, 8th November 1965: "The market street proposition"

Lincoln Tunnel *noun*
in homosexual usage, a loose anus and rectum *US, 1981*
- — *Male Swinger Number 3*, p. 45, 1981: "The complete gay dictionary"

line *noun*
1 a dose of powdered cocaine arranged in a line for snorting *US, 1973*
- "Have a line," said the doctor. "Things go better with coke." — Armistead Maupin, *Tales of the City*, p. 300, 1978
- With a razor he cuts the pile into four big lines and then he hands me a rolled up twenty and I lean down and do a line. — Bret Easton Ellis, *Less Than Zero*, p. 32, 1985

2 a vein, especially in the context of injecting drugs *US, 1938*
- I bit down on my bottom lip waiting for the stabbing plunge of the needle. He said, "Damn! You got some beautiful lines." — Iceberg Slim (Robert Beck), *Pimp*, p. 131, 1969

3 political philosophy *US, 1968*
An important term of the New Left in the US, often modified by "correct," a precursor of political correctness.
- The Strike Education Committee people were edged out of the Liberation School organization. It became more and more narrow and elitist. A teacher was told he couldn't teach courses because he didn't have the right line. — James Simon Kunen, *The Strawberry Statement*, pp. 123–124, 1968

4 collectively, the prostitutes in a brothel who are available for sex at a given moment *US, 1986–1987*
- — *Maledicta*, p. 150, Summer/Winter 1986–1987: "Sexual slang: prostitutes, pedophiles, flagellators, transvestites, and necrophiles"

5 in the business of dealing with stolen goods, twice the actual price *US, 1969*
- Folks, my ticker almost stopped when Buster cracked on you for the line on the stuff. Line means the actual price doubled. It's inside code that jewelers, pawnbrokers and fences use. — Iceberg Slim (Robert Beck), *Trick Baby*, p. 229, 1969

6 the area housing a prison's general population *US, 1989*
- — James Harris, *A Convict's Dictionary*, p. 35, 1989
- Why don't they blood test her, yank her off the line? — Seth Morgan, *Homeboy*, p. 256, 1990

7 in sports betting, the points or odds established by a bookmaker that govern the bet *US, 1977*
- Even when they're being real generous with the line, I think I can beat the spread, I lay off. — John Sayles, *Union Dues*, p. 25, 1977
- — Avery Cardoza, *The Basics of Sports Betting*, p. 44, 1991

8 money *US, 1972*
- — David Claerbaut, *Black Jargon in White America*, p. 71, 1972

▸ **do lines**
to use cocaine *US, 2001*
- — Connie Eble (Editor), *UNC-CH Campus Slang*, p. 3, Fall 2001
- Now it was, it's Wednesday night, let's do lines. — Michelle Tea, *Rent Girl*, p. 173, 2004

▸ **get lines**
in bodybuilding, to achieve definition, or well-developed and sculpted muscles *US, 1984*
- — *American Speech*, p. 199, Fall 1984: "The language of bodybuilding"

▸ **on the line**
in combat, especially aerial combat *US, 1990*
- When they were done with their first period "on the line" (in combat) and were heading back to the Philippines for a week's break, the deck housing the pilots would be locked off from the rest of the ship[.] — Robert K. Wilcox, *Scream of Eagles*, p. 37, 1990

▸ **the line**
a combat line position *US, 2002*
- [I]nsanity started to take over if you stayed on what we called "the line" too long. — Joseph W. Callaway, *Mekong First Light*, p. 133, 2004

line crosser *noun*
in the Korean war, a soldier who crossed the main line of resistance to find and retrieve prisoners of war *US, 1967*
- By chance someone, perhaps an IBM machine, turned up the fact that earlier in his career, he had been a line crosser in Korea. — David Halberstam, *One Very Hot Day*, p. 91, 1967

line dog; line doggy; line doggie *noun*
an infantry soldier *US, 1967*

- In Vietnam, he goes by an assortment of names—the Grunt, Boonie Rat, Line Dog, Ground Pounder, Hill Humper, or Jarhead. — David Reed, *Up Front in Vietnam*, p. 3, 1967
- "Hey, someone take my picture," the line doggie yelled. — Larry Chambers, *Recondo*, p. 100, 1992

line duty *noun*
in the language surrounding the Grateful Dead, the hours spent waiting in line to buy tickets or to enter a concert venue *US, 1994*
- — David Shenk and Steve Silberman, *Skeleton Key*, p. 178, 1994

line jumper *noun*
an enemy spy who sneaks across allied lines *US, 1957*
Korean war usage.
- Roving patrols snoop around anyway, hunting for linejumpers (Korean or Chinese spies that have gotten through out M.I.R. and are trying to cross the river). — Martin Russ, *The Last Parallel*, p. 148, 1957

linemaker *noun*
in a sports betting operation, the oddsmaker *US, 1976*
- — Thomas L. Clark, *The Dictionary of Gambling and Gaming*, p. 119, 1987

linen *noun*
a letter *US, 1947*
- For the last six months listeners had "knocked" 2,500 to 3,000 "hunks of linen" a week to the 1290 Club's M.C., young (28), vacant-faced Fred Robbins. — *Time Magazine*, p. 92, 20th January 1947

line rat *noun*
a soldier in the infantry assigned to the front line *US, 1968*
- One thing, this job keeps me from going out on walking missions with the line rats. — David Parks, *GI Diary*, p. 75, 1968
- "[T]hey sent me to a line rat company to be a line rat." — Dexter Jeffries, *Triple Exposure*, p. 361, 2003

liners *noun*
cash *US, 2003*
- Candy, markers, ammo, liners, stocking stuffer, sweetener, garnish, and pledges are all terms for cash. — Henry Hill and Byron Schreckengost, *A Good Fella's Guide to New York*, p. 123, 2003

line screw *noun*
a prison guard assigned to a cell block *US, 1976*
- — John R. Armore and Joseph D. Wolfe, *Dictionary of Desperation*, p. 39, 1976

line-up *noun*
1 serial sex between one person and multiple partners *US, 1913*
- Louise was a "line-up" girl. She was a girl to take down in a cellar or up on a roof and share. — Dale Krame, *Teen-Age Gangs*, p. 12, 1953
- The "line-up" is a standard part of street life. Boys often "con" a girl into having intercourse, then, regardless of her protests, invite half a dozen other adolescents to share her. — Harrison E. Salisbury, *The Shook-up Generation*, p. 32, 1958
- So this rape was in fact a line-up? Yes. It was against my will. You have been a party to line-ups on several occasions? I probably have, but if so, I was under the influence of alcohol and I can't remember them. — *Truth*, p. 39, 3rd February 1970
- An old Barnum hand remarked to me that these line-ups remind him very much of Sunday Morning scenes in front of Welsh mining town whore houses[.] — Joe McKennon, *Circus Lingo*, p. 58, 1980

2 a display of the prostitutes available for sex in a brothel at a given moment *US, 1978*
- As I inspected the lineup, she came in late from doing some shopping in town. — Gerald Paine, *A Bachelor's Guide to the Brothels of Nevada*, p. 106, 1978
- In each establishment there is always some kind of "line-up" with girls standing before one or more customers. — Sisters of the Heart, *The Brothel Bible*, p. 14, 1997
- I call a full line-up. — Lora Shaner, *Madam*, p. 6, 1999

lineup man *noun*
a member of a youth gang who carries firearms for himself and other gang members *US, 1962*
- Lineup man (he carries the pistols and initiates the war by "shooting up the rival gangs")[.] — Howard Polsky, *Cottage Six*, p. 24, 1962

line work *noun*
the addition of fine lines or other markings on the design of a card to aid a cheat *US, 1979*
- — John Scarne, *Scarne's Guide to Modern Poker*, p. 283, 1979

linguist *noun*
a person who enjoys performing oral sex *US, 1967*
Leading, inevitably, to cunning puns.
- — Dale Gordon, *The Dominion Sex Dictionary*, p. 101, 1967
- — *Maledicta*, p. 198, Winter 1980: "A new erotic vocabulary"

linguistic exercise *noun*
oral sex *US, 1964*
- — Roger Blake, *The American Dictionary of Sexual Terms*, p. 123, 1964

link *noun*
a police officer, prosecutor, or judge who has been bribed *US, 1964*
- — R. Frederick West, *God's Gambler*, p. 227, 1964: "Appendix A"

linked *adjective*
1 dating (someone) steadily and exclusively *US, 1966*
- — *San Francisco Examiner*, p. 17, 17th June 1966: "Teen slanguage: real shark"
2 bribed *US, 1964*
- — R. Frederick West, *God's Gambler*, p. 227, 1964: "Appendix A"

Link the Chink *noun*
any Vietnamese person *US, 1971*
- I had come to view the enemy in Vietnam as a real monster, as a threat to my personal security, something which had to be stopped and squashed. Phrases like "gook" and "link the chink" and "luke the gook," stuff we used in training got solidly into my head. — John Kerry, *The New Soldier*, p. 96, 1971

lion *noun*
in pool, a skilled and competitive player *US, 1990*
- — Steve Rushin, *Pool Cool*, p. 20, 1990

lion food *noun*
middle management *US, 1991*
From a joke, the punch-line of which features a lion boasting of eating one IBM manager a day and nobody noticing.
- — Eric S. Raymond, *The New Hacker's Dictionary*, p. 223, 1991

lip *noun*
1 impudence; talking back *UK, 1803*
- Don't you take any lip from him, Governor — Clive Exton, *No Fixed Abode [Six Granada Plays]*, p. 138, 1959
- We took an oath not to hurt anybody on our way up, but we said it was okay to use some lip if you started to slip. — Dan Jenkins, *Life Its Ownself*, p. 53, 1984
- You'll have plenty of lip, arguments, but get 'em outta here. — Josh Alan Friedman, *Tales of Times Square*, p. 52, 1986
- — Connie Eble (Editor), *UNC-CH Campus Slang*, p. 6, March 1986
2 a lawyer, especially a criminal defence lawyer *US, 1929*
From the image of a lawyer as a mouthpiece.
- — Lou Shelly, *Hepcats Jive Talk Dictionary*, p. 13, 1945
- I don't need a bondsman or a lip now. You don't have a "sheet." — Iceberg Slim (Robert Beck), *Pimp*, p. 114, 1969
- — Clarence Major, *Dictionary of Afro-American Slang*, p. 77, 1970

lip *verb*
to kiss *US, 1947*
- — Marcus Hanna Boulware, *Jive and Slang of Students in Negro Colleges*, 1947

lip fart *noun*
a fart-like noise made by exhaling to flap the lips *US, 1930*
- There's a one-man band parading up and down the hall making strange tuneless lip farts. — Norman Mailer, *The Executioner's Song*, p. 335, 1979

lip in *verb*
to interrupt *US, 1899*
- — Hyman E. Goldin et al., *Dictionary of American Underworld Lingo*, p. 127, 1950

lipkisser *noun*
a regular practitioner of oral sex on women *US, 1985*
- — *American Speech*, p. 19, Spring 1985: "The language of singles bars"

lip-lock *noun*
1 a sustained kiss *US, 1970*
- We were outside the Carlton when Robin pulled me close to him and put this lip-lock on me. — Annie Ample, *The Bare Facts*, p. 123, 1988
- He'd rise, cup her face tenderly, and pull her into a world-class, end–of–the–movie lip lock. — Stephanie Kallos, *Broken for You*, p. 264, 2004

2 oral sex performed on a man *US, 1976*
- Why, there's a broad there who'll whip a lip lock on you that'll scorch your shorts and curl the hairs on the back of your neck to look like pig's tails[.] — Larry Heinemann, *Close Quarters*, p. 171, 1977

lip music *noun*
bragging, boasting, teasing *US, 1992*
- — William K. Bentley and James M. Corbett, *Prison Slang*, p. 49, 1992

lip off *verb*
to speak forcefully and without tact *US, 1958*
- Dan Hamins, who runs the station, lipped off to him about the way he came into the drive. — Joe Eszterhas, *Charlie Simpson's Apocalypse*, p. 142, 1973
- "I wasn't lipping off, for once. Just curious." — Barbara Kingsolver, *The Bean Trees*, p. 53, 1988

lipper *noun*
a pinch of chewing tobacco *US, 1997*
- — Pamela Munro, *U.C.L.A. Slang*, p. 86, 1997

lippy *adjective*
impudent, impertinent; talkative *US, 1865*
- Listen, you lippy bastard. — George Mandel, *Flee the Angry Strangers*, p. 226, 1952

lip-sloppy *adjective*
talkative to a fault *US, 1962*
- — *Dobie Gillis Teenage Slanguage Dictionary*, 1962

lipstick *noun*
a grease pencil *US, 1962*
Used by first aid workers to note tourniquet time on an injured person.
- — *American Speech*, p. 270, December 1962: "The language of traffic policemen"

lipstick lesbian; lipstick *noun*
a feminine, stylish, upwardly mobile lesbian *US, 1984*
- Was it time to relent, to throw in the towel and become a lipstick lesbian? — Armistead Maupin, *Babycakes*, p. 59, 1984
- [A] beautiful Latina lipstick lesbian by the name of Janet Canarias has taken the alderman's seat away from Delvin in the Twenty-seventh[.] — Robert Campbell, *Cat's Meow*, p. 22, 1988
- People think it's cute, because they've got this fool picture in their heads about lipstick lesbians—like they all resemble Alyssa—while most of them look more like you. — *Chasing Amy*, 1997

lipstick on your dipstick *noun*
oral sex performed on a man *US, 1970*
- — *Current Slang*, p. 20, Spring 1970
- "I might even let you get some lipstick on my dipstick." — William Johnstone, *Survival in the Ashes*, p. 134, 1999
- "let me put some lipstick on your dipstick." She reached for his zipper again. — James Hall, *Bones of Coral*, p. 328, 2004

Lipton's *noun*
poor quality marijuana *US, 1964*
An allusion to a popular, if weak, tea.
- — Clarence Major, *Dictionary of Afro-American Slang*, p. 77, 1970

lip work *noun*
oral sex on a woman *US, 1967*
- — Dale Gordon, *The Dominion Sex Dictionary*, p. 101, 1967

LIQ *noun*
a liquor store *US, 1970*
- — *Current Slang*, p. 9, Fall 1970

liquid bar *noun*
a mixture of codeine-infused cough syrup and soda *US, 2006*
- With the liquid bar kicking in I was in my own zone, getting my lean on, and just about sleeping. — Linden Dalecki, *Kid B*, p. 11, 2006

liquid courage *noun*
the bravado produced by alcohol *US, 1942*
- What are you waiting for, run outta liquid courage? — *Kill Bill*, 2003

liquid ecstasy; liquid e *noun*
the recreational drug GHB *US, 1998*
- People say it's an amino acid, and it's all natural, but it's really a drug, like liquid Ecstasy. — *Los Angeles Times*, p. B1, 3rd November 1993

- GHB has been marketed as a liquid or powder and has been sold on the street under names such as Grievous Bodily Harm, Georgia Home Boy, Liquid Ecstasy, Liquid X, Liquid E, GHB, GBH, Soap, Scoop, Easy Lay, Salty Water, G-Riffick, [and] Cherry Menth. — *Morbidity and Morality Weekly Report*, p. 281, 4th April 1997

liquid grass *noun*
tetrahydrocannabinol, the purified psychoactive extract of marijuana *US, 1971*
- — *Current Slang*, p. 15, Spring 1971

Liquid Jesus *noun*
pepper spray *US, 2006*
So named because it instantly converts the unruly to compliance.
- Wesley tried to Liquid Jesus on him but the OC can was clogged and it created a pepper-spray mist in front of his own face that almost blinded him. — Joseph Wambaugh, *Hollywood Station*, p. 106, 2006

liquid sky *noun*
heroin *US, 1987*
- — Carsten Stroud, *Close Pursuit*, p. 269, 1987

liquid wrench *noun*
alcohol *US, 1996*
Like a wrench, alcohol will loosen things.
- — John Vorhaus, *The Big Book of Poker Slang*, p. 25, 1996

liquorhead *noun*
a drunkard *US, 1923*
- [T]hey shunned guys on the white stuff just like vipers shun liquorheads. — Mezz Mezzrow, *Really the Blues*, p. 248, 1946

listener *noun*
a person whose only role in conversation is to listen and verify what was said *US, 1982*
- When Angelo got there, with Charley as his listener, Hanly had brought along a police captain named Kiely from the PC's squad. — Richard Condon, *Prizzi's Honor*, p. 215, 1982

listen up!
used for commanding attention *US, 1962*
Almost always heard in the imperative.
- Listen up, don't try to sound pretty. Just belt it out. — *Reno Evening Gazette*, p. 22, 9th November 1962

lister bag *noun*
a water bag *US, 1983*
World War 2, Korean, and Vietnam war usage.
- Water bags, called "lister bags," were set up on tripods. — Robert Mason, *Chickenhawk*, p. 359, 1983
- Doc, do you have to empty all your iodine bottles into that lister bag? — William B. Hopkins, *One Bugle No Drum*, p. 67, 1986

lit *adjective*
drunk *US, 1899*
- Like I said, he was always pretty well lit back in New York. — Raymond Chandler, *The Long Goodbye*, p. 209, 1953
- [T]he euphemisms for "drunkenness," e.g., "high," and "lit," from ten or fifteen years ago, and the direction of those euphemisms toward omnipotence[.] — William and Jerrye Breedlove, *Swap Clubs*, p. 151, 1964
- Nothing is more beautiful than four lit stooges in a graveyard spieling on[.] — John Nichols, *The Sterile Cuckoo*, p. 155, 1965
- — Collin Baker et al., *College Undergraduate Slang Study Conducted at Brown University*, p. 151, 1968

little bit *noun*
a prostitute *US, 1976*
- There's always a little bit at that truck 'em up stop about this time. — Lanie Dills, *The Official CB Slanguage Language Dictionary*, p. 45, 1976

little black book *noun*
an address book containing clients' names and telephone numbers, especially in an illegal enterprise *US, 1978*
- Xaviera Hollander admits to paying "$5,000 down" for her little black book when she went out of the business and Hollander went into it. — Leonard Shecter and William Phillips, *On the Pad*, p. 34, 1973
- He found Dandolo's little black book. In it were listed major Mafia drug traffickers from New York to California. — Robert Daley, *Prince of the City*, p. 143, 1978
- Police vice squadders who raided Brandy Baldwin's bordello in Forest Hill are chortling over the Little Black Book, which contains some of the more illustrious names in local clubdom. — *San Francisco Chronicle*, p. 21, 8th January 1980

little black gun *noun*
the M-16 rifle *US, 1968*
- — Carl Fleischhauer, *A Glossary of Army Slang*, p. 31, 1968

little blues *noun*
capsules of the synthetic opiate oxycodone used recreationally *US, 2003*
- Extracts reproduced in the tabloid show Limbaugh referring to "small blue babies" and "the little blues." — *Broward Business Review*, p. 1, 18th November 2003

little boys' room *noun*
a toilet, especially one for men *US, 1935*
Juvenile and jocular.
- If I'm at your house, I can never say to you, "Excuse me, where's the toilet?" I have to get hung up with that corrupt facade of "Excuse me, where's the little boys' room?" — Lenny Bruce, *How to Talk Dirty and Influence People*, p. 152, 1965
- So I tell the connection I'll be right back, I'm goin' to the little boys room. — *Reservoir Dogs*, 1992

little casino *noun*
in a deck of playing cards, the two of spades *US, 1988*
- — George Percy, *The Language of Poker*, p. 52, 1988

little cat *noun*
in poker, a hand comprised of five cards between three and eight and no pairs among them *US, 1963*
- — Irwin Steig, *Common Sense in Poker*, p. 185, 1963

little D *noun*
a tablet of hydromorphone (trade name Dialudid™), a narcotic analgesic *US, 1986*
- — Richard A. Spears, *The Slang and Jargon of Drugs and Drink*, p. 217, 1986

little Dick; little Dick Fisher *noun*
in craps, a four *US, 1957*
- A borrowing from the early C18 language of the game of hazard. A 4 is "Little Dick" or "Little Joe from Kokomo." — Sidney H. Radner, *Radner on Dice*, p. 10, 1957
- — Thomas L. Clark, *The Dictionary of Gambling and Gaming*, p. 119, 1987

little dog *noun*
in poker, a hand comprised of five cards between two and seven and no pairs among them *US, 1963*
- — Irwin Steig, *Common Sense in Poker*, p. 185, 1963

little friend *noun*
a fighter plane *US, 1944*
- — *American Speech*, p. 310, December 1946: "More air force slang"

little girls' room *noun*
a toilet, especially one for women *US, 1949*
- She kept saying these very corny, boring things, like calling the can the "little girls' room"… — J.D. Salinger, *Catcher in the Rye*, p. 74, 1951
- "Let's go to the little girls' room and fix our faces." — Jacqueline Susann, *Valley of the Dolls*, p. 92, 1966
- I gotta go to the little girls' room — Richard Condon, *Prizzi's Money*, p. 112, 1994

little guy; little man; little people *noun*
a Japanese soldier; a Viet Cong or soldier in the North Vietnamese Army *US, 1950*
- It's kind of dark anyway, but we ain't calling in no medevac bird to tell the little guys and the world where we are, you got it? — Charles Anderson, *The Grunts*, p. 45, 1976
- A little man drags himself away with his rifle under one arm, held level, pushing at the grass with his good leg, pulling with his free arm. — Larry Heinemann, *Close Quarters*, p. 76, 1977
- Four Americans and seventeen little people. — Richard Burns, *Pathfinder*, p. 275, 2002

little Harlem *noun*
a black ghetto *US, 1931*
- Baltimore's Little Harlem—Pennsylvania Avenue—is more peaceful than the Negro section of any other large town we ever gandered. — Jack Lait and Lee Mortimer, *Washington Confidential*, p. 272, 1951
- O what times we get when I hit Frisco loaded with loot & maybe Persian hasheesh & we carry wire recorder to little Harlem & also use it to record fucking-sounds in beds, etc. — Jack Kerouac, *Letter to Neal Cassady*, p. 327, 9th October 1951

- "Wheeoo! let's go!" cried Dean, and we jumped in the back seat and clanked to the little Harlem on Folsom Street. — Jack Kerouac, *On the Road*, p. 196, 1957
- "Sometimes we go over to Little Harlem," he said, and smacked his lips. — Irving Shulman, *The Short End of the Stick*, p. 26, 1959

little help noun
a linear amplifier for a citizens' band radio *US*, 1977
- — Bill Davis, *Jawjacking*, p. 61, 1977

Little Italy noun
a neighborhood populated by a large number of Italian immigrants and Italian-Americans *US*, 1904
- A man who had hammered himself off the streets of Little Italy to a position so powerful that for years he dictated to law enforcement agencies[.] — Red Rudensky, *The Gonif*, p. 57, 1970

little Joe noun
a roll of four in craps *US*, 1890
Often elaborated with a rhyming place name, in the pattern "little Joe from Kokomo" (or Chicago, Idaho, Lake Tahoe, Mexico, Ohio, Tokyo).
- "Little Joe from Kokomo," one of the colored fellows murmured, looking at me. — Chester Himes, *If He Hollers Let Him Go*, p. 32, 1945
- "There it was—Little Joe or Phoebe, Big Dick or Eighter from Decatur, double trey the hard way and dice be nice." — Nelson Algren, *The Man with the Golden Arm*, p. 11, 1949
- There for a while all I could hear was "snake eyes," "little joes," and "carp out, Lord." It was lovely. — Guy Owen, *The Flim-Flam Man and the Apprentice Grifter*, p. 117, 1972

little Joe in the snow noun
cocaine *US*, 1992
- — William K. Bentley and James M. Corbett, *Prison Slang*, p. 49, 1992

Little Korea nickname
Fort Leonard Wood, Missouri *US*, 1968
Based on a comparison of the climates.
- — Carl Fleischhauer, *A Glossary of Army Slang*, p. 32, 1968
- Known as a "Little Korea" of climatic extremes, Fort Wood is a place where soldiers swelter in humid summers and freeze in meat-locker winters. — *Newsday (New York)*, p. 4 (Section II), 4th October 1989

little man in a boat; little man; man in the boat; boy in the boat noun
the clitoris *UK*, 1896
The "little man" or "boy" represent the clitoris as a small penis, and the vulva is imagined to be boat-shaped.
- Avoid putting pressure on the little man in the canoe until it seems very aroused. — Anka Radakovich, *The Wild Girls Club*, p. 131, 1994
- It is a small man-in-a-boat—she obviously hasn't masturbated a lot. — Clarence Major, *All-Night Visitors*, p. 8, 1998
- [R]ocking the bed in a bondage-harness bang, opening her legs for the close-up crotch shot, fast-finger her little man in the boat. — Mr. Skin, *Mr. Skin's Skincyclopedia*, p. 79, 2005

little old lady in tennis shoes noun
used as a stereotype of an energetic, quirky old woman *US*, 1961
- [N]ot the people who are in logistics and maintenance or the little old lady in tennis shoes at the Defense Genreal Supply Center. — United States Senate Committee on Appropriations, *Department of Defense Appropriations*, p. 301, 1961
- "If there's anything that's discouraging, it's the little old lady in tennis shoes crying." — Raymond Dasmann, *The Destruction of California*, p. 182, 1965
- Which is all well and good, except that the Little Old Lady in Tennis Shoes (a most dreadful symbol for a city) isn't what she used to be[.] — Bill Cardoso, *The Maltese Sangweech*, p. 113, 1984

little ploughman noun
the clitoris *US*, 1980
- — *Maledicta*, p. 184, Winter 1980: "A new erotic vocabulary"

little R noun
during the Korean and Vietnam wars, rest and rehabilitation *US*, 1960
Distinguished from the **BIG R** (rotation home).
- — *Korean Bamboo English, American Speech*, p. 121, May 1960
- — Linda Reinberg, *In the Field*, p. 129, 1991

littles noun
in pool, the solid-colored balls numbered 1 to 7 *US*, 1990
- — Steve Rushin, *Pool Cool*, p. 6, 1990

little Saigon nickname
a neigborhood with a large number of Vietnamese immigrants and businesses *US*, 1979
- Do is one of more than a dozen Vietnamese who have set up shop in Clarendon, turning a retailing center once known as "Northern Virginia's downtown" into an area often referred to by Americans as "Little Saigon," the "Mekong Delta" or even the "Ho Chi Min Trail." — *Washington Post*, p. A1, 23rd September 1979
- The neighborhood is called Little Saigon. In this one-block strip you will find four Vietnamese markets—Pacific Department Store, Mekong Center, Vietnam Market and Saigon Market. — *Washington Post*, p. E1, 17th January 1980
- They say that Vietnamese thugs from Westminster's Little Saigon can strip a radio out of a Mercedes faster than you can tune it to a Dodgers game. — Joseph Wambaugh, *The Golden Orange*, p. 177, 1990

little sisters noun
a group of US magazines aimed at women *US*, 1986
- — Rachel S. Epstein and Nina Liebman, *Biz Speak*, p. 131, 1986

little Tokyo noun
an urban neighborhood with a high concentration of Japanese people *US*, 1945
- Only in Little Tokyo they'd have to kill and be killed[.] — Chester Himes, *If He Hollers Let Him Go*, p. 77, 1945
- Filipinos are not concentrated in any section, but many live on N. LaSalle near Little Tokyo. — Jack Lait and Lee Mortimer, *Chicago Confidential*, p. 73, 1950

little woman noun
the wife *UK*, 1795
Intentionally archaic, revolting coy, and condescending.
- He still feels free to philander all over the town because he knows his little woman is keeping the home fires burning. — Sue Rhodes, *And when she was bad she was popular*, p. 35, 1968
- Comes home and the little woman sends him to the store. — Elmore Leonard, *Killshot*, p. 106, 1989

lit up adjective
drunk or drug-intoxicated *US*, 1899
- We were both lit up pretty well when we staggered up from the table that morning. — Donald Goines, *Whoreson*, p. 41, 1972

live verb
▶ live large
to enjoy a life full of material pleasures *US*, 1975
- He say he gonna be livin' large. — Stephen Cannell, *King Con*, p. 50, 1997
- — Connie Eble (Editor), *UNC-CH Campus Slang*, p. 7, Fall 1999
- The video cemented Jay-Z's reputation as hip-hop's smoothest hustler, and "big pimpin'" became slang for living large. — *New Yorker*, p. 74, 20th August 2001
- "Yeah, I been livin' large with that Larry dude." — J.T. LeRoy, *Harold's End*, p. 48, 2004

live adjective
1 (used of the potential customer of a prostitute) eager to spend money *US*, 1969
- Just like to any professional, time is money to the girls and they want to be sure they are latching on to what they call a "live John." — *Screw*, p. 12, 3rd November 1969

2 in horse racing, said of a horse that has attracted heavy betting *US*, 1975
- It's a way to have some fun—because you've got a "live" horse, one with a lot of money going for it, and you've got an overlay. — Jimmy Snyder, *Jimmy the Greek*, p. 215, 1975

3 extreme, intense, exciting, good *US*, 1987
- — *New York Times*, 12th April 1987

4 impressive *US*, 1991
- — Trevor Cralle, *The Surfin'ary*, p. 69, 1991

live bait noun
one young drug user selling drugs to other young users *US*, 1951
- — *American Speech*, p. 27, February 1952: "Teen-age hophead jargon"

lived-in look noun
a complete mess *US*, 1968

● — Collin Baker et al., *College Undergraduate Slang Study Conducted at Brown University*, p. 152, 1968

live one *noun*
a person worth noticing *US, 1896*

● "You'll grab a live one right away." — Jacqueline Susann, *Valley of the Dolls*, p. 2, 1966
● Her book was basically made up of "live ones"—which meant men who still actively patronized a brothel[.] — Xaviera Hollander, *The Happy Hooker*, p. 161, 1972
● Tell him you may have a "live one" out here. — Terry Southern, *Now Dig This*, p. 131, 2001

liver lips *noun*
plump, full lips *US, 1920*

● "He has liver lips!" — Ethan Morden, *I've a Feeling We're Not in Kansas Anymore*, p. 57, 1985

liver rounds *noun*
used in a hospital as humorous code for a drinking party to be held on hospital grounds *US, 1988–1989*

● — *Maledicta*, p. 33, 1988–1989: "Medical maledicta from San Francisco"

liveware *noun*
1 a human being *UK, 1966*
A playful evolution of "software" and "hardware."
● — Karla Jennings, *The Devouring Fungus*, p. 222, 1990
2 a living organism *US, 1991*
● Waiter, there's some liveware in my salad. — Eric S. Raymond, *The New Hacker's Dictionary*, p. 226, 1991

living color yawn *noun*
an act of vomiting *US, 1993*

● "C'mon, bro', let's go do the livin'-color yawn." — Jess Mowry, *Six Out Seven*, p. 133, 1993

living end *noun*
the very best *US, 1959*

● "I've mixed the cod liver with a Bloody Mary. It should be the living end." — Irving Shulman, *The Short End of the Stick*, p. 114, 1959

lizard *noun*
1 a prostitute *US, 2001*
● "I won't be gettin' my arm broke while you're doin' some goddamn lizard." — J.T. LeRoy, *The Heart is Deceitful Above All Things*, p. 83, 2001
2 an uncooperative, dirty hospital patient with scaly skin *US, 1978*
● — *Journal of American Folklore*, p. 568–581, January–March 1978: "The gomer"
● — Sally Williams, "*Strong" Words*, p. 149, 1994
3 the penis *US, 1962*
● — Eugene Landy, *The Underground Dictionary*, p. 121, 1971
4 a mechanical device used by card cheats to hold cards in the player's sleeve *US, 1988*
● — George Percy, *The Language of Poker*, p. 53, 1988

lizard hit *noun*
the last draw on a water pipe *US, 1997*

● It tastes bad and makes you stick your tongue out like a lizard. — Jim Emerson-Cobb, *Scratching the Dragon*, April 1997

lizards *noun*
lizard-skin shoes *US, 1980*

● — Edith A. Folb, *runnin' down some lines*, p. 245, 1980

LLDB *noun*
the special forces of the Army of the Republic of Vietnam *US, 1985*

● But in some of the camps, particularly working with the LLDB—Lousy Little Dirty Bastards—the Vietnamese Special Forces, there was a tremendous sense of frustration. — Al Santoli, *To Bear Any Burden*, p. 97, 1985

loach; loch *noun*
a light observation helicopter *US, 1971*

● — Ronald J. Glasser, *365 Days*, p. 243, 1971
● When the loach buzzed in, a CP RTO ran alway down to the pad yelling, "Pop smoke." — William Pelfrey, *The Big V*, p. 74, 1972
● I got McCaan on the command channel and told him there would be no artillery and only two loches. — Anthony Herbert, *Soldier*, p. 389, 1973
● "Man, one Dink with a forty-five could put a hurtin' on those Loaches they'd never come back from." — Michael Kerr, *Dispatches*, p. 160, 1977

load *noun*
1 an ejaculation's worth of semen *US, 1927*
● I moved my raw and swollen penis, perpetually in dread that my loathsomeness would be discovered by someone stealing up me just as I was in the frenzy of dropping my load. — Philip Roth, *Portnoy's Complaint*, p. 18, 1969
● And when she mounts him, displaying one of the roundest, hottest, most perfect butts in creation (the ancient Greeks would have deified her), it's hard to resist shooting your second load. — *Adult Video*, p. 13, August/September 1986
● They'll squirt their load and sit in it just to see how the story ends. — *Boogie Nights*, 1997
● The most honest moment in a man's life is the five minutes after he's blown a load. That's a medical fact. — *Something About Mary*, 1998
2 a state of intoxication *US, 1947*
● He seemed like one of those steady, all-day drinkers—always with a load on, but never wobbly. — Marvin Wald and Albert Maltz, *The Naked City*, 1947
● "I saw him in Joe's bar before," Steven said. "He was getting a real load on the way he looked." — Hal Ellson, *Tomboy*, p. 118, 1950
● It's pretty hard to hang around the island without taking on a load. — Jim Thompson, *The Nothing Man*, p. 194, 1954
● And then he'd go home with his load on, dreaming his dreams, pass out, get up the next day[.] — Richard Price, *Clockers*, p. 379, 1992
3 a drug addiction *US, 1970*
● "All the symptoms are present, Boyd. How big is your load?" — Burt Hirschfield, *Fire Island*, p. 283, 1970
4 a group of prisoners being transferred *US, 1954*
● These transfers, incidentally, are referred to as "loads" or "chains." — Caryl Chessman, *Cell 2456 Death Row*, p. 299, 1954
5 a dose of a drug *US, 1952*
● [O]n the day of the party he went overboard with a big load and slept through till his mother came home. — Hal Ellson, *The Golden Spike*, p. 67, 1952
6 a codeine pill combined with a Doriden™ sleeping pill, producing an opiate-like effect *US, 1989*
● — Geoffrey Froner, *Digging for Diamonds*, p. 41, 1989
7 an inept, ludicrous, stupid or unpleasant person *US, 1950*
● — Collin Baker et al., *College Undergraduate Slang Study Conducted at Brown University*, p. 152, 1968
● Bert Parks was a load! — Howard Stern, *Miss America*, p. ix, 1995

▸ **take a load off**
to sit down *US, 1922*
● I gestured to the armchair. "Take a load off." — Armistead Maupin, *Maybe the Moon*, p. 155, 1992

load *verb*
to alter (dice); to weight (dice) to score a certain point *US, 1962*
● — Frank Garcia, *Marked Cards and Loaded Dice*, p. 262, 1962
● — John S. Salak, *Dictionary of Gambling*, p. 148, 1963

load call *noun*
in a telephone swindle, a repeat call to a recent victim *US, 1985*
● — M. Allen Henderson, *How Con Games Work*, p. 221, 1985: "Glossary"
● — Kathleen Odean, *High Steppers, Fallen Angels, and Lollipops*, p. 133, 1988

loaded *adjective*
1 drunk or drug-intoxicated *US, 1879*
The abbreviated variation of a mainly obsolete range of similes beginning "loaded to."
● He's just loaded, honey. — *Rebel Without a Cause*, 1955
● The stumplifter boy, looking like a pellet regurgitated by an owl, woke her up at dawn, so she was again loaded as I shuffled into breakfast. — John Nichols, *The Sterile Cuckoo*, pp. 152–153, 1965
● Rules of the Black Panther Party No. 7: No party member can have a weapon in his possession while DRUNK or loaded off narcotics or weed. — *The Black Panther*, p. 22, 25th January 1969
● We're all loaded on acid and trying to throw this ball around as the bus goes careening down the highway at high speed and Cassady seeing how many curbs he can almost hit. — Ken Kesey, *The Further Inquiry*, p. 160, 1990
2 wealthy *US, 1948*
● Jesus, I thought, this dame is loaded, she really is. — Horace McCoy, *Kiss Tomorrow Good-bye*, p. 209, 1948
● With Boo it wouldn't have mattered; she's loaded. — Max Shulman, *Anyone Got a Match?*, p. 264, 1964
● I wish you were going to be loaded. — *Body Heat*, 1980

- Well, a lot of people are jealous because he's loaded. — *Cruel Intentions*, 1999

3 pregnant *US, 1973*
- — Malachi Andrews and Paul T. Owens, *Black Language*, p. 50, 1973

4 armed with a gun *US, 1952*
- "You loaded?" "The cops lifted my rod and P.I. ticket." — Mickey Spillane, *Kiss Me Deadly*, p. 50, 1952

5 (used of a car) equipped with every possible accessory *US, 1996*
- Yah, ya got yer—this loaded here—this has yer independent, uh, yer slipped differential, uh, yer rack and pinion steering, yer alarm and radar. — *Fargo*, 1996

loaded for bear

prepared for an emergency, heavily armed *US, 1927*
The term arose in the late C19 as a literal description of a weapon loaded with ammunition suitable for killing a bear, and then in the 1950s came to assume a figurative meaning that dominates today.
- But the O'Sheel woman is coming in loaded for bear this time. — Max Shulman, *Rally Round the Flag, Boys!*, p. 54, 1957
- We began the trip into town loaded for bear. — Oscar Zeta Acosta, *The Autobiography of a Brown Buffalo*, p. 173, 1972
- I get out there in Framingham this morning, there's old Tiger Mike Fobarty, got his yellow suit on and he's loaded for bear. — George V. Higgins, *The Rat on Fire*, p. 133, 1981
- In one minute there were seventeen blue boys there, all loaded for bear, all knowing exactly what the fuck they were doing, and they were all just there. — *Reservoir Dogs*, 1992

loader *noun*

1 in American casinos, a blackjack dealer who carelessly exposes his down card while dealing *US, 1985*
- — Steve Kuriscak, *Casino Talk*, p. 35, 1985

2 an experienced and skilled confidence swindler who makes a second sale to a prior victim *US, 1988*
- — Kathleen Odean, *High Steppers, Fallen Angels, and Lollipops*, p. 133, 1988

load exchange *noun*

the passing of semen to its maker, mouth to mouth *US, 1970s*
- — Bruce Rodgers, *The Queens' Vernacular*, p. 76, 1972

loadie *noun*

a drug user *US, 1979*
- The other mechanics were loadies who were always ragging him about his disdain for dope. — James Ellroy, *Suicide Hill*, p. 578, 1986
- — Michael V. Anderson, *The Bad, Rad, Not to Forget Way Cool Beach and Surf Disctionary*, p. 13, 1988
- Loadies generally hang out on the grassy knoll there. — *Clueless*, 1995
- [H]ence the terms "Stoners" or "Loadies" were applied to them by their "square" teen peers. — Robert Jackson and Wesley McBride, *Understanding Street Gangs*, p. 43, 2000

loadies *noun*

dice loaded with weights that affect the roll *US, 1997*
- Them metal slugs would take my loadies straight to the bottom of the glass. — Stephen Cannell, *Big Con*, p. 215, 1997

load-in *noun*

the carting in and setting up of equipment before a concert or show *US, 1999*
- They were bringing their amps and instrument cases out through the load-in door, a giant illuminated martini glass on the wall above it. — Elmore Leonard, *Be Cool*, p. 62, 1999

load plane *noun*

an aircraft loaded with illegal drugs being smuggled *US, 1992*
- There was always a "load plane," carrying pot or Mexican heroin, landing on one of the little desert airstrips, usually at night. — Joseph Wambaugh, *Fugitive Nights*, p. 37, 1992

loads *noun*

dice that have been altered with weights so as to produce a certain score *US, 1963*
- — John S. Salak, *Dictionary of Gambling*, p. 148, 1963

loafer's loop *noun*

a military aiguillette *US, 1947*
- [T]rying to keep up chitchat with Captain Carton, a beefy man with a crushing handgrip on whose right shoulder blue-and-gold "loafer's loops" blazed. — Herman Wouk, *Winds of War*, p. 172, 1971

loaner *noun*

a piece of equipment that is loaned out while the owner's piece of equipment is being repaired *US, 1926*
- So I dug the loaner out of the motel lot, found a pay phone on P.C.H. and gave old Cal a buzz. — James Ellroy, *Brown's Requiem*, p. 220, 1981
- BB: And I get a loaner if the car's got to stay? SALESMAN: As we discussed, you get a car if the car has to be kept overnight. BB: I get a loaner? — *Tin Men*, 1987

loan shark *noun*

a person who loans money privately with usurious interest rates and criminal collection procedures *UK, 1905*
- And those Monday loan sharks, the six-for-five boys, who make a fine art of collection. — John D. McDonald, *The Neon Jungle*, p. 5, 1953
- I remember once in Chicago when I was working for a loan shark, a very tough outfit, incidentally. — Jim Thompson, *Roughneck*, p. 54, 1954
- Contempt of court, refused to testify before New Jersey State Commission of Investigation on loan-shark activities, sixty days, in and out. — Elmore Leonard, *Glitz*, p. 141, 1985
- You have to understand the loan shark's in business the same as anybody else. — *Get Shorty*, 1995

lob *noun*

1 a prisoner who displays excessive zeal on his job *US, 1951*
- — *American Speech*, p. 194, October 1951: "A Study of Reformatory Argot"

2 in a gambling establishment, a hanger-on who runs errands for gamblers *US, 1979*
- — John Scarne, *Scarne's Guide to Modern Poker*, p. 283, 1979

3 in horse racing, a horse pulled back by its jockey to prevent it from finishing first, second or third in a race *US, 1935*
- — David W. Maurer, *Argot of the Racetrack*, p. 41, 1951

lobby louse *noun*

a nonguest who idles in a hotel lobby *US, 1939*
- It concerned characters inelegantly termed "lobby lice." These were loungers, loafers and larrikins who hung around annoying, and sometimes swindling, desirable patrons. — Dev Collans with Stewart Sterling, *I was a House Detective*, p. 13, 1954
- "The only thing I don't understand is where were all the lobby lice the day I registered," I said. — Robert Deane Pharr, *S.R.O.*, p. 27, 1971

lobster *noun*

in poker, an unskilled and/or inexperienced player *US, 1988*
- — George Percy, *The Language of Poker*, p. 53, 1988

lobster skin *noun*

badly sunburnt skin *US, 1982*
Hawaiian youth usage.
- — Douglas Simonson, *Pidgin to da Max: Hana Hou*, 1982

local *noun*

1 a resident of a location, contrasted to the visitor *UK, 1835*
- A woman doesn't count all the miscellaneous dick: the guy she met at the club; that time she fucked Keith Sweat; the local she dubbed in Jamaica. — Chris Rock, *Rock This!*, p. 130, 1997

2 a person who surfs in an area and asserts territorial privileges there *US, 1965*
- — John M. Kelly, *Surf and Sea*, p. 289, 1965
- Okay, so this is where you tell me all about how locals rule and uppie insects like me shouldn't be surfing your break and all that, right? — *Point Break*, 1991

3 during a massage, hand stimulation of the penis until ejaculation *US, 1972*
- — Robert A. Wilson, *Playboy's Book of Forbidden Words*, p. 162, 1972
- "I only give locals." "Locals?" "Hand jobs," she explained. "Okay," he said, "I'll have a local." — Guy Talese, *Thy Neighbor's Wife*, p. 431, 1980

localism *noun*

an attitude, defiant if not hostile, of local surfers towards visiting surfers at "their" beach *US, 1991*
- — Trevor Cralle, *The Surfin'ary*, p. 70, 1991

local talent *noun*

a pretty female *US, 1955*
- — *American Speech*, p. 304, December 1955: "Wayne University Slang"

loced out; loqued out *adjective*

exciting, crazy *US, 1995*
- Did I show you the loqued-out Jeep Daddy got me? — *Clueless*, 1995

lock *noun*

1 control; complete control *US, 1966*

- Slim was a bitch that I really had to put the locks on, or I could blow her to anyone of those rich actors. — A.S. Jackson, *Gentleman Pimp*, p. 163, 1973

2 a sure thing, a certainty *US, 1942*

- BOOGIE: Game's a lock. BAGEL: Nothing's a lock. — *Diner*, 1982
- The Mets are a fucking lock. I wanna make some money. — *The Bad Lieutenant*, 1992

3 in poker, a hand that cannot lose *US, 1990*

- — Anthony Holden, *Big Deal*, p. 302, 1990

4 in bar dice games, a perfect hand that at best can be tied *US, 1971*

- — Jester Smith, *Games They Play in San Francisco*, p. 104, 1971

lock *verb*

in prison, to reside in a cell *US, 1931*

- "As soon as I can buy a two-man cell, we'll move out of here and lock together." — James Blake, *The Joint*, p. 81, 1971
- [W]here you locking? — Miguel Pinero, *Short Eyes*, p. 25, 1975
- You get to know the guy that locks next to you, or you don't get to know him—it depends. — Herbert Huncke, *Guilty of Everything*, p. 116, 1990

lock and load *verb*

to prepare for an imminent confrontation *US, 1949*

Originally military, and originally "load and lock," then reversed for the sound (perhaps to conform with "rock and roll") and generalized.

- The team leader would then shout, "Lock 'n' load." — Gary Linderer, *The Eyes of the Eagle*, p. 107, 1991
- Accustomed to war with show-biz receptionists, and being in character, all locked-and-loaded, so to speak, Fin said, "I don't know what I said." — Joseph Wambaugh, *Finnegan's Week*, p. 113, 1993

lock-down *noun*

any situation in which your complete freedom is restricted *US, 1997*

Like "warden" (girlfriend or wife), jail slang brought home.

- Since I got a girlfriend, she has had me on lock down. — Pamela Munro, *U.C.L.A. Slang*, p. 94, 1997

locked *adjective*

tense, stressed *US, 1955*

- I've had it. This is bottoms. I'm really locked. — Max Shulman, *Guided Tour of Campus Humor*, p. 105, 1955

locker *noun*

a safe or a locked compartment within a safe *US, 1949*

- — Vincent J. Monteleone, *Criminal Slang*, p. 147, 1949

locker room *noun*

1 amyl or butyl or isobutyl nitrate as a recreational drug *US, 1998*

Popular as a sex-aid in the gay community, the name (possibly deriving from a brand name) reflects the locality of use.

- Street names [...] Amyl, liquid gold, locker room, poppers[.] — James Kay and Julian Cohen, *The Parents' Complete Guide to Young People and Drugs*, p. 144, 1998

2 the group of professional wrestlers under contract with a promoter at any given moment *US, 1999*

- I'm sure it would be no problem because there are so many talented guys in our locker room right now. [quoting Francine Fournier] — *World of Wrestling Magazine*, p. 143, June 1999
- Vince said he had confidence in his locker room. — *Chatterbox News*, 8th August 2000

lock-in-a-sock *noun*

an improvised prison weapon—a combination lock inside in a sock *US, 1996*

- — Reinhold Aman, *Hillary Clinton's Pen Pal*, p. 48, 1996

lockmate *noun*

a cellmate *US, 1962*

- Doug, the trumpet player from Lake Forest who was my lockmate for three years, has come out of the joint. — James Blake, *The Joint*, p. 296, 25th June 1961

lock-mortal cinch *noun*

in betting, the surest possible certainty *US, 1975*

- I thought this was a lock-mortal cinch, so I didn't mind taking his offer of five-to-one. — Jimmy Snyder, *Jimmy the Greek*, p. 40, 1975

lock partner *noun*

in prison, a cellmate *US, 1958*

- A complete change from the previous lock partner, he's sensitive, bright, cynical, somewhat tightly strung. — James Blake, *The Joint*, p. 188, 28th March 1958

lockpicker *noun*

an illegal abortionist *US, 1976*

- [W]e got this kid that was about sixteen and her boyfriend knocked her up and the lockpicker hurt her so she hadda go in the hospital. — George V. Higgins, *The Judgment of Deke Hunter*, p. 36, 1976

locksmith *noun*

1 in pool, a betting professional who only plays games that he is sure of winning *US, 1990*

- — Steve Rushin, *Pool Cool*, p. 20, 1990

2 a poker player who only plays excellent hands *US, 1966*

- — John D. Bell et al., *Loosely Speaking*, p. 13, 1966

lockup *noun*

1 a jail or prison *US, 1839*

- The first time I met Ed was in the county lockup in Tempe, Arizona. — *Raising Arizona*, 1987

2 in pool, a shot that cannot be missed or a game that cannot be lost *US, 1990*

- — Steve Rushin, *Pool Cool*, p. 20, 1990

lock-worker *noun*

a thief who steals from hotel rooms *US, 1954*

- If a room-rifler or a lock-worker gets away with a good score at some hotel, he'll keep quiet about it. — Dev Collans with Stewart Sterling, *I was a House Detective*, p. 47, 1954

loco *noun*

marijuana *US, 1982*

An abbreviation of **LOCOWEED**.

- You know I'm like a loco man — Busta Rhymes, *Get Out*, 2000

loco *adjective*

crazy *US, 1887*

From the Spanish.

- Here you got some loco doings goin' on here. — Chester Gould, *Dick Tracy Meets the Night Crawler*, p. 106, 1945
- "I wouldn't even be throwin' in with you, Sarge, on this loco idea if I was what a man would call sensible." — George Clayton Johnson, *Ocean's Eleven*, p. 172, 1960
- The whites didn't like the Blacks, (we were outnumbered on each shift by fifty to one) the Mexicans didn't like the whites and thought the whites were slightly loco. — Odie Hawkins, *Scars and Memories*, p. 122, 1987

locos *noun*

sunglasses *US, 1993*

- I'd open it, pull out my flag, put on my murder ones (dark shades, also called Locs or Locos), button the top button of my shirt, put my strap in my lap, and drive on to the 'hood. — Sanyika Shakur, *Monster*, p. 43, 1993

locoweed *noun*

marijuana *US, 1930*

Directly from the name given to several species of poisonous plants which may cause frenzied behavior in grazing stock; ultimately from Spanish *loco* (mad).

- Hashish was used among the ancients to stimulate armies for ruthless killing. It has since become known as locoweed[.] — Jack Lait and Lee Mortimer, *New York Confidential*, p. 102, 1948
- [P]oor Neal with his pockets full of innocent loco weed that grows wild in Texas getting an indefinite term. — Jack Kerouac, *Jack Kerouac Selected Letters 1957–1969*, p. 222, 17th April 1959: Letter to Carolyn Cassady
- If Horatio Alger had been born near a field of locoweed his story might have been a lot different. — Hunter S. Thompson, *Hell's Angels*, p. 215, 1966
- "Well, I ain't never seen no locoweed make a cow act like that," said Harold[.] — Terry Southern, *Texas Summer*, p. 37, 1991

locs; lokes *noun*

sunglasses *US, 1993*

- I'd open it, pull out my flag, put on my murder ones (dark shades, also called Locs or Locos), button the top button of my shirt, put my strap in my lap, and drive on to the 'hood. — Sanyika Shakur, *Monster*, p. 43, 1993
- — Pamela Munro, *U.C.L.A. Slang*, p. 87, 1997
- — Judi Sanders, *Da Bomb*, p. 19, 1997

log *noun*

1 a carton of cigarettes *US, 1991*
- — Lee McNelis, *30 + And a Wake-Up*, p. 9, 1991

2 the counter surface in a bar *US, 1967*
- I saw him pound the bottom of his glass against the log. — *Iceberg Slim (Robert Beck), Pimp*, p. 120, 1969

3 a bar or tavern *US, 1950*
- — Jack Lait and Lee Mortimer, *Chicago Confidential*, p. 301, 1950: "Loop lexicon"

4 a heavy, cumbersome surfboard *US, 1963*
- — Grant W. Kuhns, *On Surfing*, p. 118, 1963

▸ **behind the log**
(used of a betting style in poker) conservative, even when winning *US, 1971*
- — Thomas L. Clark, *The Dictionary of Gambling and Gaming*, p. 16, 1987

log *verb*
to send military logistics helicopters to troop units *US, 1991*
- — J.D. Coleman, *Incursion*, p. 276, 1991: Glossary

log bird *noun*
a logistical supply helicopter, used to bring fresh supplies and provisions to troops in the field *US, 1982*
- The first two log birds arrived, one behind the other. The boonierats unloaded seventy cases of C-rations, batteries for the company's fifteen radios and heavy loads of M-60 belts, fragmentation grenades and new M-16 magazines and cartridges. — John M. Del Vecchio, *The 13th Valley*, p. 321, 1982

logic bomb *noun*
code secretly included in a program that causes a computer to fail when certain conditions are met *US, 1991*
- — Eric S. Raymond, *The New Hacker's Dictionary*, p. 227, 1991
- Logic bombs are dangerous, but at least they are contained. — The Knightmare, *Secrets of a Super Hacker*, p. 134, 1994

logjam *noun*
constipation *US, 1991*
- — Trevor Cralle, *The Surfin'ary*, p. 70, 1991

logy *adjective*
lethargic, without energy *US, 1859*
- BOCKRIS: I hate Quaaludes. BURROUGHS: You really feel logy in the morning. It's terrible stuff. — Victor Bockris, *With William Burroughs [The Howard Marks Book of Dope Stories]*, p. 35, 1997

loid *noun*
a strip of celluloid, used to force locks *UK, 1958*
- [P]icking a dead gaff [empty house] and persuading the front door to yield to their trusty 'loid. — Charles Raven, *Underworld Nights*, p. 53, 1956
- — John R. Armore and Joseph D. Wolfe, *Dictionary of Desperation*, p. 39, 1976

Loisaida *nickname*
the Lower East Side of New York *US, 1981*
A Spanish adaptation of English, borrowed back into English.
- Loisada, actually, is the area between 14th and Houston Streets from Avenue A east. This sunny, flowery, Spanish-flavored name for the Lower East Side was conferred on an unpromising piece of real estate by our Puerto Rican fellow residents to cheer things up — *New York Times*, p. C8, 27th May 1981
- The sidewalk bikers of Loisaida dare you to glare at them, and too many of the dogs are pit bulls in training for their pro season. — *New York Times*, p. 4 (Section 14), 7th September 2003

LOL
used as Internet shorthand to mean "*laughing out loud*" *US, 1991*
- — Eric S. Raymond, *The New Hacker's Dictionary*, p. 342, 1991
- RUBBERBABY: Hold on ... you want me to get the vibrator? CAPTAINJAPAN: Yes [...] RUBBERBABY: Okay ... one more sec. CAPTAINJAPAN: What's going on? RUBBERBABY: ... Extension cord ... lol. — Howard Stern, *Miss America*, p. 37, 1995

lola *noun*
cocaine *US, 1993*
- — Peter Johnson, *Dictionary of Street Alcohol and Drug Terms*, p. 112, 1993

Lolita *noun*
a young teenage girl objectified sexually; a girl of any age up to the legal age of consent who dresses in a manner that is considered sexually provocative or predatory *UK, 1959*

Generic use of a proper name, after the sexually aware 12-year-old girl in Vladimir Nabokov's controversial 1955 novel *Lolita* and subsequent films in 1962 and 1998.
- One thinks of bouncing a "Lolita" on one's lap, but hardly a big-breasted pom-pom girl of one hundred and thirty pounds. — Angelo d'Arcangelo, *The Homosexual Handbook*, p. 215, 1968
- The idea of making it with a young girl—the Lolita plot—has always been a major turn-on to porno audiences. — Stephen Ziplow, *The Film Maker's Guide to Pornography*, p. 18, 1977

lollapalooza; lollapoloosa *noun*

1 an outstanding example of its type *US, 1896*
"Lollapalooza" was adopted as the title for an annual series of peripatetic music festivals that commenced in Phoenix, Arizona in July 1991.
- Lollapalooza dockwalloper, good attentive husband, caring stepfather, bowler among bowlers. — Sidney Bernard, *This Way to the Apocalypse*, p. 153, 1965

2 in bar dice games, a roll that produces no points for the player *US, 1971*
- — Jester Smith, *Games They Play in San Francisco*, p. 104, 1971

lollipop *noun*

1 a soldier removed from combat *US, 1966*
- For the men of the 33rd any man farther back—in sector, division, or corps, is a "lollipop," only slightly better than than a "Saigon commando." — Jim Lucas, *Dateline: Viet Nam*, p. 189, 1966

2 an attractive young woman seen only in terms of her sexuality *US, 1984*
- [T]he next thing Robbie Hurt knew, he was regaling three wide-eyed lollypops with a story as to how he got his "wound." — Joseph Wambaugh, *Lines and Shadows*, p. 218, 1984

lollipop artist *noun*
a male homosexual *US, 1977*
- Next to loneliness the biggest problem the trucker encounters on the highway is the "queer," the lollipop artist, the funny boys. They harrass a trucker unmercifully. — Gwyneth A. "Dandalion" Seese, *Tijuana Bear in a Smoke 'Um Up Taxi*, p. 75, 1977

lollipop stop *noun*
a rest stop on a motorway known as a place where male homosexuals may be found for sexual encounters *US, 1985*
- Lollipop means penis, the principal activity being fellatio. — Wayne Dynes, *Homolexis*, p. 85, 1985

lollygag; lallygag *verb*

1 to kiss; to have sex *US, 1868*
- — *American Speech*, p. 55, February 1947: "Pacific war language"

2 to dawdle, to dally *US, 1869*
- For the next few minutes she lollygagged about the room puffing smoke, picking things up and putting them down and adjusting her frizz in a mirror over the sofa. — Gerald Petievich, *To Die in Beverly Hills*, p. 18, 1983
- I was just taking a couple or three courses, lolly gaggin'. — Odie Hawkins, *Black Casanova*, p. 121, 1984
- You guys lollygag the ball around the infield, ya lollgag your way to first, ya lollygag in an' outta the duggout. — *Bull Durham*, 1988
- STEPHANIE: So what are you up to? ULTIMATE LOSER: Same old same old, just lollygagging around. Still unemployed. — *Slacker*, 1992

lo-lo; low-low *noun*
a custom-designed low rider car *US, 1997*
- — Pamela Munro, *U.C.L.A. Slang*, p. 87, 1997

lone wolf *noun*
a criminal who works alone *US, 1909*
- Mostly he was a loner acting the lone-world tough guy, but he was still dangerous for all that. — Brian McDonald, *Elephant Boys*, p. 19, 2000

long *adjective*

1 (used of money) a lot of *US, 1947*
- A syndicated outfit with lots of the long green. — Mickey Spillane, *I, The Jury*, p. 70, 1947
- I began to realize that to make long bread one needed to be a singer and look pretty for the girls. — Babs Gonzales, *I Paid My Dues*, p. 40, 1967
- He'd read an item about some black female theatrical star getting thousands a week for her act and bemoan the fact that a brilliant and gorgeous dude like himself was pimping his heart out on a gang of stinking street whores instead of taking off long bread from

a glamorous black performer. — Iceberg Slim (Robert Beck), *The Naked Soul of Iceberg Slim*, p. 80, 1971

- Where'd I see this blond bitch before, maybe thinking he was a pay lawyer, because he was well groomed and looked like long money. — Robert Price, *Clockers*, p. 93, 1992

2 (of a drug addiction) serious *US, 1971*

- "Sharlee's habit was oooh-long. And got longer." — Robert Deane Pharr, *S.R.O.*, p. 155, 1971

long bread *noun*
a lot of money *US, 1963*

- I had some long bread in my pockets cause I'd just finished selling some fine pot and had bought some more all rolled up. — Piri Thomas, *Down These Mean Streets*, p. 109, 1967
- I began to realize that to make long bread one needed to be a singer and look pretty for the girls. — Babs Gonzales, *I Paid My Dues*, pp. 39–40, 1967

long con *noun*
an elaborate confidence swindle in which the victim is initially allowed to profit, and then returns with a large sum of money which he loses *US, 1969*

- In long con the sucker is given a powerful play to convince him that whatever scratch he has is only a drop in the bucket compared to what he can take off from the long con proposition. — Iceberg Slim (Robert Beck), *Trick Baby*, p. 112, 1969

long-dick *verb*
to win a woman away from another; to cuckold *US, 1984*

- Poor ol' Elroy got long-dicked, and now his wife won't even look at him. — Ken Weaver, *Texas Crude*, p. 71, 1984
- Jerry was happy 'til that salesman long-dicked his woman away from him. — Michael Dalton Johnson, *Talking Trash with Redd Foxx*, p. 57, 1994

long drink of water *noun*
a very tall thin person *US, 1936*

- He was a tall, lanky man, the kind my grandma called a long drink of water, and the dog was a dachshund[.] — Louise Bernikow, *Bark If You Love Me*, p. 93, 2000

long end *noun*
a confidence game in which the victim is sent for his money, as opposed to a confidence game in which the spoils are limited to the amount on the victim's person *US, 1963*

- "You talk the lingo. What's your pitch?" "The long end. The big-con." — Jim Thompson, *The Grifters*, p. 153, 1963

long green *noun*
a large amount of money *US, 1887*

- A syndicated outfit with lots of the long green. — Mickey Spillane, *I, The Jury*, p. 70, 1947
- He didn't neglect his woman because by keeping "long green" (money) in his slide (pocket) daily, he was always copping her furs[.] — Babs Gonzales, *I Paid My Dues*, p. 97, 1967
- Leroy was trying to decide how best to go about getting his hands on some "long green"[.] — Elliot Liebow, *Tally's Corner*, p. 70, 1967
- I told you not to talk to me until you got some long greens. I might even charge you for talkin' to me like this. — Christina and Richard Milner, *Black Players*, p. 87, 1972

longhair *noun*
1 an intellectual *US, 1919*

- "I never read the Post," said Wilma Hepp. "That longhair stuff is too deep for poor little me." — Max Shulman, *The Zebra Derby*, p. 165, 1946

2 a participant in the 1960s counterculture *US, 1969*

- No one ever asks a fellow longhair how old he is. It's a counter-revolutionary question. — Jerry Rubin, *Do It!*, p. 89, 1970
- The two guys right behind me were longhairs. Acid people. They'd been picked up for vagrancy, too. — Hunter S. Thompson, *Fear and Loathing in Las Vegas*, p. 174, 1971
- he told the chicano junior and senior high school kids in the valley that if they wanted some exercise they should go into town and beat up some longhairs. — Paul and Meredith, *Chamisa Road*, 1971

3 classical music *US, 1951*

- Until the late 1940's, the jazz concerts in symphony halls and other repositories of long-hair music, had been dominated by the Old Guard. — Robert Sylvester, *No Cover Charge*, p. 279, 1956
- Man, just dig all them fine long-hair records, whole albums of operas and symphonies and stuff. — Ross Russell, *The Sound*, p. 190, 1961

longies *noun*
long underwear *US, 1941*

- "Where are you going?" "Home," said Guido, "to pack my longies." — Max Shulman, *Rally Round the Flag, Boys!*, p. 237, 1957

long john *noun*
a sleeveless wet suit *US, 1985*

- — Frank Fox, *A Beginner's Guide to Zen and the Art of Windsurfing*, p. 152, 1985: "A short dictionary of wind surfing terms"

longneck *noun*
a bottle of beer with a long neck *US, 1980*

- They sat in the living room of the house in Delray Beach drinking beer out of longnecks, the only way Dale liked to have his. — Elmore Leonard, *Maximum Bob*, p. 107, 1991

long-nose *noun*
an American or European *US, 1967*
From the Vietnamese, adopted by US soldiers.

- Off limits to me. Off limits to you. Off limits to all long noses. Colonel's orders. — David Halberstam, *One Very Hot Day*, p. 15, 1967

long shoe *noun*
a stylish shoe with a tapered toe *US, 1968*

- Y'see, long shoes are success. They're the keen-toed design, right for kickin' a whore in the behind with when she comes up with short money or gits outta line. — Nathan Heard, *Howard Street*, p. 159, 1968

longshoe *noun*
a competent, stylish person *US, 1975*

- LONGSHOE Someone who's hip, slick, and "has his act together." — Miguel Pinero, *Short Eyes*, p. 125, 1975

long-shoe game *noun*
a swindle *US, 1955*

- He lived off the hicks from out in the sticks / He was a master of the long-shoe game. — Dennis Wepman et al., *The Life*, p. 86, 1976

longshot *noun*
a venture involving great risk; in horse racing, a bet on a horse with very long odds *UK, 1869*
Originally race track slang.

- Only suckers lay it all in on more than one horse race. They finally agreed on a longshot. — Robert Sylvester, *No Cover Charge*, p. 221, 1956
- It was a long shot all the way. We gave 'em a good run at it. — *48 Hours*, 1982
- A runner at "long" odds with little chance. — David Bennet, *Know Your Bets*, p. 58, 2001

long side *noun*
in sports betting, a bet on the underdog *US, 1975*

- For some reason, if you really liked an underdog you went to Philly. You could always get a half point more on the long side. — Jimmy Snyder, *Jimmy the Greek*, p. 36, 1975

long time, no smell
used as an affectionate greeting *US, 1982*
Hawaiian youth usage.

- — Douglas Simonson, *Pidgin to da Max: Hana Hou*, 1982

Long Tom *noun*
a long-range artillery gun *US, 1991*

- It was the only U.S. Army World War II towed artillery weapon with a commonly used nickname: "The Long Tom." — Konrad F. Schreier, *Tanks and Artillery*, p. 102, 1994

long white roll *noun*
a factory-made cigarette *US, 1945*

- — Lou Shelly, *Hepcats Jive Talk Dictionary*, p. 28, 1945

long-winded *adjective*
in homosexual usage, said of a man who takes a long time to reach orgasm *US, 1981*

- — *Male Swinger Number 3*, p. 48, 1981: "The complete gay dictionary"

loogie *noun*
phlegm that has been expelled from the respiratory passages *US, 1985*

- In the middle of a French kiss, she slips a killer loogie into his face. — *San Francisco Chronicle*, 27th April 1985
- The body snatcher giggled and snuffled and hacked up a loogie, while Fortney fired up the boar and drove away, wanting to be well clear if the floater should explode. — Joseph Wambaugh, *Floaters*, p. 147, 1996

loogin *noun*
an awkward, unaccomplished person *US, 1919*

- That was the kind of man to be associating with, no McGinty and these loogins from the express company. — James T. Farrell, *Willie Collins*, p. 110, 1946

looie; louie; looey *noun*

1 a lieutenant *US, 1916*

- "What the hell do you think of this new looey?" — Norman Mailer, *The Naked and the Dead*, p. 460, 1948
- Hey, you see that new second looey? — Charles Anderson, *The Grunts*, p. 113, 1976
- The next morning some young looey stood in the doorway and called everybody's name. — Larry Heinemann, *Close Quarters*, p. 273, 1977
- A hundred times he flies the Hueys / Flown by publicity-seeking lueys. — Joseph Tuso, *Singing the Vietnam Blues*, p. 39, 1990: The Ballad of the PIO

2 a gob of phlegm or nasal mucus *US, 1970*

- He hocked such a huge looie that I had a spiderweb of saliva running from my dark glasses onto my hair. — Howard Stern, *Miss America*, p. 340, 1995

look *noun*
in the entertainment industry, the right to review and consider a script or project *US, 1999*

- "I go to another studio. Tower has first look, that's all. They turn it down I can take it anywhere I want." — Elmore Leonard, *Be Cool*, p. 6, 1999

look *verb*

▸ **look at the gate**
to near the end of a prison sentence *US, 1984*

- — Inez Cardozo-Freeman, *The Joint*, p. 513–514, 1984

▸ **look at the procter and gamble**
to cheat during an examination or test *US, 1968*
A pun alluding to the well-known corporation.

- — Collin Baker et al., *College Undergraduate Slang Study Conducted at Brown University*, p. 152, 1968

▸ **look for a hole in the fence**
(used of a racehorse) to perform very poorly, as if the horse would rather find a hole in the fence and return to the stable *US, 1976*

- — Tom Ainslie, *Ainslie's Complete Guide to Thoroughbred Racing*, p. 334, 1976

▸ **look out the window**
in horse racing, to fail to bet on a horse in a race it wins after betting on the horse in a number of previous losing efforts *US, 1951*

- — David W. Maurer, *Argot of the Racetrack*, p. 41, 1951

looker *noun*
an attractive woman *US, 1892*

- That was some looker what just trotted out of here. — Robert Campbell, *Nibbled to Death by Ducks*, p. 260, 1989

lookie *verb*
to look *US, 1972*
A diminutive that introduces a folksy tone; almost always used in the imperative.

- Lookie here, cats. Lookie here at the cat who holds the key to the whole jivin' tomorrow. — Dan Jenkins, *Semi-Tough*, p. 135, 1972

lookie-loo *noun*

1 a customer who enjoys looking at merchandise but has no intention of buying *US, 1978*

- Looky-loos, that breed of bird that made it an evening out going around drooling over items they could never afford. — Robert Campbell, *Juice*, pp. 228–229, 1988
- Hopefully there'd be a lot more when the finals got under way, but of course most of the tourists were looky-loos. — Joseph Wambaugh, *Floaters*, p. 17, 1996
- Made famous by a series of commercials for Twentieth Century real estate. — Editors of Ben is Dead, *Retrohell*, p. 115, 1997

2 an inquisitive observer *US, 1979*

- She had noticed, however, that no one, not even the nosiest Lookie-Loo, ever looked into the drier or under the bed. — Barbara Abercrombie, *Good Riddance*, p. 20, 1979
- The lookie-lous planted themselves. — John Ridley, *Everybody Smokes in Hell*, p. 136, 1999

look of eagles *noun*
in horse racing, the proud look perceived in the eyes of a great racehorse *US, 1976*

- — Tom Ainslie, *Ainslie's Complete Guide to Thoroughbred Racing*, p. 334, 1976

look-see *noun*
a viewing, an observation *US, 1854*

- Dusted off and gone home with a million dollars wortha gunge on his pecker, all the way at Michael Reese Hospital, 'cause some fucken lifer wanted to have a "look-see." — Larry Heinemann, *Close Quarters*, p. 168, 1977
- Mario Villalobos, while awaiting the arrival of the shoulder holster kids, had given his crime report another perfunctory looksee. — Joseph Wambaugh, *The Delta Star*, p. 39, 1983
- I approached slowly, slowly, and had a look-see. — Richard Marcinko and John Weisman, *Rogue Warrior*, p. 17, 1992

look that up in your Funk and Wagnalls!
used for a humorous observation about a word or fact *US, 1967*
One of the most popular catchphrases from the US television series *Laugh-In* (1967–73) and repeated referentially.

loomer *noun*
a large wave that suddenly appears seaward *US, 1964*

- — John Severson, *Modern Surfing Around the World*, p. 172, 1964

loon *noun*
a madman *US, 1823*
Abbreviation of "lunatic."

- [W]hat else could I or any other loon from my peer group ever possibly become schizoid over but a lousy rock 'n' roll album? — Lester Bangs, *Psychotic Reactions and Carburetor Dung*, p. 11, 1971
- I'm thinking, Oh, I always get these loons next to me, what is it about me? — Edward Lin, *Big Julie of Vegas*, p. 213, 1974
- To his awestruck fellow loons back on the ward he offered this modest yet manly explanation: "Just to show 'em I could take it." — Seth Morgan, *Homeboy*, p. 43, 1990

looney tune; loony tune *noun*
a crazy person *US, 1967*
From the television cartoons created by Warner Brothers beginning in 1960. The variant "looney tunes" is also used as a singular.

- Paul [Simonon]'s loony toon playfulness. — Lester Bangs, *Psychotic Reactions and Carburetor Dung*, p. 238, 1977
- He was the local looney tunes. — Edwin Torres, *After Hours*, p. 370, 1979
- We've got a top-of-the-line loony-tune either way you cut it. — *Basic Instinct*, 1992

looney tunes *adjective*
insane *US, 1971*

- I started to realize that they had decided I was loony-tunes. — Cleo Odzer, *Goa Freaks*, p. 258, 1995

loon platoon *noun*
the patients at an insane asylum *US, 1977*

- He was carted off to the state prison for the criminally insane. He referred to this experience as being drafted into the loon platoon. — Jerry McGinley, *Miles to Go Before I Sleep*, p. 46, 2002

loony *noun*
a madman *US, 1883*
An abbreviation of "lunatic."

- Which one of you claims to be the craziest? Which one is the biggest loony? — Ken Kesey, *One Flew Over the Cuckoo's Nest*, p. 17, 1962
- I smiled stupidly at people passing, as if this loony were my bereaved brother-in-law. — Leonard Cohen, *Beautiful Losers*, p. 45, 1966
- In less than 10 days we registered about 300 street-loonies who never even thought about voting. — Hunter S. Thompson, *Fear and Loathing in America*, p. 224, 6th December 1969: Letter to Warren Hinckle
- Lobotomy—isn't that for loonies? — *Repo Man*, 1984

loony *adjective*
extremely erratic; mildly crazy *US, 1841*

- "Too bad she's loony," he said to himself, a little later, "because she sure is pretty." — Max Shulman, *Rally Round the Flag, Boys!*, p. 12, 1957
- He was delighted with himself for having had the foresight to be loony and to have the papers to prove it. — Mary McCarthy, *The Group*, p. 278, 1963

- Archibald Cox (crew-cut) told me that he thought anyone who made a big thing about kids' hair was loony as hell (or something to that effect, I don't remember his exact words). — James Simon Kunen, *The Strawberry Statement*, p. 87, 1968
- "Where's that loony fruit Al Ginsbert?!?" I shouted, rushing to overtake him. — Terry Southern, *Now Dig This*, p. 121, November 1968

loony bin *noun*
a hospital (or other institution) for the treatment of psychiatric problems and mental illness *UK, 1919*
- Throwed his ass in a loonybin, called him insane. — Robert Gover, *JC Saves*, p. 172, 1968
- State Law requires the testimony of two shrinks in order to commit one psycho to the loony bin[.] — Oscar Zeta Acosta, *The Autobiography of a Brown Buffalo*, p. 151, 1972
- Got one kid in the loony bin, and my wife's headed there. — George V. Higgins, *Penance for Jerry Kennedy*, p. 141, 1985

loony bird *noun*
a person who is at least eccentric, at most mentally unstable *US, 1964*
- Boy, you pay off that hyphenated loon-bird and pack him in. — Max Shulman, *Anyone Got a Match?*, p. 79, 1964

loony farm *noun*
an insane asylum *US, 1977*
- "I think the wife checked into a loony farm up near St. Louis or something." — Nick Evangelista, *Country Living is Risky Business*, p. 37, 2000

loony house *noun*
an insane asylum *US, 1959*
- "That would have landed you right in the loony house." — LIsi Marburg Goodman, *Light at the End of the Tunnel*, p. 155, 2002

loony roost *noun*
a mental hospital *US, 1949*
- "[I]t's not enough to give me time 'n too many for the loony roost." — Nelson Algren, *The Man with the Golden Arm*, p. 275, 1949

loop *noun*
1 a short pornographic video shown on a recurring cycle *US, 1973*
- Back in the neolithic days of 1969, most sex theaters were running loops of ten-minute girlie films. — George Paul Csicsery (Editor), *The Sex Industry*, p. 165, 1973
- He took us to the company studio and we dubbed (made erotic sounds) for his peep-show loops. — Tina Russell, *Porno Star*, p. 33, 1973
- Loops are the short sex scenes usually shown at peep shows—small, individual projection booths located in the rear of many adult bookshops. — Stephen Ziplow, *The Film Maker's Guide to Pornography*, p. 12, 1977
- Why not make loops for the Fat Man? — Seth Morgan, *Homeboy*, p. 188, 1990

2 in television and movie-making, voice recordings that are used with previously recorded video *US, 1980*
- But they would talk and Julie would run to the studio where she was doing voice loops for an Italian-made film... — Elmore Leonard, *Gold Coast*, p. 151, 1980
- He recorded two versions of the statement, a thirty-second loop for radio and two fifteen-second sound bites for television. — Carl Hiaasen, *Tourist Season*, p. 143, 1986

3 an intrauterine contraceptive device *US, 1972*
- — Helen Dahlskog (Editor), *A Dictionary of Contemporary and Colloquial Usage*, p. 33, 1972
- So I'll say sure, Roddy, whatever you want, let's make a baby. I never told him about wearing the loop. — Carl Hiaasen, *Native Tongue*, p. 214, 1991

4 the people in a business or enterprise who make critical decisions; the process by which those critical decisions are made *US, 1987*
A person is either "in the loop" or "out of the loop."
- — *American Speech*, Fall 1988
- — Connie Eble (Editor), *UNC-CH Campus Slang*, p. 4, Fall 1997

▸ **out of the loop**
not part of a process or inner circle *US, 1976*

Loop *noun*
▸ **the Loop**
the core central area of Chicago *US, 1946*
From the elevated railway constructed in 1897 that loops around two square miles of central Chicago.

- He had not been in the Loop at lunchtime in several years. — James T. Farrell, *Willie Collins*, p. 101, 1946
- And the Loop is the heart of Chicago's commercial life, the capital of her civic activities, and the headquarters of her underworld. — Jack Lait and Lee Mortimer, *Chicago Confidential*, p. 11, 1950
- But we forgot that and headed straight for North Clark Street, after a spin in the Loop[.] — Jack Kerouac, *On the Road*, p. 238, 1957
- Mr. Cox, Railroad's Papa, dropped dead while shining a customer's shoes in the Loop barber shop where he had worked for twenty years. — Iceberg Slim (Robert Beck), *Mama Black Widow*, p. 193, 1969

loop-de-loop *noun*
simultaneous, reciprocal oral sex between two people *US, 1971*
- — Eugene Landy, *The Underground Dictionary*, p. 121, 1971

looped; looping *adjective*
drunk *US, 1934*
Descriptive of the inability when drunk to maintain a straight line.
- The sap sounded half looped and was only too happy to tell me that there was better than ten grand in his safe[.] — Mickey Spillane, *The Big Kill*, p. 33, 1951
- He got a little looped as the evening progressed. — John Conway, *Love in Suburbia*, p. 38, 1960
- [W]e were more than pretty well looped—we were blind. — John Nichols, *The Sterile Cuckoo*, p. 190, 1965
- "They're all pretty well looped." — Charles Whited, *Chiodo*, p. 160, 1973

looper *noun*
a wave that breaks over itself, creating a hollow through which a surfer can ride *US, 1964*
- — John Severson, *Modern Surfing Around the World*, p. 172, 1964

loop joint *noun*
an arcade showing recurring pornographic videos in private booths *US, 1986*
- A woman in San Francisco who has worked as a stripper in most of the live sex shows all over the West, including loop joints and brothels in Nevada, insists that no connection exists between sex and violence[.] — Hunter S. Thompson, *Generation of Swine*, p. 130, 16th June 1986

loop-legged *adjective*
drunk *US, 1944*
- All that beer and a stiff drink, to boot? Little wonder his head hurt. Both he and Charlie had been loop-legged when they left the bar. — Catherine Anderson, *Blue Skies*, p. 25, 2004

loop-scoop *verb*
to steal something quickly *US, 1972*
- — Bruce Jackson, *Outside the Law*, p. 58, 1972: "Glossary"
- [T]hat's when you come to the penitentiary they'll go loop-scoop your old lady and get her selling cock and they don't send you any of the money. — Bruce Jackson, *Outside the Law*, p. 157, 1972

loopy *adjective*
slightly mad; drunk *UK, 1925*
A conventional "loop" is an obvious aberration from a straight line.
- Sidney Blackpool was looking for Victor Watson in all this loopy art mix[.] — Joseph Wambaugh, *The Secrets of Harry Bright*, p. 15, 1985

loose *adjective*
1 (of a slot machine) advantageous to the gambler, both in terms of the frequency of payouts and a small house advantage *US, 1984*
- — J. Edward Allen, *The Basics of Winning Slots*, p. 58, 1984

2 romantically unattached *US, 1968*
- — Joan Fontaine et al., *Dictionary of Black Slang*, 1968

loose bump *noun*
in the military, an unsolicited and unwanted promotion *US, 1947*
- — *American Speech*, p. 55, February 1947: "Pacific war language"

loose cannon *noun*
a person whose actions or words cannot be controlled or predicted *US, 1977*
From the image of a cannon rolling loose on the deck of a fighting ship.

- Meese had added, however, that the entire operation had been run by one man working on his own in the White House basement, a "loose cannon," as Meese put it, named Oliver North. — H. Jay Riker, *The Silent Service*, p. 39, 2001

loose goose *adjective*
applied to something or someone that can be described as loose in whatever sense *US, 1958*

- That Foreman camp was totally whacked out, so uptight compared with Ali, who runs a loose-goose operation. — Bill Cardoso, *The Maltese Sangweech*, p. 299, 1984

loose wig *noun*
a wild demeanor *US, 1959*

- — *Look*, p. 49, 24th November 1959

loosey-goosey *adjective*
very loose in any sense *US, 1943*

- I'm lookin' like money, but the best kind, casual, loosey-goosey. — Edwin Torres, *After Hours*, p. 177, 1979
- You take it too serious. I wanna see you loosey goosey up there on the eighteenth tee. — Joseph Wambaugh, *The Secrets of Harry Bright*, p. 150, 1985
- "She'd just jump from one man to the next at the senior meeting," Grandma said. "And I heard she was real loosey-goosey." — Janet Evanovich, *Seven Up*, p. 17, 2001

loosie *noun*
an individual cigarette sold over the counter *US, 1981*

- — Terry Williams, *Crackhouse*, p. 150, 1992
- — John Fahs, *Cigarette Confidential*, p. 302, 1996: "Glossary"

loosie goosie *noun*
a sexually promiscuous young woman *US, 1979*

- I saw Brad weaving off through the bushes with some Loosie Goosie and I remember laughing and thinking that now I could forget about the little padlock I'd planned on getting him for his zipper. — Beatrice Sparks, *Jay's Journal*, p. 115, 1979

loot *noun*
1 money *US, 1929*

- "How much loot you got?" asked the man. "I beg your pardon?" "Money. How much?" — Max Shulman, *The Many Loves of Dobie Gillis*, p. 30, 1951
- He ran out of loot and marble at the same time. — William "Lord" Buckley, *Nero*, 1951
- Take this beat-up bovine to market and don't come back without some real loot. — Steve Allen, *Bop Fables*, p. 54, 1955
- I get 75 cents an hour and it's making more loot for me to hit road with. — Jack Kerouac, *Letter to Allen Ginsberg*, p. 494, 14th July 1955

2 a lieutenant *US, 1967*

- Chilly placed the loot's coffee at his elbow. — Malcolm Braly, *On the Yard*, p. 94, 1967

loot-in *noun*
politically motivated group shoplifting *US, 1970*

- He flipped out over Keith's suggestion that "a thousand children will stage Loot-ins at department stores to strike at the property fetish that underlies genocidal war." — Jerry Rubin, *Do It!*, p. 73, 1970

loot money *noun*
after World War 2, Chinese national currency obtained by looting *US, 1949*

- — *American Speech*, p. 31, February 1949: "A.V.G. Lingo"

lop *noun*
a nervous, timid, cautious person *US, 1992*
An elaboration of **RABBIT**.

- You can tell rabbits, you know, the lops in here. — Pete Earley, *The Hot House*, p. 141, 1992

lope *verb*
to stroke *US, 1974*

- Tompkins had such a peeny pecker he'd of had to lope it with forefinger and thumb. — Earl Thompson, *Tattoo*, p. 294, 1974

▶ **lope your donkey**
(of a male) to masturbate *US, 1985*

- "Old Chester going 'Ain't it wooooooonderful' while he's loping that old rubber donkey!" — Joseph Wambaugh, *The Secrets of Harry Bright*, p. 171, 1985

▶ **lope your mule**
(of a male) to masturbate *US, 1967*

- "Pithead's queer for soap," he told his buddies on the yard. "He sleeps with a bar under his pillow and sniffs it while he lopes his mule." — Malcolm Braly, *On the Yard*, p. 8, 1967
- "[L]oping his mule, giving free reign to his sexual fantasies." — Richard Drake, *Freedom Run*, p. 120, 2002

lop-ear *noun*
an easily duped person *US, 1950*

- — *The Annals of the American Academy of Political and Social Sciences*, p. 127, May 1950
- Figured we'd cull out, from the lopears arriving, a mark to trim on the "smack." — Iceberg Slim (Robert Beck), *Long White Con*, p. 30, 1977

lop-ear; lop-eared *adjective*
naive, gullible *US, 1863*

- It's easy to steer a lop-eared chump, so long as Mordecai Jones has sized up the mark. — Guy Owen, *The Flim-Flam Man and the Apprentice Grifter*, p. 168, 1972

lopp *noun*
a perpetually naive and ignorant person *US, 1989*

- — James Harris, *A Convict's Dictionary*, p. 35, 1989

Lord Jesus *noun*
a curly hairstyle popular with black men and women in the mid-1970s *US, 1975*

- It's goodby Afro, hello curls for scads of local hip black men who are part of the international, unisex trend to curly hair. They call the style "a Superfly," "a Lord Jesus" or just "a Curly Do" and they're spending lots of time and money to get the look. — *San Francisco Examiner*, p. 34, 13th April 1975

Los *noun*
Los Angeles, California *US, 1913*
Border Spanish used in English conversation by Mexican-Americans.

- — George Carpenter Baker, *Pachuco*, p. 42, January 1950
- And then they were offered a ride to "Los," as they refer to Los Angeles on the streets. — Joseph Wambaugh, *Lines and Shadows*, p. 78, 1984

Los Angeles turnaround *noun*
a powerful central nervous system stimulant *US, 1968*

- Some of the names describe the drugs' effects, such as "helpers," "copilots," "Los Angeles turn arounds," or their shape, color and markings—"hearts," "footballs," "blackjacks," "crossroads." — Phil Hirsch, *Hooked*, pp. 51–52, 1968

lose *verb*
1 to get rid of *US, 1931*

- — Ralph S. Singleton, *Filmmaker's Dictionary*, p. 98, 1990

2 (used of a computer program) to fail to work as expected *US, 1983*

- — Guy L. Steele et al., *The Hacker's Dictionary*, p. 87, 1983

▶ **lose a load**
to ejaculate *US, 1964*

- — *American Speech*, p. 117, May 1964: "Problems in the study of campus slang"

▶ **lose water**
in bodybuilding, to perspire *US, 1984*
Done intentionally before competition in bodybuilding in order to improve muscle definition.

- — *American Speech*, p. 200, Fall 1984: "The language of body building"

▶ **lose your lunch**
to vomit *US, 1918*

- And I think he would have lost his lunch if he knew that his wife was The Plumber's daughter[.] — Richard Condon, *Prizzi's Money*, p. 47, 1994

loser *noun*
1 a socially inept person; a person with consistently bad luck; anyone deemed unacceptable or an outcast *US, 1955*

- — *Washington Post*, 23th April 1961: "Man, dig this jazz"
- — Collin Baker et al., *College Undergraduate Slang Study Conducted at Brown University*, p. 153, 1968
- — *American Speech*, p. 62, Spring–Summer 1975

2 a convicted felon *US, 1912*

- — Hyman E. Goldin et al., *Dictionary of American Underworld Lingo*, p. 129, 1950
- Richard Douglas Wilson, white male, age thirty-four. Two-time loser with a Quentin jacket. — James Ellroy, *Blood on the Moon*, p. 83, 1984

3 a hospital patient who dies *US, 1970*

- This kid looks like a loser. — *M*A*S*H*, 1970

lossage *noun*
the ongoing effect of a computer malfunction *US, 1991*

- Thus (for example) a temporary hardware failure is a loss, but bugs in an important tool (like a compiler) are serious lossage. — Eric S. Raymond, *The New Hacker's Dictionary*, p. 228, 1991

loss-leader *noun*
something displayed prominently, and at a cut-price rate, to encourage further buying of other stock *US, 1922*

- How much of it was practically loss-leader stuff, items that we have to sell in order to compete? — Jim Thompson, *The Grifters*, p. 165, 1963

lossy *adjective*
(used of a data-compression computer program) apt to lose some data *US, 1997*

- A "lossy" algorithm (such as JPEG) therefore can't possibly be used to compress a piece of software—if even one bit is mislaid, the program just won't run—but it's just fine when it comes to compressing pictures, video, or sound. — Andy Ihnatko, *Cyberspeak*, p. 115, 1997

lost *adjective*
murdered, especially as a victim of "criminal justice" *US, 1962*

- — Joseph E. Ragen and Charles Finston, *Inside the World's Toughest Prison*, p. 808, 1962: "Penitentiary and underworld glossary"

lost-and-found badge *noun*
a US Army name tag *US, 1991*
Gulf war usage.

- — *American Speech*, p. 394, Winter 1991: "Among the new words"

lost in the sauce *adjective*
daydreaming, completely inattentive *US, 1988*

- — *Washington Post*, p. 7, 3rd January 1988: "Say wha?"

lost sailor *noun*
in the language surrounding the Grateful Dead, a follower of the band who has lost all touch with reality *US, 1994*
From the title of a Grateful Dead song.

- — David Shenk and Steve Silberman, *Skeleton Key*, p. 182, 1994

Lost Wages *nickname*
Las Vegas, Nevada *US, 1951*

- In the last two years I have lost about $40,000 at "Lost Wages, Nev." and Del Mar. — *Los angeles Times*, p. 22, 5th September 1951
- Las Vegas, or "Lost Wages," as it's known in Westside, is off limits to all Negroes—except entertainers and janitors. — Ed Reid and Ovid Demaris, *The Green Felt Jungle*, p. 136, 1963
- — Ralph de Sola, *Crime Dictionary*, pp. 199–200, 1982

losum game *noun*
in the language of carnival workers, a game that for whatever reason should be terminated immediately *US, 1985*

- — Gene Sorrows, *All About Carnivals*, pp. 21–22, 1985: "Terminology"

lot lady *noun*
in circus and carnival usage, a local woman who is attracted to and makes herself sexually available to circus or carnival employees *US, 1981*
In short, a circus or carnival **GROUPIE**.

- — Don Wilmeth, *The Language of American Popular Entertainment*, p. 162, 1981

lot lizard *noun*
a prostitute who works at truck stops *US, 1987*

- Lot lizards will often advertise on the CB by asking truckers if they need any "commercial company." — Jim Crotty, *How to Talk American*, p. 371, 1997
- That's why he's a good pimp for a lot lizard to have. — J.T. LeRoy, *Sarah*, p. 1, 2000
- Truckers who don't want solicitations from hookers, he explains, put a decal on their windshield depicting a lizard behind a red circle with a bar through it. (The creature is a reference to the slang term for truck-stop prostitutes: lot lizards.) — *Riverfront Times (St. Louis)*, 6th August 2003
- You the smallest lot lizard I ever seen, trickin' them truckers for change. — *Hustle and Flow*, 2004

lot loafer *noun*
in circus and carnival usage, a local resident who loiters as a show is assembled or taken down *US, 1981*

- — Don Wilmeth, *The Language of American Popular Entertainment*, p. 107, 1981

lot louse *noun*
a person drawn to carnivals and circuses *US, 1980*

- Twenty dollars a week didn't put me above the lot lice, as the carnival folks called the townsfolk. — Drew Page, *Drew's Blues*, p. 9, 1980
- — Joe McKennon, *Circus Lingo*, p. 59, 1980
- Other than for a few lot lice, the midway remained devoid of marks. — Peter Fenton, *Eyeing the Flash*, p. 182, 2005

Lotusland *noun*
a paradise *US, 1980*

- Florida meant exposed skin and illicit liquor, nightclubs with hot jazz and rouged lips, a Lotusland where you could lounge under palm trees[.] — Diane Roberts, *Dream State*, p. 218, 2004

lou *noun*
a lieutenant *US, 1973*

- I heard you talking to the lou. — Charles Whited, *Chiodo*, p. 129, 1973

loud handle *noun*
the mechanism controlling the ejection seat in an airplane *US, 1977*

- He grabbed the loud handle and pulled. The canopy blasted off. — Ron Karren, *Wing Commander*, p. 269, 1998

loudmouth *verb*
to speak forcefully and aggressively *US, 1938*

- He started cussing and shouting even before he stormed into the hut, loudmouthing the woman from one end of the little street to the other. — Ossie Davis, *With Ossie and Ruby*, p. 134, 1998

loud mouth lime *noun*
green signal smoke *US, 2004*
The allusion to the color of a powdered sweet drink was to throw off enemy listeners.

- — David Hart, *First Air Cavalry Division Vietnam Dictionary*, p. 37, 2004

loud pedal *noun*
the foot pedal controlling the after-burners on a military aircraft *US, 1990*

- The Marine pilot kept his foot on the loud pedal all the way and made the trip in thirty-seven minutes. — Lee Child, *Lee Child*, p. 148, 2000

loudtalk *verb*
to speak forcefully and aggressively *US, 1930*

- He did not take his eyes off me as I walked up, and he kept loud-talking me. — Louis Armstrong, *Satchmo*, p. 212, 1930

louie *noun*
a left turn *US, 1967*

- — *Current Slang*, p. 6, Spring 1968

Louisiana lottery *noun*
an illegal numbers game *US, 1949*

- — *American Speech*, p. 192, October 1949: "The argot of number gambling"

louse *noun*
a despicable person *US, 1864*

- "The louse!" Bernie exclaimed. "Did he try to push you around?" — Irving Shulman, *Cry Tough*, p. 25, 1949
- What was the louse arrested for? — C.D. Payne, *Youth in Revolt*, p. 301, 1993

louse book *noun*
an illegal betting operation that accepts only very small bets *US, 1951*

- — David W. Maurer, *Argot of the Racetrack*, p. 41, 1951

loused up *adjective*
covered with scars and abscesses from repeated drug injections *US, 1970*

- — William D. Alsever, *Glossary for the Establishment and Other Uptight People*, p. 18, December 1970

louse trap *noun*
a vermin-invested low-cost hotel or room *US, 1946*

- — Irving Lewis Allen, *The City in Slang*, p. 156, 1993

lousy *adjective*
contemptible, shoddy, bad *UK, 1386*
Because of the association with body lice, the term was deemed vulgar if not taboo in the US well into the C20.

- "Well. Go to sleep now. How was your dinner?" "Lousy." — J.D. Salinger, *Catcher in the Rye*, p. 177, 1951

- [T]hey sing the praises of the working man's red-state virtues even while they pummel the working man's economic chances with out-sourcing, new overtime rules, lousy health insurance, and coercive new management techniques. — Thomas Frank, *What's the Matter with Kansas?*, p. 151, 2004

Lousy-ana *noun*
Louisiana *US, 1942*
- When the Tide got up, 35-0, against Lousy-ana Tech, coach Gene Stallings decided to start substituting. — *The Commercial Appeal (Memphis)*, p. D7, 27th September 1993
- We used to call it Fort Puke, Lousy-ana. — *The Post-Standard (Syracuse)*, p. A5, 1st July 2003
- "It used to be Louisiana, but now we call it Lousy-ana," said Thanh, who is staying at the Buddhist temple. — *Houston Chronicle*, p. B7, 10th September 2005

love apple *noun*
a tomato *US, 1956*
- "I wouldn't eat love apples," he warned his friend. "It's a poison fruit." — Nelson Algren, *A Walk on the Wild Side*, p. 59, 1956

love bladder *noun*
a condom *US, 1968*
- I turned and saw what the wind and the tide had brought in from Brooklyn and from the city's sewers; a sub-aquatic forest of waving white rubber eels, thousands of love-bladders. — Angelo d'Arcangelo, *The Homosexual Handbook*, p. 219, 1968

love boat *noun*
phencyclidine, the recreational drug known as PCP or angel dust *US, 1983*
- Asked how may knew about the drug "Lovely" or "Loveboat"—street slang for PCP—nearly all raised their hands. — *Washington Post*, p. B3, 20th November 1983
- — US Department of Justice, *Street Terms*, October 1994

love bone *noun*
the penis *US, 1962*
- "Ya make me nervous with that death talk and my love bone goes down." — Paul Crump, *Burn, Killer, Burn!*, p. 386, 1962
- Larry's legions of enemies planned to trap him and lop off his love bone. — Iceberg Slim, *Death Wish*, p. 44, 1977
- Just me and my *** love bone. — Eric V. Copage, *SoulMates*, p. 23, 2001

love box *noun*
the vagina *US, 1985*
- "Her love box is all dried up." — Wendy Doniger, *Tales of Sex and Violence*, p. 80, 1985
- Have you ever heard the expressions precious, mound, garden, tri-angle, love box[?] — Barbara Keesling, *How to Talk Sexy to the One You Love*, p. 69, 1996
- I rubbed her pussy mound with my thumb while I slid my dick in and out of her love box. — *Penthouse International, Letters to Penthouse XII*, p. 58, 2001

love button *noun*
the clitoris *US, 1994*
- Swirl your tongue around the hood, circumscribing the love button. Then get your whole mouth around her clitoris. — Amy Goddard, *Lesbian Sex Secrets for Men*, p. 136, 2001

love canal *noun*
the vagina *US, 1987*
- — Eric V. Copage, *SoulMates*, p. 23, 2001

love cherry *noun*
a bruise from a suction kiss *US, 1951*
- When Rocky took off his shirt I saw that he had a big red love cherry on his shoulder. — Ethel Waters, *His Eye is on the Sparrow*, p. 118, 1951

love child *noun*
a member of the 1960s counterculture *US, 1970*
- The other thing that concerns us, in the Berkeley scene originally we had the flower children and the hippie and the love child. — United States Congress Committee on Internal Security, *The Black Panther Party*, pp. 392–3, 1970
- "They call themselves love children!" It was in the paper, the whole bullshit trip. — Herbert Huncke, *Guilty of Everything*, p. 169, 1990

love drug *noun*
the recreational drug methaqualone, best known as Quaaludes™ *US, 1985*
- By 1972 it was one of the most popular drugs of abuse in the United States and was known as love drug, heroin for lovers, Dr. Jekyll and Mr. Hyde, sopors, sopes, ludes, mandrakes and quacks. — Marilyn Carroll and Gary Gallo, *Methaqualone*, p. 18, 1985

love factory *noun*
a brothel *US, 1963*
- I came through the back way Papa Manny always used when the police raided the old love factory he ran. — Mickey Spillane, *Me, Hood!*, p. 25, 1963

love glove *noun*
a condom *US, 1987*
- [A]lthough their standards and practices permitted the words "prophylatctic" and "contraceptive," and even a student who calls a condom a "love glove," the word "condom" was not allowed. — *PR Newswire*, 2nd November 1987
- However, even a love glove can't always protect you from herpes simplex, genital warts or hepatitis B. — Lisa Sussman, *Sex in the City*, p. 241, 2003

love handles *noun*
a roll of fat on either side of the body, just above the waist *US, 1970*
- — *Current Slang*, p. 20, Spring 1970
- She is too well acquainted with the ridges and the valleys of my deteriorating body, and can tell right off when I have strapped the metal thing on my love handles." — George Higgins, *Kennedy for the Defense*, p. 153, 1980
- HEATHER: He's got those love handles. — *Clerks*, 1994

love hole *noun*
the vagina *US, 1986*
- The animal's penis connected with her love hole. — Maxim Jakubowski, *The Mammoth Book of Historical Erotica*, p. 390, 1998
- The feel of the fabric against my love-hole was making me cream again. — *Penthouse Magazine, Letters to Penthouse XXII*, p. 146, 2004
- I reached back down to her love hole, it was slippery with cunt-juice and she swayed slightly as I inserted my fingers gently. — Jani, *G-Gasm*, p. 92, 2006

love juice *noun*
semen *UK, 1882*
- — Donald Webster Cory and John P. LeRoy, *The Homosexual and His Society*, p. 265, 1963: "A lexicon of homosexual slang"
- To man, sperm is "nature's love juice." — Anka Radakovich, *The Wild Girls Club*, p. 110, 1994

love lips *noun*
the vaginal labia *US, 1969*
- She took it in the right spirit, but when I reached her love lips she said, blushing, "It's my period." — Michael Perkins, *The Secret Record*, p. 45, 1976

lovely *noun*
1 an attractive woman *UK, 1938*
- "When I walk down the fairway I want the lovelies to know it's me for sure," Donny once explained. — Dan Jenkins, *Dead Solid Perfect*, p. 91, 1986

2 phencyclidine, the recreational drug known as PCP or angel dust *US, 1978*
A longer variant is "lovely high."
- Asked how many knew about the drug "Lovely" or "Loveboat"—street slang for PCP – nearly all raised their hands. — *Washington Post*, p. B3, 20th November 1983
- — US Department of Justice, *Street Terms*, October 1994

love machine *noun*
an energetic lover with great stamina *US, 1969*
- It's almost too good to be true. I'm a love machine. — Mantak Ciha, *The Multi-Orgasmic Man*, 1996

love muscle *noun*
the penis *US, 1958*
- Put a lip lock on my love muscle. — Ken Weaver, *Texas Crude*, p. 81, 1984
- He fit the huge, sopping head of his love muscle to George's pucker and worked the entire seven inches inside. — Dennis Cooper, *Closer*, p. 80, 1990

- I have a well-developed love muscle. — Anka Radakovich, *The Wild Girls Club*, p. 228, 1994
- And guided my love muscle into her wet, hot box. — Firebird, *Journey to Dimension Nine*, p. 153, 2006

love nest *noun*

1 a secluded room, apartment or house where lovers rendez-vous *US, 1919*

- She had not left the apartment above the Paradise Room during the entire week, and would have stayed in the love nest for the rest of her life had Duke only asked her. — Donald Goines, *Inner City Hoodlum*, p. 85, 1975

2 the vagina *US, 1994*

- In addition to oral moves, some women occasionally like a finger or two inserted into the love nest. — Anka Radakovich, *The Wild Girls Club*, p. 131, 1994

love nuts *noun*

testicles that ache because of sexual stimulation that has not led to ejaculation; sexual frustration *US, 1971*

- — Eugene Landy, *The Underground Dictionary*, p. 122, 1971
- He then had to walk around for two days with his love-nuts trapped in glassware[.] — *FHM*, p. 250, June 2003

love pill *noun*

a capsule of MDA, a synthetic amphetamine *US, 1970*

- — William D. Alsever, *Glossary for the Establishment and Other Uptight People*, p. 19, December 1970

love pillows *noun*

the female breasts *US, 2005*

- Dr. Bess drops her scrubs, showing us her pert li'l love-pillows. — Mr. Skin, *Mr. Skin's Skincyclopedia*, p. 25, 2005

love pump *noun*

the penis *US, 1984*

Popularized if not coined for the film *This Is Spinal Tap*.

- This piece is called "Lick My Love Pump." — Christopher Guest, *This Is Spinal Tap*, 1984
- "You really want my love pump up ya, don't ya girl?" — Bettina Varese, *Erotica 1*, p. 187, 1999

lover *noun*

1 a prostitute's customer who is determined to arouse the prostitute's sexual interest *US, 1971*

- A "lover" is a customer who is determined to arouse the prostitute or to get her to respond to him. — Charles Winick, *The Lively Commerce*, p. 188, 1971

2 any sex offender *US, 1950*

- — Hyman E. Goldin et al., *Dictionary of American Underworld Lingo*, p. 130, 1950

lover's leap *noun*

in backgammon, the customary play with a first roll of 6 – 5: moving a back man 11 points *US, 1970*

- — Jacoby and John Crawford, *The Backgammon Book*, p. 242, 1970

lover's nuts *noun*

testicles that ache because of sexual stimulation that has not led to ejaculation; sexual frustration *US, 1961*

- — Helen Dahlskog (Editor), *A Dictionary of Contemporary and Colloquial Usage*, p. 8, 1972

love, security and devotion *noun*

LSD *US, 1970*

A sobriquet formed from the drug's initials.

- — William D. Alsever, *Glossary for the Establishment and Other Uptight People*, p. 18, December 1970

love steak *noun*

the penis *US, 1989*

- — Pamela Munro, *U.C.L.A. Slang*, p. 56, 1989

love stick *noun*

the penis *US, 1924*

- She let my spent love-stick slide out of her mouth and sat up. — *Penthouse Magazine, Letters to Penthouse V*, p. 130, 1995

lovey-dovey *adjective*

extremely affectionate, sentimental, romantic *US, 1886*

Heard at the turn of the century, then obsolete; heard again in the late 1940s. When not a genuine endearment, it tends to be used contemptuously.

- It's a goddam shame the helling around I do, cheating on her and writing lovey-dovey letters. — Norman Mailer, *The Naked and the Dead*, p. 553, 1948
- Well, diary, when we got all lovey-dovey who should come in but Jill. — Jess Stearn, *Sisters of the Night*, p. 39, 1956
- The HIP merchants were naturally afraid that Emmett and the Diggers might seize upon the moment to disturb their sweet, lovey dovey courtship of the media[.] — Emmett Grogan, *Ringolevio*, p. 267, 1972
- "My parents have never been so lovey-dovey... They were going at it for hours," he confided. — C.D. Payne, *Youth in Revolt*, p. 456, 1993

low and slow *adjective*

describing the manner in which lowriders drive their cars, low to the ground and at a crawl *US, 1985*

- — Jennifer Blowdryer, *Modern English*, p. 65, 1985

low bandwith *adjective*

lacking useful information *US, 1995*

- — Christian Crumlish, *The Internet Dictionary*, p. 114, 1995

low camp *noun*

a coarsely ostentatious style, often unintentional *US, 1963*

An elaboration of **CAMP** (flamboyance).

- "Cut the low camp, bitch!" Chi-Chi barked furiously at Echoes and Encores, shoving the queen's hand roughly away from her shoulder. — John Rechy, *City of Night*, p. 355, 1963

lower 48 *noun*

in Alaska, all states except Alaska *US, 1984*

- — *American Speech*, pp. 256 – 258, Fall 1984: "Terms for 'Not Alaska' in Alaskan English"

lower 49 *noun*

in Alaska, all states except Alaska *US, 1984*

- — *American Speech*, pp. 256 – 258, Fall 1984: "Terms for 'Not Alaska' in Alaskan English"

lower deck *noun*

the genitals, male or female *US, 1967*

- — Dale Gordon, *The Dominion Sex Dictionary*, p. 102, 1967

lower states *noun*

in Alaska, all states except Alaska *US, 1984*

- — *American Speech*, pp. 256 – 258, Fall 1984: "Terms for 'Not Alaska' in Alaskan English"

low-five *verb*

to slap palms below waist-level in greeting or celebration *US, 2002*

- I love-five Horse, kiss Cruella, and case the joint. — David Henry Sterry, *Chicken*, p. 211, 2002

lowgrade *verb*

to disparage with great effect *US, 1973*

- You keep talking that way bout my pardner and I'm gonna LOW GRADE you. — Malachi Andrews and Paul T. Owens, *Black Language*, p. 85, 1973

low-hung *adjective*

possessing a large penis *US, 1964*

- Because you're low-hung and she's high-strung! — Jim Thompson, *Pop. 1280*, p. 191, 1964

Lowies *noun*

Lowenbrau™ beer *US, 1982*

- — Lillian Glass with Richard Liebmann-Smith, *How to Deprogram Your Valley Girl*, p. 27, 1982

low maintenance *adjective*

(used of a person) not requiring a great deal of attention or emotional support *US, 1989*

A term that did not achieve anywhere near the fame of its cousin **HIGH MAINTENANCE**.

- And Ingrid Berman is low maintenance? — *When Harry Met Sally*, 1989

low-man feed *noun*

in pinball, an understanding among friends playing a game that the person with the lowest score on one game will pay for the next game *US, 1977*

- — Bobbye Claire Natkin and Steve Kirk, *All About Pinball*, p. 113, 1977

low man on the totem pole *noun*

in poker, the player with the worst hand *US, 1988*

- — George Percy, *The Language of Poker*, p. 54, 1988

low marble count *noun*
low intelligence *US, 1994*
- — Sally Williams, *"Strong" Words (Dissertation)*, p. 148, 1994

low neck; low neck and short sleeves *noun*
an uncircumcized penis *US, 1941*
- — *Male Swinger Number 3*, p. 48, 1981: "The complete gay dictionary"

low pass *noun*
a preliminary review of a situation *US, 1986*
US naval aviator usage.
- — *United States Naval Institute Proceedings*, p. 108, October 1986

low-rate *verb*
to denigrate; to insult *US, 1906*
- Why's he say it like that? Tryin't lowrate me? — Robert Gover, *JC Saves*, p. 77, 1968
- Now it was their turn to scoff and low-rate me. — Guy Owen, *The Flim-Flam Man and the Apprentice Grifter*, p. 63, 1972

lowrider *noun*
a young person who restores and drives a car with a hydraulic system that lowers the car's chassis to just above the ground *US, 1963*
A lifestyle and art form in the American southwest, especially among Mexican-American youth.
- Low Rider. A Los Angeles nickname for ghetto youth. — Eldridge Cleaver, *Soul on Ice*, p. 4, 1968
- — *Current Slang*, p. 33, Fall 1968
- — Oscar Zeta Acosta, *The Revolt of the Cockroach People*, 1973
- "That lowrider shit is dead." — James Ellroy, *Suicide Hill*, p. 700, 1986

lows *noun*
in pool, the solid-colored balls numbered 1 to 7 *US, 1990*
- — Steve Rushin, *Pool Cool*, p. 15, 1990

low side *noun*
in craps, all the points below seven *US, 1950*
- — *The Annals of the American Academy of Political and Social Sciences*, p. 127, May 1950

loyal to the dollar *adjective*
bribed and compliant with the intent of the bribe *US, 1989*
- Strong competition meant employing more and more backup; the police were no longer "loyal to the dollar" or to the crews they extorted money from. — Terry Williams, *The Cocaine Kids*, p. 123, 1989

LP *noun*
a listening post *US, 1987*
- The LP is next to a trail running through a bamboo thicket that grows to within 30 feet of our wire. — Ernest Spencer, *Welcome to Vietnam, Macho Man*, p. 63, 1987

L's *noun*
a driver's license *US, 2001*
- — Rick Ayers (Editor), *Slang Dictionary*, p. 12, 2001

LSD *nickname*
Lake Shore Drive, Chicago *US, 1985*
- Today the new in spot is Rush Street, located just west of LSD (Lake Short Drive), north of Chicago Avenue ad south of Division Street. — *Graphic Arts Monthly*, p. 57, April 1985
- — Jim Crotty, *How to Talk American*, p. 47, 1997

LT; eltee *noun*
a lieutenant *US, 1977*
From the common abbreviation.
- "Could you tell me where I can find the platoon leader?" "Say? The El-tee?" — Larry Heinemann, *Close Quarters*, p. 17, 1977
- The L.T. was kind enough to let us use his office. — Elmore Leonard, *Be Cool*, p. 21, 1999
- "Fuckin' ARVNs took our C's, LT." — Cherokee Paul McDonald, *Into the Green*, p. 24, 2001

L train *noun*
▶ **take the L train**
to lose, to fail miserably *US, 1993*
- — *Merriam-Webster's Hot Words on Campus Marketing Survey '93*, 1993

L train!
used for a warning that police are nearby *US, 1993*
- — *Washington Post*, p. C5, 7th November 1993

lube *noun*
a lubricant *US, 1970*
- K is for K-Y, miraculous lube! At any good drugstore, a dollar a tube. — *Screw*, p. 15, 22nd March 1970
- "So by the end of the day I totalled nine anals." "Yeeow! That must've hurt. Lotsa lube I imagine?" "Lotsa lube." — Anthony Petkovich, *The X Factory*, p. 55, 1997
- I kept asking for more lube, but finally Red said, "Honey, you have a ton of lube in your ass." — *The Village Voice*, 2nd November 1999
- That's right, just a few squirts of lube on your hand, and you'll be on your way to working his cock well. — Tristan Taormino, *Pucker Up*, p. 57, 2001

lubed *adjective*
drunk *US, 1979*
An abbreviated form of **LUBRICATED**.
- He buys me drinks up the ying yang, gets me righteously lubed, then splits. — James Ellroy, *Because the Night*, p. 485, 1984
- Sounds like his partner's all lubed up. — *Something About Mary*, 1998

lube job *noun*
sex *US, 1973*
- I'm in the mood for a Menage a Trois. This girl needs a Lube Job bad tonight. — Cameron Tuttle, *The Bad Girl's Guide to Getting What You Want*, p. 64, 2000

lubricated *adjective*
drunk *US, 1911*
- "Breda," he said, "we're both still a little lubricated. We shouldn't try to communicate right now." — Joseph Wambaugh, *Fugitive Nights*, p. 234, 1992

luck into *verb*
to be the beneficiary of good fortune *US, 1920*
- Commissioner Cameron seems O.K. is all I'm trying to say, even though he sort of lucked into the job as a compromise candidate of the owners on the forty-eighth ballot. — Dan Jenkins, *Semi-Tough*, p. 15, 1972

luck money *noun*
a tip or gratuity *US, 1948*
- If they stay through, they are besieged for "luck money," as gratuities are known among these habitues and sons of habitues. — Jack Lait and Lee Mortimer, *New York Confidential*, p. 70, 1948

lucky boy; luck boy *noun*
a swindler; a pickpocket *US, 1922*
- And the luck boys were there too. It's easy to spot them when you know what to look for. — Robert Edmond Alter, *Carny Kill*, p. 9, 1966

lucky buck *noun*
a casino gambling coupon *US, 1974*
- — Thomas L. Clark, *The Dictionary of Gambling and Gaming*, p. 123, 1987
- — Michael Dalton, *Blackjack*, p. 62, 1991

lucky Pierre *noun*
the man (or the woman) sandwiched between the outer layers of a sexually active threesome *US, 1942*
Glorified in the following lyric: "Pierre gave it to Sheila, / Who must have brought it there. / He got it from François and Jacques, / A-ha, Lucky Pierre!" (Tom Lehrer, "I Got It From Agnes," 1953). Predominately gay male usage.
- — Wayne Dynes, *Homolexis: A Historical and Cultural Lexicon of Homosexuality*, p. 105, 1985

lucky stiff *noun*
in blackjack, a poor hand that is transformed by a lucky draw into a winning hand *US, 2003*
- — Victor H. Royer, *Casino Gamble Talk*, p. 82, 2003

lu-cu-pu
good night *US, 1948*
A short-lived, but intensely used, piece of bebop slang.
- "What do 'Mop-shi-lu' and 'Lu-cu-pu' mean?" I asked Dizzy. — *San Francisco Examiner*, Pictorial Review, 3 December 1948
- — Arnold Shaw, *Lingo of Tin-Pan Alley*, p. 14, 1950

Lucy *noun*
an individual cigarette sold over the counter *US, 1996*
- — John Fahs, *Cigarette Confidential*, p. 302, 1996: "Glossary"

lude; lud *noun*
a tablet of the recreational drug methaqualone, best known as Quaaludes™; any central nervous system depressant *US,*
1973
Quaalude™ was a brand name for methaqualone, a muscle relaxant and barbiturate substitute introduced in 1965 and made illegal in the US in 1984.
- Still, millions choose to ignore the warnings, and relieve their anxieties with minor tranquilizers like Librium and Valium, or sedate their troubles with more powerful sedative phenobarbital or "purple hearts," Quaaludes or "ludes," and a host of other so called "downers[.]" — *Washington Post*, p. A7, 30th July 1978
- All right. Just relax. Take a lude. Take a lude. — *Manhattan*, 1979
- Laugh at the thought of eating ludes / Laugh at the thought of sniffing glue / Always gonna keep in touch / Never want to use a crutch / I've got the straight edge. — Minor Threat, *Straight Edge*, 1983(?)
- "You wanna lude, is that it?" He pulls out a Pez dispenser and pulls Daffy Ducks' head back. — Bret Easton Ellis, *Less Than Zero*, p. 21, 1985

lude head *noun*
a methaqualone addict or abuser *US, 1980*
- Lude-head comedian Freddie Prinze, star of TV's Chico and the Man, had taken half a dozen the day he shot himself to death in 1977. — Jim Hogshire, *Pills a Go Go*, p. 86, 1999

lude out *verb*
to experience the effects of methaqualone taken recreationally, especially combined with alcohol *US, 1973*
- Street users talk about "luding out"—that is, taking Quaaludes and wine to produce a numb, euphoric state. — Winifred Rosen, *From Chocolate to Morphine*, p. 72, 1993

luer *noun*
a glass syringe with a slip-on needle and a solid plunger *US,*
1973
- — David Maurer and Victor Vogel, *Narcotics and Narcotic Addiction*, p. 424, 1973

lug *noun*
1 a large, clumsy, dim man *US, 1927*
- Then try to get hold of me and maybe we can ambush the lug.
— Mickey Spillane, *I, The Jury*, p. 89, 1947
- I need you to run interference with the lug. Make some small talk with him or something. — *Mallrats*, 1995
- Elliot would walk in and Andy would say, "Hi, you big lug," Or he'd say, "Hi stranger. New in town?" — Elmore Leonard, *Be Cool*, p. 305, 1999
2 a woman who takes lesbian lovers in college and then reverts to heterosexuality after graduation from college *US, 1993*
An abbreviation of "*lesbian until graduation*."
- There is even a new term—"lugs," lesbians until graduation. — *New York Times*, p. 7, 5th June 1993
- — Steven Daly and Nathaniel Wice, *alt.culture*, p. 138, 1995
- — Don R. McCreary (Editor), *Dawg Speak*, 2001
3 a demand *US, 1929*
- I'm hip to the ways you pimps try to play / And the lugs you drop on a frail. — Dennis Wepman et al., *The Life*, p. 86, 1976

lugan *noun*
a Lithuanian *US, 1947*
Coined in Chicago.
- — Bill Reilly, *Big Al's Official Guide to Chicagoese*, p. 42, 1982

lugger *noun*
1 in a big store confidence swindle, somebody who is assigned to provide background ambience, an extra *US, 1931*
- "John, this is Victoria Hart. She's gonna be a lugger on this hustle." — Stephen Cannell, *King Con*, p. 114, 1997
2 a person who physically transports players to an illegal poker game *US, 1979*
- — John Scarne, *Scarne's Guide to Modern Poker*, p. 283, 1979

lug in *verb*
(used of a racehorse) to tend to run toward the rail *US, 1964*
- — Nate Perlmutter, *How to Win Money at the Races*, p. 120, 1964

luke *noun*
precoital vaginal secretions *US, 1960s*
- Luke—Female coital fluid. Corruption of "leucorrhea." — *Fact*, p. 26, January–Feburary 1965

luken *noun*
in circus and carnival usage, a naive, gullible person *US, 1981*
- — Don Wilmeth, *The Language of American Popular Entertainment*, p. 164, 1981

Luke the Gook *noun*
during the Korean war, a North Korean; during the Vietnam war, any Vietnamese person *US, 1953*
War usage.
- Yet everyone knew he was there—Old Joe Chink, Luke the Gook, the enemy. — T.R. Fehrenbach, *This Kind of War*, p. 432, 1963
- I had come to view the enemy in Vietnam as a real monster, as a threat to my personal security, something which had to be stopped and squashed. Phrases like "gook" and "link the chink" and "luke the gook," stuff we used in training got solidly into my head. — John Kerry, *The New Soldier*, p. 96, 1971
- They called him Luke the Gook, and after that no one wanted anything to happen to him. — Michael Herr, *Dispatches*, p. 126, 1977

Luke the Gook's castle *noun*
a fortified North Korean position *US, 1964*
- In fact they scoffed at one such Red fortress, as "Luke the Gook's Castle." — Don Lawson, *The United States in the Korean War*, p. 109, 1964

lullaby *verb*
to knock unconscious; to kill *US, 1990*
- Money, I want you to escort Mr. Rivera out of the court and off the block. If he tries anything, lullaby him. — *New Jack City*, 1990

lulu *noun*
something that is amazing *US, 1886*
- The funny thing was, though, we were the worst skaters on the whole goddamn rink. I mean the worst. And there were some lulus, too. — J.D. Salinger, *Catcher in the Rye*, p. 129, 1951
- James Baldwin has finally written his own "protest novel," *Another Country*, and it is a lulu. — Terry Southern, *Now Dig This*, p. 202, 1962
- In Parker Tyler's masterpiece *Magic and Myth of the Movies*, he refers to James Craig's voice as "some kind of Middle Southwest drawl, a genuine lulu." — Gore Vidal, *Myra Breckinridge*, p. 10, 1968
- He really caught himself a lulu. — Herbert Huncke, *Guilty of Everything*, p. 16, 1990

Lulu's parlor *noun*
a brothel *US, 1946*
- My ears are bent in half from the tales of woe I've listened to in Lulu's parlors on both sides of the Atlantic. — Mezz Mezzrow, *Really the Blues*, p. 88, 1946

lumber *noun*
1 the stems of a marijuana plant *US, 1982*
- — Ernest L. Abel, *A Marijuana Dictionary*, p. 64, 1982
2 a nonplaying, nonbetting observer of a game of chance *US,*
1961
- — George Percy, *The Language of Poker*, p. 54, 1988

lumins *noun*
rays of the sun *US, 1968*
Often found as "soaking up a few lumins."
- — Collin Baker et al., *College Undergraduate Slang Study Conducted at Brown University*, p. 154, 1968

lump *noun*
1 a stupid, inept person *UK, 1909*
- [O]f the 150, probably 100 were just a bunch of starkers who could pull at one end of a rope that was looped around some poor fucker's neck, while some other lump pulled at the other end. — Richard Condon, *Prizzi's Honor*, p. 118, 1982
2 a small lunch carried in your pocket *US, 1980*
- — Joe McKennon, *Circus Lingo*, p. 59, 1980

lump *verb*
▶ **lump lips**
1 to kiss *US, 1961*
- — Art Unger, *The Cool Book*, p. 109, 1961
2 to talk on the telephone *US, 1951*
Teen slang.
- — *Newsweek*, p. 28, 8th October 1951

lumper *noun*
in carnival usage, a confederate who is hired to play and win a game in order to generate business *US, 1981*
- — Don Wilmeth, *The Language of American Popular Entertainment*, p. 30, 1981

lumps *noun*

the consequences of your actions, punishment, or other unpleasantness, either physical or by reprimand *US, 1930*

- After three years of getting his lumps in the small towns, he realized that he didn't have it[.] — Babs Gonzales, *I Paid My Dues*, p. 104, 1967
- Larry is getting his lumps in Portsmouth[.] — Darryl Ponicsan, *The Last Detail*, p. 154, 1970
- "I'll talk to you after class," I said. That's when I would have to tell her the truth; that's when I would get my lumps. — Max Shulman, *The Many Loves of Dobie Gillis*, p. 171, 1981

lump up *verb*

to beat physically *US, 1952*

- "Once in a while we get a contract from one of them bootleggers to lump somebody up." — Harry Grey, *The Hoods*, p. 48, 1952
- "Niggas said you got lumped up by Kyle, so I was just looking to see if that was true." — 50 Cent, *From Pieces to Weight*, p. 182, 2005

lunar occurence *noun*

the bleed period of the menstrual cycle *US, 1968*

- — Collin Baker et al., *College Undergraduate Slang Study Conducted at Brown University*, p. 154, 1968

lunch *noun*

oral sex performed on a woman *US, 1995*

- — *Adult Video News*, p. 48, August 1995

▸ **do lunch**

to have lunch, usually a working lunch *US, 1987*

Hollywood lingo, embraced elsewhere with a sense of mocking.

- — Connie Eble (Editor), *UNC-CH Campus Slang*, p. 3, Spring 1987
- I didn't hang out with the movie crowd, didn't "do lunch" at the latest place or swing with the swingers. — Odie Hawkins, *Lost Angeles*, p. 33, 1994

▸ **out to lunch**

1 distracted, insensible, foolish, stupid, vacant; being there with the mind elsewhere *US, 1955*

A figurative use of a favorite excuse for someone not being there, in this case extended to "not all there."

- — *Washington Post*, 23rd April 1961: "Man, dig this jazz"
- He was a Neurotic Artist, almost a magician when it came to dealing with cards, but "out to lunch" on the people level. — Odie Hawkins, *Men Friends*, p. 113, 1989

2 knocked from your surfboard by a wave *US, 1977*

- — Gary Fairmont R. Filosa II, *The Surfer's Almanac*, p. 191, 1977

lunch *verb*

to fail, to do poorly *US, 1966*

- — *Current Slang*, p. 5, Winter 1966

▸ **get lunched**

to be knocked from your surfboard and thrashed by the ocean *US, 1988*

- — Michael V. Anderson, *The Bad, Rad, Not to Forget Way Cool Beach and Surf Discriptionary*, p. 13, 1988

lunch *adjective*

without a care, absent-minded *US, 1975*

- — *American Speech*, p. 62, Spring–Summer 1975: "Razorback slang"

lunch bucket *noun*

a socially inept outcast *US, 1956*

- — *Time*, p. 56, 1st January 1965: "Students: the slang bag"

lunch-bucket *adjective*

working class *US, 1956*

- Paul Maslin, who conducted the focus-group sessions, then asked the lunch-bucket Democrats and Reagan supporters for their reactions[.] — Dennis Johnson, *No Place for Amateurs*, p. 88, 2001

lunch-bucket pimp *noun*

a small-time pimp without style or standards *US, 1954*

- Playboy gave assurance he was no lunch-bucket pimp. He had no time for ordinary hustlers. — Caryl Chessman, *Cell 2456 Death Row*, p. 95, 1954
- Just a contrary fart and a cow thief at heart / And actually just a lunch bucket pimp. — Guy Logsdon, *The Whorehouse Bells Were Ringing*, p. 112, 1989

lunch hooks *noun*

the hands *US, 1896*

- "Took me ten years to learn this little honey—watch the lunch hooks now." — Nelson Algren, *The Man with the Golden Arm*, p. 11, 1949

lunching *adjective*

1 completely out of touch and unaware of what is happening *US, 1987*

An evolved **OUT TO LUNCH**.

- — *Washington Post Magazine*, p. 9, 19th April 1987: "Say wha?"
- — Connie Eble (Editor), *UNC-CH Campus Slang*, p. 7, Fall 1999

2 in touch and aware of what is happening *US, 1957*

- Of course, "lunching" is the opposite of O.T.L. (out to lunch), which plainly tells not that someone is out-of-it. — *Washington Post*, p. F1, 29th September 1957

lunchmeat *noun*

1 in the pornography industry, an extremely appealing and sexual woman *US, 1995*

- — *Adult Video News*, p. 48, August 1995

2 in poker, bad cards or a player who proceeds with a bad hand *US, 1996*

- — John Vorhaus, *The Big Book of Poker Slang*, p. 26, 1996

lunch out *verb*

1 to perform oral sex *US, 1986*

- There, finally, Anthony let down the drawbridge whereby men could touch, or in fact lunch out on the participating strippers[.] — Josh Alan Friedman, *Tales of Times Square*, p. 41, 1986
- After a while you piss. You have your shithole lunched out. — Peter Sotos, *Index*, p. 14, 1996

2 to experience a psychotic break during drug intoxication *US, 1988*

- "Everybody knows somebody who's 'lunched out' at some point," Faggett said, using street slang to refer to the psychotic reactions often produced in PCPC users. — *Washington Post*, p. B4, 22nd October 1988

lunchpail *noun*

an ugly, stupid and/or despised person *US, 1968*

- — Collin Baker et al., *College Undergraduate Slang Study Conducted at Brown University*, p. 154, 1968

lung balloons *noun*

the female breasts *US, 2005*

- Lisa busts out her lung balloons and dances for a tux-clad dandy while he's taking a dump on a toilet. — Mr. Skin, *Mr. Skin's Skincyclopedia*, p. 92, 2005

lung butter *noun*

phlegm *US, 1993*

- It's time to get serious, Wayne reasons, before he "ends up at Great America wiping up hurl and lung butter." — *San Francisco Chronicle*, p. C3, 10th December 1993

lunger *noun*

1 phlegm expelled from the lungs *US, 1946*

- very now and then a car splutters, hacks, coughs, hocks a lunga, rumbles out into the track itself for a practice run. — Tom Wolfe, *The Kandy-Kolored Tangerine-Flake Streamline Baby*, p. 139, 1965
- I'll put a fucking lunger right into the bottom of his espresso cup. — Vincent Patrick, *The Pope of Greenwich Village*, p. X, 1979

2 a person suffering from tuberculosis *US, 1893*

- — Hyman E. Goldin et al., *Dictionary of American Underworld Lingo*, p. 130, 1950

lungs *noun*

the female breasts *US, 1951*

- We decided that if she had gone to TCU, she would have come from Floydada with big lungs and skinny calves and a lot of chewing gum. — Dan Jenkins, *Semi-Tough*, p. 32, 1972
- Their secondary sex characteristics are simply too conspicuous to pass without insult, and we were unmerciful towards them: tits, boobs, knockers, jugs, bubbies, bazooms, lungs, flaps and hooters we called them, and there was no way to be polite about it. — *Screw*, p. 6, 3rd January 1972
- The voice-over said, "A nice body, but a little weak in the lungs." — Elmore Leonard, *52 Pick-up*, p. 10, 1974
- Still, it's never too late to unleash Loni's lungs. — Mr. Skin, *Mr. Skin's Skincyclopedia*, p. 16, 2005

lunk *noun*

a dolt *US, 1867*

- For they are either simpletons with cow-dung on their boots or they are a con-man's dream, the lunk with larceny in his heart. — Jack Lait and Lee Mortimer, *Washington Confidential*, p. 276, 1951

- He was already just a lunk who had gone broke as a cabaret genius.
  — Robert Sylvester, *No Cover Charge*, p. 219, 1956

lunker *noun*

any large fish, especially a large bass *US, 1867*

- "In these parts, they're not big ones, they're lunkers." — Carl Hiaasen, *Double Whammy*, p. 45, 1987

lunkhead *noun*

a dolt *US, 1868*

- When a lunkhead and his twist spat in a night club, it's etiquette for him to dash after her and slip her cab fare. — Jack Lait and Lee Mortimer, *New York Confidential*, p. 222, 1948
- An oversize mob of ignorant, lunkheaded jerks who ruled with fear and got away with it because they had money to back themselves up. — Mickey Spillane, *Kiss Me Deadly*, p. 38, 1952
- That moronic culture of macho lunkheads and pap music fem-bots[.] — Jessica Berens and Kerri Sharp, *Prada sucks! [Inappropriate Behaviur]*, p. ix, 2002

lurk *verb*

to read postings on an Internet discussion group without posting your own comments *US, 1984*

- A newbie with the nerve to post in alt.sex.bondage, without taking the time to lurk (read, not post) for several weeks, can expect to be flamed to blackened perfection. — Nancy Tamosaitis, *net.sex*, p. 75, 1995

lurker *noun*

a person who reads postings on an Internet discussion group without posting their own comments *US, 1991*

- — Eric S. Raymond, *The New Hacker's Dictionary*, p. 229, 1991

lurp *noun*

1 a misfit *US, 1955*

- — *American Weekly*, p. 2, 14th August 1955

2 a long-range reconnaissance patrol; a member of such a patrol *US, 1968*

From the initials LRRP.

- LRRPs—long range recon patrol, prounced "lerps," the elite—were strutting towards the PX[.]. — William Pelfrey, *The Big V*, p. 16, 1972
- And I wasn't going out like the night ambushers did, or the Lurps[.] — Michael Herr, *Dispatches*, p. 5, 1977
- He led Long-Range Reconnaissance patrollers, Lurps, silently harassing enemy camps and columns for weeks and months on end. — James Mills, *The Underground Empire*, p. 241, 1986

luser *noun*

a computer neophyte *US, 1995*

- — Christian Crumlish, *The Internet Dictionary*, p. 115, 1995

lush *noun*

1 alcohol *UK, 1790*

- From the way I was holding up you would have sworn I was immune to the lush. — Louis Armstrong, *Satchmo*, p. 202, 1954
- With each week of work, bombed and sapped and charged and stoned with lush, with pot, with benny[.] — Norman Mailer, *Advertisements for Myself*, p. 243, 1955
- They came into the camp lushed, but nasty lush: ethyl alcohol coming on like the sleeping bags weren't there, you know? — Richard Farina, *Been Down So Long*, p. 63, 1966

2 an alcoholic *US, 1851*

- Used to be a lush. Quit. — Philip Wylie, *Opus 21*, p. 249, 1949
- Nobody can make that shot and you know it. Not even a lucky lush. — *The Hustler*, 1961
- There had been a third child and Big Tom was a confirmed lush now from Gina's nagging. — Clancy Sigal, *Going Away*, p. 67, 1961
- [T]he rulers of the land seemed all to be lushes. — Eldrige Cleaver, *Soul on Ice*, p. 4, 1968

lush *verb*

to drink alcohol excessively *UK, 1811*

- And, if she needed any more evidence, his lushing on the 5:29 was a matter of record. — Max Shulman, *Rally Round the Flag, Boys!*, p. 76, 1957
- I was feeling so good because no lushing. — Jack Kerouac, *Jack Kerouac Selected Letters 1957–1969*, p. 35, May 1957: Letter to Allen Ginsberg
- The broads stopped talking to watch Humpty lush. — Dan Burley, *Diggeth Thou?*, p. 14, 1959
- He was there, of course, lushing it up. — Terry Southern, *Now Dig This*, p. 155, 2001

lush *adjective*

drunk *UK, 1812*

- Two years ago I was real lush and drinking a quart a day. — John Clellon Holmes, *Go*, p. 113, 1952

lushed *adjective*

drunk *US, 1927*

- "He's lushed already." — Stephen Longstreet, *The Flesh Peddlers*, p. 111, 1962
- Pineapple, a dock worker from Hawaii, was lushed and nursing a beer at a table. — Emmett Grogan, *Ringolevio*, p. 100, 1972
- He could barely walk, so lushed was he. — Bill Cardoso, *The Maltese Sangweech*, p. 173, 1984

lusher *noun*

a drunkard *US, 1848*

- — *American Speech*, p. 87, May 1955: "Narcotic argot along the Mexican border"

lush green *noun*

money *US, 1951*

- — David W. Maurer, *Argot of the Racetrack*, p. 42, 1951

lushhound *noun*

a drunkard *US, 1935*

- We liked things to be easy and relaxed, mellow and mild, not loud or loutish, and the scowling chin-out tension of the lushhounds with their false courage didn't appeal to us. — Mezz Mezzrow, *Really the Blues*, p. 94, 1946

lush-roll *verb*

to rob drunkards *US, 1957*

- "I'm appealing to you as one Razor Back to another," and he pulled out his Razor Back card, a memo of his lush-rolling youth. — William Burroughs, *Naked Lunch*, p. 177, 1957

lushroller *noun*

a person who robs drunkards *US, 1919*

- The doormen are cops, expert lushrollers like all cops of the area[.] — William S. Burroughs, *Naked Lunch*, p. 261, 1959

lushwell *noun*

a drunkard *US, 1960*

Newspaper comic genius Jimmy Hatlo's Lushwell character with his jaunts to the El Clippo nightclub was a beloved fixture in popular American culture from the 1930s through the 1960s, and the nickname "Uncle Lushwell" was reserved with affection for those whose wit increased while drinking.

- Only thing about him, he's such a lushwell his liver's probably big as his ass. — Joseph Wambaugh, *The Glitter Dome*, p. 6, 1981

lush-worker *noun*

a thief who preys on drunks who have passed out *US, 1908*

- He was a skillful lush worker, but he had no front. — William Burroughs, *Junkie*, p. 26, 1953
- [A] "lush worker" specializes in clients who are drunk. — Charles Winick, *The Lively Commerce*, p. 41, 1971

lushy *noun*

a drunkard *US, 1944*

- Besides, the lushies didn't even play good music. — Mezz Mezzrow, *Really the Blues*, p. 94, 1946

lust dog *noun*

a passionate, promiscuous female *US, 1975*

- — *American Speech*, p. 62, Spring–Summer 1975: "Razorback slang"

L'ville *nickname*

Louisville, Kentucky *US, 1981*

- — Don Wilmeth, *The Language of American Popular Entertainment*, p. 164, 1981

lye *noun*

marijuana *US, 1990s*

- Buy a nickel bag / Smoke a little lye / Get high tonight — Busta Rhymes, *Get High Tonight*, 1997

LZ *noun*

a combat aircraft landing zone, especially an improvised one *US, 1967*

- To allow minimum time in the LZ, the trial pilot called out "Trail up" even before he was on the ground. — Elaine Shepard, *The Doom Pussy*, p. 7, 1967
- It was 100 degrees when they hit the LZ. — Ronald J. Glasser, *365 Days*, p. 30, 1971

Mm

M *noun*

1 the Mexican Mafia, a Mexican-American prison gang *US, 1978*

- The "M" (or "eme," originally meaning "Mafia" but soon to be glorified as "El Mejicano Encarcelado") accepted this as a challenge and stepped up their attacks. — Joan W. Moore, *Homeboys*, p. 115, 1978

2 morphine *US, 1914*

- More specifically, it was classified as M, C, and H—Mary, Charlie, and Harry—which stood for morphine, cocaine, and heroin. — William J. Spillard and Pence James, *Needle in a Haystack*, pp. 147–148, 1945
- Heroin got the drive awright—but there's not a tingle to a ton—you got to get M to get that tingle-tingle. — Nelson Algren, *The Man With The Golden Arm [The Howard Marks Book of Dope Stories]*, p. 45, 1949
- I saw him pack in his moldy room where he'd shot M all this time. — Jack Kerouac, *Letter to John Clellon Holmes*, p. 389, 9th December 1952
- If I use at all I want the best. I want to smoke O or use good pure M or H. — William Burroughs, *Letters to Allen Ginsberg 1953–1957*, p. 105, 1st August 1955

3 marijuana *US, 1955*

Extended from the previous sense.

- Their Nazi insignia, patches with the letter M signifying use of marijuana[.] — Arthur Blessitt, *Turned On to Jesus*, p. 187, 1971

M *nickname*

Memphis *US, 2004*

- Born and raised in the M, Tennessee. — *Hustle and Flow*, 2004

ma and pa *adjective*

(used of a business) small-scale, family-owned *US, 1972*

- I pull over at a ma and pa liquor store across the street from City Lights Bookstore, a hangout for sniveling intellectuals and runaway teenyboppers out for a score. — Oscar Zeta Acosta, *The Autobiography of a Brown Buffalo*, p. 36, 1972

mac *noun*

an automated cash machine *US, 1996*

Originally from the trademarked acronym Money Access Center, then applied to any such device.

- — Claudio R. Salvucci, *The Philadelphia Dialect Dictionary*, p. 47, 1996

Mac; mac; mack *noun*

used as a term of address for a man whose name is not known by the speaker *US, 1918*

- That's right, Mac. We all been through the mill too. — Max Shulman, *The Zebra Derby*, p. 144, 1946
- "You're right, Mac." I tipped him a quarter. — Philip Wylie, *Opus 21*, p. 8, 1949

mac; mack *verb*

to eat voraciously *US, 1990*

From the Big Mac, a hamburger specialty from the McDonald's™ hamburger chain.

- — Judi Sanders, *Cal Poly Slang*, p. 6, 1990
- — Trevor Cralle, *The Surfin'ary*, 1991

macaroni *noun*

an Italian-American or Italian *UK, 1845*

From the pasta product.

- Then the guy who sent the hitter gets hit, the macaronis are shooting each other, and its hard to tell who's on whose side. — Elmore Leonard, *Glitz*, pp. 107–108, 1985

macaroni and cheese *noun*

marijuana worth $5 and cocaine worth $10 *US, 2002*

- — *Detroit News*, p. 5D, 20th September 2002

MacArthur sweep *noun*

a combing of the hair from the side of the head over a bald spot on top of the head *US, 1953*

- It was brushed sideways across his skull in a MacArthur sweep. I had a hunch there was nothing under it but bare skull. — Raymond Chandler, *The Long Goodbye*, pp. 200–201, 1953

macher *noun*

an important and powerful man *US, 1930*

Yiddish.

- So, here he is, the big macher, the committeeman, the next alderman of the Twenty-seventh, the mayor, the governor[.] — Robert Campbell, *In a Pig's Eye*, p. 50, 1991

machine *noun*

1 the penis *US, 1970*

- "About whether or not you've got a big machine or a small one," Leila said[.] — Burt Hirschfield, *Fire Island*, p. 47, 1970

2 a machine gun *US, 1995*

- — Bill Valentine, *Gang Intelligence Manual*, p. 110, 1995: "Jamaican gang terminology"

3 in horseracing, a pari-mutuel betting machine *US, 1976*

- — Tom Ainslie, *Ainslie's Complete Guide to Thoroughbred Racing*, p. 334, 1976

4 in horseracing, a battery-powered device used to impart a shock to a horse during a race *US, 1976*

- — Tom Ainslie, *Ainslie's Complete Guide to Thoroughbred Racing*, p. 334, 1976

Machine Gun Murphy *noun*

a stereotypical fearless soldier *US, 1971*

- A mad minute—everybody gets on line, everybody in the company, and you play Machine Gun Murphy. (From the Congressional Record, 7 April 1971). — John Kerry, *The New Soldier*, p. 60, 1971

machinery *noun*

the equipment used to prepare and inject narcotics *US, 1970*

- — *Congressional Record*, p. E3982, 6th May 1970
- — Eugene Landy, *The Underground Dictionary*, p. 122, 1971

macho *adjective*

excessively masculine, virile, and brave *US, 1959*

A direct loan from Spanish.

- Listen, I did my time in back seats, the Bay Ridge number, getting fucked over by some Saturday night macho moron. — *Saturday Night Fever*, 1977
- Every man wants to be a macho, macho man / To have the kind of body, always in demand. — Victor Willis, *Macho Man*, 1978
- Look, spare me the macho bullshit about your gun. — *48 Hours*, 1982
- He was a thirty-year-old brain surgeon, a sensitive guy trapped in a macho body, traveling with another doctor and having a terrible singles' cruise. — Anka Radakovich, *The Wild Girls Club*, p. 75, 1994

Macintoy; Macintrash *noun*

an Apple Macintosh™ computer *US, 1991*

- — Eric S. Raymond, *The New Hacker's Dictionary*, p. 230, 1991

mack *noun*

1 a pimp *US, 1903*

- The fee went to the pimps, or macs, who kept wandering downstairs. The girls used to fight over their macs. — Mezz Mezzrow, *Really the Blues*, p. 23, 1946
- For some of our boys was drifters and some of our boys was macks. — Bruce Jackson, *Get Your Ass in the Water and Swim Like Me*, 1964
- In being a mack, you're supposedly the supreme being of a man. Man rules woman. In being a mack, you acknowledge this fact. — Susan Hall, *Gentleman of Leisure*, p. 39, 1972
- Like every nigger mack fresh outta big foot country [the deep South], he's sizzling for young white 'ho pussy. — Iceberg Slim (Robert Beck), *Airtight Willie and Me*, p. 24, 1979

2 a person who is a smooth and convincing talker *US, 1962*

- And I'm gonna need a female mack to steer Tommy. — Stephen Cannell, *King Con*, p. 119, 1997

3 the speech a pimp makes to recruit a woman as a prostitute *US, 1972*

- The initial line a pimp uses in recruiting a girl is often referred to as Mack or Mack talk[.] — Christina and Richard Milner, *Black Players*, p. 35, 1972

4 a person's style and projected character *US, 2005*

- I'll attack any nigga who's slack in his mack. — RZA, *The Wu-Tang Manual*, p. 140, 2005

mack *verb*

1 to work as a pimp *UK, 1887*

- Ice! You ain't heard? I cut loose from that gig. I'm macking and that vision is humping for me. — Iceberg Slim (Robert Beck), *The Naked Soul of Iceberg Slim*, p. 54, 1971
- I know you're macking now, and we both know eight bills will buy a lotta cocaine or take care of anything else that's bugging you. — A.S. Jackson, *Gentleman Pimp*, p. 48, 1973
- Your broad becomes lazy, trifling and slack / And starts signifying about your not having a license to mack. — Dennis Wepman et al., *The Life*, p. 165, 1976

2 to speak with a stylish flair and flattery *US, 1967*

- "Still macking in his own intellectual way?" "Still what—?" "Macking. Macking. Oh, Margrit, you know what macking is." — John Williams, *The Man Who Cried I Am*, p. 18, 1967
- He sure can mack 'em down in five minutes. — Christina and Richard Milner, *Black Players*, p. 35, 1972
- And maybe one night me and Lunchbox'll be macking some bitch, and she'll be like, "Oooo! I want to suck youse guys's dicks off. What's your names?" And I'll be like, "Jay and Silent Bob." — Kevin Smith, *Jay and Silent Bob Strike Back*, p. 21, 2001

3 to kiss *US, 1993*

- — Judi Sanders, *Faced and Faded, Hanging to Hurl*, p. 26, 1993
- — Connie Eble (Editor), *UNC-CH Campus Slang*, p. 4, Spring 1993

mack *adjective*

stylish, socially adept *US, 2006*

- Like I already said, Dap's the Clique's mackest dancer. — Linden Dalecki, *Kid B*, p. 129, 2006

mackadocious *adjective*

excellent, stylish, fashionable *US, 1991*

- Yes, Dick, it certainly is mackadocious to have the venerable MC Hammer here with us in the studio, chilling so to speak. — *talk.bizarre*, 26th August 1992
- "We buy the clothes we see in videos. We use words like 'mackadocious.'" — William Upski Wimsatt, *Bomb the Suburbs*, p. 24, 1994

Mack Daddy *noun*

a skilled ladies' man; a pimp *US, 1959*

- So I then go into my Mack Daddy mode cause I'm getting a woodie in my cackies y'know. — *Boyz N The Hood*, 1990
- Is that that nigga Caine out there playin' Mack Daddy in the parking lot? — *Menace II Society*, 1993

macked out *adjective*

dressed in the height of street fashion *US, 1933*

- A macked out full length blue rabbit fur coat, the finest polyester suits, and the finest 6 and 1/2 inch platform Payless shoes. — *alt.music.michael-jackson*, 15th April 1998

macker *noun*

1 a man to whom the pursuit of women is more interesting than relationships that might ensue after conquest *US, 1967*

- Roger was not an ordinary macker; he gave a little more than most Negroes who were thus engaged between books or articles or showings or jazz engagements. — John Williams, *The Man Who Cried I Am*, p. 18, 1967

2 a very large wave *US, 1991*

- — Nick Carroll, *The Next Wave*, 1991

mackerel-snapper *noun*

a Roman Catholic *US, 1855*

From the practice of eating fish on Fridays.

- Me? I was raised a mackerel-snapper. — *M*A*S*H*, 1970

mack man *noun*

a pimp *US, 1954*

- Did those oldhead mackmen think they were the only ones who could drive Hogs? — Clarence Cooper Jr., *The Scene*, p. 68, 1960
- Several cons slightly older than I came in on transfer from the big joint. They claimed to be "mack men." — Iceberg Slim (Robert Beck), *Pimp*, p. 56, 1969
- A "mackman" (probably from the French maquereau, or pimp) who has more than one prostitute may be as busy[.] — Charles Winick, *The Lively Commerce*, p. 118, 1971

- I thought you were a mackman, a master at the Game; But I peeped your hole card, you're a funny-time lame. (Collected in 1954.) — Dennis Wepman et al., *The Life*, p. 39, 1976

Mack the Knife *noun*

any surgeon *US, 1980*

- — Lois Monteiro, *Maledicta*, Summer 1980: "Not sticks and stones, but names: more medical perjoratives"
- — Sally Williams, *"Strong" Words (Dissertation)*, p. 150, 1994

mac out *verb*

to eat ravenously *US, 1982*

- — Mimi Pond, *The Valley Girl's Guide to Life*, p. 59, 1982

mad *adjective*

1 exciting, good *US, 1941*

- Nero is havin' a ball, he's diggin' this mad game, he's guicin' up a storm. — William "Lord" Buckley, *Nero*, 1951
- — *American Speech*, p. 302, December 1955: "Wayne University slang"
- You don't know "Jungle Love?" That shit is the mad notes. — Kevin Smith, *Jay and Silent Bob Strike Back*, p. 9, 2001
- Seeing the Bull Roosters' mad skills just made me want to practice harder. — Linden Dalecki, *Kid B*, p. 176, 2006

2 in homosexual usage, unrestrained and ostentatious *US, 1949*

- Loosely used with many shades of meaning. — Anon., *The Gay Girl's Guide*, p. 12, 1949
- — Bruce Rodgers, *The Queens' Vernacular*, p. 129, 1972

3 used as an all-purpose, dramatic intensifier *US, 1972*

- I'm gonna get mad diesel. — *Kids*, 1995
- Vince Carter has mad hoops. — Connie Eble (Editor), *UNC-CH Campus Slang*, p. 4, Fall 1996
- We would hang out and smoke herbs and drink, have a little party. For me, I was young and having mad fun. We usually stea cars or jump somebody. — S. Beth Atkin, *Voices from the Street*, p. 86, 1996
- — *Newsday*, p. B2, 11th October 1997
- Doing this, we make mad bank. — *Gone in 60 Seconds*, 2000

madam *noun*

in a deck of playing cards, a queen *US, 1988*

- — George Percy, *The Language of Poker*, p. 55, 1988

mad ball *noun*

in circus and carnival usage, a fortune teller's glass globe *US, 1948*

- — Don Wilmeth, *The Language of American Popular Entertainment*, p. 165, 1981

mad dog *noun*

a fearless, aggressive, uninhibited criminal *US, 1956*

- The thing he soon had was a small following of other "mad dogs" each with a grievance against one mob leader or another, each with nothing to lose but his life. — Robert Sylvester, *No Cover Charge*, p. 62, 1956
- On the way back to the shack, I practiced my "mad dog" stares on the occupants of cars beside us at stoplights. — Sanyika Shakur, *Monster*, p. 8, 1993

mad-dog *verb*

to behave in an intensely aggressive fashion, giving the appearance of near insanity *US, 1991*

- Why the hell didn't he just say not to mad-dog somebody? — Leon Bing, *Do or Die*, p. 5, 1991
- When they slowed down to maddog him with hostile stares, Kevin recognized the driver as L.A. Ray[.] — Bob Sipchen, *Baby Insane and the Buddha*, p. 14, 1993
- Or, worse yet, fronting-off the Asian gangbangers who hung out at South Dove, mad-dogging any rival gang that infringed on their turf. — Joseph Wambaugh, *Floaters*, p. 22, 1996

mad-dog *adjective*

overtly aggressive *US, 2005*

- The mad-dog stares of youths, who stop cutting grass and sweeping asphalt, pierce the windows. — Colton Simpson, *Inside the Crips*, p. 56, 2005

made *adjective*

officially admitted into a crime family *US, 1966*

- Everyone knew that Hank had once been on the verge of being "made" by the Mafia—taken on by them as a permanent member. — James Mills, *The Panic in Needle Park*, p. 21, 1966
- But his uncle was a made-guy, a lieutenant with the Mulberry Street crew—a heavy hitter[.] — Edwin Torres, *Carlito's Way*, p. 22, 1975

- A fully made Mafioso. Plus, the guy is a total whackadoo. — Vincent Patrick, *The Pope of Greenwich Village*, p. 138, 1979
- As far as Jimmy was concerned, with Tommy being made, it was like we were all being made. We would now have one of our own guys as a member. — *Goodfellas*, 1990

made in the shade *adjective*
successful, accomplished *US, 1951*
- — *Newsweek*, 8th October 1951
- He's got it made in the shade with her. — Frederick Kohner, *Gidget*, p. 114, 1957
- Made in the shade? Hell, as long as any man, white or black, isn't getting his rights in America I'm in danger. — Dick Gregory, *Nigger*, p. 159, 1964
- [T]hey would moo over the view, exclaim "Holy shit" or make some comment about how he had it "made in the shade." — Richard Price, *Clockers*, p. 405, 1992

Ma Deuce *noun*
a Browning .50 caliber machine gun *US, 1982*
- Every tank and personnel carrier had one M2 caliber .50 machine gun, called a Ma Duce. — Harold Coyle, *Team Yankee*, p. 104, 1987
- I've seen these things in John Wayne movies, but this is the first time I've seen a Browning .50-caliber machine gun up close. In the GI vernacular, it's called a Ma Deuce. — *The Cincinnatti Post*, 2nd May 2000

Madison Avenue crash helmet *noun*
a kind of businessman's hat *US, 1965*
- [I]n walks a young man wearing a crease-top hat, of the genre known as the Madison Avenue crash helmet, and carrying an attache case. — Tom Wolfe, *The Kandy-Kolored Tangerine-Flake Streamline Baby*, p. 49, 1965

mad minute *noun*
an intense, short-lived burst of weapon fire *US, 1917*
- We initiated, as was customary in many of the battalions of the 1st Air Cavalry at dusk, a "Mad Minute." — Kenneth Mertel, *Year of the Horse*, p. 136, 1968
- And "mad minutes" is when everybody on perimeter, around the base camp (you have bunkers all the way around it), opens up and fires away with all their fire power for about a minute, two minutes. — John Kerry, *The New Soldier*, p. 62, 1971
- The "mad-minute," ten seconds long for want of ammunition, was over. — Nelson DeMille, *By the Rivers of Babylon*, p. 232, 1978

mad money *noun*
money set aside to use in an emergency or to splurge *US, 1922*
- I embraced her, got me a big fat juicy taste of honey, gave her some mad money and told her if I wasn't there to cab it on in. — A.S. Jackson, *Gentleman Pimp*, p. 110, 1973
- "I don't give a shit if he gets it out of the mad money he keeps in his panty girdle." — George Higgins, *Kennedy for the Defense*, p. 70, 1980
- I could rent something nice and still have a little mad money in the bank. — Armistead Maupin, *Maybe the Moon*, p. 31, 1992
- She went to the closet and reached up next to the ski cap, where she kept her mad money, and found the .32-caliber nickel-plated revolver she'd bought from the horney gas station owner who serviced her car. — Joseph Wambaugh, *Floaters*, p. 127, 1996

mad-mug *verb*
to glare, to stare with hostility *US, 2007*
- Authorities say Mao thought someone there had "mad-mugged" him. — *Monterey County Herald*, 18th November 2007

madon! *
used as a moderately profane exclamation *US, 1977*
Originally Italian-American usage.
- Madon', you guys think you're still in Red Hook. — Edwin Torres, *Q & A*, p. 146, 1977

mad props *noun*
effusive compliments *US, 1994*
- — Linda Meyer, *Teenspeak!*, p. 28, 1994

Mae West *noun*
in the language of parachuting, a partial inversion of the canopy resulting from a deployment malfunction *US, 1958*
- Two suspension lines are over my canopy, forming a Mae West. — Donald Duncan, *The New Legions*, p. 134, 1967
- — Dan Poynter, *Parachuting*, p. 169, 1978: "The language of parachuting"

mafia *noun*
used as part of a jocular formation referring to a large number or influential group of people *US, 1989*
- The "Hawaiian" mafia was a term we had that referred to the large number of Hawaiians among the Wolfhound ranks. — David H. Hackworth, *About Face*, p. 69, 1989

mag *noun*
1 a magazine, in any sense of the term *UK, 1801*
- For the rest of her career in Hollywood, while her gams are still straight and her figure otherwise, she'll pose cheesecake for fan-mags[.] — Jack Lait and Lee Mortimer, *New York Confidential*, p. 145, 1948
- He was going to publish a mag called The Rebel but it had come out only twice. — James Simon Kunen, *The Strawberry Statement*, p. 97, 1968
- Customers who flocked to the stores in 1967 allegedly asked for more explicit mags and loops. — Josh Alan Friedman, *Tales of Times Square*, p. 75, 1986
- MURTAUGH: What's it take? RIGGS: Fifteen in the mag, one up the pipe. — *Lethal Weapon*, 1987

2 a Magnum™ pistol *US, 1970*
- Thirty-eights, I'll take a three-fifty-seven mag if I have to. — George V. Higgins, *The Friends of Eddie Doyle*, p. 8, 1971
- He's got a range, he's teaching all these housewives come in how to fire three-fifty-sevens, forty-fives. Can you see it? Broad's making cookies, she's got this big fucking Mag stuck in her apron? — Elmore Leonard, *Split Images*, p. 22, 1981

Maggie *noun*
any revolver that fires a cartridge that is more powerful than standard ammunition *US, 1957*
- — *American Speech*, p. 194, October 1957: "Some colloquialisms of the handgunner"

Maggie's drawers *noun*
a red flag indicating a "miss" on a rifle range *US, 1936*
- — Carl Fleischhauer, *A Glossary of Army Slang*, p. 32, 1968

maggot *noun*
1 a white person *US, 1985*
Urban black usage.
- — Carsten Stroud, *Close Pursuit*, p. 273, 1987

2 in the US Air Force, someone who is very dedicated to service *US, 1998*
- — *Seattle Times*, p. A9, 12th April 1998: "Grunts, squids not grunting from the same dictionary"

maggot bait *noun*
a corpse *US, 1955*
- "They had their way with her and left her for maggot bait." — Jon Sharpe, *New Mexico Nightmare*, p. 241, 2003

maggot box *noun*
an Apple Macintosh™ computer *US, 1991*
- — Eric S. Raymond, *The New Hacker's Dictionary*, p. 230, 1991

maggot wagon *noun*
a catering truck *US, 1992*
- — Lewis Poteet, *Car & Motorcycle Slang*, p. 125, 1992

magic *adjective*
in computing, complicated or not yet understood *US, 1981*
- — Guy L Steele, *Coevolution Quarterly*, Spring 1981: "Computer slang"
- — Guy L. Steele et al., *The Hacker's Dictionary*, p. 88, 1983

magic mushroom *noun*
any mushroom with an hallucinogenic effect *US, 1968*
- — Walter Way, *The Drug Scene*, p. 110, 1977

magnet *noun*
a person who attracts the precedent thing or personality type *US, 1993*
- With a voice like that, he's got to be a babe magnet. — *Wayne's World 2*, 1993
- I think I'm just a weirdo magnet. — *Something About Mary*, 1998
- Here's what a guy who goes by the chick-magnet Net handle of "Wampa-One" thinks about Bluntman and Chronic. — Kevin Smith, *Jay and Silent Bob Strike Back*, p. 20, 2001
- "It's lucky you got the island thing going for you Mick, because this"—she patted the dashboard—"ain't exactly a pussy magnet." — Carl Hiaasen, *Skinny Dip*, p. 89, 2004

magnet ass *noun*
a military aviator who seems to attract enemy fire *US, 1962*

- Ther was the normal banter going on about Chuck being a magnet ass, when one of the crew chiefs found two bullet holes in the belly of White's aircraft. — Randy Zahn, *Snake Pilot*, p. 170, 2003

magoo *noun*

1 in circus usage, a cream or custard pie thrown by clowns at each other *US*, *1926*
- — Don Wilmeth, *The Language of American Popular Entertainment*, p. 166, 1981

2 a very important person *US*, *1932*
- Eddie was a CPA and a big magoo in the Elks. — Janet Evanovich, *Two for the Dough*, p. 181, 1996

mahogany *noun*
the counter in a bar *US*, *1896*
- If your timing is good, you are likely to see Chuck Coggins, bartender extraordinaire, behind the mahogany. — Gary Regan, *New Classic Cocktails*, p. 49, 1997

mahoot *noun*
in bar dice games, a roll that produces no points for the player *US*, *1971*
- — Jester Smith, *Games They Play in San Francisco*, p. 104, 1971

mahoska; hoska *noun*
an addictive drug, especially heroin *US*, *1949*
- — David Maurer and Victor Vogel, *Narcotics and Narcotic Addiction*, p. 425, 1973

maiden *noun*

1 in horse racing, a horse that has never won a race *US*, *1951*
- — David W. Maurer, *Argot of the Racetrack*, p. 42, 1951

2 by extension, a jockey who has never won a race *US*, *1971*
- She was on the bit, but a maiden was up and he came a cropper. — *San Francisco Chronicle*, p. 54, 21st April 1971

maidenhead *noun*
a woman's toilet *US*, *1968*
Punning on the hymen and **HEAD** as "a toilet."
- — Collin Baker et al., *College Undergraduate Slang Study Conducted at Brown University*, p. 154, 1968

main *noun*
any large blood vein *US*, *1952*
- They knew he was on drugs, a real horsehead who hit the main. — Hal Ellson, *The Golden Spike*, p. 68, 1952

▸ the main
to island dwellers off the coast of Maine, the mainland *US*, *1975*
- — John Gould, *Maine Lingo*, p. 174, 1975

main *verb*
to inject a drug into a main vein *US*, *1952*
- Do you know she was the first one to show him how to main? — Hal Ellson, *The Golden Spike*, p. 52, 1952

main line *noun*

1 any large blood vein, especially the median cephalic vein *US*, *1931*
- After that it was nothing but the main-line, the high of highs. — Hal Ellson, *The Golden Spike*, p. 228, 1952
- I began shooting in the main line to save stuff and because the immediate kick was better. — William Burroughs, *Junkie*, p. 34, 1953
- When you shoot C in main line—no other way of taking it gives the real C kick—there is a rush of pure pleasure to the head. — William Burroughs, *Letters to Allen Ginsberg 1953–1957*, p. 27, 7th April 1954
- He could absorb a large amount at one time—mainline—and turn on in a flash. — Herbert Huncke, *The Evening Sun Turned Crimson*, p. 189, 1980

2 at a horseracing track, the area with the greatest concentration of mutual betting machines *US*, *1951*
- — David W. Maurer, *Argot of the Racetrack*, p. 42, 1951

3 the general population of a prison *US*, *1960*
- [R]ather than stand in the thousands-long "main-line" chow lineups[.] — Neal Cassady, *Grace Beats Karma*, p. 162, 10th January 1960: Letter to Carolyn Cassady
- "They're making fair time," he said. "We'll eat mainline tonight." — Malcolm Braly, *On the Yard*, p. 28, 1967
- In the entire California penal system there's no better food than on the Tracy mainline[.] — James Carr, *Bad*, p. 26, 1975
- Whisper told the police he walked the mainline eighteen years and was never once bumped. — Seth Morgan, *Homeboy*, p. 124, 1990

▸ ride the mainline
to inject drugs intravenously *US*, *1957*
- "Dammit, Scar, I told you about riding the mainline." — Herbert Simmons, *Corner Boy*, p. 15, 1957

Main Line *nickname*
the wealthy suburbs just to the west of Philadelphia, Pennsylvania, extending from Merion to Bryn Mawr to Paoli *US*, *1918*
From the Paoli Local commuter train that ran out of the main line of the now-defunct Pennsylvania Railroad, carrying businessmen to work and future lexicographers in blue wool jerseys with five white stripes on each arm to school.
- — Laurence Urdang, *Names and Nicknames of Places and Things*, p. 158, 1987

mainline *verb*
to inject drugs, especially heroin, into a main vein *US*, *1938*
- Main-lining her. Capping her straight. — John D. McDonald, *The Neon Jungle*, p. 46, 1953
- But when you main-line, you're gone, man, clear out. — Ross Russell, *The Sound*, p. 205, 1961
- Of course all the students smoke pot and experiment with LSD but only a few main-line[.] — Gore Vidal, *Myra Breckinridge*, p. 39, 1968
- "Don't mainline him, for Chrissake," he, too, shouting at the top of his voice, "we'll have a fucking stiff on our hands." — Terry Southern, *Blue Movie*, p. 190, 1970

mainliner *noun*
a drug user who injects the drug into a vein *US*, *1934*
- While Lukey the Swede, with scars under his sleeve and a mainliner standing among junkies, laughed with his old knowledge of Nothing. — George Mandel, *Flee the Angry Strangers*, p. 313, 1952
- They are all mainliners except Nellie and Fran. They go strictly for the veins. — Willard Motley, *Let No Man Write My Epitaph*, p. 158, 1958
- A junkie, a dope addict, a hop-head, a mainliner—a dope fiend! — James Baldwin, *Blues for Mister Charlie*, p. 45, 1964
- I had jumped from being a careful snorter, content to take my kicks of sniffing through my nose, to a not-so-careful skin-popper, and now was a full-grown careless mainliner. — Piri Thomas, *Down These Mean Streets*, p. 200, 1967

main-line shooter *noun*
a drug user who injects into a blood vein *US*, *1951*
- Women are seldom "main line shooters" unless they accidentally hit a vein. — Donald Wilson, *My Six Convicts*, p. 337, 1951

main man *noun*

1 an important man *US*, *1977*
From circus jargon.
- "That's his job. He's a main man." — Malcolm Braly, *The Protector*, p. 78, 1979

2 a pimp, in relation to a prostitute *US*, *1985*
- The young man was wearing a cardigan, pants with cuffs, and penny loafers, so it never occurred to Wingnut that he could be a hooker's main man. — Joseph Wambaugh, *The Secrets of Harry Bright*, p. 63, 1985

main punch *noun*
a man's favored girlfriend *US*, *1994*
- Tommy Blue Eyes and his main punch, what's her name, Charlotte, with her ta-tas sticking out of her sundress like a couple of muskmelons[.] [Quoting James Lee Burke] — *USA Today*, p. 8D, 2nd August 1994

main queen *noun*
a man's primary girlfriend *US*, *1948*
- — Jack Lait and Lee Mortimer, *New York Confidential*, 1948: "A glossary of Harlemisms"

mainside *noun*
the main area of a military shore base *US*, *1945*
- He could then have a clerk type it up and send it over to Mainside and let it work its way through the bureaucracy. — W.E.B. Griffin, *Call to Arms*, p. 161, 1987

main squeeze *noun*
a person's primary partner in romance *US*, *1926*
- — *Current Slang*, p. 10, Fall 1970
- He remembers how each time the lovers' frequent break-ups sent Reba to him for solace, how each time his secret dream, to move from Reba's play big bro to her main squeeze, had to be deferred[.] — Iceberg Slim (Robert Beck), *Doom Fox*, p. 3, 1978

- And I'm thinking, poor guy just lost his main squeeze, feeling real sympathetic[.] — Jay McInerney, *Story of My Life*, p. 4, 1988
- I happen to think Willie's main squeeze is sexy. — Joseph Wambaugh, *Floaters*, p. 26, 1996

mainy *adjective*
fearless, crazy *US, 2004*
- You mainy, blood, and I don't want to get caught up in that. — Rick Ayers (Editor), *Berkeley High Slang Dictionary*, p. 31, 2004

Maizie *noun*
used as a term of address among male homosexuals *US, 1965*
- — *Fact*, p. 26, January – February 1965

major *noun*
a dependable, reliable person *US, 1956*
- — *American Speech*, p. 97, May 1956: "Smugglers' argot in the Southwest"

major *verb*
▸ **major in plumbing**
in college, to take nothing but easy courses *US, 1955*
An allusion to "pipes" (easy courses).
- — *American Speech*, p. 304, December 1955: "Wayne University slang"

major buck *noun*
a lot of money *US, 1992*
- His brother Danny wanted a new pair of Nikes, the major-buck kind. — Jess Mowry, *Way Past Cool*, p. 58, 1992

major-league *adjective*
prominent, accomplished, prestigious *US, 1941*
On 4th September, 2000, US presidential candidate George W. Bush leaned to his running mate Dick Cheney at a campaign stop in Naperville, Illinois, and, pointing to a reporter, said "There's Adam Clymner—major-league asshole from the *New York Times*." "Major-league" had major-league arrived.
- The whole thing happened because we both were consumed by the desire to get a top-notch front that would cause us to be two of the youngest major-league mack men in the city of Detroit. — A.S. Jackson, *Gentleman Pimp*, p. 59, 1973
- "Bunkie, I've had good blow jobs in my life, but that was major league." — Herb Michelson, *Sportin' Ladies*, p. 89, 1975
- She's trouble, Ned. The real thing. Big-time, major league trouble. — *Body Heat*, 1980
- I'm really impressed that you were such a major-league fuck-up. — Jay McInerney, *Story of My Life*, p. 99, 1988

majorly *adverb*
very much *US, 1983*
- I am majorly, totally, butt-crazy in love with Josh. — *Clueless*, 1995
- It would have been so majorly stupid of me to turn him down. — *American Beauty*, 1999

makable *adjective*
(used of a wave) in surfing, possible to catch for a ride *US, 1973*
- — William Desmond Nelson, *Surfing*, p. 222, 1973

make *noun*
an identification *US, 1950*
- Things that I'd never thought about before, like why did it take 'em so long to get a make on me? — A.S. Jackson, *Gentleman Pimp*, p. 113, 1973
- I had everything on him. Prints. Positive make. Everything. — George V. Higgins, *The Judgment of Deke Hunter*, p. 38, 1976

▸ **on the make**
in search of sexual company *US, 1929*
- She's just another of those rich wives on the make. — Philip Wylie, *Opus 21*, p. 273, 1949
- "You think I'm on the make for you, don't you?" — Mark Tryon, *Of G-Strings and Strippers*, p. 36, 1953
- "If he's interested in you, doll, you'd better keep your legs crossed. 'Cause I'd say he was strictly on the make." — Georgia Sothern, *My Life in Burlesque*, p. 299, 1972
- It's a local tradition. Every Wednesday night. And you don't even have to look like you're on the make. — Armistead Maupin, *Tales of the City*, p. 14, 1978

▸ **put the make on**
to try to seduce *US, 1963*
- An this guy gives me a ride—an that was the first guy ever put the make on me. — John Rechy, *City of Night*, p. 152, 1963

make *verb*
1 to identify (a person) *UK, 1906*
- "We still can't make her." "Could it have been a man dressed like a dame?" — Mickey Spillane, *Kiss Me Deadly*, p. 143, 1952
- "They've made us, Pat," I said. "Get going." — William Burroughs, *Junkie*, p. 80, 1953
- He's a nice, clean-cut gun dealer, is what he is, and if he wanted to, he could probably make half the hoods and forty percent of the bikies in this district. — George V. Higgins, *The Friends of Eddie Doyle*, p. 215, 1971
- This part of town, they'll make us for heat the second we walk in. — *48 Hours*, 1982

2 to seduce or have sex with *US, 1923*
- Al had had the reputation of making every girl he took out. — James T. Farrell, *Saturday Night*, p. 18, 1947
- Later that night I found out why Tino had put me in the hospital so readily. He was trying to make me. — Chester Himes, *Cast the First Stone*, p. 71, 1952
- He had decided at the start that he was going to make one or other of the Graces sooner or later. — Charles Raven, *Underworld Nights*, p. 119, 1956
- We picked up two girls, a pretty young blonde and a fat brunette. They were dumb and sullen, but we wanted to make them. — Jack Kerouac, *On the Road*, p. 34, 1957

3 to admit someone into membership in an organized crime organization *US, 1964*
- Valachi told the subcommittee that the purpose of a particular meeting in upstate New York had been to make us. — *American Speech*, p. 306, December 1964: "Lingua Cosa Nostra"

▸ **make ass**
to blunder; to make a spectacle of yourself *US, 1981*
Hawaiian youth usage.
- — Douglas Simonson, *Pidgin to da Max*, 1981

▸ **make good**
to succeed; to meet expectations *US, 1901*
- — David Burton Morris (Director), *Hometown Boy Makes Good*, 1993

▸ **make hole**
to drill for oil *US, 1984*
- Working on an oil rig, that's what you do: you make hole. — Ken Weaver, *Texas Crude*, p. 92, 1984

▸ **make it**
1 to have sex *US, 1952*
- I took her home and in her kitchen almost made it on the floor, a Marilyn Monroe type with mouth open and round hips and tight skirt[.] — Jack Kerouac, *Letter to Gary Snyder*, pp. 582–583, May 1956
- Once, because it seemed logical, Jessica and I had tried to make it, but the chemistry just wasn't there. — Clancy Sigal, *Going Away*, p. 407, 1961
- I'm a good woman; that's why he can't make it with me. — Mary McCarthy, *The Group*, p. 130, 1963
- Then what's his sex life, who was not married? He masturbates? No, probably not. Makes it with men? Who knows. — *The Digger Papers*, p. 4, August 1968

2 to leave *US, 1913*
- I'd still say now's the time, man—make it back to the Apple. — Ross Russell, *The Sound*, p. 99, 1961
- "Suppose I get into trouble and I got to make it [leave]." — Elliot Liebow, *Tally's Corner*, p. 69, 1967
- Buddy jumped quickly. "Sure, I'll do it!" "Beautiful. Let's make it[.]" — Donald Goines, *Inner City Hoodlum*, p. 108, 1975

3 to be accepted by *US, 1955*
- Laura and I marched but her friend went home because she said the whole thing made her sick—all the hatred—which was a very honest thing to say inasmuch as if you want to make it with the activists, hatred is supposed to be all right with you. — James Simon Kunen, *The Strawberry Statement*, p. 118, 1968

4 to be acceptable *US, 1955*
- Brown shoes don't make it. — Frank Zappa, *Borwn Shoes Don't Make It*, 1967

▸ **make like**
to behave in a suggested manner *US, 1954*
Used in conjunction with "and" to join a noun and a verb in a pun.
- A favorite pun is "make like a tree and leave." — *Gettysburg (Pennsylvania) Times*, 18th March 1954

- Make like an alligator and drag ass. — *American Speech*, p. 100, May 1954
- Today's expressions include "Make like the wind and blow!," "Make like a tree and leave!" — *American Weekly*, p. 2, 14th August 1955

▶ **make nice**
to be act politely *US, 1957*
- I'm gonna make nice there! I'm only gonna challenge him. — *West Side Story*, 1957

▶ **make the hole**
to rob drunks sleeping on underground platforms and in carriages *US, 1980*
- They informed me they were making the hole together as partners — Herbert Huncke, *The Evening Sun Turned Crimson*, p. 112, 1980

▶ **make tracks**
to depart hurriedly *US, 1978*
- "I know just what you mean," Jackie replied quickly as he tossed his gun on the seat. "Let's make tracks." — Donald Goines, *Crime Partners*, p. 89, 1978

make for *verb*
to steal, to obtain *US, 1936*
- Taking junk hidden by another junkie is known as "making him for his stash." — William Burroughs, *Junkie*, p. 35, 1953

make my day
used as a jocular challenge *US, 1985*
The phrase entered the popular lexicon in 1983 as a line uttered by the Clint Eastwood character "Dirty Harry" Callahan in the film *Sudden Impact*.
- "I have only one thing to say to the tax increasers," said President Reagan, delighting in a mock-tough line submitted by one of his writers. "Go ahead and make my day." — *New York Times Magazine*, p. 10, 7th April 1985

make out *verb*
to kiss with passion and in a sustained fashion *US, 1949*
- "He has finesse. No sweaty hands, no making out in drive-in movies." "Making out?" "My God, Larry, where've you been living. I guess you still call it necking." — Frederick Kohner, *Gidget*, p. 71, 1957
- Then we broke up, she telling me I didn't know enough about "making out" to keep her from wanting to date other boys[.] — Phyllis and Eberhard Kronhausen, *Sex Histories of American College Men*, p. 116, 1960
- I'm sick of these creeps who want to make out all the time. — Ann Landers, *Ann Landers Talks to Teen-Agers About Sex*, p. 117, 1963
- Who do you make-out to? Sinatra or Mathis? — *Diner*, 1982
- And now he was downstairs making out with one of the prettiest girls Griffin had ever seen. — Francesca Lia Block, *I Was a Teenage Fairy*, p. 97, 1998

make-out artist *noun*
a person who is successful in the pursuit of sexual companions *US, 1949*
- His notoriety as a make-out artist sometimes worked against him. — Ellis Amburn, *The Sexiest Man Alive*, p. 75, 2002

makeover *noun*
a complete transformation of fashion and hairstyle *US, 1999*
- SCOTT: I can't believe you'd do this on national television! DR. EVIL: They offered me a free makeover. — *Austin Powers*, 1999

make the scene with 18
used as a jingle to remind US troops in Vietnam to limit their M-16 rifles to 18 rounds because the rifle sometimes jammed when loaded to its 20-round capacity *US, 1991*
- — John Elting, *A Dictionary of Soldier Talk*, p. 193, 1984

makings *noun*
the tobacco and rolling paper needed to make a cigarette *US, 1905*
- — Frank Prewitt and Francis Schaeffer, *Vacaville Vocabulary*, 1961–1962
- [H]e fumbled with Roxy's makings and rolled a cigarette. — Peter Corris, *Pokerface*, 1985

malarkey; malarky; mullarkey *noun*
nonsense *US, 1929*
- "I told you earlier I had this date, but to show you much I care for you I ducked him all these hours to spend them with you." The malarkey! — Jack Lait and Lee Mortimer, *New York Confidential*, p. 167, 1948

male *adjective*
(said of a candy bar) with nuts *US, 1991*
- It was loaded with "vagina" (Vienna) sausages, shoestring potatoes, peanuts, a large hard salami, two jars of Tang, forty packages of presweetend Kool-Aid, and four "male" (with nuts) Hershey bars[.] — Gary Linderer, *The Eyes of the Eagle*, p. 119, 1991

male beaver *noun*
featuring shots of the naked male genitals *US, 1969*
- I was viewing two hours of male beaver films. — *Screw*, p. 7, 31st July 1969

malehouse *noun*
a homosexual brothel *US, 1963*
- I figured theres got to be that malehouse somewhere in Hollywood I heard so much about, an someone'll spot me, sign me up for it. — John Rechy, *City of Night*, p. 137, 1963

male twigs *noun*
low quality marijuana *US, 1979*
- Also known as doodley-squat, salt and pepper, and "male twigs," this female-impersonator a/k/a Headache Mary is sometimes advertised as "good commercial[.]" — *Hi Life*, p. 15, 1979

malfunction junction *noun*
any bureaucracy or inefficient organization *US, 1975*
- "Not only does Malfunction Junction send me a woman, but a New Yorker to boot." — Jessica Speart, *A Killing Season*, p. 49, 2002

mallard *noun*
a hundred-dollar bill *US, 1985*
- — Steve Kuriscak, *Casino Talk*, p. 36, 1985

mall crawl *noun*
an outing to a shopping center, slowly moving from store to store *US, 1996*
A play on PUB-CRAWL or BAR-HOP with a rhyme to boot.
- — *American Demographics*, September 1996: "Mall crawl palls"
- The Mall Crawl; Many still enjoy shopping the old-fashioned way. — *The Danbury News-Times*, 7th December 2000

mallie *noun*
a young person who spends their free time at shopping centers *US, 1985*
- The other day a friend accused me of having become a "mallie." — *Washington Post*, p. D3, 3rd August 1987
- The Time Out, besides being a classroom for sublimating foreign policy, also is headquarters for "mall rats," a subspecies of teen-ager also known as "mallies." You've seen them. Perhaps your son or daughter is one. — *New York Times*, p. B1, 4th September 1987
- — Kenn "Naz" Young, *Naz's Dictionary of Teen Slang*, 1993
- — Vann Wesson, *Generation X Field Guide and Lexicon*, p. 110, 1997

mall rat *noun*
a young person who spends a great deal of time at a shopping center *US, 1982*
- You're one of those fucking mallrats; you don't come to the mall to shop or work. You hang out and act like you fucking live here. — *Mallrats*, 1995

mama *noun*
1 used as a term of address towards a woman *US, 1959*
- Hey mama, don't you treat me wrong / Come and love your daddy all night long. — Ray Charles, *What'd I say*, 1959
- Hey, mama, what it is! — Carolyn Greene, *70 Soul Secrets of Sapphire*, p. 35, 1973

2 in motorcycle clubs and gangs, a female who is available to all the gang members and attached to none *US, 1965*
- There are mamas at any Angel gathering, large or small. They travel as part of the troupe, like oxpeckers, fully understanding what's expected: they are available at any time, in any way, to any Angel, friend or favored guest—individually or otherwise. — Hunter S. Thompson, *Hell's Angels*, p. 171, 1966
- He came and so did guys from a dozen other bike clubs, their mamas in their pussy holders[.] — Nicholas Von Hoffman, *We Are The People Our Parents Warned Us Against*, p. 157, 1967
- Each Angel looked about, checking out any movement towards his old lady, and at the same time he might be thinking of getting in line for one of those magnificent mama turn-outs. — Frank Reynolds, *Freewheelin' Frank*, p. 6, 1967

- A mama is the sexual equivalent of the public well—anyone can dip into her, at any time, as often as he wants. — Yves Lavigne, *Hell's Angels*, p. 115, 1987

3 in a deck of playing cards, a queen *US, 1988*
  - — George Percy, *The Language of Poker*, p. 55, 1988

4 the lead airplane in a combat flight formation *US, 1986*
  - — *American Speech*, p. 123, Summer 1986: "The language of Naval fighter pilots"

mama coca *noun*
cocaine *US, 1984*
  - — R.C. Garrett et al, *The Coke Book*, p. 200, 1984

mama-jammer *noun*
used as a euphemism for "motherfucker" *US, 1969*
  - I'd bought a rifle, which was not illegal at that time, and it was a sweet mama-jammer, too. — H. Rap Brown, *Die Nigger Die!*, p. 109, 1969

mama-san *noun*
in Southeast Asia usage, a woman whose age demands respect, especially a brothel madam *US, 1946*
The Japanese honorific *san* added to English "mama."
  - The typical mama-san on a typical shopping spree presents a very colorful picture [.] — William Hume, *When We Get Back Home*, p. 42, 1953
  - The Green Apple was chaired by a Mama-San who looked like a mixture of every ethnic culture that ever had passed through the Orient. — Elaine Shepard, *The Doom Pussy*, p. 137, 1967
  - "I had a drink and the Mama San told me I could get a boum-boum for 300 piasters or a sop-sop [fellatio] for 500." — Charles Winick, *The Lively Commerce*, p. 265, 1971
  - Mamasan sold me a real weird drink / Glass of that stuff hit the sink. — Sandee Johnson, *Cadences: The Jody Call Book, No. 2*, p. 63, 1986

mama's little helper *noun*
in shuffleboard, a score that is accidentally provided to you by an opponent *US, 1967*
  - — Omero C. Catan, *Secrets of Shuffleboard Strategy*, p. 69, 1967: "Glossary of terms"

mama's mellow *noun*
the calming effect of secobarbital (brand name Seconal™), a barbiturate *US, 1971*
  - — Eugene Landy, *The Underground Dictionary*, p. 127, 1971

mammy *noun*
1 a mother *US, 1942*
  - "You rich, Miss Marie?" "Puddin', I got money's mammy." — Toni Morrison, *The Bluest Eye*, p. 53, 1970

2 in a striptease act, a woman, usually older, who waits backstage, catching a stripper's clothing as she flings it offstage *US, 1981*
  - — Don Wilmeth, *The Language of American Popular Entertainment*, p. 166, 1981

3 the most; the ultimate example *US, 1971*
An English language version of the famous Arabic **MOTHER OF ALL**.
  - — Hermese E. Roberts, *The Third Ear*, 1971

mammy *adjective*
a lot of *US, 1992*
Placed after the noun.
  - A person with four cartons of cigarettes has cigarettes mammy. — William K. Bentley and James M. Corbett, *Prison Slang*, 1992

mammy-fugger *noun*
used as a euphemism for "motherfucker" *US, 1998*
  - Leroy is the dumbest, ugliest, biggest, baddest—I mean really malignant!—black mammyfugger on the playground. — Clarence Major, *All-Night Visitors*, p. 27, 1998

mammy-jammer *noun*
used as a euphemism for "motherfucker" *US, 1963*
  - "You know what that dirty mammy-jammer did to me?" — Malcolm Braly, *Shake Him Till He Rattles*, p. 95, 1963

mammyjamming *adjective*
used as a euphemism for the intensifier "motherfucking" *US, 1946*
  - Then that mammyjamming night manager put the claw on him for 60, so that left 70. — Bernard Wolfe, *The Late Risers*, p. 169, 1954
  - — Robert S. Gold, *A Jazz Lexicon*, p. 200, 1964
  - — Kenn "Naz" Young, *Naz's Underground Dictionary*, 1973

mammy-screwing *adjective*
used as a euphemism for "motherfucking" *US, 1963*

- Ma fell in a ditch, starts cussin up a mammy-screwin' storm! — John Rechy, *City of Night*, p. 147, 1963

mammy-sucker *noun*
used as a euphemism for "motherfucker" *US, 1972*
  - — Robert A. Wilson, *Playboy's Book of Forbidden Words*, p. 165, 1972

mams *noun*
the female breasts *US, 2005*
  - A-N bares her legendary mams in bed, then lights up the screen with her magnificent seat-meat as she rises to join Jack Nicholson in the shower. — Mr. Skin, *Mr. Skin's Skincyclopedia*, p. 21, 2005

man *noun*
1 used as a neutral term of address or a lexicalized hesitation phenomena *UK, 1512*
  - He's really diggin' the scene, man! — William "Lord" Buckley, *Nero*, 1951
  - Oh, you know, man. We got our kicks. — John Clellon Holmes, *Go*, p. 96, 1952
  - He even yelled at me at the table last night for saying "man." — Anonymous, *Go Ask Alice*, p. 54, 1971
  - Since "man" is commonly used as a neutral designation and since "man" is also used generically when referring to persons in authority, Ainsley Washington was made to feel like everyman on one hand and the living symbol of the police on the other. — Robert Campbell, *Juice*, p. 69, 1988

2 a drug dealer *US, 1942*
  - You better find somebody else cause I'm not your man no more. I'm not selling you. — Hal Ellson, *The Golden Spike*, p. 30, 1952
  - I'm waiting for my man / Twenty-six dollars in my hand. — Velvet Underground *I'm Waiting for the Man*, 1967
  - Well I pawned my Smith Corona / And I went to meet my man / He hangs out down on Alvarado Street / By the Pioneer Chicken Stand. — Warren Zevon, *Carmelita*, 1976
  - Posing in front of a marawanny bush is the connection—a parasite that thrives on the tragic despair of a seamy world; from which the underworld term, "If you see me with the man, cool it," was derived. — Lenny Bruce, *The Unpublished Lenny Bruce*, p. 67, 1984

3 a pimp *US, 1973*
  - Sometimes me and my man Daddy drive up Park Avenue in his car. — Susan Hall, *Ladies of the Night*, p. 17, 1973
  - They had the same man, Ronnie. — Frederique Delacoste, *Sex Work*, p. 30, 1987

▶ **the man**
a police officer; an authority figure *US, 1928*
  - My friends were now "downtown," busy, as they put it, "fighting the man." — James Baldwin, *The Fire Next Time*, p. 31, 1963
  - I never let them stop laughing, hit them hard and fast with jokes on processed hair and outer space and marijuana and integration and the numbers racket and long white Cadillacs and The Man downtown[.] — Dick Gregory, *Nigger*, p. 101, 1964
  - I got a job with the poverty program as a neighborhood worker and that's really when I began to see where "the man" was at. — H. Rap Brown, *Die Nigger Die!*, p. 75, 1969
  - The Man has got himself a "temporary" restraining order against the printer of the Berkeley Tribe (Walter Press) from further printing of the names and addresses of local narcs. — *The Berkeley Tribe*, p. 4, 15th–21th August 1969

man; mandy *noun*
in a deck of playing cards, a king *US, 1988*
  - — George Percy, *The Language of Poker*, p. 55, 1988

Manchu law *noun*
a military practice limiting the duration of noncombat duty in Washington *US, 1924*
  - In addition, it passes the "Manchu Law," which states that officers who have not served two years of line duty during the previous six years had to be returned immediately for troop duty for two years. — Raymond Bluhm, *U.S. Army: A Complete History*, p. 532, 2004

M and G track *noun*
in a pornographic film, additions to the sound track amplifying moans and groans *US, 1991*
  - They [later with editing] put in a groan. The M and G track. — Robert Stoller and I.S. Levine, *Coming Attractions*, p. 121, 1991
  - — *Adult Video News*, p. 51, October 1995

mandie *noun*
a tablet of the recreational drug methaqualone, best known as Quaaludes™ *US, 1985*
From the trade name Mandrax™.
- — Liz Cutland, *Kick Heroin*, p. 107, 1985
- I took a bunch of mandies and Apolon thought I was dying. — Cleo Odzer, *Goa Freaks*, p. 140, 1995

M and M; M & M *noun*
1 any tablet drugs used for recreational purposes: amphetamine, barbiturate, MDMA, the recreational drug best known as ecstasy *US, 1977*
Named because of the similar appearance of the candy and multicolored pills.
- — Donald Wesson and David Smith, *Barbiturates*, p. 121, 1977
- Street names [...] love doves, M and Ms, MDMA[.] — James Kay and Julian Cohen, *The Parents' Complete Guide to Young People and Drugs*, p. 136, 1998
2 a red central nervous system tablet shaped and colored like a piece of M&M chocolate candy *US, 1978*
- The M&M red was the first tablet exclusively manufactured in Mexico. — Joan W. Moore, *Homeboys*, p. 80, 1978
3 a 9 mm Pistol *US, 1999*
- Calloway asked him if a robbery was involved, if the people were dead and if "an M & M" was used, street slang for a 9mm pistol. — *Times Picayune (New Orleans)*, p. B1, 10th November 1999

man down!
used in prison for alerting the guards that a prisoner has been injured or fallen ill *US, 1990*
- His sweatslick buttocks slipped off and he was on the floor, shrieks percussing his skull; and from a great distance heard Smoothbore shouting at the bars: "MAN DOWN!" — Seth Morgan, *Homeboy*, p. 96, 1990

mandrake *noun*
1 a tablet of the recreational drug methaqualone, best known as Quaaludes™ *US, 1985*
From Mandrax™, the trade name for a synthetic nonbarbiturate sedative consisting of methaqualone and a small amount of the antihistamine diphenhydramine.
- By 1972 it was one of the most popular drugs of abuse in the United States and was known as love drug, heroin for lovers, Dr. Jekyll and Mr. Hyde, sopors, sopes, ludes, mandrakes and quacks. — Marilyn Carroll and Gary Gallo, *Methaqualone*, 1985
2 a sexually aggressive male homosexual *US, 1978*
- — Anon., *King Smut's Wet Dreams Interpreted*, 1978

manga *noun*
a central nervous system depressant *US, 1978*
- In late 1973 a new red, manga, hit the streets in Los Angeles. — Joan W. Moore, *Homeboys*, p. 80, 1978

manged *adjective*
damaged without hope of repair *US, 1991*
- — Eric S. Raymond, *The New Hacker's Dictionary*, p. 231, 1991

manhole *noun*
the vagina *US, 1916*
- Had some dope shoved in her manhole? — *alt.prisons*, 17th November 1998
- With two fingers, he pressed into her and up and down her manhole. — *alt.sex.stories*, 14th July 2000
- as her manhole swallows my fingers I ram all the meat I have left into Janelles ass. — *alt.personals.transgendered*, 5th April 2002

manhole cover *noun*
a sanitary napkin *US, 1948*
- "Hey. You Gals want to loan me a Sanitary Napkin to staunch the flow? That's right. Those Manhole Covers!" — *alt.utensils.spork*, 27th June 2000

manicure *verb*
to prepare marijuana for smoking, trimming the leaves and stems and removing foreign objects *US, 1938*
- But "manicured" and made into cigarettes, and sold at 50 cents to $1 each, the pound of "weed" will return $750 to $1500. — Phil Hirsch, *Hooked*, p. 139, 1968
- — Eugene Landy, *The Underground Dictionary*, p. 127, 1971
- Manicuring. The process used in separating the tobacco from the twigs. — Lenny Bruce, *The Unpublished Lenny Bruce*, p. 69, 1984

Manila General *noun*
used as a humorous if xenophobic nickname for any hospital with a largely Filipino staff *US, 1988–1989*
- — *Maledicta*, p. 33, 1988–1989: "Medical maledicta from San Francisco"

man in Kokomo *noun*
in horseracing, any mysterious source of inside information on a horse or race *US, 1951*
- — David W. Maurer, *Argot of the Racetrack*, p. 42, 1951

man meat *noun*
the penis *US, 1990*
- I was almost drooling at the sight of his man meat sliding in and out of Kim's glistening smooth cunt. — *alt.sex.bondage*, 29th March 1990
- I want to suck and lick every last drop of it off of his man meat. — Carol Queen, *Switch Hitters*, p. 111, 1996
- It's sort of dark (and there's a lot of man meat in the shot). — Mr. Skin, *Mr. Skin's Skincyclopedia*, p. 120, 2005
- Use "cock" instead of "man meat." — Russell Kick, *Everything You Know About Sex Is Wrong*, p. 183, 2005

mano *noun*
used as an embellished "man" as a term of address *US, 1967*
- [H]e'd try to right the situation something like this: "Oh, gee, mano," using the hip Mexican appellation. — John Rechy, *Numbers*, p. 33, 1967

mano a mano *noun*
a one-on-one confrontation *US, 1968*
- Halfway down the grade into Sausalito, Harvey had had this mano a mano with a Langendorf bread truck he was sure had his number on it. — Cyra McFadden, *The Serial*, p. 102, 1977
- The letter called up visions of heavy sport on the high seas, mano a mano with giant sailfish and world-record marlin. — Hunter S. Thompson, *The Great Shark Hunt*, p. 492, 1979
- Mano a mano. No—more like High Noon. Gunfight at the O.K. Corral. — Elmore Leonard, *City Primeval*, p. 119, 1980
- North did issue a crowd-pleasing challenge to terrorist Abu Nidal to meet anywhere, anytime and on equal terms—mano a mano. — *Los Angeles Times*, p. 6 (Calendar), 11th July 1987

man of the cloth *noun*
in pool, a skilled player who makes a living betting on his ability *US, 1990*
- — Steve Rushin, *Pool Cool*, p. 20, 1990

man oil *noun*
semen *US, 1949*
- — Captain Vincent J. Monteleone, *Criminal Slang*, p. 152, 1949

man o Manishewitz!
used as a jocular, mild oath *US, 1992*
From a commercial for Manishewitz kosher wine.
- "Man-oh-Manishewitz, they say the snatch grows fine up there." — James Ellroy, *White Jazz*, p. 111, 1992

man overboard!
1 in dominoes, used for announcing the fact that a player is forced to draw a piece *US, 1959*
- — Dominic Armanino, *Dominoes*, p. 17, 1959
2 in craps in American casinos, used for announcing that the dice or a die are off the table *US, 1985*
- — Steve Kuriscak, *Casino Talk*, p. 66, 1985

man pipe *noun*
the penis *US, 2005*
- Fast toplessness as she takes man-pipe from William Baldwin on a train. — Mr. Skin, *Mr. Skin's Skincyclopedia*, p. 122, 2005

man-size *adjective*
difficult *US, 1945*
- — Lou Shelly, *Hepcats Jive Talk Dictionary*, p. 29, 1945

man's man *noun*
a police informer *US, 1972*
From THE MAN (the police).
- — Bruce Jackson, *Outside the Law*, p. 59, 1972: "Glossary"

Manson lamps *noun*
a look full of hate, a murderous look *US, 1999*
Formed from a reference to US serial killer Charles Manson and LAMP (the eye).

- Don't give me your fucking Manson lamps, just fucking stop.
  — *Sopranos*, Episode 24, 1999
- But it was nonetheless brimming with brilliant moments, funny lines, witty scene bits, and original characterizations, most notably by David Proval, whose Richie Aprile has shut his "Manson lamps" and sported a leisure suit for the last time. — *Boston Globe*, p. D1, 7th April 2000

man-trap *noun*
an attractive, seductive woman *US, 1963*
- She would talk to a really beautiful model, a "man-trap" whom she "happened to know." — Michael Leigh, *The Velvet Underground*, p. 45, 1963

manual exercises *noun*
masturbation *US, 1964*
- — Roger Blake, *The American Dictionary of Sexual Terms*, p. 128, 1964

manual release *noun*
manual stimulation of a man's genitals *US, 1980*
- [O]nly "manual release" was allowed, and this service was automatically provided with the massage, no extra tipping was required. — Guy Talese, *Thy Neighbor's Wife*, p. 221, 1980
- The rates are $20 for the manual release, $30 for the manual release with top off, $40 for manual release with top and bottom off. — James Ridgeway, *Red Light*, p. 217, 1996

man up *verb*
to stand up to a difficult situation *US, 2004*
- man up: to toughen up, to take the blame — J.G. Narum, *The Convict Cookbook*, p. 161, 2004

man upstairs *noun*
God *US, 1948*
Always used with "the."
- Mr. McDougall says that the only thing that sustained him and kept him going through the hours in the water was the counsel he received from "the man upstairs." — *The New York Times*, p. BR11, 22nd August 1948
- [T]hinking about the Man Upstairs every once in a while. — Lewis John Carlino, *The Great Santini*, 1979
- "I believe the man upstairs will decide who's going to win this tournament," he said to the press[.] — Dan Jenkins, *Dead Solid Perfect*, p. 138, 1986

map *noun*
1 the face *US, 1899*
- Brother, you should have seen their maps when they took one peep at those strutting searchlights up above. — Mezz Mezzrow, *Really the Blues*, p. 168, 1946
- You gotta stop that grinning. Freeze your "map" and keep it that way. — Iceberg Slim (Robert Beck), *Pimp*, p. 162, 1969

2 a musical score; a piece of sheet music *US, 1970*
- — Clarence Major, *Dictionary of Afro-American Slang*, 1970
- — Arnold Shaw, *Dictionary of American Pop/Rock*, p. 223, 1982

3 a check *US, 1979*
- Don't take that guy's map. He's a paperhanger. — John Scarne, *Scarne's Guide to Modern Poker*, p. 284, 1979

map *verb*
to hit, to strike *US, 1989*
- — Terry Williams, *The Cocaine Kids*, p. 137, 1989

maracas *noun*
the female breasts *US, 1940*
- She thought it would be cute to show off her maracas in Harper's Bazaar. — Calvin Trillin, *With All Disrespect*, p. 62, 1985
- Her maracas were magnificent, more than ample, not pointed at all but full, generous. — Donald O'Donovan, *Babylon*, p. 82, 1994
- "See, Lola shakes her maracas, and Rosa bounces her bongos, while Nena is all hands." — Barbara Novak, *Down with Love*, p. 21, 2003

marathon *noun*
1 in horseracing, any race that is longer than a mile and a quarter *US, 1976*
- — Tom Ainslie, *Ainslie's Complete Guide to Thoroughbred Racing*, p. 334, 1976

2 any amphetamine, methamphetamine, or other central nervous system stimulant *US, 1980*
- — National Institute on Drug Abuse, *What do they call it again?*, 1980

marauder *noun*
a surfer who is indifferent to safety, if not reckless *US, 1985*
- — John Blair, *The Illustrated Discography of Surf Music 1961–1965*, p. 124, 1985

marble *noun*
a slow-witted person *US, 1958*
Teen slang.
- — *San Francisco News*, p. 6, 25th March 1958

▸ **all the marbles**
used as a symbol of complete success *US, 1924*
- This was for all the marbles, the African club championship. — Bill Cardoso, *The Maltese Sangweech*, p. 298, 1984

Marblehead turkey *noun*
salt cod *US, 1955*
- In the vicinity of Marblehead, Mass., cod fish is such a common food commodity that the inhabitants refer to it as Marblehead Turkey in the same sense that elsewhere cheese is dubbed Welsh rabbit. — George Earlie Shankle, *American Nicknames*, p. 282, 1955

marble orchard *noun*
a graveyard *US, 1925*
- — William K. Bentley and James M. Corbett, *Prison Slang*, 1992

marbles *noun*
1 the testicles *US, 1916*
- — James McDonald, *A Dictionary of Obscenity, Taboo and Euphemism*, p. 7, 1988

2 dice *US, 1962*
- — Frank Garcia, *Marked Cards and Loaded Dice*, 1962
- — Thomas L. Clark, *The Dictionary of Gambling and Gaming*, p. 126, 1987

marcel *noun*
a hairstyle characterized by deep, regular waves made by a heated curling iron *US, 1963*
After Marcel Grateau (1852–1936), a French hairdresser.
- Instantly Teese was on his guard, for the young "ragheads," as he called them by dint of their habits of tying kerchiefs about their marcels to keep down sweat and protect the sheens[.] — Clarence Cooper Jr., *Black*, p. 190, 1963
- Those two pimps? That style is just called a process, some call it a marcel. — Joseph Wambaugh, *The New Centurions*, p. 66, 1970
- Maurice had his hair done in a marcel, a process in a Caesar style[.] — James Carr, *Bad*, p. 110, 1975
- They flashed big smiles signifying their joy at sporting straight hair via konks or marcels. — Piri Thomas, *Stories from El Barrio*, p. 51, 1978

marching powder *noun*
cocaine *US, 1984*
A shortening of BOLIVIAN, COLUMBIAN or PERUVIAN MARCHING POWDER.
- A boatload of Marching Powder might get you through this ordeal. — Jay McInerney, *Bright Lights, Big City*, p. 25, 1984
- I find myself at the house of Hedgehopper, notoriously nefarious dealer of marching powder. — Lynn Breedlove, *Godspeed*, p. 21, 2002

Marge *noun*
the passive, "feminine" partner in a lesbian relationship *US, 1956*
- — Robert A. Wilson, *Playboy's Book of Forbidden Words*, p. 166, 1972

mari *noun*
a marijuana cigarette *US, 1933*
A clipping of "marijuana."
- [S]o too I condemn a society that has so rejected reason as to prefer seeing their children raped before allowed to smoke Mari. — Neal Cassady, *Grace Beats Karma*, p. 121, 20th August 1959: Letter to Carolyn Cassady

Maria *noun*
in a deck of playing cards, the queen of spades *US, 1950*
- — Thomas L. Clark, *The Dictionary of Gambling and Gaming*, p. 126, 1987

marihooch; marihoochie; marihootee; marihootie *noun*
marijuana *US, 1971*
- [I]t was an ace bomber of absolutely atomic North African marihooch[.] — Lester Bangs, *Psychotic Reactions and Carburetor Dung*, p. 80, 1971

marinate *verb*
to relax, to idle *US, 2000*
- — *Ebony Magazine*, p. 156, August 2000: "How to talk to the new generation"

Marine Tiger *noun*
a recent arrival in New York City from Puerto Rico *US, 1952*
From the name of a converted C4 Troopship that brought many early Puerto Rican immigrants to the US.

- They spoke only Spanish, but he would have known anyhow that they were recent arrivals—Marine Tigers—for only newcomers would play ball barefooted in the street. — Hal Ellson, *The Golden Spike*, p. 82, 1952
- The first carried so many immigrants that the slang term for a new arrival became Marine Tiger. — Dale Krame, *Teen-Age Gangs*, p. 77, 1953
- Later I called her my "marine tiger," after the ship that brought so many Puerto Ricans to New York. — Piri Thomas, *Down These Mean Streets*, p. 109, 1967

mark *noun*

1 a victim, a potential victim of a swindle *UK, 1749*

- She had her eye on a mark—a small man in a dark suit and a country haircut, who had stopped to gawk into the lighted window of a photographic-supply shop. — *Rogue for Men*, p. 45, June 1956
- The amount of bread it would cost you would stagger the mark that gigs for a living. — A.S. Jackson, *Gentleman Pimp*, p. 123, 1973
- It is alright to burn one's victims as long as they can be referred to as marks, but never—never—burn the guy you work with and who is your partner. — Herbert Huncke, *The Evening Sun Turned Crimson*, p. 138, 1980
- Uneducated as to the inner workings of the business, I was still a "mark" as we'd say in wrestling. — Gary Cappetta, *Bodyslams!*, p. 62, 2000

2 a youth gang's graffiti-style signed name *US, 1992*

- "You sayin' you never seen our marks?" — Jess Mowry, *Way Past Cool*, p. 61, 1992

mark *verb*

in casino gambling, to place in a stack chips equal to the amount of marker (a loan) extended to a gambler *US, 1980*

- — Lee Solkey, *Dummy Up and Deal*, p. 116, 1980

Mark Anthony *noun*

an exceptionally gullible victim *US, 1972*

- What I didn't know was that there was a Mark Anthony—that's a super-sucker—on the sidelines. — Robert Byrne, *McGoorty*, p. 32, 1972

marked wheel *adjective*

rigged *US, 1975*

- I learned that a "marked wheel" was a roulette table rigged to activate a pin under a heavy number. — Jimmy Snyder, *Jimmy the Greek*, p. 15, 1975

marker *noun*

in a casino or gambling enterprise, an advance with an IOU; by extension, any debt or obligation *US, 1887*

- Never sign a marker or IOU. — Mario Puzo, *Inside Las Vegas*, p. 14, 1977
- No, I owe you a favor. You got my marker. That's the way it is. — Robert Campbell, *The Cat's Meow*, p. 179, 1988
- You signed markers for a hundred and a half, you're over sixty days past due and you haven't told anybody what the problem is. — *Get Shorty*, 1995

marking *noun*

a welt or bruise produced in sadomasochistic sex *US, 1987*

- Sometimes a man will want "markings" to jog his fantasies if he travels or lives alone. — Frederique Delacoste, *Sex Work*, p. 51, 1987

marks *noun*

signs of intravenous drug use, such as scars or abcesses *US, 1983*

- Check this out. I ain't got no fucking marks. — Gerald Petievich, *To Live and Die in L.A.*, p. 221, 1983

Marlboro country *noun*

a remote place; the wilderness *US, 1968*

- Sure is marlboro country. Ain't a soul in sight. Nothin' but sand and water. — Robert Gover, *JC Saves*, p. 66, 1968

Marlboro man *noun*

a rugged, masculine, handsome cowboy type *US, 1969*
Derived from the decades-long advertising campaign for Marlboro cigarettes, featuring ultra-masculine cowboys smoking.

- If you are a boy soprano this will underscore your potential as a Marlboro Man. — *Screw*, p. 11, 15th December 1969
- "He walked in, I thought he was a farmer, or maybe a rancher. He looks like a cowboy, that raw-boned, outdoor type. Wears cowboy boots and a hat with a curled brim." "The Marlboro man," Chip said. "Yeah, except he's real." — Elmore Leonard, *Riding the Rap*, p. 102, 1995

Marley *noun*

a marijuana cigarette *US, 1997*

From Bob Marley, Rastafarian and marijuana-lover.

- — Jim Emerson-Cobb, *Scratching the Dragon*, April 1997

Marmon *noun*

morphine *US, 1945*

- "Are the Marmon and Cadillac working tonight?" "Yeah." "That Marmon's an eight, isn't it? And Cadillac's a twelve?" — William J. Spillard and Pence James, *Needle in a Haystack*, p. 145, 1945

married *adjective*

1 handcuffed together *US, 1962*

- — Joseph E. Ragen and Charles Finston, *Inside the World's Toughest Prison*, p. 808, 1962: "Penitentiary and underworld glossary"

2 (used of opium) adulterated with foreign substances *US, 1956*

- — *American Speech*, p. 101, May 1956: "Smugglers' argot in the Southwest"

married to Mary Fist *adjective*

obsessed with masturbating *US, 1950*

- — Hyman E. Goldin et al., *Dictionary of American Underworld Lingo*, p. 137, 1950

marry *verb*

in police work, to serve as partners *US, 1992*

- Subtracting the five years with Minifee and then averaging it out, he'd been married to a different cop for maybe a year and half at a time, with lots of space between marriages. — Robert Campbell, *Boneyards*, pp. 9–19, 1992

marsh *noun*

in soda fountain usage, a marshmallow *US, 1946*

- — *American Speech*, p. 88, April 1946: "The language of West Coast culinary workers"

martin-eye *noun*

a martini *US, 1969*
A jocular embellishment.

- "Fresheners," Nancy said. "Tighteners and fresheners. Sometimes drinkees or martin-eyes." — Elmore Leonard, *The Big Bounce*, p. 88, 1969

Marvin the ARVN; Marvin *noun*

a stereotyped soldier in the South Vietnamese Army *US, 1974*

- Within our first month in country we began trading our Marvin the ARVN beta boots for the tire-soled sandals favored by the VC. — Richard Marcinko, *Rogue Warrior*, p. 121, 1992

marvy *adjective*

marvelous *US, 1931*

- "Gee, that was a marvy movie," she said as we left the theater. — Max Shulman, *The Many Loves of Dobie Gillis*, p. 43, 1951
- Tons of marvy makeup, too, and a most effective hairspray. — *Screw*, p. 13, 6th November 1972
- [A]nd from perusing your marvy letters. — Leo Rosten, *Dear Herm*, p. 62, 1974

marvy-groovy *adjective*

bad *US, 1967*
A combination of two clichéd adjectives for "good," meaning "bad."

- — *Current Slang*, p. 4, Spring 1967

Mary *noun*

1 used as a term of address from one male homosexual to another *US, 1925*

- "Oh, Mary, get off it!" the fatman says impatiently with a fatwave of his hand[.] — John Rechy, *City of Night*, p. 166, 1963
- Oh! That whore! Mary, everybody's had him. — Antony James, *America's Homosexual Underground*, p. 34, 1965
- "Sure, there's a party. Now, Mary, you wouldn't want to miss it." — Joe Houston, *The Gay Flesh*, p. 61, 1965
- Oh, Mary, don't ask. — Mart Crowley, *The Boys in the Band*, p. 42, 1968

2 morphine *US, 1945*

- More specifically, it was classified as M, C, and H—Mary, Charlie, and Harry—which stood for morphine, cocaine, and heroin. — William J. Spillard and Pence James, *Needle in a Haystack*, 1945

Mary Ellen man *noun*

a pickpocket who distracts the victim by telling a sexually charged story *US, 1976*

- — John R. Armore and Joseph D. Wolfe, *Dictionary of Desperation*, 1976

Mary Fist *noun*

used as a personification of male masturbation *US, 1950*

- Many of them had been abetted by the fold-out pictures in Playboy, the magazine that, indeed, had verbally implanted the original suggestion in his just-turned-twelve mind with an article, "Doing It Without Chicks"—or, rather, doing it with a surrogate cutely identified as "Mary Fist." — Hyman E. Goldin et al., *Dictionary of American Underworld Lingo*, p. 136, 1950
- Jackie the Priest, who's got himself that good ole girlfriend, Mary Fist. — Gilbert Sorrentino, *Steelwork*, p. 39, 1970
- But I can understand some gazoony without a woman, or with the wrong woman, watching crap like this and having it off with Mary Fist. — Robert Campbell, *In La-La Land We Trust*, p. 175, 1986

Mary Jane *noun*
marijuana *US, 1928*
From the disputed presumption that marijuana is formed of two Mexican Spanish names: Maria and Juan or Juanita, hence Mary Jane, and many variants, such as Mary J, Mary Jonas, Mary Juana and so on.
- "Is that really mary-juana, Paul?" Christine asked, speaking in a shocked hush. — John Clellon Holmes, *Go*, p. 86, 1952
- I answered (and remember the pills, the liquor, the maryjane)[.] — John Rechy, *City of Night*, p. 124, 1963
- Mr. Mannheim said, "It isn't hep to call it Mary Jane any more," and the woman in the black bikini said, "Hip." — Evan Hunter, *Last Summer*, p. 117, 1968
- But everythin' is funny when your smokin' Mary Jane[.] — Tone Loc, *Cheeba Cheeba*, 1989

Mary unit *noun*
a motorcycle police officer *US, 2001*
- There's going to be a parade led by two hundred Mary units (motorcycle cops), followed by a hundred black-and-whites. — Stephen J. Cannell, *The Tin Collectors*, p. 65, 2001

Mary Warner; Mary Warmer; Mary Weaver; Mary Werner; Mary Worner *noun*
marijuana *US, 1933*
Giving a feminine identity by mispronunciation.
- — Captain Vincent J. Monteleone, *Criminal Slang*, p. 153, 1949
- Here. Try one of these. This is the real Mary Warner. — Douglas Rutherford, *The Creeping Flesh*, p. 49, 1963
- Well, that was my life and I don't feel ashamed at all. Mary Warner, honey, you sure was good — Louis Armstrong, quoted in *Waiting For The Man*, Harry Shapiro, p. 26, 1999

Mary Worthless *noun*
an older homosexual man *US, 1979*
- "Kinks and queens: linguistic and cultural aspects of the terminology for gays" — *Maledicta*, p. 222, 1979

Masarati *noun*
an improvised pipe for smoking crack cocaine, made from a plastic bottle *US, 1992*
- — Terry Williams, *Crackhouse*, p. 150, 1992

mash *noun*
1 a romantic infatuation; a sweetheart *US, 1877*
- And to me it was just another mash—that's what we called flirting in those days. We would use the expression, "The lady has a mash on you[.]" — Louis Armstrong, *Satchmo*, p. 151, 1954
- The dyke was sending Lor a hundred long-stemmed red roses a day, along with mash notes bearing her nom de plume d'amour: "Your tongue of Fire." — James Ellroy, *Hollywood Nocturnes*, p. 270, 1994

2 any homemade liquor *US, 1972*
- Talking trash, drinking mash, and snorting cocaine was a thrill, and she was just beginning to complete her education in hipness. — Nathan Heard, *To Reach a Dream*, p. 56, 1972
- The word on the yard was that the fight stemmed from a gang-related beef over the sale of mash, homemade whiskey that some inmates sold. — Nathan McCall, *Makes Me Wanna Holler*, p. 166, 1994
- — Gary K. Farlow, *Prison-ese*, p. 42, 2002

mash *verb*
1 to flirt aggressively *US, 1877*
- We're liable to get pinched for mashing on Sixty-third. I heard the Law is watching that pretty close. — James T. Farrell, *Saturday Night*, p. 38, 1947

2 to pass, to hand to someone, to give *US, 1944*
- — Jack Lait and Lee Mortimer, *New York Confidential*, 1948: "A glossary of Harlemisms"

- — Joseph E. Ragen and Charles Finston, *Inside the World's Toughest Prison*, p. 808, 1962: "Penitentiary and underworld glossary"

mash and dash *verb*
to kiss and run *US, 1996*
- — DePauw University Campus Corner, 29th January 1996: "Slang terms at DePauw"

mashed *adjective*
astonished *US, 1968*
- — Collin Baker et al., *College Undergraduate Slang Study Conducted at Brown University*, p. 155, 1968

mashed potato circuit *noun*
forums included on a speaking tour *US, 1965*
- When he left the film industry, his long years on the mashed potato circuit not only shaped his capacity as a public speaker—more on that later—but also exposed him to a wide diversity of voices and interests[.] — David Gergen, *Eyewitness to Power*, p. 159, 2000

masher *noun*
1 an unsophisticated flirt *US, 1973*
- — Sherman Louis Sergel, *The Language of Show Biz*, p. 133, 1973

2 a person who takes sexual pleasure from physical contact with strangers in crowded places *US, 1875*
- — Anon., *King Smut's Wet Dreams Interpreted*, 1978

mash list *noun*
a tally of all those with whom you have had sex *US, 1996*
- — DePauw University Campus Corner, 29th January 1996: "Slang terms at DePauw"

mash note; mash letter *noun*
a love letter *US, 1880*
- [T]hat poor bag of bones kept sending me mash notes and little presents. — Ethel Waters, *His Eye is on the Sparrow*, p. 84, 1951
- Hey! hey! now THAT'S the way to wail! a five page mash note crammed with everything[.] — Neal Cassady, *Grace Beats Karma*, p. 128, 22nd September 1959: Letter to Carolyn Cassady
- Your very elegant mash note arrived today. — Hunter S. Thompson, *Fear and Loathing in America*, p. 28, 30th January 1968: Letter to Sue Grafton
- Maureen Dowd is a superb parodist, but even she cannot compete with Harriet E. Miers's mash notes to George W. Bush, recently provided by the Texas State Library and Archives Commission. The mash notes are beyond parody. [Letter to Editor] — *New York Times*, p. A24, 14th October 2005

mash out *verb*
to complete *US, 1973*
- I had did my bit, the whole 1–3–2–6 was mashed out and there's one ting about getting outta a New York penitentiary that amazed me. — A.S. Jackson, *Gentleman Pimp*, p. 132, 1973

mask *noun*
1 a hostile, unmoving facial expression *US, 1993*
- I put on my mask (a mask is an extended version of a mad-dog stare; it's one's combat face) and prepared for a possible confrontation. — Sanyika Shakur, *Monster*, p. 90, 1993

2 oversized sunglasses *US, 1962*
- — *American Speech*, p. 270, December 1962: "The language of traffic policemen"

mass *adjective*
a lot of *US, 1981*
- I've got mass studying to do tonight. — Connie Eble (Editor), *UNC-CH Campus Slang*, p. 4, March 1981
- We have mass knives in our kitchen. — Judi Sanders, *Mashing and Munching in Ames*, p. 13, 1994

Massa Charlie *noun*
used as a stereotype of the dominant white male in relation to blacks *US, 1965*
- They didn't know Goldberg from Massa Charlies; to them, Goldberg was Massa Charlie. — Claude Brown, *Manchild in the Promised Land*, p. 298, 1965

Massachusetts driver *noun*
in the northeastern US, an inconsiderate and dangerous driver *US, 1975*
- — John Gould, *Maine Lingo*, p. 177, 1975

mass gas *noun*
a group of tanker aircraft refueling a group of receiver planes *US, 1963*
- — *American Speech*, p. 119, May 1963: "Air refueling words"

master *noun*
in a sadomasochistic relationship, a man who inflicts many forms of humiliation, including extreme pain and public displays of submission *US, 1975*
- The idea of a "mistress" or "master" taking over one's life, like the idea of a "slave" catering to one's every whim, has its appeal. — Stephen Lewis, *The Whole Bedroom Catalog*, p. 129, 1975

master blaster *noun*
1 a large piece of crack cocaine *US, 1992*
- — Terry Williams, *Crackhouse*, p. 150, 1992

2 a military pin awarded to soldiers who complete parachute training *US, 1980*
- His master-blaster "blood wings" were on his hat. — David Hackworth, *About Face*, p. 449, 1989

master key *noun*
in law enforcement, a sledge hammer *US, 1995*
- So when still no one came they used a sledgehammer—what the strike team called their master key—busted in and here was a woman standing in the living room no doubt the whole time, not saying a word. — Elmore Leonard, *Riding the Rap*, p. 37, 1995

master of your domain *noun*
a person who can refrain from masturbation for a prolonged period *US, 1992*
Coined and popularized by Jerry Seinfeld in an episode of his television comedy *The Contest* that first aired on 18th November 1992.

masturbation mansion *noun*
a movie theater showing pornographic films *US, 1970*
- [T]he early skin-flick houses became known humorously among much of the trade as "masturbation mansions." — Roger Blake, *The Porno Movies*, p. 65, 1970

mat *noun*
▸ **go to the mat**
to engage in a full-scale struggle *US, 1908*
From wrestling.
- Okay. We're going to the mat. — Edwin Torres, *After Hours*, p. 365, 1979

match *noun*
approximately half an ounce of marijuana *US, 1980*
An abbreviation of "matchbox," which contains approximately the same amount.
- — Edith A. Folb, *runnin' down some lines*, p. 246, 1980

mate *noun*
in poker, a card that forms a pair *US, 1988*
- — George Percy, *The Language of Poker*, p. 56, 1988

maternity blouse *noun*
a large, loose shirt worn untucked by a heavy man *US, 1981*
- — Male Swinger Number 3, p. 48, 1981: "The complete gay dictionary"

math out *verb*
to render a presentation beyond comprehension by virtue of dense mathematical content *US, 1991*
- — Eric S. Raymond, *The New Hacker's Dictionary*, p. 237, 1991

matinee; matinee session *noun*
a sexual encounter in the mid-afternoon *US, 1944*
- Some commuting businessmen, called matinees, reject the night hours altogether and come afternoons between two and four-thirty[.] — Judge John M. Murtagh and Sara Harris, *Cast the First Stone*, p. 2, 1957
- A matinee, and so early in the day. — Robert Leslie, *Confessions of a Lesbian Prostitute*, p. 67, 1965
- The second appointment was a "matinee" with a tried-and-true customer, a man I had known for three years[.] — Sara Harris, *The Lords of Hell*, p. 101, 1967
- Picture, if you will, two young men ... old friends, if an unsatisfactory love affair can make for friendship ... in a room, engaged in the preliminaries of a matinee. — Angelo d'Arcangelo, *The Homosexual Handbook*, p. 7, 1968

matrimonial peacemaker *noun*
the penis *US, 1967*
- — Dale Gordon, *The Dominion Sex Dictionary*, p. 105, 1967

mattel Messerschmitt *noun*
a Hughes TH-55 Cayuse aircraft *US, 1979*

- We sometimes called it the Mattel Messerschmitt because of its toylike appearance and mosquitolike agility. — Tom Marshall, *Price of Exit*, p. 41, 1988

Mattel toy rifle *noun*
the M16 rifle *US, 1986*
- I state categorically that the "Mattel toy rifle" is not fit for a grown man to fight a war with. — Ralph Zumbro, *Tank Sergeant*, p. 94, 1986

mattressback *noun*
a promiscuous woman *US, 1960*
- "Mattressback!" — John Barth, *The Sot-Weed Factor*, p. 442, 1960

mattresses *noun*
▸ **go to the mattresses; hit the mattresses**
during gang warfare, to retreat in an armed group to a fortified room, apartment, or house *US, 1964*
- Valachi quoted his boss as saying on one occasion: "We have to go to the mattress again," and explained that mattress derived from the practice of warring gangs of moving rapidly from place to place, holing up for temporary stays wherever necessary and sleeping on only a simple mattress. — American Speech, p. 306, December 1964: "Lingua Cosa Nostra"
- Sonny told his caporegimes to go to the mattresses. — Mario Puzo, *The Godfather*, p. 253, 1969
- Some of the heavies in the mob have hit the mattress, the big names are surrounding themselves with soldiers and a few have dropped out of sight entirely. — Mickey Spillane, *Last Cop Out*, p. 84, 1972
- And all we're trying to do is stop the button men from hitting the mattresses. — Joseph Wambaugh, *The Glitter Dome*, p. 181, 1981

mattress joint *noun*
a hotel catering to prostitutes *US, 1956*
- When the clerk in a mattress joint like the Beloit was reluctant to furnish the police with a guest's room number, the pressure was really on. — Rogue for Men, p. 49, June 1956

Mattress Mary *noun*
used as a personification of the stereotypical sexually loose female *US, 1955*
- — American Speech, p. 302, December 1955: "Wayne University slang"

Matty Mattel; Matty Mattel mouse gun *noun*
the M-16 rifle *US, 1978*
Named after the toy manufacturer because many soldiers in Vietnam found the M-16 to be a seriously flawed rifle.
- The following story is one that I tell with some trepidation, since my experience(s) with the "Matty Mattel Mouse Guns" were not pleasant ones. — Dick Culver, *The Saga of the M-16 in Vietnam*, 2000

Maui wowie; Maui wauie; Maui wowee; Maui *noun*
a potent marijuana cultivated in Hawaii *US, 1977*
The island of Maui plus wow (a thing of wonders).
- When Pattie Mae returned, she put her hand surreptitiously into Philo's coat pocket and said breathlessly: "One's Colombia Gold, the other's Maui wow-ee." — Joseph Wambaugh, *The Black Marble*, p. 145, 1978

mauler *noun*
a set of brass knuckles *US, 1953*
- "Get rid of the knucks," I said, watching his eyes. He looked surprisingly down at his hand. He slipped the mauler off and threw it casually in the corner. — Raymond Chandler, *The Long Goodbye*, p. 126, 1953

Mau-Mau *noun*
a black person who uses the fact that he is black to get his way with guilty white people *US, 1965*
- "Your life has been too easy for you to be making it as a jazz musician." "And too white," Mary muttered. "Miss Mau Mau." Hitchcock grinned at her. — Nat Hentoff, *Jazz Country*, p. 17, 1965
- The days of the poverty Mau-Mau were finished. No more blacks intimidating the white men with their African garb and Dark Continent souls. — Donald Goines, *Kenyatta's Last Hit*, pp. 6–7, 1975

mau-mau *verb*
to bully, especially using confrontational political arguments that play on racial guilt *US, 1970*
Coined as a verb by Tom Wolfe based on the name of a secret society organized to expel European settlers from Kenya.
- Going downtown to mau-mau the bureaucrats got to be the routine practice in San Francisco. — Tom Wolfe, *Radical Chic & Mau-Mauing the Flak Catchers*, p. 97, 1970

- Yeah, yeah it could work if Cynthia wrote the kind of proposal they needed, an airtight, fantastic piece of bureaucratic bullshit ... mau-maued into place by the right kind of militant niggerism. — Odie Hawkins, *The Busting Out of an Ordinary Man*, p. 153, 1985

maw-maws *noun*
the female breasts *US*, *2005*
- Fast toplessness as she takes man-pipe from William Baldwin on a train. Its quick but those are supermodel maw-maws. — Mr. Skin, *Mr. Skin's Skincyclopedia*, p. 122, 2005

max *noun*
1 maximum; a maximum *US*, *1851*
- I laid up there in the cell, telling myself, even if I can get this cut down to a lesser charge and stand a better chance of getting a lower max, I still end up doing that max[.] — Herbert Huncke, *Guilty of Everything*, p. 115, 1990
- A year—max—that's all I could do. — Danny King, *The Burglar Diaries*, p. 243, 2001

2 a maximum security prison *US*, *1961*
- San Quentin, although it was a prison, wasn't a max, though they had other ways of dealing with screw-ups. — Ralph "Sonny" Barger, *Hell's Angel*, p. 193, 2000

▸ **to the max**
as far as possible, to the limit *US*, *1971*
- I left that scene and returned to my room, uptight to the max! — Bobby Seale, *A Lonely Rage*, p. 121, 1978
- He was wasted to the max. — Robert Lipkin, *A Brotherhood of Outlaws*, p. 185, 1981
- My imagination's taxed to the max. — Joseph Wambaugh, *Fugitive Nights*, p. 255, 1992
- I've got a connection to the equipment and the mail order distribution, not to mention those kids I got out there who are hot-fuck-action to the max. — *Boogie Nights*, 1997

max *adjective*
maximum security *US*, *1976*
- I knew if we didn't make it Snoopy and I'd get sent here or some other max joint. — Elmore Leonard, *Out of Sight*, p. 58, 1996
- During the 1980s, when the authorities went after the Aryan Brotherhood in earnest and slammed validated AB members in Pelican Bay and other max lock-up prisons, the NLR filled the void[.] — Bill Valentine, *Gangs and Their Tattoos*, p. 9, 2000

max and relax *verb*
to take things easy, to take leisure with pleasure *US*, *1994*
- Yes, Clifton was feeling on top of the world, just maxin' and relaxin', feeling copasetic. — Karline Smith, *Moss Side Massive*, p. 188, 1994

max BBs *noun*
a tactic in aerial combat of using the highest rate of fire and filling the air with rounds *US*, *1991*
- The higher rate of fire was for air-to-air fighting where filling a block of sky with "max BBs" was the way to go. — Gerry Carroll, *North S*A*R*, p. 50, 1991

maxed to the onions *adjective*
extremely large *US*, *1982*
US military usage during the Vietnam war.
- — *Maledicta*, p. 259, Summer/Winter 1982: "Viet-speak"

maximum brilliant *adjective*
extremely good *US*, *1982*
- — Mimi Pond, *The Valley Girl's Guide to Life*, p. 60, 1982

max out; max *verb*
1 to reach a limit *US*, *1977*
- Mommie's Trust Fund was about to max out[.] — Dan Jenkins, *Life Its Ownself*, p. 124, 1984
- "Well max out with the fifty-buck-a-nighters," Lynn suggested. — Joseph Wambaugh, *Fugitive Nights*, p. 128, 1992
- Our credit cards are maxed. — *Traffic*, 2000

2 to complete a maximum prison sentence *US*, *1972*
- — John R. Armore and Joseph D. Wolfe, *Dictionary of Desperation*, 1976
- — Ralph de Sola, *Crime Dictionary*, p. 90, 1982

3 to relax *US*, *1984*
- — Bradley Elfman, *Breakdancing*, p. 41, 1984

mayo *noun*
mayonnaise *US*, *1960*

- #8 Whopper, Hold the Mayo[.] — Michael Moore, *Dude, Where's My Country?*, p. 76, 2003

Mayor Hunna; Mayor John *noun*
marijuana *US*, *1968*
- — Collin Baker et al., *College Undergraduate Slang Study Conducted at Brown University*, p. 156, 1968

maytag *noun*
a weak prisoner, especially one who does laundry for others as a sign of submission *US*, *1987*
- — Carsten Stroud, *Close Pursuit*, p. 273, 1987
- — Gary K. Farlow, *Prison-ese*, 2002

Mazatlans *noun*
beach sandals made with tire treads for soles *US*, *1965*
- — Duke Kahanamoku with Joe Brennan, *Duke Kahanamoku's World of Surfing*, p. 174, 1965

Mazola party *noun*
group sex, enhanced by the application of vegetable oil to the participants' bodies *US*, *1968*
An allusion and tribute to Mazola Corn Oil™.
- Of course there's always the group sex, the Mazola party thing. — Roderick Thorp, *The Music of their Laughter*, p. 129, 1970
- Eugene Landy, *The Underground Dictionary*, p. 129, 1971

mazoola *noun*
money *US*, *1951*
- All that mazoola, he kin be jes's dum's dum kin be! — Robert Gover, *One Hundred Dollar Misunderstanding*, p. 23, 1961

mazuma *noun*
1 money *US*, *1901*
From Hebrew to Yiddish to English.
- You've brought in a lot of mazuma. — Mickey Spillane, *One Lonely Night*, p. 74, 1951
- Jack, shekels, mazuma, simoleons, Mr. Green, filthy lucre, even spondulicks—this is other Why of prostitution. — Gail Sheehy, *Hustling*, p. 11, 1973
- A tasteful commercial emblazoned across each English breast and thigh would bring much-needed mazuma into the game. — Andrew Nickolds, *Back to Basics*, p. 140, 1994

2 a female professor *US*, *1947*
- — Marcus Hanna Boulware, *Jive and Slang of Students in Negro Colleges*, 1947

MB *verb*
to return a carnival customer's money *US*, *1985*
From "money back."
- — Gene Sorrows, *All About Carnivals*, p. 22, 1985: "Terminology"

MC; emcee *noun*
1 a master of ceremonies *US*, *1790*
- An M.C. is trying to warm us up with bad jokes. — Gore Vidal, *Myra Breckinridge*, p. 122, 1968
- The emcee had a voice that could take the paint off your car. — Carl Hiaasen, *Tourist Season*, p. 150, 1986
- SUZY SONG: And then the powow emcee called for a ladies' choice dance. — *Smoke Signals*, 1998

2 a rap artist *US*, *2000*
From "microphone controller."
- My first album is a combination of eveything I went through during my first couple of years as a frustrated emcee. — Eminem (Marshall Mathers), *Angry Blonde*, p. 3, 2000

MC; emcee *verb*
to serve as a master of ceremonies *US*, *1937*
- The owner asked my mother to m.c. She was petrified. — Lenny Bruce, *How to Talk Dirty and Influence People*, p. 28, 1965
- I'll close the room and serve them booze, and you and I will emcee, encouraging the people to talk. — Mort Sahl, *Heartland*, pp. 56–57, 1976

McFly *noun*
used as a term of address to someone who does not think often or well *US*, *1989*
From a character in the *Back to the Future* films.
- — Pamela Munro, *U.C.L.A. Slang*, p. 58, 1989

McNamara Special *noun*
a transport plane specially equipped for flying dignitaries to Vietnam during the war *US*, *1988*

- It occurred that same October of 1966 aboard a "McNamara Special" bound for Saigon, one of those windowless KC-135 jet tankers that the Air Force had fitted out for long-distance VIP travel and that the secretary used on his frequent shuttles. — Neil Sheehan, *A Bright Shining Lie*, p. 681, 1988

MD *noun*
Dr. Pepper™ soda *US*, *1967*
- — *American Speech*, p. 63, February 1967: "Soda-fountain, restaurant and tavern calls"

MDA *noun*
a synthetic halluciongen (methylenedioxy-amphetamine) that also contains a central nervous system stimulant *US*, *1978*
Used as a technical term in the late 1950s, in a slang sense later when the drug became popular, largely with gays.
- "Is my MDA still in your stash box?" "Yeah, Christ, you don't need that for a movie!" — Armistead Maupin, *Tales of the City*, p. 110, 1978

MDB *noun*
a hospital patient with an appalling lack of hygeine *US*, *1988–1989*
A "*mega* dirtball."
- — *Maledicta*, p. 33, 1988–1989: "Medical maledicta from San Francisco"

meadow muffin *noun*
cow excrement *US*, *1974*
- Be sure to keep a vigilant lookout for meadow muffins—the stuff can stay on your boots for days. — Ann Marie Brown, *Foghorn Outdoors*, p. 52, 2003

meal *noun*
a socially inept person *US*, *1949*
Youth usage.
- — *Time*, 3rd October 1949

meals rejected by Ethiopians; meals refused by Ethiopians *noun*
military MRE's (meals ready to eat) *US*, *1988*
- The Army now calls them MRSs: Meals-Ready-to-Eat. The soldiers call them Meals-Rejected-by-Ethiopians. — *Washington Post*, p. A3, 20th December 1988
- Reservist Carolyn Bowman tells me that the miserable packaged chow officially known as MRE (Meals, Ready to Eat) is translated by the troops as "Meals, Refused by Ethiopians." — *San Francisco Chronicle*, p. B1, 21st September 1990
- "Desert cherries" in "Kevlars" fly the "Sand Box Express" to the "beach" and soon are complaining about "Meals Rejected by Ethiopians" if they can't find a "roach coach" run by "Bedouin Bob." — *Houston Chronicle*, p. 15, 24th January 1991

meal ticket *noun*
a source of support, especially a person *US*, *1899*
- "As she often said, they [her breasts] were her meal ticket and if she didn't take care of them who would." — Gypsy Rose Lee, *Gypsy*, p. 282, 1957
- "All you wanted to do was latch onto a good meal ticket." — Georgia Sothern, *My Life in Burlesque*, p. 141, 1972
- She could erase Dillinger's record if she tried. I hear she's Keaton's meal ticket. — *The Usual Suspects*, 1995
- As Jack said, "her present meal ticket," & his outspoken worry was her nympho tendencies. — Tom Christopher (Editor), *Neal Cassady Volume Two*, p. 93, 1998

mean *adjective*
excellent *US*, *1919*
- The message to "Squaresville" (where nobody except possibly adults live) is that Frankie[Avalon] is "real mean, man" (very good). — *Look*, p. 49, 24th November 1959
- — Robert George Reisner, *The Jazz Titans*, 1960
- — *Time*, p. 56, 1st January 1965: "Students: The slang bag"
- "How do you lack my crib, man?" "It's mean, Bart." — Charles W. Moore, *A Brick for Mister Jones*, p. 112, 1975

mean *adverb*
very *US*, *1998*
- — Ethan Hilderbrant, *Prison Slang*, 1998

me and the devil, pretty soon just the devil
in poker, said when all players but two have withdrawn from a hand *US*, *1951*
- — *American Speech*, p. 100, May 1951

meanest *adjective*
best, fastest *US*, *1965*
- — Miss Cone, *The Slang Dictionary (Hawthorne High School)*, 1965

mean green *noun*
phencyclidine, the recreational drug known as PCP or angel dust *US*, *1981*
The "green" is from the parsley or mint on which the drug is at times sprinkled; the "mean" is reduplicative yet accurately describes the behavior of most users.
- — Ronald Linder, *PCP*, 1981

mean mugging *noun*
a glare *US*, *2004*
- mean mugging: give angry stare — J.G. Narum, *The Convict Cookbook*, p. 161, 2004
- Jackson was 17 when he and three friends were shot on March 4 in what police said then was a case of "mean mugging"—a slang term for hard stares. — *Alameda (California) Times-Star*, 1st January 2004

mean out *adjective*
good; bad *US*, *1982*
Hawaiian youth usage.
- — Douglas Simonson, *Pidgin to da Max Hana Hou*, 1982

meanwhile, back at the ranch
used as a humorous indication that a story is about to change to another thread *US*, *1956*
From a clichéd device used in cowboy films.
- "Meanwhile, back at the ranch," said Axel. Snickering. Meanwhile, I said, back at the ranch, generally speaking, things were prosperous[.] — Clancy Sigal, *Going Away*, p. 247, 1961

meany *noun*
an exceedingly mean person *UK*, *1927*
- Meany. What do you want to do, fuck? — Elmore Leonard, *Switch*, p. 113, 1978

measle map; measle sheet *noun*
a military map with a large number of small circled numbers indicating checkpoints *US*, *1966*
- On the wall of Fatum's office was a "measle" map. — Elaine Shepard, *The Doom Pussy*, p. 25, 1967
- — Carl Fleischhauer, *A Glossary of Army Slang*, p. 33, 1968

meat *noun*
1 the penis *UK*, *1595*
- — Donald Webster Cory and John P. LeRoy, *The Homosexual and His Society*, p. 265, 1963: "A lexicon of homosexual slang"
- I think a man has gotta be a bit large in the meat department to get that wash board effect. — A.S. Jackson, *Gentleman Pimp*, p. 109, 1973
- Ron Jeremy is sucked off before ramming his meat into Patti Petite in Blonde on the Run. — *Adult Video*, p. 15, August/September 1986
- Ultimately, though, it's not the meat, but the motion. — Anka Radakovich, *The Wild Girls Club*, p. 12, 1994
2 information *US*, *1996*
- They took me to an investigation bureau to see if I had any meat on me, information about the gang. — S. Beth Atkin, *Voices from the Street*, p. 75, 1996
3 a person as a sex object *US*, *2002*
- I am soon surrounded by a crowd of convicts checking out "the meat." — Jimmy Lerner, *You Got Nothing Coming*, p. 191, 2002
4 the vagina *US*, *1973*
- — Ruth Todasco et al., *The Intelligent Woman's Guide to Dirty Words*, p. 25, 1973
5 the human body *US*, *1834*
- You never played the Horseshoe in McKessport, or Christy's Four-a-day in Minneapolis where the ofay strippers threw their meat right over your head[.] — John Clellon Holmes, *The Horn*, p. 28, 1958
6 a corpse *US*, *1949*
- — Captain Vincent J. Monteleone, *Criminal Slang*, p. 154, 1949
7 in a hospital, tissue taken for a biopsy *US*, *1994*
- As in the saying "No meat, no treat," meaning, if you don't know the pathology with a biopsy, you won't know what treatment to go ahead with. — Sally Williams, *"Strong" Words: (Dissertation)*, p. 150, 1994

meat axe *noun*
in television and movie-making, a rod used on scaffolding to hold light screens *US*, *1990*
- — Ralph S. Singleton, *Filmmaker's Dictionary*, p. 103, 1990

meatball *noun*

1 a dim-witted, gullible person *US, 1939*

- "You must be the friend," "Winnie," Mitch looked at him, "who loaned this meatball the five hundred?" — Irving Shulman, *Cry Tough*, p. 158, 1949
- Well, anyhow, Grady Metcalf, who is one of the really big meatballs of our generation and I hate him like poison, he took me out riding on his motorcycle, and you know what? All of a sudden, he didn't seem like such a meatball! — Max Shulman, *Rally Round the Flag, Boys!*, p. 168, 1957
- "And there's all these assorted pimps, junkies and meatballs who don't even live here, standing around waiting[.]" — Robert Deane Pharr, *S.R.O.*, p. 28, 1971
- And Tony Parisi is nothing but a New York tenement house meatball who made good. — Gerald Petievich, *Shakedown*, p. 63, 1988

2 a false or petty criminal charge *US, 1944*

- That's a meatball rap, you'll get out tomorrow. — Hal Ellson, *The Golden Spike*, p. 240, 1952
- [E]ven Jackson Prison was used to lock-up for all the niggers the police were arresting on a lot of bullshit, meatball charges. — A.S. Jackson, *Gentleman Pimp*, p. 9, 1973
- You guys picked me up on a meatball. I ain't robbed nobody, so you ain't got no case on me. — Donald Goines, *Crime Partners*, p. 103, 1978

3 a prostitute's customer *US, 1956*

- [E]levator operators were recruited to steer the customers—the "Johns" or "meatballs"—to the selected suites. — Jess Stearn, *Sisters of the Night*, p. 5, 1956

4 a colored light that serves as a visual aid in an optical landing system for an airplane landing on an aircraft carrier *US, 1957*

- He had to see the meatball, the yellow light between the two green reference, or datum, lights of the optical landing system. — Stephen Coonts, *Final Flight*, p. 99, 1988
- [H]e could start to discern the "meatball"—a mirrored device reflecting a grapefruit-sized orange light, flanked on either side by a line of smaller green lights. — Robert Wilcox, *Scream of Eagles*, p. 35, 1990
- (Royal Canadian Navy, 1950s to 1969). Finally I broke free of the cloud layer; then all I had to do was fly the meatball down onto the deck. — Oral citation from Tom Langeste, *Words on the Wing*, 1995

5 in horseracing, a combination of cathartics administered to a horse *US, 1951*

- — David W. Maurer, *Argot of the Racetrack*, p. 12, 1951

meatball beef *noun*

a complaint or accusation without merit *US, 1976*

- It was a meatball beef, but a sketch of the circuitous reasoning behind it will illustrate one aspect of official thinking. — Malcolm Braley, *False Starts*, p. 186, 1976

meat block *noun*

any area where prostitutes, especially male prostitutes, are likely to be found *US, 1971*

- Homosexual client and prostitute meet on a "meat block," a section where men seeking such services are likely to be found, such as West 42nd Street in New York City. — Charles Winick, *The Lively Commerce*, p. 90, 1971

meat book *noun*

at a college or university, a book with the names and photographs of all incoming students *US, 1996*

- — DePauw University Campus Corner, 29th January 1996: "Slang terms at DePauw"

meat cutter *noun*

a surgeon *US, 1980*

- — *Maledicta*, p. 57, Summer 1980: "Not sticks and stones, but names: more medical perjoratives"

meat district *noun*

an area where sex is available *US, 1984*

- Down Forty-Second Street, through the meat district. — Jay McInerney, *Bright Lights, Big City*, p. 13, 1984

meat drapes *noun*

the condition that exists when a tight-fitting pair of pants, shorts, bathing suit, or other garment forms a wedge between a woman's labia, accentuating their shape; the labia *US, 2004*

- Sing, oh hairy muse of spandex and gym shorts that split in twain thin cooze Meat drapes, rent in twain. — alt.sports.football.pro.pitt-steelers, 18th November 2004

- The film is one of Signer Brass's better efforts, if for no other reason than he convinced Claudia to bare her meat drapes in several different scenes. — Mr. Skin, *Mr. Skin's Skincyclopedia*, p. 302, 2005
- You know, my "birth-giving thighs," my "third nipple," my "velvety meat drapes." — Carly Milne, *Naked Ambition*, p. 336, 2005

meat factory *noun*

a college or university that recruits athletes solely for their athletic ability and without any real expectation that they will graduate *US, 1978*

- — Bill Shefski, *Running Press Glossary of Football Language*, p. 68, 1978

meat fleet *noun*

a military hospital ship *US, 1991*

Gulf war usage.

- — *American Speech*, p. 394, Winter 1991: "Among the new words"

meathead *noun*

a stupid person; hence a general derogative implying stupidity *US, 1928*

No brains between the ears, just meat.

- Those meatheads? They don't know their rear from third base. — Max Shulman, *Guided Tour of Campus Humor*, p. 141, 1955
- When a woman's glands is actin' up and she can't control certain urges—they say she's got hot pants! Same as the meathead there. Hot trousers, hot pants, same thing! — Eugene Boe (Compiler), *The Wit & Wisdom of Archie Bunker*, p. 153, 1971
- Chiodo, and his meathead partners could be in a real jam over an incident tonight that I won't go into. — Charles Whited, *Chiodo*, p. 277, 1973

meat mag *noun*

a homoerotic, often pornographic, magazine *US, 1979*

- "Kinks and queens: linguistic and cultural aspects of the terminology for gays." *Maledicta*, p. 250, 1979

meat market *noun*

1 a bar or other public place where people congregate in search of sexual companionship *UK, 1957*

- There they rent homes, given them "gay names" like Dora's Domicile Campy Corner, loll in the sun, and at night frequent a dark corner of the beach known as "the meat market." — Antony James, *America's Homosexual Underground*, p. 30, 1965
- — Connie Eble (Editor), *UNC-CH Campus Slang*, p. 4, Spring 1983
- And we don't go to meat markets to buy drinks for dick teasers. — Dan Savage, *Savage Love*, p. 26, 1998

2 a modeling agency *US, 1972*

- — Helen Dahlskog (Editor), *A Dictionary of Contemporary and Colloquial Usage*, p. 40, 1972

meat parlor *noun*

an establishment where sex is the most important commodity *US, 1969*

- In one meat parlor, they have two massage rooms. — *Screw*, p. 14, 6th October 1969

meat puppet *noun*

a person of no substance *US, 1982*

- "I thought you had just taken your marching orders and off you went like good little meat puppets." — Mary Janice Davidson, *Undead and Unemployed*, p. 141, 2004

meat rack *noun*

1 a restaurant, bar, or other public place where people gather in search of sexual partners *US, 1962*

- Soon, we got up, walked around the west side—toward the "meat rack"—the gay part of the park. — John Rechy, *City of Night*, p. 53, 1963
- Our landlord had explained that the "meat rack" (an outdoor sex-supermarket) was only a block or so away. — *Screw*, p. 17, 31st July 1969
- "Your first years in The Pines you can't get enough of the beach parade, tea, the meat racks." — Ethan Morden, *Buddies*, p. 170, 1986
- What if the tabloids—or, worse yet, some activist—had discovered the virile young star of said movie wagging wienie at the local meat rack. — Armistead Maupin, *Maybe the Moon*, p. 274, 1992

2 a gymnasium *US, 1976*

- — *Elementary Electronics*, *Dictionary of CB Lingo*, p. 86, 1976

3 the female breasts *US, 2005*

- Check out that meat rack! — Mr. Skin, *Mr. Skin's Skincyclopedia*, p. 52, 2005

meat shot *noun*

1 a photograph or scene in a pornographic film focusing on a penis *US, 1974*

- Despite the relative absence of hard-core action in it—some oral sex and an occasional discreet meat shot—Little Sisters ran into some legal trouble[.] — Kenneth Turan and Stephen E. Zito, *Sinema*, p. 129, 1974
- Take, for example, the obsessively repeated meat shot as one such moment of solution. — Linda Williams, *Hard Core*, p. 93, 1989
- The sex mafick section contains views of actual intercourse, although meat shots are discreetly avoided. — Bill Landis, *Sleazoid Express*, pp. 173–174, 2002

2 a bullet wound in a muscle, not involving a bone or organ damage *US, 1992*

- It looked like just a meat shot—it wasn't as if he was dead or anything. — Richard Price, *Clockers*, p. 516, 1992

meat show *noun*

a striptease act or other performance featuring naked or near-naked women *US, 1943*

- — Don Wilmeth, *The Language of American Popular Entertainment*, p. 168, 1981

meat wagon *noun*

1 an ambulance *US, 1925*

- — Lou Shelly, *Hepcats Jive Talk Dictionary*, p. 47, 1945
- "How'd he get it?" "For christsake. How would I know? I don't run the meat wagon." — Audie Murphy, *To Hell and Back*, p. 96, 1949
- The meat wagon rolled on, and Sissy, unlike young Mozart, was rewarded by not so much as a lump of sugar for her experiment. — Tom Robbins, *Even Cowgirls Get the Blues*, p. 43, 1976
- And a few minutes later, the ambulance, popularly called "the meat wagon." — Odie Hawkins, *Amazing Grace*, p. 22, 1993

2 a coroner's ambulance *US, 1942*

- I saw a cluster of people on the sidewalk at the front door. There was a city meat wagon on the street. — Iceberg Slim (Robert Beck), *Airtight Willie and Me*, p. 60, 1979
- The squad-car guys didn't know for sure he's dead, so they call EMS. EMS comes, they take one look, call the meat wagon. — Elmore Leonard, *City Primeval*, p. 30, 1980
- By the time I gave it to the meat wagon, the ants had bought it. — Joseph Wambaugh, *Finnegan's Week*, p. 133, 1993
- A shitload of Hollywood division black-and-whites showed up, and the meat wagon removed Miller Treadwell and Special Agent Norris Stensland, D.O.A. — James Ellroy, *Hollywood Nocturnes*, p. 191, 1994

meat whistle *noun*

the penis *US, 1965*

- "What're you going to do on the variety show," Red wanted to know. "Perform on the meat whistle?" — Malcolm Braly, *On the Yard*, p. 81, 1967

meat with two vegetables; meat and two veg *noun*

the penis and testicles *US, 1964*

- — Roger Blake, *The American Dictionary of Sexual Terms*, p. 131, 1964

meaty *adjective*

(used of a wave) powerful *US, 1991*

- — Trevor Cralle, *The Surfin'ary*, p. 74, 1991

mechanic *noun*

1 in gambling, a cheat who manipulates the cards or dice *US, 1909*

- No better card mechanic ever lived. — Mickey Spillane, *Me, Hood!*, p. 29, 1963
- Folks said, "Precious, you still a star nine ball player and top craps mechanic?" — Iceberg Slim (Robert Beck), *Long White Con*, p. 167, 1977
- He is a dice hustler, a mechanic. — Gerald Petievich, *To Die in Beverly Hills*, p. 113, 1983
- I mean, all of Nicky's half-assed mechanics, they were all real signal happy. — *Casino*, 1995

2 in the underworld, a specialist for hire *US, 1949*

- "What I mean is I was doing him in a very different way than he said Shelley Orchid was asking about doing you." "I understood you the first time. What's this mechanic's name?" — Robert Campbell, *Boneyards*, p. 249, 1992

3 a hired killer *US, 1989*

- — James Harris, *A Convict's Dictionary*, p. 38, 1989

4 any safety device worn by a circus performer *US, 1980*

- Most all performers, both aerial and ground, are trained by aid of mechanics. — Joe McKennon, *Circus Lingo*, p. 61, 1980

5 an accomplished, skilled lover *US, 1985*

- "Mechanic"—a man who's good with his bird [penis]; a ladies' man. — *Washington Post*, p. B1, 17th January 1985

mechanized dandruff *noun*

body lice *US, 1949*

- "I thought that dame in Palermo was perfectly okay until I woke up with the mechanized dandruff." — Audie Murphy, *To Hell and Back*, p. 16, 1949

medical shot *noun*

in a pornographic movie, an extreme close-up of genitals *US, 1977*

- Use your first camera from a more or less fixed position, and your hand-held camera for the ever-important closeups, or, as some refer to them, the "medical shots." — Stephen Ziplow, *The Film Maker's Guide to Pornography*, p. 78, 1977

medicine *noun*

1 alcohol; liquor *US, 1847*

- "Let's find a place and get a shot," Powers said. "Oh, hell, forget it. that's bad medicine for us now." — James T. Farrell, *The Life Adventure*, p. 186, 1947

2 illegal drugs or narcotics *US, 1976*

- — John R. Armore and Joseph D. Wolfe, *Dictionary of Desperation*, p. 40, 1976

meditation *noun*

solitary confinement in prison *US, 1990*

- — Charles Shafer, *Folk Speech in Texas Prisons*, p. 210, 1990

meditation manor *noun*

a prison cell used for solitary confinement *US, 1962*

- — Joseph E. Ragen and Charles Finston, *Inside the World's Toughest Prison*, p. 808, 1962: "Penitentiary and underworld glossary"

meeces *noun*

mice *US, 1991*

From the *Huckleberry Hound* television cartoon series of the late 1950s, in which Mr Jinx the beatnik cat regularly described his feelings towards Pixie and Dixie, two mice, as "I hate those meeces to pieces."

- — Eric S. Raymond, *The New Hacker's Dictionary*, p. 237, 1991

meemies *noun*

a feeling of anxiety and fear *US, 1946*

A shortened form of the SCREAMING MEEMIES.

- It was a night to give you the meemies. — Mickey Spillane, *One Lonely Night*, p. 102, 1951

meet *noun*

a session in which musicians collectively improvise; a jam session *US, 1957*

- — Robert George Reisner, *The Jazz Titans*, p. 161, 1960

meet *verb*

in poker, to make a bet equal to the previous bet *US, 1990*

- — Anthony Holden, *Big Deal*, p. 302, 1990

meeting *noun*

► **take a meeting**

to attend a business meeting *US, 1977*

Entertainment industry terminology, used outside the industry in a mocking, pretentious tone.

- Well, you take a meeting with him, I'll take a meeting with you if you'll take a meeting with Freedy. — *Annie Hall*, 1977
- "I took three meetings." "Three? That's marvelous. Three! Do ourself any good?" "I took a meeting with Ivan Kipplinger." — Robert Campbell, *Alice in La-La Land*, p. 131, 1987

mega- *prefix*

used for intensifying *US, 1966*

- — *Current Slang*, p. 5, Winter 1966
- Just one little step to relieve megaboredom. — Joseph Wambaugh, *The Delta Star*, p. 126, 1983
- Heather, why can't you just be a friend? Why are you such a megabitch? — *Heathers*, 1988
- This band, "Crucial Taunt," had this megababe for a lead singer. — *Wayne's World*, 1992

megablast *noun*

a dose of crack cocaine *US, 1993*

- — Peter Johnson, *Dictionary of Street Alcohol and Drug Terms*, p. 119, 1993

megabuck *adjective*

very expensive *US, 1992*

- Its glistening polish, blood-crimson striping, and mirror-chrome Centerlines told of regular care by a megabuck detailer. — Jess Mowry, *Way Past Cool*, p. 23, 1992

megabucks *noun*
one million dollars; any large amount of money *US, 1946*

- Such a processing plant would involve the expenditure of a number of "megabucks" and probably could not be justified. — Ernest Donald Klema, *Nuclear Reactors and Radiation in Industry*, 1957

mega dirtball *noun*
a hospital patient with an appalling lack of hygeine *US, 1988–1989*

- — *Maledicta*, p. 33, 1988–1989: "Medical maledicta from San Francisco"

megalicious *adjective*
very good *US, 1992*

- "Shit, that taste megalicious! No lie!" — Jess Mowry, *Way Past Cool*, p. 87, 1992

megapenny *noun*
ten thousand dollars (one cent times ten to the sixth power) *US, 1991*

- — Eric S. Raymond, *The New Hacker's Dictionary*, p. 237, 1991

megillah *noun*
all of something *US, 1954*
For observant Jews on Purim, the reading of the entire Megillas Esther is deemed an obligation.

- Oh, come on, Frana. Not the whole megilleh. — Bernard Wolfe, *The Late Risers*, p. 134, 1954
- And gave the whole megilleh legitimacy. — *The Deep Throat Papers*, p. 17, 1973

MEGO
my *eyes glaze over US, 1977*

- — Eric S. Raymond, *The New Hacker's Dictionary*, p. 237, 1991

meig *noun*
a penny; a five-cent piece *US, 1962*

- — Joseph E. Ragen and Charles Finston, *Inside the World's Toughest Prison*, p. 808, 1962: "Penitentiary and underworld glossary"

Mekong Delta *nickname*
a neigborhood with a large number of Vietnamese immigrants and businesses *US, 1979*

- Do is one of more than a dozen Vietnamese who have set up shop in Clarendon, turning a retailing center once known as "Northern Virginia's downtown" into an area often referred to by Americans as "Little Saigon," the "Mekong Delta" or even the "Ho Chi Min Trail." — *Washington Post*, p. A1, 23rd September 1979

mel *noun*
in the language surrounding the Grateful Dead, a conventional, law-abiding citizen *US, 1994*

- — David Shenk and Steve Silberman, *Skeleton Key*, p. 190, 1994

mellow *noun*
a good friend *US, 1976*

- It came through, fellows; so tell my mellows / I'll spring 'em, 'cause I've got the price. — Dennis Wepman et al., *The Life*, p. 68, 1976

mellow *verb*
to calm *US, 1974*

- Go inside, have a drink and mellow this off, you understand? — *Boogie Nights*, 1997

mellow *adjective*
1 pleasing, relaxed, good *US, 1938*

- [T]he gauge they picked up on was really in there, and it had them treetop tall, mellow as a cello. — Mezz Mezzrow, *Really the Blues*, p. 75, 1946
- Shorty would take me to groovy, frantic scenes in different chicks' and cats' pads, where with the lights and juke down mellow, everybody blew gage and juiced back and jumped. — Malcolm X and Alex Haley, *The Autobiography of Malcolm X*, p. 56, 1964
- "The smoke [marijuana] is mellow, baby," he answered. — Donald Goines, *Whoreson*, p. 131, 1972
- Uh, not a big deal, it's just relax, just be very mellow. — *Annie Hall*, 1977

2 mildly and pleasantly drunk or drug-intoxicated *UK, 1699*

- [T]he gauge they picked up on was really in there, and it had them treetop tall, mellow as a cello. — Mezz Mezzrow, *Really the Blues*, p. 75, 1946

3 (used of a friend) close *US, 1941*

- But like I said, he's a real big man now but he was and still is my righteous mellow fellow. — A.S. Jackson, *Gentleman Pimp*, p. 88, 1973

mellow man *noun*
an attractive male *US, 1945*

- — *Yank*, p. 18, 24th March 1945

mellow yellow *noun*
fried banana skin scrapings, sold for their nonexistent psychoactive effect *US, 1966*
Brought into the mainstream by Donovan's 1967 hit song.

- At this printing, mellow yellow is legal and United Fruit Company sales are still climbing. — Mary Lay and Nancy Orban, *The Hip Glossary of Hippie Language*, June 1967
- — Eugene Landy, *The Underground Dictionary*, p. 130, 1971

melons *noun*
large female breasts *US, 1957*

- — Collin Baker et al., *College Undergraduate Slang Study Conducted at Brown University*, p. 156, 1968
- "Big tits?" "Real melons." — James Ellroy, *Brown's Requiem*, p. 106, 1981
- "What the hell you doing, Bouche?" Barcaloo whispered fiercely, "runnin' a goddamn fruit stand, sittin' around with your melons hanging out like that?" — Robert Campbell, *In La-La Land We Trust*, p. 74, 1986
- Those ripe, sweet, gravity-defying, young melons fell ripe and juicy from her shirt at last in The Invisible Circus (2001). — Mr. Skin, *Mr. Skin's Skincyclopedia*, p. 82, 2005

melt *verb*
to leave *US, 1961*

- "Melt? Will you kindly translate? I'm not good at semantics." "Melt means—get lost!" — Frederick Kohner, *Gidget Goes Hawaiian*, p. 10, 1961

meltdown *noun*
the complete and total malfunctioning of a casino slot machine *US, 1999*

- The second meltdown I ever experienced occurred when I was playing at the Stardust on a Piggy Bankin' machine of the one dollar denomination. — Charles W. Lund, *Robbing the One-Armed Bandits*, p. 115, 1999

melted butter *noun*
semen *US, 1980*

- — *Maledicta*, p. 192, Winter 1980: "A new erotic vocabulary"

melted out *adjective*
broke; without funds *US, 1948*

- — Jack Lait and Lee Mortimer, *New York Confidential*, p. 235, 1948: "A glossary of Harlemisms"

Melvin *noun*
the condition that exists when someone pulls your pants or underpants forcefully upwards, forming a wedge between buttock cheeks *US, 1989*

- And the guys suddenly pull each of the Cowboys' long underwear up, giving them "Melvins." — *Bill and Ted's Excellent Adventure*, p. 42, 1989
- "Don't that feel uncomfortable?" Leeds asked. "I mean, do you like giving yourself a Melvin all day long?" — Joseph Wambaugh, *Floaters*, p. 81, 1996

Melvin *verb*
to dupe *US, 1991*

- — *USA Today*, p. 1D, 5th August 1991: "A sterling lexicon of the lingo"

member *noun*
a fellow homosexual *US, 1960s*

- There ain't too many members in Alaska. — Bruce Rodgers, *The Queens' Vernacular*, p. 133, 1972

Memphis dominoes *noun*
dice *US, 1942*

- — *The Annals of the American Academy of Political and Social Sciences*, p. 127, May 1950

mender *noun*
in circus and carnival usage, a claims adjuster *US, 1981*

- — Don Wilmeth, *The Language of American Popular Entertainment*, p. 168, 1981

mensch; mensh; mench *noun*
an honorable person *US, 1953*
German *mensch* (a person) into Yiddish.

- As a child I often heard it said: "The finest thing you can say about a man is that he is a mensch!" — Leo Rosten, *The Joys of Yiddish*, p. 174, 1968

- She was what we call "mensch" in Yiddish[.] — Xaviera Hollander, *The Happy Hooker*, p. 79, 1972
- When the hero (Ricardo Darin) is immediately revealed as a bloated, chain-smoking, workaholic deadbeat dad, we know a tragedy and/or cardiac event will transform him into a life-loving mensch. — *The Village Voice*, 26th March 2002

mental *adjective*
insane, crazy *UK, 1927*
- I lost you two months ago! We broke up. Are you mental? — *Wayne's World*, 1992
- I know it sounds mental, but sometimes I have more fun vegging out than when I go partying. — *Clueless*, 1995

mental hernia *noun*
1 an ignorant person *US, 1970*
- — Eugene Landy, *The Underground Dictionary*, p. 130, 1971

2 an emotional breakdown *US, 1972*
- The old man fell into his study for about two weeks of mental hernia at home. — Barry Hannah, *Geronimo Rex*, p. 37, 1972

mental midget *noun*
a person with limited intelligence *US, 1951*
- They were using the Democratic candidate as a megaphone for their smear, the same as they are using the mental midget from Connecticut. — United States Congress, Senate Committee on Foreign Relations, *Nomination of Philip C. Jessup*, p. 84, 1951
- "What did you mental midgets think by strapping me in?" — Joi Brozek, *Sleeveless*, p. 179, 2002

mental pygmy *noun*
a dolt *US, 1968*
- — Mary Swift, *Campus Slang (University of Texas)*, 1968

menu *noun*
1 the list of services available in a brothel *US, 1993*
- The menu can help "break the ice" for first-timers, and is a conversation piece[.] — J.R. Schwartz, *The Official Guide to the Best Cat Houses in Nevada*, p. 27, 1993
- They had written something called a "Menu," which listed activities and prices that they used during their negotiations. — Sisters of the Heart, *The Brothel Bible*, p. 38, 1997

2 graffiti describing sex preferences and telephone numbers *US, 1972*
- — Bruce Rodgers, *The Queens' Vernacular*, p. 133, 1972

Merc *noun*
the Chicago Mercantile Exchange *US, 1985*
- "All my social plans are contingent on wind," the 48-year-old Merc trader says. — Lynn Schnaiberg, *Outside Magazine's Urban Adventure: Chicago*, p. 110, 2003

merch *noun*
merchandise *US, 1995*
- Whenever we got local merch, we'd usually send it to Palm Springs or Arizona. — *Casino*, 1995
- The merch could bring in five grand or more, depending on audience reaction, how much they like the show. — Elmore Leonard, *Be Cool*, p. 251, 1999

merchant *noun*
a prisoner who sells goods to other prisoners *US, 1958*
- [I]nmates have drawn a sharp line between selling and giving and the prisoner who sells when he should give is labeled a merchant or pedlar. — Gresham M. Sykes, *The Society of Captives*, p. 93, 1958

mercy!
used for expressing mild surprise *US, 1992*
- — William K. Bentley and James M. Corbett, *Prison Slang*, p. 46, 1992

mercy fuck *noun*
sex motivated by a sense of pity *US, 1968*
- "A mercy fuck from a goyish basket case. Jesus, why didn't I go to Harvard like my father wanted me to." — Harriet Frank, *Single*, p. 35, 1979
- "I just want you to know it wouldn't have been a mercy fuck. It would have been the real thing." — Carl Hiaasen, *Double Whammy*, p. 204, 1987
- Why hadn't she at least given Adam a decent kiss on the lips, a mercy kiss—the way Beverly bestowed her mercy fucks, or so she claimed—instead of that pathetic little vesper-service peck on the cheek? — Tom Wolfe, *I Am Charlotte Williams*, p. 335, 2004

mercy-fuck *verb*
to have sex based on pity *US, 1994*

- It's much more plausible to be mercy fucked by a lovely and kind babe in nursing mode. — *rec.arts.poems*, 23rd July 1994
- I guess Ally mercy fucks her. So what. — Lynn Breedlove, *Godspeed*, p. 75, 2002
- "She mercy fucked you and THEN moved on?! Dude, where have I been?" — Edna Lir, *The Cinderella Prophecy*, p. 22, 2003

mercy Mary!
used for expressing surprise in a melodramatic fashion *US, 1970*
- — *American Speech*, p. 58, Spring–Summer 1970: "Homosexual slang"

mercy Miss Percy!
used for embellishing any exclamation *US, 1953*
- When I peer into her peepers, mercy miss percy, I am sent one time. — Lavada Durst, *The Jives of Dr. Hepcat*, p. 9, 1953

mere gook rule *noun*
a belief during the Vietnam war that a crime committed against a Vietnamese person was not a crime *US, 1976*
- At that point the grunts allowed the "Mere Gook Rule" to enter their value system: a crime wasn't a crime if it was committed against a Vietnamese, a Mere Gook. — Charles R. Anderson, *The Grunts*, p. 207, 1976
- [A]n endemic, pervasive feeling in the military that wasting "mere gooks" was of no great consequence. — Myra MacPherson, *Long Time Passing*, p. 582, 1984

merry-go-round *noun*
the visits to many different prison offices the day before a prisoner is released *US, 1996*
- — Reinhold Aman, *Hillary Clinton's Pen Pal: A Guide to Life and Lingo in Federal Prison*, p. 50, 1996

merry widow *noun*
1 a bust-emphasizing corset *US, 1957*
- Cass emptied the contents of my bag—a spare bathing suit and the Merry Widow that goes with the spare, on account of that lousy bias-cut uplift arrangement. — Frederick Kohner, *Gidget*, p. 111, 1957

2 in pool, a cue stick with a butt made with a single, unspliced piece of wood *US, 1983*
- — Mike Shamos, *The Illustrated Encyclopedia of Billiards*, p. 149, 1993

mesc; mezc *noun*
mescaline *US, 1969*
- Since then, however, I've discovered a sporadic supply of excellent mesc. for $3 a cap. — Hunter S. Thompson, *Fear and Loathing in America*, p. 157, 3rd January 1969: Letter to Oscar Acosta
- "Poor Chessman"—he muttered, still slight zonked from a late night mesc drop[.] — Ed Sanders, *Tales of Beatnik Glory*, p. 41, 1975

mesh *noun*
on a computer keyboard, the # character *US, 1983*
- — Guy L. Steele et al., *The Hacker's Dictionary*, p. 93, 1983

meshugge; meshuga; meshuggener; meshigener *adjective*
crazy *US, 1888*
Yiddish.
- Mishuga jobs like that don't grow on trees. — Clancy Sigal, *Going Away*, p. 11, 1961
- [A]ll those meshuggeneh rules and regulations on top of their own private craziness! — Philip Roth, *Portnoy's Complaint*, p. 37, 1969
- But the case's not resolved, 'cause your meshuge counsel's trying to make history first time at bat[.] — Emmett Grogan, *Final Score*, p. 164, 1976
- "I was just telling Nora how clean you were when you were a little boy. Meshugga for clean." — Glenn Savan, *White Palace*, p. 273, 1987

meshuggener *noun*
an emotionally unstable person *US, 1946*
- "Will you please get that meshuggener back in the outfield?" — Phillip Roth, *Portnoy's Complaint*, p. 243, 1969

mess *noun*
1 a large amount *US, 1826*
- I've been to a mess of schools like that—ones you won't find on the approved list of any Parent-Teacher Association. — Mezz Mezzrow, *Really the Blues*, p. 3, 1946

2 drugs *US, 1978*
- "How do you get your mess from him?" Benson asked sharply. "You got the guy's address?" "Naw man, he comes up on the corner every day at the same time, two o'clock, you dig. If you want to cop, you had better be up there by then." — Donald Goines, *Crime Partners*, p. 9, 1978

3 in poker, a draw of replacement cards that fails to improve the hand *US, 1979*
- — John Scarne, *Scarne's Guide to Modern Poker*, p. 284, 1979

mess; mess with *verb*
to confront; to interfere; to bother; to fight *US, 1935*
- Daddy, I don't want to mess with 'em. — William "Lord" Buckley, *Nero*, 1951

mess around *verb*
to engage in sexual foreplay; to have sex *UK, 1896*
- There's a lot of girls out there and you mess around with Stacy — *Fast Times at Ridgemont High*, 1982
- Maybe you just want to mess around or something. — Kenneth Lonergan, *This is Our Youth*, p. 76, 2000

messed up *adjective*
drunk or drug-intoxicated *US, 1963*
- We could buy a cap, and just four of us all could sit down and snort it, and all of us would be messed up. — Henry Williamson, *Hustler!*, p. 74, 1965
- Man, I am so fucking messed up and ripped! I got off on the first hit, man!? — John Rechy, *The Fourth Angel*, p. 32, 1972
- Strike's father had never been a heavy drinker, and whenever he did get a little messed up, he'd never do anything mean or violent. — Richard Price, *Clockers*, pp. 65–66, 1992

messenger *noun*
a bullet *US, 1962*
- He wouldn't stop, so I sent a couple of little messengers after him. — *American Speech*, p. 270, December 1962: "The language of traffic policemen"

mess up *verb*
to beat someone up *US, 1914*
- — Maria Hinojas, *Crews*, p. 167, 1995: "Glossary"

met *noun*
methamphetamine *US, 1993*
- — Peter Johnson, *Dictionary of Street Alcohol and Drug Terms*, p. 120, 1993

metal harvester *noun*
a person who steals metal for sale as scrap *US, 1997*
- Touts, burn-artists, doctors, slingers, stash-stealers, stickup boys who never rob a citizen, who only hit dealers, metal harvesters[.] — David Simon and Edward Burns, *The Corner*, p. 160, 1997

metalhead *noun*
a lover of heavy metal music and the attendant lifestyle *US, 1982*
- You know what really bites; when people watch that cafeteria stuff on TV and see all those Geeks and Metalheads jumping around, they're going to think Uncool is the Rule at Westerburg. — *Heathers*, 1988
- One of the metalheads, Dez, raped the pumpkin girl in the backyard. — Michelle Tea, *The Passionate Mistakes and Intricate Corruption of One Girl in America*, p. 14, 1998

metal mouth *noun*
a person with orthodontia *US, 1978*
- When Arnold meets Drummond's daughter, a condescending sort who wears braces, he snaps, "Hi, metal mouth." — *Washington Post*, p. B1, 3rd November 1978
- "Fewer people make fun of me; they want to see them," Shawn said. "And they don't call me as many names as they used to, like 'brace face' and 'metal mouth.'" — *St. Petersburg (Florida) Times*, p. 2D, 9th September 1991
- For boomers, taunts like "brace-face," "tin grin" and "metal mouth" have made way for more sophisticated teasing. — *Washington Post*, p. F1, 13th January 2004

meter *noun*
twenty-five cents *US, 1945*
- — Lou Shelly, *Hepcats Jive Talk Dictionary*, p. 15, 1945
- — Jack Lait and Lee Mortimer, *New York Confidential*, p. 235, 1948

meter beater *noun*
a criminal who steals from parking meters *US, 1972*
- And there are meter-beaters. They're the guys who go around here beatin' these parking meters. Most of them get a key made. — Harry King, *Box Man*, p. 71, 1972

meter reader *noun*
in the US Air Force, a co-pilot *US, 1946*
- — *American Speech*, p. 310, December 1946: "More Air Force slang"

meth *noun*
1 methamphetamine hydrochloride, a powerful central nervous system stimulant, brand name Methedrine™ *US, 1966*
- — J. L. Simmons and Barry Winograd, *It's Happening*, p. 172, 1966: "glossary"
- Take your average Meth freak, once he's started putting the needle in his arm, it's not too hard to say, well, let's shoot a little smack. — Joan Didion, *Slouching Toward Bethlehem*, p. 116, 1967
- Scrounge food, shoot meth, hustle college kids coming to gawk and get laid, just as their father went to Fillmore when nigger wasn't spelled negro. — *The San Francisco Oracle*, 1967
- "You two 'ho's still pushing your meth?" she said conversationally. — Robert Deane Pharr, *Giveadamn Brown*, p. 48, 1978

2 methadone (a drug prescribed as a substitute for heroin) *US, 1971*
- "Nothing can be compared to meth. Not even penicillin. Why, in two hours' time methadone could eradicate the entire heroin problem in New York City." — Robert Deane Pharr, *S.R.O.*, p. 42, 1971
- So they make you pee in a cup and fill out a form. They give you some meth. — John Allen, *Assault with a Deadly Weapon*, p. 176, 1977

3 marijuana *US, 1994*
An abbreviation of **METHOD** (marijuana).
- All right, y'all get ya White Owls, get ya meth, get ya skins (cigarette papers) — Method Man (Clifford Smith), *Method Man*, 1994

meth freak *noun*
a methamphetamine addict *US, 1967*
- He is called a speed freak or meth freak. — Martin Haskell, *Crime and Delinquency*, p. 173, 1970
- "I was in a cell with a meth freak who tried to talk to his wife in the women's section by yelling into the toilet bowl." — James Lee Burke, *Crusader's Cross*, p. 53, 2005

meth head *noun*
a habitual user of methamphetamine *US, 1966*
- She's a meth head and an ex-con and stir crazy as hell. — Joseph Wambaugh, *The Blue Knight*, p. 62, 1973
- Hearn's work world is the world of the southwest county meth-heads, where crank is king, and the only rival to getting high is a pocket full of $100 bills. — *Press Enterprise (Riverside, California)*, p. B1, 14th December 1993
- He stumbled onto the answer soon after, when the meth-heads invited him to go "Dumpster diving" for junk. — *New York Times*, p. 42 (Section 6), 21st December 2003

meth monkey *noun*
an amphetamine user *US, 2001*
- "Tweaker," "cranker," "meth monkey" – A user. — *Lewiston (Idaho) Morning Tribune*, p. 6A, 20th May 2001

meth monster *noun*
1 an amphetamine addict *US, 1967*
- — Stephen H. Dill (Editor), *Current Slang*, p. 34, Fall 1968
- — William D. Alsever, *Glossary for the Establishment and Other Uptight People*, p. 30, December 1970

2 any paranoid delusion suffered after sustained methamphetamine use *US, 1989*
- — Geoffrey Froner, *Digging for Diamonds*, p. 43, 1989

meth mouth *noun*
diseased gums and decayed teeth brought on by sustained methamphetamine use *US, 1998*
- METH MOUTH: dry mouth that results from the use of methedrine. — Robert Buckhout, *Toward Social Change*, p. 465, 1971
- What kind of speech impediment does he have? I can barely understand him. Crystal meth mouth? — *alt.showbiz.gossip*, 8th October 1998
- Methamphetamine's drying effect on saliva glands leads to tooth decay and gum disease, dentists say, a trend known as "meth mouth." — *Investor's Business Daily*, 31st January 2003
- The condition, known to some as meth mouth, has been studied little in dentistry's academic circles[.] — *New York Times*, p. A1, 11th June 2005

method; method murder *noun*
marijuana *US, 1995*
- You can smell the method from across the hall. — Los Stavsky et al, *A2Z*, p. 68, 1995

Methodist hell *noun*
the epitome of heat *US, 1975*
- Steve Mitchell sold parlor heaters with the absolute guarantee that they would heat any room hotter than a Methodist Hell. — John Gould, *Maine Lingo*, p. 180, 1975

Metro Tux *noun*
in Los Angeles, the police officer's uniform except for his shirt, which is replaced by a white t-shirt *US, 1994*
With this slight modification, policemen may drink at a bar without violating the department rule against drinking in uniform.
- — *Los Angeles Times*, p. B8, 19th December 1994

Mex *noun*
1 a Mexican or Mexican-American *US, 1847*
Offensive.
- This Mex, now, was about as defenseless as a man could be. — Jim Thompson, *The Killer Inside*, p. 37, 1952
- The Mex had a black and white checked sport shirt, heavily pleated black slacks without a belt, two-tone black and white buckskin shoes, spotlessly clean. — Raymond Chandler, *The Long Goodbye*, p. 169, 1953
- Jesse was a wiry little man, about thirty, who had once killed a Mex over a game of dominoes[.] — Nelson Algren, *The Neon Wilderness*, p. 128, 1960
- Anyway, we're driving along the interstate, this Mex tells me how he's been picking oranges half the year and how he's going up to Michigan to pick sugarbeets. — Elmore Leonard, *Killshot*, p. 28, 1989

2 the Spanish language *US, 1858*
- Practically everyone in this area talks some Mex, but I do it better than most. — Jim Thompson, *The Killer Inside*, p. 37, 1952

Mex *adjective*
Mexican *US, 1854*
Offensive.
- Nice sky Mex kids with good manners. — Norman Mailer, *The Naked and the Dead*, p. 65, 1948
- I have had two women so far, one American with huge tits and a splendid Mex whore in house. — Jack Kerouac, *Letter to Allen Ginsberg*, p. 353, 10th May 1952
- [G]roups of Mex chicks swaggered around in slacks; mambo blasted from jukeboxes[.] — Jack Kerouac, *On the Road*, p. 93, 1957
- The Mex authorities keep an eye on him all the time and let him blow his loot in that little town where he lives[.] — Mickey Spillane, *Last Cop Out*, p. 10, 1972

Mexicali revenge *noun*
diarrhea *US, 1973*
- — Felix Rodriguez Gonzalez, *Spanish Loanwords in the English Language*, p. 120, 1996

Mexican bankroll *noun*
a high-denomination bill wrapped around low-denomination bills or plain paper *US, 1941*
- A pimp often has a "Mexican bankroll," a large bill on the outside covering a roll of singles. — Charles Winick, *The Lively Commerce*, p. 117, 1971
- There's no envelope full of money, just a bunch of napkins wadded up into a Mexican bankroll. — Robert Arrellano, *Don Dimaio of La Plata*, p. 177, 2004

Mexican breakfast *noun*
any combination of a glass of water, a cigarette, and the chance to urinate *US, 1960*
- — *Maledicta*, p. 165, 1979: "A glossary of ethnic slurs in American English"
- If I only stopped for a Mexican breakfast. Coffee and piss. — Dan Jenkins, *Dead Solid Perfect*, p. 239, 1986

Mexican brown *noun*
inferior heroin that originates in Mexico *US, 1975*
The adjective "Mexican" has a negative value.
- [W]here you could get top-grade smack when everybody else was dealing that Mexican brown[.] — Elmore Leonard, *City Primeval*, p. 64, 1980
- [I]t brushes up against the competition, including Mexican-produced Black Tar, known derisively as Mexican Mud because of its poor quality; the more superior Mexican Brown in powder form; and especially high-grade Colombian White, its biggest rival. — *New York Times*, p. SM29, 23rd June 2002

Mexican compromise *noun*
a decision in which you lose property but save your life *US, 1954*
- — Jerry Robertson, *Oil Slanguage*, p. 83, 1954

Mexican mud *noun*
brown heroin that originates in the Sierra Madre mountains of Mexico; heroin *US, 1977*
- [I]t brushes up against the competition, including Mexican-produced Black Tar, known derisively as Mexican Mud because of its poor quality; the more superior Mexican Brown in powder form; and especially high-grade Colombian White, its biggest rival. — *New York Times*, p. SM29, 23rd June 2002

Mexican red *noun*
a capsule of secobarbital sodium (trade name Seconal™), a central nervous system depressant *US, 1977*
- — Donald Wesson and David Smith, *Barbiturates*, p. 122, 1977
- The only way we made it was with a great big old bag of Mexican reds and two gallons of Robitussin HC [a branded cough medicine]. Five reds and a slug of HC and you can sleep through anything. — Butch Trucks of the Allman Brothers, *Jabberock*, 1997

Mexican shower *noun*
a hurried washing of the face and armpits *US, 2004*
- — Ben Applebaum and Derrick Pittman, *Turd Ferguson & The Sausage Party*, p. 44, 2004

Mexican standoff *noun*
1 a situation in which nobody clearly has the advantage or emerges a clear winner *US, 1891*
- It is a Mexican standoff. In a Mexican standoff, both parties narrow their eyes and glare but nobody throws a punch. — Tom Wolfe, *The Pump House Gang*, p. 16, 1968
- Our brothers loaded up. Every cop stopped in his tracks and stepped back. It was like the proverbial Mexican standoff. — Bobby Seale, *A Lonely Rage*, p. 213, 1978
- Looks like we got a Mexican standoff. — *Natural Born Killers*, 1994

2 the quitting of a poker game when a player is slightly ahead, slightly behind, or even *US, 1958*
- — John Scarne, *Scarne's Guide to Modern Poker*, p. 284, 1979

Mexican time *noun*
used for denoting a lack of punctuality *US, 1967*
- Like Mexican Time and the onetime JPT, Jewish People's time, C.P.T. is a phrase that draws the lines of the ghetto. — Paul Jacobs, *Prelude to a Riot*, p. 12, 1967

Mexican two-step *noun*
diarrhea *US, 1962*
- I spoke but had to leave the party with a bad case of "Montezuma's Revenge" or the "Mexican Two-Step." — Jimmie Vansickle, *A Journey Without End*, p. 141, 2003

Mexican Valium *noun*
Rohypnol™ (flunitrazepam), popularly known as the "date-rape drug" *US, 1995*
- Mexican Valium. Ruffie. Quaalude of the '90s. Nicknames abound for the illegal drug Rohypnol that's now hitting the Texas teen scene at $1 to $5 a pill. — *Newsweek*, p. 8, 3rd July 1995
- The drug is called rope, rophies, roofies, roche and Mexican Valium on the streets and is marketed as Rohypnol in South America. — *Daily Oklahoman (Oklahoma City)*, p. 1, 5th September 1995

Mextown *noun*
a neighborhood with a large population of Mexicans and Mexican-Americans *US, 1957*
- We bounced over the railroad tracks in Fresno and hit the wild streets of Fresno Mextown. — Jack Kerouac, *On the Road*, p. 93, 1957

mezz *noun*
marijuana, a marijuana cigarette *US, 1937*
An eponym honoring Milton "Mezz" Mezzrow, a jazz musician who was better known for his missionary work on behalf of marijuana than his jazz, and who is better remembered for his writing than his jazz.
- I had a trey ounce of mezz and that ain't hay. — *War Medicine*, p. 391, 1944
- New words came into being to meet the situation: the mezz and the mighty mezz, referring, I blush to say, to me and to the tea, both[.] — Mezz Mezzrow, *Really the Blues*, p. 215, 1946

mezzed *adjective*
entranced, as if marijuana-intoxicated *US, 1989*
- I was lying there vedged, mezzed by it all, but then I thought I saw something. — *Playboy*, p. 88, November 1989

- Even though it's smaller it's bigger, more forceful, like God is talking at me. I'm totally mezzed — James Blinn, *The Aardvark is Ready for War*, p. 104, 1997

mezzroll; mezz roll; Mezz's roll; meserole; messorole; mezzrow *noun*
an extra-large marijuana cigarette *US, 1944*

- [M]ezzroll, to describe the kind of fat, well-packed, and clean cigarette I used to roll (this word later got corrupted to meserole and it's still used to mean a certain size and shape of reefer, which is different from the so-called panatella). — Mezz Mezzrow, *Really the Blues*, p. 215, 1946
- The cigarettes came in three qualities: sars-fras, the cheapest kind, sold to thousands of school children at about ten cents each; the panatella, or messerole, retailed at twenty-five cents[.] — Jack Lait and Lee Mortimer, *New York Confidential*, p. 102, 1948
- Even then he had wanted to be an important jazz musician and some of the very good ones were reputed to be regular consumers of the reefer and mezziroll. — Ross Russell, *The Sound*, p. 21, 1961

MF; em ef *noun*
a motherfucker *US, 1959*

- Of all people, why'd they kill Malcolm? Why'n't they kill some of them Uncle-Tomming m.f.'s? — Eldridge Cleaver, *Soul on Ice*, p. 51, 1968
- "Then in comes this m.f. from Midtown North, our precinct." — Gail Sheehy, *Hustling*, p. 90, 1973
- The Rev. (Carl Davis) pulled out his knife and said Babs here's a tom ass m.f. all the way over in Paris tomming. — Babs Gonzales, *Movin' On Down De Line*, p. 18, 1975
- I think they're some cold mf's. — Yusuf Jah, *Uprising*, p. 168, 1995

MFIC; MFWIC *noun*
the person in charge of a situation. An abbreviation of *motherfucker (who's) in charge US, 1968*

- — Carl Fleischhauer, *A Glossary of Army Slang*, p. 33, 1968

mf-word *noun*
the word motherfuck, motherfucker or motherfucking *US, 1992*

- If you had a nickel for every time these rappers used the "F" word, the "MF" word and the like, you might be almost as rich as they are. — *Chicago Tribune*, 26th July 1992

MG *noun*
a machine gunner *US, 2001*

- "Doc, wait—we think Brown got their MG, but there's still a lot of shit flying." — Cherokee Paul McDonald, *Into the Green*, p. 109, 2001

mic *noun*
a *microphone US, 1927*
Pronounced "mike."

- I was co-hosting an open-mic for girls. — Michelle Tea, *Valencia*, p. 117, 2000
- And when he's on the mic, it still sounds like dancing. — RZA, *The Wu-Tang Manual*, p. 17, 2005

Michigan bankroll; Michigan roll *noun*
a single large-denomination bill wrapped around small-denomination bills, giving the impression of a great deal of money *US, 1914*

- — *The Annals of the American Academy of Political and Social Sciences*, p. 127, May 1950
- Put Pimp in a tailored suit, arm him with a Michigan roll faced with a $100 note, and he was good enough to go on the road. — David Simon and Edward Burns, *The Corner*, p. 320, 1997

Michigan handshake *noun*
a firm handshake that imparts a farewell *US, 1996*
Newspaper advice columnist Ann Landers used the term in a column on 27th June 1996, in which she urged "Embarrassed in Pittsburgh" to give her friend Fred "a Michigan handshake" and "tell him to hit the bricks" because he had taken a picture of her sleeping in the nude. Landers' use of the term generated a number of inquiries as to its meaning, and placed the term into the public lexicon. Landers herself pointed to Traverse City, Michigan, in the 1960s as the source of the term.

mick *noun*
1 an Irish person or Irish-American *US, 1850*

- It's funny, micks like us fighting each other. — James T. Farrell, *Saturday Night*, p. 52, 1947

- ACTION: Spics! PEPE: Micks! — *West Side Story*, 1957
- Agnew has pointed out that it's a land of opportunity for anyone, whether he's a Mick, as Polack or a Jap. — *Playboy*, p. 62, February 1969
- No sooner we was on the bus back, we had to bail out the windows on to Amsterdam Avenue, a mob of micks was comin' through the door after us. — Edwin Torres, *Carlito's Way*, p. 9, 1975

2 a prisoner *US, 1950*

- — Hyman E. Goldin et al., *Dictionary of American Underworld Lingo*, p. 139, 1950

mickey *noun*
1 a potato *US, 1936*

- After that, the junkies burn it to get at the brass pipes, and the kids do it for whatever reason kids burn things. Roasting mickeys or something. — Vincent Patrick, *The Pope of Greenwich Village*, p. 108, 1979
- "Also in spring firemen get more calls for fires in empty lots. The kids like to roast mickeys—" "Potatoes," Carlucci says. "Talk about dumb. You think an Irish kid like Jimmy here don't know what's a mickey?" — Robert Campbell, *The Cat's Meow*, p. 48, 1988

2 a flat pint bottle of alcohol *US, 1972*

- "Danny," he said, "you gotta get me a mickey. I need a mickey awful bad." — Robert Byrne, *McGoorty*, p. 144, 1972

3 an ordinary fellow *US, 1949*

- You must be new mickies 'cause you don't call a ship a boat. — Piri Thomas, *Down These Mean Streets*, p. 181, 1967

4 an alcoholic drink adulterated with knock-out drops *US, 1936*
A shortened form of MICKEY FINN.

- Theory was to feed them the sweet talk, and in between all the chit and chat slip them these mickeys[.] — Bernard Wolfe, *The Late Risers*, p. 174, 1954
- "A mickey won't hurt him any." — Gypsy Rose Lee, *Gypsy*, p. 197, 1957
- Thrills would do anything—his favorite gimmick was a peyote-methedrine mickey in the champagne[.] — Ed Sanders, *Tales of Beatnik Glory*, p. 108, 1975
- Somebody slipped the poor old cat an arsenic mickey. — Robert Campbell, *The Cat's Meow*, p. 139, 1988

mickey; mickey out *verb*
to drug someone's drink *US, 1946*

- — Robert C. Prus and C.R.D. Sharper, *Road Hustler*, p. 170, 1977: "Glossary of terms"

Mickey D's *noun*
a McDonald's™ fast-food restaurant *US, 1977*

- — Connie Eble (Editor), *UNC-CH Campus Slang*, p. 6, Fall 1987
- Dennis, my man, run over to Mickey D's and get me a Big Mac and some fries. — *Heathers*, 1988
- At Mickey D's, I earned $200 a week, and the tax man took out fifty. That was like kicking Monday and Friday in the Ass. — Chris Rock, *Rock This!*, pp. 96–97, 1997
- "I auditioned for a commercial. Mickey Dee's. A national." — Eric Jerome Dickey, *Cheaters*, p. 264, 1999

Mickey Finn; Mickey Flynn; Mickey's *noun*
an alcoholic beverage that has been adulterated with a strong tranquilizer; the narcotic that is so used *US, 1928*

- [F]or the first time in my life I had met up with a great old American institution, the Mickey Finn. — Mezz Mezzrow, *Really the Blues*, p. 294, 1946
- We knocked him out with a small and harmless Mickey Finn and we loaded his pockets with corks. — Robert Sylvester, *No Cover Charge*, p. 211, 1956
- I got back to the base a day late and told my C.O. that I'd been given a mickey finn and couldn't wake up until Monday. — Oscar Zeta Acosta, *The Autobiography of a Brown Buffalo*, p. 130, 1972
- I'm positive someone slipped me a Mickey Finn. — Ian Rankin, *The Falls*, p. 110, 2001

Mickey House *noun*
in poker, an unplayable hand *US, 1988*

- — George Percy, *The Language of Poker*, p. 56, 1988

Mickey man *noun*
a radar operator *US, 1946*

- — *American Speech*, p. 310, December 1946: "More Air Force slang"

Mickey Mouse *noun*
1 a wrist watch *US, 1959*
From the watches with the face of Mickey Mouse first popular in the 1930s.

- I peeped into my skull file and saw that "Roost" note. My "Mickey Mouse" read one-thirty A.M. — Iceberg Slim (Robert Beck), *Pimp*, p. 104, 1969

2 in American casinos, a $2.50 chip *US, 1985*
- — Steve Kuriscak, *Casino Talk*, p. 11, 1985

3 an ultra-shortwave radar used for aircraft spotting *US, 1947*
From a distance, the apparatus may be said to resemble a mouse.
- — *American Speech*, p. 153, April 1947: "Radar slang terms"

Mickey Mouse *adjective*
inferior, trivial, cheap *US, 1947*
- All that pedantic Mickey Mouse chitchat. — Richard Farina, *Been Down So Long*, p. 220, 1966
- All they know is that it feels good to swing to way-out body-rhythms instead of dragassing across the dance floor like zombies to the dead beat of mind-smothered Mickey-Mouse music. — Eldridge Cleaver, *Soul on Ice*, p. 81, 1968
- "My last tour was better though, not so much mickeymouse." — Michael Herr, *Dispatches*, p. 29, 1977
- What is this Mickey Mouse shit? — *Full Metal Jacket*, 1987

Mickey Mouse around *verb*
to fool around *US, 1961*
School usage.
- — *Washington Post*, 23rd April 1961: "Man, dig this jazz"

Mickey Mouse boots *noun*
heavy rubber boots issued to soldiers during the Korean war *US, 1952*
- But the temperatures were fast approaching zero at night, and the minute the boys got into position, their sweat-filled, heavy rubber "Mickey Mouse" boots (newly issued and so named for the striking resemblance they bore to those worn by Walt Disney's famous rodent) froze from the inside out. — David H. Hackworth, *About Face*, p. 262, 1989

Mickey Mouse mission *noun*
a simple, undemanding, relatively safe military task *US, 1990*
- — Gregory Clark, *Words of the Vietnam War*, p. 327, 1990

Mickey Mouse money *noun*
military scrip issued to soldiers in the Korean war *US, 1957*
- [O]ur US currency has been substituted by a military script referred to as Mickey Mouse money[.] — Martin Russ, *The Last Parallel*, p. 58, 1957

mickie *noun*
a bottled alcoholic drink *US, 1914*
- We stole our first mickies together from Gordon's fruit stand. — Claude Brown, *Manchild in the Promised Land*, p. 308, 1965

Microsloth Windows *nickname*
Microsoft Windows™ *US, 1991*
- — Eric S. Raymond, *The New Hacker's Dictionary*, p. 242, 1991

middle *noun*
in sports betting, a combination of bets that produce a win no matter what the outcome of the game *US, 1975*
- The wider the "middle" the more beautiful is twenty-to-one. — Jimmy Snyder, *Jimmy the Greek*, p. 208, 1975
- I was grabbing everything I could get on the Bears and giving up 10. Here was a chance for a two-point "middle" time honored gambler's trick to win coming and going, to collect on both ends. — Hunter S. Thompson, *Generation of Swine*, p. 73, 1986

middlebrow *adjective*
used for describing bourgeois taste *UK, 1925*
- Bill and Beth would say—well, probably not Bill, but definitely Beth—that your guilt, and their disapproval, is a very middlebrow, middle-class, midwestern sort of disapproval. — Dave Eggers, *A Heartbreaking Work of Staggering Genius*, p. 115, 2005

Middlesex *adjective*
homosexual *US, 1948*
A pun on the place.
- Between these two levels of honest if Middlesex entertainment are the atmospheric places gotten up to look very Left Bank[.] — Jack Lait and Lee Mortimer, *New York Confidential*, pp. 68–69, 1948

middle-sexed *adjective*
homosexual *US, 1950*
- Such habituals always draw the distorted and the perverted and that melange of middle-sexed jobs which nature started but never finished. — Jack Lait and Lee Mortimer, *Chicago Confidential*, p. 65, 1950

midget *noun*
a very young member of a youth gang *US, 1957*
- "All they got is juniors and midgets." — Herbert Simmons, *Corner Boy*, p. 140, 1957
- All the midgets and tinys in the Black Spiders had been to the Hall. most of the peewees even! — Joseph Wambaugh, *The Glitter Dome*, p. 110, 1981

midnight *noun*
in dice games, a roll of 12 *US, 1919*
- — Gil Jacobs, *The World's Best Dice Games*, p. 198, 1976

midnight cowboy *noun*
a homosexual prostitute, originally one who wears cowboy clothes; hence a homosexual man *US, 1972*
Brought from gay subculture into wider use by the movie *Midnight Cowboy*, 1969.
- The clothes chosen by the fetishists epitomize masculinity: cowboys, sailors, etc. The model acting out the cowboy then is a midnight cowboy[.] — Bruce Rodgers, *The Queens' Vernacular*, 1972
- [I]t showed triple bills of westerns to Popeyes, inner city denizens, kids playing hooky, and bored Midnight Cowboys. — Bill Landis, *Sleazoid Express*, p. 154, 2002
- Orange Julius was the spot where Midnight Cowboys copped heroin in the 60s. — Josh Friedman, *When Sex Was Dirty*, p. 53, 2005

midnight inventory *noun*
a burglary *US, 1968*
- I also ferreted out facts that, I'm glad to say, aided police in being on the spot a half-dozen times when junkies dropped by to take a "midnight inventory" of a safe's contents. — Phil Hirsch, *Hooked*, p. 136, 1968

midnight lab *noun*
a laboratory where illegal drugs are manufactured *US, 1970*
- — William D. Alsever, *Glossary for the Establishment and Other Uptight People*, p. 21, December 1970

midnight requisition *noun*
theft, especially in the military *US, 1946*
- [M]ay indeed, as rumor had it, have been "borrowed" from a PX warehouse in Saigon in a midnight requisition. — W.E.B. Griffin, *The Aviators*, p. 6, 1988

midnight revue *noun*
serial consecutive sex between one person and multiple partners, usually consensual *US, 1949*
- It was the Midnight Revue. Everybody plays jam in that park, gets their trim. We got on her. Seven of us. — Hal Ellson, *Duke*, p. 61, 1949

midnight small stores *noun*
the notional source of material that has been stolen *US, 1944*
- The numbers depended on where and how they were procured [Some by "midnight small stores"] and the deck space you had available. — William McGee, *The Amphibians are Coming!*, p. 59, 2000

midnight supply man *noun*
a person who traffics in stolen equipment *US, 1954*
- — Jerry Robertson, *Oil Slanguage*, p. 83, 1954

midrats *noun*
a meal served between midnight and 1am *US, 1973*
An abbreviation of "midnight rations."
- — Bernadette Hince, *The Antarctic Dictionary*, p. 229, 2000
- — Ethan Dicks, *English, as She is Spoke at McMurdo*, 2007

midway bonus *noun*
in circus and carnival usage, an extravagant, empty promise *US, 1981*
- — Don Wilmeth, *The Language of American Popular Entertainment*, p. 172, 1981

miff *verb*
to botch *US, 1951*
- "He miffed the job and they gave him the works." — Mickey Spillane, *The Big Kill*, p. 41, 1951

MIG alley *noun*
during the Korean war, airspace controlled by North Korea and its allies *US, 1951*
- This he did, while Sabrejets went thundering north to "MIG Alley" to recover air supremacy. — Robert Leckie, *The Wars of America, Volume II*, p. 389, 1968

mighty mezz *noun*

a generous marijuana cigarette, or simply marijuana *US, 1946*

- New words came into being to meet the situation: the mezz and the mighty mezz, referring, I blush to say, to me and to the tea, both[.] — Mezz Mezzrow, *Really the Blues*, p. 215, 1946

mighty mite *noun*

a fan used to blow gas into Viet Cong tunnels *US, 1967*

- It would be launched either by grenades or by a device known as the "Mighty Mite," a fifty-pound instrument that was originally a fumigating device but was later used to force tear gas under great pressure into Viet Cong tunnels. — Elaine Shepard, *The Doom Pussy*, p. 94, 1967
- Mighty mite—Commercial air blower used for injecting gas into tunnels. — Tom Mangold, *The Tunnels of Cu Chi*, p. 284, 1985

Mighty Mo *noun*

the USS Missouri *US, 1955*

- The Mighty Mo is best remembered for being the site of Japan's surrender to General MacArthur on September 2, 1945. — Richard Sullivan, *Driving and Discovering Oahu*, p. 32, 1993

mike *noun*

1 a microgram (1/1,000,000th of a gram) *US, 1967*

The unit of measure for LSD doses, even in the nonmetric US.

- "How many mikes?" Papa All wanted to know. "Ahh, I dunno. They'll get ya off." — Nicholas Von Hoffman, *We Are The People Our Parents Warned Us Against*, p. 26, 1967
- I had one woman that took four hundred mikes of LSD. — *Los Angeles Free Press*, p. 10, 14th-20th August 1970
- She hung out with me while I was coming on when I had been dosed by what I think was something approaching 3500 mikes[.] — Stephen Gaskin, *Amazing Dope Tails*, p. 115, 1980
- Crisis-level bummers are less likely to happen on low doses of acid—100 mikes or less—than on high doses of 150 mikes or more. — Cam Cloud, *The Little Book of Acid*, p. 22, 1999

2 a microphone *US, 1927*

- Shortly after noon the two largest national broadcasting systems installed mikes on the main walk down near the front gates. — Chester Himes, *Cast the First Stone*, p. 145, 1952

3 a minute *US, 1986*

From the military phonetic alphabet—"mike" for "m," and "m" for "minute."

- Three is inbound from the Sierra Whiskey. Should be here in two zero mikes if they don't hit any shit. — *Platoon*, 1986

4 a mercenary *US, 1972*

Prior to the US invasion of Iraq in 2003, mercenaries were disrespected, if not despised. Under President Bush, mercenaries became a respected and regular part of the American occupation of Iraq.

- I saw the house and a group of eight giggling, wide-eyed Vietnamese mercenaries, Mikes, pointing at me and talking very excitedly. — Michael Herr, *Dispatches*, p. 229, 1977

mike; mike up *verb*

to equip with a microphone *UK, 1984*

- Victoria was miked and sat in a straight-back chair opposite Ted. — Stephen Cannell, *King Con*, p. 82, 1992
- Requests to mike up any electronic keyboard should be met with diplomatic tactics. — Ben Duncan, *The Live Sound Manual*, p. 16, 2002

mike boat *noun*

a military landing craft *US, 1948*

- Catch a "Mike" boat [LCM] to the IUWG site. Conduct service about 1300. — Clifford Drury, *The History of the Chaplain Corps, United States Navy*, p. 72, 1948
- Two motor-drive "mike" boat, each with a capacity for 300 passengers, would be waiting to load them on. — Frank Snepp, *A Decent Interval*, p. 505, 1977
- The mike boat came sliding toward the quay, its diesel engine falling silent as it coasted the last few yards to the early float. — Stephen Coonts, *Final Flight*, p. 252, 1988
- The "Mike" boat was utilized for numerous operations by SEALs and UDT. — T.L. Bosiljevac, *SEALs*, p. 52, 1990

Mike Hunt *noun*

a fictitious name, used as a prank for waiting lists *US, 1981*

The announcement "table for Mike Hunt" sounds very much like "table for my cunt," thus a source of amusement. Used with great comic effect in the 1981 film "Porky's."

- — Michael Dalton Johnson, *Talking Trash with Redd Foxx*, p. 14, 1994
- Annie: I'm looking for Mike Hunt. Brian: She's looking for her cunt. — Katie Wales, *Feminist Linguists in Literary Criticism*, p. 80, 1994
- He claims to be "Mike Hunt, Beaver Falls." — Maurice Yacowar, *The Sopranos on the Couch*, p. 200, 2003

mike juliet *noun*

marijuana *US, 1977*

Vietnam war usage. The military phonetic alphabet for **MJ** (marijuana).

- Why, smoke is M.J., Mike Juliet. Ya know—grass. — Larry Heinemann, *Close Quarters*, p. 26, 1977

mike-mike *noun*

1 a millimeter, or a weapon with a caliber measured in millimeters *US, 1967*

From the military phonetic alphabet for "mm."

- The C-47 was a standard prop flareship, but many of them carried .20- and .762-mm. guns on their doors, Mike-Mikes that could fire out 300 rounds per second[.] — A.D. Horne, *The Wounded Generation*, p. 59, 1981
- We called in the 80 Mike-Mikes—mortars—because we wanted to walk the tree line with them. — Mark Baker, *Nam*, p. 62, 1981
- Listen to the small arms, hear the twenty mike-mike roar. — Joseph Tuso, *Singing the Vietnam Blues*, p. 27, 1990: The Ballad of Bernie Fisher

2 a sudden, intense, coordinated burst of fire *US, 2001*

The phonetic abbreviation for **MAD MINUTE**.

- "Three, two, one ... mike-mike ... mike-mike ..." — Cherokee Paul McDonald, *Into the Green*, p. 204, 2001

mikeside *adjective*

broadcasting on radio *US, 1977*

- "This is Curly Bill, mikeside, starting on that second cup of coffee." — Bob Cudmore, *You can't Go Wrong*, p. 100, 2000

Mike Strike *noun*

a Vietnamese mercenary *US, 1972*

- "As of tomorrow, you'll work with a squad of Mike Strikes and an ARVN interpreter." — William Pelfrey, *The Big V*, p. 78, 1972
- "The Mike Strikes work for the Brigade, not for you." — Anthony Herbert, *Soldier*, p. 297, 1973

Mikey *noun*

a person who is willing to sample an illegal drug before others use, buy or sell it *US, 2003*

An allusion to a long-running cereal commercial in which the youngest brother, Mikey, tries what the older brothers won't try.

- The tablets were seized during a probation check from a local drug user who is a so-called "Mikey" (a volunteer "guinea pig" who is willing to "test" (by self-administration) illicit drugs and drug mixtures of virtually any type.) — *Microgram Bulletin (DEA)*, p. 249, November 2003

Mile High Club *noun*

a notional club for people who claim to have had sex on an airborne plane *US, 1972*

- "Anyhow, I'm a member of the Mile High Club, and it's something I always wanted to do." — Rona Jaffe, *After the Reunion*, p. 90, 1985
- She splays wide her hairless crack before Max Hardcore (real name Max Steiner), who initiates her into the Mile-High Club. — Editors of *Adult Video News*, *The AVN Guide to the 500 Greatest Adult Films of All Time*, p. 199, 2005

milf; MILF *noun*

a sexually appealing mother *US, 1995*

- We have a term for it around here, its called "MILF" It stands for "Mothers I'd Like to Fuck." — *alt.mag.playboy*, 11th January 1995
- Dude, that chick's a MILF. What the hell is that? Mom I'd like to fuck. — *American Pie*, 1999
- — Connie Eble (Editor), *UNC-CH Campus Slang*, p. 7, Fall 2001
- You won't believe it's the M.I.L.F. from The O.C. — Mr. Skin, *Mr. Skin's Skincyclopedia*, p. 111, 2005

milk *verb*

1 to exploit, to cheat *UK, 1536*

- The boss catered mostly to Indians who struck oil on the reservation, beefy cattlemen who were sure to be milked, sugar-daddies with their sable-sporting chicken dinners, and butter-and-egg men with plenty of bacon. — Mezz Mezzrow, *Really the Blues*, p. 84, 1946
- Too many people wanna milk it for what it's worth. — *The Bad Lieutenant*, 1992

2 in card games, to draw the top and bottom cards (off a new pack) before the first shuffle *US, 1845*

- — Albert H. Morehead, *The Complete Guide to Winning Poker*, p. 268, 1967

▶ **milk a rush**

while injecting a drug, to draw blood into the syringe and slowly release the drug into the vein, controlling the immediate effect of the drug *US, 1986*

- — Richard A. Spears, *The Slang and Jargon of Drugs and Drink*, p. 340, 1986

▶ **milk it**

to squeeze the shaft of the penis towards the head of the penis *US, 1967*

- Rubber-gloved doctors pass down the rows of naked men. "Milk it down. Turn your head. Cough. Again." — Donald Duncan, *The New Legions*, p. 6, 1967

▶ **milk the anaconda**

(of a male) to masturbate *US, 1985*

- A signal meant they'd caught some guy milking the anaconda. — Joseph Wambaugh, *The Secrets of Harry Bright*, pp. 60–61, 1985

milk?

used as a tease of someone whose demeanor is just a bit catty *US, 1994*

- — Kevin Dilallo, *The Unofficial Gay Manual*, p. 242, 1994

milk-ball *noun*

any alcoholic beverage served with milk *US, 1983*

- "Ulcer?" Mario Villalobos asked. "Iron stomach," she said. "I just like milk-balls." — Joseph Wambaugh, *The Delta Star*, p. 121, 1983

milker *noun*

in poker, a player who bets only on a very good hand or with very good odds *US, 1988*

- — George Percy, *The Language of Poker*, p. 57, 1988

milk rope *noun*

a pearl necklace *US, 1956*

- — *American Speech*, p. 98, May 1956: "Smugglers' argot in the Southwest"

milk route *noun*

an easy, lucrative sales route *US, 1930*

- To use the contemptuous installment house term, I was handed a "milk route." — Jim Thompson, *Roughneck*, p. 59, 1954

milk run *noun*

1 a simple, undemanding, undangerous military task *US, 1943*

- "No sweat, my boy, it's an old time milk run." — Joseph Tuso, *Singing the Vietnam Blues*, p. 192, 1990: Tchepone

2 the first run of a ski-lift on a given morning, or the first run down the mountain of the day *US, 1963*

- Ambitious skiers will get up early to make the milk run. — *American Speech*, p. 206, October 1963: "The language of skiers"

milksop *noun*

a cowardly or effeminate man *UK, 1382*

- But Trixie, deferential as she usually was, would have none of this milksop attitude. — Jim Thompson, *Roughneck*, p. 88, 1954

milksucker *noun*

a young child *US, 1975*

- Had so fucking many milksuckers running around she forgot the police department summer camp was taking care a the little prick for a week. — Joseph Wambaugh, *The Choirboys*, p. 37, 1975

milk train *noun*

a train with an early morning schedule *US, 1853*

- She'd gone out to the rear platform for some fresh air—a rarity on the milk train—and taken a tumble. — Jim Thompson, *The Nothing Man*, pp. 268–269, 1954
- [E]ven allowing you a couple of weeks at the "lake" in Michigan, traveling on a "milk-train" or crossing the country at the rate of speed you drive thrown in, you still can't quite get away before I get out. — Neal Cassady, *Grace Beats Karma*, p. 134, 8th October 1959: Letter to Carolyn Cassady

mill *noun*

1 a *mill*ion, especially and usually a million dollars *US, 1942* Sometimes simply "mil."

- They make, what, about a quarter of a mil in a month? — George V. Higgins, *The Friends of Eddie Doyle*, p. 201, 1971

- We walk away with a mill. Does that turn you on? — Gerald Petievich, *One-Shot Deal*, p. 159, 1981
- "If Jimmy killed Marty, Jimmy would get Marty's half a mill." — Nicholas Pileggi, *Wise Guy*, p. 216, 1985
- [I]f you consider middle class a family that rakes in two-fifty to half a mil a year. — John Ridley, *Everybody Smokes in Hell*, p. 3, 1999

2 one thousand dollars *US, 1961*

- — Francis J. Rigney and L. Douglas Smith, *The Real Bohemia*, p. xx, 1961

Miller time *noun*

hours spent drinking beer after work or play *US, 1981*

An advertising slogan by the Miller Brewing Company, expanded to nonproduct-specific ironic usage.

- Every night the sun goes down and the guy that drives the bulldozer around goes back to the shack and gets his jacket on and goes home for Miller Time. — George V. Higgins, *The Rat on Fire*, pp. 80–81, 1981

millihelen *noun*

a notional unit used for measuring beauty *US, 1969*

- I therefore whiled away one lunch period by making up units and I finally came up with the "millihelen," which is enough beauty to launch one ship. — Isaac Asimov, *Asimov Laughs Again*, p. 200, 1995

million dollar wound *noun*

during war, a wound that was serious enough to get a soldier sent home but not so serious as to affect the rest of their life *US, 1947*

- "So long, you miserable sonsabitches," he yells. "I just got that million-dollar wound." — Audie Murphy, *To Hell and Back*, p. 219, 1949
- "Well, maybe it will be right for me to go home. I got a million dollar wound." — Mark Baker, *Nam*, p. 98, 1981
- Some examples of "million dollar wounds" were loss of toes, fingers, hearing, and some stomach wounds. Million dollar wounds were an "automatic ticket" back to The World. — Gregory Clark, *Words of the Vietnam War*, p. 327, 1990

milquetoast *noun*

a timid person *US, 1938*

- Somehow the dynamo that Skilling—and, after him, Lay—had met on the East Coast had become a milquetoast in Houston. — Kurt Eichenwald, *Conspiracy of Fools*, p. 174, 2005

Milwaukee goiter *noun*

a big belly produced by excessive beer consumption *US, 1941*

- The second guy is gigantic with a huge Milwaukee goiter, red suspenders, a piggy crew cut and an oversize silver-and-gold rodeo-campeen belt buckle. — Richard Ford, *Independence Day*, p. 185, 1992

mimeo *noun*

a mimeograph machine; a document produced by mimeograph *US, 1963*

- He "couldn't take too many meetings" so was running the mimeo instead. — Ann Fettamen, *Trashing*, p. 2, 1970

minch *noun*

in circus and carnival usage, an unengaged, low-spending customer *US, 1928*

- — Don Wilmeth, *The Language of American Popular Entertainment*, p. 172, 1981

mindbender *noun*

1 anything that challenges your knowledge or assumptions *UK, 1963*

- It goes through to where you're going to escape, and they escape and they're getting away, and while they're getting away clean, suddenly, Bang!—they're caught again. It was a real mind-bender. — Stephen Gaskin, *Amazing Dope Tales*, p. 148, 1980
- Walking the yard was a mind bender. — Gerald Petievich, *Money Men*, p. 35, 1981

2 a hallucinogenic drug *US, 1971*

- — Eugene Landy, *The Underground Dictionary*, p. 132, 1971

mindblower *noun*

an event, experience or situation that completely surprises or shocks *US, 1968*

- — Eugene Landy, *The Underground Dictionary*, p. 133, 1971
- I'm talking about drugs and alcohol and their use and and abuse as mind-blowers and leg-openers. — Xaviera Hollander, *The Best Part of a Man*, 1975
- "Paco form El Perro?" To Kate's discomfiture, she grinned broadly. "Now, that's a mind-blower." — Cyra McFadden, *The Serial*, p. 117, 1977

mind candy *noun*

entertainment that requires little intellectual engagement
US, 1978

- Still, for mind candy that's reasonably fair in its portrayal of magical spirituality, this is worth a watch. — Carl McColman, *The Complete Idiot's Guide to Paganism*, p. 314, 2002

mindfuck *noun*

1 anything that causes an internal paradigm shift *US, 1971*

- MINDFUCK: something which is too much to accept, more upsetting than a mindblower. — Robert Buckhout, *Toward Social Change*, p. 466, 1971

2 the mental aspects of sex *US, 1970*

- Mind fuck: A term originated by freaks to describe the experience of orgasm. — *Screw*, p. 7, 12th October 1970

mindfuck *verb*

to baffle; to manipulate psychologically *US, 1967*

- The prosecutor tried for another few minutes, until the judge called both attorneys up to the bench and politely told the prosecutor to please quit mind-fucking the court[.] — Elmore Leonard, *Swag*, p. 7, 1976
- He's really mind-fucked you. — Jack W. Thomas, *Heavy Number*, p. 105, 1976
- He mind-fucked in lyrics and in interviews and in concert[.] — Chuck Eddy, *Stairway to Hell*, p. 13, 1991

mindless *adjective*

(used of waves) immense and powerful *US, 1987*

- — Mitch McKissick, *Surf Lingo*, 1987

mine *adjective*

a "minus" attached to a grade *US, 1968*

- — Collin Baker et al., *College Undergraduate Slang Study Conducted at Brown University*, p. 157, 1968

mingy *adjective*

in pool, a shot that cannot be missed or a game that cannot be lost *US, 1990*

- — Steve Rushin, *Pool Cool*, p. 21, 1990

mini skirt *noun*

a woman *US, 1977*

- Truckers expanded the existing slang term of "beaver" into their own vocabulary and "sweet thing" and "mini skirt," two previous names used for females were discarded. — Gwyneth A. "Dandalion" Seese, *Tijuana Bear in a Smoke 'Um Up Taxi*, p. 45, 1977

mink *noun*

1 a female friend or lover *US, 1899*

- — Anthony Romeo, *The Language of Gangs*, p. 20, 4th December 1962
- — Joan Fontaine et al., *Dictionary of Black Slang*, 1968
- — David Claerbaut, *Black Jargon in White America*, p. 72, 1972

2 a female whose romantic interest in a man is overshadowed by her interest in his financial worth *US, 1960*

- — *San Francisco Examiner*, p. III-2, 22nd March 1960
- Deek had girls up all the time ... minks that would never have looked twice at Ty in school or on the street. — Jess Mowry, *Way Past Cool*, p. 33, 1992

Minnesota mule *noun*

a prostitute recently arrived in New York City from a small town or city *US, 1986–1987*

- — *Maledicta*, p. 151, Summer/Winter 1986–1987: "Sexual slang: prostitutes, pedophiles, flagellators, transvestites, and necrophiles"

Minnesota strip *noun*

an area in New York City frequented by prostitutes *US, 1977*

- For the last three years we have operated our program there, on the so-called "Minnesota Strip," a seamy fifteen-block stretch of Eight Avenue. — Senate Committee on the Judiciary, *Reauthorization of the Juvenile Justice and Delinquency Prevention Act of 1974*, p. 204, 1981
- The "Minnesota Strip"—Eighth Avenue between 34th and 55th streets—picked up its nickname in 1972. Many hookers gave Minneapolis as their home city whenever asked, to the point of it becoming a cynical retort, though some undoubtedly told the truth. — Josh Alan Friedman, *Tales of Times Square*, p. 143, 1986
- "It's a brothel, Judy, on West Forty-first Street. In the Minnesota Strip." — Michael Collins, *Minnesota Strip*, p. 6, 1987
- For the past three years, she's been under the watchful eye of "Sweetpea," a very grimy excuse for a human being who plies the sexual trade on the Minnesota Strip. — Mary Rose McGeady, *Are you out there, God?*, p. 38, 1999

Minnie *noun*

in lowball or low poker, the lowest possible hand *US, 1967*
A personification of "minimum."

- — Albert H. Morehead, *The Complete Guide to Winning Poker*, p. 268, 1967

minnow *noun*

a poker player who joins a no-stakes game without sufficient funds *US, 1978*

- — Thomas L. Clark, *The Dictionary of Gambling and Gaming*, p. 130, 1987

minny *noun*

a minimum security jail or prison; the minimum security wing of a jail or prison *US, 1976*

- — John R. Armore and Joseph D. Wolfe, *Dictionary of Desperation*, p. 40, 1976

minoo *adjective*

a "minus" attached to a grade *US, 1968*

- — Collin Baker et al., *College Undergraduate Slang Study Conducted at Brown University*, p. 157, 1968

minor-league *adjective*

mediocre, less than impressive *US, 1949*
From the minor leagues in US professional baseball.

- I'm in minor-league shock: my eyes are wide, but my gaze is blank. — James Ellroy, *Hollywood Nocturnes*, p. 5, 1994

minors *noun*

bicycle rims under 18 inches *US, 2006*

- "Y'all can't shake the block sittin' on minors." — Linden Dalecki, *Kid B*, p. 73, 2006

minors!

that's not a problem! *US, 1981*
Hawaiian youth usage.

- "But I no mo' money fo' da movies!" "Minors, brah. I get." — Douglas Simonson, *Pidgin to da Max*, 1981

mint *noun*

money *US, 1997*

- — Vann Wesson, *Generation X Field Guide and Lexicon*, p. 112, 1997

mint *adjective*

good looking, sexy, good *US, 1965*

- — Miss Cone, *The Slang Dictionary (Hawthorne High School)*, 1965
- — *USA Today*, 29 September 1983

mintie *noun*

a lesbian who plays the aggressive or dominant role *US, 1972*

- — Helen Dahlskog (Editor), *A Dictionary of Contemporary and Colloquial Usage*, p. 40, 1972

mintweed; mint *noun*

phencyclidine, the recreational drug known as PCP or angel dust *US, 1981*

- — Ronald Linder, *PCP*, pp. 9–10, 1981

minty *adjective*

1 homosexual, effeminate *US, 1965*

- — *Maledicta*, p. 238, Winter 1980: "'Lovely, blooming, fresh and gay': the onomastics of camp"

2 excellent *US, 1987*

- — *Carmel (California) High School Yearbook*, 1987

miracle *noun*

in the language surrounding the Grateful Dead, an extra ticket for that night's show *US, 1994*

- The phrase "I need a miracle!" has become the most common plea for a ticket in the parking lot, both spoken (shouted) and written (colorfully) on cardboard placards[.] — David Shenk and Steve Silberman, *Skeleton Key*, p. 194, 1994

miracle meat *noun*

a penis that is almost as large flaccid as erect *US, 1970*

- — *American Speech*, p. 58, Spring–Summer 1970: "Homosexual slang"

mirror *noun*

a military sentry's enemy counterpart *US, 1992*

- For each American sentry post there's a Cuban counterpart. They're called mirrors. — *A Few Good Men*, 1992

misdee *noun*

a misdemeanor or minor crime *US, 1992*

- You don't have anything on me. A misdee auto-theft. — *Gone in 60 Seconds*, 1992

misery lights noun

the colored lights on the top of a police car US, 1992

- The cruiser followed suit, hitting its misery lights as soon as both cars were clear of the mainstream traffic. — Richard Price, *Clockers*, p. 395, 1992

misery machine noun

a motorcycle US, 1962

- — *American Speech*, p. 269, December 1962: "The language of traffic policemen"

misery parade noun

alcoholics pacing on the pavement waiting for a bar to open in the morning US, 1998

- — Christopher Cavanaugh, *AA to Z*, p. 127, 1998

misfeature noun

in computing, a feature of a program that was carefully planned but that produces undesirable consequences in a given situation US, 1983

- — Guy L. Steele et al., *The Hacker's Dictionary*, p. 93, 1983

misfire noun

an instance of sexual impotence or premature ejaculation US, 1964

- — Roger Blake, *The American Dictionary of Sexual Terms*, p. 134, 1964
- Perhaps Al Mackey's misfire at the Chinatown motel was inevitable. — Joseph Wambaugh, *The Glitter Dome*, 1981

mish noun

the missionary position for sexual intercourse—man on top of prone woman US, 1995

- After a steamy run munch and a wicked b.j., they engage in some nut-slappin' mish capped off with—you guess it—major anal penetration. — *Adult Video News*, p. 128, August 1995
- A white guy in his early forties wearing a Gang Bang 2 T-shirt is soon fucking Jaz in the mish pazish. — Anthony Petkovich, *The X Factory*, p. 195, 1997

mishegoss noun

nonsense; craziness US, 1969

Yiddish.

- Alex, you are never going to hear such a mishegoss of mixed-up crap and disgusting nonsense as the Christian religion in your entire life. — Philip Roth, *Portnoy's Complaint*, p. 44, 1969
- Steve Beauchamp of Manhattan, a 27-year-old actor and writer, said he boxed three to five times a week at the West Side Y, mainly as an outlet for bottled up anger, frustration and "all my mishegoss." — *New York Times*, p. 49, 9th January 1983
- That's why Beavis and Butt-head are marketed like Barney the Dinosaur; Howard Stern is king of a trash pile bigger than the Twin Towers; Tonya Harding received all that attention for hatching an evil plot; and the three networks shamelessly scrambled to immortalize the Fisher-Buttafucco mishegoss. — *Newsday (New York)*, p. A34, 19th October 1994
- Joel Schumacher's Phone Booth is based on a script by Larry Cohen that, for bold mishegoss, nearly rivals the B-movie meister's Gold Me To. — *Village Voice*, p. 129, 24th September 2002

Miss Ann; Missy Ann noun

the prototype of the white southern woman US, 1925

- "You know Charlie and Miss Ann ain't going to sit still for that—their kids in the same classroom with black kids." — John Williams, *The Man Who Cried I Am*, p. 235, 1967
- Is he gonna grow up t'be a big bad see-eye-aye man an keep the world safe fo' Missy Ann's fur coat? — Robert Gover, *JC Saves*, p. 70, 1968
- He stopped, talked, and discussed he points of the ten-point platform with all the black brothers and sisters off the block, and with mothers who had been scrubbing Miss Ann's kitchen. — Bobby Seale, *Seize the Time*, p. 64, 1970
- "What about Miss Ann there?" he said. — Vernon E. Smith, *The Jones Men*, p. 14, 1974

Miss Carrie noun

a small supply of drugs carried on the person of a drug addict US, 1973

Carried to get the addict through a short incarceration in the event of an arrest.

- — David Maurer and Victor Vogel, *Narcotics and Narcotic Addiction*, p. 427, 1973

misses noun

dice that have been weighted, either to throw a seven less (for the opening roll in craps) or more (for subsequent rolls) than normal US, 1962

- — Frank Garcia, *Marked Cards and Loaded Dice*, p. 262, 1962

Miss Green noun

marijuana US, 1952

- By the way, boy, I am of course indulging in a perfect orgy of Miss Green & can hardly see straight right at this minute, whoo! 3 bombs a day. — Jack Kerouac, *Letter to Neal and Carolyn Cassady*, p. 358, 10th May 1952

missing noun

a report of a missing person US, 1985

- She called in a Missing. Morning of the day we found the body. — Elmore Leonard, *Glitz*, p. 89, 1985

mission noun

1 a search to buy crack cocaine US, 1992

Another *Star Trek* metaphor.

- — Terry Williams, *Crackhouse*, p. 150, 1992

2 an assignment given to a youth gang member US, 1995

- — Bill Valentine, *Gang Intelligence Manual*, p. 77, 1995: "Black street gang terminology"

mission bum; mission stiff noun

a tramp who frequents the dining rooms and sleeping quarters offered to the destitute by religious missions US, 1924

- We call this Mission Row, because it's where the mission stiffs hang out. — Jack Lait and Lee Mortimer, *Washington Confidential*, p. 32, 1951
- The mission bums watched the policemen, two rookies and a more experienced partner, pass them by[.] — Clancy Sigal, *Going Away*, p. 235, 1961

Mississippi flush noun

in poker, any hand and a revolver US, 1999

- — Jeffrey McQuain, *Never Enough Words*, p. 55, 1999

Mississippi marbles noun

dice US, 1920

- But I didn't exactly duck when the Mississippi marbles were rolling on the rug or a golf-betting proposition came along. — Sam Snead, *The Education of a Golfer*, p. 162, 1962

Mississippi saxophone noun

a harmonica, a mouth organ US, 1996

- Not for nothing has the blues harp long been nicknamed the "Mississippi Saxophone." Masters and definers of harp style dating back to John Lee (Sonny Boy) Williamson and Little Walter[.] — Dick Shurman, *The Hard Way (by William Clarke)*, sleeve notes, 1996

Miss It noun

used as a term of address to a person with excessive self esteem US, 1968

- "Oh, Miss It, you're too much." — Nathan Heard, *Howard Street*, p. 119, 1968
- I got myself a serious Miss It—she's a six-foot tall, blonde jazz singer with a group at the Holiday Inn in the Financial Center at Jackson and Kearney. — Oscar Zeta Acosta, *The Uncollected Works*, p. 105, 1972

Missouri bankroll noun

a bankroll with a high-denomination bill on the outside and low-denomination bills or plain paper on the inside US, 1992

- [S]he was wearing a grease-smeared apron, stuffed with what must have been a Missouri bankroll of ones and fives from generous customers. — Robert J. Thompson, *Panacea*, p. 43, 2002

Missouri marbles noun

dice US, 1962

- — Frank Garcia, *Marked Cards and Loaded Dice*, p. 263, 1962

Missouri pass noun

in the US, pulling off a road onto the hard shoulder to pass a vehicle on the right US, 1999

- — Jeffrey McQuain, *Never Enough Words*, p. 54, 1999

Miss Thing noun

used as a term of address for someone (female or homosexual male) with excessive self-esteem US, 1957

- You don't have to yell Miss Thing. — Hubert Selby Jr., *Last Exit to Brooklyn*, p. 58, 1957
- Miss Thing had told me, "why how ridiculous!—that petuh between your legs simpuhlee does not belong, dear." — John Rechy, *City of Night*, p. 115, 1963

- Every time he hit on me I would just say, "Miss Rubber I need five for my room rent," and he'd just say, "Go head Miss Thing, I ain't got no money." — Babs Gonzales, *Movin' On Down De Line*, p. 70, 1975
- "Very butch, Miss Thing," somebody else chimed in. — James St. James, *Party Monster*, p. 171, 1990

Missy noun
cocaine *US*, 1997
- They called it "girl" or "Jane" or "Missy" in feminine contrast to "boy" or "John" or "Mister" for king heroin. — David Simon and Edward Burns, *The Corner*, p. 62, 1997

mist noun
the smoke produced when crack cocaine is smoked *US*, 1994
- — US Department of Justice, *Street Terms*, October 1994

mister noun
the male manager of a homosexual brothel *US*, 1966
- There are clandestine call boy rings, operated by discreet male madams (often called "misters" in Miami) who supply male prostitutes to guests at beach hotels. — Johnny Shearer, *The Male Hustler*, pp. 123–124, 1966

Mister noun
heroin *US*, 1997
- They called it "girl" or "Jane" or "Missy" in feminine contrast to "boy" or "John" or "Mister" for king heroin. — David Simon and Edward Burns, *The Corner*, p. 62, 1997

Mister; Mr noun
a stereotype of the adjective that follows *US*, 1940
- But I know I have to talk to Chichi if I want any kind of emotional angle, a point of view, because Robbie's such a cold fish. He thinks he's Mr. Personality, but he's basically a very dull person. — Elmore Leonard, *Split Images*, p. 213, 1981

Mister Brown; Mr Brown noun
the passive male in homosexual anal sex *US*, 1950
- — Hyman E. Goldin et al., *Dictionary of American Underworld Lingo*, p. 35, 1950

Mister Charles; Mr. Charles noun
a white man *US*, 1970
- But black separatists have gone one step further, and would insist that "Mr. Charles" is even more appropriate[.] — Roger Abrahams, *Positively Black*, p. 32, 1970
- Mister Charles was going about his nocturnal business[.] — Cherokee Paul McDonald, *Into the Green*, p. 78, 2001

Mister Charlie; Mr Charlie noun
a white man *US*, 1928
A piece of slang used as a gesture of resistance by US black people.
- He talks about Mister Charlie, and he says he's with us—us kids—but he ain't going to do nothing to offend him. — James Baldwin, *Blues for Mister Charlie*, p. 40, 1964
- Goldberg's just as bad as Mr. Charlie. — Claude Brown, *Manchild in the Promised Land*, p. 295, 1965
- "Mr. Charlie, Mr. Charlie. Who the fuck is he?" "That's the name Brew calls the paddies." — Piri Thomas, *Down These Mean Streets*, p. 144, 1967
- Whenever some nigga brings in some money from Mister Charlie, all the other niggas want a piece. — Christina and Richard Milner, *Black Players*, p. 129, 1972

Mister Clean; Mr Clean; Miss Clean noun
a person in the public eye who maintains an image that is beyond reproach *US*, 1974
- Egil Krogh was the White House Mr. Clean, so straight an arrow that his friends mockingly called him "Evil Krogh." — Carl Bernstein and Bob Woodward, *All the President's Men*, p. 257, 1974
- The C.E.O. of a nonpublic Wall Street competitor sarcastically remarked that Buffet "came in as Mr. Clean, the open-eyed boy from Omaha." — Roger Lowenstein, *Buffet*, pp. 403–404, 1995

Mister Dictionary has deserted us yet again
used as a humorous comment on profanity *UK*, 1994
Popularized and varied in the US by ESPN's Keith Olberman.
- — Keith Olberman and Dan Patrick, *The Big Show*, pp. 20–21, 1997

Mister Five by Five noun
a short, heavy man *US*, 1942

- Chuck is five feet tall and five feet broad, a traditional Mr. Five-by-Five. — JoAnna Carl, *The Chocolate Puppy Puzzle*, p. 71, 2004

Mister Green; Mr Green noun
money *US*, 1973
- "Unless you're ready with the only kind of loving the pimp knows." "What's that?" "Mr. Green." — Gail Sheehy, *Hustling*, p. 49, 1973

Mister Happy; Mr Happy noun
the penis *US*, 1984
- — Connie Eble (Editor), *UNC-CH Campus Slang*, p. 6, Fall 1987
- He was wearing a black mask and black socks and his Mr. Happy hung almost to his knees. He looked like he'd been sired by Thunder the Wonder Horse. — Janet Evanovich, *Three to Get Deadly*, p. 74, 1988
- But don't concentrate on your genitals; you already know how sensitive Mr. Happy is. — K. Winston Caine, *The Male Body*, p. 180, 1996

Mister Hawkins; Mr Hawkins noun
a cold winter wind *US*, 1970
An embellishment and personification of **HAWK**.
- — Clarence Major, *Dictionary of Afro-American Slang*, p. 83, 1970

Mister Jones; Mr Jones noun
used as a personification of the dominant white culture *US*, 1971
- — Eugene Landy, *The Underground Dictionary*, p. 133, 1971

Mister Money; Mr Money noun
a Jewish person *US*, 1980
- — Edith A. Folb, *runnin' down some lines*, p. 247, 1980

Mister Nasty; Mr Nasty noun
the penis *US*, 2001
- A while back, after a short consultation with his johnson [penis], Vinnie agreed to hire Joyce [...] Mr. Nasty was still happy with the decision, but the rest of Vinnie didn't know what to do with Joyce. — Janet Evanovich, *Seven Up*, p. 37, 2001

Mister Nice Guy noun
a man who is nice to a fault *US*, 1966
- I'm finished being Mr. Nice Guy. — Mel Celbulash, *The Love Bug*, p. 113, 1970
- His sense of humor reinforced his Mr. Nice Guy image even when his administration was declaring ketchup a vegetable in school lunch programs and violating congressional mandates about selling arms to Iran. — Helen Thomas, *Thanks for the Memories, Mr. President*, p. 127, 2002

Mister Period; Mr Period noun
used of a personification of the fact that a woman has missed her normal menstrual period *US*, 1980
- — *Maledicta*, p. 242, Winter 1980: "'Lovely, blooming, fresh and gay': the onomastics of camp"

Mister Sin; Mr Sin noun
a police officer assigned to the vice squad *US*, 1980
- — Edith A. Folb, *runnin' down some lines*, p. 247, 1980

Mister Softy; Mr Softy noun
a flaccid penis *US*, 1995
- — *Adult Video News*, p. 38, September 1995

Mister Speaker; Mr Speaker noun
a handgun *US*, 1945
- — Lou Shelly, *Hepcats Jive Talk Dictionary*, p. 29, 1945

Mister Twenty-six; Mr Twenty-six noun
a hypodermic needle *US*, 1973
- — David Maurer and Victor Vogel, *Narcotics and Narcotic Addiction*, p. 427, 1973

mistress noun
in a sadomasochistic relationship, a woman who inflicts many forms of humiliation, including extreme pain and public displays of submission *US*, 1975
- The idea of a "mistress" or "master" taking over one's life, like the idea of a "slave" catering to one's every whim, has its appeal. — Stephen Lewis, *The Whole Bedroom Catalog*, p. 129, 1975

mit noun
a handle *US*, 1972
- That puts pressure on the mid [handle]. — Harry King, *Box Man*, p. 34, 1972

mites and lice *noun*

in poker, a hand with a pair of threes and a pair of twos *US,*
1967

- — Albert H. Morehead, *The Complete Guide to Winning Poker*, p. 268, 1967

mitt *noun*

1 the hand *US, 1893*

- Some day, before long, I'm going to have my rod in my mitt and the killer in front of me. — Mickey Spillane, *I, The Jury*, p. 7, 1947
- The Pachuco shivs Mace while the big stoop stands there all goofed off with a rod in his mitt. — Thurston Scott, *Cure it with Honey*, p. 160, 1951
- You're very fast with your mitts, Collie. — Jim Thompson, *After Dark, My Sweet*, p. 10, 1955
- He said, "All right, Kid, keep that 'sizzle' [drug] in your mitt, so you can down it in a hurry." — Iceberg Slim (Robert Beck), *Pimp*, p. 135, 1969

2 in poker or other card games, a hand of cards *US, 1896*

- — John Scarne, *Scarne's Guide to Modern Poker*, p. 284, 1979

mitt *verb*

to grab, to seize *US, 1915*

- The judge took one look at him that day in police court and decided that no such demure youth could have "mitted" twenty dollars from the grocer's cash drawer, then shortchanged him with his own money. — Jim Thompson, *Bad Boy*, p. 352, 1953

mitt camp *noun*

a fortune-telling booth in a carnival *US, 1980*

- — Joe McKennon, *Circus Lingo*, p. 62, 1980
- Although some MITT CAMPS stick to a simple Fortune, others are as deadly as any rigged game. — Gene Sorrows, *All About Carnivals*, p. 22, 1985

mitten money *noun*

extra money, either in the form of a tip or a bribe *US, 1975*
From the practice of sea-going pilots charging an extra fee for winter work.

- — John Gould, *Maine Lingo*, p. 182, 1975

mitt man *noun*

in gambling, a cheat who switches cards *US, 1997*

- Besides dice tats and 7UPS, there were volumes for nail nickers and crimpers (card markers), hand muckers and mit men (card switch-ers), as well as card counters and shiner players. — Stephen Cannell, *Big Con*, p. 143, 1997

mitt reader *noun*

a fortune reader who reads palms *US, 1928*

- — Don Wilmeth, *The Language of American Popular Entertainment*, p. 174, 1981
- "You ever hear of a mitt-reader calls herself Madame Miseria?" — Joe Gores, *32 Cadillacs*, p. 221, 1992

mix *noun*

an adulterant or dilutant *US, 1977*

- Eventually, I could taste different drugs and tell how much mix in it or if there's too much mix in it or what have you. — John Allen, *Assault with a Deadly Weapon*, p. 160, 1977

▸ **in the mix**

involved with criminal or drug activity *US, 1995*

- — Bill Valentine, *Gang Intelligence Manual*, p. 77, 1995: "Black Street Gang Terminology"
- Casper's in the mix. — *Kids*, 1995
- His mother is back in the mix and he's free to do what he wants. — David Simon and Edward Burns, *The Corner*, p. 512, 1997
- "Kinda old to be up the mix, dawg, know what I'm sayin'?" — Jimmy Lerner, *You Got Nothing Coming*, p. 54, 2002

mix *verb*

to fight *US, 1895*

- We're gonna mix with the PRs. — Stephen Sondheim, *West Side Story*, 1957

mix and match *noun*

attending multiple colleges in search of a degree *US, 2006*

- Officials call it swirling, mix and match, grab and go. Today's students attend two colleges, three colleges, even four. — *New York Times*, p. A1, 22nd April 2006

mixer *noun*

a woman who works in a bar, encouraging customers through flirtation to buy drinks, both for themselves and for her *US, 1950*

- — Jack Lait and Lee Mortimer, *Chicago Confidential*, p. 302, 1950: "Loop lexicon"

mixmaster *noun*

a dance music disc jockey *US, 1995*
With variant form "mixmeister."

- The Mystro, aka Sean Mather, aka a rising young producer with his first gold record on the wall and ambitions for many more, is currently the first-string varsity mixmeister for WPGC. — *Washington Post*, p. R6, 14th September 1995

mixologist *noun*

a bartender *US, 1950*

- — Jack Lait and Lee Mortimer, *Chicago Confidential*, p. 302, 1950: "Loop lexicon"

miz!

that's too bad! *US, 1997*
An abbreviation of "miserable."

- — Pamela Munro, *U.C.L.A. Slang*, p. 90, 1997

mo *noun*

1 in a prison, a prisoner subject to mental observation *US, 2000*

- — *Village Voice*, p. 68, 19th December 2000

2 a month *US, 1928*

- "How long a trip?" Carter asked. "Six moes." — George Mandel, *Flee the Angry Strangers*, p. 89, 1952

3 a homosexual *US, 1968*

- — Kevin Dilallo, *The Unofficial Gay Manual*, p. 242, 1994
- You also might want to make it clear that the Federal Wildlife Marshal's Office is also pro-'mo as well. — Kevin Smith, *Jay and Silent Bob Strike Back*, p. 79, 2001

MO *noun*

a criminal's method of operating *US, 1954*
From the Latin *modus operandi*.

- — Evan Hunter, *The Blackboard Jungle*, p. 160, 1954
- I dig your MO, West, and here's what you are, man, here's just what you are. — Evan Hunter, *The Blackboard Jungle*, p. 160, 1954
- The MO was simple. We'd spend the summer on research trips. — Val McDermid, *Keeping on the Right Side of the Law*, p. 180, 1999

mob *noun*

1 a group of friends *US, 1939*

- He introduced me to his mob, lying around of the beach, some of whom were unfriendly[.] — Clancy Sigal, *Going Away*, p. 132, 1961

2 in circus and carnival usage, the men employed by the show as a group *US, 1981*

- — Don Wilmeth, *The Language of American Popular Entertainment*, p. 175, 1981

▸ **the Mob**

organized crime; the Mafia *US, 1969*

- Her father drives a taxi during the day, and a car for The Mob at night. — Philip Roth, *Portnoy's Complaint*, p. 187, 1969
- I hooked up with a fellow named Art who was right with many of the Italian mob. — A.S. Jackson, *Gentleman Pimp*, p. 102, 1973
- The mob made their thrust into Times Square porn shops in 1968. — Josh Alan Friedman, *Tales of Times Square*, p. 75, 1986
- Those fucking mob assholes. — *The Bad Lieutenant*, 1992

mob *verb*

1 to idle, to relax with friends *US, 1995*

- — Bill Valentine, *Gang Intelligence Manual*, p. 77, 1995: "Black street gang terminology"

2 to surround, yell at and assault *US, 1998*

- — *Columbia Missourian*, p. 1A, 19th October 1998

MOB

money over bitches *US, 1998*

- — Ethan Hilderbrant, *Prison Slang*, p. 157, 1998

mobbed up *adjective*

associated with organized crime *US, 1973*

- He was mobbed up with the Pleasant Avenue outfit. — Edwin Torres, *Carlito's Way*, p. 21, 1975
- They liked to pretend they were "mobbed up"—associated with big city organized crime. — Kim Rich, *Johnny's Girl*, p. 62, 1993

mobbie *noun*

a member of an organized crime organization *US, 1994*

- She happened to know after she had done some checking around that The Plumber was a mobbie. — Richard Condon, *Prizzi's Money*, p. 91, 1994

Mobe *noun*
the Student Mobilization Committee Against the War in Vietnam (SMC), the most powerful and visible antiwar group in the US in the late 1960s and early 70s *US, 1970*
- At the convention, the "Mobe" people wanted large, disciplined demonstrations focusing on the war and racism. — J. Anthony Lukas, *The Barnyard Epithet and Other Obscenities*, p. 33, 1970

mobile *adjective*
sexually attractive *US, 1993*
- — *People Magazine*, p. 73, 19th July 1993

moby *adjective*
enormous *US, 1965*
A term brought into the world of computer programming from the model railroad club at MIT.
- — Guy L. Steele, "Computer Slang", *Coevolution Quarterly*, p. 31, Spring 1981
- "Some MIT undergrads pulled off a moby hack at the Harvard-Yale game." — Guy L. Steele et al., *The Hacker's Dictionary*, p. 94, 1983

moby bloat; moby; the mobies *noun*
a bloated feeling *US, 1971*
- MOBY BLOAT: very full feeling — Robert Buckhout, *Toward Social Change*, p. 464, 1971

mocktail *noun*
a nonalcoholic version of a cocktail *US, 1982*
- We took our turns standing at the darkened window swirling a mocktail and pretending to be mesmerized by the glittering lights of North Hills. — David Sedaris, *Naked*, p. 33, 1997

mocky; mockie *noun*
a Jewish person *US, 1893*
- Tell me, Dadier, what do you think of kikes and mockies and micks and donkeys and frogs and niggers, Dadier. — Evan Hunter, *The Blackboard Jungle*, p. 209, 1954
- One in a while you hear, "You mockie bastard!" — Lenny Bruce, *The Essential Lenny Bruce*, p. 35, 1967
- You got it all over everything, you mocky son of a bitch! — Philip Roth, *Portnoy's Complaint*, p. 203, 1969
- No one seems to know where mockie comes from. I never heard mockie until I came to New York[.] — Leo Rosten, *The Joys of Yinglish*, p. 344, 1989

moco rag *noun*
a handkerchief or bandana *US, 2000*
Moco is Spanish for mucus or **SNOT**.
- They refer to the bandana as a "moco" rag. — Robert Jackson and Wesley McBride, *Understanding Street Gangs*, p. 34, 2000

mod *noun*
1 in computing, a modification *US, 1991*
- — Eric S. Raymond, *The New Hacker's Dictionary*, p. 245, 1991
2 a modification of a video game *US, 2002*
- Meanwhile, as mods helped drive ongoing sales of "Doom," id developers were noticing how good those mods could be. — Wagner James Au, *Salon.com*, 16th April 2002
3 a percent sign (%) on a computer keyboard *US, 1991*
- — Eric S. Raymond, *The New Hacker's Dictionary*, p. 39, 1991

modder *noun*
a person who modifies video games *US, 2002*
- Or, in modder jargon, it's a "total conversion." — Wagner James Au, *Salon.com*, 16th April 2002
- After plugging the chip into a console, a modder has to delve into the game's program code to make changes, which are then often shared with others online. — *Baltimore Sun*, p. 1C, 25th July 2005

mode *verb*
to show disrespect; to exploit *US, 2001*
- — Rick Ayers (Editor), *Slang Dictionary*, p. 12, 2001

modern married *noun*
a couple that engages in spouse swapping *US, 1964*
- And for "modern marrieds" (their advertised title) it still characterizes those in the forefront of changing sexual attitudes. — William and Jerrye Breedlove, *Swap Clubs*, p. 36, 1964

mod squad *noun*
any group of black and white people *US, 1971*

An allusion to a US television series (1968–73) that featured three hipper-than-hip juvenile delinquents turned police—Julie, Linc and Pete, one black, one white and one blonde.
- — Eugene Landy, *The Underground Dictionary*, p. 134, 1971

mofo *noun*
motherfucker *US, 1965*
- — Connie Eble (Editor), *UNC-CH Campus Slang*, p. 5, Fall 1997
- These mofos [Abramoff's client] are the stupidest idiots in the land. — Al Franken, *The Truth With Jokes*, p. 128, 2005: Jack Abramoff e-mail to Mike Scanlon 4/11/02

mofuck *adjective*
used for intensifying *US, 1962*
An offspring of **MOTHERFUCKING**.
- "This mofuck division fucked up." — John Del Vecchio, *The 13th Valley*, p. 477, 1982

mo-gas *noun*
gasoline fuel used for ground vehicles *US, 1977*
Vietnam war usage.
- Our bellies bloated with water from the mechanics' Lister bag and streaked with grit and sweat, stinking of the road and grease and mo-gas. — Larry Heinemann, *Close Quarters*, p. 101, 1977

mohasky *noun*
marijuana *US, 1938*
Variants include "mohaska," "mohasty" and "mohansky."
- — Kenn "Naz" Young, *Naz's Underground Dictionary*, p. 46, 1973
- — Richard A. Spears, *The Slang and Jargon of Drugs and Drink*, p. 342, 1986

mojo *noun*
1 a spell, magic *US, 1926*
- "Does this mean that number sixteen, the hole I just bet Lard Ass Louis Huckle five thousand dollars on, has a mojo on it?" "That be the correct terminology, Balls." — Jimmy Buffett, *Tales from Margaritaville*, p. 120, 1989
2 hard drugs, especially powdered drugs: cocaine, heroin, morphine *US, 1935*
From the sense "a kind of magic"; first recorded in this sense as "morphine."
- — Haldeen Braddy, *American Speech*, p. 87, May 1955: "Narcotic argot along the Mexican Border"
3 sexuality, libido, sexual attraction *US, 1999*
The song "Got My Mojo Working" was sung on stage by Ann Cole in 1956—the lyric continues: "but it just won't work on you." In 1971, The Doors released a song entitled "Mr Mojo Risin"; the title serves as an anagram for the singer Jim Morrison and as an advertisement for his dangerous sexuality. This meaning, however, was not widely appreciated before the second *Austin Powers* film opened in 1999, but it caught on quickly thereafter.
- The mojo is the life force, the essence, the libido, the "right stuff." — *Austin Powers*, 1999
- Felix Carter has worked his mojo on a weak-at-the-knees makeup girl and the day is over. — Andrew Holmes, *Sleb*, p. 104, 2002
4 an early version of the telecopier machine *US, 1972*
Very slow, very cumbersome, but for its day a great advance, almost "magical," hence the term. Popularized by Hunter S. Thompson's writings.
- I can hear the Mojo Wire humming frantically across the room. [Tim] Crouse is stuffing page after page of gibberish into it. — Hunter S. Thompson, *Fear and Loathing in America*, p. 478, April 1972: Letter to Jan Wenner
- He installed an electric telecopier in his Palm Spring digs and, when Thompson expressed wonder at the "mojo wire," provided one for him as well. — Robert Anson, *Gone Crazy and Back Again*, p. 283, 1981

mojo juice *noun*
liquid dolophine, a drug commonly known as methadone, used for the rehabilitation of heroin addicts *US, 1987*
- Mrs. Toto at the door gives me a polite shove and tells me I can start tomorrow morning on the mojo juice. — Jim Carroll, *Forced Entries*, p. 116, 1987

moke *noun*
a dolt *UK, 1855*
From an earlier sense meaning a donkey.
- "Has that moke got the fever!" — Leo Rosten, *Silky!*, p. 100, 1979

mokus *adjective*
craving a drink *US, 1960*
- [P]imply kids with electric noserings, denial-ridden housewives and etc., all jonesing and head-gaming and mokus and grieving and basically whacked out and producing nonstopping output 24 – 7 – 365. — David Foster Wallace, *Infinite Jest*, p. 271, 1996

moldy fig *noun*
a very dull person; specifically, used by young supporters of modern jazz of any jazz aficionado who remains loyal to a traditional form *US, 1945*
- — Robert George Reisner, *The Jazz Titans*, p. 161, 1960

moldy oldie *noun*
a song from the past, especially one that does not survive the test of time well *US, 1979*
- "Oh, Mr. Wilson had us playing some moldie oldie for over half the hour." — Malcolm Braly, *The Protector*, p. 11, 1979

mole hole *noun*
the underground barracks where air attack alert crews live *US, 1963*
- — *American Speech*, p. 119, May 1963: "Air refueling words"

moll-buzzer *noun*
a thief who specializes in snatching handbags from women with children in baby carriages or strollers *US, 1859*
- "If you ain't here for jackrollin' it must be for strong-arm robb'ry—'r you one of them Chicago Av'noo moll-buzzers?" — Nelson Algren, *The Neon Wilderness*, p. 56, 1960

molly *noun*
any central nervous system stimulant *US, 1976*
- — Elementary Electronics, *Dictionary of CB Lingo*, p. 87, 1976

mollycoddle *noun*
an effeminate man, especially an effeminate homosexual man *UK, 1833*
- There were no real two-fisted drinkers any more—only molly-coddles who sipped half-heartedly at their drinks and then went on about their business. — Jim Thompson, *Bad Boy*, p. 302, 1953
- You think religion is for suckers and easy marks and mollycoddles, huh? — *Elmer Gantry*, 1960

Molly Putz *noun*
a notional foolish and/or clumsy woman *US, 1963*
- "Moose always was a fine fielder but he looked like Molly Putz for a few games." — *Washington Post*, p. D3, 1st May 1963

mom *noun*
the "feminine" or "passive" member of a lesbian relationship *US, 1957*
- — John M. Murtagh and Sara Harris, *Cast the First Stone*, p. 261, 1957: "Glossary"
- — Robert George Reisner, *The Jazz Titans*, p. 161, 1960

mom-and-pop *adjective*
small-time, small-scale *US, 1943*
From the image of a small grocery store owned and operated by a husband and wife.
- Evelle and the Cashier, a late-middle-aged man (perhaps the proprietor of this small mom-and-pop store) face each other across the check-out counter. — *Raising Arizona*, 1987
- You run a mom and pop arms smuggling ring. — Mike Judge and Joe Stillman, *Beavis and Butt-Head Do America*, p. 35, 1997

momgram *noun*
the postcard that many US Marine recruits sent home upon arriving at basic training in Parris Island, South Carolina *US, 1987*
- — Daniel Da Cruz, *Boot*, p. 295, 1987

momma-hopper *noun*
used as a euphemism for "motherfucker" *US, 1977*
- — *Maledicta*, p. 11, Summer 1977: "A word for it!"

mommy-o *noun*
used as a term of address for a woman *US, 1955*
Far rarer than **DADDY-O**.
- "Mommy-o," said Goldie, heading for the yard, "dis is de place!" — Steve Allen, *Bop Fables*, p. 4, 1955

momo *noun*
an idiot *US, 1960*

- Frank hit him in the head with a cueball, shrieking, Looka this fuckin' momo! — Gilbert Sorrentino, *Steelwork*, p. 63, 1970

moms *noun*
a mother *US, 1965*
- My moms couldn't sleep; there were four of us our there for her to worry about. — Claude Brown, *Manchild in the Promised Land*, p. 258, 1965
- My moms and pops always wanted Hector and me to go to college[.] — Terry Williams, *The Cocaine Kids*, p. 74, 1989
- I'm glad my moms ain't like your moms. My moms lets me do whatever I want, when I want. — *Mo' B etter Blues*, 1990
- Yo pale muthfucka, don't play with me, 'cause I ain't your moms. — *New Jack City*, 1990

momzer; momser *noun*
a bastard; a brute; a detestable man *US, 1947*
From the Hebrew for "bastard."
- "Momser," his mother said bitterly, "you had to be a regular actor, a comedian." — Irving Shulman, *The Amboy Dukes*, p. 90, 1947
- I'll work on the momser. — Clancy Sigal, *Going Away*, p. 17, 1961
- "The momsers serve him a paper to bring the books, lists of clients, contracts." — Stephen Longstreet, *The Flesh Peddlers*, p. 161, 1962
- Joe Licamarito, Marxie's boss, was furious that the momser thought he could get away with such a ripoff[.] — Richard Condon, *Prizzi's Honor*, pp. 113 – 114, 1982

Mon *nickname*
the Monongahela River *US, 1982*
- — Sam McCool, *Pittsburghese*, p. 25, 1982

monarch *noun*
in a deck of playing cards, a king *US, 1988*
- — George Percy, *The Language of Poker*, p. 58, 1988

Monday morning quarterback *noun*
a self-styled expert who from the safety of distance knows exactly what should have been done in a given situation in which he was not a participant *US, 1950*
- We are a race of grandstand managers, Monday morning quarterbacks and chronic, incurable kibitzers. — Robert Sylvester, *No Cover Charge*, p. 192, 1956

Monday night at the movies *noun*
used for describing the vivid dreams experienced by some US soldiers in Afghanistan after taking their weekly anti-malarial medication Lariam on Mondays *US, 2002*
- Several soldiers deployed to Afghanistan joked to UPI reporters that the night they take the once-a-week pill has been dubbed "Monday Night at the movies" because of the vivid dreams it often causes. — *United Press International*, 29th August 2002

Monday pill *noun*
the large, orange antimalarial pill (chloroquine-primaquine) taken once a week by US troops in Vietnam *US, 1990*
- — Gregory Clark, *Words of the Vietnam War*, p. 100, 1990

mondo *adjective*
large *US, 1982*
- Therein, instead of yelling "I love mondo hooters," they can yell "I love 44 DDs" or "I want a 34B." — Nancy Tamosaitis, *net.sex*, p. 85, 1995

mondo *adverb*
very *US, 1968*
- "Mondo gross!" said Ric. — Jess Mowry, *Way Past Cool*, p. 10, 1992
- The boys are back with something quite unnatural / Mondo weird. — Children on Stun, *Mondo Weird*, 1997

money *noun*
1 a close friend or trusted colleague *US, 1992*
- — William K. Bentley and James M. Corbett, *Prison Slang*, p. 50, 1992
- — Rick Ayers (Editor), *Berkeley High Slang Dictionary*, p. 31, 2004

2 in prison, anything of value in trade *US, 1976*
- — John R. Armore and Joseph D. Wolfe, *Dictionary of Desperation*, p. 40, 1976

▸ **in the money**
in horseracing, finishing first, second or third in a race *US, 1964*
- — Nate Perlmutter, *How to Win Money at the Races*, p. 120, 1964

▸ **money talks and bullshit walks**
used as a humorous suggestion that talk is cheap *US, 1984*

- Money talks and bullshit walks and if the first album was a hit then we could have pressed on them, then we could have told them yes. — *This is Spinal Tap*, 1984

money ball *noun*

in pool, a shot that if made will win a wager *US, 1990*
- — Steve Rushin, *Pool Cool*, p. 21, 1990

money from home *noun*

any money won easily, betting *US, 1951*
- — David W. Maurer, *Argot of the Racetrack*, p. 42, 1951

money-getter *noun*

the vagina *US, 1973*
- But if it was all her thing, she really had a money getter. — A.S. Jackson, *Gentleman Pimp*, p. 15, 1973

money in the bank and cattle in the hills *noun*

independently wealthy *US, 1954*
- — Jerry Robertson, *Oil Slanguage*, p. 60, 1954

moneymaker *noun*

1 the genitals; the buttocks *UK, 1896*
- Shuck my clothes an hop in that fabbroom, take a fullout shower, wash the jail off my skin an the funk outa my moneymaker. — Robert Gover, *JC Saves*, p. 78, 1968
- [P]unch him in the cocksucker and land him on his moneymaker. — *Maledicta*, p. 253, 1979

2 a success *US, 1899*
- The play had been a moneymaker for us when I had Puddin' Patterson to block for me. — Dan Jenkins, *Life Its Ownself*, p. 33, 1982

money rider *noun*

in horseracing, a winning jockey *US, 1951*
- — David W. Maurer, *Argot of the Racetrack*, p. 43, 1951

money shot *noun*

a scene in a pornographic film or photograph of a man ejaculating outside his partner *US, 1977*
Perhaps because it is the one shot that justifies the cost of the scene.
- This shot is known as the "come shot." On a porno-movie set it is also referred to as the "money shot." — Stephen Ziplow, *The Film Maker's Guide to Pornography*, p. 78, 1977
- Mark examines the flashlight he and Butch will use to distinguish each orgasm in the barely lit room, when Lev does his "money shot." — Josh Alan Friedman, *Tales of Times Square*, p. 105, 1986
- For one thing, although male actors must reach a climax, known as the "money shot," women can, and usually do, fake orgasms. — *Los Angeles Times*, p. 8, 17th February 1991
- Most spectacularly, it revolutionizes the money shot by having Cy and various stunt cocks rain male and female cum juice on girls simultaneously. — Editors of Adult Video News, *The AVN Guide to the 500 Greatest Adult Films of All Time*, p. 84, 2005

mongee *noun*

a good student who is socially inept *US, 1961*
School usage.
- — *Washington Post*, 23rd April 1961: "Man, dig this jazz"

mongo *noun*

1 scavenged material; a scavenger *US, 1984*
- The fact that he also collects mongo took me as long to find out as it did to get some answers out of the DSNY. — Ted Botha, *Mongo: Adventures in Trash*, p. 21, 1984

2 an idiot *US, 1975*
Abbreviated from the offensive usage of "mongoloid" (affected with Down's syndrome); probably used without thinking.
- [T]he mongos blowing the shit out of the Middle East. — Frank Zappa, *The Real Frank Zappa Book*, p. 293, 1989

mongo *adjective*

very large *US, 1985*
- — Connie Eble (Editor), *UNC-CH Campus Slang*, p. 7, Fall 1985
- — Judi Sanders, *Don't Dog by Do, Dude!*, p. 21, 1991
- I mean, I notice when they're dressed well or when they're fat or ugly or have mongo bazooms. — Rita Ciresi, *Pink Slip*, p. 52, 1999

Mongolian clusterfuck *noun*

an orgy *UK, 1974*
- I'm startin' to feel like the bottom man in a Mongolian cluster fuck. — James Ellroy, *Suicide Hill*, p. 699, 1986

moniker; monicker *noun*

1 a nickname or sobriquet *UK, 1851*
- From this trick he got this moniker. — William Burroughs, *Junkie*, p. 43, 1953
- True monicker was Early Gibson but he was called Early Riser. — Chester Himes, *Cotton Comes to Harlem*, p. 31, 1965
- Kid, you've outgrown "Young Blood" as a monicker. How about "Iceberg Slim?" — Iceberg Slim (Robert Beck), *Pimp*, p. 221, 1969
- They called her "Anne of a Thousand Names." That's the moniker her fellow detectives hung on her because during her police-department career she'd been Anne Zorn, Anne Barlett, Anne Sullivan, Anne Minskey, and now Anne Zorn again. — Joseph Wambaugh, *Floaters*, p. 133, 1996

2 the mark that identifies dice as being from a given casino or gambling house *US, 1950*
- — *The Annals of the American Academy of Political and Social Sciences*, p. 128, May 1950

moniker file *noun*

a list of street names or aliases maintained by the police *US, 1981*
- The field interrogation cards and moniker file had already been checked by Al Mackey and Martin Welborn for the nickname Mr. Wheels. — Joseph Wambaugh, *The Glitter Dome*, p. 123, 1981
- [T]he "monicker" files on "Bird" and "Birdy" had yielded only the names of a dozen ghetto blacks. — James Ellroy, *Blood on the Moon*, p. 192, 1984
- So what do you want to do? Go down, check the moniker file? — Richard Price, *Clockers*, p. 39, 1992

monkey *noun*

1 an addiction, especially to heroin or another drug *US, 1949*
- He'd taken the sweat cure in a little Milwaukee Avenue hotel room cutting himself down, as he put it, "from monkey to zero." — Nelson Algren, *The Man with the Golden Arm*, p. 59, 1949
- Aside from the monkey, I got room rent and meals and all that stuff to take care of. — Clarence Cooper Jr., *The Scene*, p. 67, 1960
- The only way anyone can help me is that they give me some money to get some shit and get that monkey off my back. — Claude Brown, *Manchild in the Promised Land*, p. 195, 1965
- Hitched a ride on a monkey's back / Headed west into the black. — Dada, *Dizz Knee Land*, 1992

2 in circus and carnival usage, a gullible customer who has been swindled *US, 1922*
- — Don Wilmeth, *The Language of American Popular Entertainment*, p. 175, 1981

3 a gambler who complains to the police about an illegal gambling operation after losing *US, 1950*
- — *The Annals of the American Academy of Political and Social Sciences*, p. 128, May 1950

4 a band leader *US, 1942*
A reference to the tuxedo, or **MONKEY SUIT**, worn by many band leaders.
- — Robert S. Gold, *A Jazz Lexicon*, p. 207, 1964

5 a poor poker player *US, 1988*
- — George Percy, *The Language of Poker*, p. 58, 1988

6 your boyfriend's or girlfriend's "other" person *US, 1989*
- — Pamela Munro, *U.C.L.A. Slang*, p. 59, 1989

7 the vagina *US, 1888*
- — Charles Shafer, *Folk Speech in Texas Prisons*, p. 210, 1990
- — Judi Sanders, *Da Bomb*, p. 11, 1997

8 in horseracing, a $100 bet *US, 1951*
- — David W. Maurer, *Argot of the Racetrack*, p. 43, 1951

9 in card games, a face card *US, 1985*
- — Steve Kuriscak, *Casino Talk*, p. 38, 1985

monkey *verb*

to fiddle, to tamper, to fool around with *US, 1876*
- You haven't monkeyed with his car there, have ya? — *Fargo*, 1996

monkeybars *noun*

jail *US, 1973*
- Win was broke, headed once again for the monkeybars. — Joe Eszterhas, *Charlie Simpson's Apocalypse*, p. 116, 1973

monkey bite *noun*

1 a bruise on the skin produced by a suction kiss *US, 1942*
- — Eugene Landy, *The Underground Dictionary*, p. 103, 1971
- Rule number two: no monkey bites, no hickeys—in fact no leavin' no marks of no kind. — *Kill Bill*, 2003

2 a painful pinch *US, 1997*

- The monkey bite—the most painful pinch in the history of the time. — Editors of Ben is Dead, *Retrohell*, p. 91, 1997

monkey boots *noun*

a heavy work shoe embraced as a fashion statement by punks and post-punks *US, 1997*

- Other acceptable alterna-shoes you could own were: monkey boots[.] — Editors of Ben is Dead, *Retrohell*, p. 60, 1997

monkey business *noun*

mischief; foolishness *US, 1883*

The term is powerfully etched in American culture because of revelations in 1987 that Gary Hart, then a married US Senator campaigning for the presidential nomination, had taken an overnight cruise to Bimini with a stunningly attractive woman, Donna Rice, on the aptly named yacht "Monkey Business." Hart withdrew from the race under attack as an adulterer.

- And I guarantee I know how to take care of any you guys who feel like a little monkey business[.] — Evan Hunter, *The Blackboard Jungle*, p. 34, 1954
- Any monkey business is ill-advised. — *The Breakfast Club*, 1985

monkey-chaser *noun*

an immigrant from the West Indies *US, 1924*

- "It was started by that great leader, Ras the Destroyer!" "That monkey-chaser?" somebody said. — Ralph Ellison, *Invisible Man*, p. 527, 1952
- There was antagonism from native-born blacks, who sang the rhyme: "When a monkey-chaser dies / Don't need no undertaker / Just throw him in de Harlem River / He'll float back to Jamaica." — Paul Johnson, *A History of the American People*, pp. 664–665, 1997

monkey-drill *noun*

physical exercises *US, 1895*

- But that week, while participating in the "monkey drill" in the riding hall—leaping off and back onto a galloping horse—his knee crumbled when he hit the ground. — Stephen Ambrose, *Eisenhower*, p. 11, 1990

monkey dust *noun*

phencyclidine, the recreational drug known as PCP or angel dust *US, 1981*

- — Ronald Linder, *PCP*, p. 9, 1981
- — US Department of Justice, *Street Terms*, October 1994

monkey flush *noun*

in poker, three cards of the same suit, unpaired and without value *US, 1963*

- — Irwin Steig, *Common Sense in Poker*, p. 185, 1963

monkey jacket *noun*

a men's formal dress jacket *US, 1851*

- I was beginning to think my bag with its elegant wardrobe, its Hermes neckties, its old chaser's monkey-jackets, and so forth was lost[.] — Saul Bellow, *Humboldt's Gift*, p. 406, 1975

monkey-on-a-stick *adjective*

a style of horseracing using short stirrups *US, 1949*

Popularized by jockey Ted Sloan (1874–1933), whose abnormally short legs made the style—widely used today—a necessary innovation.

- It was not all the "monkey-on-a-stick" type of riding that made the American jockey, Ted Sloan, so successful in England. — *San Francisco Examiner*, p. 17, 28th June 1949
- Tom Ainslie, *Ainslie's Complete Guide to Thoroughbred Racing*, p. 334, 1976

monkey on your back; monkey *noun*

an addiction to drugs, especially heroin *US, 1959*

A tenacious monkey is hard to shake off.

- [A] certain down-at-heel vet growing stooped from carrying a thirty-five-pound monkey on his back. — Nelson Algren, *The Man With The Golden Arm [The Howard Marks Book of Dope Stories]*, p. 43, 1949
- And gave him all the confidence he lacked / With a Purple Heart and a monkey on his back[.] — John Prine, *Sam Stone*, 1971

monkey rum *noun*

illegally manufactured alcohol colored by molasses *US, 1985*

- Moonshine with molasses is monkey rum. — *Chicago Tribune*, p. C3, 21st August 1985

monkey's fart *noun*

used as a representation of something that is completely worthless *US, 1970*

- "I wasn't there, and I don't care a monkey's fart what that bastard Oc does." — I.J. Parker, *Rashomon Gate*, p. 115, 2002

monkeyshines *noun*

foolish antics, embarrassing behavior *US, 1828*

- — Hermese E. Roberts, *The Third Ear*, 1971
- [Lou Reed] actually managed to lasso a great rock 'n' roll band to back up his monkeyshines? — Lester Bangs, *Psychotic Reactions and Carburetor Dung*, p. 169, 1975

monkey straps *noun*

a harness used by the crew chief and door gunner on a combat helicopter *US, 2002*

- While the pilots conducted a preflight inspection, he provided me a quick refresher on the M-60, basic do's and don'ts, and the use of monkey straps. — Richard Burns, *Pathfinder*, p. 128, 2002

monkey suit *noun*

a formal evening dress suit; a tuxedo *US, 1895*

- They wore monkey suits and on them the term was absolutely descriptive. — Mickey Spillane, *Kiss Me Deadly*, p. 101, 1952
- He also said I wouldn't have to wear the "monkey" suit, just stay sharp and clean. — Babs Gonzales, *I Paid My Dues*, p. 20, 1967
- Look at you in those candy ass monkey suits. — *The Blues Brothers*, 1980

monkey's uncle *noun*

used in nonprofane oaths to register surprise *US, 1926*

- "Jesus Christ in Marlboro Country, but if this here is Cherry then I'm an unkey's monocle." He tried to say it straight, and muffed it again[.] — Lawrence Block, *No Score [The Affairs of Chip Harrison Omnibus]*, p. 113, 1970

Monkey Ward *nickname*

Montgomery Ward, a department store chain *US, 1912*

A play on the sound.

- He was an open apple knocker from the West Side wearing plain Monkey Ward jeans rather than Levi's and high-top horsehide shit kickers. — Earl Thompson, *Tattoo*, p. 55, 1974
- Your little tyke can't possibly network with the right people at pre-K if he's wearing a poly-cotton blend from Monkey Ward. — *Washington Post*, p. C1, 4th October 1987
- The guy at the Foot Locker said I might find some at Monkey Ward's. — *Rocky Mountain News (Denver, Colorado)*, p. 5A, 9th January 1996
- The execs at Monkey Ward (as it was fondly known in those days) liked the story and printed 2.4 million copies that year. — *Chattanooga (Tennessee) Times Free Press*, p. E6, 11th December 2003

mono *noun*

mononucleosis glandular fever *US, 1960*

- Also, they are pooped. Many have mono. — Glendon Swarthout, *Where the Boys Are*, p. 7, 1960
- "Where's Oeuf, anyway?" "Recuperating from mono in the infirm. There was some rumor about the clap, too." — Richard Farina, *Been Down So Long*, p. 22, 1966
- The girls promised to bring me hot soup and other goodies to get over my mono. — Oscar Zeta Acosta, *The Autobiography of a Brown Buffalo*, p. 39, 1972

monolithic *adjective*

extremely drug-intoxicated *US, 1971*

- — Eugene Landy, *The Underground Dictionary*, p. 134, 1971

mono-rump *noun*

the buttocks formed into a single mass by a garment *US, 1974*

- It was tightly encased in a girdle so it was an unyielding mono-rump, with less fleshy warmth than a medicine ball. — Earl Thompson, *Tattoo*, p. 232, 1974

monster *noun*

1 a formidable piece of equipment *US, 1955*

- Tim Cahalan carried the Monster, a PRC-77. This radio was similar to the 25 except it was also a kryptographer, automatically scrambling or descrambling voice transmissions. — John Del Vecchio, *The 13th Valley*, p. 193, 1982
- Resembling a prehistoric reptile, its two huge General Electric J79 engines bulging its sides, humpbacking its 58-foot fuselage, the "brute," or "monster," as the Phantom was sometimes called, was already the talk of the Navy. — Robert K. Wilcox, *Scream of Eagles*, p. 13, 1990
- It's got four wheel drive, dual side airbags and a monster sound system. — *Clueless*, 1995

2 an immense wave, surfed by a special and small class of
surfers *US, 1987*

- — Mitch McKissick, *Surf Lingo*, 1987

- You ride the monsters, you gotta know you're ridin' a line between
life and death. — *Break Point*, 1991

3 in poker, a great hand or large amount of money bet *US, 1982*

- — David M. Hayano, *Poker Faces*, p. 186, 1982

4 used as a term of endearment *US, 1954*
Teen slang.

- — *Look*, p. 88, 10th August 1954

monster *adjective*

1 large, formidable, impressive *US, 1975*

- And use the monster cable so we don't get any drop-out. — *Airheads*,
1994

2 excellent *US, 1953*
Originally black usage.

- — Lavada Durst, *The Jives of Dr. Hepcat*, p. 13, 1953

monster shot *noun*

in pornography, a close-up shot of genitals *US, 1970*

- Ugly people in harsh, flat lighting, dominated by the same rear
master-shot, or "monster-shot" as Sid kept shouting[.] — Terry
Southern, *Blue Movie*, p. 18, 1970

- And he [Randy] is rock hard. So we go monster shots, the graphic
close-up. — Robert Stoller and I.S. Levine, *Coming Attractions*, p. 86, 1991

Montana maiden *noun*

a ewe *US, 1970s*
Sheep will be sheep and men will be men. Collected from
a former resident of Iowa, March 2001.

Montezuma's revenge *noun*

diarrhea suffered by tourists in Mexico *US, 1960*
Montezuma II (1466–1520), the ninth Aztec emperor of
Mexico, famously died as a result of his confrontation with
Spanish invaders. Former US President Ronald Reagan in 1981
exhibited what commentator David Brinkley referred to as
"excruciatingly bad taste" by telling a joke about Montezuma's
revenge at a state dinner in Mexico City.

- [T]hey admit that, like most Americans, they suffered a three-day
gastric upset described by a variety of names like the Gringo Gallop
and Montezuma's revenge. — *Washington Post, Times Herald*, p. AW8, 24th
January 1960

- And I'm afraid the wife is bringing back Montezuma's revenge.
— Gerald Petievich, *The Quality of the Informant*, p. 167, 1970

- Like a thief, traveler's diarrhea has many aliases. It is euphemisti-
cally known as "Turista," Montezuma's Revenge, "The Aztec Two
Step," "Turkey Trots," and scores more. — *The Patriot Ledger (Quincy,
Massachusetts)*, p. 16, 3rd June 1997

- Children face bigger threat from Montezuma's revenge [headline]
— *San Francisco Chronicle*, p. C8, 18th August 2002

month in Congress *noun*

a period served in solitary confinement *US, 1976*

- — Troy Harris, *A Booklet of Criminal Argot, Cant and Jargon*, p. 19, 1976

monthly bill *noun*

the bleed period of the menstrual cycle *US, 1989*

- — Pamela Munro, *U.C.L.A. Slang*, p. 60, 1989

monthly blues *noun*

the bleed period of the menstrual cycle *US, 1954*

- — *American Speech*, p. 298, December 1954: "The vernacular of menstruation"

monthly visitor *noun*

the bleed period of the menstrual cycle *US, 2001*

- — Don R. McCreary (Editor), *Dawg Speak*, 2001

month of Sundays *noun*

a long time, with time passing slowly *US, 1986*

- It's only just that minute I think maybe that Mary Ellen is more to
me in one night than any other woman's ever been to me in a
month of Sundays. — Robert Campbell, *Junkyard Dog*, p. 56, 1986

moo *noun*

money *US, 1941*

- — Clarence Major, *Dictionary of Afro-American Slang*, p. 82, 1970

mooch *noun*

1 a freeloader *US, 1955*

An abbreviation of **MOOCHER**.

- My introduction to this woman came about through an old English
mooch and drunk. — William Burroughs, *Letters to Allen Ginsberg 1953–1957*,
p. 110, 7th October 1955

2 a person who gives his money to swindlers, a dupe *US, 1927*

- If you get the right rhythm you can work it out even if the mooch
is awake. — William Burroughs, *Junkie*, p. 45, 1953

- — Frank Garcia, *Marked Cards and Loaded Dice*, p. 263, 1962

- Anyone who succumbs to a sales pitch—due to the hot stuff or
a phone call—becomes, in the yaks' slang, a mooch. — Kathleen
Odean, *High Steppers, Fallen Angels, and Lollipops*, p. 132, 1988

- Hey, sweetheart, let me handle my end of it. How I get this mooch
to cooperate is my business. — Stephen Cannell, *King Con*, p. 140, 1997

3 in the car sales business, a customer who thinks that with
arithmetic skills, a calculator, and his sharp mind he can
outsmart the salesman *US, 1975*

- — *American Speech*, p. 312, Autumn–Winter 1975: "The jargon of car salesmen"

- — Kathleen Odean, *High Steppers, Fallen Angels, and Lollipops: Wall Street Slang*,
p. 133, 1988

mooch *verb*

to beg from friends, to sponge *UK, 1857*

- "You still mooching around here?" Dopey said sarcastically.
— James T. Farrell, *Saturday Night*, p. 27, 1947

- Russell and I had already sold all our albums for cash, and after
I ran out of pocket money I went on an orching of mooching.
— Jennifer Blowdryer, *White Trash Debutante*, p. 34, 1997

moocher *noun*

a beggar; one who sponges off others, a freeloader *US, 1851*

- They never had any gum money themselves and were both great
moochers. — Larry McMurtry, *The Last Picture Show*, p. 18, 1966

- I feel like a moocher. I don't have a dime. — Darryl Ponicsan, *The Last
Detail*, p. 104, 1970

- There's more moochers on one corner in downtown San Diego than
in this whole town, I bet. — Joseph Wambaugh, *Finnegan's Week*, p. 55, 1993

- He was a moocher, a card cheat, a country-club golf hustler.
— *Casino*, 1995

moo juice *noun*

milk *US, 1942*

- They kept saying they were going to leave the milkman a note
telling him to nix our moo-juice, but they never did find a pencil
and paper at the same time[.] — Mezz Mezzrow, *Really the Blues*,
p. 122, 1946

- It is ridiculous to hear a child referring to milk as "moo juice[.]"
— *New Idea*, p. 87, 7th October 1989

mook *noun*

an incompetent person who is to be more pitied than
despised *US, 1930*

- I tell these two mooks the whole sordid and silly tale. — Jennifer Lee,
Tarnished Angel, p. 280, 1993

- MARY: He's kind of a mook. MAGDEA: What's a mook. MARY: You
know, a mookalone, a schlep. — *Something About Mary*, 1998

- "Mook" is a male, "Crude, loud, obnoxious and in-your-face."
— *San Francisco Chronicle*, 27th February 2001

moola; moolah; mullah *noun*

money *US, 1939*

- But I'm low in the dough. No moolah, and that's bad. — Hal Ellson,
Duke, p. 3, 1949

- "Don't go spending that moolah you borrowed[.]" — David Gregory,
Flesh Seller, p. 114, 1962

- Barton, of course, was strapped for moolah at the time and could
not share the expense. — Ed Sanders, *Tales of Beatnik Glory*, p. 95, 1975

- I'd love to get our mitts on that moolah!! — Al Franken, *The Truth With
Jokes*, p. 128, 2005: E-mail from Jack Abramoff to Ralph Reed 2/1/02

moon *noun*

1 used as a quaint, indefinite measure of time *US, 1988*

- I've known the sorry-assed shyster for many a moon. — Gerald
Petievich, *Shakedown*, p. 77, 1988

2 a smooth, convex wheel cover *US, 1980*

- — Edith A. Folb, *runnin' down some lines*, p. 247, 1980

3 illegally manufactured alcoholic drink *US, 1928*
An abbreviation of **MOONSHINE**.

- Fellow out in the western part of the state was using it to transport
moon. — George V. Higgins, *The Friends of Eddie Doyle*, p. 11, 1971

• Of course it wasn't aged much, and when I swallowed the raw moon, it made by eyes blink and reamed my throat out like Red Devil Lye. — Guy Owen, *The Flim-Flam Man and the Apprentice Grifter*, p. 41, 1972

moon *verb*

1 to flash your exposed buttocks at someone *US, 1963*
From the venerable sense as "the buttocks."
• — Collin Baker et al., *College Undergraduate Slang Study Conducted at Brown University*, p. 158, 1968
• — *Current Slang*, p. 4, Spring 1968
• Just two weeks ago a whore had dropped her pants and mooned a customer—he wanted to know if she had pimples on her ass—and caused a three-car collision. — Robert Campbell, *Alice in La-La Land*, p. 259, 1987

2 in a split-pot game of poker, to declare or win both high and low *US, 1988*
An abbreviation of "shoot the moon."
• — George Percy, *The Language of Poker*, p. 58, 1988

moonie *noun*

1 a follower of the Rev. Moon *US, 1974*
• Each Moonie must exist for the one goal of converting. — United States Congress, House Committee on International Relations, *Investigation of Korean-American Relations*, p. 1499, 1978
• A thin young Moonie in worn corduroys came up to the park bench and held out a bundle of red and white carnations. — Carl Hiaasen, *Skin Tight*, p. 196, 1989

2 any blind, unthinking, unquestioning follower of a philosophy or person *US, 1991*
An extension of the early 1970s labeling of followers of the Reverend Sun Myung Moon.
• I hope you're not buying into this banza-bullshit like the rest of Bodhi's moonies. — *Point Break*, 1991

moonlight requisition *noun*
the notional procedure attached to stolen materials *US, 1946*
• — *American Speech*, p. 55, February 1947: "Pacific War language"

moon rock *noun*
the combination of heroin and crack cocaine *US, 1989*
• — Terry Wiliams, *Crackhouse*, p. 150, 1992

moonshine *noun*
privately and illegally distilled alcohol *UK, 1782*
• [T]hey just talked and drank some of the Southern moonshine I left in the compartment. — Jack Kerouac, *On the Road*, p. 125, 1957

moonshot *noun*

1 anal sex *US, 1972*
• — Robert A. Wilson, *Playboy's Book of Forbidden Words*, p. 170, 1972

2 outdoor sex at night *US, 1986*
• [A]nd who was to say that they might not be able to go to the powder room simultaneously, and thereby slip off for a ten-minute moonshot? — Dan Jenkins, *Dead Solid Perfect*, p. 101, 1986

moose *noun*

1 in the Korean war, a girlfriend, mistress, or prostitute *US, 1951*
From the Japanese *musume*.
• — *American Speech*, p. 119, May 1960: "Korean bamboo English"
• I have been shacked up there now for more than two years with the prettiest little moose you ever did see. — Joseph C. Goulden, *Korea*, p. 142, 1982

2 in poker, a large pot *US, 1996*
• John Vorhaus, *The Big Book of Poker Slang*, p. 26, 1996

moose-eyed *adjective*
infatuated; in love *US, 2000*
• — Recorded by Murry A. Taylor, *Jumping Fire*, p. 457, 2000

moose farm *noun*
a college sorority whose members are perceived as not particularly attractive *US, 1968*
• — Mary Swift, *Campus Slang (University of Texas)*, 1968

moose knuckle *noun*
the condition that exists when a tight-fitting pair of pants, shorts, bathing suit, or other garment forms a wedge between a woman's labia, accentuating their shape *US, 1996*
• Always been partial to "Moose Knuckles." — *alt.tasteless.jokes*, 27th May 1996

• Everywhere you turned in 2001, it was lip gloss and glitter, moose-knuckle hot pants and sweetened vocals. — *Phoenix New Times*, 3rd January 2002

moose pasture *noun*
any worthless (or nonexistent) land sold as part of a confidence swindle *US, 1985*
• — M. Allen Henderson, *How Con Games Work*, p. 221, 1985: "Glossary"

moose pasture con *noun*
a big con in which the victim is induced to invest in a company that appears on the verge of a great secret success *US, 1997*
• It's gonna be a Big Store. We're gonna set up a trap. I'm gonna run a moose pasture con on Tommy. — Stephen Cannell, *King Con*, p. 110, 1997

moose shit!
used as an exclamation of disbelief *US, 1967*
• "They say the Mad Bomber looked like a gardener," Mrs. Norton said reflectively. "Moose shit," Susan said cheerfully. — Stephen King, *Salem's Lot*, p. 43, 1975

moosh *verb*
to shove in the face *US, 1998*
• The alleged perpetrator called him a "bitch-ass punk" and mooshed him, causing annoyance and alarm. — *The New Yorker*, p. 35, 10th August 1998

moota *noun*
marijuana *US, 1926*
The Mexican Spanish slang *mota* (marijuana) was smuggled north with the drug. Variant spellings include "moocah," "mootah," "mooter," "mootie," "mooster," "mootos," "motta," "muta" and "mutah."
• Rapp smoked his muta while he played the new guitar[.] — Mezz Mezzrow, *Really the Blues*, p. 52, 1946

mop *noun*

1 a head of hair *UK, 1821*
• He was a little bit of a guy, no chubbier than a dime and as lean as hard times, with a mop of dark hair[.] — Mezz Mezzrow, *Really the Blues*, p. 109, 1946
• What do they care if their baldheaded and crew-cut elders don't dig their caveman mops? — Eldridge Cleaver, *Soul on Ice*, p. 81, 1968
• Pop was chopping a study's mop and Mom was in her favorite squat behind the stove[.] — A.S. Jackson, *Gentleman Pimp*, p. 11, 1973

2 your date for an evening *US, 1954*
Teen slang.
• — *Look*, p. 88, 10th August 1954

MOP *adjective*
in the military, missing on purpose *US, 1985*
• DeTonq was MOP—missing on purpose. DeTonq, a Cajun from Louisiana, spoke passable French and had undoubtedly chosen to terminate his short military career before it terminated him. — Nelson DeMille, *Word of Honor*, p. 150, 1985

mop booth *noun*
a private booth where pornographic movies are shown for a fee *US, 2001*
• If public pudpulling is your thing, try a "spooge booth" or "mop booth." — Rob Cohen, *Etiquette for Outlaws*, p. 73, 2001

mope *noun*

1 a person who is not particularly bright *US, 1919*
From C16 to C19 a part of colloquial speech, "mope" reappeared 200 years later as slang.
• Alma mater for many a mope majorin' in thievery, roguery, lechery, and mopery. — Edwin Torres, *Carlito's Way*, p. 20, 1975
• Just as a couple of mopes who you knew from the Palm Springs crowd. — Gerald Petievich, *To Live and Die in L.A.*, p. 195, 1983
• I don't suppose you could ever accuse these two mopes of being on the take. — Jim Carroll, *Forced Entries*, p. 93, 1987

2 in hospital usage, a nonsurgeon physician *US, 1994*
A derogatory evolution of the term "medical outpatient."
• — Sally Williams, "*Strong*" Words, p. 151, 1994

3 a thug *US, 1998*
• [A] perp can be a "skell" or a "mope," depending on whether he's a bum or a thug. — *The New Yorker*, p. 35, 10th August 1998
• "Not bad for a couple defrocked mopes." — Jonathan Kellerman, *Rage*, p. 320, 2005

mopery *noun*
incompetence, stupidity *US, 1907*
- Alma mater for many a mope majorin' in thievery, roguery, lechery, and mopery. — Edwin Torres, *Carlito's Way*, pp. 19–20, 1975

mopp *verb*
to don protective clothing and breathing apparatus against chemical warfare *US, 1993*
From the official designation *"mission oriented protective posture."*
- — *The Retired Officer Magazine*, p. 39, January 1993

mop-squeezer *noun*
in a deck of playing cards, a queen *US, 1949*
- — *American Speech*, p. 100, May 1951

mop-up boy *noun*
a worker performing janitorial work at an arcade where men masturbate while watching videos *US, 1997*
- It's not fair. If you're the mop-up boy at a peep show, it's obvious the government is not working for you. — Chris Rock, *Rock This!*, p. 98, 1997

morale-booster *noun*
any stupid act by the authorities that has the immediate effect of lowering morale *US, 1968*
- — *Current Slang*, p. 16, Spring 1968

more *noun*
phencyclidine, the recreational drug known as PCP or angel dust *US, 1994*
- — US Department of Justice, *Street Terms*, October 1994

MORF
used as Internet shorthand to mean *"male or female" US, 1997*
- — Andy Ihnatko, *Cyberspeak*, p. 125, 1997

morgue *noun*
in circus and carnival usage, a performance or series of performances in a town that fail to attract more than a few customers *US, 1904*
- — Don Wilmeth, *The Language of American Popular Entertainment*, p. 176, 1981

Mormon buckskin *noun*
bailing wire *US, 1977*
- He secures the muffler and drives on. Bailing wire, he informs me, is Mormon buckskin. — John McPhee, *Irons in the Fire*, p. 50, 1997

Mormons *noun*
in hold 'em poker, a king and two queens *US, 1996*
An allusion to the practice of plural marriage.
- — John Vorhaus, *The Big Book of Poker Slang*, p. 26, 1996

morning glory *noun*
1 a drug addict's first injection of the morning *US, 1959*
- — J.E. Schmidt, *Narcotics Lingo and Lore*, p. 114, 1959
2 in horseracing, a horse that runs well in early morning workouts but not during races *US, 1904*
- — Robert Saunders Dowst and Jay Craig, *Playing the Races*, p. 165, 1960

morning wood *noun*
an erection experienced upon waking *US, 1997*
- — Pamela Munro, *U.C.L.A. Slang*, 1997
- — Don R. McCreary (Editor), *Dawg Speak*, 2001

moron corps *noun*
the US Army during the Vietnam war *US, 1973*
The US Armed Forces qualification test passing score was lowered substantially in the late 1960s to help swell the ranks of the army with poor urban black men, poor rural white men, and Mexican-Americans.
- Many soldiers referred to the group as the "moron corps." — Paul Starr, *Troubled Peace*, 1973
- Even members of the "moron corps," as they were sometimes called, could figure out that more from their ranks were dying. — Myra MacPherson, *Long Time Passing*, p. 560, 2001

morph *verb*
to create an electronic message in a manner that gives the appearance of having been sent by someone else *US, 1997*
- — Andy Ihnatko, *Cyberspeak*, p. 125, 1997

morphodite *noun*
a homosexual *UK, 1796*
- I remember being called a communist, morphodite, hippie-surfer bitch as I was marched with my fellow "new boys" to the academy barbershop. — Chuck Pfarrer, *Warrior Soul*, p. 6, 2004

mortal lock *noun*
in horseracing, a bet that is sure to win *US, 1951*
- — David W. Maurer, *Argot of the Racetrack*, p. 41, 1951

mortal nuts *noun*
in poker, a hand that is sure to win *US, 1979*
- — John Scarne, *Scarne's Guide to Modern Poker*, p. 284, 1979

Mortaritaville; Mortarville *noun*
any military base subjected to constant mortar attacks *US, 2004*
- But some of the thousands of soldiers and contractors who suffer daily mortar and rocket attacks have another name for it: "Mortaritaville." — *Baltimore Sun*, p. 1A, 11th October 2004

MOS *adjective*
in television and movie-making, said of a scene shot without sound *US, 1977*
- The first thing to learn about sound is the expression "MOS," which stands for "mit out sound." I was told that it derives from Otto Preminger's heavy accent. — Stephen Ziplow, *The Film Maker's Guide to Pornography*, 1977
- Legend has it that director Lothar Mendes (a German himself) was the person who coined the term when he instructed the crew to do the next shot "mit out sound." — Ralph S. Singleton, *Filmmaker's Dictionary*, p. 107, 1990

mosey *verb*
to move slowly and seemingly aimlessly; to amble *US, 1829*
Introduces a folksy tone.
- I sat down in the lobby and planned a large volume to be entitled "Profiles in Snollygostering" and ate a Suchard chocolate bar and then moseyed into the hotel record shop and asked for a Lennie Tristano. — Clancy Sigal, *Going Away*, p. 74, 1961
- Well, I know you're busy, so I'll mosey on. — Max Shulman, *Anyone Got a Match?*, p. 145, 1964
- "Guess I'll mosey along." Kitty stood. — Seth Morgan, *Homeboy*, p. 235, 1990
- Bobbie told Reggie she was going to mosey over to the post office to buy some stamps, but really, she wanted to get some fresh air. — Joseph Wambaugh, *Finnegan's Week*, p. 32, 1993

mosh *verb*
(at a rock music concert, especially hardcore, punk, or metal) to jump/dance in a violent and ungainly manner, deliberately crashing into other moshers *US, 1983*
- He got her in effortlessly, even though she was too young to drink, and escorted her to a VIP booth by the stage where Wig Starbuck, punk grandpa of the scene, was playing for the moshing youngsters. — Francesca Lia Block, *I Was a Teenage Fairy*, p. 88, 1998

mosher *noun*
a participant in slam dancing at a punk or postpunk concert *US, 1988*
- The 10-foot space between the stage and the first row became an uncontrolled mosh pit, with dozens of moshers slamming into each other, running fulll-speed from one end of the pit to the other. — *Colorado Springs Gazette Telegraph*, p. D4, 1st September 1988
- And let's pretend that Anthrax could've gone on tour this spring and gotten enough moshers to each donate $18.50 of their allowance to sell out every date. — *Phoenix New Times*, p. 99, 5th April 1989

moshky *noun*
a marijuana user *US, 1971*
- — Eugene Landy, *The Underground Dictionary*, p. 135, 1971

mosh pit *noun*
an area in a dance hall where dancers mosh *US, 1992*
- — *American Speech*, p. 417, Winter 1993: "Among the new words"
- "Are you ready for my darkness?" [...] Words that can and should only be followed by blood and feathers being launched into the moshpit. — *X-Ray*, June 2003

mosquitos; mosquitoes *noun*
cocaine *US, 1994*
- — US Department of Justice, *Street Terms*, August 1994

moss *noun*
hair *US, 1926*

- Later on he would bring the whole Austin High Gang out to Holly-wood an set them up, each one with a hand-picked harem of bath-ing beauties to manicure his toenails and shampoo his moss. — Mezz Mezzrow, *Really the Blues*, p. 131, 1946
- And did you dig that chick with moss that thick? — Dan Burley, *Diggeth Thou?*, p. 19, 1959
- Decatur said, "The black geechie with the wavy moss." — Iceberg Slim (Robert Beck), *Death Wish*, p. 112, 1977

most *noun*
the best *US, 1953*

- "And, Grandma," said Red, "your ears are the most, to say the least." — Steve Allen, *Bop Fables*, p. 44, 1955
- It was the mostest the most could be! — Clarence Cooper Jr., *The Scene*, p. 63, 1960
- Gee, this hound's-tooth is really the most. — Ross Russell, *The Sound*, p. 178, 1961

most *adverb*
very *US, 1989*

- We will have a most triumphant time. — *Bill and Ted's Excellent Adventure*, 1989

most def!; mos' def!
used for expressing emphatic agreement *US, 1998*

- — Ethan Hilderbrant, *Prison Slang*, 1998
- — Connie Eble (Editor), *UNC-CH Campus Slang*, p. 6, Spring 2003

MOT *noun*
a Jewish person identified as such by another Jewish person *US, 1989*

- Jews may ask, "Is she M.O.T. [member of our tribe]?" instead of "Is she Jewish?" — Leo Rosten, *The Joys of Yinglish*, p. 152, 1989

mota; moto *noun*
marijuana *US, 1933*
The Mexican Spanish slang *mota* (marijuana) was smuggled north with the drug.

- We wandered off campus to get a pint of rum, something to keep our mota strength at a peak 'til 10. — Odie Hawkins, *Men Friends*, p. 55, 1989

motate *verb*
to move *US, 1967*

- Man, when he said that, I needed to motate out of there. — Nicholas Von Hoffman, *We Are The People Our Parents Warned Us Against*, p. 61, 1967

motel time
used to signal that a bar is closing and that customers must leave *US, 1965*

- — *The Guild Dictionary of Homosexual Terms*, p. 30, 1965

mothball fleet *noun*
a group of inactive naval vessels *US, 1946*

- One ship after another was purged from mothball fleets on both coasts. — Kit Bonner, *Warship Boneyards*, p. 81, 2001

mother *noun*
1 a man; a thing *US, 1951*
A slightly euphemistic **MOTHERFUCKER**; sometimes a low form of abuse, sometimes merely jocular.

- Yeah, Nero was an all-high flip-out-in-orbit mother to end all mothers! — William "Lord" Buckley, *Nero*, 1951
- Drive, you puny mothers, drive! — Ken Kesey, *One Flew Over the Cuckoo's Nest*, p. 194, 1962
- You see that innocent mother with the red hair; you see him waking up in that bed? — Richard Farina, *Been Down So Long*, p. 93, 1966
- So why not put those dirty mothers in prison too? — Eldridge Cleaver, *Soul on Ice*, 1968

2 a male homosexual in relation to a man whom he has introduced to homosexuality *US, 1946*

- — Anon., *The Gay Girl's Guide*, p. 13, 1949

3 a drug dealer *US, 1970*

- — William D. Alsever, *Glossary for the Establishment and Other Uptight People*, p. 26, December 1970

mother dear *noun*
methedrine, a central nervous system stimulant *US, 1969*

A phonic pun.

- — *Current Slang*, p. 9, Fall 1969

motheren; motherin; mothering *noun*
used as a euphemism for "motherfucker," or "motherfuck-ing" *US, 1951*

- [W]hen I asked him what for, he said if the motherin' screw ever caught up to us, he'd wish he hadn't. Oh fine. — James Blake, *The Joint*, p. 27, 21st June 1951
- I can remember 'em all, every motherin' one-night stop. — Ross Russell, *The Sound*, p. 61, 1961
- Sooner or later, baby, that shakin' gonna pay off, fetch me out some big money from that motherin' lounge — Robert Gover, *Here Goes Kitten*, p. 44, 1964
- The worst word of all, a word that even sportsmen disguise as "motheren," Mark didn't even attempt to change. "You mother-fucker!" — Sara Harris, *The Lords of Hell*, p. 176, 1967

motherfather *noun*
used as a euphemism for "motherfucker" *US, 1992*
Used by comedian Redd Foxx on *The Royal Family* (CBS, 1991–92).

motherferyer *noun*
used as a euphemism for "motherfucker" *US, 1946*

- And it was in Pontiac that I dug that Jim Crow man in person, a motherferyer that would cut your throat for looking. — Mezz Mezzrow, *Really the Blues*, p. 4, 1946

motherflipping *adjective*
used as a euphemism for the intensifier "motherfucking" *US, 1961*

- I wanna find out how come nobody kin truss nobody in this mothahflippin muddlefuggin worl', how come everybody gotta ack mean. — Robert Gover, *One Hundred Dollar Misunderstanding*, p. 190, 1961

mother-for-you *noun*
used as a euphemism for "motherfucker" *US, 1957*

- "I'll be a mother-for-you!" he exclaimed, half choking, more repulsed by the sight of the cut throat than shocked. — Chester Himes, *A Rage in Harlem*, p. 182, 1957

motherfouler *noun*
used as a euphemism for "motherfucker" *US, 1947*

- Give it to him, Maceo, coolcrack the motherfouler! — Ralph Ellison, *Invisible Man*, p. 488, 1947

motherfuck *verb*
used for damning or cursing *US, 1942*

- Motherfuck you, man. — Piri Thomas, *Seven Long Times*, p. 18, 1974
- "Man, look at my door!" "Motherfuck your door," McDaniel said. — Vernon E. Smith, *The Jones Men*, p. 206, 1974
- Motherfuck JLB, they don't support no hip-hop[.] — Eminem (Marshall Mathers), *Low Down Dirty*, 1998

motherfucker *noun*
1 a despised person *US, 1918*
In 1972, the US Supreme Court reversed the conviction of a man who had used the word "motherfucker" four times during remarks at a school board meeting attended by some 40 children and 25 women, accepting "motherfucker" as constitutionally protected speech (Rosenfeld v. New Jersey, 1972).

- Will you tell these motherfuckers to get off my back? — Alexander Trocchi, *Cain's Book*, p. 166, 1960
- It's these respectable motherfuckers been doing all the dirt. They been stealing the colored folks blind, man. — James Baldwin, *Another Country*, p. 16, 1962
- Dare any dirty mother-fucker in this place to come and stop me from stomping this bitch. — Dick Gregory, *Nigger*, p. 22, 1964
- Senator Abraham Ribicoff of Connecticutt publicly decried the city's "Gestapo tactics"—to which Mayor Richard Daley responded on camera through the din, "Fuck you, you Jew son of a bitch. You lousy motherfucker! Go home." — Hunter S. Thompson, *Fear and Loathing in America*, p. 127, 2000

2 a fellow, a person *US, 1958*

- Originally, a derogatory term. Presently used as a term of either admiration or disgust, depending on the moment and the emotion-al or intellectual point of view when written or vocalized. — Robert deCoy, *The Nigger Bible*, p. 33, 1967
- Myra Breckinridge is a dish, and never forget it, you motherfuckers, as the children say nowadays. — Gore Vidal, *Myra Breckenridge*, 1968

- About that time motherfucker came into style—it came down from black Harlem in a game called "the dozens." — Edwin Torres, *Carlito's Way*, p. 10, 1975
- Check out the big brain on Brett. You a smart motherfucker, that's right, the metric system. — *Pulp Fiction*, 1994

3 a difficult thing or situation *US, 1958*

- Oh shit me! I wish I was back in Memphis now, ooh baby this is gonna be a motherfucker! — *Platoon*, 1986

4 used as a basis for extreme comparisons *US, 1962*

- He had guns for a motherfucker. — Bobby Seale, *Seize the Time*, p. 72, 1970
- We can see for a hundred miles, it's hotter than a motherfucker, and there's not a smidgen of sign. — Rad Miller Jr., *Whattaya Mean I Can't Kill 'Em?*, p. 180, 1998
- Yo, your pop groovier-than-a-motherfucker. — Paul Beatty, *Tuff*, p. 36, 2000
- Strange was higher than a motherfucker by the time he finished his beer and could muster no bad will toward anyone. — George Pelecanos, *Hard Revolution*, p. 207, 2004

5 methamphetamine hydrochloride, a powerful central nervous system stimulant *US, 1993*

- — Peter Johnson, *Dictionary of Street Alcohol and Drug Terms*, 1993

motherfuckers and beans *noun*
canned beans and frankfurters served as field rations by the US Army *US, 1980*

- — *Maledicta*, p. 255, Summer/Winter 1982: "Viet-speak"

motherfucking *adjective*
used as an emphatic intensifier *US, 1897*

- I go 3,000 motherfucking miles, sleep on railroad porches, in Salvation flops, eat out of cans—in Hickey, N.C. — Jack Kerouac, *Letter to John Clellon Holmes*, p. 381, 12th October 1952
- I lived with them all, one right after the mother-fucking other. — John Rechy, *City of Night*, p. 177, 1963
- You ain't nothin' but an old stupid God damn fool, motherfucking asshole! — Bobby Seale, *A Lonely Rage*, pp. 24–25, 1978

motherfucking A!
used for expressing dismay, surprise or strong assent *US, 1977*
An embellished **FUCKING A!**

- "Now you a fuckin' de-tective?" Valetin almost shouted back. The two men were leaning forward, their faces almost touching. "Motherfuckin'-A right." — Edwin Torres, *Q & A*, p. 40, 1977

motherfugger *noun*
used as a euphemism for "motherfucker" *US, 1948*

- "That's the motherfugger who cut up Chipper's jacket," said Peachy. — A.B. Hollingsworth, *Flatbellies*, p. 204, 2003
- The catcalls and laughter echoed through Deal's helmet. That motherfugger! — Frank Johnson, *Twice Departed*, p. 133, 2004

motherfugging *adjective*
used as a euphemism for "motherfucking" *US, 1948*

- "Of all the mother-fuggin' luck, that sonofabitch takes it all." — Norman Mailer, *The Naked and the Dead*, p. 10, 1948

mothergrabber *noun*
used as a euphemism for **MOTHERFUCKER** *US, 1963*

- "You set me up, mother-grabber." — James Blake, *The Joint*, p. 357, 7th September 1963
- "Hey, Hanover, you lazy good-for-nuthin' orbitin' mothergrabber!" — Alan Dean Foster, *Impossible Places*, p. 101, 2002

mothergrabbing *adjective*
used as a euphemism for "motherfucking" *US, 1958*

- [S]erving (i.e., in films and on TV programs) what he describes as "three mother-grabbin' years." — *Time*, p. 48, 28th June 1963

motherhopper *noun*
used as a euphemism for "motherfucker" *US, 1977*

- Maybe they're gonna set me up. Mother hopper. — Edwin Torres, *Q & A*, p. 183, 1977

motherhugger *noun*
used as a euphemism for "motherfucker" *US, 1956*

- Uptown a whore was a whore; a pimp was a pimp; a dike was a dike; a mother-hugger was a mother-hugger. — Billie Holiday, *Lady Sings the Blues*, p. 85, 1956

motherhugging *adjective*
used as a euphemism for **MOTHERFUCKING** *US, 1956*

- It doesn't matter how unlikely the couple, the mother-hugging squares always figure they're only up to one damn thing. — Billie Holiday with William Dufty, *Lady Sings the Blues*, p. 93, 1956

motherhumper *noun*
used as a euphemism for "motherfucker" *US, 1963*

- The motherhumpers who were wrong, stupid, vulgar, shallow, wrong, wrong, wrong, mothersucking bastards always had it. — Cecil Brown, *The Life & Loves of Mr. Jiveass Nigger*, p. 199, 1969
- Rock salt tore through your clothes and made your skin sting like a mother humper. — James Ellroy, *American Tabloid*, p. 351, 1995

motherhumping *adjective*
used as an intensifying euphemism for **MOTHERFUCKING** *US, 1961*

- "In two measly months I'm out of this chickenshit outfit, and no motherhumping dipshit colonel is gonna screw up my record." — Donald Gazzaniga, *A Few Good Men*, p. 152, 1986

mother-in-law *noun*
an enemy airplane *US, 1991*

- "Mother-in-law at sixteen hundred," Charbonnet responded, referring to bogies approaching from the four o'clock position. — Joe Weber, *Defcon One*, p. 268, 1991

motherjumper *noun*
used as a euphemism for "motherfucker" *US, 1949*

- "So what?" I said to Chink. "That motherjumper ought to get caught." — Hal Ellson, *Duke*, p. 140, 1949
- "David baby," he yelled happily, throwing out his arms, "you old benevolent motherjumper, I love you." — Richard Farina, *Been Down So Long*, p. 107, 1966
- I wanna tell ya I'm here—you bunch of motherjumpers. — Piri Thomas, *Down These Mean Streets*, p. ix, 1967
- Outside the Tijuana bullring waiting for my contact! — Ken Kesey, *The Further Inquiry*, p. 196, 1990

motherjumping *adjective*
used as a euphemism for "motherfucking" *US, 1950*

- Them mother-jumping Roaches are in the club room busting it up! — Hal Ellson, *Tomboy*, p. 104, 1950
- He said, "The mother-jumping bastards." — Thurston Scott, *Cure it with Honey*, 1951
- I put them packages next to you, you mother-jumping thief! — Hal Ellson, *The Golden Spike*, p. 19, 1952

mother lover *noun*
used as a euphemism for "motherfucker" *US, 1950*

- He raps me across the back. "Stand straight, you little mother-lover," he says. — Rocky Garciano (with Rowland Barber), *Somebody Up There Likes Me*, p. 202, 1955

mother loving *adjective*
used as a euphemism for "motherfucking" *US, 1951*
Also used as an infix: "abso-mother-lovin'-lutely!."

- Hydrogen fuel, it burns so clean, / throbs in the veins; a mother lovin' machine. — Bette Midler, *Oh Industry*, 1988

motherlumping *adjective*
used as a euphemism for the intensifier "motherfucking" *US, 1961*

- I feel like sayin', Baby way you go off, you musta been saving that one for a mothahlumpin lifetime. — Robert Gover, *One Hundred Dollar Misunderstanding*, p. 36, 1961

mother nature *noun*
marijuana *UK, 1969*

- The best pipes for smoking Mother Nature come form Headgear. — Emile Nytrate, *Underground Ads*, p. 38, 1971

mother of all *noun*
an epic, if not the epic, example *US, 1991*
From Saddam Hussein's somewhat hyperbolic prediction that the western invasion of the Persian Gulf in 1991 would be the "mother of all battles." Hussein's use of a common Arabic vernacular expression immediately appealed to the American and British ear, with hundreds of variations appearing over several years—"the mother of all retreats," "the mother of all confirmation hearings," "the mother of all eclipses," "the mother of all government mistakes," etc.

- Saddam Hussein said the war would be "the mother of all battles." Reporters hailed Gen. Norman Schwarzkopf's press briefing as "the mother of all briefings." Oh, brother. — *The Detroit News*, 4th March 1991

- A year ago, when Saddam Hussein predicted the Gulf War would be the "mother of all battles," little did he know what was to follow. Everyone, it seems, has jumped on the "mother of all" bandwagon. — *Los Angeles Times*, p. E1, 29th January 1992
- The mother of all rackets. The hustle to end all hustles. — John Ridley, *Love is a Racket*, p. 88, 1998

mother of pearl *noun*
cocaine *US, 1983*
- DEALER: Hey, man. You wanna cop some blow? / JUNKIE: Sure, watcha got? Dust, flakes or rocks? / DEALER: I got China White, Mother of Pearl...I reflect what you need. — Grandmaster Flash & The Furious Five featuring Melle Mel, *White Lines*, 1983

mother of shit!
used for registering surprise, rage, etc. *US, 1988*
Variation on the prayer "Mother of Christ."
- [T]he two cops run into the clearing, guns raised. Seeing the Jocks, they stop. MCCORD: Mother of Shit! MILNER: Call in! — *Heathers*, 1988

mother raper *noun*
used as a euphemism for "motherfucker" *US, 1959*
Intended as a euphemism, but one which does not leave much room for the affectionate side of **MOTHERFUCKER**.
- Once he said "the little one" but mostly he used the word mother-raper which Harlemites apply to everybody, enemies, friends and strangers. — Chester Himes, *The Real Cool Killers*, p. 104, 1959
- The Mississippi voice said furiously: "Goddamn stupid mother-raper!" — Chester Himes, *Cotton Comes to Harlem*, p. 9, 1965
- We will rob that motherraper blind. — John Sinclair, *Guitar Army*, p. 153, 1972

mother raping *adjective*
used as a euphemism for "motherfucking" *US, 1932*
- [T]hinking of how he could drive that goddam DeSoto taxicab straight off the mother-raping earth. — Chester Himes, *A Rage in Harlem*, p. 17, 1957
- THE NEW WHITE STRIPES ALBUM SUCKS, YOU SHIT LICKING, SCUM FUCKING MOTHER RAPING ASSHOLES — *Dumb Ass and the Fag (On-line Comic)*, 10th April 2003

mother robbing *adjective*
used as a euphemism for "motherfucking" *US, 1948*
- When we came out I discovered some mother-robbin' bastard had broken into my car window and taken my horn. — Wingy Manone, *Trumpet on the Wing*, p. 237, 1948

motherscratcher *noun*
used as a euphemism for "motherfucker" *US, 2001*
- — Don R. McCreary (Editor), *Dawg Speak*, 2001

mother's day *noun*
1 payday *US, 1965*
Because on payday you pay the money you owe to one mother(fucker) after another.
- — *Current Slang*, p. 17, Summer 1970
2 the day when welfare checks arrive *US, 1973*
- — Malachi Andrews and Paul T. Owens, *Black Language*, p. 51, 1973
- — James Harris, *A Convict's Dictionary*, 1989

motherseller *noun*
used as a euphemism for "motherfucker" *US, 1953*
- Cattle Baron, Oil King, and Mother Seller (Headline) — *Esquire*, p. 6, June 1953

mother's little helper *noun*
any tranquillizer; meprobamate (trade names Equanjill™, Meprospan™ and Miltown™), a habit-forming antianxiety agent *US, 1977*
- — Donald Wesson and David Smith, *Barbiturates*, p. 122, 1977

mothersucker *noun*
1 an odious person *US, 2003*
A slightly emphemized **MOTHERFUCKER**.
- Fuck that mother sucker I'ma kill that mother sucker. — Barutia Ambakiseye, *The Castle is My Heart (Voices III)*, p. 99, 2003
2 used as a somewhat defiant term of address *US, 1999*
- Not yet, mothersucker, but soon America will belong to Austria and then in some way I will be one. — *alt.flame*, 25th March 1999
3 a regular fellow *US, 2005*
- Something about that mothersucker just moved me. — Noire, *Candy Licker*, p. 184, 2005

4 an extraordinary person or thing *US, 1999*
- We're gonna tear the roof off the mothersucker. Tear the roof off. — *rec.sport.football.college*, 15th August 1999

Mother Superior *noun*
an older, experienced homosexual man *US, 1941*
- — Dale Gordon, *The Dominion Sex Dictionary*, 1967

mother thumb and her four lovely daughters *noun*
the hand in the context of masturbation *US, 1967*
- "It originates from the old Army barracks shenanigan where you hear a comrade entertaining Mother Thumb and her Four Lovely Daughters." — Ken Kesey, *Kesey's Jail Journal*, p. 4, 1967

mother wit *noun*
common sense *US, 1972*
- — David Claerbaut, *Black Jargon in White America*, p. 73, 1972

moto *noun*
a motivated self-starter *US, 1993*
- — *Washington Post*, 14th October 1993

motor *verb*
to leave *US, 1980*
- — Connie Eble (Editor), *UNC-CH Campus Slang*, p. 6, Fall 1987
- I'm going to have to motor if I want to be ready for the funeral tomorrow. — *Heathers*, 1988
- Let's motor. Be cool. — Jess Mowry, *Way Past Cool*, p. 15, 1992

Motor City *nickname*
Detroit, Michigan *US, 1943*
Because of the car manufacturing concerns in Detroit.
- Man, I'll lay it back on you as soon as we pay off in Motor City. — Ross Russell, *The Sound*, p. 135, 1961
- At six p.m. we reached the motor city. — A.S. Jackson, *Gentleman Pimp*, p. 55, 1973

motored out *adjective*
said of a scoring device in pinball which fails to register a score because the scoring register is already in use *US, 1977*
- — Bobbye Claire Natkin and Steve Kirk, *All About Pinball*, p. 113, 1977

motorhead *noun*
a fool *US, 1973*
- What the hell do you want me to do, motorhead? — *The Blues Brothers*, 1980
- But it's harder to believe her when she says that some greasy motorhead named Rick is running around South Baltimore in a custom $60,000 Lotus. — David Simon, *Homicide*, p. 436, 1991

motormouth *noun*
someone who talks without end, or when it would be better not to talk *US, 1955*
- Man, what a motormouth. — *Los Angeles Times*, p. II-5, 3rd November 1955
- That motormouth better put a hat on when he goes outside else he'll get a sunburned tongue. — Ken Weaver, *Texas Crude*, p. 118, 1984
- Courtney [Love] has motormouth trouble. (Juvenile hall social worker's report, 1978) — *Q*, p. 85, December 2001

motor mouth *verb*
to talk incessantly *US, 1985*
- The drunk also started screaming about suing for false arrest and police brutality until Prankster Frank got a headache from all the motor-mouthing. — Joseph Wambaugh, *The Secrets of Harry Bright*, p. 66, 1985

motormouth *adjective*
inclined to talk without end, or when it would be better not to talk *US, 1974*
- "I didn't know he was motor-mouth, but I brought him in and he was." — George Higgins, *Cogan's Trade*, p. 136, 1974

motor scooter *noun*
used as a euphemism for "motherfucker" *US, 1960*
- He rides through the jungle tearing limbs off of trees / Alley-oop / Knocking great big monsters dead on their knees / Alley-oop / The cats don't bug him coz they know better / Alley-oop / Coz he's a mean motor-scooter and a bad go-getter. — (Dallas Frazier) The Hollywood Argyles, *Alley-Oop*, 1960

mouly *noun*
a black person *US, 1990*

- Us Italian boys got to stick together or the spics 'n' the moulys here will be runnin' everything. — *New Jack City*, 1990

mount *verb*
▶ **mount the red flag**
to have sex with a woman experiencing the bleed period of the menstrual cycle *US, 1972*
- — Robert A. Wilson, *Playboy's Book of Forbidden Words*, p. 176, 1972

mountain goat *noun*
a comic who made his name in the Borscht Belt and then came to New York clubs to perform *US, 1973*
- — Sherman Louis Sergel, *The Language of Show Biz*, p. 141, 1973

mountain lightning *noun*
potent, homemade alcohol *US, 1962*
- Almost anybody could build a ten- or twenty-gallon-a-day still and brew mountain lightning, but our family stayed honest. — Sam Snead, *The Education of a Golfer*, p. 35, 1962

mountain oysters *noun*
lamb or calf testicles as food *US, 1857*
- If I was having special company, I might make up a delicacy. You get some money, you can get mountain oysters—that's the male parts of a lamb. — Earl Conrad, *Rock Bottom*, p. 246, 1952

mouse *noun*
a bruise *US, 1842*
- The left half sported a very human mouse under the eye and a welt as big as a fist across her jaw. — Mickey Spillane, *The Big Kill*, p. 29, 1951
- My bed was next to the door so the first thing he saw was the mouse on my cheek. — Robert Gover, *Poorboy at the Party*, p. 54, 1966
- He glanced from the wounded man to Phillips, who had a mouse under one eye. — Leonard Shecter and William Phillips, *On the Pad*, p. 93, 1973
- Nelson had a mouse under his eye and his shirt was almost torn from his body. — Joseph Wambaugh, *Fugitive Nights*, p. 305, 1992

mouse droppings *noun*
in computing, single pixels on a computer screen that do not reappear when the cursor of the mouse is moved away from the spot *US, 1991*
- — Eric S. Raymond, *The New Hacker's Dictionary*, p. 247, 1991

mousetrap *noun*
a series of exit consoles on websites that link back on themselves, creating an infinite loop *US, 2003*
- The latest tactic used by smut peddlers targeting children on the internet is the pop-up mouse trap, said Hansen. — *Salt Lake Tribune*, p. B1, 2nd November 2003

mousetrap *verb*
to ambush an enemy by drawing them into position with some sort of bait *US, 1989*
- This was to prevent a patrol from being "mousetrapped," with rescue forces, in turn, becoming entrapped. — Eric Hammel, *Khe Sanh*, p. 154, 1989

moustache *noun*
a MOUSTACHE PETE *US, 1973*
- It started out the young guys hitting the old guys, the mustaches, 'cause they wouldn't get off their ass, make a move on the gambling. — Elmore Leonard, *Glitz*, p. 107, 1985

moustache mob *noun*
first generation immigrants from Sicily or southern Italy *US, 1955*
- They never saw no fighter who brought out the "mustache mob" like I done, not even Primo Carnera who was an Italian from Italy. — Rocky Garciano (with Rowland Barber), *Somebody Up There Likes Me*, p. 339, 1955

Moustache Pete *noun*
an older Italian-American criminal, associated with outdated ways of doing things *US, 1938*
- Georgetti was of the old Mafia school, known as the Mustache Petes. — Ed Reid and Ovid Demaris, *The Green Felt Jungle*, p. 181, 1963
- Between the old Moustache Petes and the new breed bucking their way in, there were no exceptions, no excuses, and if you couldn't cut it, they'd cut you. — Mickey Spillane, *Last Cop Out*, p. 104, 1972
- The two old guys flanking Mazzone—Mustache Petes—had the shirt buttoned to the top but no tie. — Edwin Torres, *Carlito's Way*, p. 101, 1975
- Do I look like a penniless "Mustache Pete" fresh off the boat? — Iceberg Slim (Robert Beck), *Death Wish*, p. 26, 1977

moustache ride *noun*
an act of oral sex by a man *US, 2002*
- "Give her a mustache ride," Morris suggested, breaking into loud laughter. — Stella Cameron, *True Bliss*, p. 289, 2002
- While I was playing poker with the guys Boo was giving mademoiselle a free mustache ride up in his stateroom. — Hank Miller, *The Admiral's Son*, p. 340, 2007

mouth *noun*
1 back-talk, insults *UK, 1896*
- I used to give Silky mouth. In Ottawa, you could tell pimps shit. I've learned not to talk back to Silky. — Susan Hall, *Gentleman of Leisure*, p. 164, 1972

2 a play's reputation *US, 1973*
- — Sherman Louis Sergel, *The Language of Show Biz*, p. 141, 1973

▶ **in the mouth**
in poker, said of the first player to act in a given situation *US, 1979*
- — John Scarne, *Scarne's Guide to Modern Poker*, p. 281, 1979

▶ **with his mouth wide open**
said of a racehorse that easily wins a race *US, 1951*
- — David W. Maurer, *Argot of the Racetrack*, p. 69, 1951

mouth *verb*
to inform on someone to the police *US, 1965*
- Instead of throwing it away, he tried to sell it, and he got busted—and he mouthed on everybody he knew. — Claude Brown, *Manchild in the Promised Land*, p. 154, 1965

mouth bet *noun*
in poker, a bet made without putting up the funds, binding among friends *US, 1889*
- — Irwin Steig, *Common Sense in Poker*, p. 185, 1963

mouthfuck *verb*
to take the active role in oral sex *UK, 1866*
- Repp's formula was as basic as they come: cuntfuck, arsefuck, mouthfuck, not necessarily in that order. — Chris Pett, *Robinson*, pp. 162–163, 1993
- She wanted me to mouthfuck her and I kept wondering when she would want me to pull out to pull down her pants and fuck her ass from behind. — J. Price Vincenz, *Anything That Moves*, p. 184, 2001

mouthpiece *noun*
1 a lawyer *UK, 1857*
- "If I hire a mouthpiece, then they know i got dough and I'm licked." — Max Shulman, *Sleep Till Noon*, p. 29, 1950
- "The flagrantly provocational role played by Det-Constable Silver" gave his mouthpiece something to bite on[.] — Charles Raven, *Underworld Nights*, p. 99, 1956
- "He's out of town, but he's the best mouthpiece fixer in Chi." — Iceberg Slim (Robert Beck), *Long White Con*, p. 179, 1977
- TILLEY: You got a high-priced mouthpiece to speak for ya? BB: I don't need one. I don't expect to win. — *Tin Men*, 1987

2 a spokesperson *UK, 1805*
- Clifford C. H. Tavernier, close to Dawson, is the present Bronzeville mouthpiece. — Jack Lait and Lee Mortimer, *Chicago Confidential*, p. 46, 1950

mouth pig *noun*
a male homosexual who offers his mouth anonymously to any penis that is presented through a glory hole *US, 1996*
- Mouth pigs are glory hole faggots. Cocksuckers. Made, not born. — Peter Sotos, *Index*, p. 24, 1996

move *noun*
▶ **put the move on**
to make sexual advances *US, 1987*
- I'm wondering what to do if he does try to put the moves on me. — Jim Carroll, *Forced Entries*, p. 27, 1987

move *verb*
to sell, especially in bulk *US, 1938*
- Ex-pimp. Moved a couple of ounces, supposed to be a big shot. — Edwin Torres, *After Hours*, p. 190, 1979
- Though the 'vette would be easier to move. Get some plates off another car, drive up to Atlanta, and unload it. — Elmore Leonard, *Stick*, p. 67, 1983
- All I need is for you to keep bringing the stuff. I've gut a guy in here from Pittsburgh who'll move it for me. — *Goodfellas*, 1990

- Henry Santoro and Frankie Fish are moving weight in Florida.
  — *Gone in 60 Seconds*, 2000

▸ **move the line**
in sports betting, to change the point spread that is the basis for betting on one team or the other *US, 1974*

- Usually moving a line does what a BM wants, which is to balance out very uneven betting. — Gary Mayer, *Bookie*, p. 155, 1974
- When the guys at the Amorita Club noticed how I was winning they paid me the compliment of favoring the side that I liked. That is, they would move the line. — Jimmy Snyder, *Jimmy the Greek*, p. 28, 1975

move in *verb*
in poker, to bet your entire bankroll *US, 1979*

- — John Scarne, *Scarne's Guide to Modern Poker*, p. 284, 1979

movement *noun*
collectively the various organizations fighting for social justice, racial justice, economic justice, and peace in the 1960s *US, 1966*

- The Berkeley "Movement" designs, builds, set, and springs a vicious trap on itself. (Letter to the Editor) — *The Berkeley Barb*, p. 10, 6th May 1966
- He says everybody, including movement people, is completely hung up with status. — James Simon Kunen, *The Strawberry Statement*, p. 93, 1968
- [S]o for a nine-month year it ain't been bad, especially since the in-fighting between movement groups and factions had reached grating proportions. — Abbie Hoffman, *Woodstock Nation*, p. 11, 1969
- Ever since Ed and I have been active in the Movement we've always carried our guns. — H. Rap Brown, *Die Nigger Die!*, p. 81, 1969

mover *noun*
1 someone who imports drugs *US, 1995*

- — Mark S. Fleisher, *Beggars & Thieves*, p. 290, 1995: "Glossary"

2 a police ticket for a moving violation *US, 1970*

- Wish I could write a ticket. I haven't got a mover yet this month. — Joseph Wambaugh, *The New Centurions*, p. 293, 1970

3 in casino gambling, a dice cheat who places his bet after a roll has started *US, 1962*

- — Frank Garcia, *Marked Cards and Loaded Dice*, p. 263, 1962

mover and shaker *noun*
a powerful person with powerful connections *US, 1972*

- We have wax museums for historical people and show business people and sports people, but nary a thing for the movers and shakers of society. — Armistead Maupin, *Further Tales of the City*, p. 35, 1982
- Mayor Simmons became one of the movers and shakers in the state's political set up. — Odie Hawkins, *The Life and Times of Chester Simmons*, p. 172, 1991

moves *noun*
sexual advances *US, 1968*
Always used with "the."

- Nina, seeking "eternal pleasure," makes the moves on Paul Thomas as this sex pro gladly teaches her all he knows. — *Adult Video*, p. 18, August/September 1986
- You know sooner or later he's going to make the moves on her, but you don't know what she's going to do. — Elmore Leonard, *Bandits*, p. 84, 1987

movie job *noun*
sex, especially sex for pay, in cinema *US, 1966*

- "Movie jobs go for five dollars and that's too low," he said. — Johnny Shearer, *The Male Hustler*, p. 79, 1966

movin' *adjective*
good, pleasurable, fashionable, popular *US, 1997*

- — Vann Wesson, *Generation X Field Guide and Lexicon*, p. 114, 1997

mow *verb*
to eat with gusto and stamina *US, 1991*

- — Trevor Cralle, *The Surfin'ary*, p. 78, 1991
- — Judi Sanders, *Da Bomb*, p. 10, 1997

mowed lawn *noun*
a shaved vulva *US, 1964*

- — Roger Blake, *The American Dictionary of Sexual Terms*, p. 136, 1964
- — Robert A. Wilson, *Playboy's Book of Forbidden Words*, p. 176, 1972
- — *Maledicta*, p. 131, Summer/Winter 1982: "Dyke diction: the language of lesbians"

moxie *noun*
nerve, courage, gall *US, 1930*

Moxie was the first mass-marketed soft drink in the US.

- But you never had the moxie to see what his world was really like. — Ross Russell, *The Sound*, p. 174, 1961
- Poor Williams was left holding the civic bag; he had taken a gutsy stand, his image was all moxie[.] — Hunter S. Thompson, *Hell's Angels*, p. 209, 1966

mox nix
it makes no difference *US, 1955*

- The soldiers often expressed their indifference with the phrase "mox nix," a corruption of the German *machts nicht*, "it doesn't matter." — Rick Atkinson, *The Long Gray Line*, p. 389, 1989

MR *noun*
a person lacking intelligence *US, 1988*
An abbreviation of "mentally retarded."

- When we walked away together, they yelled, "There go the M.Rs." — Annie Ample, *The Bare Facts*, p. 27, 1988

MRS degree *noun*
the notional degree awarded to a woman who attends college for the purpose of marriage *US, 1957*

- Feeling very small as a result of her faux pas, Miss Boyd decided that she had made a mistake. After receiving the BA degree, she should have secured the Mrs degree. — Wayne Thompson, *Fundamentals of Communication*, p. 582, 1957
- This was the era [the 1950s] when people first began to joke about women attending college to earn an MRS degree. — Stephanie Coontz, *Marriage, a History*, p. 236, 2005

mu *noun*
used for expressing the sentiment that "your question cannot be answered because it depends on incorrect assumptions" *US, 1991*
A Japanese word borrowed by computer enthusiasts.

- — Eric S. Raymond, *The New Hacker's Dictionary*, p. 248, 1991

mucho *adjective*
much, a lot of *US, 1942*
A direct borrowing from Spanish.

- — Collin Baker et al., *College Undergraduate Slang Study Conducted at Brown University*, p. 160, 1968
- To them I say EAT MUCHO FUCK! — *Ask*, p. 46, 5th May 1979
- With what I'd done already—which apparently, although it amounted to no more than threatening violence, was mucho plenty[.] — Ken Lukowiak, *Marijuana Time*, p. 181, 2000

muck *noun*
in poker, the pile of discarded cards *US, 1990*

- — Anthony Holden, *Big Deal*, p. 302, 1990

muck *verb*
in a casino, to spread playing cards on the table and move them randomly as part of the shuffling process *US, 2003*

- — Victor H. Royer, *Casino Gamble Talk*, p. 89, 2003

muck-a-muck; muckety-muck *noun*
an important and prominent person *US, 1856*

- All the high mucky-mucks cussed and made fun of him for the way he'd cut up in politics. — Jim Thompson, *The Killer Inside*, p. 152, 1952
- Dames in the upper brackets, muck-a-mucks of dames, with upper bracket noses and knockers and legs and bank accounts. — Bernard Wolfe, *The Late Risers*, p. 48, 1954
- A lot of them are clean-cut high "muckty mucks" in the white world. — Iceberg Slim (Robert Beck), *Pimp*, p. 176, 1969
- We interviewed the university muckety-mucks on the hot school issues. — Cousin Bruce Morrow, *Cousin Brucie*, p. 44, 1987

mucked up *adjective*
in disarray; confused; spoiled *US, 1951*
A euphemism for **FUCKED UP**.

- Sure, and it's a mucked-up civilization to let a guy like that run around loose in the first place. — Thurston Scott, *Cure it with Honey*, p. 197, 1951

mucker *noun*
a person who uses sleight-of-hand to cheat at cards *US, 1996*

- — Frank Scoblete, *Best Blackjack*, p. 266, 1996

muck out *verb*
to kill *US, 1984*

- — Inez Cardozo-Freeman, *The Joint*, p. 113, 1984

muck sack *noun*

a lazy person *US, 1959*

- — *American Speech*, p. 154, May 1959: "Gator (University of Florida) slang"

muck up *verb*

to botch, to ruin, to interfere *UK, 1886*

- Nothing like a little panic to muck up an investigation. — Carl Hiaasen, *Tourist Season*, p. 60, 1986
- I don't want you—with all due respect, Jerry—I don't want you mucking this up. — *Fargo*, 1996

mud *noun*

1 coffee *US, 1875*

- Just ground this morning. — James Harris, *A Convict's Dictionary*, 1989

2 chemical fire retardant dropped from the air *US, 2000*

- — Murry A. Taylor, *Jumping Fire*, p. 457, 2000

3 in circus and carnival usage, any cheap merchandise used as a prize *US, 1981*

- — Don Wilmeth, *The Language of American Popular Entertainment*, p. 177, 1981

4 on the Internet, a multiuser dungeon, a text-based, networked, multiparticipant virtual reality system *US, 1995*

- The appeal of MUDs is really quite simple. — Nancy Tamosaitis, *net.sex*, p. 156, 1995

5 a billiard ball *US, 1993*

- — Mike Shamos, *The Illustrated Encyclopedia of Billiards*, p. 152, 1993

mud *verb*

(used of a racehorse) to run well on muddy track conditions *US, 1978*

- — Thomas L. Clark, *The Dictionary of Gambling and Gaming*, p. 132, 1987

mudder *noun*

any athlete who performs well in rainy conditions; a racehorse that performs well on wet or muddy track conditions *US, 1942*

- — David W. Maurer, *Argot of the Racetrack*, p. 43, 1951

muddlefugging *adverb*

used as a euphemism for the intensifier "motherfucking" *US, 1961*

- It was too muddlefuggin way up t'talk bout right now. — Robert Gover, *One Hundred Dollar Misunderstanding*, p. 152, 1961

muddy feet *noun*

said of someone who needs to urinate *US, 1963*

- — Carol Ann Preusse, *Jargon Used by University of Texas Co-Eds*, 1963

muddy fuck *noun*

anal sex that brings forth feces or fecal stains on the penis *US, 1972*

- — Bruce Rodgers, *The Queens' Vernacular*, p. 242, 1972

mud flaps *noun*

the condition that exists when a tight-fitting pair of pants, shorts, bathing suit, or other garment forms a wedge between a woman's labia, accentuating their shape; large labia *US, 2001*

- Mud Flaps: The meaty, hanging, larger than norm, pussy lips or labia minora. — *rec.arts.movies.erotica*, 11th February 2001
- Camel Toe and the other is Mud Flaps. — *alt.tv.big-brother*, 23rd July 2002

mudhead *noun*

a fanatic enthusiast for multiuser dungeon computer play *US, 1991*

- — Eric S. Raymond, *The New Hacker's Dictionary*, p. 250, 1991

mudkicker *noun*

a prostitute, especially of the streetwalking variety *US, 1932*

- She knew her husband Howie and his kind, the mudkickers, the stars, the stables and occasional white call-girls—she had been part of these things. — Clarence Cooper Jr., *The Scene*, pp. 91 – 92, 1960
- She was three-quarter Kelsey with mossy glossy hair / she was a stompdown mudkicker and her mug was fair. — Bruce Jackson, *Get Your Ass in the Water and Swim Like Me*, p. 106, 1964
- The only reason Lou's so good, though, is 'cause she don't turn down no money; that bitch is a real mud-kicker. — Nathan Heard, *Howard Street*, p. 40, 1968
- I remember the time we muscled a mud kicker when we was oh ten ... twelve and got our first blowjob together. — Iceberg Slim (Robert Beck), *Death Wish*, p. 174, 1977

mudlark *noun*

a racehorse that performs well on muddy track conditions *US, 1909*

- That horse is a dud on pasteboard, she's strictly a mudlark. — *San Francisco Chronicle*, p. 54, 21st April 1971
- Van Der Hum as a noted mudlark and his price shortened considerably[.] — Joe Brown, *Just for the Record*, p. 140, 1984

mud marine *noun*

a combat Marine *US, 1946*

- [A]t fifteen Danny was determined to enlist in the Marines, "ASAP" as he put it, and get into the action as a "mud Marine" in the ongoing war. — Matthew Bracken, *Enemies Foreign and Domestic*, p. 260, 2003

mud mark *noun*

in horseracing, an indication in a past performance report that a horse runs well in muddy track conditions *US, 1965*

- — George King, *Horse Racing*, p. 59, 1965

mud-mover *noun*

a military aircraft engaged in ground attack *US, 1979*

- He liked the idea of aircraft providing cover, not playing mud mover. — Harold Coyle, p. 218, 1988

mud show *noun*

a second-rate circus *US, 1909*

- "I guess I'm going to learn firsthand why circuses like Quest Brothers are called "mud shows." — Susan Elizabeth Phillips, *Kiss an Angel*, p. 258, 1996

mud slogger *noun*

a soldier in the infantry *US, 1915*

- The army sought to improve the image of the infantrymen, whom Americans saw as the dirt-eaters and mud-sloggers, the guys at the bottom of the military's pecking order. — Stephen Borelli, *How About That!*, p. 53, 2005

mud soldier *noun*

a soldier in the infantry *US, 1982*

- A dwindling number of people on the Armed Services Committees are able to reach back to their time as mud soldiers to skeptically quiz the military brass. — Thomas Ricks, *Making the Corps*, 1997

mud turtle *noun*

a black prisoner *US, 1976*

- — John R. Armore and Joseph D. Wolfe, *Dictionary of Desperation*, 1976

muff *noun*

the vulva; a woman as a sex object *UK, 1699*

- For an instant I saw Chenault standing alone; she looked surprised and bewildered, with that little muff of brown hair standing out against the white skin[.] — Hunter S. Thompson, *Songs of the Doomed*, p. 101, 1962
- "She's maybe got more moves than you or me got." "That's because she's got a pair of tits and a muff." — Robert Campbell, *Juice*, p. 92, 1988
- You know, you're sitting around the pool all day, chasing the muff around. — *Dazed and Confused*, 1993
- Then Aniko uses her foot on Melody's muff before using her tongue. — Editors of Adult Video News, *The AVN Guide to the 500 Greatest Adult Films of All Time*, p. 186, 2005

▸ **buff the muff**

to manually stimulate a woman's genitals *US, 1999*

- I even got to the point where I could pop during sex—but only if somebody was buffing the muff while we were going at it. — Amy Sohn, *Run Catch Kiss*, p. 115, 1999

muff *verb*

1 to bungle *UK, 1827*

- — Randy Voorhees, *The Little Book of Golf Slang*, p. 74, 1997

2 to perform oral sex on a woman *US, 1968*

- The man had not recognized her until after he'd muffed her. — Andrew Lindsay, *The Slapping Man*, p. 116, 2003

muff-dive *verb*

to perform oral sex on a woman *US, 1948*

- Let's get on to "muff-diving," shall we? — Angelo d'Arcangelo, *The Homosexual Handbook*, p. 209, 1968
- You muff-diving, mother-fucking son of a bitch! — Philip Roth, *Portnoy's Complaint*, p. 118, 1969
- Incidentally Jane Fonda is one piece I would be most glad to muff dive. — *Screw*, p. 5, 7th March 1969

- HOLDEN: So if we'd met a long time ago, say in high school...
  ALYSSA: I'd still be muff-diving, yes. — *Chasing Amy*, 1997

muff-diver *noun*
a person who performs oral sex on a woman *US*, *1930*

- "Yeah, speaking about hairs—you know what that muff diver does?" — Madam Sherry, *Pleasure Was My Business*, p. 147, 1963
- Only a muffdiver knows for sure (headline). — *Screw*, p. 12, 27th October 1969
- Jack said to Jimmy I could tell just by looking at you you're a muff diver[.] — William T. Vollman, *Whores for Gloria*, p. 42, 1991
- Men with big noses have the potential to be exemplary muffdivers, but most of them are still unaware of how to use their noses as a sex organ[.] — *The Village Voice*, 16th November 1999

muff-diving *noun*
oral sex performed on a woman *US*, *1970*

- They're all assholes, they got no class and I actually met one guy who thought going down on a girl was something called "muff-diving" and only perverts did it. — Eve Babitz, *Eve's Hollywood*, p. 149, 1974
- He wondered what muff-diving had to do with love. — John Gregory Dunne, *True Confessions*, p. 166, 1978
- [I]t had prompted only vile and scrubby descriptions, the most polite of which was "muff-diving." — Guy Talese, *Thy Neighbor's Wife*, p. 193, 1980

muffin *noun*
a woman objectified sexually *US*, *1870*
Probably a disguised **MUFF** (the vagina).

- "There ain't no calories in muffin," Torrey said. — George Higgins, *The Digger's Game*, p. 29, 1973

muffin top *noun*
a midriff bulging out over a pair of tight pants *AUSTRALIA*, *2004*

- And trend spotters in New York are calling out ordinary people and celebrities alike for being guilty of muffin top. — *Detroit Free Press*, 3rd August 2005

muff job *noun*
oral sex on a woman *US*, *1990*

- — Charles Shafer, *Folk Speech in Texas Prisons*, p. 210, 1990

muffler burn *noun*
a bruise on the skin caused a suction kiss *US*, *1982*
Hawaiian youth usage.

- I got dis muffler burn las' night Diamon' Head! — Douglas Simonson, *Pidgin to da Max: Hana Hou*, 1982

muff mag *noun*
a magazine featuring photographs of naked women, focusing on their pubic hair and vulvas *US*, *1972*

- (Headline) Muff Mags for the Meat and Potatoes Man — *Screw*, p. 5, 3rd July 1972

muff-noshing *noun*
oral sex on a woman *US*, *1980*

- — *Maledicta*, p. 198, Winter 1980: "A new erotic vocabulary"

mug *noun*
1 the face, especially an ugly one *UK*, *1821*

- [S]he handed me an apron. Very politely, I laid it on the back of a chair. It just wouldn't go well with my mug. — Mickey Spillane, *I, The Jury*, p. 51, 1947
- I looked at his confident mug; he was going to be a farmer. — Ralph Ellison, *Invisible Man*, p. 106, 1947
- But when he was wrestlin' the newspapers printed his mug a few times. — Marvin Wald and Albert Maltz, *The Naked City*, 1947
- I chopped the mops and shaved the mugs and cuffed the boots of about six hicks before the shop closed. — A.S. Jackson, *Gentleman Pimp*, p. 19, 1973

2 a man, a fellow *US*, *1859*

- "There are ten thousand mugs that hate me and you know it." — Mickey Spillane, *I, The Jury*, p. 7, 1947
- We won't hit anything, and if we do, it'll be the other mug's fault, and some poor bastard's tough titty. — James T. Farrell, *Saturday Night*, p. 25, 1947
- What do these muggs mean to me? I don't worry about them[.] — Horace McCoy, *Kiss Tomorrow Good-bye*, p. 265, 1948
- "Is there anything you mugs don't understand about what Doc here said?" — Donald Wilson, *My Six Convicts*, p. 62, 1951

3 a gullible fool, an easy dupe *UK*, *1857*
A "mug" is a vessel into which you can pour anything.

- Now look, kid, all we want around here is a 60–40 break. Don't say a word if you catch these mugs stealing; so long as we get sixty cents on the dollar we'll call it even. — Mezz Mezzrow, *Really the Blues*, p. 66, 1946
- [N]o mugs to skin. — Charles Raven, *Underworld Nights*, p. 9, 1956

4 a thug *US*, *1890*

- "Look kid, when you play with mugs you can't be coy." — Mickey Spillane, *The Big Kill*, p. 68, 1951

mug *verb*
1 to rob with violence or the threat of violence *UK*, *1864*

- He told how he and his brother, Calvin, 17, and Vallejo Caldwell, 16, "mugged" Farley and robbed him of twenty dollars — Louise Meriwether, *Daddy Was a Number Runner*, p. 126, 1970
- You was drinking, you ended up in the Village, you was mugged, had your wallet taken, you put up a fight and got shot, got it? — Edwin Torres, *Carlito's Way*, p. 91, 1975

2 to grimace theatrically, especially while posing for a photograph *UK*, *1762*

- Bruce, shown here with his attorney, stops and mugs for the cameraman and promises to stir a little commotion at tomorrow's hearing. — Lenny Bruce, *How to Talk Dirty and Influence People*, p. 160, 1965
- Leslie West thumped guitar [...] with broad, joyously agonized mugging, grimacing and grinning and nodding[.] — Lester Bangs, *Psychotic Reactions and Carburetor Dung*, p. 35, 1970

3 to stare at *US*, *2001*

- — *Milwaukee Journal-Sentinel*, 5th March 2001

4 to kiss *US*, *1947*

- — Marcus Hanna Boulware, *Jive and Slang of Students in Negro Colleges*, 1947
- — *American Speech*, p. 62, Spring–Summer 1975: "Razorback slang"

5 to photograph a prisoner during the after-arrest process *US*, *1899*

- We brought him up to the marshsal's office and mugged him and printed him and then we brought him here. — George V. Higgins, *The Friends of Eddie Doyle*, p. 135, 1971

mug down *verb*
to kiss *US*, *2006*

- Casee was the first girl I ever really mugged down with, so I thought all girls might taste that way. — Linden Dalecki, *Kid B*, p. 87, 2006

mug gallery *noun*
in a carnival, a concession where people pay to have their picture taken *US*, *1960*

- — *American Speech*, pp. 308–309, December 1960: "Carnival talk"

muggle *noun*
a marijuana cigarette *US*, *1933*

- "Ever smoke any muggles?" he asked me. "Man, this is some golden-leaf I brought up from New Orleans, it'll make you feel good, take a puff." — Mezz Mezzrow, *Really the Blues*, p. 51, 1946
- [I]t is commonly called "tea" and the cigarettes made therefrom are called "reefers" or "muggles." — Jack Lait and Lee Mortimer, *New York Confidential*, p. 102, 1948
- Me he charged a buck each—maybe these muggles were fatter, or maybe it's just he knows I'm ready and he's taking advantage. — Bernard Wolfe, *The Late Risers*, p. 168, 1954
- The muggles were going around like crazy, loose lip to loose lip. — Willard Motley, *Let No Man Write My Epitaph*, p. 109, 1958

mugglehead *noun*
a marijuana user *US*, *1926*

- — *American Speech*, p. 28, February 1952: "Teen-age hophead jargon"

muggles *noun*
marijuana *US*, *1928*

- "How in hell do you get away with it? The muggles, I mean." He looked around. "I only smoke when I feel extra special low." — Raymond Chandler, *Playback*, p. 123, 1958

mug joint *noun*
in circus and carnival usage, a concession where customers are photographed *US*, *1931*

- — Joe McKennon, *Circus Lingo*, p. 63, 1980
- — Don Wilmeth, *The Language of American Popular Entertainment*, p. 178, 1981

mug's game *noun*
a thankless activity *UK*, *1910*

- [T]his going with girls was a mug's game, which strong, tough blokes like Bill and Waldo couldn't be bothered with. — Norman Lindsay, *Halfway to Anywhere*, p. 37, 1947

- At the moment he disapproved thoroughly of himself, not for playing a mugg's game with Boo, or with Nineteen Meyers either, but for letting himself wallow so long in the slough of self-pity. — Max Shulman, *Anyone Got a Match?*, p. 14, 1964

mugsnapper *noun*
in circus and carnival usage, a traveling photographer *US, 1981*
- — Don Wilmeth, *The Language of American Popular Entertainment*, p. 178, 1981

mug-up *noun*
a coffee break or snack, at work or home *US, 1958*
- — John Gould, *Maine Lingo*, p. 185, 1975
- — Russell Tabbert, *Dictionary of Alaskan English*, 1991

mug up *verb*
to flirt, to kiss *US, 1947*
- — Marcus Hanna Boulware, *Jive and Slang of Students in Negro Colleges*, 1947

mujer *noun*
cocaine *US, 1994*
Spanish for "woman."
- — US Department of Justice, *Street Terms*, August 1994

mukluk telegraph *noun*
a radio show that makes announcements delivering messages to people in rural Alaska who have no telephone or mail service *US, 1945*
The "mukluk" is "an insulated boot designed for arctic wear."
- — Mike Doogan, *How to Speak Alaskan*, p. 44, 1993

mule *noun*
1 a person who physically smuggles drugs or other contraband *US, 1922*
- How? Simple, he thought, with carefully established networks of "mules" to bring it into the States. — Iceberg Slim (Robert Beck), *Death Wish*, p. 32, 1977
- We're just the mules, comprende? — *Repo Man*, 1984
- Bullshit, I ain't handling no dope. He thought about a mule, a buffer between him and the consequences. — Richard Price, *Clockers*, p. 179, 1992
- I know what the term "mule" means on the street, but I have never met one so young. — Mary Rose McGeady, *Are you out there, God?*, p. 9, 1999

2 a Vietnamese who carried supplies for the Viet Cong or the North Vietnamese Army *US, 1990*
- These mules made their way down the Ho Chi Minh Trail, or along the numerous resupply routes within South Vietnam transporting their goods on their backs or by bicycle. — Gregory Clark, *Words of the Vietnam War*, p. 357, 1990

3 marijuana that has been soaked in whiskey *US, 1955*
- — *American Speech*, p. 87, May 1955: "Narcotic argot along the Mexican border"

mule *verb*
to smuggle *US, 2003*
- "He mules crystal in the projects, too." — James Lee Burke, *Last Car to Elysian Fields*, p. 5, 2003

mulenyam; moulonjohn *noun*
a black person *US, 1967*
From the Italian, referring to an eggplant.
- Have I ever talked about the schwarzes when the schwarzes had gone home? Or spoken about the Moulonjohns when they'd left? — Lenny Bruce, *The Essential Lenny Bruce*, p. 11, 1967

mule teeth *noun*
in craps, a roll of twelve *US, 1999*
- — Chris Fagans and David Guzman, *A Guide to Craps Lingo*, p. 38, 1999

mule train *noun*
in humorous smuggler usage, a car *US, 1956*
- — "Smugglers' Argot in the Southwest", *American Speech*, p. 100, May 1956

mullet *noun*
1 a gullible person *US, 1955*
- GARY: So you're a big mover with Diane, are you? BENTLEY: Practically home and hosed. GARY: [...] Big mover with Diane! You mullet! — Alexander Buzo, *Rooted*, 1969
- — Connie Eble (Editor), *UNC-CH Campus Slang*, November 1976
- — Kathleen Odean, *High Steppers, Fallen Angels, and Lollipops*, 1988

2 a socially inept outcast *US, 1959*
- — *Time Magazine*, p. 46, 24th August 1959

mullethead *noun*
a fool, a stupid person *US, 1857*

- Durmot Mulroney is not a mullethead, but he plays one in "About Schmidt." — *Associated Press*, 1st December 2002

mulligan *noun*
1 a prison guard *US, 1939*
Used with derision by prisoners.
- — Charles Shafer, *Folk Speech in Texas Prisons*, p. 210, 1990

2 a gun *US, 1952*
- Captain John and two guards leveled their Mulligans at me. — Charles Hamilton, *Men of the Underworld*, p. 269, 1952

mulligan stew; mulligan *noun*
a stew made without a recipe, relying on ingredients that are left over from previous meals *US, 1904*
- The convicts cooked them into mulligan stews. They tasted fine. — Chester Himes, *Cast the First Stone*, p. 207, 1952
- [H]e lived on dehorn alcohol, mulligan, dayolds, misery[.] — John Clellon Holmes, *The Horn*, p. 159, 1958
- Say, "I even built jungle fires beneath the northern stars / and eaten Mulligan with the dirtiest of bums." — Bruce Jackson, *Get Your Ass in the Water and Swim Like Me*, p. 74, 1965

mullion *noun*
an ugly person *US, 1959*
- If an import is a mullion, she may have to pay her own way. — Jim Bouton, *Ball Four*, p. 252, 1970
- — David Claerbaut, *Black Jargon in White America*, p. 73, 1972

mullygrub *verb*
to sulk *US, 1984*
A venerable noun (meaning "depressed spirits"), now surviving in verb form.
- So your sister Darlene runned off with a albino motorcycle gang president. Mullygrubbin' around the house ain't gonna help. Don't you worry, Tyshonda, we'll find you somebody just as good. — Ken Weaver, *Texas Crude*, p. 118, 1984

multiples *noun*
sex involving multiple people; an orgy *US, 1968*
- The Orgy, or multiples. (Multiples has a more discreet sound, don't you think?) — Angelo d'Arcangelo, *The Homosexual Handbook*, p. 112, 1968

mum *adjective*
quiet, silent *UK, 1950*
- Lepke threatened to the last hour to "blow the roof off," but died mum. — Jack Lait and Lee Mortimer, *Chicago Confidential*, p. 186, 1950

mumblage *noun*
stuff *US, 1981*
- — *Coevolution Quarterly*, p. 31, Spring 1981: "Computer slang"

mumble
used as a verbal placeholder when an answer is either too difficult or unknown *US, 1983*
- Example: "Don't you think that we could improve LISP performance by using a hybrid reference-count transaction garbage collector, if the cache is big enough and there are some extra cache bits for the microcode to use?" "Well, mumble ... I'll have to think about it." — Guy L. Steele et al., *The Hacker's Dictionary*, p. 96, 1983

mumbler *noun*
a woman wearing a tight-fitting pair of pants, shorts, bathing suit, or other garment that forms a wedge between her labia, accentuating their shape; the pants in question. Derives from the humorous logic that you can see the lips moving but can't make out what is being said *UK, 2002*
- Mumblers: Camel toe—the crotch of obscenely tight pants. The lips move but you can't understand a word. — *Playboy*, p. 19, 1st January 2003

mumbo jumbo *noun*
1 meaningless jargon *UK, 1896*
- If you looked at it clearly without the aura of military mumbo-jumbo, it became absurd, perverted, a revolting idea. — Norman Mailer, *The Naked and the Dead*, p. 314, 1948
- Joe Bell showed me his picture in the paper. Blackhand. Mafia. All that mumbo jumbo; but they gave him five years. — Truman Capote, *Breakfast at Tiffany's*, p. 25, 1958
- All this synchronization business and mumbo-jumbo. — J.D. Salinger, *Franny and Zooey*, p. 39, 1961
- What kind of mumbo-jumbo bullshit was this? — Bobby Seale, *A Lonely Rage*, p. 134, 1978

2 any religion or religious practice, especially one that has or appears to have its roots in Africa *UK, 1956*

- I can smell that damned incense. You are trying to drive me round the bend, with your mumbo jumbo. — Charles Raven, *Underworld Nights*, p. 199, 1956
- "Jesus Christ," Princess Grace says, not liking it at all, him being very much into all kinds of Central American mumbo jumbo lately. — Robert Campbell, *In a Pig's Eye*, p. 22, 1991
- Caleb knows that was a load of mumbo jumbo. Ju-ju bollocks from Maria's dad! — Jack Allen, *When the Whistle Blows*, p. 86, 2000

mummy bag *noun*
a sleeping bag which can enclose the sleeper's head *US, 1956*

- Getting into my mummy bag became a problem. Our army sleeping bags were known as Arctic mummy bags, the name stemming from their Egyptian mummy-like shape. — Jennie Darlington and Jane McIlvaine, *My Antarctic Honeymoon*, p. 275, 1956

munch *verb*
1 to fall or be knocked from a surfboard *US, 1977*

- — Gary Fairmont R. Filosa II, *The Surfer's Almanac*, p. 190, 1977

2 in computing, to explore flaws in a system's security scheme *US, 1991*

- — Eric S. Raymond, *The New Hacker's Dictionary*, p. 251, 1991

munchie *noun*
an injury sustained in a fall from a skateboard or bicycle *US, 1987*

- — *Washington Post Magazine*, p. 11, 24th May 1987: "Say wha?"

munchies *noun*
a sensation of hunger experienced when smoking marijuana *US, 1959*

- — *Current Slang*, p. 10, Fall 1970
- We get serious munchies and decide on Ratner's for soup and blintzes. — Jim Carroll, *Forced Entries*, p. 25, 1987
- I got the munchies in a big muthafuckin' way! — *Menace II Society*, 1993
- Well-known to anyone who has ever manned the till at a late-night garage are the "munchies," which hit cannabis users after an hour or so. — *Drugs An Adult Guide*, p. 42, December 2001

munchkin *noun*
1 an acutely short person *US, 1975*
From the race of small people in Frank Baum's *Wizard of Oz*.

- There's gonna be alotta speculation about a middle-aged fat guy and red-headed munchkin in red snakeskin cowboy boots impersonating officers of the law. — Joseph Wambaugh, *Fugitive Nights*, p. 206, 1992

2 a young computer enthusiast *US, 1991*

- — Eric S. Raymond, *The New Hacker's Dictionary*, p. 252, 1991

munchy *adjective*
excellent, trendy, fashionable *US, 1961*
School usage.

- — *Washington Post*, 23rd April 1961: "Man, dig this jazz"

mundane *adjective*
unrelated to science fiction *US, 1982*

- — *American Speech*, p. 28, Spring 1982: "The language of science fiction fan magazines"

munge; mung *verb*
in computing, to destroy data, accidentally or maliciously *US, 1983*

- — Guy L. Steele et al., *The Hacker's Dictionary*, p. 97, 1983

mung-pusher *noun*
a poker player who habitually plays hands that have no chance of winning *US, 1966*

- — John D. Bell et al., *Loosely Speaking*, p. 13, 1966

mung up; mung *verb*
to botch, to blunder, to ruin *US, 1969*

- — *Current Slang*, p. 11, Summer 1969

mural *noun*
a person with many tattoos *US, 1997*

- — *Los Angeles Times Magazine*, p. 7, 13th July 1997

murder *noun*
something that is extremely good *US, 1927*

- Listen—I was a smash in that fight. Oh, Riff, Riff, I was murder! — *West Side Story*, 1957

murder board *noun*
an examining board or review board *US, 1944*

- Murder board—a panel of people who try to shoot down a new project idea. — Rita Mulcahy, *PMP Exam Prep*, p. 75, 2002

murderer's row *noun*
the top floor of a hotel catering to entertainers *US, 1957*

- In the heyday of vaudeville and burlesque, large hotels in metropolitan cities put performers in "murderer's row," as the top floor was known. — Helen Giblo, *Footlights, Fistfights and Femmes*, p. 108, 1957

murderlize *verb*
to kill; to defeat convincingly *US, 1960*

- "You squealed, you dirty rat, and I'm gonna murderlize yah." — Dennis McNally, *Desolate Angel*, p. 51, 2003

murder one *noun*
a mixture of heroin and cocaine *US, 1994*

- — US Department of Justice, *Street Terms*, October 1994

murder ones *noun*
sunglasses *US, 1993*

- I'd open it, pull out my flag, put on my murder ones (dark shades, also called Locs or Locos), button the top button of my shirt, put my strap in my lap, and drive on to the 'hood. — Sanyika Shakur, *Monster*, p. 43, 1993

murder-your-wife brick *noun*
in television and movie making, an imitation brick *US, 1990*
The imitation brick was first used in the 1965 comedy *How to Murder Your Wife*, starring Jack Lemmon and Virna Lisi.

- — Ralph S. Singleton, *Filmmaker's Dictionary*, p. 108, 1990

murgatroid *noun*
a socially inept, out-of-style person *US, 1961*

- Murgatroid—a square. — Art Unger, *The Cool Book*, p. 108, 1961

murk *verb*
to shoot with a gun *US, 2003*

- "The (expletive) made me murk him for $62," Calhoun told one of the accomplices, using street slang for "shoot." — *Milwaukee Journal Sentinel*, p. 1B, 19th November 2003

Murphy *noun*
a claim by a street drug dealer to his supplier that he lost his supply of drugs to robbers *US, 1994*

- If word got around that one person got away with running a Murphy, everybody would try it, everybody would try it and I'd be out of business in no time. — Nathan McCall, *Makes Me Wanna Holler*, p. 122, 1994

Murphy *verb*
to extort or rob a prostitute's customer *US, 1973*

- Murphied like two rube teenagers looking for their first piece, the revolutionaries left the ghetto and went back to their square. — Joe Eszterhas, *Charlie Simpson's Apocalypse*, p. 104, 1973

Murphy game; Murphy *noun*
a swindle involving a prostitute and her accomplice, usually entailing robbing the prostitute's customer *US, 1954*

- I had heard about jostling and the Murphy for a long time, but I didn't really know what it was all about. — Claude Brown, *Manchild in the Promised Land*, p. 160, 1965
- Another source of livelihood for me was a first-class Murphy game I used to run up on 111th Street with the tricks looking for hours. — Edwin Torres, *Carlito's Way*, p. 15, 1975
- If we are going to put down murphy for millions, we got to look like millions. — Robert Deane Pharr, *Giveadamn Brown*, p. 156, 1978
- Passing back into the club, she palmed Joe a twenty, his cut of the Murphy, as any bunko prostitution game was called. — Seth Morgan, *Homeboy*, p. 25, 1990

Murphy man *noun*
the prostitute's male accomplice in a Murphy swindle *US, 1966*

- He was a Murphy Man, which meant that he supported himself by posing as a pimp. — James Mills, *The Panic in Needle Park*, p. 34, 1966
- Pimps, muggers, Murphy men, narco, vice and regular fuzz haunt the area waiting for victims — *Screw*, p. 6, 19th July 1971
- By the sleight-of-hand of a Murphy man / Or the words that a con man spoke. — Dennis Wepman et al., *The Life*, p. 80, 1976

muscle *noun*

1 a person or persons using violence and intimidation, usually in the service of another *US, 1942*

- The big hotels and casinos pay a lot of muscle to make sure the high rollers don't have even momentary hassles with "undesirables." — Hunter S. Thompson, *Fear and Loathing in Las Vegas*, p. 155, 1971
- He ran the troops—period. He was muscle. — Richard Condon, *Prizzi's Honor*, p. 191, 1982
- Costello knew that to survive in our world a man had to be versatile, and thus Costello was not without his "muscle." — Joseph Bonanno, *A Man of Honor*, p. 147, 1983
- The buttons had driven over from Las Vegas where they worked as freelance muscle. — Stephen Cannell, *Big Con*, p. 251, 1997

2 physical violence *US, 1879*

- "Who's behind all the muscle, Mamie?" I was going too fast for her. "Muscle?" she repeated blankly. "Don't go stupid on me. Who's roughing up the street this time?" — *Rogue for Men*, p. 45, June 1956
- "He was a free-lance gun that did muscle for small bookies on bettors who didn't want to pay off." — Mickey Spillane, *The Snake*, p. 11, 1964

3 combat troops *US, 1986*

- Finally, with 1st Sergeant Quinton and Lieutenant Walker directly, the "muscle," or combat platoons, growled into place[.] — Ralph Zumbro, *Tank Sergeant*, p. 79, 1986

▸ **on the muscle**

free *US, 1949*

- "You know that this time it won't be on the muscle?" — Irving Shulman, *Cry Tough*, p. 137, 1949

▸ **on the muscle**

threatening, coercive *US, 1859*

- You sure get on the muscle easy. I don't care if you're union or not, long as you know melons. — Elmore Leonard, *Mr. Majestyk*, p. 18, 1974

muscle *verb*

to inject a drug intramuscularly, as opposed to intravenously *US, 1970*

- — William D. Alsever, *Glossary for the Establishment and Other Uptight People*, p. 22, December 1970

muscle boy *noun*

a hired intimidator *US, 1963*

- From Elizabeth, Jersey, y'know? Muscle boys ... docks. — Mickey Spillane, *Me, Hood!*, p. 44, 1963

muscle-dancing *noun*

a sexually suggestive dance *US, 1950*

- Muscle-dancing was introduced in the United States in a big way when the late Sol Bloom, as an entrepreneur at the Chicago World's Fair, celebrating the 400th anniversary of the discovery of America, presented "Little Egypt." — Jack Lait and Lee Mortimer, *Chicago Confidential*, p. 157, 1950

muscle-happy *adjective*

said of a prisoner who concentrates on physical fitness in jail *US, 1958*

- — Jack Webb, *The Badge*, p. 221, 1958

musclehead *noun*

an athlete *US, 1923*

- That said, we should add that we know of few accomplished muscleheads who reached their goals using nothing but free weights. — Lou Schuler, *Men's Health Home Workout Bible*, p. 203, 2002

muscle house *noun*

a house occupied by bodybuilding enthusiasts *US, 1988*

- I took a share in a muscle house, as The Pines terms it: seven tremendous men, a fair passel of free weights, and me. — Ethan Morden, *Everybody Loves You*, p. 221, 1988

muscleman *noun*

an enforcer for a criminal enterprise *US, 1929*

- Billy Mist and a heavyset muscleman came off the elevator, opened the apartment door and went in. — Mickey Spillane, *Kiss Me Deadly*, p. 110, 1952
- Bert was known as a muscleman. — William Burroughs, *Junkie*, p. 58, 1953
- They were in a glamorous business which no longer needed peepholes, locked doors, and muscle men standing by for inevitable trouble. — Robert Sylvester, *No Cover Charge*, p. 225, 1956
- He's a muscle man for a Harlem numbers-raquet operator. — Iceberg Slim (Robert Beck), *Trick Baby*, p. 213, 1969

muscle pop *verb*

to inject a drug into a muscle rather than a vein *US, 1967*

- — Elizabeth Finn, *Drugs in the Tenderloin*, 1967: Glossary of Drug Slang Used in the Tenderloin

muscle shirt *noun*

a tight, sleeveless t-shirt *US, 1972*

- On a man you would call them muscle shirts but on Wanda/Veloma, it wasn't muscle that showed. — E.L. Konigsburg, *T-backs, T-shirts, Coat, and Suit*, p. 61, 1993

mush *noun*

1 the mouth or face *US, 1859*

Sometimes seen as "moosh."

- "Boy," he went on, "would I like to give that bitch a good sock in the mush!" — Jim Thompson, *The Nothing Man*, p. 265, 1954
- I bring up my left hand and give him a looping shot in the mush. — Rocky Garciano (with Rowland Barber), *Somebody Up There Likes Me*, p. 224, 1955

2 a weak, slow wave *US, 1977*

- — Gary Fairmont R. Filosa II, *The Surfer's Almanac*, p. 190, 1977

mush *verb*

1 to kiss *US, 1926*

- Ten minutes after I made home-sweet-home and laid some Chanel Number Five and some find handmade underwear on my old lady, I mushed her and cut out for the Riverside Towers, on the West Side overlooking the Hudson, where the gang dummied. — Mezz Mezzrow, *Really the Blues*, p. 199, 1946

2 (used of an airplane) to run out of airspeed *US, 1935*

- She seemed to be mushing, running out of airspeed. — Stephen Coonts, *Flight of the Intruder*, p. 419, 1986
- He drops down, the trees blur by underneath, the overloaded choppers bump and mush through the heavy air. — Dennis Marvicsin and Jerold Greenfield, *Maverick*, p. 102, 1990

mushbrain *noun*

a person with limited intelligence *US, 1958*

- Surrender to a mushbrain, else worse would follow. — Al Dewlen, *The Bone Pickers*, p. 16, 1958
- "Triger, you are an egocentric mushbrain monster," she said. — Donald Barthelme, *Amateurs*, p. 25, 1977
- I was a fool, a mushbrain. — Chaterine Coulter, *False Pretenses*, p. 120, 1988

mushburger *noun*

in surfing, a weak, poorly formed wave *US, 1988*

- — Michael V. Anderson, *The Bad, Rad, Not to Forget Way Cool Beach and Surf Discreptionary*, p. 13, 1988

mushfake *noun*

to manufacture in defiance of prison rules and prohibitions *US, 1952*

A term originally applied to the makeshift repair of umbrellas.

- Mush-faking was the major industry within the prison. It was the manufacture of gadgets such as cigarette holders and lighters and jewel boxes and rings and pins and similar items from old bones, toothbrush handles, copper coins, and coin crowns. — Chester Himes, *Cast the First Stone*, p. 80, 1952
- — Troy Harris, *A Booklet of Criminal Argot, Cant and Jargon*, 1976

mushhead *noun*

a fool *US, 1878*

- "Don't be a mushhead all your life, will you!" — Saul Bellow, *The Adventures of Augie March*, p. 92, 1953

mushmouth *noun*

a person of no strong convictions *US, 1930*

- For months they'd been trying to sell "the Man from Maine" as a comfortable, mushmouth, middle-of-the-road compromiser who wouldn't dream of offending anybody. — Hunter S. Thompson, *Fear and Loathing on the Campaign Trail*, p. 129, 1973

mushmouthed *adjective*

unable to speak clearly *US, 1977*

- Sometimes he would be mushmouthed on morphine or pain pills[.] — Lester Bangs, *Psychotic Reactions and Carburetor Dung*, p. 219, 1977

mushroom *noun*

an innocent bystander killed in crossfire *US, 1988*

- In city after city, police report a startling rise in shootings of innocents—"mushrooms" in street slang—struck by stray bullets. — *New York Times*, p. 24 (Section 4), 24th September 1989

- That was a time when crack dealers talked nonchalantly about "mushroom killings," street slang for bystanders slain in crossfires. — *Daily News (New York)*, p. 6, 15th December 1997

mushroom *verb*
(of the felt tip on a pool cue stick) to compress and spread outward *US, 1988*
- — Mike Shamos, *The Illustrated Encyclopedia of Billiards*, p. 152, 1993

mush worker *noun*
a prostitute who steals from customers *US, 1939*
- A prostitute who steals from her clients is called a "mush worker." — Charles Winick, *The Lively Commerce*, pp. 40–41, 1971

mushy *noun*
a weak, slow wave *US, 1964*
- — John Severson, *Modern Surfing Around the World*, p. 175, 1964

muskrat *noun*
a child *US, 1976*
- — Porter Bibb, *CB Bible*, p. 100, 1976

mustang *noun*
an officer appointed from the enlisted ranks *US, 1878*
- It usually takes only thirty months to make the rank of captain, so fifteen years made Sam a "mustang," an enlisted man who was offered a commission because of his demonstrated leadership and military knowledge. — Charles Anderson, *The Grunts*, p. 30, 1976

mustard *noun*
AIDS [Acquired Immune Deficiency Syndrome], a disease that is transmitted by sexual contact *US, 1996*
There are very few synonyms for AIDS despite the huge impact of the disease; the etymology here is uncertain.
- The moral to the story is the mustard's all around / ... I ain't really got AIDS, it's just a motherfucking record. — Sadat X, Fat Joe & Diamond D, *Nasty Hoes*, 1996

mustard case *noun*
a supreme show-off *US, 2001*
The suggestion is of a **HOT DOG**, dosed with mustard.
- He never had many friends in Motors because the officers assigned there were basically "hot pilot" types—attitude junkies known on the job as "mustard cases." — Stephen J. Cannell, *The Tin Collectors*, p. 169, 2001

mustard chucker *noun*
a pickpocket who spills mustard on the victim as a diversion and excuse to approach *US, 1989*
- A mustard chucker, for instance, sprays a victim with mustard. He apologizes profusely and helps to remove it while an accomplice steals the victim's wallet. — *The New York Times*, p. B1, 13th July 1989

mustard road *noun*
▶ up the mustard road
engaging in some form of anal sex *US, 1972*
- [W]hat really hurt was being taken up the old mustard road without KY by the one individual I had actually trusted. — R.J. Pineiro, *Havoc*, p. 23, 2005

mustard shine *noun*
the application of mustard to the shoes in the hope of throwing tracking dogs off the scent *US, 1949*
- — Vincent J. Monteleone, *Criminal Slang*, p. 160, 1949

mutant *noun*
a social outcast *US, 1984*
- But it's not fair—she's a mutant, Daddy! — *Ten Things I Hate About You*, 1999

mute *noun*
in horseracing, a pari-mutuel betting machine *US, 1942*
- — Dan Parker, *The ABC of Horse Racing*, p. 147, 1947

mutt *noun*
a despicable low-life *US, 1899*
- "Forget about it," Lefty says. "The guy was a mutt, that's all." — Joseph Pistone, *Donnie Brasco*, p. 235, 1987
- [I]nterviewing an anonymous and endless stream of indigent mutts through the grills of the processing pen, haggling over jail time, accepting collect calls from the coinless phones upon the tiers[.] — Richard Price, *Clockers*, p. 445, 1992

Mutt and Jeff *noun*
1 a pair of men who are physically mismatched, especially in height *US, 1914*
From the popular comic strip.

- Baddest of the bad was Big Jeff from the "Mutt and Jeff" detective team from the Twenty-third. One was a little wop, Lil' Jeff, the other a big mick, Big Jeff; you couldn't call either one Mutt or they'd break yo' ass. — Edwin Torres, *Carlito's Way*, p. 16, 1975
- "You had ... experiences together," Sidney Blackpool said, double-teaming him with Mutt and Jeff. — Joseph Wambaugh, *The Secrets of Harry Bright*, p. 240, 1985
- And turned to see Raji first, holding a pistol in his lap, then Elliot, on the love seat. He laid the jacket over a chair, saying, "Mutt and Jeff, what can I do for you?" — Elmore Leonard, *Be Cool*, p. 339, 1999
- Andrew Hallock and Jeffrey Jones Ragona, doubling as Belshazzar's wise men and Darius's envious counselors, made a kind of Mutt-and-Jeff pair, visually and even vocally. — *Austin (Texas) American-Statesman*, p. 20, 25th December 2003

2 a police interrogation method in which one interrogator plays the role of a hardliner, while the other plays the role of a sympathetic friend *US, 1964*
- One of the FBI interrogation techniques is the old "Mutt and Jeff" routine taught by Army Intelligence. — *Washington Post*, p. A13, 30th August 1964

muttonhead *noun*
a fool *US, 1903*
- "You bastard no-good muttonhead," she shrieked. — Anita Diamant, *The Last Days of Dogtown*, p. 138, 2005

muzzle guzzle *noun*
a party organized around alcoholic drink *US, 1968*
- — Collin Baker et al., *College Undergraduate Slang Study Conducted at Brown University*, p. 160, 1968

muzzler *noun*
in circus and carnival usage, a person lacking morals *US, 1981*
- — Don Wilmeth, *The Language of American Popular Entertainment*, p. 180, 1981

my bad!
used for acknowledging responsibility for and apologizing for a mistake *US, 1989*
- — Connie Eble (Editor), *UNC-CH Campus Slang*, p. 6, Spring 1989
- Yeah, that was my bad, sorry. — *South Park*, 1999
- "I think you have the wrong number." "Oh. Whups, my bad." — Marty Beckerman, *Death to All Cheerleaders*, p. 134, 2000

my dog ate it
used as a humorous explanation of why a person does not have something that they are supposed to have *US, 1999*
From the clichéd student excuse for not having a homework assignment.
- It means, "My dog ate it." It's Latin. It's a joke. — *American Pie*, 1999

MYOB
used in colloquial speech as well as shorthand in Internet discussion groups and text message to mean "mind your own business" *US, 1915*
- — Gabrielle Mander, *WAN2TLK? ltl bk of txt msgs*, p. 48, 2002

mystery meat *noun*
cold cuts or any meat dish of suspicious heritage *US, 1918*
- Then we still have "gung ho" (all for it), "real crazy," "riot" which to teenagers means lots of fun, "fantabulous," "real nervous," "mystery meat" (meat loaf, stew or almost any meat concoction), "nervous breakdown" (rushing around too much), and "schnook" for someone you don't like. — *Washington Post*, p. F1, 29th September 1957
- — John D. Bell et al., *Loosely Speaking*, p. Addenda, 1969
- — *Verbatim*, p. 280, May 1976

mysto *adjective*
mystical *US, 1980*
- Then I heard he went mysto, and I thought he was sold out. Later on, I went mysto, and looked him up again. — Stephen Gaskin, *Amazing Dope Tails*, p. 2, 1980

my wave!
used by surfers to express "ownership" of a wave and to warn other surfers to get out and stay out of the way *US, 1991*
- — Trevor Cralle, *The Surfin'ary*, p. 78, 1991

my way or the highway
used as a declaration that only the speaker's opinion matter *US, 1986*
- Rumsfeld had already established a reputation for "my way or the highway" ruthlessness. — Jeffrey Krames, *The Rumsfeld Way*, p. 142, 2003

Nn

nab *noun*

the police; a police officer *UK, 1813*

- — Babs Gonzales, *Be-Bop Dictionary and History of its Famous Stars*, p. 9, 1949
- We'd all gotten in trouble again and the neighborhood was full of nabs, and plainclothes guys were hanging around. — Hal Ellison, *Duke*, p. 1, 1949
- He couldn't afford to have "Nab" (police) catch anything in his short[.] — Babs Gonzales, *I Paid My Dues*, p. 98, 1967

nab *verb*

to catch, to arrest *UK, 1686*

- The men stated that when they nabbed Jack Guzik in 1947, Prendergast shook his head and said, "They won't like it." — Jack Lait and Lee Mortimer, *Chicago Confidential*, p. 236, 1950
- Not because they almost nabbed us, but because of me, see? — John Clellon Holmes, *Go*, p. 122, 1952
- After watching a Catholic video mass I caught the end of "Milton the Monster," which dealt with inept motor-cycle cops trying with consistent unsuccess to nab speeders and also violence. — James Simon Kunen, *The Strawberry Statement*, p. 91, 1968
- CAMERON: We're gonna get nabbed, for sure. FERRIS: No way, Cameron. Only the meek get nabbed. — *Ferris Bueller's Day Off*, 1986

nabber *noun*

a police officer *US, 1837*

- — Lavada Durst, *The Jives of Dr. Hepcat*, p. 13, 1953
- A California nabber took me, white slavery was my charge / convicted me and in twenty-four hours in the bighouse I did lodge. — Bruce Jackson, *Get Your Ass in the Water and Swim Like Me*, p. 151, 1965

nabe *noun*

1 a neighborhood movie theater *US, 1935*

- It's time to tour the nabes, gang, and what fun that is! — *The Berkeley Barb*, p. 4, 10th June 1966
- — Sherman Louis Sergel, *The Language of Show Biz*, p. 145, 1973
- [O]ur parents, who probably saw the things at the nabes when they first came out[.] — Lester Bangs, *Psychotic Reactions and Carburetor Dung*, p. 121, 1973

2 a tavern *US, 1950*

- These work about as the nabe joints do, which will be set forth as fully hereinafter as our stomachs will allow. — Jack Lait and Lee Mortimer, *Chicago Confidential*, p. 12, 1950

naches; nakhes *noun*

proud pleasure *US, 1968*

Yiddish from the Hebrew for "contentment."

- A boyla, as we would say, who gave nothing but Naches to his parents. — Vincent Patrick, *Family Business*, p. 274, 1985
- I have such naches: My son is chief of his play group. — Leo Rosten, *The Joys of Yinglish*, p. 350, 1989

nada *noun*

nothing; none *US, 1914*

From the Spanish, used by English speakers who do not understand Spanish.

- If your late ass woulda been here you woulda missed nada. — *Mo' Better Blues*, 1990

nad alert; gonad alert *noun*

used as a warning in a hospital that an x-ray is about to be taken *US, 1994*

- — Sally Williams, *"Strong" Words (Dissertation)*, p. 151, 1994

nads *noun*

the testicles *US, 1964*

From "gonads."

- He was telling Stevie with great glee how he'd managed to kick a cop in the 'nads before they'd gotten to him. — Michael Douglas, *Dealing*, p. 33, 1971
- It's such run to read, and, Molet really pumps my nads! — *The Breakfast Club*, 1985
- "It's true. And it sucks donkey nads." — Linden Dalecki, *Kid B*, p. 162, 2006

nagware *noun*

free computer software that frequently asks the user to send a voluntary payment for further use *US, 1995*

- — Christian Crumlish, *The Internet Dictionary*, p. 131, 1995

nail *noun*

a hypodermic needle *US, 1936*

- — David Maurer and Victor Vogel, *Narcotics and Narcotic Addiction*, p. 428, 1973

nail *verb*

1 to apprehend; to arrest *UK, 1732*

- "Remember our story if we get nailed," Roy said. — William Burroughs, *Junkie*, p. 48, 1953
- They nailed him two months later shacked up in Seattle with a red-headed whore. — Darryl Ponicsan, *The Last Detail*, p. 30, 1970
- Jimmy Swaggart, a 52-year-old howler from Baton Rouge known in some quarters as "the Mick Jagger of TV evangelism," got nailed in a nasty little sting operation down in New Orleans[.] — Hunter S. Thompson, *Generation of Swine*, p. 21, 1988
- I forgot for a minute there it was Gibbs convicted Sonny and nailed you on the dope charge. — Elmore Leonard, *Maximum Bob*, p. 116, 1991

2 to kill *UK, 1824*

- She's a Commie pig. We're going to nail every last one. — *Harold and Maude*, 1971

3 to have sex *US, 1957*

- ALLISON: He nailed me. CLAIRE: Very nice. ALLISON: I don't think that from a legal standpoint what he did can be construed as rape since I paid him. — *The Breakfast Club*, 1985
- Name me one chick in our senior class that Rick Derris didn't nail, for Christ's sake. — *Chasing Amy*, 1997
- I decided not to nail her when she was too drunk to remember it. — *Ten Things I Hate About You*, 1999
- I wonder if I can nail that dumb bitch. — Marty Beckerman, *Death to All Cheerleaders*, 2000

4 (of a wave) to knock a surfer from the surfboard *US, 1977*

Always in the passive voice.

- — Gary Fairmont R. Filosa II, *The Surfer's Almanac*, p. 190, 1977

▶ **nail the core**

in the language of hang gliding, to find the centre of a thermal and ride it up *US, 1992*

- — Erik Fair, *California Thrill Sports*, p. 328, 1992

nail-biter *noun*

any situation that evokes anxiety or tension as to its outcome *US, 1971*

- Its place in Dodger mythology, however, is more interesting than that because the first three games were Series classics, nail-biters that could have gone either way[.] — Thomas Oliphant, *Praying for Gil Hodges*, p. 169, 2000

nailed *adjective*

deranged *US, 1836*

- — *American Speech*, p. 304, December 1955: "Wayne University slang"

nail-em-and-jail-em *noun*

a police officer *US, 1980*

- — Edith A. Folb, *runnin' down some lines*, p. 247, 1980

nail nicker *noun*

in gambling, a cheat who marks cards by nicking them with his fingernails *US, 1997*

- Besides dice tats and 7UPS, there were volumes for nail nickers and crimpers (card markers), hand muckers and mit men (card switchers), as well as card counters and shiner players. — Stephen Cannell, *Big Con*, p. 143, 1997

nails *noun*

a disappointment; a failure *US, 1981*

Hawaiian youth usage.

- Wow, da prom was nails dees year! — Douglas Simonson, *Pidgin to da Max*, 1981

Naked Fanny *nickname*
Nakhon Phanon, Thailand *US, 1967*
Vietnam war humor.

- His former classmate was visiting the Shiloh under an unofficial "liaison" program that brought together navy airmen and the air force types stationed at Nakhom Phanom in Thailand, a place referred to by the military as NKP or "naked fanny." — Stephen Coonts, *Flight of the Intruder*, p. 307, 1986

Nam *nickname*
Vietnam *US, 1962*
Usually used with "the." Originally military, then widespread.

- She's in love with some fool what's in the Nam. — Steve Cannon, *Groove, Bang, and Jive Around*, p. 29, 1969
- In the Nam the same gold ball drives the colonels and generals into their air-conditioned headquarters offices. — Charles Anderson, *The Grunts*, p. 6, 1976
- He likes to hear stories about Nam. — *Apocalypse Now*, 1979
- Sorry bout that boys—"sin loi" buddy, you gonna love the Nam, man. — *Platoon*, 1986
- This is not 'Nam. This is bowling. There are rules. — *The Big Lebowski*, 1998

namby-pamby *noun*
an effeminate male *US, 1968*

- — Collin Baker et al., *College Undergraduate Slang Study Conducted at Brown University*, p. 161, 1968

name *noun*
an important or famous person *US, 1975*

- We've got a lot of names coming in. — *Nashville*, 1975
- All they had at this stage was a few 8X10's off the names Rougeau presumably plans to build around. — *Herb's Wrestling Tidbits*, 17th August 1995

na-na's *noun*
the female breasts *US, 2005*

- Maddy shows off an extremely fluffy muff as her kissy sissy nuzzles her na-nas. — Mr. Skin, *Mr. Skin's Skincyclopedia*, p. 116, 2005

nance *noun*
an effeminate male or homosexual *US, 1910*

- The club-footed nance son-of-a-bitch. — Horace McCoy, *Kiss Tomorrow Good-bye*, p. 70, 1948
- Right away I spotted the nances, they were dolled up like Lady Astor's horses. — Dev Collans with Stewart Sterling, *I was a House Detective*, p. 105, 1954
- The unsophisticated who think of queers as prancing nances with rouged lips and bleached hair may not believe that all pansies do not wear skirts over their pants. — Lee Mortimer, *Women Confidential*, p. 63, 1960
- When he told the director, softly, where to get off, the nance gave him notice. — Mary McCarthy, *The Group*, p. 72, 1963

nance *verb*
to behave in an exaggeratedly feminine fashion *US, 1968*

- "Ok, Buck," he nanced in a high voice. — Earl Thompson, *Tattoo*, p. 243, 1974

Nancy Flores; Nancy *noun*
Nuestra Familia, a Mexican-American prison gang *US, 1975*

- — Report to the Senate, *California Senate Committee on Civil Disorder*, p. 230, 1975

nano *noun*
a very short period of time *US, 1991*
An abbreviation of "nanosecond," used figuratively.

- "Be with you in nano" means you really will be free shortly[.] — Eric S. Raymond, *The New Hacker's Dictionary*, p. 254, 1991

nap *noun*
the short, curly hair of a black person *US, 1969*

- He continued to rub both the broads' heads, pulled Annette's wig off, exposing her naps, and pulling Virginia's stringy hair. — Steve Cannon, *Groove, Bang, and Jive Around*, p. 133, 1969
- "I felt that motherfucker pull on my nap." Meaning his Afro. — Mark Baker, *Cops*, p. 202, 1985

nape *noun*
napalm, a mixture of gasoline and a thickening agent for use in flame throwers or incendiary bombs, used extensively by the US during World War 2 and later war
s *US, 1968*

- They gonna lay snake and nape right on the perimeter so stay tight in your holes and don't leave 'em. — *Platoon*, 1986
- But dropping nape and strafing trucks / Are two things he don't know. — Joseph Tuso, *Singing the Vietnam Blues*, p. 103, 1990: I 'Druther Be an F-4 Jock

nar *adjective*
treacherous *US, 1988*
An abbreviation of **GNARLY**.

- — Surf Punks, *Oh No! Not Them Again!* (liner notes), 1988

narc *verb*
to inform, to betray *US, 1974*

- "He wouldn't turn me, would he, June? He wouldn't narc me over?" — Robert Stone, *Dog Soldiers*, p. 83, 1974
- She got some trashy boyfriend who sold cocaine and eventually he got busted and narced on everyone to stay out of jail. — Michelle Tea, *The Passionate Mistakes and Intricate Corruption of One Girl in America*, p. 15, 1998

narc; nark *noun*
1 an undercover narcotics officer *US, 1967*

- I read how the narcs came and busted Jerry Rubin, a founder of the Yippies. — James Simon Kunen, *The Strawberry Statement*, p. 94, 1968
- He [President Nixon] announced in his very first speech, his inaugural address if I remember right, that he was adding three hundred new narks to the team. — Abbie Hoffman, *Woodstock Nation*, p. 68, 1969
- The Man has got himself a "temporary" restraining order against the printer of the Berkeley Tribe (Walter Press) from further printing of the names and addresses of local narcs. — *The Berkeley Tribe*, p. 4, 15th–21st August 1969
- They thought I was a narc (narcotics agent) out to bust them. — Arthur Blessitt, *Turned On to Jesus*, p. 110, 1971

2 a social outcast *US, 2001*

- — Pamela Munro, *U.C.L.A. Slang*, p. 95, 2001

narc ark; nark ark *noun*
an undercover narcotic officer's car *US, 1973*

- I could just picture me and her getting hauled off to jail in a nark ark. — Joseph Wambaugh, *The Blue Knight*, p. 37, 1973
- Halfway down to Sunset with the loot, the car fishtails and sideswipes a sheriff's nark ark. — James Ellroy, *Suicide Hill*, p. 597, 1986

narco *noun*
1 narcotics *US, 1954*

- Where it began, he couldn't say. Maybe on Patterson's first night with the Narco Squad. — Clarence Cooper Jr., *The Scene*, p. 21, 1960
- Do in 5 years for Sale of Narco. — Clarence Cooper Jr., *The Farm*, p. 9, 1967
- He had plastic surgery done on his face after he beat that narco rap out there and changed his base. — Mickey Spillane, *Last Cop Out*, p. 42, 1972
- Like if there was a shrink who could turn you off narco for the rest of your life, I'd turn all that bread over to him without even bothering to count it. — Robert Deane Pharr, *Giveadamn Brown*, p. 10, 1978

2 a narcotics detective *US, 1955*

- His adversaries in this continual quest are always the police: the "narcos," "The Man." — James Mills, *The Panic in Needle Park*, p. 15, 1966
- Take hippies and straights, heads and narcos, put them together for 36 hours – under a church roof. — *Berkeley Barb*, p. 3, 25th February 1967

3 the Lexington (Kentucky) Federal Narcotics Hospital *US, 1955*

- — *American Speech*, p. 87, May 1955: "Narcotic argot along the Mexican border"

nards *noun*
the testicles *US, 1970*

- — *Current Slang*, p. 21, Spring 1970
- [F]reezing my nards off every weekend. — Frank Zappa, *The Real Frank Zappa Book*, p. 35, 1989

narf!
used for expressing frustration *US, 2002*
From the television cartoon show "Pinky and the Brain."

- "Narf! I burnt the cookies!" — *Dictionary of New Terms (Hope College)*, 2002

narghile *noun*
a water pipe used for smoking marijuana or hashish *US, 1970*

- — William D. Alsever, *Glossary for the Establishment and Other Uptight People*, p. 16, December 1970

narrow yellow *noun*
a military form (OCSA Form 159) used to pass routine actions to staff agencies *US, 1986*

- — Department of the Army, *Staff Officer's Guidebook*, p. 62, 1986

nasodrain *noun*
while surfing, the sudden and violent expulsion of sea water through the nose *US, 1991*
- — Trevor Cralle, *The Surfin'ary*, p. 79, 1991

nasty *noun*
▸ **do the nasty**
to have sex *US, 1977*
A squeamish euphemism applied in a jocular manner.
- — Connie Eble (Editor), *UNC-CH Campus Slang*, p. 3, Spring 1990
- "He really dating your grandma? [...] Think they did the nasty?" I almost ran the car up on the sidewalk. "No! Yuck!" — Janet Evanovich, *Seven Up*, p. 7, 2001
- Another way to say "intercourse" [...] Doing the nasty[.] — Erica Orloff and JoAnn Baker, *Dirty Little Secrets*, p. 63, 2001
- "Malley and Cherish doing the nasty. Good old reliable human frailty." — Jonathan Kellerman, *Rage*, p. 266, 2005

nasty *adjective*
1 excellent *US, 1940*
- — Robert S. Gold, *A Jazz Lexicon*, p. 213, 1964
2 sexy, attractive, appealing; sluttish *US, 1995*
A reversal of the conventional sense.
- She be wearin' nasty gear and voguin' like Tina Turner. — Lois Stavsky, *A2Z*, p. 70, 1995
- And they're Nasty, the kind of girls who want their tasty butts spanked before they drink cum! — Peter Sotos, *Index*, p. 54, 1996
- We're a party group, we about being nasty and having parties. — Alex Ogg, *The Hip Hop Years [quoting 'Duke Bootee' Ed Fletcher]*, p. 67, 1999

nasty boat *noun*
a patrol boat developed for the coastal anti-invasion mission of the Royal Norwegian Navy *US, 1990*
The "nasty" is a technical term adopted to the vernacular.
- Dubbed a "Nasty" boat, after the Norwegian "Nasty" class PT boats, these Norwegian-built, aluminum-hulled boats were more modern than the two U.S. boats taken out of mothballs. — T.L. Bosiljevac, *SEALs*, p. 19, 1990
- [T]he Vietnamese simply couldn't master the Nasty's tricky high-speed maneuvers. — John Plaster, *SOG*, p. 26, 1997

nastygram *noun*
any unpleasant or unwanted e-mail *US, 1991*
- — Eric S. Raymond, *The New Hacker's Dictionary*, p. 255, 1991

nasty neat *adjective*
cleaner than clean *US, 1975*
- — John Gould, *Maine Lingo*, pp. 187–188, 1975

natch *noun*
▸ **on the natch**
withdrawing from drug addiction without medication to ease the pain *US, 1969*
- — Eugene Landy, *The Underground Dictionary*, p. 141, 1971

natch; nach *adverb*
naturally *US, 1945*
- — Lou Shelly, *Hepcats Jive Talk Dictionary*, p. 15, 1945
- Natch I was hip to the lay the moment I dug his joint. — Terry Southern, *Candy*, p. 212, 1958
- "You really expect me to go callously off to Hawaii while he's still here?" "Natch," my father said. "Why not?" — Frederick Kohner, *Gidget Goes Hawaiian*, p. 4, 1961
- "But Mary-Ann told me he behaved abominably at your house." "Natch!! That's what I like." — Gore Vidal, *Myra Breckinridge*, p. 218, 1968

nate *noun*
1 nothing *US, 1993*
- — *The Bell (Paducah Tilghman High School)*, pp. 8–9, 17th December 1993: "Tilghmanism: the concealed language of the hallway"
2 an Alaskan native *US, 1983*
- — Russell Tabbert, *Dictionary of Alaskan English*, p. 53, 1991

nates *noun*
the buttocks *UK, 1581*
- — J.R. Schwartz, *The Official Guide to the Best Cat Houses in Nevada*, p. 165, 1993: "Sex glossary"
- Is there anyone on earth who is outside the realm of Jennifer Lopez's magnificent nates? — Mr. Skin, *Mr. Skin's Skincyclopedia*, p. 334, 2005

native *noun*
1 a Native American Indian *US, 2000*
- Whites were seen in quiet conversations with Natives. — Bill Valentine, *Gangs and Their Tattoos*, p. 12, 2000
2 to the employee of a circus or carnival, a local patron *US, 1980*
- — Joe McKennon, *Circus Lingo*, p. 64, 1980
- — Don Wilmeth, *The Language of American Popular Entertainment*, p. 181, 1981

nato *adjective*
used for describing someone who is not sexually aggressive *US, 1961*
- N.A.T.O. No action, talk only. — Art Unger, *The Cool Book*, p. 130, 1961
- "Hey, so it was all NATO?" "Huh?" "No Action—Talk Only." — Frederick Kohner, *The Affairs of Gidget*, p. 25, 1963
- When New York girls speak of a date as N.A.T.O., they mean contemptuously, "No Action, Talk Only." — Joe David Brown, *Sex in the '60s*, p. 19, 1968

natural *noun*
1 a hairstyle embraced largely by black people, featuring longer, unprocessed, unparted hair *US, 1969*
- [S]ome with fluffy naturals like my sister Angie, some with silky naturals like my sister Betty. — George Jackson, *Soledad Brother*, p. 313, June 1970
- Her once scrawny frame was all softness and curves, and she looked like an African princess, with her hair in a then uncommon Natural. — Iceberg Slim (Robert Beck), *The Naked Soul of Iceberg Slim*, p. 83, 1971
- And take those two dudes with the naturals along with you. — Joseph Wambaugh, *The Blue Knight*, p. 67, 1973
- Wilson looked up at the tall man wearing the large shades that hid his eyes and the wide-brimmed hat that covered his natural. — Joseph Nazel, *Black Cop*, p. 37, 1974
2 in craps, a winning roll of seven on the first toss *US, 1962*
- — Frank Garcia, *Marked Cards and Loaded Dice*, p. 263, 1962
3 Seven-Up™ soda *US, 1967*
An allusion to the game of craps, where a seven is a "natural."
- — *American Speech*, p. 63, February 1967: "Soda-fountain, restaurant and tavern calls"
4 in pool, a shot that cannot be missed or a game that cannot be lost *US, 1990*
- — Steve Rushin, *Pool Cool*, p. 21, 1990

natural punk *noun*
in prison, a man who had been homosexual outside prison *US, 1972*
- — Bruce Jackson, *Outside the Law*, p. 59, 1972: "Glossary"

nature *noun*
the penis; sexual arousal *US, 2002*
- Every time I see that bitch, I feel my nature come up on me. — Gary K. Farlow, *Prison-ese*, p. 45, 2002

nature boy *noun*
a boy in need of a haircut *US, 1955*
- — *American Weekly*, p. 2, 14th August 1955

naughty *noun*
▸ **do the naughty**
to have sex *US, 1998*
- I knew we'd do the notty tonight. — Renay Jackson, *Oaktown Devil*, p. 21, 1998

nautch *noun*
a brothel; a striptease; a sex show of any kind *US, 1872*
- I'm one of the nautch girls. I do a specialty dance. — Robert Edmond Alter, *Carny Kill*, p. 5, 1966
- — Joe McKennon, *Circus Lingo*, p. 64, 1980

Nava-Joe *noun*
a member of the Navajo Indian tribe *US, 1963*
- — *American Speech*, p. 271, December 1963: "American Indian student slang"

navy brat *noun*
the child of a career member of the navy *US, 1992*
- Renee was a navy brat, born and raised in San Diego. — Armistead Maupin, *Maybe the Moon*, p. 91, 1992

Navy cake *noun*
homosexual anal sex *US, 1964*
- — Roger Blake, *The American Dictionary of Sexual Terms*, p. 139, 1964
- — Anon, *King Smut's Wet Dreams Interpreted*, 1978

Navy Junior *noun*
the child of a career member of the US Navy *US, 1934*
- Winters was a Navy junior who grew up in the service and graduated from Annapolis in 1935. — Robert Lawson, *U.S. Navy Air Combat*, p. 45, 2000

nay-nays *noun*
a woman's breasts *US, 1967*
- You know, in the backs of those "Fun Shops," you'll see guys looking through racks and racks of pictures of ladies' nay-nays wrapped in cellophane. — Lenny Bruce, *The Essential Lenny Bruce*, p. 219, 1967
- Next comes the baton-twirling face of Desiree Cousteau, whose nay-nays are uncle-handed by then-mustachioed Lou at the Melody. — Josh Alan Friedman, *Tales of Times Square*, p. 31, 1986
- She really and truly was until Baby Jewels nuked her naynay. — Seth Morgan, *Homeboy*, p. 274, 1990

Nazi *noun*
a fanatic about the preceding noun *US, 1984*
Not coined but rendered wildly popular on the "Soup Nazi" episode of Jerry Seinfeld's television comedy that first aired on 2nd November 1995.
- Barbara Jane shrugged apologetically. "Clothes Nazi." — Dan Jenkins, *Life Its Ownself*, p. 58, 1984
- SURF NAZI: Blond hair, blue eyes and a one track mind. — Michael V. Anderson, *The Bad, Rad, Not to Forget Way Cool Beach and Surf Discriptionary*, p. 20, 1988

near-beer *noun*
a beer-like product with a very low alcohol content, legal during Prohibition *US, 1909*
There is some dispute about who said the cleverest thing ever said about "near-beer"—"The guy who called that near beer is a bad judge of distance."
- Ahern said the banning is part of the current drive on "waterholes," those nonalcoholic bars serving near-beer, soft drinks, and sex. — *San Francisco Examiner*, p. 21, 9th March 1976

neat *adjective*
1 pleasing, very good *US, 1936*
Found as early as 1808, rejected late in the C19, and then returned to favor in the 1930s. Still heard; inescapably **HOKEY**.
- "Hi," I answered. "That's a neat board." — Frederick Kohner, *Gidget*, p. 27, 1957
- I was up there the other day, it's really a neat scene. — Gurney Norman, *Divine Right's Trip (Last Whole Earth Catalog)*, p. 159, 1971
- I hate to tell yuh, this is nineteen seventy-five, you know that "neat" went out, I would say, at the turn of the century. — *Annie Hall*, 1977
- We're having like a really neat open house today from like four to whenever if you care to stop by. — *Sleepless in Seattle*, 1993
2 (used of an alcoholic drink) served without ice or water *UK, 1579*
- He sweated in his shirts till the backs were rotted through, and drank his whiskey neat[.] — John Clellon Holmes, *The Horn*, p. 44, 1958
- He had taken his first drink neat. Now he poured another, dropped ice into it, sat back and smiled at her. — John A. Williams, *Sissie*, p. 24, 1963
- Buster was trying to look jaunty but his hands were shaking. "Gimme a Johnny Blc," he said. "Neat." — Joseph Wambaugh, *The Golden Orange*, p. 49, 1990
- He felt warm inside, a nice buzz warming his belly, filled with three straight neat gins and an ice-cold Guinness stout. — Odie Hawkins, *Midnight*, p. 84, 1995

neat *adjective + adverb*
(said of sex) without a condom *US, 1997*
- "I am totally shocked, let me tell you, that you fucked him neat. Just because he doesn't understand condoms doesn't—." — Ethan Morden, *Some Men Are Lookers*, p. 173, 1997

neatnik *noun*
a person with a compulsive desire for neatness *US, 1959*
- Kate, who confessed to being a neatnik, also found Harold a total slob and bitterly resented having to dispose of his crusted rice and congealed chow yuk before she could cook her own Veg-All patties. — Cyra McFadden, *The Serial*, p. 146, 1977
- Tidying up. Getting everything straight and true. What was running through this neatnik's mind right now? — James Patterson, *4th of July*, p. 324, 2005

neato *adjective*
good *US, 1901*

- I asked my sisters if they thought they saw a kid burning, melting, on the engine and they said no, did you?, neato. — Bret Easton Ellis, *Less Than Zero*, p. 76, 1985
- If they do they're probably too scared of seeming critical of those neato Latinos to even try. — Alisa Valdes-Rodriguez, *The Dirty Girls Social Club*, p. 101, 2003

neatojet *adjective*
excellent *US, 1972*
- — Helen Dahlskog (Editor), *A Dictionary of Contemporary and Colloquial Usage*, p. 42, 1972

nebbie; neb *noun*
Nembutal™, a branded central nervous system depressant *US, 1963*
- Not even a nebbie. He could have given me one at least. — Hubert Selby Jr., *Last Exit to Brooklyn*, p. 55, 1957

nebby *adjective*
inquisitive, prying *US, 1982*
- — Sam McCool, *Pittsburghese*, p. 25, 1982

Nebraska sign *noun*
a completely flat reading on an electrocardiogram *US, 1994*
An allusion to the endless flat prairies of Nebraska.
- — Sally Williams, *"Strong" Words*, p. 151, 1994

neck *noun*
1 a rural, racist white person *US, 1973*
An abbreviation of **RED NECK**.
- Consensus of opinion: watch out for pigs and necks! — Joe Eszterhas, *Charlie Simpson's Apocalypse*, p. 179, 1973
2 a white prisoner *US, 1976*
A shortened "redneck."
- — John R. Armore and Joseph D. Wolfe, *Dictionary of Desperation*, p. 41, 1976
3 in horseracing, a distance of less than half a horse length *US, 1951*
- — David W. Maurer, *Argot of the Racetrack*, p. 43, 1951

▸ **come out of the side of your neck**
to talk back, to insult *US, 2002*
- "How 'bout I clarify your sideways-talking mouth into chopped meat, you fish motherfucker! Nobody comes outta the side of their neck at me!" — Jimmy Lerner, *You Got Nothing Coming*, p. 61, 2002

neck *verb*
to kiss in a lingering fashion *UK, 1825*
- Couples began to neck publicly. — James T. Farrell, *Saturday Night*, p. 50, 1947
- A couple necking on a flat bench beside the Park wall diddled a battery radio and it began to sing through its nose. — Philip Wylie, *Opus 21*, p. 169, 1949
- We parked down by the riverbank and necked for a couple of hours. Then she said, "My name is Pearl McBride." — Max Shulman, *The Many Loves of Dobie Gillis*, p. 124, 1951
- She starts necking some bastard in the kitchen when she gets tanked up. — J. D. Salinger, *Nine Stories*, p. 117, 1953
- We were downstairs in the cellar playroom, her parents were asleep, and we decided to turn out the lights and neck a little. — Phyllis and Eberhard Kronhausen, *Sex Histories of American College Men*, p. 74, 1960

neck-stretcher *noun*
a thief *US, 1960*
- "You're a common neck-stretcher. That's my opinion." — Nelson Algren, *The Neon Wilderness*, p. 12, 1960

necktie party *noun*
a hanging, especially an extra-judicial lynching *US, 1882*
The 19th century companion "necktie social" (1888) does not appear to have survived in the later 20th century.
- Howsoever, it sure looked like I was about to be the guest of honor at a necktie party, when Myra decided to speak up. — Jim Thompson, *Pop. 1280*, p. 98, 1964
- While waiting for his special necktie party, President Woodrow Wilson commuted his death sentence[.] — Red Rudensky, *The Gonif*, p. 21, 1970
- Not wanting Earl to ruin his necktie party, Jake grabbed the rope and helped Willie pull on it. — Donald Goines, *Swamp Man*, p. 60, 1974
- All I could visualize was a lunch party waiting under some tree. But no, it is not to a necktie party he's taking me to, it's to Spanikie's home in the suburbs. — Odie Hawkins, *Black Casanova*, p. 70, 1984

necro *noun*
a necrophile *US, 1986–1987*
- — *Maledicta*, p. 180, Summer/Winter 1986–1987: "Sexual slang: prostitutes, pedophiles, flagellators, transvestites, and necrophiles"

nectar *noun*
alcohol *US, 1966*
Formerly standard English, now slumming in slang with an archaic tone.
- No sign of nectar, though. — Richard Farina, *Been Down So Long*, p. 35, 1966

nectar *adjective*
excellent *US, 1989*
- — Pamela Munro, *U.C.L.A. Slang*, p. 61, 1989

needle *noun*
▸ **on the needle**
using or addicted to drugs injected intravenously *US, 1942*
- "The dealer's on the needle," was the whisper, and overnight he was an outcast of outcasts[.] — Nelson Algren, *The Man with the Golden Arm*, p. 279, 1949

▸ **take the needle**
to be executed by lethal injection *US, 2002*
- "Two years for sure versus maybe a chance of taking the needle?" — Jimmy Lerner, *You Got Nothing Coming*, p. 23, 2002

needle *verb*
to irritate, to annoy, to provoke *UK, 1873*
- [T]he mush said he would not go until he got the denial that was coming to him. That needled the boss. — Butch Reynolds, *Broken Hearted Clown*, p. 28, 1953
- Don't give them any lip if they come by and needle you. — Iceberg Slim (Robert Beck), *Pimp*, p. 300, 1969

needle beer *noun*
beer which has been fortified with another form of alcohol *US, 1962*
- — Joseph E. Ragen and Charles Finston, *Inside the World's Toughest Prison*, p. 809, 1962: "Penitentiary and underworld glossary"

needle candy *noun*
any drug that can be injected *US, 1971*
- — Eugene Landy, *The Underground Dictionary*, p. 139, 1971

needledick *noun*
a small, thin penis; a man so equipped *US, 1970*
- You paddy motherfuckers never make me feel nothin' with yo' needle dicks. — Joseph Wambaugh, *The New Centurions*, p. 81, 1970
- "Hey Needledick, checked anybody's oil lately?" "Needledick the Bug-Fucker!" — John Sayles, *Union Dues*, p. 20, 1977

needle drop *noun*
a single playing of a recorded musical performance *US, 1970*
- They want thirty-five bucks a needle drop. — Roger Blake, *The Porno Movies*, p. 192, 1970

needle freak *noun*
an intravenous drug user *US, 1967*
- "Gypsie's a needle freak, too," someone said to him one day, while he was geezing. — Nicholas Von Hoffman, *We are the People Our Parents Warned Us Against*, p. 153, 1967
- My main horror, all afternoon, was a firm conviction that I was locked in a clutch of junkies, real needle freaks. — Hunter S. Thompson, *Fear and Loathing in America*, p. 189, 9th June 1969: Letter to Oscar Acosta

needle house *noun*
a house or apartment where needle-injecting drug users can buy sterile needles *US, 1997*
- Either that or you can walk the block or two of the established needle house—the house of some profit-minded diabetic—and get fixed for a dollar. — David Simon and Edward Burns, *The Corner*, pp. 68–69, 1997

needle jockey *noun*
a nurse or doctor who administers shots *US, 1960*
- — *American Speech*, pp. 158–159, May 1960: "The burgeoning of 'jockey'"

needleman *noun*
in a confidence swindle, an agent who inspires the victim with confidence in the scheme *US, 1988*
- — Kathleen Odean, *High Steppers, Fallen Angels, and Lollipops*, p. 133, 1988

needle park *noun*
a public park or public area where drug addicts gather and inject drugs *US, 1966*
- Back-pocket bookies get their pockets picked, hookers and Cadillac pimps get herded off the street, the needle parks and shooting galleries get swept. — Robert Campbell, *Juice*, p. 143, 1988

Needle Park *nickname*
Sherman Square (71st Street and Amsterdam Avenue and Broadway), New York *US, 1966*
So named because it was a spot favored by drug users.
- To subway riders who use the stop there, the intersection is Sherman Square. To the drug addicts it is "Needle Park." — Jack Douglas, *Observations of Deviance*, p. 267, 1970
- He came to the surface at Broadway and Seventy-second Street, and directly behind him as the patch of dried grass and ring of benches known as Needle Park. — Malcolm Braly, *The Protector*, p. 8, 1979

needle-sticker *noun*
a drug user who injects the drugs *US, 1992*
- "Ain't losin' my board to some stinkin' ole needle sticker!" — Jess Mowry, *Way Past Cool*, p. 85, 1992

negaholic *noun*
a person with a compulsion to be negative *US, 1989*
- To help her clients recognize and reverse these disastrous patterns, she coined the term negaholic as a way to describe colleagues, managers, and organizations that pull us all down. — Paul Edwards, *Getting Business to Come to You*, p. 102, 1998

negative perspiration
no problem; no need to worry *US, 1970*
- "Take her easy, Harold." "Sure! Negative perspiration!" Harold said heartily. — Stephen King, *The Stand*, p. 544, 1978

negatory
no *US, 1955*
Coined in the military, popularized in the US by truck drivers in the 1970s.
- — Connie Eble (Editor), *UNC-CH Campus Slang*, p. 7, Spring 1988
- Negatory. Okay! — *Wayne's World 2*, 1993

negotiable grass *noun*
money *US, 1951*
- — David W. Maurer, *Argot of the Racetrack*, p. 44, 1951

neighbor *noun*
the number on either side of the winning number on a roulette wheel *US, 1961*
- — Thomas L. Clark, *The Dictionary of Gambling and Gaming*, p. 135, 1987

nellie *noun*
an obviously homosexual man; an effeminate homosexual man *UK, 1916*
Recorded at least as early as 1916, but not fully emerged until the outing of gay culture.
- — Collin Baker et al., *College Undergraduate Slang Study Conducted at Brown University*, p. 161, 1968
- And if a gay cruise up and down the Hudson River does not strike you as the nadir of nellie narcissism, it was, at all events, enough to set pleated pants back ten years. — *Screw*, p. 10, 20th November 1972
- Today, for the third day in a row, I was besieged by a mob of hostile nellies midway through the feature because no one was making the reel changes up in the projection booth[.] — Jim Carroll, *Forced Entries*, p. 49, 1987
- Nellie, you're a disgrace to depression. — *As Good As It Gets*, 1997

nelly-assed *adjective*
effeminate *US, 1963*
- I may not be the Queen of Sheba, exactly, but I am The Queen of This Meat Rack—and I'll prove it to any nellyassed queen that wants to try me. — John Rechy, *City of Night*, p. 53, 1963

nelly, nellie *adjective*
extremely, even outrageously, effeminate *US, 1963*
- "Shut your nelly mouth, Mary," said the Negro queen—"or I'll have you eight-sixed out of this bar[.]" — John Rechy, *City of Night*, p. 186, 1963
- Horace had chosen show business because it was best for him since he was so obviously nellie... — Lenny Bruce, *How to Talk Dirty and Influence People*, p. 34, 1965

- Carey-Lee, secure in his knowledge that he is loved, does not throw a "bitch fit" when his nellie neighbor, Tommy (Edward Dunn) intimates that something more than a simple "visit" may have taken place while he was away. — *Screw*, p. 20, 27 October 1969
- He shed his navy-blue cotton parka, submitted to the indignity of women's skates (white, with nelly-looking tassels) and clopped his way awkwardly to the edge of the rink. — Armistead Maupin, *Tales of the City*, p. 124, 1978

nembie; nemby *noun*
a barbiturate, especially Nembutal™ *US, 1950*
- This night, Herman was knocked out on "nembies" and his head kept falling down onto the bar. — William Burroughs, *Junkie*, p. 26, 1953

nemish *noun*
a capsule of pentobarbital sodium (trade name Nembutal™), a central nervous system depressant *US, 1969*
- — Richard Lingeman, *Drugs from A to Z*, p. 182, 1969

nemmie *noun*
a capsule of pentobarbitral sodium (trade name Nembutal™), a central nervous system depressant *US, 1950*
- Nembutals are the prostitutes' favorite. Among initiates they are known as goof balls, or nemmies. — Jack Lait and Lee Mortimer, *Washington Confidential*, p. 117, 1951
- — Donald Louria, *Nightmare Drugs*, p. 25, 1966

nephew *noun*
a young, passive male homosexual in relation to his older lover *US, 1950*
- — Hyman E. Goldin et al., *Dictionary of American Underworld Lingo*, p. 144, 1950

neppy *noun*
a person from northeast Philadelphia *US, 1996*
A combination of "North East Philly."
- — Claudio R. Salvucci, *The Philadelphia Dialect Dictionary*, p. 47, 1996

'ner *noun*
dinner *US, 1969*
- — John D. Bell et al., *Loosely Speaking*, p. Appendix, 1969

nerd; nurd *noun*
a person lacking in social skills, fashion sense, or both *US, 1951*
- In Detroit, someone who once would be called a drip or a square is now, regrettably, a nerd, or in a less severe case, a scurve. — *Newsweek*, 8th October 1951
- [A]nyone who is not a nerd (drip) knows that the bug is the family car[.] — *Herald Press (St. Jospeh, Missouri)*, p. 14, 23rd June 1952
- Cats who lack grey matter are nerds or oddballs. — *Frederick (Maryland) Post*, p. 9, 8th February 1954
- "Oahu—what's that?" asked Wally. He was a real nurd. — Frederick Kohner, *Gidget Goes Hawaiian*, p. 22, 1961

nerd box *noun*
a study cubicle *US, 1997*
- — Pamela Munro, *U.C.L.A. Slang*, p. 92, 1997

nerdly *noun*
a socially inept outcast *US, 1965*
- — *Time*, p. 56, 1st January 1965: "Students: the slang bag"

nerd pack *noun*
a plastic pocket protector *US, 1981*
- We faced a smaller man with a row of Bic fine points in a plastic case in his breast pocket—otherwise known as a nerd pack[.] — Michael Lewis, *Liar's Poker*, p. 29, 1989

nerdy *adjective*
socially inept *US, 1960*
- He was a pleasant-faced balding man, mild-mannered and slightly nerdy. — Michael Crichton, *State of Fear*, p. 73, 2004

nerps *noun*
the female breasts *US, 2005*
- Little Nel shows her not-so-little nerps with Roger Daltrey and Ringo Starr. — Mr. Skin, *Mr. Skin's Skincyclopedia*, p. 94, 2005

nerts!; nertz!
used as an expression of frustration *US, 1929*
A dialect rendering of **NUTS!**
- "Nertz," said Gimlet. "It's already past lunch." — Harvard Lampsoon, *Bored of the Rings*, p. 108, 1969

nervous *adjective*
excellent, well done *US, 1926*
- — *American Speech*, p. 304, December 1955: "Wayne University slang"
- According to enthusiasts, this "cat" (man) is "real nervous" (great). — *Look*, p. 49, 24th November 1959
- — Robert George Reisner, *The Jazz Titans*, p. 161, 1960

nervous-jervis *adjective*
very nervous *US, 1982*
- I'm having a real blast and I don't have pimples, or rashes on my hands, or go home all nervous-jervis from holding back with a date. — Scott Rubin, *National Lampoon's Big Book of Love*, p. 92, 2004

nervous Nellie *noun*
an excessively nervous person *US, 1925*
- "You're being a nervous Nellie. This is a trying moment, sure." — Saul Bellow, *Humboldt's Gift*, p. 285, 1975

nervy *adjective*
nervous *US, 1891*
- I don't know a thing about her, but she seemed like a nervy kid in a jam and I didn't like the snotty way that cop acted when he stopped the car. — Mickey Spillane, *Kiss Me Deadly*, pp. 18–19, 1952

nest *noun*
a hairdo *US, 1961*
High school student usage.
- — *San Francisco Examiner*, p. 21, 12th December 1961: "Colloquialisms for your murgatroid handcutts"

nest egg *noun*
money saved for the future *UK, 1700*
- It was obvious, they both agreed, that this last, unexpected stake must somehow be built into a nest egg which would reestablish them both on the bigtime where they belonged. — Robert Sylvester, *No Cover Charge*, p. 221, 1956
- Our houses, cars, jewels, paintings, and alleged objets d'art can be sold, which will give us a nice little nest egg to dip into if we should run short in Birmingham. — Max Shulman, *Anyone Got a Match?*, p. 264, 1964

nester *noun*
a member of the Mexican-American prison gang Nuestra Familia *US, 1990*
A corrupted pronunciation of "Nuestra."
- Sworn blood brothers, allies to the death against La Nuestra Familia, or Nesters, whose membership represented California's rural chili-chokers. — Seth Morgan, *Homeboy*, p. 176, 1990
- — Russell Flores, *Gang Slanging*, p. 131, 1998

nethead *noun*
in the language surrounding the Grateful Dead, a follower of the band who is part of the Grateful Dead cyber community *US, 1994*
- — David Shenk and Steve Silberman, *Skeleton Key*, p. 201, 1994

netiquette *noun*
the protocol, implicit or explicit, observed by members of an Internet discussion group *US, 1995*
- By taking the time to see if there is a FAQ, you'll be following Usenet "netiquette," the etiquette rules that have developed over the years to let members of the on-line community peacefully interact. — Nancy Tamosaitis, *net.sex*, p. 5, 1995

netlag *noun*
an inordinate delay in an Internet relay chat *US, 1995*
A pun on the standard "jet lag."
- — Christian Crumlish, *The Internet Dictionary*, p. 134, 1995

net police *noun*
a participant in an Internet discussion group who on a self-appointed basis polices the discussion for protocol and etiquette violations *US, 1991*
- — Eric S. Raymond, *The New Hacker's Dictionary*, p. 256, 1991

neuron *noun*
a neurologist *US, 1994*
- — Sally Williams, *"Strong" Words*, p. 152, 1994

Nevada lettuce *noun*
a one-thousand-dollar bill *US, 1962*
- — Frank Garcia, *Marked Cards and Loaded Dice*, p. 263, 1962

Nevada nickel *noun*
a five-dollar gambling token *US, 1979*
- — Thomas L. Clark, *The Dictionary of Gambling and Gaming*, p. 135, 1987

never happen
used for expressing a definitive "no" *US, 1977*
- "He goes to me, 'Take a little run up to the ridge and report to me,' and I goes like, 'Never happen, sir'" — Michael Herr, *Dispatches*, p. 26, 1977

nevermind *noun*
▸ **makes no nevermind**
makes no difference *US, 1924*
- My own marriage isn't exactly a bed of roses—true—but that makes no nevermind. — Robert Gover, *JC Saves*, p. 63, 1968

never-never land *noun*
an imaginary, ideal world *UK, 1900*
From J. M. Barrie's *Peter Pan* novels.
- My heart and beliefs is out there in never-never land when it comes to religion, but I don't want to get into that. — Robert Campbell, *Junkyard Dog*, p. 19, 1986

never pitch a bitch
used in confidence swindles as a humorous rule of thumb meaning "never try to do a sales job on a woman" *US, 1985*
- — M. Allen Henderson, *How Con Games Work*, p. 217, 1985: "Glossary"

never smarten a sucker up
used by gambling cheats and confidence swindlers as a prime rule of the trade *US, 1950*
- — *The Annals of the American Academy of Political and Social Sciences*, p. 128, May 1950

never-was *noun*
a person whom actual achievement has alluded *US, 1891*
- Some guy might boast about how he is going to get out next time and stay out, and some will put him down by saying he'll soon be back, playing marbles like a hasbeen, a nerverwas[.] — Eldridge Cleaver, *Soul on Ice*, p. 43, 1968
- The first four were aging has-beens and never-weres. — Robert Campbell, *Alice in La-La Land*, p. 195, 1987

new!
used for commenting humorously on a new purchase *US, 1963*
- For example, when a boy gets a haircut, he is greeted by his friends with an emphatic new. — *American Speech*, p. 274, December 1963: "American Indian student slang"

newbie *noun*
1 a newcomer *US, 1970*
Originally military.
- Andrews had first come to the attention of the grunts because he was the newest arrival—a "newby"—which meant he couldn't really lead or command anyone[.] — Charles Anderson, *The Grunts*, p. 31, 1976
- "You guys the newbies assigned to F Company, 58th?" — Gary Linderer, *The Eyes of the Eagle*, pp. 27–28, 1991
- A Deadhead who just got "on the bus." — David Shenk and Steve Silberman, *Skeleton Key*, p. 203, 1994
- [A] scrubby teenager approaches and asks whether or not I'm a Warhammer "newbie." — Marty Beckerman, *Death to All Cheerleaders*, p. 91, 2000

2 a new user of the Internet; a new arrival to an Internet discussion group *US, 1995*
The general sense "newcomer" used condescendingly.
- If you're a Net neophyte or "newbie," you'll undoubtedly be tempted to ask questions that have been covered thousands of times before. — Nancy Tamosaitis, *net.sex*, p. 5, 1995
- — Christian Crumlish, *The Internet Dictionary*, p. 134, 1995
- Last night I e-mailed Nancy.>I'm very taken with a nut, I said. / And she e-mailed back>It's a newbie phase, sweetie. Bob was just the same. — Melanie McGrath, *Hard, Soft & Wet*, p. 55, 1998

new cock *noun*
a freshly arrived prisoner, seen as a sexual object *US, 1971*
- These coveralls had a wide white stripe down the legs, and marked us as new-cocks. — James Blake, *The Joint*, p. 65, 1971

newfer *noun*
a new participant in an activity or group *US, 1971*
- Both men with nearly a year and a half in-country were tied by old times and impatient disrespect for the newfers and for the army in general. — John M. Del Vecchio, *The 13th Valley*, p. 24, 1982

New Guinea crud *noun*
any skin rash suffered in tropical and jungle environments *US, 1946*
- "Jungle rot," "New Guinea crud" or "the creeping crud" are U.S. servicemen's names for any & every kind of tropical skin disease. — *Time*, p. 76, 13th August 1946

new guy *noun*
a freshly arrived soldier to combat *US, 1970*
Often embellished to **FUCKING NEW GUY**.
- Being a new guy is a very uncomfortable thing; it's probably the most uncomfortable thing I've ever experienced. — Malcolm Boyd, *My Fellow Americans*, p. 212, 1970
- You listen to Joker, new guy. — *Full Metal Jacket*, 1987

new jack *noun*
a newcomer, especially one likely to be a success *US, 1988*
- We were the backpack wearin', baggy pants wearin' new jacks. — William Upski Wimsatt, *Bomb the Suburbs*, p. 19, 1994
- Experienced officers, not newjacks, which we'd soon be, were getting badly beaten up. — Ted Conover, *Newjack*, p. 47, 2000

new jill *noun*
a new female participant in an activity or group *US, 1990*
- Except for the hard rocks with something to prove and the new jills who had no idea who Isoke Oshodi was, all the other inmates soon followed Esperanza's lead. — Black Artemis, *Picture me Rollin'*, 2005

new kid *noun*
in roller derby, a skater who has not yet been accepted by other skaters *US, 1999*
- A rookie may be a new kid for years—until becoming one of the "family." — Keith Coppage, *Roller Derby to Rollerjam*, p. 126, 1999

new kid on the block *adjective*
in bar dice games, a player just joining an ongoing game *US, 1971*
- — Jester Smith, *Games They Play in San Francisco*, p. 104, 1971

new lamb *noun*
a freshly arrived prisoner *US, 1973*
- "The ones who seemed scared and sore at being inside, the 'new lambs,' as they're known." — Stanley Weber, *A Study of Sex in Prison*, p. 70, 1973

new meat *noun*
1 a newly met candidate for sexual conquest *US, 1967*
- The man also sees himself performing better with "new meat" or "fresh meat" than with someone familiar to him sexually. — Elliot Liebow, *Tally's Corner*, p. 122, 1967

2 a new student at a school *US, 1962*
- — *American Speech*, p. 272, December 1963: "American Indian student slang"

3 an inexperienced prison inmate *US, 1984*
- When a new arrival is assigned to permanent housing and moves into his assigned tier, he is the "new man" or "new meat." — Wayne Wooden, *Men Behind Bars*, p. 74, 1984

new pussy *noun*
a woman unknown to gang members *US, 1966*
- Usually they were mamas, but now and then what the Angels call "a strange broad" or "new pussy" would show up. — Hunter S. Thompson, *Hell's Angels*, p. 193, 1966

news bunny *noun*
a female television reporter or anchor hired for her cute looks *US, 1990*
- And for a least two decades now, stations most everywhere have been clipping their call letters to the microphones that their news bunnies thrust at people they want to interview. — *Los Angeles Times*, p. F1, 16th July 1990

new school *adjective*
(used of rap music) current, modern *US, 2001*
The functional reciprocal of **OLD SKOOL**.
- — Pamela Munro, *U.C.L.A. Slang*, p. 95, 2001

news hound *noun*
an enthusiastic and committed newspaper reporter *US, 1918*
- Perhaps he wasn't really a news hound; perhaps he was too distracted by personal matters. — Edwin Diamond, *Behind the Times*, p. 35, 1993

newsie *noun*

1 a street vendor of newspapers *US, 1875*

- Town of the blind and crippled newsies and the pinboys whose eyes you never see at all. — Nelson Algren, *Chicago*, p. 66, 1951
- "He played chess with the blind newsie down the block every Monday night." — Mickey Spillane, *The Big Kill*, p. 27, 1951
- [T]he kid we'd set up as a lookout had wandered off to match nickels with the corner newsie. — Nelson Algren, *The Neon Wilderness*, p. 84, 1960
- Some newsie might remember an odd customer on Monday night. — Thomas Harris, *Red Dragon*, p. 315, 1981

2 a newspaper reporter *US, 1951*

- I think I've learned a lot while working from home and making the switch from full-time newsie[.] — Celia Rivenbark, *We're Just Like You, Only Prettier*, 2004

newspaper *noun*

a thirty-day jail sentence *US, 1926*

- — Troy Harris, *A Booklet of Criminal Argot, Cant and Jargon*, p. 20, 1976

newsstand *noun*

a dealer in pornographic literature and magazines *US, 1986*

- "Some S and M. Some kiddie porn. Some—" "Zabano was a newsstand?" "Only retail." — Robert Campbell, *In La-La Land We Trust*, p. 97, 1986

newsy *adjective*

nosy; too interested in gossip *US, 1996*

- — Claudio R. Salvucci, *The Philadelphia Dialect Dictionary*, p. 49, 1996

newszine *noun*

a fan magazine that does not contain any fiction, just news *US, 1976*

- — *American Speech*, p. 53, Spring 1978: "Star Trek lives: Trekker slang"
- — *American Speech*, p. 28, Spring 1982: "The language of science fiction fan magazines"

New York kiss *noun*

a punch to the face *US, 1999*

- — Jeffrey McQuain, *Never Enough Words*, p. 55, 1999

New York minute *noun*

a very short period of time *US, 1948*

A nod to the impatience associated with New Yorkers.

- Equates to a nanosecond, or that infinitesimal blink of time in New York after the traffic light turns green and before the ol' boy behind you honks his horn. — Ken Weaver, *Texas Crude*, p. 116, 1984
- You tell me yes, I'll go call him at his house right now, get you set up in a New York minute. — Richard Price, *Clockers*, p. 524, 1992
- He hesitated for a New York minute, staring at a spot between Leddy's eyes. — Robert Campbell, *Boneyards*, p. 54, 1992

New York Slime *nickname*

the *New York Times* newspaper *US, 1981*

- — *CoEvolution Quarterly*, p. 27, Spring 1981

nextish *noun*

the next issue of a single-interest fan magazine *US, 1982*

- — *American Speech*, p. 28, Spring 1982: "The language of science fiction fan magazines"

nexus *noun*

4-bromo-2,5-dimethoxyphenethyliamine, a mild hallucinogen *US, 1995*

- — Steven Daly and Nathaniel Wice, *alt.culture*, p. 256, 1995

NF *nickname*

the Nuestra Familia prison gang *US, 2000*

- NF enforcers then went after the drug dealers and other big-money crooks. — Bill Valentine, *Gangs and Their Tattoos*, p. 34, 2000

NFG *adjective*

used as shorthand to mean "no fucking good" *US, 1977*

- [T]he Lucas Opus ignition is NFG and tricky besides. — Carroll Smith, *Tune to Win*, p. 5, 1978
- — Andy Ihnatko, *Cyberspeak*, p. 135, 1997

NG *adjective*

no good *US, 1879*

- "How'd it go?" "N.G. Somebody made us." — Charles Perry, *Portrait of a Young Man Drowning*, p. 145, 1962

NHI *adjective*

used for describing a crime against a criminal, especially one involving only black people *US, 1973*

An abbreviation of *"no humans involved."*

- And he called the wagon job "the N.H.I. detail." When you asked him what that stood for he'd say "No Humans Involved," and then he let out with that donkey bray of his. — Joseph Wambaugh, *The Blue Knight*, p. 124, 1973
- As incensed as the public gets at appallingly brutal killings—the ones that blow away innocents—police expend little sympathy on criminal-to-criminal mayhem. An acronym drifts unwritten about the system; those are NHI crimes—No Human Involved. — *Los Angeles Times*, p. 1 (Metro), 14th May 1989
- The cops got an actual rubber stamp that says that. NHI. — Lynn Breedlove, *Godspeed*, p. 24, 2002
- And they recoiled at a police report documenting a prostitute's death—it was stamped "NHI"—No Human Involved. — *Kansas City Pitch Weekly*, 30th January 2003

nibshit *noun*

a person of no consequence *US, 1960*

- "Hey, mind your own business, nibshit," barked Mack. — Jason Headley, *Small Town Odds*, p. 264, 2004

Nice Nellie *noun*

a driven, fastiduous woman *US, 1936*

- Kate is reminiscent of those nice-nellie scourges who used to tyrannize the back pages of the New York Times Book Review[.] — Norman Miller, *The Time of Our Life*, p. 789, 1998

nicey nice *adjective*

extremely nice, even excessively nice *UK, 1859*

A diminutive, childish formation usually used with some degree of mocking or irony.

- Why was she so goddamn nice all the time? Nicey-nice. God. — Elmore Leonard, *Switch*, p. 9, 1978

nick *noun*

1 five dollars' worth of a drug *US, 2002*

A shortened form of "nickel" as in **NICKEL BAG**.

- — Gary K. Farlow, *Prison-ese*, p. 45, 2002
- "I need a nick," she mumbled to him. Without hesitation, he sold her a nickel bag—$5 worth of crack. — *Philadelphia Daily News*, p. Local 3, 27th December 2006

2 in craps, a winning roll of seven on the first toss *US, 1962*

- — Frank Garcia, *Marked Cards and Loaded Dice*, p. 263, 1962

3 a nickname *US, 1995*

- — Christian Crumlish, *The Internet Dictionary*, p. 137, 1995

nickel *noun*

1 a five-year prison sentence *US, 1953*

- Fritz was glad to attract so much attention and he talked complacently about his "nickel" in Lexington. — William Burroughs, *Junkie*, p. 42, 1953
- Well, it's only a nickel, even if they stick it all to you, you can still see the end of it. — Malcolm Braly, *On the Yard*, p. 80, 1967
- I just did a nickel in Terminal Island. — Gerald Petievich, *Money Men*, p. 33, 1981
- "Caught a new case outta Reno, dawg, looking at a fucking nickel." — Jimmy Lerner, *You Got Nothing Coming*, p. 27, 2002

2 five dollars *US, 1946*

- "Where's that nickel you owe me, Geo?" Lou said from where he stood at the draining board of the sink. — Alexander Trocchi, *Cain's Book*, p. 165, 1960
- "I certainly would appreciate it if you could give us some kind of room for a nickel." — Stephen Schneck, *The Nightclerk*, p. 10, 1965
- [F]ive dollars is a nickel and 40 dollars is 40 cents. — Phil Hirsch, *Hooked*, pp. 59–60, 1968

3 in American casinos, a five-dollar betting chip *US, 1980*

- — Lee Solkey, *Dummy Up and Deal*, p. 116, 1980
- — Steve Kuriscak, *Casino Talk*, p. 39, 1985

4 five hundred dollars *US, 1974*

- — *Bay Sports Review*, p. 8, November 1991

5 a mediocre object or situation *US, 1977*

- — Gary Fairmont R. Filosa II, *The Surfer's Almanac*, p. 190, 1977

6 the Republic F-103 Thunderchief military aircraft *US, 1990*

- I have seen them in their Nickels when their eyes were dancing flame. — Joseph Tuso, *Singing the Vietnam Blues*, p. 22, 1990: Air Force Lament

▶ **the Nickel**

Fifth Street, Los Angeles *US, 2006*

- We finally left the squalor of Fifth Street, known as the Nickel. — Stephen J. Cannell, *White Sister*, p. 3, 2006

nickel *adjective*
inferior *US, 1932*
- — David W. Maurer, *Argot of the Racetrack*, p. 44, 1951
- How many times am I gon' have to whip your jive, stinkin' ass before you stop tryin' to be nickel slick? — Odie Hawkins, *Ghetto Sketches*, p. 17, 1972
- Bessie working, Fred Lee chili pimpin' and trying to be nickel slick... — Odie Hawkins, *The Busting Out of an Ordinary Man*, p. 137, 1985

nickel and dime *noun*
in pool, a table that is five feet by ten feet *US, 1993*
- — Mike Shamos, *The Illustrated Encyclopedia of Billiards*, p. 154, 1993

nickel-and-dime *adjective*
small-time, operating on a small scale *US, 1941*
- This is the big time, Ira baby, not like those nickel-and-dime epics you made back in the old days. — Max Shulman, *Anyone Got a Match?*, p. 113, 1964
- But the lemonade syndicate, like copping milk bottles, was nickel and dime. — Piri Thomas, *Down These Mean Streets*, p. 75, 1967
- That trio and the woman played every nickel-and-dime base camp, every falling-down mess hall and sleazy, scruffy Enlisted Men's Club south of the 17th Parallel[.] — Larry Heinemann, *Paco's Story*, p. 11, 1986
- Rocco saw a hesitant curl coming into his brow and sensed that the guy knew something was up other than the usual nickel-and-dime bullshit. — Richard Price, *Clockers*, p. 513, 1992

nickel-and-dime pimp *noun*
a small-time pimp *US, 1972*
- I am a nickel-and-dime pimp who has been built up in the papers to be more than what I was. The only thing I've ever had was an apartment where I had three girls at one time. And that was a very short time. I mostly had one girl and that's it[.] — Bruce Jackson, *In the Life*, p. 185, 1972

nickel bag *noun*
five dollars' worth of a drug *US, 1966*
- Often the junkie pusher will deal "nickel bags" at $5 each, as well as $3 "treys." — James Mills, *The Panic in Needle Park*, p. 20, 1966
- He hit you with lids, caps, keys, tabs, nickel bags, blotters, buttons, spoons and everything from milligrams to boatloads. — Robert Sabbag, *A Way with the Spoon [The Howard Marks Book of Dope Stories]*, p. 350, 1998
- Lemme get a nickel bag. — Kevin Smith, *Jay and Silent Bob Strike Back*, p. 9, 2001

Nickel City *nickname*
Baltimore, Maryland *US, 2003*
- Baltimore was still "Nickel City" back then—cheaper than Washington. — Bill Manville, *Cool, Hip and Sober*, p. 271, 2003

nickel-dime-quarter *noun*
poker played with very small bets *US, 1968*
- — Thomas L. Clark, *The Dictionary of Gambling and Gaming*, p. 135, 1987

nickel game *noun*
a game of craps in which the true and correct odds are paid *US, 1950*
- — *The Annals of the American Academy of Political and Social Sciences*, p. 128, May 1950

nickel gouger *noun*
the operator of a dishonest carnival game *US, 1950*
- — *American Speech*, p. 235, October 1950: "The argot of outdoor boob traps"

nickel-nurser *noun*
a miser *US, 1916*
- "What's a skinflint?" he asked. Mrs. Rippee chuckled. "A nickel-nurser," she said. "Someone who is miserly with money." — Roger Lea MacBride, *Little Town in the Ozarks*, p. 180, 1996

nickel-pincher *noun*
a cheapskate *US, 1949*
A variation on the much more common "penny-pincher."
- I had always tipped too much—knowing that I had never cared because I'd been brought up amidst nickel pinchers and because I like to please the people around me[.] — Philip Wylie, *Opus 21*, p. 66, 1949

nickels *noun*
in craps, a roll of two fives *US, 1983*
- — Thomas L. Clark, *The Dictionary of Gambling and Gaming*, p. 135, 1987

nickels and dimes *noun*
in hold 'em poker, a five and ten as the first two cards dealt to a player *US, 1981*
- — Thomas L. Clark, *The Dictionary of Gambling and Gaming*, p. 135, 1987

nickel tour *noun*
a quick, cursory tour *US, 1985*
- "I'll show you your bunk and then give you the nickel tour of this joint." — David Donovan, *Once a Warrior King*, p. 38, 1985

nick joint *noun*
a dishonest gambling operation *US, 1978*
- — Thomas L. Clark, *The Dictionary of Gambling and Gaming*, p. 135, 1987

nick-nacker *noun*
an infrequent drug user *US, 1984*
- — Inez Cardozo-Freeman, *The Joint*, p. 517, 1984

niebla *noun*
phencyclidine, the recreational drug known as PCP or angel dust *US, 1994*
Spanish for "cloud."
- — US Department of Justice, *Street Terms*, October 1994

nieve *noun*
cocaine *US, 1993*
Spanish for "snow."
- — Peter Johnson, *Dictionary of Street Alcohol and Drug Terms*, p. 132, 1993

nifty *adjective*
smart, fashionable, fine, splendid *US, 1805*
Old-fashioned and affected; probably a corrupted "magnificent."
- I'm free, and I got a date tonight with the niftiest Polack. — James T. Farrell, *Saturday Night*, pp. 30–31, 1947
- [S]ome nifty tomfoolery [jewelry]. — Charles Raven, *Underworld Nights*, p. 174, 1956
- Strooby here has a couple of the niftiest damn teen-age boys you'll ever meet. — Dan Jenkins, *Semi-Tough*, p. 142, 1972
- Me and Carri got a nifty studio apartment on 85th Street between West End Avenue and Riverside Drive[.] — A.S. Jackson, *Gentleman Pimp*, p. 153, 1973

nifty-keen *adjective*
excellent *US, 1972*
- — Helen Dahlskog (Editor), *A Dictionary of Contemporary and Colloquial Usage*, p. 42, 1972

nig *noun*
a black person *US, 1828*
A shortened form of **NIGGER**, no less offensive.
- All the dirty old nigs and broken down old men. — John Peter Jones, *Feather Pluckers*, p. 60, 1964
- "How you get along with the nigs?" "Fine," I said. "They're good guys." — Dan Jenkins, *Life Its Ownself*, p. 47, 1984
- Nig—black woman's boyfriend: "Let me introduce you to my new nig." Used only by African Americans. — Connie Eble (Editor), *UNC-CH Campus Slang*, p. 6, Spring 1992

Nigerian *noun*
in homosexual usage, any black man *US, 1986–1987*
- — *Maledicta*, p. 52, 1986–1987: "A continuation of a glossary of ethnic slurs in American English"

Nigerian scam spam *noun*
a swindle that uses e-mail to solicit potential victims to help an African correspondent transfer millions of dollars into an American bank account *US, 2002*
- "Nigerian scam spam"—junk e-mail promising fabulous wealth to anyone who will help purported African officials or dignitaries handle some banking chores—is one of the Internet's fastest-growing forms of fraud. — *San Francisco Chronicle*, p. A6, 8th September 2002

nigga *noun*
a black person *US, 1989*
A deliberate misspelling, reinventing **NIGGER** for exclusive black use; widely used in gangsta rap.
- [C]razy muthafucka named Ice Cube / From the band called Niggaz With Attitude — NWA, *Straight Outta Compton*, 1989
- There's two niggas inside me. One wants to live in peace, and the other won't die unless he's free. — *Jabberrock [quoting Tupac Shakur]*, p. 64, 1997

nigger *noun*
a black person *UK, 1574*
When used by white speakers, highly offensive; used by black speakers, especially the young, with increasing frequency.

- Somewhere in the middle of Missouri, for the first time, this sailor, who never called a woman a woman if he could call her a cunt, and a Negro a nigger (I'd advertised for him in the New York Times), finally boiled over. — Clancy Sigal, *Going Away*, p. 175, 1961
- You want to get a glimpse of what it feels like to be a nigger? Let your hair grow long. — Abbie Hoffman, *Revolution for the Hell of It*, p. 71, 1968
- Aunt Sadie, long hair is our black skin. Long hair turns white middle-class youth into niggers. — Jerry Rubin, *Do It!*, p. 94, 1970
- It got so that the women's movement called women the "niggers" of our time and confused gender with class. — Mort Sahl, *Heartland*, p. 50, 1976

nigger babies *noun*
dirt specks, especially in the creases of the neck *US, 1970*
- — Claudio R. Salvucci, *The Philadelphia Dialect Dictionary*, p. 50, 1996

nigger bait *noun*
a great deal of chrome on a car *US, 1960*
- — *Maledicta*, p. 168, 1979: "A glossary of ethnic slurs in American English"

nigger bankroll *noun*
a single large-denomination bill wrapped around small-denomination notes, giving the impression of a great deal of money *US, 1980*
- — Edith A. Folb, *runnin' down some lines*, p. 248, 1980

nigger bet *noun*
an uncommon amount wagered *US, 1968*
- — Thomas L. Clark, *The Dictionary of Gambling and Gaming*, p. 136, 1987

nigger box *noun*
a portable radio *US, 1993*
- The only time he used any sort of force against my sister or myself was when he referred to her portable radio as a "nigger-box." — *bit.loisterv.politics*, 1st July 1993

nigger flicker *noun*
a small knife; a razor blade used as a weapon *US, 1980*
- — Edith A. Folb, *runnin' down some lines*, p. 248, 1980

nigger-hater *noun*
an overt racist *US, 1951*
- Honest policemen are afraid to make too many pinches in Negro neighborhoods for fear the pinkos will list them as "nigger-haters" and send their names up above—maybe even to the White House. — Jack Lait and Lee Mortimer, *Washington Confidential*, p. 42, 1951

niggerhead *noun*
a tuft of grass *US, 1859*
- — Robert O. Bowen, *An Alaskan Dictionary*, p. 23, 1965

niggerhead keister *noun*
a steel safe shaped like a ball *US, 1976*
- Leo took the cold chisel from the satchel and they both began taking turns breaking up the concrete to pound apart the niggerhead keister for what they could now smell it contained. — Emmett Grogan, *Final Score*, p. 86, 1976

nigger heaven *noun*
1 a simple, perfect happiness *US, 1906*
- — *Maledicta*, p. 165, Summer/Winter 1978: "How to hate thy neighbor: a guide to racist maledicta"

2 the highest, least expensive seats in a theater *US, 1866*
- — Don Wilmeth, *The Language of American Popular Entertainment*, p. 182, 1981

niggerize *verb*
to modify something or someone to be more like a stereotyped black person *US, 1972*
Not used kindly.
- "You're attempting to niggerize me, Macon," Burleigh said. — Adam Mansbach, *Angry Black White Boy*, p. 309, 2005

nigger-knocker *noun*
a police baton, a club *US, 1965*
- Joe got the nigger knocker wrapped around his hand real tight, dig. — Miguel Pinero, *Short Eyes*, p. 79, 1975
- An officer smacked him in the stomach with his baton—an implement that some LAPD officers openly referred to as a "nigger knocker." — Bob Sipchen, *Baby Insane and the Buddha*, p. 35, 1993

- "Take your nigger-knocker with you." I stepped out of the car, slipped my baton into its ring, and peered through the passenger window. — Norm Stamper, *Breaking Rank*, p. 94, 2005

niggerlip *verb*
to moisten the end of a cigarette with saliva *US, 1940*
- "Light me a cigarette, darling," she said, snatching off a bathing cap and shaking her hair. "I don't mean you, O.J. You're such a slob. You always nigger-lip." — Truman Capote, *Breakfast at Tiffany's*, p. 34, 1958
- — *Maledicta*, p. 168, 1979: "A glossary of ethnic slurs in American English"
- — Connie Eble (Editor), *UNC-CH Campus Slang*, p. 5, Fall 1987

nigger-lover *noun*
a white person who mixes with or admires black people; a white person who believes that all men are created equal *US, 1856*
Originally white usage, it was intended to be offensive and disparaging.
- The Southerners had called me a "nigger-lover" there. — Mezz Mezzrow, *Really the Blues*, p. 18, 1946
- "Officer, do you know who I am?" "Some nigger-lover who..." — Dick Gregory, *Nigger*, p. 67, 1964
- Here comes the nigger-lover! — James Baldwin, *Blues for Mister Charlie*, p. 143, 1964
- "We ought to beat hell out of you nigger lovers," he said. — Arthur Blessitt, *Turned On to Jesus*, p. 39, 1971

nigger-loving *adjective*
used for describing a white person who does not share the speaker's pathological hatred of black people *US, 1879*
- We'll cut your niggerlovin heart out. — Hubert Selby Jr., *Last Exit to Brooklyn*, p. 32, 1957

nigger navel *noun*
a type of daisy *US, 2002*
- [P]eople could "nigger-rig" a fence (a type of jerry-rigging) or pick "nigger-navel" flowers (a variety of African daisy with a black button center). — Dina Temple-Raston, *A Death in Texas*, p. 38, 2002

nigger pennies *noun*
an illegal lottery game *US, 1977*
- There's what's his name, Wee Willie. Hustling them numbers. Nigger pennies. — John Sayles, *Union Dues*, p. 148, 1977

nigger pool *noun*
an illegal numbers gambling lottery *US, 1949*
- — *American Speech*, p. 192, October 1949

nigger rich *adjective*
maintaining outward signs of wealth *US, 1930*
- Anyone who wanted to could be nigger-rich, nigger-important, have their Jim Crow religion, and go to nigger heaven. — Chester Himes, *If He Hollers Let Him Go*, p. 153, 1945
- [I]ts three nigger-rich occupants were his buddies and all worked at Douglas Aircraft during those hours. — Neal Cassady, *The First Third*, p. 166, 1971
- But today was Checkday, a disease that turned everyone on Welfare into mean, cantankerous, nigger-rich arrogant fools. — Robert Deane Pharr, *S.R.O.*, p. 139, 1971
- In the bleak shadow of his mother, getting "nigger rich," and buying a restaurant, going into all kinds of shady businesses—a new Cadillac, a hog, every year? — Clarence Major, *All-Night Visitors*, p. 182, 1998

nigger rig *noun*
an improvised solution to a problem *US, 1950*
- I have resorted to one method which most yachtsmen would characterize as a "nigger rig" but which nevertheless has brought consistently good results. — Harold Augustin Calahan, *Sailing Technique*, p. 111, 1950
- His dad had run its drain out through the wall with PVC pipe and then dug a little ditch so the water went down the riverbank. It was a nigger-rig. — Jess Mowry, *Six Out Seven*, p. 27, 1993

nigger-rig *verb*
to improvise in a shoddy way *US, 1965*
- — *Maledicta*, p. 168, 1979: "A glossary of ethnic slurs in American English"
- [P]eople could "nigger-rig" a fence (a type of jerry-rigging). — Dina Temple-Raston, *A Death in Texas*, p. 38, 2002

nigger-rigged *adjective*
shoddily improvised *US, 1991*

- The wiring was always overloaded and blowing fuses, and the nigger-rigged plumbing was a leaky stinking joke even when it worked. — Jess Mowry, *Way Past Cool*, p. 119, 1992

nigger-shooter *noun*
a slingshot *US, 1876*

- She'd have him so the six-year kids will be plugging him with nigger-shooters, and then not bothering to run. — Robert Penn Warren, *All the King's Men*, p. 154, 1946
- The old man fashioned him a slingshot—a "Niggershooter"—and he spent bone-cold hours lurking in ambush, waiting for a yellow-belly to swoop down within range. — Joe Eszterhas, *Charlie Simpson's Apocalypse*, p. 67, 1973

nigger stick *noun*
a reinforced baton used by police on suspected criminals, criminals, and prisoners *US, 1971*

- A hack walked over to our table and pointed with a hard-ass reinforced wooden club that I'd learn was called a "nigger stick," supposedly because it could stand against heads that were anything but white. — Piri Thomas, *Seven Long Times*, p. 72, 1974
- "Grab the nigger stick." — Linden Dalecki, *Kid B*, p. 89, 2006

nigger sticker *noun*
a long, sharp knife *US, 1969*

- — Ralph de Sola, *Crime Dictionary*, p. 102, 1982

nigger toe *noun*
1 a Brazil nut *US, 1896*

- For instance, there's this nut I used to eat when I was a kid, we called a niggertoe. It must have some other name, but I don't know what it is. Does that mean that all us kids were prejudiced because we used to eat niggertoes? — Darryl Ponicsan, *The Last Detail*, p. 78, 1970

2 a black olive *US, 1996*

- — *Maledicta*, p. 16, 1996: "Domino's pizza jargon"

niggertown *noun*
a neighborhood with a large population of black people *US, 1904*

- It's in Niggertown, on the radio alla time. I say, You know where is Niggertown? — Robert Gover, *One Hundred Dollar Misunderstanding*, p. 131, 1961
- A lot of the other kids in school used to drive over to niggertown at night to try and find black women. — James Baldwin, *Blues for Mister Charlie*, p. 87, 1964
- Every Negro that lives in a city has seen the type a thousand times, the Northern cracker who will go to visit "niggertown," to be amused at "the coons." — Malcolm X and Alex Haley, *The Autobiography of Malcolm X*, p. 147, 1964
- In the town of —— blacks came in from nigger-town when the sun rose. — Jack Henry Abbott, *In the Belly of the Beast*, p. 171, 1981

niggerville *noun*
a section of a city or town populated by black people *US, 1857*
Offensive.

- That's all Niggerville there now and wasn't much better then. — Elmore Leonard, *Maximum Bob*, p. 122, 1991

nigger work *noun*
any difficult, dirty, strenuous job *US, 1939*

- [D]own among the black beetles and the millipedes, and did the laundry. "Time to do the Nigger work," she said. — Kurt Vonnegut, *Breakfast of Champions*, p. 250, 1973

niggle *verb*
to have sex *US, 1962*

- — Joseph E. Ragen and Charles Finston, *Inside the World's Toughest Prison*, p. 809, 1962: "Penitentiary and underworld glossary"

night bull *noun*
a prison guard assigned to a night shift *US, 1967*

- Other night bulls sit out in the towers above the floodlit walls and blocks. — Malcolm Braly, *On the Yard*, p. 53, 1967

nightcap *noun*
1 the final alcoholic drink of the night *UK, 1818*

- On the evening before, I could have accepted Yvonne's invitation for a nightcap, or accepted the later invitation in her note to me. — Philip Wylie, *Opus 21*, p. 192, 1949
- Come on. Let's have a nightcap together. — *The Graduate*, 1967
- Hey, let's go have a nightcap at my place. — *The Deer Hunter*, 1978

- I was wondering if you would care to join us in a nightcap. — Terry Southern, *Now Dig This*, p. 237, 1984

2 in horseracing, the last race of the day *US, 1951*

- — David W. Maurer, *Argot of the Racetrack*, p. 44, 1951

night crawler *noun*
1 a prisoner who steals from other prisoners at night *US, 1951*

- We also have a group of prisoners called "creeps" or "night-crawlers," who prowl the dormitory at night and steal from the other sleeping prisoners. — James Blake, *The Joint*, p. 21, 15th April 1951

2 a person who enjoys night life *US, 1995*

- Betty's was the after-hours hangout for the Foxy Lady crew and the older night crawlers of the Providence area. — Heidi Mattson, *Ivy League Stripper*, p. 141, 1995

nightery; niterie *noun*
a nightclub *US, 1934*

- Crothers is grabbing five bills a week as a nitery comic. — *Capitol News*, p. 15, March 1949

nighthawk *noun*
1 a person who is active late at night *UK, 1818*

- In spite of the weather, nighthawks were finally gathering outside Gentry's[.] — Robert Campbell, *In La-La Land We Trust*, p. 32, 1986

2 a taxi driver who works late at night *US, 1868*

- We at least walk you down to the Merchandise Mart. Then we'll see. Maybe we spot a nighthawk cruising. — Robert Campbell, *Boneyards*, p. 188, 1992

night house *noun*
an illegal lottery operating at night *US, 1957*

- He put ninety dollars on numbers in the night house, playing five dollars on each. — Chester Himes, *A Rage in Harlem*, p. 23, 1957

nightime name *noun*
a person's nickname or alias *US, 1949*

- "That's me, too, Sparrow Saltskin, it's my daytime name." "What's your nighttime name?" "Solly. Account I'm half Hebe." — Nelson Algren, *The Man with the Golden Arm*, p. 5, 1949

nightingale *noun*
a police informer *US, 1968*
From the **SING** metaphor.

- — Hy Lit, *Hy Lit's Unbelievable Dictionary of Hip Words for Groovy People*, p. 51, 1968

night maneuvers *noun*
a social date *US, 1962*

- — *Dobie Gillis Teenage Slanguage Dictionary*, 1962

night nurse *noun*
a cigarette smoked in the middle of the night by an addict whose body is awakened by the craving for nicotine in the night *US, 1996*

- — John Fahs, *Cigarette Confidential*, p. 302, 1996: "Glossary"

night rider *noun*
1 a person who enjoys the wild side of life at night *US, 1951*

- I was going home now, home to my kind of people—the cons, killers, thieves and night-riders. — Red Rudensky, *The Gonif*, p. 113, 1970

2 in horseracing, someone who takes a horse out for a night workout in the hope of lessening its performance in a race the next day *US, 1951*

- — David W. Maurer, *Argot of the Racetrack*, p. 44, 1951

nights belong to Charlie
used as a rule of thumb by US soldiers in Vietnam, acknowledging the ascendancy of the Viet Cong during the dark *US, 1990*

- — Gregory Clark, *Words of the Vietnam War*, p. 350, 1990
- These kinds of nights belong to Charlie, aka, Victor Charlie, or the VC. — Lee Alley, *Back from War*, p. 49, 2007

night shift *noun*
a slumber party *US, 1961*

- — Art Unger, *The Cool Book*, p. 106, 1961

night train *noun*
suicide *US, 1984*

- He used to say if he ever took the Night Train, he'd never do it with his gun. — James Ellroy, *Because the Night*, p. 501, 1984

nighty-night; night-night; nigh'-nigh'
good night *UK, 1896*
Originally children's vocabulary but now widely used and not always ironically.

- But Keyes didn't remember shutting his eyes and going nighty-night on the cool concrete. — Carl Hiaasen, *Tourist Season*, p. 49, 1986

-nik *suffix*
a supporter or follower of the precedent activity or principle *US, 1963*

- I mean, beatniks and slutniks, they're so dull. — Douglas Rutherford, *The Creeping Flesh*, p. 84, 1963
- A few college hawkniks come by. — Elmore Leonard, *Revolution for the Hell of It*, p. 25, 1968
- Beatniks happened elsewhere—even in Australia [...] The Beats showed it was possible, even glamorous, to throw the gauntlet at the lifestyle of IBM. — Richard Neville, *Play Power*, pp. 23–24, 1970

Nike down *verb*
to dress in nothing but Nike™ clothing and shoes *US, 1998*

- — Ethan Hilderbrant, *Prison Slang*, p. 90, 1998

nimby *noun*
1 used as an acronym for *"not in my back yard,"* a description of the philosophy of those who support an idea in principle but do not want to be personally inconvenienced by it *US, 1980*
The acronym followed the phrase by only a year.

- The first time we heard of the neat acronym-like word NIMBY, it was voiced by J. Hamilton Lambert, the county executive of Fairfax County[.] — *Washington Post*, p. B2, 13th February 1983
- Not in my Back Yard—NIMBY for short—an acronym that will symbolize the psychographic marketing profile that will dominate the next decade. — *Financial Post (Toronto)*, p. 9, 17th February 1989
- Whereas NIMBIES promise the development will be Not In My Back Yard, the note says Not Over There Either. — David Rowan, *Glossary for the 90s*, p. 9, 1998

2 a capsule of pentobarbital sodium (trade name Nembutal™), a central nervous system depressant *US, 1962*

- — Richard Lingeman, *Drugs from A to Z*, p. 183, 1969

nimrod *noun*
a fool, a stupid person, a bungler *US, 1932*

- — *USA Today*, 29th September 1983
- — Connie Eble (Editor), *UNC-CH Campus Slang*, p. 4, Spring 1993
- Jules, if you give this nimrod fifteen hundred bucks, I'm gonna shoot 'em on general principle. — *Pulp Fiction*, 1994
- EDDIE: Hey, Brent, have a beer. EDDIE: Nimrod. — *Empire Records*, 1995

Nina; Nina from Carolina; Nina from Pasadena *noun*
in craps, a roll of nine or the nine point *US, 1939*

- — Vincent J. Monteleone, *Criminal Slang*, p. 44, 1949
- — *The Annals of the American Academy of Political and Social Sciences*, p. 128, May 1950
- — Steve Kuriscak, *Casino Talk*, p. 68, 1985

nine; 9 *noun*
a 9mm pistol *US, 1990*

- Keisha puts the "nine" right next to his temple, and pulls the trigger twice. Blood flies everywhere. — *New Jack City*, p. 19, 1990
- My 9's at your brain[.] — Eminem (Marshall Mathers), *Weed Lacer (Freestyle)*, 1999
- He was good with his nines, though. Three dead muthafuckas'll tell you all about that. — John Ridley, *Everybody Smokes in Hell*, p. 37, 1999
- Bolden broke into the Pony Express Sports Shop in North Hills and took about 25 guns—"nines," "deuce-deuces," and "deuce-fives," Dixon, also of North Hills testified[.] — *Daily News of Los Angeles*, p. N1, 27th April 2003

nine-day blues *noun*
the incubation period for gonorrhea *US, 1981*

- — *Maledicta*, p. 228, Summer/Winter 1981: "Sex and the single soldier"

nine-nickel *noun*
ninety-five *US, 1998*

- — Ethan Hilderbrant, *Prison Slang*, p. 90, 1998

nine of hearts *noun*
a racehorse that is not likely to win *US, 1951*

- — David W. Maurer, *Argot of the Racetrack*, p. 44, 1951
- — Thomas L. Clark, *The Dictionary of Gambling and Gaming*, p. 136, 1987

nineteen *noun*
nothing at all *US, 1975*
From the game of cribbage (a hand with no points).

- — John Gould, *Maine Lingo*, p. 190, 1975

nineteenth hole *noun*
a golf course bar where golfers retire after a round of golf *US, 1901*

- — Randy Voorhees, *The Little Book of Golf Slang*, p. 79, 1997

nine-trey *noun*
ninety-three *US, 1993*

- — *The Bell (Paducah Tilghman High School)*, pp. 8–9, 17th December 1993: "Tilghmanism: the concealed language of the hallway"

ninety days *noun*
in dice games, a roll of nine *US, 1909*

- — Frank Garcia, *Marked Cards and Loaded Dice*, p. 263, 1962

ninety-day-wonder *noun*
a recent graduate of the US Army's Officer Candidate School *US, 1917*

- The OCS course was 90 days in length, and field troops referred to OCS graduates as "90 day wonders." — Gregory Clark, *Words of the Vietnam War*, p. 359, 1990

ninety-in-ninety *noun*
in twelve-step recovery programs such as Alcoholics Anonymous, used as a prescription for starting recovery—ninety meetings in ninety days *US, 1998*

- — Christopher Cavanaugh, *AA to Z*, p. 131, 1998

ninety-six *noun*
reciprocal anal sex *US, 1949*

- — Anon., *The Gay Girl's Guide*, p. 13, 1949

ninety-weight *noun*
any strong alcohol *US, 1976*

- — Lanie Dills, *The Official CB Slanguage Language Dictionary*, p. 50, 1976

ninny *noun*
1 a fool, a dolt *UK, 1593*

- [P]aying the poor ninny six and a half cents a pound for the lot. — Max Shulman, *The Zebra Derby*, p. 84, 1946
- If you "called" a man, the ninny would have you hauled into court instead of making the proper response with fists and feet. — Jim Thompson, *Bad Boy*, p. 302, 1953

2 a small-time bettor *US, 1974*

- Ninny action is any bet of $25 or less that I take as an accommodation to my old friends and small bettors who want to get down. — Gary Mayer, *Bookie*, p. 4, 1974

nip *noun*
1 a Japanese or Japanese-American person *US, 1942*
Shortened from "Niponese." Deemed offensive by Multicultural Management Program Fellows, *Dictionary of Cautionary Words and Phrases*, 1989.

- If you ever do get a live Nip, keep him away from Daniels. — Eric Lambert, *The Veterans*, p. 143, 1954
- But if the Nips were all there were left, then the Nips it would have to be. — Earl Thompson, *Tattoo*, p. 4, 1974
- — Edith A. Folb, *runnin' down some lines*, p. 248, 1980

2 a Vietnamese person *US, 2002*

- They were referred to as gooks, slopes, dinks, and nips. — Richard Burns, *Pathfinder*, p. 366, 2002

3 a small drink *US, 1736*

- You're just in time to join me in a nip. — Chester Himes, *If He Hollers Let Him Go*, p. 80, 1945
- "A guy'd decide, he was gonna check himself in, and he would, and before he did it he'd get a couple friends of his and they'd come down every day and put ten nips in the woods where he said." — George Higgin, *Cogan's Trade*, p. 19, 1974

4 a nipple, especially a woman's *US, 1965*
The nickname given to the character Elaine Benes (played by Julia Louis-Dreyfus) on Seinfeld (NBC, 1990–98) after a snapshot that she took for a Christmas card showed a breast nipple.

- Say, Lil had nips on her titties about the size of your thumb. — Bruce Jackson, *Get Your Ass in the Water and Swim Like Me*, p. 150, 1965
- She was a healthy-looking bitch, a jogger type with a great rack ... a couple of real pointers. And I'm not talking about a bra with rubber

nipples. I'm talking about a pair of honest-to-Christ pointed nips that must have weighed as much as silver dollars. — Gerald Petievich, *To Die in Beverly Hills*, p. 93, 1983

- There's a certain kind of uniquely American girl who comes from the Midwest to Greenwich Village—cute as a button, pert derriere, full wet lips, nips in eternal distention, etc. — Terry Southern, *Now Dig This*, p. 1, 1986
- How big and brown are your nips? — Nicholson Baker, *Vox*, p. 10, 1992

nip *verb*
1 to grab *UK, 1566*
- He nipped me by my coatsleeve and lamped me with a wicked eye. — Bruce Jackson, *Get Your Ass in the Water and Swim Like Me*, p. 85, 1965

2 to open a locked door using a special pair of pliers that can grasp the key from the other side of the door *US, 1962*
- — Joseph E. Ragen and Charles Finston, *Inside the World's Toughest Prison*, p. 810, 1962: "Penitentiary and underworld glossary"

nip and tuck *noun*
cosmetic surgery *US, 1981*
- She wants a little face lift, I bought her a little nip and tuck. — George V. Higgins, *The Rat on Fire*, p. 170, 1981

nip it in the bud!
used for humorously suggesting the emerging presence of a problem *US, 1965*
A signature line of deputy Barney Fife, played by Don Knotts, on the situation comedy *Andy Griffith Show* (CBS, 1960–68). Repeated with referential humor.

nip joint *noun*
an unlicensed bar *US, 1965*
- What the hell was 5-C anyhow? Some kind of nip joint? — Robert Deane Pharr, *S.R.O.*, p. 17, 1971

nipper *noun*
1 a baby or young child *UK, 1859*
- Honey, could ya slide over a tad and raise the nipper up? — *Raising Arizona*, 1987

2 in target shooting, a shot that just nicks a ring, scoring as if it had fallen within the ring *US, 1957*
- — *American Speech*, p. 194, October 1957: "Some colloquialisms of the handgunner"

nippers *noun*
1 the female breasts *US, 1968*
- — Collin Baker et al., *College Undergraduate Slang Study Conducted at Brown University*, p. 162, 1968
2 the teeth *US, 1965*
- The nippers; I lost 'em. — John Nichols, *The Sterile Cuckoo*, p. 219, 1965
3 any cutting tool *US, 1950*
- — Hyman E. Goldin et al., *Dictionary of American Underworld Lingo*, p. 145, 1950
4 a special pair of pliers that can grasp the key from the other side of the door *US, 1962*
- — Joseph E. Ragen and Charles Finston, *Inside the World's Toughest Prison*, p. 810, 1962: "Penitentiary and underworld glossary"

nipple cripple *noun*
the act of grabbing a person's nipple between the forefinger and thumb and then twisting roughly *US, 1995*
- A variant on this theme was the NIPPLE WHISTLE, in which the victim would only be released from the Nipple Cripple if he could whistle, a task surprisingly difficult under the circumstances. — *rec.humor*, 3rd August 1995

nipple palm *noun*
a Nipa palm, found in swampy and marshy land in South Vietnam *US, 1984*
- He was in a little mound inside this real heavy stuff, nipple [Nipa] palm that grows around the rivers. — Myra MacPherson, *Long Time Passing*, p. 19, 1984

nipplitis *noun*
(used of a woman) erect nipples *US, 1997*
- — Pamela Munro, *U.C.L.A. Slang*, p. 93, 1997
- Use band-aids for nippilitis and go, or wear a strapless and something over the top. — *alt.fashion*, 10th June 2000

nippy *adjective*
chilly *US, 1985*
Almost always applied to the weather.

- "Kinda nippy out there, ain't it?" Miss Rabbit commented, attempting to cool the tension out. — Odie Hawkins, *The Busting Out of an Ordinary Man*, p. 118, 1985

nip slip *noun*
a photograph revealing at least a part of a woman's nipple *US, 1997*
The premise is that the reveal is accidental; major usage of the term on Internet photograph sites.
- Her nip-slip is merely very quick. But yes, Maureen McCornick's nipple was exposed. — *rec.arts.movies.erotica*, 4th March 1997

nip-up *noun*
a maneuver whereby someone springs from a prone position to their feet *US, 2000*
- That's a hundred nip-ups a day, which, by itself, is a pretty demanding workout. — The Rock, *The Rock Says...*, p. 170, 2000

nip up *verb*
to spring from a prone position to your feet *US, 2000*
- So my father and I agreed that every time I was down, I would get up by nipping up. — The Rock, *The Rock Says...*, p. 170, 2000

nitro *noun*
a streetlight bulb *US, 1980*
- — A.B. Chance Co., *Lineman's Slang Dictionary*, p. 12, 1980

nitro *adjective*
volatile *US, 1977*
Derived from the unstable nature of nitroglycerin.
- But with a nitro fluff like that, there's no bedrock stability. Be careful. Don't shake her up! She could blow us into the pen! — Iceberg Slim (Robert Beck), *Long White Con*, p. 90, 1977

nitrous *noun*
nitrous oxide used for recreational purposes *US, 2000*
- Hey, who has nitrous, where can I get a balloon? — Michelle Tea, *Valencia*, p. 135, 2000

nits and buggers *noun*
in poker, a hand with a pair of threes and a pair of twos *US, 1967*
- — Albert H. Morehead, *The Complete Guide to Winning Poker*, p. 268, 1967

nits and lice *noun*
in poker, a hand with two low-valued pairs *US, 1967*
- — Albert H. Morehead, *The Complete Guide to Winning Poker*, p. 268, 1967

nitshit *noun*
nonsense; pettiness *US, 1976*
- "They don't violate for that sort of nitshit." "They do now." — Malcolm Braley, *False Starts*, p. 355, 1976

nitty-gritty *noun*
the essence of the matter *US, 1942*
Coined by black people, then spread into wide use. In the early 2000s, the belief that the term originally applied to the debris left at the bottom of slave ships when the slaves were removed from the ship circulated with speed, certainty, and outrage. Whether the initial report was an intentional hoax or merely basis-free speculation, it is a false etymology. All authorities agree that the etymology is unknown yet some ill-informed politically correct types consider the word to have racist overtones.
- [W]hen it got down to the nitty-gritty, you could always go to Mister Ben. — Dick Gregory, *Nigger*, p. 35, 1964
- You finished taking our words, too? What do you know know about nitty-gritty? — Nat Hentoff, *I'm really dragged but nothing gets me down*, p. 27, 1968
- nitty gritty: the heart of the matter, the unvarnished truth. A Negro term much in use by whites during 1968 — Ethel Romm, *The Open Conspiracy*, p. 245, 1970
- Sapphire believes in gettin' down to the nitty-gritty; beating around the bush just isn't her style. — Carolyn Greene, *70 Soul Secrets of Sapphire*, p. 39, 1973

nitwit *noun*
a simpleton, a moron, a fool *US, 1914*
- But he will vote Democratic because of Bush's vice presidential candidate, Sen. Dan Quayle of Indiana. "That guy is a nitwit," Drews said. — *Newsday (New York)*, p. 7, 12th October 1988

- "Guess who Carlotta slept with last night?" "Who? Bruno Modjaleski?" "No, nitwit. Sheeni Saunders!" — C.D. Payne, *Youth in Revolt*, p. 466, 1993
- These women have talent—more than enough to survive the bashing of right-wing nitwits like Rosen, Rush Limbaugh, Jerry Falwell and hayseed country music radio stations. (Letter to editor). — *Rocky Mountain News (Denver)*, p. 53A, 9th May 2003

nix *verb*
to reject, to deny *US, 1903*
- He tried to steer me to a hangout around the corner but I nixed the idea[.] — Mickey Spillane, *One Lonely Night*, p. 23, 1951
- But you got the nerve to nix dough and cold shoulder me, Lock Jaw. — Iceberg Slim (Robert Beck), *Mama Black Widow*, p. 164, 1969

nixies *noun*
a female undergarment with a cut-out crotch permitting vaginal sex while otherwise clothed *US, 1978*
- — Anon., *King Smut's Wet Dreams Interpreted*, 1978

nizzel; nizzle *noun*
a close friend *US, 2001*
A hip-hop, urban black coinage, formed as a rhyming reduplication of **SHIZZLE** (sure, yes).
- Fa shizzle my nizzle used to dribble down in V-A — Jay-Z, *Izzo (HOVA)*, 2001
- — Rick Ayers (Editor), *Berkeley High Slang Dictionary*, p. 32, 2004

N.O.
no *US, 1913*
Spelt for emphasis, usually humorous.
- CAROL: Hey, is this what they call copping a feel? JOHN: What? No. Get up. N.O. Jesus! — *American Graffiti*, 1973

noah *noun*
a shark *US, 1963*
Rhyming slang from "Noah's ark."
- — Grant W. Kuhns, *On Surfing*, p. 119, 1963
- — Trevor Cralle, *The Surfin'ary*, p. 80, 1991

Noah's nobles *noun*
female volunteers from the American Red Cross *US, 1968*
Korean war usage; Noah is suggested by the Red Cross initials (ARC).
- — Carl Fleischhauer, *A Glossary of Army Slang*, p. 3, 1968

no biggie
don't worry about it *US, 1982*
- But NO BIGGIE / It's wo AWESOME / It's like TUBULAR, y'know. — Moon Unit and Frank Zappa, *Valley Girl*, 1982
- — Pamela Munro, *U.C.L.A. Slang*, p. 62, 1989
- "Cleo said you brought it across from the Bahamas by yourself." "No biggie," he says. — Carl Hiaasen, *Basket Case*, p. 127, 2002

no bitch!
I don't have to sit in the middle of the back seat of the car! *US, 1989*
Quickly shouted after someone else reserves the front passenger seat by shouting "shotgun!."
- — Pamela Munro, *U.C.L.A. Slang*, p. 62, 1989

noble *noun*
an influential, respected prisoner *US, 1976*
- Those real boss meals are eaten by wheels / Nobles and all of that jazz. — Dennis Wepman et al., *The Life*, p. 61, 1976

noble weed *noun*
marijuana *US, 1970*
- — *Current Slang*, p. 21, Spring 1970

no brag, just fact
used for humorously calling attention to having bragged *US, 1967*
Cavalry scout Will Sonnett, played by Walter Brennan, used this line to instill fear on the television Western *The Guns of Will Sonnett* (ABC, 1967–69). Repeated with referential humor.
- "No brag, just fact." I love it, I love it. — net.trivia, 19th August 1983
- "No brag, just fact?" he interrupted, his warm baritone gently easing. — *Sweet Tomorrow, Francine Christopher*, p. 72, 1987

no-brainer *noun*
1 an opinion so easily formed or decision so easily made that no thinking is required *US, 1977*
- According to the American Dairy Association, it is a "no brainer" that milk is necessary for proper bone health. — Rober Hermann, *Differential Geometry and the Calculus of Variations*, 1977
- "It [torturing captured prisoners of war] is a no brainer for me," Cheney replied. — *American News (South Dakota)*, p. A6, 28th October 2006

2 in croquet, a lucky shot *US, 1977*
- — James Charlton and William Thompson, *Croquet*, p. 159, 1977: "Glossary"

nobs *noun*
shoes *US, 1968*
- — Joan Fontaine et al., *Dictionary of Black Slang*, 1968
- — Charles Shafer, *Folk Speech in Texas Prisons*, p. 210, 1990

no can do
used as a humorous, mock-Pidgin declaration that something cannot be done *US, 1833*
- "No can do, buddy-boy." — Burt Hirschfield, *Fire Island*, p. 177, 1970
- "Join me." "No can do." — Jay McInerney, *Ransom*, p. 107, 1985

no can do, Madame Nhu
used as a humorous if emphatic suggestion that something cannot be done *US, 1984*
Madame Nhu was the sister-in-law of South Vietnamese President Diem.
- — John Elting, *A Dictionary of Soldier Talk*, p. 51, 1984

no chance outside *noun*
a noncommissioned officer of the US Army *US, 1968*
From the initials NCO and a healthy distrust of military authority.
- — Carl Fleischhauer, *A Glossary of Army Slang*, p. 3, 1968
- We're not all NCO's, which short-timers claim stands for "No Chance Outside" the military. — Jack Hawkins, *Chopper One #2*, p. 250, 1987

no comprende
I do not understand *US, 1971*
Partial Spanish used by English speakers without regard to their fluency in Spanish, and with multiple variations reflecting their lack of fluency.
- What wall were those Tulls coming off anyhoo? No comprende. — Lester Bangs, *Psychotic Reactions and Carburetor Dung*, p. 132, 1971

nod *noun*
in horseracing, a very small margin of victory or lead *US, 1971*
- A little twitch kept her from dwelling, and on a good cushion she took it by a nod. — *San Francisco Chronicle*, p. 54, 21st April 1971

▸ on the nod
lost in mental stupefaction brought on by heroin or other narcotics *US, 1951*
- Taking so much I keep going on the nod. — William Burroughs, *Letters to Allen Ginsberg 1953–1957*, p. 131, 26th February 1956
- She'd sit with them, they'd go on the nod, in the dead silence she'd wait[.] — Jack Kerouac, *The Subterraneans*, p. 29, 1958
- We all three got really stoned and sat talking or simply going on the nod until the early hours of the morning—finally dropping off to sleep—awakening much later in the day. — Herbert Huncke, *The Evening Sun Turned Crimson*, p. 83, 1980
- Skid rows populated by the homeless. Tenderloins strewn with winos sucking on a bottle in a bag and young dopers on the nod. — Robert Campbell, *Alice in La-La Land*, p. 2, 1987

nod *verb*
to enter a near-coma state after drug use *US, 1958*
- There were only moments to cop and moments to use and moments to nod and cop again. — Clarence Cooper Jr., *The Scene*, p. 39, 1960

noddy *adjective*
(used of a computer program) trivial, useless but illustrative of a point *US, 1991*
- — Eric S. Raymond, *The New Hacker's Dictionary*, p. 261, 1991

no dice!
positively no *US, 1931*
- Captain Black came in. "No dice." — Philip Wylie, *Opus 21*, p. 342, 1949

- No dice, Mr. Berin. They hurt me but they didn't scare me. — Mickey Spillane, *My Gun is Quick*, pp. 74–75, 1950
- I tried to make myself sleep, but it was no dice. — Jim Thompson, *Savage Night*, p. 67, 1953
- No shirts, no shoes, no dice. — *Fast Times at Ridgemont High*, 1982

no doubt!
used as a formulaic expression of agreement *US, 1988*
- — Connie Eble (Editor), *UNC-CH Campus Slang*, p. 7, Spring 1988
- — *Newsday*, p. B2, 11th October 1997

nods *noun*
a mixture of codeine-infused cough syrup and soda *US, 2000*
- In Houston, Elwood said, it has a variety of nicknames—Lean, AC/DC, barr, down, Karo and nods. "Lean because after you take it your will be definitely leaning and losing your coordination," Elwood said. — *The Commercial Appeal (Memphis)*, p. F1, 9th July 2000

no duh!
used for expressing sentiment that what was just said is patently obvious to even the casual observer *US, 1982*
- — Mimi Pond, *The Valley Girl's Guide to Life*, p. 60, 1982

NoFuck, Virginia *nickname*
Norfolk, Virginia *US, 1998*
- "NoFuck Virginia." Recruits learn to say "NoFuck" on their first Cinderella liberty when they have to be back on base by midnight without getting "any." — Maria Flook, *My Sister Life*, p. 62, 1998

noggin *noun*
the head *US, 1859*
- "That tap on the noggin ain't bothered your memory any," he said[.] — Chester Himes, *If He Hollers Let Him Go*, p. 185, 1945
- [T]his one here on my noggin is an African hat; but that don't make no difference. — Cecil Brown, *The Life & Loves of Mr. Jiveass Nigger*, p. 53, 1969
- I clapped my noggin: "What the fuck am I thinking of? That's a great song!" — Lester Bangs, *Psychotic Reactions and Carburetor Dung*, p. 9, 1971

no-go *adjective*
impossible *UK, 1825*
- "It's no go, guys," I said. — Donald Wilson, *My Six Convicts*, p. 64, 1951

no go; no-go *noun*
a failure, something that is not good; a hopeless attempt *UK, 1824*
Although the term has an undeniable US 1960s space program ring to it, it was 140 years old and had crossed the Atlantic before we heard it from NASA's lips.
- There were several dark husky men wearing hats who made Lynn's heart pump for a few seconds, but when he'd get close to them it was always a no-go. — Joseph Wambaugh, *Fugitive Nights*, p. 269, 1992
- If their [Dachshunds'] feet aren't crooked, it's no go. I've got one with front feet that are so turned you can't tell which way he's going. — *New York Daily News*, 27th February 2003

no-goodnik *noun*
a worthless person *US, 1936*
- So why in the world did she want such a no-goodnik back? — Laura Schlessinger, *Ten Stupid Things Women Do*, p. 217, 1993

no-go pill *noun*
any central nervous system depressant; a sleeping pill *US, 2003*
- The military has long prescribed amphetamines, termed go pills, and its counterpart no-go pills to control sleep deprivation in combat. — David Ross, *Some Among Them Are Killers*, p. 47, 2003

no-go zone *noun*
an area to which access is prohibited or ill-advised *US, 1979*
The term came to the attention of Americans in 2004 in the context of the US occupation of Iraq.
- Police are planning to cordon off an area between Independence Avenue and Jefferson Drive from Fourth to 14th Street as a secure "no-go" zone. — *Washington Post*, p. C1, 30th September 1979
- There are "no-go" zones in Iraq today. You can't hold an election in a "no go" zone. [Quoting John Kerry]. — *New York Times*, p. A1, 24th September 2004

noise *noun*
foolish talk; nonsense *US, 1871*

- He was giving me all kinds of noise about it and I can't take that from him, baby, I can't take it. — James Mills, *The Panic in Needle Park*, p. 140, 1966
- — Hermese E. Roberts, *The Third Ear*, 1971
- You think I need this noise? — George V. Higgins, *Penance for Jerry Kennedy*, p. 120, 1985
- Fuck that redneck noise, dude. All dem chicks be rappin' how dey losin' der ho's and how dey ain't got no bread for beer. — *Platoon*, 1986

noisemaker *noun*
a gun *US, 1979*
- "You're not packing a noisemaker, Mr. Matrobe?" — Leo Rosten, *Silky!*, p. 34, 1979

noisemaker *adjective*
producing the impression of force through loud sounds *US, 1998*
Professional wrestling usage.
- The stomps are quieter since they're putting more weight on the stomping foot and less on the noisemaker foot. — Sharon Mazer, *Professional Wrestling*, p. 165, 1998

noise pollution *noun*
in poker, excessive chatter at the table *US, 1996*
- — John Vorhaus, *The Big Book of Poker Slang*, p. 27, 1996

nomad *noun*
a member of a motorcycle gang who is not a member of any specific chapter of the gang *US, 1992*
- — Paladin Press, *Inside Look at Outlaw Motorcycle Gangs*, p. 36, 1992

no make!
stop what you are doing! *US, 1982*
Hawaiian youth usage, shortened from "no make like that."
- — Douglas Simonson, *Pidgin to da Max: Hana Hou*, 1982

no man's Nam *nickname*
Vietnam *US, 1978*
A blend of the historic "no man's land" and "Vietnam."
- "Two or three months in No Man's Nam, as a grunt anyway, and you get right lean in the flank." — *South Atlantic Quarterly*, p. 150, 1978
- — John Elting, *A Dictionary of Soldier Talk*, p. 210, 1984

no mention
you're welcome *US, 1981*
Hawaiian youth usage.
- — Douglas Simonson, *Pidgin to da Max*, 1981

no more forever *adverb*
never again *US, 1998*
Echoing the 1877 surrender speech of Chief Joseph of the Nez Perce nation—"I will fight no more forever."
- He retired young, man. He will play basketball no more forever. — *Smoke Signals*, 1998

no-neck *noun*
a person with muscular shoulders and no visible neck *US, 1955*
- He'd give you a Leather Man, a Lion Man, a Blimp, a No-Neck, and so many other types of oddities, I've lost track. — Classy Freddie Blassie, *The Legends of Wrestling*, p. 31, 2003

nonhacker *noun*
a soldier who cannot keep up with his fellow soldiers; an ineffective, incompetent soldier *US, 1976*
Coined in Vietnam and used heavily there. Back-formation from **HACK IT** (to cope with).
- I'd like to know where they get some of them non-hackers and then I'd like to know how they ever got through that OCS. — Charles Anderson, *The Grunts*, p. 113, 1976
- And my orders are to weed out all non-hackers who do not pack the gear to serve in my beloved Corps! — *Full Metal Jacket*, 1987

non-heinous *adjective*
good *US, 1991*
- — *USA Today*, p. 1D, 5th August 1991: "A sterling lexicon of the lingo"

no-no *noun*
something that ought not be done *US, 1942*
- "Did you do something, Mona?" "I was honest with a client. The Ultimate No-No." — Armistead Maupin, *Tales of the City*, p. 116, 1978

- "That's a no-no, bro." Johnny gave him the boy scout sign with both hands held high. "Profanity is not for us." — Piri Thomas, *Stories from El Barrio*, p. 5, 1978
- That's a no-no, Billy Clyde. Can't plug another network. — Dan Jenkins, *Life Its Ownself*, p. 318, 1984
- I've never seen Crash so angry and frankly, Bull fans, he used a certain word that's a "no-no" with umpires. — *Bull Durham*, 1988

nonproducer *noun*
a professional gambler who cannot be counted on to lose a great deal of money while gambling in a casino *US, 1963*
- During his stay, hieroglyphics are secretly appended to his name on the hotel register, which catalogue him as a "dropper" (businessman and heavy loser), "producer" (businessman), or "nonproducer" (professional gambler). — Ed Reid and Ovid Demaris, *The Green Jungle*, p. 2, 1963

nonseller *noun*
a plan that almost certainly will be rejected *US, 1986*
- — Department of the Army, *Staff Officer's Guidebook*, p. 63, 1986

nontrivial *adjective*
extremely complex *US, 1997*
- It's really a nontrivial solution, but it works. — Andy Ihnatko, *Cyberspeak*, p. 138, 1997

noodle *noun*
the penis *US, 1975*
- "You're just not getting enough?" "None! I got a limp noodle," he whispered. — Joseph Wambaugh, *The Glitter Dome*, p. 255, 1981
- I remembered that time she got boiling mad at me when I made a joke about Al Dante's firm noodle[.] — Rita Ciresi, *Pink Slip*, p. 13, 1999

noodle *verb*
1 to think, to ponder *US, 1942*
- How did I discover the VIP food storage lockers? Just noodlin' around with a trash bag over my shoulder, trying to look efficient. — Odie Hawkins, *Lost Angeles*, p. 102, 1994
2 to play music in a tentative, exploratory fashion *US, 1937*
- Next year you'll find me in Hollywood noodling for the sound tracks. — Ross Russell, *The Sound*, p. 207, 1961

noogie *noun*
a blow, usually repeated, to the head with a protuberant knuckle *US, 1972*
A hazing of youth. A recurring skit on *Saturday Night Live* in the 1970s vaulted the phrase "Noogie Patrol" into great popularity, with a nerdish Todd DiLaMuca (played by Bill Murray) grabbing Lisa Lupner (played by Gilda Radner) for a rash of noogies.
- Here's those fall noogies you ordered! Black and blue is going to be a big color this year, my dear! — *Saturday Night Live*, 7th October 1978
- "Kick his knees." "No, let's give him noogies." — Ethan Morden, *Buddies*, p. 45, 1986
- "Noogie time, noogie time," the morons chanted. — Seth Morgan, *Homeboy*, p. 325, 1990

nook *noun*
the vagina *US, 1973*
- Then Dove clasped her breasts and began to ease his sweeper into her hairless nook[.] — D.M. Perkins, *Deep Throat*, p. 24, 1973
- He was only half erect when she slid it into her nook and some crazy wonderful muscles inside began to pull at him, pulling him in and making him harder. — Ed Martin, *Busy Bodies*, p. 63, 2006

nookie; nooky *noun*
the vagina; hence a woman as a sex object; sexual intercourse *US, 1928*
- He wanted to be an accountant, and it troubled him that there was no accounting for the costs of nooky. — Bernard Wolfe, *The Late Risers*, p. 47, 1954
- Oh boy, I wonder who'd gimme some nookie. — Lenny Bruce, *The Essential Lenny Bruce*, p. 145, 1967
- What's the matter—got some hot nooky lined up for this afternoon? — Terry Southern, *Now Dig This*, p. 33, 1975
- "Well," said Mona, grinning at him, "a little nookie does you a world of good." — Armistead Maupin, *Tales of the City*, p. 199, 1978

nooky-nooky *noun*
sex *US, 1974*

- Man, a whole lot of men have pulled time without digging another man's behind and I'd better get my mind on something else beside nooky-nooky. — Piri Thomas, *Seven Long Times*, p. 149, 1974

nooner *noun*
a bout of sex at about noon *US, 1973*
- And you think you can dance me into a porno movie for a nooner? — Joseph Wambaugh, *The Black Marble*, p. 101, 1978
- "Nooners, for Christ sake?" I said. "Coop, I'm middle-aged." — George V. Higgins, *Penance for Jerry Kennedy*, p. 207, 1985
- Keyes hated to admit it, but that's what covered the rent; he'd gotten damn good at staking out nooner motels[.] — Carl Hiaasen, *Tourist Season*, p. 19, 1986

noonsie *noun*
sex during the lunch hour *US, 1973*
- Make a date for a "noonsie" in the office while the secretary is out to lunch. — Gail Sheehy, *Hustling*, p. 36, 1973

no-pay *noun*
a person who refuses to repay a debt or loan *US, 1982*
- The sports book handle was so tremendous, day in day out, that nobody seemed to stop and think about the losses they were taking on, weak collections and no-pays. — Richard Condon, *Prizzi's Honor*, p. 283, 1982

no problem
you're welcome *US, 1982*
At some point in the 1980s, the term "you're welcome" suddenly vanished from the vocabulary of America's young, replaced suddenly and completely with "no problem."
- STACY: Thanks for picking me up. RON: No problem. — *Fast Times at Ridgemont High*, 1982
- TEACHER: Thank you, Simone. SIMONE: No problem whatsoever. — *Ferris Bueller's Day Off*, 1986
- Yes, I'll make sure she's all right. Here's Suzanne. Bye now. No problem. — Sandra Bernhard, *Confessions of a Pretty Lady*, p. 100, 1988

no problema; no problemo
no problem *US, 1989*
A popular elaboration.
- "Richie's history," said Tina. "No problema." — Carl Hiaasen, *Skin Tight*, p. 92, 1989
- SKINNER: Er, one question remains: how do I get out of the army? BART: No problemo. Just make a pass at your commanding officer! — *The Simpsons*, 1994
- — Connie Eble (Editor), *UNC-CH Campus Slang*, p. 6, April 1997
- "Thanks for the doughnuts." "Hey, no problemo." — Janet Evanovich, *Seven Up*, p. 251, 2001

normie *noun*
someone who is not addicted to anything *US, 1998*
Used in twelve-step recovery programs such as Alcoholics Anonymous.
- — Christopher Cavanaugh, *AA to Z*, p. 132, 1998

Norwegian steam *noun*
brute physical exertion *US, 1944*
- — *Maledicta*, p. 171, 1979: "A glossary of ethnic slurs in American English"

nose *noun*
1 cocaine *US, 1980*
- Nadeau's wife, Helena, beautiful broad, had a disease, too. Cocaine. Two-hundred-dollar-a-day nose. — Robert Campbell, *Juice*, p. 23, 1988
2 in horseracing, any very short distance that separates winner from loser *US, 1908*
- — David W. Maurer, *Argot of the Racetrack*, p. 44, 1951

▸ **get your nose bent**
to be convicted of a traffic violation *US, 1962*
- — *American Speech*, p. 269, December 1962: "The language of traffic policemen"

▸ **get your nose cold**
to use and become intoxicated on cocaine *US, 1980*
- — Edith A. Folb, *runnin' down some lines*, p. 239, 1980

▸ **have a nose for someone**
to be sexually attracted to someone *US, 1958*
- Suppose I fix you up with Baby here. You always had a nose for her. — John Clellon Holmes, *The Horn*, p. 57, 1958

▶ **have your nose open**
to be strongly attracted to *US, 1957*

- That's what I intend to do, only trouble is m'nose opens up and I can't tell what I'm doing. — Jack Kerouac, *On the Road*, p. 257, 1957
- What about that gray girl in San Jose who had your nose wide open? — Eldridge Cleaver, *Soul on Ice*, p. 9, 1968
- My nose is still open for that yellow, stinking, skunk, lousy, junkie 'ho. — Iceberg Slim (Robert Beck), *Airtight Willie and Me*, p. 104, 1979
- Most working girls were like that, their noses open wider than their cunts. — Seth Morgan, *Homeboy*, p. 7, 1990

▶ **on the nose**
1 in horseracing, a bet on a horse to finish first *US, 1960*
- — Robert Saunders Dowst and Jay Craig, *Playing the Races*, p. 166, 1960

2 (used of a person's bet in an illegal numbers gambling lottery) invariably the same *US, 1949*
- — *American Speech*, p. 192, October 1949

3 at the start of a song *US, 1982*
- — Arnold Shaw, *Dictionary of American Pop/Rock*, p. 267, 1982

nose *verb*
to curry favor through obsequious conduct *US, 1968*
A shortening of **BROWN-NOSE**.
- — Collin Baker et al., *College Undergraduate Slang Study Conducted at Brown University*, p. 163, 1968

nosebleed *noun*
a stupid, inept person *US, 1951*
Teen slang.
- — *Newsweek*, p. 28, 8th October 1951

nosebleeds *noun*
the highest seats in an auditorium or a stadium *US, 1978*
Because high altitudes can cause nosebleeds.
- — Judi Sanders, *Cal Poly Slang*, p. 7, 1990
- — David Shenk and Steve Silberman, *Skeleton Key*, p. 207, 1994

nose-burner; nose-warmer *noun*
the still-lit butt of a marijuana cigarette *US, 1973*
- — Victor H. Vogel and David W. Maurer, *Narcotics and Narcotic Addiction*, p. 429, 1973

nose candy *noun*
cocaine or, rarely, another powdered drug that can be snorted *US, 1925*
- First thing, the nose candy kids'll be tryin' for the tap. — Mickey Spillane, *Me, Hood!*, p. 40, 1963
- "All you have to do, see about the grass and some candy." What? I go, Candy? He goes, "Nose candy, dummy. They like to have a little gig after, you understand?" — Elmore Leonard, *Touch*, p. 29, 1977
- We've been doing nose candy all night. — Armistead Maupin, *Babycakes*, p. 279, 1984
- I can quite easily recall her asking Michael to send her some "nose candy" many times over the years. — James St. James, *Party Monster*, p. 179, 1999

no-see-um *noun*
any small, nearly invisible insect that bites *US, 1842*
- No-see-ums are called many different things, mostly unprintable. — Mark Wheeler, *Half Baked Alaska*, p. 104, 1972
- Wiley swatted no-see-'ems in the darkness for three hours until he heard the hum of a passing motorboat. — Carl Hiaasen, *Tourist Season*, p. 359, 1986
- The bain of all those who venture into the bush, "noseeums" are also known across much of Canada, but they were named by the Indians and appear to be at their worst in the western bush. — Chris Thain, *Cold as a Bay Street Banker's Heart*, p. 107, 1987
- [A] number of kids had lit strips of newspaper, making a game of swirling them in loops, trying to smoke away the mosquitoes and no-see-ums. — Richard Price, *Clockers*, p. 384, 1992

nosefull *noun*
a strong dose of a powdered drug that is snorted *US, 1980*
- No, you my man, only man I know can do it cool, without a nose-full. — Elmore Leonard, *Gold Coast*, p. 22, 1980

nose garbage *noun*
poor quality cocaine *US, 1993*
- I have to hand it to you, this is not nose garbage, this is quality. — *True Romance*, 1993

nose habit *noun*
an addiction to a powdered drug ingested by nose *US, 1968*
- [J]ust sniffing heroin dust can increase your habit if you're a junkie or give you a "nose habit" if you aren't. — Phil Hirsch, *Hooked*, p. 22, 1968

nose hose *noun*
the tubing used for nastrogastic intubation *US, 1994*
- — Sally Williams, *"Strong" Words*, p. 152, 1994

nose job *noun*
cosmetic surgery to enhance the nose *US, 1960*
- She's admitted that she lived with Rubirosa—and brags about her boyfriends, but any mention of her age or nose job and she gets hysterical. — Lee Mortimer, *Women Confidential*, p. 83, 1960
- "Bullshit, he's too good-lookin' for a Hebe." "Maybe he got a nose job," countered Perry. — Richard Price, *The Wanderers*, p. 27, 1974

nose packer *noun*
a cocaine user *US, 1988*
- Bruce O'Hara is probably a dope addict, like everybody else in Hollywood. A nose-packer. — Gerald Petievich, *Shakedown*, p. 115, 1988

nose-picking speed *noun*
an extremely slow pace *US, 1986*
US naval aviator usage.
- — *United States Naval Institute Proceedings*, p. 108, October 1986

noser *noun*
an informer *US, 1992*
- — William K. Bentley and James M. Corbett, *Prison Slang*, p. 36, 1992

nose-ride *verb*
in surfing, to ride on the front of the board *US, 1979*
- I've admired your nose-riding for years. — *Apocalypse Now*, 1979

nosh *noun*
food *US, 1951*
From Yiddish, ultimately German *nachen* (to eat slyly), since early 1960s.
- Kate was going around the room offering everybody green tea and freakly little noshes she picked up at the Japanese Trade Center. — Cyra McFadden, *The Serial*, p. 102, 1977

nosh *verb*
1 to eat; to nibble *US, 1947*
From Yiddish.
- — Connie Eble (Editor), *UNC-CH Campus Slang*, p. 5, March 1979
- Her twins crawled among the market boxes and noshed grapes. "Stop noshing grapes!" Ellen warned. — John Clayton, *Bodies of the Rich*, p. 54, 1984
- A picnic and Chick Ottens noshing bar-b-q'd chicken with his snazzy new face. — James Ellroy, *Hollywood Nocturnes*, p. 260, 1994
- Rigorous union timekeeping meant they would materialize hungry at exactly 12:01, nosh somewhere, and then hang out at the war memorial[.] — Ethan Morden, *How's Your Romance?*, pp. 15–16, 2005

2 to kiss in a sustained fashion *US, 1994*
- — Linda Meyer, *Teenspeak!*, p. 30, 1994

no shame!
you act as if nothing embarrasses you! *US, 1981*
Hawaiian youth usage.
- — Douglas Simonson, *Pidgin to da Max*, 1981

noshery *noun*
an eating establishment, especially a delicatessen *US, 1952*
- Expect to wait for a seat in the small, conversation-friendly dining room or the other larger and much noisier noshery with bar and counter seating. — Shannon O'Leary, *Best Places Seattle*, p. 86, 2004

no shit, Dick Tracy!
used for pointing out that another person has just made an obvious statement *US, 1973*
A variant of the more common allusion to Sherlock Holmes, this based on the US cartoon detective.
- "No shit, Dick Tracy," I replied. "And just what did you expect to command?" — Anthony Herbert, *Soldier*, p. 237, 1973
- "Rats run up inside walls," Proctor said. "No shit, Dick Tracy," Fein said. — George V. Higgins, *The Rat on Fire*, p. 60, 1981
- "You're hit." "No shit, Dick Tracy." — Lynda Van Devanter, *Home Before Morning*, p. 8, 1983

no shit, Sherlock
used for pointing out that another person has just made an obvious statement *US, 1976*
Sherlock Holmes extends **NO SHIT!**
- — Pamela Munro, *U.C.L.A. Slang*, p. 62, 1989
- "But don't say a word about this." "No shit, Sherlock." — Carl Hiaasen, *Stormy Weather*, p. 218, 1995
- "I'm never gonna be able to pay you back." "No shit, Sherlock." — Stephen J. Cannell, *The Tin Collectors*, p. 265, 2001

no-shitter *noun*
a true statement; a truth *US, 1975*
- "This was a no-shitter. This was the real thing." — Richard Marcinko, *Rogue Warrior*, p. 81, 1992

no-show *noun*
1 a nonappearance at an appointed time or place *US, 1957*
- [F]ind out why he pulled a no-show on his hearing yesterday. — Janet Evanovich, *Seven Up*, p. 4, 2001

2 an organized crime scheme in which someone appears on a legitimate payroll, is paid by a legitimate business, but performs no work *US, 1985*
- Henry was given the car so that he could be put on a building contractor's payroll as a no-show and his salary divided among the Varios. — Nicholas Pileggi, *Wise Guy*, p. 24, 1985
- "He's got this phantom union set up, and half the cops working this sector have got nice no-show jobs and nice paychecks." — James Ellroy, *American Tabloid*, p. 98, 1995

no siree; no siree, Bob
absolutely no *US, 1848*
- I couldn't do that. No siree, bob, you little nut. — *Lethal Weapon*, 1987
- This ain't gonna happen! You people will not be allowed to put quality radio shows on our air waves, no siree bob! — Odie Hawkins, *Lost Angeles*, p. 141, 1994

no soap
used for signifying that the deal is off, not a hope, you're wasting your time *US, 1926*
- I tried to get transferred to a day job, but it was no soap. — Jim Thompson, *Bad Boy*, p. 405, 1953
- Terry and I tried to find work at the drive-ins. It was no soap anywhere. — Jack Kerouac, *On the Road*, p. 86, 1957
- They all gave me the same answer after they saw the medical report on me. The answer was no soap. — John Knowles, *A Separate Peace*, p. 182, 1959

no squash *noun*
irreparable brain damage *US, 1978*
- — *Maledicta*, p. 68, Summer/Winter 1978: "Common patient-directed pejoratives used by medical personnel"

nostril *noun*
in horseracing, any very short distance between winner and loser that is shorter even than a nose *US, 1951*
- — David W. Maurer, *Argot of the Racetrack*, p. 44, 1951

no sweat
no problem; no need to worry *US, 1955*
Therefore no sweat will be produced by fear or exertion.
- JOHN: Don't you have some homework or somethin' to do? CAROL: No sweat. My mother does it. — *American Graffiti*, 1973

no-sweat pill *noun*
a potent antibacterial pill *US, 1986*
- Remorse hit him the next morning; he went to the flight surgeon, asked for and got some "No Sweat" pills guaranteed to be good for what ailed you, no matter what secret Asian problem that was. — Walter J. Boyne and Steven Thompson, *The Wild Blue*, p. 476, 1986

Nosy Parker *noun*
an exceptionally inquisitive person *UK, 1907*
- "What do you want to be a nosy parker for?" — Max Shulman, *Sleep Till Noon*, p. 35, 1950

not!
used as a humorous cancellation of what has just been said in jest *US, 1893*
Coined a hundred years before it was broadly popularized by Mike Myers in the "Wayne's World" sketches on *Saturday Night Live*.

- — Connie Eble (Editor), *UNC-CH Campus Slang*, p. 6, November 1990
- I love the suburbs. Not! — *Wayne's World*, 1992
- "Yeah, but you've got a boyfriend now." "Not," I said, emphatically, appropriating one of her more asinine pop phrases. — Armistead Maupin, *Maybe the Moon*, p. 226, 1992

note from mother *noun*
official permission *US, 1986*
US Naval aviator usage.
- — *United States Naval Institute Proceedings*, p. 108, October 1986

no-tell motel *noun*
a motel with discreet management favored by prostitutes and couples seeking privacy *US, 1974*
- [T]hrowing hammerhead sharks into hotel swimming pools, blanket-tossing, building 40-foot high pyramids of empty beer cans on the beach and checking in and out of no-tell motels with handsome Ivy Leaguers. — *Washington Post*, p. B1, 20th April 1977
- It was a no-tell motel all right. It offered closed-circuit television with X-rated shows. — Joseph Wambaugh, *The Delta Star*, p. 186, 1983
- [S]he'd been at it ever since, up and down the coast from Tacoma to Tarzana; in massage parlors, for escort services, in no-tell motels, on street corners. — Seth Morgan, *Homeboy*, p. 4, 1990
- They played the one-room beer joints among the no-tell motels, pawnshops and liquor stores that line the city's shadiest thoroughfare. — *Phoenix New Times*, 11th December 2003

not even
no, not at all *US, 1984*
- — Jonathan Roberts, *How to California*, p. 173, 1984
- — Pamela Munro, *U.C.L.A. Slang*, p. 62, 1989
- MURRAY: He's gay. CHER: Not even. — *Clueless*, 1995
- What? What are you talking about? I'm not even. — *Chasing Amy*, 1997

nothing-ass bitch *noun*
used as a stern term of contempt for a woman *US, 1972*
- As he did, one of them called out after her—"nothin' ass bitch!"—to the laughter of his fellows. — Christina and Richard Milner, *Black Players*, p. 41, 1972

nothing but the bacon!
used as a stock answer when greeted with "what's shakin?" *US, 1951*
- — *Philadelphia Evening Bulletin*, 11th November 1951

nothing but the bottom of the cup; nothing but the bottom of the net
used as a humorous comment on a job well done or a remark well made *US, 1997*
Coined by ESPN's Dan Patrick to describe a great shot in golf and basketball.
- — Keith Olberman and Dan Patrick, *The Big Show*, p. 22, 1997

nothing flat *adverb*
very quickly *US, 1947*
- I went through the pile of chicken in nothing flat. — Mickey Spillane, *I, The Jury*, p. 51, 1947
- He got us to Mount Sinai in nothing flat. — Erich Segal, *Love Story*, p. 117, 1970
- I had only one thought—to get the hell out in nothing flat! — Red Rudensky, *The Gonif*, p. 90, 1970

nothing shaking *noun*
nothing happening *US, 1975*
- [I]f a wop is deported he goes crazy. There's nothin' shakin' outside the U.S.A. — Edwin Torres, *Carlito's Way*, p. 86, 1975

no time flat *adverb*
very quickly *US, 1957*
- We got there in no time flat. — Jack Kerouac, *On the Road*, p. 21, 1957

no-trump *noun*
a life prison sentence without chance of parole *US, 1976*
- — John R. Armore and Joseph D. Wolfe, *Dictionary of Desperation*, p. 41, 1976

novhere *adjective*
unattractive; unpleasing *US, 1955*
A mock German or Dutch accent.
- — *American Speech*, p. 304, December 1955: "Wayne University slang"

now *adjective*
fashionable, in style, current *US, 1955*
- "Hey, man," said the stranger, "where you goin' with that here now cow?" — Steve Allen, *Bop Fables*, p. 55, 1955
- [L]ooking uncomfortable in an outdated suit, so outdated that it is almost Now again, and a pair of canary yellow pointed toe shoes. — Odie Hawkins, *Ghetto Sketches*, p. 52, 1972

now and thener *noun*
in horseracing, a horse that is an uneven or inconsistent performer *US, 1951*
- — David W. Maurer, *Argot of the Racetrack*, p. 44, 1951

no way!
used for expressing disbelief at that which has just been said *US, 1968*
- No day, no way. No can do. — George V. Higgins, *The Friends of Eddie Doyle*, p. 74, 1971
- — Eugene Landy, *The Underground Dictionary*, p. 140, 1971
- "I suppose you have every reason to regard me as a certified nut case." "No way." — Armistead Maupin, *Further Tales of the City*, p. 162, 1982
- LINDA: I hear some surfer pulled a knife on Mr. Hand this morning. STACY: No way! He just called him a dick. — *Fast Times at Ridgemont High*, 1982
- TED: Whoa! Second base! BILL: No way! — *Bill and Ted's Excellent Adventure*, 1989

no way, Jose
used as a humorous, if emphatic, denial *US, 1977*
The catchy reduplication makes this a favorite early in a young person's process of slang acquisition.
- — Connie Eble (Editor), *UNC-CH Campus Slang*, p. 5, March 1981
- No way, Jose. First you have to get rid of this bald girl. — Jay McInerney, *Bright Lights, Big City*, p. 5, 1984
- The Rican said, "No way, Jose." — Mark Baker, *Cops*, pp. 67–68, 1985
- Joe freaks at the badge and cocked magnum in his face and starts blabbing how a hitchhiker left the stuff in the trunk. No way, Jose, the cop said. — James Ellroy, *Suicide Hill*, p. 597, 1986

nowhere *adjective*
unaware of what is happening, extremely naive, utterly at a loss *US, 1843*
- He decided that his wife was a burden to him and that the life he was leading in California was nowhere. — Chandler Brossard, *Who Walks in Darkness*, p. 6, 1952
- Man, if you hadn't heard those spools of Royo Dehn's you were not with it at all, were as square as John Home from Rome, really nowhere. — Ross Russell, *The Sound*, p. 165, 1961
- "I'm sorry," I repeated, "but this scene is nowhere." — John Rechy, *City of Night*, p. 234, 1963
- Man, your puritanical putdown of people who are trying a healthier attitude toward sex and girls is nowhere. — Murray Kaufman, *Murray the K Tells It Like It Is, Baby*, p. 54, 1966

nowhereness *noun*
the state of complete unawareness of current trends or complete lack of grounding in reality *US, 1958*
- I had never seen such nowhereness, no s-h-i-t, why don't he just go somewhere and fade, um. — Jack Kerouac, *The Subterraneans*, p. 29, 1958

Nowheresville *noun*
any remote, dull place *US, 1963*
- "Hanky and the boss in a cold truck in Nowheresville." — Bruce Firedman, *Far from the City of Class*, p. 34, 1963
- Alan was a thin, bald guy with thick glasses who lived in Nowheresville, Pennsylvania. — Jason Starr, *Lights Out*, p. 38, 2006

now what?
can you top what I just said? *US, 2001*
- — Jim Goad, *Jim Goad's Glossary of Northwestern Prison Slang*, December 2001

NOYB
used as an abbreviation for "none of your business" *US, 1915*
- Don't grill someone by asking if he is a recovering alcoholic. It's an NOYB question (none of your business). — Letitia Baldridge, *Letitia Baldridge's New Manners for New Times*, p. 441, 1990

NRC *adjective*
(by police) nobody really cares *US, 1992*
- Everybody jist wants to handle NRC calls and go home at shift change. — Joseph Wambaugh, *Fugitive Nights*, p. 95, 1992

'n stuff
used either as a substitute for "et cetera" or to complete a sentence that has run out of steam *US, 2001*
- — Pamela Munro, *U.C.L.A. Slang*, p. 95, 2001

NT *noun*
in pornography, a scene showing nipple teasing (or torture) *US, 2000*
- — Ana Loria, *1 2 3 Be A Porn Star!*, p. 166, 2000: "Glossary of adult sex industry terms"

nubbins *noun*
the female breasts *US, 2005*
- Ample nubbins and side nudity when Angela removes her top and pops onto her guy. — Mr. Skin, *Mr. Skin's Skincyclopedia*, p. 63, 2005

nubian *noun*
in homosexual usage, a black man *US, 1986–1987*
- — *Maledicta*, p. 53, 1986–1987: "A continuation of a glossary of ethnic slurs in American English"

nudge *noun*
in pinball, subtle physical force applied to the machine to affect the trajectory of the ball without activating the tilt mechanism *US, 1979*
- — Edward Trapunski, *Special When Lit*, p. 154, 1979

nudge *verb*
1 to nag; to annoy *US, 1968*
Yiddish. Various transliterations including "nudzh," "nudj" and "noudge."
- — Collin Baker et al., *College Undergraduate Slang Study Conducted at Brown University*, p. 163, 1968
- Shout he could shout, squabble he could squabble, and oh nudjh, could he nudjh! — Philip Roth, *Portnoy's Complaint*, p. 44, 1969
2 in pool, to touch the cue ball with the cue stick accidentally while preparing to shoot *US, 1993*
- — Mike Shamos, *The Illustrated Encyclopedia of Billiards*, p. 157, 1993

nudge show *noun*
a safe family comedy *US, 1973*
- Nudge shows are always viewed slightly askance by the industry but actors seldom turn down jobs in them and authors and producers wear smug little smiles as they bank their royalties. — Sherman Louis Sergel, *The Language of Show Biz*, p. 147, 1973

nudie *noun*
a performance or movie featuring naked women but no sexual activity *US, 1935*
- The nudies show naked breasts and backsides, and there can be a few double-edged lines of dialogue or narration thrown in here and there, but that's as far as they can go and still qualify for open exhibition. — Wade Hunter, *The Sex Peddler*, p. 108, 1963
- Usually the "nudies," in contrast to the old-fashioned sun-bathing, nudist colony, sex-exploitation stuff, have a male actor as the central subject or star. — Michael Milner, *Sex on Celluloid*, p. 18, 1964
- Is he making nudies? girlie films? stag films? — *Porno Films and the People who Make Them*, p. 18, 1973
- Actually, I had done several nudies before doing Strangers, both as a director and working the crew. (Quoting Bob O'Neil). — *Adam Film Quarterly*, p. 48, August 1975

nudie *adjective*
featuring naked or near-naked women *US, 1966*
- To combat a group of religious zealots hounding her nudie magazine, a female publisher calls on several former centerspread models to seduce some of them. — Kent Smith et al., *Adult Movies*, p. 52, 1982
- Only a card-carrying shithead would show his face at a nudie joint in an election year. — Carl Hiaasen, *Strip Tease*, p. 11, 1993
- [H]e [Larry King] acted like she was a whore and he'd never drooled over a nudie mag in his life. — *The Village Voice*, 25th July 2000

nudie booth *noun*
a private enclosure affording privacy while a paying customer views a nude woman or nude women, usually through a glass partition *US, 1994*
- RANDAL: You've never been in a nudie booth? DANTE: I guess not. RANDAL: Oh, it's great. You step into this little booth and there's this window between you and this naked woman, and she puts on this little show for like ten bucks. — *Clerks*, 1994

nudie-cutie *noun*

a genre of sex movie popular in the 1960s, featuring frolicking, cute, nude women *US, 1967*

- The sex exploitation film has long since replaced the "nudie-cuties" in the theatres that cater to adults across the nation. — *Adam Film Quarterly*, p. 13, November 1967
- Joyce, an ex-nudie-cutie queen, turned agent, became our agent through Rob. — Tina Russell, *Porno Star*, p. 24, 1973

nudie film *noun*

a movie featuring naked women but no sexual activity *US, 1963*

- Nudie films? Well, that was something else. — Wade Hunter, *The Sex Peddler*, p. 22, 1963

nudnik; noodnik *noun*

a pest, a fool *US, 1925*

- — Nathan Ausubel, *A Treasury of Jewish Folklore*, p. 732, 1948
- "I keep talking to myself." "Now, now," the doctor crooned, "that isn't such a bad habit. why, thousands of people do it." "But, doctor," protested Polanski, "you don't know what a nudnik I am!" — Leo Rosten, *The Joys of Yiddish*, p. 274, 1968
- Immediately that noodnick Penny Crone would broadcast my net worth all over Fox TV. — Howard Stern, *Miss America*, p. 354, 1995

nuff *adjective*

enough *US, 1840*

- [T]oday I know of one very bad thing the tea can do to you—it can put you in jail. "Nuff said." — Mezz Mezzrow, *Really the Blues*, p. 214, 1946

nuff said

used as an assertion that nothing more needs to be said *US, 1840*

- — Nina Simone, *'Nuff Said*, 1968
- I'm leavin' lame niggaz brain dead / Aww fuck it, nuff said — Kool G. Rap & DJ Polo, *Nuff Said*, 1992

nug *noun*

marijuana *US, 1997*

Variant "nugs."

- — Jim Emerson-Cobb, *Scratching the Dragon*, April 1997

nugget *noun*

1 a new, inexperienced soldier or pilot *US, 1966*

- "I hope I don't get a nugget." A nugget was a new man on his first tour of duty. — Stephen Coonts, *Flight of the Intruder*, p. 121, 1986
- Thus, "Frogman" became his nickname as a nugget pilot in the fleet. — Joe Weber, *Defcon One*, p. 21, 1989
- As a rookie or "nugget," Ruliffson felt conspicuous and apprehensive. — Robert K. Wilcox, *Scream of Eagles*, p. 29, 1994
- Welch looked at Andrews and, beaming, said, "A couple of nugget jaygees! How about that, Sam?" — Gerry Carroll, *North S*A*R*, p. 58, 1991

2 an amphetamine tablet *US, 1994*

- — US Department of Justice, *Street Terms*, August 1994

3 a piece of crack cocaine *US, 1994*

- — US Department of Justice, *Street Terms*, October 1994

nuggets *noun*

the testicles *US, 1963*

- Eyes like cold yellow stone at Mark, a regular Sonny Liston prefight hoodoo glare that would sizzle your average bleeding-heart radical's nuggets to a crisp. — John Sayles, *Union Dues*, p. 281, 1977

nugs *noun*

great waves for surfing *US, 1991*

- — Trevor Cralle, *The Surfin'ary*, p. 81, 1991

nuke *verb*

1 to lay waste, to ravage, to devastate *US, 1969*

A metaphorical, if less dramatic, sense.

- Part of the fun in preparing touring arrangements is nuking those norms. — Frank Zappa, *The Real Frank Zappa Book*, p. 185, 1989
- Something happened. You got nuked in the last quarter. — *Point Break*, 1991
- "[F]or some reason the funding got nuked in the Senate." — Carl Hiaasen, *Sick Puppy*, p. 50, 1999

2 to heat in a microwave oven *US, 1984*

- — Connie Eble (Editor), *UNC-CH Campus Slang*, p. 7, Fall 1988
- "Pizza on the second shelf, nuke that motherfucka three." — Jess Mowry, *Six Out Seven*, p. 151, 1993

3 in computing, to delete *US, 1991*

- — Eric S. Raymond, *The New Hacker's Dictionary*, p. 263, 1991

nuke; nook *noun*

a nuclear weapon *US, 1958*

- [T]here is reason to believe that two Soviet-manufactured suitcase nukes may have fallen into bin Laden's hands. — John W. Dean, *Worse than Watergate*, p. 123, 2004

nuke and pave *verb*

to reformat the hard drive of a computer *US, 2001*

- — Don R. McCreary (Editor), *Dawg Speak*, 2001

nuke-knob *noun*

a bald or shaved head *US, 1997*

- The labels were cruel: Gimp, Limpy–go-fetch, Crip, Lift-one-drag one, etc. Pint, Half-a-man, Peewee, Shorty, Lardass, Pork, Blubber, Belly, Blimp. Nuke-knob, Skinhead, Baldy. Four-eyes, Specs, Coke bottles. — *San Francisco Examiner*, p. A15, 28th July 1997

nukka *noun*

a black person *US, 1998*

Slightly less offensive than **NIGGER**.

- if that don't be eveyweah you be one dumb nukka. — *alt.music.hardcore*, 14th August 1998
- "You talking good shit. Respect, nukka." — Paul Beatty, *Tuff*, p. 151, 2000
- You lucky Nicky's my nuccah and I got to him in time. — Noire, *Candy Licker*, p. 102, 2005

number *noun*

1 a person, particularly someone attractive, originally of a woman *US, 1896*

- [A] "number" is a potential or actual or merely desired partner in vagrant sex. — John Rechy, *Numbers*, p. 16, 1967

2 a prostitute's client (especially in a male homosexual context) *US, 1967*

- I have three main trips—hustling, "numbers" and mutual contacts with certain people[.] — John Rechy, *The Sexual Outlaw*, p. 69, 1977

3 a casual sex-partner *US, 1970*

- — *American Speech*, p. 58, Spring–Summer 1970: "Homosexual slang"

4 a situation *US, 1908*

- I'll do my New York number, and you do your Akrons and your Denvers. — Dan Jenkins, *Semi-Tough*, p. 201, 1972
- Ms. Murphy said she thought it sounded fantastic and why didn't they just leave the whole number up to Pierre. — Cyra McFadden, *The Serial*, p. 29, 1977
- "Okay," he said, "now here's a funny number a couple of guys I know run from time to time." — Terry Southern, *Now Dig This*, p. 18, 1981
- An interesting number gets played out these days by fifty-year-old brothers who've had white women play prominent roles in their lives; some of them go into a deep denial mode. — Odie Hawkins, *Lost Angeles*, 1994

5 used as a vague catch-all susceptible of several meanings, usually related to sex or drugs *US, 1978*

- "I recognized him right away, because him and me did a little number last month on his houseboat in Sausalito." "A little number?" "Fucked." — Armistead Maupin, *Tales of the City*, p. 21, 1978

6 in craps, any roll except the shooter's point or a seven *US, 1950*

- He picked up the dice and throwed six numbers. — *The Annals of the American Academy of Political and Social Sciences*, p. 128, May 1950

7 a marijuana cigarette *US, 1963*

- They light another number, passing it around like tribal Indians. — John Rechy, *The Fourth Angel*, p. 22, 1972
- Think I'll roll another number for the road[.] — Neil Young, *Roll Another Number*, 1975
- [W]e both went to the "john" and knocked up a couple of numbers, which we put to good use before we hit the streets. — Ken Lukowiak, *Marijuana Time*, p. 94, 2000

8 a song *UK, 1878*

- When you take off on a number, it sounds as though you never know where you're going to come out, you just go flying off into musical space. — Mezz Mezzrow, *Really the Blues*, p. 330, 1946

▸ **do a number on**

1 to use emotional pressure, to humiliate *US, 2000*

- You really fucked me, Kim / You really did a number on me. — Eminem (Marshall Mathers), *Kim*, 2000

2 to kill *US, 1982*

- [S]he can pay back the money and a penalty, because she is Charley's wife and we don't do numbers on wives[.] — Richard Condon, *Prizzi's Honor*, p. 270, 1982

number-cruncher *noun*

an accountant or bookkeeper *US, 1977*

- A detailed explanation can put even the most ardent number cruncher to sleep[.] — Marcus Buckingham, *First, Break All the Rules*, p. 31, 1990

number one *noun*

1 yourself, your own interests *UK, 1705*

- [H]e started off thinking of number one. — Robert Rossen, *All the King's Men*, 1949
- Take care of business; look out for number one—one way or the other there'll always be hustlers. — Edwin Torres, *Carlito's Way*, p. 81, 1975

2 urination *UK, 1902*

The plural variant "number ones" is also used.

- "You know, I even used to think that teachers didn't make number one or number two, like God or the saints." — Jose Antonio Villarreal, *Pocho*, p. 70, 1959
- — Collin Baker et al., *College Undergraduate Slang Study Conducted at Brown University*, p. 164, 1968
- I feel like I am five years old. Mama, may I go to the potty? Number one? Number two? — Beatrice Sparks (writing as "Anonymous"), *Jay's Journal*, p. 137, 1979
- Liquid Gold 5 features women doing number one and (ain't that America!) getting paid for it. — *New Times Los Angeles*, 19th July 2001

number one; numba one *adjective*

the very best *US, 1838*

Although coined in the 1830s in a pure English sense, it took on a pidgin or mock pidgin tone in the C20; very popular in the Vietnam war.

- This being the proper polite form of Japanese and manners, saying good morning, and that he was number-one, the best with you. — Gregory "Pappy" Boyington, *Baa Baa Black Sheep*, pp. 293–294, 1958
- No!! Wear on Tet! T-E-T! Numbah one holiday! — Ted Zidek, *Choi Oi: The Lighter Side of Vietnam*, p. 75, 1965
- Maybe you like see number-one girl? — *The Berkeley Barb*, p. 1, 5th November 1965
- Baby-san give you number one blow job, you like? Come on G.I. Me suck you guts out. Baby'san love to eat G.I. dick. — *Screw*, p. 5, 15th February 1971

numbers *noun*

an illegal lottery based on guessing a number determined by chance each day *US, 1897*

- You got the numbers running in here? — Mickey Spillane, *I, The Jury*, p. 43, 1947
- All the people who had a little more nerve than average or didn't care would take numbers. Numbers was the thing; it sort of ran the community. — Claude Brown, *Manchild in the Promised Land*, p. 191, 1965
- It was an even bigger money-maker than numbers, and Jimmy was in charge. — *Goodfellas*, 1990
- Black people don't play the stock market. We play the numbers. But how do we determine what numbers to play? Dreams. — Chris Rock, *Rock This!*, p. 95, 1997

▶ **by the numbers**

precisely, correctly *US, 1918*

- Mace, let's make this one smooth and by the numbers. Okay? — *Airheads*, 1994

▶ **take the numbers down**

in horseracing, to disqualify a horse from a race and announce a new winner *US, 1947*

- — Walter Steigleman, *Horseracing*, p. 278, 1947

numbers banker *noun*

the operator of an illegal numbers racket or lottery *US, 1959*

- A numbers banker? — Chester Himes, *The Real Cool Killers*, p. 102, 1959
- [I]t was generally known that the numbers bankers paid off at higher levels of the police department. — Malcolm X and Alex Haley, *The Autobiography of Malcolm X*, p. 85, 1964
- They couldn't be trusted by numbers bankers any more. — Claude Brown, *Manchild in the Promised Land*, p. 191, 1965

numbers drop *noun*

a place where bets on an illegal lottery are turned in or made *US, 1957*

- [E]ntered a grimy tobacco-store which fronted for a numbers drop and and reefer shop. — Chester Himes, *A Rage in Harlem*, p. 36, 1957

numbers game *noun*

sex expressed in numeric terms *US, 1964*

The most common is, of course, **69**, with other lesser known variants.

- — Roger Blake, *The American Dictionary of Sexual Terms*, p. 141, 1964
- — Anon., *King Smut's Wet Dreams Interpreted*, 1978

number ten *noun*

an unspecified central nervous system depressant *US, 1984*

- They were mainly not really smoking grass so much anymore, but taking "number tens," which are something like Quaaludes, and speed. — Wallace Terry, *Bloods*, pp. 211–212, 1984

number ten; numba ten *adjective*

the worst *US, 1965*

- You number Ten, you crazy. — *The Berkeley Barb*, p. 3, 3rd December 1965
- I hadn't noticed him until he smiled and said, "Numbah one!" I quickly grabbed for my shirt. As soon as I got the last button fastened, he snorted: "Numbah ten." — Elaine Shepard, *The Doom Pussy*, p. 69, 1967
- "Hoa, numah fucking ten!" the kid yelled. "Cheap Charlie." — William Pelfrey, *The Big V*, p. 17, 1972
- "This grass is Number Ten," Davies said. — Michael Kerr, *Dispatches*, p. 177, 1977

number ten thousand *adjective*

worse than the very worst *US, 1966*

Vietnam war usage.

- NUMBAH TEN THOU!! Absolutely the living worst. Your orders, your promotion, and your girl are all overdue. — Ken Melvin, *Sorry 'Bout That*, p. 95, 1966: Glossary
- No, VC. VC numba fucken ten. VC numba ten thou! — Larry Heinemann, *Close Quarters*, p. 107, 1977

number two; number twos *noun*

defecation *US, 1936*

Adult usage of children's bathroom vocabulary.

- "You know, I even used to think that teachers didn't make number one or number two, like God or the saints." — Jose Antonio Villarreal, *Pocho*, p. 70, 1959
- — Collin Baker et al., *College Undergraduate Slang Study Conducted at Brown University*, p. 164, 1968
- [S]he left to do number two. — Miguel Pinero, *Short Eyes*, p. 34, 1975
- I feel like I am five years old. Mama, may I go to the potty? Number one? Number two? — Beatrice Sparks (writing as 'Anonymous'), *Jay's Journal*, p. 137, 1979

number two man *noun*

a skilled card cheat adept at dealing the second card instead of the top card in a deck *US, 1979*

- — John Scarne, *Scarne's Guide to Modern Poker*, p. 284, 1979

numbnuts *noun*

an idiot *US, 1960*

- I figured even some numbnuts could find this guy easy. — Leonard Shecter and William Phillips, *On the Pad*, p. 143, 1973
- What is your major malfunction, numbnuts? — *Full Metal Jacket*, 1987
- These numbnuts are laughing, thought Jake Harp. — Carl Hiaasen, *Native Tongue*, p. 317, 1991
- A trillion is more than a billion, numb-nuts. — *Austin Powers*, 1999

numbskull; numskull *noun*

a dolt; a fool *UK, 1742*

- Toliver and his boys were louts and numskulls propped up only by the local Communists[.] — Clancy Sigal, *Going Away*, p. 362, 1961

numerologist *noun*

a person who claims to have devised a winning system for an illegal numbers gambling lottery *US, 1949*

- — *American Speech*, p. 192, October 1949

numero uno *noun*

1 the very best *US, 1960*

Spanish for "number one."

- That moves Cush solidly up to numero uno in the draft. — *Jerry Maguire*, 1996

2 yourself *US, 1973*

- Being able to take care of yourself. Looking out for numero uno is more important now than ever. — Emmett Grogan, *Final Score*, p. 162, 1976
- [S]he'd earned the right to just look after Numero Uno. — Cyra McFadden, *The Serial*, p. 45, 1977

nummy *noun*

a fool, a dim-witted person *US, 1902*

A shortened "numbskull."

- Heh-heh-heh-heh, the nummies picked a Sunday; everybody was scattered all over the island, getting drunk or getting laid. — Philip Caputo, *A Rumor of War*, p. 39, 1977

num-nums *noun*

the female breasts *US, 1993*

- — J.R. Schwartz, *The Official Guide to the Best Cat Houses in Nevada*, p. 165, 1993: "Sex glossary"
- Like Herb's wife on WKRP in Cincinatti, we could say, "Better mow the grass, Herbie, or no num-nums tonight." — Sheila Wary Gregoire, *Honey I Don't Have a Headache Tonight*, p. 30, 2004

nunya *noun*

used for conveying that something is "none of your business" *US, 2000*

- — *Ebony Magazine*, p. 156, August 2000: "How to talk to the new generation"

nurds *noun*

the testicles *US, 1981*

- — *Maledicta*, p. 255, Summer/Winter 1981: "Five years and 121 dirty words later"

nurse *verb*

in a card game, to nervously fondle and adjust your cards *US, 1988*

- — George Percy, *The Language of Poker*, p. 59, 1988

nursery *noun*

1 a reformatory for juvenile offenders *US, 1950*

- — Hyman E. Goldin et al., *Dictionary of American Underworld Lingo*, p. 147, 1950

2 a gentle slope where beginning skiers practice *US, 1963*

- — *American Speech*, p. 206, October 1963: "The language of skiers"

nursery race *noun*

in horseracing, a relatively short distance race for two-year-olds *US, 1976*

- — Tom Ainslie, *Ainslie's Complete Guide to Thoroughbred Racing*, p. 335, 1976

nut *noun*

1 a crazy person *US, 1908*

- To them, Bob looked like a comical cartoon character, a total nut. — Bob Spitz, *Dylan*, p. 51, 1991

2 a regular and recurring expense *US, 1909*

- The Embers cost about $20,000 to open, a mild nut in these days of expensive construction. — Robert Sylvester, *No Cover Charge*, p. 283, 1956
- I asked the driver if he'd made his nut for the day and he glared at me as if I were from the vice squad. — Clancy Sigal, *Going Away*, p. 30, 1961
- She, from the daily bind of trying to crack the weekly nut. — Odie Hawkins, *Black Casanova*, p. 83, 1984
- We'll be rich. No more nut every week. — *Goodfellas*, 1990

3 an act of sexual intercourse; sex as an activity *US, 1991*

- Nut one, nut two, nut four, five, six / I lost the third nut in the mix—fuck it! — NWA, *Findum, Fuckum & Flee*, 1991
- Gimme that, gimme that, gimme that nutt — Eazy-E, *Gimme That Nutt*, 1993

4 an orgasm, especially of a male *US, 1968*

- It's not what you think. It won't take but five minutes for the guy to reach a nut. I mean, it's like takin' candy from a baby. — Donald Goines, *Daddy Cool*, p. 106, 1974
- "What exactly is a sweet nut?" I think the woman must have stared at me for five minutes. "Uhh, it'd be pretty hard to explain it to you, if you've never had one, honey." — Odie Hawkins, *The Life and Times of Chester Simmons*, p. 150, 1991

5 semen *US, 1991*

- Back up bitch unless you want nut in your eye. — NWA, *Findum, Fuckum & Flee*, 1991

6 an enthusiast *US, 1934*

- Health nuts are not necessarily, as the term may imply, fanatics. — Blythe Cameson, *Careers for Health Nuts & Others Who Like to Stay Fit*, p. 1, 2004

7 in horseracing, a horse picked by a racing newspaper to win a race *US, 1951*

- — David W. Maurer, *Argot of the Racetrack*, p. 45, 1951

8 in horseracing, the tax levied on bets by the track and the state *US, 1990*

- — Robert V. Rowe, *How to Win at Horse-Racing*, 1990

9 a bankroll *US, 1951*

- — David W. Maurer, *Argot of the Racetrack*, p. 45, 1951

▸ **crack the nut**

in gambling, to make enough money to meet the day's expenses *US, 1961*

- — Thomas L. Clark, *The Dictionary of Gambling and Gaming*, p. 53, 1987

▸ **make the nut**

to suffice *US, 1966*

- We were received in camp with cheers and shouting. Our eight cases made the nut. — Hunter S. Thompson, *Hell's Angels*, p. 184, 1966

▸ **off your nut**

deranged, crazy *US, 1946*

- He was replacement for the First Lieutenant, who had gone off his nut and had been transferred to a hospital ship. — Thomas Heggen, *Mister Roberts*, p. 215, 1946

▸ **on the nut**

in horseracing, to have lost a large amount of money betting *US, 1951*

- — David W. Maurer, *Argot of the Racetrack*, p. 46, 1951
- As facts are mattered, his luck was shattered / For he was what you'd call "on the nut." — Dennis Wepman et al., *The Life*, p. 103, 1976

nut *verb*

1 to have sex *US, 1971*

- — Eugene Landy, *The Underground Dictionary*, p. 140, 1971

2 to orgasm, especially of a male *US, 1999*

- get yo' nails out my back / Slut I'm bout to nut — Dr. Dre, *Housewife*, 1999

nutbag *noun*

a mesh restraint used by police to restrain violent people *US, 1997*

- Known as the "nut bag," the device is meant to keep the EDP restrained, calm and alive until he or she can be transported[.] — Samuel M. Katz, *Anytime Anywhere*, p. 61, 1997

nutbar *noun*

an eccentric, odd, or crazy person *US, 1978*

- So universal, in fact, that the paper once heard from a real nutbar who insisted I was plagiarizing my column from the contents of her journal. — Anna Quindlen, *Loud and Clear*, p. 4, 2004

nutbox *noun*

a mental hospital *US, 1965*

- Just because we had fought the day before and I was the only one who saw the accident, I ended up in the nutbox. — Claude Brown, *Manchild in the Promised Land*, p. 23, 1965

nutburger *noun*

an eccentric, odd, or crazy person *US, 1971*

- Most husbands, except utter nutburgers, don't cheat in the first few years of marriage. — Frank Robinson, *Sex American Style*, p. 59, 1971
- "She's a nutburger. She tracked me down at my job." — Joshilyn Jackson, *Gods in Alabama*, p. 188, 2005

nutcake *noun*

an eccentric or crazy person *US, 1967*

- "How would I know," he said. "We have nutcakes calling here every night of the week." — Tip O'Neill with William Novak, *Man of the House*, p. 128, 1987

nutcracker *noun*

1 a stern person; a strict disciplinarian, especially a woman who crushes a man's spirit *US, 1977*

- Now this Budka is notorious, worst accident record in the mine and pictures himself as a real nutcracker. Always on your back for chickenshit while the important stuff goes right past him. — John Sayles, *Union Dues*, p. 42, 1977
- I never met a broad yet named Tammy wasn't a nut cracker. — Joseph Wambaugh, *The Golden Orange*, p. 11, 1990

2 a psychotherapist *US, 1966*

- He was a medical doctor, not a nutcracker. — Jacqueline Susann, *Valley of the Dolls*, p. 404, 1966

nutcut *noun*

the critical point in an enterprise or operation *US, 1972*

- I take me a pair of dice and beat that shit, or a deck of cards, or if it comes down to the nutcut, I'll sell a sonofabitch the Brooklyn Bridge. — Bruce Jackson, *In the Life*, p. 146, 1972

nut-cutting *noun*

the most critical and distasteful stage in a project or operation *US, 1968*

An image from the West and cattle raising.

- It's getting to be, as the boys say, nut-cutting time. — Jim Bouton, *Ball Four*, p. 89, 1970
- They's one thing you always do when you're down to the nut-cutting. — Dan Jenkins, *Semi-Tough*, p. 190, 1972

nut factory *noun*

a hospital for the mentally ill *US, 1899*

- She could hardly get a job—except maybe at a nut factory. — Trevanian, *The Crazyladies of Pearl Street*, p. 131, 2005

nut farm *noun*

a hospital for the mentally ill *US, 1940*

- You see them around for a few days after the men don't want them, acting crazy before they go off somewheres else—to the House of Detention or the Bellevue nut farm. — Sara Harris, *The Lords of Hell*, p. 55, 1967

nut flush *noun*

in poker, a hand with all cards of the same suit and an ace as the high card *US, 1979*

- — John Scarne, *Scarne's Guide to Modern Poker*, p. 295, 1979

nut hatch *noun*

a mental institution *US, 1942*

- I used to know a tall young bum called Big Slim William Holmes Hubbard my buddy of the nuthouse who planned a break with me with breadknives to get to freights that ran behind the nuthatch[.] — Jack Kerouac, *Letter to Neal Cassady*, p. 307, 10th January 1951
- The next crisis occurred when they got married, at which time the family considered putting her, or him, or both, into a nuthatch. — Ed Sanders, *Tales of Beatnik Glory*, p. 20, 1975

nut house *noun*

a mental hospital *US, 1906*

- Incidentally, the girl I'd had that night is now in the nut-house, she was picked up, babbling. On the street the next morning. — Neal Cassady, *Neal Cassady Collected Letters 1944–1967*, p. 53, 9th September 1947: Letter to Jack Kerouac
- This is the man who went to see Ezra Pound at the nuthouse with Robert Lowell. — Jack Kerouac, *Letter to Allen Ginsberg*, p. 208, 16th July 1949
- They'd put you in a nuthouse, Brownie. They wouldn't give you the gas chamber. — Jim Thompson, *The Nothing Man*, p. 283, 1954
- He'd been close to a month in this nuthouse and it might be a lot better than a work farm[.] — Ken Kesey, *One Flew Over the Cuckoo's Nest*, p. 162, 1962

nut-hugging *adjective*

(said of pants) very tight *US, 2002*

- I come with long feet and big hands, nuthugging elephant bells[.] — David Henry Sterry, *Chicken*, p. 6, 2002

nut hustle *noun*

a swindle involving a prostitute and a confederate *US, 1978*

- The Murphy game is also called the nut hustle. — Burgess Laughlin, *Job Opportunities in the Black Market*, p. 16–1, 1978

nut job *noun*

someone who is mentally unstable *US, 1972*

- "I'm stuck with a hundred-dollar-a-week nut job for a guard." — Nicholas Pileggi, *Wise Guy*, p. 111, 1985
- These charges have attracted a lot of attention and it seems to be bringing all the nut jobs out of the nut jar. — *Traffic*, 2000

nut mob *noun*

a group operating three-shell games in carnivals *US, 1950*

- — *American Speech*, p. 235, October 1950: "The argot of outdoor boob traps"

nut-nut *noun*

in high-low poker, a hand that is the best possible hand either high or low *US, 1996*

- — Peter O. Steiner, *Thursday Night Poker*, p. 414, 1996

nut out *verb*

to act mentally ill; to lose emotional stability *US, 1966*

- But I nutted him out and continued my filing and staffing work. — Clarence Cooper Jr., *The Farm*, p. 233, 1967
- All the patients in the ward were basically just having a healthy reaction to the insane environment of the pen, by either nutting out or pretending to. — James Carr, *Bad*, p. 148, 1975
- I could nut out and say that I took my frustrations out on her, but that would only be half true. — Odie Hawkins, *Scars and Memories*, p. 86, 1987

nut player *noun*

in poker, a player who only plays a hand that is excellent as dealt *US, 1979*

From **NUTS** (the best possible hand in a given situation).

- — John Scarne, *Scarne's Guide to Modern Poker*, p. 295, 1979

nut role *noun*

the act of feigning eccentricity or mild insanity *US, 1969*

- I'll "nut roll" on her. I'll stay outta the pimp role until I case her. I'll go "Sweet William" on her. — Iceberg Slim (Robert Beck), *Pimp*, p. 144, 1969

nut-role; nut-roll *verb*

to feign mental instability *US, 1972*

- Buddha deadpans, nutrolls on them, as the Afro-Lords crack up around him. — Odie Hawkins, *Ghetto Sketches*, p. 81, 1972

nuts *noun*

1 the testicles; the scrotum *US, 1863*

- You ever been kneed in the nuts in a brawl, buddy? — Ken Kesey, *One Flew Over the Cuckoo's Nest*, p. 58, 1962
- Licking my nuts. Slobbering. My nuts in her face. Slobbering. Lick. — Terry Miller, *Standing By*, p. 88, 1984
- Listen you son of a bitch, if you don't let us in to see this movie I'm gonna kick you square in the nuts. — *South Park*, 1999
- If another one of these chairs hits me in the nuts, I'm gonna go postal. — *Austin Powers*, 1999

2 in poker, the best possible winning hand at a given moment *US, 1977*

- It's tough to beat that character since he won't bet unless he has the nuts. — Robert C. Prus and C.R.D. Sharper, *Road Hustler*, p. 170, 1977: "Glossary of terms"
- — John Scarne, *Scarne's Guide to Modern Poker*, p. 285, 1979

3 the advantage in a bet *US, 1990*

- If two players of equal speed are playing on an overcoat's table, the overcoat has the nuts. — Steve Rushin, *Pool Cool*, p. 21, 1990

▶ **get your nuts off**

to ejaculate *US, 1932*

- One of them noticed the hunchback and gave a derisive snort: "Wha'cha doin', Mac—gittin' yer nuts off?" — Terry Southern, *Candy*, 1958
- When I'd gotten my nuts off about six times, we got hungry. — Claude Brown, *Manchild in the Promised Land*, p. 165, 1965

nuts *adjective*

crazy *US, 1908*

- I find Terry and ask if he's ready to go, and he looks at me like I'm nuts. — Sara Paretsky, *Chicago Blues*, p. 315, 2007

nut sack *noun*

the scrotum *US, 1971*

- "Open your mouth and wiggle your tongue. Lift up your nut sack." — Sanyika Shakur, *Monster*, p. 320, 1993
- You can pull my nutsack up over my dick, so it looks like a bullfrog. — Kevin Smith, *Jay and Silent Bob Strike Back*, p. 90, 2001
- Come to think of it, grabbing your nutsack pretty much anytime is a good way to dis whoever. — Linden Dalecki, *Kid B*, p. 69, 2006

nuts and sluts *noun*

a college course on abnormal psychology or deviant behavior *US, 1980*

- A Yale undergraduate once told me that the deviance course was known about Yale students as "nuts and sluts." — Stuart Traub, *Theories of Deviance*, p. 330, 1980

- Pinto emerged from his Saturday Nuts 'n Sluts class no more enlightened about schizophrenia than ever. — Chris Miller, *The Real Animal House*, p. 125, 2006

nuts around *verb*
to idle *US, 1960*

- "What's Benkowski doin' for a living these days, Lefty?" "Just nutsin' around." — Nelson Algren, *The Neon Wilderness*, p. 58, 1960

nutso *adjective*
crazy *US, 1979*

- Lady, pardon me for saying, but I think you're goddamn fucking nutso. — Carl Hiaasen, *Native Tongue*, p. 81, 1991
- The idea of women looking down at their own breasts drives me nutso. — Nicholson Baker, *Vox*, p. 56, 1992

nuts to butts *adjective*
lined up, standing close to the person in front of you *US, 1993*

- We were herded into R&R like cattle. "nuts to butts" is how the Correctional Officer (C.O.) explained the way he wanted us lined up. — Sanyika Shakur, *Monster*, p. 319, 1993

nutsy *adjective*
eccentric, odd, crazy *US, 1923*

- You're not going nutsy on me, are you? You're not going to have one of those nervous breakdowns or anything, are you? — *Nashville*, 1975

nutty *adjective*
excellent *US, 1953*
A variation on "**CRAZY**."

- "Nutty," said the papa bear, "but you better call GAC. They booked you into the wrong room." — Steve Allen, *Bop Fables*, p. 12, 1955

nut up *verb*
1 to lose your composure completely *US, 1972*

- — Gary N. Underwood, *American Speech*, p. 63, Spring–Summer 1975: "Razorback slang"
- But he nutted up. I was tryin' to tell him where the necklace was. — Seth Morgan, *Homeboy*, p. 8, 1990
- — William K. Bentley and James M. Corbett, *Prison Slang*, p. 93, 1992

2 in poker, to shift into a more conservative mode of betting *US, 1982*

- — David M. Hayano, *Poker Faces*, p. 186, 1982

nut ward *noun*
the psychiatric ward of a prison *US, 1953*

- He was held in the nut ward of the Wayne County jail for some time[.] — John Sinclair, *Guitar Army*, p. 262, 1972
- Only a con who had just been released from the nut ward approached him at Four Gate. — Malcolm Braley, *False Starts*, pp. 187–188, 1976

nut wing *noun*
the part of a prison or hospital housing the mentally ill *US, 1998*

- Peanut butter and jelly means it's about noon, and macaroni and cheese must signify Happy Hour here on the nut wing of the Las Vegas County jail. — Jimmy Lerner, *You Got Nothing Coming*, p. 19, 2002

NWAB *adjective*
(of a girl) promiscuous, because she will neck with any boy *US, 1949*
Youth usage.

- — *Time*, 3rd October 1949

n-word *noun*
the word "nigger" *US, 1987*
This clumsy euphemism was popularized during the 1995 O.J. Simpson murder trial by F. Lee Baily's cross examination of Mark Fuhrman about a taped interview that Fuhrman had given in 1985.

- But nagging thoughts of ethnic slurs—black resentment over the "n" word, Irish resentment over the "m" word, Jewish resentment over the "k" word, etc.—held me back. — *St. Petersburg (Florida) Times*, p. 5D, 22nd March 1987
- I just said "nigger" a whole lot. You probably think I just use the N-word, but that rule is just for white folks. Any black person can say "nigger" and get away with it. It's true. — Chris Rock, *Rock This!*, pp. 22–23, 1997
- I'm afraid you need to work more on not saying the F word and the N word. — *South Park*, 1999
- Last year, she demanded that a word be removed from the 2000 census for Russian-speaking Sacramentans because it sounded too much like the N-word. — *Sacramento Bee*, 10th November 2001

nylon letdown *noun*
a descent by parachute *US, 1983*

- Both crewmen activated their ACES ejection seats and headed for a "nylon letdown" and God-knows-what on the ground. — Tom Clancy, *Fighter Wing*, p. 292, 1995

nympho *noun*
a nymphomaniac *US, 1910*
A creature of men's dreams; used to disparage a woman whose sexual appetites may threaten to make the dream come true.

- The goal of this type of dwelling is to put us in the mood, to get us turned on like crazed nymphos. — Anka Radakovich, *The Wild Girls Club*, p. 15, 1994
- Nympho is more appropriate, quite honestly. — Francesca Lia Block, *I Was a Teenage Fairy*, p. 99, 1998

Oo

O *noun*

1 opium *US, 1933*

- [O]n the floor a drunken snoring soldier who'd just eaten some O after lush. — Jack Kerouac, *Letter to Allen Ginsberg*, p. 347, 10th May 1952
- If I use at all I want the best. I want to smoke O or use good pure M or H. — William Burroughs, *Letters to Allen Ginsberg 1953–1957*, p. 105, 1st August 1955
- I don't know much about O and maybe my eyes are dilated? — Ken Kesey, *Kesey's Jail Journal*, p. 1, 1967
- He identified the meth by its effect, and the liquid O by its taste and blackness. — Terry Southern, *Blue Movie*, p. 202, 1970

2 an ovation *US, 1984*

Most commonly heard in the term "standing O."

- Ed Ray received a hero's reception at the state convention of the School Employees Association, and a tumultuous standing-O when he was presented its Man-of-the-Year Award. — Bill Cardoso, *The Maltese Sangweech*, p. 62, 1984

O *nickname*

the Nuestra Familia prison gang *US, 2000*

- By now the Nortenos, out of necessity, had formed their own prison gang, a paramilitary organization they called Nuestra Familia (Our Family), also known as the "Organization" or, more simply, the "O."
— Bill Valentine, *Gangs and Their Tattoos*, p. 24, 2000

oaktoe *noun*

the numbing of toes by cold water, creating the sensation that your toes are wooden *US, 2004*

Surfing usage.

- — *Transworld Surf*, p. 42, April 2004

Oaktown *nickname*

Oakland, California *US, 1989*

- Hammer has already produced two other releases: Oaktown's 3–5–7, an all-female rap trio, and Ace Juice, a hip-hop duo. — *Arkansas Democrat-Gazette*, 23rd June 1989
- "Shit, you really the coolest dude in Oaktown!" — Jess Mowry, *Six Out Seven*, p. 17, 1993
- "Back in Oakland?" "Yep. Out in Oaktown, as they called it." — Eric Jerome Dickey, *Milk in My Coffee*, p. 142, 1998

OAO *noun*

a girlfriend *US, 1956*

- Whether flanker (tall person) or gnome (member of a runt company), he's sure to have an O.A.O. (One and Only Her). — *Chicago Daily Tribune*, p. N4, 23rd December 1956

oasis *noun*

a bar *US, 1956*

- A whole series of Barney Gallant oases wrote history in the Village[.]
— Robert Sylvester, *No Cover Charge*, p. 247, 1956

oatburner; oatmuncher *noun*

in horseracing, a racehorse that does not perform well *US, 1916*

- — David W. Maurer, *Argot of the Racetrack*, p. 45, 1951

oater *noun*

a cowboy film, story, or song *US, 1946*

- [S]pecials and the merits of "soaps" and "oaters" (the last two were not commodities, but weepy morning serials for women and western action stories). — Stephen Longstreet, *The Flesh Peddlers*, p. 189, 1962
- I mean, yes, I did make eighteen feature-length oaters, that's true[.] — Gore Vidal, *Myra Breckinridge*, p. 51, 1968

oatmeal *noun*

a small, mushy wave *US, 1991*

- — Trevor Cralle, *The Surfin'ary*, p. 82, 1991

oats *noun*

1 money which a carnival worker steals from his boss *US, 1985*

- — Gene Sorrows, *All About Carnivals*, p. 23, 1985: "Terminology"

2 enthusiasm *US, 1831*

- — Lou Shelly, *Hepcats Jive Talk Dictionary*, p. 15, 1945

▸ **on his oats**

(used of a racehorse) racing without the benefit of a stimulant *US, 1994*

- — Igor Kushyshyn et al., *The Gambling Times Guide to Harness Racing*, p. 120, 1994

OBE *adjective*

overcome by events; overtaken by events *US, 1986*

- — Department of the Army *Staff Officer's Guidebook*, p. 63, 1986
- The plans that they had gone into Hong Kong with were now "OBE," or overcome by events, because now, at the beginning of the fall of '72, President Nixon had finally decided that enough was enough.
— Gerry Carroll, *North S*A*R*, p. 154, 1991

obit *noun*

an obituary *UK, 1874*

- I been reading the obit page for twenty years, and I haven't found one yet. — Max Shulman, *Rally Round the Flag, Boys!*, p. 134, 1957

obscure *adjective*

in computing, completely beyond all understanding *US, 1991*

- — Eric S. Raymond, *The New Hacker's Dictionary*, p. 267, 1991

OC *noun*

1 organized crime *US, 1975*

- Wops don't make parole—right away they stamp us O.C. or mafia. — Edwin Torres, *Carlito's Way*, p. 140, 1975
- Since his file had been stamped "OC" (Organized Crime) in big red letters, it was unlikely that the parole board would free him at the first opportunity. — Nicholas Pileggi, *Wise Guy*, p. 164, 1985

2 the synthetic opiate oxycodone used recreationally *US, 2001*

- "Hey, I was getting OC's prescribed to me in Pennsylvania; I'm going to get them in Las Vegas," he said. — *The New York Times Magazine*, p. 36, 29th July 2001

ocean *noun*

in pool, the expansive center of a table *US, 1993*

- — Mike Shamos, *The Illustrated Encyclopedia of Billiards*, p. 159, 1993

O club *noun*

in the US armed forces, an officer's club *US, 1985*

- "You know about the O-clubs, the BOQ's, and other privileges officers are given in this army?" — David Donovan, *Once a Warrior King*, p. 152, 1985
- Most O clubs around the country were disgraces, vending substandard food to captive clients. — Walter J. Boyne and Steven L. Thompson, *The Wild Blue*, p. 261, 1986
- "Are the beers cold in your O club, Lieutenant Ritchie?" Steve asked. — T.E. Cruise, *Wings of Gold III*, p. 226, 1989
- Any night in the O-Club you can hear how well they sing. — Joseph Tuso, *Singing the Vietnam Blues*, p. 79, 1990: Early Abort

OCS *noun*

the synthetic opiate oxycodone used recreationally *US, 2000*

- Investigators say the drug, an opiate called OxyContin, sold on the street as "Oxys" or "Ocs," has spawned a crime wave[.] — *Richmond (Virginia) Times Dispatch*, p. B1, 21st October 2000

octopus *noun*

a sexually aggressive boy *US, 1932*

- — *San Francisco Examiner* p. 2, 22nd March 1960
- — *American Speech*, p. 273, December 1963: "American Indian student slang"

OD *noun*

a drug overdose *US, 1959*

- Well, he died. The cat took an O.D., an overdose of heroin. — Claude Brown, *Manchild in the Promised Land*, p. 188, 1965
- [O]ne area in which her brilliance was widely recognized was in the treatment of an OD, an overdose—a shot that unexpectedly contains more heroin than the body can survive. — James Mills, *The Panic in Needle Park*, p. 37, 1966
- About this time the OD's started. — Herbert Huncke, *Guilty of Everything*, p. 178, 1990

OD *verb*

to overdose, to take an excessive dose of a drug, usually heroin *US, 1966*

- Frankie's OD'ing up in Marcie's room in the Reynolds. He needs help bad, honey. — James Mills, *The Panic in Needle Park*, p. 37, 1966
- When Janis Joplin O.D.'d one Sunday at the Landmark Motel, John Carpenter wrote a piece for the L.A. Free Press which clung pretty much to the theory, "What else is a Janis Joplin going to do on a Sunday afternoon alone in L.A.?" — Eve Babitz, *Eve's Hollywood*, p. 250, 1974
- I couldn't get hung up with her at that point, going over each time she called and shooting her up, having her collapse, with doubt in mind about whether she had O.D.'d or not. — Herbert Huncke, *The Evening Sun Turned Crimson*, p. 176, 1980
- The day I bring an O.D.ing bitch to your place, then I gotta give her the shot. — *Pulp Fiction*, 1994

o-dark-hundred *noun*

very early in the morning *US, 1982*

Mock military time.

- We got to Chau Doc at oh dark hundred but didn't land until first light. — Richard Marcinko and John Weisman, *Rogue Warrior*, p. 136, 1992

o'dark-thirty *noun*

a notional time after sunset or before sunrise *US, 1980*

- The next morning at "O-dark thirty" all 212 Ranger candidates were roused from the barracks bays for a brutally paced run[.] — Rick Atkinson, *The Long Gray Line*, p. 153, 1989

oday *noun*

money *US, 1928*

A pig Latin construction of **DOUGH**.

- — Don Wilmeth, *The Language of American Popular Entertainment*, p. 185, 1981

oddball *adjective*

eccentric, peculiar *US, 1957*

- "That's just the kind of odd-ball reaction I'd expect." — John D. MacDonald, *The Deceivers*, p. 121, 1958

oddball trick *noun*

a prostitute's customer who pays for fetishistic sex *US, 1973*

- "Oddball tricks are where the money is," Sugarman assures her. — Gail Sheehy, *Hustling*, p. 61, 1973

odor *noun*

a scandal, a fuss *US, 1960*

- Two hoody boys in our class put on a race one night with their cars full of kids and smashed up and the school board made a large odor. — Glendon Swarthout, *Where the Boys Are*, p. 4, 1960

OD's *noun*

a drab olive military uniform *US, 1955*

- What he threw in is the set of o.d.s I had on when I was taken from the Fifth Street station house by the MPs. — Rocky Garciano (with Rowland Barber), *Somebody Up There Likes Me*, p. 203, 1955
- "OD and khaki go with everything," said Jaworski, 23, who's majoring in geology. "Also, military clothes are rugged, hold up well and are comfortable to wear, with their drawstrings and tab closures." — *Atlanta Journal-Constitution*, p. 8M, 4th March 2001

ofaginzy *noun*

a white person *US, 1946*

An elaboration of **OFAY**.

- "May, why don't you come clean, don't nobody fault you for makin' out you's ofaginzy," talking as though he was on the girls' side and knew I was really colored. — Mezz Mezzrow, *Really the Blues*, p. 204, 1946

ofay *noun*

a white person *US, 1925*

Origin unknown. Suggestions of a pig Latin etymology (foe) are implausible. More plausible are suggestions of a basis in an African language or the French *au fait* (socially proper).

- "You mean those ofays?" — Ralph Ellison, *Invisible Man*, p. 282, 1947
- It was a pleasure house, where those rich ofay (white) business men and planters would come from all over the South and spend some awful large amounts of loot. — Louis Armstrong, *Satchmo*, p. 147, 1954
- Not like some of them ofays come here with race girls. — Willard Motley, *Let No Man Write My Epitaph*, p. 337, 1958
- I am here to tell you that ofay boy has really got sex appeal in spades! — Gore Vidal, *Myra Breckinridge*, p. 90, 1968

ofer; o-for *adjective*

used to describe a male pornography performer who either cannot achieve an erection or cannot ejaculate when needed *US, 1995*

Borrowing from sports lingo, identifying the performer as "oh" (zero) for however many tries.

- — *Adult Video News*, p. 38, September 1995

off *noun*

1 a warning given to an illegal betting operation by corrupt police of a pending raid *US, 1952*

- — *Life*, p. 39, 19th May 1952

2 in dominoes, a piece that does not contribute to the value of your hand *US, 1959*

- — Dominic Armanino, *Dominoes*, p. 17, 1959

off *verb*

1 to kill *US, 1967*

- I hoped he wouldn't bring his snitchfriend with him, because that meant I'd have to off both of them. — Clarence Cooper Jr., *The Farm*, p. 236, 1967
- Off the Pig means to kill the slave master. It doesn't mean commit murder. — Bobby Seale, *Seize the Time*, p. 404, 1970
- I mean, offin' somebody might be necessary too. — Odie Hawkins, *Ghetto Sketches*, p. 15, 1972
- There's come all over the sheets—he got off before he got offed. — *Basic Instinct*, 1992

2 to sell, especially contraband *US, 1960*

- "Maybe he's got something we can off. A watch, maybe?" — Malcolm Braly, *It's Cold Out There*, p. 69, 1966
- "I'll just off 'em to the guy down on Canal Street." — Joseph Pistone, *Donnie Brasco*, p. 76, 1987
- "You should be able to off the chips at face value, right?" Sands said. — Gerald Petievich, *Shakedown*, p. 148, 1988
- The Indians [Colombians] have so much coke they can't off [sell] it without finding new markets. — Terry Williams, *The Cocaine Kids*, p. 22, 1989

off *adjective*

not using drugs *US, 1952*

- "You mean you're off it?" "Yeah, off it. I'm kicking it." — Hal Ellson, *The Golden Spike*, p. 103, 1952
- "Anyway, I didn't want to come around because I knew you was off. You off completely?" — William Burroughs, *Junkie*, p. 118, 1953

off-brand *noun*

a member of a youth gang other than the gang the speaker belongs to *US, 1991*

- "Ask him what he wants to do when he get older." Diamond's features slide into a grin. "Kill off-brands." — Leon Bing, *Do or Die*, p. 64, 1991

off-brand cigarette *noun*

a marijuana cigarette *US, 1980*

- — Edith A. Folb, *runnin' down some lines*, p. 248, 1980

off-brand stud *noun*

a male homosexual *US, 1962*

- — Anthony Romeo, *The Language of Gangs*, p. 20, 4th December 1962

off-by-one error *noun*

in computing, any simple and basic error, such as starting at 1 instead of 0 *US, 1991*

- — Eric S. Raymond, *The New Hacker's Dictionary*, p. 267, 1991

office *noun*

a warning; a private signal *UK, 1818*

- — *The Annals of the American Academy of Political and Social Sciences*, p. 128, May 1950
- [O]ne player gives the other a prearranged signal (gives him "the office," as the hustler's argot has it). — Ned Polsky, *Hustlers, Beats, and Others*, p. 58, 1967
- "We'll rap tomorrow after breakfast." "Same office?" "Now what do you think?" — Malcolm Braly, *On the Yard*, p. 38, 1967
- Within five minutes he gave me the "office" that some action was coming down the street. — Iceberg Slim (Robert Beck), *Pimp*, p. 37, 1969

office hours *noun*

1 minor discipline issued by a US Marine Corps company commander *US, 1898*

- You tell them if anybody pulls this shit again I'm gonna rock them in office hours, and they'll never get promoted in this Company. — Charles Anderson, *The Grunts*, p. 94, 1976

2 in poker, pairs of 9s and 5s, or a straight from 9 to 5 *US, 1963*
- — Irwin Steig, *Common Sense in Poker*, p. 185, 1963

officer material *noun*
a mentally deficient enlisted soldier *US, 1945*
- — *American Speech*, p. 238, October 1946: "World War II Slang of Maladjustment"

off-trail *adjective*
unconventional, eccentric *US, 1954*
- Of all the weird, off-trail characters I have known, he was the weirdest, the most off-trail. — Jim Thompson, *Roughneck*, p. 33, 1954

OG *noun*
1 your mother *US, 1878*
An abbreviation of **OLD GIRL**.
- — David Claerbaut, *Black Jargon in White America*, p. 73, 1972

2 a founding member of a youth gang *US, 1991*
An abbreviation of **ORIGINAL GANGSTER**.
- "I ain't probably gonna reach O.G. stage for a while yet." — Leon Bing, *Do or Die*, p. 21, 1991
- We had to rush the O.G.'s for that. — *Menace II Society*, 1993
- So they recognized me as an OG homie, they put on that status as soon as I came over there. — Yusuf Jah, *Uprising*, p. 27, 1995

O.G. call *noun*
a murder ordered by an older, established youth gang member *US, 2007*
- Prosecutors said Robert Green was killed on an "O.G. call," street slang for an assassination ordered by a senior gang member. — *Arkansas Democrat-Gazette*, 7th March 2007

oh, behave
used as a catch-all catchphrase, usually in the context of a sexual innuendo *US, 1997*
Wildly popular for several years after the release of the first *Austin Powers* film in 1997.
- SUPERMODEL 1: We could have another photo session back at my flat. AUSTIN: Oh, behave! — *Austin Powers*, 1997

oh, fiddle-faddle!
used as a non-profane expression of frustration *US, 1963*
Used with regularity by the Aunt Bee character on *The Andy Griffith Show* (CBS, 1960–68). Repeated with referential humor.

Ohio bag *noun*
one hundred grams of marijuana *US, 1982*
Under Ohio's decriminalization laws, this is the maximum amount for a fine for simple possession.
- — Ernest L. Abel, *A Marijuana Dictionary*, p. 75, 1982

ohmigod!; omigod!
used for expressing surprise or horror *US, 1982*
- — Mary Corey and Victoria Westermark, *Fer Shurr! How to be a Valley Girl*, 1982
- "Omigod," she said, eyes wide, the shock obvious on her face. — Janet Evanovich, *Seven Up*, p. 239, 2001

oh my stars!
used for expressing frustration *US, 1966*
Popularized by the sexy blonde witch Samantha on *Bewitched* (ABC, 1964–72). Repeated with referential humor.

oh-shit *noun*
a criticism *US, 1997*
- You tried to frame your own prosecutor. The list of "Oh shits" is awesome. — Stephen Cannell, *Big Con*, p. 398, 1997

oh the pain, the shame!
used as a humorous comment on humiliation *US, 1997*
Coined on the television program *Lost in Space* (1965–68), and then revived and popularized by Keith Olberman on ESPN.
- — Keith Olberman and Dan Patrick, *The Big Show*, p. 22, 1997

-oid *suffix*
used as a suffix that embellishes without changing the base word's meaning *US, 1978*
- In the middle of the room was a cheesoid Formica replica-pulpit. — Frank Zappa, *The Real Frank Zappa Book*, p. 81, 1989

- Now fearing I would become the brunt of it, I vowed never to introduce another interesting factoid into the rumor mill again. — Rita Ciresi, *Pink Slip*, p. 107, 1999

oil *noun*
1 alcohol *US, 1912*
- Janet didn't drink, so I didn't really need any oil but I picked up a pint of gin anyway[.] — Donald Goines, *Never Die Alone*, p. 113, 1974

2 in pool, extreme spin imparted to the cue ball *US, 1912*
- — Mike Shamos, *The Illustrated Encyclopedia of Billiards*, p. 160, 1993

oil *verb*
▶ **oil it**
to study late into the night *US, 1975*
- — *American Speech*, p. 63, Spring–Summer 1975: "Razorback slang"

oil and water king *noun*
aboard ship, the engineer controlling fresh water distillation *US, 1986*
- — Hans Halberstadt, *USCG*, p. 129, 1986: "Glossary"

oil burner *noun*
1 a serious drug addiction *US, 1938*
- We both got oil burners, especially Nina. — Clarence Cooper Jr., *The Scene*, p. 43, 1960
- "You look like you kicked an ass wiper." "An oil burner." — Malcolm Braly, *On the Yard*, p. 31, 1967
- You better cut down on your blows, Terry, or you're going to end up with a oil burner. — Donald Goines, *Dopefiend*, p. 118, 1971
- He knew I had an oil burner but he also knew I never once tried to get him to use during all the time we were running buddies. — A.S. Jackson, *Gentleman Pimp*, p. 102, 1973

2 in horseracing, a fast horse *US, 1951*
- — David W. Maurer, *Argot of the Racetrack*, p. 46, 1951

oil-burning *adjective*
(used of a drug addiction) severe *US, 1972*
- I had this habit, a real bad oil-burning habit — Bruce Jackson, *In the Life*, p. 81, 1972
- Things were so smooth that we both got an oil-burning habit (a habit to end all habits) out of the deal. — Herbert Huncke, *Guilty of Everything*, p. 103, 1990

oil-can *verb*
(of a boat) to make a hollow booming sound striking the water *US, 1990*
- Won't go fast, but very stable. Doesn't oil-can when you go to weather. — Joseph Wambaugh, *The Golden Orange*, p. 74, 1990

oiled; oiled up *adjective*
drunk *US, 1737*
- "Sit down, Holden," Mr. Antolini said. You could tell he was a little oiled up. — J.D. Salinger, *Catcher in the Rye*, p. 182, 1951
- You know. Drunk stewed, clobbered, gone, liquored up, oiled, stoned, in the bag. — Max Shulman, *Guided Tour of Campus Humor*, p. 106, 1955
- Last Saturday night, he showed up well-oiled at Carl's place. — Jeffrey Golden, *Watermelon Summer*, p. 87, 1971
- Frank was not too oiled to miss that. — George V. Higgins, *Penance for Jerry Kennedy*, p. 47, 1985

oil in the can *noun*
in horseracing, a horse believed by its backers to be a sure winner *US, 1951*
- — David W. Maurer, *Argot of the Racetrack*, p. 46, 1951

oil merchant *noun*
a smooth-talking swindler *US, 1935*
- — Hyman E. Goldin et al., *Dictionary of American Underworld Lingo*, p. 148, 1950

oil well *noun*
in a deck of playing cards, an ace *US, 1988*
From the visual comparison of an "A" with an oil well.
- — George Percy, *The Language of Poker*, p. 60, 1988

oily *adjective*
mean-spirited, tough *US, 1958*
- — *American Speech*, p. 271, December 1958: "Ranching terms from Eastern Washington"

oink *noun*
a police officer *US, 1970*

A far less common usage than the related **PIG** (police).
- — Clarence Major, *Dictionary of Afro-American Slang*, p. 87, 1970

oink *verb*
to lure by greed *US, 1954*
- You can't oink Biff into just anything. He don't need the loot, understand. — Bernard Wolfe, *The Late Risers*, p. 193, 1954

oinkers *noun*
the police *US, 1971*
An obvious extension of **PIG**.
- OINKERS: the police — Robert Buckhout, *Toward Social Change*, p. 466, 1971

OJ *noun*
a marijuana cigarette dipped in liquid opium or heroin *US, 1970*
In other words, an "*opium joint.*" Popular with US troops in Vietnam.
- — William D. Alsever, *Glossary for the Establishment and Other Uptight People*, p. 23, December 1970
- The O-Js were thin, perfectly rolled marijuana cigarettes soaked in an opium solution. Fifty O-Js to a deck. — John Del Vecchio, *The 13th Valley*, p. 31, 1982
- The model for usage of the OJ (opium joint—heroin loaded cigarette) was that of the social group use of marijuana at home. [Referring to the war in Vietnam] — David H. Marlowe, *Psychological and Psychosocial Consequences of Combat and Deployment*, p. 93, 2001
- Opium and marijuana rolled into a cigarette is sometimes called an OJ, which is short for "Opium Joint." — Debra Moraes, *The Little Book of Opium*, p. 19, 2003

OK; okay *noun*
1 consent, approval *US, 1841*
- Do you really need Sonny Barger's O.K. to do what you feel like doing? — Hunter S. Thompson, *Fear and Loathing in America*, p. 19, 15th January 1968: Letter to Kelly Varner
- The Chancellor gave his okay to the idea[.] — Randy Neil, *The Official Cheerleader's Handbook*, p. 19, 1979
- McFarlane told Congress last week that Reagan gave his okay for the deal to proceed. — *Chicago Tribune*, p. C1, 14th December 1986
- If the rising payroll-tax burden was imposed on young working people, they would eventually revolt and Social Security would self-destruct of its own weight. The Gipper liked that, and gave his OK. — Holly Sklar, *Raise the Floor*, p. 172, 2001

2 a bribe paid by an illegal gambling establishment to the authorities to stay in business *US, 1979*
- — John Scarne, *Scarne's Guide to Modern Poker*, p. 285, 1979

OK; okay *verb*
to approve *US, 1952*
- Scotty signed it and the Judge okayed it. — Bernard Malamud, *The Natural*, p. 42, 1952
- Supervising this entire phase of the operation was a medical officer with a flair for accounting who okayed pulses and checked the figures of the tally clerk. — Joseph Heller, *Catch 22*, pp. 80–81, 1961
- McFarlane testifies that Reagan okayed first arm shipment. — *ABC World News Tonight*, 5th December 1986
- Even some of the more incurious might wonder if North okayed his wife's Philadelphia rendezvous with a total stranger who wished to offer her $70,000 because she "loved" her husband. — *Washington Post*, p. A2, 7th July 1987

OK; okay *adjective*
1 comfortable, at ease *US, 1978*
Especially common as "OK about" or "OK with."
- To be successful in it as a career ... a girl is going to have to know values as well as skills—how to feel OK about herself and what she's doing. — *Washington Post*, p. C3, 2nd April 1978
- Felt OK about it, actually, strangely enough. I don't recall too much guilt. — *The Oprah Winfrey Show*, 27th October 2004

2 safe, unhurt *US, 1839*
- Not a sound came over the intercom until a few long seconds later, and then the skipper asked if we were all OK. — Ron Smith, *Rear Gunner Pathfinders*, p. 23, 1987
- Are you okay? You don't look good. — Aaron McGruder, *Fresh for '01*, p. 96, 2001
- Are you okay Sir? How's the bird Sir? Where'd you get the feckin' bullet holes Sir? — Samuel Brantley, *Zero Dark Thirty*, p. 69, 2002

3 decent, mediocre, satisfactory *US, 1839*
In 1963, the late Allen Walker Read published his extensive and definitive research on the term, tracing its coinage to 1839 as an abbreviation of "oil korrect," itself a then-popular slang term.
- MOM: How are you? ANDY: Okay. MOM: Just okay? You sound a little down. — Helen E. Johnson, *Don't Tell Me What to Do, Just Send Money*, p. 61, 2000
- The print looked okay, but just okay. — Bruce Campbell, *If Chins Could Kill*, p. 74, 2002
- "That's okay," I told her. "I'll be fine." — Sue Monk Kidd, *The Secret Life of Bees*, p. 28, 2002
- The upshot: he hopped on the next plane to L.A. to see me and make sure everything was okay. — Janice Dickson, *Everything About Me is Fake*, p. 128, 2004

OK; okay
used for expressing assent, approval, understanding, or agreement *US, 1839*
- "Forty-five guys won this game. Okay, that's a cliche, right?" — *Washington Post*, p. F1, 20th December 1979
- I love my clients, okay? — Malcolm Gladwell, *The Tipping Point*, p. 71, 2002
- Okay, Sophie, if you must know, P.S. is a code. — Dan Brown, *The Da Vinci Code*, p. 112, 2003
- Okay, some guys might like it, but they're just lazy. — Greg Behrendt, *He's Just Not That Into You*, p. 16, 2004

OK Corral *noun*
a group of men masturbating while watching a female *US, 2002*
An extrapolation of the **GUN DOWN** image, alluding to the site of a famous American gun battle in 1881.
- — Gary K. Farlow, *Prison-ese*, p. 46, 2002

okey-doke *noun*
a swindle or deception *US, 1969*
- Ain't no nigger pimp going to put my ass in a sling. I'm too slick for that "okee doke." — Iceberg Slim (Robert Beck), *Pimp*, p. 116, 1969
- "Not one lousy bitch on 125th will go for the okey-doke!" — Robert Deane Pharr, *S.R.O.*, p. 40, 1971
- "I ain't about to go for none of their jive-ass okey-doke." — James Baldwin, *If Beale Street Could Talk*, p. 83, 1974
- So its up to all of us down people to see that cats like Brother Martin, Brother Malcolm, Brother Evers, and others did not go for the whitey oke-e-doke in vain. — Babs Gonzales, *Movin' On Down De Line*, p. 98, 1975

okey-dokey *adjective*
acceptable *US, 1942*
- He shrugs, "That's okee dokee with me." — Iceberg Slim (Robert Beck), *Doom Fox*, p. 122, 1978

okey-dokey
used for communicating agreement *US, 1932*
An old-fashioned, affected, still popular perversion of **OK**.
- KRINKILE: Now what's happened, what's going on, and what are you talking about. DIMES: Okee-dokee. It's like this. — *True Romance*, 1993
- Okee dokey. You should come back in seven days and we should have your results. — *Kids*, 1995
- Okey-dokey, thanks a bunch. — *Fargo*, 1996
- Okey-dokey, so tomorrow night? — *Something About Mary*, 1998

Oki; Okie *noun*
Okinawa *US, 1945*
Coined in World War 2, still used in Vietnam.
- I just think of that first steam bath I'm going to get on Oki. — Charles Anderson, *The Grunts*, p. 11, 1976

Okie *noun*
a poor, white resident or native of rural Oklahoma; a poor, white resident or native of the southcentral US *US, 1938*
Used with derision or pride but not neutrally.
- So after a few beers in the saloon, where sullen Okies reeled to the music of a cowboy band, Terry and I and Johnny went into a motel room and got ready to hit the sack. — Jack Kerouac, *On the Road*, p. 93, 1957
- You don't know whether she's a hillbilly or an Okie or what. — Truman Capote, *Breakfast at Tiffany's*, p. 68, 1958

- The one thing about the Row was that it was filled with okies, weary old Wobblies, drunkies and dopies far gone, whores on their last legs—they never judged you. — Clancy Sigal, *Going Away*, p. 238, 1961
- Riverbank is divided into three parts, and in my corner of the world there were only three kinds of people: Mexicans, Okies and Americans. — Oscar Zeta Acosta, *The Autobiography of a Brown Buffalo*, p. 78, 1972

Okie chrome *noun*
aluminum paint *US, 1961*
- — *American Speech*, p. 272, December 1961: "Northwest truck drivers' language"

Okie-land *noun*
any place with a large population of white southerners *US, 1971*
- Give or take a speck here and there in Canada or Monta or Okie-land California, the people who make it have come overwhelmingly from the South. — John Shelton Reed, *Whistling Dixie*, p. 108, 1990

Oklahoma toothbrush *noun*
the penis *US, 1994*
In Oklahoma, known as a "Texas toothbrush."
- — Michael Dalton Johnson, *Talking Trash with Redd Foxx*, p. 93, 1994

okole *noun*
the end of something; the buttocks *US, 1938*
- "Or else swerve and heave my okole into the breakdown lane." — Paul Theroux, *Hotel Honolulu*, p. 354, 2001

-ola *suffix*
a meaningless embellishment of a suffix *US, 1919*
- He borrowed thirty-eight bucks from me once, never paid it back. A lousola. — Marvin Wald and Albert Maltz, *The Naked City*, p. 107, 1947
- Payola — *American Speech*, pp. 104–116, May 1961
- Mickey Cohen is Skidsville, U.S.A., and he needs moolah, gelt, the old cashola. — James Ellroy, *White Jazz*, p. 7, 1992
- Schoolteachers out there teach school better than Joe Jack Billy, but they still make crapola. — Dan Jenkins, *The Money-Whipped Steer-Job Three-Jack Give-Up Artist*, p. 79, 2001

old; ol'; ole *adjective*
tiresome *US, 1864*
- I'd dismount with my AK and check them on foot, but that got old awful quick. — Larry Heinemann, *Close Quarters*, p. 248, 1977

old bag *noun*
a criminal's past associations and activities *US, 1970*
- Keeping out of the old bag is seen to be a major obstacle in making it. The old bag in this instance is a former life routine involving a great many felonious acts[.] — John Irwin, *The Felon*, p. 89, 1970

old bill *noun*
a signal, by hand or word, asking "Are there any other cheaters in this game?" *US, 1979*
- — John Scarne, *Scarne's Guide to Modern Poker*, p. 285, 1979

old country *noun*
to the US armed forces at the end of World War 2, the United States *US, 1949*
- — *American Speech*, p. 30, February 1949: "A.V.G. lingo"

old face *noun*
a chorus dancer whose long tenure makes her unmarketable *US, 1948*
- [T]here are thousands of kids who pound out the soles of their aching feet for five or six years, then discover that at 21 or 22 they've been around the Stem so long the managers call them "old faces" and they no longer can get work. — Jack Lait and Lee Mortimer, *New York Confidential*, p. 140, 1948

old fart *noun*
an old or older person, especially one who is unpleasant or disliked *UK, 1937*
Often elaborated as "boring old fart."
- [T]he old fart will be dead by the time it's a question of recommending you for general's rank. — Norman Mailer, *The Naked and the Dead*, p. 417, 1948
- [B]y old farts I mean all the pantheon of geniuses treated with such reverence: Chuck Berry, who might be the greatest songwriter of all time, is an old fart. Little Richard is an old fart[.] — Lester Bangs, *Psychotic Reactions and Carburetor Dung*, p. 72, 1971

old-fashioned *noun*
conventional vaginal intercourse *US, 1971*
- A "flat-backer" who offers only coitus ("old-fashioned" or "straight") is likely to lose customers. — Charles Winick, *The Lively Commerce*, p. 207, 1971

old folks *noun*
in circus and carnival usage, monkeys *US, 1981*
- — Don Wilmeth, *The Language of American Popular Entertainment*, p. 186, 1981

old foul dude *noun*
a seasoned veteran *US, 1992*
- Even though the average age of the so-called "old foul dudes" was only twenty, they looked more like they were in their thirties. — Larry Chambers, *Recondo*, p. 47, 1992

old head *noun*
1 a mentor, a respected figure *US, 1994*
- I had admired Scobie-D, Kenny Banks, and other old-heads not very many years before. — Nathan McCall, *Makes Me Wanna Holler*, p. 97, 1994
- "That's his old head," said one of the boys, using street slang for mentor. He was Donnie's boss. — *Philadelphia Daily News*, p. Local 3, 27th December 2006

2 an older prisoner *US, 2002*
- [S]ome of us junior types had to argue with many an oldhead[.] — *The Source*, p. 36, March 2002

3 a returning student to a school *US, 1963*
- — *American Speech*, p. 272, December 1963: "American Indian student slang"

old horsey *noun*
strong, illegally manufactured whiskey *US, 1999*
- It is called corn liquor, white lightning, sugar whiskey, skull cracker, popskull, bush whiskey, stump, stumphole, 'splo, ruckus juice, radiator whiskey, rotgut, sugarhead, block and tackle, wildcat, panther's breath, tiger's sweat, sweet spirits of cats a-fighting, alley bourbon, city gin, cool water, happy Sally, deep shaft, jump steady, old horsey, stingo, blue John, red eye, pine top, buckeye bark whiskey and see seven stars. — *Star Tribune (Minneapolis)*, p. 19F, 31st January 1999

oldie *noun*
a song from the past that is still popular *US, 1939*
A shortened form of GOLDEN OLDIE or "oldie but goody."
- We owe our thanks for these to the wonderful services of the U.S.O. Here's another oldie. — *Apocalypse Now*, 1979

old Joe *noun*
any sexually transmitted infection *US, 1967*
- — Dale Gordon, *The Dominion Sex Dictionary*, p. 111, 1967
- — Anon., *King Smut's Wet Dreams Interpreted*, 1978

old lady *noun*
1 a mother *US, 1877*
- Inspiration's old lady gave birth to a new brainchild one afternoon at a Rhythm Kings rehearsal[.] — Mezz Mezzrow, *Really the Blues*, p. 54, 1946
- About Benny Bliss's old lady having been in Doctors' Hospital for a checkup[.] — Bernard Wolfe, *The Late Risers*, p. 170, 1954
- "No, no, man," Manny says with impatience. "My old lady—my mother..." — John Rechy, *The Fourth Angel*, p. 40, 1972
- "Since my old man left," he said, "and my old lady tried to make up for it by smothering me with affection, I've always valued my friendships with men more than my relationships with women." — Helen Garner, *Monkey Grip*, p. 138, 1977

2 a wife, common-law or legal; a girlfriend *US, 1836*
- "Hey, look, baby," I said, "I know you're Capone's old lady—uh, uh, I ain't coming on this tab." — Mezz Mezzrow, *Really the Blues*, p. 24, 1946
- At twelve that night my old lady bailed me out and met me at the door with some goof balls. — William Burroughs, *Junkie*, p. 39, 1953
- Many who would ordinarily take their "old ladies" had left the girls behind in case of a serious clash with the law. — Hunter S. Thompson, *Hell's Angels*, p. 119, 1966
- [H]e began coming around inviting us out or up to his place to pick up on music and maybe smoke a little pot and keep him and his old lady company[.] — Herbert Huncke, *The Evening Sun Turned Crimson*, p. 90, 1980

3 the more passive member of a same-sex couple *US, 1937*
- After that Blocker referred to him as my old lady. — Chester Himes, *Cast the First Stone*, p. 103, 1952
- "Pretty soon, if the kid is a little weak he gives in. He becomes some con's old lady." — Charles Perry, *Portrait of a Young Man Drowning*, p. 203, 1962

- I promise not to let no one know about you being my old lady[.]
  — Piri Thomas, *Down These Mean Streets*, p. 266, 1967
- He had looked into the eyes of convicts, wondering if they saw something, and had got propositioned, proposed to and finally picked by a big colored boy, Monroe Ritchie, to be his old lady.
  — Elmore Leonard, *Glitz*, p. 132, 1985

old man *noun*
1 a father *US, 1811*
- "First I want revenge because their fathers sent my old man to die in the pen." The Crawler's eyes were blazing with hate as he spoke.
  — Chester Gould, *Dick Tracy Meets the Night Crawler*, p. 40, 1945
- My old man says them Puerto Ricans is ruinin' free ennaprise.
  — Stephen Sondheim, *West Side Story*, 1957
- The thing I wanted to avoid was suddenly and without warning meeting my old man on the subway. — Clancy Sigal, *Going Away*, p. 420, 1961
- Let him see what his old man does for a living. — Carl Hiaasen, *Tourist Season*, p. 20, 1986

2 a boyfriend or husband *UK, 1768*
- An old man is another thing. An old man is like a marriage without the legal binding[.] — Leonard Wolfe (Editor), *Voices from the Love Generation*, p. 243, 1968
- "Who's that in back there?" asked the Greek when Estelle got back to the bus. "My old man." — Gurney Norman, *Divine Right's Trip (Last Whole Earth Catalog)*, p. 67, 1971
- We don't need no piece of paper / From the city hall / Keeping us tied and true / My old man / Keeping away my blues. — Joni Mitchell, *My Old Man*, 1971
- The ho is similar in her role to the hippy chick who holds down a straight job and puts on her neat little dress and makeup in the morning to go out and face the working world, so she can bring home money to her long-haired "old man[.]" — Christina and Richard Milner, *Black Players*, p. 212, 1972

3 a commanding officer, military or police *US, 1830*
- The old man gave the order to move. — David Parks, *GI Diary*, p. 51, 1968
- [A]t which point, of course, we were called up for a little quiz-session by the Old Man. — Joey V., *Portrait of Joey*, p. 155, 1969
- There was a lifer in San Diego who was dumped for indebtedness. The old man got sick of the dunning letters so he had the man discharged and thereby made the matter a non-navy problem.
  — Darryl Ponicsan, *The Last Detail*, p. 13, 1970
- "Anyway, the captain says no more of it," Bridget continued, "and another thing the old man says is that you guys are not at any time to push cars with your police vehicle." — Joseph Wambaugh, *The New Centurions*, p. 55, 1970

4 a pimp in relation to a prostitute *US, 1891*
- Clippinger added that he knew all the pimps who had "teams" of girls in southern California, but disliked to hire girls who had "old men" for masters. "Old men" was explained to mean pimps with teams of girls. — Ed Reid and Ovid Demaris, *The Green Felt Jungle*, p. 101, 1963
- [E]ventually he became her real old man instead of her play old man and moved in with her and let her support him and go down on lots of fat cats and high rollers for lots of money[.] — Joseph Wambaugh, *The Choirboys*, p. 190, 1975

5 a shark *US, 1965*
- — John M. Kelly, *Surf and Sea*, p. 289, 1965

old man comforts *noun*
high-top shoes with ankle support and extra laces *US, 1973*
- They called them "old man comforts" and they were soft and comfortable, but ugly as hell, I guess, to most people. — Joseph Wambaugh, *The Blue Knight*, p. 44, 1973

old man's aid *noun*
in pool, a device used to support the cue stick for a hard-to-reach shot *US, 1977*
As the terminology suggests, the device is scorned by skilled players.
- — Steve Rushin, *Pool Cool*, p. 22, 1990
- — Mike Shamos, *The Illustrated Encyclopedia of Billiards*, p. 160, 1993

old navy *noun*
heroin *US, 2002*
- — *Detroit News*, p. 5D, 20th September 2002

Old Nick *noun*
mischief *US, 1817*

Nearly obsolete.
- Well, when he was young and full of the Old Nick, maybe, hadn't settled down, on the right amount of caps. — Elmore Leonard, *Stick*, p. 134, 1983

Old Reliables *nickname*
the Ninth Infantry Division, US Army *US, 1973*
- The Old Reliables had established Dong Tam in January 1967, as their primary base camp in the Mekong Delta. — Franklin Rast, *Don's Nam*, p. 69, 1999
- Our combat unit, the 9th Infantry Division, the Old Reliables, established its reputation and proud traditions in World War II[.]
  — Joseph W. Callaway, *Mekong First Light*, p. 37, 2004

old school *noun*
a past generation with an old-fashioned but reliable way of doing things *UK, 1749*
- He was an old school man by training, coming up through policeman's beat to guard, captain, warden's assistant. — Donald Wilson, *My Six Convicts*, p. 7, 1951
- [H]e's out of the old school, I think, because he looks like he's out of the old school, shorty, portly, baldy, ruddy-faced, twinkly-eyed.
  — Jim Bouton, *Ball Four*, p. 13, 1970
- Even Old School clubgoers faced up to their inform fear of being seen entering the once terminally tacky Limelight. — James St. James, *Party Monster*, p. 76, 1990
- Fuck that, I'm from the old school. — *Menace II Society*, 1993

old shaky *noun*
a C-124 long-range transport aircraft *US, 1986*
- He'd spent another profitless year driving C-124s around the globe, an ancient mariner in Old Shaky, as the aging piston-engines planes were called. — Walter J. Boyne and Steven Thompson, *The Wild Blue*, p. 28, 1986

old skool; old school *noun*
the original style of hip-hop music viewed retrospectively *US, 1989*
- — Judi Sanders, *Faced and Faded, Hanging to Hurl*, p. 29, 1993
- — Connie Eble (Editor), *UNC-CH Campus Slang*, p. 6, Spring 1994
- [T]hey're so ol' skool and simple nobody can really count them as moves these days. — Linden Dalecki, *Kid B*, p. 1, 2006

Oldsmobile *noun*
in hold 'em poker, a nine and an eight as the first two cards dealt to a player *US, 1981*
An allusion to the Oldsmobile 98, a popular model.
- — Thomas L. Clark, *The Dictionary of Gambling and Gaming*, p. 139, 1987

Old Smokey *noun*
the electric chair *US, 1929*
- — Lou Shelly, *Hepcats Jive Talk Dictionary*, p. 31, 1945

Old Sod *noun*
Ireland *UK, 1891*
- He sounded like the Old Sod. I thought to myself that all I seem to meet are Dagos and Irish[.] — Red Rudensky, *The Gonif*, p. c, 1970

Old Sparky *noun*
an electric chair, especially Florida's electric chair *US, 1971*
- Union Correctional, or UCI, is what they used to call Raiford, when they had Old Sparky there. See, wherever the 'lectric chair is, that's your state prison. — Elmore Leonard, *Maximum Bob*, p. 107, 1991

oldtimer's disease *noun*
Alzheimer's disease *US, 1988*
- A memo from a Mackay airline office to the airline's airport staff said special assistance would have to be offered to one traveler, who was suffering from "old timer's disease" and needed help changing planes. — *Courier-Mail*, p. 2, 26th January 1988
- — *Maledicta*, p. 35, 1988–1989: "More Milwaukee medical maledicta"

Old Toasty *noun*
the electric chair *US, 2001*
- "They used to ride Old Toasty in Huntsville." — Dan Jenkins, *The Money-Whipped Steer-Job Three-Jack Give-Up Artist*, p. 114, 2001

old Tom *noun*
an aggressive, "mannish" lesbian *US, 1978*
- — Anon., *King Smut's Wet Dreams Interpreted*, 1978

ole gal *noun*

a male roommate *US, 1947*

- — Marcus Hanna Boulware, *Jive and Slang of Students in Negro Colleges*, 1947

Oliver *noun*

in circus and carnival usage, a police officer *US, 1981*

- — Don Wilmeth, *The Language of American Popular Entertainment*, p. 186, 1981

Ollie, Molly, and Dolly *noun*

in poker, three queens *US, 1948*

olly; ollie *noun*

in skateboarding, a jumping maneuver, the basis of most skating tricks *US, 1989*

- — Dan Maley, *Macon Telegraph and News*, p. 9A, 18th June 1989
- — Alon Shulman, *The Style Bible*, p. 181, 1999: "Skatespeak for going airborne."
- On one side skaters hang out and do ollies off the steps[.] — Michelle Tea, *Valencia*, p. 155, 2000

omen *noun*

low grade phencyclidine, the recreational drug known as PCP or angel dust *US, 1993*

- — Peter Johnson, *Dictionary of Street Alcohol and Drug Terms*, p. 136, 1993

on *adjective*

1 protected from police action by bribes *US, 1973*

- "What's going on?" the controller said. "We're on, man." — Peter Maas, *Serpico*, p. 200, 1973

2 drug-intoxicated *US, 1946*

- "I'm on," Diane announced after four gentle hits[.] — George Mandel, *Flee the Angry Strangers*, p. 254, 1952

on *preposition*

(used of a drug) under the influence of *US, 1925*

- You don't sound too goddamn sane yourself. What are you on, anyway? — Gurney Norman, *Divine Right's Trip (Last Whole Earth Catalog)*, p. 191, 1971

oncer *noun*

a person who has sex only once with any given partner *US, 1959*

- — J.D. Mercer, *They Walk in Shadow*, p. 565, 1959: "Slang vocabulary"
- — Guy Strait, *The Lavender Lexicon*, 1964

one *noun*

▶ **in one**

in bar dice games, to make a hand in one roll of the dice *US, 1971*

- — Jester Smith, *Games They Play in San Francisco*, p. 104, 1971

one and one *noun*

a dose of heroin accompanied by a dose of cocaine *US, 1997*

- That's enough for a one-and-one each. — David Simon and Edward Burns, *The Corner*, p. 262, 1997

one-armed bandit *noun*

a slot machine *US, 1938*

- The night we were there, we saw three fancy one-armed bandits whirring and swallowing. — Jack Lait and Lee Mortimer, *Washington Confidential*, p. 65, 1951
- "What's so special about slots?" "The one-armed bandit is a dilly." — Stephen Longstreet, *The Flesh Peddlers*, p. 295, 1962

one-armed paper hanger *noun*

used as a representation of a very busy person *US, 1908*

- [H]is duties are numerous enough to keep him busier than a one-armed paper hanger. — Joe DiMaggio, *Baseball for Everyone*, p. 98, 2003

one-digit midget *noun*

during the Vietnam war, a soldier with less than 10 days to serve before his date of expected return from overseas *US, 1984*

- Something new was tried in Vietnam—fighting the war in one-year hitches, creating "short-timer's mentality." Various phrases were invented for the remaining length of time in the country. A "one-digit midget" was so "short" that he had anything under ten days left. — Myra MacPherson, *Long Time Passing*, p. 63, 1984
- They said you were a one-digit midget and talked about being so short you had to parachute into your boots every morning. — Ronald Schultz, *Jailhouse Religion*, p. 135, 2004

one-eighty *noun*

a complete reversal of course *US, 1956*

An allusion to a 180-degree turn.

- I had to do a one-eighty from the target area. — Amy Waters Yarsinke, *No One Left Behind*, p. 27, 1999

one-eye *noun*

1 the penis *US, 1961*

- I'm afraid he'll pull the stiff one-eye on me. I need you to chaperone. — *As Good As It Gets*, 1997
- When a woman looks you straight in the one-eye and says, "There's no way you're putting that near my tradesman's," she is really saying, "You're huge!" — *GQ*, p. 117, July 2001

2 in a deck of playing cards, a face card drawn in profile, the jack of hearts, the jack of spades, or the king of diamonds *US, 1967*

- — Albert H. Morehead, *The Complete Guide to Winning Poker*, pp. 268–269, 1967

3 a car with only one headlight working *US, 1962*

- — Don Dempsey, *American Speech*, p. 271, December 1962: "The language of traffic policemen"
- — Bill Valentine, *Gang Intelligence Manual*, p. 130, 1995: "Asian street gang terminology"

one-eyed jack *noun*

a car with only one headlight working *US, 1988*

one-finger salute *noun*

the extension of the middle finger in a crude gesture of defiance *US, 1966*

- Giving the one-finger salute is effective but rather limiting. — Cameron Tuttle, *The Bad Girl's Guide to the Open Road*, p. 66, 1999

one for the boy *noun*

in horseracing, a bet placed on a horse by the owner and given to the jockey before the race *US, 1951*

- — David W. Maurer, *Argot of the Racetrack*, p. 46, 1951

one for the road *noun*

a final drink before leaving a bar *US, 1943*

- Collucci stopped to have one for the road and light chitchat with Mack Rivers at the bar. — Iceberg Slim (Robert Beck), *Death Wish*, p. 234, 1977
- Buddy ordered a couple more Jim Beams with a splash, for the road. — Elmore Leonard, *Out of Sight*, p. 186, 1996

one-gutted *adjective*

cowardly *US, 1961*

- A month before they had held up a market without bothering to discover that Ardilla was one-gutted. — Malcom Braly, *Felony Tank*, p. 43, 1961

one-handed game of five-fingered jack *noun*

male masturbation *US, 1991*

- "And if an occasional trip to Missy Li's don't satisfy your sexual needs, a late-night visit on the end hole for a one-handed game of five-fingered jack will usually get the job done." — Gary Linderer, *The Eyes of the Eagle*, p. 29, 1991

one-hit wonder *noun*

a recording artist or group with a single hit song *US, 1968*

- One-hit wonders have the lucky combination of a good song and the right timing for their moment in the spotlight. — *The Des Moines Register*, p. E8, 15th May 1994
- Fucking one hit wonder, dime-store Frank Miller's. — *Chasing Amy*, 1997
- Some of rock and roll's most notorious one-hit wonders from the '50s and '60s will soon be attempting comebacks via a proposed variety series called "Rock & Roll Legends Live." — *Las Vegas Review-Journal*, p. 1E, 27th July 1999

one hundred *noun*

a marijuana cigarette dipped in an opium solution *US, 1991*

- — Gregory Clark, *Words of the Vietnam War*, p. 361, 1991

one-lunger *noun*

a counterfeit watch *US, 1973*

- We call them gaffs in the mob or one-lungers. The mob's jewelers can make any kind of watch you want. — Vincent Teresa, *My Life in the Mafia*, p. 59, 1973

one-nighter *noun*

a sexual relationship lasting a single night *US, 1969*

- He left word, no man gets near you in a serious way or as a one nighter just fooling around or anything like it as long as you live. — Elmore Leonard, *Gold Coast*, p. 45, 1980
- Too many one-nighters, too many faces without meaning. — Odie Hawkins, *Black Casanova*, p. 90, 1984

one-night stand *noun*
a sexual relationship lasting a single night *UK, 1937*
- All those guys—out for a one-night stand! — John Rechy, *Numbers*, p. 101, 1967
- I'm through with one-night stands. — *Bull Durham*, 1988

one-o-one *adjective*
basic *US, 1993*
Alluding to basic college courses such as "English 101."
- Do de name Gary Hart ring a bell? Fuckups 101—you need a refresher course? — Carl Hiaasen, *Strip Tease*, p. 11, 1993

one-percenter; two-percenter *noun*
used as a self-identification by members of outlaw motorcycle clubs *US, 1966*
When the president of the American Motorcycle Association proclaimed that 99% (or later 98%) of motorcyclists are "decent, hardworking, law-abiding citizens," outlaw bikers did the arithmetic and proclaimed themselves the remainder.
- This compact description of rancid, criminal sleaziness is substantially correct except for the hocus-pocus about the one percenters. — Hunter S. Thompson, *Hell's Angels*, p. 9, 1966
- Thirty or so hawgs are parked in front, many of their owners (One Percenters, as they're known) pissing into the night highway. — Bill Cardoso, *The Maltese Sangweech*, p. 243, 1984
- When the Hollister incident cut deep into their cred, they labeled rowdy, outlaw motorcyclists the "one-percenters." — Ralph "Sonny" Barger, *Hell's Angel*, p. 41, 2000

one-spot *noun*
a prison sentence of one year *US, 1949*
- — Vincent J. Monteleone, *Criminal Slang*, p. 168, 1949

one-step snake *noun*
a highly poisonous bamboo viper *US, 1985*
- "They would take a snake, we used to call them one-step, two-step, or three-step snakes, and they were bamboo vipers." — Tom Mangold, *The Tunnels of Cu Chi*, p. 129, 1985

one-striper *noun*
a low-level military officer *US, 1940*
- A one-striper gets screwed by a two-striper. — Chris Bunch, *Storm Force*, p. 115, 2000

one swell foop *noun*
used as a humorous reversal of "one fell swoop" *US, 1900*
- "It's being done in one swell foop." Mutters another: "And that's frequently how it comes out!" — *Forbes*, p. 84, 12th November 1979
- Diane has finally gone from the bargain basement to the penthouse, in one swell foop. (I'm partial to spoonerisms.) — Haywood Smith, *The Red Hat Club*, p. 246, 2003

one-time *noun*
the police *US, 1990*
- The youth's companion also yelled: "Hey, one time's comin', drop the gun." — *Seattle Times*, p. A1, 29th July 1990
- One-time! Break! — *Menace II Society*, 1993
- "One time!" Kevin shouted. He walked over to the wall and jabbed three small baggies of rock into a crevice. — Bob Sipchen, *Baby Insane and the Buddha*, p. 144, 1993
- While kids in Northwest refer to police as "one-time," Northeast teenagers call them "bo-deen" or "hot dog," and in Southeast they're "po-pos" or good old "feds." — *Washington Post*, p. A1, 20th August 2001

one-toke weed *noun*
marijuana of such potency that only a few inhalations induce intoxication *US, 1982*
- — Ernest L. Abel, *A Marijuana Dictionary*, p. 75, 1982
- "It's genuine one-took weed." — Erik Storlie, *Nothing on My Mind*, p. 25, 1996

one-way *adjective*
heterosexual *US, 1964*
- — Roger Blake, *The American Dictionary of Sexual Terms*, p. 145, 1964
- — Dale Gordon, *The Dominion Sex Dictionary*, p. 112, 1967

one-way ride *noun*
an execution murder *US, 1942*
- "He's the only guy to ever survive a one-way ride." — Harold Robbins, *Sin City*, p. 16, 2002

onion *noun*
the head *US, 2002*
- "I'll just reach up and snatch your old ass down here and peel your fucking onion." — Jimmy Lerner, *You Got Nothing Coming*, p. 71, 2002

onion ballad *noun*
a painfully sad song *US, 1981*
An allusion to the relationship between onions and tears.
- — Don Wilmeth, *The Language of American Popular Entertainment*, p. 188, 1981

onion church *noun*
the Greek Orthodox church *US, 1997*
From the dome on many Greek Orthodox churches.
- — Amy and Denise McFadden, *CoalSpeak*, p. 10, 1997

onionhead *noun*
a fool, an idiot *US, 1928*
- St. Paul was an outpost to him, a city of Swedes and onionheads. — Garrison Keillor, *Homegrown Democrat*, p. 160, 2004

onliest *adjective*
only *US, 1907*
- I found myself running with a literary ex-pug, a pistol-packing rabbi, and a peewee jockey whose onliest riding crop was a stick of marijuana. — Mezz Mezzrow, *Really the Blues*, p. 69, 1946
- They really do their thing, and they're the onliest ones that I really, really respect. — John Allen, *Assault with a Deadly Weapon*, p. 110, 1977

only *adverb*
very *US, 1982*
Hawaiian youth usage.
- Wow, on'y trippy! — Douglas Simonson, *Pidgin to da Max: Hana Hou*, 1982

only suckers beef
used as a catchphrase in Chicago to affirm a guiding principle of that city, that losers should not complain *US, 1982*
- Only suckers beef—Chicago is a tough town and not interested in losers. Next to "where's mine?" that's the name of the game here. If you lose, take your lumps and don't bitch. — Bill Reilly, *Big Al's Official Guide to Chicagoese*, p. 45, 1982

on my honor as a Rocket Ranger
used as a humorous oath or pledge *US, 1954*
On the US children's television program *Rod Brown of the Rocket Rangers* (CBS, 1953–54), the children in the television audience were asked to pledge on their honor, among other things, "to chart my course according to the Constitution of the United States of America." Used in following years with irony by those who had been children during the dark years of the early 1950s.

on my skin
used as a profound oath of honor by white prisoners *US, 1989*
- — James Harris, *A Convict's Dictionary*, p. 35, 1989
- "On your skin, bro?" "On my skin." — Jimmy Lerner, *You Got Nothing Coming*, p. 88, 2002

OnO
used as an Internet shorthand farewell to mean "over and out" *US, 1997*
- — Andy Ihnatko, *Cyberspeak*, p. 140, 1997

on the strength!
seriously! *US, 1989*
- — Ellen C. Bellone (Editor), *Dictionary of Slang*, p. 17, 1989

on time *adjective*
excellent *US, 1992*
- — William K. Bentley and James M. Corbett, *Prison Slang*, p. 46, 1992

oodles *noun*
a large number; a large amount *US, 1867*
- Oodles and oodles of love and kisses, Suzie. — Max Shulman, *Guided Tour of Campus Humor*, p. 71, 1955
- They have oodles of photo albums with pictures taken when they were young[.] — Frederick Kohner, *Gidget*, p. 6, 1957
- "You've got just oodles of letters." — William Johnston, *The Brady Bunch*, p. 119, 1969
- No groovey clubs, only rock joints and oodles of prejudice. — Babs Gonzales, *Movin' On Down De Line*, p. 115, 1975

• He had oodles of warm, comedic charm. — Iceberg Slim (Robert Beck), *Airtight Willie and Me*, p. 51, 1979

oogle *verb*
to openly stare *US, 1949*

• Men enjoy looking at, being aroused by, and loving women. They don't oogle, make snide remarks, or abuse. — Charlene Giannetti, *The Rollercoaster Years*, p. 230, 1997

oogley *adjective*
good, excellent *US, 1955*
Teen slang.

• — *American Weekly*, p. 2, 14th August 1955

ooh and aah *verb*
to express admiration *US, 1957*

• He made his way across the carpeted casino to where a small crowd had gathered to ooh and aah as Duffy threw his money away with stupid bets on table three. — Stephen Cannell, *Big Con*, p. 205, 1997

• People oooh and aaah. More gather to watch. — Mike Judge and Joe Stillman, *Beavis and Butt-Head Do America*, p. 25, 1997

ooh-la-la
used as an expression of admiration *US, 1957*

• What are we going to tell our friends/When they say ooh-la-la? — The Everly Brothers, *Wake Up Little Susie*, 1957

• "Ooh-la-la," Beano said and looked over at Paper Collar John. — Stephen Cannell, *King Con*, p. 119, 1997

ooky *adjective*
revolting, disgusting *US, 1964*

• Wednesday shows off her all-grown-up pumpkins, ass, and gash, while getting some guy's thing in a bath tub. Kooky and ooky! — Mr. Skin, *Mr. Skin's Skincyclopedia*, p. 336, 2005

oomphy *adjective*
powerful, sexually attractive *US, 1955*

• I had been cast as Norman, the quiet fuddy-duddy husband, helplessly watching as his oomphy wife peeled at a suburban swap party. — Merrill Markoe, *The Psycho Ex Game*, p. 303, 2004

oop-pa-a-da
used as a greeting by bebop musicians and followers *US, 1949*
A highly stylized greeting, widely publicized in the early years of bop jazz, used sparingly.

• — Babs Gonzales, *Be-Bop Dictionary and History of its Famous Stars*, p. 9, 1949

• — Arnold Shaw, *Lingo of Tin-Pan Alley*, p. 15, 1950

ooze *verb*
to move, especially slowly, carefully, without enthusiasm *US, 1929*

• Then, having discovered that my funds totaled slightly over six hundred dollars, I oozed to the floor in a moaning mound. — Max Shulman, *The Many Loves of Dobie Gillis*, p. 29, 1951

• Just on the loose—a half hour at Mary's, let's ooze over to Jo's, say Pete's got a fistful of hot new platters, so let's lend an ear. — Dick Clark, *To Goof or Not to Goof*, p. 103, 1963

op *noun*
1 opium *US, 1967*

• Slang Term: Op, "O" — Elizabeth Finn, *Drugs in the Tenderloin*, p. 38, 1967

2 an operator *US, 1930*

• The op behind the counter had the kind of mute, predatory face that belonged in a shooting gallery. — Robert Edmond Alter, *Carny Kill*, p. 2, 1966

3 a private detective; a private operator *US, 1947*

• Not only that, but she had a private op's ticket and on occasions when she went out with me on a case, packed a flat .32 automatic—and she wasn't afraid to use it. — Mickey Spillane, *I, The Jury*, p. 11, 1947

op *verb*
to operate; to do; to set up *US, 1953*

• We tried to op a pad downtown, like in the Village, but they Jim Crowed us. — Ross Russell, *The Sound*, p. 123, 1961

OP *adjective*
other people's *US, 1972*

• — Helen Dahlskog (Editor), *A Dictionary of Contemporary and Colloquial Usage*, p. 43, 1972

• "Got a cigarette?" Mannelli asked, reaching across the desk. "I gave them up two years ago. Now I only smoke O.P.'s ... other people's." — William J. Cavnitz, *One Police Plaza*, p. 81, 1984

OPB *noun*
used as an initialism for other people's brand, a mythical and humorous brand of cigarettes *US, 1970*

• — Clarence Major, *Dictionary of Afro-American Slang*, p. 88, 1970

open *noun*
in computing, a left parenthesis—the (*US, 1991*

• — Eric S. Raymond, *The New Hacker's Dictionary*, p. 268, 1991

open *adjective*
in organized crime, safe for anyone without fear of violence *US, 1963*

• Las Vegas has been an "open city" (off limits to mob violence and open to mobs with the proper credentials) since the wild days of Bugsy Siegel. — Ed Reid and Ovid Demaris, *The Green Felt Jungle*, p. 179, 1963

open at both ends *adjective*
in poker, four cards in sequence that could form a five-card straight with a draw at either end of the sequence *US, 1988*

• — George Percy, *The Language of Poker*, p. 61, 1988

open door *noun*
in surfing, a wave that breaks such that the surfer can ride away from the peak onto the shoulder *US, 1963*

• — Grant W. Kuhns, *On Surfing*, p. 119, 1963

• — Rob Burt, *Surf City, Drag City*, 1986

open-kimono *adjective*
characterized by complete honesty and full disclosure *US, 1974*
Sometimes formulated as **OPEN THE KIMONO** or a variation thereon. Ronin International, a computer consulting firm, promises "open-kimono" in its published mission statement, explaining that the term "stems from feudal Japanese times where the term signified that the party will hide nothing within his clothing [the kimono was the dominant clothing of that era] that could conceivably be used as a weapon."

• — Robert Kirk Mueller, *Buzzwords*, p. 117, 1974

• The breakup is forcing AT&T not only to get competitive, but to be willing to open its kimono and talk more thoroughly about its plans. — *Computerworld*, p. 55, 4th July 1984

• "Developers look at us and think 'corporation' and we want them to know that we embrace open source, an open kimono approach so to speak. That was the reason for our keynote," Shapanka said. — *IDG News Service*, 25th October 2000

• Laura Day Del Cotto, attorney for The United Co., Wilkinson's largest creditor, said debtors who receive court protection while reorganizing their finances have to assume an "open kimono" position when asked for financial data by their creditors. — *Lexington Herald-Leader*, 13th April 2001

open-mike *adjective*
said of a club where anybody may perform briefly and without payment *US, 1983*

• [H]e saw me at a club, it was open-mike night, and he gave me some shit about this group he's putting together. — Elmore Leonard, *Be Cool*, p. 56, 1983

open room *noun*
an establishment where it is possible to bet on sporting events and listen to or watch the event as it takes place *US, 1978*

• An open room is a gambling room where you can make a bet and then listen to the game or race you've bet on. — Burgess Laughlin, *Job Opportunities in the Black Market*, p. 11–4, 1978

open shadow *noun*
in a surveillance operation, a follower who lets himself be spotted *US, 1958*

• "I guess you know what an open shadow is." "Sure. One that deliberately lets the subject spot him, then shake him, so that another shadow can pick him up when he thinks he is safe." — Raymond Chandler, *Playback*, p. 86, 1958

open up *verb*
to recruit into prostitution *US, 1981*

- There was a square broad named Paula he'd been opening up, but he still had a way to go to catch her. — Alix Shulman, *On the Stroll*, p. 229, 1981

opera *noun*
a traveling show *US, 1980*
- — Joe McKennon, *Circus Lingo*, p. 67, 1980

operator *noun*
1 someone who is popular, crafty, and perhaps manipulative *US, 1944*
- — Collin Baker et al., *College Undergraduate Slang Study Conducted at Brown University*, p. 165, 1968
2 a drug dealer *US, 1952*
- — *American Speech*, p. 28, February 1952: "Teen-Age hophead jargon"

OPM *noun*
other people's money *US, 1901*
- — Robert Kirk Mueller, *Buzzwords*, p. 118, 1974
- When OPM is "backing" a player, he can afford to play for higher stakes. — Steve Rushin, *Pool Cool*, p. 22, 1990

orale
hello *US, 1950*
Border Spanish used in English conversation by Mexican-Americans.
- — George Carpenter Baker, *Pachuco*, p. 42, 1950

orange *noun*
a tablet of dextroamphetamine sulfate (trade name Dexedrine™), a central nervous system stimulant *US, 1967*
- — John B. Williams, *Narcotics and Hallucinogenics*, p. 115, 1967

orange-peel *verb*
(used of freshly applied paint) to wrinkle or form small ridges *US, 1998*
- Make it shiny and wet, but don't let it orange-peel or run. — Peter Coyote, *Sleeping Where I Fall*, p. 109, 1998

orb *verb*
to see *US, 2004*
- Orb the plastic saddlebags, aaa-ooo-gah born, and toy tommy gun. — James Ellroy, *Destination Morgue*, p. 33, 2004

orbit *verb*
to engage in oral sex *US, 1985*
- — *American Speech*, p. 20, Spring 1985: "The language of singles bars"

orchid *noun*
a beautiful woman *US, 1948*
- As the poisonous fumes were snuffing out the life of this Broadway orchid—bride of 29 days—the lobby of her apartment building was filling up[.] — Jack Lait and Lee Mortimer, *New York Confidential*, p. 56, 1948
- We would put up a pot of five dollars each day and the one that "copped" the most "orchids" would win. — Babs Gonzales, *I Paid My Dues*, p. 68, 1967

ordie *noun*
a soldier who handles ordinance *US, 1986*
- A true achievement, since the man was a bomb ordie on special assignment. — Dale Brown, *Dale Brown's Dreamland*, p. 48, 2003

Oregon boots *noun*
leg irons *US, 1949*
- — Vincent J. Monteleone, *Criminal Slang*, p. 169, 1949
- [B]ecause I was such an escape artist they fit me with an Oregon boot, a large steel doughnut that locks around the ankle. — Malcolm Braley, *False Starts*, p. 142, 1976

Oregon trifecta *noun*
oral, vaginal, and anal sex in the same session *US, 2003*
- Oregon Trifecta (aka "Triple Crown of Sex")—in the yapper, the snapper, and the crapper all in the same session. — *news.admin.net-abuse.email*, 4th August 2003

Oreo *noun*
a black person whose values are seen as white values *US, 1968*
Never used kindly.
- — *Current Slang*, p. 21, Spring 1970
- She's a pure Oreo. You know, like the cookie, black outside and white inside. — Iceberg Slim (Robert Beck), *The Naked Soul of Iceberg Slim*, p. 89, 1971

- LIONEL: He's what we call an Oreo cookie. ARCHIE: Oreo cookie? LIONEL: That's right. Black on the outside and white on the inside. ARCHIE: I'm glad you liked him, Lionel. — Eugene Boe (Compiler), *The Wit & Wisdom of Archie Bunker*, p. 71, 1971
- "You really know that rich Oreo motherfucka Jake Thomas?" — Jason Starr, *Lights Out*, p. 177, 2006

organ grinding *noun*
sex *US, 1972*
- We never had another around-the-clock drunken marathon, but we did a good bit of organ grinding. — Robert Byrne, *McGoorty*, p. 67, 1972

organized chicken shit *noun*
Officer Candidate School *US, 1992*
From the initials.
- He had been accepted to Organized Chicken Shit, which is how OCS is known in the fleet. — Richard Marcinko and John Weisman, *Rogue Warrior*, pp. 55–56, 1992

orgy room *noun*
a room designated for group sex *US, 1969*
- Returning to the "orgy room," I peeked through the curtains. — *The Advocate*, p. 5, March 1969
- These bars generally consist of a large open space containing a bar and dance floor, and a connected "sex room" or "orgy room" where men practice homosexual sexual acts on each other. — *The Knapp Commission Report on Police Corruption*, p. 140, 1972
- I was in the orgy room. Very late. I had smoked a little pipe of sinsemilla, and I was feeling glorious. — Armistead Maupin, *Babycakes*, p. 253, 1984

Oriental dancer *noun*
in circus and carnival usage, a sexually explicit female dancer *US, 1981*
- — Don Wilmeth, *The Language of American Popular Entertainment*, p. 190, 1981

original *noun*
a male prisoner who selects and maintains a primary sexual partner in jail *US, 1972*
- There are two classes of homos in here. You have what they call the "original" or "square" and you have what they call the "candy-bar punk." — Bruce Jackson, *In the Life*, p. 359, 1972

original gangster *noun*
a member of the founding generation of a youth gang; somebody who is so committed to a gang that he remains a gang member at all costs *US, 1995*
- — Mark S. Fleisher, *Beggars & Thieves*, p. 290, 1995: "Glossary"

originals *noun*
the clothes worn by a member of Hell's Angels when he is initiated into the gang, and worn thereafter in perpetuity *US, 1966*
- These are his "originals," to be worn every day until they rot. — Hunter S. Thompson, *Hell's Angels*, p. 47, 1966

or, in English
used as a humorous bridge between a butchered attempt at verbalization and an attempt to correct *US, 1997*
Coined as a self-parody by ESPN's Keith Olberman.
- — Keith Olberman and Dan Patrick, *The Big Show*, p. 23, 1997

O-ring *noun*
a novice surfer; a dolt *US, 1992*
- — *Surfer Magazine*, p. 30, February 1992

orphan *noun*
1 in craps, a bet on the table that a gambler has forgotten belongs to him *US, 1981*
- — N.B. Winkless, *The Gambling Times Guide to Craps*, p. 97, 1981
2 a computer that has been phased out due to technological advances *US, 1986*
- — Rachel S. Epstein and Nina Liebman, *Biz Speak*, p. 162, 1986

Oscar *noun*
1 a male homosexual *US, 1967*
Surely a reference to Oscar Wilde.
- — Dale Gordon, *The Dominion Sex Dictionary*, p. 115, 1967
2 an offensive, unlikeable person *US, 1905*
- She felt a lot better when she left, but this time I didn't get my sentence reduced for being a Boy Scout. There were a hard lot of oscars in the Bridewell. — Mezz Mezzrow, *Really the Blues*, p. 40, 1946

3 a handgun *US, 1949*
- — Captain Vincent J. Monteleone, *Criminal Slang*, p. 169, 1949

Oscar deuce; Oscar douche *noun*
a Cessna 0–2 Super Skymaster aircraft *US, 1971*
- Known as the "Oscar Deuce," the 0–2 was essentially the military version of the Cessna Skymaster[.] — Tom Yarborough, *Da Nang Diary*, p. 22, 1990
- After hearing my story, even the maintenance supervisor was overjoyed that my trusty Oscar Deuce apparently suffered little more than a write-up for being over-G'd. — Frank Borman, *Naked in Da Nang*, p. 5, 2004

oscar hock *noun*
a sock *US, 1928*
- "[T]hat's a mistake many a guy makes—they take off a few touches, get a little gold in the oscar hock, and right off they start studying a Cadillac automobile, expensive broads, and a trip to Vegas." — Malcolm Braly, *It's Cold Out There*, pp. 39–40, 1966

ossifer; occifer *noun*
a police officer *US, 1819*
An intentional metathesis, spoken in imitation of the slurred speech of intoxication.
- He was not weaving at all. Hardly at all. Watch this, Ossifer, I'm going to walk right up this white line to the stop light. — Stephen King, *Salem's Lot*, p. 227, 1975

ossified *adjective*
very drunk *US, 1901*
- "Do you ever look drunk?" "Yeah. I get ossified ever so often and don't care how I look." — Robert Deane Pharr, *S.R.O.*, p. 314, 1971
- [O]ne time they got him loaded in the terminal and they got him on the airplane. He was ossified, that's the only way they could get him on. — Edward Lin, *Big Julie of Vegas*, p. 96, 1974

OTL *adjective*
distracted, foolish, stupid *US, 1957*
An abbreviation of **OUT TO LUNCH**.
- Or if you don't want to say a friend is O.T.L. just call the "square" a "fly." — *Washington Post*, p. F1, 29th September 1957
- — Fred Hester, *Slang on the 40 Acres*, p. 12, 1968

OTOH
used as Internet shorthand to mean "on the other hand" *US, 1995*
- — Christian Crumlish, *The Internet Dictionary*, p. 145, 1995

OTR *adjective*
literally, experiencing the bleed period of the menstrual cycle; figuratively, complaining *US, 1968*
An initialism of **ON THE RAG**.
- — Collin Baker et al., *College Undergraduate Slang Study Conducted at Brown University*, p. 164, 1968
- — Pamela Munro, *U.C.L.A. Slang*, p. 64, 1989

ouch *noun*
an injury *US, 1962*
- — *American Speech*, p. 271, December 1962: "The language of traffic policemen"

ouch!
how unfortunate! *US, 1997*
- — Pamela Munro, *U.C.L.A. Slang*, p. 94, 1997

ouchy *adjective*
(used of a racehorse) sore *US, 1976*
- — Tom Ainslie, *Ainslie's Complete Guide to Thoroughbred Racing*, p. 335, 1976

ouija board *noun*
in horse racing, the official odds board at the racetrack *US, 1951*
- — David W. Maurer, *Argot of the Racetrack*, p. 47, 1951

ounce man *noun*
a drug dealer at the wholesale level, buying and selling in ounces *US, 1966*
- — Burgess Laughlin, *Job Opportunities in the Black Market*, p. 3, 1978: "Glossary"
- All the kilo men and ounce men around town talked about real estate, about getting out, but Strike knew they were all full of shit. — Richard Price, *Clockers*, p. 57, 1992

our concrete brethren *noun*
members of the US Air Force *US, 1998*

US Army usage.
- — *Seattle Times*, p. A9, 12th April 1998: "Grunts, squids not grunting from the same dictionary"

out *noun*
▸ **on the outs**
not incarcerated *US, 1991*
- "You know, on the outs, this pig was sayin', 'You shouldn't steal because then somebody steal from you.'" — Leon Bing, *Do or Die*, p. 19, 1991

out *verb*
to disclose another person's homosexuality *US, 1990*
Usually done to a public figure, and most commonly to one who is publicly antihomosexual, such as J. Edgar Hoover or the cadre of gay men who surrounded Lt. Co. Oliver North in the Reagan White House.
- He's petrified he'll be outed if this becomes an issue. — Armistead Maupin, *Maybe the Moon*, p. 216, 1992
- Meanwhile, Kia's lover, Evy (Migdalia Melendez), is outed by her ex-husband[.] — *Vogue*, p. 91, June 1994
- The term's coinage was prompted by Michelangelo Signorile's (b. 1960) "The Secret Gay Life of Malcom Forbes," a March 1990 Outweek story which appeared one month after the millionaire's death. — Steven Daly and Nathaniel Wice, *alt.culture*, p. 175, 1995

out *adjective*
publicly and openly homosexual *UK, 1979*
An abbreviation of the full "out of the **CLOSET**."
- — *American Speech*, Winter 1990
- — Jeff Fessler, *When Drag Is Not a Car Race*, p. 39, 1997

out
used in farewell *US, 1993*
- Allright. Out. — *Menace II Society*, 1993

outa here; outta here *adjective*
about to leave *US, 1980*
- "No," Dawn said, "but I wanted you to know I'm outta here." — Joseph Wambaugh, *Floaters*, p. 42, 1996

outcall service *noun*
a decentralized brothel, where prostitutes are dispatched to customers *US, 1987*
- In the last few years, a system of "escort services" has developed (originally as an "outcall" service offered by massage parlors) which works like a dating service[.] — Frederique Delacoste, *Sex Work*, p. 190, 1987

outdoors *noun*
▸ **all outdoors**
a great amount *US, 1830*
- "Goddamned place costs all outdoors," he said. — George V. Higgins, *Penance for Jerry Kennedy*, p. 172, 1985

outfit *noun*
1 a criminal organization *US, 1933*
- In one season the outfit netted $6,000,000 in Miami gambling houses. — Jack Lait and Lee Mortimer, *New York Confidential*, p. 186, 1948
- The Mafia—the Capone gang—The Syndicate—The Outfit—it's all the same. The Outfit is the Mafia's "Enforcer" in Syndicate City. — Alson Smith, *Syndicate City*, p. 83, 1954
- It was strictly a penny-ante operation, said Grana, and the Outfit let it exist because it took some heat off of their own dope syndicate. — Emmett Grogan, *Ringolevio*, p. 158, 1972
- He was mobbed up with the Pleasant Avenue outfit. — Edwin Torres, *Carlito's Way*, p. 21, 1975

2 a still used in the illegal production of alcohol *US, 1974*
- — David W. Maurer, *Kentucky Moonshine*, p. 121, 1974

3 the needle and syringe used to inject a drug *US, 1951*
- You got an outfit here? — John D. McDonald, *The Neon Jungle*, p. 73, 1953
- I said, "Please, 'Sweet,' cook it for me and load my outfit. It's inside the candy-striped tie in the closet." — Iceberg Slim (Robert Beck), *Pimp*, p. 100, 1969
- I guess they'll try and make it look like an outfit that a junkie would use, but neither me or my wife use, so I don't see how they can make a case out of it. — Donald Goines, *White Man's Justice, Black Man's Grief*, p. 153, 1973
- Anybody got an outfit up there? — *Drugstore Cowboy*, 1988

4 a vehicle *US, 1997*
Idaho usage.
- — Jim Crotty, *How to Talk American*, p. 213, 1997

out front *adjective*
direct, honest *US, 1968*
- — Lewis Yablonsky, *The Hippie Trip*, p. 368, 1968: "Glossary"
- — David Powis, *The Signs of Crime*, 1977

outgribing *noun*
a written contribution to a single-interest fan magazine *US, 1982*
- — *American Speech*, p. 28, Spring 1982: "The language of science fiction fan magazines"

outhole *noun*
in pinball, the hole beneath the flippers through which a ball leaves play *US, 1977*
- — Bobbye Claire Natkin and Steve Kirk, *All About Pinball*, p. 113, 1977

outhouse *noun*
in poker, a full house (three of a kind and a pair) that is inferior to another full house hand *US, 1996*
- — John Vorhaus, *The Big Book of Poker Slang*, p. 28, 1996

outie *noun*
an outward-turned navel *US, 1966*
- — John D. Bell et al., *Loosely Speaking*, p. 14, 1966
- Erin's mother had paid a plastic surgeon $1,500 to transform her "outie" belly button to an "innie." — Carl Hiaasen, *Strip Tease*, p. 56, 1993

outie *adverb*
▶ **be outie**
to leave *US, 1995*
- Dee, I'm outie. — *Clueless*, 1995

outlaw *noun*
a prostitute working without the services of a pimp *US, 1935*
- I don't tell them other bitzes this, but being a lone outlaw in this life, with the johnlaws up one side an the pimps down the other, everybody mouth-waterin' for a taste—well you catchin' too much mogo at once[.] — Robert Gover, *JC Saves*, p. 55, 1968
- A pimples prostitute was often called an "outlaw." — Charles Winick, *The Lively Commerce*, p. 113, 1971
- An outlaw is a ho without a proper pimp. — Christina and Richard Milner, *Black Players*, p. 41, 1972
- I have also heard that "outlaws," girls without a connection, are thrown out of that hotel bar and all others in Vegas soon as they are spotted. — Gerald Paine, *A Bachelor's Guide to the Brothels of Nevada*, pp. 129–130, 1978

outlaw *adjective*
in roller derby, outside the official Roller Derby League *US, 1999*
- — Keith Coppage, *Roller Derby to Rollerjam*, 1999

out of here
used as a farewell *US, 1991*
- — Lee McNelis, *30 + And a Wake-Up*, p. 10, 1991

out of it *adjective*
crazy, mentally ill *US, 1979*
- He's out of it, Bailey. I think the defendant should be remanded for a psychiatric examination. — Edwin Torres, *After Hours*, p. 259, 1979

out of sight; outasight *adjective*
excellent, amazing *US, 1876*
Nearly a hundred years old before being swept up as a core adjective of the 1960s hippie lexicon.
- He gave me some LSD that night and it was outasight. — Abbie Hoffman, *Revolution for the Hell of It*, p. 154, 1968
- GEORGE: Now this is supposed to be the finest whorehouse in the South. These ain't no pork chops. These are U.S. Prime. BILLY: out a site, man. — Peter Fonda, *Easy Rider*, p. 117, 1969
- The high point for me, thus far, was an unbelievable performance by The Quarry, an outasite group of very heavy musicians, Saturday night. — *East Village Other*, 20th August 1969
- "Hey, man, let me say a word about Jesus. Man, He's out of sight." — Arthur Blessitt, *Turned On to Jesus*, p. 161, 1971
- We could be a dynamite team, outasight. — *Saturday Night Fever*, 1977

- "Out of sight!" Jerry Rubin said, as the defendants began to talk among themselves. — Bobby Seale, *A Lonely Rage*, p. 237, 1978

out of sight, satellite
used as a farewell *US, 1961*
- — Art Unger, *The Cool Book*, p. 108, 1961

out of the money *adjective*
in horse and dog racing, finished below third place *US, 1988*
- "Out of the money and tiring at the finish," Ciglianni added. — Robert Campbell, *Juice*, p. 2, 1988

out of this world *adjective*
extraordinary *US, 1928*
- Tony could play the blues out of this world. — Mezz Mezzrow, *Really the Blues*, p. 45, 1946

outs *noun*
in poker, the playing of a weak hand in the hope of a drastic improvement in drawing *US, 1979*
- — John Scarne, *Scarne's Guide to Modern Poker*, p. 285, 1979

outside *noun*
1 in Alaska, anywhere in the US other than Alaska *US, 1900*
- As a salesman I had an appointment in Anchorage and spent about 10 days and $700 to get there at the appointed time and date, only to be told my customer was "outside," to which I almost replied, "Why don't you go outside and get him." — Mark Wheeler, *Half Baked Alaska*, p. 111, 1972
- — *American Speech*, pp. 256–258, Fall 1984: "Terms for 'not Alaska' in Alaskan English"
- — Mike Doogan, *How to Speak Alaskan*, p. 47, 1993

2 the world outside the armed forces *US, 1898*
- — *American Speech*, p. 288, December 1962: "Marine Corps slang"

3 the world outside prison *US, 1990*
- I hadn't heard from anyone on the outside; and it began to matter less after a while. — Herbert Huncke, *Guilty of Everything*, p. 122, 1990

outside *adjective*
1 out of the ordinary *US, 1969*
- That shit's really outside. — Steve Cannon, *Groove, Bang, and Jive Around*, p. 21, 1969

2 in surfing, seaward of the swell *US, 1963*
- — Grant W. Kuhns, *On Surfing*, p. 119, 1963
- They are just "outside," about one fifth of a mile out from the shore, beyond where the waves start breaking. — Tom Wolfe, *The Pump House Gang*, p. 23, 1968

3 not in prison *US, 1871*
- You were outside, I was inside, you were s'posed to keep in touch with the band. — *The Blues Brothers*, 1980

outside!
used for calling to the attention of other surfers the presence of an approaching series of waves seaward *US, 1964*
- — John Severson, *Modern Surfing Around the World*, p. 175, 1964

outside man *noun*
in carnival and circus usage, a person stationed outside an attraction whose job it is to attract customers *US, 2005*
- "Your job as Outside Man will be to keep a tip [crowd] from building as we work our marks," Ghost said. — Peter Fenton, *Eyeing the Flash*, p. 197, 2005

outside work *noun*
any external alteration of dice for cheating *US, 1963*
- — John S. Salak, *Dictionary of Gambling*, p. 174, 1963

outstanding *adjective*
excellent *US, 1964*
Conventional English converted to slang by attitude and a drawn-out pronunciation.
- "Out-standing!" Bobbie said. — Joseph Wambaugh, *Finnegan's Week*, p. 247, 1993
- Hey, Bea Arthur, outstanding! — *Airheads*, 1994

out there *adjective*
1 in a state of extreme marijuana-intoxication *US, 1977*
- He smokes a lot, and when he gets really out there on it makes with cartoon non sequiturs that nobody else can fathom[.] — Lester Bangs, *Psychotic Reactions and Carburetor Dung*, p. 234, 1977

2 in the alternative society; out of the mainstream *US, 1975*
- Barton decided that it would be "out there" to leave the apartment just as it was. — Ed Sanders, *Tales of Beatnik Glory*, p. 91, 1975
- — Connie Eble (Editor), *UNC-CH Campus Slang*, p. 7, April 1995

out ticket *noun*
in horse racing, a winning bet not presented for payment on the day of the race *US, 1982*
- — Bob and Barbara Freeman, *Wanta Bet? A Study of the Pari-Mutuels System in the United States*, p. 291, 1982

oven *noun*
▸ **in the oven**
pregnant *UK, 1937*
Especially in the phrase "bun in the oven."
- Poor thing has another one in the oven. — Louise Meriwether, *Daddy Was a Number Runner*, p. 51, 1970
- What about this little crumb-crusher you got in the oven here? — Edwin Torres, *After Hours*, p. 378, 1979

over *adjective*
popular with the audience *US, 1999*
Professional wrestling usage.
- Myth: Steve Austin is more over than Hulk Hogan was. Fact: It all depends on how you define the term "over." — Luke Johnston, *The Shooters*, p. 10, 2nd December 1999
- Ric Flair was the most over wrestler at this point of the night. — Herb's *Wrestling Tidbits*, 15th May 2000
- Verne always thought Crusher was selfish, wanted too much, and wasn't as over as he thought he was. — Bobby Heenan, *Bobby the Brain*, p. 33, 2002

overamp *verb*
to overdose on narcotics *US, 1967*
- — William D. Alsever, *Glossary for the Establishment and Other Uptight People*, p. 24, December 1970

overamped *adjective*
over-stimulated *US, 1979*
- My overamped brains and self-will still fought against this decision that seemed so irrational. — Peter Jenkins, *A Walk Across America*, pp. 256–257, 1979

over-and-under *noun*
1 a capsule containing both a barbiturate and an amphetamine *US, 1973*
- — David Maurer and Victor Vogel, *Narcotics and Narcotic Addiction*, p. 431, 1973
2 an M-16 rifle with an M-79 grenade launcher tube under the rifle barrel *US, 1972*
- I continued, "THE PERFORMANCE OF THE OVER AND UNDER," and proceeded to report that this Rube Goldberg wonder weapon (which was an M-16 with an M-79 fixed underneath) was an ineffective, undesirable piece of shit. — David H. Hackworth, *About Face*, p. 479, 1989

overboard *adjective*
drunk *US, 1948*
- At about nine o'clock, half overboard, Legs said he was going to the washroom. — Jack Lait and Lee Mortimer, *New York Confidential*, p. 162, 1948

▸ **go overboard**
to refuse or fail to pay a gambling debt *US, 1947*
- — Dan Parker, *The ABC of Horse Racing*, p. 146, 1947

over-boogie *verb*
to over-indulge in the pleasures of vice *US, 1982*
- [M]y ability to consume vast quantities of things that were supposed to poison me from what one rock'n'roll crowd used to call "over boogie" was tested to the hilt and I thought I was invincible. — Eve Babitz, *L.A. Woman*, p. 49, 1982

overcoat *noun*
in pool, a player who has mastered the foibles of a particular table *US, 1990*
- — Steve Rushin, *Pool Cool*, p. 22, 1990

overfix *verb*
to overdose using a drug *US, 1972*
- You all won't believe this, but I ain't ever been overfixed. — Bruce Jackson, *In the Life*, p. 223, 1972

overjolt *noun*
a drug overdose *US, 1959*

- Finally, the next morning, he said, he drove her to a patch of grass near Mission Emergency Hospital and then tipped police that she'd had "an over-jolt." — *San Francisco Examiner*, p. 12, 9th March 1962
- "Overjolt," Cabiness told her, "we've got to walk him." — Malcolm Braly, *Shake Him Till He Rattles*, p. 145, 1963

overland route *noun*
▸ **to take the overland route**
in horseracing, to race on the outside portion of the track because a horse prefers passing around a pack to accelerating through it *US, 1947*
- — Walter Steigleman, *Horseracing*, p. 274, 1947

over-much *adjective*
astonishing, difficult to believe *US, 1968*
- — Collin Baker et al., *College Undergraduate Slang Study Conducted at Brown University*, p. 166, 1968

overs *noun*
in a game of poker, the small amount of money left in the center of the table after a pot is divided among two or more players, held over for the next hand *US, 1988*
- — George Percy, *The Language of Poker*, p. 62, 1988

Oversexed Weekly *noun*
the Overseas Weekly newspaper *US, 1969*
- The paper thrived on sex and scandal; most soldiers called it the "Oversexed Weekly." — John Singlaub, *Hazardous Duty*, p. 255, 1991

owie *noun*
any minor injury *US, 1967*
Children's vocabulary.
- Toddler Has "Owie" After 3-Story Fall [Caption] — *Chicago Tribune*, p. 9C, 20th May 1988
- "Everybody has an owie," Chang said. "Everybody has a bruise, a torn something." — *Honolulu Advertiser*, p. 3D, 27th November 2002

owlhead *noun*
a revolver *US, 1927*
Originally referred to a revolver manufactured by Iver Johnson Arms, featuring an owlhead logo; later applied to any revolver.
- He pulled out his owl head all packed with lead. — Dan Burley, *Diggeth Thou?*, p. 11, 1959

owlhooter *noun*
an outlaw *US, 1942*
- Them owlhooters was in a real bind, I can tell you. They had the big bunch the posse and miners a-coming. — Robert Conley, *A Cold Hard Trail*, p. 210, 2001

owl shit *noun*
used in comparisons involving insignificance, remoteness, and slickness *US, 1862*
- "Slicker than owl shit. Two-faced. Double-dealing." — Sandra Brown, *Mirror Image*, p. 336, 1990

Owl Shit Junction *noun*
any extremely remote town *US, 1977*
- — *Maledicta*, p. 12, Summer 1977: "A word for it!"

own *verb*
to dominate; to command complete deference *US, 1997*
- No, I promise, not a chance. I own this guy. — *As Good As It Gets*, 1997

ownage *noun*
complete domination *US, 2003*
- Ownage: beating an opponent by a huge amount. — Raymond Smith, *Wi-Fi Home Networking*, 2003
- "I think it's going to be great," Chris said, because Bawls is an energy drink and it'll let us deliver the ownage." — *Orange County Register*, 22nd May 2003

Owsley; Owsley acid; owsley *noun*
high quality LSD *US, 1967*
From the name of legendary LSD manufacturer Augustus Owsley Stanley III. Other variations include: "Owsley blue dot"; "Owsley blues"; "Owsley power"; "Owsley purple"; **PURPLE OWSLEY** "pink Owsley"; "white Owsley"; "Owsley's stuff"; "Owsleys."
- The Owsleys are also given away as free samples. — Nicholas Von Hoffman, *We Are The People Our Parents Warned Us Against*, p. 35, 1967
- — William D. Alsever, *Glossary for the Establishment and Other Uptight People*, p. 24, December 1970

ox *noun*
a knife *US, 2002*
- — Jeffrey Ian Ross, *Behind Bars*, p. 182, 2002: Slammer Slang

oxy *noun*
the synthetic opiate oxycodone used recreationally; a capsule of OxyContin™ *US, 2000*
This term got national attention in 2003 when radio entertainer
Rush Limbaugh, who had made a career of criticizing and
disparaging drug addicts, revealed that he was in fact a drug
addict, and that OxyContin was his drug of choice.
- On the street, Oxys, as they are commonly called, fetch about $1 per
  milligram and usually are dosed in 20-, 40-, or 80-milligram tablets.
  — *Bangor Daily News*, 14th June 2000
- "When you get the oxy buzz," she says, "it's a great feeling. You're
  happy. Your body don't hurt." — *New York Times Magazine*, p. 34, 29th July
  2001
- Hence, Oxy has a time-release coating that gradually releases the
  drug over time. — Suroosh Alvi et al., *The Vice Guide*, p. 109, 2002
- About the article "Rush back, reborn" (Nov. 18), regarding the return
  of Rush "Oxy" Limbaugh. (Letter to Editor) — *Palm Beach Post*, p. 19A,
  5th December 2003

oy gevalt!
used for expressing a lament, protest, dismay, or delight *US,*
1921
Yiddish from German.
- — Leo Rosten, *The Joys of Yiddish*, p. 134, 1968
- Terrance and Phillip Movie! Oy gevalt! Not again! — *South Park*, 1999

oy vey!
used for expressing surprise *US, 1992*
Yiddish.
- "Oy vey!" wailed the Rabbi. "How can a Jew swallow a mouthful
  without first washing his hands?" — Nathan Ausubel, *A Treasury of Jewish
  Folklore*, p. 385, 1948
- — Judi Sanders, *Kickin' like Chicken with the Couch Commander*, p. 17, 1992

OZ; oh-zee *noun*
an ounce of marijuana or other drugs *US, 1933*
Spelling out the standard abbreviation for "ounce."
- And I'll get Verger to bring some weed to your party. He's gotten
  an o.z. from a passer up on One Hundred and Twenty-fifth Street.
  — John Clellon Holmes, *Go*, p. 83, 1952
- [A]n American hipster friend from L.A. laid 5 ozees on me free.
  — Jack Kerouac, *Letter to Neal and Carolyn Cassady*, p. 359, 27th May 1952
- I had managed with financial assistance to breathe a little life into
  the scene—had an O.Z. of good amphets to use and sell enough of
  to make up the cost and possibly even realize a little profit. — Herbert
  Huncke, *The Evening Sun Turned Crimson*, p. 126, 1980
- Unloading a single O.Z. sometimes took up to an hour. — Nathan
  McCall, *Makes Me Wanna Holler*, p. 120, 1994

ozone *noun*
phencyclidine, the recreational drug known as PCP or angel
dust *US, 1994*
- — US Department of Justice, *Street Terms*, October 1994

ozone theater *noun*
an outdoor movie theater *US, 1957*
- — *American Speech*, p. 239, October 1957: "Outdoor movie talk"

Pp

P *noun*

1 pure or nearly pure heroin *US, 1968*

- "I can get you a quarter-ounce of P (pure heroin) and two dime bags." — Phil Hirsch, *Hooked*, p. 153, 1968
- She could hardly keep her eyes open. The strong P, "pure," that Porky had given her was enough to bring the worst dopefiend into a dreamlike state. — Donald Goines, *Dopefiend*, p. 33, 1971
- The black colony was flooded with a new, much stronger grade of junk called "P." — John Sinclair, *Guitar Army*, p. 290, 1972
- "You selling P, if you wanta deal, Bernie Lee." — Vernon E. Smith, *The Jones Men*, p. 8, 1974

2 a Vietnamese piastre *US, 1965*

- — *Time*, p. 34, 10th December 1965
- But then he said, "I'm out of P's / And cannot buy you Saigon Tea's." — Ken Melvin, *Sorry 'Bout That*, p. 59, 1966
- The shopper pays in local currency, piasters, or p's, in soldier slang. — Elaine Shepard, *The Doom Pussy*, p. 21, 1967
- Having dropped the twenty P and exchanged smiles with his friend, Converse sauntered down Tu Do to the Crazy Horse. — Robert Stone, *Dog Soldiers*, p. 19, 1974

P *adjective*

pretty *US, 1982*

Hawaiian youth usage.

- "Oh, she so P, yeah?" — Douglas Simonson, *Pidgin to da Max: Hana Hou*, 1982

-p *suffix*

used for turning a word into a question *US, 1981*

- From the LISP convention of appending the letter "P" to denote a predicate (A Boolean-values function). The question should expect a yes/no answer, though it needn't. At dinnertime: "Foodp?" "Yeah." — *CoEvolution Quarterly*, p. 27, Spring 1981

P-38 *noun*

1 in Vietnam war usage, the small can opener included with individual field rations *US, 1966*

A humorous application of bureaucratic nomenclature.

- — *Army Times*, p. 1, 19th January 1966
- — Carl Fleischhauer, *A Glossary of Army Slang*, p. 8, 1968
- The Anachronism's tent was empty and we used a P-38 to take the tops off the first coke cans. — William Pelfrey, *The Big V*, p. 125, 1972

2 a police-issue .38 caliber revolver *US, 1976*

- I would climb in the ring with nothing but two P-.38's / And send either one that moved through the pearly gates. — Dennis Wepman et al., *The Life*, p. 157, 1976

PA *noun*

1 a "Prince Albert" piercing of the penis *US, 1989*

- Well, a PA is a good choice for an initial cock piercing. — *alt.sex .bondage*, 26th December 1989
- Sooooo, what do I tell my boyfriend when he asks about the PA I got "visiting my aunt in Pittsburgh" for three days? — Dan Savage, *Savage Love*, p. 216, 1998

2 a prosecuting attorney *US, 1992*

- I say, "Hey, you say that, we'll have to go to trial, because the PA ain't gonna negotiate that[.]" — Richard Price, *Clockers*, p. 450, 1992

pachook; pachuk *noun*

a pachuco *US, 1958*

- "I first joined the Pachuks—short of Pachucos—when I was stationed in California with the Navy." — Willard Motley, *Let No Man Write My Epitaph*, p. 207, 1958
- [D]ay in, day out goldtoothed pachooks scratching on its screen door hissing how they do for cooz. — Seth Morgan, *Homeboy*, p. 50, 1990

Pachuco *noun*

a young Mexican-American, especially a tough or gang member *US, 1943*

Characterized by a highly stylized fashion sense, a private language, and a rage against white oppression of the 1940s.

- [L]ike maybe Gonzalez the Mexican sort of bum or hanger-on sort of faggish who kept coming up to her place on the strength of some old friendship she'd had with some Tracy Pachucos[.] — Jack Kerouac, *The Subterraneans*, p. 43, 1958

pack *noun*

1 a *pack*age of illegal drugs, especially heroin *US, 1952*

Also variant "packet."

- — Richard Horman and Allan Fox, *Drug Awareness*, 1970
- I been feeling boogy ever since this morning. I didn't do but a five-dollar pack when I woke up. — Donald Goines, *Dopefiend*, p. 97, 1971

pack *verb*

1 (from the male point of view) to have sex with *US, 1947*

- "Are you packing her steady?" "Whenever I want." — Willard Motley, *Knock on Any Door*, p. 201, 1947

2 to carry a weapon, usually a concealed one *US, 1949*

- I'm packing no joint. — Hal Ellson, *Duke*, p. 2, 1949
- "This cat is packing a Saturday-night special," someone said. — Charles Whited, *Chiodo*, p. 60, 1973
- They're going to think you're packing something. — *Repo Man*, 1984
- He wouldn't be packing today, risk doing two years for nothing. — Elmore Leonard, *Glitz*, p. 175, 1985

3 to tuck the male genitals into the left or right pants leg *US, 1972*

- "[M]en in the armed forces are taught to pack it to the left, but you show more meat when you pack it to the right." — Bruce Rodgers, *The Queens' Vernacular*, p. 145, 1972

4 while snowboarding, to hit the snow hard *US, 1990*

- — Elena Garcia, *A Beginner's Guide to Zen and the Art of Snowboarding*, p. 122, 1990

5 to take someone along on a motorcycle cruise *US, 1966*

- On another occasion, Magoo was packing Mama Beverly on a run to Bakersfield when he ran out of gas. — Hunter S. Thompson, *Hell's Angels*, p. 171, 1966

▸ **pack a rod**

to carry a gun *US, 1940*

- "That John must have said I was packin' a rod to make hisself look good," Frankie guessed. — Nelson Algren, *The Man with the Golden Arm*, p. 327, 1949

▸ **pack double**

to carry a passenger on a motorcycle *US, 2000*

- Ernie and I had a couple of girls ("packing double"), and here I was stuck with a dead bike six hundred miles from home. — Ralph "Sonny" Barger, *Hell's Angel*, p. 30, 2000

▸ **pack fudge**

to play the active role in anal sex *US, 1987*

- He's been making a nice piece of change for himself by taking the wealthy swells of our clientele into a small sofa-filled room aside the projection booth and packing their fudge for prices only the kin of a true superstar can demand. — Jim Carroll, *Forced Entries*, p. 49, 1987

▸ **pack heat**

to carry a gun *US, 1930*

- You packing any heat, mister? — Mickey Spillane, *Last Cop Out*, p. 73, 1972

▸ **pack it in**

to retire, to quit *US, 1979*

- The day you don't feel a few butterflies in your tummy just before you go on stage, that's the time to pack it in. — Madeleine Brent, *The Capricorn Stone*, p. 207, 1979
- More often than not these days, Worden found himself talking seriously about packing it in. — David Simon, *Homicide*, p. 31, 1991

▸ **pack meat**

to recover and process the bodies of those killed in action *US, 1949*

- "Boy, am I tired," says one of the men. "We been packing meat all night. This guy got his dog tags?" — Audie Murphy, *To Hell and Back*, p. 137, 1949

▶ **pack the cracks**

to endure injections of collagen *US, 1997*

● — Anna Scotti and Paul Young, *Buzzwords*, p. 109, 1997

package *noun*

1 a corpse *US, 1951*

● "If they keep on pushing us around, we'll start leaving packages on every corner in Brooklyn." — Burton Turkus and Sid Feder, *Murder, Inc.*, p. 23, 1951

● "Harry, I didn't know there was a package in the car. You shoulda told me." — Charles Perry, *Portrait of a Young Man Drowning*, p. 255, 1962

2 a man's genitals as seen through pants *US, 1997*

● — Jeff Fessler, *When Drag Is Not a Car Race*, p. 53, 1997

3 a good-looking woman *US, 1945*

● — Lou Shelly, *Hepcats Jive Talk Dictionary*, p. 15, 1945

4 a sexually transmitted infection, especially gonorrhea *US, 1950*

● — Hyman E. Goldin et al., *Dictionary of American Underworld Lingo*, p. 151, 1950

5 AIDS or HIV *US, 2002*

● I wouldn't be associating with him if I were you. He's got the package. — Gary K. Farlow, *Prison-ese*, p. 48, 2002

pack horse *noun*

a person, usually a guard, who brings contraband into prison *US, 1984*

● — Inez Cardozo-Freeman, *The Joint*, p. 519, 1984

packie *noun*

a liquor store *US, 1973*

From states where liquor stores are known as "package stores."

● "I stopped at a packy and I bought three quarts of Beefeaters." — George Higgins, *The Digger's Game*, p. 204, 1973

● — Connie Eble (Editor), *UNC-CH Campus Slang*, p. 4, Fall 1991

pack in; pack up *verb*

to stop; to cease an activity; to retire *US, 1942*

● All croakers [doctors] "pack in" sooner or later. — William Burroughs, *Junkie*, p. 36, 1953

● Let's just pack it in an hour early. — *Heathers*, 1988

pad *noun*

1 an apartment or house; a room, especially a bedroom *US, 1938*

In the C18, "pad" referred to a bed. By the 1930s, it took on the new meaning and was spread by jazz musicians. Still heard, with a retro feel.

● Red Riding Hood opened the door, stepped inside and looked around the room. "Wowie," she said. "What a crazy pad." — Steve Allen, *Steve Allen's, Bop Fables*, p. 42, 1955

● Come in my pad, sport, look around. — Richard Farina, *Been Down So Long*, p. 21, 1966

● I quit working for this outfit when the bad shit that was coming down because too much to take—a friend of the theater-owner, whose apartment we were using to film a lez flick—attacked one of the other chicks as she was leaving the pad. — *The Berkeley Tribe*, p. 9, 22nd–28th August 1970

2 a bed *UK, 1718*

● You gotta have a date with me before you fall in my pad, darling. — Chester Himes, *If He Hollers Let Him Go*, 1945

● One day along about noon Frank Hitchcock yanked us all out of our pads and took us downstairs. — Mezz Mezzrow, *Really the Blues*, 1946

● A bed is now a pad. "I was in the pad when the phone rang." — *Philadelphia Evening Bulletin*, 11th October 1955

● "Climb out that pad, catman. It's past one o'clock and time to pick up." — Irving Shulman, *The Short End of the Stick*, p. 105, 1959

3 a prison cell *US, 1943*

● — Inez Cardozo-Freeman, *The Joint*, p. 519, 1984

4 the bribery paid by a criminal enterprise to police *US, 1970*

● The "pad" refers to regular weekly, bi-weekly, or monthly payments, usually picked up by a police bagman and divided among fellow officers. — *The Knapp Commission Report on Police Corruption*, p. 66, 1972

● He could hardly believe his ears, that Stanard would be so indiscreet about the existence of a "pad"—as the systematized police payoffs were called—that he could be that stupid. — Peter Maas, *Serpico*, p. 156, 1973

● A pad is what you're on when you're paying police not to do their job. — Leonard Shecter and William Phillips, *On the Pad*, p. 23, 1973

● How long do you think they can stand it without the pad? — Richard Condon, *Prizzi's Honor*, p. 218, 1982

▶ **on the pad**

bribed *US, 1971*

● Those who make such payments as well as policemen who receive them are referred to as being "on the pad." — *The Knapp Commission Report on Police Corruption*, p. 66, 1972

● And it seemed the lady needed some help. She wanted to go on the pad. — Leonard Shecter and William Phillips, *On the Pad*, p. 23, 1973

● Kept your mouth shut, right. Never made a wave. Kimo sabe, you was on the pad. — Edwin Torres, *Q & A*, p. 165, 1977

● It used to be a captain was on the pad, he let word filter down through the whole precinct that such and such a location was protected. — Vincent Patrick, *The Pope of Greenwich Village*, p. 38, 1979

pad *verb*

1 to reside *US, 1963*

● "And if you ain't got a pad any time, spote," he said, "you can pad there too." — John Rechy, *City of Night*, p. 43, 1963

● There's a cat in the Chicken Shack that knows where Ace is paddin at. — Charles W. Moore, *A Brick for Mister Jones*, p. 99, 1975

● He pads in the penthouse in my hotel. — Iceberg Slim (Robert Beck), *Airtight Willie and Me*, p. 161, 1979

2 (used of police) to add to the narcotics confiscated from a suspect in order to render the charge against them more serious *US, 1972*

● "[P]adding," or adding to the quantity of narcotics found on an arrested person in order to upgrade an arrest — *The Knapp Commission Report on Police Corruption*, p. 91, 1972

▶ **pad the ring**

in horseracing, to place many small bets on several horses in a race while placing a large bet on one horse away from the track, hoping that the small bets on other horses will drive the odds on your horse up *US, 1951*

● — David W. Maurer, *Argot of the Racetrack*, p. 49, 1951

paddle *verb*

▶ **paddle the pickle**

(of a male) to masturbate *US, 1967*

● — Dale Gordon, *The Dominion Sex Dictionary*, p. 117, 1967

paddlefoot *noun*

an infantryman *US, 1950*

● The shoe pac "paddlefoot shuffle" in the American infantry ranks that winter was often a sign, not just of dysfunctional bulk, but of numbed and frozen feet. — Richard Engler, *The Final Crisis*, p. 102, 1999

pad duty *noun*

sleeping *US, 1960*

● I was fresh from a lengthy rest and my squadron was scheduled for hot-pad duty. — Ed McGaa, *Rainbow Tribe*, p. 250, 1992

paddy *noun*

1 an Irish person *UK, 1780*

● Fuck me, if there's one thing we poor bloody Paddies should have learned, it is never to trust a British fucking leftie liberal bastard. — James Hawes, *Dead Long Enough*, p. 253, 2000

2 a white person *US, 1945*

● If it had come down to a point where I had to hit a paddy, I'd have hit him without any thought — Chester Himes, *If He Hollers Let Him Go*, p. 3, 1945

● We ought to beat the hell out of those paddies! — Ralph Ellison, *Invisible Man*, p. 268, 1947

● My friend Crutch had told me there were a lot of paddies out there, and they didn't dig Negroes or Puerto Ricans. — Piri Thomas, *Down These Mean Streets*, p. 81, 1967

● [S]he was in L.A. and she was tough and she wanted furniture and a paddy husband. Paddy means white in Pachuco. — Eve Babitz, *Eve's Hollywood*, p. 47, 1974

3 a police officer *US, 1946*

● I was made the lookout man and told to stick around out front with my eyes peeled for any signs of John Law. When a paddy showed himself I would tap on the window with a key, and in five seconds a billiard tournament was going full blast. — Mezz Mezzrow, *Really the Blues*, p. 20, 1946

● Every time I saw a paddy roll by in a car, I picked up one of the half-bricks, and threw it at the motherfuckers. — Bobby Seale, *Seize the Time*, p. 3, 1970

paddy *adjective*

white, Caucasian *US, 1967*

- "These niggers up here are harder on my ass than a hundred paddy cats." — John Williams, *The Man Who Cried I Am*, p. 172, 1967

paddy humping *noun*
taking part in an infantry march across rice paddies *US, 1978*
- "Nice, comfy painting job? No paddy humpin', no dinks." — Tim O'Brien, *Going After Cacciato*, p. 38, 1978

paddy hustler *noun*
a criminal who targets white people as victims *US, 1970*
- There's lesbians, masochists, hypes, whores, flim flammers, paddy hustlers, hugger muggers, ex-cons of all descriptions, and anybody else with a kink of some kind or other. — Joseph Wambaugh, *The New Centurions*, p. 174, 1970

paddy strength *noun*
in the Vietnam war, the combat strength of a unit, measured by the actual number of troops in the field *US, 1974*
- The medical research effort proved to be the most important single factor in increasing the paddy strength of the 9th Division. — House Committee on Government Operations, *Military Medical Health and Research*, p. 499, 1978

paddy wagon *noun*
a police transportation van *US, 1909*
- The Navy's shore patrol takes over most of the policing. We saw Navy paddy-wagons in front of Guy's, the Ship's Cafe and the Penguin. — Jack Lait and Lee Mortimer, *Washington Confidential*, p. 33, 1951
- I'm thinkin' about Neal, red neons, night, and instead, enroute home, get few beers in the wildest bar in America, corner 3rd and Howard, paddy wagon's there every hour[.] — Jack Kerouac, *Letter to John Clellon Holmes*, p. 338, 8th February 1952
- Three squad cars and a paddy wagon stood ready in the icy morning air[.] — Clarence Cooper Jr., *The Scene*, p. 126, 1960
- A Madera County paddy wagon was parked at the other end of the shopping center, with two cops in the front seat. — Hunter S. Thompson, *Hell's Angels*, p. 143, 1966

paddywood *noun*
a white person *US, 1980*
Not used kindly.
- — Edith A. Folb, *runnin' down some lines*, p. 249, 1980

padiddle *noun*
a car with only one headlight functioning *US, 1976*
A childish word for the childish activity of spotting cars with one broken headlight.
- — Elementary Electronics, *Dictionary of CB Lingo*, p. 91, 1976
- — Connie Eble (Editor), *UNC-CH Campus Slang*, p. 6, April 1997

padna *noun*
a close friend; a confederate in crime *US, 2007*
- Gaines denied killing Rivet, whom he called his "padna," street slang for partner. — *Times Picayune (New Orleans)*, p. Metro 1, 23rd August 2007

pad roll *noun*
a controlled roll of the dice by a skilled cheat, best made on a blanket spread on the ground *US, 1950*
- — The Annals of the American Academy of Political and Social Sciences, p. 128, May 1950

pad-roll *verb*
to roll dice in a controlled fashion *US, 1950*
So called because it can best be made on a blanket, rug, or other soft pad.
- — The Annals of the American Academy of Political and Social Sciences, p. 128, May 1950
- I could knock, shoot the turn down, or pad-roll. — Donald Goines, *Whoreson*, p. 28, 1972
- And by the time I was eleven / I could pad-roll seven. — Lightnin' Rod, *Hustlers Convention*, p. 6, 1973

pads *noun*
padding that enhances the apparent size of a female's breasts *US, 1945*
- Millions and millions of men were being deceived, hoodwinked, and betrayed by scientific gadgets known as "falsies," "gay deceivers," "pads," and "cheaters." — Earl Wilson, *I Am Gazing Into My 8-Ball*, p. 70, 1945

page *noun*
one thousand doses of LSD soaked into paper *US, 1999*
- A larger piece of paper consisting of ten unseparated sheets—a thousand hits, known as a "page"—is a unit commonly sold wholesale. — Cam Cloud, *The Little Book of Acid*, p. 34, 1999

pail *noun*
the stomach *US, 1945*
An abbreviation of "lunch pail" (a container).
- — Lou Shelly, *Hepcats Jive Talk Dictionary*, p. 15, 1945

pain in the ass *noun*
a great nuisance *US, 1934*
- "C'mon, let's get out here," I said. "You give me a royal pain in the ass, if you want to know the truth." — J.D. Salinger, *Catcher in the Rye*, p. 133, 1951
- My OCD rituals were beginning to become a real pain in the ass. — Howard Stern, *Miss America*, p. 105, 1995

pain in the net *noun*
a person who posts inflammatory attacks on Internet discussion groups *US, 1991*
- — Eric S. Raymond, *The New Hacker's Dictionary*, p. 273, 1991

paint *noun*
1 make up *UK, 1660*
- The school marm came back with a new coat of paint and a bedroom smile. — Iceberg Slim (Robert Beck), *Trick Baby*, p. 195, 1969
2 in card games, a face card or a ten *US, 1985*
- — Steve Kuriscak, *Casino Talk*, p. 41, 1985

paint *verb*
1 to apply make up *UK, 1382*
- [H]er brown hair was as tousled as a lamb's tail, and her unpainted face was drawn with sleep. — Jim Thompson, *The Killer Inside*, p. 8, 1952
- If you are (tell the truth!) the only girl your age within a fifty-mile radius who is not permitted to paint yourself as well as the town red, you have reason to gripe. — Dick Clark, *To Goof or Not to Goof*, p. 97, 1963
- Their women don't paint themselves. — Piri Thomas, *Down These Mean Streets*, p. 293, 1967
2 in lowball poker, to draw a face card to a hand of four low cards *US, 1967*
- — Albert H. Morehead, *The Complete Guide to Winning Poker*, p. 269, 1967
3 in hearts, to play a heart on a nonheart trick *US, 1987*
- — Thomas L. Clark, *The Dictionary of gambling and gaming*, 1987
4 to mark a target with laser beams *US, 1991*
Gulf war usage.
- — American Speech, p. 397, Winter 1991: "Among the new words"

▸ **paint the town red**
to have a raucous time on the town *US, 1884*
- Let's go out and paint old cow town red. — Jim Thompson, *The Killer Inside*, p. 83, 1952
- I drank liquor, smoked marijuana, painted the Big Apple red with increasing numbers of friends[.] — Malcolm X and Alex Haley, *The Autobiography of Malcolm X*, p. 78, 1964
- Yet there were thousands of girls living between Sunset and Santa Monica in between La Brea and La Cienega who painted the town red like me—and who got away with it. — Eve Babitz, *L.A. Woman*, p. 137, 1982

paint card *noun*
in a deck of playing cards, a Jack, Queen, or King *US, 1932*
- If you have this hand and everyone else has a paint card (face card), you have the best hand at that moment. — Andy Nelson, *Poker*, p. 23, 1996

painted pony *noun*
in circus and carnival usage, a zebra *US, 1981*
- — Don Wilmeth, *The Language of American Popular Entertainment*, p. 193, 1981

painter *noun*
a card cheat who marks cards for identification in another player's hand *US, 1993*
- — Frank Scoblete, *Guerrilla Gambling*, p. 320, 1993

pair *noun*
1 a pair of female breasts *US, 1957*
- She had a nice pair though. — Hubert Selby Jr., *Last Exit to Brooklyn*, p. 77, 1957
- Also she had the biggest pair at the Villa Monterey, even when they weren't pushed up by her kitty outfit. — Elmore Leonard, *Swag*, p. 44, 1976
- In Getting It Right (1989), she flashed her petite pair. — Mr. Skin, *Mr. Skin's Skincyclopedia*, p. 75, 2005

2 a pair of testicles, hence manliness or courage *US, 1985*

- You like real clangers? I'll show you a pair that gong like Big Ben! — Joseph Wambaugh, *The Secrets of Harry Bright*, p. 47, 1985
- I can't hear you! Sound off like you got a pair. — *Full Metal Jacket*, 1987

pair of panties *noun*
paragliding *US, 1992*
From the French term *parapente* (paragliding).

- — Erik Fair, *California Thrill Sports*, p. 335, 1992

paisan; paisano *noun*
an Italian-American; used as a term of address that evokes a common heritage, especially Italian *US, 1947*

- As I hung up, I spotted the two lean, tough-looking paisanos gazing at me cooped up in the booth. — Malcolm X and Alex Haley, *The Autobiography of Malcolm X*, p. 125, 1964
- Why the old lady? Why, paisan, the same reasons we killed the old man, baby, the same reason. — Donald Goines, *Black Gangster*, p. 80, 1977
- The maitre d' didn't shout, "You back again?" nor did the bartender holler, "What's your poison, paesan?" — Rita Ciresi, *Pink Slip*, pp. 88–89, 1999

pal *noun*
1 a close friend; used as a term of address, usually sarcastically *UK, 1681*
From the English, Turkish, and Transylvanian Romany tongues.

- Okay, pal, I accept the compliment. — *As Good As It Gets*, 1997

2 a studio musician *US, 1982*

- — Arnold Shaw, *Dictionary of American Pop/Rock*, p. 271, 1982

pal around *verb*
to associate with; to socialize with *US, 1879*

- All I know is that when I was a kid palling around with Mike, it never occurred to me that he was insensitive[.] — Jack Kerouac, *Letter to Neal Cassady*, p. 150, 7th May 1948
- After I'd gotten out of reception, Minetti and I started palling around, and we got tight. — Claude Brown, *Manchild in the Promised Land*, p. 142, 1965
- I was pal-ing around with a lot of wops from downtown and the west Bronx, younger guys like me, not the prejudiced old hoods. — Edwin Torres, *Carlito's Way*, p. 30, 1975

pale-face *noun*
when spoken by a black person, a white person *US, 1945*
From C18 American Indian usage.

- "Yes, I do like you palefaces," he said. — Max Shulman, *Anyone Got a Match?*, p. 60, 1964

pale, male, and stale *adjective*
used as a humorous description of many power elites *US, 1991*
A favorite phrase used by the pale and male leaders of the unions that broke away from the AFL-CIO in 2005 to describe the AFL-CIO.

- Outside their windows, life is browner, more feminine and spicier, but inside, newsrooms are too pale, too male, and often too stale. — *USA Today*, p. 13A, 12th April 1991

pally *noun*
a friend; a comrade *US, 1979*

- Pallies, damper the rapping! — Iceberg Slim, *Robert Beck Airtight Willie and Me*, p. 29, 1979

palm oil *noun*
a bribe *UK, 1627*

- — Joseph E. Ragen and Charles Finston, *Inside the World's Toughest Prison*, p. 811, 1962: "Penitentiary and underworld glossary"

palm shiner *noun*
in gambling, an object that reflects the image of cards, small enough to be held in the user's hand *US, 1997*

- The other was a "palm shiner," which he used when it wasn't his deal. It was a tiny, upside-down periscope. He could palm it, or hold it cupped in his hand on the green felt table, positioned so he could look down through the space between his fingers. — Stephen J. Cannell, *King Con*, p. 2, 1997

palm-warmer *noun*
a person who tips *US, 1951*

- The best palm-warmers are South American diplomats, who apparently have no regard for American money. — Jack Lait and Lee Mortimer, *Washington Confidential*, p. 133, 1951

palooka *noun*
a person who is mediocre at their craft *US, 1925*
Originally a boxing term.

- If you were some palooka sitting in the bleachers at a tournament, Cochran was the guy you would watch. — Robert Byrne, *McGoorty*, p. 169, 1972
- [L]ow man on the totem pole, a mere jog step above the palooka from the Bronx Home News — Bill Cardoso, *The Maltese Sangweech*, p. 281, 1984
- The Doll Theater, at Seventh and 48th, revolves around an emotionless palooka ramming his three-quarters hard-on into some broad's snatch atop a pink-spotlighted mattress tilted toward the audience. — Josh Alan Friedman, *Tales of Times Square*, p. 189, 1986

Palookaville *noun*
a notional, remote, boring town *US, 1980*

- [T]hey're lonely and homesick and they miss their little fuckin' girl friends back home in Palookaville. — Lucian Truscott, *Dress Gray*, p. 228, 1980
- I felt like I had just been handed a one-way ticket to Palookaville. — Pamela Des Barres, *I'm With the Band*, p. 153, 1988

palsy-walsy *adjective*
friendly, often with an undertone of insincerity *US, 1937*

- Only this afternoon his gin partner and palsy-walsy competitor Big Ernie had been convicted for wholesaling the main line stuff. — Morton Cooper, *High School Confidential*, p. 110, 1958
- I started shining up to Mother Jackson the best I could, trying to get palsy-walsy with him. — Joey V., *Portrait of Joey*, p. 149, 1969
- getting palsy-walsy with his fellow students to be invited to dinner and parties — Emmett Grogan, *Ringolevio*, p. 81, 1972
- [I]n other words, the world notes that sometimes we are palsy-walsy with the bad guys and sometimes we want to rip their lungs out, depending on which stance serves our perceived interests at the time. — *Milwaukee Journal Sentinel*, p. 4, 29th September 2002

pal up *verb*
to make friends *US, 1953*

- [B]ut to take me into his home—pal up with me—when there was any kind of a chance that I might mean trouble — Jim Thompson, *Savage Night*, p. 83, 1953

pamphlet *noun*
one ounce of a drug *US, 1976*

- Less than a pound, so smaller than a book. — Robert Sabbag, *Snowblind: A Brief Career in the Cocaine Trade*, p. 271, 1976

pan *noun*
the face *US, 1923*

- One day even Frankie Riccardi's pan jumped out at me. — Mezz Mezzrow, *Really the Blues*, p. 101, 1946

pan *verb*
to criticize something as unsuccessful *US, 1911*

- His novel was refused, his movie was panned / And his big Broadway show was a flop. — Loudon Wainwright III, *The Man Who Couldn't Cry*, 1973

Panama red; Panamanian red *noun*
a potent variety of marijuana cultivated in Panama *US, 1966*

- Panama Red is very good and so is Chicago Green. — *Washington Post*, pp. E1–E5, 21st August 1966: A New Drug Culture is Burgeoning
- "Gold. It's Acapulco Gold," White Rabbit corrected the doctor, who was mixing up the slang names for different kinds of marijuana. "I mean Panama Red," Goddard corrected himself[.] — Nicholas Von Hoffman, *We Are The People Our Parents Warned Us Against*, p. 23, 1967
- But when things get too confusing, honey / You're better off in bed / And I'll be searching all the joints in town for / Panama Red. — Peter Rowan (New Riders of the Purple Sage), *Panama Red*, 1971
- This is some of that Panama Red I've been saving for my exit smoke. — Odie Hawkins, *Men Friends*, p. 56, 1989

panatella *noun*
a marijuana cigarette; marijuana *US, 1944*

- About half an inch longer than mine and much thinner, and they called their product "panatella" — Mezz Mezzrow, *Really the Blues*, 1946
- The cigarettes come in three qualities: saras-fras, the cheapest kind, sold to thousands of school children at about ten cents each; the panatella, or messerole, retailed at twenty-five cents[.] — Jack Lait and Lee Mortimer, *New York Confidential*, p. 102, 1948

- "Jimmy's got the best panatella you ever smoked in your life." — Billie Holiday, *Lady Sings the Blues*, p. 44, 1956

P and P *noun*
in the military, a leave for rest and recreation *US, 2004*
Jocular.
- Commonly known as R&R in the military, or rest and relaxation, some called it P&P (Pussy and Popcorn), A&A (Ass and Alcohol). — Edmund Ciriello, *The Reluctant Warrior*, p. 254, 2004

P and Q *noun*
solitary confinement in prison *US, 1982*
Abbreviated "peace and quiet."
- — Ralph de Sola, *Crime Dictionary*, p. 110, 1982
- — William K. Bentley and James M. Corbett, *Prison Slang*, p. 11, 1992

pane *noun*
a dose of LSD on a tiny, clear gelatin chip *US, 1994*
A shortened form of WINDOWPANE.
- — US Department of Justice, *Street Terms*, October 1994

panel house *noun*
a brothel with sliding walls through which thieves steal from the clothes of customers *US, 1848*
- There are also "panel" houses. These work by having the woman help the man take his clothing off and place it in a certain position, probably over a convenient chair. While he is concentrating on thoughts other than his watch and money, a panel slides open, a dark hard comes through the opening and takes everything out of the pockets. — Jack Lait and Lee Mortimer, *New York Confidential*, pp. 98–99, 1948

panhandle *verb*
to beg *US, 1884*
- I get high drunk, drop money on floor, am panhandled, play Ruth Brown wildjump records among drunken alky whores. — Jack Kerouac, *Letter to John Clellon Holmes*, p. 338, 8th February 1952
- Shipped back to the United States for treatment, he had walked off the grounds of the Army hospital and panhandled his way south[.] — Clancy Sigal, *Going Away*, p. 233, 1961
- Panhandling really blows the mind when it's carried on by middle class drop-outs. — Abbie Hoffman, *Revolution for the Hell of It*, p. 34, 1968
- To panhandle man-to-man on the street in this country is a noble, liberating act. — Jerry Rubin, *Do It!*, p. 123, 1970

panhandler *noun*
a beggar *US, 1897*
- Squatting there on a pile of Sunday papers sat my big, red-hot date of the evening, Broadway Rose, the straggly-haired little queen of panhandlers. — Earl Wilson, *I Am Gazing Into My 8-Ball*, pp. 163–164, 1945
- Maybe a panhandler will try to mooch a quarter[.] — Jack Lait and Lee Mortimer, *New York Confidential*, p. 14, 1948
- He was a panhandler and a fruit. A disgrace to the Jewish race. — William Burroughs, *Junkie*, p. 68, 1953
- Chicago: invisible hierarchy of decorticated wops, small of atrophied gangsters, earthbound ghost hits you at North and Halstead, Cicero, Lincoln Park, panhandler of dreams[.] — William Burroughs, *Naked Lunch*, p. 11, 1957
- "I been a panhandler for ten years," he said. — Willard Motley, *Let No Man Write My Epitaph*, p. 73, 1958
- [T]he scattered junkies, the smalltime pushers, the teaheads, the sad panhandlers, the occasional lonely exiled nymphos haunting the entrance to the men's head[.] — John Rechy, *City of Night*, pp. 100–101, 1963

panic *noun*
1 a widespread unavailability of an illegal drug *US, 1937*
- Election is over and the panic is off. — George Mandel, *Flee the Angry Strangers*, p. 55, 1952
- And then if this really does turn out to be a real bad panic, well then too I'll—we'll—always have stuff. — James Mills, *The Panic in Needle Park*, p. 41, 1966
- Everything was going as good as could be expected, till the panic hit. There was a short go of heroin on account of some big wheeler-dealer with millions of dollars' worth of the stuff had gotten himself busted and this caused a bad shortage. — Piri Thomas, *Down These Mean Streets*, p. 202, 1967
- He puttin' out that weak shit like the panic was on or somethin'. — Nathan Heard, *Howard Street*, p. 117, 1968
- There's been a panic. Until this morning I couldn't cop [buy] any stuff [heroin]. — Iceberg Slim (Robert Beck), *Pimp*, p. 99, 1969

- A panic was on among the junkies. There were still a few people able to connect—but on the whole conditions were bad. — Herbert Huncke, *The Evening Sun Turned Crimson*, p. 84, 1980

2 a very good time *US, 1958*
- — *San Francisco News*, p. 6, 25th March 1958
- — Judi Sanders, *Faced and Faded, Hanging to Hurl*, p. 30, 1993

panic flip *noun*
in pinball, the premature activation of a flipper *US, 1977*
- — Bobbye Claire Natkin and Steve Kirk, *All About Pinball*, p. 113, 1977

panning *noun*
negative gossip *US, 1966*
- "Panning" is general derogatory gossip about an inmate when she is not physically present. — Rose Giallombardo, *Society of Women*, p. 110, 1966

pansy *noun*
a male homosexual; an effeminate man *UK, 1929*
- You want to get yourself down to London if you're a bloody pansy. They're all bloody pansies down there. — Geoff Brown, *I Want What I Want*, p. 71, 1966

pansy ass *noun*
a weak, effeminate man *US, 1976*
- "I can't hit this fuckin' thing no more," Jimmy said. "C'mon, pansy ass," Donald Ray complained. — William Brashler, *City Dogs*, p. 152, 1976

pansy-ass *adjective*
effeminate, weak *US, 1997*
- Son of a bitch pansy-assed stool-pusher. — *As Good As It Gets*, 1997
- [Andrew WK] loves kittens but hates "pansy-ass" music, cramming up to 90 studio tracks into his piledriver hedonist anthems. — *Uncut*, January 2002

pansy patch *nickname*
an area in west Hollywood, California, largely populated by homosexual men since the 1960s *US, 1971*
- When one thinks of gay ghettos across the country, his mind leaps to the Pansy Patch of West Hollywood[.] — John Francis Hunter, *The Gay Insider*, p. 172, 1971

pansy prattle *noun*
the snide remarks and witty insults characteristic of male homosexual banter *US, 1980*
- — *Maledicta*, p. 237, Winter 1980: "Lovely, blooming, fresh and gay: the onomastics of camp"

panther breath *noun*
strong, illegally manufactured whiskey *US, 1999*
- It is called corn liquor, white lightning, sugar whiskey, skully cracker, popskull, bush whiskey, stump, stumphole, 'splo, ruckus juice, radiator whiskey, rotgut, sugarhead, block and tackle, wildcat, panther's breath, tiger's sweat, Sweet spirits of cats a-fighting, alley bourbon, city gin, cool water, happy Sally, deep shaft, jump steady, old horsey, stingo, blue John, red eye, pine top, buckeye bark whiskey and see seven stars. — *Star Tribune (Minneapolis)*, p. 19F, 31st January 1999

panther juice *noun*
strong, homemade alcohol *US, 1960*
- Then I slurped it up like a hound laps pot likker, rolling the panther juice around on my tongue, smacking my lips over it. — Guy Owen, *The Flim-Flam Man and the Apprentice Grifter*, p. 40, 1972

panther piss *noun*
illegally manufactured, low quality alcohol *US, 1946*
- "That whiskey they make," said Dwody, "is really panther-piss. Two drinks of that will knock you on your ass like nothing you ever saw." — Thomas Heggen, *Mister Roberts*, p. 134, 1946
- Everywhere there were steam baths, massages, girls, Panther Piss, opium dens, souvenirs, clothes from India[.] — *Screw*, p. 5, 15th February 1971
- — Edith A. Folb, *runnin' down some lines*, p. 249, 1980

pantload *noun*
a great deal of something *US, 1968*
- — Collin Baker et al., *College Undergraduate Slang Study Conducted at Brown University*, p. 168, 1968

pants *noun*
1 sex *US, 1965*
- When one of Johnny's girls messed up on him—tried to hold back some money or gave somebody some pants and didn't get any

money—he sure was hard on them. — Claude Brown, *Manchild in the Promised Land*, p. 114, 1965

2 a male *US, 1966*

- — Rose Giallombardo, *Society of Women*, p. 210, 1966: Glossary of Prison Terms

▸ **get into someone's pants**

to seduce someone; to have sex with someone *US, 1952*

- I've been in more guys' pants than you could count. — George Mandel, *Flee the Angry Strangers*, p. 220, 1952
- He hoped to deflect her thoughts from the possibility of getting into her pants a bit again. — Earl Thompson, *Tattoo*, p. 473, 1974
- You know all you'd do is hump her leg for an hour and try to get in her pants. — *Mallrats*, 1995
- I threw my costume in his face and said, "You're always trying to get in my pants. Here's your chance." — Kathryn Leigh Scott, *The Bunny Years*, p. 81, 1998

pants *verb*

to pull someone's pants down as part of a prank or practical joke *US, 1989*

- They follow this by "pantsing" the Cowboys—pulling their pants down around their knees. — *Bill and Ted's Excellent Adventure*, p. 42, 1989
- Yeah, and who pantsed me at the tenth grade assembly in front of the world? — *Wayne's World 2*, 1993

pantsful *noun*

a great deal, especially of something bad *US, 1993*

A suggestion of a lot of excrement.

- All my stuff is gone. My parents think I'm a sicko. And the whole world knows I've got a crooked dick. Thanks a pantsful, Nick. — C.D. Payne, *Youth in Revolt*, p. 91, 1993

pants rabbits *noun*

pubic lice; body lice; fleas *US, 1949*

- — Vincent J. Monteleone, *Criminal Slang*, p. 171, 1949
- — Helen Dahlskog (Editor), *A Dictionary of Contemporary and Colloquial Usage*, p. 16, 1972

panty apples *noun*

the buttocks *US, 2005*

- She covers her muff, but we get an ass-tonishing shot of her naked panty-apples. — Mr. Skin, *Mr. Skin's Skincyclopedia*, p. 2, 2005

panty raid *noun*

a college fad in which male students invade the dormitories of female students, seizing underwear as trophies *US, 1952*

The practice and term faded quickly with the onset of 1960s culture.

- [L]ike breaking up a pantie raid on the girls' dorms by delivering an impassioned address on responsible citizenship to the nylon-maddened mob of boys. — Glendon Swarthout, *Where the Boys Are*, p. 19, 1960
- I am dubbed a "deranged anarchist" and Mr. Burke concludes the show with the suggestion that I stick to panty raids, which he says are "more constructive." — James Simon Kunen, *The Strawberry Statement*, pp. 64–65, 1968

panty-stretcher *noun*

a heavy woman *US, 1976*

Also recorded in UK usage.

- — Elementary Electronics, *Dictionary of CB Lingo*, p. 91, 1976

pantywaist *noun*

a weakling or coward; a homosexual man *US, 1936*

- And while the hot-shots were tough, the regulars were no panty-waists. — Jim Thompson, *Bad Boy*, p. 366, 1953
- When I first started going with girls, the guys in the gang called me a sissy and a pantywaist and like that[.] — Max Shulman, *I was a Teen-Age Dwarf*, p. 59, 1959
- There's them pantywaist Owenses with their lifted pinkies. — Max Shulman, *Anyone Got a Match?*, p. 6, 1964

pan up *verb*

to prepare a powdered drug for heating prior to injection *US, 1971*

- — Eugene Landy, *The Underground Dictionary*, p. 145, 1971

papal roulette *noun*

the rhythm method of birth control *US, 1967*

- Long in use by Catholics as the only church-approved contraceptive technique, rhythm has been facetiously called "Papal Roulette." — Jules Griffon, *Orgies American Style*, p. 24, 1967

paper *noun*

1 a free ticket for a performance *US, 1951*

- If we'd been playing to crowded houses the producer would swear on his children's bones that the house was almost all paper. — Ethel Waters, *His Eye is on the Sparrow*, p. 152, 1951

2 money *US, 1972*

- [W]hen the girl turned her head—bang—she had the paper [money] out of the drawer. — Harry King, *Box Man*, p. 71, 1972
- The bitch had to make fair paper, no matter how small a part she had on the program. — Donald Goines, *Never Die Alone*, p. 113, 1974
- You know, this "paper" [money] thing ain't gonna last forever. — Terry Williams, *The Cocaine Kids*, p. 89, 1989
- These bitches pop it for some paper. Pop that ass for some cash flow. — *Hustle and Flow*, 2004

3 personal identification papers *US, 1982*

- No running. No face jobs or new paper. — Richard Condon, *Prizzi's Honor*, p. 278, 1982

4 promotional literature produced as part of a telephone sales swindle *US, 1988*

- — Kathleen Odean, *High Steppers, Fallen Angels, and Lollipops*, p. 132, 1988

5 a free pass to a performance *UK, 1785*

- — Joe McKennon, *Circus Lingo*, p. 68, 1980

6 a check, securities *US, 1972*

- She is more upgraded, she knows how to pass paper [forged checks, credit cards], she knows the various houses to go to. — Christina and Richard Milner, *Black Players*, p. 95, 1972
- All the joints on 7th and 8th Avenues and up on Sugar Hill, Tad visited and passed out $1,600 worth of bad paper until he got so sick he had to go the hospital. — Babs Gonzales, *Movin' On Down De Line*, p. 50, 1975
- He was a con artist dealing in paper—a stocks-and-bonds type guy. — Joseph Pistone, *Donnie Brasco*, p. 54, 1987

7 a deck of cards that have been marked for cheating *US, 1977*

- — Robert C. Prus and C.R.D. Sharper, *Road Hustler*, p. 171, 1977: "Glossary of terms"
- — John Scarne, *Scarne's Guide to Modern Poker*, p. 286, 1979

8 heroin sold in a paper package; a folded paper containing any powdered drug *US, 1951*

- Like where to pick up a strip of benny or a paper of snow, or anything you want from the outside, if the price is right. — Thurston Scott, *Cure it with Honey*, p. 194, 1951
- Whenever a law needs money for a quick beer, he goes over by Lupita and waits for someone to walk out on the chance he may be holding a paper. — William Burroughs, *Junkie*, p. 101, 1953
- [A] little Negro girl roaming the shuffle restless street of winos, hoodlums, sams, cops, paper peddlers[.] — Jack Kerouac, *The Subterraneans*, p. 56, 1958

9 probation in lieu of a jail sentence; parole from prison *US, 1973*

- With his record, Chester didn't believe he'd get out on paper, but he didn't believe he'd get the same time that Willie got[.] — Donald Goines, *White Man's Justice, Black Man's Grief*, p. 127, 1973
- Marie had a habit of fucking with me late at night out in the streets because she knew I was on paper and couldn't stand to be picked up for cracking her head. — A.S. Jackson, *Gentleman Pimp*, p. 83, 1973
- — William K. Bentley and James M. Corbett, *Prison Slang*, p. 101, 1992

10 an underworld contract to have someone killed *US, 1983*

- Rick Masters has paper out on me. There's a price on my head so I asked to be put in protective custody. — Gerald Petievich, *To Live and Die in L.A.*, p. 151, 1983
- The point is, Parisi has paper on me and I'm dead, hon. — Gerald Petievich, *Shakedown*, p. 201, 1988

▸ **make paper**

to be released from jail on parole *US, 2002*

- — Jeffrey Ian Ross, *Behind Bars*, p. 190, 2002: Slammer Slang

paper *verb*

▸ **paper the house**

to fill an audience for a performance with people given free tickets *UK, 1859*

- Bernstein papered the house with business associates. — Gail Sheehy, *Passages*, p. 282, 1976
- Vince papered the house with the American servicemen, so the reaction is very much American. — *Herb's Wrestling Tidbits*, 21st May 1992
- We paper the house to assure against empty seats. The idea, keep a buzz going. — Elmore Leonard, *Be Cool*, p. 252, 1999

paper and plastic *noun*

in gambling, a combination of cash and betting chips *US, 1996*

A play on the grocery clerk's query to a customer—"Paper or plastic bag?"

- — John Vorhaus, *The Big Book of Poker Slang*, p. 28, 1996

paper boy *noun*
a drug dealer, especially a heroin dealer *US, 1970*
Because heroin is often sold in paper envelopes; punning on a newspaper delivery boy.

- — William D. Alsever, *Glossary for the Establishment and Other Uptight People*, p. 26, December 1970
- — US Department of Justice, *Street Terms*, October 1994

paper crime *noun*
a crime involving financial paper such as checks, bonds, securities, etc. *US, 1997*

- He'd made up his mind to forsake burglaries, car thefts and other property offenses in favor of forgeries, check kiting, and other so-called paper crimes, for which judges seldom dispensed state prison time. — Carl Hiaasen, *Lucky You*, p. 21, 1997

papered *adjective*
used of a stadium or an auditorium filled by people given free tickets *US, 1978*

- — Bill Shefski, *Running Press Glossary of Football Language*, p. 76, 1978

paper-hang *noun*
the passing of counterfeit money or forged securities *US, 1976*

- There's the blow-up bang and the paper-hang / Where some poor chump gets beat. — Dennis Wepman et al., *The Life*, p. 161, 1976

paper hanger *noun*
a criminal whose expertise is the use of fraudulent securities *US, 1954*

- "You're not a paper hanger, and you're not a small fry pusher, and you're not even a booster." — Evan Hunter, *The Blackboard Jungle*, p. 160, 1954
- The distrust felt toward paperhangers, for instance, is based on the nature of these offenses and on firsthand experience with the men who commit them. — *Saturday Evening Post*, p. 72, 6th October 1962
- These paper hangers—that's a disease, believe me. They have no control over themselves. — Harry King, *Box Man*, p. 83, 1972
- They grabbed a paper hanger in a bank. A broad. She's singing for a deal. — Gerald Petievich, *Money Men*, p. 140, 1981

paper laying *noun*
the passing of forged checks or checks drawn on insufficient funds *US, 1972*

- Paper laying [writing bad checks] today is done by the majority of thieves — Harry King, *Box Man*, p. 83, 1972

paper puncher *noun*
used as a jocular description of a handgun target shooter *US, 1957*

- — *American Speech*, p. 194, October 1957: "Some colloquialisms of the handgunner"

paper pusher *noun*
1 a bureaucrat; in the military, anyone with a desk job and not in combat *US, 1943*

- — Linda Reinberg, *In the Field*, p. 161, 1991

2 a person who places counterfeit money into circulation *US, 1981*

- He had learned to take the edge off the loneliness by working harder, meeting more paper pushers, pressing more strongly for the hundred-grand buys. — Gerald Petievich, *Money Men*, p. 9, 1981
- Hell, he had chased paper pushers and passers around the city for so long that few streets were unfamiliar to him. — Gerald Petievich, *The Quality of the Informant*, p. 16, 1985

papers *noun*
in prison, a person's background *US, 2000*

- A prospect's papers [background] had to be checked and approved by the group's leaders. — Bill Valentine, *Gangs and Their Tattoos*, p. 18, 2000

paper soldier *noun*
a rear-area military personnel who supported those in combat *US, 1990*

- — Gregory Clark, *Words of the Vietnam War*, p. 426, 1990

paper time *noun*
the additional years added to a prison sentence because of publicity surrounding the crime, criminal, and/or trial *US, 1962*

- — Joseph E. Ragen and Charles Finston, *Inside the World's Toughest Prison*, p. 811, 1962: "Penitentiary and underworld glossary"

paperwork *noun*
any alteration of playing cards as part of a cheating scheme *US, 1962*

- — Frank Garcia, *Marked Cards and Loaded Dice*, p. 263, 1962

papes *noun*
money *US, 2000*

- — *Ebony Magazine*, p. 156, August 2000: "How to talk to the new generation"

pappy *noun*
a father *UK, 1763*
A childish, rural ring.

- She were that teasing color of them half-chink gals that got white pappies. — Iceberg Slim (Robert Beck), *Trick Baby*, p. 50, 1969

pappy guy *noun*
an experienced if older veteran *US, 1956*

- Put the kids in with a few old pappy guys who still like to win and the combination is unbeatable. — Glenn Liebman, *Hockey Shorts*, p. 247, 1996

par *noun*
▸ **below par; under par**
less than average or less than projected *UK, 1767*
A term that migrated from conventional English into golf and then back into broader slang usage.

- I called him and told him Petey and I were under par. — Iceberg Slim (Robert Beck), *Death Wish*, p. 56, 1977

paracki *noun*
paraldehyde, an antiepileptic central nervous system depressant *US, 1974*

- "[H]e puts some of the paracki in the glass and some water and they sit there and they sip it." — George Higgin, *Cogan's Trade*, p. 19, 1974

parade *noun*
in a striptease show, the dancer's fully clothed walk across the stage before beginning to strip *US, 1945*

- In succession as the Flash or entrance; the Parade or march across the stage, in full costume; the Tease or increasing removal of wearing apparel; and the climactic Strip or denuding down to the G-String[.] — *Saturday Review of Literature*, p. 28, 18th August 1945: "Take 'em off!"

paradise stroke *noun*
a man's movement just before ejaculating *US, 1972*

- In order to let him penetrate deeper and directer for the paradise stroke, I lay over on my back with little silk pillow under my hips and my ankles over his shoulders[.] — Xaviera Hollander, *The Happy Hooker*, p. 173, 1972

parakeet *noun*
a Puerto Rican *US, 1962*

- — Anthony Romeo, *The Language of Gangs*, p. 21, 4th December 1962
- — David Claerbaut, *Black Jargon in White America*, p. 74, 1972

parallel *adjective*
lying down *US, 1982*
Hawaiian youth usage.

- — Douglas Simonson, *Pidgin to da Max: Hana Hou*, 1982

pard *noun*
partner *US, 1850*
A definite Western flavor; a highly affected shortening of "partner."

- What the hell, pard, you finally gone completely crazy or something? — *Drugstore Cowboy*, 1988
- What's happening, pard? — *Airheads*, 1994
- "Well, you just watch your pard operate," Leeds said, signaling the bartender for another round. — Joseph Wambaugh, *Floaters*, p. 113, 1996

pardner *noun*
used as a term of address, male-to-male *US, 1795*
Used with an intentional folksiness that harkens to cowboy movies.

- "You're quite a fly fisherman, pardner," he added. — Chester Gould, *Dick Tracy Meets the Night Crawler*, p. 12, 1945

parental units *noun*
your parents *US, 1982*

- — Connie Eble (Editor), *UNC-CH Campus Slang*, p. 6, Spring 1982
- The parental units called while you were out. — *Cruel Intentions*, 1999

parfait *noun*
a young male prisoner desired as a sexual object by other prisoners *US, 1975*
- — Miguel Pinero, *Short Eyes*, p. 125, 1975: Glossary of Slang

park *verb*
to engage in sexual foreplay in a parked car *US, 1968*
- — Collin Baker et al., *College Undergraduate Slang Study Conducted at Brown University*, p. 168, 1968
- — Helen Dahlskog (Editor), *A Dictionary of Contemporary and Colloquial Usage*, p. 16, 1972

▸ **park the ball**
in pool, to leave the cue ball roughly in the center of the table after an opening break shot *US, 1992*
- — Mike Shamos, *The Illustrated Encyclopedia of Billiards*, p. 167, 1993

parking lot *noun*
▸ **in the parking lot**
in gambling, without further funds *US, 1996*
- — John Vorhaus, *The Big Book of Poker Slang*, p. 24, 1996

parlay *verb*
to socialize at clubs, bars, or parties *US, 2000*
- — *Ebony Magazine*, p. 156, August 2000: "How to Talk to the New Generation"

parlor pink *noun*
a wealthy person who espouses socialist views from the safety of luxury *US, 1920*
- Born in Minneapolis in 1888, like many other parlor pinks, fellow-travelers, Communists and convicted perjurers, he attended Harvard Law School. — Jack Lait and Lee Mortimer, *Washington Confidential*, p. 104, 1951
- That showed that dirty parlor pink. — Robert Gover, *One Hundred Dollar Misunderstanding*, p. 99, 1961
- Besides, no man, not even a parlor pink, liked a girl who carried things around in old cream bottles stuffed into paper bags. — Mary McCarthy, *The Group*, p. 215, 1963

parole dust *noun*
fog *US, 1976*
A term coined at the San Quentin state penitentiary just north of San Francisco, where fog invites escape attempts.
- — John R. Armore and Joseph D. Wolfe, *Dictionary of Desperation*, p. 43, 1976

parsley *noun*
phencyclidine, the recreational drug known as PCP or angel dust *US, 1981*
Because one method of administration of the drug is to sprinkle it on parsley.
- — Ronald Linder, *PCP: The Devil's Dust*, p. 10, 1981

partied out *adjective*
exhausted from excessive party-going *US, 1992*
- Phil, you're partied out. — *Wayne's World*, 1992

partner *noun*
a very close associate who can be counted on in almost any situation *US, 1994*
- JULES: If Jimmie's ass ain't home, I don't know what the fuck we're gonna do. I ain't got any other partners in 818. — *Pulp Fiction*, 1994

partridge *noun*
a good-looking girl or woman *US, 1947*
- He ganders this partridge and goes right on the beam solid. — Harry Haenigsen, *Jive's Like That*, 1947

party *noun*
1 sex, especially with a prostitute *US, 1956*
A prostitute euphemism.
- "I couldn't hear the words, but they would come out to 'How about a little party, honey?'" — *Rogue for Men*, p. 45, June 1956
- I'm accustomed to being accosted with "Wanna have a party, Joe?" — *Screw*, p. 4, 24th November 1969
- The words used by the prostitute to describe her services are often ambiguous: "How about a date?" "Would you like to have a good time?" "Let's have a party." — *The Lively Commerce*, p. 41, 1971
- These were usually easy parties, cuz you'd have another girl helping you get the guy satisfied. — Sisters of the Heart, *The Brothel Bible*, p. 53, 1997
2 sex with more than one prostitute *US, 1973*
- "What's a party?" I'd say, "Two girls. Both of us at the same time." — Susan Hall, *Ladies of the Night*, p. 27, 1973

party *verb*
1 to have sex, especially with a prostitute and especially with more than two people involved *US, 1963*
- Stick around till this mob clears, babe; I'll party you like you never been partied before. — John Rechy, *City of Night*, p. 355, 1963
- The girl is still sitting by me and asks whether I've ever partied before. — Susan Hall, *Ladies of the Night*, p. 19, 1973
- I partied with one girl, one, and took home a dose. — Elmore Leonard, *Cat Chaser*, p. 25, 1982
- Several years ago, while I was on holiday with several girlfriends, tucked away at a seaside Florida bar, the hunky bartender poured us all vodka shots "on the house," and asked if we wanted to "party" after closing. "Define 'party,'" was my retort. — Nancy Tamosaitis, *net.sex*, p. 123, 1995
2 to use drugs *US, 1999*
- RICKY: Hey, do you party? LESTER: I'm sorry? RICKY: Do you get high? — *American Beauty*, 1999

par-ty!
used as an exhortation to relax and enjoy yourself *US, 1988*
The break between syllables is key.
- Hey guys, par-ty! — *Bull Durham*, 1988

party animal *noun*
a person dedicated to making merry and having a good time *US, 1997*
A creature born of the 1990s.
- I was more than game, since Bob's parents have a reputation as party animals. — Elissa Stein and Kevin Leslie, *Chunks*, p. 68, 1997
- "I am not a party animal," I had told her once, defensively. "Nano," she had replied [...] "you're not even a party vegetable." — Rhiannon Paine, *Too Late for the Festival*, p. 32, 1999

party central *noun*
an apartment or house where parties are frequently in progress *US, 1988*
- We had this little house in Santa Monica on Second Street which was Party Central. — Jay McInerney, *Story of My Life*, p. 52, 1988
- As usual, Golk Links was Party Central that day. — Ralph "Sonny" Barger, *Hell's Angel*, p. 107, 2000

party favors *noun*
drugs *US, 1989*
- — Pamela Munro, *U.C.L.A. Slang*, p. 64, 1989

party foul *noun*
a faux pas; a substantial breach of etiquette *US, 1993*
- — Connie Eble (Editor), *UNC-CH Campus Slang*, p. 4, Spring 1993
- — Ben Applebaum and Derrick Pittman, *Turd Ferguson & The Sausage Party*, p. 51, 2004

party girl *noun*
a prostitute *US, 1960*
- Whores are now "call girls," "party girls" or "company girls." Instead of visiting them, they come to see you. — Lee Mortimer, *Women Confidential*, p. 140, 1960

party hat *noun*
a condom *US, 1989*
- — Pamela Munro, *U.C.L.A. Slang*, p. 65, 1989

party hearty *verb*
to party in a diligent fashion *US, 1979*
The term is sometimes heard and spelled as "party hardy."
- As everyone "partied hearty" at New York, New York. — *New York Amsterdam News*, p. 28, 28 July 1979
- He waved as he popped the clutch. "You guys party hearty." — Robert Lipkin, *A Brotherhood of Outlaws*, p. 83, 1981
- "Celebrity Party, starring Sandra Bernhard, party hearty, be a party animal!" — Sandra Bernhard, *Confessions of a Pretty Lady*, p. 119, 1988
- Well, in spite of what you've heard, it is time to party! Party hearty! — *Wayne's World*, 1992

party lights *noun*
the colored, flashing lights on top of a police car *US, 1992*
- When I see those party lights, I know the party's over for me. — *San Francisco Chronicle*, p. C4, 26th December 1992
- — Bill Valentine, *Gang Intelligence Manual*, p. 130, 1995
- Any police car that flips on its party lights and accelerates is leaped upon by these news choppers[.] — *Houston Press*, 13th May 1999

party movie *noun*

a pornographic film made for and enjoyed by men *US, 1986*

- There are some movies called stag movies or party movies. These are not shown in regular theaters, but are shown in private homes or private parties or at club meetings. — *Final Report of the Attorney General's Report on Pornography*, p. 251, 1986

party nap *noun*

a nap taken in anticipation of a night of drinking and partying *US, 2004*

- — Ben Applebaum and Derrick Pittman, *Turd Ferguson & The Sausage Party*, p. 9, 2004

party on!

used as an encouragement for revelry *US, 1989*

- And ... party on, dudes. — *Bill and Ted's Excellent Adventure*, 1989
- Until then, good night and party on. — *Wayne's World*, 1992

party pack *noun*

a package of ten rolled marijuana cigarettes for sale in Vietnam during the war *US, 1991*

- — Gregory Clark, *Words of the Vietnam War*, p. 392, 1991

party pooper; party poop *noun*

a killjoy; a spoilsport *US, 1951*

- — *Newsweek*, p. 28, 8 October 1951
- The bastard. Making me look the party-pooper. — Clancy Sigal, *Going Away*, p. 358, 1961
- [A]n aural document of what happened when the greatest party poopers since Charles Manson went into overdrive. — *Pogo A Go Go*, 1993
- "Oh, don't be a party pooper," Donna said. — Jason Starr, *Lights Out*, p. 36, 2006

party reptile *noun*

an enthusiastic party-goer *US, 1986*

- — Levi Straus & Company, *Campus Slang—"Hot," "Hip" and "Wicked"*, p. 2, January 1986

pashpie *noun*

an attractive boy or girl *US, 1951*

Teen slang.

- — *Newsweek*, p. 28, 8th October 1951

pass *verb*

to seek acceptance as white because of fair skin coloring *US, 1933*

- I heard of many a cat passin' for white, but this is the first time I ever heard of a white man passin' for colored, and in jail too. — Mezz Mezzrow, *Really the Blues*, p. 312, 1946
- There is no way of calculating how many light-skinned citizens can and do "pass." — Jack Lait and Lee Mortimer, *Washington Confidential*, p. 34, 1951
- The boy (she always spoke of him as a boy) would be able to "pass." After perhaps two hundred years of outrace-breeding, after eight generations, there would be a child of her blood who could pass for white. — Jim Thompson, *The Kill-Off*, p. 48, 1957
- "This Loam," he say, "is one nigga ain't passin' nohow let me tell you." — Richard Farina, *Long Time Coming and a Long Time Gone*, p. 3, 1969

passenger *noun*

a member of a prison clique *US, 1989*

Formed from **CAR** a clique.

- — James Harris, *A Convict's Dictionary*, p. 36, 1989

passer *noun*

1 a person who places counterfeit money into circulation *US, 1981*

- He remembered searching the streets of Los Angeles years ago for a twenties passer with a star tattoo on the back of his right hand. — Gerald Petievich, *One-Shot Deal*, p. 226, 1981

2 a drug dealer *US, 1952*

- And I'll get Verger to bring some weed to your party. He's gotten an o.z. from a passer up on One Hundred and Twenty-fifth Street. — John Clellon Holmes, *Go*, p. 83, 1952

passers *noun*

dice that have been altered so as to roll a seven less often than normal *US, 1950*

- — *The Annals of the American Academy of Political and Social Sciences*, p. 129, May 1950

passion mark *noun*

a bruise caused by extended sucking *US, 1966*

- — Andy Anonymous, *A Basic Guide to Campusology*, p. 14, 1966

passion pit *noun*

a drive-in movie theater *US, 1951*

Teen slang.

- — *Newsweek*, p. 28, 8 October 1951
- The official name of an outdoor movie theater may be Starview, but the patrons will likely refer to it, because of the lovers attending, as the passion pit. — *American Speech*, p. 239, October 1957

passover party *noun*

a party where those who have been passed over for promotion drown their sorrows *US, 1998*

- — *Seattle Times*, p. A9, 12th April 1998: "Grunts, squids not grunting from the same dictionary"

passport *noun*

standing permission from a youth gang to enter the territory which they consider their "turf" *US, 1972*

- — David Claerbaut, *Black Jargon in White America*, p. 74, 1972

pasta *noun*

cocaine *US, 1984*

From "paste," a step in the production process.

- — R.C. Garrett et al., *The Coke Book*, p. 200, 1984

paste *noun*

1 finely crafted fake gems *US, 1950*

- — Hyman E. Goldin et al., *Dictionary of American Underworld Lingo*, p. 153, 1950

2 crack cocaine *US, 1994*

From an intermediary step in the production of crack.

- — US Department of Justice, *Street Terms*, October 1994

pasteboard *noun*

in horseracing, a dry track in good condition *US, 1971*

- That horse is a dud on pasteboard, she's strictly a mudlark. — *San Francisco Chronicle*, p. 54, 21st April 1971

pasties *noun*

decorative coverings for a female dancer's nipples *US, 1954*

- "Pasties"—adhesive coverings for breast points—sell at $1.50 a pair and up. — E.J. Abbot, *True Police Cases*, p. 5, 1954
- Pasties are used to cover the nipples. They can be plain or gaudy, large or small. — Lois O'Conner, *The Bare Facts*, p. 15, 1964
- [B]ush-league sex compared to L.A.; pasties here—total naked public humping in L.A. — Hunter S. Thompson, *Fear and Loathing in Las Vegas*, p. 41, 1971
- It's hard to believe Jackson's revealing finale was spontaneous, as under her breakaway leather bustier she was wearing what appeared to be a large sunburst pastie. — *Boston Globe*, p. F1, 3rd February 2004

pasture *noun*

a place where teenagers engage in various levels of sexual activity in parked cars at night *US, 1960*

- — *San Francisco Examiner*, p. III-2, 22 March 1960

▸ **out to pasture**

incarcerated *US, 1992*

- — William K. Bentley and James M. Corbett, *Prison Slang*, p. 28, 1992

pat *verb*

▸ **pat the pad**

to go to bed *US, 1955*

- Q: What will you do until then? A: I'm gonna flake out. Q: What? A: Pat the pad, sack out, lay in the sun — Max Shulman, *Guided Tour of Campus Humor*, p. 106, 1955

patch *noun*

1 a small community *US, 1997*

- — Amy and Denise McFadden, *CoalSpeak*, p. 10, 1997

2 a small piece of material covering a striptease dancer's vulva *US, 1973*

- — Sherman Louis Sergel, *The Language of Show Biz*, p. 160, 1973
- A small piece is sometimes used underneath a G-string so that when a stripper works strong, she can remove the G-string and then be "in the patch." — Don Wilmeth, *The Language of American Popular Entertainment*, p. 197, 1981

3 in computing, a temporary modification of code to repair an immediate problem *US, 1991*

- — Eric S. Raymond, *The New Hacker's Dictionary*, p. 275, 1991

4 in the circus or carnival, the person who adjusts legal problems *US, 1952*

- The "patch"—our legal adjuster—had taken care of everything as far as Johnny Law went. — Charles Hamilton, *Men of the Underworld*, p. 178, 1952
- — Joe McKennon, *Circus Lingo*, p. 68, 1980

5 an ad hoc payment to a police officer to allow a crime to take place *US, 2001*

- I think you're involved with the wrong people, vice or drugs ... some other street action. You were taking a "patch" and you took too much. — Stephen J. Cannell, *The Tin Collectors*, p. 193, 2001

6 the proceeds of a crime, confiscated, and kept by corrupt police in lieu of arrest *US, 1987*

- Instead of busting him, they took his supply as a patch or payoff and said good-bye. It was the beginning of a lot of patches for dope dealers after that. — Thomas Renner and Cecil Kirby, *Mafia Enforcer*, p. 75, 1987

patch *verb*

in carnival and circus usage, to adjust a legal problem, especially through bribes *US, 2005*

- To make that possible, Double-O paid off (or "patched") every police chief or county sheriff where Party Time Shows put down stakes. — Peter Fenton, *Eyeing the Flash*, p. 67, 2005

patched *adjective*

thirsty *US, 1968*

- — *Current Slang*, p. 10, Summer 1968

patch money *noun*

in a carnival, the money paid by concession operators to the "patch" or "fixer" for adjusting legal problems *US, 1985*

- — Gene Sorrows, *All About Carnivals*, p. 24, 1985: "Terminology"

patico *noun*

crack cocaine *US, 1994*

Spanish slang used by English-speakers who would not know what the word means in Spanish.

- — US Department of Justice, *Street Terms*, October 1994

patient zero *noun*

the first person to transmit a disease *US, 1987*

Usually used in the context of AIDS.

- Dubbing Dugas "Patient Zero," researchers for the federal Centers for Disease Control retraced his sexual exploits as he traveled throughout North America[.] — *Associated Press*, 6th October 1987

patoot *noun*

the vagina *US, 1974*

- Anyways, I get this knife an' some bread and I stuck the knife up her ol' patoot, got a nice gob of clam squirt, an' I spread it on the bread. — Richard Price, *The Wanderers*, p. 37, 1974

patootie *noun*

1 a boy's girlfriend *US, 1918*

- "Oh Olive Oyl, you is my sweet patootie." — Richard Matheson, *I Am Legend*, p. 197, 1995

2 the buttocks *US, 1967*

- "You're supposed to dress just like the troops or you'll get pinked in the patootie faster." — Elaine Shepard, *The Doom Pussy*, p. 20, 1967
- Dammit, if you're going to get a wild hair up your Mexican patootie every time I make a comment about something that's going on, I'm not even going to talk to you — Robert Campbell, *Juice*, p. 82, 1988

patsy *noun*

1 a dupe; someone blamed for a crime or accident *US, 1903*

Perhaps the most famous maybe-patsy of the C20 was Lee Harvey Oswald, who told reporters shortly before being killed: "They're taking me in because of the fact that I lived in the Soviet Union. I'm only a patsy."

- Supposed somebody took you for a patsy. What would you do? — Mickey Spillane, *Kiss Me Deadly*, p. 26, 1952
- We know they used you as a patsy, a fall guy — Edwin Torres, *Carlito's Way*, 1975
- At least I still have my money and a designated patsy to take the rap for grand theft. — C.D. Payne, *Youth in Revolt*, 1993
- We needed Brent, Justice! He was our patsy! — Kevin Smith, *Jay and Silent Bob Strike Back*, p. 47, 2001

2 in poker, a hand that requires no draw *US, 1988*

Conventionally known as a "pat hand."

- — George Percy, *The Language of Poker*, p. 65, 1988

patzer *noun*

an unskilled chess player *US, 1948*

- [H]e was just annoyed that a patzer could become influential in the chess world just because he was famous for something else. — J.C. Hallman, *The Chess Artist*, p. 320, 2003

pause *verb*

▸ **pause for a cause**

to pull off the highway to use a toilet *US, 1977*

- — Bill Davis, *Jawjacking*, p. 73, 1977

pave knife *noun*

a laser-guided bombing system *US, 1971*

- PAVE KNIFE system—I hate to keep using these terms but they do get tied up with the system. The PAVE KNIFE system will be that system. — Senate Armed Services Committee, *Investigation into Electronic Battlefield Program*, p. 159, 1971
- — Karl Eschmann, *Linebacker*, p. 271, 1989: Glossary

pavement-pounder *noun*

a prostitute who solicits customers on the street *US, 1960*

- The Mayfair pavement-pounders were the class of the crop. — Lee Mortimer, *Women Confidential*, p. 178, 1960

pavement princess *noun*

a prostitute, especially one who works at truck stops *US, 1977*

- The "pavement princess" is out there doing her "thing," also — Gwyneth A. "Dandalion" Seese, *Tijuana Bear in a Smoke 'Um Up Taxi*, p. 75, 1977
- All Glad's pavement princesses dress so comely in the most delicate silks from China, fine lace from France, and degenerate leather from Germany. — J.T. LeRoy, *Sarah*, pp. 1–2, 2000

paw *noun*

the hand *UK, 1605*

- He stuck out a skinny paw and me and I took it. — Mickey Spillane, *I, The Jury*, p. 45, 1947
- When nightclubbing, keep your paw off your lady friend's leg. There's a time and place for everything. — Jack Lait and Lee Mortimer, *New York Confidential*, p. 220, 1948
- Dynamite, baby, but get your paws out of my pocket. — Richard Farina, *Been Down So Long*, p. 119, 1966

paws up *adjective*

dead *US, 1997*

New York police slang.

- There is always a lot of second-guessing following a job where the EDP and some of his hostages end up "paws up." — Samuel M. Katz, *Anytime Anywhere*, p. 336, 1997

pay *noun*

a debtor *US, 1989*

- He knew how to convince a slow pay to come up with what was owed. This one was different, a one-shot deal, but based on the same idea: scare the guy enough and he'll pay every time. — Elmore Leonard, *Killshot*, p. 50, 1989

pay *verb*

▸ **get paid**

to commit a successful robbery *US, 1987*

- — Carsten Stroud, *Close Pursuit*, p. 272, 1987
- — *Philadelphia Inquirer*, p. C3, 12th May 1991

▸ **pay the bills**

to stab someone *US, 1975*

- — Report to the Senate, *California Senate Committee on Civil Disorder*, p. 227, 1975

▸ **pay the rent**

(said of police) to meet a quota for tickets written *US, 1995*

- Paying the rent: For police officers, the handing out of a certain number of traffic summonses and moving violations. — Samuel Katz, *NYPD*, 1995

▸ **pay your dues**

to persevere through hardship *US, 1956*

- He'd kicked his habit. He'd paid his dues. — James Baldwin, *Blues for Mister Charlie*, p. 123, 1964
- He [John Tower] spent twenty-eight years in Washington, but he never paid his dues. — Hunter S. Thompson, *Songs of the Doomed*, p. 268, 6th March 1989

pay and lay *noun*

used for describing the exchange of payment and services involved in prostitution *US, 1969*

- I heard Bessie running bath water and I couldn't help wondering if Railhead was just another pay and lay customer like the pullman porters. — Iceberg Slim (Robert Beck), *Mama Black Widow*, p. 166, 1969

pay ball *noun*
in pool, a shot that, if made, wins a wager *US, 1993*
- — Mike Shamos, *The Illustrated Encyclopedia of Billiards*, p. 168, 1993

payday pussy *noun*
a visit with a prostitute on a working man's payday *US, 1969*
- It's what I call payday pussy. — Juan Carmel Cosmes, *Memoir of a Whoremaster*, p. 122, 1969

pay-for-play *noun*
sex that is paid for *US, 1969*
- Outside of the bar scene, most S&M scenes are pay-for-play affairs. — *Screw*, p. 8, 24th November 1969

pay lawyer *noun*
a privately retained lawyer, as contrasted with one provided for indigents by the state *US, 1992*
- Where'd I see this blond bitch before, maybe thinking he was a pay lawyer, because he was well groomed and looked like long money. — Richard Price, *Clockers*, p. 93, 1992

payola *noun*
an illegal payment to a radio station or individual to encourage the playing of a particular song *US, 1938*
The word leapt into the American vocabulary in late 1959 as pay-off scandal after pay-off scandal toppled the first generation of rock 'n' roll disc jockeys. Later broadened to include other forms of bribery.
- — Arnold Shaw, *Lingo of Tin-Pan Alley*, p. 16, 1950
- — *American Speech*, pp. 104–116, May 1961: "Payola"
- If she really liked the record she might hustle it with a little extra effort, but without ever getting hyper about it. Any payola arrangements, if they were made, were left to Artie. — Elmore Leonard, *Touch*, p. 22, 1977

pay school *noun*
a school charging a tuition fee *US, 1992*
- Peanut was being cool and funny with Strike sitting there, but Peanut went to Catholic pay school, his mother was a working woman, and he was scared of her. — Richard Price, *Clockers*, p. 11, 1992

payware *noun*
commercially available computer software *US, 1991*
- — Eric S. Raymond, *The New Hacker's Dictionary*, p. 276, 1991

PB *nickname*
Pacific Beach, San Diego, California *US, 1993*
- The main street of Pacific Beach, or "P.B.," as the locals called it, fed right onto the pier, under a two-story arch that joined two whitewashed, tealshingled buildings belonging to the Crystal Pier Hotel. — Joseph Wambaugh, *Finnegan's Week*, p. 148, 1993

PB and J *noun*
a peanut butter and jelly sandwich *US, 1981*
A culinary staple of American youth for decades.
- — Connie Eble (Editor), *UNC-CH Campus Slang*, p. 5, Fall 1981
- PB & J with the crusts cut off. Well, Brian, this is a very nutritious lunch, all the food groups are represented. — *The Breakfast Club*, 1985

PC *noun*
1 protective custody *US, 2002*
- The minors went to yard with the "PC" niggas. — Earl "DMX" Simmons, *E.A.R.L.*, p. 122, 2002

2 a latex finger glove used during digital examinations *US, 1958*
A "pinkie cheater."
- "Good Lord!" said Krankeit exasperated. "If you're going to poke your finger into that girl every three minutes you could at least put a p.c. on." — Terry Southern, *Candy*, p. 97, 1958
- — *American Speech*, p. 201, Fall–Winter 1973: The Language of Nursing

3 probable cause to arrest someone *US, 1995*
- You're a known hijacker. You're sweating like a guilty motherfucker. That's my P.C. — *The Usual Suspects*, 1995

4 a percentage *US, 1956*
Applied to drug sales.
- — Terry Williams, *Crackhouse*, p. 150, 1992

PC *adjective*
politically correct *US, 1986*
Originally used of left-on-left criticism, appropriated and exploited by the right to marginalize any and all dissent from the left.
- — Connie Eble (Editor), *UNC-CH Campus Slang*, p. 7, Spring 1991
- I know not to dick with him when it comes to matters PC. — Armistead Maupin, *Maybe the Moon*, p. 163, 1992
- C'mon. Don't get all p.c. on me. — *Chasing Amy*, 1997

PCH *nickname*
the Pacific Coast Highway, US route 1 in Los Angeles *US, 1947*
- So I dug the loaner out of the motel lot, found a pay phone on P.C.H. and gave old Cal a buzz. — James Ellroy, *Brown's Requiem*, p. 220, 1981
- — Trevor Cralle, *The Surfin'ary*, p. 86, 1991

PCOD *noun*
pussy cut-off date *US, 1991*
When soldiers were returned to the US from the war in Vietnam, they were tested for sexually transmitted diseases. To be sure that any problems were identified and cured before that test, most stopped having sexual relations before the end of their rotation to avoid any delay in returning home.
- "Add ten days for the symptoms to show; and that's PCOD. No screwing around after that." — David Poyer, *The Med*, p. 89, 1991
- This was the PCOD, or pussy cut-off date. As one's DEROS approached, one was best advised to stop sampling the local talent. — David Holland, *Vietnam, A Memoir*, p. 36, 2005
- In the lexicon of army contractions, initializations, and slang there was that one mentioned in Michael Casey's poem "Syphilis and Fort Lewis," The VNPCOD (Vietnam Pussy Cut-off Date). — Dean Muelberg, *Remf War Stories*, p. 164, 2005

P'cola *abbreviation + noun*
Pensacola, Florida, home to a naval air station known as the "cradle of Navy aviation" *US, 1991*
- He had tried the old "We who are about to ..." line and failed. The blonde had been around P'cola too long and had heard that bullshit too often. — Gerry Carroll, *North S*A*R*, p. 40, 1991

PCP *noun*
phencyclidine, an anesthetic agent abused recreationally for its dissociative effect *US, 1969*
- PCP is an animal tranquilizer and anesthetic. — James Gamage, *Management of Adolescent Drug Misuse*, p. 115, 1973
- He was often high on PCP, or happy stick, a potent hallucinogen that could cause disorientation[.] — Alex Kotlowitz, *There Are No Children Here*, p. 232, 1991
- She takes PCP and jumps out the school window, falls two stories, gets up, runs around, dies. — Dave Eggers, *A Heartbreaking Work of Staggering Genius*, p. 250, 2001

PDA *noun*
a public display of affection *US, 1968*
- — *Current Slang*, p. 5, Spring 1968
- — Helen Dahlskog (Editor), *A Dictionary of Contemporary and Colloquial Usage*, p. 43, 1972

pea *noun*
1 in pool, a small tally ball used as a scoring device *US, 1993*
- — Mike Shamos, *The Illustrated Encyclopedia of Billiards*, p. 168, 1993

2 a bullet *US, 1988*
- [B]ecause if they dared do anything else they'd been warned they'd get a couple of peas each in their heads[.] — Robert Campbell, *Juice*, p. 287, 1988

pea brain *noun*
a person lacking common sense, intelligence or both *US, 1950*
- Their opinion of this character happily coincided with ours—that he was a pea brain who needed a lesson in manners[.] — Jim Thompson, *Bad Boy*, p. 345, 1953

peacenik *noun*
a person who is opposed to war or a war *US, 1963*
- I am a peacenik, but the endeavors of the many peacenik organizations with which I am associated look more and more like prayer wheels whirling in front of a bursting dam. — *Bulletin of the Atomic Scientists*, pp. 21–22, September 1963
- [A]nd toughs out after peaceniks to beat up[.] — Nicholas Von Hoffman, *We Are The People Our Parents Warned Us Against*, p. 53, 1967

He probably thought I was a peacenik intellectual disloyal commie, but if so I was a peacenik intellectual disloyal commie with two dollars for him, and that's what counts. — James Simon Kunen, *The Strawberry Statement*, p. 92, 1968

peace out
used as a farewell *US, 1992*
- — Connie Eble (Editor), *UNC-CH Campus Slang*, p. 7, Spring 1992
- — Julian Johnson, *Urban Survival*, p. 258, 2003

peace pill *noun*
a combination of the hallucinogen LSD and the stimulant methedrine *US, 1971*
- — Eugene Landy, *The Underground Dictionary*, p. 146, 1971

PeaCe Pill; peace *noun*
phencyclidine, the recreational drug known as PCP or angel dust *US, 1977*
A rather clumsy back-formation from the initials.
- — *Drummer*, p. 77, 1977
- — Ronald Linder, *PCP*, p. 10, 1981

peace tab *noun*
a tablete of psilocybin, a mushroom-based hallucinogen *US, 1971*
- — Eugene Landy, *The Underground Dictionary*, p. 147, 1971

peace up *verb*
to reconcile differences *US, 2002*
- After the battle, Bill got on the mic and started talking about unity. Now he wanted the two of us to peace up. — Earl "DMX" Simmons, *E.A.R.L.*, p. 144, 2002

peaceweed *noun*
phencyclidine, the recreational drug known as PCP or angel dust *US, 1981*
- — Ronald Linder, *PCP: The Devil's Dust*, p. 10, 1981

peach *noun*
1 an excellent person or thing *UK, 1863*
- Look, Charlotte, you've been a peach and I really mean that. — Darryl Ponicsan, *The Last Detail*, p. 106, 1970

2 the vagina *US, 1997*
- — Pamela Munro, *U.C.L.A. Slang*, p. 95, 1997

3 a tablet of amphetamine sulfate (trade name Benzedrine™), a central nervous system stimulant *US, 1967*
- — John B. Williams, *Narcotics and Hallucinogenics*, p. 115, 1967
- — *Current Slang*, p. 37, Fall 1968

peachy *adjective*
good, pleasing, attractive *UK, 1926*
If used at all, used with irony.
- Some people can be content / Playing Bingo and paying rent / That's peachy for some people. — Stephen Sondheim, *Some People*, 1960
- "Just peachy-keen, Harry baby," said Ira. "Just tickety-boo." — Max Shulman, *Anyone Got a Match?*, p. 19, 1964
- Next thing you know he'll find you keen and peachy, you know? — *Annie Hall*, 1977

peachy-keen *adjective*
excellent *US, 1960*
- [E]verything was going to be peachy keen down here in Dixie[.] — Sandra Brown, *Breath of Scandal*, p. 289, 1991

peacocky *adjective*
used of a racehorse, high-headed *US, 1976*
- — Tom Ainslie, *Ainslie's Complete Guide to Thoroughbred Racing*, p. 335, 1976

pea-eye *noun*
an English-speaking person from Canada's Maritime Provinces *US, 1975*
From, if awkwardly, "Prince Edward Island."
- — John Gould, *Maine Lingo*, p. 43, 1975

peahead *noun*
a fool *US, 1960*
- "Young man—peahead— you're not going to do anything of the kind." — Harold Keith, *Forty-Seven Straight*, p. 304, 1984

peak freak *noun*
a casino blackjack gambler who consistently tries to see the dealer's down card *US, 1981*

- — Ken Uston, *Million Dollar Blackjack*, p. 320, 1981
- — Michael Dalton, *Blackjack*, p. 67, 1991

peanut *noun*
a capsule of a barbiturate or other sedative *US, 1967*
- — John B. Williams, *Narcotics and Hallucinogenics*, p. 115, 1967

peanut butter *noun*
low quality, impure amphetamine *US, 1989*
- — Geoffrey Froner, *Digging for Diamonds*, p. 47, 1989

peanut gallery *noun*
the least expensive seats in a theater; more abstractly, an audience *US, 1888*
- Colored people could buy seats only in the peanut gallery in B.F. Keith's Alhambra Theater[.] — Ethel Waters, *His Eye is on the Sparrow*, p. 124, 1951
- Again the peanut gallery responded with nods. — Joseph Nazel, *Black Cop*, p. 96, 1974

peanut grifter *noun*
a small-time swindler *US, 1953*
- You're a piker, Marlowe. You're a peanut grifter. You're so little it takes a magnifying glass to see you. — Raymond Chandler, *The Long Goodbye*, p. 64, 1953

peanut heaven *noun*
the uppermost gallery in a theater or arena *US, 1946*
- It was fifteen minutes from the time Siki left his roost in Peanut Heaven, where for two hours his noisy Harlem admirers had been calling the crowd's attention to him, before he reached the ring. — James Fair, *Give Him to the Angels*, p. 89, 1946

peanut poker *noun*
poker played for very small stakes *US, 1988*
- — George Percy, *The Language of Poker*, p. 65, 1988

peanuts *noun*
a very small sum of money *US, 1934*
- I'd worked for those people for peanuts, and I'd have stolen from myself quicker than I would have from them. — Jim Thompson, *Savage Night*, p. 121, 1953
- Unlike the big-con operator, whose elaborate scene-setting may involve as much as a hundred thousand dollars, the short-con grifter can run on peanuts. — Jim Thompson, *The Grifers*, p. 22, 1963
- Real estate was going for peanuts in those days. That's the only way to describe it. Peanuts. — Edward Lin, *Big Julie of Vegas*, p. 68, 1974
- "Mom says $800 a month. Can you handle that, Nick?" "Peanuts, Frank." — C.D. Payne, *Youth in Revolt*, p. 466, 1993

peanut whistle *noun*
used as the epitome of cheapness and low quality *US, 1995*
- So all of a sudden, this peanut whistle, semi-worthless station was churning some real heavy money. — Wolfman Jack (Bob Smith), *Have Mercy!*, p. 86, 1995

pearl *noun*
1 an ampule of amyl nitrite *US, 1971*
- — Eugene Landy, *The Underground Dictionary*, p. 147, 1971

2 cocaine *US, 1984*
- — R.C. Garrett et al., *The Coke Book*, p. 200, 1984

pearl dive *noun*
when surfing, an occasion when you are forced deep under the water by a wave *US, 1957*
- [O]n Malibu Mac's how to get out of a "boneyard" when you're caught in the middle of a set of breakers—and on Scooterboy Miller's hot rod I learned how to avoid a pearl dive. — Frederick Kohner, *Gidget*, p. a, 1957

pearl diving *noun*
oral sex *US, 1949*
- — Vincent J. Monteleone, *Criminal Slang*, p. 173, 1949
- One orally ambidextrous boyfriend specialized in pearl diving. — Anka Radakovich, *The Wild Girls Club*, p. 130, 1994

pearlies *noun*
the teeth *UK, 1914*
A shortened form of **PEARLY WHITES**. Also variant "pearls."
- I see beginnings of bad congestion at the corners of her pearlies which would lead to decay[.] — Jack Kerouac, *The Subterraneans*, p. 69, 1958

- Since the bathroom was down the hall, Taggarty (now clothed provocatively in pale green babydolls) stood guard outside the door as Vijay and I leaned over the grungy sinks and brushed our pearlies. — C.D. Payne, *Youth in Revolt*, p. 193, 1993

pearl necklace *noun*

semen ejaculated on a woman's throat and breasts, especially after penis—breast contact *US, 1984*

- — Brigid Mconville and John Shearlaw, *The Slanguage of Sex*, p. 151, 1984
- — J.R. Schwartz, *The Official Guide to the Best Cat Houses in Nevada*, p. 165, 1993: Sex Glossary
- In the indoor sex trade, too, such safer sexual activities as massage, hand release, pearl necklace, and fantasy stimulation are common. — Wendy Chapkis, *Live Sex Acts*, p. 170, 1997
- Pearl necklace: stick you penis between her breasts and go to town (use plenty of lube). — Jamie Goddard, *Lesbian Sex Secrets for Men*, p. 46, 2000
- But she said she was familiar with the pearl necklace and agreed that in porn, women seemed to enjoy the facials. — *New York Observer*, p. 2, 26th January 2004

pearly gates *noun*

morning glory seeds, rumored to have hallucinogenic powers *US, 1971*

- — Eugene Landy, *The Underground Dictionary*, p. 147, 1971

pearly whites *noun*

the teeth *US, 1935*

- Nothing's sexier than a mouthful of pearly whites. — *Something About Mary*, 1998

peasant *noun*

in circus and carnival usage, a customer who does not show proper appreciation for a performance *US, 1981*

- — Don Wilmeth, *The Language of American Popular Entertainment*, p. 197, 1981

peashooter *noun*

1 a small-caliber handgun *US, 1950*

- — Hyman E. Goldin et al., *Dictionary of American Underworld Lingo*, p. 154, 1950
- We were carrying those peashooters like you got. — Joseph Wambaugh, *The Choirboys*, p. 49, 1975

2 a rifle, especially one with a small caliber *US, 1960*

- "Nice pea-shooter," grinned the figure, smothering Holly's gun hand in a turnip-sized fist. — Eoin Colfer, *Artemis Fowl*, p. 74, 2001

pebble *noun*

a piece of crack cocaine *US, 1989*

The **ROCK** metaphor used again; the plural means crack generally.

- — Terry Williams, *The Cocaine Kids*, p. 137, 1989
- — US Department of Justice, *Street Terms*, October 1994
- Crack is also known as PEBBLES, SCUD, WASH, STONE and ROCK[.] — Macfarlane, Macfarlane and Robson, *The User*, p. 112, 1996

peck *noun*

a poor white Southerner; any white person *US, 1924*

A shortened form of **PECKERWOOD**.

- "And a peck come right after—I was standing right there—and he signed him up right away." — Chester Himes, *If He Hollers Let Him Go*, p. 12, 1945
- "One of them pecks from down home." — Herbert Simmons, *Corner Boy*, p. 119, 1957
- — *Current Slang*, p. 4, Fall 1966
- Of course, a poor white peck will cuss. A poor white peck will cuss worse'n a nigger. — Cecil Brown, *The Life & Loves of Mr. Jiveass Nigger*, p. 6, 1969

peck *verb*

1 to eat *UK, 1536*

- "I'll tell you about it after we peck." — Herbert Simmons, *Corner Boy*, p. 151, 1957

2 to eat *UK, 1665*

- So I said to Satin, "Say, girl, feel like pecking?" And I said hi to Jim's rib. "Yeah, daddy," she said. "Order me a chicken dinner[.]" — A.S. Jackson, *Gentleman Pimp*, p. 100, 1973
- — Charles Shafer, *Folk Speech in Texas Prisons*, p. 211, 1990

pecker *noun*

1 the penis *UK, 1902*

- We had a stand and wait and watch a wild gay whore playing kittenishly with the pecker of the man she just engaged on the street[.] — Jack Kerouac, *Letter to Neal and Carolyn Cassady*, p. 359, 27 May 1952
- She'd just come into a room sometimes and my old pecker would stand up at attention. — James Baldwin, *Blues for Mister Charlie*, p. 151, 1964

- Wow! That thing's the fattest, longest, reddest pecker I've ever seen! — James Harper, *Homo Laws in all 50 States*, p. 77, 1968
- What's the bet she goes for my pecker on the first date? — *Diner*, 1982

2 by extension, a despicable person *US, 1988*

- That pecker actually scored something on his own? — *Heathers*, 1988
- We're not signing with this pecker. — *Airheads*, 1994
- [N]ow, I know I put you through hell, and I know I've been one rough pecker, but from here on end you guys are in my cool book. — Quentin Tarantino, *From Dusk Till Dawn*, p. 77, 1995

pecker checker *noun*

1 a military doctor or medic who inspects male recruits for signs of sexually transmitted disease *US, 1967*

- — Dale Gordon, *The Dominion Sex Dictionary*, p. 119, 1967

2 a member of a police vice squad targeting homosexual activity *US, 1970*

- Pecker checker pine (Headline) — *Screw*, p. 10, 27th April 1970

3 a person who stares at athletes' crotches in a locker room *US, 1994*

- "Did you see that pecker-checker in the purple pantsuit?" says one of the guys. — Jim Bouton, *Strike Zone*, p. 80, 1994

pecker-foolish *noun*

used of a woman, overly obsessed with men and sex *US, 1977*

- — *Maledicta*, p. 16, Summer 1977: "A word for it"

peckerhead *noun*

a despicable or offensive person *US, 1802*

Formed from **PECKER** "penis," not **PECKERWOOD** "racist."

- You were right about my "peckerhead romanticism." — Jack Kerouac, *Letter to Allen Ginsberg*, p. 91, 23rd August 1945
- Man, I tell you, I really put them peckerheads on! — Ross Russell, *The Sound*, p. 73, 1961
- "I know there's a war going on, you overweight peckerhead," said Jefferson to the Honorable Mr. Pettigrew. — Max Shulman, *Anyone Got a Match?*, p. 93, 1964
- No matter how worthy the cause—and let's face it, some peckerheads don't care much about the city's kids—passing any type of TIF reform isn't easy. — *Riverfront Times (Missouri)*, 20th June 2001

peckerman *noun*

a rapist *US, 1990*

- Who the hell cares about a pocketbook booster when a peckerman has gone beserk? — Robert Campbell, *Sweet La-La Land*, p. 215, 1990

pecker tracks *noun*

stains from seminal fluid *US, 1964*

- I know you're not a pansy, not the way you're leaving pecker tracks all over town. — Max Shulman, *Anyone Got a Match?*, p. 8, 1964
- [D]oing it everyway we could think of any-old place we happened to be, in fact, we did it in so many places that Denver was covered with our pecker-tracks. — Neal Cassady, *The First Third*, p. 153, 1971
- The goofy bastard borrowed my car and when I got it back there was a thirteen-inch pecker track on the back seat. — Ken Weaver, *Texas Crude*, p. 76, 1984
- [H]e also agrees to throw in two pairs of boxer shorts, which he swears on his skin are not from St. Mary's Hospice. "Ain't no pecker tracks on these, dawg!" — Jimmy Lerner, *You Got Nothing Coming*, p. 204, 2002

peckerwood *noun*

1 a white rural southerner, especially an uncouth and racist one *US, 1904*

Not praise. Also shortened variants "peck," "pecker" and "wood."

- [T]he thing I want to know is who's the peckerwood runs the poker game in this establishment. — Ken Kesey, *One Flew Over the Cuckoo's Nest*, p. 264, 1962
- And, man, you ain't seen a peckerwood until you've seen Lyle Britten. — James Baldwin, *Blues for Mister Charlie*, p. 40, 1964
- And Grandma told me what peckerwoods were. — Claude Brown, *Manchild in the Promised Land*, p. 48, 1965
- You come back here and kill one racist, red-necked, honkey camel-breathed peckerwood who's been misusing you and your people all your life and that's murder. — H. Rap Brown, *Die Nigger Die!*, p. 38, 1969

2 a non-Italian *US, 1980*

- Nick also warned against using outside hit men, especially "peckerwoods"—a term used by Kansas City mobsters for non-Italians. — *U.S. News & World Report*, p. 50, 29th September 1980

pecks *noun*
food *US, 1958*
- [F]ood is "pecks[.]" — Harrison E. Salisbury, *The Shook-up Generation*, p. 160, 1958
- — Kenn "Naz" Young, *Naz's Underground Dictionary*, p. 49, 1973

pecky *adjective*
characterized by well-developed chest muscles *US, 1997*
- — Jeff Fessler, *When Drag Is Not a Car Race*, p. 86, 1997

pecs *noun*
the pectoralis major muscles *US, 1966*
- — *American Speech*, p. 200, Fall 1984: The Language of Bodybuilding
- The obvious choice, when you think about it, given the number of Blenheim films in which he's flashed those lovely silicone pecs[.] — Armistead Maupin, *Maybe the Moon*, p. 291, 1992
- "Spread your pecs and save me a place at the bar," Fortney said. — Joseph Wambaugh, *Floaters*, p. 113, 1996

peddle *verb*
▸ **peddle your papers**
to mind your own business *US, 1947*
- Ralph shouted at them, suddenly furious. "Go peddle your papers! Mind your business!" — Stephen King, *Insomnia*, p. 67, 1994

peddler *noun*
a prisoner who sells goods to other prisoners *US, 1980*
- Cuba is what is known in present prison jargon as a peddler. He is a real hustler in the sense that if there is anything in the way of contraband to be obtained within the prison, such as eggs, meat, grease, winter overshoes, coats, shirts, tailor made pants, special hair preparations, after-shave lotions, etc., he is the man to see. — Herbert Huncke, *The Evening Sun Turned Crimson*, p. 157, 1980

pedigree *noun*
a person's background *US, 1974*
- In those cases, they check the guy's pedigree—a pedigree being an unofficial word of mouth opinion that floats around among gamblers. — Gary Mayer, *Bookie*, pp. 88–89, 1974
- Now sit down, mister, and listen to me / While I run down my pedigree. — Dennis Wepman et al., *The Life*, p. 130, 1976

pedo *noun*
trouble; nonsense *US, 1974*
Border Spanish used in English conversation by Mexican-Americans.
- — Dagoberto Fuentes and Jose Lopez, *Barrio Language Dictionary*, p. 112, 1974

Pedro *noun*
a survival winch mounted on a military helicopter *US, 1991*
- "Pedro" could be used to extract downed flyers, or a wire-basket stretcher could be attached to remove casualties when the helicopter was unable to land. — Gregory Clark, *Words of the Vietnam War*, pp. 395–396, 1991

pee *noun*
an act of urination; urine *UK, 1902*
- She flashed into consciousness, inspected herself—wrinkle-free!—in the mirror, took a pee and headed for the elevator. — Tom Robbins, *Even Cowgirls Get the Blues*, p. 68, 1976
- "I have to take a wicked pee," Jerry informed the others. — Richard Mousseau, *Roosevelt Street*, p. 63, 1998
- Moreover, she told this reporter, during the search several of the agents taunted her by asking how long she could hold her pee. — Preston Peet, *Under the Influence*, p. 37, 2004

pee *verb*
to urinate *UK, 1879*
- May or can. You can, but you may not. We've come a long way. In the old days if you had to pee, you peed on a tree with no may or can. That's progress for you. — *Avalon*, 1990

pee-eye *noun*
a pimp *US, 1960*
- He nursed a new rhythm from Kid's drums until the prostitutes were doing the funkybutt so sexy that even the pee-eyes were flashing their money. — Patrick Neate, *Twelve Bar Blues*, p. 112, 2001

peekaboo *adjective*
1 said of a garment with decorative holes or slashes *US, 1895*
- Harry turned to the problem at hand—namely, what to do when Angela came downstairs in her peek-a-boo negligee. — Max Shulman, *Rally Round the Flag, Boys!*, p. 101, 1957

- The attempt at a Monroe effect, besides the smiles, is present in the tight jeans, spun-candy hairdoes, peekaboo blouses. — Sidney Bernard, *This Way to the Apocalypse*, p. 222, 1965
- I wear peek-a-boo bras, and corsettes that give me the wildest cleavages. — Roger Gordon, *Hollywood's Sexual Underground*, p. 35, 1966
- Finally Letch noticed Rita behind him, all tarted-up for another evening on the john detail: Day-Glo green satin shorts, knee-high green plastic boots with spike heels, a white peekaboo chemise, a sequined jacket on top. — Joseph Wambaugh, *Floaters*, p. 33, 1996

2 used of a mirror, seen through from outside the room *US, 1992*
- I strolled, itchy—over to sweat box row. Standard six-by-eights, peekaboo glass. — James Ellroy, *White Jazz*, p. 110, 1992

peeker *noun*
a thief who operates by observing the numbers given at a cloakroom and then using a counterfeit check to retrieve valuable items that have been checked in *US, 1954*
- [A] couple of peekers, suitably dressed for admission to one of the zizzier places, wait across the street from the nightclub entrance. — Dev Collans with Stewart Sterling, *I was a House Detective*, p. 16, 1954

peek freak *noun*
a voyeur *US, 1967*
- — Dale Gordon, *The Dominion Sex Dictionary*, p. 119, 1967
- — *American Speech*, p. 58, Spring–Summer 1970: "Homosexual slang"

peek man *noun*
a lookout during an illegal or forbidden activity in prison *US, 1976*
- — John R. Armore and Joseph D. Wolfe, *Dictionary of Desperation*, p. 43, 1976

peel *noun*
the prying open of a safe *US, 1976*
- [O]nce a had a peel started, I continued the opening by driving in a number of softball bats I found on display. — Malcolm Braley, *False Starts*, p. 279, 1976

peel *verb*
1 to perform a striptease *US, 1948*
Originally a term used by and with athletes, later by and with stripteasers.
- I'd dropped around to the 51 Club on Fifty-second Street, where she was then peeling[.] — Earl Wilson, *I am Gazing Into My 8-Ball*, p. 14, 1945
- One gal of our acquaintance who had made a respectable and comfortable living on the road (even in Boston) peeling in night clubs and theaters, was booked into one of our larger cafes. — Jack Lait and Lee Mortimer, *New York Confidential*, p. 38, 1948
- Rosie had wanted to peel completely in the darkened house[.] — Helen Giblo, *Footlights, Fistfights and Femmes*, p. 190, 1957
- They strut their stuff, peeling, slowly, piece by piece, before the music comes to an end and so does their act. — *Adult Video*, p. 15, August/September 1986

2 to pry something open *US, 1968*
- [Y]ou know you're home free, or if you're peeling it you see that smoke come out. — *The Digger Papers*, p. 12, August 1968
- In either case, whether it's in a house or an apartment, you never try to pop the door of the safe itself by peeling it or punching it till the pin hits the back of the safe. — Emmett Grogan, *Ringolevio*, p. 91, 1972
- The rest of the guys were peeling boxes all the time or burning them with torches. — Harry King, *Box Man*, p. 12, 1972
- While one man is keeping six, two others are either peeling or blowing the safe. — Thomas Renner and Cecil Kirby, *Mafia Enforcer*, p. 38, 1987
- A couple of hard blows and he peels the steering column. — *Menace II Society*, 1993

3 (used of a pimp) to entice a prostitute away from her current pimp *US, 1993*
- Sometimes when this happens, the new pimp presents the old pimp with a banana peel wrapped in newspaper and says, "I just peeled your 'ho." — *Washington Post*, p. C5, 7th November 1993

4 to fire a gun *US, 2001*
- I've seen fifteen-year-olds roll pipe bombs under taxis and peel a clip-a'-nines at a passing squad car. — Stephen J. Cannell, *The Tin Collectors*, p. 34, 2001

▸ **peel caps**
to shoot someone *US, 1993*
- All I knew was we was gon' find some 'a them niggas, and peel they caps. — *Menace II Society*, 1993

▶ **peel wheels**
to accelerate a car quickly, squealing the tires and leaving rubber marks on the road *US, 1989*
- — Ellen C. Bellone (Editor), *Dictionary of Slang*, p. 18, 1989

▶ **peel your banana**
to pull back the foreskin of your penis for inspection or as part of masturbating *US, 2002*
- — Gary K. Farlow, *Prison-ese*, p. 49, 2002

peeler *noun*
1 a striptease dancer *US, 1948*
- The flatfeet tore down the billing and wouldn't let her work. They said she was a peeler. — Jack Lait and Lee Mortimer, *New York Confidential*, p. 163, 1948
- They're not all pimping like crazy for a peeler with the roundest heels in the Borough of Manhattan. — Bernard Wolfe, *The Late Risers*, p. 38, 1954
- "I light up. I'm the only peeler in the business who gets lit." — Monroe Fry, *Sex, Vice, and Business*, p. 62, 1959

2 a fast, well-developed wave *US, 1964*
- — John Severson, *Modern Surfing Around the World*, p. 175, 1964

peel out *verb*
to accelerate a car suddenly from a stopped position, squealing the tires on the road *US, 1973*
- I just love it when guys peel out. — *American Graffiti*, 1973
- As the Furty junkers descended into the crescent, the line of customer cars peeled out[.] — Richard Price, *Clockers*, p. 512, 1992

peep *noun*
1 a quick glance *UK, 1730*
- Brother, you should have seen their maps when they took one peep at those strutting searchlights up above. — Mezz Mezzrow, *Really the Blues*, p. 168, 1946

2 a two-way mirror *US, 1975*
- They have what they call the catwalk, and the peep—hidden mirrors—through which someone is looking down at all times at the dealers. — Jimmy Snyder, *Jimmy the Greek*, p. 218, 1975

3 a sexually desirable woman *US, 1977*
An abbreviation of "*perfectly elegant eatin' pussy.*"
- — *Maledicta*, p. 16, Summer 1977: "A word for it"

4 a PEEP SHOW *US, 2005*
- She migrated up from the nightmare alley of 42nd Street peeps to the relative sanctuary of the Harmony. — Josh Friedman, *When Sex Was Dirty*, p. 56, 2005

peep *verb*
1 to watch in a voyeuristic manner *US, 1999*
- [T]hey peeped naked chicks on cable for free. — John Ridley, *Everybody Smokes in Hell*, p. 4, 1999

2 to engage in surveillance *US, 1975*
- "What do you say we peep through the hospital. Otherwise we're a stand-out on the street." — Jim Sepe, *Cop Team*, p. 20, 1975
- "Let's go peep a lick, Salt," Little Rock said, using street slang for casing a liquor store to rob. — Bob Sipchen, *Baby Insane and the Buddha*, p. 197, 1993

3 to look at something, to discover something *US, 1992*
Variation of conventional "peep" (to look).
- Just some fools peepin' out the ride. — *Menace II Society*, 1993
- [P]eep it or weep. — *Hip-Hop Connection*, p. 24, July 2002
- Peep the "Top 10 Albums" and you'll see ya boys on that list. — *The Source*, p. 44, March 2002

4 to listen to someone or something *US, 2000*
- — *Ebony Magazine*, p. 156, August 2000: "How to talk to the new generation"

5 to read music *US, 1964*
- — Robert S. Gold, *A Jazz Lexicon*, p. 227, 1964

▶ **peep the holecard**
to gain deep insight into someone's character *US, 1981*
- — *Maledicta*, p. 266, Summer/Winter 1981: "By its slang, ye shall know it: the pessimism of prison life"

pee-pee *noun*
1 urine; urination *UK, 1923*
Childish.
- On the other hand, some corresponding euphemistic expressions (e.g., dickie, peepee, weewee, number one, number two, to move the bowels, to pass water, to make love, and so on), obviously evasive in their very structure, do have considerable usage. — *Eros*, p. 69, Autumn 1962
- [A] few finely crafted doody [excrement] jokes. Then a little pee-pee humor with a few real farts[.] — Howard Stern, *Miss America*, p. 137, 1995

2 the penis *US, 1967*
Children's toilet vocabulary. Also variant "pi-pi."
- I felt my pants zipper being pulled open and cold fingers take my pee-pee out and begin to pull it up and down. — Piri Thomas, *Down These Mean Streets*, p. 61, 1967
- Just slip in your pi-pi and fuck away! — Angelo d'Arcangelo, *The Homosexual Handbook*, p. 90, 1968
- Looking down I saw my "peepee" for the first time grow purplish as it filled with blood. — *Screw*, p. 31, 30th October 1972
- [S]he did day work and left me with a teenaged girl who had me climb up on top of her and pushed my lil' peepee into a huge, hairy, warm Something. — Odie Hawkins, *Scars and Memories*, p. 40, 1987

peeper *noun*
1 an eye *UK, 1700*
A definite old-fashioned feel to the term. Popularized in 1938 with the film *Going Places* and the song by Harry Warren: "Jeepers, creepers / Where'd you get them peepers?"
- They sure gave me the glad-hand when they laid their peepers on my new car. — Mezz Mezzrow, *Really the Blues*, p. 88, 1946
- Wait till they focused their bright peepers on that biopsy! — Philip Wylie, *Opus 21*, p. 76, 1949
- Time to wake up, kid, I mean, Bobbie. Open up your peepers. — Joseph Wambaugh, *Finnegan's Week*, p. 231, 1993

2 a voyeur *UK, 1652*
- I looked down at my own pink tipped pretties and decided that maybe the peepers wouldn't have much time for me after all. — Petra Christian, *The Sexploiters*, p. 70, 1973
- Otherwise, he comes and goes, like some goddamned peeper. — George V. Higgins, *Penance for Jerry Kennedy*, p. 202, 1985
- "Okay, peepers then." "Say what?" "Peeping Toms. Guys who get their kicks looking in windows." — James Ellroy, *White Jazz*, p. 51, 1992
- "Alfred Hitchcock did movies about peepers like you," Fortney informed him. "And they all ended up in trouble." — Joseph Wambaugh, *Floaters*, p. 158, 1996

3 a private investigator or private detective *US, 1943*
- "Who's the house peeper here now?" — Raymond Chandler, *The Little Sister*, p. 44, 1949
- "Curt Gannon." He gave a low chuckle that died in his throat. "The disillusioned peeper." — Curt Cannon, *Die Hard*, p. 24, 1953
- "He that private peeper—Fortune." — Michael Collins, *Minnesota Strip*, p. 66, 1987
- All you are is a peeper — Robert Crais, *L.A. Requiem*, p. 100, 1999

4 a card player who tries to see another player's cards *US, 1988*
- — George Percy, *The Language of Poker*, p. 65, 1988

5 a one-way eye-hole in a door allowing the person on the inside to see who is outside; a peephole *US, 1996*
- She squinted through the peeper in gloomy twilight at a spindly blonde, who knew she was being observed. — Joseph Wambaugh, *Floaters*, p. 6, 1996

peep freak *noun*
a voyeur *US, 1972*
- To tell with it / better to be a peep freak / So I turned on my side and looked at those delicious legs through the moonlit train — Charles Bukowski, *Erections, Ejaculations, Exhibitions*, p. 328, 1972
- As I've previously confessed, I was a big-time peep freak. — Ishmael Reed, *Dark Eros*, p. 215, 1999

peepholer *noun*
a person watching a sexual performance through a one-way mirror *US, 1963*
- Here, from the comfort of club chairs, the "peepholers" could enjoy themselves as they watched the exciting goings-on in each chamber. — Madam Sherry, *Pleasure Was My Business*, p. 36, 1963

peep-hole special *noun*
sex in a public toilet *US, 1966*
- The act itself, performed in the toilets, is considered a "peep-hole special" because hustlers and customers know there are special peepholes in many subway toilets for vice squad surveillance. — Johnny Shearer, *The Male Hustler*, p. 18, 1966

pee pill *noun*
a pill containing an agent that increases the excretion of urine *US, 1968*

- [S]tart taking pee-pills again to lose weight[.] — Gore Vidal, *Myra Breckinridge*, p. 22, 1968

peeping Tom *noun*
1 a voyeur; a person who spies on others *UK, 1795*

- I'm watchin' these three people in all their mess and misery. I felt like a burglar, or a peepin' Tom. — Edwin Torres, *After Hours*, p. 363, 1979
- As I lay there scrunched under the windowsill catching all the juicy action, I thought to myself, "I am a pervert. A techno Peeping Tom. I need professional help." — Anka Radakovich, *The Wild Girls Club*, p. 95, 1994

2 in poker or other card games, a player or spectator who tries to see a player's hand *US, 1996*

- — John Vorhaus, *The Big Book of Poker Slang*, p. 28, 1996

pee-poor *adjective*
very poor *US, 1964*
A variation on the much more common **PISS-POOR**.

- Will you settle for pee-poor guardians of the public gut? — Max Shulman, *Anyone Got a Match?*, p. 74, 1964

peep out *verb*
to look at something carefully; to examine something *US, 1990*

- "Peep this out." (Gee Money pulls a tiny vial from the jacket of his sweatsuit.) — *New Jack City*, p. 9, 1990

peeps *noun*
people; friends *US, 1951*

- Tammy suggested, "The peeps from the play are hanging out at the Hollywood Athletic Club." — Eric Jerome Dickey, *Cheaters*, p. 289, 1999
- "What's going on with you and my peeps," this kid named Kenny asked me. — Earl "DMX" Simmons, *E.A.R.L.*, p. 126, 2002

peep show *noun*
an arcade where it is possible to view pornographic videos or a nude woman in private booths; formerly an arcade where it was possible to view photographs of scantily clad women *US, 1947*

- This part of 9th Street is packed solid with "play lands," featuring pin-ball machines, peep show movies and souvenir stands[.] — Jack Lait and Lee Mortimer, *Washington Confidential*, pp. 30–31, 1951
- These "peep-shows" usually depict fully nude females exposing their genitals[.] — *The Presidential Commission on Obscenity and Pornography*, p. 114, 1970
- In the late 1970s, the industry expanded to include much larger "adults only" pornographic outlets, complete with peep show booths. — *Final Report of the Attorney General's Report on Pornography*, p. 345, 1986
- If you're the mop-up boy at a peep show, it's obvious the government is not working for you. — Chris Rock, *Rock This!*, p. 98, 1997

peer queer *noun*
a male homosexual who takes pleasure in watching others have sex *US, 1970*

- — *American Speech*, p. 58, Spring–Summer 1970: "Homosexual slang"

peeties *noun*
dice that have been altered with small weights to produce a desired number when rolled *US, 1898*

- — Frank Garcia, *Marked Cards and Loaded Dice*, p. 263, 1962

peeved *adjective*
angry, irritated *US, 1906*

- This friendship, plus the fact that Boo Boo was understandably peeved at Capone for ignoring his advice, resulted in Boo Boo's talking freely to O'Rourke[.] — Alson Smith, *Syndicate City*, p. 127, 1954

pee wee *verb*
in dice games with no bank, to roll the dice to see who will play first *US, 1950*

- — *The Annals of the American Academy of Political and Social Sciences*, p. 129, May 1950

peewee *adjective*
composed of children *US, 1877*

- He has volunteered to serve as coach in the local peewee football league, thus assuring another generation of gridiron mediocrity in the valley. — C.D. Payne, *Youth in Revolt*, p. 255, 1993

peewee; pee wee *noun*
1 the penis *US, 1970*

- Smith holding back the bushes for him with his peewee hanging hard as a popsicle waiting — Clarence Major, *All-Night Visitors*, p. 39, 1998
- I was sorry and didn't try to look at his peewee any more after that. — Barbara Kingsolver, *The Poisonwood Bible*, p. 191, 2003

2 a very young member of a youth gang *US, 1981*

- All the midgets and tinys in the Black Spiders had been to the Hall. Most of the peewees even! — Joseph Wambaugh, *The Glitter Dome*, p. 110, 1981
- "I was a peewee, then juniors and seniors, and then—boom—you're there, you Ladies." — Gini Sikes, *8 Ball Chicks*, p. 201, 1997

3 a small, tightly rolled marijuana cigarette *US, 1970*

- — Clarence Major, *Dictionary of Afro-American Slang*, p. 90, 1970

4 crack cocaine *US, 1994*

- — US Department of Justice, *Street Terms*, October 1994

5 in craps, a roll of three *US, 1999*

- — Chris Fagans and David Guzman, *A Guide to Craps Lingo*, p. 11, 1999

peg *noun*
1 the penis *US, 1972*

- I could have swung her over me and sat her on the peg, but I had lost all interest in that. — Robert Byrne, *McGoorty*, p. 84, 1972

2 heroin *US, 1994*

- — US Department of Justice, *Street Terms*, October 1994

peg *verb*
1 to identify someone or something *US, 1940*

- He went to the window, caught sight of what she pegged, and motioned Leo over. — Emmett Grogan, *Final Score*, p. 65, 1976
- — H. Craig Collins, *Street Gangs*, p. 223, 1979
- His Smash Hits good looks may have matured into the kind of fizzog that has him pegged for film stardom[.] — Andrew Holmes, *Sleb*, p. 103, 2002

2 in a card cheating scheme, to prepare a deck for a maneuver *US, 1962*

- — Frank Garcia, *Marked Cards and Loaded Dice*, p. 263, 1962

peg boy *noun*
in male homosexual intercourse, a passive partner *US, 1960*

- — Bruce Rodgers, *The Queens' Vernacular*, 1972

pegs *noun*
tapered pants, very fashionable in the US in the late 1950s and 60s *US, 1969*

- Get those fuckin' tweeds out of Ware Pratt's and let me see those sweet talking pegs. — Abbie Hoffman, *Woodstock Nation*, p. 27, 1969
- She watched Gus dispassionately as he moved assuredly around the table in hand-stitched baby blue pegs that must have cost twenty-five dollars[.] — Earl Thompson, *Tattoo*, p. 47, 1974

pellet *noun*
a pill or capsule of LSD *US, 1990*

- — Gilda and Melvin Berger, *Drug Abuse A-Z*, p. 107, 1990

pelt *noun*
a woman's pubic hair; sex; a woman as a sex object *US, 1980*
Building on the vulva-as-**BEAVER** image.

- — *Maledicta*, p. 181, Winter 1980: "A new erotic vocabulary"
- — Michael Dalton Johnson, *Talking Trash with Redd Foxx*, p. 71, 1994

pen *noun*
1 a jail or prison *US, 1884*
Shortened from "penitentiary."

- "First I want revenge because their fathers sent my old man to die in the pen." The Crawler's eyes were blazing with hate as he spoke. — Chester Gould, *Dick Tracy Meets the Night Crawler*, p. 40, 1945
- He's on the lam from a pen back east, crashed out with twenty years to serve of a thirty-year bank-robber rap. — Jim Thompson, *A Swell-Looking Babe*, p. 77, 1954
- Gentlemen, I've worked many pens before, and believe me when I tell you I enjoy entertaining you fellows. — Dick Gregory, *Nigger*, p. 153, 1964
- I'm sorry man, I shoulda picked you up personally at the pen. — *Reservoir Dogs*, 1992

2 a detention or holding room at a jail or courthouse *US, 1979*

- I was able to communicate with Mr. Mahoney in the pens. — Edwin Torres, *After Hours*, p. 259, 1979

penalty box *noun*
the area behind the back seat of an SUV or station wagon
US, 2004
- — Ben Applebaum and Derrick Pittman, *Turd Ferguson & The Sausage Party*, p. 52, 2004

pen bait *noun*
a girl under the age of sexual consent *US*, 1964
A variation on the more common **JAILBAIT**.
- — Roger Blake, *The American Dictionary of Sexual Terms*, p. 111, 1964
- — Dale Gordon, *The Dominion Sex Dictionary*, p. 120, 1967

pencil *noun*
in a casino, the authority to give a gambler complimentary drinks or meals *US*, 1977
Often phrased as "power of the pencil."
- Only a few Hosts have the awesome authority of "the Pencil" which authorizes a completely free stay in Vegas. The Pencil is strictly controlled. — Mario Puzo, *Inside Las Vegas*, p. 288, 1977
- — John Scarne, *Scarne's Guide to Modern Poker*, p. 286, 1979

▸ **get your pencil sharpened**
to have sex *US*, 1991
- "Where, that's where you go to get your nob polished. You know, to get your pencil sharpened." — Gary Linderer, *The Eyes of the Eagle*, p. 66, 1991

pencil dick *noun*
a thin penis; used, generally, to insult a man by attacking a perception of his masculinity *US*, 1998
- I'm more woman than you'll ever have, pencil dick. — *The Guru*, 2002

pencil-neck geek *noun*
a bookish, timid, weak man *US*, 1979
The term was popularized, if not coined, by US professional wrestler "Classy" Freddie Blassie to describe his opponents. Blassie recorded a novelty song so titled, written by Johnny Legend and Pete Cicero, in 1979.
- — Connie Eble (Editor), *UNC-CH Campus Slang*, p. 7, Fall 1985
- — Michael Dalton Johnson, *Talking Trash with Redd Foxx*, p. 98, 1994

pencil-pusher *noun*
1 a person who works with words; a clerk or secretary *US*, 1881
Usually derisive.
- — Lou Shelly, *Hepcats Jive Talk Dictionary*, p. 31, 1945
- [F]or a pencil-pusher he sure could flash plenty of Uncle Sam's I.O.U.'s. — Mezz Mezzrow, *Really the Blues*, p. 69, 1946
- — Jerry Robertson, *Oil Slanguage*, p. 95, 1954
- I just love men who work hard, I mean who work with their hands. Yeah, I hate pencil pushers. — Hubert Selby Jr., *Last Exit to Brooklyn*, p. 204, 1957
2 in the US Air Force, the navigator on a bomber aircraft *US*, 1946
- — *American Speech*, p. 310, December 1946: "More air force slang"

pencil talk *noun*
bargaining over a price in a bazaar carried on by writing down the offer *US*, 1968
Vietnam war usage.
- — Carl Fleischhauer, *A Glossary of Army Slang*, p. 6, 1968

pencil-whip *verb*
1 to file constant lawsuits and complaints against prison authorities *US*, 1992
- — William K. Bentley and James M. Corbett, *Prison Slang*, p. 103, 1992
2 to write someone a traffic ticket or notice of a criminal infraction *US*, 2001
- — Don R. McCreary (Editor), *Dawg Speak*, 2001

pend *verb*
to listen; to pay attention *US*, 1968
- — Joan Fontaine et al., *Dictionary of Black Slang*, 1968

pendejo *noun*
a fool *US*, 1974
From the Spanish of Mexican-Americans, literally translated as "a pubic hair."
- — Dagoberto Fuentes, *Barrio Language Dictionary*, p. 113, 1974
- This scrawny pendejo wheeled a mutant '65 GTO which he claimed could outjump Crystal Blue Persuasion, though the Imp and Goat had never showed down. — Seth Morgan, *Homeboy*, p. 176, 1990

penguin *noun*
a nun *US*, 1980
- You can't lie to a nun. We gotta go in and visit the penguin. — *The Blues Brothers*, 1980
- Girls get raped everyday, and now they're gonna pay 50 G just because these chicks wore penguin suits! — *The Bad Lieutenant*, 1992

▸ **go penguin**
in pool, to enter a formal tournament *US*, 1990
A reference to the tuxedo that is mandated by the dress code of some tournaments.
- — Steve Rushin, *Pool Cool*, p. 14, 1990

penguin food *noun*
anchovies *US*, 1996
Limited usage, but clever.
- — *Maledicta*, p. 17, 1996: "Domino's pizza jargon"

penguin suit; penguin outfit *noun*
a tuxedo or formal evening dress *UK*, 1967
- An effervescent nightmare of familiar faces and bodies turned into rented penguin outfits and slurpy masks. — Odie Hawkins, *Black Casanova*, p. 24, 1984

penis breath *noun*
used as a general-purpose insult *US*, 1986
- "Some of the language used by these children is gross profanity"—an allusion to Elliott's calling his older brother "Penis Breath." — Heather Botting, *The Orwellian World of Jehovah's Witnesses*, p. 86, 1984
- The movie E.T. has contributed penis breath, an aggressively weird phrase in perfect harmony with the aggressively weird psyche of the eight-year-old. — Gary Goshgarian (Editor), *Exploring Language*, p. 302, 1986

penitentiary pull *noun*
influence within a prison *US*, 1985
- — Ronald Davidson, *New York* (letter to editor), p. 10, 11 February 1985

penitentiary punk *noun*
a male who starts taking part in homosexual sex in prison *US*, 1972
- We classify them two ways: penitentiary punk and free-world punk. — Bruce Jackson, *Outside the Law: A Thief's Primer*, p. 176, 1972

penitentiary turn-out *noun*
a male who starts taking part in homosexual sex in prison *US*, 1972
- Now there's only a few natural punks in there that are free-world; the rest of them are penitentiary turnouts. — Bruce Jackson, *Outside the Law*, p. 173, 1972

penny *noun*
one dollar *US*, 1972
- — David Claerbaut, *Black Jargon in White America*, p. 75, 1972

penny *verb*
to force pennies into the space between a door and the jam near the hinges, making it difficult or, if done correctly, impossible to open the door from the inside *US*, 1989
- — Pamela Munro, *U.C.L.A. Slang*, p. 65, 1989

penny-ante *adjective*
petty, insignificant *US*, 1935
From a poker game with a one-cent "ante" or buy-in, an insignificant stake.
- Why he ever started this cheap, penny-ante Building and Loan, I'll never know. — *It's a Wonderful Life*, 1946
- Her father was a penny-ante politician on the South Side[.] — Willard Motley, *Let No Man Write My Epitaph*, p. 125, 1958
- "Anything you make teaching our guests is yours, and I can promise you it won't be penny ante." — Sam Snead, *The Education of a Golfer*, p. 11, 1962
- Killing machines like Quick Cicero were inexpendable; not so pennyante players like Frank Stutz. — Seth Morgan, *Homeboy*, p. 98, 1990

penny-nickle-nickle *noun*
an M-114 155-mm howitzer *US*, 1990
The standard infantry heavy artillery weapon during the Vietnam war.
- — Gregory Clark, *Words of the Vietnam War*, pp. 304–305, 1990

penny pimp *noun*
a small-time pimp *US*, 1953

- The pimps and whores—anyhow the penny pimps and two-bit whores—were barred. — Dale Krame, *Teen-Age Gangs*, p. 116, 1953

penny pincher *noun*
a frugal person *US, 1918*
- Knowing what penny-pinchers her parents were, she suspected they'd wait for her call instead of putting additional charges on their phone. — Janet Evanovich, *Full House*, p. 161, 2002

pennypinching *adjective*
frugal *US, 1920*
- Because—you ignor-amus—there's a big difference between his father managing big-time jobs like hospitals and airports and him offering penny-pinching housewives like your sister three rooms for the price of two[.] — Rita Ciresi, *Pink Slip*, pp. 249–250, 1999

Pentagon East *noun*
the US military command in Tan Son Nhut air base, South Vietnam *US, 1975*
- [A]bout halfway between the South Vietnamese Air Force headquarters and the huge American military complex that used to be called "Pentagon East" or "Mac V." — Hunter S. Thompson, *Songs of the Doomed*, p. 167, May 1975
- There in the bowels of a sprawling bunkerlike complex known as "Pentagon East," the American generals who made up the United States Military Assistance Command for Vietnam (MACV) had plotted the course of the war[.] — Frank Snepp, *Decent Interval*, p. 10, 1977
- These November briefings, the most elaborate of the war, were held at "Pentagon East." — Neil Sheehan, *A Bright Shining Lie*, p. 694, 1988

peon *noun*
an ordinary computer user with no special privileges *US, 1995*
- — Christian Crumlish, *The Internet Dictionary*, p. 151, 1995

people *noun*
1 narcotics police *US, 1957*
- [C]hased up Exchange Place by a baying pack of People. (Note: People is New Orleans slang for narcotics fuzz.) — William Burroughs, *Naked Lunch*, pp. 7–8, 1957
2 a prisoner's closest friends and associates *US, 1992*
- — William K. Bentley and James M. Corbett, *Prison Slang*, p. 39, 1992
- In the morning, we chilled with his peoples for a little while and then decided to get some beers. — Earl "DMX" Simmons, *E.A.R.L.*, p. 116, 2002

People *noun*
▶ **the People**
the masses, at least to the extent that the masses support the agenda advocated by the speaker *US, 1961*
Egalitarian or communist undertones.
- Ostensibly devoted to the cause of speaking to "The People" at their own level and in their own language (the other way had been tried and failed), the League had become fatally implicated in the way to say it rather than the thing that needed saying. — Clancy Sigal, *Going Away*, p. 303, 1961
- We march down Broadway, explaining in unison that "the streets belong to the People." — James Simon Kunen, *The Strawberry Statement*, p. 49, 1968
- We, as the vanguard of the oppressed masses, realize that we must and will serve the People heart and soul. — *The Black Panther*, p. 14, 6th April 1969

pep *noun*
pepperoni *US, 1996*
- — *Maledicta*, p. 17, 1996: "Domino's pizza jargon"

pep-em-up *noun*
an amphetamine or other central nervous system stimulant *US, 1980*
- — Edith A. Folb, *runnin' down some lines*, p. 249, 1980

pepper *noun*
an inexperienced, gullible victim of a gambling cheat *US, 1974*
Playing on "green" as a color and as a slang badge of inexperience.
- — John Scarne, *Scarne on Dice*, p. 475, 1974

pepperbelly *noun*
a Mexican or Mexican-American *US, 1970*
- — *Current Slang*, p. 22, Spring 1970

pepper upper *noun*
a person who energizes others *US, 1940*

- I will go into some detail about him, because several years later he was to become chief confidant, pepper-upper, and ghost-chaser when I returned to Daytona Beach[.] — Susy Smith, *The Afterlife Codes*, p. 40, 2000

pep pill *noun*
a central nervous system stimulant in a pill form *US, 1937*
A deceptive yet accurate euphemism that persisted for several decades, especially with students.
- Pep pills make you feel good. — Timothy Leary, *The Politics of Ecstasy*, p. 45, 1963
- There are those who claim the outlaws don't need food because they get all their energy from pep pills. — Hunter S. Thompson, *Hell's Angels: A Strange and Terrible Saga*, p. 175, 1966
- Pep pills and all variation of the benzedrine formulae present no valid excuse for continued existence. — *The San Francisco Oracle*, 1967
- Have reached midway ploint in new novel, full of pep pills and booze I then sat down and wrote you that silly postcard. — Jack Kerouac, *Jack Kerouac Selected Letters 1957–1969*, p. 495, 30th March 1967: Letter to John Clellon Holmes

Pepsi habit; Pepsi Cola habit *noun*
the occasional use of a drug, short of an all-out addiction *US, 1970*
- — William D. Alsever, *Glossary for the Establishment and Other Uptight People*, p. 5, December 1970

pep talk *noun*
a brief, emotional speech made to encourage or increase morale *US, 1925*
- I'm not paid to give pep talks. — Carl Hiassen, *Tourist Season*, p. 208, 1986
- Just give yourself a little pep talk, "Must try other people's clean silverware as part of the fun of dining out." — *As Good As It Gets*, 1997

pep up *verb*
to invigorate someone; to strengthen or enhance something *UK, 1925*
- After the dog-ass Jets got Dreamer Tatum, they made a stud trade with Dallas and got Jessie Luker and Gruver Allgood to pep up the offense. — Dan Jenkins, *Semi-Tough*, p. 92, 1972

per *noun*
percentage *US, 1974*
- In casino gambling, the percentage—always referred to in Las Vegas as the "per"—is everything. — Edward Lin, *Big Julie of Vegas*, p. 74, 1974

percentage dice *noun*
dice that have been altered to favor a certain roll *US, 1975*
- I learned about percentage dice that are shaved to favor an ace-six—and a plenitude of snake eyes and boxcars. — Jimmy Snyder, *Jimmy the Greek*, p. 15, 1975

percentage girl *noun*
a woman who uses her sexuality to induce customers to buy drinks at a bar *US, 1971*
- A B-girl (also called a "come-on" or "percentage girl" or "drink rustler") often spends six to seven hours in a bar every evening. — Charles Winick, *The Lively Commerce*, p. 171, 1971

percentage joint *noun*
a carnival concession that relies on volume for profit *US, 1985*
- — Gene Sorrows, *All About Carnivals*, p. 24, 1985: "Terminology"

percentage player *noun*
a gambler who appreciates odds and percentages, absorbing losses in the belief that the odds will ultimately favor him *US, 1961*
- Yeah, percentage players die broke too, don't they, Bert? — *The Hustler*, 1961

percolate *verb*
to meander; to be doing fine *US, 1945*
- — Lou Shelly, *Hepcats Jive Talk Dictionary*, p. 15, 1945

Percy *noun*
an effeminate male *US, 1955*
- — *American Weekly*, p. 2, 14th August 1955

perdue *noun*
in poker, an unplayable hand abandoned by a player *US, 1988*
From the French for "lost."
- — George Percy, *The Language of Poker*, p. 66, 1988

perfection _noun_

a break dancer's best move _US, 2006_

- "A b-boy's best move, the move he takes out the comp with, is called his perfection." — Linden Dalecki, _Kid B_, p. 105, 2006

perfecto _adjective_

first-class, perfect, wonderful _US, 1988_

A simple embellishment in the Spanish style.

- The one perfecto thing I picked up. — _Heathers_, 1988

- WAYNE: How's it working, Scotty? SCOTT: Perfecto! — _Natural Born Killers_, 1994

perfects _noun_

dice that are true to an extremely minute tolerance, approximately $\frac{1}{1000}$th of a inch _US, 1950_

- — _The Annals of the American Academy of Political and Social Sciences_, p. 122, May 1950

perico _noun_

cocaine _US, 1994_

Spanish slang, adapted by some English speakers.

- — US Department of Justice, _Street Terms_, August 1994

perk _noun_

a tablet of Percodan™, a painkiller _US, 1971_

Also variant "perc."

- Get some up in Boystown, New York Avenue, those cute guys had anything you wanted, knockout drops, percs, street ludes, all kinds of meth. — Elmore Leonard, _Glitz_, p. 131, 1985

- He remembered a thousand Soledad bull sessions about dope and dry-swallowed two perks and three dexies. — James Ellroy, _Suicide Hill_, p. 749, 1986

- Pop a Perc and have a beer and that's it, sweetness all evening. — Suroosh Alvi et al., _The Vice Guide_, p. 109, 2002

perker-upper _noun_

someone who raises spirits and confidence _US, 1960_

- Grandpa was the best boy perker-upper in the world. — Wilson Rawls, _Summer of the Monkeys_, p. 68, 1976

perk-me-up _noun_

a stimulant; coffee _US, 1977_

- "Anyone wantin' to dunk their donuts in some hundred-mile perk-me-up, how about a taste o' some real down-home Hot Coffee, the way you like it?" — E.M. Corder, _Citizens Band_, p. 36, 1977

perky _adjective_

said of a woman with large buttocks but otherwise a slender body _US, 2004_

- — Rick Ayers (Editor), _Berkeley High Slang Dictionary_, p. 33, 2004

perm _noun_

in hairdressing, a permanent wave _UK, 1927_

- He [Rev. Al Sharpton] looks like Bookman from "Good Times" with a damn perm. How can you take anyone seriously with that hair? No matter what he says, you can't take your eyes off the hair. — Chris Rock, _Rock This!_, p. 14, 1997

perm _verb_

to give hair a permanent wave hair treatment _UK, 1928_

- She was wearing a hat and had had her hair permed and looked like someone's maiden aunt[.] — Alexander Trocchi, _Cain's Book_, p. 164, 1960

permission piece _noun_

a piece of graffiti painted with permission of the owner of the surface _US, 1994_

- Futura 2000, one of Graffiti's early visionaries, who in 1986 helped paint the Detroit Art Train, a permission piece which was the first multi-car freight burner. — William Upski Wimsatt, _Bomb the Suburbs_, p. 135, 1994

perp _noun_

1 a criminal suspect _US, 1987_

From "perpetrator."

- — Carsten Stroud, _Close Pursuit_, p. 274, 1987

- He clobbered a neighbor of his last night and another person who could be one of your perps, and he's at large. — _Fargo_, 1996

- The perp(s) doused the Oakland Hills house with gasoline and set fire to the kitchen. — Ralph "Sonny" Barger, _Hell's Angel_, p. 180, 2000

- No weapon, no perp, the usual. — Ted Conover, _Newjack_, p. 7, 2000

2 wax and baking soda made to look like crack cocaine _US, 1994_

- — US Department of Justice, _Street Terms_, October 1994

perpetrate _verb_

to start a fight _US, 2001_

- — Don R. McCreary (Editor), _Dawg Speak_, 2001

perp walk _noun_

a purposeful display of a charged criminal, especially when being transported from jail to court _US, 1986_

- Throughout the country, many prosecutors also put defendants through what is called in the trade a "perp walk." The prosecutor, again before trial, alerts television stations when to bring in their cameras to get some "eyewitness shots" of the alleged malefactors. — _Washington Post_, p. A23, 29th November 1986

- [W]hat they call a perp walk, they walk the defendant in front of the cameras to assure the public that the perpetrator has been caught. — Terry Moran, _Court TV_, 20th May 1994

Persian _noun_

heroin purportedly grown in or near Iran _US, 1981_

- Well, he also uses Mexican brown. And Persian by the bead! He whiffs it. — Joseph Wambaugh, _The Glitter Dome_, p. 248, 1981

Persian brown _noun_

heroin _US, 1993_

- — Peter Johnson, _Dictionary of Street Alcohol and Drug Terms_, p. 143, 1993

Persian mafia _noun_

a group of influential Iranians _US, 1997_

- — Pamela Munro, _U.C.L.A. Slang_, p. 96, 1997

personality girl _noun_

a popular woman who works in a bar, encouraging customers through flirtation to buy drinks, both for themselves and for her _US, 1950_

- — Jack Lait and Lee Mortimer, _Chicago Confidential_, p. 302, 1950: "Loop lexicon"

persuader _noun_

1 any weapon, the more deadly the more persuasive _UK, 1796_

- — Inez Cardozo-Freeman, _The Joint_, p. 520, 1984

2 a linear amplifier for a citizens' band radio _US, 1977_

- — Bill Davis, _Jawjacking_, p. 74, 1977

Peruvian lady _noun_

cocaine _US, 1994_

- — US Department of Justice, _Street Terms_, August 1994

Peruvian marching powder _noun_

cocaine _US, 1995_

A variation of BOLIVIAN/COLOMBIAN MARCHING POWDER.

- "Peruvian Marching Powder is Peruvian coke," Ryan explained. — Stephen J. Cannell, _The Plan_, p. 374, 1995

- The dressing room was after the show was crowded with fans, celebs, shirttail cousins, groupies, and purveyors of Peruvian marching powder. — Kinky Friedman, _Kinky Friedman's Guide to Texas Etiquette_, p. 188, 2001

pervert squad _noun_

a police sex crime investigative squad _US, 1996_

- It is not uncommon to hear officers from other investigative units refer to the sex crime investigative unit as the "pervert squad," or worse, the "pussy posse." — F.D. Jordan, _Sex Crime Investigations_, p. 9, 1996

perv shop _noun_

a pornography store _US, 1992_

- Word said that a perv-shop owner had once paid him a bill to pose in black leather for a magazine, holding a whip over some old white sucker in a KKK suit. — Jess Mowry, _Way Past Cool_, p. 207, 1992

pessimal _adjective_

as bad as bad can be _US, 1983_

Computer slang.

- — Guy L. Steele et al., _The Hacker's Dictionary_, p. 101, 1983

pet _verb_

▸ **pet the bunny**

(of a woman) to masturbate _US, 1998_

- I "pet the bunny" (the female equivalent of "spank the monkey") at least three times a week about this man. — Dan Savage, _Savage Love_, p. 50, 1998

▶ **pet the cat**
to stroke the air or water while getting through a difficult moment surfing *US*, *1991*
- — Trevor Cralle, *The Surfin'ary*, p. 87, 1991

pete *noun*
1 a safe *US*, *1909*
- The dummy pete was already set up, and we rolled it into position. — Charles Hamilton, *Men of the Underworld*, p. 137, 1952
2 nitroglycerin *US*, *1949*
- — Vincent J. Monteleone, *Criminal Slang*, p. 174, 1949

pete man *noun*
a criminal specializing in breaking into safes *US*, *1931*
- Today the art of box-busting is in a fast decline, and the pete-man may soon join the ranks of forgotten criminals. — Charles Hamilton, *Men of the Underworld*, p. 143, 1952
- Pete Man wasn't anybody's name. It was slang for safecracker. — Emmett Grogan, *Final Score*, p. 18, 1976

peter *noun*
1 the penis *UK*, *1902*
- Just a while ago you were as hard as a little boy's peter in a fifty-cent cat house. — Clarence Cooper Jr., *The Scene*, p. 199, 1960
- IF YOU DON'T GIVE ME A SEX CHANGE, I'LL CUT OFF YOUR PETER AND SEW IT ON ME MYSELF!!! — John Waters, *Desperate Living*, p. 161, 1988
- Maybe it did piss Titus off, the fact that his peter was so big. — Hal Bennett, *Lord of Dark Places*, p. 37, 1997
2 a safe *US*, *1859*
- This peter's a motherfucker. — *Casino*, 1995

peter *verb*
to knock someone out using knock-out drops *US*, *1957*
- "We've been petered," he mumbled. "Petered?" "Yeah, petered. Knockout drops." — Helen Giblo, *Footlights, Fistfights and Femmes*, p. 62, 1957

peter-crazy *adjective*
obsessed with having sex with men *US*, *1972*
- I mean, she was peter-crazy anyway. — Bruce Jackson, *In the Life*, p. 399, 1972

peter-eater *noun*
a person who enjoys performing oral sex on men *US*, *1952*
- "Goddamn those peter-eaters. We ought to smack them around. Maybe that would cure them." — Harry Grey, *The Hoods*, p. 62, 1952
- — Anon., *King Smut's Wet Dreams Interpreted*, 1978

Peter Funk *noun*
used for describing a dishonest auction *US*, *1960*
- The "Peter Funk" auctioneers specialized in bait-and-switch routines[.] — Luc Sante, *Low Life*, p. 62, 1960

peter gazer *noun*
a prisoner who cannot hide his interest in other men's penises while in the showers *US*, *2001*
- — Jim Goad, *Jim Goad's Glossary of Northwestern Prison Slang*, December 2001

peter heater *noun*
an act of urination while wearing a wetsuit *US*, *1991*
- — Trevor Cralle, *The Surfin'ary*, p. 87, 1991

peter pan *noun*
a pan used by prostitutes while washing a customer's penis *US*, *1974*
A crude if smart allusion to J.M. Barrie.
- I puked in her peter pan. — Earl Thompson, *Tattoo*, p. 182, 1974

peter parade *noun*
a mass inspection of soldiers for signs of sexually transmitted infections *US*, *1947*
- — *American Speech*, p. 55, February 1947: "Pacific war language"

peter pilot *noun*
a co-pilot, especially one in training *US*, *1980*
- The co-pilot, or peter pilot, was a new man Brody had only seen around the Turkey Farm a couple times, but his jungle boots were scuffed and he needed a haircut, so he must be an OK kinda dude. — Jack Hawkins, *Chopper One #2: Tunnel Warriors*, 1987
- "He very calmly said that he had to break station because his peter pilot [copilot] has just taken a round through the chest." — Keith Nolan, *Ripcord*, p. 136, 2000

peter-puffer *noun*
a person who performs oral sex on a man *US*, *1987*
- Are you a peter-puffer? — *Full Metal Jacket*, 1987

peter tracks *noun*
stains from seminal fluid *US*, *1993*
- A few days before, Martha had sneaked into his closet and dribbled motor oil on the crotches of his pants. The stains won't wash out and now all his trousers have permanent peter tracks. — C.D. Payne, *Youth in Revolt*, p. 59, 1993

PFC *noun*
a private fucking citizen *US*, *1985*
What a private first class became upon his discharge from duty in Vietnam.
- Kalane smiled. "They don't let pfc's in here, Lieutenant." Tyson said, "They do if pfc means private fucking civilian." — Nelson DeMille, *Word of Honor*, p. 356, 1985

Pfizer riser *noun*
sildenafil citrate marketed as Viagra™, an anti-impotence drug *US*, *1998*
Viagra™ is manufactured by Pfizer, and "riser" is a convenient rhyme that suggests the drug's power to stimulate an erection.
- But men of all ages are swamping doctors' offices, claiming flaccidity and begging for that little blue pill dubbed the "Pfizer Riser." — *New York Times*, p. 15 (Section 4), 26th April 1998

p-funk *noun*
crack cocaine and phencyclidine mixed for smoking *US*, *1994*
- — US Department of Justice, *Street Terms*, October 1994

PG *noun*
paregoric elixir, a flavored tincture of opium designed to assuage pain *US*, *1953*
- Now he had no money for junk. He couldn't even raise the price of PG and goof balls to taper off. — William Burroughs, *Junkie*, p. 96, 1953
- Poor trade of tea. P.G. in the drug stores. — William Burroughs, *Letters to Allen Ginsberg 1953–1957*, p. 14, 20th January 1954
- One minor hitch—my gear is still at the hotel, so far as I know, containing an assload of barbiturates, amphetamines, T.O., PG—paregoric—and assorted shit. — James Blake, *The Joint*, p. 161, 7th January 1957
- It was a long time since he'd had that PG fix. — Phil Hirsch, *Hooked*, p. 151, 1968

PG&E *noun*
electric shock treatment *US*, *1961–1962*
From the electric utility *Pacific Gas and Electric Company*.
- — Frank Prewitt and Francis Schaeffer, *Vacaville Vocabulary*, 1961–1962

PG bag *noun*
a small bag for carrying your personal effects, your *personal gear US*, *2000*
- — Murry A. Taylor, *Jumping Fire*, p. 458, 2000

pharming *noun*
the mixing and then consumption of the mixed prescription drugs *US*, *2001*
- In ever-increasing numbers, federally sanctioned, totally licit prescription medications, everything from Adderall to Zoloft, are finding their way onto the streets and into the digestive tracts and nasal passages of the unprescribed, as college students locally and nationwide pop prescription pills for practical and recreational purposes. They call it "pharming." — *The Hartford Advocate*, 19 April 2001

pharm party *noun*
a party at which celebrants exchange and consume prescription drugs *US*, *2005*
- Nowadays, there are so-called "pharm parties," where teens gather and get high off pills. — *The Courier-Journal (Louisville)*, p. 6A, 9th August 2005
- Actually I could have quite the pharm party with my leftovers from when I was on a ton of meds. — *Suicide, Self-Injury, Depression, AbuseSupport*, 15th April 2006

phat *adjective*
stylish, admirable, fashionable, good *US*, *1963*
Suggestions that the term is an abbreviation of "pretty hips and thighs" or "pussy, hips, ass, thighs" belong in the land of false

etymologies. For centuries "fat" has meant stylish or living well, and the "ph" is nothing more than slang spelling.

- mellow, phat, stone, boss. General adjectives of approval. — *Time*, p. 5, 2nd August 1963
- — Connie Eble (Editor), *UNC-CH Campus Slang*, November 1973
- While we relax to the tight raps / And the phat tracks / That that nigga Timbaland put down. — *Ludacris, Phat Rabbit*, 2000

phatty!
great! *US*, *1997*
- — *Maybeck High School Yearbook (Berkeley, California)*, p. 29, 1997

P-head *noun*
a frequent user of phenobarbital, a central nervous system depressant *US*, *1982*
- — Ralph de Sola, *Crime Dictionary*, p. 114, 1982

pheasant *noun*
in a gambling cheating scheme, a victim *US*, *1974*
- — John Scarne, *Scarne on Dice*, p. 461, 1974

phedinkus *noun*
nonsense *US*, *1935*
Coined by Damon Runyan.
- In Joseph Wood Krutch's opinion, "ridiculous and disgusting," or in Damon Runyon's slang phrase, "strictly the old phedinkus." — Ann Douglas, *Terrible Honesty*, p. 48, 1995

phennie *noun*
a capsule of phenobarbital, a central nervous system depressant *US*, *1971*
- — Eugene Landy, *The Underground Dictionary*, p. 148, 1971
- — Stewart L. Tubbs and Sylvia Moss, *Human Communication*, p. 119, 1974
- — Walter L. Way, *The Drug Scene*, p. 112, 1977

pheno *noun*
a capsule of phenobarbital, a central nervous system depressant *UK*, *1966*
- We also dealt for red capsules of phenos, two of which, with hot water, produce a forgetting high[.] — Piri Thomas, *Down These Mean Streets*, p. 258, 1967
- — William D. Alsever, *Glossary for the Establishment and Other Uptight People*, p. 2, December 1970

Philadelphia bankroll *noun*
a single large-denomination bill wrapped around small-denomination bills, giving the impression of a great deal of money *US*, *1968*
- — Hy Lit, *Hy Lit's Unbelievable Dictionary of Hip Words for Groovy People*, p. 47, 1968

Philadelphia lawyer *noun*
a shrewd and skilled lawyer who is not guided by scruples or ethics *US*, *1788*
One of many unwarranted slurs on a fine city and a fine profession.
- What in hell are you? A Philadelphia lawyer? — Hubert Selby Jr., *Last Exit to Brooklyn*, p. 35, 1957
- Came one response, "You'll need a Philadelphia lawyer for that one." — Sidney Bernard, *This Way to the Apocalypse*, p. 22, 1968
- Ya gotta have a dozen Philadelphia lawyers to figure out them propositions anyway. — Eugene Boe (Compiler), *The Wit & Wisdom of Archie Bunker*, p. 59, 1971
- "Don't pull that Philadelphia lawyer on me," Serpico replied[.] — Peter Maas, *Serpico*, p. 241, 1973

Philadelphia mafia *noun*
recording artists, record producers, and radio personalities based in Philadelphia in the late 1950s *US*, *1982*
- — Arnold Shaw, *Dictionary of American Pop/Rock*, p. 278, 1982

Philadelphia roll *noun*
a Philadelphia bankroll *US*, *1972*
- Directly, he took out his wallet again and apologized, peeling off two new ten-spots, flashing a few coarse ones, a real Philadelphia roll. — Guy Owen, *The Flim-Flam Man and the Apprentice Grifter*, p. 172, 1972

Philadelphia sea lawyer *noun*
a sailor with a strong propensity for arguing *US*, *1973*
- [A] Philadelphia sea lawyer is one who professes to know the answers to all questions. — Horace Palmer Beck, *Folklore and the Sea*, p. 74, 1973

Philistine *noun*
a usurer *US*, *1974*
- — John Scarne, *Scarne on Dice*, p. 475, 1974

Phillies Blunt; Phillies; Philly; Phillie *noun*
a cigar remade to contain marijuana *US*, *1992*
Generic usage but originally made with a Phillies Blunt™ cigar.
- The saga of the philly blunt continues[.] — Redman, *How To Roll A Blunt*, 1992
- You got a Phillie? — Kids, 1995
- I was instrumental in introducing Phillies Blunts to the UK [...] It was LL Cool J who taught me how to roll a Phillies. I can roll Phillies, Dutch Owls and White Owls. — *Mixmag*, p. 75, April 2003

Philly *noun*
Philadelphia, Pennsylvania *US*, *1891*
- Look at a few weeks ago when he was off in Philly. — Ralph Ellison, *Invisible Man*, p. 401, 1947
- Washington wolves go to Philly to howl. — Jack Lait and Lee Mortimer, *Washington Confidential*, p. 256, 1951
- In "Philly" I ran into "Archie Moore." — Babs Gonzales, *I Paid My Dues*, p. 63, 1967
- As I explained last night, you know, we're not gonna saturate the New York market. Now Philly, now that's a real rock and roll town. — *This is Spinal Tap*, 1984

philosopher *noun*
a card cheat *US*, *1967*
- — Albert H. Morehead, *The Complete Guide to Winning Poker*, p. 270, 1967

phish *verb*
to steal credit card data on the Internet *US*, *2003*
- — *San Francisco Chronicle*, p. D2, 27th July 2003

phishing *noun*
the act of stealing credit card data on the Internet *US*, *1997*
- The scam is called "phishing"—as in fishing for your password, but spelled differently. — *Florida Times-Union*, p. G3, 16th March 1997

Phoebe *noun*
in dice games, a roll of five *US*, *1898*
- — Lou Shelly, *Hepcats Jive Talk Dictionary*, p. 15, 1945
- "There it was—Little Joe or Phoebe, Big Dick or Eighter from Decatur, double trey the hard way and dice be nice." — Nelson Algren, *The Man with the Golden Arm*, p. 11, 1949
- — Frank Garcia, *Marked Cards and Loaded Dice*, p. 263, 1962

phone call *noun*
in prison, a remark that someone wants to talk to you *US*, *1990*
- — Charles Shafer, *Folk Speech in Texas Prisons*, p. 211, 1990

phone phreak; phone freak; phreaker *noun*
a person who electronically and fraudulently manipulates telephone calls *US*, *1972*
- A man suspected of being Captain Crunch, bane of telephone companies around the world and hero of "phone phreaks" across the country, was arrested Tuesday in Jamaica, N.Y. — *San Francisco Examiner*, p. 43, 14th July 1972
- Abbie Hoffman and a phone phreak who went by the handle Al Bell used YIPL to distribute information about cracking the phone network. — The Knightmare, *Secrets of a Super Hacker*, p. 14, 1994

phone phreak; phreak *verb*
to hack into a telecommunications system *US*, *1991*
- — Eric S. Raymond, *The New Hacker's Dictionary*, p. 281, 1991

phone spot *noun*
a telephone location used in a bookmaking operation *US*, *1973*
- Zoot wants to trade a phone spot to us. — Joseph Wambaugh, *The Blue Knight*, p. 56, 1973

phoney; phony *noun*
1 a person who lacks sincerity and substance *US*, *1900*
- So I drank up all the money / Yes, I drank up all the money / With these phonies in this Hollywood bar / These friends of mine in this Hollywood bar. — Warren Zevon, *The French Inhaler*, 1973
2 a homosexual male *US*, *1947*
- The man was looking at him. Yeah, he's a phoney. — Willard Motley, *Knock on Any Door*, p. 137, 1947
3 a deck of playing cards that is either stacked or marked for cheating *US*, *1979*
- — John Scarne, *Scarne's Guide to Modern Poker*, p. 287, 1979

phoney; phony *adjective*

fraudulent; fake; without substance *US, 1894*

- They don't make up phoney backgrounds, phony schools, phony parents, to give themselves respectability. — Earl Wilson, *I am Gazing Into My 8-Ball*, pp. 13–14, 1945
- If an actor acts it out, I hardly listen. I keep worrying about whether he's going to do something phony every minute. — J.D. Salinger, *Catcher in the Rye*, p. 117, 1951

phoney-baloney *adjective*

utterly false *US, 1936*

- "It seems like a phoney-baloney deal to me." — Xaviera Hollander, *The Happy Hooker*, p. 82, 1972
- Being your own boss and having a phony-baloney job like I do affords me the great excuse of saying "I have to be alone and free from distractions in order to create." — Jimmy Buffett, *Tales from Margaritaville*, p. 4, 1989

phoney up *verb*

to fabricate *US, 1960*

- They soon had me ready to quit, with their accents so phonied up that if you just heard them and didn't see them, you wouldn't even know they were Negroes. — Malcolm X, *Autobiography of Malcolm X*, p. 63, 1965

phooey

used for registering disbelief or disgust *US, 1929*

- "Phooey. You've just been working at it." — Mickey Spillane, *I, The Jury*, p. 91, 1947

photog; fotog *noun*

a photographer *US, 1913*

- A battery of photogs will greet her at Union Station. — Jack Lait and Lee Mortimer, *New York Confidential*, p. 144, 1948
- This guy knocked off a couple of men giving her a hard time and a photog happened along who grabbed a pic for the front page of his tabloid. — Mickey Spillane, *Kiss Me Deadly*, p. 62, 1952

physical *adjective*

▸ **get physical**

to become violent *US, 1996*

- The mob collector would take the customer outside, where the collector would get physical with him[.] — James Ridgeway, *Red Light*, p. 180, 1996

PI *noun*

1 a pimp *US, 1954*

- "I just don't think I got the qualifications to be a P.I.," he said. — Caryl Chessman, *Cell 2456 Death Row*, p. 97, 1954
- "Is she having trouble with her P.I.?" — Madam Sherry, *Pleasure Was My Business*, p. 63, 1963

2 the Marine Corps Recruit Depot of Parris Island, South Carolina *US, 1958*

- I know exactly what you mean when you say that your stay at P.I. is an "educational experiment" with the lowest form of human life. — Hunter S. Thompson, *The Proud Highway*, p. 137, 26th September 1958: Letter to Paul Semonin
- Army, Navy, where you been? ? Down to PI and back again. — Sandee Johnson, *Cadences: The Jody Call Book, No. 2*, p. 136, 1986

piano *noun*

▸ **play the piano**

to search for particles of crack cocaine with your fingers in an obsessive and compulsive manner *US, 1992*

- — Terry Williams, *Crackhouse*, p. 150, 1992

pic *noun*

1 a picture *UK, 1884*

- This guy knocked off a couple of men giving her a hard time and a photog happened along who grabbed a pic for the front page of his tabloid. — Mickey Spillane, *Kiss Me Deadly*, p. 62, 1952

2 a phonograph record *US, 1960*

- — Robert George Reisner, *The Jazz Titans*, p. 162, 1960

Picasso *noun*

a card cheat who marks cards for identification in another player's hand *US, 1993*

- — Frank Scoblete, *Guerrilla Gambling*, p. 320, 1993

piccaninny *noun*

a small black child; children; occasionally any black person *UK, 1785*

From Spanish *pequeño* (small) or Portuguese *pequeno* (small). Originally applied in the West Indies and US without being considered racist; now highly offensive and derogatory or, in a black-on-black context, judgmental and negative. Also variants "piccanin," "picaninny," "pickaninny," and "pickney."

- You should have seen her—in her feed-sack dress, like scared and roll-eyed, pickaninny mud on her knees, crooning "Trouble in Mind" all breathy. — John Clellon Holmes, *The Horn*, p. 83, 1958
- I saw that there were some kinds in it with Pookie—a pickaninny who resembled a baby unicorn what with a pink-ribboned pigtail standing straight up on her head[.] — John Nichols, *The Sterile Cuckoo*, p. 188, 1965

piccolo *noun*

1 the penis, especially as the object of oral sex *US, 1967*

- — Dale Gordon, *The Dominion Sex Dictionary*, p. 124, 1967

2 a record player *US, 1953*

- We made a number of unsuccessful attempts to locate the ideal piccolo-owning host. — William Burroughs, *Junkie*, p. 30, 1953

pick *noun*

1 a pickpocket *US, 1949*

- — Vincent J. Monteleone, *Criminal Slang*, p. 175, 1949

2 an oversized comb, used for bushy hair *US, 1976*

- — Heather Doob, *Multicultural/multiethnic Studies Programs*, p. 43, 1976
- Other indicators of gang affiliation include articles of clothing, hair ties, or a pick (comb) protruding from a pocket[.] — Bill Valentine, *Gangs and Their Tattoos*, p. 77, 2000

pick *verb*

▸ **pick fruit**

to find and select a homosexual partner *US, 1950*

- — Hyman E. Goldin et al., *Dictionary of American Underworld Lingo*, p. 156, 1950

▸ **pick lint**

to focus on petty imperfections in a play or performance *US, 1973*

- — Sherman Louis Sergel, *The Language of Show Biz*, p. 128, 1973

▸ **pick up your marbles and go home**

to quit an effort, especially to do so with a lack of good sportsmanship *US, 1991*

- In politics, you have two choices if your side isn't winning: You can pick up your marbles and go home, abandoning the game to others, or you can stay, fight and try to do better next time. — *Seattle Post-Intelligencer*, p. A12, 27th September 1991
- "As long as we are meeting and talking," Bagley said, "compromise is entirely possible. But to pick up your marbles and go home, as has been suggested by some on the County Commission, makes reaching a resolution extremely difficult." — *The Orlando Sentinel*, p. B1, 21st March 1999

pick-ed wiss *noun*

urination after a period of discomfort *US, 1968*

An intentional spoonerism of "a wicked piss."

- — Collin Baker et al., *College Undergraduate Slang Study Conducted at Brown University*, p. 170, 1968

pick 'em *noun*

in sports betting, a game in which neither team is favored and the bettor must pick the winner *US, 1974*

- The odds were 10 to 11 pick-em that the fight wouldn't go ten rounds[.] — Edward Lin, *Big Julie of Vegas*, p. 179, 1974
- "I'll make the fucking game pick-em if I get drunk enough." — Gary Mayer, *Bookie*, p. 179, 1974
- — Michael Knapp, *Bay Sports Review*, p. 8, November 1991

picker *noun*

1 a finger *US, 1945*

- — Lou Shelly, *Hepcats Jive Talk Dictionary*, p. 15, 1945

2 a pickpocket *US, 1950*

- — *The New American Mercury*, p. 707, 1950

picker-upper *noun*

a person who lifts the spirits and energy of others *US, 1936*

- Maria Piais a picker-upper; she has room for everybody and people of the oddest persuasion gravitate to her[.] — Isabella Dusi, *Vanilla Beans and Brodo*, p. 201, 2001

pickle *noun*

1 a predicament; a sorry plight; an unpleasant difficulty *UK, 1562*

- What a pickle! — Lester Bangs, *Psychotic Reactions and Carburetor Dung*, p. 77, 1971
- She found herself in the pickle she'd been in a thousand times when she'd been a kid. — Robert Campbell, *Juice*, p. 129, 1988

2 a torpedo *US, 1948*
- — *American Speech*, p. 38, February 1948: "Talking underwater: speech in submarines"

3 a handgun *US, 1950*
- — Hyman E. Goldin et al., *Dictionary of American Underworld Lingo*, p. 156, 1950

pickle *verb*
to release ordinance; to drop bombs *US, 1990*
- Pickle 'em off and boot that mother for home. — Joseph Tuso, *Singing the Vietnam Blues*, p. 48, 1990: Battle Hymn of the Red River Rats

pickle button *noun*
the control on a bomber that releases ordinance *US, 1990*
- I punched the pickle button, let all those babies go. — Joseph Tuso, *Singing the Vietnam Blues*, p. 92, 1990: Hallelujah I

pickled *adjective*
drunk *UK, 1633*
- I figured they were reeling pickled. — S.E. Hinton, *The Outsiders*, p. 50, 1967
- — Connie Eble (Editor), *UNC-CH Campus Slang*, p. 1, Fall 1987

pickled punks *noun*
in a carnival, a sideshow display of jars, each with a fetus preserved in formaldehyde *US, 1960*
- — *American Speech*, pp. 308–309, December 1960: "Carnival talk"

pickle licker *noun*
a despicable person *US, 1996*
An alternative to **COCKSUCKER**.
- Sermon's over, pickle licker. — *rec.sport.pro-wrestling.fantasy*, 15th November 1996
- "What telegram you trying to deliver, pickle licker?" — Linden Dalecki, *Kid B*, p. 217, 2006

pickle, pull, and climb *verb*
to drop a load of bombs and then climb to evade groundfire *US, 1991*
- Four thousand feet was the hard deck, so the procedure was pickle, pull and climb. This meant release your weapons at 5500 feet, then pull as many g's as it took to get climbing without going below four thousand feet. — William H. LaBarge, *Hornet's Next*, p. 243, 1991

picklepuss *noun*
an overtly and infectiously unhappy person *US, 1963*
In the same vein as **SOURPUSS**, with "pickle" conveying the sour quality.
- He was laughing! Old Picklepuss Kaggs laughed out loud! — Jim Thompson, *The Grifters*, p. 167, 1963

pickle wrapper *noun*
a condom *US, 2006*
- One of the pickle wrappers even had a plastic mouth on it that said FRENCH TICKLER. — Linden Dalecki, *Kid B*, p. 89, 2006

pick-me-up *noun*
1 an alcoholic drink *US, 1867*
- Many was the shaking wino who came to them for an early morning pick-me-up. — Robert Deane Pharr, *S.R.O.*, p. 72, 1971
- He picked up the drink Moran set before him. "Thank you, I believe I will. Little pick-me-up." — Elmore Leonard, *Cat Chaser*, p. 278, 1982
- The 44 Regular fit Winnie okay, but he wasn't used to baggy trousers and big shoulders, and when he stopped at Spoon's Landing for a pick-me-up, Spoon looked him over. — Joseph Wambaugh, *The Golden Orange*, p. 61, 1990

2 a dose of a central nervous system stimulant *US, 1984*
- She's at the point of bolting when you ask her if she needs a little pick-me-up. — Jay McInerney, *Bright Lights, Big City*, p. 7, 1984

pick off *verb*
in poker, to catch a player bluffing *US, 1979*
- — John Scarne, *Scarne's Guide to Modern Poker*, p. 287, 1979

pickup *noun*
1 a short-term sexual partner *US, 1871*
- Many Baltimore Street joints are pointedly pick-up bars. — Jack Lait and Lee Mortimer, *Washington Confidential*, p. 267, 1951
- First, there are the pick-up bars for amateurs only. — *Screw*, p. 12, 3 November 1969

2 a police order to detain and bring a person to the station for questioning *US, 1977*
- She decided to bluff; she didn't believe there was a pickup out on her. — Donald Goines, *Black Gangster*, p. 279, 1977

3 in the entertainment industry, a commitment to finance production of a set number of episodes of a television program *US, 1993*
- So the job might be good for several episodes if Harbor Nights got a seven-show pickup. — Joseph Wambaugh, *Finnegan's Week*, p. 2, 1993

pick up *verb*
to smoke marijuana *US, 1952*
- It was passed around by Pasternak, who gave instructions on how to "pick up" to Kathryn, and all sipped deeply. — John Clellon Holmes, *Go*, p. 86, 1952

▸ **pick up on**
to comprehend something *US, 1959*
- — Lawrence Lipton, *The Holy Barbarians*, p. 317, 1959
- — Burton H. Wolfe, *The Hippies*, p. 205, 1968: "A hip glossary for the uptight people"

pick-up artist *noun*
a skilled seducer *US, 2005*
- Shark definitely seemed to have lost his chops as a pick-up artist, along with his best clients and his dough. — Josh Friedman, *When Sex Was Dirty*, p. 3, 2005

pickup man *noun*
in an illegal lottery, a person who takes bets from players to a central location and pays off winning bets *US, 1963*
- Teese, the pickup man. — Clarence Cooper Jr., *Black*, p. 183, 1963

picnic *noun*
1 oral sex, especially on a man *US, 1964*
- — Roger Blake, *The American Dictionary of Sexual Terms*, p. 161, 1964
- — Robert A. Wilson, *Playboy's Book of Forbidden Words*, p. 192, 1972

2 sex involving many people and many acts; an orgy *US, 1964*
- — Roger Blake, *The American Dictionary of Sexual Terms*, p. 161, 1964
- — Anon., *King Smut's Wet Dreams Interpreted*, 1978

pic pac *noun*
in the movie industry, a contract to make a set number of movies *US, 1990*
An abbreviation of "picture package."
- — Ralph S. Singleton, *Filmmaker's Dictionary*, p. 85, 1990

picture card; picture *noun*
in a deck of playing cards, any jack, queen, or king *US, 1961*
- — Irv Roddy, *Friday Night Poker: Penny Poker for Millions*, p. 217, 1961
- [T]hey would answer, after only a little thought, that it would be the tend. A picture. — Edward Lin, *Big Julie of Vegas*, p. 170, 1974

picture gallery *noun*
in circus and carnival usage, a heavily tattooed person *US, 1960*
- — Don Wilmeth, *The Language of American Popular Entertainment*, p. 200, 1981

pictures *noun*
money *US, 1972*
- The usual sentence for that [armed robbery] is ten to a quarter. How come you got only five? Pictures. The secret of getting less time is pictures [money]. — Bruce Jackson, *In the Life*, pp. 30–31, 1972

piddle *verb*
1 to steal something *US, 1952*
- He was supposed to have piddled some funds, that's what they say. — Norman Mailer, *Advertisements for Myself*, p. 178, 1952

2 in bar dice games, to roll the dice to determine who will go first in the game *US, 1971*
- — Jester Smith, *Games They Play in San Francisco*, p. 104, 1971

3 in tiddlywinks, to make a minute change in a pile *US, 1977*
- — *Verbatim*, p. 526, December 1977

4 to build something with matchsticks *US, 1989*
- The inmate, known on death row for his "piddling" ability—a phrase that refers to crafting items out of matchsticks—gave his handicrafts and remaining supplies to fellow inmates. — *Houston Chronicle*, p. 33A, 23rd March 1989

piddle around *verb*
to loaf or fool around *UK, 1545*
- Don't be piddling around with me! — Mickey Spillane, *I, The Jury*, p. 74, 1947

- How about some coffee, okay? Sets a bad example; too much piddling around here already. — Jim Thompson, *The Grifters*, p. 120, 1963
- I did piddle around a little bit with barbiturates, but I loathe them. — Herbert Huncke, *Guilty of Everything*, p. 8, 1990

piddler *noun*

in prison, a prisoner assigned to work in a craft shop *US, 1990*

- — Charles Shafer, *Folk Speech in Texas Prisons*, p. 211, 1990

pie *noun*

1 the vulva *US, 1981*

An abbreviation of **HAIR PIE** or **FUR PIE**.

- — *Maledicta*, p. 255, Summer/Winter 1981: "Five Years and 121 Dirty Words Later"
- Kaki and her other "high school" friends were showering after gym class, showing off their pseudo-'50s unshaved pies. — Mr. Skin, *Mr. Skin's Skincyclopedia*, p. 261, 2005

2 a woman as a sexual object *US, 1975*

- — *American Speech*, p. 63, Spring–Summer 1975: "Razorback Slang"

3 a pizza *US, 1997*

An abbreviation of the rarely used, full "pizza pie."

- — Amy and Denise McFadden, *CoalSpeak*, p. 11, 1997

pie car *noun*

in the circus, a dining car on the circus train *US, 1980*

- — Joe McKennon, *Circus Lingo*, p. 68, 1980

piece *noun*

1 a handgun *US, 1930*

Conventional English from C16 until the late C19, then dormant, then slang, chiefly used in the US.

- It was a bad break for Cheyenne that he had happened to be picked up with a "piece" on him. — Harrison E. Salisbury, *The Shook-up Generation*, p. 8, 1958
- I went up to him, and I said, "I got to get me a piece, baby." — Claude Brown, *Manchild in the Promised Land*, p. 176, 1965
- Then I started smoking with both pieces. — Edwin Torres, *Carlito's Way*, p. 32, 1975
- And the big kid reaches in his coat, pulls out a little piece, like a twenty-two. — Terry Williams, *The Cocaine Kids*, p. 119, 1989

2 a knife *US, 2005*

- "This shit don't look right. We need our pieces," I say. — Colton Simpson, *Inside the Crips*, p. 271, 2005

3 an ounce of drugs *US, 1936*

- "Everything, she is ready. I have da pieces —pure stuff." Pieces was an underworld term for ounces. — William J. Spillard and Pence James, *Needle in a Haystack*, p. 77, 1945
- I want to pick up a piece of H. — William Burroughs, *Naked Lunch*, p. 213, 1957
- He used to sell half a piece, a whole piece, two-three-four pieces. — Jeremy Larner and Ralph Tefferteller, *The Addict in the Street*, p. 201, 1964
- A fin for a number-five cap. A sixteenth for a "C." A piece for a grand. — Iceberg Slim (Robert Beck), *Pimp*, p. 128, 1969

4 a woman as a sexual object; sex *US, 1942*

- "She's nuts but a good piece." — Irving Shulman, *Cry Tough*, p. 32, 1949
- He had planned on a quick piece on a deserted stairwell. — Evan Hunter, *The Blackboard Jungle*, p. 73, 1954
- [A] beautiful little piece she is[.] — Gore Vidal, *Myra Breckinridge*, p. 24, 1968
- We commenced to trade drags on the Camel and fondle and neck, and then we tore off another piece[.] — Larry Heinemann, *Close Quarters*, p. 187, 1977

5 a well-executed work of graffiti art *US, 1982*

An abbreviation of "masterpiece."

- Pieces, short for "masterpieces," are the names, usually consisting of four or more letters, that are painted on the outside of subway trains. — Craig Castleman, *Getting Up*, p. 31, 1982
- I have been picked up and arrested by cops and, although they realized very well that I was King Pin, they let me only pay for the piece I did that night. — Henry Chalfant, *Spraycan Art*, p. 10, 1987
- Tey started with insides, then throw ups and outlines on the nice white trains, and soon went to pieces. — Stephen Power, *The Art of Getting Over*, p. 122, 1999
- Straddling the middle ground are men like Poke, a 27-year-old West Sider who considers himself a skilled artist—able to quickly get his name up, as well as craft more intricate "pieces," graffiti shorthand for masterpieces. — *Plain Dealer* (Cleveland, Ohio), p. L1, 29th July 2001

6 a snack *US, 1996*

- — Claudio R. Salvucci, *The Philadelphia Dialect Dictionary*, p. 52, 1996

7 a domicile, be it a room, apartment or house *US, 2001*

- — Don R. McCreary (Editor), *Dawg Speak*, 2001

piece *verb*

to paint graffiti *US, 1982*

- Everybody took their cans and we went outside and we started piecing. — Craig Castleman, *Getting Up*, p. 5, 1982

piece book *noun*

a graffiti artist's notebook containing ideas, outlines, sketches, and plans for future graffiti pieces *US, 1987*

- — Henry Chalfant, *Spraycan Art*, p. 12, 1987: Glossary
- — *Los Angeles Times*, p. B10, 5th January 1990
- Presto, who is sort of a mentor to Rox, has an airbrush store and a skilled, imaginative piecebook. — William Upski Wimsatt, *Bomb the Suburbs*, p. 45, 1994

piece man *noun*

an armed bodyguard; a hired killer *US, 1974*

- I ain't sure, but you figure at least two piece men beside the driver. I don't guess he'd move that much shit round with less than two guns guardin' it. — Vernon E. Smith, *The Jones Men*, p. 23, 1974
- So what's the use of being good at it if she's a piece man? — Richard Condon, *Prizzi's Honor*, p. 81, 1982

piece of ass *noun*

a woman as a sexual object; sexual intercourse *US, 1930*

- We'll all go down to Panama Street and get a piece [of] ass for 48c each—beautiful girls with shapely hips leaning in scabrous lovely doorways[.] — Jack Kerouac, *Letter to John Montgomery*, p. 591, 6th November 1956
- Son, here's twenty dollars; I want you to go to a good whore and get a piece of ass off her. — William Burroughs, *Naked Lunch*, p. 119, 1957
- She's fifteen, this kid—a great piece of ass. — *Raging Bull*, 1980
- I'm the best piece of ass in three states. — *American Beauty*, 1999

piece of cake *noun*

anything that is considered to be easily achieved or acquired *US, 1936*

Originally Royal Air Force usage.

- Hey, Steve, what'd "ya say! Piece o' cake! — *The Deer Hunter*, 1978
- Right. Piece of cake. I'm very happy. Read the man his rights. — *Lethal Weapon*, 1987

piece of change *noun*

a sum of money *US, 1946*

- "This place must have cost you a nice piece of change," I said. — Max Shulman, *The Zebra Derby*, p. 98, 1946
- Saved me a piece of change on this job, kid. You know paint. — *Saturday Night Fever*, 1977
- Man, I can't carry it anymore. I've made my piece of change on it. — Herbert Huncke, *Guilty of Everything*, p. 191, 1990

piece of cheese *noun*

in poker, a truly terrible hand *US, 1982*

- — David M. Hayano, *Poker Faces*, p. 186, 1982

piece of cunt *noun*

sex with a woman; a woman as a sexual object *US, 1947*

- A pat on the back and a piece of cunt without no passion? — Ralph Ellison, *Invisible Man*, p. 373, 1947
- She really was a bewitching piece of cunt. Pure cunt, that's what she was. — Henry Miller, *The Rosy Crucifixion*, p. 184, 1965
- Like smoking and using coke and trying to get a quick piece of cunt. — Claude Brown, *Manchild in the Promised Land*, p. 366, 1965

piece off *verb*

to divide an ounce of drugs *US, 1984*

From **PIECE** (an ounce).

- — Inez Cardozo-Freeman, *The Joint*, p. 520, 1984

piece of leg *noun*

sex *US, 1977*

- Apeman is more than likely gettin' him a piece of leg somewhere, and it done got too good for him to let go. — Donald Goines, *Black Gangster*, p. 222, 1977

piece of meat *noun*

a woman as a sexual object; sex *US, 1965*

- He said to use slang words like "guys" and "a piece-a meat" when talking about girls and to offer them some chewing gum and take out some cigarettes. — Claude Brown, *Manchild in the Promised Land*, p. 161, 1965
- That's some sweet piece of meat, ain't it? — *Natural Born Killers*, 1994

piece of shit *noun*
something disgusting or of very poor quality; a person who is greatly disliked *US, 1986*
- Rooney'd never believe Mr. Peterson drives that piece of shit. — *Ferris Bueller's Day Off*, 1986
- "Motherfucking piece of SHIT!" raged Gordon. — Jess Mowry, *Way Past Cool*, p. 4, 1992
- Oh man, I'm gonna need a cherry pie to get the taste of ass out of my mouth from that piece of shit movie. — *South Park*, 1999

piece of tail *noun*
a woman as a sexual object; sex *US, 1970*
- "[W]henever I was on a long cruise my old lady says it's all right if I buy a piece of tail as long as I don't bring anything home and as long as there's none of that love stuff." — Darryl Ponicsan, *The Last Detail*, p. 16, 1970
- "No, I'm down here on the floor knocking off a piece of tail." — Edwin Torres, *Carlito's Way*, p. 112, 1975

piece of trade *noun*
a male who self-identifies as a heterosexual but will let homosexual men perform oral sex on him *US, 1965*
- Making it with a "hustler" or a "piece of trade" fills this need when everything else has failed. — Antony James, *America's Homosexual Underground*, p. 14, 1965
- The humiliating position he would put himself in when some piece of trade spurned him because he was not able to lay on the requisite bread! — Gore Vidal, *Myra Breckinridge*, p. 97, 1968

piece of work *noun*
1 a contemptible person *UK, 1928*
- Your dad's a real piece of work. — Carl Hiaasen, *Tourist Season*, p. 210, 1986
- Oh, you're good, Ted. You're a real piece of work. — *Something About Mary*, 1998
- Ralph Sr. was a piece of work: a hardworking, hard-drinking functioning alcoholic. — Ralph "Sonny" Barger, *Hell's Angel*, p. 12, 2000
2 a killing *US, 2001*
- "He said if I ever needed a "piece of work" done just call him, Mr. Clean. He would take care of it," said the undercover detective[.] — *Daily News (New York)*, p. 15, 17th May 2001

piece out *verb*
to divide an illegal drug into ounce packages *US, 2005*
- [C]ooked and pieced out in Baltimore, it sold for about eight thousand. — 50 Cent, *From Pieces to Weight*, p. 155, 2005

pie-chopper *noun*
the mouth *US, 1953*
- — Lavada Durst, *The Jives of Dr. Hepcat*, p. 13, 1953

pie-eyed *adjective*
extremely drunk *US, 1904*
- He said that he had been pie-eyed last night and thrown some sugar bowls at people whose faces he didn't like in Sally Carns's restaurant. — James T. Farrell, *Saturday Night and other stories*, p. 27, 1947
- With the later Senator Karl Mundt, he "used to invent drinks and get pie-eyed." — Bill Cardoso, *The Maltese Sangweech and other herbes*, p. 74, 1984
- Sure enough, at table eight a pie-eyed Volvo salesman was trying to suck the toes off a cocktail waitress. — Carl Hiaasen, *Strip Tease*, p. 9, 1993

pie factory *noun*
a mental institution *US, 1967*
- The captain's office has him listed for transfer to the pie factory, and that's no rumor. — Malcolm Braly, *On the Yard*, p. 340, 1967

pie hole *noun*
the mouth *US, 1994*
- Look, you, shut your pie hole and get moving. — *Airheads*, 1994
- — Pamela Munro, *U.C.L.A. Slang*, p. 106, 1997
- — Connie Eble (Editor), *UNC-CH Campus Slang*, p. 7, Spring 1998

piercing *adjective*
overbearing *US, 1960*
- — Robert George Reisner, *The Jazz Titans*, p. 162, 1960

pier rat *noun*
a surfer with no regard for surf etiquette *US, 1977*
- — Gary Fairmont R. Filosa II, *The Surfer's Almanac*, p. 191, 1977

pier six brawl *noun*
an all-out brawl *US, 1929*
- Okay. It's turning into a real pier-six brawl[.] — Steve Allen, *Steve Allen's Private Joke File*, p. 361, 2000
- "It's a Pier-6 brawl," he would warn the TV audience. "We'll be back as soon as order is restored." — *Tampa (Florida) Tribune*, p. 1 (Baylife), 10th November 2003

pies *noun*
the eyes *US, 1945*
- — Lou Shelly, *Hepcats Jive Talk Dictionary*, p. 16, 1945

pie taster *noun*
a person who enjoys performing oral sex on women *US, 1981*
- — *Maledicta*, p. 255, Summer/Winter 1981: "Five years and 121 dirty words later"

pie wagon *noun*
a police transportation truck or van *US, 1904*
- Two by two they were led from bullpen to pie-wagon, thirty in all. — Hal Ellson, *The Golden Spike*, p. 240, 1952
- The clanging pie wagon finally came along, the cops in their high stiff helmets swinging their clubs. — Harry Grey, *The Hoods*, p. 15, 1952

pig *noun*
1 a police officer; in the plural it may mean a number of police personnel or the police in general *UK, 1811*
- LETTVIN: Why do you insist on calling policemen pigs? ABBIE: Cause on TV we can't call them cocksuckers. — Abbie Hoffman, *Woodstock Nation*, p. 12, 1969
- The Pigs, hogs and the boars of the racist power structure—the Pigs of the police department and the hand tool Pork Chop Nationalists are showing the "essence of swine" within their degenerate souls. — *The Black Panther*, p. 1, 25th January 1969
- In 1958 I escaped from Kern County Jail and fought the pigs, all the way back to the midwestern area of my birth[.] — George Jackson, *Soledad Brother*, p. 41, 1970
- Today's pig is tomorrow's bacon! — John Sayles, *Union Dues*, p. 341, 1977
2 a racehorse that is not likely to win *US, 1973*
- The horse he had was a stiff, a real pig from Canada. — Vincent Teresa, *My Life in the Mafia*, p. 154, 1973
3 a male chauvinist *US, 1992*
- Show the world exactly what a pig Clarence Thomas is. — Armistead Maupin, *Maybe the Moon*, p. 264, 1992
- VERONICA: You've slept with twelve different girls? DANTE: Including you, yes. DANTE: What the hell was that for? VERONICA: You're a pig. — *Clerks*, 1994
4 a chorus dancer *US, 1948*
- And "pigs" is the backstage slang for chorines. — Jack Lait and Lee Mortimer, *New York Confidential*, 1948
5 a promiscuous woman *US, 1995*
- — *American Speech*, p. 302, December 1955: "Wayne University Slang"
6 an M-60 machine gun *US, 1977*
Each squad in Vietnam was assigned an M-60, the army's general-purpose machine gun which entered the service in the 1950s. It was designed to be lightweight (23 pounds) and easy to carry. It produced a low "grunting" sound and thus the porcine allusions.
- I sat with my back to the wire, my feet in the ditch, under the tight heaviness of the flak jacket and belted ammo, worn criss-cross fashion, looking down at the M-60—the "pig," they called it. — Larry Heinemann, *Close Quarters*, p. 47, 1977
- Lighter, at fifteen pounds, than the old M-60 (that weighed twenty-three pounds dry and was sometimes called "The Pig"), which keeps the gunner feeling cheerful and refreshed after a hard day on the assault. — Hans Halberstadt, *Airborne*, p. 104, 1988
- Sugaar told me I would be carrying a "pig" (M-60) on the mission. — Gary Linderer, *The Eyes of the Eagle*, p. 74, 1991

pig board *noun*
a surfboard with a narrow, tapered point and a broad tail *US, 1963*
- — Grant W. Kuhns, *On Surfing*, p. 120, 1963
- Here, you need a rhino chaser like this one to learn on. Good board. I mean for a pig board. — *Point Break*, 1991

pig boat *noun*
a submarine *US, 1921*
- Fortunately, the pig boats with all their faults, from the outset attracted a stream of young officers and enlisted men with adventurous spirits. — David Hinkle, *United States Submarines*, p. 43, 2002

pig book *noun*
a student directory with photographs of each student *US, 1969*
- — *Current Slang*, p. 17, Spring 1971

pig drunk *adjective*
very drunk *US, 1973*
- I realized for the first time that we were both quite drunk. Not pig drunk, but unnaturally loose-tongued. — Timothy Crouse, *The Boys on the Bus*, p. 61, 1973

pigeon *noun*
1 a gullible victim of a swindle *UK, 1593*
- Now my old man is a pigeon when it comes to promoting dough for a pair of skis[.] — Frederick Kohner, *Gidget*, p. 23, 1957
- Take a seat, Hawk. We can use a fresh pigeon. — *M*A*S*H*, 1970
- I didn't lose no fortune, but I lost all the money I could get my hands on, it began in the Marine Corps, I met a lot of pigeons in Vietnam. — Joan Didion, *The White Album*, p. 105, 1970
- A "steerman" hunts for "pigeons," unsuspecting amateurs who could be steered into fixed games with professional card players. — Kim Rich, *Johnny's Girl*, p. 61, 1993
2 a young woman, especially an attractive one *UK, 1586*
- There was a pin-up pigeon. She was a twenty-twenty quail. — Harry Haenigsen, *Jive's Like That*, 1947
- When you see a friend with a squab in a cabaret, don't suggest that you and your pigeon move to his table. — Jack Lait and Lee Mortimer, *New York Confidential*, p. 223, 1948
3 an informer *US, 1849*
A shortened form of **STOOL PIGEON**.
- A little pigeon I knew shook his head just enough so I knew they weren't there[.] — Mickey Spillane, *Kiss Me Deadly*, p. 96, 1952
- Now they began contacting their pigeons, but only those on the petty-larceny circuit. — Chester Himes, *Cotton Comes to Harlem*, p. 33, 1965
- His terrible eyes accused Eddie. "You are a pigeon," Marco taunted. "You broke the code." — Sidney Bernard, *This Way to the Apocalypse*, p. 164, 1965
- Collucci said, "Is how you planted the pigeon classified?" — Iceberg Slim (Robert Beck), *Death Wish*, p. 67, 1977
4 a new participant in a twelve-step recovery program such as Alcoholics Anonymous *US, 1998*
- — Christopher Cavanaugh, *AA to Z*, p. 142, 1998
5 in horseracing, a losing ticket that someone tries to cash in for winnings *US, 1947*
- — Dan Parker, *The ABC of Horse Racing*, p. 147, 1947
6 in shuffleboard, a disk straddling the $^7/_{10}$ off line *US, 1967*
- — Omero C. Catan, *Secrets of Shuffleboard Strategy*, p. 69, 1967: "Glossary of terms"

pigeon *verb*
to betray someone; to inform on someone *US, 1950*
- While they pigeoned off to the warden we all just sat in the sun and roasted and rested, waiting to see what would happen. — Haywood Patterson, *Scottsboro Boy*, p. 112, 1950
- If I thought you'd pigeon I'd kill you. — Chester Himes, *The Real Cool Killers*, p. 50, 1959

pigeon drop *noun*
a swindle in which two confederates pretend to find a wallet and convince a third person to share in the proceeds of the find *US, 1940*
- You some kind of confidence man or dope peddler or something? You trying to work one of those pigeon drops on me? — Ralph Ellison, *Invisible Man*, p. 330, 1947
- The pigeon drop may have begun in China more than 400 years ago. — *San Francisco Examiner*, p. 40, 19th November 1976
- Spring you get your con games. Your pigeon drops, your Murphys[.] — Robert Campbell, *The Cat's Meow*, p. 47, 1988
- The victim of a "pigeon drop," an old scam that police say has resurfaced, she gave $5,000 to two people with a fake lottery ticket. — *Palm Beach (Florida) Post*, p. 2B, 31st January 2004

pigfoot *noun*
marijuana *US, 1960*
- — Robert George Reisner, *The Jazz Titans*, p. 162, 1960

pigfucker *noun*
a despicable person *US, 1965*
- Ah, this fucking rotten machine. One more strike against those pigfuckers. — Hunter S. Thompson, *The Proud Highway*, p. 509, 18th April 1965: Letter to Paul Semonin
- Throw me in jail? I'm already there, you stupid pigfucker. — *Natural Born Killers*, 1994

piggie bank *noun*
the stockings worn by an overweight woman *US, 1981*
- — Don Wilmeth, *The Language of American Popular Entertainment*, p. 200, 1981

piggies *noun*
▸ **make piggies**
to have sex *US, 1969*
- — *Kiss*, 1969: "Groupie glossary"

piggyback *verb*
in casino blackjack, to place a bet in another player's square *US, 1996*
- — Frank Scoblete, *Best Blackjack*, p. 252, 1996

piggybacking *noun*
1 the reclamation of an abandoned building, floor by floor *US, 1989*
- Landlords have all but left many buildings for dead in these areas, and dealers either rent several apartments on a floor very cheaply, or "squat" illegally without paying any rent, usually working upward, a practice called "piggybacking." — Terry Williams, *The Cocaine Kids*, p. 53, 1989
2 the use of a computer whose legitimate user has not logged out *US, 1994*
- So you see, piggybacking—the use of another's legitimate access to gain entry into a building or computer—is an on-site hacker's best friend! — The Knightmare, *Secrets of a Super Hacker*, p. 93, 1994

piggy parts *noun*
ham *US, 1996*
- — *Maledicta*, p. 17, 1996: "Domino's pizza jargon"

pig iron *noun*
a carnival ride; the metal assembly of a carnival ride *US, 1960*
- — *American Speech*, pp. 308–309, December 1960: "Carnival talk"
- — Joe McKennon, *Circus Lingo*, p. 69, 1980

pig killer *noun*
phencyclidine, the recreational drug known as PCP or angel dust *US, 1981*
- — Ronald Linder, *PCP: The Devil's Dust*, p. 10, 1981

pig meat *noun*
a prostitute *US, 1971*
- "Biffer," "prossie," "she-she," "pig-meat" are some other slang designations. — Charles Winick, *The Lively Commerce*, p. 41, 1971

pig-out *noun*
a session of gorging on food *US, 1978*
- I haven't had a good TV-and-junk-food pig-out in ages. — Armistead Maupin, *Further Tales of the City*, p. 156, 1982

pig out *verb*
to eat a lot quickly and messily *US, 1978*
- If you really want to pig out, the Old World Market next door will collaborate with the Wharf[.] — *Washington Post*, p. W5, 31st March 1978
- After leaving the Cascades, I drove down to California (pigging out at every smorgasbord place along the way). — Drew Bergman, *Going it Alone*, p. 76, 1979
- Fix up a nice big plate of sargassum. We'll pig out. — Carl Hiaasen, *Tourist Season*, p. 260, 1987
- If your daughter really is pigging out on candy and other junk food all the time, and she's genuinely overweight, you do need to address that. — Rosalind Wiseman, *Queen Bees & Wannabes*, p. 104, 2002

pigpen *noun*
an illegal gambling operation *US, 1982*
- — Thomas L. Clark, *The Dictionary of Gambling and Gaming*, p. 155, 1987

pig pile *noun*
an orgy with homosexual men *US, 1972*
- — Bruce Rodgers, *The Queens' Vernacular*, p. 148, 1972

pig's eye *noun*
used in a number of phrases to mean never *US, 1847*

- "In a pig's eye," I say. "I ain't going to cut nothin' off." — Lennox Lewis, *Muhammad Ali*, p. 300, 2001

pig's Latin *noun*
any coded language used by prison guards *US, 1984*
A truly brilliant pun.
- — Inez Cardozo-Freeman, *The Joint*, p. 521, 1984

pig slices *noun*
ham *US, 1996*
- — *Maledicta*, p. 17, 1996: "Domino's pizza jargon"

pig station *noun*
in prison, a guard control room *US, 1984*
- — Inez Cardozo-Freeman, *The Joint*, p. 521, 1984

pig-sticker *noun*
1 a knife, especially a large knife *UK, 1890*
- The pig-sticker, the switchblade, the knife, for Christ's sake. — Jim Thompson, *Savage Night*, p. 69, 1953
- I said back in my own Kentucky Blue Ridge voice, "I reckon you could hurt me real bad with that there pig sticker." — Sandra Bernard, *Confessions of a Pretty Lady*, 1988
2 a stick with a nail or sharp metal point on one end used for picking up paper litter *US, 1996*
- — Reinhold Aman, *Hillary Clinton's Pen Pal: A Guide to Life and Lingo in Federal Prison*, p. 55, 1996

pig water *noun*
weak, low quality alcohol *US, 1958*
- [W]hen he said a double bourbon he didn't mean "no one-and-a-half-ounce shot of pig-water bar whiskey either[.]" — John Clellon Holmes, *The Horn*, p. 39, 1958

pike *noun*
a glance *US, 1950*
- — Hyman E. Goldin et al., *Dictionary of American Underworld Lingo*, p. 157, 1950

pike *verb*
1 in a card game, to peek at an opponent's cards *US, 1962*
- — Frank Garcia, *Marked Cards and Loaded Dice*, p. 263, 1962
2 (of a man) to tape the penis and testicles to the body as part of an effort to pass as a woman *US, 1987*
- "Why do you pike?" Spinnerman asked. "Don't most of your customers just want you to go down on them?" — Robert Campbell, *Alice in La-La Land*, p. 217, 1987

piker *noun*
a rank amateur or beginner; a gambler who makes small, cautious bets *US, 1872*
- Willie felt impelled to demonstrate that he was something more than a piker like the others here. — James T. Farrell, *Willie Collins*, p. 107, 1946
- I gave him a quarter so he wouldn't remember me as a piker. — Mickey Spillane, *My Gun is Quick*, p. 65, 1950
- I winked at the mark and said, "What makes you think we're pikers? We're not afraid to bet even as much as ten dollars or more." — Iceberg Slim (Robert Beck), *Trick Baby*, p. 151, 1969
- Mr. Henry Booth, Donovan's owner. A real wealthy gent. And no piker. Lays out money like it grew on trees. — Wilda Moxham, *The Apprentice*, p. 30, 1969

pile *noun*
in poker, the amount of money (cash and/or chips) a player has in front of him available for betting *US, 1979*
- — John Scarne, *Scarne's Guide to Modern Poker*, p. 287, 1979

▸ **on the pile**
in prison *US, 1970*
- And half of my life would have been spent on the pile. — Red (Morris) Rudensky and Don Riley, *The Gonif*, p. 133, 1970

pile *verb*
(from the male point of view) to have sex *US, 1968*
- There is a certain type who will leave you and his wife alone and tell you to pile her real good. — Eldridge Cleaver, *Soul on Ice*, p. 170, 1968

pile driver *noun*
1 a sexual position in which the woman stands on her head and the man enters her directly and powerfully from above *US, 1995*
A term (and practice) found more commonly in pornography than real life.
- — *Adult Video News*, p. 38, September 1995

- I like pile driver, that's when you lay down and your legs are over your head. — Anthony Petkovich, *The X Factory*, p. 83, 1997
- For most of the girls, the position that makes us shudder is the pile driver. The girl is upside down with only her head and shoulders on the ground and her bits in the air, and the guy is up and over her, pounding away like a jackhammer. — *Playboy*, p. 132, 1st March 2002
2 the active participant in anal sex *US, 1979*
- — *Maledicta*, p. 232, 1979: "Kinks and queens: linguistic and cultural aspects of the terminology for gays"
- — William K. Bentley and James M. Corbett, *Prison Slang*, p. 60, 1992

pile in *verb*
to enter en masse, especially a vehicle or a bar *US, 1841*
- Once in a while, when business was slow at the Martinique, I would knock off early and Bix and I would pile into a cab, bound for the South Side in Chicago[.] — Mezz Mezzrow, *Really the Blues*, p. 82, 1946

pilgrim *noun*
a newcomer to a game of poker *US, 1988*
- — George Percy, *The Language of Poker*, p. 67, 1988

pill *noun*
1 any central nervous system stimulant *US, 1966*
- — *American Speech*, p. 281, December 1966: "More carnie talk from the west coast"
2 a pellet of opium *US, 1946*
- Then he held the pipe bowl close to the top of his special lamp and stuck the pill on the edge of the bowl, drawing the yen hok round and round to stretch the opium[.] — Mezz Mezzrow, *Really the Blues*, p. 98, 1946
3 a cigarette *UK, 1914*
- I leaned back again and lit another pill. — Raymond Chandler, *The Long Goodbye*, p. 54, 1953
4 in pool, a small tally ball used as a scoring device *US, 1993*
- — Mike Shamus, *The Illustrated Encyclopedia of Billiards*, p. 170, 1993

▸ **the pill**
the contraceptive pill *UK, 1957*
Not in practical currency until the early 1960s.
- The Pill, the cap and the I.U.D. are equally becoming very popular in this country after great success in Europe. — Jules Griffon, *Orgies American Style*, p. 25, 1967
- The pill, of course, is the big new development in the '60s. — Joe David Brown, *Sex in the '60s*, p. 18, 1968
- All I can say is Thank God for the pill! — *Screw*, p. 7, 12th January 1970
- I didn't always use protection and, I sometimes forgot to take the Pill. — *Mixmag*, p. 99, February 2002

pilled; pilled up *adjective*
under the influence of central nervous system stimulants or depressants *US, 1966*
- — *American Speech*, p. 282, December 1966: "More carnie talk from the west coast"
- I figured he was pilled up to the eyeballs. — Jamie Mandelkau, *Buttons*, p. 28, 1971
- I was all pilled up—I had a pill habit at that time with the dope habit. — Bruce Jackson, *In the Life*, p. 76, 1972

pillhead *noun*
a habitual user of amphetamines, barbiturates, or MDMA, the recreational drug best known as ecstasy *US, 1966*
- I'm not a pill head, I really need these things. Here's my prescription. — Roger Gordon, *Hollywood's Sexual Underground*, p. 46, 1966
- My "buddies" were heroin users, marijuana smokers, and "pill-heads[.]" — Phil Hirsch, *Hooked*, p. 129, 1968
- [A] wired-up pillhead, he said to himself[.] — Gerald Petievich, *Shakedown*, p. 38, 1988

pillow *noun*
a sealed polyethylene bag of drugs *US, 1970*
- — William D. Alsever, *Glossary for the Establishment and Other Uptight People*, p. 25, December 1970

pillow pigeons *noun*
bedbugs *US, 1947*
- — Marcus Hanna Boulware, *Jive and Slang of Students in Negro Colleges*, 1947
- — Helen Dahlskog (Editor), *A Dictionary of Contemporary and Colloquial Usage*, p. 45, 1972

pillow talk *noun*
intimate discussions in bed *US, 1977*
Suggests secrets shared, not sexually oriented talk.
- "That message gets delivered in pillow talk, I'm sure," Califano said. — *The Washington Post*, p. A3, 30th May 1977

- "Pillow talk," he said. "I've got a solution honey.' Yeah, makes sense, doesn't it? — Jonathan Kellerman, *Rage*, p. 274, 2005

pill party noun
execution in the gas chamber *US, 1971*
Pills of cyanide dropped into a bucket of water produce the lethal gas.
- — Eugene Landy, *The Underground Dictionary*, p. 150, 1971

pill pusher noun
a pharmacist *US, 1980*
- — *Maledicta*, p. 57, Summer 1980: "Not sticks and stones, but names: more medical perjoratives"

pill roller noun
a doctor *US, 1951*
- — *American Speech*, p. 194, October 1951: "A study of reformatory argot"

pilly noun
an abuser of drugs in pill form *US, 1970*
- — *Congressional Record*, p. E3981, 6th May 1970

pilot noun
1 a person who remains drug free to guide another through an experience on a hallucinogenic drug *US, 1966*
- Psychedelic adventurers in San Francisco who are on a bad trip can call in a friendly pilot to bring them down safely. — *Berkeley Barb*, p. 6, 9th December 1966

2 in horseracing, a jockey *US, 1983*
- — Thomas L. Clark, *The Dictionary of Gambling and Gaming*, p. 155, 1987

pilot error noun
in computing, a user's misconfiguration that produces errors that at first appear to be the fault of the program *US, 1991*
- — Eric S. Raymond, *The New Hacker's Dictionary*, p. 281, 1991

pimp noun
1 a stylized stride *US, 1994*
- The pimp was a proud, defiant, bouncy stride. You take a regular step with one leg, then sort of hop or drag the other on the second step. — Nathan McCall, *Makes Me Wanna Holler*, p. 25, 1994

2 a charming man who attracts women *US, 1997*
- — Judi Sanders, *Da Bomb!*, p. 21, 1997
- — Connie Eble (Editor), *UNC-CH Campus Slang*, p. 6, April 1997

3 in a deck of playing cards, a jack or knave *US, 1988*
- — George Percy, *The Language of Poker*, p. 67, 1988

4 cocaine *US, 1994*
- — US Department of Justice, *Street Terms*, August 1994

pimp verb
1 to work as a pimp; to exert control over a prostitute *US, 1972*
- Then I would pimp her—try to get as much out of her as I could. Sandy's not gettin' pimped. She's with a pimp. She doesn't just want to be part of the group that's getting pimped. — Susan Hall, *Gentleman of Leisure*, p. 56, 1972
- The only thing I had going for me was the fact that Ace wasn't a kid but a man who had pimped long enough to know just how the pimp game goes. — A.S. Jackson, *Gentleman Pimp*, p. 143, 1973
- Just because I didn't want to pimp Amelia or anybody else? — Bobby Seale, *A Lonely Rage*, p. 153, 1978
- Sistahs had a lot of heart and you had to be a lotta pimp to pimp 'em. — Odie Hawkins, *Black Chicago*, p. 116, 1992

2 to take advantage of *US, 1942*
- You can start pimping hard on a bitch and then sucker out and blow her, but ain't no way you can turn it around and pimp on Pepper after starting with her like a sucker. — Iceberg Slim (Robert Beck), *Pimp*, p. 65, 1969

3 to act in a stylized, fashionable way *US, 1970*
- — *Current Slang*, p. 11, Fall 1970
- The hip dudes profiled in their All Stars and pimped down the hallway at school like they owned the white man's world. — Nathan McCall, *Makes Me Wanna Holler*, p. 25, 1994

4 to win away the affection of another person's date *US, 1966*
- — John D. Bell et al., *Loosely Speaking*, p. 14, 1966

▶ **pimp your pipe**
to loan or rent a pipe used for smoking crack cocaine *US, 1994*
- — US Department of Justice, *Street Terms*, October 1994

pimp adjective
excellent, fashionable, stylish *US, 1970*
- "Pimp" as an adjective commonly means "sharp" or "beautiful." — Roger Abrahams, *Positively Black*, p. 92, 1970
- Sometimes a group of buddies who ran together, who were "stone pimp," as the phrase went, would move straight into the poverty program. — Tom Wolfe, *Radical Chic & Mau-Mauing the Flak Catchers*, p. 132, 1970

pimp-crazy adjective
psychologically controlled by a pimp *US, 1972*
- A woman who has been abused by several pimps in succession is said to be pimp-crazy. — Christina and Richard Milner, *Black Players*, p. 34, 1972

pimp dust noun
cocaine *US, 1980*
Before the era of crack cocaine, cocaine was an expensive drug enjoyed only by the wealthy, notably by pimps.
- — Edith A. Folb, *runnin' down some lines*, p. 249, 1980

pimped-up adjective
flashy; of a car, laden with flashy accessories, usually not related to the car's performance *US, 1993*
- [H]e allowed as how thin, pan-sauteed veal with wild mushroom sauce is "a pimped-up version" of that dish — *Newsday*, 18th June 1993
- Cruz says her kids, an 8-year-old son and 11-year-old daughter, loved the pimped up ride. — *Plain Dealer (Cleveland, Ohio)*, p. L1, 23rd May 2004

pimper noun
a person who walks with a stylized stride *US, 1994*
- At Waters, the best pimpers twisted their torsos slightly and swung their arms in unison with that hop. — Nathan McCall, *Makes Me Wanna Holler*, p. 25, 1994

pimping adjective
expensive, fashionable *US, 2003*
- "I wish we had a pimping grill like those guys," Kiefer said of one raft. — *Post-Crescent (Appleton, Wisconsin)*, p. 8B, 13th April 2003

pimp out verb
to embellish in an extravagant style *US, 1999*
- Found a hip-hugging black sequin dress that had the right cleavage to pimp out my twin 36C cups. — Eric Jerome Dickey, *Cheaters*, p. 41, 1999

pimp post; pimp rest noun
an armrest or console between the driver's seat and the passenger seat of a car *US, 1980*
Used for the **GANGSTER LEAN**.
- — Edith A. Folb, *runnin' down some lines*, p. 249, 1980

pimp roll noun
a highly stylized manner of walking, projecting an image of control and dispassion *US, 1970*
- Others have taken on the "soul" styles of black teenagers, wearing their hair in James Brown-style pompadours and walking with the so-called "pimp roll." — United States Congress, *Equal Educational Opportunity Hearings*, p. 10891, 1970
- Now he felt good all the way around, so he walked over to the four corners at Hollywood and Vine, practicing the pimp roll that made the black hustlers look so cool. — Robert Campbell, *Sweet La-La Land*, p. 66, 1990
- Or consider Eggy Daddy, a man on a mission, his thinned-out frame motivating away from the corner traffic in a brisk pimp roll[.] — David Simon and Edward Burns, *The Corner*, p. 317, 1997

pimp's arrest noun
used to describe a pimp causing the arrest of a prostitute who has left his control *US, 1972*
- "Pimp's arrest" occurs when a man seizes his former ho and brings her to jail, forcibly if necessary, and then reclaims his bond money. — Christina and Richard Milner, *Black Players*, p. 101, 1972

pimp shoes; pimping shoes noun
flashy, expensive shoes *US, 1972*
- A few years ago, pimpin' shoes meant expensive alligator shoes with a long and narrow cut. — Christina and Richard Milner, *Black Players*, p. 34, 1972

pimp slap verb
to strike someone forcefully, usually with the back of the hand across the face *US, 1991*
A term perhaps best known for its use as the hook in Snoop Dogg's song "Pimp Slap."

- Trying my best not to electronically pimp-slap this guy. — *rec.sport. pro-wrestling*, 11th September 1991
- — Pamela Munro, *U.C.L.A. Slang*, p. 97, 1997
- One was spewing, one was on the ground bleeding, and one was crying like he'd just got pimp-slapped. — John Ridley, *Love is a Racket*, p. 125, 1998
- "Now go back to sleep," I said and she did—without once pimp slapping me. — *Las Vegas Mercury*, 27th July 2001

pimp socks *noun*
thin, dress nylon socks with vertical patterns *US, 1970*
- We all have some sharp clothes, but Bunchy was always sharp—clean, with a sharp suit, pimp socks, and shined knobs. — Bobby Seale, *Seize the Time*, p. 269, 1970
- I wore a gold bar & looping chain, Blue suede Stacy Adams and powder blue "pimp" socks. — Renay Jackson, *Oaktown Devil*, p. 2, 1998

pimp steak *noun*
a hot dog *US, 1970*
- — Clarence Major, *Dictionary of Afro-American Slang*, p. 91, 1970

pimp stick *noun*
a cigarette holder *US, 1967*
- Society Red took the cigarette holder and waved it with his notion of elegance. "Pretty smooth pimp stick for only three packs." — Malcolm Braly, *On the Yard*, p. 155, 1967

pimp sticks *noun*
wire coathangers used by pimps to beat prostitutes *US, 1972*
- When my hand came out it was holding my pimp sticks, two coat hangers twisted together. — Donald Goines, *Whoreson*, p. 199, 1972

pimp suit *noun*
a showy, extravagant, tasteless suit *US, 1980*
- He knew he should keep still, but he didn't like Roland's bright blue pimp suit or the big Lone Ranger hat touching the roof of the car. — Elmore Leonard, *Gold Coast*, p. 34, 1980

pimp title *noun*
a pimp's claim on the loyalty, services, and earnings of a prostitute *US, 1979*
- He had taken off the 'ho's bread and most likely had massaged her tonsils with his swipe to cop legal pimp title. — Iceberg Slim (Robert Beck), *Airtight Willie and Me*, p. 65, 1979

pimp up *verb*
to add flashy touches to something; to dress something up *US, 1993*
- — Sylvia Carter, *Newsday*, p. 91, 18th June 1993
- — Pamela Munro, *U.C.L.A. Slang*, p. 97, 1997
- Every Thursday, the VIP room will be pimped up with rock decor and rock music. — *Chicago Tribune*, p. 59, 17th May 2004

pimp wagon *noun*
an extravagantly accessorized, flashy car *US, 1976*
- It glowered over the dark, dead-end street, a garbage-clogged strip of smashed-out Plymouths and gossy, spade-spangled pimp wagons with Kewpie dolls and lamb's wool. — William Brashler, *City Dogs*, p. 13, 1976

pimp without a briefcase *noun*
a man who borrows money from a girlfriend *US, 1967*
- Max had already given himself a name; he was a pimp without a briefcase. When you pimped without a briefcase, you borrowed money from the girl[.] — John Williams, *The Man Who Cried I Am*, p. 154, 1967

pin *noun*
1 a very thin marijuana cigarette *US, 1967*
- — Richard A. Spears, *The Slang and Jargon of Drugs and Drink*, p. 389, 1986
- — Pamela Munro, *U.C.L.A. Slang*, p. 97, 1997

2 a person who serves as a lookout *US, 1992*
- — William K. Bentley and James M.Corbett, *Prison Slang*, p. 40, 1992

pin *verb*
1 to scrutinize someone or something; to look at someone or something intently *US, 1965*
- The paddy boy'd just pass by you and say, "Watch it, baby, the Man is on the next corner," or "The Man is pinning you from across the street." — Claude Brown, *Manchild in the Promised Land*, p. 161, 1965
- Last night I pinned the heat, I see them. They were sitting there. — Lenny Bruce, *The Essential Lenny Bruce*, p. 202, 1967

- Shit, them whores you "pinning" ain't but half the stable. — Iceberg Slim (Robert Beck), *Pimp*, p. 119, 1969
- When this queen rolled on the scene and began to pin / With one look at her I could tell she was pure sin. — Dennis Wepman et al., *The Life*, p. 52, 1976

2 to act as a lookout *US, 1966*
- [T]he "hip square" tends to sympathize with the inmate code and adheres to some of its principles, sometimes going so far as to "pin"—to act as a lookout—for other inmates. — Rose Giallombardo, *Society of Women*, p. 116, 1966

3 to tattoo something with improvised equipment *US, 1972*
- Kenny also got himself tattooed while there; a sparkling pair of dice, showing up a winning roll of seven, was pinned into his left forearm[.] — Emmett Grogan, *Ringolevio*, p. 65, 1972

pin artist *noun*
an illegal abortionist *US, 1962*
- — Joseph E. Ragen and Charles Finston, *Inside the World's Toughest Prison*, p. 812, 1962: "Penitentiary and underworld glossary"

pinch *noun*
1 an arrest *US, 1900*
- I am glad that the newspaper boys, who later liked to refer to me as an ace narcotic inspector, never heard the story of my first big pinch. — William J. Spillard and Pence James, *Needle in a Haystack*, p. 71, 1945
- You'll be right behind me every inch of the way, but when the pinch comes I'll get shoved aside and you slap the cuffs on. — Mickey Spillane, *I, The Jury*, p. 10, 1947
- I thought it was a pinch. I didn't know it was a shakedown till I got here[.] — Horace McCoy, *Kiss Tomorrow Good-bye*, p. 71, 1948
- "After about four months, I took my first pinch for running a wire room" — Nicholas Pileggi, *Wise Guy*, p. 120, 1985

2 a technique used by a man to maintain an erection, compressing the base of his penis *US, 1995*
- — *Adult Video News September*, p. 38, 1995

3 very potent heroin, bought and used in small amounts *US, 1993*
- — Peter Johnson, *Dictionary of Street Alcohol and Drug Terms*, p. 145, 1993

4 a five-dollar bill or five-dollar betting chip *US, 1988*
- — George Percy, *The Language of Poker*, p. 67, 1988

pinch *verb*
1 to arrest someone *UK, 1837*
- We're liable to get pinched for mashing on Sixty-third. I heard the Law is watching that pretty close. — James T. Farrell, *Saturday Night*, p. 38, 1947
- The cop shrugged. "Looks like you're pinched, kid," he told me. — Max Shulman, *The Many Loves of Dobie Gillis*, p. 195, 1951
- POLICE OFFICIAL: I want to tell you that if this man ever uses a four-letter word in this club again, I'm going to pinch you and everyone in here. If he ever speaks against religion, I'm going to pinch you and everyone in here. — Lenny Bruce, *How to Talk Dirty and Influence People*, p. 146, 1965
- My kidneys ain't too good, but I don't wanna get pinched for pissin' in public. — Edwin Torres, *Q & A*, p. 36, 1977

2 to steal something *UK, 1656*
- He pinches a shoeshine box for me and we start out working the BMT trains. — Rocky Garciano (with Rowland Barber), *Somebody Up There Likes Me*, p. 28, 1955
- "Pinched. Jobbed. Swiped. Stole," he says, happily. "You know, man, like somebody boosted my threads." — Ken Kesey, *One Flew Over the Cuckoo's Nest*, p. 94, 1962
- Anything that could be pinched could be sold. — Brian McDonald, *Elephant Boys*, p. 9, 2000

▸ pinch a loaf
to defecate *US, 1994*
- — Michael Dalton Johnson, *Talking Trash with Redd Foxx*, p. 44, 1994

pinch and press *verb*
to cheat at gambling, secretly taking back chips from your bet when dealt a bad hand and adding chips when dealt a good hand *US, 1985*
- — Steve Kuriscak, *Casino Talk*, p. 43, 1985

pinche *adjective*
used as an intensifier, roughly the same as "fucking" *US, 1974* Border Spanish used in English conversation by Mexican-Americans.
- — Dagoberto Fuentes and Jose Lopez, *Barrio Language Dictionary*, p. 115, 1974

pinchers *noun*
shoes, especially tight shoes *US, 1945*
- — Lou Shelly, *Hepcats Jive Talk Dictionary*, p. 16, 1945

pinch hit *noun*
a single inhalation of marijuana *US, 1993*
- — Peter Johnson, *Dictionary of Street Alcohol and Drug Terms*, p. 143, 1993

pinch pipe *noun*
a small pipe designed to hold enough marijuana for a single inhalation *US, 1993*
Small, easily hidden from parents and teachers, and economical.
- — Peter Johnson, *Dictionary of Street Alcohol and Drug Terms*, p. 143, 1993

pineapple *noun*
1 a hand grenade, especially a MK-2 hand grenade or Type 59 grenade *US, 1918*
- — Lou Shelly, *Hepcats Jive Talk Dictionary*, p. 47, 1945
- We'd need some arms and stuff, some real factory-made heaters and a couple of machine guns and maybe some pineapples.
— Chester Himes, *The Real Cool Killers*, p. 53, 1959
- All Whiskey j. carried was a knapsack and Claymore bag filled with grenades, both the old pineapples and the newer smooth-side sort[.] — Larry Heinemann, *Close Quarters*, p. 46, 1977
- "MK-two," Franklin said, "they call a pineapple." He looked at Jack, offering him the grenade, and grinned. — Elmore Leonard, *Bandits*, p. 359, 1987
2 a combination of cocaine and heroin *US, 1973*
- At this time tooting the boy along with the girl was called "PINEAPPLE." — A.S. Jackson, *Gentleman Pimp*, p. 70, 1973

pineapple juice *noun*
a rain storm in Hawaii *US, 1991*
- — Trevor Cralle, *The Surfin'ary*, p. 88, 1991

pine box release; pine box parole *noun*
death while in prison *US, 1978*
- "Ya done flipped and gotta yen for a pine box parole 'stead of walkin' through the front gate" Percy taunts[.] — Iceberg Slim (Robert Beck), *Doom Fox*, p. 214, 1978
- — William K. Bentley and James M. Corbett, *Prison Slang*, p. 105, 1992

pine top *noun*
strong, illegally manufactured whiskey *US, 1999*
- It is called corn liquor, white lightning, sugar whiskey, skully cracker, popskull, bush whiskey, stump, stumphole, 'splo, ruckus juice, radiator whiskey, rotgut, sugarhead, block and tackle, wildcat, panther's breath, tiger's sweat, Sweet spirits of cats a-fighting, alley bourbon, city gin, cool water, happy Sally, deep shaft, jump steady, old horsey, stingo, blueye John, red eye, pine top, buckeye bark whiskey and see seven stars. — *Star Tribune (Minneapolis)*, p. 19F, 31st January 1999

ping *verb*
▸ **ping the pill**
to remove a small amount of a drug from a capsule or package for your later use *US, 1970*
- — William D. Alsever, *Glossary for the Establishment and Other Uptight People*, p. 25, December 1970

pinga *noun*
the penis *US, 1960*
Cuban-American Spanish.
- [T]hen he was pinching the tip of my pinga through the fabric of my shorts. — Junot Diaz, *Drown*, p. 12, 1996

pinhead *noun*
1 a fool; an imbecile *US, 1896*
- LISTEN YA LITTLE PINHEADS, IT [spitting]'S NAUSEATING AND MORONIC[.] — Lester Bangs, *Psychotic Reactions and Carburetor Dung*, p. 230, 1977
- — Joe McKennon, *Circus Lingo*, p. 69, 1980
- The truth was that people were determined to smoke, regardless of what any pinhead researchers had to say. — Carl Hiaasen, *Skinny Dip*, p. 470, 2004
2 a person whose interest in playing pinball approaches the level of obsession *US, 1977*
- — Bobbye Claire Natkin and Steve Kirk, *All About Pinball*, p. 113, 1977
3 an amphetamine user *US, 1971*
- — Eugene Landy, *The Underground Dictionary*, p. 150, 1971
4 in the language of snowboarding, a skier *US, 1990*
- — Elena Garcia, *A Beginner's Guide to Zen and the Art of Snowboarding*, p. 122, 1990: "Glossary"

pink *noun*
1 a liberal; a socialist; a communist sympathizer *US, 1927*
- The others got good government jobs, became "contact men" or spoke at meetings and wrote for publications sponsored by rich left-wingers to provide automobiles and other luxuries for the needier pinks. — Jack Lait and Lee Mortimer, *Washington Confidential*, p. 9, 1951
- Rumor had it that there were quite a few pinks in the publishing biz. — Mary McCarthy, *The Group*, p. 185, 1963
2 a white person *US, 1945*
- "Was she that big Gawga pink work as a tacker?" Pigmeat asked. — Chester Himes, *If He Hollers Let Him Go*, p. 103, 1945
- In no time at all Konky got on the ball / And had ten whorers—nine pinks and a shade. — Dennis Wepman et al., *The Life*, p. 103, 1976
3 the open vagina *US, 2000*
Widely used in pornography, and beyond.
- When I see a naked woman spread out in the centerfold of Playboy or a porn queen sitting atop some stud in reverse-cowgirl position or a sassy stripper showing her pink in a gentleman's all-nude club, one burning question always comes to mind: Who does her pubic hair? — *The Village Voice*, 8–14 November 2000
4 a capsule of secobarbital sodium (trade name Seconal™), a central nervous system depressant *US, 1967*
- — John B. Williams, *Narcotics and Hallucinogenics*, p. 115, 1967
5 a casino gambling token worth $2.50 *US, 1991*
- — Michael Dalton, *Blackjack*, p. 68, 1991
6 in poker, a flush consisting of either hearts or diamonds *US, 1963*
- — Irwin Steig, *Common Sense in Poker*, p. 186, 1963
7 in horseracing, a track police officer *US, 1947*
Derived from the *Pink*erton Agency.
- — Dan Parker, *The ABC of Horse Racing*, p. 147, 1947

pink *adjective*
white; Caucasian *US, 1945*
- "Was she that big Gawga pink work as a tacker?" Pigmeat asked. — Chester Himes, *If He Hollers Let Him Go*, p. 103, 1945
- I ain't pink and I got two strikes against me now. — Mezz Mezzrow, *Really the Blues*, p. 267, 1946
▸ **all pink**
in poker, a flush consisting of all hearts or all diamonds *US, 1967*
- — Albert H. Morehead, *The Complete Guide to Winning Poker*, p. 255, 1967

pink-assed *adjective*
somewhat angry *US, 1962*
- — *American Speech*, p. 271, December 1962: "The language of traffic policemen"

pink champagne *noun*
methamphetamine with a pinkish color produced by the presence of the stimulant pemoline *US, 1989*
- — Geoffrey Froner, *Digging for Diamonds*, p. 69, 1989: "Types of speed"

pink elephants *noun*
collectively, influential homosexual Republican political staffers and operatives in Washington *US, 2006*
- Known in some insider slang as the Velvet Mafia or the Pink Elephants, gay Republicans tend to be less open about their sexual orientation than their Democratic counterparts. — *New York Times*, p. A20, 8th October 2006

pinker *noun*
in poker, a timid bettor *US, 1967*
- — Albert H. Morehead, *The Complete Guide to Winning Poker*, p. 270, 1967

pink eye *noun*
special contact lenses worn by card cheats to see luminous markings on the back of cards *US, 1988*
- — George Percy, *The Language of Poker*, p. 67, 1988

pink heart *noun*
an amphetamine tablet *US, 1997*
- Also black beauties, pink hearts, et cetera, advertised in the back of magazines like Creem, High Times, Hustler. — Laurel Sterns, *Retrohell*, p. 50, 1997

pinkie *noun*
1 the little finger *UK, 1808*
- Why, those little twerps at Webster—I can handle 'em with my pinkie! — Max Shulman, *Rally Round the Flag, Boys!*, p. 48, 1957

- Krankeit took hold of the little finger and held it up. "Which is that?" "Pinky!" the patient said delightedly. — Terry Southern, *Candy*, p. 110, 1958
- Vicariousness institutionalized, dipping their pinkies in. — Clancy Sigal, *Going Away*, p. 72, 1961
- This kind of man can kill you with his pinky. — *Apocalypse Now*, 1979

2 a bruised eye *US, 1970*
- — Claudio R. Salvucci, *The Philadelphia Dialect Dictionary*, p. 52, 1996

3 a Pinkerton private guard *US, 1949*
- "How you suppose Pinkies get trainin'—in classrooms?" — Nelson Algren, *The Man with the Golden Arm*, p. 84, 1949

pinkie cheater *noun*
a latex finger glove used during digital examinations *US, 1973*
- — *American Speech*, p. 201, Fall-Winter 1973: "The language of nursing"

pinkie ring; pinky ring *noun*
a ring worn on the little finger, especially an ostentatious ring worn by a criminal *US, 1975*
- At the check-in station, prison officials took my watch, my pinky ring and $2,000 I had in my pocket. — Joseph Bonanno, *A Man of Honor*, p. 225, 1983
- Middle-aged guinea with a full head of dyed-black hair, a diamond pink ring. — Elmore Leonard, *Be Cool*, p. 109, 1999

pinkies *noun*
underwear *US, 1954*
- If you answered that sometimes it could be scraped off with a knife, in nothing flat she'd be taking her skirt off and parading around in her pinkies. — Dev Collans with Stewart Sterling, *I was a House Detective*, p. 8, 1954

pink lady *noun*
a capsule of secobarbital sodium (trade name Seconal™), a central nervous system depressant *US, 1968*
- — *Current Slang*, p. 37, Fall 1968
- — Norman W. Houser, *Drugs*, p. 13, 1969
- — *American Speech*, pp. 152–154, Summer 1982: "More on nursing terms"

pink lemonade *noun*
cleaning fluid injected intravenously *US, 1971*
An often lethal substitute for methedrine.
- — Eugene Landy, *The Underground Dictionary*, p. 150, 1971

pink mafia *noun*
any group of women banded together, especially lesbians *US, 1997*
- Isn't that grounds enough for the little pink mafia to throw you out of their club? — *Chasing Amy*, 1997

pinko *noun*
a liberal; a socialist; a communist *US, 1925*
Originally applied to Communist party members, subsequently (in the late 1950s) to anyone who disagreed with the dominant culture and politics. Also used attributively.
- Haunt of homos, pinkos, nature lovers and nuts. Chicago's version of London's Hyde Park with soap boxers and prosties. — Jack Lait and Lee Mortimer, *Chicago Confidential*, p. 289, 1950
- Kampf's thundering oration was punctuated by bloodthirsty screams and hoarse shouts of "kill them pinkos!" from a black-shirted band of Legionnaires[.] — Hunter S. Thompson, *The Proud Highway*, p. 170, 12th June 1958: Press Release
- The Old Left says we work for the CIA. Ex-Marines stomp on us as Pinkos. — Abbie Hoffman, *Revolution for the Hell of It*, p. 27, 1968
- Red Mulvaney came into Lento's, looking for ore Reds, or pinkos at least, to beat up. — Gilbert Sorrentino, *Steelwork*, p. 5, 1970

pink puffer *noun*
a patient suffering from emphysema *US, 1973*
- — *American Speech*, p. 202, Fall-Winter 1973: "The language of nursing"

pink-ribbon case *noun*
a criminal case that has been thoroughly and professionally investigated by the police *US, 1962*
It is said that the police hand the prosecutor a case like this with a pink ribbon tied around it.
- — *American Speech*, p. 271, December 1962: "The language of traffic policemen"

pink shot *noun*
a photograph or video shot of a woman's vulva that shows the inside of the labia *US, 1974*

- The November 1974 issue was a watershed, the first in which Hustler featured a so-called "pink shot." — Larry Flynt, *An Unseemly Man*, p. 91, 1996

pink tea *noun*
an effeminate male homosexual *US, 1957*
- All the fairies in her town were closet queens or pinkteas[.] — Hubert Selby Jr., *Last Exit to Brooklyn*, p. 60, 1957

pink-top *noun*
a small pial of heroin sealed with a pink plastic cap *US, 2002*
The pink plastic cap denotes a variation in purity and price.
- The pink-top I have just clumsily purchased has its particular niches, or target market: the "kids from the counties," as middle-class teenagers from the suburbs are known in Maryland. — *New York Times*, p. SM24, 23rd June 2002

pink torpedo *noun*
the penis, especially when erect *US, 1984*
Aggressive imagery.
- My baby fits me like a flesh tuxedo / I love to sink her with my pink torpedo. — Spinal Tap, *Big Bottom*, 1984

Pinkville *noun*
an area in the province of Quang Ngai, South Vietnam *US, 1970*
Either named because of the area's appearance on maps or because of the strong presence of communist forces in the area.
- One of the Task Force's main objectives would be keeping pressure on an area a few miles northeast of Quang Ngai known as "Pinkville," the name deriving from the fact that its higher population density caused it to appear red on Army maps. — Seymour Hersh, *My Lai 4*, p. 23, 1970
- My Lai 1, 2, 3, and 4 hamlets were part of the village of son My, known as Pinkville—heavily VC in the fiercely contested province of Quang Ngai. — Myra MacPherson, *Long Time Passing*, p. 581, 1984

pinky *verb*
in dice games with no bank, to roll the dice to see who will play first *US, 1950*
- — *The Annals of the American Academy of Political and Social Sciences*, p. 129, May 1950

pinky crooker *noun*
a person with affected mannerisms *US, 1951*
- "Listen, pinky crooker, this evidence stuff is all smoke and mirrors." — Marc Brown, *Binky Rules*, p. 33, 2000

pinky's out of jail!
your slip is showing! *US, 1955*
- — *American Weekly*, p. 2, 14th August 1955

pin money *noun*
spending money *UK, 1697*
Originally a C16 practice of a husband allotting to his wife a certain amount each year for personal expenses.
- For pin money Sammy did an altogether different sort of cooking. — Seth Morgan, *Homeboy*, p. 126, 1990

pinned *adjective*
(used of eyes) constricted after opiate use *US, 1966*
- When the heroin addict is high, his pupils are "pinned," constricted. — James Mills, *The Panic in Needle Park*, p. 16, 1966
- I looked in the mirror. Oh shit! Look at my eyes! They were so pinned! You could hardly see black in the middle at all. — Cleo Odzer, *Goa Freaks*, p. 65, 1995
- Consequently, on this visit, when I saw that Emmett's eyes were "pinned" and knew that he was using heroin again, I allowed myself to blow up. — Peter Coyote, *Sleeping Where I Fall*, p. 324, 1998

pinner *noun*
a lookout *US, 1966*
- And for this reason the role of the "pinner" is a very crucial and important one. — Rose Giallombardo, *Society of Women*, p. 122, 1966

pin shot *noun*
an improvised injection of a drug in which the skin is pricked and an injection made directly into the wound *US, 1949*
- — Vincent J. Monteleone, *Criminal Slang*, p. 177, 1949
- — *American Speech*, p. 28, February 1952: "Teen-age hophead jargon"

pint *noun*
a short person *US, 1997*

- The labels were cruel: Gimp, Limpy—go-fetch, Crip, Lift-one-drag one, etc. Pint, Half-a-man, Peewee, Shorty, Lardass, Pork, Blubber, Belly, Blimp. Nuke-knob, Skinhead, Baldy. Four-eyes, Specs, Coke bottles. — *San Francisco Examiner*, p. A15, 28th July 1997

pinta *noun*
a prison *US, 2000*
Spanish slang used by English-speaking Mexican-Americans.

- What was of importance now—here in la pinta [Chicano slang for prison]—was the success of the MRU. — Bill Valentine, *Gangs and Their Tattoos*, p. 27, 2000

pinto *noun*
a Mexican-American convict or ex-convict *US, 1978*
From "la pinta," slang for "penitentiary." Spanish slang used by Mexican-American English speakers.

- The donation of time and effort by pintos, both inside and outside prison, was one of the most significant features of the project. — Joan W. Moore, *Homeboys*, p. 7, 1978

pip *noun*
1 the best, the finest *US, 1897*
From "pippin" (the best).

- "That place's a pip," I said to the driver. — Horace McCoy, *Kiss Tomorrow Good-bye*, p. 198, 1948
- Well, pal, here's a pip. — Leo Rosten, *Dear Herm*, p. 180, 1974

2 a star worn by military officers as an indication of rank *UK, 1917*

- Three months later he got his "pip" as a second lieutenant. — Frederick Forsyth, *The Devil's Alternative*, p. 32, 1980

3 an unidentified spot on a radar screen *US, 1947*

- *American Speech*, p. 154, April 1947: "Radar slang terms"

4 a woman's menstrual period *US, 2001*

- Don R. McCreary (Editor), *Dawg Speak*, 2001

▸ **give someone the pip**
to annoy someone *UK, 1896*

- I'm teed off. Things like this give me the pip. — Mickey Spillane, *My Gun is Quick*, p. 16, 1950

pipe *noun*
1 a foregone conclusion *US, 1961*

- "What if you lose?" Billy asked bleakly. "I won't. That game's a pipe." — Malcom Braly, *Felony Tank*, p. 47, 1961

2 the penis *US, 1962*

- Anthony Romeo, *The Language of Gangs*, p. 21, 4th December 1962
- Like a baton twirler with lots of practice, Annette grabbed Willie's pipe[.] — Steve Cannon, *Groove, Bang, and Jive Around*, p. 7, 1969
- When she said that, my pipe jumped to attention, and I had to have her right then. — A.S. Jackson, *Gentleman Pimp*, p. 36, 1973

3 any large vein, well suited for drug injection *US, 1952*

- But keep off, better, because if you like junk you keep shmeckin and shootin, then the skin pop goes to the big pipe[.] — George Mandel, *Flee the Angry Strangers*, p. 56, 1952
- Walter L. Way, *The Drug Scene*, p. 112, 1977
- Gilda and Melvin Berger, *Drug Abuse A-Z*, p. 110, 1990
- Sally Williams, *"Strong" Words*, p. 154, 1994

4 any wind or reed instrument *US, 1964*

- Robert S. Gold, *A Jazz Lexicon*, p. 230, 1964

5 the firing chamber of a handgun; a handgun *US, 1969*

- [T]hey had fought over a woman and then over a gun, which one of the men referred to at different times as "my piece," "my thing," "my roscoe," "my jive," "my cannon," "my shit," "my pipe," and "my heater." — L.H. Whittemore, *Cop!*, p. 197, 1969
- MURTAUGH: What's it take? RIGGS: Fifteen in the mag, one up the pipe. — *Lethal Weapon*, 1987

6 the vertical bar (|) on a computer keyboard *US, 1991*

- Eric S. Raymond, *The New Hacker's Dictionary*, p. 41, 1991

7 an academically unchallenging course *US, 1968*

- Collin Baker et al., *College Undergraduate Slang Study Conducted at Brown University*, p. 171, 1968

▸ **do the pipe**
to smoke crack cocaine *US, 1996*

- Yeah, but I ain't done the needle in a long time. Lately I been doing the pipe. — Neil S. Skolnik, *On the Ledge*, p. 110, 1996

▸ **get your pipes cleaned**
(said of a male) to experience orgasm *US, 2000*

- "I've had a long, shitty day and I really need to get my pipes cleaned." — Jason Starr, *Lights Out*, p. 64, 2006

▸ **on the pipe**
1 addicted to crack cocaine *US, 1990*

- I've been on the pipe for days now, ½ way thru my college fund, but I'm not even halfway hooked yet. — *alt.drugs*, 22nd September 1990
- Judi Sanders, *Don't Dog by Do, Dude!*, p. 22, 1991
- The kids around the pool table and video game were mostly here by default, half of them living on the street or with mothers on the pipe. — Richard Price, *Clockers*, p. 26, 1992
- People had been telling her for weeks that he was on the pipe. — David Simon and Edward Burns, *The Corner*, p. 48, 1997

2 used of a conversation between two jail cells conducted through plumbing emptied of water *US, 1992*

- William K. Bentley and James M. Corbett, *Prison Slang*, p. 56, 1992

▸ **take the pipe**
to commit suicide *US, 1982*

- Ralph de Sola, *Crime Dictionary*, p. 148, 1982

pipe *verb*
to fabricate a story *US, 1976*

- John R. Armore and Joseph D. Wolfe, *Dictionary of Desperation*, p. 43, 1976

pipe course *noun*
an easy course in college *US, 1927*
From the older, largely forgotten sense of "pipe" as "easy to accomplish."

- "You are all freshmen," continued Mr. Fitzhugh, "and you may not be familiar with the term 'pipe course.' A pipe course is a course where students can get passing grades without doing much work. This is not a pipe course." — Max Shulman, *The Many Loves of Dobie Gillis*, p. 96, 1951

piped *adjective*
drunk or drug-intoxicated *US, 1949*

- Vincent J. Monteleone, *Criminal Slang*, p. 178, 1949

pipe down *verb*
to be quieter; to shut up *UK, 1965*
Often exclamatory. From the nautical sense (to dismiss by sounding the pipe).

- Miss Cone, *The Slang Dictionary (Hawthorne High School)*, 1965
- "All right, pipe down," Maraney bellowed. — Charles Whited, *Chiodo*, p. 71, 1973

pipehead *noun*
a crack cocaine addict *US, 1992*

- He looked away, seeing her two months from now, no more baby fat, stinky, just another pipehead. — Richard Price, *Clockers*, p. 3, 1992
- "With the way I was dressed, and I was talking to myself, she thought I was some crazy pipehead." — Gini Sikes, *8 Ball Chicks*, p. 47, 1997

pipe job *noun*
1 oral sex performed on man *US, 1973*

- They come around, ask what time's your meal and take you for a ride. Pipe-job specialists. — Charles Whited, *Chiodo*, p. 66, 1973

2 an elaborate, fanciful fabricated story *US, 1968*

- Carl Fleischhauer, *A Glossary of Army Slang*, p. 6, 1968

pipeline *noun*
1 in the era of analogue phone exchanges, a telephone number with a recorded message which several people could call at the same time, circumvent the recorded message, and speak to each other *US, 1997*

- Editors of Ben is Dead, *Retrohell*, p. 153, 1997

2 the rapidly spreading curl of a breaking wave *US, 1965*

- D.S. Halacy, *Surfer!*, p. 216, 1965

pipeliner *noun*
in the era of analogue phone exchanges, a person who called a number with a recording, where it was possible to communicate with others calling at the same time *US, 1997*

- All the kids at school who were into this called themselves "pipeliners." — Editors of Ben is Dead, *Retrohell*, p. 153, 1997

pipe-opener *noun*
in horseracing, a short, intense workout several days before a race *US, 1976*

- Tom Ainslie, *Ainslie's Complete Guide to Thoroughbred Racing*, p. 336, 1976

pipes *noun*
1 the vocal chords *US, 1966*
- "I'll still pay a broker fifty bucks for a pair of seats to see her. She's got a great set of pipes." — Jacqueline Susann, *Valley of the Dolls*, p. 65, 1966
- I had pitched my pipes dry. — Iceberg Slim (Robert Beck), *Pimp*, p. 165, 1969
- She had lost her pipes and all the jive bitches she'd helped on the way was curving as they thought they'd have to lay some loot on her if they went by. — Babs Gonzales, *Movin' On Down De Line*, p. 51, 1975
- Pipes aren't quite as good as old Harry Bright's, but not so bad for a hoofer. — Joseph Wambaugh, *The Secrets of Harry Bright*, p. 291, 1985
2 the upper arm muscles *US, 1997*
- — Pamela Munro, *U.C.L.A. Slang*, p. 97, 1997

pipe up *verb*
to smoke crack cocaine *US, 1992*
- Girl wants to pipe up, it's a free country. As long as she's got ten dollars. — Richard Price, *Clockers*, p. 7, 1992

pip jockey *noun*
a radar operator *US, 1947*
- — *American Speech*, p. 154, April 1947: "Radar slang terms"

pipper *noun*
the sighting dot on an aircraft gunsight *US, 1955*
- At approximately fifteen-hundred feet slant range, I put the pipper on some heavy brush one hundred feet below my team[.] — Tom Yarborough, *Da Nang Diary*, p. 198, 1990
- I rolled into my bomb run, trying to set my pipper right. — Joseph Tuso, *Singing the Vietnam Blues*, p. 71, 1990: Cruising Over Hanoi

pips *noun*
the female breasts *US, 1981*
- Her pips were hanging there because she was naked to the waist. — Joseph Wambaugh, *The Glitter Dome*, p. 164, 1981

piranha *noun*
a poker player who bets aggressively on any hand with any chance of winning *US, 1988*
- — George Percy, *The Language of Poker*, p. 68, 1988

pirate *noun*
an unlicensed taxi driver *UK, 1977*
- — David Powis, *The Signs of Crime*, 1977

pirate's dream *noun*
a flat-chested woman *US, 1972*
From the association of pirates enjoying sex with captive teenage boys, or perhaps from the punning association of a girl with "a sunken chest and a box full of treasure."
- — Robert A. Wilson, *Playboy's Book of Forbidden Words*, p. 140, 1972
- — Pamela Munro, *U.C.L.A. Slang*, p. 66, 1989

pisher *noun*
a person of no consequence *US, 1968*
Yiddish from German, literally "a bed-wetter."
- And I'd think, who is this little pisher to say no to Meyer Faust[.] — Sol Yurrick, *The Bag*, p. 218, 1968
- Call me pisher for five hundred miles. — Vincent Patrick, *Family Business*, p. 273, 1985
- Herbert Haft opens negotiations to buy the Toronto Blue Jays, saying, "I'll bury the little pisher." — *Washington Post*, p. B1, 6th July 1993
- "I'm going to nail that little cocksucking pisher prick to the goddamn Hollywood sign as a warning[.]" — John Ridley, *Everybody Smokes in Hell*, p. 144, 1999

piss *noun*
the act of urination; urine *UK, 1958*
The verb produced the noun. Late Middle English then standard English, until it was deemed vulgar during C19. The sound of the word echoes the sound of urination.
- One fact that he knew was true was that if you go into a building where most of the tenants are niggers, either the hallway or the elevator is going to smell of piss. — Richard Price, *The Wanderers*, p. 4, 1974
- Piss ran down the graffiti on our inner-city walls. — Kathy Acker, *In Memorian to Identity*, p. 59, 1998
- "I gotta take a piss," he mumbled, feeling the urge. — Jackie Collins, *Dangerous Kiss*, p. 59, 1999
- Not surprisingly, her piss had the smoky fragrance of Lapsang souchong. — Rikki Ducomet, *The Word "Desire"*, p. 48, 2005

piss *verb*
to urinate *UK, 1290*
Derives from Old French *pisser* and has been perfectly good English since C13, but from mid-C18 it has been considered a vulgarism.
- He remembered telling her once he bet that she pissed ice water. — John Gregory Dunne, *True Confessions*, p. 102, 1977
- I had watched her piss and shit, I had, when she wanted me to, watched her be fucked by Andrew. — Jerome Gold, *The Prisoner's Son*, p. 155, 1996
- She pissed hugely in a steaming flow, with dignity and nonchalance. — Gregory Maguire, *Wicked*, p. 238, 2004

▶ **piss in the wind**
to engage in a hapless, futile activity *US, 1974*
- You're all pissin' in the wind / You don't know it but you are — Neil Young, *Ambulance Blues*, 1974
- — Michael Dalton Johnson, *Talking Trash with Redd Foxx*, p. 106, 1994
- He was pissing in the wind with someone like Trevor[.] — Greg Williams, *Diamond Geezers*, 1997

▶ **piss on ice**
to be living in luxury *US, 1960*
- We'll have dinner at Chasen's twice a week, we'll be pissing on ice the rest of our lives. — Robert Towne, *Chinatown*, p. 54, 1974

piss and moan *verb*
to complain constantly *US, 1951*
- It's no use to piss and moan about it; if I made a Thing of it and let it drag me, I really would flip. — James Blake, *The Joint*, p. 38, 30th December 1951
- Six months ago you used to piss and moan something awful, I brought you anything but two-inchers. — George V. Higgins, *The Friends of Eddie Coyle*, p. 34, 1971
- Don't waste your time pissing and moaning about how shitty everything is. — John Sinclair, *Guitar Army*, p. 117, 1972
- They were pissing and moaning about not having any decent food. — Mark Baker, *Nam*, p. 88, 1981

piss and punk *noun*
bread and water *US, 1970*
- "I was on piss 'n punk for three of the eight days." "What's piss 'n punk?" asks the messenger. "Bread 'n water," Billy tells him. "They don't do that much anymore, though." — Darryl Ponicsan, *The Last Detail*, p. 18, 1970

piss and vinegar *noun*
energy, enthusiasm, vigor *US, 1942*
- Fulla piss an' vinegar, buddies; they checked my plugs and cleaned my points[.] — Ken Kesey, *One Flew Over the Cuckoo's Nest*, p. 278, 1962

pissant *noun*
a small person *US, 1946*
- Yeah, I know he's a sawed-off little ol' pissant, but you call him "Shorty" and he'll stop your heart. — Ken Weaver, *Texas Crude*, p. 121, 1984
- We'll trample on the piss ants! — Kathy Lette, *Girls' Night Out*, p. 156, 1987

pissant *adjective*
insignificant, small-time *US, 1981*
- I was ensconced in the relatively decidedly pissant environs of Creem[.] — Lester Bangs, *Psychotic Reactions and Carburetor Dung*, p. 377, 1981

piss around *verb*
to play the fool, to waste time; to make a mess of something; to inconvenience someone *UK, 1998*
- I felt kind of silly pissing around backstage with my surfboard. — *New York Observer*, 19th February 2001

piss-ass *adjective*
despicable, unworthy, inconsequential *US, 1974*
- [B]efore he would work at some pissass job all his life and still wind up on welfare, he would take a gun and rob. — Earl Thompson, *Tattoo*, p. 7, 1974
- [T]hat's when I know he's had a piss-ass day and I'm gonna end up driving him home again. — George V. Higgins, *The Rat on Fire*, p. 74, 1981
- Shit, it was only about seven miles long, I don't know what we needed it for, little piss-ass island. — Elmore Leonard, *Bandits*, p. 272, 1987

piss away *verb*
to waste or to squander something *US, 1948*

● "The result," Julie says, "is that the bankroll that should have been there to absorb his losing days, he's pissed away." — Edward Lin, *Big Julie of Vegas*, p. 252, 1974

● And they're broke on Monday, boozing, whoring, pissing away the money all weekend. — *Saturday Night Fever*, 1977

● You've got a Hall of Fame arm but you're pissing it away. — *Bull Durham*, 1988

● And if I gave her the money and her jewels now, you know what she's gonna do? She's gonna piss it all away in about a year[.] — *Casino*, 1995

piss boy *noun*
a person of no consequence *US*, 1999

● Is this guy for real or what? What're we, fuckin' piss boys? — David Chase, *The Sopranos: Selected Scripts from Three Seasons*, p. 151, 20th September 1999

piss call *noun*
1 a break so that people can use the bathroom *US*, 1947

● "Piss call," he finally said. Sherwood ran the jeep up the grassy shoulder of the road, stopping nearly before a red-lettered sign. — David Davidson, *The Steeper Cliff*, p. 68, 1947

● "Every now and then you have to yell for a pisscall otherwise you have to piss off the air and hang on, brother, hang on." — Jack Kerouac, *On the Road (The Original Scroll)*, p. 127, 1951

● "Fella has to take a leak; all men equal, gringos and Mex and whatever, when the piss call comes, right-fellas?" — Tom Wolfe, *The Electric Kool-Aid Acid Test*, p. 326, 1968

2 time to wake up *US*, 1960

● "Piss call, you little shit!" Bill cackled cruelly. "Get up and piss, the world's on fire." — Earl Thompson, *A Garden of Sand*, p. 388, 1970

piss can *noun*
a local police station or jail *US*, 1950

● — Hyman E. Goldin et al., *Dictionary of American Underworld Lingo*, p. 158, 1950

piss cutter *noun*
a clever, resourceful and tough person *US*, 1941

● He was a real piss cutter, Ol' Tonto. Going all that way into Texas alone. — Clancy Sigal, *Going Away*, p. 108, 1961

● — *Maledicta*, p. 13, Summer 1977: "A ward for it"

● Ain't Delbert a piss cutter? I've seen a lot of guys open beer bottles with their teeth, but he's the only guy I know that eats the caps. — Ken Weaver, *Texas Crude*, p. 122, 1984

pissed *adjective*
1 drunk *UK*, 1929

● I really stuffed myself, boy, and I'm pissed to the ears, too, on top of it. — Lenny Bruce, *The Essential Lenny Bruce*, p. 15, 1967

● [A]nd then you're half pissed again and useless for the rest of the afternoon. — Mart Crowley, *The Boys in the Band*, p. 41, 1968

● "That's not Dennis Conner! Blaze, you're getting pissed!" a Kiwi grinder said. — Joseph Wambaugh, *Floaters*, p. 189, 1996

2 angry, annoyed *US*, 1971
An abbreviation of **PISSED OFF**.

● "Is she pissed?" you ask. "I wouldn't put it that way," Wade says. "I like that word better the British use it—colloquial for intoxicated." — Jay McInerney, *Bright Lights, Big City*, p. 19, 1984

● The only thing that gave away how pissed she was, was the tone of her voice. — Francesca Lia Block, *I Was a Teenage Fairy*, p. 98, 1998

● You were right. She's still pissed. — *Ten Things I Hate About You*, 1999

● God'll be pissed. You'll rot in hell. — Janet Evanovich, *Seven Up*, p. 86, 2001

pissed off *adjective*
fed up; disgruntled; annoyed; angry *US*, 1946

● Roseanne Kreiner was standing on her corner, in the rain, looking totally wet and pissed off. — Janet Evanovich, *Seven Up*, p. 93, 2001

piss-elegant *adjective*
conceited, haughty *US*, 1954

● Bar No. 2 is stocked with the dreariest breed of piss elegant, cagy, queens. — William Burroughs, *Letters to Allen Ginsberg 1953–1957*, p. 14, 20th January 1954

● So this elegant faggot comes to New York from Cunt Lick, Texas, and he is the most piss elegant fag of them all. — William Burroughs, *Naked Lunch*, p. 128, 1957

● — Florida Legislative Investigation Committee (Johns Committee), *Homosexuality and Citizenship in Florida*, 1964: "Glossary of homosexual terms and deviate acts"

● That piss-elegant kooze hit me! — Mart Crowley, *The Boys in the Band*, p. 94, 1968

pisser *noun*
1 a urinal *UK*, 1961

● "I have to take a leak," I said. "Where's the pisser?" — Robert Byrne, *McGoorty*, p. 99, 1972

● Another gang of kids push some melon into the pisser and I take off. — Tim Winton, *That eye, the sky*, p. 121, 1986

● — Pamela Munro, *U.C.L.A. Slang*, p. 97, 1997

● "Where's this little lot come from then Bogey?" Hangs his head shamefaced and embarrassed. Mutters his reply: "From the pisser down the church hall sir." — Jack Allen, *When the Whistle Blows*, p. 108, 2000

2 an extraordinary person or thing *US*, 1943

● Dreamer Tatum is what we call a pisser. I mean that sumbitch will make your helmet ring when he puts it on you. — Dan Jenkins, *Semi-Tough*, p. 17, 1972

3 an annoyance *US*, 1943
Literally something that will **PISS OFF** (annoy).

● That was a pisser. If Eddie didn't hit one of the stripes, Boomer would have an easy run out. — Walter Tevis, *The Color of Money*, p. 7, 1984

● A little pisser I've known all my life. — *Goodfellas*, 1990

● I mean, the matches go off, burn the hell out of my leg, scare the shit out of me...but the real pisser was blowing a hole in a brand new pair of jeans. — *Hard Eight*, 1996

● "Well, isn't this a pisser," Grandma said. — Janet Evanovich, *Seven Up*, p. 66, 2001

4 solitary confinement in prison *US*, 1990

● — Charles Shafer, *Folk Speech in Texas Prisons*, p. 211, 1990

piss hard-on *noun*
an erection driven by a full bladder *US*, 1969

● Almost every man is hard when he wakes up in the morning. We call it a piss hard-on. — Juan Carmel Cosmes, *Memoir of a Whoremaster*, p. 29, 1969

piss-hole *noun*
1 the entrance to the urethra *US*, 1996

● Sperm spills down from my piss-hole. — Peter Sotos, *Index*, p. 149, 1996

2 an unpleasant location *UK*, 1973

● [T]his filthy piss hole we call Mother Earth[.] — Howard Stern, *Miss America*, p. x, 1995

piss house *noun*
a public restroom *UK*, 1625

● Edith (her sister) & Patricia (my love) walked out of the pisshouse hand in hand (I shan't describe my emotions). — Neal Cassady, *The First Third*, p. 190, 7th March 1947

pissing match; pissing contest *noun*
a duel of unpleasantries *US*, 1983
From the graphic if vulgar image of two men urinating on each other.

● I made it by not getting involved in pissing contests. — Gerald Petievich, *To Live and Die in L.A.*, p. 78, 1983

● They treated Strike with respect, but the Homicide was a hawk-eyed motherfucker, and anytime they were under the same roof it was a goddamn pissing match. — Richard Price, *Clockers*, p. 207, 1992

piss off *verb*
to irritate or annoy someone *US*, 1937
First recorded in the normally slang-free poetry of Ezra Pound.

● That pissed me off, and depressed me more. — Bobby Seale, *Seize the Time*, p. 8, 1991

● All she said was that she had pissed him off somehow—pissed him off pretty badly, apparently—because he ended up throwing her out of the car naked. — Hulk Hogan, *Hollywood Hulk Hogan*, p. 102, 2002

piss play *noun*
sexual behavior involving urination and urine *US*, 1999

● Red is for fisting, black for heavy s/m, light blue for oral sex, dark blue for anal sex, yellow for piss play, orange for anything goes, purple for piercing, and so on. — *The Village Voice*, 24th November 1999

piss-poor *adjective*
extremely poor or feeble *UK*, 1946
Brought into general usage from British service usage during World War 2.

- From the point of view of human interest, it was a piss-poor day, Donald. — Bernard Wolfe, *The Late Risers*, p. 243, 1954
- I have to tell you the time my father and I and a pisspoor bum from Latimer Street took a trip to Nebraska in the middle of the depression to sell flyswatters. — Jack Kerouac, *On the Road*, p. 207, 1957
- "You'd make a piss-poor lawyer," he replied. "Relax. I'll handle this." — Hunter S. Thompson, *Fear and Loathing in Las Vegas*, p. 129, 1971
- "I've played this kid before," Bo said. "He's big, he's almost sixteen. But he's got a piss-poor backhand." — Elmore Leonard, *Switch*, p. 28, 1978

pisspot *noun*

1 an extraordinary example of something *US, 1993*
- "[Y]'all start in makin' piss-pots of money and figure you can afford yourself a niggaboy, I yours, brother." — Jess Mowry, *Six Out Seven*, p. 50, 1993

2 a despicable person *US, 1973*
- "You can go now. Cheap ghinny pisspot." — George Higgins, *The Digger's Game*, p. 25, 1973

3 a terrible thing or place *US, 1964*
- Prob'ly ain't every day they get to meet a real man in a pisspot of a town like this. — Jim Thompson, *Pop. 1280*, p. 54, 1964

4 a US military M-1 helmet *US, 1987*
- We call our helmets piss pots. You can wash or even shit in a helmet. — Ernest Spencer, *Welcome to Vietnam, Macho Man*, p. 45, 1987

piss slave *noun*

the passive member of a sadomasochistic relationship in which urine is a source of pleasure *US, 1981*
- Piss-slaves can recline in bathtubs or sit on toilets. — *The World of S & M*, p. 128, 1981

piss tube; pee pipe *noun*

a metal tube partially buried in the ground, into which soldiers urinate *US, 1977*
Vietnam war usage.
- I put it in my mouth—what the hell—then turned my head and spit it out over the low sandbag wall in the direction of the piss tube. — Larry Heinemann, *Close Quarters*, p. 251, 1977
- "Don't leave here," said the staff sergeant, "unless it's to use the piss-tube." Paul Berlin nodded, fearful to ask what a piss-tube was. — Tim O'Brien, *Going After Cacciato*, p. 34, 1978
- [H]e was standing at the piss tube—those were rocket casings that were driven into the ground at an angle and you stuck your dick in them ... when they filled up, you pissed somewhere else. — Dennis Marvicsin and Jerold Greenfield, *Maverick*, p. 42, 1990

pissy *adjective*

angered, crotchety, fussy *US, 1973*
- He's all pissy these days. Won't give me nothin' hardly. — Joseph Wambaugh, *Floaters*, p. 7, 1996
- Got pissy with me because I wouldn't let her carry the bag. Started running her fuckin' mouth. — *Jackie Brown*, 1997
- I had bummed a latex glove off Laurel and she was so pissy about it. — Michelle Tea, *Valencia*, p. 78, 2000

pissy-ass *adjective*

dirty, inconsequential *US, 1975*
- How many pissy ass winos have more'n a dollar fifty anytime? — Joseph Wambaugh, *The Choirboys*, p. 308, 1975

pistol *noun*

1 the penis *US, 2002*
- — Gary K. Farlow, *Prison-ese*, p. 51, 2002

2 a hired gunman *US, 1964*
- — R. Frederick West, *God's Gambler*, p. 228, 1964: "Appendix A"

pistola *noun*

a cigarette enhanced with freebase cocaine *US, 1979*
- A pistola is a base and tobacco cigarette made by emptying out and repacking a regular cigarette, or by rolling one. — *Hi Life*, p. 78, 1979

Pistol Pete *noun*

a chronic male masturbator *US, 2002*
- — Gary K. Farlow, *Prison-ese*, p. 51, 2002

pit *noun*

1 the armpit *US, 1965*
- So kept my pits bare and hid my hairy legs with thick, black stockings. — Michelle Tea, *The Passionate Mistakes and Intricate Corruption of One Girl in America*, p. 125, 1998

- So what do you do if you suspect you have problem pits? — Joy Masoff, *Oh, Yuck*, p. 22, 2000

2 the vein at the antecubital site, opposite the elbow, commonly used for drug injections *US, 1964*
- He hasn't even used his pit, which is what they call the original mainline to the heart and one of the best veins to hit. — Jeremy Larner and Ralph Tefferteller, *The Addict in the Street*, p. 167, 1964
- — Eugene Landy, *The Underground Dictionary*, p. 151, 1971
- — Geoffrey Froner, *Digging for Diamonds*, p. 48, 1989

3 Pitocin™, a drug used for inducing labor *US, 1994*
- — Sally Williams, *"Strong" Words*, p. 154, 1994

4 phencyclidine, the recreational drug known as PCP or angel dust *US, 1994*
- — US Department of Justice, *Street Tems*, October 1994

5 the area in a club or concert hall where dancers can slam dance *US, 1995*
An abbreviation of MOSH PIT.
- Got to punk gigs by himself. Slam in the pit with the boys until the pain sweated out of him[.] — Francesca Lia Block, *Baby Be-Bop*, p. 410, 1995

6 an inside jacket pocket *US, 1958*
- — *New York Times Magazine*, p. 88, 16th March 1958

▸ **no pit**
no trouble *US, 1968*
From "armpit" to "pit" to "sweat" to "trouble."
- — Collin Baker et al., *College Undergraduate Slang Study Conducted at Brown University*, p. 172, 1968

pit *verb*

to sweat under the arms *US, 1966*
- — John D. Bell et al., *Loosely Speaking*, p. 15, 1966

PITA
used as Internet shorthand to mean "*pain in the ass*" *US, 1995*
- — Christian Crumlish, *The Internet Dictionary*, p. 153, 1995

pitch *verb*

to play the active sexual role in a homosexual relationship *US, 1966*
- I've been known to pitch, but I'm no catcher. — Malcolm Braly, *On the Yard*, p. 149, 1967
- The young man walked over and leaned in through the window. "It's thirty; head only, pitch or catch," he said. — James Ellroy, *Blood on the Moon*, p. 133, 1984
- Elaine caught his slight grin and was sure Chili did too. He said, "You pitch or catch, Elliot?" "Mostly pitch." — Elmore Leonard, *Be Cool*, p. 269, 1999

▸ **pitch a tent**
to have an erection *US, 2001*
- — Don R. McCreary (Editor), *Dawg Speak*, 2001

▸ **pitch the furies**
to become very angry *US, 1993*
- [T]he drivers had them adjusted with scientific precision and would pitch the furies if they were moved. — Jess Mowry, *Six Out Seven*, p. 4, 1993

pitcher *noun*

1 the active partner in homosexual sex *US, 1966*
- — *Maledicta*, p. 231, 1979: "Kinks and queens: linguistic and cultural aspects of the terminology for gays"
- "Everyone's a natural catcher with someone who's a pitcher," said Carlo. — Ethan Morden, *Everybody Loves You*, p. 164, 1988
- Frank found one the day he arrived at Folsom—a big black-bearded "pitcher" (in prison jargon, the active sexual partner)[.] — Lora Shaner, *Madam*, p. 74, 1999

2 in a illegal drug sales operation, the person who physically delivers the drug to the customer *US, 2003*
- Another steerer sent the customer to a pitcher, who delivered the glassines. — Adrian Nicole LeBlanc, *Random Family*, p. 46, 2003

3 a dealer in a casino card game *US, 1973*
- — Thomas L. Clark, *The Dictionary of Gambling and Gaming*, p. 157, 1987

pit girl *noun*

a female casino employee whose job is to provide company and encouragement for heavy-betting gamblers *US, 1963*
- Known as "pit girls," their job is to entertain high rollers while the house empties their pockets. — Ed Reid and Ovid Demaris, *The Green Felt Jungle*, p. 95, 1963

pit guard *noun*

an underarm deodorant *US, 1968*
- — *Current Slang*, p. 10, Summer 1968

pits *noun*

▸ **the pits**

the very bottom; the depths; the nadir; the worst *US, 1953*
Perhaps from "arm*pits*."
- — *American Speech*, p. 194, October 1965: "Notes on campus vocabulary, 1964"
- — Collin Baker et al., *College Undergraduate Slang Study Conducted at Brown University*, p. 173, 1968
- Well, the first year it wasn't so bad, but then it went right downhill. The pits. — John Sayles, *Union Dues*, p. 127, 1977
- DeDe smiled bitterly. "I do. Isn't that the pits?" — Armistead Maupin, *Tales of the City*, p. 165, 1978
- "Things aren't going so well at home, Nickie?" asked Lacey solicitously. "The pits," I replied. — C.D. Payne, *Youth in Revolt*, p. 117, 1993

pit stop *noun*

1 a short stay in prison, especially one occasioned by a parole violation *US, 1984*
- — Inez Cardozo-Freeman, *The Joint*, p. 521, 1984

2 an underarm deodorant *US, 1969*
- — *Current Slang*, p. 12, Summer 1969

pitter-patter *verb*

to walk in small, quiet steps *US, 1964*
- So I pitterpatter over an grab my pocketbook[.] — Robert Gover, *Here Goes Kitten*, p. 128, 1964

Pittsburgh feathers *noun*

coal *US, 1949*
- — Vincent J. Monteleone, *Criminal Slang*, p. 175, 1949

pitty *adjective*

messy, dirty *US, 1975*
- — *American Speech*, p. 64, Spring–Summer 1975: "Razorback slang"

pity fuck *noun*

sex motivated by pity *US, 1983*
- In his movie, "The End," he uses his impending death to get a "pity fuck" from Sally Fields. — Helen Ewald, *Writing as Process*, p. 249, 1983
- Fucko the Clown (Evan Stone) has his own theme song, which tells of the character's drinking habits and how he can only get pity-fucks. — Editors of Adult Video News, *The AVN Guide to the 500 Greatest Adult Films of All Time*, p. 60, 2005

pity fuck *verb*

to have sex motivated by pity *US, 1998*
- One of those girls should have pity fucked you. — *alt.romance*, 27th October 1998
- "If I have to be pity fucked, then you do it. Goddamnit, it wouldn't hurt nearly as bad." — Lora Leigh, *Jacob's Faith*, p. 97, 2004
- Instead of adding them to The List or pity fucking them, I'll give them a hand job or let them do the job for themselves in my presence. — Angel Adams, *I'm Easy*, p. 158, 2006

pity party *noun*

any self-indulgent feeling sorry for yourself *US, 1975*
- I can still manage to work up a good pity party. — Jonathan Lewis Nasaw, *Easy Walking*, p. 108, 1975
- Again, you have the choice of either indulging in self-pity or angrily saying to yourself, I'm not going to have a pity party. — Andre Bustanoby, *But I Didn't Want a Divorce*, p. 22, 1978
- What she couldn't stand about Gary was the pity parties he would throw for himself, the crying and complaining about how he once had it all and how he had been betrayed. — David Simon and Edward Burns, *The Corner*, p. 50, 1997
- "There's no time for a pity party." — Carl Hiaasen, *Skinny Dip*, p. 495, 2004

pity pot *noun*

used in twelve-step recovery programs such as Alcoholics Anonymous as a name for the imaginary place where the addict sits feeling sorry for himself *US, 1998*
- — Christopher Cavanaugh, *AA to Z*, p. 143, 1998

pix *noun*

photographs or films *US, 1932*
- Striking pix is enclosed and you must of course send back without fail as I love it. — Jack Kerouac, *Letter to Neal Cassady*, p. 238, 3rd December 1950

- There have been pussy-lathering scenes and bare, fleshy vulva in plenty of pix. — *Adult Video*, p. 48, August/September 1986

pixie *noun*

1 a male homosexual *US, 1941*
The term was enshrined in US popular/political culture during the McCarthy hearings in April, 1954. Joseph Welch, the lawyer for the US Army, demanded to know the origins of a doctored photograph, asking if it had come from a "pixie," alluding to a suspected homosexual relationship involving Roy Cohn, a member of McCarthy's staff. Senator McCarthy asked Mr. Welch to define the term, which he happily did: "I should say, Mr. Senator, that a pixie is a close relative of a fairy."
- "He's a pixie, isn't he? He wouldn't know what to do with a woman, let alone rape one!" — Bernard Cornwell, *Gallow's Thief*, p. 101, 2003

2 an amphetamine tablet *US, 1994*
- — US Department of Justice, *Street Terms*, August 1994

3 hair that has been chemically straightened *US, 1972*
- — David Claerbaut, *Black Jargon in White America*, p. 75, 1972

pizlum *noun*

a pig's penis *US, 1952*
- About the only part of an old pig we don't eat is his pizlum. That's his auger. — Earl Conrad, *Rock Bottom*, p. 246, 1952

pizza dude *noun*

a pizza delivery person *US, 1988*
- — Connie Eble (Editor), *UNC-CH Campus Slang*, p. 8, Spring 1988
- Most of America has their face in the fridge half the game or is busy paying the pizza dude or having their lips stapled to a beer can and are too sloshed to even knew who's winning. — *alt.slack*, 26 January 1992

pizzaface *noun*

a person with a bad case of acne *US, 1971*
- — *Current Slang*, p. 8, Winter 1971

pizzazz; pizazz; p'zazz *noun*

energy, vim, vigor, excitement *US, 1937*
- I'm not merchandising my product properly. Knuckleball. It's got no pizzaz. — Jim Bouton, *Ball Four*, p. 173, 1970
- [I]f they ever had any pizazz in the first place[!] — Lester Bangs, *Psychotic Reactions and Carburetor Dung*, p. 37, 1970
- The pizzazz had gone out of our lives. — *Raising Arizona*, 1987

PJ's *noun*

pajamas *US, 1964*
- Next thing I knew I was stuck at the door, sand in my eyes, wearing my pj's with the feet, talking to some Jehovah's Witnesses. — Chris Rock, *Rock This!*, p. 67, 1997
- AUSTIN: I'll get you some PJs. FELICITY: No, I'm ready for bed. — *Austin Powers*, 1999

PK *noun*

preacher's kid *US, 2004*
Used without regard to denomination or even religion, applied even to children of rabbis; denoting a certain bond among those who have grown up in the shadow of organized religion.
- When one participant revealed the pressures he felt growing up as a "PK—preacher's kid," George W. chuckled. "You think that's tough? Try being a VPK." — Peter Schweizer, *The Bushes*, p. 335, 2004

PL *noun*

a professional wrestler who is regularly assigned to lose to advance the careers of others *US, 1990*
- Sometimes known as fish, redshirts, or PLs (professional losers). — *rec.sports.pro-wrestling*, 17th July 1990

placa *noun*

a nickname, especially the artistic representation of the nickname on a public wall *US, 1974*
Spanish slang used by English-speaking Mexican-Americans.
- — Dagoberto Fuentes and Jose A. Lopez, *Barrio Language Dictionary*, p. 118, 1974
- After a gang worker flew a group of teenagers to Sacramento, he found that felt-tipped pens had marked the placas (gang insignia) throughout the airliner. — Joan W. Moore, *Homeboys*, p. 37, 1978
- When off brands venture into the area and flag red, it's the same thing as coming in to cross out [puto mark] the local gang members' placas. — Bill Valentine, *Gangs and Their Tattoos*, p. 113, 2000
- These gang members call their inscriptions plaquesos, or placas. — Robert Jackson and Wesley McBride, *Understanding Street Gangs*, p. 61, 2000

plague *noun*

▶ **the plague**

HIV *US, 1990*

- The reason the topmost range of Quarantine is being used, sir, is because it's an open tiered block and it's widely believed you're as scared of heights as you are of the plague. — Seth Morgan, *Homeboy*, p. 351, 1990
- "This immune-deficiency thing." "The plague," Eve said. — Robert Campbell, *Sweet La-La Land*, p. 128, 1990
- "Tuffy has developed a prodigious case of plague necrophobia." — Ethan Morden, *Some Men Are Lookers*, p. 4, 1997

plagued *adjective*

infected with HIV *US, 1990*

- You don't want no part of Nefertiti. She's plagued, yeah. — Seth Morgan, *Homeboy*, p. 256, 1990

plaguer *noun*

a person infected with HIV *US, 1990*

- Every day plaguers are being paroled to spread it in the real world. — Seth Morgan, *Homeboy*, p. 257, 1990

plain wrapper *noun*

an unmarked police car *US, 2006*

- [A] plain-wrapper detective unit pulled up in front and parked. — Joseph Wambaugh, *Hollywood Station*, p. 110, 2006

plank *noun*

a heavy surfboard, especially an older wooden one *US, 1957*

- "[N]ever seen a girl on those planks!" — Frederick Kohner, *Gidget*, p. 23, 1957
- — John Severson, *Modern Surfing Around the World*, p. 175, 1964

▶ **make the plank**

in homosexual usage, to take the passive position in anal sex *US, 1981*

- — *Male Swinger Number 3*, p. 48, 1981: "The complete gay dictionary"

plank *verb*

to have sex with *US, 1972*

- — Helen Dahlskog (Editor), *A Dictionary of Contemporary and Colloquial Usage*, p. 45, 1972
- They planked on the cinder riding track near 72nd Street on the west side of Central Park and were interrupted by police horses—again at a critical moment. — Ed Sanders, *Tales of Beatnik Glory*, p. 18, 1975
- "What's right" include planking that little Russian girl of yours on the side. — David Chase, *The Sopranos: Selected Scripts from Three Seasons*, p. 200, 20th September 1999

plant *noun*

1 a police surveillance action *US, 1984*

- Sitting on a "plant"—what cops on TV call a stakeout—is like looking at a small section of a street under a microscope. — William J. Caunitz, *One Police Plaza*, p. 58, 1984

2 a cell used for solitary confinement *US, 1976*

- — John R. Armore and Joseph D. Wolfe, *Dictionary of Desperation*, p. 44, 1976

3 an electrical generator *US, 1985*

- — Gene Sorrows, *All About Carnivals*, p. 24, 1985: "Terminology"

plant *verb*

1 to kill *US, 1985*

- "There was no question—Jimmy could plant you just as fast as shake your hand." — Nicholas Pileggi, *Wise Guy*, p. 24, 1985

2 to bury a body *US, 1855*

- At least she's having him planted decently. — George Mandel, *Flee the Angry Strangers*, p. 372, 1952

planting *noun*

a burial *US, 1977*

- He said the honors at poor Joe's planting. — John Sayles, *Union Dues*, p. 266, 1977
- GANG BOSS PLANTING THRONGED BY THOUSANDS. — Richard Condon, *Prizzi's Glory*, p. 91, 1988

plant you now, dig you later

used as a farewell *US, 1947*

- Well, so long Hank. Plant y'now, dig y'later. — Harry Haenigsen, *Jive's Like That*, 1947
- — Kenn "Naz" Young, *Naz's Underground Dictionary*, p. 50, 1973

plaster caster *noun*

a groupie who makes plaster casts of celebrities' penises *US, 1966*

The practice was the brainchild of Cynthia Plaster Caster, who in 1966 printed business cards which she handed to British rock musicians visiting Chicago. The cards read: "Plaster Casters of Chicago. Life-Like models of Hampton Wicks." The British rhyming slang (for "pricks") was designed to appeal to the British-invasion musicians.

- — *Kiss*, 1969: "Groupie glossary"
- Cynthia remained chief plaster caster, responsible for the mix and mold. — John Burks, *Groupies and Other Girls*, p. 110, 1970
- The most famous incident in the Hendrix mythos was his encounter with Cynthia Plaster Caster, a college drop-out whose thing was immortalizing cocks—rock cocks—in plaster. — *Screw*, p. 15, 5th July 1971
- The Plaster Casters were two girls so desperate to get near their rock idols that they devised an extremely enticing approach[.] — Pamela Des Barres, *I'm With the Band*, p. 101, 1988

plastered *adjective*

drunk *US, 1912*

- Fell in the river when he was plastered. — Marvin Wald and Albert Maltz, *The Naked City*, 1947
- I took the pieces out of my coat pocket and showed her. "I was plastered," I said. — J.D. Salinger, *Catcher in the Rye*, p. 163, 1951
- My mother (not wanting me to go get plastered so often in NY and me too I get sick and dirty and don't work) invites all 3 of you to come out here any time you want. — Jack Kerouac, *Jack Kerouac Selected Letters 1957–1969*, p. 220, 24th March 1959: Letter to Allen Ginsberg
- He was plastered, I didn't know how. — Clancy Sigal, *Going Away*, p. 25, 1961

plastic *noun*

1 a credit card; consumer credit in general *US, 1979*

- These were fifteen-thousand-a-year guys—not paying with plastic, either: hard-earned green. — Vincent Patrick, *The Pope of Greenwich Village*, p. 13, 1979
- Carol was the Queen of Plastic. She could have written books on how to make two grand a day from a hot American Express card. — Gerald Petievich, *Money Men*, p. 35, 1981
- It costs me fifteen bucks for the cab to LAX and a hundred twenty-nine bucks on my plastic to New Orleans. — Robert Campbell, *In La-La Land We Trust*, p. 262, 1986
- What the sponsor will do is give the kid some plastic and about $500 in cash a week[.] — Dan Jenkins, *Dead Solid Perfect*, p. 22, 1986

2 a condom *US, 1993*

- I always pack the plastic. I ain't goin' out like Willy Lump-Lump. — *Menace II Society*, 1993

3 a Glock handgun *US, 2005*

- I handle my plastic, gunplay I mastered. — RZA, *The Wu-Tang Manual*, p. 177, 2005

▶ **pull plastic**

(used of a prisoner) to place your belongings in a plastic rubbish bag when you are transferred *US, 1997*

- — Jim Crotty, *How to Talk American*, p. 57, 1997

plastic *adjective*

conventional; superficial; shallow *US, 1967*

- Plastic people! / Oh, baby, now / You're such a drag. — Frank Zappa, *Plastic People*, 1967
- Estelle's hips and her thighs were too thick for anyone ever to call her figure "beautiful" in that plastic sense that Miss America is considered "beautiful." — Gurney Norman, *Divine Right's Trip (Last Whole Earth Catalog)*, p. 41, 1971
- The music tells them to drop out of the plastic nightmare and live together in communes and communities of their own people[.] — John Sinclair, *Guitar Army*, p. 29, 1972
- She was even laid back, at least publicly, about Harvey's liaison with Marlene, the eighteen-year-old Safeway checker he was living with in that plastic condo in Greenbrae. — Cyra McFadden, *The Serial*, p. 37, 1977

plastic badge *noun*

a private security guard *US, 2001*

- They were stopped by the plastic badge guarding the east gate[.] — Stephen J. Cannell, *The Tin Collectors*, p. 226, 2001

plastic fantastic *adjective*

wonderful *US, 1970*

If not coined, widely popularized by Jefferson Airplane's 1967 song, "Plastic Fantastic Lover."

- It's a lot of bread. It's like plastic fantastic. — Fred Baker, *Events*, p. 32, 1970

plastic hippie *noun*

a person who assumes the outer trappings of the counter-culture without fully immersing himself in it *US, 1967*

- [Y]ou began to hear stories out of the Haight saying the "real" hippies were taking flight to rural communes and that ersatz plastic hippies and teeni-boppers had taken over. — Nicholas Von Hoffman, *We Are The People Our Parents Warned Us Against*, p. 119, 1967
- plastic hippie: part-time or weekend hippie. — Ethel Romm, *The Open Conspiracy*, p. 245, 1970
- Their scene in Harrisonville, he told Rise and Win, was more real than the plastic hippies' flimflamming. — Joe Eszterhas, *Charlie Simpson's Apocalypse*, p. 110, 1973

plastic job *noun*

cosmetic surgery *US, 1953*

- The skin had a glossy look along the scars. A plastic job and a pretty drastic one. — Raymond Chandler, *The Long Goodbye*, p. 3, 1953

plate *noun*

1 a phonograph record *US, 1935*

- I genuinely like all those same plates of horrid blare and them for pleasure myself[.] — Lester Bangs, *Psychotic Reactions and Carburetor Dung*, p. 376, 1981

2 a decorative tooth cap *US, 2006*

- The teeth caps are alternately called grills, fronts, shines, plates, or caps, and these glittering decorative pieces are the latest hip-hop culture trend making its way into the mainstream. — *Boston Globe*, p. C1, 31st January 2006

plater *noun*

in horseracing, a horse that competes in minor, low-paying races *US, 1923*

From the practice of awarding a silver plate instead of a cash prize.

- — Les Conklin, *Payday at the Races*, p. 207, 1974

plats *noun*

platform shoes *US, 1997*

- — Vann Wesson, *Generation X Field Guide & Lexicon*, p. 128, 1997

platter *noun*

a phonograph record *US, 1931*

- — Arnold Shaw, *Lingo of Tin-Pan Alley*, p. 17, 1950
- "I'll tell you, Kipper, everytime I hear one of these new platters, it burns me up." — Edwin Gilbert, *The Hot and the Cool*, p. 29, 1953
- Just on the loose—a half hour at Mary's, let's ooze over to Jo's, say Pete's got a fistful of hot new platters, so let's lend an ear. — Dick Clark, *To Goof or Not to Goof*, p. 103, 1963

play *noun*

a maneuver; a tactical move *US, 1982*

- You got no right for this kind of play. — *48 Hours*, 1982

2 the deception surrounding a confidence swindle *US, 1940*

- Now let's join the others at the ghost town for the final tightening up before the play. — *Long White Con*, p. 33, 1977

3 in horse racing, a bet *US, 1994*

- — Igor Kushyshyn et al., *The Gambling Times Guide to Harness Racing*, p. 121, 1994

▶ **in play**

falling into a confidence swindle *US, 1997*

- You did great. You got him here. He's in play. — Stephen J. Cannell, *Big Con*, p. 298, 1997

play *verb*

1 to engage in sado-masochistic sex *US, 2001*

- People often describe BDSM with the term "play," as in, "I'd like to play with her." — Tristan Taormino, *Pucker Up*, p. 197, 2001

2 to work as a pimp; to hustle *US, 1977*

- I had class, Grief. I never had any filthy low-life junkie bitches when I was playing. — Iceberg Slim (Robert Beck), *Death Wish*, p. 88, 1977

▶ **play ball**

to co-operate with someone else; occasionally applied to inanimate objects such as computers *US, 1957*

- His dossier contains three pages of monikers indicating his proclivity for cooperating with the law, "playing ball" the cops call it. — William Burroughs, *Naked Lunch*, p. 157, 1957

▶ **play bingo**

to try to determine the reason for a cash shortage by comparing orders with receipts *US, 1996*

- — *Maledicta*, p. 8, 1996: "Domino's pizza jargon"

▶ **play checkers**

to move from empty seat to empty seat in a cinema, looking for a sexual partner *US, 1972*

Homosexual usage.

- — Robert A. Wilson, *Playboy's Book of Forbidden Words*, p. 197, 1972

▶ **play dead**

to act dumb *US, 1953*

- — Lavada Durst, *The Jives of Dr. Hepcat*, p. 13, 1953

▶ **play faces**

in a sports betting operation, to adjust the odds for specific bettors *US, 1974*

- With iiescu, "playing faces" meant moving the line up because the word was he always bet chalk. — Gary Mayer, *Bookie*, p. 181, 1974

▶ **play for the other team**

to be homosexual *US, 1997*

- — Jeff Fessler, *When Drag Is Not a Car Race*, p. 39, 1997
- Although I am confident that I can persuade people to play for the other team—I think everyone's sexuality is a lot more fluid than they think it is or would like to be—I was content with our friendship. — *The Village Voice*, 1st July 2002

▶ **play handball**

to smoke crack cocaine *US, 1993*

A highly euphemistic code.

- — Peter Johnson, *Dictionary of Street Alcohol and Drug Terms*, p. 147, 1993

▶ **play hookey; play hooky**

to absent yourself from school or work *US, 1848*

- I played hooky more and more often, spending my school hours in burlesque houses. — Jim Thompson, *Bad Boy*, p. 347, 1953
- [W]hen she was 14 or 13 maybe she'd play hookey from school in Oakland and take the ferry to Market Street[.] — Jack Kerouac, *The Subterraneans*, p. 56, 1958
- Some days we played hooky from school, leaving at lunch time with all the other older boys[.] — Bobby Seale, *A Lonely Rage*, p. 29, 1978

▶ **play past something**

to overcome an obstacle or impediment to progress *US, 1972*

- Thus, if someone attempts phony excuses one should "play past that shit" and find out the real reasons behind their actions. — Christina and Richard Milner, *Black Players*, p. 39, 1972
- He played it so good 'til he played past the real New York finest a number of times to my knowledge. — A.S. Jackson, *Gentleman Pimp*, p. 130, 1973
- If anybody ask who you are, tell them it's none of their motherfuckin' business. Just play past that shit. — Terry Williams, *The Cocaine Kids*, p. 28, 1989

▶ **play someone cheap**

to assume that someone is stupid *US, 1947*

- — Marcus Hanna Boulware, *Jive and Slang of Students in Negro Colleges*, 1947

▶ **play the chill**

1 to act calm *US, 1920*

- Blue whispered, "Play the chill for him. Remember, son, he's not bunco, he's only robbery detail." — Iceberg Slim (Robert Beck), *Trick Baby*, p. 13, 1969

2 to snub someone *US, 1985*

- — M. Allen Henderson, *How Con Games Work*, p. 222, 1985: "Glossary"

▶ **play the kerbs**

to sell drugs on the street *US, 1989*

- — Ellen C. Bellone (Editor), *Dictionary of Slang*, p. 18, 1989

▶ **play the queens**

to have sex with a passive, effeminate male prisoner *US, 1984*

- — Inez Cardozo-Freeman, *The Joint*, p. 522, 1984

▶ **play them as they lay**

used as a wisely humorous acceptance of the need to work with what has been given to you *US, 1992*

- You gotta play 'em as they lay, Luther. — *A Few Good Men*, 1992

▶ **play too close**
to take advantage of another's good nature by excessive teasing or abuse *US, 1992*
- — William K. Bentley and James M. Corbett, *Prison Slang*, p. 93, 1992

playback *noun*
a scheme by which the odds on a particular horse race are engineered lower by heavy betting on that horse *US, 1963*
- The explanation was reasonable. Playback—knocking the odds down on a horse by heavy pari-mutuel betting—was common in big-time bookmaking. — Jim Thompson, *The Grifters*, p. 41, 1963

player *noun*
1 a person who takes pride in the number of sexual partners they have, not in the depth of any relationship; a selfish pleasure-seeker *US, 1968*
- — *Current Slang*, p. 37, Fall 1968
- They were pimps in those days and not players. — Robert Deane Pharr, *Giveadamn Brown*, p. 15, 1978
- — Edith A. Folb, *runnin' down some lines*, p. 250, 1980
- She was a player, so her friends were probably players too. — Jason Starr, *Lights Out*, p. 188, 2006

2 a pimp *US, 1972*
- He is then no longer a pimp but a player, perhaps even a boss (excellent, tops) player. — Christina and Richard Milner, *Black Players*, p. 34, 1972
- It's almost inevitable that a prostitute ends up with a player. It's hand and glove. — Susan Hall, *Gentleman of Leisure*, p. 4, 1972
- After kicking things like that around with the city's biggest pimps and players and smoking a lotta good pot, I went into the hat shop to get my stumps shined. — A.S. Jackson, *Gentleman Pimp*, p. 27, 1973

3 a schemer; an important figure in a field *US, 1995*
- Harry Zimm. The man happens to be a major Hollywood player. — *Get Shorty*, 1995
- George chats away harmlessly, telling the brothers about his days as a sinner, about his days as a player in the criminal underworld of East London and Essex. — Mark Powell, *Snap*, p. 54, 2001

4 a drug user or drug seller *US, 1971*
- — Eugene Landy, *The Underground Dictionary*, p. 152, 1971

5 in casino gambling, a craps player *US, 1974*
- In Las Vegas parlance, a blackjack player is never called anything except "a twenty-one player" and a craps player is never called anything except "a player." — Edward Lin, *Big Julie of Vegas*, p. 182, 1974

6 a hip-hop artist *US, 2002*
Also variant "playa."
- — *Touch*, January–February 2002: "Too short—the original Californian playa"

play-for-pay *adjective*
1 available for paid sex *US, 1956*
- That title must have raised plenty of eyebrows among Hollywood's play-for-pay girls [.] — *Confidential*, p. 17, July 1956

2 receiving compensation while competing as an amateur athlete *US, 2003*
- But a few days before the SEC tournament opened, Georgia administrators were forced to cancel the rest of the season and fire coach Jim Harrick because of an academic fraud and play-for-pay scandal. — *Pittsburgh Post-Gazette*, p. C1, 30th December 2003

playmate *noun*
the wingman on a military aircraft *US, 1990*
- I guessed "playmate" was a wingman and got it right. — Tom Yarborough, *Da Nang Diary*, pp. 8–9, 1990

play out *verb*
1 to reject *US, 2002*
- Oh, hell no. I'm not going to get played out again. — Earl "DMX" Simmons, *E.A.R.L.*, p. 156, 2002

2 to escape from confinement *US, 1972*
- So I was there I guess three or four months and I played out [escaped]. — Bruce Jackson, *In the Life*, p. 110, 1972

please; per-lease; puh-lease
used for humorously asking please or expressing scepticism *US, 1990*
An affectation popularized in any number of television situation comedies in the mid- to late 1980s and thereafter a staple of US popspeak.
- — Connie Eble (Editor), *UNC-CH Campus Slang*, p. 4, Fall 1990
- Puh-leeeze, Nelson! I'm getting seasick. — Joseph Wambaugh, *Fugitive Nights*, p. 134, 1992

- Oh, puh-leez, why don't you take a handful of F-off pills? — *Austin Powers*, 1999

pleasure girl *noun*
a prostitute *US, 1959*
- The whole state became rough on pleasure girls. — Monroe Fry, *Sex, Vice, and Business*, p. 99, 1959

pledges *noun*
cash *US, 2003*
- Candy, markers, ammo, liners, stocking stuffer, sweetener, garnish, and pledges are all terms for cash. — Henry Hill and Byron Schreckengost, *A Good Fella's Guide to New York*, p. 123, 2003

plier *noun*
in a confidence swindle or sales scheme, an agent who for a commission locates potential victims *US, 1988*
- — Kathleen Odean, *High Steppers, Fallen Angels, and Lollipops*, p. 133, 1988

pling *noun*
an exclamation mark (!) on a computer keyboard *US, 1991*
- — Eric S. Raymond, *The New Hacker's Dictionary*, p. 39, 1991

pling *verb*
in circus and carnival usage, to beg *US, 1981*
- — Don Wilmeth, *The Language of American Popular Entertainment*, p. 204, 1981

plink *verb*
to shoot *US, 1967*
The term suggests ineffectiveness.
- Patrol after patrol was sent out to put an end to his plinking at planes. — David Reed, *Up Front in Vietnam*, p. 33, 1967

plokta *verb*
in computing, to press keys randomly in an effort to obtain a response from the computer *US, 1991*
An acronym from of "press lots keys to abort."
- — Eric Raymond et al., *The New Hacker's Dictionary*, p. 284, 1991

ploo *adjective*
a "plus" attached to a grade *US, 1968*
- — Collin Baker et al., *College Undergraduate Slang Study Conducted at Brown University*, p. 174, 1968

plop *noun*
excrement *US, 1984*
- In yore, did farmers rush to shovel the plop? — Bill Cardoso, *The Maltese Sangweech*, p. 134, 1984

plop *verb*
to fall or to drop heavily *UK, 1839*
- I couldn't just plop down and sit on the couch. — Howard Stern, *Miss America*, p. 125, 1995
- I simply shoved him on my bed and made him stay there until I had the time to plop down at the end of the party. — Jennifer Blowdryer, *White Trash Debutante*, p. 82, 1997

plop; plop down *verb*
to lay down forcefully; to lie down with abandon *UK, 1900*
- Grover came in and plopped down on a bench and sighed. — Dan Jenkins, *Dead Solid Perfect*, p. 104, 1986
- He was about to plop into a chair; but Cosgrove was ready. — Ethan Morden, *Some Men Are Lookers*, p. 120, 1997

plotzed *adjective*
drunk *US, 1962*
From German *plotzen* (to burst) via Yiddish *plotz* (to burst).
- [S]he was drunker than she'd been in years, plotzed, zonked, a mess. — Lester Bangs, *Psychotic Reactions and Carburetor Dung*, p. 364, 1981

plow *noun*
▶ **get your plow cleaned**
to be killed in combat *US, 1968*
- — Carl Fleischhauer, *A Glossary of Army Slang*, p. 6, 1968

plow *verb*
(used of a male) to have sex *US, 1970*
- He's so horny he'd plow a dead alligator or even a live one if somebody'd hold the tail. — Joseph Wambaugh, *The New Centurions*, p. 55, 1970
- Dorsey can plow whoever he wants. — *Ten Things I Hate About You*, 1999

plowboy *noun*
a rustic; an unsophisticated person from the far reaches of the countryside *UK, 1569*

Disparaging.

- New York gets its share, but its tourists include many from fairly alive communities; the plowboys hail from New England or other points not very far away. — Jack Lait and Lee Mortimer, *Washington Confidential*, p. 3, 1951

plowed *adjective*

drunk *US, 1960*

- I didn't in high school because getting plowed then was no so much alcohol as the will to get plowed, which bored me. — Glendon Swarthout, *Where the Boys Are*, p. 25, 1960
- "It gets better the more you drink," said Joey, on his third. After a while, everyone was plowed. — Richard Price, *The Wanderers*, p. 141, 1974
- "You have one drink a year, and your low tolerance gets you plowed." — James Ellroy, *Because the Night*, p. 431, 1984
- "I did not get drunk," she said absently. "You and Frank did. You got absolutely plowed." — George V. Higgins, *Penance for Jerry Kennedy*, p. 202, 1985

plow jockey *noun*

1 a farmer *US, 1951*

- — *American Speech*, pp. 158–159, May 1960: "The burgeoning of Jockey"

2 a soldier who cannot keep cadence when marching, who appears to be walking as if behind a plow with one foot in the furrow *US, 1946*

- — *American Speech*, p. 238, October 1946: "World War II slang of maladjustment"

pluck *noun*

1 wine *US, 1964*

- We went and got some "pluck" (wine) and I told him I was in college. — H. Rap Brown, *Die Nigger Die!*, p. 24, 1969
- But the brothers passed the pluck, putting the top back on after each sip, and conjectured anyway. — Steve Cannon, *Groove, Bang, and Jive Around*, p. 154, 1969
- What about China? I missed that runnin' to the git the pluck. — Odie Hawkins, *Ghetto Sketches*, p. 81, 1972
- Sid Strove said, watching a huddle of winos in front of an abandoned store nip at pints of strong port combined with sweet sherry in a mixture known as "pluck" — Emmett Grogan, *Final Score*, p. 157, 1976

2 the recruiting of a prostitute to work for a pimp; a prostitute recruited to work for a pimp *US, 1973*

- While I was ripping and running up and down Hastings trying to catch a pluck from all the whore bars, there was a little girl named Ruth who had been watching me[.] — A.S. Jackson, *Gentleman Pimp*, p. 34, 1973

pluck *verb*

1 to steal *US, 1997*

- Her line of work is crowded with those who can't resist taking advantage of the helpless, but Rita will never pluck a patient. — David Simon and Edward Burns, *The Corner*, p. 77, 1997

2 to recruit a prostitute into the services of a pimp *US, 1973*

- A lotta outlaw girls were there and I felt I'd be able to pluck off one of 'em. — A.S. Jackson, *Gentleman Pimp*, p. 91, 1973

▸ **pluck the chicken**

to swindle a victim in a phony investment or sales scheme *US, 1988*

- — Kathleen Odean, *High Steppers, Fallen Angels, and Lollipops*, p. 133, 1988

plug *noun*

1 a piece of publicity, a promotional pitch *US, 1902*

- Getting these songs before the public, or as the trade terms it, the "plug," is perhaps the soul of the industry. — Jack Lait and Lee Mortimer, *New York Confidential*, p. 32, 1948
- When it begins to rain, the dancers begin an anti-rain dance and it stops. The leader concludes with a plug for his studio, which teaches dance, song, drums, and karate. — James Simon Kunen, *The Strawberry Statement*, p. 48, 1969

2 a poker player with a steady, competent, and predictable style of play *US, 1988*

- — George Percy, *The Language of Poker*, p. 68, 1988

3 a horse that has seen its best days *US, 1860*

- There are five half-mile tracks in Maryland, which run almost all year with unknown plugs and has-beens, raced by "Gypsy" horsemen. — Jack Lait and Lee Mortimer, *Washington Confidential*, p. 273, 1951

plug *verb*

1 to support, to endorse, to promote *US, 1927*

- — Lou Shelly, *Hepcats Jive Talk Dictionary*, p. 16, 1945

- But a late development in the business, one which suspiciously smacks of a restraint of trade violation, is the practice of some publishers of giving a stock interest in their firms to noted crooners, band leaders, and disk jockeys, who in return "plug" the latest publications of the companies in which they are interested. — Jack Lait and Lee Mortimer, *New York Confidential*, p. 32, 1948
- "I'm still plugging for you," Owens said. — Jim Bouton, *Ball Four*, p. 348, 1970

2 to shoot *US, 1870*

- "Listen, rat"—Benny's face paled—"one more word like that and I'll plug you too. They can only burn me once, and I'd just as soon knock you off to stay alive as not." — Irving Shulman, *The Amboy Dukes*, p. 85, 1947
- "Hurry up you bitch!" Vito's voice said, "or I'll plug you!" — Willard Motley, *Knock on Any Door*, p. 285, 1947
- Yeah, go on over and plug that dame in the belly! Get real kicks! — John Clellon Holmes, *Go*, p. 13, 1952

3 (of a male) to have sex with someone *UK, 1888*

- "You know Eleanor McDonald? I plugged her." — Leonard Gardner, *Fat City*, p. 93, 1969
- You'd be lookin' old as sin too, if you was floppin' up and down bein' plugged by twenty or thirty tricks a night. — Odie Hawkins, *Ghetto Sketches*, p. 20, 1972
- Then ol Buck comes around and plugs her dog fashion while she's goin' down on me. — Earl Thompson, *Tattoo*, p. 225, 1974
- I spent four fucking hours at Slater Hawkins last night, trying to plug a chick I wouldn't have sneezed at in college. — Armistead Maupin, *Tales of the City*, p. 218, 1978

4 to engage in a fist fight without any weapons *US, 1992*

- — William K. Bentley and James M. Corbett, *Prison Slang*, p. 90, 1992

5 to tease or taunt someone *US, 2002*

- — Gary K. Farlow, *Prison-ese*, p. 52, 2002

▸ **plug your mug**

to stop talking *US, 1947*

- — Marcus Hanna Boulware, *Jive and Slang of Students in Negro Colleges*, 1947
- — Clarence Major, *Dictionary of Afro-American Slang*, p. 92, 1970

plugged in *adjective*

connected to something fashionable *US, 1989*

- In order to gain status at the university, a professor or composer in residence has to be plugged into something that's really hot—something fundable[.] — Frank Zappa, *The Real Frank Zappa Book*, p. 189, 1989

plugged nickel *noun*

something of no value *US, 1988*

- But your promises aren't worth a plugged nickel, are they? — Robert Campbell, *Juice*, p. 130, 1988

plugger *noun*

a person whose job it is to promote a record, recording artist, or other work of art *US, 1945*

- This singer—he was an old-time song plugger! — William J. Spillard and Pence James, *Needle in a Haystack*, p. 77, 1945
- The song pluggers began to come after me to sing their numbers. — Ethel Waters, *His Eye is on the Sparrow*, p. 178, 1951
- Bernie G.—known to the trade as Fat Bernie the Gossip Broker, the best columns plugger in the business—starts each morning repeating the daily routine he has followed for the last nine years. — David Freeman, *U.S. Grant in the City*, p. 119, 1971

plug-ugly *noun*

a violent, rough person *US, 1856*

- Then the plug-ugly moonshiner was leaning over the tombstone and grabbing me around the neck, hard — Guy Owen, *The Flim-Flam Man and the Apprentice Grifter*, p. 68, 1972

plum *noun*

1 in pool, the plum-colored four-ball *US, 1990*

- If you're playing Nine-Ball and you've sunk the 1-, 2- and 3-balls, you'd best pick the plum. — Steve Rushin, *Pool Cool*, p. 23, 1990

2 in pool, an easy shot *US, 1970*

- [I]t was an unnecessary shot, because Al really had plums all over the table[.] — Gilbert Sorrentino, *Steelwork*, p. 161, 1970

plumber *noun*

1 a urologist *US, 1961*

- — *American Speech*, May 1961: "The spoken language of medicine; argot, slang, cant"

2 a male pornography performer *US, 1995*

- — *Adult Video News*, p. 38, September 1995

plumbing *noun*

1 the reproductive system *US, 1960*

- Helena had known about sex from a very early age, but treated it as a joke, like what she called your plumbing. — Mary McCarthy, *The Group*, pp. 102–103, 1963
- In this dive you almost have to check everybody's plumbing to know whether it's interior or exterior. — Joseph Wambaugh, *The Blue Knight*, p. 44, 1973

2 any wind instrument *US, 1935*

- — Robert S. Gold, *A Jazz Lexicon*, p. 232, 1964

plumbing problem *noun*

the inability of a male pornography performer either to maintain an erection or to ejaculate on demand *US, 1995*

- — *Adult Video News*, p. 48, September 1995

plunge *noun*

a dose of a drug to be injected *US, 1957*

- "Four cents for the plunge, and it's lemonade." — Herbert Simmons, *Corner Boy*, p. 55, 1957

plungeroo *noun*

a pinball enthusiast *US, 1945*

- — Lou Shelly, *Hepcats Jive Talk Dictionary*, p. 16, 1945

plush *noun*

stuffed animals *US, 1985*

- — Gene Sorrows, *All About Carnivals*, p. 24, 1985: "Terminology"
- "It's a piece of plush that's supposed to be that dog from that kiddie cartoon, you know- what's-its-name-," he added. — Peter Fenton, *Eyeing the Flash*, p. 155, 2005

Pluto water *noun*

a natural mineral water that acts as a strong laxative *US, 1972*

- He marched over to the dresser and poured himself another snort of painkiller, downing it like it was Pluto water. — Guy Owen, *The Flim-Flam Man and the Apprentice Grifter*, p. 179, 1972
- The name "Pluto water" was coined in the 1890s by two doctors from Louisville, presumably to shift attention from the odor. "It tastes as bad as it smells, too," grins Gail Spencer, spa director[.] — *Chicago Tribune*, p. C9, 13th January 1985
- Visitors still take mineral springs baths at the 471-room French Lick Springs Resort & Spa, where the so called "Pluto" water was once promoted with the slogan: "When nature won't, Pluto will." — *Desert Morning News (Salt Lake City)*, p. T3, 14th September 2003

PM *noun*

1 a post mortem examination of a corpse *US, 1989*

- They could find out he had a heart attack—a man his age—when they do the P.M. — Robert Campbell, *Nibbled to Death by Ducks*, p. 153, 1989

2 in horseracing, the odds listed before a race *US, 1955*

Also known as the "PM line."

- — Thomas L. Clark, *The Dictionary of Gambling and Gaming*, p. 160, 1987

PMJI

used as Internet discussion group shorthand to mean "pardon my jumping in" *US, 1997*

- — Andy Ihnatko, *Cyberspeak*, p. 154, 1997

pneumonia hole *noun*

a car window *US, 1973*

- — Kenn "Naz" Young, *Naz's Underground Dictionary*, p. 50, 1973
- Throw some glass in that pneumonia hole! — Ken Weaver, *Texas Crude*, p. 9, 1984

po *noun*

1 in pool, position *US, 1993*

A horrid contraction, but one that is in actual use.

- — Mike Shamos, *The Illustrated Encyclopedia of Billiards*, p. 174, 1993

2 a promiscuous girl, one who will "put out" *US, 1963*

- — *American Speech*, p. 273, December 1963: "American Indian student slang"

PO *noun*

a probation officer or parole officer *US, 1966*

- I says, "If the PO goes over to the house, it's going to be all over" — James Mills, *The Panic in Needle Park*, p. 53, 1966
- The P.O. asked me if I had a job. — Piri Thomas, *Down These Mean Streets*, p. 319, 1967
- Knowing he could outthink, outgame and outmaneuver any cop, judge or P.O. he got hit with and that his destiny was the dead

opposite of every man in the bus, he said, "No, Anne Vander-linden." — James Ellroy, *Suicide Hill*, p. 573, 1986

- I said to my PO, "Look, I've signed all these—sixteen things you're not supposed to do while out on parole." — Herbert Huncke, *Guilty of Everything*, p. 111, 1990

po' boy *noun*

a welfare check *US, 1971*

- — Eugene Landy, *The Underground Dictionary*, p. 152, 1971

pocho *noun*

a Mexican-American, especially one who has assimilated *US, 1944*

From the Spanish for "faded." Used in English conversation by Mexican-Americans.

- "I am a Pocho," he said, "and we speak like this because here in California we make Castillian words out of English words." — Jose Antonio Villarreal, *Pocho*, p. 165, 1959

pocket *noun*

▸ **in pocket**

in possession of drugs to be sold *US, 1989*

- — Geoffrey Froner, *Digging for Diamonds*, p. 48, 1989

▸ **in the pocket**

in poker, dealt face down *US, 1990*

- — Anthony Holden, *Big Deal*, p. 303, 1990

▸ **out of pocket**

out of line; inappropriate *US, 1972*

- If you get caught smoking pot, you're totally out of pocket, you know what I mean? — Christina and Richard Milner, *Black Players*, p. 264, 1972

pocket club *noun*

a police truncheon *US, 1962*

- — *American Speech*, p. 271, December 1962: "The language of traffic policemen"

pocket man *noun*

in a functionally compartmentalized criminal enterprise, the person who holds the cash *US, 1987*

- — Carsten Stroud, *Close Pursuit*, p. 274, 1987

pocket pool *noun*

used of a man, self-stimulation or masturbation while clothed *US, 1960*

Word play based on ball play; the title of a song by Killer Pussy on the "Valley Girl" soundtrack.

- He was playing "pocket pool" with his other hand. — Iceberg Slim (Robert Beck), *Pimp*, p. 105, 1969
- [T]hey took the Scout Manual's advice and gave up jacking off (also known as pocket pool, flogging the bishop, and polishing the pudd). — Allan Sherman, *The Rape of the APE*, p. 15, 1973
- For chrissake, I'm a cop, Phil. What do you think I do all day, hang around eating tacos with Missy and playing pocket pool? — Robert Campbell, *Juice*, p. 230, 1988

pocket rocket *noun*

an improvised syringe filled with a drug and ready for injection *US, 1989*

- — James Harris, *A Convict's Dictionary*, p. 36, 1989

pod *noun*

1 marijuana *US, 1952*

- Don't say pot, Dinch. It's the intellectuals from college and all who come on that way. They want to get their hip-cards punched. Say pod, Dincher. — George Mandel, *Flee the Angry Strangers*, p. 26, 1952
- Nice stud. He made pod but not junk. — William Burroughs, *Letters to Allen Ginsberg 1953–1957*, p. 89, 19th February 1955
- "That doesn't mean you have to tear it up, smoking pod and —" — Herbert Simmons, *Corner Boy*, p. 27, 1957
- Oh, you know, man—the score you was with that time—the one that wanted pod so bad. — John Rechy, *City of Night*, p. 140, 1963

2 the head *US, 1960*

- I nudged my pod. — William "Lord" Buckley, *The Ballad of Dan McGroo*, 1960

3 an orthopedist *US, 1994*

- — Sally Williams, *"Strong" Words*, p. 135, 1994

PO'd *adjective*

angry; pissed off *US, 1957*

- Some of the girls from the luau stood around and they were sort of p.o.'d on account of being stuck there without transportation home. — Frederick Kohner, *Gidget*, p. 136, 1957

- Oh, God ... extremely PO'ed that hubby's not getting off on the decadent ambience. — Armistead Maupin, *Tales of the City*, p. 144, 1978
- Wow. She is really PO'd. — *Romy and Michele's High School Reunion*, 1997

podgy *noun*
a girlfriend, mistress, or prostitute *US, 1968*
Korean war usage; from the Korean word for "vulva."
- — Carl Fleischhauer, *A Glossary of Army Slang*, p. 6, 1968

pods *noun*
the female breasts *US, 1968*
- — Fred Hester, *Slang on the 40 Acres*, 1968

podunk *adjective*
worthless, remote *US, 1968*
- — *Current Slang*, p. 6, Spring 1968

pogey *noun*
a male homosexual who prefers the passive role in anal sex *US, 1950*
- — Hyman E. Goldin et al., *Dictionary of American Underworld Lingo*, p. 161, 1950

pogey bait *noun*
any food with high calorific, low nutritional content *US, 1950*
In prison, candy, cigarettes, or other inducements given to men willing to play the passive role in anal sex.
- — Hyman E. Goldin et al., *Dictionary of American Underworld Lingo*, p. 161, 1950
- — William H. McMichael, *Seattle Times*, p. A9, 12th April 1998: "Grunts, squids not grunting from the same dictionary"

pogo-pogo *noun*
cocaine *US, 1970*
- — William D. Alsever, *Glossary for the Establishment and Other Uptight People*, p. 6, December 1970

pogo stick *noun*
1 a Chinese rocket launcher, used in Vietnam by the Viet Cong *US, 1966*
- — *Newsweek*, 25th July 1966
- — Carl Fleischhauer, *A Glossary of Army Slang*, 1968

2 in poker, a player with wildly fluctuating play and success *US, 1996*
- — John Vorhaus, *The Big Book of Poker Slang*, p. 29, 1996

pogue *noun*
1 a homosexual male who plays the passive role during anal sex, especially if young *US, 1941*
Deriving perhaps from Irish Gaelic *pogue* (to kiss).
- The kid was a pogue. It seemed to Hicks that if he got any drunker and his place any lonelier and more savage he might actually have some sort of a shot at him. — Robert Stone, *Dog Soldiers*, p. 85, 1974
- — *Maledicta*, p. 221, 1979: "Kinks and queens: linguistic and cultural aspects of the terminology for gays"

2 a member of the armed forces assigned to the rear echelon, safely away from combat; a soldier newly arrived in combat *US, 1975*
- You're an office pogue. You never been anything but an office pogue. You don't have the slightest idea what goes on in a working police division. — Joseph Wambaugh, *The Choirboys*, p. 10, 1975
- It was the ages-old animosity between front-line infantrymen and the staff and support personnel farther back—the "pogues," those "rear-echelon mother-fuckers!" — Charles Anderson, *The Grunts*, p. 28, 1976
- Hell, I'm used to the pogues moving because of us. — Mark Baker, *Nam*, p. 137, 1981

pogy *noun*
a jail or prison *US, 1970*
- Since I had to get to the pogy to consolidate my plans and since my every move was under suspicion because of my break record, I had to have a clear and painful injury. — Red Rudensky, *The Gonif*, p. 13, 1970

poindexter *noun*
a serious student *US, 1981*
- — Connie Eble (Editor), *UNC-CH Campus Slang*, p. 5, March 1981
- Ohmigod, like Hillary's brother is like such a total Poindexter he's skipped two grades. — Mary Corey and Victoria Westermark, *Fer Shurr! How to be a Valley Girl*, 1982
- It's facing to ask rents for money, get airmail, or hang around with poindexters. — *United Press International*, 5th January 1984
- A good student who has already met his test-score requirement and a classmate who still hasn't qualified take the test on the same Saturday

morning. Poindexter puts Sluggo's name on Poindexter's test, and Sluggo puts Poindexter's on Sluggo's. — *Sports Illustrated*, 7th July 1997

point *noun*
1 a hypodermic needle and syringe *US, 1961*
- — Francis J. Rigney and L. Douglas Smith, *The Real Bohemia*, p. xx, 1961
- History is a Scabbie Point / For putting Cash to sleep. — Leonard Cohen, *Beautiful Losers*, p. 238, 1966
- Hawaiian Chuck was handing out hepatitis-infected points to friends who'd burned him. — Nicholas Von Hoffman, *We Are The People Our Parents Warned Us Against*, p. 83, 1967
- — Geoffrey Froner, *Digging for Diamonds*, p. 48, 1989

2 a man who insures that order reigns at a brothel *US, 1986–1987*
- — *Maledicta*, p. 150, Summer/Winter 1986–1987: 'Sexual slangs prostitutes, pedophiles, flagellators, transvertites, and necrophiles"

pointer *noun*
1 a criminally inclined youth, especially a youth gang member *US, 1963*
- — *San Francisco Examiner: People*, p. 8, 27th October 1963: What a "Z"! The astonishing private language of Bay Area teenagers

2 a large facial blemish *US, 1976*
- — *Verbatim*, p. 280, May 1976

3 a graduate of the United States Military Academy at West Point, New York *US, 1985*
- "He's a Pointer, you know. He wants in for a career." — David Donovan, *Once a Warrior King*, p. 57, 1985

pointers *noun*
female breasts with prominent pointed nipples *US, 1983*
- "She was a healthy-looking bitch, a jogger type with a great rack... a couple of real pointers." And I'm not talking about a bra with rubber nipples. I'm talking about a pair of honest-to-Christ pointed nips that must have weighed as much as silver dollars. — Gerald Petievich, *To Die in Beverly Hills*, p. 93, 1983
- Boobs, zonkers, headlights, watermelons, sweater puppies, pointers, knockers, jugs, tatas—these are some of the words to describe women's breasts. — Howard Stern, *Miss America*, p. 441, 1995

point-out *noun*
a member of a confidence swindle who introduces the intended victim to someone whom he identifies as a former acquaintance with good connections, who then lures the victim further into the swindle *US, 1997*
- We'll have a separate point-out meeting in a minute, then I want you to run rehearsals. — Stephen J. Cannell, *Big Con*, p. 342, 1997

poison *noun*
a narcotic or an alcoholic drink, especially a person's favorite *US, 1805*
Used in a jocular tone.
- He sat beside me and said, "See, Honey, I remembered your poison: gin and soda." — Iceberg Slim (Robert Beck), *Mama Black Widow*, p. 25, 1969
- So what's your poison? What do you drink? — *The Breakfast Club*, 1985
- I didn't think people said, "What's your poison" anymore, but I don't hang around these joints so I wouldn't really know. — Robert Campbell, *In a Pig's Eye*, p. 115, 1991
- The maitre d' didn't shout, You back again? nor did the bartender holler, What's your poison, paesan? — Rita Ciresi, *Pink Slip*, pp. 88–89, 1999

poison shop; poison joint *noun*
a pharmacy *US, 1972*
- We would go crack some poison joints and he would get enough stuff [drug] to last him two or three months. — Harry King, *Box Man*, p. 48, 1972
- We gots to find out first just what poison shops in this town are holding. — *Drugstore Cowboy*, 1988

poke *noun*
1 a wallet or purse *US, 1859*
- When the cluck woke up, he frisked his pockets for his poke. — Jack Lait and Lee Mortimer, *Washington Confidential*, p. 268, 1951
- Fat Girl returned to the room and picked up Bernie's wallet. "Your poke, man." — Ross Russell, *The Sound*, p. 158, 1961
- Where blood was shed for the sake of bread / And drunks rolled for their poke. — Dennis Wepman et al., *The Life*, p. 80, 1976
- Phil reaching behind Bill, fingers feeling the inside breast pockets of the mark's suit jacket or perhaps the overcoat pockets searching for the wallet—or poke, as Phil referred to it. — Herbert Huncke, *The Evening Sun Turned Crimson*, p. 112, 1980

2 money; a roll of money *US, 1926*

- The other boy he had could do the running and make some poke. — Hal Ellson, *Duke*, p. 65, 1949
- — Hy Lit, *Hy Lit's Unbelievable Dictionary of Hip Words for Groovy People*, p. 30, 1968
- — Clarence Major, *Dictionary of Afro-American Slang*, p. 92, 1970
- Then the mark opens the wallet to find out that they switched the poke on him and he has a wallet full of cut paper. — Stephen J. Cannell, *Big Con*, p. 165, 1997

3 the stomach *US, 1975*

- — John Gould, *Maine Lingo*, p. 213, 1975

4 an inhalation of marijuana or opium smoke *US, 1955*

- Go ahead. Take a poke. It won't hurt you. — Thurston Scott, *Cure it with Honey*, p. 60, 1951
- Then some lame was puffing on a joint one night, got next to a kitty and said she had to take a poke. — Edwin Torres, *Carlito's Way*, p. 26, 1975

poke *verb*

(from a man's point of view) to have sex with a woman
UK, 1868

- That's pretty much the story, folks, and after everybody gets to poke each other, in the pool, on the couch, in the bathroom and living room, Mosca performs his fabulous erotic dance[.] — *Adult Video*, p. 13, August/September 1986
- BB: Hey, asshole, here's the ultimate fuck-you. I just poked your wife! — *Tin Men*, 1987
- I'd poke her myself, 'cept last time I tried white stuff I got my neck sliced. — James Ellroy, *White Jazz*, p. 52, 1992

▸ **poke squid**

(of a male) to have sex *US, 1982*

- What, Rory—you wen poke squid las' night? — Douglas Simonson, *Pidgin to da Max: Hana Hou*, 1982

poker *noun*

the erect penis *US, 1969*

- Gawd, what a poker it was! — *Screw*, p. 19, 17th November 1969

poker face *noun*

a blank expression that gives nothing away *US, 1885*

- [H]e used to give us hysterics up on the bandstand, but we had to sit through it poker-faced and act like we weren't hip. — Mezz Mezzrow, *Really the Blues*, p. 85, 1946
- When the case was called, the courtroom filled with poker-faced orientals. — Jack Lait and Lee Mortimer, *Washington Confidential*, p. 56, 1951
- My old lady, nobody can tell what she thinking about nothing or nobody. She the one and original poker face, you know. — Sara Harris, *The Lords of Hell*, p. 114, 1967
- Again, I with my progressive ideas, played poker as well as they did, losing some and winning some as they did, but rapidly reading all stud card-hands and calculating odds and betting properly against the bluffers and the slick poker faces[.] — Bobby Seale, *A Lonely Rage*, p. 269, 1978
- Dude. You gotta have a poker face, like me. — *Bill and Ted's Excellent Adventure*, 1989

pokerino *noun*

low-stakes poker *US, 1960*

- They had closed up their hanky-panks, grab joints, pitch-and-dunks, pokerino parlors, had turned off the lights and killed the music and folded up the gaudy glamour. — Dean Koontz, *Twilight Eyes*, p. 4, 1987

poker voice *noun*

an even speaking tone that does not reveal any underlying emotion *US, 1986*

- McManus didn't know if the chief's last remark was a compliment or a jibe; Braverton was a poker voice all the way. — James Ellroy, *Suicide Hill*, p. 633, 1986

pokey *noun*

a jail *US, 1919*

- I'm gonna do everything in my power to fix it up so he'll think heroin's a new dance when he gets out of the pokey. — Clarence Cooper Jr., *The Scene*, p. 122, 1960
- If it weren't for him I probably would have been thrown in a military pokey for three or six months[.] — Clancy Sigal, *Going Away*, p. 214, 1961
- As I stood on the side of the road my thoughts centered around the prospect of "Pokey"—where a state trooper had once threatened to put me when he caught me hitching at 3 a.m. — James Simon Kunen, *The Strawberry Statement*, p. 80, 1968

- They grab some fat cat who identifies himself as a lawyer and go off to the local pokey to bail out fellow Digger Peter Berg. — Abbie Hoffman, *Revolution for the Hell of It*, p. 34, 1968

pokey *adjective*

dawdling, slow *US, 1991*
From **SLOWPOKE**.

- He said it would take about half an hour. Elvin said, "If you're a pokey driver it might." — Elmore Leonard, *Maximum Bob*, p. 126, 1991
- ... Nelson Hareem, who happened to be dawdling down the street at a poky seventy miles per hour, the speed limit he ordinarily reserved for parking lots and residential driveways. — Joseph Wambaugh, *Fugitive Nights*, p. 111, 1992

pol *noun*

a politician *US, 1942*

- I don't tell him that the world of old pols and patronage is probably doomed. — Robert Campbell, *Junkyard Dog*, p. 6, 1986

Polack; Polak *noun*

a Polish immigrant or a Polish-American *US, 1898*
Disparaging.

- Come on, you yellow-bellied Polack bas— — *West Side Story*, 1957
- Eat your last can of sauerkraut, Polack, because one of us has to die unless Mister Gregory and his people get out of solitary. — Dick Gregory, *Nigger*, p. 195, 1964
- a nice dumb polack who maybe has that extra something that makes for stardom. — Gore Vidal, *Myra Breckinridge*, p. 25, 1968
- A Polack's day, my father has suggested to me, isn't complete until he has dragged his big dumb feet across the bones of a Jew. — Philip Roth, *Portnoy's Complaint*, p. 142, 1969

Polack; Polak *adjective*

Polish *US, 1964*

- I had a few before I left Lansing—them Polack chicks that used to come over the bridge. — Malcolm X and Alex Haley, *The Autobiography of Malcolm X*, p. 45, 1964

Poland-and-China *noun*

a black and white police car *US, 1962*

- — *American Speech*, p. 269, December 1962: "The language of traffic policemen"

pole *noun*

the penis *UK, 1972*

- "Bitch," I replied coldly, until you grow a pole you leave the pimping to me. — Donald Goines, *Whoreson*, p. 141, 1972

▸ **up the pole**

pregnant *US, 1958*

- "If you had been on your toes you could have told him you had Mario up the pole and with a birth imminent you needed a little nest egg." — J.P. Donleavy, *The Ginger Man*, p. 10, 1958

poleax *verb*

to stun *UK, 1959*

- Katie Battenkill had poleaxed him with her fine alert features and lusty wholesomeness. — Carl Hiaasen, *Lucky You*, p. 29, 1997

polecat *noun*

1 a police car *US, 1976*
From the animal's black and white fur.

- — Warren Smith, *Warren's Smith's Authentic Dictionary of CB*, p. 56, 1976

2 in the television and movie industries, a lamp support *US, 1990*

- — Ralph S. Singleton, *Filmmaker's Dictionary*, p. 125, 1990

poleclimbers *noun*

heavy work boots with steel-reinforced toes and arches
US, 1995

- Doc Martens may have taken over a decade to go from exotic cipher to mall staple, but poleclimbers—and their lower-cut relative, logger boots—seemed to do it overnight. — Steven Daly and Nathaniel Wice, *alt.culture*, p. 184, 1995

poledad *noun*

an annoying, new-to-the-sport skateboarder *US, 1964*

- Those hopsotch poledads and pedestrians too, will bug ya / Shout "Cuyabunga!" now and skate right on through. — Jan Berry and Dean Torrance, *Sidewalk Surfin'*, 1964

pole dance *noun*

a sexual dance performed with a vertical pole as a main prop *US, 2000*

- Sure, I appreciate a tasteful pose, an artful fuck, and an athletic pole dance as much as the next woman. — *The Village Voice*, 8th–14th November 2000

pole orchard *noun*
the half-acre of utility poles at the Fort Gordon, Georgia Signal Corps School where linemen are given climbing instruction *US, 1968*
- — Carl Fleischhauer, *A Glossary of Army Slang*, p. 7, 1968
- "Prepare to ascend the poles," Staff Sgt. Doug Foster tells a group of soldiers, each harnessed to a 30-foot pole at the fort's Pole Orchard. — *Augusta (Georgia) Chronicle*, p. A1, 15th March 1999

pole work *noun*
utilization of a pole by a dancer in a sex club *US, 2001*
- The five-day Pure Talent School allowed Burana to polish her "floor work" skills on the dance stage—skills that Burana forthrightly acknowledges she lacked in the early years of her career—and refine her "pole work." — *Denver Post*, p. E1, 10th October 2001
- There's no pole work in the series, but props include a chair. — *Los Angeles Times*, p. 1 (Part 6), 27th October 2003

polgarize *verb*
during the Vietnam war, to give unrealistic and optimistic reports of the US progress in the war *US, 1990*
Named after Thomas Polgar, CIA station chief in Saigon in the early 1970s.
- — Gregory Clark, *Words of the Vietnam War*, p. 405, 1990

po-lice *noun*
the police *US, 1956*
By stressing the first syllable, the conventional term becomes unconventional.
- "Nothing personal, but I'm taking off. You're PO-lice." — Jess Stearn, *Sisters of the Night*, p. 51, 1956
- I ain't got nothin' to hide, it just that the PO-lice is always fuckin' over me ever' time I goes outside[.] — Joseph Wambaugh, *The New Centurions*, p. 73, 1970
- Still, it took about six months before we had learned to talk enough "game" to earn their respect as non-squares, and for suspicions that we might be "po-lice" to evaporate. — Christina and Richard Milner, *Black Players*, p. 24, 1972

police discount *noun*
a great, if not complete, reduction in the price of goods or services provided to police in their area of duty *US, 1975*
- His "police discounts" had furnished his house princely. — Joseph Wambaugh, *The Choirboys*, p. 60, 1975
- Two detectives argue about whether or not to ask for a "police discount" on cookies they're purchasing for Crosetti's funeral reception. — *Star Tribune (Minneapolis)*, p. 1E, 2nd December 1994
- Reference is made to the Ledger's articles on and preceding Nov. 19, regarding police discounts at restaurants[.] (Letter to Editor). — *The Ledger (Lakeland, Florida)*, p. A22, 20th November 2003

policeman *noun*
in horseracing, a horse entered in a claiming race solely for the purpose of permitting the owner to claim another horse in the race *US, 1951*
- — David W. Maurer, *Argot of the Racetrack*, p. 52, 1951

police psychology *noun*
brute physical force *US, 1973*
- At that time they used interrogation by police psychology—a punch in the mouth, a kick in the ass, a rap in the balls. — Leonard Shecter and William Phillips, *On the Pad*, p. 85, 1973

policy *noun*
an illegal lottery *US, 1843*
Better known as the **NUMBERS** racket.
- Once he got the club over Pepper's head, he would force her to sneak in phony "hit" slips against the policy wheel. — Iceberg Slim (Robert Beck), *Pimp*, 1969
- You know when you been round policy long as me it gets in your blood. — Vernon E. Smith, *The Jones Men*, p. 91, 1974

policy banker *noun*
the operator of an illegal numbers racket or lottery *US, 1975*
- Around Harlem, he'd feed off the policy bankers. — Edwin Torres, *Carlito's Way*, p. 17, 1975

polio weed *noun*
extremely potent marijuana *US, 1982*
Marijuana so strong as to reduce the user to a "polio-like" condition.
- [W]e were quite often transformed into Fred Astaire and Noel Coward by the same polio weed[.] — Dan Jenkins, *Life Its Ownself*, p. 22, 1982
- A Garcia term from the '70s; marijuana so potent it induces a state of paralysis. — David Shenk and Steve Silberman, *Skeleton Key*, p. 228, 1994

poli sci *noun*
political science *US, 1930*
College shorthand.
- CANDY: Poli Sci. With a home ec minor. MRS. CHASEN: Eh, Poli Sci? CANDY: Political Science. It's all about what's going on. — *Harold and Maude*, 1971

polish *verb*
▸ **polish the mug**
to wash your face *US, 1962*
- — Joseph E. Ragen and Charles Finston, *Inside the World's Toughest Prison*, p. 813, 1962: "Penitentiary and underworld glossary"

Polish jew *noun*
a firecracker *US, 1991*
- This cynical name for a firecracker comes about, I presume, from German days, because when you set fire to one it leaves the world with a harmless bang, scarcely ever injuring its murderers. — William T. Vollman, *Whores for Gloria*, p. 137, 1991

Polish martini *noun*
a shot of whiskey and a glass of beer *US, 1982*
- — Bill Reilly, *Big Al's Official Guide to Chicagoese*, p. 28, 1982

Polish matched luggage *noun*
two shopping bags from Goldblatt's, a low-end Chicago department store chain *US, 1982*
- — Bill Reilly, *Big Al's Official Guide to Chicagoese*, p. 49, 1982

Polish victory lap *noun*
circling a track in the opposite direction to which a race has been run in celebration of victory *US, 1990*
A calculated creation in 1988 of driver Alan Kulwicki.
- Kulwicki resisted the urge to take another unique victory lap, similar to his self-described "Polish victory lap" when he ran backward around Phoenix International Raceway after victory No. 1. — *AutoWeek*, p. 51, 29th October 1990
- But at the end of the night, after leading the final six laps, it was Hornaday who was able to turn his Chevrolet around and take a Polish victory lap in celebration and in tribute to the man for whom the race was named. — *Milwaukee (Wisconsin) Journal Sentinel*, p. 1C, 27th June 2004

politician *noun*
in prison, a trusted prisoner given responsibilities and liberties exceeding those of normal prisoners *US, 1946*
- [I]t didn't take a day before one of the "politicians" (that was what we called the trustees) slipped me a folded piece of toilet paper. — Mezz Mezzrow, *Really the Blues*, pp. 10–11, 1946

politico; politicko *noun*
a politician either ambitious or unscrupulous, or both *UK, 1893*
From the Italian or Spanish.
- I mean he's right—you make it with some big politicko an you got a good thing goin'. — Robert Gover, *Here Goes Kitten*, p. 41, 1964
- I kept wondering whether the Pigs were concerned about Liberation News Service (politicos) or Tate Blues Band (hippies) and things like that. — Abbie Hoffman, *Woodstock Nation*, pp. 56–57, 1969
- I was a very big politico on my campus and even got asked by the president to leave. — Malcolm Boyd, *My Fellow Americans*, p. 160, 1970
- Baby Jewels gladhanding politicos, grabassing showgirls, squeezed into nightclub booths with minor celebrities, lolling in his box at Candlestick Park — Seth Morgan, *Homeboy*, p. 29, 1990

polluted *adjective*
1 drunk *US, 1900*
- Finally the group of about ten or twelve slightly polluted young men, all dressed in black tie, showed up after their formal dinner[.] — Xaviera Hollander, *The Happy Hooker*, p. 87, 1972
- One night they come home and get polluted on the beer[.] — George V. Higgins, *The Judgment of Deke Hunter*, p. 121, 1976

2 warped, perverse *US, 1988*
- You're so polluted. Talking down to people, making fake notes. — *Heathers*, 1988

polly *noun*
a politician *US, 1974*
- — John Scarne, *Scarne on Dice*, p. 475, 1974

Polski *noun*
a Polish immigrant or Polish-American *US, 1997*
- And those given a name were stuck with it forever: Svade, Svenska, Lugan, Schnapps, Moishe, Stosh, Henie, Mockie, Guinea, Canuck, Bohunk, Pork-dodger, Limey, Greaseball, Krauthead, Dutchie, Squarehead, Grick, Mick, Paddy, Goombah, Polski, Dago, Hunkie, Wop[.] — *San Francisco Examiner*, p. A15, 28th July 1997

polvo *noun*
phencyclidine, the recreational drug known as PCP or angel dust *US, 1988*
Spanish for "dust."
- Beer, wine, polvo (angel dust), reds and marijuana were consumed on a regular basis[.] — James Vigil, *Barrio Gangs*, p. 74, 1988
- — *Q Magazine*, p. 75, February 2001

poly *noun*
1 a person who loves and has sex with multiple partners *US, 2000*
An abbreviation of "*poly*amorous."
- Not all neo-pagans are polys and not all polys are neo-pagans[.] — *Nerve*, p. 78, October–November 2000
2 a surfboard manufactured with *poly*urethane *US, 1963*
- — Grant W. Kuhns, *On Surfing*, p. 120, 1963

pom-pom *noun*
sex *US, 1947*
Used by US soldiers in Japan and the Phillippines.
- — *American Speech*, p. 55, February 1947: "Pacific war language"

ponce *noun*
a pimp *UK, 1872*
- Gabriel knew Mavis was a sucker for ponces. She often had several bludging off her at the one time. — Lance Peters, *The Dirty Half-Mile*, p. 92, 1979
- A toothpick traversed his mouth in sync with the restless eye gunning the street, identifying in less time than it took to name the hookers, hustlers, thieves, and thugs; pennyweight ponces and flyweight flimflammers; diddyboppers, deadbeats and dopefiends. — Seth Morgan, *Homeboy*, pp. 12–13, 1990

pond scum *noun*
a person with no redeeming features *US, 1997*
- Because the People of the great Garden State of New Jersey wanted to put a piece of pond scum like Joe "Dancer" Rina in the yellow brick prison at Rahway? — Stephen J. Cannell, *King Con*, p. 11, 1997

pony *noun*
1 a racehorse *US, 1907*
Used especially in the phrase "play the ponies."
- He played the ponies, got his tail, smoked cigarettes incessantly, despite his bad lungs, drank, sat up at all-night poker games. — James T. Farrell, *Saturday Night*, p. 12, 1947
- "They say they go for wine, women and song but whoever said it forgot to add the ponies, too." — Mickey Spillane, *The Big Kill*, p. 97, 1951
- He was married to a woman by the name of Lisa, who had a pocketful of busted dreams of her own, but he still took what he could get, still played the ponies and still lost the farm nearly each and every time he tried to be a sport. — Robert Campbell, *Juice*, pp. 3–4, 1988
- Apparently, way it went, he invited her to come to Santa Anita to play the ponies with him. — *Get Shorty*, 1995
2 a chorus girl or dancer, especially a small one *UK, 1908*
- The whole Ziegfeld chorus, from the ponies to the showgirls, would be hired to fan us with palm leaves as we lounged around in the sun, reading H.L. Mencken and playing Louis Armstrong records[.] — Mezz Mezzrow, *Really the Blues*, p. 131, 1946
- A new crop of lovelies had come up, were displayed and went on to Hollywood. To mention one, Alice Faye—a Hollywood Restaurant pony. — Jack Lait and Lee Mortimer, *New York Confidential*, p. 28, 1948
- But here the feathers hang tired on the rumps of the floor-show ponies, and there is no self-conscious reading of Proust in satined dressing rooms. — John D. McDonald, *The Neon Jungle*, p. 6, 1953
- Rita batted her rhinestoned eyelashes seductively like the Vegas chorus pony she once, recently, was. — Iceberg Slim (Robert Beck), *Long White Con*, p. 20, 1977
3 crack cocaine *US, 1994*
- — US Department of Justice, *Street Terms*, October 1994

4 a literal, line-by-line translation of a work in a foreign (usually classical) language *US, 1827*
- Then she would produce a Virgil pony—a Latin text book with English translations set in smaller type beneath each line of Latin. — Max Shulman, *The Many Loves of Dobie Gillis*, p. 2, 1951

pony girl *noun*
an out-call prostitute *US, 1971*
- A call girl or "pony girl" is a prostitute who keeps individual dates with her clients at a place selected by mutual consent. — Charles Winick, *The Lively Commerce*, p. 176, 1971

pony pecker *noun*
sausage; unidentified pressed meat *US, 1968*
- — Carl Fleischhauer, *A Glossary of Army Slang*, p. 26, 1968

ponyplay *noun*
an animal transformation sexual fetish, in which the dominants train, ride, and groom people who dress and act like ponies *US, 2000*
- The erotic elements of ponyplay depend on the people involved. — *The Village Voice*, 28th November 2000

pony up *verb*
to contribute your share of a bet or collection *US, 1979*
- — John Scarne, *Scarne's Guide to Modern Poker*, p. 287, 1979

poo *noun*
feces; the act of defecation *UK, 1960*
Childish or jocular. Many variant forms, including "pooh," "poo poo" and "pooh pooh."
- — *Maledicta*, p. 32, 1988–1989: "Medical Maledicta from San Francisco"
- Who knew that eating cheese makes good pooh-pooh? — Howard Stern, *Miss America*, p. 245, 1995
- This projectile terd shoots right out of his butt and lands SMACK on her neck .... this poo hits her right on the neck. — *Hard Eight*, 1996

pooch *noun*
a dog *US, 1924*
Also used as a term of address for an unknown dog.
- old women with grotesque young get-ups and peroxided hair, parading their pooches — Jack Lait and Lee Mortimer, *New York Confidential*, p. 13, 1948
- Of course the pooch padded down the steps heading straight for the tree to pee over Letch's. — Joseph Wambaugh, *Floaters*, p. 12, 1996

pooch out *verb*
to purse your lips *US, 1989*
- "[M]ake the dancer face" (eyes closed; lips pooched out—you know the one[.]) — Frank Zappa, *The Real Frank Zappa Book*, p. 159, 1989

pooh-butt *noun*
a despicable person *US, 1993*
- "You pooh-butts in the Coast now." — Bob Sipchen, *Baby Insane and the Buddha*, p. 71, 1993
- Don't bring her here! I'm not even fuckin' joking with you, don't you be bringing some fucked up pooh-butt to my house! — *Pulp Fiction*, 1994

pooh-pooh *verb*
to belittle someone or something; to dismiss someone or something as inconsequential *UK, 1827*
- And he pooh-poohed her angry opinion that the stuff was too old for me. — Jim Thompson, *Bad Boy*, p. 294, 1953
- The kids all pooh-poohed her and told her not to worry so much about a fifty-dollar watch[.] — Larry McMurtry, *The Last Picture Show*, p. 79, 1966

pooky *noun*
marijuana *US, 2001*
- — Rick Ayers (Editor), *Slang Dictionary*, p. 13, 2001

poolhall cowboy *noun*
a pool player who has perfected a reckless manner *US, 1976*
- I thought he was a jock. He's a poolhall cowboy. — Elmore Leonard, *Swag*, p. 64, 1976

pool harpy *noun*
a pool player who plays for money, relying on a combination of skill and deceptive behavior *US, 1966*

- Pool-Harpies, it should be mentioned, come in all four of the Hollywood sexes; homosexual, heterosexual, lesbian, bisexual. — Roger Gordon, *Hollywood's Sexual Underground*, p. 17, 1966

poolhouse *verb*
to stay at a friend's house temporarily, literally or figuratively in their poolhouse *US, 2004*
- "My mom is a drag. Mind if I poolhouse with you a while?" — Brittany Kent, *O.C. Undercover*, p. 139, 2004

pool shark *noun*
an expert pool player who makes a living by feigning a lack of expertise and convincing strangers to play against him *US, 1908*
- Back on Chicago's street-corner haunts you tangled with gamblers and racketeers and poolroom sharks[.] — Mezz Mezzrow, *Really the Blues*, p. 206, 1946
- Why, you're a pool shark. A real pool shark. — *The Hustler*, 1961

poon *noun*
the vagina; a woman; a woman as a sex object; sex with a woman *US, 1957*
A shortened form of **POONTANG**.
- You'll find more poon per square inch in hick towns than in any big city on God's green earth. — Max Shulman, *Rally Round the Flag, Boys!*, p. 158, 1957
- You don't have to be wild with the notion to want some poon. — Elmore Leonard, *Gold Coast*, p. 19, 1980
- [I]t's hotter than a nun's poon in here! — Terry Southern, *Texas Summer*, p. 119, 1991
- [H]e was given excess gambling skim to invest as he saw best and opened a call house specializing in underaged poon dressed up as movie stars. — James Ellroy, *Hollywood Nocturnes*, p. 210, 1994

pooner
a male with sexual experience and apparent expertise *US, 1968*
- — Collin Baker et al., *College Undergraduate Slang Study Conducted at Brown University*, pp. 174–175, 1968

poonhound *noun*
a man obsessed with sex with women *US, 1998*
- My dad say Yul was a poonhound. He had the goods. — James Ellroy, *Destination Morgue*, p. 174, 2004

poon light *noun*
in the pornography industry, a light used to illuminate the genitals of the performers *US, 1995*
- — *Adult Video News*, p. 50, October 1995

poon-poon *noun*
the vagina *US, 2005*
- He didn't even stroke the poon-poon or worry whether or not it was wet. — Noire, *Candy Licker*, p. 8, 2005

poontang *noun*
the vagina; sex; a woman regarded as a sexual object *US, 1929*
Suggestions that the term comes from an American Indian language, Chinese, Bantu, Peruvian or a Filipinio dialect notwithstanding, it almost certainly comes from the French *putain* (prostitute).
- I say to you send me over a simple C.O.D. slice of poontang, and what do I get? — Bernard Wolfe, *The Late Risers*, p. 200, 1954
- He's just enervated on too much pooo-oo-nn tang. — Clancy Sigal, *Going Away*, p. 10, 1961
- Two things we always had in common—liquor and poon-tang. — James Baldwin, *Blues for Mister Charlie*, p. 103, 1964
- Say, "You got to get down on that floor on both your knees / Nibble at this poontang like a rat nibbling at cheese." [Collected in 1967]. — Roger Abrahams, *Positively Black*, p. 95, 1970
- He dug that young poontang—even though at his age I knew he was shooting blanks. — Edwin Torres, *Carlito's Way*, p. 29, 1975
- Talk about poontang / Right down to your yin ang / Down by the banks of the Ohio. — Roogalator *Cincinnatti Fatback*, 1976
- The poontang was dope and you know that I rocked her. — Kool Moe Dee, *Go See The Doctor*, 1986
- In a mere three lines, they tackle homesickness, syphilis, "hottail poontang sweetheart sweat," and creative uses for J. Paul Getty's auditory canal[.] — Chuck Eddy, *Stairway to Hell*, p. 25, 1991
- A highly sensitive condition whereby a man temporarily surrenders power to a woman; the consequence of being hypnotized by hot poontang. — Anka Radakovich, *The Wild Girls Club*, p. 18, 1994

poop *noun*
1 information, news *US, 1942*
Probably from the sense as "nonsense" (**SHIT**).
- The only catch is that the guy who could identify him is dead and they have to go from the poop he gave them. — Mickey Spillane, *My Gun is Quick*, p. 96, 1950
- The moment one of the Marines came off watch he was pumped for new aldrich poop. — William Brinkley, *Don't Go Near the Water*, pp. 251–252, 1956
- What's the old poop, David? You've been hinting. — Richard Farina, *Been Down So Long*, p. 193, 1966
- Surtees walked me down to the seven-three, talking the whole way. "Putting the poop to me," as he said. — Larry Heinemann, *Close Quarters*, p. 20, 1977

2 feces; an act of defecation *US, 1948*
Children's toilet vocabulary.
- She'd even say to Buddy, poop all over his stand, "Buddy go potty?" — Elmore Leonard, *Glitz*, p. 341, 1985
- One day, taking a poop, I noticed that "it" was not really coming out but felt suspended over the water. — Sandra Bernard, *Confessions of a Pretty Lady*, p. 19, 1988

3 a pledge to a college fraternity *US, 1955*
- — *American Speech*, p. 304, December 1955: "Wayne University slang"

poop *verb*
1 to defecate *UK, 1872*
- I mean, things were kind of better when I pooped in my pants. — Jay Jacobs, *Pretty Good Years*, p. 62, 2006

2 to brief, to inform *US, 1990*
- So the boys in TOC pooped us up on what we'd see. — Joseph Tuso, *Singing the Vietnam Blues*, p. 232, 1990: Wolf Pack's Houseboy

3 in poker, to raise a bet *US, 1951*
- — *American Speech*, p. 100, May 1951

poopadoop *noun*
the rectum *US, 1977*
- — *Maledicta*, p. 15, Summer 1977: "A word for it!"

poop-butt *noun*
a lazy person *US, 1972*
- A poop-butt is a lazy person, a "drag-ass." — Christina and Richard Milner, *Black Players*, p. 47, 1972

poop chute; poop shute; poop shooter *noun*
the rectum and anus *US, 1970*
- She said she gives around the world or straight French cause it's too much trouble to screw and she'll go right up the old poop chute if a guy wants it. — Joseph Wambaugh, *The New Centurions*, p. 238, 1970
- "Darn magazine folk'd prob'ly like to take your pitcher stark naked with your old hog-leg stuck up a Great Dane's poop-chute if they could get it that way." — Stephen King, *The Dark Half*, p. 45, 1990
- And if you inform him that your poop chute is a one-way street, he's gotta respect that, or he won't get a taste of your sweet lovin'! — *Seattle Weekly*, p. 127, 9th August 2001
- [M]uch of her oeuvre coming under the tutelage of poop-chute auteur Seymour Butts. — Mr. Skin, *Mr. Skin's Skincyclopedia*, p. 300, 2005

pooped *adjective*
exhausted *US, 1932*
- I'm half dead with looking for a place. A guy told me about a basement apartment on Kings Highway near Ninety-sixth, but it was a bum steer. So I'm pooped. — Irving Shulman, *The Amboy Dukes*, p. 194, 1947
- Another thing ... well, I guess there isn't another thing, I'm all pooped out and I have to get on with other things. — Jack Kerouac, *Letter to Allen Ginsburg*, p. 142, 2 January 1948
- A couple of cars banged bumpers backing up so they could swing around me and I was too damned pooped even to swear back at some of the stuff they called me. — Mickey Spillane, *My Gun is Quick*, p. 6, 1950
- Not tonight, Simon, I'm pooped. — Joseph Wambaugh, *Floaters*, p. 126, 1996

pooper *noun*
the rectum and anus *US, 1972*
From **POOP** (excrement).
- No more fingers up my pooper without written orders. — Robert Byrne, *McGoorty*, p. 217, 1972
- If ya can't fuck a slut-come-lately in the pooper without a rubber, why not watch strangers do it on film? — Anthony Petkovich, *The X Factory*, p. 10, 1997

- Nice bun-shot as Bridget walks away after Robert DeNiro has pounded her pooper in the kitchen. — Mr. Skin, *Mr. Skin's Skincyclopedia*, p. 183, 2005

pooper-scooper *noun*
an implement for gathering canine excrement *US, 1972*
- — *New York Times*, p. 28, 26th May 1972
- Bring your pooper-scoopers, boys. The dogs are covering the red carpet in a sea of shit. — Joseph Wambaugh, *The Black Marble*, p. 136, 1978
- To make it easier on them a pooper scooper was invented, which was like a smaller version of the "lobby pans" they clean up with at amusement parks. — Editors of Ben is Dead, *Retrohell*, p. 163, 1997
- I could drive him [a dog] to my arch enemy Joyce Barnhardt's house to poop. This way I didn't have to do the pooper-scooper thing, and I felt like I was accomplishing something. — Janet Evanovich, *Seven Up*, p. 34, 2001

poop file *noun*
a collection of (school, college, university) examinations given in the past *US, 1976*
- — *Verbatim*, p. 280, May 1976

poophead *noun*
a boring, conventional person *US, 1955*
- Couple old poopheads? — *Rebel Without a Cause*, 1955

poo-poo head *noun*
an objectionable person *US, 1995*
A variation of **SHITHEAD**.
- I was the only person who was trying to shame this poo-poo head of a husband into behaving. — Howard Stern, *Miss America*, p. 302, 1995

poop sheet *noun*
a bulletin or other document containing news and information *US, 1964*
- — *American Speech*, p. 121, May 1964: "Problems in the study of campus slang"
- — *Current Slang*, p. 18, Winter 1970

poopy *adjective*
bad, awful; of poor quality *US, 2002*
A euphemistic synonym for **SHITTY**.
- Blue birds are poopy. I want to be a black stallion. — Janet Evanovitch, *Hard Eight*, p. 270, 2002

poor-ass *adjective*
wretched, unimportant *US, 1998*
- An army of people out there thinking up ways to torture my poor-ass, gentle, loving vagina. — Eve Ensler, *The Vagina Monologues*, p. 69, 1998

poorboy *noun*
a small bottle of alcohol *US, 1952*
- I get in my double bed with bop on the radio, a poorboy half-bottle of Tokay wine, the shades drawn[.] — Jack Kerouac, *Letter to John Clellon Holmes*, p. 381, 12 October 1952
- I figured I needed a poorboy of Tokay wine to complete the cold dusk run to Santa Barbara. — Jack Kerouac, *The Dharma Bums*, p. 6, 1958

poor man's roulette *noun*
the game of craps *US, 1953*
- — Thomas L. Clark, *The Dictionary of Gambling and Gaming*, p. 164, 1987

poor pearl *noun*
an unpopular girl *US, 1960*
- — *San Francisco Examiner*, p. III-2, 22nd March 1960
- Poor Pearl—an unpopular girl. — Art Unger, *The Cool Book*, p. 105, 1961

poot *noun*
1 feces *US, 1981*
Children's vocabulary; a variation of **POOP**.
- — *Maledicta*, p. 255, Summer/Winter 1981: "Five years and 121 dirty words later"

2 a very small thing; anything at all *US, 1978*
Usually heard in the negative, as "that ain't poot."
- — Terrence M. Steele, *Streettalk Thesaurus*, p. 23, 1978

poot *verb*
1 to defecate *US, 1945*
- I'm gonna light in on him and whip im till he poot. — Chester Himes, *If He Hollers Let Him Go*, p. 12, 1945
- Now she squirmed, she scooted, she farted, and she pooted. — Bruce Jackson, *Get Your Ass in the Water and Swim Like Me*, p. 159, 1966

2 to fart *US, 1972*
- And when I held it up, their eyes stretched and the whole crowd went so still you could've heard a gnat poot across the river. — Guy Owen, *The Flim-Flam Man and the Apprentice Grifter*, p. 12, 1972
- Winston sniffed the air, then checked the bottom of his sneakers. "Hey, did you poot?" he asked Fariq. — Paul Beatty, *Tuff*, p. 13, 2000

3 (used of a hospital patient) to become suddenly more ill, especially without hope of reversing the course *US, 1988–1989*
- — *Maledicta*, p. 34, 1988–1989: "Medical maledicta from San Francisco"

poot-butt *noun*
a lazy fool *US, 1972*
- How you gonna convince this pootbutt that havin' a group that would be beneficial to anybody? — Odie Hawkins, *The Busting Out of an Ordinary Man*, p. 152, 1985

pootie *noun*
the vagina; a woman as a sex object *US, 1953*
- "Say, who's that pootie I saw sitting out there alone?" — Edwin Gilbert, *The Hot and the Cool*, p. 31, 1953
- [Y]oung supple breasts, a tight firm ass and an uncharted pootie. — *Cruel Intentions*, 1999

pop *noun*
1 an instance or occurrence *US, 1868*
- We get anywhere from three hundred to five hundred a pop, depending on how much the Sioux Falls quarterback Club—or some such thing—can afford. — Dan Jenkins, *Semi-Tough*, p. 62, 1972
- By wearing Via Spiga pumps that cost a hundred dollars a pop with fifty-nine-cent grocery-store label panty hose underneath. — Rita Ciresi, *Pink Slip*, p. 80, 1999

2 a murder *US, 1951*
- "You're lucky. It's an easy pop." — Burton Turkus and Sid Feder, *Murder, Inc.*, p. 7, 1951

3 a handgun *US, 1992*
- "We ain't nuthin but goddamn fools if we try an take Deek down with just the pussy little pops we got us now." — Jess Mowry, *Way Past Cool*, p. 255, 1992

4 an arrest *US, 1972*
- So the minute the pop comes, one of the guys that was out in front during all this, he offered a ten-flat [ten-year sentence]. — Bruce Jackson, *In the Life*, p. 170, 1972
- Since the summer moved along without a pop, I stopped annoying Barry. — Gary Mayer, *Bookie*, p. 193, 1974
- Do whatever the fuck they want—you know, street pops, raids, whatever. — Richard Price, *Clockers*, p. 269, 1992

5 an ejaculation *US, 1986*
- The eighteen-year-old blonde blew Lev to his first pop, reports Mark, and then was replaced by a short-haired brunette, who brought Larry to number two in under thirty minutes. — Josh Alan Friedman, *Tales of Times Square*, p. 105, 1986
- We want the pop. How much time is left on this cassette? Three minutes. Okay, give us the pop in two forty-five. — Robert Stoller and I.S. Levine, *Coming Attractions*, p. 55, 1991

6 one event of sexual intercourse *US, 1982*
- There were plenty of girls for that, you know, if a guy wanted a pop. — *Diner*, 1982

7 the "masculine" or "active" member of a lesbian relationship *US, 1957*
- — John M. Murtagh and Sara Harris, *Cast the First Stone*, p. 262, 1957: "Glossary"
- — Robert George Reisner, *The Jazz Titans*, p. 163, 1960

8 a drink, usually at a bar *US, 1977*
- I seen a couple of guys I know, had a couple of pops, got something down on it. — John Sayles, *Union Dues*, p. 24, 1977
- She says she stopped in there for a pop after she was through working and he was in there again. — Elmore Leonard, *Split Images*, p. 265, 1981
- You better learn to have a pop once in a while or you're gonna fall off the wagon. — *Something About Mary*, 1998

9 cough syrup containing codeine *US, 1970*
- — William D. Alsever, *Glossary for the Establishment and Other Uptight People*, p. 6, December 1970

10 an injection of a drug *US, 1952*
- You make it wit me, Diane? If I take a pop, you make it? — George Mandel, *Flee the Angry Strangers*, p. 282, 1952

11 a strong crowd reaction *US, 2000*
Professional wrestling usage.

- It really sounded like the Cat got the biggest pop of the night.
  — *Chatterbox News*, 23rd August 2000
- The first pop from the crowd, while I was still in the dressing room, scared the bejeezes out of me. — Missy Hyatt, *Missy Hyatt*, p. 37, 2001

pop *verb*

1 to ejaculate; to experience orgasm *US, 1961*
- She likes them jittery tricks cause they pop fast. — Robert Gover, *One Hundred Dollar Misunderstanding*, p. 20, 1961
- I remember the time we muscled a mud kicker when we was oh ten ... twelve and got our first blowjob together. He passed out when he popped. — Iceberg Slim (Robert Beck), *Death Wish*, p. 174, 1977
- The cocks pop and the wads fly as wide-open mouths train to catch the steaming jizz. — *Adult Video*, p. 32, August/September 1986
- First, Vijay groaned and blasted, then I popped. — C.D. Payne, *Cut to the Twisp*, p. 47, 2001

2 to have sex with someone *US, 1965*
- Well, did you pop her? You must have jugged her by now, haven't you? — Claude Brown, *Manchild in the Promised Land*, p. 363, 1965
- "Oh, man, I popped her a couple, and blam, I was in love," Bill said. — Cecil Brown, *The Life & Loves of Mr. Jiveass Nigger*, p. 113, 1969
- I'd get more thrill out of popping the dead / Than I got out of you in a nice warm bed. — Dennis Wepman et al., *The Life*, p. 143, 1976
- I'll pop a broad in a minute, but nothing to get tied down to, right, Chappie? — Edwin Torres, *Q & A*, p. 117, 1977

3 to take a pill *US, 1968*
- Also has been known to pop a greenie. — Jim Bouton, *Ball Four*, p. 212, 1970
- "Petey, I'm popping Valium like Jujubes just trying to cover to maintain." — Anne Steinhardt, *Thunder La Boom*, p. 104, 1974
- I participated in the popping of the old love drug[.] — Dave Courtney, *Raving Lunacy*, p. 73, 2000
- Painkillers—particularly Vicodin—have stormed back onto the drug scene in the States in recent months and are apparently being popped like Smarties at showbiz parties. — *Drugs An Adult Guide, FHM Bionic*, p. 25, December 2001

4 (of a number bet on in an illegal lottery) to win *US, 1968*
- "Maybe three or four years after this, 427 finally pops, but not for much." — Peter Maas, *The Valachi Papers*, p. 140, 1968

5 to arrest someone *US, 1972*
- [M]e and Dennis were getting popped in the parking lot. — John Sinclair, *Guitar Army*, p. 76, 1972
- That fool had driven across the country with a blond without them. Lucky he got popped in the Apple instead of the lowlands. — Babs Gonzales, *Movin' On Down De Line*, p. 80, 1975
- Elijah glared at him. Motherfucker! and threw the empty whiskey bottle out of the open window and held his hands up for the cuffs. Popped again. — Odie Hawkins, *Chicago Hustle*, p. 100, 1977
- There's nothing to worry about. Carmine got popped. — Gerald Petievich, *To Live and Die in L.A.*, p. 31, 1983

6 to give birth *US, 1990*
- What would rapists be doing going after a woman ready to pop? — Robert Campbell, *Sweet La-La Land*, p. 33, 1990

7 to inject a drug *US, 1952*
- I never popped in a vein, Carter. — George Mandel, *Flee the Angry Strangers*, p. 290, 1952
- They want to pop. They want company. — John D. McDonald, *The Neon Jungle*, p. 44, 1953

8 when using amyl nitrate, to break the glass ampoules containing the gas *US, 1995*
- — Steven Daly and Nathaniel Wice, *alt.culture*, p. 185, 1995

9 to fire a gun *UK, 1725*
- I go to this little firing range downtown, pop off a few rounds, and it always makes me feel better. — *American Beauty*, 1999

10 to hit someone *US, 1980*
- And he did his entire stretch in a series of thirty days at a time in solitary, for popping a guard. — Stephen Gaskin, *Amazing Dope Tales*, p. 191, 1980

11 to kill someone *US, 1952*
- You keep thinking that they wouldn't pop you out in broad daylight[.] — Mickey Spillane, *Kiss Me Deadly*, p. 90, 1952
- Armand tried to think how his brothers used to say it. They would say they were going to do a guy. Or they might say so-and-so got popped. Maybe because when you used a suppressor it made a popping sound, like an air rifle. — Elmore Leonard, *Killshot*, p. 74, 1989

12 to pay for something *US, 1953*
- Yeah, but let me pop for it. — Willard Motley, *Let No Man Write My Epitaph*, p. 73, 1958
- The records and phonograph caught his eye, too. "You pop for all this?" — Ross Russell, *The Sound*, p. 188, 1961

13 to praise or promote someone or something *US, 1984*
- You don't pop the opposition, Teddy. — Dan Jenkins, *Life Its Ownself*, p. 318, 1984

14 to applaud and cheer enthusiastically *US, 2000*
Professional wrestling usage.
- [T]he audience pops big enough to blow the roof off. — *Rampage Magazine*, p. 35, September 2000

15 in pinball, to win a replay or additional ball, activating the sound effect known as a knocker *US, 1977*
- — Bobbye Claire Natkin and Steve Kirk, *All About Pinball*, p. 114, 1977

16 to open *US, 2000*
- Pop the trunk, I need my tool. — *Gone in 60 Seconds*, 2000

▶ **pop a cap**
to shoot a gun *US, 1965*
- I'm prepared to scour the earth for this motherfucker. If Butch goes to Indo China, I want a nigger hidin' in a bowl of rice, ready to pop a cap in his ass. — *Pulp Fiction*, 1965
- Outside of the accidental shot fired by Eddie Cervantes when he used his revolver as a club, nobody had popped a single cap in the canyons. — Joseph Wambaugh, *Lines and Shadows*, p. 101, 1984

▶ **pop corn**
to engage in a swindle or dishonest scheme *US, 1995*
- — Mark S. Fleisher, *Beggars & Thieves: Lives of Urban Street Criminals*, p. 290, 1995: "Glossary"

▶ **pop junk**
to gossip *US, 1990*
- — *Frederick (Maryland) Post*, p. B2, 24th May 1990: "For home boys and zimmers; this dictionary is def!"

▶ **pop shit**
to talk nonsense *US, 2005*
- Then Ray-Ray starting popping shit about discrimination, making it even worse. — 50 Cent, *From Pieces to Weight*, p. 117, 2005

▶ **pop smoke**
to detonate a smoke grenade *US, 1978*
- "Pop smoke, sir?" — Tim O'Brien, *Going After Cacciato*, p. 10, 1978
- El Paso signals Doc Johnson to pop smoke and Doc pulls the pin on a smoke grenade. — John M. Del Vecchio, *The 13th Valley*, p. 632, 1982

▶ **pop the chute**
in sailing, to release the spinnaker *US, 1990*
- "Okay!" Winnie shouted. "Let's pop the chute!" — Joseph Wambaugh, *The Golden Orange*, p. 286, 1990

▶ **pop your nuts**
1 (of a woman) to experience an orgasm *US, 1969*
- [A] girl is more likely to pop her nuts with a prick buried in her tail than in her mouth. — Juan Carmel Cosmes, *Memoir of a Whoremaster*, p. 60, 1969

2 to ejaculate *US, 1970*
- They just want to pop their nuts as fast as they can. — John Warren Wells, *Tricks of the Trade*, p. 14, 1970

▶ **pop your pumpkin**
to lose your temper *US, 1954*
- The boss man'd just naturally pop his pumpkin if he found out about it. — Jim Thompson, *Roughneck*, p. 16, 1954

▶ **pop your rocks**
to ejaculate *US, 1977*
- [H]ere was this guy looking her in the eye like he wanted something more than to pop his rocks. — John Sayles, *Union Dues*, p. 189, 1977

popcorn match *noun*
in professional wrestling, the match immediately before the main event *US, 1997*
The suggestion is that fans will take time during this match to buy popcorn.
- This would settle zero, but I think it would be a great popcorn match. — *rec.sport.pro-wrestling*, 13th April 1997
- "Then get dressed, get back to the mic and bring the popcorn match to the ring." — Gary Cappetta, *Bodyslams!*, p. 134, 2000

- That Wrestlemania match was a popcorn match. It was right before the main event, and that's when people go out to get their popcorn. — Bobby Heenan, *Bobby the Brain*, p. 70, 2002

popcorn pimp; popcorn *noun*
a small-time pimp; a pimp who fails to live up to pimp standards *US, 1971*

- Black pimps never solicit for their women if they are "true pimps," and call a man who does a cigarette pimp, popcorn pimp, or chile pimp. — Christina and Richard Milner, *Black Players*, p. 33, 1972
- One of the bouncers pulled his wallet out. Popcorn pimp, he didn't have fifty dollars. — Edwin Torres, *After Hours*, p. 179, 1979
- He talked game with him at every chance, lectured him on the pimping code, instilled contempt for the small-time popcorns and respect for the real boss players[.] — Alix Shulman, *On the Stroll*, p. 56, 1981
- Then there are "popcorn pimps," a term of contempt for men who force women into prostitution, unlike true players who claim to operate with personal magnetism alone. — Terry Williams, *The Cocaine Kids*, p. 102, 1989

popcorn storm *noun*
a surprise, intense rainstorm *US, 1991*

- "You get more of the "popcorn" storms during the afternoon during the summer," Kramper said. — *Arkansas Democrat-Gazette*, 25th June 1991

pope's nose *noun*
the rump of a turkey or chicken *UK, 1796*
Once scandalously anti-Catholic, but not benign.

- Using a steel or aluminum wire, tie the legs and pope's nose together securely[.] — Martha Stewart, *The Martha Stewart Living Cookbook*, p. 318, 2000

po-po *noun*
the police; a police officer *US, 1990*

- — Connie Eble (Editor), *UNC-CH Campus Slang*, p. 8, April 1995
- While kids in Northwest refer to police as "one-time," Northeast teenagers call them "bo-deen" or "hot dog," and in Southeast they're "po-pos" or good old "feds." — *Washington Post*, p. A1, 20th August 2001
- The cop-call—Po-Po—was a neighborly warning sounded by whoever spotted the police, for anyone who might like to know. — Adrian Nicole LeBlanc, *Random Family*, p. 107, 2003

pop-off *noun*
someone who talks too much *US, 1951*

- To shut up the pop-off cut him down by saying he's a "jack-wise," or maybe an "odd job." — *Philadelphia Evening Bulletin*, 11th November 1951

pop off *verb*
1 to ejaculate *US, 1969*

- Sure, I wanted to pop off. Christ, did I ever! — Joey V., *Portrait of Joey*, p. 39, 1969

2 to brag, to boast; to speak out when discretion would suggest silence *US, 1940*

- I sat back a lot, I didn't pop off a lot. — Bruce Jackson, *In the Life*, p. 69, 1972
- I'ma be another rapper dead / for poppin' off at the mouth with shit I shouldn'ta said[.] — Eminem (Marshall Mathers), *Kill You*, 2000

3 to kill someone *UK, 1824*

- The arrest of serial killer David Berkowitz—who claimed he heard the voice of God through his parents' dog, and the God-Dog told him his duty in life was to pop off women—had been all over the papers that year. — Rita Ciresi, *Pink Slip*, p. 10, 1999

pop-out *noun*
a mass-produced surfboard with little or no handwork involved in the making *US, 1964*

- — John Severson, *Modern Surfing Around the World*, p. 178, 1964
- PANCHO: Eighty-five dollars would buy me a popout Tiki surfboard. Q: What's a "popout"? PANCHO: A popout, cause it was manufactured—it wasn't made custom-made. — Leonard Wolfe (Editor), *Voices from the Love Generation*, pp. 170–171, 1968

poppa *noun*
in prison, a lesbian *US, 1953*

- When she saw that I really didn't understand, she explained that "Poppa" was the jailhouse term for Lesbian[.] — Polly Adler, *A House is Not a Home*, p. 264, 1953

poppa Charlie *noun*
a military personnel carrier *US, 1968*

- If it wasn't for our Poppa Charlies (personnel carriers), it would be impossible. — David Parks, *GI Diary*, p. 103, 1968

poppa-lopper *noun*
used as a euphemism for "motherfucker" *US, 1977*

- — *Maledicta*, p. 11, Summer 1977: "A word for it!"

pop party *noun*
a party where drug users inject drugs *US, 1971*

- — Eugene Landy, *The Underground Dictionary*, p. 152, 1971

popped out *adjective*
drug-intoxicated *US, 1954*

- "Dinch, you're popped out." It had begun as reproof, but, she tied a smile to it, remembering that she was just as high as the boy. — George Mandel, *Flee the Angry Stranger*, p. 131, 1954

popper *noun*
1 a capsule containing vapors of amyl nitrate or butyl nitrate inhaled as a stimulant *US, 1967*
Often used in the plural form.

- When I use a popper, I feel as though I had ten assholes and I wanted them all filled at once. — Angelo d'Arcangelo, *The Homosexual Handbook*, p. 165, 1968
- And if you're sick of people, what about poppers? — Mart Crowley, *The Boys in the Band*, p. 31, 1968
- Amyl nitrate, or "poppers" as they are frequently known, is one of several drugs that have come to be associated with sex. — *Screw*, p. 9, 28th June 1971
- But I never took drugs all those years, just toke. No poppers or anything. — Ethan Morden, *Buddies*, p. 183, 1986

2 a finger *US, 1947*

- — Marcus Hanna Boulware, *Jive and Slang of Students in Negro Colleges*, 1947

3 a pistol *US, 1976*

- — Porter Bibb, *CB Bible*, p. 94, 1976

4 a popcorn wagon *US, 1985*

- — Gene Sorrows, *All About Carnivals*, p. 24, 1985: "Terminology"

5 a person who pretends to be that which they are not *US, 2002*

- I'm also relieved to see no swirly sideburns and goatees so favored by the teen poppers. — *St. Petersburg (Florida) Times*, p. 1D, 28th January 2002

poppy love *noun*
an older Jewish man *US, 1987*

- — Carsten Stroud, *Close Pursuit*, p. 274, 1987

poppy pad *noun*
a room or apartment where heroin users congregate *US, 1959*

- And behind the respectable facades of the apartment buildings were the plush flesh cribs and poppy pads and circus tents of Harlem. — Chester Himes, *The Real Cool Killers*, p. 61, 1959

pops *noun*
1 used as a term of address for a man, especially an older man *US, 1844*

- "Looks like pops couldn't take it," one of them shouted. — Ralph Ellison, *Invisible Man*, p. 87, 1947
- "Pops," said the stranger, "I can see that when it comes to cows you don't know a hill of beans." — Steve Allen, *Bop Fables*, p. 55, 1955
- [W]e ain't got the same hip-hop knowledge as you, pops. — *Hip-Hop Connection*, p. 9, July 2002

2 father *US, 1893*

- "My moms and pops always wanted Hector and me to go to college[.]" — Terry Williams, *The Cocaine Kids*, p. 74, 1989
- Yeah, see, you ain't goin' out like ya pops. — *Menace II Society*, 1993
- See, my pops was an artist. — Earl "DMX" Simmons, *E.A.R.L.*, p. 22, 2002

pop shot *noun*
a scene in a pornographic film or photograph depicting a man ejaculating *US, 1991*

- Pull it out of her. Wait a minute. Got to change batteries! Okay, go into the pop shot now. — Robert Stoller and I.S. Levine, *Coming Attractions*, p. 55, 1991
- Most of the guys get paid anywhere from $75 to $300 per pop shot. — James Ridgeway, *Red Light*, p. 52, 1996
- Are facials required, or are you just being polite? JULIA ANN: It's not required at all. I usually ask the director where he wants the pop shot. — *Playboy*, p. 132, 1st March 2002
- The only drawback—and it's a big one—is no pop shot that we could discern. — Editors of Adult Video News, *The AVN Guide to the 500 Greatest Adult Films of All Time*, p. 218, 2005

popsicle *noun*
used as a term of abuse *US, 1984*
- Come on you fucking popsicles, let's get that car. — *Repo Man*, 1984

popsie *noun*
an ampoule of amyl nitrate *US, 1971*
- — Eugene Landy, *The Underground Dictionary*, p. 152, 1971

popskull *noun*
strong, homemade whiskey *US, 1999*
- It is called corn liquor, white lightning, sugar whiskey, skully cracker, popskull, bush whiskey, stump, stumphole, 'splo, ruckus juice, radiator whiskey, rotgut, sugarhead, block and tackle, wildcat, panther's breath, tiger's sweat, Sweet spirits of cats a-fighting, alley bourbon, city gin, cool water, happy Sally, deep shaft, jump steady, old horsey, stingo, blue John, red eye, pine top, buckeye bark whiskey and see seven stars. — *Star Tribune (Minneapolis)*, p. 19F, 31st January 1999

population *noun*
the general population in a prison *US, 1975*
- Back in population I stayed clean, worked out every day, did some reading, a lot of rapping. — Edwin Torres, *Carlito's Way*, p. 46, 1975

pop-up *noun*
1 a hand-fired flare *US, 1968*
- I was having trouble opening my eyes until I heard Sohner shout Fire a pop-up, a pop-up! — Martin Russ, *Happy Hunting Ground*, p. 25, 1968
2 an electronic advertisement delivered to a computer via the Internet that is superimposed over the original browser window *US, 1996*
- "I think if they (AOL) are really concerned about junk mail, if they're truly concerned about members' wishes, they would stop sending pop-up (advertisement) screens," Wallace said. — *Central Penn Business Journal*, p. 1, 6th December 1996

pop-up hell *noun*
an unfriendly web-surfing environment characterized by multiple console advertisements in pop-up windows *US, 2004*
A term used frequently on the web but not in conventional print sources.
- — www.adultquarter.com, January 2004: "Glossary of adult internet terms"

Po' Rican *noun*
Puerto Rican *US, 1975*
- You had to go with a gang, 'cause if the wops caught you alone on the balcony, you was a flyin' Po' Rican. — Edwin Torres, *Carlito's Way*, p. 12, 1975

pork *verb*
to have sex with someone *US, 1968*
- — Collin Baker et al., *College Undergraduate Slang Study Conducted at Brown University*, p. 175, 1968
- That mean I can go out to where you live and feel up your wife? Maybe pork her, if she's interested? — George V. Higgins, *The Rat on Fire*, p. 127, 1981
- Nine months, and he hasn't porked you? — Marty Beckerman, *Death to All Cheerleaders*, 2000
- But I think maybe Newt [Gingrich] was having some trouble at home with his new wife, the former staffer he started porking while he was still married to his second wife. — Al Franken, *Lies*, p. 111, 2003

pork-dodger *noun*
a Jewish person *US, 1997*
From the dietary restrictions of observant Jews.
- And those given a name were stuck with it forever: Svade, Svenska, Lugan, Schnapps, Moishe, Stosh, Henie, Mockie, Guinea, Canuck, Bohunk, Pork-dodger, Limey, Greaseball, Krauthead, Dutchie, Squarehead, Grick, Mick, Paddy, Goombah, Polski, Dago, Hunkie, Wop — *San Francisco Examiner*, p. A15, 28th July 1997

porker *noun*
1 a fat person *US, 1959*
- Which is not to say that everybody's a porker — Robert Campbell, *In a Pig's Eye*, p. 12, 1991
2 a police officer *US, 1971*
An extension of **PIG**.
- Tom spent an edgy two hours down at the station, grilled over by Leesburg's total force of three porkers. — Jeffrey Golden, *Watermelon Summer*, p. 99, 1971
- [T]he other porkers were smashing me with nightsticks[.] — John Sinclair, *Guitar Army*, p. 90, 1972

- I don't hafta point my shotgun / at them pesky porkers no more[.] — Cypress Hill, *Dr. Greenthumb*, 1998

porn; porno *noun*
pornography *UK, 1962*
- — *Current Slang*, p. 11, Summer 1968
- Throughout the book are quotes from some of the people who are very much involved in the world of porno. — Stephen Ziplow, *The Film Maker's Guide to Pornography*, p. 8, 1977
- Some of my best friends are porn stars. — *Cult Movies No. 17*, p. 46, 1996

porno *adjective*
pornographic *US, 1952*
- Screw explains its new device to graphically illustrate our evaluation of sexploitation and porno films. — *Screw*, p. 15, 8th December 1969
- Russ Meyer really hit it big with his porno masterpiece Vixen[.] — Roger Blake, *The Porno Movies*, p. 68, 1970
- You know how I told you when Nellie came back to L.A. she started going with this darling guy, Stuart, who makes all those porno movies? — Eve Babitz, *Eve's Hollywood*, p. 247, 1974
- Sometimes you'll pick up a black porno flick and with luck get a real actor—some out-of-work brother that you used to see on TV. You'll be watching and you'll say, "Hey wait a minute, isn't that Sticks from 'Happy Days?'" — Chris Rock, *Rock This!*, p. 26, 1997

porny *adjective*
pornographic *US, 1969*
- The San Francisco porny movies are being busted, including the audience. — *The Berkeley Tribe*, p. 24, 22nd–28th August 1969

porpoise *verb*
in mountain biking, to ride responding to, instead of controlling, the bike *US, 1992*
- — William Nealy, *Mountain Bike!*, p. 162, 1992: "Bikespeak"

portable *noun*
a foot-patrol police officer *US, 1987*
- — Carsten Stroud, *Close Pursuit*, p. 274, 1987

Portagee *noun*
a person from Portugal, or of Portuguese heritage *UK, 1830*
- — *Maledicta*, p. 168, Summer/Winter 1978: "How to hate thy neighbor: a guide to racist maledicta"

Portagee chrome *noun*
aluminum paint *US, 1961*
- — *American Speech*, p. 272, December 1961: "Northwest truck drivers' language"

Portagee lawnmower *noun*
a goat *US, 1988–1989*
- — *Maledicta*, p. 234, 1988–1989: "The portagee in speech and joke"

Portagee lift *noun*
in manual labor, said when one worker does not carry his fair share *US, 1960*
- — *Journal of American Folklore*, p. 211, July–September 1960: "John Newhaus: wobbly folklorist"

portapotty *noun*
a portable toilet, transported to construction sites, campgrounds, outdoor concerts, etc. *US, 1993*
- WAYNE: Do you know anything about portapotties? GARTH: They look like phone booths, they're usually white, they smell funny. — *Wayne's World 2*, 1993
- Check it out Butt-Head, porta-potties. — Mike Judge and Joe Stillman, *Beavis and Butt-Head Do America*, p. 50, 1997

port-sider *noun*
a left-handed person *US, 1971*
- — Dick Squires, *The Other Racquet Sports*, p. 221, 1971: "Glossary"

Portuguese parliament *noun*
a meeting where everybody talks and nobody listens *US, 1951*
- — *Maledicta*, p. 234, 1988–1989: "The Portagee in speech and joke"

Portuguese straight *noun*
in poker, a straight formed with different suits, thus without value *US, 1982*
Hawaiian youth usage.
- — Douglas Simonson, *Pidgin to da Max: Hana Hou*, 1982

porty *noun*
a portable telephone *US, 1996*
- Is that your porty or mine? — *Jerry Maguire*, 1996

pos *noun*
position *US, 1986*
- Check your fire, check your fire, you're short on our pos! — *Platoon*, 1986

POS *noun*
a patient regarded by hospital personnel as a *piece of* shit *US, 1978*
- — *Maledicta*, p. 6, Summer/Winter 1978: "Common patient-directed pejoratives used by medical personnel"

pose *verb*
to pretend a station in life that has yet to be achieved *US, 1946*
- He gave Irving a fit posing all over the place, then cut out for Florida, where he became a bigtime bookmaker. — Mezz Mezzrow, *Really the Blues*, p. 87, 1946

poser *noun*
a person who imitates that which he is not *US, 1980*
- Highway surfer: A "poser" whose surfboard stays on the roofrack. — Abbott, Rick and Mike Baker, *Start Surfing*, p. 85, 1980
- He was turned off by what he called "posers"—"kids who shave their heads for a year and then go to N.Y.U." — *New York Times*, 27th April 1984
- — Connie Eble (Editor), *UNC-CH Campus Slang*, p. 7, November 1990

poser gear *noun*
clothing that marks the wearer as someone trying to be that which they are not *US, 1993*
- "Sides, you two burrheads done over-dressed yourselfs ... what they callin "poser-gear" out there in California." — Jess Mowry, *Six Out Seven*, p. 31, 1993

posse *noun*
1 a group of close friends *US, 1989*
- — Ellen C. Bellone (Editor), *Dictionary of Slang*, p. 18, 1989
2 a gang *US, 1994*
- He acted as lookout for the posse, an early warning system to guard against surprise raids. — Karline Smith, *Moss Side Massive*, p. 8, 1994
- I feel so happy. They want me. I'm going to be a part of their posse. — Karline Smith, *Letters to Andy Cole*, p. 139, 1998
- [Y]our Kru, or your Massive, your Thugs, or Bredrins; Dawgs, Homies, your Clique, or your Posse. — Julian Johnson, *Urban Survival*, p. 264, 2003

possible *noun*
in poker, any hand that can be completed with the draw of one card *US, 1951*
Variant "possibulletee."
- — *American Speech*, p. 100, May 1951

post *noun*
an autopsy *US, 1942*
From the more formal "post mortem."
- "What's a post? A post mortem?" "Yeah, an autopsy. They have to determine the cause of death. Even when a man's been shot four times." — Elmore Leonard, *Split Images*, p. 104, 1981

postal *adjective*
extremely angry; furious to the point of violence *US, 1994*
From a series of highly publicized workplace shootings by frustrated and furious employees of the US Postal Service.
- Like Josh thinking I was mean was making me postal. — *Clueless*, 1995
- — *American Speech*, p. 304, Fall 1996: "Among the new words"
- — Connie Eble (Editor), *UNC-CH Campus Slang*, p. 4, April 1997
- If another one of these chairs hits me in the nuts, I'm gonna go postal. — Austin Powers, 1999

poster boy *noun*
a very good example of an attitude or condition *US, 1993*
Used facetiously.
- Well, I have to admit, walkin' through the door and seein' these Soldier of Fortune poster boys made me a bit nervous. — *True Romance*, 1993

postman's knock *noun*
in pool, a shot in which the cue ball hits the object ball twice in rapid succession, producing a knock-like sound *US, 1993*
- — Mike Shamos, *The Illustrated Encyclopedia of Billiards*, p. 180, 1993

post mortem *noun*
in poker, an analysis of a hand after it has been played *US, 1988*
- — George Percy, *The Language of Poker*, p. 70, 1988

post op *noun*
a transsexual who has undergone all surgery necessary to complete a sex change *US, 1995*
- As a two-year postop MTF, I can attest life as a woman is no bowl of cherries. — Nancy Tamosaitis, *net.sex*, p. 130, 1995

post up *verb*
to idle *US, 1998*
- — *Columbia Missourian*, p. 1A, 19th October 1998

pot *noun*
1 marijuana *US, 1938*
The most popular slang term for marijuana in the 1950s. No agreement on the etymology, with competing conjectures and little supporting evidence.
- But I never blew up a joint in the folks' apartment the whole time I was on pot—that's grass, you know, marijuana. I really never did. — David Hulburi, *H is For Heroin*, p. 47, 1952
- I learned the new hipster vocabulary; "pot" for weed[.] — William Burroughs, *Junkie*, p. 120, 1953
- Marijuana will be legal some day, because the many law students who now smoke pot will some day become Congressmen and legalize it in order to protect themselves. — Lenny Bruce, *How to Talk Dirty and Influence People*, p. 129, 1965
- What do you bring to a hippie "tea party"? Your own "pot"! — Paul Laikin, *101 Hippie Jokes*, 1968
2 a combat helmet *US, 1972*
- I still saw no M-16s, no steel pots, nothing to suggest a real combat zone. — William Pelfrey, *The Big V*, p. 3, 1972
3 in poker, all of the chips or money bet on a single hand *US, 1947*
- — Oswald Jacoby, *Oswald Jacoby on Poker*, p. 138, 1947
4 a hospital patient with many trivial complaints *US, 1980*
- — *Maledicta*, p. 56, Summer 1980: "Not sticks and stones, but names: more medical pejoratives"

pot *verb*
to shoot or kill *US, 1860*
- "They were all too busy trying to pot you guys." — Malcom Braly, *Felony Tank*, p. 120, 1961
- His partner, Fred, smiled. "You goin' pot the bastard?" he asked with unwarranted glee. — Donald Goines, *Black Gangster*, p. 109, 1977

potable *noun*
drinking water *US, 1968*
- — Carl Fleischhauer, *A Glossary of Army Slang*, p. 7, 1968

potato *verb*
to hit very hard *US, 1990*
- potato v.t. To injure or knock another wrestler unconscious by hitting him on the head. — *rec.sports.pro-wrestling*, 17th July 1990
- My father had always been the kind of guy who, when he was really getting potatoed (in wrestling, when you're getting hit real hard—too hard—it's called "getting potatoed"), he would let his opponent know. — The Rock, *The Rock Says...*, p. 179, 2000

potato head *noun*
a fool, an idiot *US, 1952*
- [A]s do mocking phrases like couch potato or potato head, and such expressions aren't unique to English. — Larry Zuckerman, *The Potato*, p. 10, 1998
- "Listen, Potato Head, I've got a new parish to take care of and a yard to mow." — Jan Karon, *New Song*, p. 202, 1999

potato jack *noun*
whiskey made from potato scrapings *US, 1974*
- "He won't get enough potato jack in the can to kill him." — George Higgins, *Cogan's Trade*, p. 190, 1974

potato-masher *noun*
a German fragmentation hand grenade *US, 1919*
- He had just thrown a potato-masher grenade at the E-boat to destroy and sink her. — John Steinbeck, *Once There was a War*, p. 135, 1961
- [T]he North Viet, hunkered down on his heels and cowering, was holding a potato-masher grenade. — Martin Russ, *Happy Hunting Ground*, p. 71, 1968
- We policed up a case of Chinese potato-masher grenades. They were probably World War I German Army vintage and about as effective as cherry bombs, but they made a lot of noise and at least they were something. — David H. Hackworth, *About Face*, p. 73, 1989

potato soup *noun*
vodka *US, 1970*
- — *Current Slang*, p. 17, Summer 1970

potato wagon *noun*
a police van *US, 1970*
- — Claudio R. Salvucci, *The Philadelphia Dialect Dictionary*, p. 53, 1996

potch *verb*
to spank or smack someone *US, 1969*
- And why my mother weeps is because my father refuses to potch my behind, which she promised would be potched. — Philip Roth, *Portnoy's Complaint*, p. 95, 1969

potchkeh *verb*
to dawdle; to spend time inefficiently *US, 1954*
Yiddish from German. Also variants "potchee" and "potchky."
- Aly Kahn, supposed to be potchkying around in Paris broken-hearted on account of the Princess Margherita walking out on him, was really in this country[.] — Bernard Wolfe, *The Late Risers*, p. 35, 1954
- We got on the first tee and I watched her get over on the ball and potchee around. — Buddy Hackett, *The Truth About Golf and Other Lies*, p. 120, 1968

pot head *noun*
a user of marijuana *US, 1955*
- They send two square photographers. And one of them turns out to be a pot-head. — Jack Gerber, *The Connection*, p. 38, 1957
- Impossible, man, they move like potheads. — Richard Farina, *Been Down So Long*, p. 85, 1966
- Others came also—42nd Street hustlers—poets—simple dreamers, thieves, prostitutes, (both male and female) and pimps and wise guys and junkies and pot heads, and just people[.] — Herbert Huncke, *The Evening Sun Turned Crimson*, p. 42, 1980
- So I'm blazing with my friends, man. So I'm a fucking pot head man. What's it to you, huh? — *Dazed and Confused*, 1993

pot hook *noun*
in a deck of playing cards, a nine *US, 1967*
- — Albert H. Morehead, *The Complete Guide to Winning Poker*, p. 270, 1967

Pot. Kettle. Black.
used as Internet shorthand to criticize someone for engaging in precisely the same conduct or reasoning that they are attacking in another *US, 1995*
- — Christian Crumlish, *The Internet Dictionary*, p. 156, 1995

pot likker; pot liquor *noun*
1 tea brewed with marijuana leaves *US, 1967*
The intentional spelling error gives a rustic, moonshining feel to the term.
- It is ubiquitous and easily grown, can be smoked in "joints" (cigarettes), baked into cookies, or brewed in tea ("pot likker"). — *Time*, p. 21, 7 July 1967
- — William D. Alsever, *Glossary for the Establishment and Other Uptight People*, p. 20, December 1970
- — Ernest Abel, *A Marijuana Dictionary*, p. 81, 1982

2 strong, homemade whiskey *US, 1972*
- Then I slurped it up like a hound laps pot likker, rolling the panther juice around on my tongue, smacking my lips over it. — Guy Owen, *The Flim-Flam Man and the Apprentice Grifter*, p. 40, 1972

POTS *noun*
plain old telephone service *US, 1997*
- — Andy Ihnatko, *Cyberspeak*, p. 155, 1997

pot shot *noun*
in poker, an early and aggressive bet designed to drive other players from the field of play *US, 1951*
Borrowed from hunting and punning on "pot" as the collective bets.
- — *American Speech*, p. 100, May 1951

potted *adjective*
1 tipsy, drunk *US, 1924*
- "[A]nd we can just get potted together, which is what the hell we want to do in the first place." — Norman Mailer, *The Naked and the Dead*, p. 243, 1948
- We had one guest at the hotel where I worked during the early forties, who got well potted every Saturday night he stayed with us[.] — Dev Collans with Stewart Sterling, *I was a House Detective*, p. 67, 1954

- — Collin Baker et al., *College Undergraduate Slang Study Conducted at Brown University*, p. 175, 1968

2 in a state of marijuana intoxication *US, 1955*
- — Ernest L. Abel, *A Marijuana Dictionary*, p. 82, 1982

potty *noun*
▸ **go potty**
to use a bathroom *US, 1942*
Children's toilet vocabulary.
- I feel like I am five years old. Mama, may I go to the potty? Number one? Number two? — Beatrice Sparks (writing as "Anonymous"), *Jay's Journal*, p. 137, 1979
- Teddy got up during the night to go the bathroom. "Go potty," his mom called it; woman her age. — Elmore Leonard, *Glitz*, p. 341, 1985
- Everyone go potty—we don't want to have to stop! — *Boys on the Side*, 1995

potty mouth *noun*
a person prone to use profanity; profanity *US, 1968*
- — *Current Slang*, p. 8, Spring 1969
- It's come to my attention that you boys have a potty-mouth problem. — *South Park*, 1999
- After sixteen years of uninterrupted potty mouth from you people, I get slammed? — *The Sopranos (Episode 58)*, 2004
- Potty-mouth tirade; all those years in law school spent parsing and composing elegant phrases wasted. — Jonathan Kellerman, *Rage*, p. 399, 2005

potty talk *noun*
speech that is considered obscenely offensive *US, 2002*
- [James O'Connor's] book, which offers alternatives to public potty talk, also offers the kind of advice that could have altered the Michigan tale of the tainted tongue[.] — *The New York Times*, 7th April 2002

pot-wrestler *noun*
a restaurant cook or dishwasher *US, 1860*
- He thought he was somebody when he was nothing but a pot wrestler in a downtown restaurant and hardly able to speak English. — Hal Ellson, *The Golden Spike*, p. 83, 1952

potzie *noun*
a socially inept person *US, 1986*
- "And here's this narrow-shouldered potzie named Lance who likes to dress up on Halloween and collect candy with the eight-year-olds." — Ethan Morden, *Buddies*, p. 82, 1986

pound *noun*
1 a five-dollar bill *US, 1935*
- So I got Manny, I gave him a pound, and I said, listen, Manny, you want to get a job? — Jeremy Larner and Ralph Tefferteller, *The Addict in the Street*, p. 240, 1964
- "So will you loan Jackie a pound?" — Robert Deane Pharr, *S.R.O.*, p. 73, 1971
- My shirts were from Brooks'; my socks cost a pound / I wore solid gold cufflinks—I knew I was down. — Dennis Wepman et al., *The Life*, p. 36, 1976
- Throw Walter a pound for forgetting the dupes. — Vincent Patrick, *The Pope of Greenwich Village*, p. 15, 1979

2 a five-year jail sentence *US, 1967*
- But after you do almost a pound here, like me, you get so you can stand it. — Clarence Cooper Jr., *The Farm*, p. 128, 1967
- He give me a pound for a frown. — Miguel Pinero, *Short Eyes*, p. 16, 1975
- Even did time for a homicide. Did a pound. — Edwin Torres, *Q & A*, p. 88, 1977
- I did a pound at Coxsackie. — Vincent Patrick, *The Pope of Greenwich Village*, p. 28, 1979

3 a closed fist hand-to-hand greeting *US, 2007*
- At every step other boys extended their hands to give him a pound. — Treasure E. Blue, *A Street Girl Named Desire*, p. 113, 2007

4 a jail or prison *US, 1977*
- Federal pound. Forty-four months. — Edwin Torres, *Q & A*, p. 66, 1977

5 in poker, a heavy bet *US, 1988*
- — George Percy, *The Language of Poker*, p. 70, 1988

pound *verb*
▸ **pound cotton**
to strain the residue of a narcotic from a bit of cotton used to strain the drug for a previous injection *US, 1990*
- "I'll do you good if you lemme pound cotton." By which he meant add more water in her cooker and strain the residue from her cotton, something like percolating coffee grounds a second time. — Seth Morgan, *Homeboy*, p. 64, 1990

▶ **pound ground**
to march *US, 1977*
- But at least it isn't the straight-leg infantry. At least I won't have to pound ground. — Larry Heinemann, *Close Quarters*, p. 33, 1977

▶ **pound her pee-hole**
from the male perspective, to have energetic sex *US, 1994*
- — Michael Dalton Johnson, *Talking Trash with Redd Foxx*, p. 79, 1994

▶ **pound pavement; pound the pavement**
to look for a job *US, 1960*
- Imagine what it'd be like to perform before roaring crowds for eight years through high school and college, and then, a year later, pound the pavement alone, desperately hunting for some kind of employment. — Mel Levin, *Ready or Not, Here Life Comes*, p. 39, 2005

▶ **pound salt up your ass; pound salt**
used as a term of rejection *US, 1960*
- Christina felt secure in her job, certainly enough to tell Reynaldo Flemm to go pound salt every time he put the make on her. — Carl Hiaasen, *Skin Tight*, p. 44, 1989

▶ **pound sand**
to engage in futile behavior *US, 1981*
Usually used as a command, where the term takes on a meaning not unlike "go fuck yourself."
- And what happens if I, for once, just tell you people to go pound sand? — Gerald Petievich, *One-Shot Deal*, p. 195, 1981

▶ **pound the bishop**
(used of a male) to masturbate *US, 1977*
- I stop pounding the bishop now, lest I cross the finish-line right along with him. — *Adam Film World*, p. 60, 1977

▶ **to get pounded**
while surfing, to be knocked from your surfboard and thrashed by the wave *US, 1988*
- — Michael V. Anderson, *The Bad, Rad, Not to Forget Way Cool Beach and Surf Discriptionary*, p. 15, 1988

pound; pound down *verb*
to drink (alcohol) *US, 1995*
- We get there, we pound booze till Carlos shows up[.] — Quentin Tarantino, *From Dusk Till Dawn*, p. 79, 1995
- — Connie Eble (Editor), *UNC-CH Campus Slang*, p. 8, April 1995
- I soon found myself pounding down beers in a Dayton bar called Little Mickey's. — Larry Flynt, *An Unseemly Man*, p. 27, 1996

poundage *noun*
weight that should be lost *US, 1972*
- You'll need more exercise than sucking dick to work that poundage off. — Bruce Rodgers, *The Queens' Vernacular*, p. 153, 1972

pounder *noun*
1 a police officer assigned to foot patrol *US, 1945*
- — Lou Shelly, *Hepcats Jive Talk Dictionary*, p. 16, 1945
- We just began to eat when in breezed these two pounders on the bloodhound tip, hunting down the owner of the cab parked out front. — Mezz Mezzrow, *Really the Blues*, p. 32, 1946
- — Jack Lait and Lee Mortimer, *New York Confidential*, p. 236, 1948: "A Glossary of Harlemisms"
- — Kenn "Naz" W. Young, *Naz's Under-ground Dictionary*, p. 50, 1973

2 a powerful, hard-breaking wave *US, 1964*
- — John Severson, *Modern Surfing Around the World*, p. 178, 1964
- — Douglas Simonson, *Pidgin to da Max: Hana Hou*, 1982

3 a 16-ounce can of beer *US, 1997*
- Any true-blue region transplant should have a few pounders in the fridge at all times. — Amy and Denise McFadden, *CoalSpeak*, p. 11, 1997

pound off *verb*
(used of a male) to masturbate *US, 1969*
- But I've been pounding off over this for a week! — Philip Roth, *Portnoy's Complaint*, p. 199, 1969

pounds *noun*
money *US, 1971*
- — Hermese E. Roberts, *The Third Ear*, 1971

pour *verb*
▶ **pour on the coals**
in trucking, to drive fast *US, 1971*
- — Montie Tak, *Truck Talk*, p. 122, 1971

▶ **pour the pork**
(from the male point of view) to have sex *US, 1973*
- [S]he told him she just laid a guy across the hall and had seen a gun under his pillow while he was pouring her the pork. — Joseph Wambaugh, *The Blue Knight*, p. 167, 1973
- My dad worked for Rita Hayworth circa 1950. He told me he poured her the pork. — James Ellroy, *Destination Morgue*, p. 30, 2004

pour (it) out *verb*
to urinate *US, 1990*
- — Charles Shafer, *Folk Speech in Texas Prisons*, p. 211, 1990

poverty pimp *noun*
a person who works for a government-funded anti-poverty program *US, 1974*
- It appears that the universities are developing "poverty pimp" programs, headed by incompetents and serving only to appease ethnic students. — Thomas Linton, *Patterns of Power*, p. 330, 1974
- I could see him at the "Board" meeting, Ron Reinaldo, a voice form the community, who will pull no punches. Jive-ass poverty pimp. — Edwin Torres, *After Hours*, p. 177, 1979
- Poverty pimp. It's rough language, but it's also the perfect description of what happens when people stuff their own pockets with money that's supposed to go to the poor. — *Milwaukee Journal Sentinel*, 1st August 2000

poverty poker *noun*
a style of poker in which a player who loses their bankroll may play for free until they win a hand *US, 1988*
- — George Percy, *The Language of Poker*, p. 70, 1988

powder *noun*
a powdered narcotic, usually heroin or cocaine *US, 1975*
- There's people down here, Blacks pushing the powder and hustling the chicks, and using their own people to pad their damned pockets. — Donald Goines, *Inner City Hoodlum*, p. 23, 1975
- "He's trying to get 2 ounces of powder," a caller named Truck told Bellamy[.] — *Orlando Sentinel*, p. B2, 17th August 2002

▶ **take a powder**
1 to leave *US, 1934*
- First Mrs. Hitchcock packed up and took a powder, and there was hell to pay. — Mezz Mezzrow, *Really the Blues*, p. 66, 1946
- Well, when the cuckoo quacks a dozen she takes a fast powder but loses a slipper. — Harry Haenigsen, *Jive's Like That*, 1947
- He had been five minutes away from being killed and he was taking a quick-acting powder. — Mickey Spillane, *Kiss Me Deadly*, p. 168, 1952
- The vine [rumor-mill] said you're Lancaster the guy who took a powder thirteen years ago. — Iceberg Slim (Robert Beck), *Pimp*, p. 299, 1969

2 to inhale or ingest powdered drugs *US, 1982*
- — Ralph de Sola, *Crime Dictionary*, p. 148, 1982

powder *verb*
▶ **powder your nose**
to sniff cocaine *UK, 1983*
- Well I'll tell you what, I'll go to the bathroom and powder my nose, while you sit here and think of something to say. — *Pulp Fiction*, 1994

powdered *adjective*
under the influence of cocaine *US, 1986*
- — Sacramento Municipal Utility District, *Glossary of Drugs and Drug Language*, 1986

powder puff *noun*
an effeminate homosexual male *US, 1997*
- Now would chime in the litany of abuse: naughty sissy, baby-boy, not-really-a-boy-but-a-pussy, little faggot, secret cocksucking toy, queer-bait, boy-hole, powder-puff. — Terence Sellers, *Dungeon Evidence*, p. 58, 1997

powder puff *adjective*
in various sports, describing an event limited to female competitors *US, 1973*
- This is a Le Mans start for the powder puff class. — Ed Radlauer, *Motorcyclopedia*, p. 39, 1973
- — Phantom Surfers, *The Exciting Sounds of Model Road Racing (Album cover)*, 1997

power *adjective*
in a concentrated, intense manner *US, 1989*
Almost always used mockingly.

- powerstudy: to study hard. — Pamela Munro, *U.C.L.A. Slang*, p. 68, 1989
  - "I overslept and had to power walk to class." "I need a power nap before I study." — Connie Eble (Editor), *UNC-CH Campus Slang*, p. 5, Fall 1991
  - While I was gassing up the mower, Lacey came out on the patio in a weensy bikini for some al fresco power tanning. — C.D. Payne, *Youth in Revolt*, p. 5, 1993
  - But you can go out dancing in this too. It's a total power suit. — *Jackie Brown*, 1997

power hit *noun*
the act of inhaling marijuana smoke and then exhaling it into another's mouth as they inhale *US, 1982*
- Ernest L. Abel, *A Marijuana Dictionary*, p. 82, 1982

power lunch *noun*
a lunch meeting where business or deals, not eating, is the central focus *US, 1978*
- The name calls to mind the New York restaurant which started life as a Prohibition-era "speakeasy" but now is the venue for many a "power lunch." — Walter Herdeg, *Graphis Posters*, p. 97, 1978
- Rachel S. Epstein and Nina Liebman, *Biz Speak*, p. 174, 1986

power table *noun*
a prominent table at a restaurant, seating at which is a recognition of fame or power *US, 1984*
Used in the entertainment industry.
- So if you want to become a power luncher, it's imperative you learn which are the prime areas and power tables of the restaurants you frequent—and how to obtain them. — *Nation's Restaurant News*, 13th February 1984

power trip *noun*
any activity that is motivated by a desire for power *US, 1967*
- All these people away on power trips and ego trips. I'm almost to the point of being sick of it, sick of being a Digger. — Nicholas Von Hoffman, *We Are The People Our Parents Warned Us Against*, p. 97, 1967

pow-wow *noun*
a meeting *US, 1812*
Originally an Algonquin word for an "Indian priest" or "ceremony."
- This pow-wow right here is news inside already. — Edwin Torres, *Carlito's Way*, p. 122, 1975
- There was a big pow-wow last night to decide what to do. — Jay McInerney, *Bright Lights, Big City*, p. 100, 1984

pozzle *noun*
the vagina *US, 1962*
- I mean, whoever heard of a man gettin' too much pozzle? — *One Flew Over the Cuckoo's Nest*, 1962

PP *noun*
1 a person whose regular appearance in a hospital casualty department has earned him the label *professional patient* *US, 1978*
- *Maledicta*, p. 6, Summer/Winter 1978: "Common Patient-Directed Pejoratives Used by Medical Personnel"
2 influence within a prison *US, 1985*
A shortened form of "penitentiary pull."
- *New York* (letter to editor), p. 10, 11th February 1985

PR *noun*
1 Puerto Rico *US, 1909*
- I got bored of New York and P.R. Figure I'd check the scene over here. — Edwin Torres, *Carlito's Way*, p. 75, 1975
2 a Puerto Rican *US, 1957*
Also attributed as an adjective.
- You're gonna make nice with them PR's from now on. — *West Side Story*, 1957
- P.R.'s dig manhood, don't play sissy. — Abbie Hoffman, *Revolution for the Hell of It*, p. 30, 1968
- The tigers would go to the Cabo and the BC, the down P.R.'s would go to the Palladium. — Edwin Torres, *Carlito's Way*, p. 24, 1975
- Gus is in the hospital. Some P.R.'s got 'em. — *Saturday Night Fever*, 1977

practice bleeding *noun*
engaging in night-training flights off an aircraft carrier *US, 1986*
- *United States Naval Institute Proceedings*, p. 108, October 1986

prairie nigger *noun*
A Native American Indian *US, 1989*
- Among the townspeople, the epithet used to describe an Indian is "prairie nigger[.]" — *New York Times*, p. C7, 29th September 1989
- Mr. Campbell, a Northern Cheyenne Indian, told the Senate that "there are some places in this country yet where American Indians are called 'prairie niggers'." — *New York Times*, p. B6, 23rd July 1993
- "I've been called 'blanket ass' and 'prairie nigger' more times than I can count," he said. — *Philadelphia Inquirer*, 7th November 1999
- "There are still places in this country," he added, "where American Indians are called prairie niggers, which is about the most vulgar term I can think of for both groups of people." — *Washington Post*, p. A8, 12th December 2003

prang *verb*
to crash or crash-land an aircraft *UK, 1941*
- Woodford Agee Heflin, *United States Air Force Dictionary*, p. 398, 1956
- The half million bucks' worth of Uncle Sam's aerial hardware was rolling down the Da Nang runway instead of pranging into the South China Sea. — Elaine Shepard, *The Doom Pussy*, p. 181, 1967
- *Current Slang*, p. 17, Summer 1970
- I was pranging the Huey again. So was Len. "Pranging" was an unofficial term we learned in flight school. It was descriptive of both the sound of the deflection of a helicopter's skids during a very hard landing. — Robert Mason, *Chickenhawk*, p. 182, 1983

prat *verb*
to engage in coy or fawning behavior *US, 1969*
- The "Murphy" player will "prat" him to enhance his desire. He will say, "Man, don't be offended, but Aunt Kate, that runs the house don't have nothing but high-class white men coming to her place." — Iceberg Slim (Robert Beck), *Pimp*, p. 38, 1969

prat in *verb*
in pickpocket usage, to back into the potential victim, getting him into position for a confederate *US, 1981*
- Don Wilmeth, *The Language of American Popular Entertainment*, p. 207, 1981

pratt boy *noun*
a weak or effeminate person; an outcast *US, 1952*
- He was becoming a pratt boy for her. — George Mandel, *Flee the Angry Strangers*, p. 372, 1952

prayer bones *noun*
the knees *US, 1946*
- My prayerbones played knock-knock. Jack, I was bad off. — Mezz Mezzrow, *Really the Blues*, p. 179, 1946

prayer meeting *noun*
a private dice game *US, 1949*
- The next night the boys was having a little prayer meeting when I came by. I didn't have no mind for dice so I didn't get in on it. — Hal Ellson, *Duke*, p. 113, 1949

prayer pusher *noun*
an overtly religious person *US, 1983*
- Gina and I were teamed up with, of all people, two nuns who hadn't yet taken their final vows. "Just what we need," Gina said. "A couple of prayer pushers to ruin every party." — Lynda Van Devanter, *Home Before Morning*, p. 42, 1983

praying John *noun*
a gambler who believes that he can influence the fall of the dice by uttering the right, magical words *US, 1950*
- *The Annals of the American Academy of Political and Social Sciences*, p. 129, May 1950

preach *verb*
▸ **preach to the choir**
to talk to those who are already convinced *US, 1986*
- Department of the Army, *Staff Officer's Guidebook*, p. 64, 1986
- Instead, the rally organizers decided to preach to the choir. — *The Boston Herald*, p. 10, 1st June 1996

preacher *noun*
1 a traffic police officer who is too kindhearted to issue citations *US, 1962*
- *American Speech*, p. 271, December 1962: "The language of traffic policeman"
2 a log that is partially submerged in a river *US, 1974*
- Russell Tabbert, *Dictionary of Alaskan English*, p. 223, 1991

preacher's pasttime *noun*
the shell game *US, 1966*

- Here we are, ladies and gentlemen! Carnival croquet, the preacher's pastime. — Robert Edmond Alter, *Carny Kill*, p. 34, 1966

preemie *noun*

a premature baby *US*, 1927

- She got a new baby, one of them preemeys, jist a little tiny bug of a chil'. — Joseph Wambaugh, *The New Centurions*, p. 242, 1970

prefab *adjective*

prefabricated *US*, 1937

- The commercial little pig laid out for a few bars and then moved into a prefab joint somewhere out of the high-rent district[.] — Steve Allen, *Bop Fables*, p. 21, 1955

preg *adjective*

pregnant *US*, 1960

- Incidentally, I was preg. That's right, p.r.e.g. — Glendon Swarthout, *Where the Boys Are*, p. 235, 1960

pre-game *verb*

to engage in social activity before a sporting event or concert *US*, 2000

- "Pre-gaming," said Cunningham, 25, holding up a cold bottle of Bud Light. — *Chicago Sun-Times*, p. 4, 23rd July 2000
- — Don R. McCreary (Editor), *Dawg Speak*, 2001
- "A lot of the kids were pre-gaming," said Downs, explaining that they had been drinking before they arrived at the event. — *The News Journal (Wilmington)*, p. 3B, 8th November 2005

preggers *adjective*

pregnant *UK*, 1942

- The girl on the grass beside me is white-faced and Mona Lisa like and she's preggers. — Anonymous, *Go Ask Alice*, p. 103, 1971

pregnant duck *noun*

the B-24 Liberator bomber *US*, 1946

A nod to the plane's clumsy appearance.

- — *American Speech*, p. 310, December 1946: "More Air Force slang"

prelim *noun*

a preliminary sport's competition *UK*, 1923

- I saw him in a pre-lim at the stadium. — Iceberg Slim (Robert Beck), *Long White Con*, p. 201, 1977

premium *noun*

a brand name manufactured cigarette *US*, 1992

- — William K. Bentley and James M. Corbett, *Prison Slang*, p. 65, 1992

prenup *noun*

an agreement entered into before marriage concerning the division of property in the event of divorce *US*, 1983

Shortened from "prenuptial."

- Fierman believes clients can sidestep the pre-nup by declaring, with trembling lip, that it would "undermine the trust and love on which our relationship is built." — *Money*, p. 180, June 1983
- O.J. should have had a prenup. Everyone needs a prenup. — Chris Rock, *Rock This!*, pp. 199–200, 1997

pre-op *noun*

a transsexual who has yet to undergo all surgery necessary to complete a sex change *US*, 1986

- A Puerto Rican pre-op transsexual stabs a trick in the eye with a sharp fingernail to grab his cabfare before he pays the driver. — Josh Alan Friedman, *Tales of Times Square*, p. 51, 1986
- Pre-ops wanted for erotic encounters. — Anka Radakovich, *The Wild Girls Club*, p. 43, 1994
- A male-to-female preop posts: "On the way home from the doctor, a bunch of men driving past me shouted out of the window 'DYKE' at me, as loud and offensively as they could." — Nancy Tamosaitis, *net.sex*, p. 130, 1995

prep *verb*

to prepare someone or something *US*, 1927

- [H]e moved from chair to chair with incredible speed and finesse, instructing the nurses on what to do to prep each patient. — Jim Carroll, *Forced Entries*, p. 135, 1987
- But I've already been prepped, in fact told what to do. — Elmore Leonard, *Maximum Bob*, p. 242, 1991

preppy; preppie *noun*

a well-groomed, well-heeled, conventional young person with upper-class prep-school values *US*, 1956

- Eliot [a university dormitory] is crawling with preppies. — *Harvard Crimson*, 29th March 1956
- — Collin Baker et al., *College Undergraduate Slang Study Conducted at Brown University*, p. 176, 1968
- Ollie, you're a preppie millionaire, and I'm a social zero. — Erich Segal, *Love Story*, p. 40, 1970
- [H]e was the only person in the whole joint without an alligator on his shirt. Even the bartender had one. Keyes thought he'd died and gone to Preppie Heaven. — Carl Hiaasen, *Tourist Season*, p. 221, 1986

Presbyterian poker *noun*

low-key, low-limit, friendly poker *US*, 1996

- — John Vorhaus, *The Big Book of Poker Slang*, p. 30, 1996

prescriptions *noun*

commercially manufactured drugs used for nonmedicinal purposes *US*, 1980

- — Edith A. Folb, *runnin' down some lines*, p. 250, 1980

presence *noun*

MDMA, the recreational drug best known as ecstasy *US*, 1989

- — Bruce Eisner, *Ecstasy*, p. 1, 1989

presento *noun*

during the Korean war, a piece of merchandise used by US servicemen to trade with Koreans for services *US*, 1960

- — *American Speech*, p. 118, May 1960: "Korean bamboo English"

press *noun*

in betting, a doubling of the bet in effect *US*, 1962

- "I'll give you a press," means I will bet you the same amount as the original bet for the remaining holes. — Dawson Taylor, *How to Talk Golf*, p. 55, 1985
- Then he said we'd play Zark and Ruffin a $50 Nassau. Automatic one-down presses. — Dan Jenkins, *Dead Solid Perfect*, p. 16, 1986

press *verb*

1 to pursue criminal charges *US*, 1993

- The Korean lady and her kid moved back out of the country so they couldn't press me. — *Menace II Society*, 1993

2 to dress up *US*, 1974

- — Stewart L. Tubbs and Sylvia Moss, *Human Communication*, p. 122, 1974

▸ **press the meat; press the sausage**

while gambling, to continue betting your winnings after several consecutive wins *US*, 2003

- — Victor H. Royer, *Casino Gamble Talk*, p. 89, 2003

pressed *adjective*

dressed stylishly *US*, 1980

- — Edith A. Folb, *runnin' down some lines*, p. 250, 1980

pressed duck *noun*

a human corpse that has been flattened by traffic *US*, 1962

A truly grim comparison.

- — *American Speech*, p. 271, December 1962: "The language of traffic policeman"

pressed ham *noun*

bare buttocks pressed against a car window as a prank *US*, 1966

- — Andy Anonymous, *A Basic Guide to Campusology*, p. 20, 1966
- "Pressed Ham"—the buttocks are pressed against a car window. — *New York Folklore Quarterly*, p. 55, March 1973
- "That's not a moon, Moses; that's a pressed ham." — Chris Miller, *The Real Animal House*, p. 133, 2006

pressure out *verb*

to lose your composure completely under pressure *US*, 1981

Hawaiian youth usage.

- Ey, no tell Lance about hees girlfriend, brah—he going pressure out! — Douglas Simonson, *Pidgin to da Max*, 1981

pressurize *verb*

to intimidate; to threaten; to coerce *US*, 2001

- — Jim Goad, *Jim Goad's Glossary of Northwestern Prison Slang*, December 2001

prestiff *noun*

a patient close to death *US*, 1994

- — Sally Williams, *"Strong" Words*, p. 156, 1994

pretties *noun*

on a movie or television crew, the makeup, hair, and wardrobe departments *US*, 1997

- — *American Speech*, p. 418, Winter 1997: "Among the new words"

pretty boy *noun*
a sexually active young man *US, 2003*
- Pretty boy is a sexually active boy, someone who's been fairly promiscuous. — *Oprah Winfrey Show*, 2nd October 2003

pretty pictures *noun*
in computing, graphical representations of statistics *US, 1991*
- — Eric S. Raymond, *The New Hacker's Dictionary*, p. 287, 1991

pretty-print *verb*
in computing, to format code so that it looks attractive *US, 1983*
- — Guy L. Steele et al., *The Hacker's Dictionary*, p. 74, 1983

pretzels *noun*
a small amount of money *US, 1988*
An evolution from the more common **PEANUTS**.
- — George Percy, *The Language of Poker*, p. 71, 1988

price *noun*
1 in betting on horseracing, the approximate equivalent odds to $1 *US, 1951*
- — David W. Maurer, *Argot of the Racetrack*, p. 52, 1951

2 a discount *US, 1991*
A euphemism that saves face for both the seller and buyer.
- Also Brennan gives him a price on sandwiches and a free first round of drinks which everybody thinks is very nice of him. — Robert Campbell, *In a Pig's Eye*, p. 2, 1991

prick *noun*
1 the penis *UK, 1592*
From the basic sense, "anything that pricks or pierces"; in conventional English until around 1700. William Shakespeare (1564–1616) played word games with it, Robert Burns (1759–96) used it with vulgar good humor, and the Victorians finally hid it away.
- In his anxiety the man has even forgotten to pretend he's standing there for any purpose other than to see Johnny's prick[.] — John Rechy, *Numbers*, p. 41, 1967
- [H]is prick is small and rather dismal-looking. — Gore Vidal, *Myra Breckinridge*, p. 109, 1968
- When the prick stands up, the brain gets buried — Philip Roth, *Portnoy's Complaint*, 1969
- "Can you put your prick further in my ass, and further in my cunt." — *Final Report of the Attorney General's Commission on Pornography*, p. 438, 1986

2 a despicable person *US, 1929*
- "I've seen some awful pricks. And the funny thing is a lot of them were mustangs. Old enlisted men." — Thomas Heggen, *Mister Roberts*, p. 177, 1946
- Old men with white hair and black-ribbon glasses "look right"—no cop, no prick dares question their freedom. — Jack Kerouac, *Letter to Allen Ginsberg*, p. 213, 16 July 1949
- You ever stop to figure that, you dumb prick? — Evan Hunter, *The Blackboard Jungle*, p. 295, 1954
- What I wouldn't give to know what heavy feels like, you insensitive prick. — *Something About Mary*, 1998

prick 25 *noun*
a portable radio communications, model 25 *US, 1972*
- "What do you know about a prick twenty-five?" Fi Bait asked. — William Pelfrey, *The Big V*, p. 27, 1972

pricked off *adjective*
annoyed, angry *US, 1968*
- — Fred Hester, *Slang on the 40 Acres*, p. 11, 1968

prickface *noun*
a despicable person *US, 1974*
- "What the hell took you so long, prick-face?" — Anne Steinhardt, *Thunder La Boom*, p. 33, 1974
- "Prickface, mothafucker. You want I should spell it out for you?" — Jackie Collins, *Lady Boss*, p. 136, 1990

pricklick *noun*
a homosexual male *US, 1972*
- — Helen Dahlskog (Editor), *A Dictionary of Contemporary and Colloquial Usage*, p. 46, 1972

prick parade *noun*
a group inspection by a military doctor or medic of male recruits for signs of sexually transmitted disease *US, 1964*

- — Roger Blake, *The American Dictionary of Sexual Terms*, p. 168, 1964
- — Dale Gordon, *The Dominion Sex Dictionary*, p. 130, 1967

prick rag *noun*
a cloth used to clean a man after sex *US, 1987*
- Afterwards I stand there quietly for a moment, still holding his penis in my right hand , my left hand resting on his chest. Then I reach for a prick rag[.] — Frederique Delacoste, *Sex Work*, p. 64, 1987

prickshit *noun*
a despicable person *US, 1968*
- "[Y]our starving motherfuckers . . .kill you prickshits you." — Sol Yurrick, *The Bag*, p. 47, 1968
- Well, the little prickshit was going to be surprised. — Richard Helms, *The Valentine Profile*, p. 259, 2002

pricksmith *noun*
a military doctor or medic who inspects male recruits for signs of sexually transmitted disease *US, 1967*
- — Dale Gordon, *The Dominion Sex Dictionary*, p. 130, 1967
- And much represents powerful condescension and contempt, as in such hospital usages as pecker checker, prick smith, and penis machinist for the medical officer obliged to scrutinize genitals for signs of gonorrhea. — Paul Fussell, *Wartime*, p. 257, 1989

prick-teaser *noun*
a woman who invites sexual advances but does not fulfill that which she seems to promise *US, 1970*
- [H]e was beginning to suspect her of being one of the world's great prick-teasers. — Terry Southern, *Blue Movie*, p. 91, 1970
- "To tell you the truth, she was kind of a prick-teaser." — Xaviera Hollander, *Xaviera*, p. 112, 1973
- She was always a prickteaser. Now she stood so closely the pert tips of her tits radiated warm spots on his chest. — Earl Thompson, *Tattoo*, p. 432, 1974
- "Or 1 of them classic Society types; a prick-teaser." — Leo Rosten, *Silky!*, p. 40, 1979

pride of Deadwood *noun*
in poker, a hand consisting of aces and eights *US, 1988*
From the belief, true or legendary, that when Wild Bill Hickock was shot and killed in Deadwood, Dakota Territory, he was holding a hand consisting of aces and eights, all black.
- — George Percy, *The Language of Poker*, p. 71, 1988

pride of the morning *noun*
the erection experienced by a man upon awakening in the morning *US, 1972*
- — Robert A. Wilson, *Playboy's Book of Forbidden Words*, p. 204, 1972

prime *noun*
high-quality marijuana *US, 2004*
- But my boy Arnel say you slangin' the prime. — *Hustle and Flow*, 2004

primed *adjective*
drunk or under the influence of drugs *US, 1950*
- — Hyman E. Goldin et al., *Dictionary of American Underworld Lingo*, p. 163, 1950
- — Stephen H. Dill (Editor), *Current Slang*, p. 3, Summer 1966

prime time *noun*
time spent with a spouse or lover *US, 1976*
Trucker slang, punning on television terminology.
- — Wayne Floyd, *Jason's Authentic Dictionary of CB Slang*, p. 25, 1976

primo *noun*
1 a very high grade of marijuana, consisting of a high degree of potent flowering tops of the plants *US, 1971*
- — Ernest L. Abel, *A Marihjana Dictionary*, p. 83, 1982

2 marijuana mixed with crack cocaine *US, 1993*
- [H]e allowed his newfound taste for Primos—pot laced with cocaine—to flourish. — Bob Sipchen, *Baby Insane and the Buddha*, p. 221, 1993
- — Mark S. Fleisher, *Beggars & Thieves: Lives of Urban Street Criminals*, p. 290, 1995: "Glossary"

primo *adjective*
excellent *US, 1977*
- — Gary Fairmont R. Filosa II, *The Surfer's Almanac: An International Surfing Guide*, p. 192, 1977
- "I just like the sandwiches." He was damned if he'd let her peg him as an old preppie finding his roots. "Yeah," she said, "they are primo." — Armistead Maupin, *Further Tales of the City*, p. 99, 1982

- But old Owsley's preemo purple or even windowpane, that stuff could get you in touch with your ancestors. — Elmore Leonard, *Freaky Deaky*, p. 19, 1988
- This is primo advertising. Christ, Igor, we're all over the news! — *Airheads*, 1994

Princeton rub; Princeton style *noun*
the rubbing of the penis between the thighs of another boy or man until reaching orgasm *US, 1971*
- You know, Uncle, the Princeton Rub? — John Francis Hunter, *The Gay Insider*, p. 158, 1971
- Princeton rub—Ostensibly reflects the gentlemanly restraint of the Ivy League. — Wayne Dynes, *Homolexis*, p. 116, 1985
- "Actually, they could go to bed without fucking, couldn't they? Princeton rub, and so on. Would that count as adultery?" — Ethan Morden, *Everybody Loves You*, p. 164, 1988
- This last activity, generally referred to as frottage, also had the only slightly derogatory nickname, I was later to find out, of "the Princeton rub." — Jack Hart, *My First Time*, p. 241, 2002

print *verb*
to take the fingerprints of a prisoner during the after-arrest process *US, 1939*
- We brought him up to the marshal's office and mugged him and printed him and then we brought him here. — George V. Higgins, *The Friends of Eddie Doyle*, p. 135, 1971

prior *noun*
a prior arrest or prior conviction *US, 1896*
- The guy he killed was running on speed and trailing a lifetime of priors, destined—they told Vincent—to crash and burn or die in jail. — Elmore Leonard, *Glitz*, p. 4, 1985
- With their priors, they're looking at a serious bounce. — *Gone in 60 Seconds*, 2000

prison punk *noun*
a formerly heterosexual man who submits to homosexual sex in prison *US, 1954*
- You have the free-world homosexuals like me. You have the strictly prison punks. — John Martin, *Break Down the Walls*, p. 179, 1954
- He absolutely refused to give up his manhood and be turned into a prison punk. — Carl Prichard, *Silent Agony*, p. 4, 2007

prissy lad *noun*
a homosexual man *US, 1954*
- He and another prissy lad were in our cocktail lounge one evening, drinking, making catty and audible cracks about other patrons[.] — Dev Collans with Stewart Sterling, *I was a House Detective*, p. 105, 1954

private dance *noun*
a one-on-one sexual performance by a woman for a man *US, 1991*
- He had gone to the go-go bar to meet a buddy of his, had one beer, that's all, while he was waiting, minding his own business and this go-go whore came up to his table and started giving him a private dance he never asked for. — Elmore Leonard, *Maximum Bob*, p. 1, 1991
- A United States congressman, you're telling me it's just a private dance party? — Carl Hiaasen, *Strip Tease*, p. 280, 1993
- I knew he wanted a private dance. — Heidi Mattson, *Ivy League Stripper*, p. 162, 1995
- I wanted my girlfriend to have a full strip-club experience, complete with a private dance. — *The Village Voice*, 21st September 1999

private dick *noun*
a private detective *US, 1912*
- "You've been followed by a private dick I hired ever since last Wednesday night[.]" — David Gregory, *Flesh Seller*, pp. 115–116, 1962

private jingle *noun*
a private investigator *US, 1964*
- "An ex private jingle coming in with a big ticket isn't easy to take." — Mickey Spillane, *The Snake*, p. 75, 1964

private slick *noun*
a physician in private practice *US, 1994*
- — Sally Williams, *"Strong" Words*, p. 154, 1994

private star *noun*
a private detective *US, 1958*
- I'm a private star. I followed somebody down here last night. — Raymond Chandler, *Playback*, p. 123, 1958

privy queen *noun*
a homosexual male who searches for sexual partners in public toilets *US, 1941*
- — Bruce Rodgers, *The Queens' Vernacular*, p. 195, 1972
- Other terms such as privy-queen (one who frequents toilets looking for "trade") and top sergeant (a masculine Lesbian "who takes or is imagined to take the superior position in tribady)[.] — Jennifer Terry, *An American Obsession*, p. 456, 1999

pro *noun*
a professional prostitute *UK, 1937*
- My gal's a pro and them is just chippies. — Chester Himes, *The Real Cool Killers*, p. 100, 1959
- "Jesus, nine years old," he said, reached over and pinched Candy's nose, "and knew a lot more than a good many pros" — Ken Kesey, *One Flew Over the Cuckoo's Nest*, p. 245, 1962
- Hey, don't do that. I said I wasn't a pro, remember? — *48 Hours*, 1982
- CATHERINE: I wasn't dating him. I was fucking him. GUS: What are you—a pro? — *Basic Instinct*, 1992

prob *noun*
a problem *US, 1992*
- Got a prob with that too? — Jess Mowry, *Way Past Cool*, p. 35, 1992

process *noun*
a chemical straightening of curly hair *US, 1967*
- After observing all the "down" cats who frequent these Barber shops, he decided to get a process (Hair marcelled). — Babs Gonzales, *I Paid My Dues*, p. 94, 1967
- Those two pimps? That style is just called a process, some call it a marcel. — Joseph Wambaugh, *The New Centurions*, p. 66, 1970

procon *noun*
a *professionally* run fan *convention US, 1978*
- — *American Speech*, p. 53, Spring 1978: "Star Trek lives: Trekker slang"

procure *verb*
▸ **procure for a cause**
to steal something *US, 1970*
- — *Current Slang*, p. 22, Spring 1970

prod *noun*
1 the penis *US, 1975*
- — *American Speech*, p. 64, Spring–Summer 1975: "Razorback slang"

2 in horseracing, an illegal, battery-powered device used to impart a shock to a horse during a race *US, 1976*
- — Tom Ainslie, *Ainslie's Complete Guide to Thoroughbred Racing*, p. 336, 1976

▸ **on the prod**
looking for something; on the offensive; provoked *US, 1904*
- Once a hooligan mob was on the prod and was quick to call my bluff. — Bruce Jackson, *Get Your Ass in the Water and Swim Like Me*, p. 75, 1966
- I never see him when he ain't on the prod. Maybe this is because he's almost always the man sent out to pick up pieces too ugly for other people to pick up. — Robert Campbell, *Junkyard Dog*, p. 21, 1986

produce *noun*
food *US, 1957*
- "Got any produce?" "Food," the great Kahoona explained, noticing my puzzled expression. — Frederick Kohner, *Gidget*, p. 31, 1957

producer *noun*
a serious gambler who, like most gamblers, usually loses *US, 1963*
- During his stay, hieroglyphics are secretly appended to his name on the hotel register, which catalogue him as a "dropper" (businessman and heavy loser), "producer" (businessman), or "nonproducer" (professional gambler). — Ed Reid and Ovid Demaris, *The Green felt Jungle*, p. 2, 1963

product *noun*
illegal drugs *US, 1982*
- Jack a phone in there and make a deal, talk about the product, it's always the product now[.] — Elmore Leonard, *Cat Chaser*, p. 165, 1982
- You'll have more product day after tomorrow, right? — *The Bad Lieutenant*, 1992
- No, man, no product. This is a clean run I'm talking about. No contraband, no kind of shit of any kind like that. — Elmore Leonard, *Riding the Rap*, p. 265, 1995
- We hire drivers with nothing to lose. Then we throw a lot of product at the problem. — *Traffic*, 2000

prof noun
a professor US, 1838

- New bunch now—mess of students with arms like twigs, passel of bald-head profs with vests. — Max Shulman, *Anyone Got a Match?*, p. 225, 1964

professional scene noun
a sadomasochistic encounter for pay US, 1979

- — *What Color is Your Handkerchief*, p. 6, 1979

professor noun
1 a diligent student US, 1955

- — *American Speech*, p. 304, December 1955: "Wayne University slang"

2 a piano player in a brothel US, 1939

- — Robert S. Gold, *A Jazz Lexicon*, p. 237, 1964
- [T]he "professor" is the house musician in a brothel. — Charles Winick, *The Lively Commerce*, p. 40, 1971

3 a skilled and experienced poker player US, 1979

- — John Scarne, *Scarne's Guide to Modern Poker*, p. 287, 1979

profile verb
1 to show off US, 1997

- — *Newsday*, p. B2, 11th October 1997
- That way I could profile in a "stolen Nova" just like in the rhyme. — *E.A.R.L.*, p. 110, 2002

2 (used of the police) to stop, question, and search someone based on their race and age US, 1992

- It was only natural to look at a cop car; nothing gave a clocker away to a profiling cop like that stony, straight-ahead stare at a red light. — Richard Price, *Clockers*, p. 24, 1992

profiles noun
in a deck of playing cards, the king of diamonds, jack of spades, and jack of hearts, all one-eyed and drawn in profile US, 1963

- — Irwin Steig, *Common Sense in Poker*, p. 186, 1963

pro from Dover noun
an expert US, 1970

- We're the pros from Dover and we figure to crack that kid's chest and get out to the golf course before it's dark. — *M*A*S*H*, 1970

program noun
the twelvestep Alcoholics Anonymous program for recovery from alcoholism US, 1991

- Plus everybody there was on the frigging program anyway. — Robert Stoller and I.S. Levine, *Coming Attractions*, p. 192, 1991

program verb
in prison, to follow the rules and avoid trouble in hope of an early release US, 1981

- — *Maledicta*, p. 265, Summer/Winter 1981: "By its slang, ye shall know it: the pessimism of prison life"
- "Guys from all over the jail try to get transferred here because we run the best shop in the house," the inmate boasted. "We program hard." — Nathan McCall, *Makes Me Wanna Holler*, p. 145, 1994

prohi noun
a federal law enforcement official US, 1974
Used by those in the illegal production of alcohol.

- them goddam, low-down, sonuvabitch prohi bastards. — David W. Maurer, *Kentucky Moonshine*, p. 122, 1974

prole noun
a member of the proletariat UK, 1887

- "Good morning, fellow proles," you say, slipping into your seat. — Jay McInerney, *Bright Lights, Big City*, p. 16, 1984
- They call it the new liquid acid, and, to proles like me, it's the best drug in the world. — Suroosh Alvi et al., *The Vice Guide*, p. 91, 2002

prole adjective
proletariat; of the working class US, 1938

- Spector, while still in his teens, seemed to comprehend the prole vitality of rock and roll that has made it the kind of darling holy beast of intellectuals in the United States. — Tom Wolfe, *The Kandy-Kolored Tangerine-Flake Streamline Baby*, p. 66, 1965

promo adjective
promotional US, 1963

- Man has money, he's connected, knows people, like he must know some indie promo guys. — Elmore Leonard, *Be Cool*, p. 176, 1999

promote verb
in the circus or carnival, to obtain illegally something that is badly needed US, 1980

- — Joe McKennon, *Circus Lingo*, p. 72, 1980

prong noun
the penis US, 1968

- I suppose as the biggest stud in England, he felt it his duty to show the biggest prong. — Angelo d'Arcangelo, *The Homosexual Handbook*, p. 67, 1968
- "He's got the biggest prong I ever saw on a white man," Gorilla said in honest admiration. — Earl Thompson, *Tattoo*, p. 327, 1974
- [O]n my prong, which seemed hardy and useful and insistently hard. — Jesse Grant, *The Best of Friction*, p. 373, 2002

pronger noun
the penis US, 1977

- I doubt if there are very many gigs where he doesn't end up pogoing his pronger in some sweet honey's hive. — Lester Bangs, *Psychotic Reactions and Carburetor Dung*, p. 235, 1977

prong on noun
an erection US, 1974

- "So I go, and I'm gone a pretty long time, because I got this huge prong on and I gotta practically stand on my head if I wanna piss in the hopper and not in my own fuckin' mouth." — George Higgins, *Cogan's Trade*, p. 183, 1974

pronto adverb
immediately US, 1911
From the Spanish.

- Nelson didn't say a word. He ejected that mother, pronto. — Joseph Wambaugh, *Fugitive Nights*, p. 245, 1992
- We did what we were told to do, pronto, or else we got slammed. — Odie Hawkins, *Black Chicago*, p. 117, 1992
- We're in a car we gotta get off the road pronto! — *Pulp Fiction*, 1994

proof noun
an identification card establishing you as old enough to buy alcohol US, 1983

- — *Esquire*, p. 180, June 1983

proof verb
to show identification proving that you are old enough to be where you are, buying what you are buying US, 1987

- I still look young enough to get proofed in bars. — Jim Carroll, *Forced Entries*, p. 7, 1987

proof shot noun
a photograph, or a scene in a pornographic film, of a man ejaculating. US, 1995

- Proof Shot stems from old time producers demanding an external ejaculation of sperm so that the customer saw proof that he popped his wad. — *Adult Video News*, p. 42, August 1995

prop noun
1 in casino gambling, a casino employee who poses as a player to draw interest to a game US, 1996
An abbreviation of "proposition player."

- — Frank Scoblete, *Best Blackjack*, p. 269, 1996

2 the leg US, 1969

- If my "props" get cut off I'll wheel myself on a wagon looking for a whore. — *Pimp*, p. 103, 1969

propellerhead noun
an expert computer enthusiast US, 1997

- A geek has more profound understanding of his or her subject, but the propellerhead has a date for Friday night. — Andy Ihnatko, *Cyberspeak*, p. 157, 1997

propeller key noun
the command key on an Apple Macintosh™ computer keyboard US, 1991

- — Eric S. Raymond, *The New Hacker's Dictionary*, p. 288, 1991

proper noun
proper respect US, 1974

- These punks just don't want to give us our proper. — Donald Goines, *El Dorado Red*, p. 110, 1974

props noun
1 proper respect; due credit US, 1993

Variant "propers."

- [S]lackness (X-rated lyrics), that gave me the props, that made me stick[.] — *Chicago Tribune*, p. 6C, 3rd January 1993
- — Connie Eble (Editor), *UNC-CH Campus Slang*, p. 6, Spring 1994
- Nobody's giving me props. Nobody. — *Jerry Maguire*, 1996
- I gotta give y'all props on the whole "Power 30" issue[.] — *The Source*, p. 44, March 2002

2 false breasts *US, 1967*
- — Dale Gordon, *The Dominion Sex Dictionary*, p. 131, 1967

pros *noun*

in circus and carnival usage, a prosecutor *US, 1981*
- — Don Wilmeth, *The Language of American Popular Entertainment*, p. 210, 1981

prospect *noun*

a prospective member of a club or gang *US, 2000*
- To become a Hell's Angel, there never has been any initiation rite outside of serving as a prospect. — Ralph "Sonny" Barger, *Hell's Angel*, p. 42, 2000

pross bust *noun*

a police sweep of suspected prostitutes *US, 1973*
- In two hours, unbeknownst to her procurers, the new girl was picked up in a general pross bust. — Gail Sheehy, *Hustling*, p. 64, 1973

pross collar *noun*

an arrest of a prostitute for a direct solicitation *US, 1973*
- Even girls who are found guilty on the more serious "pross collars," involving a specific proposal for a specific price made to a plainclothesman, are rarely jailed. — Gail Sheehy, *Hustling*, p. 15, 1973

pross cop *noun*

a member of a police vice squad *US, 1973*
- The pross cop, Pete, arrests me every time he sees me. — Susan Hall, *Ladies of the Night*, p. 45, 1973
- Either an easy trick or a pros cop, thought Robin, remembering that New York City police were not allowed to remove their pants[.] — Alix Shulman, *On the Stroll*, p. 147, 1981

prossie *noun*

a prostitute *US, 1971*
- "Biffer," "prossie," "she-she," "pig-meat" are some other slang designations. — Charles Winick, *The Lively Commerce*, p. 41, 1971

pross van *noun*

a police van used in mass arrests of prostitutes *US, 1973*
- The last pross van to Night Court leaves the precinct at seven. — Gail Sheehy, *Hustling*, p. 89, 1973

prosty; prostie *noun*

a prostitute *US, 1930*
- Haunt of homos, pinkos, nature lovers and nuts. Chicago's version of London's Hyde Park with soap boxers and prosties. — Jack Lait and Lee Mortimer, *Chicago Confidential*, p. 289, 1950
- And then she was on top of me, working me up like a Paris prostie[.] — Roger Gordon, *Hollywood's Sexual Underground*, p. 140, 1966
- I don't think it's ever happened to any other male prostie[.] — Joey V., *Portrait of Joey*, p. 123, 1969
- "Think he was trying to pick up a prostie." — John Ridley, *Love is a Racket*, p. 13, 1998

protection *noun*

1 contraception, especially a condom *US, 1917*
- — Dale Gordon, *The Dominion Sex Dictionary*, p. 133, 1967
- Oh sure, we'll need protection. — Evan Hunter, *Last Summer*, p. 173, 1968
- Padre, fucking that pig without a rubber is like playing the Rams without a helmet. Hope you got protection. — Joseph Wambaugh, *The Choirboys*, p. 325, 1975
- The Stud claims to be immune from disease, refuses to wear protection. — Josh Friedman, *When Sex Was Dirty*, p. 4, 2005

2 an extortion scheme in which the victim pays the extorting party to protect him from crime, especially crime committed by the extorting party *US, 1872*
- It was his speciality, selling protection. — Elmore Leonard, *Be Cool*, p. 182, 1999

protein shake *noun*

in the pornography industry, semen that is swallowed *US, 1995*
- — *Adult Video News*, p. 51, October 1995

proto *noun*

protection from prosecution by law enforcement *US, 1945*
- Do you know why? I'll tell you. I'm working under proto. — William J. Spillard and Pence James, *Needle in a Haystack*, p. 127, 1945

prozine *noun*

a professionally published fan magazine *US, 1978*
- — *American Speech*, p. 53, Spring 1978: "Star Trek lives: trekker slang"

prune *noun*

the anus *US, 1967*

An allusion to the wrinkles found on each.
- She kept it on the mantel when she wasn't cramming it in your mammy's prune. — Malcolm Braly, *On the Yard*, p. 32, 1967
- I guess by now you know what MY FANTASY will be about: the old prune, that tight little chocolate path[.] — *Screw*, p. 6, 20th November 1972

prunes *noun*

testicles; courage *US, 1967*
- The trooper who had shown me the pants now bent down and pulled aside the crotch of the prisoner's shorts, exposing his shriveled yellow prunes[.] — Martin Russ, *Happy Hunting Ground*, p. 71, 1968
- He had prunes, they whispered to one another. Manny's prunes were big as honeydews. Manny Lopez had balls to the walls! — Joseph Wambaugh, *Lines and Shadows*, p. 141, 1984

pruno *noun*

a potent, homemade alcohol, often made with fermented prune juice *US, 1974*
- He'd had some trouble in the last year when he yanked one inmate drunk on prison-made pruno out of his cell and ran into a number of other inmates coming back from a movie. — Tim Findley, *The Rolling Stone Reader*, p. 87, 1974
- Striker had been drinking pruno, and when he does this he always without fail becomes belligerent. — Jack Henry Abbott, *In the Belly of the Beast*, p. 81, 1981
- After Lights Joe uncapped a Maxwell House coffee jar of pruno, as prison hootch was called. — Seth Morgan, *Homeboy*, p. 302, 1990
- We had just finished making a batch of pruno—jail-made wine—and were preparing to get drunk when we heard a voice. — Sanyika Shakur, *Monster*, p. 286, 1993

Prussian *noun*

a male homosexual who prefers the active role in anal sex *US, 1950*
- — Hyman E. Goldin et al., *Dictionary of American Underworld Lingo*, p. 164, 1950

P's *noun*

parents *US, 1989*
- — Pamela Munro, *U.C.L.A. Slang*, p. 68, 1989

p's and q's *noun*

▸ **mind your p's and q's**

to be careful, exact, prudent *UK, 1779*

Perhaps, from the old custom of alehouse tally, marking "p" for pint and "q" for quart, care being necessary to avoid over or undercharging. Whether the source is in printing, or "pints and quarts," or learning to read, is unknown.
- It paid to be on your ps n' qs at all times, no tellin' when someone was going to pop in the door and throw a knife, a brick, a bottle, or just simply shoot. — Odie Hawkins, *Chicago Hustle*, p. 177, 1977

psych *noun*

1 psychology; psychiatry *US, 1895*
- I would be up against all those emotional forces the psych books describe. — Erich Segal, *Love Story*, p. 58, 1970

2 a psychiatrist or psychologist *US, 1971*
- When I got down to the induction center I said I wanted to see the psych — J. Anthony Lukas, *Don't Shoot—We Are Your Children*, p. 436, 1971

psyche!

I fooled you! *US, 1990*
- Pysche! You thought I forgot about your daughter Mary's wedding. — *New Jack City*, 1990

psyched *adjective*

excited, enthusiastic *US, 1970*
- I'm so psyched for this concert. Aerosmith are going to kick ass! — *Wayne's World 2*, 1993
- My colds and sore throats disappeared. I was psyched. — Howard Stern, *Miss America*, p. 109, 1995

- I'm psyched to see the Dead in Philly on my birthday, but the tour gets postponed after the Cap theater radio show because Jerry has bronchitis or something. — Scott Meyer, *Deadhead Forever*, 2001

psychedelic martini *noun*
DMT, a short-lasting hallucinogen *US*, *1970*
- — William D. Alsever, *Glossary for the Establishment and Other Uptight People*, p. 9, December 1970

psychic energizer *noun*
an amphetamine or other central nervous system stimulant *US*, *1967*
- Amphetamine, that group of drugs which are called pep pills by squares. They are also called psychic energizers. — Ruth Bronsteen, *The Hippy's Handbook*, p. 12, 1967

psycho *noun*
1 a psychopath, or someone who is otherwise psychologically disturbed *US*, *1942*
- I was an escapee from an insane asylum, a pyscho with a gun, an ex-pug who could do plenty without a gun if he took a notion. — Jim Thompson, *After Dark, My Sweet*, p. 107, 1955
- I hated what the word meant. I hated the sound of it at once. "psycho" had a sudden mental-ward reality about it, a systematic, diagnostic sound. — John Knowles, *A Separate Peace*, p. 135, 1959
- They're a special breed of psycho. — Robert Gover, *The Maniac Responsible*, p. 211, 1963
- The way I hear it, Soze is some kind of butcher. A pitiless, psycho, fucked-up butcher. — *The Usual Suspects*, 1995
2 a psychologist *UK*, *1925*
- "They sent me to a psycho eight years ago." — Nelson Algren, *The Man with the Golden Arm*, p. 204, 1949
- "Last psycho we had here stayed six months." — Donald Wilson, *My Six Convicts*, p. 11, 1951

psycho *adjective*
1 psychiatric or psychological *US*, *1927*
- He's in the pyscho ward. He needs some horse. — Clarence Cooper Jr., *The Scene*, p. 66, 1960
- It's one of those things I hid from the psycho team all these years. — Mickey Spillane, *Last Cop Out*, p. 15, 1972
- I think Riggs is pulling for a psycho pension. — *Lethal Weapon*, 1987
- They always got those signs around hospitals that says QUIET, and if I was to go into that shimmy act, they'd probably throw me into the pyscho ward and I'll never get out. — *Drugstore Cowboy*, 1988
2 crazy *US*, *1936*
An abbreviation of "psychopathic."
- Besides being psycho, she was unintelligent and illiterate, practically, and probably wouldn't understand it anyhow. — Robert Gover, *One Hundred Dollar Misunderstanding*, p. 148, 1961

psycho block *noun*
an area in a prison where the most violent prisoners are held *US*, *1985*
- The tiers in Quentin or Folsom they call psycho blocks. — Vincent Patrick, *Family Business*, p. 244, 1985

psych out *verb*
1 to intimidate someone completely on a psychological level *US*, *1994*
- Arnold was able to totally psych out any confidence Ferigno had. — *Natural Born Killers*, 1994
2 to figure out or discover something *US*, *1978*
- You'll learn to psyche out the regulars. — Armistead Maupin, *Tales of the City*, p. 155, 1978

PT *noun*
a woman who promises more sex than she delivers *US*, *1958*
An abbreviation of **PRICK TEASER**.
- That goddamn P.T. Listen, once I was with her in this guy's car and ... — Willard Motley, *Let No Man Write My Epitaph*, p. 179, 1958
- Helen Dahlskog (Editor), *A Dictionary of Contemporary and Colloquial Usage*, p. 46, 1972
- "She's the biggest little PT in town," a tall girl who reminded Jack of one of the Andrew Sisters turned to advise him. — Earl Thompson, *Tattoo*, p. 42, 1974

PTA *noun*
a hasty washing by a female *US*, *1971*
The most common association with PTA is the school support Parent-Teacher Association. The PTA in question here refers to the woman's *pussy*, *tits* and *ass* (or *armpits*).

- — Eugene Landy, *The Underground Dictionary*, p. 155, 1971
- Speaking of half-baths and so on, anyone out there ever heard of a PTA bath? It was new to me in Montana two years ago. — *alt.usage.english*, 23rd April 1992
- sm. packet of baby wipes (for a "P-T-A" whore in the plane bathroom) — *m7voke.blogspot.com/2007/11/carry-ons.html*, 11th November 2007

ptomaine wagon *noun*
a catering truck *US*, *1937*
- — Judi Sanders, *Kickin' like Chicken with the Couch Commander*, p. 19, 1992
- It begins with a catering truck, like hundreds that ply San Diego work sites. Yes, but this is no ordinary roach coach, ptomaine wagon or gedunk truck. — *Los Angeles Times*, p. 1, 8th July 1992

P-town *nickname*
Provincetown, Massachusetts *US*, *1980*
- It's easy to treat P-town as though it were a simple summer spot where you could go and find a place for some quick and good sex. — *Drummer: America's Mag for the Macho Male*, p. 76, 1980
- — Jeff Fessler, *When Drag Is Not a Car Race*, p. 64, 1997
- The fact that Tania lived in an apartment and not in one of the skanky rooming houses that everyone else in P-Town existed in made me think she probably had money. — Michelle Tea, *The Passionate Mistakes and Intricate Corruption of One Girl in America*, p. 91, 1998

pubber *noun*
a publisher, especially of a single-interest fan magazine *US*, *1982*
- — *American Speech*, p. 28, Spring 1982: "The language of science fiction fan magazines"

pub-crawl *verb*
to move in a group from one drinking establishment to the next, drinking at each *UK*, *1937*
- They pub-crawled through the night and wound up in a twenty four hour restaurant that was Spain's version of Denny's. — Odie Hawkins, *The Life and Times of Chester Simmons*, p. 34, 1991

pube *noun*
a high school girl *US*, *1969*
- — *Current Slang*, p. 9, Winter 1969

▶ **get pube**
in the categorization of sexual activity by teenage boys, to touch a girl's vulva *US*, *1986*
- Next in order of significant intimacy was "getting silk," which meant touching panty-crotch, and then for the more successful, "getting pube." — Terry Southern, *Now Dig This*, p. 3, 1986

pubes *noun*
pubic hair *US*, *1970*
- [T]he camera (voyeur's POV) finds occasion to linger, in a desultory, almost caressing fashion, on her pubes. — Terry Southern, *Blue Movie*, p. 24, 1970
- A year has passed. I'm older. I'm wiser. Garth got pubes. — *Wayne's World 2*, 1993
- The photos in issue number 4 were a little more explicit and featured models with their pubic hair exposed—and one with her pubes dyed red, white and blue. — Larry Flynt, *An Unseemly Man*, p. 89, 1996
- Marina's hair was red and curly and she dyed her pubes to match[.] — Michelle Tea, *Rent Girl*, p. 31, 2004

pubies *noun*
pubic hairs *US*, *1968*
- — Collin Baker et al., *College Undergraduate Slang Study Conducted at Brown University*, p. 177, 1968
- He sat up and picked a few pubies like flecks of tobacco from the tip of his tongue — Richard Price, *The Wanderers*, p. 99, 1974
- I'm still missing half my pubies from the first day here and the ones I got left aren't but a half-inch long — John Sayles, *Union Dues*, p. 14, 1977

public relations *noun*
a member of a swindling enterprise who promotes the swindle *US*, *1977*
- — Robert C. Prus and C.R.D. Sharper, *Road Hustler*, p. 171, 1977: "Glossary of terms"

puck *noun*
in a number of casino games, a disk used to mark a point or position *US*, *2003*
- — Victor H. Royer, *Casino Gamble Talk*, p. 108, 2003

pucker noun
the anus *US*, *1995*

- You'll pardon me if I ask you to kiss my pucker. — *The Usual Suspects*, 1995

pucker factor noun
the degree of fear or anxiety *US*, *1957*

From the image of the sphincter tightening in a frightening situation.

- My "pucker factor" went back to normal. — Society of Experimental Test Pilots, *Technical Review*, p. 175, 1957
- I was really frightened. In the Marine Corps, they have what they call the Pucker Factor. They joke about it. You get so scared that your asshole puckers. — Mark Barker, *Nam*, p. 40, 1981
- *Maledicta*, p. 255, Summer/Winter 1982: "Viet-Speak"
- His eyes are glued to the tube in Saudi Arabia, watchful of any sinister dots that tells him a Scud is on its way and it's time to neutralize it by launching a Patriot missile. Anxieties, which he calls "the pucker factor," are high. — *USA Today*, 1st February 1991

pucker paint noun
lipstick *US*, *1961*

The title of a 1957 ode to lipstick recorded by Huelyn Duvall for Challenge Records.

- — Art Unger, *The Cool Book*, p. 107, 1961

pucker palace noun
a drive-in movie theater *US*, *1961*

High school student usage.

- — *San Francisco Examiner*, p. 21, 12th December 1961

pucker string noun
a notional mechanism for tightening the sphincter when afraid *US*, *1990*

- — Joseph Tuso, *Singing the Vietnam Blues*, p. 258, 1990

pucker up verb
to tighten your rectal and anal muscles *US*, *1972*

- Well, they like you to squeeze yourself up, you know, so it would be tighter. They call it puckering up. And they like to put it in and bring it out and you just all the time squeezing on it. — Bruce Jackson, *In the Life*, p. 399, 1972

pud noun
▶ **pound your pud; pull your pud; pull your pudding**
(of a male) to masturbate *UK*, *1944*

- Well don't just lay there in your sleeping bag pullin' your puddin', get up and fetch some water. — Jack Kerouac, *The Dharma Bums*, p. 164, 1958
- He picked up Rocky's limp cock, nursed it with his tongue back into a hard-on, and gave him the wildest, frenziedest, freakiest blow job his world had ever seen, while he pounded his own pud. — Steve Cannon, *Groove, Bang, and Jive Around*, p. 186, 1969
- I told him about the first time I pounded my pud and which hand I used. — Joseph Wambaugh, *Lines and Shadows*, p. 329, 1984
- The embers of eroticism will stoke the couples, and raincoaters will pound their puds to Stagliano's quality porn productions. — Editors of Adult Video News, *The AVN Guide to the 500 Greatest Adult Films of All Time*, p. 328, 2005

pudding wagon noun
in circus and carnival usage, an ice cream truck *US*, *1981*

- — Don Wilmeth, *The Language of American Popular Entertainment*, p. 211, 1981

puddle noun
a generous dose of liquid LSD *US*, *1994*

- — David Shenk and Steve Silberman, *Skeleton Key*, p. 239, 1994

puddy tat; puddy cat noun
a cat *US*, *1958*

From the Looney Tunes cartoons with Sylvester the cat and Tweety Bird, with Tweety Bird's constant mantra of "I taut I taw a puddy-tat" (I thought I saw a pussy cat).

- I had been informed that this large puddycat wouldn't harm humans[.] — Gregory "Pappy" Boyington, *Baa Baa Black Sheep*, p. 78, 1958
- Take a look. The puddy tat's out of the bag. — Carl Hiaasen, *Tourist Season*, p. 331, 1986

pud puller; pud pounder noun
a male masturbator *US*, *1990*

- [F]inally encounter myself at the culminating moment of every Playboy-reading pud pounder's macho dreams. — John Nichols, *The Nirvana Blues*, p. 346, 1981

- A pudpuller at the movies that night said one of them called the other Joe. — Seth Morgan, *Homeboy*, p. 206, 1990
- I saw pud pounders and parolees pounced on. — James Ellroy, *Destination Morgue*, p. 291, 2004

Puerto Rican shower noun
an improvised cleaning of the body at a sink *US*, *1999*

- Should I go up to that person and tell them to go take a Puerto Rican shower in the cockpit because the reek is bothering me and giving me a sinus infection? — *alt.tv.real-world*, 8th January 1999

puffer noun
a crack cocaine user *US*, *1994*

- — US Department of Justice, *Street Terms*, October 1994

Puff the Magic Dragon; Puff nickname
a C-47 aircraft modified as a gunship and redesignated an AC47, heavily used by the US Air Force in Vietnam *US*, *1966*

From the gentle 1963 song recorded by the antiwar folksingers Peter, Paul, and Mary.

- "Puff the Magic Dragon" is among the many kinds of weapons, old and new, serving in the war against the Viet cong. — *The Berkeley Barb*, p. 6, 28 January 1966
- Known as Puff, the Magic Dragon, it has proved very effective in close air support by delivering heavy fire against Viet Cong ground forces. — Elaine Shepard, *The Doom Pussy*, p. 55, 1967
- Belmonte recognized its silhouette; it was the type of plane known as "Puff the Magic Dragon." — Neil Sheehan, *The Arnheiter Affair*, p. 191, 1971
- With the spotting plane came the large support plane, Puff the Magic Dragon. — Charles Anderson, *The Grunts*, p. 131, 1976

pug noun
1 a boxer; a fighter *UK*, *1858*

A shortened form of the conventional "pugilist."

- Feivel was a former pug, a lightweight who had battled it out with Lew Tendler and Abe Attell[.] — Irving Shulman, *The Amboy Dukes*, p. 53, 1947
- On the main floor, facing Broadway, are two cafes—the Turf, hang-out for musicians, and Dempsey's, rendezvous of pugs. — Jack Lait and Lee Mortimer, *New York Confidential*, p. 31, 1948
- Scraggs, a thirty-seven-year-old ex-pug who once fought Bobo Olson, was the oldest Angel then riding[.] — Hunter S. Thompson, *Hell's Angels*, p. 7, 1966
- I was thinkin' myself, among other things, half a pug in them days. — Edwin Torres, *Carlito's Way*, p. 11, 1975

2 a male homosexual *US*, *1992*

- — William K. Bentley and James M. Corbett, *Prison Slang*, p. 50, 1992

pug verb
to fight *US*, *1960*

- "We want to see you through this thing so's you can get back to pugging." — Nelson Algren, *The Neon Wilderness*, p. 66, 1960
- — Ellen C. Bellone (Editor), *Dictionary of Slang*, p. 18, 1989
- — Ann Lawson, *Kids & Gangs*, p. 56, 1994: "Common African-American gang slang/phrases"

puggie noun
a hardened criminal *US*, *1965*

- Teen-age girls, first offenders, some of them merely awaiting trial, are heaped in with "institutionalized" old puggies who feel like bigger shots inside than out. — Tom Wolfe, *The Kandy-Kolored Tangerine-Flake Streamline Baby*, p. 309, 1965

puke noun
1 vomit *US*, *1952*

- Kate spews out some puke and I close my eyes and waits. — Ralph Ellison, *Invisible Man*, p. 5, 1952

2 a despised person *US*, *1966*

In the mid-C19, the term was applied with some degree of scorn to residents of the state of Missouri; it later gained a broader sense. In *Rogue Warrior*, Richard Marcinko gives a virtual litany of pukes—Academy puke, admin puke, fleet puke, jet puke, puke ensign, staff puke and Team-puke.

- — *American Speech*, p. 282, December 1966: "More carnie talk from the West Coast"
- The roof is crowded with kids, some with binoculars. One is yelling, "Scorecard! Scorecard! Can't tell the cops from the pukes without a scorecard." — James Simon Kunen, *The Strawberry Statement*, p. 49, 1968
- Anyway, there were five of us in the park that night and for fifteen minutes we all battle that puke. — Joseph Wambaugh, *The New Centurions*, pp. 218–219, 1970

- But until that day you are pukes. You're the lowest form of life on Earth. — *Full Metal Jacket*, 1987

puke *verb*

1 to vomit *UK, 1600*

- That was the year I puked on every winter holiday. — Michelle Tea, *Valencia*, p. 106, 2000

2 in street luge, to melt (a wheel) *US, 1998*

- PUKE A WHEEL: To blow up; to liquefy a wheel due to the extreme heat of traveling at high speeds. — Shelley Youngblut, *Way Inside ESPN's X Games*, p. 130, 1998

3 in the illegal production of alcohol, to allow the still to boil over *US, 1974*

- Don't throw no more wood on that fire, you'll puke the still. — David W. Maurer, *Kentucky Moonshine*, p. 122, 1974

4 while on a combat air mission, to separate out from formation while under attack *US, 1986*

- — *American Speech*, p. 124, Summer 1986: "The language of naval fighter pilots"

puke hole *noun*

a shabby, shoddy, dirty place *US, 1973*

- I spotted a paddy hustler taking a guy up the back stairs of the Marlowe Hotel, a sleazy Main Street puke hole used by whores and fruits and paddy hustlers. — Joseph Wambaugh, *The Blue Knight*, p. 203, 1973

pukepot *noun*

a despicable person *US, 1973*

- I was filled with loathing for a pukepot like Zoot[.] — Joseph Wambaugh, *The Blue Knight*, p. 56, 1973

pull *noun*

an inhalation of smoke from a cigarette or pipe *US, 2002*

- "What are you doing?" I asked him when he was still holding onto the blunt after two or three pulls. — Earl "DMX" Simmons, *E.A.R.L.*, p. 205, 2002

pull *verb*

1 to serve time in prison or in the armed forces *US, 1961*

- The "elder" man had "pulled his combat time," and this was the way many arguments ended, even arguments about religion and politics, and not about the war at all. — Russell Davis, *Marine at War*, p. 57, 1961
- The *haras* wanted to know how things had been in Comstock, how long I had pulled, and how it had been. — Piri Thomas, *Down These Mean Streets*, p. 312, 1967

2 to recruit someone into prostitution *US, 1967*

- It was there he pulled his first ofay girl. — Babs Gonzales, *I Paid My Dues*, p. 99, 1967
- I was traveling with my partner, Cocaine Smitty / On our way to pull some whores in Mexico City. — Dennis Wepman et al., *The Life*, p. 36, 1976

3 to leave *US, 1960*

- Rudy started the car. "I'm pullin." — Clarence Cooper Jr., *The Scene*, p. 35, 1960

▸ **pull on the rope**

to masturbate a man *US, 1972*

- And then you start pulling on the rope or to throw the bald-headed champ [perform oral sex], boy you have reached rock bottom in my opinion. — Bruce Jackson, *In the Life*, p. 171, 1972

▸ **pull someone's covers**

to reveal a person's true character *US, 1970*

- — William K. Bentley and James M. Corbett, *Prison Slang*, p. 33, 1970

▸ **pull the plug**

in submarining, to dive *US, 1948*

- — *American Speech*, p. 38, February 1948: "Talking under water: speech in submarines"

▸ **pull time**

to be sentenced to imprisonment *US, 1950*

- "I don't want to pull any more time," Junior tells me, "but I wouldn't take anything in the world for the experience I had in prison." — Tom Wolfe, *The Kandy-Kolored Tangerine-Flake Streamline Baby*, p. 145, 1965
- I've talked to men who have pulled time all over the country and they say it's the same everywhere. — Malcolm Braly, *On the Yard*, p. 42, 1967
- You got to be a boss crook to pull that kind of time. — Joseph Wambaugh, *The Blue Knight*, p. 71, 1973
- I'd be eighty-two years old when I got out if I pulled every day of it. — Piri Thomas, *Seven Long Times*, p. 61, 1974

▸ **pull up on**

to approach *US, 1981*

- Someone pulled up on him on the yard and told him what he knew of him. — Jack Henry Abbott, *In the Belly of the Beast*, p. 68, 1981

▸ **pull your coat**

to warn someone; to alert someone, *US, 1954*

- Last night Lovis had pulled Mort's coat about something. — Bernard Wolfe, *The Late Risers*, p. 35, 1954
- Then get thee in front on a sudden bunt and I'll pull your coat and let you know that's all she wrote. — Dan Burley, *Diggeth Thou?*, p. 25, 1959
- Look here, baby, pull my coat to what's going down! — Eldridge Cleaver, *Soul on Ice*, p. 198, 1968
- After Jim pulled my coat to Hargrave, we came up with a way to cheat him "like white folks cheat us." — Nathan McCall, *Makes Me Wanna Holler*, p. 200, 1994

pull down *verb*

1 to arrest *US, 1975*

- Slick got pulled down on another beef and one of the liquor store owners spotted him on the lineup. — James Carr, *Bad*, p. 78, 1975

2 to earn money *US, 1917*

- He's pulling down six bills a week. — *The Blues Brothers*, 1980
- You pull down four bills a week which is damn good. — *48 Hours*, 1982

3 to rob *US, 1992*

- FREDD: I robbed a few gas and sips, sold some weed, told him recently I held the shotgun while me and another guy pulled down a poker game in Portland. — *Reservoir Dogs*, 1992

pulled up *adjective*

former *US, 1972*

- She must have been a pulled-up whore or something. — Bruce Jackson, *Outside the Law*, p. 151, 1972

puller *noun*

1 a sneak thief *US, 1984*

- — Inez Cardozo-Freeman, *The Joint*, p. 523, 1984

2 a dealer in stolen or smuggled goods *US, 1956*

- — *American Speech*, p. 98, May 1956: "Smugglers' argot in the Southwest"

3 a racehorse that strains to run at full speed *US, 1994*

- — Igor Kushyshyn et al., *The Gambling Times Guide to Harness Racing*, p. 121, 1994

4 a crack cocaine user who obsessively/compulsively tugs at different body parts *US, 1992*

- — Terry Williams, *Crackhouse*, p. 150, 1992

pulleys *noun*

suspenders *US, 1945*

- — Lou Shelly, *Hepcats Jive Talk Dictionary*, p. 16, 1945

pulling time *noun*

in an illegal numbers gambling lottery, the time of day when the winning number is drawn or selected *US, 1949*

- — *American Speech*, p. 193, October 1949

pull out of *verb*

to be released *US, 1973*

- When the day came for you to pull out of Jackson they would fuck around for five or six hours before you'd be on a bus going home. — A.S. Jackson, *Gentleman Pimp*, p. 132, 1973

pull out on *verb*

to draw a firearm and aim it at someone *US, 2005*

- "Why you pullin' out on me? I thought we was cool?" — 50 Cent, *From Pieces to Weight*, p. 65, 2005

pull up *verb*

to stop (doing something) *US, 1972*

- — Bruce Jackson, *Outside the Law*, p. 59, 1972: "Glossary"

pummel *verb*

to skateboard fearlessly, without regard to the effect on the board or body *US, 1984*

- — *San Francisco Sunday Examiner & Chronicle*, p. 20, 2nd September 1984: "Say it right"

pump *noun*

1 the heart *US, 1946*

- It's funny how the toughest gorilla gets tame and whimpers like a young pup when he begins to hear his own pump riffing. — Mezz Mezzrow, *Really the Blues*, p. 87, 1946
- He's on sick leave, his pump acting up on him, and I doubt will be back. — Elmore Leonard, *Killshot*, p. 182, 1989

2 a fire hydrant *US, 1979*

- He came up 111th Street in his jalopy with the windows down and stuck. "Boys" had the pump on. — Edwin Torres, *After Hours*, p. 164, 1979

3 an illegal linear amplifier for a citizens' band radio *US, 1976*

- — Elementary Electronics, *Dictionary of CB Lingo*, p. 98, 1976

pump *verb*

1 to exert yourself in a labor *US, 1992*

- You're fuckin' out here pumping bottles, I mean, what's your problem? — Richard Price, *Clockers*, p. 522, 1992

2 to sell drugs, especially crack cocaine *US, 1989*

- "He's pumping" means he sells drugs. — *USA Today*, p. 1A, 25th April 1989
- You be pumping that rock, Tre? — *Boyz N The Hood*, 1990
- Every day when I was done pumping, I'd go home and stash my money and rocks in a shoebox in the closet. — 50 Cent, *From Pieces to Weight*, p. 34, 2005

3 in poker, to increase a bet made by another player *US, 1983*

- — Thomas L. Clark, *The Dictionary of Gambling and Gaming*, p. 168, 1987

▸ **pump the stump**

to shake hands *US, 1947*

- — Marcus Hanna Boulware, *Jive and Slang of Students in Negro Colleges*, 1947

pumped *adjective*

pregnant *US, 1969*

- — *Current Slang*, p. 9, Winter 1969

pumped; pumped up *adjective*

with muscles inflated *US, 1997*

- He looked like all the other boys, if more pumped and tattooed from time in the pen. — Gini Sikes, *8 Ball Chicks*, p. 22, 1997
- He wasn't ripped, but he was pumped. — John Ridley, *Everybody Smokes in Hell*, p. 182, 1999

pumping *adjective*

(used of surf conditions) powerful, excellent *US, 1977*

- — Gary Fairmont R. Filosa II, *The Surfer's Almanac: An International Surfing Guide*, p. 192, 1977
- [I]t's so sick out there [...] it's really sick, it's pumping. — a British surfer interviewed in Newquay *Word of Mouth*, 6th August 2004

pumpkin *noun*

used as a sentimental term of address *US, 1998*

The affectionate tone of the term of address runs counter to the earlier sense of an "ineffective, incompetent person."

- I'm guessing that's what the soprano shriek was about, pumpkin. — *Something About Mary*, 1998

pumpkin roller *noun*

a farmer; a naive rustic *US, 1951*

- Speaking of pumpkin rollers in the corridors of power, I went to see the house where Rasputin was assassinated. — P.J. O'Rourke, *Eat the Rich*, p. 137, 1998

pumpkin seed *noun*

a yellow, oblong mescaline pill *US, 1971*

- — Eugene Landy, *The Underground Dictionary*, p. 155, 1971

pumpkin time *noun*

a curfew *US, 1970*

An allusion to the Cinderella tale.

- — *Current Slang*, p. 22, Spring 1970

pumps *noun*

the female breasts *US, 1949*

- — Vincent J. Monteleone, *Criminal Slang*, p. 184, 1949

pump up *verb*

1 to increase something, to inflate something, to turn something higher *US, 1987*

- That was it for Anne and Ted and I, and we left together as we'd arrived, but pumped up from Ochs. — Jim Carroll, *Forced Entries*, p. 74, 1987
- Turn your radios up! Crank it up so's we can hear it! Come on, pump it up, man! — *Airheads*, 1994

2 when lifting weights, to engorge a muscles with blood in order to inflate and define them *US, 1984*

- — *American Speech*, p. 201, Fall 1984: "The language of bodybuilding"

3 to conduct an exhaustive and detailed briefing *US, 1986*

- — Department of the Army, *Staff Officer's Guidebook*, p. 64, 1986

4 while gambling, to lose at a steady rate *US, 1980*

- — Lee Solkey, *Dummy Up and Deal*, p. 118, 1980

punch *noun*

an act of sexual intercourse; a person viewed only in terms of sex *US, 1983*

- She was just a punch. — Gerald Petievich, *To Die in Beverly Hills*, p. 137, 1983

punch *verb*

1 to open something by force *US, 1931*

Most commonly, but not exclusively, applied to breaking into a safe.

- Billy punched a beer can for the girl[.] — Ken Kesey, *One Flew Over the Cuckoo's Nest*, p. 226, 1962
- and there's no charge in the world like when you see that smoke ... and when you're punching it and you hear that pin hit the back of the safe. — *The Digger Papers*, August 1968
- If you're getting ready to punch a safe, you need one man to hold the punch and another to hit the hammer. — Bruce Jackson, *Outside the Law*, p. 81, 1972
- He knew he couldn't risk punching it. — Emmett Grogan, *Final Score*, p. 99, 1976

2 to have sex *US, 1971*

- — Eugene Landy, *The Underground Dictionary*, p. 155, 1971

3 in a card cheating scheme, to prepare a deck for cheating *US, 1962*

- — Frank Garcia, *Marked Cards and Loaded Dice*, p. 263, 1962

▸ **punch it**

to escape (from prison) *US, 1990*

- — Charles Shafer, *Folk Speech in Texas Prisons*, p. 212, 1990

▸ **punch someone's ticket**

1 to kill someone *US, 1983*

- I've been to too many autopsies of people killed by burglars—old ladies, housewives with kids, people who had never harmed anyone—to worry about how a career burglar got his ticket punched. — Gerald Petievich, *To Die in Beverly Hills*, p. 65, 1983
- Sure punched his ticket. — Edwin Torres, *Carlito's Way*, p. 69, 1985
- — Michael Dalton Johnson, *Talking Trash with Redd Foxx*, p. 102, 1994

2 to have sex with someone *US, 1992*

- Callum, to my amazement, was managing a reasonable facsimile of a leer. "I'd punch her ticket in a minute." — Armistead Maupin, *Maybe the Moon*, p. 231, 1992

punchboard *noun*

a promiscuous woman *US, 1960*

A "punchboard" is a game which used to be found in stores, where for a price the customer punched one of many holes on the board in the hope of winning a prize.

- "They called her a punchboard. What's that?" — Glendon Swarthout, *Where the Boys Are*, p. 133, 1960
- Claymore Face, the platoon punchboard, was there too. — Larry Heinemann, *Close Quarters*, p. 69, 1977
- There's one woman handler, named Wilma. A punchboard. — Joseph Wambaugh, *The Black Marble*, p. 34, 1978
- She's a passive punchboard and a seductress. — James Ellroy, *Destination Morgue*, p. 133, 2004

punch-drunk *adjective*

of a boxer, deranged or debilitated to some degree as a result of punches received *US, 1918*

Hence the condition of being punch-drunk: "punch-drunkenness."

- He looks like a punch-drunk pug to me. — Irving Shulman, *The Amboy Dukes*, p. 55, 1947
- [H]e happened to read a newspaper article about the awful dangers of punch-drunkenness. He vowed there and then never to box again. — Charles Raven, *Underworld Nights*, p. 42, 1956

puncher *noun*

a safe cracker *US, 1949*

- — Vincent J. Monteleone, *Criminal Slang*, p. 184, 1949

punching bag *noun*

a promiscuous woman *US, 1974*

From **PUNCH** in its sexual sense.

- "Linda says she's a regular punchin bag." — Earl Thompson, *Tattoo*, p. 237, 1974

punch-in-the-mouth *noun*

oral sex on a woman *US, 1967*

- — *American Speech*, p. 229, October 1967: "Some special terms used in a University of Connecticut men's dormitory"

punch job *noun*
a safe robbery in which the combination lock is punched out to gain access to the safe *US, 1958*
- — Jack Webb, *The Badge*, p. 222, 1958
- The punch job is much faster, three minutes maybe. — Leonard Shecter and William Phillips, *On the Pad*, p. 179, 1973

punch out *verb*
1 to leave *US, 1998*
- — *Seattle Times*, p. A9, 12th April 1998: "Grunts, squids not grunting from the same dictionary"

2 to eject someone from a fighter plane *US, 1986*
- — *American Speech*, p. 124, Summer 1986: "The Language of Naval Fighter Pilots"
- Then a MiG made one more pass / Hosed a missile up my ass / Then the bird pitched up and we punched out. — Joseph Tuso, *Singing the Vietnam Blues*, p. 229, 1990: Wolf Pack's Houseboy

3 to die *US, 2002*
- Reading on, I see that Anne was correct: the man punched out at age forty-seven. — Carl Hiaasen, *Basket Case*, p. 220, 2002

punch up *verb*
to enhance something, especially to enhance a script with humor, more lively dialogue, or the like *US, 1984*
In the 1950s, the entertainment industry used the term to mean to increase the volume of the sound track or brightness of the picture. Towards the end of the century, the meaning changed to a writing term.
- The eighth team of writers had been brought in to "punch up" the script, and each page that flew out of a typewriter had made the show less humorous and less charming[.] — Dan Jenkins, *Life Its Ownself*, p. 147, 1984
- "I want you to punch up Skip's piece," Mulcahy said. "Really make it sing." — Carl Hiaasen, *Tourist Season*, p. 201, 1986
- Ian, you want to punch it up a little? You're about as spunky as a corpse up there. — *Airheads*, 1994

punishment *noun*
▶ **put to the punishment**
in horseracing, to use any physicality such as whipping or kicking to an extreme degree *US, 1951*
- — David W. Maurer, *Argot of the Racetrack*, p. 53, 1951

punk *noun*
1 a young and/or weak man used as a passive homosexual partner, especially in prison *US, 1904*
- A punk, if you want it in plain English, is a boy with smooth skin who takes the place of a woman in a jailbird's love life. — Mezz Mezzrow, *Really the Blues*, p. 15, 1946
- Punks and brats are those prisoners who take the passive role in sodomy; there is no chronological age limit. — Arthur V. Huffman, *New York Mattachine Newsletter*, p. 6, June 1961
- The hacks would hear about it and they would put Tico on A-1 tier where all the faggots were, and he'd be a jailhouse punk. — Piri Thomas, *Down These Mean Streets*, p. 266, 1967
- Four years fuckin' punks in the ass made you appreciate rib when you get it. — *Reservoir Dogs*, 1992

2 a child *US, 1985*
- — Gene Sorrows, *All About Carnivals*, p. 24, 1985: "Terminology"

3 in horseracing, a mildly talented jockey *US, 1951*
- — David W. Maurer, *Argot of the Racetrack*, p. 53, 1951

punk *verb*
1 to have anal sex with someone *US, 1949*
- I had some Vaseline for my chapped lips and the desk copper leered and asked if we punked each other. — Neal Cassady, *The First Third*, p. 193, 3rd July 1949
- "And don't go thinking I punks that Jew faggot neither." — Robert Deane Pharr, *S.R.O.*, p. 171, 1971
- That's the only time I've ever been punked. — Bruce Jackson, *In the Life*, p. 372, 1972
- Washington punked him again and took off all his clothes. The kid went running naked down the trail, his face all dirty, his body scratched up, and his ass raw and bloody. — James Carr, *Bad*, p. 57, 1975

2 to intimidate *US, 1994*
- When caught, never let them punk you or sweet-talk you into a confession[.] — William Upski Wimsatt, *Bomb the Suburbs*, p. 55, 1994

3 to assault someone *US, 1991*
- He said they shouted and joked about "punking on someone"— street slang for jumping and beating a victim. — *Post-Standard*, p. B1, 10th June 1991

punk *adjective*
poor, lousy, inferior *US, 1896*
- "Oh, man, I don't know what's the matter with me. I fell kind of punk." Jack said, "Punk, I never used the word punk in my life." — Elmore Leonard, *Bandits*, p. 1, 1987

punkfucker *noun*
a male prisoner who has sex with homosexual prisoners, especially taking the active role *US, 1972*
- My fall partner was a notorious punkfucker in the penitentiary and he got out and he just converted right over to girls with no problem whatsoever. — Bruce Jackson, *Outside the Law*, p. 174, 1972

punk-hunt *verb*
to search for homosexuals and assault them for the sole reason of their homosexuality *US, 1968*
- The young Negros rejected the homosexual, and this was Wright alluding to a classic, if cruel, example of a ubiquitous phenomenon in the black ghettos of America: the practice by Negro youth of going "punk-hunting." — Eldridge Cleaver, *Soul on Ice*, p. 106, 1968

punk in the bunk *noun*
used for expressing the fact that the speaker has an effeminate homosexual prisoner under his control *US, 1984*
- — Inez Cardozo-Freeman, *The Joint*, p. 523, 1984

punk out *verb*
1 to withdraw from a task out of fear *US, 1920*
- I made sure, but if you want to punk out, say so. — Hal Ellson, *The Golden Spike*, p. 18, 1952
- The opposite of heart is punking out. — Harrison E. Salisbury, *The Shook-up Generation*, p. 25, 1958
- The opposite of heart is "punking out." — John Gimenez, *Up Tight!*, p. 28, 1967
- [H]e just wanted to know whether the private standing in front of him was trying to punk out of that war, or was truly bat-shit. — Emmett Grogan, *Ringolevio*, p. 227, 1972

2 to inform on or betray a compatriot *US, 1976*
- — John R. Armore and Joseph D. Wolfe, *Dictionary of Desperation*, p. 44, 1976

punk pill *noun*
any central nervous system depressant *US, 1968*
- — *Current Slang*, p. 39, Fall 1968

punk ride *noun*
an amusement ride for children *US, 1985*
- — Gene Sorrows, *All About Carnivals*, p. 25, 1985: "Terminology"

punk rock; punk *noun*
a genre of basic, high-energy rock music that came to prominence in the mid-1970s *US, 1970*
- Sanders does this particularly well in his first solo album for Reprise Records, "Sanders' Truckstop," which he describes as "punk rock." — *Chicago Tribune*, p. G4, 22nd March 1970
- A big part of punk rock is the Great American (or English, really) Teen Sublimation Riff. — Lester Bangs, *Psychotic Reactions and Carburetor Dung*, p. 101, 1972

punk rocker *noun*
a musician who plays punk rock *US, 1973*
- And make no mistake about it: the J. Geils Band are punk-rockers in the truest sense of the term. — *Creem*, 1st August 1973

punk tank *noun*
a holding cell in a jail or prison reserved for homosexuals *US, 1972*
- They take and put him in the punk tank too, and those people are usually the easiest to turn out. — Bruce Jackson, *Outside the Law*, p. 177, 1972

punt *verb*
to do poorly; to give up in some fashion because you are doing poorly *US, 1968*
A metaphor from American football, where a team that has not advanced the ball ten yards after three plays will often choose to punt the ball to its opposition rather than risk giving up field position.

- — Collin Baker et al., *College Undergraduate Slang Study Conducted at Brown University*, p. 178, 1968
- — Eric S. Raymond, *The New Hacker's Dictionary*, p. 291, 1991

pup *noun*
a young person *US, 1964*
- — R. Frederick West, *God's Gambler*, p. 228, 1964: "Appendix A"

puppies *noun*
the female breasts *US, 1992*
- Previous posts about her breast size were accurate. Un-be-lievable! Those puppies wanted out of that sweater! — *rec.arts.tv.soaps*, 14th September 1992
- Mae said her puppies are real, unlike all the other women. — Herb Kunze, *Herb's Wrestling Tidbits*, 27th January 2000
- Lela Rochon's perky puppies easily upstaged Spuds McKenzie[.] — Mr. Skin, *Mr. Skin's Skincyclopedia*, p. 472, 2005

puppies in a box *noun*
in the pornography business, a group of bare-breasted women cavorting *US, 1991*
- Um-hmmm. Puppies in a box [four young women playing[.] — Robert Stoller and I.S. Levine, *Coming Attractions*, p. 150, 1991

puppy *noun*
1 a person of a specified type *US, 1984*
- "These guys are sick puppies," said Boston Fire Capt. Matthew Corbett. — *Associated Press*, 26th July 1984
- When I see the bullish (inventory) figures, I just can't see how they can be accurate. This market is a sick puppy. — *Platt's Oilgram Price Report*, 24th May 1984
2 a pit bull terrier, especially a fierce one *US, 1997*
New York police slang.
- — Samuel M. Katz, *Anytime Anywhere*, p. 389, 1997: "The extremely unofficial and completely off-the-record NYPD/ESU truck-two glossary"
3 a small penis *US, 1980*
- — Edith A. Folb, *runnin' down some lines*, p. 250, 1980
4 in pool, a shot that cannot be missed or a game that cannot be lost *US, 1990*
- — Steven Rushin, *Pool Cool*, p. 24, 1990
- — Mike Shamos, *The Illustrated Encyclopedia of Billiards*, p. 183, 1993
5 a small bottle of wine *US, 1980*
- — Edith A. Folb, *runnin' down some lines*, p. 250, 1980
6 a gun *US, 1995*
- — Bill Vallentine, *Gang Intelligence Manual*, p. 110, 1995

puppyfoot *noun*
in a deck of playing cards, a club, especially the ace *US, 1967*
- — Albert H. Morehead, *The Complete Guide to Winning Poker*, p. 271, 1967

puppy-footed *adjective*
big-footed *US, 1992*
- Of course, she'd seen some puppy-footed white boys too ... but never naked, and she doubted she ever would. — Jess Mowry, *Way Past Cool*, p. 177, 1992

puppy love *noun*
a youthful infatuation *US, 1834*
- Attracted by her extremely mature figure, I found myself in the throes of "puppy love." — Phyllis and Eberhard Kronhausen, *Sex Histories of American College Men*, p. 72, 1960
- I found it difficult to believe that almost fifteen years had passed since our puppy love affair. — Iceberg Slim (Robert Beck), *Airtight Willie and Me*, p. 58, 1979

puppy lover *noun*
a person who is completely infatuated with someone *US, 1970*
- Then we sat on a big red sofa, holding hands like puppie lovers[.] — Red Rudensky, *The Gonif*, p. 114, 1970

puppy paws; puppy feet *noun*
in craps, a ten rolled with a pair of fives *US, 1981*
- — Steve Kuriscak, *Casino Talk*, p. 69, 1985

pups *noun*
the female breasts *US, 2005*
- Laura loses her orange bra, then treats us to her pink-nosed pups and she lies back and diddles her cliddle. — Mr. Skin, *Mr. Skin's Skincyclopedia*, p. 6, 2005

pup tents *noun*
in circus and carnival usage, overshoes *US, 1981*
- — Don Wilmeth, *The Language of American Popular Entertainment*, p. 212, 1981

pure *noun*
pure, unadulterated heroin *US, 1967*
- Musta' shot some "pure," cause a lookout on the sidewalk heard him mumble before he croaked, "Well kiss my dead mammy's ass if this ain't the best smack I ever shot" — Iceberg Slim (Robert Beck), *Pimp*, p. 79, 1969
- "That'll learn you, messing with the pure." — Robert Stone, *Dog Soldiers*, p. 13, 1974
- It ain't my fault Crying Junior gave me pure 'stead a mix. — Charles W. Moore, *A Brick for Mister Jones*, p. 28, 1975

purl; pearl *verb*
(used of the nose of a surfboard) to plunge under the surface of the ocean *US, 1963*
- — Grant W. Kuhns, *On Surfing*, p. 120, 1963

purple *noun*
the recreational drug ketamine *US, 1994*
- — US Department of Justice, *Street Terms*, October 1994

purple *adjective*
sexually suggestive but not explicit *US, 1986*
Not quite BLUE.
- I saw 'em this morning, Cab, and they're not bad. A little purple, maybe, but interesting. — Carl Hiaasen, *Tourist Season*, p. 43, 1986

purple heart *noun*
a capsule of phenobarbital (trade name Luminal™), a central nervous system depressant *US, 1966*
- — Donald Louria, *Nightmare Drugs*, p. 25, 1966
- [F]or five shillings you can buy enough pills—"purple hearts," "depth bombs" and other lovelies of the pharmacalogical arts. — Tom Wolfe, *The Pump House Gang*, p. 81, 1968

purple passion *noun*
red wine *US, 1966*
- He remembered the previous Christmas with Heff. Mexican grass and birdbath martinis, stealing the D-Phi car at a purple passion party[.] — Richard Farinia, *Been Down So Long*, p. 24, 1966

purple pickle *noun*
the bar awarded to US Air Force flight officers *US, 1946*
- — *American Speech*, p. 310, December 1946: "More Air Force slang"

purple-suiter *noun*
a military officer assigned to the US Department of Defense *US, 1986*
- — Department of the Army, *Staff Officer's Guidebook*, p. 64, 1986

push *noun*
1 in betting, a doubling of the bet in effect *US, 1986*
- — Sam Snead and Jerry Tarde, *Pigeons, Marks, Hustlers and Other Golf Bettors You Can Beat*, p. 110, 1986
2 in blackjack, a tie between the dealer and a player *US, 1978*
- — Jerry L. Patterson, *Blackjack*, p. 20, 1978
3 a radio frequency *US, 1968*
As in "the battalion push." Vietnam war usage.
- — Carl Fleischhauer, *A Glossary of Army Slang*, p. 9, 1968

push *verb*
1 to sell something, especially drugs *US, 1938*
- You're pushing junk, it's murder, baby. — George Mandel, *Flee the Angry Strangers*, p. 248, 1952
- My grandma pushes tea. — *West Side Story*, 1957
- Everyone knows he pushes—and takes the stuff himself. — John Rechy, *City of Night*, p. 210, 1963
- I came storming up to him. "One of your chicks is pushing outside." — Arthur Blessitt, *Turned On to Jesus*, p. 142, 1971
2 to make a special effort to promote a professional wrestler's image and status *US, 2000*
- I know Shane McMahon likes him and has told the writing team to push him, but what does he see in him? — *Inside Wrestling*, 25th August 2000

▸ **push daisies**
to be dead *US, 1919*
- "One four bad guys to be pushing up daisies soon." — Paul Morgan, *The Parrot's Beak*, p. 81, 2000

▸ **push the bush**
(used of a male) to have sex with a woman *US, 1984*

- The bartender spoke slowly, as if to an idiot child. "You know, push the bush? Slake the snake? Drain the train? Siphon the python?" — James Ellroy, *Because the Night*, p. 415, 1984

pusher *noun*
a drug dealer *US, 1935*

- Chico slipped the watch on his wrist and they went looking for Domingo, the pusher, to see if he would want it. — Hal Ellson, *The Golden Spike*, p. 15, 1952
- What frightened the owners most were the "pushers," the traders in narcotics. — Robert Sylvester, *No Cover Charge*, p. 286, 1956
- Everyone down on the pusher, but he don't push nobody, he only push the dope. He provides a service, that's all—somebody got to do it. — Edwin Torres, *Carlito's Way*, p. 41, 1975
- I'm no pusher, Betsy. Honest. — *Taxi Driver*, 1976

push-in *noun*
a robbery accomplished by knocking on a door and pushing your way into a house or apartment *US, 1982*

- "A push-in," said Yo. "You'll have to explain," said Billy. "I don't live up here in this city." "You push 'em in the door," said Yo. — Tom Lewis, *Game of Honor*, p. 276, 1982

push in the bush *noun*
vaginal sex *US, 1980*

- — *Maledicta*, p. 199, Winter 1980: "A new erotic vocabulary"

push out
in the language of hang gliding, used as an all-purpose greeting or farewell *US, 1992*

- — Erik Fair, *California Thrill Sports*, p. 328, 1992

pushover *noun*
someone who is gullible or easily manipulated; a person who is easily persuaded into sexual activity *US, 1944*

- A curvy push-over called Three-way Rosie lived up at Tenth and Galena. — Iceberg Slim (Robert Beck), *The Naked Soul of Iceberg Slim*, p. 99, 1971
- a romance with a charming little pushover, good for a few drunken parties. — Ayn Rand, *The Fountainhead*, p. 301, 1996
- Jesus was no pushover and displayed firmness and righteous anger toward the religious establishment[.] — Greg Ogden, *Discipleship Essentials*, p. 134, 1998
- It wasn't that she was a pushover either. She had a finely tuned BS detector[.] — Jay McGraw, *Closing the Gap*, p. 42, 2001

pushy *adjective*
used of a woman, in the second stage of labor *US, 1994*

- — Sally Williams, *"Strong" Words*, p. 156, 1994

pusillanimous polecat *noun*
used as a general term of disapproval *US, 2005*
A term used by George "Gramps" Miller, played by George Cleveland, on the television drama *Lassie* (CBS, 1954–57). Repeated with referential humor.

- "Then tell this pusilanimous polecat to show himself if he's not a coward." — Clara Miller, *The Sons of the Fathers*, p. 103, 2005

puss *noun*
1 the vagina; a woman; sex with a woman *US, 1971*
An abbreviation of **PUSSY**.

- Jack Katt and Tom Smart were there, at a front table, lushing it up and keen for puss. — Terry Southern, *Candy*, p. 151, 1958
- And she had the tan around her puss region too and also her buttocks. — Richard Meltzer, *A Whore Just Like the Rest*, p. 211, 1971
- That broad can't move, I'm on her. Look at that, scratching her puss[.] — Elmore Leonard, *Split Images*, p. 192, 1981
- How did she smell? Did her puss stink? — *Kids*, 1995
- We get some bare boobage as Josie satisfies her cough syrup addiction, followed by a brief peek at the puss[.] — Mr. Skin, *Mr. Skin's Skincyclopedia*, p. 135, 2005

2 an effeminate man *UK, 1991*

- I kicked out this puss I had and said that one's mine, the cute blond — Elmore Leonard, *Maximum Bob*, p. 50, 1991
- An you stop actin' like a goddamn puss! — Jess Mowry, *Way Past Cool*, p. 9, 1992

3 the mouth; the face *US, 1891*
A term hatched simultaneously in Ireland and the US.

- I can slap someone in the puss and they can't do a damn thing. — Mickey Spillane, *I, The Jury*, p. 7, 1947

- "Get that grin off your puss." — Nelson Algren, *The Man with the Golden Arm*, p. 195, 1949
- Do you want me to explain, innocent puss? — Hal Ellson, *Summer Street*, p. 76, 1953
- Did you see the puss on Bobby Tex? — Edwin Torres, *Q & A*, p. 99, 1977
- Why the long puss? I thought that went well. — Cleo Odzer, *Goa Freaks*, p. 102, 1995

pussified *adjective*
effeminate *US, 1994*

- — Michael Dalton Johnson, *Talking Trash with Redd Foxx*, p. 115, 1994

pussy *noun*
1 the vagina *UK, 1880*

- She thought she felt a second finger slish into her pussy, but before that could be confirmed, still another finger muscled up her asshole. — Tom Robbins, *Even Cowgirls Get the Blues*, p. 88, 1976
- He wondered if Landers would make her come by licking her pussy for her. — James Jones, *Whistle*, p. 182, 1978
- Avoid touching her pussy with a glove, toy or penis that's had prior anal contact. — Nina Hartley, *Nina Hartley's Guide to Total Sex*, p. 175, 2006

2 the mouth or anus as an object of sexual penetration *US, 1972*

- — Bruce Rodgers, *The Queens's Vernacular*, p. 162, 1972

3 a weak or effeminate boy or man; a coward *US, 1942*

- — Collin Baker et al., *College Undergraduate Slang Study Conducted at Brown University*, p. 179, 1968
- If Ossie did not fight, if he turned over all Harry's narco assets and secrets, then Ossie was a pussy. — Robert Deane Pharr, *Giveadamn Brown*, p. 148, 1978
- When I got the nine millimeter, I told everybody I wanted them to know I was no pussy and not to fuck with me. — Terry Williams, *The Cocaine Kids*, p. 60, 1989
- Fight back you little pussy. — *American Beauty*, 1999

4 anchovies *US, 1996*
Based on the puerile comparison of the smell of fish and the vagina.

- — *Maledicta*, p. 19, 1996: "Domino's pizza jargon"

▶ **push pussy**
to work as a pimp *US, 1992*

- "I sold dope, and began pimping, pushing pussy at the bar." — Pete Earley, *The Hot House*, p. 61, 1992

▶ **sling pussy**
to work as a prostitute *US, 1990*

- Now that she was good for nothing else, she figured why not fulfill Sugarfoot's highest ambition for her and sling pussy on Sunset Strip. — Seth Morgan, *Homeboy*, p. 4, 1990

pussy *adjective*
weak; effeminate; not manly *US, 1986*

- [S]willing ice-cold raspberry daiquiris and vodka sours by the pitcherful—pussy drinks, bartenders call them. — Larry Heinemann, *Paco's Story*, p. 11, 1986

pussy-ass *noun*
a weak or effeminate man; a coward *US, 1995*

- I taught you, you pussy ass! — Howard Stern, *Miss America*, p. 456, 1995

pussy beard *noun*
female pubic hair *US, 1967*

- — Dale Gordon, *The Dominion Sex Dictionary*, p. 135, 1967

pussy boy *noun*
an effeminate, passive homosexual *US, 1971*

- They were known as pussyboys, galboys, fuckboys, and all had taken girls' names like Betty, Fifi, Dotty, etc. — James Blake, *The Joint*, p. 67, 1971

pussy bumping *noun*
genital-to-genital lesbian sex *US, 1949*

- Milan became so pleasantly caught up in the excitement of pussy bumping, she was taken completely off guard[.] — Allison Hobbs, *A Bona Fide Gold Digger*, p. 225, 272

pussy butterfly *noun*
an interuterine contraceptive device *US, 1974*
More gently known simply as a "butterfly IUD."

- — Kathy Acker, *Essential Acker*, p. 244, 2002

pussycat; pussy cat *noun*
the vagina *US, 1980*

- — Edith A. Folb, *runnin down some lines*, p. 250, 1980

- Don't wear panties underneath your pajamas, dear; you need to air out your pussycat — Eve Ensler, *The Vagina Monologues*, p. 6, 1998

pussy collar *noun*
a desire for sex *US, 1963*

- Yes, dopers and drugmen and dapper mocking Dans—the fuzz and pussy and pussy-collared[.] — Clarence Cooper Jr., *Black*, p. 289, 1963

pussy cop *noun*
a member of a police vice squad *US, 1971*

- "Why I could do a hell of a lot more for them broads than any pussy cop coulda done for her," Charlie declared. — Robert Deane Pharr, *S.R.O.*, p. 183, 1971
- "A pussy cop!" She blushed. — Lawrencia Bembenek, *Woman on Trial*, p. 24, 1992
- He's got this problem about supervising everybody else's life. He should have been a pussy cop. — Edward Allen, *Mustang Sally*, p. 123, 1994

pussy eater *noun*
a practitioner of oral sex on women *US, 1971*

- He had been a dedicated pussy-eater since the very first time he had indulged the pastime. — James Jone, *The Merry Month of May*, p. 53, 1971
- A bit of the old "slow-down-you're-going-too-fast-yeah-there-like-that-oh-that's-perfect" can turn even the John Wayne Bobbitt of pussy eaters into a Doug Hart. — Suroosh Alvi et al., *The Vice Guide*, p. 25, 2002
- I have been an avid pussy eater since I was sixteen and I'm now seventy—that's fifty-four years of chowing down. — Al Goldstein, *I, Goldstein*, p. 80, 2006

pussy fart *noun*
the expulsion of trapped air from the vagina *US, 1991*

- QUEEF: Pussy fart, vart, fanny fart. — *alt.tasteless!.news.answers*, 21st April 1991
- A pussy fart or cunt fart is either the sucking noise of a well-lubricated vagina as a man withdraws his penis during sexual intercourse or a sound some women can make simply by using their vaginal muscles. — Jim Dawson, *Who Cut the Cheese*, p. 2–, 1999

pussy finger *noun*
the index finger *US, 1977*

- You almost wrecked my pussy finger. — *Saturday Night Fever*, 1977
- [T]he teenagers drinking there rib him about breaking his "pussy finger." — Carolyn Russell, *The Films and Joel and Ethan Coen*, p. 13, 2001

pussyfoot *verb*
to act with such caution that your behavior appears evasive or cowardly *US, 1903*
From the cautious progress of cats.

- For Christ's sake, Walter, I can't go around pussyfooting on this. — Robert Campbell, *In La-La Land We Trust*, p. 10, 1986
- To reach the restaurant, we had to cross a corner of the paddy field, jump a ravine, and pussyfoot through a ruin. — Cleo Odzer, *Goa Freaks*, p. 28, 1995
- He said it was time for Boorman to stop pussyfooting around and to take an aggressive stance with consumers[.] — Rita Ciresi, *Pink Slip*, p. 297, 1999

pussy game *noun*
prostitution *US, 1978*

- A pimp is an organizer in the pussy game (prostitution). — Burgess Laughlin, *Job Opportunities in the Black Market*, p. 11–4, 1978
- "No freebies in the pussy game. Nope." — John Kaye, *Stars Screaming*, p. 176, 1997

pussy hair *noun*
female pubic hair *US, 1969*

- I noticed and Boomie too her pussy hair was a darker color than on her head. — Wallace Markfield, *Teitlebaum's Window*, p. 182, 1970
- So guys buy these things to look at pussyhair? — *Screw*, p. 4, 3rd July 1972
- [G]iving them men short peeks of her black, fuzzy, short-cropped pussy hair. — Tina Russell, *Porno Star*, p. 24, 1973
- One of the hottest times ever was when I told my lover I wanted to go down on her but I wanted to trim her pussy hair first. — Violet Blue, *The Ultimate Guide to Cunnilingus*, p. 63, 2002

pussy holder *noun*
the passenger seat on a motorcycle *US, 1967*

- He came and so did guys from a dozen other bike clubs, their mamas in their pussy holders[.] — Nicholas Von Hoffman, *We Are The People Our Parents Warned Us Against*, p. 157, 1967

pussy hound *noun*
a man obsessed with sex and women *US, 1976*

- "Glad to see a fellow pussy hound, hey Lonnie?" — Felix Goodson, *Sweet Salt*, p. 87, 1976
- You're the most notorious pussy hound in Robber-Homicide[.] — James Ellroy, *Blood on the Moon*, p. 144, 1984
- The Stallion was a weight lifter, a party animal—a real pussy hound—and a damn good shooter. — Richard Marcinko, *Rogue Warrior*, p. 285, 1992
- Rumor still had him as a pussyhound, and a bitter one at that. — Faye Kellerman, *Street Dreams*, p. 16, 2003

pussy juice *noun*
vaginal secretions *US, 1980*

- My pussy smells like pussy juice. — Alta, *The Shameless Hussy*, p. 140, 1980
- She bucked wildly, licking Jan's pussy juice from her chin, fingering her clit. — *alt.sex*, 21st December 1989
- [N]ude photographer Suze Randall carefully poses stripper Linda Lee Tracey and adds a few drops of "pussy juice" to her vulva. — Barry Keith Grant, *Voyages of Discovery*, p. 184, 1992
- For some women, direct stimulation of the paraurethral gland can result in the ejaculation of a clear, usually odorless fluid that is not—not—piss or pussy juice. — Dan Savage, *Savage Love*, p. 130, 1998

pussy lips *noun*
the labia *US, 1968*

- Finally, they opened and closed breathlessly around her vertically smiling pussy lips. — Barnet Rosset, *Evergreen Reader*, p. 751, 1968
- [W]ord has come down from above that the exposure of pussylips, clitorae, urethrae, etc., is lewd[.] — *Screw*, p. 4, 13th October 1969
- Gee whiz—you could see her asshole pucker and her pink pussy lips yawn open and EVERYTHING! — Curt Johnson, *The Morning Light*, p. 183, 1977
- Ugh. All that hair. Then my pussy lips be black. — Alice Walker, *The Color Purple*, p. 78, 1982

pussy man *noun*
a pimp *US, 1967*

- "You cheap pimp." She very drunk, you know, and don't know what she saying at all. "Cheap pussy man." — Sara Harris, *The Lords of Hell*, p. 20, 1967

pussy out; puss out *verb*
to back out of a task because of fear *US, 1992*

- Don't pussy out on me now, Marvin. We're just gonna sit here and bleed until Joe Cabot sticks his fuckin' head through that door. — *Reservoir Dogs*, 1992
- Don't give me that bullshit. Don't pussy out on me. — *The Bad Lieutenant*, 1992
- Prince Cheetah wasn't going to puss-out this time! — Jess Mowry, *Six Out Seven*, p. 491, 1993
- All I'm saying is if you're going to be insubordinate, you should go the full nine and not pussy out when it comes to free refreshments. — *Clerks*, 1994

pussy parlor *noun*
a sex club *US, 1987*

- "I mean, it was your idea to meet at this pussy parlor." — Carl Hiaasen, *Skin Tight*, p. 176, 1989
- Xavier was always at one Pussy Parlor or another. — Jaid Black, *Death Row*, p. 166, 2004

pussy patrol; pussy posse; pussy squad *noun*
a police vice squad focusing on prostitution *US, 1953*

- Do you want to go back on the Pussy Posse and round up the Forty-second street hookers? — Margaret Mayorga, *The Best Short Plays*, p. 396, 1953
- There was, Stanard grandly pointed out, another option that Serpico could elect—the Times Square prostitution detail, the so-called pussy posse[.] — Peter Maas, *Serpico*, p. 156, 1973
- "You ought to transfer to the vice squad. Pussy posse," Chiodo said. — Charles Whited, *Chiodo*, p. 146, 1973
- [P]olice "pussy posses" and prominent businessmen. — Gail Sheehy, *Hustling*, p. 12, 1973

pussy queer *noun*
a lesbian *US, 1982*

- "You move fast for a pussy queer." — Joseph Garber, *Vertical Run*, p. 204, 1996

pussysucker; pussysugger *noun*
the mouth *US, 1964*

- Settin' over there with that grin on his pussysugger an them love-sick eyes jes a-lickin' all over my face[.] — Robert Gover, *Here Goes Kitten*, p. 56, 1964

pussywhip *verb*

(used of a woman) to dominate a man *US, 1974*

- I ain't gone never let one of them young oversexed broads get ahold of me and pussywhip me and get off into my bankroll. — Joseph Nazel, *Black Cop*, p. 96, 1974

pussy-whipped *adjective*

dominated by a woman *US, 1956*

- White men (and square Blacks) are thought to be "pussy-whipped" by their wives, after having been brainwashed by their mothers to accept female dominance as the natural order of things. — Christina and Richard Milner, *Black Players*, p. 180, 1972
- "Brennan's pussy-whipped," the Digger said. "Afraid his wife's gonna find out." — George Higgins, *The Digger's Game*, p. 161, 1973
- Keep seeing a chick who won't fuck you, you get pussy-whipped without even seeing the pussy. — *Saturday Night Fever*, 1977
- He was very much pussy-whipped, OK? His old lady just ran the whole show[.] — William T. Vollman, *Whores for Gloria*, p. 92, 1991

pussy whisker *noun*

a pubic hair *US, 1986*

- You got a wild pussy whisker up your ass? — Robert Campbell, *In La-La Land We Trust*, p. 87, 1986

put *verb*

to dilute a drug *US, 1992*

- You put a half on it cause it's a little harder for them to get better closer. But, like if somebody's coming up from Virginia? You put a one, one and a half on it. — Richard Price, *Clockers*, p. 180, 1992

▸ **put a (number) on**

to dilute a drug by the identified numerical factor *US, 1971*

- "Give me that stuff, woman!" Sid ordered. "I got ten pieces, Porky, that you can put a six on." — Donald Goines, *Dopefiend*, p. 185, 1971

▸ **put it on**

to declare hostilities with another youth gang *US, 1953*

- A few weeks ago the Emeralds and the War Hawks had "put it on," a phrase meaning declaration of hostilities. — Dale Kramer and Madeline Karr, *Teen-Age Gangs*, p. 11, 1953

▸ **put next to**

to introduce one person to another or to acquaint one person with another *US, 1906*

- So you're thinking what if I was to put you next to my dry cleaner. — *Get Shorty*, 1995

▸ **put on**

to fool someone, to tease someone, to deceive someone *US, 1958*

- "It sounds like you're putting me on," Dawn said, "except I know you're not." — Elmore Leonard, *Riding the Rap*, p. 230, 1995

puta *noun*

a sexually promiscuous woman; a prostitute *US, 1964*

From Spanish *puta* (a whore).

- Liz had been cheating on her. Liz was becoming a tramp. A little chippy. A puta. — Sheldon Lord, *The Third Way*, 1964

put down *verb*

1 to belittle someone; to treat someone with humiliating contempt *US, 1958*

- Put-down, or ranked-out, or second-class citizen treatment as described above is what causes the daughter to say of her parents, "They don't understand." — Murray Kaufman, *Murray the K Tells It Like It Is, Baby*, p. 34, 1966

2 to implicate someone as guilty *US, 1965*

- I didn't know if he wanted to put me down or what! I was scared to go down there. — Henry Williamson, *Hustler!*, p. 115, 1965

put it there

used as a greeting, soliciting a handshake *US, 1978*

- "Me too." He extended his hand. "Put it there." — Armistead Maupin, *Tales of the City*, p. 129, 1978

puto *noun*

a male homosexual *US, 1965*

Border Spanish used by English-speakers in the American southwest.

- [T]he most derogatory are puto (homosexual), culero (coward), and relaje (informer). — George R. Alvarez, *Semiotic Dynamics of an Ethnic-American Sub-Cultural Group*, p. 9, 1965

puto mark *noun*

writing or art that defaces graffiti *US, 2000*

- A "cross-out" is a type of asterisk that covers a rival's graffiti, and in gang jargon is called a "puto mark." — Robert Jackson and Wesley McBride, *Understanding Street Gangs*, p. 65, 2000

puto mark *verb*

to cross something out *US, 2000*

Puto is Spanish slang for "a male prostitute."

- When off brands venture into the area and flag red, it's the same thing as coming in to cross out [puto mark] the local gang members' placas. — Bill Valentine, *Gangs and Their Tattoos*, p. 113, 2000

put-on *adjective*

affected, insincere *UK, 1621*

- He had listened to some of it again to hear her voice, this girl with the easy drawl, nothing put-on about her. — Elmore Leonard, *Be Cool*, p. 15, 1999

puto snizzie *noun*

a prison informer *US, 1975*

"Puto" is Spanish for "male whore."

- — Report to the Senate, *California Senate Committee on Civil Disorder*, p. 227, 1975

put out *verb*

to consent to sex *US, 1947*

- [S]he was in that profession and consequently, being a passionate actress, would "put out." — Mark Tryon, *Of G-Strings and Strippers*, p. 13, 1953
- Nobody likes a cockteaser. Either you put out or you don't. — Hubert Selby Jr., *Last Exit to Brooklyn*, p. 107, 1957
- Some of the girls said he would go out with any girl who put out. — Tempest Storm, *Tempest Storm*, p. 13, 1987
- We're in the big time now. We're freshmen, where all the girls will be putting out. — *Dazed and Confused*, 1993

put over *verb*

to portray someone or something, usually with some degree of deception *US, 1990*

- So they'll have to be put over as being tough. — *Herb's Wrestling Tidbits*, 25th October 1990
- For the first time in the WWF, a ring announcer was actively involved in putting over a wrestler's persona. — Gary Cappetta, *Bodyslams!*, p. 63, 2000

put some water on it!

used as a demand that a person using a communal toilet flush to rid the room of the smell of feces *US, 2001*

- — Jim Goad, *Jim Goad's Glossary of Northwestern Prison Slang*, December 2001

putter-offer *noun*

a procrastinator *US, 1965*

- As a world-class late sleeper and eternal putter-offer, I can only express awe at this First Lady's energy. — Margaret Truman, *First Ladies*, p. 149, 1995

putting green *noun*

in pool, the largest regulation-size table *US, 1990*

- — Steve Rushin, *Pool Cool*, p. 24, 1990

put up *verb*

to serve time in prison *US, 1976*

- I put up eight years at Sing Sing. — Troy Harris, *A Booklet of Criminal Argot, Cant and Jargon*, p. 21, 1976

putz *noun*

1 the penis *US, 1934*

- Smolka, who is always dragging drinks out of everybody else's bottle of cream soda, and grabbing with his hand at your putz! — Philip Roth, *Portnoy's Complaint*, p. 188, 1969
- With regard to the erection per se there is no relationship between the sized of a non-erect putz and its size at erection (so stop comparing schlongs in the locker room)[.] — *Screw*, p. 8, 8th December 1969
- Bet he'd be naked under the coat. Show his stubby putz to every broad he passed on the street — Joseph Wambaugh, *The Glitter Dome*, p. 176, 1981

- Dave's professional putz was just too big. — Josh Alan Friedman, *Tales of Times Square*, p. 117, 1986

2 by extension, an inept, contemptible person *US*, *1952*

- "What else can you expect from a putsy like Cockeye?" — Harry Grey, *The Hoods*, p. 6, 1952
- The poor putz had nothing to do with Sparky Harper's death[.] — Carl Hiaasen, *Tourist Season*, p. 182, 1986
- Don't be a putz—who's been to Santiago twice in a year? — *Something About Mary*, 1998
- NBC took offence when Walther Matthau called George Burns a "putz," the word to denote "penis" rather than the more common understanding of "jerk." — Aubrey Dillon-Malone, *I Was a Fugitive from a Hollywood Trivia Factory [on "The Sunshine Boys" (1975)]*, p. 44, 1999

putz around *verb*
to idle; to do nothing; to waste time *US*, *1968*

- [B]ecause we have worked for one year we do not "putz" around with each other for two weeks of the rehearsal period. — Robert Edward Gard, *Theater in America*, p. 131, 1968
- The fish was stone-cold-blooded about collecting for damages after a real accident occurred. He didn't putz around — Emmett Grogan, *Ringolevio*, p. 141, 1972
- What the man says she does, she putzes. Putzes around the house trying to think up things to be done — Elmore Leonard, *Stick*, p. 102, 1983
- They putz around, make it as a big case, call Homicide. — James Ellroy, *L.A. Confidential*, p. 228, 1990

PV *noun*
a parole violation *US*, *2002*

- "Yeah, dawg, caught a P.V. myself." — Jimmy Lerner, *You Got Nothing Coming*, p. 27, 2002

PV
used in gang graffiti to boast of perpetual control of territory *US*, *2000*
An abbreviation of "por vida," Spanish for "for life."

- Another closing inscription is p/v (for por vida), a reference to the length of time the gang will be in control of the turf: forever. — Robert Jackson and Wesley McBride, *Understanding Street Gangs*, p. 64, 2000

PW *adjective*
dominated by a female *US*, *1966*
An abbreviation of **PUSSY-WHIPPED**.

- — Andy Anonymous, *A Basic Guide to Campusology*, p. 19, 1966

p-whipped *adjective*
dominated by a female *US*, *1999*
An abbreviated and euphemized **PUSSY-WHIPPED**.

- Oh my God. You're completely p-whipped. — *Cruel Intentions*, 1999

pylons *noun*
the legs *US*, *1947*

- — *Time Magazine*, p. 92, 20th January 1947: "Dicty dictionary"

Qq

Q *noun*

1 the San Quentin state prison in San Rafael, California *US, 1951*

- If you was to run into the front end of a Mack truck on one of these corners, the dings might miss you bad over at Q. — Thurston Scott, *Cure it with Honey*, p. 62, 1951
- This would be very nice to come home to after a stretch in Q. — George Clayton Johnson, *Ocean's Eleven*, p. 43, 1960
- He had been at Q, as the prisoners called the prison, for four months[.] — Ovid Demaris, *The Last Mafioso*, p. 291, 1981
- If you were a troublemaker at Q, they'd keep you inside your cell by welding the door shut. — Ralph "Sonny" Barger, *Hell's Angel*, p. 193, 2000

2 a homosexual *US, 1968*

An abbreviation of **QUEER**.

- Collin Baker et al., *College Undergraduate Slang Study Conducted at Brown University*, p. 179, 1968

3 barbecue *US, 2001*

- The term barbecue (a.k.a. Bar-B-Q, BBQ, 'cue, or, to the real aficionados, simply Q) is often used synonymously with grilling. — Omaha Steaks, *Omaha Steaks*, 2001

4 in American casinos, a $25 chip *US, 1983*

An abbreviation of **QUARTER**.

- Steve Kuriscak, *Casino Talk*, p. 45, 1985
- Thomas L. Clark, *The Dictionary of Gambling and Gaming*, p. 170, 1987

QT *noun*

▶ **on the QT**

quietly, in strict confidence *UK, 1884*

- She told me right in front of my boyfriend and kids that she had heard from one of her stool pigeons that I was screwing four or five guys on the Q.T. — Iceberg Slim (Robert Beck), *Mama Black Widow*, p. 103, 1969
- And that's what we did I organized... on the q.t. of course, a tribal festival that involved the Asantehene. — Odie Hawkins, *The Busting Out of an Ordinary Man*, 1985
- Well, this is only my first charitable donation—$400,000—to the community; between me and you on the "Q.T.," of course. — *New Jack City*, 1990
- So everything is on the Q-T here. — Howard Stern, *Miss America*, p. 453, 1995

Q tip *noun*

in poker, a queen and a ten *US, 1996*

- John Vorhaus, *The Big Book of Poker Slang*, p. 31, 1996

quack *noun*

1 a hospital patient who feigns symptoms in order to receive attention, prescription medication, or both *US, 1978*

- *Maledicta*, p. 6, Summer/Winter 1978: Common patient-directed pejoratives used by medical personnel
- Sally Williams, *"Strong" Words: Medical Slang (Dissertation)*, p. 157, 1994

2 in poker, a player who complains loudly when losing *US, 1979*

- John Scarne, *Scarne's Guide to Modern Poker*, p. 288, 1979

3 the recreational drug methaqualone, best known as Quaaludes™ *US, 1985*

- By 1972 it was one of the most popular drugs of abuse in the United States and was known as "love drug," "heroin for lovers," "Dr. Jekyll and Mr. Hyde," "sopors," "sopes," "ludes," "mandrakes and quacks." — Marilyn Carroll and Gary Gallo, *Methaqualone*, p. 18, 1985

4 a firefighter *US, 1997*

New York police slang.

- Samuel M. Katz, *Anytime Anywhere*, p. 389, 1997: "The extremely unofficial and completely off-the-record NYPD/ESU truck-two glossary"

5 a novice surfer *US, 1977*

- Gary Fairmont R. Filosa II, *The Surfer's Almanac*, p. 192, 1977

quad *noun*

a *quad*riplegic *US, 1980*

- *Maledicta*, p. 56, Summer 1980: "Not sticks and stones, but names: more medical perjoratives"

quad-fifty *noun*

a quadruple mount .50 caliber machine gun *US, 1953*

- Two "quad-fifties"—four .50 caliber machine guns on a single mount: two of these units—are set up on the hill mass behind us. — Martin Russ, *The Last Parallel*, p. 204, 1953
- Each truck had three quad fifties. — William Pelfrey, *The Big V*, p. 21, 1972
- They put a Quad 50 on top of that big water tower. — Wallace Terry, *Bloods*, p. 122, 1984
- Lord a'mighty! They've got a freakin' quad fifty! — Stan Lee, *The 'Nam*, p. 80, 1987

quadruplets *noun*

in poker, four cards of the same rank *US, 1979*

- John Scarne, *Scarne's Guide to Modern Poker*, p. 288, 1979

quads *noun*

1 the quadriceps muscles *US, 1984*

- *American Speech*, p. 201, Fall 1984: "The language of bodybuilding"

2 in poker, a hand with all four cards of the same rank *US, 1996*

- Peter O. Steiner, *Thursday Night Poker*, p. 416, 1996

quail *noun*

1 a woman *US, 1859*

- He goes to the jukery to watch and wait and cut a rug with a solid gate: he snatches a quail with hep and class and they go to town cooking with gas! — Harry Haenigsen, *Jive's Like That*, 1947
- I fix him up with the fanciest quail in Greater Manhattan. — Bernard Wolfe, *The Late Risers*, p. 248, 1954

2 a girl under the legal age of consent *US, 1976*

A shortened form of **SAN QUENTIN QUAIL**.

- Radio Shack, *CBer's Handy Atlas/Dictionary*, p. 38, 1976

3 a twenty-five cent betting token used in of craps *US, 1983*

- Thomas L. Clark, *The Dictionary of Gambling and Gaming*, p. 170, 1987

quaking and shaking *noun*

the impact of heavy bombing *US, 1977*

- "Quakin' and Shakin'," they called it, great balls of fire. Contact. — Michael Herr, *Dispatches*, p. 63, 1977

quarked out *adjective*

under the influence of drugs *US, 1999*

- Three hours later I was in Dodie's apartment quarked out on ludes, my head hanging off the mattress[.] — Rita Ciresi, *Pink Slip*, p. 96, 1999

quart *noun*

in poker, four cards of the same suit in sequence *US, 1979*

- John Scarne, *Scarne's Guide to Modern Poker*, p. 288, 1979

quarter *noun*

1 a prison sentence of 25 years *US, 1964*

- Say, "I'm gonna see if you can't shake this quarter off your goddamn ass." — Bruce Jackson, *Get Your Ass in the Water and Swim Like Me*, p. 87, 1964
- The usual sentence for that [armed robbery] is ten to a quarter. — Bruce Jackson, *In the Life*, p. 30, 1972
- "You can also pull ten to a quarter in Jackson," Stick said. — Elmore Leonard, *Swag*, p. 16, 1976
- William K. Bentley and James M. Corbett, *Prison Slang*, p. 23, 1992

2 a quarter of an ounce of drugs, especially cocaine *US, 1968*

- *Current Slang*, p. 39, Fall 1968

3 in American casinos, a $25 chip *US, 1980*

- Lee Solkey, *Dummy Up and Deal*, p. 118, 1980
- Steve Kuriscak, *Casino Talk: A Rap Sheet for Dealers and Players*, p. 11, 1985

4 twenty-five pounds of weights used in lifting *US, 1989*

- James Harris, *A Convict's Dictionary*, p. 37, 1989

5 a cigarette *US, 1958*

- A square is a cigarette. And also a quarter. — Willard Motley, *Let No Man Write My Epitaph*, p. 148, 1958

quarter bird *noun*

one quarter pound of cocaine *US, 1999*

- Erfort then offered Korey "a quarter bird," street slang for a quarter pound of cocaine, to kill Kuhn, Logan testified. — *Pittsburgh Post-Gazette*, p. B7, 10th November 1999

quarter house *noun*
a place where mid-level heroin dealers do business *US*, *1978*
- — Burgess Laughlin, *Job Opportunities in the Black Market*, p. 6, 1978: "Glossary"

quart store *noun*
a store that sells beer on the retail level *US*, *1997*
- — Amy and Denise McFadden, *CoalSpeak*, p. 11, 1997

quater *noun*
twenty-five cents *US*, *1980*
A corruption of "quarter."
- — Joe McKennon, *Circus Lingo*, p. 74, 1980

queased out *adjective*
nauseated, sick *US*, *1993*
- I start to feel a little sick to my stomach. Queased out. — Francesca Lia Block, *Missing Angel Juan*, p. 257, 1993

queber *noun*
a social outcast *US*, *1987*
- — Mitch McKissick, *Surf Lingo*, 1987

queeb *noun*
a bisexual *US*, *1988*
- — Michael V. Anderson, *The Bad, Rad, Not to Forget Way Cool Beach and Surf Discriptionary*, p. 15, 1988

queef *noun*
the passing of air from the vagina *US*, *1991*
- One may find that prolonged doggy style can do a lot in the way introducing air into the vagina, thereby causing a "queef/vart" when the position as ceased to be assumed, or soon thereafter. — *alt.sex*, 6th June 1991
- [D]efending this limp-wristed yuppie handjob of an album as if it were High Art, and acting as if the blues were a queef emitted from the loins of Camryn Manheim—when she had a yeast infection[.] — *OC Weekly*, p. 25, 25th October 2002

queef *verb*
to expel air from the vagina, intentionally or not *US*, *1991*
- I know one woman who can queef on demand. — *alt.sex*, 6th June 1991
- I want a girl who queefs during sex to be able to laugh about it with her partner instead of blushing in embarrassment. — *Ohio University Post*, 7th November 2002

queen *noun*
1 an obviously homosexual male *UK*, *1729*
- It was assumed by the Row that because we ganged together so closely the four of us were confirmed, comradely queens. — Clancy Sigal, *Going Away*, 1961
- Old Jewish mothers never know when their sons are faggots. They just miss it somehow. Out-and-out screaming queens—mothers are never hip. — Lenny Bruce, *The Essential Lenny Bruce*, p. 162, 1967
- One of them is a Negro queen named Irving Amadeus. — Gore Vidal, *Myra Breckinridge*, p. 87, 1968
- If there's one thing I'm not ready for, it's five screaming queens singing Happy Birthday. — Mart Crowley, *The Boys in the Band*, 1968
2 a popular girl *US*, *1959*
- — *Time Magazine*, p. 46, 24th August 1959
3 a girlfriend, mistress, or prostitute *US*, *1968*
- — Carl Fleischhauer, *A Glossary of Army Slang*, p. 9, 1968
4 an enthusiast of the preceding thing or activity *US*, *1999*
- Do I look like some king of gossip queen? — *Cruel Intentions*, 1999

queen around *verb*
to act in a flamboyant, effeminate manner *US*, *1957*
- As for Willy B[urroughs], he's queening around now as ever he never bothers me with that. — Jack Kerouac, *Jack Kerouac Selected Letters 1957–1969*, p. 6, 28th January 1957: Letter to Edith Parker Kerouac

queen bee *noun*
1 the manager of a homosexual brothel *US*, *1967*
- Customers call the queen bee and specify the male they want by physical characteristics and the length of time he is wanted. — Mark Holden, *Sodom 1967 American Style*, p. 95, 1967
2 a heterosexual woman who seeks out the company of homosexual men *US*, *1957*

- A man with white tie and dress shirt, naked from the waist down except for black garters, talks to the Queen Bee in elegant tones. (Queen Bees are women who surround themselves with fairies)[.] — William Burroughs, *Naked Lunch*, p. 80, 1957

Queen City *nickname*
Cincinnati *US*, *1974*
- I mean, the "Queen City" was their home town and the Big "O" + 5 wasn't bad no matter where you lived. — Gary Mayer, *Bookie*, p. 182, 1974

queenie *noun*
a prostitute *US*, *1964*
- Rest a us queenies from them eight places up and down the street, we was left high and dry, cause they wasn't gonna open them places up no more. — Robert Gover, *Here Goes Kitten*, p. 153, 1964

Queen Mary *noun*
a surfboard that is too big for the surfer using it *US*, *1964*
Named after the ocean liner, not a royal female.
- — John Severson, *Modern Surfing Around the World*, p. 178, 1964

queen's row *noun*
an area in a prison reserved for blatantly homosexual prisoners *US*, *1967*
- If you want to stay off queen's row, you better lay low and do exactly what you're told. — Malcolm Braly, *On the Yard*, p. 296, 1967
- Studies of incarcerated persons have shown that such a person is more likely to get hurt on the "inside," since the code of "QUEEN'S ROW" inmates think that such a person is trying to make light of them by being uncooperative. — Richard Frank, *A Study of Sex in Prison*, p. 24, 1973

queen tank *noun*
a jail holding cell reserved for flamboyantly effeminate homosexual men *US*, *1988*
- I also can throw handcuffs on you and book you into the queen tank at the county jail. — Gerald Petievich, *Shakedown*, p. 191, 1988

queeny *adjective*
1 blatantly homosexual *UK*, *1961*
- — *Maledicta*, p. 234, 1979
- I mean mince—singing that hideous line, "With you two arm-in-arm again, Rome can sleep secure," in a very queen way. — Robert Tear, *Tear Here*, p. 104, 1990
- They were all very, very queeny and flamboyant. — Patrick Dilley, *Queer Man on Campus*, p. 111, 2002
2 showy, melodramatic, affected *US*, *1997*
- — Pamela Munro, *U.C.L.A. Slang*, p. 100, 1997

queer *noun*
1 a homosexual man or a lesbian *US*, *1914*
Usually pejorative, but also a male homosexual term of self-reference within the gay underground and subculture.
- I am not a fool! a queer! I am not! — Jack Kerouac, *Letter to Neal Cassady*, p. 167, 3rd October 1948
- Is he a queer? Doesn't he act like one though! — John Clellon Holmes, *Go*, p. 25, 1952
- "And a little hash," added Jean-baby. "There was a little hashish in the can, too." Frost shuddered. "Goddamn queers!" he said. — Terry Southern, *Flash and Filigree*, p. 121, 1958
- Then I remembered that was an illiberal thing to say, and argued that even if he was a queer they shouldn't hold it against him. They did. — Clancy Sigal, *Going Away*, p. 150, 1961
2 counterfeit money *UK*, *1812*
- I was sure that Hertert wanted to use this fellow as a shover of the queer, or the man who was to pass the fake currency. — William J. Spillard and Pence James, *Needle in a Haystack*, pp. 54–55, 1945
- The limo back seat is gizmoed, and I copped Jake's hundred and twenty grand in "queer" and the valises. — Iceberg Slim (Robert Beck), *Long White Con*, p. 212, 1977
- — Joe McKennon, *Circus Lingo*, p. 74, 1980

queer *verb*
to spoil something; to ruin something; to interfere with something *UK*, *1812*
- I ain't going to rap and maybe queer things. — Iceberg Slim (Robert Beck), *Pimp*, p. 253, 1969

queer *adjective*
1 homosexual *US*, *1914*

Derogatory from the outside, not from within.

- You mean—if I went and enrolled and asked for a girl teacher—nobody would think I was—queer? — Philip Wylie, *Opus 21*, p. 105, 1949
- You know, he's not queer at all. It was just an imitation. — John Clellon Holmes, *Go*, p. 9, 1952
- Rubber was queer but he weighed 240 and could whip any two cats easily. — Babs Gonzales, *Movin' On Down De Line*, p. 70, 1975
- God, these panties feel great. That don't make me queer, right? — *Bull Durham*, 1988

2 catering to or patronized by homosexuals *US, 1957*

- This is a queer bar. You are not a queer. Why do you insist on being in here? — Helen P. Branson, *Gay Bar*, p. 56, 1957

3 driven by deep and perverse sexual desires *US, 1967*

- I say, You not queer, baby. You look around you and you see, you not the only one. — Sara Harris, *The Lords of Hell*, p. 62, 1967

4 not good; out of fashion *US, 1997*

Like "gay," "queer" has been hijacked from its homosexual context.

- This is so queer! — *Chasing Amy*, 1997

5 counterfeit *US, 1951*

- These fast workers make a splendid living peddling queer securities from an office on the sidewalk in front of the Ambassador Hotel, at 14th and K. — Jack Lait and Lee Mortimer, *Washington Confidential*, p. 278, 1951
- I asked for fifties 'cause, you know, they're the hardest to counterfeit and the easiest to spot when they are queer. — Emmett Grogan, *Final Score*, p. 59, 1976
- S'posed to have done time years ago for passing queer twenties and tens. — Gerald Petievich, *Money Men*, p. 12, 1981

▶ **to be queer for**

to be fond of someone or something *US, 1953*

- "I'm queer for Jack," she said. — William Burroughs, *Junkie*, p. 28, 1953
- I'm queer for spades, Bernie, and the sounds, and that one cat. — Ross Russell, *The Sound*, p. 173, 1961

queer as a three-dollar bill *adjective*

ostentatiously homosexual *US, 1966*

- I could tell that feller was queer as a three-dollar bill—been thinking it for years. — Larry McMurtry, *The Last Picture Show*, p. 153, 1966
- Wally's a fag. Queer as a three-dollar bill. — Robert Gover, *JC Saves*, p. 105, 1968
- Big, mean bastards, and every one of them queer as a three-dollar bill. — Vincent Patrick, *The Pope of Greenwich Village*, p. 75, 1979

queerbait; queer-bait *noun*

a man who commands the attention of homosexual men, whether he is homosexual or not *US, 1957*

- She knew he wouldn't go with her while the others were there, fearing the jeers of queerbait, so was forced to wait and hope the others might leave. — Hubert Selby Jr., *Last Exit to Brooklyn*, p. 45, 1957
- Now would chime in the litany of abuse: naughty sissy, baby-boy, not-really-a-boy-but-a-pussy, little faggot, secret cocksucking toy, queer-bait, boy-hole, powder-puff. — Terence Sellers, *Dungeon Evidence*, p. 58, 1997

queer beer *noun*

weak, watery beer *US, 1976*

More commonly reduplicated as "near beer."

- — Elementary Electronics, *Dictionary of CB Lingo*, p. 99, 1976

queer jack *noun*

counterfeit money *US, 1949*

- — Vincent J. Monteleone, *Criminal Slang*, p. 187, 1949

queer's lunch box *noun*

the male crotch *US, 1964*

- — Roger Blake, *The American Dictionary of Sexual Terms*, p. 177, 1964

queeve *verb*

to experience a loss of energy *US, 1984*

- — San Francisco Sunday Examiner & Chronicle, p. 20, 2nd September 1984

ques *noun*

the question mark (?) character on a computer keyboard *US, 1991*

- — Eric S. Raymond, *The New Hacker's Dictionary*, p. 294, 1991

quick and dirty *adjective*

constructed as quickly as possible *US, 1991*

- I can have a quick-and-dirty fix in place tonight, but I'll have to rewrite the whole module to solve the underlying design problem. — Eric S. Raymond, *The New Hacker's Dictionary*, p. 294, 1991

Quickdraw McGraw *noun*

the US Secret Service agent who is closest to the president *US, 1981*

Quickdraw McGraw was a Hanna Barbera cartoon that first aired in 1959; ironically, the character Quickdraw McGraw was not a quick draw, but his name has survived, implying that which the character was not.

- That's Quickdraw McGraw, whatever guy has that job, that's what he's called. Keeps within six paces of the president at all times. — Elmore Leonard, *Split Images*, p. 77, 1981

quickie *noun*

1 a sexual encounter that is carried out quickly *US, 1950*

- We had a quickie; I didn't come & was only telling of the future where there were better bed fucks & us living contentedly as we walked slowly across town again to her home. — Neal Cassady, *The First Third*, p. 201, 5th November 1950
- We did a stand-up quickie by the refrigerator — Jefferson Poland and Valerie Alison, *The Records of the San Francisco Sexual Freedom League*, p. 60, 1971
- [S]ometimes Madeleine or even Georgette would call up and ask me could I handle a midday quickie. — Xaviera Hollander, *The Happy Hooker*, p. 92, 1972
- EBBY: Got time for another quickie? MILLIE: Jesus, you got a game to pitch! EBBY: But we got three minutes! — *Bull Durham*, 1988

2 something that is accomplished quickly *US, 1940*

- They were riding first-class on a Delta flight from Miami to Dulles; a one-day quickie. — Carl Hiaasen, *Strip Tease*, p. 210, 1993

3 an unexpected, quickly executed maneuver or piece of trickery *US, 1950*

- — Hyman E. Goldin et al., *Dictionary of American Underworld Lingo*, p. 172, 1950
- — Harry Orsman, *A Dictionary of Modern New Zealand Slang*, p. 105, 1999

quickie *verb*

to have sex in a hurry *US, 1959*

- "But I had a little matinee session with a doll who just won't be quickied." — Irving Shulman, *The Short End of the Stick*, p. 81, 1959

quickie *adjective*

carried out quickly *US, 1940*

- It had come to the attention of 60 Minutes that the progressive city of Dallas had spawned a flurry of drive-in divorce centers in which lawyers were handling as many as 175 quickie divorces a day. — Dan Jenkins, *Life Its Ownself*, p. 50, 1984

quick-turn burn *noun*

the refueling and reloading of an F-18 fighter jet in less than five minutes *US, 1991*

- — Army, p. 48, November 1991

quid *noun*

five dollars *US, 1988*

If a pound is five dollars, so must be a quid.

- — George Percy, *The Language of Poker*, p. 72, 1988

quiet-side *adjective*

secret *US, 1976*

- — John R. Armore and Joseph D. Wolfe, *Dictionary of Desperation*, p. 45, 1976

quiff *noun*

a male homosexual *US, 1939*

- We will fuck Reilly in the ass. He's probably a quiff, too. — Edwin Torres, *Q & A*, p. 58, 1977
- Some quiff said Ad Vice was operating the park, which we both know is bullshit. — James Ellroy, *White Jazz*, p. 69, 1992

quill *noun*

anything used to snort powdered drugs; the drugs themselves *US, 1935*

- — John B. Williams, *Narcotics and Hallucinogenics*, p. 115, 1967
- But he's got a solid yen for the quill if he can get it. — Iceberg Slim (Robert Beck), *Trick Baby*, p. 213, 1969
- Her fingers trembled slightly as she rolled up a dollar bill, making it into a quill. She stuck one end of the quill in her nose, while she

held the other end to the white powder in the package. — Donald Goines, *Dopefiend*, p. 32, 1971

quilty *adjective*

luxurious *US, 1976*

- Van had a straw, a Corona corona in his jaw / A beige suit looking real quilty. — Dennis Wepman et al., *The Life*, p. 45, 1976

quim *noun*

the vagina; used objectively as a collective noun for women, especially sexually available women *UK, 1735*

- There was a young girl from New York / Who plugged up her quim with a cork. — *Eros*, p. 62, Winter 162
- I'll spring for that if you can guarantee a tight back door and quim. — Iceberg Slim (Robert Beck), *Doom Fox*, p. 6, 1978
- With his pal filling her quim and Butler's dick sliding in and out of her luscious lips, Kari gets a heaping helping of the living needle from both ends at once. — *Adult Video*, p. 65, August/September 1986
- Jokingly, she gave him the finger, then stuck the same digit in her quim. — Anthony Petkovich, *The X Factory*, p. 36, 1997

quinine *noun*

in the game of craps, the number nine *US, 1950*

- — *The Annals of the American Academy of Political and Social Sciences*, p. 129, May 1950

quint *noun*

in poker, five cards of the same suit in sequence *US, 1979*

- — John Scarne, *Scarne's Guide to Modern Poker*, p. 288, 1979

quint major *noun*

in poker, a sequence of five cards, same suit, ending with the face cards *US, 1988*

- — George Percy, *The Language of Poker*, p. 72, 1988

quitter *noun*

a suicide *US, 1982*

- — Ralph de Sola, *Crime Dictionary*, p. 124, 1982

quiver *noun*

a selection of surfboards used for different surf conditions *US, 1977*

- — Gary Fairmont R. Filosa II, *The Surfer's Almanac*, p. 192, 1977

quivver-giver *noun*

an attractive person *US, 1947*

- There's that new pigeon. Boy, she's sure a quivver givver! — Harry Haenigsen, *Jive's Like That*, 1947

quiz *noun*

a roadside sobriety test *US, 1976*

- — Wayne Floyd, *Jason's Authentic Dictionary of CB Slang*, p. 25, 1976

Rr

RA *noun*
the regular Army, as distinguished from special forces
US, 1948

- The LRRP/Rangers viewed such RA lifers are fuckheads who were too afraid to do the real job of the army. — Kregg Jorgenson, *Very Crazy G.I.*, p. 152, 2001

rabbi *noun*
a mentor or protector *US, 1970*

- The translation of "I see you got the gold tin, who's your rabbi?" is "I see you have been promoted to detective. Who's your high-ranked sponsor?" — *New York Times*, 15th February 1970
- He did not have, nor did he attempt to develop, any "rabbis"—people in high places in the department—to advance his career[.] — Peter Maas, *Serpico*, p. 110, 1973
- You mean an Irish guy like you didn't have no rabbi? — Edwin Torres, *Q & A*, p. 17, 1977
- That hasn't changed. Cops still move into slots according to who their rabbis are, and you guys are paying off the rabbis. — Vincent Patrick, *The Pope of Greenwich Village*, p. 39, 1979

rabbit *noun*
1 a nervous, timid, cautious person *US, 1951*

- "Why? Because they all married rabbits." "How very odd!" I exclaimed. "Real rabbits?" "No stupid, they married guys with no drive, no gumption." — Max Shulman, *The Many Loves of Dobie Gillis*, p. 163, 1951
- You can tell rabbits, you know, the lops in here. — Pete Earley, *The Hot House*, p. 141, 1992
- This rabbit'll do anything not to do time, including wearing a wire. — *True Romance*, 1993

2 a prisoner who is known for attempting to escape prison *US, 1972*

- He said, "In spite of the rabbit in this man I want him transferred to Ramsey construction immediately." — Bruce Jackson, *In the Life*, p. 322, 1972

3 an escape *US, 2005*

- "How much time elapsed between their respective rabbits?" — Jonathan Kellerman, *Rage*, p. 458, 2005

4 a man who ejaculates with little stimulation *US, 1987*

- *Maledicta*, p. 150, Summer/Winter 1986–1987: "Sexual slang: prostitutes, pedophiles, flagellators, transvestites, and necrophiles"

5 a white person *US, 1991*

- Linda Reinberg, *In the Field*, p. 178, 1991
- Gary K. Farlow, *Prison-ese*, p. 55, 2002

6 a person who regularly borrows money from an illegal money lender and pays back promptly *US, 1950*

- Hyman E. Goldin et al., *Dictionary of American Underworld Lingo*, p. 173, 1950

7 a poor poker player *US, 1967*

- Albert H. Morehead, *The Complete Guide to Winning Poker*, p. 271, 1967

rabbit *verb*
to run away *UK, 1887*

- Frank, why did you rabbit? I can't figure it out. Was someone in camp putting pressure on you? — Malcolm Braly, *On the Yard*, p. 75, 1967
- He was trying to decide whether to rabbit or freeze. — Joseph Wambaugh, *The Blue Knight*, p. 27, 1973
- It was the old man who'd rabbited when he saw me on the ladder. — James Ellroy, *Hollywood Nocturnes*, p. 180, 1994

rabbit blood *noun*
a seemingly unstoppable urge to try to escape from prison *US, 1950*

- Hyman E. Goldin et al., *Dictionary of American Underworld Lingo*, p. 173, 1950

rabbit ears *noun*
1 a v-shaped aerial placed on top of a television set *US, 1967*

- Usually she would've gone home by now, but she was wrestling with the rabbit ears on top of the TV, trying to fix the snow on the screen. — Sue Monk Kidd, *The Secret Life of Bees*, p. 19, 2002

2 in a casino Keno game, the two clear plastic tubes through which the number balls are blown *US, 1993*

- Frank Scoblete, *Guerrilla Gambling*, p. 322, 1993

rabbit fever *noun*
the urge to try to escape from prison *US, 1962*

- Joseph E. Ragen and Charles Finston, *Inside the World's Toughest Prison*, p. 814, 1962: "Penitentiary and underworld glossary"

rabbit hunt *verb*
in poker, to look through undealt cards after a hand is completed to see what might have been *US, 1967*

- Albert H. Morehead, *The Complete Guide to Winning Poker*, p. 271, 1967

rabbit season *noun*
spring, when prisoners are inclined to try to escape *US, 1967*

- [S]pring was known as rabbit season, and four camp men ran off during the first week of good weather. — Malcolm Braly, *On the Yard*, p. 323, 1967

rabbit tracks *noun*
in craps, a six rolled with a pair of threes *US, 1985*

- Steve Kuriscak, *Casino Talk*, p. 68, 1985

rabbit turds *noun*
Italian sausage *US, 1996*
Limited usage, but graphic.

- *Maledicta*, p. 19, 1996: "Domino's pizza jargon"

race *noun*
a single game in an illegal numbers lottery *US, 1963*

- You playin' twenty dollars on 526 in the first race? — Clarence Cooper Jr., *Black*, p. 180, 1963

▸ **the race**
the game of roller derby *US, 1960s and 70s*

- [S]katers refer to "the race" the way baseball players solemnly refer to their sport as "the game." — Keith Coppage, *Roller Derby to Rollerjam*, p. 127, 1999

race bird *noun*
an enthusiastic fan of horseracing *US, 1971*

- Thomas L. Clark, *The Dictionary of Gambling and Gaming*, p. 172, 1987

racehorse *noun*
an accomplished, sought-after prostitute *US, 1972*

- [A] young what-they-call "racehorse," she'd have run in there, got her $20, and have been back in fifteen minutes. — Bruce Jackson, *Outside the Law*, p. 188, 1972

racehorse Charlie; racehorse Charley *noun*
heroin; cocaine *US, 1936*
Perhaps from the long-ago brand name White Horse.

- I've known many hypes with Racehorse Charlies as a monicker, but never knew why. — David Maurer, *Narcotics and Narcotic Addiction*, pp. 436–437, 1973

race record *noun*
a recording by a black artist; rock 'n' roll before whites discovered rock 'n' roll *US, 1927*

- The music we listened to was called race-records and then rhythm and blues. — Abbie Hoffman, *Woodstock Nation*, p. 24, 1969

racerhead *noun*
in mountain biking, someone who competes in races *US, 1992*
A mild put-down to describe riders so into competition that they have lost their perspective on the cosmic absurdity of mountain biking.

- William Nealy, *Mountain Bike!*, p. 162, 1992

race track *noun*
a hotel mezzanine *US, 1971*
From the constant flow of prostitutes seeking customers.

- The mezzanine floor in some hotels is called "the race track." — Charles Winick, *The Lively Commerce*, p. 168, 1971

race track bull *noun*
a private policeman at a race track *US, 1963*
- After all, they were race track bulls, and their jurisdiction only covered the race tracks, nothing more. — Madam Sherry, *Pleasure Was My Business*, p. 81, 1963

racetracker *noun*
in horseracing, a person who makes their living in some capacity at racetracks *US, 1951*
- — David W. Maurer, *Argot of the Racetrack*, p. 54, 1951

racing stripe *noun*
a fecal stain in the underpants *US, 1991*
- — Lee McNelis, *30 + And a Wake-Up*, p. 12, 1991

rack *noun*
1 a woman's breasts *US, 1970*
- Up there near the Section 23 sign. Check the rack on that broad. — Jim Bouton, *Ball Four*, p. 242, 1970
- — *Current Slang*, p. 22, Spring 1970
- She was a healthy-looking bitch, a jogger type with a great rack ... a couple of real pointers. And I'm not talking about a bra with rubber nipples. I'm talking about a pair of honest-to-Christ pointed nips that must have weighed as much as silver dollars. — Gerald Petievich, *To Die in Beverly Hills*, p. 93, 1983
- Two legs, nice rack. — *Ten Things I Hate About You*, 1999

2 bed *US, 1955*
- Janine had someone else in the rack—the missing technician, I guessed. — Wade Hunter, *The Sex Peddler*, p. 99, 1963
- We'll spend twenty-four hours a day in the rack. — John Nichols, *The Sterile Cuckoo*, p. 113, 1965
- I just got in the rack a few hours ago and I'm beat! — Odie Hawkins, *Ghetto Sketches*, p. 177, 1972
- I jumped right out of my fuckin' rack. — Edwin Torres, *Carlito's Way*, p. 121, 1975

3 a hotel's front desk *US, 1954*
- I rang the rack, asked what they had on Mrs. Stehiti. — Dev Collans with Stewart Sterling, *I was a House Detective*, p. 73, 1954

4 a foil-wrapped package of amphetamines *US, 1997*
- [Cross Tops] were sold by the $1 unit called a rack in tightly foiled increments of four, five, or ten, depending on the quality of the drugs or the dealer. — Don Bolles, *Retrohell*, p. 50, 1997

5 a packet of five barbiturate capsules or other drugs, give or take several *US, 1972*
- — Connie Eble (Editor), *UNC-CH Campus Slang*, October 1972
- — Kenn "Naz" Young, *Naz's Underground Dictionary*, p. 53, 1973
- — Edith A. Folb, *runnin' down some lines*, p. 251, 1980

6 a one-month supply of birth control pills *US, 1980*
- — Edith A. Folb, *runnin' down some lines*, p. 251, 1980

▸ **hit the rack**
to go to bed; to go to sleep *US, 1973*
- The night is young, and I'm not hittin' the rack 'til I get a little action. — *American Graffiti*, 1973
- — *Washington Post*, 14th October 1993

▸ **on the rack**
available for prostitution *US, 1977*
- Out on the rack nearly an hour and half and she still hadn't broke luck. — John Sayles, *Union Dues*, p. 182, 1977

rack *verb*
1 to go to sleep *US, 1993*
- — *Washington Post*, 14th October 1993

2 to shoplift *US, 1982*
- So we kept on every day, me and Mono, racking up, picking out the colors we need for outlines and fill-ins. — Craig Castleman, *Getting Up*, p. 3, 1982
- Through these media, the culture of graffiti was transplanted intact, embracing language, customs and rules, bombing, "racking" and the competitive spirit. — Henry Chalfant, *Spraycan Art*, p. 8, 1987
- "Look what I racked from Radio Shack." — William Upski Wimsatt, *Bomb the Suburbs*, p. 122, 1994
- Real graffiti writers "boost" or "rack" their paint, both slang for stealing. — *Plain Dealer (Cleveland, Ohio)*, p. L1, 29th July 2001

3 to perform well *US, 1955*
- I thought I was gonna rack on midterms, but my shovel broke—I forgot I'd even cracked a book. — Max Shulman, *Guided Tour of Campus Humor*, p. 105, 1955

4 in the television and movie industries, to adjust the camera lens in the middle of a shot to keep the subject in focus *US, 1990*
- — Ralph S. Singleton, *Filmmaker's Dictionary*, p. 135, 1990

▸ **rack it up**
to sleep *US, 1959*
- Lights Out whistle just blew, have to rack it up. — James Blake, *The Joint*, p. 227, 25th June 1959

▸ **rack the bars**
to open or close a prison cell door *US, 1992*
- — William K. Bentley and James M. Corbett, *Prison Slang*, p. 7, 1992

rack attack *noun*
a nap; sleep *US, 1975*
- — *American Speech*, p. 64, Spring–Summer 1975: "Razorback slang"

rack duty; rack time *noun*
sleep *US, 1960*
- By dawn, flapjacks with bacon for his gang of paladins, some rack time for himself, then start it all over. — Jeff Long, *The Descent*, p. 64, 1999

racked *adjective*
asleep *US, 1975*
- — *American Speech*, p. 64, Spring–Summer 1975: "Razorback slang"

racked up *adjective*
upset *US, 1970*
- — William D. Alsever, *Glossary for the Establishment and Other Uptight People*, p. 26, December 1970

racket *noun*
1 a criminal enterprise; a swindle or a means of deception *UK, 1894*
Any illicit or dubious enterprise may be termed a "racket" by prefixing the area of criminal operation, hence "narcotics racket," "loan-shark racket," etc.
- Now this gal was like me, a racket broad from the word go. — John M. Murtagh and Sara Harris, *Cast the First Stone*, p. 111, 1957

2 a private, police-only party *US, 1987*
- — Carsten Stroud, *Close Pursuit*, p. 275, 1987

3 any rigged carnival game or attraction *US, 1960*
- — Gene Sorrows, *All About Carnivals*, p. 25, 1985: "Terminology"

racket boy *noun*
a member of an organized criminal enterprise *US, 1953*
- He's a walking lesson that it is a mistake to push the racket boys too hard[.] — Raymond Chandler, *The Long Goodbye*, p. 251, 1953
- Down on the boardwalk they're getting ready for a fight / Gonna see what them racket boys can do. — Bruce Springsteen, *Atlantic City*, 1982

racket jacket *noun*
the jacket of a zoot suiter *US, 1945*
- — Lou Shelly, *Hepcats Jive Talk Dictionary*, p. 31, 1945

rackets show *noun*
a dishonest carnival *US, 2005*
- The carnival deservedly earned its reputation as a "rackets show." — Peter Fenton, *Eyeing the Flash*, p. 67, 2005

rackety *adjective*
noisy *US, 1975*
- — John Gould, *Maine Lingo*, p. 225, 1975

rackey *noun*
a boy who dresses like a gangster *US, 1955*
Teen slang.
- — *American Weekly*, p. 2, 14th August 1955

rack face *noun*
lines on your face left from a blanket, sheet, or pillow *US, 1996*
- — *DePauw University Campus Corner*, 29th January 1996: "Slang terms at DePauw"

rack monster *noun*
a person who spends a great deal of time in bed *US, 1976*
- — *Verbatim*, p. 281, May 1976

rack up *verb*
1 to inform, to bring up to date *US, 1959*
- "I'm just trying to get you racked up to the present." — Irving Shulman, *The Short End of the Stick*, p. 107, 1959

2 to accumulate things; to score points *US, 1961*
- She could of racked up points on that one. — *Diner*, 1982

3 in a casino or gambling establishment, to have your chips placed in a chip rack to be cashed in *US, 1982*
- — David M. Hayano, *Poker Faces*, p. 187, 1982

4 in prison, to return prisoners to their cells *US, 1990*
- — Charles Shafer, *Folk Speech in Texas Prisons*, p. 212, 1990

rack-up artist *noun*
an accomplished shoplifter *US, 1982*
- Wasp, an acknowledged rack-up artist, has developed a technique whereby he has only to take a marker from a display, hold it in his hand, and snap his fingers in order to have it disappear up his sleeve. — Craig Castleman, *Getting Up*, p. 48, 1982

rad *adjective*
extreme; intense; exciting; good *US, 1977*
An abbreviated "radical."
- Rad—short for radical. — *Los Angeles Times*, p. IX10, 18th September 1977
- Short for "radical," it is used by Stanford University students with "way" added for emphasis. — Levi Straus & Company, *Campus Slang*, January 1986
- There is a long list of words to say things are going well. On the West Coast, something fantastic is "rad," short for radical. — *New York Times*, 12th April 1987
- He is the biggest, fastest, raddest wide receiver in the league. — *Jerry Maguire*, 1996

radar *noun*
▶ **below the radar**
keeping a low profile; unperceived *US, 1990*
- Susan Howell says because of GoPer David Duke's "racist background," "people are reluctant to say they're for Duke. The saying is, 'he flies below the radar'—he's difficult to pick up." — *USA Today*, 26th February 1990

radar Charlie *noun*
a poker player with a strong intuitive sense of other players' hands *US, 1988*
- — George Percy, *The Language of Poker*, p. 73, 1988

radiator whiskey *noun*
strong, homemade whiskey *US, 1999*
- It is called corn liquor, white lightning, sugar whiskey, skully cracker, popskull, bush whiskey, stump, stumphole, 'splo, ruckus juice, radiator whiskey, rotgut, sugarhead, block and tackle, wildcat, panther's breath, tiger's sweat, Sweet spirits of cats a-fighting, alley bourbon, city gin, cool water, happy Sally, deep shaft, jump steady, old horsey, stingo, blue John, red eye, pine top, buckeye bark whiskey and see seven stars. — *Star Tribune (Minneapolis)*, p. 19F, 31st January 1999

radical *adjective*
extreme; outrageous; good *US, 1967*
Originally surfer slang, then migrated into the argot of the San Fernando Valley and then into mainstream US youth slang.
- — Midget Farrelly and Craig McGregor, *The Surfing Life*, p. 191, 1967
- — Connie Eble (Editor), *UNC-CH Campus Slang*, p. 6, March 1979
- "I saved those really radical chocolates from the dish that turns around." — Ethan Morden, *Everybody Loves You*, pp. 121–122, 1988
- Maybe the eighties will be radical, you know? — *Dazed and Confused*, 1993

radio *noun*
a prisoner who talks loudly and without paying attention to who might be listening *US, 1976*
- — Troy Harris, *A Booklet of Criminal Argot, Cant and Jargon*, p. 24, 1976

radio that; radio that shit!
used in prison as a demand for quiet *US, 1981*
- — *Maledicta*, p. 264, Summer/Winter 1981: "By its slang, ye shall know it: the pessimism of prison life"

'rado *noun*
a Cadillac El Dorado car *US, 1980*
- — Edith A. Folb, *runnin' down some lines*, p. 251, 1980

rag *noun*
1 a sanitary napkin *US, 1966*
- R is for rag to catch the flow from the womb / it substitutes for Kotex when menstruation is in full bloom. — Bruce Jackson, *Get Your Ass in the Water and Swim Like Me*, p. 213, 1966
- [A] loved one will rebuff you, that's you with the rags on! — Frank Hardy, *The Outcasts of Foolgarah*, p. 17, 1971

- For tomorrow she would have the rags on, and the day off. — Lance Peters, *The Dirty Half-Mile*, p. 3, 1979
- — Edith A. Folb, *runnin' down some lines*, p. 251, 1980

2 the bleed period of the menstrual cycle *US, 1971*
- Fellatia passes uptown for a woman and specializes in blowing her johns in the back seat of cabs and if they insist on taking her to their rooms, pleads the rag and blows them there. — John Francis Hunter, *The Gay Insider*, p. 90, 1971
- Many a nut got busted in her butt / For the rag didn't mean a thing. — Dennis Wepman et al., *The Life*, p. 83, 1976

3 a newspaper, especially a disreputable one *UK, 1889*
- The other rag gave me a good spread and a good going over and they didn't have my picture. — Mickey Spillane, *One Lonely Night*, p. 16, 1951
- I've got a guy coming in—used to work on the labor rag here before it folded[.] — Jim Thompson, *The Nothing Man*, p. 232, 1954

4 a despicable person *US, 1997*
- Don't be such a rag. I have to sit here and work up the desire to fuck you later. — *Chasing Amy*, 1997

5 in pool, a cushion *US, 1985*
- — Mike Shamos, *The Illustrated Encyclopedia of Billiards*, p. 186, 1993

6 in poker, a useless card in the dealt hand or a drawn card that does not improve the hand *US, 1978*
- — Edwin Silberstang, *Winning Poker for the Serious Player*, p. 219, 1992

7 in a carnival midway game, a small prize in a plastic bag *US, 1985*
- — Gene Sorrows, *All About Carnivals*, p. 25, 1985: "Terminology"

▶ **on the rag; have the rag on**
1 experiencing the bleed period of the menstrual cycle *US, 1974*
- What's wit' you, you got the rag on or somethin'? — Richard Price, *The Wanderers*, p. 188, 1974
- "He's getting rid of me because I'm on the rag!" — Anne Steinhardt, *Thunder La Boom*, p. 48, 1974
- Is she on the rag or what? — *Airheads*, 1994
- Yeah, I'm just waiting because I'm on my rag. — Ana Loria, *1 2 3 Be A Porn Star!*, p. 47, 2000

2 figuratively, to be distracted and irritable *US, 1963*
- "You see, zoll—" (That how she said doll.) "—little Flip's got the mean rag on." — John Rechy, *City of Night*, p. 50, 1963
- It's all a matter of which team don't have the rag on. — Dan Jenkins, *Semi-Tough*, p. 48, 1972
- See, he always calls me "Sergeant" when he's on the rag which is most the time. — Joseph Wambaugh, *The Choirboys*, p. 259, 1975
- Vinnie was on the rag. He'd pulled a muscle in his leg again and lost a good bust on a chickenshit technicality and then when they reported for work the Captain said they'd have to go an extra four[.] — John Sayles, *Union Dues*, p. 383, 1977

rag *verb*
to dress *US, 1994*
- Personality or not, babes flocked to guys who ragged hard. — Nathan McCall, *Makes Me Wanna Holler*, p. 90, 1994

ragbag *noun*
in circus and carnival usage, a show that has fallen on hard times or is fundamentally dishonest *US, 1981*
- — Don Wilmeth, *The Language of American Popular Entertainment*, p. 215, 1981

rag chewing *noun*
conversation *US, 1885*
- "The game was cleanly played, there being little rag-chewing and no gab fests or mid-diamond mass meetings." — J. Anthony Lucas, *Big Trouble*, p. 610, 1999

rage *noun*
a large wave *US, 1991*
- If you want to get aggro, man, this stick can handle your best rage. — *Point Break*, 1991

rage *verb*
to enjoy a party with great enthusiasm *US, 1992*
- — Connie Eble (Editor), *UNC-CH Campus Slang*, p. 7, Spring 1992
- — Linda Meyer, *Teenspeak!*, p. 30, 1994

rager *noun*
a large party *US, 1990*
- — Judi Sanders, *Cal Poly Slang*, p. 8, 1990
- — Vann Wesson, *Generation X Field Guide and Lexicon*, p. 136, 1997

ragged *adjective*
without money *US, 1990*
- — Charles Shafer, *Folk Speech in Texas Prisons*, p. 212, 1990

raggedy *adjective*
ragged; rough; disheveled *US, 1890*
- — Malachi Andrews and Paul T. Owens, *Black Language*, p. 52, 1973
- I'll need to use her raggedy ass car the rest of the day. — Donald Goines, *Never Die Alone*, p. 117, 1974
- The basketball courts in Bill Robinson are too raggedy, and the kids need a place to play when it gets cold. — *New Jack City*, 1990

raggin' *adjective*
dressed in fashionable and expensive clothing *US, 1987*
- — *Washington Post Magazine*, p. 13, 26th April 1987: "Say wha'?"

rag head *noun*
1 an Arab person, or a native of any race that wears a cloth-covering on the head; by extension a native of Muslim countries *US, 1921*
Offensive.
- — Joseph E. Ragen and Charles Finston, *Inside the World's Toughest Prison*, p. 814, 1962: "Penitentiary and underworld glossary"
- "That's how you treat a handicap? Then I quit, raghead." — Carl Hiaasen, *Lucky You*, p. 105, 1997
- Limbaugh was reacting to a wire story about Sen. Conrad Burns' most recent faux pas, in which the Republican senator described Arabs as "ragheads" during a speech to the Montana Equipment Dealers Association. — *Great Falls (Montana) Tribune*, p. A6, 15th March 1999
- In a series of racist statements that began when the World Trade Center collapsed, Roque announced his murderous plans and told a co-worker that he had been treated rudely at a gasoline station on University Drive by "a towel head or a rag head." — *The Arizona Republic*, p. 1A, 3rd September 2003
2 in circus and carnival usage, a gypsy *US, 1981*
- — Don Wilmeth, *The Language of American Popular Entertainment*, p. 215, 1981

raging *adjective*
very good; very exciting *US, 1995*
- This is raging! — *Clueless*, 1995

rag joint *noun*
a carnival concession in a canvas booth *US, 1985*
- — Gene Sorrows, *All About Carnivals*, p. 25, 1985: "Terminology"

rags *noun*
clothing *US, 1994*
- The different responses convinced us that we had to hustle because we had to lots of nice rags to run our games. — Nathan McCall, *Makes Me Wanna Holler*, p. 91, 1994

rag store *noun*
a big con swindle in which the lure is the promise of wealth from stocks traded based on allegedly inside information *US, 1969*
- The same gimmicks are used in the rag store. It's the bogus shares of stock and fake inside market information that trim the sucker in that case. — Iceberg Slim (Robert Beck), *Trick Baby*, pp. 119–120, 1969

rag town *noun*
a town built in prosperous times, bound to fall into poverty with the end of prosperous times *US, 1954*
- We had been in many of the same places—the pipeline jobs, the "rag towns" of the south and west. — Jim Thompson, *Roughneck*, p. 65, 1954

rag trade *noun*
the garment business *UK, 1907*
- September wholesale price reductions on bathing suits are not uncommon in the rag trade. — Mort Brown, *So You Want To Own The Store*, p. 88, 1997

rah-rah *noun*
spirit, enthusiasm *US, 1963*
- She's full of the old rah-rah, having been the only female member who ever played on a high school team, back in old Roseburg. — Frederick Kohner, *The Affairs of Gidget*, p. 54, 1963

rah-rah *adjective*
characterized by excessive spirit and enthusiasm, usually associated with college or high school *US, 1914*

- College kids have outgrown all that rah-rah stuff. The war, the A-bomb, the H-bomb—who's thinking about fun and jokes these days? — Max Shulman, *The Many Loves of Dobie Gillis*, p. 24, 1951
- Maybe in some rah-rah campus crowd beer joint I'd just hee-haw and let him slide, but here in the Pink Dragon the beat cops rule by force and fear. — Joseph Wambaugh, *The Blue Knight*, p. 45, 1973

rail *noun*
a line of cocaine or other powdered drug, laid out for snorting *US, 1984*
- You followed the rails of white powder across the mirror in pursuit of a point of convergence[.] — Jay McInerney, *Bright Lights, Big City*, p. 170, 1984
- They have their party, chop some rails, put a movie on. — Elmore Leonard, *Maximum Bob*, p. 52, 1991
- It would be a handy place to do rails and pour shots. — Lynn Breedlove, *Godspeed*, p. 14, 2002

▸ **on the rail**
in American casinos, observing the gambling but not playing *US, 1985*
- — Steve Kuriscak, *Casino Talk*, p. 40, 1985

rail *verb*
to arrest or detain someone *US, 1995*
- Okay, so I did a little time, does that mean I get railed every time truck finds its way off the planet? — *The Usual Suspects*, 1995

railbird *noun*
1 in horseracing, an enthusiast who watches morning workouts, carefully clocking performances *US, 1931*
- — David W. Maurer, *Argot of the Racetrack*, p. 54, 1951
2 in American casinos, a thief who steals chips from inattentive gamblers *US, 1985*
- — Steve Kuriscak, *Casino Talk*, p. 46, 1985
- "Guy's acting a little shifty," Roger said. "Could be a railbird, waiting to grab a few chips." — Elmore Leonard, *Glitz*, p. 116, 1985
3 in pool, a spectator *US, 1993*
- — Mike Shamos, *The Illustrated Encyclopedia of Billiards*, p. 187, 1993

railfield *verb*
a thief who simply grabs store merchandise and runs from the store *US, 1960*
- Then me and some more guys was railfield in a radio shop and got caught, and I got sapped up and went to the Hill for eighteen months. I was so scared I never railfielded no more. I kept stealin' but I never railfielded. — Clarence Cooper Jr., *The Scene*, p. 135, 1960
- — Clarence Major, *Juba to Jive*, p. 346, 1994

railrat *noun*
in the language surrounding the Grateful Dead, a member of the audience who prefers to see the show from as close as possible to the band, right on the rail *US, 1994*
- — David Shenk and Steve Silberman, *Skeleton Key*, p. 238, 1994

railroad *verb*
to move your jaw from side to side obsessively and involuntarily after sustained amphetamine use *US, 1989*
- — Geoffrey Froner, *Digging for Diamonds*, p. 50, 1989

railroad bible *noun*
a deck of playing cards *US, 1976*
- — Thomas L. Clark, *The Dictionary of Gambling and Gaming*, p. 175, 1987

railroad flat *noun*
an apartment consisting of connected long, narrow rooms *US, 1956*
- Red's apartment was the type known as a "railroad flat." It had no hallway. There was a succession of rooms, one telescoped into the next. — Ross Russell, *The Sound*, p. 105, 1961
- Alan lived in a railroad flat, in one large room of it, with paintings on all the walls. — Clancy Sigal, *Going Away*, p. 417, 1961
- We were freezing our asses off in a fourth-floor railroad flat on Ninety-second Street with a toilet in the hall used to freeze up overnight. — Vincent Patrick, *The Pope of Greenwich Village*, p. 166, 1979

railroad station *noun*
a criminal court *US, 1975*
- — Report to the Senate, *California Senate Committee on Civil Disorder*, p. 229, 1975

railroad tracks *noun*
the bars on a captain's uniform signifying his office *US, 1947*
- — *American Speech*, p. 55, February 1947: "Pacific War language"

railroad weed *noun*

marijuana, especially of inferior quality *US, 1974*
From the weeds that flourish alongside railroad lines.
- — John G. Cull et al., *Problems of Runaway Youth*, p. 112, 1976

rail sandwich *noun*

a surfboard between your legs *US, 1978*
- — Aaberg, Dennis and John Milius, *Big Wednesday*, p. 211, 1978

rain *noun*

▸ **make it rain**

to throw handfuls of money onto the stage in a strip club *US, 2007*
- Jones had tossed hundreds of $1 bills on the stripper stage, an action known in street slang as "making it rain." — *Las Vegas Review-Journal*, p. 1A, 21st February 2007

rainbow *noun*

1 a capsule of amobarbital sodium and secobarbital sodium (trade name Tuinal™), a combination of central nervous system depressants *US, 1966*
- — Donald Louria, *Nightmare Drugs*, p. 25, 1966
- The carpeted lobby was littered with fallen rainbows, dexis, bennies, ludes, speed, even some dust, though it had a bad rep these days[.] — Joseph Wambaugh, *The Glitter Dome*, p. 122, 1981

2 in casinos, a bet comprised of different color and different value betting chips *US, 1991*
- — Michael Dalton, *Blackjack*, p. 29, 1991

3 in oil drilling, a very small showing of oil in a hole *US, 1954*
- — Jerry Robertson, *Oil Slanguage*, p. 60, 1954

rainbow hand *noun*

a poker hand with cards of all four suits *US, 1950*
- — Thomas L. Clark, *The Dictionary of Gambling and Gaming*, p. 175, 1987

rainbow party *noun*

oral sex on one male by several females, all wearing different colors of lipstick *US, 2003*
- A rainbow party is an oral sex party. It's a gathering where oral sex is performed. And a rainbow comes from all —all of the girls put on lipstick and each one puts her mouth around the penis of the gentleman or gentlemen who are there to receive favors and make marks in a different place on the penis, hence the term rainbow. — *Oprah Winfrey Show*, 2nd October 2003

rainbow roll *noun*

a multicolored assortment of barbiturate capsules *US, 1973*
- — David W. Maurer and Victor Vogel, *Narcotics and Narcotic Addiction*, p. 437, 1973

raincoat *noun*

a condom *US, 1970*
Figurative use of waterproof wear.
- — *Current Slang*, p. 22, Spring 1970
- "Make sure you wear a raincoat when you bone them broads." — Nathan McCall, *Makes Me Wanna Holler*, p. 40, 1994
- "Because, let's face it, no one's going to slam out of your apartment just because you want to use a raincoat." — Ethan Morden, *Some Men Are Lookers*, p. 173, 1997
- But DeAndre doesn't like sex in a raincoat[.] — David Simon and Edward Burns, *The Corner*, p. 225, 1997

Raincoat Charlie *noun*

a striptease audience member who masturbates beneath the safety of his raincoat *US, 1981*
- — Don Wilmeth, *The Language of American Popular Entertainment*, p. 216, 1981

raincoater *noun*

a stereotypical perverted pornography fan *US, 2000*
- — Ana Loria, *1 2 3 Be A Porn Star!*, p. 166, 2000: "Glossary of adult sex industry terms"

raincoat job *noun*

a sexual fetish involving urination on your partner *US, 1993*
- — J.R. Schwartz, *The Official Guide to the Best Cat Houses in Nevada*, p. 164, 1993: "Sex Glossary"

rain dance *noun*

in computing, an action that is expected to be taken but will likely produce no results *US, 1974*
- — Robert Kirk Mueller, *Buzzwords*, p. 133, 1974
- I can't boot up the machine. We'll have to wait for Greg to do his rain dance. — Eric S. Raymond, *The New Hacker's Dictionary*, pp. 294–295, 1991

rainmaker *noun*

a member of an enterprise whose job includes procuring clients or business by the use of charm *US, 1985*
- "Frank is the rainmaker," I heard Edmund say one night at the annual meeting of the Massachusetts Bar Association[.] — George V. Higgins, *Penance for Jerry Kennedy*, p. 56, 1985
- — Rachel S. Epstein and Nina Liebman, *Biz Speak*, p. 186, 1986
- Beano smiled his boyish rainmaker smile. It brought rain, but only a few drops. — Stephen J. Cannell, *King Con*, p. 73, 1997

rain room *noun*

a shower room *US, 1968*
- — Carl Fleischhauer, *A Glossary of Army Slang*, p. 10, 1968
- — Lee McNelis, *30 + And a Wake-Up: A Compendium of Prison Slang Terms and Definitions*, p. 5, 1991
- — Judie Sanders, *Faced and Faded, Hanging at Hurl*, p. 32, 1993

raise *noun*

parents *US, 1972*
- — David Claerbaut, *Black Jargon in White America*, p. 77, 1972

raise *verb*

1 to identify yourself to a fellow traveler *US, 1957*
- Ever notice how many expressions carry over from queers to con men? Like "raise," letting someone know you are in the same line? — William Burroughs, *Naked Lunch*, p. 3, 1957

2 to bail someone out of jail *US, 1973*
- [S]ince the High One was an undercover bondsman he raised her each time. — A.S. Jackson, *Gentleman Pimp*, p. 121, 1973
- I want to raise. I want out. — Gerald Petievich, *To Live and Die in L.A.*, p. 133, 1983

▸ **raise sand**

to argue loudly, creating a problem *US, 1965*
- There wasn't much raisin' sand at these parties, 'cause the peoples was havin' fun! — Henry Williamson, *Hustler!*, p. 23, 1965

raiser *noun*

1 a criminal who specializes in forging increases in the amount payable to an otherwise legitimate check or security *US, 1950*
- — Hyman E. Goldin et al., *Dictionary of American Underworld Lingo*, p. 173, 1950

2 a lookout who warns confederates of approaching police *US, 1992*
- Both of the front doors flew open and two Hawaiian shirts stepped out. The raiser barked "Five-oh" and split. — Richard Price, *Clockers*, p. 441, 1992

raise up *verb*

1 to leave *US, 1998*
- "Alright, let's raise the fuck up outta here." — Renay Jackson, *Oaktown Devil*, p. 128, 1998

2 to make someone angry *US, 2001*
- — Don R. McCreary (Editor), *Dawg Speak*, 2001

3 to warn someone *US, 1992*
- Strike looked at Peanut now, sulking on the corner, demoted to raising up—looking out for the Fury—a flat twenty-dollar gig, no bottles, no commission. — Richard Price, *Clockers*, p. 4, 1992

4 to be released from prison *US, 1990*
- I'll go home to Galvaston n have it n wait on Joe to raise up. — Seth Morgan, *Homeboy*, p. 171, 1990
- — William Bentley, *Prison Slang*, p. 108, 1992

raisinhead *noun*

a black person *US, 1978*
Offensive.
- I'm so tired of being called names. I ain't no raisinhead or nothing like that. — Piri Thomas, *Stories from El Barrio*, p. 60, 1978

raisin snap; raisin jack *noun*

alcohol made from fermented raisins *US, 1986*
- [W]atching mentally impoverished lowlifes get fucked up on raisinjack[.] — James Ellroy, *Suicide Hill*, p. 574, 1986
- Later on she discovered, when a shipmate came to call, that her husband had cooked up some raisin snap in a cookpot stashed behind the boilers. — Robert Campbell, *Juice*, p. 27, 1988

raize *verb*

to annoy or harass someone *US, 1991*
- — Trevor Cralle, *The Surfin'ary*, p. 96, 1991

rake *noun*

1 a comb *US, 1960*
- — *San Francisco Examiner*, p. III-2, 22 March 1960

2 in pool, a device used to support the cue stick for a hard-to-reach shot *US, 1990*
- — Steve Rushin, *Pool Cool*, p. 24, 1990

rake *verb*

► **rake a game**
to charge card players for the privilege of playing *US, 1977*
- — Robert C. Prus and C.R.D. Sharper, *Road Hustler*, p. 171, 1977: "Glossary of terms"

rakehell *noun*
an utter scoundrel *UK, 1554*
- Liz is the rakehell from Scarsdale, who bickers her journeyman into defeat. — Sidney Bernard, *This Way to the Apocalypse*, p. 147, 1964

rake-in *noun*
the financial results of an enterprise *US, 1947*
- Dopey asked how Phil had gotten the rake-in, and Phil told him. — James T. Farrell, *Saturday Night*, p. 24, 1947

rake-off *noun*
money obtained from a crime or as a bribe *US, 1899*
- Pa recalled that the old man had made his fortune by rake-offs in the distribution of railway lines during his administration. — Miles Franklin, *My Career Goes Bung*, p. 112, 1946

rallier *noun*
a former Viet Cong who has become a scout or translator for the US Army *US, 1968*
- The civilians are fed C rations, given medical attention and lectured by the ralliers. — Martin Russ, *Happy Hunting Ground*, p. 119, 1968
- "All ralliers are untrustworthy and a waste of time." — Tom Mangold, *The Tunnels of Cu Chi*, p. 198, 1985

ralph *noun*

1 a right turn *US, 1968*
- — *Current Slang*, p. 6, Spring 1968

2 vomit *US, 1975*
- — *American Speech*, p. 64, Spring–Summer 1975: "Razorback slang"

ralph *verb*
to vomit *US, 1966*
- — *Current Slang*, p. 6, Winter 1966
- — Collin Baker et al., *College Undergraduate Slang Study Conducted at Brown University*, p. 181, 1968
- Your middle name is Ralph, as in puke. — *The Breakfast Club*, 1985
- I was really bad today. I had two moccacinos. I feel like ralphing. — *Clueless*, 1995

ram *noun*
amyl or butyl nitrite *US, 1998*
- Street names [...] poppers, ram, rock hard[.] — James Kay and Julian Cohen, *The Parents' Complete Guide to Young People and Drugs*, p. 144, 1998

-rama; -erama; -orama *suffix*
used for conveying a superlative quality or quantity *US, 1954*
From Greek *orama* (a view).
- — John Lotz, *American Speech*, pp. 156–158, May 1954: "The suffix '-rama'"
- — Pamela Munro, *U.C.L.A. Slang*, p. 64, 1989
- Upset-O-Rama! (Headline) — *San Francisco Chronicle*, p. 1, 17th March 2001

Rambette *noun*
a female Rambo—reckless, fearless, the warrior woman *US, 1992*
- He'd even formed a Pt. Mugu SWAT team—it was unusual in that it contained both men and women—which he lovingly called his Rambo and Rambette SWATs. — Richard Marcinko and John Weisman, *Rogue Warrior*, p. 296, 1992

rambling ROK's *noun*
ground troops of the Army of South Korea (the Republic of Korea) *US, 1964*
- When they arrived at their destination, South Korean ground units known as the "Rambling ROK's" were already in possession of the city. — Don Lawson, *The United States in the Korean War*, p. 69, 1964

Rambo *noun*
a soldier with too much of a sense of drama and too little intelligence *US, 1989*

After the 1982 movie starring Sylvester Stallone as an invincible if mentally unstable Vietnam veteran.
- The name "Rambo" (a movie version of an invincible Army veteran of Vietnam) is used derisively by soldiers for someone who is braver than he is intelligent. — *Houston Chronicle*, 20th March 1989
- The females often had to become surrogate mothers or big sisters out there in the patrol units at night to all those blue-suited Rambos who temporarily traded testosterone for teddy bears[.] — Joseph Wambaugh, *Fugitive Nights*, p. 49, 1990

Rambo rag *noun*
a handkerchief worn on the head *US, 1991*
Worn by Stallone in the movie.
- Other orders prohibit what had threatened to become a desert fashion trend: the wearing of head scarves knotted at the back, prized by soldiers for their anti-dust qualities but disparaged by higher-ups as "Rambo rags." — *Washington Times*, p. 11A, 11th February 1991
- — *Army*, p. 48, November 1991

ramf; RAMF *noun*
a rear-echelon support troop *US, 1984*
An abbreviation of rear-area motherfucker.
- The mess hall was full of RAMFS as Reid called them. (Rear Area Mother-Fuckers.) — Paul Morgan, *The Parrot's Beak*, p. 102, 2000

ramrod *noun*
the penis; the erect penis *UK, 1902*
- My ramrod is me, any man's rod is himself. — Clarence Major, *All-Night Visitors*, p. 4, 1998

ranch *noun*

1 a house *US, 1960*
- — Robert George Reisner, *The Jazz Titans*, p. 163, 1960

2 any place where marijuana is sold *US, 1945*
- — Lou Shelly, *Hepcats Jive Talk Dictionary*, p. 16, 1945

ranch hand *noun*

1 a C-123 aircraft equipped with tanks filled with defoliants used on the Vietnam jungle *US, 1969*
- On the other was the motto of the "Ranch Hand" pilots—the men who flew the C-123 defoliation planes: "ONLY YOU CAN PREVENT FORESTS." — Edwin Corley, *Siege*, p. 80, 1969
- My eyes have seen the Ranch Hands as they start a spray to pass. — Joseph Tuso, *Singing the Vietnam Blues*, p. 46, 1990: Battle Hymn of the Ranch Hands

2 a member of a special US Air Force defoliation unit during the Vietnam war *US, 1977*
- They were called the Ranch Hands, and their motto was "Only we can prevent forests." — Michael Kerr, *Dispatches*, p. 154, 1977

rancid *adjective*
in poor taste *US, 1989*
- — Pamela Munro, *U.C.L.A. Slang*, p. 70, 1989

random *adjective*
ordinary if unexpected *US, 1968*
A major word of the 1990s US youth, just a tad to the slang side of conventional English.
- — Collin Baker et al., *College Undergraduate Slang Study Conducted at Brown University*, p. 181, 1968
- — Connie Eble (Editor), *UNC-CH Campus Slang*, p. 4, Fall 1982
- — *Merriam-Webster's Hot Words on Campus Marketing Survey '93*, p. 3, 13th October 1993
- Oh, she met some random guys at the Foot Locker and escorted them right over there. — *Clueless*, 1995

R and R *noun*
rest and rehabilitation; rest and recovery; rest and recreation; rest and recuperation; rape and restitution; rape and ruin; rape and run *US, 1953*
Despite disagreement on the "R's," the meaning is the same —a brief stint away from combat or regular duty.
- Any man who captures a prisoner these days is promised a five-day Rest and Rehabilitation breather in Japan. — Martin Russ, *The Last Parallel*, p. 163, 1957
- He'll be on sick leave for a few weeks. We call it "R & R (Rest and Recuperation)." — Dennis Smith, *Report From Engine Company 82*, p. 46, 1972
- Walker Hill one time belong US Army that time big R and R place for soldier. R and R mean "rest and recreation." — Walter Sheldon, *Gold Bait*, p. 31, 1973
- R&R—rest and recovery leave. — William H. LaBarge and Robert Lawrence Holt, *Sweetwater Gunslinger 201*, p. 281, 1983

rang *noun*

a person who is acting very oddly *US*, 1966

An abbreviation of "orangutan."

- — *American Speech*, p. 282, December 1966: "More carnie talk from the West Coast"

rangdoodles *noun*

in poker, a temporary increase in the betting limit after a player has won a hand with an agreed-upon, rare and excellent hand *US*, 1967

- — Albert H. Morehead, *The Complete Guide to Winning Poker*, p. 271, 1967

rank *noun*

1 an insult *US*, 1972

- [T]he waitress would look at him like he got rocks in his head, you know, and I told him, "The broad is giving you a rank here man, you better lay off." — Harry King, *Box Man*, p. 88, 1972

2 a big mistake *US*, 1972

- [W]e read where a safe man had been working down a block from us and got a rank which put all the heat in the neighborhood as the guy had gotten away. — Harry King, *Box Man*, pp. 42–43, 1972

rank *verb*

1 to disparage; to insult, especially in a formulaic or ritual manner *US*, 1945

- — Lou Shelly, *Hepcats Jive Talk Dictionary*, p. 16, 1945
- — J. R. Friss, *A Dictionary of Teenage Slang (Mt. Diablo High)*, 1964
- Hey, you know; like that's what I come all the fucking way up here for, but if you gon rank me, I'll go somewhere else and spend my money. — Vernon E. Smith, *The Jones Men*, p. 165, 1974
- They knew what "ranking" and "snapping" on someone meant. — *New York Amsterdam News*, p. 34, 29th September 1979

2 to bungle or ruin something *US*, 1950

- — Hyman E. Goldin et al., *Dictionary of American Underworld Lingo*, p. 174, 1950
- He just hoped Sister Heavenly wouldn't do anything to rank his play. — Chester Himes, *Come Back Charleston Blue*, p. 49, 1966
- But the trouble began when I ranked my hand / And stopped blowing and started to hit. — Dennis Wepman et al., *The Life*, p. 84, 1976

rank *adjective*

unpleasant; stupid; bad-smelling *US*, 1955

In the world of bad-is-good alienated youth, "rank" can be good or bad.

- You always travel in this rank company? — *Rebel Without a Cause*, 1955
- — *Current Slang*, p. 6, Winter 1966
- "Kids today like things that are rank," he says. — Tom Wolfe, *The Pump House Gang*, p. 99, 1968
- I knew the punk was rank, but Jackson was crazy about him so I stayed on the dummy. — Iceberg Slim (Robert Beck), *The Naked Soul of Iceberg Slim*, p. 122, 1971

rank out *verb*

1 to offend or disgust someone *US*, 1966

- Put-down, or ranked-out, or second-class citizen treatment as described above is what causes the daughter to say of her parents, "They don't understand." — Murray Kaufman, *Murray the K Tells It Like It Is, Baby*, p. 34, 1966
- I've heard the two of you play your little rank out game where one insists the other is gay. — *Chasing Amy*, 1997

2 to back down from a confrontation *US*, 1993

- Amazingly, I never once thought of rankin' out, pleading, or otherwise backing down. — Sanyika Shakur, *Monster*, p. 133, 1993

rap *noun*

1 a criminal charge *US*, 1903

- This time I'm pinning a murder rap on him, and he won't dodge it. — Chester Gould, *Dick Tracy Meets the Night Crawler*, p. 112, 1945
- I'll go to San Quentin, 'cause, Sal, one more rap of any kind and I go to San Quentin for life—that's the end of me. — Jack Kerouac, *On the Road*, p. 185, 1957
- Just what I needed—get busted for a littering rap on top of six counts of hitchhiking with long hair. — James Simon Kunen, *The Strawberry Statement*, p. 81, 1968
- It was bullshit. The whole rap was a setup. — *The Usual Suspects*, 1995

2 blame or responsibility *US*, 1927

- "He's takin' the rap for some dame." — Donald Wilson, *My Six Convicts*, p. 51, 1951
- Y-you m-mean I—I should take the rap for you? — Jim Thompson, *The Killer Inside*, p. 119, 1952

3 a prison sentence *US*, 1927

- He's on the lam from a pen back east, crashed out with twenty years to serve of a thirty-year bank-robber rap. — Jim Thompson, *A Swell-Looking Babe*, p. 77, 1954
- They mentally calculated Murray's age, and they figured this for a prison rap. — Evan Hunter, *The Blackboard Jungle*, p. 79, 1954
- He got sent to Starke on a homicide, shot some dude he was supposed to be bringing in. Doing his rap he was the man up there among the Latinos. — Elmore Leonard, *Riding the Rap*, p. 29, 1995

4 a clever line of improvised chat, speech, or conversation *US*, 1967

Black coinage, adopted and popularized by hippies.

- His rap was boss and really got across / When they saw that his eyes were wet. — Dennis Wepman et al., *The Life*, p. 69, 1976
- Our rap was if girls could only look beyond the fact we didn't have good looks [...] they would fall in love with us. — Howard Stern, *Miss America*, p. 4, 1995

5 a meandering, unstructured discussion *US*, 1967

- Please don't dominate the rap, Jack / If you got nothin' to say. — The Grateful Dead, *New Speedway Boogie*, 1970
- The rap was two or three minutes old before D.R. even realized that a strange man and woman had taken over the bus and were driving them away. — Gurney Norman, *Divine Right's Trip (Last Whole Earth Catalog)*, p. 69, 1971
- Julie had been the only other woman on the block who was heavily into macrame, and Kate missed her and the raps they'd had on lazy summer afternoons while they sat out on Julie's patio tying knots in plant hangers. — Cyra McFadden, *The Serial*, p. 17, 1977

6 a popular music genre in which a rhythmic lyric is spoken over a musical background *US*, 2002

- Hip-hop historians have determined that the first "rap" record (the Fatback Band's "King Tim III [Personality Jock]") preceded the Sugarhill Gang's "Rapper's Delight" by a few months in 1979. — *The Source*, p. 180, March 2002

7 the way in which a person expresses himself or herself *US*, 1975

- It is true I spend all my time pursuin' good trim and, thank God, have a good rap. — Edwin Torres, *Carlito's Way*, p. 19, 1975

8 a very small amount *US*, 1973

- I just didn't give a rap anymore about school. — Leonard Shecter and William Phillips, *On the Pad*, p. 61, 1973

▸ **ride the rap**

to serve a prison sentence without losing control, or sanity *US*, 1991

- What you have to learn is how to ride the rap, do your own time, but get salty quick as you can. — Elmore Leonard, *Maximum Bob*, p. 108, 1991

rap *verb*

1 to talk without an agenda, aimlessly but honestly *US*, 1929

Found before the 1960s, but truly a word of the 60s.

- Somebody to talk to, he's intuitive and perceptive, and we walk around the ball field for hours and rap about everything. — James Blake, *The Joint*, p. 75, 15th April 1954
- In point of fact he is funny and very glib, and I dig rapping (talking) with him. — Eldridge Cleaver, *Soul on Ice*, p. 46, 19th September 1965
- As Che rapped on for four hours, we fantasized taking up rifles. — Jerry Rubin, *Do It!*, p. 20, 1970
- I readily rapped to Zelda, trying to talk cool but nicer than most boastiferous conversations I heard in the Fire Island. — Bobby Seale, *A Lonely Rage*, p. 109, 1978

2 to criticize someone *US*, 1957

- "They fed me, they clothed me, they sent me to college." "So what are you rapping 'em for?" "Because they filled me full of insecurities." — Max Shulman, *Rally Round the Flag, Boys!*, p. 10, 1957

3 to accuse someone falsely or to seek a more serious sentence for someone than their crime deserves *US*, 1949

- "Who wanted to rap a punk for a caper as guilty as that?" — Nelson Algren, *The Man with the Golden Arm*, p. 275, 1949
- I gave the officer that was pressin' charges against me ten dollars, not to turn me loose, but to not rap me. — Henry Williamson, *Hustler!*, p. 68, 1965

rap buddy *noun*

a fellow prisoner who becomes a good and trusted friend while incarcerated *US*, 1966

- Any two people who find one another compatible in this way may become "rap buddies" to one another. — Rose Giallombardo, *Society of Women*, p. 118, 1966
- "The one's name is Stony. He's my rap buddy." — David Simon, *Homicide*, p. 394, 1991
- So when you go up to Fayette and Monroe and hear that your rap buddy just fell dead after slamming some Red Tops, you barely miss a beat. — David Simon and Edward Burns, *The Corner*, p. 72, 1997

rape *verb*
in computing, to destroy a program or data without hope of recovering it *US, 1991*
- — Eric S. Raymond, *The New Hacker's Dictionary*, p. 297, 1991

rape tools *noun*
the penis and testicles *US, 1962*
- — Joseph E. Ragen and Charles Finston, *Inside the World's Toughest Prison*, p. 814, 1962: "Penitentiary and underworld glossary"

rapo; rape-o *noun*
a rapist *US, 1972*
- Your rapos, they get ahold of the Bible and they start going to church and they stay there. — Bruce Jackson, *Outside the Law: A Thief's Primer*, p. 143, 1972
- — John R. Armore and Joseph D. Wolfe, *Dictionary of Desperation*, p. 45, 1976
- Joe screamed the words, his voice breaking: "You're a rape-o!" — James Ellroy, *Suicide Hill*, p. 598, 1986

rap parlor *noun*
a brothel in disguise as a business where you pay to talk to women *US, 1975*
- — Ralph de Sola, *Crime Dictionary*, p. 126, 1982
- "I could have done better for ten bucks and a fifteen percent tip in some Forty-second Street rap parlor." — Keith Mano, *Take Five*, p. 502, 1998
- "The street ain't no Times Square rap parlor, buddy." — George Chesbro, *Shadow of a Broken Man*, p. 43, 1999

rap partner *noun*
in a criminal enterprise, a person who will accept responsibility for a venture gone poorly and serve a jail sentence *US, 1977*
- My rap partners, Pun Plamondon and Jack Forrest, are both in the federal penitentiary right now on other charges. — John Sinclair, *Guitar Army*, p. 58, 1972
- A tension that gave birth to unknown hostilities between fast friends and rap partners. — Nathan Heard, *To Reach a Dream*, p. 45, 1972
- One of the studs was my rap partner in a bit a long time ago. He took the prison sentence, Prince, just so he could cut me loose. — Donald Goines, *Black Gangster*, p. 226, 1977

rapper *noun*
1 the mouth; the voice *US, 1969*
- His voice box screwed up on him a "dime" ago. He's been the brass nuts here for a double dime, and guess how the bastard lost his "rapper?" — Iceberg Slim (Robert Beck), *Pimp*, p. 51, 1969

2 the chief witness for the prosecution in a criminal trial *US, 1962*
- — Joseph E. Ragen and Charles Finston, *Inside the World's Toughest Prison*, p. 814, 1962: "Penitentiary and underworld glossary"

rappie *noun*
a partner in crime *US, 1981*
- — *Maledicta*, p. 265, Summer/Winter 1981: "By its slang, ye shall know it: the pessimism of prison life"
- — Lee McNeils, *30 + And a Wake-Up*, p. 3, 1991
- — William K. Bentley and James M. Corbett, *Prison Slang*, p. 41, 1992

rap session *noun*
a group discussion, unstructured and uninhibited *US, 1969*
- When the Pigs left we had a heavy rap session about self-defense, land, and whether or not the chickens bar-be-cuing on the open fire were done yet. — Abbie Hoffman, *Woodstock Nation*, p. 57, 1969
- "Well, we're getting back to one of our rap sessions, aren't we?" — Jeffrey Golden, *Watermelon Summer*, p. 101, 1971
- Now dig it, we've all done enough time, or been involved in enough "git yo' soul!" rap sessions to know how to carry off a group therapy thing, right? — Odie Hawkins, *The Busting Out of an Ordinary Man*, p. 150, 1985

rap sheet *noun*
a record of a person's past arrests and convictions *US, 1960*
- For a long time, my father's FBI rap sheet was all I had by ways of a family history. — Kim Rich, *Johnny's Girl*, p. 27, 1993

ras!
used for expressing surprise *US, 2004*
- — Rick Ayers (Editor), *Berkeley High Slang Dictionary*, p. 35, 2004

raspberry *noun*
1 a sore or abcess on an intravenous drug user from repeated injections in the same spot *US, 1973*
- — David Maurer and Victor Vogel, *Narcotics and Narcotic Addiction*, p. 437, 1973

2 a male who trades sex for drugs *US, 1995*
- — Mark S. Fleisher, *Beggars & Thieves*, p. 290, 1995: "Glossary"

raspy *adjective*
1 excellent *US, 1982*
- — Mimi Pond, *The Valley Girl's Guide to Life*, p. 61, 1982

2 bad, unpleasant *US, 1977*
- — Gary Fairmont R. Filosa II, *The Surfer's Almanac*, p. 192, 1977

rasta box *noun*
a large portable stereo system associated, stereotypically, with black youth culture *US, 1988*
- Awful tapes were put on a large Rasta box. — PJ. O'Rourke, *Holidays in Hell*, p. 29, 1988

rasta weed *noun*
marijuana *US, 2001*
Marijuana is famously central to *Rasta*farian ritual.
- I loaned some Rasta weed to somebody. — Stephen J. Cannell, *The Tin Collectors*, p. 58, 2001

rat *noun*
1 a person who informs on or otherwise betrays compatriots *UK, 1902*
- [H]e stopped me at the beginning of my "pitch" to inform me, boldly and slyly, that he had been a "testifier" and that according to some people he was a rat, traitor and scoundrel. — Clancy Sigal, *Going Away*, p. 271, 1961
- I heard of spitters going down to Honduras and Panama to ice a rat. — Edwin Torres, *Carlito's Way*, p. 44, 1975
- I'm not a rat. — *The Usual Suspects*, 1995
- At the time we didn't know Tait was a rat working for the federals and just waiting for an excuse to fuck up the club. — Ralph "Sonny" Barger, *Hell's Angel*, p. 233, 2000

2 an enthusiast of the preceding activity or thing *US, 1864*
- RINK RAT, Skating rink enthusiast. — Lou Shelly, *Hepcats Jive Talk Dictionary*, p. 31, 1945
- — *Dobie Gillis Teenage Slanguage Dictionary*, 1962
- Up there in Loa Jolla you get a different breed of surf rat. — Joseph Wambaugh, *Finnegan's Week*, p. 205, 1993
- You're one of those fucking mallrats; you don't come to the mall to shop or work. You hang out and act like you fucking live here. — *Mallrats*, 1995
- In a grim twist that could fit into one of his songs, in the past year Zevon has been a gym rat ("I was working out more than Vin Diesel," he says) and assumed that his shortness of breath and the tightness in his chest were side effects of his regimen. — *Los Angeles Times*, 13th September 2002

3 a neighborhood girl *US, 2002*
- Daphne burned me, but she was more of a trophy for a young nigga than anything else; and fucking rats on the rooftop was just that—fucking rats on a rooftop. — Earl "DMX" Simmons, *E.A.R.L.*, p. 160, 2002

rat *verb*
to inform *US, 1934*
Perhaps from an earlier political sense of changing political parties.
- I mean, he's got those kids so trained now that they'll rat on their best friend if they hear him curse. — Evan Hunter, *The Blackboard Jungle*, p. 150, 1954
- He had worked for them, had done time in jail because of jobs he did for them, and had never ratted. — James Mills, *The Panic in Needle Park*, p. 21, 1966
- Luce, who had helped organize the Cuba trips and had once gone skinnydipping with Fidel, joined with the FBI and ratted on all of his friends. — Jerry Rubin, *Do It!*, p. 63, 1970
- As long as you done your time nice, you didn't rat anybody out, and you never took it in the ass. — Vincent Patrick, *Family Business*, p. 55, 1985

rat *adjective*
disloyal, untrustworthy *US, 1955*
- I was going to get out of this lousy can and catch them rat bastards who shot up Benjy if it was the last thing I did. — Rocky Garciano (with Rowland Barber), *Somebody Up There Likes Me*, p. 160, 1955

rat belt *noun*
in computing, a self-locking cable tie *US, 1991*
- — Eric S. Raymond, *The New Hacker's Dictionary*, p. 298, 1991

rat bite *noun*
a skin bruise caused by a suction kiss *US, 1982*
Hawaiian youth usage.
- — Douglas Simonson, *Pidgin to da Max: Hana Hou*, 1982

ratboy *noun*
among a group of drug users, a person who will sample any drug before the group uses it *US, 1987*
An allusion to the rat as the subject of laboratory experiments.
- — Carsten Stroud, *Close Pursuit: A Week in the Life of an NYPD Homicide Cop*, p. 275, 1987

ratchet *noun*
any weapon *US, 2003*
- In a fourth call, made to friend Larry Morrell, Manor cryptically asked about the "ratchet"—street slang for a weapon—that Morrell was holding for him. — *Rochester (New York) Democrat and Chronicle*, p. 3B, 24th October 2003

ratchet jaw *noun*
a person who talks too much and says too little *US, 1965*
- — John Lawlor, *How to Talk Car*, p. 87, 1965

ratchet-mouth *verb*
to talk incessantly *US, 1981*
- I never turn the damned CB on anymore. Too many assholes ratchet-mouthin' shit at each other. — George V. Higgins, *The Rat on Fire*, p. 14, 1981

rat-drawn *adjective*
used of shoes, pointed *US, 1976*
- Rat-drawn shoes, an old Stetson hat / A "28 Ford and payments on that. — Dennis Wepman et al., *The Life*, p. 135, 1976

ratfink; rat fink *noun*
1 a despised person *US, 1964*
- Boy, will I tell that lying rat fink! — Max Shulman, *Anyone Got a Match?*, p. 28, 1964
- — J. R. Friss, *A Dictionary of Teenage Slang (Mt. Diablo High)*, 1964
- — Hy Lit, *Hy Lit's Unbelievable Dictionary of Hip Words for Groovy People*, p. 33, 1968
- I want you to find that ratfink Eddie DeChooch, and I want you to drag his bony ass back here. — Janet Evanovich, *Seven Up*, p. 3, 2001

2 an informer *US, 1965*
- "There's a rat fink in this room," Hugel said, striding around the conference room and staring at people accusingly. — Bryan Burrough, *Barbarians at the Gate*, p. 366, 1990

rat fuck *noun*
1 a chaotic military disaster *US, 1930*
- Add the excitement of having to shoot rockets and machine guns at the same time and the stiff penalty exacted by your constant rush of adrenaline, never knowing when the routine mission will turn into a legendary Rat Fuck, and you develop a chronic emotional overdraft. — Dennis Marvicsin and Jerold Greenfield, *Maverick*, p. 113, 1990

2 a despicable person *US, 1922*
- [T]hose ratfucks in Chicago can suck my asshole[.] — Lester Bangs, *Psychotic Reactions and Carburetor Dung*, p. 199, 1976

3 a damn *US, 1971*
- — Helen Dahlskog (Editor), *A Dictionary of Contemporary and Colloquial Usage*, p. 48, 1972
- I don't give a rat fuck how much she cries! — Howard Stern, *Miss America*, p. 155, 1995

4 a prank *US, 1965*
- — *American Speech*, p. 195, October 1965: "Notes on campus vocabulary, 1964"

5 the Reaction Forces of the South Vietnamese Army *US, 1990*
- The pilots called the RF's Rat Fucks because they never knew what the hell they'd be flying into. A routine mission could turn into the worst chapter of the book of Revelation in half a second. — Dennis Marvicsin and Jerold Greenfield, *Maverick*, p. 40, 1990

ratfuck *verb*
to pull a prank *US, 1965*
- — *American Speech*, p. 195, October 1965: "Notes on campus vocabulary, 1964"

rat head *noun*
a person, especially a woman, who conveys a complete lack of taste and finesse *US, 2004*
- — Rick Ayers (Editor), *Berkeley High Slang Dictionary*, p. 35, 2004

rat hole *noun*
a small, messy, cluttered place *UK, 1812*
- During my stay at the Canal, I spent part of my time in the famous Hotel De Gink, a real rat hole. — Gregory "Pappy" Boyington, *Baa Baa Black Sheep*, p. 127, 1958
- "This week, five in a rathole built for four." — Georgia Sothern, *My Life in Burlesque*, p. 36, 1972
- I go, "How can you live in a rat hole like this and drive a Cadillac?" and he got pissed. — Elmore Leonard, *Maximum Bob*, p. 235, 1991
- [T]he UWF covered much more territory than WCCW did—which meant that the venues ranged from nice modern arenas to rat holes. — Missy Hyatt, *Missy Hyatt*, p. 45, 2001

rat-hole *verb*
to stash something away, usually secretively *US, 1948*
- Secretly, in the way of many wives—although she was not legally his wife—she had been rat-holing money for years. — Jim Thompson, *The Grifters*, p. 82, 1963

rat jacket *noun*
a reputation for being an informer *US, 1973*
- You got a rep for protecting your informants. Nobody never got a rat jacket behind your busts. — Joseph Wambaugh, *The Blue Knight*, p. 29, 1973

rat out *verb*
to inform on someone *US, 1990*
- They're all afraid I'm gonna rat them out. — *Goodfellas*, 1990
- Why would I rat myself out? — *Something About Mary*, 1998
- I rat Cecile out to mommy. — *Cruel Intentions*, 1999

rat pack *noun*
in competition surfing, competitors vying for the lead *US, 1988*
- — *Competitive Surfing: A Dedicated Approach*, 1988

rat-pack *verb*
to surround and attack someone *US, 1971*
- The batos locos get loaded and start looking for their own kind of action (burning a store, rat-packing a nigger, or stealing some cars for a night of high-speed cruising on the freeways). — Hunter S. Thompson, *Fear and Loathing in Las Vegas*, p. 230, 1971
- Even ten years ago veterans recall "rat packing" each other, kicking and beating en masse, but the guns remained in the background. — *Christian Science Monitor*, p. B2, 16th July 1981
- When we get down and somebody gets rat-packed, people think that's not fair. — Ralph "Sonny" Barger, *Hell's Angel*, p. 40, 2000
- Although such crimes aren't unusual in City Heights, "rat packing," or surrounding and beating a victim, is fairly rare[.] — *San Diego Union-Tribune*, p. B1, 23rd October 2003

rat patrol *noun*
a mine-clearing team *US, 1981*
- I started volunteering for everything: Lurps, trackers working with the dogs, the Rat Patrol—those maniacs who ride around in jeeps clearing mines from the roads. — Mark Barker, *Nam*, p. 34, 1981

rat race *noun*
any hectic and nonproductive situation, activity, or lifestyle *US, 1947*
- A going-nowhere ratrace—on a gloriously advanced, technological treadmill. — Robert Gover, *JC Saves*, p. 155, 1968

rat row *noun*
an area in a jail or prison reserved for police informers who would not be safe in the general population of the facility *US, 1982*
- — Ralph de Sola, *Crime Dictionary*, p. 126, 1982

rats *noun*
combat rations *US, 1976*
- Hey Chief, Six says we're getting birds in with mail, rats and water, Man, fucking water! — Charles Anderson, *The Grunts*, p. 84, 1976

rats!
used as an expression of annoyance or dismissal *US, 1886*
- My stars! Thunder and lightning! Rats and blue blazes! Suffering cats! — Audrey Wood, *Elbert's Bad Word*, p. 27, 1988

rat's ass *noun*

▶ **not give a rat's ass**

to not care at all *US, 1971*

- I frankly don't give a rat's ass — George V. Higgins, *The Friends of Eddie Doyle*, p. 115, 1971
- There you go. What am I tellin' you. Who gives a rat's ass about writers? — Robert Campbell, *Alice in La-La Land*, 52 1987
- I don't give a rat's ass about you or your fuckin' family. — Quentin Tarantino, *From Dusk Till Dawn*, p. 58, 1995
- I don't give a rat's ass if they're working for Jesus Christ! — Robert Crais, *L.A. Requiem*, p. 44, 1999

ratshit *noun*

a despicable person or thing *US, 1994*

- I mean, those two rat shits are a walkin' reminder of just how fucked up our system is. — *Natural Born Killers*, 1994

rat squad *noun*

1 an internal affairs police squad *US, 1995*

- Rat squad: Officers and detectives assigned to Internal Affairs Bureau[.] — Samuel Katz, *NYPD*, 1995
- "I don't want a bunch of grief from the rat squad about this later." — Stephen J. Cannell, *White Sister*, p. 21, 2006

2 a small team of American soldiers who explored Viet Cong tunnels *US, 1985*

An abbreviated reference to **TUNNEL RAT**.

- Most of the men had months of experience in Vietnam before volunteering for the rat squad. — Tom Mangold, *The Tunnels of Cu Chi*, p. 198, 1985

ratter *noun*

a police informer; a traitor to a cause or enterprise *US, 1975*

- In other words, you can rat out a ratter but you can't rat out a double-crosser. — Edwin Torres, *Carlito's Way*, p. 80, 1975

rattle *noun*

dice *US, 1983*

- — Thomas L. Clark, *The Dictionary of Gambling and Gaming*, p. 176, 1987

rattle *verb*

▶ **rattle someone's knickers**

to have sex *US, 1967*

- "I wonder who's rattling her knickers." — Elaine Shepard, *The Doom Pussy*, p. 59, 1967

ratty *adjective*

wretched, miserable, mean; stained, tattered *US, 1867*

- The blonde guy was getting out, built like a bull in a ratty suit tight on him, too small, and a brightly patterned sportshirt—the kind you saw in stores and wondered who would ever buy a shirt like that — Elmore Leonard, *Be Cool*, p. 222, 1999

raunch *noun*

in the usage of youthful model road racers (slot car racers), a slow car *US, 1997*

- — Phantom Surfers, *The Exciting Sounds of Model Road Racing (Album cover)*, 1997

raunchy *adjective*

used of music, abrasive, aggressive *US, 1982*

- — Arnold Shaw, *Dictionary of American Pop/Rock*, p. 301, 1982

rave *noun*

a party open to the public, often announced and sited clandestinely, featuring drugs, music, and sensory overload *UK, 1989*

- — Connie Eble (Editor), *UNC-CH Campus Slang*, p. 8, Spring 1992
- For those of you out there who are over 25, a rave is an illegal party generated by word of mouth. — *Empire Records*, 1995
- She sold rave music and incense and oils and people would come and hang out and talk about raves and DJs[.] — Michelle Tea, *Valencia*, p. 36, 2000

rave *verb*

1 to enjoy the music and other sensations of a rave *US, 1995*

- It starts at midnight. Rave on, everybody. — *Empire Records*, 1995
- You can rave on another night. — *Kids*, 1995

2 to persist in discussing something that does not interest anyone else involved in the discussion *US, 1981*

- — Guy L Steele, *Coevolution Quartly*, p. 34, spring 1981
- — Karla Jennings, *The Devouring Fungus: Tales of the Computer Age*, p. 223, 1990

raver *noun*

an enthusiastic participant in raves *US, 1990*

- There were raver boys and pixie girls and the plucky Baroness Sherry von Koeber-Bernstein. — James St. James, *Party Monster*, p. 75, 1990

raw *noun*

crack cocaine *US, 1994*

- — US Department of Justice, *Street Terms*, 1994

▶ **in the raw**

naked *US, 1934*

- "Haven't you ever been swimming in the raw with a girl?" — Grace Metalious, *Peyton Place*, p. 281, 1956
- I got in the sack in the raw. — Robert Beck (Iceberg Slim), *Pimp*, p. 110, 1969

raw *adjective*

1 naked *US, 1931*

- "Do you sleep raw, if you'll pardon the expression?" I asked. — Earl Wilson, *I am Gazing Into My 8-Ball*, p. 37, 1945
- Though we both wore pajamas, he had insomnia. Now at least I can sleep raw. — Mary McCarthy, *The Group*, p. 130, 1963

2 undiluted *US, 1974*

- He says he can cop me some raw stuff. That's what they call pure dope out here. It's supposed to be uncut. — Donald Goines, *Never Die Alone*, p. 116, 1974

3 exciting; excellent *US, 1987*

- — *Washington Post Magazine*, p. 9, 19th April 1987: "Say wha'?"
- — Trevor Cralle, *The Surfin'ary*, p. 96, 1991
- — Connie Eble (Editor), *UNC-CH Campus Slang*, p. 7, April 1997
- — *San Jose Mercury News*, 11th May 1999

4 unembalmed *US, 1987*

- — *Maledicta*, p. 180, Summer/Winter 1986–1987: "Sexual slang: prostitutes, pedophiles, flagellators, tranvestites, and necrophiles"

raw dog *adverb*

without a condom *US, 2007*

- "How many of you got HIV, hepatitis C or herpes because you let some man go up in you raw dog?" — Treasure E. Blue, *A Street Girl Named Desire*, p. 271, 2007

raw-jaw *noun*

verbal abuse *US, 1975*

- Smitty, a fake Muslim and a real raw-jaw artist, answered. — James Carr, *Bad*, p. 103, 1975

raw-jaw *verb*

1 to abuse verbally *US, 1975*

- [W]hen I got in there he started raw-jawing me about my "notorious reputation for this kinda shit." — James Carr, *Bad*, p. 61, 1975

2 to ignore someone; to bless someone with silence *US, 1992*

- — William K.Bentley and James M.Corbett, *Prison slang*, p. 39, 1992

raw-jaw *adjective*

brutish, thuggish *US, 1960*

- That was the only time I used raw-jaw methods. Rip-and-tear is all right for kids, but there's no future in it. — Nelson Algren, *The Neon Wilderness*, p. 89, 1960
- "And some of what you don't know is that there's many a way to cash out a little velvet without going rawjaw." — Malcolm Braly, *It's Cold Out There*, p. 40, 1966

raw meat *noun*

a new recruit in the US Army *US, 1948*

- — *American Speech*, p. 77, February 1948

rays *noun*

radiology *US, 1994*

- — Sally Williams, "Strong" Words, p. 157, 1994

▶ **bag some rays; catch some rays; cop some rays**

to sunbathe *US, 1963*

- And baby go catch some rays in the sunny surf. — Brian Wilson, *Catch a Wave (performed by the Beach Boys)*, 1963
- I learned, with the advent of the "Bennie God" to make an acceptable "bennie machine" out of aluminum foil, and use it on the flat back porch every afternoon during the spring semester to "catch a few rays" while downing some frosties. — John Nichols, *The Sterile Cuckoo*, p. 60, 1965
- — Collin Baker et al., *College Undergraduate Slang Study Conducted at Brown University*, p. 182, 1968

razoo noun

harassment US, 1949

- The big razoo I can get to home. From my wife — Raymond Chandler, The Little Sister, p. 174, 1949

razored adjective

muscular and sculpted US, 1984

- — American Speech, p. 201, Fall 1984: "The Language of Bodybuilding"

razor edges noun

dice that are true to an extremely minute tolerance, approximately 1/1000th of an inch US, 1950

- — The Annals of the American Academy of Political and Social Sciences, p. 129, May 1950

razz verb

to heckle; to show contempt; to jeer US, 1919

Short for RASPBERRY, a derisive sound.

- That was the way he and Al Herbert always razzed anybody who told them dumb stories. — James T. Farrell, Saturday Night, p. 13, 1947
- Then we went back to the house, and after a while Fay began to razz me a little. — Jim Thompson, After Dark, My Sweet, p. 32, 1955
- "Take it off, take it off!" the latecoming collegiate mafia began razzing Desdemona. — Seth Morgan, Homeboy, p. 136, 1990
- Immediately, a half-dozen sailors started razzing Miles, who looked at Anne with approval. — Joseph Wambaugh, Floaters, p. 232, 1996

razzberry noun

a jeering, derisory, farting noise US, 1922

Extends RAZZ (to jeer) back to a variation of its source: RASPBERRY.

- [D]isappointed at not soliciting more razzberries from the peanut gallery[.] — Lester Bangs, Psychotic Reactions and Carburetor Dung, p. 35, 1970
- [H]e now must endure taunts from a jury of unsympathetic razzberry experts[.] — Saturday Evening Post, March 2001

razzle-dazzle noun

1 confusion; chaos; bewilderment US, 1885

- All this hip shit. You understand what I mean? The casino business, all this razzle-dazzle — Elmore Leonard, Glitz, p. 258, 1985

2 in circus and carnival usage, a prostitute US, 1981

- — Don Wilmeth, The Language of American Popular Entertainment, p. 217, 1981

razzmatazz noun

1 old-fashioned, sentimental jazz US, 1936

The term was originally used, before use of the word "jazz" to describe an early jazz-like music.

- [H]e was huddled up more and more at his phonograph at home, listening to all kinds of symphonic razzmatazz like Holst's The Planets and Stravinsky and Ravel. — Mezz Mezzrow, Really the Blues, p. 157, 1946

2 extreme pleasure US, 1953

- [T]he way they pull their lay hips our ship that they are from the land of razz ma tazz. — Lavada Durst, The Jives of Dr. Hepcat, p. 1, 1953

RB noun

a prisoner with a large supply of things valued by other prisoners US, 2002

An abbreviation of "rich bitch."

- — Jeffrey Ian Ross, Behind Bars, p. 193, 2002

RC adjective

Roman Catholic UK, 1762

- For four years, I hitchhiked thirty miles twice a day to attend an R.C. prep school where everybody except me was rich[.] — Raymond Mungo, Famous Long Ago, p. 2, 1970

RCH noun

a tiny notional unit of measure US, 1968

An abbreviation of RED CUNT HAIR, perceived as a smaller unit even than a simple CUNT HAIR.

- — Carl Fleischhauer, A Glossary of Army Slang, p. 10, 1968

RD noun

a red-colored capsule of secobarbital sodium (trade name Seconal™), a central nervous system depressant US, 1977

An initialized RED DEVIL.

- — Donald Wesson and David Smith, Barbiturates, Their Use, Misuse and Abuse, p. 122, 1977

reach verb

to be prepared to fight US, 2004

- — Rick Ayers (Editor), Berkeley High Slang Dictionary, p. 35, 2004

▸ **reach out and touch someone**

to telephone US, 1989

From a 1982 American Telephone and Telegraph advertising slogan.

- Well, then, let's reach out and touch someone, dude! — Bill and Ted's Excellent Adventure, 1989

reach-around noun

manual stimulation of the passive partner's genitals by the male penetrating from behind US, 1987

- I'll bet you're the kind of guy that would fuck a person in the ass and not even have the goddamn courtesy to give him a reach around! — Full Metal Jacket, 1987
- Replace the "rubbing the clit" part with a reach-around while you're at it. — Suroosh Alvi et al., The Vice Guide, p. 42, 2002
- Ellen takes Al Pacino up against a wall and gives him his first reach-around since Cruising (1980)! — Mr. Skin, Mr. Skin's Skincyclopedia, p. 42, 2005

read verb

1 in poker, to try to discern an opponent's hand US, 1979

- — John Scarne, Scarne's Guide to Modern Poker, p. 288, 1979

2 in transsexual usage, to detect a person's genetic sex US, 1987

- — Maledicta, p. 173, Summer/Winter 1986–1987: "Sexual slang: prostitutes, pedophiles, flagellators, transvestites, and necrophiles"

▸ **read a shirt**

to look for signs of body lice US, 1981

- — Don Wilmeth, The Language of American Popular Entertainment, 1981

▸ **read the mail**

to listen to gossip US, 1993

- Kevin sat on his musky bunk and read the newspaper accounts of his homeboys' preliminary hearing, and he "read the mail" as gossip drifted in on the Crip grapevine. — Bob Sipchen, Baby Insane and the Buddha, p. 201, 1993

readable adjective

used of a casino blackjack gambler, sloppy in dealing or generous with body language, in either event revealing to players the strength of his hand US, 1991

- — Michael Dalton, Blackjack, p. 72, 1991

reader noun

1 a "Wanted" poster or handbill US, 1926

- I was running snow from the coast to Detroit and there was a reader out on me — Chester Himes, Cast the First Stone, p. 14, 1952

2 a counterfeit driving license US, 1985

- A popular item on any Midway, a READER usually costs twenty dollars, but it is a cheap investment for someone needing to change identities or unable to obtain his own. — Gene Sorrows, All About Carnivals, p. 25, 1985

3 a prescription for a narcotic US, 1950

- You can't work a cartwheel or a bug to get a reader because the butcher's gumptious to all that — The New American Mercury, p. 711, 1950
- — Richard Horman and Allan Fox, Drug Awareness, p. 470, 1970

4 a marked card US, 1894

- — Albert H. Morehead, The Complete Guide to Winning Poker, p. 270, 1967
- He sees through his "reader" eyeglasses Hicks' hand; space ace in hole with ten showing. — Iceberg Slim (Robert Beck), Doom Fox, p. 59, 1978

readers noun

special tinted eyeglasses used for reading marked cards US, 1959

- Those who dispensed vice often had the first crack at the boys on leave, whether they were women or card sharps with "readers." — Monroe Fry, Sex, Vice, and Business, p. 74, 1959
- — Steve Kuriscak, Casino Talk, p. 46, 1985

read my lips

pay attention to what I am saying, for it is the bedrock truth US, 1988

- This dramatic use in a formal acceptance speech sealed the phrasal intensifier "read my lips" into the language. — New York Times Magazine, p. 22, 4th September 1988
- Read my lips (as she mouths the word "no"). — True Romance, 1993

ready noun

crack cocaine US, 1997

An abbreviation of READY ROCKS.

- Ready rock, cried the Fayette Street touts. Got that ready. — David Simon and Edward Burns, The Corner, p. 62, 1997

ready *adjective*
competent *US*, 1946

- [H]e's ready, like a boxer poised to take on all comers[.] — Mezz Mezzrow, *Really the Blues*, p. 227, 1946

ready, Freddie
used for signaling readiness *US*, 1952

- He would say, "Hey, Bix Six. Everything is A-okay. We are ready, Freddie." "You know, he had to add something to whatever you said." — Wallace Terry, *Bloods*, p. 113, 1984

ready-made *noun*
a commercially manufactured cigarette *US*, 1952

- Come on down to the bunk and I'll get you a ready-made. — Chester Himes, *Cast the First Stone*, p. 10, 1952

ready rocks; redi rocks *noun*
a form of cocaine prepared for smoking *US*, 1989

- — Geoffrey Froner, *Digging for Diamonds*, p. 50, 1989
- They were selling Redi Rocks this evening, precooked nuggets ready to smoke, purer than crack and no mystery ingredients like Raid or formaldehyde. — Richard Price, *Clockers*, p. 72, 1992
- Ready rocks (cocaine) and blows (heroin) can usually be purchased from the same street drug dealers — *The Emergence of Crack Injection Among Injecting Drug Users in Chicago*, June 1995
- Fran actually cried the first time she saw him on the corner copping ready rocks. — David Simon and Edward Burns, *The Corner*, p. 48, 1997

ready-rolls *noun*
commercially manufactured cigarettes *US*, 1951

- — *Newsweek*, p. 98, 8th October 1951
- — Malachi Andrews and Paul T. Owens, *Black Language*, p. 107, 1973

ready-to-run *noun*
in the usage of youthful model road racers (slot car racers), a store-bought car that has not been modified or enhanced *US*, 1997

- — Phantom Surfers, *The Exciting Sounds of Model Road Racing (Album cover)*, 1997

real *noun*
the truth *US*, 1972

- I snarled, "Tell the real, whore." — Donald Goines, *Whoreson*, p. 159, 1972

▸ **on the real**
seriously *US*, 1993

- Now that's some shit on the real! — *Menace II Society*, 1993
- — *Milwaukee Journal-Sentinel*, 5th March 2001

real *adjective*
homosexual *US*, 1997

- Don't let Chester's tool belt and boot-cut Wrangler jeans fool you, he's as real as they come. — Jeff Fessler, *When Drag Is Not a Car Race*, p. 13, 1997
- Real girl is used to refer to someone who's not a girl (i.e., homosexual man) or a drag queen in the Polari sense. — Paul Baker, *Polari*, p. 188, 2002

real bikini *noun*
something that is excellent *US*, 1955
Teen slang.

- — *American Weekly*, p. 2, 14th August 1955

real case *noun*
a serious medical emergency *US*, 1994

- — Sally Williams, *"Strong" Words*, p. 157, 1994

real deal *noun*
1 an authentic item or person; the plain truth *US*, 1991

- Always go to where the real people go, that way you'll always know what the real deal is — Odie Hawkins, *The Life and Times of Chester Simmons*, p. 13, 1991
- This baby's the real deal. Daddy's little angel. — *Cruel Intentions*, 1999
- "Ray was the real deal, asswipe," Drucker hissed — Stephen J. Cannell, *The Tin Collectors*, p. 30, 2001

2 a youth gang member who is fully committed to the gang *US*, 1995

- — Mark S. Fleisher, *Beggars & Thieves*, p. 291, 1995: "Glossary"

real estate *noun*
in war, territory to be taken, held, abandoned, or lost *US*, 1982

- "Real estate" was irrelevant; Ridgway would not advance simply to occupy a few square miles of ground which the Chinese might seize from him a few days later. — Joseph C. Goulden, *Korea*, p. 433, 1982

reality check *noun*
in computing, a simple test of a computer's or program's operating ability *US*, 1991

- — Eric S. Raymond, *The New Hacker's Dictionary*, p. 301, 1991

really!
used for expressing emphatic agreement *US*, 1973

- "We got to take care of those people that been takin' care of us!" "REALLY!" — Malachi Andrews and Paul T. Owens, *Black Language*, p. 76, 1973
- — Connie Eble (Editor), *UNC-CH Campus Slang*, April 1977
- "Sorta grabs you, doesn't it?" "Really!" — Odie Hawkins, *The Life and Times of Chester Simmons*, p. 200, 1991

real McCoy; McCoy *noun*
the genuine article *US*, 1883

- Far as I know it's the McCoy — George V. Higgins, *The Friends of Eddie Doyle*, p. 104, 1971
- "Now," Terry said, "while Czechmate's satisfying himself that stuff is McCoy, I'm inside the South Brooklyn Bank emptying the fifties from our box[.]" — Emmett Grogan, *Final Score*, p. 60, 1976
- "Those are the real McCoys," said Kingsbury. Churrito looked perplexed. "McCoys?" "Her tits, I mean." — Carl Hiaasen, *Native Tongue*, p. 238, 1991
- A friend of mine had himself declared a minister of his own religion. A way to fuck the IRS. Is that what you're doing, or are you the real McCoy? — Quentin Tarantino, *From Dusk Till Dawn*, p. 57, 1995

real world *noun*
the nonpornographic entertainment industry; the world outside the pornography industry *US*, 1995

- — *Adult Video News*, p. 38, September 1995

ream *verb*
1 to have anal intercourse *US*, 1942

- Night after night, he rooted, rolled, and reamed. — Tom Robbins, *Jitterbug Perfume*, p. 26, 1984

2 to cheat someone *US*, 1933

- He wouldn't be reamed no sir, not him, because he wasn't the kind of a chump who allowed himself to be chumped by a cheap kike auctioneer. — James T. Farrell, *Willie Collins*, p. 107, 1946

3 to scold or punish someone *US*, 1950
From the sense of "ream" as widening a hole. "Ream out" is also used.

- And then Rags reamed her out—real hard. It was pretty rough. — Jim Thompson, *The Kill-Off*, p. 22, 1957
- If they do, they'll get reamed and they know it. — Darryl Ponicsan, *The Last Detail*, p. 22, 1970
- Yeah, Mom already reamed me, alright? — *The Breakfast Club*, 1985
- Tommy tries to explain something but Lefty won't hear it. He just wants to ream his son out. — Joseph Pistone, *Donnie Brasco*, p. 241, 1987

ream job *noun*
1 anal sex *US*, 1995

- The next time you put an add in your personals section in the back of your magazine about "ream jobs" show a nice brown or black female ass! — David Kerekes, *Critical Vision*, p. 134, 1995

2 a difficult situation *US*, 1968

- — Collin Baker et al., *College Undergraduate Slang Study Conducted at Brown University*, p. 183, 1968

ream, steam, and dry-clean *verb*
to treat poorly; to abuse *US*, 2005

- The ex-wife tried to ream, steam and dry-clean him in court. — Josh Friedman, *When Sex Was Dirty*, p. 42, 2005

rear *noun*
▸ **get your rear in gear**
to get going *US*, 1972

- — Helen Dahlskog (Editor), *A Dictionary of Contemporary and Colloquial Usage*, p. 48, 1972

rear admiral *noun*
a proctologist *US*, 1994

- — *American Speech*, p. 201, Fall–Winter 1973: "The language of nursing"
- — Sally Williams, *"Strong" Words*, p. 157, 1994

rear-area hawk *noun*
an officer stationed away from the field of battle who has strong, bellicose opinions about what should be done in battle *US, 1989*
Vietnam war usage.

- He was a rear-area hawk, one of those lily-livered saber-rattling fucks who spouted opinions from the vantage point of his air-conditioned quarters in Saigon about the strategic need for more division-sized month-long sweeps of enemy territory[.] — Lucian K. Truscott, *Army Blue*, p. 89, 1989

rear-area pussy *noun*
a support personnel safely away from combat *US, 1991*
Occasionally abbreviated to RAP.

- RAP is short for "rear area pussy," those safely out of the combat zone. — Carol Burke, *Camp All-American*, p. 108, 2004

rear door delivery *noun*
anal sex *US, 1973*

- [T]hen I was inside him with the strange device, making a "rear door delivery," as they say. — Jennifer Sills, *Massage Parlor*, p. 89, 1973

rear-echelon commando *noun*
a soldier assigned to duty safely away from combat *US, 1947*

- — *American Speech*, p. 55, February 1947: "Pacific war language"

rear-echelon motherfucker *noun*
a member of the armed forces serving behind lines well away from combat *US, 1976*
Often abbreviated to **REMF**.

- It was the ages-old animosity between front-line infantrymen and the staff and support personnel farther back—the "pogues," those "rear-echelon mother-fuckers!" — Charles Anderson, *The Grunts*, p. 28, 1976
- The troops developed a series of terms for these officers, the most derisive of which was "rear-echelon motherfucker." — Jay M. Shafritz, *Words on War*, p. 362, 1990

rear exit *noun*
a retreat or flight from danger *US, 1957*

- If the feces really hit the fan, there are three points through which a man can run for the hills—rear exits in the trench called "bug-outs." — Martin Russ, *The Last Parallel*, p. 116, 1957

rearrange *verb*
▸ **rearrange the deck chairs on the Titanic; rearrange the deck chairs**
to focus on petty matters while ignoring major problems *US, 1972*
From the image of the folly of worrying about the arrangement of deck chairs on the *Titanic* as the ship sank.

- "He's trying to rearrange the deck chairs on the Titanic out of self interest," he told AAP. — *AAP Newsfeed*, 13 February 1998
- Rather than rearrange deck chairs on a sinking ship, the Postal Service should consider more financially sound alternatives — *Business Wire, Inc.*, 26th April 2001

reat pleat *noun*
fashionable pants *US, 1947*
Usage by Mexican-American youth (Pachucos) in the south-western US.

- — *Common Ground*, p. 81, Summer 1947

reb *noun*
any poor, rural, white southerner *US, 1978*

- — *Maledicta*, p. 168, Summer/Winter 1978: "How to hate thy neighbor: a guide to racist maledicta"

rebbish *adjective*
poor, white, and racist *US, 1945*
From the shortened **REB** or **JOHNNY REB**, harkening to Confederate soldiers.

- It was a rebbish neighborhood, poor white; I'd have felt much better parked in Beverly Hills. — Chester Himes, *If He Hollers Let Him Go*, p. 139, 1945

rebel trap *noun*
in pool, the largest regulation-size table *US, 1966*
In the US, the large tables were unknown in the south, giving rise to this term in the north.

- [W]hen those southern gentlemen came to New York and tried to move around on those big tables, they looked like they just got out

of the blind men's home. We called the five-by-tens rebel traps. — Minnesota Fats, *The Bank Shot*, p. 87, 1966

rebound *noun*
a person with whom you have a romantic relationship in close proximity to the unhappy ending of a prior relation-ship *US, 1997*

- — Pamela Munro, *U.C.L.A. Slang*, p. 102, 1997

recap *noun*
a recapitulation *US, 1926*

- I mean, let's just run it down in a recap — Terry Southern, *Now Dig This*, p. 24, 1981
- REPORTER: I need a recap—Glen Tunney—two years ago—shot a kid holding a water gun. — *Copland*, 1997

recognize *verb*
to pay attention *US, 2001*

- I told him to recognize and stop talking like that to me. — Don R. McCreary (Editor), *Dawg Speak*, 2001

recon *noun*
*recon*naissance *US, 1918*
Often used in an adjectival sense.

- [C]overtly inserting four- to six-man recon teams into enemy territory via a variety of means[.] — Bob Newman, *Marine Special Warfare And Elite Unit Tactics*, p. 11, 1995

recon *verb*
to *recon*noiter *US, 1966*
Shortened for military purposes.

- Scholtes continued to insist on sending his own people in to recon the site[.] — Tom Clancy, *Shadow Warriors*, p. 10, 2002

recon by fire *noun*
in a military situation, random gunfire designed to ascertain the presence of the enemy by return fire *US, 1971*

- "Recon by fire" is when you go into an area and you're not exactly sure what is in the area. You want to find out, so you just fire into the jungle or into the surrounding vegetation in the hope you hit the enemy or something. — John Kerry, *The New Soldier*, p. 62, 1971

recovery room *noun*
a golf course's bar *US, 2000*

- — Hubert Pedroli and Mary Tiegreen, *Let the Big Dog Eat! A Dictionary of the Secret Language of Golf*, p. 71, 2000

rec room *noun*
a recreational room *US, 1962*
A mandatory feature of suburban 1960s life in the US, where the family gathered to watch television, play table tennis, set up model trains, etc.

- It was a snug, knotty-pine bar, more like somebody's rec room than a saloon, and it was cold and rainy outside. — Elmore Leonard, *Glitz*, p. 124, 1985
- We shot pool in the rec room all night the day before our perma-nent duty stations were posted on the bulletin board. — Odie Hawkins, *Scars and Memories*, p. 78, 1987

recycle *verb*
▸ **recycle the dice**
in bar dice games, to roll again after a roll that produces no points for the player *US, 1971*

- — Jester Smith, *Games They Play in San Francisco*, p. 105, 1971

red *noun*
1 any central nervous system depressant, especially a capsule of Seconal™ or another barbiturate *US, 1966*

- The next step up the scale is Seconal ("reds" or "red devils"), a bar-biturate normally used as a sedative. — Hunter S. Thompson, *Hell's Angels*, p. 216, 1966
- They walking in fours and kicking in doors; dropping Reds and busting heads. — Eldridge Cleaver, *Soul on Ice (letter dated August 15, 1965)*, p. 27, 1968
- What in the world ever became of sweet Jane / She lost her sparkle you know she isn't the same / Living on reds, vitamin C and cocaine — The Grateful Dead, *Trucking*, November 1970
- [R]eady to go pick him up from the Troubador and lie there next to him all night still in all my clothes, just to make sure nobody took many reds. — Eve Babitz, *L.A. Woman*, p. 142, 1982

2 morphine *US, 1945*

- They ordered cocaine or morphine by the pieces (ounces) and used the dope peddler's slang or code terms, red or blue identifying morphine or cocaine. — William J. Spillard and Pence James, *Needle in a Haystack*, p. 147, 1945

3 in a deck of playing cards, any heart or diamond *US, 1988*
A flush of hearts or diamonds is referred to as "all red."

- — George Percy, *The Language of Poker*, p. 74, 1988

4 in American casinos, a five-dollar betting chip *US, 1982*

- — Thomas F. Hughes, *Dealing Casino Blackjack*, p. 74, 1982

5 a penny *US, 1950*

- — Hyman E. Goldin et al., *Dictionary of American Underworld Lingo*, p. 176, 1950

red *adjective*
of a mixed (black and white) racial heritage *US, 1969*

- In between light negro america and Black negro america (in terms of color), there is a special category of people, who are assigned the name of red niggers. — H. Rap Brown, *Die Nigger Die!*, p. 7, 1969
- Yeah, she was a fine red motherfucker and if you think it was easy for me not to fuck this girl, you're dead wrong. — A.S. Jackson, *Gentleman Pimp*, p. 150, 1973

red and blue *noun*
a capsule of amobarbital sodium and secobarbital sodium (trade name Tuinal™), a combination of central nervous system depressants *US, 1969*

- — Norman W. Houser, *Drugs*, p. 13, 1969

red ass *noun*
anger *US, 1975*

- — *American Speech*, p. 64, Spring–Summer 1975: "Razorback slang"
- "They get the red-ass if they have to look at me too much." — Larry Brown, *Dirty Work*, p. 70, 1989

red-ass *verb*
to annoy or tease someone *US, 1994*

- — Michael Dalton Johnson, *Talking Trash with Redd Foxx*, p. 123, 1994

red-assed *adjective*
very angry *US, 1962*

- — *American Speech*, p. 271, December 1962: "the language of traffic policemen"
- — Helen Dahlskog (Editor), *A Dictionary of Contemporary and Colloquial Usage*, p. 48, 1972

red badge of courage *noun*
a notional badge awarded to someone who performs oral sex on a woman who is experiencing the bleed period of the menstrual cycle *US, 1994*

- — Michael Dalton Johnson, *Talking Trash with Redd Foxx*, p. 50, 1994

red bird *noun*
a capsule of secobarbital sodium (trade name Seconal™), a central nervous system depressant *US, 1953*

- [W]e have a pretty complete exhibit of the little pills downtown. Bluejays, redbirds, yellow jackets, goofballs, and all the rest of the list. — Raymond Chandler, *The Long Goodbye*, p. 230, 1953
- Well, let's see. I still got some redbirds and yellowjackets. — Emmett Grogan, *Final Score*, p. 81, 1976

red blanket *noun*
the corpse of a person who died with massive injuries *US, 1987*

- — *Maledicta*, p. 180, Summer/Winter 1987: "Sexual slang: prostitutes, pedophiles, flagellators, transvestites, and necrophiles"

red bread *noun*
payment for donating blood *US, 1971*

- — Eugene Landy, *The Underground Dictionary*, p. 35, 1971

red bullet *nickname*
a capsule of secobarbital sodium (trade name Seconal™), a central nervous system depressant *US, 1977*

- — Walter L. Way, *The Drug Scence*, p. 113, 1977

red cent *noun*
the lowest value denomination, hence the least amount possible *US, c. 1839*
A *copper* cent, thus "red."

- He bragged that he'd never give her "one red cent" and warned the merchants in town not to help her by giving her credit. — Mirian Harris, *Rape, Incest, Battery*, p. 131, 2000

red chicken *noun*
heroin, especially Chinese heroin *US, 1969*

- — Gilda and Melvin Berger, *Drug Abuse A-Z*, p. 114, 1990

red cunt hair *noun*
a very small unit of measure *US, 1968*
Sterling Johnson, in *English as a Second F*cking Language*, 1995, notes: "The term originated with the master carpenters of Cape Cod and is now universally used."

- — Carl Fleischhauer, *A Glossary of Army Slang*, p. 14, 1968
- It's a thin, red cunt hair away from the "oops" position, so I have a hard time with it. — Marc Animal MacYoung, *Fists, Wits, and a Wicked Right*, p. 25, 1991
- But my message is just a red cunt hair too complicated to be delivered by stiffs alone. — Penn Jillette, *Sock*, p. 114, 2004

red devil *noun*

1 a capsule of secobarbital sodium (trade name Seconal™), a central nervous system depressant *US, 1959*

- The next step up the scale is Seconal ("reds" or "red devils"), a barbiturate normally used as a sedative. — Hunter S. Thompson, *Hell's Angels*, p. 216, 1966
- [A] barbiturate, called Red Devils, so called because of the color of the capsule and because they are reputed to possess a vicious kick[.] — Eldridge Cleaver, *Soul on Ice*, p. 27, 1968
- Jack, you're lucky. I just remembered, my sick old man is got some red devils from a script [forged prescription] at his pad. — Iceberg Slim (Robert Beck), *Trick Baby*, p. 268, 1969
- He took red devils and thought he was big shit. — James Carr, *Bad*, p. 136, 1975

2 a woman's menstrual period *US, 1954*

- — *American Speech*, p. 298, December 1954: "The vernacular of menstruation"

red diaper baby *noun*
a person who was raised by Communist parents who instilled Communist beliefs and values *US, 1968*

- This thesis could be called the "red-diaper baby" hypothesis. — Kenneth Keniston, *Young Radicals*, p. 47, 1968
- They have developed the so-called "red diaper baby" theory to explain it. — Tom Wolfe, *Radical Chic & Mau-Mauing the Flak Catchers*, p. 38, 1970
- Radosh was what radicals call a "red-diaper baby." He grew up in a fellow-traveling household, went to communist-run summer camps, and during college was active with the Labor Youth League[.] — *Washington Post*, p. T8, 22nd July 2001
- I was a red-diaper baby. Born in 1947, the year the House Un-American Activities Committee unleashed its vengeance on the film industry, I learned secrecy at my mother's knee. — *New York Times*, p. 3–8, 8th July 2001

red dirt marijuana; red dirt *noun*
uncultivated marijuana *US, 1960*

- "That aint no ordinary loco-weed," said C.K., "...that there is red-dirt marijuana, that's what that is." — Terry Southern, *Red-Dirt Marijuana and Other Tastes*, 1967
- The two men were planning a trip to Texas to help Bill Burroughs, a friend of Allen's, harvest his crop of red-dirt marijuana. — Brenda Knight, *Women of the Beat Generation*, p. 61, 1996

red doll *noun*
a capsule of secobarbital sodium (trade name Seconal™), a central nervous system depressant *US, 1977*

- — Walter L. Way, *The Drug Scene*, p. 113, 1977

red dollars *noun*
US military scrip in Vietnam *US, 1965*

- — *Time*, p. 34, 10th December 1965
- — Carl Fleischhauer, *A Glossary of Army Slang*, p. 10, 1968

red dope *noun*
wild cannabis that has been sprayed with a bright red herbicide *US, 2001*

- The Oklahoma Bureau of Narcotics And Dangerous Drugs has issued a warning, advising people to stay away from "red dope." — *Mixmag*, p. 32, September 2001

red-eye *noun*

1 potent, impure homemade alcohol, especially whiskey *US, 1819*

- His animals needs are taken care of by a bowl of soup and as much red-eye as he can drink. — Jack Lait and Lee Mortimer, *Washington Confidential*, p. 33, 1951
- "I figure I might not be able to handle red-eye, so why take a chance?" — Sam Snead, *The Education of a Golfer*, p. 102, 1962

2 a long, aggressive stare *US, 1985*
- — Jennifer Blowdryer, *Modern English*, p. 37, 1985
- — Ann Lawson, *Kids & Gangs*, p. 56, 1994: "Common African-American gang slang/phrases"

3 fermented catsup *US, 1976*
A prison concoction.
- — John R. Armore and Joseph D. Wolfe, *Dictionary of Desperation*, p. 45, 1976

4 in pinball, an activated special scoring device, usually lit in red *US, 1977*
- — Bobbye Claire Natkin and Steve Kirk, *All About Pinball*, p. 115, 1977

5 a flashing red light on top of a police car *US, 1976*
- — Elementary Electronics, *Dictionary of CB Lingo*, p. 100, 1976

6 the anus *US, 1966*
- — Andy Anonymous, *A Basic Guide to Campusology*, p. 20, 1966
- — Collin Baker et al., *College Undergraduate Slang Study Conducted at Brown University*, p. 183, 1968
- Ben over and crack yo daddy some redeye, punk! — Seth Morgan, *Homeboy*, p. 179, 1990

red flag *noun*
1 an obvious indication that all is not well *US, 1968*
- Cap'n, the guard around that boxcar is a red flag. I don't understand why you officers don't recognize a red flag when you see one. — William B. Hopkins, *One Bugle No Drum*, p. 80, 1986

2 when injecting a drug into a vein, the practice of drawing blood up into the syringe to verify the finding of a vein and to control the pace of the injection *US, 1987*
- — Carsten Stroud, *Close Pursuit*, p. 275, 1987

red gunyon *noun*
smashed marijuana seeds or gum hashish smoked in a pipe *US, 1973*
- — David W. Maurer and Victor H. Vogel, *Narcotics and Narcotic Addiction*, p. 437, 1973

red head *noun*
a match *US, 1981*
- — *Maledicta*, pp. 266–267, Summer/Winter 1981: "By its slang, ye shall know it: the pessimism of prison life"

redheaded stepchild *noun*
a person or thing that is treated less favorably than others in its class *US, 1924*
- "In Norfolk, we were always stuck in the back like a red-headed stepchild." — *Virginian-Pilot*, 29th July 2006

red hot *noun*
a frankfurter *US, 1950*
- — Jack Lait and Lee Mortimer, *Chicago Confidential*, p. 302, 1950: "Loop lexicon"

red hot mamma *noun*
an attractive, sexual woman *US, 1924*
- "I look like Sophie Tucker. I'm not the last of the red-hot mammas, goddamit, I'm a vestal virgin in a temple!" — Marilyn Horne, *The Song Continues*, p. 218, 2004

redlegs *noun*
the artillery *US, 1900*
From the red stripes on the pants of Union artillerymen during the US Civil War.
- — Ronald J. Glasser, *365 Days*, p. 244, 1971
- "They got a red leg FO but I don't know what's he like." — William Pelfrey, *The Big V*, p. 59, 1972
- [T]oo close to get our fire support form the redlegs on Bastogne. — Gary Linderer, *The Eyes of the Eagle*, p. 48, 1991

red light *noun*
the bleed period of the menstrual cycle *US, 1954*
As in "red light—stop—there will be no sex."
- — *American Speech*, p. 298, December 1954: "The vernacular of menstruation"

red-light *adjective*
pertaining to prostitution *US, 1900*
- The District's "red-light" region may be the largest on earth. — Jack Lait and Lee Mortimer, *Washington Confidential*, p. 21, 1951

red lilly *noun*
a capsule of secobarbital sodium (trade name Seconal™); any central nervous system depressant *US, 1977*
From the color of the capsule and the name of the manufacturer.

- — Donald Wesson and David Smith, *Barbiturates*, p. 121, 1977
- — Stanley M. Aronson, *Providence (Rhode Island) Journal-Bulletin*, p. 6B, 4th August 1997: "Doctors must know the narcolexicon"

Red Mary *noun*
the bleed period of the menstrual cycle *US, 1980*
- — Edith A. Folb, *runnin' down some lines*, p. 251, 1980

redneck *noun*
a conservative, often bigoted, often ill-educated, white rural southerner *US, 1830*
- I'd have to drop everything and run to sell some redneck a dime's worth of nails or something. — William Faulkner, *The Sound And the Fury*, p. 263, 1954
- He was saying we are tired of all those young northern white kids coming down South with all their hang-ups and their guilt, bugging our redneck Mississippi. — Dick Gregory, *Write Me In!*, p. 38, 1968
- A redneck drives a Ford pickup. He has a gun rack behind his ears. — James Michener, *Texas*, p. 1132, 1987
- You might be a redneck if? Your mother has ever been involved in a fistfight at a high school event. — Jeff Foxworthy, *You Might Be A Redneck if...*, 2004

redneck radio *noun*
citizens' band radio *US, 1977*
- — Bill Davis, *Jawjacking*, p. 82, 1977

red nigger *noun*
a Native American Indian *US, 1998*
- In May 1997, the state says Cilley, 19, and Smith, 20, drove by the home of a Passamaquoddy family in Indian Township in Washington County, yelling "prairie nigger," "red nigger" and "Indian nigger[.]" — *Portland (Maine) Press Herald*, p. 6A, 15th March 1998

red one *noun*
in carnival usage, a profitable engagement *US, 1973*
- — Sherman Louis Sergel, *The Language of Show Biz*, p. 181, 1973
- — Gene Sorrows, *All About Carnivals*, p. 25, 1985: "Terminology"

red-out *noun*
a flood of the color red in your vision just before you pass out from lack of oxygen *US, 1990*
- It causes what is called "red out," a flood of red color in one's eyesight followed by a loss of consciousness. — Robert K. Wilcox, *Scream of Eagles*, p. 147, 1990

red pussy hair *noun*
a very short distance *US, 1987*
Slightly less offensive than **RED CUNT HAIR**.
- "That Benzo missed her ass by a red pussy hair." "Why red?" "Don't you know, it's the finest." — Robert Campbell, *Alice in La-La Land*, p. 11, 1987

Red Rider of Bloody Gulch *noun*
a man having sex with a woman experiencing her menstrual period *US, 1972*
- There are even Kotexes here and there—we had some Red Riders of Bloody Gulch. — Robert Byrne, *McGoorty*, p. 63, 1972

red river *noun*
the bleed period of a woman's menstrual cycle *US, 1954*
- — *American Speech*, p. 298, December 1954: "The vernacular of menstruation"

red rock *noun*
granulated heroin originating in China; heroin generally *US, 1969*
- — Gilda and Melvin Berger, *Drug Abuse A-Z*, p. 114, 1990

reds *noun*
a sense of anger *US, 1951*
- "It gives me the Reds" means it makes me angry. — *Newsweek*, 8th October 1951

red shirt *noun*
1 a troublemaker *US, 1967*
- "What's a red shirt?" "That's an old expression for troublemaker. If you fell out of line too many times they issued you a red shirt. Then whenever there was trouble on the yard the gun bulls had orders to shoot the cons in the red shirts first." — Malcolm Braly, *On the Yard*, p. 296, 1967

2 in roller derby, a skater who engages in rough, "bad guy" tactics *US, 1999*

- If the red-shirt team wins, the skaters on that team must run off the track after the final whistle, partly to make them look cowardly but also for safety reasons, especially if the crowd starts to queue menacingly toward the track. — Keith Coppage, *Roller Derby to Rollerjam*, p. 127, 1999

3 a professional wrestler who is regularly scripted to lose matches to advance the careers of other wrestlers *US, 1990*

- Sometimes known as fish, redshirts or PLs (professional losers). — *rec.sports.pro-wrestling*, 17th July 1990

redskin *noun*

in a deck of playing cards, any face card *US, 1967*
- — Albert H. Morehead, *The Complete Guide to Winning Poker*, p. 271, 1967

red snapper *noun*

in blackjack, a dealt hand of two red cards that add up to 21 *US, 1996*
- — Frank Scoblete, *Best Blackjack*, p. 272, 1996

red squad *noun*

a police unit that engages in systematic investigation and record keeping about leftist political and social action organizations unrelated to criminal conduct *US, 1970*
- The antisubversives unit of the Chicago Police Department—known popularly as the Red Squad—has become something of a legend on the shores of Lake Michigan. — J. Anthony Lukas, *The Barnyard Epithet and Other Obscenities*, p. 55, 1970
- In Chicago and Los Angeles and other big cities in the 1960s, police departments had Red Squads that were notorious for spying on leftwing political activists. — *The Progressive*, 14th March 2002

red tape *noun*

excessive formality; bureaucratic obstacles *UK, 1837*
Originally a literal term, referring to the red-colored tape used in securing legal documents; later used figuratively.
- You know what a stickler she is for procedure—"red-tape" I called it to her—I can tell you she was almost in tears. — Terry Southern, *Flash and Filigree*, p. 55, 1958
- It's a hard life down there so they learn to cut through the U.S. red tape. — Joseph Wambaugh, *Finnegan's Week*, p. 143, 1993

red wings *noun*

sexual intercourse or oral sex with a woman who is experiencing the bleed period of the menstrual cycle *US, 1967*
From motorcycle gang culture.
- He thought I was a pretty good one at scarfin' it too. I was going to get my red wings. — Frank Reynolds, *Freewheelin' Frank*, p. 7, 1967
- You got your Red Wings by eating a girl on her period and your Black Wings by eating a black girl. — Ralph "Sonny" Barger, *Hell's Angel*, p. 99, 2000

reeb *noun*

beer *UK, 1859*
Back slang.
- — David Powis, *The Signs of Crime*, 1977
- — Connie Eble (Editor), *UNC-CH Campus Slang*, p. 7, Fall 1997

reeds *noun*

long shorts, favored by surfers *US, 1985*
- — John Blair, *The Illustrated Discography of Surf Music 1961–1965*, p. 124, 1985

reef *noun*

a marijuana cigarette *US, 1958*
- I don't touch reefs that come out of the bargain basement. If they're good, then I'm hip — Morton Cooper, *High School Confidential*, p. 69, 1958

reefdogger *noun*

a marijuana cigarette *US, 1982*
- So like I hide these reefdoggers in a shoebox, like my mom finds them and she's tries to be real cas, right. — Mary Corey and Victoria Westermark, *Fer Shurr! How to be a Valley Girl*, 1982

reefer *noun*

1 a marijuana cigarette *US, 1931*
Almost certainly from the Spanish word meaning "to twist." Still used, with a nostalgic air to it.
- Later they smoked the reefers in Panama, and when World War II took them to bases in Ecuador, the hop habit they brought was the answer to a medicine man's prayers. — *Time*, pp. 40–41, 14th October 1946

- I lost ground so fast you'd think I was a juvenile delinquent trying her first reefer. — Philip Wylie, *Opus 21*, p. 287, 1949
- Shorty talked to me out of the corner of his mouth: which hustlers—standing around, or playing at this or that table—sold "reefers," or had just come out of prison, or were "second-story men." — Malcolm X and Alex Haley, *The Autobiography of Malcolm X*, p. 45, 1964
- They all take a drag on their reefers / And say prayers to St. Konky Mohair. — Dennis Wepman et al., *The Life*, p. 107, 1976

2 marijuana *US, 1931*
- It was like waiting for the accentuated heart beat of your heart when you're on a reefer jag[.] — Mezz Mezzrow, *Really the Blues*, p. 181, 1946
- Two other developments in the street—said to be normal consequences of its jazz madness—are the presence of reefer (marijuana) addicts and homosexuals, of all races. — Jack Lait and Lee Mortimer, *New York Confidential*, p. 45, 1948
- We could sell them for about three or four dollars and buy a bag of reefer. We'd roll up and get high and then go do something crazy... — Claude Brown, *Manchild in the Promised Land*, p. 130, 1965
- Man, someone's tokin' some reefer. — *Dazed and Confused*, 1993

reefer room *noun*

in a morgue, a refrigerated room where bodies are stored *US, 1997*
- She went past the reefer room where the bodies were frozen after the M.E. had opened them up. — Stephen J. Cannell, *King Con*, p. 62, 1997

reeker *noun*

a bad-smelling hospital casualty department patient *US, 1978*
- — *Journal of American Folklore*, pp. 568–581, January–March 1978: "The gomer"

reet; reat *adjective*

good, pleasing *US, 1934*
- "You're really reet," he said as he guided her closer to the curb where they could speak without obstructing the sidewalk. — Irving Shulman, *The Amboy Dukes*, p. 136, 1947
- [O]utdressing everyone on the block in the uniform of the period, pork-pie hat, satin shirt, peg pants, reat jacket. Zoot, man. — Clancy Sigal, *Going Away*, p. 462, 1961
- He leaped about in the building shouting, YEAH REET! — John Williams, *The Man Who Cried I Am*, p. 87, 1967

reggin *noun*

a black person *US, 1981*
The offensive **NIGGER** spelt backwards.
- — *Maledicta*, pp. 266–267, Summer/Winter 1981: "By its slang, ye shall know it: the pessimism of prison life"

regular *noun*

a prisoner who serves his sentence with dignity and strength *US, 1974*
- — Paul Glover, *Words from the House of the Dead*, 1974

regular *adjective*

kind; decent; honest *US, 1946*
- What a relief—here was a keeper who talked my language. I was ready to scrub that cell with my tongue for a guy as regular as that. — Mezz Mezzrow, *Really the Blues*, p. 306, 1946

rehab *noun*

rehabilitation (a medical regime for the cure of alcohol and drug addiction); also, the clinic or hospital environment where *rehabilitation* takes place *UK, 1961*
Both senses may serve concurrently.
- I don't see how in hell Phil's going to get her into rehab[.] — Jay McInerney, *Story of My Life*, p. 121, 1961
- "May we should book him into rehab." "I heard that, dude. That's a bummer idea. Those people in rehab are weird. They're like real downers. They're all, like, druggies." — Janet Evanovich, *Seven Up*, p. 72, 2001
- Vicodin first hit the news in the US when Friends star Matthew Perry's addiction saw him check in and out of rehab on an almost monthly basis. — *Drugs An Adult Guide*, p. 25, December 2001

rehash *verb*

in the circus or carnival, to resell ticket stubs to patrons and pocket the funds *US, 1980*
- — Joe McKennon, *Circus Lingo*, p. 77, 1980

rehitch *verb*

to reenlist; to remarry *US, 1953*

- Your correspondent is all fluttery at the news that Terry and Sulvia Lennox have rehitched at Las Vegas, the dears. — Raymond Chandler, *The Long Goodbye*, p. 13, 1953

reject *noun*

a socially inept person; a pathetic individual; a person who does not fit in with the fashionable, trendy majority *US, 1968*
- — Collin Baker et al., *College Undergraduate Slang Study Conducted at Brown University*, p. 183, 1968
- On their lonesomes they're not total rejects. — Kathy Lette, *Girls' Night Out*, p. 192, 1987

relate *verb*

to understand; to like or appreciate someone or something *US, 1959*

A quintessential, over-used vague verb of the 1960s.
- — Lawrence Lipton, *The Holy Barbarians*, p. 317, 1959
- A sister sent in a report that she got kicked out of the party because she refused to relate to a particular brother. — Bobby Seale, *A Lonely Rage*, p. 230, 1978

relay spot *noun*

a room with a telephone used to relay calls placing bets in a bookmaking operation *US, 1973*
- "Is it a relay spot? Are you sure?" asked Charlie. — Joseph Wambaugh, *The Blue Knight*, p. 56, 1973

release *noun*

in the coded language of massage parlors, ejaculation *US, 2002*
A 2002 Incident Report from the Sausalito (California) Police Department describes the activities at a local massage parlor as follows: "Every massage ends with some type of 'release' (orgasm). The release is accomplished by the employee masturbating the client to an orgasm."

relievers *noun*

shoes *US, 1962*
- — Joseph E. Ragen and Charles Finston, *Inside the World's Toughest Prison*, p. 815, 1962: "Penitentiary and underworld glossary"

relight *noun*

a cigarette butt retrieved and smoked *US, 1996*
- — John Fahs, *Cigarette Confidential*, p. 303, 1996: "Glossary"

religious issue *noun*

in computing, a topic that is bound to launch an endless debate which cannot be resolved *US, 1991*
- — Eric S. Raymond, *The New Hacker's Dictionary*, p. 303, 1991

Rembrandt *noun*

in poker, a hand of face cards *US, 1988*
- — George Percy, *The Language of Poker*, p. 74, 1988

remf *noun*

a solider assigned to a combat support role *US, 1982*
Acronym of a "rear-echelon *motherfucker.*"
- I been humpin ruck in those mountains while you been suckin' down whiskey at the NCO club. I know my shit. Man, and I do my job better'n any mother-fucking REMF. — John Del Vecchio, *The 13th Valley*, p. 25, 1982
- Hence those who never went to the front line, but stayed with the echelon were known as "Remfs" or Rear Echelon Mother Fuckers. — Robert McGowan and Jeremy Hands, *Don't Cry For Me Sergeant-Major*, p. 81, 1983
- You're talking like a VC. Jesus, the guy was just some hotdog REMF who wanted a reason to pop some caps somewhere beside the shooting range. — Jack Hawkins, *Chopper One #2*, p. 104, 1987
- He had gone over—become a REMF. As we wandered back toward the platoon tent, Martinez found his voice. "I'd like to have a nice safe job in the rear, but no way could I handle that sucking up business." — Robert Peterson, *Rites of Passage*, p. 473, 1997

Reno *noun*

in bar dice games, two dice that add up to seven *US, 1976*
- — Gil Jacobs, *The World's Best Dice Games*, p. 200, 1976

renob *noun*

a person who acts foolishly *US, 2001*
- — Don R. McCreary (Editor), *Dawg Speak*, 2001

rent *noun*

a youthful, attractive homosexual male prostitute *UK, 1967*
- — Bruce Rodgers, *The Queens' Vernacular*, p. 111, 1972

rent-a-cop *noun*

a private security guard *US, 1968*
A tad disparaging.
- — Collin Baker et al., *College Undergraduate Slang Study Conducted at Brown University*, p. 183, 1968
- While the sacrament was being ingested two rent-a-cops strolled onto the scene, surprising one brother with a joint in his hand. — John Sinclair, *Guitar Army*, p. 74, 1972
- Rialto started walking through the gate. A uniformed rent-a-cop asked him was he a guest. Rialto put out a folded ten. — Robert Campbell, *Alice in La-La Land*, pp. 134–135, 1987
- She had the rentacop half convinced she was looking for a job application in the narcotics box when the real heat arrived. — Seth Morgan, *Homeboy*, p. 181, 1990

rent party *noun*

a party thrown for the purpose of collecting donations from friends to pay your rent *US, 1925*
- They came and went from the apartment houses where the after-hours joints were jumping and the house-rent parties swimming, and the whores plying their trade and the gamblers clipping chumps. — Chester Himes, *A Rage in Harlem*, p. 130, 1957
- — Robert S. Gold, *A Jazz Lexicon*, p. 248, 1964
- I'm gonna play the piano at three rent parties next weekend. — Louise Meriwether, *Daddy Was a Number Runner*, p. 30, 1970
- Every Friday night Bob and Virginia had a rent party. You danced, you drank, and you brought money. — Larry Rivers, *What Did I Do?*, p. 126, 1992

rents *noun*

parents *US, 1968*
Teen slang that cuts parents down to size.
- — *Current Slang*, p. 11, Summer 1968
- — Connie Eble (Editor), *UNC-CH Campus Slang*, March 1973
- — *Concord (New Hampshire) Monitor*, p. 17, 23rd August 1983: "Slang slinging: an intense and awesome guide to prep school slanguage"

rent whore *noun*

an occasional prostitute who sells her services when cash is otherwise short *US, 1973*
- Next rung up on the prostitution ladder are rent whores, girls who turn a few tricks to buy clothes or pay the rent. — Gail Sheehy, *Hustling*, p. 37, 1973

reo *noun*

a difficult surfing maneuver on the breaking lip of a wave *US, 1988*
An abbreviation of "re-entry."
- — John Conway, *Surfing*, p. 121, 1988
- Barrel after barrel, reo after reo. I don't think I'll ever see another surfer shred that point at Avoca like Sanga did. — *Tracks*, p. 8, October 1992

rep *noun*

1 re*p*utation *US, 1705*
- "Two boys by the name of Charlie Max and Sugar Smallhouse." "They have reps." "So I hear." — Mickey Spillane, *Kiss Me Deadly*, p. 68, 1952
- A real Cool Cat is hep that he has a rep and has to get going if he plans on showing the chick the jive about loving and the turtle-doving. — Dan Burley, *Diggeth Thou?*, p. 5, 1959
- I'm gonna have to find me some strong cats to get tight with, cats with reps. — Claude Brown, *Manchild in the Promised Land*, p. 136, 1965
- I took a few guys out and my rep was made. — Edwin Torres, *Carlito's Way*, p. 21, 1975

2 a re*p*etition, or complete cycle of an exercise *US, 1984*
- — *American Speech*, p. 201, Fall 1984: "The language of bodybuilding"
- With me do the exercise for one rep, and then put the bar down correctly. — *Bodybuilding*, p. 42, 1996

repo *noun*

re*po*ssession *US, 1971*
- Slim, I been getting a little light weight bad break, so I figured out that angle to keep the repo bastards from copping [taking] my hog [Cadillac] when I ain't in it. — Iceberg Slim (Robert Beck), *The Naked Soul of Iceberg Slim*, p. 126, 1971
- And I profited; my desk was covered with repo orders, ranging in make and model[.] — James Ellroy, *Brown's Requiem*, p. 11, 1981

repo *verb*

to repossess *US, 1999*

- [T]he army of foot soldiers who marched up and down Wilshire Boulevard Bayless had sent to repo the tape by any means necessary[.] — John Ridley, *Everybody Smokes in Hell*, p. 100, 1999

repo depot *noun*
a replacement depot where soldiers arriving in combat are assigned to units and soldiers leaving combat are processed for homecoming *US*, *1968*
- — Carl Fleischhauer, *A Glossary of Army Slang*, p. 10, 1968
- I went to the Replacement Depot, the "repot-depot," and reported in as a wounded returnee[.] — Anthony Herbert, *Soldier*, p. 43, 1973
- Unfortunately, on my third day at the "Repo Depot," I found out that the 71st would be my new home. — Lynda Van Devanter, *Home Before Morning*, p. 85, 1983
- "In here buddy! I'll take you to your repo depot." — Stan Lee, *The 'Nam*, p. 11, 1987

repple-depple *noun*
a replacement depot where soldiers arriving in combat are assigned to units and soldiers leaving combat are processed for homecoming *US*, *1945*
- When a soldier gets out of an army hospital, he will most likely be thrown into a "repple depple." This institution, identified in army regulations as a replacement depot, is a sort of clearing house. — Bill Mauldin, *Up Front*, p. 125, 1945
- "I left my conscience at the repple depple." — Audie Murphy, *To Hell and Back*, p. 235, 1949
- "I don't know why the repple-depple types seemed to think that all a tank is good for is escorting convoys[.]" — Ralph Zumbro, *Tank Sergeant*, p. 2, 1986

represent *verb*
to serve as a pimp for a prostitute *US*, *1991*
- I been jumped out here, 'cause like I said my male was in the pen. I didn't have anybody representing me. — William T. Vollman, *Whores for Gloria*, p. 148, 1991

res *noun*
the oily residue in a pipe after crack cocaine has been smoked *US*, *1992*
- — Terry Williams, *Crackhouse*, p. 151, 1992

rest *verb*
▸ **rest your neck**
to stop talking *US*, *1989*
- Homeboy, rest your neck; I don't want to hear it! — James Harris, *A Convict's Dictionary*, p. 37, 1989

ret *noun*
a cigarette *US*, *1971*
- — *Current Slang*, p. 9, Winter 1971

retail therapy *noun*
shopping when considered as an empowering leisure activity *US*, *1986*
- We've become a nation measuring out our lives in shopping bags and nursing our psychic ills through retail therapy. — *Chicago Tribune*, p. C2, 24th December 1986
- [T]ogether we formulated the Law of Retail Therapy: the larger your size, the further from the city center a woman is forced to forage. — Elizabeth Buchan, *Revenge of the Middle-Aged Woman*, p. 9, 2002

retard *noun*
a slow, dim-witted person *US*, *1970*
From "mentally retarded," but not necessarily indicative of actual mental retardation.
- Like my retard little brother borrows my blow drier to like dry his model airplane, right, and so like I can't find it[.] — Mary Corey and Victoria Westermark, *Fer Shurr! How to be a Valley Girl*, 1982
- Everyone thinks I'm a retard. — *Empire Records*, 1995

retardo *noun*
a mentally challenged person *US*, *1981*
- For treating me like a slave! Like a retardo! — James Ellroy, *Brown's Requiem*, p. 190, 1981
- What are you thinking? Are you a retard-o, or what? — *Airheads*, 1994

retread *noun*
a recently divorced person *US*, *1985*
- — *American Speech*, p. 20, Spring 1985: "The language of singles bars"

retread *verb*
in the language surrounding the Grateful Dead, to tape over a tape that has been recorded once *US*, *1994*
- — David Shenk and Steve Silberman, *Skeleton Key*, p. 246, 1994

re-up *noun*
the replenishing of a stack of something; a resupply *US*, *1975*
- "It looks like a re-up," Telano said. — John Sepe, *Cop Team*, p. 64, 1975

re-up *verb*
to replenish a stack of something; to resupply something; to re-sign or reenlist *US*, *1906*
Originally a military slang term for re-enlisting.
- Harper just got out of the Air Force and they asked him if he wanted to re-up, as they call it. — Jim Bouton, *Ball Four*, p. 20, 1970
- I just might possible re-up and make a twenty-year career of it—but only if I made the rank of staff sergeant before my four-year tour ended. — Bobby Seale, *A Lonely Rage*, p. 107, 1978
- Then I re-upped for another tour. — *Apocalypse Now*, 1979
- "Splib," said Max, "thinks he's gonna re-up on my stuff when he gets the money he says he's owed him in the street." — Terry Williams, *The Cocaine Kids*, p. 38, 1989

rev *verb*
to leave, to go *US*, *1952*
- "Let's rev" means let's go, and the appropriate answer is "reet" (okay). — *Herald Press (St. Joseph, Missouri)*, p. 14, 23rd June 1952

revenoo; revenuer; revenooer *noun*
a federal law enforcement official *US*, *1962*
Used by those in the illegal production of alcohol.
- Mostly it was the revenooers against the moonshiners, and it was no joke. — Sam Snead, *The Education of a Golfer*, p. 34, 1962

reverse *adjective*
▸ **reverse gears**
to vomit *US*, *1989*
- — Pamela Munro, *U.C.L.A. Slang*, p. 71, 1989

reverse cowgirl *noun*
a sexual position in which the woman straddles the prone man, facing his feet *US*, *1991*
- There's a rough scheme before you start: oral, missionary, reverse cowgirl, doggy, then a pop. — Robert Stoller and I.S. Levine, *Coming Attractions*, p. 131, 1991
- Since many men's erections slant upward, doggy style and reverse cowgirl (when you're on top riding him while facing his feet) are ideal. — *Cosmopolitan*, p. 130, 1st January 2001
- When you're working, is there a sexual act or position you won't do? BRITTANY ANDREWS: Reverse cowgirl. I can't stand it. — *Playboy*, p. 132, 1st March 2002
- Angela Stone squirts three times while riding Billy Glide beautifully—catch those hips!—in reverse cowgirl. — Editors of Adult Video News, *The AVN Guide to the 500 Greatest Adult Films of All Time*, p. 11, 2005

Rexall ranger *noun*
someone who wears cowboy clothes but has never worked on a ranch *US*, *1970*
Rexall is a chain drugstore, giving a touch of specificity to the more common **DRUGSTORE COWBOY**.
- — *Current Slang*, p. 23, Spring 1970

rez *noun*
a Native American Indian reservation *US*, *1998*
- VELMA: Yeah, you're leaving the rez and going into a whole different country, cousin. — *Smoke Signals*, 1998

RF *verb*
to play a prank *US*, *1964*
An abbreviation of **RATFUCK**.
- — *American Speech*, p. 195, October 1965: "Notes on campus vocabulary, 1964"
- — *Current Slang*, p. 6, Summer 1967

RFB *noun*
room, food and beverage—the basic components of a complimentary pass at a casino or hotel *US*, *1996*
- — Frank Scoblete, *Best Blackjack*, p. 270, 1996

RG *noun*
in homosexual usage, a biological female *US*, *1971*

A fellow homosexual is a **GIRL**, while a woman is a "real girl," or RG.
- — Eugene Landy, *The Underground Dictionary*, p. 161, 1971

rhino *noun*
1 money *UK, 1688*
- — Joseph E. Ragen and Charles Finston, *Inside the World's Toughest Prison*, p. 815, 1962: "Penitentiary and underworld glossary"

2 a large and powerful wave *US, 1991*
- — Trevor Cralle, *The Surfin'ary*, p. 99, 1991

rhino chaser *noun*
a large surfboard made for big-wave conditions *US, 1987*
- — Mitch McKissick, *Surf Lingo*, 1987
- Here, you need a rhino chaser like this one to learn on. — *Point Break*, 1991

RHIP
rank has its privileges *US, 1968*
- — *Current Slang*, p. 8, Spring 1968

rhoids *noun*
hemmorhoids *US, 2000*
- Are these troublesome "rhoids possibly rectal cancer?" — Richard Meltzer, *A Whore Just Like the Rest*, p. 1, 2000

rhubarb *noun*
a fight; an uproar; a riot *US, 1943*
- "It was the only time in my life," remembered an anonymous chap who took part in the rhubarb, "that I was ever kicked in the head by a man spinning in the air above me." — Robert Sylvester, *No Cover Charge*, p. 254, 1956

rhythm *noun*
an amphetamine tablet *US, 1993*
- — Peter Johnson, *Dictionary of Street Alcohol and Drug Terms*, p. 159, 1993

rhythm method *noun*
a method of cheating while playing a slot machine by controlling the spins of the inner wheels *US, 1977*
Playing on the name of the least successful method of birth control.
- For some time players could beat the machines legitimately with what is called the "rhythm method." — Mario Puzo, *Inside Las Vegas*, p. 220, 1977

rib *noun*
1 a wife or girlfriend *UK, 1589*
From the Biblical creation tale, with Eve springing from Adam's rib.
- — *Current Slang*, p. 40, Fall 1968
- Two of 'em looked like apes, so I picked Walter's rib to sleep with. — A.S. Jackson, *Gentleman Pimp*, p. 32, 1973

2 Rohypnol™ (flunitrazepam), popularly known as the "date-rape drug" *US, 1995*
- On the street the drug has many nicknames; teenagers know it as rope, ribs, or roaches. — *Texas Monthly*, p. 88, September 1995

rib *verb*
1 to make fun of someone *US, 1930*
- Buck was also a close friend of Louis', and he would rib Zutty now and then about leaving Louis, so that put me on a complex even more. — Mezz Mezzrow, *Really the Blues*, p. 237, 1946
- He started to rib me, called me a square. — Iceberg Slim (Robert Beck), *Pimp*, p. 99, 1969

2 to insult someone in a semiformal quasi-friendly competition *US, 2000*
- There are many different terms for playing the dozens, including "bagging, capping, cracking, dissing, hiking, joning, ranking, ribbing, serving, signifying, slipping, sounding and snapping." — James Haskins, *The Story of Hip-Hop*, p. 54, 2000

rib artist *noun*
a person who teases constantly *US, 1972*
- He was a rib artist with a million irritating remarks. — Robert Byrne, *McGoorty*, p. 160, 1972

ribbon clerk *noun*
a poker player who withdraws from a hand at any sign of serious betting *US, 1988*
- — George Percy, *The Language of Poker*, p. 75, 1988

rib crib *noun*
a barbecued rib stand *US, 2004*

- I saw his pander poontang and cats cliqued up outside rib cribs.
- — James Ellroy, *Destination Morgue*, p. 327, 2004

Rican *noun*
a Puerto Rican *US, 1975*
- Somebody was always jumpin' off the roof too. Usually some Rican who couldn't cut it on the street. — Edwin Torres, *Carlito's Way*, p. 16, 1975
- The Rican said, "No way, Jose." — Mark Baker, *Cops*, pp. 67–68, 1985

rice-and-ring *verb*
to get married *US, 1947*
- He says, "How's about we rice an' ring it?" — Harry Haenigsen, *Jive's Like That*, 1947

rice-a-roni *noun*
in necrophile usage, a badly decomposed corpse *US, 1987*
A comparison to the branded soft-boiled rice product.
- — *Maledicta*, p. 180, Summer/Winter 1986–1987: "Sexual slang: prostitutes, pedophiles, flagellators, transvestites, and necrophiles"

rice eye *noun*
a Japanese person *US, 1982*
Hawaiian youth usage, especially in the taunt "No lie, rice eye."
- — Douglas Simonson, *Pidgin to da Max Hana Hou*, 1982

riceman *noun*
a Chinese person *US, 1945*
Offensive.
- — Lou Shelly, *Hepcats Jive Talk Dictionary*, p. 16, 1945

rice paddy Hattie *noun*
any rural Chinese prostitute *US, 1949*
- — *American Speech*, p. 31, February 1949: "A.V.G. Lingo"

rice queen *noun*
a gay man attracted to men of South Asian origin *US, 1972*
- — Bruce Rodgers, *The Queens' Vernacular*, p. 171, 1972
- A gay white male who dates Asian guys exclusively ("Rice Queen") should be differentiated IMMEDIATELY from gay white guys who date all kinds of men and who happen to date an Asian guy. — *group/soc.culture.asian.american*, 21st December 1992

ricer *noun*
a person from South Asia *US, 1980*
Offensive.
- — Edith A. Folb, *runnin' down some lines*, p. 251, 1980

rice rocket *noun*
a motorcycle or car made by a Japanese manufacturer *US, 1985*
- "I come cruisin' back from the store, some white-ass cocksuckas roll by in one of them jacked up rice-rockets." — Jess Mowry, *Six Out Seven*, p. 355, 1993
- You could push your rice rocket on Main Street, and it would be left alone. — *Orlando Sentinel Tribune*, p. A1, 28th February 1993
- The newest "rice rockets" can carry 140 horsepower to the rear wheel, and can easily do 180 miles per hour right out of the box. — Ralph "Sonny" Barger, *Hell's Angel*, p. 53, 2000

Richard *noun*
any police official, especially a detective *US, 1950*
An embellished **DICK**.
- — Hyman E. Goldin et al., *Dictionary of American Underworld Lingo*, p. 177, 1950

rich man's drug *noun*
cocaine *US, 1972*
- Cocaine is prestigious to use because it is so expensive; they call it the "rich man's drug." — Christina and Richard Milner, *Black Players*, p. 12, 1972

rickety-raw *adjective*
attractive, fashionable *US, 1987*
- — *Washington Post Magazine*, p. 11, 24th May 1987: "Say wha'?"

Ricky Racer *noun*
a fanatic mountain bike enthusiast who rarely if ever rides *US, 1997*
- — Vann Wesson, *Generation X Field Guide and Lexicon*, p. 142, 1997

ricky tick *adverb*
promptly, immediately *US, 1987*
Mock pidgin, used by US soldiers during the Vietnam war.
- Vanish, Joker, most ricky-tick, and take Rafterman with you. — *Full Metal Jacket*, 1987

- If the other enemy soldiers escaped, he would be back with reinforcements ricky-tick. — Larry Chambers, *Recondo*, p. 60, 1992

ricky-ticky; ricky-tick *adjective*

used of a jazz rhythm, old-fashioned, even, boring *US, 1952*

- [H]e had blown complex and minor in the midst of vulgar stomping swing bands, jitterbugs and ricky-ticky-too[.] — John Clellon Holmes, *The Horn*, p. 87, 1958
- [W]hat lifts Tiny Tim miles above the nostalgia, the rickey-tick[.] — Albert Goldman, *Freak Show*, p. 116, 1968
- That ole ricky-tick? That ain't even worth listen to. Ole ricky-tick like that. — Terry Southern, *Texas Summer*, p. 151, 1991

riddle *verb*

to contemplate, to ponder *US, 1963*

- The line reads "Does not everything depend on our interpretation of the silence around us?" Now you riddle this one, fans. — Frederick Kohner, *The Affairs of Gidget*, p. 35, 1963

riddle me this, Batman

answer this question *US, 1993*

From the *Batman* television series (1966–68) and one of its arch villains, The Riddler.

- Riddle me this, Batman. If you're all so much in love with each other, what the fuck are you doing here? — *True Romance*, 1993
- Well, riddle me this, Batman. How do you feel about the fact that you're never gonna see Mallory again? — *Natural Born Killers*, 1994

ride *noun*

1 a single dose of a drug *US, 1975*

- The policemen relieved the dealers of a total of forty-five decks of heroin—enough to provide "highs" for at least forty-five addicts at $5 a ride, or $225 all told. — John Sepe, *Cop Team*, p. 57, 1975

2 a companion, especially a companion who is a fellow gang member *US, 1981*

- — *Maledicta*, p. 265, Summer/Winter 1981: "By its slang, ye shall know it: the pessimism of prison life"

3 a criminal enterprise *US, 1995*

- You keep trying to lay this whole ride on Keaton. It wasn't like that. — *The Usual Suspects*, 1995

▸ **get a ride**

in circus and carnival usage, to receive unfavorable publicity *US, 1981*

- — Don Wilmeth, *The Language of American Popular Entertainment*, p. 110, 1981

ride *verb*

1 to have sex *US, 1994*

Usually from the female perspective.

- I tied him to the bed, then I rode him. He loved it! — Anka Radakovich, *The Wild Girls Club*, p. 5, 1994
- She probably got the hots so bad for those hunks she rode Al Dante like a horse for days after. — Rita Ciresi, *Pink Slip*, p. 50, 1999

2 (used of a lesbian) to straddle your prone partner, rubbing your genitals together *US, 1967*

- Riding is when one girl gets on top of another and their legs are criss-crossed and you just go up and down. — Ruth Allison, *Lesbianism*, p. 39, 1967

3 to engage in sycophantic flattery *US, 1988*

- — *Washington Post Magazine*, p. 17, 18th December 1988: "Say wha'?"

▸ **let it ride**

in gambling, to continue a bet from one play to another, increasing the bet with winnings *US, 1980*

- — Lee Solkey, *Dummy Up and Deal*, p. 118, 1980
- Let it all ride. — *Diner*, 1982

▸ **ride a beef**

to accept a charge for a crime that you did not commit *US, 1967*

- And he let you ride the beef? — Malcolm Braly, *On the Yard*, p. 292, 1967
- "No sense anybody else riding this beef," Harold said stubbornly. — Joseph Wambaugh, *The Choirboys*, p. 365, 1975
- Carol would never ride a beef for a man. — Gerald Petievich, *Money Men*, p. 35, 1981
- "If anybody gets caught for this, ride the beef, 'cause ain't no snitchin' here." — Sanyika Shakur, *Monster*, p. 10, 1993

▸ **ride a pony**

to cheat on a test in college or school *US, 1959*

- — *Time Magazine*, p. 46, 24th August 1959

▸ **ride bitch**

to sit in the middle of the front seat in a pickup truck, between the driver and another passenger *US, 1992*

- — Lewis Poteet, *Car & Motorcycle Slang*, pp. 164–165, 1992

▸ **ride dirty**

to drive under the influence of alcohol *US, 2001*

- — Don R. McCreary (Editor), *Dawg Speak*, 2001

▸ **ride ghost**

to drive at night without headlights *US, 1995*

- — Steven Daly and Nathaniel Wice, *alt.culture*, p. 120, 1995

▸ **ride old smokey**

to be executed by electrocution *US, 1950*

- — Hyman E. Goldin et al., *Dictionary of American Underworld Lingo*, p. 177, 1950

▸ **ride rubber**

to ride in a car *US, 1981*

- — Don Wilmeth, *The Language of American Popular Entertainment*, p. 222, 1981

▸ **ride shotgun**

1 to be prepared for any eventuality in business *US, 1974*

- — Robert Kirk Mueller, *Buzzwords*, p. 140, 1974

2 to oversee and control someone with a firm hand *US, 1972*

- 'Cause you did your time there and nobody wasn't constantly riding shotgun on you. — Bruce Jackson, *In the Life*, p. 122, 1972

▸ **ride the broom**

to threaten someone; to predict harm *US, 1990*

- — Charles Shafer, *Folk Speech in Texas Prisons*, p. 212, 1990
- — William K. Bentley and James M. Corbett, *Prison Slang*, p. 36, 1992

▸ **ride the circuit**

to move someone who has been arrested from stationhouse to stationhouse, making his timely release difficult *US, 1949*

- But we don't have to. We can ride the circuit with you. It might take days. — Raymond Chandler, *The Little Sister*, p. 174, 1949

▸ **ride the cotton pony; ride the cotton horse**

to experience the bleed period of the menstrual cycle *US, 1954*

This "cotton pony" is a "sanitary towel."

- — *American Speech*, p. 298, December 1954: "The vernacular of menstruation"
- Except for when she was riding the cotton pony—you know, menstruating[.] — Joey V., *Portrait of Joey*, p. 48, 1969
- — *Adult Video News*, p. 38, September 1995

▸ **ride the Hershey Highway**

to engage in anal sex *US, 1989*

- — Pamela Munro, *U.C.L.A. Slang*, p. 71, 1989
- The emphasis this time out is on stretched-out, gaping sphincters and long bouts of riding the Hershey highway with little if any plot to get in the way. — Eric Danville, *The Penthouse Erotic Video Guide*, p. 12, 2003

▸ **ride the lightning**

to be put to death by electrocution *US, 1935*

- ALL RIGHT, RUBY, YOU'RE GONNA RIDE THE LIGHTNING! — Lenny Bruce, *The Essential Lenny Bruce*, p. 206, 1967

▸ **ride the short bus**

to be mentally deficient *US, 1995*

From the literally short bus that special education students use in the US.

- Actually, I think our bass player, Frank [Cavanaugh], rode the short bus, but that was 'cause his mom drove it. — *Baltimore Sun*, p. 8, 28th September 1995

▸ **ride the showing**

to tour an area evaluating billboards for potential advertising use *US, 1980*

- — Walter Hurst and Donn Delson, *Delson's Dictionary of Radio & Record Industry Terms*, p. 95, 1980

▸ **ride the sick book**

to feign illness; to malinger *US, 1968*

- — Carl Fleischhauer, *A Glossary of Army Slang*, p. 10, 1968

▸ **ride the silver steed**

to participate in bismuth subcarbonate and neoarsphenamine therapy for syphilis *US, 1981*

- — *Maledicta*, p. 227, Summer/Winter 1981: "Sex and the single soldier"

▸ **ride the white horse**

to experience euphoria after using heroin *US, 1955*

- — *American Speech*, p. 88, May 1955: "Narcotic argot along the mexican border"

▶ **ride the wire**
to travel by trolley *US, 1970*

- We didn't trust cabbies, so we got on another trolley, and in one morning I rode the wire more than I had in five years. — Red Rudensky, *The Gonif*, p. 108, 1970

ride along *verb*
in poker, to remain in a game without betting because you have bet your entire bankroll on the hand *US, 1967*

- — Albert H. Morehead, *The Complete Guide to Winning Poker*, p. 271, 1967

ride boy *noun*
in carnival and circus usage, a person who assembles, operates, and disassemble amusement rides *US, 2005*

- Hanky Pank agents occupied the lowest rung, with little more than Ride Boys, the untouchables of carny society. — Peter Fenton, *Eyeing the Flash*, p. 123, 2005

ride man; ride jock; ride monkey *noun*
the operator of a carnival amusement ride *US, 1985*

- Most RIDE MEN make below standard wages, sleep in trucks, and seldom have facilities to bathe, but still hold a reputation for being a ladies man. — Gene Sorrows, *All About Carnivals*, p. 25, 1985

rider *noun*

1 a visible, aggressive member of a gang *US, 2001*

- I heard legends about one or two female gangbangers who were said to be "riders," an expression of respect used to describe fiercely active gang members. — *Rolling Stone*, p. 80, 12th April 2001
- "Doesn't make him a rider. Or above the law." — Colton Simpson, *Inside the Crips*, p. 228, 2005

2 a police officer *US, 2003*

- Riders was the latest street slang for police, akin to "Po-Po" and "Five-O," according to Vallimont and Miller. — *Alameda (California) Times-Star*, 12th January 2003

3 a cheater *US, 1959*
From the phrase **RIDE A PONY** (to cheat on a test).

- — *Time Magazine*, p. 46, 24 August 1959

ridge runner *noun*
any white male from the Appalachian Mountain region in the southern US *US, 1933*

- "One of these ridge runners is gonna say something to me and I'm gonna knock the top of his head off." — James Carr, *Bad*, p. 185, 1975
- — *Maledicta*, p. 125, Summer 1980: "Racial and ethnic slurs: regional awareness and variations"

ridiculous *adjective*
excellent *US, 1959*

- — Robert S. Gold, *A Jazz Lexicon*, p. 251, 1964

riding DA *noun*
the prosecutor assigned to a particular precinct *US, 1995*

- The Assistant District Attorney assigned to a particular precinct. — Samuel Katz, *NYPD*, 1995

riding Saint George; the dragon on Saint George *noun*
heterosexual sex with the woman straddling the man, her head upright *US, 1980*

- — *Maledicta*, p. 198, Winter 1980: "A new erotic vocabulary"

riff *noun*

1 a rhythmic musical phrase played repeatedly, used in jazz and rock *US, 1935*
Probably an abbreviation of "refrain."

- Do you know how he spent years watching the droopy chicks in cathouses, listening to his cellmates moaning low behind the bars, digging the riffs the wheels were knocking out when he rode the rods[.] — Mezz Mezzrow, *Really the Blues*, p. 5, 1946
- The arrangement Ernie Wilkins put behind him for Basie was so great, I used to tell Ernie to copyright his background riffs. — Babs Gonzales, *Movin' On Down De Line*, p. 64, 1975
- I know! I'll use the "may I help you" riff. — *Wayne's World*, 1992

2 a verbal embellishment that adds no meaning to what is being said *US, 1967*

- — Ruth Bronsteen, *The Hippy's Handbook*, p. 15, 1967

3 an activity or experience *US, 1952*

- "I've found a new riff." "What is it?" "Bicycling." — Chandler Brossard, *Who Walks in Darkness*, p. 103, 1952
- [H]e wasn't sure that she and Zack were not going through a sadomasochistic riff for the sake of the camera. — Ed Sanders, *Tales of Beatnik Glory*, p. 208, 1975

riff *verb*

1 to talk in a fast, persuasive way *US, 2005*

- "And most of all, Joe College," Jimmy said loudly, ignoring Cat, "you'll need to learn how to riff like me." — Peter Fenton, *Eyeing the Flash*, p. 191, 2005

2 to brag; to lie *US, 1990*

- Some of the same empty yang you riffin' to me? — *New Jack City*, 1990

3 to complain *US, 1989*

- — Ellen C. Bellone (Editor), *Dictionary of Slang*, p. 20, 1989

riffle *noun*
in a restaurant or soda fountain, to refill (an order) *US, 1967*

- — *American Speech*, p. 63, February 1967: "Soda-fountain, restaurant and tavern calls"

riff on *verb*
to tease someone; to disparage someone or something *US, 1995*

- — Maria Hinojas, *Crews*, p. 167, 1995: "Glossary"

riff-raff *noun*
the lowest class *UK, 1470*

- One is for general riffraff; the second is for old-timers; the third is exclusively for sailors. — Jack Lait and Lee Mortimer, *Washington Confidential*, p. 30, 1951
- Mr. Caraballo, the owner, don't cater to no riff-raff. — Edwin Torres, *Carlito's Way*, p. 117, 1975

rifle range *noun*
the ward in a hospital reserved for patients withdrawing from heroin addiction *US, 1973*
A pun on **SHOOTING GALLERY**.

- — David Maurer and Victor Vogel, *Narcotics and Narcotic Addiction*, p. 438, 1973

rifle spot *noun*
in the television and movie industries, a spotlight that produces a long, thin beam of light *US, 1990*

- — Ralph S. Singleton, *Filmmaker's Dictionary*, p. 141, 1990

rig *noun*

1 a car, truck or bus *US, 1938*

- And what a driver—a great big tough truckdriver with popping eyes and a hoarse raspy voice who just slammed and kicked at everything and got his rig under way and paid hardly any attention to me. — Jack Kerouac, *On the Road*, p. 16, 1957
- Well, we don't want to take any chances of missing our young friend, or allowing him to see you climb out of this rig. — Donald Goines, *El Dorado Red*, p. 171, 1974

2 a hypodermic needle and syringe *US, 1969*

- "Sweets for my sweet," Rooski softly crooned withdrawing the spent rig. — Seth Morgan, *Homeboy*, p. 64, 1990
- — Peter Johnson, *Dictionary of Street Alcohol and Drug Terms*, p. 160, 1993

3 a still used in the illegal production of alcohol *US, 1974*

- — David W. Maurer, *Kentucky Moonshine*, p. 123, 1974

4 a holster *US, 2001*

- It is a proven LAPD street-cop axiom that any officer in plain clothes who wears a shoulder rig is, by definition, an asshole. — Stephen J. Cannell, *The Tin Collectors*, p. 104, 2001

5 the penis *US, 1964*

- "In fact, I believe the reason we couldn't get his rig out [of the plaster cast] was that it wouldn't GET SOFT." — *Screw*, p. 15, 5th July 1971

6 a bad situation *US, 1997*

- — *Maybeck High School Yearbook (Berkeley, California)*, p. 28, 1997

right *noun*
in craps, a bet for the shooter *US, 1974*

- At the dice table, the professor would bet either on or against the shooter—otherwise known as do or don't, right or wrong—at $1,000 a shot on what may or may not have been a system. — Edward Lin, *Big Julie of Vegas*, p. 47, 1974

right *adjective*
understanding and accepting the mores of the underworld *US, 1950*

- — Hyman E. Goldin et al., *Dictionary of American Underworld Lingo*, p. 177, 1950

righteous *adjective*

1 very good, excellent, fine; honest; satisfactory *US, 1942*
Conventional English with a religious overtone propelled into hip slang by context and emphasis in pronunciation.

- In the late summer of 1924 I got the band together and we headed for the Martinique Inn at Indiana Harbor, righteous and ready. — Mezz Mezzrow, *Really the Blues*, p. 70, 1946
- That from all these ace-stamped studs we double our love kick to that righteous ride for which they cats hard-sounded the last nth bong of the bell of their bell. — William "Lord" Buckley, *The Gettysburg Address*, 1951
- Owsley makes righteous acid, said the heads. — Tom Wolfe, *The Electric Kool-Aid Acid Test*, p. 188, 1968
- No offense, but it sounds to me like Cincinnati ain't no healthy place for a righteous dude to be in. — Gurney Norman, *Divine Right's Trip (Last Whole Earth Catalog)*, p. 193, 1971

2 used of a drug, relatively pure and undiluted *US*, 1967

- I hear it's a very good scene there. Not much heat, beautiful people, no speed freaks, and righteous dope. — Nicholas Von Hoffman, *We Are The People Our Parents Warned Us Against*, p. 47, 1967
- In the earlier part of 1967 there was a whole lot of righteous weed and even more righteous acid floating around the rainbow colony[.] — John Sinclair, *Guitar Army*, p. 286, 1972
- Some, uh, really righteous grass. — George V. Higgins, *Penance for Jerry Kennedy*, p. 228, 1985

righteous name *noun*
a person's true name *US*, 1975

- I never gave a snitch's righteous name since I been on the job. — Joseph Wambaugh, *The Choirboys*, p. 302, 1975

righteous nod *noun*
a refreshing sleep *US*, 1947

- — Marcus Hanna Boulware, *Jive and Slang of Students in Negro Colleges*, 1947

right guy *noun*
a dependable, trustworthy, and reliable criminal *US*, 1964

- — R. Frederick West, *God's Gambler*, p. 228, 1964: "Appendix A"

rightie *noun*
in craps, a gambler who bets that the shooter will make his point before rolling a seven *US*, 1974

- — John Scarne, *Scarne on Dice*, p. 477, 1974

right numbers; right price *noun*
in horseracing, higher than normal odds that merit a wager *US*, 1968

- — Thomas L. Clark, *The Dictionary of Gambling and Gaming*, p. 181, 1987

right on *adjective*
excellent, correct *US*, 1968
Often used as an exclamation of strong agreement.

- The people dig it and they said, "Right on." — Bobby Seale, *Seize the Time*, p. 139, 1970
- RAINBOW POWER! ANN ARBOR POWER! Right on! — John Sinclair, *Guitar Army*, p. 302, 1972
- "I have some acid." "Good. Right on." — Doug Lang, *Freaks*, p. 64, 1973
- In fact, nobody had even propositioned her, except for Harvey's friend Jerry from the car pool, who had bad breath, still said "Right on," and had phoned her one night to ask her bluntly if she was "hot to trot." — Cyra McFadden, *The Serial*, p. 39, 1977

righty *noun*
someone who looks very much like someone else; a double or near double *US*, 1962

- — Joseph E. Ragen and Charles Finston, *Inside the World's Toughest Prison*, p. 815, 1962: "Penitentiary and underworld glossary"

rigid *adjective*
drunk *US*, 1972

- — Helen Dahlskog (Editor), *A Dictionary of Contemporary and Colloquial Usage*, p. 48, 1972

rigmarole *noun*
a string of incoherent statements; a disjointed or rambling speech; a trival or almost senseless harangue *UK*, 1736

- In crude code it said, "Bad Landry rigmarole.' — Iceberg Slim (Robert Beck), *Trick Baby*, p. 56, 1969

RIH
rest in hell *US*, 1999
A bitter version of RIP (rest in peace).

- All the photos had R.I.H. scribbled on with a felt-tip pen. Rest in Hell. — Elmore Leonard, *Be Cool*, p. 30, 1999

rim *noun*
the anus *US*, 1997

- "Then ... first, that delicious trembling as the head presses against your rim." — Ethan Morden, *Some Men Are Lookers*, p. 64, 1997

▸ **above the rim**
of the highest quality *US*, 2002

- — Alonzo Westbrook, *Hip Hoptionary*, p. 1, 2002

rim *verb*
to lick, suck, and tongue another's anus *US*, 1941

- "Darling, I want to rim you," she whispers. — William Burroughs, *Naked Lunch*, p. 90, 1957
- Finally, the third man advances to the side of Johnny, licking his chest as the first one did earlier, tongue flitting over his nipples now, then along his back, down, rimming him[.] — John Rechy, *Numbers*, p. 181, 1967
- This manipulation of the hungry mouth upon a tender asshole is more commonly known among sexual gourmets as rimming, sometimes pronounced reaming by the lowborn[.] — *Screw*, p. 10, 19th January 1970
- He rimmed me; I rimmed him. — John Preston, *Hustling*, p. 20, 1994

rim-jag *verb*
to make an indentation on a playing card with your fingernail or thumbnail to identify the card later in another player's hand *US*, 1988

- — George Percy, *The Language of Poker*, p. 75, 1988

rim job *noun*
the licking of a partner's anus for the purposes of sexual pleasure *US*, 1969

- Thrills shot from one end of Annette's body to the other, as his tongue ran circles around her behind, giving her a rim job. — Steve Cannon, *Groove, Bang, and Jive Around*, p. 8, 1969
- "It was the most spectacular rim job since Scheherazade." — Ethan Morden, *I've a Feeling We're Not in Kansas Anymore*, p. 7, 1985
- KYLE'S MOTHER: What was that word, young man? CARTMAN'S MOTHER: Oh, he said rim job. It's when someone licks your ass. — *South Park*, 1999

rim queen *noun*
a male homosexual who is proficient at mouth-to-anus stimulation *US*, 1970

- — *American Speech*, p. 58, Spring–Summer 1970: "Homosexual slang"

Rinehart!; Oh Rinehart!
used as a shout to announce the onset of a student disturbance, started in fun but not always ending as such *US*, 1933
Specific to Harvard University, honoring John Rinehart, Harvard Law School class of 1903.

- In 1900 a new cry, "Oh Rinehart!" first sounded through Harvard Yard and in the following years became the high-explosive summons for book-disgruntled students. — *American Speech*, p. 293, December 1958

ring *noun*
a telephone call *UK*, 1900

- Give me a ring in a couple of hours. I'll be at the office. — Mickey Spillane, *My Gun is Quick*, p. 100, 1950

▸ **get a ring in your nose**
in horseracing, to lose all your money betting *US*, 1951

- — David W. Maurer, *Argot of the Racetrack*, p. 31, 1951

ring *verb*
to open and pilfer a cash register *US*, 1965

- Butch had warned me many times to never ring a cash register when there was nobody around to keep the person on the counter busy. — Claude Brown, *Manchild in the Promised Land*, p. 31, 1965

▸ **ring the bell**
to achieve success beyond expectations *US*, 1950

- — Hyman E. Goldin et al., *Dictionary of American Underworld Lingo*, p. 179, 1950

▸ **ring your chimes**
to strike someone on the head with great force *US*, 1981

- If their wives weren't coming down after them it'd be the cops or some sonofabitch wanted to ring their chimes for them. — George V. Higgins, *The Rat on Fire*, p. 102, 1981

ring-a-ding *noun*
1 an excellent example of something *US*, 1965

- In the patois of the Rat Pack, a ring a ding of a scene. — Sidney Bernard, *This Way to the Apocalypse*, p. 153, 1965

2 an eccentric or oddball *US, 1974*

- "Jesus, what a ring-a-ding," said the manager, shaking his head. — Anne Steinhardt, *Thunder La Boom*, p. 62, 1974

ring-a-ling on the ting-a-ling *noun*
a telephone call *US, 1968*

- — Hy Lit, *Hy Lit's Unbelievable Dictionary of Hip Words for Groovy People*, p. 33, 1968
- "I did a ring-a-ling on the ding-a-ling after the old man said he would go a property bond." — James Lee Burke, *The Lost Get-Back Boogie*, p. 189, 1986

ring angel *noun*
a "blip" on a radar screen, often a flock of birds *US, 1947*

- All unidentified dots [on the radar screen] were originally dubbed "angels" by the radar men [...] Dots in circles that move outward like ripples on a pond are known as "ring-angels." — Jeffrey Boswell (Editor), *Private Lives*, 1970

ring-by-spring
the desire of a female college student to be married by the end of college or the end of a college year *US, 1977*

- We work on a university campus and have discovered a disturbing syndrome afflicting a good portion of every senior class. We call it "ring-by-spring" syndrome. — Les Parrott, *Saving Your Second Marriage Before It Starts*, p. 25, 2001
- It's a classic "ring by spring" school, where students quickly pair off and engagement announcements are commonplace. — *Texas Monthly*, p. 38, 2004

ringer *noun*
1 a perfect resemblance *US, 1891*
Often intensified with **DEAD**.

- Around 10,000 people—wearing rear-vented Brooks Brothers flannels instead of flashy pinstripes, operating out of the suites in Radio City and the Squibb Building instead of drug-store phone booth, but all of them, in essence, dead ringers for Mort Robel. — Bernard Wolfe, *The Late Risers*, p. 38, 1954

2 an athlete or horse fraudulently entered in a game or race *US, 1890*

- We can balance that by getting ourselves a ringer. — *M*A*S*H*, 1970
- Impressed with Alf's story and his overwhelming confidence, Sam passed the word to Davis that he should pull Three Gulls and back the "ringer." — Joe Andersen, *Winners Can Laugh*, p. 173, 1982
- [O]n the day after the race he was put down, but it transpired that this was destroying the evidence in another ringer case. — John McCririck, *John McCririck's World of Betting*, p. 141, 1991

3 a false vehicle registration license plate *US, 1956*

- Blackie backed the car deftly into the barn and fixed the "ringers[.]" — Charles Raven, *Underworld Nights*, p. 17, 1956

4 a single inhalation of crack cocaine with a strong effect *US, 1994*

- — US Department of Justice, *Street Terms*, October 1994

ring game *noun*
a game of poker with all seats at the table occupied *US, 1982*

- — David M. Hayano, *Poker Faces*, p. 187, 1982

ring in *verb*
to secretly introduce altered dice into a dice game *US, 1950*

- — *The Annals of the American Academy of Political and Social Sciences*, p. 130, May 1950

ring-knocker *noun*
a graduate of one of the US military academies *US, 1984*
From the school rings worn by graduates.

- "I'm just an OCS kind of lieutenant, not a ring-knocker, and I guess I had to see for myself." — Cherokee Paul McDonald, *Into the Green*, p. 38, 2001

ring-tailed snorter *noun*
a braggart and brawler *US, 1950*

- An outlandish person or thing, often as a "ring-tailed snorter." — Paul Green, *A Paul Green Reader*, p. 284, 1998

ringy *adjective*
irritable *US, 1932*

- What do you want that goddamn speed for? You know how ringy it makes you. It turns you into a different person, Bob, and I don't much like that person. — *Drugstore Cowboy*, 1988

rink rat *noun*
a young boy who hangs around ice rinks, totally involved in hockey *US, 1945*

- — Lou Shelly, *Hepcats Jive Talk Dictionary*, p. 31, 1945
- — Dobie Gillis, *Teenage Slanguage Dictionary*, 1962

rinky-dink *noun*
something that is second rate, cheap, or trivial *US, 1912*

- I had to cook my ass on them stone bleachers, with a Spike Jones band playin' rinky-dink behind me. — Edwin Torres, *After Hours*, p. 197, 1979
- Robbie was smiling sincerely now. It was a con, he was positive. These rinky-dinks were giving him the grim-cop number, Hurd, playing stone-face, and he was supposed to what, break down? — Elmore Leonard, *Split Images*, p. 278, 1981

rinky-dink *adjective*
inexpensive; poorly made; worthless *US, 1912*

- My struggle-buggy was getting to look like a rinky-dinky old tin can on wheels[.] — Mezz Mezzrow, *Really the Blues*, p. 87, 1946
- — Carol Covington, *A Glossary of Teenage Terms*, 1965
- "He was a rinky-dink dope dealer most," Boone continued. — Vernon E. Smith, *The Jones Men*, p. 124, 1974
- Not like those rinkydink toys sold in S&M shops. — Seth Morgan, *Homeboy*, p. 67, 1990

rinsebag *noun*
a plastic bag that once contained amphetamine *US, 1989*

- A trace amount of speed remains in the bag; the contents of several of these rinsebags may be combined, in the same manner as cottons, to produce enough drug to achieve a high. — Geoffrey Froner, *Digging for Diamonds*, p. 51, 1989

riot *noun*
something or someone that is very amusing or greatly funny *UK, 1933*

- — Miss Cone, *The Slang Dictionary (Hawthorne High School)*, 1965
- — Billy Bragg, *Life's a Riot with Spy Vs Spy*, 1983

Riot Hyatt; Riot House *nickname*
the Continental Hyatt House, Sunset Boulevard, Los Angeles, famous for its association with rock musicians *US, 1989*

- You just missed Russell! He says he's at the "Riot House" all week and to call him. — *Almost Famous*, 2000

riot panic *noun*
in circus and carnival usage, enthusiastic applause *US, 1981*

- — Don Wilmeth, *The Language of American Popular Entertainment*, p. 224, 1981

rip *noun*
1 a swindle, deception, or theft *US, 1989*
An abbreviation of **RIP-OFF**.

- "Not long afterwards a Purolator truck gets hit, but the robbers turn up dead three days later—without the loot. Classic mob rip." — Carl Hiaasen, *Skin Tight*, p. 21, 1989

2 a robbery *US, 2007*

- "Clanton lived right there. In our eyes, there was no way he was going to do a rip," Kelly says. — *Newsday (New York)*, p. A2, 26th March 2007

3 a current traveling seawards from shore, usually moving swiftly *US, 1990*
An abbreviation of "rip tide" or "rip current."

- He bitched about missing some rad tubes and said that old dorks shouldn't be anywhere near a rip, even a baby rip. — Joseph Wambaugh, *The Golden Orange*, p. 33, 1990

4 a method of breaking into a safe that employs mechanical force and no explosives *US, 1950*

- — Hyman E. Goldin et al., *Dictionary of American Underworld Lingo*, p. 179, 1950

5 in a cheating scheme in a dice game, the switching of tampered dice into a game *US, 1962*

- — Frank Garcia, *Marked Cards and Loaded Dice*, p. 263, 1962

6 a complaint lodged against a police officer *US, 1970*

- — *New York Times*, 15th February 1970

7 a fine or punishment imposed for breaking a police department conduct rule *US, 1958*

- I got a five-day rip (fined five days' pay). — *New York Times Magazine*, p. 88, 16th March 1958

rip *verb*
1 to cheat or swindle someone *US, 1904*

- "How much did you pay for this man?" I asked her. "Sixty-five." I pressed my lips together. "You got ripped." — Rita Ciresi, *Pink Slip*, p. 18, 1999

2 to steal something *US, 1984*

- Most cars you rip are worth two or three hundred dollars. — *Repo Man*, 1984

3 to kill someone *US, 1974*

- He probably had him ripped anyway. — Vernon E. Smith, *The Jones Men*, p. 5, 1974

4 to surf in a bold, skilled manner *US, 1988*

- — Brian and Margaret Lowdon, *Competitive Surfing*, 1988

5 to excel *US, 1994*

- CHAZZ: You like that Seattle bullshit? CALLER 1: Shroud rips, dude. — *Airheads*, 1994
- "You fully rip," Duck said. — Francesca Lia Block, *Baby Be-Bop*, p. 471, 1995

▸ **rip a new asshole**
to berate someone severely *US, 1980*

- "If I hear that you have anything more to do on this hand thing, Slaight, I'll rip you a new aswshole." — Lucian Truscott, *Dress Gray*, p. 340, 1980
- She would have some beef with me, real or imagined, and she'd rip me a new asshole or give me the silent treatment. — Howard Stern, *Miss America*, p. 168, 1995

▸ **rip off a piece (of ass)**
to have sex *US, 1971*

- "Nice piece of ass," the man said. "You ripping off some of that?" — George V. Higgins, *The Friends of Eddie Coyle*, p. 149, 1971

ripe *adjective*
1 bad-smelling *US, 1995*

- Go on in the bathroom and clean yourself up. Man, you smell ripe. — Elmore Leonard, *Riding the Rap*, p. 183, 1995

2 used of a girl, over the legal age of consent *US, 1988*

- — Michael V. Anderson, *The Bad, Rad, Not to Forget Way Cool Beach and Surf Dictionary*, p. 16, 1988

3 in the language surrounding the Grateful Dead, poised for enlightenment in the mysteries of the band *US, 1994*

- — David Shenk and Steve Silberman, *Skeleton Key*, p. 249, 1994

rip job *noun*
a safe robbery in which the front of the safe is peeled off *US, 1973*

- In the rip job you drill a hole in the corner of the safe. Then you peel the front of the door off with a big sectional jimmy or crowbar. — Leonard Shecter and William Phillips, *On the Pad*, p. 179, 1973

rip-off *noun*
1 a copy; an imitation *US, 1970*

- Ignorant people were still writing them [the Count Five] off as nothing more than a Yardbirds rip-off[.] — Lester Bangs, *Psychotic Reactions and Carburetor Dung*, p. 15, 1971

2 a robbery; a theft; a swindle; exploitation *US, 1970*

- "It's a rip-off!" Johnny whispered to Buddy. — Donald Goines, *Inner City Hoodlum*, p. 102, 1975

rip off *verb*
1 to steal something *US, 1967*
If the speaker is doing the stealing, the term suggests an act of political heroism; if not, it suggests corporate greed. The subject of this verb can be either the goods stolen, the location, or the owner; the subject can split the verb without changing the sense.

- Too bad in a way cause most of us used to rip off the Lion Supermarket when we had to eat and had no dough. — Abbie Hoffman, *Woodstock Nation*, p. 21, 1969
- I let her talk me into ripping off a few amphetamines for her. — Beatrice Sparks (writing as "Anonymous"), *Jay's Journal*, p. 25, 1979
- The hangers on, the rip-off artists, that is. — *Drugstore Cowboy*, 1988
- I'm just explaining to you what I'm doing here. Case you think I come to rob the place, rip off any of this dusty old shit the man has. — *Get Shorty*, 1995

2 to rape someone *US, 1967*

- Ray was ripping off the blond chick and I could hear screams from the bedroom as someone else ripped off the one I had ripped off first. — Frank Reynolds, *Freewheelin' Frank*, p. 120, 1967
- — Inez Cardozo-Freeman, *The Joint*, p. 526, 1984

rip-off *adjective*
exploitative; cheating *US, 1995*

- That "Dating Game" rip-off thing? Jesus, that guy knows no shame. — *Mallrats*, 1995

ripped *adjective*
1 drunk or drug-intoxicated *US, 1969*

- She assumed that she must have been stoned. Ripped. Just out of it. — Steve Cannon, *Groove, Bang, and Jive Around*, p. 109, 1969
- I was shocked. I was also ripped out of my mind. The word on this dope was no exaggeration. — Jim Carroll, *Forced Entries*, p. 48, 1987
- Now I'm gonna head over to Atlantic, drink some beers, get ripped, and—please God—get laid. — *Clerks*, 1994
- I was getting [Jack] Nicholson loaded ... [he laughs]... really good pot ... he was really ripped. — Peter Fonda, *Shaking The Cage*, 1999

2 muscular; lacking body fat; well sculpted *US, 1984*

- — *American Speech*, p. 201, Fall 1984: "The Language of Bodybuilding"
- He wasn't ripped, but he was pumped. — John Ridley, *Everybody Smokes in Hell*, p. 182, 1999
- "My body was shredded down, cut as they call it and I was totally ripped." — Robert Picarello, *Rules of the Ring*, p. 139, 2000
- Dark tan. Ripped stomach. — Missy Hyatt, *Missy Hyatt*, p. 111, 2001

ripper *noun*
1 an amphetamine or other central nervous system stimulant *US, 1984*

- — Sacramento Municipal Utility District, *Glossary of Drugs / Drug Language*, 1986
- — Gilda and Melvin Berger, *Drug Abuse A-Z*, p. 115, 1990

2 a skilled skateboarder *US, 1949*

- — *San Francisco Sunday Examiner & Chronicle*, p. 20, 2nd September 1984: "Say It Right"
- — *Macon Telegraph and News*, p. 9A, 18th June 1989

3 in pinball, a ball that is forcefully hit into play *US, 1977*

- — Bobbye Claire Natkin and Steve Kirk, *All About Pinball*, p. 115, 1977

ripping *adjective*
1 excellent *UK, 1846*

- — Michael Palin and Terry Jones, *Ripping Yarns*, 1976 – 79
- — Connie Eble (Editor), *UNC-CH Campus Slang*, p. 8, Spring 1991

2 very angry *US, 1968*

- — Collin Baker et al., *College Undergraduate Slang Study Conducted at Brown University*, p. 185, 1968

riproodling *adjective*
excellent *US, 1954*

- Frana watched them cross the street and turn the corner, chatting like a couple of riproodling debs. — Bernard Wolfe, *The Late Risers*, p. 132, 1954

ritzy *adjective*
classy, stylish, fashionable *US, 1920*
After the Ritz luxury hotels in New York, London, and Paris.

- Before long the Goldkette office steered me to a steady job, playing with a small hot band in a ritzy joint called Luigi's Cafe. — Mezz Mezzrow, *Really the Blues*, p. 92, 1946
- I understand she caters to a pretty ritzy clientele. — Mickey Spillane, *I, The Jury*, p. 13, 1947
- Then we gonna buy you a ritzy house ... "lectric lights! ... a great big slew of snazzy furniture." — Iceberg Slim (Robert Beck), *Airtight Willie and Me*, p. 116, 1979

Riv; Rivie; Rivie hog *noun*
a Buick Riviera car *US, 1980*

- — Edith A. Folb, *runnin' down some lines*, p. 252, 1980

river *noun*
▸ **up the river; upriver**
to a prison *US, 1947*

- He had been a pickpocket until a long stretch up the river gave him a turn of mind. — Mickey Spillane, *I, The Jury*, p. 15, 1947
- "He's been up the river so many times, we call him showboat." — Harry Grey, *The Hoods*, p. 91, 1952
- [T]he poor jerk from Camden you take up the river to the Crossbars Hotel[.] — Darryl Ponicsan, *The Last Detail*, p. 181, 1970
- Or maybe he's storing up memories for his trip upriver, like Butch. — Josh Alan Friedman, *Tales of Times Square*, p. 120, 1986
- Lance would have me sent upriver for a ten-year stretch. — C.D. Payne, *Youth in Revolt*, p. 355, 1993

RJR *noun*
inexpensive cigarette tobacco given free to prisoners *US, 1990*
An abbreviation of R.J. Reynolds, a major tobacco company.

- — Charles Shafer, *Folk Speech in Texas Prisons*, p. 213, 1990

roach *noun*

1 the butt of a marijuana cigarette *US, 1938*

The variant "roche" also exists.

- Satchmo making a roach of a bomber joint in two mighty drags. — Neal Cassady, *Neal Cassady Collected Letters 1944–1967*, p. 299, 20th June 1951: Letter to Jack Kerouac

- Save me the roach, man. — Willard Motley, *Let No Man Write My Epitaph*, p. 90, 1958

- [A]nd then the stick was gone, burnt to a little bit of a roach. — Piri Thomas, *Down These Mean Streets*, p. 58, 1967

- Twist up a big bomb of this serious dope / Smoke it down to tha dub or roach tip / So much damn resin it's startin' to drip — Tone Loc, *Cheeba Cheeba*, 1989

2 Rohypnol™ (flunitrazepam), popularly known as the "date-rape drug" *US, 1995*

From the manufacturer, Hoffman-La Roche. The variant "roachie" also exists.

- On the street the drug has many nicknames; teenagers know it as rope, ribs, or roaches. — *Texas Monthly*, p. 88, September 1995

- Among the New Words — *American Speech*, p. 193, Summer 1997

3 a police officer *US, 1963*

A disliked insect found nearly everywhere.

- — Marlena Kay Nelson, *Rookies to Roaches*, p. 5, 1963

4 an unpopular girl *US, 1959*

- — *Time Magazine*, p. 46, 24th August 1959

- — *American Speech*, p. 154, May 1959: "Gator (University of Florida) Slang"

roach *verb*

in computing, to destroy a program *US, 1991*

- Hardware gets toasted or fried, software gets roached. — Eric S. Raymond, *The New Hacker's Dictionary*, p. 305, 1991

roach clip *noun*

a device, improvised or manufactured, designed to hold the butt of a (marijuana) cigarette and make smoking the final portion possible *US, 1997*

- After several draws, she produces a sequined roach clip for the rest of the joint. — Darryl Ponicsan, *The Last Detail*, p. 99, 1970

- She and Dr. Baker would do it on weekends when he was still in school, using forceps for a roach clip, Keith the only person she knew who could smoke and never crack a smile. — Elmore Leonard, *Maximum Bob*, p. 237, 1991

- Yes I smoke shit, straight off the roach clip. — Cypress Hill, *I Wanna Get High*, 1993

- Roach Clips. Sure, they were mostly decorated alligator clips, but it didn't matter—they were icons, a symbol of an enlightened life. — Bruce Elliot, *Retrohell*, p. 177, 1997

roach coach *noun*

a catering truck *US, 1985*

- Another depicts workers at the motorized snack bar, which Lai has titled with the workers' slang: "Man Leaning on the Roach Coach at Lunchtime." — *Chicago Tribune*, p. 1C, 6th August 1985

- — Judi Sanders, *Kickin' like Chicken with the Couch Commander*, p. 19, 1992

- Parked in the middle is the "roach coach," purveyor of coffee and rolls. — Ted Conover, *Newjack*, p. 5, 2000

- We need Mexican Popsicle carts downtown, as well as the roach coaches selling tacos. — *Phoenix New Times*, 2nd October 2003

roached *adjective*

under the influence of Rohypnol™ (flunitrazepam), popularly known as the "date-rape drug" *US, 1996*

From the name of the manufacturer, Hoffman-La Roche.

- — *American Speech*, p. 193, Summer 1997: "Among the new words"

roach haven *noun*

a hotel/motel lacking in hygiene *US, 1995*

- We got a Winnebago. We don't need those overpriced roach havens. — Quentin Tarantino, *From Dusk Till Dawn*, p. 15, 1995

roach stomper boots; roach killers *noun*

pointed shoes or boots *US, 1974*

- Richie wore roach killers—pointy as a dangerous weapon, curving high over his ankle and low over his heel. — Richard Price, *The Wanderers*, p. 5, 1974

- Kyle, the big kid, had been wearing Texas roach-stomper boots. — Carl Hiaasen, *Double Whammy*, p. 220, 1987

roach trap *noun*

a dirty, inexpensive place *US, 1972*

- I had been living in that roach trap on Eighth Avenue back in New York[.] — Georgia Sothern, *My Life in Burlesque*, p. 59, 1972

- I wanted my own safe room for the event, not some five-dollar roach trap[.] — Josh Friedman, *When Sex Was Dirty*, p. 46, 2005

roach wagon *noun*

a catering truck *US, 1984*

- Dick Snider watched through binoculars the throngs who played soccer and baseball and bought tamales and soda pop from the Tijuana "roach wagons[.]" — Joseph Wambaugh, *Lines and Shadows*, p. 17, 1984

road *noun*

▸ **the road**

in Roller Derby, anywhere outside the nine San Francisco Bay Area counties, the home of the game *US, 1999*

- — Keith Coppage, *Roller Derby to Rollerjam*, 1999

road apple *noun*

1 a piece of horse manure *US, 1996*

- Road apples are chunks of frozen or dried horse manure, used as pucks in road hockey, also called horse hockey. — Lewis Poteet, *Hockey Talk*, p. 60, 1996

2 a touring performer *US, 1981*

- — Don Wilmeth, *The Language of American Popular Entertainment*, p. 224, 1981

road burn *noun*

in the language surrounding the Grateful Dead, the deteriorated grooming and personal hygiene that serve as physical manifestations of a long tour following the band *US, 1994*

- — David Shenk and Steve Silberman, *Skeleton Key*, p. 249, 1994

road dog *noun*

1 an extremely close friend *US, 1989*

- — *Houston Chronicle*, 9th April 1989

- So I went in search of a "road dog," or best friend. — Sanyika Shakur, *Monster*, p. 14, 1993

- Me and my road dog, Tyriqqua, used to steal cars, too, but our main thing was jumpin' people to take what they got. — *Rolling Stone*, p. 86, 12th April 2001

2 in sports betting, a team picked as the underdog playing away from home *US, 1989*

- — Wayne Alan Root, *Betting to Win on Sports*, p. 183, 1989

road game *noun*

a criminal's field of expertise *US, 1984*

- — Inez Cardozo-Freeman, *The Joint*, p. 526, 1984

road head *noun*

oral sex received while driving *US, 2001*

- — Don R. McCreary (Editor), *Dawg Speak*, 2001

road helper *noun*

an amphetamine or other central nervous system stimulant *US, 1969*

- — *American Speech*, p. 207, Fall 1969: "Truck driver's jargon"

roadie *noun*

a member of a rock band's entourage who is responsible for setting up and dismantling the band's equipment while on tour *UK, 1968*

- That's Barry. He used to be a roadie. — *Wayne's World 2*, 1993

- When he came home he was a roadie for different bands, then a roadie for the Boo-Yaa T.R.i.b.e., the famous Samoan rappers, and then hooked up with Raji as a way to get connected in the business end. — Elmore Leonard, *Be Cool*, p. 175, 1999

- VAL: These guys are musicians! STEPHIE: They're roadies, Val! There's a difference! — *200 Cigarettes*, 1999

- While I sit here mired in her bullshit, trying to be a good son, while you're off dropping acid and blowing roadies! — *The Sopranos (Episode 55)*, 2004

road kill *noun*

1 a cigarette made from many cigarette butts, especially those gathered on the side of a road *US, 2004*

- — Jeffrey Ian Ross, *Behind Bars*, p. 194, 2002: Slammer Slang

2 literally, an animal or bird carcass on the side of the road; figuratively, an unattractive mess *US, 1979*

- Here, yours is the one that looks like a road kill. Enjoy. — *Break Point*, 1991

- She dropped me like a bad habit and left me for road kill. — *Wayne's World 2*, 1993

road louse *noun*
a chorus dancer who can no longer get work in the major metropolitan dance halls *US, 1948*
- [T]hey've got to get jobs in inferior outlying clubs or in out-of-town cafes or road shows, and, typed as a "road louse," there is only one direction for them—down. — *Jack Lait and Lee Mortimer, New York Confidential, p. 141, 1948*

road map *noun*
1 multiple facial lacerations *US, 1988–1989*
- — *Maledicta, p. 34, 1988–1989: "Medical maledicta from San Francisco"*
2 in craps, the dice placed before the shooter with the point needed to win face up *US, 1983*
- — *Thomas L. Clark, The Dictionary of Gambling and Gaming, p. 182, 1987*

road rash *noun*
scraped, bruised, and/or cut skin earned in falls while skateboarding or engaging in activity on the road *US, 1976*
- — *Albert Cassorla, The Skateboarder's Bible, p. 202, 1976*

road soda *noun*
alcohol drunk in a car on the way to a party or concert *US, 2004*
- — *Ben Applebaum and Derrick Pittman, Turd Ferguson & The Sausage Party, p. 68, 2004*

roadster *noun*
a tramp *US, 1890*
- The other had spike (casual ward) written all over him, a real roadster, and a ruddy hairy one. — *Charles Raven, Underworld Nights, p. 198, 1956*

road trouble *noun*
problems encountered on the street, usually between a pimp and prostitute *US, 1973*
- It was the same nappyheaded bitch that had been giving me the road trouble. — *A.S. Jackson, Gentleman Pimp, p. 180, 1973*

roam *noun*
▸ **on the roam**
away from home *US, 1976*
- I went to see your whoring sister, but she was on the roam / I called your dope fiend brother, but the punk had pawned his phone. — *Dennis Wepman et al., The Life, p. 140, 1976*

roarer *noun*
in horseracing, a horse that coughs loudly while galloping *US, 1947*
- — *Dan Parker, The ABC of Horse Racing, p. 148, 1947*

roast *noun*
a person killed by a fire *US, 1976*
- His words made the hair prickle on the back of my neck, for I had caught the unmistakable pungent odor of burning human flesh. "Larry," I muttered, "Think we got a roast." — *John Barracato with Peter Michelmore, Arson, p. 34, 1976*

roasted *adjective*
drunk or drug-intoxicated *US, 1989*
- They can pour a whole orchestra's worth of booze in nanoseconds [...] many members were roasted—and so was my music. — *Frank Zappa, The Real Frank Zappa Book, p. 153, 1989*

rob *verb*
▸ **rob the cradle**
to be romantically involved with a young person *US, 1978*
- She even gets to robbing the cradle, a little boy or a little girl. — *Robert Deane Pharr, Giveadamn Brown, p. 120, 1978*
- — *Connie Eble (Editor), UNC-CH Campus Slang, p. 5, Spring 1983*
- His little prepubescent trophies gleamed on the shelf, reminding me that I was robbing the old cradle. — *Pamela Des Barres, I'm With the Band, p. 197, 1988*

robe *noun*
in circus and carnival usage, a judge in criminal court *US, 1981*
- — *Don Wilmeth, The Language of American Popular Entertainment, p. 225, 1981*

robo *noun*
dextromethorphan (DXM), an active ingredient in non-prescription cold and cough medication, often abused *US, 2003*

- Youths' nicknames for DXM: Robo, Skittles, Triple C's, Rojo, Dex, Tussin, Vitamin D. DXM abuse is called "Robotripping" or "Tussing." Users might be called "syrup heads" or "robotards." — *USA Today, p. 1A, 29th December 2003*

robo *verb*
to drink Robitussin™ (branded cough medicine with codeine) *US, 1993*
- The [Robitussin] trip is more of a buzz to my experience, and to that of my friends. I have been told that high dosages produce hallucinogenic effects similar to "shrooms and LSD[.] — *Nathan Bowen, alt.drugs, 13th April 1993*

robodose *verb*
to abuse cough syrups for recreational purposes *US, 1995*
From the name of the most popular syrup of abuse, Robitussen™.
- This worried me a bit because the last time I robodosed was 3 or 4 days prior. — *alt. drugs, 31st January 1995*

robodosing *noun*
the recreational abuse of dextromethorphan *US, 1994*
- Try ingesting 8 oz. of Vicks Maximum Strength cough syrup (Robodosing). Interesting experience. — *alt.drugs, 25th January 1994*
- For the uninformed, robodosing is the high school high that comes from doses of cough syrup. — *The Miami Herald, p. 1G, 24th August 1996*

robofizzing *noun*
the recreational abuse of dextromethorphan *US, 2007*
- Code names used for abusing DXM are "roboing," "robo-tripping," "robo-fizzing," "smurfing" and "skillting." — *Columbia (Missouri) Daily Tribune, 30th August 2007*

roboing *noun*
the recreational abuse of dextromethorphan *US, 1992*
- I first became interested in the articles about Roboing. I have been doing Robo for about six months. — *alt.drugs, 11th February 2002*
- Especially popular among younger people at dance "raves," DXM users feel anything from slight intoxication to intense hallucinations when "roboing" or "robotripping"—slang derived from Robitussin cough syrup that users sometimes call "tuss." — *Angela Macias, Saint Paul Pioneer Press, p. 1B, 2nd September 2002*

robotard *noun*
a person who abuses for nonmedicinal purposes nonpre-scription medication containing dextromethorphan (DXM) *US, 2003*
From the branded cough syrup, Robitussen™.
- Youths' nicknames for DXM: Robo, Skittles, Triple C's, Rojo, Dex, Tussin, Vitamin D. DXM abuse is called "Robotripping" or "Tussing." Users might be called "syrup heads" or "robotards." — *USA Today, p. 1A, 29th December 2003*

robotrip *verb*
to abuse for nonmedicinal purposes nonprescription medi-cation containing dextromethorphan (DXM) *US, 2003*
From the branded cough syrup, Robitussin™.
- Youths' nicknames for DXM: Robo, Skittles, Triple C's, Rojo, Dex, Tussin, Vitamin D. DXM abuse is called "Robotripping" or "Tussing." Users might be called "syrup heads" or "robotards." — *USA Today, p. 1A, 29th December 2003*

robotripping *noun*
the recreational abuse of cough syrup *US, 1991*
- I have found robotripping to be VERY much like tripping on acid. — *alt.drugs, 23rd December 1991*
- The buzz surrounding robotripping, fueled by both word-of-mouth and Internet postings, is persuasive. — *Agnes Blum, The Capital (Annapolis, Maryland), p. C2, 6th January 2000*

roca *noun*
crack cocaine *US, 1994*
Corrupted Spanish-English for "rock."
- — *US Department of Justice, Street Terms, October 1994*

Roche; La Roche; rochie *noun*
Rohypnol™ (flunitrazepam), popularly known as the "date-rape drug" *US, 2004*
Because Roche Pharmaceuticals markets the Rohypnol™ sleeping pill.
- — *American Family Physician, p. 2619, 1st June 2004*

rock *noun*

1 a diamond *US, 1908*

- As Duffy served them he noticed that she was ablaze with rocks, and when she reached for money to pay, that she had a roll. — Jack Lait and Lee Mortimer, *Chicago Confidential*, p. 31, 1950
- My wife's got a hundred and fifty grand in rocks and another seventy-five in furs and clothes. — Raymond Chandler, *The Long Goodbye*, p. 65, 1953
- Profacci bought hot rocks. I knew then it was rocks, phony rocks that he thought were real! — Iceberg Slim (Robert Beck), *Trick Baby*, p. 19, 1969

2 crack cocaine *US, 1983*

Describes the crystalline lumps of purified cocaine.

- I sell the rock with some shake to people who buy quarters [1/4 ounce or seven grams], and pure rock only to my very best customers. — Terry Williams, *The Cocaine Kids*, p. 37, 1989
- You look like you sell rocks. — *Boyz N The Hood*, 1990
- A $100 bag of coke could pull about $500 in rocks. — *Menace II Society*, 1993
- You want some crack? Sweet-ass rock. Get you high. — Kevin Smith, *Jay and Silent Bob Strike Back*, p. 90, 2001

3 a pool ball *US, 1990*

- — Steve Rushin, *Pool Cool*, p. 24, 1990

4 in the usage of youthful model road racers (slot car racers), a slow car *US, 1997*

- — Phantom Surfers, *The Exciting Sounds of Model Road Racing (Album cover)*, 1997

5 a solid, reliable, dependable fellow prisoner *US, 1976*

- — John R. Armore and Joseph D. Wolfe, *Dictionary of Desperation*, p. 46, 1976

6 in prison, a predatory homosexual *US, 1967*

- I was swinging my feet ever so easy when I dug three rocks watching me, funny like. — Piri Thomas, *Down These Mean Streets*, p. 251, 1967

7 a frugal and stingy person *US, 1950*

- — *The Annals of the American Academy of Political and Social Sciences*, p. 130, May 1950

8 a dollar *US, 1947*

- "Okay—half a rock." — Willard Motley, *Knock on Any Door*, p. 131, 1947
- Some old dame stopped me and without me askin' her nothin' she hands me half a rock. — Willard Motley, *Let No Man Write My Epitaph*, p. 73, 1958

9 a package of brand name manufactured cigarettes, used as a basic medium of exchange in prison *US, 1992*

- — William K. Bentley and James M. Corbett, *Prison Slang*, p. 65, 1992

10 a crystal tuning device used in a citizens' band transceiver *US, 1976*

- — Porter Bibb, *CB Bible*, p. 103, 1976

11 the Alcatraz federal penitentiary, located in San Francisco bay *US, 1970*

- You're going to the Rock, Al, a nice long ride to Alcatraz. — Red Rudensky, *The Gonif*, p. 61, 1970
- What was it like to be locked up on The Rock? Well, even if you were a "Machine Gun" Kelly or a "Scarface," at The Rock you were just a number. — Marlene Freedman, *Alcatraz*, 1983

12 Riker's Island jail, New York *US, 1975*

- They call them "rocks from The Rock," since they were baked at another jail out on Rikers Island, otherwise known as The Rock. — Ed Sanders, *Tales of Beatnik Glory*, p. 219, 1975
- "Please, I know much niggers on the rock." — Paul Beatty, *Tuff*, p. 34, 2000
- Rikers prisoners refer to their home as "the Rock," but from an archaeological point of view it's more accurate to call this place a dump. — *The Village Voice*, 13th–19th December 2000

13 Guam *US, 1990*

A nickname used by US military pilots during the Vietnamese war.

- — Gregory Clark, *Words of the Vietnam War*, p. 210, 1990

rock *verb*

1 to have sex *US, 1922*

- Who did you rock over this week? — George Mandel, *Flee the Angry Strangers*, p. 41, 1952
- you know that I rocked her / But three days later I had to see the doctor — Kool Moe Dee, *Go See The Doctor*, 1986

2 to excite someone *US, 1955*

- "In other words," I remarked, "whether or not the kid rocks you." — Max Shulman, *Guided Tour of Campus Humor*, p. 161, 1955

3 to excel *US, 1996*

- The new playhouse rocks, Dotty. — *Jerry Maguire*, 1996
- Cos it's like you're bein' done by a stranger. It rocks. — *Gone in 60 Seconds*, 2000
- "Awesome," I say, adding "you rock." — Marty Beckerman, *Death to All Cheerleaders*, p. 135, 2000

rock and roll *verb*

to begin and perform the task at hand *US, 1990*

- — Connie Eble (Editor), *UNC-CH Campus Slang*, p. 7, November 1990
- Little hand says it's time to rock and roll. — *Point Break*, 1991
- Let me make an adjustment here and we'll be ready to rock "n roll. — *Natural Born Killers*, 1994

rock and roll; rock 'n' roll *noun*

1 a genre of music with a driving rhythm; an umbrella for most simply rhythmic music produced since the 1950s *US, 1946*

The etymology is laden with sexual overtones, thus "My Man Rocks Me With One Steady Roll," sung by blues singer Trixie Smith in 1924, and a song entitled "Rock and Roll" is recorded in 1934. It is not until 1954 that the music now recognized as "rock 'n' roll" is given its identity; coinage is generally credited to US disc jockey Alan Freed, although the 1946 citation shows that Freed popularized but did not coin the term.

- It's right rhythmic rock and roll music that provides plenty of inspiration in Joe Liggins' "Sugar Lump." — *Billboard*, p. 33, 22nd June 1946

2 used of an automatic or semiautomatic weapon, full automatic fire *US, 1979*

- Then he stood up, flicked his iron to rock and roll and gave the little zero a long burst through the Playboy mag. — *Apocalypse Now*, 1979
- You peep through that skinny-ass embrasure with your M-16 on full rock and roll[.] — Larry Heinemann, *Paco's Story*, p. 10, 1986
- Sergeant said, "You're on lane four / Set that lever on 'rock and roll.'" — Sandee Shaffer Johnson, *Cadences*, p. 83, 1986
- I swear the black dudes weld their selector switches on rock and roll. — Ernest Spencer, *Welcome to Vietnam, Macho Man*, p. 56, 1987

rock candy *noun*

diamonds *US, 1970*

- — Clarence Major, *Dictionary of Afro-American Slang*, p. 98, 1970

rock crusher *noun*

in poker, a hand that is certain to win *US, 1988*

- — George Percy, *The Language of Poker*, p. 76, 1988

rockdance *noun*

walking barefoot over a rocky surface to retrieve a surfboard *US, 1963*

- — Grant W. Kuhns, *On Surfing*, p. 120, 1963

rocked out *adjective*

under the influence of crack cocaine *US, 1991*

- The guy's sitting there nodding, all rocked out, while I go get a warrant signed. — Elmore Leonard, *Maximum Bob*, p. 164, 1991

rocker *noun*

1 any of the several curved stripes below the three chevrons on the insignia of a sergeant in the US Army or Marine Corps *US, 1944*

- This morning the Duty was a staff sergeant: three stripes and one rocker underneath. — Martin Russ, *The Last Parallel*, p. 19, 1957
- — Carl Fleischhauer, *A Glossary of Army Slang*, p. 11, 1968
- Now they had to call us "sir," although, with the previous summer's experience fresh in our minds, the sight of some old salt with three stripes and a rocker on his sleeves still caused a Pavlovian reaction of terror. — Philip Caputo, *A Rumor of War*, p. 13, 1977

2 the convex curvature of the bottom of a surfboard *US, 1965*

- — D.S. Halacy, *Surfer!*, p. 216, 1965

▸ **off your rocker**

crazy *UK, 1897*

- I know it doesn't seem right, but Jake's halfway off his rocker! — Jim Thompson, *Savage Night*, p. 128, 1953
- "You're nuts, man," Tony stated flatly. "I mean you're really off your goddamn rocker," he said and burst out laughing. — Donald Goines, *Black Gangster*, p. 80, 1977
- The experience was so awful for him that he went completely off his rocker. — Herbert Huncke, *Guilty of Everything*, p. 47, 1990

- [H]e's crazy and off his rocker / Crazier than Slim Shady is off the vodka[.] — Eminem (Marshall Mathers), *The Kids*, 2000

rocket *noun*
1 a marijuana cigarette *US, 1942*
- — Vincent J. Monteleone, *Criminal Slang*, p. 195, 1949
- "Speak to Antonio," Sammy said. "He can always fix you up with a pack of rockets." — Douglas Rutherford, *The Creeping Flesh*, p. 49, 1963

2 a hypodermic needle and syringe *US, 1989*
- — Geoffrey Froner, *Digging for Diamonds*, p. 53, 1989

3 a bullet *US, 1965*
- 'Bout this time the poor bartender had gone to rest / I pumped six a my rockets in his motherfucken chest. — Bruce Jackson, *Get Your Ass in the Water and Swim Like Me*, p. 47, 1965
- — Roger D. Abrahams, *Deep Down in the Jungle*, p. 262, 1970

rocket cap *noun*
a dome-shaped cap on a vial in which crack cocaine is sold *US, 1994*
- — US Department of Justice, *Street Terms*, October 1994

Rocket City *nickname*
Tay Ninh, South Vietnam; Lai Khe, South Vietnam *US, 1983*
- Byrom told him that they were under enemy rocket attack and that he had better get used to it, because it happened so often they called Lai Khe "Rocket City." — Peter Goldman and Tony Fuller, *Charlie Company*, p. 35, 1983
- When Donald arrived at Tay Ninh, he discovered the camp was so frequently under attack it had been nicknamed Rocket City. — James Mills, *The Underground Empire*, p. 137, 1986

rocket fuel *noun*
phencyclidine, the recreational drug known as PCP or angel dust *US, 1976*
- John R. Armore and Joseph D. Wolfe, *Dictionary of Desperation*, p. 46, 1976
- — *Drummer*, p. 77, 1977

rocket man *noun*
a person who sells syringes to drug addicts *US, 1989*
Illegal in the US, but profitable.
- — Geoffrey Froner, *Digging for Diamonds*, p. 53, 1989

rocket ripple *noun*
a barrage of 144 rockets fired from a small cart *US, 1957*
Korean war usage.
- It may be ridiculous to call any barrage beautiful, but if one doesn't think about it too hard, a barrage is beautiful—to watch; especially a rocket ripple. — Martin Russ, *The Last Parallel*, p. 280, 1957

rocket scientist *noun*
used in comparisons as the epitome of intelligence *US, 1986*
- Not exactly a rocket scientist but she's a lot of fun. — Jay McInerney, *Story of My Life*, p. 104, 1988

rock-happy *adjective*
anxious to leave an island *US, 1845*
- "I can't take any more of this petty bullshit. Between that S.O.B. and Burin, I'm going rock-happy." — Philip Caputo, *A Rumor of War*, p. 213, 1977

rockhead *noun*
1 a dim-witted person *US, 1957*
- A mule. A rock-head. You know how they get. — Max Shulman, *Rally Round the Flag, Boys!*, p. 3, 1957

2 a crack cocaine addict *US, 1991*
- "I'm Department of Corrections," Kathy said. "What are you?" A rockhead for one thing, no doubt lights popping in this brain. — Elmore Leonard, *Maximum Bob*, p. 65, 1991
- The realization that he hadn't seen a rockhead in three days jolted him. Wowwww! These people ain't into crack. — Odie Hawkins, *Midnight*, p. 62, 1995

rock house *noun*
a premises used for the sale and consumption of crack cocaine *US, 1985*
- I said, "Listen homeboy, what you talkin' about? / You're mistakin' my pad for a rockhouse / Well, I know to you we all look the same / But I'm not the one slingin' caine[.]" — Toddy Tee, *Batterram*, 1985
- The rock house nigga. We done served that fool before. — *Menace II Society*, 1993

- [T]he way he'd pass slowly by a rock house and maddog gangsters suspected of doing drivebys. — Bob Sipchen, *Baby Insane and the Buddha*, p. 399, 1993
- In the ghetto, I would learn, there are hundreds of independent "rock house" franchises. — Gini Sikes, *8 Ball Chicks*, p. 13, 1997

rock jockey *noun*
in the language of paragliding, the pilot of a hang glider *US, 1992*
- — Erik Fair, *California Thrill Sports*, p. 336, 1992

rockman *noun*
a dealer in crack cocaine *US, 1989*
- And the Chief of Police says he just might / (Flatten out every house he sees on sight) / Because he say the rockman is takin' him for a fool [...] And Mister Rockman, you better stop some day — Toddy Tee, *Batterram*, 1985
- — Ellen C. Bellone (Editor), *Dictionary of Slang*, p. 20, 1989
- — Kenn "Naz" Young, *Naz's Dictionary of Teen Slang*, p. 99, 1993

rock med *noun*
medical treatment targeted for rock 'n' roll concert goers *US, 1994*
- — David Shenk and Steve Silberman, *Skeleton Key*, p. 250, 1994

rock of Gibraltar *noun*
in shuffleboard, a disk that is well hidden and guarded *US, 1967*
- — Omero C. Catan, *Secrets of Shuffleboard Strategy*, p. 71, 1967: "Glossary of terms"

rockpile *noun*
any prison job *US, 1984*
- — Inez Cardozo-Freeman, *The Joint*, p. 527, 1984

rock queen *noun*
a woman who trades sex for crack cocaine *US, 2003*
- [W]hite crack whores, called rock queens, and their black pimps, worked the street corners. — James Lee Burke, *Last Car to Elysian Fields*, p. 193, 2003

rocks *noun*
1 salt *US, 1981*
- — Don Wilmeth, *The Language of American Popular Entertainment*, p. 225, 1981

2 money *US, 1950*
- — *The Annals of the American Academy of Political and Social Sciences*, p. 130, May 1950

3 dominoes *US, 1959*
- — Dominic Armanino, *Dominoes*, p. 16, 1959

4 the testicles *US, 1948*
- Well, he's just a kid, and he always hadda pair of rocks on him, the man. — George V. Higgins, *The Friends of Eddie Coyle*, p. 192, 1971
- "I'm beat to the rocks." "You mean your socks." "I mean my rocks, my nuts, my balls, fachrissakes." — Robert Campbell, *Sweet La-La Land*, p. 24, 1990

5 courage *US, 1974*
- "Don't take no brains. Just the rocks." — George Higgin, *Cogan's Trade*, p. 22, 1974
- Oh yes, planting bombs took a lot of rocks, you had to admire that. — John Sayles, *Union Dues*, p. 176, 1977

▸ **get your rocks off**
to ejaculate *US, 1969*
- He wiped the blood away and gave her fifty slats [dollars] to get his rocks. — Iceberg Slim (Robert Beck), *Pimp*, p. 293, 1969
- At last he made vulgar use of me to get his rocks off and told me I could leave[.] — Jefferson Poland and Valerie Alison, *The Records of the San Francisco Sexual Freedom League*, p. 153, 1971
- Baths vary in character, from the Wall Street Sauna, where businessmen go to get their rocks off during the lunch hour (it's called "funch"), to the Beacon[.] — *The Village Voice*, 27th September 1976
- The sex scenes cover a wide range of lovin', from the perverse to the passionate, and everybody gets their rocks off. — *Adult Video*, p. 14, August/September 1986

▸ **on the rocks**
used of a drink, served over ice *US, 1946*
- She gave him a bourbon-on-the-rocks. — Max Shulman, *Anyone Got a Match?*, p. 245, 1964
- Sweetie, will you mix us a nice martini? Beefeater gin, no vermouth, on the rocks, with just the tiniest dash of rock salt. — Gore Vidal, *Myra Breckinridge*, p. 268, 1968

▶ **shoot your rocks**
to ejaculate *US, 1975*
- "There," Gloria said as she closed the door behind her, "don't want those fuckin' honkies to shoot their rocks 'fore they pay!" — Donald Goines, *Inner City Hoodlum*, p. 118, 1975

▶ **the rocks**
a confidence swindle involving fake diamonds *US, 1969*
- The Westside mark had been sweet as honeysuckle. He had blown ten grand on our slick version of the rocks. — Iceberg Slim (Robert Beck), *Trick Baby*, p. 11, 1969

rock star *noun*
1 a crack cocaine dealer *US, 1988*
- They say "Beam Me Up, Scotty." They say, "I Need a Beam-Me-Up Scotty. You got some? You got some?" And the rock star say, Looky here. Lookyhere. I got a dollar beamer. Dollar Beamer. Three dollar Beamer. — *St. Petersburg (Florida) Times*, p. 1F, 28th February 1988
- "It was mostly old people living there — then the rock stars moved in," Knight said, using street slang to describe the crack dealers. — *Orlando Sentinel Tribune*, p. B3, 22nd May 2001
- — Mike Haskins, *Drugs*, p. 282, 2003

2 a woman who engages in sex for payment in crack cocaine or money to buy crack cocaine; a prostitute addicted to crack cocaine *US, 1993*
- — *Washington Post*, p. C5, 7th November 1993
- "You know, a rock star, a woman hooked on crack who'll do sexual favors for drugs." — Colton Simpson, *Inside the Crips*, p. 171, 2005

rock whore *noun*
a woman who will trade sex for crack cocaine *US, 1991*
- This here's a go-go rock whore I'm talking about. Does it to buy crack and get high. — Elmore Leonard, *Maximum Bob*, p. 189, 1991
- DREXEL: You ain't seen nothing like these rock whores. They ass be young man. They got that fine young pussy. Bitches want the rock, they be a freak for you. — *True Romance*, 1993
- You send some hard-headed rock whore and she fucks things up. — *Jackie Brown*, 1997

rock wing *noun*
in the language of paragliding, the pilot of a hang glider *US, 1992*
- — Erik Fair, *California Thrill Sports*, p. 335, 1992

Rocky *noun*
Coors™ beer *US, 1967*
Coors boasts of being brewed with "pure Rocky Mountain spring water."
- — *American Speech*, p. 63, February 1967: "Soda-fountain, restaurant and tavern calls"

Rocky Mountain Kool Aid *noun*
Coors™ beer *US, 1977*
Once available only in Colorado, where it is brewed.
- — Bill Davis, *Jawjacking*, p. 83, 1977

Rocky Mountain oyster *noun*
an animal testicle, usually that of a steer formerly known as a bull, prepared for eating as a regional delicacy *US, 1986*
- — John Mariani, *Mariani's Coast-to-Coast Dining Guide*, p. 225, 1986
- "Rocky Mountain oysters is what they call 'em out West. Can you imagine eating barbecued bull's balls?" — Carl Hiaasen, *Sick Puppy*, p. 458, 1999

rod *noun*
1 the penis; the erect penis *UK, 1902*
- [Y]ou slip in your hard rod in all that squishy softness and kiss their lips[.] — Jack Kerouac, *Jack Kerouac Selected Letters 1957–1969*, p. 153, 19th June 1958: Letter to Gary Snyder
- It's all right. She's my wife. She needs black rod, is all. — Eldridge Cleaver, *Soul on Ice*, p. 170, 1968
- "The Spirit tells them that they blew the thing, that they should have gotten hold of his Rod—" "His Dick," said Doc. "Yeah." — Cecil Brown, *The Life & Loves of Mr. Jiveass Nigger*, p. 56, 1969
- The dean comes in and makes the girl perform fellatio on his "black rod" because she "pissed" on his floor. — *Final Report of the Attorney General's Commission on Pornography*, p. 437, 1986

2 a gun, usually a pistol *US, 1903*
- I still have a private cop's license with the privilege to pack a rod, and they're afraid of me. — Mickey Spillane, *I, The Jury*, p. 7, 1947

- My boys don't carry rods. — Hal Ellson, *The Golden Spike*, p. 70, 1952
- You couldn't even rob a bank, to rob a bank you needed a rod and to buy a rod you need at least twenty bucks. — Bernard Wolfe, *The Late Risers*, p. 7, 1954
- It worried me to be part of a hustle that required a rod. — Iceberg Slim (Robert Beck), *Pimp*, p. 252, 1969

3 a hired gunman *US, 1964*
- — R. Frederick West, *God's Gambler*, p. 228, 1964: "Appendix A"

rodda *noun*
a Cadillac El Dorado car *US, 1972*
- — David Claerbaut, *Black Jargon in White America*, p. 78, 1972

rodded up *adjective*
armed with a handgun or handguns *US, 1950*
- — Hyman E. Goldin et al., *Dictionary of American Underworld Lingo*, p. 180, 1950
- But Lance is by no means rodded up, because a rod is apt to create a bump in his shape when he has his tuxedo on. — James Tidwell, *A Treasury of American Folk Humor*, p. 158, 1956

rodeo fuck *noun*
used for describing sex between a man and woman; the man enters the woman from behind, insults her and then holds on *US, 2002*
A term heard mostly in jokes.
- — John-Paul Sousa, *Speaking of Sex*, p. 86, 2002

rodge *noun*
an affirmation of a message *US, 1973*
A variant of the more common "Roger that."
- "That's a rodge," Ernie said. — Anthony Herbert, *Soldier*, p. 375, 1973

Rodino *noun*
a Mexican citizen permitted to stay in the US during an immigration amnesty period in the late 1980s *US, 1993*
After Congressman Peter Rodino, sponsor of the legislation that made the amnesty possible.
- Abel knew that a real driver would be a gringo, not a former "Rodino" like himself. — Joseph Wambaugh, *Finnegan's Week*, p. 39, 1993

rod man *noun*
a gunman *US, 1949*
- "Red must be turnin' over when he sees his best rod man settin' that big free bottle down." — Nelson Algren, *The Man with the Golden Arm*, p. 146, 1949

rog *noun*
an acknowledgement that a message has been received *US, 1977*
- "Uh, that's a Rog, we mark your position, over." — Michael Kerr, *Dispatches*, p. 210, 1977

roger *verb*
to acknowledge receipt of a message *US, 2001*
- He had "rogered" the transmission but had not shown up for almost forty-five minutes. — Stephen J. Cannell, *The Tin Collectors*, p. 110, 2001

roger!
used for expressing agreement or affirmation *US, 1941*
"R" or "roger" signified that a message or command had been received.
- That's a roger. — Gerald Petievich, *Money Men*, p. 99, 1981
- "Just watch the show, smartass." "Roger." — Armistead Maupin, *Further Tales of the City*, p. 220, 1982

rogue *noun*
in surfing, a wave that appears without warning *US, 1977*
- — Gary Fairmont R. Filosa II, *The Surfer's Almanac*, p. 193, 1977

rogue's badge *noun*
in horseracing, blinkers *US, 1947*
Usually worn by horses that do not behave well, hence the label of "rogue."
- — Dan Parker, *The ABC of Horse Racing*, p. 148, 1947

rogue's gallery *noun*
a collection of photographs of criminals *US, 1859*
- The butler identified a Rogues Gallery picture of Sam ("Sammy the Hook") Entratta, alias Ippolletti. — Jack Lait and Lee Mortimer, *Chicago Confidential*, p. 18, 1950

- Any day, you can visit the office of Sheriff Ralph Lamb, and you will see on his walls a rogue's gallery of cheaters, identified by their specialties—slots, craps, cards. — Jimmy Snyder, *Jimmy the Greek*, p. 218, 1975

roid rage; 'roid rage *noun*
violently ill-tempered behavior resulting from excessive steroid use *US, 1987*
An abbreviation of "ste*roid,*" playing on **ROAD RAGE**.

- But that young athlete should know that there are dozens of other steroid reactions, and that some, such as acne and uncontrollable 'roid rages (aggressive and combative behavior), might cause immediate difficulties. — *FDA Consumer*, p. 16, November 1987

roids *noun*
anabolic steroids *US, 1980*

- Please be advised that no one uses "oids," but rather "roids," instead of steroids. [Letter to the editor] — *New York Times*, p. 78 (Section 6), 21st December 1980
- I do have that one thing against me, but I'm not on roids, and I don't drink and I've always been able to hold myself in a respectable way wherever I go. [quoting 2 Cold Scorpio] — *Wrestling Flyer*, 1st January 1994
- You probably know of how many guys tested positive on it, it doesn't take a rocket scientist to figure out who was on roids. [quoting Bill Watts] — Herb Kunze, *Herb's Wrestling Tidbits*, 23rd February 1995
- Plus, the 'roids made him pretty useless in the sack. — Missy Hyatt, *Missy Hyatt*, p. 160, 2001

rojito *noun*
a red central nervous system depressant, especially Seconal™ *US, 1971*
From the Spanish for "little red one."

- — Eugene Landy, *The Underground Dictionary*, p. 54, 1971

rojo *noun*
dextromethorphan (DXM), an active ingredient in nonpre-scription cold and cough medication, often abused for non-medicinal purposes *US, 2003*
Spanish for "red," which is the color of the cough syrup.

- Youths' nicknames for DXM: Robo, Skittles, Triple C's, Rojo, Dex, Tussin, Vitamin D. DXM abuse is called "Robotripping" or "Tussing." Users might be called "syrup heads" or "robotards." — *USA Today*, p. 1A, 29th December 2003

rojo flow *noun*
the bleed period of the menstrual cycle *US, 2001*
A use of the Spanish word *rojo* (red).

- — Don R. McCreary (Editor), *Dawg Speak*, 2001

rolf *verb*
to vomit *US, 1982*

- — Mary Corey and Victoria Westermark, *Fer Shurr! How to be a Valley Girl*, 1982

roll *noun*
1 an act of sexual intercourse *US, 1948*
An abbreviation of **ROLL IN THE HAY**.

- "She had one of the meanest rolls a man could want." — Norman Mailer, *The Naked and the Dead*, p. 5, 1948
- Hey, Billy boy, you remember that time in Seattle you and me picked up those two twitches? One of the best rolls I ever had. — Ken Kesey, *One Flew Over the Cuckoo's Nest*, p. 98, 1962

2 a roll of money *US, 1965*

- I had just got back with a load of jack / from out where the big shot reside / She lamped my roll, fell heart and soul / and wanted to dance with me. — Bruce Jackson, *Get Your Ass in the Water and Swim Like Me*, p. 101, 1965
- He invested £750 of his "roll" on a horse he considered a "good thing" in the opening race. — James Holledge, *The Great Australian Gamble*, p. 36, 1966

3 ten barbiturate capsules sold as a unit *US, 1973*

- — David W. Maurer and Victor Vogel, *Narcotics and Narcotic Addiction*, p. 438, 1973

4 a double-breasted suit *US, 1970*

- — Roger D. Abrahams, *Deep Down in the Jungle*, p. 262, 1970

▸ **on a roll**
enjoying continuing success *US, 1976*

- The scent of victory in his nostrils [...] Refreshed in mind and body. On a roll! — Jack Allen, *When the Whistle Blows*, p. 91, 2000

roll *verb*
1 to rob someone, especially with force and especially someone bemused with drink *US, 1873*

- The clip joint would roll a drunk and then toss him, unconscious, out in the parking lot. — Robert Sylvester, *No Cover Charge*, p. 82, 1956
- Adolpho had carried away the drunkie's Sterno, replying to my feeble protest, "What in hell, he's lucky, we wain't rolling him." — Clancy Sigal, *Going Away*, p. 237, 1961
- Some black crazy cat threw a cup of coffee at a white drunk and rolled him. — Abbie Hoffman, *Revolution for the Hell of It*, p. 176, 1968
- Where blood was shed for the sake of bread / And drunks rolled for their poke. — Dennis Wepman et al., *The Life*, p. 80, 1976

2 to avoid paying a bill for services provided by an establishment such as a hotel or restaurant *US, 1977*

- — Robert C. Prus and C.R.D. Sharper, *Road Hustler*, p. 171, 1977: "Glossary of terms"

3 to betray friends by changing sides; to inform on someone *US, 1997*
A variation of **ROLL OVER**.

- He knew the big, ugly steroid jockey was just smart enough to figure that Tommy would kill him inch by fucking inch if he ever rolled. — Stephen J. Cannell, *King Con*, p. 20, 1997

4 to leave *US, 1982*

- Let's roll, my man. — *Fast Times at Ridgemont High*, 1982
- C'mon, get your gear on, we're rollin'. — *Break Point*, 1991
- In the 'hood, it was easy to find someone who would roll with you to do your dirt. — Earl "DMX" Simmons, *E.A.R.L.*, p. 89, 2002

5 to ride in a car *US, 1990*

- Whose Benzo was that I saw you rolling in yesterday? — *Boyz N The Hood*, 1990
- Ty had a Benz. S-class. Snowflake white, like all Dumas boys rolled in. — John Ridley, *Love is a Racket*, p. 30, 1998

6 in prison, to open a cell *US, 1976*

- With grip in hand, Bud called the man / "Roll 'em, Cap, and don't be slow." — Dennis Wepman et al., *The Life*, p. 71, 1976

7 to take MDMA, the recreational drug best known as ecstasy *US, 2001*

- Mirranda Fernandes, 22, a waitress who lived alone with her dog, said to a neighbor one day in September 1999 that she wanted "to roll," street slang for taking the drug ecstasy. — *Tampa (Florida) Tribune*, p. 1, 14th February 2001

▸ **roll bones**
to play dice *US, 1950*

- — *The Annals of the American Academy of Political and Social Sciences*, p. 130, May 1950

▸ **roll down the windows**
in snowboarding, to wave your arms while trying to maintain balance *US, 1998*

- ROLLING DOWN THE WINDOWS When a rider is caught off balance and is fighting to stay upright with a wild rotation of the arms. — Shelley Youngblut, *Way Inside ESPN's X Games*, p. 232, 1998

▸ **roll in on someone**
to attack someone *US, 2000*

- AW soldiers would roll in on a white known to have well-off family members. — Bill Valentine, *Gangs and Their Tattoos*, p. 12, 2000

▸ **roll it up**
to gather all of your belongings from a prison cell before moving *US, 2002*

- "Roll it up," I have come to learn, means the same thing to all convicts in all jails and prisons: you are moving! Gather up your state issue—sheets, towel, blanket, mattress—and personal belongings[.] — Jimmy Lerner, *You Got Nothing Coming*, p. 27, 2002

▸ **roll the big seven**
to die *US, 1991*

- [A] thirty-eight-year-old man is lingering in a hospital bed, where three weeks later he rolls the Big Seven. — David Simon, *Homicide*, p. 173, 1991

▸ **roll the dice**
to take a chance on something *US, 1992*

- You want to investigate me, roll the dice, and take your chances. — *A Few Good Men*, 1992

▸ **roll the drums**
in betting, to double the bet in effect *US, 1986*

- — Sam Snead and Jerry Tarde, *Pigeons, Marks, Hustlers and Other Golf Bettors You Can Beat*, p. 110, 1986

▸ **roll with it**
to accept change, to adjust *US, 1981*

- [W]hat the hell, if it made the pigs feel good, might as well roll with it. — Robert Lipkin, *A Brotherhood of Outlaws*, p. 134, 1981

▸ **roll your own**
to reload your own ammunition *US, 1957*
- — *American Speech*, p. 194, October 1957: "Some colloquialisms of the handgunner"

roll deep *verb*
to go somewhere with a large group of friends; to have a large group of friends *US, 2001*
- — Pamela Munro, *U.C.L.A Slang*, p. 107, 2001
- — Connie Eble (Editor), *UNC-CH Campus Slang*, p. 9, October 2002

roller *noun*
1 a police officer *US, 1964*
- Boy, but the next day the roller may run down on ya, take you down to that lonesome old county jail. — Bruce Jackson, *Get Your Ass in the Water and Swim Like Me*, p. 123, 1965
- At noon, two "rollers" broke the door down. — Iceberg Slim (Robert Beck), *Pimp*, p. 101, 1969
- — Christina and Richard Milner, *Black Players*, p. 10, 1972
- Now I had a corner just like the rollers got a beat / Right on Eighth Avenue and a Hundred and Fifteenth Street. — Dennis Wepman et al., *The Life*, p. 52, 1976
2 a drug dealer *US, 1991*
An abbreviation of **HIGH-ROLLER**.
- "See, at first when I was workin' for a roller, I thought a hundred dollars was a lot of money." — Leon Bing, *Do or Die*, p. 57, 1991
3 a prostitute who robs customers *US, 1971*
- One kind of bar prostitute as the "roller." She is less interested in fees than in "rolling" her client and taking his wallet after he is drunk. — Charles Winick, *The Lively Commerce*, p. 173, 1971
4 a robber who relies on brute force *US, 1975*
- People were waiting to find out who the Greek was betting on, including some people who would make my Ohio River rollers look like choirboys. — Jimmy Snyder, *Jimmy the Greek*, p. 65, 1975
5 a wave *US, 1988*
- — Michael V. Anderson, *The Bad, Rad, Not to Forget Way Cool Beach and Surf Discriptionary*, p. 16, 1988
6 a vein that tends to roll away from a needle *US, 1970*
- — Walter Way, *The Drug Scene*, p. 113, 1977
- He was one of those wiry guys with veins forever; he could even fire at will into the rollers around his wrists and ankles. — Seth Morgan, *Homeboy*, p. 65, 1990
7 a tablet of MDMA, the recreational drug best known as ecstasy *US, 2002*
- Tablets of the rave-party drug ecstasy are called "rollers," he added, explaining that ecstasy users often describe their high as "feeling like they're rolling." — *Milwaukee Journal Sentinel*, p. 1B, 9th February 2002
8 a hot dog *US, 1991*
- After they had eaten in the formal wardroom (they were fortunate; the meal was real meat in the form of "sliders and rollers," cheeseburgers and hot dogs), they visited Tim's tiny stateroom. — Gerry Carroll, *North S*A*R*, p. 133, 1991

roller-rings *noun*
the police *US, 1987*
- — *Washington Post Magazine*, p. 9, 6th September 1987: "Say Wha'?"

rollers *noun*
dice with rounded edges *US, 1950*
A roller may be intentionally crafted or not; a naturally occurring roller makes a controlled shot by a cheat difficult.
- — *The Annals of the American Academy of Political and Social Sciences*, p. 130, May 1950

roll for the bowl *noun*
toilet paper *US, 1991*
- — Lee McNelis, *30 + And a Wake-Up*, p. 11, 1991

rollie *noun*
a hand-rolled cigarette. loose tobacco, used for hand-rolling cigarettes *US, 1967*
Prison usage.
- I took out a bag of rollies and rolled one and offered it to him. — Piri Thomas, *Down These Mean Streets*, p. 265, 1967
- "I'm gonna make us a righteous Cadillac so we can score a couple of rollies form my dawg Big Bear." — Jimmy Lerner, *You Got Nothing Coming*, p. 90, 2002

rolling bones *noun*
dice *US, 1950*
- — *The Annals of the American Academy of Political and Social Sciences*, p. 130, May 1950

rollings *noun*
loose cigarette tobacco *US, 1945*
- — Lou Shelly, *Hepcats Jive Talk Dictionary*, p. 48, 1945

rolling thunder *noun*
sustained, heavy bombing *US, 1977*
- He called them Rolling Thunder, and it was incessant during the nights. — Michael Herr, *Dispatches*, p. 108, 1977

roll in the hay *noun*
an act of sexual intercourse *US, 1945*
- He uses frig all over the place, and he doesn't even know what he's saying. If a girl uses that word, she knows damn well what she's saying, and you can chalk up another roll in the hay. — Evan Hunter, *The Blackboard Jungle*, p. 146, 1954
- "But this was a little more than what you gay fellows refer to as a roll in the hay." — George Clayton Johnson, *Ocean's Eleven*, p. 90, 1960
- We had a few rolls in the hay years ago—nothing much. — Mary McCarthy, *The Group*, p. 349, 1963

roll out *verb*
to leave *US, 1997*
- — Vann Wesson, *Generation X Field Guide and Lexicon*, p. 144, 1997

rollover *noun*
an informant *US, 2000*
- Manly began interviewing the rollovers and slowly put together a credible prosecution, thanks to the AW informants. — Bill Valentine, *Gangs and Their Tattoos*, p. 13, 2000

roll over *verb*
to inform, to betray, to cooperate with the police *US, 1989*
- Shortly after the Patriarca indictment, which drew front-page stories about a Mafia stool pigeon, an angry Barboza tried to explain why he'd rolled over[.] — Gerard O'Neill, *The Under Boss*, p. 84, 1989
- "You're going to give him to us." That was Partner form the wall. "You're going to roll over on him." — John Ridley, *Love is a Racket*, p. 204, 1998

roll-past *noun*
a police car driving past suspected criminal activity *US, 1997*
- The roll-past gave DeAndre something to think about, and he's thinking about it still. — David Simon and Edward Burns, *The Corner*, p. 27, 1997

Rolls *noun*
a Rolls-Royce car *US, 1928*
- You said the guy had a Rolls. You know how many fucking Rolls are parked out at Seminole? — Elmore Leonard, *Split Images*, p. 172, 1981

roll up *verb*
1 to arrive *US, 2005*
- One day, we were about sixteen, and some guys rolled up on him and a couple of the other cousins in Brooklyn with a shotgun. — RZA, *The Wu-Tang Manual*, p. 12, 2005
2 to roll a marijuana cigarette *US, 1971*
- — Eugene Landy, *The Underground Dictionary*, p. 162, 1971

roll-your-own *noun*
a handmade cigarette *US, 1947*
- "You don't smoke roll-your-owns any more, huh?" — Willard Motley, *Knock on Any Door*, p. 161, 1947

Roman candle *noun*
1 in homosexual usage, the penis of an Italian or Italian-American *US, 1987*
- — *Maledicta*, p. 58, 1986–1987: "A continuation of a glossary of ethnic slurs in American English"
2 in target shooting, a poorly loaded cartridge that produces a spray of red sparks when detonated *US, 1957*
- — *American Speech*, p. 194, October 1957: "Some colloquialisms of the handgunner"
3 a burst of tracer bullets *US, 1962*
- — *American Speech*, p. 272, December 1962: "The language of traffic policemen"

Roman culture; Roman love *noun*
group sex *US, 1964*
- "Roman," "Greek" and "Egyptian" love are, respectively, heterosexual, homosexual and bestial or sado-masochistic. — William and Jerrye Breedlove, *Swap Clubs*, p. 58, 1964
- — Dale Gordon, *The Dominion Sex Dictionary*, p. 141, 1967

romeos *noun*
high-topped loafers *US, 1975*
- Lipipo walked into the shoe shop and asked Tommy Barnes for a pair of his romeos. — James Carr, *Bad*, p. 126, 1975

romp *noun*
in horseracing, an easy victory *US, 1976*
- — Tom Ainslie, *Ainslie's Complete Guide to Thoroughbred Racing*, p. 337, 1976

romp *verb*
to excite; to excel; to be lively *US, 1946*
- It really romped. — Mezz Mezzrow, *Really the Blues*, p. 236, 1946

ron *noun*
a homosexual Mafia don *US, 2002*
- Gay Mafia dons are also called rons and davids. — *New Yorker*, p. 164, 9th September 2002

ronies *noun*
pepperoni *US, 1996*
- — *Maledicta*, p. 19, 1996: "Domino's pizza jargon"

-roo *suffix*
used as an meaningless, affected embellishment of a noun *US, 1984*
- "Pluto says a buddy-roo of his is making a movie-roo in Venice." — James Ellroy, *Blood on the Moon*, p. 129, 1984

roodle *adjective*
in poker, said of a hand in which the stakes have been temporarily raised *US, 1947*
- — Oswald Jacoby, *Oswald Jacoby on Poker*, p. 142, 1947

roody-poo *noun*
someone who is ignorant or unsophisticated *US, 1999*
- Cole has played most of this season at No. 3 singles or No. 2 doubles, but he's no tennis roody poo. — *Plain Dealer (Cleveland, Ohio)*, p. 12D, 15th May 1999
- The Rock is a finely tuned machine, and he's more than capable of laying the smack down on every single roody-poo stupid enough to enter the ring against him. — Rock, *The Rock Says*, p. 221, 2000

roody-poo *adjective*
second-rate; shallow *US, 2000*
- Laying the Smack Down on Your Roody-Poo Candy Ass! — The Rock, *The Rock Says...*, p. 305, 2000
- You mean we're not taking any crap from that roody-poo jabroni Ronald DeChooch. — Janet Evanovich, *Seven Up*, p. 211, 2001

roof *noun*
the flight deck of an aircraft carrier *UK, 1998*
- — *Seattle Times*, p. A9, 12th April 1998: "Grunts, squids not grunting from the same dictionary"

roof *verb*
to break into a building through the roof *US, 1972*
- Say it's a two- or three-story building and you've roofed it and you've come in and it's a big old soundproof place[.] — Bruce Jackson, *Outside the Law*, p. 94, 1972

roofer *noun*
Rohypnol™ (flunitrazepam), popularly known as the "date-rape drug" *US, 1995*
- One of my good friends has used a drug referred to as something like "roofer," a prescription drug called something like "rophynol." — *alt.drugs*, 8th March 1995
- Bo "got any roofer, man?" — *alt.folklore.urban*, 16th April 1996
- This drug, flunitrazepam, or Rohypnol (known on the street as "roofies" or "roofers") is a powerful sedative[.] — *Teen Magazine*, p. 68, July 1997

roofies; ruffles; roples *noun*
the recreational drug Rohypnol™ (flunitrazepam) *US, 1995*
- "Roofies" are used to pre-medicate patients before surgery. The drug is not approved for use in the U.S. — *alt.drugs*, 22nd March 1995
- See if she wasn't stoned-out on roofies. — James Lee Burke, *Cimarron Rose*, p. 277, 1997
- He'd had a few beers, a couple joints, maybe half a roofie, when he decided to tune the Impala. — Carl Hiaasen, *Lucky You*, p. 150, 1997
- "I think what he did was put something in my Seven-Up, a roofie or something." — Jonathan Kellerman, *Rage*, p. 351, 2005

rook *noun*
a beginner *US, 1905*
An abbreviation of **ROOKIE**.
- "Who's the rook?" — Herbert Simmons, *Corner Boy*, p. 125, 1957
- Hey, you're the rook I'm working with tonight. — Charles Whited, *Chiodo*, p. 27, 1973
- Check out the rook! — *Bull Durham*, 1988

rook *verb*
to cheat someone; to swindle someone; to defraud someone *UK, 1590*
- I know exactly what it was worth and that guy just rooked you. — Kenneth Lonergan, *This is Our Youth*, p. 116, 2000

roomie *noun*
1 a roommate *US, 1918*
- I finished unpacking, pushing my roomie's battery of bottles aside to make room for my own. — Frederick Kohner, *The Affairs of Gidget*, p. 10, 1963
- Guy's got n'eleven o'clock, roomie won't tell "i'm the right Jesuschris" time. — Richard Farina, *Been Down So Long*, p. 94, 1966
- "Fuck him," said Mona. "You've got a new roomie now." — Armistead Maupin, *Tales of the City*, p. 72, 1978
- We really became roomies—roommates. — Bobby Seale, *A Lonely Rage*, p. 106, 1978

2 a prison cellmate *US, 1982*
- — Ralph de Sola, *Crime Dictionary*, p. 130, 1982
- I told two of my old roomies about the coke house, but I didn't say I worked here or nothing. — Terry Williams, *The Cocaine Kids*, p. 40, 1989

room-rifler *noun*
a thief who steals from hotel rooms *US, 1954*
- If a room-rifler or a lock-worker gets away with a good score at some hotel, he'll keep quiet about it. — Dev Collans with Stewart Sterling, *I was a House Detective*, p. 47, 1954

'rooms *noun*
mushrooms *US, 1969*
- — John D. Bell et al., *Loosely Speaking*, p. Appendix, 1969

rooms *noun*
a roommate *US, 1970*
- He'd say things like, "Rooms, tomorrow we go to a bookstore and buy some of those real-estate books." — Jim Bouton, *Ball Four*, p. 227, 1970
- — Connie Eble (Editor), *UNC-CH Campus Slang*, p. 8, Spring 1992

room temperature IQ *noun*
a very low intelligence *US, 1981*
- He had a room-temperature I.Q., which made him extremely obliging, hence an excellent artist's model and a pretty fair marine. — Joseph Wambaugh, *The Glitter Dome*, p. 61, 1981
- Even someone with a room temperature IQ would know it was the type of case you could retire on. — *The National Law Journal*, p. 3, 28th November 1983
- — *Maledicta*, p. 118, 1984–1985: "Milwaukee medical maledicta"
- Either Bush is living up to the rumor of a room temperature IQ or he's getting very bad advice. — *San Diego Union-Tribune*, p. B11, 27th March 2003

room time *noun*
time spent surfing in the breaking hollow of a wave *US, 1991*
- — Trevor Cralle, *The Surfin'ary*, p. 102, 1991

rooney *noun*
the penis *US, 1968*
- — Collin Baker et al., *College Undergraduate Slang Study Conducted at Brown University*, p. 186, 1968

roost *noun*
a residence, be it room, apartment or house *US, 1945*
- — Lou Shelly, *Hepcats Jive Talk Dictionary*, p. 16, 1945
- — Clarence Major, *Dictionary of Afro-American Slang*, p. 98, 1970

rooster *noun*
1 the buttocks *US, 1946*
- "Sorry," the bossman said, not even bothering to get up off his rooster. — Mezz Mezzrow, *Really the Blues*, p. 131, 1946

2 crack cocaine *US, 1994*
- — US Department of Justice, *Street Terms*, October 1994

3 a member of the Piru youth gang *US, 1994*
- — Ann Lawson, *Kids & Gangs*, p. 56, 1994: "Common African-American gang slang/phrases"

rooster tail *noun*
a spray of water directly behind an object or person moving fast through the water *US, 1965*
- — John M. Kelly, *Surf and Sea*, p. 292, 1965

root *noun*
1 the penis *US, 1968*
- — Collin Baker et al., *College Undergraduate Slang Study Conducted at Brown University*, p. 186, 1968
- The girl unzips his fly and extracts his root. — Anne Steinhardt, *Thunder La Boom*, p. 146, 1974

2 an amphetamine or other central nervous system stimulant *US, 1971*
- — Eugene Landy, *The Underground Dictionary*, p. 162, 1971

root, hog, or die *verb*
used when difficult work is the only course of action *US, 1834*
- It was—as he put it to himself, root, hog, or die! — Malcolm Braly, *It's Cold Out There*, p. 9, 1966
- "Don't make Ruby feel worse than she does already. They've got no choice. In times like these, it's root, hog, or die." — Sandra Dallas, *The Persian Pickle Club*, p. 43, 1995

rootin' tootin' oil *noun*
semen *US, 1962*
- — Joseph E. Ragen and Charles Finston, *Inside the World's Toughest Prison*, p. 816, 1962: "Penitentiary and underworld glossary"

rope *noun*
1 a thick gold chain necklace *US, 1989*
- — Ellen C. Bellone (Editor), *Dictionary of Slang*, p. 20, 1989
- "We gonna be wearing big gold ropes, Rolexes, diamond ear studs, and you gonna be looking at your Timex, trying to figure out what time it is, cuz." — Bob Sipchen, *Baby Insane and the Buddha*, p. 142, 1993

2 Rohypnol™ (flunitrazepam), popularly known as the "date-rape drug" *US, 1995*
- On the street the drug has many nicknames; teenagers know it as rope, ribs, or roaches. — *Texas Monthly*, p. 88, September 1995
- The drug is called rope, rophies, roofies, roche and Mexican Valium on the streets and is marketed as Rohypnol in South America. — *Daily Oklahoman (Oklahoma City)*, p. 1, 5th September 1995

3 a prominent vein *US, 2002*
- But boy could he hit me and never miss, which is hard because I got the invisible veins, not the ropes he had. — Lynn Breedlove, *Godspeed*, p. 17, 2002

rope *verb*
1 to lure someone into a swindle *US, 1848*
- You've heard me brag that I had once been with the big con. I lied to you, son. I never roped or played the inside. — Iceberg Slim (Robert Beck), *Trick Baby*, p. 39, 1969
- He sends you out to rope suckers in with your ass? — Robert Campbell, *Juice*, p. 233, 1988

2 in a card game, to cheat or mislead someone *US, 1985*
- — Steve Kuriscak, *Casino Talk*, p. 48, 1985
- — George Percy, *The Language of Poker*, p. 76, 1988

rope-a-dope *noun*
a tactic of feigning weakness in order to lure an opponent into an ill-advised offensive *US, 1979*
Boxer Mohammed Ali used the term to describe his tactics fighting George Foreman in Zaire—Ali rested against the ropes, absorbing or evading blows from Foreman who soon tired from the exertion. First recorded in the boxing sense in 1975.
- Carlito, the dude pulled the rope-a-dope on you. — Edwin Torres, *After Hours*, p. 387, 1979

rope dope *noun*
low grade marijuana *US, 2002*
- — Nick Brownlee, *This Is Cannabis*, p. 153, 2002

roper *noun*
in a confidence swindle, a confederate who identifies and lures the victim into the swindle *US, 1840*
Originally used in the context of gambling houses, and then in confidence swindles.
- You've made it to become a big white con roper. — Iceberg Slim (Robert Beck), *Long White Con*, p. 16, 1977

rophie *noun*
Rohypnol™ (flunitrazepam), popularly known as the "date-rape drug" *US, 1993*

- One rophie salesman says his connection sells them by the thousand, at one dollar per tablet. — *Miami New Times*, 14th July 1993
- The drug is called rope, rophies, roofies, roche and Mexican Valium on the streets and is marketed as Rohypnol in South America. — *Daily Oklahoman (Oklahoma City)*, p. 1, 5th September 1995

ro-ro *adjective*
roll on, roll off *US, 1990*
Said of a containerization system used to ship military cargo during the Vietnam war.
- Ro-ro container method further increased the Navy's logistical support capabilities. — Gregory Clark, *Words of the Vietnam War*, p. 439, 1990

Rosa Maria; rosa maria *noun*
marijuana *US, 1938*
- — Ernest L. Abel, *A Marijuana Dictionary*, p. 89, 1982
- In the early twenties, marijuana, muggles, muta, gage, tea, reefer, grifa, Mary Warner, Mary Jane or rosa maria was known almost exclusively to musicians. — Harry Shapiro, *Waiting For The Man*, p. 29, 1999

roscoe *noun*
a handgun *US, 1914*
- Every time I meet a girl I whip out the old roscoe and pretend I'm a New York gangster and scare the hell out of them. — Jack Kerouac, *Letter to Neal Cassady*, p. 127, 13th September 1947
- Then, holding his roscoe or barker on Mr. Mach, the policeman moseyed back to the truck and peered inside. — *San Francisco News*, p. 1, 25th August 1950
- I mean, she stood up, right in the face of my Roscoe! — Robert Gover, *One Hundred Dollar Misunderstanding*, p. 180, 1961
- The dude went mad / an' started to jump bad, pulling his roscoe out his slide. — Lightnin' Rod, *Hustlers Convention*, p. 98, 1973

roscoe *verb*
to point a handgun at someone and order them not to move *US, 1974*
- Why you wants to be roscoeing me, brother? — Vernon E. Smith, *The Jones Men*, p. 115, 1974
- I heard Bailey holler, "Police," so I figured he had the suspect roscoed. — Gerald Petievich, *To Die in Beverly Hills*, p. 108, 1983

rose *noun*
a tablet of Benzedrine™ (amphetamine sulfate), a central nervous system stimulant *US, 1967*
- — John B. Williams, *Narcotics and Hallucinogenics*, p. 114, 1967

rosebud *noun*
1 the anus *US, 1965*
- — *The Guild Dictionary of Homosexual Terms*, p. 39, 1965
- — Bruce Rodgers, *The Queens' Vernacular*, p. 19, 1972

2 a textbook example of a primary lesion *US, 1981*
- — *Maledicta*, p. 227, Summer/Winter 1981: "Sex and the single soldier"

3 following a colostomy, the pink tissue that marks the opening of the intestine on the abdomen *US, 1980*
- — *Maledicta*, p. 56, Summer 1980: "Not Sticks and stones, but names: more medical pejoratives"

rose garden *noun*
a group of neurologically depressed hospital patients *US, 1978*
- — *Maledicta*, p. 69, Summer/Winter 1978: "Common patient-directed pejoratives used by medical personnel"

rosette *noun*
the buttocks *US, 1972*
- A guy came into the Woodlawn Recreation in Chicago, where I was sitting on my rosette doing nothing[.] — Robert Byrne, *McGoorty*, p. 32, 1972

rosewood *noun*
a police nightstick *US, 1970*
- — Clarence Major, *Dictionary of Afro-American Slang*, p. 98, 1970

Rosie Palm and her five sisters; Rosie Palm; Rosie *noun*
the male hand as the instrument of masturbation *US, 1977*
- When you turn out the light—I've got to hand it to me / Looks like it's me and you again tonight Rosie[.] — Jackson Browne and Donald Miller, *Rosie*, 1977
- FRIEND: why don't you be a gentleman and ask Rosey? TED: Who? FRIEND: Rosey Palm, your girlfriend. God knows you spend enough fucking time with her. — *Something About Mary*, 1998

rot *noun*
an unidentified disease or malady *US, 1947*
- — *American Speech*, p. 304, December 1947: "Imaginary diseases in army and navy parlance"

rot corps *noun*
the ROTC, or Reserve Officer Training Corps, found at many colleges *US, 1972*
- — Helen Dahlskog (Editor), *A Dictionary of Contemporary and Colloquial Usage*, p. 49, 1972

ROTF
used in computer message shorthand to mean "*rolling on the floor (laughing)*" *US, 1991*
- — Eric S. Raymond, *The New Hacker's Dictionary*, p. 342, 1991

rotgut *noun*
any unwholesome alcohol *UK, 1633*
- Indiana Harbor was a drinking town, and he must have shoved enough rotgut across the bar to fill Lake Michigan, but he never touched the juice himself. — Mezz Mezzrow, *Really the Blues*, p. 70, 1946
- Somebody passed a bottle of rotgut, the bottom of it. — Jack Kerouac, *On the Road*, p. 24, 1957
- Anything with a buzz in it was in great demand on campus. A pint of "rot gut" whiskey brought from seven and a half to ten dollars, depending on supply. — Iceberg Slim (Robert Beck), *Pimp*, p. 43, 1969
- This ain't Kentucky sipping whiskey. It's Mexican rot gut. — Quentin Tarantino, *From Dusk Till Dawn*, p. 96, 1995

rotorhead *noun*
a helicopter pilot or crew member *US, 1991*
- With introductions and handshakes all around, the pilots at the table greeted the two rotorheads warmly, as most fixed-wing guys do after one of their own has been pulled out of the water. — Gerry Carroll, *North S*A*R*, p. 36, 1991
- He calls me "grunt," and I call him "rotorhead." — Kregg Jorgenson, *Very Crazy G.I.*, p. 224, 2001

roto-rooter *noun*
a person who kisses with an active and probing tongue *US, 1963*
- — Carol Ann Preusse, *Jargon Used by University of Texas Co-Eds*, 1963

rots of ruck
lots of luck! *US, 1957*
Deliberately corrupted English, associated with Chinese or Japanese immigrants.
- "Rots of ruck, Jack." — Amalgamted Transit Union, *In Transit*, p. 9, 1957
- "Rots of ruck," he said. That's Jap for, "Don't let anybody cut your air hose." — Frank Bonham, *Deepwater Challenge*, p. 29, 1965
- "Rots of ruck!" said Freddy Muldoon, shouting back. — Bertrand R. Brinley, *Mad Scientists' Club*, p. 151, 1967
- "Well, rots of ruck," I wished him as I walked out of the door. — Xaviera Hollander, *The Happy Hooker*, p. 180, 1972

rotten squash *noun*
brain damage *US, 1984–1985*
- — *Maledicta*, p. 118, 1984–1985: "Milwaukee medical maledicta"

rotter *noun*
a despised person *UK, 1894*
- "Shut that panel, you rotter!" he rasped. — Chester Gould, *Dick Tracy Meets the Night Crawler*, p. 216, 1945

rottie *noun*
a *Rottweiler* dog *US, 1987*
- But you pay $800 for a good rottie, while you can find a Doberman for $30. — *Business Week*, p. 148, 23rd February 1987
- The Rottie is not excitable or quarrelsome; he is faithful, friendly and able. — Andrew De Prisco, *The Mini-Atlas of Dog Breeds*, p. 144, 1990

rough *verb*
to rob someone with force or threat of force *US, 1973*
- We played this thing for three years and outta all the people we busted, we only had to rough (stick up) three of 'em. — A.S. Jackson, *Gentleman Pimp*, p. 131, 1973

▸ **rough it up**
in poker, to bet heavily *US, 1979*
- — John Scarne, *Scarne's Guide to Modern Poker*, p. 289, 1979

rough *adjective*
1 excellent; fashionable, trendy *US, 1963*

- — *San Francisco Examiner: People*, p. 8, 27th October 1963: "What a 'Z&'! The astonishing private language of Bay Area teenagers"

2 in lowball poker, unfavorable *US, 1967*
- — Albert H. Morehead, *The Complete Guide to Winning Poker*, p. 271, 1967

roughhouse *verb*
to brawl in a playful if rowdy and boisterous manner *US, 1900*
- Bill, they won't stop roughhousing. — *Bill and Ted's Excellent Adventure*, 1989

rough hustle *noun*
an amateurish, unpolished swindle *US, 1977*
The term does not connote any physical roughness, simply a lack of polish.
- — Robert C. Prus and C.R.D. Sharper, *Road Hustler*, p. 171, 1977: "Glossary of terms"

roughie *noun*
a movie that combines sexual and violent exploitation *US, 1970*
- Others produced "roughies," amixture of sex and violence. — *The Presidential Commission on Obscenity and Pornography*, p. 109, 1970

roughneck *noun*
a thug, a lout, a rowdy person *US, 1836*
- I want him to be a gentleman of sorts, not a rough-neck. — Geoff Brown, *I Want What I Want*, p. 164, 1966
- Clubs seem to get a honeymoon period, but then a bunch of roughnecks attach themselves to the night and it goes downhill from there. — Dave Haslam, *Dear Colin*, p. 151, 1999

rough off *verb*
to steal something using brute force *US, 1985*
- Anyway, a couple of punks tried to rough off the kid's radio and one of them got himself stabbed. — Andrew Vachss, *Flood*, p. 342, 1985

rough stuff *noun*
violent or sadistic sexual behavior *US, 1925*
- "No rough stuff," she warned suddenly. "Rough stuff?" "Whips—and that type of crap." — Joey V., *Portrait of Joey*, p. 90, 1969
- "No rough stuff or fancy fuckin', boys; Lolita is only sixteen and just startin' out." — Edwin Torres, *Carlito's Way*, p. 15, 1975

rough trade *noun*
a tough, often sadistic male homosexual, especially as a casual sex partner *US, 1925*
In rare instances used to describe a homosexual sexual liaison.
- "Man, I want to make a score!" a young, rough-trade guy says in loud invitation to any man who wants to go. — Willard Motley, *Let No Man Write My Epitaph*, p. 203, 1958
- I had an address book a mile long, packed with tricks from "drag queens" to rough trade, old aunties, little nellie queens queens that stayed home with mother. — Antony James, *America's Homosexual Underground*, p. 78, 1965
- A street, stud, commonly referred to as "rough trade," will prostitute himself for as little as five dollars. — Johnny Shearer, *The Male Hustler*, p. 17, 1966
- Almost always rough trade is fellated first after which he turns sour. — Bruce Rodgers, *The Queens' Vernacular*, p. 173, 1972

round *verb*
to make the rounds *US, 1961*
- You can still go rounding. Some stores stay open. — Bernard Wolfe, *The Magic of Their Singing*, p. 25, 1961

round-brown *noun*
the anus *US, 1972*
- We call that a brownie queen. In prison they call it under-yonder and round-brown. — Bruce Jackson, *In the Life*, p. 397, 1972
- "Bend over and show me that round brown," Elwood Banks said. — Joseph Wambaugh, *The Choirboys*, p. 74, 1975

rounder *noun*
1 a prisoner associated with traditional Italian-American organized crime *US, 1992*
- — William K. Bentley and James M. Corbett, *Prison Slang*, p. 43, 1992

2 a highly skilled professional poker player who travels and plays less skilled players *US, 1979*
- — John Scarne, *Scarne's Guide to Modern Poker*, p. 281, 1979
- Rounders, grifters, con artists, and thieves worked the area strip bars and pool halls[.] — Kim Rich, *Johnny's Girl*, p. 48, 1993

rounder girl *noun*
a woman involved in the criminal lifestyle *US, 1972*

- If you're with a rounder girl, believe me she says what she thinks and if she's going to swear, she says swear words and she knows them all[.] — Harry King, *Box Man*, p. 137, 1972

round eye *noun*

1 the anus; by extension, a male homosexual who plays the passive role in anal sex *US, 1950*

- — Hyman E. Goldin et al., *Dictionary of American Underworld Lingo*, p. 181, 1950
- At thirty-three I was fairly safe from wholesale rape. That is unless I tipped my secret or somebody came in from the street that knew me and told that I was an experienced "round eye." — Iceberg Slim (Robert Beck), *Mama Black Widow*, p. 303, 1969
- She had a good round-eye, and that's no lie / How the trickhouse door would swing! — Dennis Wepman et al., *The Life*, p. 83, 1976

2 an American or European *US, 1960*
From the Southeast Asian perspective, adopted by US soldiers in Vietnam to describe themselves.

- The round-eyes are very expensive, they are imported for the politicians and generals[.] — William Wilson, *The LBJ Brigade*, pp. 37–38, 1966
- "My God, a round-eye," gasped a Seebee. — Elaine Shepard, *The Doom Pussy*, p. 36, 1967
- Whatever he expected to see, it wasn't a bearded "round-eye." — Donald Duncan, *The New Legions*, p. 39, 1967
- — Carl Fleischhauer, *A Glossary of Army Slang*, p. 11, 1968
- — *Current Slang*, p. 17, Summer 1970

round-eyed *adjective*

American or European, Caucasian *US, 1966*

- Now nobody is happy except the command officers; they keep the round-eyed prostitutes[.] — William Wilson, *The LBJ Brigade*, p. 43, 1966
- [A]bout half the round-eyed press corps in Saigon had seriously considered staying on, after South Vietnam finally fell and the PRG took over[.] — Hunter S. Thompson, *Songs of the Doomed*, p. 167, May 1975
- [T]he restaurant proprietor regularly engaged Asian and round-eyed B-girls to solicit drinks from customers. — Joseph Wambaugh, *The Delta Star*, p. 124, 1983

round-eye tail *noun*

an American nurse as perceived by a soldier in Vietnam *US, 1981*

- The GIs called nurses round-eye tail, and suddenly that's exactly what we were. — Mark Baker, *Nam*, p. 186, 1981

round file *noun*

a wastebasket *US, 1975*

- — *American Speech*, p. 65, Spring–Summer 1975: "Razorback slang"

roundheel *noun*

a woman who is easily talked into sexual relations *US, 1943*
Boxing slang from the 1920s for a poor fighter—a "pushover"—applied later to women of easy virtue.

- — Lou Shelly, *Hepcats Jive Talk Dictionary*, p. 16, 1945
- [N]one of these roundheels that crumb a place up just by walking through the lobby[.] — Jim Thompson, *The Grifters*, p. 18, 1963
- One can dry hump the local roundheels without fear of infection[.] — Seth Morgan, *Homeboy*, p. 44, 1990

round-heeled *adjective*

easily seduced *US, 1957*

- Jefferson Tatum, who never allowed visitors in his house, unless you count Millie and Esther McCabe, the round-heeled twins from packaging[.] — Max Shulman, *Anyone Got a Match?*, p. 95, 1964

round heels *noun*

a promiscuous or sexually compliant woman *US, 1926*
Derogatory; from the anatomical notion that a woman with round heels is more easily put on her back.

- To cap the climax he later learned that the queen had round heels for everyone else. — Glendon Swarthout, *Where the Boys Are*, p. 33, 1960
- [D]irectly on the round heels of the Food and Drug Administration (FDA) approval of the abortion pill[.] — *Insight on the News*, 23rd October 2000

roundhouse *noun*

a punch that swings round to hit your opponent side-on *US, 1920*

- I'll lift you off your feet so fast with a roundhouse / You'll think I pulled the ground out from underneath you[.] — Eminem (Marshall Mathers), *Fuck the Planet*, 2000

round robin *noun*

a story begun by one writer and completed by another or multiple writers *US, 1982*

- — *American Speech*, p. 29, Spring 1982: "The language of science fiction fan magazines"

round sound *noun*

a fashionable, current song *US, 1955*
"Round" means nothing, but contrasts with **SQUARE**.

- — *American Speech*, p. 304, December 1955: "Wayne University slang"

roundtable *noun*

in organized crime, a meeting of leaders convened to discuss and decide pressing business issues *US, 1975*

- Tommy, there was a roundtable just before you come out and Mr. A said you done the right thing—so we're gonna move you up[.] — Edwin Torres, *Carlito's Way*, pp. 48–49, 1975

round-up *noun*

in college, a notification of academic deficiency *US, 1968*

- — *American Speech*, pp. 76–77, February 1968: "Some notes on flunk notes"

roust *verb*

to subject to a thorough, often messy search *US, 1981*

- This was done because the day before, I had been rousted by pigs who pretended they were searching my cell and beaten up in the process. — Jack Henry Abbott, *In the Belly of the Beast*, p. 36, 1981

rout *noun*

a wild, rowdy party *US, 1968*

- — Collin Baker et al., *College Undergraduate Slang Study Conducted at Brown University*, p. 186, 1968

row *verb*

▶ **row down the red river**
to experience the bleed period of the menstrual cycle *US, 2001*

- — Don R. McCreary (Editor), *Dawg Speak*, 2001

rowbottom *noun*

a student disturbance, started in fun but not always ending as such *US, 1940*
Specific to the University of Pennsylvania, claimed to have been named for J.T. Rowbottom, a rowdy member of Penn's Class of 1913.

- Any provocation, particularly that of springtime, is enough to touch off mischief-making riots signaled by the cry "Oh, Rowbottom!" on the Penn campus and the adjacent main streets of Philadelphia. — *American Speech*, p. 293, December 1958
- — Claudio R. Salvucci, *The Philadelphia Dialect Dictionary*, p. 55, 1996

row dog *noun*

in prison, another prisoner whose cell is on the same tier *US, 1995*

- — Mark S. Fleisher, *Beggars & Thieves*, p. 291, 1995: "Glossary"

rowdy *noun*

a person who inhales glue for the psychoactive effect *US, 1971*

- — Eugene Landy, *The Underground Dictionary*, p. 162, 1971

rowdy dowdy *noun*

in pickpocketing, the seemingly accidental jostling of victims or potential victims by members of the gang *US, 1962*

- — Joseph E. Ragen and Charles Finston, *Inside the World's Toughest Prison*, p. 816, 1962: "Penitentiary and underworld glossary"

rowers' revenge *noun*

the ritual of throwing the coxswain into the water after a rowing team wins an event *US, 2001*

- — Judy's Enterprises, *Coxswain Postcard*, 2001

rox *noun*

crack cocaine *US, 1994*
A phonetic play on **ROCK(S)**.

- — US Department of Justice, *Street Terms*, October 1994

Roxanne *noun*

cocaine; crack cocaine *US, 1994*
A **ROCK** personification.

- — US Department of Justice, *Street Terms*, October 1994

royal shaft *noun*

monumental mistreatment *US, 1974*

- Christ, tell 'em you're out here in goddamn New Mexico gettin' the royal shaft from Clark. — Mark Medoff, *When You Comin' Back, Red Ryder*, p. 14, 1974
- — *Esquire*, p. 180, June 1983

royal wedding *noun*

in hold 'em poker, a king and queen, especially of diamonds *US, 1996*

- — John Vorhaus, *The Big Book of Poker Slang*, p. 32, 1996

RPG *noun*

1 a *role-playing game US, 1986*

- AppleCat modem information and programming, online role-playing games (RPG) such as Dungeons & Dragons. — *Washington Post*, p. N4, 11th July 1986
- "I'm really into RPGs," he says. "It's a fun thing to collect." — Marty Beckerman, *Death to All Cheerleaders*, p. 92, 2000

2 a rocket-propelled grenade *US, 1992*

- Hell, after all of that shooting right here in front of me and not hits, now I take an RPG round. — Bob Stoffey, *Cleared Hot!*, p. 89, 1992

RSN

used as Internet shorthand to mean "*real soon now*" *US, 1995*

- — Christian Crumlish, *The Internet Dictionary*, p. 172, 1995

RTFM

read the fucking manual *US, 1997*

- — Andy Ihnatko, *Cyberspeak*, p. 166, 1997

ru *noun*

a member of the Piru youth gang *US, 1994*

- — Ann Lawson, *Kids & Gangs*, p. 56, 1994: "Common African-American gang slang/phrases"

rub *verb*

▸ **rub it on your chest**

to forget about *US, 1975*

- — Miguel Pinero, *Short Eyes*, p. 126, 1975: Glossary of Slang

rubber *noun*

1 a condom *US, 1947*

- "[I]f they was to be a piece of pussy settin' up on that beach, and Ah didn't have a rubber, Ah'd just shoot myself anyway." — Norman Mailer, *The Naked and the Dead*, p. 21, 1948
- One of these inexpressible American evenings in a girl's home-parlor, with darkness pressing at the windows, and little lace panties, and little sighs, and noises that make you jump and look over your sweaty shoulder, and the final disposal of the saggy rubber in your handker-chief. — Jack Kerouac, *Letter to Neal Cassady*, p. 287, 10th January 1951
- There is an awful lot of clap loose in the U.S.—and while rubbers are a drag, the clap is something else again. — *Berkeley Barb*, p. 10, 2nd–8th June 1967
- Few men use rubbers in Nevada's clean houses, but you can if you want to. — Gerald Paine, *A Bachelor's Guide to the Brothels of Nevada*, p. 12, 1978
- This receptacle is where the studs deposit their used rubbers (perfectly placed, too, as the horrific stench its mouth emits discourages anyone from lingering onstage). — Anthony Petkovich, *The X Factory*, p. 188, 1997

2 balloons *US, 1966*

- — *American Speech*, p. 282, December 1966: "More carnie talk from the west coast"

rubber *adjective*

used of a check, unfunded *US, 1991*

A back-formation from the metaphor of an unfunded check bouncing.

- The guy says, "What can I do? They gave me a rubber check." — Robert Stoller and I.S. Levine, *Coming Attractions*, p. 93, 1991

rubber arms *noun*

the sensation experienced by a surfer paddling into a large wave *US, 1964*

- — John Severson, *Modern Surfing Around the World*, p. 180, 1964

rubber bitch *noun*

the inflatable rubber air mattress given to US troops in the field in Vietnam *US, 1984*

- — John Elting, *A Dictionary of Soldier Talk*, p. 266, 1984
- Then I fell on the unmade "rubber bitch" and slept till late afternoon. — Randy Herrod, *Blue's Bastards*, p. 7, 2004

rubber cow *noun*

in circus usage, an elephant, male or female *US, 1981*

- — Don Wilmeth, *The Language of American Popular Entertainment*, p. 36, 1981

rubber heels *noun*

meat loaf *US, 1949*

- "Rubber heels 'n' fisheyes again" was the word on the meatloaf and tapioca[.] — Nelson Algren, *The Man with the Golden Arm*, p. 208, 1949

rubber man *noun*

in circus and carnival usage, a balloon seller *US, 1981*

- — Don Wilmeth, *The Language of American Popular Entertainment*, p. 228, 1981

rubberneck *verb*

to stare with undue interest *US, 1896*

- I rubbernecked around some as we streaked along the avenue[.] — Mezz Mezzrow, *Really the Blues*, p. 174, 1946
- [H]e went on rubber-necking the speed demons. — Bernard Wolfe, *The Late Risers*, p. 183, 1954

rubberneck bus *noun*

a tour bus *US, 1958*

- Slowly the rubberneck bus groaned along Maxwell Street, lights out. — Willard Motley, *Let No Man Write My Epitaph*, p. 101, 1958

rubbernecker; rubberneck *noun*

a person who stares with curiosity, especially a motorist who slows to view an accident *US, 1934*

- [T]he blues men [meths drinkers] may become exhibitionists. Rubbernecks would attempt to photograph them from the windows of air-conditioned coaches. — Geoffrey Fletcher, *Down Among the Meths Men*, p. 22, 1966
- Back to the street—rubberneckers swarming. — James Ellroy, *White Jazz*, p. 38, 1992
- As soon as you tell people about your separation, they behave like rubberneckers at a car accident — Anka Radakovich, *The Wild Girls Club*, p. 40, 1994
- A few ordinary uniformed officers were standing around trying to disperse the rubberneckers who were disrupting the flow of traffic. — Greg Williams, *Diamond Geezers*, p. 203, 1997

rubber vag *noun*

in circus and carnival usage, someone who lives in a mobile trailer *US, 1981*

- — Don Wilmeth, *The Language of American Popular Entertainment*, p. 228, 1981

rubbins; rubbings *noun*

rubbing alcohol *US, 1980*

A drink of desperation.

- — Joe McKennon, *Circus Lingo*, p. 80, 1980

rubby *noun*

a derelict who drinks rubbing alcohol *US, 1961–1962*

The word is not to be confused with "rummy."

- — Frank Prewitt and Francis Schaeffer, *Vacaville Vocabulary*, 1961–1962
- A "rubby" drinks rubbing alcohol. He can buy it in drugstores on Sunday, when Canadian liquor stores are closed. — Bill Casselman, *Canadian Words*, p. 15, 1995

rubby-dub *noun*

an ignorant soldier from a rural mountain area, a poor candidate to be a good soldier *US, 1946*

- — *American Speech*, p. 238, October 1946: "World War II slang of maladjustment"

rube; reub *noun*

an unsophisticated, naive, inexperienced person *US, 1896*

From the older, UK "reuben" (a country bumpkin).

- Baltimore is overrun by rubes. — Jack Lait and Lee Mortimer, *Washington Confidential*, p. 261, 1951
- It used to irritate him, knowing what I had in my head, to hear me talking and acting like any other rube around town. — Jim Thompson, *The Killer Inside*, p. 28, 1952
- A few of the carnys knew who did it but they figured the rube had it coming[.] — Robert Edmond Alter, *Carny Kill*, p. 137, 1966
- I'm not a rube. I know who Tennessee Williams was. — Walter Tevis, *The Color of Money*, p. 52, 1984

rubies *noun*

the lips *US, 1947*

- — Marcus Hanna Boulware, *Jive and Slang of Students in Negro Colleges*, 1947

rub job *noun*

a planned murder *US, 1953*

- "I had agreed to do a rub job for Charlie Semmler." — Curt Cannon, *The Death of Me*, p. 106, 1953

rub joint *noun*

a dance hall where men can, for a small price, dance intimately with women *US, 1981*

- — Don Wilmeth, *The Language of American Popular Entertainment*, p. 228, 1981

rub 'n' tug *noun*

a massage that includes masturbation *US, 2000*

- If you really got lucky, maybe a wayward stripper took one of your unmarried groomsmen into the coat room of the Armpit Tavern and gave him a rub 'n' tug for an extra twenty-five bucks. — *Nerve*, p. 17, October–November 2000

rub of the brush *noun*

a beverage made from the remnants of drinks in a bar *US, 1950*

- Each got a tin-cup of this. It was called "a rub of the brush," because that was how it felt going down. — Jack Lait and Lee Mortimer, *Chicago Confidential*, p. 54, 1950
- After this rude awakening, the guest was sent out into the cold after a "rub of the brush"—a tin cup full of a mixture drawn from a slop pail in which the dregs from beer, wine, whiskey, and gin glasses had been emptied the night before[.] — Alson Smith, *Syndicate City*, p. 219, 1954

rub-out *noun*

a killing *US, 1927*

- I paid him back a month later by knocking off a punk that tried to set him for a rub-out when he refused to pay off for protection. — Mickey Spillane, *I, The Jury*, p. 43, 1947
- Had you read about the slaying of a young union leader in New Jersey, a man who was gunned down by a pair of hoods, a rub-out that was clearly tied to the victim's anti-Hoffa activities? — Sidney Bernard, *This Way to the Apocalypse*, p. 127, 1963
- "Our friend Bill O. has Reles stuck away in the Tombs for some old rubout." — Martin Gosch, *The Last Testament of Lucky Luciano*, p. 245, 1975
- They could always hold gangland rub-outs there. — Dan Jenkins, *Life Its Ownself*, p. 17, 1984

rub out *verb*

to kill someone *US, 1848*

- You're scared right now I'm gonna rub you out. — Marvin Wald and Albert Maltz, *The Naked City*, 1947
- The Hook was killed and Tony Indelicato was taken for a ride and rubbed out. — Jack Lait and Lee Mortimer, *Chicago Confidential*, p. 19, 1950
- Ribler had been "quietly rubbed out to prevent his testifying against the Hotsy Totsy Club murderers." — Robert Sylvester, *No Cover Charge*, p. 13, 1956
- Boots thinks you're an all right guy—he don't want you completely rubbed out. — Clarence Cooper Jr., *Black*, p. 279, 1963

rub up *verb*

to assault someone *US, 1952*

- There was a lot of yelling and gesticulating, and a few blows were passed. A couple of the guards got rubbed up a little. — Chester Himes, *Cast the First Stone*, p. 107, 1952

rubyfruit *noun*

the vagina *US, 1982*

- — *Maledicta*, p. 147, Summer/Winter 1982: "Dyke diction: the language of lesbians"

ruck *noun*

a rucksack or backpack *US, 1982*

- "You ever been under a ruck? You couldn't even pick my ruck up." — John Del Vecchio, *The 13th Valley*, p. 25, 1982

ruckus juice *noun*

strong, homemade whiskey *US, 1999*

- It is called corn liquor, white lightning, sugar whiskey, skully cracker, popskull, bush whiskey, stump, stumphole, "splo, ruckus juice, radiator whiskey, rotgut, sugarhead, block and tackle, wildcat, panther's breath, tiger's sweat, Sweet spirits of cats a-fighting, alley bourbon, city gin, cool water, happy Sally, deep shaft, jump steady, old horsey, stingo, blue John, red eye, pine top, buckeye bark whiskey and see seven stars." — *Star Tribune (Minneapolis)*, p. 19F, 31st January 1999

ruco *noun*

a boyfriend or husband *US, 1950*

Border Spanish used in English conversation by Mexican-Americans; also used in the feminine "ruca" (a girlfriend or wife).

- — George Carpenter Baker, *Pachuco*, p. 43, January 1950

rude *adjective*

1 intense; superior *US, 1995*

Collected from fans of heavy metal music.

2 used of a computer program, poorly designed *US, 1983*

- — Guy L. Steele et al., *The Hacker's Dictionary*, p. 111, 1983

rude!; rudeness!; how rude!; how rudeness!

used for suggesting that the speaker has crossed an etiquette line that is better not breached *US, 1989*

- — Pamela Munro, *U.C.L.A. Slang*, p. 51, 1989

ruff *noun*

1 a twenty-five cent piece *US, 1945*

- — Lou Shelly, *Hepcats Jive Talk Dictionary*, p. 16, 1945

2 pubic hair *US, 1974*

- In the fullness of time a sparse ruff was revealed, but to me the boobs were more interesting. — Anne Steinhardt, *Thunder La Boom*, p. 28, 1974

ruff *adjective*

acceptable, good, cool *US, 2001*

- — *National Education Association Today*, April 1985: "A glossary for rents and other squids"
- Consider that Fatboy Slim's real name is Norman. Which sounds more ruff? Rough? R-u-f-f: it means cool. — *Radio Times*, p. 28, 23rd June 2001

ruffie *noun*

Rohypnol™ (flunitrazepam), popularly known as the "date-rape drug" *US, 1995*

- Mexican Valium. Ruffie. Quaalude of the '90s. Nicknames abound for the illegal drug Rohypnol that's now hitting the Texas teen scene at $1 to $5 a pill. — *Newsweek*, p. 8, 3rd July 1995

ruffle *noun*

the passive participant in lesbian sex or a lesbian relationship *US, 1970*

- — *American Speech*, p. 58, Spring–Summer 1970: "Homosexual slang"

ruffneck *noun*

a tough *US, 2002*

- At Yonkers High, if you were one of the ruffnecks that didn't go to class all day, you hung out at a spot called the Castle. — Earl "DMX" Simmons, *E.A.R.L.*, p. 87, 2002

ruff-puff *noun*

a South Vietnamese local defense force *US, 1968*

RFs were regional forces, PFs were platoon-size village forces. Quick American minds took RF with PF to form "ruff-puff."

- Below the RF's and the PF's (collectively known as Ruff-Puffs) were regular national police, white suited, pistol-carrying cops known as White Mice. — Ward S. Just, *To What End*, p. 136, 1968
- They were PF's, Popular Forces, whom everybody called Ruff Puffs. — Larry Heinemann, *Close Quarters*, p. 83, 1977
- None of the Civil Guards, now called the Regional Forces or RF and referred to derisively by the advisors as "Ruff Puffs," who were supposed to be protecting Cu Chi, stirred. — Neil Sheehan, *A Bright Shining Lie*, p. 511, 1988
- The ruff-puffs (regional popular forces) took me to him[.] — Cherokee Paul McDonald, *Into the Green*, p. 218, 2001

rug *noun*

1 a hairpiece, especially a poorly executed one *US, 1940*

- At ten p.m. a makeup man from NBC dropped a curly headed rug over my short hair[.] — Mickey Spillane, *Return of the Hood*, p. 100, 1964
- "The guy who plays opposite Terry King is bald without his rug." — Jacqueline Susann, *Valley of the Dolls*, p. 78, 1966
- And despite the fact that Wilfred wore a black Burt Reynolds toupee, and had do so long before Burt bought his first rug. — Seth Morgan, *Fugitive Nights*, p. 20, 1990
- Hey, Bones, looks like you're gonna have a nice scar up there. Maybe these guys can fit you with a rug, cover it up for ya. — *Get Shorty*, 1995

2 pubic hair, especially on a female *US, 1964*

- — Roger Blake, *The American Dictionary of Sexual Terms*, p. 183, 1964
- — *Maledicta*, p. 131, Summer/Winter 1982: "Dyke diction: the language of lesbians"
- Portia and her picture-perfect pals pose for a painting, the subject of which seems to be impossibly hot chicks who show rack, rug, and rear. — Mr. Skin, *Mr. Skin's Skincyclopedia*, p. 140, 2005

3 in horseracing, a heavy horse blanket *US, 1976*

- — Tom Ainslie, *Ainslie's Complete Guide to Thoroughbred Racing*, p. 337, 1976

rug-cutter *noun*

a great time *US, 1951*

- "Hey, Brown," he would shout, "ain't this a rug-cutter?" — Norman Mailer, *Advertisements for Myself*, p. 111, 1951

rug joint *noun*
a well-appointed, even luxurious gambling operation *US, 1974*
- — John Scarne, *Scarne on Dice*, p. 463, 1974

rug munch *noun*
an instance of oral sex on a woman *US, 1995*
- After a steamy rug munch and a wicked b.j., they engage in some nut-slappin' mish capped off with—you guess it—major anal penetration. — *Adult Video News*, p. 128, August 1995

rug-muncher *noun*
a lesbian *US, 1997*
From the image of oral sex as 'munching a hairpiece.'.
- Maybe that's just what dykes like to do, fuck around with straight guys' heads, just so she can go back to her little rug-muncher club and have a good laugh with all her man-hating cronies about how fucking stupid and easily duped men are! — *Chasing Amy*, 1997

rug rat *noun*
a young child *US, 1970*
A bit derisive.
- Still in Topsiders, mind you, but driving an Audi now and sending a couple of rug rats to the French-American school and swapping notes on their Cuisinarts[.] — Armistead Maupin, *Tales of the City*, p. 245, 1978
- They fuck like minks, raise rugrats, and live happily ever after. — *Basic Instinct*, 1992
- She seems determined to get those rugrats off welfare and with your help I'll bet she does it. — *Something About Mary*, 1998
- Those rugrats sure in hell weren't mine. — Eric Jerome Dickey, *Cheaters*, p. 14, 1999

rule *verb*
used as an expression of supremacy for the preceding collective or plural noun(s) *US, 1968*
- You're on top; the greatest, the boss, the leader of the pack; your word is the law because YOU RULE! — Hy Lit, *Hy Lit's Unbelievable Dictionary of Hip Words for Groovy People*, p. 33, 1968
- This guy rules. — *Airheads*, 1994
- Fuckin' Rod Tidwell—You rule! You rule! — *Jerry Maguire*, 1996
- Cigarettes and beer rule! Huh huh. — Mike Judge and Joe Stillman, *Beavis and Butt-Head Do America*, p. 91, 1997

rum *noun*
1 an unsophisticated, unaware person *US, 1972*
- They're not a rum, you can't consider them an idiot or a rum, and you can't consider them a character[.] — Bruce Jackson, *Outside the Law*, p. 156, 1972
- — Kenn "Naz" Young, *Naz's Underground Dictionary*, p. 54, 1973
2 a prisoner deemed inferior or too odd by other prisoners *US, 1972*
- — Bruce Jackson, *Outside the Law*, p. 59, 1972: "Glossary"
3 a drunkard *US, 1960*
- If that rum is still outside, tell him I said to get the hell away from here. — Clarence Cooper Jr., *The Scene*, p. 93, 1960

rumba *verb*
to fight *US, 1957*
- "We ain't fixing to rumba with the T's, not yet we ain't." — Herbert Simmons, *Corner Boy*, p. 40, 1957

rumble *noun*
1 a fight, especially between teenage gangs *US, 1948*
- On this particular evening rumbles with other gangs had been far from Sandpaper's mind. — Dale Krame, *Teen-Age Gangs*, p. 10, 1953
- A rumble! That's the only way. — Max Shulman, *Rally Round the Flag, Boys!*, p. 230, 1957
- The second test, we had to come off with a rumble—in another town—in other words, a gang war. — Willard Motely, *Let No Man Write My Epitaph*, p. 208, 1958
- Ray was the toast of Paris and although he had a rumble coming up in London in ten weeks with a stud named Turpin, he did his rehearsing in the south of France balling on the beaches and casinos. — Babs Gonzales, *Movin' On Down De Line*, p. 16, 1975
2 a rumor *US, 1953*
- "The rumble's out already. Half the Bowery knows you're holed up here." — Curt Cannon, *The Death of Me*, p. 104, 1953
3 a wild party *US, 1968*
- — Collin Baker et al., *College Undergraduate Slang Study Conducted at Brown University*, p. 186, 1968

4 a difficult encounter with law enforcement *US, 1972*
- — Bruce Jackson, *Outside the Law*, p. 59, 1972: "Glossary"
5 a concerted police search for narcotics *US, 1958*
- — *New York Times Magazine*, p. 88, 16th March 1958

rumble *verb*
1 to fight *US, 1946*
- One guy leaning on the bar would make a friendly remark about his neighbor's tie or the style of his haircut, and in nothing flat each one was cussing up a breeze about the other's mother until they began to rumble. — Mezz Mezzrow, *Really the Blues*, p. 70, 1946
- When Ray cut out to London to rumble, he only took his key five cats and left the others at the Claridge Hotel. — Babs Gonzales, *Movin' On Down De Line*, p. 16, 1975
- One time I had to rumble a deaf-mute guy. On me like white-on-rice. — Edwin Torres, *Carlito's Way*, p. 13, 1975
2 in circus and carnival usage, to spoil something *US, 1981*
- — Don Wilmeth, *The Language of American Popular Entertainment*, p. 229, 1981

rumbleseat *noun*
the rear seat in a two-set aircraft *US, 1990*
- — Joseph Tuso, *Singing the Vietnam Blues*, p. 260, 1990

rum blossom *noun*
a red welt produced from excessive consumption of alcohol *US, 1865*
- "[H]e's the kind of guy that doesn't exactly blend into a crowd, with that big nose of his all decorated with rum-blossoms and that scar he got on his cheek[.]" — George V. Higgins, *The Judgment of Deke Hunter*, p. 30, 1976

rumdum; rum-dumb *noun*
a drunk *US, 1891*
- It was too late all right. Too late for roaches or old Skid Row rumdumbs[.] — Nelson Algren, *The Man with the Golden Arm*, p. 25, 1949
- We get up there and sure enough there's the rumdum, some old panhandler who when not mooching used to hang around the lions in front of the Public Library feeding the pigeons. — Bernard Wolfe, *The Late Risers*, p. 266, 1954
- The rum-dumbs would yank themselves together and suddenly remember they'd eaten nothing in ten hours. — Robert Sylvester, *No Cover Charge*, p. 217, 1956

rumdummed *adjective*
extremely drunk *US, 1891*
- Red can't be rumdummed up tonight. This is one night he has to blow. — Ross Russell, *The Sound*, p. 239, 1961

rummy *noun*
an alcoholic *US, 1851*
- At this rate, I'll end up being a fuckin' rummy, he warned himself. — Donald Goines, *Never Die Alone*, p. 205, 1974
- He didn't mean to scare the old fart; probably should've just let him go on thinking he was a rummy. — Seth Morgan, *Homeboy*, 1990

rummy *adjective*
1 prone to drink too much, if not alcoholic *US, 1834*
- She and Frannie Halcyon had absolutely nothing to catch up on. Why was this sweet, but rummy, society dowager talking to her like an equal? — Armistead Maupin, *Further Tales of the City*, p. 78, 1982
2 poor; inferior; bad *US, 1947*
- Anyway, it was rummy luck for the bastards in this accident. — James T. Farrell, *Saturday Night*, p. 42, 1947

rump bump *noun*
in a sexual dance, a pelvic thrust that emphasizes the buttocks moving backward *US, 1956*
- At one point, Mrs. De Carlo turned her back on the enchanted customers to give them some rump bumps that had them shouting for more. — *Confidential*, p. 17, July 1956
- Nor did she give right and left rump bumps that had the men cheering for the overweight Detroit woman who placed fourth. — *Hartford (Connecticut) Courant*, p. D1, 2nd October 1993

rump-ordained *adjective*
used for describing a preacher who has no formal theological training or denominational affiliation *US, 1974*
- An offshoot of the gambling was a five-dollar-for-ten-dollar loan-sharking business which left a rump-ordained Southern Baptist minister from Oklahoma on his way to being a rich Christian. — Earl Thompson, *Tattoo*, p. 293, 1974

rump ranger *noun*
a male homosexual *US, 1993*

- Such tsuris—Herman is grooming that rump ranger for stardom apart from me. — James Ellroy, *White Jazz*, p. 62, 1993
- "You're into that, huh, pops? A rump ranger." — Carl Hiaasen, *Sick Puppy*, p. 385, 1999
- I asked other girls out, trying to get over the irritation of being branded a rump-ranger, but nothing interesting ever came of it. — Doug Lambeth, *Runaways*, p. 16, 2007

rum-runner *noun*
an importer, transporter, and/or purveyor of illegal alcohol, especially rum *US, 1920*

- According to Carroll Mealy, capable and efficient head of the Alcoholic Tax Unit, the rum-runners take this stuff to Washington in 1940 Fords, with Cadillac or racing motors in place of original power. — Jack Lait and Lee Mortimer, *Washington Confidential*, p. 130, 1951

run *noun*
1 a crime spree moving from city to city *US, 1976*

- We were on what police call a "run," and the run provided its own internal sense and energy. We would steal a car and finance the trip with robberies. — Malcolm Braley, *False Starts*, p. 76, 1976

2 a group motorcycle excursion *US, 1966*

- A run is a lot of things to the Angels: a party, an exhibition and an exercise in solidarity. — Hunter S. Thompson, *Hell's Angels*, p. 116, 1966
- The first adventure I ever had was the first time I went on a run with the Hell's Angels. — Frank Reynolds, *Freewheelin' Frank*, p. 5, 1967
- The rest of the meeting was pretty routine, with discussions of a run that was coming up[.] — Robert Lipkin, *A Brotherhood of Outlaws*, p. 41, 1981
- A motorcycle run is a get-together; a moving power. It's a real show of power and solidarity when you're a Hell's Angel. — Ralph "Sonny" Barger, *Hell's Angel*, p. 1, 2000

3 a period of extended amphetamine use *US, 1967*

- — Ruth Bronsteen, *The Hippy's Handbook*, p. 15, 1967
- Speed runs can extend to several months, but usually they are self-limiting and last from 2–3 days. — Geoffrey Froner, *Digging for Diamonds*, p. 53, 1989

run *verb*
to associate; to socialize *US, 1946*

- I found myself running with a literary ex-pug, a pistol-packing rabbi, and a peewee jockey whose onliest riding crop was a stick of marihuana. — Mezz Mezzrow, *Really the Blues*, p. 69, 1946
- Some big Afro-wearin' gangsters. My dad used to run with 'em. — *Menace II Society*, 1993

▸ **run a batch by hand**
to masturbate *US, 1972*

- Oh, what some of those broads would do to tease you . . . suck tongues, blow in your ear, rub your organ, then send you home to run a batch off by hand. — Robert Byrne, *McGoorty*, p. 35, 1972

▸ **run a pot**
in poker, to make a sustained, preplanned bluff on a hand *US, 1967*

- — Albert H. Morehead, *The Complete Guide to Winning Poker*, p. 272, 1967

▸ **run blues**
to use blue lights in a car's tail lights *US, 1985*

- — Jennifer Blowdryer, *Modern English*, 1985

▸ **run hot**
to drive with sirens and flashing lights activated *US, 2002*

- There is in fact, no scientific proof that "running hot"—street slang for operating with lights and siren—saves lives. — *USA Today*, p. 1A, 21st March 2002

▸ **run speed limit**
to do something with great speed *US, 1982*
Hawaiian youth usage.

- — Douglas Simonson, *Pidgin to da Max Hana Hou*, 1982

▸ **run the gears**
to stab someone in the chest and then to move the knife up and down as if shifting gears in a car *US, 1992*

- There is little doubt that if the inmate had refused to turn down the radio, the murderer would have, as he said later, "run the gears"—a reference to the most effective of stabbing another human being. — Pete Earley, *The Hot House*, p. 42, 1992

▸ **run your mouth**
to talk too much *US, 1960*

- "You done already made yourself fifteen minutes late running your mouth." — William Faulkner, *The Reivers*, p. 81, 1962
- There was no way to stop the man from running his mouth, from telling one lie after another. — Odie Hawkins, *Chicago Hustle*, p. 7, 1977

▸ **run your neck**
to make threats or boasts which you are not prepared to back up with actions *US, 2001*

- — Jim Goad, *Jim Goad's Glossary of Northwestern Prison Slang*, December 2001

rundown *noun*
a complete explanation *US, 1969*

- Those pimps back in the joint sure knew basic whorology. I was glad my ears had flapped to all those rundowns. — Iceberg Slim (Robert Beck), *Pimp*, p. 80, 1969

runes *noun*
in computing, any esoteric display character or computer language *US, 1991*

- — Eric S. Raymond, *The New Hacker's Dictionary*, p. 307, 1991

run, Johnny, run *noun*
inexpensive loose cigarette tobacco *US, 1961–1962*
Formed from the initials of the R.J. Reynolds tobacco company.

- — Frank Prewitt and Francis Schaeffer, *Vacaville Vocabulary*, 1961–1962
- — Charles Shafer, *Folk Speech in Texas Prisons*, p. 213, 1990

run letter *noun*
a final deportation letter from the US Immigration and Naturalization Service *US, 2002*

- They are noncitizens who either have skipped deportation hearings or disappeared after receiving a final deportation notice—known in street slang as a "run letter," so common is that reaction to its receipt. — *Buffalo (New York) News*, p. B4, 14th January 2002

runner *noun*
1 in an illegal betting operation, a person who physically collects and pays off bets placed with sheet writers *US, 1947*

- He don't come around hisself. De runners do all the work. — Mickey Spillane, *I, The Jury*, p. 43, 1947
- The daily small army of runners got ten percent of the money they turned in[.] — Malcolm X and Alex Haley, *The Autobiography of Malcolm X*, p. 85, 1964
- I was glad Daddy was a number runner and not just hanging around the corners like those men. — Louise Meriwether, *Daddy Was a Number Runner*, p. 15, 1970
- When his runners and sheet writers called he told them to sit on their totals another day or so and he'd get back to them. — Elmore Leonard, *Pronto*, p. 44, 1993

2 someone who carries illegal drugs between dealer and purchaser *US, 1972*

- Normally, a runner makes $250 and he's on his own. — Bruce Jackson, *In the Life*, p. 164, 1972

3 in the television and movie industries, an errand-running production assistant *US, 1990*

- — Ralph S. Singleton, *Filmmaker's Dictionary*, p. 143, 1990

4 in the language surrounding the Grateful Dead, a fan who stands in line before a show and then quickly claims space for friends who will follow *US, 1994*

- — David Shenk and Steve Silberman, *Skeleton Key*, p. 252, 1994

runners *noun*
diarrhea *US, 1948*

- "I got the runners. They came on all of a sudden," I said, going inside, pushing past the men who were coming out. — Horace McCoy, *Kiss Tomorrow Good-bye*, p. 9, 1948

running buddy *noun*
a close friend and confederate in crime *US, 1969*

- Because large groups of any character tend to be undependable, a boy seeks a close running buddy to help in his fighting. — David Schulz, *Coming Up Black*, p. 72, 1969
- Her running buddy was a burnt-brown color, with red hair, of all things. — Louise Meriwether, *Daddy Was a Number Runner*, p. 26, 1970
- The dope man wants to know why I ain't doing with my running buddy[.] — Vernon E. Smith, *The Jones Men*, p. 150, 1974
- Or Dink-Dinks's running buddies, Fat Eric and Lamont. — David Simon and Edward Burns, *The Corner*, p. 53, 1997

running dog *noun*

a servant of the ruling class, subservient to counter-revolutionary powers *US, 1937*

From Chinese communist terminology originally applied to the Kuomintang.

- The People shall smash the glutton roaches running this decadent society and, along with the directing of the Black Panther Party, halt these running dogs and gain true liberation for all. — *The Black Panther*, p. 14, 6th April 1969

running partner *noun*

a close friend joined for criminal and social activities *US, 1965*

- For that whole time, I didn't hang out with any of my old running partners. — Claude Brown, *Manchild in the Promised Land*, p. 94, 1965
- Simple pimps have "running partners," and are rarely seen alone, while the boss player almost always arrives and leaves by himself. — Christina and Richard Milner, *Black Players*, p. 104, 1972
- The club, lined with billows of deep blue satin and thousands of tiny reflecting mirrors, was dotted with people from the life, including Prince's running partner, Sweet Rudy[.] — Alix Shulman, *On the Stroll*, p. 177, 1981

run-off *noun*

a prostitute who has attempted to break off from her pimp *US, 1993*

- — *Washington Post*, p. C5, 7th November 1993

run-out powder *noun*

the departure of a gambler who has not paid off his gambling debts *US, 1979*

- — John Scarne, *Scarne's Guide to Modern Poker*, p. 289, 1979

runs *noun*

▸ **the runs**

a case of diarrhea *US, 1962*

- Do you have the runs again? — Rita Ciresi, *Pink Slip*, p. 347, 1999

runt *noun*

1 in circus and carnival usage, a dwarf or midget *US, 1980*

- — Joe McKennon, *Circus Lingo*, p. 80, 1980
- — Don Wilmeth, *The Language of American Popular Entertainment*, p. 230, 1981

2 in poker, a pairless hand *US, 1963*

- — Irwin Steig, *Common Sense in Poker*, p. 187, 1963

runts and cunts *noun*

used for expressing disapproval of the composition of the US armed forces and urban police forces in the decades after Vietnam *US, 1993*

- Bad Dog, my ass. Five foot three in platforms. It's what the navy's come to: runts 'n' cunts. — Joseph Wambaugh, *Finnegan's Week*, p. 31, 1993
- Old-timers bitched constantly about the new academy graduating classes, full of "cunts and runts." — Stephen Cannell, *Cold Hit*, pp. 12–13, 2005

run up on *verb*

to attack *US, 1991*

- "But I don't do that too often, 'cause I don't feel like gettin' ran up on." — Leon Bing, *Do or Die*, p. 33, 1991

ruptured duck *noun*

the US armed forces insignia designating honorable discharge *US, 1946*

- — *American Speech*, p. 153, April 1946: "GI words from the separation center and proctology ward"

rush *noun*

1 the sudden onset of drug intoxication *US, 1966*

- Cocaine and bombitas are both stimulants and combined with heroin, a depressant, they produce an electrifying "rush" or "flash" far more pleasurable to the addict than heroin alone. — James Mills, *The Panic in Needle Park*, p. 36, 1966
- I don't get strung out on any speed; there's no chemical I need. I like the buzz. I like the rush. — Nicholas Von Hoffman, *We are the People Our Parents Warned Us Against*, p. 151, 1967

2 a sudden and powerful sense of euphoria or energy *US, 1971*

Figurative use of the drug term.

- There simply is no rushing thumbing—although I can get a rush off a car stopping for me. — Marge Piaggio, *The Last Supplement to the Whole Earth Catalog*, p. 36, March 1971
- It feels "out there." A major rush. — *Bull Durham*, 1988
- Imagine being one of those guys, legends, and the rush you'd get performing for all those people. — Elmore Leonard, *Be Cool*, p. 265, 1999

3 a capsule containing vapors of amyl nitrate or butyl nitrate inhaled as a stimulant *US, 1988*

- "May I have some rush first, mistress?" "Oh, you have rush?" I said. — Dolores French, *Working*, p. 128, 1988

4 in poker, an unusual streak of good cards *US, 1982*

- — David M. Hayano, *Poker Faces*, p. 187, 1982

rush *verb*

▸ **rush the knocks**

in drug sales, to ignore the order of customers and make a sale *US, 2002*

- An informal code of conduct mandates dealers at popular drug spots take turns catering to customers, testified Officer Jame "Mike" Gant, a police narcotics expert. Cauley was known to "rush the knocks," street slang for cutting into the rotation and snagging clients out of order. — *Oakland (California) Tribune*, 18th October 2002

rush-and-snatch job *noun*

a search and rescue mission without the complications of enemy fire *US, 1991*

- None of the survivors had been down in areas that had been heavily defended. They had been quick rush-and-snatch jobs. — Gerry Carroll, *North S*A*R*, p. 34, 1991

Rushina *noun*

in homosexual usage, a personification of amyl nitrite or butyl nitrite *US, 1980*

From **RUSH**, a popular name for amyl nitrite.

- — *Maledicta*, p. 227, Winter 1980: "'Lovely, blooming, fresh and gay': the onomastics of camp"

Russki *adjective*

Russian *UK, 1859*

- A weasel-faced guy complied; I popped one into the chamber and tucked my Russki roulette piece in my belt. — James Ellroy, *Hollywood Nocturnes*, p. 284, 1994

Russki; Russky; Rusky *noun*

a Russian *UK, 1858*

- What's the Russky doing? — Mickey Spillane, *One Lonely Night*, p. 124, 1951
- The only excitement came when Sly beat the huge Russky like a mule. — Hunter S. Thompson, *Generation of Swine*, p. 27, 16 December 1985
- They're not stable, sir. The Russkies. — John Milne, *Alive and Kicking*, p. 97, 1998

rust belt *noun*

the northern central US, highly industrialized prior to the economic decline in the US in the 1980s *US, 1987*

- Breaking the Rust Belt loose [Headline] — *Milwaukee Journal*, 13th March 1987

rusty dusty *noun*

the buttocks *US, 1942*

- — Robert S. Gold, *A Jazz Lexicon*, p. 259, 1964

rusty fuck *noun*

a notional object of no value whatsoever *US, 1969*

- — John D. Bell et al., *Loosely Speaking*, p. 9, 1969

RV; r.v. *noun*

a recreational vehicle or large motor home *US, 1967*

- You want to get out of the r.v. business, wasting your talent selling motor homes. — Elmore Leonard, *Touch*, p. 34, 1977

Ss

sachie *noun*
Versace™ clothing *US, 1998*
- — Ethan Hilderbrant, *Prison Slang*, p. 110, 1998

sack *noun*

1 a bed *US, 1942*
Probably related to the C19 sailor's use of "sack" as a "hammock."
- I started to tell her that all during the time she thought I was humped up in the sack with some other dame I was out hustling for her[.] — Horace McCoy, *Kiss Tomorrow Good-bye*, p. 204, 1948
- I left the tavern, returned to the dormitory, and put my miserable frame into the sack. — Max Shulman, *Guided Tour of Campus Humor*, p. 60, 1955
- Terry and I and Johnny went into a motel room and got ready to hit the sack. — Jack Kerouac, *On the Road*, p. 93, 1957
- I think the romance angle in your story is critically important, that it isn't simply a jump in the sack for either of them. — *Get Shorty*, 1995

2 courage *US, 1984*
A testicular reference.
- — Inez Cardozo-Freeman, *The Joint*, pp. 527–528, 1984

3 a coat or jacket *US, 1972*
- — David Claerbaut, *Black Jargon in White America*, p. 78, 1972

sack *verb*

1 to take to bed; to have sex with *US, 1967*
- "I'd have liked to sack her, though, because she had a good figure." — Robert Newton, *Bondage Clubs U.S.A.*, p. 73, 1967

2 to sleep; to spend the night *US, 1966*
- "Got a place to sack?" he asked. — Robert Emond Alter, *Carny Kill*, p. 8, 1966

sack drill *noun*
sleep *US, 1963*
- — *American Speech*, pp. 76–79, February 1963: "Marine Corps slang"

sack duty *noun*
sleep *US, 1947*
- A sailor who retires hits the sack, sacks in, sacks out, gets in some sack duty, gets in some sack drill[.] — *California Folklore Quarterly*, p. 387, 1947

sack hound *noun*
a lazy person, overly fond of sleep *US, 1959*
- — *American Speech*, p. 154, May 1959: "Gator (University of Florida) slang"

sack of garbage *noun*
in bar dice games, a roll that produces no points for the player *US, 1971*
- — Jester Smith, *Games They Play in San Francisco*, p. 105, 1971

sack of sauce *noun*
a used condom *US, 1997*
- — Pamela Munro, *U.C.L.A. Slang*, p. 104, 1997

sack of shit *noun*
an unpleasant person *US, 1965*
- You're a sack of shit. — Michael McClure, *The Beard*, 1965
- "Willa, you lying sack of shit." — Henry Van Dyke, *Blood of Strawberries*, p. 142, 1969
- "Listen, you dickless sack of shit," I said[.] — Janet Evanovich, *Seven Up*, p. 118, 2001

sack out *verb*
to go to bed *US, 1946*
- Siegel was a little tired form having met four different parties of visitors at the airfield while Griffin was sacking out. — William Brinkley, *Don't Go Near the Water*, p. 71, 1956
- On his last day in Red Canyon, while Guido was sacked out in his bunk thinking jolly thoughts about all the pleasing prospects ahead, the fly entered the ointment. — Max Shulman, *Rally Round the Flag, Boys!*, p. 18, 1957

- He's in the silk, sacked out with a concrete wig. — William "Lord" Buckley, *The H-Bomb*, 1960
- "If you were a wino," he said, "where would you pick to sack out?" — John Sayles, *Union Dues*, p. 28, 1977

sack rat *noun*
a lazy person, overly fond of sleep *US, 1947*
- — *American Speech*, p. 55, February 1947: "Pacific War language"
- — *American Speech*, p. 154, May 1959: "Gator (University of Florida) slang"

sack weather *noun*
inclement weather during which air missions cannot be flown *US, 1949*
- — *American Speech*, p. 30, February 1949: "A.V.G. lingo"

sacky dacky *noun*
a depressed misfit *US, 1946*
- — *American Speech*, p. 238, October 1946: "World War II slang of maladjustment"

sacred *adjective*
excellent *US, 1991*
- — Trevor Cralle, *The Surfin'ary*, p. 104, 1991

sad *adjective*
terrible *US, 1945*
- Anything very bad might also be called "frone" or "sad." — *Women's Digest*, p. 40, September 1945

sad apple *noun*
a pathetic person *US, 1950*
- "Those things you wear are all out of date," Fred said. "Only sad apples wear them any more." — Frank Gilbreth, *Belles on Their Toes*, p. 201, 1950

sad-ass; sad-assed *adjective*
contemptible *US, 1971*
- Girl, that's a sad-ass state of affairs. — Janet Evanovitch, *High Five*, p. 181, 1999

saddle *noun*
▸ **in the saddle**

1 engaged in sexual intercourse *US, 1979*
The term enjoyed widespread popularity in the US during discussions of the 1979 death of former Vice President and New York Governor Nelson Rockefeller.
- Both celebrities lived just long enough to realize a traditional American male fantasy—they "died in the saddle." — Allan Sherman, *The Rape of the APE*, p. 202, 1973
- Didn't women have to wait six weeks before you could get back into the saddle? — Odie Hawkins, *Black Casanova*, p. 188, 1984
- He either had a heart attack in the saddle and she had to take him to Charity, or he pulled out. — Elmore Leonard, *Bandits*, p. 338, 1987
- No old guy has looked this sturdy since Nelson Rockefeller. If you recall, Nelson died in the saddle—he didn't need any damn Viagra. — *New York Observer*, 11th January 1999

2 in control *US, 1950*
- — Hyman E. Goldin et al., *Dictionary of American Underworld Lingo*, p. 184, 1950

saddle-fuck *verb*
to have sex, the woman astride the prone man *US, 1972*
- Again a very pretty chick, this time with beautiful big boobs, is our star, saddle-fucking some weary stud. — *Screw*, p. 23, 6th November 1972

saddle tramp *noun*
a motorcycle gang member *US, 1989*
- — James Harris, *A Convict's Dictionary*, p. 37, 1989

saddle up *verb*

1 to pick up your gear and resume a combat patrol *US, 1972*
- "First platoon, saddle up and move down." — William Pelfrey, *The Big V*, p. 85, 1972
- Pretty soon Sam called again but it was the hated saddle up order. — Charles Anderson, *The Grunts*, p. 75, 1976

- "Saddle up. Let's move out." — Cherokee Paul McDonald, *Into the Green*, p. 51, 2001

2 to engage in mutual oral sex simultaneously *US, 1985*

- — *American Speech*, p. 20, Spring 1985: "The language of singles bars"

Sadie Masie *noun*
sadomasochism *US, 1965*
A jocular personification.

- — *The Guild Dictionary of Homosexual Terms*, p. 40, 1965
- It is on the outer fringes of this motorcycle set's shadow world that one finds the bizarre "Sadie-Masie" groups, also known as "Pain and Pleasure" clubs. — W.D. Sprague, *Sexual Rebellion in the Sixties*, p. 84, 1965
- A side trip to the "S. & M." (sadomasochistic) or "Sadie-Maisie" homosexual bars — G. Legman, *The Fake Revolt*, p. 30, 1967

Sadie Thompson *verb*
to rape (a man) *US, 1985*

- O.A. Jones mumbled, hoping that he would get put in the cops' tank at the county jail because a twenty-four-year-old former surfer, who was also a former cop, would be Sadie Thompson'd in the regular tank within three minutes. — Joseph Wambaugh, *The Secrets of Harry Bright*, p. 33, 1985

sad sack *noun*
a miserable and depressing individual; an inept misfit *US, 1942*
Originally US military.

- "He's a sad sack, and that's no mistake," says Kerrigan. — Audie Murphy, *To Hell and Back*, p. 217, 1949
- Jimmy said now listen I used to be a sad sack myself until I met my wife Gloria who made me so happy[.] — William T. Vollman, *Whores for Gloria*, p. 75, 1991
- Some sad sack opens the show whining an anticensorship speech[.] — Chuck Eddy, *Stairway to Hell*, p. 71, 1991
- Scott the Engineer is the Sad Sack of our show. — Howard Stern, *Miss America*, p. 221, 1995

sad sack of shit *noun*
a miserable and depressing individual *US, 1978*
Abbreviates as **SAD SACK**.

- What a theatrical bastard he was, abusing that poor little sad sack of shit until he didn't know whether he was coming or going. — James Garrett, *And Save Them For Pallbearers*, p. 104, 1958
- They've got nothing to do but go fishing, play poker, drink bonded bourbon, and wait for some sad sack of shit like you to show up in the courtroom[.] — Stephen King, *The Stand*, p. 191, 1978
- The cartoon character Sad Sack of course derives his name from the NCO's favorite term for a despised subordinate, a sad sack of shit, a bit of nomenclature reducing the addressee to a bag of noisome matter equipped, as if by some accident, with arms and legs. — Paul Fussell, *Wartime*, p. 91, 1989

safe *noun*
1 a condom *UK, 1965*

- She asked me what I meant; rubbers? safes? skins? prophylactics? contraceptives? — John Nichols, *The Sterile Cuckoo*, p. 105, 1965
- Saul muttered "Have you got a safe? A rubber, a joe, don't be stupid?" — *Islands*, p. 54, 1976
- Meaning she didn't make we wear a safe. — James Ellroy, *White Jazz*, p. 112, 1992
- She'd better have an arsenal of Trojans in her purse just in case he wasn't carrying a safe in his back pocket. — Rita Ciresi, *Pink Slip*, p. 328, 1999

2 the rectum *US, 1992*
Referring to the rectum as a depository for drugs to be smuggled into prison.

- — William K. Bentley and James M. Corbett, *Prison Slang*, p. 76, 1992

3 in a pickpocketing team, the thief who takes the wallet or object stolen by the wire and leaves the scene with it *US, 1954*

- The third partner in the trio might have been either man or woman; his (or her) function was indicated well enough by the name given this important member of the crew; he was called the "safe." — Dev Collans with Stewart Sterling, *I was a House Detective*, p. 48, 1954

safe *adjective*
hopelessly out of style *US, 1982*
Hawaiian youth usage.

- "Oh dat Renton! He so safe! Make be bahf!" — Douglas Simonson, *Pidgin to da Max Hana Hou*, 1982

safe house *noun*
a room, apartment, or house where it is safe to stay, work, and hide from the authorities, rival criminals or rival spies *US, 1963*

- Joe Loop said what the guy was doing they used to call "going to the mattress," hiding out, going to a safe house had enough mattresses for the crew to sleep on. — Elmore Leonard, *Be Cool*, p. 125, 1999

safe-'n'-soft corps *noun*
the notional collection of noncombat, support jobs in the military *US, 1985*

- This meant that many of the "good" cadets were allowed to choose the safe-'n' soft corps like Ordinance, Transportation, or Medical Services. — David Donovan, *Once a Warrior King*, p. 236, 1985

safety *noun*
1 a condom *US, 1973*

- Can't you recall telling me when I first hit the bricks to always use a safety? — A.S. Jackson, *Gentleman Pimp*, p. 45, 1973

2 a safety pin used for an improvised injection of an illegal drug *US, 1952*

- — *American Speech*, p. 29, February 1952: "Teen-age hophead jargon"

safe word *noun*
a code word, agreed between a sexual dominant and submissive masochistic partner, for use by the masochist as a signal that the current activity should stop *US, 1987*

- The submissive may feel inadequate, or chagrined, at having to use her safe-word. — Claudia Varrin, *Erotic Surrender*, p. 35, 2003

sag *verb*
to wear pants that are too big and which consequently ride very low on or below the hips *US, 1991*

- "A-WAX," (18), sporting the sagging dickies, with nearly all of his draws showing, looks like a little kid dressed up in his father's clothes. — *Menace II Society*, 1993
- A lot of guys don't know that we didn't even sag back then. — Yusuf Jah, *Uprising*, p. 29, 1995
- Now "sagging" is a sing of Cripism. — Colton Simpson, *Inside the Crips*, p. 289, 2005

saggie *noun*
a central nervous system depressant such as Seconal™ *US, 1960*

- — Robert George Reisner, *The Jazz Titans*, p. 163, 1960

Saigon commando *noun*
a rear-echelon troop *US, 1966*

- For the men of the 33rd any man farther back—in sector, division, or corps, is a "lollipop," only slightly better than a "Saigon commando." — Jim Lucas, *Dateline: Viet Nam*, p. 189, 1966
- Some Saigon-commando captain monitoring his new electronic black-box sensor device. — Larry Chambers, *Recondo*, p. 100, 1992

Saigon cowboy *noun*
a rear-echelon troop or civilian who dressed the part of a combat soldier but did not experience combat *US, 1977*

- This manifests instelf in such phenomena as the "Saigon cowboy." — U.S. Department of the Army, *Department of the Army Pamphlet*, p. 756, 1976
- Later that morning, a Chinook came in with a load of newsmen, looking so bad-ass spiffy in their Saigon-cowboy suits—starched tiger fatigues, spit-shined boots, and silly fucking bush hats. — Larry Heinemann, *Close Quarters*, p. 235, 1977
- Saigon cowboys were a breed of rear-echelon soldiers so called for their latest and greatest dressed-to-the-hilt warrior look that they took no closer to the combat zone than absolutely necessary. — David Hackworth and Julie Sherman, *About Face*, p. 579, 1989

Saigon quickstep *noun*
diarrhea *US, 1984*

- But no matter how bad the "C-rats" (combat rations) were, none produced the dreaded "Saigon quickstep" as impressively as the local street food. — Carol Burke, *Camp All-American*, p. 111, 2004

Saigon Suzie *noun*
used for describing a stereotypical Vietnamese sex worker during the Vietnam war *US, 1990*

- Like I believed Saigon Suzie when she swore she loved only me. — Joseph Wambaugh, *Fugitive Nights*, p. 21, 1990

Saigon tea noun

a whiskey-colored drink, passing for expensive whiskey, served to bar girls in Vietnam and paid for by US servicemen *US, 1966*

- I found a girl to sit with me / Who doesn't ask for Saigon Tea. — Ken Melvin, *Sorry 'Bout That*, p. 53, 1966

- Jake, Reggie, and Crunch were buying Saigon tea for four of her best girls. — Elaine Shepard, *The Doom Pussy*, p. 141, 1967

- Always use condoms; obey curfew times; don't hassle the local police (white mice); don't buy the ladies Saigon teas AND never eat the indigenous food. — Martin Cameron, *A Look at the Bright Side*, 1988

- They received a percentage from the drinks of colored water, called "Saigon tea," that the soldiers had to buy them to enjoy their company and dance to the rock 'n' roll music that blared from the bars. — Neil Sheehan, *A Bright Shining Lie*, p. 625, 1988

Saigon Tech noun

the war in Vietnam; military service in Vietnam *US, 1969*

- — *Current Slang*, p. 13, Summer 1969

Saigon warrior noun

a rear-echelon troop or civilian *US, 1969*

- My first weeks in Vietnam provided me with a quickly fleeting view of what life had been like for the Saigon Warrior. — John Steinbeck, *In Touch*, p. 9, 1969

- We had hated the "Saigon warriors" who pounded typewriters and sent us to nowhere even more than we hated the Viet Cong and Richard Nixon. — Lynda Van Devanter, *Home Before Morning*, p. 183, 1983

sailing adjective

1 drunk *US, 1968*

- — Collin Baker et al., *College Undergraduate Slang Study Conducted at Brown University*, p. 187, 1968

2 marijuana-intoxicated *US, 1993*

- — Peter Johnson, *Dictionary of Street Alcohol and Drug Terms*, p. 163, 1993

Saint Loo -nickname

St. Louis, Missouri *US, 1960*

- I've definitely got the theater job in St. Loo[.] — James Blake, *The Joint*, p. 256, 8th February 1960

- And on into St. Loo, the second or third ugliest city in America, after Indianapolis, Detroit and perhaps El Paso. — Clancy Sigal, *Going Away*, p. 261, 1961

- "He's a contract man from St. Loo." — Mickey Spillane, *The Snake*, p. 39, 1964

Saint Vitus dance verb

to move in a fidgety, jerking manner *UK, 1621*

- He Saint Vitus danced to the subway as fast as he could, painfully lugging the load and contemptuously clutching the stupid football close to his side. — Emmett Grogan, *Ringolevio*, p. 93, 1972

salad noun

1 marijuana *US, 1997*

- — Jin Emerson-Cobb, *Scratching the Dragon*, April 1997

2 a mixture of two or more drugs *US, 1970*

- — William D. Alsever, *Glossary for the Establishment and Other Uptight People*, p. 6, December 1970

salad days noun

a period of youthful inexperience and innocence *UK, 1606*

- The Tournament seems forever to remain in its salad days. — Bill Cardoso, *The Maltese Sangweech*, p. 117, 1984

- Big Momma smiled at Robert 30X, formerly called Baby June in his dope fiend salad days, feeling a maternal pride in his superneatness. — Donald Goines, *The Busting Out of an Ordinary Man*, p. 14, 1985

salad wagon noun

a garbage truck *US, 1962*

- — *American Speech*, p. 272, December 1962: "The language of traffic policemen"

salami technique noun

a computer theft scheme in which fractions of cents are stolen from many transactions *US, 1994*

- A salami technique is a method used to steal small sums of money over a long period of time, with the assumption that such small sums won't be missed. — The Knightmare, *Secrets of a Super Hacker*, p. 9, 1994

saleslady noun

a prostitute *US, 1962*

- — Joseph E. Ragen and Charles Finston, *Inside the World's Toughest Prison*, p. 816, 1962: "Penitentiary and underworld glossary"

salesman noun

1 a professional wrestler who does a good job of feigning pain, anger, or fear *US, 1999*

- In the ring, he was a skilled wrestler and a terrific salesman. When he punished an opponent, the crowd never doubted the fury in his face. When he took a beating, his jerk, falls, and cry convinced spectators of his anguish. — Larry Nelson and James Jones, *Stranglehold*, p. 57, 1999

2 in gin, a card discarded to lure a desired card from an opponent *US, 1965*

- — Irwin Steig, *Play Gin to Win*, p. 141, 1965

Sally Army; Sally Ann; Sally noun

the Salvation Army; a Salvation Army hostel *US, 1915*

- It's a hotel for the workingman run by the Sallies. — Colleen McCullough, *The Thorn Birds*, p. 65, 1977

- The Sally was Rooski's second home away from the home he never had, the first being jail. — Seth Morgan, *Homeboy*, p. 41, 1990

- The Sally was on Division Street. I didn't know where Division Street was. — John Ridley, *The Drift*, p. 68, 2002

Sally Sorority noun

a stereotypical college sorority member who looks, dresses, talks, and lives the part *US, 1963*

- So I became a G.D.I., which stands for God Damn Independent, and that's the way I like it and to hell with all the Betty Coeds, Sally Sororities and Freddy Frats. — Frederick Kohner, *The Affairs of Gidget*, p. 8, 1963

salon noun

a semiprivate area created by shrubs and trees where homosexual liaisons take place *US, 1972*

- — Bruce Rodgers, *The Queens' Vernacular*, p. 176, 1972

saloon noun

in poker, a hand consisting of three cards of the same rank and a pair *US, 1988*

Known conventionally as a "full house."

- — George Percy, *The Language of Poker*, p. 78, 1988

salt noun

1 an experienced veteran in any calling *UK, 1970*

- Serge smiled as he remembered how badly the young marines wanted to be salts. — Joseph Wambaugh, *The New Centurions*, p. 36, 1970

2 heroin *US, 1971*

From the appearance of the powdered drug.

- — Peter Johnson, *Dictionary of Street Alcohol and Drug Terms*, p. 163, 1993

salt verb

1 to make something appear to be worth more than it is *US, 1852*

Originally mining slang.

- I salted the graveyard behind St. Pat's over on the Southeast Side with Indian artifacts[.] — Robert Campbell, *Nibbled to Death by Ducks*, p. 65, 1989

2 to swindle someone by baiting them *US, 1950*

- — Hyman E. Goldin et al., *Dictionary of American Underworld Lingo*, p. 184, 1950

3 to plant or place something to be found *US, 1852*

- — Don Wilmeth, *The Language of American Popular Entertainment*, p. 232, 1981

- "You salted me!" Lopez said with his hand still clutching his shirt pocket. "I'm gonna tell my parole officer you salted me!" — Gerald Petievich, *Shakedown*, p. 92, 1988

salt and pepper noun

a police car *US, 1976*

From the black and white color scheme of many police cars.

- — Lanie Dills, *The Official CB Slanguage Language Dictionary*, p. 60, 1976

- — Edith A. Folb, *runnin' down some lines*, p. 252, 1980

salt and pepper adjective

white and black *US, 1915*

- "Hell, Boston is full of sailors." "Yeah, but how many of them are salt and pepper, toting two .45's in an AWOL bag?" — Darryl Ponicsan, *The Last Detail*, p. 160, 1970

- A salt 'n pepper neighborhood to play in, not too much danger of someone calling the pigs just because a black had been spotted on the block. — Odie Hawkins, *Chicago Hustle*, p. 65, 1977

- Her hair was done in a salt-and-pepper DA. — Armistead Maupin, *Tales of the City*, p. 25, 1978

- He's sixteen and heading to the Pendulum, the salt and pepper bar, where white guys and black guys go to pick up on each other. — Lynn Breedlove, *Godspeed*, p. 122, 2002

Salt River *noun*

▶ **go up Salt River**

to die *US, 1945*

- — Lou Shelly, *Hepcats Jive Talk Dictionary*, p. 25, 1945

salt water *noun*

a US police officer born in Ireland *US, 1982*

- — Bill Reilly, *Big Al's Official Guide to Chicagoese*, p. 50, 1982

saltwater taffy *noun*

an attractive woman on the beach *US, 1990*

- They were lying in rows, all this Golden Orange saltwater taffy, in taffy-colored French cuts and thong bikinis: lemon, licorice, tangerine, strawberry. They were soft and pliable and tasty[.] — Joseph Wambaugh, *The Golden Orange*, p. 173, 1990

salty *adjective*

1 angry, hostile *US, 1938*

- The soldiers got salty. — Chester Himes, *If He Hollers Let Him Go*, p. 75, 1945
- And they been sleepin' in crevices and shoe boxes and shelves and holes in the walls ever since and they is very salty with you, Nero. — William "Lord" Buckley, *Nero*, 1951
- "Seriously. I wasn't being salty." — Chandler Brossard, *Who Walks in Darkness*, p. 33, 1952
- All reet, all reet. No call to come on salty. — Ross Russell, *The Sound*, p. 93, 1961
- I get salty standing in a long line for my loving. — Iceberg Slim (Robert Beck), *Pimp*, p. 184, 1969

2 uncouth; unpleasant *US, 1985*

- [He] brought in twenty dry holes before he got cured. That means "get rich," in the salty lingo of the oil fraternity. — William Burroughs, *Queer*, p. 45, 1985

salty water *noun*

the recreational drug GHB *US, 1997*

Caustic soda mixed with industrial cleaner *gamma butyrolactone* produces a *salt* which is dissolved in *water* to produce the clear solution GHB.

- GHB has been marketed as a liquid or powder and has been sold on the street under names such as Grevious Bodily Harm, Georgia Home Boy, Liquid Ecstasy, Liquid X, Liquid E, GHB, GBH, Soap, Scoop, Easy Lay, Salty Water, G-Riffick, [and] Cherry Menth. — *Morbidity and Morality Weekly Report*, p. 281, 4th April 1997

sam *noun*

1 a federal narcotics agent *US, 1971*

An abbreviation of Uncle Sam, the personification of the US federal government.

- — Eugene Landy, *The Underground Dictionary*, p. 164, 1971

2 a southern Appalachian migrant *US, 1981*

- — *Maledicta*, p. 95, Summer/Winter 1981: "Acrimonious acronyms for ethnic groups"

same-day service *noun*

in computing, a lengthy response time *US, 1991*

- — Eric S. Raymond, *The New Hacker's Dictionary*, p. 313, 1991

same mud, same blood

used for explaining the absence of racism in combat troops *US, 1981*

- They shared the same mud. They spilled the same blood. Black and white soldiers soldiering together. — A.D. Horne (Editor), *The Wounded Generation*, p. 167, 1981
- Racism was a minor problem in frontline combat, where the saying went, "Same mud, same blood." In the rear it was a different story. — Myra MacPherson, *Long Time Passing*, p. 663, 1984

same old same old; some-o some-o *noun*

more of the same *US, 1952*

- "As they say in the Far East, it's 'sameo-sameo' here in Korea." — *Pacific Stars & Stripes* (magazine), 5 February 1952
- If the back fence is the conversation site for American housewives, then the hibachi in Japan is the samo-samo. (As you may have guessed, samo-samo means "not different.") — Willam Hume, *When We Get Back Home*, p. 32, 1953
- "What's he sayin' now, Thelma?" "Same-o same-o." — Odie Hawkins, *Ghetto Sketches*, p. 16, 1972
- STEPHANIE: So what are you up to? ULTIMATE LOSER: Same old same old, just lollygagging around. Still unemployed. — *Slacker*, 1992
- "What's that girl named Ramona doing these days." "She doing the same old same-old." — Nathan McCall, *Makes Me Wanna Holler*, p. 163, 1994

same old six and seven

used for expressing a certain lack of progress in life *US, 1959*

A borrowing from the game of craps—having established six as the point (the easiest point to make), the shooter rolls a seven, thus losing.

- "Oh, same old six-and-seven, Ginger," he said. — Terry Southern, *The Magic Christian*, p. 39, 1959

same shit, different day

used as a stock answer when asked how things are going *US, 1992*

- — William K. Bentley and James M. Corbett, *Prison Slang*, p. 47, 1992

samey-same; same same *adjective*

the same *US, 1956*

Korean and Vietnam war usage.

- — *American Speech*, p. 121, May 1960: "Korean Bamboo English"
- "Why, smoke is M.J., Mike Juliet. Ya know -grass. Same same smoke." — Larry Heinemann, *Close Quarters*, p. 26, 1977
- "You say it's same-same? Nam and fucking San Diego State?" — Tim O'Brien, *Going After Cacciato*, p. 245, 1978
- Yeah? Well, why go back? Here or there, samey-same. — *Full Metal Jacket*, 1987

Sam Hill *noun*

used as a very quaint euphemism for "hell" *US, 1839*

- Well, what the Sam Hill, son—it's only money. — Terry Southern, *Blue Movie*, p. 227, 1970
- [W]hat the Sam Hill is this thingumabob supposed to do? — Eric Kraft, *Herb 'n' Lorna*, p. 188, 1989

Samoan family car *noun*

a used police car bought at auction *US, 1982*

Hawaiian youth usage.

- — Douglas Simonson, *Pidgin to da Max Hana Hou*, 1982

Samurai *noun*

a Japanese man who is abundantly masculine, virile, brave, and demeaning towards women *US, 1982*

Hawaiian youth usage.

- — Douglas Simonson, *Pidgin to da Max Hana Hou*, 1982

San Antone!

used as a mild oath *US, 1951*

- — *American Speech*, p. 100, May 1951: "The vocabulary of poker"

San Bernaghetto *nickname*

San Bernadino, California *US, 2003*

- Born: San Bernaghetto (aka San Bernardino), CA. — *alt.sports.basketball.nba.la-lakers*, 24th December 2003

sanction *noun*

in organized crime, punishment by death *US, 1997*

- He was not a made guy, but an independent contractor that Joe used when he had to do sanctions outside the family. — Stephen J. Cannell, *Big Con*, p. 338, 1997

sand *noun*

1 courage *US, 1962*

- — Joseph E. Ragen and Charles Finston, *Inside the World's Toughest Prison*, p. 816, 1962: "Penitentiary and underworld glossary"

2 cocaine *US, 2002*

- The wiretaps recorded a primer of street slang for powder cocaine: white lady, white fingers, soft, fish scales and sand. — *Orlando Sentinel*, p. B2, 17th August 2002

sand *verb*

to mark the edges of playing cards with sandpaper or another abrasive for the purpose of cheating *US, 1979*

- — John Scarne, *Scarne's Guide to Modern Poker*, p. 289, 1979

s'up?

used as a greeting *US, 1981*

A very slurred "what's up?"

- — Connie Eble (Editor), *UNC-CH Campus Slang*, p. 6, Fall 1981
- — *National Education Association Today*, April 1985: "A glossary for rents and other squids"
- Lactameon smiled and flashed the Collector sign: a thumb and the first three fingers. "S'up, brothers?" — Jess Mowry, *Six Out Seven*, p. 78, 1993
- Sup boys. You on this show? — *Mallrats*, 1995

sandbag *verb*

1 to lull someone into a false sense of security, and then suddenly attack them *US, 1940*

Originally a term from poker, used to describe a betting strategy, and then expanded to broader use.

- "Now watch the son-of-a-bitch sandbag me!" — Thomas Heggen, *Mister Roberts*, p. x, 1946
- Now, General, I'm going to sandbag you. — *M*A*S*H*, 1970
- Perfect. Sandbag the father. — *Sleepless in Seattle*, 1993

2 in poker, to decline to raise a bet while holding a good hand in the hope of driving up the bet later in the play *US, 1947*

- — Oswald Jacoby, *Oswald Jacoby on Poker*, p. 142, 1947

sandbagger *noun*

a person who lulls an opponent into security, and then suddenly attacks *US, 1940*

- Robbie gave him the twelve strokes—the son of a bitch, the sandbagger—and beat him by twenty-six. — Elmore Leonard, *Split Images*, p. 158, 1981

sandbox *noun*

1 a toilet; a lavatory *US, 1968*

A reference to a cat's toilet habits, intended as cute.

- — Collin Baker et al., *College Undergraduate Slang Study Conducted at Brown University*, p. 187, 1968
- — *Complete CB Slang Dictionary*, p. 82, 1976

2 in computing, the research and development department *US, 1991*

A recognition of the playing nature of research.

- — Eric S. Raymond, *The New Hacker's Dictionary*, p. 313, 1991

3 the Middle East *US, 1990*

Coined during the first US invasion of Iraq and revived with the second.

- More than four months in the Middle East—the "sandbox" as some soldiers call it—hasn't dampened his spirits any. — *Fort Mills (South Carolina) Times*, 3rd March 2005

Sand Box Express *noun*

military transport to Saudi Arabia or Kuwait during the first Gulf war *US, 1991*

- "Desert cherries" in "Kevlars" fly the "Sand Box Express" to the "beach" and soon are complaining about "Meals Rejected by Ethiopians" if they can't find a "roach coach" run by "Bedouin Bob." — *Houston Chronicle*, p. 15, 24th January 1991

S&D *noun*

a search and destroy mission *US, 1981*

- "We just came off a fifteen-klick S&D." — Mark Baker, *Nam*, p. 93, 1981

sand flea *noun*

someone who associates with surfers at the beach but rarely if ever enters the water *US, 1985*

- — John Blair, *The Illustrated Discography of Surf Music 1961–1965*, p. 124, 1985

S and J *noun*

a beating by a police officer *US, 2001*

An abbreviation of "sentence and judgment."

- You wanna go pick up Drucker or Kono or one of Ray's other hamsters ... then go give them some S and J. — Stephen J. Cannell, *The Tin Collectors*, p. 262, 2001

S and M; s-m; S & M *noun*

1 sadomasochism *US, 1964*

- On another far-out fringe of the "gay" world are the so-called S & M bars. — *Life*, p. 68, 26th June 1964
- He attends S. & M. meetings (i.e., sado-masochist or slave-master) where truly gory doings are rumored. — Ned Rorem, *The New York Diary*, p. 13, 1967
- Much of gay S & M is strictly playacting. — John Rechy, *The Sexual Outlaw*, p. 254, 1977
- When serious S&M people in San Francisco say they are going out to the bar, this is the place they are going. — *The World of S & M*, p. 127, 1981

2 sausage and mushrooms *US, 1996*

- — *Maledicta*, p. 21, 1996: "Domino's pizza jargon"

3 Santa Monica Boulevard in Los Angeles, California *US, 1986–1987*

- — *Maledicta*, p. 145, Summer/Winter 1986–1987: "Sexual slang: prostitutes, pedophiles, flagellators, transvestites, and necrophiles"

sand nigger *noun*

an Arab; an Indian or Pakistani person *US, 1984*

Highly offensive.

- "Sand niggers," Big Ed said. "Your A-rabs cause the glut and they cause the gasoline lines." — Dan Jenkins, *Life Its Ownself*, p. 92, 1984
- I know them sand niggers got all kinda sheep and camels runnin' loose. — Seth Morgan, *Homeboy*, p. 17, 1990
- "The fucking Muslims, motherfucking sand niggers, raised so much shit about it being against their social religion, that nobody can get ham." — Jimmy Lerner, *You Got Nothing Coming*, p. 71, 2002
- "Wannabe sand niggers. Or maybe Gypsies boosting mechandise under those fucking muumuus." — Joseph Wambaugh, *Hollywood Station*, p. 46, 2006

Sandoz; Sandoz's *noun*

LSD *US, 1967*

Named after Sandoz Pharmaceuticals, the original Swiss manufacturer of the drug.

- Once, once, I had a white Sandoz. Oh, oh, I can't tell you. Such acid! — Nicholas Von Hoffman, *We Are The People Our Parents Warned Us Against*, p. 34, 1967
- — Richard A. Spears, *The Slang and Jargon of Drugs and Drink*, p. 435, 1986

sandpaper *noun*

playing cards that have been altered for cheating by minute sanding of the edges *US, 1962*

- — Frank Garcia, *Marked Cards and Loaded Dice*, p. 263, 1962

sandpaper *verb*

▸ **sandpaper the anchor**

to perform a job that need not and, in fact, cannot be performed *US, 1975*

- — John Gould, *Maine Lingo*, p. 241, 1975

sand-pounder *noun*

a member of the US Navy assigned to shore duty *US, 1960*

- That summer German saboteurs had been put ashore on Long Island and Florida, and so the "sand-pounders" had to be alert. — Charles Duffy, *A Family of His Own*, p. 69, 2003

sand toad *noun*

an Arab, a Muslim *US, 2007*

- "I got one of them sand-nigger prayer rugs the Muslims gotta use when they beg Allah for another oil well or missile or whatever the fuck those sand toads pray for." — Jimmy Lerner, *You Got Nothing Coming*, p. 197, 2002

sandwich *noun*

sex involving more than two people, the specific nature of which varies with use, usually sex between one woman and two men, one penetrating her vagina and one penetrating her anus *US, 1971*

A term given a lot of attention in 2000 when actress Cybill Shepherd dedicated a chapter of her autobiography to a description of her having taken the part of the filling in a "Cybill Sandwich" with two stuntmen.

- I have been invited home to meet one number's lover for a sandwich, have been groped accidentally by platonic acquaintances (I never liked "sister"), and have had many an ego satisfaction. — John Francis Hunter, *The Gay Insider*, pp. 102–103, 1971
- — Edith A. Folb, *runnin' down some lines*, p. 246, 1980
- It'd be so righteous to be in a Veronica Sawyer-Heather Chandler sandwich. — *Heathers*, 1988
- [T]hey'll want you to be the filling for a sandwich, being fucked by one while you fuck the other. — John Preston, *Hustling*, p. 89, 1994
- Pussy/ass penetration has always been known as a SANDWICH. — *Adult Video News*, p. 44, August 1995
- With the change in the order of the sandwich's ingredients, a new taste became evident. — Jack Boulware, *Sex American Style*, p. 157, 1997
- "The Cybill sandwich" turned out to be a positive sexual experience. Having all the pleasure points being attended to simultaneously rather than sequentially made me feel adored, emancipated, and more relaxed about sex. — Cybill Shepherd with Aimee Lee Bail, *Cybill Disobedience*, p. 226, 2000

sandwich *verb*
in poker, to surround a player with two confederates whose collusive betting tactics relieve the middle player of his bankroll and drive him from the game *US, 1973*
- — Thomas L. Clark, *The Dictionary of Gambling and Gaming*, p. 188, 1987

sandwich job *noun*
condemnation surrounded on either side by faint praise *US, 1981*
- I got my evaluation today. No Waves put it in on my desk so he wouldn't have to face me. It was a "sandwich job" as usual. — Gerald Petievich, *Money Men*, p. 45, 1981

Sandy *nickname*
a Douglas A-1E Skyraider, especially effective in providing cover for combat rescue missions in Vietnam *US, 1980*
- Sandy, the Douglas A-1E was the oldest combat airplane in the Air Force's inventory. — William C. Anderson, *Bat-21*, p. 20, 1980

San Fran *nickname*
San Francisco, California *US, 1957*
- But this is only after you and I, dear Carlo, go to Texas, dig Old Bull Lee, that gone cat I've never met and both of you've told me so much about, and then I'll go to San Fran. — Jack Kerouac, *On the Road*, p. 48, 1957

sanitary ride *noun*
in a horse race, the tactic of riding away from the rail to avoid the mud flung by the pack of racehorses near the rail *US, 1978*
- — Thomas L. Clark, *The Dictionary of Gambling and Gaming*, p. 189, 1987

sano *adjective*
used of surf conditions, excellent *US, 1988*
- — Michael V. Anderson, *The Bad, Rad, Not to Forget Way Cool Beach and Surf Discriptionary*, p. 18, 1988

San Q *nickname*
the San Quentin state prison, San Rafael, California *US, 1993*
- "My man ... takes his meals ... down at San Q," she replied. "And will be ... for the next ... 10 to 20 years." — C.D. Payne, *Youth in Revolt*, p. 182, 1993

San Quentin breakfast *noun*
a male under the age of legal consent as an object of sexual desire *US, 1976*
- The man knows he can be sent to San Quentin for having sexual relations with a minor. They are known as "San Quentin breakfast." — *San Francisco Chronicle*, p. 12, 22nd March 1976

San Quentin briefcase *noun*
a large portable stereo system associated, stereotypically, with black youth culture *US, 1990*
San Quentin is the most famous of California's state prisons.
- He cranked up his San Quentin briefcase, reawaking its raging rhymes. — Seth Morgan, *Homeboy*, p. 18, 1990

San Quentin quail *noun*
a girl under the age of legal consent *US, 1940*
In the 1940 film *Go West*, Groucho Marx played a character named S. Quentin Quale, an inside joke.
- "You ain't been fooling around that little kid, have you? Honest?" "That's San Quention quail," said Thomas, attempting to sound like a man of the world. — Jose Antonio Villarreal, *Pocho*, p. 140, 1959
- One month to go until I turn 18, free from the stigma of "San Quentin quail." — Jefferson Poland and Valerie Alison, *The Records of the San Francisco Sexual Freedom League*, p. 47, 1971
- "I'm San Quentin Quail, Mr. Winner," Rosalie says. — Oscar Zeta Acosta, *The Revolt of the Cockroach People*, p. 108, 1973
- Sightem spotted by self: middle-aged Volvo with license plates "SQQ," and you'd have to be middle-aged to remember Errol Flynn's painful experience with "San Quentin quail." Just a sec and I'll spin Artie Shaw's Gramercy Seven recording of "When the Quail Come Back to San Quentin." — *San Francisco Chronicle*, p. B1, 19th August 1994

Santa Barbara *noun*
in hold 'em poker, an ace and a king as the first two cards dealt a player *US, 1981*
- An ace and a king are a Santa Barbara. The older term for that is big slick, but a few years ago there was an oil spill off the coast and the California players started called it Santa Barbara. — Thomas L. Clark, *The Dictionary of Gambling and Gaming*, pp. 18–19, 1987

Santa Claus rally *noun*
an increase in stock prices between Christmas and the end of the year *US, 1976*
- "I think the year-end Santa Claus rally commenced on Tuesday," commented Alfred E. Goldman, vice president of A. G. Edwards & Sons, Inc. — *Wall Street Journal*, p. 19, 23rd December 1976

sap *noun*
1 a gullible fool *UK, 1815*
- What saps we were! — Max Shulman, *The Zebra Derby*, p. 83, 1946
- "Tomorrow we can go out and get a new radio—if, Wally darling, you'll be a doll and put it in for me?" "You know I will, baby," said Wally. The guy is such a sap. — C.D. Payne, *Youth in Revolt*, p. 121, 1993
2 a short club; a police officer's nightstick *US, 1899*
- The Independent has special cops hired by the company, but they don't carry guns. Only saps. — William Burroughs, *Junkie*, p. 45, 1953

sapazzola *noun*
semen *US, 1985*
- There's a little jerkoff down there going splooey all over the place! you could hydroplane on all the sapazzola in this freak show! — Joseph Wambaugh, *The Secrets of Harry Bright*, p. 61, 1985

saperoo *noun*
a complete fool *US, 1950*
- — Hyman E. Goldin et al., *Dictionary of American Underworld Lingo*, p. 184, 1950

sapfu *noun*
a badly botched situation *US, 1960*
The situation "surpasses all previous fuck-ups."
- SNAFU / FUBAR / SAPFU: Acronyms, not words, listed in ascending order of implied ineptitude or stupidity. — Marion F. Sturkey, *Warrior Culture of the U.S. Marines*, p. 187, 2003

sap gloves *noun*
gloves weighted for maximized damage when used to strike someone *US, 1975*
- He wore his old sap gloves with the lead filled palm and padded knuckles (which a sob sister sergeant had caught him beating up a drunk with and which he had been ordered to get rid of). — Joseph Wambaugh, *The Choirboys*, p. 34, 1975

sapper *noun*
a Viet Cong or North Vietnamese commando *US, 1987*
Members of the North Vietnamese Army's combat engineers, and thus the name, derived from the longstanding UK sense of the word as "a soldier in the Engineer Corps, the Royal Sappers and Miners." "Sappers inside the wire!" was a warning call that US soldiers did not want to hear.
- Now rewrite it and give it a happy ending—say, uh, one kill. Make it a sapper or an officer. — *Full Metal Jacket*, 1987
- The shelling became the worst curse of this DMZ war, worse than the infantry assaults, worse than the ambushes of the convoys, worse than the raids by the sappers (a term Americans applied to NVA and Viet Cong commando-type troops) who stripped to their undershorts and crawled through the barbed wire to toss satchel charges into bunkers and artillery revetments. — Neil Sheehan, *A Bright Shining Lie*, p. 649, 1988

sardine *noun*
a shark *US, 1965*
Surfer humor.
- — John M. Kelly, *Surf and Sea*, p. 292, 1965

sars-fras *noun*
a low-grade marijuana cigarette *US, 1948*
- The cigarettes come in three qualities: sars-fras, the cheapest kind, sold to thousands of school children at about ten cents each[.] — Jack Lait and Lee Mortimer, *New York Confidential*, p. 102, 1948

sash *noun*
anything used to tie around your arm while injecting a drug *US, 1972*
- — Helen Dahlskog (Editor), *A Dictionary of Contemporary and Colloquial Usage*, p. 50, 1972

sashay *verb*
to walk in a casual, often provocative, manner *US, 1928*

A corruption of the French *chasse*, (a gliding dance step).

- "Son, I think one of them Arin bastids jus' sashayed by and copped a gander at us" Percy whispers. — **Iceberg Slim (Robert Beck)**, *Doom Fox*, p. 227, 1978

sass *noun*

disrespectful, flippant back talk *US, 1835*

A corrupted pronunciation of the British **SAUCE**.

- Little Jeff give you sass, Big Jeff look around like he ain't even listening, but if you gave backlip—wap! — **Edwin Torres**, *Carlito's Way*, p. 17, 1975

sass *verb*

to talk back to someone; to speak to someone with disrespect *US, 1856*

- [F]inally he went to jail for sassing a cop and now he's gone[.] — **Jack Kerouac**, *Letter to Gary Snyder*, p. 582, May 1956

satchel *noun*

▶ **in the satchel**

said of a motorist who has been given a traffic ticket *US, 1958*

- The policeman who hands a summons to a motorist puts him in the satchel. — *New York Times*, p. 34, 20th October 1958

▶ **in the satchel**

corrupted; bribed; beholden to someone else *US, 1955*

A variation of the more common **IN THE BAG**.

- I got the word to watch out for action on Shank. I think this one is in the satchel. — **Rocky Garciano (with Rowland Barber)**, *Somebody Up There Likes Me*, p. 311, 1955

satellite *noun*

1 a prisoner who remains on the fringes of a prison gang without actually joining it *US, 1992*

- — **William K. Bentley and James M. Corbett**, *Prison Slang*, p. 43, 1992

2 a small-stakes poker tournament, the winning of which entitles the player to entry in a higher stakes tournament *US, 1990*

- — **Anthony Holden**, *Big Deal*, p. 304, 1990

satin *noun*

Italian Swiss Colony Silver Satin wine *US, 1980*

An inexpensive wine.

- — **Edith A. Folb**, *runnin' down some lines*, p. 253, 1980

Saturday night *noun*

in dominoes, the double blank *US, 1959*

- — **Dominic Armanino**, *Dominoes*, p. 17, 1959

Saturday night special *noun*

1 an inexpensive handgun, usually small caliber *US, 1968*

- "This cat is packing a Saturday-night special," someone said. — **Charles Whited**, *Chiodo*, p. 60, 1973
- Dough-Boy probably told you I don't carry any Saturday Night Specials or crap like that. — *Taxi Driver*, 1976
- It might have been better for him if Pedro's Saturday night special had left him dead. — **Piri Thomas**, *Stories from El Barrio*, p. 101, 1978
- "What kind of gun is that?" "No kind," Walter said. "Guy shoots the president of the United States with a fucking Saturday-night special." — **Elmore Leonard**, *Split Images*, p. 77, 1981

2 a hospital patient who regularly appears in the emergency room on weekends in search of food and a bed *US, 1978*

- — *Maledicta*, p. 6, Summer/Winter 1978: "Common patient-directed pejoratives used by medical personnel"

3 in computing, a program designed under intense time restraints *US, 1991*

- — **Eric S. Raymond**, *The New Hacker's Dictionary*, p. 313, 1991

Saturday night syndrome *noun*

1 tachycardiac fibrillation *US, 1992*

- It used to be called Saturday Night Syndrome, brought on by all-night dancing, carousing, and strenuous sexual activity. — **Larry Rivers**, *What Did I Do?*, p. 154, 1992

2 the stress and fear suffered by preachers who wait until Saturday night to write their Sunday sermon *US, 2000*

- In the preaching trade there's that thing called the "Saturday night syndrome," and what that is, is the anxiety caused by putting off the sermon until Saturday night. Fortunately, I know nothing about that issue! — **Dr. John M. McCoy**, *The Worrying Mind (sermon)*, 7th May 2000

3 the tendency of a restaurant kitchen to fail to live up to its highest potential on the busiest night of the week, Saturday night *US, 2001*

- We're not sure whether this was because of the "Saturday night syndrome" or because chicken is something Franco does particularly well. — *Improper Bostonian*, May 2001

sauce *noun*

any and all alcohol *US, 1940*

- But the first thing you have to do is cut down on the sauce and build up your health. — **William Burroughs**, *Junkie*, p. 112, 1953
- too much sauce. — **Jack Kerouac**, *Jack Kerouac Selected Letters 1957–1969*, p. 346, 17th October 1961: Letter to Philip Whalen.
- Then you make a joy-scene with some fine, hot-ass bitch and a case of sauce to celebrate that you crossed me into the joint. Right? — **Iceberg Slim (Robert Beck)**, *Trick Baby*, p. 268, 1969
- I'm off the sauce. I'm not even smoking anymore. — *Basic Instinct*, 1992

sauced *adjective*

drunk *UK, 1979*

- They went to see an Italian comedy, they ate—and eventually got sauced—at the Adriatica Cafe. — **David Gurewich**, *Travels with Dubinsky and Clive*, p. 45, 1987

saucer *noun*

1 a silver dollar coin *US, 1959*

- — **Edd Byrnes**, *Way Out with Kookie*, 1959

2 in pinball, a scoring hole with a bevelled lip *US, 1977*

- — **Bobbye Claire Natkin and Steve Kirk**, *All About Pinball*, p. 116, 1977

saucy *adjective*

attractive; desired *US, 2004*

- Those new shoes are hella saucy. — **Rick Ayers (Editor)**, *Berkeley High Slang Dictionary*, p. 36, 2004

Saudi cool *adjective*

warm to hot *US, 1991*

Gulf war usage.

- — *American Speech*, p. 400, Winter 1991: "Among the new words"

sausage fest; sausage party *noun*

a party with far more boys than girls *US, 2001*

- — **Don McCreary (Editor)**, *Dawg Speak*, 2001
- — **Connie Eble (Editor)**, *UNC-CH Campus Slang*, p. 6, November 2002

sauskee *noun*

in circus and carnival usage, fifteen dollars *US, 1981*

- — **Don Wilmeth**, *The Language of American Popular Entertainment*, p. 232, 1981

Savannah *noun*

in craps, a seven *US, 1983*

- — **Thomas L. Clark**, *The Dictionary of Gambling and Gaming*, p. 189, 1987

save *verb*

▶ **save me**

please save for me *US, 1968*

- Turning to Jimmy, he said, "Save me on that butt, Jim." — **Nathan Heard**, *Howard Street*, p. 62, 1968

saver *noun*

in a pool tournament, an agreement between two or more players to share their winnings *US, 1993*

- The effect of a saver is to reduce competitiveness, since a player will still receive money even if he loses. — **Mike Shamos**, *The Illustrated Encyclopedia of Billiards*, p. 201, 1993

savvy *noun*

knowledge; intelligence; experience *US, 1825*

From the Spanish *saber* (to know).

- Common Zen savvy tells us as much. — **Terry Southern**, *The Magic Christian*, p. 52, 1959
- "She's quite a guide. Lots of savvy." — **Frederick Kohner**, *Gidget Goes to Rome*, p. 61, 1963
- Them pimps and 'hos offa Rampart Street got their own understanding of one another's crazy shit and savvy of their thing together. — **Iceberg Slim (Robert Beck)**, *Airtight Willie and Me*, p. 24, 1979
- Everybody laughs at that one, because they think it's true, because street savvy says that everybody wears a tag. Everybody can be bought. — **Robert Campbell**, *Junkyard Dog*, p. 142, 1986

savvy *verb*
to understand *UK, 1785*
Horribly butchered Spanish *saber* (to know), used by a monoglot English speaker trying to make himself understood by a foreigner.

- He moves his leg, look for the bulge. You savvy bulge? — *Get Shorty*, 1995

saw *verb*
▸ **saw wood**
to sleep *US, 1885*
From cartoons comparing the sound of snoring to the sound of sawing wood.

- One night some of Toy Face's goons sneaked up on him while he was sawing wood. — Phil Hirsch, *Hooked*, p. 20, 1968

▸ **saw wood**
in pool, to play with an awkward stroke *US, 1990*
- — Steve Rushin, *Pool Cool*, p. 25, 1990

sawbones *noun*
a doctor, especially a surgeon *UK, 1837*
- "When that doctor asked me, Son / How'd you get in this condition?" I said, "Hey sawbones / I'm just carrying on / An ole family tradition." — Hank Williams Jr., *Family Tradition*, 1979
- Plus we're gonna send for a free specialist so you're not at the mercy of these sorryass state sawbones. — Seth Morgan, *Homeboy*, p. 288, 1990
- HEALY: I got a date tonight with that Mary girl I told you about. SULLY: The sawbones? — *Something About Mary*, 1998

sawbuck *noun*
1 a ten-dollar bill *US, 1850*
- Through Western Union the Freemans had lucked up on a sawbuck from home, so were in the chips again. — Mezz Mezzrow, *Really the Blues*, p. 135, 1946
- The two suits I had bought off the rack had had to be altered slightly, but I had given the clerk a sawbuck and he had said they would be delivered this afternoon[.] — Horace McCoy, *Kiss Tomorrow Goodbye*, p. 249, 1948
- He was a kid trying to get a fin or a sawbuck a day to keep his habit up. — Willard Motely, *Let No Man Write My Epitaph*, p. 369, 1958
- "Then Bernie should get 'something extra' every time he solos on Grand Piano Jump." "Say an extra sawbuck," red went on. — Ross Russell, *The Sound*, p. 91, 1961

2 a ten-year prison sentence *US, 1950*
- — Hyman E. Goldin et al., *Dictionary of American Underworld Lingo*, p. 185, 1950
- — Joseph E. Ragen and Charles Finston, *Inside the World's Toughest Prison*, p. 816, 1962: "Penitentiary and underworld glossary"
- — John R. Armore and Joseph D. Wolfe, *Dictionary of Desperation*, p. 47, 1976

sawdust *noun*
dynamite *US, 1949*
- — Captain Vincent J. Monteleone, *Criminal Slang*, p. 200, 1949

sawdust joint *noun*
an unassuming, barebones gambling operation *US, 1963*
- Some of the names of the sawdust joints are as direct as their actions. — Ed Reid and Ovid Demaris, *The Green Jungle*, p. 4, 1963
- [S]etting up shop in the various "carpet" joints on the Strip and "sawdust" joints downtown. — Ovid Demaris, *The Last Mafioso*, p. 57, 1981

sawski; sawsky *noun*
a ten dollar bill *US, 1957*
From **SAWBACK**.
- "We rigged his room with a one-way whorehouse mirror and charged a sawski to watch it." — William Burroughs, *Naked Lunch*, p. 2, 1957
- — Joe McKennon, *Circus Lingo*, p. 81, 1980
- The Manager was right: the Varsity Squad was reaching up, tucking sawskis in her garter belt. — Seth Morgan, *Homeboy*, p. 138, 1990

sayanora
goodbye *US, 1968*
- — Collin Baker et al., *College Undergraduate Slang Study Conducted at Brown University*, p. 187, 1968

say kids, what time is it?
used as a humorous call to action *US, 1947*
The signature opening of Howdy Doody Show (NBC, 1947–60). Repeated often with referential humor.

say now
used as a greeting *US, 1973*
- — Malachi Andrews and Paul T. Owens, *Black Language*, p. 86, 1973

say-so *noun*
1 authority *UK, 1637*
- I don't know if he's rippin' us off or not. The thing is, he has too much say-so about the money. — Donald Goines, *Black Gangster*, p. 123, 1977
- We took you to this country. We took you into the paper-hanging business. If I did't give the say-so, you'd be in the old country. — *Avalon*, 1990

2 a person's word of honor *UK, 1637*
- That's your say-so. I don't take the word of gonnifs, pimps and juicemen. — Robert Campbell, *Juice*, p. 52, 1988

say what and so what?
intended as a clever dismissal of what has just been said *US, 1992*
- I say what and so what. Too bad Wardell's dead, he'd probably want to poke her. — James Ellroy, *White Jazz*, p. 52, 1992

scab *noun*
a citizens' band radio operator *US, 1976*
A derisive term used by purist shortwave radio operators.
- — Warren Smith, *Warren's Smith's Authentic Dictionary of CB*, p. 61, 1976

scab *verb*
1 to act as a strike-breaker *US, 1806*
- A mine clerk named Herbert Smith, scabbing in a Colorado Fuel and Iron mine, was brutally beaten near Trinidad. — Russ Kick, *Everything You Know is Wrong*, p. 256, 2002
- Students earned the enmity of the working class by scabbing the jobs of strikers just for fun. — Thomas Frank, *What's the Matter with Kansas?*, p. 204, 2004

2 to search for a possible sex partner *US, 1982*
Hawaiian youth usage.
- — Douglas Simonson, *Pidgin to da Max Hana Hou*, 1982

3 in pinball, to obtain a result through luck, not skill *US, 1977*
- — Bobbye Claire Natkin and Steve Kirk, *All About Pinball*, p. 116, 1977

scad!
used in expressing anger *US, 2001*
- — Don R. McCreary (Editor), *Dawg Speak*, 2001

scads *noun*
a large quantity of anything *US, 1869*
From an earlier sense specific to money.
- "But this must cost scads." — Glendon Swarthout, *Where the Boys Are*, p. 84, 1960

scaffle *noun*
phencyclidine, the recreational drug known as PCP or angel dust *US, 1994*
- — US Department of Justice *Street Terms*, October 1994

scag; skag *noun*
1 heroin; cocaine *US, 1967*
- I was snortin' scag / while other kids played tag / and my elders went to church to pray. — Lightnin' Rod, *Hustlers Convention*, p. 8, 1973
- Only a skag high ain't but good the first few times out, then you hooked[.] — Edwin Torres, *Carlito's Way*, p. 10, 1975
- When I heard they croaked Charlie I freak out, almost went back to shootin scag. — Charles W. Moore, *A Brick for Mister Jones*, p. 105, 1975
- You copping two bills a week and freebie skag to shoot. — Iceberg Slim (Robert Beck), *Airtight Willie and Me*, p. 173, 1979

2 a cigarette *US, 1945*
- — Lou Shelly, *Hepcats Jive Talk Dictionary*, p. 48, 1945

3 inferior alcohol *US, 1947*
- — Marcus Hanna Boulware, *Jive and Slang of Students in Negro Colleges*, 1947

4 an unattractive girl or woman *US, 1962*
- — *Dobie Gillis Teenage Slanguage Dictionary*, 1962
- — J. R. Friss, *A Dictionary of Teenage Slang (Mt. Diablo High)*, 1964
- — *Current Slang*, p. 5, Spring 1967

scag-hag; skag-hag *noun*
a heterosexual woman who takes pleasure in the company of homosexual men *US, 1970*
- — *American Speech*, p. 58, Spring–Summer 1970: "Homosexual slang"

scag nasty; skag nasty *adjective*
repulsive in the extreme *US, 1994*
- — Michael Dalton Johnson, *Talking Trash with Redd Foxx*, p. 132, 1994

scallybip *verb*
to burgle a house while the housewife is outside hanging washing on the line to dry *US, 1972*
- Around Christmas of that year me and a friend was going to go up through Oklahoma bipping—scallybipping [burglarizing a home when they saw the wife out back hanging clothes], you know. — Bruce Jackson, *In the Life*, p. 82, 1972

scalp *noun*
the appearance of a pornography performer's photograph on the video box *UK, 1995*
From the sense of a "scalp" as a "trophy."
- — *Adult Video News*, p. 51, October 1995

scalp *verb*
to buy tickets for an event and resell them, usually outside the event itself *US, 1886*
Originally stock exchange slang, then passed into broader general usage.
- I tell him, picked up once for scalping tickets at the Superdome and fined two hundred books. — Elmore Leonard, *Bandits*, p. 21, 1987

scalper; scalp *noun*
a person who buys tickets for a sporting or entertainment event and resells them at a profit *US, 1869*
- [T]he hawk-eyed scalpers, the hard-boiled New York scouts for Hollywood, the agents of the players or acquisitive agents looking for clients, nervous stockholders in the theater and show and their staffs, comprise the hundreds "out front[.]" — Jack Lait and Lee Mortimer, *New York Confidential*, p. 41, 1948
- Scalper? You call me a scalper? I perform a service, my friends. The service costs money. Now do you want the tickets or not. — *Fast Times at Ridgemont High*, 1982
- As a student in Bronxville I had learned all the tricks—showing up an hour before the performance at Weill to nab five-dollar seats and waiting beneath the overhang at Lincoln Center for the ticket scalpers. — Rita Ciresi, *Pink Slip*, p. 193, 1999

scaly leg *noun*
a common prostitute *US, 1972*
- See, ordinarily I don't mess with dirty legs, or scaly legs, or whatever you want to call them. Tramps. — Bruce Jackson, *In the Life*, p. 187, 1972

scam *noun*
1 a scheme by which a legitimate business is forced into bankruptcy and taken over by organized crime *US, 1982*
- In recent years, bankruptcy has become a major source of income for the underworld. New York hoodlums call it "bust-out"; in Chicago it is known as a "scam." — Ovid Demaris, *Captive City*, p. 84, 1969
2 a scheme to defraud people *US, 1963*
- The Six Degrees of Separation scam caught up with her at a table that included writers and editors. — Melissa de la Cruz, *How to Become Famous in Two Weeks or Less*, p. 79, 2003
3 a report; the latest information *US, 1977*
- — Gary Fairmont R. Filosa II, *The Surfer's Almanac*, p. 193, 1977

scam *verb*
to cheat or defraud someone *US, 1963*
- You're my man. I knew it. I knew soon as you scammed your way in here, got the free ride. — Elmore Leonard, *Glitz*, p. 255, 1985

scamp *noun*
a rascal *UK, 1808*
- He put two and two together, remembered that his old running buddy had always been a scamp, and took me in without any questions. — Alice Walker, *The Color Purple*, p. 176, 1982
- But when you scamps get together, you're worse than a sewing circle. — *Pulp Fiction*, 1994

scan *verb*
to examine someone or something *US, 1988*
- God, scan on Martha Dumptruck. — *Heathers*, 1988

Scandahoovian *adjective*
Scandanavian *US, 1960*

- This week Margrethe and I, with help from our daughter Gerda, are giving our house and our shop a real Scandahoovian cleaning. — Robert Heinlein, *Job*, p. 435, 1984
- A big Scandihoovian Bergman madly suffering but eternally hopeful face. — David Henry Sterry, *Chicken*, p. 115, 2002

scandalous *adjective*
1 immoral *US, 1997*
- "This girl was behaving scandalously!" Gang lexicon reserves the word "scandalous" for the most amoral act. — Gini Sikes, *8 Ball Chicks*, p. 32, 1997
2 extremely competent *US, 1992*
- — William K. Bentley and James M. Corbett, *Prison Slang*, p. 33, 1992
3 mean-spirited *US, 2001*
The variant "Scan'lous" also exists.
- — Rick Ayers (Editor), *Slang Dictionary*, p. 14, 2001

scandalous!
used for expressing disbelief or shock *US, 1997*
- — *Maybeck High School Yearbook (Berkeley, California)*, p. 29, 1997

scanties *noun*
underwear *US, 1967*
- "So's Pat, but he's seen other suicides go out in their scanties. Seems to be a common practice." — Mickey Spillane, *The Body Lovers*, p. 19, 1967

scare cards *noun*
in poker, the strongest cards in a player's hand, exposed to other players accidentally on purpose *US, 1996*
- — Peter O. Steiner, *Thursday Night Poker*, p. 417, 1996

scarecrow *noun*
an empty police car parked at the side of a road to deter speeding *US, 1976*
- — "Slingo", *The Official CB Slang Dictionary Handbook*, p. 53, 1976

scarf *noun*
food *US, 1967*
- There's plenty on the shelf. Take what you need. If you want coffee or some scarf—help yourself. — Malcolm Braly, *On the Yard*, p. 247, 1967

scarf *verb*
1 to eat, especially to eat greedily and hurriedly *US, 1951*
- That, before you know it, it was scarfing time and these port cats is forty-two miles out of town and nobody's got the first biscuit. — William "Lord" Buckley, *The Nazz*, 1951
- In times of crisis, all great men scarf. — Edwin Torres, *Q & A*, p. 86, 1977
- Tell him not to eat anything. We're gonna scarf when we get there. — *True Romance*, 1993
- Probably you've been scarfing down doughnuts and all I'm allowed to eat is toast. — Janet Evanovich, *Seven Up*, p. 74, 2001
2 to lick, suck, and tongue a woman's vagina *US, 1966*
- He said, "All I have to do is scarf her a few times and I get anything I want." Nuttee asked Diehl to explain the word "scarf." "To eat her box, in other words." — Richard Honeycutt, *Candy Mossler*, p. 80, 1966
- Or some of them might turn out to scarf and rim [cunnilingus and analingus] to make it. — Bruce Jackson, *In the Life*, p. 120, 1972

▸ **scarf pussy**
to perform oral sex on a woman *US, 1972*
- Scarfing pussy gets great press, but most men know shit about eating out women. — *Screw*, p. 5, 12th June 1972

scarfer *noun*
in the usage of youthful model road racers (slot car racers), a fast car *US, 1997*
From **SCARF** (to eat), suggesting that the car "is eating up" the track.
- — Phantom Surfers, *The Exciting Sounds of Model Road Racing (Album cover)*, 1997

scarf up *verb*
to acquire *US, 1973*
Extends from **SCARF** (to eat hungrily), possibly playing on **SCARE UP** (to obtain).
- If that's your idea of entertainment, scarf up a ticket the next time Jethro Tull hit town. — Lester Bangs, *Psychotic Reactions and Carburetor Dung*, p. 131, 1973

scarlet sister *noun*
a prostitute *US, 1951*

Many pious people showed up, but so did a swarm of scarlet sisters. — Jack Lait and Lee Mortimer, *Washington Confidential*, p. 88, 1951

scary *adjective*
good *US, 1969*
- — *Current Slang*, p. 11, Summer 1969
- — Connie Eble (Editor), *UNC-CH Campus Slang*, p. 5, Spring 1983

scat *noun*
1 sadomasochistic sex play involving defecation *US, 1979*
- — *What Color is Your Handkerchief*, p. 7, 1979
- Scat is slang for coprophilia—a fetish for poop. — Dan Savage, *Savage Love*, p. 170, 1998
2 heroin *US, 1949*
- — John B. Williams, *Narcotics and Hallucinogenics*, p. 116, 1967
- — Eugene Landy, *The Underground Dictionary*, p. 164, 1971
3 low quality, low cost whiskey *US, 1950*
- — Hyman E. Goldin et al., *Dictionary of American Underworld Lingo*, p. 185, 1950

scene *noun*
1 a situation *US, 1945*
A superfluous word to describe further a person, place, thing, or happening.
- This scene of going to church on Sunday and playing with the kids, then kissing the wife good-bye Monday morning and heading down to the office to work on maximizing kill-densities or something, is what Hanna Arendt refers to as the banality of evil. — James Simon Kunen, *The Strawberry Statement*, p. 90, 1968
- While there are people camping all over—in the woods and meadows—there are basically two scenes here, the performance area and the Hog Farm / Movement City site. — *East Village Other*, 20th August 1969
- So, it would be best that the energy that flowed through our scene this summer be work oriented rather than Trip oriented—if you dig what I mean. — *The Last Supplement to the Whole Earth Catalog*, p. 78, March 1971
- Get together with your people who are waiting to split and plan a scene for when you can be together. — John Sinclair, *Guitar Army*, p. 117, 1972
2 a personal choice or taste; a favored setting or milieu *US, 1965*
Originally Black usage, then via jazz into hippy circles.
- Hitchcock suddenly scowled and got up. "Teaching life ain't my scene," he said. — Nat Hentoff, *Jazz Country*, p. 17, 1965
- I'm going to make a lot of money / Then I'm going to quit this crazy scene. — Joni Mitchell, *River*, 1971
- Joan had gone noisily down the hall, screaming at Harvey about how he was a "sickie on a power trip." "It's her scene. She's got a different lifestyle." — Cyra McFadden, *The Serial*, p. 33, 1977
- "You must admit," said another, "that the S & M scene would make a wonderful movie." — Ethan Morden, *Everybody Loves You*, p. 37, 1988
3 a sexual interlude *US, 1971*
- I saw her in front of the campfire entertaining a few brothers by having a scene with a dog. — Jamie Mandelkau, *Buttons*, p. 100, 1971
- But a scene with her boyfriend was out of the question. — Michelle Tea, *The Passionate Mistakes and Intricate Corruption of One Girl in America*, p. 50, 1998

▸ **make the scene**
1 to arrive and participate in a social gathering *US, 1958*
- If you don't embarrass easily or have a streak of the show-off, try to be the first one in town to make this particular scene with the new fads. — Art Unger, *The Cool Book*, p. 2, 1961
- Carlotta Fugatti made the scene driving a used blue La Salle coupe Bobo had given her. — Iceberg Slim (Robert Beck), *Death Wish*, p. 20, 1977
2 to go where something of interest is happening *US, 1950*
- The Fire Department makes the scene, since smoke seems to be pouring out of one of the classroom buildings, and I sit around and watch them for a while. — James Simon Kunen, *The Strawberry Statement*, p. 52, 1968
- Big-name movie and television stars make the Strip scene every night, many scouting for new shack-ups. — Arthur Blessitt, *Turned On to Jesus*, p. 117, 1971
3 to have sex *US, 1966*
- The folklore of the hustler's world has legendary stories of hustlers who supposedly made the scene with a big-time producer, satisfied the old auntie and ended up as a big star. — Johnny Shearer, *The Male Hustler*, p. 141, 1966

scenic route *noun*
in horse racing, running outside the pack on turns *US, 1978*
- — Thomas L. Clark, *The Dictionary of Gambling and Gaming*, p. 189, 1987

scheme-on *noun*
a person's regular opening line in a singles bar *US, 1985*
- — *American Speech*, p. 20, Spring 1985: "The language of singles bars"

schitz *verb*
to behave in an abnormal fashion because of sustained methamphetamine use *US, 1993*
From "schizophrenia."
- — Peter Johnson, *Dictionary of Street Alcohol and Drug Terms*, p. 165, 1993

schizo; schitzi; schizy; schizzy *adjective*
*schizo*id or *schizo*phrenic; used derogatively of anyone whose behavior is considered eccentric, illogical or mad *US, 1951*
Schizophrenia is a severe mental disorder mistakenly understood by readers of modern thriller to be little more than a split-personality.
- I was schizy for sure now. — Thurston Scott, *Cure it with Honey*, p. 177, 1951
- The Vigilante copped out as a schizo possession case. — William Burroughs, *Naked Lunch*, p. 8, 1957
- Growing up in Hyde Park, the University of Chicago's stockade on the edge of the Black Belt, Paul led a quietly schizzy life. — Albert Goldman, *Freak Show*, p. 105, 1968

schizz *noun*
a person suffering from schizophrenia *US, 1973*
- — *American Speech*, p. 208, Fall–Winter 1973: "The language of nursing"

Schneider *verb*
in gambling, to defeat someone completely *US, 1997*
- — Irwin Steig, *Play Gin to Win*, p. 141
- Zigman moved up and whispered to the Floor Manager, "We're gonna Schneider this jerk in less than an hour." — Stephen J. Cannell, *Big Con*, p. 203, 1997

school *noun*
in poker, a group of players who customarily play together *UK, 1967*
- — Albert H. Morehead, *The Complete Guide to Winning Poker*, p. 272, 1967

schoolboy draw *noun*
in poker, a draw in a highly unlikely attempt to improve a hand *US, 1988*
- — George Percy, *The Language of Poker*, p. 79, 1988

school solution *noun*
a military tactic as taught in the classroom *US, 1988*
- The whole position had been so perfectly chosen and prepared that Scanlon was later to remark that it was the Fort Benning "school solution" of how an outnumbered infantry unit ought to organize a defense. — Neil Sheehan, *A Bright Shining Lie*, p. 274, 1988
- Here lies the bones / Of Ranger Jones / A graduate of this institution / He died last night / In his first fire fight / using the school solution / Therefore, be flexible. — Charlie A. Beckwith and Donald Knox, *Delta Force*, p. 87, 274

schwag; shway *noun*
marijuana, especially low quality marijuana *US, 1995*
- — Connie Eble (Editor), *UNC-CH Campus Slang*, p. 6, Fall 1995
- — Jim Emerson-Cobb, *Scratching the Dragon*, April 1997
- Can you tell the low-thc schwag from the good pot? — Dana Larsen (editor), *Pot Puzzle Fun Book*, p. 7, 2000

schwing!
used as a vocalization of the sound a penis makes getting suddenly erect at the passing of a beautiful woman *US, 1992*
A gift to teenage slang from Mike Myers and his "Wayne's World" sketches.
- Garth holds up a poster of Claudia Schiffer. WAYNE: Schwing. GARTH: Schwing — *Wayne's World*, 1992
- — Connie Eble (Editor), *UNC-CH Campus Slang*, p. 8, Spring 1992

scissor-fingers *verb*
to shorten a performance *US, 1981*
Often accompanied by finger gestures mimicking the use of scissors.
- — Don Wilmeth, *The Language of American Popular Entertainment*, p. 233, 1981

scivvie house *noun*
a brothel *US, 1977*
- "Mayhew got himself a little number down at China Beach, little chickie workin' the scivvie houses there, she jus' love Mayhew." — Michael Kerr, *Dispatches*, p. 138, 1977

scobo *noun*
a black person *US, 1947*
- Hell, all scobos is ridiculous. — Ralph Ellison, *Invisible Man*, p. 269, 1947
- — *New York Times Magazine*, p. 62, 23rd August 1964

scody *adjective*
disagreeable *US, 1966*
- — *San Francisco Examiner*, p. 17, 17th June 1966: "Teen slanguage: real shark"

scoff *verb*
to eat *US, 1846*
- We sure used to scoff back some during those sessions—my wife Bonnie would come on with a mess of green-apple pies and buttercrust strawberry tarts that were really killers. — Mezz Mezzrow, *Really the Blues*, p. 117, 1946
- "Now, the first thing is scoff, baby, I mean, like eat," Zaida explained and she and the drummer piled into the front seat. — Ross Russell, *The Sound*, p. 15, 1961
- We might could scoff back lightly, in the most minor way, before I uptown. — Bernard Wolfe, *The Magic of Their Singing*, p. 39, 1961

scoffins *noun*
in circus and carnival usage, food *US, 1981*
If **SCOFF** is "to eat," it is only logical that "scoffins" are "that which is eaten."
- — Don Wilmeth, *The Language of American Popular Entertainment*, p. 233, 1981

sconce *noun*
the head *UK, 1567*
- I was going to kick him in the belly first, then get one of those quarter beer bottles from the case on the floor and break it over his sconce. — William Burroughs, *Junkie*, p. 27, 1953

scooch *verb*
to slide; to slide yourself *US, 1968*
- "Awright, honey," Lucille answers, scooching her ample hips around in bed. — Odie Hawkins, *Ghetto Sketches*,
- He nodded yes, yes, I dig coke and scooched himself up in bed, nostrils flared for the cocaine's reception. — Odie Hawkins, *The Busting Out of an Ordinary Man*, p. 154, 1985
- "Just scootch the seat up and go—ain't never got in an accident in my life." — Leon Bing, *Do or Die*, p. 160, 1991

scoop *noun*
1 the latest information or news *US, 1874*
- It was Lord Gallo who gave me the scoop on afternoon as I was sitting out in the surf with him waiting for a halfway decent wave to take us in. — Frederick Kohner, *Gidget*, p. 41, 1957
- [S]he had so many battle stars and could give me the straight scoop. — Glendon Swarthout, *Where the Boys Are*, p. 57, 1960
- I'm not even gonna give you a cup of coffee 'till I get the whole scoop and nothing but the scoop. — Darryl Ponicsan, *The Last Detail*, p. 56, 1970
- Sean Hartie's giving everyone the inside scoop. — *Mallrats*, 1995

2 the convex curvature of the bottom of a surfboard *US, 1965*
- — D.S. Halacy, *Surfer!*, p. 216, 1965

3 the recreational drug GHB *US, 1997*
- Health officials say mixing the drug, known on the street as "Georgia Home Boy" or "Scoop," with alcohol or other drugs can cause nausea and life-threatening breathing problems. — *Atlanta (Georgia) Journal and Constitution*, p. M1, 15th April 1993

scoop *verb*
1 to be the first to report a news story *US, 1999*
- That four-page hot-tamale sheet had scooped the A.P., the U.P., and the I.N.S., along with Reuters and Tass and all the other globe-circling know-it-all newshawks. — Mezz Mezzrow, *Really the Blues*, p. 167, 1946
- Does the president have a time machine? Have I been scooped on that? — *Austin Powers*, 1999

2 to kiss someone *US, 1997*
- — Vann Wesson, *Generation X Field Guide and Lexicon*, p. 146, 1997

3 to arrest someone *US, 1977*
- "We call in his name we got to scoop him." — John Sayles, *Union Dues*, p. 29, 1977

scoot *noun*
1 a motorcycle *US, 1943*
A shortened "scooter."
- Curtis had a big tricked-out scoot, a Harley, he kept in the house. — Elmore Leonard, *Split Images*, p. 48, 1981
- I aimed my scoot toward the curb and hit the throttle. — Robert Lipkin, *A Brotherhood of Outlaws*, p. 4, 1981

2 a dollar *US, 1981*
- I found the address of the cab company in the phone book, drove over, and left the dispatcher with an envelope containing fifty scoots. — James Ellroy, *Brown's Requiem*, p. 16, 1981

scoot *verb*
1 to leave in a hurry *US, 1882*
- You'd better scoot, hadn't you? C'mon, I'll walk you to the door. — Armistead Maupin, *Babycakes*, p. 10, 1984
- [S]he explained she was a lab technician on twenty four hour call and scooted back to the ladies room to phone her escort service and say she couldn't book any tricks that night[.] — Seth Morgan, *Homeboy*, 1990
- We scooted into the dark foyer and I closed and locked the door behind us. — Janet Evanovich, *Seven Up*, p. 44, 2001

2 to slide *UK, 1838*
- Scoot over, goddamnit. — *The Blues Brothers*, 1980

scoot around *verb*
to drive a motorcycle without a set destination *US, 1981*
- "Where you headed?" "No place particular, I'm just scooting around." — Robert Lipkin, *A Brotherhood of Outlaws*, p. 23, 1981

scooter *noun*
marijuana *US, 1997*
- — Jin Emerson-Cobb, *Scratching the Dragon*, April 1997

scooter trash *noun*
a motorcycle gang member *US, 1989*
- — James Harris, *A Convict's Dictionary*, p. 37, 1989

scoots *noun*
diarrhea *US, 1975*
- — *American Speech*, p. 65, Spring–Summer 1975: "Razorback slang"

scope *verb*
to see or to look at someone or something *US, 1974*
- Only a few people had scoped us, but they were cool. — Odie Hawkins, *Lost Angeles*, p. 191, 1994
- "Shit, scope those delts on a kid." — Ethan Morden, *Some Men Are Lookers*, p. 326, 1997
- Not much. Just, uh, scopin' the babes. — *American Pie*, 1999

scope on *verb*
to look or examine someone or something *US, 1990*
- Oooh Rene I was scoping on her man. — John Singleton, *Boyz N The Hood*, 1990

scope out *verb*
to investigate something; to examine something; to check something out *US, 1992*
- So I hassled and I hustled and I still couldn't scope it out. — Lester Bangs, *Psychotic Reactions and Carburetor Dung*, p. 132, 1973
- You go inside and talk to your dad. I'm gonna scope the place out. — *Bill and Ted's Excellent Adventure*, 1989
- The other guy, Roach, waited in the truck. They were scoping it out, right? — *Break Point*, 1991
- Strike never knew when or where they might be scoping him out. — Richard Price, *Clockers*, p. 4, 1992

scoper; scope jockey *noun*
a pathologist *US, 1994*
- — Sally Williams, *"Strong" Word*, p. 159, 1994

scope worker *noun*
in circus and carnival usage, an astrologer *US, 1981*
An abbreviation of "horoscope worker."
- — Don Wilmeth, *The Language of American Popular Entertainment*, p. 233, 1981

scorch *verb*
to stare at someone or something *US, 1991*
- — *USA Today*, p. 1D, 5th August 1991: "A sterling lexicon of the lingo"

scorcher noun

a very hot day UK, 1874

- Gonna be a scorcher today. — Marvin Wald and Albert Maltz, The Naked City, 1947
- A scorcher. It was my father's phrase and came back to me as familiarly, when I opened my eyes, as the heard reveille of my childhood. — Philip Wylie, Opus 21, p. 322, 1949
- "Ain't this a scorcher, kid?" — Jim Thompson, A Swell-Looking Babe, p. 67, 1954
- Today was a scorcher. This Chevy doesn't have air conditioning. — Point Break, 1991

score noun

1 a robbery; the proceeds of a robbery US, 1965

- I was real crazy by then. "Let's pull a score?" I said. — Hal Ellson, Duke, p. 68, 1949
- I'd say, "C'mon, man, let's go pull a score." — Claude Brown, Manchild in the Promised Land, p. 127, 1965
- Giant scores should be stored in a garage-type warehouse equipped with freezers and its whereabouts known only to the Free Food Gang. — The Digger Papers, p. 15, August 1968
- [W]e'd got away with it, hadn't we, we'd got the score, and Tony hadn't grassed and the Securicor man hadn't snuffed it. — Ted Lewis, Jack Carter's Law, p. 21, 1974

2 a one-time payment from a criminal to the police to avoid prosecution US, 1972

- A "score" is a one-time payment that an officer might solicit from, for example, a motorist or a narcotics violator. — The Knapp Commission Report on Police Corruption, p. 66, 1972

3 a sale, especially of drugs or something else illegal US, 1914

- Dincher spoke of the big score he'd make so that he might fill his life with music. — George Mandel, Flee the Angry Strangers, p. 170, 1952
- [T]hey go on looking, fabricating preposterous lies about their big scores[.] — William Burroughs, Junkie, p. 20, 1953
- Divine Right paid the man with cash he'd got from a big grass score that morning[.] — Gurney Norman, Divine Right's Trip (Last Whole Earth Catalog), p. 9, 1971

4 a prostitute's customer US, 1966

- And I could spot the scores easily—the men who paid other men sex-money[.] — John Rechy, City of Night, p. 35, 1963
- The "scores" frantically wander around the area trying to select the youngest and best-looking hustler. — Johnny Shearer, The Male Hustler, p. 44, 1966

5 a sexual conquest US, 1970

- A score like that, a man could just live on his reputation. — M*A*S*H, 1970

▸ **keep score**

to perform the paperwork required of a police team US, 1970

- "Want to drive or keep score?" asked Light after roll call[.] — Joseph Wambaugh, The New Centurions, p. 137, 1970

score verb

1 to obtain something, especially drugs and especially dishonestly US, 1914

- We covered Brooklyn, the Bronx, Queens, Jersey City, and Newark. We couldn't even score for pentapon. — William Burroughs, Junkie, p. 37, 1953
- We go outside the city and score and everything is crazy. — Jack Gerber, The Connection, p. 67, 1957
- He had heard I was in town and wanted to know if I wanted to score. — Alexander Trocchi, Cain's Book, p. 19, 1960
- I said, "Top, I'm frayed. I sure wish I had a snort of 'gir.' Can you score?" — Iceberg Slim (Robert Beck), Pimp, p. 128, 1969
- Alvy, listen, while you're in California, could you possibly score some coke for me? — Annie Hall, 1977

2 (of a police officer) to extract a one-time bribe from a criminal to avoid prosecution US, 1972

- The term is also used as a verb, as in "I scored him for $1,500." — The Knapp Commission Report on Police Corruption, p. 66, 1972
- It was not his style to score prostitutes. — Leonard Shecter and William Phillips, On the Pad, p. 24, 1973

▸ **score on**

to get the best of someone verbally US, 1963

- — American Speech, p. 275, December 1963: "American indian student slang"

score!

used as a humorous acknowledgement of a correct answer US, 1994

- IAN: So Pip's your younger brother? REX: Yup. Score! — Airheads, 1994

scorpion noun

in dominoes, the 4–4 piece US, 1959

- — Dominic Armanino, Dominoes, p. 17, 1959

Scotch screw noun

a nocturnal emission of semen US, 1986–1987

- — Maledicta, p. 60, 1986–1987: "A continuation of a glossary of ethnic slurs in american english"

Scotty noun

crack cocaine; the intoxication produced by crack cocaine US, 1992

Taken from the catchphrase "Beam me up, Scotty," first heard in cult science-fiction television series "Star Trek" (1966–69).

- — Terry Williams, The Cocaine Kids, p. 137, 1989

scout's honor noun

used as a mocking pledge or oath to tell the truth US, 1984

A reference to the Boy Scouts of America and their pledge to be truthful.

- Lloyd said "Scout's honor" and started up the car, waggling his eyebrows at Kathleen until she laughed and begged him to stop. — James Ellroy, Blood on the Moon, p. 182, 1984

scrag verb

to murder someone US, 1930

- "You know, she's hollering Muffo was scragged like Magoo." — George Mandel, Flee the Angry Strangers, p. 377, 1952

scraggy adjective

shabby US, 1946

- When we bust in on our pals we found them all kiping in one scraggy room, practically sleeping in layers. — Mezz Mezzrow, Really the Blues, p. 177, 1946

scram verb

to leave quickly US, 1928

Probably a reduction of "scramble," possibly from German schrammen (to run away).

- [A] bookkeeper, no less, who used to beat her up and who scrammed with a lot of her assets. — Jack Lait and Lee Mortimer, New York, p. 187, 1948
- The Inspector wants this fellow to scram. — Horace McCoy, Kiss Tomorrow Good-bye, p. 82, 1948
- We have some of the wheels in the Mafia dangling by their you-know-whats and they're scramming for cover. — Mickey Spillane, Kiss Me Deadly, pp. 140–141, 1952
- Scram, beat it, vamoose, out! Is that plain enough? — King of Comedy, 1976

scram bag noun

in circus and carnival usage, a suitcase that is always packed in the event that a hasty departure has become the prudent course of action US, 1981

- — Don Wilmeth, The Language of American Popular Entertainment, p. 233, 1981

scramble noun

1 adulterated heroin US, 1984

- Heroin is called either "bones," referring to a high level of purity, or "scramble," meaning a much less pure version, which is much cheaper. — Washington Post, p. B1, 29th July 1984

2 crack cocaine US, 1994

From the effect on the user.

- — US Department of Justice Street Terms, October 1994

scramble verb

1 to live hand-to-mouth by a variety of hustles US, 1989

- — Terry Williams, The Cocaine Kids, p. 137, 1989
- "Fariq, how you get that earring?" "Scrambling, nigger, you know that." — Paul Beatty, Tuff, p. 69, 2000

2 to sell drugs US, 1990

- He beat this kid who was scramblin' for him with a Louisville Slugger, poured gasoline on him and set him on fire after he shorted him $5.00. — New Jack City, 1990

scrambled eggs *noun*

1 the gold braid insignia on an officer's cap or uniform *UK, 1943*

- They have stripes on the sleeves, scrambled eggs on the peak of the cap and blue socks with yellow stripes. — Jim Bouton, *Ball Four*, p. 98, 1970
- I made him put on his hat. It had a bunch of gold braid, which he called scrambled eggs, on its visor. — Delle Brehan, *Kicks is Kicks*, p. 80, 1970
- the Commandant, with the rank of Commander and a lot of scrambled egg on his shoulders. — Duncan MacLaughlin, *The Filth*, p. 51, 2002

2 in street luge, poor road conditions *US, 1998*

- SCRAMBLED EGGS Road conditions that are bad but usable. — Shelley Youngblut, *Way Inside ESPN's X Games*, p. 130, 1998

3 mental confusion or mental illness *US, 1984*

- Fred Gil was lying there looking at his littlest daughter, perhaps a bit dazed from the medication, when she said, "Dad, you don't have scrambled eggs, do you?" — Joseph Wambaugh, *Lines and Shadows*, p. 190, 1984

scrambled eggs cap *noun*

a Captain or First Officer's cap, with gold "scrambled eggs" applique *US, 1982*

- "That famous scrambled-egg hat did not look very dashing on that day either. He [General MacArthur] was a beaten man." — Joseph C. Goulden, *Korea*, pp. 453–q, 1982

scrambler *noun*

a street-level drug seller *US, 1990*

- Fat Smitty controls the scramblers around the Carter. — *New Jack City*, 1990

scram heat *noun*

the urge to attempt escape from prison *US, 1962*

- — Joseph E. Ragen and Charles Finston, *Inside the World's Toughest Prison*, p. 816, 1962: "Penitentiary and underworld glossary"

scram switch *noun*

in computing, an off switch for use in emergency *US, 1991*

- — Eric S. Raymond, *The New Hacker's Dictionary*, p. 314, 1991

scranker *noun*

in the language surrounding the Grateful Dead, a follower of the band who has lost all touch with reality *US, 1994*

- — David Shenk and Steve Silberman, *Skeleton Key*, p. 182, 1994

scrantz *noun*

the vagina *US, 2006*

- Emboldened, I slipped a skillful, almost imperceptible hand six inches closer to her scrantz. — Chris Miller, *The Real Animal House*, p. 29, 2006

scrap *noun*

a problem; a complaint *US, 1982*

Hawaiian youth usage.

- — Douglas Simonson, *Pidgin to da Max Hana Hou*, 1982

scrap *verb*

to fight *US, 1997*

- Vann Wesson, *Generation X Field Guide and Lexicon*, p. 148, 1997

scrape *noun*

an abortion *UK, 1968*

- Touch told Mickey she drove to T.J. for a scrape. — James Ellroy, *White Jazz*, p. 295, 1992

scrape *verb*

▶ **scrape the mug**

to shave *US, 1962*

- — Joseph E. Ragen and Charles Finston, *Inside the World's Toughest Prison*, p. 816, 1962: "Penitentiary and underworld glossary"

scrape doctor *noun*

an abortionist *US, 1995*

- The scrape doctor was his kid brother, Frank. — James Ellroy, *American Tabloid*, p. 10, 1995

scrape job *noun*

an abortion, especially an illegal one *US, 1972*

- — Stephen H. Dill (Editor), *Current Slang*, p. 6, Summer 1967
- — Helen Dahlskog (Editor), *A Dictionary of Contemporary and Colloquial Usage*, p. 51, 1972

- A guess: scrape jobs made Lucille sterile. — James Ellroy, *White Jazz*, p. 113, 1992

scrap iron *noun*

1 a potent and dangerous alcoholic concoction made from wood alcohol, mothballs, and chlorine *US, 1992*

- — William K. Bentley and James M. Corbett, *Prison Slang*, p. 71, 1992

2 in prison, weights for bodybuilding *US, 1981*

- — *Maledicta*, pp. 266–267, Summer/Winter 1981: "By its slang, ye shall know it: the pessimism of prison life"

scrapper *noun*

a fighter *US, 1978*

- Alice was pound for pound one of the best scrappers around as well as the President of the Honey Debutantes[.] — Piri Thomas, *Stories from El Barrio*, pp. 92–93, 1978

scratch *noun*

1 money *US, 1914*

- "How can we make some money?" "I could use some scratch too," he says and throws the dice. — Rocky Garciano (with Rowland Barber), *Somebody Up There Likes Me*, p. 26, 1955
- "I've known of times when Miller could have made a real sackful of scratch by doing just what he's done for us, but he never bit before." — Phil Hirsch, *Hooked*, p. 72, 1968
- When he got inside the door, he would shout, "All right you poor ass bastards, it's party time and Joe Evans is in port with enough scratch to burn up a wet elephant." — Iceberg Slim (Robert Beck), *Pimp*, p. 33, 1969
- Say you cop a choice chick and you're really doing great / The scratch is right and the set up looks straight. — Dennis Wepman et al., *The Life*, p. 165, 1976

2 the vagina; a woman as a sex object; sex with a woman *US, 1962*

- "The trim, the grind, the scratch—in plain, everyday English—the pussy!" — Charles Perry, *Portrait of a Young Man Drowning*, p. 195, 1962

3 a sound or rhythmic effect created by the manipulation of a vinyl recording *US, 1995*

- He had a way of rhythmically taking a scratch and making that shit sound musical. — Lois Stavsky et al. (quoting DJ Fuze, July1994), *A2Z*, p. 89, 1995

4 a drug addict *US, 2001*

- — Don R. McCreary (Editor), *Dawg Speak*, 2001

5 an attestation by a superior that a police officer was on his beat at a given time *US, 1973*

- waiting at street corners for a sergeant to come by and make the scratch. — Charles Whited, *Chiodo*, p. 291, 1973

scratch *verb*

1 to manipulate a vinyl record to create sounds and rhythms *US, 1995*

Scratching, as a technique, was invented in the late 1970s by 13-year-old Theodore Livingstone (later Grand Wizard Theodore) and widely recognized by the mainstream in 1983 with the release of "Rockit" by Herbie Hancock which featured Grandmixer DST scratching.

- I did the scratching and he was the MC. — Lois Stavsky et al. (quoting DJ Fuze, July1994), *A2Z*, p. 89, 1995
- [T]echniques like back-spinning, cutting, which was later called scratching[.] — Alex Ogg, *The Hip Hop Years*, p. 27, 1999
- I liked the bit in the middle (of Malcolm McLarens' "Buffalo Girls") that went wucka, wucka, wucka. And he said, "that's scratching, that is." — J. Hoggarth (quoting Prime Cuts), *How To Be a DJ*, p. 81, 2002

2 to forge *US, 1962*

- — Joseph E. Ragen and Charles Finston, *Inside the World's Toughest Prison*, p. 816, 1962: "Penitentiary and underworld glossary"

3 to erase something; to withdraw something from a competition *UK, 1685*

- No, more like a Formula race car. No, scratch that one, too. — *Natural Born Killers*, 1994

4 to paddle a surfboard energetically *US, 1963*

- — Grant W. Kuhns, *On Surfing*, p. 121, 1963

▶ **scratch gravel**

to leave quickly, especially in a car *US, 1968*

- — Hy Lit, *Hy Lit's Unbelievable Dictionary of Hip Words for Groovy People*, p. 51, 1968

▶ **scratch your monkey**

(used of a drug addict) to satisfy your drug habit with an injection or other ingestion of the drug *US, 1992*

- — William K. Bentley and James M. Corbett, *Prison Slang*, p. 72, 1992

scratch bombing *noun*
to create graffiti by scratching or etching a surface rather than painting it *US, 1994*
- If there are any graffiti writers here, they haven't discovered scratch bombing. — William Upski Wimsatt, *Bomb the Suburbs*, p. 43, 1994

scratcher *noun*
1 a forger *US, 1961–1962*
- — Frank Prewitt and Francis Schaeffer, *Vacaville Vocabulary*, 1961–1962
2 a tattoo artist, especially an unlicensed amateur *US, 1997*
- — *Los Angeles Times Magazine*, p. 7, 13th July 1997

scratch house *noun*
an inexpensive boarding house, club, or brothel *US, 1960*
- The Arizona Club, where Danny Ocean and Jimmy Foster sought Vince Massler, turned out to be a place known inelegantly in theater parlance as a scratch house. — George Clayton Johnson, *Ocean's Eleven*, p. 11, 1960

scratch man *noun*
a forger *US, 1952*
- Benton's cell-mate in Atlanta was a forger named Jim Heyaward, and the two scratch-men soon became fast friends. — Charles Hamilton, *Men of the Underworld*, p. 156, 1952
- — Joseph E. Ragen and Charles Finston, *Inside the World's Toughest Prison*, p. 817, 1962: "Penitentiary and underworld glossary"

scratch off *verb*
to leave, especially in a hurry *US, 1956*
- — *American Speech*, p. 229, October 1956: "More United States Air Force slang"

scratch pad *noun*
very inexpensive lodging *US, 1946*
- You'll never toss and turn again in a Bowsery scratchpad, digging the lice and chinches out of your hide. — Mezz Mezzrow, *Really the Blues*, p. 317, 1946

scratch sheet *noun*
a leaflet or pamphlet offering "inside" tips on horse betting *US, 1972*
- — Helen Dahlskog (Editor), *A Dictionary of Contemporary and Colloquial Usage*, p. 19, 1972

scream *noun*
an extremely ridiculous or funny person or thing *US, 1888*
Originally used in theater slang, now simply melodramatic.
- Oh, Harry, you're a scream. — Max Shulman, *Rally Round the Flag, Boys!*, p. 42, 1957
- It's a scream. You'd love it. — Armistead Maupin, *Tales of the City*, p. 124, 1978
- We made a girl want to consider suicide. What a scream. What a jest. — *Heathers*, 1988

scream *verb*
to complain *US, 1984*
- — Inez Cardozo-Freeman, *The Joint*, p. 528, 1984

screamer *noun*
1 a blatant and conspicuous homosexual *US, 1960*
- The homosexual, who was playing hard to get, came to one masquerade party dressed as Tinkerbelle, the good fairy. He was what the other queers called a screamer. — Phyllis and Eberhard Kronhausen, *Sex Histories of American College Men*, p. 184, 1960
- In the summer they'd pile into convertibles and head for North Beach, a spot for bawdy screamers and butch hillbilly types. — *Screw*, p. 15, 23rd February 1970
- — Jeff Fessler, *When Drag Is Not a Car Race*, p. 14, 1997
2 a headline *US, 1946*
- Screamers (n. pl.) Newspaper headlines. — *Hit Parader*, p. 33, September 1946
3 in rock climbing, a serious fall *US, 1998*
- SCREAMER A big fall. — shelley Youngblut, *Way Inside ESPN's X Games*, p. 209, 1998
4 an arrest warrant *US, 1990*
- They haven't booked me yet. I'm beginning to think that maybe I can walk out of this when somebody comes up to me and says, "Oh, you're Huncke. We've got a screamer on you." — Herbert Huncke, *Guilty of Everything*, p. 107, 1990
5 a police siren *US, 1992*
- Course, if they come it with their screamer full on, just like now. — Jess Mowry, *Way Past Cool*, p. 15, 1992

6 a hamburger with hot sauce and onions *US, 1997*
- — Amy and Denise McFadden, *CoalSpeak*, p. 12, 1997

screamer and creamer *noun*
a woman who is vocal during sex *US, 1977*
- — *Maledicta*, p. 18, Summer 1977: "A word for it"

screaming *adjective*
1 striking; conspicuous; obvious *US, 1848*
Used as an intensifier since the mid-C19, but in a slangy homosexual sense much more recently.
- I have always made fun of the swishing, screaming, flaunting queens and you have always laughed with me. — *Mattachine Review*, p. 24, March 1960
- "You don't appreciate this bunch of screaming faggots very much, do you?" — Joe Houston, *The Gay Flesh*, p. 10, 1965
- — *Fact*, p. 27, January–February 1965
- Old Jewish mothers never know when their sons are faggots. They just miss it somehow. Out-and-out screaming queens—mothers are never hip. — Lenny Bruce, *The Essential Lenny Bruce*, p. 162, 1967
2 excellent; the best *US, 1989*
- That cup of coffee was screamin' — James Harris, *A Convict's Dictionary*, p. 37, 1989
- — Jim Goad, *Jim Goad's Glossary of Northwestern Prison Slang*, December 2001

screaming meemies *noun*
hysteria; excessive fear noisily expressed *US, 1927*
- By the time a big company got around to referring one of its employees to a psychiatrist, the screaming meemies had already set in and the patient was often receiving radio beams from Venus. — Carl Hiaasen, *Tourist Season*, p. 40, 1986
- Somebody threw a building block through the plate glass, gave Hetty the screaming meemies. — Robert Campbell, *Alice in La-La Land*, pp. 210–211, 1987

screaming shits *noun*
1 a nonexistent disease *US, 1947*
It is commonly found in expressions such as, "I'd rather die with the screaming shits."
- — *American Speech*, p. 305, December 1947: "Imaginary diseases in army and navy parlance"
2 diarrhea *US, 1971*
- — *Current Slang*, p. 19, Spring 1971
- We would probably pay a price later for our indiscretion, but just then that stream was full of the best water we had tasted in a long time. A case of the screaming shits was worth the risk. — Gary Linderer, *The Eyes of the Eagle*, p. 61, 1991

screamy *adjective*
melodramatic; exhibitionist; extremely extroverted *US, 1979*
Homosexual usage.
- — *Maledicta*, p. 235, 1979: "Kinks and queens: linguistic and cultural aspects of the terminology for gays"

screechie *noun*
in circus and carnival usage, an audio technician *US, 1981*
- — Don Wilmeth, *The Language of American Popular Entertainment*, p. 233, 1981

screw *noun*
1 a prison officer *UK, 1812*
Possibly from an obsolete sense of "screw" (a skeleton key), hence a "turnkey" or "warder," or perhaps from "thumbscrew" (an instrument of torture used in C17 prisons).
- When the screw came, I'd spit in his face. — William Burroughs, *Junkie*, p. 68, 1953
- [T]he money which his friends, outside, will bung the screws to pay for his snout [cigarettes] and other little creature comforts. — Charles Raven, *Underworld Nights*, p. 52, 1956
- Several prisoners stood in the doorway, watching him. "Somebody call the screw." — Clarence Cooper Jr., *The Scene*, p. 228, 1960
- But one day these screws got to me. — *Raging Bull*, 1980
2 an act of sexual intercourse *US, 1929*
- If you don't like sleeping, and don't want a screw / Then you should take lots of amphetamine too — The Fugs *New Amphetamine Shreik*, 1965
- After a month of these cheap screws she finally told me she had $25,000 in her personal savings account. — Oscar Zeta Acosta, *The Autobiography of a Brown Buffalo*, p. 155, 1972

screw *verb*
1 to have sex *UK, 1725*

- What are you going to screw tonight, eh? Who? Your brother-in-law? — George Mandel, *Flee the Angry Strangers*, p. 50, 1952
- [S]hore, come on with us and we'll all screw ya at ten thousand feet[.] — Jack Kerouac, *The Dharma Bums*, p. 24, 1958
- "But decent girls don't screw," Max said. — Willard Motley, *Let No Man Write My Epitaph*, p. 178, 1958
- He would've screwed this nanny goat if he couldn't find a nymph. — Tom Robbins, *Another Roadside Attraction*, p. 273, 1971

2 to ruin something *UK, 1976*

- I think they've screwed biology in this country for ever. — *Maclean's*, 17th May 1976

3 to leave *US, 1985*

- Terminology — Gene Sorrows, *All About Carnivals*, p. 26, 1985

4 in pool, to apply spin to the cue ball to affect the course of the object ball or the cue ball after striking the object ball *US, 1990*

- — Steve Rushin, *Pool Cool*, p. 25, 1990

▶ **screw the pooch**
to bungle or to ruin something *US, 1979*
A slightly cleaned up **FUCK THE DOG**.

- [H]is prayer had not been answered, and the Lord let him screw the pooch. — Tom Wolfe, *The Right Stuff*, p. 231, 1979
- You really know how to screw the pooch, Sarge! — John Culbertson, *13 Cent Killers*, p. 62, 2003

▶ **screw your brains out**
to have sex with great regularity and force *US, 1971*

- She didn't talk much but she was quite affectionate. Nearly screwed my brains out is what I'm trying to say. — Tom Robbins, *Another Roadside Attraction*, p. 32, 1971

screwage *noun*
a computer malfunction due to design error *US, 1991*

- — Eric S. Raymond, *The New Hacker's Dictionary*, p. 315, 1991

screw around *noun*
to fool around; to waste time *US, 1939*

- Shooting pool and screwing around. — Willard Motley, *Let No Man Write My Epitaph*, p. 85, 1958

screwball *noun*
an odd, eccentric, or crazy person *US, 1933*

- He had known there would be some screwball around. — Earl Wilson, *I Am Gazing Into My 8-Ball*, p. 88, 1945
- You're sure the world's prize screwball. — Irving Shulman, *The Amboy Dukes*, p. 238, 1947
- Kinsey only talked to screwballs and neurotics and people who were inventing stuff to show off. — Philip Wylie, *Opus 21*, p. 113, 1949
- And the only way you'll get me to Scranton is if some screwball hijacks the plane! — Eugene Boe (Compiler), *The Wit & Wisdom of Archie Bunker*, p. 20, 1971

screwball *adjective*
odd, eccentric *US, 1936*

- That screwball play of yours with Sugar and Max. — Mickey Spillane, *Kiss Me Deadly*, p. 109, 1952
- "Where'd you get a screwball notion like that?" asks Mule. — Darryl Ponicsan, *The Last Detail*, p. 139, 1970

screwed, blued, and tattooed *adjective*
treated very well or treated very poorly *US, 1962*

- We're screwed, blued and tattooed, man, and that's from the beginning. — Saul Bellow, *The Noble Savage*, p. 249, 1962
- "See, Bangkok's the only city in the world named after it's number one activity! You can get screwed, blued, and tattooed there and, if you're conscious, enjoy every minute of it." — Kregg Jorgenson, *Very Crazy G.I.*, p. 155, 2001

screwed up *adjective*
drunk *US, 2004*

- If you ask me, getting screwed-up and making love are just about the two most fun things in the entire world[.] — Marty Beckerman, *Generation S.L.U.T.*, p. 97, 2004

screwhead *noun*
a dolt *US, 1990*

- — Joseph Tuso, *Singing the Vietnam Blues*, p. 261, 1990: Glossary

screw job *noun*
an exploitation or other maltreatment *US, 1987*

- I think this is nothin' but a goddamn screw job. I think it's a shakedown. — *Raising Arizona*, 1987

screw-up *noun*

1 an action or circumstance that has been handled badly *US, 1998*

- First of all, was a man who had made such a thorough screw-up of his own affairs a suitable mentor for me? — Jim Thompson, *Bad Boy*, p. 335, 1953

2 an awkward person an incompetent, a blunderer; an inadequate person *US, 2002*

- When I was an undergraduate, I was described by those who knew me best as a complete screw up (that is a nice way to put it). — Frederick Frank, *Playing the Game*, p. 58, 2004

screw up *verb*
to bungle; to fail in a task; to perform something poorly *US, 1942*

- You're screwing things up. — Irving Shulman, *The Amboy Dukes*, p. 232, 1947
- Because if I feel down or screwed it up, I'd never live to fumble another one. — Jim Thompson, *Savage Night*, p. 48, 1953
- I'm not going to screw it up just because you people got hot pants. — George V. Higgins, *The Friends of Eddie Doyle*, p. 74, 1971
- If you screw up, I can promise you, you're goin' down. — *48 Hours*, 1982

screwy *adjective*
crazy, eccentric *US, 1887*

- As soon as their Hawaiian honeymoon was over, she had taken up with that screwy crowd. — John Conway, *Love in Suburbia*, p. 30, 1960

scribble *verb*
in computing, to inadvertently and detrimentally modify a data structure *US, 1991*

- Somebody's disk-compactor program went beserk and scribbled on the i-node table. — Eric S. Raymond, *The New Hacker's Dictionary*, p. 315, 1991

scribe *noun*
a letter *US, 1970*

- — Clarence Major, *Dictionary of Afro-American Slang*, p. 101, 1970
- When the door opened and in walked the man / Carrying what looked like a scribe in his hand. — Dennis Wepman et al., *The Life*, p. 139, 1976

scrilla; skrilla *noun*
money *US, 1995*

- That scandalous bitch just wanted some scrilla. — *rec.music.hip-hop*, 8th March 1995
- If they can get mo scrillah form some stupid ass City to move there, they will. — Renay Jackson, *Oaktown Devil*, p. 11, 1998

scrimy *adjective*
despicable; lowdown *US, 1952*

- Another kid cut down by a pack of scrimy hoods[.] — Mickey Spillane, *Kiss Me Deadly*, p. 151, 1952

script *noun*

1 a prescription for a narcotic, especially a forged prescription *US, 1936*

- I keep getting codeine from the Doc here. New script today. — William Burroughs, *Letters to Allen Ginsberg 1953–1957*, p. 73, 29th October 1954
- I just remembered, my sick old man is got some red devils from a script at his pad. — Iceberg Slim (Robert Beck), *Trick Baby*, p. 268, 1969
- [H]e's got a lot of doctors who gamble with him and they write him a scrip once in a while. — Bruce Jackson, *Outside the Law*, p. 107, 1972
- Joe told him he only needed to find Rooski this morning, who often cadged [begged] Demerols from Hymie's migraine script. — Seth Morgan, *Homeboy*, p. 59, 1990

2 a forged check *US, 1950*

- — Hyman E. Goldin et al., *Dictionary of American Underworld Lingo*, p. 187, 1950

script jockey *noun*
a screenwriter *US, 1964*

- The script jockey is one Stanley Shapiro, and he commands $250 Thou per flick. — Sidney Bernard, *This Way to the Apocalypse*, p. 167, 1964

script pad *noun*
a doctor's prescription pad *US, 1954*

- Met a doctor's son, he need money, and the old man's script pad right there. — William Burroughs, *Letters to Allen Ginsberg 1953–1957*, p. 25, 1st March 1954

scroat; scrote *noun*
a despicable man *US, 1975*
Probably from an abbreviation of "scrotum."

- Scrotes! That's what all people are: ignorant filthy disgusting ugly worthless scrotes. — Joseph Wambaugh, *The Choirboys*, p. 33, 1975

scromp *verb*
to have sex *US, 1993*

- — *People Magazine*, p. 72, 19th July 1993

scronies *noun*
pepperoni *US, 1996*

- — *Maledicta*, p. 19, 1996: "Domino's pizza jargon"

scrotum *noun*
▶ **on the scrotum**
alert, prepared *US, 1949*
A play on the more common "on the ball."

- — *American Speech*, p. 31, February 1949: "A.V.G. Lingo"

scrounger *noun*
a person known for their ability to beg, borrow, buy, or steal what was needed *US, 1918*
Respected and valued.

- A "scrounger" in the Marines is a highly experienced artist and not a mere thief. The scrounger's idea is that everything is basically government property, and the government belongs to its citizens. As a citizen in good standing, the scrounger feels entitled to anything he can move. — Russell Davis, *Marine at War*, p. 171, 1961
- He was a decent scrounger; had hustled Haskins for eggs and bacon and No. 10 cans of fruit, and real ground coffee. — Larry Heinemann, *Close Quarters*, p. 228, 1977

scroungy *adjective*
cheap, always in search of help *US, 1959*

- — *American Speech*, p. 154, May 1959: "Gator (University of Florida) slang"

scruff puppy *noun*
a girl as the object of social and sexual desire *US, 1988*

- — Michael V. Anderson, *The Bad, Rad, Not to Forget Way Cool Beach and Surf Discriptionary*, p. 18, 1988

scrunch up *verb*
to squeeze in; to huddle *US, 1902*

- You sit scrunched up, bent-backed, and stoop-shouldered on a plain pine plank, staring through a gun slit the size of a mail slot. — Larry Heinemann, *Paco's Story*, p. 10, 1986
- Nadeau was in the corner with Sam's Man, scrunched over into the corner, a Styrofoam cooler full of ice and canned beer on the seat between them... — Robert Campbell, *Juice*, p. 86, 1988

scrunchy; scrunchie *noun*
a circular elastic hair band covered with colorful fabric *US, 1988*

- The fashionable ponytail holders called scrunchies have been very popular for the last few years. — *Newsday (New York)*, p. II-17, 16th August 1989
- A gold scrunchie cinched her waist-length hair into a bun. — Adrian Nicole LeBlanc, *Random Family*, p. 159, 2003

scruples *noun*
crack cocaine *US, 1994*

- — US Department of Justice, *Street Terms*, October 1994

scudded *adjective*
drunk *US, 1991*
Used by US troops during the 1991 war against Iraq, playing on the missile.

- — *Army*, p. 48, November 1991
- — John Algeo and Adele Algeo, *American Speech*, p. 400, Winter 1991: "Among the new words"

scudder *noun*
a disagreeable, unlikeable person *US, 1972*

- That is, until some feisty scudder comes along begging for trouble and gets my gorge up. — Guy Owen, *The Flim-Flam Man and the Apprentice Grifter*, p. 48, 1972
- A fella did that in a movie where these six scudders wearing black suits go and rob a jewelry store and they all get killed. — Elmore Leonard, *Riding the Rap*, pp. 8–9, 1995

scuds *noun*
the female breasts *US, 2001*

A comparison with Scud missiles.

- — Don R. McCreary (Editor), *Dawg Speak*, 2001

scuff *verb*
in circus and carnival usage, to barely make a living *US, 1981*

- — Joe McKennon, *Circus Lingo*, p. 1980, 1981

scuffer *noun*
a prostitute *US, 1971*

- — Eugene Landy, *The Underground Dictionary*, p. 166, 1971

scuffle *verb*
to survive by your ingenuity, not by working *US, 1961*

- — Francis J. Rigney and L. Douglas Smith, *The Real Bohemia*, p. xvi, 1961

scuffler *noun*
a person who scrounges to earn a living on the fringes of legality *US, 1965*

- He said he was a hustler, but he really wasn't nothin' but a goddamn scuffler. — Henry Williamson, *Hustler!*, p. 137, 1965

scuff up *verb*
to engage in a fist fight *US, 1992*

- — William K. Bentley and James M. Corbett, *Prison Slang*, p. 91, 1992

scugly *adjective*
very ugly *US, 1975*

- — Carl J. Banks Jr., *Banks Dictionary of the Black Ghetto Language*, 1975

scum *noun*
1 semen *US, 1965*

- Horse, who was always talking about facts, said, "Man, that can't be scum, 'cause scum is white." "Knowing that scum was white, most of the guys said that Horse was right and that it was just dog water." — Claude Brown, *Manchild in the Promised Land*, pp. 80–81, 1965
- [A]ll the other girls are having all the fun while she has to scrub the pots, and the floors, and an occasional honied dick, or scum-smeared pussy. — *Adult Video*, p. 73, August/September 1986
- I had to make sure my mother found no stiffened, wrinkled traces of ecstasy's scum. — Larry Rivers, *What Did I Do?*, p. 51, 1992
- "No, she's too untalented for me to waste my scum over," said Fred. — Josh Friedman, *When Sex Was Dirty*, p. 106, 2005

2 a despicable, unlikeable person *US, 1971*

- "We'll see about this!" my attorney shouted as we drove away. "You paranoid scum!" — Hunter S. Thompson, *Fear and Loathing in Las Vegas*, p. 45, 1971
- You are scum. I'll be there. — *Sex, Lies and Videotape*, 1989

scumbag *noun*
1 a low, despicable person *US, 1957*
The highest profile use of the term in recent years was in late April 1998, when US Congressman Dan Burton publicly called then-President Clinton "a scumbag." This was shortly before the revelation that Burton was the father of a child born out of wedlock, a revelation that silenced his public judgments on President Clinton's morality. In May 2004, the word got another 15 minutes of fame when it was used in the family-friendly *Blondie* comic strip, provoking serious outrage among some readers.

- The rotten scumbag. — Hubert Selby Jr., *Last Exit to Brooklyn*, p. 123, 1957
- Let's get the fuck out of this town. Those scumbags were trying to kill us. — Hunter S. Thompson, *Fear and Loathing in Las Vegas*, p. 34, 1971
- When he flashed on that, on the downright outrageousness of that pack of scumbags paying somebody to snuff him, of even insinuating they'd do such a thing, Emmett began to shake with rage. — Emmett Grogan, *Ringolevio*, p. 349, 1972
- Hey, don't look at me like I'm some sort of scumbag or something. — Bret Easton Ellis, *Less Than Zero*, p. 189, 1985

2 a condom *US, 1960*

- According to him and the rest of the boys, the name of the thing was "scum bag." — Phyllis and Eberhard Kronhausen, *Sex Histories of American College Men*, p. 56, 1960
- "Do you really use scumbags?" "Yes. I use rubber Trojans every time I fuck." — *Screw*, p. 9, 12th April 1971
- I have found that some folks actually call 'em weird stuff like "rubbers" and "condoms" and even "prophylactics" when in actuality they're just talkin' about everyday garden variety scumbags. — Richard Meltzer, *A Whore Just Like the Rest*, p. 265, 1976

- Kellie returned from a vacation to find her apartment ransacked, desecrated with scumbags, all her belongings stolen. — Josh Friedman, *When Sex Was Dirty*, p. 93, 2005

3 a prostitute *US, 1973*

- — Ruth Todasco et al., *The Intelligent Woman's Guide to Dirty Words*, p. 7, 1973

scumball *noun*

a despicable person *US, 1991*

- And I thought we were scumballs. — Carl Hiaasen, *Native Tongue*, p. 353, 1991

scumbucket *noun*

a despised person *US, 1983*

- — Connie Eble (Editor), *UNC-CH Campus Slang*, p. 4, November 1983
- The deceased was a well-known scumbucket and they don't usually have the decency to kill themselves. — Carl Hiaasen, *Native Tongue*, p. 222, 1991

scumhead *noun*

a contemptible person *US, 1995*

- I know you've been listening to some scumhead[.] — Howard Stern, *Miss America*, p. 276, 1995

scummer *noun*

a despicable lowlife whose services are for hire *US, 1985*
Perhaps from the C14 sense of the word as "a pirate."

- A family deal, it was best to get outside help, scummers with no personal interest, muscle you hired by the pound. — Elmore Leonard, *Glitz*, p. 238, 1985

scummy *adjective*

unpleasant; despicable *US, 1932*
Figurative use of conventional sense (polluted).

- The old houses was empty and the outside looked real scummy and unkempt[.] — Bret Easton Ellis, *Less Than Zero*, 1985

scumpteen *noun*

a vague, large number *US, 1946*

- One night Jack "Legs" Diamond fell into the joint with scumpteen of his henchmen and ordered the doors closed, and Jim, it was on. — Mezz Mezzrow, *Really the Blues*, p. 178, 1946

scumsucker *noun*

a low, despicable person *US, 1971*

- What's going on in this country when a scumsucker like that can get away with sandbagging a doctor of journalism? — Hunter S. Thompson, *Fear and Loathing in Las Vegas*, p. 19, 1971
- Radio talk shows blistered lawmakers for holding secret budget meetings and for the income tax proposal, calling them "scumsuckeers," and other derisive terms. — *The Commercial Appeal* (Memphis, Tennessee), p. A1, 14th June 2000

scum-sucking *adjective*

despicable *US, 1982*

- Dornan vehemently denied his amendment was intended to promote discrimination, characterizing anyone who would attempt to teach racial discrimination to children as a "scum-sucking pig." — *United Press International*, 30th November 1982
- But how many times have you seen an interview of a policeman that tried to save the life of a scum-suckin' piece of slime like Earl Rimms? — Joseph Wambaugh, *The Delta Star*, p. 132, 1983
- You put yourself on the line, and you get treated like a scum-sucking pig. — *Pittsburgh Post-Gazette*, p. A8, 17th October 1993
- Conservatives must be willing to accept the fact that the English language does not require the word "liberal" to be preceded by "scum-sucking," "wooly headed" or "pathetic." — *Chattanooga Times Free Press*, p. F2, 16th November 2003

scunds *noun*

a second helping *US, 1966*

- — John D. Bell et al., *Loosely Speaking*, p. 16, 1966

scungeel *noun*

a low-life, a disreputable person *US, 1977*
From the Italian *scungili*, (squid).

- That's not the only funny fish that comes up in the net. You got two scungeel in there, too. — Edwin Torres, *Q & A*, p. 20, 1977

scup *verb*

to swing *US, 1951*
Rarely heard.

- No, I don't want no more of them Acme bushings. The shims bust off as soon as you scup 'em... — Max Shulman, *The Many Loves of Dobie Gillis*, p. 183, 1951

scurb *noun*

a suburban skateboarder who confines his skateboarding to streets and sidewalks *US, 1984*

- — *San Francisco Sunday Examiner & Chronicle*, p. 20, 2nd September 1984: "Say it right"

scurve *noun*

a graceless person; someone who is disliked *US, 1951*

- In Detroit, someone who once would be called a drip or a square is now, regrettably, a nerd, or in a less severe case, a scurve. — *Newsweek*, p. 28, 8th October 1951
- [S]ome jealous scurve (drip, again) is bound to come up with "Well, Jazz-a-boo for you." — *Herald Press* (St. Joseph, Missouri), p. 14, 23rd June 1952

scurvy *adjective*

1 unkempt; sloppy; ugly *US, 1965*

- — Miss Cone, *The Slang Dictionary (Hawthorne High School)*, 1965

2 very thin *US, 2001*

- — Don R. McCreary (Editor), *Dawg Speak*, 2001

scut duty; scut work *noun*

tedious, menial work *US, 1960*

- Scut jobs were the dirty, sometimes degrading, jobs that no one wanted, so they fell to the low men on the "totem pole" or were used as disciplinary assignments. — Gregory Clark, *Words of the Vietnam War*, p. 455, 1990
- I drank lots back then, got myself into stupid fights and spent way too many hours on scut duty, or else in the brig. — Elizabeth Mayne, *Man of the Mist*, p. 182, 1996

scuttlebutt *noun*

gossip, rumors *US, 1901*
From the name of the drinking-water cask found on board a ship, around which sailors gathered to gossip.

- Scuttlebutt down in the catacombs is that a lot of powerful Catholics, including those responsible for the Society of the Felicitator, are unhappy about those reforms. — Tom Robbins, *Another Roadside Attraction*, p. 180, 1971

scuz *noun*

a dirty, disreputable person *US, 1973*

- These guys, at least a few of them, two black guys, and one white, bearded scuz in a dirty buckskin vest and yellow headband, looked radical enough to get violent with an overweight middle-aged cop like myself[.] — Joseph Wambaugh, *The Blue Knight*, p. 64, 1973
- "This state law says to the drug dealers ... the scuz of the world, the free ride is over," D'Amato said. — *Post Standard* (Syracuse, New York), p. B3, 9th August 1984
- Indeed, he tries to lean on her as he did on his wife, meanwhile clumsily trying to dissuade her from tying the knot with her scuz of a boyfriend. — *Post and Courier* (Charleston, South Carolina), p. 9E, 5th January 2003

scuzbag; scuzzbag *noun*

a despicable, undesirable person *US, 1973*
A variation on **SCUMBAG**.

- Hit the streets, scuz bag! — John Waters, *Desperate Living*, p. 167, 1977
- "I'm your partner, scuzzbag!" Dolly yelled at Dilford. — Joseph Wambaugh, *The Delta Star*, p. 169, 1983
- If you slimeball scuzbags of piss-complected puke want to shit today, you better do some screaming. — Larry Brown, *Dirty Work*, p. 182, 1989
- Brad Rowe, playing a conservative scuzzbag in the Nixon White House, gets a phone call. — *Washington Post*, p. C7, 29th April 2000

scuz rag *noun*

during the Vietnam war, a rag used to wipe floors *US, 1987*

- Scuz rag—A cloth that is used for cleaning. — Stephen Tomajczyk, *To Be a U.S. Marine*, p. 154, 2004

scuzzball *noun*

a despicable person *US, 1986*

- "Musta scared the shit outa ya, that scuzzball." — Joseph Wambaugh, *The Delta Star*, p. 271, 1983
- "He wrote about this case," Garcia went on. "About that little scuzzball we arrested." — Carl Hiaasen, *Tourist Season*, p. 19, 1986

scuzzy *adjective*

disgusting *US, 1968*

- It's a real scuzzy joint. A beer joint that serves food be involved in real ptomaine tavern. — Joseph Wambaugh, *The New Centurions*, p. 46, 1970
- "I don't know if I'd call it dirty—Skuzzy might be more accurate terminology." — Michael Hodgson, *With Sgt. Mike in Vietnam*, p. 97, 1970
- Anyway, The Toilet is just plain flat-out scuzzy. I totaled a perfectly good pair of Bergdorf Goodman shoes[.] — Armistead Maupin, *Tales of the City*, p. 296, 1978
- Scuzzy head of hair, blue, and a lot of tattoos. — Michelle Tea, *Valencia*, p. 148, 2000

seaboard *adjective*
used of an order for takeout food at a restaurant *US, 1952*
- — *American Speech*, p. 232, October 1952: "The argot of soda jerks"

sea daddy *noun*
in the US Navy, a mentor *UK, 1899*
- If ever I had a sea daddy, it was Ev Barrett. — Richard Marcinko and John Weisman, *Rogue Warrior*, p. 51, 1992

seafood *noun*
a sailor as an object of homosexual desire *US, 1963*
- — Donald Webster Cory and John P. LeRoy, *The Homosexual and His Society*, p. 266, 1963: "A lexicon of homosexual slang"
- — Florida Legislative Investigation Committee (Johns Committee), *Homosexuality and Citizenship in Florida*, 1964: "Glossary of homosexual terms and deviate acts"
- You have plenty of clients because of the great number of military men, especially the sailors, which we commonly call "seafood." — "*The Market Street Proposition*" (KFRC radio, San Francisco), 8th November 1965

sea-going bellhop *noun*
a member of the US Marine Corps *US, 1927*
Derisive, used by other branches of the armed services to mock the USMC dress uniform.
- I hadn't even finished my second bottle of beer when I began to hear progressively louder comments about "goddamned dumb jarheads" and "sea-going bellhops." — Bruce H. Norton, *Sergeant Major U.S. Marines*, 1995
- "Oh, hell, they'll find someone else to play seagoing bellhop." — James Brady, *The Marine*, p. 58, 2003

seagull *noun*
1 a semiprofessional prostitute specializing in customers who are sailors in the US Navy *US, 1971*
- There are also lots of "sea gulls" [semi-amateurs, who follow the fleet from port to port] in the bars. — Charles Winick, *The Lively Commerce*, p. 173, 1971
2 a military aviator assigned to a nonflying job *US, 1967*
- "They're called seagulls. You know why? Because they can only eat, squawk, shit, and stand on one leg at the bar. You have to throw rocks at 'em to get 'em to fly." — Elaine Shepard, *The Doom Pussy*, p. 57, 1967
3 a person who watches what bets are being made by big spenders and then makes a small bet on the horses favored by the big spenders *US, 1966*
- — *San Francisco Examiner*, p. 52, 13th September 1966
4 a combat pilot who has become reluctant to fly *US, 1990*
- The others called them "seagulls"—you have to throw a rock to get them to fly—and "sickbay flight." The Navy let them turn in their wings, or would take them. — Robert K. Wilcox, *Scream of Eagles*, p. 39, 1990
5 chicken *US, 1945*
- — Lou Shelly, *Hepcats Jive Talk Dictionary*, p. 48, 1945

sea lawyer *noun*
a sailor with knowledge of the rules and regulations of the sea and a strong propensity for arguing *UK, 1829*
- "My kid," Hambro said, "fillibustering against going to bed. A real sea lawyer, that kid." — Ralph Ellison, *Invisible Man*, p. 486, 1952
- [A] sea lawyer is one who professes to know the answers to all questions. — Horace Beck, *Folklore and the Sea*, p. 74, 1973

seam *noun*
a ten-dollar package of a powdered drug in tin foil *US, 1993*
- He rolled each seam into a joint and we got high as we walked. — Sanyika Shakur, *Monster*, p. 247, 1993

seam shooter *noun*
a criminal who specializes in blowing up safes by placing small amounts of explosives in the safe's seams *US, 1949*
- — Vincent J. Monteleone, *Criminal Slang*, p. 202, 1949

seam squirrels *noun*
in circus and carnival usage, body lice *US, 1981*
- — Don Wilmeth, *The Language of American Popular Entertainment*, p. 217, 1981

sea pig *noun*
a fat surfer *US, 1988*
- — Surf Punks, *Oh No! Not Them Again! (liner notes)*, 1988

sea rat *noun*
a seagull *US, 1991*
- — Trevor Cralle, *The Surfin'ary*, p. 107, 1991

search *verb*
to try to buy illegal drugs *US, 1997*
- Spears said he often can't get out of his car without being approached by young men asking "Are you searching?"—street slang for buying drugs. — *Milwaukee Journal Sentinel*, p. 4, 8th January 1997

search and avoid; search and evade *verb*
used by US forces to describe the activities of the South Vietnamese Army *US, 1972*
- You see the mood is changing over there and a search and destroy mission is a search and avoid mission. — Senate Committee on Foreign Relations, *Legislative Proposals Relating to the War in Southeast Asia*, p. 208, 1971
- "Search and evade" has not gone unnoticed by the enemy. — House Committee on Internal Security, *Investigation of Attempts to Subvert the United States Armed Services*, p. 7133, 1972
- Newsweek reported that soldiers commonly thwarted the "green machine" simply by failing to carry out orders, by engaging in "search and evade" tactics. — James Clotfelter, *The Military in American Politics*, p. 44, 1973

search me
I don't know *US, 1947*
- — Marcus Hanna Boulware, *Jive and Slang of Students in Negro Colleges*, 1947

sea story *noun*
a tale about the teller's exploits, real and imagined *US, 1961*
- In the Pacific, telling "sea stories" helped to pass the time and relieve old pressures. I listened to thousands of them. I told them. — Russell Davis, *Marine at War*, p. 165, 1961

seat *noun*
a police officer assigned to ride as a passenger with another officer *US, 1970*
- — *New York Times*, 15th February 1970

seatman *noun*
in circus and carnival usage, a paid customer, employed to show enthusiasm *US, 1981*
- — Don Wilmeth, *The Language of American Popular Entertainment*, p. 234, 1981

seat meat *noun*
the buttocks *US, 2005*
- A-N bares her legendary mams in bed, then lights up the screen with her magnificent seat-meat as she rises to join Jack Nicholson in the shower. — Mr. Skin, *Mr. Skin's Skincyclopedia*, p. 21, 2005

seat-surf *verb*
to move from empty seat to empty seat in a stadium or auditorium, gradually improving your position *US, 1994*
- — David Shenk and Steve Silberman, *Skeleton Key*, p. 255, 1994

sec *noun*
a second *UK, 1909*
- Slipping a hundred G's out of the cash cage takes only a sec—but it's robbery. — Philip Wylie, *Opus 21*, p. 242, 1949
- Wait a sec. — Mickey Spillane, *Kiss Me Deadly*, p. 70, 1952
- Now, shut up a sec, Prudy Sue, and hear me out. — Armistead Maupin, *Further Tales of the City*, p. 35, 1982
- Could you hold this a sec? — *This is Spinal Tap*, 1984

seccy *noun*
a capsule of secobarbital sodium (trade name Seconal™), a central nervous system depressant *US, 1969*
- — Norman W. Houser, *Drugs*, p. 13, 1969
- She turned on once in a while; preferred doriden nembutal, seccies, any of the barbiturates and most of all, heroin. — Herbert Huncke, *The Evening Sun Turned Crimson*, p. 189, 1980
- Barbiturates are also known as BARBS, BLUES, REDS, and SEKKIES. — Macfarlane, Macfarlane and Robson, *The User*, p. 97, 1996

seco *noun*
Seconal™, a barbiturate *US, 1972*

- When he got to the car window I bought all the pills he had on him, red devils and secos and a few dexis. — Donald Goines, *Whoreson*, p. 211, 1972

second balloon *noun*
a second lieutenant *US, 1956*
- — *American Speech*, p. 227, October 1956: "More United States Air Force slang"

second banana *noun*
a person in a supporting role *US, 1953*
Originally applied to a supporting comedian.
- Not long ago, Art Carney was the most popular second banana on television as the sewer man on the Gleason Show. — *Life*, p. 53, 9th May 1960
- For years one of the most formidable second bananas in the comedy spectrum, Louis Nye comes into his own and attains premium solo status in his current nitery act. — *Variety*, p. 10, 23rd May 1962
- The actor was not the leading-man type, a second banana, maybe. The guy that doesn't get the girl, hard as he tries. — Joseph Wambaugh, *Finnegan's Week*, p. 144, 1993
- Elsa never quite gained top billing to carry an X-rated flick by herself, but figures nicely as a second banana. — Josh Friedman, *When Sex Was Dirty*, p. 96, 2005

second base *noun*
1 in a teenage categorization of sexual activity, a level of foreplay, most usually referring to touching a girl's breasts *US, 1977*
The exact degree varies by region or even school.
- He's too busy going for it with your step-mom! Whoa! Second base! — *Bill and Ted's Excellent Adventure*, 1989

2 in casino games of blackjack, the seat or player in the center of the table directly across from the dealer *US, 1980*
- — Lee Solkey, *Dummy Up and Deal*, p. 119, 1980

3 in a deck of playing cards, the card second from the bottom of the deck *US, 1988*
- — George Percy, *The Language of Poker*, p. 79, 1988

second John *noun*
a second lieutenant *US, 1956*
- — *American Speech*, p. 227, October 1956: "More United States Air Force slang"

second nuts *noun*
in poker, a good hand that is bested by a better hand *US, 1976*
- — Thomas L. Clark, *The Dictionary of Gambling and Gaming*, p. 192, 1987

seconds *noun*
1 sex with someone who has just had sex with someone else *US, 1966*
Often preceded by the adjective "sloppy."
- That would be kind of you, yes. Unless of course you plan to fall by and watch, take seconds. — Richard Farina, *Been Down So Long*, p. 153, 1966

2 playing cards that have been altered for cheating *US, 1950*
- The first offense ever prosecuted in the fledgling community at the junction of the Chicago River and Lake Michigan was running a swindling cardstore, using "seconds." — Jack Lait and Lee Mortimer, *Chicago Confidential*, p. 124, 1950

second second *noun*
in the television and movie industries, an additional second assistant director *US, 1990*
- — Ralph S. Singleton, *Filmmaker's Dictionary*, p. 149, 1990

second-story man *noun*
1 a burglar *US, 1886*
- Viciki living with second-story man in Queens — Jack Kerouac, *Letter to Neal Cassady*, p. 175, 8th December 1948
- He had been released from Riker's Island almost two months before, and had picked up a few dollars steering second-story men to a friend of his from Chicago days. a fence. — John Clellon Holmes, *Go*, p. 198, 1952
- Shorty talked to me out of the corner of his mouth: which hustlers—standing around, or playing at this or that table—sold "reefers," or had just come out of prison, or were "second-story men." — Malcolm X and Alex Haley, *The Autobiography of Malcolm X*, p. 45, 1964
- I had Sal Fusco, a great second-story guy. — *Casino*, 1995

2 a skilled card cheat who deals the second card in a deck *US, 1988*
- — George Percy, *The Language of Poker*, p. 79, 1988

second story trade *noun*
the craft of burglary *US, 1952*
- "You want to learn the second-story trade, Jake?" — Harry Grey, *The Hoods*, p. 189, 1952

see *noun*
a visual inspection *US, 1973*
- Some patrolmen started cooping as soon as the sergeant on patrol made his first "see"—police slang for a visual inspection to make sure all officers in the precinct were properly on duty. — Peter Maas, *Serpico*, p. 63, 1973

seed *noun*
1 a child *US, 1998*
- — Ethan Hilderbrant, *Prison Slang*, p. 111, 1998

2 a person who is hopelessly out of touch with current fashions and trends *US, 1968*
A shortened form of **HAYSEED**.
- — Hy Lit, *Hy Lit's Unbelievable Dictionary of Hip Words for Groovy People*, p. 34, 1968

3 in a deck of playing cards, an ace *US, 1988*
- — George Percy, *The Language of Poker*, p. 80, 1988

4 in private poker games, a one-dollar betting chip *US, 1971*
- — Thomas L. Clark, *The Dictionary of Gambling and Gaming*, p. 192, 1987

5 a dollar *US, 1961*
- It's in hock for fifty seeds. — Ross Russell, *The Sound*, p. 146, 1961

seeds and stems *noun*
the detritus of marijuana, unsmokeable but a reminder of what was *US, 1971*
- — Commander Cody and the Lost Planet Airmen, *Down to Seeds and Stems Again Blues*, 1971
- There wasn't any grass in the apartment anyway. Down to seeds and stems. — Elmore Leonard, *City Primeval*, p. 54, 1980

seek *verb*
▶ **seek the sheets**
to crawl into bed *US, 1967*
- — *McCall's*, April 1967

see seven stars *noun*
strong, illegally manufactured whiskey *US, 1999*
- It is called corn liquor, white lightning, sugar whiskey, skully cracker, popskull, bush whiskey, stump, stumphole, "splo, ruckus juice, radiator whiskey, rotgut, sugarhead, block and tackle, wildcat, panther's breath, tiger's sweat, Sweet spirits of cats a-fighting, alley bourbon, city gin, cool water, happy Sally, deep shaft, jump steady, old horsey, stingo, blue John, red eye, pine top, buckeye bark whiskey and see seven stars." — *Star Tribune (Minneapolis)*, p. 19F, 31st January 1999

see the Chaplain!
used for silencing a soldier who complains excessively *US, 1941*
- — Carl Fleischhauer, *A Glossary of Army Slang*, p. 12, 1968

see you around campus
goodbye *US, 1972*
- See you around the campus, as they say. Is that what they say? — Dan Jenkins, *Semi-Tough*, p. 127, 1972

seg; seggie *noun*
in prison, segregation; a segregation unit *US, 1967*
- If it were up to me, I'd throw him in seg and bury the key. — Malcolm Braly, *On the Yard*, p. 200, 1967

seggy *noun*
a capsule of secobarbital sodium (trade name Seconal™), a central nervous system depressant *US, 1967*
- — John B. Williams, *Narcotics and Hallucinogenics*, p. 116, 1967

self-propelled sandbag *noun*
a US Marine *US, 1991*
US Army Gulf war usage.
- — *American Speech*, p. 400, Winter 1991: "Among the new words"

self-solver *noun*
a crime in which the criminal's actions resolve the investigation into the crime *US, 2006*
- "Why would they put themselves through something like that for a self-solver? Shoulda just let the guy jump in the tub with her and bleed out the way he wanted to." — Joseph Wambaugh, *Hollywood Station*, p. 19, 2006

sell *noun*
in professional wrestling, acting as if a blow or hold was devastatingly painful *US, 1995*
- My Knockout cohorts well knew this was more than one of Heidi's good sells. — Heidi Mattson, *Ivy League Stripper*, p. 159, 1995

sell *verb*
in professional wrestling, to feign pain, to act as if a blow or hold was devastatingly painful *US, 1995*
- Of course, I would "sell" the drop, so that it appeared I had been thoroughly manhandled and abused by my opponent. — Heidi Mattson, *Ivy League Stripper*, p. 159, 1995
- I have my head on the ground, feigning pain and I'm laughing like hell. Skaaland thought he was going to get fired. I crawled out of the ring, selling big time. — Jeff Archer, *Theater in a Squared Circle*, p. 338, 1999
- I sell, you know, roll around and groan for a couple of seconds, then stand up and start rubbing my butt, but I'm fine. — Missy Hyatt, *Missy Hyatt*, p. 135, 2001

▸ **sell a hog**
to scare someone by bluffing *US, 1990*
- — Charles Shafer, *Folk Speech in Texas Prisons*, p. 213, 1990

▸ **sell Buicks**
to vomit *US, 1978*
- — Connie Eble (Editor), *UNC-CH Campus Slang*, p. 4, April 1978
- I charge for the toilet and sell a Buick all over the corner of my cell. — Suroosh Alvi et al., *The Vice Guide*, p. 174, 2002

▸ **sell tickets**
to engage in ritualistic, competitive insulting *US, 1975*
- You selling me a ticket, faggot? — Miguel Pinero, *Short Eyes*, p. 98, 1975
- — Don R. McCreary (Editor), *Dawg Speak*, 2001

sell-out *noun*
in pool, a missed shot that leaves your opponent with a good shot *US, 1978*
- — Mike Shamos, *The Illustrated Encyclopedia of Billiards*, p. 204, 1993

sell out *verb*
to betray a cause of conviction, especially for financial reward *US, 1888*
Around long before the 1960s, but promoted and glorified in the idealistic haze of the 60s.
- But the gist of it is clear enough. Kesey has sold out to keep from getting a five-year sentence or worse. — Tom Wolfe, *The Electric Kool-Aid Acid Test*, p. 336, 1968
- The gist of the talk from the people was that we had sold them out. — Jamie Mandelkau quoting Ken Kesey, *Buttons*, p. 147, 1969
- It's not selling out. How is it selling out? — Fred Baker, *Events*, p. 19, 1970
- There's two major record companies wants to sign us. Heeavy bread. We don't have to sell out, man. Just tone down the sex trip. — Tom Robbins, *Another Roadside Attraction*, p. 98, 1971

semi-retired *adjective*
unable to find work *US, 1995*
- — *Adult Video News*, p. 51, October 1995

semper fi
used as a shortened version of the US Marine Corps creed—*semper fidelis* (always faithful) *US, 1951*
Used as a greeting, an affirmation, and in practically any situation to mean practically anything.
- In the Marines, when you said Semper FI, it meant The hell with you, Jack. — Edward Newhouse, *Many are Called*, p. 380, 1951
- "Semper fi, Mac." He felt wonderful. — Keith Nolan, *The Magnificent Bastards*, p. 66, 1954
- Fun and games, amor fait. Semper Fi. "Peace," he said to Hicks. — Robert Stone, *Dog Soldiers*, p. 337, 1974
- Each time one of my men complained, a man from Weapons or a rifle company cried out "Semper Fidelis!" or sometimes the abbreviated version "Semper Fi!" — William B. Hopkins, *One Bugle No Drum*, p. 79, 1986

semper Gumby *adjective*
flexible *US, 1991*
- Gulf War usage; a play on the US Marine Corps motto and an allusion to a rubber television character. — *Army*, p. 48, November 1991
- — *American Speech*, p. 400, Winter 1991: "Among the new words"

senator *noun*
in a game of poker, a dealer who does not play *US, 1988*
- — George Percy, *The Language of Poker*, p. 80, 1988

send *noun*
▸ **put on the send**
in a confidence swindle, to send the victim off to retrieve the money that will pass to the swindlers *US, 1972*
- Then he put old Hare "on the send" for the cash, as confidence men call it, which doesn't need any lengthy explanation. — Guy Owen, *The Flim-Flam Man and the Apprentice Grifter*, p. 177, 1972

send *verb*
1 to excite someone; to please someone *US, 1935*
- Albert really sent that audience singing Some Sweet Day. — Mezz Mezzrow, *Really the Blues*, p. 26, 1946
- "Ross," the exec said, "is the only officer I know who could really do a job on this. Provided it really sends him." — William Brinkley, *Don't Go Near the Water*, p. 16, 1956
- "Oh, man," she moaned happily, "this beat does it. Man, it sends me." — Robert Gover, *This Maniac Responsible*, p. 84, 1963
2 to produce a drug intoxication *US, 1950*
- There are sufficiently strong to "send" the kids. — Jack Lait and Lee Mortimer, *Chicago Confidential*, p. 148, 1950

▸ **send a boy to do a man's work**
in poker, to make a small bet with a good hand in the hope of luring players with inferior hands to continue betting *US, 1951*
- — *American Speech*, p. 101, May 1951

▸ **send out a salesman**
in gin, to discard in a manner that is designed to lure a desired card from an opponent *US, 1965*
- — Irwin Steig, *Play Gin to Win*, p. 138

▸ **send to Long Beach**
to flush a toilet *US, 1968*
Long Beach is a community to the south of Los Angeles.
- Giving her a proper burial, I flushed the commode. As the saying goes, I sent her to Long Beach. — Eldridge Cleaver, *Soul on Ice*, p. 8, 1968
- — *Current Slang*, p. 41, Fall 1968

sender *noun*
something or someone that arouses or excites *US, 1935*
Originally (mid 1930s) a jazz term referring to a musician who excites and inspires a jazz band; in the early 1940s extended to general usage. Often emphasized as **SOLID SENDER**.
- [F]inally, he's a solid sender, he can send your spirit soaring and make you real happy[.] — Mezz Mezzrow, *Really the Blues*, p. 227, 1946
- It's a funny thing how life can be such a drag one minute and a solid sender the next. — Louis Armstrong, *Satchmo*, p. 126, 1954

send up *verb*
to sentence someone to prison *US, 1852*
- This was the master card from the files of the police in the town from which I had been sent up. — Horace McCoy, *Kiss Tomorrow Good-bye*, p. 175, 1948
- He was sent up for his first real bit when he was 16. — Hubert Selby Jr., *Last Exit to Brooklyn*, p. 42, 1957
- You're going to be arrested before you leave this building! I'm going to send you up for this! — Willard Motley, *Let No Man Write My Epitaph*, p. 95, 1958
- I was sent up to Dannemora, a much nicer place than Greenhaven. — Herbert Huncke, *Guilty of Everything*, p. 117, 1990

senior *noun*
an established member of a youth gang *US, 1949*
- A count is difficult because the larger gangs have "seniors," "juniors," and young auxiliaries known by such names as "Tiny Tims." — William Bernard, *Jailbait*, p. 80, 1949

senior moment *noun*
a short interval in which an older person succumbs to a mental or physical lack of energy or consistency *US, 1996*
- When something temporarily goes awry in her recall cells, she waves it away: "Oh, pardon me, I'm having a senior moment." — *Omaha (Nebraska) World Herald*, p. 17, 22nd November 1996
- — Walter A. Atkinson, *Forgive Us Our Senior Moments.*, 2002

sense; sens *noun*

marijuana *US, 1984*

An abbreviation of **SENSIMILLIA**.

- Loose joints. Genuine Hawaiian sens. — Jay McInerney, *Bright Lights, Big City*, p. 108, 1984
- Cause it seems a lot of times, I'm at my best / After some methical or a bowl of sense. — Tone Loc, *Cheeba Cheeba*, 1989

serenity, tranquility and peace *noun*

STP, a synthetic hallucinogen that appeared on the drug scene in 1967 *US, 1972*

Because of its claimed psychedelic powers, the drug was named STP after the engine oil additive (scientifically treated petroleum), with this trinity of virtues produced through back formation.

- — Carl Chambers and Richard Heckman, *Employee Drug Abuse*, p. 209, 1972

sergeant from K company *noun*

in a deck of playing cards, a king *US, 1988*

- — George Percy, *The Language of Poker*, p. 80, 1988

serious as a heart attack *adjective*

very serious *US, 1970*

- I looked in those eyes I had come to know so well, and I could see she was serious as a heart attack. — Jimmy Buffet, *A Salty Piece of Land*, p. 418, 2004

serve *verb*

1 to sell drugs to someone *US, 1990*

- "Yeah, loc, are you serving, cuz?" Glass asked in street slang. — *Los Angeles Times Magazine*, p. 12, 16th September 1990
- I dint serve no one, Big Chief! It's for mah mother's birthday, I swear. — Richard Price, *Clockers*, p. 14, 1992
- "Can you serve me forty dollars, Lil' Pup?" she asked Kevin. — Bob Sipchen, *Baby Insane and the Buddha*, p. 207, 1993

2 to humiliate someone; to hit someone *US, 1989*

- — Ellen C. Bellone (Editor), *Dictionary of Slang*, p. 21, 1989

3 in card games, to deal *US, 1988*

- — George Percy, *The Language of Poker*, p. 80, 1988

server *noun*

a person who hands crack cocaine to a buyer as part of a multilayered selling operation *US, 1994*

- — US Department of Justice, *Street Terms*, October 1994

service stripes *noun*

bruises, punctures, and sores visible on the skin of an intravenous drug user *US, 1973*

- — David Maurer and Victor Vogel, *Narcotics and Narcotic Addiction*, p. 440, 1973

sesh *noun*

a session *US, 1982*

- I mean we like had this way cranking bud sesh and like listened to AC/DC and watched Mommie Dearest with the sound off. — Mary Corey and Victoria Westermark, *Fer Shurr! How to be a Valley Girl*, 1982

sess; sces; sezz *noun*

potent marijuana *US, 1982*

Variations on **SENSIMILLIA**.

- — Richard A. Spears, *The Slang and Jargon of Drugs and Drink*, p. 443, 1986
- Sess. Smoke. Hash, shrooms. — *Kids*, 1995

session *noun*

1 a social dance *US, 1949*

- Session means dance. — William Bernard, *Jailbait*, p. 81, 1949

2 a series of waves *US, 1963*

- — Grant W. Kuhns, *On Surfing*, p. 121, 1963

set *noun*

1 a neighborhood; a specific place in a neighborhood where friends congregate *US, 1965*

- This was the way people in our set did things. — Claude Brown, *Manchild in the Promised Land*, p. 176, 1965
- Ya baby, I'm going up on the set. — Donald Goines, *Whoreson*, p. 95, 1972
- Everybody from Washington Square to Tompkins Square called the streets "the set"—as in "I've been looking for you all over the set, man." — Ed Sanders, *Tales of Beatnik Glory*, p. 192, 1975
- That nigga roll upon the set one more time I swear I'm gonna fuck him up. — *Boyz N The Hood*, 1990

2 a neighborhood faction of a gang *US, 1970*

- "If you're doing something for the community in the revolutionary struggle," Huey told them, "we'll join your set." — Bobby Seale, *Seize the Time*, p. 113, 1970
- Shane knew you didn't usually get a street name unless you'd been "jumped in the set[.]" — Stephen J. Cannell, *The Tin Collectors*, p. 147, 2001
- Claudia had retired from her Crip set after being blinded in a shotgun attack[.] — *Rolling Stone*, p. 77, 12th April 2001

3 a party, especially a party with music *US, 1966*

- — *Current Slang*, p. 5, Fall 1966
- The set is on the fifth floor and the floor is creaking an' groaning under the weight of all the coolies that are swinging. — Piri Thomas, *Down These Mean Streets*, p. 59, 1967

4 in prison usage, a continuance of a parole hearing *US, 1981*

- — *Maledicta*, p. 267, Summer/Winter 1981: "By its slang, ye shall know It: the pessimism of prison life"

set joint *noun*

a carnival game which is rigged to prevent players from winning *US, 1968*

- [T]he set joint is peculiar in that it is "set" after all bets are down. — E.E. Steck, *A Brief Examination of an Esoteric Folk*, p. 8, 1968

settler *noun*

in an illegal betting operation, the person who determines the final odds on an event after all bets are taken *US, 1964*

- — Thomas L. Clark, *The Dictionary of Gambling and Gaming*, p. 194, 1987

settlers *noun*

dice that have been weighted and are thrown with an altered cup with great effect by a skilled cheat *US, 1963*

- — John S. Salak, *Dictionary of Gambling*, p. 225, 1963

set trip *noun*

a conflict between factions of a youth gang *US, 1995*

- [W]e used to have a little problem with Nickerson Gardens, they're Bloods too, but there was a thing called "set trip," where gangs get into it with each other. — Yusuf Jah, *Uprising*, p. 76, 1995

set tripping *noun*

gang warfare between factions of a single gang *US, 2005*

- This inner-Crip war is expanding over South Central. It's called set tripping because if you're not from the "set" or an ally, you get tripped on—shot, stabbed, robbed, murdered. — Colton Simpson, *Inside the Crips*, p. 139, 2005

set-up *noun*

the equipment used to inject a drug *US, 1952*

- The needle had found a vein, and Paddy, with setup firm at his hip, drew his real red blood into the gleaming syringe, where it lost color in boiled heroin. — George Mandel, *Flee the Angry Strangers*, p. 230, 1952

set-up man *noun*

a criminal who identifies, plans, and organizes crimes *US, 1953*

- They are always looking for a "setup man," someone to plan jobs and tell them exactly what to do. — William Burroughs, *Junkie*, p. 20, 1953

seven and seven *noun*

a drink made by mixing equal parts of Seven-Up™ soda and Seagrams Seven Whiskey™ *US, 1976*

- Over seven-sevens and whiskey sours they remind each other in silence where they're going[.] — Charles Anderson, *The Grunts*, p. 20, 1976
- BARTENDER: What'll you have, Tony? TONY: Usual—seven and seven. — *Saturday Night Fever*, 1977
- Hey, kid! Get me a seven and seven. — *Goodfellas*, 1990
- I sat down opposite the Fireman at the fold-out kitchen table while Cat fawned over me, pouring a tall, strong 7&7. — Peter Fenton, *Eyeing the Flash*, p. 187, 2005

seven-eleven *noun*

a small amount of money given to a gambler who has lost all their money, either by a casino or his fellow gamblers *US, 1950*

- — Thomas L. Clark, *The Dictionary of Gambling and Gaming*, p. 194, 1987

seven-o *noun*

seventy; 70th Street *US, 1972*

- — David Claerbaut, *Black Jargon in White America*, p. 78, 1972

seven out *verb*

in craps, to roll a seven before making your point, thus losing *US, 1974*

- When Trish quickly sevens-out, the guy who would have been the next shooter mutters, "Cold as a witch's eyebrows," and turns away. — Edward Lin, *Big Julie of Vegas*, p. 19, 1974
- He sevened out without even throwing a number, much less a pass. — Mario Puzo, *Inside Las Vegas*, p. 261, 1977

seven-ply gasser *noun*
the very best thing *US, 1968*
- — Hy Lit, *Hy Lit's Unbelievable Dictionary of Hip Words for Groovy People*, p. 34, 1968

seventh wave *noun*
the difficulty that follows many others and proves to be climactic disaster *US, 1975*
From the belief that every seventh wave is larger than the six before or after.
- — John Gould, *Maine Lingo*, p. 249, 1975

seventy-eight; 78 *noun*
a prostitute's customer who is quickly satisfied *US, 1971*
From early vinyl records that were played on a turntable revolving 78 times per minute.
- A customer who worked quickly was called a "78" and one with a slower response was a "33." — Charles Winick, *The Lively Commerce*, p. 188, 1971

seven-up *noun*
crack cocaine *US, 1993*
A pun on "coke" as a soft drink and drug.
- — Peter Johnson, *Dictionary of Street Alcohol and Drug Terms*, p. 168, 1993

sewer *noun*
1 a vein, especially a prominent vein suitable for drug injection *US, 1994*
- — US Department of Justice, *Street Terms*, October 1994
2 in pool, a pocket that is receptive to shots dropping *US, 1990*
- — Steve Rushin, *Pool Cool*, p. 26, 1990
3 a person who cannot keep a secret *US, 1955*
- — *American Weekly*, p. 2, 14th August 1955

sewer trout *noun*
white fish of unknown origin *US, 1945*
- — Lou Shelly, *Hepcats Jive Talk Dictionary*, p. 48, 1945
- Bass there are, and pickerel, and muskelonge, not to mention such sewer trout as catfish, dog fish and pike. — Kenneth Wells, *Cruising the Georgian Bay*, p. 104, 1958
- — *Maledicta*, p. 267, Summer/Winter 1981: "By its slang, ye shall know it: the pessimism of prison life"
- — Gary K. Farlow, *Prison-ese*, p. 61, 2002

sex *verb*
to have sex with someone *US, 1966*
- "We ain't sexing and we ain't gonna sex." — Treasure E. Blue, *A Street Girl Named Desire*, p. 111, 2007

▸ **sex in**
to initiate a female member into a male youth gang by group sex *US, 1996*
- If you get sexed in, they consider you a Crip ho [whore], and the gang will give you love but no respect. — S. Beth Atkin, *Voices from the Street*, p. 8, 1996

sex appeal *noun*
false breasts *US, 1981*
- — Don Wilmeth, *The Language of American Popular Entertainment*, p. 236, 1981

sex bomb *noun*
a woman stacked with sex appeal *US, 1963*
- The 1950s also saw Brigitte Bardot of France head a list of European sex bombs who insisted upon taking it off[.] — Roger Blake, *The Porno Movies*, p. 63, 1970

sex changer *noun*
a computer cable with either two male or two female connectors *US, 1991*
- — Eric S. Raymond, *The New Hacker's Dictionary*, p. 175, 1991

sexile *verb*
to force your roommate from your shared housing while you have sex *US, 2000*
- I've been sexiled. — *Nerve*, p. 14, May–June 2000

sex kitten *noun*
an especially attractive young woman who exploits her appeal *UK, 1958*
- SOUTHERN-FRIED SEX KITTEN. Britney Spears is the most famous person I've ever interviewed. — Chuck Klosterman, *Cuck Klosterman IV*, p. 11, 2007

sexpot *noun*
a sexually exciting woman *US, 1957*
- There they were, the sex pots, grown pottier, the once muscular football stars, now into insurance premiums[.] — Odie Hawkins, *Black Casanova*, p. 128, 1984

sex tank *noun*
a holding cell reserved for homosexual prisoners *US, 1963*
- All lonesome tears and Humiliation, Miss Destiny ends up in the sex tank[.] — John Rechy, *City of Night*, p. 104, 1963

shabony *noun*
a thug *US, 1952*
- "Well, I was thinking of calling the New York office and having them send me a couple of shabonies, you know, the demotion squad from Mulberry Street, to blow the joint apart." — Harry Grey, *The Hoods*, p. 176, 1952

shack *noun*
1 a temporary live-in sexual partner *US, 1967*
- For those stationed in town the thing to do was to obtain a permanent "shack," which eliminated sitting in a bar every night. — Donald Duncan, *The New Legions*, p. 224, 1967
2 a house that exudes wealth and invites burglary *US, 1950*
- — Hyman E. Goldin et al., *Dictionary of American Underworld Lingo*, p. 189, 1950
3 a room, apartment or house *US, 1955*
- — *American Speech*, p. 304, December 1955: "Wayne University slang"
4 any room where a citizens' band radio set is housed *US, 1976*
- — Len Buckwalter, *CB Radio*, p. 66, 1976
5 a direct hit on the target by a bomb *US, 1991*
- A bulls-eye for an Air Force bomber is a "shack." — *Shreveport Journal*, p. 4B, 1st February 1991
6 a sexual episode *US, 1960*
- Tonight Dilworth, the one I had heard through the wall, had taken her to a motel for some shack and got her drunk[.] — Glendon Swarthout, *Where the Boys Are*, p. 179, 1960
- I heard about your shack with Matt last night. — Connie Eble (Editor), *UNC-CH Campus Slang*, p. 9, April 1995

shack *verb*
to live together as an unmarried couple *US, 1935*
Very often used in the variant "shack up."
- Who you been shacking with? — George Mandel, *Flee the Angry Strangers*, p. 40, 1952
- [W]e have two single couples, they are shacking together at the present time. — Thomas Wilson, *Wife Swapping*, p. 171, 1965
- I was 22 years of age and shacking with a chick named Julie, I gave her one "joint" which she stashed and later turned over to the cops—a joint that netted me one of the 5-to-life sentences. — *The Berkeley Tribe*, p. 5, 5th–12th September 1969
- Yeah, Alyssa, who've you been shacking up with? — *Chasing Amy*, 1997

shacking *noun*
a party or social gathering *US, 1972*
- — *American Speech*, p. 154, Spring–Summer 1972: "An approach to black slang"

shack job *noun*
a person with whom you are living and enjoying sex without the burdens or blessings of marriage; the arrangement *US, 1958*
- "Brief me on this shack job of yours." — John D. MacDonald, *The Deceivers*, p. 156, 1958
- "You got a shack job with you?" — Stephen Longstreet, *The Flesh Peddlers*, p. 63, 1962
- It was one of those times—when he had been gone for a couple of days, probably for a shack-job somewhere[.] — Joey V., *Portrait of Joey*, p. 33, 1969
- Poor as us, sometimes from mixed marriages and shack jobs. — Joseph Wambaugh, *The New Centurions*, p. 147, 1970

shack rat *noun*
a soldier who has with a woman *US, 1947*

- — *American Speech*, p. 5556, February 1947: "Pacific War language"
- — John T. Algeo, *American Speech*, p. 120, May 1960: "Korean bamboo English"

shack-up *noun*

1 an act of casual sex *US, 1967*

- "You'll see him look around a party and pick out the best-looking girl present, to claim he's just come back from a shack-up with her somewhere." — Elaine Shepard, *The Doom Pussy*, p. 146, 1967

2 a person with whom you are living and enjoying sex without the burdens or blessings of marriage *US, 1960*

- — *American Speech*, p. 120, May 1960: "Korean bamboo English"
- Big-name movie and television stars make the Strip scene every night, many scouting for new shack-ups. — Arthur Blessitt, *Turned On to Jesus*, p. 117, 1971

shack up *verb*

1 to take up residence, usually of a temporary nature *US, 1942*

- Besides, Lovis was handy to shack up with on the one night in ten when he felt like shacking up with somebody. — Bernard Wolfe, *The Late Risers*, p. 35, 1954
- I told him he could "shack up" with me for a couple of days so I took him home with me. — Babs Gonzales, *I Paid My Dues*, p. 52, 1967
- I'm better off shacking up at my mum's. She got plenty food, plenty love, plenty money. — Karline Smith, *Moss Side Massive*, p. 21, 1994

2 to provide living quarters for a lover *US, 1960*

- However, he might also shack her up or simply shack her. — *American Speech*, p. 120, May 1960: "Korean bamboo English"

shade *noun*

1 a black person *US, 1865*
Offensive.

- In no time at all Konky got on the ball / And had ten whorers—nine pinks and a shade. — Dennis Wepman et al., *The Life*, p. 103, 1976
- "I reckon this is down to the Brown Brothers, don't you, John." "Who?" "The Shades" I have noticed before that you have to be very current to keep up with young London coppers' slang. — John Milne, *Alive and Kicking*, p. 92, 1998

2 a legitimate business that acts as a cover for an illegal enterprise *US, 1978*

- Shade is a legal business front that keeps an illegal business out of the bright light of police scrutiny. — Burgess Laughlin, *Job Opportunities in the Black Market*, p. 13–2, 1978

3 detached superiority *US, 1994*

- — Kevin Dilallo, *The Unofficial Gay Manual*, p. 245, 1994

shade *verb*

1 to reduce something slightly and gradually *US, 1997*

- [H]e would always find a way to shade the odds in his favor. — Stephen J. Cannell, *King Con*, p. 35, 1997

2 to mark the backs of cards with a subtle shading of the existing color *US, 1979*

- — John Scarne, *Scarne's Guide to Modern Poker*, p. 290, 1979

shades *noun*

sunglasses *US, 1958*

- — Edd Byrnes, *Way Out with Kookie*, 1959
- California, Labor Day weekend ... early, with ocean fog still in the streets, outlaw motorcyclists wearing chains, shades and greasy Levis roll out from damp garages[.] — Hunter S. Thompson, *Hell's Angels*, p. 3, 1966
- Tonk breaks his "shades" and continues to wear the horn-rimmed frames minus the lenses. — Elliot Liebow, *Tally's Corner*, p. 61, 1967
- He looked at the cap in the mirror, turning his head this way and that to check it out, and pulled the peak down a hair closer to his shades. — Elmore Leonard, *Be Cool*, p. 175, 1999

shadie *noun*

a man, especially a young man, who spends his life on the edges of crime *US, 1976*

- [S]uch peripheral types as "street cats" and "shadies" are not members, though these groups frequently interact with those who truly belong to the Life. — Dennis Wepman et al., *The Life*, p. 2, 1976

shadow *noun*

a collector for an illegal money lender *US, 1950*

- — Hyman E. Goldin et al., *Dictionary of American Underworld Lingo*, p. 189, 1950

shadows *noun*

dark glasses *US, 1955*

- Dark eyeglasses are "shadows." — *Philadelphia Evening Bulletin*, 11th October 1955

shady *adjective*

detached, aloof *US, 1994*

- — Kevin Dilallo, *The Unofficial Gay Manual*, p. 245, 1994

shady lady *noun*

a prostitute *US, 1976*

- — *Complete CB Slang Dictionary*, p. 83, 1976
- The shady lady / from shady lane / is lying in my bed again[.] — Deep Purple, *A Touch Away*, 1996

shaft *noun*

1 the penis *UK, 1772*

- One bit of contemporary slang for this item, the purely descriptive Shaft, has undergone a strange decontamination, largely through the ignorance of naive people. — Frank Robinson, *Sex American Style*, p. 307, 1971

2 poor treatment *US, 1959*

- Chilly smiled at the shaft. Red was the type of stud that just when you were sure he was a fool and a clown came up with something half sharp. — Malcolm Braly, *On the Yard*, p. 79, 1967
- "Oh ... you got the shaft?" "Well, we parted amiably enough." — Armistead Maupin, *Tales of the City*, p. 70, 1978
- She got the goldmine / I got the shaft — Jerry Reed, *She Got the Goldmine*, 1982

3 the leg *US, 1970*

- — Clarence Major, *Dictionary of Afro-American Slang*, p. 102, 1970

shaft *verb*

to mistreat or abuse *US, 1959*

- Whoever coined the word shafted had me in mind. — Mickey Spillane, *Me, Hood!*, p. 49, 1963
- After all, he intended to shaft Folks for four times the fair market value of his white elephant parcel of land. — *Long White Con*, p. 54, 1977
- I'd rather be upfront about shafting somebody. — *Body Heat*, 1980

shaft artist *noun*

a person who is prone to cheat or behave unfairly *US, 1977*

- — *Maledicta*, p. 14, Summer 1977: "A word for it!"

shafts *noun*

the legs *US, 1952*

- "What a figure, what a pair of shafts." — Harry Grey, *The Hoods*, p. 239, 1952

shaftsman *noun*

a person who is prone to cheat or behave unfairly *US, 1977*

- — *Maledicta*, p. 14, Summer 1977: "A word for it!"

shafty *adjective*

(used of a thing) fashionable, popular *US, 1951*

- A Cadillac convertible is real cool or even shafty, and its driver, particularly if he be cat, or well-dressed, is cool Jonah. — *Newsweek*, p. 28, 8th October 1951

shag *noun*

the vulva and pubic hair *US, 2005*

- Diana scrubs her perky torso pups in the shower, then shows off her snazzy shag when she steps out to towel off. — Mr. Skin, *Mr. Skin's Skincyclopedia*, p. 45, 2005

shag *verb*

1 to carry, to take *US, 1953*

- "Now then, you shag word to the Acemen and the Ware Counselor to meet me at the pool hall." — Dale Krame, *Teen-Age Gangs*, p. 13, 1953

2 to have sex *UK, 1788*
Possibly from obsolete "shag" (to shake); usage is not gender-specific.

- All you've done is shag your twat, and that ain't nothin'. — *Drugstore Cowboy*, 1988

3 to leave *US, 1963*

- "Shag, man," she said roughly, "I mean, split—Barbara don't need you guys any more[.]" — John Rechy, *City of Night*, p. 158, 1963
- He was a fag, and so I had to shag. — Dennis Wepman et al., *The Life*, p. 48, 1976
- Same's all them other suckers shaggin' off to school ever goddamn mornin'. — Jess Mowry, *Way Past Cool*, p. 32, 1992

4 to run someone down; to arrest someone *US, 1973*

- I'll bet no other uniformed cop ever takes the trouble to shag him after I'm gone. — Joseph Wambaugh, *The Blue Knight*, p. 48, 1973

- I'm getting the salary of a deputy sheriff to sit here at this computer rather than shagging prisoners[.] — Gerald Petievich, *To Die in Beverly Hills*, p. 111, 1983
- "You gave the kid a five?" Nell asked. "What the hell. I shagged cards more than once. Besides, if I tipped him a buck, I might never see my car again." — Robert Campbell, *Alice in La-La Land*, p. 146, 1987

▸ **shag ass**
to leave *US, 1964*
- — *American Speech*, p. 235, October 1964: "Student slang in Hays, Kansas"
- — Collin Baker et al., *College Undergraduate Slang Study Conducted at Brown University*, p. 192, 1968
- — Helen Dahlskog (Editor), *A Dictionary of Contemporary and Colloquial Usage*, p. 52, 1972

shaka *adjective*
excellent *US, 1981*
Hawaiian youth usage.
- Dat was some shaka weed, brah! — Douglas Simonson, *Pidgin to da Max*, 1981

shaka
used as a greeting or to signify fraternity. Spoken in conjunction with a hand signal that emphasizes the little finger and thumb *US, 1981*
Hawaiian youth usage.
- — Douglas Simonson, *Pidgin to da Max*, 1981

shake *noun*
1 a blunt demand for money supported by the threat of physical force *US, 1953*
A shortened form of **SHAKEDOWN**.
- He was a heavy-set, round-faced, deceptively soft-looking young man who specialized in strong-arm routines and "shakes." — William Burroughs, *Junkie*, p. 58, 1953
2 the questioning of a suspected criminal *US, 2006*
An abbreviation of **SHAKEDOWN**.
- The FBI file was full of shakes involving Farley Ramsdale and Olive O. Ramsdale[.] — Joseph Wambaugh, *Hollywood Station*, p. 291, 2006
3 marijuana, especially the resinous matter that is shaken to the bottom during transit or what remains after the buds have been removed *US, 1978*
- A spokesman who identified himself as a "former user," said that "shake," the fine, powdery remants of marijuana processing, costs about $75 per ounce. — *Chicago Tribune*, p. C1, 13th August 1985
- On a tip, police searched Williamson's Gaston home in August, 2002, and found 13 marijuana plants, 11 gallon-sized bags of marijuana shake and some seeds. — *The Oregonian*, p. C1, 12th September 2003
4 any adulterant added to cocaine powder *US, 1989*
- [M]ost suppliers will allow up to 120 grams of shake to a kilo, or 12 percent; kilo-level buyers are usually unhappy if they find more. — Terry Williams, *The Cocaine Kids*, p. 35, 1989

shake *verb*
1 to search a person's clothing and body *US, 1972*
- I told him, "You don't search me. A matron shakes me, but not you." — Bruce Jackson, *In the Life*, p. 84, 1972
2 to get rid of someone or something *US, 1872*
- Nicky couldn't even go for a ride without changing cars at least six times before he could shake all his tails. — *Casino*, 1995

▸ **shake hands with an old friend**
used by a male as a jocular euphemism when excusing himself to go and urinate *US, 1994*
- — Michael Dalton Johnson, *Talking Trash with Redd Foxx*, p. 43, 1994

▸ **shake your skirt**
(of a woman) to go dancing *US, 1989*
- — Pamela Munro, *U.C.L.A. Slang*, p. 74, 1989

shake and bake *noun*
a noncommissioned officer fresh out of training *US, 1985*
- The sergeant in charge of rear security was a "shake 'n' bake," like all the squad leaders in the platoon. — Shelby L. Stanton, *The Rise and Fall of an American Army*, p. 314, 1985
- Sergeants who came from the NCO school were also known as "shake-and-bakes," after a television commercial for a product that promised something equally, improbably instantaneous, like fried chicken from the oven. — Lucian K. Truscott, *Army Blue*, p. 22, 1989
- A twenty-year-old Shake 'n' Bake sergeant by the name of Larry Closson had just arrived with a new batch of cherries. — Larry Chambers, *Recondo*, p. 87, 1992

- The shake 'n' bakes did their best to fill the gap, though many felt that they were in over their heads. — Keith Nolan, *Ripcord*, p. 103, 2000

shakedown *noun*
1 a search of a person or place *US, 1914*
- They put on "a shakedown" as the girls called it. Top officers went into each cottage and searched room by room for it. — Helen Bryan, *Inside*, p. 177, 1953
- — Paul Glover, *Words from the House of the Dead: Prison Writings from Soledad*, 1974
2 an act of extortion *US, 1902*
- The "security officer" (refined designation for a house dick) of one of the oldest and most famous hotels in Washington, near the White House, was recently fired because he ran a shakedown racket[.] — Jack Lait and Lee Mortimer, *Washington Confidential*, pp. 285–286, 1951

shake down *verb*
1 to search a person or a place *US, 1915*
- People with beards are shaken down thoroughly. — Hunter S Thompson, *Hell's Angels*, p. 210, 1967
2 to extort *US, 1872*
- What's changed? You're still trying to shake me down. — Elmore Leonard, *Glitz*, p. 291, 1985
- He doesn't know if this guy is shaking you down or taking advantage of you. — *Casino*, 1995

shake joint *noun*
a strip club *US, 2006*
- "We win, we can hit a shake joint." — Linden Dalecki, *Kid B*, p. 166, 2006

shaker wire *noun*
a motion-detector system used for perimeter security in prisons *US, 1996*
- As soon as they're out you know they're gonna be spotted—the hack in tower seven, or they touch the fence, the shaker wire sets off the alarm[.] — Elmore Leonard, *Out of Sight*, p. 111, 1996

shakes *noun*
any disease or condition characterized by trembling, especially *delirium tremens UK, 1782*
- Practically all the men with me were white, either lushheads or junkies, and this morning they all had the shakes and rattles real bad[.] — Mezz Mezzrow, *Really the Blues*, p. 304, 1946
- Most of them were shaving, some had the "shakes" so that it was quite a job, and so as not to cut themselves or face the agony too often, they only shaved when they were on their way uptown to hustle a dime. — Neal Cassady, *The First Third*, p. 54, 1971

sham-battle *verb*
to engage in youth gang warfare *US, 1949*
- I ain't club-fighting no more. I ain't sham-battling or nothing else. I'm out. — Hal Ellson, *Duke*, p. 144, 1949

sham dunk *noun*
in poker, a poor hand that wins a pot as a result of successful bluffing *US, 1996*
- — John Vorhaus, *The Big Book of Poker Slang*, p. 32, 1996

shameful!
used as a humorous admission that you have been cleverly ridiculed *US, 1963*
- — *American Speech*, p. 275, December 1963: "American Indian student slang"

shame out *verb*
to ridicule vociferously *US, 1963*
- — *American Speech*, p. 273, December 1963: "American Indian student slang"

shammer *noun*
a soldier who prolongs a legitimate absence from the frontline to avoid combat *US, 1970*
- The military's own estimate was that, for example, over Christmas in sixty-eight, there were four thousand shammers out of fifteen thousand men in a single division. — Malcolm Boyd, *My Fellow Americans*, p. 210, 1970

shampoo *noun*
a scene in a pornographic film or photograph depicting a man ejaculating onto a person's hair *US, 1995*
- — *Adult Video News*, p. 51, October 1995

shamus *noun*
a police detective; a private detective *US, 1925*

- What are you afraid of, this dirty two-bit shamus? — Mickey Spillane, *I, The Jury*, p. 20, 1947
- You'll get paid, shamus—if you do a job. — Raymond Chandler, *Playback*, p. 12, 1958
- I want to know so I can call up the shamuses, I want to know so I can blacklist you to the grave. — Clancy Sigal, *Going Away*, p. 265, 1961
- Hey, relax man, I'm a brother shamus. — *The Big Lebowski*, 1998

shanghai *verb*

to detail someone to a task; to enlist someone to do something that they are not entirely willing to do *US, 1915*
From US nautical slang describing a method of recruiting sailors with drugs and force.

- Meanwhile, her new boyfriend's out of town, so she's shanghaied yet another guy into her bed—a fascistic cop. — C.D. Payne, *Youth in Revolt*, p. 126, 1993

shank *noun*

a homemade knife or stabbing and slashing weapon *US, 1967*

- Picao, who I dug as no heart, squawked out, "Sticks, shanks, zips—you call it." — Piri Thomas, *Down These Mean Streets*, p. 52, 1967
- I better show you how to make a shank. I could use a spoon. The easiest kind of weapon to make, you how the end of a toothbrush and stick a razor blade in it. — Elmore Leonard, *Maximum Bob*, p. 108, 1991

shank *verb*

to stab someone, especially with a homemade weapon *US, 1955*

- E-magine that cat shanking me like that. — Piri Thomas, *Down These Mean Streets*, p. 114, 1967
- If you send me back there it's the death sentence. I'll get shanked in a week. — Gerald Petievich, *The Quality of the Informant*, p. 35, 1985

shanty *noun*

in poker, a hand consisting of three cards of the same rank and a pair *US, 1988*
Conventionally known as a "full house."

- — George Percy, *The Language of Poker*, p. 80, 1988

shanty Irish *noun*

poor Irish immigrants *US, 1970*

- She called everyone shanty Irish or nigger rich. — Gilbert Sorrentino, *Steelwork*, p. 101, 1970
- "Fucking shanty irish sot!" he called toward the bathroom[.] — Vincent Patrick, *The Pope of Greenwich Village*, p. 198, 1979

shapes *noun*

dice altered by cheats so as to be not true cubes *US, 1950*

- — *The Annals of the American Academy of Political and Social Sciences*, p. 130, May 1950
- — Frank Garcia, *Marked Cards and Loaded Dice*, p. 263, 1962
- — Thomas L. Clark, *The Dictionary of Gambling and Gaming*, p. 195, 1987

shape up or ship out!

used as a last warning to someone whose ways need mending *US, 1956*

- You're right, Michael! These folks need to shape up or ship out. — Michael Graham, *Redneck Nation*, p. 95, 2002

shareware *noun*

computer software that is freely available but for which the developer asks a voluntary payment *US, 1988*

- A $99 CD ROM with more than 3,000 PC-compatible shareware programs has been announced by Alden Publishing. — *InfoWorld*, p. 20, 18th January 1988

shark *noun*

a loan shark *US, 1990*

- And then I'd either blow the winnings in a week or go to the sharks to pay back the bookies. — *Goodfellas*, 1990

shark *verb*

in a dice game such as craps, to make a controlled (cheating) throw of the dice *US, 1950*

- — Thomas L. Clark, *The Dictionary of Gambling and Gaming*, p. 195, 1987

shark bait *noun*

a person with very pale skin *US, 1982*
Hawaiian youth usage.

- — Douglas Simonson, *Pidgin to da Max Hana Hou*, 1982

sharking *noun*

the illegal loaning of money at extremely high interest rates *US, 1973*

- "What's the business?" "Junkets and sharking," the Greek said. — George Higgins, *The Digger's Game*, p. 185, 1973
- He wore Air corps sunglasses, combed his hair into a gelatinous country pomp and tithed his pay and tithed the vigorish on his sharking. — Earl Thompson, *Tattoo*, p. 293, 1974

shark meat *noun*

an easy victim of a cheat, swindler, or hustler *US, 1990*

- — Steve Rushin, *Pool Cool*, p. 26, 1990

sharky *adjective*

used of a surfboard nose, pointed *US, 1991*

- — Trevor Cralle, *The Surfin'ary*, p. 110, 1991

sharp *noun*

1 in gambling, a cheat *UK, 1797*
A shortened from of **SHARPER**.

- At fifteen, he was an accomplished card sharp, pickpocket and ravishing female impersonator baiting tourist tricks for muggers in the French Quarter. — Iceberg Slim (Robert Beck), *Doom Fox*, p. 46, 1978
- On one wall hung ten or twelve large leather-bound photo albums that had pictures of card sharps. — Stephen Cannell, *King Con*, p. 143, 1997

2 a number sign (#) on a computer keyboard *US, 1991*

- — Eric S. Raymond, *The New Hacker's Dictionary*, p. 39, 1991

sharp *adjective*

stylish, fashionable, attractive *US, 1944*

- I wanted to look sharp but I wanted to feel comfortable too. — Chester Himes, *If He Hollers Let Him Go*, p. 136, 1945
- Neal had arrived the night before, the first time in NY, with his beautiful little sharp chick Louanne. — Jack Kerouac, *On the Road (The Original Scroll)*, p. 109, 1951
- When it came to personal matters, my mind was strictly on getting "sharp" in my zoot as soon as I left work[.] — Malcolm X and Alex Haley, *The Autobiography of Malcolm X*, p. 65, 1964
- It's, like, Santa Claus used ta have this really sharp chort, man, y'know? — Cheech Marin and Tommy Chong, *Santa Claus and his Old Lady*, 1971

sharper *noun*

in gambling, a cheater *UK, 1681*

- We got to have sharpers with private licenses hiding information[.] — Raymond Chandler, *The Little Sister*, p. 219, 1949
- The terrier was showing real signs of being a world class sharper, but that was before Beano, using a dead man's I.D., got caught cheating[.] — Stephen J. Cannell, *King Con*, p. 32, 1997

sharpie *noun*

1 a gambling cheat *US, 1942*

- Some poolroom sharpie lounging in the lobby came to a sitting position when he spotted two hustlers being pulled in by a couple soft-clothes dicks[.] — Nelson Algren, *The Man with the Golden Arm*, p. 265, 1949
- And do not think that it is the abode, the stomping ground, of only the pimp, sharpie, and floozy set. — John D. McDonald, *The Neon Jungle*, p. 6, 1953
- Just what I said: any of your sharpies here willing to take my five bucks that says that I can get the best of that woman—before the week's up—without her getting the best of me? — Ken Kesey, *One Flew Over the Cuckoo's Nest*, p. 71, 1962
- [H]is latest room had an assortment of bum dice and new-but-marked decks of cards very cleverly packaged and stamped. He was a sharpie. — Mickey Spillane, *Me, Hood!*, p. 23, 1963

2 in pinball, a player who can play for long periods of time without paying because of his ability to win free games *US, 1977*

- — Bobbye Claire Natkin and Steve Kirk, *All About Pinball*, p. 116, 1977

3 an uncircumcized penis *US, 2002*

- — Amy Sohn, *Sex and the City*, p. 157, 2002

sharps *noun*

a hypodermic needle and syringe *US, 1994*
Drug addict usage, borrowed from the medical terminology for any skin-piercing device.

- — US Department of Justice, *Street Terms*, October 1994

sharpshoot *verb*

to question a speaker after a lecture *US, 1968*

- — Carl Fleischhauer, *A Glossary of Army Slang*, p. 2, 1968

sharpshooter *noun*

an intravenous drug user who usually hits a vein on the first attempt to inject a drug *US, 1957*

- [H]e'd gotten into the sharpshooter mob, the ones who lived only for the next fix. — James Blake, *The Joint*, p. 172, 15th July 1957

sharp top *noun*
in a deck of playing cards, an ace *US, 1988*
- — George Percy, *The Language of Poker*, p. 80, 1988

shasta *noun*
a sexual partner who is not particularly attractive, but who was available at the time *US, 2001*
An allusion to Shasta™ soda, not especially liked but available and inexpensive.
- — Don R. McCreary (Editor), *Dawg Speak*, 2001

shatchen *noun*
a matchmaker *UK, 1890*
Yiddish on loan to English. Many variant spellings.
- "This ugly duckling. We'll someday have to get a schatchen to take her off our hands." — Hortense Calisher, *Sunday Jews*, p. 31, 2002

shave *verb*
to alter the edges or surfaces of dice for use by a cheat *US, 1974*
- — John Savage, *The Winner's Guide to Dice*, p. 91, 1974

▶ **shave points**
to reduce scoring during a sports contest in furtherance of a gambling conspiracy *US, 1952*
- The first admissions of "shaving" points were by players from New York City schools. — *The American Peoples Encyclopedia Yearbook*, p. 229, 1952
- This has been lightlighted recently by disclosures that for the second time in 10 years, gamblers have bribed college basketball players to shave points. — United States Congress, *The Attorney General's Program to Curb Organized Crime*, p. 6, 1961
- I'm telling you. They're shaving points on the game. This is no bullshit tip. — *Diner*, 1982
- It was like spreading rumors in Boston about Larry Bird shaving points, or priests selling fat young boys out of vans behind Fenway Park. — Hunter S. Thompson, *Generation of Swine*, p. 121, 26th May 1986

shaver *noun*
in the Korean war, a booby trap used by South Korean troops to sabotage North Korean transportation carts *US, 1982*
- When a group lifted the cart to replace the wheel the booby trap went off. This diabolical device was referred to by the ROKs as "the shaver"—for the effect it had on one's head. — Joseph C. Goulden, *Korea*, p. 129, 1982

shave-tail *noun*
a newly promoted second lieutenant *US, 1970*
- — *Current Slang*, p. 18, Winter 1970
- I looked at him, and waited, just a second looie, shavetail, butterbar, shit-assed LT. — Cherokee Paul McDonald, *Into the Green*, p. 37, 2001

shazam!; shazzam!
used for registering triumph *US, 1940*
An incantatory ritual from the comic book character created by Bill Parker and C.C. Beck in 1940—a metaphorically God-like character whose name is called on by the superhero Captain Marvel in moments of crisis; Shazam is an acronym of Solomon (wisdom), Hercules (strength), Atlas (stamina), Zeus (power), Achilles (courage), and Mercury (speed).
- Fuck, I'll finish it, send it to Luther Nichols of Doubleday, and, shazam! I'll strike it big. — Oscar Zeta Acosta, *The Autobiography of a Brown Buffalo*, p. 155, 1972

she *noun*
1 cocaine *US, 1958*
- The She. Yeah, S-h-e. Because if you take cocaine you have no need for a woman. — Willard Motley, *Let No Man Write My Epitaph*, p. 199, 1958
2 used of an effeminate homosexual man, he *UK, 1950*
- — Donald Webster Cory and John P. LeRoy, *The Homosexual and His Society*, p. 266, 1963: "A lexicon of homosexual slang"
- The world of queens and malehustlers and what they thrive on, the queens being technically men but no one thinks of them that way—always "she[.]" — John Rechy, *City of Night*, p. 105, 1963
- Florida Legislative Investigation Committee (Johns Committee), *Homosexuality and Citizenship in Florida*, 1964: "Glossary of homosexual terms and deviate acts"
- If she [Harold] doesn't like it, she can twirl on it. — Mart Crowley, *The Boys in the Band*, p. 24, 1968

shears *noun*
playing cards that have been trimmed for cheating *US, 1961*
- — Thomas L. Clark, *The Dictionary of Gambling and Gaming*, p. 195, 1987

shebang *noun*
any thing, matter or business at issue at the moment *US, 1869*
Usually as "the whole shebang." The former senses of "a hut," "vehicle," or "tavern" are all but forgotten.
- Maybe you can get to be boss of the whole shebang! — Jim Thompson, *Roughneck*, p. 114, 1954
- Helen said that after I left Detroit the whole shebang collapsed like a house of cards. — Clancy Sigal, *Going Away*, p. 299, 1961
- If I do, this whole shebang will come apart on me and I won't look too good, will I? — Elmore Leonard, *Killshot*, p. 258, 1989
- A grassy square in the middle of Old Town Plaza was the best part of the whole shebang, as far as Finnegan was concerned. — Joseph Wambaugh, *Finnegan's Week*, pp. 141–142, 1993

she-bill; she-note *noun*
a two-dollar bill *US, 1996*
- — Claudio R. Salvucci, *The Philadelphia Dialect Dictionary*, p. 57, 1996

shed *noun*
in poker, a hand consisting of three cards of the same rank and a pair *US, 1988*
Known conventionally as a "full house."
- — George Percy, *The Language of Poker*, p. 80, 1988

shed row *noun*
in horseracing, the row of barns where horses are stabled *US, 1951*
- — David W. Maurer, *Argot of the Racetrack*, p. 58, 1951

Sheena *noun*
a melodramatic black homosexual male *US, 1980*
From the comic book, *Sheena, Queen of the Jungle*.
- — *Maledicta*, p. 228, Winter 1980: "'Lovely, blooming, fresh and gay': the onomastics of camp"

sheeny *noun*
a Jewish person *UK, 1816*
- One time in Humboldt Park Leo "Bow" Gistensohn, our leader, didn't like the way a cop down by the lake called him "sheeny." — Mezz Mezzrow, *Really the Blues*, p. 6, 1946
- "Sheeny!" she is screaming. "Hebe!" — Philip Roth, *Portnoy's Complaint*, p. 203, 1969
- — Helen Dahlskog (Editor), *A Dictionary of Contemporary and Colloquial Usage*, p. 53, 1972

sheep *noun*
a woman who volunteers to take part in serial sex with members of a motorcycle club or gang *US, 1972*
- — Robert A. Wilson, *Playboy's Book of Forbidden Words*, p. 220, 1972
- Novitiates had to bring along a girl (called a "sheep"). The sheep had to fuck all the gang members present, in order of seniority, after which the initiate had to perform cunnilingus on her in front of everybody. — Allan Sherman, *The Rape of the APE*, p. 201, 1973

sheep-dipping *noun*
the use of military equipment or personnel in an intelligence operation under civilian cover *US, 1989*
- Those Air Force officers who had "sheep-dipped"—taken a temporary tour of duty with the Agency—had moved quickly up the promotional ladder. — T.E. Cruise, *Wings of Gold III*, p. 64, 1989

sheepskin *noun*
1 a college diploma *US, 1843*
- Wouldn't have a sheepskin if they paid me. — Robert Gover, *The Maniac Responsible*, p. 25, 1963
- I would cut my tongue off before I would tell them the sheepskins they wanted in their family were not worth a damn. — John A. Williams, *The Angry Ones*, p. 7, 1969
- Stevenson said we were discussing the fact that a sheepskin was a handicap in American politics. — Mort Sahl, *Heartland*, p. 51, 1976
2 an executive criminal pardon *US, 1962*
- — Joseph E. Ragen and Charles Finston, *Inside the World's Toughest Prison*, p. 817, 1962: "Penitentiary and underworld glossary"

sheet *noun*
1 a police record of arrests and convictions *US, 1958*

Probably a shortened **RAP SHEET**, but earlier sources for "sheet" than this raise questions.

- Turk had gotten a walk because his sheet wasn't too bad. — Claude Brown, *Manchild in the Promised Land*, p. 17, 1965
- I have twenty-two cases on my sheet and only eight were righteous. — Susan Hall, *Ladies of the Night*, p. 61, 1973
- I bet he got a sheet down there damn near long as mine. — Vernon E. Smith, *The Jones Men*, p. 93, 1974
- One question: Do they have a sheet on you, where you told him you're from. — *Reservoir Dogs*, 1992

2 a newspaper *US, 1956*

- "You think I, with my extensive big-city newspaper experience, want to do filler copy for a bunch of tank-town sheets?" — William Brinkley, *Don't Go Near the Water*, p. 84, 1956
- — Don Wilmeth, *The Language of American Popular Entertainment*, p. 237, 1981

3 one hundred doses of LSD soaked into paper *US, 1999*

- A "sheet" is one hundred hits on a ten-by-ten-hit piece of paper, a unit often sold on the retail level. — Cam Cloud, *The Little Book of Acid*, p. 34, 1999

sheets *noun*
a daily report of recent criminal activity, circulated among police going on shift *US, 1975*

- I read the sheets this morning … and they sounded like the same watches. — Donald Goines, *Inner City Hoodlum*, p. 55, 1975

sheet writer; writer *noun*
in an illegal sports betting operation or lottery; a functionary who takes and records bets *US, 1949*

- — *American Speech*, p. 193, October 1949
- Buda was the daughter of a race track sheet-writer, an only child. — Jack Lait and Lee Mortimer, *Chicago Confidential*, p. 15, 1950
- A "writer" (some 2,000) in Chicago alone comes to your door with his "book." He takes your bet, writes it up in his book, and gives you a ticket showing what numbers you picked and how much you bet. — Alson Smith, *Syndicate City*, p. 195, 1954
- I think the flat is a check-in station for so called runners or writers who turn in their bet books and cash, less their earned twenty percent. — Iceberg Slim (Robert Beck), *Mama Black Widow*, p. 97, 1969

she-he *noun*
a transvestite or transgender person *US, 1970*

- When she-he finally tired and left the spotlight, a girl got on the bed, undressed, and started to masturbate. — *Screw*, p. 7, 13th April 1970

shekels *noun*
money *US, 1883*
From the ancient Babylonian unit of weight and coin.

- Generally a runner made plenty for himself, taking a chance that the dough he clipped wasn't on the number that pulled in the shekels. — Mickey Spillane, *I, The Jury*, p. 46, 1947
- And I'd still sacrifice everything. All Freddy's shekels. — Mary McCarthy, *The Group*, p. 352, 1963
- Jack, shekels, mazuma, simoleons, Mr. Green, filthy lucre, even spondulicks—this is other Why of prostitution. — Gail Sheehy, *Hustling*, p. 11, 1973
- The first step was to place the all-important hat by the fountain to catch the shekels. — Ed Sanders, *Tales of Beatnik Glory*, p. 78, 1975

shelf *noun*

1 solitary confinement *US, 1967*

- Stick was confined in the second cell—a holding cell in the isolation unit known as the shelf. — Malcolm Braly, *On the Yard*, p. 61, 1967
- — William K. Bentley and James M. Corbett, *Prison Slang*, p. 11, 1992

2 in circus and carnival usage, an upper sleeping berth *US, 1981*

- — Don Wilmeth, *The Language of American Popular Entertainment*, p. 237, 1981

▶ **on the shelf**
unlikely to marry *UK, 1839*

- She didn't seem to go out on many dates, and he couldn't figure out why she was on the shelf. — James T. Farrell, *Saturday Night*, p. 19, 1947

shelfware *noun*
a computer program bought but not used *US, 1991*

- — Eric S. Raymond, *The New Hacker's Dictionary*, p. 318, 1991

shell *noun*

1 a person who is somewhat lacking in mental faculties *US, 2002*

- — Gary K. Farlow, *Prison-ese*, p. 62, 2002

2 a safe with a thin door and walls *US, 1950*

- — Hyman E. Goldin et al., *Dictionary of American Underworld Lingo*, p. 191, 1950

shellack *verb*
to physically beat *US, 1930*

- Today it's a little different, they don't shellack these guys like that. — Harry King, *Box Man*, p. 79, 1972

shellacking *noun*
a beating; a defeat *US, 1931*

- Now Frank 'n' me got our pictures in the paper, and my old man would've given me a shellacking if Sam didn't stop him. — Irving Shulman, *The Amboy Dukes*, p. 101, 1947
- Take a licking, a real shellacking and see how she likes that! — Rocky Garciano (with Rowland Barber), *Somebody Up There Likes Me*, p. 255, 1955
- [Y]ou knew you was going to get a shellacking every time they'd catch you. — Harry King, *Box Man*, p. 79, 1972

shemale *noun*
a transvestite, transsexual, or other transgender person; a person with mixed sexual physiology, usually the genitals of a male and surgically augmented breasts *US, 1954*

- In hotels these off-beat she-males don't get together in groups, wearing mannish clothes, as they sometimes do in hole-in-the-wall cafes or bohemian eating places. — Dev Collans with Stewart Sterling, *I was a House Detective*, p. 102, 1954
- Like most shemales on the Strip, Olivia's forte was B-drinking. — Seth Morgan, *Homeboy*, p. 14, 1990
- "I'm 47," he says, "and I haven't danced since I was out with a punk rock debutante year ago. She lived on Esplanade Avenue with two shemales." — *Times-Picayune (New Orleans)*, p. 1, 13th November 2003

shenanigans *noun*
trickery; mischief *US, 1855*

- That's when the shenanigans began. Kefauver had no experience with such shenanigans. — Jack Lait and Lee Mortimer, *Washington Confidential*, p. 197, 1951
- After all my shenanigans, if I'd missed that penalty, the crowd would have crucified me. — Frank Skinner, *Frank Skinner*, p. 27, 2001

sherm *noun*

1 phencyclidine, the recreational drug known as PCP or angel dust *US, 1981*

- — Ronald Linder, *PCP*, p. 10, 1981
- "From what I know out there on the street, there's some crazy people out there—and not only the ones who smoke sherm [PCP]." — Leon Bing, *Do or Die*, p. 146, 1991
- Drugs, such as Sherm, Red Devils, Old English 800, Mad Dog 20/20, and Silver Satin. — Yusuf Jah, *Uprising*, p. 238, 1995

2 a marijuana cigarette that has been supplemented with phencyclidine, the recreational drug known as PCP or angel dust *US, 1982*
From Shermans™, a cigarette brand.

- — Ralph de Sola, *Crime Dictionary*, p. 137, 1982
- One of the popular ways to get "dusted" is to dip cigarettes, specifically the Sherman brand, into a liquid form of PCP, allowing it to dry before smoking it. It is known as "SuperCool" or "Sherm." — James Vigil, *Barrio Gangs*, p. 127, 1988
- Finally Stagalee got out of prison and I was grateful, as the sherm was starting to take a toll on me. — Sanyika Shakur, *Monster*, p. 253, 1993
- This is a Blood hood. Amber live here with her baby and her mother. Her mother be smokin' Sherm all the time. — *Rolling Stone*, p. 80, 12th April 2001

3 crack cocaine *US, 1993*

- BIG D: Shit! Nigger, you smoke enough sherm, your dumb ass'll do a lot of crazy ass things. — *True Romance*, 1993

Sherman *noun*
phencyclidine, the recreational drug known as PCP or angel dust *US, 1995*

- [A]ll the brothers that were slangin' were selling "water," "Sherman," angel dust, PCP, or whatever you want to call it. — Yusuf Jah, *Uprising*, p. 180, 1995

shermed *adjective*
intoxicated with phencyclide *US, 1990*

- — Kenn "Naz" Young, *Naz's Dictionary of Teen Slang*, p. 104, 1993

sherm head *noun*
a person addicted to phencyclidine, the recreational drug known as PCP or angel dust *US, 1997*
- Bird had warned me his neighbor was a "shermhead," addicted to marijuana cigarettes dipped in PCP. — Gini Sikes, *8 Ball Chicks*, p. 53, 1997

sherms *noun*
crack cocaine *US, 1994*
- — US Department of Justice, *Street Terms*, October 1994

she-she *noun*
a prostitute *US, 1971*
- "Biffer," "prossie," "she-she," "pig-meat" are some other slang designations. — Charles Winick, *The Lively Commerce*, p. 41, 1971

shield *noun*
a police officer *US, 1965*
- He was a true disciple of the field, he never used a hammer / or cracked it by the shield while stickin' in the slammer. — Bruce Jackson, *Get Your Ass in the Water and Swim Like Me*, p. 85, 1965

shifty *noun*
sex with a prostitute *US, 1954*
- — Jerry Robertson, *Oil Slanguage*, p. 112, 1954

shikse; shiksa; shixa *noun*
a Gentile woman *UK, 1892*
- The fault lay with them, because they had never approved Lee-Simon's marrying a shikse—and a fair-haired one at that[.] — Clancy Sigal, *Going Away*, p. 375, 1961
- That Alice was so blatantly a shikse caused no end of grief in Heshie's household. — Philip Roth, *Portnoy's Complaint*, p. 60, 1969

shikse from Dixie *noun*
the ultimate in Gentile femininity *US, 1945*
The reference to Dixie is solely for the rhyme; it does not connote that the woman in question is from the south.
- — Lou Shelly, *Hepcats Jive Talk Dictionary*, p. 37, 1945

shill *noun*
1 a person posing as an enthusiastic and satisfied customer in order to boost sales by a confederate *US, 1916*
- He had the compassion of an icicle, the effrontery of a carnival shill, and the generosity of a pawnbroker. — Mardy Grothe, *Oxymoronica*, p. 152, 2004

2 in a confidence swindle, a confederate who appears to be prospering as a result of the scheme which is designed to fleece the victim *US, 1940*
- I was never even a shill. I was with it, all right. I was a mere stagehand[.] — Iceberg Slim (Robert Beck), *Trick Baby*, p. 39, 1969

shill *verb*
to pose falsely as a satisfied customer or successful gambler in order to encourage genuine customers, gamblers, etc. *US, 1914*
- I've shilled for a traveling evangelist. — Max Shulman, *The Zebra Derby*, p. 50, 1946
- You follow a man who shills for Pizza Hut-pizza[.] — Howard Stern, *Miss America*, p. 19, 1995

shim *noun*
1 a plastic strip used for forcing locks *US, 1968*
- All a thief needs is a shim to open a locking bar, Tobias said. — *Myrtle Beach (Florida) Sun-News*, p. D9, 10th September 2004

2 a person whose sex is not easily guessed on the basis of their hair and clothing *US, 1970*
- — William D. Alsever, *Glossary for the Establishment and Other Uptight People*, p. 28, December 1970

shim *verb*
to force a lock with a plastic strip *US, 1972*
- A knife and keys were stolen from a real-estate office entered by shimming a front-door lock. — *Washington Post*, p. T6, 21st August 2001

shimmy *noun*
the game *chemin de fer US, 1961*
- — Thomas L. Clark, *The Dictionary of Gambling and Gaming*, p. 196, 1987

shimmy act *noun*
a feigned seizure *US, 1988*
- They always got those signs around hospitals that says QUIET, and if I was to go into that shimmy act, they'd probably throw me into the pyscho ward and I'll never get out. — *Drugstore Cowboy*, 1988

shimmy dancer *noun*
a woman who performs sexual dances *US, 1962*
- [B]oth those girls are workin' shimmy dancers and hustlers I know from Portland. — Ken Kesey, *One Flew Over the Cuckoo's Nest*, p. 210, 1962

shindig *noun*
a party *US, 1871*
A rural term that moved to the city; it gained wide usage as a result of the musical television program *Shindig* which aired on ABC from September 1964 until January 1966.
- Man, what a shindig that was. Give me a barrelhouse joint on the South Side any day[.] — Mezz Mezzrow, *Really the Blues*, p. 136, 1946
- Well, sir, that was quite a little shindig yesterday, wasn't it? — Max Shulman, *Rally Round the Flag, Boys!*, p. 220, 1957
- At one of those shindigs, he presented Governor Ruby Laffoon of Kentucky to me. — Helen Giblo, *Footlights, Fistfights and Femmes*, p. 229, 1957
- "I heard that Gypsy Rose Lee's holding a shindig tonight." — Georgia Sothern, *My Life in Burlesque*, p. 178, 1972

shine *noun*
1 a black person *US, 1908*
Abusive in any context.
- Suddenly I heard the school superintendent, who had told me to come, yell, "Bring up the shines, gentlemen! Bring up the little shines!" — Ralph Ellison, *Invisible Man*, p. 18, 1947
- A Negro sitting opposite us smiled. "The shine is wise," said Roy in my ear. — William Burroughs, *Junkie*, p. 46, 1953
- Get the shine out of here, Carlito. — Edwin Torres, *Carlito's Way*, p. 82, 1975
- Listen, you shine, we 'bout carved up one jungle bunny t'night. — Larry Heinemann, *Close Quarters*, p. 164, 1977

2 a decorative tooth cap *US, 2006*
- The teeth caps are alternately called grills, fronts, shines, plates, or caps, and these glittering decorative pieces are the latest hip-hop culture trend making its way into the mainstream. — *Boston Globe*, p. C1, 31st January 2006

3 a government bureaucrat *US, 1987*
From the shine on the seat of the bureaucrat's pants.
- — Carsten Stroud, *Close Pursuit*, p. 275, 1987

4 alcohol *US, 1933*
- Some of Roland Crowe's buddies were still sloshing around back there in the swamp, driving air boats, guiding hunting and fishing parties, poaching alligators, making shine[.] — Elmore Leonard, *Gold Coast*, p. 33, 1980

5 a still used in the illegal production of alcohol *US, 1974*
- — David W. Maurer, *Kentucky Moonshine*, p. 124, 1974

shine *verb*
1 to speak evasively and avoid a subject, often through flattery *US, 1993*
- I'm the Finnegan that calls here twice a week hoping to at least hear Orson say there's no work, except that you shine me every time, and I never hear him say anything at all. — Joseph Wambaugh, *Finnegan's Week*, p. 5, 1993

2 to mock someone *US, 1993*
- — *Washington Post*, 14th October 1993

▸ **shine for someone**
to appeal to someone *US, 1949*
- He's kind of big and kind of ugly and he's giving the up and down. Right off he don't shine for me. — Hal Ellson, *Duke*, p. 30, 1949

▸ **shine on**
to ignore something completely *US, 1981*
- He's in there trying to pick up teenyboppers, but they've all shined him on. — Gerald Petievich, *Money Men*, p. 47, 1981
- No, I shined it on and went to Hawaii. — Sandra Bernard, *Confessions of a Pretty Lady*, p. 80, 1988

shine parlor *noun*
an establishment that sells alcohol illegally, by the drink *US, 1978*
The "shine" is an abbreviated **MOONSHINE**.
- Shot-house operators run informal (and illegal) taverns in their own homes (shot-house operators are often women). The houses go by other names too; gold mine, good-time house, blind tiger, shine parlor, or juicejoint. — Burgess Laughlin, *Job Opportunities in the Black Market*, pp. 10 – 9, 1978

shiner *noun*
1 a black eye *US, 1904*

- For a busted smeller, a couple of shiners, and a few creases in the knowledge-box, he made himself ten grand. — Mezz Mezzrow, *Really the Blues*, p. 21, 1946
- He was going to have a couple of very unlovely black eyes. I, who had seen him at a gross disadvantage, was to receive a figurative shiner. — Jim Thompson, *Roughneck*, p. 133, 1954
- But his picture was in the paper. He had quite a "shiner." — Mary McCarthy, *The Group*, p. 166, 1963
- I crawled out of it with a sprained thumb and a bloody lip, Pookie picked up a gorgeous shiner. — John Nichols, *The Sterile Cuckoo*, p. 166, 1965

2 a torch *US, 1950*
- — Hyman E. Goldin et al., *Dictionary of American Underworld Lingo*, p. 191, 1950

3 in carnival usage, a diamond *US, 1981*
- — Don Wilmeth, *The Language of American Popular Entertainment*, p. 238, 1981

4 in gambling, an object that reflects, enabling the user to cheat by seeing cards as they are dealt *US, 1997*
- He had two "shiners" working on the table; one was a money clip that he could lay on the table directly in front of him. It was shiny, but only reflected directly back. — Stephen J.Cannell, *King Con*, p. 2, 1997

shiner player *noun*
in gambling, a cheat who uses a shiny object to reflect the cards as they are dealt *US, 1997*
- Besides dice tats and 7UPS, there were volumes for nail nickers and crimpers (card markers), hand muckers and mitt men (card switchers), as well as card counters and shiner players. — Stephen J. Cannell, *Big Con*, p. 143, 1997

shin fight *noun*
a sham gang fight *US, 1958*
- The shin fight simulates gang combat except that knives and guns are now used and blows are not supposed to be struck below the belt or in the face. — Harrison E. Salisbury, *The Shook-up Generation*, p. 25, 1958

shingle *noun*

1 a name plate above a prison cell door *US, 1954*
- Above each cell door is a board, a "shingle," with the inmate's name and number. — John Martin, *Break Down the Walls*, p. 135, 1954
- The name-plate over his cell (a "shingle"), which formerly was white, now becomes blue and, as such, identifies him as someone who has committed a serious infraction of rules. — Arthur V. Huffman, *New York Mattachine Newsletter*, p. 7, August 1961

2 a car license plate *US, 1976*
- — John R. Armore and Joseph D. Wolfe, *Dictionary of Desperation*, 1976

3 a lawyer *US, 1958*
- I spoke to Iggy Fitelstein. Iggy's the best shingle in New York. — Truman Capote, *Breakfast at Tiffany's*, p. 95, 1958

shinola *noun*
used as a contrast in describing ignorance as not knowing shit from shinola *US, 1940*
Shinola was a patented name (1903) for a boot polish.
- And I don't think the guy knows shit from Shinola about my case[.] — George V. Higgins, *The Judgment of Deke Hunter*, p. 50, 1976
- Paulie, the truth is, this horse don't know shit from Shinola. None of them do. — Vincent Patrick, *The Pope of Greenwich Village*, p. 179, 1979
- His interviewees were hicks who didn't know shit from Shinola. — James Ellroy, *Because the Night*, p. 325, 1984
- Aw, he don't know a cuss word from shinola. — *Raising Arizona*, 1987

shiny buttons *noun*
money *US, 1947*
- — Marcus Hanna Boulware, *Jive and Slang of Students in Negro Colleges*, 1947

shiny wing pilot *noun*
a pilot who has just completed his flight instruction training *US, 1963*
- — *American Speech*, p. 120, May 1963: "Air refueling words"

ship *noun*
a scholarship *US, 1957*
- "Too bad all of you couldn't get ships to the same school," Scar said. — Herbert Simmons, *Corner Boy*, p. 58, 1957

ship driver *noun*
a US Navy officer *US, 1992*
Gulf war usage.
- — *American Speech*, p. 88, Spring 1992: "Gulf War words supplement"

shipfucker *noun*
a rabble rouser; a troublemaker *US, 1970*
- Now Dolomite was from San Antone / a rambling shipfucker from the day he was born. — Bruce Jackson, *Get Your Ass in the Water and Swim Like Me*, p. 58, 1970

shipoopi *noun*
a woman *US, 1954*
- Remember the halcyon days, when you could get a cheesecake shot of any shipoopi into any paper by announcing she had just been chosen Girl I'd Most Like To Be Snowed In With[?] — Bernard Wolfe, *The Late Risers*, p. 42, 1954
- But a woman who'll wait til the third time around / Head in clouds, feet on the ground / She's the girl he's glad he's found / She's his shipoopi! — Meredith Wilson, *Shipoopi (from the Music Man)*, 1957

ship-tick *noun*
in college, a notification of academic deficiency *US, 1968*
- — *American Speech*, pp. 76–77, February 1968: "Some notes on flunk notes"

Shirley *noun*
a woman who makes herself available sexually to professional baseball players *US, 1975*
- Annies, Shirleys, Groupies, Starfuckers; that's what the men call them. — Herb Michelson, *Sportin' Ladies*, p. vii, 1975

shirttail kin *noun*
distant relatives *US, 1944*
- Not to mention that some shirt-tail kin could turn up and lay claim to the whole ball of wax. — Kathleen Hills, *Past Imperfect*, p. 262, 2002

shishkebob *noun*
the penis *US, 1999*
- Women all grabbin' at my shishkebob[.] — Eminem (Marshall Mathers), *Cum On Everybody*, 1999

shisty *adjective*
cold-hearted, mean *US, 2004*
- — Rick Ayers (Editor), *Berkeley High Slang Dictionary*, p. 38, 2004

shit *noun*

1 marijuana *US, 1946*
- Enrique went off and got me about 2 ounces of shit for only $3[.] — Jack Kerouac, *Letter to Allen Ginsberg*, p. 350, 10th May 1952
- Well, of course, I been smokin' shit for about seven years now, and my knowledge is pretty fair. — Bruce Jackson, *Get Your Ass in the Water and Swim Like Me*, p. 90, 1964
- Sitting on the couch smoking shit and enjoying yourself? — Lenny Bruce, *The Essential Lenny Bruce*, pp. 111–112, 1967
- Yes I smoke shit, straight off the roach clip — Cypress Hill, *I Wanna Get High*, 1993

2 heroin *US, 1950*
- At that time, shit was relatively scarce. — Jack Gerber, *The Connection*, p. 88, 1957
- It's good shit, not like some of the stuff we've been getting lately. — Alexander Trocchi, *Cain's Book*, p. 9, 1960
- Nickie and his friend proceeded to get straight, cooking up their shit. — Herbert Huncke, *The Evening Sun Turned Crimson*, p. 144, 1980
- White people who know the difference between good shit and bad shit, this is the house they come to. My shit, I'll take the Pepsi Challenge with Amsterdam shit any ol' day of the fuckin' week. — *Pulp Fiction*, 1994
- YOUNG STUD: This is twice in two days a chick has O.D.'d on me. COLONEL: Well maybe that means you oughta think about getting some new shit, what do you think? — *Boogie Nights*, 1997

3 narcotics; drugs in general *US, 1967*
- Some kids call all dope "shit" or "junk," terms that were once synonyms for heroin. — Nicholas Von Hoffman, *We Are The People Our Parents Warned Us Against*, p. 65, 1967
- Willie's operation was very big because of the tremendous demand for the shit. — Richard Condon, *Prizzi's Family*, p. 44, 1986

4 things; possessions *US, 1969*
- They thought it was some strange shit, but glanced at one another, realizing that she liked to fuck. — Steve Cannon, *Groove, Bang, and Jive Around*, 1969
- [P]eople telling you how to do your shit. — Frank Zappa, *The Real Frank Zappa Book*, 1989
- It's the little differences. A lotta same shit we got here, they got there, but there they're a little different. — *Pulp Fiction*, 1994

5 anything at all *US, 1995*
- He didn't recognize shit. — Quentin Tarantino, *From Dusk Till Dawn*, p. 12, 1995

6 et cetera *US, 1999*
- It's so cool. Like all the cool people live here and shit. — *200 Cigarettes*, 1999

7 used as a basis for extreme comparisons *US, 1957*
- Well, sure as shit and taxes, he comes there every night just as regular as you can set your watch by him. — William Burroughs, *Naked Lunch*, p. 175, 1957
- [T]his is as cool as shit. "There can't be anything better than this." — Ted Nugent, *Ask*, p. 49, 5th May 1979

8 trouble *US, 1937*
- We troublemakers would be in deep shit if it weren't for our movement lawyers[.] — Jerry Rubin, *Do It!*, p. 160, 1970
- He's been in and outta shit since he was thirteen, and he's got a couple man-sized charges too. — Vernon E. Smith, *The Jones Men*, p. 123, 1974
- I'm extremely rebellious. I've cut every single day of school so far except one. I'm in deep shit with my mother at all times. — C.D. Payne, *Youth in Revolt*, 1993
- Listen up man, me an' my homeboy are in some serious shit. We're in a car we gotta get off the road, pronto! — *Pulp Fiction*, 1994

9 a contemptible person *UK, 1508*
Figurative use of excrement, since C16; often in combination as "regular shit," "arrogant shit," etc.
- And never believe what the police say because they're shits. — Macfarlane, Macfarlane and Robson, *The User*, p. 50, 1996

10 abuse; unfair treatment *UK, 1980*
- [The West Indian Youths] think because they've taken so much shit from the police, they're going to dole some back in court. — *New Society*, 24th January 1980

11 nonsense *UK, 1930*
- You can give me a whole ration of shit and this and that, and blah, blah, blah. — George V. Higgins, *The Friends of Eddie Coyle*, p. 75, 1971

12 used as a term of endearment *US, 1970*
Especially common in the phrase "little shit."
- "Ain't he the cutest little shit?" said Fluffy to Poppy. — Joseph Wambaugh, *The New Centurions*, p. 232, 1970

13 business *US, 1994*
- I apologize for bein' in your shit like I was. — *Pulp Fiction*, 1994

14 in the recording industry, a hit single *US, 1982*
- — Arnold Shaw, *Dictionary of American Pop/Rock*, p. 348, 1982

▸ **have your shit together; get your shit together**
to be focused, organized, self-confident *US, 1970*
- "We've just got to get our shit together," the theme ran, but the issue of "how?" was never resolved and the more important question "why?" was never asked. — Raymond Mungo, *Famous Long Ago*, p. 49, 1970
- Charlie's definitely got his shit together. — *Full Metal Jacket*, 1987

▸ **in deep shit**
in serious trouble *US, 1999*
- Val, listen to me. We are in deep shit, here. — *200 Cigarettes*, 1999

▸ **in the shit**
in combat *US, 1987*
- I am fucking bored to death, man. I gotta get back in the shit. I ain't heard a shot fired in anger in weeks. — *Full Metal Jacket*, 1987

▸ **run shit down**
to discuss something; to inform someone; to explain something *US, 1970*
- This is no "Introduction." I'm just glad for the chance to run some shit down, cur up some things, in the context of relating to Jerry. — Eldridge Cleaves, *Do It! (Introduction)*, 1970

▸ **the shit**
the best *US, 1990*
- CHRIS: If I was going to college I'd go to one of them Black colleges they got down south. MONSTER: Yeah, that's the shit. — *Boyz N The Hood*, 1990
- I wish I had a quarterback like you in Arizona. You're the shit. — *Jerry Maguire*, 1996
- You were the shit if you came to school with food from there. — Earl "DMX" Simmons, *E.A.R.L.*, p. 26, 2002
- "You think you're the shit? You're nothing." — Linden Dalecki, *Kid B*, p. 234, 2006

shit *verb*

1 to defecate *UK, 1308*
Conventional English for about 500 years from the C14, then, sometime in the C19, slipped into vulgarity.
- They were so close to each other that if one wanted to shit, the other one had to. — Oscar Lewis, *La Vida*, p. 66, 1966

2 to deceive someone; to lie to someone or stretch the truth *US, 1934*
- "You're shitting me," says Mule. "I wouldn't shit you. You're my favorite turd," says the chief. — Darryl Ponicsan, *The Last Detail*, p. 17, 1970
- "You shittin' me?" "Would I shit you? You're my favorite turd." — Richard Price, *The Wanderers*, p. 25, 1974
- "You're not shitting me," Finney said. "Officer," I said, "for all I know, I am shitting you." — George Higgins, *Kennedy for the Defense*, p. 76, 1980
- Don't shit a shitter. — Elmore Leonard, *Cat Chaser*, 1982

▸ **I shit thee not**
I am serious *US, 1967*
- "In the words of a sergeant I once had," Max said, "I shit thee not." — John Williams, *The Man Who Cried I Am*, p. 301, 1967

▸ **shit a brick**
to have a difficult time accepting something; to react with anger *US, 1971*
- When I told Woody and the brass about this coup, they practically shit a brick. I'm talkin' an adobe brick. — *Natural Born Killers*, 1994
- Yep, Gil Green shit a brick when he saw the bill. — Stephen J. Cannell, *King Con*, p. 17, 1997

▸ **shit nickels**
to be very frightened *US, 1968*
- — Collin Baker et al., *College Undergraduate Slang Study Conducted at Brown University*, p. 193, 1968

▸ **shit or get off the pot**
used for urging action *CANADA, 1961*
- Nixon went through the roof. "There comes a time in matters like this when you've got to either shit or get off the pot." — Chris Matthews, *Hardball*, p. 173, 1998

▸ **shit your pants**
to be terrified *US, 1994*
To lose control over your excretory functions is noted as a symptom of extreme terror; however, this is used figuratively (most of the time), often as an exaggeration.
- He went into this whole story and he sent the letter and he was shitting in his pants, waiting for the FCC to show up. — Howard Stern, *Private Parts*, p. 140, 1994

shit *adjective*
bad *US, 1950*
- I have had the worse shitluck possible with that book and it is the same thing all the time with whatever I do. — Jack Kerouac, *Letter to Neal Cassady*, p. 239, 3rd December 1950
- When the job was finished, Rodrigo paid us with an ounce of shit grass and some cash. — Tina Russell, *Porno Star*, p. 7, 1973
- "The fuckers [the police] are just covering the whole park." "Shit bastards!" — John Rechy, *The Sexual Outlaw*, p. 223, 1977

shit-all *noun*
nothing, nothing at all *US, 1981*
A variation of **FUCK ALL**.
- Leo never done much time and certainly didn't do any since he was just a kid that didn't know shit-all from what he was doing so he was always getting caught. — George V. Higgins, *The Rat on Fire*, p. 107, 1981
- Well, nothing recent if it was a conviction for shit-all, because a con for shit-all meant you weren't much of a villain. — Garry Bushell, *The Face*, p. 33, 2001

shit and git *verb*
to leave quickly *US, 1990*
- I've only got one engine, Jack, and if that bastard quits / It'll be up there all by itself, 'cause I will shit and git. — Joseph Tuso, *Singing the Vietnam Blues*, p. 69, 1990
- — Michael Dalton Johnson, *Talking Trash with Redd Foxx*, p. 122, 1994

shit-ass *noun*
a despicable person *US, 1942*
- I had Reggie figured—Earl is a man, a boss, uptown or downtown, where Reggie is a shitass and he knows it. — Edwin Torres, *Carlito's Way*, p. 83, 1975

- Cocky shitass doesn't quite describe him accurately enough, and I'm not sure arrogant prick does either. — Dan Jenkins, *The Money-Whipped Steer-Job Three-Jack Give-Up Artist*, p. 75, 2001

shit-ass *adjective*
despicable, of poor quality *US, 1967*

- [I]t could've been five, motherfucking shitass car, but it's four, four people in two nights, only one tonight, four. — John Rechy, *Numbers*, p. 107, 1967
- Enough of these shit-ass questions, let's fuck. (Caption) — *Screw*, p. 6, 19th January 1970
- Shit ass punk! — *Airheads*, 1994
- Awww, it's just been a shitass day. Every inch of it hot and miserable. — Quentin Tarantino, *From Dusk Till Dawn*, p. 3, 1995

shitball *noun*
a despicable person *US, 1998*

- Answer the question, shitball. — *Something About Mary*, 1998

shitbird *noun*
a despicable person *US, 1951*

- Re-assuring, somehow, in a world fraught with change, that Louie remains the Eternal Shit-Bird. — James Blake, *The Joint*, p. 36, 23rd December 1951
- "Get that shitbird out of here." — Leonard Gardner, *Fat City*, p. 155, 1969
- I deliberately ignored a staff sergeant who called me a shit-bird. — William Pelfrey, *The Big V*, p. 2, 1972
- Last time I saw this shitbird he was flying off in a green and white helicopter. — Stephen J. Cannell, *The Tin Collectors*, p. 288, 2001

shit bowl *noun*
a toilet *US, 1967*

- P.S. Tear this up and flush it down the shit bowl. — Piri Thomas, *Down These Mean Streets*, p. 266, 1967
- I was sitting crosslegged and funky on the floor, next to the shitbowl. — Clarence Cooper Jr., *The Farm*, p. 81, 1967
- Talk to the shitblow. You'll find you got a lot in common with each other. — Miguel Pinero, *Short Eyes*, p. 45, 1975

shitbrains; shit-brain *noun*
a stupid person *US, 1970*

- I before e except after c, shitbrains. — Darryl Ponicsan, *The Last Detail*, p. 115, 1970

shit bucket *noun*
a lowly, disgusting place or thing *US, 1987*

- "Last time I checked, that's still against the law, even in a shitbucket town like this." — Carl Hiaasen, *Double Whammy*, p. 88, 1987

shitburger *noun*
poor-quality food *US, 1971*

- [A] highway-side, plasticated shitburger place like that was the safest place anyone could imagine to eat in an integrated group. — Jeffrey Golden, *Watermelon Summer*, p. 40, 1971

shit-burner *noun*
a person assigned to the task of cleaning out latrines, dousing the spoils with fuel, and burning the mixture *US, 1979*
Coined during the Vietnam war.

- Mama, I'm gonna make you a little present for bein' a numbah one shit-burner. — David Berry, *G.R. Point*, p. 21, 1979

shitcan *noun*
1 any wastebasket *US, 1948*

- — *American Speech*, p. 38, February 1948: "Talking under water: speech in submarines"

2 a bathroom; an improvised outdoor toilet *US, 1981*

- "While this's going on, Mickey's in the shitcan standing on top of the sink." — Ovid Demaris, *The Last Mafioso*, p. 37, 1981
- "Build a wooden cover for it that has a hole to sit over and you have a shit can." — David Donovan, *Once a Warrior King*, p. 41, 1985

shitcan *verb*
to throw something away; to discharge someone from employment *US, 1975*

- I was working on my summation—I wrote it all down, then I shitcanned it. — Edwin Torres, *Carlito's Way*, p. 136, 1975
- I would hate to see you get shitcanned and go on welfare. — James Ellroy, *Because the Night*, p. 430, 1984

- "What do you say we shitcan the task force?" the chief said. — Carl Hiaasen, *Tourist Season*, p. 324, 1986
- [H]e has to give me a bunch of shit first and say if his boss catches him giving out free tans he'll be shitcanned. — Jay McInerney, *Story of My Life*, p. 49, 1988
- Shitcan this movie so we don't get called names on the Internet anymore. — Kevin Smith, *Jay and Silent Bob Strike Back*, p. 125, 2001

shit-chute *noun*
the rectum *US, 1977*

- "The blonde wormed his tongue up my shit-chute." — Dennis Cooper, *Closer*, p. 74, 1989
- "I like to fuck dames up the shit chute." — Charles Rosen, *Barney Polan's Game*, p. 143, 1998

shit creek *noun*
▸ **up shit creek; up shit creek without a paddle; up the creek**
stranded, in trouble *US, 1868*
Embellishments abound.

- How about writing a composition for me, for English? I'll be up the creek if I don't got the goddamn thing in by Monday, the reason I ask. — J.D. Salinger, *Catcher in the Rye*, p. 28, 1951
- I'm really up shit creek, there's just no commercial person who can understand what I'm doing. — Jack Kerouac, *Letter to Lucien Carr*, p. 562, 24th February 1956
- [T]hose fucking boogs may turn cannibal any minute! Then we'd really be up shit creek. — Terry Southern, *Blue Movie*, p. 182, 1970
- Well, then, I guess you're really up shit creek. — *The Blues Brothers*, 1980

shit disturber *noun*
a troublemaker *US, 1977*

- Miller is one of those people who calls himself a "community organizer" and whom other people, both admirers and detractors, call a "s—disturber." — *San Francisco Chronicle*, p. 19, 25th October 1977
- "Hongisto is a great — disturber," said one Feinstein aide. — *San Francisco Chronicle*, p. 20, 17th August 1979

shit-eating grin *noun*
a broad smile, ingratiating and unctuous *US, 1957*

- So he kicks it over after 5 minutes and we listen to it cough and miss and Spook went puttin' off with a shiteatin' grin on his face. — Hubert Selby Jr., *Last Exit to Brooklyn*, p. 101, 1957
- Big Boot, booty-strucked, booted it to her from behind, a shit-eating grin on his face. — Steve Cannon, *Groove, Bang, and Jive Around*, p. 193, 1969
- I don't know what happened, but she had a big shit-eating grin and kept hugging me. — Larry Heinemann, *Close Quarters*, p. 217, 1977
- He always have that shit-eating grin? — *Ten Things I Hate About You*, 1999

shitepoke *noun*
a despicable person *US, 1926*

- Shapian, you shitepoke, when you going to start doing what I'm paying for? — Max Shulman, *Anyone Got a Match?*, p. 227, 1964

shit-face *noun*
1 a despised person *UK, 1937*

- Mcginn had said you little shitface to him. — Gilbert Sorrentino, *Steelwork*, p. 17, 1970
- Take your fuckin' hands off me, shit-face, or I'll knock you out, alright? — Paul Fraser and Shane Meadows, *TwentyFourSeven*, p. 98, 1997

2 used as an intensifier of the degree of intoxication *US, 1977*

- He went out to the kitchen to rinse the dishcloth and told Elwin why didn't he, instead of standing there getting shit-face drunker than he already was, why didn't he straight up the mess in the kitchen. — Elmore Leonard, *Touch*, p. 6, 1977

shitfaced *adjective*
drunk *US, 1968*

- My balls ached, no sleep for two days, dirty, grubby and still shit faced I suffered for 24 hours. — Hunter S. Thompson, *Fear and Loathing in America*, p. 30, 31st January 1968: Letter from Oscar Acosta
- I would've been freezing my balls off except it was summer and anyway I was so shitfaced I was probably good for about twenty below. — George V. Higgins, *The Rat on Fire*, p. 17, 1981
- I hope it isn't going to be one of those nights where they get shitfaced and take us to a pasture to tip cows. — *Heathers*, 1988
- Leave it to you to use big words when you're shitfaced. — *Ten Things I Hate About You*, 1999

shitfire!
used as an oath *US, 1970*

- Shitfire! I don't know. — Darryl Ponicsan, *The Last Detail*, p. 78, 1970
- "Shits fire, boy! All we got to do is send a whistle, and when she hears it, she comes runnin'[.]" — Donald Goines, *Swamp Man*, p. 38, 1974
- "Shitfire, y'all oughta hear my own daddy cuss when he feelin' the need!" — Jess Mowry, *Six Out Seven*, p. 30, 1993

shit fit *noun*
a tantrum *US, 1968*
- She has a shit fit and calls him two or three choice names. — Angelo d'Arcangelo, *The Homosexual Handbook*, p. 230, 1968
- Coach has been having shitfits. — John Sayles, *Union Dues*, p. 47, 1977

shit-for-brains *noun*
an idiot *US, 1959*
- Hey, shit-for-brains, be careful not to scratch that thing, huh? — *Something About Mary*, 1998

shit-for-brains *adjective*
stupid *US, 2003*
- And that score was presented in the shit-for-brains 2003 editorial[.] — Al Franken, *Lies*, p. 173, 2003

shit freak *noun*
a person with a fetish for excrement *US, 1973*
- "I had an idea that he was also a shit freak, and I didn't want to get into that." — Jennifer Sills, *Massage Parlor*, p. 215, 1973
- "I know amputees and ex-cons and shit freaks and killers. But I can't say that I know any chicks with dicks." — Ethan Morden, *Some Men Are Lookers*, p. 48, 1997

shit happens
used for conveying the inevitability of misfortune *US, 1983*
A tremendously popular catchphrase in the mid-to late 1980s in the US, spawning dozens of jokes with the predictable punch-line, tee-shirts with lists of various religions' interpretations of the phrase, etc.
- — Connie Eble (Editor), *UNC-CH Campus Slang*, p. 5, Spring 1983
- He might not've hit anybody, but at least they'd know the truth of that old saying, shit happens. When you least expect, too. — Elmore Leonard, *Killshot*, p. 137, 1989

shithead *noun*
an objectionable, obnoxious, despised person *UK, 1961*
- And everybody sees him and says, "That shithead, look at him!" — Lenny Bruce, *The Essential Lenny Bruce*, p. 203, 1967
- At the sundial are 500 people ready to follow Mark Rudd (whom they don't particularly like because he always refers to President Kirk as "that shithead") into the Low Library administration building[.] — James Simon Kunen, *The Strawberry Statement*, p. 28, 1968
- I had been there with those fuzzy little shitheads—and so, I sensed, had the desk clerk. — Hunter S. Thompson, *Fear and Loathing in Las Vegas*, p. 107, 1971
- Word of advice, shithead, don't you ever wake up. — *Kill Bill*, 2003

shitheel *noun*
a despicable person *US, 1935*
- "She's on top, so let's face it—she's a shit-heel again." — Jacqueline Susann, *Valley of the Dolls*, p. 453, 1966
- Well, there's going to be a grand jury on these shitheels, and you will appear as a witness against them. — Peter Maas, *Serpico*, p. 217, 1973
- I've got no respect for a shit-heel like that. — George V. Higgins, *The Rat on Fire*, p. 115, 1981
- Keep that in mind—that I loved them—even though they were both world-class shitheels. — James Ellroy, *Hollywood Nocturnes*, p. 199, 1994
- "Why were they in a closet?" "Because my shitheel husband pulled 'em off the wall." — Carl Hiaasen, *Skinny Dip*, p. 130, 2004

shithole; shit hole *noun*
1 the anus and rectum *US, 1999*
- His spear entered the man from below, just between his balls and his shit-hole. — Julian Rathbone, *The Last English King*, p. 326, 1999
- "Don't keep my shithole waiting." I knelt behind him and smelled the exciting musk from the open crevice and asshole. — Hal Reeves, *Hard as They Come*, p. 196, 2003
- Then Suzie says, "Lick my asshole." "Damn, I need this woman's number." "I'm not too sure about this, Dark. It is still her shit hole, you know." — Dark, *The Fever*, p. 76, 2006

2 a despicable person *US, 1976*
- "Yeah, you little shithole. An' I ain't gettin' nuttin'." — William Brashler, *City Dogs*, p. 54, 1976

3 a bad place; a dirty, run-down, or disreputable place *US, 1965*
- "Well, we fixed them but good. Opened up with everything we had on the shit-hole," he continued. — *The Berkeley Barb*, p. 2, 3rd December 1965
- Fucking shithole, that place, it's like, it's like ruined. — *Saturday Night Fever*, 1977
- Or you could get Union Correctional, over west of there not too far. It don't matter which though, they're both shitholes. — Elmore Leonard, *Maximum Bob*, p. 107, 1991
- [H]e had dug in this heels, chased off my other roommate, and turned it into a reasonable replica of his Eleventh Street shithole. — James St. James, *Party Monster*, p. 183, 1999

shithook *noun*
1 the hand *US, 1970*
- — *Current Slang*, p. 20, Winter 1970

2 a thoroughly unpleasant person *US, 1968*
- — Collin Baker et al., *College Undergraduate Slang Study Conducted at Brown University*, p. 193, 1968

3 a CH-47 Chinook helicopter *US, 1972*
Vietnam war usage.
- When the loach buzzed in, a CP RTO ran away down to the pad yelling, "Pop smoke." — William Pelfrey, *The Big V*, p. 74, 1972
- Hueys were fun, but the shithooks were great because they were faster than a huey, more maneuverable. — Harry Maurer, *Strange Ground*, p. 204, 1989
- The Chinook was a huge helicopter called the "shit-hook," because it could lift anything. — Mary Reynolds Powell, *A World of Hurt*, p. 55, 2000

shit-hot *noun*
a highly skilled fighter pilot *US, 1983*
- — *American Speech*, p. 124, Summer 1986: "The language of naval fighter pilots"

shit-hot *adjective*
extremely competent and respected *US, 1984*
- We thought we were really shit-hot. — Wallace Terry, *Bloods*, p. 155, 1984
- "You're a mighty scrappy chap / You're shit hot and we know it." — Joseph Tuso, *Singing the Vietnam Blues*, p. 96, 1990: Hallelujah III

shithouse *noun*
1 a bathroom *UK, 1795*
- And I saw the Southern white man who has nothing between him and the lowest Negro except a segregated toilet. No wonder so many of them have shithouse ways. — Dick Gregory, *Nigger*, p. 170, 1964
- I wondered how some guys could take the chance of cooking up and shooting up in any public place like a shithouse[.] — Piri Thomas, *Down These Mean Streets*, p. 117, 1967
- The sound of the Temps still gitting away in the Gumbo House seeped into the shithouse. — Steve Cannon, *Groove, Bang, and Jive Around*, p. 6, 1969
- So I reached in my slide and came out with two boss threes / And said "Here, girl, go to the shithouse and get the weakness out of your knees." — Dennis Wepman et al., *The Life*, p. 52, 1976

2 a shoddy, dirty, unpleasant place *US, 1969*
- "But if you work in a shithouse like this for a while, you can go to any precinct and it would look great." — L.H. Whittemore, *Cop!*, p. 19, 1969
- At the same time he didn't want to wind up in a "shithouse" precinct like the two-eight (Twenty-eighth) or the two-five (Twenty-fifth). — Leonard Shecter and William Phillips, *On the Pad*, p. 122, 1973
- I'd have had you live like—like somebody. Not in this shithouse. — Edwin Torres, *After Hours*, p. 362, 1979

3 jail or prison *US, 1969*
- I thought, "If someone had told me a year ago I'd be back in a shit-house, I'd have thought he was nuts." — Iceberg Slim (Robert Beck), *Pimp*, p. 243, 1969

shithouse rumor *noun*
gossip *US, 1968*
A blunt version of the kinder and gentler "latrine rumor."
- — Carl Fleischhauer, *A Glossary of Army Slang*, p. 12, 1968

shitkicker *noun*
1 a tough, belligerent person *US, 1954*
- A shitkicker, you understand, is a gangly male who is all fists in the bunkhouse[.] — Bernard Wolfe, *The Late Risers*, p. 22, 1954
- But showing his scar is beautiful. That's just where he's at. He's a shitkicker. — Lenny Bruce, *The Essential Lenny Bruce*, p. 60, 1967
- Moke, wearing his new shitkicker image for all to see. — Elmore Leonard, *Stick*, p. 119, 1983
- "Well, he's a shit-kicker," they said, "he's a troublemaker." — Terry Southern, *Now Dig This*, p. 8, 1986

2 a country dweller, a rustic *US, 1966*
- Although he himself sometimes described his chain as a "bunch of shitkicker papers," he was proud of his position as a national political writer[.] — Timothy Crouse, *The Boys on the Bus*, pp. 39–40, 1973

3 a prostitute *US, 1967*
Far less common than the term **MUDKICKER**.
- Pimps also refer to the women as "cows" and "shitkickers." — Sara Harris, *The Lords of Hell*, p. 47, 1967

4 a fraudster, especially one who adopts a pose of extreme modesty *US, 1981*
- — Don Wilmeth, *The Language of American Popular Entertainment*, p. 238, 1981

shitkickers *noun*
heavy work shoes or work boots *US, 1974*
- He was an open apple knocker from the West Side wearing plain Monkey Ward jeans rather than Levi's and high-top horsehide shit kickers. — Earl Thompson, *Tattoo*, p. 55, 1974
- "You could bust your ass in those shitkickers you're wearin'," he said. — Jimmy Buffett, *Tales from Margaritaville*, p. 54, 1989
- He wore three-inch snakeskin shitkickers and walked with a swagger that suggested not brawn so much as hemorrhoidal tribulation. — Carl Hiaasen, *Lucky You*, p. 2, 1997
- Though your shitkickers are big, too, with steel toes. — Elmore Leonard, *Be Cool*, p. 8, 1999

shitless *adverb*
completely, entirely, to a great degree *UK, 1936*
- Thank you [for the applause], we needed that. This is the second time we've ever played in front of people. We're scared shitless. — Stephen Stills of Crosby, Stills and Nash, *Woodstock*, 1969
- The police were scared shitless and the massive crowds of angry protestors chased them for blocks. — *Screw*, p. 16, 25th July 1969
- Look at them now, scared shitless because for a change they're the target and they got nobody to shoot back at. — Mickey Spillane, *Last Cop Out*, p. 43, 1972
- I'm scared shitless, Ferris! What if Rooney guesses my voice? — *Ferris Bueller's Day Off*, 1986

shit list *noun*
an imagined list of those in disfavor *US, 1942*
- You're on my shit list from now on. — Norman Mailer, *The Naked & Dead*, p. 221, 1948
- If they're playing at Pine Knob usually we get them in the Sheraton, if the group isn't on the hotel's shit list. — Elmore Leonard, *Touch*, p. 28, 1977
- One was on their shit list: an old guy in a nursing home who'd boasted for years to anyone who'd listen that he'd been the Mayor of Munchkinland. — Armistead Maupin, *Maybe the Moon*, p. 56, 1992

shitload *noun*
a great deal of *US, 1992*
- I bet you won a shitload on Oakland. — *The Bad Lieutenant*, 1992
- I learn he's got money in foreign banks, plus, around five mil in hard cash, plus, loose diamonds and gold coins, a shitload of coins worth around four bills each. — Elmore Leonard, *Out of Sight*, p. 60, 1996
- And since I'm only on the set for a day, I've obviously missed a shitload of good stuff. — Anthony Petkovich, *The X Factory*, p. 14, 1997
- Jesus, you could get in a shitload of trouble for this. — *Cruel Intentions*, 1999

shitman *noun*
used as an intensifier of what follows *US, 1959*
- "Shitman. Ats a lot of bread." — Warren Miller, *The Cool World*, p. 4, 1959
- Shitman, this cat talking make me feel creepy. — Sara Harris, *The Lords of Hell*, p. 15, 1967

shitmobile *noun*
a run-down car *US, 1985*
- MAKE: SHITMOBILE. MODEL: OLD AND WEARY. — Stephen King, *Needful Things*, p. 273, 1991
- How is your truck? It's a shitmobile. — Jane Martin, *Criminal Hearts*, p. 41, 1992

shitogram *noun*
an especially virulent e-mail message *US, 1991*
- — Eric S. Raymond, *The New Hacker's Dictionary*, p. 319, 1991

shit on a shingle *noun*
chopped or creamed beef on toast *US, 1963*

- We asked what it was. "It's shit on a shingle, you stupid asshole," the counterman said. — Allan Sherman, *The Rape of the APE*, p. 69, 1973
- Outside of overhauling a diesel engine, fieldstripping a Remington typewriter, and preparing "shit-on-a-shingle" for four hundred, none of them knew the first thing[.] — Gary Linderer, *The Eyes of the Eagle*, p. 21, 1991

shit on a string *noun*
an elusive or difficult task *US, 1981*
- — *Maledicta*, p. 255, Summer/Winter 1981: "Five years and 121 dirty words later"

shit on my dick or blood on my knife
used for giving a prisoner a choice—submit to anal sex or be knifed *US, 1976*
- Always as I have heard the story the kid is caught in the bathhouse and offered the narrow choice of putting shit on someone's dick or blood on his knife. — Malcolm Braley, *False Starts*, p. 106, 1976
- You will hear a voice whisper in your ear, "shit on my dick or blood on my knife." — *alt.flame*, 4th February 1990
- After the initial gang rapes ("shit on my dick or blood on my knife") Eddie says he was lucky to find an Old Man. — Leonard Ashley, *What I Know About You*, p. 90, 2002

shit out of luck *adjective*
very unlucky *US, 1947*
- "We're as shit out of luck tonight as a barber in Berkeley," the key grip grumbles. — Grover Lewis, *Academy all the Way*, p. 24, 1974
- "So you see, my dear, you're shit out of luck." — Mario Puzo, *Fools Die*, p. 417, 1978

shitpacker *noun*
an anal-sex enthusiast *US, 1964*
- Say, there was asshole shellackers and shitpackers / and freaks who drunk blood from a menstruatin' womb. — Bruce Jackson, *Get Your Ass in the Water and Swim Like Me*, p. 146, 1964

shit paper *noun*
toilet paper *US, 1969*
- She pulled them halfway up her thighs, twisting her hips, paused, got two small pieces of shit paper and placed one inside her burned out asshole, the other inside the lips of her cunt. — Steve Cannon, *Groove, Bang, and Jive Around*, p. 13, 1969
- — *Maledicta*, p. 195, 1979: "A taboo-boo word revisited"
- Grunts in the field often carried their "shit paper" under the elastic band that secured the helmet cover or inside the helmet to provide "dry" insurance against sweat and rain. — Gregory Clark, *Words of the Vietnam War*, p. 464, 1990
- "O.G., will you holler down to the C.O. for some shit paper." — Jimmy Lerner, *You Got Nothing Coming*, p. 116, 2002

shitpicker *noun*
a notional menial, demeaning job *US, 1971*
- I wouldn't hire a shit-picker on the basis of the I Ching or whatever that book of magic speels is called[.] — Tom Robbins, *Another Roadside Attraction*, p. 129, 1971

Shitport *nickname*
Norfolk, Virginia *US, 1982*
- — Ralph de Sola, *Crime Dictionary*, p. 202, 1982

shitpot *noun*
a great deal of *US, 1968*
- — Collin Baker et al., *College Undergraduate Slang Study Conducted at Brown University*, p. 195, 1968
- Earlier, the LA Free Press let it all hang out and published the whole shitpot full of names. — *The Berkeley Tribe*, p. 4, 15th–21st August 1969
- Yeah, a shitpotful of the crew got deep-sixed. — Darryl Ponicsan, *The Last Detail*, p. 145, 1970

shit rain *noun*
a series of disastrous events *US, 1963*
- We now enter the era of the shitrain, President Johnson and the hardening of the arteries. — Hunter S. Thompson, *The Proud Highway*, p. 420, 22nd November 1963: Letter to William J. Kennedy

shits *noun*
▶ **for shits and giggles**
for no good reason *US, 2001*
Something is done, for example, for shits and giggles.
- — Don R. McCreary (Editor), *Dawg Speak*, 2001

▸ **the shits**
1 diarrhea *UK, 1947*
- I was excited by the whole thing plus the granola diet didn't do too well, and I had the shits. The first day I was squeezing my legs, I had the shits so bad. — Stephen Ziplow, *The Film Maker's Guide to Pornography*, p. 150, 1977
- Dana Andrews said prunes gave him the runs *Shits.* — Sal Piro and Michael Hess, *The Official "Rocky Horror Picture Show" Audience Participation Guide*, p. 6, 1991
- If you drink enough, you will cease to be concerned with either your piles or your inevitably on-going case of the shits. — Steven Treanor, *The Guardian*, 18th March 2002

2 the worst *US, 1971*
- "Now isn't that the shits," exclaimed Nuclear Phyllis[.] — Tom Robbins, *Another Roadside Attraction*, p. 34, 1971

shit sandwich *noun*
a troubling, odious situation *US, 1968*
- — Stephen H. Dill (Editor), *Current Slang*, Spring 1968
- The review you had on "Shark Sandwich," which was merely a two word review—just said "shit sandwich." — *This is Spinal Tap*, 1984
- In other words, it's a huge shit sandwich and we're all gonna have to take a bite. — *Full Metal Jacket*, 1987
- And "shit sandwich" is a good generic negative review for any song, movie, TV show, or music video. — Editors of Ben is Dead, *Retrohell*, p. 141, 1997

shit, shave, shower, shine
used as a jocular reminder of a man's tasks before going out on the town *US, 1985*
Multiple variants, probably coined in the US Marine Corps as a preliberty litany.
- Shit, shower 'n shave. — Donald Goines, *The Busting Out of an Ordinary Man*, p. 66, 1985

shit stain *noun*
a stupid, despicable person *US, 1997*
- I'm glad it's happened in a place like Montreal, so these bigoted shit stains who call in on sports-talk shows can't blame it all on the blacks. — George Carlin, *Brian Droppings*, p. 48, 1997

shitstain *adjective*
despicable, unpleasant, foolish *US, 1995*
- all her shitstain friends that screw with her head all year and tell her I'm a lousy husband — Howard Stern, *Miss America*, p. 155, 1995

shit-stick *noun*
a despised person *US, 1964*
- — *American Speech*, p. 298, December 1964

shit sticks!
used as a mildly profane expression of disappointment *US, 1964*
- — *American Speech*, p. 298, December 1964

shit stompers *noun*
heavy work boots *US, 1975*
- — *American Speech*, p. 66, Spring–Summer 1975: "Razorback slang"

shit stopper *noun*
a prank *US, 1981*
- — *Maledicta*, p. 255, Summer/Winter 1981: "Five years and 121 dirty words later"

shitstorm *noun*
an extremely serious situation *US, 1962*
- They finally got to arguing with each other and created such a shitstorm I lost my quarter-cent-a-pound bonus for not missin' a day[.] — Ken Kesey, *One Flew Over the Cuckoo's Nest*, p. 206, 1962
- Hoss, you ask my wife to dance one more time and you gonna dance yourself into a shit storm. — Ken Weaver, *Texas Crude*, p. 124, 1984
- Everyone looked up—GIs and zips—and knew it was every incoming round left in Creation, a wild and bloody shitstorm, a ball-busting cataclysm. — Larry Heinemann, *Paco's Story*, p. 14, 1986
- The Bone knows you can never be too prepared in prison for a shitstorm. — Jimmy Lerner, *You Got Nothing Coming*, p. 179, 2002

shitsure *adverb*
certainly, definitely *US, 1981*
- It's one thing to demand technical excellence if you're Duke Ellington or Charles Mingus for that matter for shit fucking sure[.] — Lester Bangs, *Psychotic Reactions and Carburetor Dung*, p. 373, 1981

shitter *noun*
1 a toilet or bathroom *US, 1969*
- "You left the shitter open," he said. — Leonard Gardner, *Fat City*, p. 82, 1969
- I sit on the shitter waiting for Miss Thing to do her thing. — Paul Glover, *Words from the House of the Dead*, 1974
- "It looks like a grenade blew up the shitter." — Bob Stoffey, *Cleared Hot!*, p. 85, 1992
- My life is in the shitter right about now, so if you don't mind, I'd like to stew a bit. — *Clerks*, 1994

2 a criminal, usually a burglar, who fetishistically defecates at the scene of the crime *US, 1970*
- Anyway, he's a shitter and wouldn't it be nice if somebody would wake up some night and grab a shotgun and catch the bastard squatting on their kitchen table just squeezing out a big one[.] — Joseph Wambaugh, *The New Centurions*, p. 136, 1970
- "Speaking of which, I assume you're not a shitter or anything." — George Higgins, *The Digger's Game*, p. 6, 1973
- "You ain't the shitter, are ya? We got a burglar around here hitting all over, I mean like a blanket, and I'll be damned if he ain't a shitter." — William Brashler, *City Dogs*, p. 12, 1976
- "In there leaving his calling card," Maurice said, and Kenneth laughed. "White Boy's a shitter." — Elmore Leonard, *Out of Sight*, p. 256, 1996

3 the anus and rectum *UK, 2005*
- "Wipe my shitter," the kid said to himself. He took some sort of a pass at his rear end, dropped the toilet paper on the ground, and pulled up his pants. — Jimmy Breslin, *World Without End, Amen*, p. 185, 1973
- "Ooh," she wailed, "you're tongue-fucking my shitter!" — Richard Meltzer, *A Whore Just Like the Rest*, p. 429, 1991
- I was out of my mind with excitement. "Shoot everything you've got up my shitter," I said, "right up my nasty asshole." — *Letters to Penthouse XII*, p. 124, 2001
- Kelly Star takes Big Lex's anaconda down her throat (with accompanying tsunami of drool), in her cunt, and—most impressively—up her shitter before face-fielding his man muck. — Editors of Adult Video News, *The AVN Guide to the 500 Greatest Adult Films of All Time*, p. 39, 2005

4 a liar; a braggart; a bluffer *US, 1982*
A shortened form of **BULLSHITTER**.
- Don't shit a shitter. — Elmore Leonard, *Cat Chaser*, 1982

5 a horse *US, 1958*
- — *American Speech*, p. 270, December 1958: "Ranching terms from eastern Washington"

6 a prison cell used for solitary confinement *US, 1972*
- They might put us in the shitter [solitary], but I wouldn't get into too much trouble. — Bruce Jackson, *In the Life*, p. 397, 1972
- — Charles Shafer, *Folk Speech in Texas Prisons*, p. 213, 1990

shitting in high cotton (and wiping with the leaves)
enjoying prosperous times *US, 1984*
- Since ol' Jim Ed's took over his daddy's feed store, he's shittin' in high cotton and wipin' with the leaves. Drivin' a new used car, an' got three-four pairs of shoes. — Ken Weaver, *Texas Crude*, p. 124, 1984

shit train *noun*
a great number; a lot of *US, 1989*
- I refer, of course, to the shit train of eight (8) felony-assault, etc., charges that were brought against me by a maniac neighbor at dawn on Saturday morning[.] — Hunter S. Thompson, *Songs of the Doomed*, p. 283, 1989

shitty *adjective*
awful; of poor quality *US, 1924*
- And then Jenny explained how she had been feeling "absolutely shitty" and gone back to Dr. Sheppard, not for consultation, but confrontation. — Erich Segal, *Love Story*, p. 113, 1970
- If it sounds GOOD to YOU, it's bitchen; and if it sounds BAD to YOU, it's shitty. — Frank Zappa, *The Real Frank Zappa Book*, p. 188, 1989

shitville *noun*
any remote, forsaken town *US, 1977*
- — *Maledicta*, p. 12, Summer 1977: "A word for it!"
- Yes, you found a Johnson, but you waded through Shitville to find him. — William Burroughs, *Queer*, p. 9, 1985

shitwagon *noun*
a garbage truck *US, 1999*

- "That's how come you gotta come inside for a minute, to tell her it's no bullshit, you paid me three grand to rent out the shitwagon." — Carl Hiaasen, *Sick Puppy*, p. 26, 1999

shitwrap *noun*

a despicable person *US, 2001*

- You're his wife, and you're walking around with the shitwrap who dropped him. — Stephen J. Cannell, *The Tin Collectors*, p. 75, 2001

shiv *verb*

to stab someone *US, 1951*

- The Pachuco shivs Mace while the big stoop stands there all goofed off with a rod in his mitt. — Thurston Scott, *Cure it with Honey*, p. 160, 1951
- Do you know who shived him? — Robert Edmond Alter, *Carny Kill*, p. 23, 1966

shiv; chiv; shivvie *noun*

a homemade knife-like weapon, especially one fashioned in prison *US, 1915*

Almost certainly evolved from C17 "chive" (knife).

- And I don't like you, and if you make a move for your shiv I'm going to beat the piss outa you. — Irving Shulman, *The Amboy Dukes*, p. 209, 1947
- Because they're two of 'em and they got a shiv they're the toughest mugs in the world. — Mickey Spillane, *One Lonely Night*, p. 55, 1951
- "Let's see the shiv," he said. "The what?" "The pig-sticker, the switchblade, the knife." — Jim Thompson, *Savage Night*, p. 69, 1953
- There were wild Negro queers, sullen guys with guns, shiv-packing seamen, thin, non-committal junkies, and an occasional well-dressed middle-aged detective[.] — Jack Kerouac, *On the Road*, p. 131, 1957

shivaree *noun*

a group mocking *US, 1805*

- It seemed to Manning that every prisoner in the big yard had joined in the shivaree, just as it seemed to him they were all identical—jeering mouths wrenched open under the round stiff-billed hats. — Malcolm Braly, *On the Yard*, p. 37, 1967

shivver *noun*

a criminal who attacks victims with a knife *US, 1957*

- Then Bull came out with a couple of knives and started showing us how to disarm a would-be shivver in a dark alley. — Jack Kerouac, *On the Road*, p. 154, 1957

shiznit *noun*

the very best; something of great quality *US, 1996*

Used with "the." A euphemistic embellishment of **THE SHIT**.

- — Connie Eble (Editor), *UNC-CH Campus Slang*, p. 5, Fall 1996
- Nobody has these babies, no way, not the shiznit. — *Traffic*, 2000

shizzle my mizzle fizzle dizzle!

used as a contemptuous expression of dismissal *US, 2003*

Popular hip-hop cryptography disguising "suck my mother fucking dick!"

- "Shizzle my socialist mizzle fizzle dizzle," as [Tony] Benn probably didn't say recently. — *Bang*, November 2003

shlemiel; schlemiel; schlemihl *noun*

a bungler with chronic bad luck *US, 1948*

Yiddish. During the opening montage of the US situation comedy *Laverne and Shirley* (ABC, 1976–83), the lead characters, played by Penny Marshall and Cindy Williams, skip down a Milwaukee sidewalk singing "1–2–3–4–5–6–7–8, Shlemiel, shlamazzel, Hassenpepper Incorporated," giving "shlemiel" its highest profile to date.

- In the Jewish folk-mind, however, the schlemiel is conceived of as an awkward, bungling fellow, plagued not only with "butter-fingers" but with absolutely no skill in coping with any situation in life. — Nathan Ausubel, *A Treasury of Jewish Folklore*, p. 343, 1948
- Despite having done a thousand lunch meetings at Nate 'n' Al's, Orson never got the Yiddish right. He said kvel when he meant kvetch, schmutz when he mean schvitz and schlmeil for schlemazel. — Joseph Wambaugh, *Finnegan's Week*, 1993

shlepper; schlepper *noun*

an inconsequential person; a nobody *US, 1934*

- Once I was a schlepper, now I'm Miss Mazeppa. — Stephen Sondheim, *You Gotta Get a Gimmick*, 1960
- My outfit didn't have nothing to do with this Asbury schlepper who is making all this trouble for us. — Richard Condon, *Prizzi's Money*, p. 81, 1994

shlepper bag; schlepper bag *noun*

a tote bag *US, 2000*

- Slosberg, a Boca Raton entrepreneur whose interests include the promotional materials business, recently began handing out what he calls the "schlepper bag," a burlap tote bearing his name. — *Palm Beach (Florida) Post*, p. 1B, 17th July 2000

shlimazel; schlimazel *noun*

a person with chronic bad luck *US, 1948*

A blend of German and Hebrew, literally translated as "bad luck."

- [A] wit has made the following neat distinction between these two types: "A schlemihl is a man who spills a bowl of hot soup on a schlimazel." — Nathan Ausubel, *A Treasury of Jewish Folklore*, p. 343, 1948
- Just bring me a cold drink, you old shlimazel. — Joseph Wambaugh, *The Blue Knight*, p. 12, 1973

shlock; schlack; schlock *noun*

shoddy, defective or cheaply made merchandise *US, 1915*

From German to Yiddish to American slang.

- [A] grind house of double features and a schlock store "Selling Out!" in a permanent "Giant Moving Sale!" — Stephen Longstreet, *The Flesh Peddlers*, p. 176, 1962
- He's been serving time here since 1960, greeting folks with his cane, pointing the way upstairs at the schlock tourist restaurant next to the Winter Garden. — Josh Alan Friedman, *Tales of Times Square*, p. 58, 1986

shlocky; schlocky *adjective*

shoddy *US, 1968*

- A bunch of schlocky broads, the lowest. — Albert Goldman, *Freak Show*, p. 216, 1968

shlong; schlong *noun*

the penis *US, 1969*

From the Yiddish.

- His shlong brings to mind the fire hoses coiled along the corridors at school. — Philip Roth, *Portnoy's Complaint*, p. 54, 1969
- With regard to the erection per se there is no relationship between the size of a non-erect putz and its size at erection (so stop comparing schlongs in the locker room)[.] — *Screw*, p. 8, 8th December 1969
- The only hand on your schlong is gonna be yours. — *Diner*, 1982
- There's this talking snake and a naked chick and then this dude puts a leaf on his schlong! Heh heh heh. — Mike Judge and Joe Stillman, *Beavis and Butt-Head Do America*, p. 49, 1997

shlub; schlub *noun*

an inept, slovenly person *US, 1964*

- The American male as a pussy-whipped shlub. — James Ellroy, *Destination Morgue*, p. 174, 2004

shlubby *adjective*

ill-mannered; poorly dressed *US, 1968*

Yiddish from the Slavic *zhlob* (a coarse person).

- [A] rather shlubby Steve Lawrence ("sitting in" for Johnny Carson) asked his guest what his friends called him[.] — Albert Goldman, *Freak Show*, p. 67, 1968
- And shlubby guys find a woman and get married every day. — *Playbill*, 8th October 2002

shlump *verb*

to physically beat *US, 1962*

- "Don't hurt him serious. Just shlump him enough to make him want to get it up in a hurry." — Charles Perry, *Portrait of a Young Man Drowning*, p. 125, 1962

shlumping *noun*

a physical beating *US, 1962*

- "Listen, you guys know how to do a shlumping?" — Charles Perry, *Portrait of a Young Man Drowning*, p. 124, 1962

shm-; schm- *prefix*

used for creating a Yiddish-sounding reduplication of an English word, usually with the intention of diminishing the importance of the original word *US, 1929*

- Disguise, schmisguise. So you wear also a gold earring? That's a disguise too? — Bernard Wolfe, *The Late Risers*, p. 218, 1954
- "Fancy-shmancy" was all she said to me on the phone. — Philip Roth, *Goodbye, Columbus*, p. 14, 1959
- She snarled, "Lonely, schmlonely," folded her arms, slouched deep in her seat, and went to sleep. — John Nichols, *The Sterile Cuckoo*, p. 33, 1965

- Liberal schmiberal. — Lenny Bruce, *The Essential Lenny Bruce*, p. 13, 1967
- Cover, shmover—you all hated his songs, too. — Kevin Smith, *Jay and Silent Bob Strike Back*, p. 47, 2001

shmaltz; schmaltz *noun*
excessive sentimentality, especially in music, writing, etc. *US, 1935*
From German *schmaltz* (fat, lard) via Yiddish, with a suggestion of something too greasy to be easily digested.
- Will you be content with that standard box-office schmalz? — J.D. Salinger, *Franny and Zooey*, p. 60, 1961
- Here, reducing the rockola to showbiz schmaltz (lots movie stars on the cover) proves more amusing than annoying[.] — Chuck Eddy, *Stairway to Hell*, p. 14, 1991

'shman *noun*
a first-year college student, a freshman *US, 1987*
- — *New York Times*, 12th April 1987

shmatte; schmatte *noun*
a less than elegant house dress *US, 1969*
Yiddish.
- "A very plain drab person," he said, "who dresses in shmattas." — Phillip Roth, *Portnoy's Complaint*, p. 92, 1969

shmear; schmear *noun*
a bribe *US, 1950*
- — Hyman E. Goldin et al., *Dictionary of American Underworld Lingo*, p. 185, 1950

shmear; schmear *verb*
to bribe someone *US, 1985*
- When the cops were still ticketing you schmeared them fifty a week and had your own private space. — Vincent Patrick, *Family Business*, p. 32, 1985

shmeck; schmeck; shmee *noun*
heroin; cocaine *US, 1932*
From German *schmecken* (to taste), but note an assonant similarity to SMACK (heroin).
- "Let him snort some schmeck!" said Jean-baby, wide-eyed, reaching for her purse. — Terry Southern, *Flash and Filigree*, p. 144, 1958
- "What you got?" Furg asked. "Good stuff. Schmeck." — Malcolm Braly, *Shake Him Till He Rattles*, p. 15, 1963
- Then one night zonked out of my mind on schmeck—pot—benzedrine and seconal—I met a cat I had become friendly with who was a kind of John or mark. — Herbert Huncke, *The Evening Sun Turned Crimson*, p. 46, 1980
- She knew from pumping her father that Charley was in Miami to handle a problem with a schmeck producer[.] — Richard Condon, *Prizzi's Family*, p. 120, 1986

shmecker; schmecker *noun*
a heroin user *US, 1952*
- Like a good shmecker keeps the smell in his own private nose, see? — George Mandel, *Flee the Angry Strangers*, p. 312, 1952
- I suspect her to be a schmecker but it's hard to tell with women and Chinamen. — William Burroughs, *Letters to Allen Ginsberg 1953–1957*, p. 116, 23rd October 1955
- [W]here the skinpoppers and schmeckers (those who used the needles and those who sniffed the powder), the pushers and the weeheads gathered for sex circuses and to listen to the real cool jive. — Chester Himes, *Come Back Charleston Blue*, p. 150, 1966
- O'Keefe went along, agreeing that the time seemed right for him to become a "schmecker," too. — Emmett Grogan, *Ringolevio*, p. 44, 1972

shmeckler *noun*
a heroin user or addict *US, 1988*
- Dreck written by a shmeckler. — Gerald Petievich, *Shakedown*, p. 133, 1988

shmeer; schmear *noun*
a package or deal *US, 1963*
From the Yiddish.
- "I'm almost sorry I got mixed up in this schmeer," he growled. — Wade Hunter, *The Sex Peddler*, p. 80, 1963
- You know, big hoop skirt, eight petticoats, high-button shoes, monstrous hairpiece, the whole schmear, pretty weird. — Terry Southern, *Blue Movie*, p. 152, 1970
- "What really gets me about the whole schmeer," sad one of the wives to another, dissecting her duck with surgical precision, "is what's gonna happen to the doctor–patient relationship." — Cyra McFadden, *The Serial*, p. 27, 1977

shmegegge; schmageggy *noun*
an incompetent person *US, 1975*
An American-born "Yiddish" word.
- Against a horseplayer, maybe. But against a schmageggy who ain't out of high school, I will do all right. — Jimmy Snyder, *Jimmy the Greek*, p. 16, 1975

shmendrick *noun*
a naive, cowardly person *UK, 1944*
From the name of a character in an operetta by Abraham Golfaden.
- "Clyde"—a loser, a shmendrick. — *Washington Post*, p. B1, 17th January 1985
- "But you don't know these schmendricks like I do!" — Glenn Savan, *White Palace*, p. 138, 1987
- What a schmendrick he was, sitting around and waiting for us to provide an agenda. — *Atlanta Journal-Constitution*, p. 12P, 18th December 2003

shmo; schmo; schmol *noun*
a gullible, hapless fool *US, 1943*
An American addition to Yiddish. In August 1948, just as "shmo" was coming into the American lexicon, US cartoonist Al Capp introduced the "shmoo" in the *L'il Abner* comic strip. The loveable and selfless "shmoo" loved to be eaten and tasted like any food desired.
- You copped the 400 because you're an illiterate schmo. — Bernard Wolfe, *The Late Risers*, p. 36, 1954
- The big brother. The big schmoe. — George Clayton Johnson, *Ocean's Eleven*, p. 81, 1960
- Don't be a schmoe. Go along. — Clancy Sigal, *Going Away*, p. 391, 1961
- You would be surprised how many shmoes sit behind the wheel at a time like this. — Leo Rosten, *Silky!*, p. 78, 1979

shmooze; schmooze *verb*
to gossip; to chat, to engage in idle talk; to network; to persuade someone indirectly *US, 1897*
Yiddish from the Hebrew.
- "Come on in the kitchen, Kipper. We'll schmoose." — Edwin Gilbert, *The Hot and the Cool*, p. 51, 1953
- We schmoozed around, and then a client burst in from the corridor. — Clancy Sigal, *Going Away*, p. 28, 1961
- [Y]ou automatically think it is something where Jewish widow ladies go and sit out by the swimming pool on nice days like this and schmoos a little. — George V. Higgins, *The Rat on Fire*, p. 148, 1981
- They schmooze the manager, slip him some free goods to make sure he puts the CD on the shelf, try for some in-store airplay and stick this gorgeous shot of Linda Moon in the window. — Elmore Leonard, *Be Cool*, p. 253, 1999

shmoozy *adjective*
chatty; friendly *US, 1954*
- Well, Mort's real schmoozy with Biff. — Bernard Book, *The Late Risers*, p. 9, 1954

shmozz; schmozz *noun*
in professional wrestling, a chaotic free-for-all *US, 2000*
- It wound up being a big "schmozz," which is what we call a free-for-all, when everybody gets involved in a fight and chairs are thrown and tables are tipped over, and ultimately everyone is disqualified. — The Rock, *The Rock Says...*, p. 194, 2000

shmuck; schmuck *noun*
1 a fool; an objectionable person *UK, 1892*
Taken into general usage from Yiddish; the literal meaning is "penis," hence the original Yiddish usage in this sense had a particularly derogatory tone. The variant "schmuck" seems to have been adopted in error due to a similarity in sound to Yiddish *schmuck* (jewel).
- Which means like be a schmuck. — *West Side Story*, 1957
- I thought in my arrogance and heartbreak—discarded, unread, considered junk-mail by this schmuck, this moron, this Philistine father of mine! — Philip Roth, *Portnoy's Complaint*, p. 8, 1969
- Asshole! Schmuck! How long does it take you to figure out that nobody knows what they're doing here? — *Apocalypse Now*, 1979
- Blow the schmuck out of the water! — *Something About Mary*, 1998

2 the penis *US, 1988*
- "It's like a man should stand with his schmuck out & piss in the middle of the street." — Isaac Rosenfeld, *Preserving the Hunger*, p. 438, 1988

shmuck; schmuck *verb*
to make a fool of someone *US, 2001*

- He thinks you're being schmucked. — Stephen J. Cannell, *The Tin Collectors*, p. 43, 2001

shmutz; schmutz *noun*
filth; dirt *US, 1959*
Yiddish from German.

- "It's clean enough. Look, Aunt Gladys, I'm having a wonderful time." "Schmutz he lives in and I shouldn't worry." — Philip Roth, *Goodbye, Columbus*, p. 54, 1959

shnitzel; schnitzel *noun*
the penis *US, 1967*

- — Dale Gordon, *The Dominion Sex Dictionary*, 1967
- Dick, all I want to do is make serious movies that explore social issues and turn a profit, and slip the schnitzel to Jane DePugh. — James Ellroy, *Hollywood Nocturnes*, p. 80, 1994

shnook; schnook *noun*
an inoffensive, unassertive person; a "nobody" *US, 1948*
American Yiddish coinage.

- He thinks anything peculiar or unpleasant will just go away if he turns on the radio and some little schnook starts singing. — J.D. Salinger, *Franny and Zooey*, p. 82, 1961
- Jack Benny on radio, 9 October, 1951: "Don't be such an apologetic shnook." — Leo Rosten, *The Joys of Yiddish*, p. 368, 1968
- He couldn't help feeling like a schnook, though, when he thought about Marlene and that whole bit, because he'd never even tried to get in touch with her, after he'd split from the condo[.] — Cyra McFadden, *The Serial*, p. 75, 1977
- I'm an average nobody. I get to live the rest of my life like a schnook. — *Goodfellas*, 1990

shnorr; schnorr *verb*
to freeload *US, 1968*

- [T]he housing inspectors were schnorring more than ever. — Sol Yurrick, *The Bag*, p. 121, 1968

shnorrer; schnorrer *noun*
a freeloader *US, 1948*
Yiddish from the German for "begging."

- What were the characteristics of the schnorrer? He disdained to stretch out his hand for alms like an ordinary beggar. He did not solicit aid—he demanded it. — Nathan Ausubel, *A Treasury of Jewish Folklore*, p. 267, 1948
- I had lunch with him a couple of weeks ago. A real schnorrer, but sort of likeable, and apparently he's hot over there right now. — J.D. Salinger, *Franny and Zooey*, pp. 136–137, 1961
- Those schnorer bits: "Oh, you'll do this and this, and here's a bit of schnapps for this and this." — Lenny Bruce, *The Essential Lenny Bruce*, p. 23, 1967
- FATHER PHIL: You think I'm a schnorrer, don't you? CARMELA: A who? FATHER PHIL: Yiddish. Somebody who always shows up in time for free grub. — David Chase, *The Sopranos: Selected Scripts from Three Seasons*, p. 96, 3rd November 1998

shnoz; schnoz; shnozz; scnozz *noun*
the nose *US, 1942*
A shortening of **SHNOZZLE**.

- "Go fuck yourself, buster!" Sid roared, gave him a straight shot to the snoz — Terry Southern, *Blue Movie*, p. 250, 1970
- As always, I am in love with the quality of the merchandise. Truly soft on the schnozz. — Gerald Petievich, *To Live and Die in L.A.*, p. 196, 1983
- I guess she's afraid of getting smacked in the shnaz. Can't blame 'er. Quite a hooter on her already. — Anthony Petkovich, *The X Factory*, p. 193, 1997
- "How's the shnoz?" the blackmailer asked him. "It hurts." Chaz's nose had swollen to the size of a bell pepper. — Carl Hiaasen, *Skinny Dip*, p. 285, 2004

shnozzle; shnozzola; schnozzle; schnozzola *noun*
the nose *US, 1930*

- [F]or 3 days my eyes watered with migraine pain from that swollen shnozzola[.] — Jack Kerouac, *Letter to Neal and Gabrielle Kerouac*, p. 399, 25th April 1953
- What a coddy [bad] kaffall [face] dear. Oh vada [observe] the schnozzle on it dear. — David McKenna, *Storm in a Teacup*, 1993

shock a brew!
have a beer! *US, 1989*

An intentional corruption of the Hawaiian **SHAKA**.

- — Pamela Munro, *U.C.L.A. Slang*, p. 75, 1989

shock jock *noun*
a radio personality who tests the limits and tries to win listeners by outrageous language, thoughts, or stunts *US, 1986*

- There are probably no more than a dozen truly outrageous "shock jocks" at the nation's nearly 10,000 radio stations, yet three of them have worked in Washington. — *Washington Post*, p. F8, 23rd February 1986
- New York's WNEW-FM radio pulled the plug Thursday on shock jocks Opie and Anthony over their sex stunt at St. Patrick's Cathedral. — *New York Daily News*, 23rd August 2003

shock shop *noun*
a room where electric shock therapy is administered *US, 1962*

- They didn't take me to the Shock Shop this time. — Ken Kesey, *One Flew Over the Cuckoo's Nest*, p. 8, 1962

shocky *adjective*
in shock *US, 1983*

- "Get another IV in this one, he's shocky." — Lynda Van Devanter, *Home Before Morning*, p. 9, 1983

shoddy-doo *noun*
palms slapped in greeting *US, 1976*

- "My dear hip friend," the better began / "Here's some splow and a big shoddy-doo." — Dennis Wepman et al., *The Life*, p. 69, 1976

shoe *noun*

1 a detective *US, 1988*
An abbreviation of **GUMSHOE**.

- Told the shoes where to find Robin and her buddy Skip Gibbs. They picked them up in Los Angeles and brought them back for trial. — Elmore Leonard, *Freaky Deaky*, p. 208, 1988

2 a black person *US, 1960*
A play on **BOOT**.

- — Robert George Reisner, *The Jazz Titans*, p. 164, 1960

shoe clerk *noun*
a poker player who withdraws from a hand at any sign of serious betting *US, 1996*

- — John Vorhaus, *The Big Book of Poker Slang*, p. 32, 1996

shoe laces and collar buttons *noun*
in poker, a hand consisting of a pair of aces and a pair of twos *US, 1988*

- — George Percy, *The Language of Poker*, p. 81, 1988

shoe-leather express *noun*
walking *US, 1949*

- Conveniently O'Brien lived only a few blocks from the professor, so they took the shoe leather express. — Bill Bonanno, *The Good Guys*, p. 62, 2005

shoemaker *noun*
a boy who is not particularly intelligent *US, 1955*
Teen slang.

- — *American Weekly*, p. 2, 14th August 1955

shoes *noun*
car wheel rims *US, 2003*

- Dubs, blades, shoes, sneakers, twinkies—street slang for custom wheels—are status symbols, made popular by athletes and rap stars. — *Cincinnati Enquirer*, p. 1B, 29th August 2003

shoestring *noun*
a very small amount of money; a low budget *US, 1904*

- Of these a dozen are highly successful, another half dozen do well, and the rest are mostly shoestring affairs, picking up the ragged edges and discards of the leaders. — Jack Lait and Lee Mortimer, *New York Confidential*, p. 32, 1948

shoo *adjective*
well dressed *US, 1958*
Teen slang.

- — *San Francisco News*, p. 6, 25th March 1958

shoobie *noun*
a short-term visitor to a beach resort *US, 1952*

- Lowest on most guards' desirability list for posting were beaches such as Ninth Street, which attracted hordes of "shoobies," day trippers or weekend visitors[.] — Edward Brown, *Ocean City*, p. 341, 1952

- But there are almost as may boys as girls in town form Friday night through Sunday, while the "shoobies" are here. — *Clearfield (Pennsylvania) Progress*, p. 10, 15th August 1962

shoo-fly *noun*

a police officer assigned to investigate the integrity of other policemen *US, 1958*

- — *New York Times Magazine*, p. 88, 16th March 1958
- [A]lthough Walsh's investigators—or "shoo-flies"—caught countless cops in minor violations of the department's rules and procedures, they somehow turned up very little graft. — Peter Maas, *Serpico*, p. 172, 1973
- "But now they flop you for nothing, shoofly all over," Valentin said. — Edwin Torres, *Q & A*, p. 17, 1977
- The key to it would be the Internal Affairs shooflies. — Vincent Patrick, *The Pope of Greenwich Village*, p. 113, 1979

shoo-in *noun*

a person, idea or thing with no serious competition *US, 1939*

Originally (1935) applied to a fixed horse race and four years later in a more general sense.

- — *American Speech*, October 1950

shook-up *adjective*

alienated; confused; dehumanized *US, 1914*

- Pepito isn't as shook-up as Chocolate. Not yet. But is only fourteen. — Harrison E. Salisbury, *The Shook-up Generation*, p. 53, 1958

shoot *noun*

1 in professional wrestling, a legitimate, hard-fought match *US, 1990*

- shoot n. the real thing, i.e., a match where one participant is really attempting to hurt another. — *rec.sports.pro-wrestling*, 17th July 1990
- He was pinned in an hour and a half by Lewis in 1932, but I doubt that it was a shoot. — John F. Gilbey, *Western Boxing & World Wrestling*, p. 143, 1993
- They see a legend, a guy they remember seeing beat everybody from soup to nuts and the guy's in tremendous shape and could whip three quarters of the guys in this territory in a shoot. — *Wrestling Perspective*, 20th July 1993

2 a tall wave *US, 1961*

- "You really want to try those shoots? Twenty feet high, I hear." — Frederick Kohner, *Gidget Goes Hawaiian*, p. 22, 1961

3 anything legitimate, unscripted, or unstaged *US, 1996*

- The other key event on the show saw Jim Ross deliver his much awaited hell turn, delivering a "shoot" interview that even put the heroes of that genre, Shane Douglas and Brian Pillman, to shame. — *Herb's Wrestling Tidbits*, 26th September 1996

shoot *verb*

1 in professional wrestling, to hurt your opponent intentionally *US, 1993*

- At age forty-five he shot against and beat easily Ray Steele[.] — John F. Gilbey, *Western Boxing & World Wrestling*, p. 142, 1993
- The funny thing about this match is that I've heard more talk form people who should know better than are Hogan haters who want to see the match to see Vader shoot on Hogan. Shooting doesn't exist in the pro-wrestling world. — *Herb's Wrestling Tidbits*, 26th January 1995
- It's called shooting. That's when you apply a hold for real. — Missy Hyatt, *Missy Hyatt*, p. 44, 2001
- He was so strong and he had that mentality of shooting. — Bobby Heenan, *Bobby the Brain*, p. 46, 2002

2 to inject a drug intravenously *US, 1914*

- I was shooting every day now. — William Burroughs, *Junkie*, p. 33, 1953
- This was earlier, all the junkies in Ross's room tying up and shooting[.] — Jack Kerouac, *The Subterraneans*, p. 27, 1958
- He did suggest maybe the guy would know where to score some H—asking me if I would like to shoot a little stuff. — Herbert Huncke, *The Evening Sun Turned Crimson*, p. 81, 1980

3 to flirt; to make sexual advances *US, 1967*

- All the high powered broads were "shooting" on me. — Babs Gonzales, *I Paid My Dues*, p. 39, 1967

4 to drink alcohol in shot glass units *US, 1991*

- They go down to bars, shoot tequila and go back up to buy things. — Francesca Lia Block, *Witch Baby*, p. 121, 1991

5 to pick a pocket *US, 1969*

- Livin' said, "I wouldn't have shot on you if I had been hip you knew White Folks." — Iceberg Slim (Robert Beck), *Trick Baby*, p. 175, 1969

▸ **shoot a beaver**

to look for and see a girl's crotch *US, 1966*

- — *Current Slang*, p. 4, Summer 1966

▸ **shoot a box**

to open a safe using explosives *US, 1972*

- Denver Dick was a past master at shooting a box. — Harry King, *Box Man*, p. 10, 1972

▸ **shoot a good stick**

to play pool well *US, 1961*

- You shoot a good stick. — *The Hustler*, 1961

▸ **shoot a jug; shoot a peter**

to break into a safe using explosives *US, 1950*

- — Hyman E. Goldin et al., *Dictionary of American Underworld Lingo*, p. 192, 1950

▸ **shoot a wave**

to surf a wave, especially if difficult *US, 1963*

- — Grant W. Kuhns, *On Surfing*, p. 121, 1963

▸ **shoot an air rifle; shoot an air gun**

in pool, to bet without money to back your bet *US, 1990*

- When betting an air barrel, or "shooting the air rifle," follow the stewardess's advice and take some time to acquaint yourself with the emergency exits around you. — Steve Rushin, *Pool Cool*, p. 5, 1990
- — Mike Shamos, *The Illustrated Encyclopedia of Billiards*, p. 3, 1993

▸ **shoot blanks**

(said of a male) to engage in sex with a low or nonexistent sperm count *US, 1960*

- Oh, sure, after about the third time, I was shooting blanks, but I was still hanging in there[.] — Joey V., *Portrait of Joey*, p. 122, 1969
- He dug that young poontang—even though at his age I knew he was shooting blanks. — Edwin Torres, *Carlito's Way*, p. 29, 1975

▸ **shoot cuffs**

to grab someone around the ankles and pull them to the ground *US, 1994*

- I learned how to shoot cuffs—to tackle a man and bring him down. — Nathan McCall, *Makes Me Wanna Holler*, p. 55, 1994

▸ **shoot gravy**

to inject a mixture of blood and drug solution that has been reheated after failing to make a direct hit on the vein *US, 1973*

- — David Maurer and Victor Vogel, *Narcotics and Narcotic Addiction*, p. 441, 1973

▸ **shoot off your mouth; shoot your mouth off**

to speak with a complete lack of discretion; to speak boastfully *US, 1864*

- You've been shootin' your mouth off all night, and I'm one guy who knows that he can kick the crap outa you. — Irving Shulman, *The Amboy Dukes*, p. 229, 1947
- Winston admits to shooting his mouth off at meetings, going above Sabina to her boss[.] — William Lundin and Kathleen Lundin, *When Smart People Work for Dumb Bosses*, p. 9, 1998

▸ **shoot the agate**

to walk with a style calling attention to oneself *US, 1950*

- When one shot the agate, "your hands is at your sides with your index fingers stuck out." — Gena Dagel Caponi, *Signifyin', Sanctifyin' & Slam Dunkin'*, p. 437, 1999

▸ **shoot the breeze**

to chat idly *US, 1919*

- Then the old lady that was around a hundred years and I shot the breeze for a while. — J.D. Salinger, *Catcher in the Rye*, p. 201, 1951
- "I'd like to shoot the breeze with you again, kid." — Richard Prather, *The Peddler*, p. 16, 1952
- First, we would sit on a stoop somewhere along the block—shooting the breeze about good marks to rob, about who could beat up who. — Rocky Garciano (with Rowland Barber), *Somebody Up There Likes Me*, p. 54, 1955
- Even if you just want to talk—come in and shoot the breeze. — *Rebel Without a Cause*, 1955

▸ **shoot the bull**

to engage in small talk *US, 1902*

- Well, you could see he really felt pretty lousy about flunking me. So I shot the bull for a while. I told him I was a real moron, and all that stuff. — J.D. Salinger, *Catcher in the Rye*, p. 12, 1951

- Sometimes I visit the shack to shoot the bull and get the latest drawings (news). — Eldridge Cleaver, *Soul on Ice*, p. 44, 1968
- Prince walked beside Red shooting the bull until they reached the mess hall. — Donald Goines, *Black Gangster*, p. 9, 1977

▶ **shoot the con**

to engage in goal-oriented, truth-deficient conversation *US, 1965*

- We chewed the rag for quite a while and shot the con for fair / and when it came to spreadin' jive, you could gamble that I was there. — Bruce Jackson, *Get Your Ass in the Water and Swim Like Me*, p. 131, 1965

▶ **shoot the curl; shoot the tube**

to surf through the hollow part of a wave *US, 1957*

- Shoot it, Gidget. Shoot the curl! — Frederick Kohner, *Gidget*, p. 149, 1957
- And when I get to Surf City I'll be shootin' the curl / And checkin' out the parties for a surfer girl. — Jan Berry and Dean Torrance, *Surf City*, 1963

▶ **shoot the duck**

to skateboard crouched on one leg with the other leg extended outward *US, 1976*

- — Laura Torbet, *The Complete Book of Skateboarding*, p. 105, 1976

▶ **shoot the gab**

to gossip, to talk idly *US, 1957*

- We were in there shooting the gab when in came a local boy named Herman[.] — Helen Giblo, *Footlights, Fistfights and Femmes*, p. 147, 1957

▶ **shoot the pier**

to surf, or attempt to surf, through the pilings of a pier *US, 1962*

- At Huntington and Malibu / They're shooting the pier / At Rincon they're walking the nose. — Brian Wilson and Mike Love, *Surfin' Safari (performed by the Beach Boys)*, 1962
- — Duke Kahanamoku with Joe Brennan, *Duke Kahanamoku's World of Surfing*, p. 176, 1965

▶ **shoot the shit; shoot shit**

to engage in idle conversation; to tell lies *UK, 1949*

- It sure beats working as an extra, standing out in the sun all day while the director and the star shoot the shit. — Elmore Leonard, *Freaky Deaky*, p. 11, 1988
- She sank down next to Chili on the sofa and put her hand on his knee. "You guys working or just shooting the shit?" — Elmore Leonard, *Be Cool*, p. 256, 1999

▶ **shoot your cuffs**

(used of a man wearing a suit or sports jacket) to straighten your arms so that the cuffs of the shirt extend beyond the jacket sleeves *UK, 1909*

The modern version of the older (1878) "shoot your linen."

- This bald-headed, wrinkle-necked, full bird colonel from the Officer's Candidate School stood at the tend end, shooting his cuffs between handshakes[.] — Larry Heinemann, *Close Quarters*, p. 145, 1977
- "It's a term of art," he replied, shooting his cuffs as he turned to deal with the cash register. — Hunter S. Thompson, *Songs of the Doomed*, p. 203, 1983
- He shot the jacket and shirt cuffs over his left wrist, displaying a new Timex watch. — George V. Higgins, *Penance for Jerry Kennedy*, p. 34, 1985
- This is fight night. Shoot cuffs, boy, jack-knife yo' legs. Get down. — *Buzz*, p. 76, May 1994

▶ **shoot your load**

figuratively, to exhaust your resources early in a contest *US, 1954*

- The kids were used to hot-shot principals who had shot their loads in the first month and then settled down to letting the school run itself. — Evan Hunter, *The Blackboard Jungle*, p. 78, 1954

▶ **shoot your trap**

to talk too much *US, 1947*

- I got sick of hearing him shoot his trap off. — James T. Farrell, *Saturday Night*, p. 34, 1947

▶ **shoot your wad**

to use all your resources; to reveal all *US, 1887*

- "What'd he tell you then?" "Nothing," I said. "Clown shot his wad when she was sitting there." — George Higgins, *Kennedy for the Defense*, p. 30, 1980

▶ **shoot your wad**

to ejaculate *US, 1969*

- It calms a man down, and once a man has shot his wad the first time, he can last a lot longer the second, third, or fourth times. — Juan Carmel Cosmes, *Memoir of a Whoremaster*, p. 106, 1969
- Did you get any action? Did you slam it to her? Did you stick her? Did you hump her? Did you run it down her throat? Did you jam it up her ass? Did you shoot your wad? — *Screw*, p. 6, 29th May 1972
- Candy makes studs prematurely shoot their wads left and right before they make it to the fuck altar. — Anthony Petkovich, *The X Factory*, p. 192, 1997

shoot!

1 used as a euphemism for "shit" in an exclamation *US, 1934*

- "Shoot," said Danny Pogue. He hadn't said "shoot" since the third grade, but he'd been trying to clean up his language in Molly's presence. — Carl Hiaasen, *Native Tongue*, p. 217, 1991
- Oh shoot, she's tripping [on drugs] — Eminem (Marshall Mathers), *My Fault*, 1999
- "If you are looking for a substitute for every curse word you use ... pick words that sound similar." "Shoot! is a logical substitute because it is a mere vowel away from what really wants to be said." — *The New York Times*, 7th April 2002

2 yes! *US, 1982*

Hawaiian youth usage.

- "You like manapua, Winton?" "Shoot! I grind 'um!" — Douglas Simonson, *Pidgin to da Max Hana Hou*, 1982

shoot and scoot *verb*

to engage in warfare involving brief contact with the enemy and then a quick withdrawal *US, 1987*

- It was therefore important for the artillery to keep moving. Shoot 'n' scoot was a popular way of putting it. In modern combat you're either quick or you're dead. — Harold Coyle, *Team Yankee*, p. 94, 1987
- The United States, by contrast, practices "hip shooting" or "shoot and scoot," in which guns are moved from position to position, firing at each stop. — *USA Today*, p. 4A, 20 January 1991

shoot-'em-up *noun*

an action movie, especially a western *US, 1946*

- "This ship astern of us wanted to trade us Since You Went Away—that's almost brand new—and he took this damn shoot-'em-up!" — Thomas Heggen, *Mister Roberts*, p. 8, 1946
- Their presence in a shoot-'em-up no longer guarantees giant audiences around the world. — Peter Bart, *Shoot Out*, p. 111, 2002

shooter *noun*

1 a professional wrestler who hurts his opponent intentionally *US, 1993*

- Lewis was supposed to be a great shooter. — John F. Gilbey, *Western Boxing & World Wrestling*, p. 142, 1993

2 an alcoholic drink, especially whiskey, meant to be consumed in a single gulp *US, 1971*

- [A]ll downing either crappy beer from the keg out back or multi-colored Jello-O shooters. — Marty Beckerman, *Generation S.L.U.T.*, p. 96, 2004

3 a professional killer *US, 1964*

- "They're coming in from the burgs, man. Bit shooters and they're gathering around waiting for orders." — Mickey Spillane, *The Snake*, p. 37, 1964

4 a criminal who specializes in breaking into safes *US, 1949*

- — Vincent J. Monteleone, *Criminal Slang*, p. 206, 1949

5 an intravenous drug user *US, 1991*

- [H]e could tell just by looking at her that she was a shooter, though whether she shot coke or smack he couldn't say[.] — William T. Vollman, *Whores for Gloria*, p. 83, 1991

6 in a functionally compartmentalized illegal drug enterprise, the person who holds and turns over the drugs to buyers *US, 1987*

- — Carsten Stroud, *Close Pursuit*, p. 275, 1987

7 a pinball player *US, 1977*

- — Bobbye Claire Natkin and Steve Kirk, *All About Pinball*, p. 116, 1977

8 in pinball, the device that propels a ball into the playfield *US, 1977*

Known conventionally as a "plunger."

- — Roger C. Sharpe, *Pinball!*, p. 159, 1977

9 a television camera operator *US, 1986*

- — Rachel S. Epstein and Nina Liebman, *Biz Speak*, p. 205, 1986

shooter's coast *noun*

the slow driving speed of a car about to engage in a drive-by shooting *US, 1993*

- A car bent the corner off of Normandie and onto Eightieth with a precautionary pace that should be misconstrued as a "shooter's coast." — Sanyika Shakur, *Monster*, p. 86, 1993

shooting gallery *noun*

a place where addicts congregate to buy and inject drugs *US, 1951*

- We'd drive in with Bill for groceries and Hunkey'd disappear. We'd have to go looking for him in every shooting gallery in town. — Jack Kerouac, *On the Road (The Original Scroll)*, p. 258, 1951
- When a junkie has a hotel room, the word spreads fast. All his friends and their friends stream in and the place turns into a shooting gallery. — James Mills, *The Panic in Needle Park*, p. 75, 1966
- He might rip off one of these little shooting galleries somewhere but he doesn't have the nerve to screw around with McDaniel's stuff. — Vernon E. Smith, *The Jones Men*, p. 58, 1974
- We flew from one gig to the next in this 727 that was outfitted like a kind of low-profile shooting gallery/whorehouse. — Terry Southern, *Now Dig This*, pp. 10–11, 1986

shooting gallery doctor *noun*

a person who for a fee will help a needle-using drug addict find a vein for injecting a drug *US, 1997*

- [T]he search for an honest shooting gallery doctor can be as exhausting as the quest for an honest auto mechanic. — David Simon and Edward Burns, *The Corner*, p. 77, 1997

shooting match *noun*

all of something; the entire matter *US, 1968*

- Meanwhile, if that settlement is not made by April first, I will take over the whole shooting match. — Gore Vidal, *Myra Breckinridge*, p. 107, 1968
- "Sixty-one hundred dollars, the whole fucking shooting match." — Gerard O'Neill, *The Under Boss*, p. 179, 1989

shoot it!

in surfing, used to encourage a surfer to catch a wave breaking behind them *US, 1957*

- [J]ust then his Lordship has turned his head and saw a bitchen set of waves coming up fast and he yelled, "Shoot it!" which means the wave is breaking behind you[.] — Frederick Kohner, *Gidget*, p. 43, 1957

shoot-off *noun*

ejaculation *US, 2005*

- If I had seen her in a men's magazine, it would be instant shoot-off. — Josh Friedman, *When Sex Was Dirty*, pp. 50–51, 2005

shoot off *verb*

to ejaculate *US, 1969*

- You know how it is with a lot of kids—sometimes, they barely get the head of their pricks in, and—pow!—they shoot off. — Joey V., *Portrait of Joey*, p. 39, 1969

shoot (someone) out *verb*

to train or prepare someone *US, 1972*

- — Bruce Jackson, *Outside the Law*, p. 60, 1972: "Glossary"

shoot up *verb*

to inject heroin or another drug intravenously *US, 1914*

- Every I time I shoot up, I'm saying to them: "Fuck you and your system, lames." — Nathan Heard, *Howard Street*, p. 184, 1968
- I sold my ice at a pawnshop price / And shot up all that dough. — Dennis Wepman et al., *The Life*, p. 84, 1976
- VINCENT: You don't mind if I shoot up here? LANCE: Mi casa, su casa. — *Pulp Fiction*, 1994

shoot-up; shoot-up man *noun*

a person who promotes a card game or other activity involved in a swindle *US, 1977*

- — Robert C. Prus and C.R.D. Sharper, *Road Hustler*, p. 171, 1977: "Glossary of terms"

shop *noun*

1 a police patrol car *US, 2006*

- "And don't say the sushi bar on Melrose, where I've seen your shop parked on numerous occasions." — Joseph Wambaugh, *Hollywood Station*, p. 102, 2006

2 any home or apartment where drugs are sold *US, 1997*

- "I sold drugs hand-to-hand for him until I could get a higher position," Norton said. "Then I became a lieutenant in my own shop." A shop is street slang for a home where drugs are sold. — *Baltimore Sun*, p. 1B, 31st October 1997

shore dinner *noun*

a sailor, as seen by a homosexual *US, 1965*

- — *Fact*, p. 27, January–February 1965

short *noun*

1 the unsmoked butt of a cigarette *UK, 1990*

- "Save me shorts, Homes." Joe passed over his Camel stub as they fell in walkin' and talkin'. — Seth Morgan, *Homeboy*, p. 89, 1990
- — Don R. McCreary (Editor), *Dawg Speak*, 2001
- — Gary K. Farlow, *Prison-ese*, p. 63, 2002
- The Bone declines the short. "I ain't lookin' to catch nothin' but parole." — Jimmy Lerner, *You Got Nothing Coming*, p. 175, 2002

2 a brief nap *US, 1976*

- — *Elementary Electronics*, *Dictionary of CB Lingo*, p. 105, 1976

short *adjective*

1 lacking money; lacking enough money to meet an obligation *US, 1958*

- "Oh, sure, I'm a little short," he drawled on, cruelly unaware of it. — John Clellon Holmes, *The Horn*, p. 120, 1958

2 near the end of a prison sentence or military tour of duty *US, 1966*

- — Rose Giallombardo, *Society of Women*, p. 211, 1966: Glossary of Prison Terms
- I'm so short now I can taste the street, and it's like I can't believe I'm here and the rules and regulations jus aren't meant for me any more. — Piri Thomas, *Down These Mean Streets*, p. 303, 1967
- You're sort of short now, aren't you? — Ronald J. Glasser, *365 Days*, p. 219, 1971
- Kell was the shortest man there. — William Pelfrey, *The Big V*, p. 90, 1972

3 used of an amount of a drug, underweight *US, 1989*

- Max knows there is a lot of money out there and you can't have your package short [underweight] like as far off as the last one he gave me. — Terry Williams, *The Cocaine Kids*, p. 37, 1989

▸ **get short**

to near the end of a prison sentence or military enlistment *US, 1951*

- — *American Speech*, p. 194, October 1951: "A study of reformatory argot"
- — Inez Cardozo-Freeman, *The Joint*, p. 500, 1984

short-and-curlies *noun*

pubic hair *US, 1967*

- — Dale Gordon, *The Dominion Sex Dictionary*, p. 147, 1967
- Boy, he had me by the soft curlies and he was pulling hard. — Robert Lipkin, *A Brotherhood of Outlaws*, p. 108, 1981

short arm *noun*

the inspection of a man's penis for evidence of a sexually transmitted infection *US, 1949*

- The first phase of our examination is a short arm. A young corporal glances at our organs perfunctorily. — Audie Murphy, *To Hell and Back*, p. 60, 1949

shortarm *verb*

1 to inspect a man's penis for evidence of a sexually transmitted infection *US, 1971*

- "I'll give you what you want, but we'll have to shortarm you before[.]" — Charles Winick, *The Lively Commerce*, p. 45, 1971

2 to perform a rectal examination *US, 1994*

- — Sally Williams, *"Strong" Words*, p. 159, 1994

short-arm bandit; short-arm heister *noun*

a rapist *US, 1950*

- — Hyman E. Goldin et al., *Dictionary of American Underworld Lingo*, p. 192, 1950

short-arm inspection; small-arm inspection *noun*

an inspection for a sexually transmitted infection *UK, 1919*

- After the fingerprinting routine and short-arm inspection at Pontiac, we were given numbers and sent to the barber shop[.] — Mezz Mezzrow, *Really the Blues*, p. 10, 1946
- I hear there's a correspondence course in short-arms inspections. — Norman Mailer, *Advertisements for Myself*, p. 110, 1951
- A tall silent screw, dazzling with brass buttons and gold braid on his navy-blue uniform, slashed his lead-loaded cane through the air like a vocal sword directing us to put our bundles on a long bench and to undress for "short arm" inspection[.] — Iceberg Slim (Robert Beck), *Pimp*, p. 50, 1969
- There was a crowd in the kitchen, a mob in the hall / A short-arm inspection by the shithouse wall. — Dennis Wepman et al., *The Life*, p. 110, 1976

short bus *noun*
used as a reference to the mentally retarded *US, 1998*
Referring to the smaller school buses used to transport special education students in the US.
- You know, the guys who ride the short bus. — *Something About Mary*, 1998

short buy *noun*
a purchase of a small amount of drugs *US, 1955*
- — *American Speech*, p. 88, May 1955: "Narcotic argot along the Mexican border"

shortcake *noun*
the act of shortchanging someone deliberately *US, 1974*
Used with "the."
- — John Scarne, *Scarne on Dice*, p. 478, 1974
- — Joe McKennon, *Circus Lingo*, p. 83, 1980

shortcake *verb*
to shortchange someone *US, 1961*
- "Curly," he says, "that Greek gentleman back there shortcaked me."
  — Guy Owen, *The Flim-Flam Man and the Apprentice Grifter*, p. 154, 1972
- — Thomas L. Clark, *The Dictionary of Gambling and Gaming*, p. 197, 1987

shortcake artist *noun*
an expert at shortchanging *US, 1980*
- — Joe McKennon, *Circus Lingo*, p. 83, 1980

shortchange artist *noun*
a swindler who gives customers too little change *US, 1960*
- The shortchange artist works in reverse to the change raise, and simply gives you back less change than you are supposed to get.
  — W.M. Tucker, *The Change Raisers*, p. 17, 1960

short con *noun*
a confidence game in which the victim is swindled once, without being sent home for a bigger prize *US, 1940*
- Unlike the big con operator, whose elaborate scene-setting may involve as much as a hundred thousand dollars, the short-con grifter can run on peanuts. — Jim Thompson, *The Grifters*, p. 22, 1963
- It's short con because the play for the sucker is short and we can only trim the sucker for the goddamn scratch in his pocket. — Iceberg Slim (Robert Beck), *Trick Baby*, p. 111, 1969
- According to your statement you are a shot-con operator. Run of the mill scams. — *The Usual Suspects*, 1995

short con *verb*
to engage in a short con swindle *US, 1964*
- Now all this talk about short-coinin', the Herman was a player too.
  — Bruce Jackson, *Get Your Ass in the Water and Swim Like Me*, p. 68, 1964

short dog *noun*
a half pint bottle of alcohol; cheap wine *US, 1968*
- — *Current Slang*, p. 42, Fall 1968
- Tooner Flats is the area of gangas who spend their last dime on short dogs of T-Bird wine[.] — Oscar Zeta Acosta, *The Revolt of the Cockroach People*, p. 90, 1973
- As I pulled to the curb opposite the Grand Central Market, a wino staggering down Broadway sucking on a short dog saw me, spun around, fell on his ass, dropped his bottle, and got up as though nothing had happened. — Joseph Wambaugh, *The Blue Knight*, p. 123, 1973
- The left-hand side of the street featured a grain store, a market, the front window filled with stacks of Tokay and muscatel short dogs, and a clapboard farm-machinery repair shop[.] — James Ellroy, *Hollywood Nocturnes*, p. 177, 1994

short end *noun*
in the television and movie industries, unexposed film remaining after cutting off the exposed film *US, 1990*
- Many student and experimental films are made from short ends.
  — Ralph S. Singleton, *Filmmaker's Dictionary*, p. 152, 1990

short eyes *noun*
a child molester *US, 1976*
- Punks shooting up a delicatessen on their first heist. Rapists. Short-eyes. — Emmett Grogan, *Final Score*, p. 69, 1976
- — Carsten Stroud, *Close Pursuit*, p. 275, 1987
- Foley turned the lights on and the kid hunched around to look at him, no doubt afraid he was about to get beat up again, the fate of guys with short eyes among a population that felt superior. — Elmore Leonard, *Out of Sight*, p. 14, 1996

short fuse *noun*
an impending deadline *US, 1986*
- — Department of the Army, *Staff Officer's Guidebook*, p. 65, 1986

short go; short order *noun*
a drug dose that is smaller than the addict is accustomed to *US, 1959*
- — J.E. Schmidt, *Narcotics Lingo and Lore*, p. 166, 1959

short hairs *noun*
▸ **have someone by the short hairs**
to hold someone at a disadvantage; to exercise complete control over someone *UK, 1888*
A figurative use of the literal meaning "to hold by the pubic hair."
- "We had 'im by the short hair," the little one said. — Horace McCoy, *Kiss Tomorrow Good-bye*, p. 60, 1948
- I got you by the short hairs now. I'm in and you're out. — Mickey Spillane, *Me, Hood!*, p. 27, 1963
- [C]aught by the short hairs by the fickle finger of fate[.] — Gore Vidal, *Myra Breckinridge*, p. 234, 1968
- The government still had me by the short hairs. — Odie Hawkins, *Scars and Memories*, p. 93, 1987

short heist *noun*
an act of masturbation *US, 1974*
- There was a prisoner named Tank, a former prize-fighter who was a wealth of terms, like "hack" and "screw" (guards), "undercover faggot," and "short heist" (masturbation). — Piri Thomas, *Seven Long Times*, p. 57, 1974
- Longshoe ... giving you short-heist books. — Miguel Pinero, *Short Eyes*, p. 89, 1975
- Who's that with the funny white collar band? / What's that, a short-heist book in his hand? — Dennis Wepman et al., *The Life*, p. 119, 1976

shortitis *noun*
the mental state of knowing that you have almost finished a prison sentence or military tour of duty *US, 1950*
- — Hyman E. Goldin et al., *Dictionary of American Underworld Lingo*, p. 193, 1950
- But I had "shortitis"—the impatience which makes the last few weeks unbearably long[.] — Piri Thomas, *Down These Mean Streets*, p. 301, 1967

short-long *noun*
a hairstyle in which the hair is worn short at the front and long at the back *US, 2001*
Most commonly known as a **MULLET**.
- — Don R. McCreary (Editor), *Dawg Speak*, 2001

short ones *noun*
▸ **have someone by the short ones**
to have absolute control of someone; to force submission *US, 1971*
A figurative use of the literal meaning "to hold by the pubic hair"; a variation on **HAVE BY THE SHORT HAIRS**.
- Now wonder he's got the world by the short ones! — Eugene Boe (Compiler), *The Wit & Wisdom of Archie Bunker*, p. 85, 1971
- [W]e got you by the short ones, and there's nothing you can do about it. — Jack W. Thomas, *Heavy Number*, p. 160, 1976
- Ron [Ronald Reagan] is their Kept Boy. They've got him by the short ones—he must play ball or they'll cut the PR budget[.] — Frank Zappa, *The Real Frank Zappa Book*, p. 293, 1989

short pair *noun*
in poker, a pair of tens or lower *US, 1963*
- — Irwin Steig, *Common Sense in Poker*, p. 187, 1963

short round *noun*
gunfire or artillery fired by friendly forces *US, 1985*
- We lost our fair share of people from "short rounds"—friendly fire—just plain fuckups. — Al Santoli, *To Bear Any Burden*, p. 134, 1985

shorts *noun*
1 a condition of low or no funds *US, 1932*
- The first serious signs of the shorts came late in October when I started to get my salary piecemeal. — Gary Mayer, *Bookie*, p. 198, 1974
- I was still hanging around New York, suffering a bad case of the shorts[.] — Jimmy Snyder, *Jimmy the Greek*, p. 183, 1975
2 the last portion of a cigarette *US, 1992*
- To save someone shorts on a cigarette is to save him a couple of draws at the end. — William K. Bentley and James M. Corbett, *Prison Slang*, p. 65, 1992

3 in poker, a pair that is beaten by a larger pair *US, 1988*
- — George Percy, *The Language of Poker*, p. 81, 1988

short-shorts *noun*
very brief shorts *US, 1958*
- Who wears short shorts? She wears short shorts. — *The Royal Teens, Short Shorts*, 1958
- He also didn't need her there dressed in short-shorts and heels, pissing on him in public. — Stephen Cannell, *Big Con*, p. 209, 1997

short-sleeves *noun*
in homosexual usage, an uncircumcized penis *US, 1981*
- — *Male Swinger Number 3*, p. 48, 1981: "The complete gay dictionary"

short stick *noun*
a stick notched by a US soldier in Vietnam counting the days until the end of his tour of duty *US, 1983*
- A couple of guys were unlimbering their short-sticks, the chunky batons that grunts would carry and notch day by day when their time in-country was running out. — Peter Goldman and Tony Fuller, *Charlie Company*, p. 118, 1983

shortstop *noun*
1 a temporary arrangement or relationship *US, 1972*
- Sometimes players deliberately take on a ho they knew will only last a short while. They figure they have nothing to lose, and attempt to get as much "short-stop" money as possible before she leaves. — Christina and Richard Milner, *Black Players*, p. 101, 1972
2 a gambler who makes small and conservative bets *US, 1950*
- — *The Annals of the American Academy of Political and Social Sciences*, p. 130, May 1950
- "She was shot in the head by Smitty Cocaine / A notorious short-stop and a practical lame[.]" — Dennis Wepman et al., *The Life*, p. 43, 1976
3 in pool, a very skilled player who is just below the highest tier *US, 1990*
- Sharks (who use the term pejoratively) beat shortstops, but short-stops beat just about everyone else. — Steve Rushin, *Pool Cool*, p. 26, 1990
4 in a group eating setting, to take a second helping despite an earlier request from another for seconds *US, 1947*
- — *American Speech*, p. 56, February 1947: "Pacific War language"

short time *noun*
a brief session with a prostitute, long enough for sex and nothing more *US, 1965*
- Their return English is always questioning, in the few broken phrases they know: "How much you got?" "Short time?" "All night?" "Costume show?" — Lenny Bruce, *How to Talk Dirty and Influence People*, p. 41, 1965
- She smiled as I came up. "Short time, luv?" I nodded. — Alexander Trocchi, *White Thighs*, p. 58, 1967
- A "short time" cost from $2 to $5. — Charles Winick, *The Lively Commerce*, p. 265, 1971

short-time *verb*
1 to serve the final days of a jail sentence or term of enlistment *US, 1975*
- Like when you're short-timin', waitin' on your parole, the cons will provoke you to fight—make you blow your parole. — Edwin Torres, *Carlito's Way*, p. 45, 1975
2 to engage in a quick sexual encounter with a prostitute *US, 1977*
- — John T. Algeo, *American Speech*, p. 120, May 1960: "Korean Bamboo English"
- "To short-time Claymore Face—never mind how God-awful ugly she is, boys, just slip a sandbag over her head—is to guarantee a sovereign cure for everything[.]" — Larry Heinemann, *Close Quarters*, p. 245, 1977

short-timer *noun*
1 a prisoner whose release date is approaching *US, 1966*
- — *Current Slang*, p. 7, Winter 1966
2 a soldier near the end of his tour of duty in Vietnam *US, 1968*
All but the US Marines served exactly 12 months in Vietnam; the Marines served 13 months.
- — *Harper's*, p. 51, January 1964
- — Carl Fleischhauer, *A Glossary of Army Slang*, p. 14, 1968
- Rodriguez was a genuine "short-timer," with only fourteen days remaining in the Nam. — Charles Anderson, *The Grunts*, p. 84, 1976
3 someone whose retirement date is rapidly approaching *US, 1993*

- Because Sam had the day off, Fin thought he'd better cover his old pal's ass by making the notifications. Sam had a short-timer's attitude. — Joseph Wambaugh, *Finnegan's Week*, p. 94, 1993
4 a prostitute engaged for a short period of time *US, 1960*
- — *American Speech*, p. 120, May 1960: "Korean bamboo English"

short-timer's calendar *noun*
a calendar showing the days remaining in a soldier's tour of duty in Vietnam *US, 1965*
- Most everyone has a short-timers calendar of some sort. — Tony Zidek, *Choi Oi*, p. 124, 1965
- — Carl Fleischhauer, *A Glossary of Army Slang*, p. 14, 1968

short-timer's stick *noun*
a notched stick showing the days remaining in a soldier's tour of duty in Vietnam *US, 1981*
- Big, tall, skinny guy who walked around bowleggedly like. Carried a .45 and a short-timer's stick. — Mark Barker, *Nam*, p. 35, 1981

short-timing *noun*
premature ejaculation *US, 1990*
- — Joseph Tuso, *Singing the Vietnam Blues*, p. 261, 1990: Glossary

short weight *noun*
a package of drugs that weighs less than what was bargained for *US, 1974*
- "Anyway, you don't get burned with scag by getting short weight. You get it cut on you." — Robert Stone, *Dog Soldiers*, p. 13, 1974

shorty *noun*
1 a female, especially an attractive one *US, 1997*
- — *Newsday*, p. B2, 11th October 1997
- — Connie Eble (Editor), *UNC-CH Campus Slang*, p. 7, Spring 1999
- "I'll be out of here in a minute, man, and none of y'all can touch the shorty I got at home!" — Earl "DMX" Simmons, *E.A.R.L.*, p. 136, 2002
2 in a casino, a shorter-than-expected shift at a table *US, 1980*
- I've caught two shorties already tonight. — Lee Solkey, *Dummy Up and Deal*, p. 119, 1980

shot *noun*
1 an occurrence or instance; a thing *US, 1960*
- About 2 a.m. one morning I met a prostitute downtown who wanted me to pay her fare and 5.00 for a "shot." — Phyllis and Eberhard Kronhausen, *Sex Histories of American College Men*, p. 140, 1960
- It seems curious that the first public manifestation of psychedelics was the dances at two and a half a shot. — *Berkeley Barb*, p. 6, 25th November 1966
- I've done too many of these things. Just gimme the whole shot. — Clarence Cooper Jr., *The Farm*, p. 82, 1967
- "Not bad, Molly," Gloria said after examining Leslie up and down. "She's really a fine bitch. We'll pull a hundred a shot!" — Donald Goines, *Inner City Hoodlum*, p. 119, 1975
2 an opportunity *US, 1972*
- I appreciate the shot at the lady, but you didn't introduce me to the shot. — Susan Hall, *Gentleman of Leisure*, p. 53, 1972
- You just don't realize what a shot on the Langford Show can mean. — *King of Comedy*, 1976
- All I want is a shot. Just a fuckin' shot. — *Raging Bull*, 1980
- I've been working my ass off for a shot like this, Bally's Park Place, my charts, and you want me to hide in a hotel room. — Elmore Leonard, *Glitz*, pp. 224–225, 1985
3 an instance of sexual intercourse *US, 1968*
An abbreviation of **SHOT OF COCK**.
- — Carl Fleischhauer, *A Glossary of Army Slang*, p. 14, 1968
4 an ejaculation *US, 2001*
- If it'll get me a few hundred miles across country, I'll take a shot in the mouth. — Kevin Smith, *Jay and Silent Bob Strike Back*, p. 27, 2001
5 Coca-Cola™ *US, 1946*
- — *American Speech*, p. 87, April 1946: "The language of West Coast culinary workers"
6 a single measure of spirits *US, 2000*
- Fuck shots! I hope the weed'll outweigh these drinks[.] — Eminem (Marshall Mathers), *Kill You*, 2000
7 a blow, especially a severe one *US, 1996*
- Foley said, "I never saw a fighter take as many shots as you did and keep coming back—outside of Rocky Balboa." — Elmore Leonard, *Out of Sight*, p. 6, 1996
8 an illegal move by a gambler *US, 1980*
- I had a dozen shots pulled on me today. — Lee Solkey, *Dummy Up and Deal*, p. 119, 1980

9 a competent pickpocket *US, 1976*
- — John R. Armore and Joseph D. Wolfe, *Dictionary of Desperation*, p. 49, 1976

10 an incident report describing a prisoner's misconduct *US, 1976*
- — John R. Armore and Joseph D. Wolfe, *Dictionary of Desperation*, p. 49, 1976
- — Reinhold Aman, *Hillary Clinton's Pen Pal*, p. 67, 1996

▸ **make a shot**
to secret something on your body while shoplifting *US, 1971*
- They got a blind spot right at the milk and egg department. All you got to do is carry your meat over there and make your shot under the mirror so they can't see you. — Donald Goines, *Dopefiend*, p. 101, 1971

shotcaller *noun*
the leader of a gang *US, 1995*
- — Mark S. Fleisher, *Beggars & Thieves*, p. 291, 1995: "Glossary"
- shot callers: older gang members who act as leaders, make the rules, and "call the shots" — S. Beth Atkin, *Voices from the Street*, p. 127, 1996
- I'd encountered several girls with ruthless reputations, but none was a shot-caller whose renown reached beyond her hood. — Gini Sikes, *8 Ball Chicks*, p. 178, 1997
- Skell tells me that Kansas is the Shotcaller again now that he's back in prison. — Jimmy Lerner, *You Got Nothing Coming*, p. 114, 2002

shot down *adjective*
drug-intoxicated *US, 1982*
- — Richard A. Spears, *The Slang and Jargon of Drugs and Drink*, p. 451, 1986
- — Mike Haskins, *Drugs*, p. 291, 2003

shot-for-shot *noun*
an arrangement between two homosexuals in which they switch sex roles to satisfy each other *US, 1950*
- — Hyman E. Goldin et al., *Dictionary of American Underworld Lingo*, p. 193, 1950

shotgun *noun*
1 the front passenger seat in a car *US, 1963*
Also called the "shotgun seat." The earliest use of the term, not yet applied to a car, was in the 1939 film *Stagecoach*.
- He got up and staggered to the shotgun seat and tossed me the keys[.] — Robert Gover, *Poorboy at the Party*, p. 180, 1966
- CARLOS: Shotgun! ANTS: No, I called it. BEAN: When? ANTS: Before we picked you up. BEAN: Man, you can't call it for the whole night. I got it now. Get in the back, punk. — *American Graffiti*, 1973
- Strike started to walk away, thinking about flex, when the rust-colored Caddy came rolling up again, Rodney at the wheel with his arm flung out along the back of the shotgun seat. — Richard Price, *Clockers*, p. 17, 1992

2 a pipe with air holes used for smoking marijuana *US, 1977*
The shotgun gives a **BLAST**.
- The shotgun was a tube of seven Coca-Cola cans taped together end-to-end. Grass, bulk marijuana which could be purchased by the sandbag for ten dollars MPC, was burned in the second can. — John Del Vecchio, *The 13th Valley*, p. 132, 1982

3 a potent mix of heroin, cocaine, nitroglycerine, phenol, and kola nut administered to racehorses as a stimulant *US, 1961*
- [T]he trainer gave all his horses a "shotgun" when they went to post. — Harry J. Anslinger, *The Murderers*, p. 227, 1961

4 in blackjack, the player to the immediate left of the dealer *US, 1979*
- — Thomas L. Clark, *The Dictionary of Gambling and Gaming*, p. 199, 1987

5 an unannounced test *US, 1968*
- — Collin Baker et al., *College Undergraduate Slang Study Conducted at Brown University*, p. 196, 1968

shotgun *verb*
while treating a hospital patient, to order every possible treatment to avoid being wrong *US, 1994*
- — Sally Williams, *"Strong" Words*, p. 159, 1994

shotgun *adjective*
1 used of a house or apartment, having rooms set on both sides of a central hall *US, 1903*
- It was a shotgun flat, one room opening into the other. — Chester Himes, *The Real Cool Killers*, p. 31, 1959
- And you may find yourself / living in a shotgun shack. — Talking Heads, *Once in a Lifetime*, 1980
- I was living in half a shotgun double on Magazine with hardly any furniture, a job I hated, and I was thinking on and off of getting married. — Elmore Leonard, *Bandits*, p. 20, 1987

- Rodney's apartment looked like every other seventy-five-year-old shotgun flat in Dempsy. — Richard Price, *Clockers*, p. 61, 1992

2 wide-ranging *US, 1994*
- You occasionally read about shotgun or scattershot pleadings, but there's a lot more iffy fishing alleged among litigators than gunplay or even snare-setting. — *The Lawyers Weekly*, 8th July 1994

shotgun mike *noun*
in the television and movie industries, a directional microphone *US, 1990*
- — Ralph S. Singleton, *Filmmaker's Dictionary*, p. 152, 1990

shot house *noun*
an establishment that sells alcohol illegally, by the drink *US, 1978*
- Shot-house operators run informal (and illegal) taverns in their own homes (shot-house operators are often women). — Burgess Laughlin, *Job Opportunities in the Black Market*, p. 10–9, 1978

shot of cock *noun*
sexual intercourse *US, 1968*
- — Carl Fleischhauer, *A Glossary of Army Slang*, p. 14, 1968

shot out *adjective*
in very bad physical shape *US, 1989*
- — James Harris, *A Convict's Dictionary*, p. 38, 1989

shotty-gotty!
used as a claim on riding in the front passenger seat of a car *US, 1997*
A variation on **SHOTGUN!**
- — Pamela Munro, *U.C.L.A. Slang*, p. 106, 1997

shoulder hopper *noun*
a surfer who surfs in another surfer's right of way *US, 1987*
- — Mitch McKissick, *Surf Lingo*, 1987

shoulder surfing *noun*
looking over someone's shoulder to watch the identification code they are entering into a telephone or computer *US, 1992*
- shoulder surfing—noun, slang, the theft of computer passwords or access codes, such as long distance telephone access codes, by reading the numbers over the user's shoulder. — *comp.risks*, 20th January 1992
- Shoulder surfing is when a hacker looms over the shoulder of a legitimate user as that user logs onto a computer system. — The Knightmare, *Secrets of a Super Hacker*, p. 79, 1994

shout *noun*
a greeting *US, 1998*
- As he gave his shouts out to his people, the band began playing. — Renay Jackson, *Oaktown Devil*, p. 22, 1998
- I want to send a shout out to all my friends back home. — Connie Eble (Editor), *UNC-CH Campus Slang*, p. 7, Spring 1999

shout *verb*
to write exclusively in upper case *US, 1995*
- — Christian Crumlish, *The Internet Dictionary*, p. 180, 1995

▸ **shout at your shoes**
to vomit *US, 1987*
- — *Washington Post*, p. 18, 8th November 1987: "Say Wha?"

shout-out *noun*
a greeting; a recognition *US, 1999*
- — *San Jose Mercury News*, 11th May 1999

shove *noun*
the member of a pickpocketing team who jostles the victim, diverting his attention so that a confederate can actually pick the victim's pocket *US, 1981*
- To do the job well, three persons are necessary: the shove pushed the victim and diverted his attention; the dip goes for the pocket, hip, or otherwise; and the loot is then handed to the wire so that if one of the other two are caught, they would not be caught with the evidence. — Don Wilmeth, *The Language of American Popular Entertainment*, p. 239, 1981

shove *verb*
▸ **shove it up the ass**
to reject something completely *US, 1949*

- "Shove it up your ass, you phony." — Fritz Peters, *The World Next Door*, p. 58, 1949
- He didn't particularly care about the new guy but he was glad he had shoved it up the boss's ass and broke it off. — Hubert Selby Jr., *Last Exit to Brooklyn*, p. 150, 1957

▸ **shove paper**
to pass counterfeit money or stolen or forged cheques *US*, 1962
- "Look," a friend of mine once put it, "shoving paper's too easy. You don't have to know anything but how to write your name, you're risking no danger, you're trading on the trust of gullible people, and you're shooting for nickels." — *Saturday Evening Post*, p. 72, 6th October 1962

shover *noun*
a person who passes counterfeit money *US*, 1945
- I was sure that Hertert wanted to use this fellow as a shover of the queer, or the man who was to pass the fake currency.
— William J. Spillard and Pence James, *Needle in a Haystack*, pp. 54–55, 1945
- — Frank Garcia, *Marked Cards and Loaded Dice*, p. 264, 1962
- — Joseph E. Ragen and Charles Finston, *Inside the World's Toughest Prison*, p. 817, 1962: "Penitentiary and underworld glossary"

show *noun*
a sexual performance in a brothel *US*, 1997
- "Two Girl Shows," (as opposed to "Two Girl Parties") are where two girls each do each other and the men watch, and participate later if they have paid extra for that activity. — *Sisters of the Heart*, *The Brothel Bible*, p. 54, 1997

show *verb*
to arrive; to make an appearance *US*, 1958
- Why do you think I made you wait all this time for before I showed? — Morton Cooper, *High School Confidential*, p. 69, 1958
- "How come her parents didn't show?" the woman continued, lowering her voice, "Show?" repeated Dottie, at a loss—could she mean show dogs or cats? "Turn up for the wedding." — Mary McCarthy, *The Group*, p. 22, 1963

▸ **show hard**
to reveal to other men that you have an erection *US*, 1970s
- For example, a simplified expression of the primary tearoom strategy is frequently inscribed on the walls: "Show hard-get sucked." — Laud Humphreys, *Tearoom Trade*, p. 48, 1975

▸ **show the goldfish**
to administer a beating as part of a police interrogation *US*, 1947
- "You know—they have a slang expression for their third degree. They say, 'Take the prisoner down and show him the goldfish'" — Willard Motley, *Knock on Any Door*, p. 410, 1947

show-and-tell *noun*
a public display and explanation *US*, 1948
From the name of a school activity for young children.
- I had ventured into a rest room at school, but not wanting to smoke dope, buy drugs, or converse with 20 robust fellows in Raiders jackets hosting a switchblade show-and-tell, I quickly turned around and left. — C.D. Payne, *Youth in Revolt*, p. 107, 1993

showboat *verb*
to show off; to pay attention to the performance aspects of a task *US*, 1951
From the C19 river steamers with theatrical performances and melodramatic, showy gamblers.
- The dude was hurt bad in the eleventh [round], but he showboated his way out like 't weren't nothin'[.] — Edwin Torres, *Carlito's Way*, p. 135, 1975
- It was that showboat lawyer you worked for. — Elmore Leonard, *Bandits*, p. 213, 1987

show buddy *noun*
in the language surrounding the Grateful Dead, a friend with whom you team up for Grateful Dead tours *US*, 1994
- — David Shenk and Steve Silberman, *Skeleton Key*, p. 224, 1994

showcase *verb*
to show off *US*, 1945
- — Lavada Durst, *The Jives of Dr. Hepcat*, p. 13, 1953
- I liked showcasing with her and I'd take her to all the sets with me[.] — A.S. Jackson, *Gentleman Pimp*, p. 156, 1973

showdown *noun*
1 in prison, private time for sex *US*, 1972
- It was pretty hard to get a showdown, any kind of privacy, long enough for intercourse anyway. — Bruce Jackson, *In the Life*, p. 365, 1972
2 in poker, the moment when betting is completed and the players show their hands *US*, 1982
- — David M. Hayano, *Poker Faces*, p. 187, 1982

shower cap *noun*
a condom *US*, 1969
- — *Current Slang*, p. 13, Summer 1969

shower hawk *noun*
a sexual predator who lurks near a prison shower in search of potential victims *US*, 2002
- — Jeffrey Ian Ross, *Behind Bars*, p. 195, 2002: Slammer Slang

shower-spank *verb*
(of a male) to masturbate in the shower *US*, 1989
- — Pamela Munro, *U.C.L.A. Slang*, p. 79, 1989

show house *noun*
a homosexual brothel *US*, 1981
- — *Male Swinger Number 3*, p. 48, 1981: "The complete gay dictionary"

show me the money
used as a humorous urging that a statement be backed up *US*, 1996
A key catchphrase in the US in the late 1990s.
- TIDWELL: It's a very personal, very important thing. It's a family motto. So I want to share it with you. You ready? JERRY: Yes. TIDWELL: Here it is. "Show me the money." Show. Me. The. Money. — *Jerry Maguire*, 1996

showstopper *noun*
a proposal that would lead to a breakdown in negotiations; a deal killer *US*, 1997
- "Ouch ... there's a showstopper"—he grinned—"I never thought of that." — Stephen J. Cannell, *King Con*, p. 129, 1997

showtime *noun*
time for something to begin *US*, 1992
- It's showtime. Grab your jacket. — *Reservoir Dogs*, 1992
- Some, especially those who already had guns and were way past streetwise, came on so showtime bad that they blew their chances in the first minute[.] — Jess Mowry, *Way Past Cool*, p. 99, 1992
- Showtime! — *Gone in 60 Seconds*, 2000

showtime *verb*
to dress or act ostentatiously *US*, 1993
- He'd come up from running to street-corner dealing, but had chilled with his green instead of showtiming with boomers and clothes. — Jess Mowry, *Six Out Seven*, p. 108, 1993

show-up *noun*
a process used by police to have witnesses to a crime identify the criminals *US*, 1969
- I know this black bitch is a cinch ringer for those eight larceny from the person beefs. We oughta take her down and put her on a "Show Up" or two. — Iceberg Slim (Robert Beck), *Pimp*, p. 177, 1969
- I had him in a regular show-up and I had a few private mug-shot show-ups, and I talked and coaxed and damned near threatened my victims and witnesses. — Joseph Wambaugh, *The Blue Knight*, p. 161, 1973
- Specifically, the defendant argues that the show up identification must be suppressed on the grounds that the procedure employed by the police was unduly suggestive. — *Daily Record of Rochester (New York)*, 22nd December 2003

show-up box *noun*
a room in a jail where suspects are shown for identification by witnesses *US*, 1953
- In the corner of the cell block there may be a second door that leads to the show-up box. One of its walls is wire mesh painted black. On the back wall are ruled lines for height. — Raymond Chandler, *The Long Goodbye*, p. 44, 1953

shpilkes *noun*
an inability to sit still *US*, 1982
- I should be napping, I guess, but I'm sitting on shpilkes, as Mom used to say about twice a day. — Armistead Maupin, *Maybe the Moon*, p. 289, 1992

SHPOS *noun*
a critically ill hospital patient who fails to follow medical instructions, worsening their own condition; a sub-*h*uman piece of shit *US, 1978*
- — *Maledicta*, p. 69, Summer/Winter 1978: "Common patient-directed pejoratives used by medical personnel"

shpritz; schpritz *verb*
to squirt or spray *US, 1967*
Yiddish.
- The Irish got schpritzed and schpritzed and schpritzed. — Lenny Bruce, *The Essential Lenny Bruce*, p. 20, 1967

shrapnel *noun*
the ripple effect in poker of a player completely losing his composure and infecting other players with his poor play *US, 1996*
- Brooks went broke, of course, but I caught a little shrapnel. — John Vorhaus, *The Big Book of Poker Slang*, p. 33, 1996

shred *verb*
to perform very well; to excel *US, 1977*
- — Gary Fairmont R. Filosa II, *The Surfer's Almanac*, p. 194, 1977
- — *San Francisco Sunday Examiner & Chronicle*, p. 20, 2nd September 1984: "Say it right"
- — *Carmel (California) High School Yearbook*, 1987
- — Judi Sanders, *Cal Poly Slang*, p. 9, 1990

shredache *noun*
the headache resulting from extreme exertion while surfing *US, 2004*
A punned version of the standard "headache," built on **SHRED** (performing well).
- — *Transworld Surf*, p. 42, April 2004

shredded *adjective*
1 weary; weak *US, 1986*
- FERRIS: How do you feel? CAMERON: Shredded. — *Ferris Bueller's Day Off*, 1986
2 muscular as the result of intense workouts *US, 2000*
- "My body was shredded down, cut as they call it and I was totally ripped." — Robert Picarello, *Rules of the Ring*, p. 139, 2000
- — Connie Eble (Editor), *UNC-CH Campus Slang*, p. 5, Spring 2001

shredder *noun*
a snowboarder *US, 1995*
- — Jim Humes and Sean Wagstaff, *Boarderlands*, p. 224, 1995

shredding *adjective*
extreme; exciting; good *US, 1987*
- — *New York Times*, 12th April 1987

shrewd *adjective*
attractive; popular; savvy *US, 1962*
- — *Dobie Gillis Teenage Slanguage Dictionary*, 1962

shriek *noun*
1 distilled, concentrated heroin *US, 1987*
- — Carsten Stroud, *Close Pursuit*, p. 269, 1987
2 an exclamation mark (!) *US, 1983*
- — Guy L. Steele et al., *The Hacker's Dictionary*, p. 115, 1983

shrimp *noun*
1 a short person *UK, 1386*
- A shrimp don't have to be a wimp, but a wimp is always a shrimp, that's what I always say. — Joe Bob Briggs, *Joe Bob Goes to the Drive-In*, p. 21, 1987
2 a small penis *US, 1972*
- — Bruce Rodgers, *The Queens' Vernacular*, p. 180, 1972

shrimp *verb*
to suck another's toes *US, 2002*
A sexual fetish.
- "Victor Alexander" (Spalding Gray) as El Sharif gets shrimped in Ilsa, Harem Keeper of the Oil Sheiks. — Bill Landis, *Sleazoid Express*, p. 225, 2002

shrimp queen; shrimper *noun*
a person with a fetish for the toes *US, 1971*
- His favorite territory is your feet. A Shrimp Queen of the first order—and I am not putting him down by using the old-time vernacular, because he's a groovy guy all the way around. I just

don't know of another moniker for someone who sucks toes. — John Francis Hunter, *The Gay Insider*, p. 88, 1971

shrink *verb*
to treat (someone) in psychotherapy *US, 1971*
- "You shrink me and I plug items for you?" — David Freeman, *U.S. Grant in the City*, p. 148, 1971

shrinkage *noun*
the condition of a man's genitals after swimming in cold water *US, 1994*
Coined and popularized on an episode of Jerry Seinfeld's television program (*The Hamptons*) that first aired on 24th May 1994.

shroomer *noun*
a recreational drug user who takes hallucinogenic mushrooms *US, 1993*
- At the very least, give the shroomer the remote control, and make it very clear that it's OK to turn it off if things are getting hairy. — *alt.drugs*, 24th September 1993
- I've never been a big "shroomer" though. — Columbia University's Health Education Program, *The "Go Ask Alice" Book of Answers*, p. 235, 1998

shroomers *noun*
mushrooms as a pizza topping *US, 1996*
- — *Maledicta*, p. 21, 1996: "Domino's pizza jargon"

shrooms *noun*
psychoactive mushrooms *US, 1987*
- — Connie Eble (Editor), *UNC-CH Campus Slang*, p. 6, Fall 1987
- JAY: I got hits, hash, weed, and later on I'll have shrooms. We take cash, or stolen MasterCard and Visa. — *Clerks*, 1994
- One of the grips comes up to me at the premiere and says, "Dude, shrooms." And you know, I didn't know mushrooms, so I took I don't know how many. (Quoting Pauly Shore) — *Spin Magazine*, October 1999

shroud *noun*
from the perspective of a man not accustomed to dressing up, a suit *US, 1962*
- — Joseph E. Ragen and Charles Finston, *Inside the World's Toughest Prison*, p. 817, 1962: "Penitentiary and underworld glossary"

shtarker *noun*
a strong and brave person *US, 1959*
Yiddish, from German.
- I don't want no trouble with that starker. — Chester Himes, *The Real Cool Killers*, p. 60, 1959
- With you, I agree. But Detective Canales here's a shtarker. — Emmett Grogan, *Final Score*, p. 165, 1976
- [O]f the 150, probably 100 were justs a bunch of shtarkers who could pull at one end of a rope that was looped around some poor fucker's neck, while some other lump pulled at the other end. — Richard Condon, *Prizzi's Honor*, p. 118, 1982

shtetl *noun*
a predominantly Jewish neighborhood *UK, 1949*
From the German for "village," originally applied to small Jewish villages in eastern Europe.
- He was also drawn from reality, from Mel's mother and other old-timers who had seen the world change so much it seemed like centuries since they left the shtetl. — Albert Goldman, *Freak Show*, p. 249, 1968

shtick; schtick; shtik; schtik *noun*
1 a theatrical routine, an act; hence a style, routine or behavior *US, 1961*
From German *stück* (a bit, a piece) into Yiddish, and thence more widespread.
- [T]hey had each settled on their shtik, a signature style they hoped would be as identifying as Zack's drips were. — John Updike, *Seek My Face*, p. 95, 2002
2 an area of interest *US, 1968*
From the Yiddish for "piece" or "play."
- I can't deal with them digits every day—bad numbers, runners robbing you, all that bookkeeping every day—I'd go crazy. Nah, that ain't my stick. — Edwin Torres, *Carlito's Way*, p. 84, 1975
- I was really a lousy whore. That wasn't my shtick at all. — Kate Millett, *The Prostitution Papers*, p. 116, 1976

- No way, man. Konks or marcels ain't my stick. — Piri Thomas, *Stories from El Barrio*, p. 53, 1978

shtunk; shtonk noun
a nasty person; a jerk *US, 1977*
Yiddish, from German.
- "With all due respects, he's a shtonk," Lubsin said, his puffy eyes expanding into a stare. — Edwin Torres, *Q & A*, p. 131, 1977

shtup noun
an act of sexual intercourse *US, 1986*
- He gives them all a good shtup. — Josh Alan Friedman, *Tales of Times Square*, p. 42, 1986
- Margaret's Museum (1995) offered a wet and wild shower shtup. — Mr. Skin, *Mr. Skin's Skincyclopedia*, p. 75, 2005

shtup; shtoop; schtup verb
to have sex *US, 1986*
Yiddish from the German for "to push."
- It was funny, because when we first got married, I had never slept with a woman before. I had schtupped plenty of women, but I had never slept with one. — Lenny Bruce, *How to Talk Dirty and Influence People*, p. 79, 1965
- With those legs—why of course he was shtupping her … Wasn't he? — Philip Roth, *Portnoy's Complaint*, p. 92, 1969
- The photography is as honest as a stag film and you see close-ups of the guy shtupping (fucking) the girl's hole. — *Screw*, p. 17, 12th January 1970
- Then when she finds out he [Woody Allen]'s schtupping the girl, he tells Mia [Farrow] he fucked her daughter to instill confidence in her. — Howard Stern, *Miss America*, p. 248, 1995

shuck noun
1 nonsense; something of little worth *US, 1851*
- [H]ow many times have you heard people say of bands: "Man, what a shuck! I could get up there and cut that shit." — Lester Bangs, *Psychotic Reactions and Carburetor Dung*, p. 38, 1970
- [H]e says it's the same shuck all around[.] — Lawrence Block, *No Score [The Affairs of Chip Harrison Omnibus]*, p. 153, 1970
2 a deception; a tease *US, 1959*
- — Lawrence Lipton, *The Holy Barbarians*, p. 317, 1959
- Q: I want to hear about this ethic of the street. The poverty ethic, the Indian ethic. SHIRLY: Somehow I think it's mostly a shuck. — Leonard Wolfe (Editor), *Voices from the Love Generation*, p. 238, 1968
- Well, you knew it was a shuck but what could you say? — John Sinclair, *Guitar Army*, p. 123, 1972
3 in poker, a card that may be discarded and replaced *US, 1981*
- — Jim Glenn, *Programed Poker*, p. 157, 1981

shuck verb
to deceive someone in a blustery, teasing manner *US, 1959*
Often used with "jive."
- Damn, a rifle in my mouth and him shucking around like that! — A.S. Jackson, *Gentleman Pimp*, p. 94, 1973
- She had paused to shuck and jive on the sidewalk with a grocery clerk. — Iceberg Slim (Robert Beck), *Death Wish*, p. 119, 1977
- Hunter said, "You gonna start shucking me again, Darrold? We're talking about murder, man, not a little half-assed assault." — Elmore Leonard, *City Primeval*, p. 59, 1980

shucker noun
a striptease dancer *US, 1981*
- — Don Wilmeth, *The Language of American Popular Entertainment*, p. 241, 1981

shuckman noun
a swindler *US, 1965*
- It was on that Sixth Street to Market, between Central Avenue and Plum / that's the worst old place in ragtown for a shuckman or gun. — Bruce Jackson, *Get Your Ass in the Water and Swim Like Me*, p. 85, 1965

shucks
used as a register of dismay or contempt *US, 1847*
Used where **SHIT**! might do.
- Shucks, even a hard-working nigger wouldn't shoot a white man if he come home and found him in bed with his old lady with his pants down. — Chester Himes, *The Real Cool Killers*, p. 59, 1959
- Shucks. I drove here from Phoenix in a day and a half. — Gurney Norman, *Divine Right's Trip (Last Whole Earth Catalog)*, p. 47, 1971

shuffle noun
1 the movement by a surfer forward on the board while surfing, executed without crossing the feet *US, 1965*
- — Peter L. Dixon, *The Complete Book of Surfing*, p. 215, 1965
2 counterfeit money *US, 1950*
- — Hyman E. Goldin et al., *Dictionary of American Underworld Lingo*, p. 194, 1950

shuffle verb
▸ **shuffle off to Buffalo**
to leave *US, 1986*
The reference to Buffalo, New York, is for the sake of rhyme and adds nothing to the meaning.
- The dancers high-kick one last time and go shuffling off to Buffalo off the floor. — Robert Campbell, *Junkyard Dog*, p. 132, 1986

shuteye; shut-eye noun
sleep *UK, 1896*
- Shuteye on the bus, sneakin' into the woods at the side of the road instead of goin' to a toilet. — Ross Russell, *The Sound*, p. 60, 1961
- Now take your stinking yellow ass upstairs to a bath and some shut-eye. — Iceberg Slim (Robert Beck), *Pimp*, p. 272, 1969
- "OK, you grab some shut-eye so you'll be beautiful as hell when you wake up." — Georgia Sothern, *My Life in Burlesque*, p. 115, 1972

shutout noun
any situation in which a person fails to score, literally or figuratively *US, 1957*
- There was a series of assorted gropes, some moderately successful, some shutouts. — Max Shulman, *Rally Round the Flag, Boys!*, pp. 6–7, 1957

shutter noun
the eyelid *US, 1945*
- — Lou Shelly, *Hepcats Jive Talk Dictionary*, p. 17, 1945
- — Clarence Major, *Dictionary of Afro-American Slang*, p. 103, 1970

shutterbug noun
a photography enthusiast; a photographer *US, 1940*
- The shutterbug's partner could only gape as the 25-ton yacht settled a few more inches, causing the keel to angle up. — Joseph Wambaugh, *Floaters*, p. 2, 1996

shut UP!
shut up *US, 1989*
The difference between the slang "shut up" and the colloquial is the emphasis on a drawn out "up" with register rising slightly for the "up."
- TED: Remember when she was a senior and we were freshmen? BILL: Shut up, Ted. — *Bill and Ted's Excellent Adventure*, 1989

shuzzit noun
marijuana *US, 1971*
A discreet variation of **SHIT**.
- — Ernest L. Abel, *A Marijuana Dictionary*, p. 92, 1982

shvantz noun
the penis *US, 1954*
From the Yiddish.
- "I swear to Christ his shvantz is about a foot long" — Dan Greenburg, *Love Kills*, p. 6, 1979
- Hayley-Jane begins by whipping two trussed-up fellas before swallowing their shvantzes. — Editors of Adult Video News, *The AVN Guide to the 500 Greatest Adult Films of All Time*, p. 65, 2005
- "She's got her hand just wrapped around his schvantz." — Chris Miller, *The Real Animal House*, p. 136, 2006

shvartz; schvartz noun
a black person *US, 1961*
Also seen as "schwartz," "schvartze" and "schvartza." The Yiddish term *schvartz* (from the German for "black.") is an adjective, with *schvartzer* as the noun for "a black person." "Schvartz" the adjective became an inside, "code" word among Jews for "a black person."
- As soon as they find out you're Jewish, they wanna have their daughter marry you and not one of the south-of-the-border schwartzas. — Clancy Sigal, *Going Away*, p. 355, 1961
- She irons better even than the schvartze. — Philip Roth, *Portnoy's Complaint*, p. 12, 1969
- This shagger I have at last nailed is the color of coffee and cream. A shvartzer. — Leo Rosten, *Silky!*, p. 32, 1979
- For the love of Christ, LOSE THAT SCHWARTZE! — Terry Southern, *Now Dig This*, p. 242, 2001

shvitz; schvitz *verb*
to perspire *US, 1992*
Yiddish, from German.

- Schvitzing like a pig. — Armistead Maupin, *Maybe the Moon*, p. 16, 1992

- [S]he would, unforced, shvitz like a galley slave in a "gym" three times a week. — Jimmy Lerner, *You Got Nothing Coming*, p. 326, 2002

shvontz *noun*
the penis *US, 1965*
- — *The Guild Dictionary of Homosexual Terms*, p. 40, 1965
- — Collin Baker et al., *College Undergraduate Slang Study Conducted at Brown University*, p. 189, 1968
- I think this portrays you as a good-looking, hot-headed gavonne who's probably—excuse me, ladies—got a schvanze that's a yard long. — James Ellroy, *Hollywood Nocturnes*, p. 26, 1994

shvug *noun*
a black person *US, 1999*
- "And next to him is ths big fuckin' shvug, no offense, with an Afro out to here." — Richard Price, *Samaritan*, p. 255, 2003

shy *noun*
a person who illegally loans money at very high interest rates and often has violent collection procedures *US, 1973*
An abbreviation of **SHYLOCK**.
- "You want a good shy, get a fuckin' kike." — George Higgins, *The Digger's Game*, p. 151, 1973

shy *verb*
to cook opium pellets for smoking *US, 1946*
- "This is what you call shyin', kid," the cook said. This cooks all the poison out of the pill. — Mezz Mezzrow, *Really the Blues*, p. 99, 1946

shy *adjective*
in debt; owing money *US, 1950*
- — *The Annals of the American Academy of Political and Social Sciences*, p. 130, May 1950
- — Irv Roddy, *Friday Night Poker*, p. 220, 1961

shylock *noun*
1 a person who illegally loans money at very high interest rates and often has violent collection procedures *US, 1930*
The allusion to Shakespeare's usurious money-lender in *The Merchant of Venice* cannot be missed.
- "I know a shylock that'll give you a break if you tell him I sent you." — Irving Shulman, *Cry Tough*, p. 127, 1949
- Then the Corleone family shylocks were barred from the waterfront piers. — Mario Puzo, *The Godfather*, p. 253, 1969
- And now he was in his fifties and the only blind shylock in the world. — Emmett Grogan, *Ringolevio*, p. 100, 1972
- I do collection for Harry once in a while. Harry, or different shylocks call, they want me to lean on some guy. — Elmore Leonard, *Riding the Rap*, p. 23, 1995

2 in circus and carnival usage, the show's office secretary *US, 1981*
- — Don Wilmeth, *The Language of American Popular Entertainment*, p. 241, 1981

shylock *verb*
to engage in usurious loan practices *UK, 1930*
- — *American Speech*, p. 306, December 1964: "Lingua Cosa Nostra"
- Morse had the books and Rose was handling the shylocking. — Mickey Spillane, *Last Cop Out*, p. 10, 1972
- "But," he said, convinced now that he was being shylocked, "how am I going to pay the interest?" — Edward Lin, *Big Julie of Vegas*, p. 85, 1974

shylocking *noun*
the illegal loan business *US, 1948*
- Loan shark rackets, or shylocking as it is called on the docks, follow the same terrorizing methods. — Hendrik De Leeuw, *Underworld Story*, p. 297, 1955
- "There's all kinds of angles," he says, a little impatient with me. "Shylocking, slot machines, maybe some whores" — Charles Perry, *Portrait of a Young Man Drowning*, p. 117, 1962
- The first of these was "shylocking," or the loan shark racket—the lending of money at high interest rates[.] — Peter Maas, *The Valachi Papers*, p. 165, 1968

shyster *noun*
a lawyer, especially an unprofessional, dishonest or rapacious lawyer; any dishonest professional *US, 1843*

In his *Origin of the Term Shyster*, slang lexicographer Gerald Cohen demonstrates the craft of slang etymology at its highest: "coined by New York journalist Mike Walsh."
- If we get a confession, we beat it out of the guy, they say, and some shyster calls us Gestapo in court[.] — Raymond Chandler, *The Little Sister*, p. 218, 1949
- Our girl's going to need fancier shysters than I can afford. — Truman Capote, *Breakfast at Tiffany's*, p. 94, 1958
- The next morning I had an appointment with a shyster agent[.] — Babs Gonzales, *I Paid My Dues*, p. 52, 1967
- I mean you're calling this shyster Al, like he's an old friend. — Robert Campbell, *Juice*, p. 155, 1988

shysty *adjective*
greedy, grimy *US, 1999*
- When we arrive at her apartment building, a bunch of shysty cats loll outside. — Colton Simpson, *Inside the Crips*, p. 171, 2005
- Some people give you that shiesty vibe like you better watch your back or they'll dog you. — Linden Dalecki, *Kid B*, p. 147, 2006

sib *noun*
a sibling *US, 2004*
- His two younger sibs looked up to him. — Brittany Kent, *O.C. Undercover*, p. 2, 2004

Siberia *noun*
solitary confinement *US, 1984*
- — Inez Cardozo-Freeman, *The Joint*, p. 530, 1984

sice *noun*
in craps, the point and number six *US, 1950*
- — *The Annals of the American Academy of Political and Social Sciences*, p. 130, May 1950

Sicilian price *noun*
death, usually slow and painful, as punishment *US, 1997*
- [I]f Tommy had been involved in the tat at the Sabre Bay Casino and had stolen money from the dead-drop without an overwhelming personal reason, then Tommy would have to pay the Sicilian price. — Stephen J. Cannell, *Big Con*, p. 337, 1997

sick *noun*
withdrawal symptoms suffered by a drug addict *US, 1972*
- They were just down junkies and they hit the streets, separately, each one in his own way, trying to scrape together the necessary money to keep the sick off. — Emmett Grogan, *Ringolevio*, p. 51, 1972
- With his own sick coming on Joe was too weak to withhold the junk from another sufferer. — Seth Morgan, *Homeboy*, p. 26, 1990

sick *adjective*
1 suffering the symptoms of withdrawal from a drug addiction *US, 1938*
- But even now the feeling was upon him, not that he was sick, but he would be soon enough if he didn't get it[.] — Hal Ellson, *The Golden Spike*, p. 2, 1952
- He was really sick now, and his stomach was cramping. — Clarence Cooper Jr., *The Scene*, p. 39, 1960
- Up to Lexington, 125 / Feel sick and dirty, more dead than alive. — Velvet Underground, *I'm Waiting for the Man*, 1967
- Say, you like sick, like you need a fix / Perhaps I can do some solids for you. — Dennis Wepman et al., *The Life*, p. 55, 1976

2 excellent; wonderful *US, 1987*
On the principle that **BAD** means "good."
- — Connie Eble (Editor), *UNC-CH Campus Slang*, p. 6, Fall 1987
- — *Macon Telegraph and News*, p. 9A, 18th June 1989

3 in poker, without further funds *US, 1988*
- — George Percy, *The Language of Poker*, p. 82, 1988

4 infected with HIV or suffering from AIDS *US, 1990*
- Well I ain't sick. I all skinny and shit. — *Boyz N The Hood*, 1990
- "He ain't working now. He's kind of sick." "Oh yeah?" Rocco assumed that sick meant the Virus. — Richard Price, *Clockers*, p. 224, 1992

sick and wrong!
used for conveying a strong disagreement or disapproval *US, 1989*
- — Pamela Munro, *U.C.L.A. Slang*, p. 76, 1989

sick-bay commando *noun*
a soldier who feigns illness to avoid combat duty *US, 1987*

- I understand that as a former Marine, and you are obviously not a "sick bay commando," as we say. — House Committee on Veterans' Affairs, *Persian Gulf War Veterans and Related Issues*, p. 22, 1994

sickie *noun*
a deviant *US, 1972*

- There is one other branch of the sickies or weirdos whom I definitely would prefer never to have to do business with. — Xaviera Hollander, *The Happy Hooker*, p. 246, 1972
- Joan had gone noisily down the hall, screaming at Harvey about how he was a "sickie on a power trip." — Cyra McFadden, *The Serial*, p. 33, 1977

sickler *noun*
a person suffering from sickle-cell anemia *US, 1994*

- — Sally Williams, *"Strong" Words*, p. 160, 1994

sickness *noun*
the range of symptoms experienced when a drug addict is deprived of the drug *US, 1987*

- Warding off the sickness symptoms ... thee sneezing, the flashhees of quick transfer between hot and cold ... the dancing bowels ... I hate the litany. — Jim Carroll, *Forced Entries*, p. 110, 1987

sicko *noun*
an emotionally or psycho-sexually disturbed person *US, 1963*

- She's a sicko. Some kinda fruitcake or somethin. She plays with her own clit when I'm lovin her up. — Joseph Wambaugh, *The Black Marble*, p. 290, 1978
- This torrid tribute to the joys of dark meat features a chorus line of ebony beauties bouncing and boffing through a series of raunchy, relentlessly racist, and often unbearably funny skits that mine just about every sicko cliche[.] — *Adult Video*, p. 16, August/September 1986
- And Disco 2000 certainly let a whole generation of teenagers see homos and weirdos and sickos up close and personal, in all their majesty and splendor, — James St. James, *Party Monster*, pp. 77–78, 1990
- And these assholes are making heroes outta sickos. — *Natural Born Killers*, 1994

sick pad *noun*
a sanitary towel *US, 1966*

- Then the bitch come draggin' it home with her sickpad on / she talkin' shit, "Daddy, you sure is sweet / When you go down to the store bring me back a box a Kotex." — Bruce Jackson, *Get Your Ass in the Water and Swim Like Me*, p. 129, 1966

sick puppy *noun*
a perverted person *US, 1984*

- "This is harmless sport." "You're a sick puppy." — Carl Hiassen, *Strip Tease*, p. 239, 1993
- In your recent letter to the editor of The Anchorage Daily News, you make a strong case that I'm a sick puppy who should probably be put to sleep. — Marty Beckerman, *Death to All Cheerleaders*, p. 36, 2000

side *noun*
1 a recorded tune or song *US, 1936*

- I have within my comfy shed bottles of rare red wine and lots of sides and tapes of sounds. — Dan Burley, *Diggeth Thou?*, p. 33, 1959
- Then we went up to my place and started playing some sides and smoking pot. — Claude Brown, *Manchild in the Promised Land*, p. 183, 1965
- I bought all the latest sides. — Bobby Seale, *A Lonely Rage*, p. 110, 1978
- I'd invite these dullards up to my room, offer them pot (they'd decline), and put on some sides. — Richard Meltzer, *A Whore Just Like the Rest*, p. 536, 1998

2 a girl *US, 1972*

- — *American Speech*, p. 154, Spring–Summer 1972: "An approach to Black slang"

side arms *noun*
1 in poker, the lower value pair in a hand consisting of two pairs *US, 1988*

- — George Percy, *The Language of Poker*, p. 82, 1988

2 sugar and cream *US, 1945*

- — Lou Shelly, *Hepcats Jive Talk Dictionary*, p. 48, 1945

side boob *noun*
a photograph showing the exposed side of a clothed woman's breast *US, 1997*
A voyeuristic fetish fueled by exhibitionists such as Lindsay Lohan.

- Even the side boob of Cassandra at the end of "Prophecy" didn't instigate a thread. — *alt.tv.highlander*, 20th January 1997

- "Unlike some of us, I don't stay awake until three AM watching USA Up All Night on the chance they'll flash some side boob." — Christina Bartolomeo, *The Side of the Angels*, p. 152, 2004

side-buster *noun*
a person whose deeds do not match his description of his deeds *US, 1989*

- — James Harris, *A Convict's Dictionary*, p. 38, 1989

side comb *noun*
hair parted on the side *US, 1982*
Hawaiian youth usage.

- — Douglas Simonson, *Pidgin to da Max Hana Hou*, 1982

sidehill winder; sidehill gouger *noun*
a mythical animal whose legs are shorter on one side than the other from years of grazing on a hillside *US, 1975*

- — John Gould, *Maine Lingo*, p. 255, 1975
- Ah, you're just bullywhackin' the way you was when you tried to tell me about the side-hill gouger. — George Bowering, *Caprice*, p. 159, 1987

sidekick *noun*
a close friend and accomplice *US, 1906*

- Bull Durham was his sidekick before, but he couldn't see nothing but corona-coronas now. — Mezz Mezzrow, *Really the Blues*, p. 87, 1946
- Here's this honest cop, supposedly, using what he calls leverage, holding my old sidekick, my confidant, the Moose, over my head as a threat. — Elmore Leonard, *Glitz*, p. 330, 1985

side squeeze *noun*
a partner in romance other than your primary partner; a romantic affair *US, 1991*

- Jagger's spokesman said he hadn't heard anything about Jagger's side squeeze. — *Newsday (New York)*, p. 13, 2nd May 1991

sidewalk pizza *noun*
a puddle of vomit *US, 1997*

- I laughed even harder, causing me to toss a sidewalk pizza—much to Bob's delight. — Elissa Stein and Kevin Leslie, *Chunks*, p. 37, 1997

sideways trip *noun*
a suicide in prison *US, 1984*

- — Inez Cardozo-Freeman, *The Joint*, p. 530, 1984

side work *noun*
prostitution *US, 1996*

- Despite their assertion that go-go is only a bit of "good clean fun," many strip-club owners tolerate—or even encourage—prostitution (or "side work," as the dancers call it): a blow job or hand job outside in the parking lot[.] — James Ridgeway, *Red Light*, p. 204, 1996

sidity; sididy; seditty *adjective*
arrogant, boastful, showing off *US, 1963*

- After that recent party in that exclusive Pittsburgh club, the sidity folks who rented it out the next night claimed that the joint was "dirty," "nasty" and "filthy." — *New Pittsburgh Courier*, p. 11, 27th April 1963
- Real sidity affair, you know, all them stuck-up Montclair bitches and everything. — Nathan Heard, *Howard Street*, p. 31, 1968
- I don't care what your sidity friends think of me. — Christina and Richard Milner, *Black Players*, p. 307, 1972
- It was incredible what was going on, all those sidity people in Boston and Washington of a certain economic class formed these reading groups. — *News and Observer (Raleigh, North Carolina)*, p. 10 (What's Up), 31st January 2003

sieve *noun*
a hospital or admitting physician who freely admits patients *US, 1994*

- — Sally Williams, *"Strong" Words*, p. 160, 1994

sieve *verb*
to drill holes in a safe for the placement of explosives to be used in opening it *US, 1970*

- I decided to use every trick in the drilling business I had ever heard of to sieve it for the soup. — Red Rudensky, *The Gonif*, p. 7, 1970

siff *noun*
syphilis *US, 1972*

- There was a young lawyer of note / Who thought he had siff of the throat[.] — Robert A. Wilson, *Playboy's Book of Forbidden Words*, pp. 223–224, 1972

signal-to-noise ratio; s/n ratio *noun*
the amount of useful content found on an Internet site *US, 1997*
A figurative use of a technical term.

- A Letterman newsgroup in which most of the postings are pointless discussions of the best Stupid Pet Trick and conjectures about the sexual orientations of the band has a low signal-to-noise ratio. — Andy Ihnatko, *Cyberspeak*, p. 175, 1997

signify *verb*
to engage in ritualistic insults, goading, and teasing *US, 1932*
Unlike **DOZENS**, signifying does not make a person's mother the subject of the tease.

- Mary Jack commenced signifying with some nasty remarks. — Louis Armstrong, *Satchmo: My Life in New Orleans*, p. 73, 1954
- We take him by the neck and say, "Don't signify with me!" Bad thing, to signify—y'hear me? — Jack Kerouac, *On the Road*, p. 256, 1957
- Signifying is more humane. Instead of coming down on somebody's mother, you come down on them. — H. Rap Brown, *Die Nigger Die!*, p. 27, 1969
- Signifying: Lying or putting someone down. — Bobby Seale, *Seize the Time*, p. 409, 1970

sig quote *noun*
in computing, an aphorism automatically included with the user's formatted signature *US, 1991*

- — Eric S. Raymond, *The New Hacker's Dictionary*, p. 320, 1991

silent *adjective*
of an entry in a criminal's file, unofficial; showing crimes for which the criminal was not charged but probably committed *US, 1990*

- Silent beef. When the authorities believe a man guilty of a crime or crimes which they can't prove and must settle for a conviction on a lesser charge, they attach memoranda to the man's record stipulating the uncharged offenses. — Seth Morgan, *Homeboy*, p. 140, 1990

silent captain *noun*
in shuffleboard, the scoreboard *US, 1967*

- Your SILENT CAPTAIN—the scoreboard—dictates every single shot to be made!!! — Omero C. Catan, *Secrets of Shuffleboard Strategy*, p. 16, 1967

silk *noun*
1 a white person *US, 1960*

- Every dealer had five or six silks who spent a lot of money. — Clarence Cooper Jr., *The Scene*, p. 70, 1960
- [I]n Harlem white women are known as silks, due to the legend that their pubic hair feels silky to the skin. — Chester Himes, *Pinktoes*, p. 157, 1961

2 a homosexual *US, 1972*

- — David Claerbaut, *Black Jargon in White America*, p. 77, 1972

3 in the categorization of sexual activity by teenage boys, a touch of a girl's crotch outside her underwear *US, 1986*

- Next in order of significant intimacy was "getting silk," which meant touching panty-crotch, and then for the more successful, "getting pube." — Terry Southern, *Now Dig This*, p. 3, 1986

4 money *US, 1950*

- — Hyman E. Goldin et al., *Dictionary of American Underworld Lingo*, p. 195, 1950

▸ **hit the silk; take to silk**
to open a parachute after jumping from a plane *US, 1933*

- — *American Speech*, p. 319, October/December 1948: "Slang of the American paratrooper"
- Sandy and Oscar Brice had collided when they were doing a squirrel cage, and both of them had to hit the silk. — Gregory "Pappy" Boyington, *Baa Baa Black Sheep*, p. 140, 1958

silk *adjective*
1 white-skinned *US, 1969*

- I saw the "silk" chicks crane their necks toward the door. — Iceberg Slim (Robert Beck), *Pimp*, p. 127, 1969

2 homosexual *US, 1962*

- — Anthony Romeo, *The Language of Gangs*, p. 21, 4th December 1962

silk and satin *noun*
any combination of central nervous system stimulants and central nervous system depressants *US, 1980*

- — Edith A. Folb, *runnin' down some lines*, p. 254, 1980

silk dealer *noun*
a brothel manager or pimp with white prostitutes *US, 1961*

- Now if some compatriot in Harlem had asked Jonah for the name and address of his own silk dealer Jonah would have sent him to the same house where he could meet some white women. — Chester Himes, *Pinktoes*, p. 157, 1961

silk hat *noun*
in circus and carnival usage, an egocentrist *US, 1981*

- — Don Wilmeth, *The Language of American Popular Entertainment*, p. 242, 1981

silkies *noun*
a woman's underpants *US, 1986*

- Because she gets candy all the goddamn time from every asshole tryin' to get into her silkies. — Robert Campbell, *In La-La Land We Trust*, p. 180, 1986

silks *noun*
silk or nylon socks *US, 1972*

- — David Claerbaut, *Black Jargon in White America*, p. 79, 1972

silk-stocking *adjective*
wealthy *US, 1970*

- I worked a silk stocking division out on the west side when I first came out of the academy and I never thought of a Caucasian asshole in terms of race. — Joseph Wambaugh, *The New Centurions*, p. 146, 1970

silky *adjective*
excellent; pleasing; smooth *US, 1973*

- Everything was roses. I was contented. And life itself was silky. — A.S. Jackson, *Gentleman Pimp*, p. 43, 1973

silky-straight *noun*
any hairstyle with artificially straightened hair *US, 1981*

- The brother was one of those dumb old raghead niggers, probably been in sail the last twenty years and didn't notice nobody wore silky-straights anymore, not even pimps. — Joseph Wambaugh, *The Glitter Dome*, p. 59, 1981

silly affairs *noun*
used as a humorous synonym for "Civil Affairs" *US, 1968*

- — Carl Fleischhauer, *A Glossary of Army Slang*, p. 14, 1968

sillyvillian *noun*
a civilian, seen from the cynical eyes of the military *US, 1963*

- You know you're needed as much here as among all those sillyvillians. — Herbert Tarr, *The Conversion of Chaplain Cohen*, p. 298, 1963

silly walk *noun*
in computing, an absurd procedure that must be followed *US, 1991*
A borrowing from Monty Python.

- — Eric S. Raymond, *The New Hacker's Dictionary*, p. 321, 1991

silver *noun*
1 money *US, 1966*

- — Andy Anonymous, *A Basic Guide to Campusology*, p. 22, 1966

2 in American casinos, a silver coin or $1 chip *US, 1980*

- — Lee Solkey, *Dummy Up and Deal*, p. 119, 1980
- — Steve Kuriscak, *Casino Talk*, p. 50, 1985

silver bike *noun*
a metal syringe *US, 1970*
Drug addict usage.

- — William D. Alsever, *Glossary for the Establishment and Other Uptight People*, p. 19, December 1970
- — Walter Way, *The Drug Scene*, p. 114, 1977

silver bracelets *noun*
handcuffs *US, 1991*

- If the pieces do fall into place, some unlucky citizen gets a pair of silver bracelets and a wagon ride to an overcrowded tier of the Baltimore City Jail. — David Simon, *Homicide*, p. 17, 1991
- [T]here is no sight more unwelcome than that of Officer Robert Brown, back from his vacation, laying hands upon the sinners and working the silver bracelets hard. — David Simon and Edward Burns, *The Corner*, p. 147, 1997

silver bullet *noun*
a martini *US, 1980*

- "Nother dose of them silver bullets, Chris baby," Lurleen said, waiving her martini glass. — George Higgins, *Kennedy for the Defense*, p. 123, 1980
- Five hours, he must've had twenty silver bullets. — Elmore Leonard, *Freaky Deaky*, p. 65, 1988

silver goose *noun*

a proctoscope *US, 1988–1989*
- — *Maledicta*, p. 34, 1988–1989: "Medical maledicta from San Francisco"

silver lady *noun*

a hypodermic needle and syringe *US, 1993*
- — Peter Johnson, *Dictionary of Street Alcohol and Drug Terms*, p. 170, 1993

silvermine *verb*

to patrol a casino in search of coins left in the tray of a slot machine or dropped on the floor *US, 1985*
- Finally, there's silvermining, which may not be exactly a form of cheating but might qualify as the next thing to it. — Jim Regan, *Winning at Slot Machine*, p. 68, 1985

silver spoon *noun*

used as a metaphor of wealth at birth, especially in the expression "born with a silver spoon in your mouth" *US, 1901*
- My parents were exorbitant. Filthy rich. And they'd raised me in that silver-spoon tradition. — Oscar Zeta Acosta, *The Autobiography of a Brown Buffalo*, p. 147, 1972

simoleon *noun*

a dollar *US, 1883*
- If he was to cuss you simoleons out and put you out his car you'd say he was a bad fellow. — Chester Himes, *If He Hollers Let Him Go*, p. 102, 1945
- Not far away, the loft in which I'd earned my eighteen simoleons a week with the other sweated youths. — Philip Wylie, *Opus 21*, p. 289, 1949
- Jack, shekels, mazuma, simoleons, Mr. Green, filthy lucre, even spondulicks—this is other Why of prostitution. — Gail Sheehy, *Hustling*, p. 11, 1973
- I bet you will stash away 1,000,000 bucks (or "simoleons" as we used to say at old Crane Tech.) — Leo Rosten, *Dear Herm*, p. 120, 1974

simon

emphatically yes *US, 1970*
Mexican-American Spanish slang used in English conversation.
- "Can you come tonight and bring some money?" "Simon. Where at?" — Frank Bonham, *Viva Chicano*, p. 66, 1970

simp *adjective*

fashionable *US, 1965*
- Then I'll put on my simp togs for I will have my gage. — Bruce Jackson, *Get Your Ass in the Water and Swim Like Me*, p. 124, 1965

simple pimp *noun*

a pimp who fails to live up to the high standards of his fellow pimps *US, 1972*
- See, you got so many squares out there trying to pimp, it's pathetic. Would-be pimps. You know what I mean? Simple pimp, that's what we call them. Simple pimp. — Christina and Richard Milner, *Black Players*, p. 61, 1972
- Pimps who do solicit for their women are called popcorn pimps or simple pimps by the boss pimps. — Burgess Laughlin, *Job Opportunities in the Black Market*, p. 11–4, 1978

simple Simon *noun*

psilocybin, a hallucinogenic mushroom *US, 1967*
- — Elizabeth Finn, *Drugs in the Tenderloin*, 1967: Glossary of Drug Slang Used in the Tenderloin
- — William D. Alsever, *Glossary for the Establishment and Other Uptight People*, p. 29, December 1970

simp twister *noun*

in circus and carnival usage, a carousel *US, 1981*
- — Don Wilmeth, *The Language of American Popular Entertainment*, p. 243, 1981

since Hector was a pup

for a very long time *US, 1904*
- One of the last links with the old days of burlesque in Washington is Abraham Attenson, the portly manager of the Gayety Theater, who has been in burlesque since Hector was a pup. — *Washington Post*, p. 14, 27th March 1977
- We'll go up there and prove it. We haven't lost a case since Hector was a pup. — *Union Leader* (Manchester, New Hampshire), p. A1, 29th February 2004

sin city *noun*

the neighborhood in An Khe, Vietnam, housing brothels, bars, and other vice dens *US, 1968*
- — Carl Fleischhauer, *A Glossary of Army Slang*, p. 15, 1968

- Although the prostitution corner ("Sin City" or "Disneyland") is run by the Vietnamese, American military police patrol the area to check the pass of every soldier entering it. — Charles Winick, *The Lively Commerce*, p. 265, 1971
- Outside An Khe, the 1st Cav built an area for soldiers to go relieve themselves. Bars, whorehouses. I would open at nine in the morning. We called it Sin City. — Wallace Terry, *Bloods*, p. 25, 1984

sing *verb*

1 to give information or evidence, usually to the police *US, 1929*
- I don't worry about them any more than you do about shaking a guy down and then shooting him in the back to keep him from singing[.] — Horace McCoy, *Kiss Tomorrow Good-bye*, p. 263, 1948
- When it became obvious that the Mafia had double-crossed him, he threatened to "sing his head off." — Alson Smith, *Syndicate City*, p. 94, 1954
- Been makin' it all his life singing songs for the cops. — Donald Goines, *Kenyatta's Last Hit*, p. 69, 1975
- Yeah they don't know our names, but they can sing about this place. — *Reservoir Dogs*, 1992

2 in carnival usage, to make a sales pitch *US, 1981*
- — Don Wilmeth, *The Language of American Popular Entertainment*, p. 243, 1981

▸ **sing in the choir**

to be homosexual *US, 1994*
Cute code.
- — Kevin Dilallo, *The Unofficial Gay Manual*, p. 245, 1994

▸ **sing like a canary**

to give information or evidence, usually to the police *US, 1950*
An elaboration of **SING**.
- I heard that the Mafia narcotic syndicate believed this man was "singing like a canary" to us. — Harry J. Anslinger, *The Murderers*, p. 94, 1961

sing-cerely

used as a humorous closing in letters between singers *US, 1975*
- — *American Speech*, p. 301, Autumn–Winter 1975: "The jargon of barbershop"

singer *noun*

in a confidence swindle, a participant who passes information about the false enterprise to the victim *US, 1988*
- — M. Allen Henderson, *How Con Games Work*, p. 222, 1985: "Glossary"
- — Kathleen Odean, *High Steppers, Fallen Angels, and Lollipops*, p. 132, 1988
- There were also "singers" to give background information to Tommy Rina when he was checking Beano out[.] — Stephen J. Cannell, *King Con*, p. 130, 1997

single eye *noun*

a Japanese person *US, 1982*
Hawaiian youth usage.
- — Douglas Simonson, *Pidgin to da Max Hana Hou*, 1982

single-O *noun*

a criminal, gambling cheat, or a prisoner who acts alone *US, 1962*
- — Frank Garcia, *Marked Cards and Loaded Dice*, p. 264, 1962
- As he considered it years later he might have done all right if he had stayed on the single-O, but though he had many of the characteristics of a loner he wasn't a true solitary. — Malcolm Braly, *On the Yard*, p. 229, 1967
- — Inez Cardozo-Freeman, *The Joint*, p. 531, 1984
- — Lindsay E. Smith and Bruce A. Walstad, *Sting Shift*, p. 117, 1989: "Glossary"

single-O *verb*

to operate as a criminal without confederates; to operate selfishly within a criminal enterprise *US, 1950*
- — Hyman E. Goldin et al., *Dictionary of American Underworld Lingo*, p. 195, 1950

single-O *adjective*

selfish; alone *US, 1950*
- — Hyman E. Goldin et al., *Dictionary of American Underworld Lingo*, p. 195, 1950
- "I'm single-o, man, so I follow the action." — Burt Hirschfield, *Fire Island*, p. 27, 1970

singles bar *noun*

a bar that caters to a young, unattached clientele *US, 1969*
- When I used to go to singles bars, I'd wear my San Diego Blood Bank T-shirt just to show all the lonely nurses and schoolteachers that I'm a clean donor. — Joseph Wambaugh, *Finnegan's Week*, p. 154, 1993

sink *noun*

in the language of hang gliding, falling air that increases the speed of descent *US, 1977*

- — Dennis Pagen, *Hang Gliding and Flying Skills*, p. 110, 1977: "Glossary"

▸ **behind the sink**

depleted of funds *US, 1974*

- — John Scarne, *Scarne on Dice*, p. 460, 1974

sinker *noun*

1 a doughnut *US, 1870*

- — Joseph E. Ragen and Charles Finston, *Inside the World's Toughest Prison*, p. 817, 1962: "Penitentiary and underworld glossary"
- Not even enough for a cup of coffee and a sinker. — Robert Byrne, *McGoorty*, p. 97, 1972
- — Don Wilmeth, *The Language of American Popular Entertainment*, p. 243, 1981

2 a potato pancake *US, 1953*

- Davey handed her the platter with the mound of grated potatoes. "Let's have a fast chorus on these sinkers." — Edwin Gilbert, *The Hot and the Cool*, p. 52, 1953

3 a dent on a surfboard that requires a resin filler *US, 1986*

- — George Colendich, *The Ding Repair Scriptures*, p. 88, 1986

sin loi, motherfucker

sorry about that *US, 1990*

Xin loi or *sin loi* is Vietnamese meaning something in the nature of "sorry about that." It was widely heard and widely used by US troops in Vietnam.

- — Gregory Clark, *Words of the Vietnam War*, p. 477, 1990

sip *verb*

▸ **sip at the fuzzy cup**

to perform oral sex on a woman *US, 1980*

- — Edith A. Folb, *runnin' down some lines*, p. 254, 1980

siphon *verb*

▸ **siphon the python; syphon the python**

(of a male) to have sex *US, 1984*

- The bartender spoke slowly, as if to an idiot child. "You know, push the bush? Slake the snake? Drain the train? Siphon the python?" — James Ellroy, *Because the Night*, p. 415, 1984

Sir Charles *noun*

the Viet Cong *US, 1982*

- — *Maledicta*, p. 254, Summer/Winter 1982: "Viet-speak"
- We were busting bush in III Corps, looking for "Sir Charles" in an area they called the Hobo Woods. — Lonnie Dotson, *BOOM! Another Landmine*, 2000

sis *noun*

used as a term of address for a sister *UK, 1656*

- Hey, you're gonna love this place, aren't you sis? — Elmore Leonard, *City Primeval*, p. 145, 1980

sissie shank *noun*

an improvised knife made with a toothbrush and razor blade *US, 1992*

- Lacy strutted into the lieutenant's office with a "sissie shank," a knife made by melting a toothbrush around a razor blade. "It wasn't much good for stabbing, but it could be used to slash someone's face." — Pete Earley, *The Hot House*, p. 85, 1992

sissy *noun*

an effeminate boy or man, especially a homosexual; a coward *US, 1879*

- Those who come to prison with obvious homosexual tendencies are referred to as "sissies." — *Ebony*, p. 82, July 1951
- You think Jesus was some kind of sissy, eh? — Richard Brooks, *Elmer Gantry*, 1960
- Why would anybody want to go to bed with a flaming little sissy like you? — Mart Crowley, *The Boys in the Band*, p. 159, 1968
- He had suspected the guy before, the guy so polite and sounding a little bit like a sissy the way he talked, but looked like a businessman. — Elmore Leonard, *Be Cool*, p. 174, 1999

sissy bar *noun*

a bar patronized by homosexuals *US, 1983*

- "They got a few sissy bars not too far from there," the hooker shrugged. — Joseph Wambaugh, *The Delta Star*, p. 154, 1983

sissy pants *noun*

a coward or timid person *US, 1960*

- "I promise not to tell any of the bar boys you went sissy-pants white wine on them." — Mike Lupica, *Wild Pitch*, p. 267, 2002

sissy stick *noun*

in pool, a mechanical device used to support the cue on hard-to-reach shots *US, 1970*

- — Stephen H. Dill (Editor), *Current Slang*, p. 12, Fall 1970
- — Mike Shamos, *The Illustrated Encyclopedia of Billiards*, p. 214, 1993

sissy tank *noun*

a jail holding cell reserved for homosexual prisoners *US, 1981*

- Well, they have me in the sissy tank with all the gay people[.] — Joseph Wambaugh, *The Glitter Dome*, p. 156, 1981

sister *noun*

1 a black woman *US, 1968*

- But O.J. had the "good-looking-man" factor going for him. Those middle-aged sisters came to court every day and stared at this good-looking man they'd like to fuck. — Chris Rock, *Rock This!*, p. 204
- Sitting up on the customer's seat was a big fine sister who was popping her fingers and wiggling to the music and smiling at me because our eyes had met. — Eldridge Cleaver, *Soul on Ice*, p. 28, 1968
- And some sister was stepping forward, saying, "Who got guns?!" — Bobby Seale, *A Lonely Rage*, p. 199, 1978
- There used to be a time when sisters didn't know shit about gettin' their pussy licked. — *True Romance*, 1993

2 a fellow homosexual *US, 1949*

- Sister—an intimate friend and confidant who is not a lover. — Anon., *The Gay Girl's Guide*, p. 15, 1949
- Right here—behind those trees—my "sister" will watch out for us. — John Rechy, *City of Night*, p. 194, 1963
- I have been invited home to meet one number's lover for a sandwich, have been groped accidentally by platonic acquaintances (I never liked "sister"), and have had many an ego satisfaction. — John Francis Hunter, *The Gay Insider*, pp. 102–103, 1971
- Face it, girl, Archie's a sister. — *Chasing Amy*, 1997

3 a female fellow member of a countercultural or underground political movement *US, 1968*

- Each service should be performed by a tight gang of brothers and sisters whose commitment should enable them to handle an overload of work with ability and enthusiasm. — *The Digger Papers*, p. 15, August 1968

sister act *noun*

a relationship, usually sexual, between two homosexuals with the same orientation *US, 1965*

- — *The Guild Dictionary of Homosexual Terms*, p. 41, 1965

Sister Alice Baker *noun*

the Aryan Brotherhood, a white prison gang *US, 1975*

- — Report to the Senate, *California Senate Committee on Civil Disorder*, p. 228, 1975

sister hix *noun*

in craps, a six *US, 1983*

- — Thomas L. Clark, *The Dictionary of Gambling and Gaming*, p. 202, 1987

sisterhood *noun*

the bond that unites male homosexuals *US, 1979*

- — *Maledicta*, p. 225, 1979: "Kinks and queens: linguistic and cultural aspects of the terminology for gays"

sit *verb*

▸ **sit on your hands**

to refrain from applause at a moment when applause would be appropriate *US, 1981*

- — Don Wilmeth, *The Language of American Popular Entertainment*, p. 244, 1981

sit-and-grab *noun*

in a carnival, a food concession with seating *US, 1960*

- — *American Speech*, pp. 308–309, December 1960: "Carnival talk"

sitch *noun*

a situation *US, 1967*

- — *Current Slang*, p. 5, Spring 1967

sitcom *noun*

a situation comedy *US, 1964*

A protocol for television comedies since the early 1950s in which the humor is drawn from the confluence of characters and situations.

- The fact that he [Colin Powell] was chairman of the Joint Chiefs of Staff makes him the equivalent of a sitcom in a good time slot. Is "Suddenly Susan" any good? We don't know. It's on after "Seinfeld." — Chris Rock, *Rock This!*, p. 16, 1997

sit-down *noun*

1 a meeting or conversation over a meal or while sitting *UK, 1861*

- One only had to see the newspaper photograph of Mr. Shanker as he emerged from a "sit-down" with city officials to know that this "creditor" had been the victim of a very high-class mugging. — Mario Puzo, *Inside Las Vegas*, p. 46, 1977
- At first Strike had enjoyed these sit-downs, but lately this street-corner-prince business had become a little old. — Richard Price, *Clockers*, p. 317, 1992

2 in organized crime, a discussion of a dispute between members of the crime enterprise with a final and binding decision rendered by a leader or group of leaders *US, 1975*

- [W]hat are you going to say at the sitdown—that you killed his brother because he refused a drink? — Edwin Torres, *Carlito's Way*, p. 82, 1975
- I got to go into town for a sit-down. — Richard Condon, *Prizzi's Honor*, p. 254, 1982
- Before you could touch a made guy, you had to have a good reason. There had to be a sit-down. — *Goodfellas*, 1990
- So they have the Zip call to suggest a sit-down, like there was a disagreement to discuss. — Elmore Leonard, *Pronto*, p. 345, 1993

sit down *verb*
to join a poker game *US, 1963*

- — Richard Jessup, *The Cincinnati Kid*, p. 10, 1963

sit in *verb*

1 to play by invitation with a band to which the musician does not belong *US, 1936*

- Wednesdays was celebrity night at the Palladium—all the showbiz and Jews doing cha-cha-ca-one-two-three, Marlon Brando sit in on conga (couldn't play to save his ass), out-of-town people—shit like that—all into Latin music. — Edwin Torres, *Carlito's Way*, p. 26, 1975

2 to join a poker game *US, 1967*

- — Albert H. Morehead, *The Complete Guide to Winning Poker*, p. 273, 1967

sit-still *noun*
in horseracing, a style of riding based on patience *US, 1976*

- — Tom Ainslie, *Ainslie's Complete Guide to Thoroughbred Racing*, p. 338, 1976

sitter *noun*

1 a woman who works in a bar, encouraging customers through flirtation to buy drinks, both for themselves and for her *US, 1959*

- Baltimore has an ordinance against B-girls, who are legaly termed "sitters." — Monroe Fry, *Sex, Vice, and Business*, p. 24, 1959

2 a person who monitors and comforts an alcohol or drug addict who is going through the initial stages of detoxification *US, 1998*
A term used in twelve-step recovery programs such as Alcoholics Anonymous.

- — Christopher Cavanaugh, *AA to Z*, p. 162, 1998

3 in pool, a ball perched on the lip of a pocket *US, 1924*

- — Mike Shamos, *The Illustrated Encyclopedia of Billiards*, p. 214, 1993

sitting duck *noun*
a stolen car discovered by police through serendipitous checking of license plates *US, 1970*

- "How often you pick up a sitting duck?" asked Serge, to change the subject, checking a license plate against the numbers on the hot sheet. — Joseph Wambaugh, *The New Centurions*, p. 41, 1970

six *noun*

1 a lookout during a crime *US, 1987*

- On that job I was "keeping six." That's a safecracker's code for someone who is assigned to watch at a window for cops or to check out and deactivate any alarm system that might screw up the job. — Thomas Renner and Cecil Kirby, *Mafia Enforcer*, p. 38, 1987

2 a six-pack of a beverage *US, 1992*

- Gimme a 6 of Diet Cokes and 6 of Budweiser. — *The Bad Lieutenant*, 1992

3 a unit commander *US, 1976*

- Roger that, Six, but the doc says he's in pretty bad shape. — Charles Anderson, *The Grunts*, p. 45, 1976
- Six says torch this place! — *Platoon*, 1986

▶ **behind the six**
without funds *US, 1967*

- — Albert H. Morehead, *The Complete Guide to Winning Poker*, p. 256, 1967

▶ **take six**
to reenlist in the military for six years *US, 1968*

- — Carl Fleischhauer, *A Glossary of Army Slang*, p. 20, 1968

six-by *noun*
a large flatbed truck with wooden slats enclosing the bed *US, 1981*

- We were thrown in the back of a six-by and led through processing. — Mark Barker, *Nam*, p. 39, 1981

sixer *noun*
a six-pack of beer *US, 1984*

- Deek killed his bottle, slipped it back into the sixer, and patted his belly with a satisfied sigh. — Jess Mowry, *Way Past Cool*, p. 40, 1992
- But hey man, know us, we've got a few sixers. You with us? — *Dazed and Confused*, 1993

six-for-five *noun*
loaning workers money on their wages short term for 20% interest *US, 1962*

- "You know anything about six-for-five and the numbers?" — Charles Perry, *Portrait of a Young Man Drowning*, p. 168, 1962

six-for-fiver *noun*
a moneylender who operates informally to advance workers money on their wages *US, 1953*

- At that time, Jake, a former roustabout with the Ringling Brothers Circus, had been a six-for-fiver around the pioneer tent and shack towns. That is, he bought wages from workers in advance of their due date, giving the needy borrower five dollars for each six he had coming. — Jim Thompson, *Bad Boy*, p. 324, 1953

sixie; sixie from Dixie *noun*
in craps, the number six *US, 1985*

- — Steve Kuriscak, *Casino Talk*, p. 68, 1985

six o'clock girl *noun*
a thin girl *US, 1947*

- — Marcus Hanna Boulware, *Jive and Slang of Students in Negro Colleges*, 1947

six o'clock jump *noun*
an enema given to a patient the night before surgery *US, 1946*

- — *American Speech*, p. 154, April 1946: "GI words from the separation center and proctology ward"

six-pack *noun*

1 a six-passenger truck that transports air crews *US, 1990*

- — Joseph Tuso, *Singing the Vietnam Blues*, p. 261, 1990: Glossary

2 a well-developed and defined abdominal musculature *US, 1997*
From the superficial resemblance between the muscles and a six-pack of beer cans.

- — Pamela Munro, *U.C.L.A. Slang*, p. 107, 1997
- I've got six-pack abs. I'm eight inches cut. — Tristan Taormino, *The Village Voice*, 4th April 2000

six-packs *noun*
in craps, a roll of twelve *US, 1999*

- — Chris Fagans and David Guzman, *A Guide to Craps Lingo*, p. 38, 1999

six, six, and a kick *noun*
military discipline consisting of six months imprisonment, six months forfeiture of pay, and a bad-conduct discharge from the service *US, 1987*

- I lost every case I did. All my deserts got 6, 6, and a kick. — Ernest Spencer, *Welcome to Vietnam, Macho Man*, p. 16, 1987

sixteen *noun*
an M-16 rifle *US, 1972*

- [A]nother guy with a flak jacket and a sixteen got in the cab with him. — William Pelfrey, *The Big V*, p. 16, 1972
- They made us switch to the M-16 during our tour. I liked the fourteen much better. The sixteens were unreliable, like a Mattel toy. — Al Santoli, *To Bear Any Burden*, p. 106, 1985

sixteenth *noun*
a sixteenth of an ounce (of drugs) *US, 1988*

- How about dilaudid, you got any sixteenths? — *Drugstore Cowboy*, 1988

six tits *noun*
in poker, three queens *US*, *1948*

six-to-five!; sixty-five!; sixty-fifth street!
used as a warning among criminals or swindlers that
a police officer is nearby *US*, *1950*
- — Hyman E. Goldin et al., *Dictionary of American Underworld Lingo*, p. 195, 1950

six-trey *noun*
sixty-three; 63rd Street *US*, *1972*
- — David Claerbaut, *Black Jargon in White America*, p. 79, 1972

sixty days *noun*
in dice games, a roll of six *US*, *1962*
- — Frank Garcia, *Marked Cards and Loaded Dice*, p. 264, 1962

sixty-eight *noun*
used as a humorous variation on sixty-nine—you give me
oral sex and I'll owe you one *US*, *1982*
- — *Maledicta*, p. 126, Summer/Winter 1982: "Dyke diction: the language of lesbians"

**sixty-four dollar question; sixty-four thousand dollar
question; sixty-four million dollar question** *noun*
a question that gets to the heart of the matter *US*, *1942*
The US radio quiz show *Take It or Leave It* offered a highest
prize of $64, giving rise to the catch-phrase "sixty-four dollar
question." The phrase gained currency and decimal places in
televised quiz shows on both sides of the Atlantic.
- Now for the sixty-four-dollar question, Mike. — Mickey Spillane, *My Gun is Quick*, p. 58, 1950
- The prison camp was to be visited again by some of those naval
  intelligence officers who came out to ply us with questions, with
  their $64 questions. — Gregory "Pappy" Boyington, *Baa Baa Black Sheep*, p. 304, 1958
- Why? Now here we have a $64,000,000 question. — Dick Clark, *To Goof or Not to Goof*, p. 25, 1963
- What is love? That is the 64-billion-dollar question, and as of now
  the jackpot if still unclaimed. — Ann Landers, *Ann Landers Talks to Teen-Agers About Sex*, p. 95, 1963

sixty-nine *noun*
simultaneous, mutual oral-genital sex between two people
US, *1883*
- May engage in mutual oral-genital contact ("sixty-nine") as a
  prelude[.] — Herant A. Katschadourian, *Fundamentals of Human Sexuality*, p. 290, 1975
- Earlier, Nicole gives good moan to Brad's 69. — Editors of Adult Video
  News, *The AVN Guide to the 500 Greatest Adult Films of All Time*, p. 67, 2005

sixty-nine *verb*
to engage in simultaneous, reciprocal oral-genital sex
US, *1972*
- "Where do you go to sixty-nine?" I asked. "Australia," "said Kell."
  — William Pelfrey, *The Big V*, p. 51, 1972

six up!
used as a warning in the usage of counterculturalists associ-
ated with the Rainbow Nation gatherings and the Grateful
Dead that law enforcement officials are approaching *US*, *1994*
- — David Shenk and Steve Silberman, *Skeleton Key*, p. 262, 1994
- — Jim Crotty, *How to Talk American*, p. 290, 1997

size queen *noun*
a homosexual male or a woman who is attracted to men
with large penises *US*, *1963*
- "I gotta know how big it is before buying," a fairy said to me.
  Another one with him lisps, "Mary! He'll think we're size queens!"
  — John Rechy, *City of Night*, p. 365, 1963
- So at the baths the rivalry comes out into the open, and size
  queens, young or old, have a field day. — John Francis Hunter, *The Gay Insider*, p. 152, 1971
- Two things I detest—size queens and small cocks. — Bruce Rodgers,
  The Queens' Vernacular, p. 182, 1972
- All cocks are the same. Size queens try so hard to put personality
  where it doesn't belong. — Peter Sotos, *Index*, p. 12, 1996

sizzle *noun*
an illegal drug *US*, *1969*
- You don't want to walk through the street with that package of
  "sizzle" on you. — Iceberg Slim (Robert Beck), *Pimp*, p. 133, 1969

sizzurp *noun*
a mixture of codeine-infused cough syrup and soda *US*, *2002*
- Comparable to a Southern Nat Dogg, Moe and assorted Texas MCs
  sound off about ladies, weed, and sizzurp-sipping. — *East Bay Express*,
  27th November 2002
- Izzle always ran little errands and chores for Warren's cousin
  Branford, who slang sizzurp in the Magnolia section of town.
  — Linden Dalecki, *Kid B*, p. 29, 2006
- [D]rinking what's referred to there as sizzurp, or lean, a cocktail of
  alcohol, soda, and codeine-infused cough syrup. — *Playboy*, 1st March 2006

skank *noun*
1 a girl whose sole attraction is her immorality and sexual
availability *US*, *1966*
An abusive description possibly derived from "skunk."
- If you saw her on the street when she wasn't too sick you
  probably'd most likely as not wouldn't even know she was a junkie.
  She's not like these other skanks around here. — James Mills, *The Panic
  in Needle Park*, p. 25, 1966
- That his sister was a royal skank who fucked for a dime. — Richard
  Price, *The Wanderers*, p. 33, 1974
- "Me, there was total respect, 'cause I was Nick's lady. I knew he had
  other skanks. I mean, all the gang members have skanks." — Gini
  Sikes, *8 Ball Chicks*, p. 134, 1997
- "The skank was in rollers and house shoes." — Eric Jerome Dickey,
  Cheaters, p. 34, 1999
2 nastiness, filth *US*, *1995*
- Virgins, I love 'em. No diseases, no loose as a goose pussy, no
  skank. — *Kids*, 1995
3 methamphetamine *US*, *2002*
- I seen a lot of people do a lot of skank and survive every duel with
  deal like a high-noon sheriff. — Lynn Breedlove, *Godspeed*, p. 19, 2002

skank-pit *noun*
an unpleasant, distasteful place *US*, *1999*
- I've got to be crazy letting you drag me back to this skank-pit.
  — *200 Cigarettes*, 1999

skanky *adjective*
ugly; cheap; nasty *US*, *1975*
- Here's another one I had. Real skanky-looking guy, who wants him?
  — Elmore Leonard, *Maximum Bob*, p. 164, 1991
- This is a room of about 50 skanky groupies and others. — *Wayne's
  World 2*, 1993
- The fact that Tania lived in an apartment and not in one of the
  skanky rooming houses that everyone else in P-Town existed in
  made me think she probably had money. — Michelle Tea, *The Passionate
  Mistakes and Intricate Corruption of One Girl in America*, p. 91, 1998
- Even skanky girls who had it—while they had it—possessed
  something tangible and clean. — Adrian Nicole LeBlanc, *Random Family*,
  p. 33, 2003

skate *noun*
1 an easy task *US*, *1976*
- It wouldn't be a real long hump, but it wouldn't be a real skate
  either—about six or seven clicks. — Charles Anderson, *The Grunts*, p. 80,
  1976
- Normally resupply day was a skate, a day the command cut the
  boonierats some slack. — John Del Vecchio, *The 13th Valley*, p. 351, 1982
2 a lazy and/or incompetent worker *US*, *1998*
US Army usage.
- — *Seattle Times*, p. A9, 12th April 1998: "Grunts, squids not grunting from the same
  dictionary"
3 an act of letting someone escape wrongdoing without
punishment *US*, *1992*
- So, feature, Dudley gave Johnny a skate on the fur job and confided
  some of his own crime gigs to him[.] — James Ellroy, *White Jazz*, p. 302,
  1992
4 a motorcycle *US*, *1970*
- — *Current Slang*, p. 12, Winter 1970

▷ **see: ROLLERSKATE**

skate *verb*
to get away with something; to escape punishment *US*, *1945*
- I'm saying you'll skate—if you curtail your plans with Mickey.
  — James Ellroy, *White Jazz*, p. 292, 1992
- Leeds sensed that Fortney was as indifferent and lazy as he was.
  "Wanna let 'em skate?" — Joseph Wambaugh, *Floaters*, p. 81, 1996

skate Betty *noun*

a girl who associates with skateboarders, perhaps skateboarding herself *US*, *1989*

- — *Macon Telegraph and News*, p. 9A, 18th June 1989

skate rat *noun*

a devoted, perhaps skilled skateboarder *US*, *1989*

- — Pamela Munro, *U.C.L.A. Slang*, p. 76, 1989

skaty eight *noun*

a notional number *US*, *1960*

- Charles Wainwright Jr., called Chuckie, continued to scan the skaty-eight meters and switches and disconnects[.] — Don DeLillo, *Underworld*, p. 608, 1997

skedaddle; skiddadle *verb*

to leave in a hurry *US*, *1861*

Originally US Civil War slang, with claims of Swedish and Danish origins probably disproved.

- "The ball is at Christmas. Now scadoodle!" We scadoodled.
  — Frederick Kohner, *The Affairs of Gidget*, p. 76, 1963
- Our buckboad was skedaddling down a narrow dusty road a short piece from home when a rut in the road flung off a bag of fertilizer.
  — Iceberg Slim (Robert Beck), *Doom Fox*, p. 117, 1978
- Pink Fairies: Smart Brits originally headed by widely published social criticker Mick Farren (who'd skedaddled by the time their first LP came out). — Chuck Eddy, *Stairway to Hell*, p. 44, 1991

skee *noun*

whiskey, especially low quality, low cost whiskey *US*, *1950*

- — Hyman E. Goldin et al., *Dictionary of American Underworld Lingo*, p. 195, 1950

skeet *verb*

1 to eject liquid from a syringe *US*, *1971*

- To emphasize his point, he stuck the works back down in a glass of water sitting next to him and drew up a dropper full of water. He slowly skeeted it out on the floor, making sure the needle wasn't stopped up before loaning it out. — Donald Goines, *Dopefiend*, p. 8, 1971

2 to ejaculate *US*, *2002*

- — Gary K. Farlow, *Prison-ese*, p. 64, 2002

skeeve *noun*

a disgusting individual *US*, *1976*

- You wouldn't believe what this skeeve wrote[.] — Howard Stern, *Miss America*, p. 449, 1995
- — Claudio R. Salvucci, *The Philadelphia Dialect Dictionary*, p. 58, 1996

skeeve; skeeve out *verb*

to disgust *US*, *1976*

- — Claudio R. Salvucci, *The Philadelphia Dialect Dictionary*, p. 58, 1996
- And by the way, there is no image—none—that skeeves me out more than that of the hypocritical, hairline-challenged major (Giuliani of New York) having sex with anyone. — *The Village Voice*, 30th May 2000
- That always skeeved me about Vince. — Missy Hyatt, *Missy Hyatt*, p. 75, 2001

skeevie *noun*

a disgusting person *US*, *1955*

Teen slang.

- — *American Weekly*, p. 2, 14th August 1955

skeevie; skeevy *adjective*

disgusting *US*, *1976*

- — *Philadelphia Magazine*, p. 124, March 1976
- — Connie Eble (Editor), *UNC-CH Campus Slang*, p. 7, March 1996
- Only skeever stoners fart. — Kevin Smith, *Jay and Silent Bob Strike Back*, p. 39, 2001
- As the little autistic kid hides and watches, one skeezy kidnapper rapes Candy[.] — Bill Landis, *Sleazoid Express*, p. 236, 2002

skeeze *noun*

a person with no morals and little character *US*, *1999*

- He looked over at the two skeezes on the couch bookending his boss. — John Ridley, *Everybody Smokes in Hell*, pp. 37–38, 1999

skeeze *verb*

to have sex *US*, *1990*

- So you skeezin', or what? — *New Jack City*, 1990

skeezer *noun*

a woman who will perform sex for crack cocaine *US*, *1990*

- Yo, is that the skeezer you met at Frankie's strip joint? — *New Jack City*, 1990
- — Terry Williams, *Crackhouse*, p. 151, 1992
- — Mark S. Fleisher, *Beggars & Thieves: Lives of Urban Street Criminals*, p. 291, 1995: "Glossary"
- If a girl was labeled a hoe, a skeezer, or a freak by other students, no one seemed willing to defend her. — Nelson George, *Hip Hop America*, p. 177, 1998

skeezix *noun*

a fool *US*, *1975*

After a character (a foundling, adopted by Walt and Phyllis Rumpus Blossom, who grew up to be the father of Chipper and Clovia) in Frank O. King's newspaper comic strip *Gasoline Alley*.

- Some skeezix from one of the local dailies was up here the other day to do a "human interest" story[.] — *Creem*, September 1975

skeezy *adjective*

despicable, tasteless *US*, *1992*

- If you were performing in a benefit concert for the lead singer of Queen, and you were going to be upfront singing with Queen backing you up, wouldn't you dress up a LITTLE more than skeezy pants and a football net-jersey?? — *rec.music.misc*, 23rd April 1992
- God, this is such a skeezy job. — Missy Hyatt, *Missy Hyatt*, p. 97, 2001
- "Your just a skeezy nickel slick." — Stephen J. Cannell, *White Sister*, p. 182, 2006

skeg *noun*

a fin on a surfboard *US*, *1962*

- — Grant W. Kuhns, *On Surfing*, p. 121, 1963
- — *Paradise of the Pacific*, p. 27, October 1963

skell; skel *noun*

a vagrant, especially of the thuggish sort *US*, *1957*

Seemingly related to the C17 "skelder," an honorable cant term for "a professional beggar" which was long obsolete when "skell" started to show up in New York in the early 1970s. A favorite word of police television dramas in the 1990s; the screenplay by Gardner Stern for episode 2 of season 2 of *NYPD Blue* that aired in September 1994 was titled *For Whom the Skell Rolls*.

- Of course some a the skells from the bar worked their way up and congratulated and grabbed what they could. — Hubert Selby Jr., *Last Exit to Brooklyn*, p. 102, 1957
- That's what he wanted, to be put out of his misery, like them skells you see in the middle of East Side Highway on a foggy night.
  — Edwin Torres, *After Hours*, p. 335, 1979
- The drug-pitch skells would rather tear off with a wallet than transact an actual exchange, and they make the teenage chicken fags seem like the most discreet commodity on the street. — Josh Alan Friedman, *Tales of Times Square*, p. 51, 1986
- Without me, you, personally, every fuckin' wiseguy skell around'll take a piece of your fuckin' Jew ass. — *Casino*, 1995

sketched out *adjective*

emotionally imbalanced as a result of drug use *US*, *1999*

- He figured Cookie-Puss got a little too sketched out on crack and concocted the whole story as an excuse to rob them. — James St. James, *Party Monster*, p. 138, 1999

skezag *noun*

heroin *US*, *1974*

An embellishment of the more common **SKAG**.

- "I want to move some skezag. I can sell you a key for twenty."
  — Robert Stone, *Dog Soldiers*, p. 143, 1974

ski bum *noun*

a ski enthusiast who spends as much time as possible skiing and as little time as possible working *US*, *1963*

- — *American Speech*, p. 206, October 1963: "The language of skiers"

ski bunny *noun*

a female who is learning to ski; a female who visits ski resorts for the company but does not ski *US*, *1956*

- I once heard the familiar "I am just a beginner" from a ski bunny whom I had seen snow-plowing many years before. — Mary Sennholz, *On Freedom and Free Enterprise*, p. 162, 1956
- — *American Speech*, p. 206, October 1963: "The language of skiers"
- Rom had fallen in love with a little ski bunny he met at a bar downtown. — Robert Lipkin, *A Brotherhood of Outlaws*, p. 65, 1981

skidoo *verb*

to depart hastily *US, 1905*

- [I] turned the lights off, locked the office up, and skidooed down the corridor. — Anthony Frewin, *Sixty-Three Closure*, p. 2, 2000

skid row *noun*

in any town, the run-down area where the socially disadvantaged and marginalized tend to congregate *US, 1931*

- Below this intersection, for a third of a mile, is a Skid Row as low and lousy as any in the country, with the usual in the way of flop houses, flea circuses, hoick shops, tattoo parlors[.] — Jack Lait and Lee Mortimer, *Chicago Confidential*, p. 14, 1950
- Most American big cities have a "Skid Row"—a rundown, disreputable street lined with cheap slaoons, flophouses, all-night movies, burlesque shows, and hamburger joints[.] — Alson Smith, *Syndicate City*, p. 212, 1954
- And on skid row -if you care to look—you may now and then see among the others a singularly doomed old man. — John Rechy, *The Sexual Outlaw*, p. 162, 1977

skid shot *noun*

in pool, a shot made with backspin on the cue ball *US, 1993*

- — Mike Shamos, *The Illustrated Encyclopedia of Billiards*, p. 215, 1993

skied *adjective*

drug-intoxicated *US, 1989*

A play on "sky" not "ski," as **HIGH** in the sky."

- Most of these sneaker bitches is looking to get skied, not looking for knowledge. — Terry Williams, *The Cocaine Kids*, p. 87, 1989

skim *noun*

money stolen from a business or enterprise, skimmed from the business funds like cream from milk *US, 1973*

- "Raymond Patriarca and Henry Tameleo were getting a regular piece of the skim, like other mob bosses." — Vincent Teresa, *My Life in the Mafia*, p. 212, 1973
- Then there's the secret funds the White House and the CIA control for the Freedom Fighters and their little wars all over the world. At least sixty percent of that is skim. — Richard Condon, *Prizzi's Glory*, p. 263, 1988
- Nobody interfered with the fuckin' skim. — *Casino*, 1995

skim *verb*

to divert a portion of your earnings or winnings to avoid paying taxes or to avoid paying your superiors in the enterprise their share *US, 1966*

- I'm not saying it's skimmed in Washington, but from maker to wearer it's skimmed. — Richard Condon, *Prizzi's Glory*, p. 263, 1988
- He's skimming on them. A sheet writer that used to work for Harry told a friend of mine it's a fact. Twenty years he skimmed like two grand a week over what he made for himself. — Elmore Leonard, *Riding the Rap*, p. 30, 1995

skimmer *noun*

a hat *US, 1972*

- — David Claerbaut, *Black Jargon in White America*, p. 79, 1972

skim money *noun*

money taken from an enterprise's net proceeds before any accounting of the proceeds *US, 1981*

- "I'm sure you are familiar with the IRS interest in casino ... uh ... funds." "I believe it's called skim money." Glanzmann smiled. — Gerald Petievich, *One-Shot Deal*, p. 258, 1981

skin *noun*

1 contact between hands in greeting, acknowledgement, or congratulations *US, 1942*

- Open the door and gimme some skin, pig. Or gimme some pigskin, as the case may be. — Steve Allen, *Bop Fables*, p. 25, 1955
- "Then we all gave each other some skin." — *Life*, p. 33, 11th July 1955: Teen-Age Terror on the New York Streets
- "What it is, my man," he yelled out as he came up and held his hand out for some skin. — Donald Goines, *Cry Revenge*, p. 101, 1974

2 sex *US, 1976*

- The numbers were all in, and there wasn't any skin / Crime was on a sudden decrease. — Dennis Wepman et al., *The Life*, p. 57, 1976

3 a condom *US, 1965*

- She asked me what I meant; rubbers? safes? skins? prophylactics? contraceptives? — John Nichols, *The Sterile Cuckoo*, p. 105, 1965

4 one dollar *US, 1930*

- Fifty skins was fifty skins. Fifty! For making one lousy phone call! — Bernard Wolfe, *The Late Risers*, p. 159, 1954
- Somebody found a new tailor who could make the greatest pants for 14 skins[.] — Hubert Selby Jr., *Last Exit to Brooklyn*, p. 28, 1957
- I say, Ain' you got no skins, no kale? No bread? No bones, no berries, no boys? — Robert Gover, *One Hundred Dollar Misunderstanding*, p. 22, 1961
- I've seen him take on a professional twice his size at a carnival and not only stay in for the three minutes to win the twenty-five skins but pin him. — Earl Thompson, *Tattoo*, p. 142, 1974

5 in carnival and amusement park usage, a shirt *US, 1982*

- — Don Wilmeth, *The Language of American Popular Entertainment*, p. 244, 1981

6 a wallet *US, 1950*

- — Hyman E. Goldin et al., *Dictionary of American Underworld Lingo*, p. 196, 1950

7 fist fighting *US, 1957*

- I wanna hold it like we always held it—with skin! — *West Side Story*, 1957

8 an American Indian *US, 1989*

An abbreviated form of "redskin."

- "Hey, brother, we got a new skin in the yard" means that a new Indian has been assigned to your area of the prison. — James Harris, *A Convict's Dictionary*, p. 38, 1989

skin *verb*

1 to swindle someone *US, 1819*

- As this was being written, a gypsy fortune-teller was under indictment charged with using such props as torn diapers, a red candle and a department store ladies' room, to skin three Washington housewives of $450. — Jack Lait and Lee Mortimer, *Washington Confidential*, p. 279, 1951
- To anyone he could buttonhole, he bragged about how he had "stung" this person or "skinned" that one. — Jim Thompson, *Bad Boy*, p. 308, 1953
- [N]o mugs to skin. — Charles Raven, *Underworld Nights*, p. 9, 1956
- [A]fter the patients wouldn't vote he got mad and skinned them so bad at cards that they're all so in debt they're scared to go any deeper[.] — Ken Kesey, *One Flew Over the Cuckoo's Nest*, pp. 115–116, 1962

2 to inject (a narcotic) into the skin as opposed to a vein *US, 1953*

- Even so, he had to shoot in the skin about half the time. But he only gave up and "skinned" a shot after an agonizing half-hour of proving and poking and cleaning out the needle, which would clog up with blood. — Wiliam Burroughs, *Junkie*, p. 51, 1953
- The first time I skinned, like I wouldn't hit the vein, just pick up the spike and shove it in. — Jeremy Larner and Ralph Teffertellerr, *The Addict in the Street*, p. 34, 1964
- I had been skinning morphine and that was the worst habit I ever kicked, believe me. — Bruce Jackson, *In the Life*, p. 72, 1972

3 to slap palms in greeting or agreement *US, 1967*

- "Skin me, man, skin me!" And they had smacked palms ringingly. — John Williams, *The Man Who Cried I Am*, p. 24, 1967

4 to defeat someone *US, 1958*

- — Gary K. Farlow, *Prison-ese*, p. 64, 2002

5 to surf without a wetsuit *US, 1991*

- — Trevor Cralle, *The Surfin'ary*, p. 116, 1991

▸ **skin (it) back**

to withdraw the foreskin from your penis, either as part of a medical inspection or masturbation *US, 2002*

- — Gary K. Farlow, *Prison-ese*, p. 64, 2002

skin and grin *verb*

to greet with a hand slap and a smile *US, 1994*

- I saw Debbie's family down at the elevator, skinnin' and grinnin' and congratulating her. — Nathan McCall, *Makes Me Wanna Holler*, p. 293, 1994

skin beater *noun*

a drummer *US, 1947*

- — Marcus Hanna Boulware, *Jive and Slang of Students in Negro Colleges*, 1947

skin beef *noun*

a prison sentence for an unspecified sexual crime *US, 1976*

- — John R. Armore and Joseph D. Wolfe, *Dictionary of Desperation*, p. 49, 1976

skin book *noun*

a sex-themed book *US, 1970*

- Where'd you learn that? You really ought be writing skin books. — Darryl Ponicsan, *The Last Detail*, p. 6, 1970

- Men will fly across the country to get laid by that special guy they just jerked off to in a skin book. — John Preston, *Hustling*, p. 185, 1994

skin diver *noun*
a person who performs oral sex on a male *US*, *1969*
The reverse of a "muff diver."
- — *Current Slang*, p. 10, Winter 1969

skin fighting *noun*
a fight between members of rival gangs in which weapons or at least lethal weapons are forbidden *US*, *1967*
- "A fair fight isn't rough," Two-Bit said. "Blades are rough. So are chains and heaters and pool sticks and rumbles. Skin fighting isn't rough." — S.E. Hinton, *The Outsiders*, p. 28, 1967

skin flick *noun*
1 a pornographic film *US*, *1964*
- The newest breed in skin flicks is represented by "Babette" which opened in Manhattan recently. — *Screw*, p. 9, 29th November 1968
- Exploitation films (usually known as "skin flicks"), are low-budget films which concentrate on the exotic. — *The Presidential Commission on Obscenity and Pornography*, p. 45, 1970
- When long-run skin-flicks appealing to heteros (like Censorship in Denmark), the only action is early afternoons. — John Francis Hunter, *The Gay Insider*, p. 148, 1971
- Every day this cry can be heard echoing down the halls of every distributor of skin flicks. — Stephen Ziplow, *The Film Maker's Guide to Pornography*, p. 45, 1977

2 a slide used by a dermatologist to illustrate diseases during teaching rounds *US*, *1980*
- — *Maledicta*, p. 57, Summer 1980: "Not sticks and stones, but names: more medical pejoratives"

skin-flick house *noun*
a movie theater showing pornographic films *US*, *1972*
- The early skin-flick houses became known humorously among much of the trade as "masturbation mansions." — Roger Blake, *What you always wanted to know about porno-movies*, p. 78, 1972
- Brewer is also a center of racial unrest and urban blight, and it grows more seedy through RA as palatial movie theaters become skin-flick houses. — Jack De Bellis, *The John Updike Encyclopedia*, p. 77, 2000

skin flute *noun*
the penis *US*, *1941*
Often arises in the phrase "play the skin flute" (to perform oral sex).
- Oh Christ, could I use her as an accompanist—on the old skin flute! — Gilbert Sorrentino, *Steelwork*, p. 143, 1970
- I reached down and grabbed his "skin flute" and began to blow. — *Screw*, p. 9, 17th May 1971
- I asked her if she'd play "Flight of the Bumblebee" on my skin flute and she slapped me. — Ken Weaver, *Texas Crude*, p. 73, 1984
- Now she's playin' nighttime skin flute in the Roys R Us parking lot. — Richard Price, *Clockers*, p. 193, 1992

skin full of *noun*
drunk *US*, *1985*
- Of course, a forty-nine-year-old cop with a skin full of hooch and only months away from a stroke a heart attack wouldn't be in very good shape to begin with. — Joseph Wambaugh, *The Secrets of Harry Bright*, p. 284, 1985

skin game *noun*
1 in gambling, a rigged game that honest players always lose *US*, *1962*
- — Frank Garcia, *Marked Cards and Loaded Dice*, p. 264, 1962
- I was head toward a singing career again and could soon kiss the skin game a fond farewell, Lord willing. — Guy Owen, *The Flim-Flam Man and the Apprentice Grifter*, p. 144, 1972
- — George Percy, *The Language of Poker*, p. 83, 1988

2 the science of dermatology *US*, *1980*
- — *Maledicta*, p. 57, Summer 1980: "Not sticks and stones, but names: more medical pejoratives"

skingraft *noun*
an intramuscular injection of a drug *US*, *1968*
- Time was Son only took a skingraft once a week, a little trip t'dreamsville. — Robert Gover, *JC Saves*, p. 16, 1968

skin habit *noun*
a drug addiction based on intramuscular, not intravenous, injections *US*, *1972*

- It was a skin habit, see, which I got in the last part of 43." — Bruce Jackson, *In the Life*, p. 72, 1972

skinhead; skin *noun*
a member of a youth fashion and gang movement, characterized by close-cropped or shaven scalp *UK*, *1969*
Early in the 1970s Richard Allen, a pseudonym of James Moffat (1922–93), published a series of "youthsploitation" novels under the general title *Skinhead*.
- — William D. Alsever, *Glossary for the Establishment and Other Uptight People*, p. 29, December 1970
- Fuck facist skinhead shit. — Francesca Lia Block, *Baby Be-Bop*, p. 419, 1995

skin house *noun*
a brothel or place where the entertainment is of a sexual nature *US*, *1969*
- These theaters that we used to call "skin houses" were still going in for sex films[.] — Joey V., *Portrait of Joey*, p. 156, 1969
- [T]he various "skin houses" began to flourish as the "adults only" houses of a generation before had never been able to do. — Roger Blake, *The Porno Movies*, p. 64, 1970
- I'd heard she was hanging out in the skin houses and taxi-dance joints[.] — Joseph Wambaugh, *The Blue Knight*, p. 24, 1973

skin joint *noun*
a club featuring nude entertainers *US*, *1974*
- My ride took the Broadway exit, and we drove into the city past all the skin joints, the famous strip where it all started. — Anne Steinhardt, *Thunder La Boom*, p. 194, 1974

skin magazine; skin mag *noun*
a magazine featuring photographs of nudes, usually women *US*, *1968*
- But, mainly, the source of his money has always carried a taint in traditional status terms: Playboy, a "skin magazine," as they say at Yale, and the Playboy Clubs, "those Bunny houses." — Tom Wolfe, *The Pump House Gang*, p. 56, 1968
- Calvin glanced at the rows of skin magazines[.] — Joseph Wambaugh, *The Choirboys*, p. 105, 1975
- In the coldest weather the boss would leave a pint of cheap whiskey in the drawer along with the stacks of skin magazines (All-Star Tit Queens and Bikes, Black Leather, and Big Broads). — Larry Heinemann, *Paco's Story*, pp. 40–41, 1990
- [F]irst came the skin magazines and later, in the dark of night, he found himself climbing a tree in order to peek beneath the shade into a female neighbor's shower room. — *Rocky Mountain News (Denver)*, p. 69A, 5th September 1994

skin man; skinner *noun*
a sex offender *US*, *1976*
- — Andreas Schroeder, *Shaking It Rough*, 1976
- — John R. Armore and Joseph D. Wolfe, *Dictionary of Desperation*, p. 49, 1976

skinner *noun*
1 a gambling cheat *US*, *1974*
- — John Scarne, *Scarne on Dice*, p. 479, 1974

2 a police officer *US*, *1965*
- — Miss Cone, *The Slang Dictionary (Hawthorne High School)*, 1965

skinny *noun*
1 inside information, rumor, or fact *US*, *1959*
- But I hadn't really, because it turns out the song ["Sky Pilot"] is quite long and the real skinny is at the end—a controversial line: "Thou shalt not kill." — James Simon Kunen, *The Strawberry Statement*, pp. 88–89, 1968
- Well, what's the skinny? — Darryl Ponicsan, *The Last Detail*, p. 16, 1970
- [T]he guy was fuckin' obsessed with fuckin' data, you know. obsessed with knowin' the fuckin' skinny on other peoples lives. — James Ellroy, *Because the Night*, p. 486, 1984
- These guys here have got the skinny on the happenin' after hours. — *Clueless*, 1995

2 in circus and carnival usage, a ten-cent piece *US*, *1981*
- — Don Wilmeth, *The Language of American Popular Entertainment*, p. 244, 1981

skinny-dip *verb*
to swim in the nude *US*, *1947*

- The height of daring was attained by boys who trudged miles into the country until they reached a swimming hole far from the madding crowd where skinny-dipping wouldn't offend anybody. — *Marion (Ohio) Star*, p. 6, 2nd July 1947
- Luce, who had helped organize the Cuba trips and had once gone skinnydipping with Fidel, joined with the FBI and ratted on all of his friends. — Jerry Rubin, *Do It!*, p. 63, 1970
- "They going swimming?" "Skinny-dipping," Walter said. — Elmore Leonard, *Split Images*, p. 110, 1981

skinny Dugan *noun*
in craps, any combination of seven *US, 1985*
- — Steve Kuriscak, *Casino Talk*, p. 51, 1985

skinpix *noun*
pornographic films *US, 1964*
- These "skinpix," as the movie trade paper Variety has dubbed them, have undergone a recent revitalization in terms of production values, level of good taste, and in their profit potential. — Michael Milner, *Sex on Celluloid*, p. 18, 1964

skin pop *noun*
an injection of a drug into the skin or muscle, not into a vein *US, 1952*
- Nothing like a skin pop, not scattered like a snort. — George Mandel, *Flee the Angry Strangers*, p. 379, 1952
- That was the first time I ever got high on a skin pop. — James Mills, *The Panic in Needle Park*, p. 44, 1966

skin-pop *verb*
to inject a drug into the skin or muscle, not into a vein *US, 1952*
Usually practiced in the early stages of drug use.
- But keep off, better, because if you like junk you keep shmeckin and shootin', then the skip pop goes to the big pipe[.] — George Mandel, *Flee the Angry Strangers*, p. 56, 1952
- One of them went and got some works. So I skin-popped. — Isidor Chein, *The Road to H*, p. 152, 1964
- He said he would stop using drugs altogether rather than start skin-popping. — Claude Brown, *Manchild in the Promised Land*, p. 251, 1965
- He skin pops a load of Dilaudid into a forearm, swooms for a moment under the jolt. — Iceberg Slim (Robert Beck), *Doom Fox*, p. 157, 1978

skin popper *noun*
a drug user who does not inject the drug into a vein *US, 1967*
- I had jumped from being a careful snorter, content to take my kicks of sniffing through my nose, to a not-so-careful skin-popper, and now was full-grown mainliner. — Piri Thomas, *Down These Mean Streets*, p. 200, 1967

skin-pump *verb*
to inject a drug under the skin, not into a vein *US, 1952*
- — *American Speech*, p. 29, February 1952: "Teen-age hophead jargon"

skins *noun*
drums *UK, 1926*
- Beat the skins and keep 'em thumping! Rock the joint and keep it jumping! — Harry Haenigsen, *Jive's Like That*, 1947
- I was jivin' around with the Latinos, they was bangin' on the skins as usual, timbales, conga and bongos—like a regular fuckin' band. — Edwin Torres, *Carlito's Way*, p. 46, 1975

skin shake *noun*
a thorough search of a person's body, including orifices *US, 1967*
- You take nothing—nothing—inside the walls. Any personal valuables, rings, watches, pens, lighters, will be stored here and returned to you at the time of your release. Throw your smokes away. Now come up here one at a time for a skin shake. — Malcolm Braly, *On the Yard*, p. 33, 1967
- — Paul Glover, *Words from the House of the Dead*, 1974

skin ship *noun*
an unarmed helicopter used for medical evacuations *US, 1986*
- First the "skin ship," a unarmed medevac Huey, came in and removed the wounded. — Ralph Zumbro, *Tank Sergeant*, p. 49, 1986

skin show *noun*
a show featuring nude or nearly nude women *US, 1973*
- I remember when the slime-balls used to be packed in there solid, asshole to belly button, waiting to look at the skin show in the viewer. — Joseph Wambaugh, *The Blue Knight*, pp. 26–27, 1973

- A good SKIN SHOW is a sought after attraction for a Racket Carnival, for the better the FIX, the wilder the show, often including complete nudity and a little body contact as the girls hover at the edge of the stage. — Gene Sorrows, *All About Carnivals*, p. 26, 1985
- "Even people who once went to skin shows have classier topless clubs (off the Strip) to visit now," says Sehlinger. — *USA Today*, p. 7D, 25th August 1995
- "This is not a skin show. It's a way of looking at the women and the clothes," said Alison Fenterstock[.] — *Dallas Morning News*, p. 17A, 5th June 2001

skin trade *noun*
the sex industry in all its facets *US, 1986*
- He didn't get where he was in the skin trade just by scaring pussy to death. — Robert Campbell, *In La-La Land We Trust*, p. 178, 1986

skinz *noun*
a sexually attractive woman *US, 1993*
- — *Washington Post*, 14th October 1993

skip *verb*
▸ **skip on**
to leave *US, 1989*
- — Pamela Munro, *U.C.L.A. Slang*, p. 77, 1989

skipper *noun*
1 a police chief, captain, or sergeant *US, 1929*
Jocular, from the C14 nautical sense.
- This bust feels like fat city. Any legit L.A.P.D. dick would have taken one of our guys with him on a stakeout. Let's go get the skipper. — James Ellroy, *Because the Night*, p. 375, 1984

2 a mid-level boss in an organized crime enterprise *US, 1981*
- "Then there's capiregime, captains, or skippers." — Ovid Demaris, *The Last Mafioso*, p. 21, 1981
- The Capos are the middlemen, sometimes called skippers. — Henry Hill and Byron Schreckengost, *A Good Fella's Guide to New York*, p. 8, 2003

3 a prison warden *US, 1950*
- — Hyman E. Goldin et al., *Dictionary of American Underworld Lingo*, p. 196, 1950

4 in poker, a hand with five cards sequenced by twos *US, 1963*
- — Irwin Steig, *Common Sense in Poker*, p. 187, 1963

skippy *noun*
a homosexual male *US, 1970*
- — Clarence Major, *Dictionary of Afro-American Slang*, p. 104, 1970

skirt *noun*
a woman or women objectified sexually *UK, 1899*
In conventional English usage until the late C19 when Victorians deemed it slang; not necessarily pejorative.
- The brother inebriates worried about me for a week or two, undeniably saddened that one of their members should so suddenly go to ruin over a skirt. — John Nichols, *The Sterile Cuckoo*, p. 87, 1965
- Whistler's just got over a skirt that did a number on him. — Robert Campbell, *Alice in La-La Land*, p. 166, 1987
- So what's this skirt's name? — *Chasing Amy*, 1997
- Now I want you to level with me: did you knock this skirt up? — *Something About Mary*, 1998

skitch *verb*
in icy winter conditions, to grab the bumper of a passing car and use your feet as skis as you are pulled along *US, 1997*
- — Jim Crotty, *How to Talk American*, p. 215, 1997
- I've had some "skitch" on the back of my truck on more than one occasion as I'm driving, which is accompanied by laughter and cheers from their pals. [Letter to the editor] — *Journal and Courier (Lafayette, Indiana)*, p. 10A, 5th September 2004

skittles *noun*
dextromethorphan (DXM), an active ingredient in non-prescription cold and cough medication, often abused for nonmedicinal purposes *US, 2003*
- Youths' nicknames for DXM: Robo, Skittles, Triple C's, Rojo, Dex, Tussin, Vitamin D. DXM abuse is called "Robotripping" or "Tussing." Users might be called "syrup heads" or "robotards." — *USA Today*, p. 1A, 29th December 2003

skittling *noun*
the recreational abuse of dextromethorphan *US, 2003*
- There are no significant Google results for "skittling" that are on topic. DXM is neither "new" nor a "craze." — alt.drugs.psychedelics, 22nd October 2003

- Chugging large doses of non-prescription cough syrup, such as Robitussin DM, known as Robo-tripping, or eating Coricidin tablets that mimic the appearance of the popular candy Skittles, is known as Skittling, is nothing new for those looking to alter their minds with legal substances. — *Milwaukee Journal Sentinel*, p. 1B, 24th October 2003

skivvies *noun*
underwear *US, 1918*
Originally applied to an undershirt or vest, now to underwear in general.

- All three, tired at the end of this long day, stand in their skivvies in front of the bed. — Darryl Ponicsan, *The Last Detail*, p. 52, 1970
- So Ordell would have these businessmen stumbling around in their skivvies sneezing, spilling drinks, shit, middle-aged jitterbugs trying to dance sals with the cute ladies who'd be giggling, having some fun with them. — Elmore Leonard, *Switch*, p. 60, 1978
- No, thank you. Nothing. Get your socks and skivvies and let's get out of here before your worst fears come true and we end up at the bottom of the canyon smashed into the roadway by a semi. — Robert Campbell, *Alice in La-La Land*, p. 26, 1987

skivvs *noun*
underpants *US, 2002*

- "Chill baby—It's not worth getting your skivvs in a bunch." — *Dictionary of New Terms (Hope College)*, 2002

skizziest *adjective*
the best *US, 1960*

- — *San Francisco Examiner*, p. III-2, 22nd March 1960

skoal; skol *verb*
to drink; to down a drink *US, 1957*

- They could skoal two cases of beer in no time flat. — Frederick Kohner, *Gidget*, p. 40, 1957

skoofer *noun*
a marijuana cigarette *US, 1980*

- — Edith A. Folb, *runnin' down some lines*, p. 254, 1980

skoon *noun*
one dollar *US, 1988*

- — George Percy, *The Language of Poker*, p. 83, 1988

skosh; skoshi *noun*
a small amount *US, 1970*
Korean pidgin, used by US soldiers in Korea and brought back to the US as "skosh." The word was given a second wind in the 1970s with a radio advertisement for jeans that promised "just a skosh more room" in the crotch area for men.

- — *Current Slang*, p. 23, Spring 1970
- "Skosh" is an advertising copywriter's way of spelling the Japanese word "sukoshi," meaning "a little." — *Detroit Free Press*, 19th December 1977

skoshki tiger *nickname*
the Northrop F-5 Tiger *US, 1990*

- Oh, they call them Skoshi Tiger when they come / And they come in Freedom Fighters when they come. — Joseph Tuso, *Singing the Vietnam Blues*, p. 175, 1990: Skoshi Tiger

SKP *noun*
an escaped prisoner *US, 1962*
A play on "escapee."

- — *American Speech*, p. 272, December 1962: "The language of traffic policemen"

skronky *adjective*
of an electric guitar's sound or style of playing, excitingly raw and basic; hence, applied to fans of such music *US, 2003*

- Ferociously lo-fi, they [the Tall Boys] eschew electronics for amphetamine-loaded, skronky guitar riffs, slinky basslines, and relentless, in-your-face drums. — *The Village Voice*, 7th April 2003
- [S]ix months ago, only the skronkiest, most pared-down Detroit-sounding screechrock would have engendered a response[.] — *X-Ray*, p. 35, August 2003

skull *noun*
1 oral sex *US, 1973*

- "That's what I need, a little skull," said Fuzzy[.] — Joseph Wambaugh, *The Blue Knight*, p. 139, 1973
- While Willie drove us around, I opted for her far out skull extravaganza. — Iceberg Slim (Robert Beck), *Airtight Willie and Me*, p. 9, 1979

- The Manager gave him all the free bourbon he could guzzle and, if he could still get it up, some Oblivious backbooth skull just to discourage the likes of these two Clevelands from filing complaints. — Seth Morgan, *Homeboy*, p. 25, 1990
- Lizzie's a blast; she's smart, tender, funny and gives great skull. — James Ellroy, *Hollywood Nocturnes*, p. 265, 1994

2 in circus and carnival usage, a free ticket *US, 1981*

- — Don Wilmeth, *The Language of American Popular Entertainment*, p. 244, 1981

▸ **take a skull**
in a dramatic performance, to react slowly to a line *US, 1973*

- — Sherman Louis Sergel, *The Language of Show Biz*, p. 97, 1973

skull and brains *noun*
oral sex *US, 2002*

- — Gary K. Farlow, *Prison-ese*, p. 65, 2002

skull cracker *noun*
strong, homemade whiskey *US, 1999*

- It is called corn liquor, white lightning, sugar whiskey, skull cracker, popskull, bush whiskey, stump, stumphole, "splo, ruckus juice, radiator whiskey, rotgut, sugarhead, block and tackle, wildcat, panther's breath, tiger's sweat, Sweet spirits of cats a-fighting, alley bourbon, city gin, cool water, happy Sally, deep shaft, jump steady, old horsey, stingo, blue John, red eye, pine top, buckeye bark whiskey and see seven stars." — *Star Tribune (Minneapolis)*, p. 19F, 31st January 1999

skulled *adjective*
drunk *US, 1955*

- — *American Speech*, p. 305, December 1955: "Wayne university slang"
- "He's skulled," McMurphy hissed. "Somebody's gonna have to go out and help him." — Ken Kesey, *One Flew Over the Cuckoo's Nest*, p. 287, 1962

skull-fry *noun*
chemically straightened hair *US, 1970*

- — Clarence Major, *Dictionary of Afro-American Slang*, p. 64, 1970

skullie *noun*
a skullcap *US, 1993*

- The hats also are sported at underground clubs and at "rave" parties, where, as techno or house music blasts to a peak, the hats are tossed in the air. What are the hats called? Take your pick. Some call them skullies, street slang for skullcap. — *Atlanta Journal and Constitution*, p. L1, 3rd January 1993

skull job *noun*
an act of oral sex *US, 1971*

- — Eugene Landy, *The Underground Dictionary*, 1971

skull session *noun*
a group analysis and discussion; a conference *US, 1959*

- "Afternoon—when I get back from skull session." — Frederick Kohner, *The Affairs of Gidget*, p. 61, 1963
- I buzzed Dave DePugh's office to pitch a kidnap skull session—the fucker was "out in the field." — James Ellroy, *Hollywood Nocturnes*, p. 77, 1994

skunk *noun*
a woman, especially a promiscuous woman with deficiencies in the area of hygiene *US, 1965*

- They used to call those kind of girls skunks because they were so dirty. — Claude Brown, *Manchild in the Promised Land*, p. 252, 1965
- "You might as well be a skunk," Chilly said. "What?" "A skunk. A broad." — Malcolm Braly, *On the Yard*, p. 300, 1967

skunk *verb*
in various games, to defeat an opponent by an overwhelming margin *US, 1843*

- Janie and Speedy, of course, started having fun by skunking them soundly. — Iceberg Slim (Robert Beck), *Long White Con*, pp. 62–63, 1977

skunk beer *noun*
inexpensive, bitter, poor quality beer *US, 1997*

- We listened to Black Flag, formed bands, tried chewing tobacco, threw up from chewing tobacco, got grounded for swilling skunk beer. — *News and Observer (Raleigh, North Carolina)*, p. E5, 3rd August 1997

skunked *adjective*
drunk *US, 2001*

- — Don R. McCreary (Editor), *Dawg Speak*, 2001

skunk juice; skunk juicer; skunk junker *noun*
an illegal linear amplifier for a citizens' band radio *US, 1976*

- — *Elementary Electronics, Dictionary of CB Lingo*, p. 108, 1976

skunk oil *noun*
any odorizing agent injected into natural gas *US, 1954*
- — Jerry Robertson, *Oil Slanguage*, p. 113, 1954

skunk weed; skunk *noun*
an extremely potent variety of marijuana which will produce an hallucinogenic effect; also, good quality marijuana *US, 1982*
- A small dose of the skunk weed, like it's suppose to be[.] — Cypress Hill, *Stoned Raiders*, 1995
- Fucking good skunk. — *Kids*, 1995
- I suck down a cloud of skunk and pass it on. — Lynn Breedlove, *Godspeed*, p. 47, 2002
- "Spent it all on crap tequila, skunkweed, and second-rate head from nasty L.A. skanks." — Linden Dalecki, *Kid B*, p. 207, 2006

sky *noun*
1 a hat *US, 1976*
- And his fabulous sky was broke so fly / That the city had it banned. — Dennis Wepman et al., *The Life*, p. 48, 1976
2 in a casino, the ubiquitous overhead surveillance system *US, 1991*
An abbreviated form of **EYE IN THE SKY**.
- — Michael Dalton, *Blackjack*, p. 46, 1991

sky *verb*
to leave quickly *US, 1982*
Vietnam war slang.
- I want to ask you some questions before you sky, Danny. — John Del Vecchio, *The 13th Valley*, p. 534, 1982

skygod *noun*
a highly respected sky surfer *US, 1998*
- SKYGOD A person of noted freefall ability, whether in fact or in his own inflated estimation. — shelley Youngblut, *Way Inside ESPN's X Games*, p. 65, 1998

sky hook *noun*
a citizens' band radio antenna *US, 1976*
- — Len Buckwalter, *CB Radio*, p. 66, 1976

sky man *noun*
a preacher *US, 1959*
A variant of the more common **SKY PILOT**.
- Let's dig us up a Sky Man who'll tie the knot for us[.] — Dan Burley, *Diggeth Thou?*, p. 35, 1959

sky-nest *noun*
an apartment on an upper floor of an apartment building *US, 1950*
- This sky-nest was once occupied by mayors Thompson and Cermak, and was regarded as Chicago's executive mansion. — Jack Lait and Lee Mortimer, *Chicago Confidential*, p. 182, 1950

sky-piece *noun*
a hat *US, 1948*
- — Jack Lait and Lee Mortimer, *New York Confidential*, p. 236, 1948: "A glossary of Harlemisms"

sky scout *noun*
an air force chaplain *US, 1945*
- — Lou Shelly, *Hepcats Jive Talk Dictionary*, p. 48, 1945

sky shouter *noun*
a public address system attached to an aircraft *US, 1967*
- The psy war chopper spent two hours flying over the lake, telling the men in the boats through a sky shouter to head for the shore. — David Reed, *Up Front in Vietnam*, p. 156, 1967

sky six *noun*
God *US, 1976*
From "sky" (a unit commander).
- That Sky Six ain't cutting no husses this week, Man, not one. — Charles Anderson, *The Grunts*, p. 99, 1976

sky's the limit *noun*
in poker, any game played with no limit on the amount of bets *US, 1967*
- — Albert H. Morehead, *The Complete Guide to Winning Poker*, p. 273, 1967

sky up *verb*
1 to become intoxicated on crack cocaine *US, 2005*

- One time she skyed up for over a week and missed Dom's birthday party and a major press conference. — Noire, *Candy Licker*, p. 171, 2005
2 to be released from prison *US, 1993*
- "I'm fin' to sky up and go get bent." — Sanyika Shakur, *Monster*, p. 162, 1993

slab *noun*
1 a car *US, 2006*
- "At least they got a slab." — Linden Dalecki, *Kid B*, p. 73, 2006
2 a thick, dark, cold wave *US, 1991*
- — Trevor Cralle, *The Surfin'ary*, p. 116, 1991
3 a phonograph record; any audio recording *US, 1974*
- — Robert Kirk Mueller, *Buzzwords*, p. 142, 1974
4 a package of crack cocaine *US, 1998*
- Crack isn't usually packaged in vials anymore but in miniature heat-sealed plastic bags, which the dealers call "slabs." — *The New Yorker*, p. 35, 10th August 1998
5 crack cocaine that is heavily adulterated *US, 1992*
- — Terry Williams, *Crackhouse*, p. 151, 1992

slab *verb*
in necrophile usage, to engage in sexual activity with a corpse *US, 1986–1987*
- — *Maledicta*, p. 180, Summer/Winter 1986–1987: "Sexual slang: prostitutes, pedophiles, flagellators, transvestites, and necrophiles"

slab boy *noun*
a necrophile *US, 1986–1987*
- — *Maledicta*, p. 178, Summer/Winter 1986–1987: "Sexual slang: prostitutes, pedophiles, flagellators, transvestites, and necrophiles"

slab house *noun*
a modest restaurant serving barbecued meat *US, 1975*
- — Carl J. Banks Jr., *Banks Dictionary of the Black Ghetto Language*, 1975

slack *noun*
1 less than harsh treatment *US, 1968*
- — *Current Slang*, p. 43, Fall 1968
2 money *US, 1972*
- — David Claerbaut, *Black Jargon in White America*, p. 79, 1972
3 in a military patrol, the soldier immediately behind the lead soldier in formation *US, 1971*
- The slack takes the left overhead and the 90 degrees to his right. — Ronald J. Glasser, *365 Days*, pp. 209–210, 1971
- The slack was next in line. His primary function was to pace or keep track of the distance the team moved. — Gary Linderer, *The Eyes of the Eagle*, p. 108, 1991

slack *verb*
to wear pants, especially jeans, oversized, baggy, and sagging *US, 1993*
- — *American Speech*, p. 418, Winter 1993: "Among the new words"

slacker *noun*
a person who avoids work, study, and responsibility *US, 1898*
The most recent burst of popularity for the term is not its first.
- "And the slackers get the same pay," Ernie echoed. — L.H. Whittemore, *Cop!*, p. 200, 1969
- [O]ne man returning from R&R and four slackers from the rear. — Charles Anderson, *The Grunts*, p. 140, 1976
- Don't the slackers prefer the grassy knoll over there? — *Clueless*, 1995
- Giving my ad the headline Confused Lesbian Slacker With No Saleable Job Skills wouldn't have worked. — Michelle Tea, *Rent Girl*, p. 44, 2004

slack jaw *noun*
a dolt; a stupid person *US, 1994*
- — Michael Dalton Johnson, *Talking Trash with Redd Foxx*, p. 118, 1994

slack man *noun*
in a combat march, the second man in line *US, 1989*
- Vega, the second or "slack" man in the line, was the buffer between Chavez's point position and the main body of the unit, fifty meters behind Vega. — Tom Clancy, *Clear and Present Danger*, p. 205, 1989

slag down *verb*
to slow down *US, 1997*
- A lot of gang banging has slagged down. Happened right after Rodney King—we all decided to get together in South Park. — Gini Sikes, *8 Ball Chicks*, p. 82, 1997

slaggy *noun*
a groupie who is promiscuous and sluttish, even by groupie standards *US, 1969*
- — *Kiss*, 1969: "Groupie glossary"

slake *verb*
▶ **slake the snake**
(of a male) to have sex *US, 1984*
- The bartender spoke slowly, as if to an idiot child. "You know, push the bush? Slake the snake? Drain the train? Siphon the python?" — James Ellroy, *Because the Night*, p. 415, 1984

slam *noun*
1 a salute *US, 1958*
- A salute to a superior officer is a slam, or a highball. — *New York Times*, p. 34, 20th October 1958

2 a jail or prison *US, 1960*
A shortened form of **SLAMMER** sometimes; used as a plural.
- During the Moratorium he was in the slam. — Oscar Zeta Acosta, *The Revolt of the Cockroach People*, p. 204, 1973
- Only plea I ever copped cost me three years in the slams. — Edwin Torres, *Carlito's Way*, p. 10, 1975
- I'm going to find out why they haven't got him in the slam already. — Robert Campbell, *Junkyard Dog*, p. 38, 1986
- There're some scary fucking slams you can get sent to, Marion, Lewisburg ... — Elmore Leonard, *Out of Sight*, p. 58, 1996

slam *verb*
1 to inject an illegal drug intravenously *US, 1996*
- Blaze watched Dawn pulling up the sleeves of the red polyester blouse, examining the tracks where she slammed her speedballs, a mixture of powdered cocaine and Mexican tar heroin. — Joseph Wambaugh, *Floaters*, p. 7, 1996

2 to hide prison contraband in your rectum *US, 2000*
- Like prisoners everywhere, Rikers inmates use their rectums as a sort of suitcase for weapons, concealing one or two razor blades—or sometimes even 20 or 30—by "slamming" or "boofing" them. — *Village Voice*, p. 45, 19th December 2000

3 to defecate *US, 2001*
- — Don R. McCreary (Editor), *Dawg Speak*, 2001

4 to criticize someone or something harshly *US, 1916*
- Soup kitchens slammed[.] New approach needed to tackle homelessness, says campaigner[.] — *The Guardian*, 7th January 2004

5 to refuse to work *US, 1950*
Prison usage.
- — Hyman E. Goldin et al., *Dictionary of American Underworld Lingo*, p. 196, 1950

6 while riding a surfboard or skateboard, to lose your balance and fall *US, 1984*
- — *San Francisco Sunday Examiner & Chronicle*, p. 20, 2nd September 1984: "Say it right"
- — Nick Carroll, *The Next Wave*, 1991

7 to slam dance *US, 1995*
- Go to punk gigs by himself. Slam in the pit with the boys until the pain sweated out of him[.] — Francesca Lia Block, *Baby Be-Bop*, p. 410, 1995

slambang *verb*
to successfully cheat other gamblers *US, 1950*
- — *The Annals of the American Academy of Political and Social Sciences*, p. 130, May 1950

slam-bang *adverb*
with force or noise *UK, 1840*
- I'm only trying to convince you that you can't go slam-bang into this. — Horace McCoy, *Kiss Tomorrow Good-bye*, p. 134, 1948
- I didn't find his conversation very entertaining, he was a pretty dull fellow, until slam bang in the middle of one of his sentences I said, What did you say your name was again? — Clancy Sigal, *Going Away*, p. 179, 1961

slam book *noun*
a book with a series of questions to which friends write answers *US, 1969*
- Slam books were big. You'd pass around a list of questions. "Who's the best looking boy in school." "Who'd you love to date?" "Your favorite song." — *San Francisco Chronicle*, p. 38, 15th December 1969

slam dance *verb*
to dance in a violent manner popular in punk and post-punk settings *US, 1980*
Slam dancing was good fodder for popular television in the US, with the *Chips* episode that aired on 31st January 1982 and the *Quincy* episode of 2nd December 1982, both centered around the relatively new phenomenon.
- Other club managers and regular club-goers blamed the violence on organized Huntington Beach-area punk gangs who make a practice of pummeling each other and slam dancing at area clubs. — *Los Angeles Times*, p. 3 (Calendar Section), 29th June 1980
- Robert Louis Stevenson, the original author of this class-turned-silly, may slam-dance in his coffin. — *Los Angeles Times*, p. 5, 5th July 1981
- [T]he early Saturday evening mob of U.S. teens and young adults who descend on Tijuana to get drunk, slam-dance in nightclubs, fight, bleed, vomit, and, in general, have a wonderful time. — Joseph Wambaugh, *Finnegan's Week*, p. 266, 1993

slam dancer *noun*
a person who slam dances *US, 1981*
- Among other things, slam dancers' throw themselves into other slam dancers' arms, just as if they were throwing themselves out a window. — *Washington Post*, p. B8, 3rd November 1981

slam down *verb*
to confine someone to a jail cell *US, 1989*
- — James Harris, *A Convict's Dictionary*, p. 38, 1989

slam dunk *noun*
1 in the language of wind surfing, an unintended, sudden end of a ride when the board steers too hard to windward *US, 1985*
- — Frank Fox, *A Beginner's Guide to Zen and the Art of Windsurfing*, p. 154, 1985: "A short dictionary of wind surfing terms"

2 anything accomplished with ease *US, 2001*
- Barbara Molar is my wit. This should be a slam dunk. — Stephen J. Cannell, *The Tin Collectors*, p. 18, 2001

slam-dunk *verb*
to defeat someone convincingly, if not overwhelmingly *US, 1992*
From the basketball sense of jamming the ball through the hoop.
- I want to slam-dunk this guy. — *A Few Good Men*, 1992

slam-dunk *adjective*
certain *US, 1992*
- [S]he kissed him and told him they were a rockin' slink-chunk, slam-dunk band and that it would be fine. — Francesca Lia Block, *Cherokee Bat*, p. 183, 1992

slammer *noun*
1 a door *US, 1946*
- You had to pull up in a diamond-studded limousine, with solid gold fenders and ermine upholstery, before the doorman would even reach for the twister to your slammer. — Mezz Mezzrow, *Really the Blues*, p. 84, 1946
- When he fell back through that tavern slammer / Dad, you shouldda dug the squeals and clamor. — Dan Burley, *Diggeth Thou?*, p. 14, 1959
- I took another sip of coffee and turned around to check her out and saw two of New York's finest coming in the slammer. — A.S. Jackson, *Gentleman Pimp*, p. 151, 1973

2 a jail or prison *US, 1952*
- My mother had me in the slammer. — George Mandel, *Flee the Angry Strangers*, p. 121, 1952
- He spent twenty-three years in the slammer[.] — William "Lord" Buckley, *The Bad-Rapping of the Marquis de Sade*, 1960
- Some get snuffed, some drop out, some go to the slammer and there's always new guys who've joined. — Hunter S. Thompson, *Hell's Angels*, p. 116, 1966
- But when Vic asked me how's business, well, you don't lie to man who's just done four years in the slammer for ya. — *Reservoir Dogs*, 1992

3 solitary confinement *US, 1984*
- — Inez Cardozo-Freeman, *The Joint*, p. 531, 1984

4 a person who slam dances *US, 1995*
- Then he went and stood at the edge of the slammers. — Francesca Lia Block, *Baby Be-Bop*, p. 412, 1995

5 an illegal linear amplifier for a citizens' band radio *US, 1976*
- — Elementary Electronics, *Dictionary of CB Lingo*, p. 108, 1976

slamming *noun*
slam dancing *US, 1981*
- "Slamming," the latest mode of dancing among the punks — sudden, full-tilt lunging across the floor that sometimes knocks other dancers off their feet—has also drawn some criticism and complaints. — *New York Times*, p. D11, 22nd March 1981

slamming *adjective*

excellent; beautiful; fabulous *US, 1994*

Originally late C19; current usage started in 1980s black society and spread with hip-hop music.

- The Wu[-Tang Clan] is too slammin' for these Cold Killin' labels / Who ain't had hits since I seen Aunt Mable — Genius/GZA *Protect Ya Neck*, 1994
- I thought Oberlin was magnificent. I never wanted to come home. The library was slammin' — William Upski Wimsatt, *Bomb the Suburbs*, p. 61, 1994
- A moms and pops eatery were the food was always slamming. — Eric Jerome Dickey, *Cheaters*, p. 90, 1999

slam pit *noun*

the area in a club or concert arena where dancers gather to dance in a violent manner popular in punk and postpunk settings *US, 1983*

- A spectacular slow-motion scene of a fan diving headfirst from the stage and executing a full forwardflip before landing in the slam pit. — *Los Angeles Times*, p. VI-19, 23rd December 1983

slam up *verb*

to imprison someone *US, 1990*

- Jist cuz you gonna be slammed up three years don't make her a nun. — Seth Morgan, *Homeboy*, p. 146, 1990

slang *noun*

in carnival and amusement park usage, a watch chain *US, 1981*

- — Don Wilmeth, *The Language of American Popular Entertainment*, p. 245, 1981

slang *verb*

to sell drugs, especially crack cocaine *US, 1991*

- — Judi Sanders, *Don't Dog by Do, Dude!*, p. 29, 1991
- "Do you have a job?" "Naw," he said, his head hanging down. "I slang dope." — Sanyika Shakur, *Monster*, p. 367, 1993
- His brother is gonna go down, he's steady slangin' outside the apartments. — Rick Ayers (Editor), *Berkeley High Slang Dictionary*, p. 39, 2004
- But my boy Arnel say you slangin' the prime. — *Hustle and Flow*, 2004

slangs *noun*

slang words or terms *US, 1972*

Hawaiian youth usage.

- — Elizabeth Ball Carr, *Da Kine Talk*, p. 148, 1972

slant *noun*

a South Asian person *US, 1942*

Offensive.

- Gooks could be both. Slants and slopes were civilians. Dinks could be both. — Nelson DeMille, *Word of Honor*, p. 414, 1985
- By god, when they ain't foolin' around with wars and dope traffic, them slants do pretty good on the cuisine. — Dan Jenkins, *Dead Solid Perfect*, p. 65, 1986
- Oh, there are some soldiers thought Code Six as he watched, soldiers like Jimmy and I were, fighting the fucking GOOKS and SLANTS and SLOPES, soldiers trotting single file across a smoking field. — William T. Vollman, *Whores for Gloria*, p. 36, 1991
- Everybody goes around pretending there's one set of rules. One size fits all. That's not the way. There's one set for crooks and one for coups. Another set for niggers and another for honkies and another for slants. — Robert Campbell, *Boneyards*, p. 268, 1992

slanter *noun*

the eye *US, 1970*

- — Clarence Major, *Dictionary of Afro-American Slang*, p. 105, 1970

slant-eye *noun*

a person from southern Asia *US, 1962*

Offensive.

- — Joseph E. Ragen and Charles Finston, *Inside the World's Toughest Prison*, p. 818, 1962: "Penitentiary and underworld glossary"

slantville *noun*

a neighborhood dominated by South Asian people *US, 1959*

- Slantville is the N.Y. word for Chinatown. — Richard Farina, *Letter to Peter Tamony*, 24th August 1959

slap *verb*

▸ **slap skins**

to slap palms in greeting, farewell, or approval *US, 1967*

- I slapped skin with them, playing it cool all the way. — Piri Thomas, *Down These Mean Streets*, p. 16, 1967

- We slapped skin all around on the running of our little murder game. — Edwin Torres, *Carlito's Way*, p. 55, 1975

▸ **slap the bacon in the pan**

to have sex *US, 1977*

- — Bill Davis, *Jawjacking*, p. 91, 1977

slap circuit *noun*

the underworld *US, 1963*

- If you're really a hood, then ask around the slap circuit who I am. — Mickey Spillane, *Me, Hood!*, p. 30, 1963

slap-down *noun*

a humiliating situation *US, 1986*

- — *55-Plus*, p. 13, 12th February 1986: "Today's guide to teen slang"

slap hammer *noun*

a hammer designed for pulling dents but used to break open the top of a car's steering column to obtain access to the ignition *US, 1996*

- He told them he'd spot the car a customer wanted and use a slim jim or lemon pop to get in, a slap hammer to yank the ignition, a side kick to extract steering column locks and usually liquid nitrogen to freeze the alarm system. — Elmore Leonard, *Out of Sight*, p. 56, 1996

slap-happy *adjective*

1 dazed; confused *US, mid-1930s*

- [T]hen for a while I shook Slim, who was wandering a little slap-happy in the street from all the whisky and beer[.] — Jack Kerouac, *On the Road*, p. 34, 1957

2 obsessed with masturbation *US, 1962*

- — Joseph E. Ragen and Charles Finston, *Inside the World's Toughest Prison*, p. 818, 1962: "Penitentiary and underworld glossary"

slapper *noun*

a small, heavy club *US, 1976*

- What caused Typewriter to leave his intentions unfulfilled, flopping straight down in one heap, was an eight-ounce bar of lead tightly bound in burnished leather and cradled in the broad palm of Canale's hand. He returned the slapper to his coat before anyone saw it. — Emmett Grogan, *Final Score*, p. 271, 1976
- He came up with a slapper and gave the guy a shot that went through everybody in the room. — Mark Baker, *Cops*, p. 286, 1985

slaps *noun*

plastic flip-flops (sandals) *US, 1976*

Skateboarding usage.

- — Albert Cassorla, *The Skateboarder's Bible*, p. 202, 1976

slap-slap *noun*

a small police club that fits into a police officer's hand *US, 1962*

- — *American Speech*, p. 272, December 1962: "The language of traffic policemen"

slash *noun*

1 the vagina *US, 1972*

- "Snatch," "hole," "kooze," "slash," "pussy" and "crack" were other terms referring to women's genitals, to women as individuals, or to women as a species. — *Screw*, p. 5, 3rd January 1972
- She acts like any paid hooker [...] Paid for her slash. — Peter Sotos, *Index*, p. 56, 1996

2 an attractive, white woman *US, 1987*

- — Carsten Stroud, *Close Pursuit*, p. 276, 1987

slash *verb*

to surf aggressively back and forth across the face of a wave *US, 1991*

- — Lee Wardlaw, *Cowabunga!*, p. 156, 1991

slash-and-burn *adjective*

ruthless; unconcerned with the consequences of a tactic *US, 1989*

From a term describing a jungle agricultural practice first recorded in the early 1940s.

- But I do see certain slash-and-burn tactics in the Industry now — Robert Stoller and I.S. Levine, *Coming Attractions*, p. 216, 1991

slasher *noun*

a person who takes a perverse pleasure from vandalism by slashing *US, 1954*

- A slasher is some warped individual who cuts, rips and mutilates upholstery, leather, curtains, and sometimes employees' uniforms. — Dev Collans with Stewart Sterling, *I was a House Detective*, p. 144, 1954

slat noun

a dollar US, 1969

- You want the blue too? The bite [cost] is two for fifty slats.
— Iceberg Slim (Robert Beck), *Pimp*, p. 92, 1969

slats noun

1 ribs US, 1898

- They sometimes wear skirts, but they ask no favors and are likely to kick you in the slats when you ain't looking if you make the mistake of treating them like flowers[.] — Robert Campbell, *Junkyard Dog*, p. 8, 1986

2 prison bars US, 1950

- — Hyman E. Goldin et al., *Dictionary of American Underworld Lingo*, p. 197, 1950

3 skis US, 1963

- — *American Speech*, p. 207, October 1963: "The language of skiers"

slaughtered adjective

very drunk or drug-intoxicated US, 1989

- — Pamela Munro, *U.C.L.A. Slang*, p. 77, 1989

slaughterhouse noun

a school US, 1958
Teen slang.

- — *San Francisco News*, p. 6, 25th March 1958

slave noun

1 in a sadomasochistic relationship, a person who endures many forms of humiliation, including extreme pain and public displays of submission US, 1960

- He "loved," he testified, to be his wife's "slave," to be whipped by her and forced to perform cunnilingus for a woman friend or fellatio for a visiting male, while she watched. — Michael Leigh, *The Velvet Underground*, p. 82, 1963
- "Pat didn't want to be tied up, but Jane loved to be the slave." — Robert Newton, *Bondage Clubs U.S.A.*, p. 60, 1967
- There is also jealousy among my slaves. In America, I had three slaves, a Wall Street banker, a telephone company executive and a little printer. — *Screw*, p. 5, 8th February 1971
- I assured him I wasn't slave material. — John Preston, *Hustling*, pp. 24–25, 1994

2 a submissive prisoner who performs all types of menial tasks for others US, 1988

- "In fact, they even assigned him a slave." "A slave?" Novak said. "A gofer. Somebody to carry messages, run errands for him. That kind of shit." — Gerald Petievich, *Shakedown*, pp. 85–86, 1988

3 a job US, 1946

- I didn't mind copping a slave just then because I could use the gold[.] — Mezz Mezzrow, *Really the Blues*, p. 107, 1946
- This slave is a drag, in the bag for some old hag, but strictly nowhere for me, I swear. — Dan Burley, *Diggeth Thou?*, p. 11, 1959
- You mean you just want any slave you can find? — Malcolm X and Alex Haley, *The Autobiography of Malcolm X*, p. 44, 1964
- A guy who worked in the garment center wouldn't say he had a job; he'd say, "Man, like, I got a slave." That's about what it amounted to. — Claude Brown, *Manchild in the Promised Land*, p. 184, 1965

slave verb

to work, especially at a menial job US, 1974

- "How do you make your bread?" Wilson asked. "Where do you slave? Know what I mean?" — Joseph Nazel, *Black Cop*, p. 178, 1974

slave bracelet noun

a bracelet showing romantic devotion to another US, 1947

- As she approached he took in the slave bracelet she wore around her right ankle[.] — Irving Shulman, *The Amboy Dukes*, p. 136, 1947

sleaze noun

a person with low moral standards US, 1980

- — *Verbatim*, p. 281, May 1976
- Hey you sleaze, my bed! — *The Blues Brothers*, 1980
- "What a sleaze," Alana says, shivering in mock disgust. — Bret Easton Ellis, *Less Than Zero*, p. 29, 1985

sleazebag noun

an utterly despicable person US, 1992
A useful term when you cannot decide whether to call someone a **SCUMBAG** or a **SLEAZEBALL**.

- My guess is that the FDA finally caught up with the sleazebag from Oxnard who was fronting the operation and nailed him with a cease and desist. — Armistead Maupin, *Maybe the Moon*, p. 14, 1992

sleazeball noun

an utterly despicable person US, 1983

- The sleazeball agent screamed for twenty minutes how Rossi's would be sued. — Seth Morgan, *Homeboy*, p. 292, 1990

sleazo noun

an utterly despicable person US, 1972

- [T]he outcall office window he'd blown to bits would give him a shot at some kind of file on Vandy—and the rock sleazos she might have run to. — James Ellroy, *Suicide Hill*, pp. 807–808, 1986

sleazoid noun

an utterly despicable person US, 1986

- They wondered how the hell he was going to hold together, working for a bunch of sleazoid lawyers and bail bondsmen. — Carl Hiaasen, *Tourist Season*, p. 18, 1986

sleazy adjective

cheap; inferior; low US, 1941

- Your values are pretty sleazy, Phil. — Philip Wylie, *Opus 21*, p. 336, 1949

sledgehammer noun

in pool, a stroke lacking in finesse but full of force US, 1990

- — Steve Rushin, *Pool Cool*, p. 27, 1990

sleep noun

cocaine US, 1987
Rich irony; if you do, you won't.

- — Carsten Stroud, *Close Pursuit*, p. 277, 1987

sleep verb

▸ **sleep with someone**

to have sex with someone UK, 1819

- A woman is much more comfortable taking her current man around guys she's slept with than a guy is taking his woman around women he's had sex with. ("Slept with" / "sex with." Isn't that it in a nutshell?) — Chris Rock, *Rock This!*, p. 136, 1997

▸ **sleep with the fishes**

to be dead as a result of a murder US, 1969

- So waking up in the morning is better than sleeping with the fishes. — Gerald Petievich, *Shakedown*, p. 45, 1988

sleeper noun

1 a barbiturate capsule; a sleeping pill US, 1961

- — Francis J. Rigney and L. Douglas Smith, *The Real Bohemia*, p. xvii, 1961
- — *Current Slang*, p. 43, Fall 1968
- — Carl D. Chambers and Richard D. Heckman, *Employee Drug Abuse*, p. 210, 1972
- — *American Speech*, p. 208, Fall–winter 1973: "The Language of Nursing"
- Even though the sleeper had only done half its job, Leo was still groggy. — Emmett Grogan, *Final Score*, p. 10, 1976

2 in circus and carnival usage, money that a customer overlooks US, 1981

- — Don Wilmeth, *The Language of American Popular Entertainment*, p. 245, 1981

3 in craps, a bet on the table that a gambler has forgotten is his US, 1981

- — N.B. Winkless, *The Gambling Times Guide to Craps*, p. 97, 1981

sleeper jump noun

any long distance move between performances US, 1973

- — Sherman Louis Sergel, *The Language of Show Biz*, p. 200, 1973

sleep off verb

to serve a short prison sentence without difficulty US, 1950

- — Hyman E. Goldin et al., *Dictionary of American Underworld Lingo*, p. 197, 1950

sleepy seeds noun

the deposits of mucus formed about the eyes during sleep US, 1975

- There were still sleepy seeds in his eyes. — Stephen King, *Salem's Lot*, p. 272, 1975

sleet noun

crack cocaine US, 1994
From the drug's resemblance to sleet.

- — US Department of Justice, *Street Terms*, October 1994

sleeve noun

▸ **on the sleeve**

addicted to an injected drug US, 1949

- "I been on the sleeve since I got out of the army, Doc," Frankie told him. — Nelson Algren, *The Man with the Golden Arm*, p. 203, 1949

sleeve *verb*

to tattoo the lower half of the arm *US, 1989*
- — James Harris, *A Convict's Dictionary*, p. 38, 1989

sleeves *noun*

1 a wetsuit of any style *US, 1977*
- — Gary Fairmont R. Filosa II, *The Surfer's Almanac*, p. 194, 1977

2 arms covered with tattoos *US, 2002*
- "Any righteous white boy that's been down more than a few days got full sleeves, tattoos from the neck down to the wrist, known what I'm sayin'?" — Jimmy Lerner, *You Got Nothing Coming*, p. 63, 2002

sleigh ride *noun*

the use of cocaine or heroin; cocaine or heroin *US, 1973*
Building on the **SNOW** metaphor.
- — Joseph E. Ragen and Charles Finston, *Inside the World's Toughest Prison*, p. 818, 1962: "Penitentiary and underworld glossary"
- — David Maurer and Victor Vogel, *Narcotics and Narcotic Addiction*, p. 444, 1973

slice

an act of sex *US, 2004*
An evolution of **PIECE OF ASS**.
- "How do you get a slice from a girl you've never met before?" — Marty Beckerman, *Generation S.L.U.T.*, p. 2, 2004

sliced *adjective*

1 muscular, lacking body fat, well sculpted *US, 1984*
- — *American Speech*, p. 201, Fall 1984: "The language of bodybuilding"

2 circumcized *US, 1988*
- — H. Max, *Gay (S)language*, p. 39, 1988

slick *noun*

1 an unarmed aircraft *US, 1990*
- The true transport model, which hauls seven to nine men into battle, is called "The Slick," technically "The Delta" or UF-1D. — Elaine Shepard, *The Doom Pussy*, p. 4, 1967
- The slick had just landed, and Gilmore pointed to the machine gun so that the others would silence it. — David Reed, *Up Front in Vietnam*, p. 55, 1967
- This morning they were inserted by chopper. The slicks moved them inland, keeping about 1500 feet. — Ronald J. Glasser, *365 Days*, p. 30, 1971
- They were called "slicks" because, except for an M-60 machine gun in each cargo door, they were unarmed. — Dennis Marvicsin and Jerold Greenfield, *Maverick*, p. 36, 1990

2 a fashionable, admired person *US, 1969*
- "I remember when all the slicks used to come in here," Ernie remarked to me. — L.H. Whittemore, *Cop!*, p. 131, 1969

3 a glossy magazine *US, 1953*
- Sometimes pieces fluttered rejection slips from slick to fanzine[.] — Greil Marcus, *Psychotic Reactions and Carburetor Dung*, 1987

4 a field of criminal expertise *US, 1992*
- — William K. Bentley and James M. Corbett, *Prison Slang*, p. 34, 1992

5 in pool, a skilled player who bets on his own ability *US, 1990*
- — Mike Shamos, *The Illustrated Encyclopedia of Billiards*, p. 216, 1993

slick *adjective*

1 attractive; charming *US, 2001*
- — Don R. McCreary (Editor), *Dawg Speak*, 2001

2 in lowball poker, favorable *US, 1967*
- — Albert H. Morehead, *The Complete Guide to Winning Poker*, p. 273, 1967

slick boy *noun*

an undercover police officer *US, 1991*
The title of a 1998 novel by James Martin et al.
- The windows of the car were open, and the two men could hear children in the neighborhood yell, "Slick boys!"—code words to warn of police in the area. — *Chicago Tribune*, p. C1, 9th January 1991

slick chick *noun*

an attractive girl *US, 1947*
- — Marcus Hanna Boulware, *Jive and Slang of Students in Negro Colleges*, 1947

slicked *adjective*

(said of playing cards) waxed for identification in a cheating scheme *US, 1952*
- Slicked aces were being used. They were so thoroughly waxed it was surprising no one wised up. — Harry Grey, *The Hoods*, p. 174, 1952

slicker *noun*

1 a world-wise, sophisticated, urban person *US, 1900*

- He sure wasn't scared at all, and he acted like a slicker. — Chester Gould, *Dick Tracy Meets the Night Crawler*, p. 29, 1945
- "Phil is a real slicker. He's been holding out on us all these years," Beatrice said. — James T. Farrell, *Saturday Night*, p. 23, 1947
- "You know what you are?" she said, huskily. "You're a slicker." — Jim Thompson, *Savage Night*, p. 10, 1953
- I tried to tell him a long time ago that these so-called slickers and throughbreds don't mean him no good. — Nathan Heard, *Howard Street*, p. 36, 1968

2 a police officer *US, 1998*
- Lookouts shouted warnings, yelling to the dealers inside, using slang terms for police: "Blue and white on State! Slickers on State! I still got slickers on State1[.]" — *Chicago Tribune*, p. C11, 12th April 1998

3 a stolen car with all identification markings erased or removed *US, 1950*
- — Hyman E. Goldin et al., *Dictionary of American Underworld Lingo*, p. 197, 1950

slick leggings *noun*

the rubbing of the penis between the thighs of another man until reaching orgasm *US, 1961*
- Our prison informants consider this and "slick legging" to be statistically insignificant types of release. — *New York Mattachine Newsletter*, p. 7, June 1961

slick-sleeve *noun*

a US Army private E-1; a US Air Force airman basic; a police recruit *US, 1970*
"Slick" because he has no stripes on his sleeve.
- — *Current Slang*, p. 18, Summer 1970
- Goddamn slick-sleved rookies', I said, hot as hell[.] — Joseph Wambaugh, *The Blue Knight*, p. 59, 1973

slick-wing *adjective*

used of a pilot in the air force, junior *US, 1986*
The wing insignias of the junior pilot did not have a star above them like those of senior and command pilots.
- I didn't drag my ass three thousand miles across the country to have some slick-wing major tell me I'm nuts. — Walter Boyne and Steven Thompson, *The Wild Blue*, p. 235, 1986

slicky; slickey *verb*

to obtain something through ingenious and unorthodox diligence, up to and including theft *US, 1968*
An adaptation of pidgin English by United Nations troops in Korea in the early 1950s, from "slick" (not-quite-honestly smart).
- — Carl Fleischhauer, *A Glossary of Army Slang*, p. 15, 1968

slicky boy *noun*

a thief or swindler *US, 1967*
Coined by Koreans, borrowed by US and UN troops in Korea.
- Members of the US Air Force, for example, helped with the re-education of a Korean "Slicky Boy," as the juvenile delinquents were known there. — John Hohenberg, *Between Two Worlds*, p. 95, 1967

slide *noun*

a pants pocket *US, 1932*
- With "six yards" in my slide, I wasn't about to board another bus so I took the "Grand Central" train to New York. — Babs Gonzales, *I Paid My Dues*, p. 29, 1967
- The dude went mad / an' started to jump bad, pulling his roscoe out his slide. — Lightnin' Rod, *Hustlers Convention*, p. 98, 1973
- So I reached in my slide and came out with two boss threes / And said "Here, girl, go to the shithouse and get the weakness out of your knees." — Dennis Wepman et al., *The Life*, p. 52, 1976
- I off the other nineteen, pay Max back his five hundred dollars and take the other fourteen hundred dollars for my slide[.] — Terry Williams, *The Cocaine Kids*, p. 42, 1989

slide *verb*

to ride a wave *US, 1965*
- — Ross Olney, *The Young Sportsman's Guide to Surfing*, p. 88, 1965

slider *noun*

1 a hamburger or cheeseburger *US, 1987*
Originally the small hamburgers sold by the White Tower™ chain, later any hamburger.
- After they had eaten in the formal wardroom (they were fortunate; the meal was real meat in the form of "sliders and rollers," cheeseburgers and hot dogs), they visited Tim's tiny stateroom. — Gerry Carroll, *North S*A*R*, p. 133, 1991

2 a gambler who slides rather than rolls dice in an effort to control the result *US, 2003*
- — Victor H. Royer, *Casino Gamble Talk*, p. 122, 2003

slides *noun*
shoes *US, 1962*
- — Joseph E. Ragen and Charles Finston, *Inside the World's Toughest Prison*, p. 818, 1962: "Penitentiary and underworld glossary"

slim *noun*
a handgun *US, 1950*
- — Hyman E. Goldin et al., *Dictionary of American Underworld Lingo*, p. 197, 1950

slime *noun*
heroin *US, 1994*
- — US Department of Justice, *Street Terms*, October 1994

slime *verb*
to throw urine and/or feces on someone *US, 1992*
- "At first, we put the little bastards in a four-point position when they slimed us, but after a while they just laughed at you." — Pete Earley, *The Hot House*, p. 117, 1992

slimeball *noun*
a despicable person *US, 1973*
- I remember when the slime-balls used to be packed in there solid, asshole to belly button, waiting to look at the skin show in the viewer. — Joseph Wambaugh, *The Blue Knight*, pp. 26–27, 1973
- "My friends tell me Arnold is a rat. I also hear 'slimeball' and 'sleaze' a lot," says [actor Corben] Bernsen[.] — *Chicago Tribune*, p. CN7, 8th April 1987
- Leonard, the little slimeball, had all but promised as much when he'd asked me to perform. — Armistead Maupin, *Maybe the Moon*, p. 33, 1992
- An elderly man raised his hand, indicated plaintiff's counsel James Spiering, and said, according to Mall, "I know that slimeball over there from his TV ads." — *National Law Journal*, p. 3, 22nd December 2003

slimedog *noun*
a dirty, offensive person *US, 1994*
- — Sally Williams, *"Strong" Words*, p. 139, 1994

slimemouth *noun*
a foul-talking person *US, 1985*
- Frank disposed of seven slime-mouths by booking them drunk at the county jail, arrested by U.F. Puck. — Joseph Wambaugh, *The Secrets of Harry Bright*, p. 67, 1985

slim-fast diet *noun*
HIV or AIDS *US, 2002*
- — Gary K. Farlow, *Prison-ese*, p. 65, 2002

slim jim *noun*
a device that is slipped into a car door and used to open the door's locking mechanism *US, 1987*
- He taught me how to get into a vehicle using a tool called a "slim jim" that you slide down between the outer door panel and the glass to hook the locking bar. — Joseph Pistone, *Donnie Brasco*, p. 26, 1987
- Red Haynes, having used a Slim Jim lock-picking device to gain entry, sat in the front seat of Sands' car. — Gerald Petievich, *Shakedown*, p. 113, 1988
- He told them he'd spot the car a customer wanted and use a slim jim or lemon pop to get in, a slap hammer to yank the ignition, a side kick to extract steering column locks and usually liquid nitrogen to freeze the alarm system. — Elmore Leonard, *Out of Sight*, p. 56, 1996
- And just in case you lose your keys, good sir, I can toss in a complimentary slim-jim, free of charge. — *Gone in 60 Seconds*, 2000

slim-jim *verb*
to slip a device (a **SLIM JIM**) into a car door and used to open the door's locking mechanism *US, 1987*
- "How'd you get in, anyway?" "Slim-jimmed the back door." — Carl Hiaasen, *Double Whammy*, p. 160, 1987

slim off *verb*
to strip to your underwear *US, 1958*
- "Make yourself at home." "All right, I'll slim off." — Willard Motely, *Let No Man Write My Epitaph*, p. 210, 1958

sling *noun*
▸ **in the sling**
said of a woman experiencing her menstrual period *US, 1954*
- — *American Speech*, p. 298, December 1954: "The vernacular of menstruation"

sling *verb*
to sell illegal drugs *US, 1993*
- [H]is homies went back to Fifty-fourth and Imperial, where they continued to sling rock. — Bob Sipchen, *Baby Insane and the Buddha*, p. 151, 1993
- Watch the same dealer sling vials for two hours until he turns his back, and then sneak off with his ground stash. — David Simon and Edward Burns, *The Corner*, p. 11, 1997
- When they sling—street slang for selling drugs—they do it alone or maybe with a friend. — *St. Louis Post-Dispatch*, p. F1, 29th March 2001

▸ **sling ink**
to tattoo *US, 1989*
- — James Harris, *A Convict's Dictionary*, p. 38, 1989

slinger *noun*
1 a drug dealer *US, 1997*
- [T]he slingers work ground stashes hidden in used tires, behind cinder blocks, or in the tall grass by the edge of a rear wall. — David Simon and Edward Burns, *The Corner*, p. 5, 1997
2 a striptease artist *US, 1981*
- — Don Wilmeth, *The Language of American Popular Entertainment*, p. 246, 1981

slingshot *noun*
an extremely skimpy man's bathing suit or underpants *US, 1991*
- Surrounded by ersatz Indian warriors wearing bright Brazilian slingshots, the princess proclaimed in song and mime her passionate love. — Carl Hiaasen, *Native Tongue*, p. 229, 1991
- And don't wear slingshots. That's the prison name for men's briefs. — Nathan McCall, *Makes Me Wanna Holler*, p. 165, 1994

slingshotting *noun*
in bungee jumping, a reverse jump, beginning with the cord stretched out, yanking the participant up in the air *US, 1992*
- How do I know that this, this, this slingshotting—won't splatter me up against the bottom of the cage like some big hairy bug? — Erik Fair, *California Thrill Sports*, p. 45, 1992

sling-shot T-shirt *noun*
a sleeveless, scoop neck T-shirt *US, 2005*
- A few are wearing shorts and sling-shot tee shirts, lifting weights and playing basketball. — Colton Simpson, *Inside the Crips*, p. 139, 2005

slip *verb*
1 to act inappropriately *US, 1993*
- — *The Bell* (Paducah Tilghman High School), pp. 8–9, 17th December 1993: "Tilghmanism: the concealed language of the hallway"
2 to insult someone in a semiformal quasi-friendly competition *US, 2000*
- There are many different terms for playing the dozens, including "bagging, capping, cracking, dissing, hiking, joning, ranking, ribbing, serving, signifying, slipping, sounding and snapping." — James Haskins, *The Story of Hip-Hop*, p. 54, 2000

▸ **slip a lock**
to open a locked door by sliding a plastic credit card between the door and jamb and then sliding the lock open *US, 1981*
- "Christ, I slipped the lock!" Al Mackey held up his laminated police ID card, the corners chewed by the door latch. — Joseph Wambaugh, *The Glitter Dome*, p. 21, 1981

▸ **slip it to someone**
(of a male) to have sex with someone *US, 1952*
Euphemistic and naughty, both at once.
- I'll bet she won't say no if you try to slip it to her. — Jim Thompson, *The Killer Inside*, p. 51, 1952
- He slips it to the kid good and proper[.] — Angelo d'Arcangelo, *The Homosexual Handbook*, p. 229, 1968
- Could my father have been slipping it to this lady on the side? — Philip Roth, *Portnoy's Complaint*, p. 92, 1969

▸ **slip the pork**
from the male perspective, to have sex *US, 1976*
- Never slipped her the pork—just friends!—but she once gave me a pubic hair that I still got mounted somewhere. — Richard Meltzer, *A Whore Just Like the Rest*, p. 272, 1976

▸ **slip to cogs**
to become mentally imbalanced *US, 1981*

- "Christ almighty, you've finally slipped your cogs. Lady, you're nuts!"
  — Robert Lipkin, *A Brotherhood of Outlaws*, p. 136, 1981

slip-in *noun*
any lubricant used for faciliating sex, especially anal sex *US, 1962*
- — Joseph E. Ragen and Charles Finston, *Inside the World's Toughest Prison*, p. 818, 1962: "Penitentiary and underworld glossary"

slippery Anne *noun*
in a deck of playing cards, the queen of spades *US, 1950*
- — Thomas L. Clark, *The Dictionary of Gambling and Gaming*, p. 204, 1987

slippings *noun*
any lubricant used in anal sex *US, 1979*
- — *Maledicta*, p. 233, 1979: "Kinks and queens: linguistic and cultural aspects of the terminology for gays"

slippy *adjective*
slippery *US, 1982*
- — Sam McCool, *Pittsburghese*, p. 32, 1982

slipstick *noun*
a trombone *US, 1970*
- — Clarence Major, *Dictionary of Afro-American Slang*, p. 105, 1970

slip-stick jockey *noun*
a radar technician *US, 1947*
- — *American Speech*, p. 154, April 1947: "Radar slang terms"

S list *noun*
used as a euphemism for "shit list," a list of enemies *US, 1974*
- Watergate prosecutors are on the trial of a roster of people apparently even more in disfavor with the administration known as the "S List." — *San Francisco Chronicle*, p. 6, 18th May 1974

slit *noun*
1 the vagina *UK, 1648*
- Nicole gazed up at him and pulled the lips of her slit taut and up to show him the ragged pear of pinkness inside[.] — William T. Vollman, *Whores for Gloria*, p. 15, 1991
- Shearing our slits is not just for porn stars anymore. — *The Village Voice*, 8th–14th November 2000
- Her shaggy silken slit made an excellent petting zoo. — Mr. Skin, *Mr. Skin's Skincyclopedia*, p. 192, 2005

2 a person from South Asia *US, 1980*
Offensive. From the European perception of south Asian eyes as slanted slits.
- — Edith A. Folb, *runnin' down some lines*, p. 254, 1980

slitch *noun*
a despicable and/or promiscuous girl *US, 1963*
A blend of **SLUT** and **BITCH**.
- — Carol Ann Preusse, *Jargon Used by University of Texas Co-Eds*, 1963

slob *noun*
1 anyone of Slavic heritage *US, 1978*
Offensive.
- — *Maledicta*, p. 169, Summer/Winter 1978: "How to hate they neighbor: a guide to racist maledicta"

2 used as a derogatory nickname for a member of the Bloods youth gang *US, 1991*
- "He say somethin' like 'C.K.' to me and I'm like, 'What, nigger? Fuck slobs!'" — Leon Bing, *Do or Die*, p. 23, 1991
- "Fuck all slobs!" he yelled. The Blood stumbled back, gasping for air[.] — Bob Sipchen, *Baby Insane and the Buddha*, p. 97, 1993
- — Ann Lawson, *Kids & Gangs*, p. 56, 1994: "Common African-American gang slang/phrases"
- Slobs, he said, using a derogatory term for Bloods, won't use the letter c because it stands for Crips. — Gini Sikes, *8 Ball Chicks*, p. 8, 1997

slobber *noun*
a kiss *US, 1972*
- She opened the door and pasted a big slobber on me and a minute later we were in bed. — Robert Byrne, *McGoorty*, p. 66, 1972

slock *noun*
a sock with a heavy object inside it, used as a weapon *US, 2002*
- "Slocking" is another pasttime in the joint. "Convicts who don't want to be crossed out behind having a shank use a slock." — Jimmy Lerner, *You Got Nothing Coming*, p. 96, 2002

slock *verb*
to hit someone with a heavy object inside a sock *US, 2002*
- "Slocking" is another pasttime in the joint. "Convicts who don't want to be crossed out behind having a shank use a slock." — Jimmy Lerner, *You Got Nothing Coming*, p. 96, 2002

slop *noun*
1 poorly formed waves for surfing purposes *US, 1965*
- — John M. Kelly, *Surf and Sea*, p. 294, 1965
- — Brian and Margaret Lowdon, *Competitive Surfing*, 1988

2 in pool, a shot made unintentionally *US, 1990*
- In many games, slop is forbidden. — Steve Rushin, *Pool Cool*, p. 27, 1990

3 in computing, a built-in margin of error in one direction only *US, 1983*
- — Guy L. Steele et al., *The Hacker's Dictionary*, p. 115, 1983

4 a second-year college student *US, 1947*
- — Marcus Hanna Boulware, *Jive and Slang of Students in Negro Colleges*, 1947

slop chute *noun*
an enlisted men's bar *US, 1987*
- Nearby is a slop chute (bar) for staff NCOs and officers. — Ernest Spencer, *Welcome to Vietnam, Macho Man*, p. 22, 1987
- [A]n NCO club, and a "slop-chute" or enlisted men's club. — James Kirschke, *Not Going Home Alone*, p. 4, 2001

slope *noun*
a person from South Asia *US, 1948*
- One Army intelligence specialist said the pistol slaying of his Chinese interpreter was defended by his superior who said, "She was just a slope, anyway," meaning she was an Asiatic. — Hunter S. Thompson, *Fear and Loathing in Las Vegas*, p. 73, 1971
- The belief that one Marine was better than ten Slopes saw Marine squads fed in against known NVA platoons[.] — Michael Herr, *Dispatches*, p. 102, 1977
- Yeah—classical stuff—scares the hell out of the slopes—the boys love it. — *Apocalypse Now*, 1979
- Gooks could be both. Slants and slopes were civilians. Dinks could be both. — Nelson DeMille, *Word of Honor*, p. 414, 1985

slopehead *noun*
a person from South Asia *US, 1966*
Derogatory, perjorative, offensive, demeaning.
- And if you don't like it here why don't you go to commie China or North Vietnam with all those slopeheads or Russia??!! — *East Village Other*, p. 2, 15th–21st November 1968
- After all he had been willing to treat them all the same, even niggers and slopeheads. — Joseph Wambaugh, *The Choirboys*, p. 315, 1975
- "Put your money where your mouth is, Slophead," he said. "Whip it on me!" — Larry Heinemann, *Paco's Story*, pp. 6–7, 1986
- And he'd be damned if any slopeheads were gonna put their greasy yella hands on his boy's birthright. — *Pulp Fiction*, 1994

slope-out *noun*
an easy task *US, 1957*
- If they're parked where that guy says they are it'll be a slopeout. — Hubert Selby Jr., *Last Exit to Brooklyn*, p. 185, 1957

slopey *adjective*
(used of a wave) steep *US, 1991*
- — Trevor Cralle, *The Surfin'ary*, p. 117, 1991

slopie *noun*
a Chinese person or other South Asian *US, 1949*
Offensive.
- — *American Speech*, p. 30, February 1949: "A.V.G. Lingo"

sloppy seconds *noun*
sex with someone who has just had sex with someone else *US, 1967*
- "G'wan," said Jim, pushing the sailor toward the woman. "I don't mind sloppy seconds." — Michael Rumaker, *Gringos and Other Stories*, p. 58, 1967
- Hurry up, man. You go first. I'll take sloppy seconds, anytime. — Steve Cannon, *Groove, Bang, and Jive Around*, p. 38, 1969
- Sloppy seconds I think they call it. (Not really sloppy, because she would wash up first, but even so it used to bother me.) — Lawrence Block, *No Score*, p. 82, 1970
- "Ill get you a hot-looking girl on your arm in two minutes. That's if you don't mind taking my sloppy seconds." — Jason Starr, *Lights Out*, p. 65, 2006

slopshoot *noun*
a snack bar *US, 1993*
- If they have their way, we'll next see a Gay Disco established at Quantico and a Lesbian Slopshoot at Twentynine Palms. — Gyeorgos Hatonn, *To All My Children As the World Turns*, p. 94, 1993

slopsucker *noun*
a low priority project *US, 1991*
- — Eric S. Raymond, *The New Hacker's Dictionary*, p. 322, 1991

slop up *verb*
to drink to the point of intoxication *US, 1962*
- — Joseph E. Ragen and Charles Finston, *Inside the World's Toughest Prison*, p. 818, 1962: "Penitentiary and underworld glossary"

slosh *noun*
the back-slash (\) on a computer keyboard *US, 1991*
- — Eric S. Raymond, *The New Hacker's Dictionary*, p. 40, 1991

sloshed *adjective*
drunk *US, 2002*
- But of course, the girls can't resist buying me beer, and I can't resist beer, and so I'm getting sloshed. — Lynn Breedlove, *Godspeed*, p. 69, 2002

sloshy *adjective*
drunk *US, 1993*
- — *Washington Post*, 14th October 1993

slot *noun*
1 used as a term of address among jazz lovers of the 1930s and 40s *US, 1946*
- Come on slot, get up from there, I got some good gauge you can pick up on. — Mezz Mezzrow, *Really the Blues*, p. 298, 1946

2 the perfect spot to ride a wave *US, 1964*
- — John Severson, *Modern Surfing Around the World*, p. 181, 1964

slots *noun*
slot machines *US, 1975*
- Then I asked him how many of the permanents played the slots. — Milton Sanford Mayer, *The Nature of the Beast*, p. 224, 1975
- He said the family had five hundred slots in a warehouse[.] — Joseph Pistone, *Donnie Brasco*, p. 125, 1987

slouch *noun*
a lazy nonperformer *US, 1796*
- He had hardly been a slouch his junior year, scoring fifteen touchdowns in addition to gaining over a thousand yards rush. — H.G. Bissinger, *Friday Night Lights*, p. 51, 2000

slough *noun*
a jail or prison *US, 1950*
- — Hyman E. Goldin et al., *Dictionary of American Underworld Lingo*, p. 198, 1950

slough *verb*
1 to arrest someone *US, 1962*
- — Joseph E. Ragen and Charles Finston, *Inside the World's Toughest Prison*, p. 818, 1962: "Penitentiary and underworld glossary"

2 to close down a poker game or betting operation *US, 1945*
Also used in the variant "slough up."
- [H]e told me his joint had been "sloughed," an unchurchly vulgarism meaning shut down by the law. — Earl Wilson, *I Am Gazing Into My 8-Ball*, p. 26, 1945
- — John Scarne, *Scarne's Guide to Modern Poker*, p. 290, 1979

slow *verb*
▸ **slow your roll**
to calm down *US, 1993*
- Do or die [we gives a fuck motherfucker] / So slow your roll, I'm in control. — Snoop Dogg, *For All My Niggaz Bitches*, 1993
- "Slow your roll, now," I told her. "You can't go in there and tell that white man off!" — Yolanda Joe, *Bebe's By Golly Wow*, p. 61, 1998
- But I do care about your health and you've got to slow your roll. — Van Whitfield, *Something's Wrong with Your Scale!*, p. 186, 1999
- I say "do i look like tyra banks? best slow your roll or i'll crop your soht but good!" — Douglas Kearney, *Anansi Meets Peter Park at the Taco Bellon Lexington*, p. 89, 2000

slow boat *noun*
▸ **get someone on a slow boat**
to win all of a person's money by luring them into making ill-advised bets *US, 1951*
- — David W. Maurer, *Argot of the Racetrack*, p. 31, 1951

slow-drag *verb*
to dance in the arms of your partner *US, 1994*
- The tension was so thick that nobody dared slow-drag for fear of getting blindsided if something jumped off. — Nathan McCall, *Makes Me Wanna Holler*, p. 71, 1994

slow-em-up *noun*
any central nervous system depressant *US, 1980*
- — Edith A. Folb, *runnin' down some lines*, p. 254, 1980

slow-mo *adjective*
slow-motion *US, 1993*
- But Charlie Bat smiles. It is strange and slow-mo. — Francesca Lia Block, *Missing Angel Juan*, p. 364, 1993

slow-pay *noun*
a person in debt who has been remiss in making repayment *US, 1973*
- The reason Ratnoff stalled him on money is that Xaviera was slow pay. — Leonard Shecter and William Phillips, *On the Pad*, pp. 32–33, 1973
- I had gotten into a slow-pay situation with two bookmakers in Ohio—they didn't have the money, and yet I had to square other bets I had lost. — Jimmy Snyder, *Jimmy the Greek*, p. 67, 1975
- He had put hundreds of slow-pays in the hospital using a simple trick. — Stephen J. Cannell, *Big Con*, p. 278, 1997

slow pill *noun*
in horseracing, a depressant given to a horse to decrease its performance *US, 1947*
- — Dan Parker, *The ABC of Horse Racing*, p. 149, 1947
- The Threat of Two Tests May Eventually Stop the Needling of Winners and the Feeding of "Slow Pills" to Losers [Headline]. — *San Francisco Examiner, American Weekly*, p. 17, 17th July 1949
- Witkin said in a letter to Klein last week he learned of reports that Wallace had been fed a "slow pill" and wanted Palermo's named "cleared." — *San Francisco News*, p. 29, 30th November 1955

slow-play *verb*
to stall; to delay *US, 1992*
- — William K. Bentley and James M. Corbett, *Prison Slang*, p. 15, 1992
- "This convict is slow-playing me, won't sign for his property." — Jimmy Lerner, *You Got Nothing Coming*, p. 35, 2002

slowpoke *noun*
a person who moves slowly or dawdles *US, 1848*
- Ebbie Wexler (who really does look like Nancy's not-too-bright boyfriend, Sluggo) calls back: "Catch us, slowpoke!" — Stephen King, *Black House*, p. 120, 2001

slow smoulder *noun*
a person whose career is going nowhere fast *US, 1998*
US Air Force usage; the opposite of a "fast burner."
- — *Seattle Times*, p. A9, 12th April 1998: "Grunts, squids not grunting from the same dictionary"

slow the row, papa!
take it easy! *US, 1947*
- — Marcus Hanna Boulware, *Jive and Slang of Students in Negro Colleges*, 1947

slud *verb*
to fall victim to a chemical warfare attack *US, 1991*
From the official military warning that the victim will salivate, lachrymate, urinate, and defecate.
- — *American Speech*, p. 401, Winter 1991: "Among the new words"
- — *The Retired Officer Magazine*, p. 39, January 1993

sluff *verb*
to play truant *US, 1951*
- — *Newsweek*, p. 28, 8th October 1951

slug *noun*
1 a drink *UK, 1756*
- He handed me a man-sized slug of the stuff and set up one for himself. — Mickey Spillane, *I, The Jury*, p. 22, 1947
- This noon, recalling with distaste the nineteen slugs of bourbon he had polished off yesterday, he had promised himself that he would get through one whole day without a snort. — Bernard Wolfe, *The Late Risers*, p. 16, 1954
- Dead Jane was there, had a big bottle of Tokay wine hidden in Mardou's dresser for me and got it out and poured me a big slug[.] — Jack Kerouac, *The Subterraneans*, p. 62, 1958

- [A]fter the fourth pint, and the unease manifests itself as a shudder with each swallow. Every slug brings nearer the end of the day. — Mark Powell, *Snap*, p. 38, 2001

2 a dollar *US, 1981*
- — Don Wilmeth, *The Language of American Popular Entertainment*, p. 247, 1981

3 a group of cards that have been arranged and then inserted into a deck *US, 1996*
- — Frank Scoblete, *Best Blackjack*, p. 272, 1996

4 a hospital patient who refuses to participate in therapy or self-help *US, 1988–1989*
- — *Maledicta*, p. 34, 1988–1989: "Medical maledicta from San Francisco"

5 in the television and movie industries, a piece of unusable film that is temporarily used to fill in for footage that will be added *US, 1990*
- — Ralph S. Singleton, *Filmmaker's Dictionary*, p. 155, 1990

▸ **put the slug on someone**
to hit someone with your fist *US, 1980*
- — Joe McKennon, *Circus Lingo*, p. 73, 1980

slug *verb*
to cheat playing slot machines by inserting something other than the proper coin in the machine *US, 1985*
- Next comes the more overt and obvious attempt to play a slot machine for free by inserting foreign coins or slugs, better known as slugging. — Jim Regan, *Winning at Slot Machine*, p. 68, 1985

slugger *noun*
a casino cheat who tries to play slot machines with objects other than the proper coin *US, 1985*
- The really hard-core "slugger" will counterfeit actual casino dollar tokens, a few of which look almost like the real thing. — Jim Regan, *Winning at Slot Machine*, p. 68, 1985

slugout *noun*
a fight, especially between youth gangs *US, 1962*
- — *Dobie Gillis Teenage Slanguage Dictionary*, 1962

slum *noun*
1 inexpensive costume jewelry; any low-value merchandise *US, 1914*
- The hijacker dumped that slum to the top of the dresser under a bright lamp. It was like the display at Tiffany's. — Iceberg Slim (Robert Beck), *Trick Baby*, p. 24, 1969
- — Joe McKennon, *Circus Lingo*, p. 84, 1980
- The price of a Slum can vary from a little over a dollar a gross to almost ten a gross wholesale. — Gene Sorrows, *All About Carnivals*, p. 26, 1985
- Fluorescent tubing lit an interior "flashed" with plush stuffed animals dangling on hooks and stacked boxes of "slum," or cheap giveaways. — Peter Fenton, *Eyeing the Flash*, p. 101, 2005

2 an apartment or house *US, 1969*
The Oxford English Dictionary offers several early C19 cites in this sense but deems the term obsolete. Robert Beck (Iceberg Slim) wrote the language of the streets, not C19 England, suggesting a slang life for the word in the C20 US.
- I forgot, some louse put the heist on your "slum." — Iceberg Slim (Robert Beck), *Pimp*, p. 116, 1969

3 prison food *US, 1950*
- — Hyman E. Goldin et al., *Dictionary of American Underworld Lingo*, p. 199, 1950

slum *verb*
to visit a poor neighborhood out of curiosity; to live beneath your station *UK, 1884*
- On one of my nights off, some of us went slumming. — Helen P. Branson, *Gay Bar*, p. 69, 1957
- [E]ven a few well-dressed women, slumming with their well-dressed husbands or escorts—but, usually knowingly slumming. — John Rechy, *City of Night*, p. 247, 1963
- Eating chitterlings is like going slumming to them. — Eldridge Cleaver, *Soul on Ice*, p. 29, 1968
- A guy and his wife, slumming. Radical chic, vintage 1976. — Armistead Maupin, *Tales of the City*, p. 143, 1978

slum *adjective*
cheap; shabby; in poor taste *US, 1973*
- This fellow was sharp in a black man's kinda fashion and the things he was wearing were far from being slum. — A.S. Jackson, *Gentleman Pimp*, p. 158, 1973

slumgullion *noun*
a makeshift stew made with whatever ingredients are at hand *US, 1902*
- "A room in a slumgullion boarding house." — Audie Murphy, *To Hell and Back*, p. 107, 1949
- — Charles F. Haywood, *Yankee Dictionary*, p. 154, 1963

slumlord *noun*
a landlord who rents poorly kept-up properties in the ghetto, often with a large profit margin *US, 1953*
- — *American Speech*, December 1961
- [H]e is an anal retentive which is polite for what others have called him ... a slumlord and a motherfucker. — Sol Yurrick, *The Bag*, p. 121, 1968
- We were at the mercy of the rats. The slumlord? Never laid eyes on him. — Odie Hawkins, *Scars and Memories*, p. 17, 1987
- To make matters worse, he never got enough rest because he owned property in Logan Heights and was up half the night doing slumlord collecting. — Joseph Wambaugh, *Floaters*, p. 177, 1996

slurpage *noun*
any beverage *US, 1997*
- — Vann Wesson, *Generation X Field Guide and Lexicon*, p. 154, 1997

slush *noun*
▸ **in the slush**
very drunk *US, 1991*
- Instead, the citizen rendered temporarily senseless by booze, or "in the slush" as the street slang goes, is treated more gently here. — *St. Petersburg (Florida) Times*, p. 5D, 26th May 1991

slush fund *noun*
a discretionary fund, where the source of the money and the exact way in which it is spent is not subject to any accounting or accountability *US, 1874*
- He [George H. Bush] will, of course, need a slush fund—not unlike the one Gordon Liddy and Maurice Stans put together for Nixon in 1972. — Hunter S. Thompson, *Generation of Swine*, p. 188, 8th December 1986

slush up *verb*
to drink to the point of intoxication *US, 1949*
- — Vincent J. Monteleone, *Criminal Slang*, p. 214, 1949

slut *noun*
1 a prostitute *UK, 1450*
- "I'll break his other arm if he sends another slut after me." — Curt Cannon, *Dead Men Don't Dream*, p. 38, 1953
- Now that's the kind of girl you ought to be associating with, and not with common sluts like that one. Why, she didn't even look clean. — Joseph Heller, *Catch 22*, p. 297, 1961

2 a promiscuous boy or man *US, 2002*
- I was a little slut back then, trying to taste all the flavors, so I told her, "Wow, I'd love to fuck in that thing." — Tommy Lee, *The Dirt*, p. 55, 2002

slut lamp *noun*
an improvised lamp using bacon grease as fuel *US, 1990*
- Byron called it a "slut lamp." But Fitz always said, "light the grease" and let it go at that. — Russell Banks, *A Walk on the Wild Side*, p. 12, 1990

slut-mouth *noun*
a person whose language is often coarse and vulgar *US, 2001*
- — Don R. McCreary (Editor), *Dawg Speak*, 2001

slutted out *adjective*
broken down; in disrepair *US, 1984*
- Son, you want to watch out for those "mechanic's special" cars in the want ads. Most of 'em are so slutted out it'd take a faith healer to get 'em to start. — Ken Weaver, *Texas Crude*, p. 126, 1984

sluttish *adjective*
sexual in a cheap way *US, 2004*
- Sometimes New Yorkers can be a little too direct for a demure girl like me, even one who's realized she's probably more sluttish than demure-ish. — Plum Sykes, *Bergdorf Blondes*, p. 68, 2004

slutty *adjective*
promiscuous; having a sexual appearance *US, 1970*
- "A good personality," Reeves begins, "consists of a chick who has a little hard body and who will satisfy all sexual demands without being too slutty about things, and who will essentially keep her dumb fucking mouth shut." — Bret Easton Ellis, *American Psycho*, p. 91, 1991

- "You pig," he said. "You slutty cocktease." — Wally Lamb, *She's Come Undone*, p. 131, 1992

slutwear *noun*
extremely sexually provoking clothing *US, 2000*
- — Ana Loria, *1 2 3 Be A Porn Star!*, p. 167, 2000: "Glossary of adult sex Industry terms"
- America's teen peep show: Has "slutware" gone too far? [Headline] — *San Francisco Chronicle*, 27th July 2003

sly mongoose *noun*
an extremely clever and devious person *US, 1981*
Hawaiian youth usage.
- — Douglas Simonson, *Pidgin to da Max*, 1981

smack *noun*
1 heroin *US, 1942*
Derives, possibly, from Yiddish *shmeker* (a sniffer of drugs).
- Smack, smock, stuff, horse—they're all heroin. — Clarence Cooper Jr., *The Scene*, p. 55, 1960
- Because when the smack begins to flow / I really don't care anymore — Velvet Underground *Heroin*, 1967
- Musta' shot some "pure," cause a lookout on the sidewalk heard him mumble before he croaked, "Well kiss my dead mammy's ass if this ain't the best 'smack'" I ever shot. — Iceberg Slim (Robert Beck), *Pimp*, p. 79, 1969
- He's got more money than God and twice as much coke, crank and smack. — *Boogie Nights*, 1997
2 a dollar *US, 1974*
- He is a nice guy, with lots of class, who uses Eau-de-Cologne costs 20 smacks a bottle[.] — Leo Rosten, *Dear Herm*, p. 16, 1974
3 alcohol *US, 1973*
- — Malachi Andrews and Paul T. Owens, *Black Language*, p. 101, 1973
4 disparaging talk *US, 1999*
- — *San Jose Mercury News*, 11th May 1999
- Now it's time for The Rock to lay a little smack down on another fat-ass jabroni[.] — The Rock, *The Rock Says...*, p. 282, 2000
- — Connie Eble (Editor), *UNC-CH Campus Slang*, p. 7, Spring 2000
5 slang *US, 1997*
- — Anna Scotti and Paul Young, *Buzzwords*, p. 79, 1997
6 a swindle based on matching pennies *US, 1969*
- It was our interim game between larger scores on the longer rocks, drag and smack con games we played. — Iceberg Slim (Robert Beck), *Trick Baby*, p. 27, 1969

smack *verb*
to curry favor *US, 1991*
- "You don't gotta kiss nobody's ass, you don't have to smack, you don't have to talk white." — Leon Bing, *Do or Die*, p. 127, 1991

smack *adverb*
precisely *US, 1951*
A shortened **SMACK-DAB**.
- Some new guy I'd never seen was on the car, so I figured that if I didn't bump smack into my parents and all I'd be able to say hello to old Phoebe and then beat it and nobody'd even know I'd been around. — J.D. Salinger, *Catcher in the Rye*, p. 157, 1951
- And the assignation hotels are downtown, smack in the middle of everything, very snug. — Jack Lait and Lee Mortimer, *Washington Confidential*, p. 13, 1951
- I want 'em smack in the middle when we got the yucks glued to the chair! — Max Shulman, *Rally Round the Flag, Boys!*, p. 69, 1957
- I'd blow your ass off with a Seminole air boat. Put you smack on the trailer. — Elmore Leonard, *Gold Coast*, p. 77, 1980

smack-dab *adverb*
exactly *US, 1892*
At times reversed for comic effect.
- Dab smack on the television where even the idiots who can't read will get the message! — Max Shulman, *Anyone Got a Match?*, p. 48, 1964
- I checked into the James Brown Motor Inn there and ran smack-dab into Ernie Andrews there who had a big hit[.] — Babs Gonzales, *Movin' On Down De Line*, p. 135, 1975
- But close-up pulling the trigger this morning smack-dab up in his face, I know I ain't never gonna forget him and his bloody stump neck. — Iceberg Slim (Robert Beck), *Death Wish*, p. 122, 1977
- They moved to another good groovy lil' house, a place that had a dirty driveway leading smack dab up to the front porch. — Odie Hawkins, *Black Casanova*, p. 94, 1984

smacked back *adjective*
heroin-intoxicated *US, 1981*
- Dilaudid used to be delightful, but now I've got to be smacked-back for all the pain to go. — James Ellroy, *Brown's Requiem*, p. 69, 1981
- — William K. Bentley and James M. Corbett, *Prison Slang*, p. 79, 1992

smacked in *adjective*
fogged in *US, 1972*
- We were still smacked in next morning so they didn't bother to send us to the ad. — William Pelfrey, *The Big V*, p. 85, 1972

smacker *noun*
a dollar bill *US, 1918*
- "He's got a gag he'll pay me fifty smackers to pull." — David Gregory, *Flesh Seller*, p. 45, 1962
- That-sa my horse, boy! I got fifty smackers onna his nose! — Clarence Cooper Jr., *Black*, p. 249, 1963
- We've got 902,000 smackers! — Red Rudensky, *The Gonif*, p. 107, 1970
- — Steve Kuriscak, *Casino Talk*, p. 51, 1985

smackeroo *noun*
1 a dollar bill *US, 1942*
- A check revealed that the bank was short two hundred thousand smackeroos[.] — Mickey Spillane, *The Long Wait*, p. 31, 1951
- He's homeless, but he has a hundred thousand smackeroos that he leaves in care of Michael Alig. — James St. James, *Party Monster*, p. 236, 1999
2 a kiss *US, 1946*
- Smackeroo (n) A kiss. — *Hit Parader*, p. 33, September 1946

smack freak *noun*
a heroin addict *US, 1972*
- I got sent back down here to Jackson where I talked with a lot of brothers who had been smack freaks on the street[.] — John Sinclair, *Guitar Army*, p. 285, 1972

smack head *noun*
a heroin addict *US, 1967*
- Three or four meth-freaks and a couple of smack-heads and myself just sat around all night and got stoned and stayed that way. — Elizabeth Finn, *Drugs in the Tenderloin*, p. 13, 1967
- "Want some saki?" he asked once. "No thanks." "Oh, excuse me, I forgot you were a smack head." — Cleo Odzer, *Goa Freaks*, 1995

smack up *verb*
to inject oneself with heroin *US, 1995*
- Monica and I made daily trips to smack up at Neal's. Heroin cured cocaine frazzle. — Cleo Odzer, *Goa Freaks*, p. 64, 1995

smacky lips *noun*
prolonged kissing *US, 1965*
- — *Time*, p. 57, 1st January 1965: "Students: the slang bag"

small *noun*
one hundred dollars *US, 1988*
- Two hundred bucks, two small, two dimes, two C-notes, all blown away. — Robert Campbell, *Juice*, p. 9, 1988

small *adjective*
afraid *US, 1986*
- "If I was standing there with that guy when I saw him start to get small, I could have done something." Sims meant if he'd been there when the pilot got scared about the DEW Line and the towerless field. — James Mills, *The Underground Empire*, p. 427, 1986

small nickel *noun*
fifty dollars or, in a casino, fifty dollars' worth of betting tokens *US, 1961*
- — Thomas L. Clark, *The Dictionary of Gambling and Gaming*, p. 206, 1987

small one *noun*
one hundred dollars *US, 1988*
- — George Percy, *The Language of Poker*, p. 83, 1988

small potatoes *adjective*
something of little consequence *US, 1838*
- If I'm small potatoes that's all I want to be. — Mickey Spillane, *Kiss Me Deadly*, p. 65, 1952
- Next to theirs, my sin was pretty small potatoes. — Max Shulman, *I was a Teen-Age Dwarf*, p. 121, 1959

small spuds *adjective*
small-time *US, 1976*

A variant of **SMALL POTATOES**.

- Since he was from Hollywood he thought Sacramento small spuds[.] — Malcolm Braley, *False Starts*, p. 68, 1976

small suppository in anticipation of the broom handle *noun*

the opening volley in a battle *US, 1986*

US Naval aviator usage.

- — *United States Naval Institute Proceedings*, p. 108, October 1986

smark *noun*

a professional wrestling fan who is smarter than the average gullible fan but not as smart as he thinks he is *US, 1995*

- *smark mode on* Are you SERIOUS, man?! Where did you find this. I can't believe it. Meltzer, Keller, et al have been scooped by Bill Apter. *smark mode off* — *rec.sport.pro-wrestling*, 28th January 1995
- A true smart fan, however, realizes he is only as smart as the business wants him to be and refers to himself as a smart mark or smark. — Dave Flood, *Kayfabe*, p. 30, 2000

smart alec; smart aleck; smart alick *noun*

an offensively smart person; a know-it-all *US, 1865*

- That was how Winona talked, always a little smart-alecky. — Elmore Leonard, *Pronto*, p. 64, 1993

smart-eye *verb*

to give someone a look that may be aggressive, challenging, or disapproving *US, 2000*

- Start a fight with the same guy that was smart-eyein' you[.] — Eminem (Marshall Mathers), *Drug Ballad*, 2000

smart money *noun*

in horseracing, money bet on the basis of solid, empirical data *US, 1951*

- — David W. Maurer, *Argot of the Racetrack*, p. 58, 1951

smart-mouth *verb*

to talk insolently to someone *US, 1968*

- — John Ayto, *The Oxford Dictionary of Slang*, p. 320, 1998

smarts *noun*

intelligence *US, 1970*

- Time I got back to my room I realized that I had used no smarts at all. — Robert Deane Pharr, *S.R.O.*, p. 32, 1971
- If you don't know nothin', the Joint is a great place—me, I had all my smarts long before. — Edwin Torres, *Carlito's Way*, p. 46, 1975
- There's only so many dudes that have enough smarts to pull one off. — Gerald Petievich, *Money Men*, p. 92, 1981
- He's got more learnin' than just the paperbooks ridin' his hip alla time. That Barker's got street smarts. — Seth Morgan, *Homeboy*, p. 43, 1990

smartypants *noun*

a person who is smart, but not quite as smart as they think they are *US, 1941*

- I hope you're proud, Mr. Smartypants Lawyer. — Seth Morgan, *Homeboy*, p. 279, 1990

smash *noun*

1 momentum *US, 1986*

Air combat slang.

- North Vietnamese ground controllers would lead the MiGs in behind the Phantoms at very low altitude, below radar coverage, building up energy—"smash" was the pilot's term—at supersonic speed[.] — Walter Boyne and Steven Thompson, *The Wild Blue*, p. 523, 1986

2 money; pocket change *US, 1953*

- I managed to overcome his original bad impression of me, and soon I was buying his drinks and meals, and he was hitting me for "smash" (change) at regular intervals. — William Burroughs, *Junkie*, p. 26, 1953
- — Allen Geller, *Mr*, p. 9, April 1966: "The hippie's lexicon"

3 wine *US, 1962*

- — Anthony Romeo, *The Language of Gangs*, p. 22, 4th December 1962
- — Hermese E. Roberts, *The Third Ear*, 1971
- — *American Speech*, p. 155, Spring–Summer 1972: "An approach to Black slang"
- — Edith A. Folb, *runnin' down some lines*, p. 255, 1980

smash *verb*

▶ **smash case**

in computing, to disregard any differentiation between upper and lower case *US, 1991*

- — Eric S. Raymond, *The New Hacker's Dictionary*, p. 323, 1991

smash and grab *noun*

a simplistic burglary involving very little planning or thought *US, 1969*

- The old man never fenced anything but whiskey from hijackers and clothes from smash-and-grab store burglars. — Iceberg Slim (Robert Beck), *Trick Baby*, p. 17, 1969
- We clean out two display cases and we're outta there like clockwork, thirty seconds and the smash and grab is done. — Colton Simpson, *Inside the Crips*, p. 55, 2005

smashed *adjective*

1 drunk *US, 1960*

- It was known that the squad from Cascadia College assembled there, getting smashed and carrying each other home when "The Sink" closed up. — Frederick Kohner, *The Affairs of Gidget*, p. 54, 1963
- [T]he phrases of the recent generation, e.g., "crocked," "wiped out," and "smashed[.]" — William and Jerrye Breedlove, *Swap Clubs*, p. 151, 1964
- Well, I was super-smashed, really drunk. — Herb Michelson, *Sportin' Ladies*, p. 184, 1975
- She whispers in your ear, "We go home right now, buddy, or you don't get any." You have to decide quick. You want to get smashed, have a good time? You do, you're gonna have to wait a month to get laid. — Elmore Leonard, *Killshot*, p. 249, 1989

2 drug-intoxicated *US, 1967*

- Then I turned around and one of the men passed me a joint and that was it. I wanted to be ripped, smashed, torn up as I had never wanted anything before. — Anonymous, *Go Ask Alice*, p. 71, 1971
- Oh, like the usual. Going to Nautilus, getting smashed, going to this Uva place. — Bret Easton Ellis, *Less Than Zero*, p. 15, 1985
- — Angela Devlin, *Prison Patter*, p. 106, 1996

smasher *noun*

a very attractive female *US, 1959*

- I knew if I wanted to nail down this little smasher, I would have to move fast. — Max Shulman, *I was a Teen-Age Dwarf*, p. 8, 1959

smasheroo *noun*

1 a great success *US, 1948*

An elaboration of **SMASH**.

- In the animated category, there is no smasheroo on the level of Shrek[.] — *The Guardian*, 21st March 2003

2 a good-looking female *US, 1959*

- A smasheroo she was—a real zinger. — Max Shulman, *I was a Teen-Age Dwarf*, p. 8, 1959

smash-face *adjective*

physical; aggressive *US, 1990*

- — *American Speech*, p. 88, Spring 1995: "Among the new words"

smash-mouth *noun*

prolonged kissing *US, 1965*

- — *Time*, p. 57, 1st January 1965: "Students: the slang bag"

smash-mouth *verb*

to kiss passionately *US, 1968*

- — Collin Baker et al., *College Undergraduate Slang Study Conducted at Brown University*, p. 199, 1968

smash-mouth *adjective*

physical, aggressive *US, 1989*

- — *American Speech*, p. 88, Spring 1995: "Among the new words"

smear *verb*

to drop napalm on a target *US, 1991*

- — Linda Reinberg, *In the Field*, p. 201, 1991

smears *noun*

LSD *US, 1982*

- — Ralph de Sola, *Crime Dictionary*, p. 139, 1982
- — US Department of Justice, *Street Terms*, October 1994

smeg *noun*

any viscous matter of unknown origin *US, 1995*

The variant "shmeg" also exists.

- — *Maledicta*, p. 48, 1995: "Door whore and other New Mexico restaurant slang"

smell *noun*

digital-vaginal contact *US, 1974*

- But Buck's havin' a little trouble with his. Won't give him smell. — Earl Thompson, *Tattoo*, p. 225, 1974

smell *verb*

▸ **smell Apple pie**

to be near your date of expected return from military service in Vietnam to the US *US, 1991*

- — Linda Reinberg, *In the Field*, p. 202, 1991

▸ **smell some gas**

to be transported by motor vehicle *US, 2002*

- — Gary K. Farlow, *Prison-ese*, p. 65, 2002

smeller *noun*

the nose *UK, 1700*

- For a busted smeller, a couple of shiners, and a few creases in the knowledge-box he made himself ten grand. — Mezz Mezzrow, *Really the Blues*, p. 21, 1946

smellies *noun*

anchovies *US, 1996*

- — *Maledicta*, p. 21, 1996: "Domino's pizza jargon"

smesh *noun*

in circus and carnival usage, money *US, 1981*

- — Don Wilmeth, *The Language of American Popular Entertainment*, p. 248, 1981

smidge *noun*

the smallest amount *US, 1905*

A shortened **SMIDGEN**. First recorded in 1905, but popularized by ESPN's Dan Patrick telling viewers that *Sports Center* will resume "in a smidge."

- I believe she loved that song, I'd say just a smidge behind Luckenback, Texas. — Elmore Leonard, *City Primeval*, p. 142, 1980

smidgen; smidgin *noun*

a very small amount *US, 1845*

- — Charles F. Haywood, *Yankee Dictionary*, p. 155, 1963
- Honey, don't you think you ought to have just a smidgen of coffee? — Gore Vidal, *Weekend*, p. 8, 1968

smile *noun*

something that is amusing *US, 1982*

- BOOGIE: What's up, Fen? FENWICK: Just breaking windows, Boog. BOOGIE: What for? FENWICK: It's a smile. — *Diner*, 1982

smiley *noun*

a large chain with a padlock worn around the arm or neck *US, 1997*

- — Jim Crotty, *How to Talk American*, p. 146, 1997

smiley face; smiley *noun*

a simplistic image of a smiling face, used for indicating laughter or happiness *US, 1983*

First seen as an icon and later in electronic communications formed with punctuation marks, generally as :) but with multiple variations. According to the magazine mentalfloss.com (September/October 2005), "On September 19, 1982 at 11:44 a.m., Professor Scott Fahlman introduced the familiar sideways face that would take the Internet by storm."

- By accusing people of taking Datamation articles too seriously, watmath!rggoebel has shown lack of familiarity with computer terminology, lack of care in reading articles before replying, or forgot to add the smiley face :-) at the end of his article. — *net.nlang*, 19th January 1983
- — Christian Crumlish, *The Internet Dictionary*, p. 2, 1995

smock *noun*

heroin *US, 1960*

A corruption of **SMACK** or the Yiddish **SHMECK**.

- "What are you in for? Smock?" — Clarence Cooper Jr., *The Scene*, p. 220, 1960

smog *verb*

1 to smoke marijuana *US, 2001*

- — Don R. McCreary (Editor), *Dawg Speak*, 2001

2 to execute someone with lethal gas *US, 1992*

- — William K. Bentley and James M. Corbett, *Prison Slang*, p. 105, 1992

smoke *noun*

1 a cigarette; a cigar *UK, 1882*

- "I sure need a smoke, boss," he muttered. — Chester Gould, *Dick Tracy Meets the Night Crawler*, p. 57, 1945

- [H]e said in his slowest, deepest drawl how he figured he could use one of the smokes he bought this morning, then ran his hand through the glass. — Ken Kesey, *One Flew Over the Cuckoo's Nest*, p. 190, 1962
- He pulls a wrinkled pack of smokes from his flannel shirt and lights one. — Larry Heinemann, *Paco's Story*, p. 101, 1986
- MIA: What are you doing? VINCENT: Rollin' a smoke. MIA: Here? VINCENT: It's just tobacco. — *Pulp Fiction*, 1994

2 marijuana; heroin; opium; any drug that may be smoked *US, 1946*

- Then you know what smoke is, huh, West? You did a high on smoke, boy? — Evan Hunter, *The Blackboard Jungle*, p. 159, 1954
- They passed it back and forth, getting high. "That's pretty mellow smoke," she announced after a few more hits. — Odie Hawkins, *Chicago Hustle*, p. 161, 1977
- Our smoke was gone and the next day we made plans for replenishing the supply. — Herbert Huncke, *The Evening Sun Turned Crimson*, p. 205, 1980
- He's really funny, and straight off, he offers me some smoke. — *Clueless*, 1995

3 a marijuana cigarette *US, 1967*

- Our "Sundays" we had off and if we were out of "Smokes" we'd go down to Montreal to "cop[.]" — Babs Gonzales, *I Paid My Dues*, p. 63, 1967
- Buy you a pound of grass and just put it there on the table, roll a smoke any time you want one. — Bruce Jackson, *Outside the Law*, p. 190, 1972
- We got pretty stoned too—it's an excuse to get some in and have a few smokes. — Ben Malbon, *Cool Places*, p. 268, 1998
- To provide the guys in the band with a smoke whenever they needed it, I kept in my pocket a chunk of hash[.] — Simon Napier-Bell, *Black Vinyl White Powder*, p. 3, 2001

4 crack cocaine when smoked; heroin mixed with crack cocaine when smoked *US, 2003*

- — Mike Haskins, *Drugs*, p. 293, 2003
- She let us push crack out of the spot and do what we had to do as long as we gave her smoke. — 50 Cent, *From Pieces to Weight*, p. 112, 2005

5 denatured alcohol (ethyl alcohol to which a poisonous substance has been added to make it unfit for consumption) mixed with water for drinking *US, 1950*

- — Hyman E. Goldin et al., *Dictionary of American Underworld Lingo*, p. 199, 1950

6 toxic, potentially fatal solvents used as substitutes for alcohol for the truly desperate *US, 1955*

- If we wanted to make a more legitimate type buck, we could always sell smoke to the bums down on the Bowery. We picked up the pints of smoke—which was alcohol cut with water and some "spirit" pills added—from the neighborhood guy who mixed it in his bathtub. — Rocky Garciano (with Rowland Barber), *Somebody Up There Likes Me*, p. 69, 1955
- The junkman fished a bottle of smoke from his ragged garments. — Chester Himes, *A Rage in Harlem*, p. 123, 1957
- — Ralph de Sola, *Crime Dictionary*, p. 140, 1982

7 a black person *US, 1913*

Offensive.

- And I want the five in my hand, Smoke, before I move. — Elmore Leonard, *Be Cool*, p. 127, 1999

8 a noncommissioned officer commanding an artillery battery *US, 1988*

- — Hans Halberstadt, *Airborne*, p. 130, 1988: "Abridged dictionary of airborne terms"

9 one dollar *US, 1975*

- — *American Speech*, p. 66, Spring–Summer 1975: "Razorback slang"

▸ **bring smoke**

to fire a gun *US, 1997*

- If we take them out first, it eliminates any possibility they'll bring smoke during the action. — Stephen J. Cannell, *Big Con*, p. 383, 1997

▸ **put smoke**

to fire a single round of artillery to help others mark a target *US, 1990*

- — Gregory Clark, *Words of the Vietnam War*, p. 316, 1990

smoke *verb*

1 to shoot someone *US, 1926*

- I come in the door smilin'—"Ola, Chucho"—then I started smoking with both pieces. — Edwin Torres, *Carlito's Way*, p. 33, 1975
- Somebody got smoked! Look at the holes in the wall! — *Boyz N The Hood*, 1990

- Bout the Crew gonna smoke us? — Jess Mowry, *Way Past Cool*, p. 21, 1992
- You shouldn't have smoked the guy. — *Get Shorty*, 1995

2 to defeat someone soundly, especially in a contest of speed *US, 1996*

- John Taylor, J.J. Stokes, Andre Rison—I smoke all these fools, and yet they're making the big sweet dollars. — *Jerry Maguire*, 1996

▸ **smoke a bowl**
to smoke a pipe filled with marijuana *US, 1982*
- — Richard A. Spears, *The Slang and Jargon of Drugs and Drink*, p. 463, 1986

▸ **smoke a pipe; smoke the pipe**
to surf through the hollow tube of a wave *US, 1987*
- — Mitch McKissick, *Surf Lingo*, 1987

▸ **smoke butt**
to curry favor through obsequious behavior *US, 1992*
- Other kids just figured he rode beside Deek all the time and smoked butt. — Jess Mowry, *Way Past Cool*, p. 31, 1992

▸ **smoke it**
to commit suicide by a gunshot wound in the mouth *US, 1984*
- I've heard that every sane person contemplates suicide sometime. Well, I made up for all the insane people who never did. I never thought a smoking it—that'd be too dirty, too many reports for other cops. — Joseph Wambaugh, *Lines and Shadows*, p. 329, 1984

smoked cheaters *noun*
dark glasses *US, 1959*
- Half the cats in Harlem wear their smoke cheaters all night long. — Chester Himes, *The Real Cool Killers*, p. 46, 1959

smoked out *adjective*
1 extremely intoxicated on marijuana or crack cocaine *US, 1993*
- The basehead is completely smoked out. — *Menace II Society*, 1993
- "Look at our OGs, they're all smoked out." — Yusuf Jah, *Uprising*, p. 29, 1995

2 without any crack cocaine to smoke *US, 2003*
- — *San Diego Union-Tribune*, p. B1, 23rd October 2003

smoked up *adjective*
extremely intoxicated on marijuana or crack cocaine *US, 1993*
- He was thinner than Ethan, and his eyes had that smoked-up look Corbitt had seen too many times already. — Jess Mowry, *Six Out Seven*, p. 331, 1993

smokehound *noun*
a person who abuses denatured alcohol *US, 1991*
- A smokehound from Plainfield, New Jersey, Albert Robinson had been found dead by the B&O railbed at the foot of Clifton Park, shot once in the head. — David Simon, *Homicide*, p. 383, 1991

smoke house *noun*
a room where meetings of twelve-step recovery programs such as Alcoholics Anonymous are held *US, 1998*
A term based on the heavy cigarette smoking that is often characteristic of the meetings.
- — Christopher Cavanaugh, *AA to Z*, p. 163, 1998

smoker *noun*
1 a social gathering of men featuring boxing *US, 1956*
- "I can teach ya a lot, and in a year I can put you in smokers. Make five or ten bucks a night that way." — Jose Antonio Villarreal, *Pocho*, p. 106, 1959

2 a stolen car *US, 1997*
- — Jim Crotty, *How to Talk American*, p. 51, 1997

smoker film *noun*
a pornographic movie shown at an all-male social gathering *US, 1970*
- But this was no illegal stag or smoker film[.] — Roger Blake, *The Porno Movies*, p. 30, 1970

smokestack *noun*
a pile of gambling tokens in the hands of an unskilled gambler *US, 1996*
- You know it's only time until that stack turns to smoke. — John Vorhaus, *The Big Book of Poker Slang*, p. 33, 1996

smoke train *noun*
a cigarette *US, 2001*
- — Don R. McCreary (Editor), *Dawg Speak*, 2001

smoke-up *noun*
in college, a notification of academic deficiency *US, 1961*
- Smoke-Up — W.L. McAtee, *American Speech*, p. 156, May 1961
- — *American Speech*, pp. 76–77, February 1968: "Some notes on flunk notes"

Smokey the bear *noun*
1 a drill sergeant in the US Army *US, 1965*
From the similarity between the hats worn by Drill Instructors and Smokey.
- — *Time*, p. 31, 10th December 1965
- — Carl Fleischhauer, *A Glossary of Army Slang*, p. 16, 1968
- I want to be a Drill Instructor / I want to earn that Smokey Bear. — Sandee Johnson, *Cadences: The Jody Call Book, No. 2*, p. 26, 1986

2 a military aircraft used for dropping magnesium-based flares to illuminate the ground at night *US, 1989*
- Meanwhile, with a "Smokey the Bear" flareship hovering over the battlefield, dropping flares and lighting the ground like day, Whalen's artillerymen fought like lions for their lives[.] — David Hackworth and Julie Sherman, *About Face*, p. 537, 1989
- — Gregory Clark, *Words of the Vietnam War*, p. 180, 1990

smoking *adjective*
1 excellent; thriving; exciting *US, 1975*
- We had the smokinest little seven piece group on the road. — Babs Gonzales, *Movin' On Down De Line*, p. 19, 1975
- — *Washington Post Magazine*, p. 17, 4th October 1987: "Say Wha?"
- Let's just say the cast is smokin', and not only those icky cancer sticks that show up from time to time. — Brittany Kent, *O.C. Undercover*, p. viii, 2004

2 fashionably dressed *US, 1989*
- — Terry Williams, *The Cocaine Kids*, p. 138, 1989

Smoky Joe *noun*
a military aircraft that marks targets for bomber aircraft with smoke bombs *US, 1946*
- — *American Speech*, p. 74, February 1946: "Some words of war and peace from 1945"

smooch *verb*
to kiss in a lingering manner *US, 1932*
- "Nuts," replied Dewey. "College kids are still college kids. They're still smooching and driving convertibles and cutting classes and looking for laughs." — Max Shulman, *The Many Loves of Dobie Gillis*, p. 24, 1951
- You wonder if it's all right for them to do a little smooching? — Elmore Leonard, *The Big Bounce*, p. 33, 1969
- I'm curious to know why a splendid legit gentleman like yourself, with the world smooching your keister, yens to hang it out playing the con and risking the penitentiary? — Iceberg Slim (Robert Beck), *Long White Con*, pp. 36–37, 1977

smooth *verb*
to cheat, to deceive *US, 1985*
- In Miss Titania's court, you never smooth a queen! — Ethan Morden, *I've a Feeling We're Not in Kansas Anymore*, p. 6, 1985

smooth *adjective*
1 used of a man's body, hairless *US, 1997*
- — Jeff Fessler, *When Drag Is Not a Car Race*, p. 55, 1997

2 calm *US, 1967*
- "What's your name, kid?" "That depends. 'Piri' when I'm smooth and 'Johnny Gringo' when stomping time's around." — Piri Thomas, *Down These Mean Streets*, p. 48, 1967

3 in lowball poker, favorable *US, 1967*
- — Albert H. Morehead, *The Complete Guide to Winning Poker*, p. 273, 1967

4 sophisticated, urbane *US, 1953*
- I was with Mr. Hillman all afternoon and it was very smoooooth. — Pamela Des Barres, *I'm With the Band*, p. 168, 1988
- — Connie Eble (Editor), *UNC-CH Campus Slang*, p. 9, Spring 1991

smooth
used to intensify a phrasal verb *US, 1984*
- That city boy fucked smooth up when he started makin' fun of Shorty. — Ken Weaver, *Texas Crude*, p. 126, 1984

smoothie *noun*

1 a boy who refuses to join a youth gang *US, 1962*

- [S]moothies (nondelinquents). — Howard Polsky, *Cottage Six*, p. 24, 1962
- The decision to cool myself made the next two years hardest I had done because it meant being a smoothie and staying out of trouble which in prison is difficult[.] — Piri Thomas, *Down These Mean Street*, p. 280, 1967

2 the complete removal of a woman's pubic hair; the result thereof *US, 2001*

- Completely bare: sometimes call the Full Monty, the Sphynx, or the Smoothie, this variation on the Brazilian Wax leaves the entire area hair-free. — *Real Simple*, p. 65, May 2001

3 a man who is attractive, persuasive, crafty, and a bit manipulative *US, 1929*
Often, but not always, pejorative.

- I did try and put a few flaws in but he ended up a bit of a smoothie. Anybody in their right mind would have hated him. — *Metro*, 18th November 2003

4 a skilled gambling cheat *US, 1964*

- — Dr. R. Frederick West, *God's Gambler*, p. 228, 1964: "Appendix A"

smooth operator *noun*
someone who is attractive, crafty, and a bit manipulative *US, 1951*

- How'd you come out with that smooth operator? Petey sure picked the right night to run off and join the Navy, eh? — Max Shulman, *The Many Loves of Dobie Gillis*, p. 113, 1951
- No place for beginners or sensitive hearts / When sentiment is left to chance / No place to be ending but somewhere to start / No need to ask. He's a smooth operator. — Sade, *Smooth Operator*, 1985

smooth trade *noun*
an urbane, fashion-conscious homosexual man *US, 1965*

- Hustling, or male prostitution, is widespread. Even in the major tourist hotels, where the so-called "smooth trade" operates in the plush bars, for big stakes. — *"The Market Street Proposition" (KFRC radio, San Francisco)*, 8th November 1965
- Smooth trade hustlers are often well-bred, well-dressed and they project an urban air of sophistication and their mannerisms are suave and refined. — Johnny Shearer, *The Male Hustler*, p. 18, 1966

smurf *noun*
in an Internet discussion group, a frequent poster who adds little in the way of content *US, 1997*

- Usually it's something cute and fluffy, posted chiefly to remind everyone that the smurf is part of the gang. — Andy Ihnatko, *Cyberspeak*, p. 177, 1997

smush *verb*
to crush *US, 1991*
A blending of "crush" and "smash."

- "Hey!" the kid cried. "You're smushing me!" — Carl Hiaasen, *Native Tongue*, p. 68, 1991

smuts *noun*
sexually explicit photographs or postcards *US, 1962*

- — Joseph E. Ragen and Charles Finston, *Inside the World's Toughest Prison*, p. 818, 1962: "Penitentiary and underworld glossary"

snack *noun*
a youthful, sexually inexperienced male who is the object of an older homosexual's desire *US, 1986–1987*

- — *Maledicta*, p. 156, Summer/Winter 1986–1987: "Sexual slang: prostitutes, pedophiles, flagellators, transvestites, and necrophiles"

snackpack *noun*
the male genitals as seen in a jockstrap or tight, skimpy underwear *US, 1988*

- — H. Max, *Gay (S)language*, p. 39, 1988

snafu *noun*
a chaotic mess *US, 1941*
An acronym of "situation normal, all fucked up," or the more polite "situation normal, all fouled up."

- "Not only profanity has crept into your speech," she said, "but also the peculiar jargon of the Army." "Snafu," I said, "tarfu, fubar, and weft." — Max Shulman, *The Zebra Derby*, p. 174, 1946
- It the landing schedule had not gone snafu, we would have come ashore with the assault waves. — Audie Murphy, *To Hell and Back*, p. 1, 1949

- Now everything was screwed up proper. A real snafu. — Mickey Spillane, *Return of the Hood*, p. 88, 1964

snafu *verb*
to bungle something; to reduce something to chaos *US, 2001*

- He'd ask questions I didn't want to answer. Especially since the pig-heart swap had gotten snafued. — Janet Evanovich, *Seven Up*, p. 201, 2001

snag *noun*

1 a girl, especially an ugly one *US, 1962*

- — Anthony Romeo, *The Language of Gangs*, p. 22, 4th December 1962
- — David Claerbaut, *Black Jargon in White America*, p. 80, 1972

2 a tooth *US, 1967*

- "Yank the bastards, Doc," he said. "Those snags have whipped me for a lot of action." — Malcolm Braly, *On the Yard*, p. 9, 1967

snag *verb*

1 to grab something; to acquire something *US, 1895*

- I can't find my Cranberries CD. I've gotta go to the Quad before somebody snags it. — *Clueless*, 1995

2 to outdo someone *US, 1946*

- These cutting contests are just a musical version of the verbal duels. They're staged to see which performer can sang and cap all the others musically. — Mezz Mezzrow, *Really the Blues*, pp. 230–231, 1946

snag bag *noun*
a small bag for carrying personal effects *US, 1967*
Prison usage.

- I sat down on my snag bag (a cloth bag with whatever junk you carried around) and he squatted next to me. — Piri Thomas, *Down These Mean Streets*, p. 265, 1967

snagged stag *noun*
a boy who is steadily and exclusively dating one girl *US, 1961*

- — *San Francisco Examiner*, p. 21, 12th December 1961: 'Colloquialisms for your murgatroid handcuhs'

snaggle-toothed *adjective*
possessing crooked teeth *UK, 1585*

- The oldest was a boy, probably nine, snaggle-toothed, his hair still visibly damp where she'd combed it into a pompadour just like his dad's. — Sue Grafton, *"F" is for Fugitive*, p. 67, 1989
- I bet she is wearing fringy things and is all busty and snaggle-toothed, like Jewel. — Meg Cabot, *The Highs and Lows of Being Mia*, p. 275, 2004

snail mail *noun*
mail sent by normal postal service *US, 1983*
A term that was coined after the advent of electronic mail.

- — Guy L. Steele et al., *The Hacker's Dictionary*, pp. 117–118, 1983
- Other terms, like "snail mail," for messages delivered by the United States Postal Service, as opposed to those transported electronically, are more widely comprehensible. — *New York Times*, p. C4, 13th September 1983
- — Connie Eble (Editor), *UNC-CH Campus Slang*, p. 7, April 1997

snail track *noun*
the residue of vaginal secretions, semen and/or saliva on a woman's thighs after sex *US, 1986*

- There was drying snail track on her thigh. — Robert Campbell, *In La-La Land We Trust*, p. 68, 1986
- — *Adult Video News*, p. 51, October 1995

snake *noun*

1 an AH-1G Cobra attack helicopter *US, 1986*
The US Army's primary gunship in Vietnam.

- They gonna lay snake and nape right on the perimeter so stay tight in your holes and don't leave 'em. — *Platoon*, 1986
- Don't like to me in this kind of mess / Asked the snakes for help and they said yes. — Sandee Shaffer Johnson, *Cadences*, p. 110, 1986
- You're doin' a great job, two six. I have some fast movers and snakes coming your way. — Harold Coyle, *Trial by Fire*, p. 414, 1992
- "The two man crew from the snake, Blue Max 27, is on the ground without a radio." — Paul Morgan, *The Parrot's Beak*, p. 3, 2000

2 the penis *US, 1991*

- Steve Tyler's snake, like Bull Moose Jackson's before, is a big ten-inch[.] — Chuck Eddy, *Stairway to Hell*, p. 15, 1991

- You fucking better get on my team, Gus, or you're gonna have a fucking scar down there where you snake used to play. — Stephen J. Cannell, *King Con*, p. 142, 1997

3 a long, serpentine putt *US, 1962*
- — Dawson Taylor, *How to Talk Golf*, p. 61, 1985

4 a subway, an underground system *US, 1960*
- — Robert George Reisner, *The Jazz Titans*, p. 165, 1960

5 a surfer who surfs in another surfer's right of way *US, 1987*
- — Mitch McKissick, *Surf Lingo*, 1987

6 an informer *US, 1958*
- Blood wanted to send two or three snakes (spies or intelligence agents) to check the location and strength of the Rovers. — Harrison E. Salisbury, *The Shook-up Generation*, p. 37, 1958
- — Angela Devlin, *Prison Patter*, p. 106, 1996
- Have you heard about that snake then? — *The Guardian*, 17th February 2000
- "There's an informer on the spur, lads!" he proclaimed, pointing towards the cell where Grady was installing his few intact possessions. "Sssssss," came the reply in chorus. (An informer in prison is known as a grass from the phrase "snake in the grass.") — *The Guardian*, 30th March 2000

7 a homosexual man *US, 1975*
- — Miguel Pinero, *Short Eyes*, p. 126, 1975: Glossary of Slang

snake *verb*

1 to have sex from the male perspective *US, 2001*
- She's been getting snaked by half the fuckin' department. — Stephen J. Cannell, *The Tin Collectors*, p. 9, 2001

2 in snowboarding or skateboarding, to cut in front of someone *US, 1984*
- — *San Francisco Sunday Examiner & Chronicle*, p. 20, 2nd September 1984: "Say it right"
- That Homer snaked the jump and bailed. — Mike Fabbro, *Snowboarding*, p. 95, 1996

snakebit *adjective*
cursed, unlucky *US, 1962*
- By the early spring of 1937 I was snakebit all over. — Sam Snead, *The Education of a Golfer*, p. 80, 1962

snake charmer *verb*
a nominally heterosexual prisoner who relies on homosexual prisoners as a sexual outlet *US, 1975*
- — Miguel Pinero, *Short Eyes*, p. 126, 1975: Glossary of Slang

snake-eaters *noun*
the US Army Special Forces *US, 1991*
From their jungle survival skills.
- — Linda Reinberg, *In the Field*, p. 202, 1991
- Academy grads, he was told, do not become snake-eaters. — Richard Marcinko and John Weisman, *Rogue Warrior*, p. 206, 1992

snake-eye bomb; snake-eye *noun*
during the Vietnam war, one of several aircraft bombs with descent-slowing devices to permit low-level attacks *US, 1966*
- The "snake-eye" bomb had an air brake that deployed when it is released, slowing up its fall so that the plane could escape from the resulting blast. — Frank Harvey, *Air War Vietnam*, p. 58, 1966
- The Snakes, or Snake-eyes, were conventional general-purpose bombs fitted with clamshell fins that opened when the weapons were released and acted like parachutes to retard the weapons[.] — Stephen Coonts, *Flight of the Intruder*, p. 279, 1986
- A snakeye allows the dropping aircraft to be very low over the target and yet avoid the explosion of the dropped bombs. — Bob Stoffey, *Cleared Hot!*, p. 288, 1992

snake eyes *noun*

1 in dice games, a roll of two one's *US, 1929*
A visual metaphor.
- A one turned up on each of the cubes and stayed that way. "Snake eyes!" a couple of the men yelled. — Willard Motley, *Knock on Any Door*, p. 278, 1947
- Abie the Jew bet the dice to win or lose, barring box cars and snake-eyes. — Chester Himes, *A Rage in Harlem*, p. 26, 1957
- Snake eyes! Hoooeee, Cheswicker, where does that put you? That don't put you on my Marvin Gardens by any chance? — Ken Kesey, *One Flew Over the Cuckoo's Nest*, p. 111, 1962
- So I wasn't surprised / when he rolled snake eyes. — Lightnin' Rod, *Hustlers Convention*, p. 61, 1973

2 in dominoes, the 1 – 1 *US, 1959*
- — Dominic Armanino, *Dominoes*, p. 17, 1959

3 in poker, a pair of aces *US, 1988*
- — George Percy, *The Language of Poker*, p. 84, 1988

snakehead *noun*
a smuggler of Chinese people *UK, 1982*
Direct translation from a Chinese term.
- [F]amed Manhattan immigration attorney Robert Porges will face a federal trial in March for, among other things, helping snakeheads kidnap and enslave hundreds of asylum-seekers. — *The Source*, p. 144, March 2002

Snakenavel, Idaho *noun*
a fictitious rural place *US, 1994*
- — Michael Dalton Johnson, *Talking Trash with Redd Foxx*, p. 18, 1994

snake pit *noun*
used in the US military during the conflict in Vietnam for describing any operational headquarters *US, 1966*
- — *Newsweek*, p. 30, 23rd May 1966
- — Carl Fleischhauer, *A Glossary of Army Slang*, p. 16, 1968

snake ranch *noun*
a bachelor's house *US, 1990*
- The Lafayette Escadrille had been actor Victor McLaglen's summer home—a perfect "snake ranch," as all the Miramar flyers in those days called their bachelor party houses (invite a girl over and show her your "snake"). — Robert Wilcox, *Scream of Eagles*, p. 171, 1990

snap *noun*

1 a car *US, 2006*
- No alarm in the house, but a dude always wires his snap. — Stephen J. Cannell, *White Sister*, p. 40, 2006

2 an amphetamine tablet *US, 1994*
- — US Department of Justice, *Street Terms*, August 1994

3 a negative statement or taunt, often as part of a rap performance *US, 1994*
- When Dweck walks along 125th Street in Harlem asking people "Got any good snaps?" they all know what he wants. — *The New York Times Magazine*, 15th May 1994
- quick and witty taunts known as "snaps" or "playing the dozens" — James Haskins, *The Story of Hip-Hop*, pp. 52 – 53, 2000

4 a humorous statement or person *US, 1970*
- — *Current Slang*, p. 13, Fall 1970

5 something that is simple or easy *US, 1877*
- It's no snap to explain why I was like that, but let's not try to do it on the run. — *As Good As It Gets*, 1997

6 in pool, the first shot of the game *US, 1990*
- — Steve Rushin, *Pool Cool*, p. 27, 1990

7 a photograph *US, 1894*
- of Walter having the snaps, we've got them. — Ted Lewis, *Jack Carter's Law*, p. 193, 1974

snap *verb*

1 to insult someone in a semiformal quasi-friendly competition *US, 1979*
- They knew what "ranking" and "snapping" on someone meant. — *New York Amsterdam News*, p. 34, 29th September 1979
- Peed changed his tone, dumping the irony, snapping now. — Bob Sipchen, *Baby Insane and the Buddha*, p. 352, 1993
- It was a summer night and a guy named Al was snapping on Stephan. He was snapping on his whole family—his mother, his father, the car his father was driving, the hat his father was wearing. — *The New York Times Magazine*, 15th May 1994
- There are many different terms for playing the dozens, including "bagging, capping, cracking, dissing, hiking, joning, ranking, ribbing, serving, signifying, slipping, sounding and snapping." — James Haskins, *The Story of Hip-Hop*, p. 54, 2000

2 to realize something suddenly; to experience an epiphany *US, 1967*
- He was picked up in drag and they were booking him into the woman's wing of the county jail before they snapped. — Malcolm Braly, *On the Yard*, p. 239, 1967
- — Bruce Jackson, *Outside the Law*, p. 60, 1972: "Glossary"
- She couldn't have picked up on slang or anything else because I don't use that kind of language. She just snapped after an introduction[.] — Bruce Jackson, *Outside the Law*, p. 150, 1972

3 to flex, and thus contract, the sphincter during anal sex *US*, *1972*
- — Bruce Rodgers, *The Queens' Vernacular*, p. 32, 1972

▶ **snap in**
to engage in rifle target practice *US, 1953*
Korean war usage.
- Following his week of dummy practice, referred to as "snapping-in," we will move to Chappo flats, the huge post rifle range, for qualification[.] — Martin Russ, *The Last Parallel*, p. 10, 1953

▶ **snap your cap**
to lose your sanity *US, 1973*
- — Kenn "Naz" Young, *Naz's Underground Dictionary*, p. 57, 1973
- — Charles Shafer, *Folk Speech in Texas Prisons*, p. 215, 1990

snapper *noun*
1 amyl nitrite; an ampoule of amyl nitrite *US, 1967*
- — Joe David Brown (Editor), *The Hippies*, p. 219, 1967: "Glossary of hippie terms"
- — William D. Alsever, *Glossary for the Establishment and Other Uptight People*, p. 1, December 1970
- "Amy" is a nickname for amyl nitrate (sic). Better known as "poppers." Sometimes called "snappers." — *San Francisco Examiner*, p. 27, 15th December 1976
- Street names [...] rush, snapper, stag[.] — James Kay and Julian Cohen, *The Parents' Complete Guide to Young People and Drugs*, p. 144, 1998

2 a girl or young woman *US, 1971*
- Sometimes the Mondos would spend the whole evening in front of Duchesneau's or Sparky's, watching the girls, or "snappers," as they called them. — J. Anthony Lukas, *Don't Shoot—We Are Your Children*, p. 221, 1971

3 the vagina, especially one with exceptional muscular control *US, 1972*
- The Ape Witch has these two separate things for her knobs and a long flap over her snapper. — Richard Meltzer, *Gulcher*, p. 76, 1972
- [T]here seemed to be nothing more satisfying than to tell your pals that you felt someone up at the movies, or got your finger into her snapper. — Internet: alt-sex.stories.moderated, 16th November 1997
- Tallman went on mimicking Pearl's raspy voice. "Eat my snapper! Suck harder! Harder!" — Matt Braun, *Crossfire*, p. 50, 2004

4 in blackjack, an ace and ten-point card dealt as the first two cards to a player *US, 1980*
- — Lee Solkey, *Dummy Up and Deal*, p. 120, 1980
- — Steve Kuriscak, *Casino Talk*, p. 51, 1985

5 a wooden match *US, 1970*
- — Clarence Major, *Dictionary of Afro-American Slang*, p. 106, 1970

6 the mythical ingredient in baked beans that can be removed to prevent flatulence *US, 1975*
- — John Gould, *Maine Lingo*, p. 263, 1975

snappers *noun*
the teeth, especially false teeth *UK, 1924*
- Wally, half asleep, from the mug containing the Rabbi's snappers — Charles Raven, *Underworld Nights*, p. 201, 1956

snaps *noun*
1 praise; recognition *US, 1995*
- And I must give her snaps for her courageous fashion efforts. — *Clueless*, 1995
- — Vann Wesson, *Generation X Field Guide and Lexicon*, p. 156, 1997

2 money *US, 1997*
- — Judi Sanders, *Da Bomb!*, p. 26, 1997
- — Vann Wesson, *Generation X Field Guide and Lexicon*, p. 156, 1997

3 handcuffs *US, 1949*
- — Vincent J. Monteleone, *Criminal Slang*, p. 215, 1949

snarf *verb*
1 to eat *US, 2004*
- We snarfed Cheez Whiz. My dad rooted on race and "heart." — James Ellroy, *Destination Morgue*, p. 4, 2004

2 to take something; to grab something *US, 1968*
- "Snarfing" Tricks — *American Speech*, pp. 313–314, December 1968

snarfing *adjective*
disgusting *US, 1963*
- "Isn't that snarfing!" Lucy said, making a face. "I bet you know he's married, and just play the role to get Jeff stewed." — Frederick Kohner, *Gidget Goes to Rome*, p. 65, 1963

snark *noun*
a caustic witticism *US, 2003*
- [T]hey are also major snark targets, annoying others for seeming to have so much brilliance, youth and charm. — *San Francisco Chronicle*, p. D1, 27th August 2003

snarky *adjective*
snide, sarcastic; irritable *UK, 1906*
From the Scottish snark (to find fault, to nag).
- She wasn't a cock-teaser, a cold fish, an easy lay or a snarky bitch. — Margaret Atwood, *Dancing Girls*, p. 29, 1977
- Caption on cartoon: The Snarky District — *The New Yorker*, p. 60, 15th January 2001
- We could ask them all kinds of snarky questions in the information session. Like about their interracial dating policy. — Al Franken, *Lies*, p. 261, 2003
- We asked for the more attitude-specific Snarky Pants and the woman helping us said, "Sir, you don't wear snarky. You are snarky." — *San Francisco Chronicle*, p. E1, 27th February 2003

snatch *noun*
1 the vagina; sex; a woman (or women) as a sexual object *UK, 1904*
- "A woman's snatch." "A snatch?" "The whole thing, right, all hot and dripping and ready to go." — Philip Roth, *Portnoy's Complaint*, p. 145, 1969
- It was, remember, only '62. Playboy had not yet acknowledged snatch fur, or even snatch. — *Screw*, p. 5, 12th June 1972
- He's spewing his spunk deep inside her seething snatch! — *Adam Film World*, p. 60, 1977
- Jesus God in heaven, uh, why did you kill such hot snatch. That's a joke man. — *Heathers*, 1988

2 a kidnapping *US, 1931*
- He looked at me solemnly. "Is this some kind of a snatch?" — Horace McCoy, *Kiss Tomorrow Good-bye*, p. 282, 1958
- This isn't a ransom snatch. — Mickey Spillane, *Return of the Hood*, p. 117, 1964
- So now Joe Rao decides to put the snatch on Shapiro. — Peter Maas, *The Valachi Papers*, p. 144, 1968
- The problem part of any snatch, irregardless, is always the payoff. — Richard Condon, *Prizzi's Honor*, p. 172, 1982

3 a rescue *US, 1988*
- One day in June my team went on a POW snatch. — Wallace Terry, *Bloods*, p. 244, 1984
- Anyway, long short story, we reach the snatch point right near sunset, which is a very nervous-making time to be in the air going anyplace by home, and we spot the smoke coming up. — John Skipp and Craig Spector, *The Scream*, p. 268, 1988

snatch *verb*
to kidnap someone *US, 1932*
- In one of the boldest strokes in gangland annals, he kidnapped Big Frency De Mange, Owney Maddens' top lieutenant, and with him snatched George Immerman, Connie's brother. — Robert Sylvester, *No Cover Charge*, p. 63, 1956
- After them cats from St. Louis snatched me and I had to pay fifty grand to keep them from blowing my head off, I knew I had to have some place to hide. — Charles W. Moore, *A Brick for Mister Jones*, p. 80, 1975
- The woman who was wasted when Finlay got snatched. — Richard Condon, *Prizzi's Honor*, p. 233, 1982

snatcher *noun*
1 a thief *US, 1965*
- He's a snatcher but I don't know no sting he's made recently. — Chester Himes, *Cotton Comes to Harlem*, p. 34, 1965

2 a police detective *US, 1948*
- — Jack Lait and Lee Mortimer, *New York Confidential*, p. 236, 1948: "A glossary of harlemisms"

snatch fur *noun*
female pubic hair *US, 1972*
- It was, remember, only 62." Playboy had not yet acknowledged snatch fur, or even snatch. — *Screw*, p. 5, 12th June 1972

snatch hair *noun*
the pubic hair (of either gender) *US, 1995*
- My wife would tear out EVERY SNATCH HAIR AND EYEBALL FROM ME, never mind from Sally. — Howard Stern, *Miss America*, p. 234, 1995
- Soft blonde snatch hair framed her maroon pussy lips, aglow with excitement. — *alt.sex.stories*, 10th October 1996

snatch hound *noun*
a person who is obsessed with sex and women *US, 1992*
- "Is Jonny Duhamel queer?" "Are you nuts? He is the snatch hound to end all snatch hounds." — James Ellroy, *White Jazz*, p. 145, 1992

snatch patrol *noun*
a combat mission in which the object is to capture enemy troops for interrogation *US, 1977*
- A snatch patrol. The squad would capture the two VC and bring them to the outpost. I would interrogate them[.] — Philip Caputo, *A Rumor of War*, p. 299, 1977

snatch-plug *noun*
a tampon *US, 1972*
- [M]ost gals use snatch-plugs which have no other utilitarian value that I know of. — *Screw*, p. 6, 4th December 1972

snazzy *adjective*
stylish; fashionable; smart *US, 1931*
- A gentleman gave us a ride in his snazzy car. — Jack Kerouac, *On the Road*, p. 74, 1957
- Even Sister had to admit he was pretty snazzy, after talking to him for a while. — Mary McCarthy, *The Group*, p. 210, 1963
- "Gee you're the snazziest-looking girl at the party," is a good thing to hear[.] — Dick Clark, *To Goof or Not to Goof*, p. 23, 1963
- Then we gonna buy you a ritzy house ... 'lectric light! ... a great big slew of snazzy furniture. — Iceberg Slim (Robert Beck), *Airtight Willie and Me*, p. 116, 1979

sneak *verb*
to break into a building *US, 1949*
- I figure he was planning the sneak the hotel a little. — Raymond Chandler, *The Little Sister*, pp. 58 – 59, 1949

▸ **sneak a peak**
to take a look at something or someone *US, 1999*
- Haven't you ever sneaked a peek at him in his underwear? — *American Beauty*, 1999

sneak *adjective*
▸ **on the sneak tip**
in secret *US, 1995*
- — Maria Hinojas, *Crews*, p. 167, 1995: "Glossary"

sneak-and-peak *adjective*
1 designed to be quiet *US, 1973*
- Kind of tough kicking, ain't it, Nick, in those crepe soled, sneak-and-peek shoes you guys wear? — Joseph Wambaugh, *The Blue Knight*, p. 137, 1973

2 undertaken for the purpose of reconnaissance *US, 1974*
- But this one was a sneak-and-peak mission and I was the patrol leader. — Elmore Leonard, *The Hunted*, p. 149, 1974

sneaker *noun*
1 a person engaged in an illegal enterprise who does not pay a regular bribe to the police but does when confronted *US, 1973*
- He's what you call a sneaker—isn't on the pad, isn't paying anybody. You find him, he pays; you don't, he don't pay. — Leonard Shecter and William Phillips, *On the Pad*, pp. 150 – 151, 1973

2 a smuggler *US, 1956*
- — *American Speech*, p. 97, May 1956: "Smugglers' argot in the Southwest"

3 a linear amplifier for a citizens' band radio *US, 1977*
- — Bill Davis, *Jawjacking: The Complete CB Dictionary*, p. 93, 1977

sneaker bitch *noun*
a person who is too focused on conspicuous consumption, such as high priced trainers *US, 1989*
- Most of these sneaker bitches is looking to get skied, not looking for knowledge. — Terry Williams, *The Cocaine Kids*, p. 87, 1989

sneakernet *noun*
in computing, to carry a disk from one computer to another *US, 1991*
- — Eric S. Raymond, *The New Hacker's Dictionary*, p. 327, 1991

sneakers *noun*
car wheel rims *US, 2003*
- Dubs, blades, shoes, sneakers, twinkies—street slang for custom wheels—are status symbols, made popular by athletes and rap stars. — *Cincinnati Enquirer*, p. 1B, 29th August 2003

sneak-in *noun*
a bar that surreptitiously remains open after the legal closing time *US, 1951*
- Washington has hundreds of sneak-ins that remain open all night. — Jack Lait and Lee Mortimer, *Washington Confidential*, p. 13, 1951

sneaky *adjective*
used of a recording device, easily hidden *US, 1982*
- — Ralph de Sola, *Crime Dictionary*, p. 140, 1982

sneaky Pete *noun*
1 any potent, potentially fatal, alcoholic concoction, favored by those whose need outweighs their ability to pay *US, 1947*
- Pass me the sneakypete, Muckleroy. — Ralph Ellison, *Invisible Man*, p. 490, 1947
- Down by the river there was some bums that hung around a fire and drank Sneaky Pete all day and sometimes cooked something like stew in a can. — Hal Ellson, *Duke*, p. 151, 1949
- So drink your Sneaky Pete and then hit the street cause I'm cool like the dawn and really gone! — Dan Burley, *Diggeth Thou?*, p. 45, 1959
- He drank quarts of it a day. Any kind. Gallo, sneaky pete, the distillation of canned heat. — Clancy Sigal, *Going Away*, p. 238, 1961

2 marijuana mixed in wine *US, 1955*
- — *American Speech*, p. 88, May 1955: "Narcotic argot along the Mexican border"

3 a member of a US Army long-range reconnaissance patrol unit *US, 1967*
- The Special Forces assigned to them -called "Sneaky Petes" in Army argot—are superbly trained, dedicated, and they fight like lions under attack. — Elaine Shepard, *The Doom Pussy*, p. 62, 1967

4 an unannounced in-flight examination by a crew that boards the plane just before take-off *US, 1963*
- — *American Speech*, p. 120, May 1963: "Air refueling words"

5 in pool, an expert player's custom cue, designed to look like an ordinary cue *US, 1993*
- — Mike Shamos, *The Illustrated Encyclopedia of Billiards*, p. 217, 1993

sneaky Pete *adjective*
secret *US, 1967*
- "So damn sneaky pete we're not supposed to talk about it." — Elaine Shepard, *The Doom Pussy*, p. 190, 1967
- Then I remembered Rick was part of a "sneaky-pete" flight within Covey, a small group of six pilots who flew some super-secret mission[.] — Tom Yarborough, *Da Nang Diary*, p. 48, 1990

sneeze *noun*
pepper *US, 1981*
- — *Maledicta*, p. 267, Summer/Winter 1981: "By its slang, ye shall know it: the pessimism of prison life"

sneeze *verb*
to arrest someone *US, 1950*
- — Hyman E. Goldin et al., *Dictionary of American Underworld Lingo*, p. 200, 1950
- — Sherman Louis Sergel, *The Language of Show Biz*, p. 201, 1973

sneeze and squeeze *noun*
cocaine and sex *US, 1984*
- A little too early for Odeon, but once we're downtown, it's happy hunting ground for sneeze and squeeze. — Jay McInerney, *Bright Lights, Big City*, p. 44, 1984

sneezer *noun*
1 the nose *US, 1945*
- — Lou Shelly, *Hepcats Jive Talk Dictionary*, p. 17, 1945

2 a jail or prison *US, 1953*
- [A] bit of high class fluff that couldn't stick around long enough to make sure he didn't get tossed in the sneezer by some prowl car boys[.] — Raymond Chandler, *The Long Goodbye*, p. 5, 1953

sneezing powder *noun*
heroin *US, 1958*
- "Somebody put some sneezing powder under my nose," the girl told Father Hoodak. Sneezing powder is heroin. — Harrison E. Salisbury, *The Shook-up Generation*, p. 79, 1958

snib *noun*
a small amount of a drug *US, 2002*
- It's not like I'm gonna ruin her with this one snib. — Lynn Breedlove, *Godspeed*, p. 11, 2002

sniff *noun*
1 cocaine *US, 1990*

- After some of the fellas would step away from the blackjack table, and the bar, and get ready to buy a fiddy or a hundred dollars' worth of sniff[.] — *New Jack City*, p. 9, 1990
- Fuck Ecstasy, we'll stick with the sniff. — Wayne Anthony, *Spanish Highs*, p. 4, 1999
- Presumably, said promoter then dived right on back into the massive pile of sniff that he had spent the rest of the season plowing through[.] — *Ministry*, p. 7, October 2002

2 any solvent that can be inhaled for its psychoactive effect *US, 1974*
- — Paul Glover, *Words from the House of the Dead*, 1974

3 a sycophant *US, 1968*
From an image of the sycophant's brown nose being in the near proximity of an anus.
- — *Current Slang*, p. 10, Spring 1968

sniff *verb*
▶ **sniff jocks**
to behave in a sycophantic fashion towards athletes *US, 1994*
- It was after a game in Anaheim and the former president had come down to the locker room to shake a few hands and, as one of the players said, "sniff a few jocks." — Jim Bouton, *Strike Zone*, p. 173, 1994

sniffer *noun*
1 the nose *UK, 1858*
- Several times the master of ceremonies stuck the pill close to my nose and told me to smell it. Poppa, you never laid your sniffer on anything so fine in all your life. — Mezz Mezzrow, *Really the Blues*, p. 99, 1946
- [T]hey'll go all moody and Beardsley drawing and look down their sniffers at you[.] — Derek Raymond (Robin Cook), *The Crust on its Uppers*, p. 34, 1962

2 an ampoule of amyl nitrite *US, 1970*
- — William D. Alsever, *Glossary for the Establishment and Other Uptight People*, p. 1, December 1970

3 a cocaine user *US, 1988*
- So while this sniffer's giving you head she just stops in the middle and tells you about a commerical real estate venture? — Robert Campbell, *Juice*, p. 152, 1988

4 a device placed on a vehicle's exhaust pipe to measure the pollutants in the emission *US, 1993*
- — Jim Edwards, *Auto Dictionary*, 1993

5 a computer program that surreptitiously records user passwords and other log-in data *US, 1994*
- — *American Speech*, p. 192, Summer 1996: "Among the new words"

6 an outsider who tries to be part of the pornography industry *US, 1995*
- — *Adult Video News*, p. 51, October 1995

7 a handkerchief *US, 1945*
- — Lou Shelly, *Hepcats Jive Talk Dictionary*, p. 17, 1945

sniffer bag *noun*
a small bag of heroin intended for inhaling *US, 2002*
- — *Detroit News*, p. 5D, 20th September 2002

sniffings *noun*
any industrial solvent that is inhaled for its psychoactive effect *US, 1984*
- — Inez Cardozo-Freeman, *The Joint*, p. 532, 1984

sniff queen *noun*
a homosexual who is a heavy user of amyl nitrite or butyl nitrite during sex *US, 1972*

snipe *noun*
1 the butt of a marijuana cigarette *US, 1969*
In the late C19, a "snipe" referred to the discarded stub of a cigar or cigarette. It briefly enjoyed standing in the vocabulary of marijuana users before falling victim to **ROACH**.
- — Walter L. Way, *The Drug Scene*, 1977

2 the butt of a cigarette that can still be relit and smoked *US, 1891*
- — Lou Shelly, *Hepcats Jive Talk Dictionary*, p. 17, 1945
- He had snatched snipes, on the fly, of the cigarettes that clears the mind for the making of swift decisions in sudden crises with the fire still alive in the tobacco. — Nelson Algren, *The Man with the Golden Arm*, p. 17, 1949

- Then the man whose pant-knees and hands were muddy where he had fallen, saw a cigarette snipe on the curb. — Willard Motley, *Let No Man Write My Epitaph*, p. 76, 1958
- — William K. Bentley and James M. Corbett, *Prison Slang*, p. 65, 1992

snipe *verb*
to disparage someone *US, 1980*
- — Edith A. Folb, *runnin' down some lines*, p. 255, 1980

snipe hunting *noun*
patroling and gathering cigarette butts *US, 2002*
The term also is used to describe a childhood prank where unsuspecting children are led off to hunt for imaginary "snipes."
- [H]e can be seen snipe-hunting in the yard—collecting the discarded shorts of rollies. He puts in the butts in a Bugler can and rerolls the preowned tobacco[.] — Jimmy Lerner, *You Got Nothing Coming*, p. 216, 2002

sniper *noun*
a person who posts inflammatory attacks on the Internet *US, 2001*
- Those Net snipers can be really cruel. — Kevin Smith, *Jay and Silent Bob Strike Back*, p. 124, 2001

snipe rack *noun*
a collection of partially smoked cigarette butts *US, 2002*
- I was all hunkered down at the squat with beer, cigarettes, and dumpster-dived pizza, had my snipe rack. — Lynn Breedlove, *Godspeed*, p. 79, 2002

sniping *noun*
the practice of waiting until the very last minute to enter a bid on an online auction *US, 1997*
- Sniping is okay when it works for you, but is very frustrating when it doesn't. — *rec.antiques*, 22nd August 1997

snippy *adjective*
impatient; argumentative *US, 1848*
Originally used in the UK to mean "parsimonious" (C18), and then in the US (C19) in the current sense. The term enjoyed a brief moment of fame in the early morning hours of 9th November 2000, when US Vice President Al Gore told future President George Bush, "You don't have to get snippy with me" as he retracted a concession made several minutes earlier.
- "She was a little snippy snitch," Mickey said. — Elmore Leonard, *Switch*, p. 158, 1978
- Sir, you have no call to get snippy with me. — *Fargo*, 1996
- I sat up and narrowed my eyes at him. "No need to get snippy about it." "Men don't get snippy," Morelli said. "Men get pissed. Women get snippy." — Janet Evanovich, *Seven Up*, p. 105, 2001

snips *noun*
any cutting tool, for example scissors or wire cutters *US, 1962*
- — Joseph E. Ragen and Charles Finston, *Inside the World's Toughest Prison*, p. 819, 1962: "Penitentiary and underworld glossary"

snit *noun*
a mild temper tantrum *US, 1939*
- "She's going to the same place we are!" said Fortney. "Wanna try again or are you in too much of a snit?" — Joseph Wambaugh, *Floaters*, p. 63, 1996

snitch *noun*
an informer, especially a police informer *UK, 1785*
A high profile use of the term was in the motto of the television police drama *Richard Diamond, Private Detective* (1957–60)—"A detective is only as good as his snitch."
- The snitch is comin' out. He trusts you. — Clarence Cooper Jr., *The Scene*, p. 13, 1960
- We're talking to everybody who worked with Iris, might've known her. And we got our snitches to talk to yet. — Elmore Leonard, *Glitz*, p. 89, 1985
- Not the cops. They couldn't smell a dead rat two feet away. But the damn dope fiend snitches could. — *Drugstore Cowboy*, 1988
- You'll be the lowest sort of rat, the prince of snitches, the loudest cooing stool pigeon that ever grabbed his ankles for the man. — *The Usual Suspects*, 1995

snitch *verb*
1 to inform upon someone *UK, 1801*

- I hope you aren't going to rush over there, break down the door, and tell him I snitched him off. — Gerald Petievich, *Money Men*, p. 143, 1981
- No one knew who'd snitched on her. — William T. Vollman, *Whores for Gloria*, p. 71, 1991

2 to steal something *US*, *1904*

- Some mean hack of a keeper nabs a colored boy on the coal gang for snitching a loaf of bread. — Mezz Mezzrow, *Really the Blues*, p. 314, 1946
- My friend on kitchen assignment brought some cookies she snitched. — John M. Murtagh and Sara Harris, *Cast the First Stone*, p. 26, 1957
- It helped to think of old times, carefree days in Hillsborough when she and Binky and Muffy would snitch the keys to Daddy's Mercedes and tool down to the Fillmore to tease the black studs lurking on the street corners. — Armistead Maupin, *Tales of the City*, p. 94, 1978

snitchball *noun*

any game played by prisoners in the protective unit reserved for informers *US*, *1992*

- — William K. Bentley and James M. Corbett, *Prison Slang*, p. 12, 1992

snitch box *noun*

1 a metal detector *US*, *1974*

- The metal detector—convicts call it a "snitch box"—sounded its little electronic bleeps as Bingham went through. — Tim Findley, *The Rolling Stone Reader*, p. 98, 1974

2 an in-house prison post box *US*, *1992*

- — William K. Bentley and James M. Corbett, *Prison Slang*, p. 57, 1992

snitcher *noun*

1 an informer *US*, *1966*

- In the Alderson prison, the role of the "snitcher" is the female counterpart to the "rat" in the male prison. — Rose Giallombardo, *Society of Women*, p. 107, 1966

2 a metal detector *US*, *1950*

- — Hyman E. Goldin et al., *Dictionary of American Underworld Lingo*, p. 201, 1950

snitch house *noun*

a section of a prison housing model prisoners and informers *US*, *1966*

- — Rose Giallombardo, *Society of Women*, p. 211, 1966: Glossary of Prison Terms

snitch jacket *noun*

a reputation for being an informer *US*, *1973*

- I know you got an army of snitches, but nobody never got a snitch jacket. — Joseph Wambaugh, *The Blue Knight*, p. 29, 1973
- And you'll be in jail wearing a snitch jacket. — Gerald Petievich, *To Die in Beverly Hills*, p. 259, 1983
- Wendy didn't know a snitch jacket from a cashmere sweater. — Bob Sipchen, *Baby Insane and the Buddha*, p. 27, 1993
- On November 5, 1980, while driving (lifting weights) on the lower yard, several of the Aryans spotted a white inmate who was carrying a snitch jacket[.] — Bill Valentine, *Gangs and Their Tattoos*, p. 13, 2000

snitch kite *noun*

a note sent by a prisoner to prison authorities, informing on other prisoners *US*, *2000*

- Admin was receiving far more snitch kites (notes sent up front to staff when an inmate wants to inform on others). — Bill Valentine, *Gangs and Their Tattoos*, p. 12, 2000

snitty *adjective*

bad-tempered *US*, *1978*

- I called Kathleen from the pay phone and rehearsed my snitty but controlled opening line. "Uh, didn't you forget something?" — Anne Lamott, *Hard Laughter*, p. 91, 1979

snivel *verb*

▸ **snivel a counter**

(said of an American pilot in Vietnam) to talk your way into an incursion over North Vietnam *US*, *1990*

- — Joseph Tuso, *Singing the Vietnam Blues*, p. 261, 1990: Glossary

snob mob *noun*

1 a group of friends with a very high opinion of themselves *US*, *1955*

- — *American Speech*, p. 305, December 1955: "Wayne University slang"

2 high society *US*, *1957*

- "More of the snob mob dropping in, huh?" — Gypsy Rose Lee, *Gypsy*, p. 281, 1957

snockered; schnockered; shnockered *adjective*

drunk *US*, *1955*

- — *American Speech*, p. 304, December 1955: "Wayne University slang"
- [T]oday they had gone cruising in his car all day and drinking beer in various locales and got quite snockered[.] — Glendon Swarthout, *Where the Boys Are*, p. 197, 1960
- — Collin Baker et al., *College Undergraduate Slang Study Conducted at Brown University*, p. 200, 1968
- Bellamy was so snockered he didn't even blink at the ten-dollar cover. — Carl Hiaasen, *Tourist Season*, p. 2, 1986

snog *noun*

a passionate kiss; a short but intense period of kissing and cuddling *UK*, *1959*

- If he defeats George W this week, his victory march can be traced back to the moment when the man—cheerfully considered one of the world's dullest politicians—gathered wife Tipper into a very public snog. — *Sun-Herald (Tempo)*, p. 3, 5th November 2000
- Should they try to get a snog off that woman from an equally rowdy hen party[.] — Iain Aitch, *A Fete Worse Than Death*, pp. 159–160, 2003

snog *verb*

to have sex *US*, *2002*

- Actually I have snogged more babes on this tour than any member of the band. — Lynn Breedlove, *Godspeed*, p. 150, 2002

snooked *adjective*

drunk *US*, *1971*

- When we finally settled on an obscure niche of sand a half mile from our cars, a little winy and a lot snooked, the sky fell. — Jeffrey Golden, *Watermelon Summer*, p. 91, 1971

snooker *verb*

to trick someone; to place someone in an impossible position *UK*, *1915*

From the game played with balls on a billiard table.

- Delvin, knowing he's been snookered, too, gives Cooley half a wink, thanks everybody and turns the chair and the job over to me to another round of spontaneous applause. — Robert Campbell, *In a Pig's Eye*, p. 8, 1991
- "[S]oon as we turn our backs he goes and jumps out a window. I'm telling you, you can't trust nobody anymore." "He snookered us." — Janet Evanovich, *Seven Up*, p. 12, 2001

snookums *noun*

used as an affectionate term of address *US*, *1919*

As the *Oxford English Dictionary* so gracefully puts it, "usually applied to children or lap-dogs."

- "Just thinking, Nebbice." "About what, snookums? Love?" — Max Shulman, *The Zebra Derby*, p. 91, 1946

snoop *noun*

1 a detective *US*, *1942*

From SNOOP (to pry).

- I'm a private snoop! Like you, man! — *The Big Lebowski*, 1998
- The snoop was attempting to shield his face[.] — Stewart Home, *Sex Kick [britpulp]*, p. 215, 1999
- A professional snoop in a world where most people did it as a hobby. — Malcolm Pryce, *Aberystwyth Mon Amour*, p. 11, 2001

2 a member of the Bloods youth gang *US*, *1991*

- "Regardless—fuck slobs, that's what we all sayin'. Fuck all snoops, nigger!" — Leon Bing, *Do or Die*, p. 198, 1991

snooper *noun*

an investigator *US*, *1889*

- A private snooper, eh? — Mickey Spillane, *My Gun is Quick*, p. 20, 1950

snoot *noun*

1 the nose *UK*, *1861*

- Indeed Dorothy almost poked me in the snoot in Las Vegas recently because I made disparaging remarks about Shattuck and Lewin. — Lee Mortimer, *Women Confidential*, p. 33, 1960

2 cocaine *US*, *1993*

- — Peter Johnson, *Dictionary of Street Alcohol and Drug Terms*, p. 174, 1993

3 in the television and movie industries, a cone attachment that directs light to a specific area *US*, *1990*

- — Ralph S. Singleton, *Filmmaker's Dictionary*, p. 155, 1990

▸ **give someone the snoot**

to treat someone in a condescending manner *US*, *1989*

- "I didn't know that," I says, wondering if Betancourt's trying to make chatty conversation or give me the snoot. — Robert Campbell, *Nibbled to Death by Ducks*, p. 179, 1989

▶ **to have a snoot full**
enough alcohol to make you drunk *US*, *1918*
- Does she light them when she gets a snoot full? — Philip Wylie, *Opus 21*, p. 144, 1949
- Pick up your old man. He's got a snoot full and he's spoiling Tony's wedding. — Iceberg Slim (Robert Beck), *Death Wish*, p. 177, 1977

snooty *adjective*
arrogant, unpleasant, supercilious, snobbish *UK*, *1919*
- That Purple Gang was a hard lot of guys, so tough they made Capone's playmates look like a kindergarten class, and Detroit's snooty set used to feel it was really living to talk to them hoodlums without getting their ounce-brains blown out. — Mezz Mezzrow, *Really the Blues*, p. 92, 1946
- There ain't nobody snootier than an oilman who's had to sell one of his Cadillacs. — Larry McMurtry, *The Last Picture Show*, p. 53, 1966
- "Your snooty pals are gonna miss you." "Tell them I may come down for the polo matches. I'll see." — Elmore Leonard, *Split Images*, p. 72, 1981
- Well, it's not because of her beauty / and her brand new low cut blouse / It's not because she's so snooty / or a fine famed millionaire — ZZ Top, *If I Could Only Flag Her Down*, 1983

snooze *noun*
1 a short sleep; a doze *UK*, *1793*
- [A] one-hour nap in the morning and a one- to two-hour snooze in the afternoon. — William and Martha Sears, *The Baby Book*, p. 355, 2003
2 a bore *US*, *1997*
- — Anna Scotti and Paul Young, *Buzzwords*, p. 99, 1997

snoozer *noun*
in a poker game using the joker, the joker *US*, *1950*
Perhaps related to the earlier sense of the word as "a thief."
- — Thomas L. Clark, *The Dictionary of Gambling and Gaming*, p. 208, 1987

snorbs *noun*
the female breasts *US*, *1969*
- — *Current Slang*, p. 10, Fall 1969

snore sack *noun*
a sleeping bag *US*, *1945*
- — Lou Shelly, *Hepcats Jive Talk Dictionary*, p. 48, 1945

snore shelf *noun*
a bed; a sleeping compartment in an over-the-road truck *US*, *1976*
- If I don't hit the snore shelf pretty soon I'm not going to get up in time to make it to the saltmine. — Radio Shack, *CBer's Handy Atlas/Dictionary*, p. 42, 1976

snorker *noun*
in poker, a player who berates the other players when he wins a hand *US*, *1988*
- — George Percy, *The Language of Poker*, p. 84, 1988

snort *noun*
1 a drink of an alcoholic beverage *US*, *1889*
- With 3,400 precincts in all, there is as yet no trouble digging up a snort. — Jack Lait and Lee Mortimer, *Chicago Confidential*, p. 141, 1950
- "Howdy, hoss," said Opie genially. "Have a snort." He extended a bottle of whisky to Private Roger Litwhiler. — Max Shulman, *Rally Round the Flag, Boys!*, p. 261, 1957
- There's a pint in the glove compartment. Want a snort? — Raymond Chandler, *Playback*, p. 104, 1958
- Bill reached over toward an almost empty bottle of tequilla and said—"Come on Huncke, have a little snort. It'll make you feel great." — Herbert Huncke, *The Evening Sun Turned Crimson*, p. 119, 1980
2 cocaine *US*, *1975*
- That's good snort, Vin, you got some more. — Edwin Torres, *Carlito's Way*, p. 108, 1975
- He's got everything aboard, even snort. — Edwin Torres, *Q & A*, p. 150, 1977
- The biggest problem was that there was no snort. Nor any other drugs. — Joseph Wambaugh, *The Secrets of Harry Bright*, p. 44, 1985
- Whistler bumped into Al Lister, an old extra who used to run errands for Suzy, like scoring hash or snort[.] — Robert Campbell, *In La-La Land We Trust*, p. 57, 1986

snort *verb*
to ingest drugs by nasal inhalation *US*, *1951*
- Then he introduced her to the habit of sniffing heroin—"snorting" is the word used by the addicts. — Harry J. Anslinger (US Commissioner of Narcotics), *The Murderers*, p. 178, 1961
- He's putting a thumb over each nostril and snorting like fuckin' mad to drag up any stray powder that's hangin' around. — J.J. Connolly, *Know Your Enemy [britpulp]*, p. p. 141, 1999

snort rag *noun*
a piece of cloth holding a powdered drug *US*, *1969*
- He felt in his pocket, found a snort rag, stuck it to his nose and got a sniff of some coke. — Steve Cannon, *Groove, Bang, and Jive Around*, p. 138, 1969

snot *noun*
1 nasal mucus *UK*, *1425*
- — Shere Hite, *The Hite Report on Male Sexuality*, p. 533, 1981
2 the residue produced by smoking amphetamine *US*, *1993*
- — US Department of Justice, *Street Terms*, August 1993
3 an arrogant, conceited and flippant person *US*, *1941*
- "Trouble with you young snots is you hit Skid Row and you think you're men," the fellow growled. — Willard Motley, *Knock on Any Door*, p. 150, 1947
- "Why, you lousy little snot," Hobbs burst out, "how many five-gallon cans of oil have you sold on the black market?" — Norman Mailer, *Advertisements for Myself*, p. 129, 1951
- Anyway, I was a busy lil' snot in them days. — Edwin Torres, *Carlito's Way*, p. 16, 1975
- They thought Victor was a holier-than-thou snot who was out to erase them from the planet. — Pamela Des Barres, *I'm With the Band*, p. 22, 1988

snot locker *noun*
the nose *US*, *1971*
- I feel that life has handed me one in the snot locker. — Thomas McGuane, *The Bushwacked Piano*, p. 197, 1971
- "I guess I'll just have to go hit them in the snot locker." — *St. Petersburg Times*, p. 7B, 9th August 1991
- "Clock him on the snot locker and he'll go down like a ton of bricks." — David Sedaris, *Dress Your Family in Corduroy and Denim*, p. 44, 2004

snot nose *noun*
conceit *US*, *1984*
- I'll tell you something son. If you don't straighten up, the world is gonna have a long party knockin' that snot-nose out of you. — Ken Weaver, *Texas Crude*, p. 127, 1984

snot rag *noun*
a handkerchief *UK*, *1886*
- Let's give you a bit of a mop down with a clean snot-rag! — Barry Humphries, *Bazza Pulls It Off!*, 1971
- "Say, Pogie, man, let me use your snotrag," I said[.] — Bobby Seale, *A Lonely Rage*, p. 62, 1978
- Careful where you put that snot rag. Why? Thanks to "The Hanky Code" you could be asking for man-love without even knowing it. — *Gayness Explained*, *The FHM Little Book of Bloke*, p. 144, June 2003

snotty *adjective*
1 conceited, arrogant, aloof *UK*, *1870*
- A jury is cold and impartial like they're supposed to be, while some snotty lawyer makes them pour tears as he tells how his client was insane at the moment or had to shoot in self-defense. — Mickey Spillane, *I, The Jury*, pp. 6–7, 1947
- [W]hat hurt most was not that his nose kept dripping and that the back of his head felt as if it had been rammed by a pile driver, but that the kids in the poolroom, those snotty little Tigers, were watching him take a beating from a kid[.] — Irving Shulman, *The Amboy Dukes*, p. 57, 1947
- "None of your business," she said. She can be very snotty sometimes. She can be quite snotty. "I suppose you failed in every single subject again," she said—very snotty. — J.D. Salinger, *Catcher in the Rye*, p. 167, 1951
- Snotty bitch. — *Saturday Night Fever*, 1977
2 dirty with nasal mucus *UK*, *1570*
While accepted in conventional usage, the root-word **SNOT** (nasal mucus) is considered vulgar.
- When me nose gets snotty / An me cannot feel me botty / I get de feeling it is time fe go. — Benjamin Zephaniah, *The Cold War*, p. 26, 1992

snotty-nosed *adjective*
contemptible, dirty *UK, 1964*
- Dirty little teddy boys. Snotty-nosed layabouts, just you bloody well wait. — John Peter Jones, *Feather Pluckers*, p. 16, 1964

snout *noun*
▶ **on the snout**
in horseracing, a bet on a horse to finish first *US, 1972*
- "Well, I mean do you want it on the snout, or what?" — Robert Byrne, *McGoorty*, p. 54, 1972

snow *noun*
1 a powdered drug, especially cocaine but at times heroin *US, 1914*
- You ever hear of dope? Snow? Junk? Big H? Horse? — John D. McDonald, *The Neon Jungle*, p. 61, 1953
- [T]he hemp makes me limp and I'm ready to go when the cat hollers slow. Like I'm not lame in the brain from a snort of cocaine. — Dan Burley, *Diggeth Thou?*, p. 37, 1959
- [I]t took me only a little while to locate a peddler of "snow"— cocaine. — Malcolm X and Alex Haley, *The Autobiography of Malcolm X*, p. 134, 1964
- He said that they called it "snow" then but that the real name of it was heroin. — Claude Brown, *Manchild in the Promised Land*, p. 104, 1965
2 passes for free admission to a performance; audience members who attend a performance using a free pass *US, 1981*
- — Don Wilmeth, *The Language of American Popular Entertainment*, p. 249, 1981

snow *verb*
1 to deceive someone; to flirt insincerely *US, 1943*
- You got it wrong, boy. You mean I'm not snowing you, don't you? — Evan Hunter, *The Blackboard Jungle*, p. 160, 1954
- I walked real close to her and talked to her in this kind of soft, sexy voice that I use when I snow girls. — Max Shulman, *I was a Teen-Age Dwarf*, p. 66, 1959
- I said, "Why, those slippery bastards have conned me, snowed me into holding their bag." — Ken Kesey, *One Flew Over the Cuckoo's Nest*, p. 182, 1962
- Like somebody gettin snowed? — Robert Campbell, *In La-La Land We Trust*, p. 172, 1986
2 in poker, to bluff or fake *US, 1963*
- — Irwin Steig, *Common Sense in Poker*, p. 187, 1963

snowball *noun*
1 a drug addict *US, 1949*
- "This woman's a snowball," says the cop. "She's fulla dope." — Audie Murphy, *To Hell and Back*, p. 129, 1949
2 a white person *US, 1980*
Offensive.
- — *Maledicta*, p. 125, Summer 1980: "Racial and ethnic slurs: regional awareness and variations"

snowball *verb*
to pass semen to the donor through a kiss *US, 1972*
- — Bruce Rodgers, *The Queens' Vernacular*, p. 76, 1972
- VERONICA: That was Snowball. DANTE: Why do you call him that? VERONICA: Sylvan made it up. It's a blow job thing. DANTE: What do you mean? VERONICA: After he gets a blow job, he likes to have the cum spit back into his mouth while kissing. — *Clerks*, 1994
- Dear Jenna, My girlfriend wants to snowball me. I'm a little unwise in such areas. — *FHM*, p. 63, June 2003

snowballing; snowdropping *noun*
after oral sex, passing semen to the donor by kissing *US, 1972*
Originally an exclusively homosexual use.
- Snowballing simply means you unload in your girlfriend's mouth, she swishes it about then spits in yours — *FHM*, p. 63, June 2003

snowballs *noun*
1 crack cocaine *US, 1995*
- — Bill Valentine, *Gang Intelligence Manual*, p. 75, 1995
2 dice altered for cheating with only the numbers four, five and six on the faces *US, 1993*
- — Frank Scoblete, *Guerrilla Gambling*, p. 327, 1993

snowbird *noun*
1 a cocaine user or addict *US, 1914*
- My mother sells hops to the snowbirds. — James T. Farrell, *Saturday Night*, p. 38, 1947

- The powder is called "snow" and the user a "snow bird." — Donald Wilson, *My Six Convicts*, p. 338, 1951
- The little guy's a snowbird and he's hopped. — Mickey Spillane, *Kiss Me Deadly*, p. 96, 1952
- She was one of the few snowbirds who thought she was snowing the snowman and the juiceman. She wasn't snowing anybody. — Robert Campbell, *Juice*, p. 23, 1988

2 a person from the northern US or Canada who migrates to Florida or elsewhere in the southern US during winter *US, 1979*
Originally applied to men who enlisted in the army just before winter, and then to workers who flocked south in the winter, and then to tourists.
- He was an innocuous, round little man who was jolliest when Florida was crawling with snowbirds. — Carl Hiaasen, *Tourist Season*, p. 29, 1986
- Not much traffic now, huh? The snowbirds've all gone home. I don't know why anybody wants to live up north. — Elmore Leonard, *Maximum Bob*, p. 48, 1991

snowcaine *noun*
cocaine, or a related drug such as benzocaine or lidocaine *US, 1993*
- — Peter Johnson, *Dictionary of Street Alcohol and Drug Terms*, p. 175, 1993

snow cap *noun*
cocaine combined and smoked with marijuana *US, 1995*
- — Steven Daly and Nathaniel Wice, *alt.culture*, p. 50, 1995

snowcone; snowcones *noun*
cocaine *US, 1994*
- — US Department of Justice, *Street Terms*, August 1994
- — Mike Haskins, *Drugs*, p. 281, 2003

snowdrop *noun*
a US military police officer *US, 1946*
An allusion to the white helmets, gloves, belts, and socks.
- — *American Speech*, p. 75, February 1946: "Some words of war and peace from 1945"

snowed *adjective*
cocaine-intoxicated *US, 1949*
- — Vincent J. Monteleone, *Criminal Slang*, p. 216, 1949

snowflake *noun*
1 cocaine *US, 1997*
Also used in the plural.
- — Judi Sanders, *Da Bomb*, p. 14, 1997
- The boys' antidote for feeling rough [...] was to inhale South American snowflakes. — Wayne Anthony, *Spanish Highs*, p. 90, 1999
2 a military mail control record *US, 1986*
- — Department of the Army, *Staff Officer's Guidebook*, p. 65, 1986

snow job *noun*
deception by flattery *US, 1943*
- Where Affia was holding Velda's hand and Billy mist was giving her a snow job[.] — Mickey Spillane, *Kiss Me Deadly*, p. 102, 1952
- "Mr. Dady-yay," Miller said, "s'pose we jus' forget that li'l snowjob, okay?" — Evan Hunter, *The Blackboard Jungle*, p. 92, 1954
- I started in to do a snow job on R.G.—just pour on the old con a mile a minute. — Max Shulman, *I was a Teen-Age Dwarf*, p. 66, 1959
- "Have you guys been giving us a snow job?" — Frederick Kohner, *Gidget Goes to Rome*, p. 18, 1963

snowman *noun*
1 a cocaine dealer *US, 1988*
- She was one of the few snowbirds who thought she was snowing the snowman and the juiceman. — Robert Campbell, *Juice*, p. 23, 1988
2 a handsome, popular boy *US, 1961*
High school usage.
- — *Washington Post*, 23rd April 1961: "Man, dig this jazz"

snow party *noun*
a party where cocaine is consumed *US, 1951*
- Lurid literature depicts "snow parties" which degenerate into sexual orgies. Actually a snow party is very rare. — Donald Wilson, *My Six Convicts*, p. 339, 1951

snow queen *noun*
a black homosexual who is attracted to white men *US, 1985*
- — Wayne Dynes, *Homolexis*, p. 119, 1985

snow time *noun*
the infatuation stage of a relationship *US, 1959*
- — *Time Magazine*, p. 46, 24th August 1959

snow white *noun*
cocaine *US, 1993*
- — US Department of Justice, *Street Terms*, August 1993
- — Mike Haskins, *Drugs*, p. 281, 2003

snozzled *adjective*
drunk *US, 1947*
- With a mean boat like the one you got, you'll be a menace to public safety. When you get snozzled, it'll be even worse. — James T. Farrell, *Saturday Night*, p. 23, 1947
- — Ramon Adams, *The Language of the Railroader*, p. 142, 1977

snuff *noun*
a murder *US, 1994*
- I picked him up and he copped to those Griffith Park snuffs. — James Ellroy, *Hollywood Nocturnes*, p. 67, 1994

▸ **up to snuff**
enough, sufficient, good enough *UK, 1811*
- I hated the kata, but I knew they had to be up to snuff if I wanted to get my belt. — Odie Hawkins, *Lost Angeles*, p. 63, 1994

snuff; snuff out *verb*
to kill someone *UK, 1932*
In C19 slang, "to die," and then later the transitive "to kill."
- Kenneth "Country" beamer, vice-president of the San Bernadino chapter, had been snuffed by a truck a few days earlier[.] — Hunter S. Thompson, *Hell's Angels*, p. 13, 1966
- When he flashed on that, on the downright outrageousness of that pack of scumbags paying somebody to snuff him, of even insinuating they'd do such a thing, Emmett began to shake with rage. — Emmett Grogan, *Ringolevio*, p. 349, 1972
- What are you guys gonna do, Buff? Snuff a pig? — Oscar Zeta Acosta, *The Revolt of the Cockroach People*, p. 121, 1973
- They snuffed my best friend, Peaches Supreme. — Seth Morgan, *Homeboy*, p. 278, 1990

snuffer *noun*
1 the nose *US, 1945*
- — Lou Shelly, *Hepcats Jive Talk Dictionary*, p. 17, 1945
2 a movie purporting to depict the actual killing of someone, usually a woman *US, 1990*
- They made a snuffer of her. I saw the video. — Seth Morgan, *Homeboy*, p. 278, 1990

snuff film; snuff flick; snuff movie *noun*
a movie purporting to depict the actual killing of someone, usually a woman *US, 1976*
- The film described is what is known in the trades as a "snuff film." This is a film which includes an actual death, murder, or execution scene. — *Adam Film Quarterly*, p. 42, April 1976
- Snuff films are those in which the final sexual act is murder. — Stephen Ziplow, *The Film Maker's Guide to Pornography*, p. 16, 1977
- As far as the Los Angeles Police Department knows, there's never been a snuff film actually verified. — Joseph Wambaugh, *The Glitter Dome*, p. 282, 1981
- So now those nice folks are going to read about her in the paper and maybe even see the snuff flick. — Seth Morgan, *Homeboy*, p. 279, 1990

snuff-out *noun*
a fast and violent loss of position on a surfboard, usually followed by a sudden trip below the ocean surface *US, 1977*
- — Gary Fairmont R. Filosa II, *The Surfer's Almanac*, p. 195, 1977

snuff powder *noun*
adulterated heroin or a white powdered poison used to injure or kill someone using it in the belief it is heroin *US, 1960*
Much better known as a **HOTSHOT**.
- How do you think I know which one slid the snuff powder to Flip? — Clarence Cooper Jr., *The Scene*, p. 183, 1960

snuffy *noun*
any low-ranking soldier in the US Army or Marines, performing a servile or degrading task *US, 1991*
- — Linda Reinberg, *In the Field*, p. 203, 1991

snug *verb*
in horseracing, to rein the horse in to preserve energy for a sprint later in the race *US, 1951*
- — David W. Maurer, *Argot of the Racetrack*, p. 58, 1951
- — Thomas L. Clark, *The Dictionary of Gambling and Gaming*, p. 208, 1987

SO *noun*
used as Internet discussion group shorthand to mean "significant other" *US, 1997*
- — Andy Ihnatko, *Cyberspeak*, p. 177, 1997

so *adverb*
very, extremely *US, 1979*
Attitude and pronunciation separate the slang sense from the standard sense.
- Oh, please, you know, God, you're so the opposite! — *Manhattan*, 1979
- God, I'm so sure. — *Heathers*, 1988
- We're so ready to leave. — *Clueless*, 1995
- I have been six years without one serious relationship, and I am so not bothered by it. — *New York Observer*, 20th May 2002

▸ **so many women/books/etc., so little time**
used as a humorous expression of regret for lost opportunity *US, 1953*
So many variations, so little dictionary space.
- So many things to do and so little to do it with. — Jim Thompson, *Savage Night*, p. 55, 1953
- So many social engagements, so little time. — *Raising Arizona*, 1987
- So many women, so little time. — *Austin Powers*, 1997

soak *noun*
a person who illegally lends money at usurious rates *US, 1951*
- "When you tell me who's banking the soaks along the docks I'll get out." — Mickey Spillane, *The Big Kill*, p. 41, 1951

soak *verb*
to use something as collateral for a loan *US, 1972*
- I had a old raggedy pistol and I was going to soak it to him. — Bruce Jackson, *In the Life*, p. 62, 1972

soaked *adjective*
drunk *US, 1737*
First recorded by Benjamin Franklin in 1737.
- — Collin Baker et al., *College Undergraduate Slang Study Conducted at Brown University*, p. 201, 1968
- — Pamela Munro, *U.C.L.A. Slang*, p. 78, 1989
- Again Rocco thought ahead to the possible trial, the defense bombing out his only witness for being soaked on the night of the murder. — Richard Price, *Clockers*, p. 132, 1992

soaker *noun*
1 a surfer who lingers in the water, rarely catching a wave *US, 1991*
- — Trevor Cralle, *The Surfin'ary*, p. 118, 1991
2 an extremely large halibut *US, 1997*
- — Jim Crotty, *How to Talk American*, p. 5, 1997

so-and-so *noun*
used as a euphemism for any derogatory form of address *UK, 1943*
- Cheeky so-and-so. — Caroline Aherne and Craig Cash, *The Royle Family*, 1999
- You cunning old so-and-so — Brian McDonald, *Elephant Boys*, p. 145, 2000

soap *noun*
1 a soap opera, either in the literal sense of a radio or television melodramatic series or in the figurative sense *US, 1943*
- [S]pecials and the merits of "soaps" and "oaters" (the last two were not commodities, but weepy morning serials for women and western action stories). — Stephen Longstreet, *The Flesh Peddlers*, p. 189, 1962
- The stereo won't work and there's nothing on T.V. except soaps and game shows which I hate. — Beatrice Sparks (writing as 'Anonymous'), *Jay's Journal*, p. 65, 1979
- We other three had settled down to cruise the soaps for skin. — Ethan Morden, *Buddies*, p. 123, 1986
- Senora Sarafina Sanchez Bou-Gomez sat on the worn sofa, watching a Spanish soap, knitting a bit, chewing hard chocolate with the ten

teeth she had on the top and the fifteen on the bottom. — Odie Hawkins, *The Life and Times of Chester Simmons*, p. 12, 1991

2 the recreational drug GHB *US, 1995*
- The drug's street name is GHB, or "soap," or "liquid ecstasy." — *Dallas Morning News*, p. 27A, 20th December 1995

3 ordinary soap used to fill cracks when using explosives to open a safe *US, 1970*
- I never let it impair my business judgment or my work with the soap and soup. — Red Rudensky, *The Gonif*, p. 93, 1970

4 a bribe *US, 1972*
- — Helen Dahlskog (Editor), *A Dictionary of Contemporary and Colloquial Usage*, p. 55, 1972

soap *verb*
to fill cracks when using explosives to open a safe *US, 1952*
- I was soaping the cracks when three buzzes, the danger signal, hit me like a scream out of the night. — Charles Hamilton, *Men of the Underworld*, p. 137, 1952

soapbox derby syndrome *noun*
any rapidly progressing disease or medical condition *US, 1983*
The Soap Box Derby is a downhill coasting race sponsored by the Cub Scouts.
- — *Maledicta*, p. 39, 1983: "More common patient-directed pejoratives used by medical personnel"

SOB *noun*
1 used as a term of abuse: son of a bitch *US, 1918*
- Steve looked at Shane and the younger McMahon flipped him off, revealing himself to be a no-good SOB just like his dad. — Mick Foley, *Have a Nice Day*, p. 683, 2000

2 a sober old bastard *US, 1998*
A term used with affection in twelve-step recovery programs such as Alcoholics Anonymous.
- — Christopher Cavanaugh, *AA to Z*, p. 163, 1998

SOB *adjective*
short of breath; dyspeptic *US, 1988–1989*
- — *Maledicta*, p. 34, 1988–1989: "Medical maledicta from San Francisco"

sob sister *noun*
a soft-hearted, naive person *US, 1912*
- We'd have caught holy hell from all the sob sisters, male and female, in this town if those punks had turned out to be innocent pranksters. — Chester Himes, *The Real Cool Killers*, p. 150, 1959
- He wore his old sap gloves with the lead filled palm and padded knuckles (which a sob sister sergeant had caught him beating up a drunk with and which he had been ordered to get rid of). — Joseph Wambaugh, *The Choirboys*, p. 34, 1975

sob-story artist *noun*
a swindler whose method of operating includes a sentimental narrative of misfortune and an appeal to the emotions of the victim *US, 1954*
- The sob-story artists were much more annoying pests. — Dev Collans with Stewart Sterling, *I was a House Detective*, p. 97, 1954

sociable *adverb*
in poolroom betting, for a small wager *US, 1967*
- When one player says to another "Let's just play sociable," as often as not he means that they should play for only a dollar or two[.] — Ned Polsky, *Hustlers, Beats, and Others*, p. 47, 1967

social *noun*
a government social worker *US, 1995*
- — Maria Hinojas, *Crews*, p. 168, 1995: "Glossary"

▸ **go social**
to stop fighting *US, 1968*
- — Hy Lit, *Hy Lit's Unbelievable Dictionary of Hip Words for Groovy People*, p. 19, 1968
- Another way to reduce the tension was for a gang as a whole to forswear violence and "go social." — James Haskins, *Street Gangs*, p. 102, 1974

sock *noun*
a condom *US, 1992*
- — Judi Sanders, *Kickin' like Chicken with the Couch Commander*, p. 22, 1992

sock *verb*
1 to place something somewhere; to hide something *US, 1942*
- I don't know why they sock so much dough in coats when they spend nine-tenths of their time in bed. — Jim Thompson, *Bad Boy*, p. 352, 1953

2 used for conveying encouragement and support *US, 1960s*
- Go Fidel! Do your thing! Sock it to 'em! — Abbie Hoffman, *Revolution for the Hell of It*, p. 14, 1968

3 (of a male) to have sex *US, 1969*
- Dangerously I was frantic to sock "it" into every young girl weak enough to go for it. — Iceberg Slim (Robert Beck), *Pimp*, p. 31, 1969

▸ **sock it to someone**
1 to attack someone, literally or figuratively *US, 1946*
- Flatter 'em first. Now sock it to her. — Max Shulman, *The Zebra Derby*, p. 104, 1946

2 to have sex with a woman *US, 1969*
- Jesus, look at the old bull socking it to her, and she just lies there with a grin on her face. — Lawrence Block, *No Score [The Affairs of Chip Harrison Omnibus]*, p. 115, 1970
- We got in bed and as bad as I wanted to sock it to her, I didn't. — A.S. Jackson, *Gentleman Pimp*, p. 150, 1973
- "You socking it to that girl?" he asked me ominously one night. — Anne Steinhardt, *Thunder La Boom*, p. 180, 1974

sock hop *noun*
a dance for teenagers *US, 1937*
The term was coined on account of the practice of removing your shoes and dancing in your socks. The practice changed but the term did not.
- A sock full of fun awaits those who attend the latest rage—the sock hop. Students wear school clothes or jeans and dance in their stocking feet. — Nellie Zetta Thompson, *High Times*, p. 142, 1950
- Jordan High had thrown a sock hop on a warm Friday night in November. The Stylistics had been hired, and everyone around the school had been looking forward to the dance. — Donald Goines, *Inner City Hoodlum*, p. 80, 1975

sock it to me!
surprise me!; liven things up *US, 1967*
Borrowed from the vocabulary of Black jazz musicians. Between 1968 and 1970 it was Judy Carne's catchphrase in television variety show *Rowan & Martin's Laugh-In*.
- Sock it to me, mama. — Otis Redding, *Respect*, July 1967
- Sock it to me one time. — Jimi Hendrix, *Wild Thing*, July 1967

socko *adjective*
excellent; outstanding *US, 1938*
- Now, Sid had spotted Biff right off as a socko shitkicker. — Bernard Wolfe, *The Late Risers*, p. 162, 1954
- Myrtle was a socko attraction, although his performances left much to be desired. — Antony James, *America's Homosexual Underground*, p. 136, 1965
- I didn't mind and the deputy said it was a socko idea, so we counted out the money on the hood of the car. — Hunter S. Thompson, *Hell's Angels*, p. 142, 1966

socks *noun*
a linear amplifier for a citizens' band radio *US, 1976*
From the term **FOOTWARMER** (a linear amplifier in a truck).
- — Porter Bibb, *CB Bible*, p. 105, 1976

So Co *noun*
Southern Comfort™ whiskey *US, 1997*
- — Pamela Munro, *U.C.L.A. Slang*, p. 109, 1997

Socrates' pleasure *noun*
anal sex *US, 1993*
- If you want "Socrates' Pleasures" (anal sex), and the lady of your choice declines, complaining about rectal fissures, lesions, poor sphincter control, foreign bodies in the anus, or perforated anal walls, and you're still determined, ask her to recommend someone else who will oblige you. — J.R. Schwartz, *The Official Guide to the Best Cat Houses in Nevada*, p. 18, 1993

soda *noun*
cocaine *US, 1993*
Playing on Coke™ as the most popular soda in the US.
- — Peter Johnson, *Dictionary of Street Alcohol and Drug Terms*, p. 176, 1993

soda jerk *noun*
a person, usually a teenaged boy, who works at a counter at a soda fountain, mixing drinks for customers *US, 1910*
An abbreviation of the earlier (1889) "soda jerker."

- "Coke ..." Mandon said to the soda jerk. — Horace McCoy, *Kiss Tomorrow Good-bye*, p. 244, 1948
- [T]hey go on looking, fabricating preposterous lies about their big scores, cooling off as dishwashers, soda jerks, waiters[.] — William Burroughs, *Junkie*, p. 20, 1953
- [M]y wage as a soda-jerk had been five dollars for an approximate thirty-hour week. — Jim Thompson, *Bad Boy*, p. 336, 1953
- It was cool inside, and the soda jerk looked like an angel in his clean, white uniform. — Dick Gregory, *Nigger*, p. 66, 1964

sod buster *noun*
a business that appears to be legitimate but is in fact a front for criminal activity *US, 1982*
- — Bill Reilly, *Big Al's Official Guide to Chicagoese*, p. 52, 1982

SODDI
the claim of a criminal suspect that "some other dude did it" *US, 1996*
- Zinober might be able to employ the popular SODDI—Some Other Dude Did It—defense. — Donald Davis, *Death Cruise*, p. 236, 1996
- "Are you going to use the S-O-D-D-I defense?" — Joseph Wambaugh, *Hollywood Station*, p. 268, 2006

soft *noun*
1 paper money *US, 1950*
- — Hyman E. Goldin et al., *Dictionary of American Underworld Lingo*, p. 201, 1950

2 in the usage of telephone swindlers, a cash sale *US, 1959*
- — *American Speech*, pp. 150–151, May 1959: "Notes on the cant of the telephone confidence man"

3 cocaine *US, 2002*
- The wiretaps recorded a primer of street slang for powder cocaine: white lady, white fingers, soft, fish scales and sand. — *Orlando Sentinel*, p. B2, 17th August 2002

softball *noun*
any barbiturate or central nervous system depressant *US, 1977*
- — Donald Wesson and David Smith, *Barbiturates*, p. 122, 1977

soft-clothes *adjective*
plain-clothes, not in uniform *US, 1949*
- Some poolroom sharpie lounging in the lobby came to a sitting position when he spotted two hustlers being pulled in by a couple soft-clothes dicks[.] — Nelson Algren, *The Man with the Golden Arm*, p. 265, 1949

soft con *noun*
a confidence swindle accomplished through charm and warmth *US, 1972*
- Giving him the soft con, see? Jim would pretend to be for the guy, pretend to be his friend. — Robert Byrne, *McGoorty*, p. 79, 1972
- She flashed her magnificent teeth at him. He smiled in return. "I don't need that soft con, Ruby," he said. — Donald Goines, *Black Gangster*, p. 156, 1977

softcore *noun*
sexual material that does not show insertion, penetration, an erect penis, spread labia, or ejaculation *US, 1966*
- In soft-core you can show people engaged in sex but not what they're doing it with. — Stephen Ziplow, *The Film Maker's Guide to Pornography*, p. 77, 1977
- Cheri, for example, has its annual fellatio contest (using penis replicas for the softcore market) — E.R. Mahoney, *Human Sexuality*, p. 468, 1983

soft-nose *adjective*
easily learned *US, 1974*
A term of derision applied to the "soft" sciences, for example sociology.
- — Robert Kirk Mueller, *Buzzwords*, p. 144, 1974

soft one *noun*
in necrophile usage, a corpse that has yet to stiffen with rigor mortis *US, 1986–1987*
- — *Maledicta*, p. 180, Summer/Winter 1986–1987: "Sexual slang: prostitutes, pedophiles, flagellators, transvestites, and necrophiles"

soft slugger *noun*
a casino cheat who inserts counterfeit currency into a slot machine *US, 1999*

- Soft sluggers use copying machines. In the privacy of their office, they can create choice pieces of imitation currency that will fool many bill acceptors. — Charles W. Lund, *Robbing the One-Armed Bandits*, p. 129, 1999

soft time *noun*
a relatively short jail sentence, especially one served in an easy-going prison *US, 1983*
- — Marlene Freedman, *Alcatraz*, 1983

software rot *noun*
in computing, an imaginary condition in which unused software or software features stop working if not used *US, 1981*
- — *Coevolution Quarterly*, p. 34, Spring 1981: "Computer slang"
- — Guy L. Steele et al., *The Hacker's Dictionary*, p. 118, 1983

soft white *noun*
powdered cocaine *US, 2005*
- "Gotta get some soft-white, cuz." — Colton Simpson, *Inside the Crips*, p. 162, 2005

softy *noun*
1 a flaccid penis *US, 1995*
- — *Adult Video News*, p. 51, October 1995

2 an inexperienced and/or unskilled poker player *US, 1988*
- — George Percy, *The Language of Poker*, p. 84, 1988

3 in computing, a programing expert who lacks any substantial understanding of computer hardware *US, 1991*
- — Eric S. Raymond, *The New Hacker's Dictionary*, p. 328, 1991

soixante-neuf *noun*
mutual and simultaneous oral sex *UK, 1888*
A direct translation into French of synonymous **69**; perhaps with euphemistic intention, or to lend sophistication to the act.
- [B]efore the film came smoking out of the projector we had seen episodes of lesbianism, homosexuality, soixante-neuf, and group sex. — Roger Gordon, *Hollywood's Sexual Underground*, p. 29, 1966

sojo *noun*
a television journalist who works without a supporting crew *US, 2003*
An abbreviated "solo journalist."
- They are what is known in the trade as one-man bands—or what Sites calls "sojos[.]" — *Los Angeles Times*, pp. 5–16, 16th February 2003

sol *noun*
solitary confinement *US, 1992*
- — William K. Bentley and James M. Corbett, *Prison Slang*, p. 12, 1992

soldier *noun*
1 a regular, low-level member of a criminal organization who can be counted on to follow orders *US, 1963*
- I killed one of their soldiers a few years ago. — Juan Carmel Cosmes, *Memoir of a Whoremaster*, p. 10, 1969
- The bosses are sitting on millions and they say, you no do-a this, you no do-a that—meanwhile they close the books and the soldiers have to drive trucks on the side to live. — Edwin Torres, *Carlito's Way*, p. 41, 1975
- "They gave their soldiers $200 a week to stop selling narcotics," said Valachi. — David Leon Chandler, *Brothers in Blood*, p. 213, 1975
- He ain't one of Cabot's soldiers either. He's gotta be from outta town. — *Reservoir Dogs*, 1992

2 a male lookout for a criminal operation *US, 1956*
- — *American Speech*, p. 97, May 1956: "Smugglers' argot in the southwest"

3 a bottle of alcohol; a can of beer *US, 1945*
- — Lou Shelly, *Hepcats Jive Talk Dictionary*, p. 17, 1945
- Schoons stood up and chucked his can between two trees into the river. "Look at that old soldier go," he mourned. — John Nichols, *The Sterile Cuckoo*, p. 71, 1965

solid *noun*
1 a favor *US, 1973*
- — Connie Eble (Editor), *UNC-CH Campus Slang*, March 1973
- Say, you like sick, like you need a fix / Perhaps I can do some solids for you. — Dennis Wepman et al., *The Life*, p. 55, 1976
- GIANT: "Hey, I'm allergic to smoke. Do me a solid." — *Mo' Better Blues*, 1990
- I know that, but I want to do her a solid. — James Ellroy, *Hollywood Nocturnes*, p. 45, 1994
- Come on Steven, hook me up. Do me this solid. — *Kids*, 1995

2 a trustworthy, dependable person *UK, 1997*
- solid: a person who does not inform — J.G. Narum, *The Convict Cookbook*, p. 162, 2004

solid *adjective*
very good *US, 1935*
A jazz term that arrived on the scene with "swing" in 1935.
- "That Monk is a killer." "Solid." — Irving Shulman, *The Amboy Dukes*, p. 117, 1947
- Or a hipster: "Everything was solid that year." — Jack Kerouac, *Letter to Neal Cassady*, p. 234, 6 October 1950
- My spunk came running back. "How about tonight?" said I. "Solid," said she. — Max Shulman, *The Many Loves of Dobie Gillis*, p. 211, 1951
- ALYSSA: That was the Buffalo Two-Step. HOLDEN: Very solid. — *Chasing Amy*, 1997

solids *noun*
in pool, the solid-colored balls numbered 1 to 7 *US, 1984*
- The other man won it, broke the balls wide and ran half the solids before dogging a thin cut into the corner. — Walter Tevis, *The Color of Money*, p. 114, 1984
- — Steve Rushin, *Pool Cool*, p. 28, 1990

solid sender *noun*
a person, particularly a musician, who is especially inspired or inspiring *US, 1946*
From the jive vocabulary into the rock n' roll lexicon.
- Oh my Linda, she's a solid sender / know you better surrender[.] — Buddy Holly, *Slippin' and Slidin'*, 1963

solo sack time *noun*
time spent sleeping alone *US, 1946*
- — *American Speech*, p. 310, December 1946: "More Air Force slang"
- — *American Speech*, pp. 76–79, February 1963: "Marine Corps slang"

solve *noun*
a crime that has been solved *US, 1992*
- What the fuck do I care if this goes in as a solve or a beat? — Richard Price, *Clockers*, p. 449, 1992

somatomax *noun*
the recreational drug GHB *US, 1990*
In Aldous Huxley's *Brave New World*, 1932, "soma" is the drug of social conditioning.
- The substance [GHB] is sold in Florida health food stores under such brand names as Gamma Oh, GHM, Gamma Hydrate and Somtomax. — *Orlando (Florida) Sentinel*, p. D1, 9th November 1990

some *adverb*
very *US, 1981*
- Some good. — Douglas Simonson, *Pidgin to da Max*, 1981
- We would certainly not conclude an overview of [Prince Edward] Island or Maritime English without some attention to "some" as an intensifier: some good, some hot, some terrible. — T. K. Pratt, *The Garden Transformed*, 1982
- Another word scholar, Lewis J. Poteet, describes a scale of goodness: good, some good, right some good, and right some Jesus good. — Harry Bruce, *Down Home*, p. 107, 1988

somebody up there *noun*
God; a higher power *US, 1957*
Used in a jocular and secular vein in expressions such as "somebody up there likes me."
- Somebody Up There chuckled. — Max Shulman, *Rally Round the Flag, Boys!*, p. 63, 1957

something else *adjective*
beyond description; unbelievable *US, 1968*
- — Hy Lit, *Hy Lit's Unbelievable Dictionary of Hip Words for Groovy People*, p. 36, 1968

sometime *noun*
a person who cannot be relied upon *US, 1981*
- — *Maledicta*, p. 265, Summer/Winter 1981: "By its slang, ye shall know it: the pessimism of prison life"

sometimesy; sometimey *adjective*
moody; unstable; emotionally inconsistent *US, 1972*
- — David Claerbaut, *Black Jargon in White America*, p. 80, 1972
- — Kenn "Naz" Young, *Naz's Underground Dictionary*, p. 57, 1973

son-bitch *noun*
used as a slightly jocular form of son of a bitch *US, 1981*
- If he does, he doesn't show it, because the dumb son-bitch keeps doin' it and things like that[.] — George V. Higgins, *The Rat on Fire*, p. 28, 1981

song and dance *noun*
1 an elaborate performance or presentation of a story, especially in an effort to persuade *US, 1895*
- The way the john parks his vehicle in front of you, and methodically takes off his gloves, and reaches into his pouch for his notebook and practically stretches and yawns and enjoys the scenery before condescends to come over for the full song and dance. — Clancy Sigal, *Going Away*, p. 402, 1961
- Don't I get a sales talk too, you know, your li'l song 'n dance? — Odie Hawkins, *Chicago Hustle*, p. 132, 1977
- I start giving him a song-and-dance, filling him in on the history of how the Church disposed of the cemetery full of good Catholics[.] — Robert Campbell, *The Cat's Meow*, p. 197, 1988

2 a strip search *US, 1976*
- — John R. Armore and Joseph D. Wolfe, *Dictionary of Desperation*, p. 50, 1976

songbird *noun*
1 a female singer *UK, 1886*
- At a time when it was hip to be cool and well-tailored, and female singers were still referred to as "songbirds" and "canaries," the Playboy Club became the most popular nightclub in town. — Kathryn Leigh Scott, *The Bunny Years*, p. 58, 1998

2 a police informer *US, 1970*
- It was a cheap revenge since I'd have liked to take care of that filthy songbird myself. — Red Rudensky, *The Gonif*, p. 103, 1970

songplugger *noun*
a person employed to promote a recorded song by any of a variety of means *US, 1923*
- Even though she was married to a songplugger who was extremely jealous, brooding type, did weightlifting for a hobby. — Bernard Wolfe, *The Late Risers*, p. 35, 1954

son of a bitch *noun*
1 a despicable person *UK, 1605*
- Hunt said an obviously drunken George W. approached his family's table in the restaurant and began loudly cursing at him in front of his young child. "You fucking son of a bitch." — J.H. Hatfield, *Fortunate Son*, p. 74, 2001
- "You're trying to ruin me," Rover charged. "My reputation. You son of a bitch." — James Moore, *Bush's Brain*, p. 19, 2003
- Bill O'Reilly, who likes to torment the guests on his top-rated Fox News show, The O'Reilly Factor, rebutting their arguments with sophisticated epithets such as "pinhead" and "vicious son of a bitch." — *Sunday Tribune*, p. 1, 7th September 2003
- [Joseph] Wilson called Cheney a "lying son of a bitch" during a campaign appearance for John Kerry last December. — *National Review*, 9th August 2004

2 used in extreme comparisons *US, 1953*
- We bought up guns like a son of a bitch then. — Bobby Seale, *Seize the Time*, p. 85, 1970
- We caught a train next day to Idabelle, Oklahoma. It was hotter than a son of a bitch there. — David Honeyboy Edwards, *The World Don't Owe Me Nothing*, p. 141, 1997

son of a bitch!
used as a mild expletive *US, 1953*
- You like Mickey the Mouse? (little girl kicks her) Ohhh—son-of-a-bitch! — *Paper Moon*, 1973
- Holstein glanced at Pike's shoulder tats, then his face. "Sonofabitch. You're Joe Pike." — Robert Crais, *L.A. Requiem*, p. 38, 1999

son-of-a-bitching *adjective*
used as a somewhat profane intensifier *US, 1930*
- "The best son-of-a-bitching officer in the goddamn Navy." — Thomas Heggen, *Mister Roberts*, p. 3, 1946
- Yeah, perhaps we should get on with the sonofabitchin' meeting at that. — Ken Kesey, *One Flew Over the Cuckoo's Nest*, p. 115, 1962
- It's two-thirty in the son-of-a-bitching morning. — Tom Robbins, *Jitterbug Perfume*, p. 245, 1984
- Best son-of-a-bitching division on God's green earth. — Colin L. Powell, *My American Journey*, p. 204, 1995

son-of-a-bitch with slides *noun*
an expert guest speaker at a medical meeting *US, 1984–1985*
- — *Maledicta*, p. 118, 1984–1985: "Milwaukee medical maledicta"

sope *noun*
a recreational drug methaqualone pill, best known as Quaaludes™ *US, 1985*

- By 1972 it was one of the most popular drugs of abuse in the United States and was known as love drug, heroin for lovers, Dr. Jekyll and Mr. Hyde, sopors, sopes, ludes, mandrakes and quacks. — Marilyn Carroll and Gary Gallo, *Methaqualone*, p. 18, 1985

soph *noun*
a second-year student in high school or college *US, 1778*
An abbreviation of "sophomore."

- "He was the only soph on the varsity team, too," Sandy said. — Evan Hunter, *Last Summer*, p. 148, 1968

Sophie *noun*
a girlfriend *US, 1951*
Teen slang.

- — *Newsweek*, p. 28, 8th October 1951

sophisticated lady *noun*
cocaine *US, 1980*

- — Edith A. Folb, *runnin' down some lines*, p. 255, 1980

sop joint *noun*
a Turkish bath *US, 1968*

- He decided to try the sop joint—the bathhouse and masseur's salon on Howard Street[.] — Nathan Heard, *Howard Street*, p. 66, 1968

sopor; soper; soaper *noun*
a recreational drug methaqualone pill, best known as Quaaludes™ *US, 1973*
From a brand name, ultimately from "soporific."

- — Kenn "Naz" Young, *Naz's Underground Dictionary*, p. 57, 1973
- Too many sopors was the culprit. — Richard Meltzer, *A Whore Just Like the Rest*, p. 188, 1973
- By 1972 it was one of the most popular drugs of abuse in the United States and was known as love drug, heroin for lovers, Dr. Jekyll and Mr. Hyde, sopors, sopes, ludes, mandrakes and quacks. — Marilyn Carroll and Gary Gallo, *Methaqualone*, p. 18, 1985
- [S]tinky, sweaty, graceless, tasteless, booger-eating, stash-smoking, sopor-swallowing teen-generates[.] — Chuck Eddy, *Stairway to Hell*, p. 22, 1991

sop-sop *noun*
oral sex *US, 1971*
Another gift to the vocabulary of sex from the Vietnam war.

- "I had a drink and the Mama San told me I could get a boum-boum for 300 piastres or a sop-sop [fellatio] for 500." — Charles Winick, *The Lively Commerce*, p. 265, 1971

sore *adjective*
angry; bitter; disappointed; disgruntled *UK, 1694*

- You were sore anyway 'cause you didn't want to talk to that grand jury. — Elmore Leonard, *Pronto*, p. 49, 1993

sore bitch *noun*
a member of a college sorority *US, 1968*

- — Mary Swift, *Campus Slang (University of Texas)*, 1968

sorority *noun*
a poker game or tournament limited to female players *US, 1996*

- — John Vorhaus, *The Big Book of Poker Slang*, p. 34, 1996

Sorority Sal *noun*
a stereotypical sorority member who looks, dresses, talks, and lives the part *US, 1959*

- — *American Speech*, p. 154, May 1959: "Gator (University of Florida) slang"

sorority sauce *noun*
ketchup *US, 1984–1985*

- — *Maledicta*, p. 284, 1984–1985: "Food names"

sorostitute *noun*
a member of a college sorority *US, 1998*
Derisive, suggesting sexual promiscuity.

- I looked at myself in the mirror once I sobered up and realized that continuing to pledge would end in me becoming a drunken sorostitute. — *Pitt News (University of Pittsburgh)*, 3rd June 1998
- Connie Eble (Editor), *UNC-CH Campus Slang*, p. 9, Spring 2003

sorry about that
used as a jaded response to something bad that has just happened, especially when caused by the speaker *US, 1965*

A keystone of military vernacular during the conflict in Vietnam.

- — *Army Times*, p. 10, 8th December 1965
- — Carl Fleischhauer, *A Glossary of Army Slang*, p. 17, 1968

sorry-ass *adjective*
pathetic; despicable *US, 1967*

- The Marines would try to menace them away at rifle point, shouting, "Di, di, di, you sorry-ass motherfuckers, go on, get the hell away from here." — Ted Solotaroff, *New American Review*, p. 81, 1967
- She transformed my sorry-ass coochi snorcher and raised it up into a kind of heaven. — Eve Ensler, *The Vagina Monologues*, p. 82, 1998
- If he's alive I get to kick some sorry-ass butt, and if he's dead … I'm outta there. — Janet Evanovich, *Seven Up*, p. 6, 2001

sort-edge *verb*
to trim playing cards to facilitate cheating *US, 1959*

- "You ever sort-edge a deck?" — Irving Shulman, *The Short End of the Stick*, p. 97, 1959

SOS *noun*
1 the same old stuff *US, 1963*

- — *American Speech*, p. 272, December 1963: "American Indian student slang"

2 a somewhat older student *US, 2002*
Used by college students to describe, usually unkindly, students in their late twenties or older. Collected from a Los Angeles college student, August 2002.

SOS *adjective*
unable to learn; stuck on stupid *US, 1994*

- — *Los Angeles Times*, p. B8, 19th December 1994

sosh *noun*
1 a member of upper-class society *US, 1993*

- Like the adults, they developed their own social hierarchy, carving up the town into a variety of cliques: greasers, soshes, basies, and those who feel somewhere in between. — Kim Rich, *Johnny's Girl*, p. 154, 1993

2 a student whose emphasis is on social activities *US, 1968*

- — Collin Baker et al., *College Undergraduate Slang Study Conducted at Brown University*, p. 201, 1968
- He wasn't a sosh and he wasn't an athlete and he wasn't a bad ass. — James Ellroy, *Blood on the Moon*, p. 237, 1984

sot *noun*
an alcoholic dulled by drinking *UK, 1592*

- Ill-matched sots for parents. — Edwin Torres, *Q & A*, p. 194, 1977
- Then Swaggart, crazed by hubris, tried to take out yet another of his rivals—Preacher Gorman from New Orleans, by calling him a sot, a pervert and a dangerous child molester who couldn't help himself. — Hunter S. Thompson, *Generation of Swine*, p. 21, 22nd February 1988

so? throw party!
used for dismissing the importance of what has just been said *US, 1982*
Hawaiian youth usage.

- "Dahlene! I made cheerleadah!" "So? T'row pahty!" — Douglas Simonson, *Pidgin to da Max: Hana Hou*, 1982

soul *noun*
1 the essence of black culture *US, 1965*

- "Many, what can anybody see in a gray chick, when colored chicks are so fine; they got so much soul." This was the coming of the "soul" thing too. — Claude Brown, *Manchild in the Promised Land*, p. 172, 1965

2 a black person *US, 1968*

- Five of them, three Italians and two souls, whipped up three small white boys last night. — David Parks, *GI Diary*, p. 7, 1968

soul *adjective*
pertaining to the essence of black culture *US, 1946*

- — *Current Slang*, p. 5, Fall 1966
- Soul. Most times used as an adjective—in conjunction with such activities as eating, politics, music or social exchanges. — Sidney Bernard, *This Way to the Apocalypse*, p. 57, 1968
- The use of "soul" in black parlance drives in this same direction, toward a sense of ethnic unity based on some innate, irrational sense of community, brotherhood. — Roger Abrahams, *Positively Black*, p. 149, 1970

- The AAA gave "Soul Parties." Everyone gretting with the new handshake, doing African dances that looked like overexaggerated gyrations. — Bobby Seale, *A Lonely Rage*, p. 164, 1978

Soul Alley; Soul City; Soulsville *noun*
an area in Saigon with bars and brothels patronized largely by black US soldiers *US, 1970*

- Americans stationed or spending leave in Saigon go to Soul City, a few seedy waterfront blocks. — Maxwell Boas, *The Drug Beat*, p. 149, 1970
- For example, black soldiers in Saigon prefer the Kahn Hoi river front district, formerly the hang-out of the black Senegalese troops during the French occupation, and now dubbed "Soulsville." — Helen Hughes, *Racial and Ethnic Relations*, p. 18, 1970
- Between 400 and 500 of these live in an area of Saigon which is called Soul Alley. The area is "off limits" to US personnel and one enters at his own risk. — Senate Committee on Labor and Public Welfare, *Military Drug Abuse*, p. 61, 1971
- Not too far from the main gate of Tan Son Nhut was Soul Alley, where you could find Cambodian girls in bars who could readily pass for black females. — Wallace Terry, *Bloods*, p. 164, 1984

soul brother *noun*
a black man *US, 1970*

- A certain Soul Brother passing by took out his heat and shot both of them bastards. — Babs Gonzales, *Movin' On Down De Line*, p. 54, 1975

soul food *noun*
food associated with southern black culture *US, 1964*

- The emphasis on Soul Food is counter-revolutionary black bourgeois ideology. — Eldridge Cleaver, *Soul on Ice*, p. 29, 1968
- After a huge dinner of "soul food," half-chicken and bowls of "greens," John took the wheel and drove toward the scene of the fight[.] — L.H. Whittemore, *Cop!*, p. 144, 1969
- In most European cities there is one swinging pad where there's a piano, records, etc., and good home soul food. — Babs Gonzales, *Movin' On Down De Line*, p. 106, 1975
- We don't even have our own food. Soul food is not black food. It's just some nasty shit they fed to the slaves. You think a ham hock tasted good the first time the white man shoved it in our faces? No. — Chris Rock, *Rock This!*, p. 13, 1997

soul kiss *noun*
a sustained, open-mouthed kiss *US, 1948*

- Lonely librarians unite in soul kiss of halitosis. — William S. Burroughs, *Naked Lunch*, p. 189, 1959
- They looked at a Roy Lichtenstein blowup of a love-comic panel showing a young blood couple with their lips parted in the moment before a profound, tongue-probing, post-teen, American soul kiss. — Tom Wolfe, *The Painted Word*, p. 72, 1975
- He gave her a long, lingering soul kiss. "Wow!" she said, backing off and gasping for breath. — Jackie Collins, *Dangerous Kiss*, p. 202, 1999

soul kiss *verb*
to give someone a deep and intimate kiss, usually involving tongue or tongues *US, 1968*

- She led him to the bedroom and soul-kissed him so his knees trembled. — Martin Dibner, *The Admiral*, p. 210, 1968
- He planted one hand on the back of her head, tilted her face to the side, and soulkissed her to the bottom of her feet. — Rachel Gibson, *Simply Irresistible*, p. 69, 1998

soul patch *noun*
a trimmed patch of hair in the cleft of a man's chin *US, 1986*

- Okay, I thought Luke Perry with a bad pageboy haircut and a soul patch looked funny as hell. — rec.arts.movies, 3rd August 1992
- "Wait, Mer, I want you to meet someone," she said, waving to blond gangly giant with clunky black Elvis Costello glasses and a soul patch. — Moon Unit Zappa, *America the Beautiful*, p. 142, 2001

soul sister *noun*
a black woman *US, 1967*

- I've also noticed that most of our soul sisters, they marry whitey. — Babs Gonzales, *Movin' On Down De Line*, p. 37, 1975

soulville *noun*
a part of a city inhabited largely by black people *US, 1975*

- He hired me to gig for him after I closed in soulville so we just moved downtown to whitey-ville for six more weeks. — Babs Gonzales, *Movin' On Down De Line*, p. 33, 1975

sound *noun*
1 a style of speech, including vocabulary, syntax, and attitude *US, 1958*

- Naturally, the trigger gang of San Francisco talks the same "sound" as the Rovers of Brooklyn. — Harrison E. Salisbury, *The Shook-up Generation*, p. 158, 1958

2 a taunt or tease; an insult *US, 1967*

- "Forget it, Brew. I'm sorry for the sound." — Piri Thomas, *Down These Mean Streets*, p. 122, 1967

sound *verb*
1 to speak or inform; to tease someone; to flirt; to insult someone in a semiformal quasi-friendly competition *US, 1959*

- So, when the Hepcat sounded her, she was bound to beat him down[.] — Dan Burley, *Diggeth Thou?*, p. 34, 1959
- Alfredo and I had never been too tight and we never seemed to miss a chance to sound each other. — Piri Thomas, *Down These Mean Streets*, p. 109, 1967
- I sound on Joan if she thinks she got time for me to go phone around and see what I can do, get help I guess is what I meant. — *The Digger Papers*, p. 10, August 1968
- I mean, why aren't you sounding on her? It's obvious that you want to. — Cecil Brown, *The Life & Loves of Mr. Jiveass Nigger*, p. 187, 1969

2 to glare at or intimidate someone with a look *US, 1955*

- — *New York Times*, p. 2, 15th May 1955

soundbox *noun*
the throat *US, 1946*

- When she wasn't shouting her head off she just moaned way down in her soundbox. — Mezz Mezzrow, *Really the Blues*, p. 74, 1946

sound down *verb*
to speak to someone in a probing or inquiring way *US, 1990*

- They wanted to go and get coffee but I had a habit and I knew I was wasting time with them because I'd already been sounded down for money. — Herbert Huncke, *Guilty of Everything*, p. 72, 1990

sounding *noun*
ritualistic insulting or teasing *US, 1962*

- Clubroom activities included "sounding"—the standard needling and picking on another[.] — Lewis Yablonsky, *The Violent Gang*, p. 111, 1962

sounds *noun*
recorded music *US, 1955*

- I have within my comfy shed bottles of rare red wine and lots of sides and tapes of sounds. — Dan Burley, *Diggeth Thou?*, p. 33, 1959
- I was starved for some sounds that might warp my brain a little. — Lester Bangs, *Psychotic Reactions and Carburetor Dung*, 1971
- After the club officially closed up there'd be a small group of us left and we'd sit around smoking pot and listening to sounds—Billie Holiday, Charlie Parker, he had recordings of all the greats. — Herbert Huncke, *Guilty of Everything*, p. 135, 1990
- The first thing I bought with the proceeds was a 68" Chevy and some sounds. — Sanyika Shakur, *Monster*, p. 252, 1993

sounds like a personal problem
used for silencing a complaint without sympathy *US, 1968*

- — Carl Fleischhauer, *A Glossary of Army Slang*, p. 1, 1968

soup *noun*
1 nitroglycerin, or any explosive used for opening a safe *US, 1902*

- "You man the soup man too? You got hold of him?" — George Clayton Johnson, *Ocean's Eleven*, p. 142, 1960
- What I mean, he doesn't go in for the soup and detonator bit. — Robert Emond Alter, *Carny Kill*, p. 102, 1966
- I decided to use every trick in the drilling business I had ever heard of to sieve it for the soup. — Red Rudensky, *The Gonif*, p. 7, 1970

2 in the television and movie industries, the chemicals used to develop film *US, 1990*

- — Ralph S. Singleton, *Filmmaker's Dictionary*, p. 157, 1990

3 cocaine *US, 1993*

- He knew, for instance, that the substance called rock or crack in the other American cities he'd visited in the past year and a half was called "soup" in Seattle. — Bob Sipchen, *Baby Insane and the Buddha*, p. 391, 1993
- — Mark S. Fleisher, *Beggars & Thieves*, p. 291, 1995: "Glossary"

4 foaming water left after a wave breaks *US, 1961*
- I maneuvered our board to keep out of the soup but didn't quite manage. — Frederick Kohner, *Gidget Goes Hawaiian*, p. 80, 1961
- — Grant W. Kuhns, *On Surfing*, p. 122, 1963

5 rain *US, 1945*
- — Lou Shelly, *Hepcats Jive Talk Dictionary*, p. 17, 1945

6 in shuffleboard, the scoring area of the court *US, 1967*
- — Omero C. Catan, *Secrets of Shuffleboard Strategy*, p. 72, 1967: "Glossary of Terms"

▸ **in the soup**
in grave trouble *US, 2001*
- Something's going on, right? You're in the soup, just like me, aren't ya? — Stephen J. Cannell, *The Tin Collectors*, p. 87, 2001

soup can *noun*
a gas grenade *US, 1978*
- Also in the coffin were two SN Speediheat gas grenades for outdoor use, two EN glast dispersion gas grenades, or "soup cans," for indoor work, plus gas masks. — Jon A. Jackson, *The Blind Pig*, p. 7, 1978

souped *adjective*
drunk *US, 1954*
- "You'll find her souped to the ears in the local pub." — Curt Cannon, *Deadlier Than the Mail*, p. 133, 1954

soup out *verb*
to ride a wave into the foaming water produced by the breaking wave *US, 1963*
- — Grant W. Kuhns, *On Surfing*, p. 122, 1963

soup-strainer *noun*
a moustache *US, 1946*
- With that waxed soup-strainer of his and that slick hair, Johnny took on some grotesque features in my hot mind. — Mezz Mezzrow, *Really the Blues*, p. 181, 1946

soup suit *noun*
a dinner jacket *US, 1954*
- — Jerry Robertson, *Oil Slanguage*, p. 115, 1954

soup to nuts *noun*
start to finish; all of something *US, 2002*
- I laid the whole thing, soup to nuts, for the girl now called Buttercup. — David Henry Sterry, *Chicken*, p. 153, 2002

sourball *noun*
a person with a sour disposition *US, 1900*
- Well, I just miss being a humorous author—so I just miss being a one hundred percent sourball. — Philip Wylie, *Opus 21*, p. 32, 1949

sourdough *noun*
1 a person with considerable experience in Alaska *US, 1898*
- — Russell Tabbert, *Dictionary of Alaskan English*, p. 37, 1991

2 in Alaska, homebrew alcohol *US, 1915*
- — Russell Tabbert, *Dictionary of Alaskan English*, p. 89, 1991

sour paper *noun*
a forged check *US, 1966*
- — Rose Giallombardo, *Society of Women*, p. 212, 1966: Glossary of Prison Terms

sourpuss *noun*
a grumbler: a misery: a killjoy *US, 1937*
From the "sour" look on his or her **PUSS** (face).
- It smells good to me, even if you are a hateful sourpuss. — Henry Miller, *Sexus*, p. 371, 1965

soused *adjective*
drunk *US, 1932*
- "I think I'm a little soused." So he had been drinking. — S.E. Hinton, *The Outsiders*, p. 43, 1967
- I was bombed, man. Three sheets to the wind. Soused. — Gerald Petievich, *To Die in Beverly Hills*, p. 206, 1983
- The reek of liquor spills into the patrol car—the man is soused. — Josh Alan Friedman, *Tales of Times Square*, p. 136, 1986
- Sammy started celebrating a little too early and got thoroughly soused[.] — Tempest Storm, *Tempest Storm*, p. 134, 1987

south *noun*
▸ **go south**
to palm and hide something, usually dice or cards *US, 1962*
- — Frank Garcia, *Marked Cards and Loaded Dice*, p. 262, 1962

south 48; south 49 *noun*
in Alaska, all states except Alaska *US, 1984*
- — *American Speech*, pp. 256–258, Fall 1984: "Terms for 'Not Alaska' in Alaskan English"

South Austin suitcase *noun*
a brown paper bag used to conceal a beer you want to drink on the street *US, 2001*
- Another factor these guys consider is the so-called South Austin suitcase, the small brown paper bag the beer should be put in before it leaves the building. — *Austin American-Statesman*, 4th November 2001

South County Indian *noun*
a Portuguese immigrant or Portuguese-American *US, 1989*
Rhode Island usage, alluding to the large Portuguese population.
- — *Maledicta*, p. 233, 1988–1989: "The Portagee in speech and joke"

Southern and Seven *noun*
an alcoholic drink consisting of Southern Comfort™ whiskey mixed with Seven-Up™ soda *US, 1989*
- Meanwhile he spent his leisure time drinking Southern and Sevens and watching TV with Donna pawing him or listening to her tell him how, after devoting her life to corrections, they had treated her like dirt. — Elmore Leonard, *Killshot*, p. 19, 1989

Southern engineering *noun*
a sloppy job of design or manufacture *US, 1984*
- — Ken Weaver, *Texas Crude*, p. 93, 1984

Southern love *noun*
mouth-to-penis contact immediately after the penis is withdrawn from a rectum *US, 1995*
- — *Adult Video News*, p. 40, September 1995

Southie *nickname*
an Irish-American enclave in south Boston; the neighborhood itself *US, 1967*
An area famous for its support of the Irish Republican Army, its opposition to school busing to achieve racial integration, and its antihomosexual stance.
- A native of Southie, he is no longer popular there. — Bill Cardoso, *The Maltese Sangweech*, p. 147, 1984
- Named after a rough-and-tumble Southie street, the Gustins survived in name only[.] — Gerard O'Neill, *The Under Boss*, p. 19, 1989
- He sounded like he was from Southie. — Michelle Tea, *Rent Girl*, p. 146, 2004

south of the border *adverb*
in or to the area of the genitals, especially a woman's *US, 1945*
- On the bottom of the report the doctor noted that "these women were examined from the waist up." The Stars and Stripes headlined the story: DEPENDS ON HOW YOU LOOK AT IT, SAYS JAP DOC WHO DIDN'T GO SOUTH OF BORDER. — *Newsweek*, p. 65, 19th November 1945
- [N]ot just getting hot flashes south of the border[.] — Wolfman Jack (Bob Smith), *Have Mercy!*, p. 89, 1995
- He's not packing very much south of the border. — *America's Sweethearts*, 2001

southpaw *noun*
a left-handed person, especially a left-handed athlete *US, 1891*
- [H]e almost tore my jaw off with a left cross. I hadn't figured him to be a southpaw. — Piri Thomas, *Down These Mean Streets*, p. 260, 1967

SP *noun*
the US Navy's Shore Patrol, or internal police *US, 1951*
- The Navy's shore patrol takes over most of the policing. We saw Navy paddy-wagons in front of Guy's, the Ship's Cafe and the Penguin. But the SP's seldom make a pinch unless there are fights. — Jack Lait and Lee Mortimer, *Washington Confidential*, p. 33, 1951

space *noun*
1 privacy, time alone, emotional separation *US, 1977*
- "I mean, we really flipped out when Joannie pulled that whole Moonie number, but it came out okay after we got her deprogramed. I think she just needed space, you know?" — Cyra McFadden, *The Serial*, p. 66, 1977

2 a year, especially a year in prison *US, 1950*
- — Hyman E. Goldin et al., *Dictionary of American Underworld Lingo*, p. 202, 1950

space *verb*
to daydream; to wander off mentally *US, 1995*
- Thirty-four, that's freezing, for Christ sake. Yo, Chili, you're spacin'.
— *Get Shorty*, 1995

spacebase *noun*
a cigar wrapper filled with phencyclidine and crack cocaine *US, 1992*
- — Terry Williams, *Crackhouse*, p. 151, 1992

space cadet *noun*
a heavily drugged hospital patient *US, 1988–1989*
- — *Maledicta*, p. 35, 1988–1989: "More Milwaukee medical maledicta"

space case; space cadet; space head *noun*
a person who is completely out of touch with their surroundings *US, 1974*
- — Robert Kirk Mueller, *Buzzwords*, p. 145, 1974
- Who would do that? Nobody here would give that space case a drink. — Vincent Patrick, *The Pope of Greenwich Village*, p. 14, 1979
- Like my mother is like a total space cadet. — Moon Unit and Frank Zappa, *Valley Girl*, 1982
- Oh, and you are such a superficial space cadet. — *Clueless*, 1995

space cowboy *noun*
a disoriented, distracted person *US, 1977*
- Comes back such a mindfuck he can't remember. Fuckin space cowboy. — John Sayles, *Union Dues*, p. 313, 1977

spaced *adjective*
1 in a state of drug intoxication, especially as a result of hallucinogen use but loosely of any drug *US, 1967*
- — Ruth Bronsteen, *The Hippy's Handbook*, p. 16, 1967
- "You okay?" Ted asks, noticing I'm spaced. "Yeah, i'm finee," I assure him, "I'm just stoned is all." — Jim Carroll, *Forced Entries*, p. 108, 1987
2 unaware; unfocused; highly distracted *US, 1967*
- — Joe David Brown (Editor), *The Hippies*, p. 219, 1967: "Glossary of hippie terms"
- I was just spaced, my dears, so I stayed only long enough for a sandwich. — *Screw*, p. 15, 22nd December 1969
- — *American Speech*, p. 66, Spring–Summer 1975: "Razorback slang"

spacedancing *noun*
in the language surrounding the Grateful Dead, the freeform dancing practiced by band followers *US, 1994*
- Freeform gestures involving gentle bending at knees, swaying of the arms, and rocking of the head, combined with expressive movements of the hands. — David Shenk and Steve Silberman, *Skeleton Key*, p. 267, 1994

spaced out *adjective*
1 drug-intoxicated; disoriented *US, 1970*
Conventionally "space" is beyond the frontiers of normality.
- If I didn't know better I'd never come down myself. I was just lying there spaced out in all that beauty of mountain and streams and trees. — Beatrice Sparks (writing as "Anonymous"), *Jay's Journal*, 1979
2 stupefied from anesthetic *US, 1973*
- — *American Speech*, p. 205, Fall–Winter 1973: "The language of nursing"

spacer *noun*
a mace cigarette *US, 1967*
- and come out in the hallway, lighting cigarettes and bullshittin and clinching deals for mae or "spacers" before the hack ran us back to our units — Clarence Cooper Jr., *The Farm*, p. 40, 1967

spad *nickname*
a Douglas aircraft A-1 Skyraider, used for close air support of ground troops *US, 1968*
- By that time the Skyraider had become widely known as the Spad, a name which reflected the affection in which it was held by its pilots. — Peter Bowers, *United States Navy Aircraft Since 1911*, p. 171, 1968
- "Spad" was the nickname for the prop-driven, A-1 Douglas Skyraider. The A-1 was based on a design so old it reminded the jet jockeys of the famous S.P.A.D. biplane fighter of the First World War. — T.E. Cruise, *Wings of Gold III*, p. 267, 1989
- The helicopter, a "Big Mother," was joined by two A-1 Skyraiders (also known as "Spads") for protection[.] — Robert K. Wilcox, *Scream of Eagles*, p. 59, 1990

- [T]his time flying the old "spads" as the A-1Es were nicknamed. — Harold Moore, *We Were Soldiers Once ... And Young*, p. 83, 1992

spade *noun*
a black person *US, 1928*
Used as an insider's word without racist overtones until the early 1970s.
- And down there, with something like that happening and only a few Spades (colored folks) around, it wasn't so good. — Louis Armstrong, *Satchmo*, p. 146, 1954
- In the Haight the word "Negro" is almost never used. "Black" is employed by people tinged with New Left polluted understanding, the most common word is "spade." — Nicholas Von Hoffman, *We Are The People Our Parents Warned Us Against*, p. 102, 1967
- Those of us who dropped out before acid have lived/loved with spades & know where it's at, but the new kids don't. — *Berkeley Barb*, p. 7, 3rd March 1967
- I gave away a copy of my pamphlet and wound up in conversation with the guy who took it, this young spade kid who had the most intense brown eyes I have ever seen. — Gurney Norman, *Divine Right's Trip (Last Whole Earth Catalog)*, p. 121, 1971

▸ **in spades**
to a great degree *US, 1929*
- I'm just talking about that crummy meeting and what that nurse and those other bastards did to you. Did in spades. — Ken Kesey, *One Flew Over the Cuckoo's Nest*, p. 56, 1962
- I am here to tell you that that ofay boy has really got sex appeal in spades! — Gore Vidal, *Myra Breckinridge*, p. 90, 1968
- You'll pay for what you've done! You'll pay in spades! — *Mallrats*, 1995

spades *noun*
shoes with pointed toes *US, 1955*
Teen slang.
- — *American Weekly*, p. 2, 14th August 1955

spaghetti *adjective*
Italian *US, 1969*
- The director on this great epic spaghetti picture not only barely speaks English, he hasn't the slightest fucking idea what he's doing. — Elmore Leonard, *Gold Coast*, p. 152, 1980

spaghetti and macaroni *noun*
sadomasochism *US, 1989*
Disguising the initialism **S AND M**.
- — Thomas E. Murray and Thomas R. Murrell, *The Language of Sadomasochism*, p. 125, 1989

spaghetti-bender *noun*
an Italian or Italian-American *US, 1967*
- There's all kinds of people born there. Colored people, Puerto Ricans like me, an'—even spaghetti-benders like you. — Piri Thomas, *Down These Mean Streets*, pp. 25–26, 1967

spaghetti-eater *noun*
an Italian or Italian-American *US, 1918*
- "The spaghetti-eater's picture was a failure at the Rivoli," smilingly she summed up Enrico Caruso's film. — *The New Movies*, p. 18, 1949

spaghetti strap *noun*
very thin shoulder straps on a woman's garment; the garment itself *US, 1972*
- "Sure," Maya said, "and those slippery Republican hatchet men're out there beating the bushes for another smoking bimbo in a spaghetti-strap. Is that any way to win an election?" — Joseph Wambaugh, *Finnegan's Week*, p. 112, 1993

spaghetti western *noun*
a cowboy film about the American "wild west" produced by the Italian film industry *US, 1967*
Lesser-known variants include the "Sukiyaki Western" for the Japanese equivalent and the "Chili Western" for the Mexican equivalent.
- But it is almost as familiar as pasta on Italian tongues here in Rome since the release of what have come to become known as the spaghetti Westerns. — *Syracuse Herald Journal*, p. 38, 11th October 1967
- [D]ead, shot full of holes by the new trend of "spaghetti" Westerns. That didn't match the box office figures. — Jane Pattie, *John Wayne ... There Rode a Legend*, p. 193, 2001

spam *noun*

unsolicited, unwanted, often fraudulent advertising messages sent by e-mail *US, 1994*

- Internet users suffered another "spam attack" last week, this time from a Florida public-access host user who flooded Usenet conferences with ads for a thigh-reducing cream. — *Network World*, p. 2, 30th May 1994

spam *verb*

to post e-mail in unwanted quantities, especially advertising matter to people who don't want it *US, 1994*

Ultimately from branded tinned meat Spam™ (a compound of spiced ham); popular etymology insists that this usage is inspired by the Monty Python sketch, 1970, set in a café in which nothing but unwanted Spam is served.

- In contrast, the cost to spam an advertisement in thousands of news groups, where it is potentially read by hundreds of thousands of computer users, is typically less than $50. — *New York Times*, p. 51, 7th May 1994

spange *verb*

to ask someone for spare change *US, 1994*

Originally a term associated with followers of the Grateful Dead; a contraction of the "bro, can you spare any change?"

- Now I know that this isn't the reason for all people to Spange (most are just lazy), but it is a factor with some. — *rec.music.gdead*, 13th November 1994: The Parking Lot Situation
- We told him we were going to spange (ask for spare change) until we got enough money to get the van out. — *Vashon-Maury Island Beachcomber*, p. A3, 1st November 2006

Spanish *noun*

sex with a man's penis stimulated between a woman's breasts until he ejaculates *US, 1981*

- "[S]tick to Swedish massage (by hand), or French (by mouth), and only go Spanish (between the breasts), Russian (between the thighs), American (a body roll) or Danish (inside) if it's worth the money." — Alix Shulman, *On the Stroll*, p. 133, 1981

Spanish curse *noun*

in dominoes, the 3 – 3 piece *US, 1959*

- — Dominic Armanino, *Dominoes*, p. 17, 1959

spank *verb*

1 to rob someone *US, 1976*

- — John R. Armore and Joseph D. Wolfe, *Dictionary of Desperation*, 1976

2 (used of a male) to masturbate *US, 1994*

- JAY: "Not in me." That's what she says. I gotta pull out and spank it to get it on. — *Clerks*, 1994

3 to slap the inside of the arm to draw out veins for a drug injection *US, 1997*

- — Jim Emerson-Cobb, *Scratching the Dragon*, April 1997

▶ **spank the monkey**

(used of a male) to masturbate *US, 1999*

- Spanking the monkey. Flogging the bishop. Choking the chicken. Jerking the gherkin. — *American Beauty*, 1999
- "Some real beauts I spanked the monkey to." — Josh Friedman, *When Sex Was Dirty*, p. 106, 2005

spank bank *noun*

a notional collection of fantasies to rely upon while masturbating *US, 1999*

- Yasmine Bleeth is what I call a permanent deposit in the spank bank. — *3dfx.products.voodoo3*, 5th June 1999
- The Yanks finally added Emmanuelle to their collective spank bank in 1996[.] — Mr. Skin, *Mr. Skin's Skincyclopedia*, p. 51, 2005
- Now my mother just became part of his spank bank. — Jill Ferguson, *Sometimes Art Can't Save You*, p. 22, 2005

spanky pants *noun*

sports underwear worn by cheerleaders *US, 1994*

- Her running uniform included "stupid little spanky pants—which never stay." — *GenderWatch*, p. 63, Spring 2002
- Stick a herkie in those spanky pants and get EXCITED! — *Chicago Sun-Times*, p. Show-2, 21st December 2003

spansula *noun*

a combination of central nervous system depressants and stimulants *US, 1971*

- — Eugene Landy, *The Underground Dictionary*, p. 174, 1971

spare *noun*

a friend *US, 1947*

- — Marcus Hanna Boulware, *Jive and Slang of Students in Negro Colleges*, 1947

spare tire *noun*

a roll of fat around the waist *US, 1961*

- — *Woman's Realm*, 11th March 1967

spark *verb*

1 to shoot and kill *US, 2000*

- You spark one fool, you going to smell the vapors, might as well not leave no witnesses. — Paul Beatty, *Tuff*, p. 4, 2000

2 to light a cigarette or a marijuana cigarette *US, 1995*

Also variant "spark up."

- It is one thing to spark up a dubie and get laced at parties, but it is quite another to be fried all day. — *Clueless*, 1995

3 to see something or someone *US, 1972*

Hawaiian youth usage.

- — Elizabeth Ball Carr, *Da Kine Talk*, p. 150, 1972

4 in horseracing, to use an electrical device to shock a horse during a race *US, 1951*

- — David W. Maurer, *Argot of the Racetrack*, p. 58, 1951

sparkle *noun*

strong and pure methamphetamine with a crystalline appearance *US, 1989*

- — Geoffrey Froner, *Digging for Diamonds*, p. 69, 1989: "Types of speed"

sparkle plenty *noun*

an amphetamine tablet *US, 1969*

Named after a character in the *Dick Tracy* comic strip.

- — Richard Lingeman, *Drugs from A to Z*, 1969

sparkler *noun*

1 a diamond *UK, 1822*

- There were so many buxom madams of both races jammed in there, sporting big sparklers and fancy corsages. — Mezz Mezzrow, *Really the Blues*, p. 91, 1946
- We just sat around feeling the sparklers, counting them, sorting them out according to their size, counting them again until the flashlight went dead. — Rocky Garciano (with Rowland Barber), *Somebody Up There Likes Me*, p. 66, 1955
- When he got into the room where the sparklers were he found a corpse laid out on the bed. — Charles Raven, *Underworld Nights*, p. 191, 1956

2 an amphetamine pill *US, 1994*

- — US Department of Justice, *Street Terms*, August 1994

spastic *adjective*

incompetent; uncoordinated; unfashionable *US, 1963*

A cruel allusion to spastic paralysis.

- Well, it was sort of campusy, with everyone just spastic—looking at us. — Frederick Kohner, *The Affairs of Gidget*, p. 77, 1963
- You spastic creep! — *American Graffiti*, 1973

spaz *noun*

an uncoordinated or incompetent individual; a fool *US, 1956*

Contemptuous and derogatory use of "spastic" (a person with spastic paralysis). Also used in the variants "spazz" and "spas."

- — J.R. Friss, *A Dictionary of Teenage Slang (Mt. Diablo High)*, 1964
- — Collin Baker et al., *College Undergraduate Slang Study Conducted at Brown University*, p. 202, 1968
- It's some joke, the old man has been a total spaz since the year one, the coordination of a five-year-old, and here I've got these three—jocks. — John Sayles, *Union Dues*, p. 103, 1977

spaz out; spazz out *verb*

to act in a very awkward or uncoordinated manner; to lose emotional control *US, 1957*

- They're spazzed out on ganja anyway, they don't give a shit, they're gone. — Elmore Leonard, *Glitz*, p. 113, 1985
- I didn't tell you because I knew you'd spaz out, but the last train left an hour ago. — *200 Cigarettes*, 1999

speak *noun*

a bar where alcohol is served illegally *US, 1930*

A shortened form of SPEAKEASY.

- It was during this era that a Yale student, whooping it up in one of the block's posh speaks, wandered from room to room wearing a puzzled frown. — Robert Sylvester, *No Cover Charge*, p. 71, 1956
- [T]he Feds had an uncommonly adept knack of knocking over speaks. — Red Rudensky, *The Gonif*, p. 94, 1970

speak *verb*

▶ **speak the real**

to speak the truth, unpleasant as it might be *US, 1998*

- — Ethan Hilderbrant, *Prison Slang*, p. 164, 1998

speak!

tell me what's on your mind! *US, 1975*

- He said, "Speak, speak." So I said, "Well, I want to stay." — Hunter S. Thompson, *Songs of the Doomed*, p. 170, May 1975

speakeasy *noun*

a bar that sells alcohol illegally *US, 1889*

- Bootlegging and speakeasies are out. — Jack Lait and Lee Mortimer, *Chicago Confidential*, p. 145, 1950
- Jesus wouldn't be afraid to walk into this joint or any other speakeasy to preach the gospel. — Richard Brooks, *Elmer Gantry*, 1960

speaker *noun*

a gun *US, 1970*

- — Clarence Major, *Dictionary of Afro-American Slang*, p. 107, 1970

spear *noun*

a hypodermic needle *US, 1961*

- — Francis J. Rigney and L. Douglas Smith, *The Real Bohemia*, p. xx, 1961

▶ **take the spear**

to accept responsibility *US, 1989*

Colonel Oliver North popularized the phrase during the moral collapse of the Reagan presidency in 1986 and 1987, explaining that while he had said that he would "take the spear" for the administration's misdeeds in Iran and Nicaragua, he did not mean that he would accept responsibility if criminal prosecution became a possibility.

- Those of us who were won by his performance as an articulate witness may want to rethink our opinions as we watch him perform when it is really time to "take the spear." [Letter to the editor], — *Washington Post*, p. A18, 24th February 1989
- I've taken the spear for a lot of people. — *Gone in 60 Seconds*, 2000

spear-chucker *noun*

1 a black person *US, 1967*

Offensive. An allusion to the jungles of Africa.

- Think of the thousand names hung on them trailing back into the darkest alleys of our racist past: coon; jig; darky; shine; Sambo; Jim Crow; buck; spearchucker etc. — Ken Kesey, *Kesey's Jail Journal*, p. 14, 1967
- — *Current Slang*, p. 10, Winter 1969
- "Spearchukka." "Motherfuckah, ahm gonna chuck a spear at year!" — Richard Price, *The Wanderers*, p. 160, 1974
- You're not even a name anymore. Just a spear-chucker with a goddamn number stenciled on the back of his prison fatigues. — *48 Hours*, 1982

2 a vocal, aggressive advocate *US, 1997*

- When he ran for re-election in 1992, he bragged that "Every lesbian spear chucker in this country is hoping I get defeated." — *NRC Quartler*, Winter 1997

spear phishing *noun*

an internet fraud scheme that extracts information from targeted victims *US, 2005*

- Those Internet attacks ranged from a single e-mail with an embedded virus sent to millions of Internet users to a new breed of "spear phishing" attacks designed to steal information from a single individual or company. — *Kansas City Star*, p. A1, 2nd August 2005

special a la coke *noun*

the recreational drug ketamine in powder, capsule, or pill form *US, 1994*

- — US Department of Justice, *Street Terms*, October 1994

special friend *noun*

a woman's menstrual period *US, 2001*

- — Don R. McCreary (Editor), *Dawg Speak*, 2001

Special K *noun*

ketamine hydrochloride, an anesthetic used as a recreational drug, in powder, capsule or pill form *US, 1990*

Kellogg's Special K™, a well-known breakfast cereal, is the inspiration for this variation on **κ** (ketamine).

- Special K. It's a clean smelling trip up the nose. — James St. James, *Party Monster*, p. 10, 1990

- Special K (Ketamine) Cost: $40-$50 per half gram. — *Newsweek*, p. 62, 6th December 1993
- This makes Special K look weak. — *Kids*, 1995
- It reportedly resurfaced as "Special K" last year at Manhattan "rave parties," taking users to mental territory called "K Land" and the "K hole." — *The Record [Bergen County, New Jersey]*, p. A1, 5th December 1995

speck *noun*

a black person *US, 1980*

Offensive.

- — Edith A. Folb, *runnin' down some lines*, p. 255, 1980

specker *noun*

one year of a prison sentence *US, 1950*

Used in numeric constructions such as "three-specker" or "five-specker."

- — Hyman E. Goldin et al., *Dictionary of American Underworld Lingo*, p. 203, 1950

specs *noun*

1 eye-glasses *UK, 1807*

A shortened form of "spectacles."

- "Where your specs, Rooski?" asked Penny, watching him bent two inches over his tray, trolling for vagrant shreds of fowl in the suety paste already setting like concrete. — Seth Morgan, *Homeboy*, p. 45, 1990

2 a person with poor eyesight and thick glasses *US, 1960*

- "Say, Specs, why don't you just pretend you are a doc?" — Nelson Algren, *The Neon Wilderness*, p. 31, 1960
- The labels were cruel: Gimp, Limpy-go-fetch, Crip, Lift-one-drag one, etc. Pint, Half-a-man, Peewee, Shorty, Lardass, Pork, Blubber, Belly, Blimp. Nuke-knob, Skinhead, Baldy. Four-eyes, Specs, Coke bottles. — *San Francisco Examiner*, p. A15, 28th July 1997

3 in horseracing, blinkers on a horse *US, 1951*

- — David W. Maurer, *Argot of the Racetrack*, p. 59, 1951

sped *noun*

a social outcast *US, 1997*

- — *Newsday*, p. B2, 11th October 1997

speed *noun*

1 an amphetamine, especially Dexedrine™, which is a central nervous system stimulant *US, 1966*

- — J.L. Simmons and Barry Winograd, *It's Happening*, p. 173, 1966: "glossary"
- The profits were mighty good on the pills and besides with the speed (amphetamine) family the users often got addicted, making more permanent customers. — Abbie Hoffman, *Woodstock Nation*, p. 69, 1969
- When he meets pushers of smack and speed, as he does not infrequently in his profession, he attempts to convince them that it is a vile and murderous act to peddle chemicals which can ultimately only destroy their imbibers. — Tom Robbins, *Another Roadside Attraction*, p. 58, 1971
- That's why there ain't a repo man I know that don't take speed. — *Repo Man*, 1984

2 ability in pool *US, 1967*

- The hustler exploits this fact so as to deceive his opponent as to his (the hustler's) true level of skill (true "speed"). — Ned Polsky, *Hustlers, Beats, and Others*, p. 51, 1967
- All hustlers conceal their true speed—or travel below their speed limit—as long as possible, lest they blow their cover or be forced to give weight. — Steve Rushin, *Pool Cool*, p. 27, 1990

speed *verb*

1 to be under the influence of a central nervous system stimulant *US, 1995*

- But what usually happened was that I'd be speeding like mad when the downs finally took effect. — Cleo Odzer, *Goa Freaks*, p. 148, 1995

2 in poker, to bet heavily and to bluff often *US, 1983*

- — Thomas L. Clark, *The Dictionary of Gambling and Gaming*, p. 210, 1987

speedball *noun*

1 a mixture of a central nervous system stimulant (especially cocaine) and a narcotic (especially heroin) *US, 1936*

- "I've seen 'em shootin' speedballs—half a cap of C 'n half a cap of H together." — Nelson Algren, *The Man with the Golden Arm*, p. 213, 1949
- One morning you wake up and take a speed ball and feel bugs under your skin. — William Burroughs, *Naked Lunch*, p. 19, 1971
- I started capping "H" with my "C." I'd mix them and shoot speedballs. — Iceberg Slim (Robert Beck), *Pimp*, p. 275, 1969
- He's sitting on his waterbed doing speedballs with some naked Dutch hitchhiker he picked up at the bus stop. — Kenneth Lonergan, *This is Our Youth*, p. 41, 2000

2 an alcoholic beverage fortified with a drug *US, 1962*
- — Joseph E. Ragen and Charles Finston, *Inside the World's Toughest Prison*, p. 819, 1962: "Penitentiary and underworld glossary"

3 a fast racehorse *US, 1974*
- What I'd do was look for a race with one outstanding speedball in it and then bet twenty-five, thirty dollars on it. — Gary Mayer, *Bookie*, p. 69, 1974

speed bump *noun*
a red bump on the skin sometimes suffered after injecting impure amphetamines *US, 1989*
- — Geoffrey Froner, *Digging for Diamonds*, p. 57, 1989
- Signs of long-term use: hair loss, open sores and "speed bumps," or areas on the skin that the user constantly picks. — *The Post-Standard (Syracuse, New York)*, p. B1, 6th February 2004

speed bumps *noun*
Saudi Arabian troops *US, 1991*
Gulf war usage.
- — *American Speech*, p. 401, Winter 1991: "Among the new words"

speedfreak *noun*
a person who is addicted to or compulsively uses amphetamines or methamphetamine *US, 1967*
- Sam said he was an ex-speed freak, and that may have been why he gave the impression of spiritual fragility. — Nicholas Von Hoffman, *We Are The People Our Parents Warned Us Against*, p. 15, 1967
- Speedfreaks are probably the junkies of the marijuana generation. — Hunter S. Thompson, *Fear and Loathing in America*, p. 10, Winter 1968
- We were turning into a nation of Speed Freaks and Nixon, the used-car dealer from Whittier, California, was becomin' the biggest pill pusher of them all!!! — Abbie Hoffman, *Woodstock Nation*, p. 69, 1969
- There was a lot of speed around, and a lot of obnoxious speedfreaks running around ripping people off[.] — John Sinclair, *Guitar Army*, p. 285, 1972

speed of heat *noun*
a high speed *US, 1986*
US naval aviator usage.
- — *United States Naval Institute Proceedings*, p. 108, October 1986

speedometer *noun*
in computing, a graphic depiction of a computer's current operating speed *US, 1991*
- — Eric S. Raymond, *The New Hacker's Dictionary*, p. 332, 1991

speedy dog *nickname*
a Greyhound bus; the Greyhound corporation *US, 1988*
- — Kathleen Odean, *High Steppers, Fallen Angels, and Lollipops*, p. 30, 1988

spelling flame *noun*
an inflammatory Internet posting attacking another's spelling *US, 1995*
- — Christian Crumlish, *The Internet Dictionary*, p. 184, 1995

Spenard divorce *noun*
a shooting of one spouse by the other *US, 1965*
- — Robert O. Bowen, *An Alaskan Dictionary*, p. 31, 1965
- The action is named after the Spenard district of Anchorage, where the rite is often conducted in one of the area's many watering holes. — Mike Doogan, *How to Speak Alaskan*, p. 55, 1993

spew *noun*
1 vomit *US, 1997*
- I pulled my shirt over my face, catching about a quart of liquid spew in my T-shirt, which I cradled between my arms. — Elissa Stein and Kevin Leslie, *Chunks*, p. 13, 1997

2 semen *US, 1989*
- — Pamela Munro, *U.C.L.A. Slang*, p. 79, 1989

spew *verb*
1 to vomit *US, 1988*
- I told Dennis if he gave me another topic that was political I'd spew burrito chunks. — *Heathers*, 1988
- — Pamela Munro, *U.C.L.A. Slang*, p. 79, 1989
- I'd sing the rest, but I don't want to spew. — *Wayne's World*, 1992
- One was spewing, one was on the ground bleeding, and one was crying like he'd just got pimp-slapped. — John Ridley, *Love is a Racket*, p. 125, 1998

2 to ejaculate *US, 1989*
- — Pamela Munro, *U.C.L.A. Slang*, p. 79, 1989

3 to post an excessive number of messages to an Internet discussion group *US, 1995*
- — Christian Crumlish, *The Internet Dictionary*, p. 184, 1995

sphynx *noun*
the removal by wax of all of a woman's pubic hair; the results thereof *US, 2001*
- The Sphynx—it's the name of a hairless cat from Egypt. I must tell you: The Sphynx takes guts and not everyone has a lover who deserves a Sphynx wax. — *Nerve*, p. 20, December 2000–January 2001

spic *noun*
1 a Spanish-speaking person *US, 1913*
Derogatory and offensive.
- What about Puerto Ricans? What about spics, Dadier? — Evan Hunter, *The Blackboard Jungle*, p. 208, 1954
- BERNARDO: With an "American." Who is really a Polack. ANITA: Says the Spic. — *West Side Story*, 1957
- Lemme tell you about them rumbles. The wops said no spics could go east of Park Avenue. — Edwin Torres, *Carlito's Way*, p. 8, 1975
- Julio. Great. There are 20,000 spics named "Julio." — *The Bad Lieutenant*, 1992

2 the Spanish language *US, 1946*
- [T]hese guys would crouch around their pile of shredded joy and roll muggles on a twenty-four-hour shift, jabbering away in spic and smoking up all the profits. — Mezz Mezzrow, *Really the Blues*, p. 165, 1946

3 a West Indian *US, 1945*
- — Lou Shelly, *Hepcats Jive Talk Dictionary*, p. 17, 1945

spico *noun*
a Spanish-speaking person *US, 1967*
A modestly embellished **SPIC**.
- Rocky and his fellas got to playing a way-out game with me called "One-finger-across-the-neck-inna-slicing-motion," followed by such gentle words as "It won't be long, spico." — Piri Thomas, *Down These Mean Streets*, p. 29, 1967

Spictown *noun*
a Spanish-speaking neighborhood *US, 1969*
- I copped you a sixteenth [of an ounce of heroin] in "Spic" town. You know I gotta love your stinking junkie ass to stick my neck out like that. — Iceberg Slim (Robert Beck), *Pimp*, p. 99, 1969

spider box *noun*
in the television and movie industries, an electrical junction box *US, 1990*
- — Ralph S. Singleton, *Filmmaker's Dictionary*, p. 158, 1990

spider hole *noun*
a sniper's lair in a cave *US, 1957*
Originally Korean war usage.
- Van Horn had asked Louis Bengis to carry a twelve-pound satchel charge, in case we ran across another sniper cave or spider-hole. — Martin Russ, *The Last Parallel*, p. 374, 1957
- Finally, napalm was called in, and for ten minutes the air above the spider hole was black and orange from the strike. — Michael Herr, *Dispatches*, p. 126, 1977
- This is how we used to booby trap spider holes in the war when we didn't have any demo. — Edward Lee, *Ghouls*, p. 424, 1988

spiel *noun*
1 a long-winded explanation *US, 1896*
- In the street, a blend of juke boxes created a weird cacophony, splintered by car horns and the spiel of the hawkers before each club[.] — John Clellon Holmes, *Go*, p. 49, 1952
- He had the whole cookpot spiel worked out; he practiced on Camille and me in the evenings. — Jack Kerouac, *On the Road*, p. 175, 1957
- I was all prepared for a sermon or long spiel about the Muslim thing. — Claude Brown, *Manchild in the Promised Land*, p. 234, 1965
- "We never did try it in the phone booth, did we?" I said, seeking to divert her from the spiel I could feel coming on. — John Nichols, *The Sterile Cuckoo*, p. 174, 1965

2 a speech intended to attract customers *US, 1966*
- "Carny?" "Yeah." I named a couple of outfits. "Speil?" "Um. And sleight of hand." — Robert Edmond Alter, *Carny Kill*, p. 3, 1966

spiel *verb*
to talk, especially at length; to patter *US, 1894*
- One day while he was spieling about his dope, Mike called me over to straighten this gunman out with some golden-leaf and lowrate him once and for all. — Mezz Mezzrow, *Really the Blues*, p. 94, 1946

- I've seen you around and heard you spiel, that's all. — George Mandel, *Flee the Angry Strangers*, p. 5, 1948
- "I'm starving for some carving of beef for a thief," spieled Eddie. — Dan Burley, *Diggeth Thou?*, p. 9, 1959
- Everyone in the room leaned forward a bit as Father Love opened his mouth to spiel. — Donald Goines, *The Busting Out of an Ordinary Man*, p. 76, 1985

spieler *noun*
1 a facile and smooth speaker *US, 1894*
- If they didn't have a spieler like Kleinfeld around, they would starve to death. — Edwin Torres, *After Hours*, p. 218, 1979
- A man who had a reputation as a spieler (a man who could draw a crowd around him and sell almost anything) welched on a few pounds he owed me over a snooker bet. — Brian McDonald, *Elephant Boys*, p. 206, 2000

2 a person who stands at the door of a business to lure people passing by into the business *US, 1894*
- A showman who harangues the crowd from outside is a "spieler" or "barker[.]" — Butch Reynolds, *Broken Hearted Clown*, p. 32, 1953
- "Spielers I don't need," Cochrane told me right off. — Robert Edmond Alter, *Carny Kill*, p. 6, 1966

spiff *noun*
1 a loner *US, 1987*
An articulation of the initials SBF (surrounded *by f*riends), used with irony.
- — *Carmel (California) High School Yearbook*, 1987

2 a bonus paid by a record company to a promoter who has succeeded in getting a record played *US, 1980*
- — Walter Hurst and Donn Delson, *Delson's Dictionary of Radio & Record Industry Terms*, p. 102, 1980

spiff *verb*
to dress up *US, 1979*
Coined in the UK in the 1870s, obsolete by the 1930s, and then resurfaced in the US in the 1970s, used with "up."
- Dad just got spiffed up and left the house. He has a date. With a woman! — C.D. Payne, *Youth in Revolt*, p. 299, 1993

spifflicated; spificated *adjective*
drunk *US, 1906*
- "Sylvia dead drunk, paralyzed, spifflicated, iced to the eyebrows," I said harshly. — Raymond Chandler, *The Long Goodbye*, p. 25, 1953
- "Damn, Ern," says I, somewhat spificated myself, "that's plangent." — Molly Ivins, *Nothin'But Good Times Ahead*, p. 43, 1994

spiffy *adjective*
well-dressed, elegant, sharp *UK, 1853*
- Libby MacAusland had a spiffy apartment in the Village. — Mary McCarthy, *The Group*, p. 181, 1963
- When we got to Japan and climbed down from the plane, everybody was spiffy and scruffy[.] — Larry Heinemann, *Close Quarters*, p. 169, 1977
- Gail was lookin' spiffy. I had her all dolled up in a new wardrobe. — Edwin Torres, *After Hours*, p. 375, 1979
- The Jag got to Fifteenth and turned left, went past that little park there and turned right onto Meridian. When the spiffy dark-green car all of a sudden pulled to a stop across from the Flamingo Terrace apartments, Raylan realized, Jesus, the guy was going to see Joyce Patton. — Elmore Leonard, *Pronto*, p. 84, 1999

spig *noun*
a Spanish-speaking person *US, 1969*
A corruption of the prevalent **SPIC**.
- "Sure, I see that spig before," Mr. Majestyk said. — Elmore Leonard, *The Big Bounce*, p. 45, 1969

spike *noun*
1 a syringe and needle; a hypodermic needle *US, 1936*
- There goes my last spike! — Jack Gerber, *The Connection*, p. 85, 1957
- They didn't find the heroin but they found two spikes and with his marks and the girl's evidence that was enough. — Alexander Trocchi, *Cain's Book*, p. 106, 1960
- Cause it makes me feel like I'm a man / When I put a spike into my vein. — Velvet Underground *Heroin*, 1967
- We bought two droppers and a couple of spikes—needles—No. 26-half inch and some wires for cleaning them. — Herbert Huncke, *The Evening Sun Turned Crimson*, p. 82, 1980

2 in a deck of playing cards, an ace *US, 1988*
- — George Percy, *The Language of Poker*, p. 84, 1988

spike *verb*
to adulterate a drink or ply a person with alcohol or drugs *US, 1909*
- So these barrels of near beer were trucked out to the Arrowhead to be spiked. — Mezz Mezzrow, *Really the Blues*, p. 63, 1946
- Almost immediately I was spiked with wine and acid. — Jamie Mandelkau, *Buttons*, p. 68, 1971
- "A little spiked coffee never hurt nobody's incentive," Shoat said. — Dan Jenkins, *Semi-Tough*, p. 136, 1972

spill *verb*
1 to fall off a surfboard *US, 1957*
- Do you know he's the only guy besides Duke Kahanamoku who came in on Zero break without spilling? — Frederick Kohner, *Gidget*, p. 41, 1957

2 to talk with energy and no clear agenda *US, 1970*
- — Clarence Major, *Dictionary of Afro-American Slang*, p. 107, 1970

▶ **spill the beans**
to tell that which one is not supposed to tell *US, 1919*
- Jules knew that he didn't dare have more than one photo session because Cynthia might accidentally spill the beans. — Joseph Wambaugh, *Finnegan's Week*, p. 19, 1993

▶ **spill your guts (out)**
to confess your secrets; to tell all you know *US, 1927*
- [H]e was ready to spill his guts tomorrow[!] — Budd Schulberg, *On the Waterfront*, 1954

spin *noun*
1 a tactical, revisionist interpretation of an event for public consumption *US, 1986*
Although the term came to the forefront during the Reagan presidency, it is an ancient practice that was simply taken to new heights by Reagan's handlers.
- — *American Speech*, Fall 1988

2 a single playing of a song by a radio station *US, 1999*
- Yeah, I know we lost the bullet, spins are down slightly, but that record has legs, man. — Elmore Leonards, *Be Cool*, p. 106, 1999

3 a Separation Program Number *US, 1984*
The numbers corresponded to several hundred reasons for discharge from the service. Also known as "spin number."
- Depending on command whim and caprice, a soldier could also get an even more impairing general discharge with similar "spins" for the same things. — Myra MacPherson, *Long Time Passing*, p. 679, 1984

spin *verb*
1 to play a record, especially on the radio *US, 1965*
- Right now you have the unique opportunity of being the very first station on the coast, man, to spin Roadkill, right up to the Top Forty. — Elmore Leonard, *Be Cool*, p. 165, 1999

2 in circus and carnival usage, to speak a language or dialect fluently *US, 1981*
- — Don Wilmeth, *The Language of American Popular Entertainment*, p. 251, 1981

3 in the language surrounding the Grateful Dead, to tape a concert *US, 1994*
- — David Shenk and Steve Silberman, *Skeleton Key*, p. 268, 1994

4 to deceive *US, 1952*
- Okay, Mike. I'll spin it. Don't bother calling me again, okay? — Mickey Spillane, *Kiss Me Deadly*, p. 120, 1952

5 to leave *US, 1989*
- — James Harris, *A Convict's Dictionary*, p. 39, 1989

spinal *noun*
a paraplegic *US, 1998*
- I've seen a lot of spinals, Dude, and this guy is a fake. — *The Big Lebowski*, 1998

spinal tap *noun*
falling over backwards while snowboarding *US, 1990*
- Are you perfecting your butt drop of spinal tap? — Elena Garcia, *A Beginner's Guide to Zen and the Art of Snowboarding*, p. 120, 1990

spindle *noun*
a safe *US, 1972*
- They never call them a safe, but a pete or a box. They have names like this spindle and gutbox. — Harry King, *Box Man*, p. 56, 1972

spindle-man *noun*
a game operator in a carnival *US, 1969*

- Besides, wouldn't it be at least slightly out of line for a robbery detective and a mere carny spindle-man to exchange gifts? — Iceberg Slim (Robert Beck), *Trick Baby*, p. 14, 1969

spinner *noun*

1 a radio disc jockey *US, 1950*
- — Arnold Shaw, *Lingo of Tin-Pan Alley*, p. 20, 1950

2 a person who is mentally unstable after extensive medication *US, 1989*
- — James Harris, *A Convict's Dictionary*, p. 39, 1989

3 in dominoes, a double that may be played on both ends *US, 1959*
- — Dominic Armanino, *Dominoes*, p. 20, 1959

4 in poker, a streak of good luck *US, 1988*
- — George Percy, *The Language of Poker*, p. 85, 1988

spit *noun*

1 a small sum of money *US, 1985*
- — Steve Kuriscak, *Casino Talk*, p. 52, 1985

2 something of no value *US, 1987*
- I always taught you, BB, never walk out of a place without a signed contract. Somebody's word ain't spit. — *Tin Men*, 1987

3 in some games of poker, a card turned face-up in the center of the table which may be used by all players' hands *US, 1961*
Also called a "spit in the ocean."
- — Irv Roddy, *Friday Night Poker*, p. 221, 1961

spit *verb*
to perform a rap lyric *US, 2001*
- I could've spit that line better. — Eminem (Marshall Mathers), *Angry Blonde*, p. 4, 2001
- I got my education on the streets / And I learned how to spit rhymes out with or without beats — Cypress Hill *Memories*, 2001

▸ **spit cotton**
to salivate while under the influence of heroin *US, 1953*
- My mouth was dry, and my spit came out in round white balls—spitting cotton, it's called. — William Burroughs, *Junkie*, p. 29, 1953

spit!
be quiet! *US, 1950*
- — Hyman E. Goldin et al., *Dictionary of American Underworld Lingo*, p. 203, 1950

spit and git *verb*
to accomplish a task quickly *US, 1972*
- You talk about spitting and gitting? Those two champeen razor fighters moved like twins. — Guy Owen, *The Flim-Flam Man and the Apprentice Grifter*, p. 120, 1972

spit-back *noun*
a technique of spitting a drink back into a glass to give the appearance of consuming more alcohol than you are *US, 1964*
- Go back t'my drink, take a sip a whiskey an pssst, spit it back out inta the coke chaser. That's the spit-back. — Robert Gover, *Here Goes Kitten*, p. 19, 1964

spitball *verb*
to brainstorm *US, 1955*
- The office believed I had saved her for us by spitballing and I never disenlightened them. — Clancy Sigal, *Going Away*, p. 29, 1961

spit fuck *verb*
to penetrate a rectum or vagina using only saliva as a lubricant *US, 1979*
- — *Maledicta*, p. 232, 1979: "Kinks and queens: linguistic and cultural aspects of the terminology for gays"

spit kit *noun*
in the US submarine corps, an antisubmarine vessel *US, 1948*
- — *American Speech*, p. 38, February 1948: "Talking under water: speech in submarines"

spitter *noun*

1 a killer *US, 1975*
- This little blond guy is raising hell—he's got three or four guys with him, spitters all—the maitre d' is pleading. — Edwin Torres, *Carlito's Way*, p. 27, 1975

2 a wave that sprays from its end as it collapses *US, 1964*
- — John Severson, *Modern Surfing Around the World*, p. 182, 1964

spittin' time *noun*
the bleed period of a cycle woman's menstrual *US, 1954*
- — *American Speech*, p. 298, December 1954: "The vernacular of menstruation"

spizz *noun*
a hypodermic needle *US, 1961*
- — Francis J. Rigney and L. Douglas Smith, *The Real Bohemia*, p. xx, 1961

spizzerinktum *noun*
vim, vigor, energy *US, 1950*
- [T]he boys still had enough spizzerinktum left to wallop Shelton 13 to 0 on the Mason County lads' field. — Fredi Perry, *Bremerton and Puget Sound Navy Yard*, p. 219, 2002

splack *noun*
sex *US, 1994*
- — Linda Meyer, *Teenspeak!*, p. 29, 1994

splack *verb*
to steal a car, especially by shattering the steering column *US, 1993*
- They would "splack" cars—breaking into the steering column in seconds—and joy ride all night. — *Orlando (Florida) Sentinel Tribune*, p. A1, 10th October 1993
- There's even street slang for stealing cars such as "new buckets are being splacked." Buckets refer to small cars, such as Dodge neons, and to splack is to steal a car using a screwdriver to break into the steering column and start it. — *Tampa (Florida) Tribune*, p. 1, 6th May 2000

splash *noun*

1 an amphetamine or other central nervous system stimulant *US, 1966*
- — J.L. Simmons and Barry Winograd, *It's Happening*, p. 173, 1966: "glossary"
- — Kenn "Naz" Young, *Naz's Underground Dictionary*, p. 57, 1973

2 a small amount of water added to an alcoholic drink *IRELAND, 1922*
- Buddy ordered a couple more Jim Beams with a splash, for the road. — Elmore Leonard, *Out of Sight*, p. 186, 1996

3 a bath *US, 1972*
- — David Claerbaut, *Black Jargon in White America*, p. 81, 1972

splash *verb*

1 to ejaculate *US, 1970*
- The point is that if you usually splash early and you know you're going to get laid, then jerk off. — *Screw*, p. 6, 15th June 1970

2 to take a bath *US, 1972*
- — David Claerbaut, *Black Jargon in White America*, p. 81, 1972

▸ **splash the pot**
in a game of poker, to throw betting tokens directly into the pile of chips in the center of the table instead of lining them up for other players to see before adding them to the pot *US, 1961*
- — Thomas L. Clark, *The Dictionary of Gambling and Gaming*, p. 210, 1987

splash move *noun*
in cheating at dice, a switch of the dice *US, 1997*
- The old man nodded. "I'm gonna start with a 'splash move'," indicating he was going to rehearse the switch of the dice first without actually playing them, to see if the Pit Boss would spot it. — Stephen J. Cannell, *Big Con*, p. 196, 1997

splash shot *noun*
a scene in a pornographic movie or a photograph depicting a man ejaculating *US, 1997*
- Other terms include "splash shot," "spunk shot," "pearl necklace." — Joseph Slade, *Pornography and Sexual Representation*, p. 654, 2000

splat *noun*

1 any food not subject to ready identification *US, 1968*
From the sound made when it hits the mess kit.
- — Carl Fleischhauer, *A Glossary of Army Slang*, p. 1, 1968

2 the * character on a computer keyboard *US, 1983*
- — Guy L. Steele et al., *The Hacker's Dictionary*, p. 119, 1983
- — Eric S. Raymond, *The New Hacker's Dictionary*, p. 332, 1991

splat *verb*
to be killed bungee jumping *US, 1992*
- The bungee jumping term for a fatal accident is "zeroing out" or "splatting." Take your pick. — Erik Fair, *California Thrill Sports*, p. 55, 1992

splendiferous; splendacious; splendidious; spledidous *adjective*
excellent; very splendid *US, 1843*

- Libby was not all work and no play; she was managing to have a splendiferous time for herself without overspending her allowance. — Mary McCarthy, *The Group*, p. 189, 1963
- [Y]eah, testify, how many ectoplasmic angels are on your side, give me the splendiferous images of your famous fabulous friggin' self-created self-sustained astral plane! — Anne Rice, *Blood Canticle*, p. 77, 2003
- I didn't need an office. I could afford the most splendiferous office in the city. — Walter Yetnikoff, *Howling at the Moon*, p. 264, 2004

splib *noun*
a black person *US, 1964*
Offensive.

- We got some splibs in Central too, but none too many. — Joseph Wambaugh, *The New Centurions*, p. 171, 1970
- All the splibs on the playground knew by Leroy's action that it was Fuck With Junior Time[.] — Clarence Major, *All-Night Visitors*, p. 27, 1998
- — Jim Goad, *Jim Goad's Glossary of Northwestern Prison Slang*, December 2001

spliced *adjective*
married *US, 1962*

- "She was fresh out of college when we met and got spliced." — David Gregory, *Flesh Seller*, p. 130, 1962
- — Anna Scotti and Paul Young, *Buzzwords*, p. 30, 1997

spliff *noun*
a marijuana cigarette *JAMAICA, 1936*

- It was like our friend Slim in British Honduras, who used to buy a fifteen-cent spliff from John Scorn, and turn around and sell it in front of John's house for twenty cents. — Stephen Gaskin, *Amazing Dope Tales*, p. 89, 1980
- I brew a little tea in the mini-kitchen off the living room while the "G" lights a spliff on the big velvet sofa. — Jim Carroll, *Forced Entries*, p. 25, 1987
- Smoking a spliff of high-octane chronic (street talk for pot) in the back room, he explains his bond to Dre. "He's the bomb," says Snoop. — *People*, p. 77, 23rd May 1994

spliff *verb*
to smoke marijuana and be under its influence *UK, 1977*

- Paul [Simenon] spliffing in bigeyed space monkey glee playing the new Ramones over and over[.] — Lester Bangs, *Psychotic Reactions and Carburetor Dung*, p. 243, 1977

splinters *noun*
adversity *US, 1954*

- — Jerry Robertson, *Oil Slanguage*, p. 58, 1954

split *noun*
1 the vagina *US, 1967*

- — Dale Gordon, *The Dominion Sex Dictionary*, p. 150, 1967
- I laid her down on the sofa and placed my beef directly over her soaking split. — Renay Jackson, *Oaktown Devil*, p. 32, 1998

2 a tranquillizer or other central nervous system depressant *US, 1969*

- — Richard B. Lingeman, *Drugs from A to Z*, p. 226, 1969

split *verb*
to leave *US, 1956*

- After all, I'm not locked in here. I can split in a year or two if I want to. — Nat Hentoff, *Jazz Country*, p. 139, 1965
- And as I split, I saw her cracking up with kicks. — Eldridge Cleaver, *Soul on Ice*, p. 28, 1968
- — Hy Lit, *Hy Lit's Unbelievable Dictionary of Hip Words for Groovy People*, p. 37, 1968
- WYATT: Let's split. BILLY: Split? WYATT: Yeah. — Peter Fonda, *Easy Rider*, p. 139, 1969
- The police come to break it up. We split into the subway. — Jerry Rubin, *Do It!*, p. 118, 1970
- He told Doyle he had to split in order to make the Ultimate Rendezvous. — Gurney Norman, *Divine Right's Trip (Last Whole Earth Catalog)*, p. 9, 1971
- He saw I was ready to split and asked where I was going. — Jamie Mandelkau, *Buttons*, p. 57, 1971
- I stayed with my oldest sister, 'til her husband started to give me those free-loader looks which caused me to split. — A.S. Jackson, *Gentleman Pimp*, p. 21, 1973
- We ate and split, and as we rode, I sat quietly thinking and wondering[.] — Bobby Seale, *A Lonely Rage*, p. 293, 1978
- Joe was now at the door holding it open calling his friends, saying "Come on, Huncke, le's split." — Herbert Huncke, *The Evening Sun Turned Crimson*, p. 135, 1980

- Ferris, let's split, please? — *Ferris Bueller's Day Off*, 1986
- I gotta split. It was really nice meeting you. — *Chasing Amy*, 1997
- Let's just split, Let's just split right now. — *Boogie Nights*, 1997

▸ **split a gut**
to exert yourself to the extreme, especially laughing *US, 1958*

- "He's split a gut like that every night for years. And it's his only gut." — John Clellon Holmes, *The Horn*, p. 156, 1958

▸ **split the scene**
to leave *US, 1990*

- [H]e decided the best thing to do for the time being was to split the scene rather than come to the attention of the cops. — Herbert Huncke, *Guilty of Everything*, p. 145, 1990

▸ **split the sheets**
to divorce *US, 1976*

- — Wayne Floyd, *Jason's Authentic Dictionary of CB Slang*, p. 28, 1976
- Me and the ol' lady split the sheets a year ago, and now I'm growin' a toenail on my dick from fuckin' my socks. — Ken Weaver, *Texas Crude*, p. 76, 1984
- My folks split the sheets in 55." — James Ellroy, *Destination Morgue*, p. 30, 2004

split *adjective*
said of a prison sentence including equal amounts of jail time and probation time *US, 1976*

- Five split and Big John's prophesy was fulfilled to the letter. I had hoped for a three-split, eighteen months in and eighteen months out. — Malcolm Braley, *False Starts*, p. 197, 1976

split beaver; spread beaver *noun*
the vagina displayed with lips parted *US, 1969*
A familiar cliché of pornography.

- Then came the split beaver shot, which is where the girl has lubricated her pussy so that the mons fold apart to reveal the innerlips, clitoris, urethral opening and vagina. — *Screw*, p. 4, 13th October 1969
- By 1967 or 1968, a whole group of magazines featured nude females in a manner which emphasized their genitalia in complete detail (known in the industry as "spreader" or "split beaver" magazines). — *The Presidential Commission on Obscenity and Pornography*, p. 113, 1970
- In the first, which came to be known as the split beaver, the woman spread her legs and exhibited her vagina directly to the cameras, often pulling aside the labia in order to provide a better view of what everyone had come to see. — Kenneth Turan and Stephen E. Zito, *Sinema: American Pornographic Films and the People who Make Them*, pp. 77–78, 1974
- [G]hetto-fabulous rapper Lil' Kim (known for her split beaver shots). — *Village Voice*, p. 33, 21st April 1998

split C-note *noun*
a fifty-dollar bill *US, 1954*

- As he talked he rubbed Biff's split-C note in his pocket like a rabbit's foot. — Bernard Wolfe, *The Late Risers*, p. 171, 1954

split-tail *noun*
a female *US, 1950*

- — Hyman E. Goldin et al., *Dictionary of American Underworld Lingo*, p. 203, 1950
- "These spit-tails take a long time to get unrigged just to take a pee." — Joseph Wambaugh, *Hollywood Station*, p. 297, 2006

splo *noun*
inexpensive, low quality whiskey *US, 1974*

- — David W. Maurer, *Kentucky Moonshine*, p. 125, 1974
- — Burgess Laughlin, *Job Opportunities in the Black Market*, p. 4, 1978: "Glossary"

splooge *noun*
semen *US, 1989*

- — Pamela Munro, *U.C.L.A. Slang*, p. 80, 1989
- The slobs could even kiss her (if they so dared, with all that splooge floating about her mug). — Anthony Petkovich, *The X Factory*, p. 183, 1997

splooge *verb*
to ejaculate *US, 1989*

- — Pamela Munro, *U.C.L.A. Slang*, p. 80, 1989
- That's right—there is no wacky splooging on her face or in her mouth, which is, of course, considered the Money Shot in almost all straight porn. — *The Village Voice*, 22nd August 2000

splow *noun*
palms slapped in greeting *US, 1976*

- "My dear hip friend," the letter began / "Here's some splow and a big shoddy-doo." — Dennis Wepman et al., *The Life*, p. 69, 1976

spock *verb*
to examine something or someone *US, 1991*
- — Trevor Cralle, *The Surfin'ary*, p. 120, 1991

spodiodi *noun*
wine *US, 1957*
- Dean and I had ended up with a colored guy called Walter who ordered drinks at the bar and had them lined up and said, "Wine-spodiodi!" — Jack Kerouac, *On the Road*, p. 203, 1957
- — Carl J. Banks Jr., *Banks Dictionary of the Black Ghetto Language*, 1975

spoiled water *noun*
any nonalcoholic beverage *US, 1962*
- — Joseph E. Ragen and Charles Finston, *Inside the World's Toughest Prison*, p. 819, 1962: "Penitentiary and underworld glossary"

spondulics; spondulix; sponds; spondos *noun*
money *US, 1857*
- Jack, shekels, mazuma, simoleons, Mr. Green, filthy lucre, even spondulicks—this is other Why of prostitution. — Gail Sheehy, *Hustling*, p. 11, 1973

sponge *noun*
1 a group, notional or real, opposed to the gains of the civil rights movement *US, 1965*
The vocalized abbreviation stood for "Society for the Prevention of Negroes Getting Everything." The group was more notional than real, but, for example, in 1965 the Student Council of the University of Virginia was petitioned by an organization calling itself SPONGE for status as an independent organization eligible to receive Student Council funds.
- On First Avenue there is a meeting going on of a group called SPONGE (Society for the Prevention of Negroes Getting Everything). — Sol Yurrick, *The Bag*, p. 444, 1968
- A growing Black Nationalist movement often faced off against groups like SPONGE, the acronym for the Society for the Prevention of Negroes Getting Everything. — Gregory S. Bell, *In the Black*, p. 69, 2002

2 a boogie boarder, who rides waves on a small foam board *US, 1991*
Used in a disparaging manner by surfers.
- — Trevor Cralle, *The Surfin'ary*, p. 120, 1991

sponge *verb*
1 to obtain something in a parasitic manner *UK, 1673*
- Relatively young and able-bodied, they simply sponged because they preferred not to work. — Jim Thompson, *Roughneck*, p. 144, 1954
- Wadda you think, you can sponge drinks off me all night? — Edwin Torres, *After Hours*, p. 214, 1979

2 in horseracing, to insert a sponge into a horse's nostril just before a race, impeding its breathing during the race *US, 1951*
- — David W. Maurer, *Argot of the Racetrack*, p. 59, 1951

spongies *noun*
in the usage of youthful model road racers (slot car racers), smooth, soft tires *US, 1997*
- — Phantom Surfers, *The Exciting Sounds of Model Road Racing (Album cover)*, 1997

spoo *noun*
semen *US, 1989*
- Ike had used the word "spoo"—roughly the equivalent of jizz—in a conversation. I don't know where it came from, or if he made it up. In any event "spoo" turned out to be "the mystery word" onstage that night. — Frank Zappa, *The Real Frank Zappa Book*, p. 170, 1989

spoofed *adjective*
used of an electronic message, of a suspect origin *US, 1997*
- — Andy Ihnatko, *Cyberspeak*, p. 181, 1997

spoofer *noun*
in carnival usage, a large stuffed dog offered as a game prize *US, 1985*
- The price of SPOOFERS ranges from ten to fifteen dollars wholesale. — Gene Sorrows, *All About Carnivals*, p. 26, 1985
- "It's a spoofer," Chip shouted in his face, spittle flying. — Peter Fenton, *Eyeing the Flash*, p. 155, 2005

spoofing *noun*
the sending of e-mail that claims to come from one organization but in fact comes from another *US, 1989*

Known more fully as "IP spoofing."
- Spoofing: Masquerading as another user or program (for example, intruders, worms, and viruses)[.] — *InfoWorld*, p. S6, 11th December 1989
- Spoofing usually refers to sending electronic mail in such a way that it looks like someone else was the one who sent it. — *The Knightmare, Secrets of a Super Hacker*, p. 130, 1994

spooge *noun*
1 semen *US, 1987*
- — Connie Eble (Editor), *UNC-CH Campus Slang*, p. 8, Fall 1987
- One cock in my face, one inside me, the smell of other men's spooge in my nostrils. — Amy Sohn, *Run Catch Kiss*, p. 116, 1999
- My brain was as soggy as a spooge mop in a porno booth. — Jeffrey McDaniel, *The Splinter Factory*, p. 14, 2002
- Anna alleviates her boyfriend's backed-up bozack, setting off a geyser of spooge that sends her sailing towards the ceiling. — Mr. Skin, *Mr. Skin's Skincyclopedia*, p. 173, 2005

2 any viscous matter of unknown origin *US, 1995*
- — *Maledicta*, p. 48, 1995: "Door whore and other New Mexico restaurant slang"

3 in computing, code or output which cannot be understood *US, 1991*
- — Eric S. Raymond, *The New Hacker's Dictionary*, p. 333, 1991

spooge booth *noun*
a private booth in a pornography arcade *US, 2001*
- Sex shops range from smutty bookstores with "spooge booths" to higher-end retailers specializing in erotic tools, toys and garments. — Rob Cohen, *Etiquette for Outlaws*, p. 70, 2001

spook *noun*
1 a black person *US, 1945*
Derogatory and offensive.
- Only in Little Tokyo they'd have to kill and be killed, for those spooks down there were some really rugged cats[.] — Chester Himes, *If He Hollers Let Him Go*, p. 77, 1945
- You wait until you see a spooks' dance! — Malcolm X and Alex Haley, *The Autobiography of Malcolm X*, p. 47, 1964
- Nevertheless, uneasy white males still continue to tighten their rosy sphincters at the approach of spooks. — Gore Vidal, *Myra Breckinridge*, p. 88, 1968
- I'm what a lot you spooks might think of as a red neck with a terminal case of the dumb-ass. — Dan Jenkins, *Semi-Tough*, p. 7, 1972

2 a ghost *US, 1801*
- The headmasters were Elvis Presley and the spook of Jimmy Dean, and the entrance requirements were completely democratic. — Max Shulman, *Rally Round the Flag, Boys!*, p. 57, 1957

3 a spy *US, 1942*
- The continually emphasize that they are not spooks, but in such a way as to heighten the suspicion that such activities are at least common diversions. — Donald Duncan, *The New Legions*, p. 151, 1967
- The Army was full of spooks. — Earl Thompson, *Tattoo*, p. 633, 1974
- In the spook world they use words like "departure" or "termination" in ways that would not be acceptable in the general business community. — Hunter S. Thompson, *Generation of Swine*, p. 169, 13th October 1986

4 a psychiatrist *US, 1961*
- — *American Speech*, pp. 145–148, May 1961: "The spoken language of medicine; argot, slang, cant"

5 in casino blackjack, a player who can spot the dealer's down card *US, 1991*
- — Michael Dalton, *Blackjack*, p. 79, 1991

spook *verb*
1 to frighten or startle someone *US, 1935*
Also variant "spook out."
- "That's why I need you," Raylan said, "help me find a guy I'm looking for without showing myself and spook him." — Elmore Leonard, *Riding the Rap*, p. 286, 1995

2 to follow, to surveil *US, 1979*
- "That's why Kimberley Marsh caught him spooking her," I say. — Leo Rosten, *Silky!*, p. 101, 1979

3 in blackjack, to peak and see the dealer's down card *US, 1985*
- — Steve Kuriscak, *Casino Talk*, p. 52, 1985

spooked *adjective*
used of playing cards, marked for cheating *US, 1963*
- — Richard Jessup, *The Cincinnati Kid*, p. 93, 1963

spooky *noun*
a gunship helicopter equipped with miniguns *US, 1981*

- They had Spooky standing on a column of tracers, just circling around battalion, tilling the earth. — Mark Baker, *Nam*, p. 42, 1981

spooky *adjective*

in surfing, difficult or unpredictable *US, 1963*
- — Grant W. Kuhns, *On Surfing*, p. 122, 1963

spoon *noun*

1 the handle of a hand grenade *US, 1977*
From its curved, spoon-like shape.
- He tried to throw a grenade at them, but his hand slipped off the spoon. — Philip Caputo, *A Rumor of War*, p. 204, 1977
- Then he snatched it up again, pinched the halves together, and worked the pink back in, twisting it until the pin just hung there, holding back the spoon just barely. — Larry Heinemann, *Close Quarters*, p. 45, 1977

2 the dip up at the front nose of a surfboard *US, 1963*
- — Grant W. Kuhns, *On Surfing*, p. 122, 1963

3 a sexual position in which a couple lies on their sides, man entering from behind *US, 2005*
- It can't hurt to stay tuned for cuty Poppy Morgan rotating from spoon to mish under Joel Lawrence. — Editors of Adult Video News, *The AVN Guide to the 500 Greatest Adult Films of All Time*, p. 11, 2005

spoon *verb*

1 to lie behind someone, your face towards their back *US, 1887*
- BRODIE: You know how when someone lays with their back to you and you lay behind them, really close, and you throw one arm over them. T.S.: It's called spooning. — *Mallrats*, 1995

2 to tongue a woman's vagina and clitoris *US, 1971*
- — Eugene Landy, *The Underground Dictionary*, p. 175, 1971

spooney *noun*

an effeminate male who may or may not be homosexual *US, 1978*
- — Anon., *King Smut's Wet Dreams Interpreted*, 1978

spoon up *verb*

to arrange in proper order *US, 1956*
- The low ranking plebe, who has to brace (assume correct military carriage), spoon up (put in order), tour (hour's walk),might be a hivey (quick to learn), army brat (son of officer), but he must not get B.J. (bold before June). — *Chicago Daily Tribune*, p. N4, 23rd December 1956

sport fuck *noun*

sex for the sake of sex *US, 1990*
- More often, though, lesbians who end up doing what some call a "sport fuck" with a man have been in a situation, such as travel, in which a good time with a kindred spirit just happened along. — Loraine Hutchins, *Bi Any Other Name*, p. 1990, 328

sport-fuck *verb*

to have sex for the sake of having sex *US, 2001*
- Forth Worth has these well-known, good-looking "husband helpers" around town—fortyish-type businesswomen—who like to sport-fuck rich married men. — Dan Jenkins, *The Money-Whipped Steer-Job Three-Jack Give-Up Artist*, p. 146, 2001

sport fucking *noun*

sex without any pretence of a relationship, although with a competitive edge *US, 1979*
- [W]riting their resumes for my editing and exploring the hallways for their summer intern peers for swimming, tennis, and sport-fucking. — Robert Jagoda, *Nobody Wants My Resume*, p. 6, 1979
- There were plenty of willing ladies between here and California, and a bit of sport-fucking never hurt any man or any marriage as far as he could see. — Cathy Cash Spellman, *So Many Partings*, p. 290, 1983
- I think what's happened is a recent trend among Fort Worth housewives towards neighborhood sport-fuckin'. — Dan Jenkins, *Dead Solid Perfect*, p. 46, 1986
- Lanie gave a shallow laugh. "The sportfucking, he didn't mind. A different fella each night and he'd never say a word to me." — Carl Hiaasen, *Double Whammy*, p. 235, 1987

sporting girl *noun*

a prostitute *US, 1938*
- But have you ever known a pimp to take a barmaid and make a sportin' girl outta her? — A.S. Jackson, *Gentleman Pimp*, p. 156, 1973

sporting house *noun*

a brothel *US, 1894*

- This is a sporting house. If I don't let a white john with money come here, I must have good reasons. — Chester Himes, *The Real Cool Killers*, p. 80, 1959
- "Why hell, woman, time I was his age I'd been to ever cathouse—sportin'-house,' we called 'em then—in this county." — Terry Southern, *Texas Summer*, p. 31, 1991

sporting lady *noun*

a prostitute *US, 1972*
- Ladies is the polite form, and carries the connotations of "ladies of the evening" and sportin' lady, that is, a kind of gallant euphemism. — Christina and Richard Milner, *Black Players*, p. 37, 1972

sporting life *noun*

1 the business and lifestyle of prostitution and pimping *US, 1973*
- His name was famous in sportin' life up 'til the time he died, and then he became a legend. — A.S. Jackson, *Gentleman Pimp*, p. 26, 1973

2 cocaine *US, 1978*
From *Porgy and Bess*, in which the character Sportin' Life sells cocaine. Retro and rare. The shortened form is "sporting."
- "Sportin' Life," said Mona. "Happy dust. This stuff is an American institution." — Armistead Maupin, *Tales of the City*, p. 46, 1978

sportsman *noun*

a pimp *US, 1967*
In the mid-C19, the term referred to a gambler. By mid-C20 it was a somewhat grandiose euphemism for "pimp."
- She told me one night, just after I got into the life through her, that Bible John was her sportsman. "Sportsman? What's that?" I asked. She shrugged her shoulders. "Fancy word for pimp." — Sara Harris, *The Lords of Hell*, p. 31, 1967
- Tonight we have with us one of the greatest sportsmen of the Middlewest. — Babs Gonzales, *I Paid My Dues*, p. 89, 1967

sportsman's paradise *noun*

a bar favored by pimps *US, 1978*
- — Burgess Laughlin, *Job Opportunities in the Black Market*, p. 6, 1978: "Glossary"

spot *noun*

1 a central location from which illegal drugs are distributed to street-level dealers *US, 2003*
- At first, Boy George had paid someone $50 to deliver the heroin to his store, or spot. — Adrian Nicole LeBlanc, *Random Family*, p. 46, 2003
- She let us push crack out of the spot and do what we had to do as long as we gave her smoke. — 50 Cent, *From Pieces to Weight*, p. 112, 2005

2 an apartment or house *US, 2001*
- After a while I got tired of creeping downstairs with the around-the-way girls. I had to get my own spot so I could charge it up a bit. — *Style*, p. 96, July 2001

3 a large party, a convention, or other event that is a promising source for swindle victims *US, 1977*
- — Robert C. Prus and C.R.D. Sharper, *Road Hustler*, p. 171, 1977: "Glossary of terms"

4 money *US, 1947*
- Sep, he go an give me a spot, I ain't gonna git me no three. — Robert Gover, *One Hundred Dollar Misunderstanding*, p. 25, 1961
- But from the looks of her and the spots I could get for her to work, I felt the fox would be worth the chase[.] — A.S. Jackson, *Gentleman Pimp*, p. 79, 1973

5 any of the large suit symbols printed on the face of a playing card *US, 1967*
- — Albert H. Morehead, *The Complete Guide to Winning Poker*, p. 274, 1967

6 in a deck of playing cards, an ace *US, 1988*
- — George Percy, *The Language of Poker*, p. 85, 1988

7 in poolroom betting, a handicap given in a bet-upon game *US, 1967*
- [B]etter players are always willing to give poorer ones a handicap ("spot"). — Ned Polsky, *Hustlers, Beats, and Others*, p. 47, 1967

▸ **put someone to the spot**
to kill someone who has been lured to a rendezvous *US, 1948*
- Dutch Schultz was put on the spot. No sooner had he sat down than the two men who had lured him there dived to the floor, as a man in a green hat stepped out from behind a pillar and gave Schultz all his six bullets in the belly[.] — Jack Lait and Lee Mortimer, *New York Confidential*, p. 18, 1948

spot card noun

in a deck of playing cards, any card other than an ace or face card US, 1967

- — Albert H. Morehead, *The Complete Guide to Winning Poker*, p. 274, 1967

spot play noun

in horseracing, an approach to betting in which the bettor only bets in situations where the odds seem advantageous US, 1975

- But there are occasions, that are called "spot" plays, where you can have the parimutuel odds working in your favor. — Jimmy Snyder, *Jimmy the Greek*, p. 213, 1975
- — Tom Ainslie, *Ainslie's Complete Guide to Thoroughbred Racing*, p. 338, 1976

spots noun

in circus usage, leopards US, 1981

- — Don Wilmeth, *The Language of American Popular Entertainment*, p. 253, 1981

spotter noun

a look out in a drug-selling operation US, 1990

- And if you do as good a job there as you did as a spotter, well, the sky is the limit. — *New Jack City*, 1990

spotters noun

the eyes US, 1945

- — Lou Shelly, *Hepcats Jive Talk Dictionary*, p. 17, 1945
- — Clarence Major, *Dictionary of Afro-American Slang*, p. 108, 1970

spray verb

to fart US, 2002

- — Gary K. Farlow, *Prison-ese*, p. 65, 2002

spread noun

1 an assortment of food laid out on a table or served at a social event UK, 1822

- Some spread! Grafflings and fortinaxes all over, and pertussmied down the middle. — Bernard Wolfe, *The Late Risers*, p. 257, 1954
- Meanwhile his young wife prepared a magnificent spread in the big ranch kitchen. — Jack Kerouac, *On the Road*, p. 228, 1957
- What kind of spread would they put out over to the Judge's? Some little finger bits and pieces, celery sticks stuffed with cream cheese, potato chips and green dip that worked its way up under the fingernails? — Robert Campbell, *Boneyards*, p. 2, 1992

2 in sports betting, the margin of victory incorporated into a bet US, 1973

- Even when they're being real generous with the line, I think can beat the spread, I lay off. — John Sayles, *Union Dues*, p. 25, 1977
- The spread is nine for game one, but the Celtics will probably win by 14 or 15. — Hunter S. Thompson, *Generation of Swine*, p. 120, 26th May 1986

3 a photograph of a naked woman exposing her genitals US, 1969

- For those interested in semantics, the pictures with the legs in normal position showing only the pubic bush are called "beaver pictures" but if the legs are spread apart and the camera angle shows the vaginal aperture or clitoris, then it is called "spread." — *Screw*, p. 16, 18th August 1969

4 in pool, the first shot of the game US, 1990

- — Steve Rushin, *Pool Cool*, p. 27, 1990

spread verb

to share information or cards while engaging in a cheating scheme US, 1968

- — Thomas L. Clark, *The Dictionary of Gambling and Gaming*, p. 212, 1987

▶ **spread a game**

to start a card game US, 1977

- — Robert C. Prus and C.R.D. Sharper, *Road Hustler*, p. 171, 1977: "Glossary of terms"

▶ **spread the eagle**

to escape from prison or jail US, 1950

- — Hyman E. Goldin et al., *Dictionary of American Underworld Lingo*, p. 204, 1950

▶ **spread your shot**

to speak honestly and directly US, 1976

- — John R. Armore and Joseph D. Wolfe, *Dictionary of Desperation*, p. 51, 1976

spread-eagle verb

to spread and stretch out a person's arms and legs UK, 1826

- Three squad cars answered the call and within 20 seconds a half dozen cops had Wally out of his car and spread-eagled facedown on the asphalt. — C.D. Payne, *Youth in Revolt*, p. 135, 1993

spreader noun

the vagina displayed with lips parted US, 1970

- By 1967 or 1968, a whole group of magazines featured nude females in a manner which emphasized their genitalia in complete detail (known in the industry as "spreader" or "split beaver" magazines). — *The Presidential Commission on Obscenity and Pornography*, p. 113, 1970

spreadhead noun

a devoted follower of the band Widespread Panic US, 2001

An evolution of DEADHEAD (a follower of the Grateful Dead).

- — Don R. McCreary (Editor), *Dawg Speak*, 2001

spread shot noun

a photograph or scene in a pornographic movie showing a woman's spread vagina US, 1971

- As an example, inspector Guido cited a set of glossy spread shots that sold under the counter for $8. — *Screw*, p. 14, 10th May 1971
- A few kisses, a lot of tongue action, some fondling and a lot of spread shots. — Tina Russell, *Porno Star*, p. 23, 1973

Spreewell noun

a style of spinning chrome wheels US, 2006

- Flashy, chrome wheels including some spinning ones called "Spreewels" after NBA bad boy Latrell Sprewell. — *Daily News of Los Angeles*, p. B1, 5th December 2006

spring verb

to escape, or effect someone's escape or release, from prison or detection US, 1904

- By this time Bow and Emil Burbacher were sprung from The School and showed up on the Corner again. — Mezz Mezzrow, *Really the Blues*, p. 20, 1946
- Whenever a crowd of fellows were rounded up in a raid on a gambling house or saloon the proprietor knew how to "spring" them, that is, get them out of jail. — Louis Armstrong, *Satchmo*, p. 126, 1954
- As continuity would have it, they are sprung at the same time more or less and take up residence in a flat on the Lower East Side. — William Burroughs, *Naked Lunch*, p. 129, 1957
- So now he's sprung, but he brung his brain with him and he's gonna bring down that whole country. — Edwin Torres, *After Hours*, p. 173, 1979

springbutt noun

a person who is eager to please US, 1962

- — *American Speech*, p. 288, December 1962: "Marine Corps slang"
- We called them "Spring Butts," those eager beavers whose impressive memories had them enthusiastically bouncing out of their chairs and up the road to being first in the class. — David H. Hackworth, *About Face*, p. 214, 1989

springer noun

any person in the position to get you out of jail, from a bail bondsman to a lawyer to a judge US, 1950

- — Hyman E. Goldin et al., *Dictionary of American Underworld Lingo*, p. 204, 1950
- — *Maledicta*, p. 150, Summer/Winter 1986 – 1987: "Sexual slang: prostitutes, pedophiles, flagellators, transvestites, and necrophiles"

spritz verb

to squirt, especially a mist US, 1917

- After a vigorous sponge bath, followed by an extra-heavy spritz of deodorant, I dressed quickly and counted out my remaining cash: $43.12. — C.D. Payne, *Youth in Revolt*, p. 55, 1993
- Kay squealed with her mouth full—some club soda spritzed out and hit Leigh. — James Ellroy, *Hollywood Nocturnes*, p. 25, 1994

sprung adjective

addicted US, 1992

- — Judi Sanders, *Kickin' like Chicken with the Couch Commander*, p. 23, 1992
- [A] pale white woman, clearly sprung on crack, who absently clutched a small white girl. — Bob Sipchen, *Baby Insane and the Buddha*, p. 401, 1993

sprung on adjective

infatuated with US, 1995

- CHER: Oooh, you knew what? ELTON: That you were totally sprung on me. — *Clueless*, 1995
- — Rick Ayers (Editor), *Berkeley High Slang Dictionary*, p. 39, 2004

spud noun

a SCUD missile US, 1993

An obvious rhyme that belittles the enemy's weaponry.

- — *The Retired Officer Magazine*, p. 39, January 1993

spud juice *noun*
a potent homemade alcoholic beverage produced by
fermenting potatoes *US, 1977*
- I got some good spud juice lined up, but it takes five packs to cop.
— Donald Goines, *Black Gangster*, p. 12, 1977

spun *adjective*
1 crazy; disoriented *US, 1997*
- — Vann Wesson, *Generation X Field Guide and Lexicon*, p. 158, 1997
2 very drug-intoxicated *US, 1997*
- "They'll be smoking ice and getting all spun-out tonight or he'll be
in a straitjacket." — Joseph Wambaugh, *Hollywood Station*, p. 233, 2006
3 excited, enthusiastic *US, 1984*
- That was her goal in life, to work "behind the camera." "When it's
live, I'm spun," she said. — Dan Jenkins, *Life Its Ownself*, p. 186, 1984

spunk *noun*
1 mettle, courage *UK, 1774*
A word associated with actress Mary Tyler Moore; in the initial
episode of *The Mary Tyler Moore Show* in 1970, Moore's boss
Lou Grant assesses her—"You've got spunk. I hate spunk!"
- General Peckem blessed the fates that had sent him a weakling for
a subordinate. A man of spunk would have been unthinkable.
— Joseph Heller, *Catch 22*, p. 331, 1961
- And it takes a lot of spunk and devotion to be a chaplain. — Darryl
Ponicsan, *The Last Detail*, p. 45, 1970
- But then talking to her after changed his mind, seeing this was
a good-looking girl up close with a cute figure. She had spunk,
too. — Elmore Leonard, *Maximum Bob*, p. 43, 1991
2 semen *UK, 1888*
- He's spewing his spunk deep inside her seething snatch! — *Adam Film
World*, p. 60, 1977
- The booth smelled of spunk[.] — Richard Price, *Clockers*, p. 393, 1992
- An overweight, faggy-looking Filipino in his early thirties—who was
the "floater" at Annabel's gang bang—wipes up any and all spunk
sprayed upon Jasmin today. — Anthony Petkovich, *The X Factory*, p. 190, 1997
- Missy Monroe in the closer going beyond the call of duty, taking
way more than the requisite Baker's dozen spunk blasts all over her
pretty face. — Editors of Adult Video News, *The AVN Guide to the 500 Greatest
Adult Films of All Time*, p. 26, 2005

squab *noun*
a young girl or woman *US, 1948*
- The table is so situated that the town's aging and more prosperous
squab-hunters who congregate at it nightly can case the door and
ogle the bims brought in by younger and more energetic men.
— Jack Lait and Lee Mortimer, *New York Confidential*, p. 166, 1948
- The black whore raised her hand above her head. "We got a man
wants a squab over here," she singsonged. — Robert Campbell, *Alice in
La-La Land*, p. 256, 1987

squab *verb*
to fight *US, 1986*
- — *Los Angeles Times*, p. II-6, 11th August 1986

squab job *noun*
a sexually attractive girl below the legal age of consent *US, 1964*
- — Roger Blake, *The American Dictionary of Sexual Terms*, p. 111, 1964

squack *noun*
a woman; sex with a woman *US, 1972*
- (Caption): WHEN HE GET some fine Ofay squack in the sheets,
what he make her do? She suck his joint, man. — *Screw*, p. 15,
30th October 1972

squack *verb*
to ejaculate *US, 1993*
- I'm squacking in my pants. — *Airheads*, 1993

squad *noun*
a police squad car *US, 1965*
- They came and brought the paddy wagon with them, two squads
and a paddy wagon. — Henry Williamson, *Hustler!*, p. 104, 1965

square *noun*
1 a person with a conventional job and lifestyle; an old-
fashioned person *US, 1944*
- "It's full of squares. Retired detective-story writers and women
real-estate agents." — Chandler Brossard, *Who Walks in Darkness*, p. 46, 1952

- She's gonna marry this rich jerk from Chicago, a real square. — Jack
Kerouac, *The Dharma Bums*, p. 134, 1958
- Amphetamine, that group of drugs which are called pep pills by
squares. They are also called psychic energizers. — Ruth Bronsteen,
The Hippy's Handbook, p. 12, 1967
- I had out-slicked the law / and taken off a whole lotta squares.
— Lightnin' Rod, *Hustlers Convention*, p. 29, 1973
2 a filling meal *US, 1882*
- With Vi and Uncle Bassett I learned what it was to have three
squares a day and a bed to sleep in. — Ethel Waters, *His Eye is on the
Sparrow*, p. 11, 1951
- Have a good dinner, kid. You look as though you haven't had
a square in weeks. — Antony James, *America's Homosexual Underground*, p. 46,
1965
- I love the goddam navy. I get three squares a day, a pad to lie down
on, roof over my head, tuxedo to wear. We're living high off the hog.
— Darryl Ponicsan, *The Last Detail*, p. 33, 1970
- They've been real good to your people—gettin' 'em off the streets,
givin' 'em three squares a day, all them fancy uniforms. — Eugene Boe
(Compiler), *The Wit & Wisdom of Archie Bunker*, p. 65, 1971
3 a factory-manufactured cigarette *US, 1958*
- A square is a cigarette. And also a quarter. — Willard Motley, *Let No Man
Write My Epitaph*, p. 148, 1958
- She reached in her purse and pulled out a square / She said "Don't
worry, daddy, he's no where." — Bruce Jackson, *Get Your Ass in the Water and
Swim Like Me*, p. 55, 1974
- I said, "Hey Jack, how you doing? That sure is a fine 'silk' girl, huh?
You got a square to spare?" He flashed a cigarette from his red
shirt pocket, handed it to me, and said, "Yeh Kid, she's fine as
a Valentine." — Iceberg Slim (Robert Beck), *Pimp*, p. 35, 1969
- "Got a square, Joe?" Reaching for the Camels on his bedstand, Joe
held his breath to wince in pain and was surprised instead to feel
only a tightness. — Seth Morgan, *Homeboy*, p. 109, 1990

▸ **on the square**
living a law-abiding, conventional life *US, 1949*
- "Them whole two years on the square I didn't have one good time."
— Nelson Algren, *The Man with the Golden Arm*, p. 205, 1949

square *adjective*
old-fashioned; decent and honest; conventional *US, 1946*
- The other patients were a pretty square and sorry lot. Not another
junkie in the place. — William Burroughs, *Junkie*, p. 93, 1953
- One of the little pigs was very cool, another was more on the
commercial side, and the third was, beyond the shadow of a doubt,
square. — Steve Allen, *Bop Fables*, p. 18, 1955
- Dig the square wardrobe! — *Rebel Without a Cause*, 1955
- One is Hip or one is Square (the alternative which each new generation coming into American life is beginning to feel), one is a rebel
or one conforms[.] — Norman Mailer, *Advertisements for Myself*, p. 339, 1957
- Other square situations that you might someday find yourself facing
are installation proceedings, when Dad becomes chief of his lodge[.]
— Dick Clark, *To Goof or Not to Goof*, p. 167, 1963

square as a bear *adjective*
extremely conventional *US, 1957*
The bear appears for the rhyming value, nothing else.
- "Daddy-O," she said, "you're square as a bear, but I dig you the
most." — Max Shulman, *Rally Round the Flag, Boys!*, p. 48, 1957

square bitch *noun*
any woman who is not a prostitute *US, 1972*
- — Christina and Richard Milner, *Black Players*, p. 10, 1972

squared *adjective*
craving drugs *US, 1958*
- If you're squared, it means you need some stuff. You're not feeling
good. — Willard Motley, *Let No Man Write My Epitaph*, p. 148, 1958

squared circle *noun*
a boxing or wrestling ring *US, 1914*
- These nights were spent inside of a squared circle surrounded by
a pack of howling idiots who fouled up the air with smoke and
words[.] — Gregory "Pappy" Boyington, *Baa Baa Black Sheep*, p. 373, 1958
- The monsters of the mat are not only busy breaking bones in the
squared circle. — Robert Picarello, *Rules of the Ring*, p. xi, 2000

square from Delaware *noun*
an exceptionally naive, conventional person *US, 1938*

Delaware exists for the rhyme; it is no more or less square than any other state. In the 1930s and 40s, there was a cottage industry in inventing terms along the line of this construction—a "clown from Allentown," a "pester from Chester" and so on. The "square from Delaware" was one of the few that truly worked itself into speech.

- — Lou Shelly, *Hepcats Jive Talk Dictionary*, p. 37, 1945
- Even a square from Delaware should know God ain't going to kiss your ass when you tell him no, you poor boob. — Iceberg Slim (Robert Beck), *Pimp*, p. 134, 1969

square grouper *noun*
a brick of compressed marijuana *US, 1989*
The name of a notional fish, alluding to the presence of marijuana smugglers in south Florida waters.

- Or I could take the money and invest in a shrimper heading south to do a little "square grouper" fishing and triple my money in a month. — Jimmy Buffett, *Tales from Margaritaville*, p. 172, 1989

squarehead *noun*
any Scandinavian *US, 1975*
Left from the language of the logging camps of the early C20.

- — John Gould, *Maine Lingo*, p. 43, 1975
- — *Maledicta*, p. 171, Summer/Winter 1978: "How to hate thy neighbor: a guide to racist maledicta"

square Jane *noun*
a decent and law-abiding, if naive, woman *US, 1986*

- I could read inside the heads of all those square johns. Oh yeah, I could. Square janes, too. — Robert Campbell, *In La-La Land We Trust*, p. 69, 1986

square John *noun*
a decent and law-abiding, if naive, person *US, 1934*

- "He's a Square John (non-user)." — Donald Wilson, *My Six Convicts*, p. 51, 1951
- He works longer than "square Johns" who put in their eight hours each day. — Johnny Shearer, *The Male Hustler*, p. 23, 1966
- Still he didn't consider himself a failure, simply because it had never occurred to him he could be confined in any such square john term. — Malcolm Braly, *On the Yard*, p. 4, 1967
- Vito, you're not a down-the-line square John. — Vincent Patrick, *Family Business*, p. 55, 1985

square joint *noun*
a tobacco cigarette *US, 1971*

- — Eugene Landy, *The Underground Dictionary*, p. 67, 1971

square monicker *noun*
a person's legal, given name *US, 1959*

- "What are their family names?" "I don't know none of 'em's square monicker's." — Chester Himes, *The Real Cool Killers*, p. 113, 1959

square name *noun*
a person's legal name, sometimes unknown to his associates who know him only by a nickname *US, 1955*

- My first fight was with the Golden Boy of Boxing. His square name was Milo Theodorescu. — Rocky Garciano (with Rowland Barber), *Somebody Up There Likes Me*, p. 271, 1955

square pair *noun*
in craps, an eight rolled with a pair of fours *US, 1985*

- — Steve Kuriscak, *Casino Talk*, p. 67, 1985
- — Chris Fagans and David Guzman, *A Guide to Craps Lingo*, p. 28, 1999

squarer *noun*
in circus and carnival usage, a claims adjuster and mender of legal problems *US, 1981*

- — Don Wilmeth, *The Language of American Popular Entertainment*, p. 254, 1981

square Sam *noun*
a decent and law-abiding, if naive, man *US, 1953*

- A Square Sam myself, I was known to be "strictly okay" and a "right kid." — Jim Thompson, *Bad Boy*, p. 333, 1953

square shooter *noun*
a truthful, direct, honorable person *US, 1914*

- But what with taxes and cost of living, few square shooters can afford such luxury. — Jack Lait and Lee Mortimer, *Washington Confidential*, p. 277, 1951
- I've seen people who were supposed to be square shooters that use signals, they steal money out of the pot. — Kim Rich, *Johnny's Girl*, p. 64, 1993

Squaresville *noun*
the notional hometown of extremely conventional people
US, 1956

- And—squaresville or not—I happen to believe in duty. — Peter Nichols, *Joe Egg*, p. 58, 1968
- People talked about "Squaresville in 1961." The Morning Mayor of New York could surely have gotten elected ruler of that mythical hamlet. — Cousin Bruce Morrow, *Cousin Brucie*, p. 105, 1987

square up *verb*
to return to the path of righteousness after a sojourn in sin
US, 1968

- Soon's I kick this habit I'm gon' square up and git a job. — Nathan Heard, *Howard Street*, pp. 78–79, 1968
- Mama, I haven't shot any "H" in ten years. I haven't had a whore in five years. I squared up. I work every day. — Iceberg Slim (Robert Beck), *Pimp*, p. 29, 1969
- How do women "square up" and leave prostitution, and how many do so? — Charles Winick, *The Lively Commerce*, p. 73, 1971

square weed *noun*
tobacco *US, 1959*

- Choo-Choo fished two Camels from a squashed package in his sweat shirt and lit them, passing one to Sheik. "This square weed on top of gage makes you crazy," he said. — Chester Himes, *The Real Cool Killers*, p. 53, 1959

square wife *noun*
in law enforcement, a wife in the literal sense of the word, as opposed to the sense of work partner *US, 1988*

- Monk had another wife, a square wife, a wife who'd borne his two children and kept his house and complained every once in a while about the way Wilbur spent more time with Panama than he did with his own wife and kids. — Robert Campbell, *Juice*, p. 4, 1988

square woman *noun*
a woman who is not a prostitute *US, 1967*

- But whores ain't like square women. — Sara Harris, *The Lords of Hell*, p. 124, 1967

squash *noun*

1 a kiss *US, 1981*
Circus and carnival usage.

- — Don Wilmeth, *The Language of American Popular Entertainment*, p. 254, 1981

2 the skull or brain *US, 1985*

- — *Maledicta*, p. 118, 1984–1985: "Milwaukee medical maledicta"
- But ten years after Kennedy took one in the squash, the Supreme Court ruled in Roe v. Wade that women had the right to make decisions about their own reproductive systems. — Al Franken, *The Truth With Jokes*, p. 122, 2005

squash it!
forget it! *US, 1993*

- — *The Bell (Paducah Tilghman High School)*, pp. 8–9, 17th December 1993: "Tilghmanism: the concealed language of the hallway"

squash rot *noun*
the medical condition suffered by severe stroke victims *US, 1983*

- — *Maledicta*, p. 39, 1983: More common patient-directed pejoratives used by medical personnel

squat *noun*

1 nothing *US, 1967*
A shortened form of **DOODLY-SQUAT**. Often found in double negative constructions.

- Some of them old farts out three, four days a time, you don't say squat to them. — *Saturday Night Fever*, 1977
- She's not hearing squat. — Armistead Maupin, *Babycakes*, p. 36, 1984
- After fucking 251 times on film—and getting her cunt carved and bloodied from unwashed, untrimmed claws—she walked away with squat. Nothing. Niet. Nada penny. — Anthony Petkovich, *The X Factory*, p. 202, 1997

2 a seat; a chair *US, 1973*

- Pop was chopping a study's mop and mom was in her favorite squat behind the store. — A.S. Jackson, *Gentleman Pimp*, 1973
- So we decided we'd liven up the pot / by coppin' a squat. — Lightnin liven' Rod, *Hustlers Convention*, 1973

squat *verb*
1 to execute someone by electrocution in the electric chair
US, 1950
- — Hyman E. Goldin et al., *Dictionary of American Underworld Lingo*, p. 206, 1950

2 to assemble to discuss and mediate disagreements among prisoners *US, 1976*
- — John R. Armore and Joseph D. Wolfe, *Dictionary of Desperation*, p. 51, 1976

▸ **squat through**
to lower your stance to a squat to maintain control of your surfboard while a wave is cresting over you *US, 1965*
- — Duke Kahanamoku with Joe Brennan, *Duke Kahanamoku's World of Surfing*, p. 177, 1965

squatter *noun*
a chair *US, 1945*
- — Lou Shelly, *Hepcats Jive Talk Dictionary*, p. 17, 1945
- — Clarence Major, *Dictionary of Afro-American Slang*, p. 108, 1970

squaw *noun*
a wife or girlfriend *US, 1823*
From the dialects of the Algonquin North American Indian tribes.
- Carver comes down from the third floor with his squaw[.] — Robert Byrne, *McGoorty*, p. 62, 1972

squawk *noun*
a complaint, especially a vociferous and indignant one *US, 1909*
- "I just come to spring you—what's the big squawk?" — Nelson Algren, *The Man with the Golden Arm*, p. 23, 1949
- He has therefore developed a trained police corps to protect the Quarter operation from any squawk or complaint, reasonable or otherwise. — Robert Sylvester, *No Cover Charge*, p. 34, 1956
- "Now where you got any squawk coming?" — Malcom Braly, *Felony Tank*, p. 51, 1961
- In other words, I have done all right with the fair sex. I got no squawks in that department. — Edwin Torres, *Carlito's Way*, p. 19, 1975

squawk *verb*
to complain *US, 1970*
- They don't dare squawk about our location, and the stuff is gone anyhow. — Red Rudensky, *The Gonif*, p. 106, 1970

▸ **squawk your parrot**
to set an airborne emergency signal transmitter on continuous transmission *US, 1990*
- — Joseph Tuso, *Singing the Vietnam Blues*, p. 262, 1990: Glossary

squawk box *noun*
1 a low-fidelity public address system *US, 1945*
- The guys went back to talking about the town and the women in the town, and suddenly the LCVP's squawk box burst into static, and a gravelly voice said, "Now hear this. Now hear this." — Evan Hunter, *The Blackboard Jungle*, p. 189, 1954
- The Colonel gave Guido a final scowl and flipped the key on his inter-office squawk box. — Max Shulman, *Rally Round the Flag, Boys!*, p. 120, 1957
- Rhack has the projector working, announces over the squawk box—"Sunday movie will be starting in five minutes in the mess hall." — Ken Kesey, *Kesey's Jail Journal*, p. 95, 1967
- I was brooding on these things when the pilot came on the squawk-box and said we were turning back to Denver[.] — Hunter S. Thompson, *Generation of Swine*, p. 39, 4th October 1985

2 a citizens' band radio *US, 1976*
- — Lawrence Teeman, *Consumer Guide Good Buddy's CB Dictionary*, p. 93, 1976

3 a child hospital patient who persistently cries or complains *US, 1994*
- — Sally Williams, *"Strong" Words*, p. 160, 1994

squaw piss *noun*
beer with a low alcohol content *US, 1968*
- — *Current Slang*, p. 12, Summer 1968

squeak *noun*
1 a police informer *US, 1950*
- I happen to know you're a goddam squeak. — Hal Ellson, *Tomboy*, p. 136, 1950

2 a cheapskate *US, 1963*
- — *San Francisco Examiner*, p. 8, 27th October 1963: "What a 'Z'! The astonishing private language of Bay Area teenagers"

squeal *noun*
in police work, a person who reports a crime; the call reporting the crime *US, 1977*
- We get a squeal that a nut job has got a knife. — Edwin Torres, *Q & A*, p. 71, 1977
- Fuckin' Elias, man, fuckin' squeal, that's what he is, gonna get everybody in the platoon in shit. — *Platoon*, 1986
- I just spoke to the station commander who caught the squeal. — James Ellroy, *Suicide Hill*, p. 633, 1986
- "Kramer and me caught the squeal." "Why ain't you with the victim?" — Robert Campbell, *Boneyards*, p. 37, 1992

squeal *verb*
to inform on someone; to betray someone *US, 1846*
- Charles Becker was executed in Sing for complicity in the murder of Herman Rosenthal, a big-time gambler who squealed to District Attorney Whitman about the tie-up between police and the crime syndicate. — Jack Lait and Lee Mortimer, *New York Confidential*, p. 64, 1948
- James Castle called him a very conceited guy, and one of Stabile's lousy friends went and squealed on him to Stabile. — J.D. Salinger, *Catcher in the Rye*, p. 170, 1951
- That you don't have to suck up to me. I won't squeal. — Leonard Cohen, *Beautiful Losers*, p. 134, 1966
- It's reprehensible to squeal on your own flesh and blood, but it's for his own good. — *Ferris Bueller's Day Off*, 1986

squealer *noun*
a police informer *UK, 1865*
- Frank turned to Stan. "You squealer!" he sneered. — Irving Shulman, *The Amboy Dukes*, p. 252, 1947
- A confused old man, he came to Chico's cell twice and asked for the squealer in Number Nineteen, forgetting he'd taken him to deliver his information to those waiting below. — Hal Ellson, *The Golden Spike*, p. 241, 1952
- "Why, you stoolpigeon," I said, hurt-like, "you Puerto Rican squealer." — Piri Thomas, *Down These Mean Streets*, p. 20, 1967
- "Oh, you'll have your squealer's money." — C.D. Payne, *Cut to the Twisp*, p. 54, 2001

squealers *noun*
bacon *US, 1996*
- — *Maledicta*, p. 21, 1996: "Domino's pizza jargon"

squeegie *noun*
a young person who is hopelessly out of touch with current fashions and trends *US, 1949*
Youth usage.
- — *Time*, 3rd October 1949

squeeze *noun*
a partner in romance *US, 1971*
A shortening of **MAIN SQUEEZE** (a man's primary romantic partner).
- — Hermese E. Roberts, *The Third Ear*, 1971
- Squeeze—Girlfriend; boyfriend; intimate acquaintance — James Haskins, *Street Gangs*, p. 150, 1974
- "She your woman?" "Just a squeeze." — Robert Campbell, *In La-La Land We Trust*, p. 20, 1986
- Renee is in her room now, giggling on the phone with her latest squeeze, a guy named Royal she met at The Sizzler last week. — Armistead Maupin, *Maybe the Moon*, p. 24, 1992

▸ **put the squeeze on someone**
to exert influence on someone *US, 1941*
- Elmer, honey—baby—how could I put the squeeze on you? — Richard Brooks, *Elmer Gantry*, 1960

squeeze *verb*
1 to recount or tell something *US, 1947*
- — Marcus Hanna Boulware, *Jive and Slang of Students in Negro Colleges*, 1947

2 in poker, to surround a player with two confederates whose collusive betting tactics relieve the middle player of his bankroll and drive him from the game *US, 1949*
- — Thomas L. Clark, *The Dictionary of Gambling and Gaming*, p. 188, 1987

3 while playing cards, to look only at the very edge of a card *US, 1967*
- — Albert H. Morehead, *The Complete Guide to Winning Poker*, p. 274, 1967

▸ **squeeze a lemon; squeeze the lemon**
to drive through a traffic light as it changes from yellow to red *US, 1993*

- — Connie Eble (Editor), *UNC-CH Campus Slang*, p. 5, Fall 1993
- — Anna Scotti and Paul Young, *Buzzwords*, p. 41, 1997

▸ **squeeze the cheese**
to fart *US, 1993*
- — Judi Sanders, *Faced and Faded, Hanging to Hurl*, p. 38, 1993
- — Peter Furze, *Tailwinds*, p. 54, 1998

squeeze cheese *noun*
a pasteurized processed cheese product, semisolid, sold in a plastic bottle *US, 1986*
A clever name for a nasty thing.
- They love freeze dried stroganoff, Kraft squeeze cheese, Wyler's fruit mixes, beef jerky, but they only get it when we're backpacking. — *Chicago Tribune*, p. C21, 5th October 1986

squeeze off *verb*
to fire a shot from a gun *US, 1956*
- The guy with the rug was firing at Tommy, squeezing them off like he was on a target range, the sound of gunfire hitting the air hard... — Elmore Leonard, *Be Cool*, p. 17, 1999

squeezers *noun*
dice that have been squeezed out of shape in a vice for use by cheats *US, 1950*
- — *The Annals of the American Academy of Political and Social Sciences*, p. 131, May 1950

squeezings *noun*
a gel formed with liquid ethanol and saturated calcium acetate solution; when ignited, the alcohol in the gel burns *US, 1980*
Used as a source of fuel in portable cooking stoves and as a source of alcohol for truly desperate derelicts who squeeze the gel through sponges and collect the liquid.
- — Joe McKennon, *Circus Lingo*, p. 87, 1980

squib *noun*
1 in the television and movie industries, a small explosive charge that simulates being struck by a bullet *US, 1990*
- — John Cann, *The Stunt Guide*, p. 63: "Terms and definitions"
- — Ralph S. Singleton, *Filmmaker's Dictionary*, p. 160, 1990
2 in target shooting, a hand-loaded cartridge that does not fully detonate *US, 1957*
- — *American Speech*, p. 195, October 1957: "Some colloquialisms of the handgunner"

squid *noun*
1 a despicable, spineless person *US, 1974*
- — Connie Eble (Editor), *UNC-CH Campus Slang*, March 1974
- — *National Education Association Today*, April 1985: "A glossary for rents and other squids"
- Which wasn't too hard, the guy was a real squid. — *True Romance*, 1993
2 a serious, dedicated, diligent student *US, 1987*
- At San Diego State University, a flattering term for a hard studier is a "study bunny:" less so is "squid." — *New York Times*, 12th April 1987
3 a sailor in the US Navy *US, 1985*
- I yelled at them, never thinking that that was army lingo and the grounded squids probably didn't know what the hell I was talking about. — David Donovan, *Once a Warrior King*, p. 299, 1985
- Next door there was a hotel, crawling with "squids." — Dolores French, *Working*, p. 194, 1988
- "Charge it to me, and tell the squid thanks." — Kregg Jorgenson, *Very Crazy G.I.*, p. 10, 2001
4 a Japanese person who is lacking in all social skills *US, 1982*
Hawaiian youth usage; highly insulting.
- — Douglas Simonson, *Pidgin to da Max Hana Hou*, 1982

squid *verb*
to study hard *US, 1981*
- Studying is squidding or grinding. — *Wesleyan Alumnus*, p. 29, Spring 1981

squidge *verb*
in tiddlywinks, to shoot a wink with an oversized wink *US, 1977*
- — *Verbatim*, p. 525, December 1977

squiffed off *adjective*
annoyed; angry *US, 1952*
- Nothing, except a pair of my men are highly squiffed off. — Mickey Spillane, *Kiss Me Deadly*, p. 112, 1952

squiff out *verb*
to lose consciousness as a result of excessive consumption of alcohol *US, 1953*
- You squiffed out at The Dancers in a Rolls. Your girl friend ditched you. — Raymond Chandler, *The Long Goodbye*, p. 4, 1953

squigg *noun*
a prank *US, 1988*
- — Hans Halberstadt, *Airborne*, p. 130, 1988: "Abridged dictionary of airborne terms"

squiggle *noun*
a tilde (~) on a computer keyboard *US, 1991*
- — Eric S. Raymond, *The New Hacker's Dictionary*, p. 41, 1991

squiggles *noun*
during the 1991 US war against Iraq, any writing in the Arabic script *US, 1991*
- Only 20 kilometers to "Squiggles." — *Army*, p. 48, November 1991

squinch-eyed *adjective*
with eyes half closed *US, 1946*
- At first he was squinch-eyed but now his eyes blew up like soap-bubbles and panic danced all over his face. — Mezz Mezzrow, *Really the Blues*, p. 96, 1946

squint *noun*
a person lacking in social skills, fashion, or both *US, 1978*
- "Wouldn't put it past those squints at Internal Affairs," said Montezuma Montez. — Joseph Wambaugh, *The Black Marble*, p. 238, 1978
▸ **on the squint**
on the look-out for something *US, 1970*
- Sorry was to move up the platform four or five yards and be on the squint for trouble. — Red Rudensky, *The Gonif*, p. 117, 1970

squirm seat *noun*
the chair in which witnesses sit in a courtroom *US, 1962*
- — *American Speech*, p. 272, December 1962: "The language of traffic policemen"

squirrel *noun*
1 a mentally unstable person *US, 1985*
- The guy gave me one of those looks and I said to myself, "Shit, I've got a squirrel." — Mark Baker, *Cops*, p. 88, 1985
2 a drug addict who hides drug portions for future use *US, 1957*
- Provident junkies, known as squirrels, keep stashes against a bust. — William Burroughs, *Naked Lunch*, p. 9, 1957

squirrel guy *noun*
a psychotherapist *US, 1951*
- "They all got angles, these Squirrel Guys. Some of 'em ask us to fit square blocks in round holes, some of 'em want us to talk to 'em just like we would to our old mother." — Donald Wilson, *My Six Convicts*, p. 26, 1951

squirrely *adjective*
completely obsessed with acquiring and hoarding amphetamine *US, 1989*
- A squirrely person may collect and wash rinsebags in order to salvage the residue of speed they had contained. Empty cigarette packs are often mistaken for bags. — Geoffrey Froner, *Digging for Diamonds*, p. 58, 1989

squirt *noun*
1 a person who is small in stature, character, or both *US, 1848*
- Who's the squirt down at the end? — Mickey Spillane, *I, The Jury*, p. 123, 1947
- The pavement heats up now, the Four breaking harder, screaming louder, pushing back the five little squirts, who can't seem to stay out of the way. — Josh Alan Friedman, *Tales of Times Square*, p. 56, 1986
- Little squirt, right? He's a public defender. — Elmore Leonard, *Maximum Bob*, p. 4, 1991
2 twenty-five cents or twenty-five dollars *US, 1951*
- — *American Speech*, p. 101, May 1951

squirt *verb*
in pool, to strike the cue ball off center producing a course in the opposite direction proportional to the degree to which the ball is hit off center *US, 1978*
- — Mike Shamos, *The Illustrated Encyclopedia of Billiards*, p. 229, 1993

squirter *noun*
a scene in a pornographic movie or photograph depicting a man ejaculating *US, 1995*
- — *Adult Video News*, p. 42, August 1995

squishy *adjective*
forgetful *US, 1951*
Teen slang.
- — *Newsweek*, p. 28, 8th October 1951

SRO
standing *r*oom *o*nly; completely sold-out *US, 1890*
- A month after Zenobia's funeral, the church is again S.R.O. for the wedding of Joe and Reba. — Iceberg Slim (Robert Beck), *Doom Fox*, p. 131, 1978

stab *noun*
a victim of a knife fight *US, 1984–1985*
- — *Maledicta*, p. 15, 1984–1985: "A medical Christmas song"

stab *verb*
to disparage someone with profanity *US, 2001*
- — Don R. McCreary (Editor), *Dawg Speak*, 2001

stable *noun*
1 a group of prostitutes working for a single pimp or madam *US, 1937*
- Pell was also responsible for the widespread belief that Hebert maintained a stable of whores in the hotel[.] — Jim Thompson, *Bad Boy*, p. 362, 1953
- I can rotate my regular stable of boys or, if need be, call on part-time hustlers. — Johnny Shearer, *The Male Hustler*, p. 21, 1966
- Rocky has from sixty to seventy-five full and parttime boys in his stable. — John Francis Hunter, *The Gay Insider*, p. 213, 1971
- On being taken into Madeleine's stable, I severed all professional relationship with Pearl[.] — Xaviera Hollander, *The Happy Hooker*, p. 89, 1972
2 a group of "slaves" in the control of, or at the disposal of, a dominatrix; a collection of masochists in the control of, a sadist *US, 1989*
- — Thomas E. Murray and Thomas R. Murrell, *The Language of Sadomasochism*, 1989
3 by extension, a group of people working for someone *UK, 1942*
- I have a stable of actors and actresses. — *Boogie Nights*, 1997
4 a house or apartment *US, 2000*
- — *Ebony Magazine*, p. 156, August 2000: "How to talk to the new generation"

stable *verb*
(used of a pimp) to induce a prostitute to join other prostitutes working for him *US, 1969*
- I never tried to stable her after that. — Iceberg Slim (Robert Beck), *Pimp*, p. 268, 1969

stable boy's favorite *noun*
a controlled throw of dice onto a dirt surface *US, 1974*
- — Thomas L. Clark, *The Dictionary of Gambling and Gaming*, p. 214, 1987

stable of lace *noun*
the prostitutes associated with one pimp *US, 1976*
- The women constitute a player's "stable of lace," bound to him by many and varied ties[.] — Dennis Wepman et al., *The Life*, p. 3, 1976

stable push *noun*
inside information *US, 1956*
- [T]he "stable push" was the inside dope about whether a boat might be in the works. — Nan Mooney, *My Racing Heart*, p. 189, 2002

stable sister *noun*
one prostitute in relation to the other prostitutes in a pimp's stable *US, 1972*
- Usually the player relies on one to help him recruit new additions, known as stable sisters. — Christina and Richard Milner, *Black Players*, p. 40, 1972

'stache *noun*
a moustache *US, 1972*
- I can start growing my stache back when I get out of quarantine. — John Sinclair, *Guitar Army*, p. 171, 1972
- Excellent 'stache, Smith. — *Bill and Ted's Excellent Adventure*, 1989

stack *noun*
1 one thousand dollars *US, 2007*
- He claims he could earn a "stack"—street slang for $1000—for his work. He claims he shot someone in a dispute at a drug house. — *Milwaukee Journal Sentinel*, p. 1A, 17th March 2002
- Davis is now accused of enlisting the help of others to contact Peters by phone and offering the victim "four stacks," street slang for $4,000, to change his story of the events that led up to the shooting. — *Duluth News-Tribune*, 12th December 2007
2 in pool, the balls assembled inside the rack before a game *US, 1977*
- — Mike Shamos, *The Illustrated Encyclopedia of Billiards*, p. 230, 1993
3 in pool, the clustered pack of balls left at the foot of the table after the first shot of the game *US, 1990*
- — Steve Rushin, *Pool Cool*, p. 27, 1990
4 a package of marijuana cigarettes *US, 1955*
- — *American Speech*, p. 88, May 1955: "Narcotic got along the Mexican border"
- — Richard A. Spears, *The Slang and Jargon of Drugs and Drink*, p. 480, 1986
5 a large amount of something *US, 1870*
- There could be a stack of explanations for that initial deployment of the short, sharp blow. — *The Guardian*, 22nd March 2003

stack *verb*
1 to put away, to save *US, 1991*
- What does a fifteen-year-old do with that kind of money? "Spend it. And stack it." — Leon Bing, *Do or Die*, p. 32, 1991
2 to earn a lot of money *US, 1997*
- — Vann Wesson, *Generation X Field Guide and Lexicon*, p. 160, 1997

stacked *adjective*
1 possessing large breasts *US, 1942*
Sometimes intensified with phrases such as "stone to the bone" or rhymed as in "stacked and packed" (the name of a photographic calendar produced by former Nixon operative G. Gordon Liddy, featuring nearly naked women holding guns).
- She was stacked. She was pretty. — Jim Thompson, *Savage Night*, p. 74, 1953
- Well stacked too. Nice behind. — Willard Motley, *Let No Man Write My Epitaph*, p. 297, 1958
- "If you were good-looking or stacked or something, I would," I retaliated. — John Nichols, *The Sterile Cuckoo*, p. 82, 1965
- "She was stacked, all right, and I let something like that get away from me." — Leonard Gardner, *Fat City*, p. 120, 1969
2 used of prison sentences, consecutive, not concurrent *US, 1998*
- — Ethan Hilderbrant, *Prison Slang*, p. 121, 1998

stack shoes *noun*
shoes with platform heels *US, 1994*
- All of us were dressed like pimps, with open silk Mack shirts and big stack shoes on. — Eric Davis, *The Slick Boys*, p. 57, 1998

stackup *noun*
a group of waves; a group of surfers on a single wave *US, 1977*
- — Gary Fairmont R. Filosa II, *The Surfer's Almanac*, p. 195, 1977

stag *noun*
1 at a social function, a man without a date *US, 1905*
- Stags could hang around the kitchen or sit on the bench in front of the basement steps which led to the clubroom until they picked up a date. — Irving Shulman, *The Amboy Dukes*, p. 36, 1947
- Then you rule out the women. That cuts the total down to sixty or seventy, just the stags. — Jim Thompson, *The Nothing Man*, p. 193, 1954
- Kemp was the only stag. — Hunter S. Thompson, *Songs of the Doomed*, p. 47, 1959
- In back of us, at the door, they were coming in fast, about three stags to every couple. — Mickey Spillane, *Me, Hood!*, p. 62, 1963
2 a pornographic movie *US, 1966*
An elliptical form of **STAG MOVIE**.
- This film was not the scratched, over-printed, sloppy, jerky amateur production typical of most "stags." — Roger Gordon, *Hollywood's Sexual Underground*, p. 43, 1966
- You could see better stuff in any Times Square sex joint than those stags they were turning out. — Mickey Spillane, *Last Cop Out*, p. 21, 1972
3 the butt end of a cigarette *US, 2002*
- — Gary K. Farlow, *Prison-ese*, p. 67, 2002

stag dinner *noun*
a males-only dinner featuring sexual entertainment in the form of pornographic movies, dancers, and/or prostitutes *US, 1967*
- Until roughly 1950, the pornographic movie business consisted largely in renting films for showing at stag dinners and the like[.] — Ned Polsky, *Hustlers, Beats, and Others*, p. 201, 1967

stage verb

to single someone out in front of a crowd US, 2004

- Yo, teach, stop stagin' me in front of the whole class. — Rick Ayers (Editor), Berkeley High Slang Dictionary, p. 39, 2004

stage dive noun

a jump off a stage during a concert into the arms of the audience US, 1985

- I tell him about the time I saw a kid hurt himself doing a stage dive in New Orleans. — Harvard Crimson, 10th October 1985

stage dive verb

to jump off a stage during a concert into the arms of the audience US, 1989

- When Ian was young he often stage-dived during other group's concerts. — Plain Dealer (Cleveland), 28th April 1989

stage diver noun

a person who jumps off a stage during a concert into the arms of the audience US, 1983

- From out of the Pit come the stage divers—young men who climb onto the stage, dance or sing with the band members (who welcome them). — Boston Globe, p. 1, 30th April 1983

stage diving noun

jumping off a stage during a concert into the arms of the audience US, 1983

- Slam dancing and stage diving. Can you explain what that is? — Washington Post, p. C3, 21st August 1983

stage door Johnny noun

a man waiting outside the stage door for an actress US, 1912

- In those days there were more Stage-Door Johnnies than you could shake a chorus girl at. — Helen Giblo, Footlights, Fistfights and Femmes, p. 111, 1957
- Some of the regulars send candy backstage, though "Stage Door Johnnies" seem to be an extinct species. — Screw, p. 9, 18th April 1969
- You become a stagedoor Johnnie, except that you're not waiting around in the wings, you're waiting in gambling casinos. — Edward Lin, Big Julie of Vegas, p. 136, 1974

stage mother noun

in hospital usage, a mother who coaches their child in answering questions from a doctor and who has a preconceived notion of the diagnosis and appropriate treatment US, 1978

- — Maledicta, p. 69, Summer/Winter 1978: "Common patient-directed pejoratives used by medical personnel"

stage name noun

a criminal's alias US, 1950

- — Hyman E. Goldin et al., Dictionary of American Underworld Lingo, p. 207, 1950

stag fight noun

an amateur, extra-legally staged boxing match US, 1955

- Stag fights were a cash deal. — Rocky Garciano (with Rowland Barber), Somebody Up There Likes Me, p. 141, 1955

stag film noun

a pornographic movie US, 1967

- As I said, I'd seen stag films before ... but never like these. — Jon Fowler, Anatomy of Wife-Swapping, p. 42, 1967
- "Take stag films," he said by way of example, "they're still being made in motels, by guys without any artistic sense." — Malcolm Boyd, My Fellow Americans, p. 37, 1970
- The photography is as honest as a stag film and you see close-ups of the guy shtupping (fucking) the girl's hole. — Screw, p. 17, 12th January 1970
- Stallone took it in his stride, readily admitting that he had acted in the stag film when he was broke and desperate. — Adam Film World, p. 5, March 1979

stag flick noun

a pornographic movie US, 1966

- [T]hey were going at it in one position, then another, like out of a stag flick. — Robert Gover, Poorboy at the Party, p. 156, 1966

stagger soup noun

whiskey US, 1977

- — Ramon Adams, The Language of the Railroader, p. 145, 1977

stag line noun

at a dance, a line of men without dates, waiting to dance US, 1951

- I met Clothilde at the University of Minnesota's annual Freshman Prom. I was standing in the stag line and I saw her dancing with a fellow halfway across the floor. — Max Shulman, The Many Loves of Dobie Gillis, p. 1, 1951

stag movie noun

a pornographic movie made for and enjoyed by men US, 1960

- I mean, our frat has this stag movie (which I, of course, have nothing to do with, no authority over at all). — Robert Gover, One Hundred Dollar Misunderstanding, p. 113, 1961
- Now, the stag movie, the dirty movie—the sixteen millimeter reduction print that you drag from lodge hall, the dirty movie that the Kefauver Committee would destroy and then recreate for private parties. — Lenny Bruce, The Essential Lenny Bruce, p. 177, 1967
- One night we were sitting around in Don Mincher's room waiting to look at some stag movies[.] — Jim Bouton, Ball Four, p. 241, 1970
- There are some movies called stag movies or party movies. These are not shown in regular theaters, but are shown in private homes or private parties or at club meetings. — Final Report of the Attorney General's Report on Pornography, p. 251, 1986

stag party noun

a party for men only, usually organized to view pornography, tell sexual jokes, and/or be entertained by strippers or prostitutes US, 1856

- [E]ccentric dancer, platinum in the mop and molybdenum in the left ventricle, who gave her all at smokes and stag parties[.] — Bernard Wolfe, The Late Risers, p. 37, 1954
- Within the next quarter-hour a stag party had taken over the apartment, several of them in uniform. — Truman Capote, Breakfast at Tiffany's, p. 35, 1958
- I mean the whole thing seemed like a wild post-ice cream dream, as mentioned above, or (I might as well say it) like a stag party movie. — Robert Gover, One Hundred Dollar Misunderstanding, p. 113, 1961
- College fraternities, volunteer fire companies, lodges, businessmen's associations, conventions, bachelor and stag parties comprise the most common customers for this strictly illegal film fare. — Michael Milner, Sex on Celluloid, p. 11, 1964

stained adjective

intoxicated on phencyclidine, the drug best known as PCP or angel dust US, 2005

- One of the most hectic times in Wu-Tang history was when motherfuckers was getting stained. — RZA, The Wu-Tang Manual, p. 121, 2005

stake noun

1 money needed to finance an enterprise or to contribute as a share to finance an enterprise US, 1972

- But I don't have the stake I thought I was gonna. That's why I need you to write me a check. — Elmore Leonard, City Primeval, p. 165, 1980

2 in gambling circles, money US, 1963

- — Richard Jessup, The Cincinnati Kid, p. 34, 1963

stake verb

to provide someone with money or other needed resources US, 1853

- Okay, and you can stake me to this call, right? — Gurney Norman, Divine Right's Trip (Last Whole Earth Catalog), p. 193, 1971

stakehorse noun

in pool, a person who financially backs the wagers of a professional player US, 1990

- — Steve Rushin, Pool Cool, p. 27, 1990

stakey adjective

anxious; jumpy; ready to leave US, 1965

- A term describing a man who has made his stake and doesn't want to stay on the job any longer. — Robert O. Bowen, An Alaskan Dictionary, p. 31, 1965

stalks noun

the legs US, 1972

- — David Claerbaut, Black Jargon in White America, p. 81, 1972

stall noun

a pickpocket's confederate who distracts the victim UK, 1591

- A "cannon" with a tired horse face took the vacant stool in my right. His "stall" took the one on the left. — Iceberg Slim (Robert Beck), Pimp, p. 91, 1969

- The stall is the bump man. So he's got to have a newspaper, a magazine. — Leonard Shecter and William Phillips, *On the Pad*, p. 159, 1973

stall *verb*

in pool, to intentionally miss a shot or lose a game *US, 1967*

- By "stalling" (deliberately missing some shots, leaving himself out of position, etc.) and by "lemoning" or "lemonading" an occasional game in the session (winning in a deliberately sloppy and seemingly lucky manner, or deliberately losing the game), the hustler keeps his opponent on the hook. — Ned Polsky, *Hustlers, Beats, and Others*, pp. 56–57, 1967
- — Steve Rushin, *Pool Cool*, p. 28, 1990

stallion *noun*

an attractive, sensual woman, especially a tall one *US, 1970*

- You got a white woman, a real stallion like Nez here, that's all you need to fight the world. — John Sayles, *Union Dues*, p. 190, 1977
- [T]his Margo stallion has laid some fine trim on this nephew, see? — Robert Deane Pharr, *Giveadamn Brown*, p. 34, 1978
- A real handful of lady if ever there was one, heroic dimensions, but exquisitely put together, about 38–29–42. What used to be called a "stallion" in some circles. — Odie Hawkins, *Scars and Memories*, p. 71, 1987

stall out *verb*

to leave alone *US, 1993*

- "Eh, Hog," B.T. began, turning to Hog for relief, "tell Rat to stall me out, cuz." — Sanyika Shakur, *Monster*, p. 293, 1993

stall walker *noun*

in horseracing, a nervous jockey who paces before a race *US, 1953*

A term originally for a racehorse pacing in the stall.

- — *San Francisco Chronicle*, 19th April 1953

stand *verb*

▸ **stand firm**

to remain loyal to friends and fellow youth gang members in the face of pressure *US, 1993*

- Camp is the third testing ground in a series of "tests" to register one's ability to "stand firm," the streets, of course, being the first and juvenile hall the second. — Sanyika Shakur, *Monster*, p. 27, 1993

▸ **stand point**

to serve as a lookout *US, 1972*

- Bad-Eye went up first while I stood point for him in the alley. — Harry King, *Box Man*, p. 48, 1972

stand up *verb*

to refuse to cooperate when questioned by the police; to withstand pressure to confess *US, 1971*

- I've done time and I stood up. — George V. Higgins, *The Friends of Eddie Doyle*, p. 75, 1971
- If things went bad, Paulie would stand up. — Vincent Patrick, *The Pope of Greenwich Village*, p. 20, 1979
- "I want to hear it … will he or won't he stand up?" — Gerard O'Neill, *The Under Boss*, p. 208, 1989

stand-up *adjective*

1 loyal to the end, devoted and dependable *US, 1971*

Perhaps from boxing, where a stand-up fight was one in which the fighters stood up to each without flinching or evasion. The ultimate praise in the world of organized crime.

- I need some help, I helped you. Are you a standup guy or not. — George V. Higgins, *The Friends of Eddie Doyle*, p. 100, 1971
- They gonna need distributors with brains and with heart—stand-up motherfuckers. — Edwin Torres, *Carlito's Way*, p. 21, 1975
- Tommy always was a stand-up guy. — *Raging Bull*, 1980
- What happened to you, man? I remember you used to be a stand-up kind of guy. — *Mallrats*, 1995

2 solid; pure *US, 1973*

- I knew where I could cop a stand up twenty if he wanted it. — A.S. Jackson, *Gentleman Pimp*, p. 123, 1973

3 describing someone's play in pool, at your true skill level, not below it *US, 1993*

- — Mike Shamos, *The Illustrated Encyclopedia of Billiards*, p. 230, 1993

stang *noun*

prospective goods to be stolen *US, 1965*

- The law is that who ever finds the stang gets the majority of it. — Henry Williamson, *Hustler!*, p. 130, 1965

stank *noun*

the vagina; sex *US, 1980*

Usually said unkindly.

- — Edith A. Folb, *runnin' down some lines*, p. 255, 1980
- The answer is, it's gonna be interracial, which means it'll offer a few token liberal white broads a chance to give up a lil' stank... — Odie Hawkins, *The Busting Out of an Ordinary Man*, p. 152, 1985

stankhole *noun*

a disagreeable person *US, 2006*

- But ever since he started working at the petroleum refinery over by Port Arthur he kind of became a stankhole. — Linden Dalecki, *Kid B*, pp. 36–37, 2006

stanky *noun*

sex *US, 2002*

- He insists he did have time for sex with Lucindreth. He smiles shyly when he tells us he "got some stanky on the hang-low." — Jimmy Lerner, *You Got Nothing Coming*, p. 170, 2002

stanky *adjective*

bad smelling *US, 1980s*

- stanky—Smelly — Edith A. Folb, *runnin' down some lines*, p. 255, 1980
- As you all remember, in our last meeting we discussed the reasons why the political structure started off stanky and got progressively rotten as time went on. — Donald Goines, *The Busting Out of an Ordinary Man*, p. 26, 1985

star *noun*

an asterisk sign (*) on a computer keyboard *US, 1991*

- — Eric S. Raymond, *The New Hacker's Dictionary*, p. 39, 1991

starch *noun*

semen *US, 1967*

- — Dale Gordon, *The Dominion Sex Dictionary*, p. 151, 1967

stardust *noun*

1 cocaine *US, 1967*

- — John B. Williams, *Narcotics and Hallucinogenics*, p. 116, 1967
- Because usually you only got enough stardust for one or two nice shots, and then you're out doing everything but five-dollars blow jobs on Capp Street so you can go cop some more. — Lynn Breedlove, *Godspeed*, p. 105, 2002

2 phencyclidine *US, 1977*

- — *Drummer*, p. 77, 1977

starfucker *noun*

a person who seeks sex with celebrities *US, 1970*

- Star-fuckers are lowest on the totem pole of groupiedom, badly regarded by the other girls and musicians. — John Burks, *Groupies and Other Girls*, p. 11, 1970
- Annies, Shirleys, Groupies, Starfuckers; that's what the men call them. — Herb Michelson, *Sportin' Ladies*, p. vii, 1975
- A lot of people think she's a snob or a starfucker because all she can talk about is lunch with Jack Nicholson and drinks with Sting[.] — Jay McInerney, *Story of My Life*, p. 19, 1988

starter *noun*

a gambler hired by a casino to gamble and thereby create interest in a game *US, 1977*

- Today they are used mostly at baccarat tables. They are also called "starters." — Mario Puzo, *Inside Las Vegas*, p. 195, 1977

starter cap *noun*

a condom *US, 1996*

- I put the starter cap on the bozack — Kwest Tha Madd Lad, *Lubrication*, 1996

starter kit *noun*

an initial supply of drugs given a new street dealer on consignment *US, 1997*

- But the distinction is lost on Hungry, who must be astonished that anyone on Fayette Street is still naive enough to give him a starter kit. — David Simon and Edward Burns, *The Corner*, pp. 322–323, 1997

stash *noun*

1 a hidden supply of drugs, usually marijuana; the hiding place itself *US, 1942*

- Where is it? Where's your stash, knucklehead? — Alexander Trocchi, *Cain's Book*, p. 106, 1960
- I stopped at the broom-closet stash. I hurled the "sizzle" [drugs] into the corner on the shelf. — Iceberg Slim (Robert Beck), *Pimp*, p. 155, 1969

- Lady was tipping this broad 20 a day and soon as she found her stash, she ran and told whitey. — Babs Gonzales, *Movin' On Down De Line*, p. 51, 1975
- The stock or "stash" of cocaine is kept in a bag stitched with beads worn by adherents of Santeria[.] — Terry Williams, *The Cocaine Kids*, p. 28, 1989

2 in the illegal production of alcohol, a cache of alcohol *US, 1974*

- We got ninety gallon left in the stash. — David W. Maurer, *Kentucky Moonshine*, p. 125, 1974

3 a person's hiding place *US, 1927*

- If he wasn't home or in his stash, people would say, "Tell that nigger don't come on the street any more until he's got my money." — Claude Brown, *Manchild in the Promised Land*, p. 214, 1965

4 a room, apartment, or house *US, 1946*

- No Hotel Ritz for us this time; our stash was over some kind of feed store[.] — Mezz Mezzrow, *Really the Blues*, p. 132, 1946

stash *verb*

1 to hide something, especially drugs *US, 1914*

- I got some pod stashed by the subway. — George Mandel, *Flee the Angry Strangers*, p. 26, 1952
- I was learning to hide my stuff carefully—"stash it," as they say in the trade—so Roy and Herman couldn't find it and take some[.] — William Burroughs, *Junkie*, pp. 34–35, 1953
- He could have that almost anywhere; there were works stashed at the Garden Bar, the poolroom, near a small bush off the sidewalk on Ninety-second[.] — Clarence Cooper Jr., *The Scene*, p. 12, 1960
- Did anybody see you stash it? — Ross Russell, *The Sound*, p. 239, 1961

2 (used of a prostitute) to retain some of your earnings and not turn them over to your pimp *US, 1981*

- "She musta been stashin', holdin' out on her man." — Alix Shulman, *On the Stroll*, p. 175, 1981
- "Also during this time, she had a conversation with Daniel Mitchell wherein he told (her) that he would kill her if she ever stashed on him," Corbett said in his report. — *Post-Standard (Syracuse, New York)*, p. B1, 5th January 1989

stash apartment *noun*

an apartment where drugs are hidden *US, 1992*

- And it was a lot quicker to serve up bottles out of a bar than to have everybody running in and out of the stash apartment for every ten-dollar sale. — Richard Price, *Clockers*, p. 5, 1992

stash bag *noun*

a bag where illegal drugs are hidden *US, 1971*

- STASH BAG: a bag in which to keep drugs — Robert Buckhout, *Toward Social Change*, p. 466, 1971

stash car *noun*

a car in which drugs are hidden and driven across a border as part of a smuggling operation *US, 1978*

- Stash cars (el clavo) permitted the dealers to minimize the cost of arrests. — Joan W. Moore, *Homeboys*, p. 79, 1978

stash catcher *noun*

an employee of a drug dealer whose job it is to retrieve supplies of drugs that are jettisoned in the event of a police raid *US, 1992*

- — Terry Williams, *Crackhouse*, p. 151, 1992

stash house *noun*

a house or apartment where a drug dealer keeps a supply of drugs to sell *US, 1978*

- Local law enforcement officials told me that the current going rate for transporting a van full of marihuana from the shoreline about 12 to 20 miles to a stash house is $30,000 per run. — United States Congress, *Stopping "Mother Ships"*, p. 9, 1978
- [W]hich was followed in turn by a double murder on Lucerne Street, where a gunman broke into a stash house in a dispute over drug territory and began firing wildly, killing two and wounding two more. — David Simon, *Homicide*, p. 39, 1991
- Renting a dealer a room for a mill was a better way to make money that renting our your apartment as a stash house. — Adrian Nicole LeBlanc, *Random House*, p. 46, 2003

stat *noun*

a statistic *US, 1961*

Usually used in the plural.

- I have the stats on that car, Officer Labeef. — *Repo Man*, 1984

state *noun*

a state prison *US, 1991*

- We're talking about McGuire's friendship with Baily, who's doing time in state for second degree murder. — Robert Campbell, *In a Pig's Eye*, p. 58, 1991

State and Perversion *nickname*

in Chicago, the intersection of State and Division Streets *US, 1958*

- The corner they call State and Perversion. — Willard Motley, *Let No Man Write My Epitaph*, p. 166, 1958

state college *noun*

a state prison *US, 1949*

- — Vincent J. Monteleone, *Criminal Slang*, p. 224, 1949

state electrician *noun*

the executioner in a state using electrocution in the electric chair for capital punishment *US, 1982*

- — Ralph de Sola, *Crime Dictionary*, p. 143, 1982

statement maker *noun*

a weapon *US, 1997*

- The dealer walked back to his car trunk, popped it open and pulled out a statement-maker. Sawed-off, taped, and ugly. — David Simon and Edward Burns, *The Corner*, p. 245, 1997

State of Maine bankroll *noun*

a bankroll made from a real bill folded around paper cut to the shape of currency *US, 1975*

- — John Gould, *Maine Lingo*, p. 275, 1975

state-raised *adjective*

said of a prisoner who has spent most of his life incarcerated *US, 1970*

- This is the system of the state-raised youth. — John Irwin, *The Felon*, p. 26, 1970
- — William K. Bentley and James M. Corbett, *Prison Slang*, p. 29, 1992

states *noun*

▸ **the States**

in Alaska, all states except Alaska *US, 1984*

- — *American Speech*, pp. 256–258, Fall 1984: "Terms for 'Not Alaska' in Alaskan English"

state time *noun*

a prison sentence served in a state prison *US, 1995*

More serious than time in **COUNTY**, and within the state jurisdiction as opposed to federal jurisdiction.

- His sentence wasn't on the sheet—or all the hustles he got away with that Raylan read between the lines—but Louis must have done a few years' state time. — Elmore Leonard, *Riding the Rap*, p. 214, 1995

statey; statie *noun*

a state trooper *US, 1980*

- The doctor was not popular with the cops, Staties or feds. — George Higgins, *Kennedy for the Defense*, p. 54, 1980
- Or even one of the Staties, like the one arrested you. — George V. Higgins, *Penance for Jerry Kennedy*, p. 2, 1985
- — Amy and Denise McFadden, *CoalSpeak*, p. 12, 1997

static *noun*

harassment; trouble; complications *US, 1926*

- "Hey, look! fool!" she growled into the receiver after having obviously listened to enough bullshit, "don't be givin' me all that static!" — Odie Hawkins, *Chicago Hustle*, p. 29–30
- That's enough static out of you! — *Rebel Without a Cause*, 1955
- Don't give me any static on that score. — Mart Crowley, *The Boys in the Band*, p. 37, 1968
- The pair—whose smutty antics have earned them huge ratings—drew heavy static for a contest that rewarded listeners for having sex in public places. — *New York Daily News*, 23rd August 2003

stations of the cross *noun*

a police tactic in which a person who has been arrested is moved from one precinct to another in rapid succession, making it impossible for him to be located and bailed out by his friends and family *US, 1992*

- [A]nd the warden wanted to know who was responsible for running a man around the stations of the cross who'd been picked up for nothing more serious than a drunk and disorderly. — Robert Campbell, *Boneyards*, p. 259, 1992

stay *verb*
to reside *US, 1973*

- Black People have seldom lived in one area long enough to consider it their own. Black People only STAYED in places. — Malachi Andrews and Paul T. Owens, *Black Language*, p. 101, 1973
- Everybody said we were moving to the 'burbs, and none of my friends wanted us to go where only white people stayed. — Terry Williams, *The Cocaine Kids*, p. 76, 1989

▸ **stay awake**
to use amphetamines or methamphetamine continuously *US, 1989*
A vague euphemism.

- — Geoffrey Froner, *Digging for Diamonds*, p. 58, 1989

▸ **stay loose**
to remain calm *US, 1959*

- "Well, so long, Jack," she said. "Stay loose." — Max Shulman, *I was a Teen-Age Dwarf*, p. 82, 1959

stay and pray *verb*
in poker, to stay in a hand with a large amount of money bet, hoping for a particular card to be drawn to improve your hand *US, 1988*

- — George Percy, *The Language of Poker*, p. 87, 1988

stay-awake *noun*
amphetamine sulfate or any other central nervous system stimulant *US, 1993*

- — Peter Johnson, *Dictionary of Street Alcohol and Drug Terms*, p. 180, 1993

stayer *noun*
in poker, a hand that warrants staying in the game but not raising the bet *US, 1949*

- — Thomas L. Clark, *The Dictionary of Gambling and Gaming*, p. 216, 1987

stay-out *noun*
in prison, a confrontational tactic in which prisoners refuse to return to their cells *US, 1976*

- — John R. Armore and Joseph D. Wolfe, *Dictionary of Desperation*, p. 52, 1976

stay out of the Koolaid!
mind your own business! *US, 1995*

- — Bill Valentine, *Gang Intelligence Manual*, p. 78, 1995

stay up
used as a farewell *US, 1998*

- — *Columbia Missourian*, p. 1A, 19th October 1998

stay-wag *noun*
a station wagon *US, 1991*

- — Trevor Cralle, *The Surfin'ary*, p. 122, 1991

steady *noun*
a steady boyfriend or girlfriend *US, 1897*

- Walter McGrath seemed to be another steady she was heavy on. — Mickey Spillane, *Kiss Me Deadly*, p. 61, 1952
- The Lads and I talked about girls—not their "steadies" God forbid, but the pert creatures who paraded in pairs and threes along the sea front. — Hugh Leonard, *Out After Dark*, p. 84, 1989
- Apparently you're both on the outs with your steadies. — *Mallrats*, 1995

steady Eddie *noun*
a reliable, dependable, trustworthy person *US, 2003*

- The arrest paints a portrait at odds with the middle-aged and balding Dean, a man regarded by his peers as a "very steady Eddie." — *Los Angeles Times*, p. 1 (Part 2), 23rd July 2003

steal *verb*
in poker, to win a hand with an inferior hand either through superior bluffing skills or poor estimation by other players *US, 1979*

- — John Scarne, *Scarne's Guide to Modern Poker*, p. 291, 1979

▸ **steal the ante**
in poker, to bet aggressively early in a hand, driving out other players and leaving a pot consisting mostly of the buy-in antes *US, 1975*

- I decided to slow-play it, figuring that Nick might try to steal the ante. — Jimmy Snyder, *Jimmy the Greek*, p. 198, 1975
- — Edwin Silberstang, *Winning Poker for the Serious Player*, p. 220, 1992

steam *noun*
in sports betting, a flurry of betting on one side of a bet *US, 1991*

- — Michael Knapp, *Bay Sports Review*, p. 11, November 1991

steam *verb*
in gambling, to bet increasingly larger amounts of money in a losing effort to recoup recurring losses *US, 1985*

- — Steve Kuriscak, *Casino Talk: A Rap Sheet for Dealers and Players*, p. 53, 1985

steam and cream; steam job *noun*
during the Vietnam war, a bath and sex with a prostitute *US, 1969*

- "Hey GI, you fey two hundred piasters, I gib you number-one steam job." — John Steinbeck IV, *In Touch*, p. 15, 1969
- Give him five bucks, tell him I told you could leave your cameras with him—you're going for a steam and cream. — Joshua Karton, *Films Scenes for Actors*, p. 448, 1983
- — John Elting, *A Dictionary of Soldier Talk*, p. 305, 1984

steamboat *noun*
a cardboard tube or box with a hole for a marijuana cigarette and a hole for inhaling, used to trap the smoke *US, 1967*

- This little contraption is called a steamboat because the roach looks like the smokestack in a steamboat. — *Newsweek*, p. 49, 24th July 1967
- — William D. Alsever, *Glossary for the Establishment and Other Uptight People*, p. 20, December 1970
- "Why don't you roll a five-handed joint while I prepare a steamboat for this ugly, filthy roach?" — Michael Herr, *Dispatches*, p. 239, 1977

steamer *noun*
a gambler who increases the size of his bets after losing *US, 1968*

- — Thomas L. Clark, *The Dictionary of Gambling and Gaming*, p. 217, 1987

steam-powered *adjective*
obsolete *US, 1991*

- — Eric S. Raymond, *The New Hacker's Dictionary*, p. 334, 1991

steeazick *noun*
a marijuana cigarette *US, 1947*

- My old friend Henri Cru recently blew into N.Y. with a couple of steeazicks from Panama as big as your thumb. — Jack Kerouac, *Letter to William S. Burroughs*, p. 108, 14th July 1947

steel *noun*
a knife *US, 2002*

- — Jeffrey Ian Ross, *Behind Bars*, p. 182, 2002: Slammer Slang

steel and concrete cure *noun*
the sudden and complete deprivation of drugs to a jailed drug addict, who suffers intensely *US, 1950*

- So you might as well get yourself set for the steel-and-concrete and the chuck horrors. I had 'em. — *The New American Mercury*, p. 711, 1950
- The steel and concrete cure is the only cure I recommend for stool pigeons. — David Maurer and Victor Vogel, *Narcotics and Narcotic Addiction*, p. 446, 1973

steel beach *noun*
the deck of an aircraft carrier or other warship when used for recreational purposes *US, 1982*

- On most cruises, only two days a month are declared holidays when the men can lie around on what some call "the steel beach." — *New York Times*, p. 16, 14th March 1982
- "We work hard, but we play just as hard," said Chief Petty Officer Cole Boarders, of San Francisco, who spends a day off sunning himself at "Steel Beach" on the deck of the Dallas. — *Sun-Sentinel (Fort Lauderdale, Florida)*, p. 1H, 28th March 2004

steel door *noun*
a hospital-admitting physician who admits only the sickest patients *US, 1994*

- — Sally Williams, *"Strong" Words*, p. 160, 1994

steelie *noun*
a ball bearing used in a game of marbles *US, 1978*

- We had declared that no steelies could be used as toys. — Bobby Seale, *A Lonely Rage*, p. 31, 1978

steelies *noun*
steel-toed boots, especially those made by Doc Marten *US, 2000*

- The most sought-after article of clothing, though, was the steelies, 12- to 14-hole, calf-high, steel-toed Doc Marten boots also called DMs or Docs[.] — Bill Valentine, *Gangs and Their Tattoos*, p. 58, 2000

steel pot *noun*
the US military standard-issue M-1 helmet *US, 1967*
Vietnam war usage.
- "You men take off those steel pots so you can hear what I have to say." — David Reed, *Up Front in Vietnam*, p. 160, 1967
- — Carl Fleischhauer, *A Glossary of Army Slang*, p. 19, 1968
- The uniform of the day is shirts, rifles, and steel pots. — Larry Heinemann, *Close Quarters*, p. 62, 1977
- I told the group to leave their steel pots, packs, all that stuff. — Harold Moore, *We Were Soldiers Once ... And Young*, p. 295, 1992

steen *noun*
an imaginary large number *US, 1900*
- I ain't seen you in steen million years. How you was? — James T. Farrell, *Saturday Night*, p. 20, 1947

steep *adjective*
sought by the police; wanted *US, 1995*
- — Bill Valentine, *Gang Intelligence Manual*, p. 111, 1995

steer *verb*
in confidence swindles, to direct the confederate(s) who will swindle the victim *US, 1889*
- The lush was a complete stranger, having been delivered by a cabdriver who steered for various joints, and Tappy had just gotten around to selling him the first bottle of bubbly. — Robert Sylvester, *No Cover Charge*, p. 213, 1956
- What are you steering for this craps joint? — Iceberg Slim (Robert Beck), *Pimp*, p. 94, 1969
- It's easy to steer a lop-eared chump, so long as Mordecai Jones has sized up the mark. — Guy Owen, *The Flim-Flam Man and the Apprentice Grifter*, p. 168, 1972
- He rarely failed to "steer" the mark. — Stephen Cannell, *King Con*, p. 34, 1997

steerer *noun*
a person who directs potential customers to an illegal enterprise *US, 1989*
- Many are taken on in a variety of tangential roles and work as steerers, touts, guards, runners, and "cop men"—dealers whom suppliers will only sell to on a cash basis. — Terry Williams, *The Cocaine Kids*, p. 33, 1989

steerman *noun*
1 a member of a swindling enterprise who identifies potential victims and directs them into the swindle *US, 1993*
- A "steerman" hunts for "pigeons," unsuspecting amateurs who could be steered into fixed games with professional card players. — Kim Rich, *Johnny's Girl*, p. 61, 1993

2 in tandem surfing, the person towards the rear of the surfboard *US, 1957*
- The guy behind you is called the "steerman." You're supposed to paddle all the time sort of in the same rhythm as the steerman. — Frederick Kohner, *Gidget*, p. 51, 1957

stem *noun*
1 a main street or boulevard, especially one frequented by tramps, prostitutes, pimps, and their ilk *US, 1914*
- When I hit the main stem, I went down a side street past a little hotel. — Mickey Spillane, *I, The Jury*, p. 25, 1947
- You would also be playing your girl against a half-dozen strong, jasper [lesbian] whores on this "stem." — Iceberg Slim (Robert Beck), *Pimp*, p. 102, 1969
- The stem swirls in a straight line down 47th Street, heading for Buttermilk Bottom, the Fillmore District, Crenshaw, or the dusty, crusty surface of Gwinnett Street in deepest Georgia. — Odie Hawkins, *Ghetto Sketches*, p. 25, 1972
- Yeah, had I been on the stem during the big burn, I'd be one of the many, many niggers that got over the hump. — A.S. Jackson, *Gentleman Pimp*, p. 9, 1973

2 the dominant culture in a society *US, 1995*
An abbreviation of "system."
- — Bill Valentine, *Gang Intelligence Manual*, p. 111, 1995

3 the penis *US, 1972*
- [N]obody to my knowledge spoke of "choad," "rod," "stem" or any other more strictly pornographic term. — *Screw*, p. 5, 3rd January 1972

4 a laboratory pipette used to smoke crack cocaine *US, 1992*
- — Terry Williams, *Crackhouse*, p. 152, 1992
- — US Department of Justice, *Street Terms*, October 1994

▸ **on the stem**
performing or inclined to perform oral sex on a man *US, 1976*
- — John R. Armore and Joseph D. Wolfe, *Dictionary of Desperation*, p. 42, 1976

stem *verb*
to beg on the street *US, 1958*
- Portland, Oregon's a good town to stem. — Willard Motley, *Let No Man Write My Epitaph*, p. 73, 1958
- "You gonna stem tonight?" — Malcolm Braly, *It's Cold Out There*, p. 68, 1966
- Cunningham, who lives in a local homeless shelter, used to spend his days "steming"—street slang for panhandling. — *Christian Science Monitor*, p. 12, 4th June 1992

stemmer *noun*
a beggar *US, 1962*
- — Joseph E. Ragen and Charles Finston, *Inside the World's Toughest Prison*, p. 820, 1962: "Penitentiary and underworld glossary"

stencil *noun*
a thin and long marijuana cigarette *US, 1980*
- — Edith A. Folb, *runnin' down some lines*, p. 255, 1980

stenographer *noun*
in a deck of playing cards, a queen *US, 1988*
- — George Percy, *The Language of Poker*, p. 87, 1988

step *verb*
▸ **step on**
to dilute a powdered drug *US, 1971*
- I ain't never tried to step on this much heh-rawn in my life. We got a few bags cut but the suitcase is still full. — Vernon E. Smith, *The Jones Men*, p. 48, 1974
- The dealer-in-weight sells by the piece (about an ounce) to street dealers. The street dealer (or dealer) buys the piece and then steps on it. — Burgess Laughlin, *Job Opportunities in the Black Market*, pp. 6–5, 1978
- As it is, he's been stepping on it in ever-decreasing moderation[.] — Jim Carroll, *Forced Entries*, p. 11, 1987
- You put a one, one and half on it 'cause stuff is so shitty down there you can step all over the ounce and they still bringing home the best stuff around. — Richard Price, *Clockers*, p. 180, 1992

▸ **step on your dick**
to commit a self-damaging act *US, 1951*
- Well, I tried to hang it up [escape], and with my usual flair, I stepped on my dick. — James Blake, *The Joint*, p. 26, 21st June 1951

▸ **step on your meat**
to engage in self-defeating conduct *US, 1981*
- Before you step on your meat, let me draw you a little picture. — Gerald Petievich, *One-Shot Deal*, p. 191, 1981

▸ **step up to the plate**
to rise to a challenge *US, 1997*
From the image of a batter in baseball coming up to bat.
- Republican Sen. Fred Thompson of Tennessee, chairman of the committee probing campaign financing, said it was time for Bill Clinton to step up to the plate. — *Gannett News Service*, 10th October 1997

Stepin Fetchit *noun*
a black person who curries favor with whites through obsequious behavior *US, 1994*
After the stage name of Lincoln Theodore Monroe Perry (1902–85), a black actor known for his film portrayal of stereotypical black minstrel characters.
- The one thing I knew is that I was not going to write one of those disgraceful high-tech Stepin Fetchit things. — Odie Hawkins, *Lost Angeles*, p. 29, 1994

step off *verb*
1 to go away *US, 1993*
- Bitch, step off! — *Menace II Society*, 1993

2 in carnival and circus usage, to position concessions in a deliberate fashion meant to maximize profit *US, 2005*
- I'd had my first up-close and personal encounter with a Flattie two days before in the empty Kmart parking lot, as Chip and Jackie "stepped off" the midway[.] — Peter Fenton, *Eyeing the Flash*, p. 126, 2005

stepper *noun*

a prostitute; a promiscuous woman *US, 1953*

- Mrs. Winroy is quite a stepper—not that I'm saying anything against her, understand? — Jim Thompson, *Savage Night*, p. 4, 1953
- Reba says peevishly, "Trap? Perhaps, Mama, but just briefly for this stepper." — Iceberg Slim (Robert Beck), *Doom Fox*, p. 100, 1978
- down home gossipers, snuff dippers, exotic religionists, fast steppers, high rollers and just plan ol' folks — Odie Hawkins, *The Busting Out of an Ordinary Man*, p. 141, 1985

step up *verb*

to start a fight *US, 2001*

- — Don R. McCreary (Editor), *Dawg Speak*, 2001

stern-wheeler *noun*

the passive participant in anal sex *US, 1979*

- — *Maledicta*, p. 233, 1979: "Kinks and queens: linguistic and cultural aspects of the terminology for gays"
- — William K. Bentley and James M. Corbett, *Prison Slang*, p. 58, 1992

Steve Canyon *noun*

any fighter pilot *US, 1968*
Vietnam war usage, alluding to the name of a comic strip popular in the US in the 1950s and 60s.

- — Carl Fleischhauer, *A Glossary of Army Slang*, p. 19, 1968

stew *noun*

1 a state of alcohol intoxication *US, 1965*

- I was sittin' at the table, gettin' on a might stew / a dead swell dame come sit beside me too. — Bruce Jackson, *Get Your Ass in the Water and Swim Like Me*, p. 131, 1965

2 a drunkard *US, 1950*

- Swedes are either teetotalers or wonderful stews. — Jack Lait and Lee Mortimer, *Chicago Confidential*, p. 81, 1950

3 nitroglycerin used to blow open a safe *US, 1949*

- — Vincent J. Monteleone, *Criminal Slang*, p. 225, 1949

stew bum; stewbum *noun*

an alcoholic derelict *US, 1902*

- An old stewbum, with a pinched-up face the color of the West Madison Street pavement, squints out at the darkened rows painfully[.] — Nelson Algren, *The Neon Wilderness*, p. 14, 1960
- You ain't nothin' but a skid-row stewbum. — Nathan Heard, *Howard Street*, p. 72, 1968
- He was back in Morning Sections sitting on the bench in the fenced-off section with the stew bums and colored hookers waiting to go before the same judge. — Elmore Leonard, *The Big Bounce*, p. 99, 1969
- You know how these stew bums are. — Mickey Spillane, *Last Cop Out*, p. 56, 1972

stewed *adjective*

drunk *US, 1737*
Another drunk synonym that was first recorded by Benjamin Franklin.

- But one morning she and Frankie had drunk from the same can and gotten as drunk, all by themselves, as any two twelve-year-olds in an West Side horse-and-wagon alley can get. — Nelson Algren, *The Man with the Golden Arm*, p. 62, 1949
- You know. Drunk, stewed, clobbered, gone, liquored up, oiled, stoned, in the bag. — Max Shulman, *Guided Tour of Campus Humor*, p. 106, 1955
- I was suddenly tired. Not stewed or even excited or lonely; just plain tired out. — Clancy Sigal, *Going Away*, p. 182, 1961
- "Let's you and me get stewed tonight and talk about old times." — Glenn Savan, *White Palace*, p. 257, 1987

stewed to the gills *adjective*

very drunk *US, 1949*

- Every time he came in stewed to the gills, with Sparrow holding him up by the belt, he'd mumble the minute he saw her waiting in the chair[.] — Nelson Algren, *The Man with the Golden Arm*, p. 23, 1949

stewie *noun*

an alcoholic *US, 1945*

- — Lou Shelly, *Hepcats Jive Talk Dictionary*, p. 19, 1945

stick *noun*

1 a marijuana cigarette *US, 1938*

- At seventy-five cents a stick, seventy sticks to the ounce, it sounded like money. — William Burroughs, *Junkie*, p. 30, 1953
- Seeing that we didn't know anything about ourselves, he whipped out three sticks of tea and said to go ahead, supper'd be ready soon. — Jack Kerouac, *On the Road*, p. 145, 1957

- I got just a small amount of marijuana and I got some of the paper to roll up my own sticks. — Malcolm X and Alex Haley, *The Autobiography of Malcolm X*, p. 98, 1964
- Terry began the first day with beer, had a stick of the grass at noon, then more beer, and another joint before dinner, then to red wine and a handful of bennies to keep awake[.] — Hunter S. Thompson, *Hell's Angels: A Strange and Terrible Saga*, p. 217, 1966

2 a hypodermic needle *US, 2004*

- "A cop would not hand out sticks, right?" I whisper. — J.T. LeRoy, *Harold's End*, p. 12, 2004

3 ability in pool *US, 1947*

- Nick could hold his own with Butch now. He shot a good stick. — Willard Motley, *Knock on Any Door*, p. 153, 1947
- Hermes Pavolites, one of the three brothers who shot pool in Sal's, fair sticks, hit him a hard uppercut in the Melody Room one night[.] — Gilbert Sorrentino, *Steelwork*, p. 118, 1970
- "You shoot a pretty powerful stick, Vito baby." — Nathan Heard, *A Cold Fire Burning*, p. 106, 1974
- And he would shoot a better stick here tomorrow than he had done in Florida. — Walter Tevis, *The Color of Money*, p. 23, 1984

4 desk duty in a police station *US, 1958*

- A man on desk duty has the stick. — *New York Times*, p. 34, 20th October 1958

5 a burglar's pry-bar *UK, 1879*

- — Hyman E. Goldin et al., *Dictionary of American Underworld Lingo*, p. 210, 1950
- To free the safe from its frame with only a "stick," which is not a very delicate tool, without making hell's own row, would take a little time. — Charles Raven, *Underworld Nights*, p. 18, 1956

6 a clarinet *US, 1946*
A shortened form of **LIQUORICE STICK**.

- If I could play that stick like you do I'd be out there runnin' with all them high-powered chicks in all the fines places[.] — Mezz Mezzrow, *Really the Blues*, p. 248, 1946

7 a surfboard *US, 1964*

- — John Severson, *Modern Surfing Around the World*, p. 182, 1964
- If you want to get aggro, man, this stick can handle your best rage. — *Point Break*, 1991
- — Pamela Munro, *U.C.L.A. Slang*, p. 111, 1997
- Or he has a surfboard under his arm and the only thing he can say is "Grab your stick, dude, there's a swell at Pipeline." — Dan Jenkins, *The Money-Whipped Steer-Job Three-Jack Give-Up Artist*, p. 3, 2001

8 a skateboard *US, 1984*

- — *San Francisco Sunday Examiner & Chronicle*, p. 20, 2nd September 1984: "Say it right"

9 in horseracing, the whip used by jockeys *US, 1976*

- — Tom Ainslie, *Ainslie's Complete Guide to Thoroughbred Racing*, p. 339, 1976

10 a pool player *US, 1990*

- — Steve Rushin, *Pool Cool*, p. 28, 1990

11 the game of pool *US, 1949*

- "I lived off the stick three months all the same when the heat was on 'n' that's more 'n' a lot of hustlers can say." — Nelson Algren, *The Man with the Golden Arm*, p. 11, 1949
- Abilene not only had the best car in the country, he also shot the best stick of pool. — Larry McMurtry, *The Last Picture Show*, p. 9, 1966
- I played my best stick 15 years ago—say as late as 1948 to 1950. — Minnesota Fats, *The Bank Shot*, p. 30, 1966
- — Judi Sanders, *Mashing and Munching in Ames*, p. 19, 1994

12 a set of rules for a game of pool *US, 1990*

- — Steve Rushin, *Pool Cool*, p. 28, 1990

13 a prisoner's personal influence or power *US, 1992*

- When a person has a great deal of influence and can get things accomplished, he is said to have a sharp stick. An abundance of stick is referred to as long stick. — William K. Bentley and James M. Corbett, *Prison Slang*, p. 34, 1992

14 a fighter pilot *US, 1986*

- — *American Speech*, p. 124, Summer 1986: "The language of naval fighter pilots"

15 a prostitute *US, 1972*

- — Christina and Richard Milner, *Black Players*, p. 308, 1972

16 one thousand dollars *US, 1978*
Probably an evolution of **YARD**.

- — Burgess Laughlin, *Job Opportunities in the Black Market*, p. 7, 1978: "Glossary"

stick *verb*

1 (from the male perspective) to have sex *US, 1959*

- "[Y]ou thinking of sticking him or blowing him?" — Jose Antonio Villarreal, *Pocho*, p. 112, 1959

- Did you get any action? Did you slam it to her? Did you stick her? Did you hump her? Did you run it down her throat? Did you jam it up her ass? Did you shoot your wad? — *Screw*, p. 6, 29th May 1972

2 to stab someone with a knife *US, 1975*

- I had been on probation for sticking a guy who'd busted my jaw with brass knuckles made out of ashcan handles. — Edwin Torres, *Carlito's Way*, p. 20, 1975
- Dizzy was always known as a cat that would stick a dude in a minute if they fucked with him. — Babs Gonzales, *Movin' On Down De Line*, p. 52, 1975
- I can't negotiate knives. It takes a lot of anger to stick somebody, you know? That's like real personal. — Richard Price, *Clockers*, p. 390, 1992
- Yeah. And it was in the papers and TV, too. Somebody stuck her. They say it was you. — Joseph Wambaugh, *Floaters*, p. 240, 1996

3 to urge a racehorse with a racing whip *US, 2006*

- "Stick 'im, you fuckin' munchkin! Stick 'im!" — Jason Starr, *Lights Out*, p. 48, 2006

4 to play pool *US, 1957*

- "Let's go stick a few across the green," he said. — Herbert Simmons, *Corner Boy*, p. 15, 1957

5 to inject a drug *US, 1992*

- Stick your arm for some real fun[.] — Alice in Chains, *God Smack*, 1992

▸ **stick a hit**
in snowboarding, to achieve impressive height when jumping *US, 1995*

- Stick a hit. To land a fat air. — Jim Humes and Sean Wagstaff, *Boarderlands*, p. 224, 1995

▸ **stick it to**
(from the male perspective) to have sex *US, 1975*

- "I fired Tony because he was sticking it to Suzanne?" — Brian Boyer, *Prince of Thieves*, p. 39, 1975

▸ **stick to your knitting**
to limit your efforts to doing what you know how to do; in the business world, to avoid the temptation to diversify beyond your company's expertise *US, 1991*

- — David Olive, *Business Babble*, p. 141, 1991

sticker *noun*

1 a knife *UK, 1896*

- One guy tried to hit me with a wooden Keep Off The Grass sign, which he pulled out the ground while he was running from my sticker. — Edwin Torres, *Carlito's Way*, p. 12, 1975
- [He] just stood there for a couple of seconds fingering the handle of the sticker before toppling over[.] — Greg Williams, *Diamond Geezers*, p. 213, 1997

2 a warrant or bill of detainer *US, 1976*

- — John R. Armore and Joseph D. Wolfe, *Dictionary of Desperation*, p. 52, 1976

stick hall *noun*
a pool room *US, 1958*

- [A] poolroom is a "stick hall[.]" — Harrison E. Salisbury, *The Shook-up Generation*, p. 160, 1958

stick horse *noun*
in horseracing, a horse that runs best with some encouragement from the jockey and whip *US, 1976*

- — Tom Ainslie, *Ainslie's Complete Guide to Thoroughbred Racing*, p. 339, 1976

sticking *noun*
a stabbing *US, 1992*

- "He's got a shank," whispered Bowles. "Gonna be a sticking." — Pete Earley, *The Hot House*, p. 218, 1992

stickman *noun*
a marijuana smoker *US, 1966*

- — *Mr.*, p. 58, April 1966: "The hippie's lexicon"

sticks *noun*

1 the countryside *US, 1905*

- Try to mean what you say. No wooden Hamlets. Not even in the sticks. — Charles Ludlum, *Stage Blood*, p. 151, 1974
- Ask some young blood from the sticks who goes upstate on some check forgery. — Edwin Torres, *Carlito's Way*, p. 44, 1975
- I mean, we going to set you so far back in the sticks, they going to have to use jackrabbits to bring your mail to you[.] — Bobby Seale, *A Lonely Rage*, p. 267, 1978

- I mean, it was still way too hot for me to even go near Vegas, so I set up a meeting with the guys way out in the sticks. — *Casino*, 1995

2 skis; ski poles *US, 1963*

- — *American Speech*, p. 207, October 1963: "The language of skiers"

3 furniture *US, 1956*

- It's a cleaner but he's got no D.P. so I sent him to the happy man and now I find they couldn't get together because he's got no sticks. — *San Francisco Examiner*, p. II-1, 24th February 1956
- I got this floor-pop who's looking for a roller but I can't use the OA for the DP on his old sled—I'd take him to the mouse house but he has no sticks. — *San Francisco Chronicle*, pp. 2–1, 31st October 1966
- — *American Speech*, p. 313, Autumn – Winter 1975: "The jargon of car salesmen"

sticks and stones *noun*
the game of pool *US, 1990*

- — Steve Rushin, *Pool Cool*, p. 28, 1990

stickspin *noun*
a scene in a pornographic movie in which a woman changes positions without losing her vaginal grip on the man's penis *US, 1995*

- — *Adult Video News*, p. 40, September 1995

stick time *noun*
time spent as pilot in flight *US, 1990*

- He knows every instrument, every dial / He gets occasional stick time, once in a while. — Joseph Tuso, *Singing the Vietnam Blues*, p. 52, 1990: Bear of the Sky

stickum *noun*
any sticky substance *US, 1909*

- Pasting my hair down with some stickum and putting a few drops of gents' cologne back of my ears, I kept a date with her at the Stork Club one night many months ago. — Earl Wilson, *I am Gazing Into My 8-Ball*, p. 36, 1945

stickup; stick-up *noun*
an armed hold-up *US, 1904*

- "The bandit would shove an ugly-looking .45 caliber automatic into the faces of his startled victims and growl, "This is a stick-up!" — Caryl Chessman, *Cell 2455 Death Row*, p. 274, 1996

sticky finger *verb*
to shoplift *US, 1970*

- Jesus, Mary 'n Joseph, you said all you did was sticky finger something from a store! — Darryl Ponicsan, *The Last Detail*, p. 57, 1970

sticky-fingered *adjective*
inclined to thievery *UK, 1890*

- [W]hat if dear old Gramps was a bit of a sticky-fingered felon in his youth? — Bill Bryson, *In a Sunburned Country*, p. 6, 2001

sticky fingers *noun*

1 an inclination to steal *US, 1939*

- There was nobody to run the Inn and keep the books—that is, nobody without sticky fingers. — Mezz Mezzrow, *Really the Blues*, p. 66, 1946
- So I'd like to raise a toast here to Klepto, and his fantastic sticky fingers. — Wolfman Jack (Bob Smith), *Have Mercy!*, p. 37, 1995

2 a shoplifter *US, 1982*

- — Ralph de Sola, *Crime Dictionary*, p. 44, 1982

stiff *noun*

1 a corpse *US, 1859*

- While he's struggling with a big pine box the end falls out and a stiff slides halfway out, conking him on the skull. — Mezz Mezzrow, *Really the Blues*, p. 316, 1946
- Looks more like a morgue to me. Those pool tables are the slabs they lay the stiffs on. — *The Hustler*, 1961
- A funeral detail. Wolfe is gonna escort a stiff home. — Darryl Ponicsan, *The Last Detail*, p. 178, 1970
- ALYSSA: Two months before she's going to graduate, he's got this job digging graves, and he comes across ... HOLDEN: A stiff. — *Chasing Amy*, 1997

2 an ordinary person; a person who conforms *US, 1998*

- He goes, oh it is going round the sixth form that you two are becoming lesbians, and he said, no, really, he goes I don't believe it but you know that the "stiffs"—straight people—do. — Shane J. Blackman, *Cool Places*, p. 214, 1998

3 in any endeavor, a disappointing, poor performer *US, 1890*

- The horse he had was a stiff, a real pig from Canada. — Vincent Teresa, *My Life in the Mafia*, p. 154, 1973

4 a nonplayer in a gambling establishment *US, 1979*
- — John Scarne, *Scarne's Guide to Modern Poker*, p. 291, 1979

5 a poor tipper *US, 1974*
- A stiff is a guy who comes down with a hundred or two hundred, whacks you for $1,000 or $1,500 and won't give you a tip. — Edward Lin, *Big Julie of Vegas*, p. 202, 1974

6 a disagreeable person who is likely to try to cheat *US, 1882*
- You can smell them. The big tippers, the stiffs, the trouble makers. — *Taxi Driver*, 1976

7 a tramp; a hobo *UK, 1899*
- The street is a little too fast, flighty and noisy for the old-time bums and stiffs. — Jack Lait and Lee Mortimer, *Washington Confidential*, p. 32, 1951

8 in an illegal betting operation, a person who has agreed to pose as the head of the operation to protect the actual head in the event of a police raid and arrest *US, 1952*
- — *Life*, p. 39, 19th May 1952

9 an unskilled pool player *US, 1993*
- — Mike Shamos, *The Illustrated Encyclopedia of Billiards*, p. 231, 1993

10 in horseracing, a horse that is favored to win but is not ridden in an effort to win *US, 1947*
- — Dan Parker, *The ABC of Horse Racing*, p. 149, 1947

11 in pool, the cue ball left with no easy shot *US, 1993*
- — Mike Shamos, *The Illustrated Encyclopedia of Billiards*, p. 231, 1993

12 a worthless check *US, 1950*
- — Hyman E. Goldin et al., *Dictionary of American Underworld Lingo*, p. 211, 1950

13 in the usage of telephone swindlers, a payment by check *US, 1959*
- — *American Speech*, pp. 150–151, May 1959: "Notes on the cant of the telephone confidence man"

14 in blackjack, a card with a value of two, three, four, five, or six *US, 1975*
- But suppose you have a stiff—a two-card hand that is more than eleven and less than seventeen[.] — Jimmy Snyder, *Jimmy the Greek*, p. 225, 1975
- — Thomas F. Hughes, *Dealing Casino Blackjack*, p. 75, 1982

▶ **the stiff**
money for or correspondence to a prisoner, passed to a prison warder by a prisoner's friend or relative *US, 1875*
- [A]nd for what is known as "the stiff," the money which his friends, outside, will bung the screws to pay for his snout [cigarettes] and other little creature comforts. — Charles Raven, *Underworld Nights*, p. 52, 1956

stiff *verb*

1 to cheat someone; to rob someone; to refuse to pay someone *US, 1950*
- But if she doesn't turn in a tip for every hat, she loses her job on grounds she swiped the money or she is so stupid or icky that she gets stiffed. — Jack Lait and Lee Mortimer, *Washington Confidential*, p. 282, 1951
- She stayed in the cab, what's she gonna do? But she stiffed me. A real skunk. — *Taxi Driver*, 1976
- "How about the guy you clocked [hit]?" "He tried to stiff me[.]" — Janet Evanovich, *Seven Up*, p. 94, 2001

2 to fail miserably *US, 1996*
- "So you made it and it stiffed," Tommy said. "So? Make another one." — Elmore Leonard, *Be Cool*, p. 4, 1996

stiff *adjective*
drunk *US, 1737*
- It was at Edmond's that I got stiff—for the first and last time. — Ethel Waters, *His Eye is on the Sparrow*, p. 135, 1951
- I'll talk to you when you're not half stiff. — Jim Thompson, *The Nothing Man*, p. 205, 1954
- Getting stiff on the courthouse steps while denouncing the Roman Catholic clergy was a feat which regularly attracted scoffers and true believers[.] — Nelson Algren, *A Walk on the Wild Side*, p. 9, 1956
- "A guy I know comes along, he's stiff." — George Higgins, *The Digger's Game*, p. 52, 1973

stiff-eye *verb*
to look at someone without establishing eye contact *US, 1964*
- They walked in stiff-eying the bartenders and waiters who caught their message and acted as though they never had seen them before. — Malcolm X and Alex Haley, *The Autobiography of Malcolm X*, p. 147, 1964

stiff one *noun*
any strong alcoholic drink *UK, 1813*

- Helen dropped her compact back in her purse. "C'mon darling. Let's go pour a stiff one at Jean's." — Armistead Maupin, *Tales of the City*, p. 261, 1978

stiffy *noun*
an erection *UK, 1980*
Also variants "stiffie" and "stiff."
- — Connie Eble (Editor), *UNC-CH Campus Slang*, p. 3, Fall 1991
- I got a stiffy for Miss Channel Lock Pliers there. — *Airheads*, 1994
- — Judi Sanders, *Da Bomb!*, p. 27, 1997

stifle *verb*
to silence yourself *US, 1971*
A verb popularized by the Archie Bunker character on the television series *All in the Family*.
- Edith, was I talking too fast, or have you got slow ears? Now stifle! — Eugene Boe (Compiler), *The Wit & Wisdom of Archie Bunker*, p. 20, 1971

still game *noun*
a card game held on a regular basis with regular players *US, 1977*
- — Robert C. Prus and C.R.D. Sharper, *Road Hustler*, p. 171, 1977: "Glossary of terms"

stilts *noun*
the legs *US, 1945*
- — Lou Shelly, *Hepcats Jive Talk Dictionary*, p. 19, 1945

sting *noun*

1 any crime that achieves its purpose by fraud or deception *US, 1930*
- "He boast about a sting and effen you don't believe it, he just might go to the police and confess just to prove it." — Robert Deane Pharr, *S.R.O.*, p. 223, 1971
- But when I make that big sting, I'll straighten you / If you'll save me a little on the cotton. — Dennis Wepman et al., *The Life*, p. 78, 1976
- He wanted to talk about the sting we're plotting. — *Jackie Brown*, 1997

2 a robbery *US, 1940*
- But it wasn't hard at all; it was the sweetest sting in town. — Clarence Cooper Jr., *The Scene*, p. 32, 1960
- You know why I pulled that sting? — Claude Brown, *Manchild in the Promised Land*, p. 410, 1965
- I entered the barbershop and I took a count on the sting: nine bucks and some change. — A.S. Jackson, *Gentleman Pimp*, pp. 12–13, 1973
- Of making a few stings, getting bread together, of Whitey contacting his man and connecting for weight in heroin and of pushing. — Herbert Huncke, *The Evening Sun Turned Crimson*, p. 209, 1980

3 a short, sharp chord played to make or dissolve a sense of suspense *US, 1973*
- — Sherman Louis Sergel, *The Language of Show Biz*, p. 210, 1973

sting *verb*

1 to swindle someone; to cheat, to rob someone *UK, 1812*
- To anyone he could buttonhole, he bragged about how he had "stung" this person or "skinned" that one. — Jim Thompson, *Bad Boy*, p. 308, 1953
- I saw him the day after Limpy had stung me in the hallway on 149th Street. — Claude Brown, *Manchild in the Promised Land*, p. 176, 1965
- How the hell did you rip it off, Jan? I ain't taught you how to sting. — Donald Goines, *Daddy Cool*, p. 166, 1974

2 in horseracing, to shock a horse with an electrical device during a race *US, 1951*
- — David W. Maurer, *Argot of the Racetrack*, p. 60, 1951

stinger *noun*

1 a pinched nerve *US, 1999*
- This would bring about what is commonly known as a singer, a very innocent-sounding word for a sickeningly painful injury. — Mick Foley, *Mankind*, p. 118, 1999
- In the end, the diagnosis was not as frightening as it could have been—the damage was a pinched nerve (called "a stinger"). — Lou Albano and Berg Sugar, *The Complete Idiot's Guide to Professional Wrestling*, p. 56, 1999

2 the penis *US, 1967*
- — Dale Gordon, *The Dominion Sex Dictionary*, p. 153, 1967

3 in poker, a sequence of five cards *US, 1988*
Known conventionally as a "straight."
- — George Percy, *The Language of Poker*, p. 87, 1988

4 a high velocity, hollow-nose, expanding bullet *US, 1981*

- "Stingers and yellowjackets," Parrish said. "Hyper-velocity, hollow-nose expanders. The guy knew what he was doing." — Elmore Leonard, *Split Images*, p. 97, 1981

5 an improvised heating element consisting of exposed wires attached to a small metal plate, used for heating water *US, 1984*

- "You need a stinger?" "Please." — Jimmy Lerner, *You Got Nothing Coming*, p. 137, 2002
- The stinger is an invaluable tool in prison life, and has a long prison history. — J.G. Narum, *The Convict Cookbook*, p. 23, 2004

6 an illegal vote *US, 1982*

Chicago Mayor Richard Daley was given credit for delivering Chicago and the state of Illinois to John Kennedy in the 1960 presidential election through extensive use of "stingers." Subsequent research dispelled most of these rumors, but Daley enjoyed the power the stories gave him.

- — Bill Reilly, *Big Al's Official Guide to Chicagoese*, p. 56, 1982

stingo *noun*

strong, illegally manufactured whiskey *US, 1999*

- It is called corn liquor, white lightning, sugar whiskey, skully cracker, popskull, bush whiskey, stump, stumphole, "splo, ruckus juice, radiator whiskey, rotgut, sugarhead, block and tackle, wildcat, panther's breath, tiger's sweat, Sweet spirits of cats a-fighting, alley bourbon, city gin, cool water, happy Sally, deep shaft, jump steady, old horsey, stingo, blue John, red eye, pine top, buckeye bark whiskey and see seven stars." — *Star Tribune (Minneapolis)*, p. 19F, 31st January 1999

stingy brim *noun*

a hat with a thin brim *US, 1949*

- So I slicked up, put on my new stingy brim and went downstairs and breathed deep. — Hal Ellson, *Duke*, p. 1, 1949
- Of course, he had some stingy-brim hats, and a french-styled houndstooth topcoat with raglan sleeves. — Herbert Simmons, *Corner Boy*, p. 29, 1957

stink *noun*

a commotion; a loud complaint *UK, 1812*

- She called up Jane's mother and made a big stink about it. My mother can make a very big stink about that kind of stuff. — J.D. Salinger, *Catcher in the Rye*, p. 76, 1951

stinker *noun*

1 an offensive or despicable person or thing *US, 1911*

- I think both of them are stinkers. — Philip Wylie, *Opus 21*, p. 273, 1949
- "I've been no good. I've been a real stinker." — Charles Perry, *Portrait of a Young Man Drowning*, p. 102, 1962
- "I think you're a stinker." "What it is, stinker?" "You look it up in your dictionary, bud," I said. — Frederick Kohner, *Gidget Goes to Rome*, p. 30, 1963
- You little stinker. He's given you everything. — *As Good As It Gets*, 1997

2 a corpse that has begun to decompose and, as a result, smell *US, 1996*

- Water cops claimed that floaters somehow smelled even worse than stinkers on dry land. — Joseph Wambaugh, *Floaters*, p. 147, 1996

3 an onion *US, 1962*

- — Joseph E. Ragen and Charles Finston, *Inside the World's Toughest Prison*, p. 820, 1962: "Penitentiary and underworld glossary"

4 a cigar *US, 1907*

So known because of the offensive smell the cigar emits.

- "Here, have a guinea stinker. Special tobacco, cured in Torino." — Richard Farina, *Been Down So Long*, p. 237, 1966
- The two old guys flanking Mazzone—Mustache Petes—had the shirt buttoned to the top but no tie—rumped black suits and puffing on guinea stinkers. — Edwin Torres, *Carlito's Way*, p. 101, 1975

5 in dominoes, a player who forces the next player to draw by cutting him off *US, 1959*

- — Dominic Armanino, *Dominoes*, p. 20, 1959

stinkeroo *noun*

a complete failure *US, 1934*

Coined by Damon Runyon.

- [T]his year has been a real whizbang stinkeroo[.] — John Nichols, *The Sterile Cuckoo*, p. 174, 1965
- The Grade Z blick is Daddy O—a music / hot rod / romance stinkeroo. — James Ellroy, *Hollywood Nocturnes*, p. 4, 1994

stinker squad *noun*

a police homicide investigative department *US, 1981*

- I thought all the guys that worked the Stinker Squads knew each other. — Joseph Wambaugh, *The Glitter Dome*, p. 53, 1981

stink-eye *noun*

a hateful glare *US, 1981*

Hawaiian youth usage.

- Wow, you saw da stink-eye she wen geev me? — Douglas Simonson, *Pidgin to da Max*, 1981

stink-finger *noun*

the insertion of a finger or fingers into a woman's vagina *UK, 1903*

- "They play big kids' games, and I don't mean stink-finger." — John Williams, *The Man Who Cried I Am*, p. 312, 1967
- I could see a black ugly stud playing "stink finger" with an angel-faced broad in a booth behind me. — Iceberg Slim (Robert Beck), *Pimp*, p. 105, 1969
- A lot of johns don't want to do much but stinkfinger. They like to hold me tight, cuddle up and talk. — Charles Winick and Paul Kinsie, *The Lively Commerce*, p. 53, 1971

stink-finger *verb*

to insert a finger or fingers into a woman's vagina *US, 1992*

- Papa, unsuccessfully trying to stink-finger my first girlfriend, Peppy, in the living room, heard my sister and hid behind the piano[.] — Larry Rivers, *What Did I Do?*, p. 51, 1992

stinking thinking *noun*

the rationalization of an addiction as "not that bad" or as something short of an addiction *US, 1998*

Used in twelve-step recovery programs such as Alcoholics Anonymous.

- — Christopher Cavanaugh, *AA to Z*, p. 167, 1998

stinko *adjective*

exceedingly drunk *US, 1927*

- People are always asking me what I do in night clubs. "Don't be stupid," I reply, "I get stinko." — Earl Wilson, *I Am Gazing Into My 8-Ball*, p. 85, 1945
- Can you make it? Are you stinko? — Raymond Chandler, *The Long Goodbye*, p. 6, 1953
- Papa's hair turned almost white and he got stinko more often and he was a little more stooped. — Iceberg Slim (Robert Beck), *Mama Black Widow*, p. 125, 1969
- "Oh, I just love Chicago, she moans, and the dawn comes on me that this muss if stinko." — Leo Rosten, *Dear Herm*, p. 6, 1974

stinkout *noun*

a prank in which bad-smelling material is put in a room, making it uninhabitable *US, 1967*

- — *American Speech*, p. 230, October 1967: "Some special terms used in a University of Connecticut men's dormitory"

stink pot *noun*

the vagina *US, 1980*

- — Edith A. Folb, *runnin' down some lines*, p. 256, 1980

stink stiff *noun*

a badly decomposed and smelly corpse *US, 1984*

- "Need a couple of uniforms right away on a stink stiff," the sergeant said. — Thomas Larry Adcock, *Precinct 19*, p. 16, 1984

stinkum *noun*

any bad-smelling substance *US, 1999*

- "This is one haircut I ain't charging a thin dime for." "If that's the case put some of your stinkum on it. Whatever you figger will fetch the pretty women." — *The Flim-Flam Man and the Apprentice Grifter*, p. 57, 1972
- You can bet he tried everything—smoke, mud, mastodon fat and stinkums too gross to name. — *Arkansas Democrat-Gazette*, p. F1, 2nd September 1999

stinky *noun*

▸ **go stinky**

to defecate *US, 1979*

- He knows I go stinky when I first get up in the mornings[.] — Beatrice Sparks (writing as 'Anonymous'), *Jay's Journal*, p. 72, 1979

stinky pinky *noun*

1 a finger enriched with the aroma of vagina; the insertion of a finger or fingers into a vagina *US, 1965*

- I saw all the holes she had in her pants from playing stinky pinky. — Jerome Charyn, *On the Darkening Green*, p. 202, 1965

- "So you've played stinky-pinky with other naughty little girls?" — Frank Yerby, *Devilseed*, p. 158, 1984
- My phone rang. "In Framingham, some boys call themselves the Stinky Pinky Pussy Posse," the caller said. Geeze, what happened to the Boy Scouts? As far as the posse goes, suffice it to say that the boys, students at Framingham High School, like to do things with their hands, and we're not talking about building campfires or lean-tos. — *Boston Globe*, p. 25, 7th April 1993
- Then he asked, "You at least getting any stinky pinky, Ben?" — Richard DeGrandpere, *Ritalin Nation*, p. 220, 2000

2 a party game based on rhymes *US, 1949*

An overworked prostitute is a "sore whore," excretory humor is "shit wit," etc.

- Stinky-Pinky: There's a new game going the cocktail route. — *San Francisco Examiner*, p. 21, 19th September 1949
- The "currently raging" game ranged here some ten years ago and is properly called "Stinky Pinky." — *Saturday Review of Literature*, p. 25, 4 February 1950
- — *Maledicta*, pp. 66–67, Summer 1977: "A newly printable game of stink-pink (party rhymes)"

stir *verb*

to have sex *US, 1973*

- I ain't stirred the old lady for a couple years, but I swear when I'm with Irma I get the urge like a young stallion[.] — Joseph Wambaugh, *The Blue Knight*, p. 96, 1973

stir broad *noun*

a male prisoner who while incarcerated accepts the passive role in homosexual relationships *US, 1962*

- "A stir broad and a faggot are two different things, Harry." — Charles Perry, *Portrait of a Young Man Drowning*, p. 203, 1962

stir bug *noun*

a prisoner crazed by years of incarceration *US, 1950*

- — Hyman E. Goldin et al., *Dictionary of American Underworld Lingo*, p. 213, 1950

stir-crazy *adjective*

deranged by incarceration *US, 1908*

- Something had happened to the old man in his five days at Twenty-eighth and California, he'd gone a bit stir-crazy it began to appear. — Nelson Algren, *The Man with the Golden Arm*, p. 152, 1949
- Howard was stir-crazy. He would go around the prison saying to anybody about anybody, "I kill the sonofabitch, I sure kill the sonofabitch." — Haywood Patterson, *Scottsboro Boy*, p. 101, 1950
- People are talking about you, say you're stir crazy. They're afraid of you. — Edwin Torres, *After Hours*, p. 284, 1979
- Joe only hoped the remitless heat wasn't driving him stir crazy. — Seth Morgan, *Homeboy*, p. 224, 1990

stir-simple *adjective*

mentally unstable because of incarceration *US, 1952*

- "Aw, shut up, you screwball," Glass said. "You're stir-simple." — Chester Himes, *Cast the First Stone*, p. 49, 1952
- — Troy Harris, *A Booklet of Criminal Argot, Cant and Jargon*, p. 29, 1976

stitch queen *noun*

a male homosexual wardrobe assistant *US, 1973*

- — Sherman Louis Sergel, *The Language of Show Biz*, p. 210, 1973

stitchy *noun*

in circus and carnival usage, a tailor *US, 1981*

- — Don Wilmeth, *The Language of American Popular Entertainment*, p. 258, 1981

STL *adjective*

said of a hospital patient who is in a persistent vegetative state, who is similar to *l*ettuce *US, 1994*

- — Sally Williams, *"Strong" Words*, p. 159, 1994

St. Louis *noun*

in circus and carnival usage, second helpings of food *US, 1981*

According to Wilmeth, an allusion to the fact that circus engagements in St. Louis played in two sections.

- — Don Wilmeth, *The Language of American Popular Entertainment*, p. 255, 1981

St. Louis flats *noun*

stylish shoes custom-made with a single piece of leather *US, 1960*

- "They wore what they called St. Louis Flats and Chicago Flats, made with cork soles and without heels and with gambler designs on the toes." — Bill Crow, *Jazz Anecdotes*, p. 85, 1990

St. Louis stop *noun*

a rolling stop at a traffic signal or stop sign *US, 1999*

- — Jeffrey McQuain, *Never Enough Words*, p. 54, 1999

STO *noun*

an inconsequential person *US, 1946*

- S.T.O. (n) Small time operator. — *Hit Parader*, p. 33, September 1946

stock *noun*

1 the prizes in a carnival midway game concession *US, 1985*

- — Gene Sorrows, *All About Carnivals*, p. 27, 1985: "Terminology"

2 a relatively young prostitute *US, 1971*

- Younger girls were often called "stock," and those under fifteen were "fresh stock." — Charles Winick, *The Lively Commerce*, p. 140, 1971

▸ **throw stock**

to distribute prizes in a carnival game *US, 1966*

- — *American Speech*, p. 283, December 1966: "More carnie talk from the West Coast"

stockings *noun*

female legs *US, 1971*

- — Hermese E. Roberts, *The Third Ear*, 1971

stocking stuffer *noun*

1 in poker, money bet by a player who has withdrawn from the hand *US, 1996*

- — John Vorhaus, *The Big Book of Poker Slang*, p. 34, 1996

2 cash *US, 2003*

- Candy, markers, ammo, liners, stocking stuffer, sweetener, garnish, and pledges are all terms for cash. — Henry Hill and Byron Schreckengost, *A Good Fella's Guide to New York*, p. 123, 2003

stogie *noun*

1 a cigar *US, 1873*

Derives ultimately from Conestoga, a town in Pennsylvania, and the name given to a horse-drawn freight wagon originating in that region in the C18. Conestoga (the town and the wagon) abbreviated to "Stogy"; "Stogy drivers," apparently, smoked a coarse cigar which became known as a "stogie," and by the late C19 a "stogie" was a generic cheap or roughly made cigar.

- Mandon reached in to take out some stogies[.] — Horace McCoy, *Kiss Tomorrow Good-bye*, p. 185, 1948
- "Sue me," he said, taking a good pull on the stogie. — George Mandel, *Flee the Angry Strangers*, p. 96, 1952
- There, after each of us had a mighty sip of toddy and I had been allowed a few puffs from his Pittsburgh stogie, he delivered himself of a lecture. — Jim Thompson, *Bad Boy*, p. 300, 1953
- In his mouth was a twisted stogie; in his hand was the newspaper of the White Citizens Council. — Max Shulman, *Anyone Got a Match?*, p. 208, 1964

2 an extra-large marijuana cigarette *US, 1980*

- — Edith A. Folb, *runnin' down some lines*, p. 256, 1980
- One matchbox of pot for five bucks, and man, you were really hold; you had a lot of marijuana! We used to roll them in brown paper, three or four of us smoking these stogies as we made our way down the street. — Ralph "Sonny" Barger, *Hell's Angel*, p. 21, 2000

3 a cigarette *US, 1995*

- — Lois Stavsky et al., *A2Z*, p. 97, 1995

stokaboka *adjective*

extremely enthusiastic *US, 1991*

- — Trevor Cralle, *The Surfin'ary*, p. 123, 1991

stoke *verb*

▸ **stoke the boiler**

in a swindle operated by telephone, to telephone a prospective victim *US, 1988*

- — Kathleen Odean, *High Steppers, Fallen Angels, and Lollipops*, p. 132, 1988

stoked *adjective*

1 excited *US, 1963*

A major word of the surf lexicon, it was the title and only word in the lyric of a 1963 Beach Boys song written by Brian Wilson.

- — *Paradise of the Pacific*, p. 27, October 1963
- The whole drag racing world was stoked when Don Garlits turned the first officially-timed 200 mph run. — John Lawlor, *How to Talk Car*, p. 101, 1965
- — *Time*, p. 57, 1 January 1965
- I'm just fucking stoked I don't have to pay him! — *South Park*, 1999

2 drug-intoxicated *US, 1986*

- As usual Wilson was wrapped safely behind his Carrera sunglasses and, as usual, he was stoked to the gills, having scored some prior Jamaican herb off a busboy at the hotel. — Carl Hiaasen, *Tourist Season*, p. 169, 1986

3 drunk *US, 1964*

- — J. R. Friss, *A Dictionary of Teenage Slang (Mt. Diablo High)*, 1964

stoker *noun*

a wave that excites surfers *US, 1977*

- — Gary Fairmont R. Filosa II, *The Surfer's Almanac*, p. 182, 1977

stomach Steinway *noun*

the accordion *US, 1999*

- A man gyrating with an accordion—pumping his "Stomach Steinway" for all it's worth. — James Ellroy, *Hollywood Nocturnes*, p. 3, 1994
- Some lovers of what Mark Twain dubbed "the stomach Steinway" stubbornly insist it was always stylish so it can't make a comeback. — *The Star-Ledger*, 7th February 1999

stomp *noun*

a group attack on a single person *US, 1962*

- One is when we go on a "stomp." That's when three or four guys will jump one, for no reason at all. — Lewis Yablonsky, *The Violent Gang*, p. 78, 1962

stomp *verb*

in computing, to mistakenly overwrite something *US, 1991*

- — Eric S. Raymond, *The New Hacker's Dictionary*, p. 335, 1991

stomp-down *adjective*

excellent, admirable *US, 1968*

- I'm talking about a stomp-down sophisticated thoroughbred whore like my woman. — Nathan Heard, *Howard Street*, p. 142, 1968
- She was a stomp-down mud-kicker with kelsey hair / A jive-ass bitch but her face was fair. — Dennis Wepman et al., *The Life*, p. 147, 1976

stomper *noun*

1 the foot; a shoe, especially a heavy shoe *US, 1960*

Also used in the variant "stomp."

- I started livin' and usin' drugs and buyin' clothes, strides and stomps that'd set you back a whole month's pay! — Clarence Cooper Jr., *The Scene*, p. 137, 1960
- — Janey Ironside, *A Fashion Alphabet*, p. 134, 1968
- Sucker, first booty "butt" you don't transport no "hard" [drugs] in your "stomp," keep it in your mitt [hand] so you can down [throw] it fast to the turf. — Iceberg Slim (Robert Beck), *Pimp*, p. 64, 1969
- — David Claerbaut, *Black Jargon in White America*, p. 81, 1972

2 an aggressive, "mannish" lesbian *US, 1967*

- Known variously as a bull, a stomper, a bad butch, a hard dresser, a truck driver, a diesel dyke, a bull dagger and a half dozen other soubriquets, she is the one who, according to most homosexual girls, gives lesbians a bad name. — Ruth Allison, *Lesbianism*, p. 125, 1967

stomp pad *noun*

on a snowboard, the pad between the bindings *US, 1993*

- — Doug Werner, *Snowboarders Start-Up*, p. 114, 1993: "Glossary"

stone *noun*

1 a dollar *US, 1957*

- "I'll make at least seventy-five stones every week." — Herbert Simmons, *Corner Boy*, p. 152, 1957
- "Did you get any loot?" "About twenty stones." — Malcom Braly, *Felony Tank*, p. 120, 1961

2 a state of drug intoxication *US, 1980*

- When we got to the concert, I had a strong stone on. — Stephen Gaskin, *Amazing Dope Tales*, p. 155, 1980

3 a billiard ball *US, 1990*

- — Steve Rushin, *Pool Cool*, p. 28, 1990

4 in the usage of youthful model road racers (slot car racers), a slow car *US, 1997*

- — Phantom Surfers, *The Exciting Sounds of Model Road Racing (Album cover)*, 1997

stone *verb*

to amaze or impress someone *US, 1950*

- Allen and I have worked out the pygmy singing & drumbeat that will stone you. — Jack Kerouac, *Letter to Neal Cassady*, pp. 238–239, 3rd December 1950

Stone Age *noun*

in computing, the years from 1943 until the mid-1950s *US, 1991*

- — Eric S. Raymond, *The New Hacker's Dictionary*, p. 335, 1991

stoned *adjective*

1 intoxicated on a drug, usually marijuana *US, 1952*

- To get high again, completely stoned. — Hal Ellson, *The Golden Spike*, p. 60, 1952
- With each week of work, bombed and sapped and charged and stoned with lush, with pot, with benny[.] — Norman Mailer, *Advertisements for Myself*, p. 243, 1955
- Grass is a little less common than cigarettes. When someone says "stoned," he doesn't mean drunk. — James Simon Kunen, *The Strawberry Statement*, p. 171, 1968
- So Laura came to Petrarch's party, to put it stylishly, and got stoned out of her head. — Gore Vidal, *Myra Breckinridge*, p. 59, 1968

2 drunk *US, 1952*

- I had finished the wine while Terry slept, and I was proper stoned. — Jack Kerouac, *On the Road*, p. 90, 1957
- We had come home late the night before, my old man mildly stoned from all the grape Abby's father had forced upon him. — Frederick Kohner, *Gidget Goes Hawaiian*, p. 47, 1961

3 exhilarated, unrelated to drugs *US, 1971*

- Their ignorance kept me permanently stoned. — Jamie Mandelkau, *Buttons*, p. 82, 1971

stoned out *adjective*

in a state of drug intoxication *US, 1952*

- He must be home, but like stoned out; you know? — George Mandel, *Flee the Angry Strangers*, p. 67, 1952

stone John *noun*

a jail or prison *US, 1962*

- — Joseph E. Ragen and Charles Finston, *Inside the World's Toughest Prison*, p. 820, 1962: "Penitentiary and underworld glossary"

stoner *noun*

a regular or habitual user of marijuana; a drug user *US, 1971*

- Could I get some stoners over here please! — *Heathers*, 1988
- What was that thing the little stoner pulled on the villain in the last issue? — *Chasing Amy*, 1997
- God, what a little stoner. You look so different with long hair. — Kenneth Lonergan, *This is Our Youth*, p. 63, 2000
- "You look like a stoner." "Well, yeah, but that's because you know me." — Janet Evanovich, *Seven Up*, p. 73, 2001
- Hey, can't we do something about those two stoners hanging around outside all the time? — Kevin Smith, *Jay and Silent Bob Strike Back*, p. 10, 2001

stones *noun*

1 the testicles *UK, 1154*

- They could have heard you squealing over in Cunt Lick County, just a squealing like a stoat with his stones cut off. — William Burroughs, *Naked Lunch*, p. 173, 1957
- Did you see fuckin' Monk wade into it? Man has got some hard stones on him! — John Sayles, *Union Dues*, p. 341, 1977

2 courage *US, 1974*

From "stones" as "testicles" and "testicles" as "courage."

- "Sure," Russell said, "and a guy like you, he wants something done, hasn't got the stones to do it himself." — George Higgin, *Cogan's Trade*, p. 4, 1974
- One caper I've had on the drawing board only I didn't have the stones. — Seth Morgan, *Homeboy*, p. 55, 1990

3 crack cocaine *US, 1994*

- — US Department of Justice, *Street Terms*, October 1994

4 dominoes *US, 1959*

- — Dominic Armanino, *Dominoes*, p. 16, 1959

Stones *nickname*

the Blackstone Rangers youth gang *US, 1969*

- The entire group chanted, "Stones run it[!]" — L.H. Whittemore, *Cop!*, p. 114, 1969

Stonewall Jackson *noun*

used as a soubriquet for an extremely frugal person *US, 1962*

Thomas "Stonewall" Jackson was a general in the Confederate Army, killed by "friendly fire" in 1863.

- — Frank Garcia, *Marked Cards and Loaded Dice*, p. 264, 1962

stony lonesome *noun*

prison *US, 1969*

- "I had just done a year in stony lonesome." — Juan Carmel Cosmes, *Memoir of a Whoremaster*, p. 76, 1969

- My shit was syrup and I ain't scared to say it. I don't wanna go to stony lonesome, not down in this fuckin' country. — Joseph Wambaugh, *Finnegan's Week*, p. 51, 1993

stooge *verb*
to act as someone's lackey *US, 1939*
- You ain't plannin' to stooge, is you? — Nathan Heard, *Howard Street*, p. 139, 1968

stool *noun*
a police informer *US, 1906*
A shortened version of STOOL PIGEON.
- He protested that he couldn't be a stool. — William J. Spillard and Pence James, *Needle in a Haystack*, p. 39, 1945
- Then we'll cut the word loose on the street Carlito is a stool. — Edwin Torres, *Carlito's Way*, p. 122, 1975

stool *verb*
to give information or evidence, usually to the police *US, 1911*
- If the other rats in this business would let me alone and quit stoolin' to the cops I'd get along. — William J. Spillard and Pence James, *Needle in a Haystack*, p. 192, 1945
- She's that nun who stools for them two darky dicks, ain't she? — Chester Himes, *A Rage in Harlem*, p. 150, 1957
- "Arnie stooled on the fellows who were with him in the holdup." — Charles Perry, *Portrait of a Young Man Drowning*, p. 241, 1962
- That's the problem. Nobody wants to stool on a brother officer. — Edwin Torres, *Q & A*, p. 138, 1977

stoolie *noun*
a police informer *US, 1924*
A shortened form of STOOL PIGEON.
- Well, it seems that one day some stoolie tipped off the cops that Lil was selling hop in her place[.] — Mezz Mezzrow, *Really the Blues*, p. 249, 1946
- We let you operate because you're a stooly, and that's all. — Chester Himes, *A Rage in Harlem*, p. 74, 1957
- [W]hen Willie finishes his ten year stretch, he'll have to take another city for it, as he is a marked man as a "stoolie" and to come back would mean certain death[.] — Babs Gonzales, *I Paid My Dues*, p. 102, 1967
- With the spics, if a stoolie moves from 111th Street to the Bronx he's out of the jurisdiction[.] — Edwin Torres, *Carlito's Way*, p. 44, 1975
- Collucci said, "Pretend I'm the secret Grand Jury, stoolie cocksucker!" — Iceberg Slim (Robert Beck), *Death Wish*, pp. 213–214, 1977

stoolie *verb*
to give information or evidence, usually to the police *US, 1971*
- "But I also told you that only Joey pays rent because I stoolie for Ginsburg. I tell him who's doubling up so he can charge them extra." — Robert Deane Pharr, *S.R.O.*, p. 361, 1971

stool magnet *noun*
a person with bad luck *US, 1994*
- — Sally Williams, *"Strong" Words*, p. 161, 1994

stool pigeon *noun*
a police informer *US, 1906*
- Commonly known as stool pigeons in the underworld, these men whom nobody is supposed to like are a narcotic agent's right arm in many instances. — William J. Spillard and Pence James, *Needle in a Haystack*, p. 141, 1945
- "I haven't turned stool pigeon." Actually, although I pretended that it was the furthest thing from my thoughts, I was a little worried. There had been rumors of the FBI putting the pressure on him[.] — Clancy Sigal, *Going Away*, p. 265, 1961
- You'll be the lowest sort of rat, the prince of snitches, the loudest cooing stool pigeon that ever grabbed his ankles for the man. — *The Usual Suspects*, 1995

stooper *noun*
in horseracing, a bettor who examines discarded tickets on the ground in the hope of finding a winning bet *US, 1947*
- — Dan Parker, *The ABC of Horse Racing*, p. 149, 1947

stop *verb*
▶ **stop the clock**
to permit a financially strapped debtor to pay principal and not interest *US, 1989*
- By the early 1960s, Boston's underworld had become so rabid that it seldom "stopped the clock" on debtors who were bled dry[.] — Gerard O'Neill, *The Under Boss*, p. 54, 1989

stop-over *noun*
a short jail sentence, either empirically or in proportion to the crime involved *US, 1962*
- — Joseph E. Ragen and Charles Finston, *Inside the World's Toughest Prison*, p. 820, 1962: "Penitentiary and underworld glossary"

store *noun*
1 a betting operation *US, 1951*
- — David W. Maurer, *Argot of the Racetrack*, p. 60, 1951
2 any rigged game or attraction in a carnival *US, 1985*
- — Gene Sorrows, *All About Carnivals*, p. 27, 1985: "Terminology"
3 in a big con swindle, the fake office, poolroom, or betting establishment created for the swindle *US, 1940*
- The inside man is the guts of a store. He makes one mistake and he's lost the mark and the score. — Iceberg Slim (Robert Beck), *Trick Baby*, p. 119, 1969

store-bought *adjective*
factory-manufactured cigarettes, as opposed to hand-rolled *US, 1969*
- Oh, no thanks. I got some—uh—store-bought right over here of my own. — *Easy Rider*, p. 121, 1969

store choppers *noun*
false teeth *US, 1975*
- — John Gould, *Maine Lingo*, p. 279, 1975

store dice *noun*
inexpensive store-bought dice, not milled to casino-level tolerances *US, 1962*
- — Frank Garcia, *Marked Cards and Loaded Dice*, p. 264, 1962

store dick *noun*
a department store's private detective *US, 1960*
- I got 'em from a lady store-dick in California who used 'em to scratch the ants outta her hot pants. — Clarence Cooper Jr., *The Scene*, p. 196, 1960
- Too many store dicks. — Phil Hirsch, *Hooked*, p. 144, 1968

stork bite *noun*
a flat pink birthmark or capillary hemangioma *US, 1991*
- — Barton D. Schmitt, M.D., *Your Child's Health*, 1991

storked *adjective*
pregnant *US, 1945*
- — Lou Shelly, *Hepcats Jive Talk Dictionary*, p. 19, 1945

stork mark *noun*
a birthmark *US, 1960*
- The stormark affecting the face fades before the end of the first year. — Bill Chaudhry, *Mosby's Color Atlas and Text of Pediatrics*, p. 246, 2001

stovepipe *noun*
1 a distended, gaping anus produced by recent anal intercourse *US, 1995*
- — *Adult Video News*, p. 40, September 1995
2 a revolver *US, 1957*
- — *American Speech*, p. 195, October 1957: "Some colloquialisms of the handgunner"
3 a jet aircraft *US, 1956*
- — *American Speech*, p. 229, October 1956: "More United States air force slang"
4 gossip *US, 1977*
From the image of railroadmen gathered around a stove gossiping.
- — Ramon Adams, *The Language of the Railroader*, p. 148, 1977
5 a three-part bet in an illegal numbers gambling lottery, in which the bettor must correctly guess two of the three digits in the winning number and have the third digit be one of eight bet on *US, 1949*
- — *American Speech*, p. 193, October 1949

stove up *adjective*
injured, ill or exhausted *US, 1901*
- If I weren't so stove up and ailin' critical, I'd bung yo head bigger 'n a Georgia watermelon 'bout you and that tramp. — Iceberg Slim (Robert Beck), *Doom Fox*, p. 123, 1978
- I been feelin' a little stove up all week, but if I can walk, I can work. — Ken Weaver, *Texas Crude*, p. 129, 1984
- I don't want any parts of surveillance work. Other than following some stove-up cripple walks with a cane. — Elmore Leonard, *Glitz*, p. 320, 1985

stow *verb*
▸ **stow your chant**
to stop talking *US, 1964*
- — R. Frederick West, *God's Gambler*, p. 228, 1964: "Appendix A"

STP *noun*
a type of synthetic hallucinogen *US, 1967*
Probably coined as an abbreviation of "serotonin triphosphate" and as an allusion to the trademark name of a motor oil additive, and later deabbreviated to "serenity, tranquility and peace."
- I could write behind STP, but not behind acid. — Joan Didion, *Slouching Toward Bethlehem*, p. 109, 1967
- STP: methylmethoxyamphetamine, JB314 to the Army, developed to incapcitate enemy soldiers. STP stands for Serenity/Tranquility/Peace. — Ethel Romm, *The Open Conspiracy*, p. 246, 1970
- And I put a definite HOLD on STP, I don't think there's anything wrong with it karmically but it's such a long and juiceless trip that it damages the bearings. — *The Last Supplement to the Whole Earth Catalog*, p. 83, March 1971
- Wow, man, STP! — John Sinclair, *Guitar Army*, p. 291, 1972

St. Pete *noun*
in shuffleboard, a disk hidden midway on your opponent's side of the court *US, 1967*
- — Omero C. Catan, *Secrets of Shuffleboard Strategy*, p. 72, 1967: "Glossary of terms"

str8 *adjective*
straight, in all its senses *US, 1993*
- Str8-G, a rugged L.A. rapper whose lyrics showcase him busting off with his fists and not a gun. — *Billboard*, p. 28, 3rd July 1993
- "It saved my life," the 22-year-old student said of the movement, the fingers of his left hand tattooed with the message STR8. — *Philadelphia Inquirer*, p. A1, 1st October 1995
- — Michelle Baker and Steven Tropicano, *Queer Facts*, p. 13, 2004

strack; strac *adjective*
professional; neat; clean *US, 1978*
Military slang.
- "You look strack," the E-8 whispered. "How'd you go for a rear job?" — Tim O'Brien, *Going After Cacciato*, p. 38, 1978
- You got zero five to get out of those civvie threads and make a strack troop of yourself. — John Del Vecchio, *The 13th Valley*, p. 46, 1982
- I think they take Captain Gardner for a typical HHQ commander, not up to par, not strac enough to command a line company. — Lucian K. Truscott, *Army Blue*, p. 314, 1989
- "You wanna look strac for the Disciplinary Committee." — Jimmy Lerner, *You Got Nothing Coming*, p. 143, 2002

straddle *noun*
in poker, an increased bet made without looking at your cards *US, 1988*
- — George Percy, *The Language of Poker*, p. 87, 1988

straggler *noun*
in horseracing, a winning bet that is not cashed in immediately after a race but, unlike an out ticket, is cashed in before the end of the day *US, 1982*
- — Bob and Barbara Freeman, *Wanta Bet?*, p. 295, 1982

straight *noun*
1 a conventional person, blind to the values of a counter-culture *US, 1967*
- Most of the hip population slept the mornings out, but the straights in the neighborhood arose to the harmonics of the good morning vibrations and did their straight things. — Nicholas Von Hoffman, *We Are The People Our Parents Warned Us Against*, p. 12, 1967
- There were a few straights but they looked very uptight and out of place. — *Berkeley Barb*, p. 1, 20th January 1967
- Straights shit in their pants when they hear the yippies reveal the most crucial political issue in Amerika today: pay toilets. — Jerry Rubin, *Do It!*, p. 86, 1970
- Many straights obviously felt uncomfortable patronizing establishments that abutted a church. — Arthur Blessitt, *Turned On to Jesus*, p. 7, 1971

2 a factory-made cigarette *US, 1951*
- He took one deep drag and he coughed. "Damned straights make the eyes water." — Thurston Scott, *Cure it with Honey*, p. 35, 1951
- "Naw, just some straights." He walked over to the cigarette machine and got some smokes. — Piri Thomas, *Down These Mean Streets*, p. 211, 1967

- I walked in the drugstore to cop some straight's and while the girl was getting the smokes, I enjoyed the sound of female voices[.] — A.S. Jackson, *Gentleman Pimp*, p. 68, 1973
- They give you a bag of sawdust for tobacco, so you learn to scrounge around for cigarettes—to take Joe for a couple of straights here, hit Mike for a straight there, so you've got three smokes to knock out the night. — Herbert Huncke, *Guilty of Everything*, p. 122, 1990

3 a heterosexual *US, 1941*
- [T]he pool-playing dykes and femmes sit at tables in one corner away from the juke-box, and the "straights" fill out the rest of the bar. — Roger Gordon, *Hollywood's Sexual Underground*, p. 18, 1966
- It was a table in the corner closest to the door, the one where timid straights often perched to watch the freaks at play. — Robert Campbell, *Alice in La-La Land*, p. 270, 1987

4 simple vaginal intercourse *US, 1961*
- I say, Yoo-hoo, pitty baby, you wanna lil french? Haff an haff? How about jes a straight? I say, Twenty berries an you alla roun' the mothahfuggin' worl'. — Robert Gover, *One Hundred Dollar Misunderstanding*, p. 21, 1961
- A "flat-backer" who offers only coitus ("old-fashioned" or "straight") is likely to lose customers. — Charles Winick, *The Lively Commerce*, p. 207, 1971
- At first she figured she'd play it open-and-shut, bring him off and charge him twenty for a fifteen-dollar straight without dropping anything but her panties. — John Sayles, *Union Dues*, p. 186, 1977
- Half-and-half still costs you more than straight, so if you need the girl's mouth on your dingus to get you up it will set you back a total of thirty dollars[.] — Gerald Paine, *A Bachelor's Guide to the Brothels of Nevada*, p. 26, 1978

5 in horseracing, a bet that a horse will win a race *US, 1976*
- — Tom Ainslie, *Ainslie's Complete Guide to Thoroughbred Racing*, p. 339, 1976

straight *adjective*
1 heterosexual *US, 1941*
- Back in the days when I was first in the navy, I didn't know a gay guy from a straight guy. — Willard Motley, *Let No Man Write My Epitaph*, p. 210, 1958
- Whatever a guy does with other guys, if he does it for money, that don't make him queer. You're still straight. — John Rechy, *City of Night*, p. 45, 1963
- Listen, asshole, what am I going to do? He's straight. — Mart Crowley, *The Boys in the Band*, p. 32, 1968
- One day he told me that if there was anything that could make him go straight, it was me. — Jefferson Poland and Valerie Alison, *The Records of the San Francisco Sexual Freedom League*, p. 46, 1971

2 conventional, not part of the counterculture *US, 1960*
- Of course, they were all straight. They weren't into anycrime or stuff like that, as far as I know. — Claude Brown, *Manchild in the Promised Land*, p. 185, 1965
- I walked toward them & thru them—was almost busted—but my guardian angel (temporarily acquired) looked straight enough to get us through. — *The San Francisco Orale*, 1966
- Another threat is unwanted visitors—the sightseers from "straight" society and the weekend hippies who descend upon them to freeload. — *Life*, p. 168, 18th July 1969
- Yes, some of us do have straight jobs and others devote more of their time to the movement. — *The Last Supplement to the Whole Earth Catalogue*, p. 15, March 1971

3 not currently drug-intoxicated; no longer using drugs *UK, 1967*
- The terror of facing their daily grind "straight" was unimaginable. — Lanre Fehintola, *Charlie Says...*, p. 170, 2000
- When people are straight they don't come bounding up to you[.] — Dave Haslam, *Adventures of the Wheels of Steel*, p. 114, 2001

4 under the influence of drugs, or at least not suffering from withdrawal symptoms *US, 1946*
- Main-lining her. Capping her straight. — John D. McDonald, *The Neon Jungle*, p. 46, 1953
- I've got a job tonight and I've got to get straight. — Jack Gerber, *The Connection*, p. 32, 1957
- I don't get high anymore. I just get straight; I take a cure. I'm just normal, that's all. — Jeremy Larner and Ralph Tefferteller, *The Addict in the Street*, p. 233, 1964
- Enough to keep us straight so we won't have to worry bout coppin' for awhile. — Vernon E. Smith, *The Jones Men*, p. 177, 1974

5 good, pleasing, acceptable *US, 1993*
- A-Wax: Cool, how you feelin' man? Caine: I'm straight. — *Menace II Society*, 1993
- — Don R. McCreary (Editor), *Dawg Speak*, 2001

6 of alcoholic drinks, undiluted *US, 1874*

- "I'll take it straight, with a water chaser," answered Rube. — Helen Giblo, *Footlights, Fistfights and Femmes*, p. 131, 1957

7 without a "minus" or "plus" attached to a grade *US, 1968*

- — Collin Baker et al., *College Undergraduate Slang Study Conducted at Brown University*, p. 205, 1968

straight arrow *noun*
an honest or honorable person *US, 1969*
From the proverbial expression, "straight as an arrow."

- Something about his earnestness reassured her. He was such a straight arrow. She thought, He probably will take care of me. — Michael Crichton, *Timeline*, p. 161, 2000

straight as a string *adjective*
used of a racehorse, fully exerting itself *US, 1976*

- — Tom Ainslie, *Ainslie's Complete Guide to Thoroughbred Racing*, p. 339, 1976

straight date *noun*
conventional vaginal sex with a prostitute *US, 1972*

- At the hotel, if it's a straight date it's usually $10, and a French date, a blow job, is $20. — Bruce Jackson, *Outside the Law*, p. 186, 1972

straight edge *adjective*
reflecting a philosophy that promotes hardcore rock music, abstinence from drugs, and abstinence from promiscuous sex *US, 1983*
Probably coined by Ian Mackaye in the self-titled song "Straight Edge" while Mackaye was the singer of the Washington D.C. band Minor Threat.

- I don't think about speed / That's something I just don't need / I've got the straight edge. — Minor Threat, *Straight Edge*, 1983(?)
- — Connie Eble (Editor), *UNC-CH Campus Slang*, p. 8, March 1996
- It started out hardcore, like Bad Religion, then you got straight-edge, like Minor Threat and surf punk like Agent Orange. — Elmore Leonard, *Be Cool*, p. 197, 1999
- I really need a beer, but I'm gonna try to go straightedge. — Lynn Breedlove, *Godspeed*, p. 61, 2002

straighten *verb*
to produce drug intoxication in someone *US, 1957*

- Red brought the eighteen dollars out of his pocket with his left hand. "You straight man, just straighten me." — Herbert Simmons, *Corner Boy*, p. 117, 1957
- One bag's not enough to straighten me. — Jeremy Larner and Ralph Tefferteller, *The Addict in the Street*, p. 233, 1964
- Then James Fox came in and said he had his works and that he wanted Johnny to straighten him. — Claude Brown, *Manchild in the Promised Land*, p. 118, 1965
- But when I make that big sting, I'll straighten you / If you'll save me a little on the cotton. — Dennis Wepman et al., *The Life*, p. 78, 1976

straightened out *adjective*
officially recognized as a member of an organized crime family *US, 1987*

- A true Mafia member is a "made guy" or "straightened out," or a "wiseguy." — Joseph Pistone, *Donnie Brasco*, p. 54, 1987

straighten out *verb*
1 to feel the effects of a drug, relieving any pangs of withdrawal *US, 1966*

- Like I might find old Joe Schmoe today and buy three bags from him and find that one bag straightens me out. — James Mills, *The Panic in Needle Park*, p. 46, 1966
- How about us getting some speed, see, and then after we're all straightened out, we'll all jump in the car and head down to four-fifty[.] — *Drugstore Cowboy*, 1988

2 to bring someone up to date *US, 1946*

- The man at the window there was a fellow countryman of mine downstairs who might straighten me out. — Mezz Mezzrow, *Really the Blues*, p. 191, 1946

straight flush wannabe *noun*
in poker, a sequenced hand comprised of all red or all black suits, but not a flush *US, 1996*
Impressive looking, but worth no more than any nonflush straight.

- — John Vorhaus, *The Big Book of Poker Slang*, p. 8, 1996

straight-fuck *verb*
to engage in conventional vaginal intercourse *US, 1969*

- Mr. Smith got on top of Lisa, put his prick in her, and started straight-fucking her. — Joey V., *Portrait of Joey*, p. 100, 1969
- I still enjoy straight fucking as long as the people are nice. — Xaviera Hollander, *The Happy Hooker*, p. 132, 1972

straight lay *noun*
conventional vaginal sexual intercourse *US, 1997*

- Often times a guy would come in for a "Straight Lay," then during the medical check, he would turn out to be an "Oh My God." — Sisters of the Heart, *The Brothel Bible*, p. 81, 1997
- She's had thirteen "straight lay" customers in as many hours. — Lora Shaner, *Madam*, p. 7, 1999

straight-leg *noun*
an infantry soldier, unattached to a mechanized or airborne unit *US, 1951*

- The straight legs hate us guys in the mortars. — David Parks, *GI Diary*, p. 37, 1968
- The artillery dudes and straight-leg grunts and the gooks was doin' it hand to hand. — Larry Heinemann, *Close Quarters*, p. 29, 1977
- Airborne, "straight leg," which is best? / AIRBORNE! AIRBORNE! YES! YES! YES! — Sandee Shaffer Johnson, *Cadences*, p. 91, 1986
- Without preamble, he said, "We have twelve ex-Rangers and a couple of straight legs so far." — Alfred Coppel, *Show Me A Hero*, p. 78, 1987

straight moniker *noun*
a person's legal name *US, 1966*

- No one but Pinky and Sister Heavenly knew his straight moniker[.] — Chester Himes, *Come Back Charleston Blue*, p. 51, 1966

straight name *noun*
a person's given name, often unknown in the underworld life of nicknames *US, 1969*

- I think he had a straight name, but I never knew it. — Juan Carmel Cosmes, *Memoir of a Whoremaster*, p. 29, 1969

straight puda *noun*
the complete, whole truth *US, 1968*

- — Fred Hester, *Slang on the 40 Acres*, p. 9, 1968

straights *noun*
straight pool or continuous pocket billiards *US, 1984*

- In straights, if you were hot you kept right on going[.] — Walter Tevis, *The Color of Money*, p. 146, 1984
- — Mike Shamos, *The Illustrated Encyclopedia of Billiards*, p. 234, 1993

straight shooter *noun*
a glass or metal device used to smoke crack cocaine *US, 1995*
- — Mark S. Fleisher, *Beggars & Thieves*, p. 291, 1995: "Glossary"

straight trade *noun*
homosexual sex with a man who considers himself heterosexual *US, 1972*

- One of the principal arguments that will be made, according to Martin, is that "homosexual behavior," by homosexuals, but especially also by sailors who consider themselves and are generally considered to be heterosexual—"straight trade"—is widespread. — *The Advocate*, p. 9, 19th January 1972

straight trick *noun*
vaginal sex between a prostitute and customer *US, 1972*

- In a joint most of them are straight tricks, but on call about half of them are straight and the other half a little other than straight. — Bruce Jackson, *In the Life*, p. 195, 1972

straight up *adjective*
1 honest *US, 1993*

- "Hobbes straight up with me." — Jess Mowry, *Six Out Seven*, p. 17, 1993

2 used of an alcoholic drink or a drug, undiluted *US, 1973*

- Scotch straight up and a rum and Coke for me. — *Tin Men*, 1987
- If somebody coming in from Jersey City, you give 'em a straight-up ounce 'cause they can get pretty good stuff right in town. — Richard Price, *Clockers*, p. 180, 1992

3 a prison sentence, without reduction for good behavior or other factors *US, 1969*

- He was an orphan and he had just done a two-year "bit" "straight up," his fourth, two months before. — Iceberg Slim (Robert Beck), *Pimp*, p. 36, 1969
- I get busted again, I do five years straight up and not at one of those country-club joints either. — Elmore Leonard, *Riding the Rap*, p. 78, 1995

4 pure, unadulterated *US, 1995*

- We're gonna play straight-up rock and roll. — *Empire Records*, 1995
- There was a jumble of straight-up trash at the top of the stairs, in the hall. — Michelle Tea, *Rent Girl*, p. 176, 2004

5 used of a person, especially a girl, thin *US, 1947*

- — Marcus Hanna Boulware, *Jive and Slang of Students in Negro Colleges*, 1947

straight-up *adverb*

openly, honestly *US, 2006*

- "I'm telling you straight-up what happened," Saiquan said. — Jason Starr, *Lights Out*, p. 268, 2006

strait *adjective*

conventional *US, 1966*

An unconventional spelling to emphasize the difference between conventional and unconventional.

- Lure the enemy into your own battleground by going a turn face claiming you came back to stop kids from taking acid and then when you have thousands of these strait people together turn them on to acid. — *The San Francisco Oracle*, 1966

strange *noun*

a new and unknown sexual partner *US, 1967*

- Any man figures to get something strange ever' once in a while. — Malcolm Braly, *On the Yard*, p. 110, 1967
- — Connie Eble (Editor), *UNC-CH Campus Slang*, p. 5, November 1983
- Except on days when he yearned for some strange. — Seth Morgan, *Homeboy*, p. 276, 1990
- Once qualifies as strange. More than once you might as well pop your old lady for all the surprises you get with whoo-ers. — James Ellroy, *White Jazz*, p. 111, 1992

strange *adjective*

new, fresh, unknown, especially sexually *US, 1957*

- That was what he needed. A strange piece. Been a long time since he fucked anybody but Irene. — Hubert Selby Jr., *Last Exit to Brooklyn*, p. 268, 1957
- Usually they were mamas, but now and then what the Angels call a "strange broad" or "new pussy" would show up. — Hunter S. Thompson, *Hell's Angels*, p. 193, 1966
- "I'll call Ginny up and tell here, you're scoutin' strange tail alla time." — George Higgins, *Cogan's Trade*, p. 72, 1974
- He decided to run by the Roost and see if there was some strange cunt hanging around. — Donald Goines, *Black Gangster*, p. 108, 1977

strange place *noun*

a disturbed mental state *US, 1971*

- STRANGE PLACE: unusual mental state, as, "His head has been in a strange place since he came back to Berkeley." — Robert Buckhout, *Toward Social Change*, p. 466, 1971

stranger *noun*

1 used as a form of address emphasizing the fact that the two people have not seen each other for a while *US, 1996*

- "Hell, Stranger," Helen said to him. "Hello, Helen," he said, thinking, Why do people call other people stranger when they haven't seen them for a while? Is it to instill guilt that you haven't been attentive enough? — Joseph Wambaugh, *Floaters*, p. 224, 1996

2 in poker, any card added to a hand by draw *US, 1988*

- — George Percy, *The Language of Poker*, p. 88, 1988

strangers *noun*

in gin, cards in a hand that do not and cannot form a sequence *US, 1965*

- — Irwin Steig, *Play Gin to Win*, p. 142, 1965

strange stuff *noun*

a new and different sex partner *US, 1950*

- "Do you want to bust in on the church dance?" Steven said. "It's Friday night. There ought to be some strange stuff there?" — Hal Ellson, *Tomboy*, p. 128, 1950

strangle *verb*

to turn something off; to deactivate something *US, 1963*

- — *American Speech*, p. 120, May 1963: "Air refueling words"

strap *noun*

a handgun *US, 1991*

- [P]anic ensued when someone on the steps yelled, "Get the straps"—street slang for guns—and a bottle shattered in the street,

frightening Bynoe and causing him to fire wildly, without aim. — *Boston Globe Magazine*, p. 14, 14th November 1991

- I'd open it, pull out my flag, put on my murder ones (dark shades, also called Locs or Locos), button the top button of my shirt, put my strap in my lap, and drive on to the 'hood. — Sanyika Shakur, *Monster*, p. 43, 1993
- "Well, don't just stand there, fool. Get the strap." — Colton Simpson, *Inside the Crips*, p. 148, 2005

strap *verb*

to have sex *US, 1971*

Also used in the variant "strap on."

- — Eugene Landy, *The Underground Dictionary*, p. 178, 1971

strap-hanger *noun*

a member of the armed forces, stationed well away from combat, accompanying troops into the field without having a specific role to play *US, 1967*

- Half a dozen straphangers, including a chaplain, climb up the ramp and take the seats nearest the door. — Donald Duncan, *The New Legions*, p. 146, 1967
- — *Department of the Army, Staff Officer's Guidebook*, p. 66, 1986

strap-on *noun*

a dildo that is harnessed to a person's body *UK, 1994*

- What does it mean for a woman to want to wear a strap-on and to use it with a man? — Jonathan Goldberg, *Reclaiming Sodom*, p. 2, 1994
- When will I have another prime-time opportunity to educate the masses about a particularly crucial but mostly misunderstood aspect of lesbian sexuality like strap-ons? — *The Village Voice*, 27th June 2000

strapped *adjective*

armed, especially with a gun *US, 1991*

From **STRAP** (a handgun).

- How he was always strapped down with a nine millimeter or a 44 magnum. — Leon Bing, *Do or Die*, p. xi, 1991
- Dog, you strapped? — *Menace II Society*, 1993
- No one knew I was strapped. — Sanyika Shakur, *Monster*, p. 16, 1993
- Members who weren't felons were heavily strapped. — Ralph "Sonny" Barger, *Hell's Angel*, p. 7, 2000
- Yet many of the shocked blacks, few of them strapped (armed), now cowered under tables hoping to save their lives. — Bill Valentine, *Gangs and Their Tattoos*, p. 12, 2000

straps *noun*

suspenders *US, 1945*

- — Lou Shelly, *Hepcats Jive Talk Dictionary*, p. 19, 1945
- — Clarence Major, *Dictionary of Afro-American Slang*, p. 110, 1970

strap up *verb*

to carry a pistol *US, 1998*

- — Ethan Hilderbrant, *Prison Slang*, p. 123, 1998

straw *noun*

a hat *US, 1976*

- I'll beat you for your bankroll and your wardrobe too / And I'd beat you for your straw, but all suckers don't chew. — Dennis Wepman et al., *The Life*, p. 148, 1976

strawberry *noun*

1 a woman who trades sex for crack cocaine *US, 1989*

- They would only say that they were investigating a series of crimes that involved women who traded sex for drugs. Since August, 1985, at least nine such women, known in street slang as "strawberries," have been found shot to death. — *Los Angeles Times*, p. 3, 24th February 1989
- The woman that answers is thin and emaciated, a crack addict, pipe in hand an all. This is SHERYL, a strawberry. — *Boyz N The Hood*, p. 48, 1990
- The "strawberries" or rock whores, who worked farther east on the boulevard, would blow a guy in a doorway just for a taste of rock cocaine. — Joseph Wambaugh, *Floaters*, p. 39, 1996
- [In downtown Los Angeles] Some of the local beer bars have prostitutes known as strawberries. Strawberries are anybody's for a helping of rock cocaine which (in 1994) is worth 4 or 5 dollars. — Fiona Pitt-Kethley, *Red Light Districts of the World*, p. 85, 2000

2 the female nipple *US, 1982*

Usually in the plural.

- — *Maledicta*, p. 132, Summer/Winter 1982: "Dyke diction: the language of lesbians"

strawberry jam *noun*
1 the corpse of a person who has died with massive injuries
US, *1987*
- — *Maledicta*, p. 180, Summer/Winter 1986–1987: "Sexual slang: prostitutes, pedophiles, flagellators, transvestites, and necrophiles"
2 an unspecified flammable substance *US*, *1987*
- He'd recognized the slang term "strawberry jam." It was GI jargon for gasoline, or napalm, or whatever the flame-throwing tanks were carrying this week. — Jack Hawkins, *Chopper One #2*, p. 57, 1987

straw bond *noun*
a bail bond secured only by the word of a reliable citizen
US, *1971*
- At one time a "straw bond" could be made by a "reputable" citizen who appeared at the station house and vouched for a woman arrested for prostitution. — Charles Winick, *The Lively Commerce*, p. 128, 1971

strawboss *verb*
to work as an assistant foreman *US*, *1977*
- I think if mean Mack Rivers ain't strawbossing the thieving tricky niggers dealing numbers and dope, that spaghetti-gut enforcer got to stick his ass out for me to blow it off. — Iceberg Slim (Robert Beck), *Death Wish*, p. 191, 1977

stray *noun*
a youth without gang affiliation *US*, *1962*
- [S]trays (boys without group affiliation). — Howard Polsky, *Cottage Six*, p. 24, 1962

streak *verb*
to run naked through a crowd, especially at public events, either as a protest or out of exhibitionism *US*, *1966*
Adapted from the sense "to go very fast."
- — John D. Bell et al., *Loosely Speaking*, p. 18, 1966
- — *Current Slang*, p. 21, Summer 1970

street *noun*
1 the essence of modern urban life for the poor, with suggestions of the underworld or the shadows between the underworld and the legitimate mainstream *US*, *1967*
- The street can be a classroom, a zoo, a stage, an asphalt padded cell, a whorehouse, a folksong or the traverse of Scorpio. — *The San Francisco Oracle*, 1967
- The street is where young bloods get their education. — H. Rap Brown, *Die Nigger Die!*, p. 25, 1969
- The street will wear you out if you don't take care of yourself. — Susan Hall, *Ladies of the Night*, p. 69, 1973
- It was the street that turned you old, keeping you hustling morning to night. — Alix Shulman, *On the Stroll*, p. 8, 1981
2 in stud poker, a card *US*, *1988*
For example, the fifth card dealt is known as "fifth street."
- — George Percy, *The Language of Poker*, p. 88, 1988

▶ **make the street**
to be released from jail *US*, *1949*
- "We were pinched together, if the punk makes the street I do too." — Nelson Algren, *The Man with the Golden Arm*, p. 5, 1949

▶ **on the street**
not imprisoned; released from prison *US*, *1935*
- If you ran the names of all the bad guys convicted by Judge Gibbs who are back on the street and wouldn't mind taking a whack at him, you could paper this room with the printouts. — Elmore Leonard, *Maximum Bob*, p. 89, 1991

street *adjective*
experienced in or possessing the necessary qualities for urban survival *US*, *1980*
- "I'm smart, just like you are, the judge said to the defendant, and your attorney either doesn't have her shit together or your best interest at heart." — Elmore Leonard, *City Primeval*, p. 8, 1980
- Vanilla Ice's mistake—he should have never said he was street [...] But when you come out and you say street, street is a rite of passage. Every black person isn't street. When you say you're street that means you have had to live on the street. — Alex Ogg, *The Hip Hop Years [quoting Ice-T]*, p. 131, 1999

street bookie *noun*
a bookmaker who takes bets on the street, without an established place of business *US*, *1972*

- There are "street bookies," who work in specific—usually poor—neighborhoods, collecting their bets either at fixed locations or by making rounds[.] — *The Knapp Commission Report on Police Corruption*, p. 85, 1972

street cat *noun*
a man, especially a young black man, who spends his life on the edges of crime *US*, *1976*
- [S]uch peripheral types as "street cats" and "shadies" are not members, though these groups frequently interact with those who truly belong to the Life. — Dennis Wepman et al., *The Life*, p. 2, 1976

street divorce *noun*
a domestic quarrel that ends in one spouse murdering the other *US*, *2001*
- "So you butt in and give him a fucking street divorce," Drucker hissed. — Stephen J. Cannell, *The Tin Collectors*, p. 29, 2001

street doctor *noun*
a drug dealer *US*, *1998*
- — Ethan Hilderbrant, *Prison Slang*, p. 123, 1998

streeter *noun*
a person who spends his time fraternizing and carousing on the street *US*, *1968*
- The streeters don't bother the Divine followers. They don't steal from them or try to con them out of anything. — Nathan Heard, *Howard Street*, p. 33, 1968

street law *noun*
justice based upon an extra-judicial code *US*, *1998*
- By street law, I was supposed to shoot the guy who shot me. — Eric Davis, *The Slick Boys*, p. 64, 1998

street mike *noun*
any imprecise, inaccurate measurement used by drug dealers *US*, *1970*
- street mike: what the drug seller says the dosage is. "This acid is 250 mikes." This figure is understood to be unscientific and unreliable. — Ethel Romm, *The Open Conspiracy*, p. 245, 1970

street name *noun*
a nickname by which you are known by acquaintances *US*, *1973*
- Horseface, Little Tiffany, Dutchman: the street names they assume are impersonal and sexually neutral, like their work. — Gail Sheehy, *Hustling*, p. 21, 1973
- The most she knew of any of them was their street names[.] — Alix Shulman, *On the Stroll*, p. 172, 1981
- They still call him Chucky Buck, Rainy said. It was like his street name before he moved up to his top floor condominium. Yeah, Chucky Buck. — Elmore Leonard, *Stick*, p. 8, 1983
- Sure I know her other street name. It was Felita's Mother because everybody knew me, I was so cute. — Robert Campbell, *Alice in La-La Land*, p. 290, 1987

street person; street people *noun*
a person living, or spending most of their time, on the street *US*, *1968*
A semivoluntary, semipolitical state that preceded "homeless-ness" as a label.
- A Digger event. Flowers, mirrors, penny-whistles, girls in costumes of themselves, Hell's Angels, street people, Mime Troupe. Angels ride up Haight with girls holding Now! SIGNS. — *The Digger Papers*, p. 3, August 1968
- STREET PEOPLE: non-students who live on or around Telegraph Avenue — Robert Buckhout, *Toward Social Change*, p. 466, 1971

street pizza *noun*
a bloody corpse *US*, *1992*
- "Major street pizza or what!" — Jess Mowry, *Way Past Cool*, p. 282, 1992

street shower *noun*
play in an opened fire hydrant *US*, *1977*
- During the summer we used to have a lot of street showers[.] — John Allen, *Assault with a Deadly Weapon*, p. 13, 1977

street-smart *adjective*
familiar with the human condition as played out in an urban setting *US*, *1976*
- "The trouble is," Hunter said, "like most guys like that, he really doesn't know anything. He's not street-smart." — George V. Higgins, *The Judgment of Deke Hunter*, p. 125, 1976

street smarts *noun*
an intuitive understanding of human nature as played out in urban reality *US, 1990*
- He's got more learnin' than just the paperbooks ridin' his hip alla time. That Barker's got street smarts. — Seth Morgan, *Homeboy*, p. 43, 1990
- I know. All passion, no street smarts. — *A Few Good Men*, 1992

street-snatch *verb*
to steal from a pedestrian by grabbing and running away *US, 1974*
- The watch was his talisman against street snatchers. In all the time he had been in Saigon he had been street-snatched only once, although he knew people who were street-snatched as often as twice a week. — Robert Stone, *Dog Soldiers*, p. 19, 1974

street snatcher *noun*
a street thief who grabs and runs *US, 1974*
- The watch was his talisman against street snatchers. In all the time he had been in Saigon he had been street-snatched only once, although he knew people who were street-snatched as often as twice a week. — Robert Stone, *Dog Soldiers*, p. 19, 1974

street sweeper *noun*
a machine gun *US, 2006*
- "Mustafa tells me you've got a street sweeper in that bag there." — Stephen J. Cannell, *White Sister*, p. 299, 2006

street tax *noun*
in an illegal drug-selling enterprise, the share of an individual's earnings paid to his gang *US, 1997*
- — *American Speech*, p. 422, Winter 1997: "Among the New Words"

streetwalker *noun*
a prostitute who seeks customers on the street *UK, 1592*
- It is difficult and dangerous to fall in with streetwalkers on the avenues[.] — Jack Lait and Lee Mortimer, *New York Confidential*, p. 206, 1948
- She was a streetwalker and I bought her a coffee in a hash joint. — Mickey Spillane, *My Gun is Quick*, p. 12, 1950

street-wise *adjective*
experienced in or possessing the necessary qualities for urban survival *US, 1966*
- If a cop is worth his night stick, he has to be what they call street wise. He not only has to know the area but he has to know the situation. — Minnesota Fats, *The Bank Shot*, p. 64, 1966

Street Without Joy *noun*
Vietnam National Highway 1 *US, 1964*
- This area was traversed by National Highway 1, the infamous "Street Without Joy" where the principal casualty-makers were mines, booby traps, and occasional snipers. — J.D. Coleman, *Incursion*, p. 16, 1991

strength *noun*
▸ **on the strength**
used to signify agreement, import or sincerity *US, 1995*
- Sometimes, when you really wanted people to believe what you said, "on the strength" certified your commitment[.] — Nelson George, *Hip Hop America*, p. 209, 1998
- "On the strength, just say no to drugs." — Paul Beatty, *Tuff*, p. 77, 2000

stretch *noun*
1 a prison sentence; one year's imprisonment *US, 1821*
A prison sentence of a number of years is given with the number of years preceding "stretch."
- He had been a pickpocket until a long stretch up the river gave him a turn of mind. — Mickey Spillane, *I, The Jury*, p. 15, 1947
- That's kid stuff, and anyhow them judges sent too many away for long stretches. — Hal Ellson, *The Golden Spike*, p. 73, 1952
- Arrest, petty larceny and possession—and so on, until you wind up in a prison for a real stretch[.] — Ross Russell, *The Sound*, p. 234, 1961
- I was in County Jail with a long stretch ahead of me and two good books to while away the time. — A.S. Jackson, *Gentleman Pimp*, p. 9, 1973
2 in professional wrestling, an unscripted match in which one wrestler dominates his opponent *US, 1990*
- stretch n. a form of shoot where one wrestler dominates rather than injures the other as a proof of personal superiority. — *rec.sports.pro-wrestling*, 17th July 1990
3 in poker, a hand consisting of a sequence of five cards *US, 1988*

Known conventionally as a "straight."
- — George Percy, *The Language of Poker*, p. 88, 1988

stretch *verb*
1 to put someone to death by hanging *US, 1962*
- — Joseph E. Ragen and Charles Finston, *Inside the World's Toughest Prison*, p. 820, 1962: "Penitentiary and underworld glossary"
2 to serve time in prison *US, 2002*
From **STRETCH** (a prison sentence).
- I'd be contributing my ideas for the comic strip from the joint [...] Yeah, me and The Source got real tight back when I was stretchin'. — *The Source*, p. 36, March 2002

stretched out *adjective*
addicted *US, 1970*
- "And before that I was stretched out on hard stuff. Heroin." — Burt Hirschfield, *Fire Island*, p. 473, 1970

stretcher *noun*
1 a lie *UK, 1674*
- He got all the stuff to put in his article -except the pure-stretchers he made up—by hanging around the Queen City jail[.] — Guy Owen, *The Flim-Flam Man and the Apprentice Grifter*, 1972
2 a substance added to a drug for the simple purpose of diluting it for increased profit when sold *US, 1970*
- — William D. Alsever, *Glossary for the Establishment and Other Uptight People*, p. 15, December 1970

stretchers *noun*
shoe laces *US, 1962*
- — Joseph E. Ragen and Charles Finston, *Inside the World's Toughest Prison*, p. 820, 1962: "Penitentiary and underworld glossary"

strike *verb*
▸ **strike red**
to locate a vein when injecting a drug *US, 1971*
- Now the cat tried real hard, but he was two scarred / He just couldn't hit the spot / "Oh" Honky Tonk said as he struck red. — Michael H. Agar, *The Journal of American Folklore*, p. 179, April 1971

strike-out *noun*
a hospital patient who has died or lapsed into a neurologically depressed state *US, 1977*
- — *Philadelphia Magazine*, pp. 145–151, November 1977: "Language: doctor, there's a gomer in the pit"

striker *noun*
a member of a US Army Special Forces strike force *US, 1991*
- [S]ome of the largest supply caches ever found in Vietnam were turned over by the strikers. — J.D. Coleman, *Incursion*, p. 188, 1991

string *noun*
the group of prostitutes working for a particular pimp *US, 1913*
- In macking, the mack has a "stable" or "string" of whores. — John Irwin, *The Felon*, p. 14, 1970
- Shortly before six the pimps parade their strings for all to admire. — Gail Sheehy, *Hustling*, p. 88, 1973
- Helen wasn't in my string. She was an independent. She came and went as she pleased. — Robert Campbell, *Junkyard Dog*, p. 72, 1986

string *verb*
to manipulate a wire into a slot machine to trigger the free-play mechanism *US, 1985*
- Stringing means taping, tying, gluing, or otherwise affixing a string or fine wire to a coin and then inserting and retracting it from the machine in order to get free plays. — Jim Regan, *Winning at Slot Machine*, p. 68, 1985

stringer *noun*
1 in poker, an installment bet or the person making it *US, 1988*
- — George Percy, *The Language of Poker*, p. 88, 1988
2 in poker, a hand of five cards in sequence *US, 1967*
Conventionally known as a "straight."
- — Albert H. Morehead, *The Complete Guide to Winning Poker*, p. 274, 1967
3 a narrow strip of laminated wood on a surfboard *US, 1979*
- The Yater—the clear one with the thin stringer. — *Apocalypse Now*, 1979

strings *noun*
1 the female legs *US, 1963*
- — *American Speech*, p. 273, December 1963: "American Indian student slang"

2 spaghetti *US, 1956*
- Yardbird and strings. Harlem's own vernacular for the fried chicken and spaghetti which was so common, so cheap and so utterly, unbelievably wonderful at such wrong hours—like the hours around dawn, for instance. — Robert Sylvester, *No Cover Charge*, p. 43, 1956

strip *noun*
1 in a striptease show, the portion of the show in which the dancer removes her last garments *US, 1945*
- In succession as the Flash or entrance; the Parade or march across the stage, in full costume; the Tease or increasing removal of wearing apparel; and the climactic Strip or denuding down to the G-String[.] — *Saturday Review of Literature*, p. 28, 18th August 1945: "Take 'Em Off!"

2 a thoroughfare in a town or city lined with bars, nightclubs, package stores, and restaurants *US, 1939*
- The whole strip is shrinking. Ah, you know, I remember about five years ago, take yuh a couple of hours and a tank full of gas just to make one circuit. — *American Graffiti*, 1973
- Tonight, tonight, the strip's just right / I wanna blow 'em off in my first heat. — Bruce Springsteen, *Racing in the Street*, 1978

3 a Benzedrine™-soaked strip of paper from an inhaler, removed from the inhaler and ingested as a central nervous system stimulant *US, 1951*
- Yeah, the strips couldn't feed Lefty's hunger. — Thurston Scott, *Cure it with Honey*, p. 15, 1951
- "You want a strip, Hart?" Ben asked genially as he carefully wadded a piece of benzedrine-soaked paper in a chunk of chewing gum. It was the last of his second inhaler of the weekend, each of which had contained eight strips. — John Clellon Holmes, *Go*, p. 121, 1952

▸ **the Strip**
1 the portion of Sunset Boulevard between Crescent Heights Boulevard and Doheny Drive, Los Angeles, California *US, 1951*
- [H]e emerged, propelling the wheelchair in which he sat, from the darkness of the hospital movie basement with its pitiful representation of the Strip in Hollywood[.] — Jack Kerouac, *Letter to Neal Cassady*, pp. 323–324, 31 August 1951
- Also, he had gotten into the habit of falling in love with teen-age girls, like this Chippy on the Strip, for whom he had just bought a new cloth coat. — Clancy Sigal, *Going Away*, p. 3, 1961
- [L]ooking down from the eleventh floor balcony at a police ambulance screaming down toward the Whiskey A Go-Go on the Strip, where I used to sit in the afternoon with Lionel and talk with off-duty hookers. — Hunter S. Thompson, *Songs of the Doomed: More Notes on the Death of the American Dream*, p. 119, 16th February 1969
- I suppose in this era young girls you pick up hitchhiking on the Strip would not say, "I want to be an actress." — Mort Sahl, *Heartland*, p. 59, 1976

2 Las Vegas Boulevard south of central Las Vegas, Nevada, lined with neon-signed hotels and casinos *US, 1971*
- In the middle of a National District Attorneys' Confederence at an elegant hotel on the strip. — Hunter S. Thompson, *Fear and Loathing in Las Vegas*, p. 80, 1971
- The Strip where most of the super-luxury hotels are has more neon lighting than fabulous Broadway ever dreamed of. — Mario Puzo, *Inside Las Vegas*, pp. 67–68, 1977

stripe *noun*
in the military, a promotion *US, 1968*
- — Carl Fleischhauer, *A Glossary of Army Slang*, p. 19, 1968

stripes *noun*
1 in circus usage, tigers *US, 1981*
- — Don Wilmeth, *The Language of American Popular Entertainment*, p. 261, 1981

2 in pool, the striped balls numbered 9 to 15 *US, 1984*
- "I'm going to take the stripes." A striped ball and a solid one had fallen in on the break, giving Fats his choice. — Walter Tevis, *The Color of Money*, p. 66, 1984
- — Steve Rushin, *Pool Cool*, p. 28, 1990

stripes and solids *noun*
in pool, the game of eight-ball *US, 1974*
- — Mike Shamos, *The Illustrated Encyclopedia of Billiards*, p. 235, 1993

strip pants *noun*
panties designed by be removed easily by a stripteaser *US, 1964*
- I felt for the snap on my strip panties ... soon I would be left with just my g-string, not much for warmth but the legal limit. — Lois O'Conner, *The Bare Facts*, p. 16, 1964

stripper *noun*
1 a pickpocket *US, 1950*
- — Hyman E. Goldin et al., *Dictionary of American Underworld Lingo*, p. 214, 1950

2 a car thief who targets newer cars that will be stripped for parts *US, 1962*
- — *American Speech*, p. 272, December 1962: "The language of traffic policemen"

3 a playing card that has been altered in a manner that facilitates its extraction from a full deck *US, 1962*
- — Frank Garcia, *Marked Cards and Loaded Dice*, p. 264, 1962

stripping hole; stripping pit *noun*
a strip mine *US, 1997*
- — Amy and Denise McFadden, *CoalSpeak*, p. 12, 1997

striptoosie *noun*
a stripteaser *US, 1959*
- Naturally, I could not make a study of a burlesque town without interviewing "striptoosies," the hard-working ladies who undress for the paying public[.] — Monroe Fry, *Sex, Vice, and Business*, p. 56, 1959

stroke *noun*
1 a rule *US, 1966*
- — Rose Giallombardo, *Society of Women*, p. 212, 1966: Glossary of Prison Terms

2 praise or flattery *US, 1964*
Almost always in the plural.
- You flatter somebody outrageously. Even though they know you're doing it, the person getting the strokes is gratified. You flattered them. — Robert Campbell, *Boneyards*, p. 290, 1992

stroke *verb*
1 to flatter someone *US, 1979*
- Who don't like to be stroked? — Edwin Torres, *After Hours*, p. 162, 1979

2 to masturbate *US, 1986*
Also "stroke off."
- While not the greatest menage ever taped, the action is not bad; it certainly provides material for some lazy stroking. — *Adult Video*, p. 53, August/September 1986

▸ **stroke it**
to perform badly on purpose *US, 1989*
- We've been losing so many people going up against very heavily defended targets that our squadrons have begun to back off, to stroke it. — T.E. Cruise, *Wings of Gold III*, p. 219, 1989

▸ **stroke the lizard**
(of a male) to masturbate *US, 1971*
- — Eugene Landy, *The Underground Dictionary*, p. 178, 1971

stroke book *noun*
a magazine or book viewed while masturbating *US, 1967*
- Millions of other stroke books—the antecedent to Playboy, National Geographic with the African chicks—oh yes, they're stroke books. — Lenny Bruce, *The Essential Lenny Bruce*, p. 179, 1967
- Larry may utilize fluffers, watermelons, stroke books or harems of women to summon forth the gop. — Josh Alan Friedman, *Tales of Times Square*, p. 101, 1986
- What do you think I'm going to do with them? They're stroke books. — *Chasing Amy*, 1997
- Inside were hundreds of girlie magazines. "Welcome to stroke book paradise," he said, clapping me on the shoulder. — Peter Fenton, *Eyeing the Flash*, p. 44, 1998

stroke-me-off *noun*
used as a humorous nickname for stroganoff, as in "beef stroganoff" *US, 1985*
- — *Maledicta*, p. 284, 1984–1985: "Food names"

stroker *noun*
a hospital patient who has suffered a stroke *US, 1961*
- — *American Speech*, pp. 145–148, May 1961: "The spoken language of medicine; argot, slang, cant"

stroke rag *noun*
a pornographic magazine *US, 2004*
- Playboy was a stroke rag for horny dipshits. — James Ellroy, *Destination Morgue*, p. 122, 2004

stroll *noun*
▸ **the stroll**
1 the collective activities on a street, mostly illegal, especially prostitution *US, 1946*

- My education was completed on The Stroll and I became a Negro. — Mezz Mezzrow, *Really the Blues*, p. 210, 1946
- Hello Mayann. What in the world are you doing out on the stroll tonight? — Louis Armstrong, *Satchmo*, p. 200, 1954
- In New York, there are three different big strolls—places where prostitutes go to work. — Susan Hall, *Ladies of the Night*, p. 13, 1973
- I was in the Berkeley stroll, so we hadn't gotten the word yet. — Frederique Delacoste, *Sex Work*, p. 95, 1987

2 Seventh Avenue, New York *US, 1946*

- [S]pecific places are known by special nicknames—New York City as the Apple, Seventh Avenue as The Stroll[.] — Mezz Mezzrow, *Really the Blues*, p. 221, 1946

stroller *noun*
a car *US, 1960*
- — Robert George Reisner, *The Jazz Titans*, p. 166, 1960

strong *adjective*
1 of a theatrical performance, very sexual *US, 1962*
- "This is what we call a 'strong' theater," she said, by way of explanation. "We cheat as much as we can here." — *Eros*, p. 30, Spring 1962

2 flush with money *US, 1954*
- — *This Week Magazine, New York Herald Tribune*, p. 46, 28th February 1954
- — *San Francisco News*, p. 6, 25th March 1958

strong *adverb*
(said of a carnival game) strongly rigged against the player *US, 2005*
- The entire operation revolved around the games, which were worked "strong" in order to maximize profits. — Peter Fenton, *Eyeing the Flash*, p. 67, 2005

strongarm *noun*
1 a crime involving brute physical violence; a violent criminal *US, 1901*
- In both cases he was employed by businesses who needed strong-arm boys. — Mickey Spillane, *My Gun is Quick*, p. 76, 1950
- And, one by one, three more rothstein strong-arms were burned, cut, mutilated and killed. — Robert Sylvester, *No Cover Charge*, p. 12, 1956
- Strong-arms. I did lotsa strong-arms nobody knows about. — Joseph Wambaugh, *Fugitive Nights*, p. 176, 1992

2 a person who lends physicality and a capacity for brutal physical force to the moment *US, 1907*
Also called "strongarm man."
- "But I don't wanna be a cheap hood for some guy who's gonna sit back and pay me peanuts for being a strong arm." — Irving Shulman, *Cry Tough*, p. 31, 1949
- The strong-arm men get all their money and they are broke. — Willard Motley, *Let No Man Write My Epitaph*, p. 188, 1958
- Most of these tough ones had worked as strongarm men for Dutch Schultz[.] — Malcolm X and Alex Haley, *The Autobiography of Malcolm X*, p. 87, 1964
- Bad too, big stud, used to be strongarm for the politicals in Havana. — Edwin Torres, *Carlito's Way*, p. 12, 1975

strong-arm *verb*
to rob a place roughly or violently *US, 1903*
- Schultz had strong-armed his way into control of the Harlem numbers business. — Malcolm X and Alex Haley, *The Autobiography of Malcolm X*, p. 116, 1964
- "Party" hadn't strong-armed since his last bit. The only reason he hadn't was simply that none of the Johns we had fleeced was carrying a wad. — Iceberg Slim (Robert Beck), *Pimp*, p. 40, 1969

strongarmer *noun*
a person who lends a capacity for brutal physical force to the moment *US, 1949*
- Strongarmers hesitated to pull a bandage off a man if he were wearing it near a vein. — Nelson Algren, *The Man with the Golden Arm*, p. 293, 1949

struck *noun*
a girl's steady boyfriend *US, 1963*
- — *American Speech*, p. 273, December 1963: "American Indian student slang"

strudel *noun*
the "at" sign (@) on a computer keyboard *US, 1991*
- — Eric S. Raymond, *The New Hacker's Dictionary*, p. 40, 1991

struggle *verb*
1 to dance *US, 1960*
- — Robert George Reisner, *The Jazz Titans*, 1960

2 to experience a hangover *US, 2001*
- — Don R. McCreary (Editor), *Dawg Speak*, 2001

struggle-buggy *noun*
a broken-down car *US, 1946*
- My struggle-buggy was getting to look like a rinky-dink old tin can on wheels[.] — Mezz Mezzrow, *Really the Blues*, p. 87, 1946

strum *verb*
▸ **strum heads**
to fight *US, 1990*
- — Charles Shafer, *Folk Speech in Texas Prisons*, p. 215, 1990

strummed up *adjective*
stimulated by drugs *US, 1972*
- It was the end of six or seven months, and most of these guys were strummed up on that Benzedrine too. — Bruce Jackson, *In the Life*, p. 314, 1972

strung out *adjective*
1 addicted to a drug; in a poor state of physical and mental health as a result of drug addiction *US, 1958*
Used as a participial adjective.
- When you really get strung out you don't care about anything but your next fix. — Willard Motley, *Let No Man Write My Epitaph*, p. 368, 1958
- She was too strung out. I no longer cared enough to make the effort. — Alexander Trocchi, *Cain's Book*, p. 158, 1960
- He's a little strung out right now, but he'll be all right. — Gurney Norman, *Divine Right's Trip (Last Whole Earth Catalog)*, p. 67, 1971
- Carmelita, hold me tighter, I think I'm sinking down / I'm all strung out on heroin on the outskirts of town. — Warren Zevon, *Carmelita*, 1976

2 in love; infatuated *US, 1968*
- — *Current Slang*, p. 46, Fall 1968

strychnine *noun*
in craps, the point and number nine *US, 1950*
- — *The Annals of the American Academy of Political and Social Sciences*, p. 131, May 1950

stub down *verb*
in the language surrounding the Grateful Dead, to move to better seats at a concert using ticket stubs for the better sections smuggled up by friends *US, 1994*
- — David Shenk and Steve Silberman, *Skeleton Key*, p. 274, 1994

stube *noun*
a tavern *US, 1950*
- There were half-a-hundred more drop-ins, snug beer stubes and dining rooms[.] — Jack Lait and Lee Mortimer, *Chicago Confidential*, p. 14, 1950

stuck *adjective*
of a player in a game of poker or other gambling game, losing *US, 1974*
- "I say, 'How are you doing?' They say, 'Well, we're stuck $12,000.'" — Edward Lin, *Big Julie of Vegas*, p. 121, 1974
- — David M. Hayano, *Poker Faces*, p. 187, 1982

stuck-up *adjective*
conceited; pretentious *UK, 1829*
- "Some new kid," a voice replied. "I hear he's stuck-up." "I don't know what for," answered the Zit Queen. "He looks like a monkey." — C.D. Payne, *Youth in Revolt*, p. 167, 1993

stud *noun*
1 a man, especially a manly man *UK, 1895*
- In that way with a stud, in another way with polite dignified Sand a very interesting young fellow[.] — Jack Kerouac, *The Subterraneans*, p. 85, 1958
- A bunch of cool studs were chewing their cuds at Joe's Solid Rock in the middle of the block. — Dan Burley, *Diggeth Thou?*, p. 9, 1959
- Shorty was taking lesson "with some other studs" and he intended to organize his own small band. — Malcolm X and Alex Haley, *The Autobiography of Malcolm X*, pp. 44–45, 1964
- Even when a block belongs to your people, you are still an outsider who has to prove himself a down stud with heart. — Piri Thomas, *Down These Mean Streets*, p. 47, 1967

2 used as a jocular term of address to a man *US, 1999*
- You got it, stud! — *American Pie*, 1999

3 in homosexual usage, a person who plays the "masculine" role sexually and emotionally in a relationship *US, 1961*

- "Stud" and "sissy" are expressions commonly used by Negroes to refer to their counterparts—the white "jocker" and white "brat." — Arthur V. Huffman, *New York Mattachine Newsletter*, p. 6, June 1961
- I remember once my little sister asked my mother, "Mama, is that a lady or a man." It was a stud. Mama just looked at her and said, "That's a bull-dagger, baby." — Claude Brown, *Manchild in the Promised Land*, p. 205, 1965
- Lesbians and their women were paired off and in small groups with queens and studs in the shadowy booths lining the long room. — Iceberg Slim (Robert Beck), *Mama Black Widow*, p. 30, 1969

4 loose tobacco *US, 2002*
- — Gary K. Farlow, *Prison-ese*, p. 69, 2002

stud broad *noun*
a lesbian *US, 1966*
- The complementary role to the femme is the "stud broad" or "daddy" who assumes the male role. — Rose Giallombardo, *Society of Women*, p. 124, 1966
- Jealous reaction to a dance with one of the women has caused some men to be cut, shot, and beaten up by a gang of "stud-broads," and robbed in the process. — Nathan Heard, *Howard Street*, p. 34, 1968

student *noun*
an inexperienced drug user *US, 1952*
- — *American Speech*, p. 30, February 1952: "Teen-age hophead jargon"

stud hustler *noun*
a male homosexual prostitute who projects a tough, masculine image *US, 1966*
- And malehustlers ("fruithustlers"/"studhustlers"): the various names for the masculine hustlers looking for lonely fruits to score from[.] — John Rechy, *City of Night*, p. 100, 1963
- When he arrived in Southern Florida, Jack planned to set up a call boy service utilizing stud hustlers. — Johnny Shearer, *The Male Hustler*, p. 129, 1966

studly *adjective*
1 admirable *US, 1966*
- — *Current Slang*, p. 7, Winter 1966

2 unpleasant; unpopular *US, 1960*
- — *American Speech*, p. 78, February 1960: 'Stud' and 'Studly'

stud muffin *noun*
a handsome, well-built man *US, 1992*
- Get outa here. Go call your studmuffin. — Armistead Maupin, *Maybe the Moon*, p. 26, 1992
- Anne thought Leeds was a stud muffin, especially in those cute khaki shorts and sneakers. — Joseph Wambaugh, *Floaters*, p. 219, 1996

stud puppy *noun*
an attractive person *US, 1989*
A variation of **STUD MUFFIN**.
- Dozens of such sleek stud puppies pass through Hollywood every year[.] — *Time Magazine*, p. 74, 25th December 1989
- He looked like a young Frank, so adorable, so handsome, so studly, my little stud puppy and then he starts the show. — Kathie Lee Gifford, *Larry King Live*, 5th February 2004

stud up *noun*
in prison, a prisoner who attempts to abandon homosexual activity and return to his previous state of heterosexual celibacy *US, 1990*
- — Charles Shafer, *Folk Speech in Texas Prisons*, p. 216, 1990

study bunny *noun*
a serious and diligent student *US, 1987*
- — *New York Times*, 12th April 1987

stuff *noun*
1 a drug, especially heroin *US, 1929*
- If you think you need stuff to play music or sing, you're crazy. — Billie Holiday with William Dufty, *Lady Sings the Blues*, p. 181, 1956
- He looked at me as though I were on the stuff[.] — Clancy Sigal, *Going Away*, p. 349, 1961
- "Stuff is my first love." I said, "What do you mean 'stuff'?" He said, "You've heard of shit, haven't you, duji, heroin?" — Claude Brown, *Manchild in the Promised Land*, p. 277, 1965
- Now this is Panda, from Mexico. Very good stuff. — *Pulp Fiction*, 1994

2 in prison, anything of value *US, 1967*
- Stuff was anything of value and faggots and sissies were of great value to many[.] — Malcolm Braly, *On the Yard*, p. 148, 1967

3 the female genitals *US, 1982*
- "Don't try to tell me what to wear!" she snapped back and started a slow forward stretch that exposed the hairs of her stuff. — Odie Hawkins, *Amazing Grace*, p. 102, 1993

4 a woman as a sexual object *US, 1967*
- The couple to whom he was talking blatantly asked him why he hadn't gone out and found some "strange stuff." — R.J. Hagerman, *Husband and Wife Swapping*, p. 100, 1967
- It'd been awhile since I'd had any young stuff[.] — Joey V., *Portrait of Joey*, p. 125, 1969
- Sapphire is referred to by the same man on different occasions as: mama, sister, baby, fox, stuff, and bitch. — Carolyn Greene, *70 Soul Secrets of Sapphire*, p. 35, 1973

5 the male genitals *US, 1966*
- "There's enough white stuff around." Vess grinned slyly, and as he did it occurred to me that the word "stuff" involved me more than it was comfortable to admit, since it was not oriented towards the coozies. — Phil Andros (Samuel M. Steward), *Stud*, pp. 88–89, 1966
- He freaked out the first time he saw a dude pull his stuff out and start pissing, right across from the police station. — Odie Hawkins, *Midnight*, p. 95, 1995

6 an effeminate homosexual man *US, 1975*
- You ain't stuff and you don't want to be stuff. — Miguel Pinero, *Short Eyes*, p. 28, 1975
- — John R. Armore and Joseph D. Wolfe, *Dictionary of Desperation*, p. 53, 1976

7 in pool, spin imparted on the cue ball to affect the course of the object ball or the cue ball after striking the object ball *US, 1993*
- — Mike Shamos, *The Illustrated Encyclopedia of Billiards*, p. 236, 1993

stuff *verb*
to block the pay chute of a casino slot machine with the expectation of returning later, unblocking the chute, and retrieving the interim earnings *US, 1999*
- Stuffing is exactly what it sounds like. It is a method of blocking the pay chute on a slot machine. — Charles W. Lund, *Robbing the One-Armed Bandits*, p. 125, 1999

stuffed shirt *noun*
a person who is overly formal, aloof, and out of touch *US, 1913*
- He said I had become stiff-necked, a stuffed shirt, too uncompromising in my dealings with onetime associates. — Jim Thompson, *Roughneck*, p. 116, 1954
- Awww c'mon, man, don't be such a stuffed shirt. — Odie Hawkins, *Men Friends*, p. 113, 1989

stuffer *noun*
a male homosexual who plays the active role in anal sex *US, 1949*
- — Vincent J. Monteleone, *Criminal Slang*, p. 229, 1949

stugots; stugats *noun*
the penis *US, 1962*
From southern Italian dialect, adapted/corrupted by Italian-American immigrants.
- — Anthony Romeo, *The Language of Gangs*, p. 23, 4th December 1962

stum *noun*
any central nervous system depressant *US, 1980*
- — Edith A. Folb, *runnin' down some lines*, p. 256, 1980

stumble biscuit *noun*
a tablet of the recreational drug methaqualone, best known as Quaaludes™ *US, 1993*
From the lack of coordination associated with the drug.
- — Peter Johnson, *Dictionary of Street Alcohol and Drug Terms*, p. 183, 1993

stumblebum *noun*
a poor and foolish drunk *US, 1932*
- Sweet dreams, all you flophouse grads, I said to myself. R.I.P., you stumblebums. — Mezz Mezzrow, *Really the Blues*, p. 317, 1946
- He knew a stumblebum, a wino with a criminal record. — Jim Thompson, *After Dark, My Sweet*, p. 103, 1955
- A pale, earnest young man at a lectern was praying over JD and over the winos, the stumblebums, and the broken-down rubber tramps[.] — Malcolm Braly, *It's Cold Out There*, p. 66, 1966
- Just the alias used by the stumblebum married my mom. — Seth Morgan, *Homeboy*, p. 49, 1990

stumbler *noun*

any barbiturate or central nervous system depressant *US, 1970*

- — Donald Wesson and David Smith, *Barbiturates*, pp. 122–1977
- He went back to the cell and waited for the stumblers to start turning off the lights in his skull[.] — Frank Bonham, *Viva Chicano*, p. 63, 1970
- — Edith A. Folb, *runnin' down some lines*, p. 256, 1980

stumbles *noun*

a loss of coordination, especially as the result of drug or alcohol intoxication *US, 1971*

- — Eugene Landy, *The Underground Dictionary*, p. 99, 1971

stump *noun*

1 a dolt *US, 1960*

- If this makes me a stump, tough. — Glendon Swarthout, *Where the Boys Are*, p. 78, 1960

2 a shoe *US, 1973*

- I found it impossible to get my stumps on because my feet had swollen up so much. — A.S. Jackson, *Gentleman Pimp*, p. 21, 1973

stump-break *verb*

to make someone unquestioningly obedient *US, 1974*

- "I told you boys I was goin' stump break this here filly, and I meant every word of it." — Donald Goines, *Swamp Man*, p. 54, 1974

stump-broke *adjective*

unconditionally obedient *US, 1967*

From the quaint notion of a mule trained to step forward and then backwards for sex with a man standing on a stump.

- You don't look like you could pleasure a stump-broke mule. — Malcolm Braly, *On the Yard*, p. 207, 1967
- What's wrong with my nose? I'll tell you what's wrong with my nose. I asked Gunther if he had his girl friend stump-broke yet, and he hit me on it, that's what. — Ken Weaver, *Texas Crude*, p. 129, 1984

stumpers *noun*

shoes *US, 1971*

- — Hermese E. Roberts, *The Third Ear: A Black Glossary*, 1971

stumphole whiskey *noun*

strong, homemade whiskey *US, 1971*

- Once the preacher got limbered up good he set in to telling about what a mortal sinner he'd been all his life and had made and sold stumphole whiskey all his grown days[.] — Tom Robbins, *Another Roadside Attraction*, p. 77, 1971
- Masters of moonshine prided themselves in their ancient, father-to-son recipes and the white lightning, blue John, red eye, happy Sally, and stumphole whiskey they made, Smith said. — *Chicago Tribune*, p. C-1, 15th January 1986
- — *Star Tribune (Minneapolis)*, p. 19F, 31st January 1999

stunna shades *noun*

ostentatious, over-sized dark glasses *US, 2006*

A term popularized if not coined by the hip-hop artists The Federation/E-40.

- Remember the days before hip-hop when black radio meant more than just the hyphy anthems and Bootsy Collins wore the original stunna shades? — *East Bay Express*, 15th March 2006

stunning *adjective*

in computing, incomprehensibly stupid *US, 1991*

- — Eric S. Raymond, *The New Hacker's Dictionary*, p. 336, 1991

stunt *verb*

to wear expensive clothes and jewelry as a display of conspicuous consumption; to show off *US, 2001*

- — Rick Ayers (Editor), *Slang Dictionary*, p. 15, 2001

stunt cock; stunt dick; stunt *noun*

a male pornography performer who fills in for another performer who is unable to maintain an erection or ejaculate when needed *US, 2000*

- It's ten minutes to midnight, and it became of question of running in Randy as a stunt dick[.] — Robert Stoller and I.S. Levine, *Coming Attractions*, p. 130, 1991
- A STUNT is a guy who provides the hard dick and the POP SHOT for an actor having plumbing problems. — *Adult Video News*, p. 40, September 1995

- For the most part, cum shots are only faked in dire circumstances—like when a stunt cock can't be found and no one's being paid overtime. — Ana Loria, *1 2 3 Be A Porn Star!*, p. 73, 2000
- Most spectacularly, it revolutionizes the money shot by having Cy and various stunt cocks rain male and female cum juice on girls simultaneously. — Editors of Adult Video News, *The AVN Guide to the 500 Greatest Adult Films of All Time*, p. 84, 2005

stunt pussy *noun*

a female pornography performer who fills in for another performer for the purposes of genital filming only *US, 2000*

- — Ana Loria, *1 2 3 Be A Porn Star!*, p. 167, 2000: "Glossary of adult sex industry terms"

stunts *noun*

sex *US, 1994*

- — Linda Meyer, *Teenspeak!*, p. 29, 1994

stupe; stoop *noun*

a stupid person *UK, 1762*

Often, not always, used affectionately.

- You have be refuting everything I ever learned and I'll wind up being a stupe. — Mickey Spillane, *My Gun is Quick*, p. 55, 1950
- The stupes. He didn't need guys who could believe that he had busted Sonny Tubbs, the crippled pusher. — Clarence Cooper Jr., *The Scene*, p. 11, 1960
- I might have ended up a Christian martyr—St. Eldrige the Supe. — Eldridge Cleaver, *Soul on Ice*, p. 30, 1968
- Laredo leaned up against the fire hydrant crossing her legs and waiting for some stupe to offer her money so she could write him a ticket. — William T. Vollman, *Whores for Gloria*, p. 2, 1991

stupid *adjective*

good *US, 1989*

The spelling "stoopid" is also used.

- — Connie Eble (Editor), *UNC-CH Campus Slang*, p. 8, Spring 1989
- For a while things got "stoopid[.]" — Nelson George, *Hip Hop America*, p. 209, 1998

stupid *adverb*

extremely *US, 1992*

- — Anna Scotti and Paul Young, *Buzzwords*, p. 81, 1997
- [E]ven "stoopid fresh," which could also be "def" when it wasn't "dope." — Nelson George, *Hip Hop America*, p. 209, 1998

stupid fresh *adjective*

exceptionally good *US, 1987*

- — Henry Chalfant, *Spraycan Art*, p. 12, 1987

stupid, stupid

used as an expression of utter disapproval *US, 1997*

From the cry of "stupid, stupid rat creatures!" in the *Bone* comic book.

- Stupid, stupid end-users! — Andy Ihnatko, *Cyberspeak*, p. 184, 1997

sturgeon *noun*

a surgeon *US, 1994*

- — Sally Williams, *"Strong" Words*, p. 134, 1994

style *verb*

to conduct or carry yourself in a stylish manner, especially in an exaggerated, showy way *US, 1972*

- The pimp who is "taking care of business" often prefers less flamboyant one-to-one situations for "hitting on" women and leaves the stylin' (strutting and showing off) to what he calls "half-ass pimps" and "would-be pimps." — Christina and Richard Milner, *Black Players*, p. 44, 1972
- I know how it is, dude. Awful hard to style with those goofy fucking jackets on. — Joseph Wambaugh, *Floaters*, p. 28, 1996
- "Muthafucka be styline!" exclaims Bone, who is now inexplicably sporting a clear plastic shower cap over the top of his big Afro hairdo. — Jimmy Lerner, *You Got Nothing Coming*, p. 38, 2002
- Jake knew he was styling in a beige Helmut Lang suit and a black Armani shirt. — Jason Starr, *Lights Out*, p. 13, 2006

style master *noun*

an acknowledged master graffiti artist *US, 1982*

- Stan 153 described his battle to hold on to the title of style master in early 1973[.] — Craig Castleman, *Getting Up*, p. 57, 1982

stylie *noun*

a white person with dreadlocks *US, 1994*

- — David Shenk and Steve Silberman, *Skeleton Key*, p. 274, 1994

sub *noun*

1 the *sub*missive performer in a pornographic sex scene *US,*
2000

- — Ana Loria, *1 2 3 Be A Porn Star!*, p. 167, 2000: "Glossary of adult sex industry terms"

2 a concealed pocket, used by a casino employee to hide stolen chips *US, 1980*

- — Lee Solkey, *Dummy Up and Deal*, p. 121, 1980

sub *verb*

to serve as a *sub*stitute *US, 1853*

- Once inside, she said, "You want to watch 'Midnight America'?" "Who's subbing?" — Robert Campbell, *Alice in La-La Land*, p. 151, 1987

sub-deb *noun*

a girl in her mid teens *US, 1917*

- The Debs and Sub-Debs are usually from 50 to 500 feet behind the warriors. — Jack Lait and Lee Mortimer, *New York Confidential*, p. 106, 1948
- Some East Oakland sub-deb started walking home from the bus stop on Fifteenth one dark night a few months back, and she ran into a would-be rapist on the way. — Thurston Scott, *Cure it with Honey*, p. 79, 1951

submarine *noun*

1 a surfboard that is too small for the person using it *US, 1964*
So named because the person forces the board under water.

- — John Severson, *Modern Surfing Around the World*, p. 182, 1964

2 a gambling casino scheme in which a stolen chip is slipped into the thief's trousers *US, 1977*

- They would use this as a drop by slipping a hundred dollar chip inside their trousers. This was called a "submarine." — Mario Puzo, *Inside Las Vegas*, p. 227, 1977

submarine *verb*

in tiddlywinks, to shoot a wink under another *US, 1977*

- — *Verbatim*, p. 526, December 1977

submarine races *noun*

used as a euphemism for foreplay in a car at a remote spot
US, 1968

- — Hy Lit, *Hy Lit's Unbelievable Dictionary of Hip Words for Groovy People*, p. 38, 1968
- What better thing to do on a summer night that drips with desire than take in the submarine races? Submarine races were contests that, since they couldn't be seen, were best watched while embracing—preferably in the backseat of a car. — Cousin Bruce Morrow, *Cousin Brucie*, p. 71, 1987

subway *noun*

1 the ball tray under a pool table *US, 1949*

- Bull began to empty the balls out of the subway and to place them in the rack on the table in their proper order. — Irving Shulman, *Cry Tough*, p. 40, 1949

2 in roller derby, contact between skaters who are eligible to score before they reach the back of the pack of blocking skaters, taking them to the floor of the track *US, 1999*

- — Keith Coppage, *Roller Derby to Rollerjam*, 1999

subway dealer *noun*

in a card game, a dealer who cheats by dealing some cards off the bottom of the deck *US, 1988*

- — Frank Garcia, *Marked Cards and Loaded Dice*, p. 264, 1962
- — George Percy, *The Language of Poker*, p. 89, 1988

Subway Sam *noun*

a man who is partial to sex in subway toilets *US, 1966*

- A customer who consummates the sex act in a subway toilet is called a "Subway Sam." — Johnny Shearer, *The Male Hustler*, p. 18, 1966

subway tickets *noun*

in a card game, cards that did not come off the top of the deck because of cheating in the dealing *US, 1988*

- — George Percy, *The Language of Poker*, p. 89, 1988

such-a-much *noun*

an important or self-important person *US, 1968*

- [P]eople peeped your hole card then, knew where you were at and saw that you weren't such-a-much after all. — Nathan Heard, *Howard Street*, p. 181, 1968

suck *noun*

1 an act of oral sex *US, 1870*

- She was okay. A good suck, but not a Great suck. — *Adam Film Quarterly*, p. 72, October 1973
- I mean, I've had some fabulous suck in my time, but this chick ... WOW. — Terry Southern, *Now Dig This*, p. 36, 1975
- Born and raised in Montreal, he was used to supremo suck from the "fille du roi" and this Ontario girl was going to rank. — Suroosh Alvi et al., *The Vice Guide*, p. 27, 2002

2 a sycophant *US, 1977*

- "He's still a company suck." "He's a foreman, Luther." — John Sayles, *Union Dues*, p. 18, 1977
- Sure, you might lose some good umpires along the way, but you'd eliminate some of the sucks like Sirotta. — Jim Bouton, *Strike Zone*, p. 75, 1994

suck *verb*

1 to curry favor *US, 1948*

- You just gotta start sucking Mantelli, or that fat fug first sergeant, and you win a little money in poker, slip them twenty-thirty pounds[.] — Norman Mailer, *The Naked and the Dead*, p. 500, 1948

2 to be useless, unpopular, distasteful, of no worth *US, 1963*
When the term came into currency in the US in the 1960s, sexual connotations made it a vulgar, taboo-ridden term. By the mid-1990s, all sense of taboo had vanished in the US except for older speakers for whom the sexual connotation remained inescapable.

- I wrote on the wall, "Franz Kafka sucks." — *The Joint*, p. 205, 21st February 1963
- The show is fine but the P.R. girl and her staff suck. — *Screw*, p. 2, 21st March 1969
- She looked around and announced, "You all suck." — Timothy Crouse, *The Boys on the Bus*, p. 363, 1973
- I thought it sucked, and I bet next summer'll suck too. — George V. Higgins, *The Judgment of Deke Hunter*, p. 51, 1976

3 to perform oral sex *US, 1881*

- Were you ever caught sucking a girl? — *Screw*, p. 5, 7th March 1969
- [H]ow do you say, "sucked him"? Yes? — Terry Southern, *Blue Movie*, p. 83, 1970
- "I don't need this jive suckin' guys in the booths for the twenty bucks and the bottle of water champagne." — William Brashler, *City Dogs*, p. 29, 1976

4 in pool, to hit the cue ball with backspin that appears to draw or suck the cue ball backwards after it strikes the object ball *US, 1990*

- — Mike Shamos, *The Illustrated Encyclopedia of Billiards*, p. 236, 1993

▸ **it sucks to be you**
used for expressing a trace of commiseration in a situation that might call for a bit more *US, 1993*

- — Connie Eble (Editor), *UNC-CH Campus Slang*, p. 5, Spring 1993
- I shrugged. Despite the laborious and inefficient method, I doubted Matthew had struck at it long enough to be worthy of sympathy. "Sucks to be you." — Jim Munroe, *Angry Young Spaceman*, p. 204, 2001

▸ **suck ass**
to behave subserviently *US, 1956*
A variation of **KISS ARSE/ASS**.

- As for going to NY and sucking asses to get published, dont worry, if you're any good I'll get you read by the Farting-Through-Silk set, you won't have to stir a bone. — Jack Kerouac, *Letter to Philip Whalen*, p. 565, 6th March 1956
- But it's the guys who suck ass with the caddy master who get that action. — James Ellroy, *Brown's Requiem*, p. 63, 1981

▸ **suck cock**
to perform oral sex on a man *US, 1941*

- Sharon was munching wetly, moaning all over Lenny's dick, tugging his balls and working her mouth—she was born to suck cock. — *Letters to Penthouse V*, p. 69, 1995

▸ **suck face**
to kiss, especially in a prolonged fashion *US, 1982*

- — Douglas Simonson, *Pidgin to da Max Hana Hou*, 1982
- Leonardo DiCaprio is not sucking face with Courtney Love, the Foo Fighters, or Liam Neeson. — Bill Brownstein, *Sex Carnival*, p. 41, 2000
- People had probably seen him and the girl sucking face on the dance floor[.] — Jason Starr, *Lights Out*, p. 20, 2006

▸ **suck milk**
to be knocked off your surfboard and then be thrashed by a wave *US, 1991*
- — Trevor Cralle, *The Surfin'ary*, p. 125, 1991

▸ **suck out loud**
to be very bad *US, 1994*
- — Michael Dalton Johnson, *Talking Trash with Redd Foxx*, p. 138, 1994

▸ **suck suds**
to drink beer *US, 1969*
- — Marcus Hanna Boulware, *Jive and Slang of Students in Negro Colleges*, 1947
- — *Current Slang*, p. 10, Spring 1969

▸ **suck the big one**
to be terrible *US, 1999*
- This scene sucks the big one, I thought. — Rita Ciresi, *Pink Slip*, p. 295, 1999

▸ **suck to the bulls**
to act friendly with police *US, 1992*
- — Paladin Press, *Inside Look at Outlaw Motorcycle Gangs*, p. 38, 1992

▸ **suck weight**
to drink large amounts of liquids in a short period in order to gain weight to qualify for a sporting event *US, 2001*
- — Judy's Enterprises, *Coxswain Postcard*, 2001

▸ **suck wind**
to fail; to lose out *US, 1972*
Hawaiian youth usage.
- — Elizabeth Ball Carr, *Da Kine Talk*, p. 151, 1972

▸ **suck your flavor; suck your flava**
to copy your style *US, 1993*
- — *People Magazine*, p. 72, 19th July 1993

suck
▸ **suck gas**
to breath nitrous oxide for pleasure *US, late 1960s*
- This CIA spy has brought up a tank of nitrous oxide from Childhood. I've never sucked gas before, but a nozzle in the mouth is worth truth in the moment. — *The Last Supplement to the Whole Earth Catalog*, p. 66, March 1971

sucka *noun*
a fool; a dupe *US, 2000*
Misspelling of **SUCKER** (a gullible individual).
- I'm a sucka, all I gotta say / These drugs really got a hold of me[.] — Eminem (Marshall Mathers), *Drug Ballad*, 2000

suck and blow *nickname*
a Cessna 0–2 Super Skymaster aircraft *US, 1990*
- Among some o-2 jocks, the unique engine placement spawned another nickname, "Suck and Blow." — Tom Yarborough, *Da Nang Diary*, p. 22, 1990

suck around *verb*
to loiter, to idle *US, 1949*
- "Too many people coming in and too many little stinkers who suck around and get in my way." — Irving Shulman, *Cry Tough*, p. 28, 1949

suck-ass *noun*
a sycophant who curries favor in a self-demeaning fashion *US, 1979*
- Here's a crowd of suck-asses putting out this magazine that says it's the voice of cops, which is bullshit. — Hunter S. Thompson, *The Great Shark Hunt*, p. 485, 1979
- — Elmore Leonard, *City Primeval*, p. 8, 1980

suck-ass *adjective*
subservient; sycophantic; obsequious *US, 1985*
- That witty sally brought a lot of that suck-ass hearty cuckling that the hacks around the courthouse always draw out of themselves when they draw a judge who thinks he is a regular charmer of a fellow. — George V. Higgins, *Penance for Jerry Kennedy*, p. 6, 1985
- [T]hose lightweight, suck-ass interviews that everyone does. — Howard Stern, *Miss America*, p. 60, 1995

suck back *verb*
to drink something *US, 1980*
- We may be sucking back a few beers a little later on. — *The Blues Brothers*, 1980

sucked up *adjective*
1 weak; undeveloped physically *US, 2001*
- — Jim Goad, *Jim Goad's Glossary of Northwestern Prison Slang*, December 2001

2 angry *US, 1989*
- — James Harris, *A Convict's Dictionary*, p. 39, 1989

sucker *noun*
1 a gullible individual *US, 1838*
- You think religion is for suckers and easy marks and mollycoddles, huh? — Richard Brooks, *Elmer Gantry*, 1960

2 a prostitute's customer *US, 1972*
- I don't want customers alluded to as "tricks," "johns," or "suckers." — Xaviera Hollander, *The Happy Hooker*, p. 180, 1972

3 a fellow *US, 1980*
Neutral but informal.
- I'm gonna catch that sucker, if it's the last thing I ever do. — *The Blues Brothers*, 1980

4 a thing *US, 1972*
- Instead of ripping that sucker off, as soon as you start driving away, the whole thing just springs right out of the ground. — Joe Bob Briggs, *Joe Bob Goes to the Drive-In*, p. 9, 1987

sucker life *noun*
conventional life, with a conventional job and conventional lifestyle *US, 1977*
- Bama, I've been thinking for some time about giving the sucker life a whirl. — Iceberg Slim (Robert Beck), *Death Wish*, p. 117, 1977

sucker list *noun*
a list of potential victims for a confidence scheme *US, 1949*
- Zargoza's callers worked sucker lists that cost up to fifteen bucks a name. The room hummed with the overlapping patter of con men. — Tim Dorsey, *Hammerhead Ranch Motel*, p. 28, 2001

sucker-punch *verb*
to hit someone without warning, especially in the face *US, 1947*
- He was getting set to sucker-punch her. — Clarence Cooper Jr., *The Scene*, p. 36, 1960
- He didn't feel much like defending any creep who'd sucker-punch him in a place like Pauly's. — Carl Hiaasen, *Tourist Season*, p. 50, 1986
- They talked a moment, then Joe Ham hauled off and sucker-punched one of the whites in the face. — Nathan McCall, *Makes Me Wanna Holler*, p. 166, 1994
- Then, without blinking, I sucker punched him as hard as I could. — Larry Flynt, *An Unseemly Man*, p. 57, 1996

sucker weed *noun*
faked, adulterated, or poor quality marijuana *US, 1980*
- — Edith A. Folb, *runnin' down some lines*, p. 256, 1980

sucker wild *adjective*
completely unrestrained' and uninhibited *US, 1969*
- My idiot father had come to the big city and gone sucker wild. He couldn't stay away from the high yellow whores with their big asses and bitch-dog sexual antics. — Iceberg Slim (Robert Beck), *Pimp*, p. 20, 1969

suckhole *noun*
a hole between private video booths in a pornography arcade or between stalls in a public toilet, designed for anonymous oral sex between men *US, 1986–1987*
- — *Maledicta*, p. 177, Summer/Winter 1986–1987: "Sexual slang: prostitutes, pedophiles, flagellators, transvestites, and necrophiles"

suckie-suckie *noun*
oral sex performed on a man *US, 1987*
From the patois of Vietnamese prostitutes during the war, embraced by soldiers.
- Me suckee-suckee. My love you too much. — *Full Metal Jacket*, 1987
- — Gregory Clark, *Words of the Vietnam War*, p. 172, 1990

sucking *noun*
an act of oral sex *UK, 1869*
- Then she gave me a final sucking, draining me dry. — *Letters to Penthouse V*, p. 216, 1995

suck job *noun*
an act of oral sex *US, 1969*
- Despite the thick bush of hair, she was a good suck job. — *Screw*, p. 5, 7th March 1969

- Just as jello makes a nice change from oatmeal, a suck job beats a hand job any time. — Samuel West, *Hard-headed Dick*, p. 159, 1975

suck-off *noun*

an act of oral sex *US, 1995*

- A two-way suck-off is just what the doctor ordered. — *Letters to Penthouse V*, p. 278, 1995

suck off *verb*

to perform oral sex on either a man or woman, especially to the point of orgasm *UK, 1909*

- THERE HE IS. THERE HE IS. THE SONOFABITCH TRIED TA SUCK ME OFF. — Hubert Selby Jr., *Last Exit to Brooklyn*, p. 237, 1957
- Then she took me to her apartment and for two hundred francs I let her suck me off. She wanted me to live with her but I didn't want to have her suck me off every night ... it makes you too weak. — Henry Miller, *Tropic of Cancer*, p. 238, 1961
- Amanda lowered her long lashes and smiled sweetly. "I will suck you off," she said. — Tom Robbins, *Another Roadside Attraction*, p. 4, 1971
- Bunch of guys. You all hang out together. Yeah, you're all going out on business. You're all gonna suck each other off. — *Raging Bull*, 1980

suckout *noun*

in surfing, a wave that is breaking fast in front of itself, creating a tunnel or tube *US, 1977*

- — Gary Fairmont R. Filosa II, *The Surfer's Almanac*, p. 195, 1977

suck out *verb*

1 to speed past a parked police car, drawing it into a chase *US, 1962*

- — *American Speech*, p. 272, December 1962: "The language of traffic policemen"

2 in poker, to win in the face of every known convention and probability *US, 1996*

- — John Vorhaus, *The Big Book of Poker Slang*, p. 35, 1996

suck points *noun*

imaginary credits earned by obsequious ingratiation *US, 1994*

- — Sally Williams, *"Strong" Words*, p. 161, 1994

suck-up *noun*

a sycophant *US, 1957*

- "We can always spot a suck-up." — Gabriel Fielding, *In the Time of Greenbloom*, p. 47, 1957
- That's what it was all about—be a suck-up. — John Steppling, *The Dream Coast*, p. 20, 1987
- Unlike me, George W. Bush is also a total suck-up to corporate polluters. — Paul Begala, *Is Our Children Learning*, p. 54, 2000
- They're all a bunch a' ladder-climbing suck-ups. — Stephen J. Cannell, *The Tin Collectors*, p. 44, 2001

suck up *verb*

to seek favor through obsequious behavior *UK, 1860*

- You don't have to suck up to me. I won't squeal. — Leonard Cohen, *Beautiful Losers*, p. 134, 1966
- You should take a tip from your friend here, Quint—he really knows how to suck up. — *Mallrats*, 1995
- Don't try to suck up to me! It's a little late for that. — *Austin Powers*, 1997

suck wind!

leave me alone! *US, 1981*

Hawaiian youth usage.

- — Douglas Simonson, *Pidgin to da Max*, 1981

sucky *adjective*

awful *US, 1984*

- "The Tyler Set" can be really sucky, too—no drugs, no irony, and only moderate booze, popcorn, coca, and videos on Friday nights. — Douglas Copeland, *Generation X*, p. 106, 1991
- And it's always that same shit, soft rock! That sucky, non-threatening, easy-listening pussy music. — George Carlin, *Brain Droppings*, p. 6, 1997
- I'd be lying like a cop in court if I was to tell you Sing Ha was anything but sucky beer. — Tom Robbins, *Fierce Invalids from Hot Climates*, p. 131, 2000
- I suppose by comparison, Iceland does make every other country look sucky. — Meg Cabot, *The Princess Diaries*, p. 20, 2000

sucky; suckie *noun*

1 a woman, perceived as a sex object *US, 1981*

- That Karen was a good looking bitch, but I figured she was probably just like all the other young good looking suckies that hang around with bikers[.] — Robert Lipkin, *A Brotherhood of Outlaws*, p. 45, 1981

2 oral sex on a man *US, 2001*

- So the arrogant sergeant first class was going to the sucky room with a boy dressed like a girl and didn't even know it. — Kregg Jorgenson, *Very Crazy G.I.*, pp. 165–166, 2001
- We were approached by a fast talking man offering a strip show. Then he offered us something more. "Sucky, sucky, sucky," said the busy little man. — Ted Lerner, *The Traveler and the Gate Checkers*, p. 120, 2003

sucky face *noun*

kissing *US, 2000*

- — Jackie Collins, *Lethal Seduction*, p. 284, 2000

sucky-fucky; suckie fuckie *noun*

a combination of oral and vaginal sex *US, 1981*

- "Any everyone, all talking at once or snoring or suckie-fuckie." — Howard Moss, *The Poet's Story*, p. 196, 1973
- Quiet man! People pay to hear the sucky fucky. — Frank Chin, *The Chickencoop Chinaman*, p. 39, 1981
- Suckee, fuckee, smoke cigarette in the pussy, she give you everything you want. Long time. — *Full Metal Jacket*, 1987
- She undulated over to me and whispered in my ear, "Suckee-fuckee?" I was startled. — Kirk Douglas, *The Ragman's Son*, p. 113, 1988
- "Mmmm," she said, pursuing her lips together. "Sucky-fucky, twenty dollar." — Kregg Jorgenson, *Very Crazy G.I.*, p. 157, 2001

sucrose *noun*

money *US, 1951*

- — David W. Maurer, *Argot of the Racetrack*, p. 61, 1951

suds *noun*

1 beer *US, 1904*

- This mixture was pumped into each barrel, plus thirty pounds of air, and you had a barrel of real suds. — Mezz Mezzrow, *Really the Blues*, p. 63, 1946
- Purveyors of hard booze (who also sell beer), and beer bars which depend on draft or tap beer for about 25 cents, the occasional aristocratic drinker of bottled suds, and a hell of a lot of potato chips[.] — Roger Gordon, *Hollywood's Sexual Underground*, p. 12, 1966
- It was a junkie joint. I sat sipping on a bottle of suds; I couldn't trust the glasses. — Iceberg Slim (Robert Beck), *Pimp*, p. 91, 1969
- Shoving his suds aside, Mr. Jones leans across the table. — Guy Owen, *The Flim-Flam Man and the Apprentice Grifter*, p. 217, 1972
- All but two of 'em like to sit, sip suds, and bullshit all night. — A.S. Jackson, *Gentleman Pimp*, p. 101, 1973
- We can have the suds on the base if you want. — Joseph Wambaugh, *Finnegan's Week*, p. 196, 1993

2 a large amount of money *US, 1945*

- — Lou Shelly, *Hepcats Jive Talk Dictionary*, p. 19, 1945

suede *noun*

1 a stylish, fashionable boy *US, 1961*

- Suede—a boy who wears a duck-tail haircut and rocky clothes — Art Unger, *The Cool Book*, p. 110, 1961

2 a black person *US, 1973*

- — Malachi Andrews and Paul T. Owens, *Black Language*, p. 98, 1973
- She's going to knock on the downstairs door and start yelling something unintelligible in a way-out suede dialect, and hope Terry buzzes her in. — Joseph Wambaugh, *The Blue Knight*, p. 193, 1973

sug *noun*

1 used as an affectionate term of address *US, 1947*

A shortened form of **SUGAR**.

- "That's what I want, sug. I'm dying from thirst." — Irving Shulman, *The Amboy Dukes*, p. 117, 1947

2 an attractive woman *US, 1967*

- Never one to let a sugar, or sug, get away, he walked over to whisper a little sweet talk. — Elaine Shepard, *The Doom Pussy*, p. 58, 1967

sugar *noun*

1 used as a term of endearment *US, 1930*

A distinct southern ring. Variation include "sugar-pie," "sugar-babe," "sugar-baby," etc.

- Don't get roused, sugar. — *The Blues Brothers*, 1980
- A little girl with curly blond hair and big seashell earrings next to him at the bar saying, "What's wrong, sugar?" and patting him on the back. — Elmore Leonard, *Maximum Bob*, p. 147, 1991

- Don't stop now sugar. I'm just getting warmed up. — *Natural Born Killers*, 1994

2 diabetes *US*, 1973

- "Winnie," Gypsy Pearl scolded gently, "you know the doctor told you you ain't s'poze to drink. You got sugar, girl." — Nathan Heard, *Howard Street*, p. 49, 1968
- She's got sugar, so she leaves this outfit [syringe] of hers so that whenever she comes to visit, if she should decide to stay for the night, she has her outfit so that she can take her medicine in the morning. — Donald Goines, *White Man's Justice, Black Man's Grief*, pp. 152–153, 1973
- You got sugar, right? What the doctor is always tellin' you? — John Sayles, *Union Dues*, p. 59, 1977
- He had sugar, they had to cut his toes off. — Michelle Tea, *The Passionate Mistakes and Intricate Corruption of One Girl in America*, p. 159, 1998

3 money *US*, 1951

- — David W. Maurer, *Argot of the Racetrack*, p. 61, 1951

▸ **give some sugar**
to kiss *US*, 1973

- [S]he puts my arm behind my back and says, "Give me some sugar." — Susan Hall, *Ladies of the Night*, pp. 49–50, 1973

sugar daddy *noun*
an older man who supports or helps support a young lover *UK*, 1926
With occasional playful variants.

- The boss catered mostly to Indians who had struck oil on the reservation, beefy cattlemen who were sure to be milked, sugar-daddies with their sable-sporting chicken dinners, and butter-and-egg men with plenty of bacon. — Mezz Mezzrow, *Really the Blues*, p. 84, 1946
- In Los Angeles, I used to have a multimillionaire sugar daddy. — Susan Hall, *Ladies of the Night*, p. 133, 1973
- Well, I need a sugar daddy / He could be my friend / And if I needed money / I know he would lend me a hand. — Christine McVie (Fleetwood Mac), *Sugar Daddy*, 1975
- Find out who bought it for her. Her sugar daddy. — *Lethal Weapon*, 1987

sugar down *verb*
to dilute powder narcotics, especially with powdered milk sugar (lactose) *US*, 1970

- — *Congressional Record*, p. E3982, 6th May 1970

sugarhead *noun*
strong, homemade whiskey *US*, 1999

- It is called corn liquor, white lightning, sugar whiskey, skully cracker, popskull, bush whiskey, stump, stumphole, "splo, ruckus juice, radiator whiskey, rotgut, sugarhead, block and tackle, wildcat, panther's breath, tiger's sweat, Sweet spirits of cats a-fighting, alley bourbon, city gin, cool water, happy Sally, deep shaft, jump steady, old horsey, stingo, blue John, red eye, pine top, buckeye bark whiskey and see seven stars." — *Star Tribune (Minneapolis)*, p. 19F, 31st January 1999

sugar hill *noun*
a brothel *US*, 1987

- — *Maledicta*, p. 148, Summer/Winter 1986–1987: "Sexual slang: prostitutes, pedophiles, flagellators, transvestites, and necrophiles"

sugar pimp *noun*
a pimp who controls his prostitutes through charm and attention *US*, 1972

- A pimp who uses a great deal of charm and little violence or fear is called a sweet Mack or sugar pimp. — Christina and Richard Milner, *Black Players*, p. 35, 1972

sugar tit *noun*
any cherished object or habit *US*, 1972
From the name given a sweetened baby pacifier.

- But fuck skiing. All it is, in Aspen, is a swollen sugar-tit for a gang of aging nazis who are not the local establishment. — Hunter S. Thompson, *Fear and Loathing in America*, p. 308, 30th May 1970: Letter to Mike Moore
- [E]ven further in the distance Mt. Kilimanjaro jumped up like God's own sugar-tit[.] — Tom Robbins, *Another Roadside Attraction*, p. 64, 1971
- — Helen Dahlskog (Editor), *A Dictionary of Contemporary and Colloquial Usage*, p. 58, 1972

sugar up *verb*
to curry favor *US*, 1964

- Back in the beginning, when Tom was still sugarin' up to her, he'd taken out a ten-thousand dollar insurance policy. — Jim Thompson, *Pop. 1280*, p. 133, 1964

suicide alley *noun*
in shuffleboard, a quarter of the opponent's side of the court *US*, 1967

- — Omero C. Catan, *Secrets of Shuffleboard Strategy*, p. 73, 1967: "Glossary of terms"

suicide blonde *noun*
a girl or woman who has dyed her hair blonde at home *US*, 1962
From the pun: "dyed by her own hand."

- — Dobie Gillis, *Teenage Slanguage Dictionary*, 1962

suicide circuit *noun*
the professional rodeo circuit *US*, 1943

- The spill he'd taken at last week's rodeo in Nebraska had forced him to take a leave of absence from the suicide circuit. — Carol Finch, *Not Just Another Cowboy*, p. 11, 2000

suicide club *noun*
a notional group of jockeys who ride in steeplechase races *US*, 1951

- — David W. Maurer, *Argot of the Racetrack*, p. 61, 1951

suicide king *noun*
in a deck of cards, the king of hearts *US*, 1988
It appears that he is plunging a knife into his head.

- — George Percy, *The Language of Poker*, p. 90, 1988

suicide stew *noun*
a combination of central nervous system depressants and alcohol *US*, 1966

- His once white ROTC hat was inverted next to him on the tile floor, already full of regurgitated, semi-digested suicide stew. — Richard Farina, *Been Down So Long*, p. 185, 1966

suit *noun*
an executive; a person of authority but no creativity *US*, 1979
The term usually suggests a them-against-us mentality, with "them" being the executives who wear suits; pejorative.

- More important suits have hurried in from corporation headquarters to see what the hell was going on. — Robert Campbell, *The Cat's Meow*, p. 196, 1988
- They'll want to do the Dempsy stuff in Toronto too, but that's why they're just a bunch of suits, a bunch of sweaty fucking suits. — Richard Price, *Clockers*, p. 152, 1992
- You saw suits, some with the long-legged chicks, a few with their wives. — Elmore Leonard, *Be Cool*, p. 337, 1999
- He'd been targeted as vulnerable by the national Republican Party and money was flowing in from around the country for his opponent, a suit named Norm Coleman. — Al Franken, *Lies*, p. 178, 2003

suitcase *noun*
the rectum *US*, 1992

- Referring to the rectum as a repository for the smuggling of drugs into prison. — William K. Bentley and James M. Corbett, *Prison Slang*, p. 76, 1992

suitcase *verb*
to conceal drugs inside a condom or balloon inside a body orifice *US*, 1987

- — Carsten Stroud, *Close Pursuit*, p. 276, 1987

suitcase boy *noun*
the boyfriend/"agent" of a sexual performer *US*, 1974

- He told me that he would be my "suitcase boy," so that people could call him a gigolo and a pimp. — Blaze Starr, *Blaze Starr*, p. 158, 1974

suitcase operation *noun*
a low-cost, shoddy operation *US*, 1960

- "They'll be strictly a suitcase operation when I get mine." — George Clayton Johnson, *Ocean's Eleven*, p. 163, 1960

suitcase pimp *noun*
a boyfriend, agent or other male who accompanies a female pornography performer to the set *US*, 1995
Not flattering.

- — *Adult Video News*, p. 50, October 1995
- Porsche Lynn actually came up with the term suitcase pimp, because a lot of these guys will walk behind the girl carrying her bags. They are essentially leeches. (Quoting Bill Marigold) — Ana Loria, *1 2 3 Be A Porn Star!*, p. 36, 2000

suited and booted *adjective*
dressed stylishly and fashionably *US*, 2002

- [E]verybody was stepping Chicago style as a suited and booted crowd arrived. — Tracy Funches, *Pimpnosis*, p. 114, 2002

suit up *verb*
to place a condom on a penis *US, 2000*

- The older porn performers started their careers before condoms were commonly used, so they are predictably a little reluctant to "suit up" as they say[.] — Ana Loria, *1 2 3 Be A Porn Star!*, p. 129, 2000

sumbitch; sombitch *noun*
a son of a bitch *US, 1944*

- Finally I studied up on the sumbitch and rebuilt the road myself. — Herman Wouk, *Youngblood Hawke*, p. 101, 1962
- And Barbara Jane said, "It sure as hell might. I'll be a sumbitch." — Dan Jenkins, *Semi-Tough*, p. 216, 1972
- He was a tough sombitch. — Edwin Torres, *Carlito's Way*, p. 16, 1975
- I tried to standup and fly straight, but it wasn't easy with that sumbitch Reagan in the White House. — *Raising Arizona*, 1987
- Goddamn this sumbitch is runnin' hot. — *Natural Born Killers*, 1994

sunbathers *noun*
in poker, a pair of queens dealt face-up *US, 1988*

- — George Percy, *The Language of Poker*, p. 90, 1988

sun belt *noun*
the southern states in the US *US, 1920*

- Mike's told me all about Mr. Stumpnagler wanting to sell out and go to some place in the sunbelt. — Robert Campbell, *Nibbled to Death by Ducks*, p. 230, 1989

sunburnt *adjective*
used for describing playing cards that have been left in the sun to discolor slightly to aid a cheat in identifying them in another player's hand *US, 1988*

- — George Percy, *The Language of Poker*, p. 90, 1988

Sunday *noun*
a surprise blow from the blind side *US, 1926*
An abbreviated form of "Sunday punch" (1915).

- But nothing warned him, as Pithead pivoted sideways and, winding up like Whitey Ford, copped a Sunday, smashing Red flush on the mouth. — Malcolm Braly, *On the Yard*, p. 8, 1967

Sunday *verb*
to hit someone from the blind side *US, 1993*

- He'd been hurt by fans too—stabbed; hit from the blind side, or "Sundayed"; struck with flying bottles and chairs; burned with cigars; stuck with hairpins. — Ted Lewin, *I Was a Teenage Professional Wrestler*, p. 29, 1993

Sunday-go-to-meeting *adjective*
used of clothes, suitable for wearing to church *US, 1831*
Intentionally rural.

- Just felt like putting on my Sunday-go-to-meeting suit. — Louis Armstrong, *Satchmo*, p. 153, 1954
- Then I put on my Sunday-go-to-meetin' clothes, my new sixty-dollar Stetson and my seventy-dollar Justin boots and my four-dollar Levis. — Jim Thompson, *Pop. 1280*, p. 5, 1964
- Mr. Diane Holt, almost Easter Sunday sharp, stands on the front steps of her apartment pulling on her white Sunday-go-to-meeting gloves[.] — Odie Hawkins, *Ghetto Sketches*, p. 50, 1972
- He has costumed himself as an out of fashion Sunday-go-to-meeting silk gloved elderly woman with gray riddled long wig, black bustled dress, over trousers, and ostrich feather plumed floppy chapeau[.] — Iceberg Slim (Robert Beck), *Doom Fox*, p. 71, 1978

Sunday popper *noun*
an occasional user of an addictive drug *US, 1966*

- — *Mr.*, p. 55, April 1966: "The hippie's lexicon"

Sunday punch *noun*
a blow from a person's blind side *US, 1915*

- Thomas kept saying how he was like Fitzsimmons and that his Sunday punch was a right to the solar plexus. — Jose Antonio Villarreal, *Pocho*, p. 106, 1959
- He would play the jealous lover or husband, then, faking anger at her infidelity, he'd pick a fight with the man—usually by throwing a Sunday punch. — Nathan Heard, *Howard Street*, p. 17, 1968

Sunday run *noun*
in circus and carnival usage, a long trip between engagements *US, 1981*

- — Don Wilmeth, *The Language of American Popular Entertainment*, p. 263, 1981

Sunday school show; Sunday school *noun*
a circus or carnival with no crooked games and no performances with sexual content *US, 1980*

- Charles Sparks probably ran the best Sunday School Show of all of them. — Joe McKennon, *Circus Lingo*, p. 90, 1980
- — Don Wilmeth, *The Language of American Popular Entertainment*, p. 263, 1981
- — Gene Sorrows, *All About Carnivals*, p. 27, 1985: "Terminology"

Sunday suit *noun*
no clothes at all *US, 1976*

- — Elementary Electronics, *Dictionary of CB Lingo*, p. 112, 1976

sundowner *noun*
1 a senile patient who is quiet during the day but becomes agitated at dark *US, 1983*

- — *Maledicta*, p. 39, 1983: "More common patient-directed pejoratives used by medical personnel"

2 a VF-111 combat aircraft *US, 1990*
The plane was first deployed in 1942 in the Pacific with the mission of shooting down Japanese "Suns." Deployed in Korea and Vietnam.

- Joining the "Sundowners," as VF-111 was nicknamed, in turnaround, Weigand had been one of the two new pilots Ruliffson was considering for his wingman. — Robert K. Wilcox, *Scream of Eagles*, p. 228, 1990

sun gun *noun*
in the television and movie industries, a portable, intense light *US, 1990*

- — Ralph S. Singleton, *Filmmaker's Dictionary*, p. 166, 1990

sunshine *noun*
LSD *US, 1994*

- — *Current Slang*, p. 21, Spring 1971
- — US Department of Justice, *Street Terms*, October 1994

sunspots *noun*
in computing, the purported reason for an unanticipated error *US, 1991*

- — Eric S. Raymond, *The New Hacker's Dictionary*, p. 337, 1991

suntans *noun*
a summer-weight tan military uniform *US, 1937*

- — Carl Fleischhauer, *A Glossary of Army Slang*, p. 20, 1968
- He was dressed in his office uniform, a short-sleeved shirt and trousers of tan tropical worsted, an outfit called "suntans." — Neil Sheehan, *A Bright Shining Lie*, p. 276, 1988

sup *noun*
supper *US, 1969*

- — John D. Bell et al., *Loosely Speaking*, p. Appendix, 1969

super *noun*
in carnival usage, a handsome watch displayed as a prize *US, 1981*

- — Don Wilmeth, *The Language of American Popular Entertainment*, p. 263, 1981

super *adverb*
very *US, 1968*
Adds a melodramatic, gushing flavor to the intensification.

- — Collin Baker et al., *College Undergraduate Slang Study Conducted at Brown University*, p. 207, 1968
- He dug right into the soil there, made this super-nice cave with this lovely texture[.] — Jefferson Poland and Valerie Alison, *The Records of the San Francisco Sexual Freedom League*, p. 22, 1971
- It's like so BITCHEN cuz like everybody's like super-super nice. — Moon Unit and Frank Zappa, *Valley Girl*, 1982
- You must be superbusy, though. — Armistead Maupin, *Babycakes*, p. 68, 1984

superblush *noun*
in poker, a sequence of cards in a red suit—diamonds or hearts *US, 1996*

- — John Vorhaus, *The Big Book of Poker Slang*, p. 35, 1996

super C *noun*
ketamine hydrochloride, an anesthetic used as a hallucinogen *US, 1994*

- — US Department of Justice, *Street Terms*, October 1994

SuperCool *noun*
a cigarette dipped into phencyclidine, the drug popularly known as ANGEL DUST *US*, *1988*
- One of the popular ways to get "dusted" is to dip cigarettes, specifically the Sherman brand, into a liquid form of PCP, allowing it to dry before smoking it. It is known as "SuperCool" or "Sherm." — James Vigil, *Barrio Gangs*, p. 127, 1988

super-duper *adjective*
exceptionally good *US*, *1940*
Childish, or intentionally evocative of childishness.
- — Lou Shelly, *Hepcats Jive Talk Dictionary*, p. 35, 1945
- "Probably one of those super-duper television screens like C.B.S. and NBC have been experimenting with," I surmised. — Robert deCoy, *The Nigger Bible*, p. 179, 1967

superfly *noun*
a curly hairstyle popular with black men and women in the mid-1970s *US*, *1975*
- It's goodby Afro, hello curls for scads of local hip black men who are part of the international, unisex trend to curly hair. They call the style "a Superfly," "a Lord Jesus" or just "a Curly Do" and they're spending lots of time and money to get the look. — *San Francisco Examiner*, p. 34, 13th April 1975

superfly *adjective*
extremely fashionable, attractive, and appealing *US*, *1997*
- He wore a large hat, superflied down, as did the taller man to his left. — Joseph Nazel, *Black Cop*, p. 154, 1974
- — Connie Eble (Editor), *UNC-CH Campus Slang*, p. 8, Fall 1997

super joint *noun*
phencyclidine, the recreational drug known as PCP or angel dust *US*, *1982*
- — Ralph de Sola, *Crime Dictionary*, p. 112, 1982

super kools *noun*
phencyclidine, the recreational drug known as PCP or angel dust *US*, *1997*
Because the addition of PCP makes Kools™, a brand name cigarette and hence any cigarette, "*super*ior."
- PCP. Also known as "angel dust," "sherm," and "superkools," this rhinoceros tranquilizer was the most high-risk high of all times. — Editors of Ben is Dead, *Retrohell*, p. 154, 1997

super max *noun*
a prison with the highest maximum security features *US*, *1985*
- "You can't put the super-max in Somerset, you can't put the super-max in Jessup." — *Washington Post*, p. D4, 7th February 1985

supply *noun*
drugs waiting to be sold *US*, *2006*
- "Maybe D was jackin' supply." — Jason Starr, *Lights Out*, p. 140, 2006

supremo *adjective*
excellent; extreme *US*, *1979*
- But then Cavett, whose eagerness to please bordered on the idee fixe, committed his supremo blopper of the evening[.] — *Washington Post*, p. M1, 11th February 1979
- Born and raised in Montreal, he was used to supremo suck from the "fille du roi" and this Ontario girl was going to rank. — Suroosh Alvi et al., *The Vice Guide*, p. 27, 2002

sure as shit and taxes
very certain *US*, *1957*
- Well, sure as shit and taxes, he comes there every night just as regular you can set your watch by him — William Burroughs, *Naked Lunch*, p. 175, 1957

sure off *verb*
in an illegal number gambling lottery, to insure numbers that are the object of heavy betting *US*, *1949*
- — *American Speech*, p. 193, October 1949

sure pops *noun*
dice that have been heavily weighted and are likely to produce the desired results *US*, *1950*
- — *The Annals of the American Academy of Political and Social Sciences*, p. 131, May 1950

sure-thing man *noun*
in carnival usage, a confederate who is hired to play and win a game in order to generate business *US*, *1981*
- — Don Wilmeth, *The Language of American Popular Entertainment*, p. 30, 1981

surf *verb*
▸ **surf the crimson tide**
to experience the bleed period of the menstrual cycle *US*, *1995*
- Mr. Hall, I was surfing the crimson wave. I had to haul ass to the ladies'. — *Clueless*, 1995

surface *verb*
to come out of hiding; to leave a surreptitious existence and become more public *US*, *1971*
- There is an impression, conveyed by the Interviewer, that our New Morning communique stated we should no longer be an underground... We were not "surfacing" when we shared the Senate lavatory with the Viet Cong. — *The Last Supplement to the Whole Earth Catalog*, p. 20, March 1971

surf's down
used for expressing dismay at poor surf conditions *US*, *1977*
- — Gary Fairmont R. Filosa II, *The Surfer's Almanac*, p. 196, 1977

surfboard Suzie *noun*
a stereotypical woman who spends time at the beach admiring male surfers *US*, *1990*
- These surfboard Suzies want you more than Day-Glo earrings. — Joseph Wambaugh, *The Golden Orange*, p. 175, 1990

surf bunny *noun*
a woman who spends a great deal of time at the beach, associating with surfers and/or surfing *US*, *1980*
- Just a bunch of California surf bunnies? huh? — *Washington Post*, p. B1, 21st January 1980
- He was even sick of ogling all the bikinis stuffed with surf bunnies that littered the streets of La Jolla. — Joseph Wambaugh, *Lines and Shadows*, p. 29, 1984

surf dog *noun*
an avid, veteran surfer *US*, *1991*
- — Trevor Cralle, *The Surfin'ary*, p. 130, 1991

surfing knobs; surfing bumps *noun*
calcium deposits near the knees and feet caused by extended contact with a hard surfboard *US*, *1964*
- — John Severson, *Modern Surfing Around the World*, p. 182, 1964

surf nazi *noun*
a zealous, devoted surfer *US*, *1988*
- SURF NAZI: Blond hair, blue eyes and a one track mind. — Michael V. Anderson, *The Bad, Rad, Not to Forget Way Cool Beach and Surf Discriptionary*, p. 20, 1988

surf-o *adjective*
obsessed with surfing *US*, *1991*
- — Trevor Cralle, *The Surfin'ary*, p. 46, 1991

surf rat *noun*
a beginner surfer *US*, *1990*
- — *Surfing*, p. 43, 14th March 1990

surf safari *noun*
a trip in search of good surfing conditions *US*, *1964*
- — John Severson, *Modern Surfing Around the World*, p. 182, 1964

surf silks *noun*
silk or nylon swimming trunks worn under a wetsuit *US*, *1977*
- — Gary Fairmont R. Filosa II, *The Surfer's Almanac*, p. 196, 1977

surprise party *noun*
in poker, a hand that should not win, that is not expected by its holder to win, but that wins *US*, *1996*
- — John Vorhaus, *The Big Book of Poker Slang*, p. 35, 1996

Susie College *noun*
a stereotypical female college student *US*, *1970*
- More important, he was the real enemy, we thought, since he was our competition for the hearts and minds of Joe and Susie College, who were naively jumping on his clean-cut haywagon. — Raymond Mungo, *Famous Long Ago*, p. 80, 1970

suspicion *verb*
   to suspect someone *US, 1834*
   • The best way, of course, was to murder Trueblood, but they would have suspicioned me right away. — Max Shulman, *I was a Teen-Age Dwarf*, p. 105, 1959

Suzy Robincrotch; Suzy Rottencrotch; Suzy *noun*
   during the Vietnam war, the generic girlfriend back home *US, 1991*
   • We learned management and leadership principles that many companies would kill for, while most of our civilian peers were partyin' hardy with Suzy Rottencrotch and goin' to toga parties. — Warren Bonesteel, *Morning Coffee*, p. 39, 2004

Suzy Sorority *noun*
   a stereotypical sorority member who looks, dresses, talks, and lives the part *US, 1974*
   A character in Lily Tomlin skits in the 1970s.
   • — Connie Eble (Editor), *UNC-CH Campus Slang*, Fall 1974
   • She was leaning against a far wall, a perfect "Suzy Sorority." — Ginger Lox, *Berrigan*, p. 11, 1978
   • "Suzi Sorority" and "Freddie Fraternity," if they ever existed, are not quite as clean or wholesome as might appear at first glance. — *Maledicta*, p. 133, 1995

swa *noun*
   southwest Asia *US, 1998*
   • — *Seattle Times*, p. A9, 12th April 1998: "Grunts, squids not grunting from the same dictionary"

swab *noun*
   a roll of money *US, 1965*
   • I clipped a dance moll for a swab, it paid a trey or a fin. — Bruce Jackson, *Get Your Ass in the Water and Swim Like Me*, p. 85, 1965

swab *verb*
▸ **swab the deck**
   to perform oral sex on a woman *US, 1964*
   • — Roger Blake, *The American Dictionary of Sexual Terms*, p. 51, 1964

swabbie; swabby *noun*
   a sailor *US, 1944*
   • He showed me a couple of scars on his arm from a fight he had in a Japanese market with a "swabbie." — Martin Russ, *Happy Hunting Ground*, p. 197, 1968
   • Poor little swabbie. just out lookin' for a little fun and hauled up crazy, crazy me. — Earl Thompson, *Tattoo*, p. 163, 1974
   • She hadn't really done a lot of swabbies before and thought they might not have enough money. — Joseph Wambaugh, *Floaters*, p. 102, 1996

swab jockey *noun*
   a marine *US, 1956*
   • "God damn, you swab jockeys can't think of nothing else, I'll swear to God." — William Brinkley, *Don't Go Near the Water*, pp. 252–252, 1956
   • We didn't operate from our home base except for jackrolling swab jockeys, marines. — Willard Motley, *Let No Man Write My Epitaph*, 1958
   • I bet you don't, you freaky swab jockey. — Darryl Ponicsan, *The Last Detail*, p. 99, 1970
   • "She-it, man, we should go plow them fuckin' swab jockeys," Glenn said[.] — Earl Thompson, *Tattoo*, p. 61, 1974

swacked *adjective*
   drunk or drug-intoxicated *US, 1952*
   • — Lou Shelly, *Hepcats Jive Talk Dictionary*, p. 48, 1945
   • [B]ut gets just as cornball whenever swacked. — Leo Rosten, *Dear Herm*, p. 99, 1974
   • He was swacked out of his skull. — Edwin Torres, *After Hours*, p. 285, 1979
   • The bus driver's yellin' about gettin' rear-ended and he can see the dude's swacked. — Joseph Wambaugh, *The Glitter Dome*, p. 211, 1981

swag *noun*
   1 stolen goods; loot; bounty *UK, 1794*
   Derives from the earlier sense "a shop" hence the contents seen as the object of theft; originally, especially linens and clothes rather than precious metals and stones.
   • They had mde contact with a "fence" from Philadelphia, to whom they were to turn over the swag for $150,000 in currency. — Jack Lait and Lee Mortimer, *Chicago Confidential*, p. 18, 1950
   • I just need you along to carry swag, that's all there is to it, just to help me carry swag away. — George Mandel, *Flee the Angry Strangers*, p. 388, 1952

   • He never touches the swag himself ... has it delivered to a hotel room and one of his stooges picks it up and fences it. — Gerald Petievich, *To Die in Beverly Hills*, p. 189, 1983
   • [W]e took the swag back to Allen's apartment. — Herbert Huncke, *Guilty of Everything*, p. 105, 1990
   2 contraband *US, 1951*
   Used both as an adjective and a noun.
   • — *American Speech*, p. 195, October 1951: "A study of reformatory argot"
   • — Gresham M. Sykes, *The Society of Captives*, p. 88, 1958
   3 free merchandise or tickets to concerts handed out by music recording companies *US, 1997*
   • — Jim Crotty, *How to Talk American*, p. 222, 1997
   4 money *US, 1951*
   • [H]e began once to describe where he and Jake had buried "the swag"—the twenty thousand dollars. — Donald Wilson, *My Six Convicts*, p. 168, 1951
   • I wore a hat from Disney with a fifty-dollar tag / And my snakeskin billfold was loaded with swag. — Dennis Wepman et al., *The Life*, p. 36, 1976

swag *adjective*
   stolen *US, 1979*
   • Paulie had met him a few years ago through a friend who had once handled some swag TV sets for him. — Vincent Patrick, *The Pope of Greenwich Village*, pp. 26–27, 1979

swag bag *noun*
   a bag for loot or special contraband *US, 1974*
   • Russo opened his swag bag and pulled out two quart cans of prunes and apricots. — Piri Thomas, *Seven Long Times*, p. 122, 1974

SWAK; SWALK; SWANK
   written on an envelope, or at the foot of a lover's letter, as lovers' code for "sealed with a kiss" *UK, 1925*
   Embellishments included a "loving" kiss and a "nice" kiss. Widely known, and well used by servicemen, then a nearly mandatory sign-off line in any American teenage love letter of the 1950s and 60s, now a part of the coded vocabulary of texting.
   • S.W.A.K. Sealed with a kiss. — Art Unger, *The Cool Book*, p. 131, 1961
   • — Hy Lit, *Hy Lit's Unbelievable Dictionary of Hip Words for Groovy People*, p. 52, 1968
   • — Andrew John with Stephen Blake, *The Total TxtMsg Dictionary*, p. 244, 2001

swallow *noun*
   a drink of alcohol *UK, 1822*
   • You wouldn't be grudge her bringin' me a little swallow, would you, Billy Boy[.] — Ken Kesey, *One Flew Over the Cuckoo's Nest*, p. 255, 1962

swallow *verb*
▸ **swallow a gun**
   to commit suicide by gunshot to the mouth *US, 1981*
   • He'd probably go home and swallow his Smith & Wesson. — Joseph Wambaugh, *The Glitter Dome*, p. 3, 1981
▸ **swallow spit**
   to stop talking; to be quiet *US, 1993*
   • — *The Bell (Paducah Tilghman High School)*, pp. 8–9, 17th December 1993: "Tilghmanism: the concealed language of the hallway."
▸ **swallow the anchor**
   to go ashore *US, 1960*
   • "We'll swallow the anchor and try a new life ashore." — Gary Jennings, *The Road Show*, p. 376, 1982
▸ **swallow the olive**
   to lose your composure and concentration *US, 1961*
   • It seems Lloyd's of London has finally "taken the gas." That's a golfing term for a player who chokes up or "swallows the olive." — *San Francisco Examiner*, p. 6, 5th February 1961

swami *noun*
   a poker player with the annoying habit of coaching other players *US, 1996*
   • — John Vorhaus, *The Big Book of Poker Slang*, p. 41, 1996

swamp ass *noun*
   sweaty genitals and/or buttocks *US, 1995*
   • Stations that air the Howard Stern Show were fined $27,000 to $500,000 because he joked about personal hygiene issues like "swamp ass" on different shows. — *Daily News (New York)*, p. 31, 25th January 2005

swamped *adjective*
drunk *US, 1945*
- — Lou Shelly, *Hepcats Jive Talk Dictionary*, p. 48, 1945

swamp rat *noun*
any person living near or coming from near the great swamps of the southern US *US, 1978*
- — *Maledicta*, p. 171, Summer/Winter 1978: "How to hate thy neighbor: a guide to racist maledicta"

swampy *noun*
a rural New Englander who is thoroughly and steadfastly rural *US, 1963*
An abbreviation of **SWAMP YANKEE**.
- — *American Speech*, p. 122, May 1963: "Swamp yankee"

swamp Yankee *noun*
a rural New Englander who is thoroughly and steadfastly rural *US, 1939*
- — *American Speech*, pp. 121–123, May 1963: "Swamp yankee"
- No, no, get yourself a good Swamp Yankee! A good homely Swamp Yankee! — Edwin O'Connor, *The Best and Last of Edwin O'Connor*, p. 434, 1970
- The man who sold it to me was an old swamp Yankee that farmed it on and off when he felt like it, and didn't when he didn't. — George Higgins, *The Easiest Thing in the World*, p. 132, 2005

swank around *verb*
to treat generously *US, 1985*
- "You didn't leave a wife or abandon a family for one, but you did swank them around, rent them apartments, lease them cars, and feed them regularly with racks of swag clothes and paper bags of stolen jewelry." — Nicholas Pileggi, *Wise Guy*, p. 140, 1985

swanson *noun*
a coward *US, 2004*
- — Rick Ayers (Editor), *Berkeley High Slang Dictionary*, p. 40, 2004

swanz *noun*
the penis *US, 1985*
- They wore wigs and tied their cocks up with pantyhose back toward their ass, so if the guy reached down there he couldn't feel the swanz hanging there to give the guy away. — Mark Baker, *Cops*, p. 279, 1985

swap *verb*
▸ **swap cans**
(used of a male homosexual couple) to take turns as the active participant in anal sex *US, 1965*
- — *The Guild Dictionary of Homosexual Terms*, p. 43, 1965

▸ **swap lies; swap lies and swat flies**
to engage in prolonged, aimless conversation *US, 1852*
- — Joseph E. Ragen and Charles Finston, *Inside the World's Toughest Prison*, p. 821, 1962: "Penitentiary and underworld glossary"

▸ **swap slop**
to kiss *US, 1947*
- — Marcus Hanna Boulware, *Jive and Slang of Students in Negro Colleges*, 1947

▸ **swap spit**
to kiss long and hard *US, 1947*
- "Let's swop spit?" she said. "Yeah, that's freak stuff," he answered to her surprise. — Hal Ellson, *The Golden Spike*, p. 71, ?1952
- "You come here, Benny"—she stretched out her arms—"and we'll kiss and swap spit." — Irving Shulman, *The Amboy Dukes*, p. 118, 1947
- You ever swap spit? Or are you just all talk and no cojones? — Evan Hunter, *The Blackboard Jungle*, p. 159, 1954
- "Walk This Way" gets high school right: an outrageous defjam boast-toast of psychosexual discovery, a zitkid eyeing three skimpy skirts in a gym locker room and then swapping spit with the skirt next door. — Chuck Eddy, *Stairway to Hell*, p. 15, 1991

swap out *verb*
to exchange roles in homosexual sex after one partner achieves satisfaction *US, 2002*
- — Gary K. Farlow, *Prison-ese*, p. 70, 2002

swapper *noun*
a married person who engages in spouse swapping at sex parties *US, 1967*
- Harry wasn't the slightest bit bashful with the two sexy wives of other men, and the only time he ever felt any reluctance during the

time he knew the swappers was just before he actually met the various husbands. — Frank Harris, *The Swinging Moderns*, pp. 68–69, 1967
- But not all swappers are so enthusiastic about orgiastic activities, needless to say. — R.J. Hagerman, *Husband and Wife Swapping*, p. 92, 1967

swash *noun*
foaming water after a wave breaks on shore *US, 1963*
- — Grant W. Kuhns, *On Surfing*, p. 123, 1963

swave and blaze *adjective*
suave and blasé *US, 1967*
An intentional mispronunciation, meant to be humorous.
- — *Current Slang*, p. 2, Spring 1967

sweat *noun*
a worry or difficulty *US, 1979*
Usually used in the negative, most often as "no sweat!"
- If we started planning right now it shouldn't be any sweat at all. — Beatrice Sparks (writing as 'Anonymous'), *Jay's Journal*, p. 104, 1979

sweat *verb*
1 to coerce someone through intense pressure, usually not involving physical force *US, 1947*
- The next thing I know, if I leave him here you'll be sweating him. — Irving Shulman, *The Amboy Dukes*, p. 240, 1947
- They took him to the grilling room to sweat him some more. — Willard Motley, *Knock on Any Door*, p. 351, 1947
- DIMES: Now we know something's rotten in Denmark, 'cause this dickhead had a big bag, and it's uncut too, so we're sweatin' him, tryin' to find out where he got it. Scarin' the shit outta him. — *True Romance*, 1993
- I just knew we was gon' get sweated. — *Menace II Society*, 1993

2 to disclose that a pool player is in fact a skilled betting professional *US, 1990*
- — Steve Rushin, *Pool Cool*, p. 28, 1990

3 to gamble nervously and cautiously *US, 1991*
- — Michael Dalton, *Blackjack*, p. 81, 1991

▸ **sweat bullets**
to experience a high degree of nervous tension, usually sweating profusely *US, 1949*
- There was something very intimidating about being in a dingy, smoke-filled room with a bunch of big ol' thug ass niggers, sweating bullets over a jiveass robbery. — Odie Hawkins, *Chicago Hustle*, p. 44, 1977
- He is sweating bullets as he zooms to my desk. — Leo Rosten, *Silky!*, p. 1, 1979

▸ **sweat the brass**
in horseracing, to race a horse day after day, without giving it a rest period *US, 1951*
- — David W. Maurer, *Argot of the Racetrack*, p. 61, 1951

sweatback *noun*
an illegal immigrant to the US who is working *US, 1962*
A **WETBACK** who is working, and thus sweating.
- — *American Speech*, p. 272, December 1962: "The language of traffic policemen"

sweat box *noun*
the waiting area outside the room in which a parole hearing is to take place *US, 1961–1962*
- — Frank Prewitt and Francis Schaeffer, *Vacaville Vocabulary*, 1961–1962

sweat cure *noun*
an attempt to break an addiction without any medical intervention *US, 1949*
- He'd taken the sweat cure in a little Milwaukee Avenue hotel room cutting himself down, as he put it, "from monkey to zero." — Nelson Algren, *The Man with the Golden Arm*, p. 59, 1949

sweater *noun*
1 in a casino or other gambling establishment, a person who observes but does not participate in a game *US, 1968*
- Just as much money changes hands between the "sweaters"—the spectators—as between the players, and that is where the real treachery comes in, because the players might be in cahoots. — Robert Byrne, *McGoorty*, p. 31, 1972

2 a casino employee or executive who cheats gamblers *US, 1977*
- He will try to avoid picking "bleeders" or "sweaters." That is executives who so hate to see the player win they may cheat the customer without the permission of the hotel, just out of sheer competitiveness. — Mario Puzo, *Inside Las Vegas*, p. 182, 1977

3 a person who worries *US, 1966*
- — *Current Slang*, p. 4, Summer 1966

sweater kittens *noun*
the female breasts *US, 2005*
- Not only did she expose a lungful of her fist-sized frisky sweater kittens, but she even flashed some pussy, cats! — Mr. Skin, *Mr. Skin's Skincyclopedia*, p. 180, 2005

sweater meat *noun*
the female breasts *US, 2004*
- — Ben Applebaum and Derrick Pittman, *Turd Ferguson & The Sausage Party*, p. 63, 2004

sweater puppies *noun*
the female breasts *US, 1994*
- One phrase sums up how I feel about them: Sweater Puppies. — soc.college.teaching-asst, 2nd February 1994
- Boobs, zonkers, headlights, watermelons, sweater puppies, pointers, knockers, jugs, tatas—these are some of the words to describe women's breasts. — Howard Stern, *Miss America*, p. 441, 1995
- — Vann Wesson, *Generation X Field Guide and Lexicon*, p. 162, 1997
- In the press tent, free copies of The Generation X Field Guide and Lexicon are available for those who don't already know that sweater puppies are breasts[.] — *Playboy*, p. 82, November 1997

sweater queen *noun*
a neatly and nicely dressed homosexual male *US, 1997*
- — Jim Crotty, *How to Talk American*, p. 138, 1997

sweat room *noun*
a small room in a police station where suspects are interrogated or "sweated" *UK, 1974*
- Tell them to put the Mex in a sweat room. — James Ellroy, *White Jazz*, p. 95, 1992

Sweatshop *noun*
▸ **the Sweatshop**
the Apollo Theatre, New York *US, 1949*
- — Babs Gonzales, *Be-Bop Dictionary and History of its Famous Stars*, p. 9, 1949

Swedish headache *noun*
an aching in the testicles from sexual activity that does not culminate in ejaculation *US, 1932*
- — *Maledicta*, p. 173, 1979: "A glossary of ethnic slurs in american English"

Swedish massage *noun*
masturbation of a man by another person *US, 1981*
- "[S]tick to Swedish massage (by hand), or French (by mouth), and only go Spanish (between the breasts), Russian (between the thighs), American (a body roll) or Danish (inside) if it's worth the money." — Alix Shulman, *On the Stroll*, p. 133, 1981

sweep *noun*
1 in combat, a search and destroy mission or a concerted search through an area *US, 1985*
- Romeo sat security for the howitzers and pulled search-and-destroy missions—S & Ds—day sweeps, we called them. — Larry Heinemann, *Close Quarters*, p. 73, 1977
- Very tough, very brave, I said, "Sir, please go out and sweep the area." — Al Santoli, *To Bear Any Burden*, p. 194, 1985
- The brigade was making a "Sweep," also known as a search-and-destroy mission, of the region west of Dak To. — Lucian K. Truscott, *Army Blue*, p. 112, 1989

2 a concerted effort to find someone or something illegal *US, 1974*
- They bring all those eyeball witnesses into the squad room, be like a hooker sweep out there. — Elmore Leonard, *Be Cool*, p. 21, 1999

sweep *verb*
to systematically search for surveillance devices *US, 1966*
- The electronic surveillance guys, the ones that sweep your office. Get the bugs out, you know? — George V. Higgins, *Penance for Jerry Kennedy*, p. 88, 1985
- Caruana came by after a Celtics game at the nearby Boston Garden, but never got around to sweeping the office. — Gerard O'Neill, *The Under Boss*, p. 232, 1989

sweeper *noun*
1 in mountain biking, a tree limb overhanging the trail at approximately face height *US, 1992*
- — *Mountain Bike!*, p. 161, 1992: "Bikespeak"

2 an expert hired to search for and locate surveillance devices *US, 1985*
- Where the hell're your bills from the goddamned sweepers? — George V. Higgins, *Penance for Jerry Kennedy*, p. 88, 1985

sweet *noun*
1 an effeminate male homosexual *US, 1990*
- Phillip Mayflower, the neighborhood "sweet," strolled past, his head held high[.] — Odie Hawkins, *Great Lawd Buddha*, p. 9, 1990

2 an amphetamine tablet *US, 1994*
- — US Department of Justice, *Street Terms*, August 1994

sweet *adjective*
1 said of a supplemental loan in an illegal loan business *US, 1968*
- For a loanshark like Valachi, this was where the real windfall lay—in a reloan, or as it is called in shylocking circles, the "sweet" loan. — Peter Maas, *The Valachi Papers*, p. 168, 1968

2 excellent; in style; admirable *US, 1999*
- — Connie Eble (Editor), *UNC-CH Campus Slang*, p. 7, Spring 1982
- Dude, that movie was fucking sweet! — *South Park*, 1999

3 homosexual *US, 2002*
- I never bother to think whether someone will consider me sweet. I'm confident in my masculinity. — Susan Hall, *Gentleman of Leisure*, p. 12, 1972
- — Gary K. Farlow, *Prison-ese*, p. 71, 2002

sweet daddy *noun*
a pimp *US, 1957*
- Mary could be proud indeed because she was one girl who didn't have to get along with a single wife-in-law, not to mention seven, as that sweet daddy called Jo-Jo had. — John M. Murtagh and Sara Harris, *Cast the First Stone*, pp. 16–17, 1957

sweeten *verb*
1 in poker, to increase the amount bet *US, 1963*
- — Irwin Steig, *Common Sense in Poker*, p. 188, 1963

2 in the television and movie industries, to make subtle improvements in the soundtrack *US, 1990*
- — Ralph S. Singleton, *Filmmaker's Dictionary*, p. 166, 1990

sweetened air *noun*
candy floss *US, 1981*
- — Don Wilmeth, *The Language of American Popular Entertainment*, p. 97, 1981

sweetener *noun*
cash *US, 2003*
- Candy, markers, ammo, liners, stocking stuffer, sweetener, garnish, and pledges are all terms for cash. — Henry Hill and Byron Schreckengost, *A Good Fella's Guide to New York*, p. 123, 2003

sweethead *noun*
a marijuana user *US, 1997*
- — Jim Emerson-Cobb, *Scratching the Dragon*, April 1997

sweetie *noun*
1 a sweetheart *US, 1925*
- Even further, a Bird who takes a stranger home is probably cheating on his true sweetheart, anyway, and when sweetie learns of it he is sure to raise holy hell. — Robert Sylvester, *No Cover Charge*, p. 268, 1956
- You have a touch. But then I'll bet your steady little sweetie thinks so too. — Iceberg Slim (Robert Beck), *Mama Black Widow*, p. 241, 1969

2 used as a wheedling, patronizing form of address *US, 1971*
- Get to work, sweetie. — George V. Higgins, *The Friends of Eddie Doyle*, p. 148, 1971

3 an effeminate man, usually an effeminate homosexual *US, 1972*
A pejorative, adopted by gays as an ironic endearment.
- I asked some sweetie if he ever got pregnant and he said, "How should I know? Do I have eyes in the back of my head?" — Bruce Rodgers, *The Queens' Vernacular*, p. 74, 1972

4 the drug Preludin™, a stimulant that suppresses the appetite *US, 1970*
- — William D. Alsever, *Glossary for the Establishment and Other Uptight People*, p. 30, December 1970

sweet Jesus *noun*
morphine; heroin *US, 1967*
- — US Department of Justice, *Street Terms*, October 1994

sweet limburger!

used for expressing disapproval *US, 1983*
A signature line of Colonel Sherman Potter on *M*A*S*H* (CBS, 1972–83). Repeated with referential humor.

sweet Lucy *noun*

1 muscatel wine *US, 1973*

- He started walking away from the short dog, which was rolling around on the sidewalk spilling sweet lucy all over the pavement. — Joseph Wambaugh, *The Blue Knight*, p. 123, 1973

2 any cheap wine *US, 1971*

- "Wine is good for her and it ain't no sweet lucy. Leave her have it." — Robert Deane Pharr, *S.R.O.*, p. 156, 1971

sweet mack *noun*

a pimp who controls his prostitutes through charm and attention *US, 1972*

- A pimp who uses a great deal of charm and little violence or fear is called a sweet Mack or sugar pimp. — Christina and Richard Milner, *Black Players*, p. 35, 1972

sweet-talk *verb*

to flatter someone, to convince someone through kind words *US, 1936*

- Some fly cat chased a girl up the stairs trying to sweettalk her until one of the fellows from the Cotton Pickers hit him in the jaw and knocked him right down again. — Mezz Mezzrow, *Really the Blues*, p. 91, 1946

sweet thing *noun*

an attractive young woman *US, 1971*

- So Mick [Jagger...] disengages himself from the sweet thing at his side[.] — Lester Bangs, *Psychotic Reactions and Carburetor Dung*, p. 13, 1971

sweet tooth *noun*

an addiction to morphine *US, 1961*

- — *American Speech*, pp. 145–148, May 1961: "The spoken language of medicine; argot, slang, cant"
- — Sally Williams, *"Strong" Words*, p. 161, 1994

swell *noun*

a well-dressed, fashionable man *UK, 1786*

- Them Park Avenue swells like me. — Mickey Spillane, *I, The Jury*, p. 45, 1947

swell *adjective*

good; attractive; stylish *UK, 1812*
A key piece of slang for more than a century, eventually displaced by **COOL**.

- "Morning, Doc," the attendant said, "swell car you got there." — Terry Southern, *Flash and Filigree*, p. 29, 1958
- "Harald's a swell gent," she went on, in a different voice, more thoughtful and serious. — Mary McCarthy, *The Group*, p. 22, 1963
- He ain't no swell guy and he never was. — Eugene Boe (Compiler), *The Wit & Wisdom of Archie Bunker*, pp. 19–20, 1971

swell pipes *noun*

in circus and carnival usage, a good singing voice *US, 1981*

- — Don Wilmeth, *The Language of American Popular Entertainment*, p. 265, 1981

swerve *noun*

1 a deception, practical joke, or false report *US, 1973*

- "Time we got the swerve from Maloney and them," the Digger said. — George Higgins, *The Digger's Game*, p. 159, 1973
- When asked if his actions that night toward Coraluzzo were disingenuous or dishonest, Gordon said, "Yes, we are very clever. Yes, this was a swerve." — *rec.sport.pro-wrestling*, 10th September 1994
- Women are very clear when it comes to the kind of men they like. They go for guys with a little edge, a little swerve. They want somebody who's cool and street, but sophisticated. — Chris Rock, *Rock This!*, p. 125, 1997
- Usually it was just a swerve with a guy like him if you're an unknown, but the match went so I held my own. — Jeff Archer, *Theater in a Squared Circle*, p. 89, 1999

2 intoxication *US, 2001*

- — Rick Ayers (Editor), *Slang Dictionary*, p. 16, 2001

▸ **get your swerve on**

to drink to the point of intoxication *US, 1998*

- — Megan Ferguson, *Columbia Missourian*, p. 1A, 19th October 1998
- — Connie Eble (Editor), *UNC-CH Campus Slang*, p. 4, Spring 2003

swift *adjective*

good, clever *US, 1963*

- Ollie's a swift dancer, too, and you should see him twisting—absolute boss. — Frederick Kohner, *The Affairs of Gidget*, p. 77, 1963
- — Steve Salaets, *Ye Olde Hiptionary*, 1970
- — Connie Eble (Editor), *UNC-CH Campus Slang*, p. 9, Spring 1988

Swiftie *noun*

a Swift Boat, the US Navy PCF (Patrol Craft Fast), used in coastal operations in Vietnam between 1965 and 1973 *US, 1967*

- The Swiftie picks up the junk with its searchlight at a hundred yards. — David Reed, *Up Front in Vietnam*, p. 64, 1967

swill cup *noun*

a combination of leftover alcoholic beverages *US, 2003*

- "Swill cup" is street slang for any random, potent and invariably nasty potin' of alcoholic beverages—whiskey, gin, Purple Puckerr, jug wine, backwash dregs of a warm Tequila, whatever—blended in a single container and then chugged. — *Denver Westword*, 17th July 2003

swim *verb*

to move through a stadium or auditorium, experiencing a concert from different perspectives *US, 1994*

- — David Shenk and Steve Silberman, *Skeleton Key*, p. 274, 1994

swine *noun*

1 a police officer; the police *US, 1997*

- — Pamela Munro, *U.C.L.A. Slang*, p. 112, 1997

2 a prison guard *US, 1976*

- — John R. Armore and Joseph D. Wolfe, *Dictionary of Desperation*, p. 53, 1976

swing *noun*

a consensual orgy *US, 1969*

- But walk into a swing and take a long look around the room Every broad (if you've got the time and stamina) is yours. — *Screw*, p. 10, 7th February 1969

swing *verb*

1 to enjoy frequent casual sex with different partners *UK, 1964*

- My third sex life is swinging in the group-sex kick. — Allen S. Dunhill and Roger Blake, *The Group Sex Kick*, p. 13, 1968
- So now "swinging"—or sharing sexual partners—is the new topic for discussion in "smart circles." — *Screw*, p. 19, 10th November 1969
- "I swung with him and he was a very good lover. I had a marvelous time." — Frank Robinson, *Sex American Style*, p. 31, 1971
- You know, l'amour?! I'm talkin' me'n Dot are Swingers! As in "to Swing"! Wife- swappin'! What they call nowadays Open Marriage! — *Raising Arizona*, 1987

2 to have fun, especially in a currently fashionable or unconventional activity; hence, to be fashionable *US, 1957*

- That's the craziest name in town! It swings! — *Rebel Without a Cause*, 1955
- England swings like a pendulum do. — Roger Miller, *England Swings*, 1965

3 to play jazz with feeling and a basic understanding of the medium *US, 1933*

- When we talked about a musician who played hot, we would say he could swing or he couldn't swing, meaning what kind of effect did he have on the band. — Mezz Mezzrow, *Really the Blues*, p. 142, 1946

4 to cheat or swindle someone *US, 1952*

- "I got swung, too," Chico answered, ignoring the question. "Yeah, how come?" "Icepick said he knew a guy and I gave him the money to give to him and he blew." — Hal Ellson, *The Golden Spike*, p. 44, 1952

5 to steal something *US, 1980*
Casino usage.

- — Lee Solkey, *Dummy Up and Deal*, p. 121, 1980

swinger *noun*

1 a person who freely enjoys life's pleasures *US, 1959*

- "A swinger?" "Well, it's a word a lot of people use different ways. But in the bunch I run around with it means a gal who finds her fun in sex." — John O'Day, *Confessions of a Hollywood Callgirl*, p. 91, 1964
- He [President Nixon] has said he's not what we would call a swinger, but he knows how to have a good time. — *Playboy*, p. 60, February 1969

2 a person who engages in spouse or partner swapping *US, 1964*

- Most large-group members call themselves "swingers" and are amused by the unhesitating use of the word by the uninitiated to describe someone of quite a different character[.] — William and Jerrye Breedlove, *Swap Clubs*, p. 36, 1964

- It was the same nucleus of "swingers" however, who remained at the New Year's party long after midnight. — Roger Blake, *Love Clubs, Inc.*, p. 15, 1967
- The term swinger refers to an individual, married or single, who socializes with like-minded persons under circumstances that include a variety of sexual activities. — Bernhardt J. Hurwood, *The Sensuous New York*, p. 136, 1973
- It is a vignette picture, and stories are framed by a simple plot involving the staff of a swinger's magazine. — Kent Smith et al., *Adult Movies*, p. 127, 1982

3 a person who has died by hanging *US, 1986–1987*
- — *Maledicta*, p. 180, Summer/Winter 1986–1987

swinging *noun*
consensual swapping of sexual partners as a deliberate activity *UK, 1971*
- Although the word swinging, in its specifically sexual connotation, is too new for inclusion in the dictionary, the activities it describes—indiscriminate, ultracasual copulation with relative or complete strangers in groups of two, three, four and up—are as old as the two sexes. — Frank Robinson, *Sex American Style*, pp. 29–30, 1971

swinging dick *noun*
an ordinary fellow *US, 1957*
Sometimes euphemized (barely) as "swinging Richard."
- I know you have, ain't a swingin' dick in the country escaped it. — James Blake, *The Joint*, p. 165, 7th February 1957
- There ain't a swinging dick in the camp that could do me harm and you know it. — Malcolm Braly, *On the Yard*, p. 75, 1967
- I told her to tell her folks not to let any swinging dick know. — A.S. Jackson, *Gentleman Pimp*, p. 56, 1973
- And that quick every swinging dick in the village comes lickity-split with their guns and pitchforks and scythes and such, coming flat out up that hill. — Larry Heinemann, *Close Quarters*, p. 152, 1977

swinging partner *noun*
a close friend *US, 1994*
- It was the first time that I realized I loved my swinging partners. — Nathan McCall, *Makes Me Wanna Holler*, p. 75, 1994

swingle *noun*
an unmarried person in search of a sexual partner *US, 1968*
- In some quarters, they are called—or like to call themselves—the "swingles." — Joe David Brown, *Sex in the '60s*, p. 27, 1968

swing oil *noun*
to a golfer, beer or alcohol *US, 2000*
- — Hubert Pedroli and Mary Tiegreen, *Let the Big Dog Eat!*, p. 83, 2000

swing-out *noun*
a fight between youth gangs *US, 1972*
- — David Claerbaut, *Black Jargon in White America*, p. 82, 1972
- First into the street was always me, loved a swingout — Edwin Torres, *Carlito's Way*, 1975

swing out *verb*
to take part in a youth gang fight or a group punishment of a transgressing member *US, 1962*
- "Anyone who don't swing out is gonna get it when we come back." — Lewis Yablonsky, *The Violent Gang*, p. 42, 1962

swing shift *noun*
a work schedule that begins late in the afternoon and continues into the middle of the night, traditionally from 4 pm until midnight *US, 1943*
- "What about your folks?" "They're on the swing shift this month." — Irving Shulman, *The Amboy Dukes*, p. 31, 1947

Swing Street *nickname*
an area in downtown Philadelphia known for prostitution *US, 1971*
- The only current reminder of Philadelphia's earlier fame as a prostitution center is Locust Street from 11th to 17th Streets ("Swing Street"). — Charles Winick, *The Lively Commerce*, p. 207, 1971

swipe *noun*
1 the penis *US, 1969*
- They got a double saw [$20] in one hand and their swipes in the other. — Iceberg Slim (Robert Beck), *Pimp*, p. 131, 1969
- "I told her if she wanted to see my swipe [penis] she would have to prove herself and show she was a real hustler." — Charles Winick, *The Lively Commerce*, p. 119, 1971

- But old Franky only laughed, 'cause he was coming at last / And his swipe swole twice its size. — Dennis Wepman et al., *The Life*, p. 111, 1976

2 potent, homemade pineapple-based alcohol *US, 1982*
Hawaiian usage.
- — Douglas Simonson, *Pidgin to da Max Hana Hou*, 1982

swipe *verb*
to steal something *US, 1889*
- His wife had swiped his dough, and gone off with another man[.] — Charles Raven, *Underworld Nights*, pp. 29–30, 1956

swipes *noun*
in horseracing, a groom *US, 1947*
- — Dan Parker, *The ABC of Horse Racing*, p. 149, 1947

swirling *noun*
attending multiple colleges in search of a degree *US, 2006*
- Officials call it swirling, mix and match, grab and go. Today's students attend two colleges, three colleges, even four. — *New York Times*, p. A1, 22nd April 2006

swish *noun*
a homosexual male, especially of the dramatically effeminate type *US, 1941*
- And now, it seems, they are all here: the handsome masculine ones desired alike by men and women; the gushing swishes, hands aflutter like wings[.] — John Rechy, *City of Night*, p. 221, 1963
- If I put a couple of normal boys in the line the swishes would tear them to pieces in no time. — Antony James, *America's Homosexual Underground*, p. 123, 1965
- They made a big point of acting masculine, and they never took in any swishes. — Phil Andros, *Stud*, p. 39, 1966
- These were the flaming swishes of his prison days; "Bernice" and "Joan." — Odie Hawkins, *Midnight*, p. 159, 1995

swish *verb*
(of a homosexual male) to behave in a flamboyant, camp, or effeminate manner *US, 1960*
- I have always made fun of the swishing, screaming, flaunting queens and you have always laughed with me. — *Mattachine Review*, p. 24, March 1960
- The queens swished by in superficial gayety—giggling males acting like teenage girls[.] — John Rechy, *City of Night*, p. 35, 1963
- Fuck what the guy from Tracy said, that kid came on the big yard swishing like she had a license to run wild[.] — Malcolm Braly, *On the Yard*, p. 217, 1967

swish; swishy *adjective*
blatantly homosexual *US, 1941*
- — Florida Legislative Investigation Committee (Johns Committee), *Homosexuality and Citizenship in Florida*, 1964: "Glossary of homosexual terms and deviate acts"
- Horace was a faggot, an out-and-out flaming faggot. He didn't swish, but he was sort of like an old auntie. — Lenny Bruce, *How to Talk Dirty and Influence People*, p. 34, 1965
- Walking up and down the halls were perhaps a dozen other guys—some rather handsome, some miserable, but mostly just ordinary guys. None of them seemed swishy. — *The Advocate*, p. 5, March 1969
- The story involves only four characters: two lovers, their "swishy" neighbor, and an old "straight" friend who is a boyhood buddy of one of the lovers. — *Screw*, p. 20, 27th October 1969

swish Alps *noun*
the Hollywood Hills *US, 1983*
A homosexual enclave.
- As it happens, he does live in a gay section of Los Angeles sometimes called the "Swish Alps." — *People*, p. 117, 7th March 1983
- His collection went to his adopted "son," a likable interior decorator, who sold many of the paintings to support a lavish lifestyle in the "Swish Alps" section of Los Angeles. — *Washington Post*, 19th December 1999
- We lived in West Hollywood. My dad called it the "Swish Alps." — James Ellroy, *Destination Morgue*, p. 30, 2004

swish faggot *noun*
an effeminate, melodramatic homosexual man *US, 1980*
- — *Maledicta*, p. 225, Winter 1980: "'Lovely, blooming, fresh and gay': the onomastics of camp"

swish tank *noun*
a holding cell in a jail where homosexual suspects and prisoners are kept *US, 1992*

- Down the catwalk, turn the corner: the swish tank facing the drunk tank. — James Ellroy, *White Jazz*, p. 107, 1992

swishy *noun*

an effeminate homosexual *US, 1958*

- Lucien by the way approves of you altogether, says I'm nuts and says all women afraid of manly queers who put shoulders to wheel but ain't afraid of swishies. — Jack Kerouac, *Jack Kerouac Selected Letters 1957–1969*, p. 164, 24th(?) July 1958: Letter to Allen Ginsberg

switch *noun*

1 a person willing to play any role in a sadomasochistic sexual encounter *US, 2001*

- You can be a spanking top, a bondage bottom, and a sensory-deprivation switch. — Tristan Taormino, *Pucker Up*, p. 200, 2001

2 a switchblade knife that opens with a button-operated spring *US, 1949*

- I was afraid. I was ready to pull out my switch. — Hal Ellson, *Duke*, p. 110, 1949

3 in a sexually oriented massage parlor, a massage given to the masseuse by the customer *US, 1982*

- — Ralph de Sola, *Crime Dictionary*, p. 146, 1982

4 the buttocks *US, 1949*

- Got nice legs, and a nice switch. — Hal Ellson, *Duke*, p. 73, 1949

switch *verb*

to act upon bisexual impulses *US, 1970*

- Glossary of terms used in the underground press — Robert J. Glessing, *The Underground Press in America*, p. 177, 1970

switchable *noun*

a person who is willing to play either the sadist or masochist role in a sadomasochism encounter *US, 1979*

- — *What Color is Your Handkerchief*, p. 5, 1979

switchblade *noun*

a crew member on the F-111A Aardvark *US, 1990*

- "Pilots, gentle navs, fighter pilots all / Switchblades, gentle Switchblades" / And all the pilots shouted "Balls!" — Joseph Tuso, *Singing the Vietnam Blues*, p. 97, 1990: Hallelujah IV

switchboard jockey *noun*

a telephone operator *US, 1957*

- — *American Speech*, pp. 158–159, May 1960: "The burgeoning of 'jockey'"

switcher *noun*

a bisexual *US, 1966*

- [S]ometimes they're switchers: married men whose wives held out on them the night before. They decide to play the other side of the street before going to the office. — Johnny Shearer, *The Male Hustler*, p. 149, 1966

switcheroo *noun*

a swapping; an exchange *US, 1933*

- In other words, it's a switcheroo, with the mind playing the sucker. — Max Shulman, *Guided Tour of Campus Humor*, p. 89, 1955
- But that Latah get up in feud state and put on his Santa Claus suit and make with the switcheroo. — William Burroughs, *Naked Lunch*, p. 80, 1957
- His strategy was to slip it in while fingering her, taking advantage of the darkness to pull the old switcheroo. — Richard Price, *The Wanderers*, p. 40, 1974
- "Once we got to court, she was going to pull a switcheroo and dump all over my client." — Jonathan Kellerman, *Rage*, p. 245, 2005

switchfoot *noun*

a surfer who can surf with either foot forward, depending on the conditions *US, 1964*

- — John Severson, *Modern Surfing Around the World*, p. 183, 1964

switch hitter *noun*

1 a bisexual *US, 1960*

- There was a dramatic actress, very famous, who was really a switch-hitter; in other words, bi-sexual. — John O'Day, *Confessions of a Male Prostitute*, p. 111, 1964
- Because, actually I was a switch hitter. — Joey V., *Portrait of Joey*, p. 153, 1969
- "Bread? Osca, you want bread?" Maria, the Jewish switchhitter screamed in Billie Holiday tones. — Oscar Zeta Acosta, *The Autobiography of a Brown Buffalo*, p. 44, 1972

- "Elliot's homosexual." Elaine said, "Oh, really?" with a pleasant enough tone, putting herself in the scene now, no longer just watching. "He's a switch-hitter." — Elmore Leonard, *Be Cool*, p. 269, 1999

2 a person who masturbates with first one hand and then the other *US, 2002*

- — Gary K. Farlow, *Prison-ese*, p. 71, 2002

switch-hitting *adjective*

bisexual *US, 1980*

- "A lot of guys go into the joint straight and come out switch-hitting." — George Higgins, *Kennedy for the Defense*, p. 93, 1980

switchies *noun*

sex involving more than two people *US, 1983*

- Once we did switchies with her and one of the cocktail waitresses from the Blue Peach. — Gerald Petievich, *To Die in Beverly Hills*, p. 137, 1983

swock *verb*

to thrash, to defeat *US, 1967*

- "I say swock 'em now. We've got 'em by the gonads." — Elaine Shepard, *The Doom Pussy*, p. 144, 1967

swole *adjective*

upset; provoked; angry *US, 1998*

- — Ethan Hilderbrant, *Prison Slang*, p. 7, 1998

swoles *noun*

muscles *US, 2004*
From "swollen."

- — Rick Ayers (Editor), *Berkeley High Slang Dictionary*, p. 40, 2004

swoll *adjective*

muscular *US, 1997*

- — Pamela Munro, *U.C.L.A. Slang*, p. 112, 1997
- — Connie Eble (Editor), *UNC-CH Campus Slang*, p. 7, November 2002
- Vance was chunky enough to be called swoll. — Linden Dalecki, *Kid B*, p. 32, 2006

swoller *noun*

a muscular person, a brute *US, 2006*

- I thought he'd get caught by them two swollers. — Linden Dalecki, *Kid B*, p. 108, 2006

swoontime *noun*

the approximate time when young people congregate somewhere to socialize *US, 1953*

- — Lavada Durst, *The Jives of Dr. Hepcat*, p. 13, 1953

S-word *noun*

the word "shit" *US, 1999*

- What did my son say, Principal Victoria? Did he say the S word? — *South Park*, 1999

sword swallower *noun*

a person who performs oral sex on a man *US, 1964*
The working title of the 1970s pornographic classic *Deep Throat* was *Sword Swallower*.

- — Roger Blake, *The American Dictionary of Sexual Terms*, p. 212, 1964

sXe *noun*

used as an identifying word by members of the Straight Edge youth culture *US, 2000*
The "s" and "e" are, obviously, the initials of "Straight Edge," while the "X" represents the rubber stamp marked on the hands of under-age patrons at youth clubs.

- In fact, sXe is probably the only youth subculture that actively denounces the use of alcohol, tobacco, and illegal drugs. — Bill Valentine, *Gangs and Their Tattoos*, p. 71, 2000

syndicate *noun*

a criminal organization *US, 1929*

- But pretty soon I caught up with another syndicate house at 119th and Wood, where I found what I was looking for. — Mezz Mezzrow, *Really the Blues*, p. 24, 1946
- The Syndicate is almost entirely bossed by ex-convicts whose roots are in the lowest and most violent soil[.] — Jack Lait and Lee Mortimer, *New York Confidential*, p. 179, 1948
- The gambling was unorganized—the syndicate boys who tried to move in got the fast heave-ho. — Jim Thompson, *Roughneck*, p. 142, 1954
- One of Leo's duties for the syndicate had been to pay off the cops in his territory[.] — Bernard Wolfe, *The Late Risers*, p. 210, 1954

synergy *noun*
4-bromo-2, 5-dimethoxyphenethylamine, a mild hallucinogen
US, 1995
- — Steven Daly and Nathaniel Wice, *alt.culture*, p. 238, 1995

syph *noun*
syphilis *US, 1914*
- [B]y the time she was fifteen she had been plain lousy with clap and syph, and she had had gonorrheal rheumatism, and one day she had just jumped into the Jackson Park lagoon and polluted the drinking water for the gold fish. — James T. Farrell, *Saturday Night*, p. 30, 1947
- "He died of the syph!" — Irving Shulman, *The Short End of the Stick*, p. 198, 1953
- But I'll come down with the syph from just touching the ticket.
  — Philip Roth, *Portnoy's Complaint*, p. 145, 1969

syrup *noun*
prescription cough syrup, used recreationally *US, 1995*
- — Mark S. Fleisher, *Beggars & Thieves*, p. 291, 1995: "Glossary"

syrup head *noun*
a person who abuses for nonmedicinal purposes non-prescription medication containing dextromethorphan (DXM) *US, 2003*

- Youths' nicknames for DXM: Robo, Skittles, Triple C's, Rojo, Dex, Tussin, Vitamin D. DXM abuse is called "Robotripping" or "Tussing." Users might be called "syrup heads" or "robotards." — *USA Today*, p. 1A, 29th December 2003

syrupped up *adjective*
intoxicated by cough syrup taken for nonmedicinal purposes
US, 1970
- — *Current Slang*, p. 13, Fall 1970

system *noun*
1 the criminal justice system; jail *US, 1995*
- He'd have to be awful dumb. The guy's in and out of the system.
  — Elmore Leonard, *Riding the Rap*, p. 167, 1995
2 an audio system, especially a loud car audio system *US, 1996*
- — *Washington Post*, 14th October 1993
- I got done for nicking a system — Angela Devlin, *Prison Patter*, 1996

SYT *noun*
a youthful, attractive homosexual male; a sweet young thing
US, 1979
- — *Maledicta*, p. 220, 1979: "Kinks and queens: linguistic and cultural aspects of the terminology for gays"

Tt

T *noun*

1 marijuana *US, 1950*

An abbreviated homophone of **TEA**.

- A word about yr. request for t ... no, I have no more now, except some left from the San Remo, some Brooklyn grown[.] — Jack Kerouac, *Letter to Neal Cassady*, p. 231, 6th October 1950
- Let me tell you MAN, SF's so hot every single connection has fled or is busted, NO T anywhere. — Neal Cassady, *Neal Cassady Collected Letters 1944–1967*, p. 265, 8th January 1951: Letter to Jack and Joan Kerouac

2 testosterone *US, 2002*

- I defy dualities of definition even if I don't shoot T. — Lynn Breedlove, *Godspeed*, p. 141, 2002

T9 *verb*

to send a message with a cell phone using the T9 mode *US, 2001*

In the T9 mode, the user presses the key with the desired letter only once. When the user is done typing a word, the cell phone converts it to the most likely word.

- I go back through the message editing it to shorten it is often not too difficult to edit words that you T9ed originally. — Dave English, *alt.telecom.mobile*, 17th December 2001

tab *noun*

1 a tabloid newspaper *US, 1951*

- A tabloid and a full-sized job were there. The tab was opened to a news account of the trial that was one column wide and two inches long. — Mickey Spillane, *One Lonely Night*, p. 16, 1951
- I wouldn't have called it an orgy myself, but that's what the tabs labeled it. — Dev Collans with Stewart Sterling, *I was a House Detective*, p. 52, 1954
- The tabs and the Bible notch big numbers still. — James Ellroy, *Destination Morgue*, p. 179, 2004

2 a bill, especially in a restaurant or bar *US, 1946*

- Then just before the check comes, they get mad and walk out. Leave you with a forty-two dollar tab. — Elmore Leonard, *City Primeval*, p. 27, 1980

3 an enterprise, an activity *US, 1946*

- "Hey, look, baby," I said. "I know you're Capone's old lady—uh, uh, I ain't coming on this tab." — Mezz Mezzrow, *Really the Blues*, p. 24, 1946

▸ **run a tab**

to order drinks without paying for each one, paying instead the entire bill at the end of the session *US, 1995*

- One-fifteen Harry ordered another drink and told the waiter to run a tab. — Elmore Leonard, *Riding the Rap*, p. 43, 1995

tab *verb*

to make a drug into pill form *US, 1967*

- Most chemists don't tab their own acid [LSD]. — Nicholas Von Hoffman, *We Are The People Our Parents Warned Us Against*, p. 35, 1967
- It involved a few hundred thousand dollars' worth of LSD and a machine to tab it. — Vincent Patrick, *Family Business*, p. 225, 1985

tabbed *adjective*

dressed stylishly *US, 1980*

- — Edith A. Folb, *runnin' down some lines*, p. 257, 1980

tabla *noun*

a surfboard *US, 1977*

Spanish, imported to the US from Mexico by American surfers.

- — Gary Fairmont R. Filosa II, *The Surfer's Almanac*, p. 196, 1977

table dance *noun*

in a strip club, a semiprivate sexual performance near or on a customers table *US, 1990*

- Some of the girls there aren't worth a five dollar admission charge, much the less a dance or table dance. — *alt.sex*, 7th December 1990
- Some customers request table dances. The dancer leaves the stage and goes to the customer's table, a tiny round table with spindly legs, littered with glasses. She climbs on the table and moves to the music while removing all her clothing. — Marilyn Suriani Futterman, *Dancing Naked in the Material World*, p. 129, 1992
- Unlike the other strippers, Erin refused to do table dances. — Carl Hiaasen, *Strip Tease*, p. 8, 1993
- "Catch that pretty lady for a table dance!" — Heidi Mattson, *Ivy League Stripper*, p. 163, 1995

table-dance *verb*

in a strip club, to conduct a semiprivate sexual performance near or on a customers table *US, 1994*

- "Usually ones, but off-stage they table-dance for ten dollars, plus tips, per song." — Heidi Mattson, *Ivy League Stripper*, p. 95, 1995

table grade *adjective*

used of a woman, sexually appealing *US, 1972*

A clear suggestion of oral sex, or eating.

- — Helen Dahlskog (Editor), *A Dictionary of Contemporary and Colloquial Usage*, p. 58, 1972

table-hop *verb*

to move from table to table socializing in a restaurant or club *US, 1966*

- "Dad, you shouldn't table-hop here," Allen said quietly. — Jacqueline Susann, *Valley of the Dolls*, p. 62, 1966

table-hopper; table-topper *noun*

a necrophile *US, 1986–1987*

- — *Maledicta*, p. 178, Summer/Winter 1986–1987: "Sexual slang: prostitutes, pedophiles, flagellators, transvestites, and necrophiles"

table manners *noun*

in poker, a player's mannerisms, which may provide clues as to the relative strength of his hand *US, 1981*

- — Thomas L. Clark, *The Dictionary of Gambling and Gaming*, p. 226, 1987

table muscle *noun*

the stomach *US, 1984*

- Monroe likes to brag about how strong he is, but it looks to me like that table muscle's the one gets the most workin' out. — Ken Weaver, *Texas Crude*, p. 130, 1984

table pussy *noun*

a woman with good looks and manners *US, 1970*

- A stew can come under the heading of class stuff, or table pussy[.] — Jim Bouton, *Ball Four*, p. 204, 1970

table talk *noun*

in poker, idle chatter that does not rise to the level of intentionally distracting talk *US, 1979*

- — John Scarne, *Scarne's Guide to Modern Poker*, p. 292, 1979

table time *noun*

a time-based charge for playing pool *US, 1993*

- — Mike Shamos, *The Illustrated Encyclopedia of Billiards*, p. 241, 1993

tab out *verb*

to pay a bar bill and leave the bar *US, 1992*

- Would you remember what was going on in the movie when the guy tabbed out for the night? — Richard Price, *Clockers*, p. 377, 1992

tabs *noun*

the ears *US, 1970*

- — Clarence Major, *Dictionary of Afro-American Slang*, p. 113, 1970

tacit *noun*

▸ **take a tacit**

to stop talking *US, 1947*

- This is your professor of thermodynamics taking a tacit for 24. — *Time Magazine*, p. 92, 20th January 1947

tack *noun*

a tattoo *US, 1992*

- — William K. Bentley and James M. Corbett, *Prison Slang*, p. 85, 1992

tacked *adjective*
drunk or drug-intoxicated *US, 2004*
- — Rick Ayers (Editor), *Berkeley High Slang Dictionary*, p. 40, 2004

tacked back *adjective*
covered with tattoos *US, 1989*
- — James Harris, *A Convict's Dictionary*, p. 40, 1989

tac man *noun*
a member of a police tactical patrol *US, 1969*
- The "tac" men explained me to that the white youngster had been lured into the Panhandle, a block-long extension of Golden Gate Park, under the impression that the two Negroes would sell him some marijuana. — L.H. Whittemore, *Cop!*, p. 255, 1969

taco *adjective*
Mexican *US, 1990*
Offensive.
- By the time she was twenty-six, she was scaly legging the taco trade; rented a trailer next to the wetback camp[.] — Seth Morgan, *Homeboy*, p. 50, 1990

taco bender *noun*
a Mexican or Mexican-American *US, 1992*
Offensive.
- Feature Dudley's going to film all those taco benders fucking and sell the movies to geeks like himself who dig all that voyeuristic horseshit. — James Ellroy, *White Jazz*, p. 305, 1992

Taco Hell *nickname*
a Taco Bell™ fast-food restaurant *US, 1989*
- One, I was zooming on 3 grams of some very paltable shrooms (although we had to buy some Taco Hell burritos in which to stuff them, lacking any soup-making apparatus). — *alt.drugs*, 7th July 1989
- Mingus was tending counter at Taco Hell. — Will Shetterly, *Nevernever*, p. 166, 1995

tacoland *noun*
a Mexican or Mexican-American neighborhood *US, 1981*
Offensive.
- It's 1983 Vendome. That's in Silverlake. Tacoland. — James Ellroy, *Brown's Requiem*, p. 81, 1981

tag *noun*
1 a nickname, or popular designation *US, 1950*
- The tag's my own. What do they call you besides Red? — Mickey Spillane, *My Gun is Quick*, p. 8, 1950
2 a stylized signature often confused with graffiti *US, 1982*
- Tags are the names written all over the insides of most New York subway cars. — Craig Castleman, *Getting Up*, p. 26, 1982
- I run the new tunnel, which is longer than I expect, and clean. There are no tags in it yet. — William Upski Wimsatt, *Bomb the Suburbs*, p. 5, 1994
- [N]iggas used to call me "Rza Rza Rakeem" because I wrote "Razor" as a graffiti tag. — RZA, *The Wu-Tang Manual*, p. 4, 2005
3 a police ticket or citation *US, 1985*
- There was a fire hydrant in front of the place and people used to park there while they ran in for coffee and we didn't hang tags on them for that. — Mark Baker, *Cops*, p. 307, 1985
4 a planned murder *US, 1982*
- That was how to set up a tag, he thought. — Richard Condon, *Prizzi's Honor*, p. 34, 1982
5 in the television and movie industries, a very short final scene *US, 1990*
- — Ralph S. Singleton, *Filmmaker's Dictionary*, p. 168, 1990

tag *verb*
1 to catch or arrest someone; to convict someone of a crime *US, 1951*
- "And I'm tagged." "That's right," Pat nodded. "You're tagged." — Mickey Spillane, *The Big Kill*, p. 112, 1951
- I had driven cars for twelve years, in all but four states of the nation, and had been tagged for only two running violations[.] — Hunter S. Thompson, *Hell's Angels*, p. 39, 1966
- Everybody got tagged on every count. Thirty days for investigation and sentence. — Edwin Torres, *Carlito's Way*, p. 140, 1975
2 to spray-paint or write graffiti in a signature styling *US, 1980*
- Graffiti in New York had first appeared on neighborhood walls when kids began tagging up their street names. — Henry Chalfant, *Spraycan Art*, p. 8, 1987

- It's hard to tag around here. — William Upski Wimsatt, *Bomb the Suburbs*, p. 44, 1994
- I tagged up anything I could find. We used to always tag the railroad trestle. — S. Beth Atkin, *Voices from the Street*, p. 9, 1996
- One funny by-product of the poorly funded school system was that youths would tag all over textbooks and the books would be handed down to the next class. — Stephen Power, *The Art of Getting Over*, p. 14, 1999
3 to have sex, especially as a conquest *US, 2000*
- "Any of you niggers ever tag a white bitch?" — Paul Beatty, *Tuff*, p. 156, 2000
4 to shoot and hit someone or something *US, 1992*
- Tagged a couple of cops. Did you kill anybody? — *Reservoir Dogs*, 1992
5 to strike or hit someone or something *US, 1969*
- "Anybody can get tagged the first round." — Leonard Gardner, *Fat City*, p. 47, 1969
- I didn't really know the science of the game, but I was heavy-handed, with a lot of snap in my shoulder, so when I tagged a stud, he was hurtin'. — Edwin Torres, *Carlito's Way*, p. 11, 1975
- Huey had tagged the cop again[.] — Bobby Seale, *A Lonely Rage*, p. 190, 1978
6 to bestow a nickname on someone *US, 1966*
- The fly chicks tagged "Lenore." — William "Lord" Buckley, *The Raven*, 1960
- The guy who hardly ever opens his mouth is usually tagged Gabby. — Robert Edmond Alter, *Carny Kill*, p. 6, 1966
7 to identify someone or something *US, 1951*
- "Body still unidentified and we're tracking down his dental work. No prints on file." "Think you'll tag him?" — Mickey Spillane, *One Lonely Night*, p. 65, 1951
- He got tagged smuggling a truckload of bootleg cigarettes[.] — Janet Evanovich, *Seven Up*, p. 3, 2001

tag-along *noun*
someone who joins an activity without invitation *US, 1961*
- Smart—one righteous vato, one tagalong. — James Ellroy, *Suicide Hill*, p. 619, 1986

tag and bag *verb*
to put a name tag on a corpse and place the body in a body bag *US, 1981*
Vietnam war usage.
- The bodies—five from the courtyard, one from behind the counter in the lobby, and one from the stairs—had been tagged and bagged and placed in a row. — Timothy Findley, *Famous Last Words*, p. 56, 1981
- Just like that, they were gone. They were tagged and bagged. — Daryl Paulson, *Walking the Point*, p. 19, 2005

tagger *noun*
a person who writes his signature in a stylized fashion on public walls, subways, etc. *US, 1997*
- Taggers who simply tag are not graffiti artists. — Jim Crotty, *How to Talk American*, p. 143, 1997
- Annie showed more interest in "taggers"—bands of teenage graffiti artists with no loyalty to turf—than in Lenox-13. — Gini Sikes, *8 Ball Chicks*, p. 38, 1997
- During one ceremony, more than 50 street taggers from the Kings with Style (KWS) were "jumped in." — Bill Valentine, *Gangs and Their Tattoos*, p. 109, 2000

tagging crew *noun*
a group of graffiti artists *US, 1989*
- We were a tagging crew [graffiti artists] and we would do gang banging [fight with other crews other wall turf] and other shit like that. — Terry Williams, *The Cocaine Kids*, p. 60, 1989

tag shop; tag plant *noun*
a prison license plate manufacturing shop *US, 1958*
- 7:30 A.M. Tag Shop men leave Wing for Shop upon call from Center. — Gresham M. Sykes, *The Society of Captives*, p. 138, 1958
- — William K. Bentley and James M. Crobett, *Prison Slang*, p. 13, 1992
- The tag plant [license plate factory] reported missing metal. — Bill Valentine, *Gangs and Their Tattoos*, p. 11, 2000

tag up *verb*
to write your name or initials on a public surface in a stylized, graffiti style *US, 2002*
- Maybe he carried a boom box or occasionally tagged up somewhere, but his main job was just to stay in that b-boy stance. — Earl "DMX" Simmons, *E.A.R.L.*, p. 76, 2002

tail *noun*

1 a person who is following someone else closely and secretly
US, 1914

- If he can get the killer to me you can bet your grandmother's uplift bra that he'll have a tail on me all the way[.] — Mickey Spillane, *I, The Jury*, p. 15, 1947
- Except that would have only worked if the booger could lose the tail they'd have on him. — Elmore Leonard, *Maximum Bob*, p. 312, 1991
- Nicky couldn't even go for a ride without changing cars at least six times before he could shake all his tails. — *Casino*, 1995

2 the term of a prisoner's parole or suspended sentence
US, 1967

- "Six months, five-hundred-dollar fine, three-year tail." — Ken Kesey, *Kesey's Jail Journal*, p. 110, 1967
- "He has a six month tail." This means he has to serve six months on parole. — William K. Bentley and James M. Corbett, *Prison Slang*, p. 101, 1992

3 in prison, an informer *US, 1990*

- — Charles Shafer, *Folk Speech in Texas Prisons*, p. 216, 1990

▶ **bust your tail**
to give the maximum effort *US, 1996*

- After busting his tail to get out here he wouldn't mind relaxing for a few minutes. — Elmore Leonard, *Out of Sight*, p. 23, 1996

▶ **pull a tail**
to serve out a prison sentence on parole *US, 2006*

- "I'm still pullin' a tail." — Stephen J. Cannell, *White Sister*, p. 189, 2006

tail *verb*
to follow someone closely and secretly *US, 1907*

- Pat knows you're too smart not to recognize when you're being tailed. — Mickey Spillane, *I, The Jury*, p. 15, 1947
- You didn't think the guy'd be smart enough to know he was being tailed. — *48 Hours*, 1982
- Look to see if he was being tailed, of course. — Elmore Leonard, *Maximum Bob*, p. 303, 1991

tail-end Charlie *noun*
the soldier at the rear of an infantry patrol *US, 1989*

- I was tail-end Charlie, drag man. Watchin' 'em go down this trail. — Harry Maurer, *Strange Ground*, p. 155, 1989

tail-ender *noun*
the race horse finishing last in a race *US, 1957*

- Father's gift for picking tail-enders brought about the birth of a gag which has been kicked around for more than half a century. — Helen Giblo, *Footlights, Fistfights and Femmes*, p. 15, 1957

tail gunner *noun*
the rear-most soldier on an infantry patrol *US, 1992*

- A good tail gunner can sterilize your trail so no one knows you were ever there. — Larry Chambers, *Recondo*, p. 151, 1992

tailor *noun*

1 in gin, a win without the opponent scoring *US, 1950*

- — Thomas L. Clark, *The Dictionary of Gambling and Gaming*, p. 226, 1987

2 a factory-made cigarette *US, 2002*
An abbreviation of **TAILOR-MADE**.

- "Wanna tailor, O.G.?" — Jimmy Lerner, *You Got Nothing Coming*, p. 144, 2002

tailor-made; tailor; taylor *noun*
a factory-made cigarette *US, 1924*

- — Lou Shelly, *Hepcats Jive Dictionary*, p. 19, 1945
- He picked up his Bull Durham sack from the dresser. He never smoked tailor-mades. — Willard Motley, *Let No Man Write My Epitaph*, p. 108, 1958
- Catching up either end of the cigarette paper, she rolled it into a slender cartridge, caught the ends with her tongue, licked the glued strip, and with deft movements of her fingers secured the tube—side, front, and back—crimping it expertly. "There!" she cried in a pleased little girl's voice. "Almost as good as a tailormade, hey?" — Ross Russell, *The Sound*, p. 20, 1961
- You let your tailormade hang cool between tight lips, unlit, and when you talk, your voice is soft and deep. — Piri Thomas, *Down These Mean Streets*, p. 59, 1967
- "What are these?" he yells at the top of his lungs after a con gave him five tailor mades. — Paul Glover, *Words from the House of the Dead*, 1974

taint *noun*
the perineum *US, 1955*

- 'Tain't pussy, and 'tain't ass. — Ken Weaver, *Texas Crude*, p. 77, 1984

- Extra tip: Push on his t'aint while he's cumming. — Suroosh Alvi et al., *The Vice Guide*, p. 31, 2002

take *noun*
stolen property, especially money *US, 1888*

- [H]e was arrested soon after along with his father, Thomas Conway, and his uncle for three armed robberies. Their take was less than $1,400. — Pete Earley, *The Hot House*, p. 145, 1993

▶ **on the take**
accepting bribes *US, 1930*

- I knew you were on the fucking take the minute you walked in. You still are. — Elmore Leonard, *Glitz*, p. 291, 1985

take *verb*

▶ **take it in the shorts**
to be abused or defeated *US, 1994*

- — Michael Dalton Johnson, *Talking Trash with Redd Foxx*, p. 122, 1994

▶ **take one for the team**
to accept responsibility for an unpleasant task for the greater good of a group *US, 2001*
Originally a baseball term, used as an ex post facto explanation of a batter advancing to first base after being hit with a pitch.

- — Pamela Munro, *U.C.L.A. Slang*, p. 119, 2001

▶ **take someone for a ride**
to swindle or deceive someone *US, 1925*

- "Old Sid was just beggin' to be taken for a ride." — Wade Hunter, *The Sex Peddler*, p. 97, 1963

take a little, leave a little
used as a description of the standing orders that carnival workers have for cheating customers *US, 1985*

- — Gene Sorrows, *All About Carnivals*, p. 23, 1985: "Terminology"

take a train!
used as an all-purpose insult *US, 1951*

- You don't tell somebody to drop dead twice anymore—you kill 'em with "Take a train." — *Philadelphia Evening Bulletin*, 11th November 1951

takedown *noun*
the amount earned *US, 1990*

- — Steve Rushin, *Pool Cool*, p. 29, 1990

take down *verb*
to arrest and convict someone *US, 1997*

- He says he's gonna take him down if it's the last thing he does. — *Jackie Brown*, 1997
- The soldiers from the Empire broke his ribs and crushed his hands when they took him down[.] — Suroosh Alvi et al., *The Vice Guide*, p. 175, 2002

take-down brights *noun*
the very bright lights on a police car used when ordering a driver to pull over *US, 1992*

- Buddha Hast pulled alongside a car wash and the cruiser stopped twenty feet behind them, turning on its take-down brights and training a spotlight in the Volvo's rearview mirror[.] — Richard Price, *Clockers*, p. 395, 1992

take-homes *noun*
a several-day supply of methadone *US, 1989*

- Usually clients must come in every day for their dose; if they do not show evidence of illicit drug use for a certain period of time, between 6 months and a year depending on the program, they are eligible for take-homes. — Geoffrey Froner, *Digging for Diamonds*, p. 60, 1989

take it easy, greasy
used in parting *US, 1967*

- "Take it easy, greasy, you got a long way to slide." — John Williams, *The Man Who Cried I Am*, p. 42, 1967

take money *noun*
the proceeds of a robbery or other illegal scheme *US, 1975*

- Johnny could see the gun in one of the man's hands, and he could see the other one stashing the take money into a velvet pouch. — Donald Goines, *Inner City Hoodlum*, p. 102, 1975

take-off *noun*

1 a robbery *US, 1975*

- Automatically such a person becomes a target for a "take-off." — John Sepe, *Cop Team*, p. 78, 1975

2 in a gambling operation, the amount of the bet money taken by the house *US, 1950*
- — *The Annals of the American Academy of Political and Social Sciences*, p. 132, May 1950

3 in surfing, the catching of a wave and start of a ride *US, 1970*
- — Jim Allen, *Locked in Surfing for Life*, p. 196, 1970

take off *verb*

1 to use a drug, especially to inject a drug *US, 1952*
- Peewee had cooked the stuff and was ready to take off. — Hal Ellson, *The Golden Spike*, p. 20, 1952
- They take off. They get high. — Willard Motley, *Let No Man Write My Epitaph*, p. 117, 1958
- So Pig told the other guy to give me some. Now this next old guy he took off again, and he told me, "I'll give you some now." And he fixed it up. — Henry Williamson, *Hustler!*, p. 68, 1965
- Jim was the only guy I knew that had a shooting gallery where you could cop a speedball by buying a half cap of girl and a half cap of boy and take it off right there. — A.S. Jackson, *Gentleman Pimp*, p. 98, 1973

2 to rob a place; to steal something *US, 1960*
- I don't want nobody trailin' me to my stash so's they can take it off. — Clarence Cooper Jr., *The Scene*, p. 104, 1960
- He supported his habit by taking off (robbing) connections, and almost anyone else in the junkie world who appeared to have money. — James Mills, *The Panic in Needle Park*, p. 35, 1966
- — Eugene Landy, *The Underground Dictionary*, p. 181, 1971
- So the other kids would see them doing hard time and quit taking off the grocery stores and the old peoples' social security money so they could buy those Bosalinis and support their scag jones. — Elmore Leonard, *Switch*, p. 100, 1978
- I'd been taken off a couple of times, but there'd been no beef. — Herbert Huncke, *Guilty of Everything*, p. 2, 1990

3 to bring someone to orgasm *US, 1975*
- Are you telling me she says she took him off five times? — Jimmy Snyder, *Jimmy the Greek*, p. 212, 1975

4 in surfing, to catch the momentum of a wave and begin a ride *US, 1970*
- — Jim Allen, *Locked in Surfing for Life*, p. 196, 1970

▸ **take off a piece of work**
to masturbate *US, 2002*
- — Gary K. Farlow, *Prison-ese*, p. 72, 2002

take on *verb*
to have sex with someone *US, 1972*
- But I have seen them, some guys, have to take on the whole place every time they're in there. — Bruce Jackson, *In the Life*, p. 374, 1972

take-out *noun*
in poker, the minimum number of chips that a player can buy from the bank at once *US, 1967*
- — Albert H. Morehead, *The Complete Guide to Winning Poker*, p. 275, 1967

take out *verb*
to kill someone *US, 1939*
- I took a few guys out and my rep was made. — Edwin Torres, *Carlito's Way*, p. 21, 1975
- A man by the name of Champ who packed a Walther P.38 thought he could handle Clement and Clement took him out. Remember? — Elmore Leonard, *City Primeval*, p. 118, 1980
- Yeah lets take these niggas out. — *Boyz N The Hood*, 1990
- That's the way I look at it. A choice between doin' ten years, and takin' out some stupid motherfucker, ain't no choice at all. — *Reservoir Dogs*, 1992
- I'm taking you out, Yahoo. — *Get Shorty*, 1995

talent *noun*
an intelligent, resourceful criminal *US, 1962*
- — Joseph E. Ragen and Charles Finston, *Inside the World's Toughest Prison*, p. 821, 1962: "Penitentiary and underworld glossary"
- "Who hit him?" "Outta town talent. It was a specialist kind of job." — Richard Condon, *Prizzi's Honor*, p. 20, 1982

▸ **the talent**
in the entertainment industry, the actors, the performers *US, 1991*
- He paid the talent but said he couldn't pay the crew. — Robert Stoller and I.S. Levine, *Coming Attractions*, p. 93, 1991
- [A]s the TV presenter, Wilson chose to remain the talent, "the meat" as Americans call it. — Tony Wilson, *24 Hour Party People*, p. 212, 2002

talk *verb*
to have a sexual relationship in prison *US, 1982*
- — *Maledicta*, p. 136, Summer/Winter 1982: "Dyke diction: The language of lesbians"

▸ **talk game**
to analyze the business of prostitution *US, 1972*
- To talk game is to discuss various aspects of pimping and whoring, such as how to maintain control over a woman, how to get more money out of a trick, how to steer clear of arrests, and so on. — Christina and Richard Milner, *Black Players*, p. 37, 1972

▸ **talk shit**
to disparage someone or something; to exaggerate *US, 1965*
- Sometimes we used to sit on the stoop or up on the roof and talk to Johnny or just listen to him talk shit. — Claude Brown, *Manchild in the Promised Land*, p. 113, 1965
- I used to hang out in the bars just to hear the old men "talking shit." — H. Rap Brown, *Die Nigger Die!*, p. 30, 1969

▸ **talk smack**
to disparage someone or something *US, 1976*
- "Same as usual, walking around with a pitcher fulla drumsticks and taking smack while he's supposed to be working." — Bill Hendersen, *The Pushcart Prize*, p. 218, 1976
- Talkin' that smack, in my house, in front of my employees. Shit! Your ass must be crazy. — *True Romance*, 1993
- Ian Burnham likes to talk smack. It's not that he's a mean guy, but for the first three years of his volleyball career, it was the junior's only way to support his teammates. — *Daily Bruin*, 7th February 2001

▸ **talk stink**
to malign someone or something *US, 1981*
Hawaiian youth usage.
- — Douglas Simonson, *Pidgin to da Max*, 1981

▸ **talk story**
to gossip; to engage in idle conversation *US, 1981*
Hawaiian youth usage.
- Siddown, relax, talk story wit' me. — Douglas Simonson, *Pidgin to da Max*, 1981

▸ **talk to Ralph on the big white phone**
to vomit *US, 1989*
- — Pamela Munro, *U.C.L.A. Slang*, p. 83, 1989

▸ **talk to the seals**
to vomit *US, 1997*
Surfer usage.
- — Vann Wesson, *Generation X Field Guide and Lexicon*, p. 164, 1997

▸ **talk trash**
to engage in aggressive verbal sparring; to speak offensively *US, 1967*
- She started talking trash through her hair. — Piri Thomas, *Down These Mean Streets*, p. 112, 1967
- — Hy Lit, *Hy Lit's Unbelievable Dictionary of Hip Words for Groovy People*, p. 39, 1968
- Talking trash, drinking mash, and snorting cocaine was a thrill, and she was just beginning to complete her education in hipness. — Nathan Heard, *To Reach a Dream*, p. 56, 1972
- They were trying to team play, but kept misreading each other. They talked trash, drank too much, and ended up losing five out of six hands. — Stephen Cannell, *King Con*, p. 1, 1997

▸ **talk turkey**
to speak candidly and openly about an important issue *US, 1903*
- Let's talk turkey here, how 'bout twenty-five thousand? — *Casino*, 1995

talk at *verb*
to talk to someone *US, 1999*
The "at" is a folksy affectation that decreases the formality of the statement.
- Good talking at you, man. — Elmore Leonard, *Be Cool*, p. 109, 1999

talkdown *noun*
the conversational technique used to guide an LSD user who is having a difficult time back to reality *US, 1994*
- — David Shenk and Steve Silberman, *Skeleton Key*, p. 251, 1994

talker *noun*
in the circus or carnival, a person who entices customers into the side show *US, 1960*

- — *American Speech*, pp. 308–309, December 1960: "Carnival talk"
- — Joe McKennon, *Circus Lingo*, p. 93, 1980

talking head *noun*

an expert guest on a television or radio news show *US, 1977*

- Though the hour is largely populated with the infamous "talking heads" that are supposed make documentaries dull, "Michigan" is in fact alarming and gripping. — *Washington Post*, p. B9, 4th October 1977

talking woman *noun*

a female performer who banters with the audience as she strips off her clothes *US, 1950*

- [T]he strippers have finally divided themselves into three classes: "fan-dancers," who keep up the pretense of hiding their nakedness as they enlarge it; "grinders," also known as bumpers and belly dancers, who feature undulations and various wiggles and "talking women," who utter sly, usually dirty observations about themselves and the customers, on animal subjects apropos of their anatomy as it is exposed bit by bit. — Jack Lait and Lee Mortimer, *Chicago Confidential*, p. 158, 1950

talkman *noun*

an electrical torture (enhanced interrogation) device attached to a prisoner's face *US, 1991*
Gulf war usage, punning on the Walkman™ portable music device.

- — *American Speech*, p. 402, Winter 1991: "Among the new words"

talk powder *noun*

any central nervous system stimulant *US, 1988*

- Nine fucking quarters you want for some of that talk powder. — *Drugstore Cowboy*, 1988

talk to the hand; tell it to the hand (because the face isn't listening); speak to the hand

used for expressing a complete lack of interest in what is being said *US, 1995*
Usually followed with "because the face don't give a damn" or something in a similar vein, accompanied by a gesture of a raised hand, palm facing the other person.

- — Connie Eble (Editor), *UNC-CH Campus Slang*, p. 10, April 1995

tall *adjective*

1 used of a jail sentence, lengthy *US, 1992*

- Dave, I've tried to help you out of this, but if you ask for tall time, I'm gonna file a motion to dismiss. — *A Few Good Men*, 1992

2 drug-intoxicated *US, 1946*
A play on HIGH.

- [T]he gauge they picked up on was really in there, and it had them treetop tall, mellow as a cello. — Mezz Mezzrow, *Really the Blues*, p. 75, 1946

tallboy *noun*

a 16-ounce can of beer *US, 1984*

- Joe-boy's crazy. He likes to set three tallboys next to each other, then put two regular cans on top of 'em, and then set one of them little six-ounce cans on top. Calls it a "beeramid." — Ken Weaver, *Texas Crude*, p. 64, 1984

tall grass *noun*

in circus and carnival usage, an extremely remote location *US, 1981*

- — Don Wilmeth, *The Language of American Popular Entertainment*, p. 269, 1981

tallywhacker; tallywacker *noun*

the penis *US, 1966*

- — John Trimble, *5,000 Adult Sex Words*, 1966
- [T]here was her husband, passed out on the bed, with his tallywhacker sticking up in the air. — Huges Rudd, *My Escape from the CIA*, p. 184, 1966
- "Take his mind off his tallywhacker so he don't have to come here no more." — James Lee Burke, *The Lost Get-Back Boogie*, p. 222, 1986
- What's he got—two tallywhackers? — Terry Southern, *Texas Summer*, p. 34, 1991

Tammie *noun*

a capsule of Temazepam™, a branded sleeping pill *US, 1997*

- — Jim Crotty, *How to Talk American*, p. 97, 1997

tamp *verb*

to walk *US, 1953*

- — Lavada Durst, *The Jives of Dr. Hepcat*, p. 3, 1953

Tampa; Tampa pilot *noun*

in shuffleboard, a hidden disk on your side of the court near the apex of the ten *US, 1967*

- — Omero C. Catan, *Secrets of Shuffleboard Strategy*, p. 73, 1967: "Glossary of terms"

tamping *noun*

a beating *US, 1967*

- "He's got you figured for five tampings this last year," Red said. — Malcolm Braly, *On the Yard*, p. 213, 1967

tampon *noun*

a fat marijuana cigarette *US, 1997*

- — Pamela Munro, *U.C.L.A. Slang*, p. 113, 1997

tamp up *verb*

to beat someone physically *US, 1962*

- — Joseph E. Ragen and Charles Finston, *Inside the World's Toughest Prison*, p. 821, 1962: "Penitentiary and underworld glossary"

T and A *noun*

visual depictions of sexually provocative females *US, 1986*
From TITS AND ASS.

- Nestled close to the "swingers" were magazines variously known as "soft porn," and "tits and ass," or simply "T&A." — Jack Weatherford, *Porn Row*, p. 8, 1986
- — Connie Eble (Editor), *UNC-CH Campus Slang*, p. 5, Spring 1993
- "Can you picture a bunch of unrestrained T and A flouncing around, all the girls trying to outdo each other?" — Lora Shaner, *Madam*, p. 193, 1999

T and T *verb*

to tape record and trace the origin of a phone call *US, 2001*

- Shane heard a click, so he knew the rest of the conversation was being T and T'd—taped and traced. — Stephen J. Cannell, *The Tin Collectors*, p. 322, 2001

tang *noun*

the vagina *US, 2002*

- The guy likes to look at her tang, because that's how they are, and so she spreads it and lubes it for them. — Lynn Breedlove, *Godspeed*, p. 9, 2002

tangle *verb*

▸ **tangle ass**
to brawl *US, 1950*

- — Hyman E. Goldin et al., *Dictionary of American Underworld Lingo*, p. 220, 1950
- I tangle-assed with Sabu from 104th Street and Flash from 110th Street, bad motherfuckers in the first degree, and it wasn't even my beef. — Edwin Torres, *Carlito's Way*, p. 13, 1975

▸ **tangle assholes**
to become involved in a confrontation *US, 1974*

- "I'm not going inside and tangle assholes with that monster." — George Higgins, *Cogan's Trade*, p. 50, 1974

tanglefoot *noun*

1 a clumsy, awkward person *US, 1949*

- "What's the matter with that tanglefoot?" "I tripped and—" — Audie Murphy, *To Hell and Back*, p. 269, 1949

2 strong, homemade whiskey *US, 1860*

- Well, I slurped up another sample or two of the tanglefoot while I was about it—then I decided I'd better take some back home for home consumption, in case I felt a cold coming on[.] — Guy Owen, *The Flim-Flam Man and the Apprentice Grifter*, p. 41, 1972

3 barbed wire staked to the ground as a defensive perimeter around a military camp or base *US, 1985*

- The other two walls were bordered by a moat filled with barbed wire "Tanglefoot" and punji stakes[.] — David Donovan, *Once a Warrior King*, p. 40, 1985

tango *verb*

to have sex *US, 1964*

- "You know, I go for dames, but after I seen you two tango, I got the hots for one of you, or even both," the man said, laughing. — K.B. Raul, *Naked to the Night*, p. 65, 1964

tango boat *noun*

an armored landing craft *US, 1971*

- The tango boats moved in a straight line formation down the river. — Ronald J. Glasser, *365 Days*, p. 28, 1971

tango november *noun*

a token black soldier in an otherwise white unit or corps, especially the officer corps *US, 1990*

From the military phonetic alphabet "TN," short for "token nigger."

- The senior NCOs and some of the general officers privately referred to Brooks as Tango November, their token nigger. — John Del Vecchio, *The 13th Valley*, p. 225, 1982

tango yankee
thank you *US, 1971*
From the phonetic alphabet for TY.

- We'll try to get her into you. 10 – 24. Tango Yankee. — Don Oberdorfer, *Tet!*, p. 149, 1971

tank *noun*
1 a jail cell, especially one in a local police station *US, 1912*

- SCENE: Packed jail cell generally called "the Tank" in cop talk. — Abbie Hoffman, *Revolution for the Hell of It*, p. 96, 1968
- Everybody in the tank knew that some one ... we knew what had happened. — Oscar Zeta Acosta, *The Revolt of the Cockroach People*, p. 113, 1973
- — *The (Sydney) Bulletin*, 26th April 1975
- It was Christmas Eve babe / In the drunk tank — The Pogues featuring Kirsty MacColl, *Fairytale of New York*, 1987

2 an old and heavy surfboard *US, 1988*

- — Michael V. Anderson, *The Bad, Rad, Not to Forget Way Cool Beach and Surf Discriptionary*, p. 20, 1988

3 an ugly girl *US, 1966*

- — *Current Slang*, p. 6, Fall 1966

▸ **go in the tank**
used of an athletic contest, lost on purpose *US, 1930*

- So get in there tonight and take a dump, go in the tank. — Rocky Garciano (with Rowland Barber), *Somebody Up There Likes Me*, p. 255, 1955
- [T]he lore of betting in the United States has been rife with tales of tigers who went into the tank. — Jimmy Snyder, *Jimmy the Greek*, p. 77, 1975
- People think that every fight that was ever done was in the tank, that Liston went in the tank for Ali. — Bill Cardoso, *The Maltese Sangweech*, p. b, 1984
- She threw th' fuckin' case, went in the tank, intentionally bricked it. — Stephen J. Cannell, *The Tin Collectors*, p. 156, 2001

▸ **in the tank**
drunk *US, 1975*

- It was a refrain often heard at MacArthur Park choir practice when Spermwhale was almost in the tank, a fifth of bourbon of Scotch in the huge red hand. — Joseph Wambaugh, *The Choirboys*, p. 127, 1975

tank; tank job *noun*
an intentional loss in a competition *US, 1955*
Originally boxing slang.

- To them there is only two kinds of a fight: a tank and a double-cross. — Rocky Garciano (with Rowland Barber), *Somebody Up There Likes Me*, p. 276, 1955
- Some people are saying you're going into the tank. — *Raging Bull*, 1980
- Head-hunter Reuben—near-miss hooks moving back. Lazy Reuben, bored Reuben. A snap guess: tank job. — James Ellroy, *White Jazz*, p. 143, 1992

tank-ass *noun*
buttocks that are disproportionately large *US, 2001*

- — Don R. McCreary (Editor), *Dawg Speak*, 2001

tanked *adjective*
in computing, not operating *US, 1991*

- — Eric S. Raymond, *The New Hacker's Dictionary*, p. 343, 1991

tanked; tanked up *adjective*
drunk *UK, 1893*

- They fought like this every time they got tanked up, he said, which all Hollywood knew was at least four times a week. — Harpo Marx, *Harpo Speaks!*, p. 298, 1985

tanker *noun*
a boxing match or other athletic contest that has been fixed *US, 1955*

- You know—tankers, fixed fights. You see the odds change before ringtime, and you know what's happened. — Rocky Garciano (with Rowland Barber), *Somebody Up There Likes Me*, p. 304, 1955
- There were no setups, no tankers. He met them all and beat most all. — Helen Giblo, *Footlights, Fistfights and Femmes*, p. 168, 1957

tanker's grenade *noun*
explosives wrapped with barbed wire or chain *US, 1986*

- — Ralph Zumbro, *Tank Sergeant*, p. 192, 1986: Glossary

tank time *noun*
time served in a local jail *US, 1967*

- He'd already done eight months tank time when I checked in, so he was brimful of jailhouse lore. — Ken Kesey, *Kesey's Jail Journal*, p. 5, 1967

tank town *noun*
a small, unimportant town *US, 1906*

- What's a fast guy like you doing at a tank-town teacher's college? — Jim Thompson, *Savage Night*, p. 10, 1953
- "You think I, with my extensive big-city newspaper experience, want to do filler copy for a bunch of tank-town sheets?" — William Brinkley, *Don't Go Near the Water*, p. 84, 1956
- In America he played tank towns like Waterbury, Mass, Springfield, Kingston and Albany and New York. — Babs Gonzales, *Movin' On Down De Line*, p. 52, 1975
- Any small community where a train stopped to take on water from an elevated storage tank was known as a tank town. — J. Herbert Lund, *Herb's Hot Box of Railroad Slang*, p. 110, 1975

tank up *verb*
1 to administer fluids to a dehydrated hospital patient *US, 1994*

- — Sally Williams, "*Strong" Words*, p. 162, 1994

2 to consume large quantities of something, especially alcohol *US, 1902*

- Well, Doc had been in the hospital kitchen all morning goosing the nurses and tanking up on coal gas and Klim—and just before the operation he sneaked a double shot of nutmeg to nerve himself up. — William Burroughs, *Naked Lunch*, p. 29, 1957
- She got him tanked up on booze and coke 'til he passed out[.] — John Lescroart, *The 13th Juror*, p. 107, 1995

tan valise *noun*
a blonde prostitute *US, 1960*

- The telegraphic doe is "black bag" for brunettes and "tan valise" for blondes. — Lee Mortimer, *Women Confidential*, p. 141, 1960

tap *noun*
1 a murder *US, 1963*

- That tap was somebody else's. — Mickey Spillane, *Me, Hood!*, p. 16, 1963

2 in circus and carnival usage, the admission price *US, 1981*

- — Don Wilmeth, *The Language of American Popular Entertainment*, p. 269, 1981

▸ **tap a kidney**
to urinate *US, 1975*

- Hayduke lingers behind, pausing to tap a kidney. — Edward Abbey, *The Monkey Wrench Gang*, p. 348, 1975
- Figured out what it was one night when he had to get up and tap a kidney. — Stephen King, *It*, p. 1987, 624

tap *verb*
1 to have sex *US, 1949*

- Nobody ever tapped me. — Hal Ellson, *Duke*, p. 11, 1949
- — Malachi Andrews and Paul T. Owens, *Black Language*, p. 97, 1973
- I hear he's tapping Edie Finneran. — *The Usual Suspects*, 1995
- — Don R. McCreary (Editor), *Dawg Speak*, 2001

2 to kill someone *US, 1963*

- I remember ten years back when you were talking about killing a guy by that name. Did you tap him? — Mickey Spillane, *Me, Hood!*, p. 16, 1963

3 to intercept a telephone communication *UK, 1869*
From an earlier sense of intercepting a telegraphic message.

- Since when had freedom stooped to tap the phones of prostitutes? — Philip Wylie, *Opus 21*, p. 323, 1949

4 in poker, to bet all of your chips, or an amount equal to an opponent's bet, depending on context *US, 1947*

- — Oswald Jacoby, *Oswald Jacoby on Poker*, p. 138, 1947

▸ **tap a kidney**
to urinate *US, 1997*

- Gonna go over t'that stand a'trees over there, and tap a kidney. — Stephen Cannell, *Big Con*, p. 267, 1997

▸ **tap the pot**
in bar dice games, to bet the total amount of the pot *US, 1971*

- — Jester Smith, *Games They Play in San Francisco*, p. 105, 1971

tap city *noun*
when gambling, the position of being out of funds *US, 1976*

- "[W]e were both doing lousy on the Celtics" (he pronounced it sell-ticks) "and also on the Bruins, there, and he said he was also tap city[.]" — George V. Higgins, *The Judgment of Deke Hunter*, p. 217, 1976
- "I'm Tap City, Augie," I said. — James Ellroy, *Brown's Requiem*, p. 192, 1981

tap dancer *noun*
a black person who curries favor from white people with obsequious conduct *US, 1974*
- — Stewart L. Tubbs and Sylvia Moss, *Human Communication*, p. 122, 1974

tapioca *adjective*
▸ **go tapioca**
to go broke *US, 1974*
- Dean didn't care for the old man very much, but we agreed the place might come in handy in case we went tapioca. — Gary Mayer, *Bookie*, p. 39, 1974

tapo *noun*
an inadvertent error in a taped message *US, 1982*
- — *American Speech*, p. 29, Spring 1982: "The language of science fiction fan magazines"

tap-out *noun*
a complete depletion of funds, especially in gambling *US, 1979*
- And worse, he remembered Starkey's penchant to use his pistol to reverse a tap-out. — Iceberg Slim (Robert Beck), *Airtight Willie and Me*, p. 112, 1979

tap out *verb*
1 to run out of money, usually as a result of gambling *US, 1939*
- But if you're tapped out, if you really want that double dime note back? — Ross Russell, *The Sound*, p. 159, 1961
- "It happens that I'm tapped out right now myself." — Wade Hunter, *The Sex Peddler*, p. 96, 1963
- "Five'll get you fifty he's tapped out before the next track season's over," Heath said. — Robert Campbell, *Juice*, p. 313, 1988
- But I was tapped right out. I didn't have a thing. — Herbert Huncke, *Guilty of Everything*, p. 107, 1990

2 in a casino, to relieve a dealer from duty *US, 1961*
- He had been a floorman at Tropicana, but he'd tapped out a dealer for looking away from the cards, and it turned out the dealer had more juice than he did, so listen to this, he got fired for doing his job. — Elmore Leonard, *Glitz*, p. 124, 1985

tapper *noun*
a boy who persists in asking a girl for a date when reason would dictate a strategic retreat *US, 1951*
Teen slang.
- — *Newsweek*, p. 28, 8th October 1951

tappers *noun*
dice that have been loaded with mercury that shifts when the dice are tapped *US, 1962*
- — Frank Garcia, *Marked Cards and Loaded Dice*, p. 264, 1962

tar *noun*
crude, dark, gummy heroin, usually from Mexico *US, 1992*
- The tar, or goma, as the Mexicans called it, looked like brown window putty and smelled like vinegar. — Joseph Wambaugh, *Fugitive Nights*, p. 35, 1992

tar baby *noun*
a black person *US, 1962*
Offensive. From the *Br'er Rabbit* stories by Joel Chandler Harris.
- [H]e winked, just before the door closed, and told the black boys as they backed away form him, "You'll pay for this, you damn tarbabies." — Ken Kesey, *One Flew Over the Cuckoo's Nest*, p. 13, 1962

tar beach *noun*
a flat urban rooftop, used for sleeping or drug use *US, 1970*
- — William D. Alsever, *Glossary for the Establishment and Other Uptight People*, p. 32, December 1970

tarnation *noun*
used as a euphemism for "damnation" *US, 1790*
- "What in tarnation is a folk-drama?" asked Doc. — Max Shulman, *Rally Round the Flag, Boys!*, p. 55, 1957

tart up *verb*
to dress someone up or decorate something smartly *UK, 1952*
Often with the implication of tastelessness or tawdriness.

- [T]hen send him back to Kansas City in time for a Hollywood hack screenwriter to come in and tart up the story. — Clancy Sigal, *Going Away*, p. 206, 1961
- Well, what happens is that she gives me the brutally frank version and I sort of tart it up for them. — *This is Spinal Tap*, 1984
- Even after they tried to steal a page from the film studios and tarted up the dining room ... the quality of the food, if anything, went down instead of up. — Robert Campbell, *Alice in La-La Land*, p. 44, 1987
- The dykes were as tarted up as they could get, with black pants or levis, and white go go boots. — Jennifer Blowdryer, *White Trash Debutante*, p. 52, 1997

Tarzan *noun*
sex outdoors *US, 1966*
- Studs in New York, particularly those working the Public Library and Bryant Park areas, call a frantic quickie in the bushes a "jungle job" or a "Tarzan." — Johnny Shearer, *The Male Hustler*, p. 17, 1966

tassel dance *noun*
a sexual dance focused on the woman's breasts and the tassels worn attached thereto *US, 1977*
- Carrie Finnell, for example, performed the first "Tassel Dance" on a Minsky runway. — William Green, *Strippers and Coochers*, p. 163, 1977
- Several showgirls did a tassel dance with much swinging of breasts. — Paul Schratz, *Submarine Commander*, p. 252, 1988

taste *noun*
1 a small sample *US, 1952*
- Okay, so you're off it, but a little bit won't hurt. Just a taste. — Hal Ellson, *The Golden Spike*, p. 29, 1952
- "If I could just get a taste," Fay said. — Alexander Trocchi, *Cain's Book*, p. 37, 1960
- Did you say sometin' 'bout havin' a taste? — Odie Hawkins, *Ghetto Sketches*, p. 24, 1972
- For Christmas. Your share. It's just a taste. — *Goodfellas*, 1990

2 an alcoholic drink *US, 1919*
- "Well, Marie, you buying me a taste is righteous and perhaps I'll be able to hip you to something else you can buy me." — A.S. Jackson, *Gentleman Pimp*, p. 74, 1973
- After all, they were part of a unique police experiment and a guy needed a taste or two when he'd been stumbling around for hours out there in the black of night[.] — Joseph Wambaugh, *Lines and Shadows*, p. 103, 1984

3 a short while *US, 1975*
- — Report to the Senate, *California Senate Committee on Civil Disorder*, p. 228, 1975

taste-face *noun*
a heroin user who lends his syringe to others in return for small amounts of heroin *US, 1978*
- A taste-face is an addict who loans out his works (syringe, needle) for some of the borrower's H. — Burgess Laughlin, *Job Opportunities in the Black Market*, p. 4, 1978

tastie *noun*
a sexually attractive woman *US, 2006*
- "They got this new ho house open on Argyle Road. Only been there one time, but they go some tasties there, yo." — Jason Starr, *Lights Out*, p. 167, 2006

tat *noun*
1 a tattoo *US, 1993*
- "Hey, who did the tat?" he asked. — Bob Sipchen, *Baby Insane and the Buddha*, p. 194, 1993
- It's a tiered tat. When I get some more cash I'm gonna color it in and put some leather chaps on the Reaper. — *Airheads*, 1994
- Darryl came back at him, saying, "Oh, your people never decorate themselves?" "Some tats, yeah, but black guys have 'em too." — Elmore Leonard, *Be Cool*, p. 44, 1999
- Holstein glanced at Pike's shoulder tats, then his face. — Robert Crais, *L.A. Requiem*, p. 38, 1999

2 a swindle featuring dice and doubled bets *US, 1963*
- The tat, with its rapidly doubling bets, is murder on a fool. — Jim Thompson, *The Grifters*, p. 36, 1963

ta-ta
goodbye *UK, 1823*
Highly affected.
- "God bless," said Father Paddy. "Ta-ta," said Prue. — Armistead Maupin, *Further Tales of the City*, p. 181, 1982

tatas noun
the female breasts US, 1982
- Look at them bodacious set of ta ta's. — *An Officer and a Gentleman*, 1982
- Boobs, zonkers, headlights, watermelons, sweater puppies, pointers, knockers, jugs, tatas—these are some of the words to describe women's breasts. — Howard Stern, *Miss America*, p. 441, 1995
- Great view of her little ta-tas waking up on a stretcher. — Mr. Skin, *Mr. Skin's Skincyclopedia*, p. 22, 2005

tat gun noun
an improvised tattoo needle gun US, 2002
- "Every day we confiscate two or three tat guns off the yard—from deep inside someone's kesiter." — Jimmy Lerner, *You Got Nothing Coming*, p. 52, 2002

tats noun
dice, especially loaded dice or dice marked for cheating UK, 1688
- — John S. Salak, *Dictionary of Gambling*, p. 257, 1963
- We need to get ahold of "Fit-Throwing Duffy." He's the best tat player in the family. — Stephen Cannell, *King Con*, p. 119, 1997

taw noun
money to start a venture US, 1998
A figurative use of a term for the marble a player shoots with in a game of marbles.
- "Now you have an opportunity to win it off." "I got no taw." — John Ridley, *Love is a Racket*, p. 41, 1998

tax verb
to tease or berate someone US, 2001
- — Don R. McCreary (Editor), *Dawg Speak*, 2001

tax; taxing noun
the fee paid to enter a crack house US, 1992
- — Terry Williams, *Crackhouse*, p. 152, 1992

taxi bit noun
a prison sentence of between five and fifteen years US, 1950
- — Hyman E. Goldin et al., *Dictionary of American Underworld Lingo*, p. 220, 1950

taxi dance verb
to work as a taxi dancer US, 1973
- [S]he was back down on Main Street competing with bearer movies between reels, and taxi dancing part-time down the street at the ballroom. — Joseph Wambaugh, *The Blue Knight*, p. 21, 1973

taxi dancer; taxi girl noun
a woman who will dance and talk with bar patrons, but stops short of prostitution; a prostitute US, 1930
- The mobility of the taxi dancer as increased with recent years. — Esther Neumeyer, *Leisure and Recreation*, p. 285, 1949
- She was a taxi dancer, night-club entertainer, friend of boys on the loose and anything else yo can mention where sex is concerned. — Mickey Spillane, *Kiss Me Deadly*, p. 24, 1952
- — Gregory Clark, *Words of the Vietnam War*, p. 504, 1990
- I'm a taxi dancer. I work at the Come-N-Go Retro Lounge. — Beth Goldner, *Wake*, p. 25, 2003

taxpayer noun
a building that generates enough rental income to pay the taxes on it US, 1921
- Leon Quat, oddly enough, had the general look of those fifty-two-year-old men who run a combination law office, real estate, and insurance operation on the second floor of a two-story taxpayer out on Queens Boulevard. — Tom Wolfe, *Radical Chic & Mau-Mauing the Flak Catchers*, p. 17, 1970

TB noun
1 tuberculosis US, 1912
- My kid died from the t-bees in that deathtrap[.] — Ralph Ellison, *Invisible Man*, p. 547, 1947
- I know what a person with t.b. goes through. My old lady had t.b. — Horace McCoy, *Kiss Tomorrow Good-bye*, p. 64, 1948
- On top of everything, he's got T.B. — Mickey Spillane, *Last Cop Out*, p. 10, 1972
2 in circus and carnival usage, a dull town where business is poor US, 1981
An abbreviation of **TOTAL BLANK**.
- — Don Wilmeth, *The Language of American Popular Entertainment*, p. 278, 1981

TBF noun
severe morbidity, usually terminal US, 1988–1989
A "*total body failure.*"
- — *Maledicta*, p. 35, 1988–1989: "Medical maledicta from San Francisco"

T-bird noun
1 Thunderbird™ wine US, 1973
- Tooner Flats is the area of gangs who spend their last dime on short dogs of T-Bird wine[.] — Oscar Zeta Acosta, *The Revolt of the Cockroach People*, p. 90, 1973
- Walter was probably still passed out from last night's bout with T-Bird and TV[.] — James Ellroy, *Brown's Requiem*, p. 20, 1981
2 a T-33 jet trainer aircraft US, 1956
- — *American Speech*, p. 229, October 1956: "More United States Air Force slang"
3 a capsule of amobarbital sodium and secobarbital sodium (trade name Tuinal™), a combination of central nervous system depressants US, 1993
- — Peter Johnson, *Dictionary of Street Alcohol and Drug Terms*, p. 187, 1993

TCB verb
to take care of business US, 1964
- Let's TCB—that means taking care of business. — James Baldwin, *Blues for Mister Charlie*, p. 47, 1964
- [T]here is a growing—a rapidly growing—body of black people determined to "T.C.B."—take care of business. — Stokely Carmichael and Charles V. Hamilton, *Black Power*, pp. 184–185, 1967
- We went home in her Porsche and TCB'ed. — Cecil Brown, *The Life & Loves of Mr. Jiveass Nigger*, p. 149, 1969
- Sapphire has to stand on the corner in the rain to T.C.B. while she watches her white co-worker catch tricks in a plush, warm, dry lobby. — Carolyn Greene, *70 Soul Secrets of Sapphire*, p. 29, 1972

tea noun
1 marijuana US, 1935
- Some guys were so hopped on tea they were rocking on their heels. — Irving Shulman, *The Amboy Dukes*, p. 52, 1947
- But listen, you get Verger and his tea, and I'll see if I can round up Stofsky somewhere. — John Clellon Holmes, *Go*, p. 83, 1952
- You could smell tea, weed, I mean marijuana, floating in the air, together with the chili beans and beer. — Jack Kerouac, *On the Road*, p. 86, 1957
- Once or twice a few had fallen in with pot or tea as it was called then and I picked up for the first time one morning and got so stoned I was unable to move. — Herbert Huncke, *The Evening Sun Turned Crimson*, pp. 28–29, 1980
2 in horseracing, a drug (especially cocaine or strychnine) which will stimulate a horse US, 1951
- — David W. Maurer, *Argot of the Racetrack*, p. 64, 1951

tea-bag verb
in the pursuit of sexual pleasure, to take a man's scrotum completely into the mouth, sucking and tonguing it US, 1998
- I'm gonna finger-fuck her tight little asshole! Finger-bang ... and tea-bag my balls ... in her mouth! — Kevin Smith, *Jay and Silent Bob Strike Back*, p. 50, 2001
- She tea-bags his balls before an A2M. — Editors of Adult Video News, *The AVN Guide to the 500 Greatest Adult Films of All Time*, p. 27, 2005

teabagging noun
the sucking of a man's entire scrotum US, 1998
- In gay circles, this common practice is often referred to as teabagging. This can easily be adapted into your repertoire by having the man straddle above with his testicles dangling over your mouth. — Dan Anderson, *Sex Tips for Straight Women from a Gay Man*, p. 76, 1997
- For all its references to dingleberries and tea-bagging, Pecker has nothing that approaches Mary's mock-castration or Hairdo's money shot. — *The Village Voice*, p. 137, 22nd September 1998
- When a girl is sucking on your balls (teabagging), tap the head of your cock on her forehead and ask, "Who's your daddy?" — Karl Mark, *The Comple A**hole's Guide to Handling Chicks*, p. 269, 2003

teacher noun
a traffic police officer who lectures violators instead of issuing citations US, 1962
- — *American Speech*, p. 272, December 1962: "The language of traffic policemen"

teacup queer noun
an, effeminate homosexual man US, 1957

- [S]uddenly his pet ferret rushed out and bit an elegant teacup queer on the ankle and everybody hightailed it out the door. — Jack Kerouac, *On the Road*, p. 144, 1957

tea dance *noun*
a social gathering featuring same-sex dancing *US, 1965*

- Tea dance. What a helluva name for what it really is. It got its name because the Sunday dances begin at precisely the tea hour. — Joe Houston, *The Gay Flesh*, pp. 8–9, 1965

tea'd up *adjective*
marijuana-intoxicated *US, 1959*

- "Don't cross him," Grave Digger whispered tensely. "He's teaed to the eyes." — Chester Himes, *The Real Cool Killers*, p. 141, 1959
- The General inspected the driver to see if he was gassed, teaed, or liquored. — Sol Yurrick, *The Warriors*, p. 28, 1965
- Flattop the bartender, a football-head spade if there ever was one, tead-up on weed, with a red scarf around his neck, came over to the table to take her order. — Steve Cannon, *Groove, Bang, and Jive Around*, p. 67, 1969

tea girl *noun*
a quasi-prostitute in a Vietnamese bar who cadged US servicemen into buying her drinks, especially of Saigon tea *US, 1966*

- — *Time*, p. 29, 26th May 1966
- — Carl Fleischhauer, *A Glossary of Army Slang*, p. 21, 1968
- A good Saigon tea girl could keep a GI, particularly one not familiar with their wiles, on the ropes for some time. — David Holland, *Vietnam, a Memoir*, p. 81, 2005

tea head *noun*
a user of marijuana *US, 1948*

- [U]nless we could dig up some of the wild, mad Calypso tea-head drummers. — Neal Cassady, *Neal Cassady Collected Letters 1944–1967*, p. 98, 10th August 1948: Letter to Bill Tomson
- Then I start thinking about the mad beret-characters who actually make these movies in crazy California (the tea-head Mitchums)[.] — Jack Kerouac, *Letter to John Clellon Holmes*, p. 197, 24th June 1949
- She knew a lot of teaheads. — William Burroughs, *Junkie*, p. 30, 1953
- And the negroes / And the teaheads / And the Communists. — *The Berkeley Barb*, p. 2, 19th November 1965

tea hound *noun*
a marijuana user *US, 1951*

- The subject of tea-hounds brings us quite naturally to our next chapter, juvenile delinquency, in which stimulants are a large factor. — Jack Lait and Lee Mortimer, *Washington Confidential*, p. 117, 1951

tea joint *noun*
a place where marijuana is smoked or sold *US, 1960*

- Doc had me take him to the Dreamland then, a tea joint with a cigar-store front on South Dearborn. — Nelson Algren, *The Neon Wilderness*, p. 115, 1960

team *adjective*
dressing in a style that identifies you with a particular group *US, 1989*

- — Pamela Munro, *U.C.L.A. Slang*, p. 83, 1989

team cream *noun*
an orgy *US, 1970*

- — *American Speech*, p. 58, Spring–Summer 1970: "Homosexual slang"

team Jesus *noun*
a group of zealous, proselytizing Christian students *US, 2004*

- — Ben Applebaum and Derrick Pittman, *Turd Ferguson & The Sausage Party*, p. 64, 2004

tea pad *noun*
an apartment, house, or room where marijuana is smoked *US, 1938*

- Usually, each tea pad has comfortable furniture, a radio, victrola or, as in most instances, a rented nickelodeon. The light is more or less uniformly dim, with blue predominating. An incense burner is considered part of the furnishings. — *La Guardia Report*, pp. 9–10, 1944
- There are about 500 apartments in Harlem, known as "tea pads," set up exclusively for marijuana addicts. — Jack Lait and Lee Mortimer, *New York Confidential*, p. 103, 1948
- He drove out north to a tea pad where everybody was already hopped up. — Willard Motley, *Let No Man Write My Epitaph*, p. 109, 1958

- Meanwhile Bozo and Andre split up and Bob and I took over Bozo's apartment and turned it into a tea pad and thieves' den. — Herbert Huncke, *The Evening Sun Turned Crimson*, p. 54, 1980

tea party *noun*
a social party where marijuana is smoked *US, 1968*

- What do you bring to a hippie "tea party"? Your own "pot"! — Paul Laikin, *101 Hippie Jokes*, 1968

tear *verb*
1 to leave, especially in a hurry *US, 1951*

- He was looking at his wrist watch. "I have to tear," he said, and stood up. — J.D. Salinger, *Catcher in the Rye*, p. 148, 1951

2 to surf aggressively and with skill *US, 1988*

- — Michael V. Anderson, *The Bad, Rad, Not to Forget Way Cool Beach and Surf Discriptionary*, p. 20, 1988

▸ **tear a passion to tatters**
in a dramatic performance, to over-act *US, 1973*

- — Sherman Louis Sergel, *The Language of Show Biz*, p. 48, 1973

▸ **tear off a chunk**
to have sex *US, 1973*

- Shit, before my Flossie got sick, I used to tear off a chunk every night. — Joseph Wambaugh, *The Blue Knight*, p. 98, 1973

▸ **tear off; tear off a piece**
to have sex *US, 1964*

- If old Virgil felt like tearing off a piece, why, that wasn't nobody's business but old Virgil's, was it? — Max Shulman, *Anyone Got a Match?*, p. 208, 1964
- [W]e quickly tear off several goodies, then, I go back to work. — Neal Cassady, *The First Third*, p. 153, 1971

▸ **tear someone a new asshole**
to thrash someone; to abuse someone verbally *US, 1964*

- "Fierce enough," he proclaimed, "to tear a new asshole in whatever nigger said that!" — Ken Kesey, *Sometimes a Great Notion*, p. 541, 1964
- "You want me to tear you a new asshole?" — Alvah Bessie, *Inquisition in Eden*, p. 114, 1965
- — Carl Fleischhauer, *A Glossary of Army Slang*, p. 21, 1968

▸ **tear up the pea patch**
to overwhelm an opponent or situation *US, 1960*

- "This lineup is tearing up the pea patch." — Jack Newfield, *Somebody's Gotta Tell It*, p. 26, 2002

▸ **tear your pants**
to commit a social gaffe *US, 1947*

- — Marcus Hanna Boulware, *Jive and Slang of Students in Negro Colleges*, 1947

teardrop *noun*
a dose of crack cocaine, packaged in the corner of a plastic bag *US, 1994*

- — US Department of Justice *Street Terms*, October 1994

tearjerker *noun*
a melodramatic or sentimental and sad story or song *US, 1921*

- It's Summertime is what it is. The drunks always call during the tearjerkers. — Armistead Maupin, *Further Tales of the City*, p. 21, 1982
- One day he'd write a rousing Good Samaritan column, then a funny man-on-the-street piece, then a tearjerk about some little kid with cancer[.] — Carl Hiaasen, *Tourist Season*, p. 63, 1986
- [C]omplete the evening by renting a tear-jerker movie. — Marcy Blum, *Weddings for Dummies*, p. 66, 1997
- Anyway, they were going to let him go but his mother wrote a tear-jerker letter that ended up on my desk. — *Something About Mary*, 1998

tea-room; t-room *noun*
a public toilet *US, 1932*
From an era when a great deal of homosexual contact was in public toilets; probably an abbreviation of "toilet room," a term used in reported criminal prosecutions of homosexuals in the late C19. A public toilet in Illinois was the focus of Laud Humphrey's famous sociological study *Tearoom Trade*. The term gained new life in 2006 when Idaho Senator Larry Craig was arrested for engaging in tea-room sex solicitation.

- — Donald Webster Cory and John P. LeRoy, *The Homosexual and His Society*, p. 266, 1963: "A lexicon of homosexual slang"
- "I'm Jenny and this is my tearoom"—indicating the head[.] — John Rechy, *City of Night*, p. 193, 1963

- I suppose there has been such activity since the invention of plumbing. I first started out in one of those pavilion places. But the real fun began during the depression. * * * Suddenly, it just seemed like half the men in town met in the tearooms. — Laud Humphreys, *Tearoom Trade*, pp. 5–6, 1975
- Thinking of joining the ranks? Cruising the tearooms? — Miguel Pinero, *Short Eyes*, p. 18, 1975
- "Like years ago, when guys were getting arrested just for staring at something in a tearoom?" — Ethan Morden, *Some Men Are Lookers*, p. 117, 1997

tea-room cruiser *noun*
a male homosexual prostitute who frequents public toilets *US*, 1982
- — *Maledicta*, p. 139, Summer/Winter 1982: "Dyke diction: the language of lesbians"

tearoom queen *noun*
a homosexual man who frequents public restrooms in search of sex *US*, 1941
- I"am not a tea-room queen. Besides, I am looking for a more lasting relationship. And I don't want no man who looks around toilets." — Larry Kramer, *Faggots*, p. 94, 2000

tea-room trade *noun*
a sexual partner found in a public toilet *US*, 1980
- — *Maledicta*, p. 233, Winter 1980: "Lovely, blooming, fresh and gay": the onomastics of camp"

teaser *noun*
in sports betting, a bet that ties two or more games together *US*, 1975
- The professor was the first to put up teasers, where the bettor could move the line seven points up or down, but he had to make a two-team parlay and lay eleven-to-ten. — Jimmy Snyder, *Jimmy the Greek*, p. 75, 1975
- — Avery Cardoza, *The Basics of Sports Betting*, p. 45, 1991

tea wagon *noun*
in the television and movie industries, the console used by the sound mixer *US*, 1977
- — Tony Miller and Patricia George, *Cut! Print!*, p. 155, 1977

tecate; tecatos *noun*
heroin *US*, 1982
Directly from Mexican Spanish.
- — Ralph de Sola, *Crime Dictionary*, p. 149, 1982
- — US Department of Justice *Street Terms*, October 1994

tech *noun*
1 a technician; someone employed to deal with technological devices, especially in a creative milieu *US*, 1942
Also called a "techie."
- [S]he knew this guy played with the Fugs—well he didn't play, he helped with the equipment and all, a techie. — John Sayles, *Union Dues*, p. 135, 1977
- The place was empty except for a few techies, a few stray producers. — Armistead Maupin, *Maybe the Moon*, p. 290, 1992

2 a nine-millimeter handgun *US*, 1995
- — Maria Hinojas, *Crews*, p. 168, 1995: "Glossary"

technicolor *noun*
ground-to-air anti-aircraft flak *US*, 1967
- "When the radar-controlled searchlights lock on you, when technicolor is exploding all around you, and those red-hot tracer slugs are hosing your ass off—man, you've seen the Doom Pussy." — Elaine Shepard, *The Doom Pussy*, p. 38, 1967

technodweeb *noun*
a person who is passionately interested in technology *US*, 1990
- — Karla Jennings, *The Devouring Fungus*, p. 224, 1990

teddy bear suit *noun*
heavy winter garments issued to US troops during World War 2 and later in Korea *US*, 1982
- — Frank Hailey, *Soldier Talk*, p. 60, 1982

teed off *adjective*
angry *US*, 1950
- I'm teed off. Things like this give me the pip. — Mickey Spillane, *My Gun is Quick*, p. 16, 1950
- No, buddy boy, it's not me you're teed off at; it's somebody else. — Max Shulman, *Anyone Got a Match?*, p. 112, 1964

teen *noun*
one-sixteenth of an ounce of a drug *US*, 2006
An abbreviation of TEENER.
- Farley said, "A pair of teens." The artist left him, entered a second room and returned in a few minutes with the teeners of crystal in plastic bindles. — Joseph Wambaugh, *Hollywood Station*, p. 185, 2006

teener *noun*
one sixteenth of an ounce *US*, 1993
- "My brain got fried from snortin' all that crank. Used to do a teener every night." — Joseph Wambaugh, *Finnegan's Week*, p. 40, 1993

teenie *noun*
1 a younger teenager *US*, 1968
- He would appear before a vast audience of screaming teenies and tell them that he had just received a message from God warning him against performing that night. — Albert Goldman, *Freak Show*, p. 73, 1968

2 one-sixteenth of a dollar *US*, 1992
Trader usage.
- The term "teenies," for example, dates back to 1997 when the exchanges began trading stocks in increments of 1/16 for the first time. — *New York Daily News Express*, p. 14, 27th November 2000

teensy *adjective*
tiny *US*, 1899
A childish corruption.
- "A little refreshment?" asked Frannie. The columnist flashed her syrupy little-girl smile. "It's a teensy bit early for me, thanks." — Armistead Maupin, *Further Tales of the City*, p. 17, 1982

teensy-weensy *adjective*
very small *US*, 1906
- Not an idea came to me. Not a fragment of an idea. Not a teensy-weensy glimmer of an idea. — Max Shulman, *The Many Loves of Dobie Gillis*, p. 5, 1951
- We peg the rents just a teensy-weensy bit—say twenty-five percent—if you happen to be a Negro[.] — Nelson Algren, *Chicago*, p. 45, 1951
- I don't care a teensy-weensie little bit. — Jim Thompson, *The Killer Inside*, p. 63, 1952

teeny *adjective*
very small *UK*, 1825
- "I want to come in for just a teeny minute." — J.D. Salinger, *Franny and Zooey*, p. 71, 1961

teenybopper *noun*
a young teenager, especially a girl *US*, 1965
The term was originally coined to describe young teens who gathered at the corner of Telegraph Avenue and Durant in Berkeley during the 1960s. It soon came to a much broader audience.
- Super grubby tennie boppers. — *San Francisco Chronicle*, 21st April 1965
- There are a few teenie boppers, struggling to attain middle classness but for the most part the chicks are in slacks with hair rollers. — *The Berkeley Barb*, p. 4, 20th July 1966
- Teeny Bopper, my teenage lover / I caught your waves last night. — Doug Sahm, *Mendocino*, 1969
- I pull over at a ma and pa liquor store across the street from City Lights Bookstore, a hangout for sniveling intellectuals and runaway teenyboppers out for a score. — Oscar Zeta Acosta, *The Autobiography of a Brown Buffalo*, p. 36, 1972

teenyhooker *noun*
a young female prostitute *US*, 1982
- — Ralph de Sola, *Crime Dictionary*, p. 149, 1982

teeny weeny *adjective*
tiny *US*, 1931
"Teeny" came from "tiny," and then the reduplicative "teeny weeny," which is often found in the same breath as "itsy bitsy."
- "I still don't feel it," Mickey said, "the grass. Maybe just a teeny bit." "A teeny weeny bit?" Louis said. "A teeny-weeny weeny weeny-weeny bit," Mickey said. — Elmore Leonard, *Switch*, p. 159, 1978

tees *noun*
dice on which some numbers are repeated, usually made with identical numbers on opposite sides *US*, 1950
- — *The Annals of the American Academy of Political and Social Sciences*, p. 132, May 1950

- — John S. Salak, *Dictionary of Gambling*, p. 258, 1963
- We had a set of tee with us, but they were white. — Donald Goines, *Whoreson*, p. 31, 1972

teeter-totter *noun*
a double-headed dildo *US, 1968*
Based on the visual image of two women connected by a dildo rocking up and down.
- Here in the United States it is termed "the teeter-totter."
— L. Reinhard, *Oral Sex Techniques and Sex Practices Illustrated*, 196

teeth *noun*
cocaine; crack cocaine *US, 1994*
From the resemblance of the drug to small teeth.
- — US Department of Justice *Street Terms*, October 1994

teetotaller *noun*
a person who abstains from any and all alcohol *UK, 1834*
- Swedes are either teetotalers or wonderful stews. — Jack Lait and Lee Mortimer, *Chicago Confidential*, p. 81, 1950
- [T]he bartender rousted up an odd bottle of Christian Brothers port and poured us two shots in wide wine-glasses. Morley (a teetotaler actually) and Japhy and I drank and felt it fine. — Jack Kerouac, *The Dharma Bums*, p. 37, 1958
- [T]hree sheriff's deputies had shown up and arrested Slim for being drunk and disorderly which was quite humorous when you know that Slim was a teetotaler. — Clancy Sigal, *Going Away*, p. 82, 1961
- [S]he allows him his little toddy when visitors like myself come to call and even winks an eye at the double he manages for himself with teetotalers like myself[.] — Robert Campbell, *Cat's Meow*, p. 25, 1988

telegram *noun*
a message designed for mass distribution from prisoner to prisoner, passed from one cell to the next *US, 1992*
- — William K. Bentley and James M. Corbett, *Prison Slang*, p. 57, 1992

telegraph *verb*
to inadvertently disclose or reveal your intentions to an opponent *UK, 1925*
- Junior's crafty, older opponent sees him telegraph a left hook with an almost imperceptible hitch of his left shoulder. — Iceberg Slim (Robert Beck), *Doom Fox*, p. 179, 1978

telephone booth *noun*
in poker, a player who regularly "calls" (matches the bet of the previous player) *US, 1988*
- — George Percy, *The Language of Poker*, p. 91, 1988

telephone numbers *noun*
1 a large sum of money *US, 1979*
- Charlie, there are fucking telephone numbers we're talking about here. — Vincent Patrick, *The Pope of Greenwich Village*, p. 225, 1979
2 in horseracing, a winning bet at high odds *US, 1934*
- — Robert Saunders Dowst and Jay Craig, *Playing the Races*, p. 170, 1960
3 a long prison sentence *US, 1950*
- — Hyman E. Goldin et al., *Dictionary of American Underworld Lingo*, p. 221, 1950

telescope *noun*
the penis *US, 1968*
A jocular euphemism.
- — *Current Slang*, p. 10, Spring 1968

tell *verb*
▸ **tell it like it is**
to speak directly, candidly and with a self-righteous conviction of access to a great truth *US, 1965*
- "This play is different because it's the truth," they tell you. "We go on stage and we tell it like it is." — *Los Angeles Free Press*, p. 6, 25th June 1965
- Alinksy Tells it Like It Is [Headline] — *Berkeley Barb*, p. 3, 2nd December 1966
- In Harlem, on the other hand, to tell it like it is, is to call a spade a spade. — Sidney Bernard, *This Way to the Apocalypse*, p. 57, 1968
▸ **tell the tale**
in a swindle, to explain to the victim just how he will profit from the arrangement being proposed *US, 1989*
- — Lindsay E. Smith and Bruce A. Walstad, *Sting Shift*, p. 117, 1989: "Glossary"

teller *noun*
a skateboarder whose tales of accomplishments are exaggerated *US, 1984*
- — *San Francisco Sunday Examiner & Chronicle*, p. 20, 2nd September 1984: "Say it right"

Telly *noun*
1 television *US, 1940*
- Well, sit down. Watch the telly if you like. — Elmore Leonard, *Split Images*, p. 236, 1981
2 Telegraph Avenue, the main business street adjacent to the campus of the University of California, Berkeley *US, 1966*
- Headline: Peace-Rock OK, But Not On "Avenue" / Will Rock "Off-Telly" — *The Berkeley Barb*, p. 1, 5th August 1966
- TELE, TELLY: Telegraph Avenue. — Robert Buckhout, *Toward Social Change*, p. 466, 1971

telly- *prefix*
telephone *US, 1970*
Used for constructions such as "tellypole" or "tellywires."
- — Claudio R. Salvucci, *The Philadelphia Dialect Dictionary*, p. 62, 1996

temperance punch *noun*
a nonalcoholic fruit punch drink *US, 1957*
- In a little while we're all goin' down to the Town Hall and drink some temperance punch and look over the poon. — Max Shulman, *Rally Round the Flag, Boys!*, p. 195, 1957

ten *noun*
a perfectly beautiful woman *US, 1979*
Based on a grading scale of one to ten, popularized in the 1979 film *10* starring Bo Derek.
- Can't be with a woman who's a ten? You go to two fives. Or five twos. Adds up to the same thing. — Chris Rock, *Rock This!*, p. 126, 1997

ten-cent line *noun*
in an illegal betting operation, the 10 percent charge for making a bet *US, 1973*
- — Thomas L. Clark, *The Dictionary of Gambling and Gaming*, p. 230, 1987

ten-cent pistol *noun*
a dose of heroin that is either adulterated with a poison or contains a more pure heroin than usual, sold or given to someone with the intent of injuring or killing them *US, 1966*
- Addicts call this type of hotshot a "ten-cent pistol" because the poison costs a dime but is as effective as a gun. — James Mills, *The Panic in Needle Park*, p. 39, 1966
- — David Maurer and Victor Vogel, *Narcotics and Narcotic Addiction*, p. 449, 1973

ten-cent rock *noun*
ten dollars' worth of crack cocaine *US, 1991*
- The officer asked for a "10-cent rock"—street slang for a $10 purchase of crack cocaine. Boykin allegedly then told the officer he had only "20-cent rocks." — *Texas Lawyer*, p. 10, 14th October 1991

ten-day sweat *noun*
treatment for a sexually transmitted infection, involving heat therapy and sulpha-based drugs *US, 1949*
- — *American Speech*, p. 31, February 1949: "A.V.G. lingo"

tender *adjective*
in poker, said of a hand that is probably unplayable *US, 1988*
- — George Percy, *The Language of Poker*, p. 92, 1988

tenement *noun*
in hold 'em poker, a ten and nine *US, 1996*
- — John Vorhaus, *The Big Book of Poker Slang*, p. 36, 1996

ten F *noun*
a gall bladder patient *US, 1984–1985*
Often a fat, fair, fecund, fortyish, flatulent, female with foul, frothy, floating feces.
- — *Maledicta*, p. 118, 1984–1985: "Milwaukee medical maledicta"

tenner *noun*
1 a ten-dollar bill *UK, 1845*
- Shit, man, the day they can call me queer is when I let one of those faggots suck on me for less than a tenner[.] — Hunter S. Thompson, *Hell's Angels*, p. 87, 1966
- In order to expedite the process, will I be giving away a tenner I didn't have to spend? — Robert Campbell, *Alice in La-La Land*, p. 178, 1987
2 a prison sentence of ten years *US, 1950*
- — Hyman E. Goldin et al., *Dictionary of American Underworld Lingo*, p. 221, 1950
3 in the television and movie industries, a 10,000-watt spotlight *US, 1990*
- — Ralph S. Singleton, *Filmmaker's Dictionary*, p. 170, 1990

tennies *noun*
tennis shoes *US, 1965*
- — Carol Covington, *A Glossary of Teenage Terms*, 1965
- I shuffled my feet in their black tennies and decided to seal our fate once and for all. — Oscar Zeta Acosta, *The Autobiography of a Brown Buffalo*, p. 90, 1972

tennis, anyone?
used for humorously suggesting an activity *US, 1951*
Seen as quintessentially British and enormously witty in its many variant forms.
- The director took one look at me and said, "But this is a tough guy and you look like you're about to say, Tennis anyone?" — *Dixon (Illinois) Evening Telegraph*, p. 4, 5th May 1951
- Cocktails, anyone? — *San Francisco Examiner & Chronicle*, p. 18, 6th July 1956
- Psychology, anyone (Headline) — *San Francisco Examiner*, p. 5, 26th May 1957
- Bouillabaise, Anyone? (Headline) — *San Francisco Chronicle*, p. 10, 31st May 1957

ten one hundred *noun*
the act of urination *US, 1976*
- — Elementary Electronics, *Dictionary of CB Lingo*, p. 71, 1976

ten over *noun*
a surfing stance in which the surfer's ten toes extend over the nose or front of the board *US, 1991*
- — Trevor Cralle, *The Surfin'ary*, p. 143, 1991

ten percenter *noun*
a person who buys and resells stolen goods *US, 1976*
- — John R. Armore and Joseph D. Wolfe, *Dictionary of Desperation*, p. 54, 1976

tense *adjective*
used of a computer program, smart and economical *US, 1983*
- This routine is so tense it will bring tears to your eyes. — Guy L. Steele et al., *The Hacker's Dictionary*, p. 124, 1983

tension *noun*
crack cocaine *US, 1993*
- — Peter Johnson, *Dictionary of Street Alcohol and Drug Terms*, p. 189, 1993

tensky *noun*
a ten-dollar bill *US, 1962*
The "sky" is a meaningless decorative embellishment.
- — Frank Garcia, *Marked Cards and Loaded Dice*, p. 264, 1962
- I laid some jive and a tensky on his landlady[.] — James Ellroy, *Hollywood Nocturnes*, p. 114, 1994

ten-spot *noun*
1 a ten-dollar bill *US, 1954*
- A ten-spot, too damned much—anything was too damned much—but he had an idea that it wouldn't be much longer now[.] — Jim Thompson, *A Swell-Looking Babe*, p. 119, 1954
- Reggie got out of the car and walked up the highway and gave the cop a ten-spot, and all the way to Detroit Reggie and One-Eye argued, I mean vehemently, about whether we could have gotten away with only a fiver. — Clancy Sigal, *Going Away*, p. 156, 1961
- She laid the ten spot on me and I copped. — Odie Hawkins, *Black Casanova*, p. 165, 1984
- "Sam won't touch nothing less than a ten-spot," Sam's Man kidded. — Robert Campbell, *Juice*, p. 25, 1988

2 a ten-year prison sentence *US, 1965*
- Now New York give my girl a ten-spot and the matron led her by her hand / just thinkin' of ten long years in prison just for breakin' the laws of man. — Bruce Jackson, *Get Your Ass in the Water and Swim Like Me*, p. 141, 1965

Tenth Street *noun*
a ten-dollar bill *US, 1946*
- Tenth Street isn't a city thoroughfare but a ten-dollar bill. — Mezz Mezzrow, *Really the Blues*, p. 220, 1946

'tention *noun*
in poker, a ten *US, 1951*
- — *American Speech*, p. 102, May 1951

tent pole *noun*
an erect penis *US, 1992*

From the image of an erect penis pushing up against a sheet.
- Tent pole. She's a babe. — *Wayne's World*, 1992

tent squirrel *noun*
in circus and carnival usage, a performer *US, 1981*
- — Don Wilmeth, *The Language of American Popular Entertainment*, p. 271, 1981

termination dust *noun*
the first snow of the winter *US, 1957*
Because it terminates construction in the north.
- — Robert O. Bowen, *An Alaskan Dictionary*, p. 32, 1965
- Given to eloquence, Alaskans even have a special term for Termination Dust. It is called "snow." — Mark Wheeler, *Half Baked Alaska*, p. 138, 1972

terper *noun*
a professional dancer *US, 1973*
An abbreviation of Terpischore, daughter of Jupiter and Mnemosyne, the muse of dancing.
- — Sherman Louis Sergel, *The Language of Show Biz*, p. 222, 1973

terps; turps *noun*
a cough syrup containing elixir of terpin hydrate and codeine, abused for nonmedicinal purposes *US, 1971*
- — Eugene Landy, *The Underground Dictionary*, p. 183, 1971
- "You got terp?" "I quit." — Robert Deane Pharr, *Giveadamn Brown*, p. 50, 1978

terrible *adjective*
excellent *US, 1960*
- — Robert George Reisner, *The Jazz Titans*, p. 166, 1960
- — Hermese E. Roberts, *The Third Ear*, 1971

terrif *adjective*
terrific *US, 1950*
Not a lot of thought goes into clipped adjectives, and with a few exceptions they do not last long.
- "Oh, terrif!" cried the students. — Max Shulman, *Sleep Till Noon*, p. 141, 1950
- "Terrif, Nicky," said Sid, "terrif!" — Terry Southern, *Blue Movie*, p. 75, 1970

test-tube baby *noun*
a poker player whose experience is largely limited to simulated computer poker games *US, 1996*
- — John Vorhaus, *The Big Book of Poker Slang*, p. 36, 1996

Texas head start *noun*
starting a race before the starting gun *US, 1985*
- Miles corralled a nearby skier to count off the start, and jumped between three and go—a Texas head start. — Jay McInerney, *Ransom*, p. 143, 1985

Texas roll *noun*
a single large-denomination bill wrapped around small-denomination bills, giving the impression of a great deal of money *US, 1975*
- And I carried a Texas roll—a wad of bills, mostly ones and fives with a few big bills on the outside and play money on the inside to make it fatter. — James Carr, *Bad*, p. 53, 1975

Texas stop *noun*
slowing down but not fully stopping as required by law at a stop sign *US, 1962*
- — *American Speech*, p. 266, December 1962: "The language of traffic policemen"

Texas sunflowers *noun*
in craps, a roll of two fives *US, 1983*
- — Thomas L. Clark, *The Dictionary of Gambling and Gaming*, p. 230, 1987

Texas tea *noun*
1 oil *US, 1984*
- — Ken Weaver, *Texas Crude*, p. 132, 1984

2 a mixture of chemicals used to execute a prisoner by lethal injection *US, 2001*
- Against a background of botched executions and grisly anecdotes, most states have abandoned electrocution in favor of lethal injection, which employs a sequence of chemicals known as "Texas Tea." — *Cincinnati Enquirer*, p. 1F, 2nd September 2001
- Similar findings have led eight states to suspend used of the chemical mixture—sometimes called Texas Tea—employed in most of the death-penalty states, including California. — *The New Yorker*, p. 62, 30th July 2007

Texas toothbrush *noun*
the penis *US, 1994*
In Texas, known as an "Oklahoma toothbrush."
- — Michael Dalton Johnson, *Talking Trash with Redd Foxx*, p. 93, 1994

Texas Volkswagen *noun*
a Cadillac *US, 1956*
- — *San Francisco Examiner*, p. 1 (II), 4th November 1956

Texican *noun*
a Texan *US, 1984*
- — Ken Weaver, *Texas Crude*, p. 132, 1984

TFFTR *noun*
a very fast jet *US, 2002*
- "What the hell is a TFFTR?" "Too fucking fast to recognize!"
  — Richard Burns, *Pathfinder*, p. 216, 2002

TG *noun*
a young member of a youth gang *US, 1991*
- "If I'm with a bunch of T.G.'s and they want to jack some old lady," I say, "Fuck that, man,—go for somebody else, like a man or somethin'." — Leon Bing, *Do or Die*, p. 55, 1991
- "[H]e's listed in the Gang Street Alias Index under the name Li'l Silent, so at the very least he's a TG or a known associate." TG stood for "tiny gangster" and was basically a killer in training. — Stephen J. Cannell, *The Tin Collectors*, p. 147, 2001

TGIF
Thank God it's Friday *US, 1941*
- Newcomers to Patrick Air Force Base in Florida, where missiles are tested, are usually mystified by seeing the initials TGIF on bulletin boards and notices of various kinds. They are strictly non-regulation. They stand for "Thank God It's Friday"—meaning pay-day and week-end relaxation for some in the form of beach parties, club dances, and so on. — *New York Times*, p. SM13, 8th September 1957
- — *Current Slang*, p. 7, Summer 1967
- — Helen Dahlskog (Editor), *A Dictionary of Contemporary and Colloquial Usage*, p. 59, 1972

T-grams *noun*
a grandmother *US, 1998*
- — Ethan Hilderbrant, *Prison Slang*, p. 126, 1998

Thai stick *noun*
marijuana cultivated in Thailand, soaked in hashish oil, wound on short thin sticks of bamboo which are bundled for sale; a cigarette rolled from marijuana cultivated in Thailand *US, 1975*
- He said he'd written some dynamite poems that way and generously offered Kate part of a Thai stick. — Cyra McFadden, *The Serial*, p. 147, 1977
- It seemed likely that someone had crept into the men's restroom and unloaded Captain Woofer's tamped and loaded briar, reloading it with very high grade hashish or Thai stick[.] — Joseph Wambaugh, *The Glitter Dome*, p. 75, 1981
- I also take all the Ritalin to cut through the wild hemp, which is the best in the monde, far better than those expensive Thai Sticks that were going around last winter. — Bill Cardoso, *The Maltese Sangweech*, p. 282, 1984
- "So this is what thai stick is, huh?" "Yeahhh, it's something else, ain't it?" — Odie Hawkins, *Lost Angeles*, p. 201, 1994

Thai tabs *noun*
sweet-tasting pills that are a mixture of methamphetamine and caffeine *US, 1997*
- Are the pink thai tabs scored along the horizontal axis of the pentagon? — *mis.fitness.weights*, 20th April 1997
- The Source Determination Program of the DEA Special Testing and Research Laboratory (Dulles, Virginia) recently received some "Ya-Ba" tablets (also known as "Thai Tabs" heatsealed in what appeared to be plastic drinking straws. — *Microgram Bulletin (DEA)*, p. 5, January 2004

thang *noun*
thing *US, 1977*
Slang by vowel exchange.
- That's the groovy thang about Nick, the Geech, he takes every fuckin' thang seriously. — Odie Hawkins, *Chicago Hustle*, pp. 23–24, 1977

Thank you Captain Obvious!
used for expressing disdain of a remark that is exceedingly obvious *US, 1992*

- Bob, ordered my vx 5/80 CD on 10/27/92 (92 thank you captain obvious). — *comp.sys.mac.hardware*, 12th November 1992
- I know some of you are saying "Thank you, Captain Obvious, for that enlightening bit of minutia." — David Groth, *A+ Core Module Study Guide*, p. 168, 1998

thank-you-m'am *noun*
a bump or dip in a road which produces a moment of slight uneasiness in the stomach *US, 1920*
- We recently heard bumps in a country road referred to as "thank-you-ma'ams." Could you tell us how this term originated? It was from the rider's motion resembling a genteel bow when he was jounced over one of them. — *Old Farmer's Almanac in San Francisco Examiner and Chronicle*, p. 41, 15th April 1979

thatch *noun*
a woman's pubic hair *US, 2005*
- Imagine Saturday Night Live with a trim-butt blonde with high, firm, round boobies and a moderate, light-brown thatch cracking jokes with all her sweet bits hanging out. — Mr. Skin, *Mr. Skin's Skincyclopedia*, p. 8, 2005

that had to hurt!
used as a humorous if not particularly sympathetic observation of a painful event *US, 1992*
- Ow—that had to hurt. — *A Few Good Men*, 1992

that'll happen
used as a humorous comment on something that should not happen or never happens *US, 1997*
Coined and popularized by ESPN's Keith Olberman.
- — Keith Olberman and Dan Patrick, *The Big Show: Inside ESPN's Sports Center*, p. 24, 1997

that plays
used for expressing approval *US, 1966*
- — John D. Bell et al., *Loosely Speaking*, p. 15, 1966

that's dead!
used for expressing a strong negative *US, 1991*
- — Lee McNelis, *30 + And a Wake-Up: A Compendium of Prison Slang Terms and Definitions*, p. 12, 1991

that's word!
used for expressing strong assent *US, 1992*
- — William K. Bentley and James M. Corbett, *Prison Slang*, p. 51, 1992

that time *noun*
the bleed period of a woman's menstrual cycle *US, 1954*
- — *American Speech*, p. 298, December 1954: "The vernacular of menstruation"

THC *noun*
marijuana *US, 1971*
The psychoactive chemical in marijuana is delta-9-tetrahydro-cannabinol, or THC.
- So we refrained from balling at all at the party, got really turned on (we were on THC) and really wanted to ball. — Jefferson Poland and Valerie Alison, *The Records of the San Francisco Sexual Freedom League*, p. 33, 1971

them's my orders
used as an apology for acting in accordance with orders *US, 1843*
- I'm sorry boys. But them's my orders. — Oscar Zeta Acosta, *The Revolt of the Cockroach People*, p. 30, 1973

them's the rules
used as a humorous deference to protocol or rules *US, 1997*
- I owe you. It told you today, them's the rules. — *As Good As It Gets*, 1997

them things *noun*
marijuana cigarettes *US, 1992*
- — William K. Bentley and James M. Corbett, *Prison Slang*, p. 74, 1992

the nerve of the scurve!
used as a humorous exclamation, half admiring *US, 1975*
- The hell I know what you was wearin'. The nerve of this scurve! — Edwin Torres, *Carlito's Way*, p. 133, 1975

there's a fungus among us
used as a warning that a socially inept, unfashionable person is nearby *US, 1957*

- "There's a fungus among us" is taking the place of "creepy character." — *Washington Post*, p. F1, 29th September 1957
- Fungus Among Us: a character in our midst. — Art Unger, *The Cool Book*, p. 109, 1961

there you go!
used for expressing approval *US, 1970*
- — Clarence Major, *Dictionary of Afro-American Slang*, p. 114, 1970

They *noun*
the mysterious authority over all authority, the power behind the throne *US, 1968*
Beloved in the political culture of the 1960s.
- Laura said whimsically, "You know, after we take over and rule the world, we've got to find out who They are." "Then," I said, "we'll be They." — James Simon Kunen, *The Strawberry Statement*, p. 77, 1968

thick *adjective*
sexually appealing, attractive, well built *US, 1998*
- — Connie Eble (Editor), *UNC-CH Campus Slang*, p. 10, Spring 1998
- — Gary K. Farlow, *Prison-ese*, p. 73, 2002

thief *noun*
in horseracing, a horse that runs worst when its chances seem best *US, 1976*
- — Tom Ainslie, *Ainslie's Complete Guide to Thoroughbred Racing*, p. 339, 1976

thigh-highs *noun*
stockings worn up the middle of the thigh *US, 1995*
- While some critics complained that designers were making fun of women by dressing them like children, thigh-highs also evoke images of streetwalkers and porn layouts. — Steven Daly and Nathaniel Wice, *alt.culture*, p. 249, 1995

thigh opener *noun*
a vodka gimlet *US, 1985*
- — *American Speech*, p. 20, Spring 1985: "The language of singles bars"

T. Hill *noun*
Tommy Hilfiger™ clothing *US, 1998*
- — Ethan Hilderbrant, *Prison Slang*, p. 126, 1998

thimble-titted *adjective*
small breasted *US, 1994*
- — Michael Dalton Johnson, *Talking Trash with Redd Foxx*, p. 73, 1994

thing *noun*
1 the penis *UK, 1386*
Since Chaucer, and still.
- They staked him to the ground, see with tent pegs, then burned him all over with butts. Even his thing. — Richard Farina, *Been Down So Long*, p. 64, 1966
- Junior pulled out this thing. It looked like a horse's cock—black, long and fat, with a huge pink head. — Steve Cannon, *Groove, Bang, and Jive Around*, p. 36, 1969
- An accident. Your thing just got into a box of popcorn? — *Diner*, 1982
- I know I take a girl, stick my thing in and nine months later a baby comes out. — *Boyz N The Hood*, 1990

2 the vagina *US, 1970*
- [W]e would walk along seeing whose dress was up the highest and if you could really see their thing 'cause they didn't wear no bloomers. — Louise Meriwether, *Daddy Was a Number Runner*, p. 26, 1970

3 an interest, obsession, attraction *US, 1841*
- I made up my mind then and there that my "thing" would have to be show business as my only escape. — Babs Gonzales, *I Paid My Dues*, p. 18, 1967
- Revolution is in your head. You are the Revolution. Do your thing. — Abbie Hoffman, *Revolution for the Hell of It*, p. 10, 1968
- I think he has a little thing for Annie. — *Annie Hall*, 1977
- I did not have a "thing." I was very much in love with him. Very much in love, and there's a difference. — *Romy and Michele's High School Reunion*, 1997

4 used to replace any noun that the user cannot or does not wish to specify *US, 1974*
Also called a "thingy."
- Interested MDs should write to Free City Medical Thing c/o The Differs. — *The Digger Papers*, p. 17, August 1968
- I taught a spiritual thing in San Francisco for about four years, and we met once a week. — Stephen Gaskin, *Hey Beatnik*, 1974

- As it happens the princess thing didn't work out for me, so I went to college[.] — Janet Evanovich, *Seven Up*, p. 1, 2001

5 a romantic affair *US, 1974*
- Mary Astor was keeping a diary about her thing with George Kaufman[.] — Eve Babitz, *Eve's Hollywood*, p. 17, 1974

6 heroin; a capsule of heroin *US, 1958*
- A thing is a dollar-capsule of H. — Willard Motley, *Let No Man Write My Epitaph*, p. 148, 1958
- — Richard A. Spears, *The Slang and Jargon of Drugs and Drink*, p. 507, 1986

7 an M-50A1 Ontos antitank tracked vehicle, heavily armed *US, 1990*
- "The Thing" was especially effective against enemy bunkers and entrenchments, but its light armor made it vulnerable to enemy fire and mines. — Gregory Clark, *Words of the Vietnam War*, p. 300, 1990

▶ **this thing**
organized crime *US, 1989*
- He gave the FBI an earful. "This Thing comes first," he once reminded another soldier[.] — Gerard O'Neill, *The Under Boss*, p. 181, 1989

thingamajig; thingumajig; thingummyjig *noun*
used as a pseudo-term for something the name of which is unknown, forgotten or not important *UK, 1824*
- Doesn't it impress you at all that here is a real live human being you made all by yourself?—you and your thing-a-ma-jig there? — John Nichols, *The Sterile Cuckoo*, p. 181, 1965
- Don't tell me that fool is up blowin' on that thang-a-majig again! — Odie Hawkins, *Ghetto Sketches*, p. 40, 1972
- [T]here's a thingamajig they can put on the projector that'll cut through that gunk like Bruce Lee's foot through Velveeta cheese. — Joe Bob Briggs, *Joe Bob Goes to the Drive-In*, p. 9, 1987

thing-thing *noun*
an object the name of which escapes or is unimportant to the speaker *US, 1976*
- — John R. Armore and Joseph D. Wolfe, *Dictionary of Desperation*, p. 54, 1976

thin hairs *noun*
▶ **have someone by the thin hairs**
to hold someone at a disadvantage; to exercise complete control over someone *US, 1946*
- I was really in the dumps, but fate had me by the thin hairs and wouldn't turn me loose. — Mezz Mezzrow, *Really the Blues*, p. 129, 1946

think *verb*
▶ **think outside the box**
to reject standard assumptions and strive for a creative solution to a problem *US, 1999*
From a brain teaser puzzle which can be solved only if you reject the boundaries of a box. It vaulted into cliché use quickly, and provided the inspiration for author Jim Tompkins' 2001 book *Think Outside the Box: The Most Trite, Generic, Hokey, Overused, Cliched or Unmotivating Motivational Slogans*.
- To Think Outside the Box, Get Back Into Sandbox — *The Los Angeles Times*, 11th January 1999
- This season, another phrase leaps out at me from candidate interviews, forums and public speechifying. It is the call to Think Outside the Box. — *The Cincinnati Enquirer*, p. A18, 7th October 1999

think again, dearie
used for humorously expressing the negative *US, 1987*
- — *Washington Post Magazine*, p. 16, 26th December 1987: "Say Wha?"

thinkbox *noun*
the head; the brain *US, 1946*
- Thinkbox (n) Your brain. — *Hit Parader*, p. 33, September 1946

think it ain't?
used for expressing affirmation *US, 1992*
- — William K. Bentley and James M. Corbett, *Prison Slang*, p. 47, 1992

thinko *noun*
a momentary loss of memory or disruption in a thought process *US, 1991*
A play on "typo."
- — Eric S. Raymond, *The New Hacker's Dictionary*, p. 349, 1991

thin one *noun*
a dime, or ten-cent piece *US, 1962*
- — Joseph E. Ragen and Charles Finston, *Inside the World's Toughest Prison*, p. 821, 1962: "Penitentiary and underworld glossary"
- — Steve Kuriscak, *Casino Talk*, p. 56, 1985

third base *noun*

1 in a notional hierarchy of sexual activity, intimate sexual contact short of intercourse *US, 1948*

Generally, but not always, a reference to touching of the genitals.

- I got to third base last night, I'll make her yet. — Norman Mailer, *The Naked and the Dead*, p. 551, 1948
- "I can go all the way to third base with her but I can't get home" — Phillip Roth, *Flickers*, p. 190, 1977
- Yo—did you ever get to third base with her? — Kevin Smith, *Jay and Silent Bob Strike Back*, p. 108, 2001
- And you got to third base with her by dawn. — Christina Bartolomeo, *The Side of the Angels*, p. 281, 2004

2 in casino blackjack, the seat immediately to the dealer's right *US, 1985*

- — Steve Kuriscak, *Casino Talk*, p. 56, 1985

third degree *noun*

an intense level of interrogation *US, 1880*

- [T]he kid's mother was supposed to be a third-degree artist, and new sneakers in the house probably wouldn't have gone unchallenged. — Richard Price, *Clockers*, pp. 354–355, 1992

third leg *noun*

the penis *US, 1994*

- Condoms have become an essential part of the modern man's wardrobe, an extra sock for the third leg. — Anka Radakovich, *The Wild Girls Club*, p. 83, 1994

third rail *noun*

1 a bill, especially in a restaurant *US, 1950*

A term of the 1940s music industry.

- — Arnold Shaw, *Lingo of Tin-Pan Alley*, p. 20, 1950

2 an extremely controversial political issue *US, 2000*

Like the third rail in an electric railway system, it is to be avoided.

- The Social Security program is often being called the "third rail" of politics. — *Omaha World-Herald*, p. 8, 13th June 2000
- If there is a third rail full of lethal electricity in state politics this golden summer, it is asking voters to increase stiff increases in gas and car costs. — *The Seattle Times*, p. B4, 16th July 2001

3 inexpensive, potent liquor *US, 1962*

- — Joseph E. Ragen and Charles Finston, *Inside the World's Toughest Prison*, p. 821, 1962

third sex *noun*

homosexuals as a group *US, 1896*

- Many of the third sex journey regularly to New York, where they have friends in esoteric circles. — Jack Lait and Lee Mortimer, *Washington Confidential*, p. 92, 1951
- — Dale Gordon, *The Dominion Sex Dictionary*, p. 156, 1967

third world briefcase *noun*

a large portable stereo system associated, stereotypically, with black youth culture *US, 1986*

- Be a bum in this part of town, he knew, keep rhythm with your fingers, sport a walkman or a third world briefcase — Thomas Caplan, *Parallelogram*, p. 121, 1987
- — Connie Eble (Editor), *UNC-CH Campus Slang*, p. 1, Fall 1987

thirst monster *noun*

a crack cocaine user *US, 2002*

- — *Detroit News*, p. 5D, 20th September 2002

thirsty *adjective*

intensely craving crack cocaine *US, 1992*

- — Terry Williams, *Crackhouse*, p. 152, 1992

thirteen *noun*

1 marijuana; a marijuana cigarette *US, 1966*

Because "M" is the 13th letter of the alphabet.

- Among the first to be exposed was the numeral "13" (indicating a marijuana smoker). — Hunter S. Thompson, *Hell's Angels*, p. 117, 1966

2 in a deck of playing cards, any king *US, 1996*

- — John Vorhaus, *The Big Book of Poker Slang*, p. 36, 1996

thirteen *nickname*

the Mexican Mafia prison gang *US, 2000*

- These terms were being seen with greater frequency, thrown up as graffiti throughout California's prisons along with the numeral 13, which signifies the letter M, or more precisely, La eMe. — Bill Valentine, *Gangs and Their Tattoos*, p. 23, 2000

thirty days *noun*

in poker, a hand with three tens *US, 1963*

- — Irwin Steig, *Common Sense in Poker*, p. 185, 1963

thirty dirty miles *noun*

in a game of poker, a hand with three tens *US, 1963*

- — Thomas L. Clark, *The Dictionary of Gambling and Gaming*, p. 231, 1987

thirty miles of railroad track *noun*

in poker, a hand consisting of three tens *US, 1988*

- — George Percy, *The Language of Poker*, p. 92, 1988

thirtysomething *adjective*

describing the age of the generation of baby boomers as they moved into their thirties *US, 1987*

From the name of a television drama (1987–91) focusing on **YUPPIE** angst.

- most people like myself, my sisters, my brother my cousins and some friends are now in our late-teens to thirtysomething. — *soc.culture.asian.american*, 30th October 1989
- The rest of the kids that were rapidly replacing the largely mid-thirtysomething rockies that had been thrust into the spotlight in the Stripes' wake really didn't care one way or another. — Chris Handyside, *Fell in Love with a Band*, p. 134, 2004

thirty-thirty *noun*

a central nervous system stimulant other than amphetamine packaged to look like and sold as amphetamine *US, 1993*

- — Peter Johnson, *Dictionary of Street Alcohol and Drug Terms*, p. 191, 1993

thirty-three; 33 *noun*

a prostitute's customer who is not quickly satisfied *US, 1971*

From long-playing vinyl records.

- A customer who worked quickly was called a "78" and one with a slower response was a "33." — Charles Winick, *The Lively Commerce*, p. 188, 1971

thirty-weight *noun*

strong coffee *US, 1976*

Inviting a comparison with motor oil.

- — Wayne Floyd, *Jason's Authentic Dictionary of CB Slang*, p. 32, 1976

this time it's personal

used as a humorous assertion that an issue is being taken personally *US, 1999*

A moderately popular catchphrase from *Jaws: The Revenge* (1987).

- I don't know animals, but I do know this: this time it's personal. — *Austin Powers*, 1999

thorazine shuffle *noun*

the slow, dragging walk of a patient being medicated with thorazine *US, 1978*

- Pseudo-Parkinsonism: Symptoms include tremors, shuffling walk (the "Thorazine shuffle"), drooling[.] — Bruce Ennis, *The Rights of Mental Patients*, p. 202, 1978
- — Sally Williams, "*Strong*" Words, p. 162, 1994
- After sliding the door he does the Thorazine shuffle back to his tray, sits. — Jimmy Lerner, *You Got Nothing Coming*, p. 205, 2002

thoroughbred *noun*

a drug dealer who sells high quality, pure drugs *US, 1970*

- — William D. Alsever, *Glossary for the Establishment and Other Uptight People*, p. 32, December 1970

those days *noun*

the bleed prior of a woman's menstrual cycle *US, 1954*

- — *American Speech*, p. 298, December 1954: "The vernacular of menstruation"

thou *noun*

a *thou*sand *US, 1867*

- You know, a couple of years ago, and this was in Norfolk too, a lieutenant supply officer lifted six thou and went over the hill. — Darryl Ponicsan, *The Last Detail*, p. 30, 1970
- In the majority of pictures with budgets of five hundred thou or more, studio participation in involved[.] — Terry Southern, *Now Dig This*, p. 66, 1973

thousand percent *adverb*

completely *US, 1963*

The most famous use of the term in the US came in 1972 when Democratic presidential nominee Senator George

McGovern announced that he was "one thousand percent" in support of his running mate, Thomas Eagleton, despite revelations that Eagleton had once received shock treatment; McGovern dropped Eagleton from the ticket several days after this endorsement.

- The governor is, (as the saying goes in Las Vegas), a thousand percent correct. — Ed Reid and Ovid Demaris, *The Green Jungle*, p. 5, 1963
- It summarized the Leubsdorf story, called it "utterly untrue," and then said that George McGovern was "1,000 percent for Tom Eagleton." — Timothy Crouse, *The Boys on the Bus*, p. 328, 1973
- I was a thousand percent wrong. — Vincent Patrick, *Family Business*, p. 42, 1985

thousand-yard stare; thousand-meter stare *noun*
a lost, unfocused look, especially as the result of brutal combat *US, 1974*

- [W]ould be to lapse into a catatonic gaze—what Army psychiatrists, accustomed to dealing with the fear of combat, call the "thousand yard stare." — Dan Rather, *The Palace Guard*, p. 152, 1974
- It's hard to avoid using "1,000-yard stare." What I saw in Lawrence's eyes was the horror, The Horror. — Mark Baker, *Nam*, p. 111, 1981
- He fully recognizes Pacvo's 1,000-meter stare, that pale and exhausted, graven look from head to toe. — Larry Heinemann, *Paco's Story*, p. 95, 1986
- The thousand-yard stare. A marine gets it after he's been in the shit for too long. — *Full Metal Jacket*, 1987

thrash *noun*
a style of hard rock music that appeals to disaffected suburban adolescent boys—fast, relentlessly loud and heavy *US, 1994*

- Well, it's not exactly speed or thrash or grunge or grind. — *Airheads*, 1994

thrash *verb*
1 to surf aggressively and with skill *US, 1988*
- — Michael V. Anderson, *The Bad, Rad, Not to Forget Way Cool Beach and Surf Discritionary*, p. 20, 1988

2 to skateboard aggressively and with skill *US, 1989*
- — Macon Telegraph and News, p. 9A, 18th June 1989

thrashed *adjective*
tired, worn-down, exhausted, especially as a result of excessive indulgence in hedonistic pleasures; disheveled *US, 1999*
- She looked really thrashed and kind of droopy from the heroin she was doing. (Quoting Pauly Shore) — *Spin Magazine*, October 1999

thrasher *noun*
1 a person who violently responds to the pricks of a tattoo needle *US, 1997*
- — *Los Angeles Times Magazine*, p. 7, 13 July 1997

2 a skilled and fearless skateboarder *US, 1984*
- — San Francisco Sunday Examiner & Chronicle, p. 20, 2nd September 1984: "Say It Right"

threads *noun*
clothes *US, 1926*
- It's a shame the way you treat your threads. — Ross Russell, *The Sound*, p. 46, 1961
- I was going to be a heart breaker all right. All I needed was the "threads" and a whore. — Iceberg Slim (Robert Beck), *Pimp*, p. 59, 1969
- He was always pressed; nothing but the best / Vines and kicks he had / A thirty-dollar lid and gloves of kid / Man his threads were bad. (Collected in 1958). — Dennis Wepman et al., *The Life*, p. 97, 1976
- What's with the boss threads? — *Empire Records*, 1995

three *noun*
a three-dollar bag of heroin *US, 1976*
- So I reached in my slide and came out with two boss threes / And said "Here, girl, go to the shithouse and get the weakness out of your knees." (Collected in 1966). — Dennis Wepman et al., *The Life*, p. 52, 1976

three-balls *noun*
a Jewish person *US, 1980*
An allusion to the historical signage outside a pawn shop.
- — Edith A. Folb, *runnin' down some lines*, p. 257, 1980

three-bug *noun*
in horseracing, an inexperienced jockey given a weight allowance of ten pounds *US, 1990*
- — Robert V. Rowe, *How to Win at Horse-Racing*, p. 200, 1990

three-decker *noun*
a three-storey house *US, 1990*
Coined and primarily used by Irish immigrants and then Irish-Americans in Boston.
- Of a rickety three-decker in South Boston, he unforgettably remarked that the only thing that was holding it up was the wash lines. — *The Boston Globe*, p. A27, 3rd June 1990

three-dollar bill *noun*
1 used for comparisons of something that is rare or odd *US, 1945*
- Stage money—as phony as a three dollar bill—was one of the psychological weapons used by Allied forces in the closing days of the Japanese war. — *Washington Post*, p. 4, 2nd October 1945
- As phoney as a three-dollar bill. — *Traverse City (Michigan) Record Eagle*, 4th June 1948

2 a homosexual *US, 1965*
From the expression "as strange as a three-dollar bill."
- — *The Guild Dictionary of Homosexual Terms*, p. 44, 1965
- — Dale Gordon, *The Dominion Sex Dictionary*, p. 156, 1967

three fates *noun*
in poker, three queens *US, 1988*
- — George Percy, *The Language of Poker*, p. 92, 1988

three fifty-seven; three fifty-seven Magnum *noun*
a central nervous system stimulant, the exact nature of which is unknown, sold as amphetamine on the street *US, 1993*
- — Peter Johnson, *Dictionary of Street Alcohol and Drug Terms*, p. 191, 1993

three-for-two *noun*
fifty percent interest *US, 1967*
- Oberholster, can I borrow a box at three-for-two? — Malcolm Braly, *On the Yard*, p. 91, 1967

three-hairs *noun*
a Vietnamese woman *US, 1991*
From the perception of the US soldier that the pubic hair of Vietnamese women is very sparse.
- — Linda Reinberg, *In the Field*, p. 218, 1991

three H enema *noun*
in hospital usage, an aggressive enema—*high*, *hot*, and a *hell* of a lot *US, 1980*
- — *Maledicta*, p. 56, Summer 1980: "Not sticks and stones, but names: more medical pejoratives"

three hots and a cot *noun*
room and board *US, 1969*
From the sense of **HOT** as "a meal."
- For a day's work, each youth is paid 50 cents plus earning his room and board, or "three hots and a cot," as one youth described it. — *New York Times*, p. 51, 28th September 1969
- Jes leave me what I got, three hots and a cot. — Seth Morgan, *Homeboy*, p. 311, 1990
- Such as this: a grand a week cash and three hots and cot at a Beverly Hills mansion, all legit. — James Ellroy, *Hollywood Nocturnes*, p. 243, 1994
- To the outside, it appears that all is provided for the needs of inmates of penal institutions. "Three hots and a cot." — J.G. Narum, *The Convict Cookbook*, p. 10, 2004

three-martini lunch *noun*
a leisurely business lunch paid for from an expense account, often centered around alcohol *US, 1972*
- They wore suits, and most were businessmen who indulged in the then-proverbial three-martini lunch. — Kathryn Leigh Scott, *The Bunny Years*, p. 7, 1998

three minutes *noun*
a gang punishment in which the offending member must fight another gang member for three minutes *US, 2001*
- That's a violation, and she got to get down for three minutes with another homegirl. Either with bare fists or with boxing gloves. — *Rolling Stone*, p. 82, 12th April 2001

threes *noun*
in poker, three cards of the same rank in a hand *US, 1967*
- — Albert H. Morehead, *The Complete Guide to Winning Poker*, p. 275, 1967

three-sheet *verb*
to wear theatrical makeup in public *US, 1971*

- People are friendly, however, even if you don't have a date, but start off like a Marlboro Man unless you detect your conversation partner three-sheeting. That is an old show-biz term, meaning wearing some of his makeup offstage. — John Francis Hunter, *The Gay Insider*, p. 109, 1971

three sheets in the wind *adjective*
very drunk *UK, 1821*
- "Mr. Ivers," I said, "is just about three sheets in the wind." — Jim Thompson, *Roughneck*, p. 116, 1954

three-sixty *noun*
a complete, 360-degree turn *US, 1927*
- He told how a woman pulled out in front of him and when he braked did a three-sixty, spun all the way around. — Elmore Leonard, *Out of Sight*, p. 248, 1996

threesome *noun*
group sex with three participants *US, 1972*
- I said that you, I and that girl from your acting class should sleep together in a threesome. — *Annie Hall*, 1977

three squares *noun*
three square meals a day *US, 1922*
- Life in the joint wasn't so bad, he rationalized for a moment, the sun's rays tripping him out, not if you had three squares a day, few hassles and a chance to write as much as you wanted. — Odie Hawkins, *The Busting Out of an Ordinary Man*, p. 83, 1985

three squares and a flop *adjective*
three hot meals a day and a place to sleep *US, 1957*
- You got the right idea, boy: stay on the government tit. Why not? Three squares and a flop, nothing to do, free medical care, free trips, plenty of time off, and a pension when you're ready to hang up the gloves! — Max Shulman, *Rally Round the Flag, Boys!*, p. 208, 1957

three S's *noun*
a man's preparations for going out *US, 1972*
- After the three S's—the shit, the shave, and the shower—I would put on a clean fiddle and an erky-dirk. — Robert Byrne, *McGoorty*, p. 147, 1972

three-time loser *noun*
a criminal who has been convicted of a third serious crime, probably guaranteeing life imprisonment *US, 1951*
- "He's a three-time loser. He oughtta know better." — Donald Wilson, *My Six Convicts*, p. 104, 1951
- We'll get nabbed for sure. I'm a three-time loser. I'll get life in prison. — Chester Himes, *Come Back Charleston Blue*, p. 7, 1966

three-toed sloth *noun*
a slow-thinking, slow-talking, slow-acting hospital patient *US, 1984–1985*
- — *Maledicta*, p. 118, 1984–1985: "Milwaukee medical maledicta"

three-toke killer *noun*
extremely potent marijuana *US, 1993*
Derived from the perception that the marijuana will produce extreme intoxication after only three inhalations.
- — Peter Johnson, *Dictionary of Street Alcohol and Drug Terms*, p. 192, 1993

three-two-hundred out, one-six-hundred in *adjective*
completely confused *US, 1968*
From the standard 6400-mil circular artillery chart.
- — Carl Fleischhauer, *A Glossary of Army Slang*, p. 22, 1968

three up and three down *noun*
a master sergeant in the US Army *US, 1962*
From the stripe configuration.
- [C]ould keep an unmarried supply sergeant (three up and three down) from keeping a date one payday Saturday night. — Saul Bellow, *The Noble Savage*, p. 45, 1962

three-way *noun*
sex involving three people simultaneously *US, 1965*
- "I made it with five different guys, and then we did the three- and four-way bits." — W.D. Sprague, *Sexual Rebellion in the Sixties*, p. 101, 1965
- A three-way or sexual sandwich may consist of one person penetrating anally, a second both penetrated and penetrating, and the third penetrated only. — Wayne Dynes, *Homolexis*, p. 105, 1985
- He introduced me to some model he'd gone out with and kept pushing for a three-way, but I started getting jealous at that point and told him I wanted to go home. — Sandra Bernhard, *Confessions of a Pretty Lady*, p. 92, 1988

- Marcia did some as well, and then they had a three-way with Ramona, that very night, at my house. — Michelle Tea, *Rent Girl*, p. 177, 2004

three-way *adjective*
(used of a woman) willing to engage in vaginal, anal and oral sex *US, 1963*
- She frankly admitted she was what many call girls, including myself, had not yet advanced to, or perhaps fallen to, a three-way girl. She'd say, "What difference does it make which one of your body's openings they stick their cock in—mouth, vagina or rear end?" — Sara Harris, *The Lords of Hell*, p. 71, 1967
- Sharon is a three-way girl—available to clients by vagina, mouth or anus. — John Warren Wells, *Tricks of the Trade*, pp. 18–19, 1970
- You sure she's three way? — Mickey Spillane, *Last Cop Out*, p. 48, 1972
- She was a three-way wench, played Jasper in a pinch / And took 'em around the horn. (Collected in 1963). — Dennis Wepman et al., *The Life*, p. 81, 1976

thrift *verb*
to live a frugal, if attractive, lifestyle *US, 1997*
- — Vann Wesson, *Generation X Field Guide and Lexicon*, p. 168, 1997

thrift shop *noun*
any low-limit, low-ante poker game *US, 1996*
- — John Vorhaus, *The Big Book of Poker Slang*, p. 36, 1996

thrill pill *noun*
a central nervous system stimulant in tablet form *US, 1953*
A reduplication that never really caught on; too true for a euphemism and too euphemistic for the street.
- Goofballs, yellow jackets, wild geronimos, red birds, blue heaven, idiot pills, thrill pills, red devils—what do they mean to you? — *San Francisco Examiner*, p. 18, 19th May 1953
- And he prescribed an amphetamine, which I believe is the generic term for Dexedrine, Benzedrine, Byphetamine, and the base for most diet pills, mood elevators, pep pills, thrill pills, etc. — Lenny Bruce, *How to Talk Dirty and Influence People*, p. 132, 1965
- William D. Alsever, *Glossary for the Establishment and Other Uptight People*, p. 1, December 1970

throne *noun*
a toilet seat *UK, 1922*
- [W]hen I sit on the throne at night I close the light and open the window and look out on the field in back of the house. — Jack Kerouac, *Jack Kerouac Selected Letters 1957–1969*, p. 410, 25th March 1963: Letter to Caroline Kerouac Blake
- Bill Phillips is certain, for example, that his decision to join the Police Department was made while sitting on the "throne" in the bathroom one day and reading of the fine pension benefits available. — Leonard Shecter and William Phillips, *On the Pad*, p. 75, 1973
- I get my best ideas when I'm sitting on the throne. How about you? — Anka Radakovich, *The Wild Girls Club*, p. 192, 1994
- I'm on the throne, takin' a shit. Gimme five. — Stephen J. Cannell, *The Tin Collectors*, p. 116, 2001

throttle jockey; throttle jock *noun*
a combat jet pilot *US, 1956*
- — *American Speech*, p. 229, October 1956: More United States Air Force Slang
- We've learned out lesson very well on how to be a stud / By watching all the throttle jocks who fly the Super Thud. — Joseph Tuso, *Singing the Vietnam Blues*, p. 188, 1990: Super Constellation

through-ticket *noun*
in pool, a player who continues to play and to lose money until he has lost his entire bankroll *US, 1993*
- — Mike Shamos, *The Illustrated Encyclopedia of Billiards*, p. 246, 1993

throw *noun*
the cost of an item or action, usually preceded by a specific amount *US, 1898*
Probably from the old side shows of the fair.
- White orchids go with anything, but they cost $15 a throw. — Jack Lait and Lee Mortimer, *New York Confidential*, p. 214, 1948
- Y'innarested? Five bucks a throw. Fifteen bucks the whole night. — J.D. Salinger, *Catcher in the Rye*, p. 91, 1951
- Beer was two-bits a throw. — Mickey Spillane, *The Long Wait*, p. 47, 1951
- The male prostitute can count on being paid an average of $10 a throw, which is considerably less than the average female earns. — *Screw*, p. 3, 7th February 1969

throw verb

1 to create (graffiti) US, 2000

- [M]embers do not just write on a wall, they "throw" or "toss" graffiti on the wall. — Robert Jackson and Wesley McBride, *Understanding Street Gangs*, p. 80, 2000

2 to break an addiction US, 1952

- Jail had, as always, forced him to "throw his habit," and so small amounts were sufficient in the beginning. — John Clellon Holmes, *Go*, p. 198, 1952

▸ **throw a fin; throw the fin**

while surfing, to reach the top of a wave and expose to the air the surfboard's fin(s) US, 1987

- — Mitch McKissick, *Surf Lingo*, 1987

▸ **throw a party**

to lose heavily when gambling US, 1982

- — David M. Hayano, *Poker Faces*, p. 187, 1982

▸ **throw a shine**

to ignore someone US, 1947

Usage by Mexican-American youth (Pachucos) in the south-western US.

- — *Common Ground*, p. 81, Summer 1947

▸ **throw blows**

to fight US, 1965

- — Miss Cone, *The Slang Dictionary (Hawthorne High School)*, 1965

▸ **throw hands**

to fight US, 2002

- — Gary K. Farlow, *Prison-ese*, p. 73, 2002

▸ **throw it to someone**

from a male perspective, to have sex US, 1969

- My boyfriend and I do it at least once a day, generally oftener, but ever now and then he gets a honk out of watching one of his friends throw it to me. — *Screw*, p. 16, 16th May 1969

▸ **throw one**

from the male perspective, to have sex US, 1954

- Man, would I like to throw one to her. — Bernard Wolfe, *The Late Risers*, p. 143, 1954

▸ **throw shade**

to project a defiant attitude US, 1995

- — Steven Daly and Nathaniel Wice, *alt.culture*, p. 266, 1995

▸ **throw signs**

to flash hand signals, almost always gang-related US, 2001

- When this baby moved back here, he was throwin' gang signs and talkin' just like a little gangbanger. — *Rolling Stone*, p. 85, 12th April 2001

▸ **throw the bald-headed champ**

to perform oral sex on a man US, 1972

- And then you start pulling on the rope [masturbating him] or to throw the bald-headed champ [perform fellatio], boy you have reached rock bottom in my opinion. — Bruce Jackson, *In the Life*, p. 171, 1972

▸ **throw the knockwurst**

from the male perspective, to have sex US, 1973

- Well, I shined my light in there and here's these two down on the seat, the old boy throwing the knockwurst to his girlfriend[.] — Joseph Wambaugh, *The Blue Knight*, p. 245, 1973

▸ **throw the latch**

in a hotel, to activate a mechanical device advising hotel employees to carefully watch activity in a particular room US, 1954

- So, as I say, I'd automatically signaled to the bellman to "throw the latch." This is simply a device which makes it easier for employees to keep an eye on suspected parties. — Dev Collans with Stewart Sterling, *I was a House Detective*, p. 38, 1954

▸ **throw under the bus**

to treat very poorly US, 1991

- In Andersen's perspective, every brilliant performance by Streisand was given after stepping over some poor schnook she threw under the bus on the way up. — *The Buffalo News*, p. G6, 9th April 2006

▸ **throw up your set**

to flash gang hand signals US, 1995

- — Bill Valentine, *Gang Intelligence Manual*, p. 78, 1995
- "Put Yo Hood Up" they shout on the next single, a call to throw up your "set," or neighborhood's hand signs. — *Atlanta Journal-Constitution*, p. 7D, 31st May 2001

throwaway noun

an outer garment quickly discarded by a criminal after a crime to thwart easy identification US, 1987

- — Carsten Stroud, *Close Pursuit*, p. 277, 1987

throwaway adjective

used of a gun unregistered and not capable of being traced, and thus used to place in the vicinity of someone whom the police have shot to justify the shooting US, 1981

- Then he could be shown a mug shot, given a throwaway gun, and programed to relive the century-old killing of the Kid[.] — Joseph Wambaugh, *The Glitter Dome*, p. 42, 1981
- You done that before. Written false reports, put throwaway guns in dead hands. — Seth Morgan, *Homeboy*, p. 328, 1990
- They'd pull a throwaway gun out of their boot, put a bullet in the chamber, and say, "Watch this." — Yusuf Jah, *Uprising*, pp. 159–160, 1995
- Police known the slang: "throwaway gun." A bad cop will keep an untraceable gun stashed in the cruiser in case an arrest goes bad, and the suspected perp who lies dead in the street did not have a weapon. The officer will take the gun and drop it next to the suspected but now deceased dead guy. — *Weekly Planet (Saratoga, Florida)*, 27th March 2003

throw down verb

1 to threaten someone with a weapon; to fight US, 1972

- The last one, I walked in and threw down on [pointed his gun at] the guy. — Bruce Jackson, *In the Life*, p. 152, 1972
- The one with the poncho then did his Clint Eastwood impersonation and swept back the poncho and threw down on Manny Lopez with his M-1 carbine air rifle[.] — Joseph Wambaugh, *Lines and Shadows*, p. 209, 1984
- — William K. Bentley and James M. Corbett, *Prison Slang*, p. 88, 1992
- Stunned at how ready I was to throw down, the two kids just stood in front of me with their hands at their sides looking at me like I was crazy. — Earl "DMX" Simmons, *E.A.R.L.*, p. 71, 2002

2 to kill US, 1963

- Whoever throws you down makes five grand. The word's out on you. — Mickey Spillane, *Me, Hood!*, p. 40, 1963

throw-down gun; throwdown noun

a gun that is not registered and not capable of being traced, placed by the police in the vicinity of someone whom they have shot to justify the shooting US, 1980

- "Unless it was a throw-down gun," he said, wiping his mouth with a napkin. — Gerald Petievich, *To Die in Beverly Hills*, p. 65, 1983
- Remember, I still got that gun you were carrying—I figure that's my throwdown. The story is, I had to shoot you because of the gun. — Carl Hiaasen, *Native Tongue*, p. 375, 1991
- Ray always kept a "throw-down gun" on him to drop by a body if some street character got funky and had to take a seat on the sky bus. — Stephen J. Cannell, *The Tin Collectors*, p. 9, 2001
- The Wilshire guys bought extra throw-down guns. — James Ellroy, *Destination Morgue*, p. 233, 2004

throw off verb

to perform at a skill level below your capability US, 1965

- If I couldn't beat Jesse out, he would throw off just enough to make the game look right, and let me win. — Henry Williamson, *Hustler!*, p. 79, 1965

throw-out noun

1 the prize that a carnival game operator arranges for a player to win to entice more customers to play US, 1985

- — Gene Sorrows, *All About Carnivals*, p. 27, 1985: "Terminology"

2 a trinket thrown by a parader to spectators US, 1951

- — *American Speech*, p. 111, May 1951: "The terminology of Mardi Gras"

throw-up noun

a large, simple piece of graffiti art US, 1982

- A throw-up usually consists of a two- or three-letter name that is formed, usually rounded, into a single unit that can be sprayed quickly and with a minimum of paint on the sides of a train. — Craig Castleman, *Getting Up*, p. 29, 1982

- Also sighted: one throw-up; this makes me happy. — William Upski Wimsatt, *Bomb the Suburbs*, p. 43, 1994
- Tey started with insides, then throw ups and outlines on the nice white trains, and soon went to pieces. — Stephen Power, *The Art of Getting Over*, p. 122, 1999

throw up *verb*
to create large graffiti pieces (especially on trains, walls, etc.) *US, 1994*
- Any of y'all know any handball courts where we could throw up terrible? — *The Source*, p. 52, August 1994

thrush *noun*
a female singer *US, 1940*
- Pasternak later admitted she was no world-beater as a thrush. — Jack Lait and Lee Mortimer, *New York*, p. 125, 1948
- — Arnold Shaw, *Lingo of Tin-Pan Alley*, p. 20, 1950
- — Lavada Durst, *The Jives of Dr. Hepcat*, p. 14, 1953

thrust *noun*
amyl, butyl or isobutyl nitrite *UK, 1996*
A definite suggestion of sexual vigor and therefore, probably, derives from brand marketing as a male sex-aid.
- Street names [...] stud, thrust, TNT. — James Kay and Julian Cohen, *The Parents' Complete Guide to Young People and Drugs*, p. 144, 1998

thruster *noun*
an amphetamine or other central nervous system stimulant *US, 1969*
- — Richard Lingeman, *Drugs from A to Z*, p. 236, 1969

thud *nickname*
an F-105 Thunderchief aircraft *US, 1965*
From the fact that many were shot down during the Vietnam war. A two-seated F-105 was known as a "double thud."
- — *Time*, p. 34, 10th December 1965
- — Carl Fleischhauer, *A Glossary of Army Slang*, p. 22, 1968
- "Got out and man your guns, my boys, you have a job to do." / The Thuds are coming in! — Joseph Tuso, *Singing the Vietnam Blues*, p. 45, 1990: Battle Hymn of the 85-mm Gunner
- The $2 million "Thud" was the principal air Force tactical strike aircraft, flying more missions than any other bomber but suffering more losses. — *Tulsa (Oklahoma) World*, p. G1, 20th March 2003

thugged out *adjective*
strong, violent, immersed in the criminal lifestyle *US, 2005*
- Even the most thugged-out criminals feared him like the badass hustler that he was. — Noire, *Candy Licker*, p. 5, 2005

thugsta *noun*
a strong and violent criminal *US, 2005*
- What he didn't know was why the thugsta on the ground was slumped in the corner with a bullet hole in his forehead. — Noire, *Candy Licker*, p. 256, 2005

thumb *verb*
to hitchhike *US, 1932*
- Thumbing rides is against the law in St. Paul. — Max Shulman, *The Many Loves of Dobie Gillis*, p. 185, 1951
- After that I started thumbing. — Joe Houston, *The Gay Flesh*, p. 16, 1965
- On University Avenue in Berkeley at the last light before the freeway on-ramp trip, the last place possible on University for hitchhiking out are groups of people thumbing, sitting with beautiful dogs, with signs for America. — *The Last Supplement to the Whole Earth Catalog*, p. 36, March 1971
- I must have looked strange, standing there on the highway thumbing a ride. — Herbert Huncke, *Guilty of Everything*, p. 20, 1990

thumb-check *noun*
a cursory examination of a long document or package of documents *US, 1986*
US naval aviator usage.
- — *United States Naval Institute Proceedings*, p. 108, October 1986

thump *noun*
a fight *US, 1971*
- — Hermese E. Roberts, *The Third Ear*, 1971

thump *verb*
1 to fight *US, 1994*
- The best way to guarantee respect was simply to be able to thump. — Nathan McCall, *Makes Me Wanna Holler*, p. 54, 1994

2 to defeat someone soundly *UK, 1594*
- I've played with him a few times and notice that he thumps me real bad a couple of times and that when he notices I'm losing interest he lets me come close to beating him. — Jim Bouton, *Ball Four*, p. 140, 1970

thumper *noun*
1 a street fighter *US, 1994*
- Some of the serious thumpers found ways to literally use their heads. — Nathan McCall, *Makes Me Wanna Holler*, p. 55, 1994
2 a hand grenade launcher *US, 1990*
- The thumper won't throw grenades anymore and the miniguns are constipated, but he's still got fourteen rockets left, by God. — Dennis Marvicsin and Jerold A. Greenfield, *Maverick*, p. 209, 1990
- He wanted me to carry a "thumper" (M-79 grenade launcher). — Gary Linderer, *The Eyes of the Eagle*, p. 57, 1991
3 a drummer *US, 1981*
- — Don Wilmeth, *The Language of American Popular Entertainment*, p. 273, 1981

thumper bumper *noun*
in pinball, a bumper that upon impact with a ball scores and then propels the ball back into play *US, 1977*
- — Bobbye Claire Natkin and Steve Kirk, *All About Pinball*, p. 117, 1977

thump gun *noun*
an M79 grenade launcher *US, 1982*
Vietnam war usage.
- — *Maledicta*, p. 259, Summer/Winter 1982

thump therapy *noun*
behavior modification by physical beating *US, 1992*
- [H]aving a guard tell you how he gave a belligerent convict some "thump therapy," a euphemism for hitting an inmate, makes you squirm. — Pete Earley, *The Hot House*, p. 41, 1992

thunder *verb*
to excel *US, 1989*
- — Pamela Munro, *U.C.L.A. Slang*, p. 85, 1989

Thunder Road *noun*
Highway 13, north of Saigon, South Vietnam *US, 1967*
So named because of the US Army's frequent **THUNDER RUNS** on Highway 13.
- During the war with the Viet Minh the French called Highway 13 "Route du Sang"—The Road of Blood. Now the Americans called it "Thunder Road," and it was Alpha Troop's job to supply the thunder if needed. — David Reed, *Up Front in Vietnam*, p. 23, 1967
- These are around inhabited areas; there were villages all up and down the highway. This was Highway 13, "Thunder Road." — John Kerry, *The New Soldier*, p. 62, 1971

thunder run *noun*
during the Vietnam war, a tactic of having a small armored convoy drive at high speeds shooting at both sides of the road to thwart enemy ambushes *US, 1982*
Possibly originating in the Korean war, 1950–53, where it was used figuratively for a final bar crawl before leaving a posting.
- One, nicknamed thunder run, involved the use of armored vehicles in all-night road marches[.] — Donn Starry, *Armored Combat in Vietnam*, p. 71, 1982
- They put on a bit of show for the grunts that May morning, a whole line of them roaring down Highway 13 in an open-throttle "thunder run" meant to detonate any hidden enemy mines. — Peter Goldmand and Tony Fuller, *Charlie Company*, p. 152, 1983
- They were called Thunder Runs, high-speed gauntlet races by the mechanized infantry units of the army's 1st Infantry Division along Highway 13[.] — Kregg Jorgenson, *Very Crazy G.I.*, pp. 165–166, 2001

thunder thighs *noun*
large, heavy thighs, especially on a woman *US, 1977*
- [A]s he tells his girl friend, the ravishing, all-too-human Beverley "Thunder-Thighs" Switzler, "Listen honey—if anybody in this world knows what it is to be oppressed!" — *Washington Post*, p. B1, 27th December 1977
- "We saw him, and he had those thunder thighs," Spates said. — *Daily Oklahoman (Oklahoma City)*, p. 5D, 11th January 2004

thunk *noun*
in computing, code that supplies an address *US, 1991*
- — Eric S. Raymond, *The New Hacker's Dictionary*, p. 349, 1991

thunk *verb*
used as an alternative past tense of "think" in place of "thought" *UK, 1876*
Intentionally jocular or rural.
- "Who would have thunk it?" irrepressibly remarked "Pokey" (Mary) Prothero[.] — Mary McCarthy, *The Group*, p. 6, 1963

TI *nickname*
the federal correctional institution, Terminal Island, California *US, 1981*
- He shanked an inmate during his second year in T.I. but they couldn't prove it. — Gerald Petievich, *Money Men*, p. 133, 1981

TIA
used as Internet shorthand to mean "thanks in advance" *US, 1997*
- — Andy Ihnatko, *Cyberspeak*, p. 190, 1997

tic *noun*
phencyclidine *US, 1977*
- — *Drummer*, p. 77, 1977

tick *noun*
1 a moment; a second, a minute *UK, 1879*
- From the sound of clockwork as a second hand moves between the measured increments. A Glossary of Harlemisms. — Jack Lait and Lee Mortimer, *New York Confidential*, p. 236, 1948
- I figure that there's gonna be some killing in a few ticks. — Joseph Nazel, *Black Cop*, p. 63, 1974
2 in a hospital, an intern *US, 1994*
- — Sally Williams, *"Strong" Words*, p. 142, 1994

ticked off *adjective*
angry *US, 1959*
- Also, I was slightly ticked off at the prospects. — Glendon Swarthout, *Where the Boys Are*, p. 28, 1960
- Why was he ticked off? — Frederick Kohner, *Gidget Goes Hawaiian*, p. 58, 1961
- You were sore anyway 'cause you didn't want to talk to that grand jury. I mean you were good and ticked off. — Elmore Leonard, *Pronto*, p. 49, 1993

ticker *noun*
1 a clock, especially a pocket watch *US, 1964*
- Joe, you have a short, some fronts, and a fine ticker too. — Bruce Jackson, *Get Your Ass in the Water and Swim Like Me*, p. 91, 1964
- A Elgin ticker with a solid gold band / And a egg-sized diamond flashed on his hand. — Dennis Wepman et al., *The Life*, p. 31, 1976
2 the heart *US, 1930*
Analogized to a clock ticking.
- Lee wasn't a young man any more, a thing like that could raise a lot of hell with a guy's ticker. — Mickey Spillane, *One Lonely Night*, p. 68, 1951
- With his cigarette hand, Selena's brother tapped the left side of his chest. "Ticker," he said. — J.D. Salinger, *Nine Stories*, p. 48, 1953
- If I have a bum ticker, you can bet it comes from liquor. — Dan Burley, *Diggeth Thou?*, p. 37, 1959
- My ticker rioted. A delicious stealing lust electrified my genitals. — Iceberg Slim (Robert Beck), *Airtight Willie and Me*, p. 27, 1979

ticket *noun*
1 a warrant or bill of detainer *US, 2002*
- — John R. Armore and Joseph D. Wolfe, *Dictionary of Desperation*, p. 54, 1976
- I prevailed on Dennis to okay a ticket[.] — Duncan MacLaughlin, *The Filth*, p. 113, 2002
2 an official misconduct report in prison *US, 1976*
- — John R. Armore and Joseph D. Wolfe, *Dictionary of Desperation*, p. 54, 1976
- — Hugh Morgan, *Ye Shall Know It*, pp. 266–267, Summer/Winter 1981: "By its slang"
3 an order to be locked in solitary confinement *US, 1965*
- So he saw us sittin' down and he told the officer down in the hole to write us a ticket. — Henry Williamson, *Hustler!*, p. 146, 1965
4 in prison, a contract for a killing or beating *US, 1974*
- — Paul Glover, *Words from the House of the Dead*, 1974
5 in horseracing, a betting receipt *US, 1951*
- — David W. Maurer, *Argot of the Racetrack*, p. 64, 1951
6 a playing card *US, 1961*
As in the expression "I held some good tickets."
- — Irv Roddy, *Friday Night Poker: Penny Poker for Millions*, p. 221, 1961
7 LSD; a dose of LSD *US, 1969*
Another LSD-as-travel metaphor.
- — Richard A. Spears, *The Slang and Jargon of Drugs and Drink*, p. 509, 1986

ticket agent *noun*
an LSD dealer *US, 1974*
Premised on a **TRIP** metaphor.
- — Stewart L. Tubbs and Sylvia Moss, *Human Communication*, p. 120, 1974
- — Walter Way, *The Drug Scene*, p. 115, 1977

Ticket Bastard *nickname*
the Ticketmaster ticket service *US, 1994*
- — David Shenk and Steve Silberman, *Skeleton Key*, p. 288, 1994

ticket puncher *noun*
in the military, an officer receiving nearly automatic promotion from rank to rank with short periods in combat to justify the promotion *US, 1973*
- [N]ow, just like the rest of the ticket punchers, I was to receive mine. — Anthony Herbert, *Soldier*, p. 395, 1973

ticketpunching *noun*
in the military, nearly automatic promotion from rank to rank with short periods in combat to justify the promotion *US, 1988*
- The real reason, which held true for the Marine Corps too and which explained why the practice was derisively called "ticket-punching," was a mechanistic promotion process. — Neil Sheehan, *A Bright Shining Lie*, p. 650, 1988
- So it has a name, I thought: ticket punching—the syndrome that had me chasing down that elusive degree. — David H. Hackworth, *About Face*, p. 348, 1989

tickle *verb*
to administer oral sex to a male pornographer performer before or between scenes to help him maintain an erection *US, 2000*
- — Ana Loria, *1 2 3 Be A Porn Star!*, p. 165, 2000: "Glossary of adult sex industry terms"

▸ **tickle a bug**
in computing, to activate a normally inactive malfunction *US, 1991*
- — Eric S. Raymond, *The New Hacker's Dictionary*, p. 350, 1991

▸ **tickle the pickle**
from the male perspective, to have sex *US, 1964*
- You and Myra better stop playing tickle the pickle, boy, before you bat your brains out with your balls. — Jim Thompson, *Pop. 1280*, p. 192, 1964

tickled; tickled to death; tickled pink *adjective*
very pleased *UK, 1907*
- She would have been tickled pink to get rid of Oscar and wall up the television set. — Max Shulman, *Rally Round the Flag, Boys!*, p. 71, 1957
- I'm just tickled to death to have you aboard! — Walker Percy, *The Last Gentleman*, p. 154, 1966

tickler *noun*
an office system that serves to remind of impending deadlines *US, 1905*
- "Two years ago, we created our own tickler system, because the standard vendor packages didn't do everything we wanted them to," says Connie Marmet, vice-president and manager at Bank of America's corporate trust department. — *ABA Banking Journal*, p. 102, September 1991
- This command procedure lets you prepare a tickler-file-type reminder to be received in your VMSmail on the desired day. — *Digital Systems Journal*, p. 14, March 1993

tick twenty *noun*
ten o'clock *US, 1946*
- How can any outsider latch on to the real flavor of a secret code in which tick twenty means ten o'clock[.] — Mezz Mezzrow, *Really the Blues*, p. 220, 1946

ticky *adjective*
old-fashioned, out-of-date *US, 1960*
- — Robert George Reisner, *The Jazz Titans*, p. 166, 1960

tid-bit *noun*
an appetizing and toothsome woman *US, 1973*
- When I got back to the edge, all the cats and their ribs started right in on jiving me about my young tid-bit catching 'em, and I went right along with it. — A.S. Jackson, *Gentleman Pimp*, p. 44, 1973

tiddly; tiddley *adjective*
mildly drunk *UK, 1905*

- Once a disgruntled employee got a little tiddly in "The Saratoga[.]"
  — Alson Smith, *Syndicate City*, p. 188, 1954
- Mary-Ann got tiddly on snaps and, all in all, I was right. — Gore Vidal,
  Myra Breckinridge, p. 243, 1968
- One night the designer was at the bar, a little tiddly as they used to
  say[.] — John Francis Hunter, *The Gay Insider*, p. 221, 1971

tidy whities *noun*
white, boxer-style men's underpants *US, 1994*

- But back in the beginning came tidy whities, better known as your
  father's standard boxers and Y-front Fruit of the Looms. — *Palm Beach
  (Florida) Post*, p. 3D, 12th December 1994
- You seldom see a U.S. senator with his tidy-whities above his
  pinstripes. — *Providence (Rhode Island) Journal-Bulletin*, p. 1G, 14th June 2001

tie *verb*
▶ **tie on one**
to get very drunk *US, 1951*

- The bars close at two in Detroit and Sunday you can't buy any booze
  till noon. Give everybody a chance to go to their place of worship
  before they tie one on. — Elmore Leonard, *Out of Sight*, p. 169, 1996

▶ **tie the knot**
to marry *UK, 1605*

- T.S. and Brandi tied the knot after graduation at Universal Studios,
  Florida. — *Mallrats*, 1995
- After you tie the knot, the truth about each other finally comes out.
  — Chris Rock, *Rock This!*, p. 155, 1997

tie up *verb*
to apply an improvised tourniquet, usually on the arm, preparatory to injecting a drug *US, 1990*

- The shades would be pulled down and the next thing you know there
  was a bottle of cobalt blue loaded with liquid amphetamine. Everyone
  immediately tied up. — Herbert Huncke, *Guilty of Everything*, p. 141, 1990

tiger *noun*
▶ **take a tiger for a walk**
(used of a food addict) to eat in moderation *US, 1998*
A term in twelve-step recovery programs such as Alcoholics
Anonymous.

- — Christopher Cavanaugh, *AA to Z*, p. 170, 1998

tiger cage *noun*
an underground, high security jail cell *US, 1992*

- — William K. Bentley and James M. Corbett, *Prison Slang*, p. 8, 1992

tiger country *noun*
in hospital operating room usage, any part of the body where
surgery is high risk *US, 1994*

- — Sally Williams, *"Strong" Words*, p. 162, 1994

tiger in the tank *noun*
a linear amplifier for a citizens' band radio *US, 1976*
From the 1960s Esso advertising slogan "Put a tiger in your tank."

- — Porter Bibb, *CB Bible*, p. 107, 1976

tiger lady *noun*
a female Vietnamese civilian building worker at a US facility
during the war *US, 1977*

- Those nights there was a serious tiger lady going around on a Honda
  shooting American officers on the street[.] — Michael Herr, *Dispatches*,
  p. 41, 1977

tiger piss *noun*
Tiger Paw™ Beer *US, 1985*
A south Vietnamese speciality, made with formaldehyde.

- The label of the bottles had a picture of a tiger, and for that and
  other reasons we called it "tiger piss." — David Donovan, *Once a Warrior
  King*, p. 75, 1985

tiger stripe *noun*
a scar from intravenous drug injections *US, 1958*

- Ain't no marks to show. No tiger stripes. — Willard Motley, *Let No Man
  Write My Epitaph*, p. 129, 1958

tiger stripes *noun*
camouflage worn in the jungle *US, 1971*

- You don't wear tiger stripes in Japan. — Ronald J. Glasser, *365 Days*, p. 201,
  1971

tiger suit *noun*
a jungle camouflage uniform *US, 1967*

- I wore an Army uniform of camouflaged jungle green, called a "Tiger
  suit," an Australian Go to Hell bush hat[.] — Elaine Shepard, *The Doom Pussy*,
  p. 1, 1967

tiger team *noun*
a group of computer geniuses hired to explore the weaknesses of a computer system *US, 1994*

- tiger team—A hacker or group of hackers who are engaged by an
  organization to find the security flaws in that organization's computer
  system. — The Knightmare, *Secrets of a Super Hacker*, p. 181, 1994

tight *noun*
a close and trusted friend *US, 2006*

- On the street, the circle was your group of tights—your buddies.
  — Stephen J. Cannell, *White Sister*, p. 139, 2006

tight *adjective*
1 tipsy; drunk *US, 1830*

- He was too busy to bother with kids who were half tight. — Irving
  Shulman, *The Amboy Dukes*, p. 79, 1947
- And if you get tight, I'll take you home — Philip Wylie, *Opus 21*, p. 101,
  1949
- It happened, and it was not at all what the group or even Mother
  would have imagined, not a bit sordid or messy, in spite of Dick's
  being tight. — Mary McCarthy, *The Group*, p. 31, 1963
- "I'm also a little bit tight right now." — Glenn Savan, *White Palace*, p. 174,
  1987

2 of a slot machine, disadvantageous to the gambler in terms
of the frequency of payouts *US, 1984*

- — J. Edward Allen, *The Basics of Winning Slots*, p. 59, 1984

3 friendly *US, 1956*

- I'm not tight with her. — Willard Motley, *Let No Man Write My Epitaph*, p. 111,
  1958
- I didn't get tight with anybody in the reception center. — Claude
  Brown, *Manchild in the Promised Land*, p. 135, 1965
- He was tight with Earl Bassey. — Edwin Torres, *Carlito's Way*, p. 20, 1975
- There's a lonely Hindu works at the 7-H across the street. Get in
  tight with him. — *Chasing Amy*, 1997

4 good; fashionable; in style *US, 1998*

- — *Columbia Missourian*, p. 1A, 19th October 1998

▶ **in a tight**
in serious trouble *US, 1984*

- — Inez Cardozo-Freeman, *The Joint*, p. 507, 1984

tight-ass *noun*
a highly strung, nervous person *US, 1969*

- She preferred to think that was the case, rather than that Marx Marvelous was simply another intellectual tight-ass smugly ripping at every
  cosmic curtain to expose the specter of dank feminine (irrational!!!)
  mysticism that he is certain lurks behind it. — Tom Robbins, *Another
  Roadside Attraction*, p. 185, 1971
- "Nora, you're being irrational." "And you're being a regular tight-
  ass." — Glenn Savan, *White Palace*, p. 180, 1987
- Fenster always worked with McManus. He was a real tight-ass, but
  when it came to the job, he was right on. — *The Usual Suspects*, 1995

tight-assed *adjective*
highly strung, nervous *US, 1970*

- My tight-assed smugness disappeared quickly. — Harvey Rottenburg,
  Planted, Burnt, and Busted [The Howard Marks Book of Dope Stories], p. 340, 1970

tighten *verb*
▶ **tighten the wig**
to smoke marijuana *US, 2001*

- — Don R. McCreary (Editor), *Dawg Speak*, 2001

▶ **tighten up someone's game**
to educate or coach someone *US, 1972*

- If her man hadn't tightened her game up for her, she would be an
  easy mark to switch envelopes on. — Donald Goines, *Whoreson*, p. 203,
  1972

tightener *noun*
1 any alcoholic drink *US, 1969*

- "Fresheners," Nancy said. "Tighteners and fresheners. Sometimes
  drinkees or martin-eyes." — Elmore Leonard, *The Big Bounce*, p. 88, 1969

2 in horseracing, a race seen as preparation for the next race *US, 1994*
- — Igor Kushyshyn et al., *The Gambling Times Guide to Harness Racing*, p. 124, 1994

tight laces *noun*
commercially manufactured cigarettes, especially with filters *US, 1990*
- — Charles Shafer, *Folk Speech in Texas Prisons*, p. 216, 1990

tight roll *noun*
a manufactured cigarette *US, 1984*
- I had tight rolls and a punk and I was uptown. — Inez Cardozo-Freeman, *The Joint*, p. 537, 1984

tightwad *noun*
a miserly person *US, 1906*
- Someone gets the check and McDermott puts it on his gold AmEx card, which conclusively proves that he's high on coke since he's a famous tight- wad. — Bret Easton Ellis, *American Psycho*, p. 209, 1991

tighty-whities *noun*
form-fitting men's jockey shorts *US, 1985*
- — Connie Eble (Editor), *UNC-CH Campus Slang*, p. 4, April 1985
- He had his tighty whities on. — Michelle Tea, *Rent Girl*, p. 87, 2004

tig ol' bitties; tig bitties *noun*
large breasts *US, 1995*
An intentional Spoonerism of "big old titties."
- I know you would much rather be with a girl if she had some tig bitties. — *k12.chat.junior*, 27th May 1995
- — Connie Eble (Editor), *UNC-CH Campus Slang*, p. 5, Spring 2001
- My tig old bitties and my lumpy ass. — Wendy Coakley-Thompson, *What You Won't Do for Love*, p. 265, 2006

Tijuana Bible *noun*
a pornographic comic book *US, 1947*
- I would say the most prevalent would be the type known to us, or in the language of the people who deal in it, as the Tijuana Bible, which is a small booklet, about 2 by 3 inches, of a cartoon type, that is very lewd and very obscene in its character. — United States Senate Committee on the Judiciary, *Juvenile Delinquency*, p. 374, 1955
- "Sex in the Comics will be a faithful representation of the old-time Tijuana bibles—it's funny as hell." — Carolyn See, *Blue Money*, p. 74, 1974
- For those who remember the eight-page Tijuana Bibles—filthy cartoon sequences starring your favorite comic-strip heroes—or those who've never seen them, they're back. — Stephen Lewis, *The Whole Bedroom Catalog*, p. 167, 1975
- — *Maledicta*, p. 167, 1979: "A glossary of ethnic slurs in american english"

tiles *noun*
dominoes *US, 1959*
- — Dominic Armanino, *Dominoes*, p. 15, 1959

till-tap *verb*
to steal money from a cash till *US, 1970*
- I'm always seeing his name on robbery, burglary, or till tap reports. — Joseph Wambaugh, *The New Centurions*, 1970
- He had liberated two bennys [overcoats] off hangers and was nonchalantly till tapping (rifling a cash register) men's wear bread. — Iceberg Slim (Robert Beck), *Airtight Willie and Me*, p. 5, 1979

till tapper *noun*
in a casino, a person who steals coins or tokens from a slot machine being played by someone else *US, 1893*
- They just grab it and walk out. We call these guys till-tappers. — Harry King, *Box Man*, p. 82, 1972
- I once caught a till tapper at the Tropicana in Las Vegas when he was reaching into the till on the slot machine that my wife was playing. — Charles W. Lund, *Robbing the One-Armed Bandits*, p. 122, 1999

till tapping *noun*
theft from a cash register when the cashier is distracted *US, 1964*
- But since you've been out you've learned new names for the game / such as till-tapping, the carpet, the rope, and the drag, which all leads up to one thing. — Bruce Jackson, *Get Your Ass in the Water and Swim Like Me*, p. 92, 1964

Tilly *noun*
used as a personification of the police *US, 1970*
- — *American Speech*, p. 59, Spring–Summer 1970: "Homosexual slang"

tilt *noun*
▸ **on tilt**
used of a poker player's playing, exceptionally poor *US, 1979*
- — John Scarne, *Scarne's Guide to Modern Poker*, p. 285, 1979

timber *noun*
1 a toothpick *US, 1948*
- — Jack Lait and Lee Mortimer, *New York Confidential*, p. 236, 1948: "A glossary of Harlemisms"
2 in horseracing, a hurdle in a steeplechase race *US, 1976*
- — Tom Ainslie, *Ainslie's Complete Guide to Thoroughbred Racing*, p. 340, 1976
3 in poker, the cards that have been discarded *US, 1951*
- — *American Speech*, p. 102, May 1951

timber nigger *noun*
a Native American Indian *US, 1993*
- You assume that because I can lose my job because of my boss, that would hurt me more than a child who might call me a "timber-nigger." —*group/soc.culture.native*, 28th September 1993

timber rider *noun*
in horseracing, a jockey in a steeplechase event *US, 1976*
- — Tom Ainslie, *Ainslie's Complete Guide to Thoroughbred Racing*, p. 340, 1976

time *noun*
1 a five-dollar unit in betting *US, 1974*
- [W]hen a bettor used the expression "a time" it meant $5, as in, "give me Green Bay thirty times," which even I understood meant $150. — Gary Mayer, *Bookie*, p. 77, 1974
2 time in prison; a jail sentence *UK, 1837*
- They talk' like they serious about me doin' that machine gun time. — *Jackie Brown*, 1997

▸ **do time**
1 to serve a prison sentence, especially in a manner that preserves the prisoner's sanity *UK, 1865*
- The grateful Satira, later a Page 1 sensation, did her time, got out of the can, and promptly booked herself into his opposition saloon. — Jack Lait and Lee Mortimer, *Chicago Confidential*, p. 67, 1950
- Nearly every one of them had done some time[.] — Malcolm X and Alex Haley, *The Autobiography of Malcolm X*, p. 87, 1964
- He did the time; he didn't let the time do him. — Donald Goines, *White Man's Justice, Black Man's Grief*, p. 201, 1973
- Where I was from, who I knew, how I knew Nice Guy, had I done time, shit like that. — *Reservoir Dogs*, 1992
2 to stay after school in detention *US, 1954*
- — *This Week Magazine*, *New York Herald Tribune*, p. 46, 28th February 1954

▸ **do your own time**
when in prison, to focus on your present, not the future, not the past, and not anybody else's problems *US, 1954*
- Experienced convicts and prison officials agree that the best way to get along in prison is to "do your own time." — John Martin, *Break Down the Walls*, p. 139, 1954
- Hence, expressions among the "con-wise" as, "Do your own time," meaning stay clear of another's tension. — Neal Cassady, *Grace Beats Karma*, p. 42, 20th August 1958
- "Shouldn't we help him?" Doug asked Carl. "Do your own time," Carl told him shortly. — Malcom Braly, *Felony Tank*, p. 31, 1961

▸ **for the time**
in poolroom betting, playing with the loser paying for the use of the table *US, 1967*
- When one player says to another "Let's just play sociable," as often as not he means that they should play for only a dollar or two, and at the very least means that they should play "for the time" (the loser paying the check). — Ned Polsky, *Hustlers, Beats, and Others*, p. 47, 1967

▸ **make time**
to flirt, to attempt to seduce *US, 1953*
- "Words like 'make out' or 'make time' and 'score,' and if some words stimulated me—made me feel things." — Irving Shulman, *College Confidential*, p. 27, 1960
- Here was me, with no diamond pinkie ring and walkin' around in my drawers and sneakers, making time with this doll. — Edwin Torres, *Carlito's Way*, p. 93, 1975

time-and-a-half *noun*
in blackjack, the payout to a player of one and a half times their bet when the player is dealt a natural 21 *US, 1977*

A pun using a term usually applied to an overtime rate of pay.
- — Lee Solkey, *Dummy Up and Deal*, p. 122, 1980
- — Thomas L. Clark, *The Dictionary of Gambling and Gaming*, p. 233, 1987

time out!
used for warning others of approaching police *US, 1997*
- [L]ookouts actually shout "Bob Brown," rather than the generic "Five-Oh" or "Time Out!" — David Simon and Edward Burns, *The Corner*, p. 16, 1997
- Police were in the 1100 block of N. Stockton St. about 6:25 p.m. Saturday when they heard a young male yell "Time out!"—street slang meaning police are in the area. — *Baltimore Sun*, p. 3B, 11th September 2000

time-stretcher *noun*
a prisoner whose attitude and actions serve to make the time served by others seem longer than it is *US, 2002*
- — Gary K. Farlow, *Prison-ese*, p. 74, 2002

tin *noun*
1 a police badge *US, 1949*
- — *New York Times Magazine*, p. 88, 16th March 1949
- Calvin's board took two days, and Susan got his tin. — Stephen J. Cannell, *The Tin Collectors*, p. 181, 2001

2 a police officer *US, 1950*
- — Thomas L. Clark, *The Dictionary of Gambling and Gaming*, p. 233, 1987

3 a gun *US, 1986*
- You're talking about the mob, the members of which could be carrying more tin than all the detectives on the force put together. — Robert Campbell, *Junkyard Dog*, p. 110, 1986

4 a safe *US, 1970*
- It was a strong box and tapping the tin took some finger work. — Red Rudensky, *The Gonif*, p. 82, 1970

tin can *noun*
1 a safe that is easily broken into by criminals *US, 1949*
- — Vincent J. Monteleone, *Criminal Slang*, p. 239, 1949
- — Bruce Jackson, *Outside the Law*, p. 60, 1972: "Glossary"

2 an older ship in disrepair *US, 1970*
- I know my orders are going to be for some damn tin can and I'm gonna wind up on the friggin' deck force. — Darryl Ponicsan, *The Last Detail*, p. 4, 1970

tin collector *noun*
a police officer or prosecutor involved in investigating police misconduct *US, 2001*
- She used to be their number one tin collector. — Stephen J. Cannell, *The Tin Collectors*, p. 44, 2001

tin ear *noun*
tone deafness *US, 1935*
- Who the hell is playing piano? Get that hippie out of here. He's got a tin ear. — *Nashville*, 1975

tin grin *noun*
any person with orthodontia *US, 1977*
- Adults have swollen the ranks of America's estimated four million "tin-grins" just as declining birth rate was depleting the traditional orthodontic market of young children and teen-agers. — *Washington Post*, p. B2, 10th October 1977
- For boomers, taunts like "brace-face," "tin grin" and "metal mouth" have made way for more sophisticated teasing. — *Washington Post*, p. F1, 13th January 2004

tinhorn *noun*
a cheap and offensive person *US, 1887*
- I knew those tinhorn sports didn't have fifteen cents left in their pockets after buying us a cheap meal. — Ethel Waters, *His Eye is on the Sparrow*, p. 79, 1951
- They were fairly impressed by this; well, maybe less impressed than worried that I might turn out a tin-horn. — Clancy Sigal, *Going Away*, p. 151, 1961

tinhorn *adjective*
shoddy; inconsequential; inferior *US, 1886*
- "You're just a cheap tinhorn punk, yellow to the core." — Chester Himes, *The Real Cool Killers*, p. 138, 1959

tinkle *noun*
urine, the act urination *US, 1960*

- "I gotta ... go tinkle," the big one said and went weaving and giggling toward the latrine[.] — Ken Kesey, *One Flew Over the Cuckoo's Nest*, p. 289, 1962
- ... comes bouncing up the stairs on the way to have a tinkle.
  — Robert Campbell, *Alice in La-La Land*, p. 263, 1987

tinkle *verb*
to urinate *US, 1958*
Children's vocabulary, used coyly by adults.
- "Will you tell me the one about how you used to tinkle in the water under the bridge?" — Warren Miller, *The Way We Live Now*, p. 130, 1958
- "I want to tinkle and get some very black coffee into me before I wake his lordship." — Stephen Longstreet, *The Flesh Peddlers*, p. 95, 1962
- I almost tinkled in my pajamas with the jolt of pain. — Iceberg Slim (Robert Beck), *Airtight Willie and Me*, p. 49, 1979
- "What happened to tinkle, DeDe? I taught you to say tinkle."
  — Armistead Maupin, *Babycakes*, p. 8, 1984

tinklebox *noun*
a piano *US, 1946*
- I stood by that beat-up old tinklebox in a hypnotic state[.] — Mezz Mezzrow, *Really the Blues*, p. 25, 1946

tinkler *noun*
a doorbell *US, 1946*
- Tinkler (n) The doorbell. — *Hit Parader*, p. 33, September 1946

tin plate *noun*
in circus and carnival usage, a law enforcement official in a small town *US, 1981*
- — Don Wilmeth, *The Language of American Popular Entertainment*, p. 146, 1981

tinsel-teeth *noun*
1 any person with orthodontia *US, 1979*
- I would be in school, and notice that if a girl had braces on her teeth the other kids would call her "tinsel-teeth" or "iron mouth." — *Washington Post*, p. D1, 24th November 1979
- The appearance of the devices led to the use of such pejorative terms as "metal mouth," "armor plate," "tinsel teeth," "tin-grin" and "Siberian railroad tracks." — *Washington Post*, p. Z17, 19th September 1995

2 orthodontic braces *US, 1971*
- — *Current Slang*, p. 10, Winter 1971

Tinsel Town *nickname*
Hollywood *US, 1939*

- Trembling with excitement, the voluptuous movie queen joined the ranks of other tinsel-town celebrities while her fans shouted: "C'mon sweater girl! Give!" — *Waterloo (Iowa) Sunday Courier*, p. 3, 25th May 1950

tints *noun*
1 sunglasses *US, 1972*
- — David Claerbaut, *Black Jargon in White America*, p. 83, 1972

2 tinted car windows *US, 1980*
- — Edith A. Folb, *runnin' down some lines*, p. 258, 1980

tiny *noun*
a very young member of a youth gang *US, 1981*
- All the midgets and tinys in the Black Spiders had been to the Hall. Most of the peewees even! — Joseph Wambaugh, *The Glitter Dome*, p. 110, 1981
- "I'm still a Tiny." — Leon Bing, *Do or Die*, p. 21, 1991

tiny gangster *noun*
a young member of a youth gang *US, 1989*
- in Los Angeles, where Blood and Crip membership totals about 25,000, "baby-gangsters" as young as 9 are regularly recruited and some gangs include even younger "tiny gangsters," the report said. — *UPI*, 4th August 1989
- "[H]e's listed in the Gang Street Alias Index under the name Li'l Silent, so at the very least he's a TG or a known associate." TG stood for "tiny gangster" and was basically a killer in training. — Stephen J. Cannell, *The Tin Collectors*, p. 147, 2001

Tiny Tim *noun*
a young hanger-on with a youth gang *US, 1949*
- A count is difficult because the larger gangs have "seniors," "juniors," and young auxiliaries known by such names as "Tiny Tims." — William Bernard, *Jailbait*, p. 80, 1949

Tio Taco *noun*
a Mexican-American who curries favor with the dominant white culture *US, 1969*
Literally "Uncle Taco."

- We want her replaced with a Third World person who is absolutely responsible to Third World and poor students, not to House Nigger, Uncle Tom, Tio Taco, or a Charlie Chan. — House Committee on Education and Labor, *Campus Unrest*, p. 15, 1969
- Literally, "Uncle Taco," the Mexican-American equivalent of an Uncle Tom. — *Time*, p. 18, 4th July 1969
- "All middle-class Mexicans—Tio Tacos." — Frank Bonham, *Viva Chicano*, p. 96, 1970
- But the split this time was not between the young militants and the old Tio Tacos. — Hunter S. Thompson, *The Great Shark Hunt*, p. 149, 1979

tip *noun*
1 a crowd *US, 2005*
- You and I are going to circulate around school, flash the money, and when a tip builds, talk about Vegas Night. — Peter Fenton, *Eyeing the Flash*, p. 76, 2005
2 used as a euphemism for payment for sex *US, 1987*
- The usual price (we call it a "tip") for a hand job is ten to twenty dollars[.] — Frederique Delacoste, *Sex Work*, p. 22, 1987
3 a small group with specific economic functions, such as a drug-selling enterprise *US, 1995*
- — Mark S. Fleisher, *Beggars & Thieves*, p. 292, 1995: "Glossary"
4 a gang *US, 1975*
- — Report to the Senate, *California Senate Committee on Civil Disorder*, p. 229, 1975
- [T]here is a system, a network of ties between all the tips (prison cliques), in the prisons. — Jack Henry Abbott, *In the Belly of the Beast*, p. 85, 1981
- Just remember, if you join a prison tip or click, you'll never fit in out there again. — Seth Morgan, *Homeboy*, p. 153, 1990
- He was turned down and told that Nevada would have to form its own tip. — Bill Valentine, *Gangs and Their Tattoos*, 2000
5 a crowd gathered in front of a carnival game or show *US, 1968*
- For a game, however, the operator usually grinds for his own tip, but he also has help. — E.E. Steck, *A Brief Examination of an Esoteric Folk*, p. 9, 1968
6 a steady, repeating player in a carnival midway game *US, 1985*
- — Gene Sorrows, *All About Carnivals*, p. 27, 1985: "Terminology"

tip *verb*
1 to behave foolishly *US, 1991*
Gulf war usage.
- — *American Speech*, p. 402, Winter 1991: "Among the new words"
2 to become aware of a swindle *US, 1963*
- Some marks fell for the twenties repeatedly, without ever tipping. — Jim Thompson, *The Grifters*, p. 6, 1963

▸ **tip in**
to inform, to betray *US, 1974*
- "Thought he was gonna get the street, for tipping them in." — George Higgins, *Cogan's Trade*, p. 110, 1974

tip-fiddle *noun*
a military deployment list *US, 2003*
Back-formation from TPFDL (time-phased forces deployment list).
- The tip-fiddle stipulates who is to go where, and when they are to get there. — Randeep Ramesh, *The War We Could Not Stop*, p. 301, 2003

tip off *verb*
to give information to someone, especially about an impending crime *US, 1891*
- You know we didn't go out to Riis Park like we told that dick. And the babes better be tipped off. — Irving Shulman, *The Amboy Dukes*, p. 113, 1947
- Somebody tipped off the police the other time, and I know who it was. — Lilian Jackson Braun, *The Cat Who Turned On and Off*, p. 140, 1995

tipster *noun*
in horseracing, someone who gives his opinions on various horses and their chances in a race *US, 1951*
- — David W. Maurer, *Argot of the Racetrack*, p. 65, 1951

tip up *verb*
to join a gang, especially a prison gang *US, 2000*

- White inmates who wanted to tip up with the AWs needed a sponsor. — Bill Valentine, *Gangs and Their Tattoos*, p. 11, 2000

tish note *noun*
in circus and carnival usage, counterfeit money, especially when used to pay a prostitute *US, 1981*
- — Don Wilmeth, *The Language of American Popular Entertainment*, p. 272, 1981

tit *noun*
1 the female breast *US, 1928*
- Uptown chick with a big gold cross once more rapping her soft little tits[.] — George Mandel, *Flee the Angry Strangers*, p. 403, 1952
- I have had two women so far, one American with huge tits and a splendid Mex whore in house. — Jack Kerouac, *Letter to Allen Ginsberg*, p. 353, 10th May 1952
- [S]ince I wasn't a woman, my use of the street expression for a woman's breasts, "tits," was tactless and unprintable. — Larry Rivers, *What Did I Do?*, p. 470, 1992
2 a small raised bump on a computer keyboard key, most commonly the f and j keys, to provide orientation for the user's fingers *US, 1991*
- — Eric S. Raymond, *The New Hacker's Dictionary*, p. 352, 1991

▸ **a tit full of Wild Turkey**
used for describing an alcoholic's fondest sexual fantasy *US, 1994*
- — Michael Dalton Johnson, *Talking Trash with Redd Foxx*, p. 17, 1994

▸ **get tit**
to succeed in the goal of touching or fondling a girl's breasts *US, 1974*
- "Ja get tit?" Richie whispered. "I din't try yet." "She got nice ones." — Richard Price, *The Wanderers*, p. 91, 1974

▸ **on the tit**
enjoying charity, or quasi-charity, in the form of undemanding work *US, 1957*
- You got the right idea, boy: stay on the government tit. Why not? Three squares and a flop, nothing to do, free medical care, free trips, plenty of time off, and a pension when you're ready to hang up the gloves! — Max Shulman, *Rally Round the Flag, Boys!*, p. 208, 1957

tit and clit chain *noun*
a decorative chain that connects a woman's pierced nipples and clitoris *US, 1996*
- Dawn unzipped her leather skirt, peeled it down, and showed Blaze where the second chain went. "Tit 'n' clit chains. Right now they're only clamped on, but pretty soon I'm gonna get 'em pierced." — Joseph Wambaugh, *Floaters*, p. 8, 1996

titbag *noun*
a brassiere *UK, 1961*
- — Michael Dalton Johnson, *Talking Trash with Redd Foxx*, p. 6, 1994

tit-for-tat *noun*
a reaction equal and opposite to the action *UK, 1556*
- This guy's looking to play tit for tat. That's not my game. I'm gonna play hardball. — *Tin Men*, 1987
- "I don't mean any money changed hands. I mean, there was a little quid pro quo. A little tit for tat." — Robert Campbell, *The Cat's Meow*, p. 120, 1988

tit fuck *noun*
an act of rubbing the penis in the compressed cleavage between a woman's breasts *US, 1972*
- — Robert A. Wilson, *Playboy's Book of Forbidden Words*, p. 241, 1972
- High lights: the scene where Wilder jerks off Jamie Gillis, and a magnificent tit-fuck between John Leslie and Mona Page (a startlet who had an all-too-brief career in porn). — *Adult Video*, p. 17, August/September 1986

tit-fuck *verb*
to rub the penis in the compressed cleavage between a woman's breasts *US, 1986*
- I tell her I would like to tit-fuck her and then maybe cut her arms off. — Bret Easton Ellis, *American Psycho*, p. 79–80, 1991
- I have always been well endowed (38E), so I am well aware of how men like to, to put it bluntly, tit-fuck. — Joan Elizabeth Lloyd, *Totally Private*, p. 157, 2001

tit fucking noun

stimulation of a man's penis between a woman's breasts *US, 1980*

- The guy started jabbering about belly fucking, ass fucking, tit fucking, elbow fucking, toe sucking[.] — Lucian Truscott, *Dress Gray*, p. 109, 1980
- Vicky Vette expresses her love for tit-fucking before doing just that. — Editors of Adult Video News, *The AVN Guide to the 500 Greatest Adult Films of All Time*, p. 120, 2005

tit joint noun

a bar or club featuring bare-breasted women servers *US, 1984*

- Jim Tom wanted us to stay over another night so he could take us to Honey Bun's Forth Worth's newest tit joint. — Dan Jenkins, *Life Its Ownself*, p. 330, 1984

tit magazine noun

a magazine featuring photographs of naked women *US, 1972*

- The "tit magazines" of the Fifties and Sixties, which were fit only for the garbage pail, have transformed themselves of late into "bush mags." — *Screw*, p. 4, 3rd July 1972
- "Bring me a couple of tit magazines." "I'm embarrassed to buy them," Charley said. — Richard Condon, *Prizzi's Honor*, p. 254, 1982

tit-man; tits-man noun

a male with a primary interest in a woman's breasts as a point of attraction *US, 1974*

- BERNIE: Where does she got off with those tits? DANNY: What a pair of boobs. BERINE: Not that I'm a tit man. DANNY: I Know. BERNIE: I mean, I dig tits ... DANNY: I don't blame you. BERNIE: ... but I wouldn't go out of my way for a pair of tits. — David Mamet, *Sexual Pervsity in Chicago*, p. 66, 1974
- I loved the way you went for my tits. You took your time with me and didn't rush. A tit man is a gentle man. — Gerald Petievich, *The Quality of the Informant*, p. 89, 1985

tit ring noun

a ring that passes through a pierced nipple *US, 1984*

- I show you my tit rings and you call me innocent. — Armistead Maupin, *Babycakes*, p. 254, 1984

tit run noun

a walk through a crowd in search of attractive female breasts *US, 1995*

- — *Maledicta*, p. 47, 1995: "Door whore and other new mexico restaurant slang"

tits adjective

exceptionally good *US, 1966*

- — *Current Slang*, p. 6, Fall 1966
- — Lewis Poteet, *Car & Motorcycle Slang*, p. 204, 1992

tits!

used for expressing excitement *US, 1992*

- Suddenly he cried, "Tits!" "What?" "This is absolutely tits. We got him!" — Joseph Wambaugh, *Fugitive Nights*, p. 102, 1992

tits and ass adjective

said of a movie, television program, or magazine featuring nudity *US, 1965*

- So I said, "Why don't we cut all these things right into the picture. If they want tits and ass, let's give 'em tits and ass." — *Los Angeles Free Press*, p. 5, 30th April 1965
- [S]he continued to be used at her speciality—beach and surfing movies, or "tits-and-ass flicks" as they were called. — Terry Southern, *Blue Movie*, p. 139, 1970
- And I'm embarrassed in retrospect that the chief voice of the anti-war movement in the District of Columbia clouded its message with so much of what Lenny Bruce would call "ordinary tits and ass," as distinguished from intelligent tits-and-ass[.] — Raymond Mungo, *Famous Long Ago*, p. 39, 1970
- Nestled close to the "swingers" were magazines variously known as "soft porn," and "tits and ass," or simply "T&A." — Jack Weatherford, *Porn Row*, p. 8, 1986

tit sling noun

a bra *US, 1991*

- "Can I have a 34C Auto Tit Sling please?" — *rec.humor*, 26th August 1991
- Randi Storm is in the classic blond bimbo mold, getting d.p'd out of her tit-sling and Daisy Dukes. — Editors of Adult Video News, *The AVN Guide to the 500 Greatest Adult Films of All Time*, p. 326, 2005

tittie twister noun

a pinch and twist of the breast, especially the nipple *US, 1997*

- Tittie Twisters. My dad told my sister and me that these would give you breast cancer so we wouldn't give them to each other when we were fighting. — Editors of Ben is Dead, *Retrohell*, p. 225, 1997

tit tip noun

a female nipple *US, 1982*

- — *Maledicta*, p. 131, Summer/Winter 1982: "Dyke diction: the language of lesbians"

tit tuck noun

cosmetic surgery to lift sagging breasts *US, 2005*

- "Is your tit tuck starting to sag again?" — Josh Friedman, *When Sex Was Dirty*, p. 24, 2005

titty noun

sex with a woman *US, 2006*

- "Next nigga we see we gonna bust hard, gonna get enough money for some titty for both of us." — Jason Starr, *Lights Out*, p. 170, 2006

titty bar; tittie bar noun

a bar featuring bare-breasted female servers and/or dancers *US, 1991*

- "Well, then, let's go to a tittie bar and celebrate." Danny Pogue said he knew of a place where the girls danced naked on the tables, and let you grab their ankles for five bucks. — Carl Hiaasen, *Native Tongue*, p. 179, 1991
- As you walk into most of these nudie clubs or titty bars, you see one or more stages and runways on which as many as ten or fifteen performers "dance" to music blaring from the club's sound system. — Marilyn Suriani Futterman, *Dancing Naked in the Material World*, p. 129, 1992
- I'm gonna be sittin' at the titty bar in downtown L.A. till my man over here calls me and gives me the OK sign. — Jackie Brown, 1997
- I told him he better explain those places are titty bars. Raji goes, "Not when little Minh Linh's dancing. She don't have enough to make it a titty bar. — Elmore Leonard, *Be Cool*, p. 49, 1999
- "I'm trying ta git my titty-bar freak on." — John Ridley, *Everybody Smokes in Hell*, p. 144, 1999
- I'm a bouncer in a titty bar. — *Kill Bill*, 2003

titty-deep adjective

used of a fox hole, shallow *US, 1981*

- The hole had to be big enough for three or four people in width and what we call titty deep. — Mark Baker, *Nam*, p. 77, 1981
- In the Central Highlands the ground was so hard that many times foxholes dug at an NDP were shallow, or "titty-deep." — Gregory Clark, *Words of the Vietnam War*, p. 187, 1990

titty-fuck noun

an act of rubbing the penis in the compressed cleavage between a woman's breasts *US, 1997*

- TITTY FUCK—penis is on a woman's chest between her breasts for sexual stimulation and/or cumming. — Sisters of the Heart, *The Brothel Bible*, p. 53, 1997

titty-fuck verb

to rub the penis in the compressed cleavage between a woman's breasts *US, 1998*

- I'm titty-fuckin' Bette Midler[.] — Eminem (Marshall Mathers), *Low Down Dirty*, 1998

titty pink adjective

a bright pink shade of lipstick *US, 1963*
Thought to resemble the color of a nipple.

- There's the expression titty pink. You've heard it. It must have been coined by a joker whose experience with nipples was quite limited. — Wade Hunter, *The Sex Peddler*, p. 71, 1963
- I insisted that they open the casket ... a little to the left now ... so they opened for me, and what do you think they had on Grandma's lips? TITTY PINK! — Armistead Maupin, *Further Tales of the City*, p. 74, 1982

tizz; tiz; tizzy noun

a state of panic or confused excitement *US, 1935*

- I couldn't remember having seen anybody in such a tizzy about a girl since the days of my youth—since my own tizzies. — Philip Wylie, *Opus 21*, p. 246, 1949

TJ nickname

Tijuana, Baja California, Mexico *US, 1981*

- He loves T.J. He goes down there all time. — James Ellroy, *Brown's Requiem*, p. 59, 1981

- Garcia was dressed "TJ" fashion: a cowboy-style shirt and boots, like the million or so Mexicans who filled L.A.'s run-down apartments and garment-district sweatshops. — Gerald Petievich, *The Quality of the Informant*, p. 126, 1985
- "They ain't in no hurry down in T.J.," Sam Zahn said. — Joseph Wambaugh, *Finnegan's Week*, p. 70, 1993

T-Jones *noun*
a mother *US, 1988*
- — Ethan Hilderbrant, *Prison Slang*, p. 126, 1988

TL *noun*
a sycophant *US, 1972*
From the Yiddish *tuchus leker* (ass licker).
- — Robert A. Wilson, *Playboy's Book of Forbidden Words*, p. 242, 1972

TLC *noun*
tender, loving care *US, 1945*
- [A]bout Fundevogel, who was coming along nicely under the T.L.C. (tender loving care) of Dr. Isherwood, the campus vet[.] — Frederick Kohner, *The Affairs of Gidget*, p. 24, 1963

TM *noun*
1 a commericaly rolled cigarette *US, 1976*
A shortened form of **TAILOR-MADE**.
- — John R. Armore and Joseph D. Wolfe, *Dictionary of Desperation*, p. 54, 1976
2 transcendental meditation *US, 1979*
- I wasn't trying to say TM or CR [Cosmic Realization] would take care of all the world's ills or that they should give up them own beliefs[.] — Beatrice Sparks (writing as "Anonymous"), *Jay's Journal*, p. 47, 1979

T man *noun*
1 an agent of the United States Treasury Department *US, 1954*
- The T men went down to Miami and, after a little looking around, uncovered Mr. Leslie Shumway at a local race track[.] — Alson Smith, *Syndicate City*, p. 133, 1954
2 a male with a primary interest in a woman's breasts as a point of attraction *US, 1967*
An abbreviation of **TIT-MAN**.
- "Are you a big T-man? I'm 38-C cup." — Elaine Shepard, *The Doom Pussy*, p. 152, 1967

TMI
used for expressing the sentiment that a conversation has become too personal, that the speaker is imparting *too much information US, 1986*
- In a classic case of TMI (Too Much Information), Barrymore told a reporter from Harper's Bazaar everything but her sexual preference. — *Milwaukee Journal Sentinel*, p. 1 (Cue), 7th January 1997
- — Connie Eble (Editor), *UNC-CH Campus Slang*, p. 8, Spring 1999
- "And a few of you said 'tmi, Yolanda.' All of you have been my sounding board. For those who said too much information, at least I knew you were reading and that matters to me." — *Leaf-Chronicle*, p. 1D, 5th October 2003

TNX
used as Internet discussion group shorthand to mean "thanks" *US, 1997*
- — Andy Ihnatko, *Cyberspeak*, p. 191, 1997

TO *noun*
a novice prostitute; a prostitute working in a particular brothel for the first time *US, 1999*
An abbreviation of **TURNOUT**.
- She was a "turn out" (TO), new to prostitution and, especially, to the brothel scene. — Lora Shaner, *Madam*, p. 48, 1999

toad *noun*
1 a black person *US, 1967*
- And the big toad motherfucking blabbing nigger is still down there in that bar or somewhere else throwing bottles through the air. — Frank Reynolds, *Freewheelin' Frank*, p. 20, 1967
- — James Harris, *A Convict's Dictionary*, p. 29, 1989
- "Ya see, O.G., even when we was trying to show the niggers some respect, started calling them 'toads' instead of 'niggers,' they still act like fuckin' animals." — Jimmy Lerner, *You Got Nothing Coming*, p. 63, 2002
2 a very sick, derelict hospital patient *US, 1977*
An initialism for a "*trashy old alcoholic derelict*."
- — *Philadelphia Magazine*, pp. 145–151, November 1977: "Language: doctor, there's a gomer in the pit"
3 an unattractive, older male homosexual *US, 1985*
- — Wayne Dynes, *Homolexis*, p. 140, 1985

TOAD
used for describing what happens when a surfer catches a big wave and almost immediately falls from his board *US, 1988*
An abbreviation of "*take off and die*."
- — Michael V. Anderson, *The Bad, Rad, Not to Forget Way Cool Beach and Surf Discriptionary*, p. 21, 1988

toad-stabber; toad-sticker *noun*
a knife *US, 1945*
- — Lou Shelly, *Hepcats Jive Talk Dictionary*, p. 35, 1945
- I don't trust a man carries a toadstabber, sump'n sneaky about it. — Ken Weaver, *Texas Crude*, p. 133, 1984

toast *noun*
1 a narrative poem *US, 1976*
- Perhaps the best known of all toasts, "The Signifying Monkey" is the prototype of an interrelated series of jungle poems. — Dennis Wepman et al., *The Life*, p. 21, 1976
2 something that is completely broken or inoperable *US, 1991*
- — Eric S. Raymond, *The New Hacker's Dictionary*, p. 353, 1991
- "Twin Peaks is toast. It's had it. It won't make it another season." "Toast?" He chuckled. "People say this? Where do you pick this shit up?" — Armistead Maupin, *Maybe the Moon*, p. 34, 1992

tobacco juice; tobacco stain *noun*
fecal stains in the underwear or on a toilet bowl *US, 1966*
- You can clean him down to his tobacco-stained shorts for all I care. — Robert Edmond Alter, *Carny Kill*, p. 47, 1966
- — Bill Casselman, *Canadian Sayings*, p. 44, 2002

tobaccy *noun*
tobacco *US, 1899*
- "And where do you keep the chawin' tobaccy?" — Jude Deveraux, *High Tide*, p. 109, 2002

tochis; tuckus; tochas *noun*
the buttocks *US, 1934*
Yiddish.
- She laughed. "No, he's graduated to nudes now. And poor mama, can't understand his interest in tuchuses ... rumps to you." — Frederic Wakeman, *The Hucksters*, p. 40, 1946
- Cockeye bent down and pointed to his backside said, "If I ever meet him, he can kiss my tauchess." — Harry Grey, *The Hoods*, p. 61, 1952
- I'll tell you where he's sensitive, Lionel—in his tochas. — Eugene Boe (Compiler), *The Wit & Wisdom of Archie Bunker*, p. 70, 1971
- He looked so stiff I wondered if his bayonet was stuck up his tuckus. — Anka Radakovich, *The Wild Girls Club*, p. 52, 1994

tochis-over-teakettle *adverb*
head-over-heels *US, 1991*
- — Terry Southern, *Now Dig This*, p. 171, 1991
- His helmet caught me flush on the chin and knocked me tochis over teakettle. — Jerrry Markbreit, *Last Call*, p. 87, 2001

TODDI
the claim of a criminal suspect that "*the other dude did it*" *US, 2005*
- "Weider sent me an impassioned request for bifurcation. Looks like just another TODDI defense." — Jonathan Kellerman, *Rage*, p. 74, 2005

toefoot *noun*
a numbing of the feet in cold water, creating the sensation of having no toes, only a foot *US, 2004*
Surfing usage.
- — *Transworld Surf*, p. 42, April 2004

toe jabber *noun*
a knife used for fighting *US, 1962*
- Probably one of the most favored street weapons of all time is the good old "shiv," "blade," "toe jabber" or whatever you choose to call a good sticker. — Abbie Hoffman, *Steal this Books*, p. 163, 1971

toe jam *noun*
the amalgam of dirt and sweat that gathers between the toes of unwashed feet *US, 1999*
- Toe jam (or Chee-toes) comes from bacteria dining on the fatty acids in the sweat that pours out of the foot's pores. — Greta Garbage, *That's Disgusting*, p. 21, 1999

toe-popper *noun*
a small antipersonnel mine powerful enough to blow off a hand or foot *US, 1984*

- Sheperd had stepped on a "toe-popper" mine planted in the entrance of his hootch. — Gary Linderer, *The Eyes of the Eagle*, p. 83, 1991
- There are the small "toe poppers" that can blast off a soldier's foot. — *Washington Post*, 11th February 1991

toes over *adjective*

said when a surfer has any number of toes extended over the front end of the surfboard *US, 1964*

- — John Severson, *Modern Surfing Around the World*, p. 183, 1964

toe ticket *noun*

the name tag affixed to the toe of a corpse in a morgue *US, 1962*

- — *American Speech*, p. 273, December 1962: "The language of traffic policemen"

toe up *adjective*

drunk *US, 2001*

A corruption of "torn up."

- — Don R. McCreary (Editor), *Dawg Speak*, 2001

tog *verb*

to dress *US, 1946*

Conventional English reincarnated as slang in black vernacular.

- Even before I was in the money I togged like a fashion plate so I could run with the hip cats who hung around the poolroom. — Mezz Mezzrow, *Really the Blues*, p. 25, 1946
- Big girl's earrings; you got all togged out for the break. — George Mandel, *Flee the Angry Strangers*, p. 11, 1948
- I dig the way you're togged out. — Ross Russell, *The Sound*, p. 44, 1961
- I was togged real sharp, with a fine suit, boss coat, and soft Florsheims, real dancing shoes. — Piri Thomas, *Down These Mean Streets*, p. 109, 1967

together *adjective*

having your life, career, or emotions under control; self-assured *US, 1969*

- They [members of the Hog Farm commune at Woodstock] established very good vibes, had plenty of food (the lines were sometimes long, but usually moved quickly), good food and were really together. — *East Village Other*, 20th August 1969
- I thought you were probably … like … slumming here, doing your bit for the Junior League or something … but you're not like that at all. You're really together. — Armistead Maupin, *Tales of the City*, p. 174, 1978

▸ **get it together**

to take control of your personal condition; to get your mind and emotions under control; to become organized *US, 1975*

- [M]an, we were both sort of really spaced out [drug-intoxicated] [...] but I got it together to clean up the sick. — Paul E. Willis, *Profane Culture*, p. 142, 1978

toggle jockey *noun*

in the US Air Force, a co-pilot *US, 1946*

- — *American Speech*, p. 310, December 1946: "More Air Force slang"

tohu-bohu *noun*

turmoil *US, 1951*

- And that somewhere along the line in all this tohu-bohu I've come of age. — James Blake, *The Joint*, p. 15, 25th February 1951

toilet *noun*

1 a person as a sex object *US, 1980*

- "I want him" has become "I want his ass" and people are things, receivers, sex-machines, even toilets. — *Maledicta*, p. 225, Winter 1980

2 a casino *US, 1980*

An insider term.

- — Lee Solkey, *Dummy Up and Deal*, p. 122, 1980

toilet

▸ **in the toilet**

1 lost, wasted *US, 1987*

- Do I got to sit here and listen to a sermon when I'm eighty bucks in the toilet? — Robert Campbell, *Alice in La-La Land*, p. 245, 1987

2 in serious trouble *US, 2001*

- Then Jersey legalized gambling and pretty soon the local numbers industry was in the toilet. — Janet Evanovich, *Seven Up*, p. 15, 2001

toilet-bowl *adjective*

having an inferior location or very low status *US, 1995*

- My entire career has consisted of toilet-bowl radio stations at the bottom of the barrel[.] — Howard Stern, *Miss America*, p. 54, 1995

toilet-bowl woman *noun*

a prostitute who operates on Main Street in downtown Los Angeles *US, 2000*

- They are also known as Toilet Bowl Women. The client usually follows them down the street for discretion's sake. — Fiona Pitt-Kethley, *Red Light Districts of the World*, p. 84, 2000

toilet mouth *noun*

a person who employs a vocabulary that is considered foul or obscene *US, 1976*

- — Wayne Flyod, *Jason's Authentic Dictionary of CB Slang*, p. 20, 1976

toilet queen *noun*

a homosexual male who loiters around public toilets in search of sex partners *US, 1967*

- — Dale Gordon, *The Dominion Sex Dictionary*, p. 156, 1967

toke *noun*

1 an inhalation of marijuana smoke *US, 1962*

- Just' a plain old cigarette. Hee hee, yes. You want a toke? — Ken Kesey, *One Flew Over the Cuckoo's Nest*, p. 283, 1962
- When troubled times begin to bother me / I take a toke / And all my cares / Go up in smoke. — Cheech Marin and Tommy Chong, *Up in Smoke*, 1978

2 a dose of a drug *US, 1994*

- I doubled up on my coke toke. — Odie Hawkins, *Lost Angeles*, p. 41, 1994

3 marijuana *US, 1986*

- But I never took drugs all those years, just toke. No poppers or anything. — Ethan Morden, *Buddies*, p. 183, 1986

4 in casino gambling, a gratuity either in the form of betting chips or in the form of a bet made in the name of the dealer *US, 1981*

An abbreviation of "token of gratitude."

- [H]e considered a ten-spot as nothing more than toke money for the bellman, waiters, bartenders, and cocktails waitresses who had their mitts out when they saw him coming. — Gerald Petievich, *Money Men*, p. 27, 1981
- — Avery Cardoza, *Winning Casino Blackjack for the Non-Counter*, p. 75, 1991
- — Michael Dalton, *Blackjack*, p. 84, 1991

toke *verb*

1 to inhale smoke from a tobacco cigarette, a marijuana cigarette, a crack cocaine pipe, or other drug *US, 1952*

- Man, someone's tokin' some reefer. — *Dazed and Confused*, 1993

2 to tip someone *US, 1983*

Almost exclusively casino usage.

- The notion behind taking dealers is that they are somehow responsible for a person winning a number of bets in a row. — Thomas L. Clark, *The Dictionary of Gambling and Gaming*, p. 234, 1987

toker *noun*

1 a marijuana smoker *US, 1973*

- I'm a smoker / I'm a midnight toker — Steve Miller, *The Joker*, 1973
- — Pamela Munro, *U.C.L.A. Slang*, p. 117, 1997
- [K]nowing he was a toker himself, I asked him for his address so that I could send him a little present. — Ken Lukowiak, *Marijuana Time*, p. 170, 2000

2 in a casino, a tipper *US, 1974*

Because tips in casinos are most often in the form of gambling tokens or "tokes."

- Sitting there with people that are Georges, which means a good toker, you want them to win—even though you're a house person. — Edward Lin, *Big Julie of Vegas*, p. 210, 1974

toke up *verb*

to smoke marijuana *US, 1959*

- Chili flashed the group an arrogant smile and toked up on the joint going around. — Odie Hawkins, *The Busting Out of an Ordinary Man*, p. 170, 1985

Tokyo toughies *noun*

inexpensive tennis shoes *US, 1991*

- — Lee McNelis, *30 + And a Wake-Up*, p. 13, 1991

tolley *noun*

toluene, a paint solvent inhaled by the truly desperate abuser *US, 1997*

- — Jim Crotty, *How to Talk American*, p. 97, 1997

Tom *noun*

1 a black person who curries favor with white people by obsequious and servile behavior *US, 1959*

A shortened form of **UNCLE TOM**.

- He's kind of a Tom, ain' he? — James Baldwin, *Blues for Mister Charlie*, p. 40, 1964
- It was on Madison Avenue and you had to be a real Tom. — Claude Brown, *Manchild in the Promised Land*, p. 170, 1965
- I hope your children don't grow up to be a Tom like you. — H. Rap Brown, *Die Nigger Die!*, p. 113, 1969
- They sent in the middle-class black members of the Human Rights Commission, and the brothers laughed at them and called them Toms. — Tom Wolfe, *Radical Chic & Mau-Mauing the Flak Catchers*, p. 121, 1970

2 in a casino, a poor tipper *US, 1993*

- — Frank Scoblete, *Guerrilla Gambling*, p. 330, 1993

Tom *verb*

to curry favor by acting obsequiously and in a servile manner *US, 1963*

- I "Tomed" for him and explained we were only listening to records. — Babs Gonzales, *I Paid My Dues*, p. 49, 1967
- Big grant-size money is needed, and N.C.I. is going to keep Tomming (their word) OEO and others to get it. — Jeffrey Golden, *Watermelon Summer*, p. 52, 1971

Tom *adjective*

shoddy, inferior *US, 1989*

- — James Harris, *A Convict's Dictionary*, p. 32, 1989

tomato *noun*

an attractive woman, especially a young one *US, 1929*

- There was a neat tomato down on Third Avenue who loved to play tricks herself, especially against the police. — Mickey Spillane, *I, The Jury*, p. 41, 1947
- TOMATO's TOMATO MISSING. — Truman Capote, *Breakfast at Tiffany's*, p. 109, 1958
- There were more poolrooms than hot-dog stands, and the tomatoes running on the loose were beautiful beyond compare. — Minnesota Fats, *The Bank Shot*, p. 57, 1966
- When Ralph Ginzburg began publishing Avant Garde magazine, rival editor Paul Krassner asked sardonically, "How avant garde is a man who still calls women 'tomatoes'?" — Robert A. Wilson, *Playboy's Book of Forbidden Words*, p. 242, 1972

tomato can *noun*

a mediocre boxer *US, 1955*

- He is a heavyweight named Matt, a sacrificial tomato can lined up to appease the crowd's blood lust[.] — *Washington Post*, p. 12, 28th August 1977
- In those days, the industry designated victims "guys named Joe" in sly tribute to Stribling. Today, "tomato cans" is the most popular term. — *Arkansas Democrat-Gazette*, 19th October 2004

Tombs *nickname*

the Manhattan Detention Complex or city jail *US, 1840*

Named when built in the mid-C19 because it was modeled on an Egyptian-style mausoleum. The present facility bears no resemblance to the original structure but still carries the sobriquet.

- As they flung him into the car, Angel said, "There's plenty of rooms in the Tombs." — Hal Ellson, *The Golden Spike*, p. 139, 1952
- I had big manila envelope ready for for Tombs Incarceration, including Buddhist Bible of Goddard[.] — Jack Kerouac, *Letter to Allen Ginsberg*, p. 458, 1st January 1955
- He'd earned his name from having kicked the habit cold-turkey a few times running in the Tombs City Prison. — Piri Thomas, *Down These Mean Streets*, p. 201, 1967
- We were dismissed from the courtroom, returned inside and, after a short wait, were sent downstairs to be admitted to the Tombs[.] — Herbert Huncke, *The Evening Sun Turned Crimson*, p. 164, 1980

tombstone disposition *noun*

a surly, graceless, fearless character *US, 1970*

- I've got a tombstone disposition, graveyard mind / I know I'm a bad motherfucker, that's why I don't mind dying. — Roger Abrahams, *Positively Black*, p. 80, 1970

tombstone loan *noun*

a loan made to a dead person *US, 1973*

- "I used to arrange tombstone loans with poor old Patsy, God bless him. I'd get a name off a tombstone in town." — Vincent Teresa, *My Life in the Mafia*, pp. 54–55, 1973

tom-cat; tomcat *verb*

to pursue women for the purpose of fleeting sexual encounters *US, 1927*

- "It doesn't pay to tomcat around in singles bars, not in these times," Fin said. — Joseph Wambaugh, *Finnegan's Week*, p. 155, 1993

tongue *noun*

an attorney *US, 1962*

- — Joseph E. Ragen and Charles Finston, *Inside the World's Toughest Prison*, p. 821, 1962: "Penitentiary and underworld glossary"

▸ **get tongue**

in the categorization of sexual activity by teenage boys, to kiss with tongue contact *US, 1986*

- There were several degrees of "making out." The first was "tongue." "Did you get tongue?" was a question frequently heard after a first date with an extremely nice, honor-student-type girl. — Terry Southern, *Now Dig This*, p. 3, 1986

tongue bath *noun*

oral stimulation of the body *US, 1967*

- Joe sat next to Mike and then gently eased him a tongue bath, starting at his knees and continuing up to his thighs. — Mark Holden, *Sodom 1967 American Style*, p. 95, 1967
- Tongue baths are my specialty and I love giving them to sensual women. — Emile Nytrate, *Underground Ads*, p. 96, 1971
- Ursula lies back from an awe-inspiring lesboid tongue-bath from Adriana Vega. — Mr. Skin, *Mr. Skin's Skincyclopedia*, p. 87, 2005

tongue fuck *noun*

an act of oral sex *US, 2002*

- He responded by lying down, lifting my ass off the ground and launching into a tongue fuck whose equal I had never known. — *Letters to Penthouse XVIII*, p. 116, 2002
- Eli teased with devastating intent, stroking, sucking, treating her to a delicious tongue fuck meant to drive her mad. — Lori Foster, *Unexpected*, p. 155, 2003
- I got my first tongue fuck when I was fourteen. — Noire, *Candy Licker*, p. 256, 2005

tongue-fuck *verb*

to perform oral sex, either genital or anal *US, 1972*

- She said to tongue-fuck her ass instead of sucking, since there was no come in her ass. — *Letters to Penthouse XII*, p. 349, 2001
- She kept arching her back to help me tongue-fuck her pussy. — *Letters to Penthouse XV*, p. 104, 2002

tongue wash *noun*

oral sex, especially on a woman *US, 1981*

- A tongue wash now and then made the time go faster, right? — Gerald Petievich, *Money Men*, pp. 85–86, 1981

tonsil hockey *noun*

passionate kissing *US, 1986*

- — Connie Eble (Editor), *UNC-CH Campus Slang*, p. 5, October 1986
- It's OK to give each other a peck on the cheek or a hug from time to time, but you don't want to practice your tonsil hockey with guests around. — Leah Ingram, *The Everything Etiquette Book*, p. 97, 2005

tonsil juice *noun*

saliva *US, 1946*

- I felt like I couldn't even swallow my own tonsil-juice without gagging[.] — Mezz Mezzrow, *Really the Blues*, p. 101, 1946

tonsil paint *noun*

whiskey *US, 1977*

- — Ramon Adams, *The Language of the Railroader*, p. 159, 1977

tony's *noun*

dice that have been marked to have two identical faces *US, 1950*

- — *The Annals of the American Academy of Political and Social Sciences*, p. 132, May 1950

toodaloo, kangaroo

used as a farewell *US, 1961*

- — Art Unger, *The Cool Book*, p. 106, 1961

toodle-oo

goodbye *UK, 1907*

Cute. In the US, quite affected in a British sort of way.

- He's on his way downtown in a cab. Sweet blow-off! Toodle-oo, Wonder. — Iceberg Slim (Robert Beck), *Long White Con*, p. 55, 1977

- He waved tootle-oo with the steak knife before speeding off. — Carl Hiaasen, *Strip Tease*, p. 266, 1993

tooie; tuie; tooey; toolie; toole *noun*
a capsule of amobarbital sodium and secobarbital sodium (trade name Tuinal™), a combination of central nervous system depressants *US, 1966*
- — Donald Louria, *Nightmare Drugs*, p. 25, 1966

tool *noun*
1 the penis *UK, 1553*
Conventional English at first—found in Shakespeare's *Henry VIII*—and then rediscovered in the C20 as handy slang.
- He had taught her at five to sneak her hand so smoothly under the straw hat on his lap that Ma and none of the kids ever knew she played with Pa's tool. — Iceberg Slim (Robert Beck), *Death Wish*, p. 250, 1977
- Butler, reaching the limits of human endurance, whips out his tool and obliges her craving for male meat. — *Adult Video*, p. 66, August/September 1986
- He said he wanted somebody with a reliable tool, so I hung on just to see if the scene was going to work or not. — Robert Stoller and I.S. Levine, *Coming Attractions*, p. 157, 1991
- So was Bobbit trying to prove that his tool still works? — Anthony Petkovich, *The X Factory*, p. 86, 1997

2 a diligent student *US, 1965*
- — *Time*, p. 56, 1st January 1965: "Students: the slang bag"

3 a skilled pickpocket *US, 1950*
- — Hyman E. Goldin et al., *Dictionary of American Underworld Lingo*, p. 224, 1950

4 in pool, a player's cue stick *US, 1993*
- — Mike Shamos, *The Illustrated Encyclopedia of Billiards*, p. 250, 1993

5 a surfboard *US, 1987*
- — Mitch McKissick, *Surf Lingo*, 1987

tool *verb*
1 to wander aimlessly; to do nothing in particular *US, 1932*
The variant "tool around" is also used.
- — *Current Slang*, p. 4, Summer 1966
- All I ever did in high school was tool around with the guys and a six-pack of Bud, looking for heterosexuals to beat up. — Armistead Maupin, *Tales of the City*, p. 134, 1978

2 to work hard *US, 1997*
- — Andy Ihnatko, *Cyberspeak*, p. 192, 1997

toolbox *noun*
1 the male genitals *US, 1964*
- — Roger Blake, *The American Dictionary of Sexual Terms*, p. 85, 1964
- [H]e stripped off his strides and exposed his toolbox. — *Loaded*, p. 30, June 2003

2 the vagina *US, 1967*
- — Dale Gordon, *The Dominion Sex Dictionary*, p. 157, 1967

tool check *noun*
an inspection by a military doctor or medic of male recruits for signs of sexually transmitted disease *US, 1967*
- — Dale Gordon, *The Dominion Sex Dictionary*, p. 157, 1967

tooler *noun*
a show-off *US, 1965*
- — *Time*, p. 56, 1st January 1965: "Students: the slang bag"

toolie *noun*
a handgun *US, 2000*
- "Niggers say you finally packin' a toolie." — Paul Beatty, *Tuff*, p. 227, 2000

tooling *noun*
the processing of useless information *US, 1962*
- Tooling—The ingestion of useless information. — *Voo Doo Magazine (MIT)*, pp. 10–11, January 1962

toolio *noun*
a social outcast *US, 1996*
- hey toolio, even if i didn't think KISS were a bunch of talentless glam-ass wankers, I wouldn't pay $50. — *alt.rock-n-roll.metal*, 28th January 1996
- — Pamela Munro, *U.C.L.A. Slang*, p. 116, 1997

tools *noun*
1 the syringe and other equipment used to prepare and inject drugs *US, 1966*
- — *Mr.*, p. 59, April 1966: "The hippie's lexicon"

- The rest of the tools were already in use by other addicts. — Donald Goines, *Dopefiend*, p. 8, 1971

2 the jewelry, cars, clothing, and material flourishes that support a pimp's image *US, 1972*
- My tools are also very expensive. I'm continually sharpening my cars, my jewelry, and my clothes. These are tools like a policeman has a gun. — Susan Hall, *Gentleman of Leisure*, p. 11, 1972

too much *adjective*
great, wonderful, excellent *US, 1969*
- The regular music thing [at Woodstock] is nice, but straight. The Hog Farm is just too much. We are at home and at peace with each other and ourselves. — *East Village Other*, 20th August 1969

too much!
used as a humorous commentary, suggesting that someone has gone too far *US, 1963*
- — *American Speech*, p. 275, December 1963: "American Indian student slang"

too much perspective; too much fucking perspective
used for expressing the sentiment that too much information is being shared *US, 1984*
A catchphrase from *Spinal Tap*, used with humor and referentially.
- David retors, "Too much, too much fuckin' perspective." — Editors of Ben is Dead, *Retrohell*, p. 205, 1997

toot *noun*
1 a dose of a drug, especially cocaine to be snorted *US, 1971*
- Of course I'm going to give you a toot, honey. — Donald Goines, *Dopefiend*, p. 197, 1971
- After the well wishes were over, we rapped, we smoked, and we took a toot of boy and girl. — A.S. Jackson, *Gentleman Pimp*, p. 70, 1973

2 cocaine; heroin *UK, 1977*
- — Bill Davis, *Jawjacking*, p. 100, 1977
- You drunk or on toot? Whistler said. — Robert Campbell, *In La-La Land We Trust*, p. 15, 1986
- — Macfarlane, Macfarlane & Robson, *The User*, p. xi, 1996

3 butyl nitrite *US, 1984*
- Want some toot, dude? — *Repo Man*, 1984

4 a drinking spree *US, 1891*
- Afterwards she came to me and said her husband was off on a toot and she was worried and would I find him and bring him home. — Raymond Chandler, *The Long Goodbye*, p. 230, 1953
- Twice a year he'd go off on beer toots. — Helen Giblo, *Footlights, Fistfights and Femmes*, p. 14, 1957
- Even his Uncle Brian, an alcoholic, was worried about his being on a toot for three days. — Edwin Torres, *Q & A*, p. 82, 1977

5 a prostitute *US, 2001*
- — Rick Ayers (Editor), *Slang Dictionary*, p. 16, 2001

toot *verb*
1 to inhale a powdered drug, such as cocaine *US, 1975*
- Did I ask if they're tooting cocaine, maybe blowing a little weed? No I didn't ask him that either. — Elmore Leonard, *Split Images*, p. 16, 1981
- Irrationality ruled for ten minutes while I dug under the front seat for my stuff and tooted from the spoon — Odie Hawkins, *Lost Angeles*, p. 40, 1994

2 to fart *US, 1978*
- A far-off chorus softly sang in unison, "Beans, beans, the musical fruit. The more you eat, the more you toot." — Piri Thomas, *Stories from El Barrio*, p. 34, 1978
- — Pamela Munro, *U.C.L.A. Slang*, p. 86, 1989
- The more you toot, the better you feel[.] — Peter Furze, *Tailwinds*, p. 165, 1998

toothbrush day *noun*
after a guilty verdict, the day when sentencing is announced *US, 1985*
- Is that a nice thing to be saying to a man on Toothbrush Day? — George V. Higgins, *Penance for Jerry Kennedy*, p. 29, 1985

toothpick *noun*
1 a pool cue stick that is lighter than average *US, 1990*
- — Steve Rushin, *Pool Cool*, p. 29, 1990

2 a sharp knife *US, 1945*
- — Lou Shelly, *Hepcats Jive Talk Dictionary*, p. 19, 1945

tooth-to-tail ratio *noun*
the ratio of combat troops (tooth) to rear-echelon support personnel (tail) *US, 1969*
- This relationship of numbers is not quite what is referred to in military jargon as the "tooth to tail ratio." — Nadav Safran, *From War to War*, p. 332, 1969
- The Marine Corps tooth-to-tail ratio has been running around 63 to 37 percent. — House Appropriations Committee, *Department of Defense Appropriations for 1977*, p. 564, 1976

tootie *adjective*
homosexual *US, 1999*
- Dodie was born tootie, and Lisa wasn't. — Rita *Pink Slip*, p. 9, 1999

tooting *adverb*
completely, absolutely *US, 1932*
Usually further intensified with a preceding adverb.
- "Some people have accused us of being wrapped up in [the flag]," Thomas said. "And they're darn tootin' right we are." — *Daily Nexus* (UC Santa Barbara), 6th November 2002

toots *noun*
used as an affectionate term of address, usually to a girl or woman *US, 1936*
- He headed into the hallway again, where he saluted her crisply. "Don't OD on Beer Nuts, toots." — Armistead Maupin, *Tales of the City*, p. 295, 1978

tootsie *noun*
1 a woman, a girlfriend; often used as a form of address, either humorous or affectionate *US, 1895*
- Some other tootsies tried their hand at making a strange face but were dragged off by their boy friends who chased them into the bar. — Mickey Spillane, *I, The Jury*, p. 122, 1947
- Let's face it, whore or no whore, this is a clear-cut tootsie, right? — Philip Roth, *Portnoy's Complaint*, p. 226, 1969
- Where the hell does that little Radcliffe tootsie come off rating Scott Fitzgerald and Gustav Mahler and then Heinrich Boll? — *Manhattan*, 1979
2 a toe *UK, 1854*
A baby-talk coinage; playful or affectionate usage.
- They were the cutest, daintiest tootsies you've ever seen. — Frederick Kohner, *The Affairs of Gidget*, p. 45, 1963
- Each of your tootsies is packed with about 20,000 sweat glands! — Joy Masoff, *Oh, Yuck*, p. 63, 2000
3 a capsule of secobarbital sodium and amobarbital sodium (trade name Tuinal™), a combination of central nervous system depressants *US, 1977*
Also variant "tootie."
- — Donald Wesson and David Smith, *Barbiturates*, p. 122, 1977

tootsie roll *noun*
distilled and concentrated heroin *US, 1987*
- — Carsten Stroud, *Close Pursuit*, p. 269, 1987
- — Geoffrey Froner, *Digging for Diamonds*, p. 61, 1989

tootsie-wootsie *noun*
an attractive girl or woman *US, 1952*
- But calling Irish is like talking to your tootsie-wootsie on a Hell's Kitchen party line. — Richard Marcinko, *Task Force Blue*, p. 76, 1996

top *noun*
1 the dominant partner in a homosexual or sadomasochistic relationship *US, 1961*
- If he is said to be "tops," it means that he will assume only the active partnership in sodomy, while if he is called "tops or bottoms," he will assume either the so-called male or female role in sodomy. — *New York Mattachine Newsletter*, p. 6, June 1961
- Boots could take either the top or the bottom without the least show of emotion. — Donald Goines, *Whoreson*, p. 265, 1972
- No professional top pushes the limits of a bottom much beyond this point. — Frederique Delacoste, *Sex Work*, p. 51, 1987
- According to no less an authority than the Marquis de Sade, there is only one hierarchy in the world: tops and bottoms. Those who like to administer pain and/or sexual pleasure are the tops. — Bill Brownstein, *Sex Carnival*, p. 75, 2000
2 a maximum prison sentence *US, 1968*
- — *Current Slang*, p. 48, Fall 1968
3 a first sergeant *US, 1898*
Variants include "topper" and "tap kick."

- Guys, here's a present for you. A new greenie, with top's compliments. — Stan Lee, *The Nam*, p. 15, 1987
- "Top" also announced that the CID's comments after the inteviews were somewhat interesting. — Gary Linderer, *The Eyes of the Eagle*, p. 85, 1991

▸ **over the top**
said of a score in pinball when the score exceeds the capacity of the scoring device and thus returns to zero *US, 1977*
- — Bobbye Claire Natkin and Steve Kirk, *All About Pinball*, p. 113, 1977

top *verb*
to take the dominant, controlling role in a sadomasochistic relationship *US, 1986*
- "It was like that night for a few days, and then I started to mind it when he'd roll me over for his turn to top me." — Ethan Morden, *Buddies*, p. 137, 1986
- For the man who buys the services of a dominatrix, being "topped" is attractive as long as it's a service. — Jill Nagle, *Whores and Other Feminists*, 1997

top banana *noun*
the headliner in a vaudeville show; by figurative extension, the leading figure in any enterprise *US, 1953*
- Why do you think she went out and bought this army cot? Leave it to me: I'm always top banana in the shock department. — Truman Capote, *Breakfast at Tiffany's*, p. 61, 1958
- Lenny had his mother, Sally Marr—a top banana when they all worked in burlesque—fitted out with a recorder[.] — Albert Goldman, *Freak Show*, pp. 211–212, 1968

top bitch *noun*
in a group of prostitutes working for a pimp, the latest addition to the group *US, 1967*
- Oliver had assured her that she was his top bitch but demanded to know why she couldn't catch as many dates as Alice, his bottom bitch. — Joseph Wambaugh, *Floaters*, p. 67, 1996

top dog *noun*
1 a very important person *UK, 1900*
- One of the dudes who helped me rip off the Stool later became a top dog in the government[.] — Odie Hawkins, *Great Lawd Buddha*, p. 45, 1990
2 in poker, the highest pair in a hand *US, 1996*
- — John Vorhaus, *The Big Book of Poker Slang*, p. 36, 1996

top-drawer *adjective*
well-bred, high-class, the best *UK, 1920*
- Chances are that if a call-girl is easy to meet she is not, as her boosters boast, "top-drawer stuff." — John M. Murtagh and Sara Harris, *Cast the First Stone*, p. 2, 1957
- Daisy was a top-drawer Red in Los Angeles, a big and homely woman with the largest feet I ever saw on a woman. — *Going Away*, p. 35, 1962
- The Opal I knew was a stone young lady, with top drawer parents. — Iceberg Slim (Robert Beck), *Airtight Willie and Me*, p. 54, 1979
- Claudia always stayed at a cozy hotel near the Tennis Club in the days when tennis was tops, when developers there wouldn't dream of doing a hotel, condo or country club without top-drawer tennis facilities. — Joseph Wambaugh, *Fugitive Nights*, p. 61, 1992

top-flight *adjective*
first rate *US, 1939*
- You stack up as a top-flight man in my book, but you've had not incentive here. — Jim Thompson, *The Grifters*, p. 121, 1963

top gun *noun*
1 the US Navy course in Fighter Weapons, Tactics, and Doctrine *US, 1975*
- Ironically, the Navy program was called "Top Gun." — James Canan, *The Superwarriors*, p. 31, 1975
- At Top Gun, run at Miramar Naval Air Station, near San Diego, Navy fighter crews learned the correct offensive and defensive tactics to employ[.] — Jeffrey Ethel, *One Day in a Long War*, p. 12, 1989
2 crack cocaine *US, 1994*
- — US Department of Justice, *Street Terms*, October 1994

top hats *noun*
erect nipples *US, 1997*
- — Pamela Munro, *U.C.L.A. Slang*, p. 116, 1997

topkick *noun*
a first sergeant *US, 1956*
- If he split right back, his topkick said, they might not ever know he'd been gone. — Billie Holiday with William Dufty, *Lady Sings the Blues*, p. 111, 1956

top man *noun*
in a homosexual couple, the partner who plays the active role during sex *US, 1941*
- They are usually long-terms and are familiarly known to inmates by such local cognomens as "wolves," "top men," "jockers" or "daddies." — *Ebony*, p. 82, July 1951
- [P]roclaim his role as a dominant man in "heavy sex," a good "top man," of the best. — John Rechy, *Rushes*, p. 26, 1979
- "Who would be the top man in that combination? Aren't they both natural catchers?" — Ethan Morden, *Everybody Loves You*, p. 163, 1988

topper *noun*
1 a remark or action that serves as the *coup de grace* of a conversation or series of events *US, 1939*
- It looks like old Mr. Stumpnagler, what's owned the building ever since I can remember, has had a couple of years of bad luck, his wife dying being the topper. — Robert Campbell, *Nibbled to Death by Ducks*, p. 216, 1989
2 in circus and carnival usage, a featured act *US, 1981*
- — Don Wilmeth, *The Language of American Popular Entertainment*, p. 277, 1981

tops *noun*
dice that have been marked to have two identical faces *US, 1962*
- — Frank Garcia, *Marked Cards and Loaded Dice*, p. 265, 1962

tops *adjective*
topmost in quality, the best *US, 1935*
- I really liked that chick, I thought—she was strictly tops. — Chester Himes, *If He Hollers Let Him Go*, p. 116, 1945
- The fellers all think you are tops and they envy the fact that I know you so well. — John Wynnum, *Jiggin' in the Riggin'*, p. 64, 1965
- Apart from that everything's just fabulous. Tops. Terrific. — Kathy Lette, *Girls' Night Out*, p. 89, 1987
- Yeah, it's tops. Hats off to the judges. — Roy Slaven (John Doyle), *Five South Coast Seasons*, p. 38, 1992

tops *adverb*
at the most *US, 1987*
- Tonight and tomorrow, tops. — *Raising Arizona*, 1987
- Man, I got a shelf life of ten years, tops! — *Jerry Maguire*, 1996

tops and bottoms *noun*
1 in poker, a hand consisting of a pair of aces (the highest card) and a pair of twos (the lowest card) *US, 1951*
- — *American Speech*, p. 102, May 1951

2 a combination of Taluin™, a painkiller, and the antihistamine Pyribenzamine™, abused for nonmedicinal purposes *US, 1989*
- Tops and Bottoms is street slang for T's and Blues. T's are Taluin, a painkiller, and Blues are Pyribenzamine, an antihistamine. Combined in the right dosage they make a poorman's heroin. — *Chicago Tribune*, p. 6C, 11th June 1989

top-shelf *adjective*
excellent or the best *US, 1892*
- MOE: I gotta first cousin. He's top shelf. Handles only the best. Everything first-class, all the way. — *Mo' Better Blues*, 1990

top stick *noun*
the best regular player in a pool hall *US, 1990*
- — Steve Rushin, *Pool Cool*, p. 29, 1990

topsy-turvy *adjective*
upside down; in reverse order *UK, 1530*
- One reason for the huge incidence of juvenile delinquency, but by no means the decisive one, was an idiosyncrasy of the population trend here, topsy-turvy to every other in the country during the last 10 years. — Jack Lait and Lee Mortimer, *Washington Confidential*, p. 119, 1951
- Living in a world of topsy-turvy standards and constant temptation, a boy could easily become involved in serious and long-lasting trouble. — Jim Thompson, *Bad Boy*, p. 366, 1953

torbo *noun*
the veterinary drug butorphanol, an analgesic and antitussive abused by humans *US, 2003*

From the trademarked trade name Torbutrol under which the drug is marketed.
- According to Dr. Williams, butorphanol is colloquially referred to by the students as "Torbo." — *Microgram Bulletin (DEA)*, p. 13, January 2003

torch *noun*
1 an arsonist *US, 1938*
- "Call up North," Shad said. "Get a real torch artist." — Carl Hiaasen, *Strip Tease*, p. 277, 1993
2 an act of arson *US, 1981*
- I know who instigated the Utopia torch. — James Ellroy, *Brown's Requiem*, p. 109, 1981
3 a cigarette lighter *US, 1972*
- — David Claerbaut, *Black Jargon in White America*, p. 84, 1972
4 a handgun *US, 1962*
- — Joseph E. Ragen and Charles Finston, *Inside the World's Toughest Prison*, p. 821, 1962: "Penitentiary and underworld glossary"
5 a love song or ballad *US, 1948*
- All songs of regret and revenge and love's bitter grief are "torches." — Jack Lait and Lee Mortimer, *New York Confidential*, p. 33, 1948

torch *verb*
to light a fire, especially an arson fire *US, 1931*
- He got trapped while torching a place with some other mob guys. — Vincent Teresa, *My Life in the Mafia*, p. 73, 1973
- Now somebody's torched it to clear the lot. Probably one of my clients. — *Body Heat*, 1980
- If he'd gone in there he wouldn've known right off, the way those charrings, alligator burns, showed, he would've known you torched it. — George V. Higgins, *The Rat on Fire*, p. 22, 1981
- Alright, Six says torch this place. — *Platoon*, 1986

torch artist *noun*
a skilled arsonist *US, 1973*
- We'd sell as much as we could before the Christmas rush and then we'd hire a torch artist, a good arsonist. — Vincent Teresa, *My Life in the Mafia*, p. 100, 1973
- He saw the torch artist peel rubber. — James Ellroy, *American Tabloid*, p. 427, 1995
- "Get out of here, you chicken-shit torch artist!" Robison roared. — William Fietzer, *Penal Fires*, p. 29, 2002

torch job *noun*
an enema containing a heat-inducing agent such as Vicks Vaporub™, Ben-Gay™, Heet™, or Tobasco™ sauce *US, 1972*
- — Robert A. Wilson, *Playboy's Book of Forbidden Words*, p. 243, 1972

torch man *noun*
a criminal who specializes in breaking into safes using an acetylene torch *US, 1952*
- We were going to need burners for the big stuff, but there wasn't a torch man in the mob. — Charles Hamilton, *Men of the Underworld*, p. 140, 1952

torch up *noun*
to smoke marijuana; to light up a joint *US, 1955*
- — *American Speech*, p. 88, May 1955: "Narcotic argot along the Mexican Border"
- But first The Wolf stepped into the toilet and torched up. — Willard Motley, *Let No Man Write My Epitaph*, p. 109, 1958

tore up *adjective*
1 drug-intoxicated *US, 1957*
- He stayed gassed on pod and alcohol. He and Scar stayed tore up. — Herbert Simmons, *Corner Boy*, p. 155, 1957
2 distressed *US, 1960*
- — Robert George Reisner, *The Jazz Titans*, p. 166, 1960

torn up *adjective*
hurt; upset *US, 1968*
- — Hy Lit, *Hy Lit's Unbelievable Dictionary of Hip Words for Groovy People*, p. 1, 1968

torpecker *noun*
a torpedo *US, 1944*
- — *American Speech*, p. 38, February 1948: "Talking under water: speech in submarines"

torpedo *noun*
1 a hired gunman or killer *US, 1929*
- "I'm a torpedo, and the best gun-hand livin'," the Toad answered. — Chester Gould, *Dick Tracy Meets the Night Crawler*, p. 36, 1945
- Dion O'Banion's gun hand was firmly gripped by one Capone torpedo[.] — Frederic Sondern Jr., *Brotherhood of Evil*, p. 70, 1959

- You heard his record—talk about safe streets—is any street safe with a torpedo like that on it? — Edwin Torres, *Carlito's Way*, p. 137, 1975
- And the tough torpedo in the silk tuxedo / Proving his way with a gun (Collected in 1967). — Dennis Wepman et al., *The Life*, p. 162, 1976

2 a marijuana and crack cocaine cigarette *US, 1994*
- — US Department of Justice — US Department of Justice *Street Terms*, October 1994

torpedo juice *noun*
any improvised liquor on board a submarine *US, 1948*
- — *American Speech*, p. 38, February 1948: "Talking under water: speech in submarines"
- It was laced with 90-proof torpedo juice. — Roy Boehm, *First Seal*, p. 71, 1998

torpedos *noun*
beans *US, 1977*
- — Ramon Adams, *The Language of the Railroader*, p. 159, 1977

torqued *adjective*
angered, annoyed *US, 1968*
- — *Current Slang*, p. 12, Spring 1968

toss *noun*
1 a search of a person or place *US, 1973*
- So if a policeman gets there before anybody else, he'll give the apartment a fast toss, searching for cash, jewelry, anything of value. — Leonard Shecter and William Phillips, *On the Pad*, p. 97, 1973
- He had a wild, lucid look about him, so I gave him a toss. — James Ellroy, *Brown's Requiem*, p. 49, 1981

2 an armed robbery *US, 1950*
- — Hyman E. Goldin et al., *Dictionary of American Underworld Lingo*, p. 225, 1950

toss *verb*
1 to create (graffiti) *US, 2000*
- [M]embers do not just write on a wall, they "throw" or "toss" graffiti on the wall. — Robert Jackson and Wesley McBride, *Understanding Street Gangs*, p. 80, 2000

2 to search a room, apartment, house, office, or person without regard to the condition in which the premises or person are left *US, 1939*
- I don't get tossed too often. One time I got tossed three days in a row. Usually I don't. Maybe once every two moths. But they never find anything on me. — James Mills, *The Panic in Needle Park*, p. 101, 1966
- Andy and Leaper had almost twenty-three on them when they got tossed. — George V. Higgins, *The Judgment of Deke Hunter*, p. 31, 1976
- Yeah, but when I realized someone had broken in, the way the place was tossed, I told Miss Nolan, stay in the foyer and don't move. — Elmore Leonard, *Split Images*, p. 12, 1981
- We toss the first banks today, then the broads tomorrow, the bookies Saturday, and so on. — Richard Condon, *Prizzi's Honor*, p. 217, 1982

3 to rob a place *US, 1950*
- — Hyman E. Goldin et al., *Dictionary of American Underworld Lingo*, p. 225, 1950

▸ **toss a grind**
to eat *US, 1992*
- — *Surfer Magazine*, p. 30, February 1992

▸ **toss chow**
to eat quickly and voraciously *US, 1993*
- — *Washington Post*, 14th October 1993

▸ **toss it to someone**
to have sex with a woman *US, 1964*
- You've tossesd it to her so often, you've thrown your ass of line with your eyeballs. — Jim Thompson, *Pop. 1280*, p. 191, 1964

▸ **toss salad**
to engage in oral stimulation of the anus *US, 2001*
- You know what they make you do in County? Toss the fucking salad! I don't like this fuck's asshole; I'm gonna do it for some stranger. — Kevin Smith, *Jay and Silent Bob Strike Back*, p. 14, 2001

▸ **toss the boards**
to play three card molly, a street swindle in which the object is to identify a given card among three cards that are quickly moved around *US, 1972*
- We both knew how to toss the boards, but he was better than me. — Donald Goines, *Whoreson*, p. 35, 1972

tossed salad *noun*
any of several sexual practices involving oral-anal stimulation *US, 1997*

- Havin' your salad tossed means havin' your asshole eaten out with jelly or syrup. I prefer syrup. — Chris Rock, *Rock This!*, p. 181, 1997
- OK, a tossed salad is—get ready, hold onto your underwear for this one—oral-anal sex. — *Oprah Winfrey Show*, 2nd October 2003

toss-up *noun*
1 a person who will trade sex for crack cocaine *US, 1989*
- — Geoffrey Froner, *Digging for Diamonds*, p. 61, 1989

2 a promiscuous female *US, 1995*
- — Bill Valentine, *Gang Intelligence Manual*, p. 78, 1995

TOT
used for suggesting that it is time to tell the complete truth *US, 1989*
From the Yiddish for "buttocks on the table."
- — Leo Rosten, *The Joys of Yinglish*, pp. 482–483, 1989

total *verb*
to wreck something beyond repair *US, 1954*
Originally and chiefly applied to a car.
- Anyway, The Toilet is just plain flat-out scuzzy. I totaled a perfectly good pair of Bergdorf Goodman shoes. — Armistead Maupin, *Tales of the City*, p. 296, 1978

total blank *noun*
in circus and carnival usage, a dull town where business is poor *US, 1981*
- — Don Wilmeth, *The Language of American Popular Entertainment*, p. 278, 1981

totaled; totaled out *adjective*
drunk *US, 1966*
- — *Current Slang*, p. 4, Summer 1966

totally *adverb*
completely *US, 1982*
Very close to standard English, but with the right attitude quite slangy.
- — Mary Corey and Victoria Westermark, *Fer Shurr! How to be a Valley Girl*, 1982
- DIONNE: Hello! That was a stop sign! CHER: I totally paused! — *Clueless*, 1995

totally!
used as an enthusiastic expression of agreement *US, 1982*
- SPICOLI: The mother fucker pissed me off. STONER BUDDY #2: Totally. — *Fast Times at Ridgemont High*, 1982
- — Mary Corey and Victoria Westermark, *Fer Shurr! How to be a Valley Girl*, 1982
- Like, OH MY GOD! (Valley Girl) / Like—TOTALLY (Valley Girl). — Moon Unit and Frank Zappa, *Valley Girl*, 1982
- — Connie Eble (Editor), *UNC-CH Campus Slang*, p. 5, November 1983
- RANDOM SOLDIER: This guy is the coolest! RANDOM SOLDIER 2: Totally man! — *South Park*, 1999

total out *adjective*
to an extreme; to excess *US, 1982*
Hawaiian youth usage.
- Janelle wen break up wit' Raymond she stay total out!! — Douglas Simonson, *Pidgin to da Max Hana Hou*, 1982

tote *verb*
to carry a pistol *US, 1998*
- — Ethan Hilderbrant, *Prison Slang*, p. 129, 1998

to the rack!
used by pool players for expressing dismay and utter defeat *US, 1993*
The player has no choice in this situation but to return his cue to the rack.
- — Mike Shamos, *The Illustrated Encyclopedia of Billiards*, p. 249, 1993

touch *noun*
1 a sum of money obtained at one time, especially by cadging or theft *US, 1846*
- You thought you were hooking into a soft touch, didn't you? You thought you could take me for everything I had. — Jim Thompson, *After Dark, My Sweet*, p. 29, 1955
- "[T]hat's a mistake many a guy makes—they take off a few touches, get a little gold in the oscar hock, and right off they start studying a Cadillac automobile, expensive broads, and a trip to Vegas." — Malcolm Braly, *It's Cold Out There*, pp. 39–40, 1966
- Even when I made a good touch, it would go fairly quickly. — Herbert Huncke, *Guilty of Everything*, p. 74, 1990

2 in pool, finesse *US, 1895*
- — Mike Shamos, *The Illustrated Encyclopedia of Billiards*, p. 251, 1993

▸ **put the touch on someone**
to attempt to extract money from someone with glib or coercive talk *US, 1956*
- Perce was skint when Peter tried to put the touch on him, but he had a nice little job all lined up. — Charles Raven, *Underworld Nights*, p. 44, 1956
- When I told him about my mother and father he said he apologized for putting the touch on me for money. — Clancy Sigal, *Going Away*, p. 144, 1961
- There were guys making a good buck here and there by pressing pants, cooking for other inmates, running errands, or putting the touch on anyone. — Herbert Huncke, *Guilty of Everything*, p. 122, 1990

touch *verb*
1 to swindle *US, 1952*
- More than anybody else a thief hates to be "touched," for he despises the sucker on whom he lives. — Charles Hamilton, *Men of the Underworld*, p. 115, 1952

2 to borrow from someone *US, 1955*
- Maybe he had a morning's work in the produce market, unloading fruit crates, or maybe he touched one of his old pals for a fin. — Rocky Garciano (with Rowland Barber), *Somebody Up There Likes Me*, p. 10, 1955
- There had to be somebody he could touch. — Burt Hirschfield, *Fire Island*, p. 52, 1970

3 to subject someone to extortion or bribery *UK, 1654*
- You getting touched by anybody? — Mickey Spillane, *Me, Hood!*, p. 17, 1963

▸ **touch home**
to communicate a feeling; to make sense *US, 1959*
- "Like he's close, man" (he is quite capable) and "touches home" (really makes sense). — *Look*, p. 49, 24th November 1959

touchhead *noun*
a convert to the musical cult of the Grateful Dead after the 1987 release of the song "Touch of Grey" *US, 1989*
A play on the common "**DEADHEAD**," (a Grateful Dead follower).
- "Touchhead" is a snobby elitist term that realy-truly deadheads (tm) call those fans who started after In The Dark came out (a la after hearing TOUCH of Gray on the radio). — *rec.music.gdead*, 24th August 1989
- Deadhead sociology took a hectic turn with the 1987 influex of "touchheads[.]" — Steven Daly and Nathaniel Wice, *alt.culture*, p. 59, 1995

touching *adjective*
used of playing cards adjacent in rank *US, 1996*
- — Peter O. Steiner, *Thursday Night Poker*, p. 420, 1996

touch man *noun*
a criminal who specializes in breaking into safes by manipulating the combinations until they open *US, 1970*
- If you really want to get good as a touch man, you got to study grease and explosives for a couple of years. — Red Rudensky, *The Gonif*, p. 80, 1970

touch off *verb*
to light a fire, especially if arson *US, 1979*
- [H]e buys five gallons of kerosene and touches it off again. — Vincent Patrick, *The Pope of Greenwich Village*, p. 108, 1979
- You touch off one of those joints with niggers in it, you just burn yourself one nigger, and you are on your own. — George V. Higgins, *The Rat on Fire*, pp. 22–23, 1981

touchy-feely *adjective*
overly sensitive, caring or emotional *US, 1968*
Originating in psychotherapy, now generally used dismissively to describe every state between tactile and lecherous.
- What I was writing was somewhat touchy-feely. — *Jerry Maguire*, 1996
- [W]hat I wanted from sex—that I haven't been able to get across to Kurt—is more of that touchy-feely stuff. — Sally Cline, *Couples*, p. 132, 1998
- Oh, I'm touchy-feely? I take it you never saw Forces of Nature. — Kevin Smith, *Jay and Silent Bob Strike Back*, p. 100, 2001

touch you!
used for conveying surprise and admiration *US, 1997*
- You won the wet underwear contest at the bar last night? Well, touch you! — Jeff Fessler, *When Drag Is Not a Car Race*, p. 89, 1997

tough *verb*
to inject a drug into a vein on the underside of the tongue *US, 1986*
It is not particularly difficult to guess why this practice is so named.
- — Richard A. Spears, *The Slang and Jargon of Drugs and Drink*, p. 519, 1986

tough cheeko
used for expressing a lack of sympathy *US, 1969*
- — John D. Bell et al., *Loosely Speaking*, p. Appendix, 1969

tough darts
too bad *US, 1968*
- — *Current Slang*, p. 10, Spring 1968

tougher *noun*
in poker, an increased bet *US, 1951*
- — *American Speech*, p. 102, May 1951

tough guys *noun*
in craps, the proposition bets (bets that a number will be rolled in a pair) *US, 1983*
- — Thomas L. Clark, *The Dictionary of Gambling and Gaming*, p. 6, 1987

toughie; toughy *noun*
a tough person or situation *US, 1929*
- I couldn't think of a way because it was a real toughie[.] — Jim Thompson, *The Killer Inside*, p. 155, 1952
- The summer after I opened the bar, a 22-year-old toughy sat up front in the corner. — Helen P. Branson, *Gay Bar*, p. 45, 1957
- On one side of us were bikers and toughies wearing patches that said, Road Rats, Nightingale, Windsor and hangers on. — Jamie Mandelkau quoting Ken Kesey, *Buttons*, p. 152, 1971

toughies *noun*
in craps, the proposition bets (bets that a number will be rolled in a pair) *US, 1983*
- — Thomas L. Clark, *The Dictionary of Gambling and Gaming*, p. 6, 1987

tough love *noun*
a mixture of compassion and strictness designed to affect change in destructive behavior *US, 1981*
- There are now 12 "Tough Love" groups in Pennsylvania, notes York, whose recent appearance on a nationwide talk show has swamped him with mail. — *Washington Post*, p. D5, 24th February 1981
- The ex-wife of former baseball great Steve Garvey said Friday she will block any attempt by his new wife to impose "tough love" disciplinary measures on her two daughters. — *Los Angeles Times*, pp. 2–10, 7th October 1989
- The empty [homeless] shelter coexists with the homeless people because of Montgomery County's "tough love" program, one of the nation's most far-reaching efforts to deal with the homeless. — *Washington Post*, p. B1, 2nd January 1995

tough shitski
used as a humorous embellishment of tough shit, or too bad *US, 1961*
A mock Slav or Russian suffix.
- Yeah, Jackie say weekend is one hunner, an if the trick don' stay all weekend, tough shitski, it sill cost him one hunner. — Robert Gover, *One Hundred Dollar Misunderstanding*, p. 95, 1961

tough titty; tough titties; tough tit
used for conveying a lack of sympathy with a difficult turn of events *US, 1934*
- We won't hit anything, and if we do, it'll be the other mug's fault, and some poor bastard's tough titty. — James T. Farrell, *Saturday Night*, p. 25, 1947
- "Even if you get away with it, you'll never be able to come home." "Well, so, tough titty. Anyway, home is where you feel at home." — Truman Capote, *Breakfast at Tiffany's*, p. 102, 1958
- Tough titty. You should have thought about rights when you lifted the stuff. — John Sayles, *Union Dues*, p. 322, 1977
- ROGER: Ya see, I ordered that special. MICKEY: Tough titty, it's mine now. — *Natural Born Killers*, 1994
- "If he doesn't like it, tough titties. I'm being defamed by a person who is a piece of shit." — *Miami New Times*, 18th December 2003

tour ball *noun*
in pinball, a ball that stays in play for a relatively long period without scoring many points *US, 1977*
- — Bobbye Claire Natkin and Steve Kirk, *All About Pinball*, p. 112, 1977

tour crud *noun*
in the language surrounding the Grateful Dead or Phish, a bacterial or viral infection that quickly spreads among those following the band on tour *US, 1994*
- — David Shenk and Steve Silberman, *Skeleton Key*, p. 155, 1994
- charlie (who has still got the damn tour crud... agh cough aack wheeze snort) — *rec.music.phish*, 4th January 1997

tourist disc *noun*
in shuffleboard, a shot that passes through without hitting a target disk or disks *US, 1967*
- — Omero C. Catan, *Secrets of Shuffleboard Strategy*, p. 73, 1967: "Glossary of terms"

tourniquet *noun*
an engagement or wedding ring *US, 1961*
- — *San Francisco Examiner*, p. 21, 12th December 1961: "Coloquialisms for your murgatroid handcutts"

tour rat *noun*
in the language surrounding the Grateful Dead, a fan who follows the band on tour at all costs *US, 1994*
- — David Shenk and Steve Silberman, *Skeleton Key*, p. 291, 1994

tout *noun*
1 in a drug operation with a division of labor, a person who calls out the availability of drugs for sale *US, 1997*
- Ready rock, cried the Fayette Street touts. Got that ready. — David Simon and Edward Burns, *The Corner*, p. 62, 1997
2 in horseracing, someone who sells generally worthless advice with the promise of inside information bound to help bettors win *UK, 1865*
- — *American Speech*, p. 25, February 1955
- — David Bennet, *Know Your Bets*, p. 133, 2001
3 in a confidence swindle or sales scheme, an agent who for a commission locates potential victims *US, 1988*
- — Kathleen Odean, *High Steppers, Fallen Angels, and Lollipops*, p. 134, 1988

towelhead; towel-head *noun*
an Arab; also a Sikh or other turban-wearer *US, 1979*
An offensive or derogatory term; from the traditional headwear of the various races and creeds.
- "Nuke Iran!" shouted the seething counter-demonstrators, "Towel-heads, go home!" — *Washington Post*, p. A6, 1st December 1979
- "I wouldn't bring these papers to you after that towel-head touches them." — Joseph Pistone, *Donnie Brasco*, p. 252, 1987
- In a series of racist statements that began when the World Trade Center collapsed, Roque announced his murderous plans and told a co-worker that he had been treated rudely at a gasoline station on University Drive by "a towel head or a rag head." — *The Arizona Republic*, p. 1A, 3rd September 2003
- A full-drag dune coon opened up. — James Ellroy, *Destination Morgue*, p. 328, 2004

towel jockey *noun*
a locker room attendant *US, 1977*
- "I've got a nice offer to become a towel jockey in one of the down-town Los Angeles whorehouses." — Harry Allen Smith, *The Life and Legend of Gene Fowler*, p. 277, 1977
- "We met at the Palisades Vista Country Club where her family belonged and I was working my way through the U. as a towel jockey." — Jonathan Kellerman, *Rage*, p. 304, 2005

town *noun*
city *US, 1999*
A coy term that harkens back.
- This is how you dress in this town you're in arts and entertainment. — Elmore Leonard, *Be Cool*, p. 7, 1999

town clown *noun*
a local police officer *US, 1927*
- As I was chalking my cue, who walked in the door but the town clown. — Robert Byrne, *McGoorty*, p. 99, 1972
- The box was on the balcony and we laid on the floor and watched the town-clown [local policeman] go all over the first floor but he never came near the box. — Harry King, *Box Man*, p. 43, 1972

town dollars *noun*
in horseracing, money bet at a betting operation away from the track *US, 1951*
- — David W. Maurer, *Argot of the Racetrack*, p. 65, 1951

towner *noun*
a local resident *US, 1980*
Circus and carnival usage.
- — Joe McKennon, *Circus Lingo*, p. 95, 1980

townie *noun*
a townsperson, contrasted with a visiting student or summer visitor *US, 1852*
- On the way they passed the townies, who glared at them balefully, but the girls chattered and giggled and did not even turn their heads. — Max Shulman, *Rally Round the Flag, Boys!*, p. 228, 1957
- "No women." Youngblood leaning back. "Townies, even?" — Richard Farina, *Been Down So Long*, p. 79, 1966
- They arrived in time to be scared by a group of drunken townies beating the bejabbers out of three or four hippy boys they'd caught in the lot. — Nicholas Von Hoffman, *We Are The People Our Parents Warned Us Against*, p. 67, 1967
- Sandy had intimated on the ferry ride home that night the townies tried to rape her. — Evan Hunter, *Last Summer*, p. 114, 1968

town pump *noun*
a very promiscuous woman *US, 1961*
- "Would I be jealous of the town pump?" — Malcom Braly, *Felony Tank*, p. 126, 1961

town punch *noun*
a very promiscious woman *US, 1975*
- — *American Speech*, p. 68, Spring–Summer 1975: "Razorback slang"

toxic *adjective*
amazing, powerful *US, 1987*
- — *Washington Post Magazine*, p. 7, 30th August 1987: "Say wha'?"
- — Vann Wesson, *Generation X Field Guide and Lexicon*, p. 170, 1997

Toxic Hell *noun*
a Taco Bell™ restaurant *US, 1993*
- — Connie Eble (Editor), *UNC-CH Campus Slang*, p. 6, Spring 1993
- Even offering to get me something for lunch from taco bell (affectionately referred to toxic hell). — *rec.art.poems*, 2nd October 1997

toy *noun*
1 a can in which opium is stored, whether the can is tin, tinned iron, or another metal; a small amount of opium *US, 1934*
- What you did was, you took a toy (a tin) of hop and shook it up with this medicine in a bottle and kept taking it every day. — Mezz Mezzrow, *Really the Blues*, p. 254, 1946
- All we found were some empty "toys" of opium. — Harry J. Anslinger, *The Murderers*, p. 37, 1961
- They used to sell in what the Chinese call "toys." — Jeremy Larner and Ralph Tefferteller, *The Addict in the Street*, p. 159, 1964
2 any object that is used for sexual stimulation during masturbation, foreplay, sexual intercourse, or fetish play *US, 1977*
- A significant part of the content of gay magazines is taken over by advertisements for "toys"—a revealing euphemism, evoking child-hood, for implements of "torture:" steel clamps, branding irons, whips, straps, even handcuffs. — John Rechy, *The Sexual Outlaw*, p. 255, 1977
3 a computer system *US, 1991*
- — Eric S. Raymond, *The New Hacker's Dictionary*, p. 355, 1991
4 an inexperienced or incompetent graffiti artist *US, 1982*
- "Beginners are at a disadvantage in this regard because they have to bear the label of toy or 'DGA' ('Don't Get Around')." — Craig Castleman, *Getting Up*, p. 78, 1982
- [T]hey have to bear the label of toy or "DGA" ("Dont Get Around") until they have proved themselves through long hours of work in the yards. — Craig Castleman, *Getting Up*, p. 78, 1982
- — Henry Chalfant, *Spraycan Art*, p. 12, 1987: Glossary

toy money *noun*
military script *US, 1967*
- Later, script, or toy money is obtained at the base post offices. — Elaine Shepard, *The Doom Pussy*, p. 21, 1967

TP *noun*
a scene in a pornographic film or a photograph depicting a woman having simultaneous oral, vaginal, and anal sex *US, 2000*
An abbreviation of "triple penetration."
- — Ana Loria, *1 2 3 Be A Porn Star!*, p. 167, 2000: "Glossary of adult sex Industry terms"

track *noun*

1 a street or area where prostitutes solicit customers *US, 1969*

- I might even steal her from scarface and put her back on the track tomorrow. — Iceberg Slim (Robert Beck), *Pimp*, p. 180, 1969
- Because of my concern for Jessie, I pulled Fatima up from the track before midnight. — Donald Goines, *Whoreson*, p. 62, 1972
- Niggas hatin' on me cause I got hoes on the track. — *Hustle and Flow*, 2004

2 an armored personnel carrier, especially the M-113 *US, 1971*

- The tracks had flattened the jungle but not destroyed it. — Ronald J. Glasser, *365 Days*, p. 111, 1971
- CAPTAIN: I was an FO for the 25th. WILLARD: Tracks? — *Apocalypse Now*, 1979
- It was late in the afternoon and they were in the last of several APCs (Armored Personnel Carriers), lumbering steel-plated behemoths called "tracks." — Myra MacPherson, *Long Time Passing*, p. 21, 1984

▸ **the track**

the Savoy ballroom, New York *US, 1946*

A major night spot on Lenox Avenue between 140th and 141st Streets in New York from 1927 until the 50s.

- [S]pecific places are known by special nicknames—New York City as The Apple, Seventh Avenue as The Stroll, the Savoy Ballroom as The Track[.] — Mezz Mezzrow, *Really the Blues*, p. 221, 1946
- Whenever I didn't go to the track (Savoy) I'd go down to "Minton's." — Babs Gonzales, *I Paid My Dues*, p. 33, 1967

tracked up *adjective*

scarred from regular intravenous drug injection *US, 1971*

- — Eugene Landy, *The Underground Dictionary*, p. 187, 1971

track lawyer *noun*

in horseracing, someone who constantly resorts to claims of technical rule violations, the pettier the better *US, 1947*

- — Dan Parker, *The ABC of Horse Racing*, p. 150, 1947

tracks *noun*

bruises, punctures, and sores visible on the skin of an intravenous drug user *US, 1960*

- "For another thing, your boy's got tracks up and down his left arm—" "Tracks?" "That's the spot on an addict's arm where he keeps shoving the needle in," King told him. — Clarence Cooper Jr., *The Scene*, p. 121, 1960
- In summer, they alone wear long sleeves (to cover their "tracks"—collapsed veins and needle marks). — James Mills, *The Panic in Needle Park*, p. 17, 1966
- Old needle marks—tracks—where she had tried to hit her veins and missed. — Herbert Huncke, *The Evening Sun Turned Crimson*, p. 62, 1980

▸ **make tracks**

to leave *US, 1945*

- — Lou Shelly, *Hepcats Jive Talk Dictionary*, p. 29, 1945
- — Hy Lit, *Hy Lit's Unbelievable Dictionary of Hip Words for Groovy People*, p. 27, 1968

traction *noun*

in confidence games, an amount of money used to begin an increasingly larger series of swindles *US, 1997*

- We gotta get us some traction. — Stephen J. Cannell, *King Con*, p. 32, 1997

trade *noun*

a man, self-identified as heterosexual, who engages in active anal homosexual sex or passive oral homosexual sex but will not reciprocate *US, 1919*

- All her johns and trade were the same. They were all some kind of big shot. — Hubert Selby Jr., *Last Exit to Brooklyn*, p. 204, 1957
- And I had never heard even the scores and queens, who would often in bitchiness claim that "today's trade is tomorrow's competition," say it about Chuck. — John Rechy, *City of Night*, p. 139, 1963
- The humiliating position he would put himself in when some piece of trade spurned him because he was not able to lay on the requisite bread! — Gore Vidal, *Myra Breckinridge*, p. 97, 1968
- As the men often say, "Today's trade is tomorrow's competition." — Jack Weatherford, *Porn Row*, p. 119, 1986

trade queen *noun*

a homosexual man who prefers sex with a seemingly heterosexual man who consents to homosexual sex in the "male" role, receiving orally or giving anally *US, 1970*

- Some of these "trade queens," because they're gay, think they're not as whole as other guys. They chase "straights" exclusively so they can put one over on them. — *Screw*, p. 18, 22nd June 1970

trades *noun*

the trade journals of the US entertainment industry *US, 1984*

- "The trades?" Burt volunteered. "Daily Variety and The Hollywood Reporter?" — Dan Jenkins, *Life Its Ownself*, p. 172, 1984
- His worthless swine of an agent hadn't even called him about the role and there it was in yesterday's trades. — Joseph Wambaugh, *Finnegan's Week*, p. 2, 1993
- Now, I want to start this thing off big. The Trades, MTV, the works. — *Wayne's World 2*, 1993

trade up *verb*

to escape criminal prosecution or lessen the charges against you by providing the police with information about other criminals *US, 1981*

- We might be able to let you slide this time if you're cooperative. It's called trading up. Little fish for big fish. — Joseph Wambaugh, *The Glitter Dome*, p. 151, 1981

tragic magic *noun*

heroin *US, 1990*

- — Charles Shafer, *Folk Speech in Texas Prisons*, p. 216, 1990

trailer *noun*

in a striptease performance, the preliminary march across the stage that precedes the removal of any piece of clothing *US, 1981*

- — Don Wilmeth, *The Language of American Popular Entertainment*, p. 279, 1981

▸ **pull a trailer**

to possess large buttocks *US, 1988*

- — Surf Punks, *Oh No! Not Them Again! (liner notes)*, 1988

trail hog *noun*

a skier who is inconsiderate of other skiers, monopolizing a narrow trail *US, 1963*

- — *American Speech*, p. 207, October 1963: "The language of skiers"

trail marker *noun*

an unappetizing piece of food, the identity of which is uncertain *US, 1991*

- Today's cuisine consisted of trail markers, sometimes called elephant turds, large lumps of blandly seasoned ground beef covered with a gray, tasteless gravy good only for making the things less dry. — Gerry Carroll, *North S*A*R*, p. 36, 1991

trails *noun*

while under the influence of LSD or another hallucinogen, sequences of repeating after-images trailing a moving object *US, 1999*

- Another frequent visual phenomenon is known as "trails." — Cam Cloud, *The Little Book of Acid*, p. 10, 1999

train *noun*

1 an act of serial sex with multiple partners *US, 1994*

- I knew what a train was. It was what happened when a bunch of guys got together and jammed the same girl. — Nathan McCall, *Makes Me Wanna Holler*, p. 42, 1994

2 cocaine *US, 1993*

- — Peter Johnson, *Dictionary of Street Alcohol and Drug Terms*, p. 195, 1993

3 a series of waves *US, 1963*

- — Grant W. Kuhns, *On Surfing*, p. 123, 1963

4 multiple orgasms *US, 1985*

- — *American Speech*, p. 20, Spring 1985: "The language of singles bars"

▸ **pull a train**

to serve consecutive jail sentences *US, 2002*

- — Jeffrey Ian Ross, *Behind Bars*, p. 192, 2002: Slammer Slang

▸ **pull a train; run a train**

to engage in serial sex with multiple partners, homosexual or heterosexual, usually consensual *US, 1965*

- They thought I was one of the guys who had pulled a train on their sister in the park the summer before. — Claude Brown, *Manchild in the Promised Land*, p. 165, 1965
- A girl who squeals on one of the outlaws or who deserts him for somebody wrong can expect to be "turned out," as they say, to "pull the Angel train." — Hunter S. Thompson, *Hell's Angels*, p. 194, 1966

- A gang of niggers ran a train on her down on Thirty-ninth Street. — Iceberg Slim (Robert Beck), *Trick Baby*, p. 173, 1969
- Peggy Reeves Sanday had never heard of "pulling train" until one of her students came to her office after missing class for two weeks. — *The Chronicle of Higher Education*, p. A3, 19th September 1990

train *verb*
to engage in serial sex with multiple partners *US, 1994*
- Scobe and hig gang caught her stumbling by one night and trained her in a wooded area behind the 7-Eleven. — Nathan McCall, *Makes Me Wanna Holler*, p. 42, 1994

train wreck *noun*
a horribly wounded soldier or casualty department patient *US, 1978*
Used by medical corpsmen in Vietnam.
- — *Journal of American Folklore*, p. 568–581, January–March 1978: "The gomer"
- Train wrecks were cases suffering from multiple injuries, requiring immediate surgery: Head, chest, eye, face, stomach wounds and broken bones. — Gregory Clark, *Words of the Vietnam War*, p. 519, 1990

tramp *noun*
a promiscuous man or woman *US, 1922*
- You don't—you won't think I'm a tramp, will you? — Jim Thompson, *Savage Night*, p. 35, 1953
- And everybody's had him. He's one of the Hollywood Boulevard tramps. — John Rechy, *City of Night*, p. 202, 1963
- Liz had been cheating on her. Liz was becoming a tramp. A little chippy. A puta. — Sheldon Lord, *The Third Way*, 1964
- A tramp is a girl who will have intercourse "with anybody," perhaps even without getting paid for it. — Christina and Richard Milner, *Black Players*, p. 41, 1972

tramp stamp *noun*
a tattoo on a woman's lower back, spreading up from her buttocks *US, 2005*
The term suggests that only a sexually promiscuous woman would have such a tattoo.
- Boys call the lower back tattoo a "Tramp Stamp." It is generally accepted that these tattoos mean the girls are advertising they are sexually promiscuous and enjoy rear-entry positions. — *alt.child-support*, 15th December 2005
- It's getting worse and worse they are getting more desperate and using any means necessary to draw attention to themselves—tramp stamp tattoos, fake boobs makeup botox. — *soc.men*, 2nd June 2005

trank *noun*
any central nervous system depressant *US, 1967*
Variant spelling include "trang" and "tranx."
- But just now, with these tranks they've got me on, I feel like I'm sleepwalking anyway[.] — Jay McInerney, *Story of My Life*, p. 188, 1988
- Tranks are the synthetics, like Miltown, Valium, etc. — Herbert Huncke, *Guilty of Everything*, p. 9, 1990

tranked *adjective*
sedated; under the influence of tranquillizers *US, 1975*
- [N]othing, except having our best black brothers monitored and tranked, even with a trial, or because they pleaded guilty to get out. — Roger Elwood, *Dystopian Visions*, p. 64, 1975
- Some were moaning. Some were tranked out. — Larry Brown, *Dirty Work*, p. 51, 1989
- Tranked out of her mind is more like it. — Carl Hiaasen, *Native Tongue*, p. 231, 1991

trannie; tranny *noun*
a transsexual or transvestite *US, 1983*
- Just your average, typical trailer-park trannie from Austin, Texas. — James St. James, *Party Monster*, p. 80, 1990
- Unlike so many trannies, past and present, Candy, born James Lawrence Slattery, never spoofed womanhood or the ways in which pop culture filters and distorts it. — *San Francisco Chronicle*, p. E1, 28th July 1997
- And then, queer audiences seem to have only two speeds when it comes to transwriting: a) trannies belong and gosh do they have it difficult; b) trannies should take a hike and stop trying to hijack gay and lesbian efforts. — *Lambda Book Report*, p. 36, 30th September 1997

trannie; tranny *adjective*
transsexual *US, 1999*
- I have tried to make my workshops accessible to a variety of women and men, lesbian, bi, gay, straight, trannie, young, old, sex-positive, sex-neutral, sex-curious. — *The Village Voice*, 24th August 1999

tranquilize *noun*
to beat into submission *US, 1958*
- A policeman doesn't subdue a truculent prisoner; he tranquilizes him. — *New York Times*, p. 34, 20th October 1958

trans *noun*
a car *US, 1995*
- — Bill Valentine, *Gang Intelligence Manual*, p. 111, 1995

transformer *noun*
a transsexual *US, 1991*
- [T]hat was no problem because she shared it with three other Transformers who were as smooth and pure as chocolate statues. — William T. Vollman, *Whores for Gloria*, p. 55, 1991

transit *noun*
▶ **in transit**
experiencing the effects of LSD *US, 1971*
- — Eugene Landy, *The Underground Dictionary*, p. 109, 1971

trap *noun*
1 the mouth *UK, 1776*
- "Shut yer trap or I'll lay one on it!" Calico shouted angrily. — Chester Gould, *Dick Tracy Meets the Night Crawler*, p. 192, 1945
- "From now, Patterson resolved, I'll just keep my trap shut." — Clarence Cooper Jr., *The Scene*, p. 72, 1960
- Take your feet off my chair and shut your trap. — S.E. Hinton, *The Outsiders*, p. 21, 1967
- Not if you guys keep your traps shut. — Oscar Zeta Acosta, *The Revolt of the Cockroach People*, p. 144, 1973

2 a prostitute's earnings; the earnings expected of a prostitute by her pimp *US, 1973*
A shortened form of **TRAP MONEY**.
- After I'd been checking her trap for over a week she said she wanted to be my woman. — A.S. Jackson, *Gentleman Pimp*, p. 142, 1973
- For the first time in the week since she'd been hooking she hadn't made her trap. — Alix Shulman, *On the Stroll*, p. 110, 1981

3 an electronic device that records the originating telephone number of all incoming calls *US, 1991*
A term and practice made obsolete with the advent of the "caller ID" feature on telephones in the late 1990s.
- Course they never say who it is, but we had Southern Bell put a trap on the line. It tells what number they're calling from, so then they look up to see where the phone's located. — Elmore Leonard, *Maximum Bob*, p. 218, 1991

4 a hiding place for illegal drugs *US, 1967*
- — Ruth Bronsteen, *The Hippy's Handbook*, p. 16, 1967

5 a residence *US, 1957*
- We go up to her trap, and she remove the dry goods. — William Burroughs, *Naked Lunch*, p. 119, 1957

6 in poker, a deceptive bet *US, 1979*
- — John Scarne, *Scarne's Guide to Modern Poker*, p. 292, 1979

trap *verb*
1 to install an electronic trap on a telephone line *US, 1996*
- Burdon says they've trapped her line and hung a wire. — Elmore Leonard, *Out of Sight*, p. 118, 1996

2 to land safely and accurately on an aircraft carrier *US, 1991*
- Since there were no other aircraft in the landing pattern, they both came in and trapped without problems. — Gerry Carroll, *North S*A*R*, p. 60, 1991

trap door *noun*
1 a scab under which a drug addict injects drugs *US, 1992*
- The trapdoor hid the fresh needle marks from the cops. — Joseph Wambaugh, *Fugitive Nights*, p. 35, 1992

2 a computing function that is easily performed but difficult to perform in the inverse *US, 1991*
Extremely useful in cryptography.
- — Eric S. Raymond, *The New Hacker's Dictionary*, p. 356, 1991
- And the trap doors will always be there as well. — The Knightmare, *Secrets of a Super Hacker*, p. 7, 1994

trapeze artist *noun*
a person engaged in simultaneous anal and oral sex *US, 1979*
- — *Maledicta*, p. 232, 1979: "Kinks and queens: linguistic and cultural aspects of the terminology for gays"

trap money *noun*
a prostitute's gross earnings *US, 1974*

- She was still too young to have any apprehensions over spending her trap money. Ronald didn't put her on any quota so whatever she came home with she believed he would be happy with. — Donald Goines, *Daddy Cool*, p. 147, 1974
- Chantelle who ain't gonna pull short-ass trap money shit on me. — Wilton Barnhardt, *Emma Who Saved My Life*, p. 305, 1989

trap off *verb*
to deceive or manipulate someone *US, 2002*
- — Gary K. Farlow, *Prison-ese*, p. 75, 2002

traps *noun*
the trapeziums muscles connecting the neck and shoulder *US, 1984*
- — *American Speech*, p. 201, Fall 1984: "The language of bodybuilding"

trash *noun*
1 military decorations, awards, and patches *US, 1990*
- — Gregory Clark, *Words of the Vietnam War*, p. 520, 1990
2 waves that collapse before they break, making poor surfing conditions *US, 1977*
- — Gary Fairmont R. Filosa II, *The Surfer's Almanac*, p. 197, 1977

trash *verb*
to criticize or someone malign or something *US, 1975*
- I even made two gorgeous lesbians wait outside while I trashed DeBella some more. — Howard Stern, *Miss America*, p. 297, 1995

trashed *adjective*
very drunk or drug-intoxicated *US, 1966*
- — *Current Slang*, p. 6, Fall 1966
- "I'm getting trashed." Isn't that what you're supposed to say at a party? — *Ten Things I Hate About You*, 1999
- He was twenty and loaded with cash from fishing and he bought them both tickets to Bali where they got trashed for a week and screwed themselves silly. — Tim Winton, *The Turning*, p. 137, 2005

trash hand *noun*
in poker, an unplayable hand *US, 1992*
- — Edwin Silberstang, *Winning Poker for the Serious Player*, p. 220, 1992

trash hauler *noun*
during the Vietnam war, a cargo transport pilot *US, 1988*
- They wanted to clearly demonstrate to all the trash haulers (their term for transport pilots) who the kings of the roost were. — Harold Coyle, *Sword Point*, p. 101, 1988
- A trash hauler flew overhead one dark and windy day / He passed over our runway as he flew upon his way. — Joseph Tuso, *Singing the Vietnam Blues*, p. 37, 1990: The Balld of the C-130

trash time *noun*
a short jail sentence, especially one spent on a litter cleaning duty *US, 1987*
- Ask that fucking crook his opinion. He didn't even do trash time in a country-club joint. — Elmore Leonard, *Bandits*, p. 259, 1987

travel agent *noun*
an LSD dealer *US, 1966*
A euphemism based on a **TRIP** metaphor.
- — Richard Alpert and Sidney Cohen, *LSD*, 1966

traveler *noun*
alcohol taken in a car on the way to a party or concert *US, 2004*
- — Ben Applebaum and Derrick Pittman, *Turd Ferguson & The Sausage Party*, p. 68, 2004

traveler's check *noun*
in poker or other gambling, a betting token that rolls across the table or floor *US, 1996*
From the insider slang term **CHECK** (a gambling token).
- — John Vorhaus, *The Big Book of Poker Slang*, p. 37, 1996

treaders *noun*
shoes *US, 1970*
- — Clarence Major, *Dictionary of Afro-American Slang*, p. 116, 1970

treadhead *noun*
a member of a combat tank crew *US, 1986*
- If you weren't a trained "tread head" when you came to us, Ilpha would turn you into a top-grade "bullet stabber" in no time. — Ralph Zumbro, *Tank Sergeant*, p. viii, 1986

- Shit, don't they teach you treadheads anything at Fort Knox? — Harold Coyle, *Team Yankee*, p. 231, 1987
- "Rotor heads" are helicopter pilots and "tread heads" are tankers. — *Washington Times*, p. E1, 31st January 1991

treasure hunt *noun*
the search in a gambling establishment or cardroom for someone from whom to borrow money *US, 1982*
- — David M. Hayano, *Poker Faces*, p. 188, 1982

tree; trees *noun*
marijuana *US, 2001*
An exaggerated **BUSH**.
- All the real smokers know / They ain't passin' nuttin' but dope indeed... / Real trees... / Chronic leaves — Dr. Dre, *Xplosive*, 2001
- — Connie Eble (Editor), *UNC-CH Campus Slang*, p. 11, Fall 2001
- Pot, grass, weed, herb, cheeba, chronic, trees, indo, doja—whoever they called it then, whatever they call it now, and whatever they'll call it in the future, it was marijuana. — 50 Cent, *From Pieces to Weight*, p. 5, 2005

tree-eater *noun*
a member of the US Special Service Forces *US, 1993*
Because of the constant survival training the special forces undergo.
- — *The Retired Officer Magazine*, p. 39, January 1993

tree-hugger *noun*
an environmental activist *US, 1977*
- "These days it wouldn't take much to stir up another snail-darter scenario. I mean, if some tree-hugger type really wanted to throw a wrench in this project." — Carl Hiaasen, *Sick Puppy*, p. 43, 1999

tree-jumper *noun*
a chronic sex offender *US, 1992*
- "And one day so it's 'Mike Tyson, you (expletive deleted) tree jumper,' he said. And I didn't know what a tree jumper was. I thought it meant like I was a great athlete or something, jumping out of trees, and I was, 'What's a tree jumper?'" — *Associated Press*, 14th June 1992
- — Gary K. Farlow, *Prison-ese*, p. 75, 2002

trees *noun*
broccoli *US, 1966*
- — John D. Bell et al., *Loosely Speaking*, p. 19, 1966

treetop level and all engines out *adjective*
near death *US, 1994*
- — Sally Williams, *"Strong" Words*, p. 163, 1994

Trekker *noun*
a zealous fan of *Star Trek* *US, 1978*
Preferred by the fans over the term "**TREKKIE**."
- Star Trek Lives: Trekker Slang — *American Speech*, p. 53, Spring 1978

Trekkie *noun*
a devoted fan of *Star Trek* *US, 1978*
- — Connie Eble (Editor), *UNC-CH Campus Slang*, p. 4, April 1978
- Those Star Trek conventions should be outlawed and all Trekkies sterilized. — Howard Stern, *Miss America*, p. 256, 1995
- The message to all Trekkies is that it's not real, it's only a movie. Please beam them up. — Alon Shulman, *The Style Bible*, p. 252, 1999

trench *noun*
▸ **in the trenches**
involved in the hard, dirty aspect of an enterprise *US, 1970*
- Meanwhile, I'm the guy in the trenches. Fuckin' bosses, they think it's a fuckin' free lunch out here. — *Casino*, 1995

trey *noun*
1 three *UK, 1859*
- Lay a trey on me, ole man. — Mezz Mezzrow, *Really the Blues*, p. 216, 1946
- "What'll happen after I do that trey?" he asked MacMahon. — Clarence Cooper Jr., *The Scene*, p. 184, 1960
- He croaked, "Maybe his girls are humping on 'Four Trey.'" — Iceberg Slim (Robert Beck), *Mama Black Widow*, p. 218, 1969
- After calling me three more M.F.'s, he said he'd meet her at a trey in the morning. — Babs Gonzales, *Movin' On Down De Line*, p. 22, 1975

2 a prison sentence of three years *US, 1983*

- Doing a deuce or a trey in the joint didn't seem like much of a jolt when I was thirty, but it seems like one hell of a lot at this stage in life. — Gerald Petievich, *To Die in Beverly Hills*, p. 223, 1983

3 three dollars' worth of a drug *US, 1966*

- Often the junkie pusher will deal "nickel bags" at $5 each, as well as $3 "treys." — James Mills, *The Panic in Needle Park*, p. 20, 1966

trey eight *noun*

a .38 caliber handgun *US, 1992*

- Trey eight—.38 caliber gun. — *St. Louis Post-Dispatch*, p. 1A, 2nd June 1992
- Ann Lawson, *Kids & Gangs*, p. 56, 1994: "Common African-American gang slang/phrases"

treyer *noun*

three years or three dollars *US, 1950*

- — Hyman E. Goldin et al., *Dictionary of American Underworld Lingo*, p. 226, 1950

trick *noun*

1 a prostitute's customer *US, 1925*

- They had to keep an eye on the cops all the time, because they weren't allow to call the tricks like the girls in Storyville. — Louis Armstrong, *Satchmo: My Life in New Orleans*, p. 95, 1954
- Rita and Flossie don't exactly rust but they don't look so good to the tricks seen them twenty- thirty time as they do to tricks seeing them the first time. — Sara Harris, *The Lords of Hell*, p. 14, 1967
- When you're turned out, pimps put that in your head. "You don't get off with tricks." Tricks are tricks—that's how they got the name. — Susan Hall, *Ladies of the Night*, p. 29, 1973
- Look, I got there. He was a trick just like any other for all I know. — *48 Hours*, 1982

2 an act of sex between a prostitute and customer *US, 1926*

- The girls explained to me that they got eighty cents a trick, one payment for each metal check—"turning a trick" was how they described one session with a john. — Mezz Mezzrow, *Really the Blues*, p. 23, 1946
- From this croaker up on 76th Street. He used to write for me, you know, scripts, prescriptions. I turned a trick with him. — James Mills, *The Panic in Needle Park*, p. 91, 1966
- Pimps take cops to dinner with free tricks. — *The Digger Papers*, p. 14, August 1968
- I started working as a stripper in a club in Washington and turned a few tricks on the side. — Susan Hall, *Gentleman of Leisure*, p. 59, 1972

3 a short-term homosexual sexual partner, not paying *US, 1963*

- — Donald Webster Cory and John P. LeRoy, *The Homosexual and His Society*, p. 266, 1963: "A lexicon of homosexual slang"
- If I don't get arrested, my trick announces upon departure that he's been exposed to hepatitis! — Mart Crowley, *The Boys in the Band*, p. 163, 1968
- Martin—the blond trick I introduced you to before you went in there. — John Francis Hunter, *The Gay Insider*, p. 103, 1971
- I looked like a bull dyke, or a trick of one, with handcuffs, a leather jacket, metal belts, and levi 501's, so I would try to method act. — Jennifer Blowdryer, *White Trash Debutante*, p. 56, 1997

4 any dupe *US, 1965*

- We'd shoot among ourselves, 'cause the tricks wasn't comin' in. — Henry Williamson, *Hustler!*, p. 79, 1965
- [W]e done warned this dude six or seven times about shootin' that turn-down shot on us, but he still takes us for tricks. — Donald Goines, *Cry Revenge*, p. 11, 1974

5 a swindle *UK, 1865*

Far less common in this sense, but not unheard.

- Since work was out, so also was the grift. He wouldn't dare turn a trick. — Jim Thompson, *The Grifters*, p. 124, 1963

trick *verb*

1 to engage in sex with a paying customer, usually in an expeditious fashion *US, 1960*

- Don't tell me you made it all tricking and you're saving it for your old age. — Clarence Cooper Jr., *The Scene*, p. 206, 1960
- He knew that she was Red Shirt's woman, and knowing Red Shirt, automatically assumed that she was tricking[.] — Nathan Heard, *Howard Street*, p. 83, 1968
- Vickie had tricked with his father at a convention and was embarrassed and ashamed when Andre invited her home to meet his people and they were introduced. — Herbert Huncke, *The Evening Sun Turned Crimson*, p. 53, 1980

- The first time Phyllis went out tricking she wasn't nervous because she thought she was just going along with Shawna to watch and learn. — William T. Vollman, *Whores for Gloria*, p. 54, 1991

2 to have sex with a short-term partner, without emotion or money passed *US, 1968*

- It seems to me that the first time we tricked we met in a gay bar on Third Avenue during your junior year. — Mart Crowley, *The Boys in the Band*, p. 37, 1968
- I haven't tricked like that for about a hundred years[.] — Armistead Maupin, *Maybe the Moon*, p. 76, 1992

trick baby *noun*

the offspring of a prostitute and an unknown customer, often of mixed race *US, 1951*

- I played with thieves' children and the sporting women's trick babies. — Ethel Waters, *His Eye is on the Sparrow*, p. 15, 1951
- I said, "Goddamnit, Mr. Murray, I was no trick baby. My mother was no whore. She married a white man." — Iceberg Slim (Robert Beck), *Trick Baby*, p. 15, 1969
- "Looks like you done went and got you a trick baby, honey." — Donald Goines, *Whoreson*, p. 9, 1972

trick bag *noun*

1 a bag used by a prostitute to carry tools of the trade *US, 2003* A search warrant issued by the Sausalito (California) Police Department in its investigation of a massage parlor/brothel defines a trick bag as "a large woman's handbag, which will generally enclose the following items which are used in the practice of prostitution: clothing, especially a change of undergarments such as panties, bras, camisoles and negligees, wet wipes, paper tissues, Vaseline and personal lubricants, bottles of mouth wash, rubbing alcohol, baby oil, various kinds and numbers of condoms, douches and other forms of feminine hygiene, and various cosmetics, small hand towels which are normally used in the practice of prostitution to wipe the ejaculatory excretions from the bodies of the prostitute and the customers[.]"

2 a dilemma with no clear solution *US, 1992*

- — William K. Bentley and James M. Corbett, *Prison Slang*, p. 47, 1992

trick bar *noun*

a bar frequented by prostitutes and potential customers for their services *US, 1988*

- So I tried out other trick bars in the red-light district. — Dolores French, *Working*, p. 85, 1988

trick book *noun*

a prostitute's list of customers *US, 1972*

- You may work a trick book. You may work that up yourself or you may buy it. — Bruce Jackson, *In the Life*, p. 190, 1972
- Female corpse found in bushes off Highway 1 near El Capitan Beach had pocket litter and trick book with L.A. area phone numbers. — Gerald Petievich, *To Die in Beverly Hills*, p. 139, 1983
- Even Missy Moonbeam's trick book was pathetic. — Joseph Wambaugh, *The Delta Star*, p. 78, 1983

trick bunk *noun*

in prison, a bed used for sexual encounters *US, 1990*

- So that's what the dorm tender meant warning Joe that he'd been assigned the trick bunk. Of course—it was the furthest from the door, least visible to passing guards, best suited for the quickie clandestine cigarette date. — Seth Morgan, *Homeboy*, p. 199, 1990

trick day *noun*

an agreed time when homosexuals in long-term relationships may have sex outside the relationship *US, 1964*

- — Florida Legislative Investigation Committee (Johns Committee), *Homosexuality and Citizenship in Florida*, 1964: "Glossary of homosexual terms and deviate acts"
- — Dale Gordon, *The Dominion Sex Dictionary*, p. 158, 1967

trick dress; trick suit *noun*

a dress that a prostitute can remove easily *US, 1963*

- [S]he hurried to Burbank to get her "trick suit," which she explained was a dress worn by prostitutes to facilitate their work. — Ed Reid and Ovid Demaris, *The Green Felt Jungle*, p. 100, 1963
- There was a brief break in midafternoon while the girls put on their trick suits and lined up outside the fence for pictures. — Juan Carmel Cosmes, *Memoir of a Whoremaster*, p. 149, 1969

tricked out *adjective*

elaborated decorated or accessorized *UK, 1727*

- There was also a tricked-out Vee-dub, and a battered, big-pig station wagon that probably belonged to some homeless family[.] — Jess Mowry, *Way Past Cool*, p. 146, 1992

trick flick *noun*
a pornographic movie, usually homosexual *US, 1970*
- — *American Speech*, p. 59, Spring–Summer 1970: "Homosexual slang"

trick fuck *verb*
to have sex without any emotional content *US, 2001*
- "Can't just trick fuck and let it go. Must be a white thing." — Dan Jenkins, *The Money-Whipped Steer-Job Three-Jack Give-Up Artist*, p. 214, 2001

trick house *noun*
a house or apartment where prostitutes take their customers for sex *US, 1972*
- I met a girl who was working the streets and she took us to a trick house where we could turn our tricks for a dollar. — Donald Goines, *Whoreson*, p. 74, 1972
- She had a good round-eye, and that's no lie / How the trickhouse door would swing! — Dennis Wepman et al., *The Life*, p. 83, 1976

trick name *noun*
a prostitute's business alias *US, 1991*
- Trick names often fall into one of three categories: (1) words associated with pleasure (Joy, Felicia, etc.) (2) words associated with luxurious things that the john can eat or drink up (Candy, Brandi, etc.) (3) names that sound "aristocratic" or "fancy[.]" — William T. Vollman, *Whores for Gloria*, p. 145, 1991

trick or treat *noun*
an automatic ambush *US, 2004*
- — David Hart, *First Air Cavalry Division Vietnam Dictionary*, p. 62, 2004

trick out *verb*
to decorate something, or dress somebody, elaborately *US, 1727*
- Curtis had a big tricked-out scoot, a Harley, he kept in the house. — Elmore Leonard, *Split Images*, p. 48, 1981
- The waitresses, all older women, come to work tricked out head to toe in childishly preposterous uniforms. — Larry Heinemann, *Paco's Story*, p. 105, 1986

trick pad *noun*
an apartment or room which a prostitute uses only for sex with customers *US, 1969*
- If the pimp and girl anticipate living together, typically a "trick pad" will be rented. — Stanley Plog, *Changing Perspectives in Mental Illness*, p. 563, 1969
- Vice officers arrest them when they tail them to their trick pad[.] — Joseph Wambaugh, *The New Centurions*, p. 71, 1970
- This white, middle-aged, respectable looking man took me off and we were driving to the same trick pad. — Frederique Delacoste, *Sex Work*, p. 95, 1987

trick pants *noun*
pants that are easily removed, favored by prostitutes *US, 1967*
- A man in trick pants is still a man. — Malcolm Braly, *On the Yard*, p. 88, 1967

trick parlor *noun*
a brothel *US, 1986*
- The Pink Pussy was a trick parlor when Debbie worked in it. — Jack Weatherford, *Porn Row*, p. 70, 1986

trick rag *noun*
a cloth used to clean off a prostitute's customer after sex *US, 1986*
- "Look at the goddamn mess you left in my booth! Your trick rag is on the seat, and there's newspaper stuck to the floor from where you gave that dude his blow job." — Jack Weatherford, *Porn Row*, p. 2, 1986

trick room *noun*
a room where a prostitute takes customers *US, 1969*
- Jody and Larry had installed a two-way mirror between two rooms. One of the rooms was a trick room. The other had been converted into a voyeurs' lounge. — Vance Donovan, *High Rider*, p. 125, 1969
- And so I opened a window in one of the trick rooms and went over to the other house across the way on the roof. — Bruce Jackson, *In the Life*, pp. 198–199, 1972
- The place that I took her was a speakeasy … a bootlegging joint … that rented out trick rooms. — Robert Byrne, *McGoorty*, p. 57, 1972

- I was using a Toyota Celica as a trick room out in the parking lot with a truckdriver john[.] — Richard Condon, *Prizzi's Honor*, p. 170, 1982

tricks *noun*
▸ **on the tricks**
working as a prostitute *US, 1961*
- As soon as I walked into Rima's place I knew she was on the tricks. — Clancy Sigal, *Going Away*, p. 363, 1961

trick seat *noun*
the passenger seat on a motorcycle *US, 1984*
- Like I had a cock bike with a trick seat on it! — Joseph Wambaugh, *Lines and Shadows*, p. 51, 1984

trickster *noun*
a prostitute *US, 1976*
- — *Elementary Electronics*, *Dictionary of CB Lingo*, p. 116, 1976

trick towel *noun*
a towel or wash rag used to clean up after sex *US, 1970*
- — *American Speech*, p. 59, Spring–Summer 1970: "Homosexual slang"
- Then they spray with Lysol and that's that, unless some real stinker ignores the warnings to remain on the "trick towel" on top of the bed and not, repeat not, get between the sheets. — Lora Shaner, *Madam*, p. 199, 1999

Trick Wiley *noun*
used as a generic term for any gullible victim of a swindle *US, 1965*
- Then I would come in as "Trick Wiley." Anybody come in half drunk with money in his hand is considered a trick. — Henry Williamson, *Hustler!*, p. 81, 1965

tricky Dick *noun*
the penis *US, 1984*
- — Inez Cardozo-Freeman, *The Joint*, p. 518, 1984

tricon *noun*
in poker, a hand with three cards of the same rank *US, 1967*
- — Albert H. Morehead, *The Complete Guide to Winning Poker*, p. 276, 1967

trigger *noun*
1 in a shooting, the shooter; a gunman *US, 1975*
- "That's the best trigger I ever got," Frank said. "Nobody knows him." — Brian Boyer, *Prince of Thieves*, p. 43, 1975
- [A] diffident-looking little guy I recognized as Morris Hornbeck—an accountant and former trigger for Jerry Katzenbach's mob in Milwaukee. — James Ellroy, *Hollywood Nocturnes*, p. 205, 1994
2 any prison guard carrying a gun *US, 1992*
- — William K. Bentley and James M. Corbett, *Prison Slang*, p. 97, 1992

triggerman *noun*
in a criminal venture, a criminal carrying a gun; a gunman *US, 1930*
- "Triggermen are here from out of town," the D.A.'s office cautioned publicly. — Burton Turkus and Sid Feder, *Murder, Inc.*, p. 139, 1951
- A wheel-man was considered higher than a punk, at least, but not as high as a triggerman. The guy with the sawed-off is naturally the boss. — Robert Byrne, *McGoorty*, p. 69, 1972

trigger time *noun*
time spent in combat *US, 1985*
- [L]ogging over 1500 hours of "trigger time" (combat hours, when he was firing or taking fire). — Myra MacPherson, *Long Time Passing*, p. 249, 1985
- A high school girl could do my job. I want to get out into the shit. I want to get some trigger time. — *Full Metal Jacket*, 1987

trill *verb*
1 to stroll, to strut; to leave *US, 1945*
Also "trilly." The heroine of Du Maurier's 1894 novel *Trilby* was noted for her beautiful feet; Trilbys came to mean "feet," and then "to stroll."
- — Lou Shelly, *Hepcats Jive Talk Dictionary*, p. 19, 1945
- — Kenn "Naz" Young, *Naz's Underground Dictionary*, p. 61, 1973
- I trilled on in 'bout three A.M. Lookin' clean. — Edwin Torres, *After Hours*, p. 176, 1979
2 to idle with friends, especially with drugs and/or alcohol enlightening the idling *US, 2004*
- — Rick Ayers (Editor), *Berkeley High Slang Dictionary*, p. 41, 2004

trim *noun*

1 the vagina; a woman as a sex object; sex with a woman *US, 1949*

- Didn't I say you'd get it chasing down there for some trim? — Hal Ellson, *Duke*, p. 39, 1949
- "The trim, the grind, the scratch—in plain, everyday English—the pussy!" — Charles Perry, *Portrait of a Young Man Drowning*, p. 195, 1962
- So if he gave up some bread for some trim, well, then he just can't be a faggot. — Lenny Bruce, *The Essential Lenny Bruce*, p. 164, 1967
- She has plump, juicy lips, impish eyes like dark liquid M&Ms, a smile that is eager to tease or be teased, showgirl struts, a neatly coiffed trim, and a top-of-the-line sweater shelf. — Mr. Skin, *Mr. Skin's Skincyclopedia*, p. 79, 2005

2 in the television and movie industries, sections of scene cut by an editor *US, 1990*

- — Ralph S. Singleton, *Filmmaker's Dictionary*, p. 170, 1990

trim *verb*

1 to cheat, defraud, or swindle someone *UK, 1600*

- I'll trim you babies like little lambs. — Ken Kesey, *One Flew Over the Cuckoo's Nest*, p. 12, 1962
- Somebody you can trim for a dime or a buck or a bundle. — Robert Edmond Alter, *Carny Kill*, p. 18, 1966
- I wondered just how long it was gonna be before I found a way to trim Robin outta some kinda bread. — A.S. Jackson, *Gentleman Pimp*, p. 106, 1973
- "Old Man One Pocket is still trimming suckers at the old poolroom." — Iceberg Slim (Robert Beck), *Long White Con*, p. 159, 1977

2 to have sex with a woman *US, 1972*

- And I trimmed her three or four times as I remember and just had a ball. — Bruce Jackson, *Outside the Law*, pp. 110–111, 1972

trim job *noun*

sex *US, 1953*

- He felt very sharp. He was going to get a trim job, change his luck. — Edwin Gilbert, *The Hot and the Cool*, p. 73, 1953

trims *noun*

playing cards altered for cheating by slightly trimming off the edges of certain cards *US, 1979*

- — John Scarne, *Scarne's Guide to Modern Poker*, p. 292, 1979

trinity *noun*

a style of three-story row house consisting of three rooms stacked vertically *US, 1996*

- — Claudio R. Salvucci, *The Philadelphia Dialect Dictionary*, p. 63, 1996

trio *noun*

in poker, a hand with three cards of the same rank *US, 1967*

- — Albert H. Morehead, *The Complete Guide to Winning Poker*, p. 276, 1967

trip *noun*

1 a hallucinatory drug experience *US, 1966*

Uncertainty surrounds the first slang usage of the term. US slang lexicographer Peter Tamony argued in *American Speech* (Summer 1981) that the term was first used in a slang sense by Jack Gelber in *The Connection*, a 1957 play dealing with heroin addicts. Tammony privately conceded that the usage was not "a smoking gun," and in retrospect it appears more figurative than slang. The *Oxford English Dictionary* points to Norman Mailer's 1959 *Advertisements for Myself*, in which Mailer wrote of taking mescaline and of "a long and private trip," but there is no evidence that Mailer's use reflected a colloquial understanding and was not simply literary metaphor. Similarly, in a 1963 article about LSD in *Playboy*, Allan Harrington used the term "trip," but again the context suggests metaphor, not slang. The slang sense of the word is indelibly associated with Ken Kesey and his LSD-taking Merry Pranksters. In 1964, Ken Kesey bought a soon-to-be-famous International Harvester school bus in the name of Intrepid Trips, Inc., suggesting an already current, if private, slang sense. In September 1999, Kesey wrote about his recollection of the first use of the term: "I think it came from our bus trip in 1964, when Cassady said 'This trip is a trip.'"

- A student in Berkeley walked out a third-story window, saying, "As long as I'm going to take a trip, I might as well go to Europe." — Hunter S. Thompson, *Hell's Angels*, p. 239, 1966

- Judge Karesh than asked the much-traveled defendant [Ken Kesey] to teach him what the word "trip" really meant. Kesey said it was a happening "out of the ordinary" when induced by a psychedelic drug (such as LSD or mescaline). — *San Francisco Chronicle*, 12th April 1967
- Sometimes Cassady would ... go off into the corner, still on his manic monologue, muttering "All right, I'll take my own trip, I'll go off on my own trip, this is my own trip you understand." — Tom Wolfe, *The Electric Kool-Aid Acid Test*, p. 55, 1968
- Find a beloved friend who knows where to get LSD and how to run a session, or find a trusted and experienced LSD voyager to guide you on a trip. — Timothy Leary, *The Politics of Ecstasy*, pp. 123–124, 1968

2 any profound experience *US, 1966*

- Science fiction is bad. Screws up your head. Takes you on weird trips. — Timothy Leary, *The Politics of Ecstasy*, p. 287, 1968
- Just walking around Hog Farm [at Woodstock] is an incredible trip. — *East Village Other*, 20th August 1969
- The phone was always ringing, sometimes all five at once. It was a trip just to answer them. — Jerry Rubin, *Do It!*, p. 37, 1970
- "God," said Mona, grinning at the restaurant's Neapolitan bric-a-brac. "I'd almost forgotten what a trip this place is." — Armistead Maupin, *Tales of the City*, p. 178, 1978

3 a state of mind *US, 1966*

Used in an extremely vague and amorphous way, usually suggesting something profound.

- The fame/power/money trip is the old story again, hardly central to making music or beads or flutes or any disinterested act of involvement, of worship. — *Berkeley Barb*, p. 6, 25th November 1966
- She got down to the store early because, she said, "I'm on a money trip." — Nicholas Von Hoffman, *We Are The People Our Parents Warned Us Against*, p. 15, 1967
- They had so many fucked trips going on. — Jefferson Poland and Valerie Alison, *The Records of the San Francisco Sexual Freedom League*, p. 48, 1971
- And how dare you try to lay a guilt trip on me about it—in public, no less! — *Chasing Amy*, 1997

4 interest *US, 1967*

- I mean if she comes in and tells me she wants to ball Don, maybe, I say, "O.K., baby, it's your trip." — Joan Didion, *Slouching Toward Bethlehem*, p. 97, 1967
- His main trip is anti-Establishment, and we can beat him like a gong on that one. — Hunter S. Thompson, *Songs of the Doomed*, p. 135, 1971
- Fuck no, ese. That's a hippie trip. — Oscar Zeta Acosta, *The Revolt of the Cockroach People*, p. 122, 1973
- Worst of all, when they were sitting on the sunny deck at last, he couldn't stop talking about his own trip, rapping at her in this very hyper way about how he was into corporal punishment, the latest breakthrough in child psychology. — Cyra McFadden, *The Serial*, p. 20, 1977

5 a prison sentence *US, 1952*

- "How long a trip?" Carter asked. "Six moes," Dincher sighed. — George Mandel, *Flee the Angry Strangers*, p. 89, 1952

trip *verb*

1 to engage in flights of fancy, especially while in prison *US, 1967*

- "Sorry, I thought you might have fallen asleep with your clothes on." "I'm just lying here tripping." — Malcolm Braly, *On the Yard*, p. 175, 1967
- — *Current Slang*, p. 49, Fall 1968
- You forget you've eaten shortly after they've left, and get delirious or go tripping again. — James Carr, *Bad*, p. 26, 1975
- I would lie in my cell and trip two and three hours out of every day; I could see myself walking through the Village, see the red paint, see the clothesline, the tree in the middle of the courtyard. — Bobby Seale, *A Lonely Rage*, p. 225, 1978

2 to get angry, to lose control because of anger *US, 1990s?*

- Valaida, if I had known you were going to trip out about this, I wouldn't have mentioned the subject. — Odie Hawkins, *The Life and Times of Chester Simmons*, p. 175, 1991
- DREXEL: "Why you trippin'/" We jus' fuckin' with ya. — *True Romance*, 1993
- He's been trippin' since we been in the hospital. — *Menace II Society*, 1993

3 to insult *US, 1995*

- Louis said, "Mostly when you trippin' on some motherfucker, giving him a bad time, you say it." — Elmore Leonard, *Riding the Rap*, p. 55, 1995

trip and a half *noun*

a powerful experience, positive or negative *US, 1984*

- a trip-and-a-half: a) Quite satisfactory. b) Very bad. — Sohnya Sayres, *The 60s Without Apology*, p. 361, 1984

trip book *noun*

escape literature *US, 1976*

- It became what we called a "trip" book, one where you could blunk out and simply drift through the atmosphere of the North Beach nights the sex, music and drugs[.] — Malcolm Braley, *False Starts*, p. 295, 1976

tripe *noun*

a tripod *US, 1981*

Used by traveling salesmen and itinerant swindlers to support a suitcase full of merchandise.

- — Don Wilmeth, *The Language of American Popular Entertainment*, p. 280, 1981

triple *noun*

sex involving three people *US, 1988*

- Ciglianni's dead. Keeled over with a heart attack last year doing triples with two teenage whores he picked up off the hookers' stroll at Hollywood and Vine. — Robert Campbell, *Juice*, p. 2, 1988

triple A *noun*

antiaircraft artillery *US, 1990*

- FACs flew against the same big guns that defended Hanoi, murderously accurate 23 mm, 37 mm, and 57 mm anti-aircraft artillery—"triple A" for short. — Tom Yarborough, *Da Nang Diary*, p. 14, 1990
- The triple-A is coming up / It fills the sky ahead. — Joseph Tuso, *Singing the Vietnam Blues*, p. 22, 1990: Armed Reece25

Triple C; Triple C's *noun*

Coricidin Cough and Cold tables, abused recreationally; dextromethorphan (DXM), an active ingredient in non-prescription cold and cough medication, often abused for non-medicinal purposes *US, 2001*

- "Triple C," a popular choice among teens is more commonly known as Coricidin HBP. — *alt.drugs.info*, 5th April 2001
- One of the more popular medications being abused is Coricidin HBP Cough & Cold tablets, which pupils often call "Triple C," authorities said. — *Houston Chronicle*, p. A35, 11th February 2001
- Youths' nicknames for DXM: Robo, Skittles, Triple C's, Rojo, Dex, Tussin, Vitamin D. DXM abuse is called "Robotripping" or "Tussing." Users might be called "syrup heads" or "robotards." — *USA Today*, p. 1A, 29th December 2003

triple crown *noun*

oral, vaginal, and anal sex in the same session *US, 2003*

- Oregon Trifecta (aka "Triple Crown of Sex")—in the yapper, the snapper, and the crapper all in the same session. — *news.admin.net-abuse.email*, 4th August 2003

triple jet ace *noun*

a fighter pilot who shoots down three aircraft in a single day *US, 1964*

- Captain Joseph McConnell with with 16 victories was the top jet ace. He also became the first "triple jet ace" in history when he shot down three MIG's in one day—May 18, 1953. — Don Lawson, *The United States in the Korean War*, p. 64, 1964

triple m *noun*

mutual manual masturbation *US, 1985*

- — Wayne Dynes, *Homolexis*, p. 91, 1985

triple S *noun*

the preparation a man goes through before leaving the house *US, 1979*

- So before I do my usual morning triple "S" (shave, s–t and shower), I get the jar of vitamin-enriched chopped liver out of my refrigerator[.] I unbutton my jacket and put my elbows out to the side and raise them. "Am I heeled?" — Leo Rosten, *Silky!*, p. 68, 1979

triplets *noun*

in poker, three of a kind *US, 1963*

- — Irwin Steig, *Common Sense in Poker*, p. 188, 1963

triple W *noun*

a woman as the provider of good sex *US, 1970*

The W's are "warm," "wet," and "womb."

- — *Current Slang*, p. 14, Fall 1970

trip out *verb*

1 to undergo an hallucinogenic experience as a result of drug-intoxication *US, 1967*

- — Joe David Brown (Editor), *The Hippies*, p. 220, 1967: "Glossary of hippie terms"

2 to amaze someone; to enlighten someone *US, 1968*

- I just found out the other day that my grandfather—my father's father—was a machinist for twenty years, and that really tripped me out. — Leonard Wolfe (Editor), *Voices from the Love Generation*, p. 216, 1968

3 to become involved in something in a focused and intense manner *US, 1966*

- — J. L. Simmons and Barry Winograd, *It's Happening*, p. 173, 1966: "Glossary"

tripper *noun*

a person using LSD or another hallucinogenic drug *US, 1999*

- Trippers use the word "visuals" to refer to the visual impressions and images that acid can generate. — Cam Cloud, *The Little Book of Acid*, p. 10, 1999

tripple-dipper *noun*

a veteran of World War 2, Korea, and Vietnam *US, 1966*

- — *Citizen-Journal (Columbus, Ohio)*, p. 7, 13th April 1966
- — Carl Fleischhauer, *A Glossary of Army Slang*, p. 22, 1968

trippy *adjective*

1 of psychedelic design *US, 1969*

From **TRIP** (an LSD experience) and the psychedelic imagery inspired by such drug usage.

- X is often described as less distrubingly "trippy" than LSD and more serene than cocaine[.] — *Newsweek*, p. 62, 6th December 1993
- The hallway was very traditional Haight-Ashbury, with tie-dye and trippy lights and iridescent paper covering the ceiling. — Michelle Tea, *Valencia*, p. 133, 2000

2 extremely committed to the hippie life, especially the drug aspects of it *US, 1968*

- I'm hippy and I'm trippy / I'm a gypsy on my own. — Frank Zappa, *Who Needs The Peace Corps?*, 1968
- [I]t probably surprises you to learn that I had a trippy Xmas—even when I wasn't zonked out on your culinary crazies—but I did. — Tom Robbins, *Another Roadside Attraction*, p. 162, 1971

trip room *noun*

a room designed to maximize the experience of taking LSD *US, 1971*

- Most psychedelic shops once featured trip rooms at the rear, but they were busted so often they've given up this part of their business. — Arthur Blessitt, *Turned On to Jesus*, p. 120, 1971

trips *noun*

1 LSD *US, 1969*

- [T]here was a boom in ecstasy [MDMA], speed [amphetamine], trips, the lot. — Macfarlane, Macfarlane & Robson, *The User*, p. 91, 1996

2 dice with intentionally rounded edges used for cheating *US, 1974*

- — John Scarne, *Scarne on Dice*, p. 481, 1974

trip-wire *adjective*

mentally unstable *US, 1999*

The suggestion is a slight action may set off an explosive reaction.

- Fellow recluse Reb Brown is a violence-prone, "trip wire" vet, and Dennis Arndt is a goofy alcoholic and junk food addict. — Jeremy Devine, *Vietnam at 24 Frames a Second*, p. 1999, 1999
- [T]he figure of the "trip-wire" veteran has become something of a cliche. — Andy Hollis, *Beyond Boundaries*, p. 78, 2000
- After that airing of one that involved "trip-wire"or allegedly crazy veterans, I received calls from friends and relatives asking me how I was doing[.] — Kregg Jorgenson, *Very Crazy G.I.*, p. 228, 2001

trisexual; trysexual *adjective*

willing to try anything sexually; open to any sexual experience *US, 1988*

Borrowing from "bisexual," punning "tri" with "try."

- I prefer "tri-sexual." You know—I'll try anything. — Paul Martin, *Carmen*, p. 75, 1988
- MJ calls herself "trysexual"—"I'll try anything." — *Sojourner*, p. 13, 27th February 1988
- The large one is trisexual; Bunny just does what she's told. What's trisexual? She'll do [try] anything, I suspect. — Robert Stoller and I.S. Levine, *Coming Attractions*, p. 30, 1991

triumphant *adjective*

excellent *US, 1991*

- — *USA Today*, p. 1D, 5th August 1991: "A sterling lexicon of the lingo"

trivet *noun*
in poker, a three-dollar bet *US, 1996*
- — John Vorhaus, *The Big Book of Poker Slang*, p. 37, 1996

trivial *adjective*
in computing, too simple to bother explaining *US, 1997*
- — Andy Ihnatko, *Cyberspeak*, p. 192, 1997

troglodyte *noun*
a computer enthusiast who has abandoned all contact with life outside his computer *US, 1991*
- — Eric S. Raymond, *The New Hacker's Dictionary*, p. 357, 1991

Trojan *noun*
an AT-28 aircraft, used as a ground-attack aircraft and then a fighter bomber in the Vietnam war *US, 1985*
- — Ian Padden, *U.S. Air Commando*, p. 104, 1985

Trojan horse *noun*
1 in computing, an intentionally destructive program disguised and sent in benevolent form *US, 1991*
- — Eric S. Raymond, *The New Hacker's Dictionary*, p. 357, 1991
- Of course, viruses and Trojan horses don't have to be messengers for only password information. — *The Knightmare, Secrets of a Super Hacker*, p. 134, 1994

2 in poker, an unexpectedly strong hand held by another player whose betting has successfully masked its strength *US, 1996*
- — John Vorhaus, *The Big Book of Poker Slang*, p. 37, 1996

troll *noun*
a message posted on an Internet discussion group with the hope of attracting vitriolic response *US, 1997*
- A troll typically expresses a simple and basic question in a particularly long-winded and clueless fashion, or expresses sentiments that will likely provoke an enraged response[.] — Andy Ihnatko, *Cyberspeak*, p. 194, 1997

troll *verb*
(of a homosexual man) to walk the streets in search of sexual adventure; (of a homosexual man) to walk, to wander *UK, 1967*
Familiarity of usage has resulted in the original, conventional sense being rederived, here from the specifically sexual sense.
- Trolling homosexuals, both butch and queen. — Joseph Wambaugh, *The Black Marble*, p. 94, 1978

trolley *noun*
a line used by prisoners to exchange notes *US, 1950*
- — Hyman E. Goldin et al., *Dictionary of American Underworld Lingo*, p. 227, 1950

trolley trooper *noun*
a soldier who has made his first parachute jump off a tower *US, 1967*
- It's over. I had had made my first tower jump. Now I was a "trolley trooper." — Donald Duncan, *The New Legions*, p. 129, 1967

trombone *noun*
in the television and movie industries, a hanger that can be extended from a wall to support lighting *US, 1977*
- — Tony Miller and Patricia George, *Cut! Print!*, p. 159, 1977

tromp and stomp *noun*
a marching drill *US, 1957*
- [R]ifle inspection, tromp, and stomp (drill, marching, etc.), personnel and tent inspection, classes, hikes, training problems, night problems. This is what is called "harassing the troops." — Martin Russ, *The Last Parallel*, p. 153, 1957

trooper *noun*
a person who is the ultimately stalwart good sport *US, 1951*
- Yeah, she was really a true trouper [sic] and she came close to causing me to shed a few tears. — A.S. Jackson, *Gentleman Pimp*, p. 138, 1973
- He was sentenced to fifteen years in a Florida joint. He handled it like a trooper. — Dan Jenkins, *Life Its Ownself*, p. 28, 1984
- "You marched into that tavern like a trooper," Nell said. — Carl Hiaasen, *Tourist Season*, p. 52, 1986

trophy *adjective*
used of a wife or girlfriend, young and beautiful to an extent that would not be expected with the man *US, 1990*

- Young trophy wife, I mean, in the parlance of our times, owes money all over town[.] — *The Big Lebowski*, 1990

tropical *adjective*
extremely eccentric or mildly insane *US, 1946*
- — *American Speech*, p. 238, October 1946: "World War II slang of maladjustment"

tropical crud *noun*
any skin fungus contracted while in the tropics *US, 1958*
- I knew that I was tired, and covered with what we called the tropical crud, for lack of a medical word. — Gregory "Pappy" Boyington, *Baa Baa Black Sheep*, p. 222, 1958

Tropic Lightning *nickname*
the 25th Infantry Division, US Army *US, 1979*
- Schofield that is Home of the 25th "Tropic Lightning" Infantry Division, formerly the Hawaii Division, James Jones's own division — Joan Didion, *The White Album*, p. 146, 1979
- Evans, formerly of the 25th Infantry's "Tropic Lightning" Division, said an effort was under way for some formal recognition, a possibly a war memorial, of Korean veterans' service. — *Arkansas Democrat-Gazette*, 11th March 1985
- Tropic Lightning soldiers went into combat against the North Korean army almost immediately. — Michael J. Varhola, *Fire and Ice*, p. 99, 2000
- Dima, 56, and Broce, 54, served together in the "Tropic Lightning," the 25th Infantry Division, in Vietnam in 1969. — *Belleville News-Democrat*, p. A1, 12th September 2004

trot *noun*
a line-by-line translation of a work in a foreign language *US, 1891*
- Taggarty tried to steer the conversation toward a historical analysis of Ramayana (she must have read the trot on that one), but desisted abruptly when Vijay tripped her up in a glaring factual error. — C.D. Payne, *Youth in Revolt*, p. 190, 1993

trots *noun*
diarrhea *US, 1904*
Used with "the."
- "He's not dogging it," Carbone said. "He's got a temperature and he's got a fever and he's got the trots." — George V. Higgins, *The Rat on Fire*, p. 90, 1981
- I'll tell them you've got the trots. Puerto Rican food will do it to you. — Elmore Leonard, *Glitz*, p. 347, 1985

trotter *noun*
pork *US, 1976*
- — John R. Armore and Joseph D. Wolfe, *Dictionary of Desperation*, p. 55, 1976

trou *noun*
trousers; pants *US, 1911*
- — Collin Baker et al., *College Undergraduate Slang Study Conducted at Brown University*, p. 213, 1968

trouser snake *noun*
the penis *US, 1976*
- [U]nzips his fly. Pulls out the mother of all trouser snakes and prepares to give him a Frontline Special. — Jack Allen, *When the Whistle Blows*, p. 225, 2000
- JUSTICE: Of course I like snakes. JAY: How about trouser snakes? — Kevin Smith, *Jay and Silent Bob Strike Back*, p. 43, 2001
- Soon she was pleasing trouser snakes everywhere[.] — Mr. Skin, *Mr. Skin's Skincyclopedia*, p. 41, 2005

trouser trout *noun*
the penis *US, 1987*
- But he was wicked fulled, called his thingamabob a trouser torut, a Johnson. — Geoffrey Wolff, *Providence*, p. 131, 1987
- They were tripping up my trouser trout triumphant!!! — James Ellroy, *Destination Morgue*, p. 36, 2004

truck *verb*
to stroll; to stride *US, 1938*
- Stuck my elbow out for her and went truckin' out. — Edwin Torres, *After Hours*, p. 388, 1979

truck driver *noun*
1 an aggressive, "mannish" lesbian *US, 1967*
- Known variously as a bull, a stomper, a bad butch, a hard dresser, a truck driver, a diesel dyke, a bull dagger and a half dozen other soubriquets, she is the one who, according to most homosexual girls, gives lesbians a bad name. — Ruth Allison, *Lesbianism*, p. 125, 1967

2 in prison, a prisoner or guard who delivers messages *US, 1976*
- — John R. Armore and Joseph D. Wolfe, *Dictionary of Desperation*, p. 55, 1976

3 an amphetamine or other central nervous system stimulant
US, 1967
- — John B. Williams, *Narcotics and Hallucinogenics*, p. 116, 1967

truck stop Annie *noun*
a prostitute working at a truck stop *US, 1977*
- — Bill Davis, *Jawjacking*, p. 102, 1977

truck stop cowboy *noun*
a person who looks the part of a trucker, plays the part of a trucker, but is not a trucker *US, 1976*
- — Elementary Electronics, *Dictionary of CB Lingo*, p. 116, 1976

true bull; true bool *noun*
a tested and proven leader *US, 1982*
Hawaiian youth usage.
- — Douglas Simonson, *Pidgin to da Max Hana Hou*, 1982

true that!; true dat!
used for expressing strong agreement *US, 1998*
- — Ethan Hilderbrant, *Prison Slang*, p. 130, 1998
- — Connie Eble (Editor), *UNC-CH Campus Slang*, p. 13, Fall 1999
- "Tastes good, don't it?" "True, that." — Paul Beatty, *Tuff*, p. 21, 2000

Trujillo's revenge *noun*
diarrhea *US, 1982*
Homage to Dominican dictator Rafael Trujillo.
- "I ate that chow just one time and got Trujillo's Revenge," Nolen said. — Elmore Leonard, *Cat Chaser*, p. 25, 1982

trunk job *noun*
a corpse, especially a badly decomposed corpse, found in a car trunk *US, 1993*
- They knew all about trunk jobs, John Does, Juan Does, gun-shots, accidentals and naturals. — Carl Hiaasen, *Strip Tease*, p. 100, 1993

trustafarian *noun*
a young person who lives a counterculture lifestyle on the proceeds of a trust fund *US, 1992*
- Then there's "Trustafarian," which describes a "guy who has long hair and a trust fund, drives a Saab or Jeep, listens to reggae, and doesn't let a whole lot bother him." — *Washington Times*, p. C3, 26th August 1992
- — David Shenk and Steve Silberman, *Skeleton Key*, p. 296, 1994

trying!
you are trying too hard to be something you are not! *US, 1981*
Hawaiian youth usage.
- — Douglas Simonson, *Pidgin to da Max*, 1981

TS
too bad! *US, 1957*
An abbreviation of **TOUGH SHIT**.
- "T.S.," I murmured—and you have to figure for yourself what the initials stand for. — Frederick Kohner, *Gidget*, p. 122, 1957

T's and blues *noun*
a combination of Taluin™, a painkiller, and the antihistamine Pyribenzamine™, abused for non-medicinal purposes *US, 1989*
- — Geoffrey Froner, *Digging for Diamonds*, p. 60, 1989
- Tops and Bottoms is street slang for T's and Blues. T's are Taluin, a painkiller, and Blues are Pyribenzamine, an antihistamine. Combined in the right dosage they make a poor man's heroin. — *Chicago Tribune*, p. 6C, 11th June 1989

tsatskeleh *noun*
a pretty, sexy, brainless woman *US, 1961*
Yiddish, with the Yiddish diminutive of *tsatske*.
- Next thing he knew all two tsatskillehs were both sunk down on the floor where the fold-in seats were[.] — Bernard Wolfe, *The Magic of Their Singing*, p. 88, 1961

TS card *noun*
a notional card that is punched when a person complains *US, 1948*
An abbreviation of the sympathy-lacking **TOUGH SHIT**.
- — Carl Fleischhauer, *A Glossary of Army Slang*, p. 23, 1968

tsuris; tzuris; tszoris; tsoris *noun*
trouble, strife, a problem *US, 1948*
From the Hebrew for "trouble."
- "Chosen! Chosen for tsoris!" — Norman Mailer, *The Naked and the Dead*, p. 54, 1948
- "I don't know what it is, but every time I come to New York, I got to find tsoris!" — Harold Robbins, *The Carpetbaggers*, p. 430, 1961
- It gets you there fast, and without the tszoris of all the crap in between East Coast and West—but it tends to catch up with you. — Raymond Mungo, *Famous Long Ago*, p. 110, 1970
- What tzuris Smale caused the University! One of the world's most famous mathematicians and the most renowned professor at the university, here was Smale plotting and working with nonstudent crazies! — Jerry Rubin, *Do It!*, p. 39, 1970

TTFN
goodbye *UK, 1948*
An initialism of "ta-ta for now."
- T.T.F.N. Ta-ta for now. — Art Unger, *The Cool Book*, p. 131, 1961
- — Eric S. Raymond, *The New Hacker's Dictionary*, p. 342, 1991

T-timers *noun*
dark glasses worn by marijuana smokers *US, 1952*
- — *American Speech*, p. 30, February 1952: "Teen-age hophead jargon"

T to B *noun*
a piece of graffiti art stretching from the top to the bottom of a subway car, but not end-to-end *US, 1982*
- T-to-Bs are usually done by writers who do not have the time, the paint, or the energy to paint a whole car. — Craig Castleman, *Getting Up*, p. 31, 1982

tub *noun*
1 a drum *US, 1958*
- Go easy on that tub, this time. — John Clellon Holmes, *The Horn*, p. 135, 1958
2 a seat on an amusement ride *US, 1980*
- — Joe McKennon, *Circus Lingo*, p. 97, 1980
- — Gene Sorrows, *All About Carnivals*, p. 27, 1985: "Terminology"
3 a small crap table *US, 1983*
- — Thomas L. Clark, *The Dictionary of Gambling and Gaming*, p. 240, 1987

tubby *adjective*
emphasizing low frequencies, producing poorly defined sound *US, 1987*
Used in describing a location's sound quality in television and movie-making.
- — Ira Konigsberg, *The Complete Film Dictionary*, p. 33, 1987

tube *noun*
1 an artillery piece or mortar *US, 2004*
- — David Hart, *First Air Cavalry Division Vietnam Dictionary*, p. 63, 2004
2 a marijuana cigarette *US, 1937*
- — Ernest L. Abel, *A Marijuana Dictionary*, p. 105, 1982
3 a telephone *US, 1960*
- — Robert George Reisner, *The Jazz Titans*, p. 167, 1960
4 the concave face of a wave *US, 1963*
- — Grant W. Kuhns, *On Surfing*, p. 123, 1963
- — *Paradise of the Pacific*, p. 27, October 1963
5 a shotgun *US, 1994*
- — *Los Angeles Times*, p. B1, 19th December 1994
- "Toss that tube!" Flotsam said, and Jetsam dropped the shotgun on the grass and scurried after his partner. — Joseph Wambaugh, *Hollywood Station*, p. 87, 2006
6 in a casino, the rack where betting tokens are stored at a gambling table *US, 1996*
- — Frank Scoblete, *Best Blackjack*, p. 274, 1996

▸ **down the tubes**
ruined with no chances left; done for; lost; wasted *US, 1963*
A variation of "down the drain" or "down the pan"; literally "down the toilet."
- Now we got hurt, we really took a beating in profits, our business almost went down the tubes[.] — Josh Alan Friedman, *Tales of Times Square*, p. 81, 1986

▸ **lay tube**
from the male point of view, to have sex *US, 1983*

- [A]bout eighty a them's gonna lay more tube than the motherfucking Alaska pipeline. — Joseph Wambaugh, *The Delta Star*, p. 37, 1983

► **the tube**
a television; television *US, 1959*
Originally applied to the telephone, but then much more widely to television.
- — *Swinging Syllables*, 1959
- [T]hen we watched the tube through the late movie which ended at three. — John Nichols, *The Sterile Cuckoo*, p. 125, 1965
- Back at my room I feel depressed but I can't go to bed because I only got up at 3 p.m. I'm going to be on the tube (Allen Burke called), but I'm depressed. — James Simon Kunen, *The Strawberry Statement*, p. 62, 1968
- His photograph was published frequently in the trade papers, and he often appeared on the tube for interviews or panel discussions. — Burt Hirschfield, *Fire Island*, p. 15, 1970

tube *verb*
1 to watch television *US, 1979*
- Jane and I, and Dell and Pat, and Brad and Laura (who's old enough to drive) went tubing after dinner[.] — Beatrice Sparks (writing as "Anonymous"), *Jay's Journal*, p. 56, 1979
- — *Concord (New Hampshire) Monitor*, p. 17, 23rd August 1983: "Slang slinging: an intense and awesome guide to prep school slanguage"
2 to surf below and inside the crest of the wave *US, 1979*
- LANCE: Maybe he'll get tubed. WILLARD: What? LANCE: Maybe he'll get inside the tube—where—where they can't see him. — *Apocalypse Now*, 1979
3 to fail, to do poorly *US, 1966*
- — *Current Slang*, p. 5, Summer 1966
- — Gary N. Underwood, *American Speech*, p. 68, Spring–Summer 1975: "Razorback Slang"

tubehead *noun*
an enthusiast for radio technology *US, 1995*
- He was a classic tubehead kind of a guy, always had his shirt pockets stuffed with little wires, circuit testers, and electronic whatever-the-hells. — Wolfman Jack (Bob Smith), *Have Mercy!*, p. 142, 1995

tube lube *noun*
oral sex on a man *US, 1970*
- Not only did I get three to give me a "Tube lube" but I got to French out four of the five swingers. — *Screw*, p. 6, 20th July 1970

tube steak *noun*
1 a frankfurter, a hot dog *US, 1963*
- Tube steak—a hot dog, the main part of a drag racer's usual meal. — Ross Olney, *Kings of the Drag Strip*, p. 188, 1968
- — *Current Slang*, p. 13, Summer 1968
- Tube steak a la fire, with an array of condiments. — Darryl Poncsan, *The Last Detail*, p. 134, 1970
2 by visual extension, the penis *US, 1980*
- — Edith A. Folb, *runnin' down some lines*, p. 258, 1980
- I want to slip my tubesteak into your sister. What'll you take in trade? — *Full Metal Jacket*, 1987
- About half said they were satisfied with their tubesteaks. — Anka Radakovich, *The Wild Girls Club*, p. 29, 1994
- Decker pulls out his tube steak, aims for the peach, and heaps his genetic gunk on the once-virgin fruit. — Anthony Petkovich, *The X Factory*, p. 15, 1997

tub of lard; pail of lard *noun*
a fat person *US, 1928*
- I was this little tub of lard running behind Tony. — Jenna Jameson, *How to Make Love Like Porn Star*, p. 215, 2004

tubs *noun*
drums *US, 1946*
- Ray Eisel, the drummer, was a thin and wiry fly cat who really beat his tubs. — Mezz Mezzrow, *Really the Blues*, p. 61, 1946
- — Babs Gonzales, *Be-Bop Dictionary and History of its Famous Stars*, p. 9, 1949
- "I even beat the tubs a little 'cause that's in the wrist too." — Nelson Algren, *The Man with the Golden Arm*, p. 9, 1949
- [A] big brutal Negro with a bullneck who didn't give a damn about anything but punishing his husted tubs, crash, rattle-ti-boom, crash. — Jack Kerouac, *On the Road*, p. 197, 1957

► **the tubs**
a gay bath house; the gay bath house scene collectively *US, 1964*

- — Guy Strait, *The Lavender Lexicon*, 1st June 1964
- — Bruce Rodgers, *The Queens' Vernacular*, p. 28, 1972
- At times like this, the tubs was an easy way out. Discreet, dispassionate, noncommittal. — Armistead Maupin, *Tales of the City*, p. 313, 1978

tubular *adjective*
1 used of a wave, hollow as it breaks, creating a chamber which can be surfed through *US, 1988*
- — Michael V. Anderson, *The Bad, Rad, Not to Forget Way Cool Beach and Surf Discriptionary*, p. 21, 1988
2 spectacular *US, 1982*
- — Mary Corey and Victoria Westermark, *Fer Shurr! How to be a Valley Girl*, 1982
- But NO BIGGIE / It's wo AWESOME / It's like TUBULAR, y'know. — Moon Unit and Frank Zappa, *Valley Girl*, 1982
- — Connie Eble (Editor), *UNC-CH Campus Slang*, p. 10, Fall 1985

tuck *noun*
a cosmetic operation to remove fat or skin *US, 1993*
- Fin slapped at the flesh between his chin and Adam's apple, wondering what a little tuck would cost, and whether he could make his medical insurance cover it. — Joseph Wambaugh, *Finnegan's Week*, p. 73, 1993

tuck *verb*
in transsexual usage, to tape your penis onto your groin to avoid any telltale bulge which might tip off someone as to your genetic sex *US, 1986–1987*
- — *Maledicta*, p. 174, Summer/Winter 1986–1987: "Sexual slang: prostitutes, pedophiles, flagellators, transvestites, and necrophiles"

tuck and roll *noun*
a method of shoplifting, in which the merchandise is rolled up and tucked under the shoplifter's clothing *US, 1975*
- I used the good old tuck-and-roll to steal the overalls[.] — James Carr, *Bad*, p. 37, 1975

tuck and roll; tucked and rolled *adjective*
medically transformed from a male to a female *US, 1990*
- When she paroled, Magdalena had the sex change operation at Stanford Medical Center, she's tucked and rolled, a genuine woman. — Seth Morgan, *Homeboy*, p. 301, 1990

tud *noun*
a *t*otally *u*nnecessary *d*rink that causes you to vomit *US, 2001*
- — Don R. McCreary (Editor), *Dawg Speak*, 2001

tudge boy *noun*
a criminal hired to enforce criminal rules on other criminals *US, 2002*
- Laticia says the pimps use "tudge boys," street slang for hired enforcers, not only to rough up circuit girls who get out of line, but also to patrol Colfax, looking for crack whores out of bounds. — *Denver Westword*, 2nd May 2002

tuft-hunter *noun*
a man obsessed with sex *US, 1954*
- "Jule's a regular tuft-hunter, aren't you, Jule?" — Chester Himes, *Pinktoes*, p. 54, 1961

tules; toolies *noun*
a remote rural area *US, 1974*
An extension of the name of a type of cattail that grows in the very rural San Joaquin Valley of California.
- We drove her ass out into the toolies, and she let both me and Buck fuck her pregnant ass. — Earl Thompson, *Tattoo*, p. 224, 1974
- To be "in the toolies" is to be in the bush, and also means to accidentally drive off the road. The phrase may have come from Ultima Thule, in ancient geography, the northernmost limit of the habitable world, a distant, unknown place. — Tom Parkin, *WetCoast Words*, p. 74, 1989
- — John Edwards, *Auto Dictionary*, p. 176, 1993

tumble *noun*
1 an act of sexual intercourse; an invitation to engage in sexual intercourse *UK, 1903*
- Nobody gave me a tumble, so I supposed I was to make the selection. — Mickey Spillane, *I, The Jury*, p. 64, 1947
- I knew she was belligerent; nobody had given her a tumble. — Horace McCoy, *Kiss Tomorrow Good-bye*, p. 134, 1948
- A few tumbles during the war, then eighteen years of nothing. — Max Shulman, *Anyone Got a Match?*, p. 260, 1964

- I saw at least a thousand I'd have married gladly on the spot if they'd given me a tumble. — Oscar Zeta Acosta, *The Autobiography of a Brown Buffalo*, p. 189, 1972

2 recognition by the police or the interruption of a crime *US, 1950*

- — Hyman E. Goldin et al., *Dictionary of American Underworld Lingo*, p. 227, 1950

3 a fight, especially a gang fight *US, 1960*

- You scared of a little tumble or something? — *Man's Magazine*, p. 12, February 1960

tumble *verb*

1 to seduce, to have sex *US, 1960*

- Just like the louse to forget all the times he had tried to tumble her and how she was almost ready to let him. — Irving Shulman, *College Confidential*, p. 77, 1960

2 to discover, to understand, to notice, to realize, to become aware of *UK, 1846*

- — Joseph E. Ragen and Charles Finston, *Inside the World's Toughest Prison*, p. 822, 1962: "Penitentiary and Underworld Glossary"
- "You must have known that Sid ... or somebody ... would tumble that you were broke before the picture was finished." — Wade Hunter, *The Sex Peddler*, p. 97, 1963
- Ain't a chance for their husbands to tumble to what's going on. — Iceberg Slim (Robert Beck), *Pimp*, p. 128, 1969

3 to have sex with someone *UK, 1602*
Found in Shakespeare and understood in context if not used heavily today.

- Either you're losing your grip, or you think she's tood good to tumble. She is, but I'm not! — Jim Thompson, *The Grifters*, p. 96, 1963
- There was a girl whom he and I both loved, who actually never tumbled for either of us. — Stephen Gaskin, *Amazing Dope Tails*, p. 29, 1980

4 to get married *US, 1970*

- "I'm getting married as soon as I can get a week off." "You're tumbling too?" smiled Serge. — Joseph Wambaugh, *The New Centurions*, p. 351, 1970

▸ **tumble to**
to come to understand *US, 1962*

- Arnie looks at me, wild-eyed. At once he tumbles to it. Suddenly he screams. — Charles Perry, *Portrait of a Young Man Drowning*, p. 253, 1962

tumblers *noun*
dice with rounded edges *US, 1950*

- — *The Annals of the American Academy of Political and Social Sciences*, p. 132, May 1950

tummy *noun*
the stomach *UK, 1869*

- "Your tummy acting up on you?" "Heartburn," Chip said, touching his chest. — Elmore Leonard, *Riding the Rap*, p. 246, 1995

tummy run *noun*
a ride on a surfboard in which the rider remains lying on their stomach without attempting to stand *US, 1961*

- "We'll make the first one a tummy run," I said. "And don't you dare stand up!" — Frederick Kohner, *Gidget Goes Hawaiian*, p. 80, 1961

tummy tuck *noun*
cosmetic surgery designed to reduce the fat around a person's waist *US, 1977*

- First we heard when Jimmy was governor of Georgia, Rosalyn had had a face lift—and then a tummy tuck. — *Washington Post*, p. D1, 1st June 1977
- [T]here are enough face-lifts, dental caps, transplants, and tummy tucks in this place to convince him that the plastic surgeons and dematologists and dentists constituted the power behind the thrown. — Joseph Wambaugh, *The Glitter Dome*, p. 237, 1981
- Ida, who'd never wanted children of her own, who was always scheming for a new car or a tummy tuck or a new dinette — Carl Hiaasen, *Tourist Season*, p. 109, 1986

tuna *noun*

1 the vagina *US, 1986*
Fish, as an allusion to what some claim to be the natural odor of a woman.

- Newcomer Melissa drives the submariners crazy, and Buck Adams goes way down for the horny tuna. — *Adult Video*, p. 23, August/September 1986
- He added that many women insist on using Saran Wrap when he goes down to taste the tuna. — Anka Radakovich, *The Wild Girls Club*, p. 124, 1994

2 a female *US, 1971*

- — Eugene Landy, *The Underground Dictionary*, p. 188, 1971
- There's some serious tuna at the Delta House. — Judi Sanders, *Faced and Faded, Hanging to Hurl*, p. 41, 1993

3 a young sailor as the object of desire of a homosexual man *US, 1985*

- From the advertising slogan "Chicken of the Sea." — Wayne Dynes, *Homolexis*, p. 101, 1985

tuna party *noun*
a party where girls far outnumber boys *US, 2004*

- — Ben Applebaum and Derrick Pittman, *Turd Ferguson & The Sausage Party*, p. 69, 2004

tuner *noun*
in the television and movie industries, a musical composer *US, 1977*

- — Tony Miller and Patricia George, *Cut! Print!*, p. 160, 1977

tune up *verb*
to beat a better attitude into a fellow prisoner with a poor attitude *US, 1989*

- — James Harris, *A Convict's Dictionary*, p. 40, 1989

tunnel *noun*
the mouth *US, 1975*

- "Shut your tunnel and get in the car," Telano said breathlessly. — John Sepe, *Cop Team*, p. 78, 1975

tunnel rat *noun*

1 a US soldier who explored Viet Cong tunnels and underground networks *US, 1968*

- The platoon tunnel rat. Lavery leaned down next to the tunnel entrance, cupped his hands around his mouth, and shouted, "Chieu Hoi!" — Larry Heinemann, *Close Quarters*, p. 65, 1977
- Captain Herbert Thornton was the first of the new tunnel rats. — Tom Mangold, *The Tunnels of Cu Chi*, p. 102, 1985
- Kolosowski, 36, a small, wiry man, had been a Marine "tunnel rat"— one of a few men of small stature who explored the labyrinth of underground caverns dug by the Viet Cong. — *The Houston Chronicle*, 27th October 1989
- The tunnel rats were able to crawl down into holes that were no more than 36 inches wide and possibly four feet high. — Paul Morgan, *The Parrot's Beak*, p. 28, 2000

2 a police officer working for the New York Transit Bureau; a subway police officer *US, 1995*
New York police slang.

- Tunnel Rats: NYPD Transit Bureau. — Samuel Katz, *NYPD*, 1995
- Rosato is a former tunel rat who worked the lovely-meslling confines of New York subway stations and trains. — Samuel M. Katz, *Anytime Anywhere*, p. 245, 1997

tunnel runner *noun*
a US soldier who explored Viet Cong tunnels and underground networks *US, 1985*

- [T]he 25th Infantry Division originally called them tunnel runners and the Australian army called them ferrets[.] — Tom Mangold, *The Tunnels of Cu Chi*, p. 102, 1985

tunnel shot *noun*
a photograph or shot in a movie focusing on a woman's vagina *US, 1970*

- No ugly gaping tunnel shots, no chicks fingering themselves; just beautiful men with fine three piece sets. — *Screw*, p. 9, 5th October 1970

turbo *noun*
marijuana mixed with crack cocaine *US, 1994*

- — US Department of Justice *Street Terms*, October 1994

turd *noun*
a negative comment in a personnel file *US, 1967*

- Then he dictated a "turd" to be placed in the personnel file of the officer on duty in twelve-tower. — Malcolm Braly, *On the Yard*, p. 198, 1967

turdcutter *noun*
the buttocks *US, 1977*
Imprecise and crude physiology.

- Yeah, that bitch sho' has got a helluva turdcutter on it, ain't she? — Odie Hawkins, *Chicago Hustle*, p. 24, 1977
- — Connie Eble (Editor), *UNC-CH Campus Slang*, p. 10, Spring 1998

turdhead *noun*

a despicable person *US, 1953*

- Bragg publicly addressed us as "turds" and "turdheads." — Jim Thompson, *Bad Boy*, p. 393, 1953

turdpacker *noun*

in anal sex, the active partner *US, 1941*

- — Bruce Rodgers, *The Queens Vernacular*, p. 18, 1972

turf *noun*

1 the territory controlled by a gang; a sphere of influence *US, 1952*

- I can see us in a big blue Cadillac, the biggest pushers around this turf. — Hal Ellson, *The Golden Spike*, p. 17, 1952
- I say this turf is small, but's it's all we got. — Stephen Sondheim, *West Side Story*, 1957
- Some of the guys in our gang were scared to go out of our turf and rumble because they didn't know the backyards and the roofs in other turfs. — Claude Brown, *Manchild in the Promised Land*, p. 56, 1965
- We took a beating—their turf, too many guys. — Edwin Torres, *Carlito's Way*, p. 8, 1975

2 the street *US, 1978*

- "Out on the turf folks are wondering who it was got the spic jealous enough to try offing a dude, you know how it is." — Robert Deane Pharr, *Giveadamn Brown*, p. 14, 1978

turf *verb*

in hospital usage, to transfer a patient to another's responsibility *US, 1994*

- — Sally Williams, "Strong" Words (Dissertation), p. 164, 1994

turf consultant *noun*

in horseracing, someone who makes a living selling tips to bettors *US, 1947*

- — Dan Parker, *The ABC of Horse Racing*, p. 150, 1947

turf dance *noun*

a stylized dance developed and performed by an urban youth gang *US, 2002*

- Then she asked two of Brown's friends to honor his memory by doing a "turf dance," a curious bit of choreography—part Crip walk, part break-dancing. — *San Francisco Chronicle*, p. 1A, 17th May 2002

turistas; touristas *noun*

diarrhea *US, 1972*

- — Helen Dahlskog (Editor), *A Dictionary of Contemporary and Colloquial Usage*, p. 60, 1972

Turk *noun*

1 a homosexual man who assumes the active role in anal sex *US, 1950*

- — Hyman E. Goldin et al., *Dictionary of American Underworld Lingo*, p. 228, 1950

2 a strong and aggressive young man *US, 1949*

- Then I look at this new turk. — Hal Ellson, *Duke*, p. 30, 1949

turkey *noun*

1 in movies and showbusiness, an absolute failure or disaster, critical or financial; hence, in wider usage, a failure or disaster *US, 1927*

Why the turkey, a native of America, is the symbol of spectacular failure is a mystery.

- One night, as we went in from the lobby to watch the second act of an especially bad turkey, he seemed less dour than usual, and I asked him why he was so gay. — Earl Wilson, *I Am Gazing Into My 8-Ball*, p. 81, 1945
- We're finally getting out of this turkey town. — *American Graffiti*, 1973
- "Lost Horizon" is perhaps the grandest of 1973's turkeys. — *San Francisco Examiner and Chronicle, Sunday Scene*, p. 12, 13th January 1974
- If this is going to be a turkey movie, at least I will have brought it in on time! — Dale Pollock, *Skywalking: The Life and Films of George Lucas*, p. 120, 1999

2 an incompetent, ineffective, or disliked person *US, 1951*

May be used with affection.

- And there's plenty of Polacks and fairies around here that we might have socked instead of turkeys with the name of Murphy and Garrity. — James T. Farrell, *Saturday Night*, p. 52, 1947
- [I]t had taken the public at large about three days to brand me a "turkey." — John Nichols, *The Sterile Cuckoo*, p. 50, 1965
- This is not the official goddamn threshold. Upstairs, you turkey! — Erich Segal, *Love Story*, p. 78, 1970

- That's why they all be in Lewisburg or Green Haven. Wise up, turkey. — Edwin Torres, *Carlito's Way*, p. 44, 1975

3 a member of a youth gang who is reluctant or unwilling to join in gang fights *US, 1949*

- But if you're a Jap or a turkey or you're going to punk out it's going to be bad stuff for you. — Hal Ellson, *Duke*, p. 31, 1949
- Turkeys (boys "not in the know"). — Howard Polsky, *Cottage Six*, p. 24, 1962

4 an Irishman or a person of Irish descent *US, 1982*

- — Bill Reilly, *Big Al's Official Guide to Chicagoese*, p. 63, 1982

5 a patient who has been mishandled medically *US, 1961*

- — *American Speech*, pp. 145–148, May 1961: "The spoken language of medicine; argot, slang, cant"

6 in hospital usage, a patient with a petty medical complaint *US, 1978*

- — *Maledicta*, p. 70, Summer/Winter 1978: "Common patient-directed pejoratives used by medical personnel"

7 poor quality, adulterated or counterfeit drugs *US, 1958*

- A lot of times some of those crooked dealers, new in the neighborhood, pass off baking soda as stuff or real weak H mixed with baking powder you get what's called burned: you're getting a turkey. — Willard Motley, *Let No Man Write My Epitaph*, p. 151, 1958
- [I]t was found to be "turkey"—it looked like heroin but proved to be a non-narcotic substance. — Harry J. Anslinger, *The Murderers*, p. 93, 1961
- In fact Willie didn't buy any dope, he bought a turkey. — Henry Williamson, *Hustler!*, p. 136, 1965

turkey *verb*

to inhale marijuana smoke nasally *US, 1970*

- — Ernest L. Abel, *A Marijuana Dictionary*, p. 105, 1982

turkeyhead *noun*

a dolt *US, 1955*

- Okay for you, turkey-head, when I make my pile I leave you behind. — Max Shulman, *Guided Tour of Campus Humor*, p. 40, 1955

turkey line *noun*

in the language of hang gliding, a line used by an instructor to prevent the nose from dipping during landing or take-off *US, 1977*

- — Dennis Pagen, *Hang Gliding and Flying Skills*, p. 110, 1977: "Glossary"

turkey shoot *noun*

an overwhelming slaughter of helpless victims *US, 1968* From the C19 "sport" of a shooting match in which the target was a live turkey.

- Major Hanna, the senior advisor, had what he calls a turkey shoot. — Martin Russ, *Happy Hunting Ground*, p. 82, 1968
- "They heard that Charlie Company had a turkey shoot," Colburn recalled. — Seymour M. Hersh, *My Lai 4*, p. 90, 1970
- On August 17, in a slaughter reminiscent of the Kosong Turkey Shoot, hundreds of fleeing enemy soldiers fled in daylight to the banks of the Naktong and tried to ford the river to escape a beachhead that the marines had transformed into a deathtrap. — Joseph C. Goulden, *Korea*, p. 179, 1982
- As the Basra Road turkey shoot unfolded, US General Colin Powell reportedly told other members of the war cabinet […] "We should stop now. Our pilots are just killing for the sake of it." — Stuart Jeffries, *Mrs Slocombe's Pussy*, p. 264, 2000

Turkey trot *noun*

diarrhea suffered by tourists *US, 1960*

- In Italy, Turkey, Egypt and India it is named Turkey trot, gippy tummy, and Delhi belly. — *Washington Post, Times Herald*, p. L6, 10th April 1960

Turkish culture *noun*

anal sex *US, 1972*

- — Robert A. Wilson, *Playboy's Book of Forbidden Words*, p. 246, 1972

Turkish delight *noun*

anal sex *US, 1986–1987*

- — *Maledicta*, p. 60, 1986–1987: "A continuation of a glossary of ethnic slurs in American English"

Turkish rope *noun*

a heavy gold necklace *US, 1995*

- — Bill Valentine, *Gang Intelligence Manual*, p. 78, 1995

turn *noun*

a jail sentence *US, 1995*

- You know what happens if you do another turn in the joint? — *The Usual Suspects*, 1995

turn *verb*

1 to sell something, especially stolen goods or drugs *US, 1968*
- A pusher who "turns" (sells to) anybody who wants to buy is just throwing rocks at the penitentiary. — Phil Hirsch, *Hooked*, p. 12, 1968
- — Bruce Jackson, *Outside the Law*, p. 61, 1972: "Glossary"

2 to convert a man to homosexuality *US, 1991*
- All they think about is getting dope and getting laid, looking to see who they can turn. See, once you get turned, you're pussy. — Elmore Leonard, *Maximum Bob*, p. 108, 1991

▸ **turn 'em and burn 'em**
to quickly service a fighter plane and return it to combat *US, 1991*
- — *American Speech*, p. 404, Winter 1991: "Among the new words"

▸ **turn into a pumpkin**
in transsexual usage, to dress in keeping with your genetic sex *US, 1986–1987*
- — *Maledicta*, p. 173, Summer/Winter 1986–1987: "Sexual slang: prostitutes, pedophiles, flagellators, transvestites, and necrophiles"

▸ **turn state**
to become a witness for the prosecuting authorities *US, 1990*
- "I just remembered I got in for I could fur shur parlay into probation, maybe dismissal." "You don't mean turn state?" — Seth Morgan, *Homeboy*, p. 93, 1990

▸ **turn the duke**
in circus and carnival usage, to shortchange someone *US, 1981*
- — Don Wilmeth, *The Language of American Popular Entertainment*, p. 282, 1981

▸ **turn the mit**
to shortchange *US, 1980*
- — Joe McKennon, *Circus Lingo*, p. 97, 1980

▸ **turn turtle**
(of a surfer) to pass through a wave coming at them by rolling under their surfboard *US, 1977*
- — Gary Fairmont R. Filosa II, *The Surfer's Almanac*, p. 185, 1977

turnaround *noun*
training time for navy pilots between aircraft carrier cruises *US, 1990*
- In turnaround before the second cruise, he'd met pilot Lou Page. — Robert K. Wilcox, *Scream of Eagles*, p. 23, 1990

turn around *verb*
in criminal or police usage, to persuade someone to inform or otherwise betray *US, 1975*
- And then a lot of guys with heart ain't got no smarts, so then the bulls outfox them, put them in a bind, and then turn them around. — Edwin Torres, *Carlito's Way*, p. 130, 1975

turn-off *noun*
something that disgusts or creates antipathy *US, 1983*
- I really hate all of the macho bullshit that goes along with police work. It's a real turnoff. — Gerald Petievich, *To Die in Beverly Hills*, p. 213, 1983

turn off *verb*
to disgust, to disillusion *US, 1970*
- You're a female version of the routine Regular Army clown. And that turns me off, so just leave my outfit alone and we'll get along fine. — *M*A*S*H*, 1970
- The first time I played Fun House I got very turned off. — Lester Bangs, *Psychotic Reactions and Carburetor Dung*, p. 47, 1970

turn-on *noun*
a sharing or gifting of drugs *US, 1995*
- When I'd find a turn-on in progress, I'd yank him into the circle as I chose a good spot to be the next in line for an offering. — Cleo Odzer, *Goa Freaks*, p. 39, 1995

turn on *verb*

1 to use a drug; to experience the effects of a drug *US, 1953*
- — *American Speech*, p. 88, May 1955: "Narcotic argot along the Mexican border"
- She wanted to turn on but she didn't have any bread. — Alexander Trocchi, *Cain's Book*, p. 28, 1961
- A droopy-eyed Negro hands me a tiny joint, offers what is hardly a roach now: "Turn on?" — John Rechy, *City of Night*, p. 185, 1963

- This sudden flash awakening is called "turning on." — Timothy Leary, *The Politics of Ecstasy*, p. 14, 1963

2 to introduce someone to something, especially drugs *US, 1961*
- "Bernie, do you want me to turn you on?" Zaida said. — Ross Russell, *The Sound*, p. 21, 1961
- Have to find a place though, maybe men's room in the house. Turn Pamela on later. Wouldn't dig it probably. — Richard Farina, *Been Down So Long*, pp. 33–34, 1966
- Get high and you want to turn on the world. — Jerry Rubin, *Do It!*, p. 98, 1970
- During my sophomore year at college, somebody (God bless him) turned me on to dope. — Raymond Mungo, *Famous Long Ago*, p. 3, 1970

3 to arouse an interest, sexual or abstract in someone; to stimulate someone; to thrill someone *US, 1965*
- Not that a straightforward invitation from the young Lana Turner or the young Ava Gardner might not, as they say out here, "turn me on"[.] — Gore Vidal, *Myra Breckinridge*, p. 85, 1968
- One time I was with Jim and we were balling doggie fashion and his roommate came home and got turned on watching us ball. — *Adam Film Quarterly*, p. 68, October 1973
- Breast-feeding turned me on in a way sex never did. — Sally Cline, *Couples*, p. 29, 1998

turn on, tune in, (and) drop out
used as a slogan for, and invitation to join, the hippy counterculture *US, 1966*
Credited to Timothy Leary (1920–96) the self-styled high priest of LSD.
- The quickest, healthiest most effective way to change our society is to turn on, tune in, drop out! — *The San Francisco Oracle*, 20th September 1966
- The trinity is Tim Leary's answer to the Diet of Worms. — Sidney Bernard, *This Way to the Apocalypse*, p. 56, 1968

turnout *noun*
a novice prostitute; a prostitute working in a particular brothel for the first time *US, 1967*
- Each Angel looked about, checking out any movement towards his old lady, and at the same time he might be thinking of getting in line for one of those magnificent mama turn-outs. — Frank Reynolds, *Freewheelin' Frank*, p. 6, 1967
- Til now I never had the time for a turnout. — A.S. Jackson, *Gentleman Pimp*, p. 161, 1973
- I had ignored the compulsive desire of any turn-out to flee the master who had put her new slick image together. — Iceberg Slim (Robert Beck), *Airtight Willie and Me*, p. 63, 1979
- She was a "turn out" (TO), new to prostitution and, especially, to the brothel scene. — Lora Shaner, *Madam*, p. 48, 1999

turn out *verb*

1 to recruit and convert someone to prostitution; to become a prostitute *US, 1960*
- "A broad?" Rudy raised an eyebrow. "Thinkin' about turnin' her out, huh?" — Clarence Cooper Jr., *The Scene*, p. 14, 1960
- I just ain't got the time to turn a girl out. When I get a girl, I want her to be ready made in sportin' life. — A.S. Jackson, *Gentleman Pimp*, p. 156, 1973
- When you're turned out, pimps put that in your head. "You don't get off with tricks." — Susan Hall, *Ladies of the Night*, p. 29, 1973
- After a brief attempt to turn out Bev the phone girl, he asked for a double call with Allison and Tiffany. — Michelle Tea, *Rent Girl*, p. 83, 2004

2 to engage a woman in serial sex with multiple partners *US, 1966*
- Girls who get turned out at Hell's Angels parties don't think of police in terms of protection. — Hunter S. Thompson, *Hell's Angels*, p. 195, 1966

3 to convert someone to homosexuality *US, 1952*
- Boy, that Jeep can turn 'em out. — Chester Himes, *Cast the First Stone*, p. 13, 1952
- The place a punk usually gets turned out is the county jail. — Bruce Jackson, *In the Life*, p. 368, 1972
- With the help of the homosexual, Jug had turned out a young white boy by the name of Jerry. — Donald Goines, *White Man's Justice, Black Man's Grief*, p. 163, 1973

turn out room *noun*
a room reserved for sex *US, 1981*

- They were given a complete tour of the clubhouse including the turnout room, which was set aside for any young lady who wanted to give of herself[.] — Robert Lipkin, *A Brotherhood of Outlaws*, p. 39, 1981

turtle *noun*

the replacement for a combat soldier who is due to return home *US, 1968*

Like the turtle, the replacement seems never to get there quickly enough.

- — Carl Fleischhauer, *A Glossary of Army Slang*, p. 24, 1968
- But everyone had a strange habit of referring to us as "turtles" or "FNGs." — Lynda Van Devanter, *Home Before Morning*, p. 87, 1983

turtle *verb*

(used of a boat) to turn over completely in the water, exposing the bottom of the hull to the sky *US, 1966*

- A rented motorboat had turtled and its sole occupant was clinging to the hull while two lifeguards struggled to get her into the rescue boat. — Joseph Wambaugh, *Floaters*, p. 159, 1966

tush; tushie; tushy *noun*

the backside, the buttocks *US, 1962*

Yiddish.

- Oh, Scottie Hite, you naughty boy! You kissed my tushie! — Richard Price, *The Wanderers*, p. 79, 1974
- Her tush is tight and she's got great boobs and in bed, well, I don't need to waste my time jogging to keep my weight down. — George V. Higgins, *The Rat on Fire*, p. 170, 1981
- She told him what to do with that and he gave her one on the tush. — *Get Shorty*, 1995
- Hakan, who, shortly after being picked up by his director at L.A. International, is asked if he's ready to dive into a little good o'l American tushy. — Editors of Adult Video News, *The AVN Guide to the 500 Greatest Adult Films of All Time*, p. 14, 2005

tush hog *noun*

1 an aggressive homosexual *US, 1971*

- One of them, called Fraulein, vaguely Teutonic, affected some sort of mongrel accent, which seemed to enhance her allure among the "tush hogs." — James Blake, *The Joint*, p. 67, 1971

2 a person with a short temper *US, 1946*

- Muta takes all the goddam hardness and evil out of you, cuts down the tush-hog bullying side of your personality and makes you think straight, with your head instead of your fists. — Mezz Mezzrow, *Really the Blues*, p. 96, 1946
- [H]e organized a pack of tush hogs who called themselves the Night Riders and they went all over Little Egypt looking for fights. — Minnesota Fats, *The Bank Shot*, p. 206, 1966
- — Bruce Jackson, *Outside the Law*, p. 61, 1972: "Glossary"

tusker *noun*

an all-in-all unattractive girl *US, 1968*

- — *Current Slang*, p. 14, Summer 1968

tuskie; tuskee *noun*

a marijuana cigarette *US, 1977*

- She passed the half-smoked tuskie to his outstretched fingers. — Odie Hawkins, *Chicago Hustle*, p. 74, 1977
- — Edith A. Folb, *runnin' down some lines*, p. 259, 1980

tuss *verb*

to abuse for nonmedicinal purposes nonprescription medication containing dextromethorphan (DXM) *US, 2003*

- DXM abuse is called "Robotripping" or "Tussing." Users might be called "syrup heads" or "robotards." — *USA Today*, p. 1A, 29th December 2003

tussin *noun*

dextromethorphan (DXM), an active ingredient in nonprescription cold and cough medication, often abused for non-medicinal purposes *US, 2003*

From the branded cough syrup Robitussin™.

- Youths' nicknames for DXM: Robo, Skittles, Triple C's, Rojo, Dex, Tussin, Vitamin D. — *USA Today*, p. 1A, 29th December 2003

tutu *noun*

in craps, a roll of four *US, 1999*

A homophonic pun—two, two.

- — Chris Fagans and David Guzman, *A Guide to Craps Lingo*, p. 15, 1999

TV-style *noun*

anal sex from behind a person on their hands and knees *US, 1979*

An allusion to the fact that both participants are facing the same way and can watch television during sex.

- — *Maledicta*, p. 231, 1979: "Kinks and queens: linguistic and cultural aspects of the terminology for gays"

twangie boy *noun*

a young male prostitute *US, 1987*

- Chances they might see some twangie boy down on his knees doing a sailor up from San Pedro. — Robert Campbell, *Alice in La-La Land*, p. 1, 1987

twanky *noun*

twenty *US, 2006*

- "Whatever. I dropped twanky just on vinyl last week." — Linden Dalecki, *Kid B*, p. 67, 2006

twat *noun*

1 the vagina *UK, 1656*

- Did you ever have a woman who shaved her twat? It's repulsive, ain't it? And it's funny too. Sort of mad like. It doesn't look like a twat any more. — Henry Miller, *Tropic of Cancer*, p. 139, 1961
- [H]e once remarked that "the only meat in the world sweeter, hotter and pinker than Amand's twat is Carolina barbecue." — Tom Robbins, *Another Roadside Attraction*, p. 49, 1971
- The two big babes, hips swaying, asses grinding, consume the dildo in their bare, giant twats. — *Adult Video*, p. 50, August/September 1986
- A tastefully trimmed twat doesn't happen by accident; it takes time, technique, and talent. — *The Village Voice*, 8th–14th November 2000

2 a woman *UK, 1929*

- Let's just sit here all day and have laughs at this piecy new English twat. — Evan Hunter, *The Blackboard Jungle*, p. 36, 1954
- It was little twats like her that ruined young athletes, as far as he was concerned. — Larry McMurtry, *The Last Picture Show*, p. 117, 1966
- We always come back on tat fuckin' train an' Mom's always cryin' 'cause that stupid blond twat thinks Mom's some kinda Mustache Pete and'll contaminate her kids. — Richard Price, *The Wanderers*, p. 142, 1974
- Lemme go get this twat and finish her off. — Stephen J. Cannell, *Big Con*, p. 145, 1997

3 a promiscuous homosexual man *US, 1987*

- "Disgusting the way some of these twats flaunt it, ain't it?" a tough at the next table said. — Robert Campbell, *Alice in La-La Land*, p. 4, 1987

tweak *noun*

in mountain biking, any low, destabilizing contact with a rock, root, or stump *US, 1992*

- Recovering form a good tweak requires instantaneous handlebar torque. — William Nealy, *Mountain Bike!*, p. 163, 1992

tweak *verb*

1 to bend *US, 1990*

- — Elena Garcia, *A Beginner's Guide to Zen and the Art of Snowboarding*, p. 123, 1990: "Glossary"

2 in computing or electronics, to make a minor adjustment *US, 1983*

- If a program is almost correct, rather than figuring out the precise problem you might just keep tweaking it until it works. — Guy L. Steele et al., *The Hacker's Dictionary*, p. 127, 1983

tweak; tweek *noun*

1 methamphetamine, a central nervous system stimulant *US, 1985*

- [A]mid an indescribable clutter of trash on the floor, which includes the glassine envelopes used for methamphetamine. The officers confiscate a syringe. "He's a tweak freak," the blond says spitefully. — *San Francisco Chronicle*, p. 32, 26th April 1985

2 a dose of crack cocaine *US, 1988*

- "When crack and the hubbas (cocaine) came out, that's when things started going down the drain. People were people, but that drug came out and, my goodness, it's controlling peoples' lives," she said. "They're on a mission when they get the first tweak." — *San Francisco Chronicle*, p. A1, 19th September 1988

3 crack cocaine *US, 1986*

- When you go out to buy cocaine, you're on "a tweak mission." — *San Francisco Chronicle*, p. 6, 2nd July 1986

tweak; tweek *verb*
1 to experience the effects of methamphetamine use; to use methamphetamine *US, 1989*

- Then there are wounds inflicted with knives, baseball bats and other weapons when drug users are "tweaking." — *New York Times*, p. 20, 6th August 1989
- "Tweeker Park," they call it, for all the "crank" addicts who "tweek" there after staying up for days. — *Portland Oregonian*, p. 1, 13th November 1989
- Disgusted, Blaze said, "You were better off tweaking." — Joseph Wambaugh, *Floaters*, p. 7, 1996
- "I tweaked for days. I liked all the weight I was losing—I lost about 30 pounds just like that- and I liked the high, being very much there." — *Phoenix New Times*, 18th December 1997

2 to experience the effects of crack cocaine use; to use crack cocaine *US, 1989*

- Then there are wounds inflicted with knives, baseball bats and other weapons when drug users are "tweaking," the street jargon for the volatile behavior that accompanies crack. — *New York Times*, p. 20, 6th August 1989

tweak and freak *verb*
to engage in kinky sex after injecting methamphetamine *US, 1989*

- — Geoffrey Froner, *Digging for Diamonds*, p. 63, 1989

tweaked *adjective*
methamphetamine-intoxicated; craving methamphetamine *US, 1985*

- I'm just about tweaked to the max all the time. — *Los Angeles Times*, p. V6, 4th June 1985
- By the next day he was tweaked, craving more of the substance. — Bob Sipchen, *Baby Insane and the Buddha*, p. 334, 1993
- He offers you the rig. Don't act too tweaked. — Lynn Breedlove, *Godspeed*, p. 84, 2002

tweaked out *adjective*
methampetamine-intoxicated *US, 1989*

- A drug lab used to manufacture methamphetamines was discovered early yesterday morning after a 47-year-old Tacoma man, whom police described as "tweaked out," was arrested nude near his home. — *Seattle Times*, p. B2, 9th July 1989

tweaker; tweeker *noun*
1 a crack cocaine user or addict *US, 1988*

- The boomers sell crack, the tweakers smoke it and the survivors stay out of the way. — *San Francisco Chronicle*, p. A1, 19th September 1988

2 a user of methamphetamine or amphetamines *US, 1989*

- Typical highs lasts from four to eight hours. Users call themselves "tweakers." — *Los Angeles Times*, p. 1 (Metro), 8th October 1989
- Anyways, he's this little speed tweaker, like our snitch. — Joseph Wambaugh, *The Golden Orange*, p. 50, 1990
- According to several biographers, Adolf Hitler was a major-league tweaker, taking regular injections of meth. — *Phoenix New Times*, 18th December 1997
- [O]ccassionally some elderly tweaker would be stark naked in the back, where the DJ was stuffed in his DJ closet playing Motorhead. — Michelle Tea, *Rent Girl*, p. 178, 2004

tweed; tweeds *noun*
marijuana *US, 1995*
Contraction of "the WEED," thus "t'weed," "tweed."

- Need some tweed, cuz? — Los Stavsky et al., *A2Z*, p. 105, 1995

tweeds *noun*
clothing, especially a suit *US, 1968*

- — Collin Baker et al., *College Undergraduate Slang Study Conducted at Brown University*, p. 215, 1968

tweek *verb*
▶ to get tweeked
to be knocked from your surfboard and then be pummeled by the ocean *US, 1988*

- — Surf Punks, *Oh No! Not Them Again!* (liner notes), 1988

tweetie *noun*
an effeminate male *US, 1968*
An imitation of a lisped "sweetie" and an allusion to Tweetie Pie, a cartoon character of the 1950s and 60s.

- Collin Baker et al., *College Undergraduate Slang Study Conducted at Brown University*, p. 215, 1968

twelve *noun*
in a deck of playing cards, any queen *US, 1996*

- — John Vorhaus, *The Big Book of Poker Slang*, p. 37, 1996

twelver *noun*
a twelve-pack of beer *US, 1997*

- — Pamela Munro, *U.C.L.A. Slang*, p. 117, 1997

twennie *noun*
a twenty-dollar dose of crack cocaine *US, 1989*

- I don't put but a few twennies [$20 packets] in foil anyway 'cause if you sweat too much it cakes up. — Terry Williams, *The Cocaine Kids*, p. 43, 1989
- — Terry Williams, *Crackhouse*, p. 152, 1992

twenties *noun*
a swindle featuring a twenty-dollar bill *US, 1952*

- Thus, for the tenth time that day, he had worked the twenties, one of the three standard gimmicks of the short con grift. — Jim Thompson, *The Grifters*, p. 6, 1963
- What we did, ever so often we'd pull off the pigeon drop for maybe twenty-five dollars, with me painting the leather, or work the twenties for a five. — Guy Owen, *The Flim-Flam Man and the Apprentice Grifter*, p. 151, 1972

twenty-cent bag *noun*
twenty dollars' worth of a drug *US, 1972*

- A tiny capsule [of cocaine] sells for twenty dollars (a "twenty-cent bag"). — Christina and Richard Milner, *Black Players*, p. 12, 1972

twenty-cent rock *noun*
crack cocaine worth $20 *US, 1991*

- The officer asked for a "10-cent rock"—street slang for a $10 purchase of crack cocaine. Boykin allegedly then told the officer he had only "20-cent rocks." — *Texas Lawyer*, p. 10, 14th October 1991

twenty-five *noun*
LSD *US, 1966*
From the slightly more formal LSD-25, from the most formal D-Lysergic Acid Diethlamide.

- — Donald Louria, *Nightmare Drugs*, p. 45, 1966

twenty-one days in the county jail *noun*
in poker, a hand consisting of three sevens *US, 1988*

- — George Percy, *The Language of Poker*, p. 94, 1988

twenty-twenty *adjective*
good-looking; attractive *US, 1947*
Punning, leaping from "seeing well" to "good-looking."

- There was a pin-up pigeon. She was a twenty-twenty quail. — Harry Haenigsen, *Jive's Like That*, 1947

twenty-twenty hindsight *noun*
the ability to see clearly what should have been done *US, 1962*

- Yeah, well, twenty-twenty hindsight and all that. — *Get Shorty*, 1995

twenty-two; 22 *noun*
a 22-ounce bottle of beer or malt liquor *US, 2000*

- I had to buy a 22 at the grocery store since I no longer had my girl to split a 40 with. — Michelle Tea, *Valencia*, p. 134, 2000

twerp; twirp *noun*
an idiot, a fool, a despicable person *UK, 1874*

- The guy she married—a smug, sadistic twirp. — Philip Wylie, *Opus 21*, p. 64, 1949
- As we had been teaching him slang, his dialogue was larded with a weird mixture of Spanish and American jargon, with emphasis on his favorite word, twerp. — Jennie Darlington and Jane McIlvaine, *My Antarctic Honeymoon*, p. 132, 1956
- I'm tired of breaking in these twerps. — Albert Goldman, *Freak Show*, p. 215, 1968
- You little twirp. You come one step closer to me and I'll knock your block off. — *Drugstore Cowboy*, 1988

twerpy *adjective*
idiotic, foolish *US, 1971*

- [T]he lead singer's twerpy attempts at Doctor John-ish mumbo-jumbo [...] were godawful. — Lester Bangs, *Psychotic Reactions and Carburetor Dung*, p. 98, 1971

twice-and-a-half truck *noun*
a 2.5 ton truck *US, 1968*
- — Carl Fleischhauer, *A Glossary of Army Slang*, p. 24, 1968

twice as cold as zero *adjective*
very cold *US, 1975*
The arithmetic impossibility lends an ironic charm to the expression.
- — John Gould, *Maine Lingo*, p. 302, 1975

twiddle *noun*
the tilde character (~) on a computer keyboard *US, 1983*
- — Guy L. Steele et al., *The Hacker's Dictionary*, p. 127, 1983

twig *noun*
1 a small, tightly wound hair braid *US, 1993*
- His hair was pulled back in a dozen or so braided "twigs," each tied with a small blue rubber band. — Bob Sipchen, *Baby Insane and the Buddha*, p. 25, 1993

2 marijuana *US, 1970*
- — Ernest L. Abel, *A Marijuana Dictionary*, p. 106, 1982

3 in sports betting, a half-point increment in the pointspread *US, 1984*
- — Thomas L. Clark, *The Dictionary of Gambling and Gaming*, p. 101, 1987

twilight *verb*
to lose yourself in a daydream *US, 1974*
- — Paul Glover, *Words from the House of the Dead*, 1974

twilly *noun*
a woman, especially an attractive or promiscuous one *US, 1934*
- Betsy a twilly? He wished he'd had some of that Betsy. — Bernard Wolfe, *The Late Risers*, p. 286, 1954

twin caper *noun*
a double date *US, 1960*
- — *San Francisco Examiner*, p. III-2, 22nd March 1960

twin fins *noun*
in craps, two fives *US, 1983*
- — Thomas L. Clark, *The Dictionary of Gambling and Gaming*, p. 242, 1987

twink *noun*
1 an effeminate, young, handsome homosexual male *US, 1968*
- — *Current Slang*, p. 13, Spring 1968
- Where are the twinks, anyway? They usually have the decency to provide one or two decorative twinks… Jesus, who needs to waste a night staring at these tired old Gucci queens. — Armistead Maupin, *Tales of the City*, p. 300, 1978
- Chris said, "Yeah, the twink comes up to the table, says he's gonna be our waitperson." — Elmore Leonard, *Freaky Deaky*, p. 10, 1988

2 a new military recruit *US, 1983*
- But most of the lifers had never seen Nam and most of the twinks—the new recruits—had little idea of where they were going and none whatever about what would become of them when they got there. — Peter Goldman and Tony Fuller, *Charlie Company*, p. 32, 1983

3 a coward *US, 1982*
- Rafi comes on strong, but he's a twink at heart, he caves in. — Elmore Leonard, *Cat Chaser*, p. 160, 1982

twinkie *noun*
1 a sexual partner who is pleasing at the moment but not good for the long haul *US, 2006*
- Jason had been one of those whom several other women officers had sampled, the kind they called "Twinkies," guys who aren't good for you but you have to have one. — Joseph Wambaugh, *Hollywood Station*, p. 80, 2006

2 a person who is profoundly out of touch with reality *US, 1982*
- I doubt Rafi's expectations have anything to do with the real world. He's a twinkie. — Elmore Leonard, *Cat Chaser*, p. 194, 1982

3 a youthful, sexually inexperienced male who is the object of an older homosexual's desire *US, 1979*
The spelling "twinky" is also used.
- — *Maledicta*, p. 221, 1979: "Kinks and queens: linguistic and cultural aspects of the terminology for gays"
- This term [pogey] designates an attractive youth desired by older homosexuals (mainly naval and prison use), roughly corresponding to the more recent twinky, though often somewhat younger. — Wayne Dynes, *Homolexis*, p. 112, 1985

- Ned was no fading twinkie, though, when I knew him; he wore his age with an easy, shambling grace that was completely out of sync with the desperate pretenses of most people in this town. — Armistead Maupin, *Maybe the Moon*, p. 144, 1992

twinkle-toes *noun*
a youthful, effeminate homosexual man *US, 1979*
- — *Maledicta*, p. 247, 1979: "Kinks and queens: linguistic and cultural aspects of the terminology for gays"

twins *noun*
1 two women having sex with one man or with each other for the pleasure of the man *US, 1977*
- She has a girl specially trained for her when a customer requests "twins." The two of them go into erotic ecstasies over each other's bodies for the bon vivant voyeur who has paid handsomely for such stimulating tableaux. — Mario Puzo, *Inside Las Vegas*, p. 272, 1977

2 a woman's breasts *US, 2001*
- — Pamela Munro, *U.C.L.A. Slang*, p. 121, 2001

3 the fists *US, 1998*
- — Ethan Hilderbrant, *Prison Slang*, p. 132, 1998

twins *adverb*
▸ **go twins**
to go on a double date *US, 1959*
- — Edd Byrnes, *Way Out with Kookie*, 1959

twist *noun*
the passive, "feminine" member of a lesbian relationship *US, 1970*
- — *American Speech*, p. 59, Spring–Summer 1970: "Homosexual slang"

twist *verb*
1 to arrest someone *US, 1953*
- So for the lawyer for these two cats that got twisted found out the cat was a Federal narcotics agent. — William Burroughs, *Junkie*, p. 121, 1953

2 to spend time in jail or prison *US, 1971*
- He twisted behind a hummer means he did the time but not the crime. — Hermese E. Roberts, *The Third Ear*, 1971

3 to roll a marijuana cigarette *US, 1958*
- So we all did go to Larry's and Julien sat on the floor in front of an open newspaper in which was the tea (poor quality L.A. but good enough) and rolled, or "twisted," as Jack Steen, the absent one had said to me[.] — Jack Kerouac, *The Subterraneans*, p. 5, 1958

4 in pool, to apply spin to a shot to affect the course of the object ball or the cue ball after it hits the object ball *US, 1990*
- — Steve Rushin, *Pool Cool*, p. 29, 1990

▸ **twist a braid**
to say goodbye *US, 1993*
- — *People Magazine*, p. 72, 19th July 1993

twisted *adjective*
1 perverted *US, 1900*
- You are one twisted fuck. — *American Beauty*, 1999

2 drunk or drug-intoxicated *US, 1958*
- "Man is he high!" someone whispered. "Man, he's twisted! But on what? On what?" — John Clellon Holmes, *The Horn*, p. 201, 1958
- [H]e can be twisted on narcotics. — Clarence Cooper Jr., *The Scene*, p. 55, 1960
- You know if you're smokin' in a small room—maybe two or three guys burning this pot—it just fills the whole room with smoke. You get twisted outa your mind. — John Gimenez, *Up Tight!*, p. 87, 1967
- Very soon, I knew, we would both be completely twisted. — Hunter S. Thompson, *Fear and Loathing in Las Vegas*, p. 3, 1971

twister *noun*
1 a key *US, 1940*
- We hopped into Harry Shapiro's cab and took off for the LaSalle Street station to hand Leon Rappolo the twisters to the city. — Mezz Mezzrow, *Really the Blues*, p. 50, 1946
- I didn't miss it 'til I came home that night and found that I had no twister to get in with. — A.S. Jackson, *Gentleman Pimp*, p. 20, 1973

2 a strong drug injection, especially a combination of heroin and cocaine *US, 1959*
- — J.E. Schmidt, *Narcotics Lingo and Lore*, p. 185, 1959

twist up *verb*
to roll a marijuana cigarette *US, 1997*

- SOUTHERN: I'll just twist one up [takes out pink papers] using these clitoral pinks to give it zest. BOCKRIS: Why don't you twist up another one? — Victor Bockris, *With William Burroughs [The Howard Marks Book of Dope Stories]*, p. 34, 1997

twit *noun*

an inept and ineffectual person *UK, 1934*

- — Connie Eble (Editor), *UNC-CH Campus Slang*, p. 7, Fall 1980
- Yes, he's a congenital twit and we've got no business publishing crap like that. — Carl Hiaasen, *Tourist Season*, p. 77, 1986
- That false cousin you saddled me with and that whey-faced twit of a girl who had him by the pecker was going to do me in. — Robert Campbell, *Nibbled to Death by Ducks*, p. 274, 1989
- It was Mrs. Preston, mother of a well-known affected twit[.] — C.D. Payne, *Cut to the Twisp*, p. 46, 2001

twit *verb*

to tease or taunt someone *UK, 1530*

- Bill Lee, our pitcher in the decisive game, was twitting the writers during pregame practice. — Bill Cardoso, *The Maltese Sangweech*, p. 189, 1984

twitch *noun*

1 a prostitute *US, 1962*

- Hey, Billy boy, you remember that time in Seattle you and me picked up those two twitches? One of the best rolls I ever had. — Ken Kesey, *One Flew Over the Cuckoo's Nest*, p. 98, 1962

2 a personal pleasure *US, 1984*

- "Rather have the broad," Malatesta said. "Every man's got his own twitch," the bartender said. — George V. Higgins, *The Rat on Fire*, p. 74, 1981

3 in hospital usage, a hypochondriac *US, 1994*

- — Sally Williams, *"Strong" Words (Dissertation)*, p. 164, 1994

twitchies *noun*

anxiety, nervousness *US, 1992*

- "But I tellin' ya, that sucker out there gots the terminal twitchies." — Jess Mowry, *Way Past Cool*, p. 93, 1992

twitting *adjective*

inept; unfashionable *US, 1959*

- — *American Speech*, p. 154, May 1959: "Gator (University of Florida) slang"

two and two *noun*

cocaine *US, 1974*

- He went into the men's, paid a dime for a stall and sniffed a two-and-two, scooping the coke out of the Baggy with a silver Little Orphan Annie spoon. — Elmore Leonard, *52 Pick-up*, pp. 56–57, 1974

two bad boys from Illinois *noun*

in craps, a roll of two *US, 1985*

- — Steve Kuriscak, *Casino Talk*, p. 67, 1985

two-bit *adjective*

inconsequential; of no note *US, 1932*

"Two bits" represented a quarter of a dollar, a small sum; most younger speakers who use the term would not be familiar with its monetary roots.

- "And I'm telling you," Hobbs said, "that you're a two-bit crook." — Norman Mailer, *Advertisements for Myself*, p. 129, 1951
- Look around today, in every small town and big city, from two-bit catfish and soda-pop joints into the "integrated" lobby of the Waldorf-Astoria, and you'll see conks on black men. — Malcolm X and Alex Haley, *The Autobiography of Malcolm X*, p. 54, 1964
- A rotten low-lifed racist, two-bit pig! — Bobby Seale, *A Lonely Rage*, p. 256, 1978
- Are you telling me that some two-bit auto burglar concocted this whole thing? — Carl Hiaasen, *Tourist Season*, p. 20, 1986

two bit Annie *noun*

an inexpensive prostitute or promiscuous woman *US, 1948*

- Just let there be a Two-bit Annie around the corner when he felt like company. — Norman Mailer, *The Naked and the Dead*, p. 14, 1948

two bits *noun*

1 a small amount *US, 1989*

- "They flooded the nursing care homes and shelters," Medill says, adding his two bits. — Robert Campbell, *Nibbled to Death by Ducks*, p. 59, 1989

2 twenty-five dollars *US, 1957*

An example of the "cent = dollar" mechanism in drug slang.

- I'll endorse the check to you. It's two bits. — James Blake, *The Joint*, p. 166, 7th February 1957
- — *Current Slang*, p. 50, Fall 1968

3 twenty-five thousand dollars *US, 1986*

- According to the sources, Lambesis was seen and heard on the tape as saying: "The Man was given two-bits." — *Chicago Tribune*, p. 14C, 12th January 1986

two-bottle jump; two-quart jump *noun*

a relatively long move between performances *US, 1973*

- — Sherman Louis Sergel, *The Language of Show Biz*, p. 232, 1973

two-bug *noun*

in horse racing, an inexperienced jockey with a weight allowance of seven pounds *US, 1990*

- — Robert V. Rowe, *How to Win at Horse-Racing*, 1990

two-carbon abuser *noun*

a drunkard *US, 1978*

Hospital usage. Alcohol has two carbon atoms.

- — *Maledicta*, p. 70, Summer/Winter 1978: "Common patient-directed pejoratives used by medical personnel"

two-digit midget *noun*

a soldier with less than 100 days left on his assignment to Vietnam *US, 1972*

- "Next month I'll be a mothefuckin' two-digit midget." — William Pelfrey, *The Big V*, p. 19, 1972

two dots and a dash *noun*

the male genitals *US, 1964*

- — Roger Blake, *The American Dictionary of Sexual Terms*, p. 85, 1964

twofer *noun*

1 any situation in which you obtain two of something when only one is expected or paid for *US, 1936*

A shortening and corruption of "two-for-one;" originally applied to a pair of theater tickets sold for the price of one, and then picked up in more general use.

- — Sherman Louis Sergel, *The Language of Show Biz*, p. 232, 1973
- And if the president fumbles around in his answers on the stock market, why, those underhanded jackels of the press have got themselves a "two-fer." — Sam Donaldson, *Hold On, Mr. President*, p. 158, 1987

2 in American casinos, a chip worth $2.50 *US, 1985*

- — Steve Kuriscak, *Casino Talk*, p. 11, 1985

two-for-one *noun*

double credit for time served in prison by inmates with jobs or positions as prison trustees *US, 1972*

- — Bruce Jackson, *Outside the Law*, p. 61, 1972: "Glossary"
- He was in charge of the laboratory, making teeth, drawing two-for-one, getting ready to go home. — Bruce Jackson, *Outside the Law*, p. 174, 1972

two-four *noun*

a case of beer containing 24 bottles *US, 1993*

- — *People Magazine*, p. 73, 19th July 1993

two-in-one *noun*

cocaine and heroin mixed for injection together *US, 1964*

- Said, "Let's have a party, have some fun / for God's sake, fellas, don't forget the gun / 'cause man, I want some two in one." — Bruce Jackson, *Get Your Ass in the Water and Swim Like Me*, p. 149, 1964

two lamps burning and no ship at sea

used for describing the ultimate in wastefulness *US, 1963*

- — Charles F. Haywood, *Yankee Dictionary*, p. 182, 1963

twomp *noun*

twenty dollars *US, 2001*

- — Rick Ayers (Editor), *Slang Dictionary*, p. 16, 2001

twomp *adjective*

costing twenty dollars *US, 2001*

- — Rick Ayers (Editor), *Slang Dictionary*, p. 16, 2001

two-o *noun*

a twenty-dollar chunk of crack cocaine *US, 1989*

- — Geoffrey Froner, *Digging for Diamonds*, p. 64, 1989

two-o-eight *noun*

a military discharge for mental unfitness *US, 1968*

- — Carl Fleischhauer, *A Glossary of Army Slang*, p. 24, 1968

two pi *noun*

the number of years consumed completing a doctoral thesis *US, 1991*

- — Eric S. Raymond, *The New Hacker's Dictionary*, p. 360, 1991

two-pipe *noun*
a double-barrel shotgun *US, 1949*
- — Captain Vincent J. Monteleone, *Criminal Slang*, p. 245, 1949

two-pump chump *noun*
a male who ejaculates without much stimulation *US, 2004*
- No amount of shellfish will keep you from being a two-pump chump. — Garth Fuller, *The Chick Magnet Cookbook*, p. 3, 2004
- — Connie Eble (Editor), *UNC-CH Campus Slang*, p. 7, April 2004

two rolls and no coffee *noun*
in craps, a roll of seven on the first roll after establishing your point *US, 1949*
A pun on "roll," with the player here losing after two rolls.
- — Thomas L. Clark, *The Dictionary of Gambling and Gaming*, p. 243, 1987

two-seater *noun*
an outdoor privy which accomodates two people at once *US, 1966*
- The handsome bisexual richboy from the four-house family and the socially backward poorboy from the two-seater outhouse family. — Robert Gover, *Poorboy at the Party*, p. 8, 1966

twosky *noun*
two hundred dollars *US, 1994*
The "sky" suffix is purely decorative.
- For a twosky I want satisfaction guaranteed within forty-eight hours. — James Ellroy, *Hollywood Nocturnes*, p. 206, 1994

two-spot *noun*
a two-dollar bill; two dollars *US, 1949*
- There was four dollars and twenty cents in it for the winner—the player he'd just asked for the loan of a two-spot. — Nelson Algren, *The Man with the Golden Arm*, p. 101, 1949

two-timer *noun*
a person who is unfaithful to another person or a cause *US, 1927*
- I'll keep you posted on what's going on with little Miss Two-timer. — C.D. Payne, *Youth in Revolt*, p. 212, 1993

two-toilet *adjective*
used of an Irish immigrant, relatively well-off economically and straying from the Irish cultural ties that bind *US, 1990*
A term coined in Boston and rarely used elsewhere.
- The late Patrick J. (Sonny) McDonough not only postulated the two-toilet Irish, but also once suggested to President John F. Kennedy that he not stay at Frank Sinatra's place in Palm Springs. — *The Boston Globe*, p. A27, 3rd June 1990
- Overseeing the downtown busing scheme, federal district judge W. Arthur Garrity, Jr., who did not live in the city, was derided by blue-collar Boston Irish as an uppity "two-toilet Irishman" who had forgotten his roots. — *The Calvert News Series*, Summer 1997

two-way *adjective*
said of a carnival game or attraction that can be operated either legitimately or in a crooked fashion *US, 1989*
- — Lindsay E. Smith and Bruce A. Walstad, *Sting Shift*, p. 117, 1989: "Glossary"

typer *noun*
a typewriter *US, 1982*
- — *American Speech*, p. 29, Spring 1982: "The language of science fiction fan magazines"

typewriter *noun*
a machine gun *UK, 1915*
- I guess I managed to put up a kind of feeble grin myself while I waited for their typewriters to begin pounding out their farewell notes to me. — Mezz Mezzrow, *Really the Blues*, p. 64, 1946

typewriter commando *noun*
a soldier assigned to clerical support duty far from combat *US, 1947*
- — *American Speech*, p. 56, February 1947: "Pacific War language"

typewriter mechanic *noun*
a clerk *US, 1956*
- "What are those typewriter mechanics up to now?" Admiral Boatwright said. — William Brinkley, *Don't Go Near the Water*, p. 56, 1956

typist *noun*
in a deck of playing cards, a queen *US, 1988*
- — George Percy, *The Language of Poker*, p. 94, 1988

Uu

U4Euh *noun*
the illegal drug 4-methylaminorex, a relatively uncommon central nervous system stimulant *US, 2005*
- Fort Lauderdale Police officers and Drug Enforcement Administration (DEA) agents responding to an anonymous tip seized an operational laboratory used to make three illegal drugs—4-methylaminorex (also known as U4Euh, euphoria, and intellex)[.] — *Microgram Bulletin (DEA)*, p. 31, February 2005

Ubangi *noun*
a black person *US, 1979*
Offensive.
- [I]t's five o'clock—some sixteen-year-old Ubangi looks like he should be playing center for the Knicks comes down the street on a bicycle and yanks a pocketbook off a woman's shoulder. — Vincent Patrick, *The Pope of Greenwich Village*, p. 123, 1979

u-ey; u-ee; yewie; you-ee *noun*
a u-turn *US, 1969*
- — *Current Slang*, p. 4, Summer 1969
- And this time he jumped the brakes, wrenched the wheel and spun a U-ee at the same time. — Joseph Wambaugh, *Fugitive Nights*, p. 188, 1992

ughly *adjective*
uglier than ugly *US, 1966*
- — *Current Slang*, p. 8, Winter 1966

ugly stick *noun*
a notional stick with which a person has been beaten in order to make them ugly *US, 1967*
- "Look like he got whupped wif a hugly stick," Paul said. — Bryant Rollins, *Danger Song*, p. 193, 1967
- [H]e looked like he had been beaten with an ugly stick. — Steve Cannon, *Groove, Bang, and Jive Around*, p. 83, 1969
- You must admit, she is rather mannish. No offense, but if that's a woman, it looks like she's been beaten with an ugly stick. — *Austin Powers*, 1997
- They'd been whupped with ugly sticks, many of them. — Claire Mansfield and John Mendelssohn, *Dominatrix*, p. 110, 2002

uke *noun*
a ukulele *US, 1915*
- He stood there for a time, aloof and contemptuous, with his foot on the bench, and looked back at us, strumming a soft slow melody on his uke[.] — Chester Himes, *Cast the First Stone*, p. 222, 1952
- Tiny Tim played Hubert's in 1959 as the Human Canary, up on a platform in a tux with his uke, making $50 a week. — Josh Alan Friedman, *Tales of Times Square*, p. 182, 1986

ultimate *noun*
crack cocaine *US, 1994*
- — US Department of Justice, *Street Terms*, October 1994

ultra *adjective*
elite, fashionable *US, 1971*
- "The school is very ultra, as everyone from Boston knows." — Robert Deane Pharr, *S.R.O.*, p. 151, 1971

ultra hog *noun*
an F-105 Thunderchief *US, 1990*
- "She's big and fat and ugly, she's really quite a dog / She's known around the country as Republic's Ultra Hog." — Joseph Tuso, *Singing the Vietnam Blues*, p. 167, 1990: Republic's Ultra Hog

ulysses *noun*
a u-turn *US, 1968*
- — *Current Slang*, p. 6, Spring 1968

-um *suffix*
added to words to give the impression of English as spoken by an American Indian *US, 1946*
- "Quick-um!" cried the sad Sac. "Boil-um plenty-um water-um." — Max Shulman, *The Zebra Derby*, p. 11, 1946

umbrella *noun*
in the television and movie industries, a reflector used to bounce light onto a subject *US, 1990*
- — Ralph S. Singleton, *Filmmaker's Dictionary*, p. 177, 1990

umpteen *noun*
an imprecise, large number *UK, 1918*
- That meant I wouldn't be lying around in some hospital, like so many of them at umpteen bucks a day, while they slowly took out my neck. — Philip Wylie, *Opus 21*, pp. 66–67, 1949
- But now they're married for umpteen years and real antiques[.] — Frederick Kohner, *Gidget*, p. 6, 1957
- I don't rightly know but it must be a couple umpteen trillion sextillion[.] — Jack Kerouac, *The Dharma Bums*, p. 9, 1958
- What the hell is the point of slammin' some poor little shmuck in the can for umpteen years when we allow the liquor industry carte blanche[?] — Odie Hawkins, *Great Lawd Buddha*, p. 93, 1990

umpteenhundred *noun*
a point in the yet-to-be-determined, indefinite future *US, 1988*
- — Hans Halberstadt, *Airborne*, p. 130, 1988: "Abridged dictionary of airborne terms"

umpteenth; unteenth *adjective*
used of a great but unspecific number or amount *UK, 1918*
- For the umpteenth time, I chickened. — Max Shulman, *Anyone Got a Match?*, p. 30, 1964
- Lemme tell you this for the umteenth time. — J. Ashton Brathwaithe, *Niggers—This is Canada*, p. 24, 1971
- This is like the umpteenth time I've seen you here. — *Chasing Amy*, 1997

umpty-ump *noun*
a vague, notional large number *US, 1898*
- You've been down there to the courthouse umpty-ump times. — Mark Baker, *Cops*, p. 311, 1985

unass *verb*
to stand up; to remove yourself from your immediate location *US, 1967*
- And the next thing I knew, she was screaming. I made like a dog and "un-assed the scene," but my friend tried to explain to the cops. — Robert deCoy, *The Nigger Bible*, p. 235, 1967
- "Un-ass immediately and get in tight in contact." — Anthony Herbert, *Soldier*, p. 389, 1973
- We trained on how to board a chopper prior to an insertion and during an extraction, and, more importantly, how to unass one during an insertion. — Gary Linderer, *The Eyes of the Eagle*, p. 32, 1991
- "Unass me, woman," he said. "Get back in the house and make yourself useful." — Eric Jerome Dickey, *Cheaters*, p. 60, 1999

unassing *noun*
getting out of a helicopter *US, 1967*
- [H]e has his soft camouflage hat tucked in the front of his shirt, a precaution against loss in the prop blast at "unassing" time. — Donald Duncan, *The New Legions*, p. 11, 1967

unbutton *verb*
to force or rip open a safe *US, 1949*
- — Vincent J. Monteleone, *Criminal Slang*, p. 246, 1949
- — Hyman E. Goldin et al., *Dictionary of American Underworld Lingo*, p. 231, 1950

uncle *noun*
1 a person who buys stolen goods from criminals *US, 1950*
- — Hyman E. Goldin et al., *Dictionary of American Underworld Lingo*, p. 231, 1950

2 the US federal government *US, 1971*
An abbreviation of Uncle Sam.
- "Is uncle paying?" the black man said. — George V. Higgins, *The Friends of Eddie Doyle*, p. 63, 1971
- They're going to send that money back, and Uncle's got to catch up with you. — Harry King, *Box Man*, p. 85, 1972

- It is important to you to make sure that your Uncle does not hear what you say when you talk on the telephone. — George V. Higgins, *Penance for Jerry Kennedy*, p. 89, 1985

▸ **cry uncle; say uncle; holler uncle**
to admit defeat; to beg for mercy *US, 1918*
From Irish anacol (mercy).
- "Holler uncle." "Nope," I said, struggling, but I didn't have my usual strength. — S.E. Hinton, *The Outsiders*, p. 99, 1967

uncle *verb*
to act in a passive or subservient fashion *US, 1969*
From UNCLE TOM.
- It was a wise thing I had "uncled" on him. One of those arrogant repeaters went to the "hole" for having a sassy look in his eyes. — Iceberg Slim (Robert Beck), *Pimp*, pp. 52–53, 1969

unclear on the concept *adjective*
completely and dramatically ignorant about a particular subject *US, 1988*
- I think these baby boomers, yuppies, whatever, who have suddenly dropped back in are unclear on the concept. — *Los Angeles Times*, p. 22 (Part 6), 10th April 1988
- The late Herb Caen, one of San Francisco's best-loved newspaper columnists, had a perfect put-down for people who didn't know what they were doing or whose actions or utterances were confusing. He referred to them as being "unclear on the concept." — *Business World*, p. 4, 18th February 1998
- To be unclear on the concept, in the Mr. Boffo sense, is to suffer from an overwhelming, profound disconnection between reality and your perception of reality. — *The Washington Post*, p. F2, 17th May 1998

Uncle Charlie *noun*
1 used as a representation of the dominant white culture in the US *US, 1963*
- As I was saying, the Nigger thinks Uncle Charlie owes him a living, which is false. — Clarence Cooper Jr., *Black*, p. 100, 1963
2 the Viet Cong *US, 1985*
- We controlled the daytime, but the night belonged to Uncle Charlie. — Al Santoli, *To Bear Any Burden*, p. 89, 1985

Uncle Sugar *noun*
the FBI *US, 1973*
- You figure you got Uncle Sugar [the FBI] looking for you—and there's always the chance that some innocent slob gets hurt. — Vincent Teresa, *My Life in the Mafia*, p. 68, 1973

Uncle Tom *noun*
a black person who curries favor from whites through obsequious, fawning behavior *US, 1922*
In recent US history, Supreme Court Justice Clarence Thomas has attracted the "Uncle Tom" label more than any other black American, in part due to the irresistible Tom Thomas pun.
- And I've got to find out—whether we've been friends all these years, or whether I've just been your favorite Uncle Tom. — James Baldwin, *Blues for Mister Charlie*, p. 62, 1964
- He fired us and got another band but every night we picketed in front of the joint and kept all but a few "Uncle Toms" out. — Babs Gonzales, *I Paid My Dues*, p. 14, 1967
- The bootlickers, Uncle Toms, lackeys, and stooges of the white power structure have done their best to denigrate Malcolm[.] — Eldridge Cleaver, *Soul on Ice*, p. 60, 1968
- "I've been called everything from anti-civil rights to Uncle Tom for having taken a different stand," Thomas added. — *Washington Post*, p. A1, 11th February 1986

Uncle Tom *verb*
(used of a black person) to try to curry favor with white people by obsequious behavior *US, 1937*
- We'd stand in line and wait for hours, smiling and Uncle Tomming every time a doctor or nurse passed by. — Dick Gregory, *Nigger*, p. 27, 1964
- But for two bits, Uncle Tom a little—white cats especially like that. — Malcolm X and Alex Haley, *The Autobiography of Malcolm X*, p. 47, 1964
- Of all people, why'd they kill Malcolm? Whyn't they kill some of them Uncle-Tomming m.f.'s? — Eldridge Cleaver, *Soul on Ice*, p. 51, 1968
- Blue thundered, "You ugly, shit-colored uncle-tomming motherfucker." — Iceberg Slim (Robert Beck), *Trick Baby*, p. 230, 1969

Uncle Whiskers *noun*
the federal government *US, 1962*

- "You owe a million and three hundred thousand, roundly, to Uncle Whiskers." — Stephen Longstreet, *The Flesh Peddlers*, p. 37, 1962

uncool *adjective*
unpleasant, aggressive, dangerous; excitable; tending to show your feelings more than is prudent or advisable *US, 1953*
- — J. L. Simmons and Barry Winograd, *It's Happening*, p. 174, 1966: "glossary"
- Coming on very un-cool, hassling everybody, moving into people's areas of privacy, trying to get into people's minds. — Leonard Wolfe (Editor), *Voices from the Love Generation*, p. 238, 1968
- I mean, of course we are thrilled that you're thinking of us, and I'm pretty sure that you are not going to do anything uncool like draw a map to our house. — *The Last Supplement to the Whole Earth Catalog*, p. 78, March 1971
- This is really uncool — *Pulp Fiction*, 1994

uncunt *verb*
to withdraw the penis from a woman's vagina *US, 1961*
- [H]e could actually make her change places with his wife, all without un-cunting. — Henry Miller, *Tropic of Capricorn*, p. 177, 1961
- His spunk burst into me exactly at the instant I spent myself, and we rolled over and over in the hay until he uncunted. — Harry Barr, *Rosie*, p. 134, 2004

uncut *adjective*
not circumcized *US, 1988*
- — H. Max, *Gay (S)language*, p. 44, 1988
- We never fucked, with his uncut penis. — Sandra Bernhard, *Confessions of a Pretty Lady*, p. 66, 1988
- The gay films are definitely uncut men. — Robert Stoller and I.S. Levine, *Coming Attractions*, p. 156, 1991
- He was particularly impressed that I was uncut[.] — John Preston, *Hustling*, p. 20, 1994

undercover *adjective*
used of a racehorse, trained in secret *US, 1951*
- — David W. Maurer, *Argot of the Racetrack*, p. 67, 1951

underground *noun*
a hidden counter culture *US, 1935*
Usually in a political context, although in the 1960s also in a cultural context.
- The underground is always composed of the "outs," those who are alienated from the establishment power centers[.] — Timothy Leary, *The Politics of Ecstasy*, p. 162, 1968
- In each city of the world there is a loose competitive underground composed of groups whose aims overlap, conflict, and generally enervate the desired goal of autonomy. — *The Digger Papers*, p. 15, August 1968
- The number of underground newspapers went from fifty to a hundred to three hundred in a matter of a few months[.] — Raymond Mungo, *Famous Long Ago*, p. 41, 1970
- The question of advertisements in an underground newspaper is always a sticky business. — *The Berkeley Tribe*, p. 5, 26th June–3rd July 1970

underneath guy *noun*
a professional wrestler featured in the early, less popular matches of an event *US, 1999*
- About five of the underneath guys were going to come out as I continued my assault, but upon seeing how ugly it was getting, they literally ran away. — Mick Foley, *Have a Nice Day*, p. 235, 1999
- He wasn't a star, just an underneath guy. — Bobby Heenan, *Bobby the Brain*, p. 6, 2002

under yonder *noun*
the anus *US, 1972*
- We call that a brownie queen. In prison they call it under-yonder and round-brown. — Bruce Jackson, *In the Life*, p. 397, 1972

undressed *adjective*
used of a citizens' band radio operated without a linear amplifier *US, 1976*
- — Porter Bibb, *CB Bible*, p. 108, 1976

unforgettable *noun*
a combination of cocaine, heroin, and valium *US, 1993*
- — Peter Johnson, *Dictionary of Street Alcohol and Drug Terms*, p. 199, 1993

unfragged *adjective*
not listed on the daily frag order specifying the military objectives of the day *US, 1986*

Vietnam war usage.

• Have you ever attacked an unfragged target? — Stephen Coonts, *Flight of the Intruder*, p. 361, 1986

unfucked *adjective*
reordered; having order brought out of chaos *US, 1997*

• This is a situation that needs to get unfucked right now. — *Con Air*, 1997

unglued *adjective*
out of control *US, 1962*

• She hung up the phone and bolted for her closet, wondering why she was coming unglued like this about having lunch with Carol[.] — Cyra McFadden, *The Serial*, p. 94, 1977

unhinged *adjective*
angry; emotionally unsettled *UK, 1719*

• I worked for a city editor who was an out-and-out maniac. He was unhinged. — Max Shulman, *The Zebra Derby*, p. 147, 1946

uniboob *noun*
a woman's chest clothed in a manner that presents the two breasts as a single entity *US, 1994*

• To quote Robert Hudson on FurNet's Furry echo: "It's a Uniboob™." — alt.tv.animaniacs, 19th January 1994
• — Don R. McCreary (Editor), *Dawg Speak*, 2001

uniform *noun*
a uniformed police officer, as distinguished from a detective in street clothes *US, 1969*

• Speaking of uniforms, I ran into one the other day, while hustling up business for my woman. — *Screw*, p. 3, 7th February 1969
• There is three loads of uniforms and two detectives, all of which I know. — Robert Campbell, *Junkyard Dog*, p. 21, 1986
• By the time he got to the corner both EMS and a black and white had arrived and two uniforms were telling everyone to stay where they were for the time being, don't anybody leave. — Elmore Leonard, *Be Cool*, p. 19, 1999

uninteresting *adjective*
used of a computer problem, subject to being solved with enough time, not requiring creative problem-solving skills *US, 1991*

• — Eric S. Raymond, *The New Hacker's Dictionary*, p. 361, 1991

Union Pacific *noun*
in poker, a hand consisting of three sixes and a pair *US, 1988*
The sixes are known as "boxcars," hence the railway company name.

• — George Percy, *The Language of Poker*, p. 95, 1988

unit *noun*

1 the penis *US, 1985*
The slang sense of the word gives special meaning to the nickname "The Big Unit" given to baseball pitcher Randy Johnson.

• Get back to the library, keep your unit on this! — *The Breakfast Club*, 1985
• MADONNA: Wow, look at the unit on that guy. — *Saturday Night Live*, 11th May 1991
• Without warning, the one-eyed freak stood up, unbuttoned his army trousers, whipped out his unit and—to Snapper's mortification—urinated prodigiously upon the hurricane money. — Carl Hiaasen, *Stormy Weather*, p. 308, 1995
• "I abused 'em with this under the spotlight," he said, clutching his unit. — Josh Friedman, *When Sex Was Dirty*, p. 38, 2005

2 the vagina *US, 1978*

• These detectives here can look right up a broad's unit and check her lands and grooves. — Joseph Wambaugh, *The Black Marble*, p. 50, 1978

United Parcel Service *noun*
any amphetamine, methamphetamine or other central nervous system stimulant *US, 1976*
A forced formation: the initials UPS represent stimulants as "ups" (see **UPPER**).

• — Robert Sabbag, *Snowblind*, p. 271, 1976

unkjay *noun*
a heroin addict *US, 1949*
Pig Latin for **junkie**.

• He'd seen them coming in the rain, the unkays with their peculiarly rigid, panicky walk[.] — Nelson Algren, *The Man with the Golden Arm*, p. 59, 1949

unk-unk *noun*
an unknown that is unknown or not even suspected *US, 1974*
Aerospace usage.

• — Robert Kirk Mueller, *Buzzwords*, p. 161, 1974

unload *verb*

1 in air combat, to accelerate *US, 1990*

• Cunningham told Grant to get rid of his wing tanks, to increase his speed and maneuverability. "Get rid of your tanks," he told Grant. "Unload." — Robert K. Wilcox, *Scream of Eagles*, p. 257, 1990

2 (of a male) to ejaculate *US, 1995*
Originally in gay use.

• I'd better be quick about it or else I'd get discovered. I needed to unload fast[.] — Howard Stern, *Miss America*, p. 27, 1995

unprofessional, that's what you are
used as a humorous if pointed insult *US, 1997*
Coined by ESPN's Keith Olberman to describe the level of play of strike-breaking, "replacement" baseball players in 1995.

• — Keith Olberman and Dan Patrick, *The Big Show*, p. 27, 1997

unscrewed *adjective*
out of control *US, 1962*

• — *American Speech*, p. 273, December 1962: "The language of traffic policemen"

unsliced *adjective*
not circumcized *US, 1988*

• — H. Max, *Gay (S)language*, p. 44, 1988

until the wheels fall off *adjective*
until a prison clique disbands; ultimately loyal *US, 1989*
Back-formation from a **CAR** (a clique).

• — James Harris, *A Convict's Dictionary*, p. 40, 1989

up *noun*

1 a tablet of amphetamine, methamphetamine, or other central nervous system stimulant *US, 1976*

• Amphetamine, Dexadrine, Benzedrine, Methadrine, and a few other variants. I had a monstrous stack of ups. — Malcolm Braley, *False Starts*, p. 276, 1976
• "Ups" all day and "downs" at night. — Beatrice Sparks (writing as "Anonymous"), *Jay's Journal*, p. 26, 1979
• [S]o banged on ups and cocaine she fell out on the floor[.] — Clarence Major, *All-Night Visitors*, p. 201, 1998

2 an inspiration; an elevated mood *US, 1966*

• So to make a long story short the Vietnamese were a great up in my life[.] — Raymond Mungo, *Famous Long Ago*, p. 11, 1970

▸ **on the up and up**
legitimate, honest *US, 1863*

• A viper doesn't like lies—he's on the up and up and makes you get on the ground floor with him. — Mezz Mezzrow, *Really the Blues*, p. 96, 1946
• Rocco decided that perhaps Jo-Jo was on the up-and-up after all—he was doing a lot of garbage-level grabs here. — Richard Price, *Clockers*, p. 421, 1992

up *verb*

1 to give up *US, 1975*

• Looks like the freak ain't upping the chain, Shoe. — Miguel Pinero, *Short Eyes*, p. 49, 1975

2 to increase a bet in cards *US, 1942*

• CHEESE: Up it fifty cents. LOONEY: I call. I call. I'm in on this one. I call. — *Tin Men*, 1987

▸ **up it**
to pay off a debt *US, 1980*

• — Joe McKennon, *Circus Lingo*, p. 99, 1980

up *adjective*

1 successful *US, 1990*

• — *Los Angeles Times*, p. B10, 5th January 1990

2 under the influence of a drug, especially LSD and, later, MDMA, the recreational drug best known as ecstasy *US, 1966*

• — J. L. Simmons and Barry Winograd, *It's Happening*, p. 174, 1966: "glossary"

3 used of waves, large *US, 1964*
Giving rise to the cry, "Surf's up!"

• — John Severson, *Modern Surfing Around the World*, p. 184, 1964

4 imprisoned *US, 1975*

• Up there I meet a lot of the boys, including Rocco Fabrizi, who was up for stealing cars. — Edwin Torres, *Carlito's Way*, p. 20, 1975

5 used of an actor in the television and movie industries, unable to remember lines *US, 1977*

- — Tony Miller and Patricia George, *Cut! Print!*, p. 188, 1977

up!

used for expressing agreement *US, 1992*

An abbreviated form of **WORD UP**.

- "Well, no more tricks. Word?" "Up." — Jess Mowry, *Way Past Cool*, p. 220, 1992

up against the wall

helpless, dominated by another; used for expressing power over others *US, 1968*

A catchphrase of the politically active in the US 1960s, echoing a police command.

- President Johnson's a fool anyway. The old fool's up against the wall. — James Simon Kunen, *The Strawberry Statement*, p. 67, 1968
- The deans found themselves up against the wall for the first time in Amerika. They didn't dig it. — Jerry Rubin, *Do It!*, p. 22, 1970

up-and-down *noun*

an order of Kessler ale and Stroh's beer *US, 1981*

- He ordered up-and-downs, Kessler and Stroh's looking at all the strange flavored brandy on the back bar. — Elmore Leonard, *Split Images*, p. 154, 1981

upchuck *noun*

1 vomit *US, 1953*

- You lying in doorways with sores all over your legs and bloody stubble on your chin and upchuck stuck all over all your clothes. — Margaret Mayorga, *The Best Short Plays*, p. 313, 1953
- If you do that then you'll need to have a puke bucket real handy, particularly if the smell of upchuck is something you don't want lingering around on the floor! — Richard Meltzer, *A Whore Just Like the Rest*, p. 77, 1970
- I survey the up-chuck on the floor and say, "No dessert today, Soapy?" — Leo Rosten, *Silky!*, p. 2, 1979

2 ground beef *US, 1996*

Playing on "ground chuck" for the beef as well as the slang for "vomit."

- — *Maledicta*, p. 23, 1996: "Domino's pizza jargon"

upchuck *verb*

to vomit *US, 1936*

- — Collin Baker et al., *College Undergraduate Slang Study Conducted at Brown University*, p. 218, 1968
- What about orange juice and milk? What's the upchuck factor on that? — *Heathers*, 1988
- After talking to the body snatcher, Nell wasn't sure whether she'd be better off trying to upchuck or work. — Joseph Wambaugh, *Finnegan's Week*, p. 161, 1993

up country *adjective*

South Vietnam north of Saigon *US, 1977*

- There must be over 3,000 of them out there now, 3,000 Vietnamese who worked for the consulate or for Americans "up country" or who knew someone who did. — Frank Snepp, *Decent Interval*, p. 240, 1977

up-est *adjective*

best *US, 2006*

- The up-est thing I remember 'bout that day was when I crossed the train tracks. — Linden Dalecki, *Kid B*, p. 76, 2006

uphills *noun*

dice that have been altered in a fashion that produces high numbers when rolled *US, 1962*

- — Frank Garcia, *Marked Cards and Loaded Dice*, p. 265, 1962

upholstered *adjective*

suffering from a sexually transmitted infection *US, 1949*

- — Vincent J. Monteleone, *Criminal Slang*, p. 247, 1949
- — Joseph E. Ragen and Charles Finston, *Inside the World's Toughest Prison*, p. 822, 1962: "Penitentiary and underworld glossary"

up jumped the devil!

used for expressing dismay at the toss of a seven by a craps player trying to make his point *US, 1950*

- — *The Annals of the American Academy of Political and Social Sciences*, p. 132, May 1950

up north *adverb*

to prison *US, 1989*

- — Ellen C. Bellone (Editor), *Dictionary of Slang*, p. 25, 1989

upper *noun*

an amphetamine or other central nervous system stimulant *US, 1973*

- I mean is it an upper or a downer? — Oscar Zeta Acosta, *The Revolt of the Cockroach People*, p. 192, 1973
- "I don't need no more uppers," Joanie said, "but downers I could use." — Emmett Grogan, *Final Score*, p. 81, 1976
- Somebody always had something to get loaded on. Uppers at times, inners, outers, whatever. — Odie Hawkins, *Scars and Memories*, pp. 115–116, 1987

upper deck *noun*

the female breasts *US, 1967*

- — Dale Gordon, *The Dominion Sex Dictionary*, p. 161, 1967

upper persuasion for lower invasion *noun*

foreplay *US, 1968*

- — Mary Swift, *Campus Slang (University of Texas)*, 1968
- The tongue would search out the partner's mouth, was frowned upon by adults who warned that it was a clear case of "upper persuasion for lower invasion." — Loretta Malandro, *Nonverbal Communication*, p. 261, 1983

uppity *noun*

arrogance, self-importance, haughtiness *US, 1974*

- "Gets off the bus like she owns this here town, sees us sittin' here, then got the uppity not to speak!" — Donald Goines, *Swamp Man*, p. 26, 1974

uppity; uppidy *adjective*

brash; arrogant; refusing to accept one's place in society *US, 1880*

Originally coined by southern blacks, now widely used.

- [He] snatched an uppity dame right up from her seat and waltzed her out on the dance floor, pince-nez and all. — Mezz Mezzrow, *Really the Blues*, p. 85, 1946
- Sapphire feels real uppity while shopping in the "better" department stores because she knows they don't expect her to be able to afford the prices. — Carolyn Greene, *70 Soul Secrets of Sapphire*, p. 28, 1973
- I'd been a uppity M.F. all along[.] — Babs Gonzales, *Movin' On Down De Line*, p. 34, 1975
- [w]hile the peckerwoods called me an uppidy nigger wench who was always fulla sass[.] — Donald Goines, *The Busting Out of an Ordinary Man*, p. 53, 1985

uprights *noun*

the legs *US, 1970*

- — Clarence Major, *Dictionary of Afro-American Slang*, p. 118, 1970

upside *preposition*

against *US, 1959*

- If she hollers cop, all yo do is bop her by going up side her head with your fist hard as lead! — Dan Burley, *Diggeth Thou?*, p. 5, 1959
- "Getting so you can't walk through the lobby on account of them going upside some simple bitch's head." — Robert Deane Pharr, *S.R.O.*, p. 183, 1971
- She slapped me and kicked me and threw me upside the wall. — Dennis Wepman et al., *The Life*, p. 53, 1976
- All of a sudden we're fuckin' surrounded, every goddamn kid I ever strip searched, busted, smacked upside the head coming out of the other two theaters. — Richard Price, *Clockers*, p. 44, 1992

upskirt *noun*

a type of voyeurism devoted to seeing what is beneath a woman's skirt *US, 1994*

- I made for myself a real … candid … upskirt video … using a miniature video camera. — *alt.sex.exhibitionism*, 22nd December 1994
- I think the file you have in mind is a picture I took last month, called upskirt.gif. — Jeff Lipchik, *alt.pantyhouse*, 5th September 1994
- What began as a small photo gallery on the Internet a couple of years ago has rapidly expanded to more than 40 such "Upskirt" sites, including one devoted entirely to shots taken up skirts in Maryland, said Duqueette, who has been tracking the trend. — *Washington Post*, p. B1, 7th June 1998
- Voyeuristic "upskirt" pages likewise feature photographs taken by tiny cameras placed in shopping bags at mall stores. — Clay Calvert, *Voyeur Nation*, p. 48, 2000

upslice *noun*

the vagina; a disagreeable woman *US, 2001*

- "So, how much is the upslice bitch paying you?" Chooch started, unexpectedly. — Stephen J. Cannell, *The Tin Collectors*, p. 34, 2001

upstairs *adverb*
in poker, in the form of a raised bet *US, 1996*
- — John Vorhaus, *The Big Book of Poker Slang*, p. 38, 1996

upstate *adjective*
1 in prison *US, 1934*
- Then the whole two years I did upstate nothing was on my mind but this girl Ann. — James Mills, *The Panic in Needle Park*, p. 54, 1966
- Your trip upstate was held up because you wasn't in no shape to make it. — A.S. Jackson, *Gentleman Pimp*, p. 128, 1973
- We were bullshitting a while about upstate when Earl sent his broad upstairs. — Edwin Torres, *Carlito's Way*, p. 28, 1975
- "You're referring, I believe," Jack said, "to when I was upstate that time?" "Upstate, that's good. Well, you seem to have enjoyed a successful rehabilitation." — Elmore Leonard, *Bandits*, p. 156, 1987

2 murdered *US, 2003*
- "He went upstate" meant the guy got whacked, and don't ask again. — Henry Hill and Byron Schreckengost, *A Good Fella's Guide to New York*, p. 61, 2003

up the Irons!
used as a greeting, especially between Iron Maiden fans *US, 1995*
Collected from fans of heavy metal music by Seamus O'Reilly, January 1995.

uptight *adjective*
1 nervous, anxious *US, 1934*
- There were a few straights but they looked very uptight and out of place. — *Berkeley Barb*, p. 1, 20th January 1967
- Same old American story: except this time the cop was dead and the white folks got real uptight about THAT. — *The Black Panther*, p. 7, 25th January 1969
- Then we came upon a crowd of people ahead of us being chased by police, who were obviously very uptight. — Malcolm Boyd, *My Fellow Americans*, p. 28, 1970
- "You're getting uptight, Preacher," Cora says smirkingly. — Arthur Blessitt, *Turned On to Jesus*, p. 159, 1971

2 inhibited; narrow-minded; very correct and straight-laced *US, 1968*
- Dig what you're doing! Make war on paranoia. Don't be afraid. Don't get uptight. — Abbie Hoffman, *Revolution for the Hell of It*, p. 28, 1968
- When you were a child, did you think of your family as up tight and plastic? — Leonard Wolfe (Editor), *Voices from the Love Generation*, p. 216, 1968
- Elvis Presley ripped off Ike Eisenhower by turning our uptight young awakening bodies around. — Jerry Rubin, *Do It!*, p. 18, 1970
- "You have no reason to get uptight." "I'm not uptight. I'm not, really." — Doug Lang, *Freaks*, p. 106, 1973
- Don't be so uptight. Give it a chance. — *King of Comedy*, 1976
- Wait, wait, don't get up tight. — *Apocalypse Now*, 1979
- You were just so up tight. Now you're much softer. — *When Harry Met Sally*, 1989
- No, man, what we swingers were rebelling against were uptight squares like you. — *Austin Powers*, 1997

3 addicted to a drug *US, 1967*
- I was a stinkin' no-good junkie, twisted out of my mind. Up tight. Bound by dope. A chronic addict. — John Gimenez, *Up Tight!*, p. 17, 1967

4 excellent *US, 1962*
- They admit that James Brown is out-of-sight, up-tight, all right, so groovy, and is probably the most exciting in-person performer. — Murray Kaufman, *Murray the K Tells It Like It Is, Baby*, p. 83, 1966

5 close, friendly *US, 1967*
- In toward the center are those persons he knows and likes best, those with whom he is "up tight"; his "walking buddies[.]" — Elliot Liebow, *Tally's Corner*, p. 163, 1967
- "I mean I'm not up tight with him, no one is." — John Williams, *The Man Who Cried I Am*, p. 27, 1967

uptown *noun*
1 cocaine *US, 1980*
Uptown is expensive and glamorous, as is cocaine.
- First I'll put your Uptown on the spoon, then to make it more exciting I'm gonna add some Downtown. They call this thing a speedball, honey, but then you must know that. — *The Bad Lieutenant*, 1992
- — Peter Johnson, *Dictionary of Street Alcohol and Drug Terms*, p. 200, 1993

2 the air space above Hanoi *US, 1990*
- — Joseph Tuso, *Singing the Vietnam Blues*, p. 249, 1990: Glossary

3 in pool, the area at the head of the table *US, 1993*
- — Mike Shamos, *The Illustrated Encyclopedia of Billiards*, p. 259, 1993

uptown *adjective*
upscale, prosperous *US, 1946*
- BB: Then we'd just lean on the door of the club in the alley and listen to the music. I think the girls were looking for something a bit more uptown. — *Tin Men*, 161

up your nose with a rubber hose
used as a general-purpose, nonsensical insult *US, 1975*
A signature line of Vinnie Barbarino, played by John Travolta, on the television comedy *Welcome Back, Kotter* (ABC, 1975–79). Repeated with referential humor.
- "Up your nose with a rubber hose," Lee yelled to him. "Shut the fuck up," Jasper called back. — Susan Issacs, *Lily White*, p. 131, 1997

uranium *noun*
money *US, 1961*
- Uranium—money, bread, loot. — Art Unger, *The Cool Book*, p. 106, 1961

urine express *noun*
an elevator in a public housing project *US, 1997*
New York police slang.
- — Samuel M. Katz, *Anytime Anywhere*, p. 391, 1997: "The extremely unofficial and completely off-the-record NYPD/ESU truck-two glossary"

urkel *noun*
a social outcast *US, 2003*
From the archetypal nerd character Urkel on the 1990s situation comedy "Family Matters."
- "[T]he kid is first-team all-ghetto, has like fifty college scouts at his house, cock of the walk, banging all the cheerleaders, all the Urkels are lining up to do his homework for him[.]" — Richard Price, *Samaritan*, p. 211, 2003

use *verb*
to use drugs, especially addictive drugs such as heroin *US, 1971*
Used without an object. A euphemism, but one which is crystal clear in slang context.
- She remembered the beautiful times they had had together before Teddy started using. — Donald Goines, *Dopefiend*, p. 20, 1971
- She was getting by well and we started using. — Herbert Huncke, *Guilty of Everything*, p. 103, 1990
- Listen, yewer not a fuckin' ex-junkie, mun, yewer a fuckin' junkie who's not using at the mo. — Niall Griffiths, *Sheepshagger*, p. 138, 2001

used beer department *noun*
a toilet *US, 1995*
Modified to "used coffee department" and the like for office settings.
- — Roger E. Axtell, *Do's and Taboos of Using English Around the world*, 1995
- The used beer department is down those steps over there. — Theodore Sturgeon, *When You're Smiling*, p. 239, 2002

useless smile *noun*
used for describing the happy, vacant facial expression of someone under the influence of LSD *US, 1994*
- — David Shenk and Steve Silberman, *Skeleton Key*, p. 300, 1994

ush *verb*
to work as an usher in a theater *US, 1981*
- — Don Wilmeth, *The Language of American Popular Entertainment*, p. 286, 1981

UTA *adjective*
in abundance *US, 1986*
- I learned early that "Gook," meaning any North Korean soldier, and UTA, "up to the ass," meaning abundance, were the most frequently used expressions in conversation. — William B. Hopkins, *One Drum No Bugle*, p. 41, 1986

UUUU
used as an antiauthority slogan by US soldiers during the Vietnam war *US, 1991*
- In the late 1960's, some soldiers in Vietnam began to write UUUU on their helmet liners, meaning the unwilling, led by the

unqualified, doing the immecessary for the ungrateful. — Christian G. Appy, *Working-Class War*, p. 43, 1993

UVs *noun*
sun rays *US, 1968*
An abbreviation of "*u*ltra-*v*iolet *s*un rays."
- — Collin Baker et al., *College Undergraduate Slang Study Conducted at Brown University*, p. 216, 1968
- — Mimi Pond, *The Valley Girl's Guide to Life*, p. 63, 1982
- — Anna Scotti and Paul Young, *Buzzwords*, p. 84, 1997

Uzi *noun*
a pipe used for smoking crack cocaine *US, 1994*
- — US Department of Justice, *Street Terms*, October 1994

uzzfay *noun*
a police officer *US, 1955*
Pig Latin for **FUZZ**.
- — *American Speech*, p. 88, May 1955: "Narcotic argot along the Mexican border"

Vv

V *noun*

1 Valium™ *US, 1984*
- Of course, the last time you took a V, you were wired on C. — Jay McInerney, *Bright Lights, Big City*, p. 141, 1984

2 a visit *US, 2002*
- — Gary K. Farlow, *Prison-ese*, p. 77, 2002

3 a five-year prison sentence *US, 1945*
From the Roman numeral for five.
- — Lou Shelly, *Hepcats Jive Talk Dictionary*, p. 20, 1945
- — Joseph E. Ragen and Charles Finston, *Inside the World's Toughest Prison*, p. 822, 1962: "Penitentiary and underworld glossary"
- They sent me up the river to do a little V. — Roger Abrahams, *Positively Black*, p. 48, 1970

4 five dollars *US, 1962*
- — Joseph E. Ragen and Charles Finston, *Inside the World's Toughest Prison*, p. 822, 1962: "Penitentiary and underworld glossary"

5 marijuana *US, 1979*
- Yeah, they got stoned on giggle-weed, zonked on grifa, zapped on yerba, bombed on boo, they were blitzed with snop, warped on twist, gay on hay, free on V. — *Hi Life*, p. 14, 1979

V-8s *noun*

men's shorts *US, 1972*
- How then could I run around with just my jockey shorts? V-8s don't hide fat, you know. — Oscar Zeta Acosta, *The Autobiography of a Brown Buffalo*, p. 82, 1972
- — Dagoberto Fuentes and Jose Lopez, *Barrio Language Dictionary*, p. 153, 1974

vacation *noun*

time spent in jail or prison *US, 1971*
- — Hermese E. Roberts, *The Third Ear*, 1971

vag *noun*

1 vagrancy; a criminal charge of vagrancy *US, 1859*
- I wish I knew what that charge was! Vag, probably; take all my money and charge me vag. — Jack Kerouac, *On the Road*, p. 136, 1957
- [Y]ou can't even enjoy the sights and scenery and have always to be on the watch for the policeman who will pick you up for vag[.] — Clancy Sigal, *Going Away*, p. 138, 1961
- But if you don't have a pad, they'll bust you for vag. — John Rechy, *City of Night*, p. 319, 1963
- He says he was sittin' in a cell in a Southwest jail / where he landed doin' three days for vag. — Bruce Jackson, *Get Your Ass in the Water and Swim Like Me*, p. 82, 1966

2 a vagrant *US, 1868*
- I could tell you a few more stories of how cops treat suspected vags on the road but one story would be like another. — Clancy Sigal, *Going Away*, p. 138, 1961
- "But we ain't Vag," Glenn offered. "We got money, a car. We got jobs. We're regular citizens." — Earl Thompson, *Tattoo*, p. 483, 1974

vag *verb*

to charge someone with vagrancy *US, 1859*
- If you were on the north side of the street broke you got vagged, because that's where all the nice stores were. — Robert Byrne, *McGoorty*, p. 147, 1972

vage; vag; vadge; vaj *noun*

the vagina *US, 1986*
- Another shot has Uncle Lou returning the gesture, copping a generous helping of boob and vage. — Josh Alan Friedman, *Tales of Times Square*, p. 30, 1986
- It was well nigh impossible to achieve "full-vage-pen" by breeching aside the crotch panel of this snug-fitting garment. — Terry Southern, *Now Dig This*, p. 3, 1986
- Then I buried it all the way in and turned the vibe up to full strength, stroking it in and out of my vag. — Maxim Jakubowski, *The Mammoth Book of Sex Diaries*, p. 251, 2005

vagina sausage *noun*

a Vienna sausage *US, 1991*
- It was loaded with "vagina" (Vienna) sausages, shoestring potatoes, peanuts, a large hard salami, two jars of Tang, forty packages of presweetend Kook-Aid, and four "male" (with nuts) Hershey bars[.] — Gary Linderer, *The Eyes of the Eagle*, p. 119, 1991

vagina vandal *noun*

a rapist *US, 1962*
- — Joseph E. Ragen and Charles Finston, *Inside the World's Toughest Prison*, p. 822, 1962: "Penitentiary and underworld glossary"

vajayjay *noun*

the vagina *US, 2000*
A euphemism that built great popular acceptance in large part due to Oprah Winfrey's embrace.
- So get the sand out of your vaJayJay and shut up. — *rec.roller-coaster*, 24th June 2005
- And, now, for those of you dity little bastards out there who want to see the pictures of Britney's vajayjay—click here. — *funkybrownchick.com*, 30th November 2006
- "I would never have come up with 'vajayjay' if standards and practices hadn't told me we couldn't say 'vagina' one more time in our show." — *Daily News (New York)*, 16th January 2007

val *noun*

a resident of the San Fernando Valley, Los Angeles County, California *US, 1982*
- — Sue Black, *The Totally Awesome Val Guide*, p. 23, 1982
- — Lee Wardlaw, *Cowabunga! The Complete Book of Surfing*, p. 158, 1991
- Looks like we're going to have to make a cameo at the Val party. — *Clueless*, 1995

valentine *noun*

1 a very short jail sentence *US, 1949*
- — Vincent J. Monteleone, *Criminal Slang*, p. 247, 1949
- — Marlene Freedman, *Alcatraz*, 1983

2 in college, a notification of academic deficiency *US, 1968*
- — *American Speech*, pp. 76–77, February 1968: "Some notes on flunk notes"

valet *noun*

in a deck of playing cards, a jack *US, 1988*
- — George Percy, *The Language of Poker*, p. 95, 1988

valley *noun*

the antecubital vein at the inside of the elbow, a prime site for intravenous drug injections *US, 1967*
- VALLEY: The inside of the elbow which has two large veins. — Elizabeth Finn, *Drugs in the Tenderloin*, 1967: Glossary of Drug Slang Used in the Tenderloin
- — William D. Alsever, *Glossary for the Establishment and Other Uptight People*, p. 19, December 1970

▶ **the Valley**

1 the San Fernando Valley, Los Angeles County, California *US, 1994*
- This is the Valley, Vincent. Marsellus don't got no friendly places in the Valley. — *Pulp Fiction*, 1994
- So, anyway, the whole crew is going to this party in the Valley. — *Clueless*, 1995

2 a low-lying area east of Seventh Avenue in Harlem, New York *US, 1966*
- We'd better take a look in the valley before checking in. — Chester Himes, *Come Back Charleston Blue*, p. 24, 1966

Valleyite *noun*

a resident of the San Fernando Valley, Los Angeles *US, 1985*
- "Fucking Valleyites," loudly enough for her to hear. "Go spend the rest of it at the Galleria, or wherever the hell you go to[.]" — Bret Easton Ellis, *Less Than Zero*, p. 62, 1985

vamoose *verb*

to go; to leave *US, 1834*

- For a split second I deliberated whether to vamoose but I watched Cass for a clue and the clue didn't come. — Frederick Kohner, *Gidget*, p. 113, 1957
- Beat it, flake, fug off, vamoose, split, get the everlovin' hell outa here and let me get ready t'go on! — Robert Gover, *Here Goes Kitten*, p. 40, 1964
- Scram, beat it, vamoose, out! Is that plain enough? — *King of Comedy*, 1976

V and X *noun*

in carnival usage, a five-and-dime store *US, 1981*

- — Don Wilmeth, *The Language of American Popular Entertainment*, p. 286, 1981

vanilla *adjective*

1 ordinary, simple, basic *US, 1977*

Derives from the plainest ice cream variety.

- — Guy L. Steele et al., *The Hacker's Dictionary*, p. 129, 1983
- The food is the same straight vanilla, greasy-spoon bill of fare as the Texas Lunch. — Larry Heinemann, *Paco's Story*, p. 105, 1986
- It wasn't that exotic or anything, your basic vanilla, really, but he was so young and appreciative, and he kissed like an angel. — Armistead Maupin, *Maybe the Moon*, p. X, 1992
- "You're plain-vanilla, remember?" Harper nodded. "And the plain-vanilla motive is money." — Lee Child, *The Visitor*, p. 329, 2000

2 of sex, conventional; of homosexual sex, gentle, traditional, emotional *US, 1977*

- Then again, you say that you want nothing more adventurous than straight vanilla, morning reveille, missionary-position screwing. — Larry Heinemann, *Close Quarters*, p. 171, 1977
- Vanilla is a term used by S-M people to describe conventional, non-S-M sexual intercourse. — Robert Stoller and I.S. Levine, *Coming Attractions*, p. 49, 1991
- Be ready to shift to vanilla sex if he can't handle the specialty when the real thing is actually taking place. — John Preston, *Hustling*, p. 163, 1994
- I hadn't been wrong about the people who attended these things [fetish-themed nightclubs]—they really were much better behaved than their vanilla counterparts. — Claire Mansfield and John Mendelssohn, *Dominatrix*, p. 102, 2002

3 used of pornography, relatively highbrow, designed for couples and first-time viewers *US, 2000*

- — Ana Loria, *1 2 3 Be A Porn Star!*, p. 165, 2000: "Glossary of adult sex industry terms"

4 white-skinned, Caucasian *US, 1994*

Originally black usage, now widespread.

- I noticed a lot of Jungle Fever action, with people describing themselves as "vanilla" or "chocolate" or "caramel." — Anka Radakovich, *The Wild Girls Club*, p. 43, 1994

vapor lock *noun*

a temporary loss of common sense or memory *US, 1996*

An allusion to a mechanical problem with the carburetor of an internal combustion engine.

- — John Vorhaus, *The Big Book of Poker Slang*, p. 38, 1996

vaporware *noun*

in computing, a program that is announced well before it is completed and released *US, 1991*

- — Eric S. Raymond, *The New Hacker's Dictionary*, p. 366, 1991

varicose alley *noun*

the platform that extends from a stage used by strippers out into the audience *US, 1945*

- — *Time*, 12th March 1945
- Only the soubrettes and chorines played on "Varicose Alley," as the runway was nicknamed[.] — William Green, *Strippers and Coochers*, p. 163, 1977
- — *Detroit Free Press*, 19th December 1977

Vatican roulette *noun*

birth control by the rhythm method *US, 1960*

- During a discussion of birth control and rhythm he contributed a remark about "Vatican roulette" that was as uncharitable as it was unoriginal. — *New York Times*, p. 79, 15th March 1960
- — *Maledicta*, p. 173, 1979: "A glossary of ethnic slurs in American English"

vato; bato *noun*

a guy *US, 1950*

Border Spanish used in English conversation by Mexican-Americans.

- — George Carpenter Baker, *Pachuco*, p. 40, January 1950
- I'll hotwire it. Car theft is my Vato speciality. — Stephen J. Cannell, *The Tin Collectors*, p. 326, 2001

vato loco; bato loco *noun*

a wild guy *US, 1965*

- The label implies a permanency of behavior and a prediction: once a Mexican-American becomes a vato loco, he will continue to perform those acts and engage in those activities which "fit" the label. — George R. Alvarez, *Semiotic Dynamics of an Ethnic-American Sub-Cultural Group*, p. 4, 1965
- "This parolee of mine, this bato loco, this glue-sniffer—" — Frank Bonham, *Viva Chicano*, p. 19, 1970
- And the only difference, really, is that the ex-cons are old enough to have done time for the same things the batos locos haven't been arrested for, yet. — Hunter S. Thompson, *Fear and Loathing in Las Vegas*, p. 230, 1971
- In the cities, only the lowriders, the vatos locos, are in tune with this. — Oscar Zeta Acosta, *The Revolt of the Cockroach People*, p. 67, 1973

vault *noun*

a hotel baggage checkroom *US, 1954*

- The doorman said to me, "You wanted to know when they come outa the vault, Mister Collans." — Dev Collans with Stewart Sterling, *I was a House Detective*, p. 71, 1954

va va voom *noun*

style; a powerful or seductive style *US, 1996*

- [A] beaded backless number—like ELIZABETH DOLE's frock, but with more va-va-va-voom—for the ball. — *Time*, 7th October 1996

VC *noun*

the Viet Cong; a member of the Viet Cong *US, 1966*

- Vietnamese Communists, we call them Vietcong, we call them VC and C and Charlie and all the usual names[.] — William Wilson, *The LBJ Brigade*, p. 31, 1966
- "Now, as you can clearly see, contrary to what you've heard, th' VC is clearly distinguishable form his Vietnamese counterpart in th' south." — Michael Hodgson, *With Sgt. Mike in Vietnam*, p. 32, 1970

V-card *noun*

a person's virginity *US, 1999*

- No, she plays the big V-card, and says she's glad she didn't waste her previous virginity on a guy like you. — alt.tv.felicity, 30th May 1999
- — Pamela Munro, *U.C.L.A. Slang*, p. 114, 2001
- He talks about holding his "v-card" (virginity), while other friends are "dealing" theirs. — *Christian Science Monitor*, p. 1, 4th December 2002
- "To be perfectly honest, I just lost my own V-card a few nights ago." — Marty Beckerman, *Generation S.L.U.T.*, p. 120, 2004
- I'm a sophomore in college, and at times guys try to pressure me to turn in my V-card. — *Teenpeople*, p. 121, April 2004

VCR *noun*

a vicious campus rumor *US, 1966*

- — *Current Slang*, p. 8, Winter 1966

VD bonnet *noun*

a condom *US, 1972*

A reference to the prevention of venereal disease.

- Well, before I know it she's tied a balloon on it / One of those snug little V.D. bonnets. — *Screw*, p. 7, 15th May 1972

veal cutlet *noun*

in gambling cheating schemes, a victim *US, 1962*

- — Frank Garcia, *Marked Cards and Loaded Dice*, p. 265, 1962

veddy *adverb*

very *UK, 1859*

A jocular pronunciation, approximating a child's, or an American's (attempting a "British" accent), rendering of "very."

- "Do I make myself clear?" "Veddy, and how nice." — Hal Ellson, *Summer Street*, pp. 83–84, 1953
- [A]n amusing but bizarrely simplistic clash of personalities and cultures: the veddy English old maid and the ooh-la-la French slut. — *The Village Voice (New York)*, 2nd July 2003

vee *noun*

sex involving three people, two of whom are focused on the pleasure of the third *US, 1995*

- 'Vee' is three people where the structure puts one person at the "hinge" of the vee, also called the pivot. In a vee, the arm partners are not as commonly close to each other as each is to the pivot. — Nancy Tamosaitis, *net.sex*, p. 101, 1995

veeblefetzer *noun*
a corporate manager *US, 1997*
Not a term of endearment.
- — Andy Ihnatko, *Cyberspeak*, p. 204, 1997

vegetable *noun*
a person who is mentally and physically incapacitated to a degree that renders the comparison with a plant organism fair if cruel *UK, 1921*
- Got a brother, Anthony. He's a fuckin' vegetable. In '77 he smoked a bag of dust he bought from a dago. He jumped off our roof. — *New Jack City*, 1990
- Your grandmother was a 92-year-old vegetable. Only the machines were keeping her alive. — C.D. Payne, *Youth in Revolt*, p. 206, 1993
- The prison board is blatantly railroading you into a hospital for the sole purpose of turning you into vegetables. — *Natural Born Killers*, 1994

vegetable garden *noun*
a group of neurologically depressed hospital patients *US, 1978*
- — *Maledicta*, p. 70, Summer/Winter 1978: "Common patient-directed pejoratives used by medical personnel"

vegged out *adjective*
relaxed and inactive *US, 2001*
- I was vegged out on the floor. At some point the methadone had kicked in real heavy[.] — Jason Parkinson, *Skateboards and Methadone [The Howard Marks Book of Dope Stories]*, p. 208, 2001

veggie *noun*
a vegetable *US, 1955*
- The thin lipped man worked next to him, distributing the veggies. — Odie Hawkins, *Great Lawd Buddha*, p. 113, 1990
- And I can't find an affordable restaurant in San Diego that serves any veggies except cauliflower and broccoli. If I could ever get a side order of green beans or spinach I'd stand up and cheer. — Joseph Wambaugh, *Floaters*, p. 228, 1996

veg out *verb*
to relax and do nothing *US, 1986*
- [W]ith diabetes and a crummy pump, vegging out on All My Children, As the World Turns, refusing to watch or even think about General Hospital. — Geoffrey Wolff, *Providence*, p. 89, 1986
- I know it sounds mental, but sometimes I have more fun vegging out than when I go partying. — *Clueless*, 1995

veins *noun*
▸ **get veins**
in bodybuilding, to achieve definition, or well-developed and sculpted muscles *US, 1984*
- — *American Speech*, p. 200, Fall 1984: "The language of bodybuilding"

velvet *noun*
gambling winnings *US, 1974*
- — John Scarne, *Scarne on Dice*, p. 481, 1974

▸ **on velvet**
in good shape *US, 1997*
- Now, so long as the print server doesn't go down before we have the chance to print the report, we're on velvet. — Andy Ihnatko, *Cyberspeak*, p. 140, 1997

velvet mafia *noun*
collectively, influential homosexual Republican political staffers and operatives in Washington *US, 2000*
The influence of gay Republicans in Washington first came to public attention during the Iran-Contra scandal of 1986, when it was revealed that many of the men in Oliver North's inner circle were homosexual.
- A handful of Republicans—including presidential candidate George W. Bush and former presidential candidate John McCain—reeped just $34,000 from the gay activist leaders, previously known in the popular press as "the velvet mafia." — *Washington Times*, p. C1, 28th May 2000
- Known in some insider slang as the Velvet Mafia or the Pink Elephants, gay Republicans tend to be less open about their sexual orientation than their Democratic counterparts. — *New York Times*, p. A20, 8th October 2006

vendor *noun*
a juke box *US, 1965*
- I got up, walked to the vendor, put a dime in, and told her to go back in the back. — Henry Williamson, *Hustler!*, p. 154, 1965

vent *noun*
▸ **take it to the vent**
to commit suicide *US, 1989*
- I don't want to hear about it, asshole! Take it to the vent if you can't handle your own problems. — James Harris, *A Convict's Dictionary*, p. 40, 1989

ventilate *verb*
to shoot someone *US, 1947*
From the image of bullet holes ventilating the body.
- To ventilate your foul ticker if I parted Junior's crew cut. — Harry Haenigsen, *Jive's Like That*, 1947
- "So you got to assume that he made the contact. Unless he's been ventilated." — Dale Krame, *Teen-Age Gangs*, p. 30, 1953
- [T]wo coppers who'd just as soon wing him or ventilate him or just play the carom. — William Brashler, *City Dogs*, p. 10, 1976
- Any bullshit and I'll ventilate yo ass right here. — *Menace II Society*, 1993

ventilator *noun*
a machine gun *US, 1962*
- — *American Speech*, p. 273, December 1962: "The language of traffic policemen"

versatile *adjective*
willing to play the passive role in homosexual sex *US, 1994*
- If you use the word "versatile," it means you're willing to get fucked. — John Preston, *Hustling*, p. 120, 1994

verse *verb*
to compete against *US, 1984*
A corruption of the preposition "versus," almost always heard in the progressive form.
- We're going to be versing the Brown Bombers next week. — *New York Times*, p. B3, 20th February 1984
- "It doesn't matter who I'm versing, I want to win," Hicks said after placing third in the nationals. — *Rockford (Illinois) Register Star*, p. 6D, 31st August 2004

very *adjective*
excellent *US, 1989*
- Come on, it'll be Very. The note'll give her shower nozzle masturbation material for weeks. — *Heathers*, 1989

vest *noun*
a showoff *US, 1965*
- — *Time*, p. 56, 1st January 1965: "Students: the slang bag"

vest out *verb*
to retire from police service after investing in the pension plan with 15 years of service *US, 1997*
New York police slang.
- — Samuel M. Katz, *Anytime Anywhere*, p. 391, 1997: "The extremely unofficial and completely off-the-record NYPD/ESU truck-two glossary"

vet *noun*
an ex-member of the military *US, 1848*
- Brooke Army Medical Center was the final destination for thousands of wounded Vietnam vets and was better known to the inmates as BAMC. — Bill Goshen, *War Paint*, p. 171, 2001

veterano *noun*
an experienced, respected gang member *US, 1975*
Spanish used by English-speakers.
- [H]e had fought his way through the elaborate gang hierarchy to emerge as a seasoned veterano covered with battle wounds and glory. — Joseph Wambaugh, *The Choirboys*, p. 38, 1975

veterinarian *noun*
a physician who regards his patients as of animal intelligence *US, 1978*
- — *Maledicta*, p. 70, Summer/Winter 1978: "Common patient-directed pejoratives used by medical personnel"

V girl *noun*
a woman who is attracted to men in military uniform *US, 1960*
- They had dances all over that year, it was a beginning to ease juvenile delinquency, gang rumbles, V-girls. — Gilbert Sorrentino, *Steelwork*, p. 86, 1970

vibe; vibes *noun*
the atmosphere generated by any event; mood; nuances intimately related to all senses *US, 1967*

An abbreviation of "vibration," which has the same meaning.

- — Joe David Brown (Editor), *The Hippies*, p. 219, 1967: "Glossary of hippie terms"
- I don't care for Berkeley vibes. — Leonard Wolfe (Editor), *Voices from the Love Generation*, p. 92, 1968
- [L]ead you to draw bad conclusions (or "bad vibes" as they say in the rock biz) about what happened. — Abbie Hoffman, *Woodstock Nation*, p. 4, 1969
- They [members of the Hog Farm commune at Woodstock] established very good vibes, had plenty of food (the lines were sometimes long, but usually moved quickly), good food and were really together. — *East Village Other*, 20th August 1969
- I was at an Alice Cooper thing where six people were rushed to the hospital with bad vibes. — *Annie Hall*, 1977

vibrations *noun*
the atmosphere generated by any event; mood; nuances intimately related to all senses *US, 1966*

- Words were used to sparkle eyes, break mouths into smiles, letters into tongued vibrations and meaning in-coherent. — *Berkeley Barb*, p. 3, 21st October 1966
- — Joe David Brown (Editor), *The Hippies*, p. 219, 1967: "Glossary of hippie terms"
- I limped onto the plane with no problem except a wave of ugly vibrations from the other passengers[.] — Hunter S. Thompson, *Fear and Loathing in Las Vegas*, p. 202, 1971

vic *noun*
a victim *US, 1968*

- — *Current Slang*, p. 51, Fall 1968
- I said, "Jack, your score is zero. I'm not a 'vic.'" — Iceberg Slim (Robert Beck), *Pimp*, p. 97, 1969
- I get a call telling me to come out and seal the vic's appartment until the leads show up. — Robert Crais, *L.A. Requiem*, p. 38, 1999
- "I have seen it happen, some strong-arm psycho go down and down on the same vic time after time like they're a goddamn soda machine." — Richard Price, *Samaritan*, p. 191, 2003

vice jockey *noun*
a member of a police vice squad *US, 1967*

- "I was busted a few times, but the last one looked bad because the John had turned out to be a vice jockey." — Robert Newton, *Bondage Clubs U.S.A.*, p. 55, 1967

vice president *noun*
in poker, the player with the second best hand *US, 1988*

- — George Percy, *The Language of Poker*, p. 95, 1988

vice versa *noun*
reciprocal oral sex between two lesbians *US, 1963*
The earliest known lesbian periodical in the US (1947) was named *Vice Versa*.

- — Donald Webster Cory and John P. LeRoy, *The Homosexual and His Society*, p. 266, 1963: "A lexicon of homosexual slang"
- — *The Guild Dictionary of Homosexual Terms*, p. 48, 1965
- — *Maledicta*, p. 138, Summer/Winter 1982: "Dyke diction: the language of lesbians"

vicious *adjective*
handsome *US, 1982*

- — Lillian Glass with Richard Liebmann-Smith, *How to Deprogram Your Valley Girl*, p. 29, 1982

vick *verb*
to steal *US, 1993*
Probably an evolution from "victim."

- — Kenn "Naz" Young, *Naz's Dictionary of Teen Slang*, p. 135, 1993
- "That Cad got vicked last week when I was shopping in Beverly." — Stephen J. Cannell, *White Sister*, p. 47, 2006

Victor Charlie; Victor Charles *nickname*
the Viet Cong *US, 1966*

- — *Austin (Texas) Statesman*, p. 7A, 9th January 1966
- The Viet Cong is also known as the "VC" and many American servicemen use these initials to call the Viet Cong "Victor Charlie" or just plain "Charlie." — *San Francisco Examiner and Chronicle*, p. 17, 22nd May 1966
- "Am evading possible two companies Victor Charlie." — Donald Duncan, *The New Legions*, p. 48, 1967
- Old Victor Charlie's got a pretty daughter / She's out a roamin' every night. — Joseph Tuso, *Singing the Vietnam Blues*, p. 191, 1990: Tay Ninh Mountain

victory girl *noun*
a woman whose patriotic fervor motivated sexual relationships with members of the military during World War 2 *US, 1949*

- Victory Girls are no longer with us. — William Bernard, *Jailbait*, p. 21, 1949

Viet *noun*
a Vietnamese person *US, 1966*

- The Viets don't like us. — William Wilson, *The LBJ Brigade*, p. 36, 1966
- I stood on the driver's seat, out of breath, but exhilarated, and stared back down the road at the Viets[.] — Larry Heinemann, *Close Quarters*, p. 82, 1977
- Every Viet in base camp crowded the doorways and screened windows, and such as that, gawking at Jonesy. — Larry Heinemann, *Paco's Story*, p. 8, 1986

Viet shits *noun*
diarrhea *US, 1984*

- — John Elting, *A Dictionary of Soldier Talk*, p. 732, 1984
- There are no young men in war. You're nineteen or twenty, and you become old with the first case of the Viet shits. — Paul Ruth Gilbert, *Violence and Gender*, p. 101, 2003

vig *noun*
interest owed on an illegal loan *US, 1971*
A shortened form of **VIGORISH**.

- Senator Percy: Is this also known as the vig in the New York area? Mr. Teresa. Right. The Vig. The juice. — United States Senate, *Organized Crime: Stolen Securities*, p. 834, 1971
- "What's the vig rate down here?" — Joseph Pistone, *Donnie Brasco*, p. 250, 1987
- He wants three points over the vig. From me? — *Goodfellas*, 1990
- Well, basically, this guy owes a shylock fifteen thousand, plus he's a few weeks behind on the vig, the interest you have to pay. — *Get Shorty*, 1995

vigorish *noun*
1 the interest owed on an illegal loan *US, 1966*
Yiddish slang from the Russian *vyigrysh* (winnings-out-to-pay).

- [O]btained thousands of dollars that he could put to work at the loan shark's vigorish rate of 260 percent. — Fred Cook, *The Secret Rulers*, p. 366, 1966
- He waited, but always collected his money plus the 20 percent "vigorish" (interest). — Phil Hirsch, *Hooked*, p. 101, 1968
- He wore Air corps sunglasses, combed his hair into a gelatinous country pomp and tithed his pay and tithed the vigorish on his sharking. — Earl Thompson, *Tattoo*, p. 293, 1974
- It costs a hundred a week vigorish to borrow the bone. — Robert Campbell, *Juice*, p. 20, 1988

2 courage *US, 1960*

- "I'm sorry to crap out like this, Danny," he said, "but I don't have the vigorish for this job." — George Clayton Johnson, *Ocean's Eleven*, p. 187, 1960

vikes *noun*
the prescription drug Vicodin™ *US, 1996*

- "You give him the Vike," former defensive lineman John Jurkovic is quoted as saying in Return to Glory. — *Chicago Sun-Times*, p. 2 (Sports), 7th August 1996
- Deputies said the voice on the other end asked to buy some "viks." — *St. Petersburg (Florida) Times*, p. 9, 18th December 1998
- Hence, to score Vike, they have to be fronting that they are in some serious pain. — Suroosh Alvi et al., *The Vice Guide*, p. 109, 2002
- "Vikes," he said. "But I et up the whole damn bottle the first day!" — Carl Hiaasen, *Nature Girl*, p. 148, 2006

Viking queen *noun*
in homosexual usage, a muscular, blonde man *US, 1986–1987*

- — *Maledicta*, p. 60, 1986–1987: "A continuation of a glossary of ethnic slurs in American English"

vill *noun*
a village or town *US, 1976*
Found in the poetry of the early C18, but not particularly thereafter until the war in Vietnam.

- Well, I got some [money], but not enough for the vill again. — Charles Anderson, *The Grunts*, p. 17, 1976

Village *noun*
▸ **the Village**
Greenwich Village, New York, a small neighborhood below 14th Street and west of Broadway, haven to Bohemians *US, 1929*

- They had arranged to meet at nine that evening at Freeman's, which was a Village bar. — John Clellon Holmes, *Go*, p. 79, 1952

village *adjective*
unsophisticated, out of touch with trends *US, 2002*

- — *Woman's Weekly*, p. 53, 23rd July 2002

-ville *suffix*

used for making or emphasizing an adjective; used in combination with a characteristic to describe a place or a condition *US, 1891*

Modern usage began with the beats. By the mid-1970s this form was presumed obsolete and had been replaced by "-city."

- "Weirdsville," said the baby bear. — Steve Allen, *Bop Fables*, p. 10, 1955
- "Dullsville," said Comfort, lying on her back and regarding her toes. — Max Shulman, *Rally Round the Flag, Boys!*, p. 57, 1957
- It's probably a lousy story and can't hold a candle to those French novels from Sexville[.] — Frederick Kohner, *Gidget*, p. 3, 1957
- — *American Speech*, pp. 312–314, December 1960: "The highly productive suffix '-ville'"
- What do you say about yourself when your language is strictly from Teensville? — Dick Clark, *To Goof or Not to Goof*, p. 159, 1963

Vincent *nickname*

the Viet Cong; a member of the Viet Cong *US, 1965*

- — *Life*, p. 71, 26th November 1965
- — Carl Fleischhauer, *A Glossary of Army Slang*, p. 25, 1968

vine *noun*

1 a men's suit; clothing *US, 1932*

- I wanted to see Daisy so bad—as bad as she wanted to see me—that I decided one afternoon to put on my sharpest vine. — Louis Armstrong, *Satchmo*, p. 152, 1954
- I'd walk up the stairs at number 129 cool, oh so cool, wearing my best vines. — Piri Thomas, *Down These Mean Streets*, p. 324, 1967
- It was the one who had a Thunderbird, and some clean vines. — H. Rap Brown, *Die Nigger Die!*, p. 9, 1969
- Safari shirt and pants, tan colored, I'm pressed, but not like them vines Cye Martin used to drape on me. — Edwin Torres, *After Hours*, p. 272, 1979

2 the penis *US, 1972*

- After that, Maria never bothered me again, she just told everyone at JJ's about my dead vine. — Oscar Zeta Acosta, *The Autobiography of a Brown Buffalo*, p. 46, 1972

vine down *verb*

to dress up *US, 1969*

- He'd drop by the school and be vined down. He was clean, Jim. Had him a conk then and he knew he was ready. — H. Rap Brown, *Die Nigger Die!*, p. 24, 1969

violin cases *noun*

large, heavy shoes *US, 1946*

- When you stood up and put your weight on those violin cases you thought you were standing barefoot over the iron grating of a subway ventilator. — Mezz Mezzrow, *Really the Blues*, p. 33, 1946

viper *noun*

a marijuana user *US, 1938*

A term of the 1930s with some lingering use until the 1960s.

- He was a musician from the heart, a solid viper. I hope he finally caught that Muggles Special and rode it straight on to glory, high as a Georgia pine[.] — Mezz Mezzrow, *Really the Blues*, pp. 52–53, 1946
- But she knew how easily she could relinquish that sense of responsibility with which she had this time gone to Carter, how simply she could become a Viper again and laugh at the meaning of days. — George Mandel, *Flee the Angry Strangers*, p. 27, 1952
- Light a tea and let it be if you're a viper. — Iceberg Slim (Robert Beck), *Pimp*, p. 129, 1969
- The viper. A rare snake that can be smoked. — Lenny Bruce, *The Unpublished Lenny Bruce*, p. 71, 1984

virgin *noun*

a person who has not contracted a sexually transmitted infection *US, 1947*

- — *American Speech*, p. 56, February 1947: "Pacific War language"

virgin ears *noun*

used, usually in the first person, for a claim of innocence in matters sexual or profane *US, 1935*

- — *Current Slang*, p. 26, Spring 1970
- I tried to close my virgin ears to their horrid cackling. — John Kennedy Toole, *A Confederacy of Dunces*, p. 231, 1980
- "Am I embarrassing you over there, Lorna?" Leo called. "Hurting those virgin ears of yours." — Wally Lamb, *I Know This Much Is True*, p. 192, 1998

Virginia vitamin *noun*

any central nervous system stimulant *US, 1977*

- — Bill Davis, *Jawjacking*, p. 103, 1977

Virgin Mary *noun*

a nonalcoholic version of the Bloody Mary, made with tomato juice, horseradish, Worcestershire and/or Tabasco sauce, celery, salt and black pepper; unadulterated tomato juice *US, 1976*

A tasty pun, using "virgin" as "nonalcoholic."

- She had passed the time drinking Virgin Marys and surveying the dance talent[.] — Carl Hiaasen, *Strip Tease*, p. 258, 1993

virgin pie *noun*

cherry pie *US, 1952*

- — *American Speech*, p. 233, October 1952: "The argot of soda jerks"

virgin principle *noun*

the belief among gamblers that a beginner will have good luck *US, 1993*

- — Frank Scoblete, *Guerrilla Gambling*, p. 331, 1993

virgin state *noun*

the period when a person has started using an addictive drug but is not yet fully addicted *US, 1970*

- — William D. Alsever, *Glossary for the Establishment and Other Uptight People*, p. 15, December 1970

virus *noun*

1 HIV, the human immunodeficiency virus *US, 1992*

- The Virus wasn't a disease, it was a personal message from God or the Devil. — Richard Price, *Clockers*, p. 64, 1992
- Ella is dressed in black yet again, for a neighbor's son, a man dead from the virus after years on the corner. — David Simon and Edward Burns, *The Corner*, p. 129, 1997
- She wasn't going to beat around the bush. "I caught the virus." — Treasure E. Blue, *A Street Girl Named Desire*, p. 247, 2007

2 in computing, a program that duplicates itself maliciously when it finds a host, often with a mechanism that enables it then to spread to new hosts *US, 1990*

- — Karla Jennings, *The Devouring Fungus*, p. 225, 1990
- A true hacker may release a virus if it can move harmlessly through a system, erasing itself as it goes, making sure it never backtracks to where it's been before. — The Knightmare, *Secrets of a Super Hacker*, p. 134, 1994

visit *verb*

▸ **to visit Aunt Lillian**

to experience the bleed period of the menstrual cycle *US, 1968*

- — Collin Baker et al., *College Undergraduate Slang Study Conducted at Brown University*, p. 73, 1968

visiting card *noun*

an act of defecation at the scene of the crime by the criminal *US, 1945*

- Murderers often defecate at the scene of the crime (detectives call it "the visiting card") and in some cases have been caught by chemical analysis of the feces. — *Time*, p. 90, 23rd April 1945

visitor *noun*

the bleed period of the menstrual cycle *US, 1949*

- — Vincent J. Monteleone, *Criminal Slang*, p. 13, 1949

visuals *noun*

hallucinations experienced under the influence of psychoactive mushrooms or peyote *US, 1992*

- — Connie Eble (Editor), *UNC-CH Campus Slang*, p. 9, Spring 1992
- Trippers use the word "visuals" to refer to the visual impressions and images that acid can generate. — Cam Cloud, *The Little Book of Acid*, p. 10, 1999

vitamin C *noun*

cocaine *US, 1984*

- — R.C. Garrett et al., *The Coke Book*, p. 200, 1984

vitamin D *noun*

dextromethorphan (DXM), an active ingredient in non-prescription cold and cough medication, often abused for non-medicinal purposes *US, 2003*

- Youths' nicknames for DXM: Robo, Skittles, Triple C's, Rojo, Dex, Tussin, Vitamin D. DXM abuse is called "Robotripping" or "Tussing." Users might be called "syrup heads" or "robotards." — *USA Today*, p. 1A, 29th December 2003

vitamin G *noun*

the drug gabapentin, used medically to control pain *US, 2004*

- Neurontin rarely is encountered as a diverted pharmaceutical; however, law enforcement reporting indicates that the drug (sometimes referred to as "Vitamin G") increasingly is being abused. — *Microgram Bulletin (DEA)*, p. 168, September 2004

vitamin H *noun*
haloperidol, a potent tranquillizer *US, 1989*
- — *Maledicta*, p. 35, 1988–1989: "Medical maledicta from San Francisco"

vitamin K; vit K *noun*
ketamine hydrochloride, an anesthetic used as a hallucinogen *US, 1989*
- Experts describe ketamine, which is also called "Vitamin K," as a cult drug consumed mainly in the Western states. — *New York Times*, p. C1, 24th October 1989
- The drug became known as "Vitamin K" when it emerged in under-gay clubs in the 1980s. — *The Record [Bergen County, New Jersey]*, p. A1, 5th December 1995

vitamin M *noun*
Motrin™ *US, 1994*
- — Sally Williams, *"Strong" Words*, p. 165, 1994

vitamin N *noun*
nicotine; a cigarette *US, 2004*
- — Ben Applebaum and Derrick Pittman, *Turd Ferguson & The Sausage Party*, p. 72, 2004

vitamin P *noun*
1 sex *US, 1988–1989*
"P" is for **PUSSY**.
- — *Maledicta*, p. 35, 1988–1989: "Medical maledicta from San Francisco"
2 the game of poker *US, 1996*
- — John Vorhaus, *The Big Book of Poker Slang*, p. 39, 1996

vitamin Q *noun*
the recreational drug methaqualone, best known as Quaalude™ *US, 1982*
- Vitamin Q indeed. They were Quaaludes, what the young people called "downers." — Armistead Maupin, *Further Tales of the City*, p. 59, 1982

vitamins *noun*
any central nervous system stimulant *US, 1977*
- — Bill Davis, *Jawjacking*, p. 43, 1977

vitamin V *noun*
valium *US, 1994*
- What is Vitamin V? Sorry ... those little yellow pills fabled in song and story: valium. — *alt.folklore.urban*, 21st September 1991
- — Sally Williams, *"Strong" Words*, p. 165, 1994

vittles *noun*
food *US, 1935*
An American corruption of the C14 "victual."
- They picked up on some vittles once today and then again the day after tomorrow. — Mezz Mezzrow, *Really the Blues*, p. 177, 1946

viz *noun*
visibility *US, 1989*
- "[I]t looks like the viz is substantially better a little lower." — Jeffrey Ethel, *One Day in a Long War*, p. 67, 1989

VJ; veejay *noun*
a video jockey, a television host of music videos; a visual artist who mixes lights and images in a club environment *US, 1982*
Initialism, on the model of DJ.
- Every three or four songs, a VJ—for video jockey—pops on the screen with a bit of news or banter, and then the songs resume. — *Washington Post*, p. E1, 16th September 1982

v-mail *noun*
the use of microfilm to send large amounts of mail to American troops overseas during World War II *US, 1942*
As always, "V" stood for "victory."
- But for women during the war it would have been almost un-patriotic not to regularly write V-mail expressing encouragement and hope and loving lies[.] — Guy Talese, *Thy Neighbor's Wife*, p. 61, 1980

VO *noun*
a beautiful woman *US, 1997*
An abbreviation of "visual orgasm."

- Hey, bud, check out the major babage. V.O. to the max! — Editors of *Ben is Dead*, *Retrohell*, p. 239, 1997

vod *noun*
vodka *US, 1986*
- [S]o, in the (false) security of her panty girdle, and slightly whacko on vod, she might just relax her defenses[.] — Terry Southern, *Now Dig This*, p. 3, 1986

vogue *noun*
a posture that implies, or is part of, a fashion style *US, 2003*
- Shoulders sloped and arms wrapped around his chest, it's a kind of gangsta vogue. — Patrick Neate, *Where You're At*, p. 58, 2003
- His act was a series of vogues[.] — Michelle Tea, *Rent Girl*, p. 185, 2004

vogue *verb*
to engage in a style competition that values posturing *US, 1995*
- Voguing entered the public consciousness in 1990 when Madonna's dance track, "Vogue" climbed the charts. — Steven Daly and Nathaniel Wice, *alt.culture*, p. 266, 1995

voice *verb*
to telephone *US, 1991*
- — Eric S. Raymond, *The New Hacker's Dictionary*, p. 372, 1991

volley dolly *noun*
a woman attracted to male volleyball players *US, 1989*
- It was then that a beach volleyball star aboard the ferry—a guy much bigger and fifteen years younger than Winnie—decided to impress a volley dolly cuddled next to him in his mom's Mercedes. — Joseph Wambaugh, *The Golden Orange*, pp. 5–6, 1990

vomit comet *noun*
the modified KC-135A reduced-gravity aircraft *US, 1999*
The aircraft flies parabolas in order to investigate the effects of zero gravity; passengers are often sick to their stomachs.
- Teams of engineering mechanics students are back from a wild ride on a modified KC-135A reduced-gravity aircraft nicknamed the "Vomit Comet." — *University of Wisconsin-Madison College of Engineering Perspective*, Fall 1999

vomit-dive *noun*
a confidence swindle in which a person pretends to throw up after being poisoned at a restaurant *US, 1979*
- Shotoz hollers them up about the epidemic of vomit-dives in the burger chain. — Leo Rosten, *Silky!*, p. 3, 1979

vonce *noun*
marijuana *US, 1960*
- — Robert George Reisner, *The Jazz Titans*, p. 167, 1960

voodoo *nickname*
the McDonnell F-101 fighter aircraft *US, 1990*
- — Joseph Tuso, *Singing the Vietnam Blues*, p. 264, 1990: Glossary

VPL *noun*
a visible panty line, the most heinous of fashion crimes *US, 1966*
Popularized by Paul Simon in Woody Allen's *Annie Hall*.
- VPL. Faintly "Visible Panty Line" under pantaloons worn with an ao dai. — Ken Melvin, *Sorry 'Bout That*, p. 95, 1966: Glossary
- They all wore white dresses, that was the prescribed legal uniform, but they wore them so short and tight, that it was almost obscene (So tight that the panty lines could always be seen, and the helicopter pilots, who were insane for military abbreviations, had invented the phrase VPL, for Visible Panty Line). — David Halberstam, *One Very Hot Day*, p. 109, 1967
- Low ridin', hip huggin' panties might look best for the straightforward V.P.L. statement, but why not try panties with ruffles over the bum[?] — Nina Blake, *Retrohell*, p. 239, 1997

vroom *verb*
to leave noisily *US, 1967*
- She left me standing there with my mouth dropped open, and the blue Mustang vroomed off. — S.E. Hinton, *The Outsiders*, p. 42, 1967

V spot *noun*
a five-dollar bill *US, 1949*
- — Vincent J. Monteleone, *Criminal Slang*, p. 248, 1949

Ww

wac; wack *noun*
phencyclidine, the recreational drug known as PCP or angel dust *US, 1981*
- — Ronald Linder, *PCP*, 1981
- — US Department of Justice, *Street Terms*, October 1994

wack *adjective*
inferior, unacceptable, very bad *US, 1984*
- The opposite of fresh. Bad, not bad. Everything bad is wack. — Bradley Elfman, *Breakdancing*, p. 41, 1984
- I am so over that wack stage of the life. — Francesca Lia Block, *I Was a Teenage Fairy*, p. 72, 1998
- Go run and tell your friends my shit is wack / I just don't give a fuuuuuck! — Eminem (Marshall Mathers), *Just Don't Give a Fuck*, 1999
- I knew the dude was wack. — Earl "DMX" Simmons, *E.A.R.L.*, p. 130, 2002

wacked out *adjective*
crazy, eccentric, mad *US, 1968*
- — Collin Baker et al., *College Undergraduate Slang Study Conducted at Brown University*, p. 218, 1968
- In a blaze of publicity they illuminated the secret route: collecting wacked-out art. — Tom Wolfe, *The Pump House Gang*, p. 144, 1968
- That Foreman camp was totally whacked out, so uptight compared with Ali, who runs a loose-goose operation. — Bill Cardoso, *The Maltese Sangweech*, p. 299, 1984
- Michael Jackson. He's quirky, he's wacked out[.] — Howard Stern, *Miss America*, p. 61, 1995

wacked up *adjective*
crazy, odd, irrational *US, 1947*
- So the cops've been asking us all sorts of whacked-up questions about what we did on the day our teacher got plugged and everything. — Irving Shulman, *The Amboy Dukes*, p. 119, 1947

wacker *adjective*
worse *US, 1999*
From **WACK** (bad).
- You wacker than the motherfucker you bit [copied] your style from. — Eminem (Marshall Mathers), *Just Don't Give a Fuck*, 1999

wack job; whack job *noun*
a person who is mentally ill *US, 1979*
- The real whack jobs would get mad if you said they was crazy. — Edwin Torres, *After Hours*, p. 360, 1979
- I sat in an all-night movie until some wack-job started beating off next to me. — Pamela Des Barres, *I'm With the Band*, p. 176, 1988
- I've got to get through to this wack job to get him on live television. — Howard Stern, *Miss America*, p. 73, 1995
- Now, this benefits Mankind, who is one of the craziest guys in the World Wrestling Federation, a real whack-job when it comes to risking life and limb. — The Rock, *The Rock Says...*, p. 305, 2000

wacko; whacko *noun*
a person who is crazy, eccentric, or mentally imbalanced *US, 1938*
- You're a definite wacko. You're fuckin' crazy, you know that, crazy. — *Raging Bull*, 1980
- Raven can deal with wackos in the audience, humor them perfectly. — Josh Alan Friedman, *Tales of Times Square*, p. 25, 1986
- And now I had a partner, a full-bore whacko who was definitely prepared to rumble. — Hunter S. Thompson, *Songs of the Doomed*, p. 264, 1989
- I'm talking to a possible whacko here. — *Basic Instinct*, 1992

wacky *adjective*
odd, eccentric, crazy *US, 1935*
- I'll go on seeing her occasionally, for we are both wacky in a way, and we should never have gotten married[.] — Jack Kerouac, *Letter to Carolina Kerouac Blake*, p. 88, 14th March 1945
- The only times Benny saw him were at school, and then he'd leave with some sort of whacky excuse about looking for an apartment for his family in East Flatbrush. — Irving Shulman, *The Amboy Dukes*, p. 160, 1947
- She had a nervous breakdown and was acting so wacky she got run over by a bus. — *American Graffiti*, 1973
- And I am NOT going to spend hours and pages describing in mind-numbing detail each wacky new look. — James St. James, *Party Monster*, p. 61, 1990

wacky baccy; wacky backy *noun*
marijuana *US, 1975*
- Over the past few years in New York, the magic moniker has been successively, Chiba-Chiba, wacky, red, red wacky, gold and Santa Marta. — *Hi Life*, p. 15, 1979
- I asked what did he mean wacky tobaccy. Left-handed cigarettes. Boo-shit-tea. — Larry Brown, *Dirty Work*, p. 16, 1989
- All the other kids in the hall turned and scoped me like they thought I was smoking wacky tabacky. — Linden Dalecki, *Kid B*, p. 143, 2006

wacky for khaki *adjective*
infatuated with men in military uniform *US, 1967*
- Hello, Janice Lee. Are you still whacky for khaki? Oh, you remember that. I married a Navy man. — Malcolm Braly, *On the Yard*, p. 50, 1967

wac-wac *noun*
phencyclidine, the recreational drug known as PCP or angel dust *US, 1995*
- — Bill Valentine, *Gang Intelligence Manual*, p. 78, 1995

wad *noun*
1 the semen ejaculated at orgasm *US, 1969*
- Then came adolescence—half my waking life spent locked behind the bathroom door, firing my wad down the toilet bowl[.] — Philip Roth, *Portnoy's Complaint*, p. 18, 1969
- The cocks pop and the wads fly as wide-open mouths train to catch the steaming jizz. — *Adult Video*, p. 32, August/September 1986
2 expectorated sputum *US, 1989*
- — *Maledicta*, p. 35, 1988–1989: "Medical maledicta from San Francisco"
3 a rag saturated with glue or any volatile solvent that is inhaled for the intoxicating effect *US, 1970*
- — William D. Alsever, *Glossary for the Establishment and Other Uptight People*, p. 13, December 1970
4 a roll of money; a great deal of money *US, 1951*
- — David W. Maurer, *Argot of the Racetrack*, p. 67, 1951

wad *verb*
in street luge, to crash *US, 1998*
- WAD To crash into a large group. — Shelley Youngblut, *Way Inside ESPN's X Games*, p. 130, 1998

wad cutter *noun*
a flat-nosed bullet *US, 1962*
- — *American Speech*, p. 273, December 1962: "The language of traffic policemen"

waders *noun*
shoes *US, 1945*
- — Lou Shelly, *Hepcats Jive Talk Dictionary*, p. 20, 1945

wag *noun*
1 a guess *US, 1990*
- For the fighter pilots circling the target at twelve thousand feet, however, fifty meters was an indistinguishable blur, at best a "wag"—a wild ass guess. — Tom Yarborough, *Da Nang Diary*, p. 27, 1990
2 a social outcast, especially a nonsurfer *US, 1991*
- — Trevor Cralle, *The Surfin'ary*, p. 155, 1991

wag *verb*
▶ **wag wienie; wag your wienie**
to commit indecent exposure *US, 1984*
- "It's just an arrangement to satisfy the immigration people, so Teddy can get a green card..." "... and wag weenie in San Francisco." — Armistead Maupin, *Babycakes*, p. 268, 1984

- He was arrested in Florida for wagging wienie in a porn theater.
  — Armistead Maupin, *Maybe the Moon*, p. 125, 1992

waggle *verb*
in pool, to make practice shots before actually hitting the cue ball *US, 1993*
- — Mike Shamos, *The Illustrated Encyclopedia of Billiards*, p. 261, 1993

wagon *noun*
a US Navy troop transport vessel *US, 1946*
- "I just took for granted that I'd get on a can or a wagon or a carrier right in the middle of it." — Thomas Heggen, *Mister Roberts*, p. 65, 1946

▶ on the wagon
abstaining from drinking alcohol *US, 1906*
- Frank knew immediately by her loose laugh that she had taken a stiff drink. Benny patted his hip. "You want one?" Frank's eyes were narrow slits. "I thought we were going on the wagon?" — Irving Shulman, *The Amboy Dukes*, p. 207, 1947
- Juicers on the wagon are all big coffee fiends. — James Ellroy, *Brown's Requiem*, p. 43, 1981
- So there I was drinking Stingers with this guy who doesn't even drink. Thirteen years on the wagon and looks great. — Elmore Leonard, *Be Cool*, p. 256, 1999

wagon burner *noun*
a Native American Indian *US, 1995*
Offensive.
- They'd call me "wagon burner" and "prairie nigger." They'd go right for the jugular. — *Buffalo News*, p. 3C, 7th October 1995

wagon-chasing *adjective*
used of a lawyer, unscrupulous, inclined to solicit business from those in trouble with the law *US, 1953*
- Some wagon-chasing lawyer called me up and asked if I would put up the money to buy Herman a bond. — William Burroughs, *Junkie*, p. 37, 1953

wahini *noun*
a female surfer *US, 1963*
From the Hawaiian.
- — *Paradise of the Pacific*, p. 27, October 1963

wail *verb*
1 in jazz, to perform with great feeling *US, 1955*
- [T]o be really in the groove, thus really wailing. — Peter Clayton and Peter Gammond, *Jazz A–Z*, p. 245, 1986
2 in pinball, to score a large number of points in a short period of time *US, 1977*
- — Bobbye Claire Natkin and Steve Kirk, *All About Pinball*, p. 118, 1977

wailing *adjective*
exciting *US, 1965*
- — Carol Covington, *A Glossary of Teenage Terms*, 1965

wait-a-minute vine; wait-a-minute bush *noun*
a heavy, thorny vine found in the jungles of Vietnam *US, 1976*
When it snagged you, you had to wait a minute to disentangle yourself.
- It had been "prepped," prepared by bombardment, an hour before by Navy jets, so there was no tangled vegetation, no "wait-a-minute" vines to hack through with a dull machete[.] — Charles Anderson, *The Grunts*, p. 42, 1976
- It was the wait-a-minute vines that grab you, tangles you as you move in the jungle. — Wallace Terry, *Bloods*, p. 44, 1984
- They'd endured leeches and jungle rot, constant, heavy rains and clammy clothes that chilled them in their sleep, and the "wait-a-minute" bushes that could hold a trooper as tenaciously as a strand of barbed wire. — David Hackworth and Julie Sherman, *About Face*, p. 527, 1989
- The ridge was nearly vertical and covered with large ferns, wait-a-minute vines, and huge, gnarled tree roots snaking out in all directions. — Gary Linderer, *The Eyes of the Eagle*, p. 59, 1991

waiter's delight *noun*
in poker, a hand consisting of three threes and a pair *US, 1988*
A "three" is a **TREY**, the hand is conventionally known as a "full house," hence "treys full," the waiter pun.
- — George Percy, *The Language of Poker*, p. 95, 1988

wait up!
"wait for me!" *US, 1944*
- — Claudio R. Salvucci, *The Philadelphia Dialect Dictionary*, p. 64, 1996

wake and bake; wake-n-bake *verb*
to smoke marijuana as one of the first acts of the day *US, 1997*
- I don't wake and bake like I used to. DEAN WEAN, Wean, refuting the rumour that he smokes excessive amounts of marijuana, 1995 — *Jabberrock*, p. 211, 1997
- — Connie Eble (Editor), *UNC-CH Campus Slang*, p. 13, Fall 1999

wake-up *noun*
1 a short time remaining on a jail sentence or term of military service, especially the last morning *US, 1950*
- — Hyman E. Goldin et al., *Dictionary of American Underworld Lingo*, p. 234, 1950
- — Carl Fleischhauer, *A Glossary of Army Slang*, p. 25, 1968
- "Try three-five and a wake up." — William Pelfrey, *The Big V*, p. 171, 1972
- "Shit!" John exclaimed, "you ain't got nothing but a wake-up. You can do that shit on top of your head, man." — Donald Goines, *White Man's Justice, Black Man's Grief*, p. 192, 1973
2 the day's first dose of a drug taken by an addict *US, 1954*
- This is his "wake-up," a morning shot to hold off the anxiety and sickness of withdrawal and get him "straight" enough to start the day. — James Mills, *The Panic in Needle Park*, p. 14, 1966
- We'd have our wake-ups because the drugstores aren't open at five or six in the morning before he went to work. — Bruce Jackson, *In the Life*, p. 221, 1972
- The first shot in the morning, which is called a wake-up, another in the afternoon, and one late at night. — Emmett Grogan, *Ringolevio*, p. 40, 1972
- Why don't chew lay this dime on me so I can get my wake up? — Odie Hawkins, *Men Friends*, p. 32, 1989
3 any amphetamine or central nervous system stimulant *US, 1972*
- — Carl Chambers and Richard Heckman, *Employee Drug Abuse*, 1972

wake up *verb*
1 to become aware that you are being swindled *US, 1969*
- Pocket said, "Blue, did you bring a rod just in case the crazy mark wakes up?" — Iceberg Slim (Robert Beck), *Trick Baby*, p. 224, 1969
2 in horseracing, to stimulate a horse illegally by electric shock or drugs *US, 1947*
- — Dan Parker, *The ABC of Horse Racing*, p. 150, 1947

wake-up *adjective*
used of an addictive substance taken upon waking up *US, 1981*
- I looked around for the wake-up bottle I kept by the bed when I was drinking, then realized I had been sober for four days. — James Ellroy, *Brown's Requiem*, p. 165, 1981

wake-up pill *noun*
an amphetamine or other central nervous system stimulant *US, 1979*
- Scene: Dark brown skinned lady with darker circles under her eyes offers me a couple wake up pills because I am nodding on my post office seat. — Odie Hawkins, *Scars and Memories*, p. 56, 1987
- CALL IT... Sulfate, wake-ups, whizz, whites, base JUST DON'T CALL IT... Ice — *Drugs An Adult Guide*, p. 35, 2001

wake you *verb*
to make you aware of something *US, 1953*
- — Lavada Durst, *The Jives of Dr. Hepcat*, p. 14, 1953

wakey, wakey, eggs and bakey!
used for calling someone from sleep to breakfast *US, 2000*
Used with great comic effect by Quentin Tarantino in *Kill Bill Volume 2* (2004) as Bill's brother Budd awakens The Bride to bury her alive.
- [T]his is his [Eric San] "Sgt. Pepper," filled with elliptical compositions bearing titles such as "Music for Morning People"—a medley of break beats that includes the line "Wakey-wakey, eggs and bacey." — *San Francisco Chronicle*, p. 40 (Sunday Datebook), 27th February 2000
- Thanks to Shannon, kids will be able to wake up to their own voice and personalized message. "Mine's going to say 'Wakey, wakey, eggs and bakey,'" she says. — *Chicago Tribune*, p. C10, 20th August 2002

Waldorf-Astoria *noun*
an especially spartan solitary confinement cell *US, 1976*
- — John R. Armore and Joseph D. Wolfe, *Dictionary of Desperation*, 1976

walk *noun*

a release from jail *US, 1965*

- Turk had gotten a walk because his sheet wasn't too bad. — Claude Brown, *Manchild in the Promised Land*, p. 17, 1965
- He gave them what is known in police parlance as "a walk." Or in language everyone understands—he let them go without imposing so much as five cents worth of bail[.] — John Sepe, *Cop Team*, p. 81, 1975

walk *verb*

1 to escape unpunished *US, 1979*

- He grinned. "You're going to walk, Carlito. How does it feel?" — Edwin Torres, *After Hours*, p. 165, 1979
- RACINE: You would look favorably on that? JUDGE COSTANZAQ: He can walk. — *Body Heat*, 1980

2 to quit a job or commitment *US, 1999*

- "What I'm saying to you," Raji said, "the white chick Linda, she leaves, the label's gonna cancel me out and I have to start over. They in love with Linda, and Vita. Linda walks, Vita's liable to." — Elmore Leonard, *Be Cool*, p. 111, 1999

3 to move a boat sideways *US, 1989*

- I worked on the coal barge and then this big triple-screw towboat, the Robert R. Nally, comes in sideways from out in the river—that's calling walking the boat, when they do that. — Elmore Leonard, *Killshot*, p. 198, 1989

4 (used of a military aviator) to suit up for battle *US, 2001*

From the vocabulary of fighter pilots.

- Stationed aboard the USS Carl Vinson, Lt. Ashley likes to "walk early." In the lingo of Navy aviators, "walking" means suiting up for battle. "I wake up, I breathe, I hit the head, then I walk," she says. — *Newsweek*, p. 34, 29th October 2001

▶ **walk a cat back**

to trace a missile back to its launch site *US, 1991*

Gulf war usage.

- — *American Speech*, p. 404, Winter 1991: "Among the new words"

▶ **walk the dog**

while surfing, to move frontward and backward on the surfboard to affect its speed *US, 1987*

- — Mitch McKissick, *Surf Lingo*, 1987

▶ **walk the nose**

while surfing, to advance to the front of the board *US, 1962*

- At Huntington and Malibu / They're shooting the pier / At Rincon they're walking the nose. — Brian Wilson and Mike Love, *Surfin' Safari* (performed by the Beach Boys), 1962
- — John Severson, *Modern Surfing Around the World*, p. 184, 1964

▶ **walk the yard**

to methodically walk in a prison open space *US, 1981*

- Walking the yard was a mind bender. — Gerald Petievich, *Money Men*, p. 35, 1981

▶ **walk with your Lucy**

to inject a drug *US, 1981*

- "I want to go out walking with my Lucy." He made a gesture with his hand, indicating shooting up. — James Ellroy, *Brown's Requiem*, p. 70, 1981

▶ **walk your dog**

to use the toilet *US, 1968*

- So when I went in there to "walk my dog," you know, I picked up one and decided to try it. — Robert Gover, *JC Saves*, p. 119, 1968

walkaway *noun*

1 a type of theft in which the thief walks away with another's suitcase in a public place, leaving behind his suitcase as an alibi if apprehended *US, 1954*

- The walkway has a hundred variations which all come down to a distraction at the critical time when your luggage has not yet been assigned to the charge of one particular bellman. — Dev Collans with Stewart Sterling, *I was a House Detective*, p. 15, 1954

2 the final step in a confidence swindle, in which the swindlers walk away with the victim's money *US, 1981*

- We all get a little uptight right before the walkaway. It's called an "anxiety reaction." — Gerald Petievich, *One-Shot Deal*, p. 289, 1981

walk-back *noun*

an apartment in the rear of a building *US, 1970*

- — Clarence Major, *Dictionary of Afro-American Slang*, p. 121, 1970

walkboards *noun*

a platform outside a carnival show or attraction *US, 1966*

- — *American Speech*, p. 283, December 1966: "More carnie talk from the West Coast"

walk-buddy *noun*

in prison, a close friend and steady companion *US, 1976*

- — John R. Armore and Joseph D. Wolfe, *Dictionary of Desperation*, 1976

walker *noun*

1 a prisoner who constantly paces in his cell *US, 1984*

- — Inez Cardozo-Freeman, *The Joint*, 1984

2 a striptease dancer who disrobes while walking *US, 1981*

- — Don Wilmeth, *The Language of American Popular Entertainment*, p. 290, 1981

3 in dominoes, the highest piece of its suit that is not a double and has been played *US, 1964*

- — Dominic Armanino, *Five-up Domino Games*, p. 3, 1964

walkie *noun*

a close and dependable friend *US, 1991*

- — Lee McNelis, *30 + And a Wake-Up*, 1991

walkie-talkie *noun*

1 a portable two-way radio *US, 1939*

- Lt. Buell called Lt. O'Dwyer on the prc-6 (the Army calls them "walkie-talkies") and told him that the covering squad was in position. — Martin Russ, *The Last Parallel*, p. 105, 1957

2 a prisoner who associates with guards *US, 1992*

- — William K. Bentley and James M. Corbett, *Prison Slang*, 1992

walk-in *noun*

a thief who steals from unlocked hotel rooms *US, 1954*

- A walk-in is a room-rifler who finds a guest's door unlocked and just walks in, helps himself and beats it. — Dev Collans with Stewart Sterling, *I was a House Detective*, p. 131, 1954

walking *adjective*

used of a to-go order for food at a restaurant *US, 1952*

- — *American Speech*, p. 232, October 1952: "The argot of soda jerks"

walking buddy *noun*

a dependable friend *US, 1967*

- In toward the center are those persons he knows and likes best, those with whom he is "up tight"; his "walking buddies[.]" — Elliot Liebow, *Tally's Corner*, p. 163, 1967

walking dandruff *noun*

body lice *US, 1942*

- WALKING DANDRUFF: cooties (also known as seam squirrels). — Charles Osgood, *Kilroy Was Here*, p. 12, 2001

walking money *noun*

in gambling, a small amount of money given by the house or other players to someone who has just lost all of his money *US, 1961*

- Jay shook his head as he peeled off two hundred in walking money for the four losers. — Iceberg Slim (Robert Beck), *Airtight Willie and Me*, p. 112, 1979

walking time *noun*

the portion of a prison sentence remaining when a prisoner is paroled *US, 1966*

- — Rose Giallombardo, *Society of Women*, p. 213, 1966

walking tree *noun*

in a criminal enterprise, a watchman or lookout *US, 1956*

- — *American Speech*, p. 98, May 1956: "Smugglers' argot in the Southwest"

walking writer *noun*

in an illegal numbers gambling lottery, a person who collects and records bets *US, 1949*

- — *American Speech*, p. 193, October 1949

walk of fame *noun*

the walk home or to work after spending the night with a beautiful and popular woman *US, 2001*

- — Don R. McCreary (Editor), *Dawg Speak*, 2001

walk of shame *noun*

the walk home or to work after spending the night with a date, still wearing yesterday's clothes *US, 1990*

- THE WALK OF SHAME Are you and your friends looking for something fun to do at seven AM? — Aline Brosh, *A Coed's Companion*, p. 31, 1990

- "If I recall," she says indignantly, "you were the last one to do the walk of shame." — Jillian Medoff, *Hunger Point*, p. 155, 1997
- — Amy Sohn, *Sex and the City*, p. 157, 2002
- If you're up early enough on a Sunday morning at any college across the country, you're bound to see a phenomenon known as the "walk of shame." — Aaron Karo, *Ruminations on College Life*, p. 35, 2002

walkover *noun*
in horseracing, a race in which all but one of the entries are withdrawn *US, 1965*
The lone horse starting the race can win the purse simply by walking the distance of the race.
- — George King, *Horse Racing*, p. 61, 1965

walk-up *noun*
a brothel *US, 1950*
- — Hyman E. Goldin et al., *Dictionary of American Underworld Lingo*, p. 234, 1950

wall *noun*
▸ **behind the wall**
imprisoned *US, 1989*
- — James Harris, *A Convict's Dictionary*, 1989

▸ **go to the wall**
to lose money in stock investments *US, 1988*
- — Kathleen Odean, *High Steppers, Fallen Angels, and Lollipops*, p. 94, 1988

▸ **the wall**
a maximum security prison *US, 2002*
- — Gary K. Farlow, *Prison-ese*, p. 73, 2002

wall *verb*
to lean against the wall at a party or other social gathering *US, 1997*
- — Vann Wesson, *Generation X Field Guide and Lexicon*, p. 180, 1997

wallah; walla *noun*
in the television and movie industries, indistinguishable background voices *US, 1990*
- — Ralph S. Singleton, *Filmmaker's Dictionary*, p. 182, 1990

wallbanger *noun*
a person whose impairment with central nervous system depressants has produced a marked lack of coordination *US, 1977*
- — Donald Wesson and David Smith, *Barbiturates*, 1977

walleyed *adjective*
drunk *US, 1992*
- When Rocco had come in walleyed with vodka, she had awakened in her crib. — Richard Price, *Clockers*, p. 515, 1992

wallflower week *noun*
the bleed period of the menstrual cycle *US, 1954*
- — *American Speech*, p. 298, December 1954: "The vernacular of menstruation"

wall job *noun*
sex with one of the participants standing against a wall *US, 2001*
- Tell him 'bout the wall jobs you been doin' in the division garage. — Stephen J. Cannell, *The Tin Collectors*, p. 9, 2001

wall of death *noun*
a crowd activity at heavy metal or punk concerts, where dancers separate into two groups and then rush at each other *US, 1997*
The New York hardcore band Murphy's Law wrote a song "Wall of Death" referring to this type of moshing activity.
- Before the last song Lou announces that Pete wants to see the wall of death so people on both sides join arms and crash into each other. — *alt.music.hardcore*, 28th July 1997
- On his command, there was a giant wall of death as the floor erupted into a giant pit. — *The Daily Campus*, 14th April 2004
- "Dude, is your photographer all right? I felt so bad! Caught up in the wall of death." — *Times Herald [Port Huron, Michicgan]*, p. 40E, 17th September 2004

wallopies *noun*
large female breasts *US, 1975*
- — *American Speech*, p. 68, Spring–Summer 1975: "Razorback slang"

wallpaper *noun*
a background pattern or photograph for a computer display screen *US, 1991*
- — Eric S. Raymond, *The New Hacker's Dictionary*, p. 375, 1991

wall ticket *noun*
in Keno, a big win *US, 1987*
Casinos often post large winning tickets on the wall of the Keno lounge as an enticement to bettors.
- — Thomas L. Clark, *The Dictionary of Gambling and Gaming*, p. 247, 1987

wall-to-waller *noun*
a pornographic movie shot in one day on a very low budget *US, 2000*
- — Ana Loria, *1 2 3 Be A Porn Star!*, p. 168, 2000: "Glossary of adult sex industry terms"

wallyo; wal-yo *noun*
a young man, usually an Italian-American *US, 1975*
- [T]he only two cats that was ever in my corner was Earl Bassey, a black dude, and Rocco Fabrizi, a wal-yo. Unbelievable. — Edwin Torres, *Carlito's Way*, 1975
- Let's go hear the walyo form Bucknell. — David Chase, *The Sopranos: Selected Scripts from Three Seasons*, p. 138, 20th September 1999

walnut storage disease *noun*
any unspecified mental problem *US, 1983*
A play on **NUTTY** (crazy).
- — *Maledicta*, p. 39, 1983: "More common patient-directed pejoratives used by medical personnel"

Walter Wonderful *nickname*
the Walter Reed Army Hospital in Washington D.C. *US, 1983*
- — Lynda Van Devanter, *Home Before Morning*, p. 382, 1983: Glossary

waltz *verb*
to move in a nonchalant manner *US, 1887*
- She waltzes down to Hoxton in it [a fur coat] to see her dear old mum, and takes her out for a tiddly. — Charles Raven, *Underworld Nights*, 1956
- If he goofs up, he waltzes into court, files a new motion, and fixes it. — Carl Hiaasen, *Tourist Season*, p. 222, 1986
- RANDAL: Any moron can waltz in here and do our jobs, but you're obsessed with making it seem so much more fucking important, so much more epic than it really is. — *Clerks*, 1994

waltz off *verb*
to leave in a nonchalant or cavalier manner *US, 1989*
- Great, Harry, you love me, that settles everything, now we can waltz off into the sunset together? — *When Harry Met Sally*, 1989

wampum *noun*
money *US, 1879*
An imitation of Native American Indian language.
- — Hyman E. Goldin et al., *Dictionary of American Underworld Lingo*, p. 234, 1950
- She continues to make wampum from singles during her Sonny Bono co-singing days. — Mr. Skin, *Mr. Skin's Skincyclopedia*, p. 108, 2005

wand *noun*
in pool, a player's cue stick *US, 1993*
- — Mike Shamos, *The Illustrated Encyclopedia of Billiards*, p. 261, 1993

wang; whang *noun*
the penis *US, 1935*
- Filipinos come quick; colored men are built abnormally large ("Their wangs look like a baby's arm with an apple in its fist"); ladies with short hair are Lesbians; if you want to keep your man, rub alum on your pussy. — Lenny Bruce, *How to Talk Dirty and Influence People*, p. 1, 1965
- My wang was all I really had that I could call my own. — Philip Roth, *Portnoy's Complaint*, p. 35, 1969
- Whang whipping experts voted the New York Times Sunday Magazine their favorite masturbation media. — *Screw*, p. 26, 10th November 1969
- She unbuttoned my trousers fast and pulled out my half-erect wang. — *Screw*, p. 7, 4th May 1970
- Especially when the subject matter is a blond bombshell and a wang-heavy rock star. — Editors of Adult Video News, *The AVN Guide to the 500 Greatest Adult Films of All Time*, p. 89, 2005

wangbar *noun*
an electric guitar's tremolo arm *US, 1980*

- [J]agged wangbar-bashing lines that would make people call Jimi Hendrix a genius[.] — Lester Bangs, *Psychotic Reactions and Carburetor Dung*, p. 297, 1980
- Dave Wronski, the band [Slacktone]'s inventive 6-stringer, melds surf's slurpy wang-bar bends and twangy, thrumming bass-string riffs[.] — Andy Ellis, *GuitarPlayer.com*, June 2002

wanger; whanger *noun*
the penis *US, 1939*
- His whanger wilted, and he stuffed it back inside his pants and left. — Juan Carmel Cosmes, *Memoir of a Whoremaster*, p. 137, 1969
- But if you are going to jack your whanger, make firm determination to do it well and heartily and in an infinite amount of ways and combinations. — *Screw*, p. 14, 9th May 1969
- "Aren't you going to shake your whanger at me?" — Tom Robbins, *Even Cowgirls Get the Blues*, p. 246, 1976
- If I was a guy I wouldn't let her within twenty feet of my wanger. — Janet Evanovich, *Seven Up*, p. 93, 2001

wank *noun*
the penis *US, 2004*
- I kept my eye on his wank, and continued to maneuver me and Eleanor away from his fumey breath and eventual ejaculation. — Michelle Tea, *Rent Girl*, p. 233, 2004

wank-bank *noun*
a personal collection of inspirational erotic images *UK, 1999*
Formed on **WANK** (an act of masturbation).
- Brooke creates more yanker fare for the wank bank, showing a brief bit of bubbly breastage[.] — Mr. Skin, *Mr. Skin's Skincyclopedia*, p. 2, 2005
- The whole bit of business made a deposit in my wank bank. Every time I thought of it, my cock stirred. — P.F.G. Kozak, *Passion*, p. 15, 2006

wanker's doom *noun*
the mythological disease that is the inevitable result of excessive masturbation *US, 1977*
- — *Maledicta*, p. 11, Summer 1977: "A word for it!"

wanksta *noun*
someone, especially a white person, who postures as a gangsta rapper *US, 2002*
A derisory play on **WANKER** (a despised person).
- You said you a gansta but you neva pop nuttin' / You said you a wanksta and you need to stop frontin' / You ain't a friend of mine[.] — 50 Cent and G Unit, *Wanksta*, 2002

wannabe *noun*
someone who wants to be and pretends to be that which he is not *US, 1978*
- As for motive, Droz thinks the trio might be categorized as "wannabes"—people who always wanted to be officials. — *Los Angeles Times*, p. C9, 5th January 1978
- They call the white gangs "wannabes," meaning someone who dresses and talks the part because he "wants to be" a gang member, but is actually tame. — *Los Angeles Times*, p. 4 (Metro Section), 28th July 1985
- [I]f you are a hardcore—or just a wannabe—gang member and you are sitting in the back of an L.A. County Probation Department van, the odds are that you are seeing this panorama for the first time. — Leon Bing, *Do or Die*, pp. 3–4, 1991
- Strike saw Spook and Ahmed walk away as if they had something to hide—wannabes, the only idiots who walked. — Richard Price, *Clockers*, p. 9, 1992

wanna-bet shirt *noun*
in a rowing competition, a team's shirt which is the object of a wager between competing teams, where the winner claims the opposing team's shirts which are worn as a badge of victory *US, 2001*
- — Judy's Enterprises, *Coxswain Postcard*, 2001

want *noun*
a notification that a person is wanted by the police *US, 1958*
- — Jack Webb, *The Badge*, p. 222, 1958
- I unlocked the call box and hurried up with the wants check. — Joseph Wambaugh, *The Blue Knight*, pp. 29–30, 1973
- There's no want on the license at this time. — *Gone in 60 Seconds*, 2000

war *noun*
► **go to war**
to fight *US, 2002*
- — Gary K. Farlow, *Prison-ese*, p. 25, 2002

war bag *noun*
a backpack or duffel bag containing a police officer's equipment and clothing *US, 2006*
- Mag's war bag was on wheels, jammed with helmet and gear. — Joseph Wambaugh, *Hollywood Station*, p. 60, 2006

warden *noun*
1 a parent *US, 1968*
- — Hy Lit, *Hy Lit's Unbelievable Dictionary of Hip Words for Groovy People*, p. 44, 1968

2 a school principal *US, 1954*
- — *This Week Magazine, New York Herald Tribune*, p. 46, 28th February 1954
- Back to the warden's office. You want me to give him any messages, doll? — Morton Cooper, *High School Confidential*, p. 19, 1958

3 a teacher *US, 1951*
Teen slang.
- — *Newsweek*, p. 29, 8th October 1951

war department *noun*
someone's wife or girlfriend *US, 1984*
- I've got the war department faked out. I told her I'm working overtime. — Joseph Wambaugh, *Lines and Shadows*, p. 160, 1984
- — James Harris, *A Convict's Dictionary*, 1989

warlord *noun*
a high-level member of a political organization *US, 1991*
- However, any captain can offer a candidate and it's even happened that a retiring warlord ain't been too popular, or the man or woman he chooses to take his place has made a lot of enemies, and the committeeman don't get his way. — Robert Campbell, *In a Pig's Eye*, pp. 6–7, 1991

warmer-upper *noun*
food or drink that warms a person up *US, 1944*
- A new version of an old family favorite and a great warmer-upper on chilly days. — Maryana Vollstedt, *Big Book of Easy Suppers*, p. 4, 2005

warm for someone's form *adjective*
sexually attracted to someone *US, 1953*
- "Didn't know you were still warm for her form, pal." — Curt Cannon, *Now Die In It*, p. 54, 1953
- I knowed this daddy warm for my form, but—like, too much. — Robert Gover, *Here Goes Kitten*, p. 80, 1964

warm fuzzies *noun*
the feeling when praised by a superior *US, 1986*
- — Rachel S. Epstein and Nina Liebman, *Biz Speak*, p. 244, 1986

warm one *noun*
a bullet *US, 1998*
- Jones was not there at the time, but apparently was told at some point that Caldwell had threatened to put "two warm ones"—street slang for bullets—in Jackson for running his mouth too much. — *Roanoke (Virginia) Times & World News*, p. A1, 9th October 1998

warmup *noun*
a loose-fitting, athletic warmup suit *US, 1999*
- Raji in cranberry designer warmups today with his cowboy boots, always the boots, Raji smiling at her like nothing had changed. — Elmore Leonard, *Be Cool*, p. 81, 1999

warm up *verb*
to refill a cup of coffee *US, 1996*
- Can I warm that up for you? — *Fargo*, 1996

warp *noun*
a bent card used by a card cheat to identify the value of the card *US, 1996*
- — Frank Scoblete, *Best Blackjack*, p. 275, 1996

war paint *noun*
makeup, cosmetics *US, 1869*
Originally theatrical.
- — Lou Shelly, *Hepcats Jive Talk Dictionary*, p. 35, 1945
- I had swiped Mother's warpaint and began doing my toenails, fingernails, and then worked my way up to the eyes. — Frederick Kohner, *Gidget Goes Hawaiian*, p. 58, 1961

warped *adjective*
1 perverted *US, 1993*
- "Nick, how did you get to be so warped?" "Bad home life."
  — C.D. Payne, *Youth in Revolt*, p. 395, 1993
2 drug-intoxicated *US, 1979*
- Yeah, they got stoned on giggle-weed, zonked on grifa, zapped on yerba, bombed on boo, they were blitzed with snop, warped on twist, gay on hay, free on V. — *Hi Life*, p. 14, 1979

warp one *noun*
a high speed *US, 1986*
Figurative US naval aviator usage.
- — *United States Naval Institute Proceedings*, p. 108, October 1986

warp seven *adverb*
very quickly *US, 1992*
- There be them big dudes with their full-auto Uzis, an go bailin warp-seven cause Gordy gots the balls to shoot back with this! — Jess Mowry, *Way Past Cool*, 1992

warrior *noun*
a fearless, violent member of a youth gang *US, 1995*
- — Mark S. Fleisher, *Beggars & Thieves*, p. 292, 1995: "Glossary"

warthog *noun*
a US Air Force attack plane formally known as an A-10 Thunderbolt *US, 1991*
Gulf war usage.
- — *American Speech*, p. 404, Winter 1991: "Among the new words"

warts and all
with all blemishes or imperfections unconcealed *UK, 1930*
- Warts and all, the streets was my playground. — Edwin Torres, *Carlito's Way*, p. 19, 1975

war wagon *noun*
a vehicle carrying weapons on a motorcycle gang outing when trouble is expected *US, 1992*
- The women and probates are the ones that usually drive the crash truck or war wagon during their outings[.] — Paladin Press, *Inside Look at Outlaw Motorcycle Gangs*, p. 1, 1992

war zone *noun*
an area in Washington D.C. infamous for drug sales and other crime *US, 1984*
- About two weeks ago, Marcus visited one of his regular stops, the PCP sales "war zone" around 21st Street and Maryland Avenue NE. — *Washington Post*, p. B1, 29th July 1984

wash *noun*
the effect of a drug *US, 1974*
- "How's the wash?" he said. The girl raised her head. "Nice," she said. — Vernon E. Smith, *The Jones Men*, p. 21, 1974

wash *verb*
1 to kill *US, 1941*
- If push comes to shove, we can wash him—but right now you need time, get it, time! — Edwin Torres, *Carlito's Way*, p. 33, 1975
- If I go in the prison without any relatives, and I happen to get sent over the wall to the hospital and they want to kill me, they can wash me in no time flat. — Herbert Huncke, *Guilty of Everything*, p. 117, 1990
2 to purge or expunge something *US, 1983*
- And I've got the right contacts at the courthouse. Your case is as good as washed. — Gerald Petievich, *To Die in Beverly Hills*, p. 155, 1983
3 to give money obtained illegally the appearance of legitimacy through accounting and banking schemes *US, 1997*
- I gave you strict instructions ... that money is never to leave the dead-drop until it's been washed, and then only by my instructions. — Stephen J. Cannell, *Big Con*, p. 313, 1997
4 to shuffle a deck of cards *US, 1965*
- — Irwin Steig, *Play Gin to Win*, p. 143, 1965
5 to receive favorable consideration *US, 1986*
- — Department of the Army, *Staff Officer's Guidebook*, p. 68, 1986

wash away *verb*
to kill someone *US, 1941*
- The more guys they wash away, the more they get to feeling like they're immortal or something. — Mezz Mezzrow, *Really the Blues*, p. 95, 1946

washboard *noun*
in mountain biking, an area of hard, rippled earth *US, 1996*
- Here's the perfect position for cleaning washboard bumps. Keep your butt above the saddle and weight slightly back. — *Mountain Bike Magazine's Complete Guide To Mountain Biking Skills*, p. 145, 1996

washboard *adjective*
of an abdomen, trim, muscular, defined *US, 1992*
From the appearance—solid and rippled.
- See that? A washboard gut. I have yet to observe the black male victim in this town with more than a thirty-inch waist. — Richard Price, *Clockers*, p. 137, 1992
- I suppose you wouldn't like someone with a washboard stomach like Brad Pitt. — *Something About Mary*, 1998
- Morelli had washboard abs. Morelli could actually do sit-ups. Lots of them. — Janet Evanovich, *Seven Up*, 2001

washed-up *adjective*
no longer successful, finished *US, 1923*
- [A]sking God to help you kick the ass of a washed-up loser is a bullshit thing to ask the Almighty[.] — Howard Stern, *Miss America*, p. 252, 1995

washer-dryer *noun*
a douche bag and towel *US, 1980*
- — Edith A. Folb, *runnin' down some lines*, p. 259, 1980

washing machine *noun*
1 in computing, an obsolete large hard disk found in a large floor cabinet *US, 1991*
- — Eric S. Raymond, *The New Hacker's Dictionary*, p. 377, 1991
2 a wave as it breaks over and thrashes a surfer *US, 1991*
- — Trevor Cralle, *The Surfin'ary*, p. 156, 1991

Washington *noun*
a one-dollar bill *US, 1959*
From the portrait of George Washington on the bill.
- — Edd Byrnes, *Way Out with Kookie*, 1959

Washington Monument *noun*
in poker, a hand with three fives *US, 1988*
A rather esoteric allusion to the fact that the Washington Monument is 555 feet high.
- — George Percy, *The Language of Poker*, p. 96, 1988

wash out *verb*
to fail and expel someone from a course or training *US, 1970*
- Tell me how they're going to wash me out if I don't come to the pistol range during the lunch hour and practice extra. — Joseph Wambaugh, *The New Centurions*, p. 14, 1970

washwoman's gig *noun*
in an illegal numbers gambling lottery, a bet on 4, 11 and 44 *US, 1949*
- — *American Speech*, p. 193, October 1949

washy *adjective*
used of a racehorse sweating, especially with anxiety *US, 1976*
- — Tom Ainslie, *Ainslie's Complete Guide to Thoroughbred Racing*, p. 340, 1976

wasp; wap *noun*
1 a white Anglo-Saxon Protestant *US, 1957*
The term is applied to whites without particular regard to the religious component.
- These "old" Americans are "WASPs"—in the cocktail party jargon of the sociologists. That is, they are white, they are Anglo-Saxon in origin, and they are Protestant and disproportionately Episcopalian. — *American Political Science Review*, p. 1010, 1957
- I did meet a wasp there though. — *Screw*, 4th April 1969
- Fools, boors, philistines, Birchers, B'nai Brithees, Defense Leaguers, Hadassah theater party piranhas, UJAviators, concert-hall Irishmen, WAP ignorati. — Tom Wolfe, *Radical Chic & Mau-Mauing the Flak Catchers*, p. 93, 1970
- Christ, there are dozens of firms who will kiss the ass of a WASP who can merely pass the bar. — Erich Segal, *Love Story*, p. 98, 1970
2 a white Appalachian southern Protestant *US, 1981*
- By the mid 1950s, WASP was Chicago slang and Ohio Valley social workers' jargon for white Appalachian Southern Protestants—the poor whites who migrated to the industrial cities of northern Ohio and the Great Lakes. — *Maledicta*, p. 97, Summer/Winter 1981

waspishness *noun*

the state of being distinctly white, Anglo-Saxon and Protestant *US, 1957*

- To their Waspishness should be added the tendency to be located on the Eastern seaboard or around San Francisco, to be prep school and Ivy League educated, and to be possessed of inherited wealth. — *American Political Science Review*, pp. 1010–1011, 1957

wassup?; whas up?; wassuuup?

used as a greeting *US, 1990*

A slurred "what's up?" with dozens of variant spellings. Wildly popular pop speak in 2000 in response to a series of television advertisements for Budweiser™ beer.

- Whas up, baby doll? — *New Jack City*, 1990
- "Wha's up?" the guy said to Strike, not knowing exactly who Strike was either. — Richard Price, *Clockers*, p. 324, 1992
- — *The Bell (Paducah Tilghman High School)*, pp. 8–9, 17th December 1993: "Tilghmanism: the concealed language of the hallway"
- YOU: Wassup, baby? HER (SHAKING THE [PORNOGRAPHIC VIDEO] TAPE, SCREAMING): Is this what you like? Is this what the fuck you like? — Chris Rock, *Rock This!*, p. 166, 1997

waste *verb*

1 to kill someone *US, 1964*

- I mean, you want to waste Limpy? — Claude Brown, *Manchild in the Promised Land*, p. 176, 1965
- "I guess you heard about Malcom?" "Yeah," I said. "They say he got wasted." — Eldridge Cleaver, *Soul on Ice*, p. 52, 1968
- In that war, soldier's slang for death was "wasted." So-and-so was wasted. It was a good word. — Philip Caputo, *A Rumor of War*, p. 210, 1977
- They came to do me in. To waste me. — Gerald Petievich, *Money Men*, p. 153, 1981

2 to smoke marijuana *US, 1967*

- I decided to go upstairs to my place and waste a stick of pot. — Piri Thomas, *Down These Mean Streets*, p. 229, 1967

wastebasket *noun*

in pool, a pocket that seems receptive to balls dropping *US, 1993*

- — Mike Shamos, *The Illustrated Encyclopedia of Billiards*, p. 206, 1993

wasted *adjective*

drunk or drug-intoxicated *US, 1964*

- — J.R. Friss, *A Dictionary of Teenage Slang (Mt. Diablo High)*, 1964
- There was nothing to do but go back to camp and get wasted. — Hunter S. Thompson, *Hell's Angels*, p. 169, 1966
- I'd be too tired or stoned or wasted to get up in the afternoon to even go out and sit beneath the umbrellas in the hot sun at the beach club with Blair. — Bret Easton Ellis, *Less Than Zero*, p. 59, 1985
- Oh man I'm fucking wasted. — *Dazed and Confused*, 1993

waste-time *adjective*

dull, boring, uninteresting *US, 1972*

Hawaiian youth usage.

- Man, dat one real waste-time class! — Elizabeth Ball Carr, *Da Kine Talk*, p. 156, 1972

wastoid *noun*

a worthless, dim-witted person; a person whose drug or alcohol use is ruining their life *US, 1985*

- Yo, wastoid—you're not gonna blaze up in here! — *The Breakfast Club*, 1985
- — *Washington Post*, p. 18, 8th November 1987: "Say wha'?"

watch queen *noun*

1 a homosexual man who derives sexual pleasure from watching other men having sex *US, 1970*

- — *American Speech*, p. 59, Spring–Summer 1970: "Homosexual slang"
- Customers for this sort of service are often "watch queens," men who receive gratification from watching the sexual activities of others. — George Paul Csicsery (Editor), *The Sex Industry*, p. 33, 1973

2 a lookout during anonymous homosexual sex in public places *US, 1975*

- This is the role of the lookout ("watchqueen" in the argot), a man who is situated at the door or windows from which he may observe the means of access to the restroom. — Laud Humphreys, *Tearoom Trade*, p. 27, 1975

water *noun*

1 methamphetamine or another central nervous system stimulant *US, 1989*

- — Geoffrey Froner, *Digging for Diamonds*, 1989
- — James Harris, *A Convict's Dictionary*, 1989

2 phencyclidine, the recreational drug known as PCP or angel dust *US, 1989*

- — *USA Today*, p. 1A, 25th April 1989
- [A]ll the brothers that were slangin' were selling "water," "Sherman," angel dust, PCP, or whatever you want to call it. — Yusuf Jah, *Uprising*, p. 180, 1995

▸ **go in the water**

to lose an athletic contest or other competition intentionally *US, 1955*

- Then why did anybody bother to offer you money if you went in the water? — Rocky Garciano (with Rowland Barber), *Somebody Up There Likes Me*, p. 306, 1955

▸ **in the water; out in the water**

in debt *US, 1992*

- — William K. Bentley and James M. Corbett, *Prison Slang*, 1992

water *verb*

▸ **water the vegetables; water the garden**

to administer intravenous fluids to a hospital's neurologically depressed patients *US, 1978*

- — *Maledicta*, p. 70, Summer/Winter 1978
- — *Maledicta*, p. 118, 1984–1985: "Milwaukee medical maledicta"

water buffalo *noun*

a water trailer *US, 1991*

- There's a five-hundred gallon "water buffalo" parked behind the shower stall of wash water. — Gary Linderer, *The Eyes of the Eagle*, p. 29, 1991
- Inside the aircraft, there were four jeeps and two "water buffalo," or water trailers, along with one 105-mm howitzer artillery piece. — Bob Stoffey, *Cleared Hot!*, p. 4, 1992

water dog *noun*

in circus and carnival usage, a seal *US, 1981*

- — Don Wilmeth, *The Language of American Popular Entertainment*, p. 192, 1981

waterfall *verb*

to drink from a can or bottle by cascading the liquid into your mouth without touching the can or bottle with your lips *US, 2003*

Collected from a 13-year-old in Irvine, California, April 2003.

waterhead *noun*

a person with mental problems *US, 1968*

- In descending order there were the creep, kook, screwball, shathead, crum-bum and waterhead[.] — Stephen Longstreet, *The Flesh Peddlers*, p. 49, 1962
- There is a touch of fine humor in this gunpowder game these right-wing all-american waterheads are said to be loading up like young oxen. — Hunter S. Thompson, *Fear and Loathing in America*, p. 55, 26th April 1968: Letter to Bernard Shir-Cliff
- — Gary K. Farlow, *Prison-ese*, p. 78, 2002

watering hole; watering spot *noun*

a bar or club where alcohol is served; a public hotel *US, 1955*

- The joint was a watering and feeding spot for many of America's top black sports and theatrical stars. — Iceberg Slim (Robert Beck), *The Naked Soul of Iceberg Slim*, p. 80, 1971
- "Yeah, the Stork. Meet us there." "Swell watering hole, old buddy," Rags said. — Georgia Sothern, *My Life in Burlesque*, p. 268, 1972
- I first met Lance at the outside bar of the Island Hotel, the local watering hole also featuring great food. — Jimmy Buffett, *Tales from Margaritaville*, p. 166, 1989
- Lou was the bartender down at the Silk 'n Spurs on Geary, Frank's favorite watering hole. — Seth Morgan, *Homeboy*, p. 73, 1990

watermelons *noun*

female breasts of generous dimensions *US, 1995*

- Boobs, zonkers, headlights, watermelons, sweater puppies, pointers, knockers, jugs, tatas—these are some of the words to describe women's breasts. — Howard Stern, *Miss America*, p. 441, 1995

water sports *noun*

1 sexual activity involving the giving and getting of an enema *US, 1969*

- Have you ever heard of "water sports?" No? Well, people who are into that enjoy giving, or—more commonly—receiving enemas. — *Screw*, p. 7, 6th June 1969
- In both cases all water sports addicts know that after a second or third infusion enemas need not be repellent at all, since they come out relatively clean. — Gerald and Caroline Green, *S-M*, p. 199, 1973
- Water Sports (WC)—urine and/or enemas — Stephen Lewis, *The Whole Bedroom Catalog*, p. 144, 1975
- — *What Color is Your Handkerchief*, p. 7, 1979

2 sexual activity that includes urination *US, 1969*

- "Water sports" may mean another thing too. Some people get a charge out of urinating on their sexual partners, or having their sexual partners piss on them. — *Screw*, p. 7, 6th June 1969
- A golden shower is just another name for urination. You may also hear this act referred to as water sports. — Stephen Ziplow, *The Film Maker's Guide to Pornography*, p. 16, 1977
- We have six watersports fans stationed there anxious for your piss. — *The World of S & M*, p. 130, 1981
- Lately a lot of people have made it pretty trendy to do water sports or golden shower kind of things. — Anthony Petkovich, *The X Factory*, p. 129, 1997

water-walker *noun*

a fellow aviator whose accomplishments approach the miraculous *US, 1986*

US naval aviator usage.

- — *United States Naval Institute Proceedings*, p. 108, October 1986

water works *noun*

1 tears *UK, 1647*

- Him and his phony waterworks he could turn on and off. — John M. Murtagh and Sara Harris, *Cast the First Stone*, p. 20, 1957
- She turned on the waterworks to cop her license to do me in but I was immune to her tears. — Iceberg Slim (Robert Beck), *Long White Con*, p. 12, 1977
- Hey, kid, turn off the waterworks, okay? — *Lethal Weapon*, 1987

2 the urinary system *US, 1961*

- — *American Speech*, pp. 145–148, May 1961: "The spoken language of medicine; argot, slang, cant"

wave *noun*

the semierect penis *US, 1987*

Interview of Jim Holliday, 12th June 1987.

wave *verb*

to bend the edge of a playing card for later cheating *US, 1979*

- — John Scarne, *Scarne's Guide to Modern Poker*, p. 293, 1979

▸ **wave your wig**

to comb your hair *US, 1961*

High school student usage.

- — *San Francisco Examiner*, p. 21, 12th December 1961: "Colloquialisms for your murgatroid Handcuffs"

wax *noun*

phonograph records *US, 1932*

Recordings were originally made on wax cylinders or disks; the term applied to shellac disks and, subsequently, vinyl, but is not used to refer to newer technologies such as CD, tape, etc.

- The man ain't cut a righteous hunk of wax yet! — Ross Russell, *The Sound*, p. 112, 1961

wax *verb*

1 to shoot or kill someone *US, 1960*

- They'll wax you, maybe. — Clarence Cooper Jr., *The Scene*, p. 220, 1960
- — *Time*, p. 34, 10th December 1965
- "Really waxed their ass, huh?" — Elaine Shepard, *The Doom Pussy*, p. 110, 1967
- — Carl Fleischhauer, *A Glossary of Army Slang*, p. 25, 1968
- Just because that stud got waxed, that ain't goin' stop us from having to pay protection dues. — Donald Goines, *Black Gangster*, p. 232, 1977
- After we got serious we had the hardware and we could wax their ass every day, ten to one. — Walter Boyne and Steven Thompson, *The Wild Blue*, p. 561, 1986
- I'm going to wax your ass. — Stephen Coonts, *Flight of the Intruder*, p. 140, 1986

2 to excel; to perform well *US, 2001*

- — Don R. McCreary (Editor), *Dawg Speak*, 2001

way *noun*

a familiar neighborhood; your home territory *US, 1987*

- — *Washington Post Magazine*, p. 11, 17th May 1987: "Say wha'?"
- — *Rapper's Handbook*, 1990

▸ **go all the way**

to have sexual intercourse *US, 1924*

- If a girl goes all the way, a boy doesn't have to find out. — Frederick Kohner, *Gidget*, p. 71, 1957
- What am I saying? That a girl can be nice even though she goes all the way? Yes. — Ann Landers, *Ann Landers Talks to Teen-Agers About Sex*, p. 37, 1963
- The younger and more naive kids were sure Duane went all the way[.] — Larry McMurtry, *The Last Picture Show*, p. 63, 1966
- Go all the way; after the first fuck, why should two people ever see each other again? Havng gone all the way, where else have they got to go? — Allan Sherman, *The Rape of the APE*, p. 24, 1973

▸ **that's the way (something does something)**

that's how things turn out *US, 1952*

Used in a formulaic construction of "that's the way the NOUN VERBs."

- The soldiers coined "That's the way the ball bounces," meaning what was ordained to be. — *East Liverpool (Ohio) Review*, 28th December 1952
- But that's the way the cookie crumbles. — *Independent Record (Helena, Montana)*, 27th November 1955
- One of the children had "That's the way the mop flops." — *Progress (Clearfield, Pennsylvania)*, 5th March 1956
- — *San Francisco Examiner*, p. 21, 12th December 1961: "Colloquialisms for your murgatroid handcuffs"

way *adverb*

extremely; without doubt *US, 1982*

- I mean we like had this way cranking bud sesh and like listened to AC/DC and watched Mommie Dearest with the sound off. — Mary Corey and Victoria Westermark, *Fer Shurr! How to be a Valley Girl*, 1982
- Gaping barrels! Way overhead, man! — *Break Point*, 1991
- Way cool blood, homey. — Jess Mowry, *Way Past Cool*, p. 9, 1992
- I actually have a way normal life for a teenage girl. — *Clueless*, 1995

way out *adjective*

extreme; unconventional; experimental or innovative; good *US, 1958*

- [W]hat made him a way-out guy with the the surfers was the stupendous feat he had performed on the very spot I was standing then. — Frederick Kohner, *Gidget Goes Hawaiian*, p. 49, 1961
- I guess to people who don't know the Beatles personally, this scene seems a bit "way-out." — Murray Kaufman, *Murray the K Tells It Like It Is, Baby*, p. 94, 1966
- Rocky and his fellas got to playing a way-out game with me called "One-finger-across-the-neck-inna-slicing-motion[.]" — Piri Thomas, *Down These Mean Streets*, p. 29, 1967
- Two wild, groovy, way-out couples, black and white, desire to meet other couples, interested in group love, dog training, and family relations. — Emile Nytrate, *Underground Ads*, p. 26, 1971

way past *adverb*

extremely *US, 1992*

- Wear a tank top all the time. Look way past cool, believe! — Jess Mowry, *Way Past Cool*, 1992

way up *adjective*

drunk *US, 1955*

- — *American Speech*, p. 305, December 1955: "Wayne University slang"

wazoo *noun*

1 the anus and/or rectum *US, 1965*

- Jerry Payne, you've got your head up the old wazoo! — John Nichols, *The Sterile Cuckoo*, p. 114, 1965
- An enema is an enormous GOOOOSH right up the old WAZOO. — *Screw*, p. 11, 6th November 1972
- Like, I'm sure those guys behaved themselves, right?—TVs out the windows, groupies out the wazoo. — Jay McInerney, *Story of My Life*, p. 17, 1988
- We gonna be late an get tardies out the wazoo! — Jess Mowry, *Way Past Cool*, p. 8, 1992

2 the vagina *US, 2006*

- New to wazoos, he had no operational understanding of this, but, yes, he was pretty sure that would be the move to make. — Chris Miller, *The Real Animal House*, p. 151, 2006

weakie *noun*
a poker player who lacks courage *US, 1996*
- — John Vorhaus, *The Big Book of Poker Slang*, p. 40, 1996

weak sister *noun*
1 a weak, ineffective person *US, 1857*
- He states that you have always been a weak sister and apparently that is what you are. — Herbert Huncke, *Guilty of Everything*, p. 108, 1990
2 an investor who buys a stock as an investment but sells it as soon as the price rises *US, 1988*
- — Kathleen Odean, *High Steppers, Fallen Angels, and Lollipops*, p. 48, 1988

weapon *noun*
in pool, a player's cue stick *US, 1993*
- — Mike Shamos, *The Illustrated Encyclopedia of Billiards*, p. 261, 1993

weapons-grade *adjective*
very strong *US, 2002*
- That's some weapons-grade salsa[.] — *The Washington Post*, 19th March 2002

wear *verb*
to use a name *US, 1968*
- So I dug out my purse an shows my cards. Cost me three bills for this man t'make 'em out so's I can wear my new name. — Robert Gover, *JC Saves*, p. 125, 1968

▸ **wear buttons**
to be extremely gullible *US, 1976*
- — John R. Armore and Joseph D. Wolfe, *Dictionary of Desperation*, p. 22, 1976

we are not worthy
used as a humorous recognition of accomplishment *US, 1992*
- [WAYNE AND GARTH DROP TO THEIR KNEES AND BOW.] WAYNE & GARTH: We're not worthy! We're not worthy! — *Wayne's World*, 1992

wears *noun*
clothes *US, 2007*
- But all whose wears were tight got a pass from being talked about. — Treasure E. Blue, *A Street Girl Named Desire*, p. 119, 2007

Weary Willie *noun*
a person who is perpetually tired, sad and pessimistic *US, 1947*
From the character portrayed by circus clown Emmett Kelly (1898–1979).
- And she is always flippin' the lip about him bein' such a weary Willie, the citizens of the burg, even the hepcats, mark him solid. — Harry Haenigsen, *Jive's Like That*, 1947
- I'm fed up with all these Weary Willies saying "Thou shalt not. Thou shalt not." Yes, we fuckin' shall. — Christopher Brookmyre [quoting Billy Connolly], *Not the End of the World*, p. 303, 1998

Weary Winny *noun*
a prostitute who seeks customers on the street *US, 1951*
From the title of a 1927 film.
- Yet in Washington they flourish, though they are supposedly verboten, and the Weary Winnies parade the pavements. — Jack Lait and Lee Mortimer, *Washington Confidential*, p. 21, 1951

weasel *verb*
to use ambiguous language in an attempt to equivocate on the meaning *US, 1956*
- Yeah, he weasels it, but it still says I was one of those guys and I wasn't. — Elmore Leonard, *Be Cool*, p. 103, 1999

weathervane *verb*
(said of an airplane) to align with the prevailing winds while trying to land *US, 1967*
- "There was a helluva crosswind form the right on the take-off roll. The bird weathervaned into the wind and damn near ground-looped on him." — Elaine Shepard, *The Doom Pussy*, p. 190, 1967

weave *noun*
1 real and synthetic hair woven into existing hair to hide baldness or thinning hair *US, 1993*
- These days, your haircut looks more Clint Eastwood than Cary Grant. Have you considered a weave? — Joseph Wambaugh, *Finnegan's Week*, p. 9, 1993
2 clothes *US, 1972*
- — David Claerbaut, *Black Jargon in White America*, p. 86, 1972

web *noun*
a television network *US, 1990*
- — Ralph S. Singleton, *Filmmaker's Dictionary*, p. 183, 1990

webfoot *noun*
a racehorse that performs well on a muddy track *US, 1951*
- — David W. Maurer, *Argot of the Racetrack*, p. 68, 1951

wedding *noun*
a one-on-one battle between fighter pilots *US, 1986*
- — *American Speech*, p. 125, Summer 1986: "The language of naval fighter pilots"

wedding bells *noun*
morning glory seeds, eaten for their purported hallucinogenic effect *US, 1970*
- — William D. Alsever, *Glossary for the Establishment and Other Uptight People*, p. 22, December 1970

wedding kit *noun*
the genitals *US, 1964*
- — Roger Blake, *The American Dictionary of Sexual Terms*, p. 85, 1964

wedge *noun*
a dose of LSD; LSD *US, 1971*
- — US Department of Justice, *Street Terms*, October 1994

wedged *adjective*
in computing, suspended in mid-operation and unable to proceed *US, 1983*
- — Guy L. Steele et al., *The Hacker's Dictionary*, p. 131, 1983

wedger *noun*
someone who pushes into a line *US, 1994*
- — David Shenk and Steve Silberman, *Skeleton Key*, p. 308, 1994

wedgy; wedgie *noun*
1 the condition that exists when someone pulls your pants or shorts forcefully upward, forming a wedge between buttock cheeks *US, 1988*
- A thorough listen to his [The Notorious B.I.G.] earlier material, like "Machine Gun Funk," where he gets "up in that ass like a wedgie," will reveal an undiscovered gem or two. — *The Source*, p. 218, March 2002
2 a sandal, the thong of which wedges between the toes *US, 1981*
- "What kind of shoes?" "Sandals, like wedgies." — Elmore Leonard, *Split Images*, p. 173, 1981

weebles *noun*
an ill-defined or undefined illness *US, 1947*
- Grandma has the weebles an' these goodies will make her well. — Harry Haenigsen, *Jive's Like That*, 1947

weed *noun*
1 marijuana *US, 1928*
The preferred slang term for marijuana until the 1950s, and despite the popularity of its successors it has never completely vanished from the lexicon.
- And I'll get Verger to bring some weed to your party. — John Clellon Holmes, *Go*, p. 83, 1952
- Lee in Texas growing weed, Hassel on Riker's Island, Jane wandering on Times Square in a benzedrine hallucination, with her baby girl in her arms and ending up in Bellevue. — Jack Kerouac, *On the Road*, p. 8, 1957
- Rules of the Black Panther Party No. 7: No party member can have a weapon in his possession while DRUNK or loaded off narcotics or weed. — *The Black Panther*, p. 22, 15th January 1969
- I still had a connection. Which was insane, 'cause you couldn't get weed anyfuckinwhere then. — *Reservoir Dogs*, 1992
2 a marijuana cigarette *US, 1953*
- Kip stuck the two weeds in his breast pocket. — Edwin Gilbert, *The Hot and the Cool*, p. 36, 1953
- If you dig two-for-a-nickel weeds like this, then don't let me talk you out of anything. — Morton Cooper, *High School Confidential*, p. 79, 1958
- I lit a butt. Brew offered me a whole weed. — Piri Thomas, *Down These Mean Streets*, p. 122, 1967
3 a cigarette *US, 1951*
- — *Newsweek*, p. 28, 8th October 1951
- He asked me whether I smoked a great deal and I told him that I had a weed once in a while[.] — Frederick Kohner, *Gidget*, p. 67, 1957
- Two-Bit grinned and lit a cigarette. "Anyone want a weed?" — S.E. Hinton, *The Outsiders*, p. 29, 1967
- Billy holds his cigarette pack out to Meadows. "Weed?" — Darryl Ponicsan, *The Last Detail*, p. 27, 1970
4 a beginner surfer *US, 1990*
- — *Surfing*, p. 43, 14th March 1990

▶ **get into the weeds**
to micro-manage the smallest details *US, 1991*
- In the Army, when a commander essentially flyspecks every detail, they call it "getting into the weeds." — Tom Clancy with Fred Franks Jr., *Into the Storm*, p. 460, 1991

weed *verb*
1 to break and enter a store and steal selectively, avoiding the impression that there was been a theft *US, 1976*
- He carefully "weeded" their merchandise, never taking so much it would be next the next morning[.] — Malcolm Braley, *False Starts*, p. 131, 1976

2 in a gambling establishment, to provide an employee with money to gamble in the hopes of building up business *US, 1947*
- — Thomas L. Clark, *The Dictionary of Gambling and Gaming*, p. 248, 1987

▶ **weed a poke**
to remove all money and valuable items from a stolen wallet *US, 1962*
- — Joseph E. Ragen and Charles Finston, *Inside the World's Toughest Prison*, p. 822, 1962: "Penitentiary and underworld glossary"

weeder *noun*
a burglar who breaks into a store and steals selectively, avoiding the impression that there was been a theft *US, 1976*
- I did meet and admire a genuine weeder. — Malcolm Braley, *False Starts*, p. 129, 1976

weed head *noun*
a marijuana smoker *US, 1945*
- A bunch of weed-heads were seeing how dirty they could talk[.] — Chester Himes, *If He Hollers Let Him Go*, p. 43, 1945
- All weed-heads are cop-haters. — Jack Lait and Lee Mortimer, *Washington Confidential*, p. 117, 1951
- The weedheads were really blasting the stuff. — Willard Motley, *Let No Man Write My Epitaph*, p. 109, 1958
- Then I started running around with the show people and practically all of them was homosexuals and weed-heads. — Bruce Jackson, *In the Life*, p. 74, 1972

weed hound *noun*
a regular marijuana smoker *US, 1949*
- They picked up weed hounds, shook down every peddler they spotted coming out of the Cloudland, badgered tavern hostesses and talked price with the hustling girls. — Nelson Algren, *The Man with the Golden Arm*, p. 314, 1949

weed monkey; weed mule *noun*
an old car or truck used to haul raw materials used in the illegal production of alcohol *US, 1974*
- — David W. Maurer, *Kentucky Moonshine*, p. 127, 1974

weedo *noun*
a marijuana user *US, 1958*
- What can you expect from a confirmed weedo? — Morton Cooper, *High School Confidential*, p. 80, 1958

weeds *noun*
clothes *US, 1961*
- Gee, this hound's-tooth is really the most. You been pickin up on some new weeds. — Ross Russell, *The Sound*, p. 178, 1961

weedwacker team *noun*
in law enforcement, a surveillance team *US, 1997*
- I don't know, but the Feds have a three-man Weedwhacker team on him. They took these pictures. — Stephen J. Cannell, *Big Con*, p. 310, 1997

wee hours *noun*
very early in the morning; the hours just after midnight *US, 1891*
- The long lines during the wee hours can be a turn-off, however. — Bernhardt J. Hurwood, *The Sensuous New York*, p. 77, 1973

weekender *noun*
a person serving a jail sentence for a minor offence on weekends *US, 1971*
- Weekenders—bringing the Street in to tantalize you. — Ken Kesey, *Last Whole Earth Catalog*, p. 234, 1971

weekend hippie *noun*
a person with a conventional lifestyle who at the weekend adopts a counterculture persona *US, 1968*

- Leo finds it an intriguing convenience to be stopped on the corner by some weekend hippie and asked for a quarter for an egg cream or whatever. — Angelo d'Arcangelo, *The Homosexual Handbook*, p. 77, 1968
- Weekend hippies, one-night dropouts from suburbia's Kiddieland, they are American youth come to walk for a few hours through the neon fires of an infernal region[.] — Albert Goldman, *Freak Show*, p. 25, 1968
- Another threat is unwanted visitors—the sightseers from "straight" society and the weekend hippies who descend upon them to freeload. — *Life*, p. 16B, 18th July 1969
- The weekend, after-five, and penthouse hippies arrive in Jags and Cads[.] — Arthur Blessitt, *Turned On to Jesus*, p. 114, 1971

weekend warrior *noun*
a member of the National Guard or a reserve unit *US, 1943*
Members of reserve units must typically devote one weekend a month to refresher training.
- — Lanie Dills, *The Official CB Slanguage Language Dictionary*, p. 77, 1976
- The regulars call them "weekend warriors," which is a slight to the professionalism of the people who are required to put in one weekend a month and two weeks more during the year. — Hans Halberstadt, *Green Berets*, p. 34, 1988

weenie; weeny; wienie *noun*
1 a hot dog *US, 1906*
From the German *wienerwurst*.
- [W]e cook weenies, drink Tokay—I make love to big Swedish student girl Edeltrude. — Jack Kerouac, *Letter to John Clellon Holmes*, p. 381, 12th October 1952
- Some of the stories said the victims had been roasting weenies on the beach with their two dates[.] — Hunter S. Thompson, *Hell's Angels Tarrible Saga*, p. 37, 1966
- Green nail polish at a weenie stand is not Divine Decadence. It's just plain tacky. — Armistead Maupin, *Tales of the City*, p. 189, 1978

2 the penis *US, 1978*
- "By the way, great lover, since I took you back for the baby's sake, your midget weenie hasn't moved me once." — Iceberg Slim (Robert Beck), *Doom Fox*, p. 78, 1978
- But in reality, the muff-happy mogul is merely hidden away in an upstairs chamber watching their sexual escapades via a close circuit TV system, while pulling his weenie[.] — *Adult Video*, p. 12, August/September 1986
- They were totally dedicated and devoted to every aspect of rock and roll—especially the part about guys in bands who had Big Weenies. — Frank Zappa, *The Real Frank Zappa Book*, p. 104, 1989
- It looks like a big green weenie, huh? It turns ripe you can eat it. — Elmore Leonard, *Maximum Bob*, p. 133, 1991

weenie bin *noun*
a library carrel *US, 1987*
- — *New York Times*, 12th April 1987

weenie wagger; weenie waver *noun*
a male sexual exhibitionist *US, 1970*
- Where the wienie wagger shoved it through at the old babe changing clothes and she stuck a hatpin clear through it and the son of a bitch was pinned right there when the cops arrived. — Joseph Wambaugh, *The New Centurions*, p. 179, 1970
- Two weenie wagger convictions as an adult[.] — James Ellroy, *Brown's Requiem*, p. 34, 1981

weeny; weenie; wienie *noun*
an unlikeable, weak person *US, 1963*
- Everyone has a word for weenie again. The latest one I've heard is "dweeb," as in "He's a total dweeb." — *Washington Post (reprinted from The Nation)*, p. C5, 22nd December 1985
- I spend half my life being interviewed. I end up typing memos for some weenie, I'm not even sure what he does. — Elmore Leonard, *Bandits*, p. 212, 1987
- "Most men," I said, "are wienies." — Rita Ciresi, *Pink Slip*, p. 326, 1999

weep and wait *verb*
to serve a prison sentence while awaiting news on the outcome of an appeal *US, 1962*
- — Joseph E. Ragen and Charles Finston, *Inside the World's Toughest Prison*, p. 822, 1962: "Penitentiary and underworld glossary"

weeper *noun*
a prisoner who cannot manage his incarceration and constantly complains *US, 1976*
- — John R. Armore and Joseph D. Wolfe, *Dictionary of Desperation*, p. 56, 1976

weeping Willie *noun*
a person who cries uncontrollably *US, 1949*
- "Check on that guy with the crying jag." "What you want me to do with weeping Willie?" — Audie Murphy, *To Hell and Back*, p. 269, 1949

weeps *noun*
tears *US, 1946*
- I never saw a flock of chicks who could turn on the weeps so fast when we played their favorite tearjerkers[.] — Mezz Mezzrow, *Really the Blues*, p. 60, 1946

wee-wee *noun*
1 the penis *US, 1969*
- No little "wee-wee" was able to enter my "hole." — *Screw*, p. 7, 15th December 1969
- [L]ike some overgrown and deranged schoolboy, capable at any moment of unzipping his pants and displaying with a storm of giggles what I'm sure he'd call his wee-wee[.] — George V. Higgins, *Penance for Jerry Kennedy*, p. 29, 1985
- His wee-wee had withered from 10.4 centimeters to 7.9 centimeters in its flaccid state. — Carl Hiaasen, *Native Tongue*, p. 324, 1991
- "We'd make love so much your wee-wee would have carpal tunnel syndrome." — Eric Jerome Dickey, *Cheaters*, p. 410, 1999
2 the vagina *US, 1998*
- There's [a...] "cooter," "labbe," "Gladys Siegelman," "VA," "wee wee[.]" — Eve Ensler, *The Vagina Monologues*, p. 6, 1998
3 an act of urination; urine *US, 1962*
- "May, I have to make wee-wee." — Charles Perry, *Portrait of a Young Man Drowning*, p. 45, 1962
- No, I think that people of all ages can be appreciative of dog wee-wee and other forms of wee-wee and all sorts of physical byproducts. — Richard Meltzer, *A Whore Just Like the Rest*, p. 241, 1977

wee-wee *verb*
to urinate *UK, 1937*
Children's vocabulary.
- "I've got to go wee-wee." "You're getting kind of old for that, ain't you?" — Chester Himes, *A Rage in Harlem*, p. 66, 1957
- On the other hand, some corresponding euphemistic expressions (e.g., dickie, peepee, weewee, number one, number two, to move the bowels, to pass water, to make love, and so on), obviously evasive in their very structure, do have considerable usage. — *Eros*, p. 69, Autum 1962
- Lookit here, little pigeon, you got no cause to wee-wee. — Robert Campbell, *In La-La Land We Trust*, p. 134, 1986
- At a palmed alcove opposite Glori's door she paused to appraise its occupant, a plaster toddler making weewee in a giant seashell. — Seth Morgan, *Homeboy*, pp. 5–6, 1990

we go!
"let's leave!" *US, 1981*
Hawaiian youth usage.
- — Douglas Simonson, *Pidgin to da Max*, 1981

We Ho *noun*
West Hollywood, California *US, 2001*
- — Pamela Munro, *U.C.L.A. Slang*, p. 126, 2001

weigh *verb*
▸ **weigh into someone**
to ensnare someone in a swindle *US, 1965*
- I wanted to weigh myself into him. See, you can let a guy beat you three or four games and he'll swear before damnation that he can beat you from then on! — Henry Williamson, *Hustler!*, p. 127, 1965

weight *noun*
1 blame, responsibility *US, 1960*
- You're too weak to take your own weight. — Clarence Cooper Jr., *The Scene*, p. 14, 1960
- With only a few weeks remaining in his freshman year, he'd been expelled for smoking reefers, or, as he now said, for taking "the weight" for a bunch of chumps who couldn't care less about him. — Nathan Heard, *Howard Street*, p. 50, 1968
- I'll rob trains and banks and lots of other things / And take the weight for narcotic rings. — Dennis Wepman et al., *The Life*, p. 41, 1976
- I think my brother's taking the weight for someone. — Richard Price, *Clockers*, p. 356, 1992
2 a large amount of money *US, 1964*
- — *American Speech*, p. 306, December 1964: "Lingua Cosa Nostra"
3 large quantities of a drug *US, 1964*
- I wasn't up there to buy weight, so-called, ounces. — Jeremy Larner and Ralph Tefferteller, *The Addict in the Street*, p. 111, 1964

- Enough to buy an ounce of horse—some real weight. — Emmett Grogan, *Ringolevio*, p. 44, 1972
- "You wanted to carry weight," Converse said. "I got you weight." — Robert Stone, *Dog Soldiers*, p. 54, 1974
- I used to handle the weight [pounds, half pounds, kilograms] and I still can. — Terry Williams, *The Cocaine Kids*, p. 18, 1989
4 the handicap that a skilled pool player will allow an opponent *US, 1984*
- If you want to play me anymore, my friend, you're going to have to give me some weight. — Walter Tevis, *The Color of Money*, p. 75, 1984
- — Steve Rushin, *Pool Cool*, p. 29, 1990

weight house *noun*
in an illegal drug enterprise, any place where a dealer hides his major supply of drugs *US, 2002*
- They identified the dead man as the tenant, 30 year old Jaun Alex DeLossantos, a reputed large-scale cocaine-trafficker rumored to have several so-called "weight houses" scattered throughout the city hiding his cash and drugs. — *Milwaukee Sentinel Journal*, p. 9A, 3rd June 2002

weight pile *noun*
the area where weightlifting equipment is kept *US, 1990*
Prison terminology.
- Only two other cons were mad enough to be driving iron on the weight pile beneath Tower Three. — Seth Morgan, *Homeboy*, p. 224, 1990
- — William Bentley, *Prison Slang*, p. 4, 1992

weights *noun*
loaded dice *US, 1977*
- — Robert C. Prus and C.R.D. Sharper, *Road Hustler*, p. 171, 1977: "Glossary of terms"
- — Frank Scoblete, *Guerrilla Gambling*, p. 331, 1993

weirdie *noun*
an odd person *US, 1960*
- A kind of weirdie, like Danny Ocean. — George Clayton Johnson, *Ocean's Eleven*, p. 45, 1960

weirdo *noun*
a weird person *US, 1955*
- [T]he pianist, a real weirdo, came over to talk to Tuggle. — Glendon Swarthout, *Where the Boys Are*, p. 79, 1960
- Last night a group of us weirdos sat up all night and watched what has to be the greatest TV show, in fact, the "Greatest Show on Earth," as old John Ringling North of circus fame would have put it. — Abbie Hoffman, *Woodstock Nation*, p. 40, 1969
- Those weirdos are staring at us again. — *Romy and Michele's High School Reunion*, 1997
- Geez, print two little words—ANAL SEX—and the weirdos and freaks come out of the woodwork. — *The Village Voice*, 24th August 1999

weird out *verb*
1 to begin to act weirdly *US, 1980*
- And sometimes, he just weirds out until he gets out from being weird, somehow. — Stephen Gaskin, *Amazing Dope Tales*, p. 65, 1980
2 to frighten someone; to cause someone emotional turmoil *US, 1993*
- My mom doing it with your dad. I can't believe it. Carlotta, this is weirding me out. — C.D. Payne, *Youth in Revolt*, p. 407, 1993
- They had to be doing a lot of it to be that weirded-out. — Cleo Odzer, *Goa Freaks*, p. 273, 1995
- I weirded you out the other night. — *Chasing Amy*, 1997

weirdy *noun*
an odd person *US, 1961*
- "The ones who are talking to that couple of weirdies." — Frederick Kohner, *Gidget Goes Hawaiian*, p. 15, 1961

welcome to my world
used for expressing limited sympathy when someone is complaining about something that happens to you regularly *US, 1987*
- If you are confused at this point, welcome to my world. — Charles Keating, *Who We Are is How We Pray*, p. 34, 1987
- — Connie Eble (Editor), *UNC-CH Campus Slang*, p. 8, Spring 1999

welcome to the club!
used for expressing faint sympathy for someone who is complaining about something that others suffer *US, 1993*
- "Carlotta, this is weirding me out." "Welcome to the club, Frank," I said, adjusting my brassiere. — C.D. Payne, *Youth in Revolt*, p. 407, 1993

welder *noun*

a male pornography performer *US, 1995*

- — *Adult Video News*, p. 48, September 1995

welfare bitch *noun*

a person living on welfare *US, 1971*

- "I can tell by your talk you ain't nothing but a Welfare bitch, so's you got to be living in one of these kind of hotels." — Robert Deane Pharr, *S.R.O.*, p. 179, 1971

welfare pimp *noun*

a man living off a woman's welfare check *US, 1971*

- "He lives with a white woman now. He's a Welfare pimp!" — Robert Deane Pharr, *S.R.O.*, p. 310, 1971

welfare steak *noun*

bologna *US, 1975*

- Shit, welfare steak again. — Miguel Pinero, *Short Eyes*, p. 27, 1975

well *noun*

to a pickpocket, an inside jacket pocket *US, 1979*

- He feverishly wiped the dude clean of spittle and his billfold from the well (inside breast pocket). — Iceberg Slim (Robert Beck), *Airtight Willie and Me*, p. 6, 1979

Well *nickname*

▸ **the Well**

Bridewell Jail, Chicago *US, 1976*

- I woke up in a hospital ward in a prison called "The Well." — Dennis Wepman et al., *The Life*, p. 95, 1976

well *adjective*

used of a drug addict, unaffected by withdrawal symptoms *US, 1969*

- I had to shoot three spoons [of heroin] to stay well. — Iceberg Slim (Robert Beck), *Pimp*, p. 289, 1969

welnaw

no *US, 1993*

- — *The Bell* (Paducah Tilghman High School), pp. 8–9, 17th December 1993: "Tilghmanism: the concealed language of the hallway"

wert' *noun*

worthless *US, 1982*

Hawaiian youth usage.

- You saw dat movie? Was wert', man! — Douglas Simonson, *Pidgin to da Max Hana Hou*, 1982

Wesson party *noun*

group sex enhanced by spreading vegetable oil on the participants' bodies *US, 1971*

An allusion and tribute to Wesson™ vegetable oil.

- — Eugene Landy, *The Underground Dictionary*, p. 196, 1971

western style *adjective*

used of coffee, stale and lukewarm *US, 1976*

Punning on the observation that the coffee has "been on the range all day."

- — *Elementary Electronics, Dictionary of CB Lingo*, p. 58, 1976

west side passkeys *noun*

burglary tools *US, 1982*

Coined in Chicago.

- — Bill Reilly, *Big Al's Official Guide to Chicagoese*, p. 64, 1982

wet *noun*

1 rain; wet weather *US, 1945*

- — Lou Shelly, *Hepcats Jive Talk Dictionary*, p. 26, 1945

2 a Mexican national illegally present in the US *US, 1984*

Shortened form of **WETBACK**, from the Spanish *mojado*, drawn from the image of swimming across the Rio Grande River from Mexico into Texas. Derogatory.

- "These were Mexicans. Local wets, by the accent." — Carl Hiaasen, *Basket Case*, p. 281, 2002

wet *verb*

to kill *US, 1997*

- And I just fuckin' wet a guy to help hold on to one of our stops. — David Chase, *The Sopranos: Selected Scripts from Three Seasons*, p. 37, 25th August 1997

▸ **wet your whistle**

to have a drink, especially an alcoholic drink *US, 1720*

- "We should have brought up a bottle," he said. "A little something to wet our whistle." — Robert Campbell, *Boneyards*, p. 201, 1992

wet *adjective*

1 excellent *US, 2000*

- — *Ebony Magazine*, p. 156, August 2000: "How to talk to the new generation"

2 pertaining to killing *US, 1992*

- Strike had been so overwhelmed with his decision to get wet and do this that at first he hadn't given the target more than a passing thought. — Richard Price, *Clockers*, p. 71, 1992
- The he watched as his wet team headed for the chain-link fence. — Stephen J. Cannell, *White Sister*, p. 219, 2006

3 permitting the purchase and consumption of alcoholic beverages *US, 1950*

- Voters have three choices in addition to voting all-out wet. — Jack Lait and Lee Mortimer, *Chicago Confidential*, p. 141, 1950

wet

▸ **get wet with**

to drink *US, 1966*

- "I got nowhere to flop and nothing to get wet with." — Malcolm Braly, *It's Cold Out There*, p. 68, 1966

wetback *noun*

1 an illegal immigrant to the US from Mexico *US, 1920*

An offensive and figurative term deriving from the crossing of the Rio Grande River between Mexico and the US. Displaying a candor endemic to the time, the US Border Patrol launched "Operation Wetback" in 1954 to stem the tide of illegal immigration from Mexico.

- Sometimes a Chink or wetback gets into the city with some; it doesn't last long. — Clarence Cooper Jr., *The Scene*, p. 83, 1960
- EDDIE: Now the bartender was a wetback, he was a friend of mine, his name was Carlos. — *Reservoir Dogs*, 1992
- You wanted to box, but you didn't want to train, so them li'l wetbacks wiped the ring up with your ass. — Odie Hawkins, *Midnight*, p. 9, 1995
- Is it a more hurtful racial epithet than insults such as kike, wop, wetback, mick, chink, and gook? — Randall Kennedy, *Nigger*, p. 1, 2002

2 in surfing, a large wave *US, 1957*

- [O]nce you've licked those there is only one step further to Makaha where they have the real giant wetbacks. — Frederick Kohner, *Gidget*, p. 4, 1957

wet deck *noun*

a woman who has recently had sex with several men *US, 1963*

- Men no longer seemed particular if they got a girl with a "wet deck." — Madam Sherry, *Pleasure Was My Business*, p. 134, 1963
- "Would you go to bed with me tonight?" He saw her stiffen. "If you did, you'd be a wet deck. That's the name for a girl like that." — Jacqueline Susann, *Valley of the Dolls*, p. 428, 1966

wet-finger *noun*

▸ **get wet-finger**

in the categorization of sexual activity by teenage boys, to insert a finger into a girl's vagina *US, 1986*

- It was almost axiomatic that, under "normal" circumstances, to "get wet-finger" meant the girl's defenses would crumble as she was swept away on a tide of sheer physical excitement. — Terry Southern, *Now Dig This*, p. 3, 1986

wet rag *noun*

an unpopular, socially inept person *US, 1955*

- — *American Weekly*, p. 2, 14th August 1955

wet shot *noun*

a scene in a pornographic film or photograph depicting a man ejaculating *US, 1991*

- And here's a hazard of the trade, the wet shot. You only get one shot at it. Here comes the framing of that wet shot. It's a little off. — Robert Stoller and I.S. Levine, *Coming Attractions*, p. 86, 1991
- — *Adult Video News*, p. 42, August 1995

wetware *noun*

a human being; the human brain *US, 1991*

- — Eric S. Raymond, *The New Hacker's Dictionary*, p. 381, 1991

whack *noun*

▸ **have a whack at; take a whack at**

to attempt something; to attack someone *US, 1904*

- This regime-change stuff can be tricky. Apparently Georgie Porgie [US President George W. Bush] took a whack at it a couple of months ago in Venezuela [.] — *New York Observer*, 24th July 2002

▶ **out of whack**
   not in proper shape or order *US, 1885*
- [H]is stomach is out of whack. — *As Good As It Gets*, 1997

whack *verb*
1 to kill someone, especially by gunshot *US, 1977*
- "Whack him. Kill him." — Robert Daley, *Prince of the City*, p. 134, 1978
- You got out of line, you got whacked. Everyone knew the rules. — *Goodfellas*, 1990
- They just set their minds on whacking Kobayashi. — *The Usual Suspects*, 1995
- Don't get me wrong, I always liked your cousin, but whacking Phillip's brother was a major poke in the ass. — *The Sopranos* (Episode 64), 2004
2 to cut *US, 2002*
- Some guys would travel with the blades that they used to "whack" themselves with during matches to make themselves bleed. — Bobby Heenan, *Bobby the Brain*, p. 126, 2002

whack!
   in the language of hang gliding, used for commenting on a poor landing *US, 1992*
- — Erik Fair, *California Thrill Sports*, p. 328, 1992

whackadoo *noun*
   a crazy person *US, 1979*
- A fully made Mafioso. Plus, the guy is a total whackadoo. — Vincent Patrick, *The Pope of Greenwich Village*, p. 138, 1979

whack attack *noun*
   in the language of hang gliding, a string of bad landings *US, 1992*
- — Erik Fair, *California Thrill Sports*, p. 328, 1992

whacked *adjective*
   drunk or drug-intoxicated *US, 1967*
- I hadn't counted on this: Finding my attorney whacked on acid and locked into some kind of preternatural courtship. — Hunter S. Thompson, *Fear and Loathing in Las Vegas*, p. 114, 1971
- Tooling down the highway, half whacked out of her skull on Quaaludes and Dexamyls she'd copped from an attendant servicing a station in Moline, Illionois, Joanie Brown was listening to a Merle Haggard tune on the radio[.] — Emmett Grogan, *Final Score*, p. 77, 1976
- Am I crazy, Paulie, or is Walter half-whacked? — Vincent Patrick, *The Pope of Greenwich Village*, p. 13, 1979
- Finally Marcus opened the door, looking whacked. — Jason Starr, *Lights Out*, p. 127, 2006

whacked out *adjective*
   drug-intoxicated *US, 1973*
- Nobody else seemed to notice, but they were so whacked out of their heads on grass that they couldn't care less if we were on Candid Camera. — Xaviera Hollander, *The Happy Hooker*, p. 138, 1972

whacking *noun*
   a killing *US, 2001*
- Well, okay, Jimmy Curtains once walked Two Toes Garibaldi out of his house in his pajamas and drove him to the landfill, but still, the actual whacking didn't take place in the Burg. — Janet Evanovich, *Seven Up*, p. 5, 2001

whack-off *noun*
   an act of masturbation *US, 1981*
- He couldn't afford much beyond a quick whackoff into an old hand-kerchief[.] — Lester Bangs, *Psychotic Reactions and Carburetor Dung*, p. 348, 1981

whack off *verb*
   to masturbate *US, 1969*
- Did I mention that when I was fifteen I took it out of my pants and whacked off on the 107 bus from New York? — Philip Roth, *Portnoy's Complaint*, p. 78, 1969
- He reached down and began to whack off, and I reached for his dick. — Jennifer Sills, *Massage Parlor*, p. 64, 1973
- Perry debated whether to whack off or not. Some guys must—why else would they give them their own booths. — Richard Price, *The Wanderers*, p. 151, 1974

- What does it look like I'm doing? I'm whacking off. — *American Beauty*, 1999

whack out *verb*
   to kill someone *US, 1977*
- I always said, sooner or later the wops are gonna whack out Bobby Tex. — Edwin Torres, *Q & A*, p. 95, 1977
- I had already whacked out a couple of guys here and there. — Vincent Patrick, *The Pope of Greenwich Village*, p. 193, 1979
- [H]e drew a six-month sentence at Log Cabin Reformatory for his part in the continuing forays across the Bay Bridge to whack out the Suey Sing kids. — Bill Cardoso, *The Maltese Sangweech*, p. 8, 1984
- She wants to come back, but she's afraid you're gonna whack her out. — *Casino*, 1995

whack-silly *adjective*
   obsessed with masturbation *US, 1962*
- — Joseph E. Ragen and Charles Finston, *Inside the World's Toughest Prison*, p. 822, 1962: "Penitentiary and underworld glossary"

whack up *verb*
   to divide something, especially a quantity of illegal drugs, into portions *US, 1973*
- He says, aren't you going to whack it up with the other guys? I says, nayh, they been screwing us anyway. — Leonard Shecter and William Phillips, *On the Pad*, p. 113, 1973
- I take an eighth and I whack up two ounces [56 grams] of it, and sell the whacked stuff by the gram, half-grams, like that. — Terry Williams, *The Cocaine Kids*, p. 37, 1989

whale *noun*
   a gambler who places large bets *US, 1995*
- But I knew, the trick with whales like Ichikawa was that they can't bet small for long. — *Casino*, 1995

whale *verb*
1 to have sex *US, 1967*
- There's one thing about whalin' on booze—it kills all kinds of bad taste. — Piri Thomas, *Down These Mean Streets*, p. 57, 1967
2 to play music with passion and gusto *US, 1958*
- I saying yes and the night after the Red Drum session where Art Blakey was whaling like made and Thelonious Monk sweating leading the generation[.] — Jack Kerouac, *The Subterraneans*, p. 84, 1958
- A cool cat named Nat was whaling the drums at this hot spot in the heart of the slums. — Dan Burley, *Diggeth Thou?*, p. 9, 1959
- He talked up to me and said, "Babs, I play piano. May I sit in?" I said "sure c'mon whale some." — Babs Gonzales, *I Paid My Dues*, p. 61, 1967

whale sperm *noun*
   a plexiglas cleaning agent *US, 1991*
- By the time Heath left the base five minute slater, a case of Plexiglas cleaner, commonly known as "whale sperm," had magically appeared in the offices the IG team was occupying during the inspection. — Richard Herman, *Firebreak*, p. 97, 1991

wham *noun*
   a striptease act in which the dancer ends her performance completely naked *US, 1981*
- — Don Wilmeth, *The Language of American Popular Entertainment*, p. 292, 1981

wham bag *noun*
   a bag full of explosives *US, 1988*
- We're riding around with my wham bag in the trunk. It's got five sticks of dynamite, blasting caps, and a loaded thirty-eight revolver in it[.] — Elmore Leonard, *Freaky Deaky*, p. 159, 1988

wham, bam, thank you m'am
   used for describing anything done in very short order, especially sex *US, 1942*
   Sometimes abbreviated, and sometimes embellished with other rhymes.
- Well, there goes the liberty. That sure was a wham-bam-thank you, ma'am! — Thomas Heggen, *Mister Roberts*, p. 105, 1948
- Must be the fuckin', mustn't it / All that whambam-thank-you-ma'am. — Ken Kesey, *One Flew Over the Cuckoo's Nest*, p. 64, 1962
- With us, it wasn't the all-American wham-bam, thank you, ma'am. — Xaviera Hollander, *The Happy Hooker*, p. 83, 1972
- For me, it was supposed to be a quick hit-and-forget, a slam-bam-thank-you-ma'am. — Nathan McCall, *Makes Me Wanna Holler*, p. 389, 1994

whammer *noun*
   the penis *US, 1989*
- — James Harris, *A Convict's Dictionary*, p. 41, 1989

whammy *noun*

1 a spell, a curse *US, 1940*

Popularized by Al Capp's Li'l Abner comic strip and the charcter Eagle Eye Fleegle.

- The evil eye thus averted, along with all other forms of hex, whammy and squitch, he went on to Phil Kronfield's[.] — Bernard Wolfe, *The Late Risers*, p. 36, 1954
- All those psychologists in the pit are trying to put the whammy down on you. — Edward Lin, *Big Julie of Vegas*, p. 123, 1974
- I propose to consider the following in this and subsequent pieces: the Red Sox in particular, with occasional references to the Giants; African witch doctors and whammies (a subject about which I have some knowledge). — Bill Cardisi, *The Maltese Sangweech*, p. 139, 1984
- "Do you think Mia will put a whammy on him?" "Hester Birmingham, you know Mia doesn't do whammies." — Nora Roberts, *Face the Fire*, p. 31, 2002

2 something that is upsetting or sets you back *US, 1961*

- A man can weather a little ill fortune once in a while, but a triple whammy like that was too psychologically depressing. — Robert Gover, *One Hundred Dollar Misunderstanding*, p. 9, 1961

whammy bar *noun*

a floating bridge on an electric guitar that makes tremolos, vibrators, dives, bends, and other effects possible *US, 1985*

- He has al the whammy bar tricks, the harmonics tricks and is probably the fastest (and cleanest) rocker on the earth. — Dave Blickstein, *net.music*, 18th March 1985
- There were five of them, perfectly matched white Strats, strung upside down, with a peg for the strap on the short arm of the cutaway, and the whammy bar. — Lewis Shiner, *Deserted Cities of the Heart*, p. 134, 1988
- Wow. '65 Fender Stratocaster. In classic white with a "whammy" bar and triple hummbucker pick-ups. — *Wayne's World*, 1992

wham-wham *noun*

in prison, store-bought snacks *US, 1981*

- A phrase that must have been conceived by a person with a playful imagination is zoo-zoos and wham-whams for confections, usually small packaged cakes, pieces, candy or gum obtained from a vending machine. — *Maledicta*, p. 267, Summer/Winter 1981
- When he made the canteen cart, the beaners ripped off his zuuzuus and whamwhams. — Seth Morgan, *Homeboy*, p. 152, 1990
- — William Bentley, *Prison Slang*, p. 68, 1992

whandoodles *noun*

in poker, a temporary increase in the betting limit after a player wins a hand with a rare hand *US, 1967*

- — Albert H. Morehead, *The Complete Guide to Winning Poker*, p. 276, 1967

whangdang *noun*

a fit feigned by a drug addict *US, 1968*

A variant of the more common **WINGDING**.

- When they ignored him, I finally coached him on throwing a "whangdang"—a good imitation of the worst period of withdrawal. — Phil Hirsch, *Hooked*, p. 13, 1968

wharf rat *noun*

in the language surrounding the Grateful Dead, a follower of the band who abstains from alcohol and drugs *US, 1994*

From the title of a Grateful Dead song.

- — David Shenk and Steve Silberman, *Skeleton Key*, p. 316, 1994

what a loss

used for expressing sympathy for a difficult situation *US, 1983*

- — Guy L. Steele et al., *The Hacker's Dictionary*, pp. 87–88, 1983

what do you know, Joe?

used as a greeting *US, 1947*

- — Marcus Hanna Boulware, *Jive and Slang of Students in Negro Colleges*, 1947

whatever!

used as a dismissing retort to what has just been said *US, 1989*

Said with attitude, with a pause after "what," and sometimes with thumbs and forefingers shaped like a "W."

- — Pamela Munro, *U.C.L.A. Slang*, p. 90, 1989

- — Connie Eble (Editor), *UNC-CH Campus Slang*, p. 10, Spring 1992
- ELTON: I think we both know what it feels like to be lonely. CHER: Whatever. — *Clueless*, 1995

whatever's fair

used as a nonresponsive, vague answer to a direct question *US, 1969*

- — *Current Slang*, p. 10, Fall 1969

what goes around, comes around

used as a cliche meaning that you will reap what you sow *US, 1968*

- You have helped us and yourself by keeping your black dollars in the black community and as we all know, "What goes around, comes around." — *Chicago Daily Defender*, p. 6, 14th December 1968
- "Baby, what goes around comes round, and it's his turn." 156 — Nathan Heard, *To Reach a Dream*, p. 79, 1972

what it is

used as a greeting *US, 1974*

- "What it is, what it is," Dan said quickly, as he reached over and slapped William's palm. — Donald Goines, *Cry Revenge*, p. 87, 1974

what kind?

what's the matter with you? *US, 1963*

- For example, if one student accidentally jostles another in the hall, the latter might very well say "What kind?" There is no answer to this. — *American Speech*, p. 275, December 1963: "American Indian student slang"

whatnot *noun*

anything and everything *UK, 1540*

Usually a characteristic of individual speakers, not a group, and often used with an annoying regularity.

- "Okay," Louis said, "the guy's pulling about fifty grand a month out of Detroit, the apartments and whatnot, and banking it in the Bahamas for his retirement." — Elmore Leonard, *Switch*, p. 64, 1978

what say?

used as a greeting *US, 1965*

- — Miss Cone, *The Slang Dictionary (Hawthorne High School)*, 1965

what's cooking?

used as a greeting or an inquiry as to what is happening *US, 1963*

- "What the hell's cooking?" he asked. — Wade Hunter, *The Sex Peddler*, p. 100, 1963

what's-his-name; what's-his-namey *noun*

used to refer to a person whose name is unknown, forgotten, to be avoided or hardly worth mentioning *UK, 1697*

- Five years ago that cracker governor, the one in Alabama, whatshisname? was a superduper white racist, o.k.? — Odie Hawkins, *The Busting Out of an Ordinary Man*, p. 126, 1985

what's kicking?

used as a greeting, along the lines of "what is new?" *US, 1949*

- "What's kicking?" "Everything's kind of quiet." — Hal Ellson, *Duke*, p. 26, 1949

what's my name?

used as a taunt while beating someone *US, 1997*

In 1967, boxer Muhammed Ali fought Ernie Terrell, who insisted on calling Ali "Cassius Clay"; as Ali pounded Terrell, Ali taunted "What's my name, fool? What's my name?"

- — *Maybeck High School Yearbook (Berkeley, California)*, p. 29, 1997

what's poppin?

used as a peer-to-peer greeting *US, 1995*

- — Bill Valentine, *Gang Intelligence Manual*, p. 79, 1995

what's shaking?; what's shakin'?

used as a greeting *US, 1951*

- — Earl Selby, *Philadelphia Evening Bulletin*, 11th November 1951
- So, I used to talk in a hip idiom, so I started talking. I said, "What's shakin', man?" — Lenny Bruce, *The Essential Lenny Bruce*, p. 27, 1967
- "Yo, Lise," Al said. "What's shakin'?" — Rita Ciresi, *Pink Slip*, p. 304, 1999

what's the story, morning glory?

used as a cheerful greeting *US, 1959*

- So, what's your story, Miss Morning Glory, hip me before I broom[.] — Dan Burley, *Diggeth Thou?*, p. 48, 1959

what's up?
used as a greeting *US, 1993*
- Hey Dad, Ma. What's up? — *Dazed and Confused*, 1993
- "What's sup?" Dirk asked. — Francesca Lia Block, *Baby Be-Bop*, p. 404, 1995

whatsup?
used as a greeting *US, 1990*
- Yo, man, whatsup? Looks like she wants to talk with you. — *Boyz N The Hood*, 1990

what's your song, King Kong?
used as a greeting *US, 1947*
- — Marcus Hanna Boulware, *Jive and Slang of Students in Negro Colleges*, 1947
- — Clarence Major, *Dictionary of Afro-American Slang*, p. 122, 1970

what up?
used as a greeting *US, 1990*
- What up Tre? You do your homework? — *Boyz N The Hood*, 1990
- What up Chauncy. What up ho's. — *Menace II Society*, 1993

what up, love one?
used as a greeting *US, 2000*
Used as a coded greeting by members of the Black Guerrilla Family prison gang.
- A stranger would be asked, "What up, love one?" The correct response is, "What up, love one." — Bill Valentine, *Gangs and Their Tattoos*, p. 19, 2000

what/which part of no don't you understand?
used for humorously emphasizing a previous negative answer *US, 1991*
Wildly popular, and over-used, in the 1990s; an instant favorite of US parents scolding children. First made famous by Lorrie Morgan in a 1991 song "What Part of No," written by Wayne Perry and Gerald Smith—"I'll be glad to explain it / If it's too hard to comprehend / So tell me what part of no / Don't you understand?"
- It is apparently now time for some of us to ponder which part of no we don't understand. — *The Arkansas Democrat-Gazette*, p. B11, 18th May 2000

wheel *noun*
1 a betting operation *US, 1054*
- There are about thirty books or wheels going in Chicago alone. — Alson Smith, *Syndicate City*, p. 196, 1954

2 a leader; an important person *US, 1933*
- Evidently the fellow was some kind of a wheel, checking on activities here and there[.] — Mickey Spillane, *One Lonely Night*, p. 32, 1951
- He's a wheel. So's she. It's hard to make friends with them. — *Rebel Without a Cause*, 1955

3 a mid-level employee in an illegal lottery *US, 1978*
- Next, the wheel distributes the winnings to the runners who pass it on to the winning customers. — Burgess Laughlin, *Job Opportunities in the Black Market*, p. 11–3, 1978

4 the game of roulette *US, 1993*
- — Frank Scoblete, *Guerrilla Gambling*, p. 331, 1993

5 in a carnival, any ride that is in the form of a wheel *US, 1960*
- — *American Speech*, pp. 308–309, December 1960: "Carnival talk"

6 a life prison sentence *US, 1991*
- — Lee McNelis, *30 + And a Wake-Up*, p. 13, 1991

7 in lowball poker, the lowest possible straight (five to ace) *US, 1981*
- — Jim Glenn, *Programmed Poker*, p. 158, 1981
- — Dave Scharf, *Winning at Poker*, p. 244, 2003

8 the ankle *US, 1986*
- — Chuck Wielgus and Alexander Wolff, *The Back-In-Your-Face Guide to Pick-up Basketball*, p. 231, 1986

▸ **on the wheel**
(of a police officer) assigned to motorcycle duty *US, 1958*
- [A] man on motorcycle duty is on the wheel. — *New York Times*, p. 34, 20th October 1958

wheel *verb*
to travel; to drive *US, 1975*
- And when we got into Baltimore he was gonna drop me off at the famous Ballroom and keep on wheelin' home. — Babs Gonzales, *Movin' On Down De Line*, p. 134, 1975

wheel and deal *verb*
to engage in profit-making in a flamboyant manner *US, 1961*

- You can't go downtown to wheel and deal for yourself because you aren't used to thinking like a big entertainer with a future[.] — Dick Gregory, *Nigger*, pp. 145–146, 1964

wheeler-dealer *noun*
a scheming, contriving deal-maker with many connections *US, 1960*
The reduplication of the vowel sound serves to intensify.
- The wheelers and dealers in the Tiger didn't stop wheeling and dealing, they just took their swift moving actions to a slower, more cautious place. — Odie Hawkins, *Chicago Hustle*, p. 36, 1977
- Those wheeler-dealers who didn't blow their brains out after the Hurricane of '26 or hang themselves after the real-estate bust were eventually rewarded with untold wealth. — Carl Hiaasen, *Tourist Season*, p. 315, 1986
- The wheelers and dealers were having a good time because contacts were everything to them. Appointments were gold. — Robert Campbell, *Alice in La-La Land*, p. 130, 1987

wheel gun *noun*
a revolver *US, 1993*
- "A wheel gun? In this day and age?" "The Oracle still carries a wheel gun." — Joseph Wambaugh, *Hollywood Station*, p. 3, 2006

wheelie; wheely *noun*
▸ **pop a wheelie**
to perform a wheelie *US, 1995*
- They rode their bikes and skateboards, popping wheelies, doing jumps and flips. — Francesca Lia Block, *Baby Be-Bop*, p. 394, 1995

wheel man *noun*
1 in a criminal operation, the getaway driver *US, 1935*
- I didn't take any actual part in it except to be the wheel man. In other words, the driver of the getaway car. — Willard Motley, *Let No Man Write My Epitaph*, p. 207, 1958
- "Yeah he one of the boss wheel men of all time." — Ken Kesey, *Kesey's Jail Journal*, p. 72, 1967
- Guess I'm only the second best wheel man around. — Edwin Torres, *Carlito's Way*, p. 115, 1975
- Hiram was wheelman for the famous stopwatch bandit! — Joseph Wambaugh, *The Secrets of Harry Bright*, p. 34, 1985
- Beano had heard a rumor that Tommy Rina often used disposable wheel men. — Stephen J. Cannell, *King Con*, p. 54, 1997

2 a person who brings together pool players who are willing to play for money *US, 1993*
- — Mike Shamos, *The Illustrated Encyclopedia of Billiards*, p. 261, 1993

wheels *noun*
1 a car *US, 1959*
- "Man has wheels!" Zaida exclaimed. — Ross Russell, *The Sound*, p. 15, 1961
- "Car? You don't have wheels?" "My dad got me an Impala for senior year." — Richard Farina, *Been Down So Long*, p. 26, 1966
- [S]he explained she wouldn't be needing her station wagon for a while and if I drove it back to New York, we could save our train fare. I accepted her offer and we cut out in style with wheels. — Babs Gonzales, *I Paid My Dues*, p. 44, 1967
- With this pad, the killer wheels, looks like you really cleaned up your act. — *Something About Mary*, 1998

2 shoes or boots *US, 1990*
- — Elena Garcia, *A Beginner's Guide to Zen and the Art of Snowboarding*, p. 123, 1990: "Glossary"

3 the legs, especially a woman's legs *US, 1966*
- — *Current Slang*, p. 5, Summer 1966

▸ **on wheels**
to the extreme *US, 1943*
- And don't forget that Bix, who was a bitch-on-wheels to Tesch, and all kinds of a virtuoso, was tugging hard at these kids too[.] — Mezz Mezzrow, *Really the Blues*, p. 157, 1946

wheeze *noun*
a false belief *US, 1965*
- They don't have to stay in their places. That's an old wheeze. — Antony James, *America's Homosexual Underground*, p. 118, 1965

where it is at; where it's at
the center of a situation; a place where something important is happening *US, 1965*
- — J.L. Simmons and Barry Winograd, *It's Happening*, p. 174, 1966: "glossary"
- In the car I suggested we go to Toronto because Montreal obviously wasn't where it was at. — James Simon Kunen, *The Strawberry Statement*, p. 97, 1968

- We tell each other where it's at. — Stephen Gaskin, *Hey Beatnik*, 1974
- If you say you don't want to be stolen from, then you don't buy somebody else's stolen goods. That's exactly where it's at. — Herbert Huncke, *Guilty of Everything*, p. 188, 1990

where someone is at
the person's point of view or opinion *US, 1960s*
- Gallup takes polls; I take rides to find out where people are at. — James Simon Kunen, *The Strawberry Statement*, p. 79, 1968

where the sun don't shine
in your rectum *US, 1977*
- "My first inclination, Katheirne, is to tell you to take that walkie-talkie and stick it where the sun don't shine." — Marvin Kalb, *In the National Interest*, p. 79, 1977
- There was a look in Chicklet's eye that said he'd like to tell Orchid to shove his story up there where the sun don't shine but since Orchid always picked up the check he kept his mouth shut. — Robert Campbell, *Boneyards*, p. 31, 1992

where were you when the shit hit the fan?
used as a greeting between US Marines in Korea *US, 1986*
- With all Marines now living in the bean patch, frequent visits were made between friends of different units. "Where were you when the shit hit the fan?" was the standard invitation for one to relate his personal experience up north. — William B. Hopkins, *One Bugle No Drum*, p. 213, 1986

where you're coming from
your point of view or opinion *US, 1975*
- "We got to make it to the airport fast." "Okay... I dig where you're comin' from, Johnny." — Donald Goines, *Inner City Hoodlum*, p. 209, 1975

whif *adjective*
what-if *US, 1974*
Used in "what if...?" exercises projecting possible contingencies and developing reactions to them.
- — Robert Kirk Mueller, *Buzzwords*, p. 164, 1974

whiff *noun*
cocaine *US, 1983*
- The cure didn't take, Pete's attorneys charged, and she soon went back on the whiff and also back to the pusher[.] — Hunter S. Thompson, *Songs of the Doomed*, p. 195, 1983
- — Connie Eble (Editor), *UNC-CH Campus Slang*, p. 9, Fall 1986

whiff *verb*
to inhale a powdered drug through the nose *US, 1981*
- Well, he also uses Mexican brown. And Persian by the bead! He whiffs it. — Joseph Wambaugh, *The Glitter Dome*, p. 248, 1981

whifferdill *noun*
any improvised evasive maneuver in an aircraft *US, 1957*
- It shows a combinatoin of in-plane-out-of-plane whifferdill, the like of which I hope no one ever sees again. — Society of Experimental Test Pilots, *Technical Review*, p. 27, 1957
- — Tom Yarborough, *Da Nang Diary*, p. 280, 1990: Glossary

whim-whams *noun*
a feeling of dread or anxiety; a state of anxiety or nervousness; the jitters *US, 1950*
- When you mentioned Nancy I had a pretty good idea what you were after, and I get the wim-wams when I think about getting mixed up in anything. — Mickey Spillane, *My Gun is Quick*, p. 90, 1950
- All at once I'd had a crazy idea about him, one that kind of gave me the whimwhams. — Jim Thompson, *Savage Night*, p. 17, 1953

whiney gyny club *noun*
complaining hospital patients recovering from gynecological surgery *US, 1984–1985*
- — *Maledicta*, p. 118, 1984–1985: "Milwaukee medical maledicta"

whip *noun*
1 a police squad leader *US, 1958*
- [A] lieutenant who heads a detective squad is the whip. — *New York Times*, p. 34, 20th October 1958

2 the arm; the ability to throw *US, 1956*
- "Might fine whip for a girl," Dove had conceded. — Nelson Algren, *A Walk on the Wild Side*, p. 64, 1956

3 a customized, accessorized car *US, 2006*
- They call them "whips" in street slang—personalized cars decked out and souped up with what the auto industry politely refers to as "aftermarket products." — *Daily News of Los Angeles*, p. B1, 5th December 2006

4 a boss or supervisor *US, 1984*
- Lt. Jack Weidt, the "whip" or boss of the Nineteenth Squad of detectives, was a trendy dresser. — William J. Cavnitz, *One Police Plaza*, p. 243, 1984

whip *verb*
to arrest someone *US, 1971*
- So he gets whipped in three days after the Lowell job and he's got a gun on him and they don't even have to prove he was on the Lowell thing[.] — George V. Higgins, *The Friends of Eddie Doyle*, p. 25, 1971

▶ whip it out
to release the penis from the confines of the trousers in a bold genital display *US, 1997*
- Now they're trying to get him for sexual harassment. What happened? The girl came to his hotel room, he whipped it out, she said no, and left. And she wants to sue him? He's the one who got turned down. — Chris Rock, *Rock This!*, p. 193, 1997

▶ whip your wang
(used of a male) to masturbate *US, 1969*
- Whang whipping experts voted the New York Times Sunday Magazine their favorite masturbation media. — *Screw*, p. 26, 10th November 1969

whip off *verb*
(used of a male) to masturbate *US, 1975*
- — *American Speech*, p. 69, Spring–Summer 1975: "Razorback Slang"

whip-out *noun*
1 a bankroll designed to impress when whipped out of the pocket *US, 1972*
- I happened to scare up a publisher in New York who was enthusiastic enough about it to give me a whole lot of what you call your up-front whip-out. — Dan Jenkins, *Semi-Tough*, p. 13, 1972
- Fast-paced whip-out handled it nicely. — Dan Jenkins, *The Money-Whipped Steer-Job Three-Jack Give-Up Artist*, p. 69, 2001

2 a regular payment *US, 1981*
- My fee for a repossession is the sum of the owner's monthly whip-out. — James Ellroy, *Brown's Requiem*, p. 11, 1981

whipped *adjective*
dominated by a girlfriend or wife *US, 1965*
A shortened form of PUSSY-WHIPPED.
- — Carol Covington, *A Glossary of Teenage Terms*, 1965

whipper *noun*
1 a person who enjoys being whipped in a sadomasochistic encounter *US, 1970*
- I understand that a lot of girls get customers or Johns or dates or whatever you want to call them who are perverted in one way or the other. I guess whippers are the ones you hear about the most. Men who want to be degraded. — John Warren Wells, *Tricks of the Trade*, p. 38, 1970

2 a small cartridge of nitrous oxide *US, 1986*
Designed for use in making whipped cream, but often abused for the psychoactive effects of the gas.
- "Whippers" come in ten-packs for eight bucks, and are ostensibly used as charges for whipping cream." — Josh Alan Friedman, *Tales of Times Square*, p. 176, 1986

whippersnapper; snapper *noun*
a young, impertinent person unmindful of his station in life *UK, 1700*
Still heard, but used with the effect of dating the speaker.
- "Whippersnapper," muttered Pipgrass. "I remember when they built this state capitol." — Max Shulman, *The Many Loves of Dobie Gillis*, p. 17, 1951

whippets; whippits *noun*
capsules of nitrous oxide used as a recreational drug *US, 1980*
- — Jay Saporita, *Pourin' It All Out*, p. 62, 1980
- Lisanick had inhaled six "whippits" of nitrous oxide, commonly known as laughing gas, as he was driving along busy Route 7 on Nov. 29. — *Washington Post*, p. D6, 9th June 1990
- Gray aluminum capsules filled with nitrous oxide ("whippits") are legally available[.] — David Shenk and Steve Silberman, *Skeleton Key*, p. 203, 1994
- Whippits have taken on a mythical status since the 1960s when some weirdo first stuck a can of frozen desert topping up his nose. — Suroosh Alvi et al., *The Vice Guide*, p. 89, 2002

whippy *adjective*
clever *US, 1969*
- — *Current Slang*, p. 11, Winter 1969

whips and jingles *noun*

symptoms of heroin or alcohol withdrawal *US, 1966*
Referring to the physical pain and frayed nerves suffered.

- "When you showed, I had two cents, a dry throat and a good start on the whips and jingles." — Malcolm Braly, *It's Cold Out There*, p. 156, 1966
- — David Maurer and Victor Vogel, *Narcotics and Narcotic Addiction*, p. 452, 1973

whipsaw *verb*

1 in poker, to surround a player with two confederates whose collusive betting tactics relieve the middle player of his bankroll and drive him from the game *US, 1949*

- — Thomas L. Clark, *The Dictionary of Gambling and Gaming*, p. 188, 1987

2 in horseracing, to correctly pick both the winner and second-place finisher in a race *US, 1947*

- — Dan Parker, *The ABC of Horse Racing*, p. 150, 1947

whip shot *noun*

a type of controlled toss of the dice, effective by a skilled cheat *US, 1963*

- — John S. Salak, *Dictionary of Gambling*, p. 276, 1963

whirl *noun*

an attempt *US, 1884*

- After high school, he thought he might give college a whirl. — Max Shulman, *Rally Round the Flag, Boys!*, p. 5, 1957

whirl bet *noun*

in craps, a one-roll bet on 2, 3, 7, 11 and 12 *US, 1961*

- — Thomas L. Clark, *The Dictionary of Gambling and Gaming*, p. 249, 1987

whirlies *noun*

extreme dizziness experienced when drunk *US, 1966*

- — John D. Bell et al., *Loosely Speaking*, p. 21, 1966
- I got a touch of the whirlies form the J&B. — Albert Gurney, *The Gospel According to Joe*, p. 13, 1974
- Happily, his whirlies were gone. — Chris Miller, *The Real Animal House*, p. 154, 2006

whirligig *noun*

a revolver *US, 1957*

- — *American Speech*, p. 195, October 1957: "Some colloquialisms of the handgunner"

whirlpooling; whirlpool *noun*

the assault of a girl by a group of males in a swimming pool who grope her while churning water around her *US, 1993*

- Employees at two other pools, one in Brooklyn and one in the Bronx, said they, too, had seen whirlpooling. — *New York Times*, p. A1, 7th July 1993

whirly *noun*

in the television and movie industries, a hydraulic lift used for shooting scenes from above *US, 1990*

- — Ralph S. Singleton, *Filmmaker's Dictionary*, p. 184, 1990

whirlybird *noun*

a helicopter *US, 1951*

- — *American Speech*, February 1953
- Over 100,000 people squeezed into the Meadow listening to speakers under leaden skies and the annoying obligato of Mayor Lindsay's whirlybirds. — Sidney Bernard, *This Way to the Apocalypse*, p. 55, 1968
- Hey, Fort Rucker, have you heard? / I'm gonna fly me a whirly bird. — Sandee Shaffer Johnson, *Cadences*, p. 100, 1986

whirly pig *noun*

a helicopter-borne police officer; a police helicopter *US, 1970*

- — *New York Times*, p. 24, 10th February 1970
- WHIRLYPIG: helicopter flown by the Berkeley police during student disruptions — Robert Buckhout, *Toward Social Change*, p. 467, 1971

whiskers *noun*

pubic hair *US, 1967*

- — Dale Gordon, *The Dominion Sex Dictionary*, 1967

whiskey dent *noun*

a dent on your car that you don't remember incurring while driving drunk *US, 1984*

- He's got so many whiskey dents in his car, the fenders look like washboards. — Ken Weaver, *Texas Crude*, p. 63, 1984

whiskeyleg *noun*

a drunkard *US, 1957*

- He doesn't drink any more and he used to be the biggest whiskyleg in town. — Jack Kerouac, *On the Road*, p. 216, 1957

whiskey papa; whiskey poppa *noun*

a white phosphorous flare or grenade *US, 1990*
From the military phonetic alphabet—WP.

- "Can you pop a whiskey poppa over us?" — Paul Morgan, *The Parrot's Beak*, p. 41, 2000

whiskey-rot *noun*

any unspecified illness *US, 1970*

- — *Current Slang*, p. 26, Spring 1970

whisper *noun*

1 a rumor *UK, 1596*

- Everygreen looks likes she's laced in pretty tight, but there's been whispers that she likes a bit of a wrestle now and then. — Robert Campbell, *Nibbled to Death by Ducks*, p. 129, 1989

2 the very end of a prison sentence *US, 1976*

- — Troy Harris, *A Booklet of Criminal Argot, Cant and Jargon*, 1976

whispering campaign *noun*

the covert, planned, and targeted use of gossip and rumor in a political campaign *US, 1920*

- The Kerry campaign had heard that Karl Rove was waging a whispering campaign in the Miami condos that Kerry was weak on Israel. — Evan Thomas, *Election 2004*, p. 78, 2004

whistle *verb*

▸ **whistle in the dark**

to perform oral sex on a woman *US, 1967*

- — Dale Gordon, *The Dominion Sex Dictionary*, p. 170, 1967

whistlebait *noun*

an attractive woman or girl *US, 1947*

- You're twenty-twenty whislte bait! — Harry Haenigsen, *Jive's Like That*, 1947

whistlestop *noun*

a small town *US, 1934*
From the image of a train making a brief stop at the town.

- He squatted in a whistle-stop up in the Catskill Mountains. — Harry Haenigsen, *Jive's Like That*, 1947

white *noun*

1 a capsule of Benzedrine™ (amphetamine sulfate) or any other central nervous system stimulant *US, 1966*

- Bennies ("cartwheels" or "whites") are basic to the outlaw diet—like weed, beer and wine. — Hunter S. Thompson, *Hell's Angels*, p. 216, 1966
- "The way they put it is that they 'drop whites' to get out of bed in the morning, or whenever they get up to go to work, and 'drop reds' to go to sleep," Sweeney reported at the conference. — *San Francisco Chronicle*, p. 5, 11th October 1966
- Tim was back to his old regimen of reds and whites. — Lester Bangs, *Psychotic Reactions and Carburetor Dung*, p. 109, 1972
- Reds and Ripple mixed with a bennie, a white and a toke. — Oscar Zeta Acosta, *The Revolt of the Cockroach People*, p. 90, 1973

2 in American casinos, a white betting token worth one dollar *US, 1985*

- — Steve Kuriscak, *Casino Talk*, p. 59, 1985

3 in American casinos, a white betting token worth $500 *US, 1961*

- — Thomas L. Clark, *The Dictionary of Gambling and Gaming*, p. 249, 1987

4 a day; daytime *US, 1975*

- About a deuce of long black and whites ago, a stud from the low lands came to the Apple. — Babs Gonzales, *Movin' On Down De Line*, p. 89, 1975

▸ **like white on rice**

entirely, utterly, completely *US, 1951*

- But then the marshals were all over me like white on rice and I couldn't see anything. — Lloyd Brown, *Iron City*, p. 144, 1951
- They were on my ass like white on rice. — Odie Hawkins, *Scars and Memories*, p. 73, 1987

white *adjective*

decent *US, 1893*
Usually used sarcastically and as a conscious rejection of the racism that once would have inspired the saying.

- "You can bring her out to the house if you really want to." "That's white of you," I said. "What makes you think she'd come?" "Look,

Jim, I didn't mean it that way." — Thurston Scott, *Cure it with Honey*, p. 198, 1951

- We've only met twice and you've been more than white to me both times. — Raymond Chandler, *The Long Goodbye*, p. 9, 1953
- "Well, that's darn white of you," said my old man. — Frederick Kohner, *Gidget Goes Hawaiian*, p. 9, 1961
- "Like you inviting me out for the weekend. Damned white of you." — Burt Hirschfield, *Fire Island*, p. 74, 1970

white-bread *adjective*

everyday, unexciting, respectable; representing the epitome of white middle-class values and style *US, 1991*

- — Connie Eble (Editor), *UNC-CH Campus Slang*, p. 10, Spring 1991
- It was kind of a white-bread neighborhood[.] — Wolfman Jack (Bob Smith), *Have Mercy!*, p. 31, 1995
- They were white-bread, all-American boys in all but one critical degree, which is that they didn't care fuck-all about material wealth. — Peter Coyote, *Sleeping Where I Fall*, p. 133, 1998

white cloud *noun*

crack cocaine *US, 1989*

- So, in a feew minutes, they all went back in search of the white cloud. — Terry Williams, *The Cocaine Kids*, p. 110, 1989

white cross *noun*

an amphetamine or methamphetamine tablet, sectioned with an X *US, 1965*

- I can get all the straight old white cross benny's you want at $85 a thousand. — Neal Cassady, *The First Third*, pp. 219–220, 30th August 1965
- Paul and his friend Chris Coon had a car, a skateboard, and a new drug called White Crosses, small speed pills. — Jennifer Blowdryer, *White Trash Debutante*, p. 60, 1997
- [Cross Tops] were also referred to as whites, or, for the indecisive, white crosses, and were sold by the $1 unit called a rack in tightly foiled increments of four, five, or ten[.] — Don Bolle, *Retrohell*, p. 50, 1997

white devil *noun*

cocaine *US, 1972*

- I take my Kaabar pocket knife, my own personal coke dispenser, scoop up a tipful of the white devil and suck in giant nostrils of slow, white heat through the tender veins of my Indian nose. — Oscar Zeta Acosta, *The Autobiography of a Brown Buffalo*, p. 62, 1972

white fever *noun*

used of people of color, a strong attraction towards white people *US, 1969*

The opposite of **JUNGLE FEVER**.

- I don't have white fever. Color don't mean shit to me. — Iceberg Slim (Robert Beck), *Mama Black Widow*, p. 294, 1969

white fingers *noun*

cocaine *US, 2002*

- The wiretaps recorded a primer of street slang for powder cocaine: white lady, white fingers, soft, fish scales and sand. — *Orlando Sentinel*, p. B2, 17th August 2002

white girl *noun*

cocaine *US, 1971*

- Many of us called it "girl" or "white girl" then. It helped to be in a movie studio setting to do cocaine. — Odie Hawkins, *Lost Angeles*, p. 33, 1994

white hat *noun*

a computer hacker who acts with a legal or moral justification *US, 2001*

- He said white hats used their computer skills to understand and secure systems, but black hats used their abilities to break into systems for profit or glory. — *Wired News*, 22nd May 2001

white king *noun*

heroin *US, 1968*

- Vivian had shot "White King" from time to time[.] — Phil Hirsch, *Hooked*, p. 29, 1968

white-knuckle *verb*

to persevere on courage alone, especially in the quitting of an addictive drug *US, 1974*

- She couldn't just white-knuckle it, could she? She'd need to be in a neighborhood like West Hollywood where she could get speedballs. — Joseph Wambaugh, *Floaters*, p. 68, 1996

white lady *noun*

a powdered narcotic, especially cocaine or heroin *US, 1968*

The shortened form "lady" is also used.

- Only woman I need is the White Lady that rides through my veins. — Nathan Heard, *Howard Street*, p. 185, 1968
- I wish I could cop a few blows of the Miss Pure White Lady stashed under that cushion to clear my skull. — Iceberg Slim (Robert Beck), *Death Wish*, p. 11, 1977

white lead *noun*

the lead aircraft in a formation *US, 1967*

- We were White Lead, or the front ship in the formation. — David Reed, *Up Front in Vietnam*, p. 35, 1967

white lightning *noun*

strong, if inferior, home-made whiskey *US, 1921*

- But she brought more of the white lightning and choc, and left us alone. — Jim Thompson, *Roughneck*, p. 92, 1954
- I'm drinkin moonshine cocktails or punch made with orange juice, ice, ginger ale & white lightin. — Jack Kerouac, *Letter to William Burroughs*, p. 480, May 1955
- I found Reese kicked back in his cell drinking the local brand of white lightning. — James Carr, *Bad*, p. 88, 1975
- Illicit whiskey bootlegged in, or "white lightning" brewed farther back in the hills, had been a major industry since the area was first settled. — Larry Flynt, *An Unseemly Man*, p. 4, 1996

white man's time *noun*

used for denoting punctuality *US, 1963*

- — *American Speech*, p. 276, December 1963: "American Indian student slang"

white meat *noun*

a white person as a sex object; the genitals of a white person; sex with a white person *US, 1957*

- Shoot, whyn't they try to get them some nice white meat from downtown once in a while instead of picking on us all the time? — John M. Murtagh and Sara Harris, *Cast the First Stone*, p. 11, 1957
- She sure has, white meat! — Willard Motley, *Let No Man Write My Epitaph*, p. 337, 1958

white mice *noun*

during the conflict in Vietnam, the South Vietnamese civilian police *US, 1967*

From their white helmets and gloves.

- The remaining terrorist on the balcony slumped to his knees as the White Mice, the alert, efficient, white-garbed Vietnamese police, entered. — Elaine Shepard, *The Doom Pussy*, p. 143, 1967
- Below the RF's and the PF's (collectively known as Ruff-Puffs) were regular national police, white suited, pistol-carrying cops known as White Mice. — Ward S. Just, *To What End*, p. 136, 1968
- After seven in the evening, when the curfew included Americans and became total, nothing but White Mice patrols and MP jeeps moved in the streets[.] — Michael Herr, *Dispatches*, p. 70, 1977
- If I tried I would only be mugged by the locals or shot by the "white mice" for being out after curfew. — Martin Cameron, *A Look at the Bright Side*, 1988

white money *noun*

1 in prison, actual currency *US, 1976*

Required for major purchases, such as drugs.

- — John R. Armore and Joseph D. Wolfe, *Dictionary of Desperation*, p. 56, 1976

2 coins *US, 1951*

- But first he picked up the silver for me—the white money, as it sometimes is respectfully called. — Ethel Waters, *His Eye is on the Sparrow*, p. 75, 1951

white mule *noun*

an illegally manufactured whiskey, colorless and powerful *US, 1921*

- "Tastes a good deal like North Carolina white mule." — William Brinkley, *Don't Go Near the Water*, p. 34, 1956
- [H]e drank an entire Mason jar of white mule and danced the two-step with every lady present, bar none. — Max Shulman, *Anyone Got a Match?*, p. 2, 1964

white-on-white *noun*

a white shirt that was deemed fashionable in the 1940s *US, 1976*

- He was choked up tight in a white-on-white / And a cocoa front that was down. — Dennis Wepman et al., *The Life*, p. 54, 1976

white policeman's roll *noun*
in an illegal numbers gambling lottery, a bet on 13, 37 and 70 *US*, *1949*
- — *American Speech*, p. 193, October 1949

white powder *noun*
a narcotic in white powder form, that is, heroin, cocaine, or morphine *US*, *1908*
- They had a terrible contempt for the guys on the "white stuff"—heroin, morphine, and cocaine[.] — Mezz Mezzrow, *Really the Blues*, p. 248, 1946

white rock *noun*
high quality methamphetamine in rock form *US*, *1989*
- — Geoffrey Froner, *Digging for Diamonds*, p. 69, 1989: "Types of speed"

white Russian *noun*
in homosexual usage, the passing of semen from one mouth to another *US*, *1987*
- — *Maledicta*, p. 60, 1986–1987: "A continuation of a glossary of ethnic slurs in American English"

white shirt *noun*
1 in roller derby, a skater who plays honorably and is seen as the "good guy," usually from the team designated as the home team *US*, *1999*
- White shirts fight only when first belted by someone else and only when driven beyond the limits of patience. — Keith Coppage, *Roller Derby to Rollerjam*, p. 127, 1999
2 a high-ranking police officer *US*, *1995*
- White Shirts: Term for lieutenants and above, who wear white uniform shirts. — Samuel Katz, *NYPD*, 1995

white sidewalls *noun*
the visible scalp on the side of the head after a short haircut, especially a military haircut *US*, *1968*
- — Carl Fleischhauer, *A Glossary of Army Slang*, p. 26, 1968
- — Kenn "Naz" Young, *Naz's Dictionary of Teen Slang*, p. 135, 1993

whiteskin *noun*
in poker, any card ranked ten or lower *US*, *1943*
- — Thomas L. Clark, *The Dictionary of Gambling and Gaming*, p. 250, 1987

white slave *noun*
a woman engaged in enforced prostitution *UK*, *1857*
- I was one of the dozen or so black pimps the F.B.I. kept constant tabs on to mail on a white slave beef. — Iceberg Slim (Robert Beck), *The Naked Soul of Iceberg Slim*, p. 28, 1971

whitesocks *noun*
a ferocious if tiny mosquito *US*, *1965*
- The whitesocks is a worse pest than the NO-SEE-UM. Under a magnifying glass its white feet are visible[.] — Robert O. Bowen, *An Alaskan Dictionary*, p. 35, 1965

white stuff *noun*
any powdered drug—morphine, heroin, or cocaine *US*, *1914*
- In other cities, Hip Singers must content themselves with the sale of white stuff—heroin, morphine, and cocaine—which is seldom used by Chinese. — Jack Lait and Lee Mortimer, *Washington Confidential*, p. 60, 1951

white tornado *noun*
freebase cocaine *US*, *1979*
- They were smoking free base, also known as the "white tornado"—the form of cocaine favored by those beyond the nasal stage of evolution. — *Hi Life*, p. 78, 1979
- — Gilda and Melvin Berger, *Drug Abuse A-Z*, p. 134, 1990

white trash *noun*
an impoverished white person or persons *US*, *1822*
Originally black usage; derogatory; abbreviates to "trash" (rubbish).
- When good old Buck, of Buck and Bubbles, was driving along down South in his big Cadillac and dared to challenge the supremacy of the white race by passing a couple of white trash in a dinky old rattletrap Ford, he spent the night in jail[.] — Mezz Mezzrow, *Really the Blues*, p. 207, 1946
- Hoe-hands. Cotton-pickers. White trash. — Jim Thompson, *The Kill-Off*, p. 47, 1957
- Algren's book opens with one of the best historical descriptions of American white trash ever written. — Hunter S. Thompson, *Hell's Angels*, p. 157, 1966

- "We got white trash, you ever heard anyone talk about Black trash." — Robert Deane Pharr, *S.R.O.*, p. 211, 1971

whitewash *verb*
to win a game without your opponent scoring *US*, *1971*
- — Dick Squires, *The Other Racquet Sports*, p. 220, 1971: "Glossary"
- — Pramod Shankar, *How to Win at Gin Rummy*, p. 91, 1994

white worm *noun*
an uninfected appendix removed in surgery based on an incorrect diagnosis *US*, *1994*
- — Sally Williams, *"Strong" Words*, p. 166, 1994

whitey *noun*
1 a white person or white people collectively *US*, *1942*
Insulting; a gesture of resistance.
- And then I got to see how Whitey treats his heroes. — Dick Gregory, *Nigger*, p. 72, 1964
- Shorty felt about the war the same way I and most ghetto Negros did: "Whitey owns everything. He wants us to go and bleed for him? Let him fight." — Malcolm X and Alex Haley, *The Autobiography of Malcolm X*, p. 71, 1964
- It doesn't matter, the end result, as long as trick Whitey, fuck up Boss Charley. — Lenny Bruce, *The Essential Lenny Bruce*, p. 12, 1967
- So white would get him a little taste of black gold for $10 or $15 and Black people helped him. — H. Rap Brown, *Die Nigger Die!*, p. 31, 1969
2 an amphetamine pill *US*, *1982*
- — Arnold Shaw, *Dictionary of American Pop/Rock*, p. 397, 1982
3 in pool, the cue ball *US*, *1983*
- — Mike Shamos, *The Illustrated Encyclopedia of Billiards*, p. 262, 1993

whiz *verb*
to urinate *UK*, *1929*
- — *Current Slang*, p. 21, Spring 1971
- "How are you going to whiz in a half-inch opening?" I asked, trying to drum some sense into her. — Jennifer Leo, *Sand in My Bra and Other Misadventures*, p. 159, 2003
- [M]y need to whiz, which I'd been trying to ignore, had become overwhelming. — Chris Miller, *The Real Animal House*, p. 78, 2006

whiz; whizz *noun*
1 a genius; somebody who is extremely proficient at a given activity *US*, *1914*
An abbreviation of "wizard."
- He was, undeniably, a whiz at selling Florida real estate. — Carl Hiaasen, *Native Tongue*, p. 48, 1991
2 an act of urinating *US*, *1971*
Often in a construction such as "take a whiz."
- As Steve started for the boat, Shannon called, "I got to take a whiz." — Jack W. Thomas, *Heavy Number*, p. 76, 1976
- And somewhere in here Paco gets his own breakfast, takes another whiz, refills cofee mugs, refills napkin dispenser[.] — Larry Heinemann, *Paco's Story*, p. 115, 1986
- "Got up to take a whizz and this thing comes down the hall[.]" — Ethan Morden, *Everybody Loves You*, p. 63, 1988
- Can I give it to you in the morning? I just took a whiz. — *American Beauty*, 1999
3 whiskey *US*, *1953*
- And I knew how bad the whiz was for me—I'd been told not to drink it at all—but I have to have it. — Jim Thompson, *Savage Night*, p. 72, 1953

whizbang; whizz-bang *noun*
an injected mixture of cocaine and heroin; cocaine; heroin *US*, *1933*
- — Rose Giallombardo, *Society of Women*, p. 213, 1966: Glossary of Prison Terms

whizbox *noun*
a global positioning system device *US*, *1991*
Gulf war usage.
- — *American Speech*, p. 404, Winter 1991: "Among the new words"

whiz-kid; whizz-kid *noun*
a precociously bright child; hence a young person advancing in business faster than expectations *US*, *1960*
- Ever since he was a whiz-kid eight-grade physics pupil, Marx had dreamed of becoming a great theoretical scientist[.] — Tom Robbins, *Another Roadside Attraction*, p. 125, 1971

whizzbang *noun*
a pretty girl *US, 1947*
- — Marcus Hanna Boulware, *Jive and Slang of Students in Negro Colleges*, 1947

whizzer *noun*
in poker, a successful play of an inferior hand, or the person playing it *US, 1988*
- — George Percy, *The Language of Poker*, p. 96, 1988

whizzo *noun*
in the US military, a weapons system operator or officer *US, 1993*
From a vocalization of the abbreviation WSO.
- "It gives the whizo"—weapons system officer—"a better look-angle ito the target and little more energy on the bomb." — *New York Times*, 28th June 1991
- The FLIR is mostly the wizzo's (slang for the Weapons System Officer, or WSO, the back-seater who operates the radar and other equipment while the pilot flies the airplane) toy[.] — Hans Halberstadt, *US Marine Corps*, 1993

whizzy *adjective*
used of a computer program, well designed and attractive *US, 1991*
- — Eric S. Raymond, *The New Hacker's Dictionary*, p. 382, 1991

whoa!
used for urging a serious reconsideration of the direction that the conversation is taking *US, 1981*
From the C19 command to a horse or ox to stop, and still evocative of a simple, rural world.
- — Connie Eble (Editor), *UNC-CH Campus Slang*, p. 7, Fall 1981
- McAllen, trying to smile, said, "Whoa now, you people have a misconception about the program we better clear up." — Elmore Leonard, *Killshot*, p. 154, 1989
- I want to stay here. I f'ing told you!—Whoa, calm down, calm it down. Trust me, I know what's good for you. — Mark Powell, *Snap*, p. 222, 2001

whoady *noun*
a close friend or family member *US, 2004*
- — Rick Ayers (Editor), *Berkeley High Slang Dictionary*, p. 43, 2004

whodunit *noun*
a murder mystery novel, movie, or other entertainment; a mysterious true-life murder *US, 1930*
- "Lot of who-done-its," Robbie said, "But I'm not talking about that. Here's one. A famous hunter risks his life simply to put his sights on Hitler. Great book." — Elmore Leonard, *Split Images*, pp. 29–30, 1981
- In the newspaper story a chief detective was quoted as saying, "This one's a real whodunit," which is what the detective was told to say whenever a reporter called. — Carl Hiaasen, *Tourist Season*, p. 7, 1986
- Whodunits are genuine mysteries. — David Simon, *Homicide*, p. 42, 1991

whole enchilada *noun*
all of something *US, 1966*
Popularized in the US during the Watergate scandal of 1972–1974.
- "How much information did he relay out there before we killed him?" "He had the whole enchilada on a tape recorder." — Brian Garfield, *The Last Bridge*, p. 228, 1966
- Then Rice looked straight at the Garcias, knowing they'd go for the plan: bullshit, truth, the whole enchilada. — James Ellroy, *Suicide Hill*, p. 700, 1986
- You could've just taken the five, ten million Hindy Reno would've squeezed out of Twelvetrees for you. But no, you wanted the whole goddamn enchilada. — Robert Campbell, *Alice in La-La Land*, p. 318, 1987
- DICK: Now, if you want to sell a little bit at a time—CLARENCE: No way! The whole enchilada in one shot. — *True Romance*, 1993

whole nine yards
all of something *US, 1964*
Many etymological theories, none proven, thrive. "All nine yards" is found at least as early as 1962 with the same meaning, but was soon driven from the scene by "whole."
- Never thought I'd see myself wanting to go the whole nine yards wiht any girl. — Carl Krueger, *Wings of the Tiger*, p. 55, 1966
- Slipping out of the knot was expensive but Smith was eventually able to untangle what he called "the whole nine yards." — Elaine Shepard, *The Doom Pussy*, p. 47, 1967

who loves ya, baby?
used for expressing affection in a humorous fashion *US, 1978*
The signature line of the police captain played by Telly Savalas on the television police drama *Kojak* (CBS, 1973–78). Repeated with referential humor.

whomper *noun*
a powerful, hard-breaking wave *US, 1964*
- — John Severson, *Modern Surfing Around the World*, p. 165, 1964

whoop *verb*
to beat, to thrash *US, 1976*
- "Now get up, or do I have to whoop you where you lie?" — John Ridley, *Stray Dogs*, p. 117, 1997

▸ **whoop it up**
to make a great deal of rowdy noise *US, 1884*
- A city the size of New York, with probably 20,000,000 persons within a thirty-mile radius, and untold millions more swarming in for short periods of whooping it up, today supports only one big Broadway casino[.] — Robert Sylvester, *No Cover Charge*, p. 292, 1956
- [A]n air raid sounded while we were busy whooping it up at the Silver Grill. — Gregory "Pappy" Boyington, *Baa Baa Black Sheep*, p. 68, 1958
- A lot of old me, a la Tom Waits, were grabbing the girls and whooping it up. — Sandra Bernhard, *Confessions of a Pretty Lady*, p. 73, 1988

whoop; woop *noun*
a bit; a small amount *US, 1904*
- Lucky they didn't see you; you'd be in a whole whoop of trouble by naw. — Steve Cannon, *Groove, Bang, and Jive Around*, p. 20, 1969

▸ **give a whoop in hell**
to care, generally in a negative context *US, 1970*
- His wife, he told me at one point, didn't give a whoop in hell about his life's work. — Lawrence Block, *No Score [The Affairs of Chip Harrison Omnibus]*, p. 36, 1970

whoop and holler *noun*
an indeterminate, relatively small distance *US, 1917*
- Place over on the river bank, just a whoop an" a holler from town. — Jim Thompson, *Pop. 1280*, p. 30, 1964

whoop and holler *verb*
to shout; to carry on loudly *US, 1969*
- They questioned me in teams, the first team was threatening me, whooping and hollering; the second team was going to save me from the first, only I got to tell them the truth about the murder. — Edwin Torres, *Carlito's Way*, p. 36, 1975

whoop-de-do *noun*
in horseracing, a style of racing based on the premise of establishing an early lead and then running as fast as possible with maximum whip and heel encouragement *US, 1959*
- The number of riders in America who will give a horse of any age a chance to settle into stride is pitifully few, the great majority being strictly "whoop-de-do" booters who might have been developed by the late Bill Daly. — *Daily Racing Form*, p. 4, 27th November 1959
- — Tom Ainslie, *Ainslie's Complete Guide to Thoroughbred Racing*, p. 341, 1976

whoop-de-do *adjective*
1 in horseracing, employing the strategy of riding all-out from the start of the race *US, 1948*
- Longden, for example, is famed as a "whoop-te-do" rider: a jockey who likes to get out front and stay there. — *Time*, p. 82, 17th May 1948
- The number of riders in America who will give a horse of any age a chance to settle into stride is pitifully few, the great majority being strictly "whoop-de-do" booters, who might have been developed by the late Bill Daly. — *Daily Racing Form*, p. 4, 27th November 1959
2 a loud and rowdy event or gathering *US, 1929*
- FIGS: Quiet tonight, huh? FREDDY: At that bachelor party. Across the river. FIGS: Yeah. Whoop-de-do. — *Copland*, 1997

whoop-de-doo!; woop-tee-doo!
used as an expression of strong support or celebration *US, 2000*
Often ironic.
- Well, woop-tee-doo, little puppy with a poundcake. — *Gone in 60 Seconds*, 2000

whoopee *noun*
▸ **make whoopee**
to have sex *US, 1928*

A forced and silly euphemism, but one sanctioned by television censors; it was used with annoying regularity by Bob Eubanks, host of *The Newlywed Game* television program (ABC, 1966 – 90).

- [H]er gaze holding on Bob Eubanks talking to a panel of newlywed wives, asking them what film star will their husbands say "you would most like to make whoopee with[.]" — Elmore Leonard, *City Primeval*, p. 172, 1980
- BRANDI: If you and I were making whoopie— BRODIE: What's whoopie? BRANDIE: You know, if we were, intimate. BRODIE: What, like fucking? — *Mallrats*, 1995

whoopee card *noun*
a computer punch card with all the holes punched out *US, 1991*
- — Eric S. Raymond, *The New Hacker's Dictionary*, p. 219, 1991

whoops!
used as a hurried expression of regret *US, 1937*
- He said to the sweet girl, "Whoops, you caught me playing." — Elmore Leonard, *Stick*, p. 26, 1983

whoopsie *noun*
a male homosexual *US, 1961*
- Are you a fagola, sir? My friends and me, we got to know. Are you a whoopsie? — Bernard Wolfe, *The Magic of Their Singing*, p. 128, 1961

whop *verb*
to strike someone with heavy blows *UK, 1575*
- Some of them get whopped and smacked around. — Susan Hall, *Gentleman of Leisure*, p. 44, 1972

whopper *noun*
1 something that is extremely and unusually large *UK, 1785*
The best known Whopper in the US is a hamburger introduced by the original Burger King™ restaurant in Miami in 1957.
- [S]he explained she was a lab technician on twentyfourhour call and scooted back to the ladiesroom to phone her escort service and say she couldn't book any tricks that night; she'd just started and it was a whopper. — Seth Morgan, *Homeboy*, p. 5, 1990
- She had another long phone conversation with Wally; the next phone bill should be quite a whopper. — C.D. Payne, *Youth in Revolt*, p. 109, 1993
- I needed those kinds of gifts like I needed the kind of whopper crotch infection I got after wearing those polyster birthday briefs[.] — Rita Cirtesi, *Pink Slip*, p. 1, 1999
2 a big lie *UK, 1791*
- She probably also knew that the claim of fluency in French on your resume was something of a whopper, and that you are too proud to admit it now. — Jay McInerney, *Bright Lights, Big City*, p. 20, 1984

whopping *adjective*
enormous, powerful *UK, 1706*
- I had supper down near the depot, buying a whopping big meal for Buck along with my own. — Jim Thompson, *Pop. 1280*, p. 36, 1964
- Where you make a whopping twelve thousand dollars a year. — *Jackie Brown*, 1997

whop stick *noun*
a hammer *US, 1992*
- — Lewis Poteet, *Car & Motorcycle Slang*, p. 218, 1992

whore *noun*
in a deck of playing cards, a queen *US, 1967*
- If the player (with queens) wins the pot, they are "ladies"; but if he loses the pot, they are "whores." — Albert H. Morehead, *The Complete Guide to Winning Poker*, p. 264, 1967

whore hopper *noun*
a promiscuous man *US, 1936*
- "Reckon when he grows up will he make the car thief and whore-hopper and general no-good his daddy is?" — Leon Wilson, *Sinners Come Away*, p. 206, 1949
- They called him a sot and a whore-hopper, a walking booze-barrel with three legs. — Hunter S. Thompson, *Songs of the Doomed*, p. 302, 1990
- It did not square at all, of course, and I now believed the later statement, of his having been a whore-hopper. — Paul Theroux, *Sir Vidia's Shadow*, p. 287, 2001

whore house cut *noun*
cutting a deck of cards by removing a section from the middle of the deck and moving it to the top or bottom *US, 1951*
- — *American Speech*, p. 102, May 1951: "The vocabulary of poker"

whore house game *noun*
any exotic variation of poker *US, 1952*
- "Ante five, check stud cinches, dealer's choice but no goddamn whorehouse games." — Richard Prather, *The Peddler*, p. 63, 1952

whore name *noun*
the nickname or alias used by a prostitute in her work life *US, 1994*
- Tess was her whore name, but she really became it. — Michelle Tea, *The Passionate Mistakes and Intricate Corruption of One Girl in America*, p. 124, 1998

whore note *noun*
a two-dollar bill *US, 1970*
- — Claudio R. Salvucci, *The Philadelphia Dialect Dictionary*, p. 65, 1996

whore of Babylon *noun*
an extremely promiscuous woman *US, 1992*
Originally a disparaging sobriquet for the Church of Rome, in allusion to the Book of Revelations, Chapter XVII, where she is one of several mysterious Christian allegorical figures of evil.
- Aunt Edie is so uptight she makes Marilyn Quayle look like the Whore of Babylon. — Armistead Maupin, *Maybe the Moon*, p. 149, 1992

whore's bath; whore splash *noun*
an impromptu and quick cleaning of the body at a sink, with special attention to cleaning the genitals *US, 1949*
- "Yes, a whore's bath. We call them that too." "Just cold water and a helmet?" "And, of course, a little soap." — Audie Murphy, *To Hell and Back*, p. 157, 1949
- Always travel with a ruck, because when you hit a gas station you get a chance to take a whore's bath and change some of your clothes. — Larry Heinemann, *Paco's Story*, p. 162, 1986
- He ran cold water slowly into the basin until it was pretty clear. Then he plugged it and let it fill. He stripped down and gave himself a whore's bath, balancing on one foot with the other foot in the basin so he could work the washrag around his crotch. — Robert Campbell, *Alice in La-La Land*, p. 27, 1987
- Do you like to wash up first? Top and tails? A whore's bath? — *Austin Powers*, 1997

whore scars *noun*
puncture wounds and bruises from needle use *US, 1970*
- — Clarence Major, *Dictionary of Afro-American Slang*, p. 122, 1970

whore-style *adverb*
said when a woman has sex with her underpants still around one leg *US, 1973*
- She took one leg outta her panties, whore style, and I dropped my pants to my knees and mounted her. — A.S. Jackson, *Gentleman Pimp*, p. 36, 1973

whoretel *noun*
a hotel or motel that caters for prostitutes *US, 1973*
- I got things worked out for you to get down in some of the top whoretels in Detroit. — A.S. Jackson, *Gentleman Pimp*, p. 84, 1973

whore wagon *noun*
a police van used for sweeps to arrest prostitutes *US, 1970*
- You ready to go work the whore wagon? — Joseph Wambaugh, *The New Centurions*, p. 78, 1970

Whorez *nickname*
Juarez, Mexico *US, 1970*
The phonics work and Juarez has something of a reputation for its prostitutes.
- — *Current Slang*, p. 26, Spring 1970

who-shot-John *noun*
a reproach or interrogation *US, 1969*
- Carol, Ah don want no "who shot John" bout them bootiful clothes. — Iceberg Slim (Robert Beck), *Mama Black Widow*, p. 177, 1969

whosis *noun*
used in place of a person's name which the speaker cannot remember or doesn't think is important *US, 1953*
- Go out in the kitchen and tell whosis to give her dinner early. — J.D. Salinger, *Nine Stories*, p. 33, 1953

who's your daddy?; who's the daddy?
who is in charge (of this situation)? *US, 2001*
- — Don R. McCreary (Editor), *Dawg Speak*, 2001

whuffo *noun*
in skysurfing, a person who won't jump *US, 1998*
- From "Wha'fo' you wanna go jump outta them perfectly good planes?" — shelley Youngblut, *Way Inside ESPN's X Games*, p. 65, 1998

whup *verb*
to beat someone *US, 1945*
- I'm gonna whup his ass till it ropes like okra. — Chester Himes, *If He Hollers Let Him Go*, p. 12, 1945
- He got whupped by The Greatest. — Bill Cardoso, *The Maltese Sangweech*, p. 304, 1984
- She'll start shit like she's ready to whup some ass—without thinking about what might happen to you. — Chris Rock, *Rock This!*, p. 53, 1997

why-for *noun*
the reason or cause *US, 1954*
- The "how" I never learned. But the "why-for," to use the dialect of the section, became clear. — Jim Thompson, *Roughneck*, p. 98, 1954

wicked *adjective*
excellent *US, 1966*
- I figure, you see, buddy, to be sort of the gambling baron of this ward, deal a wicked game of blackjack. — Ken Kesey, *One Flew Over the Cuckoo's Nest*, p. 18, 1962
- *San Francisco Examiner: People*, p. 8, 27th October 1963: "What a 'Z'! The astonishing private language of Bay Area teenagers"
- J.R. Friss, *A Dictionary of Teenage Slang (Mt. Diablo High)*, 1964
- Eugene Landy, *The Underground Dictionary*, p. 198, 1971

wicked *adverb*
extremely *US, 1984*
A rare instance of late C20 American slang that has stayed regional; a common term in New England ("wicked hot," "wicked cold" etc.) rarely heard elsewhere.
- Connie Eble (Editor), *UNC-CH Campus Slang*, p. 7, Spring 1984
- *55-Plus*, p. 13, 12th February 1986: "Today's guide to teen slang"
- Judi Sanders, *Faced and Faded, Hanging to Hurl*, p. 43, 1993
- But they made their drinks wicked strong. — Michelle Tea, *Rent Girl*, p. 22, 2004

wicked pisser *adjective*
extreme *US, 1997*
- Us northeastern in-ta-leck-shoe-all types don't go for that trendy west coast shit. It ain't exactly wicked pisser if you know what I mean. — *soc.motss*, 26th January 1997
- The moisture-eating socks come in a variety of colors and with sayings like "Wicked pisser" across the bottom. — *Boston Business Journal*, p. 19, 9th July 1999
- Ever had a wicked pisser keg party at your house? Has your wicked pisser of a keg party yielded a wicked piss-drunk guy puking, urinating, or otherwise staining your couch cushions? — halfbakery.com/idea/Self-Cleaning, 2nd July 2002
- I lost out on a black T-60 on eBay on friday night. Made my bid with about 20 seconds left and got outbid by 3 bucks. Wicked pisser. — undertowmusic.com/messageboards/viewtopic, 8th May 2006

wide open *adjective*
unrestrained by authority; unrestricted by the police; wild *US, 1950*
- Under the wide-open Kelly regime, police officers took up stations at each policy drawing-place to protect the money on hand for the payoffs. — Jack Lait and Lee Mortimer, *Chicago Confidential*, p. 37, 1950
- And, at this time, baseball betting books ran wide open in Oklahoma City. — Jim Thompson, *Roughneck*, p. 142, 1954
- There was a town—Covington, Kentucky—that was wide open. — Harry King, *Box Man*, p. 28, 1972
- You could party twenty-four hours a day—Olga Guilot, Benny Casino, la Playa, Cascarita—gambling, pussy, coke—wide open. — Edwin Torres, *Carlito's Way*, p. 35, 1975

wide ride *noun*
a heavy woman *US, 1994*
- Michael Dalton Johnson, *Talking Trash with Redd Foxx*, p. 69, 1994

widow *noun*
in some poker games, an extra card dealt to the table for all players to use in their hands *US, 1967*
- Albert H. Morehead, *The Complete Guide to Winning Poker*, p. 277, 1967

widow-maker *noun*
the M-16 rifle, introduced as the standard US Army infantry rifle in 1967 *US, 1990*

Early versions of the rifle were prone to jamming, thus "making widows."
- Gregory Clark, *Words of the Vietnam War*, p. 296, 1990

wiener; weiner *noun*
the penis *US, 1960*
The phallic connotations of the food item lead to this usage.
- How is the young lady to know that her own grandmother, even with her teeth ripped off, could activate a few weiners. — Anne Steinhardt, *Thunder La Boom*, p. 93, 1974
- SHE SUPER SLIDES THAT MONSTER WEINER DOWN HER THROAT EVER SO SMOOTHLY[.] — Peter Sotos, *Index*, p. 37, 1996

wife *noun*
1 in a homosexual relationship, the more passive or "feminine" partner *US, 1883*
- Donald Webster Cory and John P. LeRoy, *The Homosexual and His Society*, p. 266, 1963: "A lexicon of homosexual slang"
- Yet, overnight, Kurt turned into what is generally termed a wife. — Ethan Morden, *I've a Feeling We're Not in Kansas Anymore*, p. 65, 1985
- Soon as I was put in with the population, I started looking for a wife. — Elmore Leonard, *Maximum Bob*, p. 50, 1991
2 in law enforcement, a work partner *US, 1988*
- The thing is a cop doesn't call his partner his husband, so what you got is two wives. — Robert Campbell, *Juice*, p. 4, 1988

wife-beater *noun*
a sleeveless tee-shirt or undershirt *US, 1994*
- Preppy is in, grunge is out. Lyrcra is out, vinyl is in. Bowling shirts are in, wife beaters are out. — *The Boston Globe*, p. 35, 28th September 1994
- Connie Eble (Editor), *UNC-CH Campus Slang*, p. 7, Fall 1996
- The guy behind the registration counter—fat, unshaved, with a dirty wife-beater T-shirt—mumbled "Ten" at me. — John Ridley, *Love is a Racket*, p. 294, 1998

wifed up *adjective*
of a male, in a serious relationship with a female who appears to dominate him *US, 2004*
- Ben Applebaum and Derrick Pittman, *Turd Ferguson & The Sausage Party*, p. 74, 2004

wife-in-law *noun*
one prostitute in relation to another prostitute working for the same pimp *US, 1957*
- You can be sure when you see girls working so cooperatively that they are "wives-in-law," feeling bound to one another because they happen to be connected with the same pimp, sweet man to them. — John M. Murtagh and Sara Harris, *Cast the First Stone*, p. 10, 1957
- Silky's other girls are my wives-in-law. They refer to me as "Mother." — Susan Hall, *Gentleman of Leisure*, p. 69, 1972
- I hipped her about her wife-in-law and I also told her where she was working. — A.S. Jackson, *Gentleman Pimp*, p. 167, 1973
- "You're with Daddy? I know Suzy [a wife-in-law]." — Susan Hall, *Ladies of the Night*, p. 22, 1973

wifey *adjective*
used of a female, dowdy, mature and proper *US, 2001*
- Don R. McCreary (Editor), *Dawg Speak*, 2001

wig *noun*
the head; the mind *US, 1944*
- The ambivalence in my wig has been terrific these recent days. — James Blake, *The Joint*, p. 98, 8th August 1955
- Bernie, you got to learn that not everything can be reasoned out. I know you got a real great wig. — Ross Russell, *The Sound*, p. 102, 1961
- The word "wig" is street/drug parlance for "head." — Terry Southern, *Now Dig This*, p. 6, 1986

▸ **tighten your wig**
to use drugs and become intoxicated *US, 1986*
- To "tighten one's wig" is to get high. — Terry Southern, *Now Dig This*, p. 6, 1986

wig; wig out *verb*
to lose control of your emotions; to become angry *US, 1955*
- If the thing bites down much harder I might wig out and demand beer. — Hunter S. Thompson, *Songs of the Doomed*, p. 123, 18/19th February 1969
- Furthermore, Kate didn't wig out over the occasional Frito[.] — Cyra McFadden, *The Serial*, p. 42, 1977
- Next thing I know, the kid wigs, he turns and he shoves me, boom, right in the chest. — Richard Price, *Clockers*, p. 366, 1992

- That ain't no reason to start wiggin' and spaz out[.] — Eminem (Marshall Mathers), *My Fault*, 1999

wig-chop *noun*
a haircut *US, 1955*
Teen slang.
- — *American Weekly*, p. 2, 14th August 1955

wig city *noun*
a medical institution for the mentally ill *US, 2001*
Extended from the adjective sense.
- Wig city is exactly where an amnesia victim might show up. — Kinky Friedman, *Steppin' on a Rainbow*, p. 71, 2001

wigged *adjective*
confused, disoriented, especially as a result of drug use; drug-intoxicated *US, 1951*
- "Said he painted it one time when he was wigged." "Wigged? Christ, it looks like he flipped." — Thurston Scott, *Cure it with Honey*, p. 57, 1951
- — *American Speech*, p. 88, May 1955: "Narcotic argot along the Mexican border"

wigged out *adjective*
in an extreme state of drug intoxication, excitement, or rage; dissociated from reality *US, 1968*
- There were more young, apolitically radical, wigged-out crazies running around Vietnam than anybody ever realized. — Michael Herr, *Dispatches*, p. 235, 1977

wigger; wigga; whigger *noun*
a white youth who affects the speech patterns, fashion, and other mannerisms of black youth *US, 1988*
An elision of "white **NIGGER**."
- Wigger, "white nigger" in the high school lexicon: "a white kid who tries to act black." — *Washington Post*, p. C5, 20th July 1991
- — *Atlantic Monthly*, p. 120, February 1993
- Someone had given them my name as an expert on wiggers. You know, wiggers. White kids scorned by their peers for listening to rap. — William Upski Wimsatt, *Bomb the Suburbs*, p. 28, 1994
- — Connie Eble (Editor) *UNC-CH Campus Slang*, p. 6, Fall 1993

wiggins *noun*
an episode of anxiety or fear *US, 2001*
Coined by the writers of the television series "Buffy the Vampire Slayer" in 2001 and used outside the confines of the show with some degree of referencing.
- The scene that still gives me the wiggins. — *alt.tv.smallville*, 11th September 2003
- It gives me the wiggins that my usenet posting habits are monitored so closely. It gives me the wiggins that you just used the word "wiggins" in a sentence. — *alt.religion.kibology*, 20th January 2004
- For him to start crushing on her gave me the wiggins. — *televisionwithoutpity.com*, 1st January 2005

wiggle *noun*
an act of sex *US, 1972*
- Then I had to sit in the car and wait while Gordy gave his broad a wiggle in the front seat. — Robert Byrne, *McGoorty*, p. 84, 1972

wigglers *noun*
the fingers *US, 1970*
- — Clarence Major, *Dictionary of Afro-American Slang*, p. 122, 1970

wiggy *adjective*
crazy; outstanding; wild; creative *US, 1961*
- Like, if you wanted to get your band book together, he can write and arrange. Real wiggy! — Ross Russell, *The Sound*, p. 47, 1961
- "He could spin donuts on that hog with his feet on the pegs, and man, he was a wiggy cat," a member of the Angels recalled. — Hunter S. Thompson, *Hell's Angels*, p. 64, 1966
- The fifth member of the household was Millie, who was eighty-five years old, a lifelong Sierra Club member and indefatigable hiker and, Woman told Kate privately, "a little wiggy." — Cyra McFadden, *The Serial*, p. 139, 1977
- To say that a person is "a wig" or "is wiggy," is to say that they are insane—even though it could be in an interesting or even desirable manner. — Terry Southern, *Now Dig This*, p. 6, 1986

wig picker *noun*
a psychiatrist *US, 1961*
- — *American Speech*, pp. 145–148, May 1961: "The spoken language of medicine; argot, slang, cant"

wig-trig *noun*
an idea *US, 1946*
- And I didn't have enough wig-trigs to explain why you had to sound like Louis and Jimmy Noone. — Mezz Mezzrow, *Really the Blues*, p. 158, 1946

wigwag *noun*
in the television and movie industries, a light outside a sound stage indicating that shooting is in process *US, 1990*
- — Ralph S. Singleton, *Filmmaker's Dictionary*, p. 184, 1990

wigwagger *noun*
a lookout *US, 1971*
- The "wigwagger," also called a "lighthouse," was a lookout for police. — Charles Winick, *The Lively Commerce*, p. 122, 1971

wigwam *noun*
in a deck of cards, an ace *US, 1988*
From the visual similarity between an "A" and a wigwam.
- — George Percy, *The Language of Poker*, p. 97, 1988

wild *verb*
to act violently and irrationally *US, 2002*
- Then when I pulled up in front of his building he started wilding and tried to grab the steering wheel from me. — Earl "DMX" Simmons, *E.A.R.L.*, p. 284, 2002

wild *adjective*
1 used of film, in the television and movie industries, shot without sound *US, 1990*
- — Ralph S. Singleton, *Filmmaker's Dictionary*, p. 185, 1990

2 of prison sentences, served consecutively *US, 1972*
- "I guess you realize that if we want to, we can run your two sentences wild," he said. — Donald Goines, *Whoreson*, p. 272, 1972
- What's another bullet [one-year sentence], wild or bowlegged [concurrent]? — Seth Morgan, *Homeboy*, p. 141, 1990
- "Running wild?" "Yeah, daw—bowlegged sentences, y'unnderstan' what I'm saying?" — Jimmy Lerner, *You Got Nothing Coming*, p. 60, 2002

wild card *noun*
an enemy fighter plane *US, 1986*
- — *American Speech*, p. 125, Summer 1986: "The language of naval fighter pilots"

wildcat *noun*
strong, illegally manufactured whiskey *US, 1999*
- It is called corn liquor, white lightning, sugar whiskey, skully cracker, popskull, bush whiskey, stump, stumphole, "splo, ruckus juice, radiator whiskey, rotgut, sugarhead, block and tackle, wildcat, panther's breath, tiger's sweat, Sweet spirits of cats a-fighting, alley bouybon, city gin, cool water, happy Sally, deep shaft, jump steady, old horsey, stingo, blue John, red eye, pine top, buckeye bark whiskey and see seven stars." — *Star Tribune (Minneapolis)*, p. 19F, 31st January 1999

wildcat *adjective*
unauthorized, unlicensed, unsanctioned *US, 1870*
- I knew that he was now managing a wild cat taxi and rental car service. — Jim Thompson, *Roughneck*, p. 115, 1954

wild hair *noun*
an impulsive notion *US, 1989*
A shortened form of **WILD HAIR UP YOUR ASS** without the full connotation of annoyance.
- Something bothering you, Jimmy? You got a wild hair? — Robert Campbell, *Nibbled to Death by Ducks*, p. 68, 1989
- — Connie Eble (Editor), *UNC-CH Campus Slang*, p. 5, Fall 1990

wild hair up your ass; wild hair up your butt *noun*
the notional cause of irrational, obsessive behavior *US, 1981*
- I was over there behind your friend with the wild hair up his ass. — Thomas Harris, *Red Dragon*, pp. 184–185, 1981
- Jeez, don't get a wild hair up your butt. — Cherie Bennett, *See No Evil*, p. 147, 2002

wilding *noun*
violent youth gang activity directed towards random victims *US, 1989*
A term popularized by the "Central Park Jogger" case in 1989.
- The suspects, who were among some 20 youths questioned for hours before the charges were announced, used the term "wilding" to describe the rampage, Colangelo said. "It's not a term we in the police have heard before." — *United Press International*, 21st April 1989

- T-Loc Ainsworth had come back to San Diego to testify against some homeboys in a 1988 "wilding" spree that had left one man dead and badly injured victims all across the county. — Bob Sipchen, *Baby Insane and the Buddha*, p. 409, 1993
- Tone Loc attracted the wrath of media elements hostile to rap when the innocent party sentiments of "Wild Thing" were confused with the term "wilding," at that time a buzzword for black criminality. — Alex Ogg, *The Hip Hop Years*, p. 125, 1999

wild-out *noun*
a gang fight *US*, *1999*
- In statements detectives read in court, several victims said they heard their assailants yelling that it was a "wild-out," street slang for a brawl[.] — *Record (Bergen County, New Jersey)*, p. L1, 22nd December 1999

wild thing *noun*
▸ **do the wild thing**
to have sex *US*, *1990*
- Man, you ain't gotta take that pussy. She'll do the wild thing for $5. — *New Jack City*, 1990
- The idea of camcorder as sex toy intrigued me so much that one night I decided to film myself doing the wild thing. — Anka Radakovich, *The Wild Girls Club*, p. 94, 1994
- We were doin' the wild thing all night. I'm exhausted. — *American Pie*, 1999
- I miss doing the wild thing with you[.] — Stephen Merritt, *Come Back from San Francisco*, 1999

william *noun*
a piece of currency *US*, *1983*
A pun on "bill."
- — Thomas L. Clark, *The Dictionary of Gambling and Gaming*, p. 250, 1987

willie *noun*
a piece of currency *US*, *1983*
A pun on "bill."
- — Thomas L. Clark, *The Dictionary of Gambling and Gaming*, p. 250, 1987

Willie Fud *noun*
an F-2 aircrafter *US*, *1974*
- A grumman WF-2 "Willie Fud" early-warming aircraft being launched from the starboard catapult on the USS Randolph. — Don Hoover, *The Road to 311 North York Street*, p. 338, 2003

Willie Peter; Willie Pete *noun*
an M-34 white phosphorous antipersonnel hand grenade *US*, *1967*
Another use of the military phonetic alphabet.
- Smith released four 2.75 Willie Peter rockets. — Elaine Shepard, *The Doom Pussy*, p. 11, 1967
- "Ill go to fucking Alpha company and call willy peter in on seventeen dinks and get a direct commission." — William Pelfrey, *The Big V*, p. 49, 1972
- It was a ways off, so we fired a three-point five at him. A willy-peter round, and that's when it got all fucked up. — Philip Caputo, *A Rumor of War*, p. 151, 1977
- V.C. standing in a field of wheat / Turned to ash by Willie Pete. — Sandee Johnson, *Cadences: The Jody Call Book, No. 2*, p. 149, 1986

willies *noun*
a condition of fear or nervousness *US*, *1896*
- Cemetery squad gives the guys the willies. — Mezz Mezzrow, *Really the Blues*, p. 316, 1946
- I started to get the willies. — Mickey Spillane, *One Lonely Night*, p. 36, 1951
- But it's the eyes that give me the willies. — Robert Campbell, *The Cat's Meow*, p. 85, 1988

Willie the Shit Burner *noun*
used as a generic term for the poor soul assigned to collect and burn solid human waste collected in latrines at US military bases in Vietnam *US*, *1990*
- — Gregory Clark, *Words of the Vietnam War*, p. 463, 1990

willy *noun*
the penis *UK*, *1905*
Originally northern English, not dialect, for "a child's penis" or a childish name for any penis. Adopted by adults as a jocular reference, now widely used as a nonoffensive and broadcastable term. The spelling "willie" is also used.
- She couldn't stand the thought of my willie going limp. — Robert Byrne, *McGoorty*, p. 59, 1972

- Look, Orson, I'm not asking for a movie with a Swedish director and subtitles, but I'm as serious as a tumor on your willy. — Joseph Wambaugh, *Finnegan's Week*, p. 11, 1993

willy-nilly *adverb*
here and there, haphazardly *US*, *1934*
Not particularly related to the C17 sense of the phrase meaning "willingly or unwillingly."
- Constant exposure made him, willy-nilly, a first rate ball player. — Max Shulman, *Rally Round the Flag, Boys!*, p. 5, 1957
- Some biographers might say I lived my childhood in a willy-nilly manner. — Helen Giblo, *Footlights, Fistfights and Femmes*, p. 8, 1957
- Willy-nilly, in the course of the 12th century, these claims, backed up as they often were by dangerous revolts, had to be granted. — *The Digger Papers*, p. 20, August 1968
- Joe bolted willynilly with the rest. — Seth Morgan, *Homeboy*, p. 179, 1990

Wilson *noun*
in skateboarding, a fall producing serious injury *US*, *1984*
- — *San Francisco Sunday Examiner & Chronicle*, p. 20, 2nd September 1984: "Say it right"

Wilson Pickett *noun*
a white phosphorous flare or grenade *US*, *1991*
From the initials WP; Pickett was a popular American rhythm and blues singer.
- — Gregory Clark, *Words of the Vietnam War*, p. 559, 1991
- He had a cache of gold-tipped high explosive and white phosphorous rounds—WIlson Picketts, they called them, because they made Sir Charles dance. — Stewart O'Nan, *The Names of the Dead*, p. 132, 1996

wimp *noun*
a weak and timid person *US*, *1911*
A thorough treatment of the word may be found in "Wimp," Reinhold Aman, *Maledicta*, Volume VIII, pp. 43–56, 1984–1985. The word played a major role in the US presidential election of 1988, in which President George H.W. Bush had to overcome a widely held perception that he was "a wimp."
- Alright, you chickenshit wimps! You pansies! — Hunter S. Thompson, *Fear and Loathing in Las Vegas*, p. 17, 1971
- But if George Bush is a doomed wimp and Jack Kemp is a giddy windbag, Rev. Pat looks pretty good right now. — Hunter S. Thompson, *Generation of Swine*, p. 127, 9th June 1986

wimpish *adjective*
weak, ineffectual *US*, *1925*
- You call that wimpish asshole and say good-bye. — John Irving, *The World According to Garp*, p. 359, 1978

wimp out *verb*
to give way to timidity or fear *US*, *1981*
- She wondered if she had "wimped out" when she tried to convert Dohrn to her brand of radical feminism[.] — *Washington Post*, p. G1, 22nd November 1981

wimpy *adjective*
feeble; afraid *US*, *1967*
From **WIMP** (a weak and timid person). Although the adjective was not recorded until the late 1960s, the *Popeye the Sailor* radio program gave the US J. Wellington Wimpy, known simply as Wimpy, in 1936.
- It was the kind of poor town where the blacks are cooler, and victimize the wimpy whites. — Jennifer Blowdryer, *White Trash Debutante*, p. 60, 1997
- Carol and I stayed inside, contemplating Security Man's strange anatomy. "Who'd be scared of that wimpy thing?" — Rita Ciresi, *Pink Slip*, p. 12, 1999
- I still would have felt better if I had gotten to that wimpy Jerry Rubin. — Ralph "Sonny" Barger, *Hell's Angel*, p. 122, 2000
- Lula talks tough, but the truth is we're both pretty wimpy when it comes to actual butt kicking. — Janet Evanovich, *Seven Up*, p. 6, 2001

winchell *noun*
a trusting, unsophisticated person *US*, *1972*
- Of course, we'd relieve some winchell who could afford it of the necessary cash. — Guy Owen, *The Flim-Flam Man and the Apprentice Grifter*, p. 167, 1972

winchester *noun*
used for conveying a complete lack of ammunition or ordinance *US*, *1990*
- — Tom Yarborough, *Da Nang Diary*, p. 280, 1990: Glossary

wind *noun*

▸ **get in the wind**

to run quickly; to depart *US, 1965*

- I made up my mind when I crossed the street to get in the wind[.]
  — Henry Williamson, *Hustler!*, p. 132, 1965
- They each flashed a grin / then got in the wind / as fast as they could flee. — Lightnin' Rod, *Hustlers Convention*, p. 73, 1973

▸ **in the wind**

free from prison *US, 1992*

- — William K. Bentley and James M. Corbett, *Prison Slang*, p. 107, 1992

▸ **take someone's wind**

to kill someone *US, 1974*

- — Paul Glover, *Words from the House of the Dead*, 1974

winded *adjective*

hungover *US, 1992*

- [T]he cha ("very cool") words include: "winded" for hung over; "craftsman" for a complete idiot; and "ass" for awful. — *Washington Times*, p. C3, 26th August 1992

winder *noun*

1 a Sidewinder missile *US, 1989*

- "We had carried a 'winder' on every mission during the entire cruise, with almost no prospect of every needing it." — Jeffrey Ethel, *One Day in a Long War*, p. 104, 1989

2 a drug addict who regularly enters and leaves treatment programs *US, 1970*

- — William D. Alsever, *Glossary for the Establishment and Other Uptight People*, p. 34, December 1970

windjammer *noun*

a person who talks too much *US, 1949*

- — Vincent J. Monteleone, *Criminal Slang*, p. 252, 1949
- — Wayne Floyd, *Jason's Authentic Dictionary of CB Slang*, p. 31, 1976

window *noun*

1 in card games, the card at the end of a player's hand *US, 1967*

- — Albert H. Morehead, *The Complete Guide to Winning Poker*, p. 277, 1967

2 in American casinos, the space through which the careful observer can see the blackjack dealer's down card as he deals *US, 1985*

- — Steve Kuriscak, *Casino Talk*, p. 60, 1985

▸ **window's open**

used for describing obvious and inept cheating *US, 1979*

- — John Scarne, *Scarne's Guide to Modern Poker*, p. 293, 1979

window dress *verb*

in poker, accidentally on purpose to let other players see the end card in your hand *US, 1967*

- — Albert H. Morehead, *The Complete Guide to Winning Poker*, p. 277, 1967

window hop *verb*

to move from window to window inside a house at night, waiting for a substance-addicted spouse to come home *US, 1998*

- I'd window hop all evening and when he finally did come home, I'd run up and jump in bed and pretend to be asleep. — Christopher Cavanaugh, *AA to Z*, p. 181, 1998

windowpane; window *noun*

a dose of LSD on a tiny, clear piece of gelatin *US, 1975*

- He sold mediocre grass for ten dollars a lid, coke for fifty a gram when you could get it and a hit of windowpane acid for two bucks. — John Sayles, *Union Dues*, p. 287, 1977
- But old Owsley's preemo purple or even windowpane, that stuff could get you in touch with your ancestors. — Elmore Leonard, *Freaky Deaky*, p. 19, 1988
- Eventually, I gave up selling reefer, dumped Frog, and tried selling chemical drugs—orange sunshine, mescaline, windowpane, purple microdots, quaaludes[.] — Nathan McCall, *Makes Me Wanna Holler*, p. 123, 1994
- Street names [...] tripper, trips, window and many other names. — James Kay and Julian Cohen, *The Parents" Complete Guide to Young People and Drugs*, p. 141, 1998

Windoze *noun*

Microsoft Windows™, *US, 1997*

Not praise.

- — Andy Ihnatko, *Cyberspeak*, p. 211, 1997

Windsor ballet *nickname*

collectively, the strip and sex clubs in Windsor, Ontario, Canada *US, 1997*

- And er, yes, that's one of those places euphemistically referred to as "the Windsor Ballet," where even tutus are no-nos. — *Detroit Free Press*, 6th June 2002

windsucker *noun*

in horseracing, a horse that swallows air when running *US, 1947*

- — Dan Parker, *The ABC of Horse Racing*, p. 150, 1947
- — Nate Perlmutter, *How to Win Money at the Races*, p. 123, 1964

wind tunnel *noun*

in homosexual usage, a loose anus and rectum *US, 1981*

- — *Male Swinger Number 3*, p. 45, 1981: "The complete gay dictionary"

windy *noun*

in pool, a shot that passes the object ball without touching it *US, 1993*

Based on the image of the cue ball breezing by the object ball.

- — Mike Shamos, *The Illustrated Encyclopedia of Billiards*, p. 263, 1993

Windy *noun*

▸ **the Windy**

Chicago, Illinois *US, 1969*

From the winds that sweep the city; a short form of **WINDY CITY**.

- His plan was to cop Mama and make it to the "Windy." — Iceberg Slim (Robert Beck), *Pimp*, p. 24, 1969

Windy City *nickname*

Chicago, Illinois *US, 1860*

Texas slang lexicographer Barry Popik has relentlessly worked to debunk the myth that the term was coined in conjunction with the 1893 World's Fair.

- Chigago. The Windy City. The city of ... wind. — Richard Thomas and Stewart Lee, *Jerrry Springer—The Opera*, 2003

wine head *noun*

a drunkard who favors wine *US, 1961*

- "No replies?" He groaned again. "Sure—wineheads!" — Hunter S. Thompson, *Songs of the Doomed*, p. 71, 1962
- My name ain't Sonny, and go fuck yourself, you wine-head bastard. — Nathan Heard, *Howard Street*, p. 61, 1968
- I don't know—guy brings wine heads out, plays music for them. — Elmore Leonard, *Mr. Majestyk*, p. 24, 1974
- "Talk like yer some gangster and you ain't nothin' but an ol" winehead." — William Brashler, *City Dogs*, p. 37, 1976

wine shed *noun*

a bar *US, 1984*

- He spends so much time in that wine shed, I thought maybe he was renting a stool. — Ken Weaver, *Texas Crude*, p. 58, 1984

wing *noun*

1 the arm *UK, 1823*

- "How's the wing?" Grave Digger asked. — Chester Himes, *The Real Cool Killers*, p. 56, 1959
- I've got a busted wing, sir. — Clancy Sigal, *Going Away*, p. 233, 1961
- I'd cut off my right wing and my swipe for you. — Iceberg Slim (Robert Beck), *Airtight Willie and Me*, p. 25, 1979

2 a winning streak in poker *US, 1988*

- — George Percy, *The Language of Poker*, p. 97, 1988

wing *verb*

to shoot at someone and wound them but not seriously *UK, 1802*

- Frenchy thought he winged one of them cats. He didn't. None of them four shots went nowheres[.] — Hal Ellson, *Duke*, p. 38, 1949

▸ **wing it**

to improvise; to do something with little preparation *US, 1970*

Originally from the theater, indicating the necessity of learning a part at short notice, standing in the wings of a stage.

- Lawyers that do their homework. They can't wing it anymore. — Edwin Torres, *After Hours*, p. 214, 1979
- He doesn't wing it very often. — Elmore Leonard, *Split Images*, p. 104, 1981

wingding; wing-ding *noun*

1 a party, a celebration *US, 1949*

- "She was at the wing-ding up the river tonight," Grave Digger said thickly. — Chester Himes, *A Rage in Harlem*, p. 189, 1957
- There was one big whing-ding going on in Leo Stevens" room. — Helen Giblo, *Footlights, Fistfights and Femmes*, p. 119, 1957
- "Bring MIss Ford if you want to—she's never seen a real wing-ding—but show up and be counted." — Stephen Longstreet, *The Flesh Peddlers*, p. 69, 1962
- "Prove it, then, and come to Mrs. Madrigal's wingding." — Armistead Maupin, *Tales of the City*, p. 347, 1978

2 a fit, especially one feigned by a drug addict; a person feigning such a fit *US, 1927*

- So he is sent to the rear, and we watch him go with hatred in our eyes. "If I ever throw a whingding like that, shoot me," says Kerrigan. — Audie Murphy, *To Hell and Back*, p. 15, 1949
- — Joseph E. Ragen and Charles Finston, *Inside the World's Toughest Prison*, p. 823, 1962: "Penitentiary and underworld glossary"
- "If I had known you could throw wingdings like that I could have been using you all along as a sideline to faith healing," she said. — Chester Himes, *Come Back Charleston Blue*, p. 72, 1966
- That square chump is sure a whingding. — Iceberg Slim (Robert Beck), *Pimp*, p. 217, 1969

wingie *noun*
the wingman on a fighter plane *US, 1989*

- "Understand your wingie was hit?" "Roger, they went in." — Jeffrey Ethel, *One Day in a Long War*, p. 120, 1989

winging *adjective*
drunk or drug-intoxicated *US, 1970*

- — William D. Alsever, *Glossary for the Establishment and Other Uptight People*, p. 15, December 1970

wingnut *noun*
a person who is easily angered or flustered *US, 1990*
As a piece of hardware, a "wingnut" is easily tightened—the basis for its application to a person.

- So, all things considered, this wingnut sitting across the desk today wasn't all that bad. — Seth Morgan, *Homeboy*, p. 193, 1990

wings *noun*
insignia worn by motorcycle gang members signifying sexual conquests *US, 1966*

- True magazine [...] also explained the varicolored pilots" wings: red wings indicating that the wearer has committed cunnilingus on a menstruating woman, black wings for the same act on a Negress, and brown wings for buggery. — Hunter S. Thompson, *Hell's Angels*, p. 117, 1966

▸ **get your wings**
to use heroin for the first time *US, 1989*
A nod to aviation terminology.

- — Geoffrey Froner, *Digging for Diamonds*, p. 66, 1989

wing-wang *noun*
the rectum *US, 1970*

- "I hope you die with a hard-on." "Yeah, well if I do, it'll be up your girl's wing-wang at the time." — Darryl Ponicsan, *The Last Detail*, p. 168, 1970

wing wipe *noun*
a crew member of a military jet aircraft *US, 1990*
A term used by the infantry.

- "Gonna get yourself a MiG, wing-wipe?" — James H. Webb, *A Country Such As This*, p. 105, 1983

wingy *noun*
a person with one arm *US, 1980*

- — Joe McKennon, *Circus Lingo*, p. 105, 1980

winkie *noun*
a sideways punctuation face indicating laughter, generally formed as ;-) *US, 1995*

- — Christian Crumlish, *The Internet Dictionary*, p. 3, 1995

winky hole *noun*
the anus *US, 1986*

- "I got credit out my winky hole." — James Lee Burke, *The Lost Get-Back Boogie*, p. 190, 1986

winner *noun*
a loser socially *US, 1964*
Sardonic, cruel.

- — J.R. Friss, *A Dictionary of Teenage Slang (Mt. Diablo High)*, 1964

winners *noun*
dice that have been altered so as to roll numbers other than seven, useful to the shooter in craps *US, 1950*

- — *The Annals of the American Academy of Political and Social Sciences*, p. 132, May 1950

wino *noun*
a lowly drunk *US, 1913*

- [S]he finally got to wild Third Street among the lines of slugging winos and the bloody drunken Indians[.] — Jack Kerouac, *The Subterraneans*, p. 34, 1958
- A wino, sleeping on the floor, stirred and woke from the drunken stupor he'd been in[.] — Nathan Heard, *Howard Street*, p. 61, 1968
- He spent hours upon hours in the old public library at Bayfront Park, amid the snoring winos and bag ladies[.] — Carl Hiaasen, *Tourist Season*, p. 57, 1986

wino time *noun*
a short jail sentence *US, 1992*

- — William K. Bentley and James M. Crobett, *Prison Slang*, p. 24, 1992

winter *noun*
any period between carnival seasons, regardless of the actual time of year *US, 1966*

- — *American Speech*, p. 282, December 1966: "More carnie talk from the West Coast"

win-win *adjective*
said of a situation in which the parties involved all feel that they have done well *US, 1977*

- In recent years, managers have taken over from game theory the notion that decision-making events can be one of two types: the win-lose situation (or zero-sum game) or the win-win situation. — *Harvard Business Review*, p. 67, May/June 1977
- Recently the terms "win, win" and "win, win, win" have evolved as a favorite among bureaucrats and politicians to describe a situation where no one can lose. — *Orlando Sentinel Tribune*, p. 1, 15th May 1990
- Ninety-nine times in the past four years, someone has called something a "win-win situation" on the pages of the St. Petersburg Times. — *St. Petersburg Times*, p. 5D, 18th August 1991

wipe *noun*
a handkerchief *US, 1981*

- — Don Wilmeth, *The Language of American Popular Entertainment*, p. 294, 1981

wiped *adjective*
drunk *US, 1968*

- — *Current Slang*, p. 15, Summer 1968

wiped out *adjective*
very drunk or drug-intoxicated *US, 1964*

- [T]he phrases of the recent generation, e.g., "crocked," "wiped out," and "smashed[.]" — William and Jerrye Breedlove, *Swap Clubs*, p. 151, 1964
- We got wiped out one night and went all over the place looking for some guy to pickup and blow his mind. — Herb Michelson, *Sportin' Ladies*, p. 5, 1975

wipe out *verb*
to destroy something; to kill or wound someone *US, 1968*

- [T]here was a certain undeniable decadence in the way we sat there, drinks in hand, watching the kids in the street getting wiped out. — Terry Southern, *Now Dig This*, p. 128, November 1968
- Police cars caught alone were wiped out with rocks. — Jerry Rubin, *Do It!*, p. 171, 1970
- And if there is a, thingy, war [...] might as well get wiped out with a few sounds in your head[.] — Mike Stott, *Soldiers Talking, Cleanly*, 1978

wire *noun*
1 a rumor, gossip *US, 1977*

- Then they told me they had got the wire that my woman was next. — John Allen, *Assault with a Deadly Weapon*, pp. 62–63, 1977

2 a telegraph message; a telegram *UK, 1876*

- Shot a wire on this to Baltimore. — Marvin Wald and Albert Maltz, *The Naked City*, 1947

3 a bookmaking operation *US, 1981*

- They told me, yeah, there was a wire going, but it was strictly amateur. — James Ellroy, *Brown's Requiem*, p. 110, 1981

4 a small microphone and transmitting device worn on the person as part of law enforcement interception of oral communications *US, 1973*

- Phillips walked in, wearing wire, and said, "How're you doing, Louis?" — Leonard Shecter and William Phillips, *On the Pad*, p. 223, 1973

- On occasion, Rossi or I would wear a "wire," either a Nagra tape recorder or a T-4 transmitter. — Joseph Pistone, *Donnie Brasco*, p. 260, 1987
- This rabbit'll do anything not to do time, including wearing a wire. — *True Romance*, 1993

5 in pool, the score string *US, 1993*

- — Mike Shamos, *The Illustrated Encyclopedia of Billiards*, p. 264, 1993

▸ **on the wire**
in pool, having scored or having been awarded a score as part of the handicapping of a game *US, 1993*

- — Mike Shamos, *The Illustrated Encyclopedia of Billiards*, p. 161, 1993

wire *verb*
1 to use a small microphone or transmitting device to intercept oral communications *US, 1973*

- I thought, shit, he's wired, my life is gone, ended, obliterated by this one individual. — Leonard Shecter and William Phillips, *On the Pad*, p. 44, 1973
- [W]ondering where the Ching was calling from. Bar on Catherine Street in South Philly? He hoped to Christ not. That social club on Hutchinson? Either place could be wired. — Elmore Leonard, *Glitz*, p. 138, 1985
- I took Rossi's car because it was wired with a Nagra in the trunk. — Joseph Pistone, *Donnie Brasco*, p. 275, 1987

2 in skateboarding, to analyze and plan a difficult maneuver or trick *US, 1976*

- — Laura Torbet, *The Complete Book of Skateboarding*, p. 109, 1976

wired *adjective*
1 intoxicated on amphetamines or cocaine *US, 1966*
Also used with "up."

- Magoo is a pill freak, and when he gets wired up he does a lot of talking. — Hunter S. Thompson, *Hell's Angels*, p. 184, 1966
- [B]ut if what you really crave is the good clean thrills and light and completely dedicated positive—if perhaps, ah um, yes, possibly just a leetle bit wired (speed? horrors!)—then climb in, hang on[.] — *The Last Supplement to the Whole Earth Catalog*, p. 84, March 1971
- A wired-up pillhead, he said to himself. — Gerald Petievich, *Shakedown*, p. 38, 1988
- We'll take a thousand bucks out of the shoe bag, cab it over to Philip's house, pick up an ounce of blow, call Natalie, tell her and Jessica to come over here, we'll get them wired, I'll fuck Natalie—you do your best to fuck Jessica. — Kenneth Lonergan, *This is Our Youth*, p. 34, 2000

2 used of a pair in stud poker, dealt in the first two cards of a hand *US, 1981*

- — Jim Glenn, *Programmed Poker*, p. 158, 1981

wired up *adjective*
available for homosexual relations *US, 1961*

- — Arthur V. Huffman, *New York Mattachine Newsletter*, p. 6, June 1961: "Sex deviation in a prison community"

wirehead *noun*
a computer hardware specialist *US, 1991*

- — Eric S. Raymond, *The New Hacker's Dictionary*, p. 383, 1991
- The sensible, mature wireheads we are. — Melanie McGrath, *Hard, Soft & Wet*, p. 111, 1998

wire room *noun*
an illegal betting establishment's telephone office *US, 1950*

- Another major wire-room, operating at this writing, is at 10 North Clark Street, a block from City Hall. — Jack Lait and Lee Mortimer, *Chicago Confidential*, p. 129, 1950
- "Why doesn't the D.A. use her to get an inside track on the wire rooms?" — Mickey Spillane, *The Big Kill*, p. 45, 1951

wires *noun*
any central nervous system stimulant *US, 1977*

- — Bill Davis, *Jawjacking*, p. 109, 1977

wire store *noun*
a big con based on a supposedly corrupt telegraph official who claims he can delay the reporting of race results to the benefit of the victim *US, 1940*

- He taught me long con and how to rope suckers for a wire store he set up in Denver, Colorado. — Iceberg Slim (Robert Beck), *Trick Baby*, p. 112, 1969

wire to wire *noun*
in horseracing, the entire distance of the race, from start to finish *US, 1951*

- — David W. Maurer, *Argot of the Racetrack*, p. 69, 1951

wise *verb*
to inform or educate someone; to explain something *US, 1905*

- He wised me to a hip hotel in lower Manhattan. — A.S. Jackson, *Gentleman Pimp*, p. 114, 1973

wiseacre *noun*
a smart alec *UK, 1595*

- Young smirking wiseacres, he would have enjoyed beating each one of them with a baseball bat. — Irving Shulman, *The Amboy Dukes*, p. 72, 1947

wiseass *noun*
an obnoxious person with delusions of cleverness *US, 1971*

- IMPATIENT CUSTOMER: Such a wiseass. But go ahead. Crack wise. That's why you're jockeying a register in some fucking local convenience store instead of doing an honest day's work. — *Clerks*, 1994

wise guy *noun*
a recognized member of an organized crime enterprise *US, 1973*

- "There were some independent games in the city, but most were run or protected by some wiseguy." — Vincent Teresa, *My Life in the Mafia*, p. 73, 1973
- Funny the way the wise-guy can never make it in legit business because the square that covers for him will always rob him. — Edwin Torres, *Carlito's Way*, p. 58, 1975
- A wise guy shouldn't just fall sprawling on the dirty pavement like some square John[.] — Brian Boyer, *Prince of Thieves*, p. 28, 1975
- They're like the police department for wiseguys. — *Goodfellas*, 1990

wisepuss *noun*
an obnoxious person with delusions of cleverness *US, 1971*
A variation of **WISEASS**.

- I know they play different instruments, wisepuss[.] — Lester Bangs, *Psychotic Reactions and Carburetor Dung*, p. 63, 1971

wishing book *noun*
a mail-order catalogue *US, 1975*

- — John Gould, *Maine Lingo*, p. 319, 1975

wish-was *noun*
someone who wishes that he were something that he is not *US, 1991*

- — Trevor Cralle, *The Surfin'ary*, p. 163, 1991

wishy-washy *adjective*
weak; uncertain *UK, 1703*

- I don't want anybody to stand up and say I change my mind about things like a hundred-dollar hooker changes her shorts. I don't want anyone to be able to say George Lurgan's wishy-washy. — Robert Campbell, *The Cat's Meow*, p. 64, 1988

wit *noun*
a witness *US, 1999*

- "Any wits?" "I've got people making a house-to-house up along the ridge[.]" — Robert Crais, *L.A. Requiem*, p. 41, 1999
- Barbara Molar is my wit. — Stephen J. Cannell, *The Tin Collectors*, p. 18, 2001
- He looked for character wits. — James Ellroy, *Destination Morgue*, p. 106, 2004

wit!
"what was just said is not funny!" *US, 1986*

- — *55-Plus*, p. 13, 12th February 1986: "Today's guide to teen slang"

witch doctor *noun*
a doctor who specializes in internal medicine *US, 1984–1985*

- — *Maledicta*, p. 118, 1984–1985: "Milwaukee medical maledicta"

witch's brew *noun*
LSD enhanced with botanical drugs from plants such as deadly nightshade or jimsonweed *US, 1970*

- — William D. Alsever, *Glossary for the Establishment and Other Uptight People*, p. 3, December 1970

with authority!
used as a humorous comment on a remark made or action taken without hesitation and boldly *US, 1997*
Coined on ESPN's Sports Center while narrating footage showing a basketball slam dunk.

- — Keith Olberman and Dan Patrick, *The Big Show*, p. 27, 1997

with it *adjective*
aware of all that is happening; stylish; part of a subculture *US, 1945*

- The title (of the 1945 show "Are You With It?") is carnival slang for "Are you with the carnival?" — *Life*, p. 97, 26th November 1945
- Now "you're with it" has left "hep nothing but a three-letter word." — *Washington Post*, p. F1, 29th September 1957

without *adjective*
clueless; out of touch; out of style *US, 1999*
- Your sister is so amazingly without. She'll never read him. She has no idea. — *Ten Things I Hate About You*, 1999

wizard *noun*
1 in computing, a person who has specific and detailed expertise *US, 1983*
- — Guy L. Steele et al., *The Hacker's Dictionary*, p. 132, 1983
2 in pinball, an expert player *US, 1977*
- — Bobbye Claire Natkin and Steve Kirk, *All About Pinball*, p. 118, 1977

wizzo *noun*
the weapons officer on a military aircraft *US, 1998*
- — *Seattle Times*, p. A9, 12th April 1998: "Grunts, squids not grunting from the same dictionary"

wobblies; wobs *noun*
a powerful and deep vibration of the board while skateboarding fast *US, 1976*
- — Albert Cassorla, *The Skateboarder's Bible*, p. 204, 1976

wobbs *noun*
in street luge, a wobbling of the luge *US, 1998*
- WOBBS Speed wobbles, in which the rear suspension is improperly adjusted, causing it to veer left and right. — shelley Youngblut, *Way Inside ESPN's X Games*, p. 130, 1998

wog *noun*
any person of nonwhite ethnicity; a native of the indian subcontinent; an Arab; any (non-British) foreigner, as in "the wogs begin at Calais" *UK, 1929*
Popular, unproven etymology has "wog" as an acronym of "Western(ised) [or] Wily Oriental Gentleman."
- Do you know what I'm going to do to those wogs? — Richard Farina, *Been Down So Long*, p. 164, 1966

woke-up *adjective*
informed; up-to-date *US, 1968*
- — Hy Lit, *Hy Lit's Unbelievable Dictionary of Hip Words for Groovy People*, p. 1, 1968

wolf *noun*
1 a sexually aggressive man *US, 1945*
- It was parked on a sofa, a full six feet long. It gave me ideas, which I quickly ignored. It was no time to play wolf. — Mickey Spillane, *I, The Jury*, p. 30, 1947
- As he walked before her he was proud of the stares and whistles Betty received from the wolves who sat at the tables. — Irving Shulman, *The Amboy Dukes*, p. 202, 1947
- Never enthuse to a fellow wolf about your latest conquest—unless you're trying to lose her. — Jack Lait and Lee Mortimer, *New York Confidential*, p. 129, 1948
- "Let go of my arm," she replied. "The last wolf that made a pass at me is now eating through a tube." — Max Shulman, *The Many Loves of Dobie Gillis*, p. 162, 1951
2 in prison, an aggressive, predatory homosexual *US, 1950*
- Old guys, they called them wolves, they saw me looking at this stuff and thought I might be a gal-boy. — Haywood Patterson, *Scottsboro Boy*, p. 65, 1950
- [H]e made no attempt to hide his lights when a rouged and predaory "wolf," having insinuated himself here and there on the primrose path, ultimately stood before him. — Donald Wilson, *My Six Convicts*, p. 150, 1951
- Everyone was either a wolf or a fag. The wolf is the so-called male of the species, a rare and almost obsolete animal. — Chester Himes, *Cast the First Stone*, p. 72, 1952
- [W]hen the riot began his cell door had been unlocked and pack of fourteen "prison wolves," as aggressive homosexuals are called, had raped him. — John Martin, *Break Down the Walls*, p. 10, 1954
3 a prison sentence of 15 years *US, 1990*
- — Charles Shafer, *Folk Speech in Texas Prisons*, p. 217, 1990

wolf *verb*
to act in a sexually aggressive manner *US, 1949*
- "That was how I found out the best place for wolfin' ain't the taverns." — Nelson Algren, *The Man with the Golden Arm*, p. 84, 1949

- A kid dressed up in his big brother's uniform out wolfin chicks. — Earl Thompson, *Tattoo*, p. 161, 1974

wolf bait *noun*
an attractive young woman *US, 1960*
- Day in and day out, year in and year out, eager young wolf-bait bangs against the big city doors, unaware that beauty and even glamor is often a drug on the market. — Lee Mortimer, *Women Confidential*, p. 88, 1960

wolf in the pack *noun*
a traffic police car in the midst of other cars *US, 1962*
- — *American Speech*, p. 273, December 1962: "The language of traffic policemen"

wolf pack *noun*
a group of friends who play poker at cardrooms, taking advantage of unskilled strangers *US, 1996*
- — John Vorhaus, *The Big Book of Poker Slang*, p. 40, 1996

wolf ticket *noun*
a threat or other act of intimidation used to coerce *US, 1974*
- It's plenty people selling wolf tickets, you know. — Vernon E. Smith, *The Jones Men*, p. 165, 1974
- If you two came here on a wolf ticket, it's time for you to leave. — Robert Deane Pharr, *Giveadamn Brown*, p. 138, 1978
- Let's face it, this girl comes right back to the situation where they're selling drugs and starts selling wolf tickets and they don't do nothing about it. — Mark Baker, *Cops*, pp. 117–118, 1985
- Wolf Tickets: What Baker accused Tony LaRussa of selling when the St. Louis Manager charged that Cubs pitchers were throwing at Cardinals pitchers. — *Chicago Tribune*, p. C10, 9th September 2003

wombat *noun*
in computing, a waste of money, brains and time *US, 1991*
- — Eric S. Raymond, *The New Hacker's Dictionary*, p. 386, 1991

womb broom *noun*
the penis *US, 1973*
- I went to the bathroom and washed the animal smell of sex from my womb broom. — A.S. Jackson, *Gentleman Pimp*, p. 166, 1973

womb duster *noun*
the penis *US, 1977*
- She caressed it and whispered, "Billy, your womb duster is heroic." — Iceberg Slim (Robert Beck), *Long White Con*, p. 98, 1977

womb sweeper *noun*
the penis *US, 1978*
- She mouths in to tow out his cable veined womb sweeper. — Iceberg Slim (Robert Beck), *Doom Fox*, p. 156, 1978

women and children off the street!
in shuffleboard, used as a humorous commentary on a hard shooter *US, 1967*
- — Omero C. Catan, *Secrets of Shuffleboard Strategy*, p. 74, 1967: "Glossary of terms"

womp; whomp *verb*
to beat someone *US, 1964*
- — J.R. Friss, *A Dictionary of Teenage Slang (Mt. Diablo High)*, 1964
- — Hy Lit, *Hy Lit's Unbelievable Dictionary of Hip Words for Groovy People*, p. 52, 1968

wong *verb*
in casino blackjack, to play several hands at a table where the count of cards played favors the player, and then to move on to another table *US, 1991*
Named after Stanford Wong, a blackjack expert.
- — Michael Dalton, *Blackjack*, p. 90, 1991

wonk *noun*
a student who studies harder than contemporaries consider necessary; a political professional who is studious and therefore well informed *US, 1962*
- — Collin Baker et al., *College Undergraduate Slang Study Conducted at Brown University*, p. 223, 1968
- Some musical wonk? — Erich Segal, *Love Story*, p. 26, 1970
- I almost never call anyone a nerd—I'm partial to the term "wonk." — *Washington Post (reprinted from The Nation)*, p. C5, 22nd December 1985

wonkey; wonky *adjective*
broken *US, 2001*
- — Don R. McCreary (Editor), *Dawg Speak*, 2001

wonk out *verb*
to study excessively *US, 1987*
- — *New York Times*, 12th April 1987

wonky *adjective*
intellectual; out of touch with reality *US, 1970*
- "Jenny Cavilleri," answered Ray. "Wonky music type." — Erich Segal, *Love Story*, p. 15, 1970

wood *noun*
1 heroin *US, 1973*
- "Wood?" Like oil in an overheated engine, the heroin makes her feel better[.] — Gail Sheehy, *Hustling*, p. 65, 1973

2 the fully erect penis *US, 1991*
- This guy has trouble with wood [erections] and if he does, I'd give you a hell of a lot to step in and do the scene. — Robert Stoller and I.S. Levine, *Coming Attractions*, p. 82, 1991
  — *Adult Video News*, p. 48, September 1995
- But whether that enthusiasm translates into on-screen "wood" is another story. More often than not, a male who has never experienced the harsh conditions of onscreen sex will not be able to "rise" to the occasion. — Ana Loria, *1 2 3 Be A Porn Star!*, p. 65, 2000
- "He's putting heavy wood to her, Lar," I said tersely, "from behind." — Terry Southern, *Now Dig This*, p. 241, 2001
- He must have been extra thorough with his genitals because he had wood on. — Ethan Morden, *How's Your Romance?*, p. 180, 2005

3 in a casino or other gambling establishment, a person who watches without playing *US, 1950*
An abbreviation of **DEADWOOD**.
- — John Scarne, *Scarne on Dice*, p. 482, 1974
- — Thomas L. Clark, *The Dictionary of Gambling and Gaming*, p. 251, 1987

▶ **on the wood**
in horseracing, racing along the rail *US, 1994*
- — Igor Kushyshyn et al., *The Gambling Times Guide to Harness Racing*, p. 120, 1994

wood burner *noun*
an attractive female *US, 1990*
A suggestion that the woman consumes **WOOD** in the "erect" sense of the word.
- All those wood burners on the beach? Yeah, I'd pay to do this job. — Joseph Wambaugh, *The Golden Orange*, p. 176, 1990

wooden *adjective*
in poker, said of a hand that is unplayable *US, 1951*
- — *American Speech*, p. 102, May 1951

wooden Indian *noun*
a poker player who does not talk or display emotion *US, 1996*
- — John Vorhaus, *The Big Book of Poker Slang*, p. 40, 1996

woodfoot *noun*
numbing of the foot in cold water *US, 2004*
Surfing usage.
- — *Transworld Surf*, p. 42, April 2004

woodpile *noun*
1 a xylophone *US, 1945*
- — Lou Shelly, *Hepcats Jive Talk Dictionary*, p. 20, 1945

2 the area in a prison yard where white prisoners exercise *US, 1989*
Formed from **PECKERWOOD** (a white person) and **IRON PILE** (weight lifting equipment).
- — James Harris, *A Convict's Dictionary*, p. 41, 1989

woodpile cousin *noun*
an actual, if distant, blood relative *US, 1975*
- — John Gould, *Maine Lingo*, p. 320, 1975

woods *noun*
the vulva; a woman's pubic hair *US, 1968*
- — Collin Baker et al., *College Undergraduate Slang Study Conducted at Brown University*, p. 223, 1968

woodshed *verb*
1 to break a drug addiction *US, 2000*
- PAGE: Where he'd gone to woodshed. TOOEY: Woodshed? PAGE: Like George said, to clean up. — Ken Kesey, *The Further Inquiry*, p. 198, 1990

2 to rehearse, especially in private *US, 1936*
- [...]that exile in the soul that jazzmen know as "woodshedding" — John Clellon Holmes, *The Horn*, p. 59, 1958
- You got a long way to go, a lot to learn, but I think that with some woodshedding you can get our book down. — Nat Hentoff, *Jazz Country*, p. 120, 1965

woodsman *noun*
a male pornography performer who can be counted upon to maintain an erection as long as needed and to ejaculate more or less on demand *US, 1995*
- — *Adult Video News*, p. 48, September 1995
- The real elite woodsman can also stand in as a "penis" for $50 to $100 bucks a scene (depending on the situation at hand) in case a younger or more inexperienced performer can't make wood. — Ana Loria, *1 2 3 Be A Porn Star!*, p. 68, 2000

woodster *noun*
a male pornography performer whose erections can be counted on *US, 2000*
- It's easier to use the same five guys because those five guys are guaranteed woodsters. — Ana Loria, *1 2 3 Be A Porn Star!*, p. 106a, 2000

woodsy *noun*
a party held in the country *US, 1967*
- — *Current Slang*, p. 2, Spring 1967

woody; woodie *noun*
an erection *US, 1985*
US pornographer Joey Silvera is given credit for coining this term, which did not stay within the confines of pornography for long.
- Old Desmond had sprouted a woody! — Joseph Wambaugh, *The Secrets of Harry Bright*, p. 47, 1985
- — Pamela Munro, *U.C.L.A. Slang*, p. 91, 1989
- So I then go into my Mack Daddy mode cause I'm getting a woodie in my cackies y'know. — *Boyz N The Hood*, 1990
- Who's the old guy with the big woody? — *Airheads*, 1994
- Woodrow was inspired by Knut himself, bragging that a lingerie ad was all it took for him to produce "a woodie a cat can't scratch." — Dan Jenkins, *The Money-Whipped Steer-Job Three-Jack Give-Up Artist*, p. 59, 2001

woof *verb*
to threaten or intimidate someone; to engage someone in ritualistic, quasi-friendly insulting *US, 1967*
- "Ain't you about to freeze to death, Pony?" "You ain't a woofin'," I said[.] — S.E. Hinton, *The Outsiders*, p. 49, 1967
- Just plain woofing pure and simple. — John Sinclair, *Guitar Army*, p. 345, 1972
- "You too new here to be woofin' that shit, Monster." — Sanyika Shakur, *Monster*, p. 153, 1993
- "The seas part, the assholes in the back rows start woofing you out, you bite the bullet and you split." — Richard Price, *Samaritan*, p. 167, 2003

woof!
used as a shout of approval, especially as a male declaration of appreciation for a sexually desirable female *US, 1992*
Originated by television talk show host Arsenio Hall in 1989; the barking is accompanied by a pumped raised hand, fist clenched.
- The woof chorus went through the roof, everybody high-fiving, bopping in glee. — Richard Price, *Clockers*, p. 203, 1992

woofie *noun*
a promiscuous woman *US, 1981*
- Raunchy sent a prospect over to the massage parlor that the club owned to get a couple of woofies for Treb and Dick while they were there[.] — Robert Lipkin, *A Brotherhood of Outlaws*, p. 39, 1981

wool *noun*
pubic hair; by extension, sex *US, 1972*
- He looks like he could get hisself some good wool if he put his mind on it. — Dan Jenkins, *Semi-Tough*, p. 10, 1972
- — *Maledicta*, p. 131, Summer/Winter 1982: "Dyke diction: the language of lesbians"

woola; woolas *noun*
crack cocaine or phencyclidine sprinkled over marijuana which is then smoked in a cigarette; a hollowed-out cigar filled with marijuana and phencyclidine *US, 1989*
- — Terry Williams, *The Cocaine Kids*, p. 138, 1989
- She flushed the woola down the john. — Lois Stavsky et al., *A2Z*, p. 112, 1995
- Started smokin woolas at sixteen. — RZA, *The Wu-Tang Manual*, p. 150, 2005

woolie *noun*
a marijuana cigarette laced with crack cocaine *US, 2002*
- But when Ready Ron spoke of the great high I could get from a "woolie," the "new thing on the block," he didn't tell me how differenlty it would affect my life. — Earl "DMX" Simmons, *E.A.R.L.*, p. 93, 2002

woolies noun

winter clothing US, 1945

• — Lou Shelly, *Hepcats Jive Talk Dictionary*, p. 50, 1945

Woolworth noun

in hold 'em poker, a five and a ten as the first two cards dealt to a player US, 1981

Woolworth's was the most famous five and dime store in the US.

• — Thomas L. Clark, *The Dictionary of Gambling and Gaming*, p. 252, 1987

Woolworth's finest noun

in shuffleboard, a ten US, 1967

• — Omero C. Catan, *Secrets of Shuffleboard Strategy*, p. 74, 1967: "Glossary of terms"

wooly noun

a black person US, 1969

Variants include "wooley head."

• — Iceberg Slim (Robert Beck), *Trick Baby*, p. 276, 1969

wooter noun

the penis US, 1981

• — *Maledicta*, p. 255, Summer/Winter 1981: "Five years and 121 dirty words later"

woozy adjective

unsteady; dizzy; disoriented; intoxicated with drugs or drink US, 1897

• For it wasn't the easiest thing in the world to visit a victim still too woozy to know what had hit him. — Nelson Algren, *The Man with the Golden Arm*, p. 73, 1949

• I was a little woozy and needed sugar[.] — Jack Kerouac, *The Dharma Bums*, p. 167, 1958

• She arched her back a trifle, and, with her mouth a trifle open, she put her hand on top of her head. "I feel so woozy and funny." — J.D. Salinger, *Franny and Zooey*, p. 29, 1961

• I am by now halfway between hallucination and coma, and somewhat woozy, as though I've gone too long without food. — Philip Roth, *Portnoy's Complaint*, p. 193, 1969

wop noun

an Italian immigrant or Italian-American US, 1914

• Then the stockboy—a hot-looking wop with long hair—took me out in his department to show me the new materials—and the place was deserted. — Philip Wylie, *Opus 21*, p. 298, 1949

• PEPE: Micks! INDIO: Wop! — Stephen Sondheim, *West Side Story*, 1957

• Eventually I relinquished presidency of the Knights to a fat loquacious slob named Richard who led us one night into a riot with the wops from east of Sacramento Boulevard. — Clancy Sigal, *Going Away*, p. 351, 1961

• Lemme tell you about them rumbles. The wops said no spics could go east of Park Avenue. — Edwin Torres, *Carlito's Way*, p. 8, 1975

wop adjective

Italian US, 1961

• "He's into weight-lifting and wop haberdashery," Endicott said. — Bernard Wolfe, *The Magic of Their Singing*, p. 15, 1961

• Is that the new car out there? The little red Wop job? — *The Graduate*, 1967

wop-jawed adjective

in circus and carnival usage, amazed by an act or demonstration US, 1981

• — Don Wilmeth, *The Language of American Popular Entertainment*, p. 294, 1981

word noun

▸ **take the word**

in the illegal production of alcohol, to warn someone about a pending law enforcement raid US, 1974

• Yeah, he took the word, else they'd got ketched Friday. — David W. Maurer, *Kentucky Moonshine*, p. 126, 1974

▸ **the word**

1 gossip, rumors US, 1961

• Milt came by with a rumor about a package delivery. Milt always had what the Marines called "the word"—the latest rumor. — Russell Davis, *Marine at War*, p. 119, 1961

2 an order US, 1962

• — *American Speech*, p. 288, December 1962: "Marine Corps slang"

word!

used for expressing assent US, 1987

• — Connie Eble (Editor), *UNC-CH Campus Slang*, p. 8, Spring 1987

• But now, word! Hey, I be selling thirty-forty caps in a few minutes. — Terry Williams, *The Cocaine Kids*, p. 57, 1989

• "I get myself shot, I want it be in the arm, Gor-DEN!" "Word!" agreed Rac. — Jess Mowry, *Way Past Cool*, p. 6, 1992

• "Word" was once a powerful affirmation that you were "dropping science" [making sense][.] — Nelson George, *Hip Hop America*, p. 209, 1998

word up

used for expressing agreement or as a greeting US, 1986

• — Connie Eble (Editor), *UNC-CH Campus Slang*, p. 6, October 1986

• Rac nodded. "Word up! By rules!" — Jess Mowry, *Way Past Cool*, p. 13, 1992

• Word up: two weeks. "It be like these." — David Simon and Edward Burns, *The Corner*, p. 73, 1997

work noun

1 cosmetic surgery US, 2001

• I said the mothers were the threat. They'd had work done. — Dan Jenkins, *The Money-Whipped Steer-Job Three-Jack Give-Up Artist*, p. 208, 2001

2 in professional wrestling, a completed scripted and stage event US, 1990

• work n. a deception or sham — *rec.sports.pro-wrestling*, 17th July 1990

• Maybe no one told Zybysko that the feud was a work[.] — Jeff Archer, *Theater in a Squared Circle*, 1999

• The con, or what we refer to in wrestling as "the work," is to knowingly misrepresent the truth, to lie, to deceive or mislead someone. — Gary Cappetta, *Bodyslams!*, p. 179, 2000

3 a prostitute with steady earnings US, 2002

• Most of his girls were white and what pimps called "work." They were tawdry-looking hos, but they kept him in minks and finger rocks. — Tracy Funches, *Pimpnosis*, p. 83, 2002

4 killing US, 1987

• [H]e had done a lot of "work" for the Colombos, meaning he had participated in hits. — Joseph Pistone, *Donnie Brasco*, p. 69, 1987

• "Tell you to put in work; give you a gun and tell you to shoot so-and-so." — Gini Sikes, *8 Ball Chicks*, p. 44, 1997

5 the betting slips in an illegal lottery or gambling operation US, 1974

• Another common method of scoring numbers operators consisted of policemen confiscating the gambler's numbers slips, which are known as "work." — *The Knapp Commission Report on Police Corruption*, p. 84, 1972

• [N]ext in the intricately structured racket is the pickup man, who brings the "work"—the betting slips—from various collectors to a controller. — Peter Maas, *Serpico*, p. 164, 1973

• He said all the things that a bookmaker, grabbed with the "works" on his person, might very well say. — Leonard Shecter and William Phillips, *On the Pad*, p. 120, 1973

• I flick the four o'clock game on the tube, make black coffee, and start going over the work. — Gary Mayer, *Bookie*, p. 7, 1974

6 cheating in gambling, especially in craps US, 1950

The statement "There's work down" means that altered dice or cards are in play.

• — *The Annals of the American Academy of Political and Social Sciences*, p. 133, May 1950

7 dice or cards that have been altered for the purpose of cheating US, 1963

• — John S. Salak, *Dictionary of Gambling*, p. 278, 1963

8 crack cocaine US, 1989

• A dealer on the street might chant, "Hey, hey, want some work?" — Geoffrey Froner, *Digging for Diamonds*, p. 66, 1989

9 sex US, 1959

• — Lawrence Lipton, *The Holy Barbarians*, p. 318, 1959

▸ **do the work on someone**

to kill someone US, 1994

• So if he did the work on the plumber he would be sending the only woman he had ever really loved to a boneyard. — Richard Condon, *Prizzi's Money*, p. 90, 1994

work verb

1 to cheat at gambling US, 1963

• One day he sat in with us and I caught him working and cut him loose. — Mickey Spillane, *Me, Hood!*, p. 30, 1963

2 to have sex with someone US, 1957

• Finally he came out with it: he wanted me to work Marylou. I didn't ask him why because I knew he wanted to see what Marylou was like with another man. — Jack Kerouac, *On the Road*, p. 131, 1957

3 to sell drugs *US, 1993*
- That holdup occurred shortly after 9:10 p.m. on Passaic Street, when Miller allegedly approached an Aspen Place man and asked if he was "working," the street slang for dealing drugs, police said. — *Record (Bergen County, New Jersey), p. A4, 13th November 1993*

4 to dilute a powdered drug *US, 1989*
- Masterrape and me played with that package forever, we worked it to death [cut it as far as they could]. — Terry Williams, *The Cocaine Kids*, p. 37, 1989

▶ **to get worked**
to be knocked from your surfboard and pummeled by the ocean *US, 1987*
- — Mitch McKissick, *Surf Lingo*, 1987

▶ **work at McDonalds**
to be a member of the Mexican Mafia, a Mexican-American prison gang *US, 1975*
- — Report to the Senate, *California Senate Committee on Civil Disorder*, p. 229, 1975

▶ **work in Frisco**
to serve time at the San Quentin Prison, San Rafael, California *US, 1975*
- — Report to the Senate, *California Senate Committee on Civil Disorder*, p. 229, 1975

▶ **work the cuts**
(used of a prostitute) to solicit customers on the streets *US, 1986–1987*
- — *Maledicta*, p. 150, Summer/Winter 1986–1987: "Sexual slang: prostitutes, pedophiles, flagellators, transvestites, and necrophiles"

▶ **work the glory road**
to affect religious conversion while in prison in the hope of receiving an early parol *US, 1959*
- There are seven other inmates on the Chaplain's staff, a few of whom are engaged in what the cons call "Working the glory road," that is, evincing an extreme degree of piety which they hope will lead to an early parole. — James Blake, *The Joint*, p. 231, 30th July 1959
- — John R. Armore and Joseph D. Wolfe, *Dictionary of Desperation*, p. 57, 1976

▶ **work the hole**
to rob drunks sleeping on subway platforms cars *US, 1953*
- Now he peddled from time to time and "worked the hole" (rolling drunks on subways and in cars) when he couldn't make connections to peddle. — William Burroughs, *Junkie*, p. 40, 1953

▶ **work the nuts**
to operate a shell game in a circus midway or carnival *US, 1980*
- — Joe McKennon, *Circus Lingo*, p. 65, 1980

▶ **work the other side of the street**
to be on opposing sides of a bipolar situation; to make a living as a criminal *US, 1982*
- Well, I been workin' the other side of the street for the law few years. — *48 Hours*, 1982

workaround *noun*
in computing, a temporary fix of a problem *US, 1991*
- — Eric S. Raymond, *The New Hacker's Dictionary*, p. 386, 1991

worker *noun*
1 a professional wrestler who puts on a good performance *US, 1993*
- As a matter of fact, I looked forward to the challenge of coming up with a good match with an opponent who was injured—it was one of the signs of a good worker (wrestler). — Mike Foley, *Mankind*, p. 3, 1999
- The singles wrestlers, even from the undercard, boasted strong workers[.] — Gary Cappetta, *Bodyslams!*, p. 141, 2000
- There's a very small margin of wrestlers that are actually what they call a good worker. There are only a handful of them left that you can go in with night after night. — *Off the Record (TSN)*, 4th April 2000
- He wasn't a great worker, but he had the size and great facial expressions[.] — Missy Hyatt, *Missy Hyatt*, p. 21, 2001

2 a member of a drug-selling enterprise who sells drugs on the street *US, 1995*
- — Mark S. Fleisher, *Beggars & Thieves*, p. 292, 1995: "Glossary"

3 a gambling cheat *US, 1962*
- — Frank Garcia, *Marked Cards and Loaded Dice*, p. 265, 1962

4 in the circus or carnival, a large blown-up balloon shown by the concession selling packages of balloons *US, 1980*

- Do not expect to inflate the purchase to more than half the size of the "worker." — Joe McKennon, *Circus Lingo*, p. 106, 1980

working *adjective*
in craps, said of a bet that will be in effect on the next roll *US, 1981*
- — N.B. Winkless, *The Gambling Times Guide to Craps*, p. 99, 1981

working boy *noun*
a male prostitute *US, 1987*
- [S]he has breasts that are actually quite large, yet, sans bra, they hang, elusive and low, concealed in her oversized T-shirts; thus, she is mistaken constantly for one of the working boys. — Jim Carroll, *Forced Entries*, p. 7, 1987

working end *noun*
the dangerous end of a tool or weapon *US, 1992*
- I submit to you that whoever wrote that memo has never served on the working end of a Soviet-made Cuban M1-A16 Assault Rifle. — *A Few Good Men*, 1992

working fifty *noun*
a large piece of crack cocaine bought at a wholesale price *US, 1990*
- At one,point, Lewis referred to "a working 50," a term he said referred to buying crack at a wholesale rate. Instead of buying cocaine by the $20 bag, Lewis said, it was possible to spend $50 and get one large rock bigger than an oversized marble[.] — *Washington Post*, p. A1, 21st June 1990

working girl *noun*
a prostitute *US, 1968*
- I could see a girl shopping with curlers in her hair and still tell she was a working girl. — Susan Hall, *Gentleman of Leisure*, p. 4, 1972
- The Vegas term working girl I find a bit snobbish. — Mario Puzo, *Inside Las Vegas*, p. 256, 1977
- Mid Edna's staff of working girls was in a constant state of flux. — Jan Hutson, *The Chicken Ranch*, p. 81, 1980
- Don't tell me she's a working girl! — Robert Campbell, *Nibbled to Death by Ducks*, p. 260, 1989
- All the men are fascinated by dancers, prostitutes, and models. They are like groupies. They think working girls are the most amazing thing on the planet. — Marilyn Suriani Futterman, *Dancing Naked in the Material World*, 1992

work out *verb*
to masturbate *US, 1975*
- Soon everybody on the tier knew that I was working out cause soon everybody's voices is with me. — Miguel Pinero, *Short Eyes*, p. 77, 1975
- — Gary K. Farlow, *Prison-ese*, p. 81, 2002

works *noun*
the equipment used to prepare and inject drugs *US, 1934*
- I cooked up a grain and got my works ready to take the shot. — William Burroughs, *Junkie*, p. 38, 1953
- "You got your works, Joe?" I gave her the spike and dropper. — Alexander Trocchi, *Cain's Book*, p. 243, 1960
- He's got the works, gives you sweet taste. — Velvet Underground *I'm Waiting for the Man*, 1967
- Meanwhile one of the others had already found our works and the stash of junk[.] — Herbert Huncke, *The Evening Sun Turned Crimson*, p. 40, 1980

▶ **the works**
the complete treatment *US, 1899*
- And we had a raving great dinner of baked potatoes and porkchops and salad and hot buns and blueberry pie and the works. — Jack Kerouac, *The Dharma Bums*, p. 74, 1958
- "He gave Genevie the works!" — Jose Antonio Villarreal, *Pocho*, p. 88, 1959
- So I ducked into a barbershop and ordered the works, shave, shine, shampoo. — Clancy Sigal, *Going Away*, p. 398, 1961
- He ate breakfast. He visited a barber shop, indulged himself in "the works" and went back to his two-room suite. — Jim Thompson, *The Grifters*, p. 117, 1963

world *noun*
▶ **the world**
during the war in Vietnam, back home, the US, life outside the military *US, 1970*
- "Don't tell me, let me guess—You're th' guy who wuz due t' rotate back t' th' world prior to us losin' your orders." — Michael Hodgson, *With Sgt. Mike in Vietnam*, p. 65, 1970

- "Henry, what's gonna happen when we go back to the world?" — William Pelfrey, *The Big V*, p. 53, 1972
- Before he joined the Corps, Andrews had a completely safe job in the World. — Charles Anderson, *The Grunts*, p. 31, 1976
- "I just can't hack it back in the World," he said. — Michael Herr, *Dispatches*, p. 5, 1977

world of shit *noun*
a very dangerous situation *US, 1984*
- Anybody messes around with J.L.'s wife gonna find hisself in a world of shit. — Ken Weaver, *Texas Crude*, p. 136, 1984

worlds *noun*
commerically manufactured cigarettes *US, 1990*
- — Charles Shafer, *Folk Speech in Texas Prisons*, p. 217, 1990

worm *noun*
1 a computer program that maliciously duplicates itself repeatedly in a host computer until it clogs and crashes the system *US, 1990*
- — Karla Jennings, *The Devouring Fungus: Tales of the Computer Age*, p. 225, 1990
- I say a true hacker will never release a worm, because they are too destructive with no purpose. — The Knightmare, *Secrets of a Super Hacker*, p. 134, 1994

2 a coiled condenser used in the illegal production of alcohol *US, 1974*
- — David W. Maurer, *Kentucky Moonshine*, p. 127, 1974

3 phencyclidine, the recreational drug known as PCP or angel dust *US, 1981*
- — Ronald Linder, *PCP*, p. 10, 1981

worm dirt *noun*
chewing tobacco *US, 2001*
An obvious visual comparison.
- — Don R. McCreary (Editor), *Dawg Speak*, 2001

worry *verb*
(said of a jockey in horseracing) to ride a horse *US, 1951*
- — David W. Maurer, *Argot of the Racetrack*, p. 70, 1951

would you believe...?
used for humorously probing for a statement that can be believed *US, 1965*
The signature line of spy Maxwell Smart, played by Don Adams, on the television comedy *Get Smart* (1965–70). Adams had used the line earlier on *The Bill Dana Show* (NBC, 1963–65). Repeated with referential humor.

wow *noun*
an exclamation mark (!) *US, 1983*
- — Guy L. Steele et al., *The Hacker's Dictionary*, p. 133, 1983

wrap *noun*
1 a wrapped roll of coins *US, 1977*
- — Thomas L. Clark, *The Dictionary of Gambling and Gaming*, p. 253, 1987

2 the end of a session *US, 1972*
Originally from the entertainment industry, extended to general situations.
- — Dan Jenkins, *Semi-Tough*, p. 55, 1972

wrap *verb*
▸ **wrap it up**
to kiss while parked *US, 1961*
- — Art Unger, *The Cool Book*, p. 107, 1961

wrapper *noun*
▸ **in the wrapper**
drunk *US, 1985*
- Sitting there half in the wrapper, on the outs with my good wife[.] — George V. Higgins, *Penance for Jerry Kennedy*, p. 128, 1985

wraps *noun*
cigarette rolling papers *US, 1994*
- A pack of wraps, my good man. It's time to kick back, drink some beer, and smoke some weed. — *Clerks*, 1994

wrap up *verb*
to complete the final days of a prison sentence *US, 1976*
- — John R. Armore and Joseph D. Wolfe, *Dictionary of Desperation*, p. 57, 1976

wrecked *adjective*
very drunk or drug-intoxicated *US, 1968*

- — *Current Slang*, p. 15, Summer 1968
- My friends just got wrecked all the time and complained how dull everything was, which was a major drag. — John Sayles, *Union Dues*, p. 135, 1977
- [I]t was a strange book even if you weren't wrecked on smack. — Jay McInerney, *Ransom*, p. 217, 1985
- We'd be totally wrecked with tangled hair and black lipstick, scaring the wealthy. — Michelle Tea, *The Passionate Mistakes and Intricate Corruption of One Girl in America*, p. 19, 1998

wrecking crew *noun*
theater insiders who watch a show's early performances and spread negative comments about the show *US, 1973*
- — Sherman Louis Sergel, *The Language of Show Biz*, p. 247, 1973

wrench *verb*
to disrupt or upset someone *US, 1976*
- — John R. Armore and Joseph D. Wolfe, *Dictionary of Desperation*, p. 57, 1976

wrestle; rassle *verb*
to play a game of bar dice *US, 1971*
- — Jester Smith, *Games They Play in San Francisco*, p. 105, 1971

wring *verb*
▸ **wring out your mule**
to urinate *US, 1974*
- I gotta ring my mule out. — Paul Glover, *Words from the House of the Dead*, 1974

▸ **wring out your sock**
to urinate *US, 1988*
- "Maybe he's got to wring out his sock," Heath said, showing no interest. — Robert Campbell, *Juice*, p. 255, 1988

wringer *noun*
a bankruptcy petition *US, 1954*
- — Jerry Robertson, *Oil Slanguage*, p. 53, 1954

wrinkleneck *noun*
in horseracing, a seasoned and experienced horse handler *US, 1951*
- — David W. Maurer, *Argot of the Racetrack*, p. 70, 1951

wrinkle room *noun*
a bar frequented by older homosexual men *US, 1980s*
- — Wayne Dynes, *Homolexis*, p. 140, 1985

write *verb*
to write a prescription for a narcotic which will not be used for medicinal purposes *US, 1953*
- There are several varieties of writer croakers. Some will write only if they are convinced you are an addict, others only if they are convinced you are not. — William Burroughs, *Junkie*, p. 33, 1953
- I had some doubts as to my ability to convince the doctors to write. — Herbert Huncke, *Guilty of Everything*, p. 54, 1990

▸ **write numbers**
to take bets on an illegal policy game (numbers lottery) *US, 1975*
- Then there was boostin' in department stores—and there was dice, cards, writin' numbers (single action) for Jake Cooperman[.] — Edwin Torres, *Carlito's Way*, p. 14, 1975

writer *noun*
1 a doctor who writes prescriptions without an excess of questions asked *US, 1954*
- The Feds had cracked down on the dolly writers. — William Burroughs, *Letters to Allen Ginsberg 1953–1957*, p. 68, October 1954

2 a graffiti artist *US, 1982*
- All the writers were there for the morning rush. — Craig Castleman, *Getting Up*, p. 10, 1982
- Do you know any other writers? — William Upski Wimsatt, *Bomb the Suburbs*, p. 44, 1994
- They call themselves writers because their paintings are often manipulations of letters. — *Plain Dealer (Cleveland, Ohio)*, p. L1, 29th July 2001

3 in a casino, an employee who accepts and records bets on Keno *US, 1972*
- — John Mechigian, *Encyclopedia of Keno*, p. 112, 1972

writing doctor *noun*
a doctor who for a price will write prescriptions without the formality of a medical exam or diagnosis *US, 1974*

• "Holy-o," Marge said, "you know a writing doctor, don't you?"
— Robert Stone, *Dog Soldiers*, p. 64, 1974

writ-writer *noun*
a prisoner with a claimed knowledge of criminal law and procedure *US, 1978*
• The Chicano jailhouse lawyers or writ-writers (as they are known in prison) are the predecessors of the more generalized pinto movement. — Joan W. Moore, *Homeboys*, p. 132, 1978

wrong *noun*
in craps, a bet against the shooter *US, 1974*
• At the dice table, the professor would bet either on or against the shooter—otherwise known as do or don't, right or wrong—at $1,000 a shot on what may or may not have been a system. — Edward Lin, *Big Julie of Vegas*, p. 47, 1974

wrong *adjective*
known to inform the police *US, 1953*
• By and large, the reason a man can't score is because he is known to be "wrong." — William Burroughs, *Junkie*, p. 52, 1953

wrongle *noun*
in craps, someone who bets against the shooter *US, 1974*
• — Thomas L. Clark, *The Dictionary of Gambling and Gaming*, p. 253, 1987

wrong number *noun*
an untrustworthy person *US, 1972*
• [H]e was a wrong number, an informer. — Emmett Grogan, *Ringolevio*, p. 54, 1972

wrong-o *noun*
a bad person *US, 1970*
• He drank when and whatever he could, begging, borrowing, wheedling credit. The Doc is a wrong-o, Pepper said, fuck him. — Gilbert Sorrentino, *Steelwork*, p. 156, 1970

wrong time *noun*
a woman's menstrual period *US, 1954*
• — American Speech, p. 298, December 1954: "The vernacular of menstruation"

wrong-way English *noun*
in pool, spin imparted on the cue ball such that the angle of refraction off a cushion is different, if not opposite, from what would be expected *US, 1993*
• — Mike Shamos, *The Illustrated Encyclopedia of Billiards*, p. 266, 1993

WS *noun*
a sadomasochist encounter involving enemas or urination *US, 1979*

An abbreviation for **WATER SPORTS**.
• — What Color is Your Handkerchief, p. 7, 1979

WTF
used in computer message shorthand to mean "what the fuck?" or "who the fuck?" *US, 1991*
• — Eric S. Raymond, *The New Hacker's Dictionary*, p. 342, 1991

wuffo; whuffo *noun*
in the language of hang gliding and parachuting, anyone other than a fellow expert *US, 1978*
Purportedly derived from the question, "Wuffo they do that?"
• — Dan Poynter, *Parachuting*, p. 170, 1978: "The language of parachuting"
• — Erik Fair, *California Thrill Sports*, p. 328, 1992

wuss *noun*
a weak, timid person *US, 1982*
A blend of **WIMP** and **PUSSY**, both meaning "a weak and timid person."
• You are a wuss. Part wimp. Part pussy. — *Fast Times at Ridgemont High*, 1982
• After Carol asked Mama, "Why'd you waste your money on that useless piece of wuss?" my mother wrinkled up her nose, not because she disapproved of the word wuss, but because it was yet another Americanism she didn't understand. — Rita Ciresi, *Pink Slip*, p. 5, 1999
• [I] felt ashamed of myself for being such a little wuss[.] — Claire Mansfield and John Mendelssohn, *Dominatrix*, p. 68, 2002

wussie; wussy; wossie *noun*
a weak, timid, passive person *US, 1982*
• With some guys you have to make the first move. A lot of guys are just wussies. — *Fast Times at Ridgemont High*, 1982

wussy *adjective*
weak, timid, passive *US, 1995*
• I figure if I sounded like a wussy momma's boy, he will trust me. — Howard Stern, *Miss America*, p. 83, 1995

Wyamine *noun*
a Benzedrine™ inhaler *US, 1967*
The Wyamine™ inhaler was manufactured by Wyeth Laboratories; it became a generic name for any inhaler with Benzedrine-infused cotton strips, valued by amphetamine users.
• Dope's not always easy. I've even shot Waymine. — Nicholas Von Hoffman, *We Are The People Our Parents Warned Us Against*, p. 223, 1967

Xx

X *noun*

1 MDMA, the recreational drug best known as ecstasy *US, 1988*
Generally an abbreviated "ecstasy," specifically any MDMA tablet stamped with a symbol that may be read as an X.

- Party invitations are often superimposed with an "X," a symbol for ecstasy, indicating what will be served or should be taken before arriving. — *New York Times*, p. 58 (Part 2), 11th December 1988
- "GOD YOU ARE SO IMPATIENT. I'm just feeling my X." — James St. James, *Party Monster*, p. 126, 1990
- X is often described as less disturbingly "trippy" than LSD and more serene than cocaine[.] — *Newsweek*, p. 62, 6th December 1993
- But she's here tonight, and I think if we all begged, or maybe offered her some X, she'd get up here and treat us to some of her vocal stylings. — *Chasing Amy*, 1997

2 in blackjack, any card worth ten points *US, 1991*
A Roman numeral used by card counters.

- — Michael Dalton, *Blackjack*, p. 91, 1991

3 a grip on all illegal gambling *US, 1974*

- — John Scarne, *Scarne on Dice*, p. 482, 1974

▸ **put the X on**
to mark for murder *US, 1973*

- — Vincent Teresa, *My Life in the Mafia*, p. 360, 1973: A Glossary of Mob Terminology

▸ **the X**
in the circus or carnival, exclusive rights for an item or concession *US, 1980*

- — Joe McKennon, *Circus Lingo*, p. 108, 1980
- — Gene Sorrows, *All About Carnivals*, p. 27, 1985: "Terminology"

X *verb*
to take MDMA, the recreational drug best known as ecstasy *US, 1985*

- KIDS ASKED EACH OTHER, "ARE YOU X-ING?" — *Life*, p. 88, August 1985
- I think yuppies everywhere will love "X-ing" (taking ecstasy). — *Chicago Tribune*, p. C1, 23rd June 1985

x-double-minus *adjective*
very bad *US, 1968*
Alluding to a nonexistent grading scale.

- — *Current Slang*, p. 11, Spring 1968

X queen *noun*
a homosexual male who is a frequent user of MDMA, the recreational drug best known as ecstasy *US, 1994*

- — Kevin Dilallo, *The Unofficial Gay Manual*, p. 246, 1994

x-ray eyes *noun*
the sense of intuition of a poker player who can ascertain the hands held by other players *US, 1988*

- — George Percy, *The Language of Poker*, p. 98, 1988

X-row *noun*
the area in a prison housing inmates condemned to death *US, 1992*

- — William K. Bentley and James M. Corbett, *Prison Slang*, p. 8, 1992

x's and o's *noun*
the basic elements of a plan *US, 1984*
From play diagrams in basketball, football or other sports, in which the x's represent the players of one team, and the o's represent players of the other.

- His mental x's and o's were settling around back mail, but his eyes kept straying back to the phone. — James Ellroy, *Because the Night*, p. 343, 1984
- Winters always keen on X's, O's and jumpers [Headline] — *San Francisco Chronicle*, p. C1, 25th December 2001

XTC *noun*
MDMA, the recreational drug best known as ecstasy *US, 1985*
Pronounced "ecstasy."

- Pamphlets promoting the use of the drug include such titles as "How to Prepare for an Ecstasy Experience," "Flight Instructions for a Friend Using XTC[.]" — *States News Service*, 31st May 1985
- Street names [...] white doves, X, XTC and many others. — James Kay and Julian Cohen, *The Parents' Complete Guide to Young People and Drugs*, p. 136, 1998

X vid *noun*
a sexually explicit video *US, 1992*

- That doesn't make any member of one group more right about what makes a good X-vid. — rec.arts.movies.erotica, 18th August 1996
- You and me are sitting side by side on my couch, watching X-vid, not touching. — Nicholson Baker, *Vox*, p. 99, 1992

XYL *noun*
a wife *US, 1976*
A partial acronym: "*ex-young lady*."

- — Wayne Floyd, *Jasons Authentic Dictionary of CB Slang*, p. 32, 1976

Yy

Y *noun*

▸ **the Y**

a premises of the Young Men's Christian Association (YMCA) or Young Women's Christian Association (YWCA) *US, 1915*

- I arrived in Chi quite early in the morning, got a room in the Y, and went to bed with a very few dollars in my pocket. — Jack Kerouac, *On the Road*, p. 14, 1957
- "I'm going to the Y right now," I announced. — Frederick Kohner, *Gidget Goes Hawaiian*, p. 90, 1961
- "They don't call this Y the French Embassy for nothing," the merchant marine laughs. — John Rechy, *City of Night*, p. 25, 1963
- The all-male group of guests make the Y's a perfect hang-out for queers. — Johnny Shearer, *The Male Hustler*, p. 25, 1966

yaba tablets *noun*

sweet-tasting tablets that are a mixture of methamphetamine and caffeine *US, 1999*

- "But Yaba comes directly to Thailand, which we regard as the real threat to our national security." — *Reuters*, 23rd July 1999
- The Source Determination Program of the DEA Special Testing and Research Laboratory (Dulles, Virginia) recently received some "Ya-Ba" tablets (also known as "Thai Tabs") heatsealed in what appeared to be plastic drinking straws. — *Microgram Bulletin (DEA)*, p. 5, January 2004

yabba-dabba doo!

used as a cry of exultation *US, 1960*

The Flintstones, a US television animation-comedy, first broadcast in 1960, introduced "yabba-dabba-doo!" as a catchphrase. "A yabba-dabba doo time" (an excellent time) comes directly from the theme song, "The Flintstones: Rise and Shine," written by William Hanna and Joseph Barbera, the show's creators. As a noun, "yabba-dabba doo" means "exuberance."

- Golf could use a little yabba-dabba-doo. — *Seattle Post-Intelligencer*, 26th August 2002
- YABBA-DABBA-DOO! NO, ME AND ZINN ARE WORKING ON THE NOVEL. — Larry Keveson, *Before We Croak!*, p. 116, 2003

yabbos *noun*

the female breasts *US, 2005*

- A fast look at Susan's yabbos as she chit-chats in bed with Gene Hackman. — Mr. Skin, *Mr. Skin's Skincyclopedia*, p. 111, 2005

yack; yak *noun*

1 voluble talk *US, 1952*

Echoic of idle chatter.

- Having made such a rash promise, we'll get down to some serious yak on the subject of the wet stuff you pour into your gas tank. — Oscar J. Gude, *Hot Rod Comics*, June 1952
- So I grabbed a dictionary and slowly learned words and tried them out in our yaks. — Piri Thomas, *Down These Mean Streets*, p. 257, 1967

2 a joke *US, 1951*

- You see, boychick, I can spike any script with yaks, but the thing I can't do is heartbreak. — Norman Mailer, *Advertisements for Myself*, p. 159, 1951

3 a telephone sales solicitor, either for a legitimate business or for a confidence swindle *US, 1985*

- — M. Allen Henderson, *How Con Games Work*, p. 224, 1985: "Glossary"
- — Kathleen Odean, *High Steppers, Fallen Angels, and Lollipops*, p. 132, 1988
- Most yaks paced to keep their energy level up when doing phone freaks. — Stephen Cannell, *Big Con*, p. 64, 1997

yack; yak *verb*

1 to talk volubly and either idly or stupidly or both *US, 1949*

- Lying with a guy on a good inner-spring mattress and listening to him yak about pine needles! — Philip Wylie, *Opus 21*, p. 297, 1949
- I don't want to appear to be the ungrateful brother-in-law guest yakking in behind their backs which I aint, I was happy and secure for the first time in years[.] — Jack Kerouac, *Letter to Allen Ginsberg*, p. 350, 10th May 1952

- MIA: Why do we feel it's necessary to yak about bullshit in order to be comfortable? — *Pulp Fiction*, 1994
- Yeah, I was going to give him some, but he started talking. Just talking, yakkety, yak. I hate a yakking man. — Chris Rock, *Rock This!*, p. 125, 1997

2 to vomit *US, 1986*

- "So then I started to open up his pants, but he bolted out of the car and ran into the trees and yakked his guts out." — Ethan Morden, *Buddies*, p. 207, 1986
- — Connie Eble (Editor), *UNC-CH Campus Slang*, p. 10, Spring 1992
- And if I yack, chances are someone else will chunder. — *Wayne's World 2*, 1993

yacker *noun*

a swindler working on a phony investment scam by telephone *US, 1988*

- — Kathleen Odean, *High Steppers, Fallen Angels, and Lollipops*, p. 132, 1988

yadda yadda yadda

used for suggesting meaningless conversation *US, 1967*

- I finally go to the doctor who gives me this big lecture on AIDS—yada yada yada. — Jay McInerney, *Story of My Life*, p. 9, 1988
- Unless you notify us by telegram or facsimile ... no phone calls, stating that you wish to yadda yadda yadda Wayne yadda yadda yadda Garthy yadda yadda yadda yadda yadda Aerosmith. — *Wayne's World 2*, 1993
- — Connie Eble (Editor), *UNC-CH Campus Slang*, p. 9, Fall 1997

yahoo *noun*

1 an unrefined, loutish, uncultured person *UK, 1726*

An imaginary race of brutes created by Swift in *Gulliver's Travels*.

- What the hell is wrong with a bunch of yahoos that'll stand around for hours on account of a hope like that? — Philip Wylie, *Opus 21*, p. 343, 1949
- And it's a dead heat which—Washington or Los Angeles—has more yahoos from dull places. — Jack Lait and Lee Mortimer, *Washington Confidential*, p. 3, 1951
- [T]he walk was faced with a camp-out among the yahoos or perhaps a forced march throughout the night to reach another country. — Ed Sanders, *Tales of Beatnik Glory*, p. 245, 1975
- Obviously the yahoos were more curious than afraid of lethal reptiles. — Carl Hiaasen, *Native Tongue*, p. 306, 1991

2 crack cocaine *US, 1994*

- — US Department of Justice, *Street Terms*, October 1994

yahoos *noun*

the female breasts *US, 2005*

- Sue's yahoos spill into view as some buddies decide to throw a surprise gang-bang. — Mr. Skin, *Mr. Skin's Skincyclopedia*, p. 61, 2005

Yale *noun*

a commercial hypodermic needle, whether or not it is manufactured by Yale *US, 1973*

- — David Maurer and Victor Vogel, *Narcotics and Narcotic Addiction*, p. 454, 1973

Yalie *noun*

a student or alumnus of Yale University *US, 1952*

- [Crossword puzzle clue: Yalies] — *New York Times*, p. 25, 27th August 1952
- He's a Yalie, Ol. — Erich Segal, *Love Story*, p. 114, 1970
- He's a Jew-boy, Norwachefsky. A Yalie like me. — Edwin Torres, *After Hours*, p. 391, 1979

yam *verb*

to talk too much *US, 1951*

- — *American Speech*, p. 155, May 1951: "Hermann Collitz and the language of the underworld"

yamp *noun*

an attractive girl *US, 2006*

- "Dang. That Oriental yamp be scoping your bone zone." — Linden Dalecki, *Kid B*, p. 169, 2006

yang *noun*

1 the penis *US, 1983*

From the masculine principle in the Chinese philosophy of yin-yang.

- "I got my old pard by the yang, ain't I?" Moke said. — Elmore Leonard, *Stick*, p. 295, 1983

2 the rectum *US, 1974*

- Hey, did you hear about that guy in F or E wing that stuffs things into his yang? — Paul Glover, *Words from the House of the Dead*, 1974

yank and bank *verb*

to execute a turn in a fighter plane *US, 1986*

- — *American Speech*, p. 125, Summer 1986: "The language of naval fighter pilots"

yankee dime *noun*

a kiss *US, 1900*

- We will save our "Yankee Dimes" til we meet again. — *Daily Oklahoman*, p. 31, 26th April 1995

- I told him I didn't have a Yankee dime and he said, "Yes, you do," and he leaned over and kissed me. And that was a Yankee dime. — *Dallas Morning News*, 18th May 2001

yap *noun*

1 the mouth *US, 1900*

- I was led back to the deputy, who asked what the trouble was and then, before I had a chance to open my yap, said, "Shut up or I'll bust you in the nose." — Mezz Mezzrow, *Really the Blues*, p. 35, 1946

- "But I told this house that if he opened his yap I'd cut his tongue out." — Irving Shulman, *Cry Tough*, pp. 30–31, 1949

- Their worst fears were realized the minute he opened his big yap. — Evan Hunter, *The Blackboard Jungle*, p. 78, 1954

- All I hoped was that old Mindzenty would keep his yap shut for seven straight days. — Clancy Sigal, *Going Away*, p. 164, 1961

2 inconsequential talk *US, 1907*

- Don't think, despite the annual yaps for more assistance, the Washington police force is radically undermanned. — Jack Lait and Lee Mortimer, *Washington Confidential*, p. 226, 1951

- So what's your point with all this yap? — Raymond Chandler, *The Long Goodbye*, p. 236, 1953

3 in circus and carnival usage, a naive, gullible local resident *US, 1952*

- "John (all the yaps called me 'Yankee John'), if ah ever gist a chance, it'll take two men to see me, one to say 'yere he comes' and another to say 'dere he goes.'" — Charles Hamilton, *Men of the Underworld*, p. 268, 1952

yap *verb*

to talk incessantly *UK, 1886*

The term existed in this sense in C19 English dialect, and then independently arose in the US in the 1920s.

- They're special shoes, and I needed them now. And quit your yapping. I'll get you there on time. — Max Shulman, *The Many Loves of Dobie Gillis*, p. 188, 1951

- When women get together, we sometimes drink, often eat, and always yap. — Anka Radakovich, *The Wild Girls Club*, p. 4, 1994

yapper, snapper, and crapper *noun*

oral, vaginal, and anal sex with a woman *US, 2003*

A clever phrase heard in jokes but rarely in real life.

- Oregon Trifecta (aka "Triple Crown of Sex")—in the yapper, the snapper, and the crapper all in the same session. — *news.admin.net-abuse.email*, 4th August 2003

yar!

used as a general-purpose interjection, usually conveying excitement about something *US, 1989*

- Yar! Dude! Check out that sweet car! — Pamela Munro, *U.C.L.A. Slang*, p. 92, 1989

yard *noun*

1 one hundred dollars *US, 1926*

- They entered and after routine questioning they asked how much money I had. I showed them six "yards[.]" — Babs Gonzales, *I Paid My Dues*, p. 27, 1967

- Give me a yard and a half and take the bitch back. — Iceberg Slim (Robert Beck), *Pimp*, p. 105, 1969

- "How much?" "A yard. Hundred bucks and she's happy." — Mickey Spillane, *Last Cop Out*, p. 48, 1972

- I lent him a yard / and copped him a rod. — Lightnin' Rod, *Hustlers Convention*, p. 14, 1973

2 one thousand dollars *US, 1932*

- You can make a couple of yards a week and be cool about it. — Piri Thomas, *Down These Mean Streets*, p. 322, 1967

3 a prison sentence of one year *US, 1950*

- — Hyman E. Goldin et al., *Dictionary of American Underworld Lingo*, p. 242, 1950

4 a prison sentence of 100 years *US, 1969*

- "Party" went back to the joint for a "yard" after he got out of City Hospital. — Iceberg Slim (Robert Beck), *Pimp*, p. 41, 1969

- — William K. Bentley, *Prison Slang*, p. 24, 1992

5 a member of the Montagnard tribes, the aborigine hill tribes of Vietnam's Central Highlands *US, 1967*

- The report had come form a Montagnard, or "Yard" as the soldiers call them. — Elaine Shepard, *The Doom Pussy*, p. 26, 1967

- "I wouldn't give no Milky Ways to no Yards." — William Pelfrey, *The Big V*, p. 65, 1972

- Here a "Yard" aidman attends to the team leader's wound. [Caption] — Hans Halberstadt, *Green Berets*, 1988

- From old I Corps / To the Delta / To the highlands / Filled with "yards." — Thomas Bowen, *The Longest Year*, p. 14, 1990: Buddha Bless Saigon

yard *verb*

to be sexually unfaithful *US, 1960*

- She told him she didn't like to yard on her man, who was living in New York. — Clarence Cooper Jr., *The Scene*, p. 34, 1960

- Or have you been out yarding somewhere? — Donald Goines, *Whoreson*, p. 159, 1972

- I ain't saying she's yarding but we both know she could very well be kicking the gong around. — A.S. Jackson, *Gentleman Pimp*, p. 90, 1973

yardage *noun*

1 money *US, 2005*

- Money mules made okay cash, but not no high yardage. — Noire, *Candy Licker*, p. 41, 2005

2 a big penis *US, 1972*

- — Bruce Rodgers, *The Queens' Vernacular*, p. 217, 1972

yard-and-a-half *noun*

one hundred and fifty dollars *US, 1962*

- — Frank Garcia, *Marked Cards and Loaded Dice*, p. 265, 1962

yardbird *noun*

1 a chicken *US, 1956*

- Yardbird and strings. Harlem's own vernacular for the fried chicken and spaghetti which was so common, so cheap and so utterly, un-believably wonderful at such wrong hours—like the hours around dawn, for instance. — Robert Sylvester, *No Cover Charge*, p. 43, 1956

2 a prisoner, a convict *US, 1949*

- Yardbirds who couldn't quite be trusted in a bakery or a laundry. — Nelson Algren, *The Man with the Golden Arm*, p. 207, 1949

- For the next two weeks, K.B. was Claiborne's yardbird. He had to go everywhere Claiborne went from morning till night. — Claude Brown, *Manchild in the Promised Land*, p. 83, 1965

3 a newly arrived military recruit *US, 1941*

- — Lou Shelly, *Hepcats Jive Talk Dictionary*, p. 50, 1945

yard buddy *noun*

a close friend in prison *US, 1974*

- All he did was call up an old yard buddy and ask him if he could turn him on to somebody with some good stuff. — Vernon E. Smith, *The Jones Men*, p. 149, 1974

yard out *verb*

to exercise in a prison yard *US, 1984*

- — Inez Cardozo-Freeman, *The Joint*, p. 543, 1984

yard rat *noun*

a prisoner who is aggressive while on the yard *US, 2002*

- Sooner or later all new fish receive a "Heart Check" from the Yard Rats. — Jimmy Lerner, *You Got Nothing Coming*, p. 170, 2002

yard sale *noun*

in snow-based sports, the result of an accident in which equipment is deposited over a wide area *US, 1988*

- I responded to her praise with a "face plant" and "yard sale"—falling flat while my skis and poles went in four directions. — *Boston Globe*, p. 18, 31st January 1988

- Skiers put on the best yard sales, sometimes spreading their skis, poles, and hats over hundreds of vertical feet. — Jim Humes and Sean Wagstaff, *Boarderlands*, p. 225, 1995

yardstick *noun*
the penis *US, 1975*

- John's friend goes down on her while she scarf's some of John's yardstick. — Stephen Lewis, *The Whole Bedroom Catalog*, p. 35, 1975

yawn *verb*
▸ **yawn in technicolor**
to vomit *US, 1981*

- — Connie Eble (Editor), *UNC-CH Campus Slang*, p. 7, March 1981
- — *The Washington Post*, 24th May 1987

yay; yayoo; yeah-O; yeyo; yeo *noun*
crack cocaine *US, 1991*

- "I sell Yay-o, Cavvy—caviar crack—fo' my money, and on a good day I can make like six, seven hundred dollars." — Leon Bing, *Do or Die*, p. 63, 1991
- That girl couldn't say nay to yay. — Lois Stavsky et al., *A2Z*, p. 115, 1995

ya-ya *noun*
the vagina *US, 2005*

- [I]ncluding three wiggling worms and numerous fingers in her ya-ya. — Mr. Skin, *Mr. Skin's Skincyclopedia*, p. 8, 2005

ya-ya's *noun*
the female breasts *US, 2005*

- The brunette hard body's ya-yas did get a nice workout as one of Baywatch's first luscious lifeguards[.] — Mr. Skin, *Mr. Skin's Skincyclopedia*, p. 70, 2005

yazoo *noun*
the anus and rectum *US, 1990*

- — Joseph Tuso, *Singing the Vietnam Blues*, p. 265, 1990: Glossary

yegg *noun*
a criminal, especially a burglar or safecracker *US, 1903*

- In his category were yeggs, who roved in packs, lived in roadside jungles, cased small-town banks and robbed them. — Jack Lait and Lee Mortimer, *Chicago Confidential*, p. 55, 1950
- You wouldn't have been surprised to learn that this man, for all his yegg's physiognomy, spent his spare hours carving cherubs and penguins out of Ivory soap[.] — Bernard Wolfe, *The Late Risers*, p. 48, 1954
- I was a yegg and one of the toughest of yeggs. — Bruce Jackson, *Get Your Ass in the Water and Swim Like Me*, p. 100, 1965
- Formerly he'd been a yegg, safecracker, the best on the coast. — Seth Morgan, *Homeboy*, p. 26, 1990

yellow *noun*
a capsule of pentobarbital sodium (trade name Nembutal™), a central nervous system depressant; any barbiturate *US, 1944*

- — Norman W. Houser, *Drugs: Facts on Their Use and Abuse*, p. 13, 1969
- He said, "Kid, I put a couple 'yellows' in your bag so you can 'come down' and get some 'doss' [sleep]." — Iceberg Slim (Robert Beck), *Pimp*, p. 133, 1969

yellow *adjective*
1 cowardly, afraid *US, 1856*

- You act mighty yellow about this. — Chester Gould, *Dick Tracy Meets the Night Crawler*, p. 208, 1945
- "Stop being so yellow," she said, "and tell these apes to pay me for my bag." — Irving Shulman, *The Amboy Dukes*, p. 236, 1947
- Yellow? Afraid of trial by combat? — William Bernard, *Jailbait*, p. 89, 1949
- I think you're yellow not because you didn't kill him, but because you didn't want to kill him. — Piri Thomas, *Down These Mean Streets*, p. 191, 1967

2 light-skinned; of mixed race *US, 1934*

- It was easy to see that the ape who was sleeping with her or married to her wouldn't be one to let a mere hundred and seventeen dollars stand in the way of something this yellow bitch had her heart set on. — Clarence Cooper Jr., *The Scene*, p. 33, 1960
- You just like most yellow nigger sissies. You don't fuck nothing but paddies and half-white niggers. — Iceberg Slim (Robert Beck), *Mama Black Widow*, p. 32, 1969

yellow bam *noun*
methamphetamine hydrochloride, a powerful central nervous system stimulant *US, 1994*

- — US Department of Justice, *Street Terms*, August 1994

yellow-bellied *adjective*
cowardly *US, 1924*

- What I wouldn't give for five minutes with you alone, you yellow-bellied bastard. — Charles Raven, *Underworld Nights*, p. 43, 1956

yellow-belly *noun*
a coward *US, 1930*

- "You chicken punk!" Lucky had said. "You don't belong in the Harps. We don't want a yellowbelly." — Hal Ellson, *Tomboy*, p. 9, 1950
- My buddies around town who were betting on Hite would have called me a yellowbelly if I'd dodged the match. — Sam Snead, *The Education of a Golfer*, p. 92, 1962

yellow bullet *noun*
a capsule of pentobarbital sodium (trade name Nembutal™), a central nervous system depressant *US, 1977*

- — Walter L. Way, *The Drug Scene*, p. 116, 1977

yellow doll *noun*
a capsule of phentobarbital sodium (trade name Nembutal™), a central nervous system depressant *US, 1977*

- — Walter L. Way, *The Drug Scene*, p. 116, 1977

yellow jacket *noun*
1 a barbiturate or other central nervous system depressant, especially Nembutal™ *US, 1952*

- [W]e have a pretty complete exhibit of the little pills downtown. Bluejays, redbirds, yellow jackets, goofballs, and all the rest of the list. — Raymond Chandler, *The Long Goodbye*, p. 230, 1953
- They also take Amytal ("blue heaven"), Nembutal ("yellow jackets") and Tuinal. — Hunter S. Thompson, *Hell's Angels*, p. 216, 1967
- Two bottles of yellow jackets are on the floor. — Arthur Blessitt, *Turned On to Jesus*, p. 151, 1971
- Well, let's see. I still got some redbirds and yellowjackets. — Emmett Grogan, *Final Score*, p. 81, 1976

2 a high-velocity, hollow-nose, expanding bullet *US, 1981*

- "Stingers and yellowjackets," Parrish said. "Hyper-velocity, hollow-nose expanders. The guy knew what he was doing." — Elmore Leonard, *Split Images*, p. 97, 1981

yellow legs *noun*
the US Marines *US, 1968*
Korean war usage; coined by the North Koreans alluding to the marine leggings.

- Forty-seven minutes later the "yellow-legs," as the Reds called the Marines after the leggings they wore, raised the American flag over Wolmi. — Robert Leckie, *The Wars of America, Volume II*, p. 359, 1968

yellow pages *noun*
in poker, a play or a bet made strictly for the purpose of creating an impression *US, 1996*

- — John Vorhaus, *The Big Book of Poker Slang*, p. 41, 1996

yellow rock *noun*
methamphetamine in rock form, yellow in color either because of incomplete processing or the presence of adulterants *US, 1989*

- — Geoffrey Froner, *Digging for Diamonds*, p. 69, 1989: "Types of speed"

yellow sheet *noun*
a criminal record *US, 1985*
From the color of the New York Police Department document at the time of coining.

- "Looking back it sure was a dumb way to start a yellow sheet." — Nicholas Pileggi, *Wise Guy*, p. 30, 1985

yen *noun*
an intense craving, especially for a drug; an addiction *UK, 1876*

- Suppose some glamorous dame and you met. Suppose you got a yen for her? — Philip Wylie, *Opus 21*, p. 23, 1949
- Most of us walked around that day like zombies, our yens in total eclipse. — Bernard Wolfe, *The Late Risers*, p. 4, 1954
- He was roaring through Las Cruces, New Mexico, when he suddenly had an explosive yen to see his sweet first wife Maylou again. — Jack Kerouac, *On the Road*, p. 112, 1957

- I was, however, a guy that had an insane cocaine yen, and that, my dear reader, is far worse than a horse habit, because it costs ten times as much bread. — A.S. Jackson, *Gentleman Pimp*, p. 75, 1973

yen *verb*
to crave a drug intensely *US, 1919*
From the Chinese; originally applied to opium users.
- You know yourself when a guy is yenning, he doesn't look behind him. — William Burroughs, *Junkie*, p. 56, 1953

yen pock *noun*
an opium pellet *US, 1934*
- If you want an introduction to Herbert Hoover, or a few yen pok of opium, speak up. — Bernard Wolfe, *The Late Risers*, p. 23, 1954

yen pox *noun*
opium ash *US, 1957*
- The old Chinaman dips river water into a rusty tin can, washes down a pen pox hard and black as a cinder. (Note: Yen pox is the ash of smoked opium.) — William Burroughs, *Naked Lunch*, p. 7, 1957
- [W]hile in Aruba we had picked up on yen-pox and had stayed knocked out the whole time we were there. — Herbert Huncke, *The Evening Sun Turned Crimson*, p. 100, 1980

Yenshee baby *noun*
an extremely constipated bowel movement that is the product of opiate addiction *US, 1938*
Yenshee is Chinese for "opium residue."
- And then came ripping down his intestines that glacial fecal boulder compacted by months of bowel paralysis, and through gritted teeth he cried, "Christ! The Yenshee baby." — Seth Morgan, *Homeboy*, p. 96, 1990

yen sleep *noun*
a drowsiness encountered by many LSD users after the effects of the drug have worn off *US, 1972*
- — Carl Chambers and Richard Heckman, *Employee Drug Abuse*, p. 211, 1972

yenta *noun*
a gossip; a busybody; a scold *US, 1923*
Yiddish.
- He's a very wealthy guy, he owns a big business, he's a smart fellow and everything, but his behavior—in Jewish they'd call him a yenta—he never stops talking and does things that just don't make sense. — Edward Lin, *Big Julie of Vegas*, p. 103, 1974
- I think her idea of a good time was learned out of "Amos 'n Andy's" Sapphire, nurtured by Good Times and developed to the fullest yenta state possible by the Jefferson's. — Odie Hawkins, *Black Casanova*, p. 108, 1984
- You want me to get up in front of all your Long Island housewife yenta pals and confess my love? — Howard Stern, *Miss America*, p. 155, 1995

yesca; yesco *noun*
marijuana *US, 1949*
Directly from Spanish *yesca* (tinder), "a fuel that is burnt."
- Tea. Grifa. Yesca. Marijuana. Whatever you want to call it. — Thurston Scott, *Cure it with Honey*, p. 4, 1951
- — *American Speech*, p. 88, May 1955: "Narcotic argot along the Mexican border"
- "Smoking yesca, you end up, it gets you in a good mood[.]" — James Vigil, *Barrio Gangs*, p. 127, 1988

yes siree (Bob)
yes indeed *US, 1846*
- "Oh, it's happened all right," he said nodding, "yessiree bob!" — Terry Southern, *Blue Movie*, p. 57, 1970
- BUD: A repo man goes it alone. LITE: Yes siree bob. — *Repo Man*, 1984

yes sir, yes sir, three bags full
used for mocking unquestioning, blind obedience *US, 1986*
US naval aviator usage, from the children's song "Ba Ba Black Sheep."
- — *United States Naval Institute Proceedings*, p. 108, October 1986

yesterday *adjective*
out-dated; unaware of current fashions and trends *US, 1968*
- — Hy Lit, *Hy Lit's Unbelievable Dictionary of Hip Words for Groovy People*, p. 46, 1968

yes way!
used for humorously rebutting someone who has just said "No way!" *US, 1989*
- NEW TED: We're you, dude! TED: No way. No way. NEW TED: Ted, Yes way, Ted. — *Bill and Ted's Excellent Adventure*, 1989

YGBSM
used for expressing disbelief *US, 1990*
An abbreviation for "you've got to be shitting me."
- — Joseph Tuso, *Singing the Vietnam Blues*, p. 265, 1990: Glossary

Yid *noun*
a Jewish person *US, 1874*
Offensive.
- But a pair of racially pure Nordic behemoths from Minnesota, sent proudly to the team by scouting old grads, decided that, although they had nothing personal against the yid, no yid would call their signals. — Philip Wylie, *Opus 21*, p. 230, 1949
- "I never heard of no starving Yid," I'd hear as we flopped down in this carpeted den. — Gary Mayer, *Bookie*, p. 41, 1974
- "This isn't back when we were kids, beating up on the yids and ginzos," Pat said. — Robert Campbell, *Juice*, p. 171, 1988

yiddel; yiddle *noun*
a Jewish person *US, 1946*
- I made up a little doggerel song about him that went, "Don't fiddle with the Yiddle, or he'll riddle you in the middle." — Mezz Mezzrow, *Really the Blues*, p. 70, 1946
- Yes, I was one happy yiddel down there in Washington. — Philip Roth, *Portnoy's Complaint*, p. 262, 1969

Yiddish highway *noun*
US Highway 301, which runs between New York and Miami, Florida *US, 1979*
- — *Maledicta*, p. 165, 1979: "A glossary of ethnic slurs in American English"

Yid kid *noun*
a young Jewish person *US, 1950*
- "Talk to a little Yid kid, and he is studying for what he's gonna be ten years form now." — Theodor Adorno, *The Authoritarian Personality*, p. 832, 1950
- I mean they can't bear the thought of a yid kid living it up there in Washington. — Sasthi Brata, *The Sensuous Guru*, p. 57, 1980

yikes!
used in surprise, pain, or shock *US, 1971*
Possibly a variant of conventional "yoicks!" or "crikey!" (Christ!).
- Two [bullets] hit the pavement beside my car and one zinged off my front bumper. Yikes. — Janet Evanovich, *Seven Up*, p. 30, 2001

ying yang *noun*
1 the anus and/or rectum *US, 1968*
- [I]t lubricates the shaft with splittle, excites the person about to be sucked, thereby dilating the yingyang[.] — Angelo d'Arcangelo, *The Homosexual Handbook*, p. 110, 1968
2 the penis *US, 1981*
- — *Maledicta*, p. 255, Summer/Winter 1981: "Five years and 121 dirty words later"

▶ **up the ying yang; out the ying yang**
to excess *US, 1976*
The suggestion of "ying-yang" is "the rectum."
- We got pictures up the ying-yang, and they're good pictures, too. — George V. Higgins, *The Judgment of Deke Hunter*, p. 28, 1976
- He buys me drinks up the ying yang, gets me righteously lubed, then splits. — James Ellroy, *Because the Night*, p. 485, 1984
- You got a serious jones that won't let go, and you got energy coming out the yin-yang. — Nathan McCall, *Makes Me Wanna Holler*, p. 184, 1994

yip *verb*
to bark in a piercing and shrill manner *US, 1907*
- The schnauzer probably didn't give a shit one way or the other, but recognized a tone that could mean a doggie treat, sat up in the chair, pointed her little ears up and yipped once. — Elmore Leonard, *Switch*, p. 109, 1978

yippee!; yippy!
used as a declaration of excitement and assent *US, 1920*
- KATHRYN: I don't think she'll be giving you any more problems. SEBASTIAN: Yippy. — *Cruel Intentions*, 1999

yippie *noun*
a member of, or adherent to, the principles of the Youth International Party, a short-lived blend of 1960s counter-culture values and New Left politics *US, 1967*

- Coincidental with the Democrats' Convention there's going to be a Youth International Party—YIP—and Chicago will be invaded by a mass of yippies. — *The Realist*, p. 21, August 1967
- There never were any Yippies and there never will be. It was a slogan YIPPIE! and that exclamation point was what it was all about. It was the biggest put-on of all time. If you believe Yippies existed, you are nothing but a sheep. — Abbie Hoffman, *Revolution for the Hell of It*, p. 121, 1968
- All of us in the room that New Year's Eve knew, when we heard it, that in a few months "yippie" would become a household word. — Jerry Rubin, *Do It!*, p. 81, 1970
- We were knocked out by the total assault tactics of the yippies. — John Sinclair, *Guitar Army*, p. 100, 1972

yo *noun*
a dolt *US, 1991*
- Calyvon Jones is simply a dead yo with a quality weapon he never got to use. — David Simon, *Homicide*, p. 324, 1991

yo!
used as a greeting *US, 1944*
Both Italian-American and black communities lay claim to "yo!" First recorded in 1944 among Philadelphia's Italian-Americans and popularized by Sylvester Stallone in the 1976 film *Rocky*.
- BOCCO: Yo! — Nat Hiken, *Sergeant Bilko*, p. 159, 1957
- — Connie Eble (Editor), *UNC-CH Campus Slang*, November 1976
- Yo! We don't score school lunch. — Jess Mowry, *Way Past Cool*, p. 12, 1992
- — Claudio R. Salvucci, *The Philadelphia Dialect Dictionary*, p. 66, 1996

yo; Yolanda *noun*
in craps, a roll of eleven *US, 1999*
- — Chris Fagans and David Guzman, *A Guide to Craps Lingo*, p. 36, 1999

yo-bo *noun*
a member of the Korean Service Corps *US, 1957*
Korean war usage.
- The supply column, or "yo-bo train" as it is called, is usually composed of ten members of the Korean Service Corps (yo-bos) escorted by a fire team of marines, that is, four marines. — Martin Russ, *The Last Parallel*, p. 226, 1957

yochie *noun*
in the language surrounding the Grateful Dead, a follower of the band who has lost all touch with reality *US, 1994*
- — David Shenk and Steve Silberman, *Skeleton Key*, p. 182, 1994

yock *noun*
a laugh *US, 1938*
- All right, all right, gentlemen, have your yocks, but then let's get down to work. — John Clellon Holmes, *The Horn*, p. 124, 1958
- He paused until somebody chuckled. But this was way too serious a matter for real yocks. — Ross Russell, *The Sound*, p. 47, 1961

yock *verb*
to laugh *US, 1938*
- You boys get your kicks, go ahead, yock it up. — John Clellon Holmes, *The Horn*, p. 125, 1958
- The crowd yocked. The crowd roared. — James Ellroy, *The Cold Six Thousand*, p. 523, 2001

yogi *noun*
a poker player with the annoying habit of coaching other players *US, 1996*
- — John Vorhaus, *The Big Book of Poker Slang*, p. 41, 1996

yoke *noun*
1 robbery by force *US, 1951*
- Three young colored boxers, aged 14, 16, and 17, terrorized Washington a few months ago, committing at least 19 yoke robberies, netting more than $2,000. — Jack Lait and Lee Mortimer, *Washington Confidential*, p. 53, 1951
2 a choke hold *US, 1987*
Originally military slang embraced by the police.
- — Carsten Stroud, *Close Pursuit*, p. 277, 1987

yoke *verb*
to grab around the neck *US, 1977*
- So Cub, a friend of mine who's still a very young teenager at the time, came up behind the man and yoked him. — John Allen, *Assault with a Deadly Weapon*, p. 82, 1977

yoked; yolked *adjective*
muscular *US, 1993*
- — Judi Sanders, *Faced and Faded, Hanging to Hurl*, p. 44, 1993
- — Jim Goad, *Jim Goad's Glossary of Northwestern Prison Slang*, December 2001

yokel *noun*
an unsophisticated, gullible person, especially one with a rural background *UK, 1812*
- Generally speaking, the kinds of yokels we spell with a capital Y prefer inns in the Times Square district. — Jack Lait and Lee Mortimer, *New York Confidential*, p. 202, 1948
- They put him on his mettle, added zest to his existence in a way that the yokels never could. — Jim Thompson, *Bad Boy*, p. 353, 1953
- I'm no yokel. Why, I was all the way to Miami once. — *Body Heat*, 1980

yoke robbing *noun*
stealing a purse from over a woman's neck *US, 1977*
- Like, I believe all ghetto kids start off yoke robbing or snatching pocketbooks or something like that. — John Allen, *Assault with a Deadly Weapon*, p. 50, 1977

yola *noun*
a light-skinned black female *US, 1947*
- — Marcus Hanna Boulware, *Jive and Slang of Students in Negro Colleges*, 1947

yomo; yom *noun*
a person, a fellow *US, 1977*
- Meanwhile I already had four hundred and fifty in my pockets on accounta I had glommed it earlier from the yom. — Edwin Torres, *Q & A*, p. 121, 1977
- I got this yomo down, knee in the back, cuffin' him up, the kid's crying. — Richard Price, *Clockers*, p. 366, 1992

yoni *noun*
the vulva and vagina *UK, 1799*
From the sanskrit word for the symbolic depiction of the the the vagina.
- At the same time, he gently slips a finger into her yoni. — Lana Holstein, *Your Long Erotic Weekend*, p. 210, 2004
- Toni goes from thonged butage in a leotard to showing off her yoni when she full frontally takes it off. — Mr. Skin, *Mr. Skin's Skincyclopedia*, p. 7, 2005

yoo-hoo *noun*
a poker player who engages in excessive needless table talk *US, 1996*
- — John Vorhaus, *The Big Book of Boker Slang*, p. 41, 1996

yoo-hoo *verb*
to try to get someone's attention by calling "yoo-hoo" *US, 1948*
- Not wave or yoo-hoo at him, he'd have to be cool, but make sure the cop saw him. — Elmore Leonard, *Glitz*, p. 227, 1985

yoot; yut; yout *noun*
a youth; a youth gang member *US, 1949*
West Indian.
- I thought of the pot-bellied yuts I'd met[.] — Philip Wylie, *Opus 21*, p. 14, 1949
- — *New York Herald Tribune*, p. 47, 28th February 1954
- — Kenn "Naz" Young, *Naz's Dictionary of Teen Slang*, p. 145, 1993

york *verb*
to vomit *US, 1966*
- — John D. Bell et al., *Loosely Speaking*, p. 22, 1966

you ain't said nothing
used for expressing contempt for what has just been said *US, 1968*
- — Joan Fontaine et al., *Dictionary of Black Slang*, 1968

you can't stop him, you can only hope to contain him
used as a humorous comment on a high achiever *US, 1997*
Popularized by ESPN's Dan Patrick.
- — Keith Olberman and Dan Patrick, *The Big Show*, p. 27, 1997

you don't even know
used as an intensifier when words fail *US, 1984*
- We went cruising in her dad's Alfa Spider and you-don't-even-know. — Jonathan Roberts, *How to California*, p. 174, 1984

you go, girl!

used as an encouragement or exhortation *US, 1993*
Popularized by several black entertainers relatively simultaneously in the 1990s, and widely repeated, usually in a woman-to-woman context.

- But in a city with problems as desperate as Detroit's it remains to be seen if the strategy, which extends down to Ms. McPhail's "You Go, Girl," a street-slang slogan for "go get 'em," will override more pragmatic judgments. — *New York Times*, p. A1, 18th October 1993
- — Connie Eble (Editor), *UNC-CH Campus Slang*, p. 6, Spring 1993
- HOLLY: Well, I don't know, but I certainly didn't like his attitude and I'm going to think long and hard before I take him back. JANE: You go, girl! — *Boys on the Side*, 1995

you have some explaining to do

used for humor when there is in fact some explanation owed *US, 1989*
A catchphrase from the *I Love Lucy* television series (1951–61), with the "explaining" often butchered with a pseudo Desi Arnaz Cuban accent to "splaining."

- "You've some some "splaining to do." — Lowell Streiker, *Fathering, Old Game, New Rules*, p. 159, 1989
- I'm sure he's got a lot of explaining to do. — *Hard Eight*, 1996
- I had some 'splaining to do. — April Sinclair, *I Left My Back Door Open*, p. 191, 2000

you know

used as a verbal pause for indicating that the speaker assumes that the listener is listening, understanding, and agreeing *UK, 1599*
An annoying discourse marker if ever there was one.

- — Miss Cone, *The Slang Dictionary (Hawthorne High School)*, 1965
- Instead of using Cockney or Liverpool slang for humorous effect, narked, knickers-job and all that, he began using American hip-lower-class slang, like, I mean, you know, baby, and a little late Madison Avenue. — Tom Wolfe, *The Pump House Gang*, p. 44, 1968

you like?

used as a humorous mock pidgin version of "do you like this?" *US, 1990*

- Yeah, I get a discount on clothes and shit. You like? — *Boyz N The Hood*, 1990

youngblood noun

a young man, especially a young black man and especially an impetuous one; used as a term of address to a young man *US, 1946*

- Does all this sound like I'm making it up, youngblood? — Eldridge Cleaver, *Soul on Ice*, p. 160, 1968
- Now Youngblood, about Pepper. You don't know anything about her. — Iceberg Slim (Robert Beck), *Pimp*, p. 66, 1969
- Hey, youngblood, pretty fancy place you living in. — Cecil Brown, *The Life & Loves of Mr. Jiveass Nigger*, p. 118, 1969
- Young bloods wanted to be like these brothers. — H. Rap Brown, *Die Nigger Die!*, p. 15, 1969
- "I wouldn't jive you, youngblood," he answered his critic with a deadpan under his cap. — Odie Hawkins, *The Busting Out of an Ordinary Man*, p. 88, 1985

young, dumb, and full of come adjective

used for describing a young man with great hopes and little experience *US, 1966*

- Because we were young, dumb and full of come, and all there for the same fun and games[.] — Robert Gover, *Poorboy at the Party*, p. 53, 1966
- "Didn't you used to go with Bart?" "Yeah," Frances answered. "When I was young, dumb, and full of come." — Nathan Heard, *To Reach a Dream*, p. 79, 1972
- — Michael Dalton Johnson, *Talking Trash with Redd Foxx*, p. 33, 1994

you're right, you fox

used as a tease when someone has finally stumbled over the obvious *US, 1966*

- — John D. Bell et al., *Loosely Speaking*, p. 16, 1966

yow!

used as an expression of surprise *US, 1991*
Popularized in the *Zippie the Pinhead* cartoon.

- — Eric S. Raymond, *The New Hacker's Dictionary*, p. 390, 1991

yo-yo noun

1 a fool *US, 1955*

- I'll bet you're a real yo-yo. — *Rebel Without a Cause*, 1955
- What would I do with a yo-yo like him all Saturday evening? — Frederick Kohner, *The Affairs of Gidget*, p. 54, 1963
- Jimmy, we got to straighten this yo-yo out. — Vincent Patrick, *The Pope of Greenwich Village*, p. 180, 1979
- [H]e gets a phone call from some yo-yo named Liddy, whom he barely knows, saying that four Cubans he's never even met have just been caught in the act[.] — Hunter S. Thompson, *The Great Shark Hunt*, p. 390, 1979

2 in air combat, a steep climb and dive in an attempt to gain a more favorable position *US, 1989*

- The other bandit was doing a high yo-yo, a vertical roller-coaster maneuver, three miles behind Fairly, trying to kill his high overtake speed and fall in behind the first bandit by trading forward momentum for altitude. — Richard Herman, *The Warbirds*, p. 57, 1989
- One tactic was the "High-speed Yo-Yo,"—the ball on a string to which Smith referred. — Robert K. Wilcox, *Scream of Eagles*, p. 174, 1990

yo-yo verb

to perform a tactic in aerial combat resembling a roller coaster ride *US, 1983*

- After a few minutes of yo-yoing up and down I was able to keep the machine about where the IP wanted it. — Robert Mason, *Chickenhawk*, p. 33, 1983
- He went supersonic, and pulled back up in a yo-yo maneuver, arming his cannon as he climbed. — Walter Boyne and Steven Thompson, *The Wild blue*, p. 568, 1986

yuck noun

1 a laugh *US, 1971*

- Toxic chock your idea of a big yuck, Larry? — Armistead Maupin, *Further Tales of the City*, p. 238, 1982

2 a fool *US, 1943*

- Always some John Family or silk moll with bookoo toadskins playing around with a yuk who'll ante to keep the knockdown from the bundleman or headache. — *The New American Mercury*, p. 708, 1950
- Honestly, I've never met such a yuk. You'll never get caught, you poor goof. — Max Shulman, *The Many Loves of Dobie Gillis*, p. 13, 1951

3 in gambling cheating schemes, a victim *US, 1962*

- — Frank Garcia, *Marked Cards and Loaded Dice*, p. 265, 1962

4 crack cocaine *US, 1993*

- "All I could hear was, 'Where was the yuck?'" he testified. Yuck is street slang for crack. — *Pittsburgh Post-Gazette*, p. B1, 4th September 1993

5 an idiot *US, 1958*

- "I'm an assistant buyer at Gliddens. Sportswear. At least I was before that yuk bounced me into the air." — John D. MacDonald, *The Deceivers*, p. 18, 1958

yuck verb

to laugh *US, 1974*
Echoic.

- He'd been giggled out of Georgetown, howled out of Harvard, yuk-yukked out of Yale, snickered out of Stanford, and chuckled out of Chattanooga State Technical Community College. — Dav Pilkey, *Captain Underpants and the Perilous Plot of Professor Poopypants*, p. 50, 2000

▶ **yuck it up; yuk it up**
to behave in a foolish, time-wasting way *US, 1964*

- The sedan pulled past, two men in the front, both with sunglasses and both yucking it up and doing their best to pretend that they weren't interested in me. — Robert Crais, *L.A. Requiem*, p. 105, 1999

yucky; yukky; yukkie adjective

disgusting *US, 1970*

- Then had taken the girl to a Japanese place where the girl said she was totally turned off by all the yukky stuff. — Elmore Leonard, *Glitz*, p. 313, 1985
- He was criticized by a lot of yukkie downmarket press people. — John Lahr, *Dame Edna Everage and the Rise of Western Civilisation*, p. 31, 1991
- Okay. I have the yuckiest taste in my mouth from those taquitos. — *Romy and Michele's High School Reunion*, 1997

yuk verb

to vomit *US, 1997*

- [M]y friend and I stuck our fingers down our throats and yukked into it for the freshman to chug. — Elissa Stein and Kevin Leslie, *Chunks*, p. 48, 1997

yummy *noun*
an attractive woman who is not easily seduced *US, 1985*
Often embellished to **KANSAS YUMMY**.

- — *American Speech*, p. 20, Spring 1985: "The language of singles bars"

yummy mummy *noun*
a sexually attractive mother *CANADA, 1993*

- Which restaurateur sent a pushy female friend into the Manlo Blahnik store on Fifth Avenue to tie up a loose end after he broke up with a yummy mummy he was dating? — *New York Post*, p. Page Six-12, 30th August 1998
- And this was way before magazines like Vogue did a motherhood issue with Amber Valetta toting her giant putti on the cover and stories of chic yummy mummies filled the glossed pages. — Carrie Karasyov, *The Right Address*, p. 116, 2004

yum-yums *noun*
any illegal drug in capsule form *US, 1980*

- — Edith A. Folb, *runnin' down some lines*, p. 260, 1980

yup *noun*
a yuppie (*young upwardly mobile professional*) *US, 1984*
A sneering abbreviation of a sneering initialism.

- Both writers are accredited Yups: Piesman, 32, is a lawyer, and Hartley, 38, is an editor. — *Time Magazine*, p. 66, 9th January 1984

yuppie *noun*
an individual socially categorized as a *young upwardly mobile professional US, 1981*
An acronym, often used derogatively, probably coined by several people independently. Many lesser variations were spawned, but none with the holding power of yuppie.

- Some are rich and healthy—Beverly with its mostly white population, Pill Hill with its mostly black professionals, Lincoln Park with its Yuppies (Young Urban Professionals). — *Chicago Tribune*, p. 1, 13th May 1981
- While he and Abbie Hoffman once led the Yippies—the Youth International Party—one social commentator has ventured that Rubin is now attempting to become the leader of the Yuppies— Young Urban Professionals. — *Chicago Tribune*, p. 4, 23rd March 1983
- And especially not by some slit-eyed yuppie who gets his salary paid out of Chronicle ad revenues and wallows (at company expense) in white wine and pesto in the finest high-dollar sports in San Francisco, Sonoma, and Tiburon. — Hunter S. Thompson, *Songs of the Doomed*, p. 252, 11th September 1987
- Let the goddamn yuppie Mormon affirmative action assholes handle it. — *Point Break*, 1991

yuppie scum *noun*
an arrogant young professional *US, 1992*
A favorite epithet of the 1980s.

- And naturally, there was a "Die, Yuppie Scum!" bumper sticker plastered to the bar mirror. — Joseph Wambaugh, *Fugitive Nights*, p. 212, 1992

yupster *noun*
a *young upwardly mobile professional US, 1986*
A variation of **YUPPIE**.

- The Hippies are now the Yupsters and they want to return. — *Phoenix (Arizona) Business Journal*, p. 1 (Section 1), 17th February 1986
- All those senior citizens in those condos, those conservative Cubans down on Eighth Street, those idealistic young yupsters on the beach. — Carl Hiaasen, *Strip Tease*, p. 12, 1993

yutz *noun*
a fool *US, 1991*
From Yiddish *yutz* (the penis).

- The guy's a total yutz, Kingsbury thought. — Carl Hiaasen, *Native Tongue*, p. 393, 1991

Zz

Z *noun*

1 an outcast; a despised person *US, 1963*

- Because a "Z" at Aragon High is a dolt, oaf, jerk, clown. — *San Francisco Examiner, p. 8, 27th October 1963*

2 an ounce of narcotics *US, 1975*

- We're buying a Z for a thousand dollars. — Kenneth Lonergan, *This is Our Youth, p. 36, 2000*

▶ **the Z**

a demilitarized zone *US, 1977*

An abbreviation of DMZ.

- In the first place, the Z was the reason the grunts were in Vietnam. — Charles Anderson, *The Grunts, p. 124, 1976*
- And what could be funnier, really, given all that an eighteen-year-old boy could learn in a month of patrolling the Z? — Michael Herr, *Dispatches, p. 103, 1977*
- Where you at? Up north. Been up by the Z? Yeah, Con Thien. — Robert A. Anderson, *Cooks & Bakers, p. 148, 1982*

za *noun*

pizza *US, 1966*

- John D. Bell et al., *Loosely Speaking, p. 22, 1966*
- *Current Slang, p. 15, Summer 1968*
- *Concord (New Hampshire) Monitor, p. 17, 23rd August 1983: "Slang slinging: an intense and awesome guide to prep school slanguage"*

zaftig; zoftig *adjective*

sexy; buxom *US, 1932*

From German/Yiddish for "juicy."

- The carhops—all zoftig numbers—wore tight space-cade outfits[.] — James Ellroy, *Hollywood Nocturnes, p. 208, 1994*

zag *verb*

when faced with two courses of action, to take the right one *US, 1948*

Most commonly used in variations of "I zigged when I should have zagged."

- He zigged when he should have zagged, that is he bet banker when he should have bet player and then switched when the shoe switched. — Mario Puzo, *Inside Las Vegas, pp. 261–262, 1977*

zags *noun*

thin papers used for rolling cigarettes *US, 1970*

From the branded name Zig Zag™, the dominant rolling papers during the hippie years.

- Steve Salaets, *Ye Olde Hiptionary, 1970*

zank *suffix*

to lose your mental composure *US, 1961*

- Zank—to flip your wig over something. — Art Unger, *The Cool Book, p. 106, 1961*

zap *noun*

an electrical shock *US, 1979*

- 'Cause when the good doctors get through givin' you the zap, you won't know where the hell you are. — *Natural Born Killers, 1994*

zap *verb*

1 to kill someone *US, 1942*

A major piece of slang from the Vietnam war.

- "I hate like hell to see the ground troops got zapped[.]" — Elaine Shepard, *The Doom Pussy, p. 9, 1967*
- "We can be sure of three kills in the firefight, and counting the two we zapped on the path later, that would be five thousand piastres." — Donald Duncan, *The New Legions, p. 76, 1967*
- All overhung with the corrosive uncertainty about when the next firefight would happen and who would get zapped in it, the men and men–children of Bravo moved into a time when they could taste relief. — Charles Anderson, *The Grunts, p. 154, 1976*
- So what am I going to do? Get one of my guys zapped so some fuckface fresh from the world can get his beauty fucking sleep! — *Platoon, 1986*

2 to give someone an electrical shock; to administer electric shock treatment to someone *US, 1973*

- They never know what hit them. And if and when they do find out they just got zapped by a cattle prod, they wish they really did have a heart attack. — *Casino, 1995*

3 to overwhelm someone *US, 1967*

- Joe David Brown (Editor), *The Hippies, p. 220, 1967: "Glossary of hippie terms"*

4 to move quickly *US, 1974*

- Robert Kirk Mueller, *Buzzwords, p. 167, 1974*
- As soon as the first bullet comes your way, your head is zapped into what I can only describe as another dimension. — Ken Lukowiak, *Marijuana Time, p. 20, 2000*

5 to have sex *US, 1985*

- *American Speech, p. 20, Spring 1985: "The language of singles bars"*

6 to present, to give *US, 1967*

- Ruth Bronsteen, *The Hippy's Handbook, p. 17, 1967*

7 to heat something up in a microwave oven *US, 1977*

- Place this dish in the oven, select and given temperature and zap away. — Victor Papanek, *How Things Don't Work, p. 94, 1977*
- We need to zap this, quick! — *South Park, 1999*

8 to give a student in college a notification of academic deficiency *US, 1968*

- *American Speech, pp. 76–77, February 1968: "Some notes on flunk notes"*

zapped *adjective*

1 drug-intoxicated *US, 1979*

- Yeah, they got stoned on giggle-weed, zonked on grifa, zapped on yerba, bombed on boo, they were blitzed with snop, warped on twist, gay on hay, free on V. — *Hi Life, p. 14, 1979*

2 spicy *US, 1983*

- Guy L. Steele et al., *The Hacker's Dictionary, p. 134, 1983*

Z-bag *noun*

the bed *US, 1968*

- Collin Baker et al., *College Undergraduate Slang Study Conducted at Brown University, p. 225, 1968*

zebra *noun*

a cadet officer in the US Air Force *US, 1946*

An allusion to how conscious the officer is of his stripes.

- *American Speech, p. 310, December 1946: "More Air Force slang"*

zebra *adjective*

racially mixed *US, 1971*

- Eugene Landy, *The Underground Dictionary, p. 203, 1971*

zeek freak *noun*

a person who greatly enjoys sex while under the influence of crack cocaine *US, 1989*

- Terry Williams, *The Cocaine Kids, p. 138, 1989*

zeke *noun*

in circus usage, a hyena *US, 1981*

- Don Wilmeth, *The Language of American Popular Entertainment, p. 56, 1981*

Zelda *noun*

a high school girl who is a socially inept outcast *US, 1961*

- *Washington Post, 23rd April 1961*

zeller *noun*

an over-devoted surfer *US, 1988*

- Michael V. Anderson, *The Bad, Rad, Not to Forget Way Cool Beach and Surf Discriptionary, p. 23, 1988*

Zen *noun*

MDMA, the recreational drug best known as ecstasy *US, 1989*

- Bruce Eisner, *Ecstasy, p. 1, 1989*

zen in *verb*

to grasp completely through intuition *US, 1967*

- Ruth Bronsteen, *The Hippy's Handbook, p. 17, 1967*

zeppelin *noun*

a poker player who contemplates long and hard before every bet or play *US, 1996*

- — John Vorhaus, *The Big Book of Poker Slang*, p. 41, 1996

zero *noun*

a gambler who is a chronic loser *US, 1996*

- — Frank Scoblete, *Best Blackjack*, p. 275, 1996

zero *verb*

1 to kill someone *US, 1990*

- You didn't know she watched you zero Gloria Monday. — Seth Morgan, *Homeboy*, p. 118, 1990

2 to identify or locate someone or something *US, 1955*

- We just zeroed three kids in a heap. Crest Drive and Observatory. — *Rebel Without a Cause*, 1955

zero-dark-thirty *noun*

very early in the morning *US, 1959*

- Began at "zero dark thirty" before dawn (and shaving in the field at that hour is quite a task.) — United States Bureau of Yards and Docks, *U.S. Navy Civil Engineer Corps Bulletin*, 1957–1959
- It was, by then, what is often referred to in the Marine Corps as zero-dark-thirty, or way past the middle of the night. — Alex Lee, *Force Recon Command*, p. 213, 1995
- We had one more night, and by God, we were going on that hill at zero dark thirty and set in. — Ed Kugler, *Dead Center*, p. 290, 1999

zero out *verb*

1 to kill someone *US, 1989*

Korean war usage.

- It was really a matter of luck and probability: the more missions, the more point duty, the more hot engagements, the higher the probability of getting zeroed out. — David H. Hackworth, *About Face*, 1989

2 to be killed *US, 1992*

- So far, not one bungee jumping customer—and only one careless instructor—has "zeroed out" in the State of California. — Erik Fair, *California Thrill Sports*, p. 55, 1992

zero week *noun*

the orientation week preceding eight weeks of basic military training *US, 1968*

- — Carl Fleischhauer, *A Glossary of Army Slang*, p. 27, 1968

Z-game *noun*

the game with the lowest betting limits in a gambling operation or cardroom *US, 1988*

There need not be 26 tables to arrive at the Z-game; it is the lowest-stakes table in the place.

- — George Percy, *The Language of Poker*, p. 98, 1988

zhlub; zhlob *noun*

a hapless misfit *US, 1972*

- "What's the matter, they can't find the guy who did it so they're picking on this poor zhlub again?" — Lawrence Block, *Small Town*, p. 88, 2003

zig *verb*

1 when faced with two courses of action, to take the wrong one *US, 1948*

Most commonly used in some variation of "I zigged when I should have zagged."

- He zigged when he should have zagged, that is he bet banker when he should have bet player and then switched when the shoe switched. — Mario Puzo, *Inside Las Vegas*, pp. 261–262, 1977

2 to shoot down an enemy fighter plane *US, 1986*

- — *American Speech*, p. 125, Summer 1986: "The language of naval fighter pilots"

ziggerboo *noun*

an eccentric or crazy person *US, 1947*

- — Marcus Hanna Boulware, *Jive and Slang of Students in Negro Colleges*, 1947

zig-zag *noun*

1 cigarette rolling papers *US, 1968*

A brand name that acquired a generic meaning.

- — Edward R. Bloomquist, *Marijuana*, 1968

2 sex with a prostitute *US, 1954*

- — Jerry Robertson, *Oil Slanguage*, p. 112, 1954

zilch *noun*

1 nothing *US, 1940*

- I have absolutely zilch in the bank, and I'm already accepted. — Erich Segal, *Love Story*, p. 68, 1970
- His value as an undercover man would be zilch. — Leonard Shecter and William Phillips, *On the Pad*, p. 49, 1973
- No class. Everythin' he ever did on the street, el zilch-o. — Edwin Torres, *After Hours*, p. 215, 1979
- A real heavy investigation. Zilch. — *Basic Instinct*, 1992

2 a socially inept outcast *US, 1965*

- — *Time*, p. 56, 1st January 1965: "Students: the slang bag"

zillion *noun*

an almost unimaginably large number *US, 1944*

One of several invented numbers used to convey a large number; probably coined by Damon Runyon.

- I bet a hunnert zillion dollars o'l wilfire cain't fling me off. (Barney Google and snuffy Smith comic strip). — *San Francisco Examiner*, 29th July 1951
- The way he explained it to me is that I'm suffering from an inferiority complex on account of my old man having zillions of books around the house and reading like a maniac. — Frederick Kohner, *Gidget*, p. 12, 1957
- Read the little book. It says United flies about sixty zillion people every year and about twenty zillion every day. — James Simon Kunen, *The Strawberry Statement*, p. 75, 1968
- It was a zillion times worse than the summer I tried to join Up With People! — Armistead Maupin, *Tales of the City*, p. 4, 1978
- And she knew a zillion old jokes her grandfather, an old vaudevillian, taught her. — *Pulp Fiction*, 1994

zimmer *noun*

a girl *US, 1990*

- For home boys and zimmers; This dictionary is def! — *Frederick (Maryland) Post*, p. B2, 24th May 1990

zine *noun*

an inexpensively self-published magazine devoted to such topics as hobbies, music, movies, or politics *US, 1978*

An abbreviation of **FANZINE**, ultimately "magazine."

- — *American Speech*, p. 53, Spring 1978: "Star Trek lives: Trekker slang"
- The newest player in the dirty magazine business is the "zines"—inexpensive publications usually put out by one or two people. — James Ridgeway, *Red Light*, p. 69, 1996
- The independent character of zines gives them significant value, allowing subjects outside of mainstream fashion to receive coverage. — Marion Leonard, *Cool Places*, p. 105, 1998

zined *noun*

a fan magazine editor *US, 1976*

- — *American Speech*, p. 53, Spring 1978: "Star Trek lives: Trekker slang"

zing *noun*

1 energy, vigor *US, 1918*

- But there is a zip and a zing here, a supercivilized, metropolitan method of behavior, unique and indescribable. — Jack Lait and Lee Mortimer, *New York Confidential*, p. 11, 1948

2 an amphetamine tablet *US, 1997*

- — *Providence (Rhode Island) Journal-Bulletin*, p. 6B, 4th August 1997: "Doctors must know the narcolexicon"

Z-ing *noun*

the practice of targeting tourists as victims of crime by the "Z" as the first letter on the car number plate, designating a rental car *US, 1994*

- — *American Speech*, p. 186, Summer 1994: "Among the new words"

zing *verb*

1 to injure, to hurt *US, 1985*

- What happened was, one of the reporters had a fight with one of the cops. Now he wants to zing him. — Mark Baker, *Cops*, p. 246, 1985

2 to travel quickly *US, 1920*

- Well, from the way I zinged through Laramie you would think I didn't like it, either. — Clancy Sigal, *Going Away*, p. 166, 1961

3 to affect someone suddenly and forcefully *US, 1975*

- The plan was to zing the pastor at a special meeting in mid-week to be arranged by Reverend Owens[.] — Iceberg Slim (Robert Beck), *Mama Black Widow*, p. 196, 1969
- "He's a cop. Right?" It zinged her, caught her by surprise and she raised her eyebrows, stared at him. — Elmore Leonard, *Glitz*, p. 157, 1985
- It was best to let that one zing past. — Joseph Wambaugh, *Fugitive Nights*, p. 6, 1992

► **zing it in**
to bet heavily *US, 1979*
- — John Scarne, *Scarne's Guide to Modern Poker*, p. 293, 1979

zingaro *noun*
in circus and carnival usage, a gypsy *US, 1981*
- — Don Wilmeth, *The Language of American Popular Entertainment*, p. 299, 1981

zinger *noun*
1 a surface wound *US, 1992*
- I got one little zinger up my back, nothing serious, just a grazing wound[.] — Harold Moore, *We Were Soldiers Once ... And Young*, p. 245, 1992

2 the punchline of a joke; the last word *US, 1964*
- "Ah!" said Polly. "Here comes the zinger." "Not, not quite yet," said Ira. — Max Shulman, *Anyone Got a Match?*, p. 111, 1964
- And he threw in a zinger. He tells me he don't like the guys I'm associatin' with. — Martin Gosch, *The Last Testament of Lucky Testamant*, p. 53, 1975
- "Except family," Carmody says, like he's handing me the fatal zinger. — Robert Campbell, *Nibbled to Death by Ducks*, p. 98, 1989

3 an arranged ending to a competition *US, 1959*
- And finally a fix—or zinger, as it was called in those days—was in with the Commission as well[.] — Terry Southern, *The Magic Christian*, p. 60, 1959

4 a surprise, an awkward or unexpected turn of events *US, 1973*
- Of course, he has a couple of zingers in there which we'll have to work around. — Ronald Reagan, *Ronald Reagan*, p. 651, 1990

5 an exceptionally good example of something *UK, 1955*
- I'm gonna crack off a zinger this afternoon. — Darryl Ponicsan, *The Last Detail*, pp. 58–59, 1970

6 a very attractive woman *US, 1959*
- A smasheroo she was—a real zinger. — Max Shulman, *I was a Teen-Age Dwarf*, p. 8, 1959

7 an amphetamine tablet *US, 1993*
- — Peter Johnson, *Dictionary of Street Alcohol and Drug Terms*, p. 208, 1993

8 a hot pepper *US, 1996*
- — *Maledicta*, p. 24, 1996: "Domino's pizza jargon"

9 a hard stare that is intended to impart bad luck on the recipient *US, 1979*
- — John Scarne, *Scarne's Guide to Modern Poker*, p. 293, 1979

zingy *adjective*
exciting, energetic *US, 1948*
- TONY: How ya doing? PETE: Zingy. Steady at sixty-five percent. — *Saturday Night Fever*, 1977

zip *noun*
1 an Italian or Sicilian criminal brought to the US for criminal purposes, especially murder *US, 1987*
- He said the zips are Sicilians being brought into the country to distribute heroin and carry out hits[.] — Joseph Pistone, *Donnie Brasco*, p. 131, 1987
- Tommy's a Zip. You know what I mean? One of those guys they used to import from Sicily to handle the rough stuff. Guy could be a peasant right out of the fucking Middle Ages, looks around, and he's in Miami Beach. Can't believe it. They hand the Zip a gun and say, "There, that guy." And the Zip takes him out. — Elmore Leonard, *Pronto*, pp. 16–17, 1993

2 a Viet Cong; a Vietnamese; any South Asian person *US, 1970*
- — *Current Slang*, p. 19, Summer 1970
- "You be lucky Mayhew don't think you a Zip an' blast your fuckin' head off." — Michael Herr, *Dispatches*, p. 129, 1977
- This term was used by U.S. troops to connote the "worthlessness" of these people (zip = zero). — *Maledicta*, p. 126, Summer 1980
- [S]ome zonked-out zip crawled up sneaky-close in the mangled underbrush[.] — Larry Heinemann, *Paco's Story*, p. 6, 1986
- Be advised I've got zips in the wire down here, over. — *Platoon*, 1986

3 energy *UK, 1900*
- But there is a zip and a zing here, a supercivilized, metropolitan method of behavior, unique and indescribable. — Jack Lait and Lee Mortimer, *New York Confidential*, p. 11, 1948
- They had shown no zip. They weren't hitting. They weren't alert. — Dan Jenkins, *Life Its Ownself*, p. 111, 1984

4 nothing at all; zero *US, 1900*
- — *Current Slang*, p. 12, Winter 1969
- "Well, I didn't want to fuck him for zip," she said. — Dan Jenkins, *Dead Solid Perfect*, p. 78, 1986

5 a hand-made gun, a zip gun *US, 1949*
- "Ain't safe to walk around without a zip or knife and some friends." — William Bernard, *Jailbait*, p. 87, 1949
- Picaeo, who I dug as no heart, squawked out, "Sticks, shanks, zips—you call it." — Piri Thomas, *Down These Mean Streets*, p. 52, 1967

zip *verb*
1 to move quickly *US, 1852*
- A few cars zipped by. — Jack Kerouac, *On the Road*, p. 15, 1957
- I was quite a spectacle zipping around Hollywood and Los Angeles at night with my turban on the scooter. — Babs Gonzales, *I Paid My Dues*, p. 21, 1967
- His fist zipped up, caught Greystone on the cheek. — *The Sweeney*, p. 30, 1976
- Then zip ahead and let the cop follow. — Elmore Leonard, *Glitz*, p. 227, 1985
- He stood in the doorway, freezing in his paisley caftan, and watched her zip away over patches of ice and tainted snow. — Odie Hawkins, *The Busting Out of an Ordinary Man*, p. 134, 1985
- A blue-uniformed nurse came in and zipped down the centre of the ward[.] — Mary Hooper, *(megan)2*, p. 9, 1999

2 to kill someone *US, 1982*
- I zip her husband while she's out tracking down specials in the supermarket, and she wants to marry me. — Richard Condon, *Prizzi's Honor*, p. 70, 1982

► **zip it**
to stop talking *US, 1999*
From the image of zipping your mouth shut.
- Zip it! Unveil the time portal. — *Austin Powers*, 1999

► **zip your lip; zip your mouth**
to stop talking *US, 1942*
- "Listen, you animated bass horn, you're welcome to stay on condition you zip your lip." — Elaine Shepard, *The Doom Pussy*, p. 45, 1967

zip ball *noun*
in pinball, a ball that leaves play without having scored *US, 1977*
- — Bobbye Claire Natkin and Steve Kirk, *All About Pinball*, p. 118, 1977

zip-five *noun*
a prison sentence of a maximum of five years *US, 1964*
- I was sent to Elmire for zip-five and I did forty-eight months. — Jeremy Larner and Ralph Tefferteller, *The Addict in the Street*, p. 96, 1964

zip gun; zipper gun *noun*
an inexpensive, homemade gun, usually consisting of a tube, a grip, and a rudimentary striking device *US, 1949*
- He accused suspects of using daggers, bayonets, ice picks—along with revolvers and what he officially called "zipper guns." — William Bernard, *Jailbait*, p. 82, 1949
- Unless they use a zip gun on you someday. — Evan Hunter, *The Blackboard Jungle*, p. 304, 1954
- Bottles, knives, zipguns, tire chains, bricks. — Willard Motley, *Let No Man Write My Epitaph*, p. 208, 1958

zipper *noun*
1 a short but well-formed wave *US, 1988*
- — Michael V. Anderson, *The Bad, Rad, Not to Forget Way Cool Beach and Surf Discriptionary*, p. 23, 1988

2 a trap play in poker *US, 1996*
- — John Vorhaus, *The Big Book of Poker Slang*, p. 42, 1996

zipperhead *noun*
a Vietnamese person. Offensive *US, 1967*
- "Get these zipperheads off the runway," Harry called over the radio to the Special Forces camp[.] — Elaine Shepard, *The Doom Pussy*, p. 62, 1967
- There were a lot of wounded and a lot of dead / But most of them were Zipperheads. — Sandee Johnson, *Cadences: The Jody Call Book, No. 2*, p. 128, 1986
- Can you believe they're actually payin' us to do this—to waste these zipperhead motherfuckers! — Jack Hawkins, *Chopper One #2*, p. 197, 1987

zipper ripper *noun*
in craps, a roll of ten *US, 1999*
Evolved from the more common **BIG DICK** (a roll of ten).
- — Chris Fagans and David Guzman, *A Guide to Craps Lingo*, p. 33, 1999

zippity-doo-dah *noun*
nothing at all *US, 1977*

An elaboration of **ZIP** (zero).

- You get zippity-doo-dah. — Neil Simon, *The Goodbye Girl*, 1977

zippity-doo-dah!

used as a nonsensical, all-purpose utterance *US, 1992*
From the lyrics of a song in the 1946 Walt Disney film *Song of the South*.

- Well zippity-doo-dah. You and your code plead not guilty and you'll be in jail for the rest of your life. — *A Few Good Men*, 1992

zippo *noun*

1 nothing *US, 1993*
An embellished form of **ZIP**.

- "Not a damn thing," he said. "I swear, I told him zippo." — Carl Hiaasen, *Strip Tease*, p. 233, 1993
- "Other than that, zippo to report." — Jonathan Kellerman, *Rage*, p. 110, 2005

2 energy *US, 1981*

- But when he managed to bounce back into big bucks with real zippo, as they say, he'd stocked the campaign larders of front-runners in state and local elections. — Joseph Wambaugh, *The Glitter Dome*, p. 34, 1981

3 a tank-mounted flame thrower *US, 1966*
An allusion to the branded cigarette lighter.

- — *Newsweek*, p. 31, 25th July 1966
- — Carl Fleischhauer, *A Glossary of Army Slang*, p. 27, 1968

zippo *verb*

to set something on fire and burn it *US, 1966*
An allusion to the branded cigarette lighter.

- "Okay, Zippo the joint." Nobody reacts. He walks to the closest hut, takes a cigarette lighter from his pocket and snaps the lid open[.] — William Wilson, *The LBJ Brigade*, p. 28, 1966

zippo job *noun*

the burning of a village as part of a military sweep through the area *US, 1988*

- "Zippo jobs" on Vietnamese hamlets by American soldiers had become so common that television audiences in the United States were no longer scandalized by them. — Neil Sheehan, *A Bright Shining Lie*, 1988

zippola *noun*

nothing at all *US, 1994*

- — Sally Williams, *"Strong" Words*, p. 167, 1994

zip top *noun*

A Jewish person *US, 1987*
Offensive.

- — Carsten Stroud, *Close Pursuit*, p. 277, 1987

zirconia flush *noun*

in poker, four diamonds *US, 1996*
Named after the synthetic diamond.

- — John Vorhaus, *The Big Book of Poker Slang*, p. 42, 1996

zit *noun*

1 a Vietnamese person *US, 1983*

- — Lynda Van Devanter, *Home Before Morning*, p. 382, 1983: Glossary

2 an acne pimple *US, 1966*

- the zit-pocked lumpen of Madison Square Garden — Lester Bangs, *Psychotic Reactions and Carburetor Dung*, p. 209, 1977
- The policeman who dropped her off at Barbary Lane was so young that he had zits — Armistead Maupin, *Tales of the City*, p. 244, 1978
- So in the ninth grade Sherry Dewitt threw me over because I had zits. — *Wayne's World 2*, 1993
- Zits were the least of my worries. — C.D. Payne, *Cut to the Twisp*, p. 7, 2001

zizzy *adjective*

fancy, showy *US, 1954*

- [A] couple of peekers, suitably dressed for admission to one of the zizzier places, waits across the street from the nightclub entrance. — Dev Collans with Stewart Sterling, *I was a House Detective*, p. 16, 1954

zloty *noun*

in poker, low-stakes betting *US, 1996*
Named after the lowest value coin in the Polish monetary system.

- — John Vorhaus, *The Big Book of Poker Slang*, p. 42, 1996

zob *noun*

an unlikeable, despicable person *US, 1911*

- "It'd be worth paying your taxes just to get clear of that zob," Francine said. — Bernard Wolfe, *The Late Risers*, p. 131, 1954

zod *noun*

someone who is socially inept to the extreme *US, 1982*

- I just got my hair streaked, OK, and like Brian throws me in the pool, and like the chlorine turns my hair like totally green, I mean I look like such a zod! — Mary Corey and Victoria Westermark, *Fer Shurr! How to be a Valley Girl*, 1982

zog *noun*

the US federal government *US, 1987*
A basic piece of paranoid, racist, right-wing political vocabulary in the US.

- Mathews and Pierce referred to the United States government as ZOG (the Zionist Occupation Government). — David Harry Bennett, *The Party of Fear*, p. 349, 1988
- Berg's murder was supposed to be the first in a series of assassinations by members of The Order in their self-declared war against ZOG. — Pete Earley, *The Hot House*, p. 325, 1992
- They refer to the U.S. government as the "Zionist Occupational Government," or "ZOG," and following the tenets of the Christian Identity philosophy, believe it is controlled by the state of Israel. — Bill Valentine, *Gangs and Their Tattoos*, p. 55, 2000

zoinks!

used for expressing fear or surprise *US, 1972*
Popularized as a signature line of the character Shaggy, voiced by Casey Kasem, on the television cartoon *Scooby Doo, Where are You?* (CBS, 1969–72). Repeated with referential humor.

- "Zoinks, Shaggy!" I answered. "Shut up, you smart aleck," he said. — Rett MacPherson, *Killing Cousins*, p. 182, 2003

zol *noun*

a marijuana cigarette *US, 1955*

- — *American Speech*, p. 88, May 1955: "Narcotic argot along the Mexican border"

zombie *noun*

1 a dull, personality-free person *US, 1941*
From the belief of certain west African religions that corpses can be revived to walk the earth without souls.

- No Jules, you're gonna be like those pieces of shit out there who beg for change. They walk around like a bunch of fuckin' zombies, they sleep in garbage bins, they eat what I throw away, and dogs piss on 'em. — *Pulp Fiction*, 1994

2 in poker, an expert player who shows no emotion, no matter how good or bad his hand is *US, 1979*

- — John Scarne, *Scarne's Guide to Modern Poker*, p. 293, 1979

zombie job *noun*

during the Korean war, a night patrol *US, 1957*

- A volunteer was needed from our group to do a zombie job and I was chosen. The general mission of the unit was to capture a prisoner. — Martin Russ, *The Last Parallel*, p. 98, 1957

zombie weed *noun*

phencyclidine, the recreational drug known as PCP or angel dust *US, 1981*

- — Ronald Linder, *PCP*, p. 10, 1981

zone *noun*

▸ **below the zone**
(used of a military promotion) unexpectedly early *US, 1989*
Vietnam war usage.

- All of my guys from the $\frac{1}{327}$ —Peeping Tom Hancock, Ben Willis, Wayne Dill, Don Chapman, Glynn Mallory—had made it "below the zone" to major. — David H. Hackworth, *About Face*, p. 606, 1989

▸ **on the zone**
lost in a daydream *US, 1974*

- — Paul Glover, *Words from the House of the Dead*, 1974

▸ **the Zone**
an unsavory area in downtown Boston, dominated by sex shops, bars, and drug dealers *US, 1984*
An abbreviation of **COMBAT ZONE**.

- By 1979, I thought that nothing in the Zone could surprise me. — Lauri Lewin, *Naked is the Best Disguise*, p. 15, 1984

zoned *adjective*

mentally absent *US, 2005*

- Half-dead, totally zoned fiends were roaming the streets day and night like survivors of a nuclear blast. — 50 Cent, *From Pieces to Weight*, p. 30, 2005

zoned out *adjective*
mentally absent *US, 1968*
- "You're zoned out," said Adam from behind his face. — Joan Baez, *Daybreak*, p. 96, 1968
- The freaky, zoned-out style being developed on the misty slopes of the Haight had still made few inroads into intense, political Berkeley. — J. Anthony Lukas, *Don't Shoot—We Are Your Children*, p. 386, 1971
- It was due to a system full of codeine. I discontinued their use after two days. I couldn't afford to be zoned out. — James Ellroy, *Brown's Requiem*, p. 249, 1981
- But pretty soon his wife, Yolie, would find him zoned out in front of the television with a drink in his hands. — Joseph Wambaugh, *Lines and Shadows*, p. 212, 1984
- Massey was a medium-size, twenty-something black man who was zoned out, like a zombie. — Ted Conover, *Newjack*, p. 143, 2000

zone out; zone off; zone *verb*
to absent yourself mentally, with or without the aid of drugs *US, 1982*
- Erroll zoned out for a second, his eyes going dim, a tiny high moan escaping his cracked lips. — Richard Price, *Clockers*, p. 423, 1992
- Deek would zone out on the ratty old sofa and Ty would finally drag him to bed and strip off his clothes. — Jess Mowry, *Way Past Cool*, p. 30, 1992
- Especially if all they ever did was to zone outon Daffy Duck cartoons. — Wolfman Jack (Bob Smith), *Have Mercy!*, p. 62, 1995
- I'm zonin' off on one joint[.] — Eminem (Marshall Mathers), *Still Don't Give a Fuck*, 1999

zoner; zonie *noun*
someone from Arizona *US, 1991*
- — Trevor Cralle, *The Surfin'ary*, p. 166, 1991

zonk *verb*
1 to hit or strike, literally or figuratively *US, 1969*
- It ain't been too busy a year, but maybe that's cause I was zonked with the help for three months. — Abbie Hoffman, *Woodstock Nation*, p. 11, 1969

2 to fall asleep, especially as a result of drugs or drink *US, 1970*
Also used with "out."
- Patrice coaxes her back, wanting to perform for men at large, who are too zonked out to give a shit. — Josh Alan Friedman, *Tales of Times Square*, p. 121, 1986
- Once we got up to my room, he zonked out in my bed. — Amy Sohn, *Run Catch Kiss*, p. 109, 1999

3 to intoxicate *US, 2002*
- She emptied no less than twenty caps into Benny's grouper chowder, enough to zonk a buffalo. — Carl Hiaasen, *Basket Case*, p. 393, 2002

zonked *noun*
the recreational drug GHB *US, 2000*
From the drug-intoxicated sense of ZONKED.
- Liquid X, Grievous Bodily Harm, Easy Lay, Georgia Home Boy, Soap, Cherry Meth, Nature's Quaalude and Zonked are just a few. — *Augusta (Georgia) Chronicle*, p. A1, 16th April 2000

zonked *adjective*
1 intoxicated on a drug, especially marijuana; drunk *US, 1958*
Also used with "out."
- You must be zonked out completely. — Terry Southern, *Flash and Filigree*, p. 150, 1958
- Everybody high on something: balloons, acid, bananas, kids, sky, flowers, dancing, kissing. I had a ball—totally zonked. — Abbie Hoffman, *Revolution for the Hell of It*, p. 23, 1968
- An old lady with a Macy's bag sitting across from you looks around as if to ask what the world is coming to between these Dracula Jews and zonked-out Africans[.] — Jay McInerney, *Bright Lights, Big City*, p. 57, 1984
- The user sits approximately eighteen inches from the stalk and inhales the fumes. Zonked. — Lenny Bruce, *The Unpublished Lenny Bruce*, p. 71, 1984

2 exhausted *US, 1968*
- At 4 A.M., I just blinked. Man, I was zonked. — Albert Goldman, *Freak Show*, p. 91, 1968

zonkers *noun*
the female breasts *US, 1995*
An abbreviation of BAZONKAS.

- During a [radio] show on breasts, Infinity was fined because I said: "Boobs, xonkers, headlights, watermelons, sweater puppies, pointers, knockers, jugs, tatas"—these are some of the words to describe women's breasts. — Howard Stern, *Miss America*, p. 441, 1995

zoo *nickname*
▸ **the zoo**
the North Vietnamese prisoner of war camp formally known as the Cu Loc Prison in Vietnam *US, 1984*
- After two weeks they took me to a camp we called the Zoo. — Wallace Terry, *Bloods*, p. 134, 1984
- From the Zoo I went to Briarpatch, and then I went to Son Tay and came back to the Annex, which was right next to the Zoo. — Harry Maurer, *Strange Ground*, p. 414, 1989

zoo book *noun*
a student directory with photographs of each student *US, 1968*
- — *Current Slang*, p. 15, Summer 1968

zoobs *noun*
the female breasts *US, 1968*
A blend of BOOB(S) and BAZOOMS.
- — Collin Baker et al., *College Undergraduate Slang Study Conducted at Brown University*, p. 227, 1968

zoo doo *noun*
compost made from multispecies feces *US, 1981*
- Each of the zoo's elephants can produce up to a wheel barrow load of "Zoo Doo" daily that can be converted into fuel through a biomass digester. — United Press International, PM cycle, 24th June 1981

zooed *adjective*
crowded *US, 1988*
Surfer usage.
- — Michael V. Anderson, *The Bad, Rad, Not to Forget Way Cool Beach and Surf Discriptionary*, p. 23, 1988

zooly *adjective*
excellent *US, 1961*
- It came soon and we all got up and had the first joyride of the day. It was zooly. — Frederick Kohner, *Gidget Goes Hawaiian*, p. 50, 1961

zoom *noun*
phencyclidine, the recreational drug known as PCP or angel dust *US, 1994*
- — US Department of Justice, *Street Terms*, October 1994

zoom *verb*
1 to move very quickly *US, 1946*
From aviation slang.
- When you passed over 110th Street it was like zooming off to another planet where they didn't build any brick walls between wanting and doing[.] — Mezz Mezzrow, *Really the Blues*, p. 204, 1946
- We were zooming past Cleveland Avenue, and I brightened a little. — Max Shulman, *The Many Loves of Dobie Gillis*, p. 188, 1951
- [I]t was strange sitting in their brand-new comfortable car and hearing them talk of exams as we zoomed smoothly into town. — Jack Kerouac, *On the Road*, p. 17, 1957
- I was laboring along behind a fire truck when the untracked outlaw came zooming past. — Hunter S. Thompson, *Hell's Angels*, p. 125, 1966

2 to induce someone to commit a crime that they were not otherwise inclined to commit *US, 1970*
- But she told me you zoomed her. — Joseph Wambaugh, *The New Centurions*, p. 175, 1970

zoom bag *noun*
a military flier's flight suit *US, 1991*
- — *Army*, p. 48, November 1991

zoomer *noun*
a person who sells fake crack cocaine and then quickly disappears *US, 2002*
- — *Detroit News*, p. 5D, 20th September 2002

zoomers *noun*
the female breasts *US, 1968*
- — Fred Hester, *Slang on the 40 Acres*, 1968

zoomie *noun*
a crew member of a military jet aircraft *US, 1948*
A term used by the infantry and navy.

- — *American Speech*, p. 38, February 1948: "Talking under water: speech in submarines"
- — Carl Fleischhauer, *A Glossary of Army Slang*, p. 27, 1968

zooms *noun*

the female breasts *US, 1968*

A shortened form of **BAZOOMS**.

- — Collin Baker et al., *College Undergraduate Slang Study Conducted at Brown University*, p. 227, 1968

zoot *noun*

a **ZOOT SUIT** *US, 1947*

- So why're you wearin' that circus zoot? I'm gonna have to burn it. — Irving Shulman, *The Amboy Dukes*, p. 139, 1947
- Swing skirts are circling, zoot-tails flying[.] — William Sansom, *A Public for Jive [The Public's Progress]*, p. 58, 1947
- [O]utdressing everyone on the block in the uniform of the period, pork-pie hat, satin shirt, peg pants, reat jacket. Zoot, man. — Clancy Sigal, *Going Away*, p. 462, 1961
- I remarked that I had saved about half enough to get a zoot. — Malcolm X and Alex Haley, *The Autobiography of Malcolm X*, p. 51, 1964

zooted; zooted up *adjective*

drug-intoxicated *US, 1986*

- — *Rutgers Alumni Magazine*, p. 21, February 1986
- At first people came after they left the first house, and most of them was already zooted up[.] — Terry Williams, *The Cocaine Kids*, p. 108, 1989
- So I went down to 123rd Street, got a bag of Red Devil Angel Dust, smoked, and got crazy zooted. — *New Jack City*, 1990
- He come here, my Ace Cool, he be zooted up, he say here's de plan, Amp. — Stephen Cannell, *King Con*, p. 50, 1997

zooter *noun*

a **ZOOT SUITER** *US, 1994*

- Over on Sunset and Figueroa, knots of zooters were assembling in violation of the Zoot Suit Ordinance, no doubt figuring that today it was anything goes. — James Ellroy, *Hollywood Nocturnes*, p. 123, 1994

zootie *adjective*

emotionally unbalanced or drug-intoxicated *US, 1990*

- — *Frederick (Maryland) Post*, p. B2, 24th May 1990

zoot up *verb*

to dress in a zoot suit and accessories *US, 1947*

- What're you doin' all zooted up? — Irving Shulman, *The Amboy Dukes*, p. 139, 1947

zooty *adjective*

fashionable, stylish *US, 1946*

Derived from, and an allusion to, **ZOOT SUIT**.

- Fashion note: colored kids working in the tailor shop tired of corny prison outfits, go to work on their dungarees, pegging the legs till they're real sharp and zooty. — Mezz Mezzrow, *Really the Blues*, p. 313, 1946
- The goose thereafter laid up a storm, and Jack, who was no astute galoot, went on a toot with a local beaut, bought himself a zooty suit and still had a little loot to boot. — Steve Allen, *Bop Fables*, pp. 66–68, 1955

zoo-zoo; zuu-zuu *noun*

in prison, sweets, snacks, soda or any other special treat *US, 1967*

- Got your own private locker that you can keep your zu-zu's in[.] — Ken Kesey, *Kesey's Jail Journal*, p. 25, 1967
- A phrase that must have been conceived by a person with a playful imagination is zoo-zoos and wham-whams for confections, usually small packaged cakes, pieces, candy or gum obtained from a vending machine. — *Maledicta*, p. 267, Summer/Winter 1981
- When he made the canteen cart, the beaners ripped off his zuuzuus and whamwhams. — Seth Morgan, *Homeboy*, p. 152, 1990
- You aren't a hostage, you're my zoo-zoo, my treat after five months of servitude. — Elmore Leonard, *Out of Sight*, p. 40, 1996

zorch *verb*

in computing, to move or process quickly *US, 1983*

- — Guy L. Steele et al., *The Hacker's Dictionary*, p. 135, 1983

zort *verb*

to shoot or destroy *US, 1990*

- That's when Charlie tries to zort me / When I'm shootin' guns and droppin' bombs. — Joseph Tuso, *Singing the Vietnam Blues*, p. 170, 1990: Shootin' Guns and Droppin' Bombs

zot *noun*

zero; nothing *US, 1964*

- — *American Speech*, p. 195, October 1965: "Notes on campus vocabulary, 1964"
- — Helen Dahlskog (Editor), *A Dictionary of Contemporary and Colloquial Usage*, p. 66, 1972

zotz *noun*

a planned murder; an assassination *US, 1988*

- Santo Calandra is gonna try for a zotz on Matty and Van when they come outta the bank. — Richard Condon, *Prizzi's Glory*, p. 80, 1988

zotz *verb*

to kill someone *US, 1982*

- "You are the only one who can get close enough to her to do it," his father said. "Zotz her? Clip Irene?" — Richard Condon, *Prizzi's Honor*, p. 304, 1982

zotzed *adjective*

drunk or drug-intoxicated *US, 1992*

- Roc, listen, it's OK, believe me. She's totally fucking zotzed. — Richard Price, *Clockers*, p. 132, 1992

zowie *noun*

vigor, vim, energy *US, 1946*

- "Charlie is still full of zip and zowie!" — Stephen King, *The Waste Lands*, p. 202, 1991

z's *noun*

sleep *US, 1963*

From Z's as the representation of snoring in comic strips used with a verb such as "catch," "cop," "cut," "get," "grab" or "rip."

- And now I, Billy Clyde Puckett, am going off to stack me up some Z's. — Dan Jenkins, *Semi-Tough*, p. 127, 1972
- Can't you talk to me later? I'm tryin' to cop some ZZZs. — Odie Hawkins, *Ghetto Sketches*, p. 176, 1972
- Half of them are sitting on a hill watching us and laughing, and the rest of them are blowing fucking Zs in a fucking hammock is what they're doing. — Charles Anderson, *The Grunts*, p. 60, 1976
- Okay. Don't catch no z's on me buddy or I'll sling your motherfucking ass. — *Platoon*, 1986

zuke *noun*

in American casinos, a gratuity *US, 1985*

- — Steve Kuriscak, *Casino Talk*, p. 61, 1985
- — Michael Dalton, *Blackjack*, p. 91, 1991

Zulu *noun*

1 an impulsive, undisciplined, violent person *US, 1952*

- "We don't need help from them wild zulus." — Harry Grey, *The Hoods*, p. 176, 1952

2 a black person *US, 1960*

Offensive.

- — William K. Bentley and James M. Corbett, *Prison Slang*, p. 56, 1992

3 a large marijuana cigarette *US, 1973*

- While standing at the rear of the hotel taking long pulls on the Zulu, a car pulled up with New York tags on it. — A.S. Jackson, *Gentleman Pimp*, p. 76, 1973

Zululand *noun*

enemy territory *US, 1992*

- We patched him up and now we knew we were in Zululand. — Harold Moore, *We Were Soldiers Once ... And Young*, p. 164, 1992

Zulu princess *noun*

in homosexual usage, a young and attractive black man *US, 1986–1987*

- — *Maledicta*, p. 53, 1986–1987: "A continuation of a glossary of ethnic slurs in American English"

Bibliography

50 Cent (Curtis Jackson) with Kris Ex.
From Pieces to Weight: Once Upon a Time in Southside Queens, Pocket Books, New York, 2006

Aaberg, Dennis and John Milius
Big Wednesday, Bantam Books, New York, 1978

Abbott, Jack Henry
In the Belly of the Beast, Vintage Books, New York, 1982

Abbott, Rick and Mike Baker
Start Surfing, Stanley Paul, Melbourne, 1980

Abernathy, Francis Edward
The Bounty of Texas (Publication of the Texas Folklore Society #49), University of North Texas, Denton, Texas, 1990

Abood, Ken and Tony Ranfone
How to Live in Vietnam for Less than 10 Cents a Day, Wayward Press, Tokyo, 1967

Abrahams, Roger D.
Deep Down in the Jungle: Negro Narrative Folklore from the Streets of Philadelphia (Revised Edition), Aldine Publishing, Chicago, 1970
Positively Black, Prentice-Hall, Englewood Cliffs, New Jersey, 1970

Ackroyd, Dan and John Landis
The Blues Brothers, Universal Pictures, 1980

Acosta, Oscar Zeta et al.
The Revolt of the Cockroach People, Straight Arrow Books, San Francisco, 1973
The Autobiography of a Brown Buffalo, Vintage Books, New York, 1989

Adams, Ramon
The Language of the Railroader, University of Oklahoma Press, Norman, Oklahoma, 1977

Addington, Deborah
A Hand in the Bush: The Fine Art of Vaginal Fisting, Greenery Press, San Francisco, 1997

Adler, Polly
A House is Not a Home, Rinehart & Company, New York, 1953

Ainslie, Tom
Ainslie's Complete Guide to Thoroughbred Racing (3rd Edition), Simon and Schuster, New York, 1976

Albano, Captain Lou and Berg Randolph Sugar
The Complete Idiot's Guide to Pro Wrestling, Alpha Books, New York, 1999

Alexander, Don
The Racer's Dictionary, Steve Smith Autosports, Santa Ana, California, 1980

Alexander, George
Escapades of a Porno King, Carlyle Communications, New York, 1973

Alexie, Sherman
Smoke Signals, Miramax, 1998

Alfange, Dean
The Horse Racing Industry, Kensington Publishing Corporation, New York, 1976

Algren, Nelson
The Man with the Golden Arm, Doubleday & Company, Garden City, New York, 1949
A Walk on the Wild Side, Fawcett, Greenwich, Connecticut, 1957
The Neon Wilderness, Berkley Publishing, New York, 1965
Chicago: City on the Make, McGraw Hill, New York, 1983

Allen, J. Edward
The Basics of Winning Slots, Gambling Research Institute, New York, 1984

Allen, Jim
Locked in Surfing for Life, Barnes and Noble, New York, 1970

Allen, John
Assault with a Deadly Weapon: The Autobiography of a Street Criminal, McGraw-Hill, New York, 1978

Allen, Woody and Marshall Brickman
Manhattan, United Artists, 1979

Allison, Ruth
Lesbianism: Its Secrets and Practices, Medco Books, Los Angeles, 1967

Alpert, Richard and Sidney Cohen
LSD, New American Library, New York, 1966

Alter, Robert Edmond
Carny Kill, Black Lizard Books, Berkeley, California, 1986

Alvarez, George R.
Semiotic Dynamics of an Ethnic-American Sub-Cultural Group, unpublished paper prepared for the International Conference on General Semantics, Los Altos, California, 1965

Aman, Reinhold
Hillary Clinton's Pen Pal: A Guide to Life and Lingo in Federal Prison, Maledicta Press, Santa Rosa, California, 1996

Ample, Annie
The Bare Facts: My Life as a Stripper, Key Porter Books, Toronto, 1988

Anderson, Charles R.
The Grunts, Berkeley Books, New York, 1986 (1976)

Anderson, Douglas
All About Cribbage, Winchester Press, New York, 1971

Anderson, Michael V.
The Bad, Rad, Not to Forget Way Cool Beach and Surf Discriptionary, Oceanside Printers, 1988

Anderson, Paul Thomas
Hard Eight, Goldwyn Entertainment, 1996
Boogie Nights, New Line Cinema, 1997

Andrews, Alice
Hooked on Bingo, Aecila Publishing, St. Louis, Missouri, 1988

Andrews, Malachi and Paul T. Owens et al.
Black Language, Seymour-Smith, West Los Angeles, California, 1973

Andros, Phil (Samuel M. Steward)
Stud, Alyson Publications, Boston, 1982 (1966)

Andrus, Mark and James L. Brooks
As Good As It Gets, TriStar Pictures, 1997

Anonymous
Shine and the Titanic; The Signifying Monkey; Stackolee and Other Stories from Down Home, More Publishing, San Francisco, 1970
Go Ask Alice, Avon Books, New York, 1971

Anonymous, Andy
A Basic Guide to Campusology, Campus Humor Publications, Austin, Texas, 1966

Anthony, Earl
Winning Bowling, Contemporary Books, Chicago, 1977

Applebaum, Ben and Derrick Pittman
Turd Ferguson and the Sausage Party: An Uncensored Guide to College Slang, iUniverse, Inc., New York, 2004

Archer, Jeff
Theater in a Squared Circle: The Mystique of Professional Wrestling, White Boucke Publishing, Lafayette, Colorado, 1999

Armanino, Dominic
Dominoes: Popular Games, Rules & Strategy, Cornerstone Library, New York, 1959
Five-up Domino Game, Five-Up Company, San Francisco, 1964

Armore, Joseph R. and Joseph D. Wolfe
Dictionary of Desperation, National Alliance of Businessmen, Washington D.C., 1976

Armstrong, Louis
Satchmo: My Life in New Orleans, Da Capo Press, New York, 1986 (1954)

Atkin, S. Beth (Editor)
Voices from the Street: Young Former Gang Members Tell Their Stories, Little, Brown and Company, Boston, 1996

Ausubel, Nathan (Editor)
A Treasury of Jewish Folklore, Crown Publishers, New York, 1968

Ayers, Rick (Editor)
Slang Dictionary, Communication Arts and Sciences, Berkeley High School, Berkeley, California, 2001
Berkeley High Slang Dictionary, North Atlantic Books, Berkeley, California, 2004

Babitz, Eve
Eve's Hollywood, Dell Publishing, New York, 1974
L.A. Woman, Linden Press, New York, 1982

Baker, Collin et al.
College Undergraduate Slang Study Conducted at Brown University Semester II, 1967-1968, College Undergraduate Slang Study, Providence, Rhode Island, 1968

Baker, Fred
Events: The Complete Film Scenario, Grove Press, New York, 1970

Baker, Mark
Nam: The Vietnam War in the Words of the Men and Women Who Fought There, William Morrow and Company, New York, 1981
Cops: Their Lives in Their Own Words, Pocket Books, New York, 1986

Baker, Nicholson
Vox, Random House, New York, 1992

Baldwin, James
Blues for Mister Charlie, Dell Publishing, New York, 1964
If Beale Street Could Talk, Dial Press, New York, 1974

Ball, Alan
American Beauty, Dream Works, 1999

Ball Carr, Elizabeth
Da Kine Talk: From Pidgin to Standard English in Hawaii, University Press of Hawaii, Honolulu, Hawaii, 1972

Bangs, Lester
Psychotic Reactions and Carburetor Dung, Serpent's Tail, London, 2001

Banis, Victor J.
Small Town Sex Today, Medco Books, Los Angeles, 1966

Banks, Carl J.
Banks Dictionary of the Black Ghetto Language, self published, Los Angeles, California, 1975

Barger, Ralph "Sonny"
Hell's Angel: The Life and Times of Sonny Barger and the Hell's Angels Motorcycle Club, William Morrow, New York, 2000

Barrett, Pat
Everybody Down There Hates Me: The Traumas and Dramas Inside the Incredible World of Professional Wrestling, Fleur Press, Gulf Breeze, Florida, 1990

Barth, Violet
Porno Films and the People who Make Them, Academy Press, San Diego, 1973

Beatty, Paul
Tuff, Anchor Books, New York, 2000

Beckerman, Marty
Death to All Cheerleaders, Infected Press, Anchorage, Alaska, 2000
Generation S.L.U.T. (Sexually Liberated Urban Teens), Pocket Books, New York, 2004

Bell, John D. et al.
Loosely Speaking: The Centennial Lexicon of Carleton Neologisms, Carleton College, Northfield, Minnesota, 1966
Loosely Speaking: A Lexicon of Carleton Neologisms (2nd Edition), Carleton College, Northfield, Minnesota, 1969

Bellisimo, Lou
The Bowler's Manual (2nd Edition), Prentice-Hall, Englewood Cliffs, New Jersey, 1969

Bellone, Ellen C. (Editor)
Dictionary of Slang, Delcastle Technical High School, Wilmington, Delaware, 1989

Bentley, William K. and James M. Corbett
Prison Slang: Words and Expressions Depicting Life Behind Bars, McFarland & Company, Jefferson, North Carolina, 1992

Berger, Gilda and Melvin
Drug Abuse A-Z, Enslow Publishers, Hillside, New Jersey, 1990

Bernard, Sidney
This Way to the Apocalypse: The 60s, Horizon Press, New York, 1969

Bernard, William
Jailbait: A Realistic Study of Juvenile Delinquency, Popular Library, New York, 1949

Bernhard, Sandra
Confessions of a Pretty Lady, Harper & Row, New York, 1988

Bibb, Porter
CB Bible, Dolphin Books, Garden City, New York, 1976

Bing, Leon
Do or Die, HarperCollins, New York, 1991

Birdiett, Sandra Combes
Dictionary of Cautionary Words and Phrases, University of Missouri, School of Journalism, Columbia, Missouri, 1989

Black, Shane
Lethal Weapon, Warner Brothers, 1987

Black, Sue
The Totally Awesome Val Guide, Price/Stern/Sloan, Los Angeles, California, 1982

Blair, John
The Illustrated Discography of Surf Music 1961 – 1965 (2nd Edition, Revised), Pierian Press, Ann Arbor, Michigan, 1985

Blake, James
The Joint, Doubleday & Company, New York, 1971

Blake, Roger
The American Dictionary of Sexual Terms, Century Publishing, Hollywood, California, 1964
Love Clubs, Inc., Century Books, Cleveland, 1967
The Stimulators: Swinging Set's Newest Rage, Century Books, Cleveland, Ohio, 1968
What You Always Wanted to Know about Porno-Movies* *but Were Afraid to Ask, Eros Publishing, Wilmington, Delaware, 1972

What You Always Wanted to Know about Porno-Shops* *but Were Afraid to Ask, Eros Publishing, Wilmingotn, Delaware, 1972

Blessitt, Arthur
Turned On To Jesus, Hawthorn Books, New York, 1971

Block, Francesca Lia
Dangerous Angels: The Weetzie Bat Books, HarperCollins, New York, 1998
I Was a Teenage Fairy, Joanna Cotler Books, New York, 2000

Block, Lawrence
The Affairs of Chip Harrison Omnibus, No Exit Press, Harpenden, Hertfordshire, U.K., 2001

Bloomquist, Edward R.
Marijuana, Glencoe Press, Beverly Hills, California, 1968
Marijuana: The Second Trip, Glencoe Press, Beverly Hills, California, 1971

Blowdryer, Jennifer
Modern English, Last Gasp, Berkeley, 1985
White Trash Debutante, Galhattan Press, Beverly Hills, California, 1997

Blue, Treasure E.
A Street Girl Named Desire, Ballantine Books, New York, 2007

Boe, Eugene (Compiler)
The Wit & Wisdom of Archie Bunker, Popular Library, New York, 1971

Bonanno, Joseph
A Man of Honor: The Autobiography of "The Boss of Bosses", Pocket Books, New York, 1984

Bond, Alison
The Glove Compartment Book, Stonesong Press, New York, 1979

Bonham, Frank
Viva Chicano, E.P. Dutton & Co., New York, 1970

Bosiljevac, T.L.
SEALs: UDT/SEAL Operations in Vietnam, Ivy Books, New York, 1991

Boulware, Jack
Sex American Style, Feral House, Venice, California, 1997

Boulware, Marcus Hanna
Jive and Slang of Students in Negro Colleges, Hampton, Virginia, 1947

Bouton, Jim and Eliot Asinof
Strike Zone, Viking, New York, 1994

Bowen, Robert O.
An Alaskan Dictionary, Nooshnik Press, Spenard, Alaska, 1965

Bowen, Thomas and Lydia Fish
The Longest Year: A Collection of Songs by Advisors and Civilians in the Vietnam War, Vietnam Veterans Oral History and Folklore Project, Buffalo, New York, 1990

Boyd, Malcolm
My Fellow Americans, Holt, Rinehart and Winston, New York, 1970

Boyer, Brian David
Prince of Thieves: The Memoirs of the World's Greatest Forger, Dial Press, New York, 1975

Boyington, Gregory "Pappy" et al.
Baa Baa Black Sheep, G.P. Putnam's Sons, New York, 1958

Boyne, Walter J. and Steven L. Thompson
The Wild Blue, Ivy Books, New York, 1986

Bradley, Matt
Queer St. U.S.A., Century Books, Los Angeles, California, 1965

Bradley, William J.
CB Fact Book and Language Dictionary, DMR Publications, Milwaukee, Wisconsin, 1977

Braithwaite, Freddy, Fred
Fresh Fly Flavor: Words and Phrases of the Hip-Hop Generation, Longmeadow, Stamford, Connecticut

Braly, Malcolm
It's Cold Out There, Fawcett, Greenwich, Connecticut, 1966
On the Yard, Little, Brown and Co., Boston, 1967
Shake Him Till He Rattles, Belmont Books, New York, 1971
Felony Tank, Pocket Books, New York, 1976
False Starts: A Memoir of San Quentin and Other Prisons, Penguin Books, New York, 1977
The Protector, Jove Publications, New York, 1979

Brandonstiel, Mark
Breaker, Breaker, 10-4: A Complete Guide to CB Radio, Grosset & Dunlap, New York, 1976

Branson, Helen P.
Gay Bar, Pan-Graphic Press, San Francisco, 1957

Brashler, William
City Dogs, Signet, New York, 1977

Brathwaithe, J. Ashton
Niggers – This is Canada, 21st Century Books, Toronto, Ontario, 1971

Breedlove, Lynn
Godspeed, St. Martin's Griffin, New York, 2003

Breedlove, William and Jerrye
Swap Clubs: A Study in Contemporary Sexual Mores, Sherbourne Press, Los Angeles, 1964

Brehan, Delle
Kicks is Kicks, Holloway House, Los Angeles, 1970

Brewer, Craig
Hustle and Flow, Paramount Pictures, 2004

Briggs, Joe Bob
Joe Bob Goes to the Drive-in, Delacorte Press, New York, 1987

Brinkley, William
Don't Go Near The Water, Signet, New York, 1957

Bronsteen, Ruth
The Hippy's Handbook, Canyon Book Company, New York, 1967

Brossard, Chandler
Who Walks in Darkness, Lancer Books, New York, 1952

Brown, Cecil
The Life & Loves of Mr. Jiveass Nigger, Farrar, Straus & Giroux, New York, 1969

Brown, Claude
Manchild in the Promised Land, Signet Books, New York, 1966

Brown, Geoff
I Want What I Want, G.P. Putnam's Sons, New York, 1966

Brown, H. Rap
Die Nigger Die!, Dial Press, New York, 1969

Brown, Joe David
Sex in the '60s: A Candid Look at the Age of Mini-Morals, Time Life Books, New York, 1968

Brown, Joe David (Editor)
The Hippies, Time Incorporated, New York, 1967

Brown, Larry
Dirty Work, Vintage Books, New York, 1989

Brownstein, Bill
Sex Carnival, ECW Press, Toronto, 2000

Bruce, Lenny
How to Talk Dirty and Influence People, Playboy Press, Chicago, 1965
The Essential Lenny Bruce, Bell Publishing, New York, 1970
The Unpublished Lenny Bruce, Running Press, Philadelphia, 1984

Bryan, Frank
Tackle Tenpin Bowling This Way, Stanley Paul, London, 1962

Bryan, Helen
Inside, Houghton Mifflin Company, Boston, 1953

Buckhout, Robert (Editor)
Toward Social Change: A Handbook for Those Who Will, Harper & Row, New York, 1971

Buckwalter, Len et al.
CB Radio: A Complete Guide, Grosset & Dunlap, New York, 1976

Buffett, Jimmy
Tales from Margaritaville, Ballantine Books, New York, 1993

Burke, James Lee
Last Car to Elysian Fields, Pocket Star Books, New York, 2004
The Lost Get-Back Boogie, Pocket Star Books, New York, 2006

Burks, John and Jerry Hopkins
Groupies and Other Girls, Bantam, New York, 1970

Burley, Dan
Diggeth Thou? Burley, Cross & Co., Chicago, 1959

Burns, Richard R.
Pathfinder: First In, Last Out, Ballantine Books, New York, 2002

Burroughs, William
Junkie, Ace Books, New York, 1953
Naked Lunch, Grove Press, New York, 1966 (1957)
Letters to Allen Ginsberg 1953–1957, Full Court Press, New York, 1982

Burt, Rob
Surf City, Drag City, Blandford Press, Poole, Dorset, U.K., 1986

Byrne, Robert
McGoorty: The Story of a Billiard Bum, Lyle Stuart, Secaucus, New Jersey, 1972

Byrnes, Edd
Way Out With Kookie, Warner Brothers, 1959

California Senate Subcommittee on Civil Disorder
Report to the Senate, State of California, Sacramento, 1975

Camhi, Morrie and James Harris
The Prison Experience ("A Convict's Dictionary"), Tuttle-IPC, Rutland, Vermont, 1989

Campbell, Robert
Junkyard Dog, Signet, New York, 1986
Alice in La-La Land, Pocket Books, New York, 1987
In La-La Land We Trust, Mysterious Press, New York, 1987
Juice, Pocket Books, New York, 1988
Nibbled to Death by Ducks, Pocket Books, New York, 1990
In a Pig's Eye, Pocket Books, New York, 1991
Sweet La-La Land, Pocket Books, New York, 1991
Boneyards, Pocket Books, New York, 1992

Cann, John
The Stunt Guide, Paul Flatterey Productions, Los Angeles

Cannell, Stephen J.
Big Con, William Morrow, New York, 1997
The Tin Collectors, St. Martin's, New York, 2002
White Sister, St. Martin's Paperbacks, New York, 2007

Cannon, Curt
I Like 'Em Tough, Fawcett, Greenwich, Connecticut, 1958

Capitol Records
Hot Rod Jargon, Capitol Records, Los Angeles, California, 1963

Capote, Truman
Breakfast at Tiffany's, Vintage Books, New York, 1958

Cappetta, Gary Michael
Bodyslams! Memoirs of a Wrestling Pitchman, Little Bro', Ltd., Jackson, New Jersey, 2000

Caputo, Philip
A Rumor of War, Ballantine Books, New York, 1977

Cardoso, Bill
The Maltese Sangweech and Other Heroes, Atheneum, New York, 1984

Cardoza, Avery
The Basics of Sports Betting, Gambling Research Institute, New York, 1991
Winning Casino Blackjack for the Non-Counter, Gambling Research Institute, New York, 1992

Cardozo-Freeman, Inez
The Joint: Language and Culture in a Maximum Security Prison, Charles C. Thomas, Springfield, Illinois, 1984

Carlisle, Norman
The Modern Wonder Book of Trains and Railroading, John C. Winston, Philadelphia, Pennsylvania, 1946

Carmichael, Stokely and Charles V. Hamilton
Black Power: The Politics of Liberation in America, Vintage Books, New York, 1967

Carpenter Barker, George
Pachuco: An American-Spanish Argot and Its Social Functions in Tucson, Arizona, University of Arizona Press, Tucson, Arizona, 1958

Carroll, Gerrt
North S*A*R, Pocket Books, New York, 1991

Carroll, Jim
Forced Entries: The Downtown Diaries 1971–1973, Penguin Books, New York, 1987

Carroll, Nick
The Next Wave: The World of Surfing, Abbeyville Press, New York, 1991

Carroll, Sidney and Robert Rossen
The Hustler, 20th Century Fox, 1961

Cassady, Carolyn
Heart Break, Creative Arts Books, Berkeley, 1978

Cassady, Neal
The First Third and Other Chronicles, City Lights, San Francisco, 1981
Grace Beats Karma: Letters from Prison 1958–1960, Blast Books, New York, 1993

Cassady, Neal (edited by Dave Moore)
Neal Cassady Collected Letters 1944-1967, Penguin, New York, 2004

Cassorla, Albert
The Skateboarder's Bible, Running Press, Philadelphia, 1976

Castleman, Craig
Getting Up: Subway Graffiti in New York, MIT Press, Cambridge, Massachusetts, 1982

Catan, Omero C.
Secrets of Shuffleboard Strategy, Great Outdoors Publishing, Fort Lauderdale, Florida, 1967

Cavanaugh, Christopher
AA to Z: Addictionary of the 12-Step Culture, Doubleday, New York, 1998

CB Roadrunner
CB Lingo Handbook, Self-published, Charlotte, North Carolina, 1976

Chambers, Larry
Recondo: LRRPs in the 101st Airborne, Ivy Books, New York, 1992

Chandler, David Leon
Brothers in Blood: The Rise of the Criminal Brotherhoods, E. P. Dutton & Co., New York, 1975

Chandler, Raymond
The Little Sister, Pocket Books, New York, 1951
The Long Goodbye, Pocket Books, New York, 1955
Playback, Pocket Books, New York, 1960
Farewell My Lovely, Folio Books, 1989

Chase, David
The Sopranos: Selected Scripts from Three Seasons, Warner Books, New York, 2002

Chein, Isidor
The Road to H: Narcotics, Delinquency, and Social Policy, Basic Books, New York, 1964

Chessman, Caryl
Cell 2456 Death Row: A Condemned Man's Own Story, Carroll & Graf, New York, 2006

Christopher, Tom
Neal Cassady Volume One, Tom Christopher, Vashon, Washington, 1995
Neal Cassady Volume Two, Tom Christopher, Vashon, Washington, 1998

Cimino, Michael and Deric Washburn
The Deer Hunter, Universal Pictures, 1978

Ciresi, Rita
Pink Slip, Dell Publishing, New York, 1999

Claerbaut, David
Black Jargon in White America, William B. Eerdmans, Grand Rapids, Michigan, 1972

Clancy, Tom with General Fred Franks
Into the Storm: A Study in Command, G. P. Putnam's Sons, New York, 1991

Clark, Dick
To Goof or Not to Goof, Fawcett Publications, Greenwich, Connecticut, 1963

Clark, Gregory
Words of the Vietnam War: The Slang, Jargon, Abbreviations, Acronyms, Nomenclature, Nicknames, Pseudonyms, Slogans, Specs, Euphemisms, Double-talk, Chants, and Names and Places of the Era of United States Involvement in Vietnam, McFarland & Company, Inc., Jefferson, North Carolina, 1990

Clark, Kenneth B.
Dark Ghetto: Dilemmas of Social Power, Harper & Row, New York, 1965

Clark, Larry and Harmony Korine
Kids, Shining Excalibur Films, 1995

Clark, Thomas L.
The Dictionary of Gambling and Gaming, Lexik House Publishers, Cold Springs, New York, 1987

Clause, Frank and Patty McBride
Strike! The Complete Handbook of Junior Bowling, Scholastic Book Services, New York, 1964

Claussen, Jim
Keno Handbook, Gamblers Book Club Press, Las Vegas, 1982

Cleaver, Eldridge
Soul on Ice, Dell Publishing, New York, 1968

Cline, Sally
Couples: Scene From the Inside, Little, Brown and Co., London, 1998

Cloud, Cam
The Little Book of Acid, Ronin Publishing, Berkeley, California, 1999

Coen, Joel and Ethan
Raising Arizona, 20th Century Fox, 1987
Fargo, Gramercy Pictures, 1996
The Big Lebowski, Gramercy Pictures, 1998

Cohen, Daniel
Wrestling Renegades: An In-Depth Look at Today's Superstars of Pro Wrestling, Archway Paperbacks, New York, 1999

Cohen, Daniel and Susan
Wrestling Superstars II, Archway Paperbacks, New York, 1986

Cohen, Leonard
Beautiful Losers, Bantam Books, New York, 1967 (1966)

Cohn, Nik and Norman Wexler
Saturday Night Fever, Paramount Pictures, 1977

Coleman, J.D.
Incursion, St. Martin's Press, New York, 1991

Colendich, George
The Ding Repair Scriptures: The Complete Guide to Surfboard Repair, Village Green Publications, Soquel, California, 1986

Collans, Dev with Stewart Sterling
I Was a House Detective, Pyramid Books, New York, 1954

Collins, H. Craig
Street Gangs: Profiles for Police, City of New York Police Department, New York, 1979

Collins, Michael
Minnesota Strip, Donald L. Fine, New York, 1987

Condon, Richard
Prizzi's Honor, Berkley Books, New York, 1983
Prizzi's Family, G. P. Putnam's Sons, New York, 1986
Prizzi's Money, Crown Publishers, New York, 1994

Conklin, Les
Payday at the Races, Wilshire Book Company, North Hollywood, California, 1974

Conover, Ted
Newjack: Guarding Sing Sing, Random House, New York, 2000

Conway, John
Love in Suburbia, Monarch Books, Derby, Connecticut, 1964
Surfing, Stackpole Books, Harrisburg, Pennsylvania, 1988

Cooper, Jr., Clarence
The Scene, Crest Giant, New York, 1961 (1960)
The Farm, Payback Press, Edinburgh, 1996 (1967)
Black, Payback Press, Edinburgh, 1998 (1963)

Cooper, Morton
High School Confidential, Avon Books, New York, 1958

Coppage, Keith
Roller Derby to Rollerjam, Squarebooks, Santa Rosa, California, 1999

Corder, E.M.
Citizens Band, Pocket Books, New York, 1977

Corey, Mary and Victoria Westermark
Fer Shurr! How to be a Valley Girl, Bantam Books, New York, 1982

Cory, Donald Webster
The Lesbian in America, Citadel Press, New York, 1964

Cory, Donald Webster and John P. LeRoy
The Homosexual and His Society: A View from Within, The Citadel Press, New York, 1963

Cosmes, Juan Carmel
Memoirs of a Whoremaster, Century Books, Cleveland, 1969

Covington, Carol
A Glossary of Teenage Terms, Macy's, Hillsdale, California, 1965

Cox, Alex
Repo Man, Universal Pictures, 1984

Coyote, Peter
Sleeping Where I Fall, Counterpoint, Washington D.C., 1998

Crais, Robert
L.A. Requiem, Orion Books, London, 2000 (1999)

Cralle, Trevor
The Surfin'ary: A Dictionary of Surfing Terms and Surfspeak, Ten Speed Press, Berkeley, California, 1991

Crouse, Timothy
The Boys on the Bus, Random House, New York, 1973

Crowe, Cameron
Fast Times at Ridgemont High, MCA/Universal Pictures, 1982
Jerry Maguire, TriStar Pictures, 1996

Crowley, Mart
The Boys in the Band, Dell Publishing, New York, 1970 (1968)

Cruise, T.E.
Wings of Gold III, Popular Library, New York, 1989

Crumlish, Christian
The Internet Dictionary, Sybex Inc., San Francisco, 1995

Csicsery, George Paul (Editor)
The Sex Industry, New American Library, New York, 1973

d'Arcangelo, Angelo
The Homosexual Handbook, Ophelia Press, New York, 1969 (1968)

Dahlskog, Helen (Editor)
A Dictionary of Contemporary and Colloquial Usage, Avenel Books, New York, 1972

Daigon, Arthur and Ronald T. LaConte
dig u.s.a., Bantam Books, New York, 1970

Dalecki, Linden
Kid B, Graphia, Boston, 2006

Dalton, Michael
Blackjack: A Professional Reference, Spur of the Moment Publishing, Merritt Island, Florida, 1991

Danesi, Marcel
Cool: The Signs and Meanings of Adolescence, University of Toronto Press, Toronto, 1994

Davis, Bill
Jawjacking: The Complete CB Dictionary, self-published, Canoga Park, California, 1977

Davis, Eric
The Slick Boys, Simon & Schuster, New York, 1998

de Laclos, Choderlos and Roger Kumble
Cruel Intentions, Columbia Pictures, 1999

De Sola, Ralph
Crime Dictionary, Facts on File, New York, 1982

Dean, Miss
The Slang Dictionary (Hawthorne High School), self-published, Hawthorne, California, 1965

deCoy, Robert
The Nigger Bible, Holloway House, Los Angeles, 1967

Del Vecchio, John
The 13th Valley, Bantam Books, New York, 1982

Delacoste, Frederique and Priscilla Alexander (Editors)
Sex Work: Writings by Women in the Sex Industry, Cleis Press, Pittsburgh, 1987

Demaris, Ovid
Captive City, Pocket Books, New York, 1970
The Last Mafioso: "Jimmy the Weasel" Fratianno, Bantam Books, New York, 1981

Department of the Army
Staff Officer's Guidebook (5th Edition), Department of the Army, Washington D.C., 1986

Des Barres, Pamela
I'm With the Band: Confessions of a Groupie, Jove Books, New York, 1988

Dew, Josie
The Sun In My Eyes, Little, Brown and Co., London, 2001

Didion, Joan
The White Album, Pocket Books, New York, 1980
Slouching Towards Bethlehem, Washington Square Press, New York, 1981 (1968)

Dilallo, Kevin
The Unofficial Gay Manual: Living the Lifestyle, Main Street Books, New York, 1994

Dillon-Malone, Aubrey
I Was A Fugitive From A Hollywood Trivia Factory, Prion, London, 1999

Dills, Lanie
The Official CB Slanguage Language Dictionary, Louis J. Martin, New York, 1976

Dinkel, John
The Road and Track Illustrated Auto Dictionary, W.W. Norton, New York, 1977

Divale, William Tulio
I Lived Inside the Campus Revolution, Cowles Book Company, New York, 1970

Donleavy, J.P.
The Ginger Man, Berkley Publishing, New York, 1958

Donovan, David
Once a Warrior King: Memories of an Officer in Vietnam, Ballantine Books, New York, 1986

Donovan, Vance
High Rider, Paperback Library, New York, 1969

Doogan, Mike
How to Speak Alaskan, Epicenter Press, Seattle, Washington, 1993

Dowst, Robert Saunders and Jay Craig
Playing the Races: A Guide to the American Tracks, Dodd, Mead & Company, New York, 1960

Draigh, David
Behind the Screen, Abbeville Press, New York, 1988

Duncan, Donald
The New Legions, Random House, New York, 1967

Dunhill, Allan S. and Roger Blake
The Group Sex Kick, Ambassador Books, Cleveland, Ohio, 1968

Durst, Albert Lavada
The Jives of Dr. Hepcat, Austin History Center, Austin, Texas, 1953

Dynes, Wayne
Homolexis: A Historical and Cultural Lexicon of Homosexuality, Gay Academic Union, New York, 1985

Earley, Pete
The Hot House: Life Inside Leavenworth Prison, Bantam Books, New York, 1992

Eddy, Chuck
Stairway to Hell: The 500 Best Heavy Metal Albums in the Universe, Harmony Books, New York, 1991

Editors of Elementary Electronics
Dictionary of CB Lingo, Davis Publications, New York, 1976

Edmonds, I.G.
Drag Racing for Beginners, Bobbs-Merrill, Indianapolis, 1972

Edwards, John (Editor)
Auto Dictionary, HP Books, Los Angeles, 1993

Elfman, Bradley
Breakdancing, Avon Books, New York, 1984

Ellis, Bret Easton
Less Than Zero, Vintage Books, New York, 1998 (1985)

Ellison, Ralph
Invisible Man, Vintage Books, New York, 1995 (1947)

Ellroy, James
Brown's Requiem, Avon Books, New York, 1981
American Tabloid, Ballantine Books, New York, 1996
L. A. Noir: The Lloyd Hopkins Novels (Blood on the Moon; Because the Night; Suicide Hill), Arrow Books, London, 1997
Hollywood Nocturnes, Delta Books, New York, 1998
White Jazz, Vintage Books, New York, 2001

Ellson, Hal
The Golden Spike, Ballantine Books, New York, 1952

Summer Street, Ballantine Books, New York, 1953
Tomboy, Bantam Books, New York, 1965

Elting, Mary
Trucks at Work, Garden City Publishing, Garden City, New York, 1946

Engel, Lyle Kenyon
The Dodge Book of Performance Cars, Pocket Books, New York, 1967
The Complete Book of Fuel and Gas Dragsters, Four Winds Press, New York, 1968

Ephorn, Nora, David S. Ward and Jeff Arch
When Harry Met Sally, Columbia Pictures, 1989
Sleepless in Seattle, TriStar Pictures, 1993

Epstein, Rachel S. and Nina Liebman
Biz Speak: A Dictionary of Business Terms, Slang and Jargon, Franklin Watts, New York, 1986

Esch, Natasha
Wilhelmina's Modeling and Acting Dictionary, Career Press, Hawthorne, New Jersey, 1994

Eszterhas, Joe
Charlie Simpson's Apocalypse, Random House, New York, 1973
Basic Instinct, TriStar Pictures, 1992

Ethell, Jeffrey and Alfred Price
One Day in a Long War: May 10, 1972, Air War, North Vietnam, Random House, New York, 1989

Evanovich, Janet
Seven Up, Headline, London, 2001

Everhart, Jim
CB Slanguage Illustrated, Centennial Press, Lincoln, Nebraska, 1976

Fabbro, Mike
Snowboarding: The Ultimate Free Ride, McClelland & Stewart, Toronto, 1996

Fagans, Chris and David Guzman
A Guide to Craps Lingo, self-published, Burlington, Iowa, 1999

Fahey, Tom
net.speak: the internet dictionary, Hayden Books, Indianapolis, Indiana, 1994

Fahs, John
Cigarette Confidential: The Unfiltered Truth About the Ultimate Addiction, Berkley Books, New York, 1996

Fair, Erik
California Thrill Sports, Foghorn Press, San Francisco, 1992

Farina, Richard
Been Down So Long It Looks Like Up To Me, Dell Publishing, New York, 1966
Long Time Coming and A Long Time Gone, Dell, New York, 1969

Farnsworth, Ross N. and Frank Brimhall
Let's Do Golf! Games that Make Golf Fun, self-published, Mesa, Arizona, 1992

Farrell, James T.
Saturday Night and Other Stories, Signet Books, New York, 1950
French Girls are Vicious and Other Stories, Signet Books, New York, 1956

Farrelly, Midget and Craig McGregor
The Surfing Life, Arco Publishing, New York, 1967

Fats, Minnesota (Rudolph Wanderone) with Tom Fox
The Bank Shot and Other Great Robberies, Playboy Press, Chicago, 1966

Fensch, Thomas
Smokeys, Truckers, CB Radios & You, Fawcett Publications, Greenwich, Connecticut, 1976

Fenton, Peter
Eyeing the Flash: The Education of a Carnival Con Artist, Simon & Schuster, New York, 2005

Ferrara, Abel and Zoe Lund et al.
The Bad Lieutenant, Aries Films, 1992

Fessler, Jeff
When Drag Is Not a Car Race: An Irreverent Dictionary of Over 400 Gay and Lesbian Words and Phrases, Fireside Books, New York, 1997

Fettamen, Ann
Trashing, Straight Arrow Books, San Francisco, 1970

Finn, Elizabeth
Drugs in the Tenderloin, Central City Multi-Service Center, San Francisco, 1967

Fitzgerald, Frances
Fire in the Lake, Little, Brown and Co., Boston, 1972

Fleischhauer, Carl
A Glossary of Army Slang, unpublished manuscript in the Western Historical Manuscript Collection, Columbia, Missouri, 1968

Fleisher, Mark S.
Beggars & Thieves: Lives of Urban Street Criminals, University of Wisconsin Press, Madison, Wiscsonsin, 1995

Flood, David
Kayfabe: The Secret World of Professional Wrestling, Gambit Publishing, Chicago, 2000

Flood, Wayne
Jason's Authentic Dictionary of CB Slang (3rd Edition), Jason Press, Fort Worth, Texas, 1976

Flynt, Larry
An Unseemly Man, Dove Books, Los Angeles, 1996

Folb, Edith A.
Running Down Some Lines: The Language and Culture of Black Teenagers, Harvard University Press, Cambridge, Massachusetts, 1980

Foley, Mick
Mankind: Have a Nice Day, Regan Books, New York, 1999

Folger, John
Black on White: A Study of Miscegenation in America, Viceroy Books, Canoga Park, California, 1967

Fonda, Peter
Easy Rider, Signet, New York, 1969

Fontaine, Joan
Dictionary of Black Slang (McClymond's High School, Oakland, California), unpublished manuscript in the Western Historical Manuscript Collection, Columbia, Missouri, 1968

Foss, Rene
Around the World in a Bad Mood: Confessions of a Flight Attendant, Hyperion, New York, 2002

Fowler, Jon
Anatomy of Wife-Swapping, Pad Library, Aqoura, California, 1967

Fox, Frank
A Beginner's Guide to Zen and the Art of Windsurfing, Amberco Press, Berkeley, California, 1985

Foxman, Sherri
Classified Love: A Guide to the Personals, McGraw-Hill, New York, 1982

Frank, Richard
A Study of Sex in Prison, Gallery Press, Los Angeles, California, 1973

Franken, Al
The Truth with Jokes, Penguin, London, 2005

Fredericks, Vic
Who's Who in Rock 'n Roll, Frederick Fell Inc., New York, 1958

Freeman, Bob and Barbara
Wanta Bet? A Study of the Pari-Mutuels System in the United States, self-published, 1982

Freeman, David
U.S. Grant in the City and Other True Stories of Jugglers and Pluggers, Swatters and Whores, Viking Press, New York, 1971

Freeman, Kerry A.
Chilton's CB Handbook, Chilton Book Company, Radnor, Pennsylvania, 1977

Freeman, Marlene
Alcatraz: No Good for Nobody, Smith Novelty Company, San Francisco, 1983

Friedman, Josh Alan
Tales of Times Square, Feral House, Portland, Oregon, 1993
When Sex Was Dirty, Feral House, Los Angeles, 2005

Friedman, Kinky
Steppin' on a Rainbow, Faber and Faber, London, 2001

Friss, J. R.
A Dictionary of Teenage Slang (Mt. Diablo High), self-published, Walnut Creek, California, 1964

Froner, Geoffrey
Digging for Diamonds: A Lexicon of Street Slang for Drugs and Sex, self-published, San Francisco, 1989

Fry, Monroe
Sex, Vice and Business, Ballantine Books, New York, 1959

Funches, Tracy and Rob Marriott
Pimpnosis, Harper Entertainment, New York, 2002

Funtes, Dagoberto and Jose A. Lopez
Barrio Language Dictionary: First Dictionary of Calo, El Barrio Publications, La Puente, California, 1974

Gaghan, Stephen
Traffic, USA Films, 2000

Gagnon, John H. and William Simon
The Sexual Scene (2nd Edition), Transaction Books, New Brunswick, New Jersey, 1973

Garcia, Elena
A Beginner's Guide to Zen and the Art of Snowboarding, Amberco Press, Berkeley, California, 1990

Garcia, Frank
Marked Cards and Loaded Dice, Bramhall House, New York, 1962

Gardner, Leonard
Fat City, Vintage Books, New York, 1986

Garrett, R.C. et al.
The Coke Book: The Complete Reference to the Uses and Abuses of Cocaine, Berkley Books, New York, 1984

Gaskin, Stephen
Heat Beatnik: This is the Farm Book, The Book Publishing Company, Summertown, Tennessee, 1974
Amazing Dope Tales and Haight Street Flashbacks, Book Publishing Company, Summertown, Tennessee, 1980

Gerber, Jack
The Connection, Grove Press, New York, 1960

Giallombardo, Rose
Society of Women: A Study of a Woman's Prison, John Wiley & Sons, New York, 1966

Giblo, Helen
Footlights, Fistfights and Femmes: The Jimmy Lake Story, Vantage Press, New York, 1957

Gifford, Barry (Editor)
As Ever: The Collected Correspondence of Allen Ginsberg and Neal Cassady, Creative Arts Book Company, Berkeley, California, 1977

Gilbert, Edwin
The Hot and the Cool, Popular Library, New York, 1954

Gilbey, John F.
Western Boxing and World Wrestling, North Atlantic Books, Berkeley, California, 1993

Gimenez, John
Up Tight!, Word Books, Waco, Texas, 1967

Glenn, Jim
Programmed Poker: The Inside System for Winning, Rutledge Press, New York, 1981

Glessing, Robert J.
The Underground Press in America, Indiana University Press, Bloomington, Indiana, 1970

Glover, Paul (Technical Advisor)
Words from the House of the Dead: Prison Writings from Soledad, Crossing Press, Trumansburg, New York, 1974

Goines, Donald
Dopefiend, Holloway House, Los Angeles, 1971
Whoreson, Holloway House, Los Angeles, 1972
White Man's Justice, Black Man's Grief, Holloway House, Los Angeles, 1973
Cry Revenge, Holloway House, Los Angeles, 1974
Daddy Cool, Holloway House, Los Angeles, 1974
Never Die Alone, Holloway House, Los Angeles, 1974
Swamp Man, Holloway House, Los Angeles, 1974
Inner City Hoodlum, Holloway House, Los Angeles, 1975
Kenyatta's Last Hit, Holloway House, Los Angeles, 1975
Black Gangster, Holloway House, Los Angeles, California, 1977
Crime Partners, Holloway House, Los Angeles, 1978

Golden, Jeffrey
Watermelon Summer, J.B. Lippincott, Philadelphia, 1971

Goldin, Hyam E. et al.
Dictionary of American Underworld Lingo, Twayne Publishers, New York, 1950

Goldman, Albert
Freak Show, Atheneum, New York, 1971

Gonzales, Babs
Be-Bop Dictionary and History of its Famous Stars, Arlain Publishing, New York, 1949
I Paid My Dues, Expubidence Publishing, East Orange, New Jersey, 1967
Movin' On Down De Line, Expubidence Publishing, Newark, New Jersey, 1975

Goodman, Alexander
Summer on Fire Island, Guild Press, Washington D.C., 1968

Gordon, Dale
The Dominion Sex Dictionary, Van Nuys, California, 1967

Gordon, Roger
Hollywood's Sexual Underground, Medco Books, Los Angeles, California, 1966

Goren, Charles H.
Goren's Modern Backgammon Complete, Doubleday, New York, 1974

Gosch, Martin and Richard Hammer
The Last Testament of Lucky Luciano, Dell Books, New York, 1975

Goshgarian, Gary (Editor)
Exploring Language, Little, Brown and Co., Boston, Massachusetts, 1986

Gould, Chester
Dick Tracy Meets the Night Crawler, Whitman Publishing, Racine, Wisconsin, 1945

Gould, John
Maine Lingo: Boiled Owls, Billdads and Wazzats, Down East Magazine, Camden, Maine, 1975

Goulden, Joseph C.
Korea: The Untold Story of the War, Times Books, New York, 1982

Gover, Robert
One Hundred Dollar Misunderstanding, Grove Press, New York, 1961
Here Goes Kitten, Dell Publishing, New York, 1965 (1964)
Poorboy at the Party, Pocket Books, New York, 1967
JC Saves, Pocket Books, New York, 1969

Graziano, Rocky with Rowland Barber
Somebody Up There Likes Me, Pocket Books, New York, 1956

Greene, Carolyn
70 Soul Secrets of Sapphire, Sapphire Publishing Company, San Francisco, 1973

Greene, Gerald and Caroline
S-M: The Last Taboo, Grove Press, New York, 1973

Greenwald, Harold
The Call Girl: A Social Psychological Investigation, Decision Books, San Diego, California, 1978

Gregory, David
Flesh Seller, Art Enterprises, Hollywood, 1962

Gregory, Dick with Robert Lipsyte
Nigger: An Autobiography, Pocket Books, New York, 1968

Grey, Harry
The Hoods, Signet Books, New York, 1959

Griff, Ricky and Ron Church
Surfer in Hawaii: A Guide to Surfing in the Hawaiian Islands, John Severson Publications, Dana Point, California, 1963

Griffiths, Niall
Grits, Vintage Books, London, 2000

Griffon, Jules
Orgies American Style, Triumph-Fact Books, Van Nuys, California, 1967

Grissim, John
Pure Stoke, Harper Collins, New York, 1982 (1980)

Grogan, Emmett
Final Score, Holt, Rinehart and Winston, New York, 1976

Guest, Christopher and Michael McKean
This is Spinal Tap, Embassy Pictures Corporation, 1984

Gutman, Bill
Strange and Amazing Wrestling Stories, Archway Paperbacks, New York, 1986

Hackett, Buddy
The Truth About Golf and Other Lies, Doubleday, New York, 1968

Hackworth, David H.
About Face, Simon & Schuster, New York, 1989

Haenigsen, Harry
Jive's Like That: Being the Life and Times of Our Bill, Procyon Press, New York, 1947

Hagerman, R.J.
Husband and Wife Swapping, Medco Books, Los Angeles, 1967

Halacy, D.S.
Surfer!, Macmillan, New York, 1965

Halberstadt, Hans
USCB: Always Ready, Presidio Press, Novato, California, 1986
Airborne: Assault from the Sky, Presidio Press, Novato, California, 1988
Green Berets: Unconventional Warriors, Berkley Books, New York, 1989

Hale, Constance
Wired Style: Principles of English Usage in the Digital Age, Hardwired, San Francisco, 1996

Hall, Susan
Gentleman of Leisure: A Year in the Life of a Pimp, Signet Books, New York, 1972
Ladies of the Night, Trident Press, New York, 1973

Hamilton, Charles
Men of the Underworld, Macmillan, New York, 1952

Harper, James
Homo Laws in All 50 States, Publishers Export Company, San Diego, California, 1968

Harris, Frank
The Swinging Moderns, privately printed, Canoga Park, California, 1967

Harris, Sara and Lucy Freeman
The Lords of Hell, Dell Books, New York, 1967

Harris, Troy
A Booklet of Criminal Argot, Cant and Jargon, self-published, Somerset, Ohio, 1976

Hart, David
First Air Cavalry Division Vietnam Dictionary, Troop Quartermaster, Maple Grove, Minnesota, 2004

Harvey, Reginald
Park Beat, Castle Books, New York, 1959

Hasford, Gustav and Michael Herr
Full Metal Jacket, Warner Brothers, 1987

Haskins, James
Street Gangs Yesterday and Today, Hastings House, New York, 1974
The Story of Hip-Hop, Penguin, London, 2002

Hawkins, Jack
Chopper One #2: Tunnel Warriors, Ivy Books, New York, 1987

Hawkins, Odie
Ghetto Sketches, Holloway House, Los Angeles, 1972
Chicago Hustle, Holloway House, Los Angeles, 1977
Black Casanova, Holloway House, Los Angeles, 1984
The Busting Out of an Ordinary Man, Holloway House, Los Angeles, 1985
Scars and Memories, Holloway House, Los Angeles, 1987
Great Lawd Buddha, Holloway House, Los Angeles, 1990
The Life and Times of Chester Simmons, Holloway House, Los Angeles, 1991
Black Chicago, Holloway House, Los Angeles, 1992
Amazing Grace and Other States of Mind, Holloway House, Los Angeles, California, 1993
Midnight, Holloway House, Los Angeles, 1995

Hayano, David M.
Poker Faces: The Life and Work of Professional Card Players, University of California Press, Berkeley, California, 1982

Haywood, Charles F. et al.
Yankee Dictionary: A Compendium of Useful and Entertaining Expressions Indigenous to New England, Jackson & Phillips, Inc., Lynn, Massachusetts, 1963

Heard, Nathan
Howard Street, Signet Books, New York, 1970 (1968)
To Reach a Dream, Signet, New York, 1973
A Cold Fire Burning, Simon and Schuster, New York, 1974

Heckerling, Amy
Clueless, Paramount Pictures, 1995

Heenan, Bobby
Bobby the Brain: Wrestling's Bad Boy Tells All, Triumph Books, Chicago, 2002

Heggen, Thomas
Mister Roberts, Houghton Mifflin, Boston, 1946

Heikkinen, Carol
Empire Records, Warner Brothers, 1995

Heimer, Mel
Inside Racing: An Introduction to the Sport of Kings, Van Nosrand, New York, 1967

Heinemann, Larry
Close Quarters, Warner Books, New York, 1983 (1977)
Paco's Story, Farrar Straus Giroux, New York, 1986

Hemmings, Fred
Surfing: Hawaii's Gift to the World of Sports, Grosset & Dunlap, New York, 1977

Henderson, M. Allen
How Con Games Work, Carol Publishing Group, New York, 1994 (1985)

Henry, George
Sex Variants, Paul B. Hoeber, Inc., New York, 1941

Hentoff, Nat
I'm Really Dragged but Nothing Gets Me Down, Simon & Schuster, New York, 1968
Jazz Country, Dell Publishing, New York, 1968

Herbert, Anthony B. with James T. Wooten
Soldier, Holt, Rinehart and Wilson, New York, 1973

Herr, Michael
Dispatches, Alfred A. Knopf, New York, 1977

Hester, Fred
Slang on the 40 Acres, unpublished manuscript, Western Historial Manuscript Collection, Columbia, Missouri, 1968

Hiaasen, Carl
Tourist Season, Warner Books, New York, 1987
Skin Tight, G. P. Putnam's Sons, New York, 1989
Native Tongue, Ballantine Publishing, New York, 1992
Strip Tease, Warner Books, New York, 1994
Lucky You, Pan Books, London, 1998
Sick Puppy, Pan Books, London, 2001
Basket Case, Warner Books, New York, 2003
Double Whammy, Warner Books, New York, 2003
Nature Girl, Alfred A. Knopf, New York, 2006
Skinny Dip, Warner Books, New York, 2006

Higdon, Hal
Finding the Groove, G.P. Putnam's Sons, New York, 1973

Higgins, George V.
The Friends of Eddie Coyle, Bantam Books, New York, 1973
Cogan's Trade, Alfred A. Knopf, New York, 1974
The Judgment of Deke Hunter, Ballantine Books, New York, 1978
The Rat on Fire, Alfred A. Knopf, New York, 1981
Penance for Jerry Kennedy, Abacus, London, 1986
Kennedy for the Defense, Henry Holt and Company, New York, 1995

Hiken, Nat
Sergeant Bilko, Ballantine Books, New York, 1957

Hilderbrant, Ethan
Prison Slang, Allusion Entertainment, Port Arthur, Texas, 1998

Hill, Henry with Byron Schreckengost
A Good Fella's Guide to New York, Three Rivers Press, New York, 2003

Himes, Chester
The Primitive, Signet Books, New York, 1955
Pinktoes, Dell, New York, 1966
Cast the First Stone, Signet Books, New York, 1972
Come Back Charleston Blue, G.P. Putnam's Sons, New York, 1972
If He Hollers Let Him Go, Thunder's Mouth Press, New York, 1986
The Real Cool Killers, Vintage Books, New York, 1988
Cotton Comes to Harlem, Vintage Books, New York, 1998
A Rage in Harlem, Canongate, Edinburgh, 2000 (1957)

Hinojosa, Maria
Crews: Gang Members Talk to Maria Hinojosa, Harcourt Brace & Company, San Diego, California, 1995

Hinton, S.E.
The Outsiders, Dell Publishing, New York, 1984 (1967)

Hirsch, Phil
Hooked, Pyramid Books, New York, 1968

Hodgson, Michael T.
With Sgt. Mike in Vietnam, Army Times Publishing, Washington D.C., 1972

Hoffman, Abbie
Revolution for the Hell of it, Dial Press, New York, 1968
Woodstock Nation, Vintage Books, New York, 1969

Holden, Anthony
Big Deal: A Year as a Professional Poker Player, Viking, New York, 1990

Holden, Mark
Sodom 1967 American Style, Edka Books, Los Angeles, 1967

Holiday, Billie (Eleanora Fagan) with William Duffy
Lady Sings the Blues, Lancer Books, New York, 1972

Hollander, Xaviera
Xaviera, Warner Paperback Library, New York, 1973
The Happy Hooker, Dell, New York, 1974

Holledge, James
The Flower People, Scripts, London, 1967

Holmes, John Clellon
Go, Ace Books, New York, 1952
The Horn, Random House, New York, 1958

Hooker, Richard and Ring Lardner
*M*A*S*H,* 20th Century Fox, 1970

Hopkins, William B.
One Bugle No Drums, Avon Books, New York, 1986

Horman, Richard and Allan Fox
Drug Awareness, Discus Books, New York, 1970

Horsley, Fred
The Hot Rod Handbook, J. Lowell Pratt & Company, New York, 1965

Hoskyns, Barney
Waiting For The Sun, Viking, New York, 1996

Houppert, Karen
The Curse: Confronting the Last Unmentionable Taboo: Menstruation, Farrar, Straus & Giroux, New York, 1999

Houser, Norman W.
Drugs: Facts on Their Use and Abuse, Scott, Foresman and Company, Glenview, Illinois, 1969

Houston, Albert
The Big Dummy's Guide to C.B. Lingo, The Book Publishing Company, Summertown, Tennessee, 1976

Houston, Joe Leon
The Gay Flesh, Argyle Books, Los Angeles, 1965

Hudson, Kenneth
A Dictionary of the Teenage Revolution and its Aftermath, Macmillan Reference Books, London, 1983

Hughes, John
The Breakfast Club, Universal Studios, Los Angeles, 1985
Ferris Bueller's Day Off, Paramount Pictures, 1986

Hughes, Thomas F.
Dealing Casino Blackjack, Gamblers Book Club Press, Las Vegas, Nevada, 1982

Humes, Jim and Sean Wagstaff
Boarderlands, HarperCollins, New York, 1995

Humphreys, Laud
Tearoom Trade: Impersonal Sex in Public Places, Aldine de Gruyter, New York, 1975

Huncke, Herbert
The Evening Sun Turned Crimson, Cherry Valley Editions, Cherry Valley, New York, 1980
Guilty of Everything: The Autobiography of Herbert Huncke, Paragon House, New York, 1990

Hunt, J.L. and A.G. Pringle
Service Slang, Faber and Faber, London, 1943

Hunter, Evan
The Blackboard Jungle, Pocket Books, New York, 1955
Last Summer, Doubleday, New York, 1968

Hunter, John Francis
The Gay Insider: A Hunter's Guide to New York and a Thesaurus of Phallic Lore, The Other Traveller, New York, 1971

Hunter, Wade
The Sex Peddler, Playtime Books, Las Vegas, 1963

Hurst, Walter E. and Donn Delson
Delson's Dictionary of Radio & Record Industry Terms, Bradson Press, Thousand Oaks, California, 1980

Hurwood, Bernhardt J.
The Sensuous New Yorker, Award Books, New York, 1973

Hutchinson, Sean
Crying Out Loud, John Daniel, Santa Barbara, California, 1988

Hutson, Jan
The Chicken Ranch: The True Story of the Best Little Whorehouse in Texas, A.S. Barnes and Company, Cranbury, New Jersey, 1980

Hyatt, Missy
Missy Hyatt: First Lady of Wrestling, ECW Press, Toronto, 2001

Ihnatko, Andy
Cyberspeak: An Online Dictionary, Random House, New York, 1997

Irwin, John
The Felon, Prentice-Hall, Englewood Cliffs, New Jersey, 1970

Jack (Bob Smith) with Byron Laursen, Wolfman
Have Mercy: Confessions of the Original Rock 'n' Roll Animal, Warner Books, New York, 1995

Jackson, A.S.
Gentleman Pimp, Holloway House, Los Angeles, California, 1973

Jackson, Bruce
In the Life: Versions of the Criminal Experience, Holt, Rinehart and Winston, New York, 1972
Outside the Law: A Thief's Primer, Transaction Books, New Brunswick, New Jersey, 1972
Get Your Ass in the Water and Swim Like Me: Narrative Poetry from Black Oral Tradition, Harvard University Press, Cambridge, Massachusetts, 1974
Killing Time: Life in the Arkansas Penitentiary, Cornell University Press, Ithaca, New York, 1977

Jackson, George
Soledad Brother: The Prison Letters of George Jackson, Coward-McCann, New York, 1970

Jackson, Renay
Oaktown Devil, LaDay Publishing, Oakland, 1998

Jackson, Robert K. and Wesley McBride
Understanding Street Gangs, Thomas Wadsworth, Belmont, California, 2000

Jacobs, Gil
The World's Best Dice Games, Dixon Press, Cupertino, California, 1976

Jacobs, Michael
Complete CB Slang Dictionary, Success Publciations, North Miami Beach, Florida, 1978

Jacoby, James and Mary
The New York Times Book of Backgammon, New American Library, New York, 1973

Jacoby, Oswald
Oswald Jacoby on Poker, Doubleday, New York, 1947

Jacoby, Oswald and John Crawford
The Backgammon Book, Bantam Books, New York, 1973 (1970)

Jah, Yusuf and Sister Shah'Keyah
Uprising, Touchstone, New York, 1997

James, Antony
America's Homosexual Underground, L.S. Publications, New York, 1965

Jenkins, Dan
Semi-Tough, Signet Books, New York, 1972
Life Its Ownself, Signet Books, New York, 1984
Dead Solid Perfect, Price Stern Sloan, Los Angeles, California, 1986
The Money-Whipped Steer-Job Three-Jack Give-Up Artist, Broadway Books, New York, 2002

Jennings, Karla
The Devouring Fungus: Tales of the Computer Age, W.W. Norton, New York, 1990

Jessup, Richard
The Cincinnati Kid, Little, Brown and Co., Boston, Massachusetts, 1963

Joe Brennan, Duke Kahanamoku with
Duke Kahanamoku's World of Surfing, Grosset & Dunlap, New York

Johnson, George Clayton
Ocean's Eleven, Pocket Books, New York, 1960

Johnson, Michael Dalton
Talking Trash with Redd Foxx, Emery Dalton Books, Del Mar, California, 1992

Johnson, Peter
Dictionary of Street Alcohol and Drug Terms (4th Edition), School of Medicine, University of South Carolina, Columbia, South Carolina, 1993

Johnson, Sandee Shaffer
Cadences: The Jody Call Book, No. 1, Daring Books, Canton, Ohio, 1986
Cadences: The Jody Call Book, No. 2, Darling Books, Canton, Ohio, 1986

Johnston, William
The Brady Bunch, Lancer Books, New York, 1969

Jones, John Peter
Feather Pluckers, Eyre & Spottiswoode, London, 1964

Jorgenson, Kregg P.J.
Very Crazy G.I. (Beaucoup Dinky Dau), Ballantine Books, New York, 2001

Judge, Mike and Joe Stillman
Beavis and Butt-Head Do America: The Official Script Book, MTV Books/Pocket Books, New York, 1997

Katz, Samuel M.
Anytime Anywhere, Pocket Books, New York, 1997

Kaufman, Murray
Murray the K Tells It Like It Is, Baby, Holt, Rinehart and Winston, New York, 1966

Kay, James and Julian Cohen
The Parents' Complete Guide to Young People and Drugs, Vermilion, London, 1998

Kellerman, Jonatrhan
Rage, Penguin, London, 2006

Kelly, John M.
Surf and Sea, A. S. Barnes and Company, New York, 1965

Kennedy-Martin, Troy
The Italian Job, Paramount Pictures, 1969

Kent, Brittany
O.C. Undercover: An Unofficial Guide to the Stars and Styles of The O.C., St. Martin's Press, New York, 2004

Kerouac, Jack
On the Road, Viking, New York, 1957
The Subterraneans, Grove Press, Inc., New York, 1958
The Dharma Burns, Signet Books, New York, 1959 (1958)
Beat Generation, Thunder's Mouth Press, New York, 2005

Kerouac, Jack (edited by Ann Charters)
Jack Kerouac Selected Letters 1957–1969, Penguin Books, New York, 1999

Kerouac, Jack (edited by Douglas Brinkley)
Windblown World: The Journals of Jack Kerouac 1947–1954, Penguin, New York, 2006

Kerry, John and Vietnam Veterans Against the War
The New Soldier, Collier Books, New York, 1971

Kesey, Ken
One Flew Over the Cuckoo's Nest, Penguin Books, New York, 1976 (1962)
The Further Inquiry, Penguin, New York, 1990
*Kesey's Jail Journal: Cut the M*********** Loose,* Viking, New York, 2003

King, George
Horse Racing: How to Win the Vegas Way, Gambling International, Las Vegas, Nevada, 1965

King, Harry as told to Bill Chambliss
Box Man: A Professional Thief's Journey, Harper Torchbooks, New York, 1972

King, Rick and W. Peter Iliff
Break Point, 20th Century Fox, 1991

Kirschke, James J.
Not Going Home Alone: A Marine's Story, Ballantine Books, New York, 2001

Klein, Naomi
No Logo, Harper Collins, New York, 2001

Kneitel, Tom
Tomcat's Big CB Handbook, CRB Research, Commack, New York, 1992

Knowles, John
A Separate Peace, Macmillan, New York, 1959

Kohner, Frederick
Gidget Goes Hawaiian, Bantam, New York, 1961
Gidget Goes to Rome, Bantam, New York, 1963
The Affairs of Gidget, Bantam, New York, 1963
Gidget, Berkley Books, New York, 2001 (1957)

Konigsberg, Ira
The Complete Film Dictionary, New American Library, New York, 1987

Kovac, Steve
Learn to Bowl, Rand McNally, Chicago, 1969

Kramer, Dale and Madeline Karr
Teen-Age Gangs: The Frank, Inside Story of Juvenile Delinquency in America, Popular Library, New York, 1957 (1953)

Kronhausen, Phyllis and Eberhard
Sex Histories of American College Men, Ballantine Books, New York, 1960

Kuhns, Grant W.
On Surfing, Charles E. Tuttle, Rutland, Vermont, 1964 (1963)

Kunen, James Simon
The Strawberry Statement, Avon Books, New York, 1968

Kuriscak, Steve
Casino Talk: A Rap Sheet for Dealers and Players, Self-published, 1985

Kushyshyn, Igor et al.
The Gambling Times Guide to Harness Racing, Lyle Stuart, Secaucus, New Jersey, 1994

Laikin, Paul
101 Hippie Jokes, Pyramid Books, New York, 1968

Lait, Jack and Lee Mortimer et al.
New York Confidential, Dell Publishing, New York, 1948
Chicago Confidential, Crown Publishers, New York, 1950
Washington Confidential, Crown Publishers, New York, 1951

Landers, Ann
Ann Landers Talks to Teen-Agers About Sex, Fawcett, New York, 1965

Landis, Bill and Michelle Clifford
Sleazoid Express: A Mind-twisting Tour Through the Grindhouse Cinema of Times Square, Fireside Books, New York, 2002

Landy, Eugene
The Underground Dictionary, Touchstone, New York, 1971

Lanklater, Richard
Slacker, St. Martin's Press, New York, 1992

Larner, Jeremy and Ralph Tefferteller
The Addict in the Street, Grove Press, New York, 1966 (1964)

Larsen, Shana
200 Cigarettes, Paramount Pictures, 1999

Laughlin, Burgess
Job Opportunities in the Black Market, Loompanics Unlimited, Port Townsend, Washington D.C., 1978

Lavigne, Yves
Hell's Angels, Carol Publishing Company, Secaucus, New Jersey, 1987

Lawlor, John
How to Talk Car, Topaz Felsen, Chicago, Illinois, 1965

Lawson, Ann
Kids & Gangs: What Parents and Educators Need to Know, Johnson Institute, Minneapolis, Minnesota, 1994

Lawson, Don
The United States in the Korean War, Scholastic Books, New York, 1964

Lay, Mary and Nancy Orban
The Hip Glossary of Hippie Language, Self-published, San Francisco, 1967

Leap, William
Word's Out: Gay Men's English, University of Minnesota Press, Minneapolis, Minnesota, 1996

Leary, Timothy
The Politics of Ecstasy, College Notes & Texts, New York, 1968

LeBlanc, Adrian Nicole
Random Family, Scribner, New York, 2003

Lecike, Robert
The Wars of America, Volume II, Bantam Books, New York, 1968

Lee, Gypsy Rose
Gypsy: A Memoir, Dell Books, New York, 1959

Lee, Stan
The 'Nam, Marvel Comics, New York, 1987

Legman, G.
The Fake Revolt, Breaking Point, New York, 1967

Leigh, Michael
The Velvet Underground, McFadden, New York, 1963

Leonard, Elmore
Mr. Majestyk, Dell Books, New York, 1974
Touch, Avon Books, New York, 1977
The Switch, Bantam Books, New York, 1978
City Primeval, Avon Books, New York, 1980
Gold Coast, Bantam Books, New York, 1980
Split Images, Avon Books, New York, 1981
Stick, Avon Books, New York, 1983
Cat Chaser, Avon Books, New York, 1983 (1982)

Swag, Dell Books, New York, 1984
Glitz, Warner Books, New York, 1985
The Big Bounce, Mysterious Press, New York, 1986
Killshot, Warner Books, New York, 1989
Freaky Deaky, Warner Books, New York, 1989 (1988)
Maximum Bob, Dell Publishing, New York, 1991
Rum Punch, Dell Publishing, New Yrok, 1992
Pronto, Dell Publishing, New York, 1993
Riding the Rap, Dell Publishing, New York, 1995
Out of Sight, Dell Publishing, New York, 1996
Be Cool, Dell Publishing, New York, 1999

Leonard, Elmore and Quentin Tarantino
Jackie Brown, Miramax, 1997

Leonard, Elmore and Scott Frank
Get Shorty, Metro-Goldwyn-Mayer, 1995

Lerner, Jimmy
You Got Nothing Coming: Notes from a Prison Fish, Corgi Books, London, 2003

LeRoy, J.T.
Sarah, Bloomsbury, New York, 2001
The Heart is Deceitful Above All Things, Bloomsbury, New York, 2002
Harold's End, Last Gasp Publishers, San Francisco, 2004

Leslie, Robert
Confessions of a Lesbian Prostitute, Dalhousie Press, New York, 1965

Levinson, Barry
Diner, MGM, 1982

Lewin, Lauri
Naked is the Best Disguise: My Life as a Stripper, Pandora, London, 1986

Lewin, Ted
I Was A Teenage Professional Wrestler, Hyperion Paperbacks, New York, 1993

Lewis, Stephen
The Whole Bedroom Catalog, Zebra Books, New York, 1975

Liberman, Jethro K.
The Complete CB Handbook, Avon Books, New York, 1976

Liebling, A.J.
The Wayward Pressman, Doubleday & Company, Garden City, New York, 1946

Liebmann-Smith, Richard, with Dr. Lillian Glass
How to Deprogram Your Valley Girl, Workingman Publishing, New York

Liebow, Elliot
Tally's Corner: A Study of Negro Streetcorner Men, Little, Brown and Company, Boston, 1967

Lin, Edward
Big Julie of Vegas, Fawcett Publications, Greenwich, Connecticut, 1975 (1974)

Linder, Ronald
PCP: The Devil's Dust: Recognition, Management and Prevention of Phencyclidine Abuse, Wadsworth Publishing, Belmont, California, 1981

Linderer, Gary
The Eyes of the Eagle: F Company LRPS in Vietnam, 1968, Ivy Books, New York, 1992

Lingeman, Richard
Drugs from A to Z: A Dictionary, McGraw-Hill, New York, 1969

Linklater, Richard
Dazed and Confused, Gramercy Pictures, 1993

Linton, E.R.
America's Newest Sex Cult, Medco Books, Los Angeles, California, 1966

Lipkin, Robert "Bob Bitchin"
A Brotherhood of Outlaws, FTW Publishing, Redondo Beach, California, 1981

Lipton, Lawrence
The Holy Barbarians, Julian Messner Inc., New York, 1959

Lit, Hy
Hy Lit's Unbelievable Dictionary of Hip Words for Groovy People, Hyski Press, Philadelphia, Pennsylvania, 1968

Lonergan, Kenneth
This is Our Youth, Overlook Press, Woodstock, New York, 2000

Longstreet, Stephen
The Flesh Peddlers, Dell, New York, 1963

Loria, Ana
1 2 3 Be a Porn Star!, InfoNet Publications, Malibu, California, 2000

Lowdon, Brian and Margaret
Competitive Surfing: A Dedicated Approach, Movement Publications, Ithaca, New York, 1988

Lucas, George and Gloria Katz
American Graffiti, MCA/Universal Pictures, 1973

Lucas, J. Anthony
The Barnyard Epithet and Other Obscenities: Notes on the Chicago Conspiracy Trial, Harper & Row, New York, 1970
Don't Shoot – We Are Your Children, Dell Publishing, New York, 1971

Ludlum, Charles
The Mystery of Irma Vep and Other Plays, Theatre Communications Group, New York, 2001

Lund, Charles W.
Robbing the One-Armed Bandits: Finding and Exploiting Advantageous Slot Machines, RGE Publishing, Oakland, California, 1999

Lund, J. Herbert
Herb's Hot Box of Railroad Slang, Jay Herbert Publishing, Chicago, Illinois, 1975

Luntz, Karen and Kirsten Smith
Ten Things I Hate About You, Touchstone, 1999

Maas, Peter
The Valachi Papers, Bantam Books, New York, 1972
Serpico, Bantam Books, New York, 1974 (1973)

MacDonald, John D.
The Neon Jungle, Fawcett Publications, Greenwich, Connecticutt, 1953
The Deceivers, Fawcett, Greenwich, Connecticut, 1958

MacLaughlin, Duncan
The Filth, Mainstream, Edinburgh, 2002

MacPherson, Tom
Dragging and Driving, Scholastic Book Services, New York, 1960

Mailer, Norman
The Naked and the Dead, Rinehart & Company, New York, 1948
Advertisements for Myself, G.P. Putnam's Sons, New York, 1959
Miami and the Siege of Chicago, Signet, New York, 1968
The Faith of Graffiti, Praeger, New York, 1974

Major, Clarence
A Dictionary of Afro-American Slang, International Publishers, New York, 1970
Juba to Jive, A Dictionary of African-American Slang, Penguin Books, 1994
All-Night Visitors, Northeastern University Press, Boston, 1998

Mandel, George
Flee the Angry Strangers, Bantam Books, New York, 1953 (1952)

Mander, Gabrielle
WAN2TLK? ltl bk of txt msgs, St. Martin's Griffin, New York, 2001

Mangold, James
Copland, Miramax, 1997

Mangold, Tom and John Penycate
The Tunnels of Cu Chi, Random House, New York, 1985

Mann, Peter
How to Buy a Used Car Without Getting Gypped, Harper & Row, New York, 1975

Marcinko, Richard and John Weisman
Rogue Warrior, Pocket Books, New York, 1992

Marlowe, Kenneth
The Gay World of Kenneth Marlowe, self-published, 1966

Martin, John Bartlow
Break Down the Walls, Ballantine Books, New York, 1954

Martin, Mark
NASCAR for Dummies, IDG Books, Foster City, California, 2000

Masoff, Joy
Oh, Yuck, Workman Publishing, New York, 2000

Mason, Robert
Chickenhawk, Penguin Books, New York, 1983

Matheson, Chris and Ed Solomon
Bill and Ted's Excellent Adventure, Orion Pictures, 1989

Mattson, Heidi
Ivy League Stripper, Arcade Publishing, New York, 1995

Maupin, Armistead
Tales of the City, HarperCollins, New York, 1978
Maybe the Moon, Black Swan, London, 1993
Babycakes, HarperPerennial, New York, 1994 (1984)

Maurer, David W.
The Big Con, Bobbs-Merrill, Indianapolis, 1940
The Argot of the Dice Gambler, American Academy of Political and Social Science, Philadelphia, 1950
Argot of the Racetrack, American Dialect Society, Tuscaloosa, Alabama, 1951
Kentucky Moonshine, University of Kentucky Press, Lexington, Kentucky, 1974
The American Confidence Man, Charles C. Thomas, Springfield, Illinois, 1974

Maurer, David M. and Victor H. Vogel
Narcotics and Narcotic Addiction (4th Edition), Charles C. Thomas, Springfield, Illinois, 1973

Maurer, Harry
Strange Ground: Americans in Vietnam 1945–1975, An Oral History, Henry Holt and Company, New York, 1989

Max, H.
Gay (S)language: A Dic(k)tionary of Gay Slang, Banned Books, Austin, Texas, 1988

Mayer, David and Kenneth Richard
Western Popular Theatre, Metheun, London, 1977

Mayer, Gary
Bookie: My Life in Disorganized Crime, Ballantine Books, New York, 1974

Mazer, Sharon
Professional Wrestling: Sport and Spectacle, University of Mississippi Press, Jackson, Mississippi, 1998

McCall, Nathan
Makes Me Wanna Holler: A Young Black Man in America, Random House, New York, 1994

McCarthy, Mary
The Group, Harcourt, Brace & World, New York, 1963

McCarthy, Pete
McCarthy's Bar, Hodder & Stoughton, London, 2000

McCool, Sam
Pittsburghese: How to Speak Like a Pittsburgher, Goodwill Industries, Pittsburgh, Pennsylvania, 1982

McCoy, Horace
Kiss Tomorrow Good-bye, Random House, New York, 1948

McCreary, Don R. (Editor)
Dawg Speak: The Slanguage Dictionary of the University of Georgia, University of Georgia, Athens, Georgia, 2001

McDonald, Cherokee Paul
Into the Green: A Reconnaissance by Fire, Plume Books, New York, 2001

McFadden, Amy and Denise
CoalSpeak: The (Un)Official Dictionary of the Schuylkill County, PA Anthracite Coal Region, CoalRegion Enterprises, Marlboro, Massachusetts, 1998

McFadden, Cyra
The Serial: A year in the Life of Marin County, Pan Books, London, 1990

McFedries, Paul
Word Spy, Broadway Books, New York, 2004

McGeady, Mary Rose
Are You Out There, God? Covenant House, New York, 1999

McInerney, Jay
Bright Lights, Big City, Vintage Books, New York, 1984
Ransom, Vintage Books, New York, 1987
Story of My Life, Vintage Books, New York, 1989

McKennon, Joe
Circus Lingo, Carnival Publishers of Sarasota, Sarasota, Florida, 1980

McKissick, Mitch
Surf Lingo: A Complete Guide to a Totally Rad Vocab, Coastline Press, Balboa, California, 1987

McMullin, Edith
Adventures in Duplicate Bridge, American Contract Bridge League, Memphis, 1988

McMurtry, Larry
The Last Picture Show, Dell Publishing, New York, 1971 (1966)

McNelis, Lee
30 + And a Wake-Up: A Compendium: Prison Slang Terms and Definitions, Self-published, 1991

McQuain, Jeffrey
Never Enough Words, Random House, New York, 1999

McQuarrie, Christopher
The Usual Suspects, Gramercy Pictures, 1995

Mechigian, John
Encyclopedia of Keno: A Guide to Successful Gambling with Keno, Funtime Enterprises, Fresno, California, 1972

Meltzer, Richard
A Whore Just Like the Rest: The Music Writings of Richard Meltzer, Da Capo Press, 2000

Melvin, Ken
Sorry 'Bout That: Cartoons, Limericks, and Other Diversions of GI Vietnam, Wayward Press, Tokyo, 1966

Meriwether, Louise
Daddy Was a Number Runner, Pyramid Books, New York, 1974

Merriam, Kendall
The Illustrated Dictionary of Lobstering, Cumberland Press, Freeport, Maine, 1978

Mertel, Kenneth
Year of the Horse—Vietnam: 1st Air Cavalry in the Highlands, Bantam Books, New York, 1990

Metalious, Grace
Peyton Place, Dell, New York, 1957

Meyer, Kathleen
How to Shit in the Woods, Ten Speed Press, Berkeley, California, 1994

Meyer, Linda
Teenspeak! A Bewildered Parent's Guide to Teenagers, Peterson's, Princeton, New Jersey, 1994

Meyer, Scott
Deadhead Forever, Running Press, Philadelphia, 2001

Michelson, Herb
Sportin' Ladies: Confessions of the Bimbos, Chilton Book Company, Radnor, Pennsylvania, 1975

Milius, John and Francis Ford Coppola
Apocalypse Now, United Artists, 1979

Miller, Chris
The Real Animal House, Little, Brown and Company, New York, 2006

Miller, Jerry
Fast Company: The Men and Machines of American Auto Racing, Follett Books, Chicago, Illinois, 1972

Miller, Tony and Patricia George
Cut! Print! The Language and Structure of Filmmaking, F.I.W. Press, Van Nuys, California, 1977

Miller, Warren
The Cool World, Little, Brown and Company, Boston, 1959
The Way We Live Now, Pawcett Crest, New York, 1968

Millett, Kate
The Prostitution Papers, Ballantine Books, New York, 1976

Mills, James
The Panic in Needle Park, Signet Books, New York, 1967 (1966)

Milner, Christina and Richard
Black Players: The Secret World of Black Pimps, Little, Brown and Co., Boston, Massachusetts, 1972

Milner, Michael
Sex on Celluloid, McFadden-Bartell, New York, 1969 (1964)

Monteleone, Vincent J.
Criminal Slang: The Vernacular of the Underworld Lingo (Revised Edition), Christopher Publishing, Boston, Massachusetts, 1949

Moore, Harold and Joseph Galloway
We Were Soldiers Once ... And Young, Random House, New York, 1992

Moore, Joan W.
Homeboys: Gangs, Drugs, and Prison in the Barrios of Los Angeles, Temple University Press, Philadelphia, 1978

Morden, Ethan
Buddies, St. Martin's Press, New York, 1986
I've a Feeling We're Not in Kansas Anymore: Tales from Gay Manhattan, Plume, New York, 1987
Everybody Loves You, St. Martin's Press, New York, 1989
Some Men Are Lookers, St. Martin's Press, New York, 1997
How's Your Romance: Concluding the "Buddies" Cycle, St. Martin's Press, New York, 2005

Morehead, Albert H.
The Complete Guide to Winning Poker, Simon & Schuster, New York, 1967

Morgan, Paul
The Parrot's Beak: U.S. Operations in Cambodia, Hellgate Press, Central Point, Oregon, 2000

Morgan, Robert
Main Event: The World of Professional Wrestling, Dial Press, New York, 1979

Morgan, Seth
Homeboy, Random House, New York, 1990

Morley, Paul
Ask, Faber and Faber, London, 1986

Morrow, Cousin Bruce
Cousin Brucie: My Life in Rock 'n' Roll Radio, Beech Tree Books, New York, 1987

Mortimer, Lee
Women Confidential, Julian Messner Inc., New York, 1960

Motely, Willard
Let No Man Write My Epitaph, Signet Books, New York, 1959 (1958)

Mowry, Jess
Way Past Cool, HarperPerennial, New York, 1993
Six Out Seven, Anchor Books, New York, 1994

Mueller, Robert Kirk
Buzzwords: A Guide to the Language of Leadership, Van Nostrand Reinhold, New York, 1974

Muirhead, Desmond
Surfing in Hawaii, Northland Press, Flagstaff, Arizona, 1962

Mungo, Raymond
Famous Long Ago: My Life and Hard times with Liberation News Service, Beacon Press, Boston, Massachusetts, 1970

Munro, Pamela (Editor)
U.C.L.A. Slang 3: U.C.L.A. Occasional Papers in Linguistics Number 18, Department of Linguistics, Los Angeles, California, 1997
U.C.L.A. Slang 4: U.C.L.A. Occasional Papers in Linguistics Number 22, Department of Linguistics, Los Angeles, 2001

Murphy, Audie
To Hell and Back, Permabooks, New York, 1955

Murray, Thomas E. and Thomas R. Murrell
The Language of Sadomasochism, Greenwood Press, Westport, Connecticut, 1989

Murtagh, John M. and Sara Harris
Cast the First Stone, Pocket Books, New York, 1958 (1957)

Music City Wordman
CBers Guide & Glossary, Zebra Books, New York, 1976

Myers, Mike
Austin Powers: International Man of Mystery, New Line Cinema, 1997

Myers, Mike and Bonnie and Terry Turner
Wayne's World, Paramount Pictures, 1992

Myers, Mike and Michael McCullers
Austin Powers: The Spy Who Shagged Me, New Line Cinema, 1999

Napolitano, George
Championship Wrestling: Masters of Mayhem, Mallard Press, New York, 1991
This is Wrestling: Today's Stars, Tomorrow's Legends, Smithmark Publishers, New York, 1993

Nash, Jay Robert
Dictionary of Crime, Paragon House, New York, 1992

Natkin, Bobbye Claire and Steve Kirk
All Aaout Pinball, Grosset & Dunlap, New York, 1977

Nazel, Joseph
Black Cop, Holloway House, Los Angeles, 1993

Nealy, William
Mountain Bike! A Manual of Technique, Menasha Ridge Press, Birmingham, Alabama, 1993 (1992)

Nelson, Larry and James Jones
Stranglehold: An Intriguing Behind the Scenes Glimpse into the Private World of Professional Wrestling, Chump Change Publishing, Denver, Colorado, 1999

Nelson, Marlena Kay
Rookies to Roaches: The Police Force and Its Folklore, unpublished manuscript in the Historical Manuscript Collection, Columbia, Missouri, 1963

Nelson, William Desmond
Surfing: A Handbook, Auerbach Publishers, Philadelphia, 1973

Neville, Richard
Play Power, Exploring the International Underground, Random House, New York, 1970

Newland, Courttia
Society Within, Abacus, London, 1999

Newton, Robert
Bondage Clubs U.S.A., Wee Hours Books, Buffalo, New York, 1967

Nichols, John
The Sterile Cuckoo, Avon Books, New York, 1970 (1965)

Niemann, Linda
Boomer: Railroad Memoirs, Cleis Press, Pittsburgh, Pennsylvania, 1990

Noire
Candy Licker, Ballantine, New York, 2005

Nolan, Keith W.
Ripcord: Screaming Eagles Under Siege, Vietnam 1970, Presidio Press, Novato, California, 2000

Norman, Gurney
Divine Right's Trip, Last Whole Earth Catalog, Menlo Park, California, 1971

Nytrate, Emile
Underground Ads, Pocket Books, New York, 1971

O'Brien, Tim
Going After Cacciato, Dell Publishing, New York, 1992

O'Conner, Lois
The Bare Facts: Candid Confessions of a Stripper, McFadden-Bartell, New York, 1964

O'Day, John
Confessions of a Hollywood Callgirl, Shelbourne Press, Los Angeles, 1964

O'Neill, Gerard and Dick Lehr
The Under Boss, St. Martin's Press, New York, 1989

Odean, Kathleen
High Steppers, Fallen Angels, and Lollipops: Wall Street Slang, Dodd, Mead & Company, New York, 1988

Odzer, Cleo
Goa Freaks: My Hippie Years in India, Blue Moon Books, New York, 1995

Ogg, Alex
The Hip Hop Years, Channel 4 Books, London, 1999

Olberman, Keith and Dan Patrick
The Big Show: Inside ESPN's Sports Center, Pocket Books, New York, 1997

Olive, David
Business Babble: A Cynic's Dictionary of Corporate Jargon, John Wiley & Sons, New York, 1991

Olney, Ross
The Young Sportsman's Guide to Surfing, Thomas Nelson & Sons, New York, 1965
Kings of the Drag Strip, G.P. Putnam's Sons, New York, 1968

Orloff, Erica and JoAnn Baker
Dirty Little Secrets, St. Martin's Griffin, New York, 2001

Oswald, Russell G.
Attica – My Story, Doubleday & Company, Garden City, New York, 1972

Owen, Guy
The Flim-Flam Man and the Apprentice Grifter, Crown Publishers, New York, 1972

Pagen, Dennis et al.
Hang Gliding and Flying Skills, self-published, State College, Pennsylvania, 1977

Paine, Gerald
A Bachelor's Guide to the Brothels of Nevada, Eros Publishing, Wilmington, Delaware, 1978

Paine, Rhiannon
Too Late for the Festival, Academy Chicago Publishers, Chicago, Illinois, 1999

Paladin Press et al.
An Inside Look at Outlaw Motorcycle Gangs, Paladin Press, Boulder, Colorado, 1992

Parker, Dan
The ABC of Horse Racing, Bantam Books, New York, 1948 (1947)

Parker, Elliott
What You Always Wanted to Know About Sodomy and Perversion, Eros Goldstripe, Wilmington, Delaware, 1972

Parker, Trey and Matt Stone
South Park: Bigger Longer & Uncut, Paramount Pictures, 1999

Parks, David
GI Diary, Howard University Press, Washington D.C., 1984

Patrick, Vincent
The Pope of Greenwich Village, Seaview Books, New York, 1979
Family Business, Poseidon Press, New York, 1985

Patterson, Haywood and Earl Conrad
Scottsboro Boy, Bantan Books, New York, 1962

Patterson, Jerry L.
Blackjack: A Winner's Handbook, Ecehlon Enterprises, Vorhees, New Jersey, 1978

Payne, C.D.
Youth in Revolt, Doubleday, New York, 1993
Cut to the Twisp, Avia Press, Sebastapol, California, 2001

Peace, David
Nineteen Seventy-Four, Serpent's Tail, London, 1999

Pelfry, William
The Big V, Avon Books, New York, 1984

Percy, George
The Language of Poker: The Jargon and Slang Spoken Around the Poker Table, self-published, 1988

Perkins, D.M.
Deep Throat, Dell, New York, 1973

Perlmutter, Nate
How to Win Money at the Races, Collier Books, New York, 1964

Perry, Charles
Portrait of a Young Man Drowning, Old School Books, New York, 1996

Peter, Ed Decter, John Strauss and Bobby Farrelly
Something About Mary, 20th Century Fox

Peter Occhiogrosso, Frank Zappa with
The Real Frank Zappa Book, Poseidon Press, New York

Peterkin, A.D.
The Bald Headed Hermit and the Artichoke, Arsenal Pulp Press, Vancouver, Washington, 1999

Petievich, Gerald
Money Men, Harcourt Brace Jovanovich, New York, 1981
One-Shot Deal, Harcourt Brace Jovanovich, New York, 1981
To Die in Beverly Hills, Arbor house, New York, 1983
To Live and Die in L.A., Arbor House, New York, 1983
The Quality of the Informant, Arbor House, New York, 1985
Shakedown, Simon and Schuster, New York, 1988

Petkovich, Anthony
The X Factory: Inside the American Hardcore Film Industry, Critical Vision, Manchester, U.K., 1997

Petty, R.D.
Encylopedia of Sexual Fetishes, Scandia Productions, Stockholm, 1973

Pharr, Robert Deane
Giveadamn Brown, Payback Press, Edinburgh, 1997 (1978)
S.R.O., W.W. Norton & Company, New York, 1998

Phillips, Louis and Burnham Holmes
The Complete Book of Sports Nicknames, Renaissance Books, Los Angeles, 1998

Phillips and Burnham Holmes, Louis
The Complete Book of Sports Nicknames, Renaissance Books, Los Angeles, 1998

Picarello, Robert
Rulers of the Ring: Wrestling's Hottest Superstars, Berkeley Boulevard Books, New York, 2000

Pileggi, Nicholas
Wise Guy: Life in a Mafia Family, Pocket Books, New York, 1987

Pileggi, Nicholas and Martin Scorsese
Goodfellas, Warner Brothers, 1990
Casino, Universal Pictures, 1995

Pincus, Arthur
How to Talk Football, Dembner Books, New York, 1984

Pintero, Miguel
Short Eyes, Hill and Wang, New York, 1975

Piro, Sal and Michael Hess et al.
The Offical "Rocky Horror Picture Show" Audience Participation Guide, Starbur Press, Plymouth, Connecticut, 1991

Plant, Sadie
Writing on Drugs, Faber and Faber, London, 1999

Plaster, John L.
SOG: The Secret Wars of America's Commandos in Vietnam, Onyx Books, New York, 1998

Poland, Jefferson and Valerie Alison
The Records of the San Francisco Sexual Freedom League, Olympia Press, London, 1971

Pollack, Bruce
The Disco Handbook, Scholastic Book Services, New York, 1979

Polsky, Howard W.
Cottage Six: The Social System of Delinquent Boys in Residential Treatment, Russell Sage Foundation, New York, 1962

Polsky, Ned
Hustlers, Beats, and Others, Adleine Publishing Company, Chicago, 1967

Pond, Mimi
The Valley Girl's Guide to Life, Dell Publishing, New York, 1982

Ponicsan, Darryl
The Last Detail, W.H. Allen, London, 1971 (1970)

Powers, Stephen J.
The Art of Getting Over, St. Martin's Press, New York, 1999

Poynter, Dan
Parachuting: The Skydivers' Handbook, Parachuting Publications, Santa Barbara, California, 1978

Prather, Richard S.
The Peddler, Fawcett, Greenwich, Connecticut, 1963

Preston, John
Hustling: A Gentleman's Guide to the Fine Art of Homosexual Prostitution, Masquerade Books, New York, 1997

Preusse, Carol Ann
Jargon Used by University of Texas Co-Eds, unpublished manuscript in the Western Historical Manuscript Collection, Columbia, Missouri, 1963

Price, Richard
The Wanderers, Houghton Mifflin, Boston, 1974
Clockers, Avon Books, New York, 1992
Samaritan, Alfred A. Knopf, New York, 2003

Prus, Robert C. and C.R.D. Sharper
Road Hustler: Grifting, Magic, and the Thief Subculture, Richard Kaufman and Alan Greenberg, New York, 1991 (1977)

Puzo, Mario
The Godfather, Fawcett Crest, Greenwich, Connecticut, 1970
Inside Las Vegas, Charter Books, New York, 1977

Radakovich, Anka
The Wild Girls Club: Tales From Below the Belt, Fawcett Columbine, New York, 1994

Radio Shack
CBer's Handy Atlas/Dictionary, Tab Books, Blue Ridge Summit, Pennsylvania, 1976

Radlauer, Ed
Drag Racing Pix Dix: A Picture Dictionary, Bowmar, Glendale, California, 1970
Motorcylopedia, Bowmar, Glendale, California, 1973

Radlauer, Ed and Ruth
Truck Tech Talk, Elk Grove Books, Chicago, Illinois, 1986

Radner, Sidney H.
Radner on Dice, Key Publishing, New York, 1957

Ragen, Joseph E. and Charles Finston
Inside the World's Toughest Prison, Charles C. Thomas, Springfield, Illinois, 1962

Ramsey, Frederic
Chicago Documentary, Jazz Music Books, London, 1944

Raul, K.B.
Naked to the Night, Paperback Library, New York, 1964

Raymond, Eric S.
The New Hacker's Dictionary, MIT Press, Cambridge, Massachusetts, 1991

Rechy, John
City of Night, Grove Press, New York, 1963
Numbers, Grove Press, New York, 1967
The Sexual Outlaw, Dell, New York, 1978
Rushes, Grove Press, New York, 1979
The Fourth Angel, Seaver Books, New York, 1983

Reed, David
Up Front in Vietnam, Funk & Wagnalls, New York, 1967

Regan, Jim
Winning at Slot Machines: A Guide to Making Money at the Most Popular of All Casino Games, Citadel Press, Secaucus, New Jersey, 1985

Reid, Ed and Ovid Demaris
The Green Felt Jungle, Pocket Books, New York, 1964 (1963)

Reinberg, Linda
In the Field: The Language of the Vietnam War, Facts on File, New York, 1991

Reinhard, L.
Oral Sex Techniques and Sex Practices Illustrated, Donti Enterprises, Baltimore, 1968

Reisner, Robert George
The Jazz Titans: Including "The Parlance of Hip", Doubleday, New York, 1960

Reynolds, Frank as told to Michael McClure
Freewheelin Frank: Secretary of the Angels, Grove Press, New York, 1968

Rich, Kim
Johnny's Girl: A Daughter's Memoir of Growing Up in Alaska's Underworld, Alaska Northwest Books, Seattle, Washington, 1993

Ridgeway, James
Red Light: Inside the Sex Industry, Powerhouse Books, New York, 1996

Ridley, John
Stray Dogs, Ballantine Books, New York, 1997
Love is a Racket, Ballantine Books, New York, 1999
Everybody Smokes in Hell, Ballantine Books, New York, 2000

Rigney, Francis J. and L. Douglas Smith
The Real Bohemia: A Sociological and Psychological Study of the "Beats", Basic Books, New York, 1961

Rivers, Larry with Arnold Weinstein
What Did I Do? The Unauthorized Autobiography, HarperCollins, New York, 1992

Robbins, Tom
Even Cowgirls Get the Blues, Bantam, New York, 1977
Another Roadside Attraction, Ballantine Books, New York, 1981

Roberts, Hermese E.
The Third Ear: A Black Glossary, English-Language Institute of America, Chicago, Illinois, 1971

Roberts, Jonathan
How to California, Dell Publishing, New York, 1984

Robertson, Jerry
Oil Slanguage, Petroleum Publishers, Evansville, Indiana, 1954

Robinson, Frank and Nat Lehrman
Sex American Style, Playboy Press, Chicago, 1972

Rock, Chris
Rock This!, Hyperion, New York, 1997

Rock with Joe Layden et al.
The Rock Says..., Avon Books, New York, 2000

Rod, Lightin'
Hustlers Convention, Harmony Books, New York, 1973

Roddy, Irv
Friday Night Poker: Penny Poker for Millions, Simon and Schuster, New York, 1961

Rodgers, Bruce
The Queens' Vernacular, Straight Arrow Books, San Francisco, 1972

Romeo, Anthony
The Language of Gangs, unpublished manuscript, New York, 1962

Romm, Ethel Grodzins
The Open Conspiracy: What America's Angry Generation is Saying, Stackpole Books, New York, 1970

Roos, Don
Boys on the Side, Warner Brothers, 1995

Root, Wayne Alan
Betting To Win on Sports, Bantam Books, New York, 1989

Rorem, Ned
The New York Diary, George Brazillier, New York, 1971

Rose, Joel
Kill Kill Faster Faster, Rebel Inc., Edinburgh, 1997

Rosenberg, Scott
Gone in 60 Seconds, Buena Vista Pictures, 2000

Ross, Jeffrey Ian and Stephen C. Richards
Behind Bars: Surviving Prison, Alpha Books, Indianapolis, 2002

Rosten, Leo
Dear "Herm"—with a cast of dozens, McGraw-Hill, New York, 1974
Silky!, Bantam Books, New York, 1980
The Joys of Yinglish, Signet, New York, 1992 (1989)

Rote, Kyle
The Language of Pro Football, Random House, New York, 1966

Roth, Eric
Forrest Gump, Paramount Pictures, 1992

Roth, Philip
Goodbye, Columbus, Bantam Books, New York, 1968 (1959)
Portnoy's Complaint, Bantam Books, New York, 1970 (1969)

Rowe, Robert V.
How to Win at Horse-Racing, Cardoza Publishing, New York, 1990

Royer, Victor H.
Casino Gamble Talk: The Language of Gambling and New Casino Games, Lyle Stuart Books, New York, 2003

Rubin, Jerry
Do It! Scenarios of the Revolution, Simon & Schuster, New York, 1970

Rudensky, Red
The Gonif, The Piper Company, Blue Earth, Minnesota, 1970

Rudgely, Richard
The Encyclopaedia of Psychoactive Substances, Abacus, London, 1999

Rushin, Steve
Pool Cool, Pocket Books, New York, 1990

Russ, Marin
Happy Hunting Ground, Atheneum, New York, 1968

Russ, Martin
The Last Parallel, Zebra Books, New York, 1957

Russell, Ross
The Sound, E.P. Dutton, New York, 1961

Russell, Tina
Porno Star, Lancer Books, New York, 1973

Rutherford, Douglas
The Creeping Flesh, Fontana Books, London, 1965 (1963)

RZA with Chris Norris
The Wu-Tang Manual, Berkley Publishing, New York, 2005

Sahl, Mort
Heartland, Harcourt Brace Jovanovich, New York, 1976

Salak, John S.
Dictionary of Gambling, Philosophical Library, New York, 1963

Salinger, J.D.
Catcher in the Rye, Little, Brown and Company, New York, 1951
Franny and Zooey, Bantam Books, New York, 1969 (1961)
Nine Stories, Bantam Books, New York, 1977 (1953)

Salisbury, Harrison E.
The Shook-up Generation, Crest Books, New York, 1958

Salvucci, Claudio R. et al.
The Philadelphia Dialect Dictionary, Evolution Publishing, Bucks County, Pennsylvania, 1996

Sanders, Ed
Tales of Beatnik Glory, Stonehill Publishing, New York, 1975

Sanders, Judi
Cal Poly Slang, Department of Communications, Cal Poly Pomona, Pomona, California, 1990
Don't Dog my Do! A Collection of Cal Poly Argot, Communications Department, Pomona, California, 1991
Kickin' Like Chicken with the Couch Commander: A Collection of Cal Poly Argot (3rd Edition), Department of Communication, Cal Poly Pomona, Pomona, California, 1992
Faced and Faded, Hanging to Hurl: A Collection of Cal Poly Argot (4th Edition), Department of Communication, Cal Poly Pomona, Pomona, California, 1993
Mashing and Munching in Ames: A Dictionary of ISU Slang, Department of Communications, Iowa State University, Ames, Iowa, 1994
Da Bomb! Dis is Dope, Dude! Dig It! A Dictionary of Cal Poly Slang (5th Edition), Department of Communication, Cal Poly Pomona, Pomona, California, 1997
Da Bomb: The Summer Supplement, Department of Communication, Cal Poly Pomona, Pomona, California, 1997

Saporita, Jay
Pourin' It All Out, Citadel Press, Secaucus, New Jersey, 1980

Saslaets, Steve
Ye Olde Hiptionary, Self-published, Las Vegas, Nevada, 1970

Savage, Dan
Savage Love, Penguin, New York, 1998

Savage, John
The Winner's Guide to Dice, Grosset & Dunlap, New York, 1974

Savan, Glenn
White Palace, Bantam, New York, 1987

Sayles, John
Union Dues, Little, Brown and Co., Boston, 1977

Sayres, Sohnya
The 60s Without Apology, University of Minnesota Press, Minneapolis, 1984

Scarne, John
Scarne on Dice, Stackpole Books, Mechanicsburg, Pennsylvania, 1974
Scarne's Guide to Modern Poker, Simon & Schuster, New York, 1979

Schiff, Robin
Romy and Michele's High School Reunion, Touchstone Pictures, 1997

Schmidt, J.E.
Narcotics Lingo and Lore, Charles C. Thomas, Springfield, Illinois, 1959

Schneck, Stephen
The Nightclerk, Grove Press, New York, 1966

Schock, Jim
Life is a Lousy Drag, Unicorn Publishing, San Francisco, 1958

Schrader, Paul J.
Taxi Driver, Columbia Pictures, 1976

Schultz, Mari Helen
May I Have This Dance? A Social Dance Digest, Vantage Press, New York, 1986

Schwartz, J.R.
The Official Guide to the Best Cat Houses in Nevada, Self-published, Boise, Idaho, 1993

Scoblete, Frank
Guerrilla Gambling: How to Beat the Casinos at their own Games, Bonus Books, Chicago, Illinois, 1993
Best Blackjack, Bonus Books, Chicago, Illinois, 1996

Scott, Kathryn Leigh
The Bunny Years, Pomegranate Press, Beverly Hills, California, 1998

Scott, Thurston
Cure it with Honey, Harper & Brothers, New York, 1951

Seale, Bobby
Seize the Time, Vintage Books, New York, 1970
A Lonely Rage, Bantam Books, New York, 1979 (1978)

See, Carolyn
Blue Money: Pornography and the Pornographers, David McKay Company, New York, 1974

Seese, Gwyneth A. "Dandalion"
Tijuana Bear in a Smoke 'Um Up Taxi, Pollock Enterprises, Grove City, Pennsylvania, 1977

Segal, Erich
Love Story, Harper & Row, New York, 1970

Selby, Hubert
Last Exit to Brooklyn, Calder & Boyers Ltd., London, 1970 (1957)

Sellers, Terence
Dungeon Evidence, Velvet, London, 1997

Sepe, John and Louis Telano
Cop Team, Pinnacle Books, New York, 1975

Sergel, Sherman Louis
The Language of Show Biz: A Dictionary, Dramatic Publishing Company, Chicago, 1973

Severson, John
Modern Surfing Around the World, Doubleday, New York, 1964

Shakur (Kody Scott), Sanyika
Monster: The Autobiography of an L.A. Gang Member, Atlantic Monthly Press, New York, 1993

Shamus, Mike
The Illustrated Encyclopedia of Billiards, Lyons & Burford, New York, 1993

Shaner, Lora
Madam: Chronicles of a Nevada Cathouse, Huntington Press, Las Vegas, Nevada, 1999

Shankar, Pramod
How to Win at Gin Rummy: Playing for Fun and Profit, Lyle Stuart, Secaucus, New Jersey, 1994

Sharpe, Roger C.
Pinball!, E. P. Dutton, New York, 1977

Shaw, Arnold
Lingo of Tin-Pan Alley, Broadcast Music, Inc., New York, 1950

Shearer, Johnny
The Male Hustler, Century Books, Cleveland, Ohio, 1966

Shecter, Leonard and William Phillips
On the Pad: The Underworld and its Corrupt Police, G.P. Putnam's Sons, New York, 1973

Sheehan, Neil
A Bright Shining Lie, Random House, New York, 1988

Sheehy, Gail
Hustlin: Prostitution in our Wide-Open Society, Dell, New York, 1974
Hustling, Dell Publishing, New York, 1974 (1973)

Shelly, Lou
Hepcats Jive Talk Dictionary, T.W.O. Charles Company, Derby, Connecticut, 1945

Shelton, Ron
Bull Durham, Orion Pictures, 1988

Shenk, David and Steve Silberman
Skeleton Key: A Dictionary for Deadheads, Main Street Books, New York, 1994

Shepard, Elaine
The Doom Pussy, Pocket Books, New York, 1967

Sherman, Allan
The Rape of the APE (American Puritan Ethic): The Official History of the Sex Revolution, Playboy Press, Chicago, 1973

Sherry as told to Robert Tralins, Madam
Pleasure Was My Business, Paperback Library, New York, 1963

Shulman, Alix Kates
On the Stroll, Academy Chicago Publishers, Chicago, 1987

Shulman, Irving
Cry Tough, Avon Publishing, New York, 1950
The Short End of the Stick and Other Stories, Doubleday & Company, Garden City, New York, 1959
College Confidential, Fawcett, Greenwich, Connecticut, 1960

Shulman, Max
Sleep Till Noon, Doubleday & Company, Garden City, New York, 1950
The Many Loves of Dobie Gillis, Bantam Books, New York, 1951
Max Shulman's Guided Tour of Campus Humor, Hanover House, Garden City, New York, 1955
The Zebra Derby, Doubleday, New York, 1956 (1946)
I Was a Teen-Age Dwarf, Bantam Books, New York, 1960
Anyone Got a Match? Harper & Row, New York, 1964

Siegel, Hy
All About CB Two-Way Radio, Radio Shack, Fort Worth, Texas, 1976

Sigal, Clancy
Going Away: A Report, A Memoir, Houghton Mifflin, Boston, 1961

Sikes, Gini
8 Ball Chicks: A Year in the Violent World of Girl Gangs, Anchor Books, New York, 1997

Silberstang, Edwin
Winning Poker for the Serious Player, Gambling Research Institute, New York, 1992

Sills, Jennifer
Massage Parlor, Ace Books, New York, 1973

Simmons, Earl and Smokey Fontane
E.A.R.L.: The Autobiography of DMX, Harper Entertainment, New York, 2002

Simmons, Herbert
Corner Boy, W.W. Norton & Company, New York, 1996

Simmons, J.L. and Barry Winograd
It's Happening: A Portrait of the Youth Scene Today, McNally and Loftin, Santa Barbara, California, 1967 (1966)

Simon, David
Homicide: A Year on the Killing Streets, Ivy Books, New York, 1993

Simonson, Douglas
Pidgin to da Max, Peppovision, Honolulu, Hawaii, 1981
Pidgin to da Max: Hana Hou, Peppovision, Honolulu, Hawaii, 1982

Simpson with Ann Pearlman, Colton
Inside the Crips: Life Inside L.A.'s Most Notorious Gang, St. Martin's Press, New York, 2005

Sinclair, John
Guitar Army: Street Writings/Prison Writings, Douglas Book Corporation, New York, 1972

Singleton, John
Boyz N The Hood, Columbia Pictures, 1990

Singleton, Ralph S.
Filmmaker's Dictionary, Lone Eagle Publishing, Beverly Hills, California, 1990

Sipchen, Bob
Baby Insane and the Buddha, Bantam Books, New York, 1994

Sisters of the Heart
The Brothel Bible: The Cathouse Experience, Brothel Books, Las Vegas, 1997

Skilbeck, Oswald
ABC of Film and TV Working Terms, Focal Press, New York, 1960

Skolnik, Neil S.
On the Ledge, Faber and Faber, Winchester, Massachusetts, 1996

Slim, Iceberg (Robert Beck)
Mama Black Widow, Holloway House, Los Angeles, California, 1969
Pimp: The Story of My Life, Holloway House, Los Angeles, 1969
Trick Baby, Halloway House, Los Angeles, California, 1969
The Naked Soul of Iceberg Slim: Robert Beck's Real Story, Holloway House, Los Angeles, California, 1971
Death Wish, Holloway House, Los Angeles, California, 1977
Doom Fox, Payback Press, Edinburgh, 1978
Airtight Willie and Me, Payback Press, Edinburgh, 1979

"Slingo"
The Offical CB Slang Dictionary Handbook, Communication Books, Milwaukee, Wisconsin, 1976

Smith, Alson J.
Syndicate City: The Chicago Crime Cartel and What To Do About It, Henry Regnery Company, Chicago, 1954

Smith, Jester
Games They Play in San Francisco, Tri-City Printing, Sausalito, California, 1971

Smith, Kent et al.
Adult Movies: Rating Hundreds of the Best Films for Home Video & Cable, Beekman House, New York, 1982

Smith, Kevin
Clerks, Miramax, 1994
Mallrats, Gramercy Pictures, 1995
Chasing Amy, Miramax, 1997
Jay and Silent Bob Strike Back, Hyperion, New York, 2001

Smith, Lindsay E. and Bruce A. Walstad
Sting Shift: The Street-Smart Cop's Handbook of Cons and Swindles, Street-Smart Communications, Littleton, Colorado, 1989
Keeping Carnies Honest: A Police Officer's Field Guide to Carnival Game Inspections, Street-Smart Communications, Littleton, Colorado, 1990

Smith, Vernon E.
The Jones Men, Payback Press, Edinburgh, 1997 (1974)

Smith, Warren
Warren Smith's Authentic Dictionary of CB, Award Books, New York, 1976

Snead, Sam and Jerry Tarde
Pigeons, Marks, Hustlers and Other Golf Bettors You Can Beat, Golf Digest, Trumbull, Connecticut, 1986

Snead with Al Stump, Sam
The Education of a Golfer, Fawcett, New York, 1962

Snowden, Roger
Gambling Times Guide to Bingo, Lyle Stuart, Secaucus, New Jersey, 1986

Snyder, Jimmy
Jimmy the Greek, Playboy Press, Chicago, Illionis, 1976 (1975)

Soderbergh, Steven
Sex, Lies and Videotape, Miramax, 1989

Sohn, Amy
Run Catch Kiss, Simon & Schuster, New York, 1999
Sex and the City: Kiss and Tell, Melcher Media, New York, 2002

Solanas, Valerie
S.C.U.M. Manifesto, Olympia Press, New York, 1968

Solkey, Lee
Dummy Up and Deal, Gamblers Book Club Press, Las Vegas, Nevada, 1980

Sondern, Jr., Frederic
Brotherhood of Evil: The Mafia, Manor Books, New York, 1972

Sondheim, Stephen
West Side Story, 1957

Sorkin, Aaron
A Few Good Men, Columbia Pictures, 1992

Sorrentino, Gilbert
Steelwork, Pantheon Books, New York, 1970

Sorrows, Gene
All About Carnivals, American Federation of Police, North Miami, Florida, 1985

Sothern, Georgia
Georgia: My Life in Burlesque, Signet, New York, 1972

Sotos, Peter
Index, Velvet, London, 1998 (1996)

Southern, Terry
Now Dig This: The Unspeakable Writings of Terry Southern 1950–1995, Methuen Publishing, London
Candy, Putnam, New York, 1958
The Magic Christian, Penguin Books, Harmondsworth, Middlesex, 1969 (1959)
Texas Summer, Arcade, New York, 1993 (1991)
Flash and Filigree, Grove Press, New York, 1996 (1958)
Blue Movie, Grove Press, New York, 1996 (1970)

Sparks, Beatrice (writing as 'Anonymous')
Jay's Journal, Dell Publishing, New York, 1979

Spears, Richard A.
The Slang and Jargon of Drugs and Drinks, Scarecrow Press, Metuchen, New Jersey, 1986

Speight, Johnny
It Stands to Reason, M&J Hobbs, Walton-on-Thames, Surrey, U.K., 1973

Spencer, Ernest
Welcome to Vietnam, Macho Man: Reflections of a Khe Sanh Vet, Bantam Books, New York, 1991
Welcome to Vietnam, Macho Man, Bantam Books, New York, 1991

Spillane, Mickey
My Gun is Quick, Signet Books, New York, 1950
The Big Kill, Signet, New York, 1951
Kiss Me Deadly, Signet Books, New York, 1952
The Long Wait, Signet, New York, 1952
I, The Jury, Signet Books, New York, 1958 (1947)
The Snake, Signet, New York, 1964
The Body Lovers, Signet, New York, 1967
Me, Hood!, Signet Books, New York, 1969 (1963)
Return of the Hood, Signet Books, New York, 1969 (1964)
Last Cop Out, Signet Books, New York, 1973 (1972)
One Lonely Night, Signet Books, New York, 1979 (1951)

Spillard, William J. and Pence James
Needle in a Haystack: The Exciting Adventures of a Federal Narcotic Agent, Whittlesey House, New York, 1945

Spottiswoode, Roger and Walter Hill
48 Hours, Paramount Pictures, 1982

Sprague, W.D.
Sexual Rebellion in the Sixties, Lancer Books, New York, 1965

St. James, James
Party Monster (Previously published as Disco Bloodbath), Simon & Schuster, New York, 2003

Starr, Blaze and Huey Perry
Blaze Starr: My Life as Told to Huey Perry, Pocket Books, New York, 1989

Starr, Jason
Lights Out, St. Martin's Minotaur, New York, 2006

Stavans, Ilan (Editor)
Oscart "Zeta" Acosta: The Uncollected Works, Arte Publico Press, Houston, 1996

Stavsky, Lois et al.
A2Z: The Book of Rap and Hip-Hop Slang, Boulevard Books, New York, 1995

Stearn, Jess
Sisters of the Night: The Startling Story of Prostitution in New York Today, Gramercy Publishing Company, New York, 1956

Steck, E.E.
A Brief Examination of an Esoteric Folk, unpublished manuscript in the Western Historical Manuscript Collection, Columbia, Missouri, 1968

Steele, Guy L. et al.
The Hacker's Dictionary: A Guide to the World of Computer Wizards, Harper & Row, New York, 1983

Steig, Irwin
Common Sense in Poker, Cornerstone Library, New York, 1963
Play Gin to Win, Cornerstone Library, New York, 1971

Steigleman, Walter
Horseracing, Prentice Hall, New York, 1947

Stein, Elissa and Kevin Lerslie
Chunks: A Barfology, St. Martin's Griffin, New York, 1997

Steiner, Paul and Meredith Maran
Chamisa Road with Paul & Meredith: Doin' the Dog in Taos, Random House, New York, 1971

Steiner, Peter O.
Thursday Night Poker: How to Understand, Enjoy—and Win, Random House, New York, 1996

Steinhardt, Anne
Thunder La Boom, Viking Press, New York, 1974

Stern, David H.
Surfing Guide to Southern California, Fitzpatrick Company, Malibu, California, 1963

Stern, Howard
Miss America, Regan Books, New York, 1995

Stern, Stewart
Rebel Without a Cause, Warner Brothers, 1955

Sterry, David Henry
Chicken: Self-Portrait of a Young Man for Rent, Regan Books, New York, 2002

Stoffey, Bob
Cleared Hot! A Marine Combat Pilot's Vietnam Diary, St. Martin's Press, New York, 1992

Stoller, Robert and I.S. Levine
Coming Attractions: The Making of an X-Rated Video, Yale University Press, New Haven, Connecticutt, 1991

Stone, Oliver
Platoon, Orion Pictures, 1986

Storm, Tempest and Bill Boyd
Tempest Storm: The Lady is a Vamp, Peachtree Publishers, Atlanta, Georgia, 1987

Stott, Mike
Soldiers Talking, Cleanly, Eyre Methuen, London, 1978

Strait, Guy
The Lavender Lexicon: Dictionary of Gay Words and Phrases, self-published, San Francisco, 1964

Strandemo, Steve and Bill Bruns
The Racquetball Book, Pocket Books, New York, 1977

Stroud, Carsten
Close Pursuit: A Week in the Life of a NYPD Homicide Cop, Bantam Books, Toronto, 1987

Sugar, Bert Randolph and George Napolitano
Wrestling's Great Grudge Matches: Battles and Feuds, Gallery Books, New York, 1985

Sullivan, George
Harness Racing, Fleet Publishing Corporation, New York, 1964

Swarthout, Glendon
Where the Boys Are, Random House, New York, 1960

Swift, Mary
Campus Slang: Slang on the University of Texas Campus, unpublished manuscript, Western Historical Manuscript Collection, Columbia, Missouri, 1968

Sykes, Gresham M.
The Society of Captives: A Study of a Maximum Security Prison, Princeton University Press, Princeton, New Jersey, 1972

Sylvester, Robert
No Cover Charge: A Backward Look at the Night Clubs, Dial Press, New York, 1956

Tabbert, Russell
Dictionary of Alaskan English, Denali Press, Juneau, Alaska, 1991

Tak, Montie
Truck Talk: The Language of the Open Road, Chilton Book Company, Philadelphia, 1971

Talese, Guy
Thy Neighbor's Wife, Doubleday & Company, Garden City, New York, 1980

Tamosaitis, Nancy
net.sex, Ziff-Davis Press, Emeryville, California, 1995

Taormino, Tristan
Pucker Up: A Hands-on Guide to Ecstatic Sex, Regan Books, New York, 2001

Tarantino, Quentin
Reservoir Dogs, Artisan Entertainment, 1992
Pulp Fiction, Miramax, 1994
From Dusk Till Dawn, Hyperion, New York, 1995
Kill Bill, Miramax Films, 2003

Tarantino, Quentin, David Veloz, Richard Turowski and Oliver Stone
Natural Born Killers, Warner Brothers, 1994

Taylor, Dawson
How to Talk Golf, Galahad Books, New York, 1985
How to Talk Bowling, Dembner Books, New York, 1987

Taylor, Emma and Lorelei Sharkey
Em and Lo's Rec Sex: An A–Z Guide to Hooking Up, Chronicle Books, San Francisco, 2006

Taylor, Murray A.
Jumping Fire: A Smokejumper's Memoir of Fighting Wildfire, Harcourt, Inc., Orlando, Florida, 2001 (2000)

Tea, Michelle
The Passionate Mistakes and Intricate Corruption of One Girl in America, Smart Art Press, New York, 1998
Valencia, Seal Press, New York, 2000

Teeman, Lawrence
Consumer Guide Good Buddy's CB Dictionary, Consumer Guide, Skokie, Illinois, 1976

Teresa, Vincent with Thomas Renner
My Life in the Mafia, Doubleday & Company, Garden City, New York, 1973

Terry, Wallace
Bloods: An Oral History of the Vietnam War by Black Veterans, Ballantine Books, New York, 1985

Tevis, Walter
The Color of Money, Abacus, London, 1985

Tewkesbury, Joan
Nashville, Paramount Pictures, 1975

Thigpen, Janet
Power Volleyball, William C. Brown, Dubuque, Iowa, 1985

Thomas, Jack W.
Heavy Number, Bantam Books, New York, 1976

Thomas, Piri
Down These Mean Streets, Alfred A. Knopf, New York, 1967
Seven Long Times, Praeger Publishers, New York, 1974
Stories from El Barrio, Alfred A. Knopf, New York, 1978

Thompson, Dave
Play Backgammon Tonight, Gambler's Book Club, Las Vegas, Nevada, 1976

Thompson, Hunter S.
Hell's Angels: A Strange and Terrible Saga, Random House, New York, 1966
Fear and Loathing in Las Vegas, Fawcett Popular Library, New York, 1971
The Great Shark Hunt: Gonzo Papers, Vol. 1, Fawcett, New York, 1980
A Generation of Swine: Tales of Shame and Degradation in the '80s, Vintage Books, New York, 1988
Songs of the Doomed: More Notes on the Death of the American Dream, Pocket Books, New York, 1991 (1990)
Fear and Loathing in America: The Brutal Odyssey of an Outlaw Journalist 1968-1976, Touchstone Books, New York, 2001
Kingdom of Fear: Loathsome Secrets of a Star-Crossed Child in the Final Days of the American Century, Simon & Schuster, New York, 2003

Thompson, Hunter S. (Edited by Douglas Brinkley)
Fear and Loathing in America: The Brutol Odyssey of an

Outlaw Journalist 1968–1976, Touchstone Books, New York, 2001
The Proud Highway: Saga of a Desperate Southern Gentleman 1955–1967, Touchstone Books, New York, 2001

Thompson, Jim
The Grifters, Vintage Books, New York, 1963
Savage Night, Black Lizard Books, Berkeley, California, 1985 (1953)
Bad Boy [Hardcore: Three Novels], Donald I. Fine, New York, 1986 (1953)
A Swell-Looking Babe, Black Lizard Books, Berkeley, California, 1986 (1954)
The Nothing Man [Hardcore: Three Novels], Donald I. Fine, New York, 1986 (1954)
The Kill-Off [Hardcore: Three Novels], Donald I. Fine, New York, 1986 (1957)
Roughneck, Mysterious Press, New York, 1989 (1954)
After Dark, My Sweet, Black Lizard, New York, 1990 (1955)
Pop. 1280, Black Lizard, New York, 1990 (1964)
The Killer Inside, Vintage Books, New York, 1991 (1952)

Thompson, Jon F.
The Official CB Book: A Consumer's Guide, Ballantine Books, New York, 1976

Thrush, Paul W.
A Dictionary of Mining, Mineral and Related Terms, U.S. Department of the Interior, Washington D.C., 1968

Todasco, Ruth et al.
The Intelligent Woman's Guide to Dirty Words, Loop Center YWCA, Chicago, Illinois, 1973

Tolbert, Candace
Tilt: The Pinball Book, Creative Arts Books, Berkeley, California, 1978

Torbet, Laura
The Complete Book of Skateboarding, Thomas Y. Crowell, New York, 1976

Torres, Edwin
Q & A, Dial Press, New York, 1977
Carlito's Way, Avon Books, New York, 1993 (1975)
After Hours, Avon Books, New York, 1993 (1979)

Townsend, Larry
The Leatherman's Handbook, Le Salon, Beverly Hills, California, 1972

Trapunski, Edward
Special When Lit: A Visual and Anecdotal History of Pinball, Dolphin Books, Garden City, New York, 1979

Tri-Star Pictures
Avalon, 1990

Trocchi, Alexander
Cain's Book, Grove Press, New York, 1960
White Thighs, Brandon House, North Hollywood, 1967

Truscott, Lucian K.
Army Blue, Warner Books, New York, 1989

Tubbs, Stewart L. and Sylvia Moss
Human Communication: An Interpersonal Perspective, Random House, New York, 1974

Tucker, W.M.
The Change Raisers, Street-Smart Communications, Littleton, Colorado, 1992 (1960)

Turan, Kenneth and Stephen E. Zito
Sinema: American Pornographic Films and the People who Make Them, Praeger Publishers, New York, 1974

Turkus, Burton B. and Sid Feder
Murder, Inc.: The Inside Story of the Mob, Manor Books, New York, 1972

Tuso, Joseph
Singing the Vietnam Blues: Songs of the Air Force in

Southeast Asia, Texas A&M University Press, College Station, Texas, 1990

Tyron, Mark
Of G-Strings and Strippers, Beacon Books, Canada, 1953

Universal Pictures
Mo' Better Blues, 1990

Unknown/Uncredited et al.
Street Terms: Drugs and the Drug Trade, Drugs and Crime Data Center and Clearinghouse, United States Department of Justice, Washington D.C.
Encyclopaedia Britannica (11th Ed), 1911
Hot Rod Comics Featuring Clint Curtis, Fawcett Publications, Greenwich, Connecticut, 1952
Swinging Syllables, Kimbrough Publishing, Memphis, Tennessee, 1959
Guide to Drag Racing, Fremont Drag Strip Inc., Fremont, California, 1960
Dobie Gillis Teenage Slanguage Dictionary, Twentieth Century-Fox Television, Los Angeles, California, 1962
The Guild Dictionary of Homosexual Terms, Guild Press Ltd., Washington D.C., 1965
The Market Street Proposition, KFRC Radio, San Francisco, 1965
The Last Supplement to the Whole Earth Catalog, The Realist, New York, 1971
The Knapp Commission Report on Police Corruption, George Braziller, New York, 1972
CB Slang Dictionary, Canyon House, 1976
CBer's Five-Star 10 Pounder Wordbook, Hayden Book Company, Rochelle Park, New Jersey, 1977
King Smut's Wet Dreams Interpreted: An Erotic Lexicon and Number Guide, Komar Ltd., Baltimore, 1978
The ABC's of CB Slang, Dell Publishing, New York, 1978
What Color is Your Handkerchief: A Lesbian S/M Sexuality Reader, SAMOIS, Berkeley, California, 1979
Lineman's Slang Dictionary, A.B. Chance Co., Centralia, Missouri, 1980
Concise Spanish Dictionary, Harrap, London, 1991
Addictions & Life Organisation, www.addictions.org, 1999

Uston, Ken
Million Dollar Blackjack, Carol Publishing, Secaucus, New Jersey, 1981

Valentine, Bill
Gang Intelligence Manual, Paladin Press, Boulder, Colorado, 1995
Gangs and Their Tattoos, Paladin Press, Boulder, Colorado, 2000

Van Devanter, Lynda with Christopher Morgan
Home Before Morning: The True Story of an Army Nurse in Vietnam, Warner Books, New York, 1984

Van Sant, Gus and Dan Yost
Drugstore Cowboy, Avenue Pictures, 1988

Vidal, Gore
Myra Breckinridge, Bantam Books, New York, 1968
Myron, Penguin Books, New York, 1997

Vigil, James Diego
Barrio Gangs: Street Life and Identity in Southern California, University of Texas Press, Austin, 1988

Villarreal, Jose Antonio
Pocho, Anchor Books, New York, 1989

Vollman, William T.
Whores for Gloria, Penguin Boos, New York, 1994 (1991)

Von Hoffman, Nicholas
We Are The People Our Parents Warned Us Against, Fawcett Publications, Greenwich, Connecticutt, 1968 (1967)

Voorhees, Don and Bob Benoit
Railbird Handbook, Hollywood Turf Club, Inglewood, California, 1968

Vorhaus, John
The Big Book of Poker Slang, Poker Plus Publications, Las Vegas, Nevada, 1996

Wald, Marvin and Albert Maltz
The Naked City, Southern Illinois University Press, Carbondale, Illinois, 1979 (1947)

Wallace, Frank R.
Poker: A Guaranteed Income for Life, I & O Publishing Company, Wilmington, Delaware, 1968

Wambaugh, Joseph
The Black Marble, Dell Publishing, New York, 1979 (1978)
The Glitter Dome, Bantam Books, New York, 1982 (1981)
Lines and Shadows, Bantam Books, New York, 1984
The Secrets of Harry Bright, Bantam Books, New York, 1986 (1985)
The New Centurions, Dell Publishing, Newe York, 1987 (1970)
The Blue Knight, Sphere Books, London, 1987 (1973)
The Golden Orange, Bantam Books, New York, 1991 (1990)
Fugitive Nights, Bantam Books, New York, 1992
Finnegan's Week, Bantam Books, New York, 1993
Floaters, Bantam, New York, 1996
Hollywood Station, Little, Brown and Company, New York, 2006

Wardlaw, Lee
Cowabunga! The Complete Book of Surfing, Avon Books, New York, 1991

Waters, Daniel
Heathers, New World Pictures, 1988

Waters, Ethel
His Eye is on the Sparrow, Doubleday & Company, Garden City, New York, 1951

Waters, John et al.
Trash Trio: Three Screenplays, Vintage Books, New York, 1988

Way, Walter L. et al.
The Drug Scene: Help or Hang-up? (2nd Edition), Prentice-Hall, Englewood Cliffs, New Jersey, 1977

Weatherford, Jack McIver et al.
Porn Row: An Inside Look at the Sex-for-sale District of a Major American City, Arbor House, New York, 1986

Weaver, Ken
Texas Crude, E.P. Dutton, New York, 1984

Webb, Charles and Calder Willingham
The Graduate, Embassy Pictures Corporation, 1967

Webb, Jack
The Badge, Crest, New York, 1958

Weber, Stanley
A Study of Sex in Prison, Gallery Press, Los Angeles, 1973

Wells, John Warren
Tricks of the Trade: A Hooker's Handbook of Sexual Techniques, New American Library, New York, 1970

Wepman, Dennis et al.
The Life: The Lore and Folk Poetry of the Black Hustler, University of Pennsylvania Press, Philadelphia, 1976

Werner, Doug
Snowboarders Start-Up! A Beginner's Guide to Snowboarding, Pathfinder Publishing, Ventura, California, 1993

Wesson, Donald and David Smith
Barbiturates: Their Use, Misuse and Abuse, Human Sciences Press, New York, 1977

Wesson, Vann
Generation X Field Guide & Lexicon, Orion Media, San Diego, California, 1997

West, R. Frederick
God's Gambler, Prentice-Hall, Englewood Cliffs, New Jersey, 1964

Wheeler, Mark
Half Baked Alaska, Self-published, Ketchikan, Alaska, 1972

Whited, Charles
Chiodo: Undercover Cop, Playboy Press, Chicago, 1974 (1973)

Whittemore, L.H.
Cop!, Fawcett Publications, New York, 1970

Wice, Nathaniel and Steven Daly
alt.culture, Harper Perennial, New York, 1995

Wilcox, Robert K.
Scream of Eagles, John Wiley & Sons, New York, 1990

Wilkes, Rich
Airheads, 20th Century Fox, 1994

Williams, John A.
The Angry Ones, Pocket Books, New York, 1970
Sissie, Thunder's Mouth Press, New York, 1988
The Man Who Cried I Am, Quality Paperback Book Club, New York, 1994

Williams, John B.
Narcotics and Hallucinogenics – a handbook [Revised Edition], Glencoe Press, Beverly Hills, California, 1967

Williams, Linda
Hard Core: Power, Pleasure and the "Frenzy of the Invisible", University of California Press, Berkeley, California, 1989

Williams, Sally
"Strong" Words: Medical Slang (Dissertation), University of North Carolina Press, Berkeley, California, 1994

Williams, Stanley "Tookie" and Barbara Cottman Becnel
Life in Prison, Chronicle Books, San Francisco, 1998

Williams, Terry
The Cocaine Kids: The Inside Story of a Teenage Drug Ring, Addison-Wesley, Reading, Massachusetts, 1989
Crackhouse: Notes from the End of the Line, Addison-Wesley, Reading, Massachusetts, 1992

Williamson, Henry
Hustler!, Avon Books, New York, 1965

Wilmeth, Don
The Language of American Popular Entertainment: A Glossary of Argot, Slang, and Terminology, Greenwood Press, Westport, Connecticut, 1981

Wilson, Earl
I Am Gazing Into My 8-Ball, Sun Dial Press, Garden City, New York, 1945

Wilson, Robert A.
Playboy's Book of Forbidden Words, Playboy Press, Chicago, Illinois, 1972

Wilson, Sophie
Teen Speak: the Definitive Lexicon 2001, The Observer, London, 2001

Wilson, Thomas
Wife Swapping, Counterpoint, New York, 1965

Wilson, William
The LBJ Brigade, Pyramid Books, New York, 1966

Wimsatt, William Upski
Bomb the Suburbs, Soft Skull Press, Brooklyn, 2000

Winick, Charles and Paul Kinsie
The Lively Commerce: Prostitution in the United States, Quadrangle Books, Chicago, 1971

Winkless, N.B.
The Gambling Times Guide to Craps, Lyle Stuart, Secaucus, New Jersey, 1981

Wiseman, Rosalind
Queen Bees & Wannabes: Helping Your Daughter Survive Cliques, Gossip, Boyfriends & Other Realities of Adolescence, Three Rivers Press, New York, 2002

Wolf, Leonard (Editor)
Voices From the Love Generation, Little, Brown and Co., Boston, 1968

Wolfe, Bernard
The Late Risers: Their Masquerade, Random House, New York, 1954
Book, MacFadden Books, New York, 1962

Wolfe, Burton H.
The Hippies, Signet Books, New York, 1968

Wolfe, Tom
The Electric Kool-Aid Acid Test, Bantam Books, New York, 1968
The Pump House Gang, Bantam Books, New York, 1969 (1968)
The Kandy-Kolored Tangerine-Flake Streamline Baby, Farrar, Straus & Giroux, New York, 1987 (1965)

Wright, Thomas Lee and Bayr Michael Cooper
New Jack City, Warner Brothers, 1991 (1990)

X, Malcolm and Alex Haley
The Autobiography of Malcolm X, Ballantine Books, New York, 1992 (1964)

Yablonsky, Lewis
The Hippie Trip, Pegasus, New York, 1968
The Violent Gang, Penguin Books, Baltimore, 1973

Yarborough, Tom
Da Nang Diary: A Forward Air Controller's Year of Combat Over Vietnam, St. Martin's Press, New York, 1990

Young, Kenn "Naz" et al.
Naz's Dictionary of Teen Slang, National Book Company, Portland, Oregon, 1993

Young, Kenn W.
Naz's Underground Dictionary, Naz Enterprises, Vancouver, Washington, 1973

Youngblut (Editorial Director), Shelley
Way Inside ESPN's X Games, Hyperion, New York, 1998

Yurrick, Sol
The Warriors, W.H. Allen, London, 1966
The Bag, Trident Press, New York, 1968

Zidek, Ted
Choi Oi: The LIghter Side of Vietnam, Charles E. Tuttle, Rutland, Vermont, 1965

Zimmerman, Paul
King of Comedy, 20th Century Fox, 1976

Ziplow, Stephen
The Film Maker's Guide to Pornography, Drake Publishers, New York, 1977

Zumbro, Ralph
Tank Sergeant, Presidio, Novato, California, 1986

The Concise New Partridge Dictionary of Slang and Unconventional English

Tom Dalzell and Terry Victor

Praise for the two-volume *New Partridge Dictionary of Slang and Unconventional English:*

'The king is dead. Long live the king!... The old Partridge is not really dead; it remains the best record of British slang antedating 1945... Now, however, the preferred source for information about English slang of the past 60 years is the New Partridge.'   – James Rettig, *Booklist, American Library Association*

'Most slang dictionaries are no better than momgrams or a rub of the brush, put together by shmegegges looking to make some moola. *The New Partridge Dictionary of Slang and Unconventional English*, on the other hand, is the wee babes.'   – Ian Sansom, *The Guardian*

The Concise New Partridge presents, for the first time, all the slang terms from *The New Partridge Dictionary of Slang and Unconventional English* in a single volume.

With over 60,000 entries from around the English-speaking world, the *Concise* gives you the language of beats, hipsters, Teddy Boys, mods and rockers, hippies, pimps, druggies, whores, punks, skinheads, ravers, surfers, Valley girls, dudes, pill-popping truck drivers, hackers, rappers and more.

The Concise New Partridge is a spectacular resource infused with humour and learning – it's rude, it's delightful, and it's a prize for anyone with a love of language.

ISBN10: 0-415-21259-6 (hbk)

ISBN13: 978-0-415-21259-5 (hbk)

Related titles from Routledge

Sex Slang
Tom Dalzell and Terry Victor

Are you a beaver cleaver or the office bike? Would you rather pack fudge or munch carpet? Do you content yourself with paddling the pickle as you're still a cherry boy?

Sex Slang will not only give you 3,000 words to talk about your favourite pastimes, but also open your eyes to practices you didn't even know existed.

All words are illustrated by a reference from a variety of sources to prove their existence. This naughty book will give you a spectacular sexual vocabulary from all over the English speaking world, as well as hours of reading pleasure.

ISBN10: 0-415-37180-5
ISBN13: 978-0-415-37180-3

Available at all good bookshops
For ordering and further information please visit:
www.routledge.com

Related titles from Routledge

Vice Slang
Tom Dalzell and Terry Victor

Are you a bit of a chairwarmer? Do you use the wins from a country straight to get scudded on snakebite in a blind tiger? Do you ride the waves on puddle or death drop?

Vice Slang gently eases you into the language of gambling, drugs and alcohol, providing you with 3,000 words to establish yourself firmly in the world of corruption and wickedness.

All words are illustrated by a reference from a variety of sources to prove their existence in alleys and dives throughout the English speaking world. This entertaining book will give you hours of reading pleasure.

ISBN10: 0-415-37181-3
ISBN13: 978-0-415-37181-0

Available at all good bookshops
For ordering and further information please visit:
www.routledge.com

Related titles from Routledge

Origins
A Short Etymological Dictionary of Modern English

Eric Partridge

This dictionary gives the origins of some 20,000 items from the modern English vocabulary, discussing them in groups that make clear the connections between words derived by a variety of routes from originally common stock. As well as giving the answers to questions about the derivation of individual words, it is a fascinating book to browse through, since every page points out links with other entries. It is easy to pursue such trails as the longer articles are written as continuous prose clearly divided up by means of numbered paragraphs and subheadings, and there is a careful system of cross-references. In addition to the main A – Z listing, there are extensive lists of prefixes, suffixes, and elements used in the creation of new vocabulary.

ISBN10: 0-415-05077-4 (hbk)
ISBN10: 0-415-47433-7 (pbk)

ISBN13: 978-0-415-05077-7 (hbk)
ISBN13: 978-0-415-47433-7 (pbk)

Related titles from Routledge

A Frequency Dictionary of Spanish
Core vocabulary for learners

Mark Davies

A Frequency Dictionary of Spanish is an invaluable tool for all learners of Spanish, providing a list of the 5,000 most frequently used words in the language. Based on a 20-million word corpus which is evenly divided between spoken, fiction and non-fiction texts from both Spain and Latin America the dictionary provides the user with a detailed frequency based list plus alphabetical and part of speech indexes.

All entries in the rank frequency list feature the English equivalent, a sample sentence plus an indication of major register variation. The dictionary also contains thirty thematically organised lists of frequently used words on a variety of topics.

A Frequency Dictionary of Spanish aims to enable students of all levels to maximize their study of Spanish vocabulary in an efficient and engaging way.

ISBN10: 0-415-33428-4 (hbk)
ISBN10: 0-415-33429-2 (pbk)

ISBN13: 978-0-415-33428-0 (hbk)
ISBN13: 978-0-415-33429-7 (pbk)

Available at all good bookshops
For ordering and further information please visit:
www.routledge.com